# HART (시 차 표)

GREENLAND
+3 +4
Nome ALASKA
60°
CANADA
−12.30
NEW FONUDLAND
Vancouver
Seattle
Montreal
Chicago
New York
San Francisco
elphia
ton
MIDWAY IS.
30°
MINICAN REP.
PUERTO RICO
Hoi
HAWAII
AKE IS.
Today
Yesterday
−12.15
GUYANA
SURINAM
−12.30
0°
SAMOA IS.
PERU
Lima
BRAZIL
BOLIVIA
FIJI IS.
Rio de Janeiro
CHILE
PARAGUAY
30°
Santiago
−12
URUGUAY
Buenos Aires
ARGENTINE
NEW ZEALAND
SOUTH GEORGIA
180° 135° 90° 45°

| +2 | +3 | −20 | −19 | −18 | −17 | −16 | −15 | −14 | −13 | −12 | −11 |
|---|---|---|---|---|---|---|---|---|---|---|---|
| 2 | 3 | 4 | 5 | 6 | 7 | 8 | 9 | 10 | 11 | 12 | 13 |
| 3 | 4 | 5 | 6 | 7 | 8 | 9 | 10 | 11 | 12 | 13 | 14 |
|  | 5 | 6 | 7 | 8 | 9 | 10 | 11 | 12 | 13 | 14 | 15 |
| 5 | 6 | 7 | 8 | 9 | 10 | 11 | 12 | 13 | 14 | 15 | 16 |
| 6 | 7 | 8 | 9 | 10 | 11 | 12 | 13 | 14 | 15 | 16 | 17 |
| 7 | 8 | 9 | 10 | 11 | 12 | 13 | 14 | 15 | 16 | 17 | 18 |
| 8 | 9 | 10 | 11 | 12 | 13 | 14 | 15 | 16 | 17 | 18 | 19 |
| 9 | 10 | 11 | 12 | 13 | 14 | 15 | 16 | 17 | 18 | 19 | 20 |
| 10 | 11 | 12 | 13 | 14 | 15 | 16 | 17 | 18 | 19 | 20 | 21 |
| 11 | 12 | 13 | 14 | 15 | 16 | 17 | 18 | 19 | 20 | 21 | 22 |
| 12 | 13 | 14 | 15 | 16 | 17 | 18 | 19 | 20 | 21 | 22 | 23 |
| 13 | 14 | 15 | 16 | 17 | 18 | 19 | 20 | 21 | 22 | 23 | 24 |
| 14 | 15 | 16 | 17 | 18 | 19 | 20 | 21 | 22 | 23 | 24 | 1 |
| 15 | 16 | 17 | 18 | 19 | 20 | 21 | 22 | 23 | 24 | 1 | 2 |
| 16 | 17 | 18 | 19 | 20 | 21 | 22 | 23 | 24 | 1 | 2 | 3 |
| 17 | 18 | 19 | 20 | 21 | 22 | 23 | 24 | 1 | 2 | 3 | 4 |
| 18 | 19 | 20 | 21 | 22 | 23 | 24 | 1 | 2 | 3 | 4 | 5 |
| 19 | 20 | 21 | 22 | 23 | 24 | 1 | 2 | 3 | 4 | 5 | 6 |
| 20 | 21 | 22 | 23 | 24 | 1 | 2 | 3 | 4 | 5 | 6 | 7 |
| 21 | 22 | 23 | 24 | 1 | 2 | 3 | 4 | 5 | 6 | 7 | 8 |
| 22 | 23 | 24 | 1 | 2 | 3 | 4 | 5 | 6 | 7 | 8 | 9 |
| 23 | 24 | 1 | 2 | 3 | 4 | 5 | 6 | 7 | 8 | 9 | 10 |
| 24 | 1 | 2 | 3 | 4 | 5 | 6 | 7 | 8 | 9 | 10 | 11 |
| 1 | 2 | 3 | 4 | 5 | 6 | 7 | 8 | 9 | 10 | 11 | 12 |

# 엣센스한영사전

민중서림 편집국 편

제 4 판

특장판

전면개정판

民衆書林

# 머 리 말

—제4판을 내면서—

우리가 처음으로 "엣센스 한영사전"을 펴낸 것이 1972년이었으며, 이를 다시 개정하여 제2판을 1986년에, 제3판을 1996년에 각각 간행하였다. 그동안 이 "엣센스 한영사전"은 영어 학도들에게는 물론이고 영어를 다루는 많은 직장인들로부터 호평을 받아 꾸준히 중쇄(重刷)를 거듭하여 왔다.

그러나 동서의 냉전 구조가 붕괴되고 국제화·정보화가 일일이 감지할 수 없을 정도의 속도로 진행되며, 많은 분야에서 국경선이 소멸되어가고 있는 '새 밀레니엄(millennium)의 시대'—21세기 정보화 시대를 맞게 되는 현시점에서는 기존의 한영사전 내용만으로는 충분히 대응할 수 없다고 느끼게 되었다.

이 개정판은 이러한 시대적 흐름에서, 세계 공통어로 자리잡은 영어를 '독자들이 어떻게 하면 보다 쉽고 유연성 있게 각 분야에서 올바르게 활용할 수 있을까' 하는 점에 초점을 맞춰 편집 작업을 진행하였다. 이를 위해 그동안 수집한 많은 새로운 자료들을 실용 위주로 선별 보충하였고, 기존의 내용들을 새로운 시각에서 일일이 검토하여 다듬고 보완하였다.

특히 이번 개정 작업에서 역점을 둔 점은 아래와 같다.

1. 활자의 크기를 최대한으로 확대하여 보기 쉽게 하였다.
2. 새로 나온 과학·전자·경제·사회·시사·일상 생활 등에 관한 중요 신어·어구 등을 대폭적으로 보충·보강하였다.
3. 실무 영작문·회화 등에 그대로 활용할 수 있는 살아있는 예문들을 많이 실었다.
4. 한 표제어에 여러 개의 역어가 있어, 그 쓰임새에 혼동이 염려되는 낱말에는 그 용법, 뜻의 차이를 구분할 수 있도록 **용법**, (★…)란을 신설하거나, 《 》안에 그 용도를 명기하였다.
5. 표제어에 관련된 **참고**란을 증설해서, 관련 사항에 대한 폭넓은 지식을 얻을 수 있도록 하였다.
6. 부록에는 최신 자료를 토대로, 여러 분야에서 참고가 될 수 있는 다양한 내용을 갖추게 하였다.

이제 개정 작업을 마치고 나니, 언제나처럼 '좀더 알차고 완벽한 사전을 만들어야 했는데'라는 아쉬움이 남는다. 최선을 다했지만, 예상 못한 미비한 점도 있을 것이라 생각된다. 독자 여러분의 따뜻한 교시와 비판을 기대하면서, 앞으로 더욱 노력, 헌신할 것을 약속드리는 바이다.

2000년 1월

민 중 서 림 편 집 국

# 2판 머리말

지난 1972년에 우리가 편찬한 『엣센스 韓英辭典』의 개정판을, 자매편인 『엣센스 英韓辭典』의 제3판의 간행에 뒤이어 오늘에야 비로소 펴내게 되었다. 실로 14년 만의 일이다. 그동안 『엣센스 韓英辭典』은 우리 나라의 대표적인 한영 사전으로서 국내외적으로 절대적인 호평을 받아 여러 차례 중쇄(重刷)를 거듭하여 왔거니와, 그때그때 우리가 발견한 오식이나 미비한 점, 독자 여러분이 편지로 혹은 전화로 지적해 주신 잘못들을 바로잡아, 정확하고 충실한 사전이 되도록 늘 유의해 오기는 했다. 다만 10여 년이 되도록 전면적인 수정 증보를 베풀지 못한 것이 못내 아쉽고 안타까웠던 차에 늦게나마 이렇게 새로운 면모를 갖추어 세상에 선을 보이게 되니, 한편으로 무거운 짐을 던 듯한 안도감을 느낀다.

이번 개정판에서 우리가 목표로 삼은 점은 다음과 같다.

(1) 활자의 크기를 종전의 5.2포인트에서 5.4포인트로 대폭 키워서 조정하였다. 그리하여 눈의 피로를 훨씬 경감시키고, 언뜻 보기에도 시원한 느낌이 들게 하였다.

(2) 전체 지면을 2천여 면으로 크게 늘려, 포켓형 사전으로서 최대한의 양을 담도록 하였다.

(3) 표제어는 『엣센스 국어 사전』 제2판을 준거하고, 다시 거기에 새로운 최신 용어를 많이 추가하되, 어디까지나 활용도가 높은 일상 생활 용어를 중심으로 한 현대 국어 위주의 사전으로 마련하였다. 이것은 우리가 5,6년에 걸쳐서 꾸준히 수집해 온 자료를 효과적으로 활용함으로써 얻어진 결과로서 자부하는 바이다.

(4) 문례도 일상성이 짙은 것으로 대폭 증가하였다. 또 표현을 풍부히 하기 위하여 같은 원문을 2가지 또는 3가지 영문으로 옮겨 놓은 예도 많다.

(5) 우리가 외국어로서의 영어를 쓰는 데 가장 틀리기 쉬운 점은 관사의 용법이다. 이 사전에서는 Ⓒ(가산 명사), Ⓤ(불가산 명사)와 같은 기호는 특별히 사용하지 않았지만, 가산 명사에는 표제어의 명사에 a 또는 an을 명기하여 이 구별을 확연히 나타내도록 배려하였다.

(6) 참고 사항 · 어법(語法) · 주의 사항의 해설을 폭넓게 확충하였다.

이상과 같은 취지로 엮어진 이 새 『엣센스 韓英辭典』은 말이 개정판이지 처음부터 전면적으로 다시 쓰다시피한 신판이다. 아무쪼록 이 사전이 애용자 여러분에 의해 충분히 활용되어 살아 있는 영어 학습과 실지 응용에 유용한 길잡이가 된다면 더 바랄 나위가 없겠다. 아울러 여러분의 기탄없는 교시와 비판을 바라 마지 않는다.

1986년 5월 2일

민중서림 편집국

＊1986년 문교부 고시의 '외래어 표기법', 1988년 문교부 고시의 '한글 맞춤법'과 '표준어 규정' 및 1990년 문화부 고시의 '표준어 모음'에 따라서 우리말 표제어와 내용을 완전히 수정하여 다시 간행한다.

1993년 1월

민중서림 편집국

# 초판머리말

우리가 엮어 펴낸『포켓 韓英辭典』은『포켓 英韓辭典』의 자매편으로서 1958년 4월에 발간한 것이다. 그 뒤 15년이 지나는 동안, 이 사전은 우리 나라의 단 하나의 한영 사전으로서, 학생은 물론이요, 학계와 일반 사회인의 절대적인 애용 속에 꾸준히 판을 거듭하여 왔다. 수록 어휘가 10만에 육박하고, 당시 국어 사전에도 채 수록되지 않은 알뜰한 일상어를 망라하였으며, 적확(的確)한 역어(譯語)와 풍부한 용례(用例)로써, 영어를 통한 의사 표현에 있어서 다시없는 반려(伴侶)가 되어 왔던 것이다.

그러나 언어는 끊임없이 유동하고 변천한다. 민족이 해방된 지 어언 4반세기가 지난 오늘날, 국어의 변모는 실로 놀랄 만한 것이었다. 특히 옛투의 어려운 한자어(漢字語)의 굴레에서 많이 벗어나, 일상 생활에서는 평이(平易)한 말이 폭넓게 쓰이게 되었다. 뿐만아니라, 해외와의 제반 교류로 말미암아 학술·예술의 발전은 말할 것도 없고, 정치·경제·문화·군사 등의 면에서도 눈부신 비약이 이루어졌으니, 이러한 여건 아래서 언어 생활에도 현저한 변화가 초래되었음은 당연한 일이라 하겠다.

더구나, 격동하는 국내외 정세 속에서 우리는 지금, 보다 적극적인 자세로써 시야를 넓히고, 보다 진지한 태도로써 대화의 장(場)에 참여하여야 할 처지에 놓여 있다. 이러한 시점에서 국제어로서의 영어, 그 중에서도 산 영어를 담은 보다 충실한 한영 사전의 필요성은 자못 큰 바 있다.

이제 우리는 시대의 대세에 알맞게 체제와 내용을 완전히 일신(一新)하여 새로운 한영 사전을 내놓게 되었다. 때늦은 감이 없지 않으나, 우리의 충실(充實)한 편집진의 총력을 결집(結集)한, 문자 그대로 완벽되고 알찬 한영 사전임을 자부하는 바이다.

이『엣센스 韓英辭典』을 꾸미는 데 특히 주력한 점은 아래와 같다.

(1) **최대한의 어휘 수록** 최대한의 어휘를 담기 위하여 포켓형(型) 사전으로는 그 면수에 있어서 극한이라 할 수 있는 1,700여 면으로 전체 지면을 증면(增面)하고, 복합어(複合語)와 파생어(派生語)를 포함한 우리말 수록 어휘를 최대한으로 대폭 늘려서 눈부시게 변천하는 내외 정세에 대응할 수 있는 각 분야의 어휘를 총망라하였다. 특히 우리의 현대 생활에 긴밀하게 밀접되어 있는 정치·과학·경제·군사 관계 용어의 채록에 용심(用心)하였다. 따라서 어휘 수록의 넓이와 깊이의 면에서, 이 사전은 앞으로 한국어를 중심으로 하는 각종 사전을 편찬하는 데에도 크게 유조(有助)할 것으로 믿는 바이다.

(2) **기본 어휘의 충실** 우리말 중에서도 사용 빈도(頻度)가 높은 중요 기본 어휘에는 되도록 지면을 크게 벌려서, 세밀하고도 다각적인 분류를 베풂으로써, 실지 이용에 폭넓은 활용도를 발휘할 수 있게 하였다.

(3) **활용 위주의 편찬** 우리말을 영어로 옮기는 데, 가장 알맞은 역어를 엄선하였음은 물론이려니와, 가능한 한 다각적이고 다양한 용례를 풍부하게 실어, 활용 사전(活用辭典)으로서의 면모도 아울러 갖추게 하였다.

(4) **살아 있는 영어 표현** 모든 영어 표현은 쉽고도 세련된 표준 영어를 구사할 수 있도록 각별히 배려하였다. 이를 위해서, 우리는 Yale 대학의 S.E. Martin, Yang Ha Lee, Sung-Un

Chang 공편(共編)의 *A Korean-English Dictionary*를 많이 참고하였다.

(5) 영미어 차이의 철저한 구명(究明) 철자(綴字)에 있어서는 주로 미어(美語)를 중심으로 하였으나 역어에서는 그 때마다 미식(美式)과 영식(英式)의 차이를 철저하게 명시하였다.

(6) 어떤 동사가 취하게 될 목적어의 명시

(7) 관사 용법의 철저한 명시

(8) 어떤 동사가 취하게 될 전치사와 그 목적어의 명시

(9) 참고사항 · 어법(語法) · 주의 사항의 해설 문법 · 어법 · 용법상 영어를 배우거나 실지로 사용하는 데, 꼭 알아야 할 사항, 틀리기 쉬운 사항, 주의해야 할 사항은 수시로 ★로 묶어 해설함으로써, 영어 지식을 높이도록 하였다.

(10) 실용적인 부록(附錄) 영작문에 유용한 기본 문형(基本文型)을 비롯하여, 일기 쓰기 · 편지 쓰기 · 전보문 쓰기 등 실무에 필요한 지식을 다방면으로 수집하여 수록하였다.

위와 같은 면밀하고 다양한 편집 방침 아래 엮어진 『엣센스 韓英辭典』은, 본래의 의도를 벗어나, 가히 대사전에도 필적할 만한 방대한 것이 되었다. 이것이 이용자 여러분의 학습 · 실무에 크게 이바지할 것으로 기대한다. 다만, 뜻하지 않게 남은 미비하고 미흡한 점은, 앞으로 이 사전을 쓰는 이들의 끊임없는 편달(鞭撻)에 따라서 더욱 훌륭하고 완전한 사전으로 키워 나갈 것을 다짐하는 바이다.

끝으로 이 사전을 엮어 나가면서, 난관에 부닥칠 적마다 수시로 협조를 의뢰했을 때, 기꺼이 귀중한 자료를 제공해 주신 여러 관공서 · 군 기관 · 언론 기관 · 학계 · 업계 등의 관계자 제위께 지면으로나마 심심한 감사를 드린다.

1972년 10월

편 자 씀

# 일 러 두 기

## 1. 표 제 어

(1) 자 체(字體) 표제어는 고딕체의 활자로 표시하였으며 그것이 한자어(漢字語)인 경우에는 그 한자를 병기하였다.

보기 : **참새, 참모(參謀).**

(2) 배열 순서

(a) 표제어의 배열은 가나다 순(順)으로 하였다.

(b) 동음 이의어는 우리말, 한자어, 외래어, 부사, 접두어, 접미어 등의 순으로 하였다.

보기 : ㉠ **공**[1], **공(工)**, **공(公)**, **공**[2].

㉡ **당(黨)**, **당-(當)**, **-당(當)**.

(c) 우리말이나 외래어 중 글자와 음이 같은 말에는 그 말 오른편 어깨에 각각 1, 2, 3…의 차례를 매겨 딴 낱말에서 참조시킬 때 편리를 도모했다.

보기 : ㉠ **고비**[1], **고비**[2], **고비**[3].

㉡ **마**[1], **마**[2], **마**[3], **마(麻)**, **마(馬)**.

(3) 철 자(綴字) 표제어의 철자는 1988년 문교부 고시의 '한글 맞춤법'과 '표준어 규정' 및 1990년 문화부 고시의 '표준어 모음'에 따랐다.

(4) 접두어·접미어 표제어 중 접두어·접미어에는 그 앞뒤에 '-'을 붙여 주었다.

보기 : **준-(準)**, **-가(家)**.

(5) 표제어 중 일부가 한자어이고 일부가 우리말인 경우에는 '—'를 넣어 한자와 병기하였다.

보기 : **냉가슴(冷—)**, **달력(—曆)**.

## 2. 본 문

(1) 어의(語義)의 분류

(a) 한 표제어가 몇 가지 다른 말뜻을 가지고 있는 경우에 이것을 ①, ②, ③… 등의 번호로 분류하였다.

보기 : **나물** ①《먹는 풀》herbs; ....... ②《무친 것》cooked potherbs; .......

(b) 말뜻이 ①,②,③… 등으로 분류된 것을 다시 세분할 필요가 있을 경우에는 (***a***), (***b***), (***c***)… 등으로 갈라 놓았다.

보기 : ㉠ **-게** ① ……. ② (***a***) 《(…하게) 되다, 하다, 만들다》 into being 〔*do*ing〕; ....... (***b***) 《하게 하다》 causing 〔making, getting, letting〕 《it》 to happen. ...... (***c***) 《…되다》 turning out 〔getting to be, coming to pass, happening〕 so that...; ....... ③ …….

㉡ **차다**[2] ① 《가득 차다》 (***a***) 《사물이》 fill; become full 《of》; ....... (***b***) 《달이》 wax.

(c) 어의를 분류함에 있어 그 내용이 복잡하지 않을 때에는 ①,②,③… 등을 쓰지 않고 다만 《 》로 구분한 경우도 있다.

보기 : **왕자(王者)** 《임금》 a king; a monarch; 《통치자》 a sovereign; a ruler; 《경기의》 a champion.

(2) 본문 중에 있는 ～하다는 표제어의 형용사꼴이나 동사꼴을 나타낸 것이다.

보기 : ㉠ 동사꼴 **수정(修正)**……. ～하다 amend; revise; .......

㉡ 형용사꼴 **수상(殊常)**……. ～하다〔스럽다, 쩍다〕 (be) suspicious; doubtful-looking; .......

(3) 역　어(譯語)

(a) 역어는 현대 영어를 표준으로 하였으며 필요에 따라 구어나 속어 등을 아울러 보였다.

보기 : ㉠ 고리(高利) high interest; a high rate of interest; …….

◉ ～대금 moneylending; usury: ～ 대금업 usury / ～ 대금업자 a usurer; moneylender; a loan shark 《미구어》 …….

㉡ 총각(總角) an unmarried man; a bachelor; a celibate; a bach 《미속어》.

(b) 용례의 순서는 원칙적으로 그 표제어의 형용사구 · 절, 명사구 · 절, 부사구 · 절, 문장의 순으로 배열했다.

(c) 역어가 미국, 영국의 어느 한 쪽에서만 쓰이는 경우에는, 《미》, 《영》과 같이 표시하였다.

보기 : 화물(貨物) 《운송화물》 freight 《미》; goods 《영》; …….

(d) 역어에 대하여 특정의 연결 관계를 보이는 관계어는 《 》로 싸서 보였다. 특히 기본적 또는 중요 표제어의 역어에는 그 수식어, 목적어, 주어, 술어, 관련 전치사 따위로 될 수 있는 대표적인 것을 열기하여 collocation의 이해를 돕게 했다.

보기 : ㉠ 좋아하다 ① 《기호》 like; 《사랑》 love; be fond 《of》; …… ; 《선택》 prefer 《*a thing*》 to 《another》; 《주로 부정문, 의문문에》 care 《for *something*, to *do*》. ② …….

㉡ 참획(參劃)……. ～하다 participate 〔have a hand〕 《in》; take part 《in》.

(e) 표제어가 형용사인 경우에는 (be)를 역어 앞에 붙임으로써 형용사임을 밝혔다. 다만, 우리말 품사는 형용사이나 영어로는 동사로 밖에 새길 수 없는 것은 동사를 역어로 했다. 또한 서술적으로 쓰이는 경우에는 괄호 없이 be를 달아 주었다.

보기 : ㉠ 싱겁다 ① 《간이》 be not properly salted; 《맛이 없다》 (be) flat; tasteless; insipid ……. ② 《언행이》 (be) flat; dull; pointless; tedious; …….

㉡ 싱숭생숭하다 scatter; wander; (be) distracted.

(f) 불가산 명사(uncountable noun)에는 관사를 붙이지 않았고, 역어가 가산 명사(countable noun)일 때에는 복수형을 제외하고는 부정관사를 달았다. 또한 가산 또는 불가산 양쪽으로 쓰이는 명사는 부정관사를 ( ) 안에 기입하였다. 또 언제나 정관사를 필요로 하는 말에는 the를 붙여 보였다.

보기 : ㉠ 노작(勞作) 《일》 a hard work; a job involving much labor; 《작품》 the product of hard work.

㉡ 참관(參觀) a visit; inspection; 《입회》 witnessing.

㉢ 문호(門戶) the door.

㉣ 간청(懇請) …; an earnest request; (an) entreaty; ….

(g) 원래 하이픈이 붙는 단어가 줄 끝에 왔을 경우는 다음과 같이 보였다.

보기 : 막상막하(莫上莫下) ……. ¶ ～의 열전 a well=
matched contest; ……. 이 경우 같은 줄에 있으면 a well-matched contest로 된다.

(h) 역어 앞에 《게시》, 《표시》 따위를 붙여 그 역어의 용도를 보였다.

보기 : ㉠ 구인(求人) a job offer; an offer of a situation; 《게시》 "Help Wanted".

㉡ 등기(登記) ……. ¶ ～필 《표시》 Registered. / …….

(4) 역어의 철자

(a) 표제어의 역어에 있어서 철자는 주로 미식을 보였다. 간혹 영식 철자를 ( ) 안에 표시한 것도 있다. 용례·복합어에서는 미국식만을 따랐다.

보기 : 노동(勞動) labo(u)r (=labor 《미》, labour 《영》).

판단(判斷) (a) judg(e)ment (=judgment 《미》; judgement 《영》).

(b) 〔 〕로 다음과 같이 나타낸 것도 있다.

〔 〕…미식은 괄호 밖의 것이고, 영식은 괄호안의 것이다. 또, 철자가 아주 다른 것도 표시했다.

보기 : ㉠ 섬유(纖維) a fiber 〔fibre 《영》〕 (=a fiber 《미》, a fibre 《영》).

㉡ 쟁기 a plow 〔plough 《영》〕 (=a plow 《미》, a plough 《영》).

(5) 용 례 중요 표제어의 역어의 활용과 이해를 돕기 위하여 용례를 보였다.

(a) 표제어의 용례는 '¶'표로 시작하였다.

보기 : 감흥(感興) fun; interest; inspiration. ¶ ～을 돋우다 arouse 〔stimulate, excite〕 *one's* interest《in》/ ～이 일어나다 get 〔become〕 interested《in》; be inspired 〔deeply stirred〕《by》/ …….

(b) 복합어에 있어서의 용례는 그 역어 뒤에 ':'표를 붙이고 보였다.

보기 : 거짓말 ……. ◉ ～탐지기 a lie detector; a polygraph: ～탐지기로 조사하다 give a lie (detector) test《to》; lie-test.

(c) 큰 항목 표제어의 용례 중, 표제어에 「～에, ～을, ～이」 따위가 붙는 용례가 여럿 있는 경우, 찾는 이의 편의를 위해 이를 고딕체로 한 다음 ':'표로 구분하고 동일 어구의 예문을 한 데 몰아서 표기한 것도 있다.

보기 : 말[5] ……. ②《담화》a talk; a speech; a conversation; a chat;《언사》what *one* says 〔said〕; …….

말에 : 말에 궁하다 be at a loss for words / 말에 가시가 있다 have a harsh tongue;《words》carry a sting / …….

말을 : 말을 하다 ⇨ 말하다 / 말을 걸다〔건네다〕 speak 〔call〕 to; address; accost; hail《*a person*》/ 말을 꺼내다 begin to talk; start a talk; broach a subject; break the ice / …….

말이 : 말이 거칠다 be rough of 〔in〕 speech; be rough-spoken / 말이 격해지다 argue with increasing vehemence; …….

(6) 이탤릭체 역어 중 다음과 같은 경우에는 이탤릭체 활자로 표시하였다.

(a) 미국·영국에서 보아 아직 완전히 영어화되었다고 볼 수 없는 외래어는 이탤릭체로 하고 뒤에 (F.), (L.) 따위를 붙여 그 어원을 밝혔다.

보기 : ㉠ 축포(祝砲) a cannon salute; ……; a *feu de joie* (F.).

㉡ 지양(止揚) 『철학』 sublation; *Aufheben* (G.).

㉢ 직권(職權) ……. ¶ ～에 의하여 in virtue of *one's* office; *ex officio* (L.).

(b) 지명·인명을 제외한 우리말로서 아직 영어화되지 않은 말을 로마자로 표기할 때

보기 : *paduk; yut; kisaeng*…….

(c) 동·식물의 학명을 표기할 때

보기 : ㉠ 참치 ……. ◉ ～방어 『어류』 *Elagatis bipinnulatus* (학명).

㉡ 더덕 『식물』 *Codonopsis lanceolata* (학명).

(d) 책 이름을 표기할 때

보기 : 국부(國富) ……. ◉ ～론《저서명》*The Wealth of Nations.*

(e) 역어 및 용례 중에서 주어 자신을 가리키는 one, 주어 이외의 사람을 가리키는 a person, 하나의 사물을 가리킬 경우의 a thing, 어떤 물건을 가리킬 경우의 something, 어떤 일을 가리킬 경우의 a matter, an affair 따위 부정대명사와 모든 동사를 대표하는 일반형 do.

보기 : ㉠ 언제까지 ……. ¶ ～고 as long as *one* likes; forever《미》; for ever《영》/ …….

㉡ 사다 ……. ¶ 사주다 buy 〔get〕《*something*》for《*a person*》/ …….

㉢ 모시다 ……. ¶ 부모를 ～ have *one's* parents with *one;* …….

㉣ 교묘(巧妙) ……. ¶ ～하게 처리하다 manage《*a matter*》cleverly / …….

㉤ 별명(別名) ……. ¶ ～으로 부르다 call《*a person*》by *his* nickname / …….

㉥ 능히(能―) ……. ¶ ～ 할〔해낼〕 수 있다 be easily able to *do;* …….

(7) 명사의 복수형 명사의 역어로서 그 복수형이 불규칙 변화를 하거나 틀리기 쉬운 것 따위는 (*pl.*) 안에 그 변화형을 표시하였고 복수형에 대한 단수형은 (*sing.*)로 표시하였다.

보기 : ㉠ 부록(附錄) an appendix (*pl.* -dixes, -dices) …….

㉡ 데이터 data (*sing.* -tum) …….

(8) 어 원

(a) 우리말에 들어와 있는 외래어는 가능한 한 그 어원을 다음과 같이 보였다.

보기 : ㉠ 카스텔라 a sponge cake. [< *pão de Castella* (Port.)]
㉡ 즈크 [< *doek* (D.)] duck; canvas.

(b) 생략어에 대한 어원 표시
보기 : ㉠ 카투사 KATUSA. [< *K*orean *A*ugmentation *T*roops to the *U*nited *S*tates *A*rmy]
㉡ 티엔티 T.N.T.; TNT. [< *tri**ni*tro*t*oluene]

(9) 복합어
(a) 복합어는 원칙적으로 그 기본어의 용례 다음에 고딕체 활자로 넣었고 '◉' 표로 시작했다.
(b) 표제어에 해당되는 부분은 '～' 표로 간략화하였다.
(c) 복합어의 배열은 '표제어+명사', '명사+표제어', '명사+표제어+명사'의 유형의 순서로 각기 가나다순으로 하였다.
보기 : 개발(開發) ……. ◉ ～계획 a development project 〔program, plan〕. ～교육 developmental education. 경제～ economic development 〔exploitation〕. 유엔～계획 the United Nations Development Plan (생략 UNDP).

## 3. 기호의 용법

(1) ～의 용법
표제어를 대신한다.
보기 : ㉠ 감식(鑑識) ……. ～하다(=감식하다).
㉡ 고치다 ……. ¶ 기계를 ～ (=기계를 고치다).
㉢ 고체(固體) ……. ◉ ～연료 (=고체 연료).
단, 외자로 된 표제어와 접두어, 접미어 따위는 그대로 다 써 주었다.

(2) ( )의 용법
(a) 한자를 병기할 때
보기 : 공해(公害).
(b) 그 부분이 생략될 수 있음을 나타낸다.
보기 : 낮잡다 ……. ¶ 아주 낮잡아도 at the lowest estimate; on a conservative basis (of appraisement) / …….
(c) 역어의 약자 또는 기호를 표시할 때
보기 : ㉠ 공배수(公倍數) ……. ◉ 최소～ the least common multiple (생략 L.C.M.).
㉡ 동(銅) copper (기호 Cu).
(d) 역어에서 영어나 우리말에 대한 설명이 필요할 때
보기 : ㉠ 오미(五味) the Five Tastes (*i.e.* sour, bitter, pungent, sweet, salty).
㉡ 근(斤) a *kŭn* (=600 g).
(e) 외래어가 어느 나라 말인가를 보이는 데 썼다.
보기 : ㉠ 대리(代理) ……. ◉ ～공사(公使) a *chargé d'affaires* (F.).
㉡ 좌선(坐禪) 〖불교〗 ……; *Dhyāna Pāramitā* (Sans.).
(f) 표제어에 대한 말뜻을《 》속에 보이고 또한 보충 설명이 필요할 때
보기 : 각(角) ① 《뿔》 a horn; an antler (사슴의); a feeler (촉각). ② …….

(3) 〔 〕의 용법
(a) 그 부분이 대체될 수 있음을 표시할 때
보기 : ㉠ 내리깎다 《값을》 knock 〔beat〕 down the price.
{ =knock down the price.
{ =beat down the price.
㉡ 강매(強賣) ……. ～하다 force 〔press〕 《*a person*》 to buy 《*a thing*》.
{ =force 《*a person*》 to buy 《*a thing*》.
{ =press 《*a person*》 to buy 《*a thing*》.
(b) 구·절·문장 안에서 〔 〕 괄호가 사용되었을 때, 어느 것을 대체하는 것인지 혼란을 줄만한

것에는「표를 사용하여 그 한계를 명백히 하였다.

보기 : 감독(監督) ……. ～하다 …;「be in charge 〔take charge〕 of.

{ =be in charge of.
{ =take charge of.

(4) [ ]의 용법

(a) 표제어나 역어가 특히 그 품사 표시를 필요로 할 때 또는 앞뒤 역어의 총칭을 나타낼 때

보기 : ㉠ 에[1] [감탄사] well; well now; let me see; uh.

㉡ 각자(各自) each 〔every〕 one; every individual; [부사적] each; individually; .......

㉢ 멍석 a straw mat; [총칭] straw matting.

(b) 필요에 따라 《 》에 앞서 대전제를 표시했다.

보기 : 몇 [의문문에서] 《얼마나》 how many 《days》 (수); how much (양·금액); how far (거리); how long (시일); at what time (시간); how old (연령); 《다소》 some; several.

(c) 형용사적 표제어의 역어가 서술적으로 표현되거나 기타 문법적·어법적 지시가 필요할 때.

보기 : ㉠ 면구스럽다, 면구하다(面灸—) (be) shamefaced; abashed; [서술적] feel awkward .......

㉡ 보증(保證) ……. ¶～할 수 없다 [사람이 주어] be not sure of; cannot vouch for; [사물이 주어] be unwarrantable / .......

(d) 어원(語源)을 표시할 때 (2의 (8) 어원 참조).

(5) 《 》의 용법

표제어의 뜻을 설명할 때

보기 : ㉠ 기화(奇貨) ① 《진품》 a rare treasure; a rarity; .......

② 《좋은 기회》 a rare 〔good〕 opportunity.

㉡ 다래 ① 《다래나무 열매》 fruit of the *Actinidia arguta.*

② 《목화의》 a cotton boll.

(6) 《 》의 용법

(a) 문법상, 어법상의 관계를 보이기 위해 관련 보충어를 기입할 때

보기 : ㉠ 문초(問招) ……. ～하다 question 《a criminal》; .......

㉡ 각성(覺醒) ……. ～하다 《무지에서》 awake 《from, to》; wake up 《to》; .......

㉢ 내항(來航) ……. ～하다 《a ship》 come on a visit.

㉣ 초사(焦思) ……. ～하다 be impatient 《to *do*》; .......

㉤ 상기(想起) ……. ¶ ～시키다 remind 《*a person* of *a matter*》; .......

㉥ 중독(中毒) ……. ◉ ～증상 《show》 toxic symptoms.

{ =～ 증상 toxic symptoms.
{ =～ 증상을 나타내다 show toxic symptoms.

(b) 용법상의 참고 사항을 기입할 때

보기 : ㉠ 감옥(監獄) a prison; a jail 《미》; a gaol 《영》.

주의 : 《미》, 《영》, 《속어》 따위의 위치는 그에 해당하는 역어가 하나일 때에는 역어 뒤에, 두 개 이상일 때에는 역어 앞에 위치하게 했다.

㉡ 아니 ……. ¶ ～ 땐 굴뚝에 연기날까 《속담》 Where there is smoke, there is fire. *or* (There is) no smoke without fire.

(c) 여러 역어 가운데의 어떤 생략된 말이 외래어이어서 그 원말을 보일 때

보기 : 주의(注意) ……. ◉ ～사항 matters that demand special attention; N.B. 《*nota bene* (L.)》.

(7) 〖 〗의 용법

학술어 기타 전문 용어임을 나타낼 때

보기 : 고슴도치 〖동물〗 a hedgehog; a porcupine.

(8) ⇨의 용법

(a) 어감(語感)상 큰말과 작은말, 센말과 여린말, 준말과 본디말 등에 붙여 '참조하라'의 뜻을 나타낸다.

보기 : 가무스름하다 ⇨ 거무스름하다.

(b) 참고할 표제어를 표시할 때

보기 : ㉠ 담대하다(膽大—) ⇨ 대담(大膽).

㉡ 내홍(內訌) an internal strife 〔trouble〕; domestic discord. ⇨ 내분(內紛).

(9) =의 용법

동의어임을 표시하여 그 쪽으로 참조시켰음을 보일 때

보기 : ㉠ 단합(團合) = 단결(團結).

㉡ 나변(那邊) ① = 거기. ② …….

(10) ★의 용법

앞에 나온 역어의 어법, 문법에 관한 지식 또는 영어 학습에 필요한 사항과 틀리기 쉬운 문법 사항을 해설했다.

보기 : 만일(萬一) ① …….

② …….

(*a*) [현재 · 장래에 관해서의 바람 · 가정] 《직설법 현재 또는 가정법 현재를 써서》 ¶ ~ 괜찮으시다면 if you 「like 〔don't mind〕/ ~ 내일 비가 오면 나는 안 갑니다 If it rains 〔rain〕 tomorrow, I will not go there. (★ 조건절 속에서는 미래형 대신 현재형이 쓰이므로 If it rains...로 하는 것이 보통임) / ~ 그 소문이 사실이라면 신문이 보도할 테지 If the rumor is true, the papers will report it. (★ 구어에서는 직설법 현재로 나타내는 것이 보통임).

★ *a*) *if*-clause 안에서는 단순미래를 보이는 will, shall은 생략되지만, 의지미래의 will은 남김 : If you *will* cook the dinner, I'll wash the dishes. 「당신이 음식을 만들면 나는 접시를 닦겠다」. *b*) 습관적인 일을 말할 때에는 주절 속에도 현재 시제가 쓰임 : If he has plenty of time, he usually *does* very well in his exams. 「시간이 충분하면 대개 그는 시험을 잘 친다」.

(11) ¶ 의 용법

용례가 시작됨을 가리킨다.

보기 : 갈채(喝采) ……. ¶ 우레와 같은 ~ a storm 〔thunder〕 of applause; ......

(12) ◉의 용법

복합어가 시작됨을 가리킨다.

보기 : 천하(天下) ……. ◉ ~명창 a great 〔an excellent〕 singer in the world. ~일색 a woman of matchless beauty.

(13) / 의 용법

표제어 · 복합어의 용례가 둘 이상일 때 그 사이를 구분하였다.

보기 : ㉠ 공적(功績) ……. ¶ ~ 있는 사람 a man of merit / 과학상의 ~ scientific achievements / .......

㉡ 결정(決定) ……. ◉ ~권 the decisive power; (the) authority to decide 《*a matter*》; the say 《in *a matter*》 《구어》: ~권을 쥐다 have the decisive power / 대표자에게 ~권을 주다 delegate 「authority 〔the say〕 in the matter to the representative / .......

(14) ①, ②, ③…의 용법

참조 표제어의 역어의 해당 번호를 나타내며 그 쪽으로 참조시켰을 때

보기 : 치아(齒牙) the teeth. ⇨ 이[1] ①.

## 4. 전 문 어

모든 전문어는 알기 쉽도록 〖건축〗, 〖전기〗, 〖사회〗, 〖인쇄〗, 〖조류〗처럼 약기하지 않고 〖 〗 안에 그대로 모두 표기하였다. 대표적인 몇 개만을 아래에 열거한다.

〖고고학〗 考古學 〖그神〗 그리스神話 〖컴퓨터〗

『고생물』 古生物 『로神』 로마神話 『TV』
『고제도』 古制度 『역사』 『한의』

## 5. 약 어 표

| | | | | | | | |
|---|---|---|---|---|---|---|---|
| D. | Dutch | F. | French | G. | German | It. | Italian |
| L. | Latin | Port. | Portuguese | Russ. | Russian | Sans. | Sanskrit |
| 日 | Japanese | 中 | Chinese | 《고》 | 고어 | | |

## 국어의 로마자 표기법

문화관광부고시 제2000-8호, 2000. 7. 7.

### 제1장 표기의 기본 원칙

제1항 국어의 로마자 표기는 국어의 표준 발음법에 따라 적는 것을 원칙으로 한다.

제2항 로마자 이외의 부호는 되도록 사용하지 않는다.

### 제2장 표기 일람

제1항 모음은 다음 각 호와 같이 적는다.

1. 단모음

| ㅏ | ㅓ | ㅗ | ㅜ | ㅡ | ㅣ | ㅐ | ㅔ | ㅚ | ㅟ |
|---|---|---|---|---|---|---|---|---|---|
| a | eo | o | u | eu | i | ae | e | oe | wi |

2. 이중모음

| ㅑ | ㅕ | ㅛ | ㅠ | ㅒ | ㅖ | ㅘ | ㅙ | ㅝ | ㅞ | ㅢ |
|---|---|---|---|---|---|---|---|---|---|---|
| ya | yeo | yo | yu | yae | ye | wa | wae | wo | we | ui |

(붙임1) 'ㅢ'는 'ㅣ'로 소리 나더라도 'ui'로 적는다.

보기 광희문 Gwanghuimun

(붙임2) 장모음의 표기는 따로 하지 않는다.

제2항 자음은 다음 각 호와 같이 적는다.

1. 파열음

| ㄱ | ㄲ | ㅋ | ㄷ | ㄸ | ㅌ | ㅂ | ㅃ | ㅍ |
|---|---|---|---|---|---|---|---|---|
| g,k | kk | k | d,t | tt | t | b,p | pp | p |

2. 파찰음

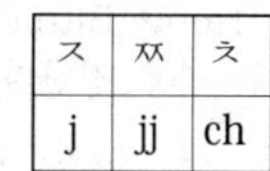

| ㅈ | ㅉ | ㅊ |
|---|---|---|
| j | jj | ch |

3. 마찰음

| ㅅ | ㅆ | ㅎ |
|---|---|---|
| s | ss | h |

4. 비음

| ㄴ | ㅁ | ㅇ |
|---|---|---|
| n | m | ng |

5. 유음

| ㄹ |
|---|
| r,l |

(붙임1) 'ㄱ, ㄷ, ㅂ'은 모음 앞에서는 'g, d, b'로, 자음 앞이나 어말에서는 'k, t, p'로 적는다.([ ]안의 발음에 따라 표기함.)

보기 구미 Gumi 영동 Yeongdong 백암 Baegam
옥천 Okcheon 합덕 Hapdeok 호법 Hobeop
월곶[월곧] Wolgot 벚꽃[벋꼳] beotkkot 한밭[한받] Hanbat

(붙임2) 'ㄹ'은 모음 앞에서는 'r'로, 자음 앞이나 어말에서는 'l'로 적는다. 단, 'ㄹㄹ'은 'll'로 적는다.

보기 구리 Guri 설악 Seorak 칠곡 Chilgok
임실 Imsil 울릉 Ulleung 대관령[대괄령] Daegwallyeong

### 제3장 표기상의 유의점

제1항 음운 변화가 일어날 때에는 변화의 결과에 따라 다음 각 호와 같이 적는다.

1. 자음 사이에서 동화 작용이 일어나는 경우

보기 백마[뱅마] Baengma 종로[종노] Jongno 왕십리[왕심니] Wangsimni
별내[별래] Byeollae 신문로[신문노] Sinmunno 신라[실라] Silla

2. 'ㄴ, ㄹ'이 덧나는 경우

보기 학여울[항녀울] Hangnyeoul 알약[알략] allyak

3. 구개음화가 되는 경우

보기 해돋이[해도지] haedoji 같이[가치] gachi 맞히다[마치다] machida

4. 'ㄱ, ㄷ, ㅂ, ㅈ'이 'ㅎ'과 합하여 거센소리로 소리 나는 경우

보기 좋고[조코] joko 놓다[노타] nota 잡혀[자펴] japyeo 낳지[나치] nachi

다만, 체언에서 'ㄱ, ㄷ, ㅂ' 뒤에 'ㅎ'이 따를 때에는 'ㅎ'을 밝혀 적는다.

보기 묵호 Mukho 집현전 Jiphyeonjeon

(붙임) 된소리되기는 표기에 반영하지 않는다.

보기 압구정 Apgujeong 낙동강 Nakdonggang 죽변 Jukbyeon
낙성대 Nakseongdae 합정 Hapjeong 팔당 Paldang
샛별 saetbyeol 울산 Ulsan

제2항 발음상 혼동의 우려가 있을 때에는 음절 사이에 붙임표(-)를 쓸 수 있다.

보기 중앙 Jung-ang 반구대 Ban-gudae
세운 Se-un 해운대 Hae-undae

제3항 고유 명사는 첫 글자를 대문자로 적는다.

보기 부산 Busan 세종 Sejong

제4항 인명은 성과 이름의 순서로 띄어 쓴다. 이름은 붙여 쓰는 것을 원칙으로 하되 음절 사이에 붙임표(-)를 쓰는 것을 허용한다.(( )안의 표기를 허용함.)

보기 민용하 Min Yongha (Min Yong-ha)
송나리 Song Nari (Song Na-ri)

(1) 이름에서 일어나는 음운 변화는 표기에 반영하지 않는다.

보기 한복남 Han Boknam (Han Bok-nam)
홍빛나 Hong Bitna (Hong Bit-na)

(2) 성의 표기는 따로 정한다.

제5항 '도, 시, 군, 구, 읍, 면, 리, 동'의 행정 구역 단위와 '가'는 각각 'do, si, gun, gu, eup, myeon, ri, dong, ga'로 적고, 그 앞에는 붙임표(-)를 넣는다. 붙임표(-) 앞뒤에서 일어나는 음운 변화는 표기에 반영하지 않는다.

보기 충청북도 Chungcheongbuk-do 제주도 Jeju-do
의정부시 Uijeongbu-si 양주군 Yangju-gun
도봉구 Dobong-gu 신창읍 Sinchang-eup
삼죽면 Samjuk-myeon 인왕리 Inwang-ri
당산동 Dangsan-dong 봉천1동 Bongcheon 1(il)-dong
종로 2가 Jongno 2(i)-ga 퇴계로 3가 Toegyero 3(sam)-ga

(붙임1) '시, 군, 읍'의 행정 구역 단위는 생략할 수 있다.

보기 청주시 Cheongju 함평군 Hampyeong 순창읍 Sunchang

제6항 자연 지물명, 문화재명, 인공 축조물명은 붙임표(-) 없이 붙여 쓴다.

보기 남산 Namsan 속리산 Songnisan
금강 Geumgang 독도 Dokdo
경복궁 Gyeongbokgung 무량수전 Muryangsujeon
연화교 Yeonhwagyo 극락전 Geungnakjeon
안압지 Anapji 남한산성 Namhansanseong
화랑대 Hwarangdae 불국사 Bulguksa

| | |
|---|---|
| 현충사 Hyeonchungsa | 독립문 Dongnimmun |
| 오죽헌 Ojukheon | 촉석루 Chokseongnu |
| 종묘 Jongmyo | 다보탑 Dabotap |

제7항 인명, 회사명, 단체명 등은 그동안 써 온 표기를 쓸 수 있다.

제8항 학술 연구 논문 등 특수 분야에서 한글 복원을 전제로 표기할 경우에는 한글 표기를 대상으로 적는다. 이때 글자 대응은 제2장을 따르되 'ㄱ, ㄷ, ㅂ, ㄹ'은 'g, d, b, l'로만 적는다. 음가 없는 'ㅇ'은 붙임표(-)로 표기하되 어두에서는 생략하는 것을 원칙으로 한다. 기타 분절의 필요가 있을 때에도 붙임표(-)를 쓴다.

| 보기 | | | |
|---|---|---|---|
| | 집 jib | 짚 jip | 밖 bakk |
| | 값 gabs | 붓꽃 buskkoch | 먹는 meogneun |
| | 독립 doglib | 문리 munli | 물엿 mul-yeos |
| | 굳이 gud-i | 좋다 johda | 가곡 gagog |
| | 조랑말 jolangmal | 없었습니다 eobs-eoss-seubnida | |

## 부 칙

① (시행일) 이 규정은 고시한 날부터 시행한다.

② (표지판 등에 대한 경과 조치) 이 표기법 시행 당시 종전의 표기법에 의하여 설치된 표지판(도로, 광고물, 문화재 등의 안내판)은 2005.12.31.까지 이 표기법을 따라야 한다.

③ (출판물 등에 대한 경과 조치) 이 표기법 시행 당시 종전의 표기법에 의하여 발간된 교과서 등 출판물은 2002.2.28.까지 이 표기법을 따라야 한다.

### 로마자 표기법 조견표

| 모음 | ㅏ | ㅑ | ㅓ | ㅕ | ㅗ | ㅛ | ㅜ | ㅠ | ㅡ | ㅣ | | ㅐ | ㅒ | ㅔ | ㅖ | ㅘ | ㅙ | ㅚ | ㅝ | ㅞ | ㅟ | ㅢ |
|---|---|---|---|---|---|---|---|---|---|---|---|---|---|---|---|---|---|---|---|---|---|---|
| | a | ya | eo | yeo | o | yo | u | yu | eu | i | | ae | yae | e | ye | wa | wae | oe | wo | we | wi | ui |
| 자음 | ㄱ | ㄴ | ㄷ | ㄹ | ㅁ | ㅂ | ㅅ | ㅇ | ㅈ | ㅊ | ㅋ | ㅌ | ㅍ | ㅎ | | ㄲ | ㄸ | ㅃ | ㅆ | ㅉ | | |
| | g,k | n | d,t | r,l | m | b,p | s | ng | j | ch | k | t | p | h | | kk | tt | pp | ss | jj | | |

### **McCune-Reischauer System** (Simplified Table)

| Initial / Final | ㅇ | ㄱ | ㄴ | ㄷ | ㄹ | ㅁ | ㅂ | ㅅ | ㅈ | ㅊ | ㅋ | ㅌ | ㅍ | ㅎ |
|---|---|---|---|---|---|---|---|---|---|---|---|---|---|---|
| | *[1] | K | N | T | (R) | M | P | S[2] | CH | CH' | K' | T' | P' | H |
| ㄱ K | G | KK | NGN | KT | NGN | NGM | KP | KS | KCH | KCH' | KK' | KT' | KP' | KH |
| ㄴ N | N | N'G | NN | ND | LL | NM | NB | NS | NJ | NCH' | NK' | NT' | NP' | NH |
| ㄹ L | R | LG | LL | LT | LL | LM | LB | LS | LCH | LCH' | LK' | LT' | LP' | RH |
| ㅁ M | M | MG | MN | MD | MN | MM | MB | MS | MJ | MCH' | MK' | MT' | MP' | MH |
| ㅂ P | B | PK | MN | PT | MN | MM | PP | PS | PCH | PCH' | PK' | PT' | PP' | PH |
| ㅇ NG | NG | NGG | NGN | NGD | NGN | NGM | NGB | NGS | NGJ | NGCH' | NGK' | NGT' | NGP' | NGH |

1. A consonant between two vowels is transcribed with its initial value except that ㄱ is G, ㄷ is D, ㅂ is B, and ㅈ is J.
2. 쉬 is romanized SHWI.

| ㅏ | ㅑ | ㅓ | ㅕ | ㅗ | ㅛ | ㅜ | ㅠ | ㅡ | ㅣ | ㅘ | ㅝ | ㅐ | ㅔ | ㅚ | ㅟ | ㅢ | ㅙ | ㅞ | ㅒ | ㅖ |
|---|---|---|---|---|---|---|---|---|---|---|---|---|---|---|---|---|---|---|---|---|
| a | ya | ŏ | yŏ | o | yo | u | yu | ŭ | i | wa | wŏ | ae | e | oe | wi | ŭi | wae | we | yae | ye |

**[참고] 박스 기사 색인**



**엣센스 한영 사전 부록**

## 차 례

ㄱ

**ㄱㄴ순**(一順) the order of the Korean alphabet. ⇨ 가나다.

**ㄱ자**(一字) the first letter of the Korean alphabet. ¶ ～꼴 an L shape / ～꼴의 L-shaped / ～집 an L-shaped house.

**가**[1] 〖음악〗 la. ¶ 가음 A / 가조(調) the tone A / 내림 가 A flat (기호 A♭) / 올림 가 A sharp (기호 A#).

**가**[2] ① 《끝》 the end; the limit; the bounds. ¶ 가없는 바다 the boundless sea / 그의 야망은 가없다 There are no bounds to his ambition.
② 《변두리·주변》 -side; the edge; the margin; the rim; the verge; brim; hem; border; the brink. ¶ 길가 the roadside / 바닷가 the seaside / 물가 the water's edge; the waterside / 연못가 the margin of a pond / 입가에 on *one's* lips / 바로 강가에 있는 집 a house by the very edge of the river / 창가에 앉다 sit by 〔at〕 a window / 벼랑가에 서다 stand on the edge of a precipice 〔cliff〕 / 난롯가에 둘러앉다 sit around the stove 〔fireplace〕.

**가**(可) 《성적》 F; fail; 《찬성》 approval; yes; yea; aye; 《옳음》 (fairly) good. ～하다 (be) right; good. ¶ 가(可) 30 부(否) 5, 30 ayes against 5 noes.

**가-**(假) ① 《임시의》 temporary; provisional; interim; tentative. ¶ 가계정 a suspense 〔temporary〕 account / 가시설 temporary facilities / 가처분 a provisional disposition. ② ＝가짜.

**-가**(家) ① 《사람》 a specialist; professional; an authority; a person noted for. ¶ 공상가 a daydreamer; a visionary / 낙천가 an optimist / 염세가 a pessimist / 사상가 a 《profound》 thinker; a man of thought / 경세가 a statesman; an administrator / 문학가 a literary man; a man of letters / 자본가 a capitalist. ② 《집안》 a family. ¶ 록펠러가 the Rockefeller family; the Rockefellers.

**-가**(哥) 《성씨 밑에》 ¶ 내 성은 남가요 My family name is Nam. / 그 늙은 홍가가 또 다녀갔다 That old Hong has been here again.

**-가**(街) ① 《거리》 a street. ¶ 월가 the Wall Street. ② 《구역》 a business district. ¶ 은행가 the banking area. ③ 《주소의》 a (numbered) section of a street 〔district〕. ¶ 동숭동 2가 Tongsung-dong 2-ga.

**-가**(歌) 《…노래》 song. ¶ 농부가 a farmer's song / 애국가 the national anthem 《of Korea》 / 자장가 a lullaby.

**-가**(價) 《…값》 price. ¶ 공정가 an official price / 최저가 the lowest price / 도매가 a wholesale price.

**가가대소**(呵呵大笑) ～하다 guffaw; laugh loudly 〔heartily〕; roar with laughter.

**가가호호**(家家戶戶) each 〔every〕 house; [부사적] house by house; from door to door; at every door. ¶ ～ 찾아다니다 〔방문하다〕 make a house-to-house visit / ～ 찾아다니며 돈을 거두다 make a house to house call for collecting money.

**가감**(加減) 《수학의》 addition and subtraction; 《증감》 increase and decrease; 《조절》 adjustment; moderation. ～하다 add and 〔or〕 subtract; increase and decrease; moderate; adjust the proportion.
◉ ～법 〖수학〗 method of addition and subtraction. ～승제 〖수학〗 addition, subtraction, multiplication and division; the four rules of arithmetic.

**가건물**(假建物) 《build》 a temporary building.

**가게** a store 《미》; a shop 《영》 (★ 미국에서는 통상 상품을 소매하는 상점을 store라고 함. shop은 소규모의 전문점, 이발소 따위 서비스업이나 대형 점포 안의 매장 등을 말할 때 씀. 영국에서는 소매점을 모두 shop이라 하고 stores라고 하면 백화점을 지칭함); 《매장》 a booth; a stand; 《노점》 a stall.
¶ ～ 보는 사람 a shopkeeper; a storekeeper; a shop assistant 《영》; a (sales) clerk 《미》 / 잘 되는 ～ a popular store / ～를 내다〔벌이다〕 open 〔start〕 a shop; keep a store / ～를 비우다 leave *one's* store / ～를 닫다 《저녁 때 문을》 close a shop; close the store; 《폐업》 wind up 〔give up, close〕 *one's* business; go out of business; shut 〔close〕 up the shop / ～를 열다 open the store; open business / ～를 보다

keep a shop 〔store〕; tend 〔mind〕 a shop / ～문이 벌써 닫혀 있었다 I found the doors of the store closed. / 저 ～는 비싸게 판다 They sell everything at a high price at that store. *or* The price at that store is very high. (★ The store… 처럼 가게를 주어로 하지 않음).
◉ ～채 a building with a shop in it; the shop part of a building. 가겟방 a shop room. 가겟집 a house used as a store. 모퉁이～ a corner shop. 술～ a liquor store; a wineshop.

**가격**(價格) price; cost; 《가치》 value; worth. ¶ ～이 오르다 the price rises 〔goes up〕; [물건이 주어] rise 〔advance, go up〕 in price / ～이 내리다 the price falls 〔goes down〕; [물건이 주어] fall 〔decline, go down〕 in price / ～이 비싸다 be high in price; be expensive; be high-priced / ～이 싸다 be low in price; be inexpensive; be low-priced / ～으로 치면 백만원이 된다 be worth 〔valued at〕 a million won / ～을 말하다 give 〔quote〕 a price / …에 ～을 매기다 put a price on… / 터무니없는～을 부르다 ask 〔demand, name〕 an extravagant price 《for》 / ～은 변동한다 Prices fluctuate 〔go up and down〕. / 우리는 ～을 내렸다〔올렸다〕 We lowered 〔raised〕 the price. / 이것은～이 얼마입니까 What's the price of this one? / 일용품의 ～이 급등하고 있다 Prices of daily necessities are soaring 〔skyrocketing〕. / ～은 예고 없이 변경될 수 있습니다 《게시》 Prices are subject to change without notice. / 이것은 내가 제의할 수 있는 최선의 ～이다 It's the best price that I can offer. / 그 ～으로는 살 수 없다 I can't buy it at that price.
◉ ～구조 price structure. ～동결 price freeze. ～변동 fluctuation of price: ～변동 조항 《노동 계약의》 an escalator clause. ～수준 a price level. ～안정 price stability. ～인상 a price advance. ～인하 price reductions 〔undercutting〕. ～조건 price terms. ～조작 price manipulation. ～조정 price adjustment. ～차 a price margin. ～책정 pricing. ～체계 a price structure 〔system〕. ～통제 price control. ～파괴 price destruction 〔slash〕. ～폭 the price range. ～표 a price list. ～협정 price cartel; agreement on prices. ～형성 price formation. 시판～ a selling price. 허가〔묵인〕～ the approved 〔permitted〕 price.

**가결**(可決) passage; decision; approval; adoption. ～하다 pass 〔adopt〕 《a bill》; carry 《a motion》; vote; approve. ¶ 원안대로 ～하다 pass a bill as drafted / 거수로 ～하다 decide 《on a bill》 by a show of hands / ～되다 be passed 〔carried〕; pass; be approved / 그 동의는〔결의안은〕 만장일치로 ～되었다 The motion 〔resolution〕 was 「carried 〔adopted〕 unanimously. / 예산안은 95대 80으로 ～되었다 The budget was passed by 95 to 80. / ～되었습니다 《의장의 말》 So ordered.

**가결의**(假決議) a temporary decision; a provisional resolution.

**가경**(佳景) fine scenery; a lovely 〔beautiful, charming, nice, picturesque〕 scene; a wonderful view.

**가경**(佳境) ① 《고비》 a pleasant 〔beautiful〕 spot; a delightful 〔an amusing, an interesting〕 part 《of a story》; a climax. ¶ 이야기가 점입 ～이다 Now we 「got into 〔have reached〕 the most interesting part of the story. ② ＝가경(佳景).

**가경지**(可耕地) arable 〔cultivable〕 land.

**가계**(家系) a family line; lineage; pedigree; genealogy; ancestry. ◉ ～도 a family tree; a genealogical chart; a pedigree (chart).

**가계**(家計) 《살림살이》 household 〔domestic〕 economy; a family budget; family finances; 《생계》 living; livelihood. ¶ ～가 넉넉지 못하다 be badly off; be in straitened 〔narrow〕 circumstances; be in need / ～에 보탬을 하다 add some to the family earnings / ～를 돕다 help the family budget / ～를 유지해 나가다 maintain domestic economy; 《생계》 earn a living; make *one's* livelihood / 우리 집 ～는 매우 궁하다 Our family finances are tight. / 어머니께서는 ～를 10% 줄이셨다 Mother cut the family budget 〔expenses〕 by ten percent. / 차 외판원으로 ～를 꾸려나가다 earn 〔gain, make〕 a living as a car salesman.
◉ ～부 a housekeeping 〔domestic〕 account book: ～부를 기록하다 keep household accounts. ～비 household expenses; housekeeping money. ～수표 a household check. ～조사 a family budget survey.

**가계약**(假契約) 《make》 a provisional 〔temporary〕 contract 〔agreement〕 《with》.

**가계정**(假計定) 《부기의》 a suspense 「account.

**가곡**(歌曲) 《곡조》 a melody; a tune; an air; an aria; 《노래》 a song. ¶ 옛 아일랜드 ~ old Irish melodies. ◉ ~집 a collection of songs. 소~ an arietta.

**가공**(加工) 《상품화의》 processing; 《대규모의》 manufacturing; 《화학·약품·열 따위로》 treatment; 《보석의》 cutting. ~하다 process; manufacture; treat; 《세공하다》 work upon 《a ring》. ¶ ~ 치즈 processed cheese / 이 천은 방수~이 되어 있다 This cloth is processed to make it waterproof.
◉ ~공장 a processing plant. ~무역 processing [improvement] trade. ~비 processing costs [charges]. ~산업 the processing industries. ~시설 processing facilities. ~식품 processed food (-stuffs). ~업자 a processor; a process manufacturer. ~원료 worked material. ~품 manufactured [processed] goods; finished goods [articles]. 보세~(무역) bonded processing (trade).

**가공**(可恐) ¶ ~할 fearful; fearsome; terrible; dreadful; formidable; terrifying / ~할 전쟁의 실태 the terrifying truth about [of] the war / 핵무기의 ~할 파괴력 the annihilating power of nuclear weapons.

**가공**(架空) building in the air; 《가설》 overhead construction. ~하다 build overhead; build a castle in the air. ¶ ~의[적인] 《허구·공상의》 fictitious; fictional; imaginary; 《공중의》 overhead; aerial / ~의 인물 a fictitious character 《in a novel》; an imaginary personage 《in a play》.
◉ ~명의(名義) a fictitious [false] name: ~명의의 은행 구좌 a bank account under a false name. ~삭도 an aerial cableway. ~선(線) an overhead [aerial] line (전신·전화의). ~철도 an elevated [aerial] railroad.

**가공사**(假工事) provisional construction work.

**가공의치**(架工義齒) a (dental) bridge; a bridgework.

**가관**(可觀) a sight; a spectacle; something to see. ¶ 그것 참 ~이다 It really is something to see. *or* It is a sight to see [to be seen]. / 그가 화내는 모습은 참 ~이었다 His face was quite a sight (to see) when he got mad.

**가교**(架橋) bridge-building; bridging. ~하다 build [construct] a bridge 《over, across》. ◉ ~공사 bridge construction; bridgework.

**가교**(假橋) a temporary [makeshift] bridge.

**가교사**(假校舍) a temporary schoolhouse.

**가구**(家口) a household; 《식구》 a family; 《집》 a house. ¶ 일곱 ~가 사는 동네 a village of seven families / 그 마을의 거의 모든 ~에서는 남자 한 사람이 군대에 가 있다 Almost every family in the village has a man in the army. ◉ ~수 the number of households [families]. ~주 a householder; the head of a family.

**가구**(家具) furniture; household goods [utensils, articles]; furnishings.

> (용법) **furniture** 식탁, 탁자, 옷장, 의자 따위의 이동 가능한 가구들을 뜻하는 집합명사. 복수형을 쓰지 않으며, 단수라도 관사 a를 붙이지 않는다. 한 개 또는 여러 개의 가구를 나타낼 때는 a piece [two pieces] of furniture로 한다. **furnishings** furniture 보다 넓은 의미를 가진 말로 방, 집안의 모든 비품, 가스, 수도설비 등도 포함된다.

¶ ~가 딸린[안 딸린] 방 a furnished [unfurnished] room / ~ 딸린 셋집 a furnished house to let [for rent] / ~ 5점 five pieces of furniture / ~ 한 세트 a set of furniture; a suite of furniture (색깔을 맞춘) / ~가 많다[적다] have much [little] furniture / 방에 ~를 들여놓다 furnish [upholster] a room; fit up a room / 이 책상은 내 방에서 가장 오래된 ~다 This desk is the oldest piece of furniture in my room.
◉ ~상 《점포》 a furniture [furnishing goods] store [shop]; 《사람》 a furniture dealer. ~장이 a furniture maker. 외제~ foreign furniture.

**가권**(家眷) *one's* family; *one's* dependents.

**가규**(家規) the rules [customs] of a family.

**가극**(歌劇) an opera; a lyric drama. ¶ ~을 좋아하다 be fond of opera / ~을 보러 가다 go to the opera; go to see an opera. ◉ ~가수 an opera singer. ~단 an opera company. ~대본 a libretto. ~작가 an opera composer. ~장 an opera house. 소~ an operetta.

**가금**(家禽) a domestic fowl; [총칭] poultry. ¶ ~을 치다 keep fowls [poultry] / ~을 치고 있다 The poultry are being fed.

**가급적**(可及的) as... as possible; as... as one can [may]. ¶ ~이면 if (it is) possible; if circumstances allow [admit] / ~ 빨리 as soon as possible; at the first opportunity; at *one's* earliest convenience; at the earliest possible opportunity / ~ 조속한 회답을 바랍니다 Please let me have your answer as soon as 「possible 〔you can〕. *or* It's required to answer at your earliest convenience (상업문 등에서).

**가긍스럽다**(可矜―) (be) pitiful; sad; sorry; miserable. ¶ 가긍스런 정상 miserable condition 〔plight〕 / 가긍스럽게 여기다 take 〔have〕 pity on 《*a person*》.

**가기**(佳期) ① 《좋은 때》 a favorable 〔good〕 season; an auspicious time. ② 《혼기》 marriageable age (of girls).

**가기**(家忌) (a period of ) family mourning; a service to the memory of *one's* parents 〔ancestors〕.

**가까스로** with difficulty; laboriously; barely; narrowly. ¶ ~ …하다 barely manage to *do* / ~ 연명해 가다 eke out a living; make a bare living; live from hand to mouth / 영어 시험에 ~ 합격하다 (just) scrape through the English examination / ~ 모면하다 make a narrow escape 《from》; escape narrowly 〔barely〕; escape by a hair's breadth / ~ 죽음에서 벗어나다 be snatched from the jaws of death / ~ 기차 시간에 대었다 I caught the train just in (the nick of) time. *or* I almost missed the train. *or* I barely had time to catch the train. / ~ 싸움을 말렸다 I had a hard time stopping the fight.

**가까워지다** ① 《때·거리》 approach; draw 〔get, come〕 near. ¶ 봄이 가까워지면(서) with the approach of spring / 종말에 ~ draw to 「a close 〔an end〕 / 육지에 ~ approach land; draw near the shore / 설날이 가까워진다〔가까워졌다〕 The New Year's Day 「is drawing near 〔is close at hand〕. ② 《관계가》 make friends with; become friendly 〔familiar〕 《with》; get 〔become〕 acquainted 《with》; become intimate 《with》 (★ intimate란 단어는 「이성과 성교섭을 할 정도로 가깝다」란 뜻이 있으므로 사용시 주의를 요함). ¶ 얼마 안 되어 둘 사이는 매우 가까워졌다 They soon became familiar with each other. / 우리 사이는 더욱 가까워졌다 Our relations have grown 〔gained〕 in intimacy.

**가까이** ① 《시간》 shortly. ¶ 정오 ~ toward noon / 그는 간밤에 11시 ~ 되어 돌아왔다 He came home shortly before eleven last night. ② 《거리》 near 《to, by》; in the neighborhood; close 《to, by》. ¶ 우리 집 ~ 교회가 있다 There is a church near my house. / 바로 ~에서 희미한 소리가 들렸다 There was a faint sound close by 〔nearby〕. / 위험! 가까이 오지 마시오 《게시》 Danger! Keep away! ③ 《거의》 nearly; almost; about; approximately. ¶ 천 명 ~ nearly a thousand people / 한 백 리 ~ about a hundred miles / 이것은 만 원 ~ 들었다 This cost me almost 〔a little less than〕 a ten thousand won. / 어머니가 돌아가신 지 5년 ~ 된다 It is almost 〔nearly〕 five years since my mother died. / 우리는 30년 ~ 이곳에서 살아왔다 We've lived here for nearly 30 years.

**가까이하다** ① 《친하게 지내다》 make *one's* acquaintance; associate 〔keep company〕 with 《*a person*》; make friends with; approach 《to》. ¶ 가까이하기 쉬운 〔어려운〕 여자 a woman who is easy 〔hard〕 to get along with / 그는 여자를 가까이하지 않는다 He 「doesn't associate with 〔keeps aloof from〕 women. / 나쁜 친구를 가까이하지 않다 keep bad company at a distance; avoid bad companions / 그런 나쁜 사람과는 가까이 하지 마라 Keep away from such bad company. / 가까이하는 친구를 보면 그 사람의 인품을 알 수 있다 A man is known by the company he keeps. ② 《즐기다》 ¶ 책을 ~ enjoy reading books; spend lots of time reading books / 자연을 ~ commune with nature / 술을 가까이하게 되다 take to drink 〔drinking〕.

**가깝다** ① 《거리가》 (be) near; close; 《장소가》 near 〔close〕 by; not far off 〔away〕; (close) at hand. ¶ 가까운 집 a nearby house; a house close by / 성당은 이곳에서 ~ The church is 「not far 〔just a little way〕 from here. / 우체국은 이 길로 가는 것이 ~ This is a 「nearer road 〔short cut〕 to the post office. / 행운은 흔히 가까운 데 있다, 꼭 멀리서 찾을 필요는 없다 Luck often lies at your very door—you need not travel far to find it.

② 《시간이》 (be) near (at hand); immediate; early; soon. ¶ 가까운 장래에 in the near future; at an early date; before long / 벌써 자정이 ~ It's nearly 〔almost〕 midnight. / 크리스마스가 ~ Christmas is 「near at hand 〔just around the corner〕.

③ 《사이·관계 등이》 (be) close 《to》; near; akin to; friendly. ¶ 가까운 친척 a near relative / 가까운 친구 a good 〔close, best〕 friend; a bosom buddy /

가깝게 지내다 be on the friendly terms《with》; be friends with (★ 이때의 friends는 항상 복수형) / 먼 사촌보다 가까운 이웃이 낫다 《속담》 A good neighbor is better than a brother far off. / 이제까지 꽤 여러 해 동안 한국과 일본은 '가깝고도 먼 나라'라는 관계에 있다고 이야기되어 왔다 For years now Korea and Japan have been said to have "close yet distant" relations.
④ 《거의 같은》 (be) nearly; almost; close to; border 〔verge〕 on; approach; resemble; be allied to; be in the neighborhood 《of》. ¶ 무모에 가까운 용기 courage verging on foolhardiness / 나이 육십에 ~ be close to sixty years old / 완전에 ~ be almost perfect / 총비용은 백만 원에 ~ The total expense is in the neighborhood of one million won. / 그의 사상은 허무주의에 ~ His thought verges on nihilism. / 원숭이는 사람에 ~ The ape is closely allied 〔related〕 to man. / 질투는 선망에 가까운 감정이다 Jealousy is a feeling similar to envy. / 그의 행동은 야만에 ~ His conduct borders on barbarism. / 그 일은 완성에 ~ The work is near completion.

**가꾸다** ① 《식물 따위를》 cultivate; raise; grow; rear. ¶ 야채를 ~ raise 〔grow〕 vegetables. ② 《치장》 dress (*oneself*) up; 《얼굴을》 make *oneself* up; 《장신구로》 adorn; 《방 따위를》 decorate. ¶ 외양을 ~ dress up; deck up; adorn *oneself*. ③ 《손질》 care for; take care of; tend. ¶ 잘 가꾼 정원 a well-kept 〔=tended〕 garden.

**가끔** ① 《종종》 occasionally; at times; sometimes; from time to time; now and then; between times. ¶ ~ 들르다 drop in from time to time. ② 《이따금》 once in a while; at long 〔rare〕 intervals; on rare occasions. ¶ 그는 ~ 오지 자주는 오지 않는다 He comes here once in a while but not often. / 나는 ~ 그로부터 소식을 듣는다 I hear from him once in a while. ③ 《자주》 often; many 〔several〕 times; frequently; repeatedly; time after time; again and again; every so often 《미》. ¶ 작년에는 ~ 큰 화재가 있었다 We had frequent big fires last year. / 요즘 그를 ~ 만납니다 I see quite a lot of him these days. / 너희들은 ~ 만나느냐 Do you see much of each other?

**가나** 《서아프리카의 독립국》 Ghana; Gana. ¶ ~의 Ghanaian. ◉ ~사람 a Ghanaian.

**가나다** 《한글》 the Korean alphabet 〔syllabary〕; 《초보》 the ABC 《of》; the rudiments 《of》. ¶ ~순으로 in Korean alphabetical order / ~순으로 하다 alphabetize; arrange in alphabetical order; file alphabetically.

**가나오나** everywhere you turn; making no difference; always; all the time; constantly; continually. ¶ 그는 ~ 말썽이다 He makes trouble wherever he may be. *or* He is a constant troublemaker.

**가난** poverty; want; indigence (궁핍); penury (빈궁); destitution (극빈); 《부족·결핍》 a dearth; scarcity. ~하다 (be) poor; needy; poverty-stricken; destitute; impecunious; indigent; be in (dire) need; be in straitened circumstances; be badly off.
¶ ~한 사람 a poor person / ~해지다 become poor; be reduced to poverty / ~ 속에 죽다 die poor; die in want 〔poverty〕 / ~하게 살다 live in poverty 〔need, want〕; be in needy 〔straitened〕 circumstance; be badly off; eke out a scanty living / 찢어지게 ~하다 be extremely poor; be poverty=stricken; be as poor as a church=mouse / ~한 집에 태어나다 be born poor; be born of a poor family / ~한 집에 제사 돌아오듯 하다 seem to come round as often as the anniversary of a poor man's ancestors; come as often as the bill collectors / 모진 ~에 시달리다 suffer dire 〔extreme〕 poverty; be poverty-stricken / 그는 ~하게 자랐다 He was raised in poverty. / ~ 구제는 나라도 못한다 There is no remedy for poverty. / 우리는 언젠가 ~한 생활을 할지도 모른다 We may one day be in want. ◉ ~살이 living in poverty. 인재~ a dearth of talented men.

**가난들다** be short 《of》; lack; want; be in need of; suffer a dearth 〔shortage, scarcity, need〕 of. ¶ 우리는 인재에 가난들었다 We suffer a dearth of talented people.

**가난뱅이** a poor person; 《극빈자》 a pauper; [집합적] the poor (★ the poor는 복수동사를 취함); the indigent. ¶~ 쉴 새 없다 Poor men have no leisure.

**가납**(假納) a deposit; provisional payment 《of a tax》. ~하다 deposit; pay 《a tax》 provisionally. ◉ ~금 a deposit; a cover.

**가납**(嘉納) acceptance; approval; appreciation. ～하다 accept 《a present》 with pleasure; approve; appreciate.

**가납사니** 《수다꾼》 a chatterbox; 《말다툼꾼》 a quarrelsome person; 《입 가벼운 사람》 a glib speaker; a gasbag 《구어》. ¶ ～ 같다 be a chatterbox.

**가내**(家內) a family; a household; members of *one's* family. ¶ 온 ～ the whole family 〔household〕. ◉ ～공업 home 〔household, domestic〕 industry; home manufacturing. ～공장 a domestic factory. ～노동자 a family worker. ～문제 a family 〔household〕 affair.

**가냘프다** (be) slender; slim; thin; feeble; fragile. ¶ 가냘픈 사람 a slender person / 몸매가 가냘픈 여자 a woman with a slender figure / 가냘픈 목소리로 in a feeble voice / 가냘픈 여자 손으로 with the weak hands of a woman / 허리가 ～ have a slim waist.

**가년스럽다** (be) shabby.

**가누다** control; keep under control; handle; hold up; keep steady; keep 〔get〕 a grip on *oneself*. ¶ 정신을 ～ take 〔pick up〕 heart; collect *oneself*; collect *one's* senses / 몸을 가누지 못하다 lose *one's* bodily control; lose control of *one's* body / 그는 비틀거렸으나 곧 몸을 가누었다 He staggered but soon recovered himself. / 그는 몹시 취해서 몸을 가누지 못한다 He is so drunk he can't keep himself steady.

**가느다랗다** (be) very slender; very thin; very fine. ¶ 가느다란 팔〔손, 목〕 a slender arm 〔hand, neck〕 / 가느다란 목소리 a thin voice / 가느다란 실 a very fine thread 〔line〕 / 목이 ～ have a slender neck.

**가느스름하다** (be) rather slender 〔thin, fine〕.

**가는귀먹다** become somewhat hard of hearing; be a little deaf; lose some of *one's* hearing; get slightly deaf.

**가늘다** ① 《폭·굵기가》 (be) thin; slender; slim; fine; narrow (좁다). ¶ 가는 목〔팔〕 a slender neck 〔arm〕 / 가는 허리 a slim 〔slender〕 waist / 가는 모래 fine sand / 가는 실 a fine thread 〔string〕 / 가는 잎 a narrow leaf / 가늘어지다 become thin 〔slender〕; taper; slim / 끝이 점점 가늘어지다 taper off to the point / 가늘게 하다 make thin 〔slender〕; narrow; slenderize; slim down; taper / 눈을 가늘게 뜨고 보다 look with eyes half-shut; squint.

② 《목소리 따위가》 (be) thin; feeble; weak; faint. ¶ 가는 목소리로 말하다 speak in a thin 〔weak〕 voice.

③ 《촘촘하다》 (be) fine; close. ¶ 가는 모시 fine ramie fabric / 가는 체 a fine sieve.

④ 《흔들림이 약하다》 (be) slight. ¶ 그녀의 입술은 노여움으로 가늘게 떨고 있었다 Her lips were trembling slightly with anger.

**가늠** ① 《겨냥》 aim; sight. ～하다, ～보다 aim; sight; take aim 《at》. ¶ 총을 잘 ～해 쏘다 take a good aim and fire the gun / ～이 틀리다 aim badly / 표적을 신중히 ～하다 take careful aim at the target / 발사 전에 신중히 ～해라 Take a careful sight before firing.

② 《판단·어림》 good 〔studied〕 aim; discernment; sense of proportion. ～하다, ～보다 use *one's* sense of proportion on; watch; study; weigh. ¶ ～ 있는 사람 a man of good judgment; a good estimater; a studied guesser / ～을 잡을 수가 없다 have no idea 《of》; be unable to figure 《it》 out / 형세를 ～하다 watch the situation; see how the wind blows; see how things develop / 그 일이 언제 끝날지 아직 ～할 수 없다 The end of the task is not yet in sight. ◉ ～쇠 the bead; the foresight; the front sight. ～자 the sight(s); a gunsight.

**가능**(可能) possibility. ～하다 (be) possible; practicable; feasible; be within the realm of possibility.

¶ 실행 ～한 계획 a feasible 〔practicable, workable〕 plan / 실행 ～한 방법 a practical method / ～하다면 if possible; if I can; if convenient / ～한 한 as much 〔far〕 as possible; within the limits of the possibility / ～하게 하다 make 《*a matter*》 possible / 불가능을 ～케 하다 turn an impossibility into a possibility / 나는 그 일이 ～하다고 믿는다 I believe that it is possible. / ～한 범위 내에서 너를 돕겠다 I'll help you as far as possible. / 비용의 개략적인 계산이 ～하다 It is possible for us to make a rough estimate of the cost. (★ 사람을 주어로 하여, We are possible to make... 라고는 할 수 없음) / 이 지역은 아직 대대적인 개발이 ～한 곳이다 This area still has a lot of potential for development.

◉ ～법 『문법』 the potential mood.

**가능성**(可能性) possibility; 《잠재적인》 potentialities.

¶ 매상을 크게 올릴 ～이 있는 발명품 an invention with a big sales potential / ~이 있는 possible / (…할) ~이 있다〔크다, 없다, 거의 없다〕 there is some 〔every, no, little〕 possibility of *doing* 〔that…〕; there is some 〔good, no, little〕 chance of *doing* 〔that…〕 / ~이 충분히 있다 be quite within the realms of possibility / 전혀 ~이 없다 be absolutely impossible / (아무의) ~을 개발하다 develop *a person's* potential 〔potentialities〕 / 중국은 큰 ~을 가진 나라이다 China is a country with great potentialities 〔potential〕. / 사고가 일어날 수 있는 ~은 부정할 수 없다 We cannot deny the possibility of an accident. / 성공할 ~은 반반이다 There is an even chance of success. / 그가 회복할 ~은 전혀 없다 He has no chance 〔hope〕 of getting better.

**가다** ① 《…을 향해》 go; come; proceed; travel 《to…》; frequent 《*a place*》; attend 《school》; 《a road》 lead to 《the station》; leave for 《Busan》; be bound for 《Seoul》. (★ go는 현재의 장소에서 떠나는 것, come은 어떤 장소로의 접근을 뜻함. 따라서 「너의 집에 가다」는 상대를 중심으로 해서 I'll *come* to your house.가 됨. 보통 「상대에게로 가다」는 모두 come을 쓰며, go는 3인칭에서 씀: I'll go to his house.) ¶ 학교에 가는 지름길 a short cut leading to the school / 서울 가는 기차 a train for Seoul / 일본 가는 배 a ship bound for Japan / 문인들이 잘 가는 다방 a café frequented by writers / 미국에 ~ go over to America 〔the United States〕 / 시골에 ~ go out into the country / 걸어~ go on foot; walk / 지하철로 ~ go by subway / 말 타고 ~ go 〔travel〕 on horseback / 모임에 ~ attend 〔go to〕 a meeting / 오른쪽으로 ~ turn to the right / 곧바로 ~ go 「straight on 〔ahead〕 / 동대문까지 ~ go as far as Tongdaemun / 하루 40리 길을 ~ make 〔do〕 forty *ri* a day / 그 거리를 5시간에 ~ cover 〔travel, do〕 the distance in five hours / 2등으로 ~ travel 〔go〕 second (class) / 다리를 건너면 거기에 갈 수 있다 Cross 〔Go across〕 the bridge, and you will come to the place. / 이 길로 가면 역에 갑니다 This street leads 〔goes〕 to the station. / 나는 당신과 같은 방향으로 갑니다 I am going your way. / 다시는 그 놈 집에 안 간다 I shall never 「darken his door 〔visit him〕 again. / 저리 가거라 Get 〔Go〕 away! *or* Away 〔Be off, Get along〕 with you! *or* Be gone! / 걸어서 20분이면 간다 It's only twenty minutes' walk. / 가서 뵙겠습니다 I will come and see you. / 곧 갑니다 I am coming right away. / 시골 갔다 왔다 I have (just) been to the country. / 미국에 간 일이 있습니까 Have you ever been to the United States? / 그는 강으로 낚시를 갔다 He went fishing in the river. (★ He went fishing to the river.라고는 쓰지 않음. go fishing이 「낚시를 하다」라는 구(句)이며 「간다」는 뜻이 적기 때문임. 마찬가지로 I went boating on the lake.) / 그 도시까지는 열차로 2시간이면 갈 수 있다 You can get to the city in two hours by train.

② 《죽다》 die; pass away. ¶ 그는 가고 없다 He is no more. *or* He is dead and gone.

③ 《전깃불 따위가》 go out; be out. ¶ 전깃불이 갔다 The electric lights are out 〔have gone out〕.

④ 《없어지다》 vanish; disappear; go away. ¶ 옷의 때가 ~ dirt 「comes out of 〔comes off〕 clothes / 나물 맛이 ~ a vegetable dish loses its flavor / 맥주 맛이 ~ beer gets flat.

⑤ 《시간이》 pass; go by. ¶ 얼마 안 가서 before long / 시간이 감에 따라 as time passes / 이 달도 다 갔다 This month is up. / 세월이 물 흐르듯이 간다 Time flies. *or* The years speed on. / 겨울이 갔다 Winter is over 〔past, gone〕.

⑥ 《필요로 하다》 be required 〔needed〕; take; require; need. ¶ 그것은 손이 많이 가야 한다 It requires a great deal of work 〔care〕.

⑦ 《값이 나가다》 cost; be worth; weigh. ¶ 집이 1억 원은 간다 The house costs 〔is worth〕 one hundred million won. / 쌀 한 가마에 17만 원 간다 The market price of rice is 170,000 won a bag.

⑧ 《지탱하다》 wear; last; hold; keep; endure. ¶ 오래~ wear well; last 〔keep〕 long; be durable; stand long use (기계 등이) / 구두가 오래~ shoes wear well / 그 환자는 오래가지 못하겠다 The patient won't live long. / 이런 날씨가 얼마나 갈는지 모르겠다 I don't know how long this weather will hold 〔last, go on〕. / 그 건물은 앞으로 백 년은 더 갈 것이다 The building will stand another century.

⑨ 《짐작·이해가》 come about; have in mind. ¶ 이해가 가는 처사 an understandable 〔a comprehensible〕 measure / 짐작〔판단, 납득〕이 ~ come 「to form an idea 〔to draw a conclusion, to reach an appreciation〕 / 이해가 ~

be comprehensible 〔understandable〕/ 당신 시계를 누가 훔쳤는지 짐작이 갑니까 Have you any idea who stole your watch?

⑩《등급》 appear; come《in an order》. ¶ 첫째 ~ come first / 세계적으로 으뜸가는 단거리 선수 a sprinter who ranks among the best in the world.

⑪《…하러》 go to《*do*》. ¶ 산책(을) ~ go for a walk / 영화(를) 구경 ~ go to「a movie 〔the movies〕;《영》 go to the cinema 〔pictures〕.

⑫《기타》 ¶ 결국〔결말〕에 가서는 in the long run; in the end; at last; after all / 금이 ~ crack; have a crack; be cracked / 마음이 ~《물건에, 사람에게》 become fond of; take a fancy to; feel inclined toward / 손해가 ~《사람에게》 lose; suffer 〔sustain〕 a loss / 주름(살)이 ~ get creased; get wrinkled / 허물이 ~ get blemished / 줄이 ~ a line runs; have a line in 〔on〕 it / 그것으로 네게 손해 가는 일은 없다 You will lose nothing by it. / 그 때문에 그들의 우정에 금이 갔다 That「has impaired 〔caused a crack in〕 their friendship. / 일주일 이내로 통지가 갈 것이다 You'll receive a notice within a week.

**가다가** ①《때때로》 sometimes; once in a while; occasionally; on occasion; at intervals; off and on; (every) now and then. ¶ ~ 실수도 하다 sometimes make a mistake; make an occasional slip / ~ 아들과 테니스를 칠 때도 있다 I have an occasional game of tennis with my son. ②《도중에》 on *one's* way《to》; on the way; halfway; midway. ¶ ~ 되돌아오다 turn back halfway.

**가다귀** oak-brush firewood.

**가다듬다** set 〔put〕 in good order; order; arrange; tidy (up); make neat. ¶ 몸을 ~ straighten 〔tidy〕 *one's* clothes; make *oneself* presentable; spruce up / 정신을 ~ steady *one's* wits; brace *oneself* up / 목소리를 ~ clear *one's* throat; modulate *one's* voice / 기억을 가다듬어 내 질문에 대답해라 Refresh your memory and answer my questions. 「bonito.

**가다랑어**〖어류〗 a bonito; an oceanic

**가다루다**〖농업〗 plow a field down.

**가다리**〖농업〗 ~하다, ~맡다 plow paddy land for wages paid by the strip.

**가닥** a piece; a cut(ting); a strip; a strand; a fork (of a road). ¶ ~수 the number of strips 〔pieces〕/ 실 한 ~ a piece of string / 한 ~ 길 a fork of a road / 한 ~의 빛〔희망〕 a ray of light 〔hope〕/ 두 ~으로 꼰 실 two-ply thread / 세 ~으로 꼰 밧줄 a rope of three strands. 「malleable.

**가단성**(可鍛性) malleability. ¶ ~이 있는

**가단(주)철**(可鍛(鑄)鐵) malleable iron.

**가담**(加擔) ①《원조》 help; aid; assistance; support;《편듦》 siding with. ~하다《…에》 help; assist; aid; support; take sides with; side with; cast *one's* lot in with. ¶ 그는 어느 쪽에도 ~하지 않는다 He is neutral. *or* He is (sitting) on the fence. / 이러한 계획에는 ~ 못 하겠다 I can not「support 〔lend myself to〕 such a project.

② 《참여》 participation;《관계·공모》 conspiracy; complicity. ~하다 take part in; participate in; be involved in; be a party to; conspire with. ¶ 그는 이 음모에 ~했다 He was a party to the plot. / 그는 폭동에 ~한 혐의로 구속되었다 He was arrested on a charge of taking part in the riot.

◉ ~자 a conspirator;《공범자》 an accomplice.

**가당**(加糖) ¶ ~한 sweetened. ◉ ~분유 sugared powder 〔pulverized〕 milk. ~연유 sweetened condensed milk.

**가당찮다**(可當—)《부당하다》 (be) unjust; unfair; unreasonable; improper; unsuitable; unworthy《of》; be not right; be not justified;《지나치다》 (be) undue; excessive;《터무니없다》 (be) absurd; preposterous; outrageous;《대단하다》 (be) awful; unbearable. ¶ 가당찮은 요구 an excessive 〔preposterous〕 demand / 가당찮은 값 an outrageous 〔unreasonable〕 price; an absurd figure / 노파가 젊은 남자와 결혼하는 것은 ~ It is improper for an old woman to marry a young man. / 가당찮은 말을 마라 Don't talk nonsense.

**가대**(家垈) a homestead; a home and its site; a house and a lot.

**가댁질** a game something like tag. ~하다 play tag.

**가도**(家道)《가계》 family livelihood;《가규》 family customs 〔traditions, morality〕.

**가도**(街道) a highway; a thoroughfare; a road. ¶ 상승 ~를 달리다 gain 〔win〕 successive victories; be ever-victorious / 출세 ~를 달리다 march the royal road to success; cruise *one's* way up the social ladder. ◉ 경인~ the Kyŏng-In highway.

**가도관**(假導管)〖식물〗 a tracheid.

**가돌리늄** 〖화학〗 gadolinium.

**가동**(可動) ¶ ～의 movable; mobile. ◉ ～관절 〖해부〗 diarthrosis (*pl.* -ses). ～교 a movable bridge. ～댐 a movable dam. ～성 mobility; movability. ～장치 movable equipment.

**가동**(稼動) operation; work. ～하다 operate; run; put into operation. ¶ 완전 ～ full(-scale) operation / ～ 능력 the operating capacity / 주야 ～ around-the-clock 〔24-hour〕 operation / ～을 시작하다 start 〔come into〕 operation / ～중이다 be in operation; be at work / ～을 중단하다 stop operation / ～ 시간 the hours of operation. ◉ ～시설 available 〔working, operative〕 equipments. ～인구 the manpower; the work force: 추정 ～인구 the potential manpower; potential working labor. ～일수 the number of workdays 〔days worked, working days〕. ～중지 a shutdown 《of a factory》.

**가동거리다** kick (the legs); make (the legs) kick; squirm. ¶ 어린애 다리가 ～ the legs of a baby kick (in the air).

**가동률**(稼動率) the rate of operation; the working ratio; the capacity utilization rate. ¶ ～ 백 퍼센트이다 operate at a 100 percent capacity.

**가두**(街頭) a street. ¶ ～에서 on 〔in〕 the street / ～ 선전하다 propagandize on 〔in〕 the street / ～ 서명을 받다 collect signature on the street / 후보자가 ～에서 선거 연설을 하고 있었다 An election candidate was making a campaign speech on the street. ◉ ～검색 the on-the-street search 《of a criminal by the police》. ～녹음 a street-corner transcription 《unit》; 《라디오 프로그램의》 a "Man on the Street" interview. ～모금 a street fund raising; collecting contributions on the street: ～모금을 하다 collect contributions on the street. ～시위 《stage》 a street demonstration. ～연설 a wayside speech; soapbox oratory; a stump speech: ～연설가 a stump orator / ～연설을 하다 speak on a soapbox. ～인터뷰 a curbside interview.

**가두다** shut in 〔up〕; coop up; lock in 〔up〕; confine; throw 《*a person*》 into prison; imprison 《*a person*》; put 《*a person*》 behind the bars; 《우리에》 pen (up). ¶ 방안에 ～ confine 《*a person*》 to 〔in〕 a room; shut 《*a person*》 up in a room / 감방에 ～ put 《*a person*》 into a cell; put 《*a person*》 behind the bars.

**가두리** 《모자·그릇의》 a brim; 《둥근 것의》 a rim; 《천·옷 따위의》 a hem; a fringe; 《장식》 a frill. ◉ ～양식장 a fish-raising farm (in the river).

**가둥가둥** swaying *one's* hips.

**가둥거리다** sway *one's* hips.

**가드** a guard. ◉ ～레일 a guardrail.

**가득** full; to the full; to capacity. ¶ 사람을 ～ 태운 버스 a jampacked bus / 돈이 ～ 든 지갑 a purse filled with money / 가구를 ～ 실은 트럭 a truck heavily loaded with furniture / ～ 차다 be filled up; be full 《of》; be chock-full / 한 잔 ～ 붓다 fill a glass full 〔to the brim〕 / 방에는 사람들이 ～ 차 있었다 The room was packed 〔crammed〕 with people. / 장내를 ～ 메운 관객이 열광적으로 박수했다 The capacity audience applauded enthusiastically. / 나는 탱크에 물을 ～ 채웠다 I filled the tank with water. / 바구니에 사과가 ～ 담겨져 있다 The basket is full of apples.

**가득률**(稼得率) 《외화의》 a rate of foreign exchange earning.

**가득하다** (be) full 《of》; filled 《with》; brimful; be full to the brim; be chock-full; be full up. ¶ 가득해지다 become full; be filled up; be packed 《with》; be crammed 《with》 / 가득하게 하다 fill (up); make overflow; cram; pack / 앞날은 희망이 ～ The future is full of hope. / 그의 눈에 눈물이 가득하였다 His eyes were 「filled 〔brimming〕 with tears. / 그녀의 마음은 자식들의 행복을 비는 생각으로 가득했다 All her thoughts were occupied with the happiness of her children.

**가득히** full; to the full. ⇨ 가득.

**가등기**(假登記) provisional registration.

**가뜩이나** besides; moreover; furthermore; in addition (to that); what is worse 〔more〕; to make matters worse; worse still; on top of that…. ¶ ～ 곤란한데 to add to *one's* misery; to make matters worse / ～ 피로한데 또 일을 하란다 I am dog-tired and still, they want me to work. / ～ 더운데 어떻게 뜨거운 것을 먹겠나 I am already so hot, how can I eat hot food? / 날은 어두워졌는데 ～ 비까지 오고 있었다 The day was dark, and moreover it was raining. / 그녀는 예쁘지도 않은데 ～ 다리까지 전다 She is plain looking, and on top of that, she limps.

**가뜬하다** 《복장이》 (be) light; casual; 《몸

놀림이》(be) light; sprightly; nimble; agile; 《심신이》 feel light〔good〕; (be) lighthearted; relaxed. ¶ 가뜬한 동작 a nimble movement / 가뜬한 복장을 하다 be lightly dressed; wear a light 〔casual〕 suit / 마음이 ~ feel lighthearted 〔relieved〕/ 중책을 벗어나 마음이 가뜬해졌다 I was relieved of my heavy responsibility. / 그 약을 먹고 나니 몸이 가뜬해졌다 I am 〔feel〕 easy after taking that medicine.

**가뜬히** lightly; nimbly; with agility. ¶ ~ 차리다 be lightly dressed; wear a light suit / ~ 여행하다 travel light / ~ 들어올리다 lift 〔hold〕《*something*》 up without difficulty / 말은 냇물을 ~ 뛰어넘었다 The horse jumped clean over the brook.

**가라말** 〖동물〗 an all-black horse.

**가라사대** as 《a saint, a wiseman》 says.... ¶ 예수 ~ As Jesus says... / 성경에 ~ The Bible says....

**가라앉다** ① 《밑으로》 sink; go down; go to the bottom; settle down; descend; be submerged. ¶ 가라앉고 있는 배 a sinking vessel / 가라앉은 배 a sunken ship; a submerged boat / 깊이 ~ sink deep / 물 속으로 ~ sink 〔dip, be submerged〕 under water / 바다 밑으로 ~ sink 〔be sent〕 to the bottom (of the sea) / 배와 함께 ~ go down with the ship / 가라앉지 않게 해 두다 keep 《*a thing*》 afloat.
② 《잠잠해지다》 become quiet 〔calm, still〕 down; quiet down; grow still; 《풍파가》 go 〔die〕 down; subside; abate. ¶ 바람이 가라앉았다 The wind ⌈has died down 〔has blown itself out〕. / 폭풍은 곧 가라앉을 게다 The storm will soon blow over. / 폭동이 가라앉았다 The rebellion was put down. / 사태가 가라앉을 때까지 기다립시다 Let's wait until things cool off.
③ 《마음·성질이》 recover *one's* composure; restore the presence of mind; become calm; calm down. ¶ 흥분이 가라앉았다 The excitement has quieted down. / 그의 형식적인 사죄로는 나의 분이 쉽사리 가라앉지 않는다 His perfunctory apology is not enough to glut my ire. / 그 그림을 보면 마음이 가라앉는다 The picture has a calming effect upon my soul.
④ 《고통·부기 따위가》 abate; subside; go down; be quelled; be subdued; be put down. ¶ 부기가 ~ the swelling subsides 〔goes down〕/ 아픔이 ~ the pain stops 〔abates〕/ 종기가 ~a boil collapses 〔goes down〕/ 그의 열은 가라앉았다 The fever has left him. / 약을 먹었더니 통증이 가라앉았다 The medicine relieved me of the pain. *or* The medicine gave me relief.

**가라앉히다** ① 《물체를》 sink; send 《it》 to the bottom; make 《dregs》 settle. ¶ 배를 ~ sink a vessel; send a ship to the bottom.
② 《기분·마음 따위를》 calm 〔quiet〕 (down); soothe; pacify; compose; pacify; appease; 《아픔·고통을》 relieve; allay; soothe; subdue; alleviate; mitigate; 《진압하다》 suppress; put down; quell 《a riot》. ¶ 화를 ~ soothe *one's* anger / 마음을 ~ calm *oneself* down; compose *oneself* / 신경〔흥분〕을 ~ quiet *one's* nerves 〔*one's* mental excitement〕/ 진통을 ~ allay 〔relieve〕 labor pains / 아스피린은 두통을 가라앉힌다 Aspirin will relieve a headache.

**가락**[1] ① 《물레의》 a spindle; a distaff. ② 《가늘고 긴 물건》 a long slender object; a stick. ¶ 젓~ chopsticks / 엿 한 ~ a stick of rice candy.

**가락**[2] ① 《음조》 a tune; a tone; a key; a pitch (높낮이의); 《박자》 time; rhythm; an accent (억양의); 《노래》 a melody. ¶ ~이 고운 melodious; harmonious / 높은 ~으로 in a high key / ~이 안 맞는 노래 a song out of tune / ~을 맞추다 keep (good) time with 〔to〕 《the music》/ ~에 맞춰〔안 맞게〕 노래 부르다 sing in 〔out of〕 tune. ② 《솜씨》 (*one's* optimum) dexterity; skill; effectiveness. ¶ 일에 ~이 나다 get into the swing of *one's* work; hit *one's* stride.

**가락국수** noodles. ¶ 가락국숫집 a noodle ⌈shop.

**가락떼다** get something amusing under way; start dancing 〔singing〕.

**가락지** a ring; a set of twin rings. ¶ ~를 끼다 put 〔slip〕 a ring on (*one's* finger) / ~를 빼다 take 〔slip〕 a ring off (*one's* finger).

**가람**(伽藍) 〖불교〗 a (Buddhist) temple; ⌈a cathedral.

**가랑눈** a fine 〔powdery〕 snow.

**가랑니** a baby louse; a nit.

**가랑머리** a hairdo with two pigtails. ¶ ~ 소녀 a pigtailed girl; a girl in pigtails / ~를 하다 wear *one's* hair in two pigtails 〔braids〕.

**가랑무** a forked radish.

**가랑비** a drizzle; a misty 〔drizzling〕 rain; a fine rain. ¶ ~가 오고 있다 It is drizzling. / 온종일 ~가 왔다 It drizzled all day.

**가랑이** a fork; a crotch. ¶ 바짓～ the crotch of (a pair of) pants / ～지다 get forked; divide into two branches; bifurcate / ～를 벌리다 set *one's* legs apart / ～를 벌리고 서다 stand with *one's* feet 〔legs〕 apart.

**가랑잎** 《마른 잎》 a dead 〔withered〕 leaf; 《떡갈잎》 an oak leaf. ¶ ～에 불 붙듯 하다 flare up like tinder; be quick to take offense; get mad 〔be ready to fight〕 at the drop of a hat.
◉ ～조개 〖조개류〗 a jingle shell.

**가래**[1] 〖도구〗 a *karae;* a kind of shovel 〔spade〕 (with a long handle and a rope attached to either side of the blade). ◉ ～질 shovel 〔spade〕 work with a *karae.*

**가래**[2] 《긴 토막》 a slender stick 〔bar〕 《of「rice cake 〔taffy〕》. ¶ 엿〔떡〕 한 ～ a stick of taffy 〔rice-cake〕. ◉ ～떡 slender sticks of rice-cake; rice-cake in form of rounded stick. ～엿 taffy in the form of rounded stick.

**가래**[3] 〖생리〗 《담》 phlegm; sputum (*pl.* -ta); mucous discharge.
¶ 피가 섞인 ～ bloody phlegm; sputum with a little blood / ～ 삭이는 약 an expectorant / ～ 덩어리 a clot of phlegm / ～를 뱉다 cough out 〔bring up〕 phlegm; spit phlegm (out); expectorate / 목에 ～가 끓다 have a hard, obstructive phlegm in *one's* throat; rattle in *one's* throat / 으흠하고 목의 ～를 트다 clear *one's* throat (of phlegm) / ～가 목에 걸렸다 The phlegm has stuck in my throat.

**가래**[4] 〖식물〗 a wild walnut. ◉ ～나무 a wild-walnut tree.

**가래침** spit; spittle. ¶ ～을 뱉다 spit; expectorate / ～을 뱉지 마시오 《게시》 No spitting. / 길에 ～을 뱉어서는 안 된다 You should not spit on the street.

**가래톳** inflammation 〔swelling〕 of a lymphatic gland in the groin; a bubo (*pl.* ～es). ¶ ～이 서다 have a bubo.

**가량**(假量) ① 《쯤》 about; some; almost; more or less; approximately; or so; something like. ¶ 만 원 ～ about 10,000 won / 5마일 ～ about 〔some〕 five miles; five miles or so; around five miles 《미》 / 50살 ～의 남자 a man about 50 years of age / 두 시간 ～ 지나면 in about two hours / 여기서 얼마 ～이나 되겠습니까 About how far is it from here?
② 《어림·짐작》 a guess; (a) conjecture; an estimate. ～하다 guess; make a (random) guess; hazard a conjecture; make an estimate 《of》. ¶ ～해서 말해 보다 try a shot in the dark; hazard a guess.

**가량가량하다** 《face》 rather scrawny but very lively.

**가량스럽다** (be) unstylish; unbecoming.

**가량없다**(假量—) 《어림짐작이 없다》 be poor at guessing; have poor judgment; 《당찮다》 be wide of the mark; (be) outrageous; absurd; preposterous. ¶ 가량없는 사람 a man of very poor judgment / 가량없는 값 an exorbitant price / 가량없는 짓 outrageous conduct / 가량없이 beyond measurement; without judgment; absurdly; preposterously / 가량없는 수작 마라 Don't talk nonsense. / 가량없이 굴지 마라 Be reasonable! / 눈이 가량없이 왔다 We had a tremendous snow.

**가려내다** sort out; assort; pick 〔single〕 out; separate; winnow. ¶ 작은 귤을～ sort out small tangerines / 모래에서 금을 ～ separate gold from sand / 진위를 ～ winnow the false from the truth / 그들 속에서 낯익은 얼굴을～ pick out a familiar face among them / 불량품을 가려내기란 매우 어렵다 It is very difficult to sort out inferior goods.

**가려쓰다** use properly; make proper use of. ¶ 말을 잘～ pick *one's* words; be careful about the use of words.

**가려잡다** choose; select; pick out.

**가련하다**(可憐—) (be) poor; pitiful; pathetic; miserable; pitiable; piteous; sad. ¶ 가련한 정경 a pitiful sight / 가련히 여기다 take 〔have〕 pity on 《*a person*》; feel pity for 《*a person*》 / 가련한 친구로군 What a poor fellow he is!

**가렴**(苛斂) ～하다 exact heavy taxes 《from》; impose heavy 〔unjust〕 taxes 《on》. ◉ ～주구(誅求) extortion 〔exaction〕 (of taxes); laying 〔imposing〕 crushing taxes 《on》: ～주구를 일삼다 extort 〔exact〕 heavy taxes 《from》; impose heavy 〔unjust〕 taxes 《on》.

**가렵다** ① 《피부가》 itch; be 〔feel〕 itchy 〔itching〕; have an itch. ¶ 가려운 곳을 긁다 scratch an itchy spot / 가려운 곳을 긁어주다 [비유적] be very attentive to 《*a person's*》 want; attend on people with scrupulous care; leave nothing to be desired / 내 등이 ～ My back itches. / 어린애가 부스럼을 가려워한다 The child finds the eruption itchy. / 가렵거든 긁어라 Scratch yourself if you itch. ② 《좀스럽다》 (be) petty; mean; stingy. ¶ 가려운 녀석 a shallow fellow; a stingy fellow.

**가령**(假令) 《이를테면》 if; suppose (that); supposing 〔admitting, granting〕 that ...; in case; even if; (even) though; 《예를 들면》 for instance. ¶ ~ 그렇다 하더라도 admitting 〔granting〕 it to be so; even if it is 〔were〕 so; even so / ~ …라고 한다면 if; suppose 〔supposing〕 (that...); provided (that ...) / ~ 한 권에 2천 원이라 치고 two thousand won per book, for example / ~ 이렇게 한다면 어떻게 될까 What if we did it this way? / ~ 자네가 내 처지에 있다면 어떻게 하겠나 Suppose you were in my position 〔shoes〕, what would you do?

**가례**(家禮) the etiquette of a family; formalities within the home.

**가례**(嘉禮) an auspicious ceremony at court; 《왕실의 결혼식》 a royal wedding; 《즉위식》 an enthronement.

**가로** ① 《폭》 width; breadth; 《옆으로 퍼진 모양새》 (being) horizontal. ¶ ~ 석 자에 세로 다섯자 되는 방 a room 3 *cha* 〔feet〕 in width and 5 *cha* in length. ② [부사적] 《옆으로》 across; crosswise; sideways; transversely; horizontally. ¶ ~ 보나 세로 보나 every inch 《a gentleman》; to all appearance 《a soldier》; from top to toe / ~ 눕다 lie (down); lie 〔stretch out〕 at full length / ~ 늘어놓다 arrange sideways / ~ 건너다 go across; traverse; cut across / ~ 쓰다 write laterally; write from left to right / 고개를 ~ 젓다 say no; answer in the negative; shake *one's* head / ~ 지나 세로 지나 매한가지다 Either way you look at it, it is still the same thing. *or* There is nothing to choose between the two.
◉ ~다지 sideways; a thing facing sideways: ~다지로 놓다 lay 《*a thing*》 sideways. ~닫이 a sliding window 〔door〕. ~대 《가로장》 a cross-stick; a wooden bar; the crossbar between the legs of a loom; the crossbeam of a ceiling; 《횡축(橫軸)》 an abscissa (*pl.* ~s, -cissae). ~쓰기 horizontal writing. ~장 a wooden bar. ~줄 a horizontal line; a dash.

**가로**(街路) a street; a road; an avenue 《미》. (★ 미국의 대도시에서는 동서로 뻗은 것을 street, 남북으로 뻗은 것을 avenue라 함).
◉ ~등 a street lamp 〔light〕. ~수 street 〔roadside〕 trees; trees along 〔bordering〕 a street: ~숫길 a tree-lined street; a street bordered 〔lined〕 with trees. ~청소부 a street cleaner; a scavenger; a whitewing 《미》.

**가로놓이다** lie; lie sideways; lie across. ¶ 앞에 난관이 ~ difficulties lie ahead; have difficulties ahead / 긴 막대가 길에 가로놓여 있다 A long pole lies across the road.

**가로누이다** lay 《*a thing*》; lay 《*a thing*》 down 〔across〕; place 《*a thing*》 across 〔horizontally〕.

**가로되** as 《*someone*》 says. ¶ 속담에 ~ a proverb says 〔has it〕 that….

**가로막다** obstruct 《the view》; block 《the passage》; bar 《the way》; intercept 《*a person*》; cut off; interrupt. ¶ 길을 ~ block the way; stand in *one's* way / 가는 사람을 ~ cross 《*a person's*》 path / 사람의 말을~ interrupt 《*a person*》; cut 《*a person*》 short 〔off〕 / 강을 가로막고 둑을 쌓다 build a dam across a river / 빛을 ~ block 〔shut〕 off the light / 그들은 굴의 입구를 큰 돌로 가로막았다 They blocked up the entrance to the cave with big rocks.

**가로막히다** get obstructed; get blocked 〔barred〕; be intercepted; be interrupted; be cut off. ¶ 산에 가로막혀 동네가 보이지 않는다 The village is blocked from view by the mountain.

**가로맡다** take over 《*a matter*》; take 《*a matter*》 into *one's* own hands; take charge of; take upon *oneself;* assume. ¶ 책임을 ~ assume 《*a person's*》 responsibility / 그는 싸움을 가로맡았다 He made the fight his own.

**가로새다** get away; escape; slip out 《of a room》; sneak away from 《company》. ¶ 수업중 ~ cut a lesson and beat it 《미속어》 / 그는 어느새 가로새고 말았다 He got away unnoticed.

**가로서다** stand looking aside 〔the other way〕; stand sideways; stand aside.

**가로세로** ① [명사적] length and breadth. ② [부사적] lengthwise and crosswise; vertically and horizontally. ¶ ~ 열십자로 crosswise; breadthwise and lengthwise / ~ 줄을 긋다 draw lines vertically and horizontally. ③ 《사방으로》 in all directions; in every direction; every which way; to all points. ¶ ~ 뻗은 철도망 a network of railways.

**가로지르다** 《건너지르다》 put 《a bar》 across; 《가로긋다》 draw 《a line》 across; 《교차하다》 intersect; 《건너다》 cross; traverse; go 〔cut〕 across. ¶ 선

로를 ~ cross 〔go across〕 a track / 철도가 사막을 수백 마일 가로질러 뻗쳐 있다 The railroad traverses hundreds of miles of desert.

**가로짜기** 〖인쇄〗 horizontal typesetting. ¶ ~로 하다 compose 〔set〕 type horizontally.

**가로채다** take 〔snatch, steal〕 《*a thing*》 out of 《*a person's*》 possession 〔hands〕; intercept; snatch away; usurp (권력·지위를). ¶ 아무에게서 지갑을 ~ snatch *a person's* purse away / 남의 아이디어를 가로채는 일을 아무렇지 않게 생각하다 think nothing of stealing other people's ideas / 남의 손님을 ~ win customers away from another / 왕위를 ~ usurp a throne.

**가로채이다** be snatched 〔intercepted, usurped〕. ¶ 이익을 ~ have *one's* share snatched by another / 여편네를 ~ be made a cuckold of.

**가로퍼지다** widen out; spread out; grow broad; fill out; get pudgy; be thickset. ¶ 가로퍼진 사람 a stocky 〔pudgy, thickset〕 man; a humpty-dumpty.

**가뢰** 〖곤충〗 a tiger beetle; a meloid.

**가료**(加療) giving medical treatment 〔care〕. ~하다 treat 《a patient》; give medical treatment. ¶ ~중이다 be under medical treatment / 두 주의 ~를 요하다 require two weeks' treatment / 그는 T 병원에서 ~중에 있다 He is receiving medical treatment in T Hospital.

**가루** 《분말》 powder; dust; 《곡식가루》 flour; meal. ¶ 옥수수 ~ corn flour / 밀을 ~로 빻다 grind wheat into flour.
◉ ~붙이 bakery goods; pastry. ~비누 soap powder; detergent. ~약 medicinal powder; powdered medicine. ~우유 powdered 〔dried〕 milk; milk powder. ~음식 flour food. ~체 a flour shifter. ~치약 tooth powder.

**가르다** ① 《분할》 split; cut (up); cut in two; divide; part. ¶ 배를 ~ open 〔cut across〕 the abdomen / 다섯 부분으로 ~ divide into five parts / 머리를 가운데로 ~ part *one's* hair in the middle / (배가) 파도를 가르며 나아가다 sail cleaving the waves / 이익을 반씩 ~ split the profit half and half / 이익을 둘〔셋〕이서 ~ divide the profit 「between the two 〔among the three〕/ 패를 여럿 갈라서 그를 찾으러 갔다 We went in search for him in parties.
② 《분류》 classify; sort (out); assort; group 《into》. ¶ 선인과 악인을 ~ sort out the good men from the bad / 크게 둘로 ~ classify into two large groups / 식물을 종류별로 ~ classify 〔distribute〕 plants into orders.
③ 《분배》 distribute 《among》; share 《*a thing* with》; allot 《to》; divide. ¶ 다섯 몫으로 ~ divide into five shares / 음식을 갈라 먹다 share food with others / 자식에게 재산을 갈라주다 distribute *one's* possessions among children; settle property on *one's* children.
④ 《두 사람 사이를》 sever 《the two, A and B, A from B》; estrange. ¶ 둘 사이를 ~ keep 《them》 apart; estrange A from B / 부부의 의를 ~ sever husband and wife; cut a husband from his wife.

**가르마** 《머리의》 a part (in *one's* hair). ¶ ~(를) 타다 part 〔split〕 *one's* hair 《in the middle, on the left》.

**가르치다** 《지식을》 teach; instruct; give lessons 《in》; initiate; school; 《교육하다》 educate; 《지도하다》 guide; coach; 《계몽하다》 enlighten; 《알아듣게》 show; tell; inform; explain; point out.
¶ 영어를 ~ teach English; give lessons in English / 비결을 ~ initiate 《*a person*》 into a secret / 길을 ~ show 《*a person*》 the way 《to a place》/ 저 학교에서 중국어를 가르친다 They teach Chinese at that school. / 어찌된 일이오, 까닭을 가르쳐 주시오 What is the matter? Tell me. / 헤엄치는 법을 좀 가르쳐 주시오 Show me how to swim. / 어머니는 딸에게 세상일을 가르쳐야 한다 A mother must school her daughter in the ways of the world. / 그 선생은 잘 가르친다 He has tact in teaching. / 그녀는 나에게 호신술을 가르쳐 주었다 She instructed me in the art of self-defense. / 아이들은 본데 있게 가르쳐야 한다 You should educate your children to behave well.

**가르친사위** a person too stupid to do anything without first being shown how.

**가르침** 《교훈》 teaching(s); instruction; a lesson; (a) precept (계율); guidance (지도); 《교의》 (a) doctrine; (a) dogma. ¶ 공자〔부처〕의 ~ the teachings of Confucius 〔Buddha〕/ ~을 받다 receive 《*a person's*》 instruction; take lessons 《in English》; study under 《*a person*》; be taught 《by》; put *oneself* 〔learn〕 under the guidance 《of》/ 부모의 ~에 따르다 obey *one's* parent's precepts / 그 사고는 우리에게 귀중한 ~

이 되었다 The accident「served as〔was〕a valuable lesson to us.

**가름** 《쪼갬》 cutting; dividing; 《분류》 classifying; 《분배》 distributing; 《분리》 separating. ◉ ~대 the crossbar dividing the upper and lower sections of an abacus.

**가리**[1] 《고기 잡는》 a (fish)weir; a fish trap. ◉ ~질 trap-fishing: ~질하다 trap-fish.

**가리**[2] 《더미》 a heap; a pile; a stack. ¶ ~를 짓다 make a pile; heap; pile. ◉ 건초~ a haystack.

**가리가리** to〔in〕pieces; into〔in, to〕shreds. ¶ ~ 찢다 tear 《*a thing*》 to pieces〔ribbons, shreds〕; tear 《a piece of cloth》 into strips〔pieces〕.

**가리개** 《병풍》 a two-fold screen; 《가리는 물건》 a cover.

**가리나무** tinder of pine needles and「twigs.

**가리다**[1] 《보이지 않게》 hide; conceal; cloak; veil; cover; bury; shelter; shield; screen; shade; keep off; obscure. ¶ 얼굴을 손으로 ~ hide *one's* face in *one's* hands / 손수건으로 얼굴을 ~ bury〔hide〕*one's* face in *one's* handkerchief / 구름이 해를 ~ a cloud veils〔obscures〕the sun / 나무가 해를 ~ a tree keeps the sun off / 아무의 눈을 ~ cover up *a person's* eyes; 《속이다》 pull〔draw〕the wool over *a person's* eyes; hoodwink; deceive / 결점을 ~ draw a veil over *one's* fault.

**가리다**[2] ① 《고르다》 choose; select; pick out; sort. ¶ 수단을 가리지 않고 by fair means or foul; by hook or by crook / 낯을 ~ be afraid〔shy〕of strangers / 수단을 가리지 않다 be unscrupulous about methods; never question the means; stop at nothing / 물불을 가리지 않다 go through fire and water; be willing to take any risk; dare the dangers of / 친구는 잘 가려서 사귀어야 한다 You must be careful in choosing your friends. / 나는 먹는 것을 그다지 가리지 않는다 I am not so particular about what I eat. / 왜 그다지 가리는 게 많은가 Why do you have so many likes and dislikes? / 장소를 가리지 않고 그는 크게 웃었다 Disregarding the place, he laughed aloud. ② 《분별하다》 discriminate; distinguish 《between》; tell *A* from *B*. ¶ 선악을 ~ distinguish〔know difference〕between good and evil; tell good from evil / 시비(是非)를 ~ tell right from wrong; argue over who is right / 앞뒤를 ~ weigh the consequences / 공사(公私)를 분명히 ~ draw a sharp line between public and private affairs / 남녀 노소를 가리지 않고 irrespective of age and sex. ③ 《빚·손익 따위를》 do accounts; make a calculation of debts and credits〔profits and losses〕; square account with. ¶ 빚을 ~ settle with *one's* creditors; clear off〔up〕*one's* debts / 셈을 ~ pay *one's* bill; square〔settle〕*one's* accounts 《with》/ 손익을 ~ make a calculation of profit and loss. ④ 《머리를》 give (*one's* hair) a rough combing; untangle (*one's* hair). ¶ 머리를 ~ run a comb through *one's* hair.

**가리다**[3] 《쌓다》 pile up; heap 《up》; stack. ¶ 장작을 ~ pile up firewood / 벼를 산더미처럼 가려 놓다 heap up a mountain of rice plants.

**가리맛** 〖조개류〗 a kind of razor clam. ◉ ~살 razor-clam meat.

**가리비** 〖조개류〗 a scallop; a scollop.

**가리사니** ① 《판단력》 discretion; prudence; good sense; 《지각》 knowledge; wisdom. ② 《실마리》 a clue; the drift of an affair. ¶ ~를 잡을 수 없다 can't get〔understand〕what it's all about.

**가리새**[1] 《갈피》 the drift〔thread, direction〕of an affair. ¶ ~를 모르다 don't know what it is all about.

**가리새**[2] 〖조류〗 a spoonbill.

**가리어지다** become hidden〔concealed〕; be cloaked〔veiled〕; get covered〔buried〕; be sheltered〔shielded, screened, shaded, kept off, obscured〕. ¶ 안개에 ~ be「enveloped in〔veiled in, wrapped in, shrouded by〕mist / 달이 구름에 가리어졌다 The moon was「veiled by〔hidden behind〕the clouds. / 그의 짧은 생애는 비밀에 가리어져 있다 His brief life is shrouded in mystery.

**가리온** 《말》 a white horse with a black「mane.

**가리키다** point at〔to〕; point out; indicate; show; denote; tell. ¶ 방향을 ~ point〔indicate〕the direction / 시계 바늘은 5시를 가리키고 있다 The hands of the clock point to〔stand at〕five. / 그 도시를 지도에서 가리켜 보시오 Point out the town in the map. / X 기호는 미지수를 가리킨다 The sign X denotes an unknown quantity. / 그것은 너를 가리켜 한 말이다 It means you. / 저런 사람을 가리켜 알랑쇠라고 한다 We call a man like him a sycophant 〔an applepolisher〕. / 그는 그 집 쪽을 가리켰다 He pointed toward the house. / 그녀는 떨리는 손가락으로 그 사람을 가리켰다 She pointed at the man with shaking fingers.

**가리틀다** ①《요구》 demand a share of 《*a person's*》 unexpected gain. ②《훼방》 thwart; interfere with 《a plan》; work against 《some cause》.

**가린스럽다** (be) stingy; niggardly; miserly; tight.

**가린주머니** a miser; a scrooge; a pinchpenny.

**가마**[1] ①《빵·숯을 굽는》 an oven; 《화덕》 a stove; a furnace; 《질그릇·벽돌 굽는》 a kiln. ¶ 벽돌 ~ a brick-kiln / 기와〔질그릇〕 굽는 ~ a tile-〔porcelain-〕kiln / 빵을 굽는 ~ a baker's oven. ②《가마솥》 an iron pot; a cauldron; a kettle. ¶ ~(솥) 밑이 노구솥 밑을 검다 한다《속담》 The pot calls the kettle black.

**가마**[2] 《머리의》 the vortex 〔whirl〕 of hair on the head; a hair whirl.

**가마**[3] 《가마니》 a bag; a sack. ¶ 쌀 두 ~ two bags of rice.

**가마**[4] 《타는》 a palanquin; a sedan chair. ¶ ~를 타다 ride in a palanquin / ~를 메다 carry a sedan chair on the shoulders. ◉ ~꾼 a sedan chair 〔palanquin〕 bearer. ~채 the shafts of a sedan chair; the fourpole carrying frame of a sedan chair.

**가마노르께하다** be a dark yellow.

**가마니** a (straw) bag; a bag made of straw. ¶ 쌀 ~ a rice bag. ◉ ~때기 a worn-out bag. ~틀 a bag-maker (machine).

**가마득하다** be far off. ⇨ 까마아득하다.

**-가마리** a person who is the butt 〔target, mark, object〕 of ridicule 〔beating, criticism, scolding〕. ◉ 걱정~ a source of anxiety; the butt of scoldings. 웃음~ a laughing stock; the butt of derision.

**가마솥** a cauldron. ⇨ 가마[1] ②.

**가마우지** 〖조류〗 a cormorant.

**가막사리** 〖식물〗 a kind of cosmos plant (*Bidens tripartita*).

**가막조개** 〖조개류〗 a corbicula.

**가만** ① =가만히. ②《가만 있자》 just a minute; hold on. ¶ ~, 누가 온다 Soft 〔Hush〕! Someone comes.

**가만가만** softly. ⇨ 가만히.

**가만두다** leave 〔let〕 alone; leave 《*a thing*》 as it is; leave undisturbed; leave intact. ¶ 애를 울리지 말고 가만둬라 Leave the child alone—you will make him cry. / 이러한 행위는 가만 둘 수 없다 I cannot suffer 〔tolerate〕 such conduct.

**가만있다** remain still 〔quiet〕; keep silent; stay motionless; sit still; stand idle. ¶ 그들은 숨을 죽이고 가만 있었다 They kept still, hardly daring to breathe. / 이 애는 한시도 가만 있질 않는다 This child can't keep still for a minute. *or* This child is 「quite restless 〔always fidgety〕. / 그는 아무 일도 하지 않고 집에 ~ He is staying home without doing any business.

**가만히** ①《조용히》 still; quietly; softly; calmly; silently; gently; motionlessly. ¶ ~ 있다 keep still 〔quiet〕; be silent / 움직이지 않고 ~ 있다 stay put; sit tight; remain motionless / 가만~ 이야기하다 speak in a calm tone / ~ 걷다 tread 〔walk〕 lightly; go with soft steps / ~ 자리에서 일어나다 leave *one's* seat quietly / 문을 ~ 두드리다 knock at 〔on〕 the door gently / ~ 있을 수 없다 cannot stay 〔keep〕 still; be 〔feel〕 restless / 사진을 찍을 동안 ~ 계십시오 Please 「keep still 〔don't move〕 while I take your picture. / 그는 ~ 누워 있었다 He lay there motionless. / 날씨가 너무 좋아서 집안에 ~ 있을 수 없었다 The weather was too fine for me to stay indoors. / 그는 회의중 내내 말하지 않고 ~ 있었다 He kept silent throughout the meeting.
②《몰래》 secretly; in secret; stealthily; furtively; privately; in confidence; on the sly. ¶ ~ 들어가다〔나가다〕 steal 〔slip〕 into 〔out of〕 / ~ 엿보다 peep furtively / ~ 귀띔하다 give a tip in confidence / ~ 돈을 쥐어 주다 slip money into 《*a person's*》 hands / ~ 떠나다 leave 《Korea》 secretly / ~ 남의 속을 떠보다 sound (out) another's view.
③《마음속으로》 inwardly; in *one's* heart. ¶ 그녀는 ~ 웃었다 She laughed in her sleeve.
④《그대로》 ¶ ~ 놔두다 leave 《*a thing*》 as it is 〔stands〕; leave 《*a thing*》 intact 〔untouched〕; leave 〔let〕 《*a person*》 alone.
⑤《기타》 ¶ 왜 지금까지 내게 알리지 않고 ~ 있었느냐 Why haven't you told me before (now)? *or* Why have you kept it from me? / 나는 ~ 모욕을 당하고 있지는 않겠다 I'm not going to take insults lying down.

**가말다** take care of 《*a matter*》; give free hand to 《*a matter*》; manage.

**가망**(可望) 《유망》 promise; hope; 《전망》 a prospect; 《가능성》 possibility; likelihood; probability; chance.
¶ ~ 있는 promising (사람이); hopeful (사물이) / ~이 있는 청년 a promising young man / ~ 없다 have no 〔not a ray of〕 hope; be hopeless 《of》 / ~ 없는 일을 하다 try a hopeless venture / 성공할 ~이 있다 stand a good chance of success; have bright prospects / 성공할 ~은 반반입니다 There is an even chance of success. / 그 의안이 통과될 ~은 없다 There is no possibility that the bill will be passed. *or* There is no likelihood of the bill passing. / 날씨가 갤 ~은 없다 There is no likelihood of fine weather. / 그는 회복할 ~이 없다 There is no hope 〔chance〕 of his recovery. *or* He is past 〔beyond〕 hope of recovery. / 핵실험 금지가 실현될 ~은 보이지 않는다 There is no hopeful sign that the nuclear test ban will come into effect.

**가말다** ⇨ 「까마(아)득하다.

**가맣다** ① 《검다》 (be) black; dark. ② =

**가매장**(假埋葬) temporary burial 〔interment〕. ~하다 bury temporarily.

**가맹**(加盟) joining; affiliation; participation. ~하다 join; become a member 《of》; affiliate 《with》; get affiliated 《with》; take part 《in》; participate 《in》. ¶ 유엔에 ~하다 join the United Nations / ~이 수락되다 be admitted to 《the United Nations》; gain membership in 《the NATO》.
◉ ~국 a member nation 〔state〕 《of the U.N.》; a signatory nation 《to a treaty》: 1996년 8월 현재, 유엔의 ~국은 185개국이었다 As of August 1996, the United Nations had a membership of 185 nations. ~단체 an affiliated body 〔member〕; a member organization. ~자 a participant; a member. ~점 a member store 《of a chain=store association》. ~ 조합 an affiliated union. 비~국 a nonmember (nation).

**가면**(假面) a mask; a cloak.
¶ (…의) ~ 밑에 under the cloak 〔mask〕 of; under the pretense of / ~을 쓰다 《탈을》 wear 〔put on〕 a mask; be masked; 《변장》 disguise *oneself* 《as》; 《위선》 dissemble; play the hypocrite / ~을 벗기다 unmask 〔take off the mask of〕 《a villain》; debunk (명사 등의) / ~을 벗다 unmask *oneself;* take 〔throw〕 off *one's* mask; show *one's* true colors / 그는 자선 사업의 ~을 쓰고 사리를 도모하였다 He furthered his own interest under the pretense of philanthropy. / 그는 친구라는 ~을 쓰고 나를 배신했다 He betrayed me under a 〔the〕 mask of friendship.
◉ ~극 a mask drama; a masque. ~무도회 a masked ball; a masquerade.

**가면허**(假免許) a temporary 〔provisional〕 license.

**가멸다** (be) rich; wealthy; affluent; 「opulent.

**가명**(佳名) a good reputation 〔name〕.

**가명**(家名) the family name; the good name of a family. ¶ ~을 더럽히다 disgrace *one's* family name / ~을 드높이다 raise the reputation of *one's* family (name); bring honor to *one's* family.

**가명**(假名) a false name; an assumed name; an alias; 《필명》 a penname; a pseudonym. ¶ …라는 ~으로 under the name 〔pseudonym〕 《of》; 《미》 under *one's* cover name 《of...》 / 그는 한백호란 ~으로 행세하고 있다 He goes by the pseudonym of Han Paekho. / 그는 김만호라는 ~으로 호텔에 묵었다 He stayed at the hotel under the name 〔alias〕 of Kim Manho. ◉ ~계좌 a false-name (bank) account.

**가묘**(家廟) a family shrine.

**가무**(歌舞) singing and dancing; songs and dances. ¶ 정부는 ~ 음곡의 공연을 일체 금지시켰다 The Government ordered a suspension of all public performances in music and dancing.

**가무러지다** ⇨ 까무러지다.

**가무리다** make away with surreptitiously; steal when no one is looking.

**가무스름하다** ⇨ 거무스름하다.

**가문**(家門) *one's* family 〔clan〕. ¶ ~이 좋은 사람 a man of good family / 한 ~의 명예 a credit 〔an honor〕 to a family / ~을 더럽히다 bring disgrace 〔dishonor〕 on *one's* family / 좋은 ~에 태어나다 come of a good stock 〔family〕 / ~을 자랑하다 be proud of *one's* birth / 그의 출세는 ~ 덕택이다 His rise in the world is due to the standing of his family.

**가문비나무** 『식물』 a spruce; a silver fir.

**가물** a drought. ⇨ 가뭄. ¶ ~에 콩나기다 be few and far between; be very rare 〔scarce〕. ◉ ~철 the dry season.

**가물가물** flickering(ly); blurred(ly); hazy 〔hazily〕.

**가물거리다** ① 《불빛이》 flicker; glimmer; blink. ¶ 가물거리는 불빛 a flickering light; a blink of light / 먼 데서 불빛이 가물거렸다 I saw a blink of light in the distance. ② 《희미하다》 (be) dim; misty; hazy; dreamy; 《정신이》 have an indistinct consciousness 〔memory, *etc.*〕. ¶ 눈이 ~ *one's* eyes are dim 〔blurred〕 / 정신이 ~ *one's* mind grows hazy; *one's* memory is blurred / 조그만 섬이 안개 속에 가물거린다 A small island appears dimly through the haze.

**가물다** ① 《날씨가》 be dry 〔arid, rainless〕. ¶ 날씨가 ~ have 〔suffer, be in〕 a drought. ② 《인재가》 ¶ 인재가 ~ suffer a shortage of talented people.

**가물들다** ① 《날씨가》 turn arid; enter a period of drought; a drought sets in. ② 《피해》 suffer from a drought.

**가물음** = 가뭄. ◉ ~못자리 a seedbed made during a dry spell.

**가물치** 〖어류〗 a snakehead (mullet); a snake-headed fish.

**가물타다** be apt to suffer from a drought; be susceptible to (spells of) dry weather. ¶ 상추는 가물타기 쉽다 Lettuce is apt to suffer from a drought.

**가뭄** a drought; a dry spell; dry weather. ¶ 오랜〔계속되는〕 ~ a long drought; a long spell of dry weather / ~에 단비 a rainfall eagerly longed for / ~이 가장 심한 지역 the most seriously drought-stricken 〔drought-hit〕 areas / 오랜 ~에 바닥이 갈라진 논 a rice paddy cracked by the prolonged drought / 오랜 ~으로 농사를 망쳤다 Owing to the long drought, the crops have failed. ◉ ~피해 drought damage.

**가뭇가뭇하다** be dotted 〔speckled〕 with black.

**가뭇없다** be nowhere to be seen; have left no clue 〔trace〕 behind.

**가뭇하다** (be) blackish; darkish.

**가미**(加味) 《맛》 seasoning; flavoring; 《한약에서》 adding 《*something*》 to a regular medical prescription; doctoring (up); 《부가》 an addition; an additive; a blend(ing). ~하다 season 《with》; flavor 《with》; add 《*a thing*》 to a regular medical prescription; doctor (up); fix (up); reinforce 《with an additive》; blend 〔mix〕 in. ¶ 해학을 ~한 담화 a conversation seasoned with humor 〔with a touch of humor〕 / 법에 인정을 ~하다 temper justice with mercy / 외부 의견을 ~하다 take external opinion into consideration.

**가발**(假髮) a wig; false hair. ¶ ~을 쓰다 wear 〔put on〕 a wig. ◉ ~공 a wig maker.

**가방** a bag; 《여행용》 a suitcase; 《멜빵이 있는》 a satchel; 《서류 가방》 briefcase; 《손가방》 a handbag 〔valise 《미》, grip 《미》〕; 《큰 가방》 a trunk. ¶ ~을 들다 carry a bag / ~에 넣다 put 《*things*》 in(to) a bag.

**가법**(加法) 〖수학〗 addition. ⇨ 덧셈.

**가법**(家法) household etiquette; family tradition; family rules.

**가변**(可變) variableness; [형용사적] variable. ◉ ~비용 variable expenses. ~익 variable wings. ~자본 variable capital. ~저항기 a variable resistor. ~전압발전기 a variable voltage generator. ~차선 a reversible lane.

**가볍다** ① 《무게가》 (be) light; be not heavy. ¶ 가벼운 짐 a light load; light baggage / 체중이 ~ weigh little; *one's* weight is light / 그는 나보다 5킬로 ~ He is five kilograms lighter than I. ② 《정도가》 (be) slight; light; trifling; be not serious; 《중요치 않다》 (be) insignificant; unimportant; light. ¶ 가벼운 감기 a slight cold / 가벼운 상처 a slight wound 〔injury〕; a mere scratch / 가벼운 범죄 a minor offense / 가벼운 형벌 a light punishment / 가볍게 여기다 make light of; think little of; attach little importance to / 가벼이 보아 넘기다 overlook; pass over 《*something*》 lightly / 나는 그때 가벼운 실망을 느꼈다 I felt mild disappointment then. / 너의 책임은 결코 가벼운 것이 아니다 Your responsibility is by no means light. ③ 《경쾌·간편하다》 (be) easy; simple; light. ¶ 가벼운 독서 (a) light reading / 가벼운 식사 a light meal; a snack / 가벼운 일 an easy work / 가벼운 마음으로 without taking it too seriously; with a light heart / 가벼운 걸음으로 with springy 〔light〕 steps. ④ 《경박하다》 (be) undignified; frivolous; flippant. ¶ 가벼운 사내 a frivolous 〔flippant〕 man / 입이 ~ be talkative; be loquacious; have a loose tongue / 가볍게 굴다 act imprudently. ⑤ 《기타》 ¶ 가벼운 상대 a poor 〔weak〕 rival / 가벼운 일 easy 〔light〕 work; a soft job / 문을 가볍게 노크하여라 Knock softly on the door.

**가보** 《노름》 9 points in gambling; a lucky nine. ¶ ~를 잡다 make nine / ~로 먹다 win the stakes with the number nine.

**가보**(家譜) a family tree; a genealogy; a genealogical table.

**가보**(家寶) an heirloom; a family 〔an ancestral〕 treasure. ¶ 대대로 내려오는 ～ an heirloom handed down for generations 〔from generation to generation〕/ 그 그림은 그 가문의 ～로서 비장되고 있다 The picture is treasured as an heirloom in the family.

**가본**(假本) a spurious edition 《of books, calligraphy, pictures》.

**가봉**(加俸) an additional 〔an extra, a special〕 allowance; a (salary) supplement. ¶ 연 백오십만원의 ～을 받다 get a special allowance of 1,500,000 won per year in addition to the regular pay. ◉ 연공(年功)～ a long service allowance.

**가봉**(假縫) a fitting; basting; tacking. ～하다 baste; tack; have a (first) fitting. ¶ 당신 옷의 ～이 되었습니다 Your suit is ready for trying on. / ～은 언제 됩니까 When will it be ready for a first fitting?

**가봉** 《아프리카의 공화국》 Gabon.

**가부**(可否) ① 《옳고 그름》 right or wrong; good or bad; 《적부》 proper or improper; propriety; advisability. ¶ 남녀 공학의 ～를 논하다 argue whether coeducation is proper or improper; argue about the advisability of coeducation.

② 《찬부》 yes 〔ayes〕 and no 〔noes〕; pros and cons; for and against. ¶ ～간 whether yes or no 〔right or wrong〕; in any case / ～ 투표 votes for and against 《a bill》/ ～를 논하다 argue for and against; argue pros and cons / ～를 묻다 vote on; take a vote on; put to vote; put 《a question》 to a vote / 투표로 ～를 결정하다 decide by vote; take a vote / ～가 상반이다 The vote is a tie. *or* The votes are equally divided. / ～간 곧 좀 알려 주시오 Please let me know soon whether it is yes or no. / ～ 동수인 경우 의장이 이를 결정한다 In case of a tie, the president shall decide the issue.

**가부**(家父) my 〔our〕 father. ◉ ～장 a patriarch: ～장 정치 patriarchal government / ～장 제도 patriarchal system; patriarchy; patriarchism.

**가분가분** lightly; nimbly; easily; airily; gently. ～하다 (be) light; nimble.

**가분수**(假分數) an improper fraction.

**가분하다** (be) light; be not heavy. ¶ 몸이 ～ feel good / 마음이 ～ *one's* mind is relieved of *one's* burden 〔anxiety〕/ 그 소식에 그의 마음은 가분해졌다 The news lightened his gloom.

**가불**(假拂) payment in advance. ～하다 (pay in) advance; make an advance. ～받다 borrow in advance; get an advance; receive 〔draw〕 *one's* wages in advance. ¶ 봉급을 ～해 주다 advance wages 《to》/ 월급에서 50만원 ～받다 get an advance of 〔borrow〕 500,000 won on *one's* salary / 그는 ～받은 돈으로 기일내에 빚을 갚을 수 있었다 An advance on salary permitted him to pay his debt on time. / 퇴직금을 ～하여 그 토지를 샀다 I had my severance pay paid in advance and bought the land. ◉ ～금 a temporary advance.

**가붓가붓** all light (in weight); very light. ～하다 (be) all light; very light.

**가붓하다** (be) rather light.

**가빈하다**(家貧—) be of a poor 〔an indigent〕 family; be in needy circumstances.

**가뿐하다** ⇨ 가분하다.

**가쁘다** 《숨이》 pant 〔gasp〕 (for breath); be out of breath; breathe with difficulty; 《속이》 (be) uncomfortable; hard; trying; heavy. ¶ 숨이 ～ be short of breath / 밋밋한 비탈을 오르는 데도 숨이 ～ I pant for breath even when going up a gentle slope. / 밥을 많이 먹었더니 속이 ～ I've eaten so much I'm uncomfortable.

**가사**(家事) household affairs; domestic duties; housekeeping; running a house. ¶ ～ 형편으로 for family reasons; owing to family matters / ～를 돌보다 take care of household affairs / ～에 얽매이다 be occupied with household cares.

**가사**(袈裟) a surplice; a cope; a priest's robe.

**가사**(假死) syncope; suspended animation; apparent death. ◉ ～상태 a coma: ～ 상태에 있다 be in a syncopic state / ～ 상태에 빠지다 fall into a state of suspended animation.

**가사**(歌詞) the words of a song; lyrics; lyric lines (유행가); a libretto (오페라). ¶ 곡이 ～에 꼭 어울린다 The tune exactly fits the words. / 나는 ～를 모른다 I don't remember the words of the song. ◉ ～집 a wordbook.

**가산**(加算) addition. ～하다 add; include 《interest》. ¶ 원금에 이자를 ～하다 add interest to principal / 특별 요금이 ～된다 An extra charge 〔A surcharge〕 will be added. / 10%의 서비스료와 10%의 정부세금이 요금에 ～됩니다 《게시》 A 10%

service charge and a 10% government tax are added to the total price. ◉ ~금 additional dues. ~기 an adding machine; a calculating machine. ~세 an additional tax.

**가산**(家産) family property 〔estate〕; *one's* fortune. ¶ ~을 탕진하다 squander 〔dissipate〕 *one's* fortune; go through *one's* (inherited) fortune / ~을 일으키다 make *one's* fortune / ~이 기울다 *one's* fortune begins to fall 〔ebb〕; *one* sinks in fortune.

**가살** a hateful stuck-up attitude. ¶ ~떨다〔빼다, 부리다, 피우다〕 behave in a hateful stuck-up way / ~스럽다 be stuck-up and hateful. ◉ ~(쟁)이, ~꾼 a hateful stuck-up person.

**가삼**(家蔘) cultivated ginseng.

**가상**(家相) the aspect 〔physiognomy〕 of a house.

**가상**(假想) supposition; assumption; imagination. ~하다 suppose; assume; imagine. ¶ ~적 imaginary; assumed; supposed / 적으로 ~하다 suppose 《a country》 to be the enemy.
◉ ~국 a given country; a hypothetical power. ~원자전 a simulated atomic war. ~적(국) an imaginary 〔a hypothetical, a potential, a supposed〕 enemy (country). ~현실(감) 《컴퓨터의》 virtual reality.

**가상**(假像) a false image; a ghost; an appearance; a pseudomorph (mineral).

**가상히**(嘉尙—) ¶ 선행을 ~ 여기다 commend 《*a person*》 for *his* good deed.

**가새지르다** make into a scissors shape; join crosswise; cross; cut across. ¶ 깃대를 ~ join flagpoles crosswise.

**가새풀** =톱풀.

**가석방**(假釋放) parole; 《가출옥》 (a) release on parole. ~하다 release 〔put〕 《*a person*》 on parole. ¶ 특별~ special release on parole / ~되다 be paroled. ◉ ~자 a criminal on parole; a parolee 《미》.

**가석하다**(可惜—) (be) regrettable; lamentable; deplorable; pitiful; sad; be too bad; be a shame.

**가선**(—線) ① 《바느질의》 a hem; a border; a frill. ¶ 저고리의 ~(을) 두르다 hem a jacket. ② 《눈의》 the wrinkles of a double eyelid fold.

**가선**(架線) 《공사》 overhead 〔aerial〕 wiring; 《선》 an overhead (power) line; a wire; 《전동차의》 a trolley wire. ◉ ~공 a lineman. ~공사 wiring work.

**가설**(架設) (a) construction; building; 《전화·전등의》 installation. ~하다 construct; build; install; lay 《a cable》. ¶ ~중이다 be under construction; be being installed / 교량을 ~하다 construct 〔build〕 a bridge 《over》 / 전화를 ~하다 install 〔put in〕 a telephone; have a telephone installed / 전선을 ~하다 put up 〔string〕 electric wires; do 〔install〕 the wiring. ◉ ~공사 building 〔construction〕 work. ~비 the installation 〔building〕 cost.

**가설**(假設) 《임시의》 temporary construction 〔installation〕. ~하다 put up temporarily; install for the time being. ¶ ~의 provisional; temporary; transient. ◉ ~교 a temporary bridge. ~극장 a temporary theater. ~무대 《put up》 a makeshift stage.

**가설**(假說) 〖논리〗 a hypothesis; 《가정》 an assumption; a supposition. ¶ ~의 hypothetical; assumed / ~을 세우다 set up a hypothesis; hypothesize / …란 ~에 근거하여 on the hypothesis that… / 그 ~은 증명〔실증〕 되었다 The hypothesis was proved 〔verified〕.

**가성**(苛性) 〖화학〗 causticity; corrosiveness; corrosive action. ¶ ~의 caustic. ◉ ~석회 quicklime. ~소다 caustic soda. =수산화나트륨. ~알칼리 caustic alkali. ~알코올 caustic alcohol. ~칼리 caustic potash.

**가성**(假性) ¶ ~의 false; pseud(o)-. ◉ ~근시 false 〔temporary〕 nearsightedness; pseudomyopia. ~비대 pseudohypertrophy. ~빈혈 pseudoanemia. ~수막염 pseudomeningitis. ~콜레라 pseudocholera.

**가성**(假聲) falsetto; a feigned 〔disguised〕 voice. ¶ ~으로 with 〔in〕 a feigned voice; in an affected tone / ~을 내다 disguise *one's* voice; feign 〔imitate〕 《other's》 voice.

**가성대**(假聲帶) 〖해부〗 a false vocal cord.

**가세**(加勢) ① 《도움》 help; aid; assistance; support; backing up. ~하다 lend help 《to》; back 《*a person*》 up; support; assist; aid; take sides with; side with. ¶ 약한 쪽에 ~하다 「take sides with 〔stand by, support〕 the weaker / ~하러 가다〔오다〕 go 〔come〕 to 《*a person's*》 assistance. ② 《병력의》 reinforcements. ¶ 병력을 ~하다 reinforce the military potential.

**가세**(苛稅) a heavy 〔high〕 tax; a heavy burden of taxation. ⇨중세(重稅). ¶ ~에 시달리다 labor 〔groan, grovel〕

under a heavy load 〔burden〕 of taxation; suffer from heavy taxes.

**가세**(家勢) a family's「financial condition 〔economic circumstances, credit rating〕. ¶ ～가 넉넉하다 be well off; be amply provided for / ～가 넉넉지 못하다 be badly off; be poorly provided for / ～가 기울다 the economic circumstances of the family are on the wane 〔at a low ebb〕.

**가소**(可塑) ¶ ～의 plastic. ◉ ～물 plastics. ～성 plasticity. ～제 a plasticizer.

**가소롭다**(可笑―) (be) laughable; ridiculous; ludicrous; absurd; foolish. ¶ 가소롭기 짝이 없다 be highly ridiculous; be quite absurd / 그가 작가가 된다니 ～ He wishes to become a writer? It's huge joke. / 그가 프랑스어를 가르치다니 가소롭군 He is teaching French? What a joke!

**가속**(加速) acceleration. ～하다 accelerate; increase speed; speed up. ¶ ～적(인) accelerative; accelerating / ～적으로 with increasing speed; at an accelerating pace / 열차는 서서히 ～이 붙었다 The train gradually speeded up.
◉ ～기〔장치〕 an accelerator. ～력 an accelerating force. ～로켓 a booster. ～운동 accelerated motion. 순간～《자동차의》 lightning acceleration. 등～운동 a uniformly accelerated motion.

**가속도**(加速度) (degree of ) acceleration. ¶ ～로 with accelerated velocity; at an increasing tempo; with increasing speed / 중력～ acceleration of gravity.
◉ ～계〖항공〗 a G-meter. ～계수〖경제〗 an acceleration coefficient. ～원리〖경제〗 the acceleration principle. ～지진계 an accelerograph. 내(耐)～복(服)〖항공〗 an anti-G suit; a G suit.

**가솔**(家率) *one's* family; members of *one's* family. ¶ 많은 ～을 거느리고 있다 have a large family to support.

**가솔린** gasoline; gas 《미구어》; petrol 《영》. ¶ 자동차의 ～이 떨어졌다 We have run out of gas 〔petrol〕. ◉ ～엔진 a gasoline engine. ～차 a gasoline car.

**가송장**(假送狀)〖무역〗 a pro forma 〔provisional〕 invoice.

**가수**(假數)〖수학〗 a mantissa.

**가수**(歌手) a singer; a songstress (여자); a vocalist (성악가); a soloist (독창자). ◉ 유행가～ a singer of popular songs; a pop singer.

**가수금**(假受金) a suspense receipt.

**가수분해**(加水分解)〖화학〗 hydrolysis. ～하다 hydrolyze. ¶ 수산화나트륨을 ～하다 hydrolyze caustic soda.

**가수요**(假需要) disguised demand; speculative demand. ¶ ～의 급증 a sudden increase of disguised demand.

**가스** 《기체》 gas. ¶ 천연〔도시, 프로판〕～ natural 〔city, propane〕 gas / 연료용〔배기〕～ fuel 〔exhaust〕 gas / ～ 모양의 gaseous 《body》 / ～를 켜다〔끄다〕 turn on 〔off〕 the gas / ～불을 크게〔작게〕 하다 turn the gas up 〔down〕 / ～의 메인 밸브를 잠그다 turn off the gas at the main / ～불로 요리하다 cook (food) by gas / 뱃속에 ～가 차다 have gas 〔wind〕 in the bowels / ～가 이 파이프에서 샌다 Gas is leaking from this pipe. / ～ 냄새가 나다 smell gas / 한 달에 ～를 얼마나 쓰느냐 How much gas do you use 〔burn〕 a month? (분량) *or* What is your monthly gas bill? (요금) / 이 근처에는 아직 ～가 들어오지 않았다 No gas is served here yet. / 우리 집에는 도시 ～가 들어와 있다 We have city gas laid on in the house.
◉ ～검침원 a gas-meter reader. ～경보기 a gas alarm. ～계량기〔미터〕 a gas meter; a gasometer. ～관〔파이프〕 a gas pipe 〔line〕. ～기관〔엔진〕 a gas engine. ～기구 gas fittings. ～난로 a gas stove; a gas heater. ～누출 a gas leak. ～등 a gas lamp. ～라이터 a gas lighter. ～레인지 a gas range 〔stove, cooker〕. ～발동기 a gas motor. ～상(商) a gasman. ～연료 gas fuel. ～온도계 a gas thermometer. ～요금 gas rate: ～요금 수금원 a gas-bill collector. ～용접 gas 〔autogenous〕 welding. ～자살 suicide by inhaling gas. ～정(井) natural gas bed. ～중독 gas poisoning. ～(처형)실 a gas chamber. ～탄 a gas shell. ～탱크 a gas tank; a gasholder 《영》. ～ 터빈 a gas turbin. ～폭발 a gas explosion. ～회사 a gas company.

**가스러지다** ⇨ 거스러지다.

**가슬가슬하다** ① 《성질이》 (be) intractable; stubborn; willful. ② 《살결이》 (be) rough; chappy; bristly; sharp.

**가슴** ① 《흉부》 the breast; the chest; 《유방》 the breasts; 《가슴둘레》 the bust; 《품》 the bosom. (★ the chest는 심장·폐를 둘러싼 흉부 전체를, the breast는 대흉근의 튀어 나온 부분을 가리킴. 여성의 경우는 유방을 지칭하나, 노골적인 표현을 피하고 싶을 때는 bosom이나 bust를 사용함). ¶ ～이 풍만한 여자 a full-bosomed 〔full-breasted, bosomy〕 woman / ～을 펴다 throw out *one's* chest / ～을 펴고 걷다 walk with *one's* head held high / ～이

답답하다 *one's* chest feels tight; have a tightness in *one's* chest / ～이 아프다 have a pain in *one's* chest / ～의 X선 사진을 찍었다 I've had a chest X-ray (photo) taken.
② 《심장》 the heart. ¶ ～이 두근거리다 *one's* heart throbs 〔beats fast, leaps〕 / 흥분으로 ～이 두근거린다 My heart is 「beating fast 〔pounding〕 with excitement.
③ 《마음》 *one's* heart; *one's* mind. ¶ ～ 깊이 deep in *one's* heart / ～속 깊이 간직한 생각 an idea cherished deep in *one's* heart / ～이 내려앉다 be greatly surprised; be startled / ～이 미어지다 〔터지다〕 have *one's* heart break; be heartbroken 〔broken-hearted〕 / (격정 등으로) ～이 메다 feel a lump in *one's* throat; A lump came into *one's* throat. / ～이 터질 것 같다 feel as if *one's* heart would break 〔rend〕 / ～이 뿌듯하다 be satisfied 〔gratified〕 《with》 / ～이 후련해지도록 울다 weep *oneself* out; weep *one's* fill / 애인이 보고 싶어서 ～을 태우다 be dying 〔yearning〕 to see *one's* lover / ～ 깊이 묻어두다 bury 《a secret》 within *one's* heart; hug 《a secret》 to *one's* bosom / ～속을 털어놓다 unbosom *oneself;* make a clean breast of / 그의 말은 나의 ～을 찔렀다 His words went home to my heart. / ～이 벅차서 아무 말도 못 했다 My heart was too full for me to speak a word. / 그 소식을 듣고 기쁨에 ～이 두근거렸다 My heart leaped with joy at the news. / 그 말은 그녀 가슴에 깊이 새겨졌다 The words were deeply etched in her mind. / 그녀는 아들의 일로 ～을 태우고 있다 She is deeply worried about her son. / 너의 말은 내 ～을 후련하게 했다 Your remarks were a breath of fresh air to me. / 슬픔으로 ～이 메어졌다 My heart was choked with sorrow.
◉ ～걸이 《말의》 a girth; a cinch; a bellyband. ～앓이 (a) chest trouble; a chest disorder 〔ailment〕; a pain in the chest; heartburn; 《실연》 heartbreak. ～지느러미 〖어류〗 the pectoral fin. ～털 chest hair: ～털이 난 hairy-chested. ～통 the chest: ～통이 좁다 〔넓다〕 have a narrow 〔broad〕 chest.

**가슴둘레** the girth of the chest; 《양장의》 bust. ⇨ 흉위. ¶ 넓은〔좁은〕 ～ a broad 〔narrow〕 chest / ～를 재다 measure the chest / ～가 얼마가 되느냐 What are your chest's measurements?

**가슴츠레하다** ⇨ 거슴츠레하다.

**가습**(加濕) humidification. ～하다 humidify. ◉ ～기 a humidifier.

**가시**[1] ① 《장미 따위의》 a thorn; 《풀잎 따위의》 a prickle; 《덤불의》 a bramble; 《밤송이 따위의》 a bur; 《나뭇조각의》 a splinter. ¶ ～ 많은 thorny; spiny / 손가락에 ～가 박이다 get a splinter in *one's* finger / ～를 빼다 pull out a thorn.
② 《물고기의》 a fish bone; a spine. ¶ 잔 ～가 많은 《a fish》 full of fine bones / 목에 ～가 걸리다 have 〔get〕 a bone stuck in *one's* throat.
③ [비유적] a sting; a thorn in *one's* flesh. ¶ ～ 돋힌 stinging 〔sharp〕 《words》; harsh 《language》 / ～가 있다 be thorny; be prickly; be spined; be bony / ～ 돋힌 말을 하다 have a sharp 〔biting〕 tongue / 그의 말에는 ～가 있다 His words carry a sting. / 그는 나를 눈엣～로 여긴다 He always looks on me as a thorn in his flesh.
◉ ～덤불 a thorn thicket 〔bush〕; a bramble. ～면류관 a crown of thorns. ～밭 brambles: ～밭 길을 걷다 tread a thorny path. ～철망 barbed wire entanglement. ～철사 barbed wire.

**가시**[2] 《구더기》 a maggot; a grub; a worm. ¶ 간장에 ～가 생겼다 The soy sauce is infested with maggots.

**가시**(可視) visibility. ¶ ～의 visible. ◉ ～거리 a visibility range. ～광선 a visible ray. ～도 visibility. ～스펙트럼 a visible spectrum.

**가시나무** a thorny plant; a bramble; a brier. ¶ ～ 울타리 a hedge of thorny bushes.

**가시다** ① 《부시다》 wash (off, out); 《입을》 rinse (off, out). ¶ 그릇을 ～ wash dishes / 입을 ～ rinse out *one's* mouth.
② 《뒷맛을》 take away the aftertaste from (*one's* mouth). ¶ 사과를 먹어서 약의 쓴맛을 ～ take away the bitter taste of medicine with an apple. ③ 《고통 등이》 go away; leave; disappear; pass off. ¶ 두통이 가셨다 Headaches passed off. / 이 약을 먹으면 아픔이 곧 가신다 This medicine will give instant relief from pain.

**가시랭이** a pricker; a sticker; a thorn; a splinter.

**가시목** 〖식물〗 a white oak.

**가시버시** husband and wife; a (married) couple.

**가시세다** (be) tough and stubborn; unyielding.

**가식**(假植) tentative planting. ～하다 plant 《a tree》 tentatively.

**가식**(假飾) hypocrisy; dissembling; dissimulation; pretence; falsity. ～하다 dissemble; dissimulate; pretend; play; play the hypocrite; be two-faced. ¶ ～적인 hypocritical; false; affected / ～없는 unaffected; plain; natural; unpretentious; 《솔직한》 artless; frank.

**가심** 《부심》 washing; rinsing; 《뒷맛을》 taking away the aftertaste from (*one's* mouth). ～하다 wash; rinse.

**가심끌** a finishing chisel.

**가심질하다** apply a finishing chisel to.

**가십** gossip 《about》. ¶ ～을 좋아하는 사람 a gossip 〔gossipmonger〕. ◉ ～기사 a gossip item. ～기자 a gossip writer. ～난 a gossip column.

**가압**(加壓) pressurization. ～하다 pressurize; apply 〔give〕 pressure 《to》. ◉ ～솥 an autoclave. ～장치 a pressure device.

**가압류**(假押留) 〖법〗 temporary 〔provisional〕 seizure 〔attachment〕. ～하다 put under temporary attachment; attach 〔seize〕 《*a person's*》 property provisionally. ◉ ～영장 a writ of provisional attachment.

**가야금**(伽倻琴) a *kayagŭm;* the *Kaya* harp; a twelve-stringed Korean harp. ¶ ～탄주자 a *kayagŭm* player.

**가약**(佳約) ① 《만날 언약》 a lover's rendezvous. ② 《혼약》 a marriage vow. ¶ 백년 ～을 맺다 exchange marriage vows; get married; become man and wife.

**가양주**(家釀酒) home-brewed 〔bathtub〕 liquor.

**가언**(假言) 〖논리〗 a hypothesis. ¶ ～적 hypothetical; conditional. ◉ ～명제 a hypothetical proposition.

**가업**(家業) 《집안의》 a family business 〔trade〕; the traditional occupation of a family; 《세업》 a hereditary occupation 〔business〕. ¶ ～을 게을리하다 neglect *one's* family business / ～에 힘쓰다 pursue *one's* family trade with diligence; be engrossed in *one's* family business / ～을 이어 의사가 될 생각이다 intend to be a physician, following in *one's* father's footsteps / ～은 그의 차남이 계승했다 His second son succeeded him in the family business.

**가없다** (be) boundless. ¶ 가없는 바다 boundless ocean.

**가역**(可逆) 〖화학·물리〗 ¶ ～의 reversible. ◉ ～기관〔전지〕 a reversible engine 〔cell〕. ～반응〔변화〕 a reversible reaction 〔change〕.

**가연성**(可燃性) combustibility; inflammability. ¶ ～의 combustible; (in-)flammable / ～ 물질 combustibles; (in)flammable materials. ◉ ～가스 flammable gas. ～시험 an inflammability test.

**가열**(加熱) heating. ～하다 apply heat 《to》; heat. ¶ 물을 ～하다 apply heat to water; heat water / ～하여 살균하다 sterilize by heating; heat-treat 《milk》. ◉ ～건조 ustulation. ～기〔장치〕 a heater; a heating device 〔apparatus〕. ～분해 decomposition by heating. ～프레스〔압착기〕 a hot-press.

**가엾다** 《불쌍하다》 (be) pitiful; pitiable; 《애틋하다》 (be) pathetic; sad; sorry. ¶ 가엾은 고아 a poor orphan / 가엾은 신세 a miserable state; a sad plight / 가엾게 여기다 feel pity 〔sorry〕 for; take pity on; pity 《*a person*》; sympathize with / 가엾기도 해라 What a pity! *or* Poor thing 〔fellow〕! / 가엾어 볼 수 없었다 It was too pitiful to watch. / 가엾으니 살려 주어라 For pity's sake save the poor fellow.

**가영수증**(假領收證) an interim 〔a temporary〕 receipt.

**가영업소**(假營業所) ＝임시 영업소.

**가오리** 〖어류〗 a stingray; a stingaree.

**가옥**(家屋) a house; a building; 〖법〗 a messuage. ◉ ～대장 a house register 〔ledger〕. ～매매 dealing in real estate.

**가옥**(假屋) a temporary shed 〔shelter〕; a shanty; a shack; a tabernacle.

**가온음**(一音) 〖음악〗 a mediant. ◉ ～자리표 a C-clef.

**가외**(加外) extra. ¶ ～의 extra; spare; excessive / ～에 in addition to; besides over and above / ～ 사람 an extra member 〔person〕 / ～ 일을 하다 do extra work / ～ 비용이 약간 들 게다 You will need some additional money. ◉ ～수입 extra income.

**가요**(歌謠) a song; a ballad; an air. ◉ ～곡, 대중～ a folk song; a popular song. 국제 ～제 the international song fete 〔festival〕.

**가용**(家用) ① 《비용》 family expenses; household expenditures. ¶ ～을 절약하다 cut down family expenses. ② 《자가용》 home 〔domestic〕 consumption; use at home. ¶ 이것은 ～으로 남겨 두었다 I have kept this for use at home.

**가용물**(可溶物) a soluble substance.

**가용물**(可鎔物) a fusible metal.

**가용성**(可溶性) solubility. ¶ ～의 soluble.

**가용성**(可鎔性) fusibility. ¶ ～의 fusible.

**가우스** 〖전기〗 a gauss (자력의 단위).

**가운**(家運) the fortunes of a family. ¶ ~이 기울다 the fortunes of the family are on the wane 〔decline〕/ ~을 돌이키다 restore the (fallen) fortunes of *one's* family; retrieve the family fortunes.

**가운** a gown.

**가운데** ① = 안¹. ② 《복판·중간》 the middle; the center; the midst; the mean. ¶ ~형 the middle brother / 가운뎃손가락 the middle finger / ~ 토막 the center cut 《of a fish》/ 방 ~에 in the middle 〔center〕 of the room / ~를 잡다 hold the middle of 《*a thing*》; hold 《*a thing*》 in the middle / 길 ~로 걸어가다 walk in 〔keep to〕 the middle of the road / ~를 싹둑 자르다 cut in two in the middle. ③ 《중에·속에》 in; in the midst of; in the heart 〔center〕 of; between; among; of; out of. ¶ 학급 ~서 가장 우수한 학생 the best student in the class / 둘 ~ 하나를 택하다 choose between the two; choose one of the two / 많은 ~서 하나를 가지다 take one of many / 이 ~서 어떤 것이든지 셋을 취하라 Take any three of these. / 이것은 많은 예 ~ 하나에 불과하다 This is only one instance out of many. ④ 《…하는 중(에)》 while 〔in the process of〕 *do*ing. ¶ 가난한 생활 ~ while living in poverty / 바쁘신 ~와 주셔서 고맙습니다 It's very kind of you to call on me in spite of your being pressed with work.

**가운데열매껍질** 〖식물〗 a mesocarp.

**가웃** and a half. ¶ 석자 ~ three feet and a half; three and a half feet / 두 말 ~ two and a half pecks.

**가위** scissors; shears (큰); clippers (털 깎는). ¶ ~ 한 자루 a pair of scissors / ~로 자르다 cut 《*a thing*》 with scissors; clip 《hair》; prune 〔trim〕 《a tree》; shear 《sheep》. ◉ ~질 cutting with scissors; scissoring: ~질하다 scissor; do the cutting. ~춤 working 〔rattling〕 a pair of scissors in the air; playing with *one's* scissors. 가윗밥 waste scraps from cutting; scraps.

**가위**(可謂) 《과연·참》 truly; really; indeed; literally; 《가히 이르자면》 as can (well) be said; as might truly be said; so to speak; as it were; what you call; what is known as; what is well named. ¶ ~ 신사다 can truly be called a gentleman / 그것은 ~ 놀랄만한 뉴스였다 It was really surprising news.

**가위눌리다** have a nightmare 〔horrible dream〕; be hagridden; be tortured with terrible dreams.

**가위바위보** paper-scissors-stone〔rock〕.

**가위표**(—票) a check mark 《×》; the multiplication symbol 《×》; an '×'. ¶ ~를 긋다 make a check (mark); write an '×'.

**가으내** throughout the autumn; all through the fall.

**가을** ① 《계절》 autumn; fall 《미》 (★ 가을은 영국에서는 8, 9, 10월을 말하며, 미국에서는 9, 10, 11월을 가리키는데 낙엽기와 일치하므로 fall이 많이 쓰임. autumn은 미국에서 딱딱한 시적인 말임.). ¶ 맑은 ~ 날씨 fine autumn weather; clear 〔fine〕 weather peculiar to autumn; a clear autumn(al) day / 독서의 계절 ~ autumn, the best season for reading / 초~ early autumn; the beginning of autumn / 늦~ late autumn / 낙엽 한 잎이 ~을 알린다 A single leaf falling is a sign of autumn coming. ② 《추수》 harvest; reaping. ~하다 harvest; reap (a harvest). ¶ ~하기에 분주하다 be busy harvesting. ◉ ~걷이 autumn reaping: ~걷이하다 = ~하다. ~경치〔단풍〕 autumn scenery 〔tints〕. ~바람 an autumn wind 〔breeze〕. ~볕 the warm sunshine in autumn; autumn sunshine. ~보리 autumn-sown barley. ~비 an autumn rain. ~철 autumn (season).

**가을갈이** 〖농업〗 ① 《추경》 fall plowing. ~하다 plow 《a field》 in fall; do fall plowing for 《a crop》. ② 《파종》 autumn planting. ~하다 plant in autumn.

**가을일** harvest; harvesting; gathering 《in》; reaping. ~하다 (reap a) harvest.

**가이거계수**(—計數) 〖물리〗 Geiger count. ◉ ~기 a Geiger counter.

**가이거뮐러계수기**(—計數器) a Geiger-Müller counter.

**가이드** 《사람》 a guide; 《행위》 guiding.

**가이아나** 《남아메리카의 공화국》 Guyana.

**가인**(佳人) a beautiful woman; a beauty. ¶ 당대의 재사 ~ the wit and beauty of the age. ◉ ~박명(薄命) Beauty and long life seldom go hand in hand. *or* Beautiful flowers are soon picked.

**가인**(家人) 《가족》 *one's* family; *one's* people; 《가족의 일원》 one of a family.

**가일**(佳日) an auspicious day. ¶ ~을 택하여 성례하다 choose an auspicious day to solemnize a marriage.

**가일층**(加一層) all the more; the more; even 〔still, much〕 more. ¶ ~ 노력하다 make greater efforts; redouble *one's* efforts / 그녀는 머리가 검어 ~ 아름답다 Her black hair adds to her beauty.

**가입**(加入) 《회·클럽 따위에》 joining; entry; admission; affiliation; 《전화 따위의》 subscription. ～하다 enter 《into》; join 《a club》; become a member 《of》; be affiliated 《with》; belong 《to》; subscribe 《to, for》. ¶ 협회에 ～하다 become a member of the society 〔association〕/ 야구부에 ～하다 join the baseball club / 새로 독립된 나라를 유엔에 ～시키다 admit a newly independent country to the United Nations / 그 클럽에 ～하기란 매우 어렵다 It is very difficult to 「get into 〔enter, be admitted into〕 the club. / 그녀는 나에게 2천만 원 보험에 ～해 달라고 부탁했다 She asked me to be insured for twenty million won.
◉ ～금 an entrance fee. ～신청 application for admission; subscription (전화 등의): ～ 신청자 an applicant for membership. ～자 a member; a (telephone) subscriber. 공동 ～선 〚전화〛 a party line. 조약 ～국 a signatory (power) to a treaty; treaty participants.

**가입학**(假入學) admission of students on probation. ¶ ～을 허가하다 admit 《a student》 on probation.

**가자미** 〚어류〛 a flatfish; a sole; a plaice.

**가작**(佳作) a good piece (of creative work); a work of merit.

**가장**(家長) ① 《가구주》 the head of a family; a patriarch (남자); a matriarch (여자). ② 《남편》 my husband. ◉ ～제도 patriarchal system; patriarchy.

**가장**(家藏) storing in *one's* own house (행위); things stored in *one's* house (물건). ◉ ～집물(什物) household furnishings.

**가장**(假葬) 《임시의》 temporary burial 〔interment〕; 《어린이의》 burial of a child. ～하다 bury temporarily; bury a child.

**가장**(假裝) ① 《변장》 disguise; masquerade; a fancy dress. ～하다 disguise *oneself* 《as》; be disguised 《as》; wear a disguise. ¶ ～하여 in disguise / 여자로 ～하다 dress up 〔be disguised〕 as a woman. ② 《거짓꾸밈》 (a) pretense; a sham; semblance; make-believe. ～하다 feign 《illness》; pretend 《to be ill》; make believe 《to *do*》; make a show 《of》; assume the appearance 《of》. ¶ …을 ～하고 under pretense 〔cover, the guise, the cloak〕 of / 양민으로 ～하다 counterfeit 〔pose as〕 a good citizen / 그의 친절은 ～이다 His kindness is a mere show 〔pretense〕. ◉ ～무도회 a fancy-dress 〔masked〕 ball; a masquerade. ～행렬 a fancy-dress parade.

**가장** most; extremely; exceedingly; to the utmost 〔extreme〕. ¶ ～ 빨리 most rapidly / ～ 많이 extremely much / ～ 새〔헌〕 것 the newest 〔oldest〕 thing / ～ 위대한 사람 the greatest man / ～ 좋다〔나쁘다〕 be best 〔worst〕/ ～ 중요하다 be most important; be of the greatest importance / ～ 용감히 싸우다 fight most bravely / 나는 이것을 ～ 좋아한다 I like this best (of all). *or* I like this better than the others.

**가장귀** 《가지의 아귀》 the crotch of branches; a notch; a fork; 《가지》 a branch. ¶ ～가 진 나뭇가지 a forked branch / ～창 a forked spear.

**가장이** a twig; a branch; a limb.

**가장자리** the edge; the brink; the verge; the brim; the hem; the border; the margin 《of a leap》. ¶ 책상 ～ the edge of a desk.

**가재** 〚동물〛 a crawfish; a crayfish. ¶ ～는 게 편이라 《속담》 Like attracts like.

**가재**(家財) ① 《가구》 household effects 〔belongings〕; furnishings. ¶ ～를 꾸려 이사가다 move 〔remove〕 《to a town》 with all *one's* belongings; pack up *one's* belongings and move 《to a new home》. ② 《가산》 the family property 〔estate〕; *one's* entire fortune.

**가재걸음** walking 〔crawling〕 backward. ～치다 walk 〔crawl〕 backward.

**가전**(家傳) something handed down in a family; a family recipe 〔technique, secret〕. ¶ ～의 hereditary; 《techniques》 handed 「on within the family 〔down from father to son〕 / ～의 비방약 a medicine prepared from a family recipe; an old family remedy 〔cure〕/ ～의 보물 a family heirloom 〔treasure〕.

**가전제품**(家電製品) (electric) home appliances; a household electric appliance.

**가절**(佳節) ① 《명절》 a happy 〔an auspicious, a festive〕 occasion. ¶ 중추 ～ the midautumn festival. ② 《때》 a beautiful season. ¶ 양춘 ～ a pleasant springtime.

**가정**(苛政) despotic rule. ⇨ 학정.

**가정**(家政) home 〔household〕 management; housekeeping; running a house. ◉ ～과 the Department of Domestic Science; a course in domestic science. ～대학 the College of

Home Economics. ～학 domestic science; home economics.

**가정**(家庭) a home; a family; a household. ¶ ～의 home; domestic; family / ～용의 for home 〔domestic〕 use / ～에서 at 〔in the〕 home / 원만한 ～ a harmonious household / 즐거운 〔단란한〕 ～ a sweet home / 불화한 ～ a family in disorder; a disordered family / ～의 붕괴 the break-up 〔collapse〕 of a family / ～의 행복 domestic happiness / ～을 가지다 make 〔start, build, establish〕 a home; get married and settle down / ～을 방문하다 visit 〔call at〕 《*a person's*》 home / ～을 꾸려나가다 manage *one's* household / 가난한 ～에 태어나다 be born into a poor family 〔of poor parents〕 / 엄격한 ～에서 자라다 be brought up 〔raised〕 in a strict family / ～ 풍파가 끊이지 않는다 There's constant domestic discord in the family. / 청소년 범죄는 대체로 ～에 그 책임이 있다 The home is mostly responsible for juvenile delinquency.
◉ ～경제 household 〔domestic〕 economy. ～교육 home training 〔education〕; training at home. ～교훈 home teaching; family precepts. ～내 폭력 family 〔domestic〕 violence; violence in the home. ～란〔면〕 a domestic column 〔page〕; a homemaker's section 〔page〕 (주부의); a home life section (가정 생활의). ～방문 a home visit; making a round of calls 《at homes》; paying visits 《to homes》: 학생의 집을 ～ 방문하다 make a round of calls at *one's* pupils' homes. ～법률상담소 the Family Legal Advice and Counseling Center. ～법원 a domestic relation court; a family court: 서울 ～법원 the Seoul Family Court. ～부인 a housewife (주부); a housemaker 《미》. ～불화 domestic discord 〔troubles〕; friction between man and wife (부부의). ～비극 a tragedy in a family; a domestic tragedy. ～사정 family circumstances; family matters 〔affairs〕: ～사정으로 for family reasons. ～상비약 a household medicine; a domestic remedy 《for diarrhea》. ～생활 home life; domesticity. ～소설 a domestic novel. ～요리 home cooking. ～용수 water for domestic use. ～용품 housewares; household articles 〔commodities〕; household furnishings 〔appliances, utensils (도구)〕. ～ 의례 준칙 《observe》 the (simplified) family ritual standards. ～의학 home-doctoring. ～쟁의 a family dispute; 《cause, make》 domestic troubles. ～파괴범 a family-destroying criminal; a criminal who destroys family happiness (by raping women after robbing). ～평화 《disturb》 domestic peace. ～폭력 domestic violence. ～환경 a home background 〔environment〕.

**가정**(假定) (a) supposition; (an) assumption; a hypothesis (가설). ～하다 suppose; assume; presume.
¶ ～적 assumed; imaginary; hypothetical / …이라고 ～하고 on the assumption that…; supposing 〔assuming〕 that… / 평화가 왔다고 ～하자 Suppose that peace has come…. / 그렇다고 ～하더라도 네가 잘못이다 Granting that it is so, you are still (in the) wrong. / 그녀가 살아 있다고 ～하자 Let us suppose that she's living.
◉ ～법 〖문법〗 the subjunctive mood.

**가정관**(假定款) the provisional articles 《of an association》.

**가정교사**(家庭教師) a private teacher; a (private) tutor; a governess (여자); 《영》 a grinder (수험 준비를 위한).
¶ ～를 하다 teach 《a boy》 at 《his》 house; (act as a) tutor / ～를 두다 engage a tutor 〔private teacher〕 / ～ 밑에서 공부하다 study under a tutor / ～ 자리를 찾다 look out for a tutor's position / 그녀는 주 2회씩 그 소년에게 영어 ～ 노릇을 하고 있다 She teaches the boy English at his home twice a week.

**가정부**(家政婦) a kitchen maid; a maidservant; a housemaid; a domestic help 《미》. ¶ ～를 두다 keep a housemaid / ～ 구함 《광고》 Wanted a maid. *or* Domestic help needed.

**가정적**(家庭的) ¶ ～인 homely 《atmosphere》; domestic 《type》; family-oriented 《men》 / ～인 남자 a family man; a homebody / ～인 여자 a domestic 〔home-loving〕 woman / 그녀는 사교적이기보다는 오히려 ～이다 She is rather domestic than sociable. / 그는 결코 ～으로는 축복받지 못했다 His home life was anything but blissful. / 그 식당의 ～인 분위기가 마음에 든다 I like the homely atmosphere in that restaurant.

**가제** [< *Gaze* (G.)] ⇨ 거즈.

**가제목**(假題目) a tentative title.

**가제본**(假製本) ① 《견본쇄》 a dummy; a sample binding. ② 《임시제본》 temporary binding.

**가져가다** take (with *one*); take along; carry; take 〔carry〕 away. ¶ 이 책을 네 형한테 가져가거라 Take this book to your brother. / 누가 내 연필을 가져갔지 Who walked off with my pencil?

**가져오다** ①《지참》 bring; bring 《*a thing*》 with *one;* fetch; carry. ¶ 가서 우산을 가져오너라 Go and fetch my umbrella. / 우산을 가져왔습니다 I have brought the umbrella. / 물을 한 잔 가져오너라 Get me a glass of water. / 돈을 얼마나 가져왔느냐 How much money have you brought with you? / 아버지께서 술을 가져오라신다 Father is calling for wine. ② 《초래》 bring about 〔on〕; cause; incur; result 〔end〕 in. ¶ 집안에 불행을 ~ bring misfortune on *one's* family / 좋은 결과를 ~ bring 〔produce〕 satisfactory results.

**가조**(一調) 『음악』 A. ◉ 가단조 A minor. 가장조 A major.

**가조약**(假條約) a provisional treaty. ¶ ~을 맺다 conclude 〔make up, enter into〕 a provisional treaty 《with another country》.

**가조인**(假調印) an initial signature; initialing. ~하다 initial 《a treaty》. ◉ ~식 an initialing ceremony.

**가족**(家族) a family; members of a family; *one's* people 〔folks 《미》〕; a household (세대). ¶ ~ 동반 여행 a family trip / ~이 많다〔적다〕 have a large 〔small〕 family / ~의 일원으로 대하다 treat 《*a person*》 as a member of *one's* family / …~의 일원이 되다 enter the family of 《Mr. Smith》 / 너의 ~은 몇 사람이나 되느냐 How many members are there in your family? / ~은 모두 6명이다 We are a family of six in all. / 나는 부양할 대~이 있다 I have a large family to support.
◉ ~계획 a family planning: 한국 ~계획 협회 The Planned Parenthood Federation of Korea / 국제 ~ 계획 연맹 International Planned Parenthood Federation (생략 IPPF). ~구성 family structure. ~묘지 a family burial ground. ~법 family laws: 여성에게 불리한 ~법을 개정하도록 정부측에 요구하다 call for the government to amend the Family Law which is disadvantageous to women. ~ 부양 의무 family responsibility. ~수당 a family allowance. ~제도 the family system. ~ 지향〔중심〕적인 제도 the family-oriented system. ~탕 a private compartment in a public bath; a family bath. ~회의 a family council. 복합~ a composite family.

**가주소**(假住所) a temporary address.

**가죽**《살에 대하여》 skin; a skin (짐승의); a hide (특히 마소의); leather (무두질한); a fur (모피); a pelt (날가죽). ¶ ~제의 leather 《belt》; leather-made / ~을 벗기다 skin 《an animal》 / ~을 다루다 tan 〔dress, taw, treat〕 leather / 사람 ~을 쓴 짐승이다 be a brute in human form / 뼈와 ~만 남다 be all skin and bones; be reduced to a (mere) skeleton.
◉ ~가방 a leather bag; a briefcase. ~구두〔신〕 (leather) shoes; boots. ~끈 a (leather) strap. ~띠〔혁대〕 a leather belt. ~부대 a leather bag; a wineskin (포도주용). ~숫돌 a razor strap; a strop. ~옷 leather garments. ~장갑 leather gloves. ~점퍼 a leather jumper. ~제품 a leather; leather goods. ~채 a rawhide whip. ~표지 a leather cover; 《제본》 leather binding: ~ 표지의 책 a leather-bound book.

**가죽나무** 『식물』 a tree-of-heaven; an ailanthus.

**가중**(加重) 《무겁게 함》 weighting; adding an extra weight; 《형량》 aggravation; increasing 〔worsening〕 《punishment》. ~하다 weight; add an extra weight; aggravate; increase; worsen. ¶ 형을 ~하다 raise 〔aggravate〕 the penalty. ◉ ~과세 surcharge; additional tax: 사치품에 대한 10% ~ 과세, 10 per cent surcharge on luxurious articles. ~평균 『통계』 a weighted average.

**가중하다**(苛重一) (be) severely heavy 〔burdensome〕. ¶ 가중한 세를 부담시키다 impose a severely heavy tax burden / 가중한 과세에 시달리다 groan under the harsh and heavy burden of taxation.

**가즈럽다** (be) conceited; complacent; smug; self-satisfied.

**가증서**(假證書) a scrip; an interim bond.

**가증하다**(可憎一) (be) hateful; detestable; abominable; despicable; contemptible. ¶ 가증스럽다=가증하다 / 가증한 처사 spiteful conduct / 이제 와서 나를 배반하다니 참으로 가증스런 녀석이다 It is a despicable thing for him to betray me now.

**가지**[1] 《나무의》 a branch [일반적]; a bough (큰); a limb (큰); a twig (작은); a sprig (작은). ¶ ~를 꺾다 break off a branch / ~를 뻗다 「put out

〔spread〕 branches / ～를 자르다〔다듬다〕 cut off 〔lop off〕 branches; prune a tree / (나무가) ～를 치다 spread its branches out / ～ 많은 나무가 바람 잘 날이 없다《속담》A mother with a large brood has not a day of peace.

**가지**[2] ①《종류》a kind; a sort; a variety. ¶ ～ 수가 많다 There are many different kinds. / 이 꽃에는 두 ～가 있다 This flower comes in two varieties. / 이것은 그것과 한 ～ 책이다 This is the same sort of book as that.
②《꼽을 때》a kind; a sort; an item. ¶ 한 ～ 청이 있습니다 I have a favor to ask of you. / 그의 잘못은 한 두 ～가 아니다 He has a good many more than one or two faults. / 여러 ～로 괴로움을 끼쳤다 I caused you much trouble. / 몇 ～ 말할 것이 있다 I have a few things to talk to you about.

**가지**[3] 〚식물〛 an eggplant. ◉ ～(산)적, ～누름적 an eggplant shish kebab; an barbecued eggplant.

**가지가지** various kinds of; all sorts of; all manner of; of every kind 〔sort〕. ¶ ～ 경험 a varied experience / ～ 이유로 for various reasons / 담배도 ～다 There are all kinds of cigarettes.

**가지각색**(一各色)《of》every kind and description. ¶ ～의 sundry; miscellaneous; various / ～의 사람들 all sorts and conditions of people / ～이다 be various; be all different / 그 가게에선 ～의 물건을 판다 They sell all sorts of things in that store.

**가지고** ①《…을》¶ 그 사람 ～ 너무 그러지 마시오 Don't pick on him so! / 가뜩이나 성난 사람 ～ 왜 그래 Are you trying to make him still angrier?
②《…으로》with; by means of. ¶ 공을 ～ 놀다 play with a ball / 무얼 ～ 그리 싸우느냐 What are you quarreling about? / 한 달에 백 불을 ～ 어떻게 삽니까 How can you live on a hundred dollars a month?

**가지고야** only with. ¶ 이 돈 ～ 살 수 없지 You certainly can't buy it with this amount of money.

**가지다** ①《손에》have; take; hold; 《몸에》carry; have with 〔on〕 *one*. ¶ 돈 가진 것이 있느냐 Do you have any money with you? / 손에 무엇을 가지고 있느냐 What do you have in your hand? / 강도는 식칼을 가지고 있었다 The burglar was armed with a kitchen knife. / 꼭 가지고 있어라 Take firm hold of it. *or* Hold it fast.
②《소유》have; have got《구어》; own; possess; be in possession of; keep. ¶ 가게〔자동차〕를 가지고 있다 keep 〔own〕 a shop 〔car〕.
③《인격·자질》possess; be endowed《with》. ¶ 그녀는 여러 가지 덕을 가졌다 She possesses many virtues. / 사람은 이성을 가지고 있다 Man is endowed with reason.
④《품다》have; hold; entertain; harbor; cherish; embrace. ¶ 의견을 ～ have 〔hold〕 an opinion / 원한을 ～ harbor hatred; bear a grudge / 큰 야심을 ～ cherish a great ambition / 진보주의 사상을 ～ embrace progressivism.
⑤《임신》conceive; be pregnant. ¶ 애를 ～ be with child; be pregnant / 새끼를 ～ be with young (동물이).

**가지런하다** be of equal 〔uniform〕 size 〔height, *etc.*〕; be in order; be arrange neatly. ¶ 가지런히 trimly; evenly; neatly; uniformly; in order / 높이가 ～ be of uniform height / 책을 가지런히 하다 put books in order / 구두를 가지런하게 놓다 arrange shoes (in order).

**가지방**(加地枋) 〚건축〛 a doorsill.

**가직하다** (be) rather near; be not far off; be near 〔close〕 by. ¶ 가직하게, 가직이 within reach; near by.

**가진급**(假進級) passing on probation. ¶ ～시키다 pass《a student》on probation; condition a student《미》.

**가집행**(假執行) 〚법〛 provisional execution; a temporary injunction. ～하다 place under a temporary injunction; execute provisionally. ¶ 집을 ～하다 place the house under a temporary injunction.

**가짜**(假一) 《모조품》an imitation; a sham; a fake; a spurious article; 《위조품》a forgery; a counterfeit; a phony. ¶ ～의 sham; imitative; spurious; faked; forged; bogus / 이 물건은 ～다 This is a spurious article. / 이 서명은 ～다 This signature is a forgery. / ～에 조심하시오 Beware of imitation. / ～를 속아 샀다 I was palmed off with such a fake. / 추사(秋史)의 글씨에는 ～가 많다 There are many imitations in the works with Ch'usa's signature. *or* Many of the writings bearing the signature of Ch'usa are spurious imitations.
◉ ～도장 a forged seal. ～돈《지폐》a counterfeit note 〔bill〕. ⇨ 위조지폐. ～박사학위 a faked doctoral degree. ～보석 an imitation stone. ～위스키 spu-

rious whisky. ~의사 a quack (doctor); a (medical) charlatan. ~증서 a counterfeit bond. ~차량번호판 a fraudulent car number plate. ~편지 a forged letter: ~편지를 쓰다 write a letter in a disguised hand. ~형사〔학생〕 a bogus detective 〔student〕.

**가차압**(假差押) = 가압류.

**가차없다**(假借—) (be) relentless; ruthless. ¶ 가차없이 relentlessly; ruthlessly; without mercy; mercilessly / 가차없이 처분하다 handle 《a culprit》 without gloves 〔reserve〕 / 가차없이 나무라다 censure 《*a person*》 roundly 〔without mercy〕 / 가차없는 철퇴를 내리다 mete out stringent punishment; take rigorous disciplinary action; crack down rigorously / 가차없이 그를 처벌해야 한다 You should punish him relentlessly.

**가책**(呵責) scolding (책망); torment (정신적 고통). ~하다 scold; torment. ¶ 양심의 ~ compunction; qualms; the pangs 〔pricks, stings〕 of (a guilty) conscience / 양심의 ~을 받다 be conscience-stricken; be troubled by pangs of conscience / 양심의 ~으로 죄를 자백하다 be driven to confess 〔admit〕 *one's* guilt by the pangs of conscience.

**가책**(苛責) violent scolding; torment. ~하다 scold severely; torment.

**가처분**(假處分) provisional disposition; a temporary injunction. ~하다 arrange temporary 〔make provisional〕 disposition 《of》. ¶ 사태 수습을 위해 ~ 신청을 하다 apply for provisional disposition to settle the matter.

**가처분소득**(可處分所得) a disposable income.

**가철**(假綴) paper binding; (a) temporary binding. ~하다 bind in paper; put a temporary binding on.

**가청**(可聽) [형용사적] audible; audio. ◉ ~거리 《within》 earshot. ~성 audibility. ~신호 audio signals. ~역 〖생리〗 the threshold of audibility. ~음 audible sounds. ~주파수 audio frequency. ~주파 증폭기 an audio frequency amplifier. ~한계 the audible limit.

**가축**(家畜) a domestic 〔farm〕 animal; cattle (소); [집합적] livestock. ¶ ~의 개량 improvement of livestock / 식육용 ~ fat stock / ~의 떼 a herd of cattle 《미》 / ~을 치다 raise 〔breed〕 livestock / ~들은 목장에서 풀을 뜯고 있었다 Cattle were grazing in the pasture. ◉ ~병원 a veterinary hospital; 《애완동물의》 a pets' hospital. ~사료 feedstuff; feeding stuff. ~상인 a dealer in livestock; a cattle dealer. ~우리 a shed. ~운반차 a cattle-van〔-truck〕; 《철도의》 a stock car; a cattle cage 《미》.

**가출**(家出) leaving home; (an) elopement. ~하다 run away from home; leave home. ¶ 요즈음 많은 아이들이 ~한다 Nowadays 〔These days〕, many young boys and girls run away from home. ◉ ~소년〔소녀〕 a runaway boy 〔girl〕. ~인 a runaway.

**가출옥**(假出獄) (a) parole; (a) provisional release. ~하다 be released provisionally 〔on parole〕; be paroled. ¶ ~중이다 be on parole. ◉ ~자 a parolee; a man on parole.

**가치**(價値) value; worth; merit.

> 용법 **value** 주로 유용성·중요성이란 점에서 사람에 따라 그 평가가 달라질 수 있는 상대적인 가치. **worth** 본질적·영속적인 가치, 특히 추상적·정신적·도덕적 가치. 그러나 금전적인 척도를 나타내는 가치란 뜻에서는 value와 worth가 거의 동일하게 쓰인다. **merit** 「뛰어나다, 우수하다」, 「장점」이 있어서 좋다란 뜻이 함축된 의미의 가치를 뜻함.

¶ 교육의 ~ the value of education / 이용 ~ utility value / ~ 있는 valuable; worthwhile; worthy 《of praise》 / ~ 없는 valueless; worthless; of no value / 매우 ~ 있는 invaluable; priceless / 읽을 〔문화적〕 ~가 있는 책 a book 「worth reading 〔of literary merit〕 / 볼 만한〔백만 원의〕 ~가 있는 그림 a picture worth 「seeing 〔a million won〕 / ~를 알다 know 〔appreciate, acknowledge〕 the value 《of a painting》 / 한푼의 ~도 없다 be entirely useless; be not worth a cent 〔a red penny〕 / 비평할 만한 ~가 없다 be beneath criticism / ~가 더하다〔떨어지다〕 increase 〔diminish〕 in value / 달러의 ~가 많이 달라졌다 The value of the dollar has varied greatly. / 이것은 증거로서 ~가 없다 This is of negative value as proof. / 그 고지는 전략적 ~가 크다 The height 〔hill〕 possesses great strategic value.

◉ ~관 a sense of values. ~기준 a standard of value. ~론 the theory of value; axiology. ~분석 value analysis (생략 VA). ~척도 a measure of value. ~체계 a value system. ~판단 value judgment; valuation; evaluation. 경제～ commercial 〔economic〕 value. 실제적 ～ practical 〔actual〕 value: 실제적 ～가 있는 발견 a discovery of practical value. 영양～ dietetic 〔nutritive〕 value. 예술적 ～ artistic value. 정신적 ～ a spiritual value. 효용～ utility value.

**가친**(家親) my father.

**가칠**(加漆) additional coating with lacquer. ～하다 give an added coat of lacquer to; lacquer once again; recoat.

**가칭**(假稱) 《잠정의》 a tentative 〔provisional〕 name; 《사칭》 an assumed name 〔title〕; a false name 〔title〕. ～하다 designate tentatively; assume a false name. ¶ ～「민중 재단」 tentatively named "Minjung Foundation".

**가탄하다**(可嘆―) be lamentable 〔regrettable, deplorable〕.

**가탈**[1] ⇨ 까탈.

**가탈**[2] 《말의 걸음걸이》 jogging; jolting. ～거리다 jog; keep jolting. ¶ ～가탈 jogging; jolting. ◉ ～걸음 a jogging pace.

**가택**(家宅) a (private) house; a residence. ◉ ～방문 a house call; a visit to a home. ～연금 house arrest; confinement.

**가택수색**(家宅搜索) a house 〔domiciliary〕 search; a raid 《구어》. ～하다 search 《*a person's*》 house 《for illegal goods》. ¶ ～을 당하다 have *one's* house searched. ◉ ～영장 a search warrant.

**가택침입**(家宅侵入) trespassing in another's house; unlawful entry. ～하다 trespass on 《*another's*》 premises; break into 《*a person's*》 residence.
◉ ～자 a trespasser; a housebreaker. ～죄 (a) trespass; (the charge of) housebreaking: 그 사내는 ～죄로 고발되었다 The man was charged with housebreaking 〔trespass(ing)〕.

**가터** ① 《양말대님》 a garter. ② 《편물》 ¶ ～뜨기 a garter stitch. ③ 《가터 훈장》 the Order of the Garter.

**가토하다**(加土―) put on (fresh) earth; cover with (fresh layer of) earth.

**가톨릭** 《천주교》 Catholicism; the Roman Catholic Church (교회). ¶ ～의 Catholic / ～을 믿다 believe in Catholicism. ◉ ～교도 a Catholic.

**가트** 《관세와 무역에 관한 일반 협정》 GATT. [<the *G*eneral *A*greement on *T*ariffs and *T*rade] (WTO의 전신).

**가파르다** (be) precipitous; steep. ¶ 가파른 길 a steep path; a sharply rising road / 가파른 절벽 a precipitous cliff / 계단이 ～ The stairs are very steep.

**가편**(可便) pro(s); aye(s); yes-vote; (vote) for. ¶ ～과 반대편 pros and cons; ayes and noes; yes-votes and no-votes; for and against (votes) / 최후의 투표는 ～이 30, 반대편이 18이었다 The final vote was: for 30, against 18.

**가편**(加鞭) whipping; lashing. ～하다 apply the whip; whip up; 《독려하다》 spur 〔urge〕 《on》. ¶ 주마(走馬) ～하다 《말을》 whip 〔lash〕 a galloping horse; 《사람을 독려하다》 spur 〔urge〕 《*a person*》 on 《to *do*》.

**가표**(可票) an affirmative vote. ¶ ～를 던지다 cast an aye vote for 《a bill》 / ～ 20, 부표 15였다 There were 〔The vote stood at〕 twenty ayes and fifteen noes.

**가풀막** a precipice. ～지다 (be) precipitous; steep.

**가풍**(家風) a family custom 〔tradition〕; the ways of a family. ¶ ～에 맞지 않다 be not in keeping with the customs of the family; fail to conform to the family's traditions.

**가필**(加筆) correction; retouching; revision. ～하다 add some (correcting) touches 《to》; correct; touch up; revise. ¶ 초고에 ～하다 add some touches to *one's* manuscript / 이 논문은 ～ 수정할 필요가 있다 This essay 〔paper〕 needs revision(s) and correction(s).

**가하다**(可―) 《옳다》 (be) right; good; be all right; 《좋다》 (be) fairly good; passable. ¶ 네 말이 ～ What you say is right. / 그렇게 말해도 ～ You may (rightly) say so. / 그를 합격시켜도 ～ You may pass him. / 둘 다 ～ Either will do.

**가하다**(加―) ① 《가산》 add; 《합계》 add 〔sum〕 up. ¶ 다섯에 셋을 ～ add three to five; add five and three / 모든 수를 ～ add up all the numbers / 원금에 이자를 ～ add interest to the principal.
② 《덧붙이다》 add 〔annex〕 《one thing to another》; 《포함시키다》 include. ¶ 보충적인 설명을 ～ add a supplementary explanation / 약간의 손질을 가해서 with minor improvements / 어떤 여관에서는 방값에 식사대를 가한 것이 숙박요금이 된다 In a certain style hotel, the rate includes both the room charge and the meal charge.
③ 《증가하다》 increase; gather 〔pick up〕 《speed》. ¶ 박차를 ～ spur *one's* horse; [비유적] spur 〔urge〕 《*a person*》 《to *do*》 / 열차는 속력을 가했다 The train gathered 〔picked up, increased〕 speed.
④ 《주다》 give; inflict; deliver; deal; apply. ¶ 압력을 ～ give 〔apply〕 pres-

sure 《to》 / 제재〔위해〕를 ～ inflict「a punishment 〔an injury〕《on》/ 열을 ～ apply heat / 적에게 맹격을 ～ deliver 〔make〕 fierce attack against the enemy / 그는 상대에게 일격을 가했다 He gave 〔dealt〕 a blow to his opponent.

**가해**(加害) doing harm; inflicting injury; violence; an offense; wrong (doing). ～하다 do harm 《to》; inflict injury 《on》; do violence 《to》.
◉ ～자 an injurer; an assailant; a wrongdoer; an offender: ～자는 그 자리에서 체포되었다 The assailant was arrested on the spot. ～행위 harm; a harmful act; a wrong.

**가헌**(家憲) household regulations; a family tradition.

**가형**(家兄) my elder brother.

**가호**(加護) divine protection; providence; guardianship. ¶ 신의 ～로 by the protection of Heaven / 신의 ～를 빌다 call upon 〔pray to〕 God for help.

**가혹**(苛酷) severity; harshness; cruelty; brutality. ～하다 (be) severe; harsh; merciless; relentless; cruel; brutal.
¶ ～한 조건으로 on merciless terms / ～한 법률 a severe law / ～한 대우 harsh treatment / ～한 비평 severe 〔harsh〕 criticism / ～한 형벌을 가하다 inflict a severe punishment / 그렇게 어린 아이에게 매질을 하다니 ～하다 It's cruel of you to lash such a little child. / ～한 기상 조건하에서도 나무는 자라고 있었다 The trees kept growing in (spite of) the severe climate.

**가화**(佳話) a good 〔an interesting〕 story.

**가환**(家患) 《병》 sickness in *one's* family; 《걱정》 family cares 〔misfortune〕.

**가황**(加黃) 〖화학〗 vulcanization. ～하다 vulcanize. ◉ ～고무 vulcanized India rubber. ～유 vulcanized oil.

**가효**(佳肴) delicacies to be eaten with wine; a tasty side dish to go with wine.

**가훈**(家訓) family precepts.

**가희**(歌姬) a songstress; a female singer.

**가히**(可―) (may) well; fairly well; (might) well; (can) rightly 〔suitably〕.
¶ ～ 일대의 석학이라 할 만한 사람 a man who might well be called the greatest scholar of the age / ～ 짐작할 수 있다 It may easily be perceived 〔presumed〕 that.... / ～ 그렇다 할 수 있다 You may well say so. / 이로 보아 그가 얼마나 부지런한지 ～ 알 수 있다 From this you can well imagine how diligent he is.

**각**(各) each; every; all. ¶ 각 사람에 하나씩 one piece each / 각 열 사람씩 every ten people / 각 방에 두 사람씩 들어 있다 Two people are (living) in each room.

**각**(角) ① 《뿔》 a horn; an antler (사슴의); a feeler (촉각). ② 《네모·사각》 a square. ③ 〖수학〗 an angle. ¶ 내〔외〕각 an interior 〔an exterior〕 angle / 직〔예, 둔〕각 a right 〔an acute, an obtuse〕 angle. ④ 〖음악〗 the middle note of the Korean pentatonic scale.

**각가지**(各―) all sorts 〔kinds〕; every sort 〔kind〕; various kinds. ¶ ～의 various (kinds of); all sorts of; a variety of; miscellaneous / ～ 물건 all sorts of things; things of every sort.

**각각**(各各) each; every; all; respectively; severally; separately; individually.
¶ ～ 책상을 하나씩 가지고 있다 Each of us has a desk to himself. / 사람은 ～ 제 할 일이 있다 Every man has his own duty to perform. / ～ 제 할 일을 해라 Go to your respective jobs. / ～ 500원씩 줘라 Give them 500 won each. / 우리 형제들은 ～ 따로 산다 Each of my brothers lives by himself. / 갈 때는 같이 갔으나 돌아올 때는 ～ 따로 왔다 We all went together but returned our separate ways. / 일등과 이등 상품이 톰과 프랭크에게 ～ 수여되었다 The first and second prizes were awarded to Tom and Frank respectively.

**각각으로**(刻刻―) from moment to moment; every moment 〔hour, minute〕; momentarily. ⇨ 시시각각(時時刻刻).

**각개**(各個) each; every one; one by one. ◉ ～격파 defeating one by one 〔one after the other〕: ～격파하다 defeat the enemy one by one; 《반대자 등을》 argue down one after another. ～교련 〖군사〗 individual drill.

**각개인**(各個人) each; each 〔every〕 individual; each person. ¶ ～의 소유품 the belongings of each person / ～의 문제 a matter of private concern for each individual.

**각거하다**(各居―) live in separate houses.

**각계**(各界) each 〔every〕 field 〔circle of society〕; all fields 〔circles〕; every walk of life. ¶ ～의 대표자 representatives of every sector of society / ～각층의 사람들 all sorts and conditions of people / ～의 명사 eminent persons from various circles / ～의 인사가 여기 다 모였다 People from all walks of life are gathered here.

**각고**(刻苦) hard work; arduous labor; close application. ～하다 work hard

〔laboriously〕; apply *oneself* closely to 《*one's* studies》. ¶ ~ 십년 끝에 그는 초지를 관철하였다 He accomplished his purpose after ten years of hard work.

**각골난망**(刻骨難忘) remembering forever; cherishing the memory of. ~하다 indelibly engrave in *one's* memory; will never forget; [사물이 주어] be 「engraved in 〔deeply impressed on〕 *one's* mind. ¶ 베푸신 은혜 실로 ~입니다 I'll never forget all the favors you have done for me.

**각과**(殼果) a caryopsis (*pl.* -opses, ┌-opsides).

**각광**(脚光) footlights; floats; spotlight. ¶ ~을 받다 be highlighted; be in the limelight; be spotlighted / ~을 받고 등장하다 move into 〔enter〕 the limelight / 그는 매스컴의 ~을 받고 있다 He is in the spotlight 〔limelight〕 of mass communication. / 그는 세계 외교 무대에서 ~을 받았다 He stood in the spotlight of world diplomacy.

**각국**(各國) 《각 나라》 every 〔each〕 country 〔nation〕; 《여러 나라》 various 〔all〕 countries 〔states〕. ¶ 세계 ~ all countries of the world / 세계 ~의 대표 representatives from all over the world / ~에서 대표 한 사람씩 a representative from each country / ~의 무역 사정을 시찰하러 가다 go to various countries to observe commercial affairs / ~은 2명의 대표를 대회에 파견한다 Each country sends two delegates to the rally. / ~의 주한 대사가 그 파티에 참석했다 All foreign ambassadors to Korea were present at the party.

**각군데**(各—) each place; everywhere. ¶ ~ 사람이 다 함께 모였다 People from all parts of the country gathered together.

**각기**(脚氣) beriberi. ¶ ~에 걸리다 get beriberi; have an attack of beriberi.

**각기**(各其) [명사] each (one); every one; [부사] each; individually; respectively; severally; in *one's* own way. ¶ 사람은 ~ 장점과 단점이 있다 Each man has his merits and demerits.

**각기둥**(角—) 『수학』 a prism.

**각내**(閣內) ¶ ~의〔에서〕 in 〔inside〕 the Cabinet / ~의 분열을 초래하다 invite Cabinet disunity.

**각다귀** ① 『곤충』 a striped mosquito. ② [비유적] a sponge; a parasite; a bloodsucker. ◉ ~판 a state of mutual parasitism; a dog-eat-dog situation.

**각다분하다** 《a job》 prove difficult; (be) hard and tedious.

**각단** the drift and shape of an affair.

**각도**(角度) ① 『수학』 an angle; degree of an angle. ¶ 40 도의 ~로 at an angle of 40 degrees / ~를 재다 take 〔measure〕 the angle 《of》. ② 《관점》 a standpoint; a point of view; an angle. ¶ 이러한 ~에서 본다면 (looked at) from this point of view; viewed from this angle / 여러 가지 ~에서 보다 view from different angles / 모든 ~에서 검토하다 survey 〔study〕 《a problem》 from all angles. ◉ ~계 a goniometer.

**각도기**(角度器) a (graduated) protractor; a graduator. ◉ 반원〔전원〕~ a semicircular 〔circular〕 protractor.

**각등**(角燈) a square hand-lantern; a bull's eye lantern.

**각뜨다**(脚—) cut up a carcass in parts; draw and quarter.

**각령**(閣令) a Cabinet ordinance.

**각로**(脚爐) a foot-warmer.

**각론**(各論) the particulars (on a subject); the details; a detailed treatise. ¶ ~에 들어가다 go into details 《of》 / 총론에서 ~으로 들어가다 go from generals to particulars. ◉ 해부학~ special anatomy; a detailed treatise on a special branch of anatomy.

**각료**(閣僚) the Cabinet 〔Ministerial〕 colleagues [총칭]; a Cabinet member 〔minister〕; a member of the Cabinet (개인). ¶ ~급의 ministerial (level); of cabinet level / ~급 회의 a ministerial meeting; a conference of ministerial level. ◉ ~회의 a Cabinet meeting. 경제~ Cabinet ministers in charge of economic affairs; economic ministers. 전(前)~ an ex-minister. 한일~회담 the ROK-Japan ministerial meeting.

**각루**(刻漏) a water clock.

**각립**(各立) ~하다 part 《with》; separate 《from》; break 〔split〕 up; withdraw 《from a party》; secede in a group.

**각막**(角膜) 『해부』 the cornea. ◉ ~렌즈 a corneal lens. ~백반(白斑) a leucoma; a leukoma; keratoleucoma. ~염 corneitis; keratitis. ~은행 an eye bank. ~이식 transplantation of the cornea; a corneal transplant. ~절개 keratotomy. ~혼탁 corneal opacity.

**각모**(角帽) an academic 〔a square, a college〕 cap; 《예복용》 a mortarboard; 《학위 수여식 때의》 a graduation cap.

**각목**(角木) a square wooden club 〔stick〕.

**각박**(刻薄) 《몰인정》 severity; harshness; hardheartedness; 《인색》 stinginess; miserliness. ～하다 (be) severe; harsh; hardhearted; stingy; miserly; closefisted; tight(-fisted). ¶ ～한 세상 the hard 〔tough〕 world; hard 〔stern〕 life / ～한 세상이다 This is a rough world we are living in. / ～한 시절이다 These are hard times.

**각반**(脚絆) gaiters; spats; leggings.

**각방**(各方) everywhere; every direction; all directions. ¶ ～으로 수색하다 search everywhere / ～으로 사람을 보내다 send messengers in all directions.

**각방**(各房) each 〔every〕 room; all rooms. ¶ 우리는 ～을 쓰고 있다 We live in separate rooms. *or* Each one of us has a room to himself. *or* We each have our own room.

**각방면**(各方面) everywhere; 《in》 every direction 〔quarter〕; 《in》 all directions 〔quarters〕. ¶ ～으로부터 from all quarters; from many sources / 사업은 ～에서 발전하고 있다 The business is expanding in every direction. / 이 대학의 졸업생은 실업계의 ～에서 활약하고 있다 The graduates of this university are taking an active part everywhere in the business world.

**각배**(各一) ① 《짐승의》 different litters from the same mother. ② 《이복》 (two half-siblings) having different mothers.

**각벌**(各一) 《옷》 separate garments; 《서류》 separate copies.

**각별하다**(各別一) ① 《특별》 (be) especial; special; particular; 《현저》 (be) marked; noticeable; 《파격적》 (be) exceptional. ¶ 각별히 especially; particularly; markedly; remarkably; exceptionally / 각별한 호의〔사랑〕 special favor 〔love〕 / 각별한 차이 marked difference / 각별히 조심하다 take special care; take every caution; be very careful 《of *one's* health》; take special precautions 《against fire》 / 각별한 용무가 없다 have nothing particular to do / 그 추위란 또 ～ The cold (spell) is exceptional. ② 《깍듯하다》 (be) polite; decorous; courteous. ¶ 각별히 politely; civilly; courteously / 각별히 대우하다 treat with kindness 〔courtesy〕; give a warm reception.

**각본**(脚本) a play(book); a drama; a (play) script; 《영화의》 a (movie) scenario; a (film) script. ¶ ～으로 만들다 dramatize; adapt for the stage 〔movies〕; make a stage 〔screen〕 version of / ～을 쓰다 write a play / ～을 무대에 상연하다 stage a play. ◉ ～가 a scriptwriter; a playwright (연극의); a scenario writer (영화의). ～낭독 a dramatic reading. 가극～ (opera) libretto.

**각봉하다**(各封一) seal 《a letter》 separately; send under separate cover.

**각부**(各部) 《부분》 each 〔every〕 part; all parts; the parts; 《각 부서》 each 〔every〕 department 〔section〕; all departments; the departments; 《정부의》 every ministry 〔department〕. ¶ 인체 ～의 구조 the structure of the parts of a body. ◉ ～장관 the minister of each department.

**각 부분**(各部分) each 〔every〕 part; various parts.

**각빙**(角氷) an ice cube.

**각뿔**(角一) 〖수학〗 a pyramid.

**각살림**(各一) living separately; living apart. ～하다 live separately; live apart; maintain separate residences.

**각상**(各床) ① 《각각의》 each dinner table. ② 《독상》 separate tables; dinner laid separately for each person. ～하다 set individual tables. ¶ ～해서 먹다 dine at individual tables.

**각색**(各色) ① 《종류》 all sorts 〔kinds〕; various kinds. ¶ 각양～의 various; diverse / ～의 물건 all sorts of things; things of every sort and variety / 각인 ～ "every man to his own taste". ② 《빛깔》 each 〔every〕 color; all 〔various〕 colors.

**각색**(脚色) dramatization. ～하다 dramatize 《a novel》; adapt 《a novel》 for the stage 〔a play〕. ¶ 이 영화는 춘향전을 ～한 것이다 This movie was adapted from the Tale of *Ch'unhyang*.

**각서**(覺書) a memorandum (*pl.* ～s, -da); a memo; a note (외교상의); a protocol (의정서). ¶ ～의 교환 an exchange of notes 〔memoranda〕 / ～를 보내다 send a note 《to》.

**각선미**(脚線美) beautiful shape of legs; a nice leg line; "a well-turned ankle". ¶ ～가 좋은 여자 a woman with shapely legs. ◉ ～대회 a leg-beauty contest.

**각설**(却說) ① 《화제를 돌림》 changing the subject in narration. ～하다 change the subject (in narration). ② [부사적] 《딴 말을 꺼낼 때》 apart from; setting 《this question》 aside; 《본래의 이야기로 돌아갈 때》 now to resume our story; to return to the topic. ～하다 return to the subject; get back from a digression.

**각설이**(却說一) 〖민속〗 a singing beggar

(at the marketplace).
**각설탕**(角雪糖) cube 〔lump〕 sugar; sugar cubes. ◉ ～집게 sugar tongs.
**각섬석**(角閃石) 〖광물〗 amphibole.
**각성**(各姓) different 「surnames 〔family names〕; people with different 「surnames 〔family names〕. ◉ ～바지 「half brothers 〔individuals〕 with different surnames.
**각성**(覺醒) awakening. ～하다 《무지에서》 awake 《from, to》; wake up 《to》; come to *one's* senses; 《잘못에서》 be disillusioned. ¶ 영적(靈的) ～ spiritual awakening / ～시키다 awaken 《*a person*》 to 《*something*》; disabuse 〔rid〕 *a person* 《of *his* mistaken idea》; open 《*a person's*》 eyes. ◉ ～제 a stimulant; a pep pill 《미구어》.
**각세공**(角細工) hornwork; hornware; manufacturing 《*things*》 from horns. ◉ ～품 horn manufactures.
**각속도**(角速度) 〖물리〗 angular velocity.
**각수**(刻手) a carver; a sculptor; a wood engraver.
**각시** ① 《인형》 a doll; a doll bride. ② 《새색시》 a bride; a newly married woman. ◉ ～놀음 playing with dolls.
**각아비자식**(各—子息) sons of different fathers; half brothers (with the same mother).
**각양**(各樣) various ways; all manners; all sorts. ◉ ～각색 = 각색(各色) ①.
**각오**(覺悟) 《마음 준비》 readiness; preparedness; 《결심》 (a) resolution; determination; 《체념》 resignation. ～하다 be 「ready 〔prepared〕 for 《the worst》; have *one's* mind made up 《to》; be 「resolved 〔determined〕 《to *do*》; be resigned 《to *one's* fate》.
¶ 그것은 ～한 바이다 I expect nothing less than that. *or* I am prepared for it. / 그 일을 완수할 ～가 되었느냐 Do you have the firm determination to accomplish the job? / 나는 최선을 다할 ～이다 I am determined to do my best. / 그는 죽음을 ～하고 있었다 He was resigned to death. / 낙방해도 좋다는 ～로 S대에 응시해 보겠다 I will apply for admission to S University though I may fail the entrance exam.
**각외**(閣外) ¶ ～의〔에서〕 outside the Cabinet.
**각운**(脚韻) 《시가에서》 an end rime; a rime at the end of a line. ¶ ～을 밟다 rime lines (at the end).
**각원**(閣員) a Cabinet 「minister 〔member〕.
**각위**(各位) each 〔every〕 gentleman; all gentlemen; 《서신에서》 Gentlemen; Sirs. ¶ 관계자 ～ To whom it may concern (★ 공문서·회람 따위의 서두에서 불특정 관계자를 지칭하는 문구) / 내빈 ～의 건강을 위하여 축배를 올립니다 I drink to the health of all the guests present.
**각의**(閣議) a Cabinet 「meeting 〔conference〕. ¶ ～에 부치다 lay 《a problem》 before a Cabinet council / ～를 열다 call 〔hold〕 a Cabinet council 〔meeting〕. ◉ 임시〔정례〕～ an 「extraordinary 〔ordinary〕 Cabinet meeting.
**각이하다**(各異—) be different from each other.
**각인**(各人) each 〔every〕 person; every one of you; everybody. ◉ ～각색 "So many men, so many minds.": ～각색으로 in all their respective ways. ～각성(各姓) every individual; each man with each surname.
**각인**(刻印) carving a seal. ～하다 carve a seal.
**각일각**(刻一刻) = 시시각각.
**각자**(各自) each 〔every〕 one; every individual; [부사적] each; individually; respectively; severally. ¶ ～는 의무를 다하라 Each of you fulfill your own duty. / ～는 최선을 다하라 Let every one do his best. / ～ 점심을 가져올 것 Each (is) to bring his own lunch. / 우리는 ～ 자기 생각을 말했다 We each expressed our ideas. *or* Each of us expressed his idea. / ～ 자기 부서로 가라 Go to your posts. / 「저녁 식대는 내가 낼게」—「아냐 ～ 부담으로 하자」 "I'll pay for dinner, OK?"—"No, let's 「split the bill 〔go Dutch 《구어》〕."
**각재**(角材) square 「lumber 〔timber 《영》〕; rectangle lumber 《미》; 《작은》 a scantling.
**각적**(角笛) a horn; a bugle.
**각조**(各條) each 〔every〕 article; each 〔every〕 item; all 「articles 〔items〕; the articles.
**각종**(各種) each 〔every〕 kind; all sorts 〔kinds〕; various kinds; the varieties. ¶ ～의 of every kind; of all 「sorts 〔kinds〕; all 「sorts 〔kinds〕 of; various / 저희 상점에는 ～ 모자가 있습니다 We have all kinds of hats (in stock). ◉ ～ 경기 all sorts of 「sports 〔games〕. ～사물 all sorts of things; things of every sort and variety. ～직업 occupations of various kinds: 모임에는 ～ 직업의 사람들이 모였다 People of various occupations gathered for the meeting.
**각주**(角柱) ① 《네모 기둥》 a square pillar 〔column〕. ② = 각기둥.
**각주**(脚註) a footnote. ¶ ～를 달다 put

in 〔add, append〕 a footnote; give footnotes 《to a book》.

**각죽**(刻竹) a pipe carved of bamboo.

**각지**(各地) = 각처.

**각질**(角質) horny substance; 〖생화학〗 keratin; collagen. ¶ ~의 horny; corneous; keratinous. ◉ ~조직 corneous 〔horny〕 tissue. ~층 horny layer; stratum corneum. ~화 cornification; keratinization.

**각처**(各處) each 〔every〕 place; all places; various places 〔quarters〕. ¶ ~에 everywhere; in every place; in several places; 《여기저기에》 here and there / 전국 ~에서 from every corner 〔all parts〕 of the country / ~에 사람을 보내다 send a messenger to each place / ~ 사람이 다 모였다 People from all over are here.

**각체**(各體) 《글씨의》 (various) forms of a written character; 《활자의》 (various) print types; fonts 〔founts 《영》〕; (various) styles of writing.

**각추렴**(各—) collecting from each; contributing jointly; pooling; splitting; Dutch treat (회식에서). ~하다 collect from each; contribute jointly; pool; defray jointly; split; go Dutch. ¶ 비용을 ~하였다 Each paid his own share of the expenses. *or* They split the expenses. / ~하자 《구어》 Let's split the tab. *or* Let's go Dutch.

**각축**(角逐) competition; rivalry; struggle 《for mastery》. ~하다 compete; vie 《with》; contend 《against》; struggle 《for mastery》. ¶ 선거에서 다른 입후보자와 ~을 벌이다 compete with other candidates at an election. ◉ ~장(場) the arena of competition. ~전(戰) a hot 〔sharp〕 contest; keen competition.

**각층**(各層) each 〔every〕 floor 〔stratum〕; all floors 〔strata〕. ¶ 각계 ~의 《people》 of all social standings; all levels of society / 사회 ~의 사람들 people of all social strata / ~마다 서다 《승강기가》 stop at every floor.

**각치다** ① =할퀴다. ② 《부아를 지르다》 needle 《*a person*》 《구어》; get 《*a person*》 mad.

**각테**(角—) a horn rim. ◉ ~안경 horn-rimmed glasses.

**각통**(各通) 《문서·통신문의》 each copy; all copies; separate 〔respective〕 copies.

**각통질** bloating an ox with fodder and water before selling it. ~하다 force fodder and water down 《an ox》.

**각파**(各派) 《정당의》 each 〔every〕 party; 《파벌》 each faction; 《종교》 each 〔every〕 sect 〔denomination〕; 《유파·학파》 each school. ◉ ~ 교섭 단체 an interparty liaison group (정당간의); an intraparty liaison group (당내의).

**각판**(刻版) ① 《판목》 a printing block; a woodblock; a woodcut(ting). ② 《각판본》 a book printed from a block 〔plate〕.

**각피**(角皮) 〖해부〗 cuticle. ◉ ~소(素) cuticula.

**각필**(擱筆) laying down *one's* pen; closing a letter; concluding a book. ~하다 lay down *one's* pen; close a letter; conclude a book.

**각하**(却下) (a) rejection; turning down; 〖법〗 (a) dismissal. ~하다 reject; turn down; dismiss. ¶ 청원을 ~하다 reject 〔turn down〕 a petition / 그는 대법원에 상고하였으나 ~되었다 His appeal to the Supreme Court was quashed 〔dismissed〕.

**각하**(閣下) 《2인칭》 Your Excellency; 《3인칭》 His 〔Her〕 Excellency (*pl.* Their Excellencies). ¶ 대통령 ~ Mr. President.

> 참고 「각하」의 호칭: 우리 나라에서 「…각하」란 경칭은 대통령에게나 붙이는 최고의 호칭으로 인식되어 있으나, 영어에서는 여러 종류의 높은 지위·관직에 있는 사람에 대한 경칭으로 사용되며, 그 종류도 다양하다. **Excellency** 장관·대사·지사·주교·총독 및 그 부인 등에 대한 호칭으로 쓰이는 경칭: 주한 미국 대사 각하 His Excellency the American Ambassador to Korea. Excellency 대신으로 영국에서는 다음 호칭들도 쓰인다. **My Lord** [milɔ́ːrd], **Your** 〔**His**〕 **Lordship** 후작 이하의 귀족·고등법원 판사·주교 등에 대한 경칭. **Your** 〔**His**〕 **Worship** 사법권을 가진 행정장관·지사·시장 등에 대한 경칭. **Your** 〔**His**〕 **Eminence** 로마 가톨릭의 추기경에 대한 경칭.

**각항**(各項) each 〔every〕 item 〔article〕; all items 〔articles〕.

**각혈**(咯血) =객혈(咯血).

**각형**(角形) ① 《모난 형상》 square shape. ② 《사각형》 a quadrilateral.

**각화**(角化) 〖의학〗 cornification; keratinization. ◉ ~증 keratodermia; hyperkeratosis.

**간** 《짠맛》 saltiness; a salty taste; 《짠 정도》 seasoning with salt; 《짠 조미료》 a salty seasoning. ¶ 간을 하다 apply 〔add〕 salt 《to》 / 간이 짜다 be too salty / 간이 싱겁다 be not salty enough; be not well salted / 간이 맞다〔맞지 않

다〕 be well 〔badly〕 seasoned with salt / 간을 보다 taste 《soup》 to see how it is seasoned with salt / 생선에 간을 하다 salt fish / 국의 간이 꼭 맞는다 The soup is just salty enough.

**간**(艮) 〖민속〗 《간괘》 the trigram 《☶》.

**간**(肝) the liver; [비유적] courage; guts 《구어》. ¶ 간농양(膿瘍) hepatic abscess / 간동맥 the hepatic artery / 간이 크다 be daring 〔bold, plucky〕 / 간이 작다 be chicken-hearted; be cowardly / 간이 콩알만해지다 be scared stiff; be terrified; be panic-stricken / 간이 철렁하다 be shaken 〔shocked, frightened〕 / 간에 기별도 안 가다 be hardly enough to be worth eating; barely begin to satisfy *one's* stomach / 간에 붙었다 쓸개에 붙었다 하다 be two-faced; be not constant; be fickle.
◉ 간암 liver cancer. 간엑스 liver extract. 간이식 liver transplantation. 간절개 hepatotomy. 간종창(腫脹) enlargement 〔swelling〕 of the liver.

**간**(間) ① 《가옥 면적의 단위》 ⇨ 칸.
② 《길이》 a unit of length (＝180 cm).
③ 《관계》 relationship; 《관계의, 관계에서》 between; among. ¶ 형제간 the relationship of brothers / 모자간의 사랑 the love between mother and child / 그 둘은 부자간이다 They are father and son. / 과학자들간에서 그것은 상식으로 통한다 That's a matter of common knowledge among scientists. / 그 조약은 한국, 독일, 영국, 미국간에 조인되었다 The treaty was signed between Korea, Germany, Great Britain and the United States.
④ 《…중에서》 out of; either ... or.... ¶ 부자간에 한 사람은 올 것이다 Either father or son will come.
⑤ 《어느 쪽이든 관계없이》 ¶ 비가 오든지 안 오든지 간에 (너에게) 가겠다 Rain or shine, I will come. / 가부간에 알려주기를 바란다 I hope you will let me know whether it is yes or no.
⑥ 《…동안》 for; during; in. ¶ 과거 10년간 during 〔for〕 the past 〔last〕 ten years / 5분간의 휴식 a five minutes' recess 〔intermission〕 / 1주일간 머물다 stay for a week / 3일간 계속해서 for three days 「running 〔on end〕 / 그는 5일간에 그 일을 끝냈다 He finished the work in five days.
⑦ 《장소의 사이》 between; among. ¶ 서울 부산간의 거리 the distance between Seoul and Pusan / 산간의 작은 부락 a small village among the mountains.

**간간이**(間間—) ① 《이따금》 at times; now and then; occasionally; once in a while; at intervals; from time to time. ¶ ～ 오는 손님 a casual visitor / ～ 그런 일이 일어난다 It happens once in a while. / 그는 ～ 편지를 보낸다 He writes to me at some intervals. / ～ 소나기가 오겠습니다 There will be showers from time to time. ② 《듬성듬성》 at intervals; here and there. ¶ ～ 일정한 간격으로 심다 plant them at regular intervals.

**간간짭짤하다** (be) pleasantly salty; good and salty; (be) well-seasoned; (be) properly salted.

**간간하다**[1] 《맛이》 (be) pleasantly salty; nicely salted. ¶ 간간한 게 맛있다 be nicely salty / 좀 ～ be a bit salty.

**간간하다**[2] 《재미있다》 (be) thrilling; fascinating. ¶ 이야기의 간간한 대목 the thrilling part of a story.

**간거르다**(間—) leave an interval 《between》; skip a time 〔place〕 《in》.

**간격**(間隔) ① 《공간·거리》 a space; an interval; a distance; a gap. ¶ 최소 200미터의 ～ a space of at least 200 meters / 일정한 ～을 두고 at regular intervals / 3미터의 ～을 두고 at three-meter intervals; three meters apart / ～을 두다 leave spaces / ～을 죄다 lessen the distance between; move closer together / 5분 ～으로 운행하다 operate at an interval of five minutes / 버스는 몇 분 ～으로 떠납니까 How often does the bus leave? / 버스는 3분 ～을 두고 온다 Buses come at intervals of three minutes.
② 《틈·사이》 a crevice; a chink; a gap; an opening; 《끊김》 an intermission; 《불화》 a breach of friendship (친구간의); an estrangement; a difference; discord 《between》. ¶ ～이 생기다 [사물이 주어] cause an estrangement 《between them》.

**간결**(簡潔) brevity; conciseness. ～하다 (be) brief and to the point; concise; terse; compendious; pithy.
¶ ～히 concisely; tersely; briefly / ～한 문체〔문구〕 a concise style 〔phrase〕 / ～하고 요령 있다 be brief and to the point / 그는 그 문제를 ～히 설명하였다 He explained the issue briefly and to the point. / 저자는 ～한 문체로 잘 알려져 있다 The author is famous for his concise style. / 질문에 ～히 답하시오 Answer briefly to the question.

> **용법** **concise** 문장·문체·연설 등이 말수가 적으며, 작은 공간에 많은 정보를 제공하고 있다는 뜻: a concise explanation (간결한 설명). **brief** concise와 거의 같은 뜻이나, 「짧다」는 데 중점을 둔 말. **terse** 문장·문체·연설 따위가 간결·솔직하면서도 요령 있게 핵심이 잘 나타나 있다는 뜻: terse headlines (핵심을 찌르는 표제). **compendious** 논문·책 따위 포괄적인 것이 본질을 벗어나지 않으면서 매우 간명하다는 뜻: a compendious history of Korean literature (간명한 한국 문학사).

**간경변증**(肝硬變症) 〖의학〗 cirrhosis of the liver.

**간계**(奸計) a trick; a plot; an evil [a crafty] design; wiles; an intrigue. ¶ ~를 꾸미다 make crafty designs; concoct tricks / 적의 ~에 빠지다 play into the enemy's hand / ~로 아무를 속이다 deceive 《*a person*》 with a scheme; trick 《*a person*》.

**간고**(艱苦) 《고생》 hardship; suffering; privations; affliction; 《곤궁》 misery; poverty; destitution. ~스럽다, ~하다 (be) poor; destitute; afflicted. ¶ ~스럽게 지내다 be badly off; live in poverty; be in dire need / ~를 겪다 undergo hardship; go through hardship / ~를 이기다 overcome hardship.

**간곡**(懇曲) kindness; cordiality; warmth. ~하다 (be) kind; cordial; hospitable. ¶ ~히 kindly; cordially; warmly / ~한 권고 kind advice / ~한 편지 a kind letter / ~한 인사 cordial greetings / ~히 타이르다 give 《*a person*》 a good talking-to; reason 《with *a person*》 earnestly 《on》; persuade 《*a person*》 earnestly.

**간과**(干戈) 《병장기》 shields and spears; arms; weapons; 《전쟁》 warfare. ¶ ~를 들다 take up arms.

**간과**(看過) 《묵인》 overlooking; connivance; 《빠뜨림》 passing over. ~하다 overlook; condone; connive at; let 《*a thing*》 go [pass]; turn a blind eye to; pass 《*a thing*》 unnoticed. ¶ 과실을 ~하다 overlook a fault / 물가 상승은 ~할 수 없는 중대 문제다 The rise in prices is a serious problem not to be overlooked.

**간교**(奸巧) craft; cunning; wiliness. ~스럽다, ~하다 (be) crafty; cunning; wily; sly. ¶ ~한 녀석 a sly [crafty] guy [fellow]; an old fox.

**간구**(懇求) requesting earnestly; soliciting; begging. ~하다 earnestly request; solicit; beg; sincerely hope.

**간국** 《짠물》 salty liquids; a salt solution; brine.

**간균**(桿菌) 〖생물〗 a bacillus (*pl.* bacilli); a bacterium (*pl.* bacteria).

**간극**(間隙) ① 《틈》 a gap; an aperture; an opening; a chink; a crevice. ¶ ~을 메우다 stop [fill up, bridge] a gap. ② 《불화》 a split; an estrangement. ¶ ~이 생기다 fall out 《with each other》; arise a difference 《between the two》.

**간기**(肝氣) (a kind of) baby colic.

**간기**(刊記) a colophon; an imprint.

**간기능검사**(肝機能檢査) a liver-function exam(ination).

**간기능부전**(肝機能不全) hepatic insufficiency.

**간나위** a cunning [sly] person.

**간난**(艱難) hardships; difficulties; troubles; affliction; adversity; ordeal. ~하다 (be) hard; difficult; troublesome. ¶ 인생의 ~ the troubles [hardships] of life / ~을 겪다 undergo [go through] hardships; have a rough time [hard life, rugged life] / ~을 참고 견디다 endure [bear] hardships; endure [stand] adversity / ~을 극복하다 overcome difficulties.

**간뇌**(間腦) 〖해부〗 the diencephalon; the interbrain.

**간다개** the headstall of a bridle.

**간단**(間斷) interruption; intermission; a break; a pause. ~없다 (be) ceaseless; incessant; continuous. ¶ ~없이 incessantly; ceaselessly; unceasingly; continuously; without a break / ~없이 전화가 걸려오다 have telephone calls almost without a break.

**간단**(簡單) simplicity; brevity; 《용이》 ease. ~하다 (be) simple; brief; short; easy. ¶ ~히 simply; briefly; in brief; easily; with ease / ~한 일 light [easy, simple] work; a cinch / ~한 절차로 through a simple procedure / ~히 말하면 to put it simply [briefly]; in brief; to be brief; in a nutshell 《구어》; to make a long story short / ~히 말하다 give a short account 《of》; explain briefly / ~한 식사를 하도록 하자 Let's have a light meal, shall we? / 이유는 매우 ~하다 The reason is simple [plain] enough. / 이 기계는 조작이 ~하다 This machine is easy [simple] to operate. / 네가 생각하는 것처럼 일이 그렇게 ~히 진행되지는 않을 게다 Things won't go on as smoothly as you expect.

**간단명료**(簡單明瞭) simplicity and clarity; conciseness. ～하다 (be) plain and simple; clear and concise. ¶ ～하게 plainly and simply; briefly and clearly / ～하게 말하다 speak briefly and to the point; make *one's* explanation short and clear / 글은 ～함이 그 생명이다 Brevity is the soul of writing.

**간담**(肝膽) 《간과 담》 liver and gall; 《속마음》 *one's* innermost heart. ¶ ～을 서늘케 하는 광경 an appalling [a gruesome] sight / ～이 서늘해지다 be extremely frightened [appalled]; *one's* blood runs cold / ～을 서늘케 하다 freeze 《*a person's*》 heart with terror; make 《*a person*》 shiver.

**간담**(懇談) a familiar talk; a friendly chat; a confabulation. ～하다 have a friendly [familiar] talk 《with》; chat 《with》. ¶ ～식으로 이야기하다 have an informal talk 《with》 / 홍 선생님을 모시고 ～하다 have a talk with Mr. Hong as its central figure. ◉ ～회 an informal gathering for discussion(s) 《on, about》; a get-together for friendly talk.

**간대로** 《not》 so easy [cheap]; 《none》 too easy [cheap].

**간댕간댕** shaking; trembling.

**간댕거리다** shake; tremble.

**간데라** a metal hand lamp [lantern].

**간데족족** everywhere[wherever] *one* goes.

**간독**(懇篤) kindness; cordiality. ～하다 (be) kind; cordial; warm; genial.

**간동간동** bundling 《it》 up neat.

**간동그리다** bundle 《it》 up neat.

**간동하다** (be) neatly bundled.

**간두**(竿頭) the greatest extreme. ¶ ～지세(之勢) the most critical situation.

**간드랑간드랑** dingle-dangle; wavering; swaying.

**간드랑거리다** dangle; sway; waver. ¶ 나뭇잎이 ～ leaves sway on a tree / 초롱이 바람에 ～ a lantern dangles in the breeze.

**간드러지다** ① 《모양이》 (be) coquettish; willowy; be full of flirtation. ② 《음성·노래가》 have a fascinating lilt; be modulated in a charming [bewitching] way; be haunting. ¶ 간드러진 노래 a lilting song / 노래를 간드러지게 부르다 sing a song with a charming lilt / 간드러지게 웃다 laugh coquettishly [fascinating].

**간드작거리다** sway slightly.

**간들간들** 《바람이》 《the wind blows》 gently; softly; 《흔들림》 with swaying [swinging, shaking] motion; 《매혹적》 charming(ly); flirting(ly); coquettish(-ly); 《소리》 lilting(ly).

**간들거리다** ① 《바람이》 blow gently [softly]. ② 《흔들리다》 sway; swing; shake; dangle; wobble; waver; tremble. ¶ 나뭇잎이 바람에 ～ the leaves tremble in the breeze. ③ 《매혹적》 put on coquettish airs; act coquettishly; play the flirt.

**간디** 《인도의 지도자》 Mohandas Karamchand Gandhi (1869-1948). ◉ ～주의 Gandhiism; Gandhian principles; passive resistance.

**간디스토마**(肝—) 〖동물〗 a liver fluke; a flukeworm; *distoma hepaticum* (L.); 《병》 distomatosis; liver rot.

**간략**(簡略) 《간단》 simplicity; conciseness; terseness; brevity; 《약식》 informality. ～하다 (be) simple; concise; terse; brief; informal. ¶ ～히 simply; briefly / ～한 기사 a short news story / ～한 보고 a brief report / ～하게 하다 make simple [brief]; simplify; abbreviate; abridge 《a process》.

**간릉**(幹能) being sly [wily]. ～하다, ～스럽다 (be) sly; wily; insidious.

**간리**(奸吏) a wicked [crafty] official.

**간만**(干滿) ebb and flow; flux (and reflux); tide. ¶ ～의 차 the difference between the rise and fall of the tide / (조수의) ～이 없는 tideless / 조수에는 ～이 있다 The tide rises and falls.

**간망**(懇望) an earnest request [entreaty]. ～하다 earnestly request; make an earnest request.

**간맞다** be well salted [seasoned]; be salted [seasoned] properly.

**간맞추다** season well; salt properly.

**간물** salty water; 《간국》 brine.

**간물**(奸物) a cunning fellow; a sly guy; a fox.

**간물**(乾物) ⇨ 건물(乾物).

**간밤** last night; yesterday evening. ¶ ～에 난 불 last night's fire / ～에 곳곳에 도둑이 들었다 There were many burglaries last night.

**간방**(間方) an in-between direction.

**간병**(看病) nursing. ～하다 nurse; tend; look after; sit up with *a person.* ¶ ～인 a (sick) nurse / 헌신적으로 ～하다 attend on a sick person with devotion / 장기간의 ～으로 몹시 지치다 become exhausted from a long period of nursing / 그들은 극진히 부친을 ～하였다 They tenderly nursed [looked after, attended] their sick father. / 어

머니는 잠을 안 자고 아들을 ～했다 The mother sat up with her sick son.

**간보다** taste; see how the food is salted 〔seasoned〕.

**간부**(姦夫) an adulterer; a paramour. ¶ ～를 두다 be unfaithful to *one's* husband; commit adultery; cuckold *one's* husband.

**간부**(姦婦) an adulteress. ¶ ～의 남편 a cuckold.

**간부**(間夫) a married woman's secret lover.

**간부**(幹部) a leading 〔principal〕 member; an executive; [집합적으로] the managing staff; the management; the executive members. ¶ 회사의 ～ the executives of a company; 《경영진》 the management / ～급에 있는 사람 a person in an executive position / 최고 ～ the top executive / 중견 ～ a middle-class executive / 민주당 ～ the executive members of the Democratic Party. ◉ ～직원 officials in responsible posts. ～회 《기관》 an executive board. ～회의 an executive council; a staff conference 〔meeting〕; a meeting of the managing staff. ～후보생 《군대의》 a military cadet.

**간비대(증)**(肝肥大(症)) hypertrophy of the liver.

**간사**(奸詐〔邪〕) cunningness; slyness; foxiness; deceitfulness; craft; guile; deceit. ～하다〔스럽다〕 (be) cunning; sly; foxy; deceitful; crafty; wily; fawning; toadying. ¶ ～한 놈 a foxy fellow / ～하게 cunningly; slyly; foxily; deceitfully; craftily / ～부리다 play a sly game; be a wily customer.

**간사**(幹事) ① 《일처리》 administering affairs. ② 《사람》 a manager; an executive secretary; a managing treasurer. ◉ ～장 a secretary-general; a chief secretary.

**간사**(諫死) ～하다 remonstrate at the risk of *one's* life.

**간살** fawning; toadying; (a) flattering. ¶ ～부리다 fawn upon; toady; flatter; curry favor 《with *a person*》; court another's favor; cringe 〔truckle〕 to / ～을 잘 부리다 have a well-oiled tongue. ◉ ～쟁이 a flatterer; a sycophant; a toady; an apple polisher 《미》.

**간상**(奸商) a dishonest merchant; a crooked dealer; an illicit trader. ◉ ～배 (a gang of) dishonest merchants.

**간색**(看色) 《표본 관찰》 sampling; 《물건》 a sample. ～하다 sample. ◉ ～대 a sharp-edged metal scoop.

**간색**(間色) an intermediate 〔in-between〕 shade; a compound 〔secondary〕 color; halftone.

**간석지**(干潟地) a beach at ebb tide; dry beach; a tideland. ¶ ～를 개간하다 reclaim tidal land. ◉ ～개간사업 a tidal land reclamation project.

**간선**(看―) 《선을 봄》 meeting 〔interview〕 preliminary to a marital engagement. ～하다 pay a preliminary visit to the prospective bride(groom).

**간선**(幹線) a main 〔trunk〕 line. ¶ 이 도로는 양국간 교통의 ～이다 This highway is an artery of communication between the two countries. ◉ ～도로 a trunk 〔main〕 road; a highway; an arterial road; a main route.

**간섭**(干涉) interference; meddling; intervention. ～하다 interfere 《in *a matter*, with *a person*》; meddle 《in》; intervene 《in》; 《쓸데없이》 put 〔stick, poke〕 *one's* nose 《into》; poke 《into》.

> **용법** 아래 세 낱말 모두 「간섭하다」란 뜻이지만, 함축되어 있는 특징을 구별하면 다음과 같다. **interfere** 간섭하여 방해한다는 뜻. **meddle** 남의 일에 관심을 가지고 참견한다는 뜻. **intervene** 나쁜 결과가 발생치 않도록 어떤 사건, 일, 시기 등에 개입한다는 뜻.

¶ ～하기 좋아하는 사람 a meddler; a busybody; an officious person; a meddlesome fellow / ～받다 be interfered with / ～을 받지 않고 free from intervention / 타국의 ～을 초래하다 invite 〔lead to〕 foreign intervention / 남의 일에 ～하다 meddle in another's business; 《사생활에》 step into *a person's* private life / 내정에 ～하다 intervene in the internal affairs of a country / 아무의 ～도 받지 않다 be *one's* own master / 쓸데없이 ～하다 make uncalled-for meddling / 내 일에 ～하지 마라 Leave me alone. *or* Hands off my business. *or* Don't put 〔poke〕 your nose into my affairs. / 아무에게도 집안 일에 관해 ～받고 싶지 않다 I don't want others to meddle 〔interfere〕 in my family affairs.

◉ ～굴절계 『물리』 interference refractormeter. ～상(像) 『물리』 interference figure. ～색 『물리』 interference color. ～주의 a policy of intervention 〔interference〕. 공동～ collective 〔joint〕 intervention. 학원～ government interference in campus activities.

**간성**(干城) a bulwark; a defender; a safeguard. ¶ 국가의 ～ the bulwarks of the state.

**간세포**(間細胞) an interstitial cell.

**간소**(簡素) simplicity; plainness. ~하다 (be) simple 〔plain〕. ¶ ~한 생활 《lead》 a simple life / ~한 식사 a plain 〔homely〕 meal / ~한 옷차림을 하다 be plainly dressed / ~하게 simply; plainly / ~하게 하다 simplify 《a ceremony》 / 우리는 결혼식을 매우 ~하게 치렀다 We held our wedding in a very small way.

**간소화**(簡素化) simplification. ~하다 simplify. ¶ 정부 기구를 ~하다 simplify the Government setup 〔structure〕 / 관공서의 수속이 ~되었다 The public office procedures have been simplified.

**간수**(一水) salt water; brine.

**간수**(看守) a (prison) guard; a jailer 《미》; a prison officer. ⇨ 교도관.

**간수하다** take care of; keep; put 《goods》 aside 〔away〕 for future use; have 《*a thing*》 in *one's* keeping 〔custody〕. ¶ 소중히 ~ treasure (up); lock away / 여름에는 음식을 잘 간수하지 않으면 상한다 In summer food is easily spoiled unless it is kept well. / 그것을 안전한 장소에 간수해 둬라 Keep it in a safety place. / 그것은 내가 간수하고 있다 I have it in my custody 〔keeping〕.

**간식**(間食) eating between meals; a snack. ~하다 eat between meals; have a snack. ¶ ~으로 감자튀김을 먹다 eat potato chips 「for *one's* snack 〔between meals〕 / ~을 안 먹기로 하다 give up snacks.

**간신**(諫臣) a councilor 〔an adviser〕 to the king; a privy councilor; a devoted retainer.

**간신**(奸臣) a villainous retainer; a treacherous subject; a traitor.

**간신히**(艱辛—) barely; narrowly; hardly; with difficulty; under the wire. ¶ ~ 도망하다 have a narrow escape; barely escape; escape by a hair's breadth / ~ 이기다 win 《a game》 by a shave 〔narrow margin〕 / ~ 합격하다 just manage to pass the test; scrape through the examination / ~ 살아가다 barely manage to make a living 〔to get along〕; eke out a scanty livelihood; make a bare living / 그는 ~ 당선되었다 He was elected by a narrow majority. / 우리는 ~ 적의 포위를 뚫었다 We succeeded in breaking the enemy's siege by the skin of our teeth.

**간악**(奸惡) wickedness; treachery. ~하다〔스럽다〕 (be) wicked; treacherous. ¶ ~한 무리 a gang of scoundrels; rogues; rascals.

**간언**(間言) mischief-making remarks; sowing discord; malicious gossip.

**간언**(諫言) a remonstrance; remonstration; admonition. ~하다 remonstrate 《with》; admonish. ¶ ~을 듣다 listen to remonstrances / ~에 따르다〔따르지 않다〕 follow 〔reject〕 advice / ~을 받아들이지 않다 give no ear to *one's* expostulations / ~은 귀에 거슬리는 법이다 Good advice is 〔sounds〕 harsh to the ear.

**간염**(肝炎) 〖의학〗 inflammation of the liver; hepatitis. ◉ ~ 예방 접종 the anti-hepatitis inoculation. 바이러스성 ~ viral hepatitis. B형~ hepatitis type B. 전염성~ infectious hepatitis. 혈청 ~ serum hepatitis 〔jaundice〕.

**간엽**(肝葉) 〖해부〗 the lobe of the liver.

**간요**(肝要) importance; necessity. ⇨ 긴하다.

**간웅**(奸雄) a villainous hero; a great villain.

**간원**(懇願) an earnest appeal; (an) entreaty; solicitation; supplication. ⇨ 간청. ~하다 entreat; beseech; implore; earnestly beg; solicit; make an earnest appeal; plead 《with *a person* to *do*》. ◉ ~자 a solicitor; a supplicant.

**간유**(肝油) (cod-)liver oil.

**간음**(姦淫) adultery; illicit intercourse; sexual misconduct. ~하다 commit adultery; have illicit intercourse 《with》; 《미혼자와》 fornicate 《with》. ¶ 여자를 보고 음욕을 품는 자마다 마음에 이미 ~하였느니라 Every one who looks at a woman lustfully has already committed adultery with her in his heart (마태복음 V: 28). ◉ ~범 《범행》 adultery; 《사람》 an adulterer(남자); an adulteress(여자). ~죄 adultery.

**간이**(簡易) 《간단함》 simplicity; handiness; 《쉬움》 easiness; ease. ~하다 (be) simple; handy; easy; plain. ◉ ~(생명)보험 postal life insurance. ~세율 simplified customs rate. ~수도 a provisional 〔small-scale, private〕 water-supply system. ~숙박소 a cheap lodging 〔rooming〕 house; a flophouse 《미속어》. ~식당 a snack bar 《미》; a cheap eating house. ~재판소 a summary court. ~주택 a simple frame house; 《조립식의》 a prefabricated house. ~화(化) simplification: 생활의 ~화 the simplification of living / ~화하다 simplify.

**간자**(間者) a spy. ⇨ 간첩(間諜).

**간자말** a horse with white forehead and cheeks.

**간작**(間作) 《작물》 intercropping; 《간접 소작》 sharecropping. ~하다 intercrop; sharecrop.

**간잔지런하다** *one's* eyelids are heavy with sleep 〔drunkenness〕.

**간장**(—醬) soy 〔soya〕 sauce. ¶ ~을 치다 put 〔pour〕 soy sauce 《on, over》/ ~은 메주콩과 소금으로 만든다 Soy sauce is made from soy beans and salt.

**간장**(肝腸) 《간과 창자》 the liver and bowels 〔intestines〕; 《마음》 heart. ¶ ~이 타다 burn up with love 《for》; be dying 《for》; *one's* heart bleeds 〔breaks〕; feel *one's* heart rent 〔torn to pieces〕/ ~을 녹이다 captivate; bewitch; enslave / 그는 늘 부모의 ~만 태운다 He keeps his parents worried sick all the time. / 그녀의 미소는 뭇남자의 ~을 다 녹여 버린다 Her smile captivates every man.

**간장**(肝臟) 〖해부〗 the liver. ⇨ 간(肝). ¶ ~의 hepatic. ◉ ~병 liver trouble 〔disease〕.

**간재**(奸才) trickiness; cunning; craft; a talent for evil. ¶ ~에 능한 skillful in deceiving others; crafty; full tricks.

**간저냐**(肝—) pan-fried liver slices.

**간절**(懇切) earnestness; ardentness; sincerity; cordiality. ~하다 (be) earnest; eager; ardent; sincere; cordial. ¶ ~한 마음 an ardent passion / ~한 부탁 *one's* earnest request / ~히 earnestly; sincerely; cordially / ~히 권하다 urge 《*a person*》 strongly; strongly advise 《*a person* to *do*》/ ~히 바라다 sincerely hope; eagerly wish; earnestly desire / 대학 가기를 ~히 바라다 be most anxious to enter the college / ~히 부탁하다 entreat 《*a person* to *do*》/ 가고 싶은 마음이 ~하다 be anxious 〔mad〕 to go; have a great mind to go / 한 잔 생각이 ~하다 I'm thirsty for a drink.

**간접**(間接) indirectness. ¶ ~적인 indirect; second hand; roundabout / ~으로 indirectly; at second hand; in a roundabout way / ~으로 듣다 have the news at second hand; learn 《about *something*》 indirectly / 나는 그 사건에 ~적으로 관계되어 있다 I am indirectly concerned in the affair. / 그것은 우리나라 경제에 ~적인 영향을 미치게 될 것이다 It will have an indirect influence on our economy. ◉ ~경험 indirect experience. ~국세 an indirect national tax. ~목적어 〖문법〗 an indirect object. ~무역 indirect commerce 〔trade〕. ~비 indirect cost; overhead costs: ~비로 천만 원을 책정하다 earmark 〔set aside〕 ten million won for overhead costs. ~사격 indirect fire. ~선거 an indirect election. ~세 an indirect tax. ~손해 consequential damage. ~전염 infection. ~조명 indirect illumination 〔lighting〕. ~증거 indirect 〔collateral〕 evidence. ~촬영 《X선의》 fluoroscopy. ~추리 mediate 〔indirect〕 inference. ~통제 indirect control. ~화법 〖문법〗 indirect discourse 〔speech 《영》〕. ~환 indirect exchange. ~흡연 secondhand smoke.

**간정되다** settle down; quiet down.

**간조**(干潮) (an) ebb tide. = 썰물.

**간종간종** orderly; neatly; tidily.

**간종그리다** put 〔set〕 《*things*》 right 〔in order〕; order; even up.

**간주곡**(間奏曲) 〖음악〗 an interlude; an intermezzo.

**간주하다**(看做—) regard 〔think of〕 《as》; consider (to be); count 《as, for》; look upon 《as》; take 《for》. ¶ 다 해결된 것으로 ~ look upon 《*a matter*》 as settled / 계약이 취소된 것으로 ~ consider the contract canceled / 위대한 학자로 간주되다 be regarded as a great scholar / 그는 그 운동의 지도자로 간주되고 있다 He is looked upon as a leader of the movement. / 불참자는 불합격으로 간주된다 Those who absent themselves will be considered to have failed in the examination.

**간지**(干支) the sexagenary cycle.

**간지**(奸智) craft; cunning; wiles; guile. ¶ ~에 능하다 be cunning; be crafty; be a sly old fox.

**간지**(諫止) dissuasion. ~하다 persuade 《*a person*》 not to *do;* dissuade 《*a person*》 from *do*ing.

**간지**(簡紙) stationery; writing paper.

**간지럼** ticklishness. ~타다 be ticklish; be sensitive to tickling.

**간지럽다** ① 《몸이》 feel a tickle. ¶ 발이 〔귀가, 코가〕 ~ my foot 〔ear, nose〕 tickles / 그만 해라, ~ Stop! It tickles! / 간지럽히지 마라 Don't tickle me. ② 《낯·양심이》 (be) tickled; pricked. ¶ 낯이 ~ *one's* face is ticklish from 「undue flattery 〔a pricked conscience〕; *one's* face blushes with 「shame 〔uneasiness〕/ 그 문제를 언급하였을 때 나는 몹시 낯간지러웠다 My conscience was pricked when he referred to that question.

**간직하다** 《보관하다》 keep; have 《*a thing*》 in *one's* custody 〔keeping〕; 《챙겨두다》 put 《*a thing*》 away 〔in〕; put aside; store (away); 《마음에》 harbor; cherish 《a secret》; keep; hold; entertain. ¶ 가슴속 깊이 ~ keep 《*something*》 in *one's* heart 〔bosom〕 / 그것은 그녀가 간직하고 있다 She has it in her custody. / 이것은 금고에 간직해 두어라 You had better put this away in the safe. / 훗날 쓰게 잘 간직해 두어라 Store it away for future use. / 훌륭한 선물, 길이 간직하겠습니다 I shall long treasure your nice present. / 가엾은 그 소녀는 그 일을 홀로 가슴에 간직하고 있었다 The poor girl kept it all to herself.

**간질**(癎疾) 〚의학〛 epilepsy. ¶ ~ 발작을 일으키다 have an epileptic fit 〔seizure〕. ◉ ~환자 an epileptic.

**간질간질** with a tickling sensation. ¶ 등이 ~하다 feel a tickle on *one's* back.

**간질거리다** ① 《간지럽다》 feel a tickle; be ticklish. ② 《간질이다》 tickle; make ticklish.

**간질이다** tickle 〔irritate〕 《*a person*》. ¶ 겨드랑이를 ~ tickle 《*a person*》 under the arm; tickle the armpit / 발바닥을 ~ tickle the soles of 《*a person's*》 foot / 간질여서 웃기다 tickle a laugh out of 《*a person*》.

**간책**(奸策) a shrewd 〔dirty〕 trick; a crafty scheme 〔design〕; a sly artifice. ¶ ~을 부리다 use wiles; play a dirty trick 《on》; resort to a trick / ~에 걸리다 fall victim to a scheme.

**간척**(干拓) reclamation of land by drainage. ~하다 reclaim (land) by drainage. ◉ ~계획〔사업〕 a land reclamation program 〔project〕. ~공사 reclamation works. ~지 reclaimed land.

**간첩**(間諜) a spy; a secret agent; an (espionage) agent. ¶ ~을 보내다 send out a spy / ~ 노릇을 하다 be engaged in espionage / ~을 색출하다 hunt 〔seek〕 out spies; dig up spies / ~ 혐의로 잡히다 be arrested under suspicion of being a spy / ~은 경찰에 자수했다 The spy surrendered 〔delivered〕 himself to the police.
◉ ~교육 espionage training: ~교육을 받다 undergo espionage training. ~망 a network of spies; an espionage chain 《that works for North Korea》. ~선 a 《north Korean》 spy boat. ~자수 기간 a spy self-surrender period. ~죄 the crime of espionage. ~행위 (an act of) espionage. ~활동 《conduct》 espionage activities / ~활동 혐의로 출국 명령을 받다 be orderded to leave 《the United States》 for engaging in espionage. 경제~ an economic spy. 대~ 대책 본부 the Counter-Espionage Operations Headquarters (생략 CEOH).

**간첩**(簡捷) promptness and simplicity. ~하다 (be) prompt and simple.

**간청**(懇請) begging earnestly; an earnest request; (an) entreaty; solicitation. ~하다 beg earnestly; make an earnest request; entreat; solicit. ¶ ~에 의하여 at 《*a person's*》 earnest request / ~을 들어주다 listen to 《*a person's*》 entreaty; comply with 《*a person's*》 earnest request / 허가해 주기를 ~하다 solicit 《the authorities》 for permission / 원조를 ~하다 implore 《*a person*》 to give help.

**간추리다** sum up; summarize; digest; epitomize; abridge. ¶ 간추린 summarized; abridged; epitomized / 간추리면 to sum up; in short 〔brief〕; in a word.

**간치다** salt; season.

**간친**(懇親) friendliness; sociability; fraternization. ◉ ~회 a social gathering 〔meeting〕; a get-together (meeting) 《미》: ~회를 열다 hold a social meeting; get together 《미》.

**간통**(姦通) adultery; illicit intercourse. ~하다 commit adultery 《with》; have illicit intercourse 《with》; misconduct *oneself* 《with》. ¶ 독신자와 기혼자의 ~ single adultery / 기혼자간의 ~ double adultery. ◉ ~자 adulterer (남자); adulteress (여자). ~죄 adultery: ~죄로 고소하다 sue 《*one's* husband and Miss A》 on charges of adultery.

**간투사**(間投詞) 〚언어〛 an interjection.

**간파**(看破) seeing through; penetration. ~하다 see through 《a fraud》; penetrate 《*a person's* disguise》; pierce into 《*a person's* motive》; read 《*a person's* thought》. ¶ 한눈에 그가 협잡꾼임을 ~했다 I saw at a glance that he was an impostor. / 나는 그의 생각을 ~하지 못했다 I could not read his mind. / 나는 그의 의도를 곧 ~했다 I penetrated into his design at once.

**간판**(看板) ① 《상점의》 a signboard; a sign; a billboard (게시판). ¶ 옥상 ~ a roof sign; a sky sign 《미》 / 영화〔제과

점] ~ a theatrical [bakery's] signboard / 세워 놓은 ~ a standing signboard / ~을 내걸다 set up [hang out] a signboard / ~을 내리다 《폐점·폐업하다》 close down *one's* store; give up *one's* business / 그 건물 옥상에는 큰 ~이 세워져 있다 There's a large signboard on the roof of the building.
② 《인기를 끄는 것》 a draw; an attraction. ¶ 그녀는 그 가게의 손님을 끄는 ~ 같은 아가씨이다 She is what draws customers into the store.
③ 《명목상의 장》 a figurehead; a front man; 《허울》 a front; a mask; a pretext. ¶ 실권이 없는 ~ 사장 a mere figurehead in a company with no clout at all / 그들은 식당 ~을 내걸고 스파이 활동을 했다 They ran a restaurant merely as a front for spy activities.
④ 《학벌》 a school career; an academic [background]. ¶ ~이 좋다 have a good academic career [background].
◉ ~장이 a sign painter [maker].

**간편**(簡便) handiness; convenience; simplicity. ~하다 (be) handy; simple; easy; convenient. ¶ ~한 방법 an easy [a simple] method / ~하게 handily; conveniently; simply; easily / 짐을 ~하게 꾸리다 pack things conveniently; pack things so they will be handy.

**간하다** apply salt 《to》; add seasoning 《to》. ⇨ 간.

**간하다**(諫—) remonstrate [expostulate] 《with》; admonish; exhort; warn; advise 《a king, *one's* superior》. ¶ 하지 않도록 ~ dissuade 《*a person*》 from *doing* 《*a thing*》; remonstrate [reason] with 《*a person*》 against 《*a matter*》 / 간하는 말을 듣지 않다 turn a deaf ear to 《*a person's*》 counsel.

**간행**(刊行) publication. ~하다 publish; issue; bring out. ¶ 신문을 ~하다 publish a newspaper / 새 잡지가 ~되었다 A new magazine came out. ◉ ~물 a publication: 정기 ~물 a periodical. ~본 a (published) book.

**간헐**(間歇) intermittence. ¶ ~적 intermittent / ~적으로 intermittently; off and on; by fits and starts. ◉ ~열 intermittent fever. ~(온)천 an intermittent spring; a geyser. ~유전(遺傳) intermittent heredity; atavism.

**간호**(看護) nursing (care); tending. ~하다 nurse; tend; care. ¶ 침식을 잊고 ~하다 nurse 《a sick person》 devotely [forgetting *one's* sleep and food] / 그는 극진히 ~한 보람도 없이 어젯밤에 죽었다 He died last night, all the care taken of him proving of no avail. / 그녀는 병원에서 극진한 ~를 받았다 She was well attended (to) in the hospital.
◉ ~과장 a director of nursing service. ~법 the art of nursing. ~병 a hospital corpsman; an orderly; a military nurse. ~보조원 a nurse's aid. ~사 a (sick) nurse; a hospital nurse (병원의); a trained nurse 《미》: 수~사 a chief [head, supervising] nurse / 정식 ~사 a registered nurse 《미》 / 파출 ~사 a visiting [hired] nurse / ~사회(會) a nurses' agency. ~실습생 a practical nurse; a student nurse ~인 a person tending the sick. ~학 the science [study] of nursing: ~학과 the department of nursing science. ~학교 a nurses' school [college]; a nursing school.

**간혹**(間或) ① 《이따금》 sometimes; occasionally; once in a while; (every) now and then; at times; on occasion; off and on. ¶ ~ 오는 손님 a casual visitor; a stray customer / ~ 들르다 drop in once in a while / 그는 ~ 늦는다 He is sometimes late. / 나는 ~ 그녀를 거리에서 만난다 I sometimes see her on the street. ② 《띄엄띄엄》 in places; at (long) intervals; few and far between; sparsely; thinly. ¶ 그 곳엔 인가가 ~ 가다 하나둘 있다 The place is sparsely dotted with cottages.

**간힘 쓰다, 간힘 주다** hold *one's* breath to withstand pain.

**갇히다** be shut up [confined, imprisoned]; be behind bars. ¶ 유치장에 ~ be locked up in a (police) cell / 비에 ~ be kept in 《*one's* room》 by the rain / 눈으로 산막에 3일간 ~ be 「snowed up [snowbound] in the mountain hut for three days / 그는 한 달 동안 갇혀 있었다 He was confined [imprisoned] for a month.

**갈** 《「…학」, 「…론(論)」의 뜻》 science of; study of; -ology. ◉ 소리갈 phonology. 한글갈 Koreanology; the study of the Korean language.

**갈**(碣) a small stone monument with rounded top.

**갈가리** ⇨ 가리가리.

**갈가마귀** 〖조류〗 a jackdaw.

**갈가위** a greedy [grasping] person.

**갈갈이** ⇨ 가을갈이.

**갈개** a small ditch made for draining [as a boundary].

**갈개꾼** a person who skins paper mulberries; 《훼방꾼》 a meddler; an interferer.

**갈개발** ① 《연의》 wedge-shaped tags attached to the two lower corners of a kite. ② 《사람》 an hanger-on; an ass in a lion's skin.

**갈강갈강하다** 《얼굴이》 look hardy; (be) thin; lean.

**갈거미** 〖동물〗 a long-legged spider.

**갈건**(葛巾) a hood made of kohemp fiber. ◉ ∼야복(野服) the hood and clothes worn by a hermit; plain dress of a hermit.

**갈겨먹다** snatch; seize; extort.

**갈겨쓰다** write carelessly 〔hurriedly〕; scribble; scrawl; scratch 《down, off》. ¶ 편지를 ∼ dash off a letter; scribble 《a few lines》.

**갈고랑막대기** a hooked stick.

**갈고랑쇠** ① 《쇠》 an iron hook. ② 《사람》 a perverse person; a cross-minded person.

**갈고랑이, 갈고리** a hook; a gaff. ¶ 갈고리 사용금지 《게시》 No hooks.

**갈고쟁이, 갈고지** a hook.

**갈구**(渴求) an eager 〔earnest〕 desire 《for》; an ardent wish 《for》; thirst 《for knowledge》. ∼하다 thirst for; be thirsty for 〔after, of〕 《knowledge》; desire eagerly 〔earnestly〕.

**갈근**(葛根) the root of the arrowroot 〔of Pueraria〕.

**갈기** a mane. ¶ ∼ 있는 짐승 an animal with a mane.

**갈기갈기** to pieces; to shreds. ¶ ∼ 찢다 tear to pieces 〔ribbons, shreds〕.

**갈기다** ① 《치다》 beat; strike; knock; hit; thrash. ¶ 몽둥이로 ∼ club; cudgel / 채찍으로 ∼ lash; whip; flog; administer a whipping / 찰싹 ∼ spank 《on the buttocks》; beat 《*a person* on the head》 / 콧등을 ∼ punch 《*a person's*》 nose / 따귀를 ∼ slap 《*a person's*》 cheeks 〔face〕 / 호되게 ∼ give a sound thrashing 《to》; give 《*a person*》 a good licking; beat 《*a person*》 up / 녹초가 되게 ∼ pommel 〔beat〕 to a jelly. ② 《베다》 cut; strike a blow 《with a sharp instrument》; slash. ¶ 도끼로 ∼ cut with an axe. ③ 《쏘다》 fire 《a gun》.

**갈다**[1] 《바꾸다》 change 《A for B》; put 《A》 in place of 《B》; replace 《A with B》. ¶ 이름을 ∼ change *one's* name / 낡은 부품을 새것으로 ∼ replace old parts with new ones / 어항의 물을 ∼ change the water in the fish bowl.

**갈다**[2] ① 《칼붙이를》 whet; grind; sharpen 《a knife》; file 《a saw》; strop 《a razor》. ¶ 도끼를 ∼ grind an axe 《on the grindstone》. ② 《문지르다》 polish; rub; file. ¶ 옥돌을 ∼ polish jade / 먹을 ∼ rub an ink-stick / 손톱을 줄로 ∼ file *one's* fingernails. ③ 《가루로》 grind (up); refine. ¶ 커피 원두를 ∼ grind coffee beans. ④ 《이 따위를》 grind down; grind away at; grate; gnash. ¶ 이를 ∼ gnash *one's* teeth; [비유적] be eager for revenge; grind *one's* teeth with vexation.

**갈다**[3] 《땅을》 plow 《a rice field》; cultivate; till. ¶ 밭을 ∼ plow 〔till〕 a (dry) field / 땅을 ∼ till the soil; cultivate land.

**갈대** 〖식물〗 a reed. ¶ ∼가 많은 reedy / 인간은 생각하는 ∼다 Man is a thinking reed. ◉ ∼발 a hanging screen made of reeds. ∼밭 ⇨ 갈밭. ∼피리 a reed (pipe).

**갈등**(葛藤) discord; disagreement; (a) trouble; (a) conflict. ¶ 마음〔감정〕의 ∼ 《undergo》 mental 〔emotional〕 conflict / ∼이 생기다 [사물이 주어] cause trouble; breed discord; give rise to complications / 그것 때문에 부자 사이에 ∼이 생겼다 That caused complications 〔trouble〕 between the father and the son. / 두 나라 사이에는 오랜 ∼이 있다 There is a long-standing feud between the two countries.

**갈라내다** sort out. ¶ 우편물을 목적지별로 ∼ sort mail according to destinations.

**갈라놓다** ① 《분할》 divide 《into》; part; partition; 《떼어놓다》 draw 〔pull, set〕 apart; separate. ¶ 갈라놓을 수 없는 indivisible; inseparable / 반으로 ∼ divide 《*a thing*》 into halves / 두 사람을 ∼ separate the two people. ② 《이간》 estrange 《from》; make unfriendly; alienate; put a barrier 《between》. ¶ 그 다툼은 그 부부 사이를 갈라놓았다 The dispute estranged him from his wife.

**갈라붙이다** divide and assign 〔allocate〕; divide; part; split up.

**갈라서다** ① 《따로》 stand apart; line up separately. ¶ 두 줄로 ∼ stand apart in two rows; line up into two groups; from a double file 〔two lines〕. ② 《헤어짐·이혼》 separate; get a divorce. ¶ 남편과 갈라선 지 오래다 It is a long time that she has been separated from her husband. / 저 부부는 노상 갈라서자는 말을 한다 The couple are always talking of divorce.

**갈라지다** ① 《물체가》 split; part; branch off; 《분기》 fork. ¶ 두 조각으로 ∼ it splits into two pieces / 길이 두 갈래로 갈라진다 The road branches off 〔divides〕 into two. ② 《사람 사이가》 split 《with》; be estranged 《from》; be divided; 《이혼하다》 be divorced 《from》. ¶ 갈라져서 살다 live apart 《from *one's* wife》; live separately / 그 점에 관하여 의견이 갈라졌다 The opinions were divided on the point. / 그는 아내와 갈라졌다 He has separated from his wife. *or* He divorced his wife.

**갈락토오스** 〖화학〗 galactose.

**갈래** 《구분》 a division; a section; 《분파》 a branch; 《갈림》 a fork. ¶ 네 ～길 a crossroad(s) / 세 ～진 three-forked / 여러 ～로 나누다 divide into several parts 〔sections〕 / 두 ～길이 되다 fork off in two.

**갈래다** ① 《혼동·혼란》 be confused; 《마음이》 wander; roam; 《길이》 split up confusingly. ② 《짐승이》 run about aimlessly; roam; wander.

**갈륨** 〖화학〗 gallium (기호 Ga.).

**갈리다**[1] ① 《갈게 하다》 make 《*a person*》 change 《one thing for another》; have 《*a person*》 replace 《*one* for another》. ¶ 구두창을 ～ have *one's* shoes resoled. ② 《바뀌다》 be changed 《for another of the same kind》; be replaced. ¶ 교육부 장관이 새로 갈렸다 The Minister of Education has been replaced. / 내각은 갈려도 외교 방침에는 변함이 없다 The Ministerial change will not affect the foreign policy of the Government.

**갈리다**[2] ① 《숫돌에》 make 《*a person*》 whet; make 《*a person*》 grind 《an axe》; have 《*a person*》 sharpen; 《옥돌 따위를》 make 《*a person*》 polish; have 《*a person*》 rub; get 《*a person*》 to file; 《가루로》 make 《*a person*》 grind (up). ② 《갈려지다》 be whetted; 《도끼 따위가》 be ground; be sharpened; be polished; be rubbed; be filed; 《콩 따위가》 be ground.

**갈리다**[3] 《논밭을》 ① 《갈게 하다》 make 〔let〕 《*a person*》 plow 〔plough〕; have 《*a person*》 cultivate; make 《*a person*》 till. ¶ 아들에게 감자밭을 ～ have *one's* son till the potato farm. ② 《갈려지다》 be plowed; get cultivated; be under cultivation; be tilled.

**갈리다**[4] 《분열》 be split; be divided; be parted; 《분기》 branch off 《from》; be forked. ¶ 두 패로 ～ be divided into two groups / 그 당은 여러 파로 갈렸다 The party was split into factions. / 샛길은 이 큰길에서 갈린다 Here the side road branches off from the main road.

**갈릴레이** 《이탈리아의 천문학자》 Galileo Galilei (1564-1642).

**갈림길** a side 〔forked, branch〕 road; 《운명의》 a turning point 《in *one's* career》. ¶ ～로 접어들다 come to the fork of a road / 너는 지금 인생의 ～에 서 있다 You are now standing at the turning point in your life. / 이것이 성패의 ～이다 Success depends on this point.

**갈림목** a corner at a juncture of streets.

**갈마**(羯磨) 〖불교〗 《업·숙명》 *karma* 「(Sans.).

**갈마들다** take turns 《in *doing*》; alternate; come on by turns; be employed 〔replaced〕 by turns.

**갈마들이다** change turns; employ by 「turns.

**갈마바람** 《서남풍》 a southwest wind; a sou'wester (뱃사람 말).

**갈마쥐다** ① 《옮겨 쥠》 shift 《*a thing*》 from hand to hand. ② 《이것저것을》 grasp one thing after another.

**갈망** 《일을 수습·처리함》 carrying out; fulfilling; discharging; coping with 《a problem》; setting 《*matters*》 right; settling. ～하다 carry 《*one's* project》 through; carry out 《a plan》; pull 〔bring〕 《*something*》 off; cope with; square away; set 《*matters*》 right. ¶ 뒷 ～ winding up; settling; squaring away / 빚 ～을 하다 pay off 〔settle, take care of 〕 debt / 제 앞 ～도 못하면서 남의 일에 참견한다 Unable to handle his own business, he pokes his nose into another's.

**갈망**(渴望) a craving 《for》; an earnest 〔eager〕 desire 《for》; an ardent wish 《for》; thirst 《for》; a longing 《for》. ～하다 thirst 〔hunger, long, crave, yearn〕 《for》; have a thirst 《for》; desire eagerly 〔earnestly〕. ¶ 지식에 대한 ～을 만족시키다 satisfy *one's* 「hunger 〔thirst, craving〕 for knowledge / 그들은 자유를 ～하고 있다 They have intense aspirations toward liberty. / 사람들은 위대한 지도자의 출현을 ～하고 있다 People are yearning for the appearance of a great leader.

**갈매** 〖식물〗 fruit of the (Dahurian) buckthorn; 《갈매빛》 a deep green (color). ◉ ～나무 the Dahurian buckthorn.

**갈매기** 〖조류〗 a seagull; a gull; 《무늬》 a chevron; a stripe (기호 ∧).

**갈무리** 《간수》 putting 《*a thing*》 away

in order; 《마무리》 finishing touches. ～하다 put 《*a thing*》 away in order; finish 《*a thing*》 up; put the finishing touches on 《*a thing*》.

**갈묻이** 〚농업〛 turning over the soil 《of a paddy》; tilling. ～하다 turn over the soil of 《a paddy》.

**갈미** 〚동물〛 a sea cucumber.

**갈바람** 《가을 바람》 a west wind.

**갈바래다** turn over 《the soil》 and expose it to the sun and wind.

**갈밭** a field of reeds.

**갈보** 《매춘부》 a prostitute; a harlot. ¶ ～ 노릇을 하다 prostitute *oneself;* practice prostitution; be on the streets / 돈이 궁하여 ～가 되었다 Poverty led her to prostitution.
◉ ～집 a brothel; a whorehouse; a house of prostitution.

**갈보리** 《가을보리》 autumn barley.

**갈보리** 〚성서〛 Calvary.

**갈분**(葛粉) arrowroot starch.

**갈붙이다** 《이간하다》 poison 《*a person's*》 mind against 《another》; alienate 〔estrange〕 《*a person* from another》.

**갈비**[1] 《뼈》 a rib; the ribs; 《요리》 (broiled) ribs. ¶ 소의 ～ ribs of beef / ～가 휘다 *one's* ribs feel as if they were bent under a heavy load.
◉ ～구이 roasted ribs. ～뼈＝갈빗대. ～새김 rib meat. ～적(炙) skewered beef= ribs. ～찜 steamed short-ribs; beef= rib stew. ～탕 beef-rib soup (and rice). 갈빗대 a rib-bone; the rib cage: 갈빗대를 부러뜨리다 get a rib broken; break a rib.

**갈비**[2] 〚건축〛 the width of a roof.

**갈색**(褐色) brown. ¶ ～의 brown; suntanned / 햇볕에 탄 ～ 피부 skin browned by the sun. ◉ ～인종 the brown race.

**갈수**(渴水) a water shortage; (a) drought. ◉ ～기 a period of water shortage; a dry season (건기).

**갈수록** as time goes by. ¶ ～ 태산이다 Things get worse and worse. *or* One calamity followed close on the heels of another. / 세월이 ～ 고향이 그립다 As time goes on, I long for home more and more. / 형세가 ～ 나빠진다 Matters are going from bad to worse.

**갈씬거리다** almost reach 〔touch〕.

**갈씬하다** 《치마 따위가》 almost touch 《the floor》. ¶ 갈씬갈씬 almost touching.

**갈아내다** replace; take out an old one (with intent to replace); supplant. ¶ 묵은 기왓장을 ～ replace an old tile.

**갈아대다** replace 《with》; substitute; put in a new one (as a replacement). ¶ 돗자리를 ～ change the mats / 사람을 ～ replace 《one man with another》; change people 〔personnel〕 / 구두창을 ～ resole a shoe.

**갈아들다** move in (as a replacement); take 《another's》 place; serve as a replacement 〔substitute, relief〕. ¶ 새 요리사가 갈아들었다 A new cook has replaced the old one.

**갈아들이다** change 《*a person*》; replace 《with *a person*》; substitute 《*a person*》. ¶ 저 회사는 매달 마케팅 직원을 갈아들인다 That company change its marketing personnel every month.

**갈아붙이다** ① 《이를》 grind (*one's* teeth) spitefully. ② 《바꾸어 붙임》 renew; replace; change 《for a new *one*》; attach 〔fix〕 anew. ¶ 표지를 ～ re-cover 〔renew the cover of〕 a book / 상처에 반창고를 ～ put a new adhesive plaster on a cut.

**갈아입다** change 《clothes》. ¶ 옷을 ～ change clothes / 옷을 갈아입고 in different clothes / 여름옷으로 ～ change into a light summer suit / 갈아입을 옷을 준비해 가다 take with a change of clothes / 갈아입으러 가다 go for a change (of clothes) / 갈아입을 것이 아무것도 없다 I have nothing to change into. / 목욕 후 옷을 갈아입고, 그녀는 외출했다 Having bathed and changed, she went out.

**갈아주다** ① 《새것으로》 change; renew. ¶ 아기의 기저귀를 ～ change the baby's diaper. ② 《이문을 붙여 사주다》 buy up 《*things*》 from a retailer giving him due profit.

**갈아타다** change 《cars, trains》; change 《to another train》; transfer 《to an express》. ¶ 말을 ～ change horses / 대전에서 목포행〔호남선〕으로 ～ change at Taejŏn for Mokp'o 〔to the Honam Line〕 / 지하철을 세 번 ～ change subways three times / 용산서 갈아타는 게 빠르다 It takes less time to change trains at Yongsan. / 갈아타지 못함 《게시》 No transfer. / 수원 방면 승객은 갈아타시오 《게시》 Change here for Suwon.

**갈음** 《바꿈》 substituting; replacing; changing; switching. ～하다 substitute; replace; change.

**갈음질** grinding; whetting; sharpening. ～하다 grind; whet; sharpen; do the grinding.

**갈이**[1] ① 《논밭의》 plowing; cultivating; tilling. ② 《넓이》 the acreage that can be plowed by one person in a given number of days. ¶ 열흘 ~ the acreage that can be plowed by one person in ten days. ◉ ~질 plowing [cultivating] the fields.

**갈이**[2] 《목기 제작》 making round-shaped wooden utensils on a turning lathe. ◉ ~기계 a turning lathe; lathe equipment. ~장이 a turner. ~질 lathing; lathe work; turning on a lathe: ~질하다 operate a lathe. ~칼 a knife used in making round wooden utensils; a lathe knife. ~틀 a turning lathe.

**갈이**[3] 《갈아댐》 changing; remodeling. ¶ 구두창 ~ resoling shoes.

**갈잎** fallen leaves (of the oak tree). ⇨「가랑잎.

**갈증**(渴症) thirst. ¶ ~이 나다 feel thirsty / ~이 심하다 be very thirsty / ~을 풀다 quench [slake] *one's* thirst 《with a bottle of beer》 / ~이 나게 하다 cause [produce] thirst / ~을 호소하다 complain of thirst.

**갈지개** 〖조류〗 a year-old hawk.

**갈지자걸음**(一之字一) staggering; unsteady [reeling] steps. ¶ ~을 걷다 walk drunkenly; reel along; weave *one's* way (along).

**갈지자형**(一之字形) a zigzag; a shape like the character Z. ¶ 길이 ~으로 구불구불하다 The road zigzags.

**갈참나무** 〖식물〗 a white oak.

**갈채**(喝采) applause; cheers; acclamation; ovation. ~하다 applaud; acclaim; cheer; give applause 《to, at》; give cheers; give an ovation. ¶ 우레와 같은 ~ a storm [thunder] of applause; a thunderous [tremendous] applause / ~를 받다 win [get, receive] applause; draw a cheer 《from》; receive an ovation 《from》 / 만장의 ~를 받다 bring down [carry] the house; win the plaudits [applause] of the whole house / ~에 답하다 acknowledge the cheers 《of the audience》 / ~를 받으며 등단하다 mount a platform amid cheers / ~로써 맞이하다 greet [receive] 《*a person*》 with (loud) applause; receive 《*a person*》 with acclamations [with an ovation] / 박수 ~로 환영하다 welcome with cheers / 훌륭한 연주에 ~를 보내다 applaud a marvelous performance / 그들은 우레와 같은 박수 ~로 그 용사를 환영했다 They received the war hero with thunders of hand-clapping and cheers. ◉ 대~ a great ovation; a rousing cheer.

**갈철광**(褐鐵鑛) 〖광물〗 limonite.

**갈초**(一草) winter hay.

**갈취**(喝取) blackmail(ing); extortion [exaction] by threats; 《미속어》 a shakedown; racketeering. ~하다 extort 《money from *a person*》 (by threats); practice extortions; blackmail; racketeer 《미속어》. ¶ 돈을 ~하다 blackmail 《*a person*》 of *his* money; wring [screw, bully] money out of 《*a person*》.

**갈치** 〖어류〗 a hairtail; a scabbard [cutlass] fish.

**갈퀴** a rake; a bamboo rake (대나무제의). ¶ ~로 그러모으다 rake up 《the dead leaves》. ◉ ~나무 small firewood. ~질 raking (up): ~질하다 rake. 갈퀫발 the hooked end of the tine of a rake.

**갈퀴다** rake (up).

**갈타다** make dovetails [forks] at (the end of a column).

**갈탄**(褐炭) 〖광물〗 brown coal [lignite]; subbituminous coal.

**갈파**(喝破) 《꾸짖음》 outshouting 《others》; 《설파》 proclamation; pronouncement 《of truth》. ~하다 outshout; proclaim; shout out; pronounce; declare.

**갈팡질팡** 《헤매는 모양》 flustered; confused; bewildered; hesitating; wavering; at a loss; nonplused; incoherent. ~하다 fluster *oneself;* be confused; be bewildered; be at a loss; be in a nonplus; be flurried; become incoherent. ¶ ~하는 통에 일이 벌어졌다 This happened in the midst of all our confusion and bewilderment. / 그의 대답이 ~하여 갈피를 잡을 수 없었다 His answer was so incoherent (that) I couldn't make anything of it.

**갈포**(葛布) kohemp cloth.

**갈품** reed blossoms (which have not fully come out).

**갈피** ① 《책 따위의》 a space between folds [layers, pages]. ¶ 책~에 사진을 끼워 두다 put a picture between the leaves of a book. ② 《요점》 the point; the sense; the drift; the thread 《of meaning》. ¶ ~를 잡을 수 없다 cannot make head nor tail 《of》; cannot get the point 《of》; cannot grasp the meaning 《of》 / 그가 하는 말은 전혀 ~를 잡을 수 없다 I can't get the point of his argument at all.

**갈피갈피** (between) leaf after leaf; page after page; layer after layer; fold after fold. ¶ 옷을 ～ 뒤져 보다 search through the clothes one by one.

**갈화**(葛花) 〖한의〗 arrowroot 〔kohemp〕 blossoms.

**갉다** gnaw; scrape 《off, away》; bite (at). ¶ 쥐가 판자를 갉아 구멍을 냈다 Rats gnawed a hole through the board. ⇨ 긁다.

**갉아먹다** nibble 《at, on, away》; gnaw 《at》; crunch on 《hard crackers》; 《재물을 뜯어먹다》 squeeze; exploit; extort. ⇨ 긁어먹다. ¶ 개가 뼈다귀를 갉아먹고 있다 The dog is gnawing a bone.

**감**[1] 《과일》 a persimmon. ◉ 감나무 a persimmon tree.

**감**[2] ① 《재료》 stuff; material; [비유적] a suitable person 《for》; good "material" 《for》. ¶ 옷감 cloth; (dress) material / 기둥감 wood for a pillar; wood suitable for making a pillar / 땔감 firewood; fuel / 사윗감 a man who would make a good son-in-law; a likely son-in-law / 그 감이 좋다 That is good material. ② 《옷감의 단위》 a pattern.

**감**(減) 《빼기》 subtraction; 《줄임》 reduction; 《감소》 diminution; decrease; drop; 《할인》 reduction. ¶ 5할 감 a decrease of 50 percent.

**(-)감**(感) ① 《감각·느낌》 (a) feeling; (a) sensation; (a) sense; 《인상》 an impression. ¶ 행복〔고독〕감 a feeling of happiness 〔loneliness〕/ 공포감 a sensation of fear / …한 감을 주다 strike 〔impress〕 《*a person*》 as…; give 《*a person*》 an impression of…; it feels 〔seems〕 like… / 그것이 좀 작은 감이 있다 It gives the feeling it's rather small I'd say. / 규칙 개정의 제안은 아직 이른 감이 있다 Their proposal to revise the regulation strikes us as premature. ② 《감도》 sensitivity; reception. ¶ 감이 좋다 be highly sensitive 《to》 / 감이 좋습니까 《무선 통신 등에서》 How do you read me? Over.

**감가**(減價) 《할인》 price reduction 〔discount〕; 《가치 하락》 depreciation. ～하다 reduce 〔discount〕 the price; depreciate. ◉ ～상각 depreciation: ～상각 기금 a depreciation fund / ～상각률 depreciation rate / ～상각비 depreciation expenses / ～상각비 보험 depreciation insurance / ～상각액 depreciation (amount) / ～상각 자산 depreciable assets / ～상각 적립금〔계정〕 a depreciation reserve 〔account〕.

**감각**(感覺) a sense; (a) sensation; (a) feeling; sensibility (감수성).
¶ ～적 sensual / ～이 둔하다 be insensitive; have dull senses / ～이 예민하다 have a keen sense 《of distance, time》; have a keen feeling 《for color》; be highly sensitive 《to》 / ～을 잃다 lose sensibility; become insensible; be benumbed / 그의 손은 전혀 ～이 없었다 He lost all feeling in his hands. / 화가는 색채에 대한 ～이 있어야 한다 An artist should have an eye for color. / 그는 국제 문제에 대하여 예리한 ～을 가지고 있다 He has a keen sense of international affairs. / 그녀는 문학에 대한 섬세한 ～을 가지고 있다 She has a delicate sensibility for literature. ◉ ～기관 a sensory 〔sense〕 organ. ～기능 a sense; a faculty of perception. ～력 sensibility; sensitivity. ～론 〖철학〗 sensationalism; sensualism. ～마비 sensory paralysis. ～묘사 sensual description. ～세포 a sensory cell. ～식물 a sensitive plant. ～신경 a sensory nerve. ～주의 〖미술〗 sensualism. ～중추 the sense center; the sensorium. ～탈실(脫失) anaesthesia. ～파 the sensualist. 잔류(殘留)～ aftersensation.

**감감(무)소식**(─(無)消息) no news for a longtime.

**감감하다** ① 《소식이》 hear nothing from 《*a person*》 (for a longtime); have no news 〔words〕 from 《*a person*》. ¶ 그는 떠난 이래 소식이 ～ Nothing has been heard from him since he left. ② 《시간·차이 등이》 be far above 〔beyond〕; be long before. ¶ 우리가 그의 식견을 따라 가려면 아직 ～ He is so far above us in his knowledge, we are no match for him. / 이 일이 끝나려면 아직 ～ It will be long before this works is done. ③ 《아득하다》 be far off (and gone).

**감개**(感慨) deep emotion; strong feelings. ¶ ～무량하다 be full of deep emotion; be deeply moved / 졸업을 맞이하니 ～무량하다 My heart is full in leaving school. / 지난날을 생각하니 정말 ～가 무량합니다 When I look back upon the past, a thousand emotions crowd on 〔well in〕 my mind. / 무사히 집에 돌아왔을 때는 정말 ～무량하였다 My heart was too full for words when I got back home safely.

**감격**(感激) ① 《감사》 (a) deep gratitude. ～하다 be very grateful. ② 《감동》 deep 〔strong〕 emotion; impression. ～하다 be deeply moved

〔touched, affected〕《by, with》; be deeply 〔very〕 impressed《with, at, by》; be in the grips of a strong emotion. ¶ ~적(인) impressive; moving; touching / ~적인 장면 a heart moving scene / ~적인 연설 an inspiring 〔a touching, an impressive〕 speech / ~케 하다 move 〔touch, affect〕《*a person's*》 heart deeply; give a deep impression《to *a person*》/ 그 책을 읽고 그녀는 ~의 눈물을 흘렸다 The book moved her to tears. / 그녀의 진심어린 환영에 우리는 크게 ~했다 We were very much moved 〔impressed〕 by her hearty welcome.

**감관**(感官) a sense 〔sensory〕 organ; the senses. ¶ ~적 착각 sensory illusion.

**감광**(感光) 〖사진〗 sensitization; exposure (to light). ¶ ~시키다 expose《the film》(to light); sensitize / ~되다 be exposed to light. ◉ ~계 a sensitometer. ~도 photosensitivity. ~약〔제〕 a sensitizer; a photosensitizer. ~재료 sensitive materials. ~지 sensitive 〔sensitized〕 paper. ~판 a sensitive 〔dry〕 plate. ~필름 (a) sensitive film.

**감군**(減軍) a cut in the armed forces; a military manpower reduction; arms 〔armament〕 reduction. ~하다 reduce 〔cut〕 armed forces.

**감극**(減極) 〖전기〗 depolarization. ◉ ~전지 a depolarized cell. ~제 a depolarizer.

**감금**(監禁) imprisonment; confinement; detention; incarceration. ~하다 imprison; confine; detain; lock up. ¶ 방에 ~하다 confine《*a person*》 in a room / 자택에 ~하다 place《*a person*》 under house arrest / ~당해 있다 be kept in confinement; be held prisoner.

**감기**(感氣) a cold; influenza; flu《구어》. ¶ 가벼운〔지독한〕 ~ a slight 〔bad〕 cold / ~ 들다, ~에 걸리다 catch 〔take, get〕 cold (★ take 〔catch〕 cold는 보통 무관사. 단, 한정적 형용사가 올 때는 반드시 a가 붙음.) / ~로 누워 있다 be in bed with a cold / ~기가 있다 have a slight cold; have a touch of cold / ~에 걸려 열이 있다 「get a fever 〔be feverish〕 with a cold / ~에 걸리기 쉽다 catch cold easily; be sensitive to colds / ~가 떨어지지 않다 can't 「get rid of 〔shake off〕 *one's* cold / ~ 걸리지 않도록 조심해요 Mind you don't catch cold. / ~가 유행하고 있다 Colds are raging. / 그에게서 ~가 옮았다 I got my cold from him. *or* He gave me his cold. ◉ ~약 a cold remedy; cold medicine 〔pills〕.

**감기다**[1] ① 《눈이》《*one's* eyes》 be shut 〔closed〕 of their own accord. ¶ 졸려서 눈이 ~ be so sleepy (that) *one's* eyes are falling shut. ② 《눈을》 shut 〔close〕《*a person's*》 eyes; make《*a person's*》 eyes fall shut. ¶ 죽은 사람의 눈을 감겨 주다 close the eyes of a dead person.

**감기다**[2] 《씻기다》 wash《*a person*》; bath《*a person*》. ¶ 머리를 ~ wash《a baby's》 hair / 멱 ~ bath; give a bath《to》.

**감기다**[3] ① 《감겨지다》 be wound (up); be rolled (up); be coiled《around》(실 따위가); cling《to》(거치적거림); 《걸림》 be caught《in a roller》. ¶ 실이 실패에 ~ thread is wound on a reel / 젖은 옷이 몸에 ~ wet clothes cling to *one's* body / 코트 자락이 바퀴에 ~ the end of *one's* coat is caught in a wheel. ② 《감게 하다》 make 〔let〕《*a person*》 wind; make《*a person*》 coil《*something*》 around. ¶ 시계 태엽을 ~ have《*one's* son》 wind the clock.

**감내**(堪耐) enduring; endurance; perseverance. ~하다 endure; persevere; bear up; put up with. ¶ 불행을 ~하다 bear up under misfortune / 그것은 내가 ~할 수 없는 일이다 It is more than I can bear. *or* It is too much for me.

**감농하다**(監農—) supervise 〔manage〕 the farming; oversee farmhands.

**감다**[1] 《눈을》 shut; close《*one's* eyes》. ¶ 눈을 굳게 감고 with *one's* eyes shut tight / 눈을 ~ close *one's* eyes; [비유적] die / 나도 모르게 눈을 감았다 I instinctively shut my eyes.

**감다**[2] 《휘휘》 wind 〔roll, coil〕《*a thing*》. ¶ 실을 실패에 ~ wind thread on a reel / 비단옷만 몸에 ~ wear nothing but silk / 붕대를 ~ roll bandage; apply a bandage; bandage《a finger》; dress / 감은 것을 풀다 unwind; unroll; uncoil.

**감다**[3] 《씻다》 wash; bathe. ¶ 머리를 ~ wash *one's* hair / 미역 ~ wash *oneself;* have a swim (in the river) / 멱감으러 가다 go for a swim.

**감당하다**(堪當—) be capable of 「carrying out 〔discharging, performing〕; be up to《*doing*》; cope 〔deal〕 with; take care of. ¶ 난국을 감당해 내다 cope with a difficult situation / 그는 병이 낫더라도 힘든 일은 감당할 수 없을 것이다 Even if he recovered, he 「would be incapable of 〔would not be up to〕 hard work. / 그는 워낙 재간이 있는 사

람이니 능히 그 일을 감당해 낼 것이다 He is a man of such ability that we are sure he is competent for the task. / 나의 급료로는 높은 생활 수준을 감당하지 못한다 My income does not take care of the high standard of living.

**감도**(感度) (degree of) sensitivity; (radio) reception. ¶ ~가 좋다 be highly sensitive / ~가 나쁘다 be insensitive / 마이크의 ~는 어떠냐 How sensitive is the microphone?

**감독**(監督) 《일에 대한》 superintendence; supervision; control; direction; 《사람》 a superintendent; a supervisor; 《직공·죄수 등의》 an overseer; 《직공·인부의》 a foreman; 《영화의》 a director 《of a film》; 《스포츠의》 a manager. ~하다 superintend; supervise; oversee; control; direct; 「be in charge 〔take charge〕 of. ¶ 존 포드 ~의 영화 a film directed by John Ford / (…의) ~ 아래 under the 「supervision 〔direction, control〕 《of…》 / 학생을 ~하다 look after pupils; take charge of *one's* class 〔pupils〕 / 시험을 ~하다 preside over an examination / 직공을 ~하다 oversee workers / ~을 한층 엄중히 하다 supervise more strictly; enforce a more strict control / 누가 이 일의 ~을 하고 있느냐 Who is supervising 〔overseeing〕 this job? / 그는 ~ 소홀로 좌천 당했다 He was relegated to a lesser position because of his failure to supervise effectively. / 그 기관은 정부의 ~을 받게 되었다 The agency was placed under government control.
◉ ~관 an inspector; a superintendent: 근로 ~관 a labor supervisor. ~관청 the competent authorities; the supervisory office. ~교회 the Episcopal 〔《영》 Anglican〕 Church. ~기관 the competent institutions.

**감돌다** ① 《빙빙 돌다》 circle around; keep circling; 《감아돌다》 make a curve 《around》. ¶ 강이 산모퉁이를 감돈다 The river curves around the bend of the mountain. ② 《분위기·표정·형세 등이》 hang in the air; drift 《about》; hang low. ¶ 주변에는 희미한 봄기운이 감돌고 있다 There is a faint suggestion of spring in the air. / 그녀의 시들에는 달콤한 애수의 정이 감돌고 있다 Her poems have a touch of sweet melancholy. / 중동에는 전운이 감돌고 있다 War threatening clouds hang 〔hover〕 over the Middle East.

**감돌아들다** make a bend. ¶ 양덕 맹산 흐르는 물은 부벽루로 감돌아 든다 The river flowing through *Yangdŏk* and *Maengsan* makes a big bend at *Pubyŏngnu*.

**감돌이** a person who will cooperate if it is favorable to his own interest.

**감동**(感動) being moved 〔touched, affected, impressed〕; deep emotion. ~하다 be moved 〔touched, affected〕 《by》; be impressed 〔struck〕 《with, by》. ¶ ~적인 impressive; touching; moving / ~시키다〔을 주다〕 move 《*a person* to tears》; touch 《*a person's*》 heart; make a deep impression 《on》 / ~하기 쉬운 사람 an emotional man / …을 보고〔듣고〕 크게 ~했다 be affected at 〔by〕 the sight 〔news〕 of… / 나는 이 책에서 큰 ~을 받았다 I am much impressed by this book. / 그는 매우 ~하여 말이 나오지 않았다 His heart was too full for words. / 그 노래는 ~없이는 들을 수가 없다 I cannot hear the song without emotion. / 관객은 ~하여 눈물을 흘렸다 The spectators were moved to tears.

**감득하다**(感得—) realize; perceive; become aware of; acquire a clear idea of; be inspired.

**감등**(減等) 《낮춤》 lowering the grade; 《감형》 commutation. ~하다 lower the grade; commute.

**감때사납다** (be) very rough 〔tough〕; unbending; coarse. ¶ 그 사내는 난폭하고 ~ The man is intractably wild.

**감람**(橄欖) 『식물』 an olive. ◉ ~나무 an olive tree. ~산 the Mount of Olives. ~색 olive color 〔green〕. ~석 『광물』 olivine; peridot. ~암 peridotite. ~유 olive oil.

**감량**(減量) a loss in quantity 〔weight〕; 《운동 선수의》 reduction of *one's* weight. ~하다 reduce the quantity; 《체중을》 reduce *one's* weight. ¶ (운동 선수 등이) ~에 애를 먹다 have a hard time losing weight; have difficulty reducing *one's* weight / 나는 5킬로 정도 ~하여야 한다 I have to lose five kilograms. ◉ ~경영 belt-tightening management. ~식품 diet 〔low-caloried〕 food.

**감로**(甘露) 《이슬》 sweet dew; refreshing dew; 『불교』 *amrita;* nectar. ¶ ~맛이 나다 taste like 〔be as sweet as〕 nectar. ◉ ~수 sugared 〔sweet〕 water.

**감루**(感淚) tears from deep emotion; tears of gratitude. ¶ ~를 흘리다 be moved to tears; shed tears of grat-

itude; be choked with gratitude.
**감률**(甘栗)〖식물〗sweet chestnuts.
**감리**(監理)《감독》supervision; superintendence; control; management.
◉ ~교 the Methodist Church: ~교회 a Methodist church.
**감마선**(―線)〖물리〗gamma rays.
**감마제**(減摩劑)〖공업〗a lubricant.
**감면**(減免)《세금의》reduction and exemption; 《형벌의》mitigation and remission; commutation. ~하다 exempt; remit. ¶ 관광객은 소비세가 ~된다 Tourists are exempt from paying the consumption tax. ◉ ~조건 conditions of reduction and exemption.
**감명**(感銘) (a deep) impression. ¶ ~을 받다 be deeply 〔strongly〕 impressed 《with, by》; be (deeply) moved 〔touched〕 《by》/ ~을 주다 impress 《*a person*》; make an impression on 《*a person'*》/ 그의 연설은 청중들에게 깊은 ~을 주었다 His speech struck 〔made〕 a deep impression on the audience. / 나는 그에게 아무런 ~을 줄 수 없었다 I could make no impression on him. / 이 책은 내게 거의 감명을 주지 못했다 This book left little impression on me.
**감미**(甘味) a sweet taste; sweetness. ¶ ~롭다 be sweet / ~(가) 돌다 taste sweet. ◉ ~료 sweetening materials; sweetenings.
**감미**(甘美) sweetness. ¶ ~로운 음악 sweet music / ~로운 목소리 honey=sweet voice / ~로운 사랑 sweet love.
**감발**《발감개》leggings made of a strip of cloth; puttees; 《차림새》wearing leggings. ~하다 wear leggings. ¶ 짚신 ~하고 길을 나서다 set out on a journey wearing leggings and straw sandals.
**감방**(監房) a cell; a ward. ¶ ~에 처넣다 throw 〔cast〕 《*a person*》 into a cell; land 〔run〕 《*a person*》 in a ward.
**감배**(減配) 《배당의》 (a) reduction in a dividend; 《배급의》 (a) reduction 「in ration 〔of distribution quota〕. ~하다 reduce a dividend; reduce 〔cut〕 the ration.
**감법**(減法)〖수학〗subtraction. ⇨ 뺄셈.
**감별**(鑑別) discrimination; discernment; judgment. ~하다 discriminate; discern; judge. ¶ A와 B를 ~하다 discriminate 〔distinguish〕 「between A and B 〔A from B〕/ 병아리의 암수를 ~하다 discern the sex of fowls.
**감복**(感服) admiration; wonder. ~하다 be struck with admiration 《for, at》; wonder 《at》; admire. ¶ ~할 만한 업적 admirable results; praiseworthy achievements / ~시키다 excite *one's* admiration; strike 《*a person*》 with admiration / 그의 수완에 ~하였다 I was struck with his ability.
**감복숭아**〖식물〗an almond.
**감봉**(減俸) a pay 〔salary, wage〕 cut; a punitive wage cut; reduction of 《*a person's*》 salary 〔pay〕. ~하다 reduce 〔cut〕 《*a person's*》 salary.
¶ ~당하다〔되다〕 have *one's* salary reduced 〔deducted〕 《by 20,000 won》; have *one's* pay cut down / 90만 원에서 85만 원으로 ~되다 be reduced in pay from 900,000 won to 850,000 won / 그는 5% ~당했다 He had his pay cut 〔reduced〕 by five percent. *or* He had a salary cut of five percent.
**감비아** 《서아프리카 독립국》 the Republic of Gambia. ¶ ~의 Gambian.
◉ ~사람 a Gambian.
**감빨다** ① 《맛있게 먹다》 enjoy licking 〔sucking〕 ② 《이익을 탐내다》 be bent upon gain; seek *one's* own interests.
**감빨리다** ① 《입맛당기다》 have a sharp appetite; *one's* appetite is whetted. ② 《욕심이 생기다》 become covetous; get greedy.
**감사**(感謝) thanks; gratitude; appreciation. ~하다 thank; be thankful 〔grateful〕 《to *a person* for...》; appreciate 《*a person's* kindness》; give *one's* thanks. ¶ ~의 표시로서 as a token of gratitude / ~의 눈물을 흘리다 shed tears of gratitude; weep for gratitude / 당신의 조언에 대해 진심으로 ~합니다 Thank you very much for your advice. *or* I am very grateful 〔thankful〕 (to you) for your advice. / 협력해 주신 데 대해 충심으로 감사합니다 I very much appreciate your cooperation. / 경청해 주셔서 ~합니다 I thank you for your kind attention. / 무어라고 ~해야 할지 모르겠습니다 I don't know how to 「thank you 〔express my thanks〕. *or* I can never thank you enough. / ~합니다 《일반적》 Thank you. *or* Much obliged (to you). *or* 《친한 사이에》 Many thanks. *or* Thanks a lot. 《미》 (★ Thank you.는 감사의 뜻을 나타낼 때에는 [θǽŋkjuː]↘, 의례적으로 가볍게 말할 때에는 [-kju]↗로 발음함. Many thanks.를 Very thanks.라고는 하지 않으며 Much thanks.도 좀처럼 쓰지 않음. Thanks. 또는 Thanks a lot.은 무간한 처지에 쓸 수 있는 구어로서 손윗사람에게 쓰지 않는 것이 좋음).

◉ ～장 a letter of thanks 〔appreciation〕; a testimonial. ～패 a plaque of thanks; an appreciation plaque.

**감사**(監事) ① 《회계의》 an auditor; an inspector. ② 〖불교〗 a monk in charge of the property of a Buddhist temple.

**감사**(監査) inspection; 《회계의》 audit; auditing. ～하다 inspect; 《회계를》 audit. ¶ 엄중한 ～ a strict inspection; 《회계의》 a strict 〔full〕 audit.
◉ ～과 the inspection department. ～보고 an audit report. ～역 an inspector; an auditor. ～원 the Board of Audit and Inspection: ～원장 the Chairman of the Board of Audit and Inspection. ～증명 an audit certificate.

**감사납다** (be) tough; rough; coarse; intractable; unmanageable.

**감산**(減産) 《자연적인》 a decrease 〔fall〕 in output 〔production〕; 《인위적인》 a cut in 〔(a) reduction of〕 production 〔output〕. ～하다 cut 〔reduce, curtail〕 production. ¶ 1할을 ～하다 reduce 〔cut〕 production by 10 percent / 이 달에는 3%가 ～되었다 Production decreased by three percent this month. / 올해는 냉해로 인해 쌀이 20% ～되었다 Because of the cold weather, rice production fell by 20 percent this year. ◉ ～체제 《introduce》 a policy of reducing production.

**감산**(減算) 〖수학〗 subtraction. ～하다 subtract.

**감상**(感想) thoughts; impressions; *one's* sentiment(s). ¶ ～을 말하다 give 〔state〕 *one's* impressions 《of》; give *one's* thoughts 《on》 / ～을 묻다 ask 《*a person's*》 opinion 《about》; sound 《*a person*》 on a subject / 한국에 대한 ～은 어떻습니까 How does Korea strike 〔impress〕 you? *or* What is your impression of Korea? / 나는 그녀에게 그녀의 최신작에 관하여 ～을 말했다 I gave her my impressions of her latest work. ◉ ～문 a description (record) of *one's* impressions.

**감상**(感傷) sentiment; sentimentality. ¶ ～적인 sentimental; emotional / ～적인 소설 a sentimental novel / ～적이 되다 become 〔get, grow〕 sentimental / 그런 ～적인 생각은 그만둬 Put such sentimental feelings out of your mind. / 외교 협상에서는 ～ 따위가 끼어들 여지가 없다 There's no room for sentiment in diplomatic negotiations.
◉ ～주의 sentimentalism: ～주의자 a sentimentalist.

**감상**(鑑賞) appreciation. ～하다 appreciate; relish; enjoy. ¶ 명화 ～회 a special show of well-known films / 영국 시를 ～하다 appreciate English poetry; read English poetry appreciatively / 나의 취미는 음악 ～이다 My hobby is listening to music.
◉ ～가 an appreciator. ～력 an appreciative power: ～력이 있다〔없다〕 have a keen 〔no〕 appreciation 《of》; have an 〔no〕 ear 《for music》; have an 〔no〕 eye 《for painting 〔beauty〕》. ～비평 appreciative criticism.

**감색**(紺色) navy blue; dark 〔deep〕 blue.

**감성**(感性) 《감각력》 sensitivity; sensibility; sensitive faculty; 《감수성》 susceptibility. ◉ ～론 (a)esthetics. ～지수 〖심리〗 Emotional Quotient (생략 EQ).

**감성돔** 〖어류〗 a black porgy.

**감세**(減稅) a tax reduction 〔cut〕; reduction of taxes. ～하다 reduce 〔cut, lower〕 taxes. ¶ 대폭적인 ～ a drastic cut in taxes / 이들 품목은 5% ～되었다 The tax on these articles was reduced by 5 percent.
◉ ～안 a tax reduction bill. ～운동 a tax reduction campaign.

**감소**(減少) (a) diminution; (a) decrease; a fall; a drop; (a) reduction. ～하다 diminish; decrease; lessen; drop; fall off; be reduced.
¶ 수입〔인구〕의 ～ a decrease 〔reduction〕 in income 〔population〕 / ～하고 있다 be on the decrease / 전년보다 십억 원의 ～ a decrease of one billion won compared with the previous year / 수출이 작년의 3분의 2로 감소하였다 Exports have fallen off 〔decreased〕 to two-thirds of last year's total. / 식량 생산은 8퍼센트 ～하였다 The food production has decreased by 8 percent. / 화물 자동차의 수요가 급격히 ～되었다 Demand for trucks has shrunk drastically.

**감속**(減速) reducing speed; speed reduction 〔dropping〕; deceleration. ～하다 reduce speed 《of》; slowdown; decelerate. ¶ 눈비 올 때 ～ 운행 《게시》 Low gear when wet. ◉ ～운동 deceleration; negative acceleration. ～장치〔기어〕 reduction gear; a speed reducer. ～재 《원자로에서 중성자의》 a moderator.

**감손**(減損) 《줆》 decrease; diminution; 《손해》 loss; 《마손》 wear; 《경제적 가치의》 depreciation. ～하다 decrease; diminish; wear; depreciate. ◉ ～액

(the amount of) depreciation.
**감쇄**(減殺) diminution; reduction; attenuation; detraction. ～하다 diminish; lessen; reduce; attenuate; deaden 《force》; detract 《from *one's* merits》; impair 《the beauty》. ～되다 get reduced; be attenuated. ¶ 활동력을 ～하다 diminish the (vigor of) activity / 효과를 ～하다 lessen 〔weaken〕 the effect.
**감수**(甘受) uncomplaining acceptance 《of *one's* lot》; readiness to suffer 〔endure〕. ～하다 be ready to suffer; willingly submit 《to》. ¶ 비난을 ～하다 submit to reproach / 자기의 쓰라린 운명을 ～하다 accept *one's* bitter fate without complaining / 모욕을 ～하다 swallow 〔put up with〕 an insult / 이런 대우는 ～할 수 없다 I cannot submit myself to be treated in this way.
**감수**(減水) the receding 〔subsiding〕 of water. ～하다 《water》 fall; subside; recede; go down; sink. ¶ 강물이 3피트 ～되었다 The water in the river has fallen (by) three feet.
**감수**(減收) a fall 〔decrease〕 in income 〔yield, output〕. ～하다 《income, crop》 decrease. ¶ 금년의 쌀 수확은 200만 톤의 ～를 보았다 The rice crop this year shows a decrease of 2,000,000 tons.
**감수**(減數) 〖수학〗 subtrahend; the number to be subtracted. ◉ ～분열 〖생물〗 reduction division; (a) meiosis.
**감수**(減壽) shortening *one's* life. ～하다 shorten *one's* life. ¶ 그 사고를 당했을 때는 꼭 십년 ～하는 느낌이었다 I felt as if my life were shortened by ten years when I met with the accident.
**감수**(感受) impression; reception. ～하다 receive (an impression); be susceptible 《of》; be impressed 《with》; 《무전을》 pick up 《a wireless message》. ◉ ～성 sensibility; susceptibility; 〖심리〗 sensitivity: ～성이 예민한 (be) sensitive 《to》; susceptible 《to, of》 / ～성이 둔한 dull; insusceptible 《to》.
**감수**(監修) editorial supervision. ～하다 supervise the compilation 《of》. ¶ 한 교수 ～하에 편집되다 be compiled under the supervision of Professor Han. ◉ ～자 an editorial supervisor.
**감숭감숭** 《sprouting》 darkly here and there; dotted sparsely. ～하다 be 「sparsely dotted 〔sprouting darkly〕 here and there. ¶ 털이 ～ 나다 sprout dots of dark hair here and there.
**감숭하다** (be) dark; blackish; be dark here and there. ¶ 감숭한 얼굴 a darkish complexion.
**감시**(監視) ① 《망봄》 watch; lookout; 《관찰》 observation; 《감독》 supervision. ～하다 watch; keep watch 〔an eye〕 on; be on the lookout; observe; keep 《*a person*》 under observation. ¶ 행동을 ～하다 watch 〔keep an eye on〕 《*a person's*》 movements / ～를 두다 set a watch 《on》 / ～를 게을리하다 neglect to watch / 엄중히 ～당하다 be (kept) under close observation; be closely watched / 정전 명령의 실행을 ～하다 police a cease-fire / 군축 협정의 이행을 ～하다 monitor a disarmament agreement / 대기 오염에 대하여 엄격한 ～가 필요하다 We must keep (a) close watch 〔lookout〕 on air pollution. / 그들은 포로를 엄중히 ～하라는 명령을 받았다 They were ordered to keep a close watch over the P.O.W.'s.
② 《형법상의》 surveillance; police supervision. ～하다 conduct surveillance 《of》; exercise surveillance 《over》. ¶ ～의 눈을 피하다 elude the vigilance 《of the police》; break through police surveillance / 그는 현재 ～를 받고 있다 He is now under police surveillance. ◉ ～국 a monitor station. ～기구 a supervisory organization. ～망 a surveillance network 〔system〕. ～병〔인〕 a guard; a watch; lookout man. ～선(船) a guard 〔patrol〕 boat; a monitoring vessel (로켓 등의). ～선(線) a picket line. ～소 a watchhouse; a lookout. ～신호 a supervisory signal. ～장치 〖통신〗 a monitor. ～전류 a pilot current. ～제어 supervisory control. ～초(哨) 《공습의》 a spotting station; 《군의》 an observation post; 《보초의》 a guard box. ～탑 a watchtower. 우선 ～ 대상국명단 the priority watch list (생략 PWL).
**감식**(減食) reduction of food intake; a diet; dieting. ～하다 reduce *one's* diet; cut down on *one's* food; diet; eat less; underfeed *oneself*; go on a diet. ◉ ～요법 a reduced diet cure: 환자에게 ～요법을 하다 reduce a patient's intake of food. ～주의 dieting; underfeeding *oneself*.
**감식**(鑑識) judgment; discernment; discrimination; 《범죄의》 (criminal) identification. ～하다 judge; discern; discriminate; identify. ¶ 미술품 ～에 뛰어나다 「be a good judge of 〔have an eye for〕 objects of art; be a good

connoisseur of works of art.
◉ ～가 a discerner; a judge; 《미술의》 a connoisseur. ～과 《경찰의》 the (Criminal) Identification Section. ～안〔력〕 a discerning 〔critical〕 eye 《for》: ～안이 있다 have a good judge 《of jewelry》; have an eye 《for the beautiful》.

**감실**(龕室) a niche; a shrine 《for a Buddhist image》; a tabernacle.

**감실감실** ① 《털이》 ～하다 (be) sparsely dotted 《with black hair》. ¶ 털이 ～ 나다 short black hair sprout out sparsely; be thinly haired here and there. ② 《가물거림》 gleaming faintly.

**감실거리다** glimmer; gleam faintly. ¶ 감실거리는 불빛 a faint gleam of light / 먼 바다 위에 배가 감실거린다 A ship is faintly discerned far at sea.

**감싸다** 《싸다》 wrap; envelop; 《비호·보호하다》 protect 〔shield〕 *a person* 《from harm》; take 《*a person*》 under *one's* wing; 《허물을》 cover up 《for *a person*》; 《변호하다》 plead 《for *another*》; take 《*a person's*》 part. ¶ 머리를 감싸 쥐고 with *one's* head between *one's* hands / 담요로 몸을 ～ wrap *oneself* in a blanket / 죄인을 ～ shelter a culprit / 아버지는 언제나 나를 감싸 주셨다 My father always took me under his wing. / 아무도 나를 감싸 주는 사람이 없다 No one 「pleads for me 〔takes my part〕. / 침묵이 주위를 감싸고 있었다 Silence reigned 〔prevailed〕 all around.

**감아 올리다** wind up; hoist. ¶ 닻을 ～ heave 〔weigh〕 the anchor / 돛을 ～ furl 〔hoist〕 a sail / 발을 ～ roll up a screen.

**감안하다**(勘案—) take 《a matter》 into consideration 〔account〕. ¶ 그가 어리다는 점을 감안해야 한다 You must take his youth into consideration. / 교통 체증을 감안해서 일찍 출발하겠다 I will start early, allowing for traffic congestion.

**감압**(減壓) reduction of pressure; decompression. ～하다 reduce the pressure; decompress. ◉ ～밸브 a reducing valve. ～장치 a decompression device.

**감액**(減額) a reduction; a curtailment; a cut. ～하다 reduce; curtail; cut down; make a reduction. ¶ 보너스가 20%나 ～되었다 Our bonuses were reduced by as much as twenty percent.

**감언**(甘言) sweet-talk 《미구어》; honeyed 〔sugared, coaxing〕 words; (words of) flattery. ¶ ～으로 처녀를 꾀다 entice 〔allure, seduce〕 a girl with fair 〔sweet〕 words / ～으로 속이다 deceive with honeyed words / 그는 쉽게 ～에 말려든다 He is easily taken in by flattery.
◉ ～이설(利說) soft and seductive language; flattery; cajolery; blarney: ～이설로 꾀다 talk 〔cajole, wheedle〕 《*a person*》 into / ～이설에 속다 be imposed upon by honeyed words / ～이설로 돈을 우려내다 wheedle money 《out of *a person*》.

**감연히**(敢然—) daringly; boldly; bravely; fearlessly; resolutely; defiantly. ¶ ～ 일어서다 stand up bravely 《against the enemy》; rise fearlessly 《against the oppressor》 / ～ 난국에 임하다 meet the difficult situation bravely.

**감염**(感染) 《물듦》 contamination; influence; 《병원체의》 infection (공기·물에 의한); contagion (접촉에 의한). ～되다 《물들다》 get contaminated; get influenced; 《전염되다》 be infected 《with cholera》; catch 《a disease from》; contract 《a disease》 by infection. ¶ ～성의 infectious; contagious / 병에 ～된 사람 an infected person / 위험한 사상에 ～되다 be influenced by dangerous ideas / 나쁜 풍습에 ～되다 catch bad manners / ～되지 않다 《면역이 되어》 be immune 《from》 / 그 병은 ～된다 The disease is infectious 〔contagious〕. ◉ ～경로 an infection route. ～원(源) the source of infection. 공기～ aerial infection. 원내(院內)～ hospital infection.

**감염**(減塩) ～하다 cut down on salt. ¶ 감염 식사를 하다 reduce 〔cut down on〕 the amount of salt in *one's* diet. ◉ ～식 a low salt diet. ～식품 food with a reduced 〔low〕 salt content.

**감옥**(監獄) a prison; a jail 《미》; a gaol 《영》. ⇨ 교도소(矯導所). ◉ ～살이 serving *one's* term; a prison life.

**감우**(甘雨) ＝단비.

**감원**(減員) a reduction in force; a cutting down of staff; a personnel cut; a manpower cut-down; 《일시적》 a layoff. ～하다 lay off; cut down personnel. ¶ 공무원을 대폭 ～하다 reduce the number of public officials drastically; skeletonize public officials 《미》. ◉ ～바람 a sweeping reduction of the personnel.

**감은**(感恩) gratefulness; gratitude 《for kindness》. ～하다 feel gratitude.

**감음정**(減音程) 『음악』 a diminished

interval.

**감읍하다**(感泣—) be moved to tears 《by, with》; shed grateful tears 《for》.

**감응**(感應) ① 《생리상의》 sympathy; response; 《신불의》 response; answer; 《영감》 inspiration. ～하다 sympathize 《with》; respond 《to》; hear 《our prayer》 (신불이). ② 〖물리·전기〗 induction. ～하다 induce; act upon.
◉ ～기전기 an induction machine. ～기전력 induced power. ～도 sensitivity. ～도체 an induction conductor. ～유전(遺傳) telegony. ～작용 inductivity; a responsive effect. ～전기 induced electricity. ～전동기 an induction motor. ～전류 induced electric current: ～ 전류 요법 faradism; faradization. ～코일 an induction coil.

**감자** a potato; a white potato 《미》; an Irish potato. ¶ 햇～ a new potato / ～ 껍질을 벗기다 peel 〔pare〕 potatoes / ～ 튀김 a fried potato; 《얇게 썬》 a potato chip. 「당 cane sugar.

**감자**(甘蔗) sugar cane. ⇨사탕수수. ◉ ～

**감자**(減資) a decrease in capital; (a) reduction of capital; capital reduction. ～하다 reduce the capital 《from ... to...》. ◉ ～잉여금 〖경제〗 a reduction surplus. ～차익(差益) gains from stock retirement.

**감작**(減作) 〖농업〗 a crop that is off; lessened 〔reduced, curtailed〕 crops; a short crop; a poor crop.

**감잡이** ① 《거멀쇠》 a large metal staple; iron fastenings. ② 《수건》 a cloth-piece used in bed (after sexual intercourse).

**감잡히다** 「get caught up 〔trip〕 on a weak argument.

**감장** getting along without depending on others. ～하다 get along independently (on *one's* own).

**감전**(感電) (receiving) an electric shock. ～되다 get shocked; receive an electric shock. ¶ ～되어 죽다 be killed by an electric shock. ◉ ～사(死) electrocution: 가선공이 동력선을 잘못 만져 ～사했다 The line man was electrocuted when he happened to touch a power wire.

**감점**(減點) a demerit mark. ～하다 give 《*a person*》 a demerit mark; deduct 〔take off〕 points. ¶ ～당하다 receive a cut in marks. ◉ ～법 〖스포츠〗 a bad mark system; a penalty count system.

**감접이** the selvage 〔selvedge〕.

**감정**(感情) 《이성에 상대되는》 feelings; (an) emotion; (a) sentiment (정서); 《열정》 passion; 《충동》 (an) impulse. ¶ ～적인 sentimental; emotional / ～의 노예 a slave of passion / ～의 충돌 a conflict of sentiment 〔feelings〕 / 일시적인～에 이끌리어 prompted by an impulse; on the impulse of the moment; driven by a passing emotion / ～을 상하게 하다 hurt 〔do violence to〕 《*a person's*》 feelings / ～을 드러내다 betray *one's* emotions / ～을 억누르다 control *one's* feelings; suppress *one's* rising passion / ～을 자극하다 stir 〔excite〕 《*a person's*》 emotion / 남의 ～을 무시하다 have no regard for *another's* feelings / ～을 표현하다 express *one's* feelings / ～에 치우치기 쉽다 be apt to be swayed 〔influenced〕 by sentiment / 인간은 감정의 동물이다 Man is a creature of impulse. / 나는 ～을 감추려고 애썼다 I tried to hide 〔conceal〕 my feelings. / 나는 그녀의 ～을 상하게 한 것 같아 걱정이다 I'm afraid I have hurt her feelings. *or* I'm afraid I have offended her. / 그는 나에 대해 ～적인 편견을 갖고 있다 He has an emotional bias toward me. / 그녀는 우리들의 이성보다는 오히려 ～에 호소했다 She appealed to our emotions 〔feelings〕 rather than to our reason.
◉ ～감각 〖심리〗 feeling sensation. ～도착 perversion of feelings. ～론 an argument charged with emotion; an impassioned debate. ～미학 〖철학〗 aesthetic feelings. ～이입 〖철학〗 empathy. ～전이(轉移) 〖정신분석〗 displacement.

**감정**(憾情) displeasure; ill feeling; ill blood; a grudge. ¶ ～을 사다 court displeasure / ～이 나다 get displeased; become angry / ～을 내다 show displeasure / ～이 있다 have 〔bear, cherish〕 a grudge 〔an ill will〕 against 《*a person*》 / 나는 그에게 아무 ～도 없다 I bear him no grudge.

**감정**(鑑定) 《판정》 judgment; an expert opinion (전문가의); 《소송의》 legal consultation 〔advice〕; 《평가》 appraisal; estimation; 《진위의》 authentication. ～하다 judge; give an (expert) opinion 《on》; 《가격을》 appraise; estimate; 《필적을》 identify. ¶ ～을 의뢰하다 ask an expert opinion / 필적을 ～하다 give an expert opinion on 《*a person's*》 handwriting / …의 ～을 잘하다〔못하다〕 be a good 〔poor〕 judge of... / 허위～을 하다 give a false appraisal / ～을 받다 have 《a painting》 appraised

〔authenticated〕《by》; have an expert look at 《a painting》/ 그 필적의 ~을 전문가에게 의뢰했다 We asked an expert to identify the handwriting. / 전문가가 나의 골동품의 가치를 ~했다 An expert appraised the value of my antiques.
◉ ~가〔인〕 a judge; an appraiser; 《미술품의》 a connoisseur; 《법정의》 an expert witness. ~가격 an appraised value; an appraisal. ~료 a fee for an expert opinion; a valuation fee. ~서 a written statement of an expert opinion; a certificate of authenticity. 한국~원 the Korea Appraisal Board.

**감주**(甘酒) rice nectar; a sweet drink (made from rice).

**감지**(感知) perception; sensing; becoming aware. ~하다 perceive; sense; become aware 《of》. ¶ 위험〔지진〕을 ~하다 sense danger 〔an earthquake〕/ 동물에게는 위험을 ~하는 특별한 능력이 있는 것 같다 Animals seem to be endowed with a peculiar capacity for sensing danger. ◉ ~장치 a sensor.

**감지덕지**(感之德之) very gratefully; with many thanks. ~하다 be 〔feel〕 very grateful; be 〔feel〕 thankful. ¶ ~ 받을 것이지 무슨 불평이냐 You should accept it gratefully without grumbling.

**감질**(疳疾) ① 〖한의〗 a disease of childhood, characterized by swelling of the belly and diarrhea. ② 《걸근댐》 an insatiable appetite; a never satisfied desire. ~(이) 나다 feel insatiable; never feel satisfied; feel eager to eat 〔have〕 more; feel 〔be〕 dying for more; feel tantalized. ¶ ~나 하다 (show that) *one* feels insatiable 〔never satisfied〕; (show that) *one* is eager to eat 〔have〕 more / ~나게 하다 make 《*a person*》 feel insatiable; tantalize / 젖이 부족해서 어린애가 ~나 한다 The baby is showing its displeasure that there isn't more milk. / 한 잔으론 ~만 난다, 한 잔 더 하자 One drink makes me all the more thirsty, let's have another drink.

**감쪽같다** 《고친 것이》 (be) perfect; be as good as new; be just as it was; 《꾸민 일·거짓 따위가》 (be) perfect; complete. ¶ 감쪽같이 perfectly; completely; successfully; nicely; fairly / 감쪽같이 속다 be completely 〔fairly, nicely〕 「taken in 〔deceived〕; fall an easy victim to another's trick / 감쪽같이 속이다 trick 〔deceive, cheat〕 nicely 〔fairly〕 / 세탁을 하니 감쪽같았다 When washed, it was as good as before. / 부러진 담뱃대를 감쪽같이 고쳐 놓았다 He has mended the pipe so you can't tell it was ever broken. / 나는 감쪽같이 속아 가짜 그림을 샀다 I was palmed off with a counterfeit picture.

**감찰**(監察) inspection. ~하다 inspect; supervise. ◉ ~감 〖군사〗 an inspector general. ~관 an inspector.

**감찰**(鑑札) a license; a permit; a license plate. ¶ 무~의 unlicensed / ~을 교부하다〔받다〕 grant 〔take〕 a license / ~을 받지 못해 아직 영업을 못하고 있다 I cannot start business, as the license has not yet been given. ◉ ~료 a license fee.

**감채**(減債) partial payment of a debt; reducing *one's* debt; amortization.
◉ ~기금 an amortization 〔a sinking〕 fund: ~ 기금으로 상환하다 amortize. ~적립금 a sinking-fund reserve.

**감천**(感天) ¶ 지성(至誠)이면 ~이라 Sincerity moves Heaven. *or* Faith will move a mountain.

**감청**(紺青) deep 〔dark, navy〕 blue.

**감초**(甘草) 〖식물〗 licorice root. ¶ 약방에 ~ 《불가결의 인물》 an indispensable man; a key person; 《참섭꾼》 a man who meddle in everything; a person active in all sorts of affairs. ◉ ~즙 licorice extract.

**감촉**(感觸) (the sense of) touch; the feel; a feeling (느낌). ~하다 touch; feel; sense; perceive through the senses. ¶ 꺼칠꺼칠한 ~ rough feeling / ~이 좋다 be agreeable to the touch / ~이 부드럽다 feel soft; be soft to the touch.

**감추다** 《숨기다》 hide; conceal; put 《*a thing*》 out of sight; keep 《*a thing*》 from sight; 《덮어두다》 cover; veil; cloak; 《비밀로 하다》 keep 《*a matter*》 secret 〔back〕 《from *a person*》; 《속이다》 disguise 《*one's* sorrow》. ¶ 감추지 않고 without concealing; openly / 문 뒤로 몸을 ~ hide *oneself* behind the door / 보이지 않는 곳에 ~ hide 〔conceal〕 《*a thing*》 from view / 나이를 ~ conceal 〔hide〕 *one's* age; make a secret of *one's* age / 놀람〔슬픔, 실망〕을 ~ hide 〔conceal〕 surprise 〔sorrow, disappointment〕 / 사실을 ~ cover up 〔suppress〕 a fact / 잘못을 ~ cover *one's* mistake / 신분을 ~ conceal *one's* identity / 행방〔모습〕을 ~ disappear; go out of sight; hide 〔conceal〕 *one-*

*self* / 그녀는 마음의 동요를 감출 수 없었다 She could not veil her confusion completely.

**감축**(減縮) reduction; diminution; retrenchment. ～하다 reduce; diminish; retrench; curtail; cut down. ¶ 군비의 ～ the reduction of armaments / 경비를 ～하다 curtail 〔cut (down)〕 the expenses; retrench expenditures.

**감축하다**(感祝—) celebrate 〔congratulate〕 (*a person* on *a thing*) enthusiastically.

**감치다** ① 《꿰매다》 hem; put a hem 《in》; sew up. ¶ 옷 가장자리를 ～ hem the edge of a garment. ② 《잊혀지지 않다》 linger 〔haunt〕 in *one's* mind.

**감칠맛** ① 《음식의》 savory taste; a good flavor. ¶ ～이 있다 be flavory 〔tasty, savory, palatable〕; 《술이》 have good body; be full of body; be rich in flavor / ～이 없다 《술이》 be flat 〔tasteless, vapid〕; have little taste; have no body; taste watery / ～이 있는 술 rice wine of good 〔excellent〕 body; full-bodied rice wine / ～이 있는 국 very tasty soup. ② 《당기는》 attraction; magnetism. ¶ ～ 있는 말 magnetic words / 그의 문장에는 ～이 있다 There is something attractive in his sentence. 「다 =감치다.

**감침질** hemming; putting in hems. ～하

**감탄**(感歎) admiration; wonder; exclamation. ～하다 admire; be struck with admiration 《for》; wonder 〔marvel〕 《at》; exclaim 《over》. ¶ ～할 만한 admirable; wonderful; marvelous / ～할 만한 솜씨 an admirable performance / ～해 마지 않다 be「full of 〔filled with〕 admiration 《for》; be struck with wonder / 그의 성실성에 ～했다 I was struck by his sincerity. ◉ ～문 an exclamatory sentence. ～부호 an exclamation mark 〔point〕. ～사 an exclamation; an interjection.

**감탕** ① 《곤죽》 slime; liquid mud; a mire; a quagmire. ¶ ～에 빠지다 fall into the mire. ② 《끈끈이》 birdlime. ◉ ～밭 a field of mud; a quagmire.

**감탕질** = 요분질.

**감퇴**(減退) a decline 《in energy》; failing 《of memory》; loss 《of appetite》; (a) decrease. ～하다 decline; decrease; recede; fall off. ¶ 시력〔기억력〕 ～ failing of eyesight 〔memory〕 / 식욕〔체력〕이 ～하다 lose *one's*「appetite 〔physical strength〕 / 더위로 기력이 ～되다 The heat saps our energy. / 수요는 전반적으로 ～되어 있다 The demand remains generally in a slump.

**감투** a horsehair cap formerly worn by gentry 〔officials〕; 〔비유적〕 a government position; a distinguished post. ¶ ～를 쓰다 wear a horsehair cap; 〔비유적〕 become a government official / ～를 노리다 hunt for a leading place. ◉ ～싸움 a struggle for getting an influential post.

**감투**(敢鬪) fighting courageously 〔bravely〕. ～하다 fight courageously 〔bravely, gamely〕; fight a gallant fight. ◉ ～상 a fighting-spirit prize. ～정신 (a) fighting spirit.

**감표**(減標) 〖수학〗 the sign of subtraction; a minus sign (기호 —).

**감풀** a low-tide sandbar.

**감하다**(減—) ① 《빼다》 subtract; take off; 《줄이다》 reduce; diminish; decrease; lessen. ¶ 30 에서 20 을 ～ subtract 20 from 30 / 값을 ～ reduce prices / 10 에서 6 을 감하면 4 가 남는다 Six from ten leaves four. *or* Ten less 〔minus〕 six leaves four. / 현금이면 얼마쯤 감해 드립니다 We allow a discount for cash. ② 《줄다》 reduce; diminish; decrease; drop; dwindle. ¶ 3 분의 1 로 ～ reduce to one-third.

**감행**(敢行) decisive 〔resolute, daring〕 action. ～하다 take decisive action; dare 〔venture〕 《to *do*》. ¶ 지금은 그런 대규모 사업을 ～할 시기가 아니다 Now is not the time to venture on such an ambitious project.

**감형**(減刑) mitigation 〔reduction〕 of a sentence; commutation. ～하다 reduce 〔mitigate〕 a penalty; commute a sentence. ¶ 사형에서 종신형으로 ～하다 commute 〔reduce〕 a death sentence to life imprisonment / ～의 은전을 입다 be granted a commutation by special favor / 우리들은 그의 ～을 위해 탄원하였다 We petitioned for a reduction in his sentence.

**감호조치**(監護措置) 〖법〗 preventive custody; a measure for care and custody. ¶ 십년 징역에 십년 ～를 선고하다 sentence 《a convict》 to 10 years in jail plus 10 years in preventive custody.

**감홍**(甘汞) 〖화학〗 calomel.

**감화**(感化) influence; conversion; reforming. ～하다 influence; inspire; reform; exert influence on. ¶ ～되기 쉬운 (be) easily influenced 《by》 / …의 ～를 받아 under the influence of... / ～를 받다 be influenced 〔affected〕

《by》; be under the influence 《of》/ 그는 불교의 ~를 받고 있다 He is under the influence of Buddhism. / 젊은이는 친구들의 ~를 받기 쉽다 Young men are susceptible to influence of their friends. / 내가 시를 좋아하게 된 것은 양 교수의 ~를 받아서이다 Professor Yang inspired me with a love of poetry. ◉ ~교육 reformatory instruction 〔training〕. ~력 power to influence. ~원 a reformatory; a house of correction; a reform school.

**감회**(感懷) 《느낀 생각》 deep emotion; impressions; 《회상》 sentimental recollection; reminiscences. ¶ ~를 말하다 express 〔give〕 *one's* feelings 〔sentiments〕 《about》/ ~가 깊다 be deeply moved 《by》/ ~에 젖다 become sentimental 《over, about》; feel emotion 《at》/ 그는 벅찬 ~를 안고 학교를 떠났다 He left school with the fullness of his heart.

**감흥**(感興) fun; interest; inspiration. ¶ ~을 돋우다 arouse 〔stimulate, excite〕 *one's* interest 《in》/ ~이 일어나다 get 〔become〕 interested 《in》; be inspired 〔deeply stirred〕 《by》/ ~을 깨뜨리다 spoil fun 〔interest〕; kill *one's* interest / 이 소설은 나에게 아무런 ~도 주지 않는다 This novel「has no interest for 〔does not appeal to〕 me.

**감히**(敢—) daringly; boldly; without hesitation. ¶ ~ …하다 dare 〔venture, presume〕 《to *do*》; make bold 《to *do*》; lend *oneself* to 《a deed》/ ~ 나에게 그런 말을 하다니 How dare you say such a thing to me? / 어디서 ~ 그런 말이 나오느냐 How could you have the face to say so? / 그들은 ~ 공격을 못했다 They did not dare to attack. /아무도 ~ 그 유령이 나오는 집에 들어가려 하지 않았다 No one dared to venture into the haunted house.
(★ dare는 조동사·동사 양쪽으로 쓰이며 동사로서는 보통 동사와 같이 3인칭 단수 현재에 s를 붙이고 부정·의문문에는 do를 사용하여 to있는 부정사를 수반함: 《동사》 She dares to laugh at me.; 《동사로서 부정문》 She does not dare to go.; 《조동사》 She dare not go).

**갑**(甲) ① 《천간(天干)의》 the first of the 10 Heaven's Stems. ② ⇨ 갑방(甲方). ③ ⇨ 갑시(甲時). ④ 《성적》 the first grade; "A". ⑤ 《갑옷》 (a coat of) mail; (a suit of) armor. ⑥ 《등딱지》 a shell; a tortoise shell; a carapace. ⑦ 《여럿 중의 하나》 A; the former; the one. ¶ 갑과 을 A and B; the former and the latter; the one and the other / 갑지에서 을지로 from one place to another; from one place to the other.

**갑**(匣) a case; a box; 《담배 등의》 a packet. ¶ 담배 한 갑 a packet 〔pack 《미》〕 of cigarettes.

**갑**(岬) a cape; a promontory; a headland.

**갑각**(甲殼) a shell; a crust; a carapace. ◉ ~류 〖동물〗 *Crustacea:* ~류의 crustaceous / ~류학 crustaceology / ~류의 동물 a crustacean.

**갑갑증**(—症) boredom; *ennui* (F.); tedium.

**갑갑하다** 《지루하다》 (be) boring; tedious; tiresome; dull; monotonous; feel bored; have a dull time; 《답답하다》 (be) stuffy; close; stifling; suffocating. ¶ 가슴이 ~ feel heavy in the chest 〔stomach〕/ 갑갑해 죽겠다 be bored to death; be bored stiff / 매우 갑갑하시죠 I am afraid you find it a bore. / 방이 갑갑해 못 견디겠다, 창문 좀 열어라 Please open the window, I feel stifled in this room.

**갑골문자**(甲骨文字) inscriptions on bones and tortoise carapaces.

**갑근세**(甲勤稅) the income tax of Grade A; the Grade A income tax. ¶ 월급에서 ~를 공제하다 deduct the income tax of Grade A from *one's* salary.

**갑년**(甲年) 《회갑의 해》 the sixty-first anniversary of *one's* birth; *one's* 61st year.

**갑론을박**(甲論乙駁) the pros and cons. ~하다 argue pro and con; argue for and against 《a matter》. ¶ ~으로 결론이 나지 않았다 No conclusion was reached in the heated arguments for and against.

**갑문**(閘門) a sluice; a floodgate; a lock. ¶ ~식 운하 a lock canal.

**갑방**(甲方) 〖민속〗 east-by-northeast.

**갑부**(甲富) the wealthiest 〔richest〕 (in a community); a magnate; a millionaire. ¶ 장안의 ~ the richest man in the town.

**갑사**(甲紗) fine gauze.

**갑상선**(甲狀腺) 〖해부〗 the thyroid gland. ◉ ~ 기능항진증 hyperthyroidism. ~염 thyroiditis. ~절제술 thyroidectomy. ~정맥 the thyroid vein. ~종(腫) goiter. ~호르몬 thyroid hormone; thyroxin(e).

**갑시**(甲時) 〖민속〗 the 6th of the 24 hour periods (=4:30—5:30 a.m.).

**갑오**(甲午) the 31st binary term of the sexagenary cycle. ◉ ~개혁 the Reformation of *Gabo.*

**갑옷**(甲—) (a suit of) armor; (a coat of) mail. ¶ ~을 입은 무사 an armored warrior / ~을 입다 buckle 〔put〕 on armor. ◉ ~미늘 the metal scales on a coat of armor.

**갑자**(甲子) 《민속》 the first year of the sexagenary cycle; the Year of the Rat. ¶ 육십 ~ the sexagenary cycle.

**갑자기** 《별안간》 suddenly; all of a sudden; all at once; abruptly; 《뜻밖에》 unexpectedly; without warning. ¶ ~ 나타나다 burst on the scene / ~ 웃음을 터뜨리다 burst into laughter / ~ 돌아오다 return unexpectedly / ~ 죽다 drop dead / ~ 돌아서다 turn back abruptly / ~ 방문하다 pay 《*a person*》 a surprise visit / ~ 공격하다 attack without warning / ~ 시험을 치르다 give an examination without notice / ~ 일이 생겨서 참석을 못 합니다 I cannot attend owing to an unexpected business.

**갑작스럽다** (be) sudden; unexpected. ¶ 갑작스러운 일 an unexpected thing 〔happening〕 / 갑작스러운 질문 an unexpected question / 갑작스러운 죽음 a sudden death / 갑작스러운 초대 〔방문〕 a surprise invitation 〔visit〕 / 그 일이 너무나 갑작스러워서 우리는 더욱더 당혹했다 The suddenness of it confused us all the more.

**갑절** ① [명사로서] two times; twice; double; twofold; 《셀 때》 times; as much. ~하다 double; redouble. ¶ ~ 반 twice and a half; two and a half times / 그 ~되는 수〔양〕 twice as many 〔much〕 as that; twice the number 〔quantity〕 / 크기〔길이〕가 ~이다 be twice as large 〔long〕 as; be as large 〔long〕 again as; be twice the size 〔length〕 《of》 / 그는 나보다 나이가 ~이다 He is twice my age. / 나의 수입은 이전의 ~이나 늘었다 My income is double what it was. / 이것은 그것보다 ~이나 좋다 This is twice as good as that. ② [부사로서] ¶ ~ 비싸다 cost twice as much / 남보다 ~ 일하다 work twice as hard as others.

**갑종**(甲種) grade A; top-grade.

**갑주**(甲胄) armor and helmet; a panoply. ⇨갑옷. ¶ ~ 한 벌 a suit of armor.

**갑충**(甲蟲) 〖곤충〗 a beetle.

**갑판**(甲板) the deck. ¶ ~으로 가다 go on deck / ~에 나가 있다 be on deck / ~에 실을 것 《게시》 On deck. / 파도가 ~을 쓸었다 Waves washed 〔swept〕 the deck. ◉ ~사관 a deck officer. ~선실 a deck cabin. ~선원 a deck hand. ~승강구 a hatchway. ~실 a deckhouse. ~여객 a deck passenger. ~일지 a deck log. ~장 a boatswain. 앞~ the forecastle deck. 주〔상, 중, 하〕~ the main 〔upper, middle, lower〕 deck.

**갑피**(甲皮) the uppers of leather shoes; shoes without soles.

**값** ① 《가치》 value; worth; merit (진가). ¶ 값이 있다 (be) worth; valuable; worthy; be of value / 값이 없다 《따질 수 없다》 (be) priceless; invaluable; 《무가치》 (be) valueless; worthless; unworthy; be of no value 〔merit〕 / 값이 오르다 rise 〔go up〕 in value / 값이 내리다 fall 〔go down〕 in value / 최근 몇년 사이 달러 값이 상대적으로 하락했다 There has been a relative decline in the value of the dollar in recent years. / 그것은 천금의 값이 있다 It is worth its weight in gold. / 건강은 값으로 따질 수 없는 은혜이다 Good health is a priceless blessing.
② 《가격》 a price; (a) cost; value. ¶ 값이 싼 low-priced; low in price; inexpensive; cheap / 값이 싸다〔비싸다〕 be cheap 〔expensive, dear, costly〕; be low 〔high〕 in price; be low-〔high-〕priced (★ dear는 영국에서 쓰이고, costly는 주로 귀중한 물건에 대해서 쓰임: a costly jewel (값이 비싼 보석). 「값이 싸다〔비싸다〕」를 The price is cheap 〔dear〕.로는 하지 않음. 왜냐하면 cheap나 dear는 그것만으로 「값이 싸다〔비싸다〕」의 뜻이 있기 때문임. price를 쓸 경우는 low, high로 함.) / 값이 오르다〔내리다〕 go up 〔down〕 in price; rise 〔fall〕 in price; the price goes up 〔down〕 / 값을 유지하다 maintain 〔keep up〕 the price / 터무니 없는 값으로 팔다 sell at an exorbitant price / 값을 올리다〔내리다〕 raise 〔lower〕 the price / 값을 매기다 set a price 《on》; price 《*a thing* at 10,000 won》; mark 《*a thing*》 with *its* price / 값을 깎다 beat down the price; haggle over (the price) / 값을 묻다 inquire 〔ask〕 the price / 값을 좀 깎아 주세요 Could you give me a discount? *or* Will you reduce the price? / 그 값으로는 본전도 안 됩니다 Your figure is below the cost. / 값이 얼맙니까 What is the price? *or* How much is it? / 값이 맞으면 팔겠다 I will sell it if you name a moderate price. / 값이 얼마면 되겠습니까 About what price would you like, Sir?

값가다, 값나가다 be valuable; be ex-

pensive; be costly; be of value. ¶ 값나가는 물건 a valuable article; an expensive article; valuables / 값나가는 물건을 몽땅 도둑맞았다 All the valuable articles were stolen.
값닿다 《the bid》 reach a price *one* has in mind; 《the price》 be reasonable 〔satisfactory〕. ¶ 값이 닿지 않아 사지 못했다 The price was too high and I couldn't buy it. / 값이 닿지 않아 팔지 않았다 The price was not satisfactory and I didn't sell it.
값보다 《어림짐작》 value; appraise; estimate; 《값부르다》 bid; offer a price. ¶ 이 물건값을 좀 보아 주오 Please appraise this article. *or* Tell me what this is worth, please. / 상당한 값을 봤는데 그 사람은 팔지 않았다 I made a good offer, but he wouldn't sell it.
값치다 fix the price of 《*a thing*》; value 《*something* at》. ¶ 그의 집과 가재를 통틀어 8,000 달러로 값쳐서 내가 맡기로 했다 I have decided to take his house and its contents, valuing them at eight thousand dollars in all.
값놓다, 값부르다 《the buyer》 name a price; bid; make a bid; 《the seller》 demand 〔ask〕 a price.
값치르다 pay 《for》. ¶ 물건값을 치르다 pay for an article.
값하다 be worth; be worthy 《of 》; deserve; merit. ¶ 밥먹은 값하다 render a service for what *one* has eaten; sing for *one's* supper; earn *one's* bread 〔board〕.

**값어치** worth; value. ¶ 3억 원의 ~가 있는 집 a house with a value of three hundred million won / 한번 읽어 볼~가 있다 be worth reading; be worthy of a perusal / 백 원의 ~도 못 된다 It isn't worth 100 won. / 「이 그림의 ~는 얼마나 됩니까」―「적어도 1천만 원은 됩니다」 "How much is this picture 〔painting〕 worth?"―"It 「will cost 〔is worth〕 at least ten million won."

**값지다** (be) expensive; costly; valuable; be of great value. ¶ 값진 선물 an expensive 〔a costly〕 gift 〔present〕 / 이 책은 내게 매우 값진 것이다 This book is very valuable to me. *or* This book is of great value to me. / 그녀는 이미 가지고 있던 값진 물건들을 모두 팔아버렸다 She had already sold everything of value that she possessed.

**갓**[1] 《쓰는》 a Korean traditional hat made of bamboo 〔horsehair〕.

**갓**[2] 〖식물〗 leaf mustard. ◉ 갓김치 mustard leaf kimchi.

**갓**[3] 《말림갓》 a forest 〔pasture〕 preserve.

**갓**[4] 《수량 단위》 a bundle 〔string〕 of ten handfuls of dried things tied together. ¶ 고사리 한 갓 a bundle of ten handfuls of dried bracken / 굴비 두 갓 two strings of ten dried corvina.

**갓**[5] 《방금》 《be done or made》 just now; a moment ago; newly; fresh from; recently. ¶ 대학을 갓 나온 (청년) (a young man) fresh from college / 갓 지은 집 a newly built house / 갓 지은 밥 rice hot from the pot / 갓 구운 빵 bread fresh from the oven / 시골서 갓 올라온 처녀 a girl fresh 〔new〕 from the country / 갓 결혼한 부부 a newly wedded couple; newlyweds / 갓 들어온 뉴스를 전해드리겠습니다 We have another item of news received right now.

**갓-** 《나이 앞에서》 just; neither more nor less than. ¶ 저 처녀는 나이가 갓스물이다 The girl is just twenty years old.

**갓끈** a Korean traditional hat string (tied under the chin).

**갓나다** be newly 〔just〕 born.

**갓난아이, 갓난애** a newborn baby; a baby (★ baby는 성별이 분명치 않으므로 흔히 it로 받지만 확실한 때에는 he나 she로 받음); an infant; a babe. ¶ 갓난애 같은 babylike / 갓난애 취급을 하다 treat 《*a person*》 as a baby.

**갓도래** the binding 〔rim〕 of a Korean traditional hat.

**갓돌** a copestone.

**갓양(태)** the brim of a Korean traditional hat.

**강**(江) a river; 《시내》 a stream. ¶ 강 건너에 across a river / 강을 끼고 along a river / 강을 따라 내려가다〔거슬러 올라가다〕 go down 〔up〕 the river; go downstream 〔upstream〕 / 강을 건너다 cross a river / 이 강은 황해로 흐른다 The river finds its way to the Yellow Sea. / 강은 서쪽으로 흘러 바다로 들어간다 The river flows westward to the sea.

**강**(鋼) steel.

**강**(綱) 〖생물〗 《분류의 단위》 a class.

**강**(講) 《글외기》 recitation; 《강의》 a lecture.

**강-** 《호됨·억지스러움》 forced; severe; harsh; rough; unreasonable; trying; terrible; awful. ¶ 강더위 a spell of intense heat with no rain at all / 강추위 severe cold weather / 강새암 unreasonable jealousy.

**-강**(強) 《우수리가 있을 때》 a little 「over 〔more than〕 《fifty》; something over

《2 pounds》; and a fraction. ¶ 3홉강 three *hob* and a fraction / 3퍼센트강 a little over three percent.

**강가**(江―) a riverside; a riverbank. ¶ 맞은편 ~ the opposite side of a river / ~의 버들 a riverside willow / ~의 호텔 a riverside hotel; a hotel by the riverside / 그녀의 집은 ~에 있다 Her house stands on 〔by〕 the riverside.

**강간**(強姦) rape; violation; outrage; assault. ~하다 rape; assault; violate; outrage; ravish. ◉ ~미수 an attempted criminal assault. ~범 a rapist. ~죄 rape; criminal assault. 미성년~ 《미》 statutory rape.

**강강술래** 《원무》 a Korean circle dance (usually played by girls under the bright full moon); the song which goes with the dance (노래).

**강건**(剛健) sturdiness; manliness. ~하다 (be) strong and sturdy; virile; manly. ¶ ~한 정신 a virile spirit / ~한 기상을 기르다 cultivate the spirit of fortitude and manliness.

**강건**(強健) ~하다 (be) robust; healthy; strong. ¶ ~한 사람 a person of robust health / 그는 신체 ~하다 He has a strong 〔robust〕 constitution.

**강견**(強肩) a strong 〔powerful〕 arm. ¶ ~의 외야수 an outfielder with a 「powerful throw 〔good arm〕.

**강경**(強硬) ~하다 (be) strong; tough; firm; resolute; positive; unyielding; uncompromising. ¶ ~히 strongly; firmly; stoutly; resolutely / ~한 결의문 a strongly-worded resolution / ~한 태도를 취하다 take a firm 〔stiff, hard-line〕 attitude 《toward, against》; take a tough line 《with, on》; take a tough stand 《on a problem》 / ~히 의견을 주장하다 maintain *one's* opinion firmly; insist on *one's* opinion uncompromisingly 〔unyieldingly〕 / ~히 반대하다 oppose 《*something*》 stubbornly; offer 〔raise〕 strong opposition.
◉ ~노선 a hard line. ~수단 drastic 〔strong〕 measures; a resolute step: ~한 수단을 취해야 한다 We should take strong measures. ~자세 a hard-line stance. ~파 the hardliners; the hawks: 미국 의회에는 한국에 대한 ~파가 다수를 차지하고 있다 The U.S. Congress is dominated by hardliners on the subject of Korea.

**강계**(疆界) the boundaries (of a country); a border; the frontier.

**강관**(鋼管) a steel pipe 〔tube〕.

**강구**(江口) an estuary. ⇨ 강어귀.

**강구**(講究) study; consideration; deliberation. ~하다 study; consider; deliberate; devise. ¶ 적당한 수단을 ~하다 devise a proper measure; take a proper step.

**강국**(強國) a (great) power; a strong nation 〔country〕; a powerful state. ¶ 세계의 ~들 the powers of the world; the world powers / 5대 ~ the Big Five; the five big 〔great〕 powers of the world.

**강굽이**(江―) a river bend; the crook of 「a river.

**강권**(強勸) recommending against 《*a person's*》 will; a persistent 〔an insistent〕 recommendation; urging; pressing. ~하다 recommend against 《*a person's*》 will; urge; press.

**강권**(強權) 《강한》 (the power of) authority; influence; 《법적인》 legal authority; state power. ¶ ~적 authoritarian / ~을 발동하다 invoke the power of (the) law 《against》; take strong measures. ◉ ~발동 the invocation of the state power. ~정치 power 〔a high-handed〕 politics. ~주의 authoritarianism.

**강기**(剛氣) firmness; strength 《of disposition》; fortitude; sturdiness. 「綱).

**강기**(綱紀) official discipline. = 기강(紀

**강기슭**(江―) a riverbank; a riverside.

**강남**(江南) the south of a river; 《서울의》 the south of the Han River. ◉ ~지역 the district south of a river; the areas south of the Han River.

**강낭콩** 〚식물〛 a kidney bean; a haricot (bean); a French bean.

**강다짐** ① 《국물 없이 먹음》 forgoing the soup or other liquid *one* usually drinks while eating rice. ~하다 eat rice without soup or other beverage. ② 《부림》 forcing 《*a person*》 to work without pay. ~하다 force 《*a person*》 to work without pay. ③ 《꾸짖음》 scolding *a person* without listening to *his* side of the story. ~하다 scold 《*a person*》 without listening to *his* side of the story.

**강단**(剛斷) ① 《결단력》 decisiveness; determination; resolution. ¶ ~이 있다 be decisive; be a decisive person. ② 《끈덕짐》 tenacity; pertinacity; perseverance; stick-to-itiveness 《미》. ¶ ~이 있는 tenacious; persevering.

**강단**(講壇) a (lecture) platform; a rostrum; 《설교단》 a pulpit. ¶ ~에 서다 stand on a platform; teach school;

preach a sermon / ～에서 내리다 leave 〔descend from〕 the platform.

**강당**(講堂) a lecture hall; an auditorium (*pl.* ～s, -ria); an assembly hall. ¶ 졸업식은 ～에서 거행되었다 The graduation ceremony was held in the hall.

**강대**(強大) being big and strong 〔powerful, mighty〕. ～하다 (be) big and strong 〔powerful〕; mighty. ¶ ～한 권력 great authority 〔power〕 / ～한 해군국 a mighty naval power / ～해지다 become powerful. ◉ ～국 a powerful country; a Big Power.

**강도**(強度) 《물체의》 strength; 《빛 따위의》 intensity. ¶ ～의 strong 《glasses》; powerful 《lenses》; intense 《light》 / ～높은 훈련 intensive training / 그의 비평의 ～ the strength of his criticism / 암반의 ～를 조사하다 examine the strength of the rock. ◉ ～시험 a strength test 《on a sample of steel》.

**강도**(強盜) 《사람》 a robber; a burglar; a holdup man 《미구어》; 《행위》 robbery; burglary; mugging. ¶ 은행〔열차〕 ～ a bank 〔train〕 robber / ～를 당하다 be robbed / 우리 집에 ～가 들었다 A burglar broke into my house. / 요즈음 여러 은행들이 ～를 당했다 A number of banks have been robbed lately. ◉ ～용의자 a robber-suspect. ～질 burglary; robbery: ～질하다 commit burglary 〔robbery〕. 무장～ 《사람》 an armed robber; 《행위》 armed robbery. 살인～(죄) burglary and murder. 삼인조～ a trio of burglars.

**강독**(講讀) reading; translation. ～하다 read. ¶ 원서를 ～하다 read original texts in class.

**강동강동** jumping up and down lightly; hopping 〔skipping〕 briskly. 「hop.

**강동거리다** jump up and down lightly;

**강둑**(江—) a river embankment; a bank; a dike; a levee. ¶ ～을 쌓다 construct 〔build〕 a bank / ～이 터져서 홍수가 났다 The riverbank collapsed and we had a flood.

**강등**(降等) demotion. ～하다 demote; reduce to a lower rank.

**강똥** hard stools; turds.

**강력**(強力) being strong 〔powerful〕. ～하다 (be) strong; powerful; mighty. ¶ ～한 폭발물 a powerful explosive / ～한 지지자 a powerful supporter / ～한 엔진 a high-powered engine / 정치 개혁 운동을 ～히 추진하다 vigorously push forward a campaign for political reform / 그 운동은 대중의 ～한 지지를 얻었다 The movement obtained strong 〔powerful〕 support from the public. ◉ ～범 『법』《죄》 a violent 〔major〕 crime; a felony; 《사람》 a felonious 〔major〕 criminal. ～비타민제 a high-potency 〔concentrated〕 vitamin preparation. ～접착제 a high-strength adhesive.

**강렬**(強烈) being strong; being intense. ～하다 (be) strong; intense. ¶ ～한 색채 loud 〔hot〕 colors / ～한 자극 a strong stimulus / ～한 인상을 주다 make a strong impression 《on》 / 이 액체는 ～한 냄새가 난다 This liquid has a strong smell. / ～한 빛으로 눈이 부셨다 An intense light dazzled me.

**강령**(綱領) 《기본 방침》 general principles; 《정당의 정강》 a platform; 《정당의 정책 방침》 party lines. ¶ 정당의 ～ a party platform 《미》; a party programme 《영》 / 십대～ a 10-point (party) platform.

**강론**(講論) 《학술의》 exposition; discussion; 《교리의》 preaching; teaching. ～하다 expound; discuss; preach; teach.

**강림**(降臨) descent from Heaven; 《예수의》 Advent; Christ's coming. ～하다 descend; come down. ¶ 성령이 ～하셨다 The Holy Ghost 〔Spirit〕 descended upon them. 「마르다.

**강마르다** (be) dried up; parched. ⇨ 깡

**강매**(強賣) high-pressure selling; aggressive peddling 《of goods》. ～하다 force a sale 《on *a person*》; force 〔press〕 《*a person*》 to buy 《*a thing*》; force 《*a thing*》 upon 《*a person*》. ¶ ～하는 사람 a high-pressure 〔pushy〕 salesman / ～하는 식의 상법 aggressive 〔high-pressure〕 salesmanship; the hard sell / 그는 그 책을 그녀에게 ～했다 He pressured her into buying the book. *or* He forced the book on her.

**강모** 《호미모》 young rice plants planted in a dry paddy. 「있는 bristled.

**강모**(剛毛) a bristle; a stiff hair. ¶ ～가

**강목** 『광산』 waste 〔unproductive, fruitless〕 mining operations. ～치다 make fruitless 〔vain〕 effort; waste labor.

**강목**(綱目) main points and details; divisions and subdivisions; 《분류》 classification. ¶ ～을 나누다 classify; arrange in classes.

**강물**(江—) river water; the river. ¶ ～이 붇다 the river rises. 「bed.

**강바닥**(江—) the river bottom; the river-

**강바람** 《마른 바람》 a strong wind bringing no rain; a dry wind.

**강바람**(江—) a wind blowing from 〔around〕 a river; a breeze from the river; a river breeze 〔wind〕.

**강박**(強迫) compulsion; coercion. ~하다 compel; coerce; force. ◉ ~관념 a persistent idea; an obsession: ~관념에 시달리다 be obsessed 《by, with》; suffer from an obsession / 그녀는 항상 감시당하고 있다는 ~관념에 사로잡혀 있다 She is obsessed with the idea that she is always being watched.

**강반**(江畔) 《강가》 a riverside; a riverbank. ¶ ~에서 at the riverside / ~에 by 〔on〕 a river; on the bank of a river.

**강배**(江—) a river boat.

**강변**(江邊) the riverside. ¶ ~의 식당 a riverside restaurant. ◉ ~도로 a riverside road. ~ 도시고속도로 the riverside urban expressway.

**강변**(強辯) quibble; sophistry. ~하다 quibble; insist obstinately; reason against reason.

**강변화**(強變化) 〖문법〗 《동사의》 strong conjugation. ◉ ~동사 strong verbs.

**강병**(強兵) a strong army.

**강보**(襁褓) swaddling clothes. ◉ ~유아 a baby in swaddling clothes.

**강보합**(強保合) 〖증권〗 ¶ ~의 《be》 firm 〔steady〕 with an upward tendency.

**강복**(降福) 〖가톨릭〗 blessing. ~하다 bless.

**강북**(江北) the north of a river; 《서울의》 the north of the Han River. ◉ ~지역 《서울의》 the areas north of the Han River.

**강사**(講士) a speaker.

**강사**(講師) a lecturer; an instructor. ¶ S 대학교 ~ a lecturer at 〔of〕 S University / 대학의 영어 ~ a university lecturer in English / ~로 임명되다 be appointed a lecturer 〔to lectureship〕.

**강삭**(鋼索) a cable; a wire 〔steel〕 rope.

**강산**(江山) rivers and mountains; 《강토》 *one's* native land. ¶ 삼천리 금수 ~ the beautiful land of Korea, far and wide / ~풍월 natural beauty / 십년이면 ~도 변한다 Ten years is an epoch.

**강상**(江上) 《강가》 《on》 the riverbank; 《물위》 《on》 the surface of the river.

**강샘** unreasonable 〔intense〕 jealousy. ~하다 feel a surge of unreasonable jealousy; become intensely jealous. ¶ 아내의 ~에는 두 손 다 들었다 My wife's jealousy has gone beyond the limit.

**강서리** a heavy frost.

**강선**(鋼線) a steel wire.

**강설**(降雪) snowing; a snowfall. ¶ ~이 1미터에 이르렀다 Snow fell 「one meter deep 〔to a depth of one meter〕. / 대관령 일대에는 엄청난 ~이 있었다 A heavy snowfall was experienced at Taegwallyŏng and neighborhood. ◉ ~량 the (amount of) snowfall.

**강설**(講說) a lecture; a talk. ~하다 lecture 〔talk〕 on 《a subject》; expound.

**강성**(剛性) hardness; stiffness; rigidity.

**강성하다**(強盛—) (be) powerful; thriving; flourishing.

**강세**(強勢) 《음의》 (a) stress; (an) emphasis (*pl.* -ses); an accent; 《시세의》 a strong 〔firm〕 tone; a bullish tendency. ¶ ~(가) 있는 음절 an emphatic syllable / ~를 두다 emphasize; accent; lay 〔put〕 emphasis 〔stress〕 《on》 / ~로 나오다 take an aggressive attitude; lead with trumps / 시황은 ~를 보이고 있다 The market is looking bullish. ◉ ~시장 a bull market. ~주 bull shares.

**강속**(江—) in the river.

**강속구**(強速球) 《야구에서》 a fast 〔speed〕 ball; a fireball. ¶ ~ 투수 a fast-ball pitcher / ~를 던지다 throw a fast 〔speed〕 ball.

**강쇠바람** an east 〔easterly〕 wind which blows in early autumn.

**강수**(降水) rainfall; precipitation. ◉ ~확률 a rainfall probability.

**강수량**(降水量) the amount of rainfall; (a) precipitation. ¶ 이곳의 ~은 30밀리미터였다 Thirty millimeter of rain fell here. / 올 여름에는 ~이 적었다 We have had little rain during this summer.

**강술** a drink without any food; just liquor. ¶ ~을 마시다 drink liquor without food 〔snack〕.

**강술**(講述) lecturing; expounding. ~하다 lecture 《on》; expound.

**강습**(強襲) an assault; a storm; a violent attack. ~하다 assault; storm. ¶ 3루를 ~하는 땅볼 《야구에서》 a terrific grounder baffling the third baseman / 3루 ~의 히트를 치다 《야구에서》 slug a hit too hot for the third baseman to handle / ~하여 점령하다 take 《a fort》 by storm; carry 《a fort》 by assault.

**강습**(講習) a (short) training course 〔class〕. ¶ ~을 받다 take 〔receive〕 a short course 《of English》; attend a lecture class. ◉ ~생 a student; a trainee. ~소 an institute giving short courses; a training school. ~회 a short course; a class; 《연구 집회》 a workshop: 여름〔겨울〕 ~회 《attend》 a summer 〔winter〕 school 〔course〕 / 프랑스 요리 ~회 French cooking class /

~회를 열다 offer courses 《in》.

**강신술**(降神術) spiritualism; mediumism; spiritism; typtology.

**강심**(江心) the center 〔very middle〕 of a river.

**강심제**(強心劑) heart medicine 〔stimulant〕; a cardiotonic drug; cardiotonics [총칭].

**강아지** a little dog; a pup; a puppy; a doggie.

**강아지풀** 『식물』 a foxtail.

**강안**(江岸) a riverside; a riverbank. ¶ ~의 풍경 the scenery along the river.

**강압**(強壓) oppression; pressure; coercion. ~하다 put pressure 《on *a person*》; bring pressure to bear 《on *a person*》; coerce 《*a person*》 《into *do*ing》. ¶ ~적인 high-handed; coercive. ◉ ~수단 high-handed 〔coercive〕 measures; a strong-arm method. ~정책 a high-handed policy; a big-stick policy.

**강약**(強弱) 《셈과 약함》 strength and weakness; 《강자와 약자》 the strong and the weak; 《음의》 stress; (a) rhythm. ◉ ~격 『시』 trochee. ~법 『음악』 dynamics.

**강어귀**(江―) a river mouth; an estuary (큰 강의). ¶ 낙동~의 하구언(河口堰) 건설 공사 the construction of an estuary barrage at the mouth of the Naktong river.

**강연**(講演) a lecture; an address; a talk. ~하다 give 〔deliver〕 a lecture 《on》; address 《a meeting》; give a talk 《on》; lecture 《on Shakespeare》. ¶ 학회에서의 ~ a lecture to a learned society / 라디오로 ~하다 talk 〔make a lecture〕 over the radio / ~을 청탁하다 ask 〔invite〕 《*a person*》 to give a lecture; ask 《*a person*》 to address 〔speak to〕 《students》 / 그는 도덕 교육에 관하여 ~하게 되어 있다 He is to give a lecture on moral education. ◉ ~료 a lecture 〔lecturer's〕 fee. ~여행 a lecture tour. ~자 a lecturer; a speaker. ~회 a lecture meeting.

**강옥석**(鋼玉石) 『광물』 corundum; ruby; sapphire.

**강온**(強穩) toughness and moderateness. ◉ ~ 양면정책 a carrot-and-stick policy. ~양파 the tough elements 〔hardliners〕 and the moderates; the hawks and the doves.

**강요**(強要) forcible demand; coercion; exaction; extortion. ~하다 demand forcibly; force; compel; coerce; exact; extort. ¶ 뇌물〔약속, 기부〕을 ~하다 exact 〔extort〕 「bribes 〔a promise, a subscription〕 from *a person* / 사직을 ~하다 force 〔coerce〕 《*a person*》 to resign; press 《*a person*》 to retire / 지급을 ~하다 demand payment with importunity / ~하여 …하게 하다 force 〔compel〕 《*a person*》 to *do;* coerce 《*a person*》 into *do*ing / …을 ~ 당하다 be compelled 〔forced, driven〕 to 《*do*》 / 그는 사직을 ~당했다 He was forced 〔compelled〕 to resign. / 그는 나에게 돈을 ~했다 He pressed me for money. / 자백을 ~당해서는 안 된다 Confessions must not be forced 〔coerced〕. / 그는 ~에 못이겨 그 계약서에 서명했다 He was coerced into signing the contract.

**강요**(綱要) elements; essentials; an outline; a summary; a synopsis. ◉ 심리학~ *the Elements of Psychology* (책이름).

**강우**(降雨) (a) rainfall; rain. ~하다 it rains; rain falls. ¶ 어제의 ~ 범위는 경기 일대에 미쳤다 The rain area yesterday spread over most of Kyŏnggi Province. / ~ 부족으로 농작물이 자라지 않는다 The crops are suffering from little 〔deficient〕 rain. ◉ ~기 a rainy season. ~대 a rain belt. ~도 a rain chart 〔map〕. ~량 the (amount of) rainfall; a rainfall 《of 20mm》; precipitation: 이 지역의 연평균 ~량 the average annual rainfall in this region. ~전선 a rain front.

**강울음** forced 〔pretended〕 tears; crocodile tears. ¶ ~을 울다 shed feigned 〔crocodile〕 tears.

**강의**(講義) a lecture; 《해설》 a discourse; an exposition. ~하다 lecture 《on》; give a lecture 《on》; give a course 《in French》. ¶ ~를 시작하다 open *one's* course of lecture / ~ 준비를 하다 prepare *one's* lecture / 영어로 ~하다 give a lecture in English / ~를 받으러 나가다〔나가지 않다〕 attend 〔cut〕 a lecture / ~를 노트하다 take notes on the lecture / 나는 남 선생님 ~를 받고 있다 I am in Mr. Nam's class. / 김 교수는 다음 학기에 셰익스피어를 ~한다 Professor Kim will give lectures on Shakespeare next term. ◉ ~록 a transcript of lectures. ~방법 the manner of lecturing. ~실 a lecture room.

**강인**(強靭) toughness. ~하다 (be) strong and tough; tenacious; stiff; unyielding. ¶ ~한 의지 a tough spirit; an iron will / 그는 ~한 정신력으로 그

난관을 극복했다 He endured the difficult circumstances with 「a tenacious spirit [great mental fortitude].

**강자**(強者) a strong man; [총칭] the strong; the powerful. ¶ ～와 약자 the strong and the weak.

**강자성**(強磁性) 〖물리〗 ferromagnetism. ¶ ～의 ferromagnetic / ～체 a ferromagnetic body [substance] / 반～체 an antiferromagnetic body [substance].

**강장**(強壯) robustness; vigorousness. ～하다 (be) robust; vigorous; strong; sturdy. ◉ ～음료 a tonic drink. ～제 a tonic; a bracer 《미구어》: ～제 주사를 맞다 have a tonic shot 《in the arm》.

**강장거리다** take short, quick steps.

**강장동물**(腔腸動物) a coelenterate.

**강재**(鋼材) steel materials; structural steel (건축용); 《압연강》 rolled steel. ¶ 재생 ～ rerolled steel.

**강적**(強敵) a powerful [strong, formidable] enemy; 《경쟁 상대》 a tough competitor [rival]. ¶ ～을 패배시키다 defeat a powerful rival / ～이 나타났다 A powerful rival came to the front. / 우리들은 ～과 상대해야 했다 We had to confront a formidable enemy. / 한국 팀은 준결승에서 ～ 일본 팀과 대전한다 In the semifinals the Korean team faces tough opposition from the Japanese team.

**강점**(強占) occupation [possession] by force. ～하다 occupy [possess] 《*a person's* house》 by force.

**강점**(強點) a strong point; *one's* strength [forte]; an advantage (이점). ¶ …하다는 ～이 있다 have the advantage of… / (상대에 대해) ～을 갖고 있다 have an 「advantage over [edge on] 《*a person*》 / 그의 ～은 …이다 His strength lies in…. / 그의 유일한 ～은 그 굉장한 재력이다 His only strong point is his immense wealth.

**강정** 《한식 과자》 a cake made of glutinous rice (찹쌀로 만든); rice candy seasoned with sesame seeds [pine nuts, beans] (엿으로 만든).

**강정제**(強精劑) a tonic.

**강제**(強制) compulsion; coercion; constraint; enforcement. ～하다 force 《*a person* to *do*》; compel; coerce.

> **용법** **force** 힘으로 어떤 일을 억지로 시킨다는 뜻. **compel** force보다는 좀 약한 뜻. **coerce** 폭력·협박 따위의 수단을 써서 강제한다는 뜻.

¶ ～적인 compulsory; coercive; forced / ～로 by force [compulsion]; forcibly / ～로 결혼시키다 force 《*a person*》 into a marriage with 《*another*》 / 노동을 ～로 시키다 force 《*a person*》 to work (against *his* will) / ～로 수용하다 put 《*a person*》 into custody; confine 《foreign nationals》 in a camp / 나는 ～로 여기에 끌려 왔다 I was brought here forcibly [by force].

◉ ～가격 a forced price. ～결혼 a forced marriage; a marriage by force; a shotgun wedding. ～경매 forced [compulsory] sale by auction; execution sale by auction. ～관리 compulsory administration. ～력 compelling force; 《법률상》 legal force. ～보험 compulsory insurance. ～소개(疎開) (an) enforced evacuation. ～송환 enforced repatriation; deportation: ～송환하다 repatriate… under compulsion. ～수단 a coercive measure; compulsory measures: ～수단을 쓰다 resort to coercive measures. ～수사 a compulsory investigation. ～수색권 the official right to search. ～수용소 a concentration camp. ～이행 compulsory performance. ～저축 forced saving. ～조정 compulsory mediation. ～중재 compulsory arbitration; legal intervention. ～집행 compulsory execution: ～ 집행 영장 a writ of compulsory execution; a writ of attachment (압류의) / ～ 집행 절차 execution proceedings / ～ 집행 정지 the stay of execution. ～처분 legal disposition: ～ 처분하다 dispose of 《*something*》 by legal force; resort to compulsory measures. ～철거 forced removal [dismantlement, demolition] 《of》. ～퇴직 a forced retirement. ～할당 a mandatory quota.

**강제노동**(強制勞動) forced [compulsory] labor; slave labor. ◉ ～자 수용소 a labor camp; a slave pen.

**강제착륙**(強制着陸) forced landing. ¶ ～시키다 force 《a plane》 to land.

**강조**(強調) emphasis; stress. ～하다 emphasize; give emphasis [weight] to; stress; place [lay, put] emphasis [stress] on; underscore; point up. ¶ 평화를 ～한 연설 a speech stressing peace / 크게[특별히] ～하다 lay [place, put] great [special] emphasis 《on》 / 지나치게 ～하다 overemphasize; lay [place] excessive emphasis 《on》 / 국방[저축]의 필요성을 ～하다 stress the need [necessity] of 「national defense

〔saving〕/ 안전 보장 문제를 ~하다 accentuate the idea of national safety and security / 선생님은 예습의 중요성을 ~하셨다 The teacher emphasized 〔stressed〕 the importance of making preparations for lessons. / 이 책의 가치는 아무리 ~하여도 지나치지 않다 You can't overemphasize the value of this book. ◉ 방화〔방범〕 ~주간 (a) fire 〔crime〕 prevention week.

**강종거리다** ⇨ 껑충거리다.

**강좌**(講座) 《강의》 a lecture; a course (라디오의); 《학과 담임》 a professional chair; lectureship. ¶ 라디오 영어 ~ a radio English course / 음악 ~ lectures on music / 특별 ~ a special course 《of》/ ~를 개설하다 establish 〔create〕 a chair 《of》/ 영문학 ~를 맡고 있다 hold the chair of English literature.

**강주정**(一酒酊) feigned intoxication. ~하다 pretend drunkenness.

**강줄기**(江一) a river course.

**강직**(強直) 〖의학〗 rigidity; stiffness. ¶ ~되다 stiffen; get stiff; become rigid. ◉ ~성 경련 tetanus.

**강직**(剛直) rectitude; integrity; uprightness; moral courage. ~하다 (be) upright; incorruptible; have moral courage. ¶ ~한 사람 a man of integrity 〔moral courage〕.

**강진**(強震) a violent 〔severe〕 earthquake; a severe shock. ¶ 근년에 없던 ~ the sharpest 〔severest〕 earthquake in recent years; one of the most terrific earthquake shocks ever felt in years / 간밤 이곳에 ~이 있었다 We had a very strong earthquake here last night. ◉ ~계 a strong-motion seismograph.

**강짜** (unreasonable) jealousy. ¶ ~를 부리다 be jealous 《of》; burn with jealousy / 연애를 하면 여성은 ~가 심해진다 Love make a woman jealous.

**강참숯** pure charcoal.

**강철**(鋼鐵) steel. ¶ ~ 같은 의지 an iron will / 전부 ~로 된 all-steel 《bridge, car》/ ~제(製)의 배 a steel-bound ship / ~을 입힌 a steel-clad〔-plated〕. ◉ ~관 a steel pipe 〔tube〕. ~봉 a round steel bar. ~선(線) a steel wire. ~제품 steel products. ~판 a steel plate: 컬러 ~판 colored steel sheets.

**강청**(強請) 《강요》 a persistent demand; importuning; exaction. ~하다 demand persistently; importune 《*a person* to *do*》.

**강촌**(江村) a riverside village.

**강추위** a spell of cold dry weather.

**강치** 〖동물〗 a sea lion.

**강타**(強打) a heavy 〔hard〕 blow; 《크리켓의》 a swipe; 《야구의》 a heavy hit; a blast; 《테니스·골프의》 a drive. ~하다 deal 《*a person*》 a heavy blow; hit 《*a person*》 hard 《on the head》; hit hard (야구에서); drive (테니스에서). ¶ ~를 퍼붓다 rain hard blows 《on》/ 가슴을 ~당하다 receive a hard blow on the chest. ◉ ~자 〖야구〗 a hard 〔powerful〕 hitter; 《미구어》 a slugger: 야구계 최고의 ~자 the most powerful hitter in the baseball world.

**강탄**(降誕) nativity; birth. ~하다 be born; become incarnate. ¶ 그리스도의 ~ the Nativity (of Christ); the birth of Jesus Christ. ◉ 석존 ~제 the celebration of the nativity of Buddha.

**강탈**(強奪) (a) seizure (토지·배 등의); (a) hijacking (차·비행기 등의); (a) robbery; looting. ~하다 seize; rob 〔plunder〕 《*a person*》 of 《*a thing*》; wrest 《*a thing*》 from 《*a person*》; hijack; loot. ◉ ~물 plunder; spoils; loot; booty. ~자 a plunderer; a looter; a robber; a hijacker.

**강태공**(姜太公) an angler; a Waltonian.

**강토**(疆土) a territory; a domain; a realm.

**강파르다** (be) gaunt and fiery; have a lean and hungry look.

**강판**(降板) ¶ ~시키다 〖야구〗 knock (a pitcher) out (of the box).

**강판**(薑板) a grater. ¶ ~에 갈다 grate 《a radish》.

**강팔지다** (be) narrow-minded.

**강펄**(江一) bottom lands 《미》; a muddy field by a river.

**강평**(講評) (a) comment; (a) criticism. ~하다 comment on; criticize; review. ¶ 나는 그녀의 연구에 대한 ~을 부탁받았다 I was asked to comment on her research.

**강포**(強暴) wildness; brutality; ferocity. ~하다 (be) wild; violent; brutal; ferocious.

**강폭**(江幅) the width of a river; river width 〔span〕. ¶ ~ 200미터의 강 a river 200 meters wide; a two-hundred=meter-wide river / ~이 약 백 미터는 된다 The river is about 100 meters across 〔in width〕.

**강풀** thick paste 〔starch〕 not tempered with water. ~치다 add a coat of paste 〔starch〕 to.

**강풍**(江風) ⇨ 강바람.

**강풍**(強風) a strong 〔high〕 wind; a gale. ◉ ~주의보 a strong-wind warning.

**강하**(降下) falling; dropping; (a) descent; a fall; a drop. ～하다 fall; drop; descend. ¶ 기온의 ～ a drop in temperature / 비행기가 고도 1천 피트로 ～하였다 The airplane glided down 〔descended〕 to a height of 1,000 feet.

**강하다**(強—) (be) strong; powerful; hard; intense. ¶ 강한 감정 an intense feeling / 강한 나라 a strong country 〔nation〕; great powers / 강한 색채 a strong 〔intense〕 color / 의지가 강한 사람 a man of strong will / 강하게 나오다 show 〔assume〕 a firm 〔strong〕 attitude 《toward》; take a firm stand 《against》 / 전쟁은 강한 자가 이긴다 The battle is to the strong.

**강행**(強行) ～하다 enforce; force. ¶ 호우속에서 경기를 ～하다 keep playing a game in the downpour / 저물가 정책을 ～하다 enforce a low-price policy.

**강행군**(強行軍) a forced march; [비유적] a「hard 〔very rigorous〕 schedule. ～하다 go on a forced march. ¶ 이 일을 내일 아침까지 ～해서 끝내자 Let's rush this work through by tomorrow morning.

**강호**(江湖) 《강과 호수》 rivers and lakes; 《세상》 the public; the world; 《은둔처》 a retreat. ¶ ～의 제현 the general public; people at large / ～의 제현에게 호소하다 appeal to the public; call the attention of the general public to 《a fact》 / ～ 제현에게 권하다 recommand 《a book》 to the public.

**강호**(強豪) a veteran (player). ¶ 전국에서 뽑힌 ～ 팀 powerful teams selected all over the country.

**강화**(強化) strengthening; reinforcement. ～하다 strengthen 《the nation's defense》; reinforce 《a bank》; step up 《an advertising drive》; build 〔beef〕 up 《the country's military strength》; intensify 《propaganda》; consolidate 《*one's* position》; 《식품을》 fortify 〔enrich〕 《food with vitamins》. ¶ 근육을 ～하다 strengthen *one's* muscles / 경비를 ～하다 strengthen the guard / 훈련을 ～하다 intensify training / 군비를 ～하다 build up armament / 시 당국은 경찰에 단속을 ～해 줄 것을 요청했다 The city authorities asked the police to enforce the regulations rigidly.

◉ ～미(米) enriched rice. ～식품 enriched foods. ～유리 tempered glass. ～제(劑) 〖화학〗 a reinforcing agent. ～ 플라스틱 reinforced plastics. ～훈련 intensified training.

**강화**(講和) peace; reconciliation. ～하다 make 〔conclude〕 peace 《with》. ¶ 굴욕적인 ～ a humiliating peace / ～를 제의하다 make overtures of peace; sue for peace / 양국간에 ～가 성립되었다 The two countries made peace.

◉ ～담판 peace negotiations. ～사절 a peace envoy 〔deligate〕. ～제의 peace proposals. ～조건 conditions 〔terms〕 of peace. ～조약 《conclude》 a peace treaty 《with》; a treaty of peace. ～회의 a peace conference.

**강회**(—蛔) a roundworm that wriggles out of the bowels by itself.

**강회**(—膾) a small roll of boiled dropwort 〔scallion〕 (eaten with hot sauce).

**강회**(剛灰) limestone; quicklime.

**갖**《가죽》 fur; leather; (ox-)hide. ¶ 갖두루마기 a Korean robe lined with fur.

**갖가지** all kinds. ⇨ 가지가지.

**갖다**[1] 《구비하다》 have all sorts; have everything; be furnished with everything. ⇨ 갖은.

**갖다**[2] ⇨ 가지다. ¶ 그는 사업상의 지식을 충분히 갖고 있다 He has enough knowledge of business.

**갖다주다** bring (as a favor). ¶ 맥주 좀 갖다주시오 Bring us some beer, please.

**갖바치** a maker of leather shoes. ¶ ～ 내일 모레 《속담》 Don't count on the date that was promised. *or* Jam tomorrow and never jam today.

**갖신** leather shoes.

**갖옷** fur clothes.

**갖은** 《모든》 all; all sorts 〔kinds〕 of; every (possible); 《빠짐없는》 complete; perfect. ⇨ 온갖. ¶ ～것 all sorts of things; everything / ～양념 all sorts of spices / ～ 떡 all sorts of cakes / ～ 고생을 하다 go through all kinds of hardships 〔troubles〕 / ～ 수단을 다 쓰다 try every means conceivable; try every possible means; use all the means in *one's* power / ～ 욕을 다 보다 suffer all sorts of humiliation.

**갖은소리** 《온갖》 every (possible) 〔all kinds of〕 words; 《주제넘은》 (self-)conceited words.

**갖저고리** a fur coat.

**갖추** (all-)inclusively; completely; fully; with no omissions; leaving nothing (out); thoroughly; all. ¶ 점포에 물건을 ～ 벌여 놓다 put out all kinds of goods in a store / 음식을 ～ 차리다 prepare a complete 〔full-course〕 dinner; fix the utmost variety of dishes.

**갖추다** ① 《예비하다》 get 〔have, keep〕 《*something*》 ready 〔in stock〕 《for》;

prepare 〔make preparation〕《for》; provide 〔make provision〕《for, against》; 《구비하다》 have; possess; be possessed of; be endowed with 《talents》; stock 《a library with books》. ¶ 위엄을 ~ have (a certain) dignity / 교과서를 빠짐없이 ~ get all the necessary textbooks / 가구를 ~ get a complete suite of furniture / 그 상점은 갖가지 상품을 고루 갖추고 있다 The store keeps a rich assortment of goods in stock. / 그녀는 영문학에 관해 상당한 지식을 갖추고 있다 She has a good knowledge of English literature. / 그는 음악에 천재적 재능을 갖추고 있다 He is endowed with genius in music. / 회의 준비를 갖추어 놓아라 Get ready for the meeting. / 나는 그 대학 지원에 필요한 서류를 다 갖췄다 I got all the papers ready for applying to the college.
② 《설비하다》 provide 〔furnish〕 《with》; equip 〔fit〕 《with》; install. ¶ 이 건물에는 화재 경보 장치가 갖춰져 있지 않다 This building is not provided 〔equipped〕 with fire alarms. / 그 구축함에는 대공 미사일이 갖춰져 있다 The destroyer is armed with anti-aircraft missiles.

**갖추쓰다** write (a character) without omitting any stroke; omit nothing.

**갖풀** glue (made from ox-hide). ¶ ~로 붙이다 glue (one thing to another).

**같다** ① 《동일》 be (one and) the same 《as》; be the self-same; (be) identical 《with》. ¶ 거의 ~ be much 〔almost〕 the same 《as》 / 같은 말을 몇 번이나 하다 say the same thing again and again; repeat *oneself;* harp on the same string / 같은 높이다 be (of) the same height; be as high as... / 자네 것과 같은 시계를 가지고 있다 I have the same watch as 「you have 〔yours〕. / 마크 트웨인과 사무엘 클레멘스는 같은 인물이었다 Mark Twain and Samuel Clemens were one and the same person. / 이것은 10년 전에 들었던 이야기와 ~ This is the same story that I heard ten years ago. / 나도 너와 같은 생각이다 Your thoughts echo mine.
② [동등] 《수량이》 (be) equal 《to》; 《가치 따위가》 (be) equivalent 《to》. ¶ 수〔무게, 크기〕가 ~ be equal in number 〔weight, size〕 / 죽은 거나 ~ be as good as dead / 도둑이나 ~ be no better than a thief / 같은 조건에서 교섭하다 negotiate on equal terms / 거절하지 않는 것은 용인하는 것과 ~ Giving no refusal is equivalent to acceptance. / 이들 도형은 면적이 모두 ~ These figures are equal in area.
③ 《보기에》 be like; be alike. ¶ 샛별 같은 눈 eyes like stars / 악마 같은 사람 a man like a devil; a devil of a man / 무엇 같은가 What is he 〔it〕 like? / 그 사진은 나 같지 않다 The picture doesn't look like me. / 어느모로 보나 그는 교사 ~ He is a teacher to all appearance(s).
④ 《닮다》 (be) similar 《to》; alike; like. ¶ 그 자매는 얼굴이 거의 ~ The sisters look very similar. / 형과 나는 식성이 ~ My brother and I have similar tastes in food. / 당신들 사내는 다 ~ You men are all alike. / 누이와 나는 성격이 ~ My sister and I are of like disposition.
⑤ 《부류》 ¶ … 같은 such; like (*one*); such... as / 그 같은 자 a man like him / 그는 네가 생각하고 있는 것 같은 대학자가 아니야 He is not such a great scholar as you think. / 나는 그와 같은 말을 할 사람이 아니다 I am not the man to say such a thing. / 그녀는 이 같은 노래를 부르지 않는다 She never sings such a song.
⑥ 《추측》 it seems 〔looks〕 「like 〔as if, as though〕. ¶ 비가 올〔오는, 온, 오던, 왔던〕 것 ~ It looks as though it 「were going to rain 〔were raining, has rained, has been raining, had been raining〕.
⑦ 《가정》 if it were. ¶ 나 같으면 if it were me; if I were you / 옛날 같으면 if these were the old days.
⑧ 《…다운》 ¶ 사람 같은 사람 a real man / 집 같은 집 a house that 「is really 〔can really be called〕 a house.
⑨ 《공통》 common. ¶ 같은 취미를 가지다 have a common interest / 삶을 사랑하며 죽음을 두려워하는 것은 사람이나 짐승이나 다 ~ Love of life and fear of death are common to man and beasts.

**같은 값이면** the price 〔distance, trouble, time〕 being equal; other things being equal. ¶ ~ 큰 것이 좋다 I will take the larger one, if I must take either. / ~ 흰 것을 사겠다 Since the price is no more, I will take the white one. / ~ 영어를 배우겠다 As long as the other things are equal, I would rather learn English. / ~ 다홍치마 《속담》 Other things being equal, choose the better one.

**같이** ①《같게》 as; like; in the same way 〔manner〕; similarly; in a similar way; alike; likewise. ¶ 형 하는 것 ~ 해라 Do as your brother does. ②《공평하게》 equally; impartially; indiscriminately; alike. ¶ 돈을 똑~ 분배하다 divide money equally / 모든 사람을 ~ 대우하다 treat all men alike. ③《…처럼》 as if 〔though〕; like; as; as... as; 《not》 so... as. ¶ 평상시와 ~ as usual / 제 아들~ 사랑하다 love 《a child》 like *one's* own / 그는 나를 어린애~ 취급한다 He treats me as (if I were) a child. / 나는 너~ 빨리 걸을 수 없다 I can't walk so fast as you. / 그는 모든 것을 아는 것~ 떠벌린다 He talks as if he knew everything. ④《함께》 together; with; together with; along with; in company with. ¶~ 살다 live together; live in the same house 《with another》 / 편지와 ~ 보내다 send 《*a thing*》 together with *one's* letter / 나하고 ~ 가자 Let's go together. *or* Come along with me. / 자 다들 ~ 사진을 찍읍시다 Let's have our photo taken all in a group. ⑤《동시에》 at the same time; together. ¶ 둘이 ~ 도착했다 The two have arrived at the same time. / 두 가지 일을 ~ 해서는 안 된다 You must not do two things at a time.

**같이하다** do 《*a thing*》 together; share ... with; have the same.... ¶ 고락을 ~ share *one's* joys and sorrows; share *one's* fortune with / 일생을 ~ share *one's* life; get married / 운명을 ~ share *one's* fortune; face the same fate 《as》 / 이해를 ~ have the same interests; have common interests / 의견을 ~ share *one's* opinion; have the same views / 때를 ~ be of the same time 〔date〕; be contemporary 《with》; date 《with》; be of a period; be of the same period / 마음을 ~ be of one 〔the same〕 mind.

**같잖다** (be) trivial; insignificant; be of no account; (be) worthless; useless; good-for-nothing; foolish; silly; absurd; unseemly; nonsensical; improper; bothersome. ¶ 같잖은 인간 a worthless fellow; a good-for-nothing / 같잖은 일 a matter of no importance; a trivial 〔trifling〕 thing 〔matter〕; a bothersome 〔thankless〕 task / 같잖은 일로 소란을 피다 make a fuse about trifles / 같잖은 말을 하다 talk nonsense; say silly 〔absurd〕 things; say unseemly things.

**갚다** 《돈을》 pay; settle *one's* account; 《물건을》 repay; pay back; give 《*a thing*》 in return; 《보상》 recompense 《*a person*》 for; compensate for; 《보답》 reward 《*a person*》 for; 《보복》 retaliate 《against *a person*》 with; return; requite; 《원수를》 revenge; avenge. ¶ 빚을 ~ pay *one's* debts / (금전이 아닌) 물품으로 ~ pay 《*a person*》 back in kind / 품으로 ~ do (a day's) work in return 《for *something*》 / 받은 것만큼 ~ give as good as *one* gets / …을 갚아주기 바라다 want 《*something*》 back / 여섯 배로 쳐서 ~ repay 《*a person*》 sixfold / 손해 본 것을 갚아 주다 compensate 〔indemnify〕 《*a person*》 for the loss / (부모한테) 은혜를 ~ repay (*one's* parents) for their favors / 은혜를 원수로 ~ return evil for good; bite the hand that feeds *one* / 주먹은 주먹으로 ~ give measure for measure; give blow for blow; meet force with force / 형의 원수를 갚기 위해 무기를 들다 take up arms to revenge *one's* brother / 내게서 꾸어간 돈을 갚게 Pay me the money you owe me.

**갚음하다** = 갚다.

**개**[1] 《강에 조수가 드나드는 곳》 an inlet; a tidewater 〔tidal〕 inlet; an estuary; the mouth of a river.

**개**[2] 〚동물〛 a dog; a bitch (암캐). ¶ 사냥개 a hunting dog; a hound / 들개 a cur; a stray dog / 똥개 a mongrel (잡종) / 개자식 a son-of-a-bitch; a dog; a bitch / 개의 감찰(鑑札)〔목걸이〕 a dog tag 〔collar〕 / 재주를 부리는 개 a performing dog / 개 돼지 같은 놈 a brute; a beast; an utter pig / 개에게 재주를 가르치다 teach a dog tricks / 개가 짖다 A dog barks. / 그는 나를 개 취급하듯 했다 He used 〔treated〕 me like a dog. / 그런 것은 개도 안 먹는다 Even a dog will turn up its nose at it. / 개조심《게시》 Beware of the Dog. *or* Beware—Fierce Dog. ◉ 개집 a kennel.

**개**(介·個·箇) a piece; a unit; an item. ¶ 책상 두 개 two desks / 복숭아 세 개 three peaches / 비누 세 개 three pieces 〔cakes〕 of soap.

**개가**(改嫁) remarriage 《of a woman》. ~하다 remarry; marry again. ¶ ~를 권하다 advise 《a woman》 to remarry / ~한 여자 a woman married second time.

**개가**(凱歌) 《개선가》 a triumphal 〔victory] song; a paean; 《환성》 a shout of triumph. ¶ 현대 과학의 ~ a triumph of modern science / ~를 올리다 win a triumph 〔victory〕 《over the enemy》; triumph 《over the enemy》 / 그들은 승리의 ~를 올렸다 They raised 〔gave〕 a shout of triumph 〔victory〕. *or* They exulted in their victory.

**개각**(介殼) shells. ◉ ~류 the crustacea; shellfish.

**개각**(改閣) a cabinet reshuffle; a cabinet shake-up. ¶ 전면〔일부〕 ~ a sweeping 〔partial〕 cabinet reshuffle / ~을 단행하다 effect a cabinet reshuffle; reshuffle the cabinet portfolios.

**개간**(改刊) reprinting; a reprint; a revised printing. ~하다 reprint; print a revised edition.

**개간**(開墾) bringing 《wasteland》 under cultivation; land reclamation; clearing. ~하다 bring 《land》 under cultivation; reclaim 《wasteland》; clear 《land》. ¶ 우리는 황무지를 ~했다 We cultivated the wasteland.
◉ ~사업 a land development project; reclamation (work). ~지 developed land; a cultivated 〔reclaimed〕 land: 미~지 a virgin soil; wild land; wasteland. 산림~ forest clearing.

**개강**(開講) 《강의의 시작》 beginning a series of lectures; opening a course; 《대학의》 beginning school. ~하다 begin a series of *one's* lectures 《on》; open a course 《in History》; begin school. ¶ 3월 4일에 ~ 《게시》 Lectures will begin on March 4th.

**개개**(箇箇) 《낱낱이》 one by one; piece by piece; individually; 《모두》 all; every one; everyone; 《각자》 being individual; each one. ¶ ~의 individual; separate; several / 그는 일반론에서부터 ~의 문제에까지 논급했다 He reasoned from the general to the particulars.

**개개다** 《닳거나 해지다》 abrade; rub 《off》; wear 《off》; 《성가시게 달라붙다》 trouble 〔annoy〕 《*a person*》 by tagging along.

**개개비** 〖조류〗 the reed warbler.

**개개인**(箇箇人) each and every person.

**개개풀어지다** 《국수 따위가》 lose its stickiness; come unstuck 〔loose〕; 《눈이》 get bleary; come dull. ¶ 개개풀어진 눈 bleary eyes; dull 〔sleepy, drowsy〕 eyes.

**개거**(開渠) an open sewer.

**개고**(改稿) 《행위》 rewriting *one's* manuscript; 《원고》 a rewritten manuscript. ~하다 rewrite *one's* manuscript.

**개고기** 《고기》 dog meat; 《막된 사람》 a pest; a nuisance; a hooligan; a scamp.

**개골** another's temper; anger; hot temper; rage. ¶ ~ 내다 snap 〔snarl〕 at; get angry.

**개골개골** ¶ 개구리가 ~ 울다 frogs croak.

**개골창** a gutter; a drain; a ditch; a sewer.

**개과**(改過) correction of erroneous ways; repentance; penitence; contrition (회한). ~하다 correct *one's* ways; repent 《of》; be repentant 〔penitent〕. ¶ ~천선(遷善)하면 죄는 용서된다 Repentance wipes out sin.

**개관**(開館) the opening of a hall 〔museum, theater, *etc.*〕. ~하다 open 《a building》. ¶ 오전 9시부터 오후 6시까지 개관함 《게시》 Open from 9 a.m. to 6 p.m. / 10시에 ~한다 The doors open at 10 o'clock. ◉ ~식 an opening ceremony: ~식을 하다 inaugurate a hall.

**개관**(概觀) 《대충 살핌》 a general survey 〔observation〕; an outline; 《윤곽》 a general outlook 〔perspective〕. ~하다 survey; take a bird's-eye view 《of》.

**개괄**(概括) 《대충 뭉뚱그림》 a summary; 〖논리〗 generalization. ~하다 sum up; generalize. ¶ ~적인 general / ~해서 말하면 on the whole; in a word; generally speaking; in short; to sum up.

**개교**(開校) the opening 〔foundation〕 of a school. ~하다 open 〔found, establish〕 a school. ¶ 이 학교는 100년 전에 ~되었다 This school was founded 〔established〕 a hundred years ago. / 저 학교는 ~한 지 50년이 된다 That school has been open for fifty years.
◉ ~기념일 an anniversary of the opening of a school. ~식 the opening 〔inauguration〕 ceremony of a school.

**개구리** a frog; a bullfrog (황소개구리). ¶ 우물안의 ~ a man of narrow views; a man who has a limited outlook / ~가 울기 시작했다 Frogs started 「to croak 〔croaking〕. / ~ 올챙이 적 생각을 못 한다 People who gain prosperity are apt to forget their early days.
◉ ~헤엄 the breaststroke. 식용~ an edible frog.

**개구리매** 〖조류〗 a marsh harrier.

**개구리밥** 〖식물〗 a great duckweed.

**개구리참외** 〖식물〗 a spotted cantaloup(e).

**개구멍** a doghole. ◉ ~바지 baby trousers with a slit in the bottom. ~받이 a child abandoned on a doorstep; a foundling.

**개구쟁이** a naughty boy; a brat; an urchin; an imp; a mischievous boy.

**개구하다**(開口—) open *one's* mouth; begin to speak.

**개국**(開國) 《건국》 the founding [foundation] of a country [state]; 《개방》 the opening of the country. ～하다 found a country; establish a state; open the country (to the world). ◉ ～정책 the open-door policy.

**개그** a gag. ¶ ～를 하다 crack jokes. ◉ ～맨 a gagman; a gagster.

**개근**(皆勤) perfect [regular] attendance; nonabsence 《throughout a year》. ¶ 그는 학교를 1년 동안 ～했다 He attended school regularly without missing a single day this year. *or* He was not absent from school a single day this year. ◉ ～상(賞)[상장] a prize [certificate] for perfect attendance. ～자 《학교·회사의》 a person who has not missed a day 《at school [work]》.

**개기**(皆旣) 〖천문〗 a total eclipse. ◉ ～식 시간 a totality. ～월식 a total eclipse of the moon. ～일식 a total eclipse of the sun; a total solar eclipse.

**개기름** 《얼굴의》 (natural) grease on *one's* face; 《피부의》 (skin) oil; oiliness. ¶ ～이 흐르는 얼굴 an oily complexion.

**개골** 《엉망이 된 체면》 disgrace; shame; humiliation. ¶ ～이 되다 be put to shame; bring disgrace upon *oneself;* disgrace *oneself;* experience a hot agony of shame; lose face.

**개꽃** 〖식물〗 the scentless false-camomile.

**개꿀** comb honey.

**개꿈** a wild [silly] dream; an empty dream.

**개나리** 〖식물〗 ① 《목서과의》 a forsythia; the golden bell. ¶ 새 봄의 전조로 ～가 벌써 활짝 피었다 Forsythias are already in full bloom to herald the coming spring. ② 《들나리》 a wild lily. ◉ ～꽃 (the blossom of) a golden bell.

**개념**(槪念) a notion; a general idea; a concept; a conception.
¶ ～적(인) conceptional; notional; general / ～적 사고 conceptual thinking / 행복의 ～ the concept [idea] of happiness / 문제를 ～적으로 파악하다 get a general idea of the matter / ～화(化)하다 conceptualize; generalize / 우리는 자유에 대한 명확한 ～을 가지고 있어야 한다 We should have a clear conception [concept] of freedom. / 전후, 가족과 결혼의 ～이 크게 달라졌다 Since the war, there has been a remarkable change in the concepts of the family and marriage. ◉ ～론 conceptualism. 기본～ fundamental notions.

**개다**[1] 《날씨·하늘이》 clear (up); become clear; 《비·눈이》 stop raining [snowing]; 《안개가》 lift; clear off [away]. ¶ 갠 날씨 clear weather / 하늘은 정오경부터 개기 시작했다 It began to clear up around noon. / 내일은 날씨가 갤 것 같다 It is likely to clear up tomorrow.

**개다**[2] 《물에》 soften [mix] with water; temper; pug; work. ¶ 풀을 ～ temper paste with water / 진흙을 ～ work [knead] clay.

**개다**[3] 《개키다》 fold; fold up 《bedding》. ¶ 이부자리를 ～ fold up quilts; put away [aside] a bed / 옷을 ～ fold (up) clothes / 다시 ～ refold.

**개다래** 〖식물〗 fruit of the silvervine. ◉～나무 a silvervine.

**개다리** a dog's legs. ◉ ～밥상 a poorly made dinner table. ～상제 an improper mourner. ～질 hateful kicking; detestable behavior.

**개두릅** sprouts of thorny ash. ¶ ～나물 seasoned sprouts of thorny ash.

**개떡** a cake made of some rough flour; a bran cake.

**개떡같다** be rubbish; be good-for-nothing; be nonsense. ¶ 개떡같은 수작 nonsense; rubbish / 개떡같은 놈 a good-for-nothing fellow; a worthless fellow / 개떡같은 소리를 하다 talk nonsense [rot, rubbish].

**개똥** dog dung [turd, droppings]. ◉ ～상놈 a vulgar [mean] fellow; a good-for-nothing; a dirty tramp. ～참외 a wild melon. ～철학 a mockery of philosophy.

**개똥같다** be not worth a damn; be trash. ¶ 개똥같은 수작 bull(shit); nonsense; utter trash [rubbish] / 개똥같이 여기다 do not think much of; make light of; hold 《*a person*》 cheap; don't care a bit 《about》.

**개똥밭** ① 《건 밭》 a rich [fertile] field. ② 《더러운 곳》 a place all dirty with dog droppings. ¶ ～에 이슬 내릴 때가 있다 《속담》 Every dog has his day.

**개똥벌레** 〖곤충〗 a glowworm; a firefly.

**개똥지빠귀** 〖조류〗 a thrush; a dusky ouzel.

**개략**(槪略) a summary; an outline; 《논문 등의》 a *résumé* (F.). ¶ ～적인 rough / ～해서 말하면 roughly [generally] speaking / ～을 보이다[적다] give 「an outline [the gist, a general idea〕《of》; make a summary《of》; summarize / ~을 보고하다 make a summarized report《of》/ 이상이 그 사건의 ~이다 Such are the facts of the case in broad outline.

**개량**(改良) (an) improvement; betterment; a reform. ~하다 improve; reform; better; make《*something*》better. ¶ 품종~《가축의》improvement of a breed;《식물의》plant breeding / 공상적 사회~주의자 a do-gooder / 품질을 ~하다 improve the quality《of the products》/ 이 기계에는 ~의 여지가 없다〔크게 있다〕There is no〔ample〕room for improvement in this machine. / ~될 가망이 있느냐 Are there any prospects of improvement? / 이 컴퓨터는 많이 ~되었다 Great improvements have been made in this computer. / 우리는 이 소프트웨어를 ~하여야 한다 We must make this software better. *or* We must reform this software. ◉ ~농지 improved〔reclaimed〕farmland. ~복 reformed dress. ~종 a select〔an improved〕breed. ~주의 reformism. ~품 an improved product. ~형 an improved model.

**개런티**《보증이 되는 것》a guarantee.

**개론**(概論) an introduction《to》; an outline《of》; a survey. ~하다 give a survey; survey. ¶ 영문학 ~ an introduction to English literature.

**개막**(開幕) raising the curtain; beginning a performance; the opening. ~하다 open; the curtain rises; raise the curtain; begin the performance. ¶ 오후 6시에 ~한다 The curtain rises at 6 p.m. / 체육 대회는 4월 1일에 ~된다 The athletic meeting will be started on the 1st of April. ◉ ~시간 the time of the rising of the curtain. ~식 the opening ceremony《of the Olympic Games》. ~일 the opening day. ~전〔경기〕an opening game〔match〕.

**개망나니** a tough《구어》; a rowdy; a roughneck《미구어》.

**개망신**(―亡身) a deep disgrace; a sore indignity; a burning〔crying〕shame. ~하다 disgrace *oneself* in public; bring burning shame on *oneself*.

**개맹이** sprightliness; spirit; pep; vigor; liveliness. ¶ ~가 없다 be spiritless〔languid, dull, lackluster〕.

**개머루**〖식물〗wild grapes.

**개머리**《소총 따위의》a butt; a butt end. ◉ ~판 a butt plate.

**개먹다** get worn down; abrade; wear 「out.

**개명**(改名) changing *one's* name; rechristening. ~하다 change *one's* name《to》; rename《the shop》. ¶ A를 B로 ~하다 change *one's* name from A to B. ◉ ~신고 a report of *one's* changed name.

**개명**(開明) civilization; enlightenment. ~하다 be〔become〕civilized; be enlightened. ¶ ~한 나라 a civilized country.

**개무**(皆無)《there is》nothing (in life);《there is》none (at all);《have》no《knowledge》whatever;《be》all gone. ¶ 거래가 ~하다 There has been no trading at all. / 그는 법률 지식이 ~하다 He has not the least knowledge of law. *or* He is utterly ignorant of law.

**개문**(開門) opening a gate. ~하다 open the gate. ¶ 오전 7시에 ~한다 The gate opens at 7 a.m. ◉ ~발차(發車) starting《of a bus》with doors open.

**개미**[1]《연줄의》powdered porcelain〔glass〕mixed with glue. ¶ ~ 먹이다 strengthen (kite strings) with *kaemi*.

**개미**[2]〖곤충〗an ant. ¶ ~ 금탑 모으듯 saving up little by little / ~ 쳇바퀴 돌듯 한다 go〔turn〕round and round. ◉ ~구멍 an ant hole; an ant's nest. ~굴 an ant tunnel. ~떼 a swarm of ants. 개밋둑 an ant hill.

**개미귀신**〖곤충〗an ant lion.

**개미산**(―酸) formic acid. ⇨ 포름산(―「酸).

**개미핥기**〖동물〗an anteater.

**개미허리** a small〔narrow, wasp〕waist. ¶ ~같은 몸매의 여인 a wasp-〔slim-〕waisted lady.

**개발** a dog's paw. ¶ ~에 편자《속담》Casting pearls before swine.

**개발**(開發)《개척》development; exploitation (자원의); cultivation (재능의). ~하다 develop; exploit; cultivate. ¶ 새로 ~한 기술 a newly-developed technique / 바다 자원의 ~ exploitation of the resources in the sea / ~ 단계에 있는 기계 a machine which is「under development〔in the development stage〕/ ~을 촉진하다 facilitate development / 광물자원을 ~하다 exploit mineral resources / 우주 병기를 ~하다 develop space weapons / 신제품을 ~하다 develop a new product / 음악적 재능을 ~하다 cultivate《*a person's*》talent for music / 어학의 잠재 능력을 ~하다 develop《*a person's*》latent ability for languages.

◉ ~계획 a development project〔program, plan〕: 우주 ~ 계획 a space

development program. ～교육 developmental education. ～금융 development credit. ～도상 국가 a developing country 〔nation〕: ～도상 국가간 기술 협력 technical cooperation among developing countries (생략 TCDC). ～비 development costs. ～사업 development works. ～업자 《토지의》 a land developer. ～원조 development aid. ～유보 지역 a reserved development district. ～융자 development loan. ～은행 a development bank: 아시아 ～은행 the Asian Development Bank. ～자 a developer; an exploiter. ～자금 a development fund. ～전략 development strategies. ～제한 지역 limited development district. ～차관 기금 a development loan fund (생략 D.L.F.). ～ 촉진 지역 development promoted district. 경제～ economic development 〔exploitation〕: 경제～ 5개년 계획 a 5=year economic development plan. 유엔～계획 the United Nations Development Plan (생략 UNDP). 한국 ～ 연구원 the Korea Development Institute (생략 KDI).

**개발코** a snub nose; a pug nose.

**개밥** dog's food. ¶ ～에 도토리 an outcast; an ostracized 〔a left-out〕 person. ◉ ～바라기 〖천문〗 《저녁의 금성》 the evening star; Venus; Hesperus.

**개방**(開放) 《문호 따위》 opening; throwing open; leaving 《the door》 open; 《금했던 것의》 lifting the ban. ～하다 open; throw open; leave 《the door》 open; lift the ban 《on》. ¶ ～적인 《성질이》 frank and easy; candid; open=hearted / 일반에게 ～된 교정 a school ground open to the public / 정원을 일반에게 ～하다 throw open a garden to the public / …에 대하여 문호를 ～하다 open doors to... / 그 대학의 도서관은 일반에게 ～되어 있다 The university library is open to the public.
◉ ～경제 open economy: ～경제 정책 the open-economy policy. ～대학 an open college. ～도시 an open city. ～사회 the open societies. ～성 결핵 〖의학〗 open tuberculosis. ～요법 open=air treatment. ～주의 *laisser-aller* (F.); *laisser-faire* (F.); unrestraint. ～현(弦) 〖음악〗 an open string.

**개방**(開方) 〖수학〗 evolution; extraction of roots. ～하다 extract the root of the number. ⇨ 제곱근 풀이.

**개백장** a dog catcher; a dog killer; a dog seller.

**개버딘** gabardine. ¶ 순모～ all woolen gabardine.

**개벽**(開闢) the Creation; the beginning of the world. ～하다 《the world》 be created. ¶ ～이래 since the beginning of the world; since the world began; from time immemorial / ～ 이래 처음 보는 사건 an unprecedented event.

**개변**(改變) (a) change; (an) alteration; reformation. ～하다 change; alter; reform.

**개별**(個別) individualization. ¶ ～적 individual / ～적으로 individually; separately; one by one / ～적으로 이야기를 나누다 talk 《*the matter*》 over separately / ～행동을 취하다 act independently / ～지도를 받다 be given personal guidance / 우리는 면접실에서 ～적으로 면접을 받았다 We were interviewed individually in a reception room. ◉ ～심사 individual screening. ～절충 a separate negotiation.

**개병**(皆兵) ◉ 국민 ～제(도) a universal conscription system.

**개복**(開腹) 〖의학〗 ～하다 cut the abdomen open. ◉ ～수술 an abdominal operation; laparotomy.

**개봉**(開封) 《편지 등의》 opening 《a letter》; opening a seal; unsealing; 《영화의》 (a) release. ～하다 open 《a letter》; open a seal; unseal; release 《a film》. ¶ 파라마운트사의 ～작 Paramount releases / 편지를 ～하지 않고 돌려보내다 return a letter unopened. ◉ ～관 a first-run movie house; a first runner: ～관으로 유명하다 be noted for new releases. ～영화 a first-run 〔a newly released〕 film.

**개비** a piece of split wood. ¶ 장작 두～ two pieces of split firewood / 성냥 한～ a matchstick; a match.

**개산**(開山) ① 《절을 세움》 founding a Buddhist temple. ② ＝～조사(祖師).
◉ ～날〔일〕 the Foundation Day of a temple. ～조사(祖師) the founder of a Buddhist temple; the originator.

**개산**(概算) a rough estimate 〔calculation〕. ⇨ 어림셈. ～하다 estimate 〔calculate〕 roughly; make a rough estimate 《of》. ¶ ～으로 roughly; in round figures / 주택 건축비를 ～하다 make a rough estimate of the cost for building a house / ～하여 그 나라의 인구는 5천만에 달한다 As roughly estimated, the country has a population of fifty million. ◉ ～가격 an approximate price. ～불(拂) payment by rough estimate. ~서(書) a written rough estimate.

**개살구** 〖식물〗 a wild apricot. ¶ 빛좋은 ~다 be not so good as it looks; be deceptive.

**개새끼** ① 《개의》 a pup (of a dog). ② 《욕》 a son of a bitch.

**개서**(改書) rewriting; 《어음·증서 따위의》 (a) renewal. ~하다 rewrite; renew 《a bill, a bond》. ◉ ~어음 a renewed bill.

**개선**(改善) improvement; a reform; betterment. ~하다 improve; make better; better. ¶ 생활 수준의 ~ the betterment of living; an improvement in living standards / 두드러진〔미미한〕 ~ a marked 〔minor〕 improvement / 근로 조건의 ~을 외치다 cry for better working conditions / 생활을 ~하다 better 〔improve〕 *one's* living; reform *one's* mode of living (양식을) / 그는 교수법을 ~하였다 He improved upon the method of teaching. / ~의 흔적이 조금도 안보인다 It shows no sign of improvement. / ~의 여지가 있다〔없다〕 There is room 〔It leaves no room〕 for improvement.
◉ ~책 a reform measure.

**개선**(改選) reelection. ~하다 reelect 《the members》. ¶ 3년마다 임원의 반을 ~하다 reelect half the members of the board every three years. 「옴[1].

**개선**(疥癬) 〖의학〗 the itch; scabies. =

**개선**(凱旋) a triumphal return. ~하다 return in triumph 〔with glory〕; make a triumphant return 《to》. ◉ ~가 a triumphal song; a paean. ~군 victorious returning troops. ~문 a triumphal arch; 《파리의》 the *Arc de Triomphe*. ~ 사열식 a triumphal military review. ~식 a triumphal celebration. ~장군 a victorious general. ~행렬 a triumphal procession 〔parade〕.

**개설**(開設) 《개최》 opening; 《창립·설립》 establishment; foundation; 《설치》 installation. ~하다 open (up); establish; set up; found; install. ¶ 전화 ~ installation of a telephone / 학교를〔병원을〕 ~하다 establish a school 〔hospital〕 / 연구소를 ~하다 set up a research institute / 당좌계정을 ~하다 open a current account 《with a bank》 / 본 주문에 대하여 5천 불의 취소 불능 신용장을 귀사 앞으로 외환은행에 ~하였습니다 To cover this order, we have established an irrevocable L/C for $5,000 in your favor with KEB.

**개설**(概說) a summary; an outline; an introduction 《to a subject》. ~하다 make a summary 《of》; make an introduction 《to》; give an outline 《of》.

**개성**(改姓) ~하다 change *one's* surname.

**개성**(個性) individuality; personality; individual character.

> 용법 **individuality** 어느 한 사람과 다른 사람을 구별하는 특징을 말하는 개성. **personality** 어느 한 사람 특유의 육체적·정신적 특징을 말하는 개성.

¶ ~이 없는 lack individuality / ~이 강한 사람 a man of marked 〔strong〕 individuality / ~을 존중하다 respect 《*a person's*》 personality / ~을 계발하다 develop 〔cultivate〕 *one's* personality / ~을 발휘하다 show 〔display〕 *one's* individuality / ~을 잃지 않다 preserve *one's* individuality / 고흐의 자화상에는 그의 강렬한 ~이 나타나 있다 The self-portrait of Van Gogh expresses his intense personality. / 옷은 그 사람의 ~을 나타낸다 Dress expresses the wearer's individuality. / 그녀는 매우 ~적인 사람이다 She has a very strong 〔clear-cut〕 personality.

**개세**(蓋世) overall power 〔influence〕. ~하다 reign supreme; hold sway over.

**개소**(個所) 《곳》 a place; a spot; a point (지점); 《부분》 a part; a portion; a passage (문장의). ¶ 수 ~에 침수하다 be flooded in several places / 도로에는 위험한 곳이 몇 ~있다 There are a few dangerous points on the road.

**개소리** nonsense; stupid talk; rubbish. ¶ ~하는군 You talk nonsense. / ~마라 Nonsense! *or* Don't talk rubbish!

**개수**(一水) = 설거지. ◉ ~통 a dishwater bucket; a dishpan. 개숫물 = 설거지물.

**개수**(改修) 《수정》 revision; 《수축》 repair; improvement. ~하다 revise 《a manuscript》; repair 《a building》; improve 《a road》. ¶ 하천의 ~ river improvement / 도로는 지금 ~ 중이다 The road is now under repair. / 막대한 비용을 들여 다리를 ~했다 They improved 〔repaired〕 the bridge at huge cost. ◉ ~공사 repair work.

**개수**(個數·箇數) the number of article.

**개수**(概數) round numbers. ⇨ 어림수.

**개수작** a foolish remark; silly words; idle talk; nonsense. ¶ ~ 마라 Nonsense! *or* Stuff and nonsense!

**개술**(概述) giving an outline 〔a summary〕; summarizing. ~하다 give an outline《of》; summarize.

**개시**(開市) ①《시장을 엶》 opening a market. ~하다 open a market; begin to sell. ②《마수걸이》 an opening sale; a first sale. ~하다 make a first sale. ¶ 오늘 아침에는 아직 ~도 못했다 We haven't made a sale yet this morning. *or* We've sold nothing so for this morning. ◉ ~손님 the first customer 〔buyer〕 of the day: 오늘 아침의 ~ 손님이시니 싸게 드리겠습니다 We'll give you a good price since you are the first customer this morning.

**개시**(開始) beginning; commencement; start; opening; inauguration. ~하다 begin; commence; start; open; inaugurate. ¶ 교섭을 ~하다 open negotiations / 영업을 ~하다 start business / 시판을 ~하다 begin to sell 〔market〕; put 〔place〕 goods on the market / 은행과 거래를 ~하다 open an account with the bank.

**개신**(改新) renewing; renovation; reformation. ~하다 renew; renovate; reform. ◉ ~교 ⇨신교.

**개심**(改心) reform; amendment. ~하다 mend *one's* ways; reform *oneself;* be penitent; turn over a new leaf. ¶ ~시키다 reclaim 〔reform〕《a criminal》/ 그는 도저히 ~할 가망이 없다 He is past praying for. *or* He is beyond 〔past〕 reform. / 그는 이제 아주 ~했다 He is quite penitent now. ◉ ~자 a reformed man; a penitent.

**개악**(改惡) a change for the worse. ~하다 change《*something*》for the worse; make《*something*》worse. ¶ 헌법의 ~ an undesirable amendment of 〔to〕 the Constitution / 노동법의 ~ the detrimental revision of the labor law.

**개안**(開眼) ①《눈을 뜸》 opening *one's* eyes; 《눈이 보임》 gaining eyesight. ② 〖불교〗 a Buddhist ceremony on consecrating a newly made image; 《깨달음》 a spiritual awakening; enlightenment. ~하다 be awakened《to a fact》; be (spiritually) enlightened; open *one's* eyes to《the beauty of...》. ◉ ~수술 an eyesight recovery operation.

**개암** ①《열매》 a hazelnut; a filbert. ②《매 먹이의》 a small wad of cotton put in a falcon's feed. ¶ ~(을) 도르다 《매가》 throw up the cotton wad after digesting the meat it was with. ◉ ~나무 the hazel (tree). ~죽 rice gruel boiled in hazelnut juice.

**개암들다** have complications after childbirth.

**개어귀** an estuary; an entry to a river; the mouth of a river.

**개업**(開業) the opening 〔commencement〕 of a business 〔trade〕; establishment in business. ~하다 start (a) business; establish *oneself* in business; set up as《a bookseller》; open a store; 《의사·변호사가》 start 〔go into〕 practice. ¶ 그는 식료품점을 ~했다 He started 〔opened〕 a grocery store. / 그 상점은 내일 ~한다 The store opens for business tomorrow. / 그녀는 변호사〔의사〕로 ~하고 있다 She has her own legal 〔medical〕 practice. ◉ ~비 the initial cost of business. ~식 a ceremony to open a business. ~의(醫) a medical practitioner; a practicing physician; a general practitioner (★ 전문의(specialist)에 대한 '일반 개업의'를 말함. G.P.로 약함).

**개역**(改譯) a revision of a translation; a revised 〔corrected〕 version. ~하다 revise 〔correct〕 a translation. ◉ ~성경 the Revised Version of the Bible. ~판 a revised version.

**개연성**(蓋然性) probability. ¶ ~이 높다 be highly 〔very〕 probable.

**개오**(改悟) remorse; reformation; repentance. ~하다 reform (*oneself*); repent 《at》. ¶ ~한 reformed《criminal》; repentant / 네가 진실로 ~한다면, 용서받을 수 있을 것이다 If you are truly repentant you will be forgiven.

**개오**(開悟) 〖불교〗 attainment of divine enlightenment; a spiritual awakening. ~하다 attain divine enlightenment; be spiritually awakened.

**개요**(概要) an outline; a summary; a synopsis. ¶ 사건의 ~를 말하다 give an outline of the event; outline the event / ~를 말하면 roughly 〔generally〕 speaking.

**개운**(開運) opening up of good luck 〔fortune〕; the betterment of *one's* fortune. ~하다 have fortune open up for *one;* fortune turns in *one's* favor. ¶ ~하기를 빌다 pray for better fortune.

**개운하다** feel well; feel all right; feel relieved; (be) refreshed. ¶ 개운해지다 feel refreshed / 자고 나니 머리가 ~ I 〔My head〕 was refreshed by the sleep. / 더운 물에 목욕을 하면 개운할 것이다 A hot bath will refresh you./(답답한 마음을) 털어놓으면 개운해질 것이다

Make a clean breast of it, and you will feel relieved.

**개울** a brook; a (small) stream; a rivulet; a creek《미》; a brooklet.

**개원**(改元) changing the name of an era; the change of an era. ~하다 change the name of an era.

**개원**(開院)《국회의》the opening of the「National Assembly〔House〕;《기관·병원 따위의》the opening of an institution〔an academy, a hospital〕. ~하다 open the「National Assembly〔House〕; open an institution〔an academy, a hospital〕. ◉ ~식 the opening ceremony of「the National Assembly〔the House, an institution, *etc.*〕.

**개의**(改議) a motion〔discussion〕for amendment. ~하다 move an amendment《to》.

**개의하다**(介意—) care about; concern〔trouble〕*oneself* about; worry about; mind;《돌보다》give heed〔attention〕to; have a regard for; have〔pay〕regard to. ¶ 개의치 않다 do not care〔mind〕; be indifferent《to》; be careless《about》; pay no attention《to》/ 사람들이 무어라고 하든 개의치 않는다 I don't mind〔care〕what people say (about me). / 그녀는 옷차림에 개의치 않는다 She doesn't care about her dress. *or* She pays no attention to her appearance. / 그는 남의 이익 따위는 개의치 않는다 He has no regard for others' interests. / 그런 일에 너무 개의할 것 없다 Don't trouble yourself about such things.

**개인**(改印) a change of *one's* seal. ~하다 change *one's* (registered) seal. ◉ ~신고 a report of *one's* changed seal.

**개인**(個人) an individual;《사인(私人)》a private person〔individual, citizen〕. ¶ ~의〔적〕《개개의》individual;《사적》private;《일신의》personal;《이기적》self-centered / ~적으로 individually; personally; in person / ~으로서(는) as an individual; individually; personally; for myself; in private / ~ 자격으로《attend the meeting》in *one's* private〔personal〕capacity; in the capacity of a private person / ~용의 for individual〔private, personal〕use / 나 ~의 의견으로는 in my personal opinion; individually (speaking) / ~적인 문제 a private affair; a personal matter / ~적 감정에 지배되다 be affected by personal prejudice / ~적으로 면담하다 talk personally《with》; have a personal interview《with》/ 이것은 나 ~의 재산이다 This is my personal property. / 그는 ~적으론 좋은 사람이다 He is, personally, a nice fellow. / 그와 ~적인 관계는 없다 I have no personal relations with him. / 나 ~으로서는 그렇게 생각지 않는다 Personally, I don't think so.

◉ ~감정 personal feelings. ~경영 private management: ~경영 회사 a firm under private management. ~경제 private economy. ~공격 personal criticism. ~교섭 individual bargain. ~교수《take》private lessons; individual instruction; tutoring. ~기업 a private〔an one-man〕enterprise. ~ 문제 a personal matter. ~소득 a personal income. ~소식란《신문의》personal columns. ~승용차 a privately owned car; a private (passenger) car. ~수표〔어음〕a personal check〔bill〕. ~숭배 a personality cult. ~심리학 personal psychology. ~용 컴퓨터 a personal computer (생략 PC). ~의견 *one's* personal opinion; *one's* private views. ~전(展)《hold》a private exhibition: 미술 ~전 a personal art exhibition. ~전(戰) a tournament series in singles; an individual match. ~정보 personal information《in the data bank》: ~정보에 대한 보호 the protection of personal information. ~ 종합경기《체조의》individual combined exercises. ~주의 individualism: ~주의적 individualistic / ~주의자 an individualist. ~주택 an individual home《미》; a private house〔residence〕. ~지도 personal guidance: ~지도를 하다 give personal guidance《to》. ~차(差) individual variation〔difference〕: 학생들의 능력에는 ~차가 있다 There is a difference in ability among students. ~택시 a privately-owned taxi; an owner-driven taxi: ~택시 운전기사 an owner=driven cabdriver. ~플레이 individual play; a selfish play (제멋대로의). ~휴대통신 personal communications service (생략 PCS): ~휴대 통신은 값싸고, 때와 장소를 안 가리고 이용할 수 있는 무선 통신 서비스이다 The PCS is a low=cost, anywhere-anytime wireless communications service.

**개입**(介入) intervention. ~하다 intervene《in》. ¶ 분쟁에 ~하다 intervene in a dispute / 적극적으로 ~하다 take an active hand 《in a dispute》/원화를 안정시키려고 정부가 ~했다 The government intervened to stabilize the won.

**개자리**[1] 〖식물〗 a medic; a trefoil; a snail-clover; alfalfa.

**개자리**[2] 《화살의》 a trench in front of the archery target (from which one observes and judges the accuracy of the shots).

**개자식** a son of a bitch. ⇨ 개새끼 ②.

**개작**(改作) (an) adaptation; (a) recomposition; a rewrite 《미》. ~하다 adapt 《a play》; recast 《a story》. ¶ ~한 adapted; recasted / 한국 무대에 알맞게 ~한 연극 a play adapted for Korean stage / 셰익스피어 작품 중의 하나를 어린이에게 알맞게 ~한 것 an adaptation from one of Shakespear's works for children / 그는 그 소설을 연극으로 ~했다 He adapted the novel for the stage. *or* He recasted the novel as a play. ◉ ~자 an adapter.

**개잘량** a dog-skin cushion.

**개잠** sleeping curled up (like a dog). ¶ ~자다 sleep curled up (like a dog).

**개잠**(改—) dozing off again after waking up in the morning. ¶ ~들다 drop off to sleep again (after waking up).

**개장**(改葬) reburial; reinterment. ~하다 rebury; reinter.

**개장**(改裝) remodeling; redecoration; a refit (특히 배의). ~하다 remodel; redecorate; refurbish; refit; convert 《*a thing* into》. ¶ 상점을 ~하다 redecorate 〔refurbish〕 a store / 다방을 ~하여 식당을 만들다 remodel 〔convert〕 a tearoom into a restaurant.

**개장**(開場) 《엶》 opening. ~하다 open 《*a place*》; open (the doors). ¶ ~중이다 be open / 오후 5시 ~ 《게시》 Doors open at 5 p.m.

**개장국**(—醬—) dog-meat soup.

**개재**(介在) 《개입》 interposition; intervention. ~하다 lie 〔stand〕 between; intervene 《between》. ¶ 이면(裏面)에 ~하다 lie behind 《*a matter*》/ 제3국의 ~를 불허하다 permit no third power intervention / 두 사람 사이에는 무언가 복잡한 사정이 ~하고 있는 것 같다 Some complicated circumstances seem to stand between the two.

**개전**(改悛) 《개심》 reform; mending *one's* mistaken ways; 《뉘우침》 repentance; penitence. ~하다 mend *one's* ways; reform *oneself;* feel remorse; repent; be penitent 《of》. ¶ 그에게는 ~의 정이 보이지 않는다 He shows no signs of repentance. / 그는 자기가 저지른 일에 대해 ~의 정이 현저하다 He shows sincere repentance for what he has done.

**개전**(開戰) the opening of hostilities; the outbreak of war. ~하다 open war 〔hostilities〕 《against》; start 〔make, wage, go to〕 war 《on, against》. ¶ ~을 선포하다 declare war 《on, against》.

**개점**(開店) the opening of a store. ~하다 open a store; the store opens. ¶ 새로 ~한 가게 a newly opened store / 오늘 ~ 《게시》 Opening 〔Opened〕 Today. / 이 상점은 9시에 ~한다 This store opens at nine. / ~시간은 9시부터 5시까지 《게시》 Open 9 to 5. / 그녀는 지난 주에 식료품점을 ~했다 She opened 〔set up, established〕 a grocery store last week. / 그 상점은 ~휴업 상태다 The store is open, but no customers come in. ◉ ~시간 the opening hour of a store. ~안내 the announcement of opening a store.

**개정**(改正) 《수정》 (a) revision; an amendment; (a) reform; 《변경》 (an) alteration; change; 《개량》 improvement. ~하다 amend; revise; alter; change. ¶ ~할 수 있는 amendable; correctable; rectifiable / ~된 시행령의 발효 the effectuation of the revised enforcement regulations / 헌법을 ~하다 amend 〔revise〕 the Constitution / 민법의 일부를 ~하다 make a partial amendment of the Civil Code / 다음 처럼 ~되다 be amended as follows / 시급한 연금제도의 ~이 필요하다 An immediate revision of the annuity system is needed. *or* It is necessary to revise the annuity system without delay. ◉ ~안 a reform bill 〔plan〕; a bill 〔proposal〕 to revise.

**개정**(改定) fixing 《a date》 anew; (a) revision. ~하다 fix anew; revise. ¶ 운임〔가격〕의 ~ a revision of fares 〔prices〕. ◉ ~세율 the revised tax rates. ~시간표 the revised 〔new〕 timetable: ~시간표는 이달 1일부터 실시된다 The revised timetable will be put into force on and after the 1st inst. ~요금 revised rates. ~정가 a revised price.

**개정**(改訂) revision. ~하다 revise. ¶ 그 책은 지금 ~ 중이다 The book is now under revision. / 그 사전은 부분적으로 〔전면적으로〕 ~되었다 The dictionary was partly 〔completely〕 revised. ◉ ~증보판 a revised and enlarged edition. ~판 《issue》 a revised edition.

**개정**(開廷) the opening of a court. ～하다 open the court; hold a court 〔a trial〕. ¶ 법정은 오후 1시에 ～되었다 The court was opened at 1:00 p.m. *or* The trial was held from 1:00 p.m. / 지금 ～ 중이다 The court is now sitting 〔in session〕. ◉ ～기일 the date fixed for a hearing. ～일 a court day.

**개제**(改題) retitling; a change of the title. ～하다 change the title 《of a book》; retitle. ¶ 그 잡지는 「문학과 예술」로 ～하여 재발행되었다 The magazine was reissued under the new title of "Literature and Art".

**개조**(改造) remodeling; reconstruction; rebuilding. ～하다 remodel; reconstruct; rebuild. ¶ 창고를 공장으로 ～하다 remodel a warehouse into a factory / 사회를 ～하다 reconstruct society / ～ 중이다 be under reconstruction / 이것은 주택을 사무실로 ～한 것이다 This is a residence turned into an office building.

**개조**(改組) ＝ 개편(改編).

**개조**(開祖) ① 《종파의》 the founder 《of a sect》; 《원조》 an originator; an initiator. ② 《개종조》 the founder of a Buddhist sect. ③ 《절의》 the founder of a Buddhist temple. ¶ 본산(本山)의 ～는 원효 대사이다 The founder of this temple is Saint Wŏnhyo Daesa.

**개조**(箇條) 《조항》 an article; a clause; 《항목》 an item. ¶ 이 계약서는 10～로 되어 있다 The contract consists of ten articles.

**개종**(改宗) (a) conversion. ～하다 convert to 《Islam》; be converted to 《Christianity》. ¶ ～시키다 convert *a person* 《to Christianity》; proselytize *a person* / 그는 기독교로 ～했다 He has turned Christian (★ 구어적 표현임). *or* He has (been) converted to Christianity. ◉ ～자 a convert.

**개종**(開宗) 『불교』 founding a Buddhist sect. ～하다 found a sect.

**개주**(改鑄) recoinage (of money); 《총포 따위의》 recasting; remolding. ～하다 recoin; recast; remint; remold.

**개죽음** useless 〔purposeless〕 death. ～하다 die 「in vain 〔uselessly〕; die to no purpose; throw away *one's* life. ¶ 그런 일로 죽는 것은 ～이다 To offer your life for such a cause is nothing more than throwing it away. / ～하고 싶지 않다 I don't want to die in vain.

**개중**(個中) ① 《여럿 중》 among them; among others. ¶ ～에는 among (them) / ～에는 좋은 책도 있고 나쁜 책도 있다 Some books are good and some bad. ② 『불교』 within the scope of Buddhism.

**개지랄** ¶ ～한다 Pig! *or* You act like a pig! / ～ 마라 Don't be such a pig!

**개진**(開陳) statement. ～하다 state 〔give, express〕 《*one's* opinion》; make a statement; set forth *one's* views.

**개집** a doghouse; a kennel.

**개차반** 《행세가 더러운 사람》 trash; scum; an undesirable person.

**개착**(開鑿) excavation; cutting; digging; 《우물 따위의》 sinking. ～하다 excavate 《a tunnel》; cut 《a road, canal》; sink 《a well》. ¶ 운하의 ～ excavation of a canal. ◉ ～공사 excavation works. ～용 펌프 a sinking pump.

**개찬**(改竄) correction; revision (of writing). ～하다 correct; revise.

**개찰**(改札) the examination 〔checking〕 of tickets. ～하다 examine 〔punch, check〕 tickets (at the barrier).
◉ ～구 a ticket gate 〔barrier〕. ～원 a ticket examiner 〔collector〕.

**개찰**(開札) opening of the bids 〔tenders〕. ～하다 open (the bids).

**개척**(開拓) 《토지의》 cultivation; reclamation; 《산림의》 deforestation; 《자원의》 development; exploitation; 《식민지의》 colonization; 《새 분야의》 pioneering; pathfinding. ～하다 reclaim; cultivate 《wasteland》; open up; put 《virgin land》 to the plow; clear 《forests》; pioneer; blaze a trail 《in》. ¶ 황무지를 ～하다 reclaim wasteland; bring waste land under cultivation / 새로운 분야를 ～하다 「open up 〔break〕 a new field / 운명을 ～하다 improve *one's* lot / 새로운 시장을 ～하다 seek 〔find, open up〕 a new market 《for》 / 자원을 ～하다 exploit 〔develop〕 natural resources / 오랫동안 방치되어 있던 토지가 ～되었다 The long-abandoned land was reclaimed 〔opened up〕. / 미국에 새로운 시장을 ～하지 않으면 안 된다 We should find 〔seek〕 a new market in America. / 그 팀은 반도체 연구에서 새로운 분야를 ～했다 The team blazed a trail in the field of semiconductor research.
◉ ～민 《이주자》 a settler. ～사업 reclamation 〔colonization〕 work. ～자 a pioneer; a frontiersman; a trail blazer; 《식민자》 a colonist: ～자적 노력 a trail-blazing effort / ～자 정신 the pioneer 〔frontier〕 spirit. ～지 reclaimed

land: 미~지 undeveloped land.

**개천**(開川) a streamlet; a rivulet; an open sewer [ditch]. ¶ ~에서 용나다 《속담》 It is a case of 「a black hen laying white eggs [a kite breeding a hawk].

**개천절**(開天節) the National Foundation Day (of Korea); *Tangun's* Accession Day.

**개체**(個體) an individual. ◉ ~개념[관념]〖논리〗an individual concept. ~발생〖생물〗ontogeny. ~변이 individual variation.

**개초**(蓋草) 《이엉》 thatch; 《이엉잇기》 thatching. ~하다 thatch 《a house, a roof》; roof 《a house》 with thatch. ◉ ~장이 a roofer; a thatcher.

**개최**(開催) holding 《a meeting》. ~하다 hold 《a meeting》; open 《an art exhibition》. ¶ ~ 중이다 be open; 《회의 등이》 be in session; be sitting; be under way / 그 회의는 지금 파리에서 ~ 중이다 The conference is now meeting [sitting] in Paris. / 체육 대회는 9월 3일에 ~된다 The athletic meet(ing) will be held on Sept. 3.
◉ ~국 the host country 《for》. ~기간 the period in which 《an exhibition》 is held. ~일 the date(s) 《of [for] the exhibition》. ~지 the site 《of [for] an exposition》; the place where 《a meeting》 is held; a venue 《for a conference》 (★ 보통, the date [site] for …는 개최 예정일[지]를, the date [site] of …는 개최가 이미 끝난, 과거의 개최일[지]이란 뜻이 함축되는 경우가 많음): 다음 동계 올림픽 ~지는 어디입니까 Where is the site for the next Winter Olympics?

**개축**(改築) rebuilding; reconstruction; remodeling. ~하다 rebuild; reconstruct; remodel. ¶ ~중이다 be under reconstruction. ◉ ~공사 rebuilding [reconstruction] works.

**개칠하다**(改漆―) ① 《글씨 획을》 correct [redo] a badly written stroke. ② 《칠을》 relacquer; revarnish.

**개칭**(改稱) renaming; changing a name [title]. ~하다 rename; change a name [title] 《to》; retitle.

**개키다** fold (up) carefully [neatly]. ¶ 옷을 ~ fold the clothes up (neatly).

**개탄**(慨嘆) deploring; lamentation; regret. ~하다 deplore; lament (over); regret. ¶ ~할 만한 deplorable; lamentable; regrettable / ~을 금할 수 없다 be most deplorable [regrettable] / ~해 마지 않는 바이다 It is a matter for great regret.

**개탕**(開錫) 《홈》 a groove; a quirk. ~치다 make a groove in; groove. ◉ ~대패 a grooving plane; a groover.

**개통**(開通) opening 《a new highway》 to traffic; opening. ~하다 《새롭게》 be opened to [for] traffic; open up; 《막혔던 것이》 be reopened for [to] traffic. ¶ 새 터널은 내일 ~된다 The new tunnel will be opened to traffic tomorrow. / 사고 구간은 5시간 후에 다시 ~되었다 The damaged section was reopened [The train service in the damaged section was restored] to traffic five hours later. ◉ ~구간 a section open to [for] traffic. ~식 an opening ceremony 《of a bridge》.

**개판** a mess; topsy-turvy; utter confusion. ¶ ~이 되다 fall into utter confusion.

**개판**(改―) 《씨름 등에서》 a run-off bout (to settle a wrestling match).

**개판**(改版) a revised edition. ⇨ 개정판.

**개펄** slime along the bank of an inlet; silt (at an estuary).

**개편**(改編) reorganization. ~하다 reorganize; revise. ¶ 정부 기구 ~ reorganization of government setups / 부(部)내 ~을 단행하다 carry out the reorganization of Ministry / 사전을 ~하다 revise a dictionary / 오케스트라를 ~하다 reorganize an orchestra.

**개평** a (free) share of the winnings; the winner's tip; a cut; something free. ¶ ~ 떼다 take a (free) cut of the winnings / ~ 주다 give away a share of *one's* winnings; give a cut. ◉ ~꾼 onlookers expecting some of the money given away by the gamblers.

**개평**(概評) a general comment [review, criticism]; an overall criticism. ~하다 give a general comment 《on》; give an overall criticism 《of》.

**개폐**(改廢) alteration(s) and abolition(s); reorganization; a change. ~하다 reorganize; make a change 《in》. ¶ 회사의 조직을 ~하다 reorganize the structure of a firm.

**개폐**(開閉) opening and shutting. ~하다 open and shut 《a window》. ¶ (전기의) 회로를 ~하다 make and break a circuit / 문은 자동 ~식이다 The door opens and shuts automatically. ◉ ~교 a drawbridge; a swing bridge. ~기 a switch; a circuit breaker: ~기 상자 a switch box / 복식 조정 ~기 a multiple-tuning switch (무전의) / 자동~기 an automatic switch. ~신호기 a switch signal.

**개표**(改票) = 개찰(改札). ◉ 자동 ~기 a ticket punching machine.

**개표**(開票) the counting 〔opening〕 of votes 〔ballots〕; ballot 〔vote〕 counting. ~하다 open the ballots; count the votes 〔ballots〕. ¶ 투표는 선거 당일로 ~되었다 The ballots were counted on the day of the election. / 나도 ~에 입회했다 I was among the witnesses when the votes were counted.
◉ ~결과 the results of the vote count. ~소 a ballot counting office 〔place〕. ~속보 a quick 〔flash〕 report of votes counted. ~율 the percentage of votes counted so far. ~ 참관인 a ballot-counting witness.

**개피떡** a rice-cake stuffed with bean jam.

**개학**(開學) starting school (after a vacation); the beginning of school. ~하다 begin school; school begins.

**개함**(開函) ~하다 open the ballot boxes.

**개항**(開港) ~하다 open a port 〔an airport〕. ¶ 인천은 1883년에 ~되었다 Inch'on became an open port to foreign vessels in 1883. ◉ ~장 an open 〔a treaty〕 port 〔airport〕.

**개헌**(改憲) amendment of a constitution; a constitutional amendment 〔revision〕. ~하다 amend a constitution. ¶ ~안을 제출하다 present 〔submit〕 a bill for amending the constitution. ◉ ~운동 a movement for the constitutional amendment. ~저지 투쟁 a fight against the constitutional amendment 〔revision〕.

**개혁**(改革) 《혁신》 reform; reformation; innovation; 《개선》 improvement. ~하다 reform; make 〔carry out〕 a reform 《in》; innovate; improve. ¶ ~에 착수하다 initiate 〔start〕 a reform / ~의 기치를 높이 들다 hoist the banners of reform / 교육 제도의 ~을 제안하다 propose a reform in the educational system / 그들은 근본적인 당의 ~을 단행하였다 They made 〔carried out〕 a drastic reform of their party. ◉ ~안 a reform bill. ~자 a reformer. 갑오~ 〖역사〗 the Reformation of *Kabo*. 대~ a shakeup 《미》. 사회~ social reform.

**개호주** 《범의 새끼》 a tiger cub.

**개화**(開化) civilization; enlightenment. ~하다 get 〔be〕 civilized 〔enlightened〕. ¶ ~한 civilized; enlightened / 문명 ~의 시대 the age of civilization; an enlightened age. ◉ ~국 a civilized country. ~인 civilized people.

**개화**(開花) blooming; flowering; efflorescence. ~하다 (come into) bloom; effloresce. ¶ ~되어 있다 be in flower 〔bloom〕 / 벚꽃의 ~는 4월이다 The cherry blossoms will come out in April.
◉ ~기 the flowering season.

**개활하다**(開豁—) 《시야가》 (be) wide open; 《마음이》 (be) broad-minded; open-hearted; liberal. ¶ 개활한 땅 an open land / 조망(眺望)이 ~ command extensive views.

**개황**(槪況) the general situation 〔condition〕; a survey. ◉ 경제~ an economic survey.

**개회**(開會) the opening of a meeting 〔session〕. ~하다 open the meeting; begin 《its》 session. ¶ ~중이다 be 「open 〔in session〕 / ~를 선언하다 announce 〔declare〕 《the meeting》 open; call 《the meeting》 to order 《미》 / 국회는 내일 ~된다 The House opens tomorrow. ◉ ~사 《give, deliver》 an opening address 〔speech〕. ~식 the opening ceremony. ~일 the opening day.

**개흘레** 〖건축〗 an alcove (in a room).

**개흙** mud 〔slime〕 on the bank of an inlet; silt (at an estuary).

**객**(客) ① 《손님》 a guest; a visitor; a lodger. ¶ 일등객 a first-class passenger; a cabin passenger (기선의). ② 《여분의·쓸데없는》 extra; superfluous; uncalled-for. ¶ 객소리 an uncalled-for 〔unnecessary, impertinent〕 remark. ③ 《지난》 last 《year, season, *etc.*》. ¶ 객년 last year.

**객거**(客居) staying away from home; living in a strange place. ~하다 stay 〔live〕 away from home.

**객고**(客苦) discomforts (of a person who is away from home). ¶ ~에 지치다 be travel-worn.

**객공**(客工) ① 《임시의》 a temporarily hired worker. ② 《객공잡이》 a person who is paid 「by piecework 〔by the hour〕.

**객관**(客觀) 〖철학〗 《객관성》 objectivity; 《대상》 the object; the material world (물질계). ¶ ~적 objective / ~적으로 objectively / ~적으로 보다 look at 《*a thing*》 objectively; take an objective view 《of》 / 그의 의견은 ~적이지 않다 His opinion is not objective. / ~적으로 말해서, 그의 결정은 공평하지가 않다 Objectively speaking, his decision is unfair. ◉ ～성 objectivity: ～성을 부여하다 objectify; objectivize / 그녀의 말에는 ～성이 거의 없다 Her statement has little objectivity. ～식 시험〔문제〕 an objective test 〔question〕. ～적 묘사 objective description. ～적 방법 an objective method. ～적 정황 『법』 the objective situation 〔circumstance〕. ～적 타당성 objective validity. ～주의 objectivism. ～화 objectification: ～화하다 objectify.

**객기**(客氣) bravado; ill-advised bravery; (a) bluff; an empty boast; an uncalled-for show of spirit 〔courage〕. ¶ ～를 부리다 be「carried away 〔driven〕 by a rash impulse.

**객년**(客年) last year.

**객담**(客談) (an) idle 〔empty〕 talk; gossip; tittle-tattle; chitchat. ～하다 gossip; engage in idle talk; tittle=tattle; chatter; shoot the bull 《미구어》.

**객담**(喀痰) expectoration; spitting. ◉ ～검사 the examination of *one's* sputum.

**객비**(客費) ① 《객쩍은 비용》 wasteful expenses. ② 《객지에서 드는 비용》 expenses of a traveler.

**객사**(客舍) a hotel; an inn.

**객사**(客死) dying away from home; dying in a strange 〔foreign〕 land. ～하다 die away from home; die in a strange 〔foreign〕 land; die abroad.

**객상**(客商) a (traveling) merchant.

**객석**(客席) a seat for a guest.

**객선**(客船) a passenger boat 〔ship〕.

**객소리**(客—) (a) useless 〔silly, idle〕 talk; bosh; nonsense. ～하다 talk nonsense; say silly things. ¶ ～를 해대는 사람 an idle talker; a gasbag 《속어》 / ～ 마라 Quit your idle talk! *or* Don't talk bosh!

**객수**(客水) ① 《비》 unwanted 〔unwelcome〕 rain. ② 《겉물》 unwanted water. ③ 《때없이 마시는》 water drunk at times other than mealtimes.

**객수**(客愁) sentimental thoughts while away from home; homesickness; nostalgia.

**객스럽다**(客—) look 〔seem〕 useless; (be) out of place; uncalled-for. ¶ 객스러운 말 a useless 〔an impertinent, an uncalled-for〕 remark.

**객식구**(客食口) a dependent not a member of *one's* own family; a hanger=on; a parasite; a freeloader 《미구어》. ¶ ～ 노릇을 하다 be a dependent 《on》.

**객실**(客室) 《호텔의》 a guest room; 《배·비행기의》 a passenger cabin; passenger quarters; a stateroom (특등의); 《집의》 a parlor; a drawing room; 《손님방》 a spare 〔guest〕 room. ◉ ～계(원) 《호텔의》 a room clerk.

**객원**(客員) a guest member; an honorary 〔associate〕 member; a non=regular member. ◉ ～교수 a visiting 〔guest〕 professor. ～지휘자 a guest conductor.

**객월**(客月) last month; *ultimo;* ult.

**객정**(客情) a traveler's feelings; *one's* feeling when away from home; feeling *oneself* a stranger. ¶ ～을 달래다 beguile tedious journey 《with》.

**객주**(客主) ① 《거간》 a commission agent 〔merchant〕. ② 《객줏집》 a peddler's inn; a commission agent's house.

**객중**(客中) while *one* is away from home; on a trip; on the road.

**객지**(客地) a strange land (where *one* is staying on a trip). ¶ ～에서 away from home; in a strange land / ～ 생활을 하다 live far away from home / ～에서 죽다 die while staying away from home; die in a strange land.

**객쩍다**(客—) (be) uncalled-for; useless; [서술적] be out of place. ¶ 객쩍은 소리 마라 Don't talk nonsense!

**객차**(客車) 《열차》 a passenger car 〔train〕; 《침대차와 구별하여》 a (day) coach 《미》; a railway 〔passenger〕 carriage 《영》. ¶ ～편(에, 으로) (by means of ) a passenger train.

**객체**(客體) ① 『법·철학』 the object. ¶ 범죄의 ～ the object of a crime / 영토와 국민은 국가의 ～다 The territory and people are the object of the state. ② 《객지에 있는 몸》 a person away from home; *one's* existence in a strange place.

**객초**(客草) tobacco 〔cigarettes〕 for「guests.

**객토**(客土) soil brought from another place (to improve the soil).

**객향**(客鄕) a foreign land 〔town〕; a place where *one* stays as a stranger 〔guest〕.

**객혈**(喀血) hemoptysis; blood-spitting; coughing up 〔spitting〕 blood; a lung hemorrhage. ～하다 cough up 〔spit〕 blood; have hemoptysis.

**객회**(客懷) traveler's sentiment; 《향수》 homesickness; nostalgia.

**갠지스강**(—江) 《인도의》 the Ganges.

**갤러리** a gallery.

**갤런** 《액체 용적》 a gallon. ¶ (차가 휘발유) 1 ～당 25마일 달리다 get 25 miles「to the 〔per〕 gallon.

**갤럽** ¶ ~ 여론 조사 the Gallup polls 〔survey〕.
**갬대** a wooden weeding knife.
**갭** a gap. ¶ ~을 메우다 fill 〔bridge, stop〕 a gap.
**갭직하다** (be) a bit light.
**갯가** the shore of an estuary 〔inlet〕.
**갯가재** 〚동물〛 a squilla (*pl.* ~s, -lae); a mantis crab.
**갯값** dirt-cheap 〔dog-cheap〕 price. ¶ ~으로 at a sacrifice; for a mere song / ~으로 팔다 sell 《*a thing*》「dirt-cheap 〔very cheap(ly)〕; sell for the mud / 나는 그 고물 자전거를 ~으로 샀다 I bought the old bicycle very chief(ly).
**갯고랑, 갯골** a small channel of tide-water on the shore of an inlet.
**갯나리** 〚동물〛 a crinoid; a sea lily.
**갯물** salt water in an inlet 〔estuary〕.
**갯바람** a sea breeze.
**갯밭** a field along the shore of an inlet.
**갯벌** a sandbar; a sandbank.
**갯지렁이** 〚동물〛 a lugworm; a lobworm; a nereid.
**갱**(坑) a (mining) pit; a shaft; 《갱도》 a gallery; a drift; 《도랑》 a drain.
**갱** a gangster 《미》. ¶ ~패거리 a gang (of hoodlums) / ~영화 a gangster movie 〔film〕.
**갱구**(坑口) a pithead; a minehead; a pit mouth.
**갱내**(坑內) 《in》 the pit 〔shaft〕. ◉ ~가스 mine gas. ~부 a pit worker; an underground miner. ~사고 an underground mine accident. ~수 mine water. ~침수 mine-flooding. ~화재 an underground fire.
**갱년기**(更年期) the change 〔turn〕 of (*a person's*) life; 《여성의》 the menopause. ¶ ~의 변화 climacteric changes / 그녀는 지금 ~다 She is going through her menopause. ◉ ~장애 climacteric suffering; a menopausal disorder.
**갱도**(坑道) ① 〚광산〛 《가로의》 a drift; a (mining) gallery; 《세로의》 a pit; a shaft. ② 《땅속의》 a tunnel. ◉ ~작업 drift work. ~지주(支柱) timbering.
**갱목**(坑木) a pit prop.
**갱부**(坑夫) a miner; a mine worker; a pitman. ¶ ~로 일하다 work in a mine. ◉ ~병 miner's disease.
**갱생**(更生) revival; rebirth; regeneration; rehabilitation; rejuvenation. ~하다 revive; be born again; come to life again; be regenerated 〔rehabilitated〕. ¶ 범죄자의 ~ the rehabilitation of an offender / ~시키다 regenerate 〔rehabilitate, reform〕 《*a person*》 / ~한 기분이다 feel like a new man. ◉ ~고무 rejuvenated rubber. ~보호시설 relief and rehabilitation facilities. ~사위 an opportunity for revival.
**갱소년**(更少年) rejuvenation; restoration of youth. ~하다 be rejuvenated; be restored to youth.
**갱신**(更新) (a) renewal; (a) renovation. ~하다 renew 《*one's* driver's license》; renovate. ¶ 기록을 ~하다 break 〔renew〕 a record; make 〔establish〕 a new record / 여러가지 제도를 ~하다 renovate many institutions / 계약을 ~하다 renew a contract / 그녀는 100미터 평영에서 한국 기록을 ~했다 She bettered 〔broke〕 the Korean national record for the 100-meter breaststroke.
**갱신못하다** be too afflicted to move about; be too tired 〔exhausted〕 to stir; cannot stir an inch 《from exhaustion》.
**갱외**(坑外) ¶ ~에(서)〔의〕 out of the pit. ◉ ~부 an out-of-pit worker.
**갱지**(更紙) pulp paper; rough 〔low-grade〕 printing paper.
**갱충쩍다, 갱충맞다** (be) careless and stupid. ¶ 갱충쩍은 짓 imprudent conduct.
**갸기** haughtiness. ⇨ 교기(驕氣).
**갸륵하다** (be) admirable; exemplary; praiseworthy; commendable. ¶ 갸륵하게도 in an admirable manner; admirably / 갸륵한 일 nice work; a fine job; a good deed / 갸륵한 행실 exemplary behavior; good conduct / 갸륵한 정신 a commendable spirit / 그의 효성을 갸륵히 여겨 in reward for 〔in consideration of〕 his filial heart.
**갸름하다** (be) small and longish; pleasantly oval; nicely slender. ¶ 갸름한 얼굴 a nicely tapered face; a slender 〔an oval〕 face.
**갸웃-** ⇨ 기웃-.
**갹금**(醵金) collection of funds; raising money 〔funds〕; 《기부금》 a contribution; a subscription. ~하다 collect funds; raise money; collect contributions; pass the hat around. ¶ 유족을 위해 100만 원을 ~하다 raise a million won for a bereaved family.
**갹출**(醵出) offering a share of money; chipping in; contributing. ~하다 chip in; contribute. ¶ 그 선물을 사기 위해 돈을 ~하다 chip in「for 〔to buy〕 the present.
**갿쭉-** ⇨ 길쭉-.
**거** 《그것, 그거》 Why!; Well!; Uh…. ¶ 거 참 좋다 Why that's fine! / 거 누구냐

Uh, who is there? / 거 우습지 않은가 Why, isn't that funny!

**거가**(車駕) 《수레》 the royal carriage 〔coach〕; 《행차》 a trip by the king.

**거가**(擧家) the whole family.

**거가대족**(巨家大族) a distinguished family; a powerful family.

**거간**(居間) ① 《행위》 brokerage. ② 《사람》 a broker; a go-between; a middleman. ~하다 do (the) brokerage; broker. ¶ ~노릇을 하다 act as a broker 〔go-between〕. ◉ ~꾼 = 거간 ②.

**거개**(擧皆) almost all; nearly everyone; the greater part; the vast majority. ¶ 참석한 사람은 ~가 대학생이었다 Those who were present were almost all college students.

**거거익심**(去去益甚) ~하다 (be) worse and worse (as time goes on).

**거골**(距骨) the anklebone; the talus; the astragalus.

**거괴**(巨魁) a ringleader.

**거구**(巨軀) a big figure 〔body〕; a large 〔massive〕 frame. ¶ 280 파운드의 ~ a massive figure of 280 pounds in weight.

**거국**(擧國) the whole country 〔nation〕. ¶ ~적(인) nationwide / ~ 일치하여 국난에 맞서다 consolidate a united effort against the national crisis / ~적으로 정부의 경제 정책을 지지했다 The whole nation supported the Government's economic policy. *or* The people gave solid support to the Government's economic policy. ◉ ~일치 내각 a cabinet supported by the whole nation.

**거금**(巨金) a large sum 〔amount〕 of money; a lot 〔great deal〕 of money; big money 《구어》. ¶ ~을 투자하다 invest a large sum of money 《in factory equipment》 / ~을 요하다 cost a great deal of money / 그는 ~을 들여 그 빌딩을 샀다 He bought the building at a great cost 〔price〕.

**거금**(距今) ago; (dating) back from today. ¶ ~ 삼백 년 전 three hundred years ago / ~ 50년 전의 일이다 It dates back fifty years.

**거기** 《장소》 that place; there; 《거기에》 in that place; there; thereupon; 《그 일, 그것》 that; 《그 범위》 so far; to that extent; that far. ¶ ~서 from there; thence / 여기서 ~까지 from here to there / ~에다가 besides; moreover; 《설상가상으로》 what is worse / ~까지는 좋았으나… So far, so good, but… / ~가 문제다 That is the trouble. / ~를 좀 긁어라 Please scratch there 〔that spot〕 for me. / ~ 가는 게 누구냐 Who goes there? / 이봐 ~ 가는 친구 Hi! you there! / ~까지는 인정한다 I admit as much. / ~까지는 생각 못 했는걸 I never thought of that. / ~까지는 알고 있다 I know that much.

**거꾸러뜨리다** 《엎어지게 하다》 make fall head first; make fall flat 〔headlong〕; throw down; bring down; trip 《*a person*》 up 《with *one's* foot》; 《물리치다》 beat; defeat; 《뒤엎다》 overthrow; topple; subvert; 《죽이다》 kill; fell; take the life 《of》. ¶ 아무를 ~ throw *a person* to the ground; get *a person* down / 아무를 때려서 ~ knock *a person* down / 강적을 ~ beat a strong opponent / 정부를 ~ overthrow a government / 그는 어퍼컷으로 챔피언을 거꾸러뜨렸다 He floored the champion with a uppercut.

**거꾸러지다** 《엎어지다》 fall head first; fall (down); tumble 〔topple〕 down; collapse; 《싸움에 지다》 be beaten 〔defeated〕; 《죽다》 die 《of, from》; be killed; 《망하다》 fall; be ruined; collapse; become bankrup (파산하다). ¶ 앞으로〔뒤로〕 ~ fall forward 〔backward〕 / 술에 취하여 ~ fall down dead-drunk / 기진하여 ~ sink down on the ground / 그 악당은 총상으로 거꾸러졌다 The rascal died of gunshot wounds.

**거꾸로** 《아래 위를》 upside down; bottom (-side) up; with the wrong end up; 《안팎을》 wrong side out; 《곤두박혀》 head foremost; headlong; head over heels; 《역으로》 the wrong way; the other way round; wrong way 〔end〕 to; 《오히려》 instead; on the contrary. ¶ ~ 세운 병 an upended bottle / ~ 떨어지다 fall headlong; fall head over heels; fall upside down / ~ 되다 be inverted; be turned upside down / 아무를 ~ 매달다 hang *a person* upside down; hang *a person* by *his* heels / 우산을 ~ 세우다 stand an umbrella wrong end up / 펜을 ~ 쥐다 hold a pen by the wrong end 〔upside down, wrong end up〕 / 우표를 ~ 붙이다 put a stamp the wrong side up / 알파벳을 ~ 말하다 say the alphabet backward / 일을 ~ 하다 put 〔set〕 the cart before the horse / 비행기가 논바닥에 ~ 박혔다 An airplane 「made a nose dive 〔fell nose-first〕 into a paddy-field. / ~ 하지 마시오 《게시》 No upside down.

**-거나** ① 《설사 …하더라도》 whatever;

whenever; however, *etc.* ¶ 네가 뭐라고 말하거나 난 곧이듣지 않겠다 I won't believe you, whatever you may say. / 누가 오거나간에 빨리만 왔으면 좋겠다 Whoever comes, I just hope they come soon. ② 《…든 …아니든》 whether ... or .... ¶ 오거나 말거나 whether *one* comes or not / (너야) 하거나 말거나 whether you do it or not / 날씨야 춥거나 말거나 예정 시간에 떠나자 Whatever the weather may turn out, let's leave on scheduled time. ③ 《…한다든지》 or. ¶ 손뼉을 치거나 큰소리로 웃거나 하지 마시오 Don't slap your hands or laugh loudly.

**거나하다** (be) tipsy; partly drunk 〔intoxicated〕. ¶ 거나하게 취하다 be pleasantly drunk; get mellow with drink; get merry over *one's* cup / 집에 돌아갈 때 그는 이미 거나했다 He was already tipsy when he started for home.

**거냉**(去冷) ~하다 warm; heat; take the chill off. ¶ ~되다 be warmed 〔heated〕.

**거년**(去年) last year. ¶ ~ 칠월 in July last year; last July.

**거년스럽다** (be) shabby.

**거느리다** 《이끌다》 lead; head 《a party》; be at the head 《of 》; 《지휘하다》 command 《an army》; be in command 《of an army》; 《부양하다》 have; take care of. ¶ 김 장군이 거느리는 군대 the army 〔troops〕 under the command of General Kim / 일군(一軍)을 거느리고 at the head of an army / 십만 대병을 거느리고 쳐들어 오다 invade 《a country》 leading an army of hundred thousand strong / 많은 가족을 ~ have 〔take care of 〕 a big family.

**거느림채** 『건축』 a detached house 〔building〕; an annex.

**-거늘** ① 《…한데 유독》 although; while. ¶ 사람이 다 형제가 있거늘 나 홀로 없구나 While all others have brothers, I alone have none. ② 《…하므로》 now that; as; since; when; upon. ¶ 시비(柴扉)에 개 짖거늘 임만 여겨 나가 봤네 When the dog barked at the twig door I went out expecting my beloved.

**-거니** ① 《…한데》 since; as; so; but. ¶ 나는 젊었거니 돌인들 무거우랴 Since I am young, can any stone be heavy (for me)! ② 《생각·추측·기대》 with the thought that... probably 〔surely〕; with confidence 〔assurance〕 that. ¶ 지금쯤 편지가 와 있겠거니 하는 생각에 빨리 돌아왔다 I have rushed home with the thought that the letter would surely be here by now. / 내일이면 그를 만날 수 있겠거니 생각하면 몹시 기쁘다 Assured of seeing him tomorrow, I am very happy. ③ 《교대로》 what with *do*ing one thing and another 《in alternation》; now... now...; sometimes... sometimes...; by turns. ¶ 말을 주거니 받거니 하다 exchange words (with each other) / 그와 얘기를 주거니 받거니 끝이 없었다 What with my telling him and his telling me, there was no end to our talking.

**-거니와** as well as; besides; admitting that; but (even so); not only... but also.... ¶ 얼굴도 곱거니와 마음씨도 곱다 have not only a pretty face but also a lovely disposition / 그건 그렇거니와 Be that as it may.... / 그 학생은 운동도 잘 하거니와 공부도 잘 한다 That student is a fine scholar as well as a good athlete. / 돈도 없거니와 틈도 없다 Not only do I lack money, but I don't have the time. / 산도 높거니와 물도 맑다 The mountains are high and the waters are clear, as well.

**거니채다** sense; perceive; suspect.

**거닐다** take a walk 〔stroll〕; stroll. ¶ 공원을 ~ saunter about a park; take a walk in a park / 해변을 ~ take a stroll on the beach.

**거담**(祛痰) the discharge of phlegm. ◉ ~제〔약〕 an expectorant.

**거당**(擧黨) the whole party. ¶ 당수의 성명을 ~적으로 지지했다 The whole party supported the leader's statement.

**거대하다**(巨大―) (be) huge; enormous; gigantic; titanic; colossal. ¶ 거대한 체구 a great bulk of a man; a huge body / 거대한 대포 a big 〔monster〕 gun / 거대한 유조선 a supertanker / 거대한 파도 a gigantic wave.
◉ ~도시 a megalopolis. ~세포 a giant cell.

**거덕치다** (be) awkward; be out of place.

**거덜거덜하다** (be) unsteady; shaky; be about to fall.

**거덜나다** be ruined; become 〔go〕 bankrupt; go broke. ¶ 은행이 거덜났다 A bank was bankrupt. / 불경기로 그 가게는 거덜나고 말았다 Owing to the business depression that store has failed.

**거독**(去毒) detoxication; detoxification. ~하다 detoxicate; detoxify.

**거동**(擧動) ① 《처신》 conduct; behavior; manner; carriage; movements; doings. ~하다 behave; conduct *oneself.* ¶ ~이 수상한 사내 a man of suspicious behavior / ～이 신사답다 behave *oneself* like a gentleman; have 〔show〕 gentlemanly conduct / ～이 수상하다 act suspiciously / ～을 감시하다 watch 《*a person's*》 movement / 점잖게 ～하다 conduct *oneself* seriously 〔maturely〕; behave *oneself*. ② ⇨ 거둥.

**거두**(巨頭) a leader; a prominent figure; a magnate; a (big) wheel; a big shot 〔bug, whale, name〕 《미속어》. ¶ 재계의 ～ a leading financier; a tycoon / 정계의 ～ a political leader / 실업계의 ～들 big businessmen; the plutes 《미속어》. ◉ ～회담 a top level conference; a parley at the summit: 3 ～ 회담 a Big Three talks 〔conference〕.

**거두다** ① 《널린 것을》 take 〔gather〕 in; 《추수하다》 harvest; reap; reap a harvest; gather up; 《돈을》 collect 《money》; call in 《debts》; 《수납》 accept; receive. ¶ 곡식을 ～ harvest crops / 기부금을 ～ collect contributions / 세금을 ～ collect taxes; levy taxes / 빨래를 거두어 들이다 take in the washing.
② 《성과·이익 등을》 gain; obtain. ¶ 효과를 ～ realize 〔achieve〕 satisfactory results; obtain good results / 대단한 이익을 ～ gain a great benefit / 승리를 ～ gain 〔win〕 the victory / 훌륭한 성과를 ～ obtain excellent results.
③ 《복장 등을》「tidy (up) 〔dress〕 *oneself*; fit *oneself* out 《for an outing》.
④ 《돌보다》 take care of; look after; care for; mind; see to (일 따위를); tend (이바지하다). ¶ 고아를 거두어 기르다 take an orphan and bring him up / 집안을 ～ take care of a household / 거두어 먹이다 feed with care / 아이들은 할머니가 거두기로 했다 The children were left in the care of their grandmother.
⑤ 《끝내다》 stop; end; quit. ¶ 눈물을 ～ stop crying; dry *one's* tears / 간과(干戈)를 ～ lay down arms; sheathe the sword.
⑥ 《숨을》 breathe *one's* last; expire; die; pass away.

**거두절미**(去頭截尾) cutting off the head and tail; 《요점》 making a short story of 《it》. ～하다 cut off the head and tail of 《it》; leave out the introduction and the conclusion of; make a short story of 《it》. ¶ ～하면 to make 〔cut〕 a long story short.

**거둠질** gathering; harvesting; collecting. ～하다 do the harvesting 〔collecting〕; harvest; collect.

**거둥** a royal procession 〔visit〕. ～하다 pay a (royal) visit 《to》; 《왕이》 proceed outside the palace.

**거드럭거리다** swagger; strut; show off; behave in a cocky way; assume 〔put on〕 airs; behave with an air of importance. ¶ 거드럭거리면서 말하다 speak「with an air of importance 〔in a lordly manner〕 / 거드럭거리며 걷다 strut about; walk with a dignified air.

**거드름** a haughty attitude 〔air〕; haughtiness; arrogance; overweening pride. ¶ ～ 부리다〔피우다〕 have an air of importance; stand upon *one's* dignity; give *oneself* 〔put on〕 airs / ～ 피우는 dignified; self-important / 그녀는 ～을 피워서 아무도 좋아하지 않는다 She has such an air of importance that nobody likes her. / 그는 늘 ～을 떨며 이야기한다 He always speaks with an air of importance. ◉ ～쟁이 a high hat; a high-hatter; a swaggerer.

**-거든** ① 《가정·조건》 provided (that); if; when. ¶ 선생님을 만나거든 그렇게 말하자 If we run into the teacher, let's tell him so. / 그것이 네 것이거든 가져라 Take it if it is yours. ② 《더구나》 if; given that; (still) more. ¶ 네가 그토록 공부해야 하거든 하물며 나야 If you must work so hard, how much more must I? ③ 《까닭》 as; so; since. ¶ 내 눈으로 똑똑히 보았거든 다를 리가 없다. As I ascertain it with my own eye, it cannot be otherwise. ④ 《놀라움》 sure(ly); indeed; certainly. ¶ 비가 참 많이 왔거든 It certainly did rain!

**거든그리다** wrap up lightly.

**거들다** lend a (helping) hand 《to》; help; assist; aid. ¶ 거들어 주는 사람 a helper; an assistant / 남의 말을 ～ second another's words / 일을 ～ help 〔assist〕 《*a person*》 with *his* work; lend a hand with 《*a person's*》 work / 옷 입는〔벗는〕 것을 거들어 주다 help 《*a person*》 on 〔off〕 with *his* clothes.

**거들떠보다** lift *one's* eyes and look at 《*a person*》; glance up 《at》; notice; take notice 《of》; pay attention 《to》. ¶ 거들떠보지도 않고 without taking any notice 《of》 / 거들떠보지도 않다 ignore completely; give no heed 〔regard〕 《to》; pay no attention 《to》; be indifferent 《to》; do not care at all 《for》 / 찾아갔으나 그는 거들떠보지도 않았다 I went to see him but he didn't even glance up at me. / 그녀는 너 따위를 거들떠보지도 않을 거다 She will not even look 〔glance up〕 at you.

**거들먹거리다** assume airs. ⇨ 거드럭거리다.

**거듬거듬** skipping about; in a cursory 〔desultory〕 way; roughly.

**거듭** repeatedly; again; over again; once more; anew. ～하다 repeat; do again. ～되다 be repeated.
¶ 실패를 ～한 끝에 after repeated failures / ～ 묻다 ask once more; ask the same question again; ask another question / ～ 읽다 read over again / 고생을 ～하다 go through many hardships / 판(版)을 ～하다 go through another edition 〔more editions〕; run into several editions / 못된 짓을 ～하다 commit a crime after another / 손해에 손해를 ～하다 sustain loss upon loss / 모임을 ～하다 hold several meetings / ～ 말하지만 I repeat (that...) / ～ 폐를 끼쳐 미안합니다 I am sorry to give you so much trouble.

**거듭거듭** repeatedly; over and over (again); again and again; many times.

**거듭나다** be born again; be reborn; come to life again; resuscitate.

**거듭제곱** 『수학』 involution; power. ～하다 involve. ◉ ～근(根) a radical root.

**거뜬-** ⇨ 가뜬-.

**거란**(契丹) 『역사』 the Kitan 〔Ch'itan, Khithai〕; a Tungustic people in Manchuria.

**거란지(뼈)** the tailbone of an ox.

**거래**(去來) transactions; dealings; business; trade; a deal 《구어》. ～하다 have dealings 《with》; do 〔transact〕 business 《with》; trade 《in cotton with *a person*》; make a deal 《with》.
¶ 현금～ cash transactions / 국내〔국외〕 ～ home 〔foreign〕 trade / 부정〔불법〕 ～ shady 〔illegal〕 transactions / 주류의 부정 ～ illicit liquor traffic / 신규 ～ new business relations / 신용 ～ dealings on credit / 위장 ～ a camouflaged transaction / 장내 ～ transactions on exchanges / 장외 ～ off-board transactions / 큰 ～ a big deal / 정당 간의 ～ a deal between the political parties / 유리한 ～ a profitable bargain / ～를 개시하다〔트다〕 enter into business relations 《with》; start dealings 《with》; open accounts 《with》 (은행과) / ～를 끊다 break off business connections 〔relations〕 《with》; close accounts 《with》 (은행과) / ～를 계속하다 maintain business relationships 《with》 / ～를 제의하다 propose to open business 《with》 / ～를 맺다 strike 〔drive〕 a bargain 《with》 / H은행과 ～를 하다 have an account with Bank H / A회사와 큰 규모의 농산물 ～를 하다 do a large (volume of) business in crops with company A / 당사는 A사와 ～를 하고 있다 Our company is doing a business with A company. / H은행과 3월에 ～를 시작할 예정이다 We are to open an account with Bank H in March. / 그는 그 ～로 한밑천 잡았다 The transaction afforded him a good profit. / 당사는 그 회사와 10년 이상의 ～가 있습니다 We have been dealing 〔doing business〕 with the firm for more than ten years. / 유감스럽게도 당사는 그 지역에 이렇다 할 ～처가 없습니다 Unfortunately we have no good connection in that area. / 그 회사와는 몇 차례 양모 제품의 ～를 한 적이 있습니다 We have had several dealings with that firm regarding woolen products.
◉ ～가격 the market price. ～관계 business relations 〔connections〕. ～량〔고〕 a turnover; the volume of business 〔dealings, traffic〕. ～방법 the mode of dealing 〔transaction〕. ～선 ⇨ 거래처. ～소 an exchange; a stock exchange (주식의): 미곡〔면화〕 ～소 a rice 〔cotton〕 exchange. ～안내 a store bulletin. ～액 the amount of business 〔dealings〕; a turnover: ～액은 500만 원에 달했다 The transaction 〔deal〕 amounted to five million won. ～연기 carrying over. ～은행 *one's* bank; a correspondent bank: 주～ 은행 *one's* major correspondent bank. ～일 a business day. ～제한 restraint of trade. ～조건 terms and conditions of business.

**거래처**(去來處) 《고객》 a customer; a client; 《거래 관계자》 a business acquaintance; 《전체》 a business 〔trade〕 connection. ¶ ～가 많다 have a large connection 《in》.

**거론하다**(擧論—) make 《it》 a subject of discussion; make 《it》 an object of criticism.

**거룩하다** (be) holy; sacred; great; grand; glorious. ¶ 거룩하신 하느님 holy God / 거룩한 자기 희생 sublime self-sacrifice.

**거룻배** a lighter; a barge. ◉ ～사공 a lighterman; a bargeman.

**거류**(居留) residence; residing. ～하다 reside 〔dwell, live〕 《in》. ¶ 6개월 이상 ～한 외국인 a foreigner of more than six months' residence / 브라질에 ～하는 한국인 Korean residents in Brazil. ◉ ～민 residents. ～민단 a settlement corporation. ～외국인 a foreign resident. ～지 a concession 〔settlement〕.

**거르다**[1] 《여과하다》 put 《*a thing*》 through; strain; filter; percolate; strain out. ¶ 거른 물 filtered water / 모래로 물을 ～ filter 〔percolate〕 water through sand / 명주로 팥소를 ～ strain bean jam through a silk strainer / 간장을 체로 ～ strain soy sauce through a sieve / 커피 찌꺼기를 걸러내다 strain out coffee grounds.

**거르다**[2] 《건너뛰다》 skip 〔jump〕 《over》; omit. ¶ 하루〔이틀〕 걸러 every other 〔third〕 day / 하루 걸러 다음날 the day after next / 한 집 걸러 이웃집 (the) next door but one / 점심을 ～ go without lunch / (책의) 어려운 부분을 ～ skip over difficult passages / 하루 ～ skip a day / 한 줄씩 걸러 쓰다 write on every other 〔second〕 line / 식사를 거르지 않도록 해라 Try not to skip meals.

**거름** fertilizer (화학 비료); dressing (혼합의); manure (자연의); compost (퇴비); muck (마소의). ～하다 manure; fertilize; dress. ¶ 똥～ dung; 《마소의》 muck / ～을 주다 spread manure 《on》; apply fertilizer 《to vegetables》 / 밭에 ～을 하다 cover a field with compost 〔manure〕.

**거리**[1] 《재료》 material; matter; stuff; makings; 《근거·핑계》 basis; excuse; pretext. ¶ 국～ soup makings; soup stock / 웃음～ a laughingstock; a butt of ridicule; a subject of laughter / 이야깃～ a subject of talk; a subject to talk on; a topic / 일～ a piece of work / 그에게 말할 ～가 없다 I can't find any excuse 〔pretext〕 to approach him.

**거리**[2] ① 《길거리》 a road; a street. ¶ ～마다 on every street / 큰 ～ a main street; a thoroughfare / ～의 천사 a homeless child; a street urchin / ～의 불량배 a street roughs 〔hooligans〕 / ～의 여자 a streetwalker; a woman of the town 〔streets〕; a street girl / ～를 걷다 walk on the street / 거릿송장이 되다 die 「on the road 〔in a ditch〕 / ～를 깨끗이 합시다 《게시》 Keep the town tidy. ② 《항간》 a downtown area; a town; a quarter. ¶ ～의 소문 the talk of the town.

**거리**[3] 《단위》 a group of 50 《cucumbers, eggplants》. ¶ 오이 두 ～ 100 cucumbers.

**거리**(巨利) a huge 〔an enormous〕 profit; a big 〔huge〕 gain. ¶ ～를 얻다〔거두다〕 make 〔reap〕 a big profit.

**거리**(距離) distance; range (착탄의); 《간격》 an interval; 《차이》 (a) difference. ¶ 비행 ～ fly; a flight / 순항 ～ a cruising distance / 장～ 전화 a long-distance call 《미》; a trunk call 《영》 / 활공 ～ a gliding distance / 활주 ～ 《비행기의》 a taxiing distance / 일정한 ～에 at a certain distance / 그 지점에서 같은 ～에 at equal distances from the point / 좀 ～를 두고 (at) a (short) distance / 상당한 ～ a good distance / 저쪽까지의 ～ the distance across / 한 시간의 ～ an hour('s) distance 《from, between》 / ～를 재다 measure 〔calculate〕 the distance 《of, between》 / 안전 ～를 유지하다 keep a safe distance 《from》 / ～에 따라 다르다 《요금 따위가》 vary with the distance / 여기서 인천까지의 ～는 얼마나 되는가 How far is it (from here) to Inch'ŏn? / 엎어지면 코 닿을 ～다 It's only a stone's throw away. / 비행기는 그 ～를 2시간에 갔다 The plane covered 〔did〕 the distance in two hours. / 여기에서 걸어서 15분 ～에 있다 It is a 15-minute walk from here. / 우리들의 의견에는 상당한 ～가 있다 We are 「very different 〔poles apart〕 in our opinions. ◉ ～감 a sense 〔feeling〕 of distance. ～측정기 a range finder (착탄·사진 따위의). ～표 《철도의》 a distance post; 《이정표》 a milestone; a mile marker.

**거리끼다** 《망설이다》 hesitate 《to *do*》; have scruples about 《*do*ing》; 《마음에 걸리다》 weigh 《on *one's* mind》; trouble *one*; 《방해가 되다》 (be) obstructive; [서술적] be a hindrance 《to》. ¶ 거리낌없이 with no hesitation 〔restraint, reserve〕; 《남에게 신경을 안 쓰고》 regardless of the others / 거리낌없이 말하다 speak out; be outspoken 《in *one's* opinion》 / 누구 앞이라도 거리낌없이 소신을 말하다 give *one's* opinion in anybody's presence / (앞에) 거리끼는 것을 제거하다 get rid of an obstacle; get an obstacle out of the way / 마음에 거리낀다 It haunts me.

**거마**(車馬) horses and vehicles. ¶ ～통행 금지 《게시》 No thoroughfare for horses and vehicles. *or* Vehicular traffic (is) suspended. ◉ ～비 transportation expenses; carriage.

**거만**(巨萬) millions; a vast 〔fabulous〕 fortune. ¶ ～의 재산을 쌓다 make fortunes; amass millions / ～의 돈을 투입

하다 spend millions ⟪on a project⟫.
**거만**(倨慢) haughtiness; arrogance; pride. ∼하다〔스럽다〕 (be) haughty; arrogant; proud; stuck-up; high-hat; have *one's* nose in the air. ¶ ∼한 태도 a haughty attitude 〔air〕 / ∼을 떨다 give *oneself* airs; ride the high horse / 그는 출세하더니 ∼해졌다 He is stuck-up by his success.
**거머들이다** drive ⟪it⟫ in greedily; rake ⟪them⟫ in; gather 〔collect〕 ⟪them⟫ greedily.
**거머리** ⟪동물⟫ a leech; ⟪사람⟫ a bur; a nuisance.
**거머무트름하다** (be) dark and chubby.
**거머삼키다** gulp (down); swallow greedily.
**거머안다** hug; clasp; fold tightly; embrace.
**거머잡다** grab 〔clutch, take hold of〕 greedily.
**거머쥐다** ＝ 거머잡다.
**거멀** a clamp; a cramp; a metal reinforcement for a joint. ∼(장)하다 clamp; cramp. ◉ ∼못 a clamp; a cramp; a clincher. ∼장식 an ornamental metal reinforcing piece.
**거멓다** (be) black; dark.
**거메지다** get dark; darken; become 〔turn〕 black; blacken; ⟪별에 타서⟫ get tanned; tan ⟪in the sun⟫.
**거목**(巨木) a great 〔large, big〕 tree.
**거무스름하다** (be) blackish; darkish; swarthy. ¶ 피부가 거무스름한 dark-skinned / 거무스름해지다 get 〔become〕 darkish.
**거문고** 〖악기〗 a *kŏmungo;* a Korean harp with six strings.
**거물**(巨物) ⟪사람⟫ a person of large caliber; a big 〔an important〕 figure; a bigwig ⟪구어⟫; a big bug 〔wheel, shot〕 ⟪구어⟫; ⟪사물⟫ a big thing. ¶ 정계의 ∼ a leading 〔prominent, great〕 figure in politics; a conspicuous figure in political world / 실업계의 ∼ a big businessman; a tycoon ⟪미⟫ / 당대의 ∼ the lion of the day.
**거뭇하다** ⇨ 가뭇하다.
**거미** a spider. ¶ ∼ 알슬듯 propagating vigorously everywhere. ◉ ∼발 ⟪보석의⟫ a jewel chain shaped like a spider's legs. ∼집 a spider's web; a cobweb.
**거미줄** ① ⟪거미의⟫ a spider's thread 〔web〕; a cobweb. ∼치다 weave 〔spin〕 a web. ¶ ∼에 걸리다 be caught in a spider's web / ∼을 걷다 clean ⟪the ceiling⟫ of cobwebs / 목구멍에 ∼치다 starve; go hungry. ② ⟪수사망⟫ a dragnet; a search apparatus (to comb a locality for a criminal). ∼치다〔늘이다〕 draw 〔post, place〕 a strict 〔police〕 cordon; cast a close dragnet.
**거미치밀다** be overwhelmed with envy 〔greed〕; get covetous.
**거반**(居半) ⇨ 거지반.
**거방지다** be dignified; have a commanding presence.
**거병**(擧兵) raising an army; rising in arms. ∼하다 raise an army; rise in arms; take up arms ⟪against⟫.
**거보**(巨步) a giant step; ⟪공적⟫ a brilliant achievement. ¶ ∼를 내디디다 make long strides ⟪in⟫; take a giant step ⟪toward⟫.
**거봐라** Look!; You see!; I told you so! ¶ ∼ 내 말이 맞았지 Look! What I told you is true. / ∼ 내 말대로 했으면 이런 잘못은 없었을 것 아냐 I told you so! You would not have made this mistake if you had done as I told you.
**거부**(巨富) a very wealthy person; a millionaire; a Croesus. ¶ ∼가 되다 become a millionaire.
**거부**(拒否) (a) refusal; (a) rejection; (a) denial; ⟪법안 따위의⟫ veto. ∼하다 refuse; reject; deny; veto ⟪a bill⟫; put 〔set〕 a veto ⟪on a proposal⟫; turn down ⟪a request⟫; disapprove ⟪of⟫. ¶ 요구를 ∼하다 refuse 〔turn down〕 a request / 지급을 ∼하다 refuse payment; decline to pay / 제안을 ∼하다 veto 〔refuse to accept〕 a proposal / 딱 잘라〔단호히〕 ∼하다 refuse roundly; give ⟪*a person*⟫ a flat refusal.
◉ ∼권 the veto right ⟪of the Big Powers⟫; a veto: ∼권을 행사하다 veto ⟪a proposal⟫; exercise *one's* veto (power) / ∼권을 휘두르다 wield *one's* veto power. ∼반응 rejection symptoms.
**거북** ⟪바다의⟫ a turtle; ⟪민물의⟫ a tortoise. ◉ ∼선 the "Turtle Boat 〔Ship〕"; an ironclad warship shaped (like) a tortoise.
**거북스럽다, 거북하다** ⟪마음이⟫ (be) awkward; unhandy; embarrassing; feel awkward 〔embarrassed〕; (be) uncomfortable; uneasy; embarrassed; be ill at ease; ⟪몸이⟫ have difficulty ⟪in⟫; out of condition 〔order〕; (be) unwell. ¶ 거북한 입장 an awkward position / 거북한 표현 an awkward 〔a clumsy〕 expression / 거북한 자리 an uncomfortable seat; an awkward meeting / 거북한 듯이 웃다 smile sheepishly / 거

북하게 하다 make 《*a person*》 self-conscious; put 《*a person*》 out of countenance / 숨쉬기가 ~ have difficulty in breathing / 그들은 만나기를 서로 거북해 한다 They feel awkward about seeing each other. / 두 사람 사이가 거북해졌다 They don't get on so well as before. / 그 사람 앞에 있으면 어쩐지 거북하다 I feel rather awkward in his presence. / 아무래도 과식했나 봐, 배가 거북한데 It seems that I overate myself. I feel quite unwell.

**거북점**(—占) 《거북의》 divination by burning tortoise shells; 《골패의》 divination by using a set of dominoes of tortoise shapes. ~하다 divinate 〔tell fortunes〕 by burning tortoise shells.

**거비**(巨費) an enormous expenditure; a great cost.

**거사**(居士) ① 《불교도》 a Buddhist devotee. ② 《처사(處士)》 a retired scholar; an anchorite; a hermit.

**거사**(擧事) taking 〔initiating〕 an action; launching an undertaking; starting 《*a matter*》. ~하다 take 〔initiate〕 an action; launch an undertaking; undertake 《a riot》; set 《a plan, a movement》 on foot 〔afoot, agoing〕; start 《a rising, a revolt, an insurrection》; rise 《in rebellion》; raise 〔foment, create〕 《a rebellion, a commotion》.

**거상**(巨商) a wealthy 〔rich〕 merchant; a merchant magnate 〔prince〕.

**거상**(巨像) a huge statue; a colossus; a gigantic 〔mammoth〕 image.

**거상**(居喪) 《상중》 (being in) mourning; 《상복》 a mourning attire. ~하다 be in mourning.

**거석**(巨石) a huge stone; 《유사 이전의》 a megalith. ◉ ~문화 megalithic culture.

**거선**(巨船) a big 〔huge, mammoth〕 ship; a leviathan.

**거성**(巨星) 《큰 별》 a giant star; 《큰 인물》 a great man; a luminary; a leading light. ¶ 문단의 ~ a leading light of the literary world.

**거세**(去勢) 《가축 등의》 castration; emasculation; 《세력의》 weakening (약화); a purge (숙청); exclusion (배제). ~하다 《가축 등의》 castrate; emasculate; geld; 《세력 등의》 weaken the power 《of the oppositions》; purge 《disroyal elements》; destroy 《*a person's*》 influence; tame; enervate.

◉ ~계(鷄) a capon. ~마(馬) a gelding. ~술(術) castration; gelding. ~양 a wether. ~우(牛) a bullock; a steer.

**거세다** ① 《거침》 (be) strong; tough; coarse; rude; fierce; violent; wild. ¶ 거센 여자 an unruly woman; a spirited woman / 거센 목소리 a coarse voice / 거센 물결 rough waves / 거센 바람 a strong wind / 거센 세파에 시달리다 be tossed about in the storms of life. ② 〖음성〗 be aspirated; have rough breathing. ¶ 거센 소리 aspirated sounds; an aspirate.

**거소**(居所) a dwelling place; *one's* residence 〔abode, whereabouts〕; *one's* address. ¶ ~를 정하다 take up *one's* quarters 〔residence〕 《at》.

**거수**(擧手) raising 〔lifting〕 *one's* hand; 《표결의》 a show of hands. ~하다 raise 〔show〕 *one's* hand. ¶ ~로 표결하다 take (a) show of hands; decide 《on a bill》 by (a) show of hands / 그 안건은 토의를 거쳐 ~로 가결되었다 After a course of discussion that bill was approved by (a) show of hands. / 찬성하시는 분은 ~해 주십시오 Let those in favor show their hands.

◉ ~경례 a military salute: ~경례하다 make a military salute. ~기 《국회 따위의》 a rubber stamp: 행정부 정책의 ~기 노릇을 하다 be amenable rubber stamps for an administration policy. ~투표 voting by (a) show of hands.

**거스러미** 《손톱의》 an agnail; a hangnail; 《나무의》 a splinter. ¶ 손~가 생기다 have a hangnail.

**거스러지다** ① 《성질이》 become unmanageable; grow stubborn; become intractable. ② 《털이》 bristle; get ruffled.

**거스르다** ① 《역행·거역하다》 go 〔act〕 against; act contrary to; run 〔act〕 counter to; oppose; disobey; defy; contradict. ¶ (…을) 거슬러 against; contrary to; in defiance of; in the face 〔teeth〕 《of the wind》 / 뜻을 ~ resist 《*a person's*》 will / 신경을 ~ rub 《*a person*》 the wrong way / 부모의 말을 ~ contradict *one's* parents; disobey *one's* parents / 운명을 ~ strive against fate / 시대의 조류를 ~ go against the tide 〔current〕 of the times / 바람을 거슬러 나아가다 go in the teeth of the wind. ② 《돈을》 give change. ¶ 잔돈을 거슬러 받다 get the change / 돈을 거슬러 주다 give (back) the change / 만 원짜리를 거슬러 줄 수 있겠습니까 Can you give me change for a 10,000 won bill?

**거스름돈** (the) change. ¶ 만 원짜리 지폐를 내고 받은 ~ the change from a ten-thousand won note / ～을 주다〔받다〕 give 〔get〕 the change / ～은 가지세요 (You may 〔can〕) Keep the change. / ～ 여기 있습니다 Here's your change. / ～이 80원입니다 That makes eighty won change.

**거슬거슬하다** 《성질이》 (be) intractable; stubborn; willful; 《살결이》 (be) rough; bristly. ¶ 성질이 ～ have a rough disposition / 손이 ～ have rough hands.

**거슬러올라가다** 《흐름을》 go 〔row, sail〕 up 〔against〕 《a stream》; go 〔swim〕 upstream; 《과거로》 go 〔trace〕 back (to the past); 《소급하다》 be retrospective 〔retroactive〕 《to》.
¶ 당시로 거슬러올라가 생각하면 when I look back on that time / 4월로 거슬러 올라가 《be effective》 retrospectively 〔retroactively〕 to April / 과거로 ～ go back to the past; retrace the past / 근원으로 ～ trace 《*a thing*》 back to *its* origin / 그는 배로 강을 거슬러 올라갔다 He rowed up the river.

**거슬리다** 《마음·비위에》 offend; get on 《*a person's*》 nerves; hurt 《*one's* feelings》; be against 「the grain 〔*a person's* taste〕; be unpleasant; give offense 《to *a person*》. ¶ 귀에 ～ be harsh 〔offensive, grating〕 to the ear / 눈에 ～ be unpleasant to the eye / 뜻에 ～ be not congenial; be not to *one's* taste 〔liking〕 / 그 말이 내 비위에 거슬렸다 That remark 「hurt my feelings 〔offended me〕. / 그 소음이 내 신경에 거슬린다 The noise gets on my nerves.

**거슴츠레하다** (be) sleepy; dull; heavy; drowsy. ¶ 거슴츠레한 눈 sleepy 〔drowsy, heavy〕 eyes.

**거시기** ① [대명사적] what-do-you-call=it; what-you-may-call-it; whatchamacallit; thingamajig; thingamabob; whatsits; dodad; whatnot; hootenanny; whozits 《속어》; so-and-so; what's=his-name. ¶ 내 ～ 어디 갔나 Where is my whatchamacallit 〔thingamajig〕? ② [감탄사적] what was it 〔he〕 called —that…. ¶ ～ 그게 무어라더라 That— what was it called?—that thingama- jig….

**거시시하다** 《눈이》 (be) dim.

**거시적**(巨視的) 『경제·물리·수학』 macroscopic; 《견해의》 all-inclusive; comprehensive. ¶ ～으로 macroscopically / ～으로 보다 take a broad 〔bird's-eye, macroscopic〕 view 《of》; see 《*a thing*》 in broad prospective / 그는 무슨 일이나 ～인 관점에서 사물을 파악한다 He is good at seeing things in broad perspective. ◉ 거시(적) 경제학 macroeconomics. ～ 물리학 macrophysics. ～ 분석 『경제』 macroscopic analysis. ～ 이론 a macroscopic theory.

**거식하다** ① [동사로서] do something=or-other 《with》. ¶ 네 친구 중 돈을 거식한 사람이 있지 않았니… 저… 언젠가 돈을 잃어버린 사람 말야 Didn't you have a friend who... uh... did something-or-other with some money... oh yes, that man who once lost some money, you know. ② [형용사로서] be some sort of; be somehow—I don't know—; so be *je-ne-sais-quoi* (F.); be hard to describe; 《거북함》 be reluctant 《to say》; be uncertain whether *one* should 《say》. ¶ 말하기 거식해서 말하지 않았다 I was in some doubt whether I should bring it up, so I said nothing.

**거식하다**(擧式—) hold a ceremony; give 「(a) celebration.

**거실**(居室) 《자기의》 *one's* own 〔private〕 room; 《가족의》 a sitting room; a parlor; a living room 《미》.

**거액**(巨額) 《금액》 a huge 〔an enormous〕 amount (of money); a colossal sum. ¶ ～의 부채 a large debt / ～에 달하다 reach 〔amount to〕 a huge 〔colossal〕 sum (of money).

**거여목**(—木) 『식물』 a (snail) clover.

**거역**(拒逆) insubordination; disobedience; opposition; objection. ～하다 disobey; protest 《against》; object 《to》; oppose. ¶ 부모〔윗사람〕에게 ～하다 contradict *one's* parents 〔superior〕 / 상관 명령을 ～하다 「object to 〔protest against〕 the order of *one's* superior; disobey commands of *one's* superior / 신의 뜻에 ～하다 give offense to the will of God.

**거우다** provoke; vex; irritate; anger; 「tease.

**거울** ① 《비춰 보는》 a mirror; a (looking) glass; a hand mirror (손거울). ¶ ～을 보다 look into a mirror; see *oneself* in a mirror / ～ 같다 be glassy; be smooth / ～같은 바다 the glassy (surface of the) sea. ② 《모범·교훈》 a pattern; a model; an example; a paragon. ⇨귀감. ¶ 신문은 사회의 ～이다 The press is the mirror of society.

**거울삼다** 《모범으로 삼다》 pattern 〔model〕 《after》; follow the example 《of》; make an example 《of》; 《경계하다》 take warning; take a lesson 《from》. ¶ 선인의 덕행을 ～ take the virtuous conduct of old sages for *one's* model / 다른 사람의 잘못을 ～ take a lesson from another man's mistakes / 실패를 ~ take warning by *a person's* failure.

**거웃**[1] 《음모》 pubic hair; pubes.

**거웃**[2] 《두둑》 a plowed furrow in a field 〔paddy〕.

**거위**[1] a goose (*pl.* geese); 《수컷》 a gander. ◉ ~새끼 a gosling. ~영장 a tall skinny person; a beanpole 《구어》.

**거위**[2] 《회충》 an intestinal worm; an ascarid; a roundworm. ¶ (뱃속에) ~가 생기다 get worms / ~를 없애다 expel 〔drive out〕 worms. ◉ ~배 stomach trouble caused by worms: ~배를 앓다 be troubled by roundworms.

**거유**(巨儒) a learned Confucianist; a great *literatuse* 〔scholar〕 (of Confucianism).

**거의** 《대체로》 almost; nearly; practically; all but; next to; well-nigh; as good as; 《약》 about; around; 《대부분》 for the most part; mostly; [부정적] few; little; hardly (ever); scarcely (any).

> (용법) **almost**, **nearly** 아주 조금만 더 있으면 「어떤 수·양·상태·수준에 이르다」란 뜻의 부사. almost는 nearly 보다 접근 정도가 더 가까운 뜻. **practically** 「실질적으로 어떤 수·양·수준 등에 이른 것이나 같다」는 뜻. **all but** 「…이외에는 모두」가 본래의 뜻이나, 형용사 앞에 쓰여 almost의 뜻이 된다 : be all but dead. **next to** 「…에 매우 가까운」의 뜻이나, 부정어 앞에 쓰여 almost의 뜻이 된다 : be next to nothing. **well=nigh** almost와 같은 뜻의 문어적인 말. **about**, **around** 어떤 수·양·상태에 약간 미달하거나 초과하는 경우에 쓰이는 말. **little**, **few** 「거의 …없다」란 뜻의 준부정어. little은 양·정도에, few는 수에 쓰인다. 둘 다 관사 a를 붙이지 않는다. **hardly**, **scarcely** 정도·가능성·빈도수 등이 「거의 …없다」란 뜻의 준부정어. 둘 다 be동사·조동사의 직후, 일반동사의 직전에 위치한다. ever, any 따위와 함께 쓰이기도 한다.

¶ ~ 전부 almost 〔nearly〕 all; mostly; the greater part 《of》 / ~ 2천 명에 달하는 종업원 nearly 〔a little less than〕 2,000 employees / ~ 대개의 경우 in most cases / ~ 불가능하다 be 「next to 〔almost〕 impossible / ~ 죽어 가다 be dying; be all but dead; be on the verge of death / 그 건물은 ~ 완성되었다 The building is almost 〔nearly, practically〕 finished. / 「내 리포트 타자는 다 끝났느냐」―「~ 다 끝나 간다. 세 페이지만 더 치면 돼」 "Are you through typing my paper?"―"Just about. I only have three more pages to go." / 그것을 믿는 사람은 ~ 없다 Scarcely anybody believes that. / 희망은 ~ 없다 There is little 〔scarcely any〕 hope. / 그는 ~ 책을 읽지 않는다 He hardly ever reads. / 조카는 나와 ~ 같은 체격이다 My nephew is about my size. / ~ 아무 것도 남아 있지 않았다 There was practically nothing left. / 3일간이나 애쓴 끝에 우리가 얻은 것은 ~ 아무것도 없었다 After three days' labor, we got next to nothing. / 그는 ~ 거지나 다름없다 He is next to a beggar. / 나는 ~ 그를 못 만난다 I hardly 〔seldom〕 see him. / 그의 성공은 ~ 기적에 가까운 일이다 His success is little short of a miracle. / 이것으로 준비는 ~ 끝난거나 다름없다 The preparations are now as good as over.

**거인**(巨人) a giant; a Titan; a colossus; 《위인》 a great man. ◉ ~국 a land of giants; 《걸리버 여행기의》 Brobdingnag.

**거장**(巨匠) a great artist 〔master〕 《of painting, of music》; a *maestro* (*pl.* ~*s, -tri*) (It.). ¶ 그는 금세기 음악계의 최대 ~이다 He is the greatest musician of this century.

**거재**(巨財) a huge 〔an enormous〕 fortune; great wealth. ¶ ~를 투입하다 invest millions 《in an enterprise》.

**거저** ① 《일을 안 하고》 without doing anything (in particular); 《빈손으로》 without bringing anything; with nothing (in hand 〔mind〕); 《무턱대고》 without giving any reason; just because 《*one* wants to》; arbitrarily; just like that. ¶ ~ 앉아 있다 be sitting down doing nothing.
② 《공짜로》 without paying anything; gratis; free (of charge); gratuitously; for nothing; as a gift. ¶ 남의 것을 ~ 가져가다 take away another's belongings without paying for them / ~ 일하다 work for nothing / 영화를 ~ 구경하다 see the movie free / ~ 주어도 싫다 I would not have 〔take〕 it as a gift. / ~드리겠습니다 You may have it for nothing. / 그 일은 ~ 해 드리겠습니다 I will make no charge for the work. / 천 원이니 ~죠 It is one thousand won and a present at that. / 이 물건은 ~나 마찬가지다 This is quite a bargain.

**거저먹기** an easy thing to do 〔achieve〕 / a job there is nothing to; a snap; a piece of cake 《구어》. ¶ ~

다 It's a snap. 《미구어》/ 그런 일은 ～다 There's nothing to a job like that. *or* It's an easy task. *or* That's nothing. *or* Nothing could be easier.

**거적** a straw mat; 《총칭》 straw matting. ¶ ～에 싸다 wrap 《*a thing*》 in straw matting / ～을 깔다 spread a straw mat / (…에) ～을 덮다 cover 《*a thing*》 with straw matting.
◉ ～눈 eyes with drooping eyelids: 피로하여 ～눈이 되다 *one's* eyelids droop with tiredness. ～때기 a piece of a straw mat. ～문 a door made of matting: ～문에 돌쩌귀 Don't use a nail when string will do. ～송장 a corpse wrapped in straw matting. ～ 자리 a straw-mat seat.

**거절**(拒絶) (a) refusal; (a) rejection; 《언명·책임 따위의》 disapproval; 『법』 repudiation; 《단호한》 a rebuff; brush=off 《미속어》. ～하다 refuse; reject; decline; rebuff; turn down; turn thumbs down 《on》; say no 《to》; pass up 《미구어》. ¶ 정중하지만 단호한 ～ a polite but decided rejection / 딱 ～하다 give a flat 〔square〕 refusal; refuse point-blank / 면회를 ～하다 refuse to see 《*a person*》 / 요구를〔신청을〕 ～하다 turn down 〔reject〕 《*a person's*》 request 〔application〕 / 약속을 ～하다 pass up the engagement / 입장을 ～당하다 We were refused entry. ◉ ～증서 a protest: 인수〔지급〕 ～ 증서 a protest for nonacceptance 〔nonpayment〕.

**거점**(據點) a position; a (strong=) point; a base (of operations); a foothold. ¶ ～을 만들다 establish a strongpoint / ～을 확보하다 secure a strongpoint 《for》 / 당사는 아프리카에 튼튼한 영업 ～을 가지고 있다 This company has a strong business foothold in Africa.
◉ 군사 ～ a strategic 〔key〕 position.

**거족**(巨族) a distinguished 〔a powerful, an influential〕 family; a mighty clan.

**거족적**(擧族的) nation-wide. ¶ ～인 축제일 a day of national celebration / ～으로 on a national scale; throughout the nation.

**거주**(居住) 《삶》 dwelling; residence; abode; habitation; 《사는 곳》 =거주지. ～하다 dwell; reside; live; inhabit; make *one's* home; take (up) residence. ¶ 6개월 이상 ～한 외국인 a foreigner of more than six months' residence / ～의 자유 the freedom of residence.
◉ ～권(權) the right of residence. ～성(性) livability; habitability. ～인구 the resident population 《of an area》. ～자 a resident; a dweller; an inhabitant. ～ 증명서 a certificate of residence. ～지 *one's* place of residence. ～지역 the residential district.

**거죽** 《표면》 the surface; the face; the right side (옷의); 《외면부》 the exterior; the head (화폐의); the external appearance. ¶ 이 천은 어느 쪽이 ～입니까 Which is the face 〔the right side〕 of this cloth?

**거중조정**(居中調停) mediation; intermediation; intervention; intercession; arbitration; good offices (주선). ～하다 intermediate; intervene 《between》; arbitrate; play an arbitrating role; mediate 《between two countries》; provide good offices. ¶ ～을 맡다 assume a mediation role.

**거즈** [<*Gaze* (G)] (cotton, antiseptic) gauze. ¶ 소독～ sterilized gauze.

**거증**(擧證) the establishment of a fact (by evidence). ～하다 establish a fact (by evidence); present evidence.
◉ ～책임 『법』 the burden of proof.

**거지** 《걸인》 a beggar; a mendicant; a panhandler 《미》. ¶ ～꼴 shabby looks; beggarly 〔miserable〕 appearance / ～처럼 되다 be reduced to beggarly condition; go to the dogs 《구어》 / 옷이 ～꼴이 되다 *one's* clothes get shabby / ～생활을 하다 go begging; beg *one's* bread 〔meals〕; beg for a living / ～ 취급을 하다 treat 《*a person*》 as a beggar. ◉ ～근성 a mean spirit; the beggar: 가난해지면 ～근성이 나온다 When a man becomes poor, the beggar in him will come out.

**거지반**(居之半) over half; the greater part 《of》; nearly all; almost; nearly. ¶ 건물이 ～ 완성되었다 The building is nearly finished. / 이 주일도 ～ 다 갔다 This week is almost over now.

**거짓** ① [명사적] a lie (거짓말); untruth; a falsehood; a fabrication (지어낸 일); a deceit (허위). ¶ ～의 false; untrue; fictitious / ～이 없는 honest; true; sincere / ～ 웃음 a feigned 〔forced〕 smile 〔laugh〕 / ～이다 be false 〔untrue, dishonest, deceitful〕 / ～ 눈물을 흘리다 shed crocodile 〔false, sham〕 tears / 그의 말엔 ～이 없다 All he said is true. / 그의 행동은 그의 말이 ～임을 말한다 His deed gives the lie to his words. / 이 광고에는 ～이 있다 There is something untrue in this advertisement. ② [부사적] falsely; fictitiously; deceitfully; dishonestly. ¶ ~ 아프다고 하다 feign illness; pretend to be ill / ~ 친절한 체하다 feign kindness; pretend to be kind.

**거짓말** a lie; a falsehood; an untruth; a fabrication. ~하다 tell a lie; lie; tell an untruth 〔a falsehood〕; don't tell the truth. ¶ 새빨간 ~ a barefaced lie; a downright lie; a pure fabrication / 엄청난〔터무니없는〕 ~ a whopping lie; a lie made out of whole cloth / 그럴 듯한 ~ a plausible lie / 빤히 들여다 보이는 ~ a lie that can be seen through clearly; a transparent 〔a palpable, an obvious〕 lie 〔falsehood〕 / 악의 없는 ~ a white lie; a fib / ~ 투성이 a pack of lies; a tissue of lies / 천연스럽게 ~하다 lie as though telling the truth; lie with a straight face / ~이 아니다 It is no lie. *or* I mean everything I say. / 그것은 ~ 같이 들린다 That sounds incredible. / ~할 사람이 아니다 He is not a man to tell a lie. ◉ ~쟁이 a liar: 상습적 ~쟁이 an inveterate liar. ~탐지기 a lie detector; a polygraph: ~탐지기로 조사하다 give a lie (detector) test 《to》; lie-test.

**거찰**(巨刹) a big Buddhist temple.

**거참** Indeed!?; O my!; O dear!; (O) dear me!; Bless me!; 《속어》 By crikey! ¶ ~ 야단났는데 O dear! What shall I do? *or* What a jolly mess I am in. / ~ 또 비야 Gee, it's raining again! / ~ 안됐군 Indeed, that was too bad.

**거창하다**(巨創—) be on a large scale; (be) large-scale; big; tremendous.

**거처**(居處) ① 《삶》 dwelling 〔living〕 《in》. ~하다 dwell 〔live〕 《in》. ② = 거소(居所). ¶ ~를 알아내다 locate; follow up 《*a person's*》 residence / ~를 자주 바꾸다〔옮기다〕 change *one's* address frequently.

**거칭숫돌** a rough grindstone.

**거초**(据礁) 〖지질〗 a fringing reef.

**거추꾼** a protector; a person who keeps an eye on another; a sponsor.

**거추없다** (be) out-of-place and silly.

**거추장스럽다** (be) burdensome; cumbersome; troublesome; tiresome; annoying. ¶ 거추장스러운 일 a troublesome job / 다루기가 거추장스러운 짐 a cumbersome parcel / 매우 거추장스럽게 여기다 think 《it》 very troublesome; think 《*a thing*》 is a real drag 《on》 / 거추장스럽게 굴다 trouble 〔burden〕 《*a person*》; give 《*a person*》 trouble; bother; annoy / 우산 가지고 다니는 것이 ~ It is burdensome to carry an umbrella. / 그는 어린애 데리고 다니는 것을 몹시 거추장스럽게 여긴다 He finds it such a burden to take the children around with him.

**거추하다** keep an eye on; look after; stand by to help.

**거춤거춤** roughly; in cursory fashion 〔way〕.

**거취**(去就) *one's* course of action; 《태도》 *one's* attitude 〔position〕. ¶ ~를 결정하다 decide *one's* course of action / ~를 분명히 하다 make it clear where *one* stands; make *one's* attitude 〔position〕 《on a topic》 clear / ~를 못 가리다〔못 정하다〕 「do not know 〔be at a loss〕 what to do.

**거치**(据置) 《지급 등의》 deferment; 《대부금 등의》 leaving 《a loan》 unredeemed. ~하다 leave 《a loan》 unredeemed; defer 〔put off〕 《the payment of a loan》. ¶ ~의 unredeemed; unredeemable; deferred / 3년 ~의 보험 insurance deferred for three years / 10년 ~의 차관 a loan unredeemable for ten years / 3년 ~ 5년 상환 repayment in five years with a three-year grace period / 5년 ~이다 be uncallable for five years. ◉ ~공채 deferred bonds. ~기간 a period of deferment. ~연금 a deferred annuity. ~저금 deferred savings.

**거치다** pass 〔go〕 through; go by way of...; drop in on *one's* way; stop 〔call, touch〕 at on *one's* way. ¶ 하와이를 거쳐 via 〔by way of〕 Hawaii / 시험을 거쳐〔거치지 않고〕 on 〔without〕 examination / 많은 사람의 손을 ~ pass through many hands / 정규 절차를 ~ go through the usual procedures / 그 기차는 대전을 거쳐서 간다 The train passes through Taejŏn. / 우리는 홍콩을 거쳐 런던으로 갔다 We flew to London 「by way of 〔via〕 Hong Kong.

**거치적거리다** be 〔stand, get〕 in 《*a person's*》 way; keep getting in the way; be a drag to 〔on〕 《*a person*》; obstruct; hamper; be an encumbrance 《to》; 《옷 따위가》 cling 《to》. ¶ 거치적거리는 cumbersome / 거치적거리는 가족이 없다 [비유적] have no dependents; be 〔remain〕 single / 책상이 거치적거린다 The desk gets in the way (when you want to go by). / 치맛자락이 거치적거려 걷기 힘들다 I have trouble in walking with my skirt clinging to my legs.

**거칠다** (be) rough; rugged; coarse;

gross; rude; wild; violent; harsh; [동사적] lack smoothness 〔sleekness〕. ¶ 거친 살결 a rough skin / 거친 종이 coarse-grained paper / 거친 사내 a rude 〔coarse〕 fellow / 거친 목소리 a harsh voice / 거친 바다〔물결〕 a high 〔heavy〕 sea; wild waves; raging waters / 거친 성미 a violent temper / 거친 천 《짜임이》 loose fabric; 《표면이》 a harsh cloth / 살결을 거칠게 하다 roughen 〔coarsen〕 the skin / 거칠게 짜다 knit with large stitches / 거친 말투를 쓰다 employ rough 〔harsh〕 language / 바다가 거칠어지다 The sea gets up 〔grows rough〕. / 바람이 거칠게 분다 The wind rages. *or* It blows hard 〔violently〕. / 그녀의 손은 고된 일로 ~ Her hands are rough with hard work. / 문장이 ~ This is written in an unpolished style.

**거칠하다** ⇨ 꺼칠하다.

**거침** something in the way; an obstacle; a hitch; a snag; an impediment; (a) hesitation; (a) hindrance. ~없다 be free from obstacles 〔obstruction〕; (be) unobstructed; be without a hitch; (be) untroubled; free and easy. ¶ ~없는 대답 a ready answer / ~없이 smoothly; without a hitch; without any trouble; readily; 《서슴지 않고》 with no hesitation / 일이 ~없이 진행되어 간다 The business is running along smoothly. ◉ ~새 a hindrance; an impediment; an obstacle; a snag: ~새가 많다 be full of snags.

**거칫거리다** keep feeling rough; snag; keep getting in the way; get caught 《on》.

**거탄**(巨彈) ① 《폭탄》 a large bomb; a heavy shell. ② [비유적] a sensation; a bombshell; a sensational feature (영화의). ¶ ~을 던지다 cause a sensation; drop a bombshell / 본 영화사가 내보내는 최초의 ~ the first sensational feature by our company 〔studio〕.

**거탈** only the outward appearance; only the surface. ¶ ~만 보고 사람을 판단하다 judge 《*a person*》 only by appearances.

**거포**(巨砲) a big gun 〔cannon〕; a huge 〔mammoth〕 gun; 《강타자》 a slugger.

**거푸** again and again; repeatedly; time after time; in succession. ¶ 두 잔의 커피를 ~ 마시다 drink two cups of coffee in rapid succession / 불행한 사건이 ~ 일어났다 Unfortunate incidents happened one after another.

**거푸집** ① 《외관》 the outer appearance of *one's* body; *one's* figure. ② 《도배의 뜬 곳》 a blister 〔an air bubble〕 left when pasting. ③ 《주형》 a matrix; a mold; a cast; a die.

**거풀거리다** flutter 〔flap〕 slowly.

**거품** a bubble; foam; froth; 《발효의》 barm; 《곤충의》 spit; spittle. ¶ 물~ a water bubble; foam on water / 맥주 ~ beer foam; froth 〔barm〕 of ale / 비누 ~ soap bubbles 〔froth〕; (soap) suds; lather / ~ 이는 foamy; frothy; bubbly; lathery; sudsy / ~이 생기다 a bubble forms; a lather is worked up / ~이 꺼지다 a bubble breaks 〔bursts〕 / ~을 떠내다 scum / ~처럼 사라지다 come to nothing 〔naught〕; end in smoke / 입에서 ~을 내뿜다 froth 〔foam〕 at the mouth. ◉ ~경제 bubble economy.

**거피하다**(去皮―) skin; rind 《mellons》; shell 《pears》; peel 《an orange》; pare 《an apple》; hull 《rice, peas》; strip off the bark of 《a tree》; bark.

**거하다** ① 《산이》 (be) steep; lofty. ② 《초목이》 (be) dense; thick; rampant.

**거한**(巨漢) a giant; a large-built person; a big man.

**거함**(巨艦) a mighty man-of-war; a super dreadnought; a big warship.

**거해궁**(巨蟹宮) 『천문』 the Crab; Cancer.

**거행**(擧行) ① 《명령대로》 acting in accordance with an order; carrying out (an order). ~하다 act in accordance with an order; carry out; put into effect. ¶ ~되다 be carried out / 분부대로 ~하겠습니다 I will carry out your order. *or* I will do as I am told. ② 《의식의》 performance; celebration; solemnization. ~하다 《모임 따위를》 hold; give; perform; 《식 따위를》 celebrate; observe; solemnize 《a wedding》. ¶ ~되다 be held; take place; come off / 졸업식을 ~하다 hold the graduation ceremony / 결혼식을 ~하다 celebrate a wedding 〔marriage〕 / 결혼식은 교회에서 ~되었다 The marriage was solemnized in the church. / 식전은 예정대로 ~되었다 The ceremony went off as planned.

**걱실거리다** bubble over with good cheer; behave buoyantly.

**걱정** ① 《염려》 care; worry; trouble; anxiety; solicitude; concern; apprehension. ~하다 worry; care; trouble; concern *oneself* 《about》; be anxious 〔concerned, solicitous, worried〕 《about》; feel uneasy 《about》; be ill at ease.

용법 **care** 비교적 가벼운 걱정, 종종 복수형으로 「걱정거리」를 뜻함. **worry** 「근심·걱정」을 뜻하는 일상어. 특히 「공연한 걱정·기우」를 뜻하는 경우가 많다. **trouble** 「성가신 일·자질구레한 걱정」을 뜻한다. **anxiety** 「무언가 좋지 않은 일이 일어날지도 모른다는 불안」을 나타내는 말. **solicitude** 「행복·건강 등에 대한 염려, 배려」 따위로 생기는 「걱정」을 뜻하는 격식차린 말. **concern** 매우 마음과 신경이 쓰이는 일을 뜻하지만, 그 정도가 anxiety만은 못함. **apprehension** 미래에 대한 불안감.

¶ 나라 ~ concern about state affairs / 돈 ~ money troubles; worries about money / 살림 ~ cares 〔worries〕 about daily livelihood / 집안 ~ domestic 〔family〕 cares / 쓸데없는 ~ idle cares; needless 〔useless〕 anxiety / ~ 없는 easy 《circumstance》; carefree 《life》 / ~ 없이 at ease; free from care / ~ 끝에 병이 들다 get sick in an excess of anxiety / ~되다 feel uneasy; be anxious 〔worried〕 about / ~ 없다 be carefree; be free from worry; have nothing to worry about / ~을 끼치다 trouble 《*a person*》; cause anxiety to 《*a person*》 / 사소한 일에 ~하다 worry about little things / ~이 그치지 않다 be always worrying 《about》; have plenty of worries / ~이 되어 견딜 수 없다 be worried sick / ~해 주셔서 고맙습니다 Thank you for being so concerned. / 그는 ~이 돼 잠을 못 잤다 He lost sleep for his troubles. / 그건 ~할 만한 일이 못 된다 It's nothing to worry about. / 무슨 ~이 있느냐 Do you have any trouble? / ~ 마라 Don't worry. *or* Never mind. / 그는 부모에게 ~만 끼치고 있다 He is a constant source of anxiety to his parents.

② 《꾸중》 a reproof; a reprimand; a rebuke; a lecture. ~하다 reprove; reprimand; give a rebuke; chide; lecture; call 《*a person*》 on the carpet. ¶ ~을 듣다 receive a reprimand / 돈을 많이 쓴다고 아버지께서 밤낮 ~하신다 My father is always jumping on me for spending too much money.

◉ ~거리 a source of anxiety; a cause for anxiety; a headache: ~거리가 끊이지 않다 always have something to worry about. ~꾸러기 《늘 걱정하는》 a worrywart; a person who is always worrying; 《걱정을 끼치는》 (a person who is) a headache; a constant worry.

**걱정스럽다** feel uneasy 〔concern〕; be anxious 《about, for》; be worried 《about》; (be) troubled. ¶ 걱정스러운 듯이 with a concerned 〔worried〕 air / 걱정스러운 일 cares; troubles / 걱정스러운 얼굴 a worried look; a careworn face / 걱정스런 태도 a concerned air / 걱정스러운 얼굴을 하다 look worried 〔concerned〕 / 그녀는 걱정스러운 듯 말없이 그들을 바라보았다 She looked at them in silent anxiety.

**건**(巾) ① 《헝겊의》 a head-cover made of cloth. ② 《두건》 a hemp cap worn by a mourner.

**건**(件) 《항목》 an item; 《일·사건》 a case; a matter; an affair. ¶ 예의 건 the matter in question / 오늘 아침 교통 사고는 몇 건 보고 되었느냐 How many cases of traffic accidents have been reported this morning? / 그 도난에 관한 건은 어떻게 되었느냐 What became of the theft case?

**건**(腱) 〖해부〗 a tendon. ¶ 아킬레스건 the Achilles' tendon.

**건**(鍵) a key 《of a piano, a typewriter》.

**건각**(健脚) 《튼튼한 다리》 strong legs; 《잘 걷는 사람》 a good walker. ¶ 그는 ~이다 He is a good walker.

**건강**(健康) health; fitness. ~하다 (be) healthy; sound; well; wholesome; healthful. (★ healthy는 장기간의, well은 일시적인, healthful은 「건강이 좋은」의 뜻). ¶ ~이 나빠서 owing to ill health / 썩 좋은 ~ 상태 excellent physical condition / ~에 좋다 be good for (the) health; be wholesome; be beneficial to health; be of benefit to *one's* health / ~에 해롭다 be bad for (the) health; be injurious to health (★ good과 bad의 다음에서만 for (the) health 이며, 그 밖의 형용사일 때에는 to health로 되는 점에 주의) / ~이 시원치 않다 be unhealthy; be out of health 〔condition〕; suffer from bad 〔ill〕 health; be in bad 〔poor〕 health / ~에 주의하다 take care of *oneself* / ~을 해치다 injure 〔ruin, lose〕 *one's* health / ~을 유지하다 keep 〔preserve〕 *one's* health / ~을 증진하다 promote *one's* health / ~을 회복하다 be restored to health; regain 〔recover〕 *one's* health / 나는 ~이 좋다〔나쁘다〕 I'm in good 〔poor〕 health. (★ 보통 I'm healthy 〔unhealthy〕 라고는 하지 않음) / 그는 ~상의 이유로 그 직을 사임했다 He quit the job for reasons of health. / 사람들은 ~을 잃고 나서야 비로소 그 고마움을 안다 One does not appreciate the value of good health until one has lose it. ◉ ~관리 health care《for the aged》: 환절기의 ~ 관리 control of *one's* health 〔health care〕 at the change of season. ~미 healthy beauty. ~법 how to maintain *one's* health; how to keep fit. ~보험 health insurance: ~ 보험에 가입하다 join a health insurance plan. ~ 보험증 a health insurance card. ~상담 a health consultation. ~상담소 a health clinic. ~상태 the condition 〔state〕 of *one's* health: ~상태가 나쁘다 be in a bad state of health. ~식품 a health food: ~ 식품점 a health food store. ~아 a healthy child. ~용품 health products. ~제(劑) a tonic. ~증명서 a medical certificate; 《선원의》 a bill of health. ~진단 a health 〔medical〕 examination; a (physical) checkup 《미》: 정기 ~ 진단 regular health checkups / ~ 진단을 받다 undergo 〔go through〕 a physical checkup. ~체 a healthy body; a healthy condition.

**건건찝질하다** (be) a bit salty; quite 「brackish.

**건건하다** (be) salty; brackish.

**건곡**(乾穀) dried grain(s).

**건곤**(乾坤) heaven and earth; the universe. ◉ ~일척 playing a game of "all or nothing"; sink or swim; neck or nothing: ~일척하다 stake all 《on》; play for all or nothing; take *one's* chance 《on (*do*ing) *something*》.

**건과**(乾果) dry 〔dried〕 fruits.

**건국**(建國) foundation 〔establishment〕 of a country. ~하다 found 〔establish〕 a country. ¶ ~의 아버지들 〖미국사〗 the Founding Fathers of America. ◉ ~ 공로훈장 the Order of Merit for National Foundation. ~기념일 National Foundation 〔Founding〕 Day. ~대본(大本) the principles upon which the state is established. ~이념 the national ideal envisioned on the founding of a country. ~포장(褒章) the National Foundation Medal.

**건군**(建軍) the founding of the armed forces. ~하다 found the armed forces. ¶ ~ 50돌을 맞다 mark the fiftieth anniversary of the founding of the Armed Forces.

**건기**(乾期) the dry season.

**건깡깡이** ① 《매나니로 하는 일》 slapdash; perfunctory workmanship. ② 《사람》 a person who does 「a slapdash job 〔a job without technical skill〕.

**건너** the other 〔opposite〕 side 《of》. ¶ 건넛집〔방〕 the opposite house 〔room〕; a house 〔room〕 on the opposite side / 건넛마을 a village on the other side; a village at the opposite side / 강 ~(에) 《live》 across the river; on the opposite 〔other〕 side of the river / 길 ~(에) the other side of a road; across the street.

**건너가다** go over; go 〔cut〕 across; cross (over) 《a bridge》; traverse 《a desert》; sail across (배로). ¶ 길을 ~ 「go across 〔cross〕 a road / 바다를 ~ sail across a sea / 미국으로 ~ go over to America.

**건너긋다** draw 〔trace〕 《a line》 across; write a horizontal stroke.

**건너다** cross; go 〔pass〕 over; go across; walk 〔run, ride, drive, sail〕 across; 《나룻배로》 ferry. ¶ 강을 ~ go 〔get〕 across a river / 다리를 ~ cross a bridge / 바다를 ~ cross 〔sail across〕 a sea / 좌우를 살핀 후 길을 건너라 Look both ways before crossing a road.

**건너다보다** ① 《저쪽을》 look across at. ② 《남의 것을》 covet; look at covetously; cast a jealous eye on. ¶ 남의 것을 ~ covet another's possession.

**건너뛰다** jump 〔leap〕 over 〔across〕; 《생략하다》 skip (over); leave out; omit. ¶ 개울을 ~ jump over a ditch / 담을 ~ leap over a wall; clear a wall (말이) / 페이지를 ~ skip over pages.

**건너오다** come across 《to this side》; come over 《the sea》; cross over 《to Korea》; 《도래》 be imported; be brought over 〔from abroad〕; be introduced 《from China》; 《철새가》 migrate. ¶ 다리를 ~ come across a bridge / 이리 건너오세요 Come over here. / 불교는 4세기에 한국에 건너왔다 Buddhism found its way to Korea in the fourth century.

**건너지르다** lay 〔put〕 《it》 across. ¶ 빗줄을 마당에 ~ hang a line 〔rope〕 across the yard.

**건너짚다** ① 《팔을 내밀어》 put *one's* hand 〔finger〕 over one thing and on something else; reach across 《*a thing*》 to touch 《*a thing else*》. ② 《넘겨짚다》 put *one's* finger on 《what *a person* is thinking》; anticipate; guess. ¶ 아무의 뜻을 ~ read *a person's* mind; guess what *a person* is thinking.

**건너편**(一便) the other side; the opposite end. ¶ ~의 opposite; on the other side / ~ 마을 a village on the other side; a village at the opposite end.

**건넌방**(一房) a room on the opposite side of the main living room.

**건널목** 《도로의》 a road crossing; 《철도의》 a railway 〔railroad 《미》〕 crossing; a level 〔grade 《미》〕 crossing. ¶ ~ 개폐기 없음 《게시》 Level crossing without gates. *or* Crossing—No gates. ◉ ~지기 a gateman; a watchman (at a crossing); a flagman 《미》. ~차단기 a crossing bar.

**건네다** ① 《건너게 하다》 carry across; pass 《*a person*》 over; 《배로》 take 〔row〕 over; carry over. ¶ 나룻배로 ~ carry across a river by a ferryboat; take 《*a person*》 over a river on a ferryboat. ② 《교부하다》 hand over; deliver; give; pay; transfer; make over; turn over. ¶ 돈을 ~ hand over 〔pay〕 money / 현품을 ~ give 〔deliver〕 an article. ③ 《말을》 address; speak 〔call〕 to 《*a person*》; accost.

**건네주다** 《배로》 pass 〔take, row〕 《*a person*》 over 《a river》; 《나룻배로》 ferry 《*a person*》 over; 《물건을》 hand (over) 《to》; deliver 《goods》; give. ¶ 가만히 ~ slip 《*a thing*》 to 《*a person*》 / 나룻배로 ~ take 《*a person*》 over a river by ferryboat.

**건달**(乾達) a penniless rake; a libertine; 《불량배》 a scamp; a good-for-nothing. ◉ ~패 a group of scamps.

**건담**(健啖) strong appetite; gluttony. ◉ ~가(家) a heavy eater; a glutton.

**건답**(乾畓) a rice field that dries easily; a dry paddy field.

**-건대** when; if; according to. ¶ 보건대 On inspection…; According to my observation… / 듣건대 As I hear…; According to the rumor…; According to what people say… / 생각하건대 Come to think of it… / 듣건대 그는 사업에 실패했다고 한다 As I hear tell, he failed in business. / 비유하건대 인생이란 길 가는 나그네다 To speak figuratively, life is a passing stranger.

**건대구**(乾大口) a dried codfish.

**건더기** solid ingredients in a mixture of liquid food; pieces of meat and vegetables 《in soup》; 《내용》 ground; substance. ◉ 국~ solid stuff in soup.

**건드렁타령**(一打鈴) staggering; reeling (drunkenly).

**건드레하다** (be) half-tipsy; somewhat intoxicated; be a bit high. ¶ 그는 건드레하게 취했다 He looks gay with drink.

**건드리다** touch; give 《*a thing*》 a jog; 《성나게 하다》 stimulate; irritate; goad; incite; provoke; vex; 《여자를》 have an affair 《with》. ¶ 아무의 신경을 ~ get on *a person's* nerves / 이 물건을 건드리지 마라 Don't touch this article. *or* Hands off!

**건들거리다** ① 《바람이》 blow gently 〔a bit strong〕. ② 《물체가》 sway; swing; shake; dangle; wobble; waver; tremble. ③ 《빈둥거리다》 lead an idle life; idle *one's* time away; fiddle about 〔around〕 (doing nothing).

**건들건들** 《바람이》 gently; softly; 《사람이》 idly; indolently; 《건물·물건 등이》 shakily; totteringly.

**건들바람** a cool wind blowing in early autumn.

**건들장마** a rainy season in early autumn in which it rains off and on.

**건듯** cursorily; hurriedly; quickly; hastily. ¶ 일을 ~ 해 치우다 make a quick job of it; get the work out of the way quickly.

**건듯건듯** briefly; cursorily. ¶ ~ 설명하다 explain briefly / ~ 읽다 glance over a letter.

**건등** 〚광산〛 the part of an ore vein near the surface.

**건땅** rich 〔fertile〕 soil.

**건락**(乾酪) cheese. ◉ ~소(素) casein.

**건랭**(乾冷) ~하다 (be) dry and cool. ¶ ~한 곳에 두다 keep 《*a thing*》 in a cool and dry place; keep 《*a thing*》 in the cool shade free from moisture / ~한 곳에 보관하시오 《게시》 Store in a cool, dry place.

**건량**(乾量) dry measure.

**건류**(乾溜) 〚화학〛 dry distillation; carbonization (석탄의). ~하다 dry (up) by distillation; carbonize.

**건립**(建立) erecting; building; establishment. ~하다 erect; build; set up; establish. ¶ ~중이다 be under construction; be in course of erection.

**-건만, -건마는** even though; although; however; but; while. ¶ 최선을 다 했건마는 실패했다 I did my best, however, I failed. *or* He failed, for all his efforts. / 나는 그를 사랑하건만 그는 나를 좋아하지 않는다 Although I love him, he does not care for me. / 형은 돈이 많건만 내겐 없다 While my brother has lots of money, I have none. / 그 친구 돈은 많건마는 그다지 행복하지는 못하다 He is none the happier for his wealth.

**건망증**(健忘症) forgetfulness; a short memory; a loss 〔slip, lapse〕 of memory; 〖의학〗 amnesia (병명). ¶ 어쩌면 ~이 이렇게 심할까 How forgetful I am! / 그는 ~이 심하다〔있다〕 He is forgetful. *or* He has a short 〔poor〕 memory.

**건면**(乾麵) 《말린》 dried noodles; 《요리하지 않은》 uncooked 〔raw〕 noodles.

**건목** a rough job 〔thing〕; rough-finishing an article; a rough-finished article. ~치다 《나무를》 cut (trees) into timber; 《일을》 do a rough job of 《it》; rough-finish 《it》.

**건목**(乾木) dried timber.

**건몸달다** get all heated up 「to no avail 〔for nothing〕; run madly about to no purpose; sweat 〔struggle〕 in vain; fret and fume; go off in vain pursuit(s). ¶ 그는 그녀에게 건몸달아 있다 He is mad about her in vain.

**건물**(建物) a building; a structure; 《큰 건물》 an edifice. ¶ 높은 ~ a tall 〔high〕 building / 르네상스 풍의 훌륭한 ~ a fine specimen of Renaissance architecture / 세계 최고(最古)의 목조 ~ the oldest wooden structure in the world / 동양 최대의 ~ the largest structure in the Orient / 새 교사는 아주 견고한 ~이다 The new school building is a very solid construction. ◉ ~유지비 building maintenance expenses.

**건물**(乾物) dry foods 〔provisions〕; groceries. ◉ ~상 《상점》 a grocery (store) 《미》; a grocer's (shop); a drysaltery 《영》; 《상인》 a grocer; a drysalter.

**건물로**(乾—) 《까닭없이》 without knowing why; without good reason; blindly; 《쓸데없이》 uselessly; in vain; 《힘 안 들이고》 without effort; easily.

**건반**(鍵盤) a keyboard; a clavier; a manual (오르간의). ◉ ~악기 keyboard instruments; a clavier. ~음악 keyboard music.

**건반사**(腱反射) 〖생리〗 a tendon reflex.

**건밤** a sleepless night. ¶ ~(을) 새우다 pass a sleepless night.

**건방지다** (be) (self-)conceited; impertinent; impudent; cocky; forward; fresh; saucy; pert (주로 여성이). ¶ 건방진 대답 a pert answer; a saucy reply / 건방진 계집애 a saucy 〔pert〕 young girl / 건방진 녀석 an impertinent 〔insolent〕 fellow; a cocky guy / 건방진 태도 an impudent attitude / 건방지게도 …하다 have the cheek 〔face, impertinence〕 to *do* / 건방지게 굴다 behave impertinently; act fresh / 건방진 수작을〔소리를〕 하다 talk fresh; give 《*a person*》 cheek 〔some lip〕; be full of lip / 건방진 수작 마라 None of your lip 〔impudence, cheek〕. *or* Don't be so fresh. *or* Don't be smart with me 《미구어》. / 정말 건방지구나 What a cheek!

**건배**(乾杯) a toast. ~하다 drink a toast 《in honor of *a person*》; drink 《*a person's* health》; toast 〔drink to〕 《*a person*》. ¶ ~를 제의하다 propose a toast 《to》 / ~ Bottoms up! *or* Toast! *or* Cheers! / 자, 그녀의 건강〔성공〕을 위해 ~합시다 Let's drink to her health 〔success〕. 「⇨ 건의(建議).

**건백**(建白) a petition; representations.

**건빵**(乾—) hardtack; a cracker 《미》; a (hard) biscuit 《영》.

**건사하다** ① 《보살피다》 take care of; look after; attend on. ¶ 어린애를 ~ take care of *one's* child. ② 《간수하다》 keep carefully; put aside carefully. ¶ 물건을 건사해 두다 put 《*a thing*》 aside 〔away〕 carefully 〔for future use〕 / 그것은 내가 건사하고 있다 I have it in my custody 〔keeping〕. ③ 《일을 처리하다》 manage; supervise; direct; deal 〔cope〕 with; 《준비하다》 make arrangements 《for》; arrange 《for》. ¶ 집안일을 ~ manage the household affairs / 장례를 ~ direct funeral service; take charge of a funeral.

**건삼**(乾蔘) a dried ginseng (with its fibrils cut off).

**건선**(乾癬) 〖의학〗 《마른 버짐》 psoriasis; scaly tetter.

**건선거**(乾船渠) ⇨ 건식 선거.

**건설**(建設) construction; building; erection; establishment (설립). ~하다 construct; build; erect; establish. ¶ ~적(인) constructive 《opinion》 / ~적으로 《discuss》 constructively / ~중이다 be under construction / 복지 국가를 ~하다 establish 〔build up〕 a welfare state / 이 마을에 댐이 ~될 예정이다 A dam is going to be 「constructed 〔built〕 in this village. / 지금 시내 중심가에 90층짜리 고층빌딩이 ~되고 있다 A ninety-story high-rise building is now being built 〔under construction〕 in the center of the city. / 좀 더 ~적인 의견을 주실 수 없겠습니까 Can't you offer 〔deliver〕 more constructive opinion 〔idea〕?
◉ ~계획 a construction plan 〔project〕. ~공사 construction work. ~교

통부 the Ministry of Construction & Transportation: ～교통부 장관 the Minister of Construction & Transportation. ～비 construction costs 〔expenses〕. ～업 the construction 〔building〕 industry: ～업자 a building contractor. ～용지 a building lot 〔plot, site〕. ～자 《건물 등의》 a constructor; a builder; 《창설자》 a founder. ～장비 construction machinery 〔equipment〕. ～현장 a construction site 〔field〕. ～회사 a construction company 〔firm〕. 한국 ～협회 the Construction Association of Korea.

**건성** absent-mindedness; half-heartedness; [부사적] absent-mindedly; vacantly; inattentively; halfheartedly. ¶～으로 듣다 listen to 《*a person*》 「absent-mindedly 〔inattentively〕; pay almost no attention to 《*a person's*》 talk / ～으로 대답하다 answer in a half-hearted way / ～으로 덤벼들다 try to do 《*a thing*》 without knowing anything about it / ～으로 분주하게 돌아다니다 be busy running about for nothing / 그는 내 말을 ～으로 듣고 있었다 He paid little attention to what I said. / 내가 ～으로 여기에 와 있는 줄 아느냐 Do you think I am here without any purpose? ◉ ～꾼 a rash person; a man who never thinks before he leaps.

**건성**(乾性) dryness. ¶～의 dry. ◉ ～늑막염 dry pleurisy. ～유 drying oil. ～피부 (a) dry skin.

**건성건성** in a casual 〔superficial, desultory, hit-or-miss, catch-as-catch=can〕 way. ¶일을 ～ 해치우다 get *one's* work done in a casual 〔hit-or-miss〕 way / …을 ～하다 do 《*a thing*》 in a slipshod way.

**건수**(件數) the number of items 〔cases〕. ¶도난～ the number of cases of theft / 취급～ the number of cases handled / 교통사고～ the number of traffic accidents.

**건수**(乾水) a temporary spring giving water only during the rainy season.

**건습**(乾濕) dryness and moisture; (degree of) humidity. ◉ ～계 a wet and dry bulb hygrometer 〔thermometer〕; a psychrometer.

**건승**(健勝) (good) health. ¶～을 빕니다 I wish you good health. *or* 《건배하며》 (To) your health! *or* Good health!

**건시**(乾柹) a dried persimmon. ¶～나 감이나 They are practically the same.

**건식선거**(乾式船渠) a dry dock. ¶～에 넣다 dry-dock.

**건실**(健實) steadiness; steadfastness; soundness; reliableness. ～하다 (be) steady; steadfast; sound; solid; reliable. ¶～한 사업〔투자〕 a sound enterprise 〔investment〕 / 사업을 ～하게 하다 do business on a sound basis.

**건아**(健兒) a vigorous youth 〔boy〕. ◉ 대한 ～ a virile son of Korea.

**건어**(乾魚), **건어물**(乾魚物) dried fish; stockfish(간을 안한).

**건울음** shedding false 〔sham〕 tears; make-believe crying. ¶～ 울다 pretend to weep; shed crocodile 〔false, sham〕 tears; feign weeping.

**건원**(建元) 『역사』 establishment as the name of an era; naming an era. ～하다 establish as the name of an era.

**건위**(健胃) a strong stomach; making *one's* stomach strong. ～하다 make digestion 〔*one's* stomach〕 strong. ◉ ～정 a peptic tablet. ～제 a digestive; a stomachic; a peptic.

**건육**(乾肉) dried meat; jerky.

**건으로**(乾—) 《공연히》 for no reason; without cause; 《맨손으로》 empty=handed; with empty hands. ¶～ 장사를 시작하다 start a business with practically no capital.

**건의**(建議) 《제의》 a proposal; a suggestion; 《진언·건백》 a memorial 《to the government》. ～하다 propose; make a proposal; suggest; 《진언하다》 memorialize; present a memorial 《to》. ¶한 씨의 ～로 on Mr. Han's proposal 〔motion〕 / 그 ～는 많은 표 차로 채택〔부결〕되었다 The proposal was 「adopted 〔defeated〕 by a large majority. / 우리는 도지사에게 새 교량의 건설을 ～했다 We 「memorialized 〔presented a memorial to〕 the Governor for the construction of a new bridge. ◉ ～서 a proposal; 『법』 a memorial. ～안 a proposition: 대정부 ～안 a proposition 〔recommendation〕 to the government. ～자 a proposer. ～함 a suggestion box.

**건잠머리하다** provide necessary informations and means to do the job.

**건장하다**(健壯—) (be) sturdy; strong; healthy; robust; stalwart. ¶건장한 체격의 《a man》 with 〔of〕 strong 〔good〕 physique 〔build, constitution〕 / 건장한 젊은이 a robust young man.

**건재**(健在) being well. ～하다 be well; be in good health 〔condition, shape〕.

¶ 양친께서는 ～하시다 Both of my parents are「in good health〔alive and well〕. / 그녀는 90세이지만 아직 ～하다 She's ninety and is still going strong.

**건재**(建材) building〔construction〕materials. ◉ ～상《상점》a building materials store;《상인》a building materials dealer.

**건재**(乾材) dried medicinal herbs. ◉ ～약국 a wholesale medicinal-herb store.

**건전**(健全) healthiness; soundness. ～하다 (be) healthy; sound; wholesome. ¶ ～한 발달 sound development〔growth〕/ ～한 사상 wholesome ideas / ～한 상식 sturdy〔hard〕common sense / ～한 읽을거리 healthy〔wholesome〕reading / ～한 경제 풍토 a sound economic climate / ～한 오락 healthy amusement〔recreation〕/ ～한 판단 sound judgment / ～한 생활을 하다 live a healthy, sensible life / ～한 정신은 ～한 신체에 깃든다 A sound mind (dwells) in a sound body. ◉ ～재정 sound finance; a healthy〔balanced〕budget (예산). ～통화 sound currency.

**건전지**(乾電池)《replace》a dry cell〔battery〕.

**건제**(乾製) preparing dry. ～하다 prepare dry.

**건조**(建造) construction; building. ～하다 construct; build. ¶ ～중이다 be「under〔in course of〕construction;《선박이》be on the stocks《at》/ 이 조선소에서는 지금 유조선을 ～중이다 We are building〔making, constructing〕a tanker in this shipyard. ◉ ～계획 a construction〔building〕plan. ～물 a building; a structure; a construction.

**건조**(乾燥) dryness; drying. ～하다 [형용사적] be〔become〕dry〔parched〕; arid (땅이); [동사적] dry (up); season (목재가); desiccate. ¶ (이상) ～주의보 a dry-weather warning〔alert〕/ 잘 ～된 목재 well-seasoned wood / ～한 데 둘 것《표시》Keep dry. *or* Must be kept dry. / 공기가 매우 ～하다 The air is exceedingly dry. ◉ ～기(期) the dry season. ～기〔장치〕drier; a drying machine. ～냉동법 dehydrofreezing. ～식품 dried〔dehydrated〕foods. ～실 a drying room; a drying oven (도자기의). ～야채 dehydrated vegetables. ～제 desiccant. ～증〖의학〗xerosis. ～지 dry land: ～지 농업 dry farming. ～지대 an arid region. ～혈장〖의학〗dried plasma.

**건주정**(乾酒酊) feigned drunkenness. ～하다 feign drunkenness; pretend to be drunk.

**건지** a plumb〔sounding〕line (to test the depth of water).

**건지다** ①《물에서》pick up; take〔bring〕out of water. ¶ 시체를 ～ bring a dead body to the land / 물에 빠진 시계를 건져내다 pick up a watch sunk in the water / 뜰채로 물고기를 건져내다 scoop fish with a landing net.
②《위험·어려움에서》save〔rescue〕《*a person*》from《danger, death》; help《*a person*》out of《a difficulty》; relieve《*a person*》from《suffering》;《죄에서》redeem〔reclaim, save〕《*a person*》from《a life of sin》. ¶ (간신히) 목숨을 ～ have〔make〕a narrow escape from death / 물에 빠진 사람을 ～ rescue a drowning person; rescue《*a person*》from drowning / 의사는 그 소녀의 생명을 건졌다 The doctor saved the girl's life. / 암의 조기 발견으로 나는 목숨을 건졌다 Early discovery saved my life from cancer. / 그는 이미 죄의 구렁에서 건져낼 수 없는 사람이다 He is past〔beyond〕redemption. / 경제적인 곤경에서 너를 건질 수 있는 사람은 나 뿐이다 I'm the only person who can help you out of financial difficulties.
③《손해를》recover; retrieve; take〔get〕《*something*》back; regain. ¶ 손해본 것을 ～ recover a loss / 회사는 그 제품의 개발 비용을 1년 내에 건지려고 한다 The company tries to recover the cost of developing the product within a year. / 그녀는 파산 직전에 있던 회사로부터 그녀의 대출금을 건질 수 있었다 She was able to get back her loan from the company which was on the brink of bankruptcy.

**건책**(建策) suggestion; advice. ～하다 suggest a plan; make suggestion.

**건천**(乾川) a stream that dries up during spells of dry weather; a dry stream.

**건초**(乾草) hay; dried grass〔herb〕. ◉ ～더미 a haycock; a haystack (큰 것). ～열〖의학〗hay fever.

**건축**(建築)《건조》construction; building; erection;《건축물》a building; a structure; architecture [총칭]. ～하다 build; construct; erect; set〔put〕up. ¶ 현대 ～ modern architecture / ～상의 architectural / 르네상스 양식의 ～ a specimen of Renaissance architecture / 한국에서 가장 오래된 목조〔콘크리

트] ~(물) the oldest wooden [concrete] building in Korea / 이것은 그리스 ~의 걸작이다 This is a masterpiece of Greek architecture. / 그의 전공은 ~이다 His field is architecture. / 지금 여러 곳에서 아파트 ~이 진행중이다 Apartments are now being built all over the place.

◉ ~가 an architect; 한국 ~가 협회 the Korea Association of Architects. ~공사 construction work. ~공학 architectural engineering. ~기사 a building engineer; an architect. ~물 a building; a structure. ~법규 the building code. ~부지 a building [housing] lot. ~비 construction [building] costs [expenses]. ~사(士) a registered [qualified] architect. ~사(史) (a) history of 《Korean》 architecture; an architectural history 《of Korea》. ~설계 architectural design: ~설계 사무소 an architectural designer's office. ~양식 a style of architecture [building]. ~업 building industry: ~업자 a builder; 《도급업자》 a building contractor. ~자금 a building [construction] fund. ~자재 building [construction] materials. ~학[술] architecture. ~허가(서) a building [construction] permit: ~허가가 나오다 be given a construction permit. ~회사 a building company. 평당 ~가격 the per-*p'yong* construction cost.

**건투**(健鬪) a good [brave] fight; 《노력》 strenuous efforts. ~하다 fight well [bravely]; fight [put up] a good fight; 《노력하다》 make strenuous efforts. ¶ 우리 팀은 ~했지만 결승에서 패했다 Our team made a good fight, but was defeated in the finals. / ~를 빕니다 We wish you good luck.

**건판**(乾板) 〖사진〗 a dry (photographic) plate; 〖인쇄〗 a gelatin dry plate.

**건평**(建坪) floor space [area]; floorage. ¶ ~이 30평이다 have a floor space of 30 *p'yŏng* in all / ~ 25평의 아파트 an apartment with a floor space of 25 *p'yŏng*.

**건폐율**(建蔽率) the building-to-land ratio; building coverage.

**건포**(乾布) a dry towel. ¶ ~ 마찰을 하다 have a rubdown with a dry towel.

**건포**(乾脯) dried meat [fish].

**건포도**(乾葡萄) raisins; currants (씨 없는). ¶ ~가 든 케이크 a raisin cake.

**건필**(健筆) a good [facile] pen; vigorous writing. ¶ ~을 휘두르다 wield a facile [powerful] pen. ◉ ~가 a prolific writer.

**건함**(建艦) naval construction; building warships. ~하다 build warships.

**걷다**[1] ① 《덮인·가린·늘어진 것을》 remove; take away; take off. ¶ 상보를 ~ take the tablecloth off / 빨래를 ~ remove the laundry from a clothes-line; gather up the laundry.

② 《말다·개키다》 gather up; fold up; roll up; tuck up. ¶ 자리를 ~ fold up a mat / 커튼을 ~ open the curtains; 《옆으로》 draw aside a curtain; 《위로》 gather up a curtains / 셔츠 소매를 걷어 올리다 hitch [roll] up the shirt sleeves / 바짓자락을 걷어 올리다 roll up *one's* trouser legs / 옷자락을 걷어 올리고 내를 건너다 wade across a stream with *one's* skirt tucked up.

③ 《치우다》 remove; take away; take off; 《천막·돛 따위를》 take [pull] down; strike. ¶ 간판을 ~ remove the shop sign / 천막을 ~ strike a tent; break camp / 돛을 ~ take in [furl] sailes / 기를 ~ take [pull] down a flag.

④ 《일 따위를》 settle 《*a matter*》; bring 《*a matter*》 to a conclusion. ¶ 일을 ~ settle *one's* affairs.

**걷다**[2] 《걸음을》 go on foot; walk 《미》; stride (성큼성큼); totter (비실비실); 《으스대며》 strut; swagger. ¶ 아장아장 ~ toddle; waddle / 비틀비틀 ~ walk with faltering steps; stagger along; hobble along / 터벅터벅 ~ plod along; trudge along; shuffle / 거리를 ~ walk along the street / 걸어서 귀가하다 walk home; go home on foot / 걸어서 돌아다니다 walk around [about 《영》] / 걷게 되다 《어린애가》 start 「walking [to walk]; (환자가) find [get back on] *one's* feet; start to walk again / 역까지 걸어서 10분 걸린다 It is 「ten minutes' [a ten-minute] walk to the station. / 학교에서 내내 걸어왔느냐 Did you walk all the way from your school? / 나는 걸어서 학교에 다닌다 I walk to school. *or* I go to school on foot. / 그 건물은 걸어서 쉽게 갈 수 있는 곳에 있다 The building is within easy walking distance. / 여기서 우체국까지는 걸어서 몇 분 걸리느냐 How many minutes does it take to walk from here to the post office? / 곧 일어나서 걸어다니게 될 것이다 You will soon be up and walk around again. / 나는 차를 타는 것보다 걷는 것이 더 좋다 I prefer walking to driving. / 너는 회사까지 걸어서 가느냐

버스로 가느냐 Do you go to your company on foot or by bus?

**걷어붙이다** roll 〔tuck〕 up. ¶ 셔츠의 소매를 ~ roll 〔tuck〕 up the sleeves of *one's* shirt / 걷어 붙인 소매를 내리다 roll down *one's* sleeves.

**걷어잡다** hold up. ¶ 치맛자락을 ~ hold up (the ends of) *one's* skirt.

**걷어차다** kick hard; give a hard kick 《to》. ¶ 정강이를 ~ give 《*a person*》 a hard kick on the shin / 문을 걷어차 열다 kick the door open / 자리를 걷어차고 나가다 storm indignantly out of the room / 상자를 걷어차서 뒤집어 엎다 kick the box over / 공을 필드 밖으로 ~ kick the ball out of the field.

**걷어채다** be kicked (hard); get a (hard) kick. ¶ 옆구리〔배〕를 ~ get a kick in the side 〔belly〕.

**걷어치우다** ① 《치우다》 put away; clear away; put in order. ¶ 흩어진 물건을 ~ clear away littered 〔scattered〕 things / 이부자리를 ~ put away the bedding. ② 《일을》 leave off; stop; wind 〔give〕 up. ¶ 하던 일을 ~ stop doing a job; leave off *one's* work / 장사를 ~ wind up a business; give up business / 가게를 ~ shut up 〔close down〕 *one's* store / 사업을 걷어치우고 시골로 가다 give up *one's* business and go to the country.

**-걷이** harvesting; gathering. ¶ 가을~ autumn harvest / 가을 ~가 끝나면 추수감사절이 온다 When the autumn harvest is finished there will be Thanksgiving Day.

**걷잡다** hold; stay; stop; 《쓰러지는 것을 붙잡다》 hold; keep 《*something*》 from falling down; stop; 《억제하다》 control; check; restrain; keep 《*something*》 under control; take measures to keep down. ¶ 걷잡을 수 없는 uncontrollable / 걷잡을 새 없이 very quickly; before you know it / 걷잡을 수 없는 혼란에 빠지다 get into uncontrollable confusion / 눈물이 걷잡을 수 없이 흘렀다 I couldn't keep back my tears. / 그는 격렬한 감정을 걷잡을 수 없었다 He couldn't control his strong emotion.

**걷히다** ① 《구름·안개》 be lifted 〔dispelled〕; be cleared off; be broken away. ¶ 구름이 바람에 ~ the cloud is dispelled by the wind / 안개가 걷히니 멀리 있는 산들의 아름다운 모습이 드러났다 The fog cleared up and we were given a magnificent view of the distant mountains. ② 《곡식·돈 따위》 be gathered; be collected. ¶ 나락이 ~ crops are gathered / 돈이 ~ money is collected / 돈이 잘 걷히지 않는다 The result of collecting money is far from satisfactory.

**걸** a girl. ◉ ~ 프렌드 a girl friend.

**걸객**(乞客) a beggar (dressed decently); a hanger-on.

**걸걸거리다** behave greedily; be greedy 「〔gluttonous〕.

**걸걸하다**(傑傑—) (be) open(-hearted); candid; cheerful; bright(-spirited). ¶ 걸걸한 남자 an open-hearted man.

**걸귀**(乞鬼) 《암퇘지》 a mother hog; a sow that littered; 《식탐하는 사람》 a glutton; a gormandizer. ¶ ~ 들린 gluttonous; voracious / ~같이〔들린 듯이〕 먹다 eat voraciously.

**걸근거리다** ① 《욕심내다》 covet; feel an inordinate longing for something which belongs to another. ¶ 남의 것을 먹고 싶어 ~ covet another's possession. ② 《목구멍이》 be scratchy; be tickled with phlegm. ¶ 목이 ~ have a scratchy throat.

**걸근걸근** 《욕심이 나서》 covetously; greedily; 《목구멍이》 scratchily; ticklishly; having a frog in *one's* throat.

**걸기**(傑氣) a heroic temper; a sturdy spirit. ¶ ~있는 of a heroic temper.

**걸기대**(乞期待) 《게시》 Coming soon! (영화 선전 등에서).

**걸기질** leveling a rice paddy. ~하다 level 〔rake〕 a rice paddy.

**걸까리지다** (be) big; burly; husky.

**걸다**[1] ① 《땅이》 (be) rich; fertile. ¶ 건 땅 rich soil / 땅이 ~ the soil is rich 〔fertile〕 / 땅을 걸게 하다 make soil fertile; fertilize soil.

② 《액체가》 (be) thick; heavy. ¶ 건 죽 thick gruel / 이 수프는 너무 ~ This soup is too thick.

③ 《솜씨가》 (be) dexterous; skillful; [서술적] be a good hand at; have a good hand with. ¶ 정원 가꾸는 손이 ~ have a green thumb / 그는 손이 걸어서 도박해도 잃는 일이 없다 With his lucky hand, he never loses a gamble.

④ 《식성이》 (be) gluttonous; greedy; omnivorous. ¶ 입이 ~ be apt to mouth any odd thing / 그는 입이 걸어 아무 것이나 잘 먹는다 He is such a glutton he will eat anything. *or* He is not particular 〔fastidious〕 about what he eats.

⑤ 《말이》 (be) foulmouthed; abusive. ¶ 입이 건 사람 a foulmouthed fellow /

입이 건 여자 a fishwife / 그는 입이 걸어 남의 욕을 잘한다 His mouth breeds ready slander. *or* He is always ready to say something bad about someone. ⑥《먹을 것이》(be) heavy; rich; sumptuous. ¶ 잔치가 ~ It is a sumptuous 〔rich〕 feast.

**걸다**[2] ①《매달다》suspend; hang; hook (고리에). ¶ 모자를 못에 ~ hang 〔hook〕 *one's* hat on a peg / 간판을 ~ put 〔hang〕 up a signboard / 문패를 ~ put up a nameplate (at the gate) / 옷걸이에 코트를 ~ put a coat on the hanger / 그림을 눈 높이에 ~ hang a picture on the line.

②《계약금을》pay; deposit; advance; 《내기를》bet《on a horse》; bet 〔stake, put〕《₩10,000 on a horse》; wager; lay 〔have〕 a wager《on》. ¶ 계약금을 ~ pay 〔make〕 a 「deposit 〔down payment〕; place deposit money《on》/ 돈을 걸고〔걸지 않고〕 카드놀이를 하다 play cards 「for money 〔for love〕/ 있는 돈을 몽땅 ~ bet *one's* bottom dollar / 어느 팀이 이기는지 우리 2만원씩 걸자 Let's bet twenty thousand won on which team would win. / 그는 그가 좋아하는 말에 만 원을 걸었다 He bet 〔staked〕 ten thousand won on his favorite horse. / 그것에 10 달러를 걸겠다 I will wager ten dollars on it.

③《목숨·명예·재산 등을》stake; risk. ¶ 목숨을 걸고 싸우다 fight at the risk of *one's* life / 그는 그 사업에 전 재산을 걸었다 He staked all his fortune on that business. / 그는 선거 결과에 정치 생명을 걸었다 He staked his political future on the outcome of the election.

④《말을》speak 〔talk〕 to《*a person*》; address《*a person*》; accost《*a person*》; start conversation with《*a person*》. ¶ 농을 ~ play a joke on《*a person*》/ 거리에서 외국인이 말을 걸어왔다 A foreigner spoke to me on the street. *or* I was 「spoken to 〔addressed〕 by a foreigner on the street.

⑤《전화를》(tele)phone《*a person*》; call《*a person*》(up); make a (phone) call to《*a person*》; dial; ring《*a person*》(up)《영》. ¶ 회사에 전화를 ~ make a phone call to a company; telephone a firm / 나는 그녀에게 전화를 걸었다 I telephoned 〔phoned〕 her. *or* I called her (up). / 거기 도착하는 대로 전화를 걸어다오 Phone me 〔Give me a ring〕 as soon as you get there. / 112〔경찰〕에 전화를 걸어라 Dial 112 〔the police〕.

⑥《시비를》pick 〔seek〕《a quarrel》 with《*a person*》; provoke《*a person* to a quarrel》; challenge《*a person*》. ¶ 아무에게 시비를 ~ pick a quarrel with *a person;* provoke *a person* to a quarrel.

⑦《재판을》¶ 재판을 ~ put《a case》 on trial; take《*a matter*》 into court; bring《*a person*》 to justice; institute legal proceedings《against》.

⑧《함정·술책을》apply; use; lay《on》; set《to》. ¶ 올가미를 ~ lay a snare; set a trap / 다리를 ~ trip *a person.*

⑨《잠그다》lock; fasten; lock with; bar with. ¶ 대문을 ~ fasten 〔lock〕 the gate / 문에 자물쇠를 ~ fasten a door《with a lock》; lock the door / 대문에 빗장을 ~ bar 〔bolt〕 the gate.

⑩《희망을》¶ 희망을 ~ set *one's* hopes on《*a person*》; anchor 〔rest〕 *one's* hope《in, on》/ 아무의 장래에 기대를 ~ have trust in *a person's* future.

⑪《작용시키다》turn 〔switch〕 on《the radio》; start《the engine》 going. ¶ 시동을 ~ start an engine (going) / 제동을 ~ apply 〔put on〕 the brake / 개혁에 제동을 ~ put a brake on reform / 최면술을 ~ mesmerize; hypnotize; exercise a mesmeric power over.

⑫《상금 등을》offer《a prize for》; put 〔set〕《a price on *a person's* head》. ¶ 상금을 건 경쟁 a prize competition.

⑬《국기 등을》hoist 〔put up〕《a flag》; hang out《a large sign》.

**걸대** a bamboo 〔reaching〕 pole used in hanging something up high.

**걸때** the size of the body; frame. ¶ ~가 크다 have a large body; be bulky.

**걸뜨다** float under the water.

**걸러** skipping; at intervals; apart. ¶ 십 분 ~ at 10-minute intervals / 하루 ~ every other day / 이틀 ~ every third day; every three days / 한 줄 ~ 쓰다 write on every other line.

**걸러뛰다** skip; leave out; omit. ¶ 다섯 페이지를 ~ skip five pages / 이야기의 재미없는 대목을 ~ skip the dull part of a story.

**걸레** ① a dustcloth; a rag; 《마른 것》a duster; 《마루용》a floorcloth; 《자루걸레》a mop; 《갑판용》a swab. ~치다 wipe with a (damp) cloth; mop《the floor》; swab《the deck》. ¶ 마른 ~ a dry duster / 물~ a damp 〔wet〕 cloth / 방바닥을 ~로 훔치다 wipe 〔mop〕 the floor / ~용 양동이 a mob bucket.

② = ～ 부정. ¶ ～ 같은 worthless.
◉ ～부정 《물건》 shabby 〔worthless〕 stuff; 《사람》 a good-for-nothing.

**걸레질** wiping; mopping; swabbing. ～하다 wipe; mop; swab. ¶ 마루를 깨끗이 ～하다 wipe 〔scrub〕 the floor clean with a damp cloth.

**걸리다**[1] ① 《매어 달리다》 be hung; be hooked; be suspended 《on, from》; hang. ¶ 모자가 못에 걸려 있다 A hat is hang on a peg. / 연이 나뭇가지에 걸려 있다 A kite is hanging from a branch. / 벽에 달력이 걸려 있었다 A calendar was hanging on the wall.
② 《하늘에 걸리듯하다》 ¶ 달이 동쪽 하늘에 걸려 있다 The moon hangs in the eastern sky. / 산꼭대기에 구름이 걸려 있다 A cloud hangs over the summit of a mountain.
③ 《돈·생명이》 be deposited 《as a guarantee》; be bet; be staked. ¶ 목숨이 걸린 문제 a life-and-death matter; a matter of life and death / 큰 돈이 ～ big money is at stake / 우리 나라의 국운이 걸려있다 Our national destiny is at stake.
④ 《전화가》 a (phone) call is made; get through; be connected. ¶ 전화가 걸려 오다 be called up; be wanted on the phone / 전화가 안 걸렸어요 I did not get my call through.
⑤ 《술책·함정 따위에》 be caught; be trapped; be cheated. ¶ 덫에 ～ be ensnared 〔entrapped〕; fall into a trap / 쥐가 덫에 ～ a rat is trapped / 책략에 ～ fall into a trap; be caught in the wiles 《of》 / 사기에 ～ be swindled; fall a victim to fraud.
⑥ 《목·장애물에》 be caught 《in, on》; get stuck; be stuck (목구멍에). ¶ 돌에 걸려 넘어질 뻔하다 stumble 〔trip〕 on 〔over〕 a stone / 바지가 가시 철망에 ～ *one's* trousers 〔pants〕 get caught on barbed wire / 가시가 목에 ～ have 〔get〕 a bone stuck in *one's* throat; have a bone (caught) in the throat / 방에서 뛰어나가다가 의자에 걸렸다 In rushing out of the room I tripped against a chair. / 가시덤불에 옷이 걸렸다 A bramble has caught my coat. / 연이 전깃줄에 걸렸다 The kite got caught on an electric line.
⑦ 《잡히다》 be caught. ¶ 물고기가 그물에 ～ fish is caught in a net / 잠자리가 거미줄에 ～ a dragonfly is 〔gets〕 caught in a spider's web / 물건을 훔치려다가 경찰관에게 ～ be caught at the act of filching a thing by a policeman.
⑧ 《법 따위에》 be against 《a law》. ¶ 법망에 ～ fall into the meshes 〔clutches〕 of the law / 세관 검사에 ～ fail to pass the customs examination / 그는 주차 위반으로 걸렸다 He got pinched for parking violation. / 그는 법망에 걸렸다 He was caught by the law 〔in the clutches of the law〕.
⑨ 《병에》 be attacked 〔seized, afflicted〕 with; contract; catch; suffer from. ¶ 병에 ～ fall ill; be taken ill / 감기에 ～ catch 〔get〕 (a) cold / 폐병에 걸려 죽다 die of tuberculosis / 감기에 걸리기 쉽다 be susceptible to cold / 그는 갑자기 열병에 걸렸다 He was suddenly taken ill with fever. / 그는 중병에 걸려 있다 He is suffering from a serious illness.
⑩ 《시간이》 take. ¶ 시간이 ～ it takes time / 그 책을 읽는 데 사흘 걸렸다 It took me three days to read the book. / 학교까지 몇분 걸리느냐 How many minutes does it take to get to the school? / 걸어서 10분 걸린다 It's ten minutes' walk from here. / 그 일을 마치는 데 나흘이나 걸렸다 It took me no less than four days to finish the work.
⑪ 《관계하다》 be involved 〔implicated〕 in; be entangled 《with》. ¶ 사건에 ～ be implicated in an affair / 나쁜 여자에게 ～ get entangled with a bad woman / 그 장관은 부정 사건에 걸려 있다 The minister is involved in the scandal.
⑫ 《잠기다》 be locked 〔fastened〕; 《빗장이》 be barred; catch. ¶ 빗장이 ～ a bolt catches 〔is barred〕 / 문이 ～ the door is fastened 〔locked〕.
⑬ 《작동되다》 work; start. ¶ 시동이 ～ start / 제동이 ～ the brake is put on / 엔진이 잘 걸리지 않는다 The engine does not start well.
⑭ 《마음에》 worry; weigh. ¶ 마음에 ～ weigh on 〔upon〕 *one's* mind; *one* feels uneasy about; be anxious about; be concerned / 그 일이 자꾸 마음에 걸린다 That worries me. *or* That weighs heavy on my mind. / 그녀의 건강이 몹시 마음에 걸린다 I'm much concerned about her health.

**걸리다**[2] 《걷게 하다》 make 《*a person*》 walk; make 《*a person*》 go on foot; walk 《*a person*》; 〚야구〛 walk a batter (사구로). ¶ 어린애에게 걸음을 ～ walk a child.

**걸림돌** a stumbling block; an obstacle. ¶ 높은 관세는 자유 무역의 큰 ～이다 High tariffs are the chief obstacles to free trade.

**걸망**(—網) a Buddhist monk's knapsack.

**걸맞다** 《양쪽이》 (be) well-mated; well-matched; well-met; nicely paired; well-balanced; 《어울리다》 suitable 《for》; suited 《for, to》; fit 《for》; becoming; proper 《for》. ¶ 걸맞는 부부 a well-paired couple; a well-matched pair / 걸맞지 않은 부부 an ill-matched couple / 걸맞은 혼인 a well-met marriage / 걸맞지 않은 혼인 an ill-advised marriage / 신분에 걸맞게 살다 live within *one's* means / 그는 교사로서 걸맞지 않다 He is not suited to be a teacher. / 당신의 옷은 파티에 걸맞지 않다 Your dress is not suitable 〔good〕 for the party.

**걸머잡다** catch hold of; clutch at; grasp; seize. ¶ 머리채를 ～ grasp 《a woman》 by the hair / 목덜미를 ～ seize 《*a person*》 by the neck.

**걸머지다** ① 《짐·책임을》 carry on *one's* back; shoulder; bear. ¶ 짐을 멜빵으로 ～ strap a bundle on *one's* back / 중요한 임무를 ～ shoulder 〔take on〕 an important task / 책임을 ～ shoulder 〔bear〕 a responsibility / 죄를 혼자 ～ bear a blame alone / 그는 그 회사의 운명을 걸머지고 있다 He bears the destiny of the company on his shoulders. ② 《빚을》 contract 〔incur〕 a debt; run into debt; be in debt. ¶ 많은 빚을 ～ incur a welter of debts; run heavily into debt; be deep in debt.

**걸메다** shoulder; 《a gun》 strap 《a burden》 on *one's* shoulder.

**걸물**(傑物) a great man; an extraordinary 〔a great〕 character; a giant; a master spirit.

**걸상**(—床) a bench; a form (등받이 없는).

**걸쇠** ① 《문 거는》 a hasp; a latch; a door fastener. ¶ 문에 ～를 걸다 latch 〔hasp〕 a door; fasten a door / 문의 ～가 벗겨졌다 The door was unlatched 〔off the latch〕. ② ＝다리쇠.

**걸스카우트** the Girl Scouts; 《영》 the Girl Guides. ◉ ～단원 a girl scout; 《영》 a girl guide.

**걸식**(乞食) begging; mendicancy. ～하다 go begging; beg 《*one's* bread》. ¶ 문전～하다 beg from door to door / ～하며 살다 live as a beggar.

**걸신**(乞神) a hungry demon; a hunger; a greed. ～들리다 get possessed by a hungry demon; have a wolf in *one's* stomach; have a voracious appetite. ¶ ～들린 사람 a man greedy for food; a glutton / 음식에 ～(이) 들리다 get greedy for food / ～들린 듯이 먹다 eat greedily; eat like a hog 〔cormorant〕; wolf down. ◉ ～쟁이 a glutton; a gormandizer; a voracious person.

**걸싸다** (be) quick; brisk; prompt. ¶ 일에 ～ be quick in doing *one's* work.

**걸쌈스럽다** (be) unyielding; persistent; adamant.

**걸쌍스럽다** (be) hearty 〔charming, attractive〕 《in working, eating》.

**걸어가다** walk 《to》; go on foot; pace *one's* way 《to》. ¶ 시골길을 ～ walk along a country lane / 걸어갑시다 Let's walk it. / 아침마다 회사까지 걸어간다 I walk to the office 〔go to the office on foot〕 every morning. / 이 길을 걸어가면 역에 닿습니다 If you walk down 〔along〕 this way you will come to the railroad station.

**걸어오다** come on foot; 《다가오다》 walk 〔step〕 up 《to》. ¶ 집으로 ～ walk home / 낯선 사람이 내게로 걸어와서 길을 물었다 A stranger walked up to me to ask the way.

**걸어총**(—銃) 『군사』 a pile 〔stack〕 of arms; 《구령》 Pile 〔Stack〕 arms! ～하다 stack arms.

**걸우다** fertilize; manure; enrich 《the soil》. ¶ 밭을 ～ manure a field; make a field fertile.

**걸음** walking; a step; 《속도》 pace. ¶ 첫～ the first step / 빠른〔느린〕 ～ a quick 〔slow〕 pace / 한～ 한～ step by step; by degrees / 느긋한 ～으로 at an easy pace / 황소 ～으로 at a snail's pace / ～을 걷다 walk; go on foot / ～이 빠르다〔느리다〕 be swift 〔slow〕 of foot; be quick 〔slow〕 on *one's* legs / ～을 빨리〔느리게〕 걷다 go at quick 〔slow〕 pace / ～을 재촉하다 quicken *one's* pace / ～을 늦추다 relax *one's* pace / ～을 멈추다 stop walking / 한～ 나서다〔물러서다〕 take a step forward 〔backward〕 / 한～ 앞서다〔뒤지다〕 be a step ahead 〔behind〕 / 그는 갑자기 ～을 멈췄다 He came to a sudden stop. / 그 ～으로는 해질녘까지 목적지에 닿지 못하겠다 At your pace you can never reach your destination before dark. / 천릿길도 한～부터 To reach the top you must ascend step by step. ◉ ～새＝걸음걸이. ～짐작 pacing; measuring 《a distance》 by pace.

**걸음걸이** a 〔*one's*〕 walk; *one's* manner of walking; gait; pace. ¶ 묘한 ~로 걷다 walk with a queer gait / ~가 어색하다 have 〔walk with〕 an awkward gait / 나는 ~로 그를 알아볼 수 있다 I can recognize him by his walk.

**걸음나비** a step; a pace; a stride. ¶ ~가 길다〔짧다〕 walk with long 〔short〕 steps.

**걸음마** a toddle. ¶ ~를 하다 toddle; find *one's* feet / ~《아기에게》 Step firm! *or* Steady! Steady!

**걸음발타다** 《a baby》 try its feet; start to toddle; 《a toddler》 get its legs.

**-걸이** a hanger; a peg; a rack. ¶ 옷걸이 a clotheshanger / 모자걸이 a hat=rack / 팔걸이 an arm 〔elbow〕 rest.

**걸인**(乞人) a beggar; mendicant.

**걸작**(傑作) ① 《작품》 a masterpiece; a masterwork; great work. ¶ 이 그림은 샤갈의 ~이다 This is a Chagall at his best. *or* This is one of Chagall's best works. / 이것은 그의 일생의 ~이다 This is the crown of his life's work. ② 《언행의》 a ridiculous talk; funny behavior; 《사람》 a buffoon. ¶ 그 재담은 정말 ~이다 That pun is really capital. ◉ ~집 a collection of masterpieces.

**걸쩍거리다** be active; be a real "live wire"; be always ready and daring 《to do *something*》; never know a dull moment; be always on the jump 〔go〕.

**걸쩍걸쩍** actively; free-heartedly.

**걸쩍지근하다** 《먹새가》 (be) omnivorous; gluttonous; 《말이》 (be) foulmouthed; abusive.

**걸쭉하다** 《액체가》 (be) thick; heavy. ¶ 죽이 ~ The gruel is thick.

**걸차다** 《기름지다》 (be) very fertile; 〔rich, productive〕. ¶ 걸찬 땅 a fertile 〔productive〕 land; rich soil.

**걸채** a mat-like rack (put on a beast of burden); a loading 〔saddle〕 rack.

**걸쳐두다** suspend; hang up; leave 《*a matter*》 in suspense; leave 《*an affair*》 unsettled; leave hanging. ¶ 교섭을 걸쳐 두(고 결말을 짓지 않)다 leave a negotiation in suspension.

**걸출**(傑出) 《뛰어남》 prominence; eminence; excellence; 《사람》 a distinguished character; a master spirit (걸물). ~하다 (be) prominent; eminent; outstanding; distinguished; excel; stand out 《from, against》; outdo 《others》. ¶ 사업가 중에서 ~하다 be prominent among businessmen / 그는 정치가로서 어느 누구보다 ~하다 He towers above others as a statesman. / 그는 어학자로서 ~한 인물이다 He stands out as a linguistic scholar.

**걸치다** ① 《시간·공간적으로 미치다》 extend 《over》; range 《from A to B》; stretch; spread 《over》; cover; last (계속하다). ¶ 6개월에 걸쳐 over a six=month period / 월요일에서 금요일에 걸쳐 extending from Monday to Friday; Monday through Friday / 몇 해에 ~ extend over several years / 양대륙에 ~ stretch over two continents / 여러 차례에 걸쳐 강연하다 deliver a series of lectures / 수차례에 걸쳐 뇌물을 받다 receive a bribe in installments / 장장 3시간여에 걸쳐 강연하다 make a lecture (extending) over three hours. / 그의 지식은 다방면에 걸쳐 있다 His knowledge extends into many fields. ② 《…에 놓다》 put 《*a thing*》 on 〔over〕 《another》; span 《with》. ¶ 어깨에 손을 ~ put *one's* hand on another's shoulder / 책상에 다리를 ~ rest *one's* feet on a table top / 양다리를 ~ sit 〔stand〕 on the fence; play double / 벽에 사다리를 ~ put up a ladder against a wall.
③ 《입다》 throw on; slip on. ¶ 누더기를 걸치고 있다 be clad in rags / 외투를 ~ throw on an overcoat (over *one's* shoulders) / 급히 잠옷을 ~ slip on *one's* pajamas hurriedly / 몸에 실오라기 하나 걸치지 않다 be stark-naked.

**걸태질** raking in money 〔property〕 shamelessly. ~하다 rake in money 〔property〕 shamelessly.

**걸터듬다** grope 〔fumble〕 for.

**걸터앉다** sit astride 〔astraddle〕. ¶ 말 위에 ~ sit astride a horse; straddle a horse. 「〔ride〕 astride.

**걸터타다** 《말에》 straddle; mount; sit

**걸프** 〖지리〗 the Gulf. ¶ ~ 협력 회의 the Gulf Cooperation Council (생략 GCC). ◉ ~전(쟁) the Gulf war.

**걸핏하면** (too) often; frequently; as often as not. ¶ ~ 때리다 hit 《*a person*》 at the drop of a hat / ~ 성내다 get angry on the slightest provocation at trivial things / ~ …하다 be apt 〔prone, liable〕 to *do;* [사람이 주어] be inclined 〔disposed〕 to *do;* it (too) often happens that…. / 그는 ~ 갖고 올 물건을 잊고 온다 As often as not, he forgets to bring something. / 나는 ~ 소화불량에 걸린다 I am prone to indigestion. / 그녀는 이 핑계 저 핑계로 ~ 친정에 간다 She frequently goes

to her parents' home in some pretext or other.
**검**(劍) 《칼》 a sword; 《군도》 a saber; 《총검》 a bayonet; 《단검》 a dagger. ¶ 검을 차다〔빼다〕 wear 〔draw〕 a sword.
**검객**(劍客) a (master) swordsman; a fencer.
**검거**(檢擧) (an) arrest; 《일제 검거》 a roundup. ~하다 arrest; take up; round up 《a narcotics ring》. ¶ 일제 ~하다 make a wholesale roundup 《of》 / ~되다 get arrested / 독직〔선거법 위반〕으로 ~되다 be arrested 「for corruption in *one's* office 〔for violation of the election law〕/ 경찰은 데모대를 ~했다 The police arrested the demonstrators. / 다수의 마약 중독자가 ~되었다 A large number of drug addicts were arrested. *or* The police rounded up a large number of drug addicts. ◉ ~자 a person in custody.
**검경**(檢鏡) a microscopic examination 〔study〕; 《검사경》 a speculum (*pl.* -la). ◉ ~판 an object plate; a slide.
**검극**(劍戟) swords and spears; arms; weapons. ◉ ~물 a sword swinger.
**검극**(劍劇) a fighting play; a sword play. ◉ ~영화 an action film featuring sword fighting.
**검기다** blacken; soil.
**검뇨**(檢尿) urinalysis; urine analysis; uroscopy. ~하다 examine 《*a person's*》 urine; 《검뇨시키다》 have *one's* urine examined.
**검누렇다** be blackish yellow; be dark yellow.
**검누르다** be a dark yellow.
**검다** ① 《빛이》 (be) black; dark. ¶ 검은 머리 black hair / 검은 옷 a black robe 〔suit〕; (a suit of) black clothes / 검은 눈동자 dark eyes / 검은 점 a black spot / 검게 되다 become 〔get〕 black / 검게 타다 《볕에》 be 〔get〕 tanned 〔sunburnt〕/ 검게 하다 black; blacken; make 《*a thing*》 black / 검게 칠하다 paint 《*a thing*》 black / 얼굴이 ~ have a dark complexion; be dark-complexioned / 그녀는 검은 옷을 입고 있다 She is dressed in black. ② 《마음이》 (be) black-hearted; evil-minded; wicked. ¶ 속 검은 사람 a black-hearted person.
**검당계**(檢糖計) 〖화학〗 a saccharimeter.
**검댕** soot. ¶ ~투성이의 sooty; sooted; soot-laden / ~이 끼다〔앉다〕 become sooty 〔sooted〕; soot collects / ~이 묻다 be smeared 〔stained〕 with soot / ~을 털다 sweep away 〔wipe off〕 the soot / 난로의 ~을 없애다 clear the soot out of the fireplace.
**검덕귀신**(一鬼神) a person with a dirty looks 〔appearance〕.
**검도**(劍道) (the art of) fencing; swordsmanship. ¶ ~ 5단 a fencer of the fifth grade. ◉ ~도장〔사범〕 a fencing school 〔master〕.
**검둥개** a black dog. ¶ ~ 멱감듯 there is no improvement at all.
**검둥이** ① 《낯이 검은》 a dark-faced person; 《검게 탄》 a well tanned person; 《흑인》 a black 〔Black〕; a Negro (*pl.* ~es); a Nigress (여자); a colored 〔black〕 person; a darky 《구어》; a nigger 《경멸》. ② 《동물》 a blackie; a black dog; 《호칭》 Blackie.
**검뜯다** 《조르다》 pester; badger; importune.
**검량**(檢量) measuring; 《적화의》 metage. ◉ ~기 a gauging rod. ~세 metage.
**검룡**(劍龍) 〖고생물〗 a stegosaur.
**검루기**(檢漏器) 〖전기〗 a ground detector.
**검류계**(檢流計) 《전류》 a galvanometer.
**검류기**(檢流器) a galvanoscope.
**검무**(劍舞) a sword dance. ¶ ~를 추다 perform a sword dance.
**검문**(檢問) a check(-up) 《미》; (an) inspection. ~하다 check up; inspect; search. ¶ 통행인을〔자동차를〕 ~하다 check up passers-by 〔cars〕/ 교차로 바로 앞에서 ~을 받았다 Just before the crossing, we were ordered to stop for a check. / 뺑소니차가 ~에 걸렸다 The hit and run car was caught at a checkpoint. / 그 차는 ~을 뚫고 달아났다 The car broke through the check and ran away. ◉ ~소 a checkpoint.
**검박**(儉朴) = 검소(儉素).
**검버섯** dark spots (on an old person's skin); the skin discoloration of age; a blotch. ¶ 얼굴에 ~이 돋다 have blotches on *one's* face.
**검변**(檢便) examination of the feces; stool examination; 〖의학〗 scatoscopy. ~하다 examine *a person's* feces 〔stool〕; make a stool test 〔examination〕. ¶ ~용 변 a sample of feces.
**검부나무** dried grass 〔leaves〕 used for fuel.
**검부러기** remnants 〔bits, odd ends〕 of dry grass 〔leaves〕. ¶ 짚 ~ bits of straw.
**검분**(檢分) = 검사(檢査).
**검불** dry grass 〔leaves〕.
**검붉다** (be) blackish red; dark-red. ¶ 검붉은 장미 a dark-red rose.
**검사**(檢事) a (public) prosecutor; a prosecuting attorney 《미》; a public prosecutor 《영》. ¶ ~는 피고인에게 종신형을 구형하였다 The public pros-

ecutor proposed life imprisonment for the accused. ◉ ~장 the director of the 《Seoul District》 Prosecutors Office; a superintendent public prosecutor. ~직무 대리 a probational prosecutor.

**검사**(檢査) (an) inspection; (an) examination; a test; a check (간단한); checkup; 《기계 따위의》 an overhaul; 《회계의》 audit. ~하다 inspect; examine; test; overhaul; audit; check up 《미》; condition (생사·양모 따위를). ¶ ~를 받다 have 〔undergo〕 an examination; be inspected 〔examined〕 / 눈을 ~받다 have *one's* eyes tested / ~에 통과되지 않다 fail to pass the inspection; be rejected / 시력을 ~하다 test *a person's* eyesight / 성병을 ~하다 examine 《*a person*》 for venereal disease / ~필 《표시》 Inspected. *or* Checked. *or* O.K.; 《견사 따위의》 Conditioned. / 이 우물물은 수질 ~를 받아야 한다 The water of this well must be examined. / 입국하기 위해서는 세관 ~를 받아야 한다 We must undergo customs inspection when entering a country. / 이 기계는 ~에 합격할 수 있을까 Does this machine stand up to (pass) the test?
◉ ~관 《세관 따위의》 an inspector; an examiner; 《회계의》 an auditor. ~기 a tester. ~소 an inspecting office: 생사~소 a silk conditioning house / 국립농산물 ~소 the National Agricultural Products Inspection Center. ~증명서 an inspection certificate. ~필증 a certificate of (safety) inspection.
안전~ safety inspection. 위생~ a sanitary inspection: 위생과에서 식당에 위생~하러 나왔다 A health inspector came to the restaurant to examine its standard of hygiene. 자동차~ an automobile inspection.

**검산**(檢算) verification of accounts; checking. ~하다 check 〔go over, verify〕 *one's* accounts; 〖수학〗 prove. ¶ 답을 ~하다 prove *one's* answer.

**검색**(檢索) reference; 《수색》 (a) search. ~하다 refer to 《a dictionary》; look up 《a word in a dictionary》; search 《for》; make a search 《for》. ¶ ~에 편리하다 be easy 〔handy, convenient〕 of reference / 책명을 컴퓨터로 ~할 수 있게 되었다 The titles of books can now be searched for by computer.
◉ 컴퓨터~ 《run, do》 a computer search 《for》.

**검세다** (be) very tough; stubborn; unyielding; dogged.

**검소**(儉素) frugality; thrift; economy; simplicity. ~하다 (be) frugal; thrifty; economical; austere; simple; plain. ¶ ~한 생활 a frugal life / ~하게 simply; frugally; economically; in a frugal manner / 그는 ~한 사람이다 He is of simple tastes. / 그녀는 옷차림이 ~하다 She is dressed simply 〔plainly〕. / 결혼식은 가까운 친척만이 초대된 ~한 것이었다 The wedding was a simple one, to which only the immediate families were invited. / 그녀는 시골에서 ~하게 산다 She lives simply 〔plainly〕 in the country. *or* She lives a simple 〔plain〕 life in the country.

**검속**(檢束) (an) arrest; (a) detention; custody. ~하다 arrest; detain; take 《*a person*》 into custody; place 〔put〕 《*a person*》 under arrest. ¶ 경찰의 용의자 일제 ~ a police roundup of suspects. ◉ 보호~ (a) protective arrest.

**검수**(檢數) counting; (a) tally. ~하다 count; tally; take a count of goods. ◉ ~인 a tallyman; a checker.

**검술**(劍術) the art of fencing; swordsmanship. ¶ ~이 능하다〔서투르다〕 be a good 〔bad〕 swordsman.

**검시**(檢屍) a post-mortem (examination); an autopsy; a coroner's inquest; an inquest. (★ autopsy나 post-mortem은 시체를 해부하여 사인을 밝힘을 뜻하고, inquest는 autopsy 〔post-mortem〕의 결과로 얻어진 사인에 대한 심리를 뜻함.) ~하다 autopsy; examine a corpse; make an autopsy 《on》; hold an inquest 《over a corpse》. ¶ ~결과 교살로 판명되었다 After an autopsy, it was found that he had been strangled. ◉ ~관 a coroner; 《미》 medical examiner.

**검실거리다** glimmer; gleam faintly; flicker in the distance. ⇨ 감실거리다.

**검쓰다** (be) very bitter; be as bitter as gall.

**검안**(檢案) 〖법〗 examination. ~하다 examine. ¶ 시체를 ~하다 examine a corpse. ◉ ~서 a certificate of death; a death certificate.

**검안**(檢眼) an eye examination 〔test〕; optometry (시력계에 의한); ophthalmoscopy (검안경에 의한). ~하다 examine 《*a person's*》 eyes; 《시력을》 test 《*a person's*》 eyes 〔eyesight〕; 《검안받다》 have *one's* eyes examined. ◉ ~경 〖의학〗 an ophthalmoscope. ~법 ophthalmoscopy. ~의 an optometrist.

**검압기**(檢壓器) a pressure gauge; a

manometer (기체·액체의).

**검약**(儉約) economy; thrift; frugality. ~하다 economize 《on》; use 《energy》 carefully; be thrifty 〔frugal〕; save 《fuel》. ◉ ~가 a thrifty 〔frugal〕 person; an economizer.

**검역**(檢疫) quarantine; (a) medical inspection. ~하다 quarantine; inspect. ¶ ~을 받다 be quarantined / ~중이다 be in quarantine / ~을 마치다 be out of quarantine / 그 배는 입항하자 바로 ~을 받았다 The ship was quarantined immediately after it entered port.
◉ ~관 a quarantine officer. ~기간 a quarantine period. ~선 a quarantine ship; a lazaretto (*pl.* ~s). ~소 a quarantine station 〔office〕; a lazaretto (*pl.* ~s). ~증명서 a quarantine certificate. ~항(港) a quarantine port.

**검열**(檢閱) 《점검》 inspection; 《군대의》 a review; 《간행물·영화의》 censorship. ~하다 inspect; examine; review; censor. ¶ ~을 받다 be inspected; 《영화의》 be censored; be submitted for censorship / ~을 폐지하다 remove the censorship / ~을 필한 censored; released by censorship / ~에 통과하다〔걸리다〕 pass 〔fail to pass〕 censorship / 지난날 신문은 엄한 ~을 받았다 In past years the newspapers were strictly censored. / 이 영화는 ~을 필했다 This film has already been censored.
◉ ~관 《검사관》 an inspector; a censor: 영화 ~관 a film censor. ~제도 the censorship system. 신문~ press censorship.

**검영법**(檢影法) 〖안과〗 skiascopy; retinoscopy.

**검온**(檢溫) 〖의학〗 thermometry. ~하다 take 《*a person's*》 temperature.
◉ ~기 a clinical thermometer.

**검유**(檢乳) examination of milk.
◉ ~기 a lactoscope; a lactometer.

**검은깨** black sesame.

**검은방울새** 〖조류〗 a siskin.

**검은자위** the dark part of the eye; the iris.

**검은콩** a black soybean.

**검이경**(檢耳鏡) an auriscope 〔otoscope〕.

**검인**(檢印) a seal 〔stamp〕 of approval. ¶ ~을 찍다 put *one's* seal 〔stamp〕 of approval 《on》; affix a seal 〔stamp〕 (of approval) 《to》; seal (품질보증의) / 이 책에는 저자의 ~이 없다 This book does not have the author's seal. / ~필 《표시》 Approved and sealed.
◉ ~증 an approval certificate.

**검인정**(檢認定) =검정(檢定). ¶ 교육부 ~필 《표시》 Approved by the Ministry of Education.

**검전기**(檢電器) an electroscope; a rheoscope; 《누전의》 a detector.

**검정** black; black color. ¶ ~색의 black / ~ 저고리 a black coat.

**검정**(檢定) 《면허》 (an) official approval 〔sanction〕; 《검사》 (an) examination. ~하다 approve; authorize; give official approval 《to》; examine. ◉ ~교과서 a textbook approved by the Ministry of Education; an authorized textbook. ~료 an authorization fee; an official examination fee.

**검정고시**(檢定考試) qualification 〔license〕 examination. ¶ 대학 입학 자격 ~에 합격하다 pass the qualification examination for college entrance.
◉ 교원자격 ~ the examination for the license of school teachers.

**검조의**(檢潮儀) a tide gauge 〔register〕.

**검증**(檢證) 〖법률〗 verification; inspection; 《유언의》 probate. ~하다 verify; inspect; probate. ¶ ~된 유언장 a probated will / 실험결과가 그 가설을 ~하였다 Experimental results verified the hypothesis. / 사고 현장에서 현장 ~이 행해졌다 An on-the-spot inspection was made 〔held〕 at the scene of the accident. ◉ ~물 data for verification.

**검진**(檢診) a medical 〔physical〕 examination; a medical 〔physical〕 checkup. ~하다 examine; check up 《on *a person's* health》. ¶ ~을 받다 be examined; have an examination 《for breast cancer》; be checked up / 치과 ~을 받다 have a dental checkup / 사원은 매년 1회씩 집단 ~을 받는다 Once a year the employees of our company undergo a group medical examination. ◉ ~날 a medical examination day. 성병~ a V.D. check. 종합 ~ a comprehensive medical testing.

**검질기다** (be) tenacious; persevering; 《구어》 stick-to-itive. ¶ 검질긴 사람 a patient man / 적의 검질긴 저항 the enemy's tenacious resistance.

**검차다** = 검질기다.

**검찰**(檢札) = 검표(檢票).

**검찰**(檢察) prosecution. ¶ ~측과 변호인측 the prosecution and the defense / 나는 ~측 증인으로 소환되었다 I was summoned as a witness for the prosecution.
◉ ~관 a (public) prosecutor; a prosecuting attorney 《미》. ~당국 the prosecutory authorities; the prose-

cution: ～당국에 의하면 according to the procuratory authorities. ～사무 procuration affairs. ～총장 the Public Procurator General; the Attorney General 《미》.

**검찰청**(檢察廳) the Public Prosecutors Office. ◉ 고등～ the 《Seoul》 High Public Prosecutors Office.

**검출**(檢出) 〖화학〗 detection. ～하다 detect 《poison, a chemical substance》. ¶ ～할 수 있는 detectable 《from》/ 그의 혈액에서 알코올이 ～되었다 Alcohol was detected in his blood. ◉ ～기〔장치〕 a detector.

**검측스럽다** (be) tricky; sly; wily; crafty; 《욕심 많다》 (be) greedy.

**검측측하다** 《색이》 (be) darkish; 《마음이》 (be) black-hearted; wicked; crafty; greedy.

**검치다** attach 《metal, *etc.*》 around a corner; cap a corner with.

**검침**(檢針) meter-reading; inspection of a meter. ～하다 check 〔read〕 a 《gas》 meter. ◉ ～원 a 《gas》 meterman; a 《gas-》meter reader.

**검토**(檢討) (an) examination; (an) investigation; study. ～하다 examine 《a theory》; investigate; inquire into; study; discuss. ¶ ～중이다 be (now) under examination 〔investigation〕/ 자세히 ～하다 examine thoroughly; sift 《*a matter*》/ 철저하게 ～되다 be thrashed out / (더) ～를 요하다 require (further) examination / 재～하다 re-examine 《a problem》; reconsider 《a plan》/ 정세를 재～하다 review the situations / 더 ～할 필요가 있다 require further examination / 정부측은 지금 그 대책을 ～하고 있다 Government is now studying 〔reviewing〕 what measures should be taken. / 이미 결정이 난 일이니 더 이상 ～할 여지가 없다 The matter is already decided, and there is no scope for any further consideration.

**검파**(檢波) 〖물리〗 detection; demodulation. ～하다 detect; demodulate. ◉ ～기 a (wave) detector; a cymoscope: 자기 ～기 a magnetic detector / 트랜지스터〔진공관〕 ～기 a transistor 〔vacuum-tube〕 detector.

**검표**(檢票) examination of tickets. ～하다 examine 〔punch〕 tickets. ◉ ～원 a ticket examiner.

**검푸르다** (be) dark blue; blueblack. ¶ 검푸른 바다 a dark-blue sea.

**검호**(劍豪) a skilled 〔master〕 swordsman.

**겁**(怯) 《공포》 fear; fright; dread; 《소심》 cowardice; timidity. ¶ 겁(이) 많다 be timid 〔cowardly, chicken-hearted, fainthearted〕/ 겁(이) 없다 be fearless 〔dauntless, bold, intrepid〕/ 겁(을) 먹다 be frightened 〔scared〕 《at》; be seized with fear; lose *one's* nerve 《at》; 《구어》 get 〔have〕 cold feet; get into a (blue) funk; have the jitters / 겁(을) 주다 scare; threaten; frighten; terrify; give 《*a person*》 a 「fright 〔good scare〕/ 그는 잔뜩 ～을 먹고 있었다 He was stiff with fright. / 그녀는 ～을 먹고 떨었다 She trembled with fright. / 그는 ～이 많아서 나무에도 오르지 못한다 He is too timid to climb up a tree.

**겁**(劫) 〖불교〗 a kalpa; an (a)eon.

**겁간**(劫姦) rape; assault; violation. ～하다 rape; assault; violate; commit rape 《upon》.

**겁결**(怯—) ¶ ～에 driven by fear; in 「*one's* horror.

**겁나다**(怯—) be frightened 《at, of》; be afraid 《of》; be seized with fear; be overcome with fright; be scared. ¶ 겁나서 울다 cry for fear / 선생님에게 들킬까봐 겁났다 I was afraid lest I should be found by the teacher. / 잘못한 것이 없으니 나로서는 겁날 것 없다 My conscience is perfectly at ease, as I am quite innocent.

**겁내다**(怯—) fear; dread; be frightened 〔scared〕 《at》; stand 〔be〕 in fear 《of》; be in a fright; be afraid 《of》. ¶ 겁내지 않고 without fear; feel no fear / 고양이는 물을 겁낸다 Cats dread water. / 아무것도 겁낼 것이 없네 You have nothing to fear.

**겁약**(怯弱) ～하다 (be) fainthearted; chicken-hearted; timid; cowardly.

**겁쟁이**(怯—) a coward; a mouse; 《속어》 a chicken. ¶ 그는 아주 ～다 He is as timid as a rabbit 〔mouse〕.

**겁탈**(劫奪) 《약탈》 robbery; plunder; 《강간》 rape; violation. ～하다 rob; plunder; rape; violate. ¶ 여자를 ～하다 rape 〔violate〕 a woman.
◉ ～자 a robber; a plunderer; a rapist.

**것**[1] ① 《사람·물건》 a one; the one. ¶ 이〔그, 저〕것 this 〔that〕 one; this 〔that〕/ 새것 a new one / 미련한 것 a stupid fellow / 어느것을 택하겠어요 Which one do you prefer? ② 《…한〔할〕 것》 the one that…. ¶ 본 것 the one that 《*someone*》 saw / 볼 것 the one to see / 어린 것이 둘 있다 I have two young ones 〔children〕. / 시간보다 중요한 것은 없다 Nothing is more precious 〔valuable〕 than time. ③ 《소

유》 the one of; -'s. ¶ 우리 것 ours / 선생님 것 the teacher's / …의 것이 되다 come into *one's* possession / 전재산은 그의 후처의 것이 되었다 The whole property went to his second wife.

**것**[2] ①《일·사실》 the fact that…; the act of《*do*ing》; the *do*ing; being. ¶ 비가 오는 것을 알다〔보다〕 know 〔see〕 that it is raining / 아침 일찍 일어난다는 것은 쉬운 일이 아니다 It is not easy to get up early in the morning. / 내 말대로 하는 것이 좋다 You'd better do just as I told you.

②《추측·가능성》 likely 〔probable〕 fact; the real likelihood; the strong probability. ¶ 내일은 날이 갤 것이다 I think it will clear up tomorrow. / 그리 말하면 그는 성낼 것이다 He's likely to get angry if you say that. / 이것으로 충분할 것이다 This will probably be enough.

③《의무·금지 등의 행위》 the thing to *do;* the thing one *does;* a thing required 〔requested〕. ¶ 법은 미성년자들이 담배 피우는 것을 금지했다 The law prohibits minors from smoking. / 그에게 사과할 것까지는 없다 You need not apologize to him. *or* You don't have to 〔need to〕 apologize to him. (★ 이 문장의 need는 본동사, 앞 문장의 need not의 need는 조동사). *or* There is no need to apologize to him. / 잔디밭에 들어가지 말 것《게시》 Keep off the grass.

**-것다** ①《사실의 다짐》 be; do; I assume 〔suppose, think〕. ¶ 너 이 동네 살것다 You must live in this village (I assume). ②《은근한 협박》 surely 〔certainly〕 be 〔do〕; you will do it (understand?). ¶ 네가 그리했것다 You certainly did do so! ③《원인·조건을 갖춤》 given this and that. ¶ 돈 있것다 힘 있것다 무슨 걱정이오 You've got money, you've got power, so what's your worry?

**겅그레** a steamer rack. ¶ ~(를) 놓다 fix a steamer rack at the bottom of the oven.

**겅더리되다** get lean and bony (after *one's* illness).

**겅성드뭇하다** (be) sparse; thin.

**겉** 《표면》 the face; the surface; the right side (옷의); 《외면》 the outside; the exterior; the (outward) appearance (외관). ¶ 겉으로(는) outwardly; in appearance; on the surface; to all appearance(s); seemingly / 겉만 보다 look only at the outside; look only at the surface of things / 겉만 보고 판단하다 judge by appearances / 겉으로는 태연한 체하다 remain 〔keep〕 calm outwardly / 겉을 꾸미다 put on a show; make outward show; keep up appearances / 겉으로 보아서는 훌륭하다 It looks fine from what you can see of it. ◉ 겉표지《책의》 a cover.

**겉가량**(―假量) a rough estimate (based on outward appearances); 《눈대중》 eye measurement. ~하다 make a rough estimate; estimate roughly. ¶ ~으로 at a rough estimate; by eye measure; by guess.

**겉겨** chaff; outer hulls 〔husks〕 of grain.

**겉곡식**(―穀―) unhulled grain.

**겉꺼풀** an outer cover 〔film, membrane〕.

**겉껍질** an outer cover 〔skin, bark〕; 《곡물의》 a hull; a husk; shuck; 《피부의》 the cuticle; 《외곽》 a crust; a shell.

**겉꾸리다** improve the looks; keep up appearances; put on a good face.

**겉꾸림** (a) pretense; a makeup; saving 〔keeping up〕 appearances; putting on a good face.

**겉나깨** buckwheat chaff.

**겉날리다** do《*one's* work》 in a careless manner; scamp 《a job》. ¶ 일을 ~ scamp *one's* work; do a slapdash job.

**겉놀다** 《못·나사 따위가》 slip; do not fit; 《겉돌다》 do not get along well.

**겉눈감다** pretend to close *one's* eyes.

**겉눈썹** an eyebrow.

**겉늙다** get old before *one's* time; look old(er) for *one's* age; be prematurely gray.

**겉대**[1] 《푸성귀의》 an outer stalk 〔leaf〕.

**겉대**[2] 《대나무의》 the outer hard part of bamboo.

**겉대중** = 겉가량.

**겉더껑이** the film; the scum. ¶ 우유의 ~를 걷어내다 skim the scum from 〔off〕 the milk.

**겉더께** surface scum.

**겉돌다** ①《잘 섞이지 않다》 do not mix 《freely》; do not blend 〔mingle〕《with》; 《바퀴·나사가》 do not gear 〔engage〕 《with》. ¶ 기름과 물은 서로 겉돈다 Oil does not mix with water. ②《잘 어울리지 않다》 do not get along well; be out of keeping 《with》; stay out of the party; have a certain reserve; 《이야기 따위가》 go around in circles.

**겉똑똑이** a superficially bright person.

**겉마르다** get dry on the surface.

**겉말** mere words; lip service; shallow

compliments. ¶ ～로만 좋게 이야기하다 talk just fair words; be a little too ready with compliments.

**겉맞추다** show a surface friendliness 《to》; flatter; gloss over; smooth over; temporize.

**겉면**(—面) the surface side; the face; the exterior.

**겉모양**(—模樣·—貌樣) outward appearance 〔show〕; appearance; front; look. ¶ ～내다 dress up; keep up personal appearances; put up a (good) front / ～은 훌륭하다 It is fine in appearance. / 사물은 반드시 ～과 같지는 않다 Things are not always what they seem. / ～만으로 사람을 판단하지 마라 Never 〔Don't〕 judge a man by his appearance 〔looks〕.

**겉물** a liquid floating on another liquid and no mixing with it. ¶ ～돌다 float on the surface without mixing.

**겉바르다** put up a good front; make outward show; put a good face 《on a matter》.

**겉발림** insincere flattery.

**겉밤** chestnuts with their shells on.

**겉보기** the outer appearance; show; look. ¶ ～에는 outwardly; on the surface; apparently; seemingly; on the face of it / 그는 ～에 정직한 것 같다 He seems to be honest.

**겉보리** unhulled barley.

**겉봉**(—封) an envelope; an outer envelope 〔wrapper〕. ¶ ～을 뜯다 cut 《a letter》 open.

**겉살** bare skin.

**겉수수** unhulled sorghum 〔kaoliang〕.

**겉싸개** an outer wrapper; a cover; a wrapper.

**겉씨식물**(—植物) 〖식물〗 gymnosperm.

**겉약다** be clever in a superficial way; be clever only on the surface; be too clever by half.

**겉어림** a rough guess. ⇨겉가량.

**겉여물다** be ripe only to outer appearances.

**겉열매껍질** 〖식물〗 an exocarp; an epicarp.

**겉옷** an outer garment.

**겉잎** the outer leaves.

**겉잠** a nap; a doze; a light 〔surface〕 sleep; a snooze 《구어》. ¶ ～들다 doze; take a nap.

**겉잡다** ① 《겉어림》 estimate roughly; make a rough estimate. ¶ 겉잡아 이틀이면 족하다 In my estimation, two days will be enough. ② 《헤아림》 make some sense of; get a rough idea of. ¶ 네 말은 통 겉잡을 수 없다 I can't make head or tail of what you're saying.

**겉잣** pine nuts with their shells on.

**겉장**(—張) ① 《일면》 the first 〔front〕 page 《of a newspaper》. ② 《표지》 the cover of a book.

**겉저고리** an outer coat.

**겉절이** vegetables pickled 〔salted〕 right before eating.

**겉절이다** salt 《vegetables》 before seasoning elaborately; pickle 〔"wilt"〕 《vegetables》 right before eating.

**겉조** unhulled millet.

**겉짐작** a rough guess (based on appearances); a random guess; a (mere) conjecture. ～하다 make a random guess 〔rough estimate〕 《at》. ¶ ～으로 판단하다 judge by guess / ～으로 알아맞히다 make a lucky shot 〔guess〕 at the answer.

**겉치레** dressing up; a (mere) show; a sham; ostensible decoration; outward show. ～하다 dress up; make outward show; put on a fair show. ¶ ～로 for show; just for appearance's sake; ostentatiously / ～를 좋아하다 be fond of display / ～를 좋아하는 사람 a showy 〔an ostentatious〕 person / 그녀의 친절은 ～에 불과하다 Her kindness is a mere show 〔pretense〕. / 그것은 결코 ～가 아니다 It was not put on at all.

**겉치마** an outer skirt.

**겉치장**(—治粧) dressing up 〔decorating〕 the outside; making outward show; improving *one's* personal appearance. ～하다 dress up 〔decorate〕 the outside; make outward show; improve *one's* personal appearance.

**겉핥다** just scratch the surface 《of a situation》; have a superficial knowledge 《of economics》; have 〔get〕 a smattering 《of Latin》. ¶ 그녀는 많은 것을 알고 있지만 모두가 겉핥기다 She knows a lot of things, but only superficially.

**게**[1] 〖동물〗 a crab. ¶ 게의 집게발 claws; nippers / 게 통조림 canned 〔tinned〕 crab; a can of crab meat / 게 가공선(加工船) a crab-canning boat / 게에 물리다 be nipped by a crab.

**게**[2] ① 《거기》 there. ¶ 게 가는 건 누구냐 Who goes there? / 게 누구 있느냐 Is anybody there? / 게서 자게 You sleep there! ② 《사람을 얕잡아》 ¶ 너까짓 게 such a guy as you / 그까짓 게 a man like him / 저까짓 게 무슨 학생이냐 How could a guy like him be called a student?

**게**[3] 《고장·집》 《*one's*》 place; home; part of *one's* country. ¶ 우리 게는 겨울에 몹시 춥다 In winter it is very cold in our part of the country. / 자네는 내게서 자게 You sleep at my house! / 그 짐을 자네 게로 보내도 괜찮겠나 May I send the baggage to your home?

**-게** ① 《전성어미》 (in a way) so that…; so that it is *or* does; so that *one* can; in a manner such that…; -ly. ¶ 적지 않게 to no small extent; considerably / 쉽게 말하면 To put it simply… / 크게 말하다 speak loud(er) / 빠르게 걷다 walk fast / 짧게 설명하다 explain briefly / 재미있게 보다 look at 《it》 with pleasure / 이상하게 생각하다 think 《it》 strange.
② (***a***) 《(…하게) 되다, 하다, 만들다》 into being 〔*do*ing〕; becoming 〔making〕 so that…. ¶ 재미있게 만들다 make 《it》 (so that it is) interesting; make 《it》 in an interesting way / 서늘하게 하다〔만들다〕 make 《it》 cool(er) / 우리의 생활을 넉넉하게 하다 enrich our lives / 아이가 크게 자랐다 The child grew 〔became, got〕 big(ger). (***b***) 《하게 하다》 causing 〔making, getting, letting〕 《it》 to happen. ¶ 그들은 나에게 춤을 못 추게 한다 They don't let me dance. / 나는 아이한테 우유를 마시게 했다 I got the child to drink his milk. / 학생을 앉게 하시오 Have the student sit down. (***c***) 《…되다》 turning out 〔getting to be, coming to pass, happening〕 so that…; getting to; being arranged so that…. ¶ 음악을 좋아하게 되다 come to be fond of music / 한국에 대해 관심을 갖게 되다 come to have an interest in Korea / 그러하게 생각된다 That's the way it seems to me. / 무슨 자격으로 미국에 가게 됩니까 In what capacity are you going to America? / 그는 할 수 없이 같이 가게 됐다 He had no choice but to go along. / 그들은 기관지를 가지게 됐다 They acquired publication organs. / 차차 아시게 됩니다 You will gradually come to understand. / 학교에 가게(만) 되면 좋겠다 How nice it would be if only I could get to go to school!
③ 《친밀한 명령》 *do*! ¶ 이리 오게(나) Come here. / 자네들끼리 가게 You guys go on. / 그 일은 자네가 맡게 You take care of that matter.
④ 《가정 어미》 then won't 《it》 turn out that…?! ¶ 그랬다간 매맞게 I do that and then I'll get whipped, won't I? / 그만한 돈이 있으면 좋게 It would be grand to have so much money, wouldn't it?

**게거품** ① 《게의》 foam gathering at the mouth of a crab. ② 《사람의》 froth; foam. ¶ 그는 입에 ~을 뿜으며 이야기한다 He foams at the mouth as he talks.

**게걸** greed for food; insatiable appetite. ~들(리)다 become greedy for food; get an insatiable appetite; have voracity; be gluttonous. ~떼다 get rid of *one's* insatiable appetite; eat *one's* fill. ~스럽다 (be) gluttonous; voracious; greedy. ¶ ~스럽게 먹다 guzzle; devour; eat like a hog 〔wolf〕; eat greedily; make a pig of *oneself*.

**게걸거리다, 게걸대다** grumble; growl; grouse; mutter; murmur (with discontent).

**게걸음** side-crawl (of a crab); walking sideways. ¶ ~치다 walk sideways.

**게걸쟁이** a grumbler; a grouch; a malcontent.

**게꽁지** [비유적] a stupid person; a dull clod.

**게꽁지만하다** (be) shallow; superficial. ¶ 게꽁지만한 학문 가지고 무얼 안다고 그래 What do you think you know, with your two-bits' worth of education?

**-게끔** so that *one* 〔it〕 may 《*do*》; so as to 《*do*》. ¶ 뒤탈이 없게끔 잘 처리하시오 Manage the matter carefully so that there will be absolutely no trouble in the future.

**게놈** 〖유전〗 a genom(e). ¶ 인간 ~ the human genome. ◉ ~ 분석 genome analysis.

**게눈** ① a crab's eye. ¶ ~ 감추듯 하다 eat 《food》 up in no time at all. ② 〖건축〗 a swirl decoration on the end of a roof beam.

**게다(가)** ① 《장소》 there; in that place; over there. ¶ 책을 게다 놓아라 Put the book there. ② 《그 위에 또》 in addition (to that); moreover; besides; on top of that; what is more; into the bargain; to boot; else; 《설상가상으로》 to make matters 〔things〕 worse; what is worse. ¶ 비가 오고 게다가 바람까지 불었다 It rained and there was wind to boot. / 게다가 병까지 걸렸다 To make him more miserable, he fell ill. / 게다가 술까지 잔뜩 마셨다 To crown it all, he was beastly drunk. / 게으른 놈이 게다가 거짓말까지 한다 He is lazy, and lies into the bargain.

**게딱지** the shell 〔crust〕 of a crab. ¶ ~만하다 be small as a crab shell; be tiny / ~만한 방 《live in》 a tiny room.

**게라** 〖인쇄〗 a (printing) galley. ◉ ~쇄(刷) a galley proof 〔sheet〕.

**게르만** the German (people). ¶ ~의 Germanic. ◉ ~(민)족 the Germanic race.

**게릴라** a guer(r)illa. ◉ ~부대 a guerilla band. ~전 guerilla war(fare) 〔fighting〕: ~전을 펴다 launch guerilla warfare. ~전술 guerilla tactics. 대~작전 counter-guerilla operations. 대~전 counter-guerilla warfare.

**게마인샤프트** 《공동 사회》 a gemeinshaft (*pl.* -shaften).

**게발** a crab's claws. ¶ 글씨를 ~ 그리듯 하다 scribble; write in poor hand; write a crabbed hand.

**게슈타포** 《나치스의 비밀 경찰》 Gestapo.

**게스트** a guest. ◉ ~멤버 a guest member. ~ 싱어 a guest singer.

**게시**(揭示) a notice; a bulletin; a posting. ~하다 put up 〔post〕 a notice; post 《a date, a fact, a name》. ¶ ~를 벽에 붙이다 pin up a notice on the wall / …라는 ~가 있다 There is a notice up saying 〔reporting〕 that… / "좌석 만원"의 ~가 그 극장에 나붙어 있었다 The sign "Standing Room Only" was displayed at the theater. ◉ ~판 a notice 〔bulletin〕 board; a billboard.

**게알젓** pickled spawn of crabs.

**게양**(揭揚) hoisting; raising; flying. ~하다 put up; hoist; raise; fly. ¶ 국기를 ~하다 hoist 〔put up〕 a national flag.

**게염** 《탐욕》 covetousness. ¶ ~나다〔내다〕 become 〔get〕 covetous / ~ 부리다 behave covetously; covet / 너 정말 ~스럽구나 How covetous you are!

**게우다** ① 《먹은 것을》 vomit; bring 〔fetch〕 up; throw 〔cast〕 up. ¶ 먹은 것을 ~ throw up what *one* has eaten / 게울 것 같다 feel sick 〔nausea, queasy〕; retch. ② 《부당한 이익을》 refund 〔replace, repay〕 《ill-gotten money》; disgorge. ¶ 그는 횡령한 돈을 다시 게웠다 He repaid what he had seized unlawfully.

**게으르다** (be) lazy; idle; indolent; slothful. ¶ 게으른 사람 an idle 〔a lazy〕 fellow; a lazybones 《구어》; an idler / 게으른 버릇이 들다 form 〔fall into, get into〕 (the) habits of laziness 〔indolence〕 / 게을러지다 get 〔grow〕 lazy; become lazy.

**게으름** laziness; idleness; indolence. ~

---

참고 **각종 게시문의 영어 표현**

**1**. 금지를 나타내는 게시
Do not use(사용 금지) Do not disturb(입실 금지, 취침중) Post no bills (광고물 부착 금지) Commit no nuisance (소변 금지) Keep off the grass (잔디를 밟지 마시오) Take off your shoes(신발을 벗으시오) No litter *or* No Dumping (쓰레기 버리지 마시오) No Smoking (금연) No Loitering(배회 금지) No Trespassing *or* Off Limits(출입 금지) No visitors allowed(면회 사절) No Spitting(침 뱉지 마시오) Private (property)(사유지 출입 금지) No admission except on business (무용자 출입 금지) No fishing here (이곳에서 낚시 금지)

**2**. 제한을 나타내는 게시
Staff 〔Employees〕 only(종업원 전용) Members only *or* No admittance except for members(회원 이외 입장사절) Room for standing only(입석만 가능) Adults only(성인 전용) Exit only(출구 전용)

**3**. 장소·주의를 나타내는 게시
Information (안내소) Entrance (입구) Exit (출구) Emergency Exit (비상구) Toilet (화장실) Gentlemen (남자용 화장실) Ladies (여자용 화장실) Private (내실) Caution (주의) Danger (위험) Watch your step (발밑 조심) Wet 〔Fresh〕 paint (칠 주의) Watch out for your head (머리 조심) Beware of the dog (개조심) Liquid (액체물 요주의) Inflammables *or* Flammables (화기주의) Restricted area (제한 구역) Warning (경고) Dead End (막다른 골목) Dead Slow (아주 천천히)

**4**. 상점·회사·병원·공사장 따위의 게시
Hours 9:00—5:00 *or* Business hours 9(A.M.)—5(P.M.)(영업시간 9시—5시) Open 24 hours (24시간 영업) For sale (매물) Not for sale(비매품) Clearance sale(재고정리 판매) Year-end sale (연말 대매출) Bargain (sale) day(염가 매출일) (We are) open (개점중) Closed (폐점) Now in session (회의중) No consultations today (오늘 휴진) Admission free(입장 무료) Under repairs(수리중) Under construction (공사중) Out of order(고장) In mourning (기중(忌中)) Open to the public (출입 개방) Welcome to beginners (초보자 환영)

부리다〔피우다〕 be idle; be 〔get〕 lazy; neglect 《*one's* lessons》; idle away 《*one's* time》; slow down 《*one's* work》. ◉ ~뱅이〔쟁이〕 an idler; a lazybones 《구어》; a sluggard; a bum 《미구어》: 타고난 ~뱅이다 He is a born idler.

**게을러빠지다** (be) very lazy; quite indolent. ¶ 사람이 게을러빠져 못 쓰겠다 He is a good-for-nothing lazybones.

**게을리** lazily; idly; indolently; negligently. ~하다 neglect; shirk; slight; be negligent 〔neglectful〕 《of duty》; be unmindful of. ¶ 공부〔직무〕를 ~하다 neglect *one's* studies 〔duties〕 / 일을 ~하다 slight *one's* work / 경계를 ~하지 마라 Keep your eyes open.

**게이** 《동성애자》 a gay. ¶ ~바 a gay bar.

**게이지** a gauge. ¶ 표준 ~ the standard gauge.

**게이트** 《문·탑승구》 a gate. ¶ 2번 ~ Gate 2.

**게임** a game. ¶ ~을 하다 play a game / ~에 이기다〔지다〕 win 〔lose〕 a game / 이길 가망이 없는〔있는〕 ~을 하다 play a losing 〔winning〕 game / 일방적인 ~ a one-sided game / 두 ~차가 있다 be two games 「ahead of 〔behind〕 《the Tigers》. ◉ ~세트 The game is over. *or* 《테니스의》 Game and set. ~이론 the game theory.

**게자리** 〖천문〗 the Crab; the Cancer.

**게장**(—醬) ① 《간장》 soy sauce in which crabs are preserved. ② =게젓.

**게재**(揭載) publication; insertion (신문에). ~하다 publish; print; insert; report; run 《미》; carry 《the news》. ¶ 연일〔격일〕 ~되는 appearing daily 〔every other day〕 / 신문에 광고를 ~하다 run an ad in the paper; insert an advertisement in a newspaper / 기사를 ~하다 《the magazine》 carry an article / ~되다 appear 〔be reported〕 《in a newspaper》 / 내 논설이 B지(誌) 5월호에 ~되었다 My article was printed in the May issue of B. ◉ ~금지 a press ban; a 「ban on 〔suppression of〕 publication.

**게저분하다** be laden 〔loaded〕 with superfluous 〔dirty〕 things. ¶ 포스터가 게저분하게 붙은 벽 a wall disorderly pasted with posters / 주(註)가 게저분하게 달리다 be loaded heavily with superfluous notes.

**게적지근하다** feel leery; feel uneasy 《about》; be not quite happy 《about》.

**게접스럽다** = 구접스럽다.

**게젓** pickled 〔salted〕 crabs.

**게정** grumbling. ¶ ~내다〔부리다〕 grumble; complain / ~스럽다 be grumbly. ◉ ~꾼 a grumbler.

**게트림** an arrogant belch; belching in haughty manner. ~하다 belch arrogantly 〔in haughty manner〕.

**겔** 〖화학〗 gel. ¶ ~화(化) gelation / ~화하다 gel; gelate.

**겔렌데** 〔< *Gelände* (G.)〕 〖스키〗 a slope.

**-겠-** ① 《미래·필연성》 will *do* 〔be〕. ¶ 나는 그 일을 내일 하겠다 I will do it tomorrow. / 그 동안에 다 늙겠다 I will get quite old in the meantime. / 그만 먹겠습니다 That's all I'll eat. ② 《추측 등》 probably *do* 〔be〕. ¶ 얼굴을 보니 좀 게으르겠다 To judge from his appearance, he must be a bit lazy. / 재미있겠다 I bet it's fun. ③ 《가능성》 can; possible. ¶ 그것쯤이야 나도 들겠다 I can lift it up, too. ④ 《기타》 ¶ 나는 모르겠다 I would't know. *or* I don't know. / 별소리 다 듣겠다 Now I've heard everything.

**겨** chaff; hulls 〔husks〕 of grain. ¶ 겉겨 (outer) husks; hulls; chaff / 속겨 bran / 쌀겨 rice bran / 똥 묻은 개가 겨 묻은 개를 나무란다 《속담》 The pot calls the kettle black.

**겨냥** ① 《조준》 aim; aiming. ~하다 (take) aim 《at》; make a target 《of》; set *one's* sights 《on》. ~ 대다 bring into aim; take aim 《at》. ~ 보다 =겨눠보다. ¶ 바로 ~하다 take good aim 《at》 / 잘못 ~하다 aim wrong; misaim / ~이 빗맞다 miss *one's* aim; miss the mark / ~이 틀리다 *one's* aim is wrong; be wide of the mark. ② 《치수》 measure; dimensions; size. ~하다 take dimensions; measure off the size. ~ 내다 take the measure 〔dimensions〕 《of》; measure; size / ~을 재다 take measure. ◉ ~대 a measuring rod; a yardstick. ~도 《make, take》 a sketch.

**겨누다** ① 《겨냥하다》 aim 《at》; take aim 《at》; sight 《a target》. ¶ 총으로 나무 위에 있는 새를 ~ aim *one's* gun at a bird in the tree / 잘 겨누고 쏘다 take good 〔careful〕 aim and fire. ② 《대보다》 take the measure 〔dimensions〕 《of》; take the size 《of》.

**겨눠보다** ① 《표적을》 take tentative aim 《at》; try aiming 《at》. ② 《치수를》 take rough measurements.

**겨드랑이** ① 《몸의》 the armpit(s). ¶ ~에 끼다 carry 〔hold〕 《*a thing*》 under *one's* arm / ~를 간질이다 tickle 《*a person*》 under the arms / ~에 땀이 나다

sweat under the arms. ②《옷의》 the armhole.

**겨레** 《민족》 a race; a nation; a people; 《동포》 offspring of the same forefather; brothers; brethren; fellow countrymen. ◉ ~붙이 members of a people 〔nation〕.

**겨루다** compete 〔contend, vie〕 《with》; match 〔oppose〕 with 《*one's* strength》; rival 〔emulate〕 《each other》. ¶ 솜씨를 ~ compete 《with *a person*》 in some art; match *one's* skill 《with *a person*》/ 패권을 잡으려고 서로 ~ compete with each other for supremacy / 두 사람이 서로 힘을 겨룬다 Two people pit their strength against each other. / 영어 회화에서 나는 그와 겨룰 수가 없다 I am no match for him in speaking English.

**겨룸** (a) competition; a contest; rivalry; a struggle (for supremacy); measuring 〔pitting〕 *one's* strength 〔talent〕 《with, against》. ¶ 힘~ a contest of physical strength; a strength contest.

**겨를** 《여가》 leisure; free time; time to spare; spare time. ¶ ~이 있다 have time to spare; be at leisure / ~이 없다 have no time to spare; be busy; be pressed for time / 책 읽을 ~이 없다 I have no time 「for reading 〔to read〕.

**겨리** a plow drawn by a yoke of two oxen. ◉ ~질 working a 2-ox plow. 겨릿소 an ox on a *kyŏri.*

**겨반지기** rice with husks 〔hulls〕 in it.

**겨우** 《가까스로》 barely; narrowly; with difficulty; barely manage to; 《고작》 only; merely; no more than; 《근소한 차이로》 by the skin of *one's* teeth. ¶ ~ 스무 살 된 여자 a girl just out of her teens / ~ 살아가다 make a bare living; barely manage to earn *one's* living / ~ 합격하다 barely pass an examination / ~ 기차 시간에 대다 be barely in time for the train / ~ 십만 원을 모으다 barely manage to collect 100,000 won / ~ 도망치다 escape narrowly; have a narrow escape / 우리 회사는 시장의 우위를 ~ 유지하고 있었다 We maintained our market lead by the skin of our teeth.

**겨우내** throughout the winter; all through the winter; all winter long. ¶ ~ 서울에 있었다 I stayed at Seoul all last winter.

**겨우살이**[1] ①《옷》 winter clothes; winter wear. ¶ ~를 장만하다 make winter clothes. ② = 월동.

**겨우살이**[2] 〖식물〗 the mistletoe; a parasite plant.

**겨울** (a) winter; the winter season. ¶ ~의 winter 《sports》; wintry 《scene》/ ~용 for winter use / 한 ~(에) (in) midwinter; (in) the midst of winter / 추운 ~ a cold 〔severe, hard〕 winter / ~ 준비를 하다 prepare for the (coming) winter / ~을 지내다 pass the winter; winter 《in, at》/ 본격적인 ~이 되었다 The winter has come in real earnest. ◉ ~날 a winter day; winter days. ~날씨 wintry 〔winter〕 weather. ~방학 the winter vacation 〔holidays〕. ~잠 wintering; hibernation. ~철 winter (time); the winter season.

**겨워하다** feel 《*something*》 to be too much for *one;* feel 《*something*》 is more than *one* can manage 〔control〕. ¶ 일이 많아 힘에 ~ feel the job is too much for *one.*

**겨이삭** 〖식물〗 a kind of bent grass.

**겨자** 《양념》 mustard; 〖식물〗 a mustard (plant). ¶ ~를 친 음식 food dressed with mustard. ◉ ~단지 a mustard pot. ~씨 mustard seed. ~채 mustard salad.

**격**(格) ①《지위·신분》 standing; status; a rank; 《등급》 a class; a grade; order; 《환경에 어울리는 격식·품위》 a manner; formality; a rule; a style. ¶ 격이 높다 be high in social standing; be of a distinguished style / 격이 떨어지다 fall in rank; be degraded / 격이 올라가다 rise in rank; be promoted to a higher grade / 격에 맞다 be regular; be in (proper) style; be in accord with a rule 〔form〕/ 격을 올리다 raise 〔promote〕《*a person*》 to higher status 〔to a higher rank〕; upgrade / 격이 다르다 be in 〔belong to〕 a different class 《from》; be on different levels / 이 호텔은 다른 호텔과는 격이 다르다 This hotel is in a different class from the rest.

②《자격》 capacity; 《인격》 character. ¶ 격에 맞지 않는 짓〔일〕을 하다 go out of *one's* character; do 《*something*》 unbecoming; play an unbecoming part / 그 일은 그녀의 격에 맞는다 That is just her job.

③ 〖문법〗 a case. ¶ 목적격 the accusative 〔object〕 case / 격변화 〖문법〗 declension.

④ 〖논리〗 figure; schema (*pl.* -mata).

⑤《셈》 ¶ 소 잃고 외양간 고치는 격이다 That is an instance of shutting the

stable door after the horse is stolen. / 그것은 공중에 누각을 짓는 격이다 That is, as it were, building a castle in the air.

**격감**(激減) a marked decline; a sharp decrease. ～하다 decline remarkably; decrease sharply. ¶ 지원자가 ～했다 There was a big drop in the number of applicants. / 매출이 ～했다 Sales have plunged 〔plummeted, dropped sharply〕.

**격검**(擊劍) fencing. ～하다 do 〔practise〕 「fencing; fence.

**격나다**(隔―) break relations《with》; split《with》; have a rupture《of relations》; be estranged《from》.

**격납고**(格納庫) a hangar; an airplane 〔aviation〕 shed. ◉ ～갑판《항공 모함의》 a hangar deck.

**격년**(隔年) every other 〔second〕 year; 《in》 alternate year. ¶ ～의 biennial / ～에 열매를 맺다 bear fruit 「biennially 〔every second year〕.

**격노**(激怒) violent anger; rage; fury; furor. ～하다 become 〔get〕 very angry; get enraged; be furious 〔infuriated〕; blow *one's* top《구어》. ¶ ～하여 떨리는 목소리 a voice quivering with rage / ～케 하다 enrage; infuriate / 그는 그녀에게 모욕을 당하고 ～했다 He was furious at her insult. / 그녀는 ～하여 그 편지를 찢었다 She tore up the letter in a fury.

**격돌**(激突) a crash; a clash. ～하다 crash《into》; clash《against》; collide violently《with》. ¶ 버스가 열차에 ～했다 A bus crashed into a train. / 국회에서 자유당과 민주당의 ～은 피할 수 없을 것 같다 A clash between the Liberals and the Democrats in the National Assembly seems unavoidable.

**격동**(激動)《격렬한 변화·동요》 violent shaking 〔change〕; turbulence; excitement. ～하다 shake violently;《사회 따위가》 be thrown into turmoil. ¶ ～하는 사회 정세 turbulent social conditions; a rapidly changing social situation / ～의 해 a year of violent 《political》 change; a tumultuous year / ～의 시대 an age of convulsions; turbulent times.

**격랑**(激浪) raging waves; a heavy sea. ¶ ～에 휩쓸리다 be swept away 〔gulped down〕 by the angry waves.

**격려**(激勵)《고무》 (an) encouragement. ～하다 encourage《*a person* to *do*》; cheer《*a person*》 up; stimulate. ¶ 아무의 말에 ～되어 encouraged 〔spurred〕 by *a person's* words / ～하여 행하게 하다 spur《*a person*》 into action / 더욱 노력하도록 ～하다 inspire《*a person*》 to further efforts. ◉ ～사〔연설〕 words 〔a speech〕 of encouragement; a pep talk.

**격렬**(激烈) violence; severity; intensity; vehemence. ～하다 (be) violent; severe; intense; vehement; acute. ¶ ～하게 violently; severely; vehemently; intensely / ～한 말 violent language; harsh words / ～한 경쟁 a keen 〔cutthroat〕 competition; a sharp 〔hot〕 contest / ～한 감정 a violent passion / ～한 싸움 a fierce battle / 논쟁은 ～해졌다 The dispute became hot. / 생존 경쟁이 점점 더 ～해지고 있다 The struggle for life is gathering its intensity. / 등줄기를 따라 ～한 통증이 오는 것을 느꼈다 I felt an acute 〔a terrible〕 pain shoot across my back.

**격론**(激論) a heated 〔stormy〕 argument 〔discussion〕; a hot 〔violent〕 controversy. ～하다 argue 〔discuss〕 hotly《about *a matter*》; get into 〔have〕 a heated discussion. ¶ 국회에서 ～이 있었다 A very vehement debate took place in the National Assembly. / 그 초고속 열차의 안전성에 관하여 ～이 벌어졌다 They were engaged in a heated controversy as to the safety of the bullet train.

**격류**(激流) a rapid 〔swift〕 current; a violent stream; a torrent. ¶ ～를 건너다 cross a rushing stream / ～에 휩쓸리다 be swept away by a torrent / 그 보트는 ～에 휩쓸렸다 The boat was caught in the torrent.

**격리**(隔離) isolation; insulation; (a) segregation;《전염병 환자의》 quarantine. ～하다 isolate; separate; quarantine; set《*a person*》 apart《from》; keep 〔put〕《a patient》 in quarantine. ¶ 문명과 ～된 작은 마을 a tiny village that has been isolated from civilization / 그는 성홍열에 걸렸으므로 ～해야 한다 He has scarlet fever and must be isolated. / 흉악범은 사회로부터 완전히 그리고 영원히 ～되어야 한다 The felon should be separated from society perfectly and eternally. ◉ ～기간《전염병 환자의》 a quarantine period. ～병동〔실〕 an isolation ward. ～병원 an isolation 〔a detention〕 hospital. ～환자 an isolated patient; a patient kept in isolation.

**격막**(隔膜) 〖해부〗 the diaphragm; 《생물의》 the septum. ◉ ~염 inflammation of the diaphragm.

**격멸**(擊滅) annihilation; extermination. ~하다 annihilate; destroy completely; wipe out.

**격무**(激務) 《직무》 a busy office 〔post〕; 《일》 hard 〔taxing〕 work; an arduous task 〔duty〕; pressing work. ¶ ~를 맡다 undertake 「an arduous 〔a difficult〕 task / ~에 시달리다 feel hard pressed; be pressed with hard work; be extremely busy with pressing duties / ~에 쓰러지다 become ill from overwork; 「break down under 〔succumb to〕 the strain of hard work.

**격문**(檄文) a written appeal; a declaration; a manifesto. ¶ ~을 내다 issue a manifesto / 전국에 ~을 띄우다 make a nationwide appeal in writing.

**격발**(激發) an outburst 《of emotion》; a sudden fit 《of passion》; explosion 《of anger》. ~하다 burst out; explode. ¶ 사람들에게 계급 의식을 ~시키다 awake people suddenly to class consciousness. ◉ ~화약 a high explosive.

**격발**(擊發) percussion. ¶ 권총에 ~장치를 하다 make a revolver ready for firing. ◉ ~신관 a percussion fuse.

**격변**(激變) a sudden 〔violent, sea〕 change; 《사회의》 an upheaval; 《감정의》 a revulsion; 〖지질〗 a cataclysm. ~하다 undergo a sudden change; change suddenly 〔violently〕. ¶ 감정의 ~ an outburst of emotion / 사회의 ~ (a) social upheaval 〔revolution〕; rapid changes in society / 사태의 ~ a sudden turn of events / 물가의 ~ a wild 〔sharp〕 fluctuation in prices / ~하는 국제 정세에 대처하다 provide for rapid changes of the international situation / 기상의 ~에 주의하시오 Be careful of sudden changes in the weather. / 그 전쟁은 사회적 ~의 원인이 되었다 The war caused 「a rapid change in society 〔a social upheaval〕.

**격분**(激憤) violent anger; indignation; resentment; flaring up. ⇨ 격노, 분개. ~하다 become 〔get〕 very angry; resent; be indignant 《at, about》; burn with indignation; flare 〔blow〕 up. ¶ ~시키다 arouse the resentment of 《*a person*》 / ~하여 in a rage 〔fury〕.

**격상**(格上) ~하다 raise 〔elevate〕 the status 《of》; raise to higher status; promote to a higher rank; upgrade. ¶ ~되다 be raised to higher status; have *one's* status elevated / 그 사무소는 지점으로 ~되었다 The office was upgraded to a branch status. / 그는 최근 품질관리 부장으로 ~되었다 He was recently promoted to quality control manager.

**격세**(隔世) ① 《딴 세대》 generations being far apart; a different age. ¶ ~지감 the impression of being poles apart in generations / ~지감이 있다 It seems as if it belonged to a completely different age. *or* I feel as if I were living in quite a different age 〔world〕. ② 《세대 걸러》 every second generation. ¶ ~유전 atavism; (a) reversion / ~유전의 atavistic.

**격식**(格式) (a) formality; social rules; formalities; an established form; ceremony. ¶ ~을 차리는 ceremonious / ~을 차리지 않고 without formality 〔ceremony〕 / ~상 for form's sake / ~을 중히 여기다 be correct in observance of formalities / ~을 차리다 stick to formality; stand on ceremony / 옛날 집안에는 으레 집안 ~이라는 게 있다 Every old family has its own established formalities. 「기의).

**격실**(隔室) a compartment; a bay(항공

**격심하다**(激甚—) (be) severe; vehement; violent; intense; keen. ¶ 격심한 추위 a severe cold / 격심한 경쟁 a keen 〔severe〕 competition / 격심한 고통 a violent 〔an acute〕 pain / 격심한 불황 a severe economic depression / 격심한 빈부의 차 the big gap 〔gulf〕 between the rich and the poor / 요즈음은 취직난이 어느 때보다 더 ~ The difficulty of securing employment is now felt more keenly than ever.

**격앙**(激昂) excitement; exasperation; a fit of passion. ~하다 get 〔be〕 excited; be enraged; flare up; lose *one's* temper. ¶ ~하기 쉬운 excitable; hot-headed; hot-tempered / ~시키다 excite; exasperate; provoke / ~된 어조로 말하다 speak in an excited 〔a fiery〕 tone.

**격야**(隔夜) every other 〔second〕 night; 《on》 alternate nights.

**격양가**(擊壤歌) a farmer's ballad celebrating the good harvest and peaceful reigns.

**격언**(格言) a proverb; a maxim; a saying. ¶ ~에 이르기를 A 〔The〕 proverb says that… / ~에도 있듯이, 「시간은 돈」이다 Time is money, as proverb goes.

**격원하다**(隔遠—) (be) distant; far (away); remote; be a long way off.

**격월**(隔月) every other 〔second〕 month; 《in》 alternate months. ¶ ～발행의 잡지 a bimonthly (magazine). ◉ ～간행물 a bimonthly.

**격의**(隔意) reserve; standoffishness. ¶ ～없는 unreserved; frank; candid; open / ～없는 의견 교환 a frank exchange of views / ～없이 이야기하다 have a heart-to-heart talk 《with》; talk 「without reserve 〔unreservedly〕 / 나는 그와 ～없이 지낸다 I have no reserves with him.

**격일**(隔日) every other 〔second〕 day; 《on》 alternate days. ¶ ～제로 근무하다 shift once in two days; work on one day and off the next. ◉ ～열 〖의학〗 a tertian (fever). ～제운행 《차량의》 an alternate-day driving ban.

**격자**(格子) ① 《창·문의》 a lattice; 《창문 따위의》 a grille; 《천장의》 a coffer; 《무늬》 fretwork; 《철제 따위》 grating. ② 《갓끈의》 beads attached to the strings of a Korean hat. ¶ ～로 된 latticed; of lattice; coffered. ◉ ～무늬 cross stripes; a checkered pattern; a tartan check. ～문〔창문〕 a lattice door 〔window〕. ～세공 latticing; latticework.

**격전**(激戰) a hot 〔heavy〕 fight; a fierce battle; heavy fighting; 《선거 따위의》 a hot 〔close〕 contest. ～하다 have 〔engage in〕 a bad 〔fierce〕 fight; fight a terrible battle. ¶ 지난번 선거는 ～이었다 The last election was a hot contest. ◉ ～지 the scene of a hard-fought battle; 《선거의》 a closely contested constituency.

**격정**(激情) a strong 〔violent〕 emotion; (a) passion. ¶ ～에 이끌려 carried away by a fit of passion; with a gust of passion; out of temper / ～을 (억)누르다 hold the passion in check / 그는 ～을 억누를 수 없었다 He could not hold back his strong emotion 〔passion〕.

**격조**(格調) 《문장 따위의》 a tone; a style. ¶ ～높은 연설 a high-toned speech / ～높은 문장 a literary composition written in 「a lofty 〔a classical, an elevated〕 style / 그의 연설은 ～가 높다 His speech has a full, deep note.

**격조하다**(隔阻―) hear nothing; have no news 《from *a person*》; neglect 〔fail〕 to write; be silent. ¶ 오랫동안 격조한 것을 사과하다 apologize for *one's* long silence / 오랫동안 격조하여 죄송합니다 Please excuse me for my long silence.

**격주**(隔週) every other 〔second〕 week; a weekly interval. ¶ ～의〔로〕 biweekly; fortnightly; every other week / 우리는 ～로 월요일에 여기 모인다 We meet here on Monday every other week.

**격증**(激增) a sudden 〔rapid〕 increase; a heavy swell. ～하다 increase suddenly 〔rapidly, markedly〕; rise 〔swell〕 suddenly(강물 따위가). ¶ 범죄의 ～ the rapid increase of crime / 인구가 ～했다 The population swelled 〔increased〕 remarkably. / 주택의 수요가 ～했다 The demand for houses has shown a marked 〔remarkable〕 increase. / 차량 사고가 ～하고 있다 The number of vehicle accidents is sharply increasing.

**격지**《켜》(many) layers; manifold.

**격지**(隔地) a distant 〔remote〕 place 〔area〕.

**격지**(隔紙) a paper inserted between 「two layers.

**격지다**(隔―) get 〔be〕 estranged 〔alienated〕 《from》; be at outs 〔odds〕 《with》; be on bad terms 《with》.

**격진**(激震) a severe earthquake; a severe 〔violent〕 shock.

**격차**(格差·隔差) difference (in quality); a differential; a gap; a 《technical》 disparity. ¶ 기술의 ～ a technological gap / 도시와 농촌의 생활 수준 ～ a gap between the urban and rural standards of living / 학교간의 ～ the difference in quality of schools / 소득의 ～를 없애다 abolish earning differentials / 그 두 나라 사이에는 경제력에 큰 ～가 있다〔거의 없다〕 There is a wide 〔narrow〕 gap in economic power between the two countries. / 임금의 ～는 시정되어야 한다 Wage disparities must be corrected.

**격찬**(激讚) high praise 〔tribute〕. ～하다 praise 《*a person*》 highly 《for》; extol; rave 《about》 speak highly of; pay a high tribute 《to》. ¶ 용감한 행위를 ～하다 speak 〔praise〕 highly of 《*a person's*》 heroic act.

**격철**(擊鐵) the cock 《of a gun》; the hammer 《of a rifle》. ¶ ～을 당기다 cock a gun.

**격추**(擊墜) ～하다 shoot 〔bring〕 down 《a plane》; down 《a plane》. ¶ 그 비행기는 영일만 상공에서 ～되었다 The plane was shot down over Yeongil Bay.

**격침**(擊沈) ～하다 sink 《a ship》; send 《a ship》 to the bottom. ¶ 어뢰로 ～하다 torpedo (and sink) 《a ship》 / 잠수

함에 의해 ～당하다 be torpedoed and sunk by a submarine.

**격통**(激痛) an acute 〔intense〕 pain; a severe 〔sharp〕 pain; a pang. ¶ ～을 느끼다 feel an acute pain《in the chest》.

**격퇴**(擊退) a repulse. ～하다 repulse 〔repel〕《an invader, the enemy》; drive 〔beat〕《the enemy》back. ¶ 공격을 ～하다 drive back an attack / ～당하다 be driven back; meet with 〔suffer〕 a repulse.

**격투**(格鬪) a (hand-to-hand) fight; a grapple; a tussle; a scuffle. ～하다 grapple 〔tussle〕《with a burglar》; fight (hand to hand)《with》. ¶ ～끝에 강도를 잡다 arrest the burglar after a scuffle.

**격투**(激鬪) a fierce fight. ～하다 fight ｢fiercely.

**격파하다**(擊破―) defeat; beat off; smash (up); crush; rout. ¶ 전차가 적의 방어 시설을 격파했다 The tanks crushed enemy defenses.

**격하**(格下) degradation; downgrading; demotion《미》. ～하다 lower the status《of》; drop《*a person*》in rank; demean (*oneself*); downgrade; demote《*a person*》; reduce《*a person*》to a lower rank. ¶ 외교 관계를 ～하다 downgrade diplomatic ties 〔relations〕《with》/ 그는 스캔들 때문에 지위가 ～되었다 He was demoted 〔dropped〕 to a lower rank 〔post〕 because of the scandal.

**격하다**(隔―)《가르다》part; separate; set apart;《사이에 두다》interpose;《막다》screen; shield;《시간을》make intervals《between》. ¶ 2시간을 격하여 한 번씩 once every two hours / 10미터씩 격하여 at intervals of 10 meters / 벽 하나를 격하고 on the other side of the wall; with a wall between / 두 마을이 강 하나를 격하고 있다 The two villages lie facing each other across a river.

**격하다**(激―)《급하고 거세다》(be) intense; violent; radical; fierce;《흥분하다》get 〔be〕 excited; be agitated;《화를 내다》be enraged 〔provoked〕; fly into a passion; get angry. ¶ 격한 감정 an intense 〔a violent〕 feeling 〔emotion〕 / 격한 논쟁 a hot dispute / 격한 사상 radical ideas / 격하기 쉬운 excitable; hot-tempered / 말이 격해지다 words run high / 격한 어조로 말하다 speak in a ｢harsh 〔fierce〕 tone / 나는 격한 나머지 말도 안 나왔다 I got too excited for words. / 그 말에 그의 감정은 격해졌다 He grew excited at the words.

**격화**(激化) becoming intense 〔violent〕; aggravation. ～하다 intensify; become 〔get〕 more intense 〔violent〕; be aggravated《by》. ¶ 반전운동이 ～되었다 An antiwar campaign has grown more intense. / 두 나라 사이에 긴장이 ～됐다 The tensions between the two countries intensified.

**격화소양**(隔靴搔癢) scratching through the sole of *one's* shoes; having an itch *one* can't scratch; leaving much to be desired 〔done〕. ¶ ～의 감이 있다 [사람이 주어] feel unsatisfied 〔impatient〕; [사물이 주어] leave much to be done 〔desired〕.

**겪다** ①《경험》undergo; suffer; experience; pass 〔go〕 through; meet with. ¶ 겪어 본 일이 있다 have experience of / 갖은 고초를 ～ undergo all sorts of hardships; have a rough time of it / 대단한 고통을 ～ suffer a severe pain / 여러 가지 일을 ～ experience a lot of things / 그 도시는 지난 10년간 큰 변화를 겪었다 The city has undergone a great change during the last ten years. ②《대접하다》entertain; feast; regale. ¶ 손님을～ entertain a guest; play host《to》.

**견**(絹) ① silk. ② ＝견본(絹本).

**견갑**(肩胛) the shoulder. ◉ ～골 the shoulder blade. ～관절 the shoulder joint. ～탈구 dislocation of the shoulder joint.

**견강부회**(牽强附會) a farfetched interpretation; a distortion. ～하다 give a farfetched interpretation; distort; force the meaning 〔opinion〕. ¶ ～의 farfetched《opinions》; forced《views》; distorted《facts》.

**견고**(堅固) being strong 〔solid, firm, durable〕. ～하다 (be) strong; solid; firm; durable. ¶ ～히 strongly; solidly; firmly; securely / ～한 기초 a solid foundation / ～한 의지 (a) strong will / ～한 진지 a strong position 〔fortress〕; a stronghold / ～히 하다 strengthen; solidify / 적의 방비는 예상외로 ～했다 The defense of the enemy was much stronger than expected.

**견과**(堅果)〖식물〗a nut.

**견디다** ①《생활을 유지하다》make a living; subsist; keep the pot boiling. ¶ 간신히 ～ support *oneself* barely; just manage to get by / 그럭저럭 견뎌

가다 manage to live somehow; get along somehow.
② 《오래가다》 wear; last (long); keep (음식물이); 《저항·지탱하다》 hold (out); stand 《against》; stand up to; withstand; resist 《감당·적합하다》 be fit [good] 《for》; be competent 《for the task》. ¶ 유혹에 ~ resist temptation / 어떤 날씨에도 ~ be proof against all weathers / 무거운 짐을 견디지 못하다 give way under the burden / 구두가 한두 달은 견디겠다 The shoes will wear for a couple of months. / 밧줄이 끊어지지 않고 견딜까 Will the rope hold? / 그의 약한 몸으로는 여행의 피로와 어려움을 견뎌낼 수가 없었다 His feeble frame was unable to resist the fatigue and hardships of the journey.
③ 《참다》 endure 《hardships》; bear; stand; put up with; suffer. ¶ 견딜 수 있는 bearable; endurable; tolerable / 견디기 어려운 unbearable; intolerable / 견딜 수 없어서 unable to bear [endure] any longer / 끝까지 ~ hold fast to the end / 견디기 어려운 고통이다 My suffering is more than I can bear. / 어머니를 뵙고 싶어 못 견디겠다 I am dying to see my mother. *or* I miss my mother a great deal. / 아파서 못 견디겠다 The pain is unbearable. *or* It is too painful to bear. / 이러한 더위는 견딜 수 없다 I cannot stand such intense heat. / 추워서 못 견디겠다 It is unbearably cold.

**견딜성**(一性), **견딜힘** endurance; perseverance; patience. ¶ ~있는 patient; persevering / ~없는 lacking in patience.

**견마**(犬馬) ¶ ~지로(之勞) *one's* humble service 《to country》; *one's* bit of service / ~지로를 아끼지 않다 spare no effort; render what little service *one* can; do the best *one* can.

**견문**(見聞) 《지식》 information; knowledge; 《경험》 experiences; 《관찰》 observation. ~하다 see and hear; observe; experience. ¶ ~이 넓다[좁다] have wide [little] experience; be well-informed [ill-informed] / ~을 넓히다 widen [extend] *one's* knowledge; enrich *one's* stock of information; enlarge *one's* experience / 그는 ~을 넓히기 위해 여행을 떠났다 He went on a tour to see more of the world.

**견문발검**(見蚊拔劍) drawing the sword at a mosquito; making a fuss about trifles.

**견물생심**(見物生心) Seeing is wanting; The object gives rise to the desire.

**견본**(見本) 《상품의》 a sample; 《표본》 a specimen; 《무늬·천의》 a pattern; 《서적·잡지의》 a sample copy; 《본보기》 a model.
¶ ~만 못하다 be below the sample; do not come up to the sample / ~과 같다 be [come] up to (the) sample / ~과 다르다 differ from sample / 이것은 ~과 같지 않다 This does not correspond with [to] the samples. / ~과 같은 것은 겨우 두 세개 뿐이다 Only a few come [are] up to (the) sample. / 이것이 신제품의 ~입니다 These are samples of our new products. / 귀사가 청구하신 ~을 가격표와 함께 소포로 발송했습니다 We have dispatched the sample you requested by parcel post together with a price list.

> 용법 **sample** 어떤 물건 전체가 어떠한 상태인가를 알아보기 위해 임의로 추출한 현물의 하나 또는 한 부분: a sample of yarn(털실의 견본). **specimen** 과학적인 용어로, sample이 과학적·기술적 목적으로 쓰일 때 「표본」이란 뜻으로 사용되는 말: a specimen of iron ore(철광석의 표본). **pattern** 조그맣게 자른 양복지 따위의 견본.

◉ ~검사인 a sampler. ~매매 sale by sample. ~쇄(刷) an advance copy (신간의); a specimen page (발췌한). ~시(市) a sample [trade] fair: 국제 ~시 an international trade fair. ~조판 specimen-page composition. ~주문 order by sample. ~진열실 a sample room. ~책 a sample book. ~추출 sampling. ~카드 a sample card. 임의 ~ a random sample.

**견본**(絹本) a sheet of silk (used for painting, writing).

**견사**(絹紗) silk and gauze.

**견사**(絹絲) silk yarn [thread]. ◉ ~방적 silk-reeling [spinning].

**견사**(繭絲) raw silk-thread.

**견습**(見習) apprenticeship. ⇨ 수습(修習).

**견식**(見識) 《의견》 an opinion; views; 《판단력》 judgment; 《안식》 insight; discernment; 《지식》 knowledge; information. ¶ ~이 풍부한 사람 a man of insight [judgment] / ~이 있다 have a broad vision / 자기 나름의 ~을 가지고 있다 have opinions of *one's* own.

**견신례**(堅信禮) 『가톨릭』 (the order of)

confirmation.

**견실**(堅實) solidity; steadiness; steadfastness; soundness; reliableness. ～하다 (be) solid; steady; steadfast; sound; reliable. ¶ ～하게 steadily; soundly / ～한 사람 a steady 〔reliable〕 person / ～한 사상〔투자〕 a sound idea 〔investment〕 / 사업을 ～하게 하다 do business on sound basis.

**견우성**(牽牛星) 〖천문〗 the Altair.

**견우직녀**(牽牛織女) 〖천문〗 the Altair and the Vega. ¶ ～의 상봉 the meeting of the two lovestars.

**견원**(犬猿) a dog and a monkey; 《앙숙》 mutual dislike 〔enmity〕. ¶ ～지간이다 be on bad terms 《with》; 《부부 사이가》 lead a cat-and-dog life.

**견유**(犬儒) a Cynic. ◉ ～주의 Cynicism. ～학파 Cynics.

**견인**(牽引) pulling; hauling; traction. ～하다 pull; drag; draw; haul; tow. ◉ ～력 pulling capacity; (force of) traction; tractive force. ～차 a tow truck; a tractor; a wrecker: ～차 역할을 하다 play the role of locomotive.

**견인불발**(堅忍不拔) untiring patience; indomitable perseverance; fortitude. ～하다 have untiring patience; have endurance 〔perseverance〕. ¶ ～의 persevering; indomitable / ～의 정신 an iron 〔adamant〕 will; an indomitable spirit.

**견장**(肩章) shoulder strap 〔ensign〕; 《주로 군복의》 an epaulet(te).

**견적**(見積) an estimate; (an) estimation; valuation; a quotation. ～하다 estimate 〔calculate, value〕 《at》; make 〔form〕 an estimate 《of》. ¶ 여유있게 본 ～ a liberal estimate; an estimate on the high side / ～이하로 below the estimate / ～을 웃돌다 exceed the estimate / 아무리 싸게 ～하여도 at the lowest estimate / 비싸게〔싸게〕 ～하다 estimate 《the cost》 high 〔low〕; overestimate 〔underestimate〕 / 대략〔줄잡아〕 ～하다 make a rough 〔moderate〕 estimate / 집수리를 위한 ～을 내다 estimate 〔give a quotation〕 for the repair of a house / 비용은 대략 50만원의 ～이 나온다 The cost are roughly estimated at 500,000 won. ◉ ～ 가격 an estimated cost. ～서 an 〔a written〕 estimate; a pro forma statement: ～서를 작성하다 draw 〔make〕 up an estimate 《for》 / ～서를 자세히 살펴 본 뒤에, 그녀는 그 거래를 진행시키기로 결정했다 After taking a good look at the pro forma statement, she decided to proceed with the transaction. ～송장(送狀) a pro forma invoice. ～액 an estimated sum. 가(假)～ a preliminary estimate. 개산(概算)～ an approximate 〔a rough〕 estimate. 세목～ a detailed estimate 정밀～ a close estimate.

**견제**(牽制) 《억제》 (a) restraint; a check; curbing; 〖군사〗 containment; 〖야구〗 a pick-off throw. ～하다 check; hold in check; restrain; curb; 〖군사〗 contain; 〖야구〗 peg a runner 《on the base》. ¶ ～와 균형 check and balance / 서로 ～하다 hold each other in check / 권력을 남용하지 못하도록 아무를 ～하다 check *a person* so that he will not abuse his power / 적의 전진을 ～하기 위해 대군을 보내다 send a large number of troops to contain the enemy's advance. ◉ ～공격 a containing attack. ～구 〖야구〗 a pick-off throw; a feint ball: ～구를 던지다 throw a ball to peg a runner on the base. ～작전 diversionary tactics. ～행동 diversionary move; delaying tactics.

**견주다** ① 《비교하다》 compare 《the two, A and B》. ¶ 견줄 수 있는 comparable / 견주어 보면 by comparison; (as) compared with... / 길이를 견주어 보다 compare length / 견주어 판단하다 judge 〔decide〕 by comparison. ② 《겨루다》 rival; compete 《with》. ¶ 힘〔기술〕을 ～ measure *one's* strength 〔skill〕 with 〔against〕 《*another's*》 / 견줄 만한 것이 없다 be unique; be unparalleled; stand unrivaled.

**견지** a fishing troll 〔reel〕. ¶ ～질하다 fish with a troll; troll (for) fish.

**견지**(見地) a viewpoint; a standpoint; a point of view; an angle. ¶ 정치적〔도덕적〕 ～ the political 〔moral〕 point of view / 이 ～에서 보면 from this point of view; viewed 〔seen〕 「in this light 〔from this angle〕 / 모든 ～에서 검토하다 study from all angles 〔points〕 / 사물을 대국적 ～에서 보다 look at things from larger point of view; take a broad view 《of *matters*》 / 다른 ～에서 고찰하다 consider 《*a matter*》 from a different standpoint / 소비자 ～에서 보면 우유값이 충분히 내린 것이 아니다 From the consumer's point of view milk prices have not gone down enough.

**견지하다**(堅持—) adhere to; stick to;

hold fast to; hold on to; maintain firmly. ¶ 민주주의를 ~ hold on to 〔adhere to〕 the idea of democracy / 정책〔원칙〕을 ~ hold fast 〔stick〕 to the policy 〔principle〕 / 찬성〔반대〕의 태도를 ~ maintain *one's* support 〔opposition〕 firmly.

**견직물**(絹織物) silk fabrics 〔goods〕; silks; mercery 《영》. ◉ ~공장 a silk mill. ~상 a silk merchant.

**견진**(堅振) 〖가톨릭〗 confirmation. ◉ ~성사 the sacrament of confirmation: ~성사를 받은 사람 a confirmed man / ~성사를 베풀다 confirm.

**견책**(譴責) a reprimand; a rebuke; a reproof; a censure. ~하다 reprimand; rebuke; reprove; censure. ¶ ~을 받다 be reprimanded 《for》; receive a rebuke. ◉ ~처분 《receive》 an official reprimand 《for》.

**견치**(犬齒) a canine (tooth). ⇨ 송곳니.

**견학**(見學) study by observation. ~하다 visit 〔tour〕 《a factory》 for 「study 〔information〕. ¶ ~하러 가다 make a field trip to 《a shipyard》 / 우리는 텔레비전 방송국을 ~했다 We visited a television station for study.
◉ ~여행 a field 〔an observation〕 trip; a tour for study.

**견해**(見解) an opinion; a view; an outlook (전망); 《관점》 a slant.
¶ ~가 일치하다, ~를 같이 하다 agree 《with》; hold the same view 《with *a person*》; have the same opinion 《as》 / ~를 달리하다 disagree 《with》; differ in opinion; have 〔hold〕 a different opinion 〔view〕 《from》 / 문제에 관하여 잘못된 ~를 가지다 have the wrong slant on the problem / ~를 나타내다 express *one's* opinion 〔view(s)〕 《on, about》 / ~를 구하다 ask 《*a person's*》 opinion 《for, about》 / 그것에 대한 너의 ~는? What's your opinion about it? / 이 문제에 대해서는 ~가 구구하다 Opinion is divided on this question. / 그것은 ~의 차이다 It's a matter of opinion. / 이 점에서 명확한 ~의 차이가 드러났다 At this point a clear divergence of views emerged.

**견고틀다** persist 〔hold out〕 to the end; struggle 〔dispute, compete〕 over.

**겯다**[1] ① 《기름에 배다》 become greasy; be oiled. ¶ 땟국에 겯은 옷 a garment greasy with grime / 종이가 (기름에) 잘 겯었다 The paper has been well oiled. ② 《일에 익다》 become experienced 《in》; be quite at home 《in》. ③ 《기름에 배게 하다》 oil; infiltrate 《*a thing*》 with oil. ¶ 종이를 기름에 ~ oil paper.

**겯다**[2] ① 《엮다》 weave; braid. ¶ 삿자리를 ~ weave 〔make〕 a reed mat. ② 《어긋매끼다》 stack; pile up crisscross. ¶ 총을 ~ stack arms.

**겯지르다** place 《*a thing*》 〔put 《*a thing*》 up〕 crosswise; cross; entwine; intersect.

**겯질리다** ① 《물건이》 be crossed 〔intersected〕; be placed 〔put up〕 crosswise. ② 《일이》 get entangled with each other. ③ 《힘에 겹다》 get exhausted 《at a hard task》; be strained.

**결**[1] ① 《물의》 a wave (in the water); 《숨결의》 waves of breath; breathing. ② 《나무·돌 따위의》 grain; 《피부·천 따위의》 (a) texture. ¶ 비단결 a silky 〔velvety〕 texture / 결이 거칠다 be rough; be coarse-grained; be of coarse texture / 결이 곱다 be fine; be fine-grained; be of close texture / 살결이 곱다 have smooth 〔delicate〕 skin. ③ 《마음의》 disposition; temper (-ament).

**결**[2] ① 《언뜻·우연히》 incidental 《to》; happening (to) in passing; (on) the wave of. ¶ 눈결에 보다 see out of the corner of *one's* eye; catch a glimpse / 귓결에 종소리를 들었다 My ears happened to catch the sound of the bell. / 바람결에 파도 소리가 들려 온다 The wind brings with it the sound of the waves.
② 《…하는 길》 (in) the course of; in passing while 《*do*ing》; at the same time as; when; while; while at it. ¶ 지나가는 결에 잠깐 들르다 drop in for a moment on *one's* way 《for》.
③ 《사품》 (as) an incidental result of. ¶ 잠결에 in *one's* sleep; while asleep / 꿈결에 듣다 listen half asleep / 꿈결 같다 be like a dream; be dreamlike; be illusory.

**결가부좌**(結跏趺坐) 〖불교〗 sitting with *one's* legs crossed (as in Buddhist statues).

**결강**(缺講) ~하다 do not give *one's* lecture; cut a lecture. ¶ K교수는 오늘 ~입니다 Professor K is not giving his lecture today.

**결격**(缺格) disqualification; 〖법〗 incapacity. ¶ ~이 되다 be disqualified 《for a position》. ◉ ~사유 a disqualification. ~자 a disqualified person.

**결과**(結果) a result; a consequence; an effect; an outcome; 《성과》 fruit(s); a

product; 《결말》 an end.
¶ 최종 ~ a final 〔an end〕 result / 원인과 ~ cause and effect / 그 ~(로서) as a result (of...); in 〔as a〕 consequence (of...) / 필연적 ~로서 as a necessary consequence / 지금까지 ~로 보아 in view of the results so far achieved / 좋은 ~를 낳다〔얻다〕 produce 〔obtain〕 good results / …한 ~가 되다 result 〔end〕 in...; come 〔turn〕 out ...; lead to... / ~가 신통치 않다 the result does not come up to *one's* expectation 〔is not quite satisfactory〕 / 당연한 ~로서 …하게 되다 as a natural consequence it follows that ... / 뜻밖의 ~가 되다 reach 〔come to〕 an unexpected result / 실상 …와 같은 ~가 되다 reach substantially the same result as... / ~에 대해 책임을 지다 take 〔answer for〕 the consequence / 반대 ~를 가져오다 bring (about) a reverse effect 〔an opposite result〕 / 바라는 ~를 얻다 attain a looked-for 〔desired〕 effect; yield 〔produce〕 desirable results / 수술 ~는 어떠했느냐 How did the (surgical) operation come out? / 결국 그것은 어떤 ~가 되었느냐 How did it finally turn out? / 선거 ~는 예측할 수 없다 No one can foresee 〔foretell〕 the outcome of the election. / 중대한 ~가 될 것이다 It may have serious consequences. / 시험 ~는 오늘 발표된다 The results of the examination will be published today. / ~적으로 그녀는 한 달도 못되어 파직되었다 As things turned out, she was fired before the month was out. / 이 발명은 그의 오랜 노력의 ~로 완성된 것이다 This invention is the fruit of many years of his hard work 〔effort〕.

> 용법 **result** 어떤 행위·사건의 결과를 뜻하는 가장 일반적인 말. **consequence** 원인에 대한 직접적인 결과가 아니라, 어떤 일·사건 등과 관련되어 나타나는 필연 또는 논리적인 결과를 뜻함. **effect** 어떤 원인·작용으로 인해 생기는 직접적인 결과. **outcome** result보다 「결말」의 뜻이 강한 말로, 문제점을 포함한 사건 따위의 결과를 뜻함.

◉ ~론 criticism 《on past events》 based on the result; second-guessing: ~론자 a second-guesser.

**결구**(結球) 〖식물〗 a head.

**결구**(結構) 《얽거나 짜서 만듦》 structure; construction; fabrication; 《구성》 constitution. ~하다 put 〔fit〕 together; frame; construct.

**결구**(結句) the concluding line of a verse; the end; the last part of a piece of writing; the conclusion; 〖문법〗 apodosis.

**결국**(結局) 《마침내》 after all; finally; ultimately; eventually; in the end; in the long run; in the final analysis; when it comes down to it; 《끝장》 end; conclusion; close.

> 용법 **after all** 「여러 모로 생각되었거나, 말이 있었거나, 일이 있었지만, 결국은 …」의 뜻. 과거형, 완료형과 함께 흔히 쓰이며 지나온 과거의 경과를 말함. **in the long run** 「도중에 여러 가지 일이 있더라도 긴 안목으로 보면」의 뜻. 미래의 가능성을 나타내며, 주로 미래형과 함께 쓰임. **in the end** 「사물이 진행되고 난 최후의 단계에서는」의 뜻. after all과 같은 뜻으로 쓰일 때도 많음.

¶ ~ …하게 되다 prove 〔turn out〕 to be...; end 〔result〕 in... / ~ 비싼 셈이다 It doesn't pay in the long run. / ~ 어떻게 될까 How will the matter come out? / 그것이 ~ 제일 싸게 먹힌다 It is the cheapest in the long run. / ~ 내가 옳았다 I was right after all. / ~ 기차를 놓치고 말았다 The result was that I missed the train. / ~ 모두 경찰서에 연행되었다 In consequence, all were taken to the police station. / 우리들의 시도는 ~ 실패로 끝났다 Our attempt 「failed after all 〔resulted in failure〕. / ~은 돈 문제로 귀착된다 When it comes down to it, money's what it's all about. *or* In the end it's a question of money. / ~ 어찌 됐느냐 How did it 「end 〔turn out〕?

**결궤하다**(決潰—) collapse; break (down); give way. ⇨ 무너지다, 터지다.

**결근**(缺勤) absence; nonattendance; 《계획적인》 absenteeism. ~하다 absent *oneself* 《from office》; be absent 《from duties》; be away 《from work》; stay home 《from the office》; take a day off (하루의). ¶ 나는 어제 회사를 ~했다 I was absent 〔stayed away〕 from my office yesterday. / 오늘은 열이 있어서 ~하겠습니다 《전화로 말할 경우》 I cannot come to work today because I feel feverish.
◉ ~계 a report 〔notice〕 of absence:

~계를 내다 report *one's* absence 《to》; give notice that *one* is going to take a day off. ~율 the rate of nonattendance. ~일수 the number of absences. ~자 an absentee. 장기~ a long-term absence: 장기 ~하다 absent *oneself* for a long term.

**결기**(一氣) impetuosity; vehemence; hot temper; bravery. ¶ ~ 있는 사람 a man of impetuous temper; a hot-headed man / ~에 아무를 때리다 beat *a person* up in a fit of anger.

**결나다** get angry; flare 〔flame〕 up; burst 〔fly〕 into a passion. ¶ 결나서 싸우다 fight in a fit of passion.

**결내다** give vent to *one's* anger; vent *one's* pique; get out of temper; flare up; fly 〔burst〕 into a passion; fly into a rage 〔passion, temper〕. ¶ 쉽게 ~ be apt to flare up.

**결단**(決斷) (a) decision; determination; (a) resolution. ~하다 decide 《on》; determine 《to》; resolve 《to》. ¶ ~력이 있는 사람 a man of decision / ~을 내리다 reach 〔come to〕 a definite decision / ~을 못 내리다 be unable to make up *one's* mind; hesitate / ~력이 있다〔없다〕 be decisive 〔indecisive〕; be a decisive 〔an indecisive〕 person / 그는 ~이 빠르다〔느리다〕 He is quick 〔slow〕 to make decisions. / 아무런 ~도 내리지 못했다 No decision was reached. / ~력이 없는 사람은 책임자 자리에 앉을 수 없다 A man who lacks decision cannot hold a position of responsibility.

**결단**(結團) ~하다 organize 〔form〕 《a team, a group》. ¶ 한국 대표 팀이 ~되었다 A Korean national team was formed. ◉ ~식 an inaugural meeting (to celebrate the formation 〔organization〕) 《of a baseball team》.

**결단코**(決斷一) never; by no means; on no account. ¶ ~ 그런 일은 없다 I positively deny it. *or* It is an impossibility. / ~ 그런 일은 않겠다 I would not do it for the world. / 그는 ~ 그런 짓을 할 사람이 아니다 He is the last person to do such a thing. / ~ 양보 않겠다 Never will I make a concession! / ~ 허용 않겠다 I won't allow it on any account. / 그녀를 ~ 버리지 않겠다 I will never leave her.

**결당**(結黨) the founding 〔formation〕 of a party. ~하다 found 〔form, organize〕 a party. ◉ ~식 the inaugural ceremony of a party.

**결딴** ruin; destruction; collapse; fall; downfall; 《파산》 bankruptcy. ~나다 go to ruin; meet destruction; be ruined 〔spoilt〕; fail; go wrong; fall through (계획 등이). ¶ ~을 내다 spoil; ruin; bring ruin 〔destruction, bankruptcy〕 《to》 / 건강〔집안〕이 ~나다 *one's* health 〔family〕 is ruined / 은행이 ~나다 a bank goes bankrupt / 몸을 ~내다 ruin *one's* health / 기계를 ~내다 put a machine out of order / 폭풍으로 곡물 수확이 ~났다 The storm has spoiled 〔damaged〕 the crop.

**결렬**(決裂) (a) rupture; a breakdown. ~하다 break down; be broken off; come to 〔end in〕 (a) rupture. ¶ 교섭〔협상〕의 ~ rupture of negotiations / ~시키다 break off 《negotiations, the engagement》; rupture / 노사간의 교섭은 ~됐다 The talk between management and labor came to a rupture.

**결례**(缺禮) lack of courtesy; negligence 〔neglect〕 of etiquette; failure 〔omission〕 to pay *one's* respect 〔compliments, greetings〕. ~하다 neglect 〔fail, omit〕 to pay *one's* compliments.

**결론**(結論) a conclusion; concluding remarks. ~하다〔짓다〕 conclude; draw 〔form〕 a conclusion. ¶ ~적으로 in conclusion; to conclude / ~에 도달하다 reach 〔come to, arrive at〕 a conclusion / 조급하게 ~을 내리다 jump to a conclusion; form a hasty conclusion / 그가 유죄라는 ~에 이르다 come to the conclusion that he is guilty / 우리는 그 배가 틀림없이 침몰했다고 ~을 내렸다 We concluded that the ship must have sunk. / 어떤 ~에 이를지 아무도 모른다 Nobody knows what kind of conclusion they will reach.

**결리다** ① 《아프다》 have a pain 〔stitch〕. ¶ 어깨가 ~ feel stiff in the shoulders / 옆구리가 ~ have a stitch in the side / 숨을 쉬면 가슴이 결린다 It pains me to breathe. ② 《기를 못 펴다》 be cowed; be shrunk; flinch 《from》.

**결막**(結膜) 〖해부〗 the conjunctiva. ¶ 급성 출혈성 ~염 acute hemorrhagic conjunctivitis (생략 AHC).
◉ ~염 conjunctivitis. ~충혈 hyperaemia conjunctivae.

**결말**(結末) 《끝》 an end; a close; a conclusion; 《결과》 a result; an outcome; 《낙착》 settlement. ~나다 come to a conclusion 〔an end〕; be settled. ¶ 행복〔불행〕한 ~ a happy 〔an unhappy〕 ending / ~을 내다 bring 《*some-*

*thing*》 to an end 〔a conclusion〕; put an end to 《*something*》; settle 《a problem》 / 학원 분쟁은 아직 ~이 나지 않았다 The campus dispute has not been settled yet. / 그 사건의 ~을 알고 있느냐 Do you know the end of the affair? / 속히 이 문제의 ~을 짓자 Let's settle this problem quickly.

**결박**(結縛) binding; tying; pinioning. ~하다〔짓다〕 bind; tie; pinion; 《수갑 채우다》 shackle the hands. ¶ 뒷짐 ~을 당하여 with *one's* hands tied behind / 도둑을 ~하다 tie a thief with cords; pinion a thief.

**결백**(潔白) 《순결》 purity; 《청렴》 integrity; 《무죄》 innocence; guiltlessness. ~하다 (be) pure; stainless; innocent; not guilty; clean(-handed). ¶ ~한 사람 a man of integrity; a man with a clean record / 완강히 ~을 주장하다 persist in pleading *one's* innocence / 자신의 ~을 입증하다 prove *one's* innocence; clear 〔vindicate〕 *oneself* 《from a charge of theft》.

**결번**(缺番) a missing number. ¶ 목록에서 4번은 ~이다 The number four is blank on the roll.

**결벽**(潔癖) 《청결을 좋아하는 성질》 fastidiousness; a love of 〔an obsession with〕 cleanliness; 《부정을 혐오하는 성질》 uprightness; scrupulousness. ~하다 (be) fastidious 《about》; cleanly; scrupulous; upright. ¶ ~한 사람 a fastidious 〔scrupulous〕 person / 돈에 ~하다 do not touch tainted money / 정직하고 ~한 정치가란 극히 드물다 Honest and upright politicians rarely exist. ◉ ~증 〖의학〗 mysophobia: ~증의 particular 〔fussy〕 about cleanliness.

**결별**(訣別) = 이별(離別).

**결본**(缺本) a missing volume; a lacking book (in a series).

**결부**(結付) linking; tying together; connecting. ~하다 link; tie; connect. ¶ …와 ~시켜 생각하다 consider 《A》 in relation to 〔in connection with〕 《B》.

**결빙**(結氷) freezing; ice formation. ~하다 freeze 〔be frozen〕 over; be icebound. ¶ ~을 방지하다 prevent ice formation. ◉ ~기 the freezing season. ~점 the freezing point.

**결사**(決死) ¶ ~의〔적인〕 desperate; at the risk of *one's* life / ~적인 싸움 a desperate battle / ~의 각오로 with desperate courage / ~ 반대하다 desperately oppose 《a bill》 / ~의 각오로 전진하다 advance in the face of death / 그는 ~의 각오로 스카이다이빙에 도전했다 He challenged skydiving at the risk of his life. ◉ ~대 a commando (unit); a suicide corps: ~대를 적진에 공중 투입하다 airdrop a suicide squad into the enemy positions.

**결사**(結社) forming an association 〔a society, a fraternity〕. ~하다 form an association 〔a society〕. ¶ ~의 자유 freedom of association.

**결삭다** *one's* temper softens; be mollified 〔soothed〕.

**결산**(決算) settlement 〔closing〕 (of accounts). ~하다 settle 〔balance〕 the accounts; close the books. ¶ 본사의 ~은 3월과 9월에 있다 We settle accounts in March and September. ◉ ~기 a settlement term. ~보고 a statement of accounts: ~보고하다 make a report on closing accounts. ~액 settled accounts. ~위원회 a committee on accounts. ~일 a settling day. 1·4분기 ~ the first quarter settlement.

**결석**(缺席) absence; nonattendance; 《구어》 a cut (수업의 무단 결석); 〖법〗 default. ~하다 be absent 《from》; absent *oneself* 《from》; fail to attend; do not appear; 〖법〗 default. ¶ ~이 잦다 be irregular in *one's* attendance; have a poor attendance record / 오후 수업에 ~하다 cut the afternoon class / 그 선생님의 강의에는 한 번도 ~한 적이 없다 I never missed his lecture. / 그는 석달이나 학교에 ~하고 있다 He has been absent from school for three months. / ~입니다 《학생의 대답》 Absent, sir. ◉ ~계 a notice 〔report〕 of absence 〔nonattendance〕. ~률 (the rate of) absenteeism. ~자 an absentee; 《재판의》 a defaulter. ~재판 a trial by default. ~판결 judgment by default. 병고~ absence on account of illness.

**결석**(結石) 〖의학〗 a calculus (*pl.* -li); a stone 《in the bladder》. ¶ 신장 ~ a kidney stone. ◉ ~증 lithiasis.

**결선**(決選) a final election; a runoff. ~하다 elect (by final vote). ◉ ~투표 a final vote 〔ballot〕; a decisive vote: ~투표를 하다 take a final vote 《on》; hold a final ballot 《for an office》.

**결성**(結成) formation; organization. ~하다 form 《a club》; organize 《a union》. ◉ ~대회 an inaugural meeting 〔rally〕.

**결속**(結束) 《묶음》 binding 〔banding〕

together; 《사람의 결합》 union; unity; solidarity. ～하다 band 〔stick〕 together; be united; unite. ¶ ～하여 in a body; in union 〔unity〕/ ～을 굳히다〔강화하다〕 strengthen the solidarity 〔unity〕; tighten the union 《of》/ ～이 안 되다 fail to present a united front / ～해서 일에 임하다 unite in *do*ing; make a united effort to *do* / 당내의 ～을 도모하다 solidify a party.

**결손**(缺損) 《손실》 (a) loss; deficiency; 《부족》 shortage; a deficit(적자). ¶ 100만 원의 ～ a loss of a million won / ～을 메우다 cover the loss 〔deficit〕; make up (for) the loss / ～(을) 보다, ～(이) 나다 suffer 〔result in〕 a loss 《of one million won》/ 이 때문에 1,000만원의 ～이 생겼다 This caused a deficit of 10 million won. / 회사는 2년간 계속해서 ～을 보았다 Our company suffered a series of losses for two years. ◉ ～금 the amount of loss. ～처분 deficits disposal.

**결승**(決勝) the decision of a contest; 《결승전》 the finals. ～하다 decide victories; fight to a finish. ¶ ～(전)에서 이기다〔패하다〕 win 〔lose〕 the finals / ～에 진출하다 go into the finals; reach 〔make〕 the finals.
◉ ～전 the final game 〔match, round, contest〕; the finals; 《동점자간의》 a runoff; a play-off: 데이비스 컵 ～전 the Davis Cup finals / ～전 출장 선수 a finalist. ～점 the goal; the finishing line; 《야구의》 the winning 〔deciding〕 run: ～점에 도달하다 reach 「the goal 〔the finishing line〕; breast 〔break〕 the (finishing) tape. ～홈런 《야구의》 the game-winning〔-deciding〕 homer.

**결승문자**(結繩文字) a quipu.

**결식**(缺食) going without a meal. ～하다 「go without 〔miss, skip〕 a meal. ◉ ～아동 undernourished 〔poorly-fed〕 children; pupils without lunch (점심을).

**결실**(結實) 《열매》 bearing fruit; fruition; [비유적] fruition; realization. ～하다 bear 〔produce〕 fruit; fruit; [비유적] bear fruit; be realized; produce (good) results; come to fruition. ¶ ～하지 못하다 be fruitless; be sterile; bear no fruit / 금년은 사과의 ～이 매우 좋았다 The apples fruited well 〔bore a lot of fruit〕 this year. / 그 정책은 ～을 맺었다 The policy bore fruits. / 그의 노력은 ～을 보았다 He was rewarded for his efforts. *or* His efforts produced good results. ◉ ～기 the fruit season.

**결심**(決心) determination; resolution. ～하다 make up *one's* mind 《to *do*》; decide 《to *do*, upon》; form a resolution 《to》; be determine 《to *do*》; resolve. ¶ 굳은 ～ a firm 〔determined, an unshakable〕 resolution / 아직 ～이 서지 않다 be still undecided 《about what to do》; be still in two minds 《about *something*》/ ～을 굳게 하다 make a firm determination / 자기의 ～을 굳게 지키다 stand fast to 〔stick to〕 *one's* resolution / ～을 번복하다 give up *one's* resolution; change *one's* mind / ～이 약해지다 get weakened in *one's* resolution / 그녀는 그의 프로포즈를 받아들이기로 ～했다 She has determined to accept his proposal. / 우리는 끝까지 싸워 나갈 ～이다 We are determined to fight it out. / 그의 ～이 흔들리고 있다 His resolution is shaken 〔staggered〕. / 그는 담배를 끊기로 ～했다 He resolved to quit smoking.

**결심**(結審) the conclusion of a hearing 〔trial〕; the decision. ～하다 close (a hearing); decide (a case). ◉ ～공판 the final trial.

**결여**(缺如) (a) deficiency; (a) lack; (a) want. ～하다 be lacking; be deficient; be wanting in; [자동사] lack; want. ¶ 경험〔상식, 자제심〕의 ～ a lack of experience 〔common sense, self-control〕/ 동정과 이해의 ～ a lack of sympathy and understanding / 그의 답변에는 성의가 ～되어 있다 I doubt his sincerity in his answer.

**결연**(結緣) 《관계를》 forming a relationship; making a connection; 《불교와》 becoming a believer in Buddhism. ～하다 form a relationship; be converted to 〔embrace〕 Buddhism.

**결연하다**(決然―) (be) determined; firm; resolute; decisive. ¶ 결연히 firmly; resolutely; in determined 〔decisive〕 manner / 결연한 태도 a determined attitude / 나는 결연히 감행했다 I crossed the Rubicon.

**결원**(缺員) a vacancy; a vacant position 〔post〕; an opening. ¶ ～을 채우다 fill (up) a vacancy / ～이 생겼다 A post has been vacated. *or* A vacancy occured. / ～이 생기면 채용하겠다 I will employ you if there is a vacancy. / 그 자리는 아직 ～인 채로 있다 The position is still vacant 〔open〕.

**결의**(決意) (a particular) determination; resolution; a firm will. ¶ 단호한〔확고한〕 ~ inflexible determination; firm resolution / ~의 표명 a declaration of resolve / ~를 굳히다 confirm *one's* determination / ~를 새로이 하다 make a fresh determination; renew *one's* resolve《to》/ 중대한 ~를 하다 take a decisive step; cross〔pass〕the Rubicon.

**결의**(決議) a decision; a resolution. ~하다 resolve; pass〔adopt〕a resolution; decide; vote. ¶ 부대(附帶) ~ an additional resolution / 국회의 ~ a resolution of the House / 총괄적인 ~ an omnibus〔a catchall〕resolution / 불신임안을 ~하다 pass a vote of nonconfidence《in the cabinet》/ 지난 회의에서 그 계획은 찬성〔반대〕~되었다 The last meeting decided for〔against〕the plan. / 회의에서 ~된 사항은 다음과 같다 The following has been resolved at the meeting.
◉ ~권 the right to vote. ~기관 a decision-making body〔organ〕. ~문 a (written) resolution: ~문을 수교하다 hand〔present, submit〕a resolution《to》. ~사항 resolutions.

**결의**(結義) ~하다 swear to be《brothers》; take an oath of brotherhood. ◉ ~형제 sworn brothers.

**결의안**(決議案) a resolution. ¶ 전쟁 반대의 ~ a resolution against war / 절충(折衷) 단일 ~ a single compromised resolution / 구속력이 없는 ~ a nonbinding resolution / …을 요구하는 ~ a draft resolution calling for… / ~을 제출하다 move〔introduce〕a resolution / ~은 절대 다수로 통과되었다 The resolution was carried by a large majority.

**결자**(缺字) an omitted word;《인쇄의》a blank type. ¶ 이 교정쇄에는 ~가 많다 Those proof sheets are full of blanks.

**결장**(結腸)〘해부〙the colon. ◉ ~부 the colic region. ~염 colonitis.

**결재**(決裁) decision; approval; sanction. ~하다 decide《on》; make a decision《on, about》. ¶ ~를 바라다 submit《*a matter*》for《*a person's*》approval / ~를 받다 obtain《*a person's*》approval〔sanction〕/ 회장의 ~를 아직 못 받았다 It remains to be sanctioned by the chairman. ◉ ~권 the right of decision; decisive power.

**결전**(決戰) a decisive〔final〕battle;《분쟁 따위의》a showdown;《경기의》the deciding match〔game, race〕; finals;《동점자간의》a runoff〔play-off〕. ~하다 fight a decisive battle; fight to a finish. ¶ ~ 단계 the decisive stage; the zero hour / ~ 단계에 들어가다 reach〔enter into〕a decisive stage / 적과 ~에 임하다 wage a decisive battle with the enemy.

**결절**(結節)《마디》a knot;〘의학〙a tuber; a tubercle; a node.

**결점**(缺點) a fault; a defect;《흠》a flaw; a blemish;《약점》a weak point; a weakness; a shortcoming; a drawback. ¶ ~이 있는 defective; faulty / ~이 없는 flawless; faultless; perfect / ~을 보충하다 cover〔make〕up《*a person's*》faults / ~을 숨기다 conceal a defect / ~을 찾다 find fault with《*a person, a thing*》/ 나는 늘 내 ~을 고치려고 노력하고 있다 I always try to correct my faults. / 욕심 많은 것이 그의 유일한 ~이다 Avarice is the only weak point in his character. / 도시 생활에도 ~은 있다 Urban life has its faults, too. / ~이 없는 사람은 없다 No one is free from faults. *or* There is no man but has some faults.

**결정**(決定) (a) decision; (a) determination; (a) conclusion; (a) settlement(해결). ~하다 decide; determine; conclude; settle; fix. ¶ ~적(으로) definite(ly); final(ly); decisive(ly); conclusive(ly) / ~적인 증거 decisive proofs / ~적 순간 a crucial moment / ~적 승리 a decisive victory / 방침을 ~하다 decide on a course of action / 날짜를 ~하다 fix〔set〕the date《for *a thing*》/ ~을 미루다 put off〔postpone, delay〕*one's* decision / ~이 내려지다 the decision is reached《as to, about, on》/ 그의 후임은 이미 ~되었습니까 Has his successor been chosen already? / ~을 서두를 필요는 없다 There is no (need for) hurry in reaching a decision. (★ need for의 생략은 구어 용법) / 승전에는 우리 공군이 ~적인 역할을 했다 Our air force was decisive in winning the war. / 위원회는 그 건에 관하여 중대한 ~을 내렸다 The committee made an important decision on that matter.
◉ ~권 the decisive power; (the) authority to decide《*a matter*》; the say《in *a matter*》《구어》: ~권을 쥐다 have the decisive power / 대표자에게 ~권을 주다 delegate「authority〔the say〕in the matter to the represen-

tative / ～권은 너에게 있다 The decision is in your hands. ～론 determinism: ～론자 a determinist. ～서 a written decision. ～타 〖야구〗 a winning hit. ～투표 the decisive vote. ～판(版) a definitive edition; 《번역의》 an authentic version: 한영 사전의 ～판 a definitive Korean-English dictionary.

**결정**(結晶) 《작용》 crystallization; 《결정체》 (a) crystal; 《성과》 fruit(s). ～하다 crystallize 《into》; be crystallized; bear fruit (노력 등의). ¶ 노력의 ～ the fruit of *one's* efforts. ◉ ～계 〖광물〗 system of crystallization. ～수 〖화학〗 water of crystallization. ～질 crystalline structure. ～형 (a) crystal form.

**결제**(決濟) settlement; liquidation. ～하다 settle 〔square〕 (accounts) 《with》; liquidate. ¶ 미～의 계정 outstanding accounts / 그 계정의 ～는 끝났다 I've settled the bill. / 그 부채는 아직 ～되지 않았다 The debts are still left outstanding. / 어음 ～를 재촉당하고 있다 I've been urged to honor the draft. ◉ ～일 a settlement day. ～자금 a settlement fund. 삼각～ the triple settlement.

**결집**(結集) ① 《모음》 concentration; focus. ～하다 concentrate; gather together. ¶ 그들은 총력을 ～하여 난국 극복에 임했다 All of them joined forces in an all-out effort to surmount the crisis. ② 〖불교〗 *Samgiti* (Sans.).

**결착**(決着·結着) conclusion; end; settlement; decision. ⇨ 결말(結末).

**결체**(結滯) 〖의학〗 acrotism; pause 〔intermittence〕 in the pulse.

**결체**(結締) tying up. ～하다 tie up. ◉ ～조직 connective tissue.

**결초보은**(結草報恩) ～하다 carry *one's* gratitude beyond the grave.

**결코**(決—) definitely 〔absolutely〕 not...; never; by no means;... on no account; in no way; not... in the least; not... at all; not in any sense; under no circumstances. ⇨ 결단코.

> 용법 **never, by no means, on no account**는 문장 중에 다른 부정어가 없을 때 사용된다. 다른 부정어가 따로 있으면 by any means, on any account 처럼 쓰인다. **under no circumstance** 「어떤 상태〔상황〕하에서도 …아니다」, **not in any sense**는 「어떤 의미로도 …아니다」란 뜻.

¶ ～ 그렇지 않다 No, never, it isn't so. *or* I am positive that it is not so. *or* That is absolutely wrong. / 그는 ～ 나쁜 사람은 아니다 He is by no means a bad man. / ～ 그를 용서할 수 없다 I can't forgive him on any account. / 사태는 ～ 위급하지 않다 The situation is in no way serious. / 그런 일은 ～하면 안 된다 You should never do such a thing. / 결과는 ～ 만족할 만한 것이 아니었다 The result was far from satisfactory. / 그는 ～ 바보가 아니다 He is by no means a fool. / 그런 행위는 ～ 용납되지 않는다 Such conduct is forbidden under any circumstances. / 그는 ～ 자네를 속일 사람이 아니다 He is the last person to deceive you.

**결탁**(結託) collusion; conspiracy. ～하다 conspire 〔collude〕 《with》; be in collusion 〔cahoots, league〕 with. ¶ …와 ～하여 in conspiracy 〔collusion〕 with / 업자와 ～하다 conspire with a trader.

**결투**(決鬪) a duel; a shoot-out (총잡이의). ～하다 fight a duel 《with》; duel 《with》. ¶ ～용 권총 a dueling pistol / ～를 신청하다 challenge 《*a person*》 to a duel / ～에 응하다 accept a challenge to a duel. ◉ ～입회인 a second. ～자 a duelist. ～장 a (written) challenge (to a duel).

**결판**(決判) ～나다 be settled 〔decided〕; be brought to an end. ¶ ～(을) 내다 settle 《a quarrel》; bring 《*a matter*》 to an end / 그것은 이제 ～이 났다 It's over and done with. / 이제 ～을 내도 될 때다 It's about time we are through with it.

**결핍**(缺乏) want; lack; 《부족》 shortage; deficiency; scarcity. ～하다 want; lack; be lacking 〔wanting〕 《in》; 《부족하다》 be 〔run〕 short 《of》; be deficient 《in》. ¶ 식량의 심각한 ～ a desperate shortage of food / 계획은 자금～으로 실패했다 The plan did not work well for want of funds. ◉ ～증 a 《vitamin》 deficiency disease.

**결하다**(決—) ① ＝결정하다. ② 《승부를》 decide 《a contest》; play off 《a tie》. ¶ 자웅을 ～ fight a decisive battle 《with》; fight 〔battle〕 it out 《with》; come to a showdown.

**결하다**(缺—) (be) lacking; deficient; wanting; missing.

**결함**(缺陷) 《결점》 a defect; a fault; a flaw; shortcomings; a gap; 《부족》 (a) deficiency; a deficit. ¶ 성격상의 ～ a defect in *one's* character / 사회 제도의

～ the vices of the social system / ～ 있는 defective; faulty / ～ 없는 perfect; complete / 인격적인 ～을 많이 지닌 사람 a person with numerous personal defects / ～을 드러내다 betray *one's* weakness / ～을 지적하다 point out defects《in》/ 그것은 기계상의 ～이었다 It was a defect in the mechanism.
◉ ～상품 a defective commodity; defective merchandise. ～제품 a faulty product. ～차(車) a defective car; a car with a《structural》defect. 무～운동 a Zero Defect campaign.

**결합**(結合) union; combination; cohesion;〖화학〗bonding;《원자핵의》fusion;《우주선의》docking. ～하다 unite《with》; combine《with》; join《with, together》; link《together》; bond《with, together》. ¶ 분자의 ～ the bonding of molecules / A와 B를 ～하다 unite〔combine〕A with B / 공통된 이해 관계에 의해 ～되다 be linked together by common interest / 기름과 물은 쉽사리 ～하지 않는다 Oil and water do not readily combine〔mix〕. ◉ ～력 coherence. ～체 a corporate body. ～효과〖물리·화학〗the packing effect.

**결항**(缺航)《선박의》the cancelation of a sailing;《항공기의》a flight cancelation; the cancelation of a flight. ～하다 cancel the sailing〔flight〕《on a line》. ¶ 706편은 ～됩니다《비행기》Flight 706 will be canceled. / 폭풍 때문에 부산 제주간 연락선은 ～됐다 The Busan-Jeju ferryboat service was canceled owing to the storm.

**결핵**(結核)〖의학〗《폐결핵》tuberculosis (생략 T.B.); consumption. ¶ ～성의 tubercular; tuberculous / ～에 걸리기 쉬운 소질 a predisposition to tuberculosis / ～에 걸리다 get T.B.; contract tuberculosis / ～을 박멸하다 eradicate〔uproot〕tuberculosis.
◉ ～균 tuberculosis〔tubercle〕bacilli. ～약 an antituberculosis drug. ～예방 prevention of tuberculosis: ～ 예방 운동 an antituberculosis campaign / ～ 예방 대책 antituberculosis measures. ～요양소 a T.B. sanatorium. ～환자 a tuberculosis〔consumption〕patient; a T.B. patient.

**결행**(決行) decisive action; a resolute step. ～하다 carry out resolutely; take a decisive〔resolute〕step; carry into effect. ¶ 미국 정부는 이라크에 대한 공습을 ～했다 Washington has taken the plunge and carried out an air raid on Iraq. / 파업 ～중 The strike is on.

**결혼**(結婚) (a) marriage; matrimony; a union. (★ matrimony는 법적·종교적으로 인정된 정식의 결혼생활을 말함. union은 「결합·화합」이란 뜻에서 연유되어 생긴 말. 「결혼」의 뜻으로는 매우 격식차린 말). ～하다 marry《*a person*》; get〔be〕married《to *a person*》; be united in matrimony. ¶ ～의 matrimonial; marital / 행복한 ～ a happy marriage〔union〕/ ～전의 관계 *one's* premarital relations / 잘 어울리는〔어울리지 않는〕～ a well-matched〔an ill-matched〕marriage / 신분의 차이가 있는 ～ (a) left=handed marriage; (a) misalliance / ～시키다 marry《*one's* daughter to a rich man》; give《*one's* daughter away in marriage》《to》; make《them》man and wife (신부·성직자 등이) / ～ 이야기를 꺼내다 bring up the subject of marriage; speak of marriage / 돈을 노려 ～하다 marry for money / ～하지 않고 아이를 낳다 have children outside marriage / ～한 지 3년 되다 have been married (for) three years / 그녀는 의사와 ～했다 She got married to a doctor. / 그녀는 좋은 상대와 ～했다 She married well. / 그녀는 작년에 스미스씨와 ～했다 She married Mr. Smith last year. / 그는 25세에 ～했다 He married at the age of twenty-five. / 그 어머니는 딸들을 모두 ～시켰다 The mother has married off all her daughters. / 그는 평생 ～하지 않았다 He remained single all his life. / 그 ～은 깨졌다 The marriage broke up.
결혼의: ～의 신청 a proposal (of marriage) / ～의 상대 *one's* fiancé(남자); *one's* fiancée(여자); *one's* marriage partner / ～의 법적 절차를 밟다 legalize a marriage.
결혼에: ～에 실패하다 make an unfortunate marriage《with》/ ～에 이의를 제기하다 forbid the banns.
결혼을: ～을 승낙하다 accept the proposal (of marriage) / ～을 약속하다 promise to marry《*a person*》; become engaged to《*a person*》/ ～을 축하하다 congratulate《*a person*》on *his* marriage / ～을 신청하다 propose《to》; ask《*a person*》to marry《*one*》; make a proposal of marriage《to》/ ～을 주선하다 arrange a marriage between《A and B》; act as go-between.
◉ ～기념일 a wedding anniversary. ～답례품 presents given to the participants in wedding. ～반지 a mar-

riage〔wedding〕ring. ~비용 wedding expenses. ~사진 a wedding picture. ~상담 marriage〔marital〕counseling. ~상담소 a marriage agency; a public love-maker's office. ~선물 a wedding present〔gift〕. ~의상(衣裳) the outfit of《a girl》on *her* marriage; a wedding dress. ~자금 a marriage fund; the money to marry on. ~적령기 (a) marriageable age. ~제도 a marriage system. ~중매 matchmaking: ~ 중매를 서다 act as (a) go-between; serve as a matchmaker. ~청첩장 an invitation card for wedding. ~피로연 a wedding dinner〔reception〕; an after-wedding celebration. ~행진곡 a wedding march.

**결혼사기**(結婚詐欺) a matrimonial〔marriage〕fraud; a false〔fake〕marriage. ¶ ~꾼 a matrimonial swindler / ~에 걸려든 미망인 a widow who has been swindled《out of her money》under promise of marriage.

**결혼생활**(結婚生活) married life. ¶ 권태를 모르는 ~ married life without boredom / ~ 30년 thirty years of married life / 그녀는 스미스와 20년간이나 행복한 ~을 하고 있다 She has been happily married to Smith for twenty years.

**결혼식**(結婚式) a wedding〔marriage〕(ceremony). ¶ ~을 올리다 hold〔perform, celebrate〕a wedding〔marriage〕/ 몰래 ~을 올리다 have a quiet wedding / ~에 초대하다 invite《*a person*》to a wedding / ~날 a wedding day. ◉ ~장 a wedding hall. ~참석자 the guests at a wedding.

**결후**(結喉) the Adam's apple.

**겸**(兼) and (also); in addition; as well; at the same time. ¶ 총리 겸 외무부 장관 Prime Minister and concurrently Minister of Foreign Affairs / 서재 겸 응접실 a study-cum-drawing room; a room used both as a study and for receiving visitors / 나는 내 방을 침실 겸 서재 겸 객실로 쓴다 I use my room as a combined bedroom, study, and parlor.

**겸무**(兼務) an additional job assignment; an extra post; plural offices. ⇨겸임. ~하다 hold the additional〔concurrent〕post《of》; hold the post concurrently; serve concurrently《as》. ¶ 두 직책을 ~하다 hold two offices〔posts〕concurrently.

**겸비하다**(兼備—) combine (one thing with another); have both; have《A and B》at the same time. ¶ 지용(智勇)을 겸비한 무인 a warrior with both wisdom and courage / 재색을 ~ have both wit and beauty / 이 학교는 근대적 설비와 전통적 분위기를 겸비하고 있다 This school has modern facilities and a traditional atmosphere at the same time.

**겸사**(謙辭) ① 《말》 humble speech. ② 《사양》 declining humbly. ~하다 decline humbly; be humble〔modest〕.

**겸사겸사** for a double purpose; for two reasons; with both things in mind; partly on... and partly for.... ¶ 일도 보고 구경도 할겸 ~해서 서울에 가다 go to Seoul partly on business and partly for sightseeing / 만나도 보고 이야기도 하려고 ~왔다 I have come with a double purpose of seeing you and of having a talk with you.

**겸상**(兼床) a table for two. ~하다 prepare a table〔meal〕for two;《two》eat at the same table.

**겸손**(謙遜) humility; modesty; humbleness. ~하다 (be) humble; modest; unassuming. ¶ ~한 사람〔태도〕a modest person〔attitude〕/ ~하게 with modesty; in a modest way / 그는 행동이〔말씨가〕~하다 He is modest in his behavior〔speech〕. / 너무 ~해 하시는군요 You're too modest!

**겸양**(謙讓) humbleness; humility; modesty; diffidence. ~하다 (be) humble; modest; diffident; compliant. ¶ ~의 미덕 the virture of modesty / ~의 미덕을 발휘하다 behave modestly.

**겸업**(兼業) a side job; a sideline; business on the side. ~하다 pursue《another trade》「as a side job〔on the side〕; have two jobs at the same time. ¶ ~ 금지 prohibition of side trade / 저 집은 식당과 여관을 ~하고 있다 That house combines restaurant and hotel business. ◉ ~농가 a farmer with a side job.

**겸연쩍다**(慊然—) be〔put〕out of countenance; (be) embarrassed; disconcerted; ashamed; feel abashed. ¶ 겸연쩍어 하며 bashfully; shyly; awkwardly / 겸연쩍은 듯 쓴웃음 지으며 grinning sheepishly / 겸연쩍게 만들다 make《*a person*》self-conscious; put《*a person*》out of countenance / 겸연쩍어 하다 feel ashamed; feel awkward〔embarrassed〕/ 너무 추켜올리지 마라, 내가 겸연쩍잖아 You praise me too much. Spare my blushes.

**겸영**(兼營) combining the management of another business. ～하다 operate 《a hotel》 in addition to some other business.

**겸용**(兼用) a combined 〔double, multiple〕 use. ～하다 use 《*a thing*》 both as... and.... ¶ 남녀 ～의 for both men and women / ～이 되다 serve both as ... and... / 이 방은 거실과 서재 ～으로 쓰인다 This room is used both as a living room and a study.

**겸유**(兼有) having both; doing both 《A and B》. ～하다 possess both; do both. ¶ 그는 문무(文武)를 ～하고 있다 He is proficient both in literature and military arts.

**겸임**(兼任) ⇨겸무, 겸직. ¶ 총리가 교육부장관을 ～하다 The Prime Minister serves concurrently as Education Minister.

**겸자**(鉗子) 〖의학〗 a forceps (*pl.* ～, -cipes).

**겸전하다**(兼全—) be perfect in both; be good at both. ¶ 문무가 ～ be good at both literary and military arts.

**겸직**(兼職) an additional job 〔post, office〕; holding two offices at the same time. ～하다 hold the additional office of; hold two offices at the same time. ¶ 공무원은 ～이 금지되어 있다 Civil servants are not allowed to have other jobs.

**겸치다**(兼—) combine; unite 《one thing with another》; add 《one thing to another》; put 〔do〕 together. ¶ 두 가지 일을 겸쳐 하다 do two things at the same time.

**겸하다**(兼—) 《구비》 combine; possess both; serve both as 《A and B》; 《겸직》 hold 《a post》 as an additional office. ¶ 서재와 객실을 겸한 방 a room serving both as a study and a drawing room / 점심을 겸한 아침 식사 a cross between a breakfast and a lunch / 김 선생님은 영어와 음악 선생을 겸하고 있다 Mr. Kim is both an English teacher and a music teacher.

**겸행**(兼行) 《아울러 함》 doing more than one job at the same time; 《쉬지 않음》 double duty; working overtime. ～하다 do (more than one job) at the same time; work a double shift; work overtime at. ¶ 주야～으로 일하다 work 「day and night 〔round the clock〕 / 주야～으로 가동시키다 set 《a machine》 on the 24-hour job.

**겸허**(謙虛) humbleness; modesty; humility. ～하다 (be) humble; modest. ¶ ～하게 in a humble way; with modesty / ～한 태도 a modest attitude / ～한 태도로 부탁하다 make a modest request / ～하게 잘못을 인정하다 humbly admit *one's* mistake 〔fault〕; eat humble pie.

**겹** ① 《포개진》 fold; 《켜》 a layer; a fold; 《쌓아올린》 a pile; 《가닥》 a ply. ¶ 두 겹 twofold / 여러 겹 many folds / 종이 한 겹 a single fold 〔thickness〕 of paper / 종이를 여러 겹으로 접다 fold a piece of paper several times. ② 《거듭》 double; twofold; twin; duplication; doubleness; duplexity. ¶ 겹문 double doors 〔windows〕.

**겹것** 《겹으로 된》 something made of two or more plies 〔layers〕; 《옷》 lined clothes.

**겹겹이** in many folds; fold on fold; ply on ply; layer upon layer; row on row; range on range. ¶ 종이로 ～ 싸다 wrap 《*a thing*》 in several sheets of paper / ～ 둘러싸다 surround 《the enemy》 thick and threefold / ～ 쌓아올리다 lay one upon another; lay in piles 〔layers〕 / 산으로 ～ 둘러싸이다 be surrounded by range after range of mountains / 도착하자마자 신문 기자들에게 ～둘러싸였다 On arriving, I was besieged by the reporters.

**겹눈** 〖동물〗 compound eyes; an ommateum (*pl.* -tea). ¶ ～의 ommateal.

**겹다** be too much for one; be more than one can manage; be out of hand; be extreme 〔excessive〕. ¶ 힘에 겨운 일 work beyond *one's* power 〔ability〕 / 눈물겨운 노력 pathetically sincere efforts / 설움에 겨워 in passion of grief / 눈물～ be moved to tears; can't hold back *one's* tears / 힘에 ～ 「be beyond 〔exceed〕 *one's* power.

**겹두루마기** a lined overcoat.

**겹말** redundant words; a pleonasm.

**겹사돈**(—查頓) a person doubly related (by marriage).

**겹살림** maintaining more than one household.

**겹세로줄** 〖음악〗 double bar.

**겹옷** clothes with a lining; lined clothes.

**겹음정**(—音程) 〖음악〗 a compound interval.

**겹저고리** a lined jacket.

**겹질리다** 《힘줄·관절 따위가》 be sprained.

**겹집** 〖건축〗 a house with several wings.

**겹창**(—窓) a double 〔storm〕 window.

**겹쳐지다** be piled up; be overlapped each other; lie one upon another;

come one after another. ¶ 지붕의 기와는 서로 겹쳐져 있다 The tiles on the roof overlap each other.

**겹치다** ① 《물건을》 pile 〔heap〕 up; put 〔lay〕 one upon another; fold so that there is more than one fold 〔ply, layer〕. ¶ 종이를 네 번 겹쳐 접다 fold a piece of paper in four folds / 내의 두 벌을 겹쳐 입다 wear two undershirts one over the other / 책이 겹쳐 놓여 있다 Books lie in piles. ② 《날·시간이》 fall on. ¶ 두 모임이 겹쳤다 Two meetings coincided. / 이 달도 또 공휴일이 일요일에 겹친다 The red-letter day falls on Sunday again this month. ③ 《일·불행 등이》 ¶ 불행이 ~ have misfortune after misfortune; have a series of misfortunes / 손해가 ~ sustain loss upon loss.

**겹치마** a lined skirt.

**경**(京) 《서울》 the capital; the metropolis.

**경**(更) 《시간》 a night watch; one of the five watches of the night.

**경**(景) ① 《경치》 a view; a scene [총칭]; scenery. ¶ 관동 팔경 the eight famous spots in Eastern Korea / 삼경 the scenic trio. ② ⇨ 경황.

**경**(卿) ① 《고관》 a high officer; a minister; a lord. ② 《그대》 You my liege (임금이 신하에게). ③ 《호칭》 Lord; Sir. ¶ 월터 스코트 경 Sir Walter Scott.

**경**(經) ① ⇨ 경서. ② 《불경》 the sutras; the Buddhist scriptures. ¶ 경을 읽다 chant 〔recite, intone〕 a sutra; read a service. ③ 《주문》 spells 〔incantations〕 of sorcerers. ¶ 경을 외다 chant a spell; make an incantation. ④ 《피륙의 날》 the warp. ⑤ ⇨ 경도(經度).

**경**(庚) 『민속』 ① 《십간의》 the 7th of the 10 Heaven's stems. ② ⇨ 경방(庚方). ③ ⇨ 경시(庚時).

**경-**(輕) light; light-weight; simple; easy. ¶ 경기관총 a light machine gun / 경화학 공업 light chemical industry.

**-경**(頃) about; around. ¶ 세 시경에 (at) about three o'clock / 그것은 1940년경에 일어났다 It took place in 1940 or thereabouts.

**경가극**(輕歌劇) a light opera 〔musical〕; an operetta.

**경가파산**(傾家破産) 《탕진》 squandering of *one's* fortune; 《파산》 bankruptcy.

**경각**(頃刻) an instant; a moment. ¶ ~간에 in a moment; in an instant; in the twinkling of an eye / ~도 지체 못한다 There is not a moment to lose.

**경각**(傾角) (angle of) inclination.

**경각하다**(警覺—) warn; bring 《*a person*》 to an awareness (of the error of *his* ways).

**경감**(輕減) (a) reduction; (a) decrease; mitigation; 《고통·불안 등의》 (a) relief. ~하다 reduce; lessen; lighten; relieve; mitigate 《an offense》; alleviate 《pain》. ¶ 세금을 ~하다 reduce 〔lighten, lower〕 taxes / 형을 ~하다 reduce 〔commute〕 a sentence / 그렇게 되면 우리의 부담이 크게 ~될 것이다 It will greatly lighten 〔alleviate〕 our burden.

**경감**(警監) a senior inspector.

**경개**(梗概) an outline; a summary; a sketch; a digest 《of a book》.

**경거**(輕擧) rash 〔hasty〕 action; an ill-considered attempt; a heedless 〔reckless, thoughtless〕 undertaking. ~하다 commit a rash act; act on impulse; act rashly 〔recklessly〕. ◉ ~망동 rash and thoughtless action: ~망동을 삼가다 behave 〔act〕 carefully; behave prudently.

**경건**(敬虔) piety; devotion; reverence. ~하다 (be) pious; devout; godly; God-fearing. ¶ ~하지 않은 impious; profane / ~한 불교 신자 a pious believer in Buddhism; a pious Buddhist / ~한 마음을 품다 feel reverence 《for》 / ~한 기도를 드리다 offer a most reverential prayer; pray devoutly 《to God》. ◉ ~주의 Pietism.

**경결**(硬結) congealment; solidification; coagulation. ~하다 congeal; solidify; coagulate; harden; clot.

**경경**(耿耿) ~하다 《불빛이》 flicker; glimmer; blink; 《마음이》 feel ill at ease; be disturbed; (be) restless; fitful. ¶ ~불매(不寐)하다 can not have a good sleep; have a broken sleep; pass a bad night.

**경경하다**(輕輕—) (be) rash; heedless; careless; frivolous. ¶ 경경히 rashly; heedlessly; carelessly.

**경계**(境界) ① 《접한 곳》 a boundary; a border 〔frontier〕; 『법』 metes and bounds(토지의). ¶ ~분쟁 a boundary 〔frontier〕 dispute / …와의 ~ the border with 《China》 / ~를 접하다 border 《on》 / ~를 접하고 있지 않다 share no common boundary 《with》 / ~를 정하다 fix 〔define〕 the boundary (line) 《between》 / ~를 봉쇄하다 close the borders / 이 강이 우리 도시와 인접 도시의 ~를 이룬다 This river forms the boundary between our town and the neighboring one. ② 〖불교〗 *one's* condition given by *karma*.

> 용법 **boundary** 지리(地理)적인 경계선. **border** 경계선 그 자체를 가리키기도 하며, 또 경계선을 따라 펼쳐진 어느 정도의 넓은 지역을 나타내기도 한다. **frontier** 정치적·군사적으로 본 타국과의 국경 지역을 뜻하나, 이 모두가 절대적인 구별은 아니다.

◉ ∼선 a boundary 〔demarcation〕 line; a border line: ∼선을 긋다 draw a line of demarcation. ∼설정 demarcation; delimitation. ∼지대 the borderland; a frontier (국경). ∼표 a landmark 《미》; a boundary stone 〔marker, post〕.

**경계**(警戒) ① 《경고》 a caution; (a) warning; (an) admonition; 《조심》 (a) caution; (a) precaution. ∼하다 《경고하다》 warn; give warning of; caution 《*a person*》 against; 《조심하다》 be cautious about 《*doing, something*》; take precautions 《against》. ¶ 지진이 일어나면 화재와 해일을 ∼해야 한다 When an earthquake occurs, we should take precautions against fire and tsunami 〔tidal waves〕.
② 《감시·경비》 watch; vigilance; (a) lookout; guard. ∼하다 watch 《for a thief》; look out 《for pickpockets》; be on the watch 《for》; guard 《against》; be on *one's* guard 《against》. ¶ 적에 대한 ∼를 엄중히 하다 keep strict watch 〔guard〕 against the enemy / ∼를 강화하다 tighten *one's* guard 《against》 / ∼를 태만히 하다 be off *one's* guard 《against》 / ∼를 늦추다 lower *one's* guard 《against》; relax *one's* vigilance 《against》 / 재계는 새로운 정책에 대해 매우 ∼적이다 Financial circles are very wary of the new policy. / 저 사람에 대해서는 ∼를 게을리하지 마라 Guard against 〔Keep an eye on〕 that man.
◉ ∼경보 《공습에 대한》 an air defense alarm; a precautionary warning 〔alert〕. ∼망〔선〕 《경찰의》 a police net 〔cordon〕: ∼망을 펴다〔뚫다〕 place 〔slip through〕 a police net. ∼색 《변색》 warning 〔sematic〕 coloration; 《색깔》 a warning color. ∼수위(水位) the danger level 《of a river》. ∼신호 a warning signal. ∼심 cautiousness. ∼태세 an alert: ∼태세에 들어가다〔있다〕 be on the alert / 우리는 어제부터 24시간 ∼태세에 들어갔다 We have been on 24-hour alert since yesterday. 특별 ∼태세 special alertness 《against》: 전군에 특별 ∼ 태세를 취할 것을 명령하다 order the armed forces to be put on special alertness 《against》.

**경계**(驚悸) 《잘 놀람》 susceptibility to fright; 《두근댐》 sudden palpitation(s).

**경고**(警告) (a) warning; (a) caution; (an) admonition. ∼하다 warn 〔caution〕 《*a person*》 of 〔against〕; give 《*a person*》 a warning 《of, that...》. ¶ ∼ 없이 without warning 〔notice〕 / ∼를 받다 take warning 《from》; be warned 《against》 / 엄중한 ∼를 내리다 issue 〔send out〕 a stern warning 《to》 / 그에게 잘못을 되풀이하지 말라고 ∼했다 I cautioned him against repeating errors. / 그들은 나의 ∼를 무시하고 산에 올랐다 They ignored my warning and climbed the mountain. ◉ ∼등 a warning light 〔flare〕. ∼발사 《fire》 a warning shot.

**경골**(脛骨) 〖해부〗 the shinbone; the tibia. ¶ ∼의 tibial. ◉ ∼동맥 the tibial artery.

**경골**(硬骨) ① 《뼈의》 (a) hard bone. ② 《강직》 a firm character; inflexibility; stubbornness. ¶ ∼의 staunch; uncompromising; inflexible. ◉ ∼어(魚) a teleost; a bony fish. ∼어류(魚類) *Teleostei* (L.). ∼한(漢) a man of firm 〔strong〕 character; a man of 「principle 〔unyielding spirit〕.

**경골**(頸骨) the neck bone(s); the cervical vertebrae.

**경공업**(輕工業) light industries. ◉ ∼생산품 light industry goods 〔products〕.

**경과**(經過) 《시간의》 passage; lapse; 《기한의》 expiration; 《사물의 진행·변화》 progress; course; development. ∼하다 《시간》 pass; elapse; go by; expire; 《사건·사물이》 progress; develop. ¶ ∼ 시간 the time elapsed / 시간이 ∼함에 따라 as time passes / 10년이란 세월이 ∼한 후 after a lapse of ten years / 유효 기간이 ∼하다 the term 〔period〕 of validity expires / 사태의 ∼를 지켜보다 watch the course of things / 교섭의 ∼ the progress of the negotiations / 사건의 ∼ the development of an affair / 수술 후의 ∼ the progress after an operation / (환자의) ∼가 양호하다 be making satisfactory progress; be doing well 〔fine〕 / 그 후 20년이 ∼했다 Twenty years have passed 〔gone by〕 since then. / 그가 죽은 지 5시간이

~했다 He has been dead these five hours. ◉ ~보고 a report on proceedings 〔developments〕. ~조치 a temporary measure.

**경관**(景觀) a view; a scene; a spectacle; scenery [총칭]. ¶ 일대 ~ a grand view.

**경관**(警官) a police officer; a policeman; 《순찰하는》 a patrolman; a constable 《영》; a cop 《구어》; the police [총칭]. ¶ 30 명의 ~이 사고 현장에 파견되었다 Thirty policemen were dispatched to the scene of the accident. ◉ 여자~ a policewoman.

**경교**(景教) 〖종교〗 Nestorianism. ¶ ~의 Nestorian.

**경구**(經口) 〖약〗 ¶ ~의 oral. ◉ ~소아 마비 백신 oral polio vaccine. ~투여 《doses for》 oral administration. ~피임약 an oral contraceptive pill; a birth control pill; the pill: 나는 ~ 피임약을 먹고 있다 I am on the pill.

**경구**(硬球) 〖야구〗 a hard 〔regulation〕 ball.

**경구**(警句) a witty remark; a witticism; an epigram; an aphorism. ◉ ~가 an aphorist. ~집 a collection of epigrams.

**경구개**(硬口蓋) 〖해부〗 the hard palate.

**경국**(經國) running a country; administration. ¶ ~지재 the capacity of a statesman; administrative talent / ~지책 administrative policy.

**경국대전**(經國大典) the *Kyŏngguk-Taejŏn;* National Code promulgated in 1471 to define the administrative structure of the *Chosŏn* Dynasty.

**경국지색**(傾國之色) a woman beautiful enough to cause the downfall of a country; a Helen of Troy.

**경금속**(輕金屬) light metals.

**경기**(景氣) ① 《일반 형편》 the times; things. ¶ ~가 좋다〔나쁘다〕 The times are good 〔bad, hard〕. / ~가 어떤가 How are you getting on? *or* How's everything? ② 《시황(市況)·상황(商況)》 business (conditions); (the tone of) the market. ¶ ~의 과열 overheating of economic activities / 조작된 ~ borrowed 〔false, artificial〕 prosperity 〔boom〕 / 시장의 ~ the tone of the market / ~가 회복되다〔후퇴하다〕 business is recovering 〔declining〕 / ~후퇴를 수출 부진에 돌리다 attribute the business setbacks to sluggish exports / ~가 좋다〔나쁘다〕 Business 〔The market〕 is brisk 〔dull〕. / 어느 시장이나 ~가 활기를 띠고 있다 Every market is booming. / 시장 ~가 좋아지고 있다 The market is looking 〔picking〕 up. / 국내 ~는 뚜렷한 회복의 조짐을 보이고 있다 The domestic business shows clear signs of recovery. / 정부는 ~ 부양책을 검토하고 있다 The Government is studying plans to stimulate business.
◉ ~대책 stimulative measures. ~동향 the trend of economic performance. ~변동 business fluctuations. ~부양책 measures to boost the economy. ~상승 a business upturn. ~수축 business contraction. ~순환 a business 〔trade 《영》〕 cycle. ~ 예고지표 the business warning index (생략 BWI). ~예측 business forecasting. ~ 조정 economic 〔cyclical〕 adjustment. ~지수〔지표〕 a business index 〔barometer〕. ~침체 economic 〔business〕 stagnation 〔slowdown, doldrums〕; a slump. ~활성화 시책 an economy-invigorating policy. ~회복 a business recovery. ~후퇴 (a) business recession: ~ 후퇴 방지책 an anti-recession measure. 벼락~ a boom.

**경기**(競技) a game; a (competitive) sport; 《시합》 a match; a contest; a competition; a tournament; 《종목》 an event; sporting events. ~하다 have 〔play〕 a match 〔game〕. ¶ ~에 이기다〔지다〕 win 〔lose〕 a match 〔game〕 / ~에 참가하다 take part 〔participate〕 in a contest / ~를 포기하다 throw up a game / 내주에 테니스 ~대회가 열린다 A tennis tournament will be held next week. ◉ ~대회 《기술 등의》 a competition; a contest; 《운동의》 an athletic meet(ing). ~자 a contestant; a player. ~장 a sports ground; a sports field(육상경기의); a stadium: 국립 ~장 the National Athletic Stadium. 실내~ indoor games. 칠종~ the heptathlon. 학교 대항 ~ an inter-school match.

**경기**(驚氣) 〖한의〗 convulsions.

**경기관총**(輕機關銃) a light machine gun.

**경기구**(輕氣球) a (dirigible) balloon; a hot-air balloon.

**경기병**(輕騎兵) 《부대》 light cavalry; 《병사》 a light cavalryman 〔horseman〕.

**경내**(境內) the precincts; the grounds; the compound.

**경년**(經年) the elapse of a year. ~하다 pass a year.

**경노동**(輕勞動) light labor 〔work〕. ◉ ~자 a light worker.

**경뇌유**(鯨腦油) sperm oil; spermaceti.

**경단**(瓊團) a rice-cake dumpling covered with powdered soybean, sesame and syrup.
**경대**(鏡臺) a mirror stand; a dressing 〔toilet〕 table; a dresser; a vanity.
**경도**(硬度) (degree of) hardness; solidity. ◉ ~계(計) a durometer.
**경도**(傾度) degree of inclination or deflection; gradient.
**경도**(傾倒) 《넘어짐》 falling down; toppling 《over》; 《기울여 쏟음》 tilting; tipping; 《마음을》 devoting *oneself;* concentration. ~하다 fall down; topple; tilt; tip; devote *oneself* to; concentrate 《*one's* mind》 on.
**경도**(經度) ① =월경(月經). ② 〖지리〗 longitude. ¶~를 재다 calculate the longitude 《of》.
**경동**(驚動) ~하다 be startled; be frightened; be terrified. 「tery).
**경동맥**(頸動脈) 〖해부〗 the carotid (ar-
**경락**(經絡) 〖한의〗 special nerve parts around the body which shows the signs of illness for acupuncture.
**경락**(競落) auctioning. ~하다 be auctioned off 《to》. ◉ ~기일 time for objectification. ~물 objects knocked down. ~인 a successful bidder.
**경량**(輕量) light weight. ◉ ~급 a lightweight class: ~급 선수 a lightweight.
**경력**(經歷) *one's* career 〔record〕; *one's* personal history; *one's* (personal) antecedents. ¶다채로운 ~을 가진 사람 a man of varied career / ~이 좋다〔나쁘다〕 have a good 〔bad〕 career 〔record〕 / 어떤 ~을 가진 사람이냐 What is his past career? ◉ ~고시(告示) 《입후보자의》 a career bulletin; a bulletin of candidates' careers. ~소개 a biographical introduction. ~퇴직 증명 career and retirement certificates.
**경련**(痙攣) convulsions; a spasm; a spasmodic contraction; 《근육의》 (a) cramp; a jerk; 《안면의》 a tic; a twitch. ~하다 be convulsed; go into convulsions; have a convulsive fit; get cramp 《in *one's* leg》; be siezed with cramp. ¶~성의 convulsive; spasmodic / ~을 일으키다〔이 일어나다〕 =~하다 / 어린아이가 ~을 일으켰다 The baby fell into a fit of convulsions.
**경례**(敬禮) salutation; a salute; a bow; 《구령》 Salute! ~하다 salute 《an officer》; make 〔give〕 a salute 〔bow〕 《to》; bow 《to》. ¶~를 받다 take the salute 《of *one's* men》; receive a salute 《from》 / 모자를 들어 ~하다 raise *one's* hat to *a person* / ~에 답하다 acknowledge 〔return〕 《*a person's*》 salute.
**경로**(經路) a course; a channel; a route; 《단계》 a stage; 《과정》 a step; a process. ¶발달의 ~ the process of growth / 정식 ~를 밟다 go through the official channels / 같은 ~를 밟다 follow the same course / 민주 사상 발달의 ~를 더듬다 trace the growth of democratic ideas / 감염 ~는 아직 판명되지 않았다 The route of infection is not yet known. / 성공한 사람들은 모두 이런 ~를 밟아 온 것이다 This is the path trodden by all successful men of the world. ◉ 외교~ a diplomatic channel.
**경로**(敬老) respect for the old 〔aged〕. ~하다 respect the aged; be kind to old folks. ¶~의 날 Respect-for-the Aged Day / ~정신을 발휘하다 show *one's* respect for the old / ~하는 마음에서 in 〔out of〕 deference to 《*a person's*》 age. ◉ ~당 a hall for the aged. ~석 a seat for the aged. ~우대권 a complimentary ticket 〔pass〕 for the old. ~우대증 《미》 the Golden Age Passport. ~잔치 a feast 〔party〕 in 「honor of 〔deference to〕 the aged. ~회 a respect-for-age association. ~ 효친사상 《promote》 the spirit of filial piety and respect for the old.
**경륜**(經綸) government; administration; management; 《국가의》 statecraft; statesmanship. ~하다 govern; administer; manage. ¶~지재 statesmanship; executive 〔administrative〕 ability / ~지사 a person of great administrative ability.
**경륜**(競輪) a bicycle 〔cycle〕 race. ◉ ~선수 a 《professional》 bicyclist; a cycle racer. ~장 a cycling stadium; a cycle-race track; a velodrome.
**경리**(經理) 《회계 처리》 accounting; the accountants' business; 《사람》 an accounting clerk. ~하다 take care of accounting. ¶그녀는 A 회사의 ~를 담당하고 있다 She is in charge of accounting for A company. ◉ ~과〔부〕 the accounting section 〔department〕. ~사무 accountant's 〔paymaster's〕 business. ~사원 an accounting clerk. ~주임 a chief accountant. ~학교 a paymasters' school.
**경마** a rein to lead a mounted horse with; a halter. ¶~ 잡다 lead a horse with 《*a person*》 on it / ~ 잡히다 have

a groom lead a horse by the halter.
**경마**(競馬) horse racing; the race; a horse race (1회의). ~하다 race horses; hold 〔have〕 a horse race. ¶ ~로 한몫 잡다 carry off a big race / ~에 돈을 걸다 bet on a horse; play the horses 《미》/ ~에서 돈을 잃다〔따다〕 lose 〔make〕 money on the horses / ~에서 요행수로 횡재하다 pick 〔hit〕 a dark horse. ◉ ~계 the racing world. ~광 a turf fan; a racing man. ~기수 a jockey. ~말 a racehorse. ~장 a race track 《미》; a racecourse 《영》.
**경망**(輕妄) frivolousness; flippancy; rashness. ~하다〔스럽다〕 (be) frivolous; flippant; rash; light. ¶ ~하게〔스럽게〕 lightly; rashly; imprudently / ~스런 남자 a reckless man / ~한 짓을 하다 act imprudently / ~한 짓을 하지 않다 use *one's* own discretion; be prudent; be discreet.
**경매**(競賣) (an) auction; a public 〔an open〕 sale. ~하다 sell 《*a thing*》 at 〔by 《영》〕 auction; put up 《an article》 「to auction 〔for sale〕; auction 《an article》 (off). ¶ 그 그림은 200만 원에 ~되었다 The picture was sold at auction for 2 million won. / ~는 언제 실시됩니까 When will the auction take place? / 나는 그것을 ~에서 샀다 I bought it at auction.
◉ ~가격 a price offered by a successful bidder. ~공고 an auction notice. ~기일 the date of auction. ~대금 the amount of money obtained for 《an article》 sold by auction. ~물 articles sold by auction. ~수속 public auction procedure. ~수수료 an auctioneer's commission. ~인 an auctioneer; a bidder. ~장 an auction house 〔room〕. ~중개인 an auction broker. ~처분 disposition by public sale 〔auction〕. ~품 an article for sale at auction.
부정〔사기〕~ a mock 〔fake〕 auction.
**경멸**(輕蔑) contempt; scorn; slight (-ing); disdain. ~하다 despise; scorn; disdain; slight; look down (up)on; look down *one's* nose at; make light of; hold in contempt.

> **용법** **despise** 상대를 무가치한 존재로 여기고 깔보다. **scorn** 감정을 노골적으로 나타내어 상대를 조소하다. **disdain** 우월한 기분을 겉으로 나타내어 상대를 경멸하다. **look down on** 상대를 「깔보다, 경멸하다」의 구어적 표현.

¶ ~적(인) contemptuous; disdainful / ~할 만한 mean; contemptible; despicable / ~하는 표정〔태도〕 a contemptuous look 〔air〕 / ~하는 눈으로 보다 eye 《*a person*》 with contempt; look at 《*a person*》 contemptuously / ~을 당하다 be held in contempt; be treated with contempt / ~하는 투로 말하다 talk 〔speak〕 disrespectfully 《of》; speak in contempt / ~을 나타내다 be expressive of contempt / 그는 정말로 ~해야 할 녀석이다 He is a most contemptible fellow. / 가난한 사람을 ~하지 마라 Don't despise the poor. / 그는 거짓말쟁이라고 심하게 ~당했다 He was much looked down on as a liar.
**경모**(敬慕) deep 〔profound〕 respect; adoration. ~하다 adore; revere; venerate. ¶ 마을 사람들은 그를 ~하고 있다 The townspeople have a great reverence and affection for him.
**경묘하다**(輕妙—) (be) light and pleasant 〔easy〕; witty; clever; smart. ¶ 그것은 매우 경묘한 필치다 It is written in a light and easy style.
**경무**(警務) police duties 〔affairs, administration〕. ◉ ~과 the police administration division. ~관 a superintendent general.
**경문**(經文) 『불교』 the Buddhist scriptures; (the text of) a sutra; 《도교의》 the Taoist scriptures 〔classics〕; 《가톨릭의》 Catholic prayers.
**경문학**(硬文學) metaphysical literature.
**경문학**(輕文學) light literature.
**경물**(景物) the scenery 〔natural features〕 of the season. ◉ ~시 a seasonal poem.
**경미하다**(輕微—) (be) slight; trifling; negligible; be not serious. ¶ 경미한 문제 a trifling 〔trivial〕 matter / 경미한 손해 a slight damage / 경미한 부상을 입다 be slightly injured.
**경박**(輕薄) 《부박》 frivolity; flippancy; levity; 《변덕》 fickleness; inconstancy; 《천박》 thoughtlessness; shallowness. ~하다 (be) frivolous; flippant; fickle; shallow. ¶ ~한 사람 a frivolous character / ~한 생각 a shallow idea / 그는 똑똑하지만 ~한 데가 있다 He is clever, but rather frivolous. / 그녀는 ~하고 머리는 텅 빈 소녀다 She is a frivolous, empty-headed girl.
**경방**(庚方) 『민속』 west-by-southwest.
**경배**(敬拜) a respectful bow. ~하다 bow respectfully.
**경백**(敬白) Respectfully yours.

**경범죄**(輕犯罪) a misdemeanor; a minor 〔light〕 offense. ¶ ～ 전과가 있다 have a record of minor offenses.
◉ ～처벌법 the Minor Offense Law.
**경변증**(硬變症) 〖의학〗 cirrhosis.
**경보**(競步) 〖스포츠〗 competitive walking; a walking race; 《모금을 위한》 a walkathon. ◉ ～선수 a walker.
**경보**(警報) an alarm; a warning. ～하다 give an alarm. ¶ ～를 내리다 warn; give「an alarm 〔a warning〕; issue a 《flood, storm》 warning / ～를 울리다 sound the alarm 《for a fire》/ ～를 해제하다 cancel a 《typhoon》 warning; 《공습 경보를》 give 〔sound〕 the all clear / ～장치가 제대로 작동되지 않았다 The alarm system did not work well. ◉ ～기 an alarm (signal). ～장치 an alarm system 〔device〕. 스모그～ a smog alert. 원거리 조기～망 the (distant) early warning networks. 조기～기 〖군사〗 an early-warning plane; a radar picket plane.
**경복**(敬服) respect; admiration; esteem. ～하다 admire; respect; think highly of 《*a person*》; hold 《*a person*》 in high esteem. ¶ ～할 만한 admirable; worthy of admiration / 나는 항상 일에 대한 그녀의 열성에 ～하고 있다 I always admire her enthusiasm for her job.
**경부**(京釜) Seoul and Pusan. ◉ ～ 고속도로 the Seoul-Pusan expressway 〔superhighway, speedway, freeway 《미》〕. ～ 고속철도 the Seoul-Pusan high-speed railroad. ～선 the Seoul-Pusan line.
**경부**(頸部) 〖해부〗 the neck (area); the「cervical region.
**경비**(經費) 《비용》 expense(s); cost(s); up-keep (유지비); 《지출》 expenditure(s); (an) outlay. ¶ 총～ over-head expenses / 차의 ～ the upkeep of a car / ～ 관계로 owing to the expenses involved; for financial reasons / ～가 (많이) 들다 be expensive; cost much / ～를 들이다 go to the expenses of 《*doing*》; make outlay 《on》/ 많은 ～를 들여서 at a great cost / ～를 줄이다〔삭감하다〕 cut down 〔reduce〕 the expenses; curtail 〔retrench〕 expenditures / 갑작스레 ～가 늘어났다 The expenses ran up suddenly. / 그것에 소요된 ～는 지급하겠다 I'll pay 〔cover〕 the expenses involved in it. / 자동차를 유지하는 데는 많은 ～가 든다 It costs a lot (of money) to maintain a car. / 이 기획의 성공을 위해서는 ～를 아끼지 않을 생각이다 I will spare no expense to make this project a success.
◉ ～절감 reduction of expenditure. ～절감 계획〔수단〕 a cost-cutting 〔cost-reduction〕 program 〔measure〕. 생활〔여행〕～ living 〔traveling〕 expenses. 일반～ general 〔overhead〕 expenses.
**경비**(警備) defense; guard. ～하다 guard 《against》; keep 〔stand〕 guard 《at, over》; defend; police. ¶ ～(를) 서다 be on guard / ～를 엄중히 하다 guard strictly 〔tightly〕 / ～가 엄중하다 be strictly guarded / ～를 해제하다 call off the guard / 끊임없이 해안을 ～하다 police a coast constantly / 국경의 ～를 강화하다 strengthen the defenses of frontiers / 총리 공관은 경찰관이 엄중히 ～하고 있었다 The premier's official residence was strictly guarded by policemen.
◉ ～과 the security division. ～병 a guard. ～실 a guardroom; a guardhouse; a gatekeeper's house. ～원 a guard; a security man. ～정 a patrol boat. ～함 a guardship. ～회사 a security company 〔agency〕.
**경비대**(警備隊) a garrison; guards.
◉ 해안～ the coastguard.
**경사**(傾斜) a slant; a slope (사면의); (an) inclination; (배의) a list; 《도로·철도의》 a grade 《미》; 《지층의》 a dip. ～지다 incline; slant; lean; tilt; 《도로가》 slope; 《배가》 list; 《지층이》 dip. ¶ 40도의 ～ an inclination 〔incline〕 of 40 degrees / 지붕의 ～ the slant 〔inclination〕 of a roof / ～진 inclined; slanting; slopping / 급한〔완만한〕 ～ a steep 〔gentle〕 slant 〔slope〕 / ～지게 하다 slope 《the ground, a roof》; give a slope to / 그 땅은 해변쪽으로 완만하게 ～져 있다 The land slopes gently toward the seashore. / 그 건물은 북쪽으로 3도 ～져 있다 The building leans northward by three degrees.
◉ ～각 an angle of inclination. ～계 a clinometer. ～도 a gradient. ～로 a slope way; a ramp (고속도로, 건물사이의). ～면 a slope; an incline. ～생산(방식) the priority production (system).
**경사**(經史) Chinese classics on ethics, politics, and history.
**경사**(經絲) 《날실》 warp.
**경사**(慶事) a matter calling for congratulation; a happy 〔an auspicious〕 event. ¶ ～스런 날 a happy day / ～롭다〔스럽다〕 《an event》 be happy 〔felicitous〕 / ～가 겹치다 have a series

of matters for congratulation.

**경사**(警査) 《한국의》 an assistant inspector; 《미》 a police sergeant.

**경산부**(經産婦) a multipara (*pl.* -rae).

**경상**(經常) ¶ ∼의 ordinary; current; working; operating. ◉ ∼계정 a current account. ∼비 operating [working, running] expenses [costs]; ordinary expenditure: ∼비를 줄이다 reduce running costs. ∼세입 current [ordinary] revenue. ∼세출 ordinary expenditure [outlay]. ∼손실 ordinary loss. ∼수지 current account; balance of current accounts: ∼수지 흑자 current account surplus. ∼예산 the working [ordinary] budget. ∼이익 ordinary profit.

**경상**(輕傷) a slight injury [wound]. ¶ ∼을 입다 be slightly injured [wounded] 《in the head》; suffer [receive] a slight injury. ◉ ∼자 a slightly wounded [injured] person; [집합적] the slightly wounded [injured].

**경색**(梗塞) getting blocked [stopped up]; stoppage; blocking; 《핍박》 tightness; stringency; 〖의학〗 infarct; 《증세》 infarction. ¶ ∼상태의 증권 시장 a stringent stock market / ∼상태에 있다 be in a「fix [tight box 《구어》]; 《금융이》 be hard pressed for money.

**경서**(經書) Chinese classics (of Confucianism).

**경석**(輕石) pumice stone.

**경석고**(硬石膏) 〖광물〗 anhydrite.

**경선**(經線) 〖지리〗 《자오선》 the meridian; a line of longitude; 《경도》 longitude.

**경선**(頸腺) 〖해부〗 the cervical gland.

**경성**(硬性) hardness. ¶ ∼의 hard. ◉ ∼세제 a hard detergent. ∼암 scirrhus. ∼하감 〖의학〗 chancre.

**경세**(經世) governing; administration. ∼하다 govern 《a country》; administer (the affairs of state). ¶ ∼지재(之才) statesmanship; ability to run a government. ◉ ∼가 an administrator; a statesman. ∼제민 national administration and relief.

**경세**(警世) a warning to the world [public]; a reproof to society. ∼하다 warn to the world; awaken the public. ¶ ∼의 서(書) a book which reproves society; an admonitory book. ◉ ∼가 a prophet; a seer.

**경솔**(輕率) frivolity; flippancy; rashness; hastiness; 《부주의》 thoughtless; carelessness. ∼하다 (be) frivolous; flippant; rash; hasty; thoughtless; careless. ¶ ∼히 frivolously; flippantly; rashly; hastily; carelessly; thoughtlessly / ∼한 판단 a hasty judgment / ∼한 짓을 하다 commit a rash act; take a rash step; act hastily; do something rash / 좀 ∼하다 be a little rash / ∼하게 믿다 be too ready [hasty] to believe / ∼하게 행동하다 behave lightly; act hastily [rashly] / ∼히(도) 언질을 주다 give a precipitate commitment / 그런 짓을 하다니 제가 ∼했습니다 It was hasty of me to do such a thing.

**경쇠**(磬―) ① 《아악기》 an ancient kind of musical instrument made of stone or jade. ② 《종》 a handbell used by Buddhist monks (before the altar); 《방울》 a handbell used by fortunetellers.

**경수**(硬水) 《센물》 hard water.

**경수**(輕水) light water. ◉ ∼로 《원자로》 a light-water reactor: 한국형 ∼로프로젝트 the "South Korean-model" light=water reactor power project.

**경승**(景勝) beautiful [picturesque] scenery. ◉ ∼지 a scenic spot; a place of scenic beauty.

**경시**(庚時) 〖민속〗 the 18th of the 24 hour periods (=4:30-5:30 p.m.).

**경시**(輕視) contempt; negligence. ∼하다 make light [little] of; think little of; slight; neglect. ¶ 문제를 ∼하다 treat a matter lightly / 그녀는 사소한 일도 결코 ∼하지 않았다 She never made light even of small [little] things. / 너의 생명을 ∼해서는 안 된다 You should not make light of your life. / 그들은 그 프로젝트에서의 나의 역할을 ∼했다 They played down my part in the project.

**경식**(硬式) hard [rigid] type. ¶ ∼의 rigid; hard. ◉ ∼야구 hardball [regulation-ball] baseball. ∼테니스 tennis.

**경식**(輕食) a light meal; a snack; a (light) lunch; a light diet.

**경식당**(輕食堂) a snack bar; a lunchroom 《미》; a luncheonette 《미》.

**경신**(更新) renewal. ⇨ 갱신.

**경신**(敬神) respect [reverence] for God; piety; devoutness. ∼하다 worship [revere] god; be pious [devout]. ¶ ∼하는 마음 a pious feeling; fear of God.

**경신**(輕信) credulity; ready belief. ∼하다 believe readily; be credulous [gullible] enough to believe 《that...》; be too ready to believe 《that...》.

**경실련**(經實聯) 《경제정의 실천 시민연합》 the Citizens Coalition for Economic Justice (생략 CCEJ).

**경심**(傾心) 〚물리〛 metacenter.

**경아리**(京一) a shifty Seoulite; a city 「slicker.

**경악**(驚愕) astonishment; amazement; (a) shock. ～하다 be astonished 〔shocked, stunned〕 《at》; be taken aback. ¶ 세상을 ～하게 한 사건 a world-shaking incident / ～하여 말도 못하다 be struck dumb with astonishment / 그 소식을 듣고 내 귀를 의심할 정도로 ～을 금치 못했다 I was thunderstruck by the news, unable to believe my own ears.

**경애**(敬愛) loving and respecting. ～하다 love and respect; hold 《*a person*》 in high 「esteem 〔regard〕; adore; venerate. ¶ ～하는 dear; respectable; adorable / ～하는 송군 my dear Mr. Song / 우리 모두는 그녀를 ～한다 All of us love and respect her.

**경야**(經夜) passing a (sleepless) night; staying up all night; 《상가에서의》 a wake. ～하다 stay 〔sit〕 up all night; stay 〔keep〕 awake the whole night; hold a wake.

**경어**(敬語) an honorific (expression); a term of respect. ¶ ～로 이야기하다 use 「respect language 〔polite expressions〕.

**경역**(境域) 《경내의 땅》 the precinct(s); the grounds; 《경계 지역》 the borders; the boundaries.

**경연**(競演) a contest; a competitive performance. ～하다 compete 《with》; play opposite 《another actor》.
◉ 민요～대회 a folk song *concours*.

**경연극**(輕演劇) a light theatrical performance.

**경염**(競艶) ～하다 vie 〔compete〕 with one another in beauty.
◉ ～대회 a beauty contest.

**경영**(競泳) 《경기》 a swimming race 〔match, competition〕; 《종목》 a swimming 〔swim〕 event. ～하다 swim a race 《with》; have a swimming race.
◉ ～대회 a swimming meet. ～선수 a (competitive) swimmer. 장거리～ a marathon 〔long-distance〕 swim.

**경영**(經營) 《관리》 management; administration; 《운영》 operation; running 《a business》. ～하다 manage 《a firm》; run 《a company》; carry on 《an enterprise》; keep 《a store, a hotel》; operate 《a mine, a factory》. ¶ ～이 잘 되지 않아서 because of bad 〔poor, incompetent〕 management / ～이 잘 되다 be well managed / 사업을 ～하다 run 〔operate〕 a business / 그것은 미국인이 ～하는 식당이다 It is an American-operated restaurant. / 그녀는 어머니를 대신해서 그 기업을 ～하고 있다 She manages the business for her mother. / 그의 뛰어난 ～으로 사업은 크게 발전하였다 Under his capable 〔excellent〕 management the business has grown more and more prosperous.
◉ ～경제학 business economics. ～계획 management planning. ～공학 management engineering. ～권 a management right; a right of management. ～난 financial difficulty: 그 대학은 ～난에 빠져 있다 The college is in financial difficulties. ～대리 제도 a managing agency system. ～대학 a college of business administration. ～대학원 a graduate school of business administration. ～방침 management 〔business〕 policy. ～법 management. ～분석 business analysis. ～비 working 〔running〕 expenses 《영》; operating costs 《미》. ～수완〔능력〕 administrative 〔executive〕 ability; a talent for managing 《a bank》. ～전략 business strategy. ～정보 시스템 the management information system. ～지표 management index. ～진 the board of directors; the management. ～참가 《근로자의》 worker participation (in management). ～학 business 〔industrial〕 administration: ～학과 the faculty 〔department〕 of business administration / ～학 석사 Master of Business Administration (생략 M.B.A.). ～합리화 rationalization of management: 우리 회사는 ～합리화가 필요하다 Our company needs the rationalization 〔streamlining〕 of management. ～협의회 《노사간의》 a joint management council. ～형태 forms of management. ～환경 business environment.

**경영자**(經營者) a manager; an executive; [집합적] the management; 《영업주》 a proprietor. ¶ ～측 the management 《of a company》 / ～와 노동자의 분쟁 the conflicts between labor and management / 한국 ～ 총협회 the Korea Employers' Federation (생략KEF).
◉ 공동～ a joint manager; a business partner.

**경옥**(硬玉) 〚광물〛 jadeite; jade.

**경우**(境遇) 《형편》 circumstance(s); a situation; 《때》 an occasion; a time; a moment; 《사례》 a case; an instance. ¶ 이〔그〕 ~ in this 〔that〕 case / 필요한 ~ in case of need; when (it is) necessary / 지금의 ~ in the present circumstances / 어떤 ~에는 in some cases; sometimes / 어떤 ~에도 in all cases; on all occasions; 《부정》 under no circumstances; in no case / 대개의 ~ in most cases 〔instances〕 / ~에 따라서 according to circumstances; as the case may be / 그런 ~에는 in such a case; under such circumstances / 최악의 ~에는 in the worst case / 비가 올 ~ 소풍은 취소한다 「In case of rain 〔If it rains〕, the excursion will be called off. / 긴급한 ~에는 비상계단을 이용하시오 Use the fire escape in case of an emergency. / 이 규칙은 모든 ~에 적용된다 This rule applies to all cases. / 너의 ~는 예외로 한다 We make an exception in your case. / 그것과 이것은 ~가 다르다 We must discriminate between the two cases. / 낸시의 ~는 사정이 다르다 It's different in Nancy's case. *or* It is not the case with Nancy.

**경운기**(耕耘機) a cultivator; a power 「tiller.

**경원**(敬遠) ~하다 respect but keep at a distance; keep 《*a person*》 at a (respectful) distance; give 《*a person*》 a wide berth. ¶ 그는 너를 ~하고 있다 He gives you a wide berth. / 그는 우리들 모두에게 ~되고 있다 He is kept by us all at a respectful distance.

**경위**(涇渭) 《옳고 그름》 right and 〔or〕 wrong; 《적부》 proper or improper; the propriety 《of》. ¶ ~에 벗어난 짓 an improper act; unreasonable doings / ~야 어떻든 whether it is right or wrong / ~를 모르다 don't know what is right and what is wrong; be unreasonable / ~를 가리다 tell right from wrong / ~에 어긋나다 be out of reason / 그는 ~가 밝은 사람이다 He is a man of fair judgment.

**경위**[1](經緯) 《경도와 위도》 longitude and latitude; 《직물의 날과 씨》 warp and woof 〔weft〕. ◉ ~도 the longitude and latitude. ~선 lines of longitude and latitude. ~의(儀) a theodolite; an altazimuth.

**경위**[2](經緯) ① 《전말》 details; particulars; 《사정》 circumstances; 《일어난 순서》 the sequence of events. ¶ 사건의 ~ the details 〔particulars, whole story〕 of the case / 사건의 ~를 말하다 tell 《*a person*》 all that happened; talk all about the case / 그 간의 ~를 말씀드리죠 I'll tell you what happened during this period. / 그것이 어떤 ~인지 잘 모르겠다 I don't know how it came about. ② = 경위(涇渭).

**경위**(警衛) ① 《경호》 guard; patrol; escort; convoy. ~하다 guard; escort; patrol; convoy. ② 《한국 경찰의 직위》 an inspector; 《미》 a lieutenant. ③ 《국회의》 an Assembly guard.

**경유**(經由) ① 《통과》 ~하다 go by way of 〔via〕; pass 〔go〕 through. ¶ …을 ~하여, … ~로 by way of…; via… / 노량진 ~ 영등포로 가는 버스 a bus for Yŏngdŭngp'o via Noryangjin / 하와이를 ~하여 미국에 가다 go to America via 〔by way of〕 Hawaii. ② 《…을 통해서》 ¶… ~로 through… / 교육부 ~로 through the Ministry of Education / 불교는 한국을 ~하여 일본에 전해졌다 Buddhism reached Japan through Korea.

**경유**(輕油) light oil; diesel fuel. ◉ ~발동기 a light oil 〔a diesel〕 motor.

**경유**(鯨油) whale oil; whale fat. 「fortis.

**경음**(硬音) 〖음성〗 a strong sound; a

**경음**(鯨飮) swig; swill; heavy drinking; drinking like a fish. ~하다 drink heavily; drink like a fish; swig.

**경음악**(輕音樂) light 〔popular〕 music.

**경의**(敬意) respect; regard; homage. ¶ …에 ~를 표하여 in honor of; as a mark of respect for; in deference to / ~를 표하다 pay 〔show〕 *one's* respects; regard with respect; do 〔pay, offer〕 homage 《to》 / 그의 용감한 행동에 ~를 표했다 We showed respect for his courageous behavior. / 너의 노력에 대해 ~를 표한다 I take my hat off to you for your effort.

**경이**(驚異) a wonder; a miracle; a marvel. ~하다 wonder 《at》; marvel 《at》. ¶ ~롭다 be wondrous 〔miraculous〕 / ~적(인) wonderful; miraculous / 대자연의 ~ nature's wonders 〔miracles〕 / ~적인 현상 a very rare phenomenon / ~적인 발전을 이룩하다 make wonderful 〔marvelous〕 progress / ~의 눈으로 보다 stare in wonder 《at》; open *one's* eyes in astonishment 〔surprise〕.

**경인**(京仁) Seoul and Inch'ŏn. ◉ ~ 고속도로 the Seoul-Inch'ŏn Expressway. ~ 공업지대 the manufacturing district (stretching) between

Seoul and Inch'ŏn; the Kyŏng-In manufacturing district. ～선 the Seoul-Inch'ŏn Line. ～지방 the Seoul=Inch'ŏn district.

**경작**(耕作) cultivation; tillage; farming. ～하다 cultivate; farm; till 《fields》; plow 《land》. ¶ ～에 알맞은 arable; tillable / 그는 2헥타의 농지를 ～하고 있다 He works his farm of two hectare. ◉ ～면적 arable acreage. ～물 farm products 〔produce〕. ～자 a tiller; a farmer. ～지 arable land; cultivated land.

**경장**(更張) 《쇄신》 a reform. ～하다 reform 《the government》.

**경장**(輕裝) light dress 〔clothing, attire, clothes〕; casual clothes (평상복). ～하다 be lightly dressed 〔attired, outfitted, equipped〕. ¶ 그는 ～하고 여행을 떠났다 Lightly dressed, he set forth on a trip.

**경장**(警長) 《경찰의》 a senior policeman.

**경쟁**(競爭) competition; a contest; rivalry; struggle. ～하다 compete 《with》; contest; rival. ¶ 미일간의 경제 ～ the US-Japanese economic competition / 선의의 ～ competition in good faith / ～에 이기다〔지다〕 win 〔lose〕 in a contest / 우승배를 놓고 서로 ～하다 「compete with 〔rival〕 each other for the cup 〔trophy〕 / 아무를 …와 ～시키다 put *a person* into competition with… / ～을 피하다 avoid competition / ～에 응하다 meet competition / 선거에서 ～은 격심했다 The election was sharply contested. / 회사들은 가격인하 ～을 하고 있다 The companies are competing in price reduction. / 가격과 품질에 있어서 폐사의 상품과 ～할 수 있는 것은 없다고 확신합니다 It is our firm belief that no other goods can compete with ours in both price and quality. / 나는 그와 ～이 되지 못한다 I'm no match for him. *or* I can't compete with him.
◉ ～가격 a competitive price. ～국 a competing 〔rival〕 country. ～률 the competition rate. ～사회 competitive society. ～상대 a competitor; a rival. ～시험 a competitive examination: ～시험으로 선발하다 select by competitive examination. ～심 a competitive spirit; a spirit of competition: ～심이 강하다 be full of competitive spirit 〔ardor〕 / ～심을 북돋우다 arouse 〔stir up〕 a spirit of competition 〔rivalry〕 《in》. ～의식 competitive consciousness. ～입찰 a competitive bid; a public tender: ～입찰하다 make a competitive bid 《for》. ～자 a competitor; a contestant; 《상대》 a rival; 《선거의》 a rival candidate: ～자를 물리치다 outdo (all) competitors. 공개～ 〖경제〗 open competition. 국내〔대외〕～ domestic 〔foreign〕 competition.

**경쟁력**(競爭力) the competitive power 〔edge〕; competitiveness. ¶ 국제 ～ international competitiveness / 약화된 ～ the weakened competitive edge / 고도의 ～이 있다 be highly competitive / ～을 높이다〔낮추다〕 increase 〔weaken〕 *one's* competitiveness / 국제 시장에서 우리 상품의 ～을 강화하다 strengthen 〔sharpen〕 the competitiveness of our commodities on international markets / 수출 가격의 상승은 세계 시장에서의 ～을 약화시킨다 Higher export prices will weaken our competitive position in world markets.

**경쟁이**(經—) 〖민속〗 a person chanting a spell to dispel misfortune; an exorcist.

**경적**(輕敵) ① 《약한 적》 a weak enemy 〔foe, adversary, antagonist〕. ② 《적을 깔봄》 underrating the enemy's force. ～하다 belittle an enemy; underrate a rival. ¶ ～필패 Don't crow too much over your enemy.

**경적**(警笛) an alarm whistle; a warning horn; 《자동차의》 a (car) horn; a honk. ¶ ～을 울리다 whistle a warning; give an alarm whistle; sound 〔blow〕 a horn; honk / ～을 세 번 울려 신호하다 signal three times with *one's* horn. ◉ ～금지 《게시》 No honking 〔horn〕! ～금지구역 no-horn zone.

**경전**(經典) the scripture; the sacred books; 《불교의》 the Sutra; the Scripture; 《기독교의》 the Bible; 《이슬람교의》 the Koran.

**경정**(更正) revision; correction; rectification. ～하다 revise; correct; rectify.

**경정**(警正) 《경찰의》 a superintendent.

**경정맥**(頸靜脈) 〖해부〗 the jugular (vein).

**경제**(經濟) economy; economics(경제상태); 《재정》 finance; 《절약》 thrift; frugality. ～하다 economize; practice economy; be frugal 〔economical〕 《of》. ¶ ～적인 economic; economical; financial; thrifty; frugal (★ economic 「경제의, 경제학상의」란 뜻: economic policies of the President-elect. economical

「(사람이) 낭비를 피하는, (물자를) 선용하는」의 뜻: an economical housekeeper) / ～적으로 economically; financially / ～적 난관 an economic deadlock 〔impasse〕 / ～적 견지 an economic point of view / ～성이 있는 commercially=viable 《oil bed》 / 세계 ～의 중심지 the economic center of the world / 제2의 ～ 도약 the second take-off of the economy / ～ 및 외교 전쟁 the economic and diplomatic battle / 국내 ～의 회복 추세 the recovery trend of the domestic economy / ～관계를 단절하다 break off economic relations / …하는 것은 ～〔비～〕적이다 it is good 〔bad〕 economy to *do* / 싸구려를 사는 것은 실제로는 비～적이다 There is no real economy in buying cheap things. / 가스는 전기보다 ～적이다 Gas is more economical than electricity. / 우리 ～는 몇 년 안에 고도 성장에서 안정 성장으로 전환될 것이다 Our economy will be switched from fast growth to stable expansion within a few years. / 값싼 유가는 한국 ～의 고도 성장을 가능케 했다 Cheap oil made possible the Korean economy's high growth rate. / 그녀는 ～에 대한 관념이 전혀 없다 She hasn't got any sense of economy. / ～의 재건이 현정부의 급선무다 It is of urgent necessity for the present government to revitalize our economy.

◉ ～가 《학자》 an economist; 《경제 성향의 사람》 a man with a strong sense of economy. ～각료 Cabinet ministers in charge of economic affairs; economic ministers. ～각료 회의 an economic ministers' meeting 〔conference〕. ～개발 economic development: ～개발 5개년 계획 a five=year economic development plan. ～계 the economic world; economic 〔financial〕 circles. ～계측학 statistical economics. ～공황 a financial 〔an economic〕 crisis. ～과학 심의회 the Economic-Science Council. ～과학 위원회 《국회의》 the Economy-Science Committee. ～관념 a sense of economy. ～관료 economic bureaucrat. ～교서 《미국 대통령의》 an Economic Report to Congress. ～구조 economic structure. ～구조조정〔개혁〕 economic structural adjustment 〔reform〕; economic restructuring. ～권 an economic bloc. ～기반 the economic infrastructure 《of a country》. ～기사 《신문 따위의》 financial news. ～기자 a financial reporter. ～단체 an economic 〔a business〕 organization 〔group〕. ～대국 a great economic nation; a major economic power. ～동향 economic trend 〔performance〕. ～란 the financial column. ～력 economic strength; financial power. ～림 lucrative trees. ～마찰 economic friction 〔strain〕. ～면 the financial page 《of a newspaper》. ～문제 an economic problem 〔question〕. ～백서 an economic white paper. ～봉쇄 an economic blockade. ～부 《신문사의》 the economics department. ～부양책 an economic stimulus package. ～사 an economic history: ～사관 the materialistic view of history. ～사범 《죄》 an economic offense 〔crime〕; 《사람》 an economic criminal; an offender of economic laws. ～사상 economic thought 〔ideas〕. ～사절 the economic mission. ～사정〔상태〕 economic conditions 〔situation〕; financial conditions; economics; 《개인의》 the state of *one's* finances: 지금과 같은 ～ 상태로는 with the economic condition as it is / ～사정이 좋다〔나쁘다〕 be well 〔badly〕 off; be in easy 〔needy〕 circumstances. ～사회 이사회 《유엔의》 the Economic and Social Council. ～성 economical efficiency: ～성이 있는 commercially viable. ～성장 economic growth: ～성장률 the economic growth rate / 고도의 ～ 성장 high growth of economy; high level of economic growth. ～속도 an economical speed. ～수역 an economic sea zone; a maritime economic zone: 200해리 배타적 ～수역 a 200-nautical mile exclusive (maritime) economic zone. ～수준 economic standard 〔level〕. ～안정 economic stabilization; stabilization of economy. ～예속 economic subordination. ～외교〔자립, 활동, 협력〕 economic diplomacy 〔self=supporting, activities, cooperation〕. ～원론 the principles of economics. ～원조 financial support 〔aid, help〕: ～원조 계획 an economic aid program. ～원칙 economical principles. ～위기 an economic 〔financial〕 crisis. ～윤리 economic ethics; business ethics: ～윤리 강령 the Economic Ethics Charter 〔Code〕 / ～윤리 위원회 the Economic Ethics Commission. ～인 an economic man; businessmen: 전국 ～인 연합회 the Federation of

Korean Industries (생략 FKI). ~전 an economic war; economic warfare [competition]. ~정의 economic justice: ~ 정의 실천 시민 연합 the Citizens Coalition for Economic Justice. ~정책 an economic policy. ~제도[체제] an economic system. ~ 제재 《impose》 economic sanctions 《on》. ~조정관(실) (Office of) Economic Coordinator. ~지리학 economic geography. ~지표 an economic indicator. ~질서 《paralyze》 the economic order. ~차관 a loan floated to improve the financial situation of a country. ~통계 economic [financial] figures [statistics]. ~파탄 financial failure; bankruptcy. ~행위[활동] economic action [activities]. ~협력 economic cooperation. ~협력 개발 기구 the Organization for Economic Cooperation and Development (생략 OECD). ~협력 증진 the enhancement of economic cooperation. ~회복 economic recovery. 복합 ~ plural economy. 수렵~ (a) hunting economy. 이중~ dual economy. 정치~ political economy. 쇄국 ~주의 economic nationalism. 연차 ~계획 annual economic plan. 제5차 ~사회 발전 5개년 계획 the fifth five-year economic and social development plan.

**경제상**(經濟上) economically; financially. ¶ ~의 economic; financial / ~의 이익[손실] economic gains [losses] / ~의 이유로 for economic [financial] reasons; for reason of economy.

**경제연착륙**(經濟軟着陸) an economic soft landing. ¶ 그는 정책의 최우선 순위는 물가 안정과 ~을 이루는 일에 주어질 것이라고 보고하였다 He reported that top policy priority would be placed on attaining price stability and an economic soft landing.

**경제특구**(經濟特區) 《중국 등지의》 a special economic zone.

**경제학**(經濟學) (the science of) economics. ¶ 경영 ~ business economics [administration] / 계량 ~ econometrics / 미시[거시] ~ micro-[macro-] economics / 순수 ~ pure economics. ◉ ~과 the economics department. ~박사 《사람》 a doctor of economics; 《학위》 Doctor of Economics. ~자 an economist.

**경조**(慶弔) an occasion for celebration or sorrow. ◉ ~비 expenses for gifts of celebration or condolence. ~전보 a telegram for celebration or condolence.

**경조**(競漕) a boat race; a regatta. ~하다 have a boat race; row a race. ◉ ~용 보트 a racing boat.

**경조부박**(輕佻浮薄) frivolity. ⇨ 부박.

**경종**(警鐘) an alarm bell; 《경고》 a warning. ¶ ~을 울리다 ring [sound] an alarm bell / 이것은 오늘날의 한국에 대한 ~이다 This is a warning to the present-day Korea.

**경죄**(輕罪) a minor offense; a misdemeanor. ⇨ 경범죄.

**경주**(競走) a race; a run; 《단거리의》 a dash; a sprint. ~하다 have [run] a race 《with》; race against 《*a person*》. ¶ 100미터 ~ a 100-meter dash [race] / ~에 이기다[지다] win [lose] a race / 누가 ~에 이겼느냐 Who (has) won the race? ◉ ~마(馬) a racehorse. ~용 자동차[자전거] a racing car [bicycle]; a racer. ~자 a runner; 《단거리》 a sprinter. ~장 the track; the course.

**경주하다**(傾注―) 《집중하다》 devote *oneself* 《to》; concentrate 《on》. ¶ 연구에 전력을 ~ 「concentrate *one's* energies on [devote *oneself* entirely to] *one's* research.

**경중**(輕重) ① 《무게》 weight. ② 《일의 중요도》 (relative) importance; value; seriousness; gravity. ¶ 병의 ~ the relative seriousness of an illness / 죄의 ~ the gravity of the offense / ~을 재다 weigh (the importance) / 사물의 ~을 헤아리다 know what is important and what is not.

**경증**(輕症) a slight illness [attack]; a mild case. ¶ 그의 위경련은 ~이었다 His stomach cramps were not serious. ◉ ~환자 a mild case 《of measles》.

**경지**(耕地) cultivated land [area]; plowed land; land under cultivation; 《경작에 알맞은 땅》 arable land. ¶ ~의 확대 the expansion of arable land. ◉ ~면적 cultivated acreage. ~정리 the readjustment [consolidation] of arable land (holdings).

**경지**(境地) ① 《상태》 a stage; a condition; a state. ¶ …의 ~에 이르다 reach [attain] a stage of… / 그는 무아의 ~에 있었다 He was in a state of perfect selflessness. *or* He was in the stage of absolute altruism. ② 《분야》 a sphere; territory; ground. ¶ 새로운

～를 개척하다〔열다〕 break new 〔fresh〕 ground 《for, in》; open up new path 《in literature》 / 독자적 ～를 개척하다 find *one's* own way.

**경직**(硬直) stiffness; rigidity. ⇨ 강직(強直). ～하다 stiffen; get rigid 〔stiff〕. ¶ 차갑게 ～된 사체 a stark and cold (dead) body / 그녀의 얼굴은 공포로 ～되었다 Her face froze with terror.

**경진**(輕震) a weak earthquake.

**경질**(更迭) a change; replacement; a shift; a shakeup; a reshuffle; 《면직》 (a) dismissal. ～하다 change; replace; switch; reshuffle. ¶ 내각의 ～ a reshuffle of the Cabinet 〔Ministry〕; a Cabinet shakeup / 두 각료를 ～하다 reshuffle two Cabinet ministers / 수회로 ～되다 be dismissed from *one's* post for bribery.

**경질**(硬質) a hard 〔strong, tough〕 variety of constitution. ¶ ～의 hard. ◉ ～고무 hard rubber. ～비누 hard 〔insoluble〕 soap. ～섬유 hard fiber. ～유리 hard glass.

**경찰**(警察) the police; the police force.

> **용법** **police** 「기구로서의 경찰」, 「경찰관들」이란 두 가지 뜻으로 쓰이며, 항상 the를 붙이고 복수 취급이 원칙이나, 신문 영어에서는 the를 생략하는 경우가 많음. 따라서 「세 사람의 경찰관」은 three police 〔policemen〕. **police force**는 특정 지역의 기구로서의 경찰을 말함.

¶ ～의 날 the Police Day / ～의 보호 police protection / ～에 신고하다〔호소하다〕 report 〔complain〕 to the police / ～에 넘기다 hand over 《*a person*》 to the police / ～에 연행하다 haul 〔bring〕 《*a person*》 before the police; take 《*a person*》 off to a police station / ～에 연행되다 be taken to the police / ～에 자수하다 give *oneself* up to the police / ～에 알릴 테다 I'll report you to the police. / 그는 ～의 감시를 받고 있다 The police are keeping an eye on him. ◉ ～견 a police dog. ～관 a police officer; a policeman; a cop 《미》; a (police) constable 《영》; the police [총칭]: ～관 파출소 a police box; a police substation (지서). ～관할구역 a police region 〔district〕. ～국가 a police state. ～권 police power 〔authority〕: ～권을 발동〔남용〕하다 exercise 〔abuse〕 the police authority. ～기동 순찰대 the mobile patrol police squad. ～대학 the National Police College. ～력 police force. ～명령 a police order. ～범 a police offense. ～법규 the police laws. ～병원 a police hospital. ～봉 a policeman's billy 〔club〕; a truncheon; a baton. ～서 a police station: ～서장 the chief of a police station; a 《town, city》 marshal 《미》. ～수첩 a policeman's pocketbook 〔identification〕. ～의 a police surgeon 〔medical officer〕. ～제도 a police system. ～처분 police dispositions. ～청 the National Police Agency: 서울 지방 ～청 the Seoul Metropolitan Police Agency / ～청장 the Director of the National Police Agency; the NPA director / 서울 지방 ～청장 the Commissioner of the Seoul Metropolitan Police Agency. ～출입 기자 a (news) reporter on the police; a police reporter. ～학교 a police academy: 국립～대학교 the National Police College / ～ 종합학교 the Police Comprehensive Academy. ～행위 a police 〔policing〕 action. ～행정 police administration. 국제 ～군 an international police force.

**경척**(鯨尺) a cloth measure 《14.91 inches》; a "tailor's foot".

**경천**(敬天) worship of Heaven. ～하다 worship Heaven.

**경천동지**(驚天動地) ～하다 astonish 〔astound, startle〕 the whole world; make a sensation in the world. ¶ ～할 대사건 an astounding 〔earthshaking〕 event.

**경천위지하다**(經天緯地一) (have the statesmanship necessary to) govern the world; show great statesmanship.

**경첩** a hinge. ¶ ～을 달다 put on a hinge; hinge / 문이 ～으로 여닫히다 a door turns on its hinges / 문의 ～이 빠져 있다 The door is off its hinges.

**경청**(傾聽) listening closely 〔attentively〕. ～하다 listen (attentively) to 《*a person's* talk》; give ear to; be all ears 〔attention〕. ¶ ～할 만하다 be worth listening to / 그들은 연사의 이야기를 ～했다 They gave the speaker all their attention. *or* They were attentive to the speaker. / 나는 한 마디도 놓치지 않으려고 열심히 ～했다 I listened devouring every word.

**경축**(慶祝) celebration; congratulation. ～하다 celebrate; congratulate 《*a person* on *his* success》. ¶ ～ 일색인 full of festive mood. ◉ ～일 a national 〔red-letter〕 holiday; a 「festival 〔fest, fête〕 day. ~행사 festivities.

**경치**(景致) scenery; a scene; a landscape(육지의); a seascape (바다의); a view; a prospect.

> **용법** **scenery** 어느 한 지역 전체의 풍경으로 사람이 보거나 보지 않거나를 불문하고 실존하고 있는 것. **scene** 사람의 시야에 비친 scenery의 한 부분으로 그림처럼 아름다움을 갖추고 있음을 암시함. **view** scenery의 한 부분에 대한 조망으로, 특히 멀리서 눈에 들어오는 경치. **landscape** 산천·계곡·들·숲·해안 등을 포함하는 넓은 경치. **seascape** 바다의 경치. **prospect** 넓고 큰 조망·전망.

¶ 시골 ~ rural scenery / 겨울 ~ a wintery scene / 아름다운 ~ beautiful scenery; a 「picturesque 〔lovely, charming〕 view / 산꼭대기에서 바라본 ~ the prospect from the top of a mountain / ~ 좋은 곳 a place of scenic beauty; a 「scenic 〔beauty〕 spot / 서울 근처의 ~ the scenery about Seoul / ~가 좋다 command a fine view / ~를 보러 여행 가다 go on a trip to see the scenery / 확 트인 ~를 내려다보다 look out over the wide view / 창문에서 내다보는 ~는 장관이다 The view from the window is magnificent.

**경치다** ① 《벌을 받다》 suffer torture; suffer severe punishment; be heavily punished. ¶ 예끼 경(을) 칠 자식아 God damn you! *or* The deuce take you! / 경(을) 칠 것 같으니 Damn it! ② 《혼나다》 have a 「hard 〔rough〕 time (of it); go through an ordeal; pay dearly; go through hell. ¶ 너 그런 짓하면 경친다 If you do (that), you'll have to pay dearly for it.

**경칭**(敬稱) 「an honorific 〔a courtesy〕 title; a term of respect. ¶ ~을 생략하다 dispense with the titles; cut out prefixes / ~을 생략해서 부르다 call 《*a person's*》 name without *his* title.

**경쾌**(輕快) ~하다 《몸이》 (be) light; nimble; jaunty; 《마음이》 (be) light= hearted; buoyant; cheerful. ¶ ~한 동작 nimble movement / ~한 리듬 a jaunty rhythm / ~한 가락 a lilting tune / ~한 발걸음으로 with 「light 〔jaunty〕 steps; light-footedly / ~한 복장을 하고 있다 be lightly dressed; be in casual wear.

**경탄**(驚歎) admiration; wonder. ~하다 admire; marvel 〔wonder〕 at. ¶ ~의 소리 a cry of wonder; a sigh of admiration / ~할 만한 wonderful; admirable; marvelous / ~할 만큼 능숙하게 with wonderful skill / 자연의 아름다움에 ~하다 wonder at the beauty of nature / 영문학에 대한 그녀의 깊은 조예에 ~했다 Her knowledge of English literature struck us with admiration. / 그것은 ~할 만한 과학상의 새로운 발견이다 It is a new and wonderful scientific discovery.

**경편**(輕便) ~하다 (be) handy; convenient; light. ¶ ~한 복장 a light dress. ◉ ~철도 a light rail train (생략 LRT).

**경품**(景品) a (free) gift; a giveaway 《미》; a premium. ¶ ~부 대매출 a sale with gifts 〔giveaways, premiums〕 / ~을 주다 offer gifts 〔giveaways〕 / ~증정 《게시》 Premiums offered. ◉ ~권 a gift 「coupon 〔voucher 《영》〕.

**경풍**(驚風) 〖한의〗 (children's) fits; convulsions. ~하다 have 〔suffer from〕 fits.

**경하**(慶賀) congratulation; felicitation. ~하다 congratulate 〔felicitate〕 《*a person* on *his* success》; offer *one's* congratulations on the occasion of. ¶ ~해 마지 않다 It is a matter for (hearty) congratulation that...; Let me offer you my hearty congratulation 《on your success》.

**경하다**(輕—) 《무게가》 (be) light; not heavy; 《정도가》 (be) slight; trifling; not serious; 《중요도가》 (be) light; insignificant; 《언행이》 (be) rash; precipitate; imprudent; frivolous; flippant. ¶ 경한 죄〔과실〕 a minor 「offense 〔error〕 / 책임이 ~ be not in a responsible position.

**경합**(競合) concurrence; competition; conflict (충돌). ~하다 concur; compete 〔conflict〕 《with *a person* for *a thing*》; 《값을》 bid against each other. ¶ 그들의 이익은 서로 ~했다 Their interests 「conflicted 〔were in conflict〕 with each other. / 그 두 상사는 서로 ~하고 있다 The two trading companies 「are competing 〔are in competition〕 with each other. ◉ ~죄〔과실〕 〖법〗 concurrent 「offenses 〔negligence〕.

**경합금**(輕合金) 〖화학〗 a light alloy.

**경향**(京鄕) the capital and the country. ¶ ~ 각지에 「all over 〔throughout〕 the country; in every nook and corner; far and wide.

**경향**(傾向) 《추세》 a tendency; a trend;

a drift; 《성향》 an inclination; a disposition; a turn of mind; a leaning. ¶ 물가 상승의 ~ the upward tendency 〔trend〕 of prices / 현대 사상의 ~ the trend of modern thought / 여론의 일반적 ~ the general trend of public opinion / 유행의 최근 ~ the latest trends in fashion / 좋은〔나쁜〕 ~ a good 〔bad〕 trend / 급격한 인플레 ~ an acute inflationary trend / …한 ~이 있다 have a tendency 《to》; be disposed 《to *do*》; be apt 〔inclined, liable〕 《to *do*》 / …의 ~을 나타내다 exhibit 〔show〕 a tendency to 〔toward〕 / 점차 …한 ~이 높아가고 있다 there is growing tendency that… / 쇠퇴하는 ~이 있다 have a declining tendency / 노인들은 흔히 보수주의로 기우는 ~이 있다 The old trend toward conservatism. / 한국인의 평균 수명은 해마다 늘어나는 ~이 있다 The average life span of the Koreans tends to increase from year to year. ◉ ~극〔소설〕 a tendency play 〔novel〕. ~문학 tendency literature. ~조사 a trend study.

**경험**(經驗) (an) experience. ~하다 experience; go through; undergo. ¶ 쓰라린〔즐거운〕 ~ a bitter 〔pleasant〕 experience / ~이 있는〔없는〕 간호사 an experienced 〔inexperienced〕 nurse; a competent 〔an incompetent〕 nurse / 내 ~으로는 in 〔from〕 my experience; so far as my experience goes / ~이 많다〔적다〕 have a wide 〔narrow〕 experience / ~을 얻다〔쌓다〕 gain 〔acquire〕 experience; add to 〔increase, build up〕 *one's* experience / ~을 살리다 make good use of *one's* experience / ~으로 알다 know 《*a thing*》 from experience / 영어 교수의 ~이 있다 have (some) experience in teaching English / 이런 일에는 ~이 없다 I have had no experience in this kind of work. / 실패가 좋은 ~이 되었다 The failure was a good lesson to me. / ~이 제일이야 Experience is a good teacher. / 나는 외국에서 많은 어려움을 ~했다 I experienced 〔went through〕 many hardships abroad. / 내 ~으로 판단하면 그것은 불가능에 가깝다 It is next to impossible, as I know from my own experience. / 조수 구함, ~은 불문 《광고》 Help wanted. No experience necessary.
◉ ~담 a narrative 〔story〕 of *one's* personal experiences. ~론 〘철학〙 empiricism: ~론자 an empiricist. ~연수 the years of experience. ~자 a man of experience; an experienced person; an expert (숙련자). ~철학〔과학〕 empirical philosophy 〔science〕.

**경혈**(經穴) 〘한의〙 spots on the body suitable for acupuncture.

**경호**(警護) guard; escort; convoy(군함 등의). ~하다 guard 《the president》; escort; convoy. ¶ ~ 아래 under guard 〔escort, convoy〕 / ~를 맡다 act as escort; be on guard; stand 〔keep〕 guard 《over》 / 그녀는 경찰의 엄중한 ~하에 그 식에 참석했다 She attended the ceremony under heavy police guard. ◉ ~원 a guard; a bodyguard; a security guard: ~원을 배치하다 post 〔place〕 guards 《on》.

**경화**(硬化) 《물질의》 hardening; vulcanization; 《태도 등의》 stiffening. ~하다 harden; stiffen; become hard 〔stiff〕. ¶ 태도를 ~시키다 stiffen *one's* attitude / 늙으면 동맥이 ~한다 The arteries harden with age.
◉ ~고무 ebonite; vulcanite. ~유〔지방〕 hardened oil 〔fat〕. ~작용 a hardening process. ~제 a hardener; a hardening agent. ~증 〘의학〙 sclerosis 《of the arteries》.

**경화**(硬貨) a coin; hard currency 〔money〕; metallic currency. ¶ ~로 지불하다 pay in coins.

**경화기**(輕火器) 〘군사〙 light firearms 〔weapons〕.

**경화학공업**(輕化學工業) light chemical industry.

**경황**(景況) an interesting situation; the state of things; conditions. ¶ ~이 없다 have no mind 〔time〕 for; have no interest in; be 「too busy 〔preoccupied〕 for; be lacking in interest / 바빠서 친구를 찾아 볼 ~이 없다 be too busy to find time to visit friends.

**곁** 《옆》 a side; 《부근》 neighborhood. ¶ 곁의 nearby; neighboring / 곁에 by the side; by; beside; at *one's* side; 《바로 곁에》 near 〔close, hard〕 by; at hand / 곁으로 다가가다 come 〔go, draw〕 near 《to》 / 곁에 앉다 sit by 《*a person*》 / 곁에 살다 live in the neighborhood / 곁에 놓다 put 〔leave〕 at *one's* side / 곁에 두다 have 〔keep〕 at hand / 곁에 서다 stand by the side of / 곁을 지나다 pass by 《*a thing, a person*》 / 부모 곁을 떠나다 leave *one's* parents / 어린애를 곁으로 부르다 call a child to *one's* side / 곁에서 보듯이 그렇게 쉽지는 않다 be not so easy as it may seem to outsiders / 곁에서 보는

눈에는 우습게 보인다 It looks funny to bystanders 〔outsiders〕. / 내 곁을 떠나지 말아라 Don't leave my side. / 너 따위는 그의 곁에도 못 간다 You are no match for him.

**곁가닥** a side piece 《of string, thread, etc.》.

**곁가지** a side branch.

**곁노**(一櫓) sculls; sculling oars. ◉ ～질 sculling.

**곁눈** a side(long) glance. ¶ ～으로 보다 look out of the corner of *one's* eyes 《at》; cast a sidelong glance 《at》/ ～주다 《눈짓》 give a suggestion with a look; 《추파》 give a wink; make eyes at 《*a person*》/ 그는 힐끔 ～으로 그녀를 보았다 He took a side glance at her.

**곁눈질** looking aside 〔askance〕; winking; looking away. ～하다 look aside 〔askance, sideways〕 《at》; leer 《at》; ogle 《at》; wink 《at》.

**곁다리** a secondary thing; someone other than the party concerned. ¶ ～끼다 participate as an outsider; join in a party as a special member / ～(를) 들다 remark 〔say〕 from the sidelines.

**곁두리** snacks for farmhands at work.

**곁들다** 《돕다》 give 〔lend〕 a helping hand 《to》; help; aid; assist; side with. ¶ 일을 곁들어 주다 help out with the work / 곁들어 싸우다 take *one's* part in a fight / 약한 자를 ～ support 〔side with〕 the weak 《against the strong》.

**곁들이다** ① 《음식을》 garnish 《with》; add 《some vegetable》 as a relish; dress. ¶ 생선 요리에 야채를 ～ garnish fish with a green vegetable / 그녀는 마실 것에다 치즈와 비스켓을 곁들여 내놓았다 She served cheese and crackers with the drinks. ② 《일을》 do 《*things*》 at a time; do 《*something*》 along with; accompany. ¶ 연설에 몸짓을 ～ accompany *one's* speech with gestures / 그녀는 항상 강연에 재치 있는 유머를 곁들인다 She always seasons her lecture with wit and humor.

**곁땀** sweat from the armpits. ¶ ～이 나다 sweat under the arm.

**곁마름** an assistant manager 〔agent〕 for farming lands.

**곁말** an allusive 〔a periphrastic〕 remark (with a bantering simile or metaphor).

**곁매** a by-blow. ¶ ～ 맞다 catch 〔get〕 a by-blow in other people's fight / ～질하다 deal blows 《at *a person*》 to help 《the other in a fight》.

**곁방**(一房) 《곁간》 a side chamber; 《셋방》 a rented room. ◉ ～살이 living in a rented room.

**곁부축** ① 《몸을》 helping 《*a person*》 to stand up holding his arms. ② 《거들다》 backing 《*a person*》 up 《with words》.

**곁붙이** distant relatives.

**곁비우다** leave *one's* post unmanned.

**곁상**(一床) a side table; a small (dinner-)table set at the side of the main one.

**곁쇠** a passkey; a duplicate 〔spare〕 key; a master key(맞쇠). ¶ ～질하다 unlock with a passkey.

**곁순**(一筍) sprouts 〔buds〕 from the side. ¶ ～을 자르다 nip off extra sprouts.

**곁자리** a side seat; seats on either side.

**곁줄기** 〖식물〗 a side stalk 《of a vine》.

**곁집** a neighboring 〔an adjoining〕 house; the house next door.

**곁채** an annex 《of a house》; an attached house; an outhouse.

**계**(戒) ① 《규정》 a command; an admonition. ② 〖종교〗 《계율》 (Buddhist) commandments; religious precepts; discipline. ¶ 계를 지키다 observe the commandments; practice 〔act up to〕 the precepts / 계를 어기다 violate the commandments 〔precepts〕.

**계**(計) ① 《총계》 the (sum) total; the total amount 〔sum〕. ¶ ～를 내다 add up; find the total of. ② 《계략》 a scheme; a stratagem; 《계획》 a plan. ¶ 백년지계 a far-sighted policy 〔program〕 / 국가의 백년지계를 세우다 draw up a long-range plan for the nation.

**계**(係) 《부서》 a section 《in an office》; 《담당자》 a clerk 〔an official〕 in charge. ¶ 출납계 the cashier's section; 《사람》 a cashier.

**계**(癸) 〖민속〗 《십간의》 the 10th of the 10 Heaven's Stems.

**계**(契) a (mutual) loan club; a mutual financing association; a credit union; a mutual assistance society. ¶ 계에 들다 join a loan club / 계를 모으다 found a loan club / 계를 타다 get *one's* loan 〔share〕 from the mutual loan club.

**-계**(系) ① 《계통》 a system. ¶ 태양〔은하〕계 the solar 〔galactic〕 system. ② 《당파》 a faction; a clique; a party. ¶ K씨계의 정치가 a politician of the K clique / 혁신계의 후보자 a progressive candidate. ③ 《혈통》 a family line; lineage; descent. ¶ 한국계의 미국인 an American of Korean descent 〔extraction〕; a Korean-American / 그녀는 라틴계다 She is of Latin origin 〔descent〕. ④ 《계열·경향》 ¶ 힐튼계의 호텔 one of the hotels in the Hilton chain / 기독교계 학교 a missionary school.

**-계**(屆) a notice; a report. ⇨ 신고.

**-계**(界) a world; circles; a community; 〖생물〗 a kingdom. ¶ 각계의 대표 representatives from 「all walks of life 〔all sections of society〕 / 실업계 business circles; the business world / 사교계 fashionable society; society circles / 동물〔식물〕계 the animal 〔vegetable〕 kingdom.

**-계**(計) a meter; a gauge. ¶ 온도계 a thermometer / 우량계 a rain gauge.

**계가**(計家) 〖바둑〗 taking count of crosses 〔each territory〕.

**계간**(季刊) 《간행》 quarterly publication; 《계간지》 a quarterly (magazine).

**계간**(鷄姦) sodomy. ⇨ 비역, 남색(男色). ~하다 commit sodomy. ◉ ~자 a sodomite; a bugger.

**계고**(戒告) a caution; a warning; a notification. ⇨ 경고(警告).

**계곡**(溪谷) a valley; a ravine; a dale.

**계관**(桂冠) a laurel wreath. ◉ ~시인 a poet laureate.

**계관**(鷄冠) ① 《볏》 a cock's crest; a cockscomb. ② 《맨드라미》 a cockscomb (plant). ◉ ~석 〖광물〗 realgar; sandarac. ~초 a cockscomb. ~화 a cockscomb flower.

**계교**(計巧) a trick; a scheme. ⇨ 계략(計略).

**계구우후**(鷄口牛後) Better be the head of an ass than the tail of a horse.

**계궁역진**(計窮力盡) exhaustion of *one's* resources; coming to the end of *one's* tether.

**계급**(階級) 《신분》 class; estate; caste; 《지위》 a rank; 《등급》 a grade. ¶ 모든 ~의 사람들 people of all classes / ~이 없는 사회 a classless society / 상류~의 가족 an upper-class family / 지배〔특권〕~ the ruling 〔privileged〕 classes / 지식~ the intellectual 〔educated〕 classes / 노동자~ the working class(es) / 상류〔중류, 하류〕~ the upper 〔middle, lower〕 class / ~이 높다〔낮다〕 high 〔low〕 in ranks / ~이 다르다 belong to different classes / ~을 형성〔타파〕하다 set up 〔level〕 classes / ~이 오르다 be promoted; be raised in rank / (…보다) ~이 위이다 be senior by rank; outrank 《another》 / ~의 차별을 철폐〔타파〕하다 abolish 〔break down〕 class distinctions / 그는 2~ 특진했다 He was promoted by two ranks. ◉ ~독재 class dictatorship. ~문학 proletarian literature. ~사회 a class society. ~의식〔감정〕 class consciousness 〔feeling〕: ~의식이 강하다 be strongly class-conscious. ~장 a badge of rank; an insignia; an ensign: 중장 ~장을 달아 주다 pin the insignia of lieutenant general 《on the shoulder of *a person*》. ~제도 the class system. ~조직 the hierarchy 《of the Civil Service》. ~층 classes; social strata. ~타파 class leveling; demolishing the distinction of classes. ~투쟁 class strife 〔conflict〕; class struggle 〔war〕.

**계기**(計器) a meter; a gauge; a scale; an instrument. ¶ 항해〔공업〕용 ~ a nautical 〔an industrial〕 instrument / 고도의 ~를 장치한 인공 위성 a highly instrumented satellite. ◉ ~반 《비행기의》 an instrument panel; 《자동차의》 a fascia (board); a dash (board). ~비행 an instrument 〔a blind〕 flight: ~비행 규칙 an instrument flight rule (생략 IFR) / ~비행을 하다 fly 〔go〕 on instruments. ~착륙 an instrument 〔a blind〕 landing.

**계기**(契機) 《기회》 an opportunity; a chance; 《철학에서》 a moment. ¶ 이것을 ~로 taking 〔availing (*oneself*) of〕 this opportunity; with this as a momentum 〔turning point〕 / ~가 되다 serve as a momentum / ~를 마련하다 provide a momentum 《for》 / 그것을 ~로 나는 담배를 끊었다 Taking that opportunity, I stopped smoking.

**계단**(階段) ① 《층층대》 (a flight of) stairs 〔steps〕; a staircase; a stairway; 《현관의》 doorsteps; 《노천 광산의》 a bench. ¶ ~식 객석 《극장 따위의》 seats arranged in tiers / ~을 오르다 ascend 〔go up〕 the stairs; go upstairs / ~을 내려가다 descend 〔go down〕 the stairs; go downstairs / ~을 총총걸음으로 오르다〔내리다〕 hurry upstairs 〔downstairs〕 / ~을 헛디디다 miss *one's* footing on the stairs; slip on the stairs / ~에서 떨어지다 fall downstairs / ~주의 《게시》 Watch your step. / ~을 2개씩 뛰어 올라가다 run up the stairs, two steps at a time / 이 ~을 올라가면 그의 방이 나온다 This

staircase leads to his room. ② 《단계》 a stage; phase. ③ 《순서》 steps.
◉ ～식 교실 a (lecture) theater. ～식 농지 a terraced farmland: ～식 농지를 개발하다 reclaim 〔cultivate〕 the terraced fields 〔paddies〕. ～통 〖건축〗 a stairwell.

**계도**(系圖) genealogy; lineage; pedigree.

**계도**(啓導) guidance; leading; instruction; teaching; enlightenment. ～하다 guide; lead; instruct; teach; enlighten.

**계란**(鷄卵) an egg; a chicken 〔hen's〕 egg. ◉ ～덮밥 a bowl of rice topped with scrambled eggs. ～지 〖사진〗 albumenized paper. ～탕 egg soup.

**계략**(計略) 《계획》 a plan; a scheme; a design; 《책략》 a trick; a ruse; a plot; an artifice; a stratagem; a policy. ¶ ～에 능한 사람 a resourceful man; a man of resources / ～을 부릴 줄 모르는 사람 a man of no resources; a shiftless man / ～을 짜다〔꾸미다〕 lay a plan; form 〔devise〕 a stratagem 〔scheme〕; hatch a plot; invent a trick; try tricks 《to deceive *a person*》/ ～에 빠지다〔걸리다〕 fall into a snare; be entrapped; be caught in a trap / 적의 ～에 빠지다 play into the hands of the enemy / ～에 빠뜨리다 entrap; ensnare / ～을 간파하다 see through 《*another's*》 design.

**계량**(計量) measuring; weighing. ～하다 measure; weigh. ◉ ～경제학 econometrics. ～기 a meter; a gauge; a scale: 수도 ～기 a water gauge 〔meter〕. ～단위 a measuring unit. ～컵 a measuring cup.

**계뢰**(界雷) 〖기상〗 a frontal thunderstorm.

**계루**(係累) ① 《연루》 involvement. ⇨ 연루(連累). ② 《딸린 식구》 encumbrance(s); dependents. ¶ ～가 많다 have 〔be encumbered with〕 a large family / ～가 없다 have no dependents.

**계류**(溪流) a mountain stream.

**계류**(繫留) ① mooring. ～하다 moor 《at, to》. ¶ ～를 풀다 cast off the moorings / (배가) ～중이다 be (rigging) at her moorings. ② 《미해결》 ¶ ～중인 pending 〔outstanding〕 《problems》; unsolved; unsettled / 그 사건은 아직도 법원에 ～중이다 The case is still pending in court.
◉ ～기구 a captive balloon. ～부표 a mooring buoy. ～선 a moored vessel; a laid-up vessel. ～장 moorings; moorage. ～주 a shoreline post; a mooring post. ～탑 a mooring tower 〔mast〕: 비행선을 ～탑에 매다 moor a dirigible 〔airship〕 to a mast.

**계륵**(鷄肋) chicken ribs; [비유적] something that *one* hesitates to give up even though it is of little interest; a superfluity; a redundancy.

**계림**(鷄林) Kyongju; Shilla; Korea.

**계면**(界面) the interface. ◉ ～장력 〖물리〗 interfacial 〔surface, phase, boundary〕 tension. ～화학 surface chemistry. ～활성제 a surfactant.

**계명**(戒名) 〖불교〗 *one's* Buddhist name (생전의); a posthumous Buddhist name(사후의). ¶ ～을 지어주다 give a posthumous Buddhist name 《to the deceased》.

**계명**(階名) 〖음악〗 syllable names. ◉ ～창법 solmization.

**계명**(誡命) 〖종교〗 a commandment.

**계모**(繼母) a stepmother.

**계몽**(啓蒙) enlightenment; illumination; education. ～하다 enlighten; illuminate; instruct 《the children, the ignorant》; educate. ¶ ～적 illuminating; enlightening; 《초보의》 elementary / 무지한 사람들을 ～하다 enlighten the ignorant.
◉ ～대 an enlightenment squad. ～문학 literature of enlightenment. ～시대 the (Age of) Enlightenment. ～운동 a campaign for enlightenment; an education(al) 〔enlightenment〕 movement; an enlightenment campaign: 국민 ～ 운동 a mass-education drive 〔campaign〕/ 농촌 ～ 운동 a rural enlightenment drive. ～철학 philosophy of enlightenment.

**계발**(啓發) enlightenment; illumination; development. ～하다 enlighten; develop; edify; educate; illuminate. ¶ 지능을 ～하다 develop the intellectual faculties. ◉ ～교육 development education. ～자 a developer.

**계방**(癸方) 〖민속〗 north-by-northeast.

**계보**(系譜) pedigree; genealogy; lineage. ¶ 한국 문학의 ～ genealogy of Korean literature / ～를 조사하다 look into 〔trace〕 《*a person's*》 genealogy 〔pedigree〕.

**계보**(季報) a quarterly bulletin.

**계부**(繼父) a stepfather.

**계사**(繫辭) 〖문법·논리〗 a copula.

**계사**(鷄舍) a chicken house; a henhouse.

**계삭**(繫索) 〖항해〗 a fast; a lasher. ◉ 이물〔고물〕～ a head 〔stern〕 fast.

**계산**(計算) (a) calculation; computation; reckoning; figure work; 《회계》

accounts; 《견적》 an estimation; 《결산》 balancing. ～하다 count; calculate; reckon; compute; 《합계》 sum 〔add〕 up; figure (up); 《견적》 estimate. ¶ 그들의 ～으로는 in their reckoning / ～에 넣다 take 《*a thing*》 into account 〔consideration〕 / ～에 안 넣다 leave 《*a thing*》 out of account / ～이 느리다 be slow at figures / ～을 잘못하다 miscalculate; miscount / ～이 빠르다 be quick at accounts / 이자를 ～하다 compute interest / ～을 잘 하다〔이서툴다〕 be good 〔poor〕 at figures / 손익을 ～하다 balance profit 〔gain〕 and loss / 요금은 거리로 ～한다 Charges are reckoned by distance. / 네 ～과 꼭 들어맞는다 My figures tally (up) with you. / ～은 따로따로 하시겠습니까, 함께 하시겠습니까 《식당 따위에서》 Is this separate or together?
◉ ～기 a calculator; a calculating 〔an adding〕 machine; a computer: 전자 ～기 an electronic computer. ～법 a method of computation 〔calculation〕. ～서 a statement of accounts; 《견적서》 an estimate. ～자〔척〕 a slide rule; a calculating scale. ～착오 miscalculation; an error in calculation: ～착오를 하다 miscalculate; calculate wrongly; make an error in calculation. ～표 a ready reckoner.

**계상**(計上) ～하다 《충당》 appropriate 《a sum for》; 《계산》 sum up. ¶ 예산에 ～하다 appropriate 《a billion won》 in the budget.

**계선**(繫船) mooring; 《배》 a laid-up 〔an idle〕 ship. ⇨ 계류(繫留). ¶ ～ 중인 선박 a ship in lay-up; a laid-up ship.
◉ ～료 moorage; quayage.

**계속**(繼續) continuation; continuance. ～하다 continue 《*doing*, to *do*, the work》; keep up 〔go on〕 《with the work, *doing*》; hold on; carry on 《the work》 (★ go on with는 보통 한번 그쳤다가 다시 계속할 때에, go on doing은 중단 없이 내리 계속하는 경우에 씀. 또 go on의 뒤에 부정사가 와서 예컨대 go on to say로 되면 「다시 말을 계속하여 …라고 하다」가 됨). ¶ ～적(으로) 《시간·공간의》 continuous(ly); continual(ly); uninterrupted(ly) / ～하여 in succession; continually; without interruption; 《내리》 (all) through; throughout; without a break / ～되는 장마 a long spell of rainy weather / 10년간이나 ～해서 for ten years 「at a stretch 〔on end, together, running〕 / ～해서 세 번 three times 「in succession 〔in a row〕 / ～해서 부지런히 걷다 keep walking at a rapid pace / 불행이 ～되다 have a run of ill luck / 일을 ～해서 하다 proceed 〔go on〕 with *one's* work / 이야기를 ～하다 go on talking; keep up a conversation / 5일 동안이나 비가 ～해서 내렸다 It rained for five consecutive 〔straight〕 days. / 학업을 ～하다 continue *one's* attendance at school; 《중단했다가》 resume *one's* study / ～ 토론하다 make a continued debate 《on》 / 이야기를 ～하게 Go on 〔Proceed〕 with your story. / 이 영화는 두 달 동안 ～ 상영되었다 This film has had a run of two months. / 전투는 종일 ～되었다 The battle went on all day. / 쌀 시세가 ～ 보합 상태이다 The market-price of rice continues firm. / 이런 날씨가 오래 ～되었으면 싶다 I hope this weather will hold much longer. / 전람회는 5월 20일까지 ～ 열린다 The exhibition remains open until May 20. / 앞 페이지에서 ～ Continued from (the) previous page. / 다음 난〔20페이지〕에 ～ Continued 「in next column 〔on page 20〕. / 뒷면에 ～ Over. *or* P.T.O. [<*P*lease *t*urn *o*ver] / 다음 호에 ～ To be continued.
◉ ～기간 a (period of) duration. ～범 a continuing crime. ～비 a continuing expenditure.

**계수**(季嫂) *one's* younger brother's wife.

**계수**(係數) 〖수학·물리〗 a coefficient; a modulus (*pl.* -li); a factor.
◉ 노동～ a labor coefficient. 증발～ the evaporation factor. 탄성～ the modulus of elasticity.

**계수**(計數) calculation; computation; figures. ～하다 calculate; compute; count. ¶ ～에 밝다 be good at figures.
◉ ～관 《방사능의》 a counter. ～기 a calculating machine; a comptometer; an arithmometer. ～회로 〖원자물리〗 a scaling circuit.

**계수나무**(桂樹—) a cinnamon 〔cassia〕 tree.

**계수법**(繼受法) 〖법〗 an adopted law.

**계승**(階乘) 〖수학〗 a factorial. ¶ 4의 ～ factorial 4; the factorial of 4.

**계승**(繼承) succession; accession; inheritance. ～하다 succeed to; accede to; come into; inherit; take over. ¶ 스페인 왕위 ～ 전쟁 the Spanish Succession War / 왕위를 ～하다 succeed to the throne 〔crown〕 / 대대로 ～하다 be succeeded from generation to generation. ◉ ～자 a successor; an heir.

**계시** an apprentice (to a craftsman 〔to an artisan〕). ＝도제(徒弟).

**계시**(癸時) 〖민속〗 the 2nd of the 24 hour periods (＝0:30-1:30 a.m.).

**계시**(計時) clocking. ～하다 《경기 따위에서》 check time; time. ◉ ～기 a timer. ～원 a timekeeper; a timer.

**계시**(啓示) 〖종교〗 (a) revelation; 《신의 존재에 관한》 an epiphany; 《예언적인》 Apocalypse. ～하다 reveal. ¶ 신의 ～ a revelation of God. ◉ ～록 the Book of Revelation; the Apocalypse. ～문학 apocalyptic literature; apocalypses. ～종교 a revealed religion.

**계시다** 《someone esteemed》 be; there be; be located; stay. ¶ 여기 계십시오 Stay here.

**계씨**(季氏) your esteemed younger brother.

**계약**(契約) a contract; a promise; an agreement; a compact; a covenant. ～하다 contract; make 〔enter into, place〕 a contract 《with》; make 〔fix up〕 an agreement 《with》; 《매매의》 close 〔conclude, settle〕 a bargain 《with》. ¶ 형식상의 ～ a formal contract / 법률상 유효한 ～ a legally binding contract / 날인한 ～증서 a written contract under seal / …을 공급하는 ～ a contract for a supply of... / 4년 ～으로 on a four-year contract / ～ 이행중 during the execution of a contract / ～을 지키다 abide by 〔observe〕 *one's* contract; keep *one's* bargain 〔promise〕 / ～을 어기다 break 〔violate〕 a contract 〔an agreement〕 / ～을 이행하다 perform 〔carry out, fulfil〕 a contract; meet *one's* engagements (채무의) / ～을 무효로 하다 vitiate a contract / ～을 취소〔해제〕하다 cancel 〔annul, break off, dissolve〕 a contract 〔an agreement〕; declare an agreement off / ～을 갱신하다 renew 〔refresh〕 a contract / ～중이다 be under contract 《to build a ship》 / KBS와 2년간 출연 ～을 맺고 있다 be under a booking of two-year to KBS / 3년 ～으로 고용되다 be engaged on a three-year contract / ～은 5년간 유효하다 The contract holds good for five years. / 이 ～은 이제 무효다 This contract is no longer valid 〔binding〕. *or* This contract no longer stands. / 나는 그 아파트를 2년간 빌리기로 ～했다 I am to take the apartment on a lease of two years.

◉ ～가격 the contract price. ～고 contract amount. ～금 a contract deposit; bargain money; 《청약금》 down payment. ～급 contract wage. ～기간 the term of a contract. ～노동 contract labor. ～농업 contract farming. ～(당사)자 contractor(s); 《한쪽》 a contracting party; 《쌍방》 contracting parties. ～문서 a charter; a contract document; a deed of contract. ～불이행 nonfulfillment 〔nonperformance〕 of a contract. ～서식 a contract form. ～설 ⇨ 사회 계약설. ～위반 (a) breach of contract. ～이민 indentured immigrants. ～조건 the conditions 〔terms〕 of a contract. ～조항 contract clause(s). ～해제 cancelation of a contract.

**계약서**(契約書) a (written) contract; an agreement; a bond; a contract document; a deed of contract. ¶ ～를 작성하다 draw up a contract 〔an agreement〕 / ～를 교환하다 exchange written contracts 《with each other》; make a written agreement 《with》 / ～에 명기하다 specify in a contract / ～에 서명하다 sign a contract 《with》.

**계엄**(戒嚴) guarding against the threat of danger; exercising vigilance.

◉ ～령 martial law: ～령을 펴다〔선포하다〕 place 〔put〕 《a city》 under martial law; proclaim martial law / ～령을 해제하다 lift 〔withdraw〕 martial law / ～령하에 있다 be under martial law. ～사령관 the martial law commander; the chief martial law administrator. ～사령부 the Martial Law Command.

**계열**(系列) 〖생물〗 a system; an order of descent; 〖물리〗 a series; 《기업체 등의》 a group; 《호텔·점포 등의》 a chain; 《단체의 제휴관계》 an affiliation; 《유파 등의》 a category.

¶ 기업의 ～화 the grouping of enterprises; the process of forming or strengthening the interrelationships among enterprises (in a financial conglomerate) / 저것은 힐튼 ～의 호텔이다 That is one of the hotels in the Hilton chain. ◉ ～회사 a business firm of the group; an affiliated company: 현대의 ～ 회사 a business firm of 〔belonging to, affiliated with〕 the Hyundai group; an affiliate of the Hyundai group.

**계원**(係員) a clerk; an official 〔a clerk〕 in charge 《of》. ¶ 접수 ～ an information clerk; a receptionist.

**계원**(契員) a member of a credit union 〔loan club, mutual aid association〕.

**계율**(戒律) ⇨ 계(戒) ②.

**계인**(契印) a tally impression 〔seal〕. ~하다 seal the two papers. ¶ ~을 찍은 서류 documents with a tally impression / ~을 찍다 affix 〔put〕 a seal「over two edges 〔at the joint of two leaves〕《of a deed》.

**계자**(界磁) =장자석(場磁石).

**계장**(係長) a chief (*pl.* ~s); a chief 「clerk.

**계쟁**(係爭) 〖법〗 dispute; contention; controversy; 《소송》 a lawsuit. ~하다 dispute; contend; engage in controversy. ¶ ~중이다 be at issue 〔in dispute〕; 《법정에서》 be pending in court. ◉ ~문제 a matter 〔an issue〕 in dispute. ~물 property under dispute. ~사건 a contentious case. ~사실 a fact in dispute; an issue; an item of controversy. ~점 a point at issue; a disputed point.

**계전기**(繼電器) 〖전기〗 a relay. ◉ ~식 자동 전화교환 방식 the relay automatic telephone system.

**계절**(季節) a season. ¶ ~의 변화 the turn(ing) 〔change〕 of the season / ~의 꽃 flowers of the season / ~에 관계 없이 in all seasons; in and out of season / ~적으로 seasonally; according to the season / ~에 맞는 suitable for the season; seasonable / ~과 동떨어진 out of season; unseasonable / ~의 별미 the best tasting 〔flavoring〕 dish(es) of the season / 가을은 여행하기 좋은 ~이다 Autumn is a good season「for travel(ing) 〔to make a trip〕. ◉ ~감 a sense of the season. ~고용 seasonal employment. ~노동자 a seasonal laborer. ~산업 a seasonal industry. ~상품 seasonal goods. ~요금 《호텔 등》 a seasonal rate. ~요리 a seasonal dish. ~풍 = 철바람.

**계정**(計定) an account (생략 a/c). ¶ …의 ~에 넣다 place 〔pass〕 to the account of…. ◉ ~과목 a title of account.

**계제**(階梯) ① 《단계·순서》 steps; stages; the course 《of things》. ② 《기회》 an opportunity; an occasion; a chance. ¶ 이 ~에 taking this opportunity; with this as a turning point / 언젠가 ~를 보아 at some convenient time / ~ 사납게 inopportunely; unfortunately; at an unfortunate moment; unluckily / ~를 보아 …를 하다 pick *one's* moment to *do*.

**계좌**(計座) an account. ¶ (은행에) ~를 트다 open an account (with a bank). ◉ ~번호 an account number.

**계주**(契主) the organizer of a mutual finance association 〔credit union〕.

**계주경기**(繼走競技) a relay race. ⇨ 릴레이.

**계진기**(計塵器) a dust counter.

**계집** ① 《여자》 a woman; a female; the gentle 〔fair〕 sex; a girl. ¶ ~에 미치다 have an insane passion for a girl / ~에 빠지다 be infatuated with a woman; be hooked on a girl. ② 《아내》 a wife; 《정부》 a mistress; a dame 《속어》. ¶ ~ 자식 *one's* wife and children; *one's* dependents. ◉ ~아이 a girl; a lass. ~종 a maid (servant); a woman-servant. ~질 a woman〔skirt〕-chasing; womanizing; 《오입》 whoring; 《난봉》 debauchery: ~질하다 whore (around); womanize; run after women; commit adultery.

**계책**(計策) a scheme; an artifice; a trick; a design; a stratagem. ¶ ~을 쓰다 adopt 〔use〕 a stratagem / 남의 ~을 알아내다 see through another's design / ~이 다하다 be at *one's* wit's end; be at the end of *one's* resources 〔tether〕.

**계체량**(計體量) the weigh-in. ¶ ~통과에 실패하다 fail to pass the weigh-in 《in *one's* first try》.

**계출**(屆出) a report. = 신고(申告).

**계측**(計測) (a) measurement. ~하다 measure; 《토지 따위를》 survey. ◉ ~공학 instrumentation engineering. ~기(器) a measuring instrument 〔machine〕. ~기학(器學) instrumentology.

**계층**(階層) a class; a social stratum; 《소득의》 a bracket. ¶ 온갖 ~의 사람들 people「of every class 〔on every social level〕; people from「every walk 〔all walks〕 of life / 고소득 ~ people in the high income bracket.

**계통**(系統) ① 《조직》 a system; 《경로》 a channel. ¶ 지휘〔명령〕~ a channel 〔chain〕 of command / 신경〔소화, 생식〕~ the nervous 〔digestive, reproductive〕 system / ~적(으로) systematic(ally) / ~을 세우다 systematize; make systematic; organize / 그의 연구는 ~이 서 있지 않다 He lacks 〔has not〕 system in his study. / 나는 영어를 ~적으로 연구하고 싶다 I'd like to make a systematic study of English. / 그는 처음으로 법의 ~을 세운 사람이다 He was the first man to systematize the law. ② 《계도》 a family line; 《혈통》 descent; lineage; origin; 〖생물〗 genealogy. ¶ …의 ~을 캐다

trace the descent of... / ～을 잇다 be descended from; 《기질 등이 주어》 be inherited 《from》; run in the family. ③ 《당파》 a party; a clique; 《언어·인종 등》 a family; 《유파》 a school. ¶ 영어는 인도유럽어 ～이다 English is of the Indo-European family.
◉ ～도(圖) 《조직 등의》 a distribution diagram; 《혈통의》 a genealogical chart. ～발생 phylogeny. ～수(樹) a genealogical 〔family〕 tree. ～오차 system errors. ～출하 route sales. ～학 systematics.

**계표**(界標) a boundary mark.

**계피**(桂皮) cinnamon; cassia (bark). ◉ ～유 cinnamon oil. 계핏가루 cinnamon powder.

**계획**(計劃) a plan; a project; a scheme; a design; a program(me); 《의도》 intention. ～하다 plan; make a plan; project; intend; contemplate.

> 용법 **plan** 「머리에 떠오른 착상」에서 이를 「실행에 옮기기 위한 세부적이고 구체적인 계획」을 뜻하는 가장 일반적인 말. **project** 장기에 걸친 대규모의 구상·기획으로 사회성이 큰 계획. **scheme** 이익을 얻으려고 면밀하게 짜여진 계획. 종종 나쁜 뜻으로 「술수·음모」 등의 의미로도 쓰임. **design** 어떤 목적을 이루기 위해 사용되는 수단에 관한 자세한 고안·준비. **program** 행사나 프로그램 따위의 실시 계획.

¶ ～적(인) intentional; deliberate; calculated; systematic / ～적으로 intentionally; deliberately; on purpose / 10년 ～으로 on a ten years' program / 국가적 ～ a national plan / 대체적인 ～ a rough plan / 작전 ～의 변경 changes in the operational plans / (경제 개발) 5개년 ～ a five-year (economic development) program / 포괄적인〔광범위한〕 장기 ～ a comprehensive long-term project / ～중인 intended 《journey》; under contemplation / ～ 중이다 have 《*a matter*》 in contemplation; be under 〔in〕 consideration / ～대로 실행하다 carry out 《a plan》 as planned 〔previously arranged〕 / ～을 세우다 plan (for); make 〔draw up, formulate〕 a plan 〔project〕 / 장래의 ～을 세우다 plan (up) *one's* future / 고가 철도를 부설할 ～이 서 있다 A project is afoot to construct an elevated railway.
◉ ～경제 planned economy. ～목표 a planned goal 〔target〕. ～생산 planned production. ～성 《lack》 planning. ～안 a plan; a blueprint; a schedule. ～자 a planner; a projector.

**곗돈**(契—) money for 〔from〕 the mutual aid society 〔the credit union〕.

**곗술**(契—) wine provided by a mutual aid society. ¶ ～에 낯내기 playing the big shot with other people's money.

**고**[1] 《고리》 a loop 《of string》; string 〔ribbon〕 ties.

**고**[2] 《그》 that little 《*thing*》. ¶ 고놈 that little man 〔guy, so-and-so〕 / 고 버릇 that little habit / 고 모양이다 be (the same little old thing) as usual; be just the same as before; be (always) like that / 그 집 살림은 밤낮 고 모양이다 They are badly off as ever.

**-고**[3] 《용언에 붙어서》 ¶ 방문하겠다고 약속하다 promise to visit / 가난하다고 남을 업신여겨서는 안 된다 You should not look down on others (only) because they are poor.

**고**(苦) hardship(s); difficulty; suffering(s); pain; affliction. ¶ 생활고 the hardships of life; a hard life.

**-고**(高) ① ＝높이[1]. ② 《수량》 an amount; (a) volume; 《금액》 an amount; a sum. ¶ 매상고 the amount sold; the sales / 생산고 an output; a yield.

**고**(鼓) a drum.

**-고**(膏) plaster; paste; ointment. ¶ 반창고 《미》 an adhesive bandage; 《영》 a sticking plaster.

**고**(故) 《죽은》 the late; the deceased; the late lamented; of blessed 〔happy〕 memory. ¶ 고 A씨 the late Mr. A.

**-고** ① 《동작·성질·상태의 잇닮》 and also. ¶ 붉고 큰 꽃 a huge red flower / 크고 달고 값싼 참외 a melon that is big, sweet and cheap / 바쁘고 피곤하다 be busy and tired / 비가 오고 바람도 분다 It rains and the wind blows too.
② 《두 동작의 대등한 연결》 《*do*》 and then; *do*ing and then. ¶ 문을 열고 손님을 맞다 open the door and welcome a visitor / 말을 타고 가다 go on horseback / 안경을 쓰고 보다 look at 《it》 with *one's* glasses on.
③ (***a***) 《동작의 진행》 -고 있다 be *do*ing. ¶ 모자를 쓰고 있다 be wearing 〔have on〕 a hat / 기다리고 있다 be waiting / 입원하고 있다 be in the hospital. (***b***) 《동작의 완료》 -고 나다 just finish *do*ing. ¶ 밥을 먹고 나다 have just finished dinner / 며칠 전에 앓고 나서 입맛을 잃었다 I just got over being sick a few days ago and I lost my

appetite. (*c*) 《동작의 욕망》 -고 싶다 *one* wants to *do*. ¶ 관광을 좀더 하고 싶다 I'd like to do a bit more sightseeing. / 집에 가고 싶다 I want to go home.

**고가**(古家) an old house. ¶ 유형 문화재로 지정된 ~ an old house designated [registered] as a tangible cultural properties [assets].

**고가**(古歌) an old song [poem].

**고가**(故家) an old family; a family of great antiquity. ◉ ~대족(大族) an illustrious family of good lineage.

**고가**(高架) ¶ ~의 elevated; overhead; high-level. ◉ ~교 an elevated bridge; a viaduct; an overpass. ~도로 an elevated road; an elevated expressway. ~선 《전선》 overhead wires [wiring]; 《노선》 an overhead [elevated] line. ~전차 an elevated 「electric car [train 《미》]. ~철도 《미》 an elevated (railroad); an L [el] 《미구어》; an overhead railway 《영》.

**고가**(高價) a high price; costliness; expensiveness. ¶ ~의 expensive; costly; dear / ~의 옷 a costly dress / ~로 팔다 sell 《*a thing*》 at a high price / 고본[옛날 우표] 고가 매입 《게시》 Best [High] prices offered for used books [old stamps].

**고각**(高角) a high angle. ◉ ~발사 a high-angle fire. ~포 『군사』 ⇨ 고사포.

**고갈**(枯渴) 《물이》 drying up; running dry; 《돈·물건이》 exhaustion; drain. ~하다, ~되다 be dried up; run dry; be exhausted [drained]. ¶ 나라의 자원을 ~시키다 drain a country of her natural resources / 그의 창작력은 ~ 되었다 His imagination has dried up.

**고개** ① 《목》 the back of the neck; the nape [scuff, scruff] of the neck; the head (머리). ¶ ~를 가로젓다 answer in the negative / ~를 갸웃하다 put *one's* head [a little to] one side / ~를 끄덕이다 nod (*one's* head) 《to, at》; nod (in) assent / ~를 (쳐)들다 raise [hold up] *one's* head / ~를 숙이다 bow [lower] *one's* head 《with awe or shame》; droop *one's* head / ~를 처뜨리다 hang [drop] *one's* head / ~를 돌리다 turn *one's* head / ~를 흔들다 shake *one's* head / ~를 들지 못하다 cannot hold up *one's* head 《for shame》.
② 《비탈》 a pass; a ridge. ¶ ~를 넘다 cross a pass [ridge]; cross over the pass; pass over the peak / ~에 접어들다 come to a mountain pass.
③ 《고비》 the crest; the height; the summit. ¶ 70 ~를 넘다 pass *one's* seventy-year milestone / 물가가 ~를 숙였다 The prices are going [coming] down. *or* The prices are falling. / 그는 벌써 50 ~를 넘었다 He is on the shady side of fifty.
◉ ~턱 the head of a pass [slope]. ~티 a steep winding road [path] over a mountain ridge. 고갯길 an uphill [ascending] pass.

**고객**(顧客) a customer; a buyer; a client; a patron; custom [총칭]. ¶ 오랜 ~ an old customer; a customer of long standing / ~이 많다 have a large custom / 외국인을 ~으로 하다 be patronized by foreigners / ~ 만족도 customer satisfaction measurement.

**고갯짓** moving *one's* head about; shaking *one's* head (좌우로); a nod (상하로). ~하다 move *one's* head about; shake [nod] *one's* head.

**고갱이** 《식물의》 the heart (of a plant); the pith; 《핵심》 the core; the kernel; the essence. ¶ 양배추 ~ the heart of a cabbage.

**고것** 《그것》 that (little) one; it; 《사람》 the fellow [man]; that guy; he. ¶ ~ 좀 집어주세요 Please pick it up for me. *or* Will you pass it to me, please?

**고견**(高見) ① 《뛰어난 의견》 an excellent [a capital] idea; a farsighted view. ② 《남의 의견》 your (respected) opinion [view, idea]. ¶ 그 문제에 대한 선생의 ~을 듣고자 합니다 Please let me know your views about the matter.

**고결**(高潔) noble-mindedness; loftiness. ~하다 (be) noble-minded; high=minded; noble; lofty; pure. ¶ ~한 사람 a man of lofty character; a high=souled person.

**고경**(苦境) a painful position; a difficult situation; distressed [adverse] circumstances; difficulties; a predicament; a fix; a dilemma.

**고계**(苦界) 『불교』 the (mundane) world; this troubled [suffering] world.

**고고**(呱呱) a baby's cry at its birth. ¶ ~의 소리를 울리다 first see the light (of day); come into being [life].

**고고**(孤高) a proud loneliness [isolation, aloofness]. ~하다 stand in lofty solitude; remain aloof from others. ¶ ~한 생활 a life of proud loneliness.

**고고** the go-go [gogo] dance; go-go; gogo. ¶ ~를 추다 dance go-go.

**고고학**(考古學) arch(a)eology. ¶ ~의

archeological / ～상으로 archeologically; from the archeological point of view. ◉ ～자 an archeologist. ～자료 archeological specimens (실례) 〔evidence (증거)〕.

**고공**(高空) a high sky; a high altitude. ¶ ～을 날다 fly high up in the air; fly at an altitude 〔a height〕 of 《6,000 feet》. ◉ ～병 altitude sickness. ～비행 high-altitude flying.

**고과**(考課) consideration of services; evaluation of merits. ◉ ～표 a business report (회사의); an efficiency report; a personal service record (개인의).

**고관**(高官) a high(-ranking) official; a dignitary; a high office (직위). ◉ ～대작 《직위》 a high office 〔rank〕; honors; 《사람》 a high and distinguished official; dignitaries.

**고광나무** 〖식물〗 a mock orange; a syringa.

**고굉**(股肱) *one's* right-hand (man); *one's* trusted henchman. ¶ ～지신(之臣) a king's right-hand man; a trusted retainer.

**고교**(高校) a (senior) high school. ¶ ～에 입학하다 enter high school / 그녀는 ～1년생이다 She is a first-year student in high school. ◉ ～ 내신 성적 high school records. ～생 a (senior) high school student; 《미》 a senior high student; a high schooler. ～야구 (senior) high school baseball. ～평준화 the academic standardization of high schools. ⇨ 고등학교.

**고교회파**(高教會派) 〖종교〗 the High Church.

**고구마** a sweet potato (*pl.* ～es). ¶ 군～ roasted 〔baked〕 sweet potatoes / 찐～ steamed sweet potatoes / ～탕 fried sweet potatoes mixed with glutinous starch syrup.

**고국**(故國) *one's* homeland; *one's* native 〔home〕 country; the country of *one's* birth. ¶ ～에 돌아오다 return to *one's* native 〔home〕 country; return home / ～을 영영 떠나다 leave *one's* home 〔native〕 land for good and all / ～을 그리워하다 long 〔pine〕 for *one's* home. ◉ ～산천 (the mountains and rivers of) *one's* homeland.

**고군**(孤軍) an isolated force; a forlorn garrison. ¶ ～분투하다 fight alone 〔unsupported〕; put up a solitary struggle.

**고궁**(古宮) an old 〔ancient〕 palace.

**고귀하다**(高貴―) 《신분》 (be) noble; high; exalted; 《가치》 (be) expensive; valuable; rare. ¶ 고귀한 사람 a person of high rank 〔noble birth〕 / 고귀한 집안에서 태어나다 be born into a noble family; be high-born.

**고금**(古今) ancient and modern times; any age; all ages. ¶ ～의 ancient and modern; of all ages / ～에 유례 없는 unprecedented / ～ 미증유의 대해전 the greatest naval battle on record / ～을 통하여 through 〔in〕 all ages / 동서～에 걸쳐 《be true》 for all ages and in all places; 《be applicable》 to all times and places / ～의 문학에 환하다 be well versed in literature, ancient as well as modern / ～에 그 유례를 볼 수 없다 have no parallel 〔equal〕 in history 〔in any age〕. ◉ ～독보 having no equal throughout the ages; unique for all time.

**고금리 정책** the dear money policy.

**고급**(告急) sending an urgent 〔emergency〕 message; raising an alarm. ～하다 send an urgent 〔emergency〕 message; raise an alarm.

**고급**(高級) ¶ ～의 high-class〔-grade, -ranking〕; higher; advanced; quality 《magazine》; 《구어》 posh 《hotels》; classy 〔expensive〕 《restaurants》 / 저 호텔은 뉴욕에 있는 최～ 호텔 중의 하나이다 That hotel is one of the classiest 〔plushiest〕 hotels in New York. / 그 식당은 ～이다 The restaurant is very exclusive. ◉ ～공무원 higher 〔high-ranking〕 (government) officials. ～상점 a high-class 〔a quality, an exclusive〕 shop. ～선원 an officer (of a ship); [총칭] the quarterdeck. ～인력 high-quality human resources. ～장교 a high-ranking officer; brass 《미구어》. ～지 a quality newspaper. ～차 a deluxe car; a high-class 〔an expensive〕 car. ～참모 a senior staff officer. ～품 (high-)quality goods 〔articles〕; an article of quality.

**고급**(高給) a high 〔big〕 salary. ¶ ～의 high-salaried; high-paid / ～을 받다 be highly paid; draw a big salary.

**고기** meat (식용); beef (소); pork (돼지); mutton (양); chicken (닭); fowl, poultry (조류의); fish (물고기). ¶ ～한 점 a piece of meat / 다진 ～ minced meat; hashed meat / ～ 저미는 기계 a meat grinder; a mincing machine / (물)～ 잡으러 가다 go fishing. ◉ ～깃 plants used as fish-lures. ～덮밥 rice topped with seasoned beef.

～떼 a school 〔shoal〕 of fish. ～만두 a meat-bun. ～밥 《먹이》 fish food; food given to fish; 《미끼》 fish bait; food used to lure fish. ～붙이 meats: ～붙이를 먹지 않다 abstain from meat(s). ～요리 a meat dish. ～잡이 fishing; 《어부》 a fisherman; a fisher. ～전골 a hot beef casserole. ～칼 a butcher knife; a carving knife. 고깃간 a butcher shop; the butcher's. 고깃국 broth; gravy; meat soup. 고깃덩어리 a lump 〔hunk〕 of meat; 《사람》 a plump fellow; a fatty. 고깃배 a fishing boat 〔vessel〕; a fisherboat.

**고기**(古記) an old record 〔chronicle〕.

**고기압**(高氣壓) high atmospheric pressure; high (air) pressure. ¶ ～이 발달하다 a high pressure develops itself 《over》. ◉ ～권 a high pressure area: 북태평양 ～권 the north Pacific atmospheric pressure zone. 대륙성 ～ the continental high pressure.

**고깃고깃-** ⇨ 구깃구깃-.

**고까짓** such; so 「trifling 〔small, trivial〕. ¶ ～ 일로 화내지 말게 Don't get angry at such trifles.

**고깔** a peaked hat (worn by Buddhist monks and nuns). ◉ ～해파리 〖동물〗 a Portuguese man-of-war.

**고깝다** (be) vexing (짜증나다); disagreeable; unpleasant; disgusting; feel bad 《about *a person's* lack of kindness》. ¶ 고깝게 여기다 be 〔feel〕 disgusted 《at》; feel unpleasant; take 《it》 ill / 고만한 돈도 빌려 주지 않아 고까웠다 I felt bad that he would not lend me that little amount of money. / 악의는 없었던 것이니 고깝게 여기진 말게 Please don't take it ill. I meant no harm.

**고꾸라뜨리다, 꼬꾸라지다** ⇨ 거꾸러-.

**고난**(苦難) suffering(s); hardship(s); distress; affliction(s); ordeal. ¶ ～을 견디다 bear 〔withstand〕 hardships 〔a trial〕 / ～을 극복하다 overcome the difficulty / ～의 길을 걷다 muddle through the bitters of life.

**고녀**(雇女) a maid; a woman servant; a hired girl 〔woman〕.

**고녀**(鼓女) a woman who has underdeveloped genitals.

**고념**(顧念) ① 《돌봄》 looking after; taking care of; patronizing. ② 《감싸다》 covering 《faults》.

**고뇌**(苦惱) suffering; distress; affliction; anguish; agony; trouble. ～하다 suffer; be afflicted; be distressed; be in agony. ¶ ～의 생활 a suffering life / ～의 빛을 띠다 a look of distress comes over *one's* face.

**고니** 〖조류〗 a swan. ◉ 큰～ a whooper swan. 흑～ a black swan.

**고다** ① 《끓이다》 boil; cook; boil down; boil dry. ¶ 고기를 흐무러지게 ～ boil meat to pulp / 생선을 ～ stew fish to pulp / 지나치게 ～ overdo; overboil / 엿을 ～ make Korean taffy / 과일즙을 고아 과당을 만들다 boil down the fruit juice into syrup. ② 《양조》 brew; distill. ¶ 소주를 ～ distill *soju*.

**고단자**(高段者) a high-rank holder; a high-ranking 《*baduk*》 player.

**고단하다** (be) tired; fatigued; exhausted; weary; worn out. ¶ 고단한 일 exhausting 〔tiring〕 work / 몸이 몹시 ～ have a real weary body; feel all worn out 〔all done in〕 / 그들은 고단해 보인다 They look tired. / 고단하신가봐요 You look done up.

**고달** 《괴통》 a metal cap; a ferrule; 《승「베》 a tang.

**고달이** an attached finger-loop.

**고달프다** (be) very tired; utterly exhausted; quite weary; tiring; exhausting; be tired out; be done up. ¶ 고달픈 일 tiring work; hard work / 고달픈 인생 a weary 〔hard〕 life / 몸이 ～ have a tired body; be all worn out.

**고담**(古談) an old story 〔tale〕; folklore.

**고담준론**(高談峻論) ① 《언론》 a stern and lofty discourse; high and mighty talk. ～하다 discourse loftily and severely. ② 《흰소리》 big talk; a loud boast; bragging. ～하다 talk big.

**고답**(高踏) keeping aloof from madding crowd; transcending the mundane world. ¶ ～적(인) high-toned; "tony"; highbrow; 《시적으로》 Parnassian; Olympian / ～적인 사람들 the highbrows / ～적 문학 highbrow literature. ◉ ～주의 transcendentalism. ～파 the Parnassian school; transcendentalists: ～파 시인 a Parnassian.

**고당**(高堂) 《집》 a lofty 〔fine〕 house; a mansion; 《양친》 parents; 《남의 집》 your 〔his〕 esteemed house.

**고대**(古代) ancient 〔old〕 times; antiquity; the remote past; remote ages. ¶ ～의 ancient; of antiquity / ～로부터 from ancient times; from time immemorial / ～에 있어서의 in the days of old / ～의 유물 antiquities; ancient relics. ◉ ～문학 ancient literature. ～사 ancient history. ～소설 a story of ancient times. ～인 ancient people; the ancients (★ the ancients는

고대 문명 국민, 특히 그리스·로마인을 뜻함).

**고대**《지금 막》 just now; just a minute 〔only a moment〕 ago; right now; soon; in a minute. ¶～ 다녀갔다 He has just been here. / ～ 들었다 I have just heard it.

**고대광실**(高臺廣室) a grand 〔tall and spacious〕 house; a lordly mansion.

**고대하다**(苦待—) wait eagerly 〔impatiently〕 for; be impatient for; eagerly look forward to; long for. ¶ 고대하던 소식 the long-awaited news / 그녀가 오기를 ～ long for her to come / 학수 ～ look forward to 《*a matter, doing*》; be on the tiptoe with expectation / 고향에서 소식이 오기를 고대하고 있다 I am dying for news from home. / 조속한 회신을 고대합니다 I am looking forward to your earliest reply.

**고도**(古都) an ancient city; a former capital (옛 수도).

**고도**(孤島) a remote and lonely island; an isolated 〔a desert〕 island. ¶ 절해 ～ a solitary island in the far-off sea. (★ 혼자 외롭게 있는 섬은 a solitary island, 사람이 잘 찾지 않는 섬은 a lonely island).

**고도**(高度) ① 《높이》 altitude; height. ¶ (비행기가) ～를 낮추다 lower its altitude; fly lower / ～를 재다 measure altitude / 3천 미터의 ～를 유지하다 keep 〔maintain〕 the altitude 〔height〕 of 3,000 meters / 그 비행기의 ～는 어느 정도였는가 What altitude did the plane reach? ② 《정도》 a high degree 〔power〕. ¶ ～의 high; highpower; intense; strong / ～의 문명 a high level of civilization / ～의 경제 성장률 rapid economic growth rate / ～로 기동화된 육군 a highly mechanized army / 그것에는 최～의 정밀 작업이 필요하다 It requires precision work of highest order. ◉ ～계 an altimeter 〔altometer〕; a height indicator. ～기록 an altitude record. ～비행 an altitude flight. ～성장 high 〔rapid, speedy〕 growth. ～측량술 altimetry.

**고도리** 〖어류〗 a young mackerel.

**고독**(孤獨) 《외로움》 solitude; loneliness; isolation. ～하다 (be) solitary; lonely; friendless; lonesome; isolated. ¶ ～벽(癖)의 shut-in / ～한 사람 a solitary 〔lonely〕 person; a solitary / ～을 느끼다 feel lonely 〔alone〕 / ～을 사랑하다 love 〔be fond of〕 solitude / ～을 참다 bear solitude / ～한 생활을 하다 lead a solitary life; live in solitude. ◉ ～공포증 monophobia. ～단신 a solitary 〔lonely〕 person.

**고동** ① 《장치》 a switch; a handle; a key; a stopcock. ¶ ～을 틀다 turn on 《the water》 / ～을 잠그다 turn off 《the gas》. ② 《요점》 a main 〔vital〕 point; the point; a pivot; the crux. ¶ 모든 것이 이 ～ 하나에 달렸다 This is the crux of the whole thing. ③ 《기적》 a (steam) whistle; a siren. ¶ ～이 울다 a siren blows / ～을 울리다 blow 〔sound〕 a whistle; whistle. ④ 《물레의》 the two bell-like rotating rings (on the) spindle of a spinning wheel.

**고동**(鼓動) a beat; pulsation (맥박); (a) palpitation (병적인); throbbing (격렬한). ～하다 beat; pulsate; palpitate; throb. ¶ 심장의 ～ heartbeats / ～치다 =～하다 / 심장의 ～이 들리다 hear 《*a person's*》 heart throbbing / 그의 심장 ～이 멎었다 His heart stopped beating.

**고동색**(古銅色) reddish brown.

**고되다** (be) hard; trying; tough. ¶ 고된 생활 a hard life / 일이 ～ a work is hard / 고되게 일하다 work like a dog; toil and moil.

**고두**(叩頭) a kowtow; a bow. ～하다 kowtow; bow; make a bow.
◉ ～사죄(謝罪) a humble 〔kowtow〕 apology: ～사죄하다 make a humble apology; kowtow 〔kneel down〕 and beg for forgiveness.

**고두리** 《뭉뚝한 끝》 a blunt tip; 《화살》 a blunt-headed arrow used to shoot small birds; 《활》 a bow equipped with blunt-headed arrows.

**고두밥** hard-steamed〔-boiled〕 rice.

**고둥** 〖조개류〗 conch; a snail.

**고드래, 고드랫돌** warp weights; stones attached to keep the warp ends in place while weaving. ¶ 고드래뽕(이다) 《a job is》 all over and done with.

**고드름** an icicle. ¶ 처마에 ～이 달리다 an icicle hangs from the eaves; an icicle forms along the eaves.

**고들빼기** 〖식물〗 a Korean wild lettuce.

**고등**(高等) ¶ ～의 high; higher; advanced; 《고급》 high-class; high-grade. ◉ ～교육 higher 〔liberal〕 education. ～동물 a higher animal; animals of the higher orders. ～법원 a high court of justice. ～비행 high-flying; stunt flying 〔flights〕; aerobatics. ～수학 higher 〔advanced〕 mathematics. ～생물 higher forms of life. ～식물 higher plant life 〔vegetation〕. ～정책 higher policies. ～판무관

a high commissioner.

**고등어** a mackerel (★ 단·복수 동형). ¶ 생~ a fresh mackerel / 자반~ a salted mackerel.

**고등학교**(高等學校) a (senior) high school; an upper secondary school. ¶ 인문〔공업, 상업, 여자〕~ an academic 〔a technical, a commercial, a girls'〕 high school / 내 동생은 ~에 다니고 있다 My brother 「goes to 〔attends〕 a (senior) high school.

**고딕** Gothic. ◉ ~건물 a Gothic building. ~(식) 건축 Gothic architecture. ~체(體) 〖인쇄〗 Gothic type.

**고라니** 〖동물〗 a kind of roe deer.

**고락** 《낙지 먹물》 (cephalopod) ink; 《먹물집》 the ink bag 《of an octopus》; 《낙지배》 the belly of an octopus. ¶ ~을 뿜다 《an octopus》 ejects 〔spurts〕 ink.

**고락**(苦樂) pain and pleasure; joys and sorrows; weal and woe. ¶ 인생의 ~ the pleasures and pains of life; the sweets and bitters of life / ~을 같이하다 share *one's* joys and sorrows 《with》; share *one's* fortunes 《with》 / 세상의 ~을 다 겪다 have tasted sweets and bitters of life.

**고람**(高覽) your inspection; your perusal 〔checking, reading〕. ¶ ~을 바랍니다 I take pleasure in submitting it for your inspection.

**고랑**[1] 《두둑 사이》 a furrow. ¶ ~을 짓다 make furrows. ◉ ~창 a narrow deep furrow; a ditch.

**고랑**[2] ⇨ 쇠고랑.

**고래**[1] 〖동물〗 a whale. ¶ 그는 술~다 He drinks like a fish. / ~ 싸움에 새우 등 터진다 《속담》 get a by-blow 《in their fight》; be struck by a chance blow; be embroiled 〔caught up〕 in 《a quarrel》. ◉ ~고기 whale meat. ~기름 whale oil. ~새끼 a whale calf. ~수염 whale fin; whalebone; a baleen. ~자리 〖천문〗 the Whale; the constellation Cetus. ~작살 a harpoon; a gaff. ~잡이 whale fishing; 《사람》 a whaleman: ~잡이 배 a whaling vessel 〔boat〕; a whaler.

**고래**[2] 《방고래》 hypocaust (heating= system) flues. ◉ 고랫당그래 a rake for cleaning out hypocaust ashes. 고랫등 the ridges where hypocaust flues are laid.

**고래**(古來) ¶ ~의 (age-)old; ancient; time-honored / ~로 from old 〔ancient〕 time; from time immemorial / ~의 관습 a time-honored custom / 인생 칠십 ~희(稀) Man seldom lives to be seventy years old. / ~로 그런 일은 허다하다 Since ancient times, there have been many examples of this kind. *or* Many examples of this kind can be found in history.

**고래고래** at shouting pitch; in 〔with〕 a loud voice. ¶ ~ 소리지르다 raise a shout; be shouting out.

**고래등같다** (be) magnificent; grand; stately; be very large. ¶ 고래등같은 기와집 a huge 〔palatial〕 tile-roofed house / 그는 고래등같은 집에 살고 있다 He lives in a stately mansion.

**고량**(高粱) = 수수. ◉ ~주(酒) Kaoliang wine.

**고량진미**(膏粱珍味) rich fare; luxurious viands; all sorts of delicacies.

**고려**(考慮) consideration; deliberation; reflection; careful thought. ~하다 consider; think over; give consideration to; take 《*a matter*》 into consideration 〔account〕; deliberate on. ¶ ~하여야 할 점 a point to be considered / 충분히 ~하여 after due consideration / ~중이다 [사람이 주어] have 《*a matter*》 under consideration; [사물이 주어] be under consideration / ~하지 않다 take no thought 《of》; have no regard 〔consideration〕 《for》; pay no regard 《to》 / ~에 넣다 take 《*a matter*》 into consideration 〔account〕 / 신중히 ~하다 give 《*a matter*》 a serious consideration / 상대편의 편의를 충분히 ~하다 pay due regard to the other party's convenience / ~할 가치가 없다 be not worth deliberation; deserve little consideration / ~할 여지가 없다 There is no room for consideration. / 아직 ~할 여지가 있다 It leaves some room for consideration.

**고려**(高麗) Koryŏ, an ancient Korean state (918-1392). ◉ ~대장경 the Tripitaka Koreana. ~자기 Koryŏ porcelain 〔pottery〕. ~장(葬) an ancient burial practice whereby an old 〔a dying〕 person is abandoned to meet his 〔her〕 death in an open tomb.

**고려**(顧慮) 《잘 생각함》 consideration; thinking over; 《걱정》 concern; solicitude. ~하다 consider; think over; be concerned about.

**고령**(高齡) an advanced age; a (good) ripe age. ¶ ~의 aged; old; advanced in years / ~에도 불구하고 in spite of 《his》 great age / 90의 ~으로 at the great age of ninety. ◉ ~자 an old 〔aged〕 person; a person of advanced age; [집합적] the old people; the aged. ～자 세대 a family of elderly people. ～출산 late child-bearing. ～화 사회 an aging society.

**고령토**(高嶺土) kaoline.

**고례**(古例) an old custom 〔practice〕; a tradition.

**고로**(故—) 《그러므로》 and so; consequently; accordingly; therefore; 《까닭에》 for the reason that….

**고로**(古老·故老) an old person; old folks; an elder; a senior; the aged. ¶ 마을의 ～ elders of the village; village seniors.

**고로**(高爐) a shaft 〔blast〕 furnace.

**고로롱거리다** suffer from a long 〔protracted〕 illness.

**고로여생**(孤露餘生) a man orphaned early in life; a lonely person who has lost the parents at an early age.

**고론**(高論) ① 《높은 의견》 an exalted view; a lofty opinion. ② 《남의 의견》 your 〔his〕 esteemed opinion.

**고료**(稿料) a fee for a manuscript 〔an article〕; a manuscript fee; copy money; remuneration for writing. ¶ ～가 많다〔적다〕 [사람이 주어] be paid well 〔poorly〕 for *one's* writing; [원고가 주어] be paid for high 〔low〕 / ～를 페이지〔1매〕당 얼마로 지급하다 pay for 《*one's*》 manuscript at so much per page 〔sheet〕.

**고루**(固陋) bigotry; intolerance; conservativeness; narrow-mindedness. ～하다 (be) bigoted; intolerant; conservative; hidebound; narrow-minded.

**고루**(高樓) a tall 〔lofty〕 building. ◉ ～거각(巨閣) tall and spacious buildings.

**고루** evenly; uniformly; equally; impartially; fairly; without omitting anything 〔anyone〕; indiscriminately. ¶ ～ 나누다 divide 《*a thing*》 equally / ～ 대접하다 treat all equally.

**고르다**[1] 《한결같다》 (be) even; uniform; equal; fair (공평하다). ¶ 고르게 evenly; equally; all alike; impartially / 고르지 않은 uneven; unequal; irregular; 《울룩불룩한》 rugged / 복장이 ～ be dressed all alike; be uniformed / 키가 고르지 않다 be of uneven height / 땅이 ～ the ground is even / 몫이 고르지 못하다 the share is not equal / 요즘 날씨가 고르지 못하다 The weather is changeable these days.

**고르다**[2] ① 《평평하게》 make 《*a thing*》 even; level 〔smooth〕 (off). ¶ 땅을 ～ make the ground even; level the ground off / 롤러로 ～ level 《the ground》 with a roller; roll 《court》. ② 《가려내다》 choose; select; pick 〔single〕 out; fix upon (선정하다). ¶ 가장 좋은 것을 ～ select the best one / 며느리를 ～ choose a future daughter-in-law / 쌀에서 돌을 ～ pick sand out of the rice / 자기가 고른 사람과 결혼하다 marry a man 〔woman〕 of *one's* own choice / 좋은 날을 ～ select 〔fix upon〕 an auspicious day.

**고름**[1] 《농즙》 pus; purulent matter. ¶ ～이 잡히다 form pus; gather head; fester / ～을 짜다 press 〔squeeze〕 the pus out of 《a boil》 / ～이 나오다 the pus oozes out. ◉ ～집 a pustule.

**고름**[2] ⇨ 옷고름.

**고리**[1] 《둥근》 a ring; a link; a loop (실 따위의). ¶ 귀～ an earring / 열쇠～ a key ring / ～ 모양의 ring-shaped / ～를 만들다 form a ring; make a loop 《of a string》; loop. ◉ ～던지기 quoits; ringtoss: ～던지기하다 play quoits; quoit.

**고리**[2] ① 《버들가지》 osier twigs; an osier; a wicker. ② 《고리짝》 a wicker basket 〔trunk〕. ◉ ～버들 『식물』 an osier; a red osier. ～장이 a maker of wicker baskets 〔trunks〕; a wicker worker.

**고리**(高利) high interest; a high rate of interest; usury. ¶ ～로 at high interest / ～로 빌려주다〔빌리다〕 lend 〔borrow〕 at a high rate of interest. ◉ ～대금 moneylending; usury: ～ 대금업 usury / ～대금업자 a usurer; moneylender; a loan shark 《미구어》 / ～ 대금업을 하다 practice usury. ～채(債) usurious loan.

**고리눈** an eye with a white-ringed iris. ◉ ～이 a person 〔horse〕 with a white-ringed iris.

**고리다** ⇨ 고리타분하다.

**고리삭다** too old for *one's* age; prematurely decrepit.

**고리짝** 《고리》 a wicker basket 〔trunk〕; 《짐》 baggage 《미》; luggage 《영》.

**고리타분하다** ① 《냄새가》 (be) foul-smelling; stinking; fetid; rank; rancid. ¶ 치즈가 상해 고리타분한 냄새가 난다 The cheese smells rancid. / 고리타분한 하수 냄새가 코를 찔렀다 The stench from the ditches assailed my nostrils. ② 《성질·행동이》 (be) old-fashioned; hackneyed; stale; trite; commonplace; banal; 《케케묵다》 worn-out; 《옹졸하다》 narrow-minded. ¶ 고리타분한 생각 a stereotyped 〔hackneyed〕 idea; a narrow view / 고리타분

한 수작 a trite 〔banal〕 remark / 고리타분한 말 a hackneyed phrase; threadbare expressions; 《상투어》 a cliché / 고리타분한 짓 a low act; pettifoggery; banalities.

**고린내** a foul 〔nasty, fetid〕 odor; a stinking smell; a stench; a stink. ¶ ~ 나는 양말 stinking socks / ~가 나다 have a foul odor; stink; smell bad / ~를 피우다 emit a foul odor.

**고릴라** 〖동물〗 a gorilla.

**고림보** ① 《허약자》 a weakling; a person of weak constitution; an invalid. ② 《옹졸한 사람》 a stingy fellow; a miser; a mean 〔cheap〕 fellow; 《미》 a tightwad.

**고립**(孤立) isolation; helplessness. ~하다 stand alone; be isolated; be helpless; be friendless; 《정치·경제상》 be quarantined. ¶ ~한 isolated; solitary; helpless / ~무원의 군대 isolated forces / 국제적〔경제적〕 ~(을 피하다) (avoid) international 〔economic〕 isolation / ~무의(無依)하다 be utterly helpless / ~시키다 isolate 《*a person*》 from / 외계로부터 ~하다 be cut off from the outside world / 사회로부터 ~하다 isolate *oneself* from society / 침략국을 ~시키다 quarantine an aggressor nation / 그 마을은 대설로 ~되었다 The village was isolated by the heavy snow. ◉ ~어(語) an isolating language. ~정책 a policy of isolation; an isolationist policy. ~주의 isolationism: ~주의자 an isolationist.

**고마움** 《감사》 gratitude; thankfulness; 《가치》 value; blessing 《of health》. ¶ 돈의 ~을 알다 know what it means to have money / 이제서야 부모님의 ~을 알았다 Now I understand how much I owe to my parents. / 병이 나야 비로소 건강의 ~을 안다 It is only after we get ill that we know how blessed it is to be healthy. / 그는 돈의 ~을 모른다 He is a stranger to the value of money.

**고마워하다** be thankful 〔grateful〕 《to *a person* for *his* kindness》; appreciate; be appreciative 《of》; be obliged 〔indebted〕 《for》. ¶ 그것을 알면 그는 매우 고마워할 것이다 He will be very grateful to know that.

**고막** 〖조개류〗 an ark shell.

**고막**(鼓膜) 〖의학〗 the tympanum (*pl.* ~s, -na); the tympanic membrane; the eardrum; the drumhead. ¶ ~의 tympanic; tympanal / ~이 찢어질 것같은 earsplitting; ear-blasting / ~이 터지다 have *one's* eardrum split 〔ruptured〕. ◉ ~염(炎) myringitis.

**고만** ⇨그만[1,2].

**고만고만하다** be much 〔nearly〕 the same; be much of a muchness; 《크기》 be of even size; 《능력》 be of even ability; 《종류》 be of a sort. ¶ 고만고만한 나이의 아이들 children much of an age.

**-고말고** it is needless to say that…; there is no doubt about it that…; it is a matter of course that…; Indeed (*one* does 〔is〕); So (*one* does 〔is〕). ¶ 가고말고(요) Of course I will go. / 기억하고말고요 Of course I remember. / 위인이고말고 여부가 있나 He is, without a doubt, a great man. / 「급하냐」―「암 그렇고말고」 "Are you in a hurry?"―"So I am." / 「나는 그가 시인이라고 생각한다」―「그렇고말고」 "I think he is a poet."―"So he is."

**고맙다** [사람이 주어] (be) thankful; appreciative; grateful; obliged; indebted; 《대상이》 (be) appreciated; welcome; kind; nice; obliging; gracious; benevolent; merciful. ¶ 고마운 말씀 *one's* kind 〔gracious〕 words / 고마운 선물 a much appreciated present / 고마운 설교 an edifying sermon / 고마운 주인 a kind landlord; a benevolent master / 아이 고마워라 Thank Goodness! *or* Heaven be praised! / 고맙지만 사양하겠습니다 Thanks, but no thanks. / 만 원만 꾸어주시면 고맙겠는데요 I should be much obliged to you if you would lend me ten thousand won. / 계속된 가뭄 끝의 고마운 비였다 After a spell of dry weather it was a welcome rain. 고맙게 생각하다〔여기다〕 be thankful 〔grateful〕; appreciate: 당신이 찾아 주신 것을 내 아내도 고맙게 생각합니다 My wife also appreciates your visit. / 원조를 해 주셔서 고맙게 여기고 있습니다 I am grateful for the help you have given me.

**고맙게도** kindly; graciously; benevolently. ¶ ~ 돈을 빌려주었다 He has kindly lent me money. *or* He was kind enough to lend me some money. / ~ 전쟁이 끝났다 Thank God, the war is over.

**고매**(故買) receiving; fencing; buying stolen goods. ~하다 fence; receive 〔buy, deal in〕 stolen goods. ◉ ~자 a receiver (of stolen goods);

《구어》 a fence. ～품 hot goods.
**고매하다**(高邁—) (be) noble; lofty; high-minded. ¶ 고매한 기상 a noble spirit / 고매한 이상 a lofty ideal / 정신이 고매한 사람 a lofty-〔high-〕minded person / 식견이 ～ have exalted ideas.
**고명** 《양념》 decorative 〔colorful〕 seasonings; a relish; fixing 《미》; trimmings 《구어》; a garnish.
**고명**(古名) an old 〔ancient〕 name.
**고명**(高名) ① 《명성》 a famous name; fame; renown; reputation. ～하다 (be) famous; famed; noted; celebrated; renowned. ¶ ～한 지휘자 a noted conductor / 식물학자로서의 그의 ～은 세계적이다 As a botanist he enjoys worldwide fame. ② 《경어》 your famous name; your fame 〔reputation〕. ¶ ～은 익히 듣고 있습니다 I have heard much of you. *or* Your name is quite familiar to me.
**고명**(顧命) the king's last will 〔dying injunction〕; orders issued from the king's deathbed. ◉ ～대신 ministers entrusted with the last words of the king.
**고명딸** *one's* only daughter among *his* many sons.
**고명하다**(高明—) 《현명하다》 (be) noble and wise; 《밝다》 (be) well-grounded; well-versed.
**고모**(姑母) *one's* father's sister; an aunt; a paternal aunt. ◉ ～부 the husband of *one's* father's sister 〔a paternal aunt〕; an uncle.
**고목**(古木) an old 〔aged〕 tree.
**고목**(枯木) a dead tree; a withered tree.
**고무** ① 《탄성 고무》 rubber; India rubber; gum elastic; 《수액》 gum. ¶ ～를 입힌 rubber(-coated); gummed; rubberized / ～ 바닥의 (신) rubber-soled (shoes) / ～ 모양의 gummy; rubbery. ② 《지우개》 an eraser; 《영》 a rubber. ◉ ～공 a rubber ball. ～공업 the rubber industry. ～관〔호스〕 a rubber tube 〔hose〕. ～나무 a gum tree; a rubber tree 〔plant〕: ～나무 농장 a rubber plantation. ～도장 a rubber stamp. ～밴드 a rubber band. ～보트 a rubber boat 〔raft〕; a rubber dinghy. ～신〔장화〕 rubber shoes 〔boots〕. ～액(液) gum. ～제품 rubber goods. ～줄 (a piece of) elastic; an elastic string 〔cord, tape〕; 《둥근》 a rubber band. ～풀 gum (arabic); mucilage; rubber cement. ～풍선 a rubber balloon.
**고무**(鼓舞) encouragement; inspiration; incitement; stimulation. ～하다 encourage 《*a person*》; stir 〔cheer〕 up; incite; inspire; stimulate. ⇨ 북돋우다. ¶ ～되다 get encouraged / 사기를 ～하다 stimulate 〔stir up〕 the morale (of the men) / 기계 공업의 장래는 매우 ～적이다 The future of the machine industry is very bright 〔encouraging〕.
**고무라기** 《떡의》 odd bits of rice cake; rice cake leavings.
**고무래** a solid wooden rake.
**고문**(古文) ancient writings; archaic texts; classics [총칭]. ◉ ～체 an archaic 〔a classical〕 style. ～학 the study of ancient classics.
**고문**(拷問) torture; the rack; 《구어》 the third degree. ～하다 torture; give 《*a person*》 the third degree; put 《*a person*》 to torture 〔the rack〕; rack. ¶ ～당하여 죽다 die on the rack; be tortured to death / 죄수의 대부분이 ～을 당했다 Most of the prisoners were tortured. / 어떤 ～도 그의 말문을 열지 못했다 No torture could make him talk. ◉ ～대 a rack. ～치사 torture resulting in death.
**고문**(顧問) ① 《물음》 asking advice. ② 《사람》 an adviser 〔advisor〕 《to the Foreign Office》; a counselor; a consultant; a brain truster. ¶ ～ 노릇하다 act as consultant 《on》; act in an advisory capacity / 외국인 전문가를 ～으로 초빙하다 employ a foreign expert as adviser / 우리에겐 ～이 필요하다 We must have an adviser at our elbow. *or* We need some brains to trust. ◉ ～관 a councilor; an adviser. ～기사 a consulting engineer. ～단 an advisory group; 《미》 a brain trust; 《구어》 a think tank: 군사 ～단 Military Advisory Group. ～변호사 a consulting lawyer; 《회사의》 a corporation lawyer. 기술～ a technical adviser.
**고문서**(古文書) old 〔ancient〕 documents; ancient 〔old〕 manuscripts. ◉ ～학 paleography.
**고물**[1] 《선미》 the stern. ¶ ～ 쪽으로 aft; astern; abaft / 이물에서 ～까지 fore and aft / ～ 쪽부터 가라앉다 sink by the stern.
**고물**[2] 《가루》 soybean 〔red bean, *etc.*〕 flour 〔crumbles〕 (for powdering rice cake). ¶ 떡에 콩 ～을 묻히다 powder rice cake with soybean flour 〔crumbles〕.
**고물**(古物) ① ⇨ 골동품(骨董品). ② 《헌것》 an old article; used 〔secondhand〕 goods; worn-out articles. ¶ ～ 구두

well-worn 〔tired〕 shoes that has seen long service / ～차 an old beat-up car; 《구어》 a jalopy. ◉ ～상 《사람》 a secondhand dealer; 《가게》 a secondhand store. ～시장 the flea market.

**고미** 〖건축〗 a (kind of) plaster panel ceiling. ¶ ～ 누르다 lay 〔put in〕 a plaster panel ceiling. ◉ ～다락 a kind of attic. ～받이 a support beam for a *komi*. ～집 a house with an attic. ～혀 rafters between support beams and crossbeams.

**고미**(苦味) bitterness; a bitter taste. ◉ ～팅크〔정기〕 〖약〗 bitter tincture.

**고민**(苦悶) 《마음의》 agony; anguish; trouble; worry. ～하다 be in agony 〔anguish〕; worry (*oneself*) 〔be worried〕 《about, over》; be troubled (in *one's* mind) 《about, over》. ¶ 마음의～ mental agony / 사랑의 ～ agony of ardent love / 아내로서의 ～ the trouble with being a wife / 큰 ～이 있다 be immensely troubled in mind / ～ 끝에 병들다 worry *oneself* sick / ～을 잊으려고 술을 마시다 take a drinking to drown *one's* agony / 자네 무슨 큰 ～이 있어 보이네 You seem to be immensely worried. / 그의 얼굴에 ～하는 빛이 나타났다 A look of distress came over his face.

**고발**(告發) complaint; denunciation. ～하다 lodge 〔file, make〕 a complaint 《against》; report 〔denounce〕 《*a person* to the authorities》; inform 《the authorities against *a person*》. ¶ …의 ～에 따라 on complaint of… / 경찰에 정식으로 ～하다 lay a formal complaint before the police / 그는 강도로 경찰에 ～당했다 He was denounced to the police as a robber. ◉ ～인 a complainant; a denouncer; an informant; an informer; 〖법〗 a relator.

**고방**(庫房) a storeroom; 《영》 a lumber room.

**고배**(苦杯) a bitter cup; a defeat (승부에서). ¶ ～를 마시다 drink a bitter cup; drink the cup of sorrow 〔humiliation〕; have 〔undergo〕 a bitter experience; 《경기에서》 suffer a defeat.

**고백**(告白) (a) confession; a profession. ～하다 confess; admit; own (up) 《to》; make a clean breast 《of》; make a confession 〔an admission〕 《of》. ¶ 사랑의 ～ a declaration of love / 신앙의 ～ a confession of faith / 죄상을 ～하다 confess *one's* guilt; confess a crime / 나는 그녀에게 사랑을 ～했다 I confessed my love to her. / 나는 깨끗이 ～하지 않으면 안 되었다 I had to make a clean breast 〔a full confession〕 of it. ◉ ～서 a written confession. ～성사 (the sacrament of) confession.

**고백반**(枯白礬) 〖약〗 burnt alum.

**고법**(高法) 《고등 법원》 a high court.

**고변하다**(告變—) report 〔bring news of〕 treason; inform 《the government》 of an uprising.

**고별**(告別) leave-taking; farewell; valediction; parting; (a) good-bye. ～하다 take (*one's*) leave 〔farewell〕 《of》; say good-by(e) 《to》; bid farewell 《to》. ¶ ～하러 가다 go for a parting call. ◉ ～사 a farewell address; a valediction; 《조사》 a memorial 〔funeral〕 address. ～식 《송별식》 a farewell ceremony; 《영결식》 a funeral service. ～연주회 a farewell concert. ～회 a farewell party 〔reception〕.

**고본**(古本) ① 《옛 책》 an old book. ② 《헌 책》 a used 〔secondhand〕 book. ¶ ～을 사다 buy a book secondhand / 지금 이 책은 ～밖에 살 수 없다 You can only get this book secondhand now. ◉ ～점 a secondhand bookstore; an old book store.

**고본**(稿本) a manuscript; an MS. (*pl.* MSS.); an original draft.

**고봉**(高峰) a high mountain 〔peak〕; a lofty peak. ◉ ～절정(絶頂) the top of a high peak. ～준령 high mountains and steep peaks.

**고봉**(高捧) a heap 《of》. ¶ ～밥 a bowlful of rice / ～으로 담다 heap (up) / 밥을 ～으로 담아 주다 serve rice heaped up in the bowl.

**고부**(告訃) ＝부고(訃告).

**고부**(姑婦) a mother-in-law and a daughter-in-law. ¶ ～간의 갈등은 한국 가정의 특성이라 생각된다 Wife and mother-in-law conflicts are thought to be characteristic of Korean households.

**고부스름하다**, **고부슴하다** (be) somewhat bent; slightly curved.

**고부장하다** ⇨ 꼬부장하다.

**고부조**(高浮彫) high relief; alto-relievo. ¶ ～의 상 a sculpture in high relief / ～로 하다 carve 《*a thing*》 in high relief; bring 《*a thing*》 into high relief.

**고분**(古墳) an old 〔ancient〕 tomb; an old mound; a tumulus (*pl.* ～es, -li). ¶ ～을 발굴하다 unearth 〔dig up〕 an ancient tomb.

**고분고분** obediently; submissively; tamely; docilely; meekly. ～하다 (be) obedient; submissive; tame; meek. ¶ 부모님의 말을 ~ 잘 듣다 be obedient to *one's* parents.

**고분자**(高分子) a macromolecule. ◉ ~물질 a (high) polymer; a macromolecule substance. ~화학 high polymer chemistry. ~화합물 a highly polymerized compound.

**고비**[1] 《절정》 the climax; the crest; the peak; the height; 《위기》 the crisis (*pl.* crises); a critical point 〔stage〕; the worst; the turning point 《of an illness》. ¶ ~를 넘기다 pass the crisis 〔critical point〕; be over the hump; turn the corner (병 등이) / 한 ~ 넘다 the crisis is over; the worst is over / 환자는 ~를 넘겼다 The patient has passed through the crisis. / 그 환자는 지금 가장 위험한 ~에 있다 The patient is now in a most critical stage. / 물가 고는 이제 한 ~ 넘었다 We have now passed the peak of high prices. / 폭동은 이제 중대한 ~를 넘어섰다 The riot has now passed its critical moment. ◉ ~판 a turning point; a critical moment.

**고비**[2] 《편지꽂이》 a letter file 〔rack〕.

**고비**[3] 『식물』 a royal 〔flowering〕 fern; an osmund.

**고비사막**(―沙漠) the Gobi Desert.

**고뿔** 『한의』 a cold. ⇨ 감기.

**고삐** reins. ¶ ~ 풀린 말 a runaway horse; a riderless horse / ~를 잡다 hold 《a horse》 by the bridle; hold the reins 《of a horse》 / ~를 당기다 pull the reins / ~를 잡아 죄다 tighten 〔pull up, draw in〕 the reins / ~를 잡아당겨 말을 멈추다 rein up 〔back〕 *one's* horse / ~를 늦추다 loosen 〔slacken〕 the reins / ~를 늦추지 않다 [비유적] keep a tight rein 《on》 / 그녀는 ~를 당겨 말을 세웠다 She reined up her horse. / 때로는 부하들에게 ~를 늦추어 주는 것이 필요하다 It is sometimes necessary to slacken the reins on your men.

**고사**(古史) ancient history.

**고사**(古事·故事) 《전설》 (a) tradition; 《내력》 a historical fact; a source; an origin. ¶ ~ 내력 the origin and history 《of》 / ~를 인용하다 allude to a historical event 〔fact〕. ◉ ~성어 사전 a dictionary of fables and phrases.

**고사**(考査) (an) examination; a test; 《간단한》 a quiz 《미》. ~하다 test; examine; quiz; put 《*a person*》 through a test. ⇨ 시험. ¶ 학생의 학력을 ~하다 test the proficiency of students / ~를 치르다 take 〔go in for, 《영》 sit for〕 an examination. ◉ ~과목 the subjects for 〔of〕 examination. ~장 an examination room 〔hall〕.

**고사**(告祀) *kosa;* a shamanistic practice of worshiping gods or spirits. ~하다 〔지내다〕 hold 〔perform〕 the "*kosa*" rites. ◉ ~떡 rice cake offered to spirits 〔household gods〕.

**고사**(固辭) a firm refusal. ~하다 refuse 〔decline〕 firmly. ¶ ~하고 받지 않다 firmly decline to accept 《an offer》 / 그는 외무 장관직을 ~했다 He firmly declined the post of Foreign Minister.

**고사**(苦辭) ~하다 humbly refuse; decline with regret; send *one's* regrets.

**고사**(枯死) (withering to) death. ~하다 wither and die; be dead; be blighted. ¶ ~한 나무 a dead tree.

**고사**(高士) a noble character; a high-minded person.

**고사기관총**(高射機關銃) an antiaircraft 〔AA, ack-ack〕 machine gun.

**고사리** 『식물』 bracken; (fern)brake. ¶ ~ 같은 손 the cute little hands 《of a baby》 / ~를 뜯다 gather young bracken.

**고사본**(古寫本) an old manuscript; a codex (*pl.* -dices).

**고사포**(高射砲) an antiaircraft 〔AA, ack-ack〕 gun. ◉ ~대(隊) an anti-air(craft) artillery. ~진지 an AA battery position; an antiaircraft emplacement. ~탄 an antiaircraft shell. ~화 antiaircraft (fire); flak.

**고사하고**(姑捨―) 《제쳐두고》 apart from; let alone; setting aside; 《말할 것도 없이》 to say nothing of; not to speak of; not to mention. ¶ 사치는 ~ 먹고 살기도 곤란하다 He has nothing to live on, to say nothing of luxuries. / 친구들은 ~ 형제들도 오지 않았다 Even his brothers did not come, to say nothing of his friends. / 그는 택시는 ~ 전철도 안 탄다 He does not take a subway, let alone a taxi. / 나는 프랑스 말은 ~ 영어도 모른다 I don't know English, not to speak of French. / 저금은 ~ 그날그날 생활하기도 어렵다 Far from saving money, I can hardly make my living.

**고산**(高山) a high 〔lofty〕 mountain; an alp. ¶ ~의 alpine. ◉ ~대(帶) an alpine belt 〔zone〕. ~동물 an alpine animal; 《동물상》 alpine fauna. ~병 mountain sickness. ~생활 an alpine life. ~식물 an alpine plant; 《식물상》 alpine flora.

**고살**(故殺) (willful) murder; 『법』 manslaughter(고살죄). ~하다 murder; commit manslaughter 〔murder〕. ◉ ~자 a person guilty of murder 〔manslaughter〕; a murderer.

**고상하다**(高尙—) (be) noble; high; lofty; refined; elegant; high-toned; elevated. ¶ 고상한 문체 a refined style / 고상한 소설 a novel for the highbrows / 고상한 잡지 a high-toned journal / 고상한 취미 a well-cultivated 〔refined〕 taste / 고상하게 하다 ennoble; refine; elevate / 고상한 체하다 assume a lofty air / 그는 취미가 ~ He is a man of refined taste. / 학문은 인격을 고상하게 한다 Learning ennobles 〔elevates〕 the character. / 고상한 취미는 사치한 생활을 의미하는 것은 아니다 Elevated taste does not mean high living.

**고색**(古色) an antique 〔a hoary〕 look 〔appearance〕. ¶ ~을 띠다 wear a look of age; have a note of antiquity / ~을 띤 antique-looking; time-worn; hoary / ~이 창연하다 look hoary; look very old.

**고생**(苦生) 《고난》 a hard life; hardship(s); suffering(s); trouble(s); 《애씀》 labor; toil; pains. ~하다 have a hard time (of it); suffer 〔go through〕 hardships; be hard put to it; 《애쓰다》 take great pains 《to *do*》; toil. ¶ 삶의 ~ the troubles of life / 가난으로 인한 ~ the hardships of poverty / ~해서 번 돈 hard-earned money / ~을 견디다 bear 〔suffer〕 hardship / ~을 같이 하다 share 《with *a person*》 in his hardships 〔distress〕 / ~이 많다 be full of hardships; have plenty of hardships / 온갖 ~을 겪다 undergo 〔go through〕 all sorts of hardships 〔troubles〕; experience 〔taste〕 the bitters of life / 가난으로 ~하다 suffer from poverty / 가족을 부양하느라 ~하다 be hard put to it to support *one's* family / 병으로 ~하다 suffer from illness / 어머니는 지금까지 숱한 ~을 겪어왔다 My mother has been through a lot of troubles. / 그는 ~이란 것을 모른다 He is an utter stranger to the grim realities of life. / ~한 보람이 있었다 We have not suffered in vain. ◉ ~길 a hard row to hoe. ~살이 a hard life; a life full of hardships. ~주머니 a person who has plenty of hardships. ~티 signs of 〔traces of, scars from〕 a hard life: 그의 얼굴에는 ~티가 역력했다 Hardship had left traces upon his features.

**고생대**(古生代) 『지질』 the Pal(a)eozoic (era). ¶ ~의 Paleozoic.

**고생물**(古生物) animals and plants of past geological periods; life on earth in earlier times. ◉ ~학 pal(a)eontology: ~학자 a pal(a)eontologist.

**고생스럽다**(苦生—) (be) hard; tough; trying; distressful; afflicting. ¶ 고생스러운 일 a hard 〔tough〕 job / 살아가기가 ~ It is hard to get along.

**고서**(古書) 《옛 책》 an old 〔ancient〕 book; 《헌 책》 a secondhand book; 《옛 글씨》 an old handwriting. ◉ ~전(展) an exhibition of rare old books.

**고성**(古城) an old 〔ancient〕 castle.

**고성**(高聲) a loud 〔stentorian〕 voice; a high-pitch voice. ¶ ~으로 loudly; aloud / ~으로 말하다 talk in a loud voice; talk loudly / ~방가(放歌)하다 sing loudly 〔noisily〕.

**고성능**(高性能) high efficiency 〔effectiveness〕. ¶ ~의 highly efficient 《car》; high-powered 《gasoline》 / 그 보트는 ~ 엔진을 갖추고 있다 The boat is equipped with a high-powered engine. ◉ ~기계 a highly efficient machine. ~수신기 a high-fidelity receiver. ~폭약 a high explosive; TNT. ~항공기 a high-performance aircraft.

**고소**(告訴) 『법』 a complaint; an accusation; legal proceedings; a legal action. ~하다 accuse 《*a person* of a crime》; bring a charge 〔a suit, an action〕 《against》; lodge a complaint 《against》; take legal steps 《against》; sue 《*a person* for damages》. ¶ ~를 수리〔기각〕하다 accept 〔reject〕 a complaint / ~를 취하〔철회〕하다 withdraw 〔drop〕 a complaint / 절도죄로 ~하다 accuse 《*a person*》 of theft / 주거 침입으로 ~하다 bring a complaint against 《*a person*》 for trespass / 사기로 ~당하다 be accused of fraud / 그녀는 그를 자동차 절도죄로 ~했다 She accused him of stealing her car. / 그는 그들이 저작권을 침해했다고 ~했다 He charged that they had infringed his copyright. / 그녀는 명예훼손으로 그 신문을 ~했다 She sued the paper for libel. ◉ ~인 an accuser; a complainant; 《원고》 a plaintiff. ~장 a letter 〔bill〕 of complaint; a written accusation. ~절차 an accusatorial procedure.

**고소**(苦笑) a forced 〔bitter, wry, sardonic〕 smile; a strained laugh. ~하

다 force a smile; give a forced 〔strained〕 laugh; smile bitterly 〔grimly〕. ¶ 그의 엉뚱한 설명에 ~를 금할 수 없었다 I couldn't resist a smile at his irrelevant explanation.

**고소**(高所) a high place; an elevation; high ground; a height; (the) heights; an eminence. ◉ ~공포증 a fear of heights; 〖심리〗 acrophobia: ~공포증이 있다 have acrophobia; fear heights.

**고소하다** ① 《맛·냄새가》 taste 〔smell〕 like roasted sesame; (be) tasty; sweet; savory. ¶ 참깨를 볶는 고소한 냄새 the aroma of sesame being roasted. ② 《남의 일이》 be pleased to see a disliked person make a mistake 〔get punished〕. ¶ 고소한 듯이 gloatingly / 남의 불행을 고소해 하다 gloat over another's misfortunes / 아이 고소해라 《구어》 Serve(s) you right! / 그 녀석 경치는 것을 보니 ~ It serves him right to get punished. *or* I am glad to see him punished. / 그는 자못 고소해하는 표정이었다 He looked on as if 〔though〕 to say "Serves you right!"

**고속**(高速) (a) high speed. ¶ ~으로 at high speed / 최~으로 달리다 run at (the) maximum speed; run at full 〔top〕 speed. ◉ ~기관(機關) a high-speed engine. ~버스 an expressway 〔a superhighway〕 bus. ~수송 rapid transit. ~열차 a rapid-transit train. ~중성자로 a fast neutron reactor. ~증식로 a fast breeder reactor (생략 FBR). ~철도 a high-speed railway; a rapid-transit railroad. ~촬영 high=speed photographing.

**고속도**(高速度) a high speed. ◉ ~강(鋼) high-speed steel. ~사진술 high=speed photography. ~필름 a high=speed film.

**고속도로**(高速道路) an expressway; a freeway; a speedway; a superhighway; 《영》 a motorway; 《유료의》 a turnpike. ¶ 경부 ~ the Seoul-Pusan Expressway / ~망 the superhighway networks. ◉ ~ 입체교차로 an interchange. ~ 진입로 a ramp. ~ 통행료 a toll. ~ 통행료 징수소 a tollgate.

**고수**(固守) adhesion; persistence; tenacity. ~하다 adhere 〔cling, stick〕 to; hold fast to; 《진지 따위를》 defend stubbornly; hold out. ¶ 의견을 ~하다 hold fast to *one's* view; stick to *one's* gun / 주의를 ~하다 hold fast to 〔stick to〕 *one's* principle / 진지를 ~하다 defend *one's* position stubbornly.

**고수**(高手) 《수가 높음》 superiority (in ability); excellent skill; mastery; 《사람》 a good hand; a master-hand; a superior; a high-grade 〔superior〕 player (고단자); a master. ¶ 바둑의 ~ a high-ranking *paduk* player.

**고수**(鼓手) a drummer. ¶ 소년 ~ a drummer boy. ◉ ~장(長) a drum major 〔majorette (여자)〕.

**고수레**[1] 〖민속〗 (a magic word said when) throwing away a bit of *one's* food in the open to propitiate the local spirits. ~하다 throw away a bit of *one's* food saying "*kosure!*"

**고수레**[2] mixing hot water in rice flour to make dough. ~하다 make dough mixing hot water. ◉ ~떡 a kind of steamed rice cake.

**고수련** nursing ⇨ 병구완.

**고수머리** curly 〔frizzled, wavy〕 hair; naturally wavy hair; curls; 《사람》 a curly-haired〔-headed〕 person; a curlyhead; a curly-pate. ¶ 그녀는 ~다 Her hair is naturally wavy. *or* She was born with curly hair.

**고수부지**(高水敷地) the high-water-level land by the river. ⇨ 둔치.

**고수위**(高水位) high-water level; flood stage.

**고스란하다** (be) intact; undamaged; whole; be just as it was; be left 〔remain〕 (untouched); be as sound 〔safe〕 as ever. ¶ 그릇이 깨지지 않고 ~ The dish did not break—it's good as new. / 간밤에 도둑이 들었으나 옷만은 고스란했다 A burglar broke into my house last night but he went on his way leaving my clothes untouched.

**고스란히** 《그대로》 just as it was; with nothing missing; with nothing damaged; 《남김없이》 all; everything; entirely; completely (완전히). ¶~ 남다 remain just as it was; remain intact 〔undamaged〕; 《이익이》 get a clear gain 《of》 / ~ 다 가져가다 take away everything; leave nothing behind / 도둑맞은 물건은 ~ 그대로 돌아왔다 The stolen things were all recovered in their original condition.

**고스러지다** 《an ear of grain》 get scraggly.

**고슬고슬** 《rice》 properly cooked. ~하다 be cooked just right; be neither too hard nor too soft.

**고슴도치** 〖동물〗 a hedgehog; a porcupine. ¶ ~ 외 따 지듯하다 be heavily in debt / ~도 제 새끼가 함함하다면 좋아한다 《속담》 No one is immune to flattery. *or* Everyone expects compli-

ments whether they are deserved or not. 「(high) virtue.
고승(高僧) a high priest; a priest of
고시(古詩) 《옛 시》 ancient poetry 〔poems〕; 《고체시》 free verse in ancient China.
고시(考試) examination; a test. ～하다 examine; give a test to. ¶ 검정～ a certificate 〔qualification〕 examination / ～를 치르다 take an examination. ◉ ～관 an official examiner. 국가～ state examinations.
고시(告示) a notice; a bulletin; a notification; an announcement. ～하다 give notice 《of》; issue a notification 《of》; announce; notify. ¶ 그 ～는 신문에 났다 The announcement appeared in the newspapers. ◉ ～가격 an official price.
고식(姑息) a mere makeshift. ¶ ～적인 stopgap; temporizing; makeshift; patch-up / ～적인 수단 a temporizing 〔half〕 measure; a makeshift / ～적인 해결 halfway solution / ～책을 쓰다 make (a) shift 《to *do*》; take a half measure; employ a stopgap policy.
고실(鼓室) 『해부』 the atrium (*pl.* -ria); the tympanic cavity. ◉ ～신경 nervous tympanicus.
고심(苦心) pains; labor; efforts; hard work. ～하다 take pains; labor; work hard; have hard work; make every possible effort. ¶ ～하여 by hard work; with great pains / ～한 끝에 after great pains / ～참담하다 take great pains; toil and labor; make strenuous efforts 《to *do*》/ 이 저작에는 저자가 많이 ～한 흔적이 보인다 The author seems to have taken great pains over this work. / ～한 만큼의 보람은 있었다 It was worth the effort.
고아(古雅) classical grace; classicality; 《고색》 antiquity. ～하다 (be) classical; antique and elegant.
고아(孤兒) an orphan (★ 한 쪽 어버이가 없는 아이도 orphan이라고 함). ¶ ～가 되다 be orphaned; be left 〔made〕 an orphan / 그는 교통사고로 부모를 잃고 ～가 되었다 He lost his parents in a traffic accident and was orphaned.
◉ ～원 an orphanage; an orphan asylum 〔home〕; a home for orphans.
고아(高雅) elegance; refinement. ～하다 (be) elegant; refined; chaste. ¶ ～한 필치 an elegant stroke (with a writing brush).
고안(考案) a device; a contrivance; an idea; a plan; a design. ～하다 devise; contrive; design; plan; originate. ¶ ～중이다 [사람이 주어] be working on a plan; [사물이 주어] be under consideration 〔contemplation〕 / 신종 엔진을 ～하다 contrive a new kind of engine / 폐기물을 재활용하는 방법을 ～하다 devise a method for recycling waste products / 그는 그것을 화학적으로 만드는 방법을 ～했다 He worked out a way to manufacture it chemically. / 그것은 홍씨의 ～이다 The idea originated with Mr. Hong. ◉ ～자 a designer; a deviser; an inventor.
고압(高壓) ① 『전기』 high tension; high voltage; 《압력》 high pressure: 위험, ～전류 《게시》 Warning. High voltage! ② 《억압》 highhandedness; oppression. ¶ ～적인 highhanded; oppressive / ～적으로 highhandedly; with the strong hand / ～적으로 나오다 take a highhanded policy; act highhandedly 〔in a highhanded manner〕 / 그는 처음부터 ～적인 태도로 나왔다 He took highhanded 〔oppressive〕 manners from the beginning.
◉ ～가스 high-pressure gas. ～보일러 a high-pressure boiler. ～선 a high-tension wire 〔line〕; a high-voltage cable; a power cable. ～수단 high-handed measures. ～전기 high-tension electricity. ～전류 a high-tension〔-voltage〕 current. ～정책 a highhanded policy. ～ 증기기관 a high-pressure steam engine.
고액(高額) a large amount 〔sum〕 (of money). ¶ ～의 소득이 있다 have a large income. ◉ ～권(券) high denomination note 〔bill〕. ～납세자 a high 〔an upperbracket〕 taxpayer. ～소득자 a large-income earner.
-고야 ① 《어찌》 considering that…; when we just take into account…; with…. ¶ 그렇게 헤프게 쓰고야 어떻게 돈 모으기를 바랄 수 있으리 The way you throw your money around, how can you expect to accumulate anything! / 그러고야 성공할 수 있나 The way you act, how can you expect to succeed!
② 《결심》 (**a**) 《끝까지》 *do* 《it》 all the way; really *do* 《it》; simply have (got) to *do* 《it》. ¶ 하고야 마는 사람 a man 「who simply must do 《it》 〔who really does 《it》〕 / 그는 공부한다고 하면 꼭 하고야 만다 If he says he studies, he really studies. / 기어이 하고야 말겠다 I

will do it come what may. / 끝까지 싸우고야 말겠다 I've just got to 〔I am determined to〕 fight it out. (***b***) 《끝장》 end in *do*ing; finally *do;* wind up by *do*ing. ¶ 그도 마침내 총으로 자살하고야 말았다 He wound up by shooting himself too.

**고약**(膏藥) a plaster; a patch; 《연고》 a salve; (an) ointment. ¶ ~을 붙이다 plaster; stick a plaster 《on a cut》; salve; apply a plaster 《to the wound》; dress with an ointment / ~을 떼다 take off 〔remove〕 a plaster.

**고약하다** 《생김새가》 (be) ugly; unseemly; 《마음이》 (be) wicked; evil; crooked; 《성질이》 (be) bad; mean; ill-natured; nasty; vile; vicious; 《냄새·맛이》 foul; stinking; offensive; disgusting; repulsive. ¶ 고약한 감기 a bad 〔nasty〕 cold / 고약한 냄새 a foul 〔nasty〕 smell / 고약한 놈 an unsavory 〔immoral〕 character; a disgusting 〔an odious〕 fellow / 고약한 말 vicious words; foul language / 고약한 성미 an ugly temper; a devious 〔perverse〕 mind / 저런 순진한 어린애를 속이다니 자네도 참 고약한 사람이네 How wicked you are to tell an untruth to such an innocent child! / 그는 술을 마시면 종종 고약해진다 He often gets mean when he drinks.

**고양이** a cat; a pussy 〔pussycat〕 《소아어》. ¶ 샴〔페르시아〕 ~ a Siamese 〔Persian〕 cat / ~ 새끼 a kitten; 《소아어》 a kitty / ~같은 catlike; feline / ~ 낯짝만하다 be of the size of a postage stamp; 《옹졸하다》 be narrow-minded / 나는 ~를 한 마리 기른다 I have 〔keep〕 a cat. / ~가 야옹야옹 운다 A cat is meowing 〔miaowing, mewing〕. / ~를 쓰다듬어 주니 가르랑거렸다 I stroked the cat, and it gave a short purr. / ~가 기지개를 켰다 The cat stretched itself. / ~ 목에 방울을 단다 《속담》 bell the cat; attempt something formidable or dangerous / ~보고 반찬가게 지키라는 격이다 《속담》 It is like setting a wolf to guard sheep.

**고양하다**(高揚―) exalt; raise; enhance; uplift. ¶ 팀의 사기를 ~ raise the morale of the team / 애사심을 ~ exalt company loyalty.

**고어**(古語) 《옛말》 an archaic word; an archaism; ancient language. ◉ ~사전 a dictionary of an ancient language.

**고언**(古諺) an old proverb 〔saying〕. ¶ ~이 그르지 않구나 I am now convinced 〔I now saw the truth〕 of the old saying.

**고언**(苦言) bitter counsel; candid 〔frank, outspoken〕 advice. ¶ ~을 하다〔드리다〕 give candid advice 《to *a person*》; exhort 《*a person* to *do*》; give unpleasant but wholesome advice / ~을 받아들이다 swallow the bitter pill.

**고역**(苦役) hard work 〔task〕; a labor; toil; drudgery; slavery. ¶ ~을 치르다 have a hard time of it; sweat / 리포트 쓰는 일은 ~이다 It is a labor to write out a (research) paper.

**고열**(高熱) (an) intense heat; 《신열》 a high fever 〔temperature〕. ¶ ~이 나다 have a high fever / ~과 싸우다 fight 〔struggle〕 with a feverish disease / ~에 시달리다 suffer from a high fever / ~로 헛소리하다 babble 〔mutter〕 deliriously in a high fever.

**고엽**(枯葉) a dead 〔withered, dry〕 leaf. ◉ ~제 defoliant: 51세의 한 남자가 ~제로 인한 병으로 죽었다고 한다 A 51-year-old man allegedly died of a disease caused by defoliant.

**고옥**(古屋) an old house. ¶ 낡은 ~들을 헐다 pull down dilapidated old houses.

**고온**(高溫) a high temperature. ¶ 이 자기는 ~에서 구운 것이다 This chinaware was fired at a high temperature. ◉ ~계(計) 『물리』 a pyrometer. ~다습 《a climate of》 high temperature and high humidity.

**고요** silence; calm(ness); quiet(ness); stillness; serenity. ¶ (달의) ~의 바다 the Sea of Tranquility / 쥐죽은 듯한 ~ a dead 〔death-like〕 silence; silence like the grave / 폭풍 전의 ~ the calm before the storm / 밤의 ~를 깨고 사이렌 소리가 울렸다 A siren sounded, breaking the silence of the night.

**고요하다** (be) quiet; still; silent; calm; tranquil; peaceful. ¶ 고요한 마음 a tranquil 〔serene〕 mind / 고요한 바다 a calm 〔placid〕 sea / 고요한 밤 a silent night / 고요한 산사 a quiet mountain temple / 고요히 calmly; peacefully / 고요히 눈을 감다 die a peaceful death / 쥐죽은 듯이 ~ be silent as the grave / 청중은 쥐죽은 듯이 고요해졌다 A dead silence fell over the audience.

**고욤** 『식물』 a lotus persimmon. ¶ ~ 일흔이 감 하나만 못하다 《속담》 Quantity is no substitute for quality. *or* Number is no substitute for size. ◉ ~나

무 a lotus-persimmon tree.

**고용**(雇用) 《부림》 employment; hire. ~하다 employ; hire. ¶ 재~하다 call back to work / 나는 그녀를 비서로 ~했다 I employed her as (a) secretary. ◉ ~주 an employer.

**고용**(雇傭) 《피고용》 employment; being employed 〔hired〕; engagement. ~하다 be employed; be hired. ¶ 완전 ~ full employment / 불완전 ~ underemployment / ~의 최저 연령 the minimum age of employment / ~을 안정시키다 secure 〔stabilize〕 employment / 그가 하는 일은 근로자를 ~하고 해고하는 것이다 His job is hiring and firing workers. / 여성의 ~ 기회가 매우 많아졌다 Employment opportunities for women have greatly expanded. ◉ ~계약 a contract of employment 〔hire, engagement〕: ~계약서 the written employment contract. ~관계 employment relationship. ~기간 the period of employment. ~대책 employment measures. ~률 hiring rate. ~보험 unemployment insurance. ~살이 the life of an employee. ~상태 조사 a survey of employment conditions; an employment status survey. ~인 an employee. ~정책 a hiring policy. ~조건 employment terms 〔conditions〕. ~촉진 the promotion of employment. 장기〔단기〕~ long-term 〔short-term〕 employment.

**고용인**(雇傭人) an employee. ¶ 임시 ~ a temporary employee / ~을 채용하다 hire an employee / ~을 해고하다 discharge 〔cast, dismiss〕 an employee / ~이 많다 [사람이 주어] have many workers in 《*one's*》 employ / [회사가 주어] have a lot of workers on its employment list.

**고우**(故友) an old friend; a long-time friend; a friend of long-standing.

**고운때** a bit of inoffensive dirt 《on *one's* clothes》.

**고원**(高原) a plateau (*pl.* ~s, ~x); a tableland; a highland. ¶ 개마 ~ the Kaema Heights. ◉ ~지대 a plateau area; highlands.

**고원**(雇員) a government employee.

**고원하다**(高遠—) (be) lofty; noble; high; exalted; high-minded. ¶ 고원한 이상을 품다 have a lofty ideals.

**고위**(高位) a high rank. ¶ ~ 정책협의 high-level policy consultations / ~에 있다 be highly placed / ~직에 오르다 attain 〔rise to〕 a high rank. ◉ ~관리 a high 〔high-ranking, high=level〕 official; people 〔persons〕 of (high) rank and office; dignitaries. ~급 안보회의 a high-ranking security meeting. ~급 회담 a high-level talk. ~성직자 a religious dignitary. ~인사 ranking personalities 〔officials〕; dignitaries. ~층 highranking officials; persons holding high positions.

**고위도**(高緯度) a high latitude. ¶ ~ 지방 high latitudes; a district in a high latitude; 《한랭 지방》 cold latitudes.

**고유**(固有) 《특유》 characteristics; peculiarity; 《천성》 inherence. ~하다 be peculiar 《to》; be *one's* own; be characteristic 《of》; be proper 《to》; be inherent 《in》; be indigenous 《to》; (be) native. ¶ 한국 ~의 음악 music native to Korea / 그 지방 ~의 식물 plants indigenous 〔native〕 to the district / 그들의 ~한 말 a language of their own / 동양 ~의 풍속 a custom peculiar to the Orient / 인간의 ~한 속성 attributes characteristic of humans / 이 풍습은 우리나라 ~의 것이다 This custom is proper to our country. ◉ ~명사 a proper noun. ~성(性) a characteristic; a peculiarity.

**고육지계**(苦肉之計) ¶ ~를 쓰다 have recourse to the last resort; take a desperate measure 《under the pressure of necessity》.

**고율**(高率) a high rate. ¶ ~의 이자 a high rate of interest; high interest. ◉ ~관세 a high tariff. ~배당 a high=rate dividend. ~세 high rate 〔percentage〕 taxes.

**고을** a district; a county. ¶ ~의 원님 a county magistrate 《in old days》.

**고음**(高音) 〖음악〗 a high tone; a high=pitched sound; a note in the high key. ◉ ~부 the treble: ~부 기호 a treble 〔G〕 clef.

**고의**(故意) deliberation; intention; design; purpose; willfulness. ¶ ~의 intentional; designed; deliberate; willful; studied / ~로 intentionally; with design; purposely; on purpose; deliberately / ~가 아닌 unintentional / 미필적 ~ 〖법〗 willful negligence / ~적인 행위 an intentional 〔a deliberate〕 action / ~인지 우연인지 intentionally or accidentally / ~로 의무를 태만히 하다 willfully neglect *one's* duty / ~로 살인하다 kill a man with malice aforethought; commit willful murder / ~로 한 짓이 아니니 용서하게나 Pardon me, for I meant no harm (to you). / 그는 ~로 그랬다. 사고가 아니다 He did it 「deliberately 〔on purpose〕. It was no accident. ◉ ~범《죄》 a deliberate 〔an intentional〕 offense; 《사람》 a deliberate 〔an intentional〕 offender.

**고의**(袴衣) summer shorts 〔short pants〕. ¶ ~춤에 손을 넣다 stick *one's* hand(s) into *one's* waistband.

**고이**《곱게》 nicely; well; beautifully; 《가만가만》 carefully; gently; quietly; 《편안히》 peacefully. ¶ ~ 잠들다 fall gently to sleep; 《죽음》 pass away peacefully / ~ 말을 듣다 obey nicely; carefully do as *one* is told / ~ 다루다 handle carefully / 영령이여 ~ 잠드소서 May your noble soul rest in peace!

**고인**(古人) the ancients; ancient people; men of old; men of other days.

**고인**(故人) the dead; the deceased; the departed; the lamented; the decedent 《미》. ¶ ~의 유족 the family of the deceased / ~이 된 K씨 the late Mr. K / ~이 되다 die; pass away.

**고인돌** 〖고고학〗 a dolmen.

**고입선발고사**(高入選拔考査) 《국가의》 the state-run high school entrance examinations.

**고자**(告者) an informer; a talebearer. ◉ ~쟁이 a telltale; a talebearer; a tattletale 《소아어》; an informer.

**고자**(鼓子) a man with underdeveloped genital organs; an impotent man; 《거세된 남자》 a eunuch.

**-고자** 《욕망》 wanting to; ready 〔prepared〕 to; intending to; going to; 《목적》 to; in order to; so as to; with the intention of; (so) that... may. ¶ …고자 하다 intend 〔want, wish, plan, mean, be going〕 to 《*do*》 / 그것이 내가 말하고자 했던 바다 That is what I was going to say.

**고자누룩하다** 《떠들다가》 (be) newly quiet; be calm 〔still〕 again; 《병세가》 (be) soothed; assuaged; alleviated.

**고자세**(高姿勢) an overbearing 〔a high-handed〕 attitude; a high posture. ¶ ~를 취하다 assume a high-handed attitude / 그들은 협상에서 ~로 나왔다 They took an aggressive attitude in the negotiations.

**고자질** taletelling; talebearing; tattling; informing. ~하다 tell 〔tattle〕 on 《*a person*》; let on 《to *a person* about, that》; tell tales 《about *a person*》; inform 《*a person* against another》; carry tales 《to *a person*》. ¶ 엄마한테 ~하지 마라 Don't tell mother on me.

**고작**《기껏해야》 at (the) most; at (the) best; at the highest 〔greatest, largest〕; at the outside; as much as *one* can 《*do*》; no more than. ¶ ~ 3년 가다 last 〔wear〕 for three years at most 〔at the outside〕 / ~하여 하루 5천 원밖에 벌지 못하다 earn at most 5,000 won a day; get no more than 5,000 won a day / 그는 ~ 그 정도의 사람이다 He is worth no more than (that) he looks. / ~ 20세밖에 안 된다 He is twenty at the most. / 그것이 ~이다 That is the limit. / 애들 먹여 살리는 것이 ~이다 It is all 〔as mush as〕 I can do to feed my children. / 이 극장의 수용 인원수는 ~ 200명에 불과하다 This theater seats 200 at the outside.

**고장**《지방》 a locality; a district; a place; 《산지》 a producing center 〔district〕; 《서식지》 the home; the habitat; the native place. ¶ 그 ~의 사람 a native (of the place) / 그 ~의 특산품 well-known local products / 말의 ~ a horse-breeding district / 담배의 ~ a tobacco-growing district / 대구는 사과의 (본)~이다 Taegu is the home of the apple. / 나는 이 ~에서 자랐다 I was raised here.

**고장**(故障) 《탈》 a breakdown; a fault; trouble; a malfunction; 《장애》 a hindrance; an obstacle; a hitch; 《게시》 Out of order. ¶ ~ 없이 without trouble 〔a hitch〕; smoothly; well; all right / ~이 없는〔나지 않는〕 trouble-free 《machine》 / 기관 ~으로 due to engine trouble / 기계의 ~ mechanical trouble; a mishap 〔an accident〕 to the machine / ~이 나다 get 〔go〕 out of order; break (down); go wrong 《with》 / ~이 없다 be in (good) order; work well / ~(난 곳)을 찾다 trace a fault 《in》 / 모터에 ~이 있다 Something is wrong 〔There is some trouble〕 with the motor. / 기관 ~으로 열차가 연착했다 The train was delayed owing to some trouble in the engine. / 배가 기관 ~을 일으켰다 The ship developed engine trouble. / 「이 차는 어디가 ~났습니까」—「연료가 떨어졌습니다」 "What has gone wrong with the car?"—"It's simply run out of gas."
◉ ~ 발견장치 〖전기〗 a faultfinder. ~차 a disabled 〔broken-down〕 car.

**고장난명**(孤掌難鳴) It takes two to wrestle. *or* One needs assistance to accomplish anything.

**고장애물**(高障礙物) ◉ ~경주 the high hurdles.

**고쟁이** women's underpants 〔panty 「bloomers〕.

**고저**(高低) 《기복》 rise and fall; unevenness; undulations; 《음성》 pitch; 《시세》 fluctuations. ¶~ 있는 undulating; uneven; fluctuating / ~ 없는 even; level / 음성의 ~ the modulation 〔pitch〕 of a voice / 토지의 ~ undulations.

**고적**(古蹟) a historic spot; a place of historical interest; an ancient landmark; 《유적》 historic remains; ruins. ¶~을 찾다 visit places of historical interest / 후세의 사람들을 위해 ~을 보존하다 preserve historical sites for future generations / 경주 일대에는 ~이 많다 There are many historic remains in Gyeongju and its vicinity. ◉ ~보존회 a historic spot preservation society.

**고적**(孤寂) solitude; loneliness; lonesomeness. ~하다 (be) solitary; lonely; lonesome. ¶~한 생활을 하다 lead a solitary 〔lonely〕 life; live in solitude.

**고적대**(鼓笛隊) a drum and fife band 〔corps〕. ◉ ~장 a drum major 〔majorette (여자)〕. 「(*pl.* -li).

**고적운**(高積雲) 『기상』 an altocumulus

**고전**(古典) 《작품》 a classic; the classics; 《고전 문학》 classical literature. ¶~적인 classic; classical. ◉ ~극 classical drama. ~문학 classical literature; (the) classics. ~물리학 classical physics. ~미 classical beauty. ~어 a classical language. ~음악 classical music. ~주의 classicism: ~주의자 a classicist. ~파 경제학 classical economics. ~학 (study of) classics: ~학자 a classical scholar; a classicist / ~학파 the classical school; the classicists.

**고전**(古錢) an ancient 〔old〕 coin. ◉ ~수집가 a collector of old coins. ~학 numismatics. ~학자 a numismatist.

**고전**(苦戰) a hard 〔severe〕 fight; a desperate battle; 《경기·경쟁의》 a close game 〔contest〕; a tight 〔tough〕 game; 《선거의》 a difficult campaign. ~하다 fight against heavy odds; have a tough 〔close〕 game. ¶~ 끝에 이기다 win a bitter fight 〔hard-fought game〕 / 선거에서 상당한 ~을 하다 have a close contest in the election / 경기는 상당한 ~이었다 The game was close and tough.

**고전장**(古戰場) an old 〔ancient〕 battlefield; the scene of an ancient battle.

**고정**(固定) fixing; fixation. ~하다 fix; be fixed; 《자본 따위가》 be tied 〔locked〕 up. ¶~된 fixed; stationary; regular; immovable / 그 작가는 ~ 독자를 가지고 있다 The writer has a fixed circle of readers. / 그는 그것을 못으로 벽에 ~시켰다 He nailed it to the wall. ◉ ~가격 a fixed 〔firm〕 price. ~간첩 a resident spy 〔agent〕. ~관념 a fixed idea; a stereotyped idea. ~금리 a fixed interest rate. ~급(給) regular pay; a fixed salary. ~독자 《신문·잡지의》 a regular subscriber. ~부채 fixed liabilities. ~비 fixed charges 〔cost(s)〕. ~석 a fixed seat. ~세율 general tariff. ~손님 a regular customer. ~수입 a fixed income. ~자본 fixed capital. ~자산 fixed property 〔assets〕: ~자산세 the fixed property tax. ~표 solid votes; loyal votes. ~환시세 fixed exchange rate. 「statute.

**고제**(古制) an old law; an ancient

**고조**(高祖) ① 《왕실 등의》 the founder of a dynasty 〔sect〕. ② ⇨ 고조부.

**고조**(高調) 《곡의》 a high tone; 《의기의》 elation; high spirits. ¶기운이 ~되다 be elated; get into high spirits / ~된 사기로 경기장에 입장하다 enter the arena in high spirits.

**고조**(高潮) ① 《조수의》 high tide 〔water〕; flood tide. ¶~에 달하다 rise to its floodmark. ② 《정점》 the climax; the culmination; the acme. ¶~된 장면 the climax; a thrilling scene / 최~에 달하다 reach the climax; rise to its floodmark; arrive at its culmination. ◉ ~선 the high-water line. ~시 the (hour of) high tide. ~점 a high-water mark.

**고조고**(高祖考) *one's* deceased great-great-grandfather. 「mother.

**고조모**(高祖母) *one's* great-great-grand-

**고조부**(高祖父) *one's* great-great-grandfather. 「great-grandmother.

**고조비**(高祖妣) *one's* deceased great-

**고종사촌**(姑從四寸) a child of *one's* father's sister; a cousin. 「*one's* sins.

**고죄**(告罪) a confession. ~하다 confess

**고주**(孤舟) a lone(ly) 〔solitary〕 boat.

**고주망태** dead drunkenness. ¶~가 되다 get 〔be〕 dead drunk; be boozy.

**고주파**(高周波) 『물리』 high frequency (생략 H.F.). ◉ ~가열 radio heating. ~발전기 a high-frequency generator. ~전류 high-frequency current. ~전파 high-frequency radio waves.

**고증**(考證) (a) historical research 〔investigation, inquiry〕. ～하다 study 〔ascertain〕 historical evidence 《for》. ¶ 고조선 시대의 풍속을 문헌을 통해 ～하다 study the manner and customs of the old *Choson* period by referring to literature / 이 영화는 시대 ～이 잘 되어 있다 The historical background of the film is very well researched. ◉ ～학 a bibliographical study 《of Chinese classics》; the methodology of historical research.

**고지**[1] 《호박·가지 따위의》 chopped and dried squash 〔eggplant〕.

**고지**[2] 《메주 따위의》 a wooden mold for shaping malt, bean paste, *etc.*

**고지**(告知) a notification; a notice; a bulletin; an announcement. ～하다 notify 《*a person*》 of 《*a matter*》. ¶ 시민에게 5월 15일까지 납세하도록 ～하다 notify the citizens to pay their taxes before May 15. ◉ ～서 a (written) notice; a bulletin: 납세 ～서 a notice for payment of tax. ～판 =게시판.

**고지**(高地) high ground; highlands; an upland; a hill; 《고원》 a plateau; a tableland. ¶ 200 ～, a 200-meter hill / ～사람 a highlander / ～에 살다 inhabit high-land / 적의 ～를 점령하다 capture an enemy-held hill. ◉ ～훈련 high altitude training.

**고지기**(庫―) a warehouse-keeper; a guard of a warehouse.

**고지대**(高地帶) the high elevated areas.

**고지새** 〖조류〗 a grosbeak.

**고지식하다** (be) simple and honest; guileless; naive; honest to a fault; literal-minded; very earnest 〔serious〕. ¶ 고지식한 사람 a 「simple and honest 〔very serious〕 person / 고지식하게 일하다 work earnestly / 고지식해서 남의 말을 곧잘 곧이 듣다 be naive and gullible / 그는 너무 ～ He is stupidly honest.

**고지자리품** 〖농업〗 working a paddy through a season for money 〔grain〕 (paid by the *majigi*).

**고진감래**(苦盡甘來) Sweet after bitter. *or* No gains 〔pleasure〕 without pains.

**고질**(痼疾) an inveterate 〔a chronic〕 disease; a deep-seated disease 〔trouble〕. ¶ 그는 ～로 결국 쓰러졌다 He fell a prey to his chronic disease. / 악성 인플레는 그 나라 경제의 ～이 되어 있다 Vicious inflationary spiral has been chronic economic trouble of the country. ◉ ～환자 a chronic sufferer 〔invalid〕; a confirmed invalid.

**고집**(固執) stubbornness; obstinacy; obduracy; pigheadedness; steadfastness; stick-to-itiveness. ～하다 stick to; adhere to; hold fast to; stand firmly by; persist in; insist upon. ¶ ～이 세다 be stubborn 〔obstinate, self-opinionated, pigheaded〕 / 제 ～대로 하다 act perversely 〔wilfully〕; have *one's* own way / 자기 의견을 ～하다 assert *oneself;* stick to *one's* opinion; stand by *one's* opinion firmly / 네가 정 ～한다면, 이 돈은 은행에 넣겠다 I'll put this money in a bank, if you insist. ◉ ～쟁이〔통이〕 a stubborn 〔an obstinate〕 person; a self-opinionated 〔pigheaded〕 person.

**고집불통**(固執不通) extreme obstinacy 〔stubborness, persistence, bigotry, perversity〕. ¶ ～인 extremely obstinate; stubborn; persistent; bigoted; perverse.

**고차방정식**(高次方程式) 〖수학〗 an equation of higher degree.

**고착**(固着) adherence; sticking. ～하다 adhere 〔stick, cohere〕 to. ◉ ～관념 a fixed idea. ⇨ 고정 관념.

**고찰**(古刹) an ancient 〔old〕 temple.

**고찰**(考察) (an) investigation; an examination; consideration; (an) inquiry; (a) study. ～하다 investigate; examine; consider; inquire into; study. ¶ 사회 문제에 관한 ～ a study of the social problem / 윤리적 ～ ethical contemplation / 사건의 역사적 의의를 ～하다 consider the historical significance of an event / 그것은 여러 각도에서 ～할 필요가 있다 It requires consideration from various angles.

**고참**(古參) seniority; 《사람》 a senior; an old-timer; a veteran. ¶ ～의 senior / 그는 나보다 훨씬 ～이다 He is many years my senior in service. / 그는 이 회사에서는 ～이다 He is an old-timer in this company. ◉ ～병 a veteran conscript; a senior comrade. 최～자 the doyen.

**고창하다**(高唱―) ① 《노래를》 sing loudly; cry out. ② 《주창하다》 advocate; urge; promote; speak up for; 《강조하다》 emphasize.

**고천문**(告天文) an announcement to Heaven 〔God〕.

**고철**(古鐵) scrap iron; steel scraps; (pieces of ) old metal. ¶ 자동차를 ～로 팔다 sell *one's* car for scraps. ◉ ～상(商) a junk dealer.

**고체**(古體) archaism; archaic style 〔form〕.

**고체**(固體) a solid (body); solid matter. ¶ ～의 solid / ～화하다 solidify 《water》. ◉ ～ 물리학 solid-state physics. ～연료 solid fuel.

**고쳐** ¶ ～ 쓰다 rewrite; write over 《again》 / 집을 ～ 짓다 rebuild a house.

**고초**(苦楚) hardship(s); privation; trials (and tribulations); sufferings; troubles; distress; afflictions. ¶ ～를 겪다 suffer (hardships); have *one's* trials / 난 그것 때문에 ～를 겪고 있다 I'm having trouble with it. *or* I'm having difficulties in it.

**고추** (a) red 〔hot, cayenne〕 pepper. ¶ 이 ～는 참 맵다 This red pepper really bites. / ～는 작아도 맵다 《속담》 Though small in body one is strong or fierce. *or* He may be little, but when he gets mad, watch out!
◉ ～바람 a cutting 〔biting〕 wind. ～박이 a low woman's husband. ～상투 a small topknot (worn by old men). ～잠자리 a red dragonfly. ～장 Korean hot pepper paste 〔sauce〕. 고춧가루 powdered red pepper.

**고충**(苦衷) difficulties; 《고뇌》 mental suffering 〔anxiety, conflicts〕; 《곤경》 a predicament; a dilemma; a painful 〔an awkward〕 position; 《걱정》 solicitude; distress. ¶ 남의 ～을 헤아리다 〔알아주다〕 appreciate *a person's* painful situation 〔position〕; sympathize with *a person* in a predicament / 그의 ～은 이해하고도 남음이 있다 His awful predicament deserves 〔calls for〕 our sincere sympathy.

**고충실도**(高忠實度) 《전축 따위의》 high fidelity (생략 hi-fi).

**고취**(鼓吹) 《장려》 inspiration; instillation; inculcation; 《창도》 advocacy; propagandism (선전). ～하다 inspire; instil; inculcate; advocate; propagandize; 《환기시키다》 stir up; arouse. ¶ 국민에게 애국심을 ～하다 inspire 〔infuse〕 patriotism into the hearts of the people / 독립 자존의 정신을 ～하다 inculcate in 《*a person*》 the doctrine of independence and self-respect / 예술 취미를 ～하다 stir up interest in art.
◉ ～자 an advocate.

**고층**(高層) 《건물의》 higher stories; upper floors; 《대기의》 a high layer. ¶ ～의 high-storied; tall; lofty.
◉ ～건물〔건축〕 a high-rise 〔tall, multistory〕 building; a skyscraper. ～기류 the upper air current. ～ 기상학 aerology. ～운 〖기상〗 altostratus (*pl.* -ti).

**고치** a cocoon. ¶ ～에서 실을 잣다 reel silk off cocoons / 누에는 ～를 짓는다 The silkworm spins a cocoon. ◉ 빈 ～ a pierced cocoon.

**고치다** ① 《수선하다》 mend; repair; patch up; fix (up) 《미》; put in order; get in working order. ¶ 기계를 ～ fix a machine; put a machine in order; get a machine in working order / 시계를 ～ fix a watch; have *one's* watch repaired / 새는 지붕을 ～ patch up the leaky roof.
② 《바로잡다》 correct; remedy; reform; redress; cure; mend; rectify; 《개선하다》 improve. ¶ 잘못을 ～ correct errors / 나쁜 버릇을 ～ correct 〔get rid of, get over〕 a bad habit; break 〔cure〕 *oneself* of a bad habit / 결점을 ～ correct 〔overcome〕 *one's* shortcomings / 버릇〔행실〕을 ～ mend *one's* ways; improve *one's* conduct / 폐단을 ～ rectify evils; redress abuses / 문장을 ～ improve a composition.
③ 《치료하다》 cure; heal; remedy; make well; set 〔make〕 right. ¶ 고칠 수 있는〔없는〕 병 a curable 〔an uncurable〕 disease / 병을 ～ cure a disease.
④ 《변경하다》 alter; change. ¶ 시간표를 ～ alter the schedule / 제도를 ～ alter institutions.
⑤ 《조정하다》 adjust; set right; put 《*a thing*》 in order. ¶ 복장을 ～ adjust *one's* coat; tidy *oneself.*

**고침**(高枕) 《높은 베개》 a high pillow; 《편히 잠》 sleeping in peace. ◉ ～단명 High pillow, short life.

**고칭**(古稱) an old name 〔designation〕; an archaic term.

**고탑**(古塔) an old tower; an ancient pagoda.

**고태**(古態) an antique (and unchanged) appearance.

**고토**(苦土) 〖화학〗 magnesia.

**고토**(膏土) rich 〔fertile〕 soil.

**고토**(故土) *one's* homeland 〔native place, soil〕.

**고통**(苦痛) (a) pain; (an) agony; anguish; (a) suffering; throes; 《격통》 pang(s). ～스럽다 (be) agonizing; painful. ¶ 정신적〔육체적〕 ～ mental 〔physical〕 pain / ～을 느끼다 feel pain; feel painful; suffer (pain) / ～을 참다 endure 〔bear〕 a pain; stand the pain / ～을 주다 cause pain; give 《*a person*》 pain; pain / ～을 덜다 relieve 〔ease, allay〕 the pain / ～을 호소하다 complain of pain / ～ 없이 죽다 die without pain / ～을 없애다 remove 〔take away〕 a pain; put 《*a person*》 out of pain 〔suffering〕 / ～스

러운 나머지 신음 소리를 내다 give a moan of pain; moan in *one's* pain / ～이 사라졌다 The pain 「has gone 〔has left me〕. / 그것은 내게 있어서 큰 ～이다 It's great torture to me. / 한 시간 동안 꼼짝 않고 서 있는 것은 ～이다 It's painful to keep standing for one hour. ◉ ～거리 a thorn in the side 〔flesh〕.

**고투**(古套) an old style; a conventional form.

**고판**(古版) 《책》 old books 〔editions〕; 《옛 목판》 an old printing block.

**고패** a pulley. ¶ ～ 떨어뜨리다 a servant bows to his master. ◉ ～우물 a wheel well. 고팻줄 a pulley rope 〔cord〕.

**고팽이** ① 《새끼줄의》 a coil. ② 《왕복》 a round-trip route; a complete circle 〔circuit〕. ¶ 연못을 한～ 돌다 walk around a pond.

**고평**(考評) commenting; reviewing; criticism. ～하다 comment on; review; criticize.

**고평**(高評) your 〔his〕 esteemed opinion 〔criticism〕. ¶ ～을 바랍니다 With the author's compliments (저서 증정의 문구).

**고풍**(古風) ① 《옛풍》 old fashions 〔manners, customs〕; an antique style; ancient 〔old〕 ways. ¶ ～의 old-fashioned; out-of-date; antique; antiquated; archaic / ～스러운 건물 an antique building / ～을 지키다 stick to the old customs; keep the traditions 《of》; follow the old ways. ② 《고시체》 an archaic style (in Chinese poetry).

**고프다** (be) hungry; famished 《미》. ¶ 배(가) ～ be 〔feel〕 hungry / 배가 고파 죽겠다 I'm awfully hungry. *or* I am dying of hunger.

**고하**(高下) 《위아래》 up and down; 《지위》 rank; grade; 《귀천》 the upper and lower classes; 《품질의》 (relative) quality; 《가격의》 rise and fall; fluctuations. ¶ 지위의 ～를 불문하고 irrespective 〔regardless〕 of rank / 시세의 ～가 심하다 The fluctuations in price are violent. / 값은 ～간에 내가 사겠다 I'll buy it irrespective of its price.

**고하다**(告―) inform 《*one's* superior》 of; tell 《*one's* superior》; 《통고하다》 announce. ¶ 사실을 ～ tell 〔reveal〕 the truth / 마지막을 ～ come to an end / 일반에게 ～ announce to the public.

**고학**(苦學) paying 〔working〕 *one's* own way through school. ～하다 support *oneself* while studying; study under adversity. ¶ 그는 ～으로 대학을 나와 변호사가 되었다 He worked his way through university and into the legal profession. ◉ ～생 a self-supporting student; a student who is paying *his* own way.

**고함**(高喊) a shout; a yell; a roar; a howl. ～지르다〔치다〕 shout; yell; roar; howl. ¶ 성나서 ～치다 roar with anger / 오라고 ～지르다 shout 《to *a person*》 to come / 목청껏 ～지르다 shout at the top of *one's* voice.

**고해**(苦海) 〖불교〗 this (bitter) world. ¶ 인생은 ～다 Life is full of hardships.

**고해**(告解) 〖가톨릭〗 penance; confession. ◉ ～성사 (the sacrament of) confession. ～신부 a confessor.

**-고 해서** saying that…; on the ground(s) that…; with the excuse that…. ¶ 그는 뇌물을 먹었다고 해서 해고되었다 He got fired (on the ground) that he had taken a bribe.

**고행**(苦行) penance; asceticism; an ascetic practice; religious austerities; self-mortification; a religious penance. ～하다 do penance; practice asceticism; mortify *one's* flesh 〔body〕. ◉ ～자 an ascetic.

**고향**(故鄕) *one's* (old) home; *one's* hometown; *one's* native place 〔province, country, village〕; 《출생지》 *one's* birthplace. ¶ ～에 계신 부모님 *one's* parents at home / 제2의 ～ *one's* second home; *one's* adopted land / ～을 멀리 떠나서 far from home; in a far-off land / ～을 떠나다 leave *one's* native place; leave *one's* hometown / ～을 등지다 leave *one's* home behind 《*one*》 / ～에 돌아가다 return to *one's* native place; go home / 만년을 ～에서 보내다 pass 「*one's* last days 〔the remainder of *one's* life〕 in *one's* old home / ～을 그리워하다 be homesick; pine 〔long〕 for home / ～은 어디십니까 Where 「are you 〔do you come〕 from? / ～을 떠난 지 몇년이나 되느냐 How many years is it since you left your home? ◉ ～방문 a home visit. ～방문단 a hometown-visiting group.

**고혈**(膏血) sweat and blood. ¶ 백성의 ～을 짜다 exploit 〔squeeze〕 the people; put the people under the screw.

**고혈압**(高血壓) 〖의학〗 high blood pressure; hypertension. ¶ 나는 ～이다 I have high blood pressure. *or* I am suffering hypertension. ◉ ～증 hyperpiesia. ～ 환자 a hypertensive.

**고형**(固形) solidity. ¶ ～의 solid / ～화하다 solidify; be solidified. ◉ ～물 a solid (body). ～산업폐기물 solid industrial wastes. ～수프 a soup cube. ～식량 compressed food. ～식품 solid food. ～알코올〔연료〕 solid alcohol〔fuel〕.

**고혹**(蠱惑) seduction; bewitchment; fascination. ～하다 bewitch; enchant; fascinate; allure; seduce. ¶ ～적인 fascinating; attractive; alluring.

**고혼**(孤魂) a lonely spirit〔soul〕of the deceased (wandering about in the other world). ¶ ～을 달래다 appease〔pray for the repose of〕the lonely soul of the deceased / 수중 ～이 되다 be buried in a watery grave.

**고화**(古畫) an old〔ancient〕painting「〔picture〕.

**고환**(睾丸) 《불알》 the testicles; the testes. ¶ ～의 testicular. ◉ ～염 orchitis. 부～ the epididymis.

**고희**(古稀) seventy years of age; *one's* 70th birthday; three score and ten. ¶ ～잔치 the celebration of *one's* 70th birthday / ～ 잔치를 하다 celebrate *one's* seventieth birthday.

**곡**(曲) music; a tune; a piece of music; an air; a melody. ¶ 한 곡 부르다 sing an air / 한 곡 연주하다 play〔render〕a tune 《on the violin》/ 시에 곡을 붙이다 set a poem to music / …곡에 맞춰서 to the tune of... / 그녀는 우리에게 피아노를 한 곡 쳐 주었다 She played a tune for us on the piano.

**곡**(哭) bewailing; lamentation; keening. ◉ 곡소리 a wail; a wailing cry.

**곡가**(穀價) the price of grain; cereal prices. ◉ ～변동 fluctuation in grain prices. ～정책 a grain price policy. 이중 ～제 a double-tiered grain price system.

**곡경**(曲境) difficult〔hard〕circumstances; adverse conditions. ⇨ 곤경.

**곡괭이** a hoe; a pick; a pickaxe. ¶ ～로 땅을 파다 hoe (up) the soil; dig the earth with a hoe.

**곡구**(曲球) ① 〖야구〗 a curve (ball). ② 〖당구〗 a fancy shot.

**곡기**(穀氣) food. ¶ ～를 끊다 go without meals 《for》/ 환자는 이틀간이나 ～를 끊었다 The patient was unable to take any food for two days.

**곡두** a mirage; a phantom; a vision; an illusion; a dream. ¶ ～ 같은 visionary; phantom; dreamlike / ～를 보다 see a vision〔phantom〕.

**곡론**(曲論) a devious〔biased〕argument; sophistry; casuistry.

**곡류**(曲流) a meander; a winding watercourse; a meandering stream. ～하다 meander.

**곡류**(穀類) cereal(s); corn; grain 《미》.

**곡률**(曲率) 〖수학〗 curvature. ◉ ～중심〔반경〕 the center〔radius〕of curvature. 공간～ space curvature.

**곡마**(曲馬) a circus; equestrian feats. ◉～단 a circus troupe〔company〕. ～사 a circus rider; a stunt rider.

**곡면**(曲面) a curved surface.

**곡목**(曲目) (an item on) a musical program; a (musical) number; the selection 《for a concert》; *one's* repertoire. ¶ 다음 ～은 …입니다 Our next number is....

**곡물**(穀物) cereal(s); corn 《영》; grain 《미》. ◉ ～건조기 a grain drier. ～상 《상인》 a grain dealer 《미》; a corn dealer 《영》; 《상점》 a shop dealing in grain. ～시장 the grain〔corn〕market. ～ 운반선 a grain carrier. ～창고 a granary; 《대형》 a grain elevator 《미》.

**곡보**(曲譜) a musical score. ＝악보.

**곡사**(曲射) high-angle fire. ～하다 fire at a high angle. ◉ ～포 〖군사〗 a howitzer; a high-angle gun.

**곡선**(曲線) a curved line; a curve. ¶ 연속 ～ a continuous curve / ～으로 된 curvilinear; curvilineal / ～을 그리다 curve; draw a curved line / ～을 그리며 날다 fly through the air forming a curve. ◉ ～도표 〖통계〗 a curve. ～운동 movement along a curve. ～좌표 curvilinear coordinates.

**곡선미**(曲線美) the beauty of「contour〔line, curves〕; curvaceousness; linear beauty (건축물 등의). ¶ ～가 있는 여자 a woman with a beautiful figure; a curvaceous woman 《구어》/ 허리의 ～ the beauty of *one's* waist line / 그 여신상은 ～가 뛰어나다 The statue of a goddess shows beautiful curves.

**곡성**(哭聲) the sound of keening〔mourning〕. ⇨ 곡소리.

**곡식**(穀—) corn 《영》; cereals; grain 《미》.

**곡신**(穀神) the God of Cereals; Ceres.

**곡예**(曲藝) acrobatics; an acrobatic feat; a stunt; a trick (동물의); fancy performances. ¶ 줄타기 ～ a tightrope feat; tightrope walking / 말타기 ～ equestrian tricks / ～를 하다 do〔perform〕stunts; perform acrobatic feats; [비유적] run a risk; make a venture; take chances〔risks〕. ◉ ～비행 an acrobatic flight; a fancy〔stunt〕flying. ～사 an acrobat; a tumbler; a circus performer.

**곡절**(曲折) ①《까닭》(a) reason; cause; the whys and hows; 《자세한 내용》 details; particulars. ¶ 무슨 ~인지 for some unknown reason / 여러 가지 ~이 있어서 for many reasons combined / ~을 설명하다 give a detailed 〔particular〕 account 《of the matter》/ 거기에는 반드시 무슨 ~이 있을 것이다 There must be「some reason for it 〔something in it〕. ② 《복잡한 사정》 intricacies; complications; 《우회》 meandering; turns and twists; sinuosity; 《파란》 vicissitudes; ups and downs. ¶ 사건의 ~ the complications of an affair / 인생의 파란~ the vicissitudes 〔the ups and downs〕 of life / 많은 ~이 있은 후에 협상이 성립되었다 After much parley the negotiation was settled. ③ 〖언어〗 inflection.

**곡조**(曲調) a tune; an air; a melody; strains; music. ¶ ~가 안 맞는 노래 a song out of tune / 한 ~ 부르다 sing a tune / 시에 ~를 붙이다 set a poem to music.

**곡직**(曲直) right and wrong; good or bad; the merits (of a case). ¶ 불문~하고 without inquiring into the right or wrong / ~을 가리다 distinguish 〔judge〕 right from wrong; inquire into the rights and wrongs.

**곡창**(穀倉) ① 《창고》 a granary; a grain elevator 《미》; a silo. ② 《지대》 a rich grain district; a breadbasket; a granary. ¶ 우리 나라의 ~인 호남 평야 Honam plain, a granary of our country.

**곡척**(曲尺) a carpenter's square.

**곡필**(曲筆) falsification; misrepresentation; perversion (of facts). ~하다 pervert; falsify; misrepresent. ¶ 사실을 ~하다 pervert the truth; falsify the facts.

**곡하다**(哭—) bewail; lament; weep.

**곡학**(曲學) ① 《바르지 못한 학문》 perverted study; diabolical studies; studies made with questionable intentions. ② 《사이비 학문》 pseudo-learning. ¶ ~아세지도(阿世之徒) charlatans and pseudo-scholars; a sycophant scholar; an academic flatterer.

**곡해**(曲解) (a) distortion; misconstruction; (a) perversion; a biased 〔strained〕 interpretation. ~하다 distort 〔pervert〕 《the meaning of a passage》; twist 《*a person's* words》. ¶ 그는 나의 말을 ~했다 He has misconstrued my words. / 신문은 사건을 ~해서 전했다 The newspaper gave a distorted account of what had happened.

**곡향**(穀鄕) a granary; a rich grain district.

**곤경**(困境) straitened 〔adverse〕 circumstances; a fix; straits; a sad plight; a predicament; a difficult 〔hard〕 situation; a dilemma. ¶ ~에 놓이다 be in a fix 〔dilemma〕; be in trouble 〔hot water〕; be in great difficulties 〔straits〕 / ~에 빠지다 fall into a difficult situation; get into hot 〔deep〕 water / ~에서 구해내다 help 《*a person*》 out of difficulties / ~을 벗어나다 get 〔find a way〕 out of difficulties 〔troubles〕.

**곤고**(困苦) hardships; privations; trials; distress; suffering.

**곤궁**(困窮) poverty; destitution; needy circumstances; distress. ~하다 (be) very poor; destitute; distressed; miserable; be hard up. ¶ ~한 사람들 the poor; the needy / 아주 ~하다 be in extreme distress; be in abject poverty / 그 가정은 아주 ~한 생활을 하고 있었다 The family was in great need.

**곤대** stripped taro stalks.

**곤댓질, 곤댓짓** nodding in a cocky manner. ~하다 nod in a cocky way.

**곤돌라** a gondola.

**곤두박질** falling headlong 〔head-over-heels〕. ~하다〔치다〕 topple; nosedive; fall (upside) down; fall head foremost 〔head-over-heels〕; 《물가 따위가》 drop sharply. ¶ 계단에서 ~치다 fall headlong down a flight of stairs / 지붕에서 ~쳤다 I fell head over heels from the roof. / 술 취한 사람이 배수구에 ~쳤다 A drunkard fell head first into the ditch. / 물가가 ~쳤다 The prices dropped sharply.

**곤두서다** stand on end; stand wrong end to; stand upside down; bristle up; 《신경이》 (*one's* nerves) become edgy; 《사람이 주어》 become touchy. ¶ 그 얘기에 머리털이 곤두서는 것 같았다 That story made my hair stand on end.

**곤두세우다** set 《it》 upside down; set on end; bristle up; 《신경을》 have *one's* nerves on edge; get nervous. ¶ 깃털을 ~ ruffle 〔bristle〕 up 《its》 feathers / 성이 나서 눈썹을 ~ raise *one's* eyebrows with anger.

**곤드기장원**(—壯元) a tie game; a draw (in gambling).

**곤드라지다** fall asleep dog-tired 〔dead-drunk〕; drop off to sleep; sink into a slumber. ¶ 술에 취해 ~ drink *one-*

*self* to sleep; lie with liquor / 술로 상대를 곤드라지게 하다 drink 《*a person*》 down 《under the table》/ 어찌나 고단한지 방에 들어서자 이내 곤드라졌다 I was so exhausted that I sank into a slumber as soon as I got into my room.

**곤드레만드레** dead-drunk; so tired *one* can't see straight; staggering 《from drunkenness》. ~하다 stagger; become unsteady; lose *one's* grip on things; lose *one's* sense of balance. ¶ ~ 취하다 be 〔get〕 dead 〔blind, rolling〕 drunk; be loaded 《속어》; be plastered 《속어》/ 그는 ~가 되어 집에 돌아왔다 He came home dead drunk.

**곤들매기** 〖어류〗 char(r).

**곤란**(困難) (a) difficulty; 《성가신 일》 (a) trouble; 《어려움》 suffering(s); hardship(s); 《곤궁》 distress; 《난처》 embarrassment. ~하다 (be) difficult; hard; tough; onerous; 《난처하다》 (be) troublesome; embarrassing; perplexing; delicate; awkward. ¶ ~한 문제 a difficult problem; a troublesome question / ~한 사람 a troublesome 〔an impossible〕 person; a tough egg 《속어》; a hard nut to crack / ~한 사정 a difficult 〔tight〕 situation / ~한 일 a tough job; a hard 〔difficult〕 task / 생활이 ~하다 be hard up; be in needy circumstances; live in poverty; live from hand to mouth / 호흡에 ~을 느끼다 have difficulty (in) breathing / ~을 극복하다 overcome 〔surmount〕 difficulties /이해하기 ~하다 be hard to understand / 식량 부족으로 ~을 당하다 suffer from lack of food / …하기가 ~하다 it is hard 〔difficult〕 for *one* to *do;* [사람이 주어] find difficulty 《in》; find it hard 〔difficult〕 to *do* / 그게 ~한 점이다 That's where the trouble comes in. / 양자를 구별하기란 ~한 일이었다 We found it difficult to distinguish one from the other. / 그는 많은 ~을 겪었다 He's been through a lot of difficulties 〔hardships〕. / 그 분쟁은 해결하기 ~하다 The dispute is difficult to settle. / 그런 짓을 하면 너의 입장이 ~해 진다 That would put you in an awkward 〔a difficult〕 position. ◉ 재정~ financial difficulties 〔embarrassment〕.

**곤룡포**(衮龍袍) an Imperial 〔a Royal〕 robe.

**곤봉**(棍棒) a club; a cudgel; 《체조용》 an Indian club; 《경찰용》 a billy 《미》; a truncheon 《영》. ¶ ~으로 때리다 club 〔cudgel〕 《*a person*》; beat 《*a person*》 with a club. ◉ ~체조 an Indian-club exercise.

**곤욕**(困辱) bitter insult; contempt; extreme affront. ¶ ~을 당하다 〔치르다〕 suffer a bitter insult / ~을 참다 bear 〔put up〕 with an insult; bear an extreme affront / 참기 어려운 ~을 치르다 be sulted 〔disgraced〕 more than one can bear.

**곤이**(鯤鮞) hard roe.

**곤장**(棍杖) a club (for flogging criminals). ¶~을 안기다 flog.

**곤쟁이** 〖동물〗 a kind of tiny shrimp. ◉ ~젓 tiny shrimps preserved with salt.

**곤죽**(一粥) ① 《진창》 a quagmire; muddiness; sloppiness; messiness; 《죽모양》 mushiness. ¶ ~이 되다 《길 따위가》 become sloppy 〔muddy〕; 《푹끓어서》 be reduced to pulp. ② 《뒤범벅》 a mess; a messy state of affairs. ¶ 일을 ~으로 만들다 make a mess of an affair.

**곤줄박이** 〖조류〗 a varied tit; a titmouse.

**곤지** the red spot on a bride's brow. ¶ ~(를) 찍다 put a rouge spot on *one's* forehead.

**곤충**(昆蟲) an insect; a bug 《미》. ◉ ~류 the insect species. ~망 an insect net. ~채집 insect collecting; 《미속어》 bugging; bug hunting: ~채집하러 가다 go hunting for insects. ~학 entomology; insectology: ~학자 an entomologist.

**곤핍하다**(困乏—) (be) exhausted; fatigued; weary.

**곤하다**(困—) (be) tired; weary; fatigued; exhausted. ¶ 곤히 tired; fatigued; exhausted / 곤히 자다 sleep like a log 〔top〕/ 곤히 잠들다 fall asleep exhausted / 몹시 ~ be worn out; be dog 〔dead〕 tired.

**곧**[1] ① 《바로》 at once; straightway; straight off; immediately; directly; instantly; in an instant; in a moment; in no time (at all); right away; 《머지않아》 soon; before long; shortly; close at hand; (at) any minute now; 《그 자리에서》 on the spot; then and there. ¶ 집으로 곧 가거라 Go home at once. *or* Go right home. / 지금 곧 간다 I am coming in a moment. *or* I am coming right away. / 곧 또 뵙겠지요 We'll be seeing soon. / 그 자리에서 곧

대답했다 I answered on the spot. / 서울 가거든 곧 편지해라 Write to me as soon as you get to Seoul. / 그는 곧 돌아올 것이다 He will be right back. *or* I expect him any minute now. / 곧 봄이다 Spring is just around the corner. / 곧 시험이다 The examination is near 〔close〕 at hand.
② 《쉽게》 easily; readily; with ease. ¶ 곧 배울 수 있다 be easy to learn / 그런 유리 그릇은 곧 깨진다 That sort of glass ware breaks easily.

**곧**[2] 《즉》 that is (to say); namely; or; in other words; i.e.; viz.

> 용법 앞에 쓰인 말을 되받아 「다시 말하면」, 「즉」이란 뜻으로 쓰이는 **that is (to say)**는 흔히 문장 전체를 다시 바꿔 말할 때, **namely**, **or**는 어구를 바꿔 말할 때 쓰인다. **i.e.**는 라틴어 *id est*의 준말로 [ðǽtíz] 또는 [ái íː]로 읽으며, 문서나 전문서적 등에서 쓰인다. **viz**는 라틴어 *videlicet*의 준말로 보통 namely로 읽는다.

¶ 이곳이 구세주 곧 그리스도가 태어난 곳이다 This is the place where the Savior, that is, Christ was born. / 그 일을 할 수 있는 사람은 단 한 사람, 곧 자네다 Only one person can do the job, namely you.

**곧날대패** a straight-blade plane.

**곧다** ① 《사물이》 (be) straight; upright. ¶ 곧은 길 a straight road. ② 《마음이》 (be) straight; straightforward; upright; honest. ¶ 곧은 사람 an upright person / 곧은 말 honest 〔straightforward〕 words / 곧은 성격 a upright character / 곧은 길로 나가다 go straight; tread the right path; lead an honest life / 아무리 가난해도 곧게 살아야 한다 However poor we may be, we must live an honest life.

**곧바로** straight; straightway; at once. ¶ ~ 집에 돌아가다 go home straight.

**곧바르다** (be) straight and right.

**곧은창자** ① 〖해부〗 the rectum (*pl.* -ta). ② 《사람》 a naive 〔tactless〕 person. ③ 《우스개》 a person who goes to the toilet right after eating.

**곧이곧대로** honestly; straightforwardly; frankly. ¶ ~ 말(을) 하다 speak out in a straightforward manner; tell the truth; tell 〔give〕 it straight.

**곧이듣다** 《남의 말을》 take 《*a person*》 at *his* word; believe *one's* ears; take seriously; take 《*a thing*》 for truth; accept 《*a thing*》 as true; swallow (whole); be gullible. ¶ 농담을 ~ take a joke seriously / 이야기를 ~ accept a story (at the face value) / 나는 그의 말을 곧이들었다 I took him at his word. / 그는 남의 말을 곧잘 곧이듣는다 He is (too) ready to take people at their word. *or* He is gullible. / 그러한 이야기는 곧이듣기 힘들다 Such stories are hard to swallow.

**곧잘** 《꽤 잘》 pretty 〔fairly〕 well; well enough; quite well; 《자주》 quite readily; often; frequently; habitually. ¶ 청년들이 ~ 저지르는 잘못 a blunder (that) young men are apt to make / ~…하곤 했다 used to 《*do*》; would 《*do*》 / 어른 말을 ~ 듣다 obey *one's* elders quite nicely / 책을 ~ 읽다 read pretty well / 그는 영어를 ~ 한다 He speaks English fairly good. / 그 여자는 노래를 ~ 부른다 She sings pretty well. / 미스 김은 ~ 웃는다 Miss Kim is ready to laugh. / 약이 ~ 듣는다 A medicine works perfectly all right. *or* A drug is fairly effective. / 그 녀석이 ~ 쓰는 수법이다 That's his usual trick.

**곧장** 《똑바로 곧게》 straight 《미》; direct (-ly); straightway; 《지체 없이》 without delay; straight off; right away. ¶ ~ 집으로 돌아가다 go straight home / ~ 떠나다 leave without delay / ~ 앞을 봐라 Look straight ahead. / 모퉁이를 오른편으로 돌아 ~ 가십시오 Turn sharp to the right and follow your nose. / 역이 보일 때까지 ~ 가십시오 Keep straight (on) till you see the station.

**곧추** straight; in a straight line; perpendicularly; vertically; upright. ¶ ~ 안다 hold 《a baby》 out straight / ~ 앉다 sit up straight 〔erect〕 / ~ 세우다 erect; set upright; set on end / 몸을 ~ 세우다 hold *oneself* erect; straighten *one's* body / 책을 ~ 세우다 place a book on end 〔upright〕 / ~ 서다 stand upright 〔on end〕.

**골**[1] 〖해부〗 《골수》 the marrow; the pith; 《두뇌》 the brain. ¶ ~이 아프다 have a headache / ~이 비다 have no sense. ◉ 작은골 the cerebellum.

**골**[2] 《성》 anger; temper; dander. ¶ 골이 나서 in anger; in heat; angrily / 골나다, 골내다 get 〔become, grow〕 angry 《with *a person*, at *a matter*》; lose *one's* temper; get *one's* dander up; blow *one's* top 〔stack〕; get mad 《at》 《미구어》 / 골나게 하다 make 《*a person*》 angry 〔mad 《미구어》〕; anger 《*one's* father》; provoke 《*a person*》 to anger; displease; offend; give offense / 골이 나 있다 be angry; be mad 《미구어》; be in a bad temper; be miffed 《at, with》.

**골**[3] 《틀》 a mold; a cast; a block. ¶ 신〔구둣〕골 a shoe last / 모잣골 a hat block / 그 상(像)은 골에 부어 만들어졌다 The statue is cast in a mold.

**골**[4] 《접는 금》 the line to fold 《paper, cloth》 into two equal parts.

**골**[5] ① =골목. ② 《구멍》 a cave; a hollow. ③ 《골짜기》 a gully; a valley.

**골**[6] the goal; 《경마의》 the winning post; 《농구의》 a basket. ¶ 골밑슛 under-the-basket shots / 골을 넣다〔얻다〕 make 〔score, get, win〕 a goal; 《농구에서》 make a basket; sink a shot / 골밑 수비를 강화하다 strengthen the under-the-basket defense. ◉ 골라인 a goal line. 골키퍼 a goalkeeper. 골킥 a goal kick. 골포스트 a goalpost.

**골간**(骨幹) ① 《뼈대》 physique; framework. ② 《골자》 the gist; the substance; essentials; the basis. ¶ 조정안의 ~ the basis of a mediation plan.

**골갱이** the core; the heart; 《골자》 the pith; the gist; the substance.

**골걷이** 〖농업〗 weeding the planted furrows. ~하다 weed the furrows.

**골격**(骨格) 《체격》 (a) frame; physique; build; 《동물학상의》 skeleton; 《건물의》 a framework. ¶ ~이 건장한 사람 a man of stout 〔sturdy〕 build; a stalwart person.

**골고래** 《방고래》 a hypocaust system with several flue entries.

**골고루** ⇨ 고루.

**골골** suffering from a lingering illness. ~하다, ~거리다 suffer from a chronic disease; stay ill all the time; have one sickness 〔sick spell, siege of sickness〕 after another. ¶ ~하는 사람 a chronic invalid; a weak 〔sickly〕 person / ~ 앓다 have an illness that just won't go away; be sick all the time.

**골다** 《코를》 snore. ¶ 코를 ~ snore; be snoring / 코를 드렁드렁 ~ snore loudly / 코를 골며 자다 snore in *one's* sleep / 코를 골기 시작하다 fall to snoring.

**골다공증**(骨多孔症) 〖병리〗 osteoporosis.

**골답**(一畓) 《수답》 a rich 〔productive〕 paddy.

**골동품**(骨董品) a curio; an antique; bric-a-brac; antique objects. ¶ 가짜 ~ a faked antique / ~ 수집 취미를 갖다 take pleasure in collecting rare old objects. ◉ ~상 《상점》 a curio 〔an antique〕 shop; 《사람》 a curio 〔an antique〕 dealer. ~수집 antique 〔curio〕 hunting 〔collecting〕. ~ 수집가 a collector of antiques. ~애호가 a curioso; a virtuoso. ~취미 antiquarianism.

**골덴** corduroy; corded velveteen. ¶ ~ 바지 corduroy pants.

**골든골** 《연장전에 첫골》 a golden goal.

**골드러시** a gold rush.

**골든아워** a golden hour; 〖라디오·TV〗 the peak listening 〔viewing〕 hour; (the) prime time.

**골똘하다** be absorbed 〔engrossed, lost〕 《in》; be intent 〔keen〕 《on》; be given 《to》; be completely taken up 《with》; be concentrated 《on》. ¶ 골똘히 intently; absorbedly; with concentration / 공부에 ~ be absorbed in study / 골똘히 생각에 잠기다 be lost in thought / 사업에 ~ be engrossed in business.

**골라잡다** select; choose; take (as *one's* choice). ¶ 골라잡아 천 원 One thousand won a piece at your choice.

**골마루** 〖건축〗 a narrow hallway 〔corridor〕.

**골마지** scum. ¶ ~가 끼다 scum.

**골막**(骨膜) 〖해부〗 the periosteum (*pl.* -tea). ◉ ~염 〖의학〗 periostitis. ~종(腫) periosteal tumor.

**골막이** 〖건축〗 plastering between rafters.

**골목** a side street; an alley; a lane; a byway. ¶ 막다른 ~ a blind alley; a dead end / ~어귀 an alley entrance / 뒷~ a backlane / 그 집은 막다른 ~에 있다 The house is at the end of the lane. ◉ ~대장 the boss of the kids; the cock of the walk; a bully.

**골몰**(汨沒) absorption; engrossment; immersion. ~하다 be immersed 〔engrossed〕 《in》; be absorbed 《in work》. ¶ 그는 매일밤 연구에 ~해 있다 He is absorbed in his study every night.

**골무** a thimble.

**골무꽃** 〖식물〗 a skullcap.

**골무떡** a thin-sliced white rice-cake.

**골밀이** 〖건축〗 a groove in the sash of a door or window.

**골반**(骨盤) 〖해부〗 the pelvis (*pl.* -ves). ¶ ~부 the pelvic region.

**골방**(一房) a back room; a closet; a small room attached to the main room.

**골배질** making a ferry channel through the ice to let boats reach a ferry point. ~하다 let the ferryboats go through a frozen river by making a channel through the ice.

**골병들다** get injured internally; get a symptomless deep-seated disease; have *one's* vital parts affected; suffer from a chronic illness.

**골분**(骨粉) bone meal; bone dust; powdered bones. ◉ ~비료 bone manure.

**골상**(骨相) physiognomy; the bony frame; *one's* features. ¶ ~을 보다 look into 《*a person's*》 future phrenologically. ◉ ~학 phrenology; physiognomy; craniology: ~학의 phrenological; physiognomical / ~학상 phrenologically; physiognomically; from a phrenological point of view / ~학자 a phrenologist; a physiognomist.

**골생원**(—生員) ① 《옹졸한》 a narrow-minded man. ② 《골골하는》 a weak 〔delicate〕 person.

**골속** ① 《머릿골 속》 the brains. ② 《골풀 속》 the heart of a rush. ③ 《왕골속》 the heart of a sedge.

**골수**(骨髓) 〖해부〗 the marrow (of a bone); the bone marrow; the medulla. ¶ ~ 공산주의자 a communist to the core / ~에 사무치다 cut 〔go〕 deep into *one's* heart / 병이 ~에 박히다 the disease has taken hold of 《*a person*》 to the marrow / 그에게 ~에 사무치는 원한이 있다 I have a deep grudge against him. *or* I bear him a bitter grudge. ◉ ~기증 bone-marrow donation: ~기증자 a (compatible) bone-marrow donor. ~분자 a hard core; an ingrained 〔out-and-out〕 ...ist. ~염 osteomyelitis. ~이식 a marrow transplant. ~정보은행 the Bone-Marrow Information Bank.

**골안개** the mist in the valley.

**골암**(骨癌) 〖의학〗 cancer of a bone.

**골연화증**(骨軟化症) 〖의학〗 osteomalacia.

**골염**(骨炎) 〖의학〗 osteitis.

**골오르다** get angry. =약오르다 ②.

**골올리다** make angry; provoke.

**골육**(骨肉) 《뼈와 살》 flesh and blood; 《혈족》 *one's* own flesh and blood; kith and kin; blood relations; kindred. ¶ ~지친 *one's* blood relations / ~지간의 사랑 love of *one's* own flesh and blood / ~상쟁하다 carry on a family feud; be engaged in a domestic 〔an internecine〕 feud. ◉ ~종(腫) 〖의학〗 osteosarcoma.

**골인** scoring a goal; 《경주에서》 a finish; breasting of the tape. ~하다 《구기에서》 make 〔score〕 a goal; 《농구에서》 score a basket; 《육상 등에서》 reach the goal (line); reach the finish line; breast the tape; 《성공하다》 succeed. ¶ 결혼에 ~하다 be happily married.

**골자**(骨子) the pith; the essentials; the main point(s); the gist; the substance. ¶ 논쟁의 ~ the gist 〔the main points〕 of an argument / 문제의 ~ the gist of the question / 계획의 ~를 설명하겠습니다 I will outline the essential features of the plan.

**골재**(骨材) (an) aggregate. ¶ ~를 채집하다 collect aggregate.

**골절**(骨折) 〖의학〗 (a) fracture (of a bone). ~하다 suffer a fracture; break a bone; have a bone broken 〔fractured〕. ¶ 팔을 ~하다 break 〔fracture〕 *one's* arm. ◉ 단순〔복잡〕~ simple 〔compound〕 fractures. 분쇄~ a comminuted fracture.

**골절**(骨節) 〖해부〗 a (bone) joint.

**골질**(骨質) bony 〔osseous〕 tissue. ◉ ~연화(軟化) osteomalacia.

**골짜기** a gully; a dale; a valley; a ravine; a gorge.

> 용법 **gully** 흐르는 물에 의해 생긴 작은 계곡. **dale** 문어적인 말. **valley** 산 사이를 흐르는 강을 끼고 넓게 펼쳐진 분지. **ravine**, **gorge** 양쪽이 절벽으로 되어 있는 협곡. 그 규모가 큰 것을 미국에서는 **canyon**이라고 한다.

¶ 산~ a mountain valley / 깊은 ~ an abysmal ravine / ~를 흐르는 물 a mountain stream / 산을 넘고 ~를 건너서 up hill and down dale.

**골초**(—草) ① 《담배》 poor-quality tobacco. ② 《사람》 a heavy smoker.

**골치** the brain. ¶ ~ 아픈 문제 a troublesome question; a knotty problem / ~ 아픈 일 a headache; a troublesome task; an annoying business / ~ 아프다 have a headache / ~(를) 앓다 suffer from head 〔brain〕 trouble; [비유적] be troubled; be annoyed / 그 사람일로 ~(가) 아프다 I have a headache on his account. *or* He is troublesome 〔annoying〕.
◉ 골칫거리 a pain in the neck; a headache; a nuisance; a bother: 그것은 정말 골칫거리예요 It's a real pain in the neck. / 그는 골칫거리야 He is a headache 〔nuisance〕.

**골치다** put《it》on the mold〔block, last〕for shaping.
**골켜다** cut the pith out of (wood).
**골타다** furrow (a field).
**골탄**(骨炭) boneblack; animal〔bone〕charcoal.
**골탕**(一湯) ①《골국》a soup made of fried ox-brain〔ox-marrow〕coated with flour. ②《손해》great injury〔loss〕; heavy〔serious〕damage. ¶ ~(을) 먹다 have a hard〔bad〕time (of it); suffer a big loss; be cheated; be taken in / 지난 번 경마에서는 ~을 먹었다 I lost a lot of money in the last horse race. / 그놈을 믿었다가 ~먹었다 I was taken in, trusting that guy. / 그 일을 해내느라 ~먹었다 I had an awful time getting the job done.
**골통** the head; the skull;《속어》the noggin; the (old) bean. ¶ ~(이) 터지다 hurt *one's* head; smash *one's* skull / ~이 터지게 싸우다 fight hard.
**골통**(骨痛)〖의학〗bone aches; ostalgia.
**골통대** a pipe (with an earthenware bowl).
**골틀리다** get angry; get upset《with *a person,* at *a thing*》; become displeased〔cross〕;《구어》get out of sorts.
**골파**〖식물〗a spring onion; leek.
**골판지**(一板紙) corrugated cardboard.
**골패**(骨牌) dominos.
**골퍼** a golfer.
**골풀**〖식물〗a rush.
**골풀무** foot bellows.
**골풀이** giving vent to *one's* anger〔pique, wrath, rage, *etc.*〕;《구어》letting off (a bit of *one's*) steam; taking *one's* anger out. ~하다 (give) vent to *one's* anger; take *one's* anger out《on *a person*》;《구어》let off (some of *one's*) steam; work off *one's* bad temper《on》. ¶ 그는 화가 나면 동생들에게 ~를 한다 He works off his bad temper on younger brothers.
**골프** golf. ¶ ~를 치는 사람 a golfer; a golf player / ~를 치다 play golf; golf / ~에서 한 라운드 돌다 play a round of golf / ~치러 가다 go golfing.
◉ ~공 a golf ball. ~바지 plus fours《미》. ~백 a golf bag. ~연습장 a golf practice range; a driving range. ~장 a golf course; golf-links (★ 언제나 복수형). ~채 a golf club; an iron (철제); a driver; a wood (목제). ~클럽 a golf club: ~클럽 회원권 a golf club membership.

> 참고 골프의 기본 용어
> 파(par): 표준 타수. 한 홀(hole)을 플레이하는 데 필요한 타수로 지형·거리 등을 고려하여 설정됨. 3~5 타수가 보통임. 버디(birdie): 파(par) 보다 1타수 적게 홀아웃(hole out)시키는 경우. 이글(eagle): 파(par)보다 2타수 적게 홀아웃시키는 경우. 앨버트로스(albatross): 파(par) 보다 3타수 적은 경우. 보기(bogey): 파(par) 보다 1타수 많은 경우. 더블보기(double bogey): 파(par) 보다 2타수 많은 경우. 트리플보기(triple bogey): 파(par) 보다 3타수 많은 경우. 홀아웃(hole out): 공을 홀에 넣는 일. 홀인원(hole in one): 첫번째로 친 공이 그대로 홀(hole)에 들어가는 경우. 캐디(caddie): 골프채를 운반해 주면서 골퍼(golfer)를 돕는 사람. 티(tee): 각 홀의 출발점 및 제1타를 칠 때 공을 올려 놓는 작은 받침대. 그린(green): 푸른 초지 또는 잔디밭. 페어웨이(fairway): 티(tee)와 퍼팅그린(putting green) 사이의 잔디 구역. 벙커(bunker, sand trap): 모래를 깔아놓은 우묵히 패인 곳. 러프(rough): 잡초가 우거진 곳.

**골필**(骨筆) a stencil pen; a stylus.
**골학**(骨學)〖해부〗osteology.
**골함석** a corrugated iron sheet.
**골혹**(骨一)〖의학〗a bone tumor.
**골회**(骨灰) bone ashes.
**곪다** ①《상처가》form pus; gather; come to a head; fester. ¶ 종기가 ~ a boil festers〔comes to a head〕/ 상처는 곪지 않고 나았다 The wound healed without festering. ②《사물이》come to a head; ripen.
**곬**《물 흐르는》a (water)course; a channel; a waterway;《한 방향으로의》a (set) route; a (fixed) direction;《유래》(a direction of) origin; a source. ¶ 외곬으로 생각하다 see things from only one point of view.
**곯다**[1] ①《덜 차다》remain unfilled; lack being full; be still not full; be short (of being full); get but partly filled; be half-empty. ¶ 자루가 좀 곯았다 The (cloth) bag is only partly filled. ②《굶주리다》(*one's* stomach) gets but partly filled; be underfed; be half=empty; go hungry; be empty. ¶ 배를 ~ be still hungry; have not had enough to eat; have an empty stomach / 곯은 배를 채우다 satisfy *one's* hunger / 배가 곯아 가지고는 일을 할 수가 없다 I can't work on an empty

stomach. / 돈이 없어서 이틀이나 배를 곯아야했다 I had to go hungry for two days as I had no money.

**곯다**[2] ① 《상하다》 go bad (from the inside); rot; putrefy; spoil; get stale. ¶ 달걀이 ~ an egg spoils 〔goes bad, addles〕 / 멜론이 ~ a melon spoils / 죽이 ~ porridge gets stale. ② 《언걸들다》 suffer secret injury 〔damage〕; suffer a secret loss. ¶ 그 놈들 농간에 나는 되게 곯았다 I suffered heavily from their tricks. ③ 《골병들다》 suffer internal injury.

**곯리다**[1] ① 《그릇을》 fill short of the full measure; fill under-measure; under-fill; leave half-empty. ② 《배를》 underfeed; leave 《*a person*》 still hungry. ¶ 간신히 식구들의 배나 안 곯릴 정도이다 I barely support my family.

**곯리다**[2] ① 《썩이다》 rot 〔putrefy, spoil, turn, addle〕 《it》; make 《it》 stale. ② 《골병들게 하다》 inflict secret injury 〔damage〕 upon; do secret harm to; 《애먹이다》 vex; embarrass; addle; put in a fix; put in a quandary; put in an awkward position. ¶ 그런 놈은 힘든 문제를 내서 좀 곯려 주어야 한다 It serves him right to addle him with difficult questions. / 어찌나 거만하게 구는지 한 번 곯려 주었다 We played a trick on him to put down his pride.

**곯아떨어지다** 《잠에》 fall fast asleep; be dead asleep; sleep like a log; 《술에》 be overcome with liquor; be dead drunk; be helplessly drunk; pass out 《구어》. ¶ 술에 취해서 ~ drink till all is blue; drink *oneself* insensible / 잠자리에 들자마자 그는 곯아떨어졌다 No sooner had he gone to bed than he fell asleep.

**곯아빠지다** ① 《사물이》 become utterly rotten 〔spoiled, stale〕; be badly addled. ② 《몹시 빠지다》 wallow in vice; be thoroughly dissipated; be given up to dissolute living. ¶ 주색잡기에 ~ be given up to wine, women, and dice.

**곰**[1] ① 〖동물〗 a bear. ¶ 곰새끼 a (bear's) cub / 곰가죽 a bearskin / 곰쓸개 bear's gall / 흰〔북극〕곰 the white 〔polar〕 bear. ② 《우둔한 사람》 a slow-witted 〔thick-headed〕 person.

**곰**[2] 《국》 a thick broth made of thoroughly cooked meat.

**곰곰(이)** mulling 〔thinking〕 over; deliberating; musing. ¶ ~ 생각하다 think it over; mull 《*the matter*》 over; deliberate; consider carefully; muse; chew *one's* cud; ruminate.

**곰국** a thick beef soup.

**곰바지런하다** (be) punctilious and diligent.

**곰방대** a smoking pipe; a pipe.

**곰배** ⇨ 곰배팔이. ◉ ~말 a sway-back horse. ~팔 a deformed arm.

**곰배팔이** a person with a mutilated 〔deformed〕 arm.

**곰보** a pockmarked person; a person with a pitted face. ◉ ~유리 crackled glass.

**곰비임비** 《잇달아》 in rapid succession; one after another; one upon the heels of another. ¶ 불행이 ~ 닥쳐 왔다 One misfortune followed on the heels of another.

**곰삭다** ① 《옷이》 (old and untouched cloth) reach the point where it will fall apart at a touch. ② 《젓갈이》 (pickled stuff) get well 〔thoroughly〕 pickled.

**곰살갑다** 《마음이 넓다》 (be) generous; magnanimous; broad-minded; 《다정스럽다》 (be) tender; good; kind; cordial; gentle.

**곰살궂다** (be) gentle; kind; meek; good; warm(-hearted); cordial. ¶ 곰살궂게 kindly; kind-〔warm-〕heartedly; cordially / 그는 곰살궂은 사람이다 He is a warm-hearted man.

**곰상스럽다** (be) punctilious; scrupulous.

**곰솔** 〖식물〗 = 해송(海松) ①.

**곰실거리다** wiggle; wriggle; writhe; twist; squirm. ¶ 곰실곰실 squirming; wriggling about.

**곰지락** 《move》 sluggishly. ⇨ 꼼짝.

**곰취** 〖식물〗 a kind of groundsel.

**곰탕** thick beef soup served with rice.

**곰팡나다, 곰팡슬다** grow 〔become, get〕 moldy 〔musty, fusty〕; mildew. ¶ 곰팡난 책 a mildewed book / 곰팡난 음식 moldy food / 곰팡스는 것을 막다 keep 《*a thing*》 from getting musty / 장마철에는 곰팡슬기가 쉽다 In the wet season things easily gather mold.

**곰팡냄새** ① 《냄새》 mustiness; fustiness; frowziness; a stale 〔stuffy〕 smell. ¶ ~ 나다 be musty; be fusty; be frowzy; be stale-smelling; be stuffy; be mildewed / ~ 나는 방 a stuffy room. ② 《진부》 commonplaceness; triteness. ¶ ~ 나다 be stale 〔trite, hackneyed, commonplace, banal, ordinary〕 / ~ 나는 사상 a mossgrown idea / ~ 나는 수작 a trite remark; a stale talk 〔comment〕; a chestnut 《구

어》/ ~ 나는 학설 an outmoded theory; a dated 〔an out-of-date〕 hypothesis.

**곰팡이** mold; mildew; must. ¶ 푸른~ green mold / ~슨 musty; fusty; moldy; mildewed / ~를 제거하다 remove the mold / ~를 막다 keep 《*something*》 from getting moldy / ~투성이다 be covered with mold; get mildewed all over / 온통 ~가 슬었다 There is a film of mold all over it.

**곱**[1] 《상처 따위의》 a film of pus; a mucous 〔filmy〕 discharge (ususally on a skin wound). ¶ 헌데에 곱(이) 끼다 a mucous discharge forms on a wound.

**곱**[2] 《곱절》 times; fold; 《두 배》 double. ¶ (…의) 한 곱 반 one and a half times / 두 곱 double; twice; twofold; two times / 2의 곱은 4. Twice two is 〔makes, equals〕 four. (★ 이때 동사는 복수형이라도 됨) / (두) 곱 크다 be twice as large 〔tall〕; be twice the size 〔height〕 of; be as large 〔tall〕 again as / (두) 곱 무겁다 be twice as heavy; be as heavy again as / 값이 두 곱 나가다 cost twice as much / (두) 곱하다 (make) double / (두) 곱(이) 되다 double; become 〔grow〕 double; be doubled / 세 곱 triple; treble; three times; thrice; threefold / 세 곱하다 treble / 네 곱 four times; quadruple / 네 곱하다 quadruple / 값을 곱으로 요구하다 charge double prices.

**곱걸다** ① 《돈을》 double (*one's* bet). ② 《겹쳐 얽다》 bind double; double-bind.

**곱꺾다** 《관절을》 bend and then strech 《a joint》; flex 《*one's* knee》.

**곱꺾이** bending and then stretching 〔flexing〕 a joint.

**곱끼다** form a 「filmy discharge 〔film of pus〕.

**곱놓다** double (*one's* bet).

**곱다**[1] bend. ⇨ 굽다[1].

**곱다**[2] 《손발이》 (be) numb 〔stiff, numbed〕 《with cold》; go numb 《with cold》. ¶ 추위로 곱은 손가락 fingers numb with cold / 추위로 손가락이 곱아 숟가락을 잡을 수 없었다 My fingers were so stiff 〔numbed〕 with cold that I couldn't hold my spoon.

**곱다**[3] 《손해보다》 end up with a loss rather than a profit.

**곱다**[4] ① 《아름답다》 (be) pretty; beautiful; nice-looking; nice; fine; fair; lovely. ¶ 고운 꽃 a pretty 〔beautiful〕 flower / 고운 말 refined language / 고운 목소리 a sweet 〔nice〕 voice / 고운 얼굴 a fair face / 고운 여자 a pretty 〔beautiful, lovely〕 woman / 곱게 차려 입다 dress *oneself* beautifully; be finely dressed / 살결이 ~ have a fine 〔delicate〕 skin / 곱게 피어 있다 be in beautiful bloom. ② 《마음이》 (be) sweet; gentle; tender-〔soft-〕hearted; pure-minded; kindhearted. ¶ 마음씨가 ~ be kindhearted 〔sweat-tempered, tender-hearted〕 / 나는 마음씨 고운 처녀와 결혼하고 싶다 I want to marry a gentle-hearted girl.

**곱다랗게** ① 《매우 곱게》 quite prettily; beautifully; nicely; finely; handsomely. ¶ ~ 생긴 소년 a handsome boy / ~ 하다 make 《*something*》 beautiful; beautify. ② 《온전하게》 safely; intactly; without any damage; as it was. ¶ 집이 ~ 그냥 있다 The house is kept quite as it was. *or* The house stands intact 〔undamaged〕. ③ 《완전히》 perfectly; all; entirely; completely. ¶ ~ 달아나다 made a perfect escape / ~ 잊어버리다 forget all about 《*something*》; clean forget 《*something*》 《구어》.

**곱다랗다** ① 《예쁘다》 (be) rather pretty 〔beautiful, nice, lovely〕. ② 《온전하다》 (be) whole; intact; safe; undamaged.

**곱돌** 『광물』 pagodites; agalmatolite.

**곱드러지다** stumble 《over, upon, against》. ¶ 돌에 채어 ~ stumble over a stone.

**곱들다** 《갑절들다》 cost twice as much (as); take twice as much (as). ¶ 그렇게 하면 돈이 곱든다 It would cost 「twice as much 〔as much again〕 as that.

**곱들이다** spend 〔put out〕 twice as much (as); consume twice as much (as). ¶ (…보다) 공을 ~ take twice as much trouble (as…).

**곱디디다** twist 〔sprain〕 *one's* ankle.

**곱똥** mucous feces.

**곱빼기** ① 《음식의》 double measure 《of 》; a double-the-ordinary dish. ¶~잔 a double-size glass. ② 《거듭》 double; twice.

**곱사등이** a hunchback; a humpback; a stooped person. ¶ ~의 hunchbacked; humpbacked; crookbacked.

**곱살끼다** 《보채다》 fret; be fretful. ¶ 오늘은 하루 종일 애가 곱살꼈다 The child has been in a fret all day.

**곱살스럽다, 곱살하다** 《얼굴이》 (be) pretty; fair; beautiful; comely; 《마음씨가》 (be) tender; soft; gentle; meek.

**곱새기다** ① 《오해》 misconstrue; misunderstand. ② 《남을》 think ill of. ③ 《생각을》 repeatedly consider.

**곱셈** 〖수학〗 multiplication. ～하다 multiply. ◉ ～표 the multiplication sign.

**곱슬곱슬하다** (be) kinky; curly; frizzled; frizzly; wavy. ¶ 곱슬곱슬한 머리 curly 〔kinky, frizzled, crisp〕 hair; crimps.

**곱씹다** 《거듭 씹다》 rechew; 《말을》 repeat 《the same thing》; dwell 《on a subject》; harp on 《*a matter*》; 《생각을》 think 《it》 over; ponder on 〔over〕.

**곱자** 《곡척》 a carpenter's square; a metal foot-measure.

**곱장다리** bowlegs; 《사람》 a bowlegged person.

**곱쟁이** 《곱절》 double; doubled amount. ¶ 무게가 ～가 되다 The weight doubles. *or* The weight is 〔becomes〕 doubled.

**곱절** double; times. ～하다 double 《it》. ⇨갑절. ¶ 두 ～의 양 twice as much as / 세 ～의 수 three times as many as / 네 ～의 크기〔길이〕 four times as large 〔long〕 as / 다섯 ～ quintuple / 여섯 ～ sextuple / 몇 ～이나 many times over / 몇 ～의 노력을 하다 redouble *one's* efforts / 값의 ～을 지불하다 pay double 〔twice〕 the price / 1,000은 100의 몇 ～이냐 How many times a hundred is a thousand? / 2의 세 ～은 6이다 Three times two is (equal to) 6. / 그는 다른 사람의 ～이나 일한다 He works twice as hard as others.

**곱창** the small intestine of a cow. ◉ ～구이 broiled (pieces of) small intestine of a cow.

**곱치다** 《반으로 접다》 fold; 《곱절하다》 double. ¶ 값을 ～ double a price / 담요를 ～ fold 〔double〕 a blanket.

**곱하다** 〖수학〗 multiply. ¶ 3에 2를 ～ multiply 3 by 2 / 2에 2를 곱하면 4가 된다 Two times two is 〔are〕 four. (★ 또는 Two twos 〔Two 2's〕 are four.).

**곳** ① 《장소》 a place; a spot (좁은); a scene (현장); a site (터); a seat (소재지); 《지방》 a locality; a district; 《공간》 space; room.

> **용법** **place** 「장소」를 뜻하는 가장 일반적인 말. 아래 열거된 낱말 대용으로 두루 쓰임. **spot** 특정의 한정된 매우 좁은 지점. **scene** 사건·사고 따위의 현장. site 보다 불명확한 장소. **site** 사건이 있었던 장소. 또 도시·건물이 있던 자리, 건축 예정지를 뜻하기도 함. **seat** 활동의 소재지·중심지.

¶ 불편한〔편리한〕 곳 an inconvenient 〔a convenient〕 place / 사고가 일어난 곳 the scene of the accident / 안전한 곳 a place of safety / 경치가 좋은 곳 a scenic spot / 담배를 재배하는 곳 a tobacco-growing district / 옛 성채가 있던 곳 the site of an old castle / 이곳 저곳 here and there / 남이 있는 곳에서 in the presence of others / 곳에 따라 다르다 be different in localities / 여기가 내가 사는 곳이다 This is the place where I live. / 아픈 곳을 보여다오 Show me the place where it hurts. / 자네 좋은 곳으로 가게 You can go anywhere you like. ② 《주소》 *one's* place 〔house, address〕; *one's* home. ¶ 사는 곳을 알리다 give 〔tell〕 *one's* address / 사는 곳이 어디요 Where is your home? *or* What is your address?

**곳간**(庫間) a storeroom; a storage; a warehouse. ¶ ～에 넣다 store; put 《goods》 in storage. ◉ ～차 a boxcar.

**곳곳** place after place; here and there; several places; everywhere. ¶ ～마다 in place after place; everywhere / ～에서 모여들다 flock from far and near; come from all quarters / ～을 여행하며 다니다 travel from place to place / ～에 군인이다 There are soldiers all around.

**곳집** ① ＝곳간. ② 《상엿집》 a funeral equipment shed.

**공**[1] a ball; a handball; a football. ¶ 공을 던지다 throw a ball / 공을 치다 hit 〔strike〕 a ball / 공을 차다 kick a ball / 공을 튀기다 bounce a ball / 공을 던지다 throw 〔pitch〕 a ball / 공을 잡다 catch a ball / 공 던지기를 하다 play catch.

**공**(工) 《공업》 industry; 《일꾼》 a worker; a workman; a mechanic. ◉ 금속공 a metalworker. 인쇄공 a pressman.

**공**(公) ① 《공사》 public matters; public affairs. ¶ 공과 사를 구별하다 draw the line between public and private matters. ② 《공작》 a duke; a prince. ¶ 에든버러공 the Duke of Edinburgh.

**공**(功) ① 《공로》 merits; a meritorious service; credit. ¶ 뛰어난 공 distinguished services / 특히 공이 있는 사람 a person of exceptional merit / 공을 치하하여 for 〔in recognition of〕 *one's* services / 공을 세우다 render distinguished services 《for the country》; perform a meritorious deed / 공을 다투다 try to get credit 《for》; claim credit 《for an invention》 / 자기 공으로 하다 take credit to *oneself* / …을 아무

의 공으로 하다 give 《*a person*》 credit for 《*doing*》 / 모든 것이 자네 공일세 All the credit goes 〔belongs〕 to you. ② 《수고》 labor; efforts. ¶ 공들이다 elaborate; exert *oneself;* take pains; labor assiduously.

**공**(空) ① 《영》 (a) zero; (a) cipher; 《무》 (a) nought; nothing (허사). ¶ 나의 모든 노력은 공으로 돌아갔다 All my efforts have come to naught. ② 《동그라미》 a circle; an 'O'. ¶ 공을 치다 draw a circle; write an 'O'; mark down a zero / 공을 하나 붙이다 put a zero to. ③ 《텅빔》 void; emptiness; vacancy. ④ 《거저》 free of charge.

**공**[2] a gong. ¶ 공이 울렸다 〖권투〗 There is the bell.

**공가**(空家) an empty 〔an unoccupied, a vacant〕 house; a deserted house.

**공간**(空間) space; 《자리·여지》 room; 《빈틈》 a (vacant) space; a gap. (★ space는 「시간」과 대비되는 공간; 「어떤 목적」을 위한 특정의 장소(=place)를 뜻하고, room은 space의 일부로, 사람·물건이 차지하기에 충분한 「자리·여지」를 뜻한다). ¶ ～적인 spacial; spatial / 시간과 ～ time and space / 무한의 ～ the infinite / 시간과 ～을 초월하다 neglect 〔take no notice of〕 time and space / 이 세상은 시간과 ～ 속에 존재한다 This world exists in time and space. / 또 한 대의 차가 들어갈 만한 ～이 있느냐 Is there enough room for another car? / 이 책상은 그리 많은 ～을 차지하지 않는다 This desk won't take up too much room. ◉ ～감각 a sense of space. ～개념 〖철학〗 the concept 〔notion〕 of space. ～성 〖심리〗 extensity. ～역(閾) 〖심리〗 the space threshold. ～예술 a spatial art. ～지각 〖심리〗 space perception.

**공갈**(恐喝) a threat; a menace; blackmail; intimidation. ～하다 threaten; menace; blackmail; intimidate; browbeat 《into》. ¶ ～하여 돈을 빼앗다 blackmail 《*a person*》 of his money / 죽이겠다고 ～치다 threaten to kill 《*a person*》; threaten 《*a person*》 with death / 아무를 ～쳐서 제안을 받아들이게 하다 browbeat 《*a person*》 into accepting the proposal / 그는 ～ 혐의로 체포되었다 He was arrested on a charge of blackmail(ing). ◉ ～자 a black mailer. ～죄 (the crime of) blackmail. ～취재(取財) extortion by threats.

**공감**(共感) sympathy; a response; consensus (의견의 일치). ～하다 sympathize 《with *a person*》; feel sympathy 《toward》; respond to 《an appeal》. ¶ ～을 느끼다 feel sympathy 《for, toward》 / ～을 불러일으키다 evoke 〔excite, rouse〕 《*a person's*》 sympathy / ～을 얻다 win 〔gain〕 the sympathy 《of》 / ～을 표시하다 express sympathy with 《*a person's*》 view / ～의 폭을 넓히다 widen the belt of consensus / 아무런 ～도 얻을 수 없었다 No response came to the appeal on our side. / 그녀의 호소는 대중의 폭넓은 ～을 일으켰다 Her appeal aroused (a) public response everywhere. ◉ ～각(覺) 〖심리〗 synesthesia.

**공개**(公開) opening to the public. ～하다 open to the public; make 《*a thing*》 public; 《전시하다》 exhibit; put 《*a thing*》 on view (to the public); 《개봉하다》 release 《a movie》; 《발명품 등을》 unveil; 《기업을》 go public. ¶ ～의 open (to the public); public 《exhibition》 / 주식의 ～ public offering of stocks; a public sale of shares / ～석상에서 연설하다 speak in public / 신문에 ～하다 open to the press / 재산을 ～하다 make public *one's* personal assets / ～가 금지되다 be closed to the public / 그는 ～ 석상에 나가는 것을 좋아하지 않는다 He does not like to attend public functions. / 많은 건전 기업이 내년에는 ～될 것이다 Many healthy companies will go public next year. / 주민들은 정보의 ～를 요구하고 있다 The residents require that the information be made public. / 그 공원은 일반에게 ～되어 있다 The park is open to the public. ◉ ～강연 a public lecture. ～강좌 《대학의》 an extension lecture. ～녹음 a public recording. ～방송 open broadcasting. ～수사(搜査) an open criminal investigation. ～수업 a workshop class. ～시장 an open market. ～시합 an open game. ～연설 a public address. ～입찰 a public 〔an open〕 bidding. ～장 an open letter. ～재판 a public trial. ～처형 an execution in public. ～청문회 a public hearing. ～토론회 an open forum. ～회의 an open session.

**공개념**(公槪念) the public concept. ¶ 토지의 ～ the public concept of land ownership.

**공것**(空—) something free; what can be had for nothing; a thing got for nothing; an article obtained without cost; a gift; a windfall. ¶ ～으로 얻다

get〔gain〕《*a thing*》「as a gift〔without efforts〕/ ～이나 다름없이 사다 buy for almost nothing / 그 따위는 ～이라 해도 안 갖겠다 I would not have it even as a gift. / (이) 세상에 ～이란 없다 There is nothing that can be had free in this world. / ～이라고 낭비해서는 안 된다 You should not waste something just because you didn't have to pay for it. / ～이라면 양잿물도 마신다 《속담》 Anything given as a gift is welcome at any time.

**공격**(攻擊) ① 《적을 침》 an attack; an assault; a raid; an onslaught; the offensive. ～하다 attack; assault; charge; storm; make a raid on. ¶ 적의 ～하에 under the attack of the enemy / ～을 가하다 deliver〔launch〕 an attack against〔on〕/ ～을 막다 defend *oneself* against an attack / 적의 ～을 저지하다 check the advance of the enemy / ～은 최선의 방어이다 A good offense is the best defense. / 적은 미사일 ～을 개시했다 The enemy launched a missile attack. / 그 유조선은 국적 불명기의 ～을 받았다 The tanker was attacked by a plane of unknown nationality. ② 《비난》 a verbal attack; a charge; (a) censure; denunciation; (a) criticism. ～하다 attack; charge; denounce; criticize; speak〔write〕 against. ¶ 정부 방침을 ～하다 denounce the government's policy / 그들은 시장의 무능을 ～했다 They charged the mayor with incompetence. ③ 〖야구〗 batting (side). ～하다 go to bat. ¶ ～측 the team at bat.

> 용법 **attack** 공격을 나타내는 가장 일반적인 말. **assault** 갑작스런 격렬한 공격. **raid** 상대를 제압하기보다는 손해를 끼치게 하기 위한 일시적인 습격이란 뜻이 강함. **onslaught** 상대를 제압·굴복시키기 위한 맹렬한 공격. **offensive** 지속적인 군사적 공격이란 뜻으로 공격적 태도, 공세란 뜻이 내포되어 있음.

◉ ～군 an attacking force. ～기(機) an attack plane. ～력 striking power〔ability〕; offensive power. ～로 a route of attack. ～목표〔점〕 objective〔point〕 of attack. ～용 무기 offensive weapons〔arms〕. ～자세 an offensive posture. ～정신 a fighting〔an offensive〕 spirit. 기습～ a surprise〔sudden〕 attack.

**공격적**(攻擊的) (being) offensive; aggressive. ¶ ～인 태도를 취하다 adopt an offensive attitude 《toward》.

**공경**(公卿) a court noble.

**공경**(恭敬) respect; reverence; veneration; deference. ～하다 respect; revere; venerate; pay respect to. ¶ ～할 만한 respectable; venerable / 스승을 ～하다 respect〔pay respect to〕 *one's* teacher〔master〕/ 어른을 ～하다 be respectful to *one's* elders.

**공고**(工高) ⇨ 공업고등학교.

**공고**(公告) a public notice〔notification〕; an (official) announcement. ～하다 give (out) a public notice 《of》; give notification; proclaim; notify〔announce〕 publicly. ¶ 입시 날짜는 내일 ～될 것이다 The date of the entrance examination will be publicly announced tomorrow. ◉ 경매〔특허〕～ an auction〔a patent〕 announcement.

**공고**(鞏固) 《튼튼함》 solidity; stability; firmness; soundness. ～하다 (be) solid; stable; firm; sound; strong. ¶ ～한 의지 a firm〔a strong, an iron〕 will / ～한 지반 firm ground / 기초를 ～히 하다 solidify the foundation / 두 정상은 양국간의 우호 관계를 ～히 하기로 약속했다 The two summits promised to strengthen the bonds of friendship between the two countries.

**공공**(公共) the public (society); the community. ¶ ～의 public; common / ～을 위하여 힘쓰다 do public service; do *one's* best in the public interest; render services to the public / ～의 이익을〔복지를〕 도모하다 promote public interests〔welfare〕.

◉ ～경제 public economy. ～교통요금 public transport(ation) fares. ～기관 a public institution. ～기업체 a public corporation. ～단체 a public body〔organization〕. ～복지 public welfare. ～사업 a public undertaking〔enterprise〕; public works: ～사업비 expenditure for public work / ～사업체 a public-service corporation. ～생활 communal life. ～시설 public〔community〕 facilities. ～심 public spirit; a sense of public duty. ～요금 public utility charges〔rates〕: ～요금의 인상을 억제하기 위해 노력하다 exert *one's* efforts to curb the hikes of public utility charges. ～위생 public health. ～재산 public property: ～재산을 소중히 해라 Take good care of public properties. ～차관 public loan: ～차관 도입 public loan inducement. ～투자 (a) public investment.

**공공**(空空) ① 《○○》 zeroes; blanks; asterisks; X's. ¶ 007, double O seven. ② [형용사적] unnamed; undisclosed; "XX"; a certain; unidentified. ¶ ○○기지 an ○○ 〔XX〕 base; an undisclosed base / ○○부대 an unnamed unit / 18○○년 eighteen hundred something / ○○사건 a certain affair.

**공공연하다**(公公然—) (be) open; public; open and public; overt; avowed. ¶ 공공연한 비밀 an open secret / 공공연한 사실 a matter of common knowledge; a fact patent to the public / 공공연한 적대 open 〔avowed〕 hostilities / 공공연히 openly; publicly; in public; in the open; officially / 공공연히 비난하다 assail openly; score 〔denounce〕 in public / 그는 그 계획에 공공연히 반대했다 He openly opposed the plan. / 그 흉악한 범죄는 백주에 공공연히 자행되었다 The atrocious crime was committed in broad daylight.

**공과**(工科) the engineering department. ◉ ～대학 an engineering 〔a technical〕 college; an institute of technology: 매사추세츠 ～대학 Massachusetts Institute of Technology (생략 MIT).

**공과**(功過) merits and demerits. ¶ 그 정책의 ～는 서로 반반이다 The merits and demerits of that policy are balanced against each other.

**공과금**(公課金) public imposts 〔charges〕; taxes; the public utilities' charge.

**공관**(公館) a public hall; an official residence. ¶ 총리 ～ the official residence of the Prime Minister / 재외～ diplomatic offices 〔establishments〕 abroad.

**공관복음서**(共觀福音書) 『성서』 the Synoptic Gospels.

**공교롭게**(工巧—) ① 《교묘히》 elaborately; with fine detail; skillfully; deftly; dexterously; cleverly. ② 《뜻밖·우연》 unexpectedly; accidentally; casually; at a likely 〔an unlikely〕 time; luckily 〔unluckily〕; fortunately 〔unfortunately〕; by a lucky 〔an unlucky〕 coincidence; as luck would have it; as it happens. ¶ ～ 그날 비가 내렸다 Unfortunately it rained that day. / ～ 그날따라 그는 집에 없었다 It so happened that he was away from home on that particular day. / 그녀는 ～ 내가 없을 때 왔다 She had the misfortune to come when I was out. / 그때 주머니엔 ～도 돈이 한푼 없었다 Unfortunately, 〔As it happened,〕 I had not a penny with me on that occasion.

**공교롭다**(工巧—) ① 《물건이》 (be) elaborate; fine; minutely detailed; ingenious; 《솜씨가》 (be) skillful; dexterous; clever. ¶ 공교로운 장식 elaborate decorations / 공교로운 솜씨 dexterity; deftness; cleverness with *one's* fingers. ② 《뜻밖의·우연의》 (be) coincidental; quite accidental; opportune 〔inopportune〕; timely 〔untimely〕. ¶ 공교로운 때 an opportune 〔inopportune〕 time; a likely 〔an unlikely〕 time / 정말 공교로운 일치로군 It's quite a coincidence. *or* What a coincidence!

**공구**(工具) a tool; an instrument; an implement. ¶ ～ 한 벌 a set of tools. ◉ ～상자 a toolbox. ～점(店) a machine-parts supplier. 정밀～ a precision tool.

**공구**(工區) a section of works.

**공국**(公國) a dukedom; a (grand) duchy; a principality. ¶ 모나코 ～ the principality of Monaco.

**공군**(空軍) an air force; a flying corps. ¶ ～의 우세 air superiority. ◉ ～기 an air-force plane. ～기지 an air (force) base. ～력 air power 〔might〕. ～본부 the Air Force Headquarters. ～사관학교 the Air Force Academy. ～참모총장 the Air Force Chief of the General Staff. 미국～ the United States Air Force (생략 USAF). 한국～ the Republic of Korea Air Force (생략 ROKAF).

**공권**(公權) civil rights; citizenship. ¶ ～을 박탈당하다 be deprived of *one's* civil rights. ◉ ～박탈 deprivation of civil rights; disfranchisement. ～정지 suspension of civil rights.

**공권**(空拳) a bare hand; a naked fist. ¶ ～으로 with *one's* naked 〔bare〕 hands / 그는 적수 ～으로 엄청난 돈을 벌었다 Having nothing to start with, he has made a colossal fortune.

**공권력**(公權力) governmental authority; government power; law enforcement authorities. ¶ ～의 행사 the exercise of governmental authority 《against》.

**공규**(空閨) the bedchamber of a neglected 〔deserted〕 wife. ¶ ～를 지키다 《홀어머니가》 lead the lonely life of a deserted 〔bereaved〕 wife; 《남편 출타중》 be a lonely wife; remain true to *one's* husband in *his* absence.

**공그르다** blindstitch; whip a seam.

**공극**(空隙) a gap; an opening; a crevice; an aperture.

**공글리다** ① 《다지다》 harden; make hard; consolidate; solidify; firm up; strengthen; stabilize. ② 《끝맺다》 finish up neatly.

**공금**(公金) public 〔government〕 money 〔funds〕. ¶ ～을 낭비하다 waste 〔squander〕 the public purse / ～을 유용하다 peculate 〔misappropriate〕 public funds / 그는 ～을 착복〔횡령〕했다 He embezzled public money. ◉ ～횡령 embezzlement 〔misappropriation〕 of public money 〔funds〕.

**공급**(供給) supply; provision (식료품 등의); 《전기·수도 따위의》 service. ～하다 supply; provide; furnish. ¶ 수요와 ～ demand and supply / 전력 ～ electric power supply / ～을 끊다 cut off the supply 《of》 / 기름 ～을 받다 be supplied with oil 《by》; get *its* supply of oil 《from》 / 인력을 ～하다 supply with manpower; man up / 석탄의 ～이 부족하다 There is a short supply of coal. / 수요와 ～의 균형을 유지하는 것이 중요하다 It is important to keep a balance between supply and demand. / 사우디아라비아는 한국에 원유를 ～하고 있다 Saudi Arabia supplies Korea with crude oil. *or* Saudi Arabia supplies crude oil for Korea. ◉ ～가격 a supply price. ～과다〔과잉〕 an excessive supply; an oversupply. ～구역 《수도 등의》 a service area. ～로(路) a channel of supply. ～부족 a deficiency in supply; a short supply. ～원(源) a source of supply. ～자 a supplier; a provider.

**공기** 《돌》 a jackstone; a pebble; 《놀이》 jackstones; marbles. ～ 놀다 play marbles 〔jackstones〕. ～ 놀리다 《농락하다》 make sport 〔a toy〕 of 《*a person*》; twist 《*a person*》 round *one's* little finger; have 《*a person*》 perfectly under *one's* control.

**공기**(公器) 《공공기관》 a public organ 〔institution, instrument〕. ¶ ～를 남용하다 abuse public instruments / 매스미디어는 사회의 ～이다 Mass media are public organs of society.

**공기**(空氣) air; 《분위기》 (an) atmosphere. ¶ ～의 air; aerial; pneumatic; atmospheric / ～가 든 pneumatic; inflated / ～의 마찰 air friction / ～의 압력 atmospheric pressure; air pressure (압축 공기의) / ～의 저항 air resistance / 신선한 ～ fresh air / 탁한 ～ impure 〔foul〕 air / 험악한 ～ grave 〔serious〕 atmosphere / ～ 중의 산소 atmospheric oxygen / ～가 안 통하는 airproof; airtight / ～ 유통이 잘 되는 well-ventilated / ～가 빠진 flat 《tires》 / ～를 넣다 《방에》 let air in; ventilate; 《타이어 따위에》 fill 《a tire》 with air; inflate; pump up / ～를 갈아넣다 air out 《a room》 / ～를 뺀 evacuated 《glass bulbs》 / ～를 빼다 deflate 《a tire》; let the air out of 《a tire》 / ～에 쐬다 expose 《*something*》 to the air; aerate / 신선한 ～를 마시다 breathe 〔have〕 fresh air / 신선한 ～를 마시러 외출하다 go out for a breath of fresh air / 사내 ～가 매우 험악하다 There is something tense in the air at the office. / 이것이 실내 ～를 정화하는 장치이다 This is an apparatus for purifying the air in the room. / 장내의 ～가 긴장되어 있었다 The atmosphere in the hall was strained.
◉ ～가열〔냉각〕기 an air heater 〔cooler〕. ～구멍 an air vent 〔hole〕. ～기중기 a pneumatic crane. ～방석 an air cushion. ～배수기 a pneumatic ejector. ～베개 an air cushion 〔pillow〕. ～압축기〔제동기〕 an air compressor 〔brake〕. ～여과기 an air filter. ～역학 aerodynamics. ～요법 the air cure; aerotherapy; pneumatotherapy. ～욕 an air bath. ～저항 air resistance. ～전염 infection by air; aerial 〔airborne〕 infection. ～정화기 an air purifier 〔cleaner〕. ～조절 air conditioning. ～조절장치 an air conditioner. ～주머니 《새의》 an air sac. ～총 an air gun 〔rifle〕. ～터빈 an air turbine. ～펌프 an air pump.

**공기**(空器) 《빈 그릇》 an empty vessel 〔dish〕; 《식사용》 a bowl. ¶ 밥 한 ～ a bowl of rice / 밥을 ～에 담아 내오다 serve boiled rice in a bowl.

**공기업**(公企業) a public 〔government, state〕 enterprise 〔undertaking〕.

**공기오염**(空氣汚染) air 〔atmospheric〕 pollution. ¶ 이 도시의 ～은 매우 심하다 The air pollution in this city is terrible. / ～은 자동차의 배기 가스가 주원인이다 Air pollution is mainly caused by automobile exhaust fumes.

**공납**(公納) tax. ◉ ～금 《학교의》 regular school payments; 《부과금》 taxes; public imposts.

**공납**(貢納) a tribute; a tributary payment. ～하다 pay 〔offer〕 a tribute.

**공단**(工團) an industrial complex.

**공단**(公團) a public corporation.
**공단**(貢緞) woven silk without patterns; satin.
**공답**(公畓) a state-owned rice field.
**공대**(工大) an engineering college.
**공대**(恭待) 《대접》 respectful treatment; 《존대》 respectful address; polite language. ~하다 《대접》 treat respectfully; treat 《*a person*》 with courtesy; 《존대》 use polite language; address respectfully.
**공대공**(空對空) air-to-air. ◉ ~미사일〔유도탄〕 an air-to-air (guided) missile.
**공대지**(空對地) air-to-surface. ◉ ~미사일〔유도탄〕 an air-to-surface (guided) missile.
**공덕**(公德) public morals 〔morality〕; civil virtues. ⇨ 공중도덕. ◉ ~심 public spirit 〔sense〕; a sense of public duty 〔morality〕: ~심에 호소하다 appeal to 《*a person's*》 sense of public morality.
**공덕**(功德) 《공과 덕》 merit and virtue; 〖불교〗 Buddhist merit; charity; piety; a charitable deed. ¶ ~을 베풀다 practice charity; do an act of charity / ~을 쌓다 do charitable act 〔deeds〕.
**공도**(公道) 《도로》 a public way 〔road〕; a highway; 《정의》 justice; equity. ¶ 천하의 ~ 《대의》 universal justice / ~를 밟다 tread 〔take〕 the path of justice; act with justice / ~에서 벗어나다 stray from the right path.
**공돈**(空—) windfall income; easy-gotten money; easy money; 《부정한》 filthy lucre; gravy 《미속어》. ¶ ~은 오래 못 간다 Light 〔Easy〕 come, light 〔easy〕 go.
**공돌다**(空—) ① 《차의 타이어가》 skid; 《엔진 등이》 race; 《기계가》 idle; run idle. ¶ 엔진이 공돌았다 The engine idled. ② 《의론·행동 등이》 ¶ 의론이 공돌아 결론이 나지 않았다 The discussion went round in circles and never reached a conclusion.
**공동**(共同) cooperation (협력); collaboration (문예·과학 등의 공동 제작); association (연합); partnership (공동 경영); union (결합). ¶ ~의 common; communal (공용의); joint; concerted / ~으로 jointly; in concert 〔collaboration, cooperation, association〕 《with》 / ~의 이익을 위하여 for common benefit / ~의 적 a common enemy 《of Korea and Japan》 / ~으로 (일)하다 cooperate 《with》; work together; team up 《with》; join forces 〔hands〕 《with》; act in union 〔concert〕 《with》 / ~으로 경영하다 run 《a hotel》 in partnership 《with》 / ~으로 부담하다 share 《the losses》 with 《another》 / ~ 보조를 취하다 take joint steps; take concerted action / 같은 방을 ~으로 쓰다 share the same room. / 그들은 ~으로 문제 해결에 노력하였다 They combined their efforts to solve the problem. *or* They made united efforts to solve the problem. / 나는 아내와 ~ 명의의 예금 계좌를 개설했다 My wife and I opened a joint bank account. / 나는 친구와 ~으로 사업을 하기로 했다 I decided to do a business in association with my friend.
◉ ~결의 a joint resolution. ~경영 joint management: ~경영자 a business partner. ~관리 joint control; 〖국제법〗 condominium. ~관심사 matters of mutual concern; issue of mutual interest. ~구입 《do》 cooperative buying. ~권리 joint rights. ~규제수역 a jointly controlled waters 〔fishing zone〕. ~기업체 a joint enterprise 〔venture〕. ~모금(운동) a community chest (campaign). ~모의 〖법〗 (a) conspiracy. ~목적 a common object. ~묘지 a public cemetery; a common burial ground. ~변소 a public lavatory 〔convenience〕; a (public) comfort station 《미》. ~보증인 a cosurety; a joint surety. ~보험 joint insurance; coinsurance. ~사업 a joint enterprise 〔undertaking〕. ~사회 a community. ~상속 joint inheritance. ~선언 a joint declaration. ~성명 《issue》 a joint statement 〔*communiqué* (F.)〕: 7·4 남북 ~성명 the South=North Joint Communiqué announced on July 4, 1972. ~소유(권) joint ownership; coproprietorship: ~소유자 a joint owner; a co-owner. ~숙박소 a public boarding house; a laborers' home. ~시설 public facilities; facilities for common 〔communal〕 use. ~시장 a common market. ~원고〔피고〕 a co-plaintiff 〔co-defendant〕. ~의무 joint obligations. ~작업 joint 〔group〕 work. ~작전 concerted 〔united〕 operations. ~재산 joint 〔common〕 property. ~전선 an united 〔a common〕 front 《against》; joint forces 《with》: ~전선을 펴다 form 〔put up〕 a united front 《against》. ~정범(正犯) 〖법〗 an accomplice. ⇨ 공범. ~정신 cooperative spirit. ~주최 joint aus-

pices; cosponsorship: ～ 주최하다 cosponsor; host 《an event》 under the joint auspices 《of》. ～주택 a community of dwelling houses; an apartment house. ～책임 corporate 〔collective〕 responsibility; joint liability: ～책임을 지다 answer jointly for 《*something*》; be jointly responsible for 《a failure》; hold joint liability for 《the debt》. ～출자 joint investment; pooling of funds: ～출자하다 jointly invest 《in》; pool funds 《for》. ～취사장 a community 〔communal〕 kitchen. ～판매 a joint sale. ～행위 common action; a cooperative action.

**공동**(空洞) 《동굴》 a cave; a cavern; a cavity; 《빈 속》 a hollow; 《폐결핵의》 a vomica (*pl.* -cae).

**공동가입**(共同加入) 〖전화〗 joint subscription. ¶ ～선 a party wire 〔line〕 / ～자 a joint subscriber / ～ 전화 a party-line telephone; a telephone on a party line.

**공동개발**(共同開發) joint development. ¶ 이 제품은 두 회사가 ～한 것이다 This product is the fruit of joint development by the two companies.

**공동생활**(共同生活) 《사회의》 community 〔communal〕 life; communal living; 《단체의》 collective life; living together; 《남녀의》 cohabitation. ～하다 live together; 《남녀가》 cohabit 《with》.

**공동연구**(共同硏究) joint research(es); a joint study. ～하다 study jointly; make 〔conduct〕 joint researches 《into》; join hands 《with another》 in making researches 《into》.

**공동제작**(共同製作) joint production; co=production. ～하다 produce 《a film》 jointly 《with》; co-produce. ◉ ～자 a joint producer; a co-producer.

**공동체**(共同體) a community; a communal society. ◉ ～의식 community spirit. 도시～ an urban 〔a town〕 community. 촌락～ a rural 〔village〕 community.

**공동투쟁**(共同鬪爭) a joint struggle. ～하다 struggle jointly 《against, for》; present a united 〔common〕 front 《against》. ◉ ～ 위원회 a joint struggle committee.

**공동해손**(共同海損) 〖보험〗 general average (생략 G.A.). ¶ ～ 부담보(不擔保) free of general average / ～ 분담〔희생〕 a general average contribution 〔sacrifice〕.

**공동협찬**(共同協贊) joint auspices. ～하다 cosponsor; sponsor jointly. ¶ ～프로 a cosponsored program.

**공동화**(空洞化) ～하다 become hollow; lose substance; get emptied of all 《*its*》 contents. ¶ 일본의 산업 ～ the deindustrialization of Japan.

**공들다**(功―) take 〔require〕 much labor 〔trouble〕; cost strenuous effort. ¶ 공드는 일 hard 〔laborious〕 work; work that requires much labor / 공든 탑이 무너지랴 《속담》 Hard work is never wasted.

**공들이다**(功―) take trouble 《for》; labor 《for》; work hard 《for》; do careful 〔elaborate〕 work. ¶ 공들인 작품 an elaborate work / 공들여 with great effort 〔care, detail〕 / 화장을 공들여 하다 make *one's* toilet 「carefully 〔with special care〕 / 그는 그 일을 위해 10년 동안 공들였다 He has labored for it ten years. / 이 책상은 매우 공들여 만든 것이다 This desk is an elaborate piece of work / 이제껏 공들인 보람이 없어졌다 All my labors have been in vain. / 이 작품은 퍽 공들인 것 같다 This work 「smells of the lamp 〔bears traces of labor〕.

**공떡**(空―) a cake won for nothing; a godsend; a windfall. ¶ 이게 웬 ～이냐 What a welcome windfall! / ～만 바라고 있지 마라 Don't sit there (idle) waiting for someone to drop a fortune in your lap!

**공란**(空欄) a blank; a vacant 〔an empty〕 column (on a page); empty space; margin. ¶ ～에 기입하다 fill space / ～을 메우다 fill in blanks.

**공람**(供覽) ～하다 submit 《*things*》 to public inspection; exhibit 《*things*》 before the public.

**공랭**(空冷) ¶ ～식의 air-cooled. ◉ ～식 엔진 an air-cooled engine. ～장치 air=cooling devices.

**공략**(攻略) attack; invasion; capture; conquest. ～하다 attack; invade; capture 《a city》; conquer 《a country》; take 《a fortress》 by storm; carry 《the enemy's position》. ¶ ～하기 어려운 진지 a impregnable fortress / 적의 진지를 ～하다 capture an enemy position.

**공력**(功力) ① 《노력》 effort; labor; elaboration. ¶ 그의 ～이 허사로 끝났다 All his efforts ended in vain. ② 〖불교〗 Buddhist merit acquired by practicing austerities.

**공로**(公路) a highway; a (public) route.

**공로**(功勞) (meritorious) service(s); a

meritorious deed; merits. ¶ ~가 있는 meritorious; of merit; distinguished / ~를 세우다 distinguish *oneself* in 《war》; render distinguished services 《to the country》 / ~를 인정하다 recognize 《*a person's*》 service / ~로 상을 받다 be awarded 「for 〔in recognition of〕 *one's* services / 자네의 ~는 충분히 보답될 걸세 Your services shall be well rewarded. / ~를 세운 군인들이 표창받았다 Commendation was given to those who performed meritorious military services. ◉ ~상 a medal for distinguished services. ~자 a man of merits; a person who has done distinguished services: 문화 ~자 a man of meritorious cultural service. ~주(株) a stock bonus (to employees). ~훈장 a distinguished service medal.

**공로**(空路) an airway; an air route 〔lane〕. ¶ ~로 by air 〔airplane〕 / ~로 부산에서 서울로 돌아오다 fly back to Seoul from Pusan / ~ 수송하다 send 〔carry〕 《cargo》 by plane; ship by aircraft / ~로 일본에 가다 go to Japan by air / 그는 김포에서 ~로 뉴욕에 갔다 He left Kimp'o by air for New York. *or* He flew from Kimp'o to New York.

**공론**(公論) ① 《공평한 의론》 an unbiased view; an impersonal 〔a disinterested〕 opinion; fair criticism. ② 《여론》 public opinion; the consensus. ¶ 모든 국사를 ~에 부치다 refer all state affairs to public opinion.

**공론**(空論) an empty 〔impractical〕 theory; an academic discussion. ¶ 그것은 탁상~에 지나지 않는다 It is only an armchair theory. ◉ ~가 an armchair philosopher 〔critic〕; a doctrinaire.

**공뢰**(空雷) an aerial torpedo.

**공룡**(恐龍) 〖고생물〗 a dinosaur. ¶ ~ 시대 the age of the dinosaurs.

**공률**(工率) rate of production; 〖물리〗 power.

**공리**(公吏) a public official 〔servant〕; 「an officeholder.

**공리**(公利) the public 〔common〕 interest. ¶ ~를 도모하다 promote public interests.

**공리**(公理) 〖수학〗 an axiom; a maxim; 《도리》 a self-evident truth.

**공리**(功利) utility. ¶ ~적인 utilitarian; practical; unsentimental; hard-nosed 《미구어》 / ~적인 사람 a businesslike man; a matter-of-fact fellow / 사물을 ~적으로 생각하다 take a utilitarian view of things; view things in a practical 〔down-to-earth〕 way. ◉ ~주의 utilitarianism: ~주의자 a utilitarian.

**공리**(空理) an empty 〔academic, impracticable〕 theory; doctrinairism. ◉ ~공론 doctrinarianism; academicism: ~공론에 흐르다 indulge in academic discussion; stick to isms and ics.

**공립**(公立) a public institution. ¶ ~의 public (사립에 대한); municipal (시립의); prefectural (도립의) / 이 학교는 ~이 아니다 This school is not a public institution. ◉ ~학교 a public school.

**공막**(鞏膜) 〖해부〗 the sclera; the sclerotica. ◉ ~염(炎) sclerotitis.

**공매**(公賣) (a) public sale 〔auction〕. ~하다 sell at 〔by〕 auction; auction off. ¶ ~에 부치다 put 《*a thing*》 up for public 「sale 〔auction〕; sell 《*a thing*》 by 〔at〕 auction / 그의 집은 ~에 부쳐졌다 His house was 「put up for public sale 〔offered at public auction〕. ◉ ~장 an auction house. ~처분 disposition by public sale; tax sale. 강제~ forced sale.

**공매**(空賣) 〖증권〗 a short sale; short 「selling.

**공맹**(孔孟) Confucius and Mencius. ¶ ~지도(之道) the doctrines of Confucius and Mencius. ◉ ~학 Confucianism.

**공명**(公明) fairness; justice; impartiality. ~하다 (be) fair; just; open; aboveboard; square; impartial. ◉ ~선거 a clean election: ~선거 운동 a campaign for clean elections.

**공명**(功名) a great exploit 〔achievement〕; a glorious deed; distinguished services; 《명성》 fame; honor; distinction; 《무공》 feats 〔deeds〕 of arms. ¶ ~을 세우다 achieve a great exploit; distinguish *oneself* 《in》. ◉ ~심 desire for fame: ~심에 불타다 be eager 〔thirsty〕 for fame.

**공명**(共鳴) 〖물리〗 resonance; 《반향》 an echo; 《공감》 sympathy. ~하다 《물체가》 be resonant 《with》; resonate; 《사람이》 sympathize 〔feel〕 《with》; respond 《to》; be in sympathy 《with》. ¶ ~을 일으키다 cause 〔produce, set up〕 resonance(s); 《사람의 마음에》 strike a sympathetic chord 《in》; arouse a response 《in *a person's* heart》 / 나는 그녀의 생각에 ~했다 I sympathized with her idea. ◉ ~관 a resonance tube. ~기 a resonator. ~자 a sympathizer. ~판(板) 《악기의》 a sound(-ing) board; a resonator.

**공명정대**(公明正大) fairness and justice; fair play. ～하다 (be) fair and just; fair and square; straight; open. ¶ ～하게 open and aboveboard; fair and square; openly / ～한 조치 《take》 impartial measures / ～한 심판 a fair and square judge / ～하게 하다 play fair / 그는 거래에서 언제나 ～하다 He is always「fair and upright 〔open and aboveboard〕 in his dealings.

**공모**(公募) an appeal for public subscription; public advertisement of a post. ～하다 《주식을》 offer shares for public subscription; 《기부를》 raise 《a fund》 by public subscription; 《사람을》 advertise for 《candidates for a post》. ¶ 현상 소설을 ～하다 invite the public to join in the prize contest for the best novel / 그는 신문에 비서를 ～했다 He advertised in the newspaper for a secretary.

**공모**(共謀) (a) conspiracy; collusion; a plot. ～하다 conspire 〔collude〕 《with》; 「plot together 〔join in a plot〕 《to *do*》. ¶ …와 ～하여 in conspiracy 〔collusion〕 with… / 그들은 내 재산을 횡령하기 위해 ～했다 They conspired together to usurp my property. ◉ ～자 a conspirator; an accomplice; a plotter.

**공무**(工務) engineering works. ◉ ～국 an engineering office; 《신문사 등의》 the printing bureau. ～소(所) an engineering firm 〔agency〕.

**공무**(公務) public 〔official〕 duties 〔business〕; government 〔official〕 affairs. ¶ ～로 인한 부상〔질병〕 an injury 〔a disease〕 incurred in the line of duty / ～에 다망하여 owing to the pressure of official business / ～로 여행하다〔출장가다〕 travel 〔be away〕 on official business / ～를 집행하다 execute *one's* official duties; exercise *one's* public duty / ～를 태만히 하다 neglect *one's* public duty / ～ 외 출입금지 《게시》 Official business only. ◉ ～재해보상 compensation for accidents in the line of duty. ～집행 execution of *one's* official duties: ～집행방해 interference with a government official in the exercise 〔performance〕 of his duties.

**공무원**(公務員) 《개인》 a public 〔civil〕 servant 〔official〕; a government employee; 《전체》 the public 〔civil〕 service (personnel) (★ 《미》에서는 public, 《영》에서 civil이 사용됨). ¶ 고급～ high-ranking public officials / 국가～ a government official / 지방～ a local (government) official / ～(사회)의 나태성 easy-goingness in officialdom / 복지부동하는 ～의 근무 자세 the lying-down-on-the-job attitudes of public servants / ～이 되다 enter into public service / ～으로 채용되다 be employed in government service. ◉ ～급여법 the Public Officials Pay Law. ～ 보수규정 Public Officials Remuneration Law. 기술〔기능〕직～ a public official in technical 〔skill〕 post. 국가〔지방〕～법 the National 〔Local〕 Public Service Law. 중앙～교육원 the Central Officials Training Institute.

**공문**(公文) 《문서》 =공문서; 《통신》 an official notice 〔correspondence, dispatch〕. ¶ ～으로 조회하다 make inquiries officially 〔in an official note〕. ◉ ～서식 formalities for official documents. ～전보 an official telegram.

**공문**(孔門) the Confucian school. ¶ ～의 십철(十哲) the ten leading disciples of Confucius.

**공문**(空文) a dead letter; a mere scrap of paper; a meaningless document. ¶ ～화하다 turn out to be a dead letter; end in a mere scrap of paper.

**공문서**(公文書) an official document 〔paper, note〕; 《보존된》 archives. ◉ ～위조 forgery of an official document: ～ 위조 및 사기 혐의로 구속되다 be arrested on charge of having forged public documents and committing fraud.

**공물**(供物) an offering; a votive offering. ¶ 부처님께 ～을 바치다 present 〔make〕 an offering to Buddha.

**공물**(貢物) a tribute; a tributary payment; an article of tribute. ¶ ～을 바치다 pay 〔offer〕 a tribute 《to》/ ～을 바치게 하다 impose tribute 《upon》.

**공미**(貢米) 〖고제도〗 rice offered as a tribute; rice paid as taxes.

**공민**(公民) a citizen; a member of the community. ¶ ～의 civic; civil / ～의 의무 civil 〔civic〕 duties. ◉ ～교육 civic education. ～권 citizenship; civil rights; the franchise: ～권을 부여〔박탈〕하다 enfranchise 〔disfranchise〕 《*a person*》. ～권 운동 a civil rights movement. ～도덕 civic virtues. ～생활 a civil life.

**공박**(攻駁) refutation; a charge; denunciation. ～하다 refute 《*a person's* argument》; argue against; charge 《at,

that》; denounce; denunciate.
**공밥**(空—) a free meal; meals *one* has not paid 〔worked〕 for. ¶ ~(을) 먹다 eat idle bread; [비유적] take *one's* reward without working for it.
**공방**(工房) a workshop.
**공방**(攻防) offense and defense. ◉ ~전 an offensive and defensive battle.
**공방**(空房) ① 《빈 방》 a vacant room; an unoccupied room. ② =공규(空閨).
**공배**(空排) 《바둑》 a blank. ¶ ~를 서로 메우다 fill blanks together.
**공배수**(公倍數) 〖수학〗 a common multiple. ◉ 최소~ the least common multiple (생략 L.C.M.).
**공백**(空白) 《인쇄물 등의》 a blank; blank space; marginal space; [비유적] a gap; a vacuum; a void. ¶ ~을 메우다 fill up 〔in〕 a blank / 정치적〔힘의〕 ~이 생기다 create 〔cause〕 a political 〔power〕 vacuum / 그의 외과의 경력에는 5 년간의 ~이 있다 There is a gap of five years in experience as a surgeon.
**공범**(共犯) ① 《행위》 complicity 《in a crime》. ② 《사람》 an accomplice; a confederate 《in a robbery》. ¶ ~으로 체포되다 be caught as a party to the crime / ~으로 기소되다 be accused of complicity 《in the case》 / 그는 그 범죄의 ~이다 He ｢has a hand 〔is a partner〕 in the crime. ◉ ~죄 complicity.
**공법**(工法) an engineering method; a method of construction. ¶ 실드 ~ the shield method.
**공법**(公法) public law. ◉ ~위반 breach of public law. ~인 a public judicial person; a public corporation. ~학 the study of public law: ~학자 a publicist.
**공병**(工兵) a military engineer; a sapper 《영》; [총칭] the (military) engineers. ◉ ~대 an engineer(ing) corps: 건설 ~대 a construction engineer corps. ~학교 the Engineering School.
**공보**(公報) an official report 〔dispatch, bulletin〕; an official gazette (관보). ¶ 선거 ~ an election bulletin. ◉ ~국 the Public Information Bureau. ~ 비서 《미》 a press secretary. ~실 the Information Office. 미국 ~원 the U.S. Information Service (생략 USIS).
**공복**(公僕) a public servant.
**공복**(空腹) hunger; an empty stomach. ¶ ~이다〔을 느끼다〕 be 〔feel〕 hungry / ~을 채우다 fill *one's* stomach; satisfy *one's* hunger / ~을 면하기 위해 쿠키를 먹다 eat cookies to stave off the pangs of hunger / ~으로는 일할 수 없다 cannot work on an empty stomach / ~에는 맛없는 것이 없다 Hunger is the best sauce.
**공부**(工夫) study; learning; work 《on *one's* studies》. ~하다 study; work at 〔on〕 《*one's* studies》; learn. ¶ 법률을 ~하다 study law / 시험 ~를 하다 study for an exam / ~를 잘〔잘 못〕 하다 be good 〔poor〕 at *one's* studies / ~를 게을리하다 neglect *one's* studies / ~를 너무해서 병이 나다 fall ill 〔sick〕 through overwork; work *oneself* ill 〔sick〕 / 영어를 열심히 ~하다 work hard at *one's* English; study English hard / 그녀는 시험 준비로 벼락 ~를 하고 있다 She's cramming for the examination. / 그는 매일 밤늦게까지 ~한다 He studies till late every night. / 그녀는 주립대학에서 ~하고 있다 She is studying at the state university. / 나는 대학에서 영문학을 ~했다 I majored in English literature at college. ◉ ~방 a study (room). ~벌레 a hard worker; a greasy grind; a grinder; 《미구어》 a dig. ~시간 *one's* study hours 〔time〕; 《수업시간》 class (time).
**공분**(公憤) public rage 〔resentment〕; 《의분》 righteous 〔moral〕 indignation. ¶ ~을 느끼다 be morally indignant at 〔over〕 《*a thing*》 / ~을 일으키다 raise public indignation 《over》 / 나는 그 정치인의 행태에 ~을 느꼈다 I was morally indignant at the politician's way of doing things.
**공비**(工費) = 공사비.
**공비**(公費) public expense 〔expenditure〕. ¶ ~로 at public expense / ~를 절감〔낭비〕하다 curtail 〔waste〕 public expenditure / 그녀는 ~로 해외 유학을 갔다 She went abroad for study at public expense.
**공비**(共匪) red 〔communist〕 guerrillas. ¶ 잔존 ~를 소탕하다 sweep 〔mop up〕 the remnants of red guerrillas.
**공사**(工事) construction 〔engineering〕 work; construction. ~하다 construct; do construction work 《on》. ¶ ~를 시작하다 start 〔begin〕 (construction) work / ~중이다 be under 〔in course of〕 construction / ~를 감독하다 supervise 〔direct〕 (construction) work / 이 공사는 완성에 약 5년이 걸렸다 It took about five years to complete the work. / ~중—접근 금지 《게시》 Keep out: Under construction. / 전방에 ~중 《게시》 Construction Ahead.

◉ ～감독 a superintendent 〔an overseer〕 of the construction site. ～비 the cost of construction. ～사무소 a construction work office; a site office. ～입찰 a bid for construction work. ～현장 a construction site. 부정～ faulty work.

**공사**(公私) public and private affairs 〔matters〕; official and personal affairs. ¶ ～의 public 〔official〕 and private / ～를 구별하다 make a proper distinction between the public and private domain; keep *one's* private and public life separate / ～를 혼동하다〔분명히 하다〕 mix up 〔draw the line between〕 public and private matters / ～간으로 많은 도움을 주셔서 정말로 고맙습니다 I have to express my deepest gratitude to your help, both in my public and my private life.

**공사**(公事) public business; public 〔official〕 affairs 〔duties〕. ¶ ～다망하여 owing to the pressure of *one's* official duties.

**공사**(公使) a (diplomatic) minister. ¶ 주한 프랑스 ～ the French Minister to Korea / 멕시코 주재 한국 ～로 근무하다 hold the post of the Korean Minister to 〔in〕 Mexico. ◉ ～관 a legation: ～관원 a legation *attaché;* (a member of) the legation staff / ～관 무관 a military 〔naval〕 *attaché* to a legation.

**공사**(公社) a public corporation.

**공사채**(公社債) bonds; public bonds and corporate debentures. ◉ ～시장 the bond market. ～투자신탁 an open=end bond investment trust.

**공산**(公算) probability; likelihood. ¶ …할 ～이 크다 There is 「a strong probability 〔every likelihood〕 that…. *or* The chances are that…. / 그는 대통령으로 선출될 ～이 크다 There is every probability that he will be elected President. ◉ ～오차 a probable error. ～인수 a probability factor.

**공산**(共產) common property; community of property. ◉ ～군 the Communist army 〔force〕. ～권 the Communist bloc. ～분자 a Communist fraction: 골수 ～분자 a hardcore Communist element. ～제 a communistic system. ～진영 the Communist camp. ～측 the Communist side. 비적성 ～국가 a nonhostile Communist country.

**공산당**(共產黨) the Communist Party; the Communists. ◉ ～기관지 a communist paper. ～비밀당원 a crypto=Communist. ～선언 the Communist Manifesto. ～세포 a communist cell. ～원 a Communist; a commie.

**공산명월**(空山明月) ① 《달》 the moon shining on a lone mountain. ② 《대머리》 a bald head.

**공산주의**(共產主義) communism. ¶ ～의〔적인〕 communist(ic) / ～에 물든 pink tinted / ～에 물든 사람 a pink.

◉ ～국가 a communist country 〔nation〕. ～사회 a communist community. ～운동 a communist(ic) drive; a drive for the spread of communism. ～자 a communist; commies《미구어》.

**공산품**(工產品) industrial products.

**공산화**(共產化) communization. ～하다 《남을》 communize; 《자기가》 become 〔turn〕 communist(ic). ¶ ～를 막다 defend 〔safeguard〕 《a country》 against Communists / 그 나라가 ～된 이래 since the Communist take over the country / 무력으로 ～하려고 하다 try to communize 《the region》 by force.

**공상**(工商) 《공업과 상업》 industry and commerce; 《계층》 the classes of artisans and merchants.

**공상**(公傷) an injury sustained 〔incurred〕 while 「on duty 〔at work〕; injury resulting from official work.

**공상**(空想) a 〔an idle〕 fancy; a daydream; (a) fantasy; a vision; imagination. ～하다 fancy; daydream; imagine. ¶ ～적(인) fanciful; imaginary; visionary / ～에 잠기다 be lost in (a) reverie 〔daydreaming〕; indulge in idle fancies / ～과 현실을 구별 못하다 confuse the imaginery with the real / 그것은 단지 네 ～에 불과하다 That is only your fancy. / 아이들은 ～의 세계를 좋아한다 Children like a fantasy world. / 나는 유명한 야구 선수가 되는 것을 ～해 보았다 I tried to imagine myself as a famous baseball player.

◉ ～가 a daydreamer; a visionary; a Utopian. ～과학소설 science fiction (생략 S.F.): ～ 과학소설가 a science fictionist. ～ 과학영화 a science fiction film. ～(적)사회주의 Utopian socialism.

**공생**(共生) 『생물』 commensalism; symbiosis. ～하다 live together 〔symbiotically〕. ◉ ～관계 a symbiotic relationship. ～ 동물〔식물〕 a commensal.

**공서양속**(公序良俗) (good) public order and customs 〔morals〕.

**공석**(公席) 《공적인 좌석》 the presence of the public; 《공무를 보는》 a place where public affairs are attended to.

**공석**(空席)《빈 좌석》a vacant [an unoccupied] seat;《결원된 자리》a vacant post; an opening; a vacancy. ¶ ~을 채우다 fill a vacancy / ~으로 있다 remain vacant / 그의 사임으로 그 자리는 ~이 되었다 His resignation left a vacancy.

**공선**(公選)《공중 선거》a public election; an election by popular vote;《공명 선거》a fair election. ~하다 elect by popular [open] vote; freely elect. ◉ ~ 의원 an elective member. ~ 지사(知事) a publicly-elected prefectural governor.

**공설**(公設) public installation. ¶ ~의 public;《시립의》municipal. ◉ ~기관 a public institution. ~시장 a municipal [public] market. ~운동장 a public stadium.

**공성**(攻城) a siege. ~하다 siege; besiege.

**공세**(攻勢) the offensive; the aggressive. ¶ ~적인 offensive; aggressive / ~로 나오다[를 취하다] take [assume] the offensive《against》/ ~로 전환하다 change [switch] to the offensive / ~를 강화하다 step up the offensive / 질문 ~를 받다 be pestered [persecuted] with questions; face a barrage of questions. ◉ 테러~ an upsurge of terrorism.

**공소**(公訴) arraignment; prosecution; accusation; public action; a criminal action. ~하다 arraign; prosecute; accuse. ¶ ~를 제기하다 institute a public action; prosecute a case / ~를 기각[철회]하다 dismiss [withdraw] a public action. ◉ ~권 the right of arraignment. ~사실 a charge. ~유지 institution and support of a public action; maintenance of a public action. ~장 a written arraignment.

**공손**(恭遜) politeness; civility; courteousness. ~하다 (be) polite; civil; courteous. ¶ ~한 태도 a reverent [respectful, polite] attitude / ~히 politely; civilly; courteously; with respect [reverence]; respectfully / ~히 대하다 treat《*a person*》with respect [civility] / ~히 절하다 bow [salute] politely / ~히 말하다 speak politely.

**공수** 〖민속〗a message from the dead delivered by a shaman. ¶ ~받다 get a message from the dead through a shaman / ~주다 bring [give] a message from the dead.

**공수**(空手) ⇨빈손. ¶ ~래 공수거《사람이》come into this world with empty hands and go to the other with empty hands also; the vanity of life.

**공수**(空輸) air transport(ation); transportation by air; an airlift; air delivery. ~하다 carry [transport]《*a thing*》by air [plane]; fly《goods to remote town》; airlift《troops》. ¶ 대규모~ an airlift on a large scale; a massive airlift / ~ 가능의 airtransportable / 그들은 눈으로 고립된 마을에 구호 물자를 ~했다 They airlifted relief goods to the town isolated by snow.
◉ ~기동사단 an air mobile division. ~부대 airborne troops; an airborne unit [corps];《수송부대》an air transport corps (생략 A.T.C.). ~사단 an airborne division《미》. ~작전 airlift operations. ~화물 airfreight.

**공수**(攻守) offense and defense; 〖야구〗 batting and fielding. ¶ 그 팀은 ~가 다 강하다 The team is powerful both in batting and fielding. ◉ ~동맹 an offensive and defensive alliance.

**공수병**(恐水病) 〖의학〗 hydrophobia; rabies. ⇨광견병.

**공수표**(空手票) a fictitious [bad] bill; a bouncing check [cheque]; a kite《속어》; a bad check; [비유적] an empty promise. ¶ ~를 떼다 issue [draw] a fictitious bill [note]; write a bad check; fly a kite; [비유적] give [make] an empty [a hollow] promise / ~로 끝나다 end in an empty pledge.

**공수하다**(拱手—) cross *one's* hands in respect.

**공순**(恭順) obedience; submission. ~하다 (be) submissive; gentle; meek.

**공술**(空—) free liquor; a free drink. ¶ ~먹고 취하다 get drunk on《*a person's*》liquor.

**공술**(供述) testimony. ⇨진술.

**공습**(空襲) an air raid [attack]; an airstrike. ~하다 make an air raid《on》; attack《a city》from the air; carry out an air strike《against》. ¶ ~받다 undergo [suffer] an air raid / ~으로 집이 불타 없어지다 be burnt out in an air raid; be bombed out.
◉~경보 an air-raid alarm [warning]; a red alert (★ a yellow alert (경계경보)에 상대되는): ~경보 사이렌 an air-raid siren / ~경보를 발하다 issue [put out, sound] an air-raid warning / ~경보를 해제하다 sound the "all clear".

**공시**(公示) (a) public announcement; an official [a public] notice. ~하다

publish; announce publicly; make 《*something*》 known to the public. ¶ 총선거 투표일이 ~되었다 The voting day for the general election was announced publicly. ◉ ~가격 the publicly assessed value 《of land》. ~사항 (government) notices. ~송달 conveyance by public announcement. ~최고(催告) a public summons.

**공식**(公式) ① 〖수학〗 a formula (*pl.* ~s, -lae). ② 《정식》 formality; an official ceremony. ¶ ~의 state; formal; official / ~으로 formally; officially / ~적인 사고방식 a stereotyped way of thinking / ~적인 환대를 받다 be officially feted 《by》 / 그것은 아직 ~적으로 발표되어 있지 않다 It has not been officially announced yet / 그것은 ~대로 행해질 수가 없다 That cannot be done out of a textbook.

◉ ~경기 a regular game 〔match〕: 비~ 경기 an exhibition game. ~기록 an official record. ~대표단 an official delegation. ~반응 an official response: ~반응을 보이다 show an official response 《to》. ~발표〔성명〕 an official announcement 〔statement〕. ~방문 a formal 〔an official〕 visit; 《국가 원수의》 a state visit: ~방문을 하다 pay a formal 〔an official〕 visit 《to》. ~사과 an official apology. ~접촉 a formal contact. ~주의 formalism. ~통보 a formal notification. ~회합 an official meeting.

**공신**(公信) public confidence 〔trust〕. ◉ ~력 public trust 《in banking institutions》: 은행의 ~력 the credit-worthiness of banks / ~력을 잃다 lose public confidence.

**공신**(功臣) a meritorious retainer; a vassal of merit. ¶ ~을 포상하다 reward deserving retainers.

**공안**(公安) public peace (and order); public security 〔safety〕. ¶ 철도 ~원 a security officer on the train / ~을 유지하다〔해치다〕 keep 〔disturb〕 public peace and order. ◉ ~경찰 a public peace police; a security police. ~사범 a public safety 〔security〕 offender. ~통치 security rule.

**공안**(公案) ① 《공문의》 the drafting of a public document. ② 《여론의》 a bill drafted in accordance with public opinion. ③ 〖불교〗 a catechism.

**공알** 《음핵》 the clitoris.

**공약**(公約) a public promise 〔pledge, commitment〕. ~하다 commit 〔pledge〕 *oneself* (publicly); make a public commitment. ¶ 정당의 ~ the public commitment of a party / ~을 지키다 〔어기다〕 keep 〔break〕 the public promises 〔pledges〕 / 선거 ~처럼 믿을 수 없는 것은 없다 Election promises always prove to be a gross deception.

**공약**(空約) an empty 〔irresponsible〕 promise; pie in the sky 《구어》.

**공약수**(公約數) a common measure 〔divisor〕. ¶ 최대~ the greatest common divisor (생략 G.C.D.); the highest common factor (생략 H.C.F.).

**공양**(供養) ① 《대접》 providing 《*one's* elders》 with food. ~하다 provide 《*one's* elders》 with food. ② 〖불교〗 an offering; service of food to Buddha. ~하다 offer food to Buddha. ③ 《스님의 식사》 having 〔taking〕 a meal. ~하다 eat a meal. ◉ ~미 rice offered to Buddha. ~주(主) a person who gives alms to a Buddhist temple.

**공언**(公言) declaration; profession. ~하다 declare openly 〔in public〕; tell the world 《미》; profess. ¶ …라고 서슴없이 ~하다 have no hesitation in 「declaring 〔stating〕 that… / 그는 자기가 휴머니스트라고 ~했다 He professed himself to be a humanist. / 나는 …라고 ~할 수 있다 I can publicly declare that….

**공얻다**(空—) get 《*a thing*》 「for nothing 〔as a gift〕.

**공업**(工業) (an) industry; the manufacturing industry. ¶ ~의 industrial; manufacturing / ~용의 for industrial use 〔purposes〕; industrial / ~적으로 industrially / 가내~ home 〔domestic〕 industry / 수~ handicraft / ~의 발달 development of industry; industrial development / ~ 기술 industrial technology / ~의 중심지 a manufacturing 〔an industrial〕 center / ~을 진흥시키다 promote the industries / ~의 발전을 촉진하다 spur 《the countrys》 industrial growth / 스위스 경제는 정밀~과 관광에 의존한다 Switzerland's economy relies on precision machinery industries and tourism.

◉ ~계 industrial circles; the industrial world. ~고등학교 a technical high school. ~교육 technical education. ~국 an industrial nation 〔country〕: 선진 ~국 advanced industrial nations; industrially-advanced nations. ~규격 ⇨ 산업규격. ~기술 지원센터 the Industrial Technology Services Center. ~단지 an industrial complex:

임해(臨海) ~단지 a coastal industrial complex. ~도시 an industrial 〔a manufacturing, a factory〕 city 〔town〕. ~디자이너 an industrial designer. ~력 industrial potential. ~분석 technical analysis. ~생산 industrial production: ~생산고 《Korea's》 industrial output. ~소유권 industrial property. ⇨지적재산권. ~시험소 an industrial laboratory 〔experimental station〕. ~약품 industrial chemicals. ~용수 water for industrial use: ~용수 문제 the water problem for industrial use. ~용지 an industrial site. ~원자재 industrial raw materials. ~의장 an industrial design. ~정책 industrial policy. ~제품 industrial goods 〔products〕. ~지대 an industrial area; a manufacturing district. ~폐수 industrial waste water. ~화학 industrial chemistry; technochemistry.

**공업화**(工業化) industrialization. ~하다 industrialize 《a country》; manufacture 《goods》 on a commercial basis 〔scale〕. ¶ 아직 ~되지 않은 지역 a non-industrialized area / 그 나라는 급속히 ~되고 있다 The country is becoming rapidly industrialized.

**공여**(供與) 《공급》 provision. ~하다 provide; give; grant; make a grant 《of》. ¶ 기술 ~ the provision of technology / 무기를 ~하다 provide weapons 《for》 / 차관을 ~하다 give 〔grant〕 《*a person*》 a loan 《of 10 billion won》; extend credit to 《a firm》.

**공역**(公役) public service. ¶ ~에 복무하다 join 〔enter〕 public service / ~을 기피하다 evade 〔shirk〕 public service.

**공역**(共譯) (a) joint translation. ~하다 translate 《a book from the English into Korean》 jointly 〔in collaboration〕 《with》. ¶ A씨와 B씨가 ~한 소설 a novel translated jointly by Messrs. A and B / 네 사람의 전문가에 의해 ~되다 be translated jointly by four specialities. ◉ ~자 joint translators.

**공연**(公演) a public performance. ~하다 perform publicly; present 〔give, stage〕 《a play》; put 《a play》 on (the stage). ¶ 첫~ a first public performance / 위문 ~ a consolatory performance / 정기 ~ the regularly scheduled performance / ~중인 연극 햄릿 "Hamlet" on the stage / 그 연극은 30일간 계속 ~되었다 The play had a run of thirty days. *or* The play has had a thirty-day run. ◉ 한국 ~ 예술 진흥 협의회 the Korea Council for Performing Arts Promotion.

**공연**(共演) coacting; costarring. ~하다 costar 《with》; play 〔feature〕 together 《in a film》. ¶ A양과 B씨 ~의 영화 a film 「costarring 〔jointly featuring〕 by Miss A and Mr. B. ◉ ~자 a co-star; a coactor; 《동료들》 fellow members of the cast.

**공연스레**(空然—) in vain; vainly; to no avail; to no purpose 〔end〕; fruitlessly; idly; without reason. ¶ ~ 애쓰다 struggle in vain 〔for nothing〕 / ~ 울다 cry for no reason (at all).

**공연하다**(空然—) (be) vain; fruitless; futile; unavailing; ineffectual; empty; useless; serve no purpose. ¶ 공연한 일 a vain attempt; a futile thing; a futility; a trifle / 공연한 노력 a fruitless effort / 공연히 소란을 피우다 make a great fuss about nothing; make much ado about nothing; have a storm in a teacup / 공연한 참견 마라 Thank you for nothing.

**공염불**(空念佛) a fair but empty phrase. ¶ ~을 하다 chant empty prayers / ~에 그치다 end in 〔prove to be〕 nothing but empty talk / 시장의 행정 개혁 약속은 ~로 그칠 것 같다 I'm afraid the Mayor's promise to carry out the administration reforms will prove to be nothing but empty talk.

**공영**(公營) public management. ~하다 place 〔bring〕 《an undertaking》 under public management. ¶ ~의 public; national (국가의); municipal (지방공공단체의). ◉ ~기업 《국가의》 a government enterprise; 《지방자치체의》 a municipal enterprise; 《전체》 a public enterprise. ~주택 a public 〔municipal〕 housing [총칭]; 《개개의》 an unit of public housing.

**공영**(共榮) mutual prosperity; co-prosperity.

**공영**(共營) joint management 〔operation〕. ¶ ~화 collectivization / ~화하다 collectivize.

**공예**(工藝) industrial arts; (artistic) handicraft(s). ¶ 전통~ a traditional craft / 미술~ arts and crafts. ◉ ~가 a craftsman. ~기술 craft skills; craftsmanship. ~미술 applied fine arts. ~품 craftwork [집합적]; a craft item 〔object, product〕; an art work: ~품점 a handicraft shop.

**공용**(公用) 《일》 official 〔government〕 business; an official duty 〔mission〕;

《공공용》《for》 public use. ¶ 그는 ～으로 해외에 나갔다 He went abroad on official business. ◉ ～물 objects for public use. ～어 an official language. ～지 land for public use. ～차 《회사》 a company car; 《관공서》 an official vehicle.

**공용**(共用) common use. ～하다 use 《*something*》 in common; share 《the bathroom》 with *a person*. ¶ ～의 for common use / 이 수도전은 ～이다 This tap 〔water faucet〕 is for common use. / 나는 그녀와 이 방을 ～한다 I use this room in common with her. ◉ ～물 public property. ～화기(火器) a crew-served weapon.

**공원**(工員) a (factory) worker 〔hand〕; a machine operator; an operative.

**공원**(公園) a park; a public garden; 《시가지의 작은 공원》 a square 《영》. ¶ 사직～ Sajik Park (★ 공원 이름에는 보통 정관사가 붙지 않음) / 자연～ a natural 〔wilderness〕 park / 국립～ a national park / ～을 만들다 lay out a park; provide a park 《for a city》 / ～으로 산책 가자 Let's go for a walk in the park. ◉ ～구역 a park district 〔area〕. ～묘지 a park cemetery.

**공위**(空位) ① 《빈》 a vacant post; a vacancy; an opening. ② 《이름뿐인》 a nominal position; a position in name only.

**공유**(公有) public ownership. ¶ ～의 public; public(ly)-owned. ◉ ～재산 public assets 〔property〕. ～지 public (=owned) land.

**공유**(共有) joint 〔common〕 ownership. ～하다 own 《*a thing*》 jointly; hold 《*a thing*》 in common. ¶ ～의 common; joint / 자연은 인류의 ～재산이므로 소중히 보전해야 한다 We must take care of nature, for it is the common property of all mankind. ◉ ～결합 〖화학〗 a covalent bond. ～자 a joint owner; a co-owner. ～재산 common property; property in co=ownership. ～지 the common (land).

**공으로**(空―) for nothing; free (of charge); gratis; gratuitously. ¶ ～ 얻다 get for nothing; get free of charge / ～ 일하다 work for nothing / ～ 표를 입수하다 obtain a ticket gratis.

**공의**(公醫) a community doctor.

**공이** a pounder; a pestle; firing pin (총의). ◉ ～치기 a hammer (of a rifle); the cock.

**공익**(公益) the public good 〔benefit, interest(s)〕; common good 〔weal〕. ¶ ～을 위하여 in the interest 〔cause〕 of the public; for public good / ～을 도모하다 「work for 〔promote〕 the public good; serve for the common good / ～을 해치다 be prejudicial 〔detrimental〕 to the public interest; be injurious to the public good 〔welfare〕 / ～을 위해 힘쓰다 take an active part in the cause of the community. ◉ ～단체 a public corporation. ～대표 representatives of public interests; public welfare delegates. ～법인 a non-profit 〔public-service〕 corporation; a juridical person for the public benefit 〔welfare〕: ～ 사단 법인 a public utility association. ～사업 an enterprise for the public good; public utilities 〔works〕: ～사업 회사〔단체〕 a public utility 〔service〕 corporation. ～우선 The public interest 「must come first 〔must take priority〕. ～재단 a public utility foundation.

**공익**(共益) common benefit 〔interest, profit〕. ◉ ～비용 〖법〗 expenses for common profit.

**공인**(公人) a public person 〔figure〕. ¶ ～으로서의 생활 *one's* public life / ～으로서 발언하다 express *one's* opinion in *one's* official capacity.

**공인**(公認) official recognition 〔approval〕; authorization; certification. ～하다 recognize 〔approve〕 officially; authorize; 《법률로》 legalize. ¶ ～의 authorized; official / ～을 받다 gain official approval / 이 기록은 아직 ～되지 않았다 This record has not yet been officially recognized. ◉ ～(세계)기록 an official (world) record: 비～기록 an unofficial record. ～중개사 a licensed real estate agent. ～회계사 《미》 a certified public accountant (생략 CPA, C.P.A.); 《영》 a chartered accountant. ～후보(자) a nominated 〔a recognized, an authorized〕 candidate.

**공인수**(公因數) 〖수학〗 a common 「factor.

**공일**(空―) 《공짜일》 free service; work for nothing; a job in vain.

**공일날**(空日―) 《일요일》 Sunday.

**공임**(工賃) wages; cost of labor; pay. ¶ ～을 올리다 raise 〔increase〕 wages / ～을 줄이다 reduce 〔cut down〕 the cost of labor.

**공자**(孔子) 《중국의》 Confucius (552-479 B.C.). ¶ ～의 Confucian / ～의 가르침 Confucianism; the teachings of Confucius.

**공자**(公子) a little 〔young〕 prince; a young nobleman.

**공작**(工作) ① 《제작》 construction; engineering work; 《수공》 handicraft. ~하다 construct; make; manufacture. ¶ ~ 시간에 책꽂이를 만들다 make a bookshelf in the handicraft hour. ② 《책동》 maneuvering; a move; activities; operations. ~하다 maneuver; scheme. ¶ 정치 ~ political maneuvering / 지하 ~ underground activities / 뒤에서 ~하다 maneuver 〔pull the wires〕 behind the scenes / (…의) 준비 ~을 하다 prepare the ground in advance 《for》; pave the way 《for》 / 평화 ~을 하다 make a peace move. ◉ ~금 operational funds. ~기계 a machine tool. ~대(臺) a worktable. ~물 《구조물》 a structure. ~선(船) 《수리·가공용의》 a factory 〔repair〕 ship. ~실 a workshop. ~원 an espionage operator; an agent: 북한 ~원 a north Korean agent. ~품 handicraft.

**공작**(孔雀) 〖조류〗 a peacock (수컷); a peahen (암컷); a peafowl. ◉ ~고사리 〖식물〗 a maidenhair fern. ~석 〖광물〗 malachite.

**공작**(公爵) a duke; a prince (영국 이외). ¶ 웰링턴 ~ the Duke of Wellington / 비스마르크 ~ Prince Bismarck / ~을 제수받다 be created prince. ◉ ~부인 a duchess; a princess.

**공장**(工匠) 《장인》 an artisan; a handicraftsman.

**공장**(工場) a factory; a plant; a mill; a workshop; a works.

> 용법 **factory** 물건을 생산·가공하는 공장에 대한 일반적인 호칭. **(work)shop** 특히 수리공장: 자동차 수리~ an auto (repair) shop. **plant** 대규모 시설을 갖춘 공장: 자동차~ an automobile assembly plant / 석유화학~ a petrochemical plant. **mill** 특히 제분·제지·제철·방적 관계 등의 공장: 제분~ a flour mill / 제지~ a paper mill / 제철~ a steel mill. **works** 가스 공장 등 특정 생산 공정을 갖춘 공장: 가스~ gasworks / 유리~ glassworks.

¶ ~에서 일하다 work in a factory / ~을 폐쇄하다 close down a factory 《미》; 《파업으로》 lock out / 그는 자동차 수리 ~을 경영하고 있다 He runs an auto (repair) shop.
◉ ~경영 〔관리〕 factory management. ~근로자 a factory worker 〔hand〕. ~도(渡) 〖상업〗 ex factory 〔works, mill, plant〕; free at factory: ~도 가격 the factory 〔ex-works〕 price. ~설비 plant and equipment. ~용지 a factory site. ~위생 factory sanitation 〔hygiene〕. ~주〔장〕 a factory owner 〔manager, superintendent〕. ~지대 a factory district; an industrial area. ~폐기물 industrial 〔factory〕 waste; industrial effluent (액체의). ~폐쇄 closure of a factory (불경기로); a lockout (노동쟁의로). ~폐수 industrial sewage 〔waste water〕: ~ 폐수 처리 장치 a waste water disposal plant.

**공저**(共著) 《책》 a joint (literary) work; 《일》 collaboration; joint authorship. ~하다 coauthor; collaborate 《on》. ¶ …와 ~로 《write a book》 in collaboration with 《Mr. Han》; under joint authorship of 《Mr. Han》. ◉ ~자 a coauthor; a joint author; a collaborator.

**공적**(公的) (being) public; official. ¶ ~ 지위 a public position / ~으로 publicly; officially / ~ 성격을 띠고 있다 be of 〔have〕 a public character / ~으로 책임을 지다 answer publicly 《for》; be held publicly responsible 《for》 / ~ 융자를 받다 get an official loan / ~ 장소에서는 말을 삼가야 한다 You should be careful of what you say on a public occasion. / ~ 입장과 사적 입장을 구별할 줄 알아야 한다 You must make a clear distinction between your public and private roles. ◉ ~생애 a public career. ~생활 public life.

**공적**(公敵) a public 〔common〕 enemy. ¶ 인류의 ~ an enemy of mankind.

**공적**(功績) an achievement; a meritorious deed; distinguished service; credit (영예). ¶ ~ 있는 사람 a man of merit / 과학상의 ~ scientific achievements / ~을 세우다 render distinguished services 《to the country》 / 자기의 ~이라고 주장하다 claim (the) credit 《for》 / … 의 ~이다 the credit goes to 《*a person*》 / 그녀의 ~은 학계에서 인정받았다 Her achievements were recognized among the academic world. / 그는 한국 경제 회복에 큰 ~을 세웠다 He 「made a great contribution 〔rendered distinguished services〕 to the recovery of Korea's economy.

**공전**(工錢) wages; pay.

**공전**(公轉) 〖천문〗 revolution 《of the earth around the sun》. ~하다 revolve; move 〔go〕 around 《the sun》.

¶ 지구의 ~과 자전 the earth's revolution and rotation / 지구는 1년에 한 번 태양의 주위를 ~한다 The earth goes round the sun in a year. ◉ ~속도〔주기〕 an orbital speed 〔period〕.

**공전**(空前) unprecedentedness. ¶ ~의 unprecedented; unexampled; unheard-of; unparalleled; epochal; epoch-making; record-breaking / 모임은 ~의 성황을 이루었다 The meeting was an unprecedented success.
◉ ~절후(絶後): ~절후의 the first and probably the last… / ~절후의 명화 the greatest film of all time / 그것은 ~절후의 장거였다 It is the first and probably the last brilliant achievement.

**공전**(空電) 〖통신〗 static; atmospherics; strays. ◉ ~장애 atmospheric disturbance. ~ 제거장치 a static eliminator.

**공전**(空轉) ① 《바퀴의》 skidding; 《엔진의》 racing. ~하다 《바퀴가》 skid; 《기계가》 race; run idle. ② 《일 따위의》 ~하다 《의론 따위가》 argue in a circle; 《회의가》 stall; be at a deadlock. ¶ 토론이 ~하다 the argument goes round and round and gets nowhere / 국회는 개회 첫날부터 ~을 거듭하고 있다 The National Assembly has remained idle since the first day of the session.

**공전식**(共電式) 〖전기〗 the common-battery system. ◉ ~ 교환기〔전화기〕 a common-battery switchboard 〔telephone set〕.

**공정**(工程) 《일의 진행》 the progress 〔stage〕 of work; 《과정》 a (manufacturing) process. ¶ 여러 ~을 거치다 go through various processes / ~을 단축하다 reduce 〔shorten〕 the length of the process / ~은 약 80%에 달했다 The work is about 80 percent finished. ◉ ~관리 process 〔production〕 control. ~표 a progress 〔work〕 schedule; a time schedule of works.

**공정**(公正) justice; fairness; equity; impartiality (공평). ~하다 (be) fair; just; equitable; impartial. ¶ ~한 fair; fair-minded; impartial; just; righteous / ~한 거래 fair trade 〔transactions〕/ ~한 조처 a fair and impartial measure; a fair 〔square〕 deal / ~을 기하기 위해 in order to do (full) justice 《to》; to ensure fairness 《in》/ ~하게 처신하다 act fairly 《toward》/ 심판은 ~한 판단을 내렸다 The referee made a fair and impartial judgment. / 거래는 ~하게 행해졌다 The transaction went on fairly.
◉ ~가격 a fair price. ~거래 square 〔fair〕 deal 〔transactions〕: ~거래법 Fair Trade law 〔Act〕/ ~거래위원회 the Fair Trade Commission. ~증서 a notarial deed; an attested 〔an authentic, a public〕 document.

**공정**(公定) public decision; official fixing. ~하다 decide publicly; fix 《a price》 officially. ¶ ~의 official; officially fixed; legal.
◉ ~가(격) an official 〔authorized〕 price; an officially fixed price: ~가격으로 팔다〔사다〕 sell 〔buy〕 《articles》 at established 〔official〕 prices. ~이율 an official 〔a legitimate〕 rate of interest. ~할인율 an official rate of discount. ~환율 an official exchange rate.

**공정(부)대**(空挺(部)隊) air-borne troops; paratroops.

**공제**(共濟) mutual aid 〔benefit〕. ◉ ~사업 a mutual-aid project. ~조합 a mutual-aid association; a (mutual) benefit society; a friendly society.

**공제**(控除) deduction; subtraction. ~하다 subtract; take off 〔away〕; deduct 《from》. ¶ 기초 ~ basic deduction / 부양가족 ~ deduction for dependents / 세금·경비를 ~한 순수입 a net income; take-home pay 《미》/ 봉급에서 ~하다 take 《a sum》 off *one's* pay; deduct 《a sum》 from *one's* salary / 세금에서 보험료 ~를 신청하다 apply for an insurance premium tax exemption / 필요 경비로 30%를 인세에서 ~하다 deduct 30 percent from royalties as necessary expenses. ◉ ~액 an amount deducted; a subtracted amount.

**공조**(共助) mutual assistance; cooperation. ~하다 mutually assist; cooperate. ◉ ~체제 a mutual-assistance system 〔structure〕.

**공존**(共存) coexistence. ~하다 coexist; exist together; live and let live. ¶ 평화 ~ peaceful coexistence. ◉ ~공영 coexistence and co-prosperity; mutual prosperity in coexistence: 모든 이웃 나라와 ~공영을 실현하자는 것이 우리의 이상이다 It is our ideal to realize the coexistence with all our neighboring nations in mutual prosperity.

**공주**(公主) a (royal) princess.

**공중**(公衆) the general public; the public (at large); 《일반 대중》 masses. ¶ ~의 public; communal / ~ 앞에서 in public / ~을 위하여 for the benefit

〔interest(s), welfare〕 of the public / ～ 앞에서 연설하다 speak in public / 관계 당국은 일반 ～의 편리를 도모해야 한다 The authorities concerned should consider the convenience of the public at large.

◉ ～도덕 public morality 〔morals〕: ～도덕을 지키다 observe public morals / ～도덕을 중하게 여기다 pay respect to 〔make much of〕 public morality. ～목욕탕 a public bath 〔bathhouse〕. ～변소 a public lavatory; a comfort room 〔station〕《미》. ～보건의 a public health doctor. ～위생 public hygiene 〔health〕; public sanitation. ～전화 a public 〔pay〕 telephone; 《미》 a telephone booth (공중전화 박스).

**공중**(空中) the air; the sky; midair. ¶ ～의 aerial; air / ～에(서) in the air 〔sky〕; in midair / ～을 날다 fly in 〔through〕 the air / ～으로 사라지다 disappear into the air 〔sky〕/ ～ 높이 떠오르다 soar up to the sky; soar skyward.

◉ ～감시 (an) air surveillance; aerial inspection. ～곡예 《서커스의》 an aerialist act; an aerial stunt performance; 《곡예 비행》 aerobatics; aerial acrobatics; stunt flying: ～ 곡예사 an aerialist; an aerial acrobat 〔stunt performer〕. ～관측 aerial observation. ～광고 advertising by airplane; a sky sign (빌딩 옥상의). ～급유 refueling in the air; air-to-air refueling. ～ 기동훈련 the air maneuvers. ～방전 atmospheric discharge. ～ 발사 순항 미사일 air-launched cruise missile (생략 ALCM). ～ 발사 탄도미사일 air-launched ballistic missile (생략 ALBM). ～보급 an airlift: ～보급 물자 an airdrop. ～부유 미생물 aeroplankton. ～사진 an air photo; an aerial photograph: ～사진 측량 aerial photogrammetry. ～사찰 an aerial 「investigation 〔inspection〕. ～살포 《농약의》 crop spraying 〔dusting〕 (★ 농약 공중 살포비행기는 a crop duster). ～쇼 an aerial pageant 〔show〕. ～어뢰 《discharge》 an aerial torpedo. ～엄호 an air cover 〔umbrella〕. ～ 정보 통신망 public switched data network. ～정찰 air 〔aerial〕 reconnaissance. ～조기 경계 an airborne early warning. ～충돌 a midair 〔an in-flight〕 collision. ～케이블 an aerial ropeway 〔cableway〕. ～투하 airdrop. ～폭발 explosion in midair. ～활주 gliding; volplane: ～활주하다 (vol)plane; glide (in the air).

**공중납치**(空中拉致) hijacking of an airplane; sky-jacking. ～하다 hijack a (passenger) plane. ◉ ～범 a hijacker.

**공중누각**(空中樓閣) a castle in the air; an air castle. ¶ ～을 그리다〔짓다〕 build castles in the air; build air castles / ～을 그리는 사람 a daydreamer; a visionary.

**공중분해**(空中分解) disintegration in the air. ～하다 disintegrate in midair; break up into pieces in the air. ¶ 로켓은 발사 직후 ～됐다 The rocket broke up into pieces in the air immediately after it was launched (from the pad). / 새로운 기획은 계획 단계에서 ～되었다 [비유적] The new project was aborted in the planning stage.

**공중수송**(空中輸送) air service; air transportation; airlift. ～하다 carry by air 〔airplanes〕; fly 《goods》. ◉ ～부대 an air transportation unit 〔corps〕. ～작전 『군사』 an airlift operation 《미》. ～화물 air cargo; airlift (goods).

**공중전**(空中戰) an air battle; an airfight; an aerial combat 〔dogfight〕. ¶ 1대 1의 ～ (a) plane-to-plane combat; an air duel / 대 ～을 펼치다 stage 〔present, wage〕 a big air battle.

**공중제비**(空中―) a somersault; a handspring; 《비행기의》 a loop-the-loop. ～하다 turn 〔throw, make〕 a somersault; 《비행기가》 loop the loop. ¶ 멋지게 앞〔뒤〕～를 하다 turn a beautiful forward 〔backward〕 somersault / 비행기가 2번 ～했다 The airplane made two loops in the air.

**공증**(公證) a notarial act; official endorsement; authentication. ～하다 notarize; authenticate; attest.

◉ ～료 a notary fee. ～인 a notary (public): ～인 사무소 a notary's office / ～인의 인증을 받다 be tested by a notary public.

**공지**(公知) common 〔universal〕 knowledge. ¶ ～의 known to all 〔everybody〕; universally 〔widely, well〕 known / ～ 사항 the (items of ) official announcement.

**공지**(空地) vacant land 〔ground〕; 《미》 a vacant 〔an empty〕 lot; 《영》 an empty 〔a vacant〕 plot (of land). ¶ ～에서 야구를 하다 play baseball on a vacant lot / 이 도시에는 아직 ～가 좀 남아 있다 This town still has some vacant land.

**공직**(公職) (a) public office; an official

position 〔post〕. ¶ ～에 있는 사람 an office-holder; a holder of public office / ～에 있다〔취임하다〕 hold 〔take up〕 (a) public office; be in 〔enter〕 government service / ～에서 추방하다 purge 《*a person*》 from public office / ～에서 추방되다 be divested of public office; be purged from public service / ～을 떠나다 leave office; leave public life / ～에서 물러나다 resign 〔retire〕 from public office / 아버지는 ～에 계시다 My father works for the government. *or* My father is in the civil 〔government〕 service.
◉ ～생활 a public career. ～추방 a purge from public service; screening of undesirable personnel: ～추방자 a purgee (from public service).

**공직자**(公職者) a public official; a government official; a public post holder. ¶ ～ 사회 the bureaucratic society / ～ 윤리법 the Public Servant's Ethics Law / ～들의 무사 안일주의와 수동적인 자세 the「easy-going 〔peace-at-any-price〕 principle and passive attitude on the part of government officials / ～의 재산을 공개하다 make public the property of public officials.

**공진**(共振) 〖물리〗 resonance; sympathy.

**공진회**(共進會) a competitive exhibition; a fair; a 《cattle》 show.

**공짜**(空―) an article got for nothing; a thing obtained without cost; gratuitousness. ¶ ～의 free (of charge) / ～로 free (of charge); gratis; for nothing / ～ 손님 《극장》 a free spectator; 《기차》 a free passenger; a deadhead 《미》 / ～로 술을 마시는 손님 a free-loader / ～로 일하다〔얻다〕 work 〔get〕 for nothing / 나는 그것을 친구에게 ～로 주겠다 I'll give it away to one of my friends.

**공차**(公差) ① 〖수학〗 a common difference. ② 《조폐·도량형의》 allowance; 《기계의》 legal remedy; tolerance.

**공차**(空車) ① 《빈차》 an empty carriage 〔car, coach〕; 〖철도〗 an idler; 《게시》 Vacant. ② 《무료로 타는 차》 a free ride; a stolen ride. ¶ ～ 타다 steal a ride on; get a free ride.

**공창**(工廠) 《철공장》 an ironworks; 《병기창》 an arsenal.

**공창**(公娼) 《사람》 a licensed 〔registered〕 prostitute; 《제도》 licensed prostitution. ¶ ～을 나쁘다고〔괜찮다고〕 하다 condemn 〔support〕 registered prostitution. ◉ ～가 a redlight district. ～제도 (the system of ) licensed 〔state-regulated〕 prostitution. ～폐지 abolition of licensed prostitution: ～폐지 운동 a purification movement.

**공채**(公採) 《공개 채용》 open 〔public〕 invitation of applications for employment 〔job, position〕. ～하다 invite openly 〔publicly〕 《*a person's*》 applications for 《position》; invite the public to apply for 《job》.

**공채**(公債) a public loan 〔debt〕; a government bond; 《증권》 a (public loan) bond; government securities. ¶ ～를 모집하다 raise 〔float〕 a loan / ～를 사다〔발행하다〕 buy 〔issue〕 bonds / ～를 상환하다 redeem 〔sink〕 a loan. ◉ ～상환자금 a sinking fund. ～시장 the bond market. ～증서소지자 a bondholder.

**공책**(空冊) a notebook.

**공처**(恐妻) (servile) submission to *one's* wife. ◉ ～가 a henpecked 〔submissive〕 husband.

**공천**(公薦) public recommendation 〔nomination〕; 《선거》 party nomination of parliamentary candidates. ～하다 recommend publicly; nominate 《a candidate》. ¶ ～받은 사람 a nominee / 민주당 ～ 후보자 a candidate nominated by the Democrats / 후보자를 ～하다 officially adopt 〔nominate〕 a candidate.

**공첩**(公牒) an official dispatch.

**공청회**(公聽會) a public 〔an open〕 hearing; 《공개 토론》 a public forum. ¶ ～를 열다 hold a public hearing / ～는 3월 10일에 열린다 The public hearing will be held on March 10.

**공출**(供出) delivery 《of rice to the government》. ～하다 deliver. ¶ 쌀을 ～하다 deliver rice 《to the government》 / ～을 할당하다 allot 〔allocate〕 a fixed quantity 《of rice》 to be delivered.
◉ ～가격 a delivery price. ～할당 allocation of delivery quota.

**공치기** a ball game; playing ball.

**공치다**(空―) ① 《허탕치다》 be unsuccessful; be fruitless; be (in) vain; be futile. ② 《○표를 하다》 draw a circle; mark down an "○".

**공치사**(功致辭) self-praise〔-laudation〕 of *one's* good conduct; admiration of *one's* own merit. ～하다 praise 〔laud〕 *oneself;* admire *one's* own merit.

**공치사**(空致辭) an empty 〔insincere〕 compliment; flattery; 《구어》 blarney. ～하다 pay compliments 《to》; say nice things 《to》; flatter.

**공칙하다, 공칙스럽다** (be) amiss; unfortunate; unhappy; ill planned 〔timed, chosen〕.

**공칭**(公稱) ¶ ～의 nominal; authorized. ◉ ～가격 a nominal price. ～능력 authorized capacity. ～마력 a nominal horsepower. ～자본금 nominal 〔authorized〕 capital.

**공탁**(供託) 《보관》 deposit; trust; lodgment. ～하다 deposit 《in, with》; lodge 《with》; post 《with》. ¶ …에 보증금을 ～하다 deposit a bond with… / 은행에 돈을 ～하다 deposit money in a bank. ◉ ～금 deposit money: ～금을 몰수당하다 forfeit a deposit. ～물 a deposit; deposited articles. ～법 the Deposit Law. ～서 a document that goes with a deposit. ～소 a deposit office; a depository. ～자 a depositor.

**공터**(空―) a vacant lot. ⇨공지(空地).

**공통**(共通) commonness. ～하다 be common 《to》. ¶ ～의 common / ～의 이해〔목적〕 a common interest 〔purpose〕 / 전체에 ～되는 성질 a characteristic common to all / 그들은 ～의 이해로 묶여있다 They are bound together by common interests. ◉ ～법 the common law. ～분모 『수학』 a common denominator. ～성〔점〕 a common feature; something in common: ～점이 있다〔없다〕 have something 〔nothing〕 in common 《with》. ～어 a common tongue 〔language〕. ～의식 common consciousness. ～인수 ＝공인수.

**공판**(公判) a public trial 〔hearing〕. ～하다 hold a court. ¶ 살인 사건의 ～ the trial of a murder case / ～을 열다 hold (a) court / ～에 부치다〔회부하다〕 bring 《a case, *a person*》 to trial; put 《a case》 on trial / ～에 회부되다 be brought to trial; come to trial; be tried / ～중이다 be on (*one's*) trial; be under public trial. ◉ ～기록 the record (of a trial). ～기일 a fixed day for public trial; a date for hearing; a court day. ～절차 procedure in a public trial. ～정 the court; the public trial court. ～조서 protocol for a public trial. ～청구 a demand for a trial.

**공판장**(共販場) a joint market. ¶ 농협〔수산물〕 ～ an agricultural cooperative's 〔a fishery〕 joint market.

**공편**(共編) coeditorship. ¶ A씨와 B씨의 ～ edited by Mr. A and Mr. B. ◉ ～자 a coeditor; a joint editor.

**공평**(公平) equity; equitability; impartiality; fairness; fair play. ～하다 (be) fair; just; fair and square; impartial; equitable; unbiased. ¶ ～한 fair (and square); unbiased; impartial 《opinions》; evenhanded 《treatment》; unprejudiced 《views》; just; equitable 《treatment》 / ～하게 impartially; fairly; justly; without partiality / ～하게 말하면 to do 《*a person*》 justice / ～을 결하다 (it will) be unfair / ～을 기하다 try to be fair; endeavor to see justice done / ～히 말하면 이것은 그의 허물이 아니다 To do him justice, he is not to blame for this. ◉ ～무사 fairness and disinterestedness.

**공포**(公布) promulgation; (a) proclamation; official announcement. ～하다 promulgate; proclaim; make public; announce officially. ¶ 본칙(本則)은 ～한 날로부터 이를 시행한다 The present regulations shall come into force on and after 〔as from〕 the day of promulgation.

**공포**(空胞) 『생물』 a vacuole. ◉ ～형성 vacuolation.

**공포**(空砲) a blank cartridge; a blank shot; blank fire. ¶ ～를 쏘다 fire a blank shot.

**공포**(恐怖) (a) fear; terror; (a) fright; (a) horror; (a) dread; (a) panic. ¶ ～를 느끼다 be frightened 〔terrified〕 《at》; be terror-stricken / ～를 느끼게 하다 strike a terror into 《*a person's*》 heart; scare; frighten / ～에 떨다 tremble with fear / ～에 싸이다 be seized with fear; be struck with horror / ～의 빛〔기색〕을 보이다 look scared 〔frightened〕. ◉ ～관념 a fear complex. ～시대 the Reign of Terror. ～심 fear; terror. ～정치 terrorism. ～영화 a horror film. ～증 morbid fear 〔dread〕; (-)phobia (★ -phobia는 「…공포증」의 뜻을 가진 명사 어미: 고소 공포증 acrophobia / 대인 공포증 anthrophobia).

**공폭**(空爆) bombardment from the air; (aerial) bombing; an air raid. ～하다 bomb; make an air raid 《on》. ¶ ～을 받다 be bombed; suffer air raids.

**공표**(公表) publication; (a) proclamation; (a) public 〔(an) official〕 announcement. ～하다 publish; make public; proclaim; announce publicly 〔officially〕; give publicity 《to》. ¶ 보도를 ～하다 make a report public / 시험 성적을 ～하다 make public the result of an examination.

**공피병**(鞏皮病) 〖의학〗 dermatosclerosis; scleroderma.

**공하**(恭賀) congratulations. ¶ ~신년 I wish you a happy New Year.

**공하다**(供—) offer; submit. ¶ 열람에 ~ submit 《a document》 to 《*a person's*》 inspection.

**공학**(工學) engineering; engineering science. ¶ 응용〔기계, 정밀, 전기, 화학, 토목〕~ practical 〔mechanical, precision, electrical, chemical, civil〕 engineering. ◉ ~박사 《칭호》 Doctor of Engineering (생략 D. Eng.); 《사람》 a doctor of engineering. ~부 the department 〔school〕 of technology 〔engineering (science)〕. ~사 《칭호》 Bachelor of Engineering (생략 B. Eng.); 《사람》 a bachelor of engineering. ~석사 《칭호》 Master of Engineering (생략 M. Eng.); 《사람》 a master of engineering. ~자 an engineer.

**공학**(共學) 《남녀의》 coeducation 《미》; mixed education 《영》. ~하다 have coeducation; be coeducational. ¶ ~의 학교 a coeducational school / (흑백의) ~을 실시하다 carry out school integration / 「너의 학교는 (남녀)~이냐」— 「아니, 남자 학교야」 "Is your school coeducational?"—"No, It's a boys' school."
◉ ~여학생 a coed; a co-ed 《미구어》. ~제 the coeducationalism.

**공한**(公翰) an official letter.

**공한지**(空閑地) idle land; land lying idle; land in fallow. ◉ ~세 an idle land tax.

**공항**(空港) an airport; an aviation field; an airdrome; an aerodrome 《영》. ¶ 국제 ~에 착륙하다 land at an international airport / 그 비행기는 ~을 떠났다 The plane took off from the airport. / 내가 당신을 마중하러 ~에 나가겠소 《미》 I'll meet your plane. / 나는 5시 비행기로 도착하는 사람을 마중하러 ~에 가야 한다 《미》 I have a plane to meet at five.
◉ ~버스 an airport bus. ~빌딩 an airport building, a terminal building. ~출입국관리소 the airport immigration office. ~택시 an airport taxi. ~호텔 an airport hotel; an airtel.

**공해**(公害) 《환경 오염》 environmental pollution; 《대기·수질 오염》 air 〔water〕 pollution; 《소음·악취 따위에 의한》 a public nuisance; (a) menace 〔a threat〕 to public health; public hazard; contamination (오염). ¶ 소음~ noise pollution / ~ 피해자 a pollution victim / 저~차 a low-pollution car / ~가 없는 pollution-free / ~에 시달리는 도시 a city festered with public nuisances / ~를 일으키다 cause harm to the public / ~를 제거하다 remove 〔wipe out〕 (air and water) pollutants / ~를 방지〔규제〕하다 prevent 〔control〕 environmental pollution / 서울은 소음 ~로 시달리고 있다 Seoul suffers from noise pollution. / 우리 도시에서 ~를 없애자 Let's get rid of pollution from our town. / 우리는 ~를 추방했다 We did away with pollution.
◉ ~대책 antipollution measures. ~문제 a pollution problem. ~물질 a pollutant; a pollutional material. ~방지 prevention of environmental pollution: ~방지법 the Public 〔an Anti-public〕 Nuisance Law; an antipollution ordinance / ~방지 시설물 antipollution facilities. ~배출 업소 industrial firms discharging air and water pollutants. ~병 pollution-caused 〔-related〕 disease 〔illness〕: ~병 환자 victims of pollution-caused disease. ~산업 an industrial polluter. ~추방운동 an antipollution campaign.

**공해**(公海) the high seas; 〖국제법〗 the open sea; international waters. ¶ ~의 자유 freedom of the seas / ~상에서 핵실험을 하다 conduct nuclear tests over international waters / 우리는 ~를 항해하는 중에 습격당했다 We were attacked while sailing in international waters. ◉ ~어업 high-sea fishery; fishery in the high seas.

**공허**(空虛) emptiness; voidness; hollowness; vacancy. ~하다 (be) empty; void; hollow; vacant. ¶ ~한 생활 an empty life; a life without meaning / 인생의 ~를 느끼다 feel the emptiness of life / 내 마음은 ~했다 My mind was blank. ◉ ~감 a sense of emptiness.

**공헌**(貢獻) (a) contribution; service. ~하다 contribute 《to》; make a contribution 《to, of》; render services 《to》; go a long way toward 《solving the problem》; do (a lot) for 《national welfare》; be helpful 《to, in》. ¶ 대외무역에 크게 ~하다 render great services to foreign trade / 그는 스포츠 발전에 많은 ~을 했다 He contributed much to the development of sports.

**공현축일**(公顯祝日) 〖가톨릭〗 (Feast of) the Epiphany.

**공혈**(供血) =헌혈.

**공화**(共和) 《화합》 universal harmony; 〖정치〗 republicanism; republican. ◉ ~국 a republic; a commonwealth. ~당 the Republican Party; 《미국 공화당의 별칭》 the Grand Old Party (생략 G.O.P.); the Elephant: ~당원 a Republican / ~당 정부 the Republican Administration. ~정체 a republican form 〔system〕 of government. ~정치 republican government 〔administration〕. ~제도 republicanism.

**공황**(恐慌) 《두려움·당황》 a panic; a scare; consternation; 《경제·금융계의》 a financial panic 〔crisis〕. ¶ ~에 휩쓸린 panic-stricken〔-struck〕/ ~을 초래하다 cause 〔bring on〕 a panic; get up a panic / ~ 상태에 있다 be in a state of panic / ~을 극복하다 get over a crisis / ~으로 일부 은행들도 파산했다 Even some of the banks smashed due to the panic. ◉ ~가격 a panic price. ~시대 a panic age.

**공회**(公會) a public meeting 〔assembly〕. ◉ ~당 a public 〔town〕 hall; a community center.

**공훈**(功勳) merits; exploits; distinguished services; meritorious deeds. ¶ 혁혁한 ~ brilliant exploits / ~을 세우다 render distinguished services.

**공휴일**(公休日) 《일반의》 a day off; a vacation 《미》; a holiday 《영》; 《법정의》 a legal holiday; a bank holiday 《영》. ¶ ~은 1년에 며칠 있느냐 How many days off do you have a year? / 다음 ~에는 어디로 갈 겁니까 Where are you going away for your next vacation?

**-곶**(串) 《갑(岬)》 a cape; a promontory; a headland; a point. ¶ 장산~ Changsan Cape; the cape 〔headland〕 of Changsan.

**곶감** a dried persimmon. ¶ ~ 빼먹듯 하다 eat away 〔up〕 *one's* savings; spend up *one's* savings bit by bit.

**과**(科) 《학과》 a course; a department; a faculty; 《생물학상의》 a family; 《병과》 arm and service. ¶ 고양잇과 the cat family / 국화과 the chrysanthemum family / 보병과 the infantry arm / 영어과 an English course 〔department〕.

**과**(課) 《학업에서》 a lesson; 《업무기구에서》 a section; a department (큰 규모). ¶ 제5 과 《학과》 Lesson 5; the fifth lesson / 경리과 the accounts 〔accounting〕 section / ~원 the staff of a section / ~장 the chief 〔head〕 of a section; a section chief.

**과** ① 《함께》 with; together with; in company with. ¶ 아버님과 가다 go with *one's* father / 어머님과 여행하다 travel with *one's* mother / 내일 홍군과 오시오 Come (together) with Mr. Hong tomorrow. / 아들과 살겠다 I will live with my son.
② [연결사] and. ¶ 딸과 어머니 daughter and mother / 술과 담배를 샀다 I bought liquor and tobacco.
③ 《대항》 with; against. ¶ 적과 싸우다 fight against the enemy / 물리학과 씨름하다 struggle with physics.
④ 《합치·협력》 with. ¶ 중국과 손을 잡다 go hand in hand with China.
⑤ 《접촉》 with. ¶ 적과 내통하다 be in 〔hold〕 secret communication with the enemy.
⑥ 《분리》 with; from. ¶ 그 사람과는 완전히 손을 끊었다 I have done with him. *or* I'm through with him 《미》.
⑦ 《관계》 with. ¶ 은행과 거래하다 have business connections 〔relations〕 with a bank; bank with / 나는 너희들과 아무 관계가 없다 I have nothing to do with you.
⑧ 《비교》 with. ¶ …과 비교〔대조〕해서 as compared 〔in contrast〕 with.
⑨ 《이동(異同)》 (the same) as; like; (similar) to; (different) from. ¶ 저 사람과 같이 the same as him; like him; together with him / 저 사람과 달리 in contrast with him; different from him / 전과 마찬가지로 대답하다 answer the same as before.
⑩ 《혼합》 with. ¶ 물과 섞다 dilute 《a solution》 with water.

**과감**(果敢) boldness; daring; resoluteness; determination. ~스럽다〔하다〕 (be) bold; daring; resolute; determined. ¶ ~히 resolutely; in a decisive manner; boldly / ~한 조처를 취하다 take up a drastic measure; take a decisive 〔bold, resolute〕 step.

**과객**(過客) a passer-by; a foot passenger; 《나그네》 a wayfarer; a transient.

**과거**(科擧) 《고제도》 "*Kwagŏ*," the highest-level state examination to recruit ranking officials during the *Chosŏn* Dynasty. ¶ ~에 급제하다 pass "*Kwagŏ*," the old state examination (during the *Chosŏn* Dynasty).

**과거**(過去) the past (days); times past; bygone days. ¶ ~의 past; bygone / ~10년간 during the past 〔for the last〕

ten years / ～가 있는 여자 a woman with a past / ～를 생각하다 think of the past 〔bygone days〕 / ～를 회고하다〔되돌아보다〕 look back into the past; look back upon the past 〔*one's* life, *one's* career〕 / ～를 묻지 말자 Let bygones be bygones. / 이제 그것은 ～사가 된 일이다 It is a thing of the past now. *or* It is water under the bridge. ◉ ～분사 〖문법〗 a past participle (생략 p.p.). ～사(事) past affairs; bygones. ～시제 〖문법〗 the past tense; the preterite (생략 pret.). ～완료 〖문법〗 the past perfect tense; the pluperfect. ～장(帳) 〖불교〗 an obituary.

**과격**(過激) being extreme 〔radical, drastic, excessive〕. ～하다 (be) extreme; radical; drastic; violent; excessive. ¶ ～한 운동 strenuous exercise / ～한 말을 쓰다 use 〔employ〕 violent language / 그것은 ～하다 That's going too far. ◉ ～분자 a radical element; radicals. ～사상 radical 〔extremist〕 ideas; revolutionary thought; bolshevism. ～주의 extremism; radicalism; bolshevism: ～주의자 an extremist; a radical; a bolshevik. ～파 extremists; radicals.

**과꽃** 〖식물〗 a China aster.

**과납**(過納) ～하다 pay in excess. ◉ ～액 an amount paid in excess.

**과냉(각)**(過冷(却)) supercooling. ～하다 supercool 《water》; superfuse. ◉ ～액체 a supercooled liquid.

**과녁** a target; a mark. ¶ ～을 맞히다, ～에 맞다 hit the mark 〔target〕 / ～에 빗맞다 miss the mark / ～을 넘어가다 overshoot the mark / 나이프를 던져 ～을 맞히다 hurl a knife on target. ◉ ～빼기 the right opposite side; the place *one* faces right ahead; the place directly opposite: ～빼기집 the house on the right opposite side; the house in the right opposite direction; the house *one* faces right ahead. ～판 a target board.

**과년**(瓜年) the marriageable 〔pubescent〕 age.

**과년**(過年) (getting) past (the) marriageable age. ～하다 (be) past (the) marriageable age.

**과년도**(過年度) the past fiscal 〔financial〕 year. ◉ ～지출 defrayment belonging to the preceding financial year.

**과다**(過多) excess; superabundance; superfluity; plethora. ～하다 (be) too much 〔many〕; excessive; superabundant. ¶ 인원 ～의 over-staffed 《office, *etc.*》 / 공급 ～ an excess of supply; oversupply / 지방 ～ excess of fat.

**과단**(果斷) (prompt) decision; resolution. ～하다 decide 〔determine, resolve〕 promptly. ¶ ～한 decisive; resolute; drastic; bold. ◉ ～성 firmness of character; promptness in action; decisiveness: ～성 있는 사람 a man of decision / ～성이 없다 lack decision; be irresolute / ～성 있는 조처를 취하다 take a drastic measure 〔resolute steps〕.

**과당**(果糖) fructose; levulose; fruit sugar.

**과당**(過當) ～하다 (be) excessive; be more than needed; 《부당한》 undue; undeserved; 《터무니없는》 exorbitant. ◉ ～경쟁 an excessive competition 《in sales》; overheated vying 《for》: ～경쟁을 삼가다 refrain from excessive competitions 《among themselves》.

**과대**(誇大) (an) exaggeration; magnification; (an) overstatement; (a) hyperbole. ～하다 exaggerate; magnify; overstate. ¶ ～한 exaggerated; magnified; stretched; extravagant; bombastic / 사실을 ～하게 말하다 exaggerate matters; stretch the truth; 《신문이》 play up. ◉ ～광고 an exaggerative 〔extravagant〕 advertisement; a puff. ～망상 delusions of grandeur: ～망상증 megalomania; 《사람》 a megalomaniac.

**과대**(過大) being too big 〔great〕; exaggeration; 《과도》 being excessive. ～하다 (be) too big 〔great〕; exaggerative; excessive; exorbitant. ¶ ～한 요구 an unreasonable 〔exorbitant〕 demand / ～하게 excessively; exorbitantly; exaggeratedly / ～하게 말하다 overstate; exaggerate. ◉ ～평가 overestimation: ～평가하다 overestimate.

**과도**(果刀) a fruit knife.

**과도**(過度) excess; immoderation; immoderateness. ～하다 (be) excessive; immoderate; inordinate. ¶ ～하게 excessively; inordinately; too much 〔hard〕; to 〔in〕 excess / ～하게 공부하다 overwork 〔overstudy〕 *oneself* / ～한 운동을 하다 take excessive exercise / ～한 음주는 해롭다 Too much drinking is harmful. / 부모는 흔히 자식들에게 ～한 기대를 걸기 쉽다 Parents are apt to expect too much of their children.

**과도**(過渡) transition. ¶ ～적인 transitional. ◉ ～기 a period 〔an age〕 of transition; a transitional period 〔stage〕: ~기의 문화〔문학〕 culture 〔literature〕 in a transition(al) period / 사춘기는 어린이에서 어른으로 이르는 ~기이다 Adolescence is a transitional period from childhood to adulthood 〔between childhood and adulthood〕. ~내각 a caretaker 〔an interim〕 cabinet. ~정부 an interim government; a caretaker government.

**과도** ¶ 형과도 의논해 봐라 Talk it over with your elder brother too. / 내 마음은 촛불과도 같다 My heart is just like a candle's flame.

**과동**(過冬) passing the winter. ⇨ 월동(越冬).

**과두정치**(寡頭政治) oligarchy. ¶ ~의 oligarchic(al).

**과람하다**(過濫—) undeserved; unmerited; more 〔greater〕 than *one* deserves.

**과량**(過量) an excess (of quantity).

**과로**(過勞) overwork; overexertion; excessive labor; strains of work. ~하다 work too hard; overwork *oneself;* overexert *oneself.* ¶ ~로 인해 탈이 나다 get 〔fall〕 ill from overwork; break down 〔get sick〕 through overwork / 아버지는 ~로 쓰러지셨다 My father fell 〔got〕 ill from overwork. *or* My father got sick through overwork. *or* My father suffered a physical breakdown from overwork. / 신경 쇠약은 흔히 정신 ~ 때문에 일어난다 Excessive mental labor often causes nervous prostration 〔breakdown〕. / 여러 해의 ~가 그의 건강을 몹시 해쳤다 The strain of many years told severely on his health. ◉ ~사 death from overwork.

**과료**(科料) 〖법〗 a fine. ¶ ~에 처하다 fine; impose a fine 《upon》 / 약간의 ~로 면하다 get off with a light fine / 그는 경범죄로 삼만 원의 ~에 처해졌다 He was fined thirty thousand won for a minor offense 〔a misdemeanor〕.

**과립**(顆粒) a little 〔small〕 grain 〔particle〕; a granule; 〖의학〗 granulation(s); a rash.

**과망간산**(過—酸) 〖화학〗 permanganic acid.

**과명**(科名) 〖생물〗 a family name.

**과목**(果木) a fruit tree.

**과목**(科目) ① 《학과》 a subject; 《과정》 a course (of study); a curriculum (전과목). ② 《항목》 an item.

**과묵**(寡默) taciturnity; reticence. ~하다 (be) taciturn; reticent. ¶ ~한 사람 a man of few words; an oyster of a man; a taciturn 〔reticent〕 person / 그는 평소에는 ~하다 He is usually a man of few words.

**과문**(寡聞) little 〔scanty〕 knowledge; limited information. ~하다 (be) unread; ill-informed; be limited in knowledge. ¶ ~한 탓으로 아직 그것에 대해 모르고 있습니다 I'm afraid I haven't heard anything about it yet.

**과물**(果物) fruit. ⇨ 과실(果實).

**과민**(過敏) oversensitiveness; nervousness; hypersensitivity. ~하다 (be) too keen; (over)sensitive; touchy; too nervous. ¶ 신경 ~ morbid sensitiveness; neurosis. ◉ ~성 hypersensitiveness: ~성의 hypersensitive. ~증 〖의학〗 erethism; anaphylaxis; hypersensitiveness: ~증의 hypersensitive; anaphylactic; hyperesthetic.

**과밀**(過密) 《사람·물건 등》 overcrowding; 《인구의》 overpopulation; 《밀집상태》 congestion. ¶ 서울 같은 ~지대 an overcrowded 〔a congested〕 area like Seoul. ◉ ~도시 an overpopulated city. ~학급 an overcrowded class.

**과반**(過半) the greater part 〔number〕 《of》; the majority; more than half 《the members》. ¶ ~은 합격했다 The majority have passed the examination. / 목적의 ~은 성취했다 Our purpose has practically been accomplished. / 학생의 ~은 지방 출신이다 The students are mostly from the country.

**과반수**(過半數) the majority; the greater part 〔number〕 《of》; more than half 《the numbers》. ¶ ~의 투표에 의해 결정하다 decide by the majority of votes / (간신히) ~를 얻다 win 〔gain〕 a (slim) majority / ~를 차지하다〔얻지 못하다〕 hold 〔lack〕 a majority 《in the Assembly》 / 출석인원 2/3 이상의 ~로 선출되다 be elected 《chairman》 by a majority of two thirds or more of those present / 의결은 ~로 한다 The decision will be made by majority. / 그 제안은 ~의 찬성을 얻지 못했다 The proposal failed to find a majority. / 합격자의 ~는 지방 출신자들이었다 The greater part of the successful candidates were from the rural country.

**과보호**(過保護) overprotection; overprotectiveness. ~하다 overprotect. ¶ ~ 어린이 an overprotected 〔a pampered〕 child / 그녀는 아들을 ~한다 She overprotects 〔is too protective toward〕 her son. / 그들은 외아들에 대해 좀 ~하

는 것 같다 They seem to be a bit protective toward their only son.

**과부**(寡婦) a widow; a widowed lady. ¶ ~가 되다 be widowed; lose *one's* husband; be bereaved of *one's* husband / ~ 생활을 하다 live in widowhood / 그녀는 25세에 ~가 되었다 She was widowed at the age of 25. / 전쟁으로 많은 ~가 생겼다 The war widowed many women. / ~ 사정은 ~가 안다 《속담》 It takes a widow to know a widow's difficulties. / ~는 은이 서 말이고 홀아비는 이가 서 말이다 《속담》 Widows are thrifty and can be counted on to save money, but a widower is apt to remain poor.

**과부족**(過不足) overs and shorts; excess and / or deficiency. ¶ ~ 없는 just enough; neither 「more 〔too much〕 nor 「less 〔too little〕 / ~ 없이 하다 avoid extremes; be moderate / ~ 없이 나누다 divide 《the profits》 equally.

**과분**(過分) being above *one's* deserts; being excessive. ~하다 be above *one's* deserts; (be) excessive; undue; unmerited; undeserved. ¶ ~하게 excessively; more than *one* deserves; unduly; immoderately / ~한 사례를 받아 송구스럽습니다 I am afraid I hardly deserve this sort of remuneration.

**과불**(過拂) overpayment. ~하다 overpay.

**과불급**(過不及) excess and / or deficiency.

**과산화**(過酸化) ◉ ~납 lead peroxide. ~물 peroxides. ~석회 superphosphate of lime. ~수소 hydrogen peroxide: ~수소수 oxygenated water. ~작용 peroxidation. ~철 peroxide of iron; crocus.

**과세**(過歲) celebrating the New Year season. ~하다 celebrate 〔observe〕 the New Year.

**과세**(課稅) taxation; imposition of taxes; 《세》 a tax; a duty; a levy. ~하다 tax; levy 〔impose〕 「a tax 〔duties〕 《on》. ¶ ~해야 할 taxable; leviable / ~가 면제되다 be exempt(ed) 〔immune〕 from taxation / 수입품에 ~하다 tax imported goods / ~의 대상이 되다 be subject to taxation; be taxable; be an object of taxation / 무겁게 ~하다 tax 《luxury goods》 heavily; impose 〔levy〕 heavy taxes on 《an article》 / 개인소득에 ~하다 tax the income of an individual / 대부분의 나라에서 술과 담배는 ~된다 Alcohol and tobacco are taxed in most countries. ◉ ~가격 the taxable amount; the assessed value. ~기간 taxable period. ~단위 a unit of assessment. ~대상 an object of taxation; a taxation article. ~대장 a tax roll. ~범위 the scope of assessment. ~소득 taxable income. ~율 tax rates. ~표준 a standard of assessment; tax basis. ~품 a taxable article; articles subject to taxation; 《세관에서의》 a dutiable 〔customable 《미》〕 article: 신고할 ~품이 있습니까 《세관에서 묻는 말》 (Do you have) anything to declare? 배당~ 《주식의》 levying tax on stock dividends. 인정~ optional taxation. 중(重)~ heavy taxation.

**과소**(過小) being too small 〔little〕. ~하다 (be) too small 〔little〕; be not large enough. ◉ ~평가 underestimation: ~평가하다 underestimate; underrate; belittle; set too low a value on 《*a person*》 / 자신을 ~평가하지 마라 Don't belittle yourself. / 정부는 그 사건이 지닌 의미를 ~평가하고 있다 The government underestimated the significance of the incident.

**과소**(過少) being too little 〔few〕. ~하다 (be) too little 〔few〕. ¶ 수입을 ~ 신고하다 understate *one's* income. ◉ ~생산 underproduction. ~소비 underconsumption.

**과소**(寡少) littleness; smallness; fewness; scantiness. ~하다 (be) very little 〔few〕; scant(y).

**과소비**(過消費) overconsumption; conspicuous consumption.

**과속**(過速) overspeed. ¶ ~으로 달리다 overspeed / ~ 위험. 안전 제일 《게시》 Speeding is dangerous. Safety first. ◉ ~시험 an overspeed test. ~차량 an overspeeding vehicle: ~차량을 단속하다 regulate 〔keep strict control over〕 the overspeeding vehicles.

**과수**(果樹) a fruit tree. ¶ ~를 재배하다 grow fruit trees. ◉ ~원 an orchard; a fruit farm 〔ranch〕. ~재배 fruit growing 〔cultivation〕: ~ 재배자 a fruit grower 〔farmer〕.

**과수**(寡守) =과부. ◉ ~댁 an esteemed widow.

**과시**(誇示) ostentation; display; showing off; parade. ~하다 make a display of; parade; show off. ¶ 권력을 ~하다 show off *one's* authority / 그는 언제나 자기 지식을 ~한다 He always makes a display of his knowledge.

**과식**(過食) overeating; eating too much. ~하다 eat too much; overeat *oneself;* eat more than (it) is good for one. ¶ ～하여 병이 나다 overeat *oneself* sick / ～은 지나치게 체중을 늘린다 Eating too much causes overweight. / ～한 게 아닌가 걱정된다 I am afraid I have overeaten myself.

**과신**(過信) excessive confidence. ～하다 place too much confidence《in technology》; be overconfident《in *a person*》. ¶ 자기의 능력을 ～하다 have too much confidence in *oneself;* overestimate *one's* own abilities.

**과실**(果實)《열매》a fruit; fruit [총칭]; 〚법〛fruit(s) (집세 따위 이익). ¶ 작은 ～ a fruitlet / ～을 맺다《나무가》bear 〔produce〕 fruit;《꽃이》develop into fruit; fructify; fruit. ◉ ～선별기 a fruit grader. ～주(酒) fruit wine 〔liquor〕. 법정〔천연〕～ legal 〔natural〕 fruits.

**과실**(過失)《과실》a fault;《과오》a mistake; an error; a blunder; 〚법〛《태만》negligence;《불의의 사고》an accident. ¶ ～의 accidental / ～로 by accident 〔mistake〕; through *one's* fault / 업무상의 ～ professional negligence; negligence (in the performance of *one's* duties) / ～을 범하다 blunder; commit an error; make a mistake 〔blunder〕/ ～을 인정하다 admit *one's* error; acknowledge *one's* fault / …의 ～을 너그럽게 보다 pass over 〔wink at〕 *a person's* fault / ～을 아무의 죄로 돌리다 lay a fault「to *a person's* charge 〔at *a person's* door〕/ 나의 ～이다 I am to blame for it. *or* It's my fault. / 그건 ～이 아니라 고의로 한 짓이다 It was not done by accident, but by design. / 그것은 아무의 ～도 아니다 Nobody is to blame. ◉ ～범 criminal negligence. ～상해죄 accidental infliction of injury. ～죄 an accidental offense. ～치사(죄) an accidental 〔involuntary〕 homicide: 업무상의 ～치사 professional negligence resulting in death. 중(重)～ 〚법〛gross negligence.

**과언**(過言) saying too much; going too far (in *one's* talk); intemperate language; exaggeration. ¶ …라고 해도 ～이 아니다 It is no exaggeration to say that…. *or* It may fairly be said that…. / 그는 전형적인 신사라고 해도 ～이 아니다 It is not too much to say that he is a typical gentleman.

**과업**(課業)《학과》lessons; school work;《할일》a task; a duty. ¶ 내일 ～의 준비를 마치다 finish preparing *one's* lessons for tomorrow / ～을 맡기다 assign a task to《*a person*》; impose a task on《*a person*》; set《*a person*》to a task / 과업을 실행하다 carry out *one's* task. ◉ ～관리 task management.

**과연**(果然)《생각한 대로》as expected; really; truly; indeed; sure enough. ¶ ～ 그럴까 Can it be so? *or* Are you sure of 〔about〕 it? / ～ 그는 실패했다 He failed, as I feared he would. / ～ 사실이었다 It was really the case. *or* It proved to be true. / ～ 그 아버지에 그 아들이다 He is a son worthy of his father.

**과열**(過熱) overheating; superheating. ～하다 overheat; superheat. ¶ ～된 과외 교육 the overheated out-of-class lessons / 경제의 ～을 막기 위한 방안을 찾다 seek ways to prevent the economy from overheating / 보일러가 ～됐다 The boiler overheated. / 오늘날 항공회사간의 경쟁은 매우 ～되어 있다 Competitions among the airlines is quite fierce nowadays.
◉ ～경기(景氣) an excessive (economic) boom. ～경쟁 overheated vying《for》: ～ 입시 경쟁 excessive 〔hot〕 competition for entrance tests; excessive preparation for entrance tests. ～기 a superheater. ～붐 an excessive boom. ～증기 a superheated vapor. ～투자 excessive investment.

**과염소산**(過塩素酸) 〚화학〛 perchloric acid. ◉ ～염 perchlorate.

**과오**(過誤)《잘못》a mistake; an error;《과실》a fault; a blunder;《죄과》an offense. ¶ ～를 범하다 make a mistake 〔an error〕; blunder; commit an offense / ～를 깨닫다 see the error of *one's* ways / ～를 고치다 mend *one's* ways; correct the errors of *one's* past / 그녀는 자신의 ～를 인정하려 하지 않았다 She wouldn't admit her fault.

**과외**(課外) extracurricular work. ¶ ～의 extracurricular; extracurriculum.
◉ ～강의 an extracurricular lecture. ～공부 out-of-school studies. ～수업 an extracurricular lesson《in English》; the off-campus tutoring; extra classes《within and without schools》; after-class study. ～활동 extracurricular activities.

**과욕**(過慾) avarice; greed; greediness; covetousness. ～하다 (be) avaricious; greedy; covetous.

**과욕**(寡慾) unselfishness; disinterestedness. ～하다 (be) unselfish; disinterested. ¶ ～한 사람 a man of few wants.

**과용**(過用) spending too much; excessive expenses. ∼하다 spend too much 《money on cosmetics》; be extravagant 〔prodigal〕 with; 《약을》 take an overdose (of medicine 〔a drug〕).

**과원**(課員) a member of the section staff; the staff of a section [총칭].

**과유불급**(過猶不及) Too much is as bad as too little.

**과육**(果肉) 〖식물〗 flesh; pulp; sarcocarp.

**과음**(過淫) lustful excesses; overindulgence in sensual pleasure; sexual intemperance. ∼하다 overindulge in sex.

**과음**(過飮) drinking too much; intemperance in drinking; excessive drinking. ∼하다 drink too much 〔to excess〕; overdrink *oneself;* be intemperate (in drinking). ¶ ∼하여 병나다 drink *oneself* ill; drink too much and fall ill.

**과인산**(過燐酸) 〖화학〗 superphosphate. ◉ ∼석회 superphosphate of lime.

**과일** a fruit; fruit [총칭]. ¶ ∼의 껍질을 벗기다 peel 〔pare〕 fruit / ∼칼 a fruit knife. ◉ ∼가게 a fruit store 〔shop〕. ∼바구니 a fruit basket. ∼장수 a fruit dealer 〔seller〕; a fruiterer 《영》.

**과잉**(過剩) (an) excess; a surplus; overabundance. ∼하다 (be) too much; excessive; superfluous; surplus; more than enough. ¶ 인구∼ overpopulation / 사과 생산의 ∼으로 시장 가격이 폭락하였다 The market price of apples has plummeted due to overproduction. ◉ ∼노동력 surplus 〔redundant〕 labor. ∼방위 excessive self-defense. ∼보호 overprotection: ∼ 보호되는 아이들 overly-protected children. ∼생산 overproduction. ∼인구 overpopulation; surplus population. ∼인원 supernumeraries; superfluous personnel. ∼충성 excessive devotion; overloyalty. ∼투여 overdosage: ∼투여하다 overdose. ∼투자 overinvestment.

**과자**(菓子) 《파이 따위》 (a) pie; pastry; 《케이크류》 (a) cake; 《당과》 sweets; candy; confectionery [총칭]. ¶ ∼를 만들다〔굽다〕 make 〔bake〕 a cake / 손님에게 차와 ∼를 내놓다 serve tea and cake to the guest. ◉ ∼그릇 a pastry tray; a cake dish; a candy bowl. ∼상자 a box of cake. ∼장수 a confectioner. ∼점 a confectionery; a candy store 《미》; a sweet shop 《영》.

**과작**(寡作) ∼하다 produce *one's* works at rare intervals. ¶ ∼하는 작가 an unprolific writer.

**과장**(誇張) (an) exaggeration; (an) overstatement. ∼하다 exaggerate; overstate. ¶ ∼된 exaggerated; bombastic; high-flown / ∼된 문장 a grandiloquent style / ∼ 광고 an exaggerated advertisement; a puff / ∼하여 exaggeratedly; in 〔with〕 exaggeration / 사실을 ∼하다 stretch the truth; overstate a fact / 터무니없이 ∼하다 exaggerate out of proportion; grossly exaggerate 《*one's* story》 / 그가 완전한 실패라고 한 것은 ∼된 말이었다 He went too far when he called it a complete failure. / 그는 ∼하는 버릇이 있다 He is given to exaggeration. / 그녀를 천재라고 말해도 ∼이 아니다 It is no exaggeration to say that she is a genius. ◉ ∼법 〖수사학〗 hyperbole.

**과장**(課長) the head 〔chief〕 of a section 〔department〕; a section(al) chief 〔head〕. ◉ ∼대리 the acting chief of a section.

**과적**(過積) overload(ing); overcharge. ∼하다 overload 《a car, a steamer》; overfreight; overburden; overcharge. ¶ ∼ 차량 진입 금지 《게시》 No overloaded vehicles. / 이 트럭은 ∼이다 This truck is overloaded.

**과전압**(過電壓) overvoltage.

**과점**(寡占) 〖경제〗 oligopoly. ◉ ∼가격 an oligopoly price. ∼경제 oligopolistic economy. ∼시장 an oligopolistic market.

**과정**(過程) (a) process; a course; a stage. ¶ 몰락 ∼에 있는 사회 a society in a decadent stage / ∼을 밟다 go through the process 〔stage〕 of... / 이들 동물은 흥미 있는 진화의 ∼을 밟아왔다 These animals have passed through an interesting process of evolution. / 심의 ∼에서 그것은 밝혀질 것이다 It will become clear in the process of discussion. ◉ 생산〔제조〕∼ production 〔manufacturing〕 process.

**과정**(課程) a course (of study); 《전과정》 a curriculum (*pl.* ∼s, -la). ¶ 고등학교 ∼ the whole course of a high school / 의무 교육 ∼을 마치다 finish 〔complete, go through〕 *one's* compulsory education course / 위의 사람은 본교 소정의 ∼을 수료하였음 The above= mentioned has completed the prescribed course of this school. ◉ ∼표 a school timetable; a (course) schedule.

**과제**(課題) ① 《제목》 a subject; a theme;

a thesis. ¶ …란 ~로 글을 쓰다 write a composition 〔an essay〕 on the subject of…. ② 《숙제》 homework; a home task; an assignment 《미》; exercises (연습 문제); 《임무》 a task. ¶ 여름 방학 ~ summer homework / ~를 주다 set a task 《to》; give an assignment 《to》 / 그는 맡겨진 ~를 다 했다 He did the task assigned to him. ③ 《해결할 문제》 a question; a problem. ¶ 정부가 해결해야 할 커다란 ~ an important problem for the Government to solve / 우리는 당면한 ~ 해결에 전력을 다해야 한다 We must do our best to solve the problems which confront us now.
◉ ~장 an exercise book; a (home-) work book.

**과줄** 《유밀과》 a cake made of wheat flour, honey, and oil.

**과중**(過重) overweight. ~하다 (be) too heavy; burdensome. ¶ ~한 노동 overwork / ~한 책임 too heavy a responsibility / 그는 ~한 짐에 신음하였다 He groaned under the heavy burden. / 높은 수입을 올린 사람들은 ~한 세금 부담에 직면한다 People on high incomes face a huge tax burden.

**과즙**(果汁) fruit juice.

**과찬**(過讚) overpraise; excessive compliment. ~하다 overpraise; give an undeserved compliment.

**과태료**(過怠料) a fine for default; a negligence fine; a penalty. ¶ ~를 부과하다 impose a fine (for default) on 《*a person*》 / ~를 부과받다 be fined 《ten thousand won》 for 《*doing*》.

**과테말라** 《나라 이름》 (the Republic of) Guatemala. ¶ ~의 Guatemalan.

**과표**(課標) a standard of assessment.
◉ ~액 the taxable amount.

**과피**(果皮) the rind (of a fruit); the seedcase.

**과하다**(科―) 《형벌을》 impose 《a penalty, a fine》 on 《*a person*》; inflict 《a punishment》 on 《*a person*》. ¶ 속도 위반으로 2만 원의 벌금이 과해지다 be fined twenty thousand won for violation of the speed limit.

**과하다**(過―) 《지나치다》 (be) too much 〔heavy, good, severe, *etc.*〕 《for》; excessive; be beyond all bounds 〔limits〕. ¶ 과하게 too much; excessively; to excess 《미》; 《과분하게》 unduly; undeservedly; unreasonably / 과한 형벌 an excessive 〔oversevere〕 punishment / 술을 과하게 마시다 overdrink *oneself;* drink too much; drink to excess / 농담이 ~ carry a joke too far / 저에겐 너무 과한 칭찬이십니다 Your praise is more than I deserve. / 검약도 너무 과하면 인색이 된다 Frugality, if carried too far, becomes miserliness. / 과한 것은 부족한 것이나 다름이 없다 Too much is just as bad as too little. / 그녀는 그 남자에게는 너무 ~ She is too good for him.

**과하다**(課―) 《세금 등을》 impose 〔levy, assess〕 《a tax on》; 《일·책임 등을》 assign; task; set; give. ¶ 세금을 ~ impose 〔levy〕 a tax / 일을 ~ assign a task to 《*a person*》; impose a task on 《*a person*》 / 학생에게 숙제를 ~ give a student some homework.

**과학**(科學) science. ¶ ~적(으로) scientific(ally) / 비(非)~적 unscientific / ~의 진보 development 〔advance〕 of science / ~을 응용하다 apply science / 근년에 ~은 눈부신 발전을 이룩했다 In recent years science has made remarkable progress. / ~적인 조사로 사고 원인이 밝혀졌다 A scientific investigation cleared up the cause of the accident.
◉ ~계(界) scientific circles; the world of science. ~기술 scientific technique; (science and) technology: ~ 기술 공포증 the technophobia / ~ 기술 용어 technical and scientific terms / ~기술 협력 협정 the agreement on cooperation in science and technology. ~기술부 the Ministry of Science and Technology: ~ 기술부 장관 the Minister of Science and Technology. ~만능(주의) scientism; almighty 〔omnipotence of〕 science. ~박물관 a science museum. ~서(書) a scientific book. ~소설 a science fiction (생략 SF); sci-fi. ~수사 scientific crime detection. ~시대 a scientific age. ~연구 scientific research. ~영화 a science film: 공상 ~ 영화 a science fiction film. ~용어 scientific terms. ~자 a scientist. ~잡지 a science magazine. ~전 scientific warfare. ~지식 scientific knowledge. 국립~박물관 the National Science Museum. 전국~전람회 the National Science Exhibition. 한국~기술 연구원 the Korea Institute of Science and Technology (생략 KIST). 한국~기술원 the Korea Advanced Institute of Science and Technology (생략 KAIST). 한국 ~ 재단 the Korea Science and Engineering Foundation.

**과히**(過―) 《너무》 too (much); excessively; to excess; overly; extremely; 《부정과 함께》 (not) very; (not) so much. ¶ 나는 ~ 바쁘지 않다 I'm not so busy. / ~ 걱정 마라 You worry too much! *or* You don't have to worry too much. / 나는 그것을 ~ 좋아하지 않는다 I do not like it so much.

**곽란**(癨亂·霍亂) 〚한의〛 an intestinal convulsion.

**관**(官) ⇨ 관청. ¶ 관에 있다 be in government service / 관을 물러나다 resign from government service.

**관**(冠) a four-pointed horsehair cap with an open top (formerly worn by the gentry); 《왕관》 a crown; 《귀족 등의》 a coronet. ¶ 왕관 a crown; a diadem / 관을 쓰다 wear 〔put on〕 a crown / 이하(李下)에 부정관(不整冠)이라 Avoid every cause of suspicion.

**관**(貫) ① 《본관》 *one's* ancestral home. ② 《무게》 a unit of weight (= 3.75kg).

**관**(棺) a coffin; a casket 《미》. ¶ 관에 넣다 lay in a coffin / 사람의 가치는 관 뚜껑을 덮고 나서야 안다 A man's worth is settled only when he is laid to rest. *or* Call no man great before he is dead. *or* Posthumous fame is a real fame.

**관**(款) 《조항》 an article; a subsection.

**관**(管) a tube; a pipe; a duct; a conduit. ¶ 유리관 a glass tube / 가스관 a gas pipe / 배수관 a drainage pipe.

**관**(館) ① 《음식점》 a fancy restaurant. ② 《큰 건물》 a large building; 《회관》 a hall. ¶ 한국관 《박람회 등의》 the Korean Pavilion.

**-관**(觀) 《견해》 an outlook; a view. ¶ 세계관 an outlook on the world; a world view / 인생관 an outlook on life / 그의 사회관 his view of society.

**관가**(官家) a public building; a district office (of the government).

**관가**(官街) = 관계(官界).

**관개**(灌漑) 〚농업〛 irrigation; watering. ~하다 irrigate; water (land). ¶ ~ 시설이 되어 있다 have irrigation facilities; be irrigated. ◉ ~공사 irrigation works. ~용수 irrigation water. ~용 수로 an irrigation canal 〔ditch〕. ~지 irrigated (crop) land.

**관객**(觀客) a spectator; a onlookers(구경꾼); [총칭] an audience; [집합적] the house. ¶ 다수의 ~ a large audience / 그 연극은 ~이 대단히 많았다〔적었다〕 The play drew 〔had〕 a large 〔thin〕 house. / 그 패션쇼에는 ~이 많았다 There were a number of spectators at the fashion show. ◉ ~석 the seats 《for the audience》. ~수 attendance. ~층 a type of audience.

**관건**(關鍵) ① 《빗장》 a bolt; a bar. ② 《핵심》 a pivotal 〔key〕 point; an important 〔a vital〕 point 〔post〕. ¶ 사건 해결의 ~을 쥐고 있다 hold the key to (the solution of) the case / 그것이 문제 해결의 ~이 된다 It furnishes a key for the solution of the problem.

**관견**(管見) 《좁은 소견》 a narrow view; 《사견》 *one's* (personal) view 《on》.

**관계**(官界) the official world; officialdom; official 〔government〕 circles. ¶ ~에 있는 사람 a man (who is) in official life 〔in the government service〕 / ~에 들어가다 enter government service / 그는 여러 해 동안 ~에 있었다 He was in public life for many years. ◉ ~쇄신 a renovation of officialdom.

**관계**(關係) ① 《관련》 relation; relationship; (a) connection; 《교제 관계》 relations; 《이해 관계》 (an) interest; (a) concern. ~하다 relate 〔be related〕 《to》; be connected 《with》; have relation 《to》; concern. ¶ 한미 ~ the relationship 〔relations〕 between Korea and the United States; Korean-American relations / 인간 ~ human relationships / 스트레스와 ~되는 병 stress=related diseases / 인과 ~ the relation between cause and effect / …에 ~없이 regardless 〔irrespective〕 of... / ~가 있다〔없다〕 have something 〔nothing〕 to do 《with》 / ~를 끊다 sever 〔break, cut off 〕 connections 《with》; wash *one's* hands of 《*a person, a thing*》 / 우호 ~를 맺다〔유지하다〕 form 〔maintain〕 friendly relations 《with a country》 / 수요는 공급과 ~가 있다 Demand bears a relation to supply. / …사이에는 끊을래야 끊을 수 없는 ~가 있다 There is an indissoluble connection between.... / 너는 그와 어떤 ~냐 How are you related to him? (친척 관계일 때) *or* How are you connected with him? (교제 관계일 때) / 그것은 한미 ~에 중요한 의미를 갖고 있다 It has an important bearing on the relations of Korea to the United States. / 이집트는 리비아와 외교 ~를 단절하였다 Egypt broke off diplomatic relations with Libya. / 농작물의 수확은 날씨와 밀접한 ~가 있다 The crops are closely connected with the weather. / 그녀는 그의 자살과 아무런 ~도 없다 She has nothing to do with his suicide.

② 《관여》 participation; concern; involvement. ~하다 participate 〔take part〕 《in a plot》; be concerned 《in, with, about》; have a hand 《in》; be involved 《in》. ¶ 그 일에 ~가 있다 have a hand in the affair / 나는 그 범죄와 ~가 없다 I am not concerned in the crime. / 이것은 자네가 ~할 일이 아닐세 It is no concern of yours. *or* It's none of your business. / 나는 그 추문과는 ~가 없다 I am not concerned with the scandal. *or* The scandal doesn't concern me. / 현직 시장이 그 수회 사건과 ~되어 있었다 The incumbent mayor was involved in the bribery case.

③ 《영향》 influence; effect. ~하다 affect; influence; have influence 《on》; matter 《to, with》. ¶ ~가 크다 [일이 주어] exert a wide influence 《over, upon》; have far-reaching effect upon / 누가 당선되든지 나에게는 별 ~가 없다 It matters little to me who is elected. / 물가 상승은 일반 국민 생활에 직접 ~된다 A rise in prices has a direct influence on people's way of life.

④ 《성 관계》 (sexual) relations; relationship; an affair. ~하다 have (sexual) relations 《with》; have an affair 《with》; be intimate 《with》. ¶ 불의의 ~ an illicit relationship / 그는 유부녀와 ~하고 있는 것 같다 He seems to have relationships with a married woman.

◉ ~각료 the Cabinet ministers concerned. ~관청 the government office concerned; the competent authorities. ~국 the nation(s) concerned. ~기관 organizations 〔agencies〕 concerned. ~당국 the authorities concerned; the relevant authorities. ~당사자 the parties 〔people〕 concerned. ~대명사〔형용사, 부사〕 〖문법〗 a relative pronoun 〔adjective, adverb〕. ~법규 the related laws and regulations. ~부처 the relevant authorities 〔government offices〕. ~서류 related papers 〔documents〕. ~자 《개인》 a person concerned; 《전체》 a party concerned; 《이해관계의》 an interested party: ~자 일동 all the parties concerned; all interested parties / ~자 각위(各位) To Whom It May Concern (★ 서류 따위를 회람할 때 쓰임) / ~자 외 출입 금지 《게시》 Authorized personnel only. ~제국(諸國) the nations interested 《in》; the countries concerned. ~회사 a concern interested. ⇨ 관련 회사.

**관골**(顴骨) 〖해부〗 the cheekbone; the zygoma (*pl.* -mata). ⇨ 광대뼈.

**관공리**(官公吏) government and municipal officials; public 〔civic〕 officials 〔servants〕.

**관공립**(官公立) government and public 《institutions》. ◉ ~학교 government and public schools.

**관공서**(官公署) government and municipal 〔public〕 offices.

**관광**(觀光) sightseeing; tourism. ~하다 go sightseeing; see 〔do〕 the sights 《of a town》. ¶ 경주로 ~을 가다 go to Kyŏngju to see the sights / 한국에 ~하러 왔나요 Did you come to Korea for sightseeing? / 그녀는 하와이에 ~하러 갔다 She went on a sightseeing trip to Hawaii. / ~산업이 이 도시의 주요 수입원이다 The tourist industry is this town's main source of revenue.

◉ ~객 a tourist; a sightseer: ~객 상대의 상점 a tourist shop / ~객의 유치 inducement of tourists 〔sightseers〕 / 외국인 ~객을 노리는 각종 범죄 various kinds of crimes aiming at foreign tourists. ~국 a country of tourist attraction; a tourist country. ~기념품 a tourism souvenir: ~ 기념품 매장 a souvenir shop. ~단 a sightseeing 〔tourist〕 party 〔group〕. ~도시 a tourist city 〔town〕. ~명소 a scenic spot. ~버스 a sightseeing 〔tourist〕 bus: 종합 ~ 버스 터미널 an integrated tourist bus terminal. ~사업〔산업〕 tourism; the tourist business 〔industry〕. ~사증(査證) a tourist visa. ~선 a sightseeing boat. ~시설 tourist facilities. ~시즌 the tourist season. ~안내(서) a travel brochure. ~안내소 a tourist information center; 《게시》 Tourist Information. ~여행 a sightseeing tour; a pleasure trip. ~자원 tourism resource 〔attractions〕: ~ 자원 개발 tourism resource cultivation. ~지 a tourist 〔sightseeing〕 resort. ~학원 a tourism training institute. ~호텔 a tourist hotel. ~회사 a tourism company. 시내~ city sightseeing. 세계~기구 the World Tourism Organization (생략 WTO). 한국~공사 the Korea National Tourism Organization (생략 KNTO). 한국~협회 the Korea Tourist Association(생략 KTA).

**관구**(管區) the district under 《its》 jurisdiction; 《경찰의》 《미》 a 《police》 precinct.

**관군**(官軍) the government forces 〔troops〕.

**관권**(官權) government authority. ¶ ～을 남용하다 abuse government authority; make an improper use of government power.

**관극**(觀劇) theatergoing; playgoing. ～하다 see a play; enjoy a theatrical performance.

**관급**(官給) government issue (생략 G.I.) 《미》; government supply. ◉ ～품 government issue articles; articles supplied by the government.

**관기**(官紀) official 〔government〕 discipline. ¶ ～를 확립하다 establish rigid discipline among officials.
◉ ～문란 corruption 〔deterioration〕 of official discipline. ～숙정 enforcement of official discipline: ～숙정을 하다 enforce strict official discipline. ～해이 laxity of official discipline.

**관내**(管內) (an area) within the jurisdiction 〔district〕 《of》. ¶ ～를 순시하다 make a tour of inspection through *one's* (area of) jurisdiction.

**관념**(觀念) ① 《생각》 an idea; a concept; a notion; thought. ¶ ～적(인) ideal; abstract; ideological / ～적인 의론 an ideal argument / 잘못된 ～을 가지다 have the wrong idea about 《death》. ② 《감각·의식》 a sense; a spirit. ¶ 책임〔의무, 국가〕 ～ a sense of responsibility 〔duty, nationality〕 / 시간 ～이 없다 have no sense of time.
◉ ～론〔학〕 idealism. ～소설 an ideological novel. ～연합 〖심리〗 association of ideas. ～주의 idealism. ～형태 ideology.

**관노**(官奴) 〖역사〗 a man slave in government employ.

**관능**(官能) 《육체적 감각》 the senses; 《육체의 기능》 organic 〔physical, natural〕 functions; 《육욕》 carnal desire. ¶ ～적(인) functional (기능적); sensuous (감각의); sensual (육감적) / ～적 쾌락 sensual pleasures / ～을 만족시키다 satisfy *one's* carnal desire. ◉ ～미 voluptuous beauty. ～장애 a functional impediment. ～주의 sensualism.

**관다발**(管—) 〖식물〗 a vascular bundle.

**관대**(寬大) generosity; leniency; magnanimity; liberality; broad-〔large-〕 mindedness; tolerance (관용). ～하다 (be) generous; magnanimous; liberal; broad-minded; lenient; tolerant. ¶ ～하게 magnanimously; generously; tolerantly; liberally / ～한 태도 generous attitude / ～한 처벌〔판결〕 lenient punishment 〔sentence〕 / ～하게 다루다 deal with 《*a person*》 leniently / 아이들에게 ～하다 be tolerant toward children / 반대파에 대하여 ～하다 be liberal to the opponents / 재판관의 ～함에 감명을 받다 be impressed by the judge's generosity 〔broad-mindedness〕 / 그는 ～한 사람이다 He has a generous nature 〔spirit〕.

**-관데** ¶ 네가 무엇이관데 그런 짓을 하느냐 What on earth do you mean, doing such a thing? / 무슨 일이관데 그런 곳에 갔느냐 What did you go there for?

**관등**(官等) official rank; civil service grade. ¶ ～이 높다〔낮다〕 be high 〔low〕 in rank; hold a high 〔low〕 position in government service. ◉ ～성명 *one's* official rank and name.

**관등**(觀燈) 〖민속〗 the Festival of Lanterns; the celebration of the birthday of Buddha. ～하다 have the Festival of Lanterns; celebrate Buddha's birthday. ◉ ～놀이 merrymaking at the Lantern Festival. ～절 the Lantern Festival.

**관람**(觀覽) viewing; inspection. ～하다 see; view; watch. ¶ 일반의 ～을 허가하다〔허가하지 않다〕 be open 〔closed〕 to 〔for〕 the public / ～ 시간 09:00—17: 50 《게시》 Opening hours 9:00 a.m.—5:50 p.m. / ～ 무료 《게시》 Admission Free. / 우리는 야구 경기를 ～했다 We watched a baseball game.
◉ ～객〔자〕 a spectator; a visitor. ～권 an admission ticket. ～료 an admission fee; admission. ～석 《극장 등의》 a seat; a chair; a box; 《야구장 등의》 a stand; bleachers 《미》. ～세 the entertainment tax.

**관련**(關聯) connection; relation; association. ～하다 be related 《to》; be connected 《with》; be associated 《with》.
¶ …와 ～하여 in connection 〔conjunction〕 with; in relation to; in 〔with〕 reference to / 그 사건에 ～된 문제 matters connected with 〔related to〕 the incident / 미묘하게 ～된 사실 facts subtly linked together / ～된 질문 《국회 등에서》 an interpellation on related matters / 두 사건은 서로 ～되어 있다 The two cases are 「related to 〔connected with〕 each other. / 폐암과 흡연 사이에는 밀접한 ～이 있다 There is a close connection between smoking and lung cancer. *or* Lung cancer has a close relation to smoking. / 그가 한 이야기와 ～하여 한마디 하고자 합니다 I would like to say a few words in connection with what he said.

◉ ～기사 a related story. ～도 the degree of association. ～부서《정부》 the relevant government ministries. ～사항 related matters; matters relevant to the subject. ～산업 related 〔associated〕 industries 〔businesses〕. ～성 relevance; relevancy: ～성이 있다〔없다〕 be relevant 〔irrelevant〕 《to》/ 자네 질문은 우리가 논의 중인 문제와 아무런 ～성이 없네 Your question has no relevance to the matter we are talking about now. ～자 the persons concerned; those who have something to do 《with》. ～회사 an associated 〔affiliated〕 company.

**관례**(冠禮) the ceremony of doing up *one's* hair; the coming-of-age ceremony. ¶ ～를 치르다 celebrate *one's* coming of age.

**관례**(慣例) (a) custom; (a) usage; a usual practice; 《전례》 a precedent; (a) convention(관습). ¶ ～의 customary; conventional; usual; time-honored / 사회의 ～ a social custom 〔code〕/ ～에 따라 in accordance with custom / ～를〔에〕 따르다 conform to the custom; follow the custom / 사회의 ～를 깨뜨리다 break 〔violate〕 the social custom / …하는 것이 ～이다 It is customary 〔the custom〕 with us to *do* …. *or* The precedents indicate that we should *do*…. / 악수는 오른손을 사용하는 것이 ～이다 Using the right hand to shake hands is a convention. / 신입 회원을 위해 환영회를 여는 것이 우리의 ～이다 It is our custom to welcome the new members by giving a reception. ◉ 국제～ internationally-accepted norms and practices: 국제 ～ 위반 violation of generally recognized international norms.

**관록**(官祿) official salary; a stipend. ¶ ～을 먹다 receive a stipend.

**관록**(貫祿) dignity; presence; weight of character; importance. ¶ ～이 있는 사람 a man of great presence; an imposing figure / ～이 없다 lack dignity / ～이 있다 be 〔look〕 dignified; have 「a lot of 〔great〕 presence / ～이 붙다 gain an air of confidence 〔dignity, presence〕 《as a politician》/ 그는 사장으로서 ～이 있다〔없다〕 He has 〔lacks〕 dignity as president of the company. / 그는 3관왕의 ～을 보였다 He showed what the winner of a triple crown can do.

**관료**(官僚) a government official; a bureaucrat; 〔집합적〕 (the) bureaucracy; officialdom. ¶ ～적(인) bureaucratic / ～출신의 정치가 a politician from officialdom / ～의 독선 the self-righteousness of the bureaucracy / 그의 사고 방식은 ～적이다 He has a bureaucratic way of looking at things. ◉ ～내각 a bureaucratic ministry 〔Cabinet〕. ～정치 bureaucratic government; bureaucracy. ～주의 bureaucracy: ～주의자 a bureaucrat. ～파 a bureaucratic group; the Bureaucrats. 직업～ a career official.

**관류**(貫流) flowing 〔running〕 through. ～하다 flow 〔run〕 through 《a plain》.

**관리**(官吏) a government official 〔employee〕; a public 〔civil〕 servant. ¶ 유능한 ～ an able official / ～가 되다 enter the government service / ～로 있다 be in government service.

**관리**(管理) ① 《지배·감독》 administration; management; control; supervision; superintendence. ～하다 administer 《the foreign affairs of a country》; manage; control 《foreign exchange》; superintend 《a private institution》; supervise. ¶ ～상의 managerial; administrative / 정부 ～의 공장 a government-controlled factory / 학교를 ～하다 manage 〔administrate〕 a school / 회사 사무를 ～하다 manage the business affairs of a company / …의 ～를 명령받다 be put 〔placed〕 in charge of… / 정부 ～하에 두다 place 《*a matter*》 under government control / 정부 ～하에 있다 be under government control / 이 운동장은 시에서 ～하고 있다 This playground is under the supervision of the city. / 이 아파트는 ～가 잘 되어 있다 This apartment house is well looked after. / 서투른 인사 ～가 그가 도산한 큰 원인이다 Poor personnel management is the principal reason for his bankruptcy. ② 《보관》 charge; care. ～하다 take 〔have, assume〕 charge of; care for. ¶ 남의 재산을 ～하다 take 〔have〕 charge of another's property / 재산의 ～를 맡기다 entrust 〔confide〕 *one's* property to 《*a person's*》 care; place 〔have〕 *one's* property under 《*a person's*》 care; put *one's* property in 《*a person's*》 charge.

◉ ～가격 〖경제〗 an administered price. ～검사 control inspection. ～권 the right of management. ～기관 a managing agency. ～능력 capacity of management. ～비 management expenses. ～사무소 a superintendent's 〔control〕 office. ～직 an administrative 〔a managerial〕 position 《in an office》; [총칭] (the) management. ～태만 negligence of administration.

**관리인**(管理人) an administrator; a manager; 《사무실·공장·공사장 등의》 a supervisor; a superintendent; 《유산의》 an executor; 《아파트 등의》 a caretaker; a concierge; a janitor 《미》; 《재산의》 a property custodian. ¶ 아파트 ～ an apartment house manager / 「열쇠를 방 안에 두고 문을 잠갔어요」—「그럼 ～에게 도움을 청하세요」 "I shut 〔locked〕 the key inside."—"Then you'd better talk to the caretaker."

**관립**(官立) a government institution.

**관망**(觀望) observation; watching; fence-sitting. ～하다 observe; watch; wait and see; sit on the fence. ¶ 사태를 ～하다 calmly watch the development of the situation / ～적 태도를 취하다 assume a wait-and-see attitude / 좀더 ～해 보세 Let's wait a little longer and see. ◉ ～주의 a wait-and-see policy.

**관명**(官名) an official title. ¶ ～을 사칭하다 assume an official title.

**관명**(官命) official orders; 《관용》 an official mission 〔business〕. ¶ ～에 의하여 by government 〔official〕 order; by order of the government / ～을 띠고 under official orders; on official business 〔mission〕.

**관모**(冠毛) ① 〖식물〗 a pappus (*pl.* pappi). ② 〖조류〗 a crest.

**관목**(灌木) shrubs; a bush. ◉ ～숲 shrubbery. ～지대 a shrubbery zone.

**관문**(關門) ① 《통과해야 할 난관》 a barrier 〔hurdle〕 《to success in life》; 《문호》 a gateway 《to the Far East》. ¶ ～을 통과하다 get over a barrier; pass a gateway / 입학 시험의 ～을 통과하다 pass (the barrier of) the entrance examination / 김포 국제 공항은 한국의 ～이다 Kimp'o International Airport is the gateway to Korea. / 인생에는 극복해야 할 많은 ～이 있다 Life has many hurdles in store for us which we must overcome. ② 《요새·국경 등의》 a boundary 〔barrier〕 gate; a checkpoint (검문소).

**관물**(官物) government issues; government property.

**관민**(官民) the government and the people; officials and private individuals. ¶ ～이 협력하여 by the united efforts of government and people / ～이 일치하여 부정부패를 근절시켜야 한다 The government and the people must unite and root out corruption.

**관변측**(官邊側) 《in》 official 〔government〕 circles 〔quarters〕; government sources. ¶ 그 정보는 ～에서 나온 것 같다 The information seems to have come from an official source.

**관보**(官報) ① 《정부 인쇄물》 an official gazette; a gazette 《영》 (★ 기관지일때는 대문자로 시작). ¶ ～로 발표하다 publish 〔announce〕 in 〔by〕 the official gazette; gazette / ～에 실리다〔나다〕 be published in the Official Gazette. ② 《공용 전보》 an official telegram.

**관복**(官服) an official outfit 〔uniform〕.

**관불**(灌佛) 〖불교〗 the rite of pouring perfume on Buddha's statue.

**관비**(官費) government expense(s). ⇨ 국비. ◉ ～생 a holder of a government scholarship; a government student. ～유학생 a government student abroad.

**관비**(官婢) 〖역사〗 a woman slave in government employ.

**관사**(官舍) an official residence. ¶ ～를 배당받다 be provided with an official residence. ◉ 장관～ a Minister's official residence.

**관사**(冠詞) 〖문법〗 an article. ¶ 이 낱말은 ～가 붙지 않는다 This word takes no article before it.

**관상**(冠狀) coronal (in) shape; crown-shape(d). ◉ ～동맥〔정맥〕 coronary arteries 〔veins〕: ～동맥혈전증 (a) coronary thrombosis; a coronary 《구어》. ～봉합 〖해부〗 a coronal suture.

**관상**(管狀) ¶ ～의 tubular; tubulous; tube-shape(d). ◉ ～기관 〖곤충〗 a fistula. ～화 〖식물〗 a tubular flower.

**관상**(觀相) phrenological interpretation. ¶ ～을 보다 judge 〔read〕 《*a person's*》 fortune by the face; tell 《*a person's*》 fortune by physiognomy. ◉ ～가〔쟁이〕 a physiognomist; a phrenologist. ～술〔학〕 (the art of) physiognomy; phrenology.

**관상**(觀賞) viewing with admiration; enjoyment. ～하다 view with admiration; enjoy; admire. ¶ 열대어를 ～하다 enjoy observing tropical fish. ◉ ～식물 an ornamental 〔a decorative〕 plant. ～어 an aquarium fish.

**관상**(觀象) meteorological observation. ～하다 observe the weather; make meteorological observations. ◉ ～대 ⇨ 기상대.

**관서**(官署) a government office. ◉ 중앙~ the offices of the central government. 지방~ local government offices.

**관선**(官選) ¶ ~의 chosen 〔appointed〕 by the government. ◉ ~변호인 a court-appointed lawyer 〔attorney〕; a public defender. ~이사 a government-appointed trustee.

**관설**(官設) a government facility 〔installation, establishment〕. ¶ ~의 established by the government.

**관성**(慣性) 『물리』 inertia. ¶ ~의 법칙 the law of inertia. ◉ ~비행 《우주선 따위의》 inertial navigation. ~유도 inertial guidance: ~유도의 inertia-guided; guided by inertia. ~항법장치 『항공』 the inertial navigation system (생략 INS).

**관세**(關稅) a tariff; customs; customs duties. ¶ ~의 일괄 인하 across-the-board reduction of tariffs / 다국간 ~ (인하) 교섭 the multilateral tariff negotiations (생략 MTN) / ~가 붙는 dutiable; customable 《미》/ ~가 붙지 않는 duty-free; undutiable / ~를 부과하다 levy 〔impose〕 (customs) duties 《on imported goods》/ ~를 치르고 화물을 인수하다 clear goods / 외국 상품에 대한 ~가 10% 인상되었다 Customs duties on foreign goods have been raised by ten percent. /「이 TV세트에 ~가 부과됩니까」—「아니, 부과 안 됩니다」 "Is there (a) customs on this TV set?"—"No, there isn't."
◉ ~개정 a tariff reform. ~동맹 a customs union. ~면세품 a duty-free article; an article on the free list. ~법 the Customs (Tariff) Law. ~수입(收入) tariff revenue. ~율 a tariff rate. ~장벽 a tariff wall 〔barrier〕: 외래품에 대해 ~ 장벽을 높이다 raise tariff walls against foreign goods / ~ 장벽을 설치〔제거〕하다 erect 〔remove〕 a tariff wall 〔customs barrier〕. ~정책 a tariff policy. ~조약 a tariff treaty. ~청 the Customs Service: ~청장 Commissioner of the Customs Service. ~협정 customs agreement. ~환급 customs refund. 호혜(互惠)~ a reciprocal tariff. 탄력(彈力)~제(制) elastic tariff system.

**관세음보살**(觀世音菩薩) the Buddhist Goddess of Mercy; Avalokitesvara 《Sans.》.

**관솔** resinous part of pine wood; a pine knot. ◉ ~불 a fire set to pine knots.

**관수**(官需) an official demand. ◉ ~물자 《medical》 supplies for government use.

**관수**(灌水) ~하다 sprinkle water; irrigate. ◉ ~장치 a sprinkler.

**관수지대**(冠水地帶) a submerged 〔flooded〕 zone 〔area〕.

**관습**(慣習) (a) custom; (a) usage; 《관례》 (a) usual 〔common〕 practice; 《인습》 convention. ¶ ~적(인) customary; usual; conventional / ~에 의하여 according to the usage 〔custom〕 / 일반화된 ~ accepted usage / 오랜 ~을 지키다 keep 〔adhere〕 to old customs / 오랜 ~을 깨다 break an old custom / 그 마을에는 오래된 ~이 꽤 많이 있다 Many old customs are kept alive in that village. / 한국에서 이것은 일상의 ~이다 In Korea this is the convention of daily life. ◉ ~법 the conventional 〔common, customary〕 law.

**관심**(關心) concern; (an) interest. ¶ (…에) ~을 갖다 be concerned about; take 〔have〕 (an) interest 《in》; be interested 《in》/ (…에) ~이 없다 be indifferent to; be unconcerned with / ~을 끌다 arouse 〔awake〕 《*a person's*》 interest 《in》/ 깊은 ~을 갖고 보다 watch with deep concern / 일반의 ~의 대상이 되다 become the center of public interest / 젊은이들은 새로 나온 차에 강한 ~을 보인다 Young people show a keen interest in the new car. / 그들은 환경 문제에 ~이 없다 They are indifferent to environmental issues. / 우리는 선거 결과에 ~이 있다 We are interested in the result of the election. / 나는 그녀에 대한 ~이 없어졌다 I have lost interest in her.
◉ ~사 a matter of concern (and interest): 최대〔중대〕~사 a matter of primary 〔grave〕 concern / 공동 ~사 a matter of common interest / 우리의 최대 ~사는 이 불황을 어떻게 극복하느냐이다 Our greatest concern is how to tide over the present recession.

**관아**(官衙) 《옛 관청》 a government office; a government agency.

**관악**(管樂) 『음악』 wind(-instrument) music; pipe music. ◉ ~기 a wind instrument.

**관여**(關與) participation. ~하다 take part 《in》; have 〔take〕 a hand 《in》; participate 《in》; be concerned 《in》. ¶ 사건에 ~하다 be involved in a case; take part 〔participate〕 in an affair /

정부의 정책 결정에 ～하다 participate in the decision-making of the Government / 그들은 수회 사건에 ～했다는 의혹을 받고 있다 They are suspected of having been connected with the bribery case. / 네가 ～할 바가 아니다 You have nothing to do with this. *or* This is none of your business.

**관엽식물**(觀葉植物) a foliage plant.

**관영**(官營) government management 〔control, operation〕. ¶ ～의 government-controlled〔-managed, -operated, -financed〕/ ～으로 하다 nationalize; put《an enterprise》under government management. ◉ ～사업 a government enterprise〔undertaking〕.

**관외**(管外) ¶ ～의 outside the jurisdiction〔control〕《of》.

**관용**(官用)《용도》official use;《일》government〔official〕business. ¶ ～의 for official use / ～으로 on official business. ◉ ～차 an official vehicle.

**관용**(慣用) common use; usage. ¶ ～의 common; usual; in common〔everyday〕use;《습관적인》customary;《어구의》idiomatic / ～되고 있다 be in common use / ～에 어긋나다 be contrary to usage. ◉ ～구〔어〕an idiom; an idiomatic phrase〔word〕. ～수단 an old trick; the same old trick. ～어법 colloquialism. ～영어 idiomatic〔colloquial〕English. ～음 『언어』 the traditional pronunciation. ～(적) 표현 an idiomatic expression.

**관용**(寬容) toleration; tolerance; leniency; generosity. ～하다 (be) generous; tolerant; forgive〔pardon〕with generosity; tolerate; show leniency《toward *a person*》. ¶ ～의 정신 the spirit of tolerance / ～해 주시기 바랍니다 Please be more generous to us. / 행복한 결혼 생활을 유지하기 위해서는 ～과 인내가 필요하다 Tolerance and patience are necessary to maintain a happy marriage.

**관원**(官員) a government official; a public official.

**관위**(官位) official rank. ¶ ～를 박탈하다 divest〔deprive〕《*a person*》of *his* official rank.

**관유**(官有) government〔state〕ownership.

**관음보살**(觀音菩薩) ⇨ 관세음보살.

**관인**(官印) an official〔a government〕seal. ¶ ～을 찍다 put〔affix〕an official seal《to》.

**관인**(官認) ＝ 관허(官許).

**관인**(寬仁) generosity; benignancy. ～하다 (be) generous; liberal; broad-minded; benignant; lenient.

**관자**(貫子) gold or jade beads on the two strings on either side of a horsehair hat.

**관자놀이**(貫子—) the temples of *one's* head.

**관작**(官爵) government office and court rank.

**관장**(管掌) management; control; charge. ～하다 manage; control; take charge of; have《*a matter*》in charge. ¶ 국가의 공중 위생을 ～하다 manage the public health of the state / 사무를 ～하다 take charge of〔supervise〕business affairs. ◉ ～업무 the business duties in *one's* charge.

**관장**(館長) a superintendent; a director; a chief〔head〕librarian (도서관의); a curator (박물관의).

**관장**(灌腸) (an) enema. ～하다 give〔administer〕an enema《to》; clyster. ◉ ～기 an enema pipe. ～제 an enema; clyster.

**관재**(管財) 『법』 administration of property; custodianship;《파산 때의》receivership. ～하다 manage〔have custody of〕property; administer; put《property》under *one's* custody. ◉ ～국 the bureau of property custody. ～인《유산의》an administrator;《파산 시의》a〔an official〕receiver;《공공물의》a trustee.

**관저**(官邸) an official residence. ◉ 수상～ the Prime Minister's official residence.

**관전**(觀戰)《군 작전 등을》observation of military operations;《경기의》watching a game〔contest, match〕. ～하다《군 작전을》observe military operations;《경기를》watch a game〔contest, match〕. ◉ ～기(記) an on-the-spot report《of a game》; a witness' account《of》.

**관절**(關節) a joint; an articulation. ¶ ～의 articular / 팔꿈치 ～을 삐다 sprain *one's* elbow joint / 나는 오른쪽 어깨 ～이 탈골되었다 I dislocated my right arm. / 그녀는 넘어져서 무릎 ～이 탈골되었다 She fell and put her knee out of joint. ◉ ～강직 ankylosis; a stiff joint. ～동물 an articulate animal. ～류머티즘 articular〔joint〕rheumatism. ～신경통 articular neuralgia. ～염 arthritis; inflammation of a joint. ～통 arthralgia.

**관점**(觀點) a point of view; a viewpoint; a standpoint; an angle (of vision). ¶ 모든 ～에서 from all angles /

다른 ～에서 보다 consider 《*a matter*》 from a different standpoint / ～이 다르다 have a different point of view; differ in opinion 《from》 / 실용적인 ～에서 보면, 그의 안이 너의 것보다 더 좋다 From a practical point of view 〔viewpoint〕, his plan is better than yours. / 다른 ～에서 이 문제를 보도록 하자 Let's look at the problem from a different angle.

**관정**(管井) a tube well.

**관제**(官制) government organization 〔setup〕; official regulations. ¶ ～를 정하다 establish a government organization. ◉ ～개편 reform of government organization; reorganization of the government offices.

**관제**(官製) government manufacture. ¶ ～의 manufactured by the government; government-manufactured 〔=made〕; of government make.
◉ ～데모 a government-inspired demonstration. ～민의(民意) a government-fabricated (public) opinion. ～엽서 a postal card; a postcard.

**관제**(管制) 《통제》 control; controlling. ～하다 control; place 《*something*》 under (government) control. ¶ ～하에 두다 place 〔bring〕 《*something*》 under control. ◉ ～사 a 〔an air-traffic〕 controller. ～장치 a controlling gear. ～탑 《비행장의》 a control tower.

**관조**(觀照) contemplation; meditation. ～하다 contemplate; meditate. ¶ 자연〔인생〕을 ～하다 contemplate nature 〔life〕.

**관족**(官足) 〖동물〗 a tube 〔an ambulacral〕 foot.

**관존민비**(官尊民卑) respect for the officials and disrespect for the people; putting government above 〔before〕 people; the preponderance of official power. ¶ ～의 폐풍 the deplorable custom of making much of the government and little of the people / ～의 습관 custom of putting the government above the people.

**관중**(觀衆) spectators; onlookers; 《a member of》 the audience. ¶ 야구장의 ～ the audience in the ballpark / ～이 많다〔적다〕 have a large 〔small〕 audience / 그는 ～의 우레 같은 박수를 받으며 등장했다 He appeared on the stage amid a thunderous handclapping of the audience. / 모든 ～이 일제히 일어섰다 The whole audience got up on its feet all at once.

**관직**(官職) a government office 〔job〕; an official post. ¶ ～에 앉다 enter government service; take up a government post / ～에 있다 be in the government service; hold an office under government.

**관찰**(觀察) observation; survey. ～하다 observe; make an observation; look at; watch. ¶ 정확한 ～ an accurate observation / 개미의 습성에 대한 ～ observations on the habits of ants / 나의 ～에 의하면 according to my observation; as I look at it / 내 ～에 잘못이 없다면 unless my observation deceives me / ～을 그르치다 make an incorrect observation.
◉ ～기록 a record of *one's* observations. ～력 (the power of) observation: ～력이 예리한〔부족한〕 사람 a man of keen 〔narrow〕 observation / ～력을 기르다 foster *one's* power of observation. ～안 an observing 〔observant〕 eye. ～자 an observer.

**관찰사**(觀察使) 〖역사〗 a (provincial) governor.

**관철**(貫徹) accomplishment; fulfillment; realization. ～하다 accomplish; achieve; attain; realize; carry out 〔through〕. ¶ 목적을 ～하다 realize 〔carry through〕 *one's* purpose; attain *one's* object / 초지를 ～하다 carry out *one's* original intention / 끝까지 요구를 ～하자 Let us push on our demand to the last. / 너는 네 사업을 ～해야 한다 You must carry through your business.

**관청**(官廳) a government office. ¶ ～의 형식적인 사무방식 red-tapism; officialism / …사무의 감독 ～ the authorities supervising the affairs of... / ～에 근무하다 attend 〔serve in〕 a government office. ◉ ～가 the district where (most of) the government offices are located. ～용어 official terminology 〔jargon〕; officialese. ～집무시간 official hours of work.

**관측**(觀測) 《관찰》 observation; a survey; 《생각·의견》 opinion. ～하다 observe; make an observation; survey. ¶ 희망적인 ～ wishful thinking / 나의 ～으로는 in my opinion / 기상〔천문〕을 ～하다 make meteorological 〔astronomical〕 observations / 일식을 ～하다 make observations of a solar eclipse / 정부는 경기가 곧 회복될 것이라고 ～하고 있다 The Government predicts that the economy will pick up soon.
◉ ～기구 an observation balloon; [비유적] 《send up》 a trial balloon. ～기록 a record of *one's* observations 《of,

on》. ～망 an observation network. ～소 an observatory; an observation post 〔station〕. ～자 an observer. ～자료 observational data. ～지점 an observation point 〔site〕. ～통 《사람》 an observer: …라고 ～통은 말하고 있다 Observers say that….

**관통**(貫通) piercing; penetration. ～하다 pass 〔go〕 through; pierce; penetrate; 《총알 따위가》 shoot 〔go〕 through. ¶ 터널이 산을 ～하고 있다 The mountain is pierced by a tunnel. / 탄알이 심장을 ～했다 A bullet went through 〔penetrated〕 the heart. / 철도가 대평원을 ～하고 있다 The railroad goes all the way across the great plain.
◉ ～상(傷) a piercing bullet wound.

**관포지교**(管鮑之交) an extremely close friendship; a Damon and Pythias 〔David and Jonathan〕 friendship.

**관하**(管下) ¶ ～의〔에〕 under the jurisdiction 〔control〕 of. ⇨관할.

**관하다**(關—) ① 《관계되다》 refer to; be connected with; be about; relate to; be related to; concern. ¶ 내게 관한 한 so 〔as〕 far as I am concerned / 전쟁〔군인〕에 관한 책 a book about war 〔servicemen〕 / 원예에 관한 책 a book on gardening / 환경 위생에 관한 법률 laws regarding 〔concerning〕 environmental sanitation / 그 사람에 관해서 말하다 speak concerning 〔about〕 him / 경제 문제에 관한 논문을 쓰다 write a treatise on economic problems / 한국전에 관한 조사자료를 모으다 collect research materials 「on 〔relating to〕 the (1950-53) Korean War / 그 모임에서는 과학에 관한 문제가 토의될 예정이다 Matters pertaining to 〔touching upon〕 science are to be discussed at the meeting. ② 《영향을 미치다》 affect; have to do with; have influence 〔bearing〕 on. ¶ 건강에 관한 대책 measures that bear on 〔affect〕 *one's* health / 명예에 관한 문제 a question of 〔affecting〕 *one's* honor / 생사에 관한 문제 a matter of life and death / 그것은 국가의 위신에 관한 문제다 It is a problem in which national honor and prestige are involved.

**관학**(官學) a government school.

**관할**(管轄) jurisdiction; control; competence. ～하다 exercise the jurisdiction 〔control〕 《over》; have competence over; govern. ¶ ～ 내〔밖〕의 within 〔outside〕 the jurisdiction 《of》 / …의 ～에 속하다 fall under the jurisdiction of…; be within the province of…; be under the control of / 그 업무는 본사의 ～에 속한다 The business is within 〔under〕 the jurisdiction of the head 〔main〕 office.
◉ ～관청 the competent authorities 〔offices〕. ～구역 the sphere 〔extent, district〕 of jurisdiction; 《경찰의》 a police district 〔precinct 《미》〕. ～권 jurisdiction: ～권 다툼 a jurisdictional dispute / 그 섬은 우리 나라가 ～권을 갖고 있다 Our country has jurisdiction over the island. ～법원 a competent court. ～서 the police station concerned; the competent police authorities.

**관함식**(觀艦式) a naval review.

**관행**(慣行) traditional 〔usual, customary, habitual〕 practice; a custom; routine. ¶ ～의 habitual; customary; practical / 국제적 ～ an international practice / ～에 따라 in accordance with (the) custom.

**관향**(貫鄕) the birthplace of *one's* first ancestor.

**관허**(官許) government permission; (government) license. ～하다 give a government permit 〔license〕 for; officially license. ¶ ～의 licensed / ～를 얻어 with government permission; under government license. ◉ ～요금 (government-)licensed charge.

**관헌**(官憲) 《관리》 government officials; 《당국》 the (administrative, government) authorities; 《경찰》 the police authorities. ¶ ～의 간섭 the government interference / ～의 압력 the pressure of the authorities.

**관현**(管絃) wind and stringed instruments. ◉ ～악 an orchestra; orchestral music: ～악 반주 an orchestral accompaniment / ～악단 an orchestra (band).

**관형사**(冠形詞) 〖문법〗 a pre-noun.

**관혼상제**(冠婚喪祭) 《사례(四禮)》 ceremonial occasions; the ceremonies of coming-of-age (=doing up the hair), marriage, funeral, and ancestor memorial.

**관후**(寬厚) generosity; liberality; magnanimity. ～하다 (be) generous; liberal; magnanimous; large-hearted. ¶ ～한 태도 an air of magnanimity / ～하게 generously; liberally. ◉ ～장자(長者) a magnanimous gentleman.

**괄괄하다** ① 《풀기가》 (be) too stiff. ¶ 이 셔츠는 풀이 너무 ～ This shirt is starched too stiff. ② [성미가] 《맹렬한》 (be) virile; spirited; fiery; 《성급한》 impetuous; hot-tempered; hotheaded. ¶ 괄괄한 사람 a spirited person; a hothead; a person of impetuous disposition.

**괄다** 《불이》 (be) high; strong. ¶ 불이 너무 괄아 밥이 탔다 The rice is burnt because the fire was too high.

**괄대**(恝待) a cold reception; cool treatment; inhospitality. ⇨ 냉대(冷待).

**괄목**(刮目) looking at 《*a person*》 carefully rubbing *one's* eyes; watching with 「keen interest 〔great expectations, close attention〕. ～하다 look at 《*a person*》 carefully rubbing *one's* eyes; watch 〔look〕 with keen interest. ¶ ～상대(相對)하다 look at each other with astonishment (at the progress each has made during their separation); each rubs his eyes in wonder / ～할 만하다 be worthy of close attention / 산업에서 ～할 만한 발전을 이룩하다 make a remarkable 〔an eye-catching〕 growth of industry.

**괄시**(恝視) maltreatment; inhospitability; negligence; cold treatment. ～하다 treat 《*a person*》 coldly; be inhospitable 《toward》; neglect; slight. ¶ 너무 ～하지 마라 Don't hold me so cheap. / 그녀는 회사에서 ～받고 있다 She is left out in the cold in the company.

**괄약근**(括約筋) 〖해부〗 a sphincter; a constrictor; sphincteral muscles. ¶ 항문의 ～ the sphincter anal.

**괄태충**(括胎蟲) a slug.

**괄호**(括弧) 《둥근 괄호》 a parenthesis (*pl.* -ses); 《각괄호》 a (square) bracket; 《중괄호》 a brace. ¶ ～ 안의 글자 the words in the brackets / ～로 묶다 put 《a word》 in brackets 〔parentheses〕; parenthesize / ～를 벗기다 remove brackets 〔parentheses〕. ◉ 이중～ double parentheses.

**괌** 《태평양 서부의 섬》 Guam (생략 GU).

**광** a storeroom; a storehouse; a cellar (지하실); a granary (곡창).

**광**(光) ① ＝빛. ② 《광택》 gloss; luster; polish; brilliance(보석 등의); (a) sheen(천·광물의). ¶ 광이 나는 glossy; lustrous; polished / 광이 없는 dim; dull; lusterless / 광을 내다 gloss; bring out the luster; polish (up); put a glaze on; burnish 《metal》 / 광을 죽이다 dim 〔take off, tone down〕 the shine 〔luster, gloss〕; dull the finish / 번쩍번쩍 광이 나도록 부드러운 가죽으로 마루를 닦다 buff the floor to a high polish.

**광**(壙) 《무덤 구덩이》 the hollow of a grave; a burial hole.

**광**(鑛) ① 《덩어리》 a (mineral) ore. ② 《갱》 a pit; a mine.

**-광**(狂) 《성벽》 a mania; 《사람》 a maniac ; a fan. ¶ 정치〔스포츠〕광 an enthusiast for politics 〔sports〕 / 야구광 a baseball fan; a craze 〔mania〕 for baseball / 장서광 bibliomania.

**광각**(光角) 〖물리〗 an optic angle.

**광각**(光覺) 〖생리〗 the optic sense; sensation of light; photoreceptivity; photosensitivity.

**광각**(廣角) a wide angle. ◉ ～렌즈 a wide-angle lens; a pantoscope.

**광갱**(鑛坑) a mine pit 〔shaft〕; a mine.

**광견**(狂犬) a mad dog; a rabid dog. ◉ ～병 rabies; hydrophobia: ～병에 걸리다 be affected with rabies / ～병 공포증 lyssophobia / ～병 예방 주사 an antirabies serum injection; (an) antihydrophobia inoculation.

**광경**(光景) a spectacle; a scene; a sight; a view.

> 용법 **spectacle** 눈이 번쩍 뜨일 정도의 아름답고 인상적인 광경. **scene** 넓게 펼쳐진 경치 중에서 눈앞에 보이는 좁은 범위의 한 장면. 흔히 사람의 움직임을 암시하는 뜻으로도 쓰임. **sight** 하나의 구체적인 광경, 관찰자의 관심을 끄는 인공적인 명소·사건·사물의 광경. **view** 한 장소에서 바라본 광경. 가장 일반적인 뜻으로 쓰이는 말.

¶ 끔찍한 ～ a terrible 〔disastrous〕 sight 〔scene〕 / 장엄한 ～ a very impressive scene / 아름다운〔애처로운〕 ～을 보여 주다 present a 「fine spectacle 〔pitiful sight〕 / 하늘에서 본 서울의 ～은 아름답다 The air view of Seoul is very beautiful. / 그 ～은 필설로 다 표현할 수 없다 The sight is beyond description. / 나는 사고의 처참한 ～에 충격을 받았다 I was shocked by the horrifying scene of the accident.

**광고**(廣告) an advertisement; an ad 《구어》; 《고지》 a notice; an announcement; 《선전》 publicity. ～하다 advertise 《for》; give publicity 《to》; announce; publicize 《미》; 《게시판 등에》 put up a bill 〔poster〕; make 《*a thing*》 widely known. ¶ 3단짜리 ～ a three-column advertisement / 전면 ～ a full-page advertisement / 대대적으로 ～하다 advertise extensively / 신문에 ～를 내다 advertise 〔put an ad〕 in a newspaper / 구직 ~를 내다 advertise ┌for employment 〔a position〕/ 신문에 구인 ~를 내다 run 〔put〕 a want ad in a paper / 방송에 ~를 넣다 insert a commercial in a radio 〔TV〕 program / ~를 보고 사다 buy 《*a thing*》 from an advertisement / 미아〔분실〕 ~를 내다 advertise for the recovery of a missing child 〔a lost article〕/ 최신형 냉장고를 TV에 광고하다 advertise the latest model refrigerator on television / 그것은 우리 회사의 좋은 ~가 된다 That will make our company better known to the public. / ~를 붙이지 마시오 《게시》 Post no bills. ◉ ~권유원 an ad(vertising) canvasser 〔solicitor, man〕; an adman 《미》. ~기구〔풍선〕 an ad balloon. ~(대리)업 an advertising agency 〔business〕: ~(대리)업자 an ad(vertisement) agent; an ad collector; an adman 《미》; a publicity agent. ~등(燈) a sign lamp; advertising lighting 〔lights〕. ~란 an advertisement column; an ad column; 《사람 찾는》 an agony column 《영》. ~료 ad(vertisement) rates; 《영》 advertising rates 〔charges〕. ~매체 the advertising media. ~문 a written advertisement. ~방송 a commercial broadcast; a commercial; a plug 《미구어》: ~ 방송 프로 a commercial (radio) program; a sponsor(ed) program / ~ 방송의 스폰서가 되다 sponsor 《a program》. ~부 the publicity department. ~비 an outlay for advertisement. ~산업 advertising industry. ~수입 advertising revenue. ~스폰서〔주〕 a sponsor(라디오·TV의); an advertiser: ~ 스폰서 제공의 프로 a sponsor(ed) program / ~ 감소로 경영난에 빠지다 suffer from financial difficulties owing to a loss of advertising. ~업 the advertising business: ~업자 an advertising agent. ~쪽지〔전단〕 a bill; a handbill; a poster (붙이는 것). ~탑 an advertisement tower; a poster column (가두의); an ad pillar (옥상의). ~판 a billboard; a signboard. ~효과 effectiveness of advertisement; advertising impact.

**광공업**(鑛工業) the mining and manufacturing industries.

**광구**(光球) 〖천문〗 a photosphere.

**광구**(鑛區) a mining area 〔field, concession〕; a mine lot. ¶ 제 6 ~《석유의》 the continental shelf Block 6. ◉ ~세 a mine-lot tax.

**광궤**(廣軌) a broad gauge; the standard gauge. ◉ ~철도 a broad-gauge railroad 〔railway 《영》〕.

**광기**(狂氣) madness; craziness; insanity; (a) frenzy. ¶ ~의 insane; mad; crazy / ~로 저지른 행동 an act of sheer madness / 그의 열성은 ~에 가깝다 His zeal verges on madness.

**광꾼**(鑛—) 《광부》 a miner; a mine worker; 《경멸》 a grubby miner.

**광나다**(光—) 《윤이 나다》 be glossy 〔shiny, lustrous, polished〕; have a gloss 〔shine, luster, glaze〕. ¶ 구두가 ~ the shoes are shiny.

**광내다**(光—) shine; make 《*a thing*》 glossy; give luster 《to》; bring out the luster 《of》; polish; burnish; put a gloss 《on》. ¶ 광내는 가루약 polishing powder / 구두를 ~ shine shoes / 금속편을 ~ burnish a piece of metal.

**광녀**(狂女) a madwoman.

**광년**(光年) 〖천문〗 a light-year.

**광대** 《옛날의 연예인》 a performer; an entertainer; a feat singer (창극의); a comedian; 《어릿광대》 a clown; a jester; a buffoon; 《곡예사》 an acrobat; a ropewalker. ¶ ~가 되다 go on the stage / ~노릇을 하다 play the jester 〔fool〕. ◉ ~놀음 《광대의 연기》 a low comedy; a farce; acrobatic feats. ~등걸 a hollow face.

**광대나물** 〖식물〗 a henbit; a bee nettle.

**광대무변**(廣大無邊) ~하다 (be) boundless; unbounded; vast and boundless; infinite. ¶ ~한 우주 the boundless universe.

**광대버섯** 〖식물〗 a fly agaric.

**광대뼈** a cheekbone; a malar (bone). ¶ ~가 나오다 have high 〔prominent〕 cheekbones.

**광대수염** 〖식물〗 a (white) dead nettle.

**광대하다**(廣大—) (be) vast; extensive; immense; boundless; be broad and wide.

**광도**(光度) 〖물리〗 intensity of light; luminous intensity; (the degree of) brightness; luminosity. ¶ 별의 ~ the magnitude 〔brightness〕 of a star / ~ 0.2, a magnitude of 0.2. ◉ ~계 a light meter; a photometer. ~측정 photometry.

**광독**(鑛毒) mineral pollution; mineral poisoning. ¶ ~의 피해 damage from mine pollution.

**광란**(狂亂) frenzy; craziness; madness. ~하다 be frenzied; be 〔become〕 frantic; go 〔be driven〕 mad. ¶ 반(半) ~

의 half-mad; half-crazy / 그녀는 너무 슬퍼서 ～ 상태가 되었다 She went mad 〔crazy〕 with grief.

**광력**(光力) 〖물리〗 illuminating power; light; 《촉광》 candlepower. ◉ ～계(計) an actinometer.

**광림**(光臨) your esteemed visit 〔call, presence〕. ～하다 condescend to come 〔be present〕; honor 〔favor〕 us with a visit. ¶ ～의 영광을 얻고 싶습니다 I will be glad to be honored with your presence.

**광막하다**(廣漠—) (be) vast; wide; spacious; extensive; boundless. ¶ 광막한 땅 a wide spread of country; a vast 〔an extensive〕 tract of land / 광막한 평원 a vast expanse of plains.

**광망**(光芒) 〖물리〗 a beam 〔shaft〕 of light.

**광맥**(鑛脈) a mineral vein; a vein (of ore); a deposit; a lode. ¶ 큰 ～ immense deposits; a mother lode / ～을 발견하다 strike a vein of ore. ◉ ～층 a seam 〔vein〕 of ore.

**광명**(光明) 《빛》 light; a sunbeam; 《희망》 hope; a bright prospect 〔future〕. ¶ 인생에 한 줄기 ～을 찾아내다 find a ray 〔gleam〕 of hope in life / 맹인에게 ～을 찾아주다 [비유적] restore sight to the blind / 어둠 속에서 ～을 찾다 see the silver lining in the dark / 그녀의 앞날에는 ～이 있다 She has a bright future before her.

**광목**(廣木) white cotton (broad) cloth.

**광물**(鑛物) a mineral. ¶ ～(성, 질)의 mineral / 풍부〔빈약〕한 ～ 자원 rich 〔poor〕 mineral resources. ◉ ～계 the mineral kingdom 〔world〕. ～성 섬유 a mineral fiber. ～성 수지〔연료〕 mineral resin 〔fuel〕. ～유(油) mineral oil. ～질 mineral matter. ～학 mineralogy: ～학자 a mineralogist.

**광반**(光斑) 〖사진〗 a flare (spot).

**광배**(光背) 《원광·후광》 a halo; a nimbus. ¶ ～가 있는 부처의 그림 a painting of Buddha with his head surrounded by a halo.

**광범**(廣範) ～하다 (be) extensive; broad; wide; far-reaching; wide-ranging; comprehensive (포괄적인). ¶ ～한 영향을 미치다 exert a far-reaching influence 《on, over》 / 태풍의 피해는 ～한 지역에 미쳤다 The typhoon caused damage over an extensive area.

**광범위**(廣範圍) 《지역》 a large 〔wide〕 area; 《넓은 범위》 a large extent; a wide range. ⇨범위. ～하다＝광범하다. ¶ ～한 지식 extensive knowledge / ～한 개혁 a far-reaching reform / 세계 평화에 관한 보다 ～한 여러 문제 wider issues of world peace / ～에 걸치다 cover a wide range 〔area〕 / ～한 권한을 부여받다 be given wide power / 안보 협력을 강화하기 위한 방안에 관해서 ～한 의견을 교환하다 exchange a wide range of views on ways to beef up the security cooperation 《against》 / 그의 지식은 ～하다 His knowledge is very wide-ranging. / 그의 교제는 ～하다 He has a wide circle of acquaintances.

**광복**(光復) glorious restoration; the restoration of independence 《to a country》. ～하다 regain 《a country's》 independence. ¶ 8·15～ the 1945 Liberation of Korea. ◉ ～절 National Liberation Day. ～회 the Association of Independence Fighters.

**광부**(鑛夫) a miner; a mine worker; a pitman; a digger.

**광분하다**(狂奔—) ① 《매우 분주하다》 make desperate 〔frantic〕 efforts 《to *do*》; be very busy in *do*ing; busy *oneself* about 《*something*》. ¶ 돈 마련하느라 ～ be busy raising money / 전쟁 준비에 ～ make a frantic effort to prepare a war. ② 《미친듯이 날뛰다》 run about madly 〔wildly〕; rage about; be on the rampage.

**광산**(鑛山) a mine; a mine field. ¶ ～을 채굴하다 work 〔exploit〕 a mine / ～을 경영하다 run 〔operate〕 a mine / ～에 투자하다 invest *one's* capital in mines / ～을 개발〔폐쇄〕하다 develop 〔shut down〕 a mine. ◉ ～근로자 a mine worker; a miner. ～기사 a mining engineer. ～업 the mining industry: ～업자 a speculator in mines; a mine operator. ～주(株) mining stocks 〔shares〕. ～채굴권 mining concessions 〔rights〕. ～촌 a mining town. ～학 mining science.

**광산물**(鑛産物) a mineral product. ¶ ～이 풍부한 mineral-rich 《provinces》; 《area》 rich in mineral resources.

**광산지**(鑛産地) a mineralized area; a district full of mineral deposits.

**광상**(鑛床) a 〔an ore〕 deposit; a mineral deposit.

**광상곡**(狂想曲) 〖음악〗 a rhapsody.

**광석**(鑛石) an ore; a mineral; 《라디오의》 crystal. ¶ 철～ an iron ore. ◉ ～검파기 a mineral 〔crystal〕 detector. ～분쇄기 an ore crusher. ～수신기 a crystal (radio) receiver 〔set〕. ～운반차 a hutch. ～표본 mineralogical specimens.

**광선**(光線) light; 《빛의 줄기》 a ray 〔beam〕 of light. ¶ 태양 ~ the rays of the sun; sunbeams / 레이저 ~ laser beams / X~, X-rays / 살인 ~ a death ray / ~의 굴절〔반사〕 the refraction 〔reflection〕 of light / ~을 차단하다 cut off light; 《덮어서》 shade from the direct rays (of the sun) / …에 ~을 집중시키다 bring the rays to focus upon… / 이 필름은 ~이 들어갔다 This film is affected. ◉ ~분색기 a disperser. ~분석 spectrum analysis. ~여과기 a light filter. ~ 요법 phototherapy. ~총 a ray gun.

**광섬유**(光纖維) optical fiber. ¶ ~ 케이블 an optical fiber cable; a fiber-optic cable / ~통신 optical fiber (tele)communication.

**광속**(光束) a pencil of light 〔rays〕; 〖전기〗 light 〔luminous〕 flux.

**광속(도)**(光速(度)) 〖물리〗 the velocity 〔speed〕 of light; light speed.

**광시**(狂詩) a comic poem; an irregular poem. ◉ ~곡 a rhapsody.

**광신**(狂信) a (religious) fanaticism. ~하다 fanatically believe 《in》; be devoted blindly 《to》. ¶ ~적(으로) fanatic(ally) / 그의 신앙은 ~에 가깝다 His religious belief is almost fanatic(al). ◉ ~자〔도〕 a fanatic; a religious zealot 〔cult〕; a fanatic believer.

**광심**(光心) 〖물리〗 an optical center.

**광야**(廣野) a wide 〔vast〕 plain; 《미국의 대초원》 a prairie. 「ness; the wilds.

**광야**(曠野) a desolate plain; a wilder-

**광양자**(光量子) 〖물리〗 a photon; a light quantum. ◉ ~설 the quantum theory of light.

**광어**(廣魚) a flatfish; a flounder.

**광언**(狂言) mad talk; crazy remarks. ◉ ~망설(忘說) absurd nonsense; incoherent ravings.

**광업**(鑛業) mining (industry). ◉ ~가 a mine owner; a mine-operator 《미》. ~권 a mining right 〔concession〕. ~기계 mining machinery. ~법 the Mines Act; the Mining Law. ~세(稅) the mining tax. ~소 a mining station 〔office〕. ~회사 a mining company. 대한 ~ 진흥 공사 the Korea Mining Promotion Corporation (생략 KMPC).

**광역**(廣域) a wide 〔large〕 area. ¶ ~수사 a search (for a suspected criminal) conducted over a very wide area; a search across a number of police districts / ~ 지방 의회 선거 a large-unit local election. ◉ ~경제 great-sphere economy. ~(도)시 a metropolitan city. ~행정 integrated administration of a large region.

**광열**(光熱) light and heat. ◉ ~비 light and fuel 〔heat〕 expenses.

**광염**(光焰) a flame.

**광영**(光榮) = 영광.

**광우병**(狂牛病) (the) "mad-cow" disease.

**광원**(光源) 〖물리〗 a source of light; a luminous source.

**광유**(鑛油) mineral oil.

**광음**(光陰) 《세월》 time (and tide). ¶ ~은 살같이 흐른다 Time flies like an arrow.

**광의**(廣義) a broad 〔wide, large〕 sense. ¶ ~로 해석하다 interpret 《*a matter*》 in a broad sense.

**광인**(狂人) a madman; an insane 〔a demented, a crazy〕 person; a lunatic.

**광자**(光子) 〖물리〗 a photon.

**광장**(廣場) an open space 〔ground〕; a (public) square; 《큰》 a plaza. ¶ 만남의 ~ 《이산 가족의》 the plaza for family reunion / 여의도 ~ Yŏuido Plaza / 역전 ~ a station square / 토론의 ~ a place for debating 〔discussion〕. ◉ ~공포증 agoraphobia.

**광재**(鑛滓) dross; slag. 「pea.

**광저기** 〖식물〗 a cowpea; a black-eyed

**광적**(狂的) (being) mad; insane; lunatic; frantic; wild. ¶ ~으로 madly; frantically; wildly / ~인 신앙 fanatical belief / ~인 행위 an insane act / ~인 열의 wild enthusiasm / 그의 동작은 ~이다 His conduct borders on insanity.

**광전**(光電) 〖전기〗 photoelectricity. ◉ ~관 〖전기〗 a phototube; 〖TV〗 a cathode ray tube. ~방사 photoemission. ~자 a photoelectron. ~지(池) a photoelectric cell. ~효과 the photoelectric effect.

**광전리**(光電離) 〖물리〗 photoionization.

**광점**(光點) 〖물리〗 a radiant; a luminous point; 《태양의》 a facula.

**광정**(匡正) correction; remedy; reform. ~하다 correct; remedy; reform.

**광주**(鑛主) the owner of a mine.

**광주리** a round basket (made of bamboo, wicker, twigs or the like).

**광주리 장수** a peddler who carries her wares in a basket on her head.

**광중성자**(光中性子) 〖물리〗 photoneutron.

**광증**(狂症) madness; insanity; lunacy.

**광채**(光彩) luster; brilliancy; splendor. ¶ ~가 나다 show luster; be brilliant /

～를 내다 shed luster; shine bright 《in society》; [비유적] cut a brilliant figure 《in society》; stand out 《among others》/ …에 ～를 더하다 add luster to… / 그녀의 눈은 ～를 잃었다 Her eyes lost their luster.

**광천**(鑛泉) a mineral spring; a spa (온천). ◉ ～수 mineral water. ～요법 balneotherapy.

**광체**(光體) a luminous body; a luminary.

**광축**(光軸) 〖물리〗 an optic(al) axis.

**광층**(鑛層) an ore bed.

**광치다**(光―) 《광내다》 glitter; polish; 《떠벌리다》 show off; talk big; brag 《about》; boast 《of》; be boastful.

**광케이블**(光―) a fiber-optic 〔an optical〕 cable. ¶ 해저 ～ undersea fiber-optic cables / 한국·러시아·일본을 연결하는 총 1,761km의 해저 ～선이 어제부터 운용되기 시작했다 A 1,761km submarine fiber-optic cable line linking South Korea, Russia and Japan started operations yesterday.

**광태**(狂態) shameful 〔disgraceful〕 conduct; crazy behavior. ¶ ～를 부리다 behave disgracefully; make a scandalous scene.

**광택**(光澤) luster; gloss; glaze; shine; polish. ¶ ～ 있는 glossy; lustrous / ～ 없는 dull; lusterless / ～을 내다 make 《*a thing*》 glossy; polish; shine / ～을 없애다 take off the luster 〔shine〕; gray(사진의); mat (금속·사진의) / ～을 잃다 lose luster 〔brilliance〕 / 이 금속은 닦으면 ～이 난다 Good polishing gives a luster 〔shine〕 to this metal.
◉ ～사진 a glossy photograph. ～지 glossy 〔slick〕 paper; art paper; glazed paper.

**광통신**(光通信) an optical communication.

**광파**(光波) 〖물리〗 a light wave.

**광포**(狂暴) wildness; frenzy; violence; brutality (잔인). ～하다 (be) wild; violent; frenzied. ¶ ～한 살인자 a violent 〔fierce〕 killer / ～하게 violently; frenziedly; like mad / ～성을 드러내다 show 〔display〕 *one's* brutality / 그는 술만 마시면 ～해진다 He gets violent when he is drunk. / 그녀는 자주 앞뒤를 못가릴 정도로 ～해진다 She often flies into a frenzy of anger. *or* She often gets so angry (that) she doesn't know what she's doing.
◉ ～성 환자병동 《정신 병원의》 a violent ward.

**광풍**(狂風) a violent gale.

**광학**(光學) 〖물리〗 optics; optical science. ◉ ～기계 an optical instrument. ～기계상 an optician. ～병기 optical weapons. ～현미경 an optical microscope.

**광합성**(光合成) 〖생물〗 photosynthesis. ◉ ～물 a photosynthate.

**광행차**(光行差) 〖천문〗 an aberration. ◉ 행성〔연주(年周), 일주(日週)〕～ planetary 〔annual, diurnal〕 aberration.

**광화학**(光化學) 〖화학〗 photochemistry. ¶ ～ 반응 (a) photochemical reaction / ～ 스모그 photochemical smog.

**광활하다**(廣闊―) (be) wide; spacious; vast; extensive. ¶ 광활한 평야 a vast open field / 광활한 대양(大洋) an expanse of the ocean.

**광휘**(光輝) brilliance; glory; splendor. ¶ ～로운 brilliant; splendid; radiant; glorious.

**광희**(狂喜) wild joy; extreme delight; exultation; ecstasy. ～하다 be mad 〔frantic, wild〕 with joy 〔delight〕; be beside *oneself* with joy; go into raptures 《at, over》; be ecstatic.

**괘**(卦) 《주역의》 a trigram from the Book of Changes; a divination sign.

**괘경**(掛鏡) a hanging 〔wall〕 mirror.

**괘그르다**(卦―) have bad luck 《in》; suffer reverses; have everything go wrong 〔fail〕.

**괘꽝스럽다** be most peculiar 《in behavior》; (be) odd; queer.

**괘념**(掛念) minding; concern; solicitude. ～하다 mind; be concerned 《over》; be solicitous 〔worried, anxious〕 《about》. ¶ 조금도 ～하지 않다 do not care a bit 《about》/ 그 점에 관해서는 일체 ～치 마십시오 You may set your mind at rest on that point.

**괘다리적다, 괘달머리적다** (be) boorish; unmannerly; crude; 《뻔뻔하다》 (be) impertinent; impudent; brazen.

**괘도**(掛圖) 《지도》 a wall map; 《두루마리》 a hanging scroll; a wall chart.

**괘력**(掛曆) a wall calendar.

**괘사** a prank; a joke; a prankster; a jokester. ¶ ～를 떨다〔부리다〕 pull a prank; crack a joke; play the fool / ～스럽다 (be) droll 〔comic, amusing〕.

**괘선**(罫線) a rule; a ruled line; 〖인쇄〗 a rule mark.

**괘씸하다** 《무례하다》 (be) rude; impolite; insolent; 《밉살스럽다》 (be) hateful; execrable; disgusting; damnable; 《건방지다》 (be) impertinent; impudent; cheeky; 《발칙하다》 outrageous; 《용서할 수 없다》 inexcusable; unpardonable; 《믿을 수 없다》 (be) untrustworthy; unfaithful; 《은혜를 모르다》 have no sense of obligation; (be) ungrateful. ¶ 괘씸한 놈 a disgusting 〔an impertinent, a saucy〕 fellow / 괘씸한 짓 an「unpardonable 〔inexcusable〕 conduct 〔behavior〕 / 괘씸하게 굴다 behave impertinently 〔outrageously〕; be rude 《to》; act disrespectfully / 나의 사과를 요구하다니 ~ It is outrageous that he should insist on my apology. / 그는 어른한테 인사도 할 줄 모르는 괘씸한 놈이다 He is an insolent fellow who doesn't know how to greet his elders properly.

**괘장** a sudden switch 〔reversal〕 in *one's* attitude. ~부치다 suddenly switch *one's* position; reverse *oneself* 《about, over》. ¶ 무슨 ~인지 알 수 없다 God knows what's got into him (that he should change so suddenly).

**괘종**(掛鐘) a wall clock.

**괘지**(罫紙) ruled 〔lined〕 paper. ¶ 양면 ~ ruled 〔lined〕 paper on both sides.

**괜찮다** ① 《나쁘지 않다》 (be) not (so) bad; tolerable; passable; 《좋다》 (be) good; fine; all right; fair; OK. ¶ 괜찮은 값 a good price; a price that's not bad / 괜찮은 사람 a good 〔fine〕 man / 괜찮은 여자 a good woman; a fairly pretty woman / 괜찮은 수입 a fair income / 괜찮은 집 a rather fine house; a fairly good house / 맛이 ~ taste good (enough); taste all right / 그만하면 ~ That is good enough (for me). *or* That will do. *or* That will serve the purpose.

② 《무방하다》 may *do;* can *do;* will *do;* (be) all right; be allowed to *do;* be justified in *do*ing; 《개의치않다》 do not mind *do*ing; 《선약이 없다》 be free; be not engaged; 《어려움이 없다》 have no trouble 〔difficulty〕 《in *do*ing》; 《이의없다》 have no objection 《to it》. ¶ 괜찮으시다면… 《지장이 없다면》 if it is convenient for you; if it is all right with you; 《개의치 않는다면》 if you don't mind; 《이의가 없다면》 if you have no objection / …라고 말해도 ~ One may safely say that….; It is not too much to say that…. / 고맙다는 인사 정도는 있어도 괜찮을 법한데 You might at least say "Thank you." / 남들이 뭐라고 하든 ~ I don't mind 〔care〕 what people say of me. / 홍차가 없으면 커피도 ~ Coffee is all right 〔I don't mind having coffee〕 if you don't have any tea. / 괜찮으시다면 내일 찾아뵙고 싶습니다 I want to call on you tomorrow if it is convenient to you. / 내일 오후는 괜찮습니다 I will be free tomorrow afternoon. / 창문을 닫아도 괜찮겠습니까 Do you mind my closing the window? / 어느 것이라도 ~ Either will do. / 내가 없어도 이젠 괜찮겠지 You'll be able to get along without me now. / 괜찮으시다면 댁의 주소와 전화번호를 알려 주십시오 Please tell me your address and phone number if you don't mind. / 약간의 술이나 담배는 마시거나 피워도 ~ A little alcohol or tobacco will do you no harm. / 이런 수단을 써도 괜찮을지 모르겠다 I hope I am justified in taking this step.

③ 《허가하다》 may; can; be at liberty to 《do》. ¶ 이젠 가도 ~ You may go now. / 질문을 해도 괜찮습니까 May I ask you a question? / 내일 다시 와도 괜찮겠습니까 May I come again tomorrow? (★ 긍정일 때는 Yes, you may. 부정할 때는 No, you must not.보다 No, you may not.이 정중한 말투) / 이 방은 마음대로 쓰셔도 괜찮습니다 You are at liberty to make use of this room in any way you please.

④ 《안전하다》 (be) safe; secure; good; all right; O.K. ¶ 이 물은 마셔도 괜찮습니까 Is this water good enough to drink? / 이 곳은 어떤 위험이 닥쳐도 ~ This place is safe from any danger. *or* We are out of danger here.

**괜하다** (be) useless; pointless; empty; idle; gratuitous. ¶ 괜한 말 useless word; idle talk / 괜한 욕 groundless censure; a gratuitous insult.

**괜히** 《공연히》 in vain; uselessly; pointlessly; gratuitously; with no call; without reason 〔ground〕; for nothing; to no purpose; 《왠지 모르게》 somehow; without knowing why; for some reason or other; vaguely; indefinably. ¶ ~ 나무라다 blame 《*a person*》 without reason / ~ 떠들다 make a row over nothing / ~ 싸우다 fight for no reason at all / ~ 애쓰다 labor in vain / ~ 왔는 걸 I regret that I came. / 나는 저 사람이 ~ 무섭다 I have a vague fear of him. / ~ 울고 싶은 기분이다 Somehow I feel like crying.

**괭이** 《땅 파는》 a hoe; a pick. ¶ ~의 날 a hoe blade / ~로 파다 dig with a hoe; hoe up the soil / ~질하다 hoe; dig with a hoe.

**괴**(塊) 《덩이》 a lump; 〖한의〗 a tumor.

**괴걸**(怪傑) an extraordinary man; a wonder(man) 《미》.

**괴경**(塊莖) 〖식물〗 a tuber; 《감자 따위의》 a seed. ◉ ～식물 a tuber plant.

**괴괴망측**(怪怪罔測) ～하다 《이상야릇하다》 (be) very strange; weird; uncanny; 《흉측하다》 (be) monstrous. ¶ ～한 소문 a wild 〔scandalous〕 rumor / ～한 일 a strange thing; an odd thing.

**괴괴하다** (be) still; quiet; silent; deserted. ¶ 괴괴한 거리 a quiet 〔deserted〕 street / 괴괴한 밤 a very still 〔silent〕 night.

**괴근**(塊根) 〖식물〗 a tuberous 〔tuberose〕 root; a root tuber.

**괴기**(怪奇) (a) mystery; (a) wonder. ～하다 (be) mysterious; strange; grotesque; bizarre. ◉ ～소설 a mystery 〔ghost〕 story.

**괴까다롭다** ① 《문제가》 (be) tricky; intricate; difficult (to cope with); troublesome. ¶ 괴까다로운 문제 a tricky problem; a difficult question. ② 《성미가》 (be) particular; fastidious; fussy; finicky; choosy 《about》; be hard to please; be difficult (to deal with). ¶ 괴까다로운 사람 a person hard to please; a difficult 〔fussy〕 person / 괴까다로운 취미 fastidious 〔finicky〕 taste(s) / 그는 무척 괴까다로운 주인이다 He is a difficult master to please. / 그녀는 옷에 ～ She is choosy 〔particular〕 about her clothes.

**괴나리**(**봇짐**) a backpack to carry *one's* things while on the road; a traveler's knapsack.

**괴다**[1] 《액체가》 collect; gather; form a puddle; stand; stay; stagnate. ¶ 괸 물 stagnant 〔standing〕 water / 빗물이 웅덩이에 ～ rainwater collects 〔forms a puddle〕 in a hollow / 눈물이 ～ tears gather 〔form〕 in *one's* eyes.

**괴다**[2] 《발효하다》 ferment; undergo fermentation; be in a ferment. ¶ 술이 괼 때는 거품이 인다 When wine is fermented it gives off bubbles of gas.

**괴다**[3] ① 《받치다》 prop; support. ¶ (손으로) 턱을 ～ rest *one's* chin 〔cheeks〕 on 〔in〕 *one's* hand(s) / 테이블 다리를 돌로 ～ support the leg of a table with a piece of stone / 쓰러져 가는 벽을 기둥으로 ～ prop a leaning wall with a post / 바퀴 밑을 ～ prevent 《a wheel》 from slipping. ② 《쌓다》 arrange 〔pile up〕 food on a table. ¶ 잔칫상에 음식을 ～ pile up food on a banquet table. ③ 《담다》 carefully fill bowls with food for *one's* elders.

**괴다**[4] 《사랑하다》 love; adore; favor. ¶ 굄을 받다 be loved 〔adored〕; enjoy 《*a person's*》 favor.

**괴담**(怪談) 《무서운》 a ghost 〔spooky〕 story; 《이상한》 a strange story.

**괴도**(怪盜) a mysterious 〔phantom〕 thief. ¶ ～뤼팽 Lupin the phantom thief.

**괴력**(怪力) 《대단한 힘》 marvelous (physical) strength; Herculean 〔prodigious, superhuman〕 strength. ¶ ～을 발휘하다 put forth 〔out〕 Herculean 〔a giant's〕 strength.

**괴로움** 《어려움·고난》 troubles; hardships; difficulties; sufferings; 《성가심·귀찮음》 (a) trouble; worries; annoyance; 《고뇌》 agony; anguish; distress; affliction; 《고통·병고》 pain; pangs; throes; 《시련》 trials; ordeals. ¶ 육체적〔정신적〕인 ～ physical 〔mental〕 pain / 가난의 ～ hardship of poverty / 마음의 ～ anguish of heart; mental affliction 〔troubles〕 / 삶의 ～ worries 〔troubles〕 of life / 양심의 ～ pangs of conscience / 육신의 ～ physical suffering 〔anguish〕 / 아무에게 ～을 끼치다 trouble; give 〔cause〕 *a person* trouble; annoy; afflict *a person* with / ～이 많다 have a lot of trouble; be full of woe; have many difficulties / ～을 겪다 suffer troubles; undergo 〔go through〕 hardship / ～을 견디다 bear *one's* sufferings / ～을 덜다 alleviate 〔relieve〕 *one's* sufferings / 그녀는 마침내 그 ～을 이겨냈다 She overcame the hardship at last. / 그 같은 부자는 가난의 ～을 알지 못한다 A rich person like him cannot understand the hardship 〔sufferings〕 of poverty. / 한국의 자동차 산업은 최악의 불황으로 심한 ～을 겪고 있다 The Korean automobile industry is in the throes of its worst depression.

**괴로워하다** ① [육체적으로] 《고통을 느끼다》 suffer 《from》; feel 〔be in〕 pain; be tormented 《by》; be afflicted 《with》. ¶ 치통〔기침〕으로 ～ suffer from a toothache 〔cough〕 / 갈증으로 ～ be tormented by thirst / 환자는 몹시 괴로워했다 The patient was 「suffering severely 〔in great pain〕.
② [정신적으로] 《고통을 받다》 be troubled 《with》; be in trouble; be distressed 《by》; be worried 《by》; suffer 《from, for》; worry *oneself* 《about, over》. ¶ 압제에 ～ groan under oppression / 무거운 세금에 ～ suffer from heavy taxes / 자기가 저지른 일로 ～

suffer for something one has done / 사랑 때문에 ~ be lovesick; languish for [with] love / 생활 문제로 ~ be troubled with the question of living / 빚 때문에 ~ be harassed with debts; be suffering because of *one's* debt / 그는 남모르게 괴로워하고 있다 He is eating his heart out. / 그녀는 내게 거짓말을 한 일로 괴로워하고 있는 것 같다 She seems to be troubled by her conscience for telling me a lie.

**괴롭다** [육체적으로] 《고통스럽다》 (be) painful; strenuous; 《힘들다》 (be) hard; difficult; tough; [정신적으로] 《고통스럽다》 (be) trying; distressing; tormenting; 《귀찮다》 (be) troublesome; onerous; 《난처하다》 (be) awkward; embarrassing; [경제적으로] (be) needy; poor; straitened.
¶괴로운 나머지 driven by pain [distress]; out of desperation / 괴로운 일 hard work; a hard [tough] job / 괴로운 세상 a troubled [troublesome, difficult] world / 괴로운 생활 a hard life; a needy [“hand-to-mouth”] existence / 괴로운 입장에 있다 be in「a difficult [an awkward] position / 괴로운 처지를 당하다 have a hard [trying] time (of it) / 경제적으로 ~ suffer from economic distress / 숨쉬기가 ~ have difficulty in breathing; breathe with difficulty / 그것은 괴로운 여행이었다 It was a painful trip. / 그녀의 중상 모략으로 나는 매우 괴로웠다 Her backbiting caused me a great deal of trouble. / 그 회사는 매우 괴로운 상황에 있다 The firm is in「serious trouble [financial difficulties]. / 그때가 나의 인생에서 가장 괴로운 시기였다 That was the worst time of my life.

**괴롭히다** [육체적으로] 《고통을 주다》 give 《*a person*》 pain; torment; torture; cause [inflict] pain 《to, on》; [정신적으로] 《고통스럽게 하다》 worry; distress; trouble annoy; harass; 《못살게 굴다》 bully; treat 《*a person*》 harshly; be cruel 《to》. ¶동물을 ~ be cruel to an animal / 마음을 ~ worry *oneself* about; be concerned about 《*a matter*》; wring *one's* heart / 적을 ~ harass the enemy / 경찰을 ~ give the police trouble / 약자를 ~ bully the weaker / 어머니, 존에게 나를 괴롭히지 말라고 말 좀 해주세요 Mom, tell John to stop picking on me. / 그 문제는 나를 매우 괴롭혔다 That affair greatly ailed me. / 자식들이란 종종 부모를 여러 가지로 괴롭힌다 Children often bother their parents in many ways. / 밤새 모기가 우리를 괴롭혔다 Mosquitoes kept annoying us all night long.

**괴뢰**(傀儡) 《꼭두각시》 a puppet; a marionette; a dummy; 《앞잡이》 a tool; a cat's-paw; 《허수아비》 a robot. ¶~노릇을 하다 act as another's tool / ~가 되다 be made a puppet of 《*a person*》 / ~로 삼다 make a cat's-paw of 《*a person*》. ◉ ~정권 a puppet regime.

**괴리**(乖離) estrangement; alienation. ~하다 be estranged [alienated] 《from》. ◉ ~개념 〚논리〛 a disparate concept.

**괴멸**(壞滅) demolition; destruction; ruin; annihilation. ¶~시키다 destroy; demolish; ruin; wipe out; annihilate / ~적 타격 a deadly [fatal] blow; a deathblow / 핵전쟁에 의한 세계의 ~ the annihilation of the world by (a) nuclear war / 집중폭격으로 그 도시는 ~되었다 The town was utterly destroyed by the intensive bombing.

**괴문서**(怪文書) a mysterious [an anonymous muckraking] document; a document of obscure origin; (politically) defamatory literature. ¶그를 중상하는 ~가 유포됐다 Defamatory literature were circulated to slander him.

**괴물**(怪物) 《물체》 a monster; a goblin (유령); 《사람》 a mysterious figure. ¶바다의 ~ a sea monster / 정계의 ~ a political sphinx / ~의 정체를 밝히다 unmask the apparition.

**괴발개발** with “hen scratches”; sloppily (writing); scribbling. ¶~ 그리다 scribble; scrawl; write an awful scrawl.

**괴벽**(乖僻) eccentricity; fastidiousness. ~하다[스럽다] (be) eccentric; fastidious; queer; odd. ¶~스러운 노인 an eccentric old man / ~스러운 취미 fastidious taste(s) / 그는 ~하기로 유명했다 He was pretty well known for his eccentricity.

**괴벽**(怪癖) a strange habit.

**괴변**(怪變) 《사고》 a strange accident; 《이변》 an odd mishap.

**괴병**(怪病) a mysterious disease; an unidentified disease.

**괴사**(怪死) death from an unknown cause; a mysterious death. ~하다 die a mysterious death. ◉ ~사건 a case of mysterious death.

**괴사**(怪事) a weird happening; a mystery; strange goings-on; a scandal.

**괴사건**(怪事件) a mystery; a mysterious [strange] event [case].

**괴상**(塊狀) ¶ ～의 massive / ～암(岩) a massive rock / ～용암 block lava / ～조직 a massive structure. ◉ ～광상(鑛床) a massive deposit.

**괴상야릇하다**(怪常―) (be) very odd; quite strange; most peculiar.

**괴상하다**(怪常―) (be) odd; strange; queer; uncanny; monstrous; grotesque. ¶ 괴상한 물건〔일〕 a strange thing; an oddity / 괴상하게 보이는 사내 an odd looking man / 괴상하게 여기다 think strange / 괴상하게 보이다 look queer 〔strange〕.

**괴석**(怪石) an oddly shaped stone.

**괴수**(怪獸) a monster; a monstrous animal. ¶ ～가 나오는 영화 a monster film.

**괴수**(魁首) the ringleader; the leader; the chief; the boss; the head man. ¶ 도둑의 ～ the head 〔boss〕 of the robbers / 폭도의 ～ the ringleader of a mob.

**괴이다** ① 《받쳐지다》 get propped; be supported. ② 《쌓이다》 be stacked; be piled up.

**괴이쩍다**(怪異―) ＝ 괴이하다.

**괴이찮다**(怪異―) (be) not strange; natural; be in no way peculiar. ¶ 그가 성내는 것도 ～ It is quite natural that he should get angry.

**괴이하다**(怪異―) (be) strange; queer; mysterious; monstrous; grotesque; weird; uncanny. ¶ 괴이한 이야기 a strange 〔weird〕 story / 괴이한 죽음 a mysterious death / 괴이한 사람 a mysterious 〔strange〕 person / 괴이한 행동 strange behavior; extraordinary conduct / 괴이한 소문 a strange 〔wild〕 rumor / 괴이한 현상 a strange 〔mysterious〕 phenomenon / 괴이한 광경 a grotesque sight.

**괴인**(怪人) a monster 〔mystery〕 man.

**괴인물**(怪人物) a mystery man; a Mr. X.

**괴조**(怪鳥) a mysterious 〔a monstrous, an ominous〕 bird.

**괴질**(怪疾) 《원인 불명의 병》 disease of unknown cause; a mystery disease. ¶ ～이 번지고 있다 An unidentified epidemic is prevalent.

**괴짜**(怪―) an eccentric person; a strange 〔an odd〕 fellow; a queer 「fish 〔sort of fellow〕; a crackpot; a screwball 《미》. ¶ 그는 ～다 He is quite a character 〔a queer fish〕.

**괴철**(塊鐵) 《쇳덩이》 an iron ingot.

**괴탄**(塊炭) lump coal.

**괴팍하다, 괴팍스럽다**(乖―) 《성미가》 (be) hard to please; difficult; cross; 《음식·옷 따위에》 (be) particular 〔choosy, fussy, fastidious〕 《in, about》; 《완고하다》 (be) obstinate; bigoted. ¶ 괴팍한 노부인 a difficult 〔bad tempered〕 old lady / 괴팍스러운 성미 a fussy temperament / 취향이〔기호가〕 ～ be fastidious in taste / 그녀는 옷〔음식〕을 매우 괴팍스럽게 가리는 사람이다 She is very particular 〔choosy, fussy, fastidious〕 about her dress 〔food〕. / 나의 부친은 매우 성미가 괴팍하시다 My father is very hard to please.

**괴한**(怪漢) a suspicious fellow; a strange(-looking) character. ¶ ～이 우리집 주위를 어슬렁거리고 있다 A suspicious fellow is loitering around our house.

**괴현상**(怪現象) a strange phenomenon; an extraordinary phenomenon. ¶ ～을 나타내다 present a strange 〔an extraordinary〕 phenomenon.

**괴혈병**(壞血病) 〖의학〗 scurvy; scorbutus. ◉ ～약 an anti-scorbutic. ～환자 a scorbutic.

**괴화**(怪火) a mysterious fire; a fire of suspicious origin.

**괸** 《받침》 a prop; a stay; a support.

**괸대** a prop (stick); a support; a strut.

**괸돌** a stone prop 〔support〕.

**괸목** a wooden prop 〔support〕.

**괸새** 《받쳐놓은 모양》 the shape 〔way〕 something is propped up; 《쌓아올린 솜씨》 skill at stacking cakes on plates.

**괸질** stacking 〔piling up〕 cakes on plates.

**굉굉하다**(轟轟―) (be) thunderous; roaring; rumbling; deafening.

**굉연하다**(轟然―) (be) roaring; thundering; ear-rending; deafening. ¶ 굉연히 with a roar; with a roaring 〔terrific〕 sound; thunderously.

**굉음**(轟音) a roaring sound; a deafening roar; an ear-splitting sound. ¶ ～을 내다 make 〔produce〕 a thundering noise / ～을 내며 《run, start》 with a roaring 〔booming〕 sound.

**굉장하다**(宏壯―) 《크고 당당하다》 (be) grand; imposing; (be) splendid; magnificent; wonderful; excellent; marvelous; great 《구어》; fantastic 《구어》; 《엄청나다》 (be) terrible; awful; tremendous. ¶ 굉장히 splendidly; marvelously; magnificently; awfully; terribly / 굉장한 건물 a magnificent 〔an imposing〕 structure; a gigantic building / 굉장한 미인 a strikingly beautiful woman; a knockout / 굉장한 저택 a palatial residence; a stately mansion / 굉

장한 부자 an awfully rich man / 굉장한 성찬 a wonderful 〔scrumptious〕 dinner / 굉장한 인파 a tremendous turnout of people; a mammoth crowd / 굉장한 착상 a capital 〔good〕 idea / 굉장히 덥다〔춥다〕 be terribly 〔unbearably〕 hot 〔cold〕 / 굉장히 나쁘다 be awfully 〔terribly〕 bad / 그녀는 굉장히 좋은〔나쁜〕 사람이다 She is an awfully nice 〔bad〕 person. / 불이 굉장한 기세로 퍼졌다 The flames spread with a fearful rapidity. / 저 영화 배우는 굉장히 인기가 있다 The movie star is amazingly popular.

**교**(教) a religion. ¶ 교를 믿다 believe in a religion.

**교가**(校歌) a school 〔college〕 song; an 「alma mater.

**교각**(交角) 〚수학〛 an angle of intersection.

**교각**(橋脚) 〚토목〛 a (bridge) pier; a 「bent.

**교각살우**(矯角殺牛) "The remedy is worse than the disease."

**교감**(交感) rapport; 〚생리〛 consensus; (mutual) sympathy. ¶ ～적인 sympathetic; consensual. ◉ ～성 associability. ～신경 the sympathetic nerve. ～작용 sympathy.

**교감**(校監) a vice-principal 《미》; an acting 〔an assistant, a deputy〕 principal; a deputy head teacher 《영》.

**교갑**(膠匣) 〚약〛 a capsule.

**교과**(教科) 《과목》 a (school) subject. ◉ ～과정(課程) a course of study; a curriculum: ～과정 위원회 the Curriculum Committee / ～과정에 있다 be on the curriculum / 4년의 ～과정을 마치다 finish (up) 〔complete〕 a 4-year course of study. ～서 a textbook; a schoolbook: 역사 ～서 a history text(book) / ～서판(版) a text(-book) edition / ～서 검정 제도 the 〔a〕 textbook screening system / 국정 ～서 state-designated textbooks.

**교관**(教官) 《특히 군대에서》 a drillmaster; a teacher; an instructor; drill instructor.

**교교하다**(皎皎―) (be) bright; brilliant. ¶ 교교히 brightly; bright / 달빛이 ～ The moon shines bright(ly).

**교구**(教具) teaching tools; training aids.

**교구**(教區) 《기독교의》 a parish; a diocese (주교(主教)의). ¶ 원주 ～ the Wonju Diocese / ～의 교회 a parish church. ◉ ～목사 a parish priest; a rector 《영》. ～민 a parishioner; the parish [총칭].

**교군**(轎軍) 《가마》 a palanquin; 《가마꾼》 a palanquin bearer.

**교권**(教權) 《종교상의》 ecclesiastical authority; 《교육상의》 educational authority; teachers' privileges. ¶ ～을 확립하다 establish educational authority.

**교근**(咬筋) 〚해부〛 the masticatory muscle; the masseter.

**교기**(校紀) school discipline.

**교기**(校旗) a school flag 〔banner〕.

**교기**(驕氣) a proud air; haughtiness; arrogance. ¶ ～ 부리다 behave arrogantly; assume a haughty attitude.

**교내**(校內) the school grounds; 《대학 따위의》 the campus. ¶ ～의 interclass; intramural / ～에서 in the school (grounds); 《미》 on (the) campus (대학의) / ～를 안내해 드리죠 I'll show you around (the) campus. / ～에서는 조용히 하여라 Be quiet on (the) campus. ◉ ～방송 the school radio service; the school PA system (★ PA는 public address의 약자). ～운동〔웅변〕 대회 an interclass athletic 〔oratorical〕 meet: ～ 운동회는 10월에 열린다 The intramural athletic meet is held in October. ～폭력 school 〔campus〕 violence; 《학급 내의》 classroom violence.

**교단**(教團) a religious body 〔order〕; an order. ¶ 프란체스코 ～ the Franciscan Order.

**교단**(教壇) 《학교의》 a (teacher's) platform; 《목사의》 the pulpit. ¶ ～에 서다 stand on the platform; teach at school; be a teacher / 나는 ～에 서기를 바라고 있다 I want to be a teacher. / ～에 선 경험이 있느냐 Have you ever taught (at) school? *or* Have you any teaching experience? ◉ ～생활 a teacher's life: ～ 생활 20년 a 20-year experiences of teaching; a teaching career of twenty years.

**교대**(交代) (an) alternation; (a) change; a relief (경비원 등의); a shift (직공의); (a) rotation (세 사람 이상간의). ～하다 take turns; take *one's* turn 《at, in》; rotate; 《교대를 하다》 take another's place; relieve 《each other》; change places 《with》. ¶ ～로 by turns; in turn; in shifts 〔relays〕; alternately; in rotation 《with》 / 2시간 ～로 하다 take turns at two-hour shifts / 1일 3 ～제로 일하다 work on a three-shift(-a-day) basis / 주야 ～로 일하다 work in shifts day and night; work in relays around the clock / 그들은 8시간씩 3 ～로 일했다 They worked in 「three shifts of eight hours 〔three eight-hour shifts〕. / 그들

은 ～로 핸들을 잡았다 They took turns in driving. / 비행기 승무원은 김포에서 ～했다 The flight crew changed at Kimp'o. / 누구 나와 ～해 줄 사람 없느냐 Is there anyone who will take my place? / ～자가 올 때까지 나는 여기를 떠날 수 없다 I cannot leave my post till my relief comes. / 간호사는 8 시간마다 ～한다 The nurses rotate every eight hours. / 다음 ～시간까지 나는 여기서 꼼짝 못한다 I'm tied down here until I am relieved. ◉ ～근무 shift work. ～병 a (military) relief. ～시간 the changing 〔relief〕 time. ～자 a shift; a relief: 주간〔야간〕 ～자 men on the day 〔night〕 shift. ～제 the shift system: 2～제 a two=shift system; a double shift. ～조업 shift operation; working in shift.

**교도**(教徒) a believer 《in》; a follower 《of》; an adherent 《to》. ¶ 기독～ a Christian / 이슬람 ～ a Mohammedan; a Moslem / 불～ a Buddhist.

**교도**(教導) (moral) instruction; teaching; guidance. ～하다 instruct; teach; guide. ¶ 비행 청소년을 ～하다 guide 〔reform〕 a juvenile delinquent.

**교도관**(矯導官) a (prison) guard 《미》; a jailer 《미》; a prison officer 《영》; a (prison) warder 《영》. ¶ 여성 ～ a female guard 《미》; a (prison) wardress.

**교도소**(矯導所) a prison; a jail; a penitentiary 《미》; a gaol 《영》; a pen 《속어》; a jailhouse. ¶ ～에서 나오다 leave prison; be released from prison / ～에 수감하다 put 〔throw〕 《a criminal》 into prison; send 《a criminal》 to jail; imprison / ～에 수감되어 있다 be in prison 《on a murder charge》; be behind (the) bars / 그는 그녀를 면회하러 ～에 갔다 He went to the prison to visit her. ◉ ～장 the governor 〔warden 《미》〕 of a prison.

**교두보**(橋頭堡) a bridgehead; 《해안의》 a beachhead. ¶ ～를 확보하다〔구축하다〕 secure 〔establish〕 a bridgehead 〔beachhead〕.

**교란**(攪亂) (a) disturbance; derangement. ～하다 disturb; stir up; upset; throw 《the enemy》 into confusion. ¶ 평화를 ～하다 disturb peace (and order) / 후방을 ～하다 harass the rear 〔backs〕 《of the opposite team》 / 민심을 ～하다 perturb 〔upset〕 the people. ◉ ～작전 harassing tactics.

**교량**(橋梁) a bridge. ¶ ～을 놓다 construct 〔build〕 a bridge 《over》 / ～ 역할을 하다 play a bridge role 《for》 / ～ 통행 금지 《게시》 Bridge closed. ◉ ～ 공사 bridge building 〔construction〕.

**교련**(教鍊) 《단련》 training; (military) drill. ～하다 train; drill. ¶ ～을 받다 drill; be drilled. ◉ ～교관 a drill instructor. 사격～ target practice.

**교령**(教令) 《임금의 명령》 a king's ordinance; 《가톨릭의》 a decree.

**교료**(校了) 〖인쇄〗 final proofreading; 《기호》 OK. ～하다 finish proofreading. ¶ ～가 되다 be OK'd. ◉ ～쇄 an OK'd proofs; a press proof. 책임～ O.K. with corrections.

**교류**(交流) ① 《문화·사상 등의》 interchange; exchange (교환). ¶ 스포츠 및 문화의 ～ sports and cultural exchange 〔interchange〕 《between》 / 동서 문화의 ～ the cultural exchange between the East and the West / 학자의 ～ an exchange of scholars 〔specialists〕 / 부서간의 활발한 인사 ～를 하기로 결정됐다 It was decided to promote an active interchange of personnel between sections. ② 〖전기〗 alternating current (생략 A.C.). ◉ ～ 발전기 an alternating current 〔A.C.〕 generator. ～암페어계 an alternating current ammeter. ～전동기 an alternating current motor.

**교리**(教理) 〖종교〗 a doctrine; a tenet; a creed; a dogma. ◉ ～론 dogmatism. ～문답 catechism: ～문답서 a catechism. ～신학 dogmatics; dogmatic theology.

**교린정책**(交隣政策) a good-neighbor policy.

**교만**(驕慢) haughtiness; arrogance; pride. ～하다〔스럽다〕 (be) haughty; arrogant; proud; stuck-up; puffed=up. ¶ ～ 무례한 insolent / ～한 사람 a conceited 〔stuck-up〕 person; smart aleck 《미》 / ～하게 굴다 act haughtily; take 〔assume〕 an overbearing attitude / ～한 코를 납작하게 하다 humble 《*a person's*》 pride; knock 《*a person*》 off his high horse; 《구어》 make 《*a person*》 eat dirt 〔humble pie〕 / 그의 ～한 태도를 참을 수 없다 I cannot bear his arrogance.

**교모**(校帽) a school cap.

**교모**(教母) 〖가톨릭〗 a Catholic sister; a nun.

**교목**(喬木) a tall 〔forest〕 tree; an arbor. ◉ ～대(帶) the forest-tree zone. ～세가(世家) a family that has been holding prominent posts for many generations.

**교묘**(巧妙) skill; dexterity; cleverness;

ingenuity; adroitness. ～하다 (be) skil(l)ful; dexterous; clever; ingenious; deft; adept. ¶ ～하게 skillfully; with skill 〔dexterity〕; cleverly; dexterously; adroitly; ingeniously / ～하게 만든 cleverly-made〔-wrought〕/ ～한 답변 a tactful 〔masterly〕 answer / ～한 고안 an ingenious device / ～한 사기 a subtle deception / ～한 세공 elaborate workmanship / ～한 솜씨 a deft performance / ～하게 처리하다 manage《*a matter*》 cleverly / ～히 환심을 사다 wind *one's* way into《*another's*》 affections 〔favor〕/ 나는 그의 ～한 속임수에 넘어갔다 I was cheated by his cunning tricks.

**교무**(教務) 《학교의》 academic 〔school〕 affairs 〔administration〕;《종교의》 religious affairs. ◉ ～과 the academic 〔educational〕 affairs section; registrar's office (대학의). ～실 the staff 〔teachers'〕 room. ～주임 a curriculum 〔an educational affairs〕 coordinator. ～처 the office of academic affairs: ～처장 the dean of academic affairs.

**교문**(校門) the gate of a school; a school-gate. ¶ ～을 나오다 leave school; leave the school grounds.

**교미**(交尾) copulation. ～하다 copulate; couple; mate; pair. ◉ ～기 the mating 〔pairing〕 season 〔time, period〕: ～기에 들다 get on 〔in〕 heat.

**교반**(攪拌) ～하다 agitate《the liquid》; stir (up)《cream》; churn《milk》; beat《eggs》. ◉ ～기 a mixer; an agitator; a stirrer; a shaker (칵테일용); an eggbeater (계란의); a whisk.

**교배**(交配) interbreeding; hybridization;《식물의》 cross-fertilization. ～하다 interbreed; hybridize; cross; crossbreed; cross-fertilize (식물을). ¶ 범과 사자를 ～하다 cross a tiger and 〔with〕 a lion. ◉ ～종 a hybrid; a crossbreed.

**교번**(交番) change of shift; alternative; duty relief.

**교범**(教範) a model for teaching; 〖군사〗 a drill book 〔manual〕; a textbook. ◉ 기술～ technical manual (생략 TM). 야전～ field manual (생략 FM).

**교법**(教法) 《교의》 the teachings of Buddha; a doctrine; 《가르치는 법》 teaching method. ◉ ～사(師) a Catholic missionary.

**교복**(校服) a school uniform. ¶ ～의 자율화 the liberalization of the dress code (for students).

**교본**(教本) a textbook《on, in》; a manual《of》; 〖음악〗 a school.

**교부**(交付) delivery; grant. ～하다 hand《to》; deliver; grant; issue. ¶ 통지서를 ～하다 serve a notice on《*a person*》/ 백만원의 보조금을 ～하다 grant a one-million-won subsidy / …에게 여권을～하다 issue a passport to 〔for〕《*a person*》. ◉ ～금 a subsidy; a grant; a bounty; a grant-in-aid. ～자 a deliverer.

**교부**(教父) 《고위성직자》 a Catholic prelate; 《초기 그리스도교의》 a Church Father. ◉ ～철학 patristic philosophy.

**교분**(交分) acquaintance(ship); friendship. ¶ ～이 두텁다 be good friends with / ～이 두터워지다 get 〔become〕 more friendly 〔familiar〕《with》/ ～을 맺다 make *a person's* acquaintance; form a friendship《with》/ 옛 ～을 새로이 하다 renew *one's* old acquaintance with / 우리는 오랜 ～이 있는 사이다 We have been long acquainted with each other. *or* We have known each other for many years.

**교사**(校舍) a school building; a schoolhouse. ¶ 무너질 듯한 ～ a ramshackle schoolhouse / ～를 증축하다 build an annex to the schoolhouse.

**교사**(教師) a teacher; a schoolteacher; 《영》 a schoolmaster; 《영》 a schoolmistress (여교사); a mentor; a preceptor; 《스승》 a master. ¶ 영어 ～ a teacher of English; an English teacher / ～ 노릇을 하다 teach (at a) school / 그녀는 초등학교 ～이다 She is a primary school teacher. *or* She teaches in a primary school. / 나는 미국인 ～한테 영어를 배웠다 I learned English from an American teacher. / ～가 되려고 결심한 동기는 무엇이냐 What has made you decide to be a teacher? ◉ ～상 the image (and authority) of teachers. ～용 지도서 a teacher's manual. ～직 the teaching profession; schoolteaching.

**교사**(教唆) 〖법〗 instigation; incitement; abetment. ～하다 instigate; incite; abet. ¶ 남의 ～를 받아 at another's instigation / 범죄를 ～하다 abet a crime / 노동자를 ～하여 파업에 이르게 하다 instigate workers to a strike. ◉ ～방조죄 (the crime of ) aiding and abetting. ～자 an instigator; an abettor. ～죄 instigation: ～죄로 체포되다 be arrested on a charge of instigating《the riot》.

**교살**(絞殺) strangulation. ～하다 stran-

gle; throttle 《*a person*》 (to death); murder 《*a person*》 by strangulation. ¶ ~의 흔적 marks of strangulation / ~되다 be strangled 《to death》.
◉ ~시체 the body of a strangled man 〔woman〕.

**교상**(咬傷) a bite. ¶ ~을 입다 be injured by biting 〔a bite〕. 「⇨ 교육실습생.

**교생**(敎生) a student 〔trainee〕 teacher.

**교서**(敎書) 《대통령의》 a message; 《교황의》 a (papal) bull. ¶ 대통령의 ~ 《미》 the President's message to Congress.

**교섭**(交涉) 《담판》 negotiation(s); bargaining; a parley. ~하다 negotiate; bargain; confer; parley. ¶ 남북한간의 ~ negotiations between South and North Korea / 외교적인 ~ diplomatic negotiations / ~의 대상 a subject for negotiation / ~의 결렬 rupture of negotiations / ~에 의한 해결 a negotiated solution 《of a dispute》 / ~ 단계에 있다 be in the negotiation stage / ~이 매듭지어지다 come to terms / ~을 시작하다 enter into 〔open, start〕 negotiations 《with》 / ~을 계속하다 carry on negotiations 《with》 / ~을 중단하다 break off negotiations 《with》 / ~은 합의를 못 봤다 The negotiations fell through. / 상여금 지급에 관하여 회사측과 ~했다 We negotiated with the company about the allowance of the bonus. / 그 일에 관해서 지금 ~중이다 That matter is now under negotiation. / 우리는 ~을 재개할 용의가 있다 We are ready to reopen the negotiations. / 그들은 제조회사와 제품의 도매가격에 대해서 ~했다 They bargained with the manufacturer over the wholesale price of the product. / 가격에 관하여는 ~의 여지가 있다 The price remains negotiable. / 그 협약은 오랜 ~의 결과였다 The treaty was the result of long negotiations.
◉ ~단체 a bargaining body; 《국회의》 a negotiation body. ~위원 (a member of ) a negotiating committee; a delegate. 「(young) women.

**교성**(嬌聲) gay 〔coquettish〕 voices of

**교수**(敎授) ① 《사람》 a professor; the faculty [총칭]. ② 《가르침》 teaching; instruction. ~하다 teach; instruct. ¶ 그는 S대학 영문학 ~이다 He is a professor of English literature at S University. / 그녀는 외국인에게 한국 무용을 ~하고 있다 She gives lessons to foreign people in Korean dance.
◉ ~법 a teaching method; pedagogics: ~법을 모르다 do not know how to teach 《English》. ~직 professorship; the professorate. ~진 the professors; 《미》 the faculty; the teaching staff 《of a college》; the professorate; the professoriate: ~진을 강화하다 strengthen the teaching staff 《of the university》. ~회 a faculty meeting 〔council〕. ~휴게실〔식당〕 a faculty lounge 〔dining hall〕.

**교수**(絞首) hanging; strangulation. ~하다 hang; strangle. ◉ ~대 the gallows; a gallows tree; a scaffold: ~대의 이슬로 사라지다 die on the gallows. ~형 (death 〔execution〕 by) hanging; the punishment of hanging; the gallows: ~형을 받다 be「put to death 〔executed〕 by hanging; be hanged; come 〔go, be sent〕 to the gallows / ~형에 처하다 hang 《a criminal》; put to death by hanging.

**교습**(敎習) training; teaching; instruction. ~하다 train; teach; instruct. ¶ 피아노 ~을 받다 take piano lessons / 무용 ~을 하다 give *a person* lessons in dancing; teach dancing / 한국어 ~ 《게시》 Korean instruction 〔lessons〕 given. ◉ ~소 a training school 〔institute〕: 댄스〔자동차〕 ~소 a dancing 〔driving〕 school.

**교시**(敎示) instruction; teaching. ~하다 instruct; teach; enlighten. ¶ …을 ~하다 enlighten 《*a person*》 on 〔about, as to〕….

**교신**(交信) an exchange of messages; communication; 《서신 교환》 correspondence. ~하다 communicate 《with》; exchange (radio) messages 《with》; communicate 《with》. ¶ 무전으로 ~중이다 be in radio communication 《with》 / 우리는 정찰대와의 ~이 두절되었다 We lost contact with the patrol.

**교실**(敎室) a classroom; a schoolroom. ¶ 215호 ~ Room 215 / 우리 ~은 2층에 있다 Our classroom is on the second floor. / 외국어는 ~ 안의 수업만으로는 익혀지지 않는다 Foreign languages cannot be learned in class alone.

**교안**(敎案) a teaching 〔lesson〕 plan. ¶ ~을 짜다 form 〔make〕 a「teaching program 〔lesson schedule〕 / 그는 ~을 짜기에 바쁘다 He is busy working out a teaching plan.

**교양**(敎養) culture; refinement; education. ¶ ~이 있는 cultured; well=educated; refined / ~이 있는 신사 an accomplished gentleman / ~이 있는

사람들 men of culture; well-educated classes; cultured circles; highbrows 《미》/ ~ 없는 사람 an uneducated 〔uncultured〕 person; a lowbrow 《미》/ ~을 위한 독서 reading for culture / ~을 높이다 raise *one's* cultural level; cultivate *oneself* / ~을 높이려면 고전을 읽어라 If you want to cultivate yourself, read the classics. / 그녀는 꽤 ~이 있어 보인다 She seems to be a person of some culture 〔refinement〕.
◉ ~과목 cultural studies; the liberal arts. ~과정 a general education course; the liberal arts course. ~프로 《라디오·TV의》 a cultural program; an educational program. ~학부 the college of general education 〔liberal arts〕; the liberal arts school.

**교언**(巧言) flattery; fair 〔fine, honeyed〕 words; blarney; soft soap. ~하다 flatter; use fine words; say nice things 《to *a person*》. ◉ ~영색(令色) fair words; flattery.

**교역**(交易) trade 《with》; commerce; barter (물물교환); interchange. ~하다 trade; barter; exchange. ¶ 외국과 ~하다 trade with foreign countries / 최근 한국과 중국의 ~이 활발해졌다 The Korea-China trade has become active recently. ◉ ~소 a (trading) post. ~조건 terms of trade; trade 〔trading〕 conditions. 비~품목 NTC 〔nontrade concerns〕 items.

**교역**(教役) 〖종교〗 religious work.
◉ ~자 a religious worker.

**교열**(校閱) reading (and correcting); revision. ~하다 read (and correct); revise; look over 《a manuscript》. ¶ 스미스 박사 ~ Revised by Dr. Smith. / 원고는 지금 ~중이다 The manuscript is under revision now. ◉ ~부 《신문사의》 the proofreading department. ~자 a reviser; 《신문사의》 a proofreader.

**교외**(郊外) 《in》 the suburbs 《of》; 《on》 the outskirts 《of》; the environs.

> **용법** **suburbs** 시가지에 인접한 주택지. 어떤 도시의 교외 전체를 뜻할 때는 the suburbs, 교외의 한 지구를 뜻할 때는 a suburb를 쓴다. **outskirts** 도심지에서 떨어진 변두리 땅. **environs** 도시를 둘러싸고 있는 환경이란 뜻에서 나온 도시 근교를 나타내는 격식차린 말.

¶ 대구와 그 ~ Taegu and its environs / ~의 suburban / ~에 in the suburbs; on the outskirts / ~로 산책가다 go for a walk in the suburbs / 서울 ~에 살다 live 「in the suburbs 〔on the outskirts〕 of Seoul.
◉ ~거주자 a suburban resident; a suburbanite; the suburbia [총칭]. ~생활 life in the suburbs; suburban life. ~선 열차 〖철도〗 a suburban train; the circular line running around the metropolitan zone (교외 순환선).

**교외**(校外) ¶ ~의 extramural / ~에(서) outside (the) school; out of school; off campus. ◉ ~생 an extramural 〔an extension course, a correspondence course〕 student. ~수업 teaching given outside a school. ~지도 the extramural 〔off-campus〕 guidance. ~활동 extramural activities.

**교우**(交友) 《사귐》 making friends 《with》; 《친구》 a friend; a companion; an acquaintance. ~하다 make friends 《with》; keep company 《with》. ¶ 넓은 ~ 범위 a large circle of friends / ~가 많다〔적다〕 have a large 〔small, limited〕 circle of friends 〔acquaintances〕.
◉ ~관계 *one's* associates 〔company〕: ~ 관계가 나쁘다 keep bad company / ~ 관계를 조사하다 check up on *a person's* associates; find out 〔investigate〕 what company 《*a person*》 keeps.

**교우**(校友) a schoolmate; a schoolfellow; 《동창생》 a graduate; 《미》 an alumnus (*pl.* -ni) (남자); an alumna (*pl.* -nae) (여자); an old boy 〔girl〕 《영》. ◉ ~회 《단체》 an alumni 〔old boys'〕 association; 《회합》 an alumni 〔old boys'〕 meeting 〔reunion〕.

**교우**(教友) a fellow believer; 「a brother 〔brethren〕 in the same faith; a fellow Christian 〔Buddhist〕.

**교원**(教員) a teacher; a schoolteacher; 《남자》 a schoolmaster; 《여자》 a schoolmistress; 《전체》 the teaching staff. ◉ ~노조 a teachers' union. ~실 a teacher's room. ~ 양성계획 a teacher-training program. ~자격검정고시 a teacher's licensing examination. ~자격증 《obtain, get》 a teacher's license 〔certificate〕: ~ 자격증을 따다 obtain 〔get〕 a teacher's certificate. 한국 ~대학교 Korea National University of Education.

**교유**(交遊) friendship; companionship. ~하다 associate 《with》; keep company 《with》. ¶ K씨와의 ~를 즐기다 enjoy the companionship of Mr. K.

**교육**(教育) education; schooling; teaching; training; instruction; upbringing

(가정교육). ~하다 educate; instruct; train; bring up.

> **용법** **education**은 가르침을 받는 사람의 능력이 개발됨을 뜻하는 가장 넓고 일반적인 말이며, **schooling**은 특히 학교 교육을, **teaching**은 지식이나 기술을 가르침을 뜻한다. **training**은 기능 훈련 따위 양성 목적을 갖고 하는 실제적인 교육이고, 전문 과목에서 이루어지는 조직적인 교육은 **instruction**이다. **upbringing**은 가정교육을 뜻한다.

¶ ~의 educational; educative / ~의 기회균등 equal educational opportunity / 엄한 가정~ a strict upbringing / ~을 받은 educated / ~을 받지 못한 uneducated; illiterate / 상당한 ~을 받다 receive 〔get〕 a fair 〔good〕 education / ~을 보급하다 extend school education / ~에 종사하다 engage 〔be engaged〕 in education; be a teacher / 가정 교사에게 아이들 ~을 맡기다 entrust a tutor 〔governess〕 with the education of *one's* children / 그녀는 정식 ~을 거의 받지 못했다 She has had little formal schooling. / 나는 아들에게 좋은 ~을 받게 하고 싶다 I want my son to get a good education. / 그녀는 자식 ~에 열성적인 어머니이다 She's enthusiastic about her children's education. / 이 책은 ~상 바람직하지 못하다 The book is undesirable from an educational point of view.

◉ ~가[자] an educator; an educationist; an educationalist. ~감(監) the superintendent of education. ~개혁 educational reform: ~ 개혁 심의회 Educational Reform Deliberative Commission. ~계 the educational world; educational circles. ~공무원 the educational public service [총칭]; an educational public service employee. ~과정 a curriculum (*pl.* -la, ~s). ~기관 an educational institution 〔establishment〕; an institution of learning: 고등 ~기관 a higher institution of learning; an institution for advanced learning. ~기금 an education fund. ~대학 a Teachers' College; a college of education. ~대학원 a graduate school of education. ~방송국 the Educational Broadcasting System (생략 EBS). ~법 《방법》 an educational 〔a teaching〕 method; 《법률》 the Law of Education. ~보조 자료 teaching aids. ~보험 educational endowment insurance. ~부 the Ministry of Education: ~부 장관 the Minister of Education. ~비 school 〔educational〕 expenses. ~사업 educational work. ~수준 a standard of education: ~ 수준이 높다 《전반적으로》 have a high standard of education; 《개인이》 stand 〔be〕 on a high level of education; be highly educated / …보다 ~수준이 낮다 have a standard of education lower than…; be beneath 《another》 in education. ~시설 educational facilities. ~실습 teaching practice; student teaching: ~실습생 a student 〔trainee〕 teacher. ~심리학 educational psychology: ~ 심리학과 the department of educational psychology. ~연도 an academic 〔a school〕 year. ~영화 an educational film. ~위원 a member of the Board of Education: (지방)~ 위원회 a board of education; a school board 《미》 / 서울시 ~ 위원회 the Education Board of Seoul. ~제도 an education(al) 〔a school〕 system. ~지도 education and guidance. ~철학 educational philosophy. ~프로그램 an educational program. ~학 pedagogy; pedagogics: ~학과 the department of education / ~학자 a pedagogist / ~학 박사 a doctor of education (생략 Ed. D.). ~행정 educational administration. ~회 an educational association.

국민 ~ 헌장 the National Charter of Education. 한국 ~ 개발원 the Korea Educational Development Institute (KEDI).

> **참고** 각종 교육의 영어 표기
> 초등교육 elementary 〔primary〕 education. 중등〔고등〕교육 secondary 〔higher〕 education. 의무교육 compulsory education. 영어교육 English teaching. 어학교육 language training. 전문교육 professional 〔specialized〕 instruction. 성교육 sex education. 대학교육 college education. 통신교육 correspondence education 직업교육 vocational education 〔training〕. 기술교육 technical education 〔training〕. 평생교육 lifelong education. 정서교육 the cultivation of aesthetic sentiments.

**교의**(交誼) friendship; companionship; friendly relations. ¶ ~를 맺다 cultivate 〔promote〕 friendship with 《*a* *person*》.

**교의**(校醫) a school doctor 〔physician〕.

**교의**(教義) a doctrine. = 교리(教理).

**교인**(教人) 〖종교〗 a believer; a follower; an adherent; 《교회원》 a member of a church. ¶ 기독교 ~이 되다 become a Christian / 그는 같은 교회의 ~이다 He is a fellow member of the same church.

**교자**(交子) food set on a large table. ◉ ~상 a large (dining) table.

**교잡**(交雜) ① 《뒤섞임》 being interlaced and intertwining; disorder; confusion. ~하다 interlace and intertwine; be tangled 〔confused〕. ② 〖식물〗 crossing; 〖동물〗 hybridization. ~하다 cross; hybridize.

**교장**(校長) 《중·고교의》 a principal; 《초등 학교의》 a headmaster; a schoolmaster; 《여자》 a headmistress; a schoolmistress. ¶ 그는 ~으로 적임이다 He is well fitted for the post of principal. ◉ ~실 the principal's office.

**교장**(教場) a (military) drill ground; a drill field; a training field.

**교재**(教材) teaching materials 〔aids〕. ¶ ~를 준비하다 provide materials of instruction / 영어 신문을 ~로 사용하다 use an English newspaper for teaching materials. ◉ ~비 expenses for teaching materials. ~연구 a study of teaching materials.

**교전**(交戰) 《전쟁》 (a) war; hostilities; 《전투》 a battle; combat; an action; an engagement. ~하다 fight 《against, with》; engage in a battle; join battle 《with》. ¶ ~ 상태에 있다 be in a state of hostilities 〔war〕 / ~중이다 be fighting 《against, with》; be at war 《with》 / 적과 ~하다 engage 〔fight with〕 the enemy troops / ~을 중지하다 break off the engagement; cease fire / ~을 회피하다 avoid action / 비무장 지대에서 산발적인 ~이 보고되었다 Sporadic skirmishes were reported in the demilitarized zone.
◉ ~국 warring 〔belligerent〕 countries 〔powers〕; the belligerents. ~권 the right of belligerency; belligerent rights. ~단체 a belligerent body 〔community〕 ~상태 《be in》 a state of war 《with》. ~지 a battlefield; a field of battle. ~지대 a war zone; a zone of hostilities.

**교점**(交點) an intersection; a point of intersection; 〖천문〗 a node.

**교접**(交接) ① 《접촉》 contact. ~하다 contact; make contact 《with》. ② 《성교》 sexual intercourse; copulation. ~하다 have sexual intercourse 《with》; copulate 《with》. ◉ ~기관 《동물》 a copulatory organ. ~불능 impotency: ~불능자 an impotent man.

**교정**(校正) proofreading; correction of the press. ~하다 proofread; read 〔correct〕 proofs; do proofreading. ¶ ~(자)의 잘못 a proofreader's error / 세밀히 ~을 보다 read proofs with care / ~중에 정정하다 make corrections in 〔on〕 the proof / ~에서 오자를 놓치고 넘어가다 overlook errors in proof / ~ 단계에서 삭제하다 delete 《the words》 at the proof stage / ~을 세 번 보다 read the proofs three times; make corrections in three proofs.
◉ ~기호 proof-correction marks; proofreader's marks. ~쇄〔지〕 a proof sheet; proofs; a galley (proof); 잘못된 ~쇄 a foul proof / 완료된 ~쇄 O.K.'d proofs; proofs marked O.K. / ~쇄를 내다 print a proof. ~원〔자〕 a proofreader. ~필 Corrected.

**교정**(校訂) revision. ⇨ 교열(校閱).
◉ ~본 a revised edition 〔text〕; a recension. ~자 a reviser. ~판 a revised edition.

**교정**(校庭) a schoolyard; a school playground (초등학교의); 《구내》 the school grounds; the campus (대학의).

**교정**(教程) a course of study; a curriculum. ⇨ 교육 과정.

**교정**(矯正) correction; reform; rectification; remedy. ~하다 reform; correct; cure; remedy; set 〔put〕 《*a thing*》 right. ¶ ~할 수 없는 incurable; incorrigible; irreclaimable / 나쁜 버릇을 ~하다 cure 〔break〕 《*a person*》 of a bad habit / 치열을 ~하다 straighten *one's* teeth / 근시를 ~하다 cure 《*a person*》 of nearsightedness. ◉ ~법 a cure; a remedy. ~시력 corrected sight. ~시설 a correctional institution.

**교제**(交際) association; company; society; friendship; acquaintance. ~하다 associate 《with》; keep company 《with》; go about 〔around〕 《with》. ¶ ~상 for company; for the sake of friendship / ~를 잘하는〔잘 못하는〕 사람 a sociable 〔an unsociable〕 person; 《구어》 a good 〔bad〕 mixer / ~를 좋아하다 be sociable; be fond of society 〔company〕 / ~가 넓다 know a lot of people; have a large 〔wide〕 circle of acquaintances / ~가 좁다 do not

know many people; do not have many acquaintances / ~를 맺다 form a friendship with《*a person*》; get acquainted《with》/ ~를 끊다 break (off)〔cut, sever〕relations《with》/ ~를 피하다 avoid company; keep to *oneself;* avoid another's society / 좋은〔나쁜〕사람과 ~하다 keep good〔bad〕company / ~상 골프 치는 일이 많다 I often play golf socially. / 그는 그 여자와 3년 동안이나 ~하고 있다 He has been going about with her for three years.
◉ ~가 a sociable person; a good mixer. ~범위 a circle of acquaintance(s): ~범위가 넓다〔좁다〕have a wide〔narrow〕circle of acquaintance(s). ~비 social expenses. ~술 the art of association.

**교조**(教祖)〖종교〗the founder《of a religion》; the head《of a religious sect》. ¶ 신흥 종교의 ~ the founder of a new religion.

**교조**(教條) a tenet; a dogma; a doctrine. ◉ ~주의 dogmatism; doctrinairism;《미》doctrinism. ~주의자 a dogmatist; a doctrinist; a doctrinarian.

**교졸**(巧拙) skill; proficiency; dexterity;《공예의》workmanship.

**교종**(教宗)〖불교〗non-Zen〔doctrinal, dogmatic〕Buddhism.

**교주**(校主) the proprietor of a school. ¶ 그 학교의 ~는 민씨다 The school is run〔kept〕by Mr. Min.

**교주**(教主) the founder of a religion. the head of a religious sect.

**교지**(校紙) a school paper.

**교지**(校誌) a school magazine.

**교지**(教旨) ①〖고제도〗a writ of appointment. ②《교리》a doctrine (of a religion). ¶ 기독교의 ~ the Christian doctrine. ③《교육》the principle of education.

**교지기**(校—) a school janitor.

**교직**(交織) a combined〔mixed〕weave; a blended fabric; a blend. ◉ ~물 union (cloth). 면모~ wool-cotton〔half-wool〕fabric.

**교직**(教職)《교사의》the teaching profession;《대학의》professorship;《종교의》the ministry; (holy) orders; the priesthood. ¶ ~에 몸을 담다 enter the teaching profession; become a teacher / ~에 있다 follow the teaching profession; be a teacher.
◉ ~과정 a「teacher-training〔teaching〕course. ~원 the staff of a school; school personnel. ~자 a (school) teacher.

**교질**(交迭) a switch; a change. ⇨ 교체「(交替).

**교질**(膠質) a colloid. ¶ ~의 gluey; glutinous; colloid(al) / ~화하다《용액이》gel; gelatinize. ◉ ~용액 a colloidal solution; a hydrosol. ~화학 colloid chemistry.

**교차**(交叉) crossing; intersection;〖유전〗crossing-over (염색체 교차). ~하다 cross〔intersect〕《each other》. ¶ 직각으로 ~하다 intersect at right angles.
◉ ~개념 cross〔intersecting〕concept. ~로 a crossroad(s): ~로를 건너다 cross (the street) at the crossing. ~선 a cross line. ~승인 the cross=recognition《of the North and the South Korea》. ~점 a point of intersection; an intersection; a crossing;《선로의》a junction: 두 거리의 ~점에서 at the intersection of two streets.

**교착**(交錯)《뒤얽힘》complication;《뒤섞임》mixture; blending. ~하다 get〔be〕complicated; cross〔mingle with〕each other. ¶ 명암의 ~ a mixture of light and shade / 희비가 ~하여 with mingled joy and sorrow.

**교착**(膠着) agglutination; adhesion; stalemate. ~하다 agglutinate; adhere《to》; stick《to》; glue《to》;《사태가》come to a deadlock〔standstill〕.
◉ ~상태 a deadlock; a standstill; a stalemate: ~ 상태에 있다 be deadlocked; be at a standstill〔deadlock〕/ ~ 상태에 빠지다 reach (a) deadlock; be brought to a stalemate / 새로운 제안이 ~ 상태를 타개할까요 Will the new proposal break the deadlock? ~어 an agglutinative language.

**교체**(交替·交遞) a shift; (a) change (of personnel); replacement. ~하다 replace《A with〔by〕B》; change《B for A》; shift《personnel》. ¶ 선수 ~ a change of players / 투수를 ~하다 change pitchers / 낡은 타이어를 새것으로 ~하다 replace a worn tire by〔with〕a new one / ~할 사람이 올 때까지 나는 이 자리를 떠날 수 없다 I can't leave my post till my relief comes.
◉ ~자 a shift; a relief.

**교칙**(校則) school regulations. ¶ ~을 지키다〔어기다〕observe〔violate〕the school regulations. ◉ ~위반 a breach〔violation〕of the school regulations.

**교칙**(教則) rules for teaching.
◉ ~본 a manual.

**교탁**(教卓) a teacher's 〔teaching〕 desk.

**교태**(嬌態) coquetry; coquettish 〔flirtatious〕 behavior. ¶ ～를 부리다 coquet 《with》; play the coquette 〔coquetry〕; behave coquettishly 〔flirtatiously〕.

**교통**(交通) 《왕래》 traffic; 《연락》 communication; 《운수》 transport; transportation. ¶ 중심가의 번잡한 ～ the dense 〔heavy〕 traffic of a main street / ～이 편리한〔불편한〕 곳 a place easy 〔hard〕 to get to; a place conveniently 〔inconveniently〕 situated / ～혼잡을 덜다 relieve (the) traffic congestion / ～을 정리하다 control 〔regulate〕 traffic / ～을 차단하다 block (up) 《the street》 / 고장난 트럭이 ～을 방해했다 The broken-down truck obstructed the traffic. / 사고로 ～이 몇시간 동안 두절되었다 The accident tied up the traffic for hours. / 이 마을은 지금 외부와 ～이 완전히 두절되어 있다 This village is now entirely isolated 〔cut off〕 from the outside world. / 이 거리는 ～이 번잡하다 Traffic is heavy on this street. *or* There is a great deal of traffic on this street. / 심한 ～ 체증으로 1시간 늦었다 I was an hour late because of a terrible traffic jam. / ～사정은 시급히 개선되어야 한다 Traffic conditions must be improved without delay.
◉ ～경제 traffic economy. ～경찰 traffic police. ～과 the traffic division. ～규칙〔법규〕 traffic regulations 〔rules〕. ～기관 a means of transportation; transport facilities; public transport. ～난 difficult conditions of traffic. ～도덕 traffic morality 〔morals, manners〕: ～도덕을 지키다 follow traffic morals. ～량 (the volume of) traffic: ～량이 가장 많은 시간 the heaviest traffic hours / 이 거리는 ～량이 많다 The traffic of this street is heavy 〔busy〕. *or* There is much traffic in this street. ～로 a traffic route; 《병참선》 a line of communication. ～마비 the traffic paralysis. ～망 a traffic 〔communication〕 network. ～문제 a traffic problem. ～사고 a traffic 〔street, road〕 accident: ～사고를 일으키다 cause 〔bring about〕 a traffic accident / ～사고로 죽다 be killed in a traffic accident / ～사고로 인한 사망자 traffic deaths; (the number of) deaths on the road. ～순경 a traffic cop 《미구어》; a traffic policeman. ～ 신고센터 a traffic report center. ～신호 a traffic signal 〔light〕: ～신호가 바뀌기를 기다리다 wait for the traffic light(s) to change. ～ 안전운동 a traffic safety campaign 〔drive〕. ～안전주간 Traffic Safety Week. ～안전지대 a traffic safety zone. ～위반 a traffic offense: ～ 위반 딱지 a traffic ticket / ～법원 a traffic court. ～인구 traffic population. ～정리 traffic control 〔regulation〕: ～ 정리하는 경관 a policeman directing traffic. ～정책 a traffic policy. ～지옥〔정체〕 a traffic jam 〔mess〕. ～질서 a traffic order. ～차단 cutting off communications; a traffic blockade: ～ 차단구역 a closed 〔blockaded〕 area. ～참사 a traffic disaster. ～체증 traffic holdups; a traffic gridlock 〔tieup, snarl, backup, jam〕: 도심 지역의 ～체증을 덜다 ease traffic jams 〔congestion〕 in the downtown area. ～ 통제센터 a traffic control center. ～표지 a traffic (control) sign. ～혼잡 《ease》 traffic congestion; a traffic jam.

**교통방송국**(交通放送局) the Traffic Broadcasting Station (생략 TBS). ¶ TBS는 우리 나라의 전문 ～이다 TBS is the specialized traffic broadcasting station in our country.

**교통비**(交通費) carfare (차삯); traffic 〔transportation〕 expenses. ¶ ～를 지급하다 provide commutation allowances / ～가 많이 든다 It costs me a lot for my traffic expenses.

**교파**(教派) 〖종교〗 a (religious) sect; a denomination (★ sect는 극단적이거나 이단적이라는 뜻이 내포되어 있어서 교도가 자기파를 말할 때는 쓰지 않음). ¶ ～적 sectarian; denominational / 온갖 ～의 성직자 clergy of all denominations / 새로운 ～를 형성하다 form a new denomination. ◉ ～심 sectarianism.

**교편**(教鞭) a birch (rod). ¶ ～을 잡다 teach at a school; be a teacher; stand on the platform.

**교포**(僑胞) a Korean resident 〔national〕 abroad; a Korean residing abroad; overseas Koreans [총칭]. ¶ 재미〔재일〕 ～ a Korean resident in America 〔Japan〕; a Korean (residing) in America 〔Japan〕.

**교풍**(校風) school spirit 〔tradition〕; traditions of a school. ¶ ～을 세우다 establish 〔form〕 the traditions of a school / ～에 어긋나다 be against the best traditions of the school.

**교합**(交合) sexual union 〔intercourse〕.

~하다 unite sexually.

**교향곡**(交響曲) a symphony. ¶ 베토벤의 5번 ~ Beethoven's fifth symphony / ~의 symphonic.

**교향시**(交響詩) a symphonic poem.

**교향악**(交響樂) a symphony. ◉ ~단 a symphony orchestra: ~단원 a symphonist / 국립〔시립〕 ~단 the National 〔Municipal〕 Symphony Orchestra.

**교호**(交互) alternation; reciprocality. ~하다 alternate 《with》; be reciprocal. ¶ ~의 mutual; alternate / ~로 mutually; alternately. ◉ ~개념 alternating concepts. ~계산 an account current (생략 A/C): ~계산서 a statement of account current. ~작용 reciprocal action; (an) interaction.

**교화**(敎化) education; enlightenment; edification; culture; civilization; 《야만인에 대한》 domestication; reclamation; taming. ~하다 educate; enlighten; civilize; domesticate. ¶ 토인을 ~하다 civilize the wild tribes / 일찍이 원주민을 ~하기 위해 많은 선교사가 파견되었다 A lot of missionaries were once sent there to enlighten the natives. ◉ ~사업 an enlightenment project; educational work. ~운동 an educational movement; a drive for people's enlightenment.

**교환**(交換) (an) exchange; (an) interchange; give-and-take; barter (물물의); a swap 《구어》; commutation; clearing (어음의). ~하다 exchange 《A for B》; make an exchange of; trade 〔barter〕 《A for B》; give and take; swap 《구어》; clear 《bills》. ¶ (전화의) 자동〔수동〕 ~ automatic 〔manual〕 switching / 포로 ~ an exchange of prisoners / ~할 수 있는 exchangeable; interchangeable / ~으로 in exchange 〔return〕 《for》 / 의견을 ~하다 exchange views 〔opinions〕 with 《*a person* on a subject》 / 중고차에 웃돈을 주고 새 차와 ~하다 trade in a used car for a new one / 새해 인사를 ~하다 wish one another "A Happy New Year" / 사신 물건은 ~해 드립니다 Articles bought are changed. ◉ ~가격 the exchange price. ~가치 exchange 〔exchangeable〕 value; value in exchange; exchangeability. ~교수 《강의》 an exchange lecture; 《사람》 an exchange professor. ~국 central 《미》; a telephone exchange. ~대 a switchboard: 우리 회사에는 ~대가 있다 There is a switchboard service in our office. ~렌즈 〖사진〗 an interchangeable lens. ~물자 barter goods. ~방문 the exchange of visits: 나이 든 이산 가족들의 ~방문 the exchange of visits by aged dispersed 〔separated〕 families. ~선 a repatriation 〔an exchange〕 ship. ~소 《어음의》 a clearing house. ~실 《전화의》 an operating room; a telephone switchboard room; telephone operators' room. ~원 《전화의》 a telephone 〔switchboard〕 operator. ~전화 회선 operator-assisted circuits. ~조건 a bargaining point. ~품 an exchange; a barter; a swap 《미》. ~학생 an exchange student.

**교환**(交歡·交驩) an exchange of courtesies 〔visits, greetings, good wishes〕 《between》. ~하다 exchange courtesies 〔visits, greetings, good wishes〕 《with》. ¶ 한일 학생간의 ~ an exchange of greetings between Korean and Japanese students. ◉ ~경기 a goodwill game. ~비행 a courtesy flight.

**교활**(狡猾) cunning; guile. ~하다 (be) cunning; crafty; wily; artful; foxy; sly. ¶ ~한 사람 a crafty 〔cunning〕 person; an old fox 《구어》 / ~한 수단 a sharp practice; a shrewd trick / ~하게 cunningly; slyly; with a trick / ~한 짓을 하다 act craftily.

**교황**(敎皇) 〖가톨릭〗 the Pope; a pope; the (Supreme 〔Sovereign〕) Pontiff. ¶ ~의 papal / ~ 요한 바오로 2세 Pope John Paul Ⅱ / 로마~ the Pope; the (Supreme) Pontiff; 《경칭》 His Holiness the Pope. ◉ ~사절 a nuncio (대사); a papal deligate; a pope's envoy. ~정치 papacy; papal government. ~제도 the papacy; the papal system. ~청 the Vatican (Palace); the (Roman) Curia.

**교회**(敎會) 《교파》 Church; 《예배당》 a church; a chapel. ¶ ~에서 하는 결혼식 a church wedding / ~에 나가다 go to church / ~에서 기도하다 pray in 〔at〕 church. ◉ ~당 a church; a chapel; 《대성당》 a cathedral. ~음악 church music.

**교회**(敎誨) (an) admonition; preaching. ~하다 admonish; preach. ◉ ~사(師) a (prison) chaplain.

**교훈**(校訓) school precepts; a motto for school discipline.

**교훈**(敎訓) 《가르침》 the teaching; instruction; 《훈화》 a precept; a lesson; 《우화적인》 a moral. ~하다 teach;

instruct. ¶ ~적 instructive; moral; edifying / 산 ~ a living lesson 〔witness〕/ ~을 주다 teach 〔give〕《*a person*》 a lesson / ~을 얻다 learn a lesson 《from》/ ~에 따르다 follow *a person's* precepts / 다른 사람에게 ~이 되다 be a lesson 〔beacon〕 to others / 좋은 ~이다 be a good lesson 〔warning〕 《to》/ 스승의 ~을 어기다 act contrary to *one's* teacher's instruction / 실패는 그에게 ~이 되었다 He has learned a lesson from his failure. / 그것을 ~삼아 앞으로 더욱 조심하는 게 좋겠다 Let it be a lesson to you. I hope you will be more careful in future. ◉ ~극 a morality play.

**구**(九) nine. ¶ 제9, the ninth; No. 9(9번) / 9분의 1, a 〔one〕 ninth / 10분의 9 nine tenths.

**구**(句) 《구절》 a phrase; a clause (절); 《문구》 an expression; 《시구》 a line; a verse. ¶ 구를 절로 바꾸다 expand a phrase into a clause.

**구**(灸) 《뜸》 moxibustion. ⇨ 뜸.

**구**(區) ① 《행정상의》 a ward. ¶ 종로구 Chongno-gu; Chongno Ward / 구립 도서관 a ward library. ② 《구역》 a district; a section; an area. ¶ 지역구 an Electoral District; a Local Constituency; a (Local) District / 전국구 《선거의》 Nationwide Proportional Seats.

**구**(球) 《구체》 a sphere; a globe; 《공》 a ball; 《전구 따위》 a bulb. ¶ 제5구 〖야구〗 the fifth pitch.

**구**(具) a body. ¶ 여러 구의 시체 several bodies.

**구-**(舊) 《옛》 old; former; past; ex-; outgoing (퇴임하는). ¶ 구세대 the old generation / 구사상 old 〔antiquated〕 ideas / 신구 시장 the outgoing and incoming mayors.

**-구**(口) an opening; a window; a hole; a wicket. ¶ 개찰구 a wicket; a ticket gate / 분화구 a crater / 접수구 a reception window / 출납창구 《은행의》 a teller's window / 출입구 an entrance; a gateway; a doorway.

**-구**(具) a tool; an implement. ¶ 문방구 stationery / 운동구 sport goods.

**구가**(舊家) 《집안》 an old family; 《집》 *one's* former house. ¶ 그 고장의 ~ an old family of the place.

**구가**(謳歌) glorification; eulogy; a pean. ~하다 glorify; eulogize; extol; sing 〔chant〕 the praises of. ¶ 인생을 ~하다 openly enjoy the joys of life / 자유〔평화〕를 ~하다 sing the praises of liberty 〔peace〕.

**구각**(舊殼) ¶ ~을 벗다〔탈피하다〕 cast off the old skin; discard 〔break with〕 the worm-eaten customs; shake off the fetters of old customs and manners.

**구간**(區間) a section (between two points); a block (of railroad track); a serviced area. ¶ 불통 ~ a damaged 〔disrupted〕 section / 지하철 요금은 1~에 500원이다 The subway fare is five hundred won (for) a section.

**구간**(舊刊) 《서적의》 an old edition 〔printing〕; an old publication; 《잡지의》 a back number 《of a magazine》.

**구간**(軀幹) 《동체》 the torso; the trunk of a body; 《몸》 the body.

**구갈**(口渴) thirst. ¶ ~을 느끼다 feel thirsty.

**구감**(口疳) 〖한의〗 stomatitis.

**구강**(口腔) the mouth; the oral cavity. ¶ ~ 위생 oral 〔dental〕 hygiene. ◉ ~경(鏡) 〖의학〗 a stomatoscope. ~근 〖해부〗 the muscles of the mouth. ~병학 stomatology; oralogy. ~암 cancer of the mouth. ~외과 oral surgery. ~정형 외과 stomatoplasty.

**구개**(口蓋) 〖해부〗 the palate; the roof of the mouth. ¶ 연〔경〕~ the soft 〔hard〕 palate. ◉ ~골 〖해부〗 the palatine 〔palatal〕 bones. ~음 a palatal (sound): ~음화 palatalization.

**구걸**(求乞) begging. ~하다 beg (for) 《food, money》. ¶ ~하고 다니다 go begging; beg from door to door (집집마다) / 그는 지나가는 사람들에게 돈을 ~했다 He begged money from people passing by.

**구경** seeing; 《관광》 sightseeing; visiting; a visit. ~하다 see 《a play》; watch 《a game》; visit 《a museum》; have a look over; see 〔do〕 the sights 《of Cheju》; look around (돌아다니다); look on (방관하다). ¶ 한번 ~할 만한 경관 a sight worth seeing / ~이 나다 a spectacle takes place / 영화를 ~하다 see a movie / 서울 ~ 가다 go to see the sights of Seoul; go sightseeing to Seoul / 세계 박람회 ~을 가다 take in the World's Fair / 싸움을 ~하다 watch a fight / ~하며 돌아다니다 tour 《a exhibition》; make a tour of 《a city》; look around 《the market》 / 경주에는 ~할 만한 유적이 많다 There are many historic remains to see in Kyŏngju. / 영화~ 안 갈래 What do you say to taking in a movie? ◉ ~가마리 a laughingstock; an object of ridicule: ～가마리가 되다 become a laughingstock 〔an object of ridicule〕. ～감 ⇨ 구경거리.

**구경**(口徑) 《총·포의》 a caliber; a bore; 《렌즈 등의》 an aperture. ¶ 38 ～ 권총 a 38-caliber pistol; a 38 / ～ 16인치의 포 a 16 in. gun / 대〔중, 소〕～의 대포 a large-〔medium-, small-〕caliber gun.

**구경**(球莖) 〖식물〗 a (plant) bulb; a corm. ◉ ～식물 a bulbous plant.

**구경거리** an attraction; a sight; a spectacle; a show; an exhibition. ¶ ～가 아냐, 썩 물러들 가지못해 Go away! This isn't a side show! / ～가 되고 싶지 않다 I don't like to be exposed to public view. *or* I don't like to make a show of myself before strangers. / 그 서커스는 볼 만한 ～였다 The circus was a great spectacle. / 그것은 참 멋진 ～였지 It was a sight to see.

**구경꾼** 《관객》 a spectator; audience [총칭]; 《명소 따위의》 a sightseer; a visitor; a tourist; 《방관자》 an onlooker; a looker-on (*pl.* lookers-); a bystander. ¶ ～들이 인산인해를 이루었다 Crowds of curious people gathered around, all rubbernecking (to see what happened). / 그 행렬에는 수많은 ～이 모였다 The procession drew crowds of spectators.

**구고**(舊稿) an old manuscript. ¶ ～를 고쳐 쓰다 rewrite *one's* manuscript.

**구곡**(舊穀) last year's grain; old grain.

**구과**(毬果) 〖식물〗 a cone. ◉ ～식물 a conifer.

**구관**(舊官) a former magistrate. ¶ ～이 명관이다 《속담》 Better the devil you know than the devil you don't know.

**구관**(舊館) the old 〔older〕 building.

**구관조**(九官鳥) 〖조류〗 a myna(h); a myna bird; a hill myna.

**구교**(舊交) old friendship 〔acquaintance〕; an old friend (오랜 벗). ¶ ～를 새롭게 하다 renew *one's* (old) friendship 《with》.

**구교**(舊教) (Roman) Catholicism; the (Roman) Catholic Church. ◉ ～도 a (Roman) Catholic.

**구구** 《닭 부르는 소리》 cluck! cluck!; chuck-chuck-chuck.

**구구**(九九) ① 〖수학〗《구구법》 the rules of multiplication. ～하다 calculate by the multiplication table. ② 《궁리》 ～하다 think over; consider carefully; ponder; mull. ◉ ～표 the multiplication table / ～표를 5단까지 알〔외〕다 say the multiplication tables up to 5.

**구구하다**(區區—) ① 《각기 다르다》 (be) various; diverse; conflicting. ¶ 구구한 보도 various 〔conflicting〕 reports / 그것에 관한 소문이 ～ There are conflicting rumors about it. / 이 점에 관해서는 의견이 ～ Opinions vary widely on this point. ② 《변변찮다》 (be) petty; meticulous; insignificant; trivial. ¶ 구구한 잔소리 an insignificant lecture. ③ 《용렬하다》 (be) poor; awkward; clumsy. ¶ 구구한 변명 a poor 〔lame, clumsy〕 excuse.

**구국**(救國) national salvation. ～하다 save *one's* country. ◉ ～운동 a save-the-nation drive 〔movement〕. ～지사 a patriot who is devoted to the salvation of his country.

**구균**(球菌) a coccus; a micrococcus.

**구근**(球根) a tuber; a bulb. ◉ ～식물 a bulbous plant.

**구금**(拘禁) 〖법〗 detention; confinement; custody; imprisonment. ～하다 detain; confine; hold 〔keep〕 《*a person*》 in custody; put 《*a person*》 in detention; lock 《*a person*》 up; intern. ¶ 자택에 ～되다 be detained in *one's* home 〔under house arrest〕 / 그는 경찰서에 ～되었다 He was detained at the police station. *or* He was taken into custody at the police station.

**구급**(救急) first aid. ¶ ～용의 first-aid / ～ 조치를 하다 administer first aid 《to》. ◉ ～붕대 (an) emergency dressing. ～상자 a first-aid kit 〔box〕. ～신호 an SOS (call); a hurry call. ～약 a first-aid medicine; an emergency remedy. ～차 an ambulance. ～책 emergency measures. ～치료 a first-aid treatment. ～환자 an emergency case.

**구기** 《작은 국자》 a ladle; a dipper; 《셈으로》 a dipperful; a ladling (of oil). ¶ ～로 뜨다 scoop (up) with a ladle; dip 〔ladle〕 out.

**구기**(球技) a ball game.

**구기다**[1] 《형편이》 take a turn for the worst; grow bad 〔unfavorable, difficult〕. ¶ 살림이 구기기 시작했다 My economic circumstances are taking an unfavorable turn. *or* I'm beginning to find it hard to get along.

**구기다**[2] 《주름지게 하다》 wrinkle; crumple; rumple; crease; 《주름지다》 be crumpled 〔wrinkled〕; get rumpled. ¶ 구겨진 종이 조각 a crumpled piece of paper / 치마를 ～ wrinkle a skirt / 구겨지지 않는 옷감 wrinkle-free 〔wrinkle-proof〕 fabric / 이 천은 잘 구겨진다

This cloth wrinkles easily.
**구기박지르다** wrinkle all up.
**구기자**(枸杞子) 〖식물〗 a Chinese matrimony vine; 〖한의〗 fruit of a Chinese matrimony vine.
**구기적거리다** crumple 〔rumple, wrinkle〕 up 《a piece of paper》.
**구기적구기적** crumpling 〔rumpling, crushing〕 up. ¶ 옷을 가방에 ~ 넣다 crush the clothes into a bag.
**구기지르다** wrinkle 〔crumple〕 up.
**구김살** wrinkles; creases; rumples; folds. ¶ ~이 진 crumpled; rumpled / ~이 잡히다 be wrinkled 〔creased, rumpled, crumpled〕 / ~을 펴다 unrumple; smooth 〔press〕 out wrinkles / 이 옷감은 ~이 잘 간다 This material creases very easily. / 거기에 앉지 마라, 옷에 ~이 진다 Don't sit on there. It will leave wrinkles.
**구깃구깃하다** (be) crumpled; wrinkled; be full of wrinkles. ¶ 구깃구깃한 저고리 a coat full of wrinkles / 구깃구깃한 지폐 a crumpled bank note.
**-구나** 《감탄》 how; what; indeed. ¶ 참 불쌍하구나 What a pity! *or* Poor thing 〔fellow〕! / 참 아름답구나 How beautiful it is! / 저 집은 크기도 하구나 What a large house that is!
**구난**(救難) rescue; salvage (난파선의).
**구내**(區內) ¶ ~에 in the ward; within the section 〔district, area〕.
**구내**(構內) premises; precincts; a compound; grounds; an enclosure; 《on》 the campus (대학의). ¶ 역 ~ the station yard / 대사관 ~ the embassy compound / ~에 on the premises; in the compound 〔grounds〕 / 학교 ~에서 on the school grounds / ~ 출입 금지 《게시》 Keep off the premises.
◉ ~식당 《학교 등의》 a refectory; a cafeteria (직접 가져다 먹는); 《역 등의》 a refreshment room. ~전화 an interphone; an (internal) office telephone: ~ 전화번호 an extension number.
**구내염**(口內炎) 〖의학〗 stomatitis.
**구년**(舊年) the past year(s); an old year; 《작년》 last year.
**구단**(球團) 〖야구〗 a (professional) baseball team. ¶ ~주 the owner of a baseball team.
**구대륙**(舊大陸) the Old World. ¶ ~의 old-world.
**구더기** a grub; a maggot. ¶ ~가 끓다 maggots hatch 〔breed〕; be infested with maggots.
**구덥다** (be) reliable; dependable; trustworthy.
**구덩이** ① 《구멍》 a hollow (place); a depression; a hole in the ground. ¶ 김치 ~ a kimchi hole; a hole for a kimchi jar / ~에 빗물이 괴었다 The rain water has gathered in a hollow. ② 〖광산〗 =갱(坑).
**구도**(求道) 〖종교〗 seeking 〔a search〕 after truth. ~하다 seek after truth. ¶ 열심히 ~하는 eager to seek after truth. ◉ ~자 a seeker after truth.
**구도**(構圖) 〖미술〗 composition 《of a painting》; 《소설의》 plot. ¶ ~가 좋다 〔나쁘다〕 It is well 〔ill〕 composed / 이 그림의 ~는 좋지 않다 The composition of this painting is poor.
**구도**(舊都) an old 〔a former〕 capital.
**구도(로)**(舊道(路)) an old 「road 〔highway〕.
**구독**(購讀) subscription. ~하다 subscribe to 《a newspaper, a magazine》; 《미》 take 《a newspaper》; 《영》 take in 《a newspaper, a magazine》. ¶ ~을 갱신하다 renew *one's* subscription / ~을 신청하다 subscribe for 《a magazine》; take out a subscription 《to a magazine》. ◉ ~료 subscription (rates). ~자 a subscriber; a reader: 이 신문은 ~자가 많다 This paper has a large circulation.
**구동**(驅動) drive. ¶ 4륜 ~ 차 a four-wheel-drive vehicle / 전륜 ~ 차 a front-wheel-drive car. ◉ ~력 driving power. ~륜 《자동차의》 a driving wheel. ~장치 running 〔driving〕 gear. ~축 a drive shaft; a driving axle.
**구두** 《단화》 《a pair of》 shoes; 《반장화》 half boots; 《장화》 (high, long) boots; 《가죽》 leather shoes.
¶ 굽 높은〔낮은〕 ~ high-〔low-〕heeled shoes / ~를 맞추다 have a pair of shoes made / ~를 신다〔벗다〕 put on 〔take off〕 *one's* shoes / ~를 잡아당겨 신다〔벗다〕 pull on 〔off〕 *one's* boots / ~를 닦다 shine 〔polish〕 *one's* shoes; 《시켜서》 have *one's* shoes shined / ~를 수선하다 repair shoes; 《수선시키다》 have shoes mended / ~에 죄여 발을 쓸리다 get a shoe sore / 이 ~는 너무 꼭 낀다 These shoes 「are too tight 〔pinch me〕. / 이 ~는 오래 신습니다 These shoes wear long 〔well〕. *or* You can wear these shoes long. / 아저씨 ~ 닦으세요 Give your shoes a shine, sir?
◉ ~골 a shoe 〔boot〕 tree. ~끈 a shoelace; a shoestring 《미》; a bootlace: ~끈을 매다 lace 〔tie〕 (up) *one's* shoes. ~닦기 《닦음》 shoe polishing: ~닦기 헝겊 a shoe rag. ~닦이 a

shoeshiner; a bootblack 《미》; a shoeblack: ~닦이 소년 a shoeshine boy. ~약 shoe 〔boot〕 polish: ~약을 칠하다 black 〔apply polish to〕 *one's* shoes. ~장이 a shoemaker. ~창 the sole (of a shoe): ~창을 갈다 put a new sole on shoes; 《해받다》 have *one's* shoes resoled 《by》. ~칼 ⇨ 구둣주걱; 《칼》 a shoe maker's knife. ~코 the toe of a shoe. 구둣발: 구둣발로 방에 들어가다 go into a room with *one's* shoes on; enter a room without taking off *one's* foot gear / 구둣발로 밟다 tread 《*a person*》 underfoot / 구둣발로 차다 kick 《*a person*》 with *one's* boots. 구둣방 a shoe store 〔shop 《영》〕. 구둣솔 a shoe brush. 구둣주걱 a shoehorn.

> 참고 **shoes**(구두)의 용법과 그 규격
> 1. 단순히 「구두」라고 할 때는 shoes라고 복수형을 쓰는 것이 일반적: my shoes(내 구두). 그러나 「한 쪽의 구두」를 말할 경우는 this shoe처럼 단수형을 씀. 한 켤레, 두 켤레라고 셀 경우는 a pair of shoes, two pairs of shoes로 표현. 경우에 따라서는 두 켤레 이상일 때도 two pair of shoes라고 pair의 단수형을 쓸 때도 있다.
> 2. 영미의 구두 사이즈는 세로를 3분의 1인치씩 차이를 두고 남성용은 대개 7에서 13까지, 여성용은 5에서 11까지로 구분되어 있다. 또 폭은 좁은 쪽에서 넓은 쪽으로의 순서로 AAA, AA, A, B, C, D, E, EE, EEE로 구분되어 있다. 따라서 eight B라든가 nine C처럼 자기의 구두 사이즈를 말하게 된다.

**구두**(口頭) word of mouth. ¶ ~의 oral; verbal; spoken / ~ 약속 a verbal promise / ~로 orally; verbally; by word of mouth / ~로 전하다 communicate a fact 《to *a person*》 verbally; give a verbal message / ~로 신청하다 make an application by word of mouth; apply verbally 《for a position》 / ~로 보고하다 make an oral report 《to the section chief》 / 보고서는 나중에 내고 즉시 ~ 보고하시오 The written report can wait until later. First of all give me an oral report.
◉ ~계약 an oral 〔a verbal〕 contract. ~변론 oral pleadings 〔proceedings〕: ~변론하다 plead orally. ~선(禪) an empty slogan; fair words; a mere talk: 한낱 ~선에 그치다 become a mere empty slogan. ~시험 an oral test. ~심리(審理) a verbal trial; a (personal) hearing. ~지시 verbal instructions.

**구두법**(句讀法) punctuation; pointing.

**구두쇠** a miser; a stingy 〔closefisted〕 person; a pinchpenny; a niggard; a cheapskate 《미구어》; a tightwad 《미구어》. ¶ ~의 stingy; miserly; close-fisted / 그는 ~라서 기부하지 않을 것이다 Because he is stingy, he won't contribute any money.

**구두점**(句讀點) a punctuation mark 〔point〕. ¶ ~을 찍다 punctuate.

**구드러지다** become hard and dry; dry up. ¶ 과자가 구드러졌다 The cake has dried up (hard).

**구들** 《방구들》 a Korean hypocaust; a Korean underfloor heating system. ¶ ~을 놓다〔고치다〕 install 〔repair〕 a hypocaust.
◉ ~방(房) an *ondol* room; a room with underfloor heating installed. ~장 a flat stone for flooring a room over a Korean hypocaust: ~장을 놓다 floor a room with flat stones (to make a Korean hypocaust). ~직장(直長) a stay-at-home; a shut-in.

**구들동티** ¶ ~가 나다 die suddenly from no apparent cause.

**구랍**(舊臘) last December; the end of 「last year.

**구래**(舊來) ¶ ~의 old; from olden times; ancient; long-established; customary / ~의 누습을 타파하다 do away with 「old abuses 〔the conventionalities of the past〕.

**구럭** a straw-net bag; a mesh bag.

**구렁** 《패인 곳》 a hollow; a cavity; a pit; a hole; [비유적] a chasm; an abyss; the depths. ¶ 헤아릴 수 없이 깊은 ~ an infinite 〔a bottomless〕 abyss / 가난의 ~에서 살다 live in extreme poverty / 절망〔가난〕의 ~에 빠져 있다 be in the depths of despair 〔poverty〕 / 자기가 판 ~에 빠지다 fall into a pit of *one's* own digging. ◉ ~텅이 = 구렁.

**구렁이** ① 《뱀》 a (huge) serpent; a large snake. ¶ ~ 담 넘어가듯 하다 realize *one's* aim 〔intention, attempt〕 in an unnoticed way. ② 《사람》 a deep 〔sly〕 one; a crafty 〔tricky〕 person; an old fox.

**구렁찰** 《늦 찰벼》 a late-ripening variety 「of glutinous rice.

**구레나룻** (side-)whiskers. ¶ ~이 있는 사내 a whiskered man / ~이 있다 wear whiskers.

**-구려** ¶ 올테면 오구려 You may come if you want to. / 좋도록 하구려 Do as you please.

**구력**(舊曆) the lunar 〔old〕 calendar. ¶ 일부 지방에서는 아직도 ∼을 쓰고 있다 In some parts of the country they still use the old calendar.

**구령**(口令) a (word of) command; a verbal order. ∼하다 command; give a verbal order.
¶ ∼을 내리다 give 〔shout〕 an order; give a (word of) command / ∼이 떨어지자 차려 자세를 취하다 stand at attention at the word of command / 그가 「차려」하고 ∼을 내렸다 He ordered, "Attention!"

> 참고 구령의 종류
> **stand at attention** 「차려」 자세로 있다. 구령은 Attention! [ətènʃʌ́n]. **stand at ease.** 「열중쉬어」 자세로 있다. 구령은 At ease! **stand easy** 「편히 쉬어」 자세로 있다. 구령은 Stand easy!

**구루**(傴僂·佝僂) a hunchback; a humpback. ◉ ∼병 〖의학〗 rickets: ∼병에 걸린 rickety.

**구류**(拘留) detention; custody; 〖법〗 commitment. ∼하다 detain; take 《*a person*》 into custody; hold 〔keep〕 《*a person*》 in custody; lock up 《*a person*》. ¶ ∼중이다 be in detention; be (kept) in custody / 그는 5일간의 ∼처분을 받았다 He was sentenced to 5 days' detention.

**구르다**[1] 《데굴데굴》 roll (over); tumble 《in, about》; 《굴러넘어지다》 tumble 〔fall〕 down. ¶ 공이 ∼ a ball rolls / 공이 구멍으로 굴러들어갔다 A ball rolled into the hole. / 뜻밖의 재산이 굴러 들어왔다 I unexpectedly came into a large fortune. / 구르는 돌에는 이끼가 끼지 않는다 《속담》 A rolling stone gathers no moss.

**구르다**[2] 《발을》 stamp 〔stomp〕 *one's* feet 《on the floor》; tread noisily; thump 〔beat〕 *one's* shoes 《on the floor》. ¶ 발을 구르며 울다 cry stamping *one's* feet 《on the floor》 / 발을 구르며 분해하다 stamp with vexation 〔chagrin〕; be hopping mad.

**구름** ① a cloud; the clouds [총칭]. ¶ 엷은 ∼ filmy clouds / 검은 ∼ a dark 〔black〕 cloud / ∼이 많은 cloudy 《days》 / ∼이 없는 cloudless; unclouded / ∼에 가린 달 the clouded moon / ∼ 위로 솟은 봉우리 a cloud-piercing mountain peak / ∼에 가리다 be covered with clouds; be clouded over / ∼이 낮게 끼어 있다 Clouds hang low. / 해가 ∼속으로 들어갔다 The sun went behind the clouds. / 푸른 하늘에 ∼한 조각이 두둥실 떠 있다 A cloud is sailing in the blue sky. / ∼이 활짝 걷혔다 The clouds have cleared away. / 하늘에는 ∼ 한 점 없다 There is not a speck of cloud in the sky.
② 《관용적 표현》 ¶ ∼을 잡는 듯한 vague; fantastic; visionary / ∼을 잡는 듯한 이야기 a vague 〔fantastic〕 story / 구름을 잡는 것 같은 계획 a visionary scheme.
◉ ∼다리 an overpass; a viaduct; an elevated bridge.

**구릉**(丘陵) a hill; a hillock. (★ hill 보다 hillock이 크기가 작다). ◉ ∼지(대) hilly districts.

**구리** 〖화학〗 copper. ¶ ∼가 함유된 coppery / ∼를 입힌 coppered / ∼를 입히다 copper 《*a thing*》; plate 《*a thing*》 with copper. ◉ ∼철사 copper wire 〔wiring〕. 구릿빛 copper color: 구릿빛의 copper-colored / 햇볕에 구릿빛으로 타다 《살갗이》 be suntanned; be browned by the sun.

**구리다** ① 《냄새가》 smell (bad); stink; (be) fetid; stinking; foul-smelling. ¶ 구린 냄새 a bad 〔an offensive〕 smell; a stench / 구려서 숨을 쉴 수가 없다 The bad odor stifles me. ② 《행동이》 (be) suspicious; 《구어》 fishy; shady. ¶ 제 밑이 ∼ have something on *one's* conscience / 무언가 구린 짓을 하고 있다 be engaged in something shady / 저 사내는 무언가 구린 데가 있다 There is something suspicious 〔fishy〕 about him. *or* That man looks suspicious. / 뭔가 좀 구린데 《부정 등을 낌새 채고》 《구어》 I smell a rat.

**구리터분하다, 구리텁텁하다** (be) foul-smelling; stinking; fetid.

**구린내** a foul 〔fetid〕 smell; a stink. ¶ ∼를 풍기다 have 〔give out〕 a bad smell; emit an offensive smell; smell nasty; stink / ∼가 코를 찌른다 An offensive smell greets my nose.

**구매**(購買) purchase; buying. ∼하다 purchase; buy; procure. ¶ ∼욕을 일게 하다 induce 《a customer》 to buy; arouse 〔excite〕 customers' interest; whet the customer(s)' appetite.
◉ ∼가격 a purchasing price. ∼계원 a purchasing agent 〔clerk〕. ∼관습 the buying habit. ∼부 the purchasing department 〔division〕. ∼사절(단) a purchasing mission. ∼자 a purchaser; a buyer. ∼조합 a consumers'

association; a cooperative (society); a co-op 《미구어》.

**구매력**(購買力) purchasing 〔buying〕 power; 《화폐의》 the buying value. ¶ ～을 흡수하다 absorb purchasing power / ～이 늘고〔줄고〕 있다 Purchasing power is increasing 〔decreasing〕. ◉ ～평가설 the theory of purchasing power parity. 부동〔잉여〕～ floating 〔excess〕 purchasing power. 실질～ real purchasing power.

**-구먼** ① 《사실의 발견·확인·추측·놀라움》 ¶ 아 그렇구먼 Indeed, that's right. *or* I see what you mean. *or* So it is. / 참 덥구먼 How hot it is! *or* What a hot day it is! / 비가 오겠구먼 I see it's going to rain! / 내일은 그녀가 오겠구먼 Perhaps she will come tomorrow. / 똑같구먼 Why it looks just like it! / 그 동네는 외국촌 같겠구먼 That part of town must be a kind of foreign colony! / 화려한 빛깔이 좋겠구먼 I guess a fancy color would be nice! / 그는 40이 넘었겠구먼 I should say he is over forty. / 그럼 문제는 간단하구먼 Then the question is simple. / 자넨 그녀를 알고 있겠구먼 You know her, don't you! / 참 좋은 책이구먼 This is a nice book indeed.
② 《-는, -더 다음에》 ¶ 비가 오는구먼 Well, I see it's raining! / 그렇다는구먼 So they say. *or* So he 〔she〕 says. / 특별히 김치맛이 유명하더구먼요 I found the flavor of the kimchi in particular is famous.

**구멍** ① 《뚫리거나 패인 구멍》 a hole; an opening(개구부); 《갈라진 틈새》 an aperture; a gap; a chink; 《공동》 a hollow; a slit.
¶ 뻥 뚫린 ～ a gaping hole / 직경〔깊이, 주위〕 3미터의 ～ a hole three meters across 〔deep, around〕 / 벽의 ～ an opening in the wall / ～을 내다〔파다〕 make 〔dig〕 a hole / ～을 막다 stop 〔fill〕 (up) a hole / 판자에 ～을 뚫다 bore a hole through the plank / 법에서 빠져나갈 ～을 찾다 find a loophole in the law / ～을 보아 가며 쐐기를 깎는다 take measures suited to the occasion / 이 포대는 ～투성이다 This bag is full of holes. / 그는 ～이 뚫린 양말을 신고 있다 He is wearing socks with holes in them. / 폭발로 선체에 ～이 뚫렸다 An explosion blew a hole in the hull. / 쥐～이라도 있으면 들어가고 싶었다 I wished I could sink through the floor. *or* I wished the floor would open and swallow me.

> 용법 **hole** 「구멍」을 나타내는 가장 일반적인 말. 크기·관통 여부에 관계없이 천연·인공의 모든 구멍에 사용된다. **opening** 「열린, 벌어진 부분」이란 뜻으로 천연·인공·크기에 관계없이 두루 쓰인다. **aperture** 빛·공기 따위가 통하는 「구멍」이란 뜻에서, opening의 뜻도 된다. **gap**, **chink**, **slit** 가늘고 길게 갈라진 「틈새」를 뜻하는 말. **hollow** 고체의 표면 위에 생긴 「공동(空洞)」이나 지면 위에 패인 웅덩이 등을 뜻하는 말.

② 《결손》 a loss; a deficit; 《결함》 a defect; a fault. ¶ ～을 내다 make a hole 《in *one's* capital》/ ～을 메우다 make up 《a deficit》; make up for 《a loss》/ 그 계획은 ～투성이다 The plan is full of faults 〔defects, holes〕.

**구멍가게** a mom-and-pop store; a penny candy store; a small store (in a corner of someone's house). ¶ ～를 하고 있다 keep 〔run〕 a mom-and-pop store.

**구메구메** now and then; at odd moments; from time to time.

**구메농사**(一農事) 《소농》 small-scale farming; 《농작》 an irregular crop.

**구메밥** food supplied to a prisoner through an opening of the cell door.

**구면**(球面) 〖수학〗 a spherical surface. ◉ ～각(角) a spherical angle. ～다각형 a spherical polygon. ～삼각법 spherical trigonometry. ～수차(收差) spherical aberration. ～천문학 spherical astronomy. ～투영법 spherical projection.

**구면**(舊面) an old acquaintance; a familiar face. ¶ 그와 나는 ～이다 He is an old acquaintance of mine. *or* We have known each other many years.

**구명**(究明) study; (an) inquiry; (an) investigation. ～하다 study; investigate; look into 《*a thing*》; bring 《*a matter*》 to light. ¶ 문제를 ～하다 bring a subject to light / 그 사고의 원인～을 위해 조사단이 결성됐다 A research group was organized to investigate the cause of the accident.

**구명**(救命) lifesaving; sparing 《*a person's*》 life; 《죄수의》 clemency. ～하다 save (a life); spare 《*a person's*》 life. ¶ ～을 요청하다 ask for 《*a person's*》 life; appeal for mercy; ask for quarter. ◉ ～구(具) a life preserver; survival equipment [총칭]. ～대(帶) a life belt. ～망(網) a life net. ～보트 a lifeboat. ～삭(索) a lifeline. ～장비 rescue equipment. ～정(艇) a lifeboat. ～조끼〔재킷〕 a life「vest〔jacket〕.

**구명**(舊名) the old「name〔designation〕.

**구무럭거리다** move (*one's* body) slowly〔lazily, sluggishly〕; delay; linger; dillydally; hesitate; dawdle. ⇨ 꾸물거리다. ¶ 구무럭거리지 말고 without delay; without hesitation; straight off / 구무럭거리며 시간을 보내다 dally〔potter〕 away *one's* time / 뭘 구무럭거리고 있느냐 Stop dillydally, will you?

**구문**(口文) (a)「commission; brokerage (fee). ¶ 사 주는〔팔아 주는〕 ～ buying〔selling〕 commission / 서 푼의 ～ 3% commission / ～을 받다 take〔receive〕 a commission《on the sale of》.

**구문**(構文) the「construction〔syntax〕 of a sentence; (sentence) structure. ¶ 문법상의 ～ grammatical construction / 분사 ～ a participial construction. ◉ ～론 syntax.

**구문**(舊聞) an old story; twice-heard〔stale〕 news. ¶ 그것은 이미 ～에 속한다 It is now an old story.

**구문서**(舊文書) an old document.

**구물**(舊物) ①《옛 물건》 old things. ②《세전지물》 heirlooms; things handed down from generation to generation.

**구미**(口味) appetite; taste; 《흥미》 *one's* interest. ¶ ～가 당기다 appeal to *one's* appetite / ～를 돋우다 《입맛을》 stimulate〔sharpen, whet〕 *one's* appetite; 《흥미를》 arouse〔excite〕 *one's* interest 《in》/ ～에 맞다 be (pleasant) to *one's* taste; suit *one's*「taste〔palate〕; be nice to the palate.

**구미**(歐美) Europe and America; the West. ¶ ～의 European and American; Western / ～의 여러 나라 Western countries. ◉ ～인 Europeans and Americans; Westerners; Occidentals.

**구미호**(九尾狐) an old fox; 《사람》 a「tricky〔cunning〕 person.

**구민**(區民) the inhabitants of a *gu*〔ward〕. ¶ ～ 대회 a ward rally.

**구박**(驅迫) harsh〔cruel〕 treatment; abuse; mistreatment; bullying. ～하다 treat「harshly〔cruelly〕; be hard (up) on《*a person*》; mistreat; ill-treat; bully (약한 자를); abuse; handle《*a person*》 roughly. ¶ ～을 받다〔당하다〕 suffer abuse; be「abused〔bullied〕/ 남편을 ～하다 treat *one's* husband badly; mistreat *one's* husband / 의붓딸을 ～하다 be「cruel to〔hard on〕 *one's* step-daughter / 며느리를 ～하여 내쫓다 drive *one's* daughter-in-law away with abuse / 나를 그리 ～하지 마시오 Don't be so hard upon me.

**구배**(勾配) an incline; a slope; 《철도·도로의》 a gradient; a grade《미》; 《지붕 등의》 a pitch. ¶ 가파른〔가파르지 않은〕 ～ a「steep〔gentle〕 grade / 올림〔내림〕 ～「an acclivity〔a declivity〕;「an up〔a down〕 grade / 15도의 ～ an incline of 15 degrees / 가파른 ～의 지붕 a steeply pitched roof. ◉ ～표(標) a「grade〔gradient〕 post.

**구법**(舊法) an old law; an old method「(방법).

**구변**(口辯) speech; tongue; eloquence. ¶ ～ 좋게 fluently; eloquently; glibbly / ～이 좋은〔없는〕 사람 a「good〔poor〕 speaker〔talker〕/ ～이 좋다 have a「ready〔glib〕 tongue.

**구별**(區別) 《차별》 (a) distinction; discrimination; 《차이》 a difference; 《분류》 (a) classification. ～하다 distinguish; make a distinction《between》; tell《one from another》; discriminate. ¶ ～ 없이 indiscriminately; irrespectively / 남녀 노소의 ～ 없이 irrespective of age and sex / …와 ～하여 in distinction from… / 공사를 분명히 ～하다 draw a sharp line between public and private affairs / 양서와 악서를 ～하다 discriminate between good and bad books; discriminate good books from bad (ones) / …와〔를〕 ～하기 힘들다 be indistinguishable from…; be difficult to tell the difference between《real and false》/ ～을 하지 않다 make no distinction《between》/ 나무는 상록수와 낙엽수로 ～된다 Trees are「divided〔classified〕 into evergreens and deciduous trees. / 본회(本會)는 남녀의 ～ 없이 모든 사람에게 입회를 허가한다 This society admits all persons without distinction of sex. / 선악을 ～할 수 있다 I can distinguish right from wrong.

**구보**(驅步) [일반적] a run; 《말의》 a canter; a gallop; 《군대의》 double-time (march). ¶ ～로 at a「run〔canter〕; 《march》 on the double / 그는 ～로 왔다 He came running.

**구복**(口腹) the mouth and the stomach. ¶ ～지계(之計) a means of living / ～이 원수라 Hunger is the source of *one's* humiliation.

**구부리다** ①《몸을》 stoop (down); bend forward; crouch; bow. ¶ 허리가 구부러

진 노인 a man bent (down) with age / 앞으로 구부리고 걷다 walk with a stoop / 책상 위에 몸을 ~ bend over *one's* desk / 몸을 구부려 꽃을 꺾다 stoop 〔bend〕 (down) to pick up a flower / 그녀는 소형차에 허리를 구부려 올라탔다 She「crouched 〔bent herself down〕 to get into the small car. ② 《물건·팔다리를》 bend; curve; twist (비틀어서). ¶ 철근을 직각으로 ~ bend the iron bar into a right angle / 철선을 구부려 고리를 만들다 bend an iron wire into a ring / 무릎을 ~ bend *one's* knees / 쇠는 뜨거워지면 잘 구부러진다 Iron becomes「pliable 〔flexible〕 when heated.

**구부정하다** ⇨ 구붓하다.

**구분**(區分) 《분할》 (a) division; 《구획》 a section; 《분류》 classification; sorting; grouping. ~하다 《분할하다》 divide 《into》; section 〔partition〕 《off》; 《분류하다》 classify; sort (out). ¶ 네 개의 큰 그룹으로 ~하다 classify 〔divide〕 《them》 into four large「groups 〔divisions〕 / 그의 서재에 있는 서적들은 주제별로 ~되어 있다 The books in his study are「divided 〔classified〕 according to subjects. / 한국에서는 학년이 두 학기로 ~되어 있다 The school year in Korea is divided into two terms.

**구붓하다** (be) slightly「bent 〔curved, twisted〕.

**구비**(口碑) (an) oral tradition; a legend; folklore. ¶ ~로 전하여지다 be handed down「orally 〔by tradition, by word of mouth〕.

**구비**(具備) having 〔possessing〕 all. ~하다 have 〔possess〕 all; be fully「furnished 〔equipped〕 《with》; be endowed with (재능 따위를). ¶ 모든 조건을 ~하다 fulfill all the conditions; satisfy all the requisites / 타고 난 음악적 재능을 ~하고 있다 be endowed by nature with a genius for music.

**구빈**(救貧) relief of the poor; poor relief. ◉ ~대책〔사업〕 poor-relief「measures 〔work〕. ~원(院) a poorhouse; a workhouse. ~제도 a relief system.

**구쁘다** feel an appetite; (be) hungry.

**구사**(驅使) ① 《부림》 driving 《*a person*》; ordering about. ~하다 drive 《*a person*》; have 《*one's* men》 at *one's* beck and call; order 《*a person*》 about. ② 《능숙히 다룸》 free use; commanding. ~하다 command; have a command of; use freely. ¶ 풍부한 어휘를 ~하다 command a large vocabulary / 영어를 자유로이 ~하다 have a「good 〔perfect〕 command of English / 그녀는 수 개 국어를 자유롭게 ~한다 She has several languages at her command.

**구사상**(舊思想) old-fashioned ideas; outdated 〔antiquated〕 notions.

**구사일생**(九死一生) a narrow escape from death. ~하다 have a narrow escape from death; escape by the skin of *one's* teeth. ¶ 나는 동사 직전에 구조대에 발견되어 ~으로 살아났다 I was found dying from cold by the rescue team and escaped death by a hairbreadth.

**구상**(求償) (claim for) compensation; reparation; indemnification. ◉ ~권 the 〔a〕 right of indemnity. ~무역 trade on a barter system; compensation 〔barter〕 trade. ~자 a claimant.

**구상**(具象) concreteness; embodiment. ~하다 embody; express concretely. ¶ ~적인 concrete; figurative; tangible / ~화하다 exteriorize; reify. ◉ ~개념 a concrete concept. ~성 concreteness. ~예술 the plastic arts. ~화(畫) a representational painting.

**구상**(球狀) a globular shape. ¶ ~의 ball-shaped; spherical; globular. ◉ ~(세)균 a micrococcus (*pl.* -cocci). ~체(體) a spheroid; a globoid.

**구상**(鉤狀) hook-shaped; hook-like. ◉ ~골(骨) 〖해부〗 an unciform bone. ~돌기 an uncinate「protuberance 〔projection〕.

**구상**(構想) 《생각》 (a) conception; an idea; 《작품의》 a plot; a plan. ~하다 map out 《a plan》; work over *one's*「ideas 〔plan, plot〕; formulate 〔elaborate〕 a「plan 〔plot〕. ¶ 소설의 ~ the plot of a novel / 유럽 연합이란 새로운 ~ the new「conception 〔idea〕 of the European Union / ~이 웅대하다 be grand in conception / ~이 떠오르다 conceive「an idea 〔a plan〕 / 그는 원대한 ~을 갖고 있다 He has far-reaching 〔grand〕 plans.

**구상나무** 〖식물〗 the Korean fir.

**구상유취**(口尙乳臭) 《젖내남》 having the smell of mother's milk. ~하다 《유치하다》 (be) green; inexperienced; be still wet behind the ears.

**구새(통)** 《구새 먹은 통나무》 a hollow tree-trunk; 《나무 굴뚝》 a wooden chimney. ¶ ~먹다 《a tree》 get hollow; be eaten hollow.

**구색**(具色) an assortment 《of goods》. ¶ ~을 갖추다 assort; provide an assortment 《of》 / ~이 갖추어져 있다

have an assortment of goods; have a well-assorted stock. ◉ ~친구 a wide and varied acquaintance.

**구석** ① an inside corner; 《드러나지 않는 곳》 a corner; a nook; recesses. ¶ 마음 한 ~(에) (in) the innermost recesses of the heart / 방 한 ~에 앉다 take a seat in the corner of a room. ② 《외딴 곳》 a remote 〔an out-of-the-way〕 place 〔corner〕. ¶ 시골 ~ a remote 〔an out-of-the-way〕 spot in the country. ③ 《…한 면·점》 a side; an aspect; a point; a way. ¶ 나쁜 ~도 있다 It has its bad sides 〔points〕 too. / 모르는 ~이 없다 know 《*a thing*》 down to the last detail / 그는 어린 ~이 많다 He has many childish ways. ◉ ~방 an innermost 〔a sequestered〕 room; a room way off to itself. ~장 a triangular chest of drawers.

**구석구석** every nook and corner; everywhere. ¶ 세계의 ~까지 to the four corners of the globe / ~ 찾아보다 look in every nook and corner; leave no corner unsearched / 이 도시를 ~ 다 잘 알다 know every inch of this town.

**구석기**(舊石器) a paleolith; a paleolithic stone implement. ◉ ~시대 『고고학』 the Old Stone Age; the Paleolithic Age 〔Era〕. ~인 Paleolithic man.

**구석지다** (be) secluded; recessed; sequestered; inmost; be off to one side. ¶ 구석진 곳 a recess; a nook; a secluded place / 건물의 가장 구석진 방 the innermost room of the building.

**구설**(口舌) malicious gossip; heated words; 《비방》 abuse; slander. ¶ ~에 오르다 be talked about by people; be the talk of the town. ◉ ~수 the bad luck to be verbally abused.

**구성**(構成) composition; organization; constitution; construction; formation; (a) make-up. ~하다 compose; constitute; organize; make up; form. ¶ 가족 ~ family structure / 문장의 ~ construction of a sentence; sentence structure / (극·영화 등의) 이야기의 ~ the framework of a story / ~되(어 있)다 be made up 《of》; consist 《of》 / 범죄를 ~하다 constitute a crime / 하나의 이론을 ~하다 construct a theory / 사회를 ~하다 form 〔constitute〕 society / 물질은 원자로 ~되어 있다 Matter is composed of atoms. / 이 부대는 전원 한국 병사로 ~되어 있다 The troop is composed entirely of Korean soldiers. / 특별 위원회는 6 명의 위원으로 ~되어 있다 The ad hoc committee consists of six members. ◉ ~개념 『심리』 a construct. ~단위 a constituent unit; a group unit: 사회의 ~ 단위 a group 〔unit〕 of society. ~분자 constituent elements; components. ~비(比) 『통계』 the component ratio. ~요소 a component. ~원 a constituent; a member. ~주의 『미술』 constructivism.

**구성없다** 「be in 〔belong to〕 a different class; be on different levels; be ill-matched to *one's* 「status 〔standing〕.

**구성지다** (be) plausible and elegant 〔artistic〕; tasteful. ¶ 구성진 목소리로 노래하다 sing in a well-trained specious voice.

**구세** 『광산』 porous rock-ore.

**구세**(救世) salvation 〔redemption〕 of the world. ◉ ~군 『기독교』 the Salvation Army (단체); a Salvationist (개인): ~군 사관 a Salvation Army officer.

**구세계**(舊世界) the Old World; the Old 「Continent (유럽).

**구세대**(舊世代) the old generation.

**구세주**(救世主) the savior of the world; 《예수》 the Savior; the Redeemer; the Messiah.

**구속**(拘束) binding; restraint; (a) restriction; 《감금》 confinement; custody (구류); 《체포》 arrest. ~하다 bind; restrict; restrain; put restraints 《on》; put 《*a person*》 under control; arrest; take 《*a person*》 into custody. ¶ ~이 없는 free; unrestrained / 언론의 자유를 ~하다 gag the press; restrict the freedom of speech 〔press〕 / 용의자의 신병을 ~하다 detain the suspect; hold the suspect in custody / ~되다 be placed under arrest; be brought into custody / 옳은 법률은 결코 선한 사람의 자유를 구속하지 않는다 Just laws are no restraint upon the freedom of the good. / 이 조례는 집회의 자유를 ~하는 것이다 This ordinance restricts the freedom of assembly. ◉ ~력 《have》 binding force 〔power〕: ~력이 있는 binding; restrictive / 법적 ~력이 없다 carry no legal binding force. ~시간 『노동』 portal-to-portal hours 〔time〕; actual working hours. ~영장 a warrant of arrest; an arrest warrant: ~ 영장을 신청하다 request an arrest warrant 《for》. ~자 a person under restraint. ~ 적부 심사 review of the legality for confinement.

**구속**(球速) 〖야구〗《a pitcher's》 pace; the speed of a pitched ball. ¶ ～이 있는 공을 던지다 pitch a very fast ball / ～을 바꾸어 던지다 change *one's* (pitching) pace.

**구속**(救贖) 〖기독교〗 the Redemption.

**구송**(口誦) ～하다 recite; read aloud.

**구수**(口授) oral instruction 〔teaching〕. ～하다 instruct 〔teach〕 orally; dictate. ¶ 그 전설은 대대로 ～되어 왔다 The legend has been handed down orally from generation to generation.

**구수하다** ① 《맛·냄새 등이》 (be) pleasant; tasty; good. ¶ 구수한 냄새 a savory odor; an appetizing smell / 고기 굽는 냄새가 ～ The roasting beef smells good. / 군고구마 맛이 ～ A roasted sweet potato tastes good. ② 《이야기가》 (be) interesting; humorous; delightful. ¶ 구수한 이야기 an interesting 〔a humorous〕 story / 구수한 사람 a delightful man.

**구수회의**(鳩首會議) a conference laying heads together to deliberate 《on the emergent problem》. ～하다 put 〔lay〕 《their》 heads together 《about》; get together to deliberate in a conference; talk 〔counsel〕 together 《over》.

**구순하다** (be) harmonious. ¶ 둘 사이가 ～ They are on good terms.

**구술**(口述) an oral statement; dictation. ～하다 state orally; dictate. ¶ ～의 oral / 사장은 편지를 ～하여 타이피스트에게 치게 했다 The president dictated a letter to the typist.
◉ ～녹음기 a dictating machine; 《상표명》 Dictaphone. ～서 a verbal note; an oral statement. ～시험 an oral examination. ～증거 a verbal evidence; a signed confession.

**구슬** glass beads; 《진주》 a pearl; 《보석》 a precious stone; a gem; a jewel. ¶ ～이 구르는 것 같은 고운 목소리 a silvery 〔sweet〕 voice / ～로 꾸미다 gem; ornament with jewels / ～을 갈다 cut 〔polish〕 a gem / ～이 서말이라도 꿰어야 보배라 《속담》 It takes more than pearls to make a necklace. *or* Nothing is complete unless you put it in final shape.
◉ ～덩 a sedan chair 〔a palanquin〕 furnished with beaded screens. ～땀 beads of sweat 〔perspiration〕; sweat in beads: ～땀을 흘리며 일하다 work with sweat running down in beads. ～백 a beaded handbag. ～세공 beading; beadwork.

**구슬구슬하다** (be) cooked just right; neither too hard nor too soft. ¶ 밥이 구슬구슬하게 잘 되었다 The rice cooked 「just right 〔properly〕.

**구슬리다** 《그럴 듯한 말로》 wheedle; cajole; coax; talk 《*a person*》 into 〔out of〕 *do*ing; win 《*a person*》 to *one's* side; seduce. ¶ 구슬려 빼앗다 wheedle 〔cajole, coax〕 《*a person*》 out of 《*his* money》 / 구슬려 …하게 하다 cajole 〔coax〕 《*a person*》 into 《giving consent》 / 슬슬 구슬려 돈을 기부하게 하다 cajole 〔talk〕 《*a person*》 into donating some money / 아이를 구슬려 장난감을 빼앗다 talk a child out of his toy; coax a child to give up his toy / 나는 그녀를 구슬려서 쇼핑을 가게 했다 I coaxed her to go shopping.

**구슬붕이** 〖식물〗 a squarrose gentian.

**구슬프다** (be) sad; sorrowful; plaintive; melancholy; mournful. ¶ 구슬픈 노래〔이야기〕 a sad song 〔story〕 / 구슬피 sadly; sorrowfully; mournfully; plaintively / 구슬프게 울다 weep 「with sorrow 〔sadly〕 / 어쩐지 구슬픈 느낌이 드는 밤이다 I don't know why, but I feel so melancholy 〔sad〕 this evening.

**구습**(舊習) old 〔time-honored〕 customs; old-fashioned 〔out-of-date〕 practices; former ways. ¶ ～을 지키는 사람 a conventionalist / ～을 고집하다 stick to old customs 〔practices〕 / ～을 타파하다 do away with old customs.

**구승**(口承) (an) oral tradition. ⇨ 구비(口碑). ◉ ～문학 oral literature.

**구시대**(舊時代) the old era. ¶ ～의 정치인 an old-school 〔old-era〕 politician / ～의 비리 청산을 바라는 국민적 여망 the national call for liquidating the ill practices of the old era.

**구시렁거리다** grumble 〔nag〕 repeatedly; keep 〔dwell〕 on grumbling.

**구식**(舊式) an old style 〔fashion, school〕. ¶ ～의 of the 〔an〕 old style 〔type〕; old-fashioned; out-of-date; outdated / ～의 교육법 an old-fashioned teaching method / 그 옷은 ～이다 The clothes are out of date.
◉ ～쟁이 an old-fashioned person; an old fogey. ～혼인 a traditional Korean wedding; an old-fashioned wedding.

**구신**(具申) reporting to 《a superior》; on 《a *matter*》 in detail. ～하다 report 《on a *matter*》. ¶ 의견을 ～하다 offer *one's* opinion 《to *one's* superior》.
◉ ～서 a written report.

**구실** ① 〖역사〗《벼슬》 public office; a

post in the government. ②《조세》 taxes to the government. ③《소임·역할》 *one's* function; *one's* duty; *one's* obligation; what is expected of *one; one's* share 〔bit, part, role〕. ¶ 제 ～을 하다 perform *one's* 「function 〔part, duty〕 worthily; do what *one* has to be done / 사람 ～을 하다 behave 「as a person should 〔as befit *one*〕; live up to *one's* role 〔name〕 / 병신 ～을 하다 play the part of a defective; act the fool / 대명사는 명사 ～을 한다 A pronoun serves in place of a noun. / TV는 선거운동에서 중요한 ～을 했다 Television played an important role in the election campaigns. / 자네는 자네 ～이나 잘 하게, 나머지는 내가 하겠네 You do your part effectively and I shall do the rest. ◉ ～길 a trip on official business. ～아치 〖역사〗 a minor 〔junior, lower-level〕 official.

**구실**(口實) an excuse; a pretext; a pretense. ¶ 좋은〔서툰〕 ～ a good 〔poor, flimsy〕 excuse / 그럴듯한 ～ a plausible excuse; a specious pretense / …을 ～로 on the pretext of...; with the excuse that... / ～을 만들다〔삼다〕 make 〔find〕 「an excuse 〔a pretext〕《for being late》/ 그는 아버지의 병을 ～로 회사에 나오지 않는다 He uses his father's illness as an excuse not to come to the office. / 그는 언제나 이 ～ 저 ～을 붙여 할 일을 안 하려고 한다 He always tries to shirk his duty on one pretext or another. / 그런 것은 ～이 될 수 없다 That doesn't justify your behavior. / 그녀는 가난을 ～로 삼는다 She pleads poverty as her excuse. / 그것은 ～에 불과하다 That is just an excuse.

**구심**(求心) ①〖물리〗¶ ～적(으로) centripetal(ly). ②〖불교〗 meditation for seeking an honest mind. ◉ ～력 centripetal force. ～성 centripetalism; centripetal tendency: ～성 신경 an afferent 〔a centripetal〕 nerve. ～운동 a centripetal motion.

**구심**(球審) 〖야구〗 plate 〔chief〕 umpire; an umpire-in-chief.

**구십**(九十) ninety; 《제 90》 ninetieth. ¶ ～ 노인 a ninety-year-old; an old man of ninety / ～대의 사람 a nonagenarian / ～춘광(春光) the ninety days 〔the three months〕 of spring; the happy springtime.

**구악**(舊惡) a past 〔former〕 misdeed 〔crime〕; an old crime; 《사회의》 the old evil. ¶ ～을 일소하다 make a clean sweep of the old evil; stamp 〔root〕 out the old evil / ～을 들춰내다 expose 〔rake up〕《*a person's*》 past misdeed / 그의 ～이 드러났다 His past crime came to light.

**구악**(舊樂) old 〔ancient〕 music.

**구애**(拘礙) ～하다 stick 〔adhere, keep〕 to 《formalities》; be particular 〔scrupulous〕 about 《trifles》; split hairs; be hairsplitting. ¶ ～하지 않고 freely; irrespective of / 규칙에 ～하다〔되다〕 be tied to the rules; stick to the rules 《in》/ 오랜 관습에 ～되다〔받다〕 be wedded to the old customs 〔ways〕 / 그녀는 세속적인 일에 ～받지 않는다 She is 「free from 〔indifferent to〕 worldly cares. / 그는 형식 같은데는 조금도 ～하지 않는다 He is no stickler for formalities. / 법의 자구(字句)에 ～되어 그 정신을 몰각해서는 안 된다 You must observe the spirit, not the letter of the law. / 그는 사회적인 지위 따위에는 ～받지 않는 사람이다 He is not one to bother 〔worry himself〕 about social status.

**구애**(求愛) courtship; courting; wooing. ～하다 try to win 《a woman's》 love; woo; court. ¶ 그녀에게 ～했으나 퇴짜를 맞았다 I courted her but met with rebuff.

**구약**(舊約) ①《옛 약속》 an old 〔a former〕 promise. ②《성서》 the Old Testament. ◉ ～성서 the Old Testament. ～시대 the Old Testament era; Old Testament days.

**구어**(口語) the spoken language; colloquial speech 〔language〕; (a) colloquialism. ¶ ～의 spoken; colloquial / ～로 in spoken language; colloquially / 그것은 ～적인 표현이다 That is a colloquial expression. ◉ ～문 a composition written in the colloquial. ～체 《write in》 colloquial style.

**구어박다** ①《틀어박히다》 stick at home; stay inactive in *one's* place; be confined to *one's* place. ②《쐐기를 달구어 박다》 heat 《a wedge》 and drive it in. ③《돈을》 hoard 〔store up〕《money》.

**구역**(區域) 《지역》 an area; a zone; a district; 《행동권》 a territory; 《한계》 the limits 〔boundary〕. ¶ 배달～ a delivery zone / 주택～ a residential zone 〔area, district, quarter〕 / 자기의 순찰 ～을 돌고 있는 경관 a policeman walking his round / …의 ～내에서 within the limits of ...; inside the boundary of / 이곳은 남부 서울의 인구 밀집 ~이다 This is a thickly populated district in south Seoul.

> 용법 **area** 어떤 경계에서 다른 곳과 구별된 지역. **zone** 어떤 특색을 가진 구역. **district** 행정·사법상의 목적으로 명확히 구분된 구역. **territory** 일차적으로는「영토」,「지역(region)」의 뜻이나, 이차적으로는「동물의 행동권」,「학문의 영역」「분야」란 뜻의 구역.

**구역질**(嘔逆—) nausea; a sickly feeling; qualms. ~하다 nauseate. ¶ ~나는 광경 a nauseating 〔sickening〕 sight / ~ 나다 have nausea; feel sick; feel like vomiting; have a sick stomach / ~을 나게 하다 cause nausea; turn *one's* stomach / 그 냄새에 ~이 난다 The smell makes me sick.

**구연**(口演) an oral narration. ~하다 narrate orally; recite.

**구연**(舊緣) old ties; (an) old 〔a former〕 relationship.

**구연산**(枸櫞酸) 〖화학〗 citric acid (시트르산).

**구열**(口熱) a fever 〔temperature〕 in the mouth.

**구옥**(舊屋) an old house 〔building〕.

**구왕실**(舊王室) the Royal Household of the Chosŏn dynasty. ◉ ~재산 the estate of the ex-Royal Household.

**구외**(構外) ¶ ~에(서) outside the compounds 〔premises〕.

**구우**(舊友) an old friend 〔pal〕; a friend of long standing.

**구우일모**(九牛一毛) a mere fraction; a drop in the bucket 〔ocean〕.

**구운석고**(—石膏) 〖화학〗 plaster of Paris; calcined gypsum.

**구움일** 《재목 말리기》 drying lumber 《in a kiln》.

**구워지다** 《음식물이》 be baked (빵·과자가); be toasted (토스트·김이); be grilled (석쇠로); be roasted (고기가); be broiled (생선 등이). ¶ 잘〔너무〕 ~ be well-done 〔overdone〕; be well-toasted 〔over-toasted〕 / 설 ~ be underdone 〔half-done〕 / 빵이 알맞게 구워지다 be done 〔toasted〕 just right.

**구원**(久遠) eternity; permanence; perpetuity. ~하다 (be) eternal; perpetual. ¶ ~의 평화 a ever lasting peace / ~의 정화(情火) the everlasting fire of passion.

**구원**(救援) ① 《구조·도움》 relief; rescue; aid (특히, 국제적인). ~하다 relieve; rescue; aid. ¶ ~을 청하다 ask for help; call on 《*a person*》 for help / ~하러 가다 go to 《*a person's*》 rescue 《of》 / 난민을 ~하다 provide aid 〔relief〕 for refugees / 홍수 피해지역에 전국으로부터 ~의 손길이 뻗어졌다 A helping hand was extended to the flood-stricken area from all over the country. ② 《건져 냄》 salvation; redemption. ◉ ~군 reinforcements (증원군). ~대 a relief party; a rescue squad. ~투수 〖야구〗 a relief pitcher 〔hurler〕; a fireman 《속어》.

**구원**(舊怨) old enmity; old scores; an old grudge 〔grievance〕. ¶ ~을 풀다 pay off 〔settle〕 old scores.

**구월**(九月) September (생략 Sep., Sept.).

**구유** a trough; a manger.

**구은**(舊恩) old favors; old 〔bygone, past〕 kindnesses. ¶ ~을 갚다 repay *one's* old favors.

**구음**(口音) an oral sound.

**구읍**(舊邑) an old town 〔county〕.

**구의**(舊誼) old friendship. ¶ ~를 존중하여 for old acquaintance's sake / ~를 두터이 하다 renew *one's* acquaintance 《with》; renew old friendship.

**구이** meat roasted 〔fish baked〕 with seasonings. ◉ 갈비~ roasted ribs. 돼지고기~ roast pork.

**구인**(求人) a job offer; an offer of a situation; 《게시》 "Help Wanted". ~하다 offer a job; seek help. ¶ ~측의 요구조건 hiring requirements 〔terms〕. ◉ ~광고 a help-wanted 〔situations-vacant 《영》〕 advertisement; a want ad 《미》: ~ 광고란 the help-wanted columns / 비서 ~광고를 신문에 내다 put a want ad for a secretary in the newspaper /「나는 친구의 소개로 입사했는데, 자네는」—「나는 신문의 ~광고를 보고 응모했어」 "I entered the company after being introduced by a friend. How about you?"—"I answered a help-wanted ad in the newspaper." ~난(難) (a) labor shortage; (a) shortage of labor: 세기의 전환기에는 심각한 ~난이 있을 것이다 There will be a serious labor shortage at the turn of the century. ~신청 application for workers.

**구인**(拘引) arrest; apprehension. ⇨ 구속(拘束). ~하다 arrest; apprehend; take 《*a person*》 into custody. ¶ ~되어 있다 be held in custody; be under arrest. ◉ ~장 a warrant of arrest.

**구일**(九日) ① 《초아흐레》 the ninth (day) of a month. ② 《9일간》 nine

days. ◉ ～장(葬) a burial on the ninth day after death.
**구입**(購入) purchase; buying. ～하다 purchase; buy; make a purchase. ¶～ 도서 books purchased / 이것이 이 달의 ～ 도서 목록이다 This is a list of books purchased this month. ◉ ～가격 the purchase price. ～명세서 a purchase specification. ～원가 purchase cost. ～자 a purchaser 〔buyer〕.
**구입장생** a bare living; a scanty livelihood. ～하다 eke out (a living).
**구작**(舊作) *one's* old 〔earlier〕 work. ¶～을 고쳐 쓰다 rewrite *one's* old work 《for broadcasting》.
**구잠정**(驅潛艇) a submarine chaser.
**구장**(球場) a ball ground 〔park〕; 〖야구〗 a baseball field 〔ground〕; a ball park 《미》; a (baseball) diamond.
**구저분하다** = 구접스럽다.
**구적**(舊蹟) ruins; a historic spot; a place of historic interest. ⇨ 고적.
**구적법**(求積法) 〖수학〗 mensuration; stereometry (체적); planimetry (면적의).
**구전**(口傳) information by word of mouth; oral transmission 〔tradition〕. ～하다 inform by word of mouth; hand down orally. ¶～심수(心授)하다 impart by lips and heart.
**구전**(口錢) (a) commission. = 구문.
**구전**(舊典) an ancient code of law.
**구절**(句節) a phrase; a passage (of writing); a paragraph.
**구절양장**(九折羊腸) = 양장(羊腸) ②. ¶그 길은 ～이다 The path is full of turns and twists.
**구절초**(九折草) 〖식물〗 Siberian chrysanthemum.
**구절판**(九折坂) a nine sectioned lacquerware serving plate; a nine sectioned dish.
**구접스럽다** ① 《사물이》 (be) shabby; dirty; messy; untidy; be a mess. ② 《하는 짓이》 (be) mean; low; nasty; dirty.
**구정**(舊正) the New Year's Day by the lunar calender; the lunar New Year.
**구정**(舊情) old friendship; old sentimental ties. ¶오랜만에 김군을 만나 ～을 새롭게 했다 I met Mr. Kim after a long interval and renewed my (old) friendship with him.
**구정물** ① 《더러워진 물》 dirty 〔filthy〕 water; used dishwater 〔laundry water〕; (kitchen) slops. ¶～통 a slop pail. ② 《종기의》 liquid discharge from a tumor 〔boil, *etc.*〕; seepage from a wound.
**구제**(救濟) 《구원》 relief; succor; help; 《원조》 aid; 《영혼의》 salvation; redemption. ～하다 relieve; give relief 〔aid〕 to; help; save. ¶～할 수 없는 unrelievable; unremediable; beyond remedy / 빈민을 ～하다 relieve the poor / 정부는 난민을 ～했다 The government 「gave relief 〔extended a helping hand〕 to the refugees. ◉ ～금융 relief financing. ～비(費) relief expenses. ～사업 relief work. ～자 a reliever; a savior (영혼의). ～자금 relief funds. ～조치 relief steps. ～책 a relief measure; a remedy: 실업자 ～책이 강구되어야 한다 Something should be done for the relief of the unemployed. *or* Relief measures should be taken for the jobless people.
**구제**(舊制) the old 〔former〕 system; the old order. ¶～의 학교 교육 school education under the old system. ◉ ～대학 a university 〔college〕 under the former 〔old〕 system.
**구제**(驅除) extermination; destruction; stamping out. ～하다 exterminate; stamp out; destroy; get rid of; clear off; clean up. ¶쥐를 ～하다 get rid of 〔exterminate〕 rats / 해충을 ～하다 stamp out noxious insects.
**구조**(救助) rescue; relief; help; aid. ～하다 rescue; relieve; save; aid; help.

> 용법 **rescue** 절박한 위험에서 구조하는 것. **save** 사람의 생명을 구하는 것. **help** 「돕다」란 뜻의 가장 일반적인 말.

¶～에 임하다 go to 《*a person's*》 rescue / ～를 요청하다 ask 〔call〕 for help / 물에 빠진 사람을 ～하다 save 〔rescue〕 《*a person*》 from drowning / 인명을 ～하여 표창을 받다 be rewarded in recognition of *one's* saving a life / 난파선 선원들은 어선에 의해 ～됐다 The shipwrecked crew were picked up by a fishing boat.
◉ ～기(機) a 〔an air〕 rescue plane 〔aircraft〕. ～대(袋) an escape chute (고층건물 화재시 쓰이는). ～대(隊) a rescue 〔relief〕 team 〔party, unit, squad〕. ～망 a safety net. ～선 a rescue boat; a lifeboat. ～신호 an SOS (call); a distress call 〔signal〕; a Mayday (call). ～작업 rescue 〔relief〕 work; salvage work (배의). ～작전 a rescue operation.
**구조**(構造) 《꾸밈새》 structure; con-

struction; (a) make-up; 《조직》 organization; frame; constitution; 《꾸며 만듦》 building; constructing; organizing. ～하다 construct; build; fix 〔set〕 up. ¶ ～상의 structural; organic / 인체의 ～ the structure of the human body / 문장의 ～ sentence structure / 사회의 이중 ～ the dual structure of the society / 우리 사회의 ～적인 모순 a structural contradiction in our society / ～적 불황 a structural recession / ～적 불황 업종 a structurally-weak industry / ～는 간단하다〔복잡하다〕 It is simple 〔complicated〕 in construction. / 한국식 ～이다 It is Korean in structure 〔style〕. / 이 기계는 ～상의 결함이 틀림없이 있다 There must be a structural defect in this machine. ◉ ～개혁 structural reform 《of a political party》. ～공학 structural engineering. ～식 〖화학〗 a structural formula 〔diagram〕. ～ 언어학 structural linguistics. ～역학 〖기계〗 structural mechanics. ～조정 〖경제·경영〗 restructuring. ～주의 〖언어·철학〗 structuralism. ～지질학 tectonic 〔structural〕 geology. 상부～ superstructure. 하부～ substructure.

**구존**(俱存) having *one's* parents alive. ～하다 have *one's* parents still alive. ¶ 그의 양친은 ～하신다 His parents are both alive.

**구좌**(口座) an account. ⇨ 계좌(計座).

**구주**(救主) 〖기독교〗 the Savior; the Redeemer; the Messiah; Christ.

**구주**(歐洲) Europe. ＝ 유럽.

**구주**(舊主) *one's* former lord 〔master〕.

**구주**(舊株) 〖증권〗 an old stock 〔share〕.

**구죽** a pile of oyster shells (on the beach). ◉ ～바위 a rock made up of oyster shells.

**구중**(九重) ① 《아홉 겹》 ninefold. ② 《구중궁궐》 the Royal Palace.

**구중중하다** (be) nasty; wet; dirty and dampish; be in a filthy 〔disgusting〕 state. ¶ 구중중한 방 a filthy room / 구중중한 날씨 nasty 〔wet〕 weather.

**구지**(舊址) historic remains; ruins.

**구지레하다** (be) filthy; dirty and untidy; be squalid and in disorder. ¶ 구지레한 방 a dirty and untidy room / 옷차림이 ～ be slovenly 〔shabbily〕 dressed.

**구직**(求職) seeking employment 〔work〕; job hunting. ～하다 seek employment; look 〔hunt〕 for a job. ¶ ～신청을 하다 apply for employment 〔work〕 / ～신청이 쇄도하다 have a flood of applications for vacancies 〔positions offered〕. ◉ ～광고 a situations-wanted ad; a want ad 《for a job》: ～ 광고란 a "Situation-Wanted" column / 신문에 ～광고를 5일간 계속해서 냈다 I put a want ad in a newspaper for five consecutive days. ～인구 the number of persons seeking employment. ～자 a job seeker (★ 「구직」은 job hunting이지만, 「구직자」를 job hunter라고는 잘 하지 않음); an applicant 《for a position》.

**구질구질하다** ① 《모양이》 (be) dirty; untidy; nasty; squalid; slovenly. ¶ 구질구질한 옷차림의 사나이 a man wearing dirty 〔filthy〕 clothes / 구질구질하게 늘어선 판잣집 a row of squalid shacks. ② 《날씨가》 (be) wet; damp. ⇨ 구중중하다.

**구차스럽다, 구차하다**(苟且—) ① 《가난》 (be) very poor; needy; destitute; be badly off; be hard up. ¶ 살림이 ～ be in poverty; be badly off; be in needy circumstances / 구차한 집안에서 태어나다 be born 「poor 〔in a poor family〕 / 그들은 구차하게 살고 있다 They are badly off. *or* They live in poverty. ② 《구구하다》 (be) ignoble; humiliating; unworthy; 《군색하다》 (be) clumsy; poor. ¶ 구차한 목숨 an ignoble existence; a humiliating life / 구차한 변명 a clumsy 〔poor〕 excuse / 구차히 poorly; humiliatingly / 남에게 구차한 소리를 하다 beg 〔plead〕 for *a person's* mercy 〔sympathy〕.

**구창**(口瘡) a sore in the mouth.

**구채**(舊債) an old debt. ¶ ～를 갚다 pay 〔clear〕 off *one's* old debt.

**구척장신**(九尺長身) a giant; a person of extraordinary stature.

**구천**(九天) ① 《하늘》 the highest heavens. ② 《불교》 the nine celestial bodies.

**구천**(九泉) 《황천》 Hades; the nether world 〔regions〕.

**구청**(區廳) a ward 〔district〕 office. ¶ 강남～ the Kangnam Ward Office. ◉ ～장 the ward head 〔chief〕; the chief of a ward. ～직원 a ward official.

**구체**(球體) a sphere; a globe.

**구체**(具體) being concrete; concreteness. ◉ ～성 concreteness. ～안(案) a concrete 〔definite〕 plan: ～안을 제시하다 show 《*a person*》 a concrete plan 《of》.

**구체적**(具體的) concrete; physical; definite; 《상세한》 specific; detailed.

> 용법 **concrete** 좀 딱딱한 표현이기는 하지만,「구체적」이란 뜻의 역어로서 가장 일반적인 말. **definite**「명확한」이란 뜻이, **specific**, **detailed**「세밀한」이란 뜻이 각각 함축된 말.

¶ ~으로 concretely; in the concrete; definitely / ~으로 말하면 to put it concretely / ~인 개념 a concrete concept / ~인 사실 a concrete fact / ~인 예를 들다 give a specific 〔actual〕 example / 좀더 ~으로 말해 주세요 Please be more specific. *or* Please explain it in more detail. / 나는 그가 유죄라는 ~인 증거를 가지고 있다 I have concrete proof of his guilt. / 나는 아직 ~인 계획을 세우지 않았다 I have not formed any concrete 〔definite〕 plan for it. / 그는 ~으로 밝히지 않은 비상 조치들을 취할 계획을 하고 있다 He is planning the adoption of unspecified emergency measures. / 아직 아무 것도 ~으로 결정되어 있지 않다 So far nothing definite has been decided on. / 「나는 무역회사에 근무하고 있습니다」—「~으로 무슨 일을 하십니까」—「회계과에서 출납업무를 보고 있습니다」 "I work for a trading company."—"What do you do there exactly?"—"I'm a cashier in the accounting section."

**구체제**(舊體制) the old structure 〔system, organization, constitution〕.

**구체화**(具體化) embodiment; materialization; giving 〔taking〕 shape. ~하다 take (concrete) shape; shape up; materialize. ¶ 계획을 ~하다 give shape to a plan / 그 계획은 곧 ~될 것이다 The plan will take concrete shape soon. *or* The plan will be realized 〔materialized〕 soon. / 그의 이론은 이 책에서 ~되어 있다 His theory takes form in this book.

**구축**(構築) construction. ~하다 construct; build. ¶ 기반을 ~하다 establish 〔build up〕 the foundation 《of》.

**구축**(驅逐) driving away; expelling; expulsion; ousting. ~하다 drive (away); expel; oust. ¶ 영토에서 적을 ~하다 drive away the enemy from *one's* territory / 악화(惡貨)는 양화(良貨)를 ~한다 Bad money drives out good. ◉ ~함 a destroyer: ~함대 a destroyer flotilla.

**구출**(救出) rescue; helping out; save. ~하다 rescue; help out; save. ¶ 물에 빠진 사람을 ~하다 rescue 〔save〕 《*a person*》 from drowning / 부서진 집더미 밑에서 부상자를 ~하다 rescue the injured persons from under rubble / 위기에서 ~되다 be saved from an imminent danger; be snatched from the jaws of death / 어린아이를 ~하려다 희생되다 sacrifice *oneself* in an attempt to save a child. ◉ ~작업〔작전〕 a rescue work 〔operation〕.

**구충**(驅蟲) extermination of insects; getting rid of intestinal worms (회충을). ~하다 exterminate insects; get rid of worms. ◉ ~약〔제〕 an insecticide; an insect powder; a vermicide.

**구취**(口臭) foul 〔bad〕 breath; 〖의학〗 halitosis. ¶ ~가 나다 have foul 〔bad〕 breath.

**구치**(臼齒) 〖해부〗 《큰》 a molar (tooth); 《작은》 a false molar; a premolar.

**구치**(拘置) custody; confinement; detention. ~하다 keep 《*a person*》 in custody; confine 《*a person*》; detain. ◉ ~소 a detention house 〔cell〕; a prison: 서울 ~소 《be put into》 the Seoul Detention House.

**구칭**(舊稱) the old name; the former title.

**구타**(毆打) beating; 〖법〗 battery. ~하다 beat; hit; strike; assault (폭행); give 〔deal〕 《*a person*》 a blow. ¶ 머리를 ~하다 beat 〔strike, hit〕 《*a person*》 on the head.

**구태**(舊態) the old 〔former〕 state of affairs 〔things〕. ¶ ~의연한 사고 방식 obsolete way of thinking / ~의연하다 be 〔remain〕 unchanged 〔as *it* was〕 / 알아볼 수 없을 정도로 ~를 벗다 be changed beyond recognition; leave no trace of *its* former state / 그들의 하는 짓거리는 ~의연하다 Their attitudes remains just as they have always been.

**구태여** 《일부러》 deliberately; intentionally; especially; 《*one* need not》 go to all the trouble of 《*doing something*》; go out of *one's* way to 《*do something*》. ¶ ~ 서두를건 없네 There is no hurry 〔rush〕. / ~ 회의에 출석할 필요는 없다 You need not trouble yourself to attend the meeting. / 그것을 사러 ~ 종로까지 갈 것은 없다 You do not have to take the trouble of going as far as Chongno just to get that. / 그렇다면 ~ 말리지 않겠다 If you insist, I wouldn't press you to stop it.

**구택**(舊宅) *one's* old house; *one's* former residence.

**구토**(嘔吐) vomiting; emesis. ~하다

vomit; 《구어》 throw 〔bring〕 up 《*one's* food》. ¶ ~감이 일다 feel like vomiting; feel sick 〔nausea〕. ◉ ~방지제 an antinausea drug. ~설사 vomiting and diarrhea. ~제 an emetic.

**구투**(舊套) an old fashion 〔custom〕; (a) convention(alism). ¶ ~를 벗다 get free from conventionalism.

**구파**(舊派) the old school 〔style〕. ¶ ~의 of the old school; old-style; 《보수적》 conservative; old-line. ◉ ~(연)극 a play of the old school; a classical drama.

**구판**(舊版) an old 〔earlier〕 edition. ¶ ~을 개정하다 revise an old edition.

**구폐**(舊弊) old abuses; an old 〔a standing〕 evil. ¶ ~를 고치다 reform old abuses.

**구포**(臼砲) 《옛 화포》 a mortar.

**구푸리다** bend (*one's* body) forward; stoop; bend. ¶ 몸을 ~ stoop; bow / 책상 위에 몸을 ~ lean 〔bend〕 over *one's* desk.

**구피**(狗皮) a dogskin.

**구필**(口筆) writing with the brush held in *one's* mouth.

**구하다**(求—) ① 《찾다》 look for; search for 〔after〕; seek (for); pursue 《happiness》; 《원하다》 want; wish for; desire; 《요청하다》 demand; call for; request; claim. ¶ 방을 ~ look for a room / 설명을 ~ call for an explanation / 조언을 ~ ask 《*a person*》 for advice / 점원을 ~ want a clerk / 인재를 ~ look out for talent / 아르바이트할 사람을 구함 《게시》 Part-timers Wanted / 그 회사는 숙련공을 구하고 있다 The company is looking for skilled workers. / 그 문제에 관해 전문가의 의견을 구했다 We asked the opinion of experts on the subject. / 그녀는 일자리를 구하기 위해 상경했다 She came up to Seoul 「in search of 〔to look for〕 a job. / 어떤 일자리를 구하느냐 What kind of job are you after? / 실업계는 새로운 사람을 구하고 있다 The business world demands new men. / 구하라, 그러면 얻을 것이다 Ask, and 「you shall receive 〔it shall be given you〕.
② 《사다·얻다》 buy; get; obtain; purchase. ¶ 서울에서 구한 물건 a thing bought in Seoul / 차표가 매진되기 전에 미리 구해라 Please try to buy 〔get〕 the tickets well in advance before they sell out.

**구하다**(救—) save 《*a person*》 from 《death》; rescue 《*a person*》 from 《a fire》; help 《*a person*》 out of 《difficulties》; relieve 《*a person*》 from 《suffering》; give relief to; 《죄에서》 redeem. ¶ 인명을 ~ save a man's life; rescue 《*a person*》 from death / 병에서 ~ release 《*a person*》 from a disease; cure 《*a person*》 of a disease / 가난한 사람을 ~ relieve 〔give relief to〕 the poor / 영혼을 ~ save a soul / 구할 도리가 없다 be hopeless 〔helpless〕; be beyond remedy; be past 〔beyond〕 redemption 〔salvation〕.

**구학문**(舊學問) classical studies; (study of the) Chinese classics.

**구현**(具現) embodiment; materialization; realization. ~하다 embody 《an idea》; materialize; realize 《a dream》; express tangibly. ¶ 그 조각상은 조각가의 감정을 ~하고 있다 The statue embodies the sentiment of the sculptor.

**구형**(求刑) 『법』 prosecutor's demand 〔proposal〕 of punishment for the accused. ~하다 demand 〔propose〕 punishment for the accused. ¶ 극형을 ~하다 demand 〔propose〕 capital punishment for 《the accused》.

**구형**(矩形) a rectangle. ⇨ 직사각형.

**구형**(球形) a globular shape 〔form〕; [형용사적] globular; spherical; globe-shaped.

**구형**(舊型) an old model 〔type, style〕. ¶ ~의 outmoded 《cars》; old-fashioned; out-of-date 《model》.

**구호**(口號) 《표어》 a slogan; a motto; a catchword; a catchphrase; a rallying word; 《군호》 a password. ¶ …의 ~를 내걸고 under the slogan of... / 한낱 ~에 그치다 end in mere gesture.

**구호**(救護) relief; aid; help; rescue. ~하다 relieve; aid; give aid 〔help〕 to. ¶ 따뜻한 ~의 손길을 뻗다 extend a warm helping hand 《to》. ◉ ~물자 relief goods 〔supplies〕. ~미 relief rice; emergency rice. ~반 a relief squad; a rescue party; an ambulance corps. ~사업 relief work. ~소 a first-aid station; an aid station. ~시설 relief facilities. ~(자)금 relief 〔charity〕 funds. ~활동 relief activities.

**구혼**(求婚) a proposal 〔an offer〕 of marriage; courtship. ~하다 propose (marriage) 《to》; ask 《a girl》 to marry 《*one*》; ask for 《a lady's》 hand; court. ¶ 돈을 목적으로 ~하다 seek 《a woman's》 hand for money / ~을 승낙〔거절〕하다 《여자가》 accept 〔decline〕 《a man's》 「hand 〔proposal of marriage〕 /

그는 그녀에게 ~했다 He asked her to marry him. *or* He proposed to her. ◉ ~광고 an advertisement for a spouse. ~자 a suitor; a wooer: 딸의 ~자 a suitor to *one's* daughter / 돈을 목적으로 하는 ~자 a fortune hunter; 《여자》 a gold digger 《미속어》.

**구황**(救荒) the relief of the famine victims; helping famine-stricken people. ~하다 relieve the sufferers from famine. ◉ ~대책 a measure for the relief of the famine victims. ~식물 hardy wild plants (capable of being used as food in a famine).

**구획**(區劃) 《구분》 division; demarcation; 《한 구획》 a section; a division; a compartment; a block (시가의); 《토지의》 a lot 〔plot〕; 《구역》 a lot; a block; an area; 《경계》 a boundary; the limits. ~하다 divide; partition; draw a line 《between》; mark off 《one lot from another》; mark out 《land》; demarcate. ¶ 행정~ an administrative division 〔boundary〕 / 세 구역으로 ~하다 partition off 《an area》 into three districts / 그 택지 조성지는 50 개로 ~되어 있다 The developed housing land is divided into fifty lots.
◉ ~분양지 a (subdivided) lot 〔plot〕 of land. ~정리 land readjustment; 《도시의》 replanning of streets; readjustment of town lots; rezoning (of land): ~ 정리하다 readjust town lots.

**구휼**(救恤) the relief (of the poor); aid. ~하다 relieve; aid; help. ¶ 이재민을 ~하다 relieve the sufferers / 빈민을 ~하다 give 〔administer〕 relief to the poor 〔indigent〕. ◉ ~금 relief money; a relief fund. ~사업 relief work.

**구희**(球戲) a ball game; bowling (볼링); billiards (당구); pinball (핀볼).

**국** ① 《먹는》 soup; broth. ¶ 국을 먹다 〔마시다〕 eat 〔sip〕 soup. ② 《국물》 the watery part of soup. ¶ 국말이 boiled rice with soup; soup on rice.

**국**(局) 《관청의》 a bureau; a board; an office; a department; 《전화국》 a telephone office; 《우체국》 a post office; 《방송국》 a broadcasting 〔radio, TV〕 station; 《바둑·장기의》 a game. ¶ 1국 3과로 나누다 divide 《an office》 into one department and three sections.

**국가**(國家) a state; a country; a nation; a body politic; a political community; a polity. ¶ ~적(인) national; state / 초~적(인) ultra〔super〕national / ~적 견지 a national point of view / ~적 운동 a national movement / ~적인 행사 a national event; 《on》 a state occasion / ~의 주권을 침해하다 infringe on a nation's sovereignty / ~에 이바지하다〔봉사하다〕 serve *one's* country / 조림(造林)은 ~의 백년지대계이다 Forestation is a grand plan for the long-term future of the nation. / ~는 재정 위기에 직면해 있다 The nation is in a financial crisis.
◉ ~경륜(책) statecraft. ~경제 state 〔national〕 economy. ~공무원 a government official; a national public servant 〔official〕: ~ 공무원법 the National Public Service Law. ~ 과학기술자문회의 the Presidential Advisory Council for Science and Technology. ~관념〔사상〕 patriotic sentiment; a spirit of nationalism. ~관리 state 〔government〕 control. ~권력 state power. ~기관 the apparatus 〔organs〕 of the nation. ~대표팀 the national team. ~론 the theory of the State. ~보안법 the National Security Law. ~보조〔보상〕 national assistance 〔indemnities〕. ~보훈처 the Patriots and Veterans Administration Agency. ~비상사태 《declare》 a state of national emergency. ~사업 a national enterprise 〔undertaking〕. ~사회주의 national 〔state〕 socialism. ~시험 a state 〔national〕 examination. ~ 안전〔안보〕 national safety 〔security〕: ~ 안전 보장법 the National Security Act 《미》. ~연합 a federation 〔union, league〕 of nations. ~재정 national finance(s); the finances of the state. ~정보원 the National Intelligence Service. ~주의 nationalism: ~주의자 a nationalist. ~총동원 a national mobilization. ~통제주의 statism.

**국가**(國歌) a national anthem. ¶ ~를 연주하다〔부르다〕 play 〔sing〕 the national anthem.

**국거리** soup makings; materials for soup.

**국건더기** the ingredients 〔solid stuff〕 in soup.

**국경**(國境) the boundary; the border 〔boundaries〕 (of a country); 《주로 영》 the frontier (★ 《미》에서는 보통 「변경」의 뜻으로 씀). ¶ ~ 내에〔밖에〕 within 〔outside〕 the border / ~을 굳게 지키다 fortify the border / ~을 넘다 cross the border 《into another country》 / ~을 획정하다 delimit the border line / 사랑에는 ~이 없다 Love has 〔knows〕 no national boundaries. / 캐

나다는 미국과 ~을 접하고 있다 Canada borders on the United States.

◉ ~경비대 the border garrison 〔guard〕. ~경비병 border 〔frontier〕 guards. ~도시 a border town. ~문제 a boundary 〔border〕 problem. ~분쟁 a boundary 〔border〕 dispute. ~선 a boundary line; a borderline. ~지대 the border (land); a border area 〔region〕. ~침범 (a) border violation. ~표 a boundary marker 〔stone〕.

**국경일**(國慶日) a national holiday.

> 참고 우리 나라의 국경일과 공휴일
> 1. 국경일(National Holiday)
> 3·1절 the anniversary of the *Samil* Independence Movement. 제헌절 Constitution Day. 광복절 National Liberation Day. 개천절 National Foundation Day.
> 2. 공휴일(Public Holiday)
> 신정 the New Year's Day. 설날 the lunar New Year's Day. 식목일 Arbor Day. 어린이날 Children's Day. 석가 탄신일 Buddha's Birthday. 현충일 Memorial Day. 추석 *Chusŏk,* the Korean Thanksgiving Day; the Full moon Day. 크리스마스 Christmas.

**국고**(國庫) the National Treasury; the coffers of the State. ¶ ~의 수입이 되다 go to the national treasury / ~에서 부담하다 defray 〔be defrayed〕《the expenses》 out of the National Treasury; be paid from the National Treasury / 의무 교육비는 전액 ~에서 부담해야 한다 The National Treasury should cover all the costs of the compulsory education.

◉ ~금〔준비금〕 national 〔a treasury reserve〕 funds. ~보조 a state 〔government〕 subsidy: ~(의) 보조를 받고 있다 be subsidized by the national treasury; be supported by state subvention. ~부담 state liability. ~수입 national revenues; national treasury receipts: ~수입이 되다 go to the national revenues. ~예금 treasury deposits. ~지출 defrayment out of the national treasury: ~지출금 National Treasury disbursements. ~차입금 a national loan. ~채권 a Treasury bond 〔bill〕《미》; an exchequer bond.

**국공채**(國公債) national 〔government〕 bond and public bond. ¶ ~를 발행〔상환〕하다 issue 〔redeem〕 government and public bonds.

**국교**(國交) diplomatic relations; national friendship; intercourse between nations. ¶ ~를 맺다〔단절하다〕 enter into 〔sever, break (off)〕 diplomatic relations《with》/ 긴밀한 ~를 수립하다 establish a closer relationship《between two countries》/ ~를 정상화하다 normalize diplomatic relations.

◉ ~단절 a severance 〔breaking-off, rupture, cessation〕 of diplomatic relations; a diplomatic break. ~회복 a restoration of diplomatic relations.

**국교**(國教) a state religion. ¶ 비~도 a nonconformist / 영국~회 the Church of England; the Anglican Church.

**국구**(國舅) the king's father-in-law.

**국군**(國軍) a nation's armed forces; the Korean 〔ROK〕 army. ¶ ~의 날 (ROK) Armed Forces Day / 내일 다채로운 ~의 날 행사가 거행된다 There will be a variety of festivities to celebrate Armed Forces Day tomorrow.

◉ ~ 기무사령부 the Defense Security Command (생략 DSC). ~ 모범용사 an exemplary military serviceman. ~장병 officers and men of the armed forces 〔services〕. ~통합병원 the Armed Forces Combined Hospital.

**국궁**(鞠躬) a bow of reverence. ~하다 bow reverently.

**국권**(國權) national 〔sovereign〕 rights; state 〔national〕 power. ¶ ~의 회복 restoration of its sovereignty / ~을 신장하다 expand 〔extend〕 national power 〔rights〕; enhance national prestige / ~을 발동하다 exercise the right of the state.

**국그릇** a soup bowl.

**국금**(國禁) national prohibition. ¶ ~의 서책 a book banned 〔forbidden〕 by state law / ~을 범하다 violate the national 〔legal〕 prohibition.

**국기**(國技) a national sport 〔game〕. ¶ 태권도는 우리 국기의 하나이다 T'aekwondo is one of the national sports of Korea.

**국기**(國基) the foundation of a nation.

**국기**(國旗) the national flag. ¶ 한국 ~를 단 선박 a ship sailing under the Korean flag / ~를 게양하다 hoist 〔put up〕 the national flag / ~를 모독하다 insult the national flag / ~에 대하여 경례하다 salute the national flag / 미국~ the American flag; the Stars and Stripes; the Star-Spangled Banner / 영국~ the British flag; the Union Jack / 한국~ ⇨ 태극기.

◉ ~게양식 a flag-hoisting ceremony.

**국난**(國難) 《위기》 a national crisis 〔danger, peril〕; 《재난》 a national disaster 〔trouble〕. ¶ ~에 처하여 무기를 들고 일어서다 take up arms for *one's* country; respond to *one's* country's call / ~을 구하다 deliver *one's* country out of difficulty; save the nation in a great crisis.

**국내**(國內) ¶ ~의 internal; domestic; home / ~에 in 〔within〕 the country. ◉ ~경제 domestic 〔home〕 economy. ~공안 public peace and order; internal 〔domestic〕 security. ~관세 internal customs; domestic tariff. ~문제 domestic problems 〔issues〕. ~방송 domestic broadcasting. ~법 municipal 〔civic〕 law. ~사정 domestic 〔internal〕 affairs. ~산업 domestic industries. ~선 《항공》 domestic lines 〔flights〕; domestic 〔internal〕 air service. ~소비 home 〔domestic〕 consumption. ~수요 《meet》 domestic needs 〔demands〕. ~시장 the domestic market. ~우편 domestic mail. ~정세 the domestic situation. ~총생산 《경제》 the gross domestic product (생략 GDP). ~ 항공 수송 internal 〔domestic〕 air transportation.

**국내외**(國內外) the inside and outside of the country; home and abroad. ¶ ~가 다사 다난한 때에 in 「these eventful days 〔these times of storm and stress〕 at home and abroad.

**국도**(國都) the capital (of a country).

**국도**(國道) a state road 《미》; a national road; a highway.

**국란**(國亂) a national disturbance 〔upheaval〕; 《반란》 a rebellion; 《내란》 a civil war.

**국력**(國力) national strength 〔power〕; 《자원》 national resources; 《부》 national wealth. ¶ ~의 고갈 the exhaustion of national resources / ~의 배양 the nurturing of national strength / ~의 신장 continued buildup of national strength / ~의 쇠퇴〔증대〕 the decline 〔growth〕 of national power / ~을 기르다 build up national power; develop national resources / ~을 증진하다 〔신장시키다〕 increase 〔expand〕 national power.

**국련**(國聯) ⇨ 국제연합.

**국록**(國祿) a government 「salary 〔stipend〕. ¶ ~을 먹다 receive a stipend; be in government service.

**국론**(國論) national 〔public〕 opinion 〔view, sentiment〕. ¶ ~을 자극하다 excite public opinion; lead to heated public discussions / ~을 통일하다 create 〔achieve〕 a national consensus / ~을 환기하다 arouse public opinion / ~의 분열을 막다 prevent disunion 〔(a) division〕 in national opinion / ~을 2분하다 split 〔divide〕 public opinion in two.

**국리**(國利) national interests. ◉ ~민복 《promote》 national interests and the welfare of the people.

**국립**(國立) ¶ ~의 national; state; government. ◉ ~공원 a national 〔state〕 park. ~극장 a national theater. ~대학〔도서관, 박물관〕 a national university 〔library, museum〕. ~묘지 a national cemetery. ~은행 a national 〔state〕 bank. ~학교 a national 〔government〕 school.

**국면**(局面) 《바둑·장기의》 the situation on a board; the state of the game; 《형편》 the situation; an aspect 〔a state〕 of affairs; a phase (단계). ¶ 전쟁〔정치〕 ~ the war 〔political〕 situation / ~이 일변하다 enter upon a new phase; the situation assumes 〔takes on〕 a new aspect / ~을 일변시키다〔뒤바꾸다〕 change the situation; turn the tables / ~을 타개하다 break the deadlock; bring the deadlock to an end / 중대한 ~을 맞다 reach 〔enter〕 a critical phase / ~은 아직 호전되지 않았다 The state of affairs is yet to be improved. / 세계 정세는 위험한 ~에 접어들고 있다 The world situation is entering into a perilous phase. / 우리는 전개되어 가는 ~을 주시하고 있다 We are watching the development of the situation. *or* We are keeping an eye on development 〔on how things develop〕.

**국명**(局名) the name of a (broadcasting) station; 《무전의》 a call sign.

**국명**(國名) the name of a country.

**국명**(國命) 《명령》 a government order; 《사명》 a national mission.

**국모**(國母) the Mother of the State; the Empress; the Queen.

**국무**(國務) (the) affairs 〔matters〕 of state; state affairs. ¶ ~를 관장하다 administer the affairs of state / ~를 보다 attend to state affairs / ~를 수행하다 carry out state affairs / ~에 다망하다 be busy with state affairs. ◉ ~부 the State Department 《미》. ~위원 a minister of state. ~장관〔차관, 차관보〕 the Secretary 〔Undersecretary, Assistant Undersecretary〕 of

State《미》. ～조정실《총리 산하의》the Office for Government Policy Coordination. ～총리 the Prime Minister; the Premier: ～총리 비서실 Prime Minister's Secretariat. ～회의 the State Council: ～회의에 회부하다 submit《*a matter*》to the State Council; lay《*a matter*》before State Council.

**국문**(國文)《문자》the national script; 《한글》the Korean alphabet; 《한국어》the Korean language; 《문학》Korean literature. ◉ ～법 Korean grammar. ～학 Korean literature: ～학을 전공하다 specialize〔major〕in Korean literature / ～(학)과 the department of Korean Literature / ～학자 a scholar of Korean literature / ～학사(史) the history of Korean literature.

**국물** ①《국의》the liquid part of a dish; the "soup"; the "broth"; the "juice". ¶ 김칫～ kimchi juice / ～이 많은 juicy; succulent. ②《부수입》a perquisite; side benefits; an (additional) emolument; 《구어》perk. (★ perk, perquisite는 흔히 복수형으로 쓰임). ¶ ～있는 paying; remunerative / ～있는 자리에 앉다 get a job with some side benefits / 그 일에는 여러 형태의 ～이 있다 The office carries various perquisites / 봉급은 많지 않으나 ～이 많이 생기는 자리다 Though it pays badly, the post has a lot of perks.

**국민**(國民)《전체》a nation; a people; 《인민》the people; the nation; 《개인》a《British》national; a citizen《of the United States》.

> **용법** **nation** 주로 정치적 관점에서 한 나라를 이루는 인간 집단을, **people** 주로 문화적·지리적 관점에서 한 민족을 나타내는 집단을, **citizen** 국적·시민권을 가진 사람으로서의 국민, **national**은 외국 거주자의 국적을 문제로 할 경우.

¶ ～의 national / 한국 ～ (전체) the Korean nation / ～의 소리 the voice of the nation / ～의 심판 people's judgment / ～의 의무 a national obligation / ～의 후원 a national backing〔support〕/ ～의 화합과 단결 national harmony and unity / ～의 축제일 a national holiday / 세계 여러 ～ 사이의 문화 교류를 촉진한다 promote cultural exchanges between different peoples of the world / ～을 계몽하다 enlighten *one's* fellow countrymen / ～에게 호소하다 appeal to the nation / 주권은 ～에게 있다 Sovereign power resides in the people. / 한국인은 예의바르고 근면한 ～이다 The Koreans are a polite and hardworking people.

◉ ～가요 national folk songs. ～감정 national sentiment〔feeling〕: ～감정을 도발〔자극〕하다 provoke the national sentiment. ～개병(제도) universal conscription (system). ～건강보험 national health insurance. ～경제 the national economy. ～고충처리 위원회 the Ombudsman of Korea. ～교육 national education: ～교육 헌장 the National Charter for Education. ～대회 a national convention. ～도덕 national morality〔morals〕; civic virtues. ～병 a militiaman. ～복지연금 the citizen's welfare pension: ～복지연금법 the Law on National Welfare Pension. ～생활 national life; the life of the people; the people's living: ～생활의 안정과 그 질의 향상을 보증하다 ensure stability and improve the quality of people's lives. ～성 the character〔characteristics〕of a nation; the national traits〔character〕《of》: 미국인의 ～성 the American character〔traits〕. ～소득 the national income: 1인당 ～소득 the national income per head; national per capita income. ～순생산 net national product (생략 NNP). ～연금 national pension: ～연금 제도 national pension〔annuity〕system. ～외교 people-to-people diplomacy. ～운동 a popular〔national〕movement〔campaign〕. ～의례 national ceremony. ～자본 national capital. ～장(葬) a national funeral; a public〔an official〕funeral: 합동 ～장 the joint national funeral service. ～저축 national savings. ～정신 a national spirit. ～주권 the sovereignty of the people. ～주의 nationalism. ～총생산 gross national product (생략 GNP). ～총소득 gross national income (생략 GNI). ～총지출 gross national expenditure (생략 GNE). ～투표 a plebiscite; a (national) referendum. ～화합 the national harmony〔reconciliation〕.

**국민학교**(國民學校) ⇨ 초등학교.

**국밥** cooked rice served in soup.

**국방**(國防) national defense; the defense of a country. ¶ ～상 for defensive reasons / ～완비〔충실〕the completion of national defense / 자주～

independent 〔self-reliant〕 national defense capability / ～을 강화하다 strengthen the national defense.
◉ ～계획 a national defense program; a national security plan. ～ 과학연구소 the National Defense and Science Institute. ～군 national defense forces; a State guard 《미》. ～대학원 the National Defense College. ～부 《미국의》 the Department of Defense; the Pentagon; 《한국의》 the Ministry of National Defense; the Defense Ministry: ～부 장관 the Minister of National Defense; the Defense Minister; the Secretary of Defense 《미》 / ～부 차관 the Deputy Secretary of Defense 《미》. ～비 national defense expenditures. ～예산 a national defense budget. ～ 위원회 《국회의》 the National Defense Committee. ～태세 national defense readiness.

**국법**(國法) national laws; the laws of the country. ¶ ～에 따르다〔을 어기다〕 obey 〔violate〕 the national law / ～에 저촉되다 come into conflict with the law of the country / ～으로 금지하다 prohibit by (national) law.

**국보**(局報) 《국(局)의》 an official bulletin; 《우체국간의》 a service telegram.

**국보**(國寶) a national treasure 〔heirloom〕; an asset to the nation. ¶ ～적 인물 a living national treasure / ～로서 보존하다 preserve as a national treasure / ～로서 등록되다〔지정되다〕 be listed as 〔designated〕 a national treasure / 그는 ～적 인물이다 He is a national asset. / 이 그림은 ～급이다 This picture ranks with the national treasures.

**국부**(局部) ① 《일부》 a (limited) part; a section; 《환부》 an affected 〔diseased〕 part of the body. ¶ ～적(으로) local(ly); sectional(ly) / 전염을 ～적으로 저지하다 localize infection / 폭우는 ～적이었다 The rainstorm was confined to a very small area. ② 《음부》 the genital area; the privates; the private parts. ◉ ～마취〔치료〕 local anesthesia 〔treatment〕. ～묘사 the local description (in a piece of writing). ～운동 local movement. ～진찰 examination of the part affected. ～화(化) localizing; localization.

**국부**(國父) the father of *one's* country; the founder of *one's* country.

**국부**(國富) national wealth 〔resources〕. ◉ ～론 *The Wealth of Nations.*

**국비**(國費) national expenditure 〔expenses, outlay〕. ¶ ～로 at (the) government 〔national〕 expense / ～를 절감하다 cut 〔slash〕 governmental spending / ～로 유럽 유학을 가다 be sent to Europe for study at the expense of the government. ◉ ～유학생 a student sent abroad at state expense. ～장학생 a state scholarship student; a student receiving state scholarship.

**국빈**(國賓) a guest of the state; a national 〔state〕 guest. ¶ ～ 대우를 하다 accord 《*a person*》 the treatment of a national guest; give 《*a person*》 full state honors / ～으로 맞이하다 be received as a state guest / 그는 ～ 대우를 받았다 He was treated as a state guest.

**국사**(國史) a national history; the history of a nation; 《한국의》 Korean history; the history of Korea. ◉ ～연표 a historical calendar of Korea. ～자료 historiographical materials.

**국사**(國事) a national affair; public matters; the affairs of state. ¶ ～를 논하다 discuss the affairs of a nation / ～에 다망하다 exert *oneself* in the interests of *one's* country / ～에 참여하다 take part in the affairs of state. ◉ ～범 《행위》 a political offense; (high) treason; a crime against the state; 《사람》 a political offender; a treason felon.

**국사**(國師) 『불교』 the Most Reverend Priest.

**국산**(國産) home 〔domestic〕 production; 《제품》 home products. ¶ ～의 home-made; domestic; 《한국산》 《wine》 made in Korea / 오늘 ～술 한 병을 샀다 I bought a bottle of domestic 〔Korean〕 wine today. / 이 위스키는 ～이다 This whisky was made in Korea. ◉ ～원료 indigenous materials. ～자동차 a motorcar of Korean make; a home-manufactured motor vehicle. ～화 localization: ～화하다 localize; begin home production of... / ～화율 the localization rate 《of major items》.

**국산품**(國産品) a home 〔domestic〕 product; a homemade article; products of domestic industry; 《한국산의》 an article of Korean make. ¶ 순～ an all-Korean product / ～을 쓰다 use 〔buy〕 homemade articles / ～ 장려 encouragement of the use of home products; a "Buy-Korean" campaign (운동) / 미국에서는 ～ 장려 운동이 한창

이다 The Buy-American Movement is strong in the U.S. / 이들 ~은 가격과 품질에 있어 수입품과 필적할 수 있다 Both in price and quality, these domestic goods can sufficiently stand comparison with the imported goods.

**국상**(國喪) national mourning for a deceased royalty.

**국새**(國璽) the Great Seal (of the King); the Seal of State.

**국서**(國書) ① 《외교 문서》 a sovereign's message (to a foreign state) (국가 원수의 친서); credentials (신임장). ② 《서적》 (works of) national history and literature.

**국선**(國選) ¶ ~의 chosen 〔appointed〕 by the government. ◉ ~변호인 a court-appointed lawyer 〔attorney〕; a public defender.

**국세**(局勢) ① 《형세》 the situation; a phase; the state 〔condition〕 of affairs 〔things〕. ¶ ~가 일변하다 take a new turn; enter upon a new phase. ② 《장기 판국》 the game (on a board); the situation (in a game of chess). ¶ 승부가 뚜렷하지 않은 ~ a situation whose outcome is uncertain / 승패를 가릴 수 없는 ~이다 The game is anybody's guess.

**국세**(國稅) a national tax. ¶ ~를 징수하다 collect national taxes.
◉ ~부가세 a surtax on the national tax. ~사정(査定) assessment of a national tax. ~업무 tax affairs. ~징수법 the National Tax Collection Law. ~청 the National Tax Service; the Internal Revenue Service 《미》: ~청장 the administrator of the National Tax Service / 지방 ~청 the regional office of national tax administration. ~체납 arrears 〔delinquency in payment〕 of national taxes: ~ 체납 처분을 하다 make an attachment on 《*somebody's*》 property for unpaid national taxes; take proceeding 〔institute a process〕 against 《*somebody*》 for the recovery of national taxes in arrears.

**국세**(國勢) the state 〔condition〕 of a country. ◉ ~조사 a (national) census: ~ 조사를 하다 take a (national) census 《of the population》 / ~ 조사표 a census form / ~ 조사원 a census taker 〔enumerator〕.

**국소**(局所) 《국부》 a part; an affected part (환부); 《관절》 joints (of the body).

**국수** noodles; vermicelli. ¶ ~를 말다 prepare a dish of noodles (with soup). ◉ ~사리 a coil of boiled noodles. ~장수 a noodle vendor. ~틀 a noodle(-making) machine; a vermicelli-press set. 국숫가락, 국숫발 a strip of noodle. 국숫물 noodle broth. 국숫집 《공장》 a noodle factory; 《식당》 a noodle shop 〔restaurant〕; a noodle stand 〔stall〕 (이동식의).

**국수**(國手) ① 《바둑·장기의》 a national champion (of *baduk, etc.*); a master player of the game of *baduk*. ¶ ~전(戰) the professional *baduk* players' championship series. ② 《명의》 a noted 〔excellent〕 physician 〔healer〕; a great doctor.

**국수**(國粹) ¶ ~ 적(인) nationalistic.
◉ ~주의 (ultra-)nationalism: ~주의자 an ultranationalist.

**국시**(國是) the national 〔state〕 policy. ¶ ~를 정하다 fix 〔formulate〕 the national 〔state〕 policy; orientate a government policy.

**국악**(國樂) national 〔Korean〕 classical music. ¶ 국립~원 the National Classical Music Institute / 국립~학교 the National Classical Music and Art School. ◉ ~인 a Korean classical musician.

**국어**(國語) 《한 나라의 말》 a language; 《자국어》 *one's* native 〔mother〕 tongue; the vernacular; 《한국말》 the Korean language; Korean. ¶ 2개 ~의 bilingual / 수개 ~를 말하는 사람 a multilingual person; a polyglot / 수개 ~로 번역되다 be translated into several languages / 그는 수개 ~를 자유로이 말한다 He has a free command of several languages.
◉ ~교과서 a Korean language schoolbook 〔text(book)〕. ~교사 a teacher of Korean. ~ 국문학과 the Department of Korean Language and Literature. ~사 the history of the national 〔Korean〕 language. ~사전 《한국어의》 a Korean dictionary. ~심의회 the National 〔Korean〕 Language Deliberative Council. ~학 Korean philology 〔linguistics〕.

**국영**(國營) nationalization; government 〔state〕 management 〔operation〕; management by state. ¶ ~의 state-operated; state-run; state-owned / ~으로 하다 put 〔place〕 《an enterprise》 under government 〔state〕 management; nationalize 《the railroads》.
◉ ~기업〔사업〕 a state 〔national〕

enterprise; a government enterprise 〔undertaking〕: ～기업체 a state policy corporation 〔company〕; a government-run 〔state-run〕 firm. ～방송국 a government-run broadcasting station. ～화 nationalization.

**국왕**(國王) a king; a monarch; a sovereign; a ruler. ¶ 스웨덴 ～ the King of Sweden.

**국외**(局外) an independent position; the outside. ¶ ～의 outside; external / ～에 서다 stand outside; keep aloof 《from》 / ～에서 관찰하다 observe from the outside. ◉ ～자 an outsider; a third party 〔person〕; a bystander; an onlooker. ～중립 neutrality; neutralism: ～중립국 a neutral country / ～중립을 지키다 observe neutrality; stand 〔be〕 neutral.

**국외**(國外) ¶ ～로〔에〕 outside the country; abroad; overseas; beyond the sea / ～로 추방하다 expel 《*a person*》 from the country; expatriate; be deported / ～로 도망가다 flee abroad / 그 제품은 국내 ～할 것 없이 잘 팔린다 The products sell well both at home and abroad. ◉ ～추방 deportation; banishment; exile: ～추방자 an expellee.

**국욕**(國辱) a national humiliation 〔disgrace〕; a disgrace to the nation.

**국운**(國運) national fortunes 〔luck〕; the fate 〔destiny〕 of a country. ¶ ～의 성쇠 the prosperity and decline of a country; the rise and fall of a nation / ～을 개척하다 explore *one's* national destiny / ～을 걸다 stake the national destiny; stake the destiny of the nation / ～이 기울었다 Fortune deserted the country.

**국원**(局員) 《관청의》 a member of a bureau 〔an office〕 (한 사람); the staff of a bureau [집합적]; 《우체국의》 a post-office clerk; the staff of a post office [집합적].

**국위**(國威) national prestige 〔dignity, honor, glory〕. ¶ ～에 관한 문제 a matter of national prestige 〔honor〕 / 해외에 ～를 떨치다 〔선양하다〕 boost 〔enhance〕 the national prestige abroad / ～를 손상시키다 impair 〔damage〕 the national dignity.

**국유**(國有) state ownership. ¶ ～의 state-〔government-〕owned.
◉ ～림 a national 〔state〕 forest. ～산업 nationalized industry. ～재산 national property 〔assets〕; government property: ～재산법 the National Property Law. ～지 《sell, dispose of 》 government-owned land. ～철도 the national railways; a government 〔state〕 railway. ～화 nationalization: ～화하다 nationalize; make 《*a thing*》 a national possession / 기간 산업의 ～화 the nationalization of key industries.

**국으로** within keeping 《of *one's* position》; within *one's* limitations; suitable to *one's* ability. ¶ ～ 가만히 있어 Know your own place. *or* Stick to 〔Stay with〕 what you can do.

**국은**(國恩) what *one* owes to *one's* country. ¶ ～에 보답하다 repay what *one* owes to *one's* country.

**국익**(國益) the national interest(s). ¶ ～을 도모하다 further 〔promote〕 the national interest / ～을 우선하다 give priority to national interests / ～이 되다 serve the best interests of the nation.

**국자** a (soup) ladle; a scoop; a dipper. ¶ ～로 국을 뜨다 ladle 〔dip up〕 soup.

**국장**(局長) the director of a bureau; the chief of an office.

**국장**(國章) a national emblem.

**국장**(國葬) a national 〔state〕 funeral. ¶ ～으로 하다 give 〔accord〕 《*a person*》 a state funeral; hold a state funeral for 《*a person*》; inter 《*a person*》 at state expense.

**국적**(國賊) a traitor 《to a country》; a rebel; an insurgent; an insurrectionist. ¶ ～이라는 낙인이 찍히다 be branded as a public enemy.

**국적**(國籍) (*one's*) nationality; citizenship. ¶ 무～자 a stateless person / 이중～ dual 〔double〕 nationality / ～불명의 《a ship》 of unknown nationality / ～의 포기 renunciation of nationality / ～을 취득하다〔상실하다〕 acquire 〔lose〕 *one's* nationality 〔citizenship〕 / ～을 속이다 disguise *one's* nationality / 너의 ～은 어디냐 What is your nationality? / ～은 미국인이지만 혈통은 한국 사람이다 He is American by nationality, but of Korean ancestry.
◉ ～법 the Korean Nationality Act. ～변경 change of nationality. ～상실 loss of nationality; denationalization: ～상실자 a denationalized person. ～회복 reinstatement of citizenship.

**국전**(國展) an art exhibit(ion) sponsored by the nation 〔state〕; the National Art Exhibition.

**국정**(國定) ¶ ～의 national; state. ◉ ～

교과서 a school textbook compiled by the state; a government designated textbook. ~세율 the statutory tariff.

**국정**(國政) national administration; state politics; statecraft; 《국무》 (the) affairs of state; state affairs. ¶ ~에 참여하다 participate in the (national) administration / ~을 맡다 assume the reins of government; take the helm of state (affairs); administer the affairs of state / ~을 담당하고 있다 be at the helm of state.
◉ ~방향 the direction of state politics. ~ 자문회의 the National Advisory Council on State Affairs. ~조사권 《국회의》 the right to conduct investigation in relation to government: ~조사권을 발동하다 exercise the right of parliament to investigate 《*a matter*》 in relation to government. ~홍보처 the Government Information Agency.

**국정**(國情) 《나라 사정》 the conditions of a country; 《국내 정세》 the state of affairs in a nation. ¶ ~을 시찰하다 inspect the actual condition of a country / ~에 밝다〔어둡다〕「be well versed in 〔be ignorant of〕 the state of affairs of a country / 일본 ~에 어둡다〔밝다〕 be ignorant of 〔well informed of〕 Japanese affairs / 그것은 한국의 ~에 안맞는다 It does not fit in with the actual situation in Korea.

**국정감사**(國政監査) parliamentary inspection of the 「administration 〔government offices〕. ¶ ~를 실시하다 inspect the government offices; conduct inspection of the government offices. ◉ ~권 authority to inspect the government offices. ~반 a parliamentary team for inspection of the administration affairs.

**국제**(國際) [형용사적] international 《relationship》. ¶ ~간의 분규 international complications 〔disputes〕 / ~간의 정보 유통 transborder date flow / ~적으로 internationally; universally / ~적 견지 an international point of view / ~적인 문제 an international problem / ~적인 명성을 얻다 win an international reputation / ~ 관리하에 두다 place 《a mandatory state》 under international control 〔authority〕 / 이 사건은 ~적 관점에서 볼 필요가 있다 We have to look at this incident from an international point of view. / 그녀는 ~적으로 유명한 여배우다 She is an internationally famous actress.
◉ ~가격 an international price. ~감각: ~감각이 풍부한 사람 an internationally-minded man / ~감각을 몸에 익히다 acquire an international way of thinking. ~감시단 the International Observer Group. ~ 개발협회 the International Development Association (생략 IDA). ~견본시 an international trade fair. ~ 결제은행 the Bank of International Settlement (생략 B.I.S.). ~결혼 an international marriage; a mixed marriage. ~경기 international game 〔match, competition〕: ~ 경기단체 총연합 the General Association of International Sports Federations (생략 GAISF). ~경쟁력 international competitiveness. ~경제 international economy. ~공무원 an international civil servant. ~공법 public international law. ~공산당 the Comintern; the Communist International. ~공항 an international airport: 김포 ~공항 Kimp'o International Airport. ~관계 international relations. ~관리 international control 〔trusteeship〕. ~관용(慣用) (an) international usage. ~관행(慣行) an international practice. ~교섭 international negotiation. ~금리 international interest rates. ~ 금융공사 the International Finance Corporation (생략 IFC). ~기구 international organization 〔body〕. ~ 기념물 유적 회의 the International Council on Monuments and Sites (생략 ICOMOS). ~기능올림픽 대회 the International Vocational Training Competition. ~ 난민기구 the International Refugee Organization (생략 IRO). ~ 노동기구 the International Labor Organization (생략 ILO). ~ 노동회의 the International Labor Conference. ~농업 개발기금 the International Fund for Agricultural Development (생략 IFAD). ~단체 an international organization. ~도시 a cosmopolitan city. ~무대 international stage. ~무역 international trade. ~문제 an international problem 〔issue〕; a diplomatic issue. ~ 문화협회 the International Cultural Society (of Korea). ~민간항공 international civil aviation: ~ 민간항공 협정 the International Civil Aviation Agreement 〔Convention〕 / ~ 민간항공 기구 the International Civil Aviation Organization. ~박람회 a world's fair. ~방송 international broadcasting. ~법 inter-

national law. ～부흥 개발은행 the International Bank for Reconstruction and Development (생략 IBRD). ～분쟁 international disputes; an international conflict. ～사법(私法) private international law. ～ 사법재판소 the International Court of Justice(생략 ICJ). ～사회 the community of nations; international society: ～사회의 냉엄한 현실 the grim reality of international society. ～ 상품협정 the International Commodity Agreement. ～ 석유자본 the oil majors. ～선 《항공로》 an international air route. ～시장 an international market. ～신기록 a new international record. ～ 아동의 해 the International Year of the Child (생략 IYC). ～어 an international 〔a world, a universal〕 language; Esperanto. ～언론인 협회 the International Press Institute (생략 IPI). ～연맹 the League of Nations. ～연합 the United Nations (생략 UN): ～연합 식량 농업 기구 the International Food and Agriculture Organization. ～ 원자력기구 the International Atomic Energy Agency (생략 IAEA). ～ 의회연맹 the Inter-Parliamentary Union (생략 IPU). ～인(人) a cosmopolitan; a citizen of the world. ～ 인권연맹 the International League for Human Rights (생략 ILHR). ～인도주의법 the International Humanitarian Law. ～ 자연보호 연합 The World Conservation Union. ～저작권 international copyright. ～적십자 the International Red Cross (생략 IRC). ～ 전기통신 연합 the International Telecommunication Union (생략 ITU). ～전화 an international 〔overseas〕 (phone) call. ～정세 the international 〔world〕 situation. ～정치 international politics. ～조약 an international treaty. ～주의 internationalism. ～ 중소기업 연합회의 the International Conference on Small & Medium Enterprises. ～ 지구관측년 the International Geophysical Year (생략 IGY). ～차관〔투자〕 international loans 〔investment〕. ～친선 《promote》 international goodwill. ～통화기금 the International Monetary Fund (생략 I.M.F.). ～펜클럽 the International Association of PEN (Poets, Playwrights, Editors, Essayists & Novelist). ～ 표준 간행물 일련번호 the International Standard Serial Number (생략 ISSN). ～ 표준 도서번호 the International Standard Book Number (생략 ISBN). ～ 표준화 기구 the International Standards Organization. ～하천 an international river. ～ 항공운송 협회 the International Air Transportation Association (생략 IATA). ～ 해사기구 the International Maritime Organization (생략 IMO). ～ 해사위성 지구국 an international marine satellite earth station. ～해사위성 지방국 a regional satellite station for international onsea affairs. ～협력 international cooperation: 한국 ～협력단 the Korea International Cooperation Agency (생략 KOICA). ～협정 an international agreement; an accord. ～ 형사경찰 기구 the International Criminal Police Organization (생략 ICPO); Interpol. ～회의 an international conference: ～회의장 an international conference hall.

**국제수지**(國際收支) international balance of payments; the balance of international payments 〔accounts〕. ¶～ 흑자국 a country with a favorable balance of international payments / ～적자국 a country with international payments deficit / ～를 개선하다 improve 《*its*》 balance of payments / ～의 불균형을 시정하다 correct the imbalance of international payments / 일본의 ～는 내내 흑자가 계속되고 있다 Japan's balance of payments has long been in the black.

**국제화**(國際化) internationalization. ～하다 internationalize; become 〔go〕 international. ¶～시대 an era of internationalization / 서울은 ～되고 있다 Seoul is going international. / 그 문제는 ～될 염려가 있다 The issue is likely to become international.

**국지**(一紙) shavings (of paper); edge scraps of cut paper.

**국지**(局地) a locality; a local 〔limited〕 area 〔region〕. ¶～적인 local; regional / ～적으로 locally; regionally / ～화하다 localize / 그 호우는 ～적인 것이었다 The heavy rain was localized. / ～적인 호우가 있었다 We had much rain regionally. ◉ ～전쟁 localized 〔limited〕 warfare; a local war.

**국창**(國唱) the national singer; the best *p'ansori* singer in Korea.

**국채**(國債) 《부채》 a national debt; 《공채》 a public loan; 《증권》 national bonds; government bonds 《미》 〔securities 《영》〕. ¶내〔외〕～ a domestic 〔foreign〕 loan / 중기 ～ 펀드 medium-term national bond investment trust / ～를 모집하다 float 〔raise〕 a national loan《of 50 billion won》/ ～를 상환하다 redeem 〔sink〕 a national loan / ～를 발행하다 issue a national loan. ◉ ～발행고 the amount of government bond issue. ～상환기금 a sinking fund; the consolidated fund 《영》.

**국책**(國策) a national 〔state, government〕 policy. ¶ ～에 따라 in line with the national policy; along the line of national policy / ～을 수립〔수행〕하다 fix 〔carry out〕 the national policy / 수출은 ～으로 장려된다 Exports are being encouraged as a matter of national policy. ◉ ～은행 a government=run bank. ～회사 a national policy concern 〔company〕.

**국체**(國體) ①《국가 형태》 the structure of a state; the national polity《of a country》. ¶ ～를 유지하다 retain the fundamental character of the state. ②《전국 체육대회》 the National Athletic Meet.

**국치**(國恥) a national disgrace 〔dishonor, humiliation〕; a disgrace to the nation. ¶ ～를 초래하다《일이》 bring disgrace upon *one's* country / 그것은 한국의 ～이다 It is a matter of national humiliation for Korea. *or* It is a disgrace to Korea. ◉ ～일 National Humiliation Day.

**국태민안**(國泰民安) the prosperity and welfare of a nation. ～하다 enjoy national prosperity and welfare.

**국토**(國土) a country; 《영토》 a territory; a realm; a domain. ¶ 인구가 많고 비좁은 ～ a small, overpopulated country / ～를 개발하다 develop the national land / ～의 협소함을 느끼다 feel confined within *one's* small 〔narrow〕 country / 한국은 좁은 ～에 비해 인구가 너무 많다 Korea has too many people for its limited land space.
◉ ～개발 national land development: ～개발 계획 a program for land development; a national land development program. ～방위 national defense: ～방위 계획 a national defense program. ～보전 maintenance of the territorial integrity. ～분단 territorial division. ～ 이용관리법 the National Territory Utilization and Management Act; the National Land Utility Control Act. ～ 정보센터 the National Land and Information Center.

**국판**(菊判) 〖인쇄〗《책의》 a small 〔demy〕 octavo (22×15cm); 《미》 a medium octavo; 《종이의》 a sheet of printing paper (93×63cm). ¶ ～ 300페이지의 책 a 300-page octavo volume.

**국풍**(國風) national manners and customs.

**국학**(國學) (study of) the national literature 〔classics〕; Korean classical literature. ◉ ～자 a classical scholar of the country; a scholar of Korean literature.

**국한**(局限) localization; limitation. ～하다 localize; limit; set limits to. ¶ …에 ～되다 be limited 〔restricted〕 to... / 전염병은 그 지역에 ～되어 있다 The epidemic is limited to that area.

**국한문**(國漢文) Korean and Chinese characters. ¶ ～을 혼용하다 use Korean (alphabets) together with Chinese characters; mix Korean and Chineses characters in use. ◉ ～체 a mixed style of writing Korean and Chinese characters.

**국헌**(國憲) the national constitution; the laws of a country. ¶ ～을 준수하다 respect the national constitution.

**국호**(國號) the name of a country.

**국혼**(國婚) a royal marriage.

**국화**(國花) the national flower. ¶ 무궁화는 한국의 ～이다 The rose of Sharon is regarded as the national flower of Korea.

**국화**(菊花) a chrysanthemum (flower); a mum 《미구어》. ◉ ～잠 an ornamental hairpin shaped like a chrysanthemum.

**국회**(國會) 《한국·프랑스의》 the National Assembly; 《일본·스웨덴의》 the (National) Diet; 《영국의》 Parliament; 《미국의》 Congress (★ 영·미가 다 무관사). ¶ 정기〔특별, 임시〕～ an ordinary 〔a special, an extraordinary〕 session of the National Assembly / 제 10차 정기 ～ the 10th regular 〔ordinary〕 session of the National Assembly / 우루과이 라운드의 ～ 승인 the National Assembly approval of the Uruguay Round / ～의 국정 감사 a parliamentary inspection of the administration 〔government offices〕 / ～회기 중 during the session of the National Assembly; while the House of Representatives is in session / ～를 소집〔해산〕하다 convene 〔dissolve〕 the National Assembly / 내일 ～가 열린다 The House meets tomorrow. / ～가 개회〔폐회〕 중이다 The National Assembly is now in 〔out of〕 session.

◉ ~도서관 the National Assembly Library. ~법 the National Assembly law. ~본회의 the Assembly plenary session. ~(부)의장 《일반적》 the (Vice-)Chairman; 《하원의》 the (Vice=) speaker; the (Vice-)President; 《한국의》 the National Assembly (Vice=) Speaker. ~사무처 the Secretariat of the National Assembly. ~ 사무총장 the Secretary-General of the National Assembly. ~ 상임위원회 the National Assembly Standing Committee. ~ 예산결산 위원회 the National Assembly Budget Settlement Committee. ~ 운영위원회 the National Assembly Steering Committee. ~윤리위원회 the National Assembly Ethics Committee. ~의사당 the National Assembly Building (한국의); the Capitol 《미》; the House of Parliament 《영》. ~의사록 the National Assembly record; Hansard 《영》. ~의원 a member of the National Assembly; an assemblyman; a Diet member; a Dietman; a Congressman 《미》; a Member of Parliament (생략 an MP) 《영》: ~의원 선거구 a parliamentary electoral district / ~의원 입후보자 a candidate running for an parliamentary seat. ~ 임시회기 an extraordinary session of the National Assembly. ~ 전문위원 a specialist. ~청원 a petition to the National Assembly.

**군**(君) ① 《호칭》 Mr.; Mister (★ 쓸 때에는 반드시 약어인 Mr.). ¶ 김 군 (Mr.) Kim (★ 보통 「…군」으로 부르는 상대에게는 Mr.를 붙이지 않음. 또 성(姓)이 아니라 「복남군」처럼 이름을 부를 때는, Mr. Boknam이라 하지 않고 그냥 Boknam이라고 함). ② 〚역사〛 Lord; Sir. ¶ 연산군 Lord Yŏnsan. ③ 《자네》 You. ¶ 그것은 군의 잘못이다 You are to blame for that.

**군**(軍) 《군부》 military authorities; the military; 《군대》 armed forces; an army; a force; troops. ¶ 군 본연의 임무 the military's proper duty / 정규〔상비(常備), 예비〕군 a regular 〔standing, reserve〕 army / 미 제8군 the Eighth United States Army / 제1군 the first (R.O.K.) Army / 진주〔점령〕군 the occupational army 〔forces〕 / 군에 입대하다 enter 〔enlist in, join〕 the army / 군에 복무하다 serve in the army / 군에서 제대하다 leave 〔be discharged from〕 military duty.

**군**(郡) a *gun;* a county; a district. ¶ 양주군 Yangju-gun; Yangju County.

**군** 《가외의·객쩍은》 extra; needless; unnecessary; uncalled-for. ¶ 군 비용 extra 〔unnecessary〕 expenses / 군 걸음 needless steps / 군 걱정 needless worry / 군 식구 a hanger-on; a dependent; a sponge / 군걱정을 하다 worry (*oneself*) unnecessarily 〔needlessly〕 / 군소리를 하다 say unnecessary things; make an uncalled-for remark / 군짓을 하다 do unwanted things; gild refined gold.

**군가**(軍歌) a war song; a military 〔martial, marching〕 song.

**군거**(群居) gregarious life. ~하다 live gregariously 〔together, in flocks〕.
◉ ~동물 a gregarious animal. ~본능 a herd 〔gregarious〕 instinct. ~성 gregariousness; sociability.

**군것** superfluous 〔unnecessary〕 things.

**군것질** buying and eating of sweets 〔eatables〕 between meals. ~하다 spend *one's* pocket money on sweets 〔candy〕.

**군견**(軍犬) ⇨ 군용견.

**군경**(軍警) the military and the police.
◉ ~유가족 the surviving 〔bereaved〕 families of the dead soldiers and policemen.

**군계**(群鷄) a flock of chickens. ◉ ~일학 the only figure among ciphers; a Triton among the minnows.

**군고구마** roast 〔baked〕 sweet potatoes.
◉ ~장수 a roast sweet potato seller 〔vendor〕.

**군공**(軍功) = 전공(戰功).

**군관구**(軍管區) a military district. ¶ 6~사령부 the 6th Military District Command.

**군국**(君國) a monarchy; *one's* sovereign and country.

**군국**(軍國) a militant nation. ◉ ~주의 militarism: ~주의적 militaristic / ~주의자 a militarist.

**군기**(軍紀) military discipline; troop morals. ¶ ~를 지키다〔어기다〕 maintain 〔offend against〕 military discipline / ~가 문란하다 The military discipline is slack 〔lax〕. / ~가 문란하면 싸우기도 전에 패배한다 If the soldiers' morals were corrupted, they would be defeated before the battle.

**군기**(軍旗) the (regimental) colors; a battle flag; a standard; an ensign.
◉ ~호위병 a color party 〔guard〕.

**군기**(軍機) a military secret. ⇨ 군사기밀. ¶ ~상 for reasons of military secrecy / ~를 누설하다 divulge 〔disclose, let out〕 a military secret.
◉ ~누설 disclosure 〔leakage〕 of military secrets: ~ 누설사건 a military secret betrayal case / 의원들은 어제 최

근의 ~ 누설사건에 대하여 국방부를 격렬히 비난〔공격〕하였다 Lawmakers lashed out at the Defense Ministry yesterday over the recent leakage of classified military information.

**군기지**(軍基地) ⇨ 군사기지.

**군납**(軍納) delivery 〔supply〕 of goods to the military. ~하다 provide 《goods, supplies》 for an army; purvey for an army. ¶ 고기를 ~하다 provide 〔supply〕 meat for an army. ◉ ~불(弗) Korean Post Exchange dollar (생략 KPX dollar). ~업자 《물품의》 a military goods supplier; a purveyor to an army; 《용역의》 service contractors for the military. ~품 supplies provided by a purveyor. ~회사 a military supply contract firm.

**군내** an unwanted 〔unpleasant〕 smell.

**군눈** eyes too curious 〔inquisitive〕 for their own good. ¶ ~ 뜨다 become conscious of undesirable way; stray from orthodoxy (into profligacy).

**군단**(軍團) 〖군사〗 an army corps; a corps. ¶ 제3~ the 3rd Corps. ◉ ~사령부 the corps headquarters. ~장 the commander of an army corps.

**군대**(軍隊) an army; troops; (armed) forces; the military [집합적].

> (용법) **army** 좁은 뜻으로는 육군을 가리키지만 넓은 뜻에서는 군대 전부를 뜻함. **troops** 군인 즉 병력에 중점을 두어 군대를 말할 때, **forces** 무력·병력을 수반한 군대의 뜻으로, **armed forces** 육·해·공군을 포함하는 한 나라 또는 수개국의 군대를 말할 때, **military** 앞에 the를 붙여 집합적인 뜻으로 「군대」, 「군부」를 뜻한다. 통상 복수취급.

¶ ~식으로 in military fashion 〔way〕 / ~에 들어가다 join 〔enter, enlist in〕 the army / 그는 ~에 있다 He serves in the army. / 폭동을 진압하기 위해 ~가 파견되었다 Troops 〔Armed forces〕 were sent to control the riot. ◉ ~생활 an army 〔a military〕 life. ~행진곡 a military march.

**군더더기** 《물건》 an excrescence; a superfluous 〔an unnecessary〕 thing; 《사람》 an unwanted follower.

**군던지럽다** (be) foul; nasty; low; mean.

**군데** 《곳》 a place; a spot; a point; a part. ¶ 한~ 오래 머물다 stay long in a place / 사람을 여러 ~ 보내다 send people to several places / 아직도 얼굴에 몇 ~ 흉터가 남아 있다 There still remain a few scars on the face.

**군데군데** in places; in some 〔several〕 places; here and there; at places; sporadically. ¶ ~ 눈이 쌓이다 be covered with snow here and there / 옷이 ~ 떨어지다 *one's* clothes are threadbare in places / 장지문에 ~ 구멍이 나 있다 There are several holes in the paper sliding door.

**군도**(軍刀) a saber; a (military) sword.

**군도**(群島) a group of islands; an archipelago (*pl.* ~(e)s). ¶ 말레이 ~ the Malay Archipelago / 하와이 ~ the Hawaiian Islands.

**군도**(群盜) a group 〔gang〕 of robbers.

**군돈** money spent unnecessarily; extra expenses. ¶ ~을 쓰다 waste money 《on》.

**군락**(群落) 《많은 촌락》 a group of villages; 〖식물〗 a community; a colony.

**군란**(軍亂) an army insurrection 〔rebellion, revolt〕.

**군략**(軍略) 《전략》 (a) strategy; a stratagem; 《전술》 tactics. ¶ ~을 쓰다 resort to a stratagem. ◉ ~가 a strategist. ~전 a general's battle.

**군량**(軍糧) military supplies 〔provisions〕; rations. ¶ ~이 떨어지다 be short of provisions.

**군령**(軍令) a military command 〔order〕.

**군림**(君臨) reigning. ~하다 reign 〔dominate, rule〕 《over a country》; lord it over. ¶ 재계에 ~하다 dominate 〔be dominant in〕 the financial world / 영국에서는 왕이 ~하나 통치하지는 않는다 In Great Britain the sovereign reigns, but does not rule.

**군마**(軍馬) ① 《군사와 말》 the soldiers and horses. ② 《말》 a warhorse; a military horse; a steed; a charger (장교의).

**군만두**(一饅頭) a toasted bun 〔dumpling〕.

**군말** an unnecessary 〔uncalled-for〕 remark; redundant 〔superfluous〕 words. ~하다 say unnecessary things; make an uncalled-for remark.

**군매점**(軍賣店) 《미육군》 a post exchange; a PX; a canteen.

**군명**(君命) the orders of *one's* lord; the royal command. ¶ ~을 받들어 in obedience to the royal command.

**군모**(軍帽) a military cap; 《육군모》 an army cap; 《해군모》 a navy cap.

**군목**(軍牧) a chaplain.

**군무**(軍務) military affairs; military service 〔duty〕. ¶ ~에 종사하다 serve in the army; perform military duties;

do military service. ◉ ~원 a civilian employee; a civilian attached to the army; a civil service employee. ~이탈 desertion from military service.

**군문**(軍門) a military camp. ¶ ~에 들어가다 enlist in the army; enter the service; join the colors [army].

**군민**(軍民) the military and the people; the fighting services and the civilians.

**군민**(郡民) inhabitants of a county; ⌈county people.

**군밤** a roast(ed) chestnut. ¶ ~ 둥우리 같다 *one's* attire looks baggy [sloppy].

**군밥** 《군식구의》 food for uninvited guests; 《남은 밥》 extra cooked rice; cooked rice left over.

**군번**(軍番) 〖군사〗 serial number (생략 S.N.); service number; 《인식표》 an identification [a dog 《속어》] tag.

**군벌**(軍閥) a military clique [caste]. ◉ ~정치 military dictatorship; militaristic government; warlordism.

**군법**(軍法) martial law; military law. ◉ ~회의 a court-martial: ~회의에 회부하다 try 《a soldier》 by court-martial; court-martial 《a soldier》 / ~회의를 소집하다 call a court-martial.

**군법무관**(軍法務官) a military judicial ⌊officer.

**군법정**(軍法廷) a military court.

**군복**(軍服) a service [military, naval] uniform. ¶ ~ 차림의 강도 a robber in military uniform / ~ 차림의 장교 an officer in uniform; a uniformed officer / ~을 입고 있다 be in (military) uniform / ~을 벗다 leave the army; get out of uniform.

**군부**(君父) *one's* lord [king].

**군부**(軍部) military authorities; the military [총칭]. ¶ ~의 횡포 militarists' despotism / 최근에 그 나라에서는 ~ 세력이 대두하고 있다 Recently the military authorities have been gaining power in that country.

**군불** a fire for the purpose of heating the floors. ¶ ~ 때다 heat the floor; burn firewood to heat *ondol.*

**군비**(軍備) armaments; military [war] preparedness. ¶ ~를 확장[축소, 강화, 제한]하다 increase [reduce, reinforce, limit] armaments / ~를 갖추고 있다 be prepared for war. ◉ ~경쟁 an armaments [arms] race. ~제한 limitation of armaments; arms control. ~증강 military [arms] buildup. ~철폐 disarmament; demilitarization. ~축소 disarmament; reduction of armaments; arms reduction: ~ 축소 회의 a disarmament [an arms reduction] conference. ~확장 expansion of armaments; military expansion.

**군비**(軍費) war expenditure [funds].

**군사**(軍士) soldiers; the men; the ranks; troops. ¶ ~를 모으다 raise [recruit] troops.

**군사**(軍使) a military envoy.

**군사**(軍事) military affairs. ¶ ~상의 military; 《작전상의》 strategic / 준(準)~적인 paramilitary / 이 섬은 국가 방위를 위해 ~상 중요하다 This island is of strategic importance for national defense. / 그들은 ~ 목적으로 그 부지를 이용하고 있다 They use the site for military purposes.

◉ ~개입 (an) armed intervention; (a) military intervention: 다른 나라에 ~ 개입하다 intervene militarily in another country. ~고문 a military adviser: ~ 고문단 the Military Advisory Group (생략 MAG). ~교류 military exchange. ~교육 military education [instruction]. ~ 기동훈련 military maneuvers. ~기밀 military secrets. ~기지 a (military) base; an army [a naval, an air] base. ~동맹 a military alliance. ~력 military strength [might]; armed strength; armaments: ~력 증강 military buildup; buildup in military strength. ~분계선 the Military Demarcation Line (생략 MDL). ~비 war expenditure [funds]: 막대한 ~비 a large expenditure of money on armaments. ~시설 military installations [establishments]. ~예산 an arms budget. ~용어 a military term: ~ 용어사전 a dictionary of military terms. ~우편 military mail. ~원조 military aid. ~위성 a military satellite. ~작전 military operations. ~재판 a military trial [court, tribunal]; a courtmartial (군법회의). ~전략 military strategy. ~정권 a military regime [government]. ~정보 military information. ~ 정전위원회 the Military Armistice Commission (생략 MAC). ~첩보 military intelligence. ~평론가 a military commentator. ~학 military science. ~행동 military action [operations, activities]; hostilities: ~ 행동을 개시하다 open hostilities 《against》; undertake armed operations. ~행정 military administration. ~협정 a military pact. ~훈련 military training [drill].

**군사람** an extra [unnecessary] person

〔hand〕; a dispensable employee.

**군사령관**(軍司令官) an army commander; a commander in chief.

**군사령부**(軍司令部) the military 〔army〕 headquarters.

**군사설**(—辭說) redundant words; a long and uncalled-for lecture.

**군살** 《군더더기살》 superfluous 〔extra〕 flesh; flab; 《지방》 fat. ¶ ~이 붙다 put on 〔pick up〕 extra flesh / ~을 빼다 get rid of flab 〔extra flesh〕; wear 〔work〕 off surplus fat (운동 따위로) / 매일 운동하면 허리의 ~이 빠질 것이다 Daily exercise will get rid of the flab around your waist.

**군상**(群像) a large group of people; 〖조각〗 a sculptured group. ¶ 실업자의 ~ a crowd of jobless people / 라오콘 ~ 《미술》 the Laocoön group.

**군색**(窘塞) 《구차함》 poverty; destitution; indigence; 《곤경》 straits; a fix. ~스럽다, ~하다 (be) indigent; poor; destitute; be in a fix. ¶ ~한 변명 a lame 〔poor, clumsy〕 excuse / 살림이 ~하다 make a poor living; be badly off / ~한 집안에 태어나다 be born poor; be born in a poor family.

**군생**(群生) ~하다 grow gregariously; grow in colonies 〔crowds〕. ◉ ~식물 gregarious plants.

**군서**(群書) various books; many books.

**군서**(群棲) 〖생물〗 gregariousness. ~하다 live gregariously; live in herds (소·돼지 따위가); live in flocks (새·양이); hive (벌이). ◉ ~동물 gregarious 〔social〕 animals.

**군세**(軍勢) 《병력수》 the number of soldiers; 《형세》 the military situation 《of a country》; 《군사력》 military strength 〔power〕; 《군대》 (military) forces; troops; an army.

**군소**(群小) ¶ ~의 minor; lesser; petty; insignificant. ◉ ~국가 minor 〔smaller〕 nations. ~작가 minor writers. ~정당 petty 〔minor〕 political parties.

**군소리** ① 《헛소리》 talking in *one's* sleep 〔delirium〕. ~하다 talk in *one's* sleep 〔delirium〕; utter meaningless words. ② 《쓸데없는 소리》 empty 〔idle, silly〕 talk; nonsense; rubbish. ~하다 talk nonsense 〔rubbish〕.

**군속**(軍屬) 〖군사〗 a civilian employee of the army 〔navy〕; a civilian attached to the army 〔navy〕; a civilian war worker. ⇨ 군무원.

**군손질** unnecessary handling 〔care〕.

**군수**(軍需) military demands 〔supplies〕; 《군수품》 munitions (특히, 무기·탄약). ◉ ~경기 a munitions 〔war〕 boom. ~공업〔산업〕 war industries; the munitions industry. ~공장 a munitions 〔an arms〕 factory 〔works, plant〕; a war plant. ~ 보급기지 a depot; a railhead; a supply complex. ~품 war supplies; munitions. ~회사 a munitions company.

**군수**(郡守) the magistrate of a county 〔*gun*〕; a county chief.

**군시럽다** feel itchy 〔creepy, crawly〕.

**군식구**(—食口) a hanger-on (*pl.* hangers-on); a sponge(r); a parasite; 《미구어》 a freeloader. ¶ 나는 숙모댁에 ~로 있다 I live at my aunt's without paying board or rent.

**군신**(君臣) sovereign and subject.

**군신**(軍神) the god of war; 〖로神〗 Mars; 〖그神〗 Ares.

**군신**(群臣) all vassals 〔retainers〕.

**군실거리다** itch; feel itchy 〔creepy〕.

**군실군실** all itchy; all crawly.

**군악**(軍樂) 《play》 military music. ◉ ~대 a military band: ~대원 a bandsman / ~대장 a band master / 해군 ~대 a naval band.

**군역**(軍役) 《군복무》 military service.

**군영**(軍營) a military camp; an encampment.

**군용**(軍用) ¶ ~의 military; for military use 〔purpose〕; war (전쟁용의). ◉ ~견 an army 〔a military〕 dog. ~기 a military plane; a warplane; combat aircraft [총칭]. ~도로 a military road. ~비둘기 a carrier pigeon in military service. ~열차 a troop train. ~전화 (a) military telephone. ~지 land for military use. ~지도 a military map. ~철도 a military 〔strategic〕 railroad. ~품 military stores.

**군용**(軍容) 《진용》 a formation of troops; 《군장》 military equipment. ¶ ~을 정비하다 marshal troops for a battle; complete military preparations.

**군웅**(群雄) rival leaders 〔barons〕. ¶ 그 시대에는 ~이 할거하고 있었다 In those days there were a number of local military leaders competing with each other for power. ◉ ~할거 rivalry of local barons: ~할거 시대 the age of rival warlords 〔chiefs〕.

**군원**(軍援) military aid 〔assistance〕. ◉~이관 transfer of a military assistance program.

**군율**(軍律) 《군법》 the articles of war; martial law; 《군기》 military discipline. ¶ ~을 지키다 observe military discipline / ~이 엄하다 Military discipline is strictly enforced.

**군은**(君恩) royal favor 〔benevolence〕.

**군음식**(一飮食) a between-meals snack; a snack (between meals). ¶ ~을 먹다 have a snack.

**군의**(軍醫) 《군의관》 an army 〔a naval, a flight〕 surgeon. ◉ ~장교 a medical officer. ~학교 a military 〔naval〕 medical college.

**군인**(軍人) a serviceperson; 《남자》 a serviceman; 《여자》 a servicewoman; a military man; a soldier (육군); a marine (해병); a sailor (해군); an airman (공군); an officer (장교); a member of the armed forces [총칭]. ¶ 직업~ a professional soldier; a career officer (장교) / 재향〔퇴역〕~ a veteran 《미》; ex-serviceman 《영》 / ~다운 soldierly; soldierlike / 그의 말투로 그가 ~ 출신이라는 것을 바로 알았다 I immediately recognized him to be a veteran by his speech. ◉ ~사회 military circles. ~생활 a military life. ~연금 a soldier's pension. ~정신 the military spirit. ~출신 an ex-soldier.

**군인원**(一人員) superfluous personnel 〔staff〕; a supernumerary (member). ¶ ~이 많다 be overmanned; be overstaffed / ~을 정리하다 dismiss 〔weed out〕 supernumeraries.

**군일** unnecessary 〔needless〕 work. ¶ ~을 하다 do unnecessary work; work uselessly 〔for nothing〕.

**군입정질** eating 〔"stuffing *oneself*"〕 between meals; snacking. ~하다 eat 〔snack〕 between meals.

**군자**(君子) a (true) gentleman; a man of virtue 〔noble character〕. ¶ ~의 덕 true gentlemanship / ~의 나라 a land of gentlemen / ~연하다 assume a virtuous air.

**군자금**(軍資金) war funds; a war chest; campaign funds (선거 자금 따위). ¶ ~을 대다 supply the sinews of war / 선거전의 ~이 부족하다 be short of election-campaign funds.

**군자란**(君子蘭) 〖식물〗 a kaffir lily.

**군장**(軍葬) a military funeral. ¶ ~으로 하다 bury 《a soldier》 with military honors.

**군장**(軍裝) 《평시의》 military uniform; 《전시의》 combat uniform; a war outfit; battle dress 〔kit〕. ¶ 완전 ~으로 in full kit 〔gear〕.

**군적**(軍籍) 《병적》 the army 〔navy〕 register. ¶ ~에 들다 enlist in the army 〔navy〕 / ~에 몸을 두다 serve in the army 〔navy〕; be on the military list.

**군정**(軍政) military administration 〔government〕. ¶ ~을 펴다 establish military administration; impose military rule 《on》 / ~하에 두다 put under a military administration. ◉ ~청 the Military Government Office.

**군제**(軍制) military organization; a military system. ¶ ~ 개편 military reorganization.

**군졸**(軍卒) a (common) soldier; a private; troops.

**군주**(君主) a monarch; a sovereign; a king; a ruler. ◉ ~국 a monarchy: 입헌~국 a constitutional monarchy / 전제~국 a despotic monarchy / 절대~국 an absolute monarchy. ~정체 monarchy; monarchism. ~정치 monarchy. ~제 monarchism.

**군중**(群衆) a crowd 〔throng〕 (of people); the multitude; a mob (무질서한); the masses. ¶ ~을 헤치고 나아가다 push (*one's* way) through the crowd / ~ 속에 뒤섞이다 mingle with the crowd / 사고 현장에 ~이 모여 들었다 A throng gathered at the site of the accidents. / ~은 조금씩 흩어지고 있었다 The crowd was gradually dispersing. / 경찰은 ~을 해산시켰다 The police dispersed the crowd. ◉ ~공포증 〖심리〗 ochlophobia. ~심리 mob 〔mass, crowd〕 psychology; the group 〔crowd〕 mind.

> 참고 군중의 수: 군중을 하나의 집합체로 보면 단수 취급, 군중 속의 한 사람 한 사람에 중점을 두고 말을 하게 되면 복수 취급이 된다. crowd와 throng은 서로 같은 뜻이지만, throng은 서로 밀치고 떠밀려서 이동하는 무리라는 뜻이 내포되는 경우가 있다.

**군집**(群集) a large group of people; a mob; 〖생태〗 a 〔an ecological〕 community. ~하다 crowd together; throng; gather; swarm. ◉ ~본능 the herd instinct.

**군짓** doing unnecessary 〔useless〕 things; things done unnecessarily 〔in vain〕. ~하다 do unnecessary 〔useless〕 things. ¶ 지금 다시 가는 것은 ~이다 It is useless to go again now.

**군청**(郡廳) a *gun* 〔county〕 office.

**군청(색)**(群青(色)) ultramarine (blue); sea blue.

**군체**(群體) 〖생물〗 a colony; a stock. ¶

개미〔산호(珊瑚)〕 ~ a colony of 「ants 〔corals〕.

**군축**(軍縮) disarmament; armament 〔arms〕 reduction; reduction of armaments. ~하다 reduce armaments. ¶ 점진적 ~ progressive arms reduction / 완전~ total 〔complete〕 disarmament / 우리는 ~협정에 등을 돌릴 수 없다 We cannot turn our back on a disarmament agreement.
◉ ~회담 disarmament 〔arms reduction〕 talks. ~회의 a disarmament conference: 양국 정상이 ~회의 석상에 앉았다 The leaders of both countries sat down at the disarmament conference table.

**군침** an excessive flow of saliva; slaver. ¶ ~이 도는 mouth-watering 《steak, offers》; appetizing 《dish》; tempting 《offer》; attractive 《woman》 / ~을 삼키다 swallow *one's* saliva / ~을 흘리다 slaver; drivel; let saliva dribble from *one's* mouth; slobber (at the mouth); 《욕심내다》 covet 〔crave〕 《for, after》; slaver 《after》 / ~이 돌게〔흐르게〕 하다 make 《*a person's*》 mouth water / 그 요리를 보자 나는 ~을 삼켰다 The sight of the dish made my mouth water. / 보기만 해도 ~이 도는 물건이다 Only a momentary sight of the article will make you crave for it. / 그녀는 ~을 흘릴 정도로 그 그림을 탐내고 있다 She is slavering after the picture.

**군턱** a double chin; a jowl. ¶ ~이 있는 double-chinned.

**군티** a slight flaw 〔defect〕.

**군표**(軍票) military scrip; occupation currency. ◉ 미~ an American MPC. [<*M*ilitary *P*ayment *C*ertificate]

**군함**(軍艦) a warship; a man-of-war (*pl.* men-); a battleship. ¶ ~ 승무원 the crew of a warship / ~을 건조〔폐기〕하다 construct 〔scrap〕 a warship / ~을 파견하다 dispatch a warship.
◉ ~기 a naval ensign.

**군항**(軍港) a naval port 〔station〕.
◉ ~사령부 the headquarters of a naval station.

**군호**(軍號) a (military) password; a watchword; a countersign. ¶ ~를 대다 give the password 〔countersign〕.

**군화**(軍靴) military 〔GI〕 shoes; combat 〔military〕 boots.

**굳건하다** (be) strong and steady; solid; firm; steadfast; secure. ¶ 굳건히 strongly; firmly; solidly / 굳건한 결심 a firm resolution / 굳건한 기초 a solid foundation / 굳건한 사람 a firm character / 굳건한 전진의 결의 *one's* strong resolve to continue the march forward / 토대가 ~ The foundation is solid 〔secure〕. / 그는 신념이 ~ He is steadfast in his faith.

**굳기** hardness; solidity; firmness. ¶ 그녀의 결심은 ~가 보통이 아니다 Her determination is unusually strong.

**굳다**[1] ① 《물체가》 (be) hard; solid; firm (지반이). ¶ 굳은 연필 a hard pencil / 굳은 땅 hard 〔tough〕 soil / 굳은 지반 위에 서다 stand on firm ground.
② 《정신·태도가》 (be) firm; strong; adamant; unyielding; steadfast; unshakable. ¶ 굳은 결심 a firm resolution 〔resolve〕 / 굳은 신념 strong conviction / 굳은 의지 strong 〔iron〕 will / 굳은 맹세 a solemn oath / 굳은 결속 strong solidarity / 굳게 결심하다 be firmly resolved / 굳게 믿다 firmly believe 《that...》; have a firm belief 《in》 / 굳게 약속하다 give 《*a person*》 a solemn promise / 굳은 악수를 교환하다 shake hands with a firm grip.
③ 《단단히 죄다》 (be) tight. ¶ 입을 굳게 다물다 shut *one's* mouth tight / 문은 굳게 닫혀 있었다 The door was shut tight.
④ 《경직하다》 (be) stiff; rigid. ¶ 굳은 표정 a stiff look / 뻣뻣하게 굳은 몸 a rigid body / 굳고 창백한 얼굴 a face rigid and pale / 그녀의 얼굴은 시무룩하게 굳어 있었다 Her face was set in a sulky look.

**굳다**[2] ① 《굳어지다》 harden; get 〔go, become〕 hard 〔firm, solid〕; stiffen; get 〔go, grow, become〕 stiff; set (유동체가); 《엉기다》 congeal; 《우유 따위가》 curdle; clot. ¶ 일을 해서 손이 굳다 *one's* hands harden 〔toughen〕 with work / 젤리가 굳었다 The jelly has set. / 비온 뒤엔 땅이 굳는다 The ground hardens after the rain. / 시멘트는〔진흙은〕 마르면 굳는다 Cement sets 〔Mud cakes〕 as it dries. / 석고는 빨리 굳는다 Plaster of Paris sets quickly. / 풀이 굳었다 The paste has become hard.
② 《몸이 긴장 등으로》 get nervous; freeze (up); become stiff 〔rigid〕. ¶ 무대에서 몸이 ~ get stage fright; freeze up on the platform / 그가 키스를 했을 때 그녀는 몸이 굳었다 She went rigid when he kissed her.

**굳세다** 《몸이》 (be) strong; firm; solid; steadfast; 《마음이》 (be) strong-minded; stouthearted. ¶ 굳세게 firmly;

solidly; strong-mindedly; stoutheartedly / 굳센 결심 a strong resolution / 굳센 마음 strong mind; a heart of adamant / 굳센 신념 a firm 〔strong〕 conviction / 굳센 저항 stubborn resistance / 굳세게 엄한 현실에 맞서다 face the grim reality of life with firm determination; meet bravely the grim reality of life / 마음이 굳세어 유혹에 넘어가지 않다 be adamant to temptation.

**굳어지다** get 〔become〕 hard; harden. ¶ 마침내 사임할 결심이 굳어졌다 My determination to quit the post finally hardened. / 여러 번 만남으로써 그들의 결혼 의사는 굳어졌다 Over several meetings, their wishes to marry each other become firm.

**굳은살** hardened skin; 《손·발의》 a callus; a corn (주로 발의). ¶ ~이 생기다 thicken into callus; get 〔become〕 callused / 손바닥에 ~이 박혔다 A callus has formed on my palm.

**굳이** strongly; firmly; solidly; decisively; 《완강히》 persistently; stubbornly. ¶ ~ 원하신다면 if you particularly wish it; if you insist (upon it) / ~ 사양하다 decline firmly / ~ 반대하다 oppose stubbornly / ~ 의견을 우기다 stick to *one's* opinion / 그는 사례를 ~ 받지 않았다 He would not accept the reward offered. / ~ 돌아가겠다면 말리지는 않겠다 If you insist on going home, I will not stop you.

**굳히기** 〖유도〗 a hold which renders 《*one's* opponent》 immobile on the floor. ¶ 무릎〔팔, 십자〕 ~ the knee 〔arm, cross〕 lock 〔hold〕.

**굳히다** ① 《부드러운 것을》 harden; make hard; 《응결시키다》 congeal; coagulate; solidify 《water into ice》. ¶ 가열하여 진흙을 ~ harden clay by heat / 치즈를 만들기 위해 우유를 ~ set milk for cheese / 젤리를 차게 해서 ~ set jelly by cooling it. ② 《강화하다》 strengthen; solidify; consolidate 《*one's* power》; (make) secure; cement. ¶ 결심을 ~ make a firm determination 〔resolve〕 / 신념을 ~ strengthen *one's* faith / 결속을 ~ strengthen the unity 《of the party》 / 논거(論據)를 ~ strengthen *one's* argument 《by adding more evidence》 / 우정을 ~ cement a friendship / 기반을 ~ consolidate the foundation 〔*one's* social standing〕 / 그녀는 작가로서의 지위를 굳혔다 She secured her position in the world of letters.

**굴** 〖조개류〗 an oyster. ¶ 생굴 a raw oyster / 깐 굴 shelled oysters / 굴튀김 fried oysters. ◉ 굴껍질 oyster shells. 굴양식 oyster farming 〔culture〕: 굴양식업자 an oyster culturist 〔farmer〕 / 굴양식장 an oyster bed 〔farm〕.

**굴**(窟) ① 《터널》 a tunnel. ¶ 굴을 파다 build 〔bore, dig, cut〕 a tunnel 《through》; tunnel 《a hill》 / 열차가 굴에 들어가다〔굴을 지나다〕 a train goes into 〔goes through〕 a tunnel. ② 《짐승의》 a hole; a burrow (토끼의); a lair; a den (야수의); an earth (여우의). ¶ 토끼가 굴을 파다 a rabbit digs a hole; a hare burrows 《into the ground》 / 굴에 숨다 run to earth; hide in a hole 〔burrow〕. ③ 《동굴》 a cave; a cavern (큰 것); an excavation (판 것). ¶ 굴 속에 사는 사람 a cave dweller / 굴에 살다 dwell in a cave. ④ 《소굴》 a den; a nest. ¶ 도둑굴 a den of thieves / 아편 굴 an opium den.

**굴갓** a hat of an office-holding Buddhist monk.

**굴검**(掘檢) an inquest of an exhumed corpse. ~하다 autopsy an exhumed corpse.

**굴곡**(屈曲) bending; winding; 《해안선 등의》 indentation. ~하다 (be) bent; winding; indented; zigzagging; crooked. ¶ ~이 많은 도로 a bendy road / 한국의 남해안은 ~이 심하다 The southern coast of Korea frequently runs in and out. / ~지역: 과속추월 금지 《게시》 Many curves: No speeding. No passing. ◉ ~부 a bend; a turn; an elbow; an elbow-shaped bend. ~작용 《관절 따위》 flection; flexion.

**굴광성**(屈光性) 〖식물〗 phototropism. ¶ ~의 phototropic.

**굴근**(屈筋) 〖해부〗 a flexor (muscle).

**굴기성**(屈氣性) 〖생물〗 aerotropism. ¶ ~의 aerotropic.

**굴다** 《행동하다》 act; behave 《toward *a person*》; conduct 〔bear, behave, carry〕 *oneself*. ¶ 고맙게 ~ act kindly 《toward *a person*》; treat 《*a person*》 kindly / 못살게〔심하게〕 ~ act harshly 《toward *a person*》; treat 《*a person*》 severely / 못견디게 ~ behave unbearably 《toward *a person*》 / 밉게 ~ behave most hatefully / 사나이답게 ~ act like a man; play the man / 신사답게 ~ behave *oneself* like a gentleman / 친절하게 ~ deal kindly toward 〔with〕 《others》 / 천연덕스럽게 ~ be *oneself;* behave naturally / 그 아이는 언제나 제 멋대로 군다 The child always has his own way. / 그는 상관한테 욕을 먹으면 하급자를 못살게 군다 When scolded by his senior, he works off his vexation on his juniors.

**굴다리**(窟—) an overpass; a bridge (over a roadway); a flyover 《영》; a crossover; a girder bridge.

**굴대** 《축》 an axis; an axle. ¶ 바퀴의 ~ a wheel axle.

**굴도리** 『건축』 a round 〔cylindrical〕 beam.

**굴때장군**(—將軍) a huge 〔burly〕 person with a dark complexion.

**굴똥** the axis of a spinning wheel.

**굴뚝** a chimney; a smokestack. ¶ 난로의 ~ a stovepipe / ~을 세 개 갖춘 기선 a three-funneled steamer 〔steamship〕 / ~ 청소부 a chimney sweep(er) / ~을 청소하다 sweep a chimney / …의 생각이 ~ 같다 be quite anxious 〔eager〕 to *do;* strongly wish to *do;* want to *do* very much / ~이 검댕으로 막힌 것 같다 The chimney seems to be clogged 〔choked〕 (up) with soot. / 사고 싶은 마음은 ~ 같지만 돈이 모자란다 I really want to buy it, but I don't have enough money.

**굴뚝새** 『조류』 a wren; a jenny wren 「(암컷).

**굴러 들어오다** roll in; 《뜻하지 않은 것이》 come into 《a fortune》; receive 《a windfall》; realize 《a windfall profit》. ¶ 많은 유산이 ~ come into a big fortune; be left rich 〔well-off〕 《by the death of...》.

**굴러떨어지다** fall 〔tumble〕 down (off). ¶ 그는 층계에서 굴러 떨어졌다 He fell 〔tumbled〕 down the stairs. / 그 차는 벼랑에서 굴러 떨어졌다 The car fell over the cliff.

**굴렁쇠** a hoop. ¶ ~를 굴리다 roll 〔drive, trundle〕 along a hoop.

**굴레** ① 《소·말의》 a bridle; a headstall. ¶ ~를 씌우다 bridle; put on a headstall / ~를 벗기다 take off a bridle; unbridle. ② 《속박》 restraint; fetters (구속물); (a) restriction (제한). ¶ ~에서 벗어나다 get released; become free; free *oneself* from restraint / ~ 벗은 말 같다 be free as an unbridled horse.

**굴레미** a wooden wheel.

**굴리다** ① 《굴러가게 하다》 roll. ¶ 구슬을 굴리는 듯한 목소리 a sweet silvery voice / 공을 ~ roll a ball / 눈알을 ~ roll *one's* eyes / 바위를 언덕에서 내리 ~ roll a rock down a hill / 눈을 굴려 큰 눈사람을 만들다 roll snow into a huge snowball. ② 《한구석에》 throw 《*a thing*》 to one side; leave 《*a thing*》 negligently; handle 《*a thing*》 carelessly 〔roughly〕. ¶ 책을 함부로 내 ~ toss a book to one side / 함부로 굴리면 못 쓰게 된다 If you leave it unattended, it will not last. ③ 《돈을》 lend out; invest. ¶ 돈을 ~ lend *one's* money out 《at 10 percent interest》; invest *one's* money wisely 〔profitably〕. ④ 《운영하다》 run. ¶ 그는 버스를 세 대 굴린다 He has three buses running for business purposes. ⑤ 《깎다》 slice the edge off 《timber》; smooth 〔even〕 a log; round 《an edge》.

**굴밥** rice boiled with oysters.

**굴복**(屈服·屈伏) (a) surrender; submission; yielding. ~하다 submit 《to》; surrender 《to》; yield 《to》; give in 《to》; succumb 《to》; knuckle under. ¶ ~시키다 force 《*a person*》 to give in; bring 《*a person*》 to *his* knees / 유혹에 ~하다 succumb to temptation / 남의 의사에 ~하다 submit to *a person's* will / 압력에 ~하다 yield under pressure / 그는 남의 의견에 순순히 ~할 위인이 아니다 He is the last man to give in tamely to another's opinion.

**굴비** a dried croaker.

**굴성**(屈性) 『생물』 (a) tropism. ◉ ~반응 a tropistic response.

**굴속**(窟—) the inside of a cave 〔tunnel〕. ¶ ~ 같다 be as dark as the inside of a cave; (be) very dark.

**굴수성**(屈水性) 『식물』 hydrotropism.

**굴신**(屈伸) extension and contraction; bending and stretching. ~하다 extend and contract; bend and stretch; 《관절 등이》 flex. ¶ ~이 자유자재한 elastic; flexible; pliable. ◉ ~운동 bending (and stretching) exercises: 무릎 ~운동을 하다 do knee bends. ~율 the flexible rate.

**굴신**(屈身) 《굽힘》 bending the body; 《겸손함》 a modest 〔humble〕 attitude. ~하다 bend *one's* body 《forward》; behave humbly 〔modestly〕.

**굴왕신같다** (be) old and shabby 〔dirty, filthy, squalid〕.

**굴욕**(屈辱) (a) humiliation; (a) disgrace; (an) indignity; dishonor; (a) shame; (an) insult. ¶ ~을 느끼다 feel insulted 《by》; feel mortification 《at》 / ~을 당하다 undergo 〔be subjected to〕 humiliation; be humiliated 〔insulted〕; be disgraced; kiss 〔lick, bite〕 the dust / ~을 주다 humiliate; disgrace; dishonor; insult / ~을 참다〔감

수하다] eat dirt [humble pie]; pocket [stomach] an insult; take an insult lying down; (swallow *one's* pride and) sit down quietly under a humiliation / 그는 뇌물 수수 혐의로 체포되는 ~을 겪었다 He suffered the indignity of arrest for suspected bribery.
◉ ~감 a sense of humiliation: 패배에 대한 ~감을 가지다 have the humiliating sense of defeat. ~외교 humiliating [crow-eating] diplomacy; a submissive foreign policy.

**굴욕적**(屈辱的) humiliating; disgraceful; shameful. ¶ ~인 양보 a humiliating concession / ~인 생활을 하다 live in dishonor / ~인 강화조약을 맺다 conclude a humiliating peace treaty 《with》/ 포로들은 ~인 취급을 받았다 The captives were subjected to humiliating treatment.

**굴우물**(窟—) an unfathomable well.

**굴절**(屈折) 《꺾임》 bending; a turn; 〖물리〗 refraction; 《어형의》 inflection. ~하다 bend; turn; be refracted; undergo a reflection bend. ¶ ~된 해안선 a crooked coastline; a deeply indented coastline / 물은 빛을 ~시킨다 Water refracts light.
◉ ~각 a refracting angle. ~계 a refractometer. ~광선 a refracted ray of light. ~광학 dioptrics. ~렌즈 a refractive lens; a refractor. ~력 《렌즈의》 refractive power; 《눈의》 refraction. ~률 the refractive index. ~망원경 a refracting telescope; a refractor. ~부 《강의》 a bend. ~어 〖언어〗 an inflectional [inflective] language.

**굴젓** pickled oysters preserved with salt.

**굴조개** 〖조개류〗 an oyster.

**굴종**(屈從) (servile) submission; subservience. ~하다 submit [yield, succumb, give in] 《to》; bend the knees 《to》. ¶ ~시키다 bring 《*a person*》 to *his* knees; make [force] 《*a person*》 submit meekly 《to》/ ~적인 submissive; subservient / 그는 사장에게 ~한다 He is subservient to his boss.

**굴지**(屈指) ~하다 count on *one's* fingers; be eminent [preeminent, prominent]. ¶ ~의 leading; prominent; preeminent; outstanding / ~의 실업가 a leading businessman / 세계 ~의 대도시 one of the largest cities in the world / 그는 나라 ~의 부자다 He is one of the richest men in the country. / 부산은 한국 ~의 양항이다 Busan is one of the best seaports in Korea.

**굴지성**(屈地性) 〖식물〗 geotropism.

**굴진** oily soot that collects in a chimney [hypocaust].

**굴진**(掘進) ~하다 dig (*one's* way) through [into].

**굴착**(掘鑿) digging; excavation. ~하다 dig out [through]; excavate.
◉ ~기 an excavator; a [an earth] scraper. ~장치 drilling rigs. ~탑 《유전(油田)의》 a derrick.

**굴참나무** 〖식물〗 an oriental oak.

**굴총하다**(掘塚—) excavate a mound; dig a mound open.

**굴타리먹다** get worm-eaten; become wormy.

**굴퉁이** a gimcrack; a trumpery; a gewgaw. ¶ ~다 be not so good as it looks.

**굴피**(—皮) 《빈 돈주머니》 an empty purse; 《나무 껍질》 oak bark.

**굴하다**(屈—) 《굽히다》 bend; stoop 《to》; 《굴종》 yield 《to》; submit 《to》; give in 《to》; bow 《to》; succumb 《to》. ¶ 굴하지 않고 undauntedly / 실패에 굴하지 않고 nothing daunted by a failure / 무력[권력]에 ~ yield [bow] to force [power] / 유혹에 ~ yield to temptation / 역경에 굴하지 않다 bear up well under adverse circumstances.

**굴혈**(窟穴) a den of thieves; 《굴속》 the inside of a cave.

**굴회**(—膾) raw oysters; a dish of fresh oysters.

**굵기** thickness; depth 《of a voice》. ¶ 밧줄의 ~ the thickness of a rope.

**굵다** (be) thick; big; 《올·낟알 따위》 (be) coarse; large; 《목소리가》 (be) deep. ¶ 굵은 몽둥이 a big stick / 굵은 실 a thick thread / 굵은 팔 a thick [stout, big] arm / 굵은 손가락[목, 가지] a thick finger [neck, bough] / 올이 굵은 천 coarse cloth / 굵은 줄무늬 large stripes / 굵게 하다 make a thing thick; thicken / 굵어지다 get [become] big [thick]; thicken / 목소리가 ~ *one's* voice is deep; have a deep voice / 굵은 글씨로 쓰다 write in bold strokes / 세상을 굵고 짧게 살다 live a short life and merry [honorable] one / 그녀는 다리가 ~ She has pudgy legs.

**굵다랗다** be rather thick [big, deep, *etc.*]. ¶ 굵다란 밧줄 a thick rope.

**굵직굵직** ~하다 be all thick [big, deep]. ¶ 고기를 ~하게 썰다 cut meat on the big side.

**굵직하다** be somewhat thick [big, deep]; (be) thickish. ¶ 굵직한 막대기 a biggish stick.

**굶기다** starve; let [make] 《*a person*》 go hungry. ¶ 굶겨 죽이다 starve 《*a person*》 to death / 처자식을 ~ let 《*one's*》 family starve [go hungry].

**굶다** go without food [eating]; skip a meal; fast (일부러); starve; go hungry; famish. ¶ 굶어 죽다 starve to death; die of [from] hunger / 흉년이 들어 많은 사람이 굶는다 Many people are starving in the famine. / 종일 굶었다 I haven't eaten anything all day. / 지금도 세계에는 굶어죽는 사람이 많다 Many people starve to death in the world even today. / 욕을 보느니차라리 굶어 죽겠다 I prefer death by starvation to an insult.

**굶주리다** starve; go [be] hungry; famish; 《갈망하다》 hanker 《after, for》; hunger [thirst] 《for》. ¶ 굶주린 사람 a hungry person / 사랑에 굶주린 아이 a love-starved child / 음식에 ~ be hungry for food; hunger for food / 권력에 ~ yearn for power / 지식에 ~ thirst after knowledge / 애정에 ~ be 「starved of [hungry for] affection.

**굶주림** hunger; starvation. ¶ ~을 면하다 keep [stave] off *one's* hunger / ~에 시달리다 suffer from hunger / 전쟁 통에 많은 어린이가 굶주림으로 죽었다 Many children 「died of hunger [starved to death] during the war.

**굼닐다** bend and stretch; work in bending waists.

**굼뜨다** (be) slow; sluggish; dull. ¶ 굼뜬 동작 sluggish behavior / 일에 ~ be slow at [in] *one's* work / 동작이 ~ be slow in motion.

**굼벵이** 《벌레》 a (white) grub; a maggot; 《사람》 a sluggard; a slow person. ¶ ~처럼 (느릿느릿) at a snail's [slack] pace; idly; leisurely / ~도 구르는 재주가 있다 《속담》 Every man for his own trade.

**굼슬겁다** (be) kindly.

**굼실거리다** creep about 《over *one's* body》; crawl over 《*one*》.

**굼실굼실** creeping; crawing. ~하다 = 굼실거리다.

**굼틀** with a wiggle [wriggle]. ~하다 give a wiggle [wriggle]; twist *oneself;* make a short writhing motion. ¶ ~굼틀 wiggling; wriggling; twisting.

**굼틀거리다** wriggle; wiggle; squirm. ¶ 몸을 ~ wriggle *one's* body / 굼틀거리며 나아가다 wriggle [squirm] *one's* way; wriggle along / 뱀은 굼틀거리며 구멍 속으로 들어갔다 The snake wriggled into its hole.

**굽** ① 《마소의》 a hoof. ¶ 굽이 있는 hoofed / 갈라진 굽 cloven hoofs / 말굽 소리 the sound [clatter] of hoofs; hoofbeats / 발굽 자국 hoof prints [tracks]. ② 《신·그릇의》 a foot (잔의); a stem (긴 것); a heel (구두의). ¶ 굽이 높은[낮은] 구두 high-[low-]heeled shoes / 양주 잔의 굽 the stem of a glass / (양주용) 굽 달린 유리잔 stem ware [총칭].

**굽다**[1] 《휘다》 bend; curve; (be) bent; stooped; crooked. ¶ 굽은 나무 a crooked tree / 굽은 길 a curved road; 《꼬불꼬불한》 a winding path / 허리가 ~ be bent 《with age》; be stooped; have a bent back / 허리가 굽지 않다 have a straight back / 굽도 젖도 할 수 없다 be left 「with nowhere to turn [with no escape]; be driven into a corner; have [see] no way out / 길은 거기서 왼쪽으로 굽어 있었다 The road made a turn to the left there.

**굽다**[2] ① 《음식을》 roast (고기); broil (생선); bake (빵); toast (겉만 살짝).

> (용법) **roast**는 비교적 큰 고기를 오븐 등에서 굽다. **broil** 《미》, **grill**은 작은 고기 등을 직화(直火)로 굽다. 고기 이외의 빵·과자 등을 오븐에서 굽는 것은 **bake**, 양념한 고기를 통째로 또는 큰 덩어리로 굽는것은 **barbecue**. **toast**는 얇은 빵조각이나 김 따위를 불에 겉만 살짝 굽다.

¶ 잘 구워진 well-done; 《빵이》 well baked / 덜 구워진 《중간》 medium; 《설 구워진》 rare / 김을 ~ toast dried laver / 고기를 (잘) ~ roast beef thoroughly / 너무 ~ overdo; overcook; overbake / 생선을 ~ broil fish / 빵을 ~ bake bread / 토스트를 ~ toast bread / 통닭을 ~ roast a chicken whole.
② 《말리다》 dry 《wood》 at fire; season. ¶ 재목을 ~ season timber.
③ 《숯·벽돌을》 make; burn; bake. ¶ 벽돌을 ~ burn [make, bake] bricks / 숯을 ~ burn [make] charcoal / 숯 굽는 사람[가마] a charcoal burner [kiln].

**굽달이** a footed plate [dish]; a stemmed glass.

**굽도리** the base molding of a wall; the lower parts of walls of a room. ◉ ~지 paper used as base molding around a room. ~판자 〖건축〗 a baseboard; a mopboard; a skirting board.

**굽실** with a low [deep] bow. ~하다 bow down low; bow from the waist; give [make] a bow 《to》. ¶ ~굽실 crawlingly; in a servile manner.

**굽실거리다** truckle [kowtow] 《to》; cringe 《to》; 《구어》 crawl 《to》; be obsequious 《to》. ¶ 윗사람에게 ~ cringe to *one's* superiors / 그는 지점장에게 항상 굽실거린다 He is always kowtowing to the office manager.

**굽어보다** ① 《아래를》 look down; overlook; command; take a bird's-eye view of. ¶ 골짜기를 ~ look down into a valley / 그 언덕에서 읍내를 굽어볼 수 있다 The hill commands 〔overlooks〕 the town. ② 《굽어살피다》 look into the circumstances of *one's* subordinate with a view to helping him; be considerate 《towards *one's* subordinate》; condescend to help.

**굽어살피다** ⇨굽어보다 ②. ¶ 민정을 ~ 「look into 〔consider〕 the living conditions of the people / 하느님이시어 굽어살피소서 God be my witness!

**굽이** a bend; a turn; a curve. ¶ ~마다 at every turn 〔bend〕 / 배는 강~를 돌았다 The boat turned a bend in the river.

**굽이감다** wind; twist.

**굽이굽이** ① 《휜 곳마다》 at every bend 〔turn, curve〕. ② 《물의 굽이침》 winding; meandering; sinuous; tortuous; serpentine. ¶ ~ 흐르는 강 a winding 〔meandering, serpentine〕 river / 들판을 ~ 흐르는 시냇물 a stream meandering through the plains / 그 강은 ~ 흘러 바다로 들어간다 The river winds down (its way) to the sea.

**굽이돌다** wind around; turn a bend 《in the river》.

**굽이지다** bend; curve; be bent; be curved. ¶ 시내의 굽이진 곳 a crook in a stream / 굽이진 해안선 an indented coastline.

**굽이치다** run 〔flow〕 in and out; wind; meander; 《파도가》 roll; surge; billow. ¶ 파도가 굽이치는 바다 the billowing 〔heaving〕 sea; surging seas / 냇물이 골짜기를 굽이쳐 흐른다 A stream winds its way through the valley.

**굽잡다** keep 《*a person*》「under control 〔under *one's* thumb〕; hold 〔keep〕 《*a person*》 down.

**굽잡히다** be under 《*a person's*》 thumb; be held 〔kept〕 down.

**굽정이** a bent 〔curved〕 thing; a crooked article; something bent.

**굽죄이다** cannot look 《*a person*》 straight in the face; feel embarrassed 〔small〕 in 《*a person's*》 presence.

**굽질리다** strike 〔come up against〕 a snag; 《*a matter*》 fail to go smoothly.

**굽창** a top lift of a straw sandal.

**굽통** ① 《화살대의》 the bamboo butt (of an arrow). ② 《마소의》 a hoof.

◉ ~줄 cords connecting the harrow and the yoke.

**굽히다** ① 《구부리다》 bend 《over》; bow 《down》; stoop. ¶ 허리를 ~ bend 〔stoop〕 over; bow (down) / 팔꿈치를 ~ hook *one's* elbow / 무릎 굽히기 운동을 하다 do a knee bend / 무릎을 굽히지 말고 발가락에 손을 대시오 Touch your toes without bending your knees. ② 《굴하다》 yield 《to》; submit 《to》; give in. ¶ 의지를 ~ act against *one's* will; yield 〔submit〕 to another's view / 주의를 ~ sacrifice 〔depart from〕 *one's* principles / 주장을 ~ concede a point / 주장을 굽히지 않다 hold fast to *one's* own views; stick to *one's* guns / 부득이한 경우에는 자기를 굽혀야 한다 We must bow to necessity.

**굿** ① 《무당의》 an exorcism; practices of an exorciser; a shaman ritual to exorcise evil spirits from a person 〔place〕. ~하다 exorcise; perform an exorcism. ② 《구경거리》 a spectacle; a show; something to see. ¶ 굿 뒤에 날장구 친다 《속담》 flog 〔mount on〕 a dead horse; useless talk on a matter which has already been decided / 굿들은 무당 a person who is only too happy to be of service.

**굿거리** a shaman song; a tune performed during exorcism.

**굿바이히트** 〖야구〗 a game-ending hit.

**굿보다** 《굿을》 witness 〔watch〕 an exorcism; 《방관하다》 look on; sit 〔stand〕 by and watch; remain a spectator; be an idle onlooker.

**궁**(宮) ① 《궁전》 a palace. ② 《점성》 (any one of) the 12 zodiacal signs. ③ 〖음악〗 the lowest note of the pentatonic scale(=D#). ④ 《장기의》 the king; the chess position of the king or queen (궁밭).

**궁경**(窮境) ① 《곤궁》 《in》 straitened circumstances. ② =궁지.

**궁계**(窮計) a last resort; a final expedient; a desperate measure.

**궁굴다** 《그릇이》 be larger than it looks; hold more than *one* might expect.

**궁굴리다** think 《it》 leniently; do not mind 〔blame〕; forgive with kind words; be tolerant.

**궁궐**(宮闕) 《대궐》 the royal palace. ¶ ~ 같은 집 a palatial mansion.

**궁극**(窮極) extremity; eventuality; finality. ¶ ~의 final; ultimate / ~의 목적 a final object; an ultimate aim / ~의 승리 a final victory / ~적으로 after all; ultimately; when all is said and done; in the end; in the long run; in the last 〔final〕 analysis / 그의 ~적인 목적은 달성되었다 His ultimate purpose was attained.

**궁글다** 《속이 비다》 (be) hollow; empty; be hollowed out; be left empty. ¶ 속이 궁근 나무 a hollow tree.

**궁금증**(一症) curiosity (호기심); (an) anxiety; a worry; concern (관심). ¶ ~을 참지 못해 드디어 그 상자 안을 들여다보았다 Finally curiosity got the better of me and I looked into the box.

**궁금하다** be eager 〔curious〕 to know; be curious 〔anxious, concerned〕 《about》; wonder 《about, what, why, who, whether, where, if, how》. ¶ 시험 결과가 ~ be anxious about the result of the examination / 개표 결과가 ~ be concerned about the result of the ballot counting / 집에서 소식이 없어 ~ I am anxious at hearing nothing from home. / 그들의 안부가 ~ I am anxious to know how they are. / 그에게 무슨 일이 일어났는지 ~ I wonder what has happened to him. / 그가 시험에 합격했는지 ~ I wonder whether he has passed the exam or not. / 그 사고 소식을 들었을 때 우리는 그의 안부가 궁금했다 We were concerned for him when we heard of the accident.

**궁기**(窮氣) a wretched 〔needy, destitute〕 look. ¶ ~가 흐르는 poor-looking.

**궁끼다**(窮一) suffer impoverishment; be hemmed in by poverty; be destitute.

**궁내**(宮內) 《in》 the royal palace; 《in》 court.

**궁녀**(宮女) a court lady; a lady of the court; a lady-in-waiting.

**궁노**(宮奴) a male servant of the palace; a court servant.

**궁노루** 〖동물〗 a musk roe deer.

**궁도**(弓道) archery; bowmanship. ◉ 대한 ~ 협회 Korea Archery Association.

**궁도련님**(宮一) a green youth 《of noble birth》; a young buck; a greenhorn. ¶ 그는 ~이다 He knows nothing of the world.

**궁둥이** the buttocks; the backside; the behind; the bottom 《구어》; the butt; the hips; 《동물의》 the rump; the haunches; the seat 《of *one's* pants》. ¶ ~가 가볍다 《동작이》 be quick in *do*ing; 《경솔하다》 be rash; be hasty / ~가 무겁다 be slow in *do*ing; be lazy 〔sluggish〕 / ~가 질기다 stay too long; outstay 〔overstay〕 *one's* welcome / 여자 ~를 쫓아다니다 chase after a girl / ~를 걷어차다 kick 《*a person's*》 butt.

> 용법 **buttocks** 앉았을 때 의자에 닿는 부분. 궁둥이 한 쪽만을 말할 때는 buttock. **behind**, **backside**, **bottom** 등은 모두 buttocks를 에둘러 말하는 표현. bottom은 《구어》. 일반적인 대화에서 「궁둥이」를 말할 때, buttocks란 직접적인 표현은 가급적 피하고 behind, backside 따위를 사용함. **hips**는 허리 밑에 좌우로 퍼진 부분. 따라서 「그녀는 궁둥이가 매우 크다」는 She has a fat backside.가 되나, hips를 사용해서 표현하려면 She has broad hips.가 된다. 또, He patted the girl's behind 〔backside〕.에서 behind, backside를 hips로 바꿔 쓸 수는 없다.

◉ 궁둥잇바람 lively hip-swinging. 궁둥잇짓 swinging *one's* hips; hip-swinging: 궁둥잇짓하다 swing 〔sway〕 hips.

**궁둥짝** both buttocks; the buttocks; the hips.

**궁따다** 《시치미떼다》 pretend not to know; make irrelevant remarks (with an innocent look).

**궁뚱망뚱하다** (be) neglected and shabby(-looking); rustic; mean; miserable.

**궁륭**(穹窿) a dome; a vault. ¶ ~형의 dome-shaped; vaulted. ◉ ~천장 a vaulted ceiling; a vault.

**궁리**(窮理) 《연구》 study of the laws of nature; 《생각》 thought; meditation; consideration; deliberation. ~하다 《연구하다》 study the laws of nature; 《생각하다》 think about; ponder; think 〔mull〕 over; devise 《methods》; contrive 《a means》; use *one's* brains. ¶ 그는 좋은 수가 없을까 하고 ~했다 He cast about in his mind for a good plan. / 아무리 ~해도 더 좋은 수가 없다 I can think of no better plan. / 그는 어떻게 하면 돈벌이가 될까 하고 ~했다 He mulled over ways and means of making money.

**궁박**(窮迫) straitened 〔necessitous, needy〕 circumstances; destitution; distress. ~하다 (be) poor; destitute; poverty-stricken; be in needy 〔straitened〕 circumstances; be in distress. ¶ 재정적으로 ~하다 be in financial difficulties; be in difficulties for want of money; be pressed for money.

**궁벽하다**(窮僻一) (be) out-of-the-way; secluded. ¶ 궁벽한 시골 a remote corner of the country; an out-of-the=

way place; the back country 《미》/ 궁벽한 산골 마을 a secluded mountain village / 궁벽한 시골에 살다 live far from town; live in a remote country place; live remote.

**궁상**(窮狀) a sad 〔distressed〕 plight; a distressed state; straitened 〔needy〕 circumstances; a wretched condition; distress. ~떨다 behave like a poor person; act poor; pretend poverty; complain of 〔grumble at〕 *one's* sad plight. ~맞다, ~스럽다 (be) miserable-looking; poor-looking; seedy=looking. ¶ 농민의 ~ the farmers' difficulties 〔distress〕 / ~스러운 사람 a poor-looking man / 옷차림이 ~스러운 여자 a seedily 〔shabbily〕 dressed 〔clad〕 woman. 「seedy.

**궁상**(窮相) a meager face. ¶ ~이다 look

**궁색**(窮塞) poverty; distress; straitened circumstances. ~하다 (be) poor; destitute 《of》; distressed. ¶ 살림이 ~하다 be in needy 〔straitened〕 circumstances; be badly off.

**궁수**(弓手) an archer; a bowman.

**궁술**(弓術) archery; bowmanship. ¶ ~을 배우다 practice archery. ◉ ~가 an archer. ~대회 an archery match. ~사 an archery master.

**궁시**(弓矢) a bow and arrow.

**궁실**(宮室) a royal chamber; a chamber (in the palace).

**궁여지책**(窮餘之策) the 〔a〕 last resort; a desperate measure. ¶ ~으로서 as a (means of ) last resort 〔expedient〕; as a desperate measure 〔shift〕 / 그는 ~을 생각해 냈다 He thought out a plan as a last resort.

**궁인**(宮人) a court lady; a lady of the court; a lady-in-waiting (*pl.* ladies-); a maid of honor.

**궁전**(宮殿) a palace. ⇨궁궐.

**궁정**(宮廷) the (Royal) Court. ◉ ~문학 court literature. ~생활 court life. ~시인 a court poet. ~화가 a court painter.

**궁중**(宮中) 《within》 the (Royal) Court. ¶ ~에서 at Court. ◉ ~문학 court literature. ~어 court language; a court(ly) term. ~예복 a court dress. ~요리 the (Korean) court cuisine.

**궁지**(窮地) a predicament; an awkward position; a fix 《구어》; a corner. ¶ ~에 몰리다 get into a fix 〔hole〕; get into trouble 〔hot water〕; be cornered; be driven to the wall; be brought 〔driven〕 to bay; be forced into a corner / ~에 몰아넣다 drive 〔force, put〕 《*a person*》 into a (tight) corner; put 《*a person*》 in a hole 〔fix〕; have 《*a person*》 over a barrel 《미구어》/ ~에 처하다 be in a hole 〔fix〕; be 〔stand〕 at bay; be in a (tight) corner; be in hot water 《구어》/ 그는 ~에 몰려 있다 He is in a predicament. *or* He is in a fix 〔tight corner〕. / 그녀는 가까스로 ~에서 벗어났다 She narrowly got out of difficulty. / 그는 ~에 몰리면 무슨 짓을 할지 모른다 He will stick at nothing if cornered. 「calligraphy.

**궁체**(宮體) the court style of *Hangul*

**궁촌**(窮村) a poverty-stricken village. ◉ ~벽지 a poor remote village.

**궁터**(宮—) the site of an old palace.

**궁핍**(窮乏) poverty; want; destitution; indigence; privation; penury. ~하다 (be) poor; destitute; [서술적] be badly off; be in needy 〔straitened〕 circumstances. ¶ ~한 생활 a life of distress 〔poverty, want〕; a needy life / ~한 생활을 하다 lead a needy existence; live in dire want 〔need〕 / ~해지다 become poor; be reduced to poverty; sink into privation / 홍수 피해 지역의 주민은 수도도 가스도 없는 ~한 생활을 하고 있다 The residents in the flood=stricken area have been suffering privations, without water and gas supply. / ~은 흔히 범죄를 저지르게 한다 Poverty will often drive a man to crime.

**궁하다**(窮—) ① 《곤궁하다》 get 〔grow, become〕 poor; be in want; be reduced to poverty; (be) destitute; be hard up; be badly off. ¶ 궁한 때에 in time of need / 살림이 ~ be hard to make a living / 돈이 ~ be in need 〔want〕 of money; be pressed 〔hard up〕 for money / 용돈에 ~ cannot afford small expenses. ② 《몰리다》 be driven to the wall; be cornered. ¶ 궁하면 통한다 There is always some way out of difficulty if you really look for one. ③ 《할 바를 모르다》 be at a loss; be at *one's* wit's end. ¶ 대답이 ~ be at a loss for an answer.

**궁합**(宮合) 〖민속〗 marital harmony as predicted by a fortuneteller. ¶ ~을 보다 predict marital harmony; 《보게 하다》 get 《*a person*》 to tell a couple's marital harmony; have 《their》 marital harmony predicted 《by》/ ~이 맞는〔안 맞는〕 부부 a well-matched

〔an ill-matched〕 couple 〔pair〕 / ～이 맞다 the horoscopes of a couple agree 〔assure married bliss〕.

**궁형**(弓形) an arch; an arc; 〖수학〗 a segment of a circle; a lune. ¶ ～의 arched; bow-shaped.

**궂기다** ① 《일이》 go amiss; be thwarted; fail. ② 《죽다》 die; a death occurs 《in *a person's* family》.

**궂다**[1] ① 《언짢다》 (be) bad; ill; disagreeable; undesirable; 《불길하다》 (be) ominous; 《성질이》 (be) cross; bad. ¶ 심술～ be illnatured; be perverse; be cross-mined / 암상～ be jealous. ② 《날씨가》 (be) bad; foul; nasty; rainy; rough (거친). ¶ 궂은 날씨 bad 〔nasty, unfavorable〕 weather; 《거친》 rough 〔stormy〕 weather.

**궂다**[2] 《눈이 멀다》 go 〔become〕 blind; lose *one's* sight.

**궂은고기** carrion.

**궂은비** a long and nasty rain; an unfavorable 〔untimely〕 rain.

**궂은살** proud flesh; granulation tissue in a healing wound.

**궂은일** 《언짢은 일》 an ugly 〔a foul〕 job; an untoward event; an unlucky affair; a misfortune; an unfortunate affair.

**궂히다** ① 《죽게 하다》 be bereaved of 《*a person*》; lose 《*a person* in death》; have 《*a person*》 die; cause 《*a person*》 to die. ¶ 아버지를 ～ lose *one's* father. ② 《방해하다》 disturb; trouble; frustrate; thwart; put a spoke in 《*a person's*》 wheel. ¶ 계획을 ～ counteract 〔cross〕 《*a person's*》 design.

**권**(卷) ① 《책의》 a volume; a book; a copy (부수). ¶ 책 한 권 one book / 제1권 the first volume; book one / 세 권으로 된 저서 a work in three volumes. ② 《한지의》 twenty sheets of Korean paper; a (Korean) quire. ¶ 한지 두 권 forty sheets of Korean paper. ③ 《영화 필름의》 a reel (of film). ¶ 5권으로 된 영화 a five-reel picture 〔film〕.

**권**(勸) recommendation; suggestion; advice; urging; prompting. ⇨ 권하다.

**-권**(券) a ticket; a coupon; a token; a card. ¶ 우대권 a complimentary ticket / 도서상품권 a book token.

**-권**(圈) a circle; a radius; a range; a sphere. ¶ 북극〔남극〕권 the Arctic 〔Antarctic〕 Circle / 태풍권 내에 있다 be within the typhoon area / 당선권 내에 있다 be in the running.

**-권**(權) 《권리》 right; 《특권》 privilege; 《권력》 authority. ¶ 입법권 legislative power / 재산권 the right of property.

**권고**(勸告) advice; counsel; recommendation. ～하다 advise; counsel; urge; give advice 〔counsel〕 《to》; recommend. ¶ 의사의 ～로 on a doctor's advice / 친구의 ～로 at the urging of a friend / ～ 사직을 하다 resign at the official suggestion / 사직을 ～하다 urge 〔advise〕 《*a person*》 to resign. ◉ ～문 a written advice; a letter of advice. ～안 a recommendation.

**권내**(圈內) [부사적] within the range 〔sphere〕. ¶ 사정 ～의〔에서〕 within range / 폭풍우 ～에 있다〔들다〕 be in 〔enter〕 the range of a violent storm / 세력 ～에 있다〔들다〕 be in 〔fall into〕 《*somebody's*》 sphere of influence / 합격〔우승〕 ～에 있다 have a good chance of 「passing the examination 〔winning the championship〕.

**권농**(勸農) encouragement of agriculture. ～하다 promote agriculture; promote farming. ◉ ～일 Farmer's Day. ～정책 the farm encouragement policy.

**권능**(權能) authority; power; function; competence. ¶ ～을 부여하다 authorize; empower / ～을 부여받다 be invested with the power 《of *doing*》; be authorized 〔empowered〕 《to *do*》.

**권두**(卷頭) the beginning 〔opening page〕 of a book. ◉ ～논설 the opening article 《of a journal》. ～사 a foreword; a preface; prefatory note.

**권력**(權力) power; authority; 《세력》 influence. ¶ ～이 있는 powerful; influential / ～이 없는 powerless; uninfluential; without power 〔authority〕 / 국가 ～ state authority 〔power〕 / ～과 재력 power and money; the powerful and the wealthy; political and financial powers / ～에 대한 욕심 a desire for power / ～에 굴하다 succumb to authority / ～을 제멋대로 휘두르다 exercise 〔wield〕 *one's* authority at will / ～을 남용하다 abuse *one's* power / ～을 장악하다 come into 〔seize〕 power / ～을 다투다 struggle for power / 그는 대통령으로서 국민에게 강력한 ～을 행사했다 He wielded the great power of the President over the people. ◉ ～가〔자〕 a man of power 〔influence〕. ～구조 power structure. ～균형 the balance of power. ～분립 ＝ 삼권분립. ～세습 the hereditary succession of power 《to》. ～욕 desire 〔lust〕

for power. ~주의 authoritarianism. ~투쟁 a struggle for supremacy 〔power〕; a power struggle.

**권리**(權利) a right; a claim (청구권); a privilege (특권); a prerogative (관직에 따르는); a title (소유권); authority (권능). ¶ ~와 의무 rights and duties; claims and obligations / 기득의 ~ a vested right / 법률상의 ~ legal rights / 인간 고유의 ~ the inalienable rights of man; natural 〔inherent〕 rights of man / ~를 행사〔남용〕하다 exercise 〔abuse〕 *one's* rights / ~가 있다 have a right《to》; be entitled《to》/ ~를 부여하다 invest《*a person*》with rights / ~를 요구〔주장〕하다 claim *one's* rights / ~를 주장하다 assert 〔insist upon〕 *one's* rights / ~를 다투다《법정에서》contest with《*a person*》for a claim / ~를 무시하다 ignore 〔disregard〕《*a person's*》rights / ~를 취득〔상실〕하다 acquire 〔lose〕 a right / ~를 침해하다 infringe on 〔upon〕 *another's* rights / ~에는 의무가 뒤따른다 Rights carry 〔entail〕 duties. / 모든 사람은 각기 자기자신의 생명, 자유, 행복을 누릴 ~를 갖고 있다 Everyone has the right to enjoy his own life, freedom, and happiness. / 너는 무슨 ~로 나를 못 하게 하느냐 On what authority 〔By what right〕 do you dare to stop me? / 채권자는 대출금의 반환을 요구할 ~가 있다 A creditor has the right to demand payment of debts owed to him. / 누가 이 건물을 가질 ~가 있느냐 Who has the title to this building?
◉ ~금 a premium《for occupancy》; key 〔concession〕 money: 비싼 ~금이 붙은 임대점포 a rented store 〔shop〕 with a high premium. ~능력 capacity of enjoyment of rights. ~락(落)〖증권〗ex rights. ~자 a rightful person. ~장전〖역사〗the Bill of Rights. ~정지 lapse 〔suspension〕 of rights. ~주(株) potential shares; promoter's shares. ~증서 a certificate of title.

**권말**(卷末) the end of a book 〔volume〕.
◉ ~부록 an appendix added at the end of a book.

**권면하다**(勸勉—) admonish; encourage.

**권모**(權謀) machination; a scheme; an artifice; wiles; a trick. ¶ ~에 능하다 be full of wiles; be resourceful.
◉ ~가 a crafty 〔wily〕 person; a Machiavellian. ~술수 machinations; trickery; Machiavell(ian)ism: ~술수를 쓰다 resort to trickery 〔machinations〕; use diplomacy; employ every possible form of tactics; appeal to Machiavellian diplomacy. ~외교 Machiavellian diplomacy.

**권문세가**(權門勢家) an influential family.

**권법**(拳法) boxing (as one of the Korean martial arts).

**권불십년**(權不十年) Every flow has its ebb. *or* Pride goes before a fall.

**권선**(勸善) promotion of virtue; exhortation to righteousness;〖불교〗soliciting contributions. ◉ ~징악 encouraging the good and punishing the evil: ~징악극 the morality (play) / ~징악 소설 a didactic novel / ~징악하다 reward 〔encourage〕 the good and punish the wicked.

**권세**(權勢) power; influence; authority. ¶ ~를 얻다 rise to power / ~(를) 부리다 wield 〔exercise〕 power 〔authority〕《over》.

**권속**(眷屬)《식구》*one's* family; *one's* dependents; my wife (아내). ◉ 일가~ a whole family; *one's* kith and kin.

**권솔**(眷率) *one's* whole family; *one's* dependents.

**권수**(卷數) the number of volumes.

**권수**(卷鬚)〖식물〗a tendril. ⇨ 덩굴손.

**권신**(權臣) a powerful 〔an influential〕 vassal 〔courtier〕.

**권업**(勸業) encouragement of industry. ~하다 promote 〔encourage〕 industry.

**권외**(圈外) ¶ ~의〔에〕 outside the circle; out of the range 〔sphere〕;《반경의》beyond the radius / 대기~ outer space / 정치 ~에 outside the sphere of politics; away from politics / 통신 ~에 있다 be out of the radius of communication / 당선 ~로 떨어지다 be outside 〔out of〕 the running; have no chance of being elected.

**권운**(卷雲) a cirrus. = 새털구름.

**권위**(權威)《권세》authority; power;《위엄》dignity; prestige;《권위자》an 〔a leading〕 authority; a (big) wheel《미속어》. ¶ 어버이의 ~ parental authority / ~ 있는 authoritative; authentic / ~ 있는 잡지 a magazine of authority《on education》/ ~ 있는 소식통 an authoritative source / 영문학의 세계적 ~ a world authority on English literature / 당대〔그 방면〕의 최고 ~ the highest authority 「of the day 〔in that line〕 / ~가 있다 have (great) authority《over, with》/ ~가 없다 have little authority 〔power, control〕; have little weight / 부하들에게 ~가 없다 have

no authority over *one's* subordinates / ~를 잃다〔회복하다〕 loss 〔reassert〕 *one's* authority / ~에 반항하다 rebel against authority / 이 주제에 관한 ~있는 책이 필요하다 I want to get an authoritative book on this subject. / 요즘 선생님들은 학생들에게 예전같은 ~가 없다 These days teachers no longer have the same authority over their students as in the past.
◉ ~자 an authority; 《전문가》 an expert; a specialist; 《대가》 a master. ~주의 authoritarianism.

**권유**(勸誘) 《권하기》 invitation; exhortation; 《설득》 persuation; (an) inducement; 《운동》 canvassing; 《간청》 solicitation. ~하다 invite; persuade; induce; exhort; canvass; solicit. ¶ 기부를 ~하다 canvass for subscription / 가입을 ~하다 invite 《*a person*》 to join 《a club》 / 보험 가입을 ~하다 persuade 《*somebody*》 to buy an insurance policy / 나는 입회를 끈질기게 ~받았다 I was asked repeatedly to be a member of the society. ◉ ~자 《선거 등의》 a cavasser; a solicitor.

**권익**(權益) (rights and) interests. ¶ ~을 보호〔옹호〕하다 protect *one's* interests / 국가 ~ national interests / 기득 ~ vested rights 〔interests〕 / 특수 ~ special interests.

**권장**(勸奬) encouragement; urging; exhortation; promotion; stimulation. ~하다 encourage; urge; exhort; promote; stimulate. ¶ 지방 산업을 육성하도록 ~하다 encourage 《*the people*》 to promote local industries / 그것은 조림을 ~하는 데 이바지할 것이다 It will 「serve as an incentive 〔give a stimulus〕 to the forestation. 「구름.

**권적운**(卷積雲) a cirrocumulus. = 비늘

**권좌**(權座) (the seat of) power. ¶ ~에 있는 사람들 men in power / ~에 오르다 come to 〔into〕 power; rise to power / ~에 있다 hold the seat of power / ~에서 물러나다 resign *one's* power / ~에서 쫓겨나다 be driven 〔forced, removed〕 from power.

**권주**(勸酒) offering (a glass of) wine 《to *a person*》. ◉ ~가 a song to offer wine; a drinking song.

**권척**(卷尺) a tape measure. = 줄자.

**권총**(拳銃) a pistol; a gun; a revolver; a handgun 《미》. ¶ 38 구경 ~ a 38=caliber revolver / 6연발 ~ a six shooter 《미》; a six-chambered revolver / 장난감 ~ a toy pistol / (베리의) 신호용 ~ a Very pistol / ~을 겨누다 point 〔level〕 a gun at 《*a person*》 / ~을 들이대다 aim 〔poke〕 a pistol at 《*a person*》 / ~을 쏘다 fire 〔discharge〕 a pistol 〔gun〕 《at》 / ~으로 위협하다 threaten 《*a person*》 with a revolver.
◉ ~강도 a burglar (armed) with a pistol; a holdup; 《사람》 a holdup man; a gunman 《미》: ~강도 사건 a case of armed robbery 〔holdup〕. 「구름.

**권층운**(卷層雲) a cirrostratus. = 햇무리

**권태**(倦怠) fatigue; languor; weariness; tedium; ennui; tiredness; boredom. ¶ ~를 느끼다 become fatigued; be 〔feel〕 tired 〔weary〕 《of》; be bored 《by, with》. ◉ ~기 《부부의》 a stage of weariness in the married life: ~기에 빠지다〔들다〕 get into the state of ennui in married life; become weary of *one's* married life.

**권토중래**(捲土重來) ~하다 make another attempt with renewed energies; resume *one's* activities with redoubled energy 〔efforts〕. ¶ ~를 기하다 determine to make a comeback.

**권투**(拳鬪) boxing; pugilism. ~하다 box 《with》; spar; put on the gloves 《구어》. ◉ ~경기 a boxing match 〔bout〕; 《현상금 붙은》 a prize ring. ~계 fistic 〔boxing〕 circles. ~글러브 boxing gloves. ~선수 a boxer; a pugilist; 《프로의》 a prize fighter. ~장 a (boxing) ring; a fistic arena. 세계~연맹 the World Boxing Association (생략 WBA). 세계~평의회 the World Boxing Council (생략 WBC). 한국~위원회 the Korea Boxing Commission. (생략 KBC).

**권패**(卷貝) a snail; a conch (*pl.* ~(e)s).

**권하다**(勸—) ① 《권고하다》 ask; suggest; exhort; counsel; advise; persuade. ¶ 동아리에 가입하라고 ~ ask 《*a person*》 to join a society / 담배를 피우지 말라고 ~ advise against smoking; advise 《*a person*》 not to smoke. ② 《추천하다》 recommend. ¶ 책을 ~ recommend a book 《to *a person*》 / 그를 ~ recommend him 《to *a person*》. ③ 《장려하다》 encourage; urge. ¶ 그는 나더러 참으라고 권했다 He urged me to be patient. ④ 《강요하다》 press; force. ¶ 달가워하지 않는 것을 그에게 억지로 권해 봤자 소용없다 It would be no use forcing it on him. ⑤ 《먹기를》 offer. ¶ 담배를 ~ offer a cigarette / 술을 ~ offer liquor; ask 《*a person*》 to have some liquor / 권커니 잣거니 술을 마시

다 exchange glasses with each other while drinking; pass the cup(s) back and forth / 손님에게 억지로 음식을 권하지 마라 You must not press food on your guest.

**권학**(勸學) the encouragement of learning. ∼하다 encourage 〔promote〕 learning.

**권한**(權限) 〚법〛 competence; competency; power; authority; the authorized limit of rights; 《법원의》 jurisdiction. ¶ 관청의 ∼ the function 〔competence〕 of a government office / ∼의 위임 delegation of power / ∼내〔외〕에 within 〔outside〕 *one's* competence 〔authority, right, power〕 / 자기 단독의 ∼으로 on *one's* own sole authority / ∼을 주다 empower; authorize; invest 《*a person*》 with authority / ∼을 넘다 exceed *one's* competence 〔authority〕 / …할 ∼이 있다 be competent 〔qualified〕 to *do;* have the right to *do;* be authorized to *do* / ∼을 지키다 observe the limits of competence / ∼을 (잘) 활용하다 make good use of *one's* authority / ∼을 대행하다 act 〔serve as proxy〕 for 《the party presidency》 / 나에게는 그것을 할 ∼이 없다 I have no authority to do that. ◉ ∼대행 [형용사적] the 〔an〕 acting: 대통령〔총재〕 ∼대행 the acting President / 학교장 ∼대행 an acting principal.

**권화**(權化) the incarnation; the personification; the embodiment; avatar. ¶ 악마의 ∼ devil incarnate 〔personified〕; the incarnation of a devil / 탐욕의 ∼ a perfect picture of avarice.

**궐기**(蹶起) ∼하다 rise 〔rouse *oneself*〕 to action; rally 《around》; rise against. ¶ ∼하게 하다 rouse 《*a person*》 to action / 지금이야말로 우리는 ∼하여 저항해야 할 때이다 It's time we roused ourselves and put up some resistance. ◉ ∼대회 an indignation meeting; a rally: 반정부 ∼대회 an antigovernment rally.

**궐련** a cigarette. ¶ ∼ 한 갑 a pack(et) of cigarettes / ∼을 입에 물고 with a cigarette between *one's* lips / ∼을 피우다 smoke a cigarette. ◉ ∼갑 a cigarette case; a pack of cigarettes. ∼물부리 a cigarette holder.

**궐석**(闕席) 〚법〛 nonappearance; default. ∼하다 make a default. ◉ ∼재판 judgement by default.

**궐위**(闕位) a vacancy; a vacant post 〔position〕; 《왕위의》 the interregnum. ∼하다 become vacant; a vacancy occurs. ¶ ∼가 생길 때 on the occurrence of a vacancy.

**궐하다**(闕—) 《빠짐》 be omitted; be missing; 《자리가 빔》 be left out.

**궤**(櫃) a chest; a box; a case. ¶ 옷 궤 a clothes chest.

**궤**(軌) ¶ ∼를 같이 하다 have the same way of doing.

**궤간**(軌間) a gauge; the gauge of a track. ¶ 표준 ∼ the standard gauge.

**궤도**(軌道) ① 《철도의》 a track 《미》; the line 《영》. ¶ 전차의 ∼ an electric tramway / 단선〔복선〕 ∼ a single 〔double〕 (railroad) track / ∼를 깔다 lay a track / ∼를 벗어나다 run off the track / ∼에 오르다 make steady headway; 《일 따위의》 be started along right lines 〔in the right direction〕; 《사물이》 get on the right track; 《일이 차츰》 get warmed into 《*one's* work》 / ∼에 올리다 《사물을》 set 《*a matter*》 in the right direction. ② 《천체의》 an orbit; an orbiting 〔orbital〕 path. ¶ ∼에 오르다 《인공 위성이》 go into orbit / (인공 위성이) ∼에 올라 있다 be in orbit / (인공 위성을) ∼에 쏘아 올리다 launch 〔lift〕 a satellite into orbit / ∼를 이탈시키다 bring 《a space capsule》 out of orbit / (역추진 로켓으로) ∼를 이탈하다 leave 〔go out of〕 (its) orbit / 지구 주위를 ∼를 그리며 돌고 있는 위성 a satellite orbiting the earth; an earth orbiting satellite.
◉ ∼면 the plane of the orbit. ∼부설 track construction 〔laying〕. ∼비행 《우주선의》 an orbital flight. ∼속도 orbital speed 〔velocity〕. ∼수정 an orbital adjustment. ∼운동 an orbital motion. ∼축 the axis of an orbit. ∼폭탄 an orbital bomb.

**궤멸**(潰滅) 《파괴》 destruction; 《전멸》 annihilation. ∼하다 be destroyed; be demolished; be annihilated. ¶ ∼시키다 destroy; ruin; wipe out; annihilate.

**궤범**(軌範) an example; a model; a pattern; 《판단 등의 기준》 a standard; a criterion; a norm.

**궤변**(詭辯) sophistry; (a) sophism; a quibble. ¶ ∼적(인) sophistic(al) / ∼을 늘어놓다 use 〔employ〕 sophistry; chop logic 《with *somebody*》.
◉ ∼가 a sophist. ∼학파 the sophists.

**궤양**(潰瘍) 〚의학〛 an ulcer. ¶ ∼성의 ulcerative 《diseases》 / 악성∼ a malignant ulcer / 위∼ a gastric ulcer; an ulcer of the stomach.

**궤적**(軌跡) ① 《바퀴 자국》 the trace of

wheels; wheel tracks. ②《행적》 the deeds of *one's* predecessors. ③ 〖수학〗《find》 a locus.

**궤주**(潰走) a rout; a debacle; a stampede. ~하다 be routed; be put to rout; stampede. ¶ 적을 ~시키다 rout the enemy; put the enemy to flight; send 《the enemy》 flying.

**궤짝**(櫃—) a box 《of apples》. ¶ ~에 담다 put 《*a thing*》 in a box / ~으로 사다 buy 《*things*》 by the box.

**귀** ①《듣는》 an ear. ¶ 귀가 어둡다〔잘 안 들리다〕 have poor hearing; be hard of hearing / 귀가 밝다 be quick to hear; be sharp-eared; have good 〔keen〕 hearing / 잠귀가 밝다 be a light sleeper / 귀가 먹다 grow hard of hearing; go 〔get〕 deaf; 《일시적으로》 be deafened / 귀에 들려오다 reach 〔fall on, come to〕 *one's* ears / 귀가 아프다 have an earache; have a pain in the ear / 귀가 따갑다 《듣기에 창피하다》 be ashamed to hear 《*something*》 / 귀를 막다 stop *one's* ears / 귀를 가리다 cover *one's* ears / 귀를 우비다 pick *one's* ears / 귀를 기울이다 listen 《to》; give ear 《to》; bend an ear 《to》 / 귀담아 듣다 listen carefully / 귀를 쫑긋 세우다 strain *one's* ears; listen (attentively) for; cock 〔prick up〕 *one's* ears / 귀에 거슬리다 sound harsh to the ear; grate 〔jar〕 upon *one's* ear; offend the ear / 귀에 익다 be familiar to *one's* ears; be something *one* is used to hearing / 귀에 익히다 get *oneself* used to hearing; train *one's* ear 《for》 / 귀에다 손을 대고 듣다 listen with a hand cupped to *one* 〔*one's*〕 ear / 귀에 온 신경을 쏟다 listen with all *one's* ears / 귀에 못이 박이도록 듣다 be sick 〔tired〕 of hearing 《*something*》; hear more than enough of 《*something*》 / 귀에 걸면 귀고리 코에 걸면 코고리 can be taken two ways; It differs with the circumstances. / 귀에 익은 목소리다 I remember hearing that voice. / 아직도 귀에 쟁쟁하다 It still rings in my ears. / 귀좀 잠깐 May I have a word in your ear? / 한쪽 귀로 듣고 한쪽 귀로 흘려 버린다 It goes in one ear and right out of the other. / 벽에도 귀가 있다 《속담》 The walls have ears. / 귀가 보배다 《속담》 You have a valuable pair of ears.
② 《귀때》 a pouring spout.
③ 《모퉁이·끝》 an edge; a strip; a border; a corner; a loop; a selvedge; a list 《of cloth》. ¶ 천 귀 the border 〔edge〕 of a fabric / 자릿귀 the end 〔corner〕 of a mat / 책 귀를 접다 dog-ear a book; turn down the corner 〔edge〕 of a page.
④ 《바늘구멍》 the eye of a needle; an eye. ¶ 바늘 귀에 실을 꿰다 run 〔pass〕 a thread through a needle's eye; thread a needle.
⑤ 《아귀》 slits 〔openings〕 at both sides of a Korean overcoat for putting *one's* hands through.
⑥ 《바둑판의》 a corner of a paduk board.
⑦ 《우수리》 an additional 〔odd〕 amount; an odd sum 〔fraction〕. ¶ 값이 만 원하고 귀가 달린다 The price is ten thousand won and a little in addition.

**귀-**(貴) 《당신의》 your esteemed; valuable; noble; distinguished. ¶ 귀정부 your government / 귀사 your company.

**귀가**(歸家) returning home; (a) homecoming. ~하다 return 〔come, go〕 home; get home (도착하다). ¶ ~ 도중에 on *one's* way home / ~ 후 after *one's* returning home / ~가 늦다 come home late / ~ 준비를 하다 get ready 〔prepare〕 to go home / 어머니는 머지않아 ~하실 겁니다 (I expect) Mother will be home before long. / 몇 시에 ~하느냐 What time will you come 〔go〕 home? / 아버님은 ~하셨느냐 Has your father come home?

**귀감**(龜鑑) a paragon; a pattern; a model; a good example; a mirror; an exemplar. ¶ 군인의 ~ a model soldier; a pattern of soldiery / 남의 ~이 되다 exemplify *oneself;* set an example to the world / 여성의 ~으로 칭송받다 be praised as a model of womanhood.

**귀갑**(龜甲) a tortoise shell.

**귀객**(貴客) an important 〔honored〕 guest; a distinguished visitor.

**귀거래**(歸去來) homecoming after *one's* resignation from a government office.

**귀거칠다** be unpleasant 〔disagreeable, offensive〕 to hear; be bitter to hear; be distasteful to *one's* ears. ¶ 귀거친 말 unpleasant words 〔advice〕; a flea in *one's* ear.

**귀걸이** ① 《귓집》 earmuffs; an earcap. ¶ ~를 하다 wear earmuffs. ② 《안경의》 eyeglasses with strings for bows. ③ 《장식용》 an earring; an eardrop; a pendant.

**귀결**(歸結) a conclusion; an end; 《결과》

a result; a consequence. ～하다 end; result; come to a conclusion. ¶ ～짓다 bring to a conclusion / 당연한 ～로서 as a natural consequence 〔result〕/ …은 당연한 ～이다 It naturally follows that…; It is a foregone 〔logical〕 conclusion that….

**귀경**(歸京) ～하다 come back 〔go back, return〕 to Seoul; be back in Seoul.

**귀고리** an earring; an eardrop.

**귀골**(貴骨) 《골상》 noble features; a noble physiognomy; 《귀인》 a noble man; an aristocrat; [총칭] the aristocracy; the nobility.

**귀공자**(貴公子) a young nobleman; a scion of the nobility. ¶ ～다운 noble looking 〔princely〕《young men》.

**귀교**(歸校) ～하다 come back 〔go back, return〕 to school.

**귀국**(貴國) your (esteemed) country.

**귀국**(歸國) homecoming. ～하다 return 〔come back〕 to *one's* country; go 〔come, get〕 home. ¶ ～길에 오르다 leave 〔start〕 for home / ～ 중에 있다 be on *one's* journey 〔way〕 home; be on *one's* homeward voyage 〔trip〕/ ～ 명령을 받다 be ordered 〔called〕 home / 그는 곧 ～할 예정이다 He is expected home shortly. ◉ ～자녀 school children who have returned from abroad; returnee children 〔students〕: ～ 자녀의 교육 문제 the educational problems of children who have returned from abroad.

**귀금속**(貴金屬) precious 〔noble〕 metals. ◉ ～상 《상인》 a dealer in jewelry; a jeweler 《미》; 《상점》 a jewelry shop.

**귀기울이다** listen 《to》; bend an ear 《to》; listen attentively 〔carefully〕 《to》.

**귀꿈스럽다** be out-of-the-way; be remote and seldom.

**귀나다** ① 《모가》 be irregular; be uneven. ¶ 귀나는 천 irregular cloth. ② 《의견이》 differ in opinion; disagree with each other. ¶ 의견이 서로 ～ have differences of opinion; disagree with each other.

**귀납**(歸納) 〖논리〗 induction. ～하다 induce 《A from B》; make an induction 《from the facts》. ¶ ～적 논리 inductive logic 〔philosophy〕/ ～적 추리 (an) inductive reasoning / ～적으로 추리하다 reason inductively. ◉ ～법 induction; an inductive method.

**귀넘어듣다** listen carelessly; pay little 〔no〕 heed to 《*a person's* talk》; take no notice of; let 《a question》 by. ¶ 아무의 말을 ～ pay no attention to what *a person* says.

**귀농**(歸農) returning 〔a return〕 to the farm 〔farming〕. ～하다 return to the farm 〔farming〕; go back to the soil; return to the agricultural pursuits. ◉ ～민 the farmers returned to the soil. ～운동 a return-to-the-soil〔-land〕 movement.

**귀담아듣다** listen 《attentively》 to 《*somebody's* talk》; be all ears 〔attention〕.

**귀대**(歸隊) ～하다 return to *one's* unit; rejoin *one's* unit 〔command (장교)〕. ¶ ～ 명령을 받다 be called in; be ordered back into the ranks 〔command〕.

**귀댁**(貴宅) your esteemed home 〔house〕.

**귀돌** a corner 〔an angle〕 stone.

**귀동냥** learning by the ear; information 〔knowledge〕 picked up by listening to others (without real study). ～하다 learn by the ear; pick up knowledge by listening to others. ¶ 그의 지식은 ～한 것에 지나지 않다 His knowledge is merely the result of learning by the ear. / 그녀는 ～으로 많은 것을 알고 있다 She has learned 〔picked up〕 a lot of things by listening to others. / 그녀는 학교에 다니지 않았지만 ～으로 알고 있는 것이 많다 She is not formally educated but knows a lot by listening to others.

**귀동이**(貴童—) a precious 〔beloved〕 child.

**귀동자**(貴童子) a precious 〔beloved〕 son.

**귀두**(龜頭) 〖해부〗 the glans (of the penis). ¶ 음경〔음핵〕 ～ the glans penis 〔clitoris〕. ◉ ～염 〖의학〗 balanitis.

**귀때** a spout 〔lip〕 (for pouring). ◉ ～그릇 a jar with a lip (for pouring) or a spout. ～항아리 a pot with a spout.

**귀때기** an ear. ⇨ 귀싸대기

**귀뚜라미** 〖곤충〗 a cricket. ¶ ～가 울다 a cricket chirps / ～ 풍류하다 the paddy fields are neglected 〔deserted〕.

**귀뚤귀뚤** chirring; chirping; 《우는 소리》 chirp! chirp! ～하다 《a cricket》 chirp.

**귀뜨다** 《a baby, a young animal》 start to hear for the first time.

**귀뜨이다** have *one's* attention drawn 《to》; be brought to *one's* attention 〔ears〕. ¶ 귀뜨이는 제안〔조건〕 a tempting 〔an inviting〕 offer 〔term〕/귀뜨이는 소식 welcome 〔encouraging, good〕 news.

**귀띔** a tip; a hint; a suggestion; a pointer (or two). ～하다 give a tip; hint; give 〔drop〕 a hint; suggest; give a suggestion; tip 《*a person*》 off; let 《*a person*》 in on a little secret; put a word or two into 《*a person's*》 ear 《about》. ¶ 그는 나에게 먼저 가라고 ～했다 He suggested that I go first. / 나는 그만두게 될지도 모른다는 것을 그에게 ～해 주었다 I gave him a hint that I might resign.

**귀로**(歸路) *one's* way home; the road back; 《여행의》 a return journey 〔trip〕. ¶ ～에 on *one's* way home 〔back〕; on *one's* return trip / ～에 들르다 drop in on *one's* way home / ～에 오르다 leave 〔start〕 for home; start on *one's* way home / ～를 서두르다 hurry back home / 방콕에서 오는 ～에 홍콩에서 일박했다 I stopped over in Hongkong for a night on my way home from Bangkok.

**귀룽나무** 〖식물〗 *Prunus padus* (학명).

**귀리** 〖식물〗 oats. ¶ ～죽 oatmeal.

**귀마개** an earplug.

**귀머거리** a deaf (person). ¶ ～가 되다 become deaf; lose *one's* hearing / ～이다 be deaf; be hard of hearing.

**귀먹다** become 〔go〕 deaf; lose hearing; 《일시적으로》 be deafened. ¶ 귀먹은 욕 abuse behind *one's* back / 귀먹은 체하다 feign deafness; pretend to be deaf / 귀먹은 중 마 캐듯 as if deaf; pretending to be deaf.

**귀명**(貴命) your esteemed orders 〔command, request, instruction〕. ¶ ～에 따라 according 〔in obedience〕 to your orders.

**귀물**(貴物) a rare 〔precious〕 thing; a treasure; 《진품》 a rare article; a rarity; a curiosity.

**귀밑** the roots of *one's* ears. ¶ ～까지 빨개지다 blush to the roots of *one's* ears; blush up to the ears.

**귀밑머리** hair parted and braided so that there is a pigtail over each ear.

**귀밝다** (be) sharp-eared; be quick of hearing; have good 〔sharp, long, keen〕 ears.

**귀밝이**(술) 〖민속〗 wine drunk on the 15th of January (by the lunar calendar) for the purpose of "quickening *one's* ears".

**귀부**(龜趺) a monument base in the shape of a turtle.

**귀부인**(貴夫人) your esteemed wife.

**귀부인**(貴婦人) a lady; a noble woman. ¶ ～다운 태도 ladylike manner.

**귀빈**(貴賓) an honored 〔a distinguished〕 guest; a guest of honor; a very important person (생략 VIP). ◉ ～석 seats reserved for honored guests; 《왕족을 위한》 a royal box. ～실 a VIP room 〔suite〕; a room reserved for special guests 〔VIPs〕.

**귀뿌리** the root of the ear.

**귀사**(貴社) your esteemed firm 〔company〕.

**귀살** ¶ ～(머리)스럽다, ～(머리)적다 be all messed up; be tangled 〔scattered〕; be complicated 〔worrisome, troublesome〕.

**귀상어** 〖어류〗 a hammerhead (shark).

**귀서**(貴書) your esteemed letter.

**귀설다** (be) unfamiliar to *one's* ear; unaccustomed to hearing; strange. ¶ 귀선 이야기 an unfamiliar tale / 귀선 목소리 a strange voice / 암만해도 귀선 이름인데 The name sounds strange to me, I am sure.

**귀성**(歸省) homecoming; going 〔coming〕 home; visiting *one's* parents in *one's* hometown 〔village〕. ～하다 go 〔come, return〕 home; visit 〔return〕 to *one's* hometown 〔village〕. ¶ 휴가로 ～중이다 be home for the vacation 〔holidays〕 / 3년 만에 ～하다 go home after three years' absence. ◉ ～객 people 〔passengers〕 going home: 기차는 많은 ～객들로 붐비고 있었다 The train was crowded with many people 〔passengers〕 going home. / ～객들을 위한 특별 수송 계획을 발표하다 announce a special transportation plan for homegoing passengers. ～(임시)열차 a (special) train for passengers going home on holidays.

**귀소본능**(歸巢本能) the homing instinct.

**귀속**(歸屬) 《복귀》 reversion; return; 《소관》 jurisdiction; 《소속》 belonging. ～하다 revert; be restored 《to》; come under jurisdiction 《of》; belong 《to》. ¶ 남극 대륙의 ～문제 the question of the title to the Antarctica / 국고에 ～하다 revert 〔fall〕 to the national treasury. ◉ ～의식 a sense of belonging. ～재산 properties reverted to the government; government-vested properties.

**귀순**(歸順) submission; surrender; defection. ～하다 submit 《to》; return to *one's* former allegiance; defect 《to》. ¶ 북한의 ～가족 a North Korean defector family / 적은 우리에게 ～했다 The enemy surrendered 〔submitted〕 to us. ◉ ～간첩 a surrendered espionage agent. ~병 a defecting soldier. ~자 a defector.

**귀신**(鬼神) 《혼령》 a ghost; a departed 〔disembodied〕 soul; 《악령》 a demon; an evil spirit. ¶ ~이 곡할 일이다 be something disagreeably surprising 〔unexpected〕; It is novel and strange. / ~도 울리다 make even the evil gods weep / ~같다 《생김새가》 be frightful 〔unsightly〕; be shocking in appearance; 《재주 등이》 be a demon 〔fiend〕; be an outstandingly talented / 일에는 ~이다 be a demon for work / ~도 모른다 No one knows.

**귀싸대기** ¶ ~를 올려붙이다 give 《*a person*》 a slap on the cheek.

**귀아프다** 《귀에 거슬리다》 be painful 〔distressing, distasteful〕 to *one's* ears; be disagreeable 〔unpleasant, offensive〕 to 「hear 〔the ear〕; 《듣기에 싫증나다》 be 〔get, grow〕 tired 〔sick〕 of hearing. ¶ 귀아픈 소리 distasteful 〔offensive〕 remarks; a flea in *one's* ear / 시끄러워 ~ be so noisy that it hurts *one's* ears / 귀아프도록 잔소리를 하다 give 《*a person*》 a long lecture; give 《*a person*》 a good scolding / 그건 귀아프도록 들어왔네 I have heard enough of it. *or* I am fed up with it.

**귀앓이** an earache; 〖의학〗 otalgia.

**귀약**(—藥) an ear(ache) remedy; eardrops. ¶ ~을 넣다 apply eardrops.

**귀얄** 《풀비》 a paste 〔paint〕 brush.

**귀얄잡이** a bewhiskered 〔stubbly beard〕 person.

**귀양** exile; banishment; ostracization. ¶ ~보내다 exile; condemn to exile; banish; ostracize / ~ 가다〔오다〕 go 〔come〕 into exile / ~ 살다 live in exile / ~ 보내지다 be 「sent into 〔condemned to〕 exile 《to an island》; be banished 〔exiled〕 《to a remote province》 / ~을 풀어 주다 rescind 《*a person's*》 exile; release 《*a person*》 from banishment / ~이 풀리다 have *one's* exile rescinded 〔lifted〕 / 그는 먼 섬으로 ~ 갔다 He was sent in exile on a remote island. ◉ ~다리 an exile. ~살이 living in exile: ~살이 하는 곳 a place of exile; a penal colony 〔settlement〕 / ~살이 하는 사람 an exile.

**귀엣말** whispering; a whisper. ~하다 whisper in(to) 《*a person's*》 ear; speak in 《*a person's*》 ear; put a word or two into 《*a person's*》 ear. ¶ ~로 in a whisper / 서로 ~을 하다 whisper to each other; talk in whispers.

**귀여겨듣다** listen carefully 〔attentively〕 《to》; listen with attention. ¶ 내 말을 귀여겨듣고 명심해라 Listen to what I say and bear it in your mind.

**귀여리다** (be) credulous; gullible; [서술적] have overcredulous ears; be easily convinced; believe what *one* hears too easily.

**귀여워하다** love; pet; make a pet of; hold dear; be affectionate to; treat 《*a person*》 with love 〔affection〕. ¶ 귀여워하는 사람 *one's* pet 〔beloved〕 person; the object of *one's* affection / 어린아이를 ~ love a child; fondle 〔caress〕 a child / 개를 ~ pet a dog; make a pet of a dog / 자식을 지나치게 ~ be overfond of *one's* child.

**귀염** love; affection; attachment. ¶ ~(을) 받다 be beloved 《of》; be loved 〔petted, liked〕 《by everybody》; be a favorite 《with *a person*》 / 그는 모두에게 ~을 받고 있다 He is beloved of 〔by〕 all. / 그는 선생님의 ~을 받고 있다 He is a favorite with his teacher. *or* He is his teacher's pet.

**귀염성** charm; attractiveness; amiability; sweetness; lovableness. ~스럽다 = 귀엽다. ¶ ~ 있는 얼굴 a lovely 〔sweet〕 face / ~ 있다 be charming 〔sweet, lovable〕.

**귀엽다** (be) cute; charming; attractive; fetching; amiable; lovable; sweet; yummy 《미》. ¶ 귀여운 아이 a lovable 〔sweet, charming〕 child / 귀여운 목소리 a sweet voice / 귀여운 태도 a charming manner; fetching ways / 얼굴이 귀엽게 생긴 소녀 a sweet-faced girl; a cute little girl.

**귀영**(歸營) return(ing) to barracks. ~하다 return to *one's* barracks. ◉ ~나팔 《미군》 a call to quarters. ~시간 the hour for returning to barracks.

**귀울다** *one's* ears ring; have a ringing 〔buzzing〕 in *one's* ears.

**귀울음** = 이명(耳鳴).

**귀의**(貴意) your esteemed will; your opinion 〔request, pleasure〕.

**귀의**(歸依) devotion; 《개종》 conversion 《to Buddhism》. ~하다 embrace 《Christianity》; become a 《devout》 believer 《in Buddhism》. ¶ ~시키다 make a convert of 《*a person*》; convert 《*a person*》 to 《Christianity》 / 그는 불교에 ~하여 중생 제도를 위해 신명을 바쳤다 He believed devoutly in Buddhism and devoted his whole life to the salvation of the world. ◉ ~자 a convert《to》; a new man.

**귀이개** an earpick.

**귀인**(貴人) a noble man; a noble; a man of rank; a high personage; a dignitary. ◉ ~상(相) a noble face〔visage〕. ~성 (the quality of) nobility: ~성스럽다 look〔be〕noble.

**귀일**(歸一) ~하다 be unified into one; be reduced to one. ¶ 한 원인에 ~하다 be reduced to one cause. ◉ ~법 the unitary method.

**귀임**(歸任) returning to *one's* post. ~하다 return〔go back, come back〕to *one's* post. ¶ ~ 도중에 on *one's* way back to *one's* post / 서울에 ~하다 return to *one's* post in Seoul.

**귀잠** a deep〔sound〕sleep. ¶ ~ 들다 drop off to〔into〕a deep sleep; fall fast asleep.

**귀재**(鬼才)《재능》remarkable talent; unusual ability;《사람》a singular genius; an outstandingly talented person.

**귀저**(貴著) your (esteemed) book〔work〕; the book you wrote.

**귀접스럽다** ①《사물이》(be) dirty; untidy; filthy. ②《사람됨이》(be) menial; base; mean; lowly; vulgar.

**귀접이** ~하다 round the edges off.

**귀젖** a skin adhesion near the ear.

**귀제비**〖조류〗a striated swallow.

**귀족**(貴族)《한 사람》a noble; a nobleman; a noblewoman(여자); a peer; a peeress(여자); [총칭] the nobility; the aristocracy; the peerage;《혈통》blue blood. ¶ ~의 noble; aristocratic / ~ 출신의 blue-blooded / ~의 반열에 오르다 be raised to the peerage〔nobility〕/ 그의 부인은 ~ 태생이다 His wife is of noble birth. ◉ ~계급 the aristocratic class. ~기질 aristocratism. ~사회 aristocracy; aristocratic circles. ~원(院) the House of Lords《영》. ~정치 aristocracy. ~취미 an aristocratic taste.

**귀중**(貴中) Messrs. …(★ 프랑스어 monsieur의 복수형인 messieurs의 간약형). ¶ 스미스 형제 회사 ~ Messrs. Smith Bros. & Co. / 서울 대학교 ~ (To) Seoul National University.

**귀중**(貴重) preciousness. ~하다 (be) precious; valuable; invaluable; priceless. ¶ ~한 시간 valuable time / ~한 인명 precious human lives / 건강은 ~한 재산이다 Health is a precious possession. / ~한 시간을 할애해 주셔서 고맙습니다 Thank you for sparing your precious time for me. / 거기서 나는 많은 ~한 체험을 했다 I learned many valuable lessons there. / 고전은 ~한 문화 유산이자 우리 마음의 고향이기도 하다 Classics are both a precious cultural heritage and our spiritual home. ◉ ~품 an article of value; valuables [총칭]: ~품실 a strongroom.

**귀중중하다** (be) filthy; dirty; sordid; unclean; untidy. ¶ 옷차림이 ~ be shabbily clothed〔clad〕.

**귀지** earwax;〖의학〗cerumen. ¶ ~를 후벼내다 clean *one's* ears.

**귀지**(貴地) your place; your district.

**귀지**(貴紙) your (esteemed) columns; your (news)paper. ¶ ~를 통하여 through the medium of your columns / 5월 10일자 ~ 보도와 같이 as stated in your paper dated May 10.

**귀지**(貴誌) your magazine.

**귀질기다** (be) insensitive; unresponsive; be slow to catch on〔to understand〕.

**귀착**(歸着) ①《돌아감》return; coming back. ~하다 return; come〔get〕back. ②《귀결》conclusion. ~하다 arrive at《a conclusion, a result》; result〔end〕in; resolve *itself* into〔to〕. ¶ 토론의 ~점 the logical conclusion of an argument / 같은 결론에 ~하다 arrive at the same conclusion / 그것은 결국 돈 문제로 ~된다 In the end it is〔comes down to, resolve *itself* into〕a question of money.

**귀찮다**《성가시다·번거롭다》(be) troublesome; annoying; bothersome; bothering; irksome; pesky;《끈덕지다》(be) persistent; importunate. ¶ 귀찮은 듯이 with an annoyed look; as if *one* is irritated / 귀찮은 일 troublesome〔irksome〕work / 귀찮은 사람 an annoying person; a nuisance; a bore / 귀찮은 소리 annoying remarks; nonsense / 귀찮게 굴다 behave in an annoying way; annoy〔bother, trouble〕people; make a nuisance of *oneself;* bug《*a person*》/ …하기를 무척 귀찮아하다 think it too much trouble to *do;* be〔feel〕much annoyed〔bothered〕《at, by》/ 귀찮게 질문하다 pester〔plague〕《*a person*》with question; be inquisitive / 귀찮게 졸라대다 ask importunately for《money》/ ~ 저리 가거라 Don't bother me—go away! / 정말 귀찮은 파리로군 What a nuisance fly is! / 귀찮게 굴지 말고 내버려 두게 Don't bother me. Just leave me alone! *or*

Get out of my hair.

**귀천**(貴賤) the high and the low; the noble and the base. ¶ ~의 차별 없이 irrespective of rank; without distinction of rank; high and low alike / 직업에 ~ 없다 All「occupations〔honest trades〕are equally honorable.

**귀청** the eardrum. ¶ ~이 터질 듯이 요란한 deafening; ear-splitting〔-rending〕.

**귀체**(貴體) your health; you.

**귀추**(歸趨) a trend; a drift; a tendency; the course〔turn〕《of events》; 《결과》 consequence. ¶ 당연한 ~로서 as a natural course of events; as a natural consequence / ~를 지켜보다 watch the development〔course〕of events; wait for the turn of events; wait and see how things will turn out; ascertain how 《the issue》 will develop / ~를 보고 결정하도록 하자 Let's see how things turn out before we decide.

**귀축축하다** (be) low; nasty; mean; base; 「filthy.

**귀태**(貴態) a noble〔princely〕figure. ¶ ~ 나다 be〔look〕noble〔elegant, graceful〕; be charming〔attractive〕.

**귀퉁이** ①《귀언저리》 the rim〔root〕of the ear. ②《모퉁이》 a corner; an edge. ¶ 탁자 ~ the corner of a table.

**귀틀** a log frame. ¶ ~집 a log cabin.

**귀하**(貴下) ①《당신》 you. ②《께》 Mr.; Esquire; Esq(r).; Mrs. (기혼 여성에게); Miss (미혼 여성에게); M(d)me (부인에게). (★ Esquire는 편지의 수취인 이름 뒤에 붙임. 공문서 이외는 보통 Esq., Esqr.를 씀: Thomas Jones, Esq. 《영》; Mr. Thomas Jones 《미》. 미국에서는 Esquire를 변호사에만 쓰는 일이 있음).

**귀하다**(貴—) ①《신분이》 (be) noble; high; exalted; honorable; venerable. ¶ 귀한 사람 a high〔noble〕personage; a person of noble birth; a person of position〔rank〕/ 귀한 집안의 사람 a man of noble family. ②《가치가》 (be) precious; valuable; highly prized; 《드물다》 (be) rare; scarce. ¶ 귀한 물건 a valuable〔precious〕thing; a rare thing / 귀한 경험 a valuable experience / 귀한 보석 precious stones / 물건이 ~ a thing〔an article〕is rare〔hard to get〕/ 귀한 시간을 내주셔서 감사합니다 Thank you for sparing your precious time for me. ③《귀엽다》 (be) dear; lovable; sweet. ¶ 귀한 자식 *one's* beloved child.

**귀한**(貴翰) your (esteemed) letter. ¶ 10월 5일자 ~을 잘 받았습니다 I acknowledge receipt of your letter dated October 5th.

**귀함**(歸艦) returning to *one's* warship. ~하다 return to *one's* warship; rejoin *one's* ship.

**귀항**(歸航) a homeward〔return〕voyage〔trip, flight〕. ~하다 make a return〔homeward〕voyage〔flight〕. ¶ ~길에 오르다 start on a return voyage〔flight〕. ◉ ~선 a homeward-bound vessel.

**귀항**(歸港) returning to port. ~하다 return to port; sail back to port.

**귀향**(歸鄕) returning to *one's* hometown〔birthplace〕; going home; homecoming. ~하다 return to *one's* home town; go〔come〕home. ¶ ~여비 fare for returning home / 휴가로 ~중에 있다 be vacationing at *one's* home town; be back home for the vacation. ◉ ~보고〔활동〕《정치인의》 report「to〔activity at〕*one's* constituency.

**귀화**(歸化) naturalization. ~하다 be(come) naturalized 《as a Korean citizen》. ¶ ~ 미국 시민 an American citizen by naturalization / ~를 허가하다 confer citizenship 《upon》/ 그는 한국에 ~했다 He was naturalized as a Korean citizen. ◉ ~식물 a naturalized plant. ~인 a naturalized citizen〔person〕. ~증명서 a naturalization certificate.

**귀환**(歸還) a return (home); 《본국으로》 repatriation. ~하다 return; return〔come〕home; be repatriated. ¶ 전선에서 무사히 ~하다 come back from the front in safety. ◉ ~병 a returned〔repatriated〕soldier. ~자 a returnee; a repatriate: 가족들은 ~자들을 눈물로 기꺼이 맞이했다 The returnees were welcomed by their families in tears.

**귀휴**(歸休) ~하다 be released before the expiration of *one's* term of service. ¶ ~중이다 be on leave from the service. ◉ ~병 a soldier on (terminal) leave. ~제 〖군사〗 a long furlough plan; 〖경제〗 the layoff system.

**귓가** the rim of the ear.

**귓결** hearing by chance; [부사적] unexpectedly. ¶ ~에 듣다 just happen to hear.

**귓구멍** auditory canal; an earhole; the opening of the ear. ¶ ~을 후비다 pick *one's* ears / ~이 막히다 *one's* ears are clogged up〔blocked off〕.

**귓등** the back of the ear. ¶ ~으로 듣다 do not listen carefully; take no

notice of; pay no attention 《to》.
**귓문**(—門) the outer orifice of the ear.
**귓바퀴** 〖해부〗 an auricle; a pinna.
**귓밥** ① (the thickness of) an earlobe. ② earwax. = 귀지.
**귓병**(—病) an ear ailment; ear trouble.
**귓불** ① 《귀의》 an earlobe. ¶ ~만 만지다 be in a quandary; be at a loss (what to do next); be confused / ~이 두툼하다 have thick lobes to *one's* ears. ② 《신관(信管)》 a gunlock.
**귓속** the inside of the ear; the inner ear. ◉ ~다짐 a whisper of assurance in *one's* ear.
**귓속말** = 귀엣말. ¶ ~로 in a whisper / ~을 하다 whisper in(to) 《*a person's*》 ear / ~을 주고 받다 whisper to each other; talk in whispers.
**귓전** (around) the ear rims. ¶ ~에 대고 소리치다 yell into 《*a person's*》 ear.
**귓집** earmuffs.
**규격**(規格) a standard; 《표준 치수》 a gauge (못의 굵기·철판 두께 따위); 《부품 등의 설계 명세서의》 (a) specification. ¶ 한국 산업 ~ Korean Industrial Standards / ~ 미달의 non-standardized; sub-standard; below 〔not up to〕 the standard 〔specification, specs〕 / ~에 맞다 meet standard requirements / ~을 통일하다〔규격화하다〕 standardize / 이 상품은 ~에 맞지 않는다 This goods are not up to the standards. ◉ ~판(判) a standard size. ~품 standardized goods; a standardized article: ~미달품 an article below standards. ~화 standardization.
**규례**(規例) rules and regulations; a standard.
**규명**(糾明) a close examination. ~하다 examine 《*a matter*》 closely; look 〔inquire〕 into 《*a matter*》 minutely. ¶ 죄상을 ~하다 make a close inquiry 〔investigation〕 into 《*a person's*》 guilt / 진상을 ~하다 inquire into the true state of things; find out the (real) truth of an affair / 그 사건은 아직 충분히 ~되어 있지 않다 The case has not yet been properly investigated.
**규모**(規模) ① 《규범》 a rule; a pattern. ② 《짜임새》 a scale (정도·크기); a scope (범위); a structure (구조). ¶ 대〔소〕~로 on a large 〔small〕 scale; in a large 〔small〕 way / 전국적〔세계적〕인 ~로 on a nationwide 〔world, global〕 scale / ~를 확장〔축소〕하다 enlarge 〔reduce〕 the scale 《of》 / ~의 경제 economy of scale / 사업의 ~가 축소되었다 The business was reduced in scale. / 저 공장은 상당히 ~가 크다 That factory is run on a very extensive scale. ③ 《씀씀이의 한도》 a budget limit. ¶ ~ 있게 돈을 쓰다 make effective use of *one's* money.
**규방**(閨房) 《안방》 women's quarters; a woman's living room; a boudoir. ◉ ~문학 literature written about women's life in *Chosŏn*.
**규범**(規範) 《본보기》 a model; a pattern; 《판단 등의》 a standard; a norm; a criterion. ¶ ~적인 normative / 건전한 사회 ~ a sound social norm 〔ethos〕 / 도덕 ~ a moral standard / 행동의 ~이 되다 be a model of (good) behavior. ◉ ~문법 prescriptive 〔normative〕 grammar. ~법칙 a normative law.
**규사**(硅砂) 〖광물〗 silica.
**규산**(硅酸) 〖화학〗 silicic acid. ◉ ~염 a silicate. ~점토 siliceous clay.
**규석**(硅石) 〖광물〗 silicon dioxide; silica.
**규소**(硅素) 〖화학〗 silicon (기호 Si). ◉ ~강(鋼) silicon steel. ~수지 silicone resins.
**규수**(閨秀) ① 《처녀》 a maiden; a girl from a good family. ¶ 김씨 댁 ~ Mr. Kim's young daughter. ② 《학식 있는 여자》 an accomplished lady 〔woman〕. ◉ ~시인 a female poet; a poetess. ~작가 a lady 〔woman, female〕 writer; an authoress; a literary woman. ~화가 a lady 〔woman〕 painter.
**규암**(硅岩) 〖지질〗 quartzite.
**규약**(規約) ① 《규정》 rules; regulations. ¶ ~을 정하다 lay out 〔down〕 rules / ~을 어기다〔지키다〕 break 〔keep〕 the rules. ② 《협약》 an agreement; a covenant; 《정관》 the statute; the article. ¶ ~을 맺다 make 〔enter into〕 an agreement 《with》 / ~을 어기다〔지키다〕 break 〔fulfill〕 an agreement.
**규율**(規律) ① 《규정》 rules; regulations. ¶ ~을 깨뜨리다〔지키다〕 break 〔observe〕 the rules. ② 《질서》 discipline; order. ¶ ~ 있는 disciplined; orderly / ~ 없는 disorderly; undisciplined / ~ 있게 in good order; 《act》 in an orderly manner / ~을 지키다〔유지하다〕 observe 〔maintain〕 discipline / 그 학교는 ~이 엄하다〔느슨하다〕 Discipline is strict 〔loose〕 in that school.
**규정**(規定) 《규칙》 rules; regulations; 《지정》 prescription; 《법률 조항》 provisions; 《계약 조항》 stipulations. ~하다 prescribe; provide 〔stipulate〕 《that ...》. ¶ 개정 ~ revised regulations / 현

행 ~ the existing regulations; the regulations now 〔at present〕 in force / ~에 밝은〔정통한〕 사람 a rubrician / ~의 prescribed; regular / ~대로〔에 따라〕 according to the rules; in conformity with the rules / ~을 만들다 make a rule / ~에 반하다 be 〔go〕 against the rule / ~에 따르다 obey the rules / …라고 회칙에 ~되어 있다 it is prescribed in the rules of the association that… / ~된 서식대로 작성하다 draw up 《a document》 in due 〔prescribed〕 form / 제5조의 ~에 따라 그녀는 처벌되었다 She was punished with the provisions of Articles 5.
◉ ~론 〖철학〗 determinism. ~식 《환자의》 a (prescribed) diet. ~액(液) a normal solution. ~요금 the regulation 〔standard〕 charge. ~종목 《체조 경기의》 compulsory exercises. ~서 a directory. ~타석 regulation at bats. ~타수 《골프의》 regulation figures.

**규제**(規制) regulation; restriction; control. ~하다 regulate; restrict; control. ¶ 교통을 ~하다 regulate traffic / 법적 ~를 가하다 impose legal controls 《on》/ ~를 해제하다 remove the controls 〔restrictions〕 on 《the price of oil》; deregulate 《air fares》/ 소비성 품목의 수입을 ~하다 restrict imports of consumer items / 보수를 위해 이 도로의 교통이 ~되어 있다 Traffic is restricted on this road due to road repairs.
◉ ~해제〔완화〕 deregulation; removal 〔easing〕 of (official) restrictions.

**규조**(硅藻) 〖식물〗 a diatom. ◉ ~류 *Diatomaceae* (학명). ~토 diatomite.

**규준**(規準) 《establish, set》 a standard; a basis; a criterion. ⇨ 기준.

> 용법 **standard** 같은 종류의 것과 비교할 때 쓰이는 일정한 표준. **basis** 이론 따위의 기초·근거. **criterion** 어떤 사물의 적부를 나타내는 기준.

**규중**(閨中) a woman's living room; a boudoir. ◉ ~처녀 a maiden; a girl brought up with tendercare (in a good family).

**규칙**(規則) a rule; a regulation.

> 용법 **rule** 일상 생활에서 질서유지를 위해 지켜야 할 규칙이란 뜻의 구어적 표현: traffic rules(교통 규칙). **regulation** 공공단체 따위가 정하는 법규란 뜻: traffic regulations(교통 법규).

¶ ~적(인) regular; methodical; orderly / ~대로 according to the rules; in conformity with the rules; 《go》 by rule / ~을 지키다 observe 〔obey〕 the rules; conform to the regulations / ~을 깨뜨리다〔위반하다〕 go against 〔break, disobey, violate〕 the rules / ~적인 생활을 하다 lead a regular 〔well-regulated〕 life / ~을 정하다 make 〔lay down〕 a rule / ~을 무시하다 disregard the established rules / 이 ~은 아직도 유효한가 Does this rule still hold good? / 일하는 시간에 잡담하는 것은 ~위반이다 It is against the rules to chatter while on duty. / 예외 없는 ~은 없다 Every rule has its exceptions. / 만사가 다 ~대로 이루어지는 것은 아니다 Not everything goes by the rules. / 이 방에서는 금연이 ~이다 It is the rule that you shouldn't smoke in this room. ◉ ~동사 〖문법〗 a regular verb. ~서 a prospectus. ~위반 violation of regulations; a breach of the rules.

**규탄**(糾彈) (a) denunciation; censure; 《법률》 (an) impeachment. ~하다 denounce; censure; impeach.

> 용법 **denunciation** 「신랄한 비판」에서 「고소」에 이르기까지 매우 넓은 뜻이 함축된 말. **impeachment** 특히 《미》에서 공직에 있는 사람에 대해 공무상의 죄상을 묻는 「기소·탄핵」이란 뜻이 내포된 말.

¶ 북한 만행 ~ 대회 a rally denouncing the treacherous act by North Korea / 부정을 ~하다 impeach 〔denounce〕 《*a person*》 for an injustice / 정부의 실정을 ~하다 impeach 〔censure, denounce〕 the Government for maladministration.

**규토**(硅土) 〖화학〗 silica; silex.

**규폐(증)**(硅肺(症)) 〖의학〗 silicosis; 《구어》 the dust disease. ◉ ~환자 a silicosis sufferer 〔victim〕.

**규합**(糾合) rally; muster. ~하다 rally; muster; call 〔gather〕 together. ¶ 그는 함께 사업에 참여할 동지를 ~했다 He mustered 〔rallied〕 「kindred spirits 〔people of like mind, like-minded people〕 to do work together.

**규화**(硅化) 〖화학〗 silicification. ~하다 silicify; become silicified. ◉ ~물 a silicide.

**규화**(硅華) 〖광물〗 siliceous sinter; geyserite.

**규환**(叫喚) an outcry; a cry; a shout;

a shriek. ¶ 아비~ agonizing cries / 아비~의 수라장 the veriest hell; a (veritable) pandemonium. ◉ ~지옥 *Raurava* (Sans.); the 4th of the 8 burning hells in Buddhism.

**균**(菌) ① 《균류》 a fungus. ② ⇨ 세균.

**균등**(均等) equality; evenness; uniformity; parity. ~하다 (be) equal; even; uniform. ¶ 기회 ~주의 the principle of equal opportunity / ~하게 equally; evenly; uniformly / ~히 하다 equalize; even; make equal 〔alike〕; render uniform / 비용을 ~하게 부담하다 share the expenses equally. ◉ ~대표제 《선거의》 an equal representation. ~할(割) per capita rate.

**균류**(菌類) fungi. ◉ ~학 fungology: ~학자 a fungologist.

**균배**(均排·均配) division into equal parts. ~하다 divide into equal parts; divide equally.

**균분**(均分) dividing equally. ~하다 divide equally; equalize.

**균사**(菌絲) a spawn; a hypha (*pl.* 「-phae).

**균산**(菌傘) 《버섯의》 a pileus (*pl.* pilei).

**균열**(龜裂) 《물체의》 a crack; a cleft; a fissure; a crevice; a fissure; 《관계의》 a failure; a break; a rupture. ~하다 crack; be cracked; split; break up 《with》. ¶ ~을 깊게 하다 deepen the split 《between A and B》 / 지진으로 도로면에 여기저기 ~이 생겼다 The roads were cracked 〔fissured〕 in places owing to the earthquakes.

**균일**(均一) uniformity; equality. ~하다 (be) uniform; equal; flat. ¶ 만원 ~ a flat rate 〔uniform price〕 of 10,000 won / 천원 ~ 상점 a 1,000 won store / ~하게 하다 unify; make 《*a thing*》 uniform; standardize / 시내버스의 요금은 500원 ~이다 A flat fare of 500 won 〔uniform 500-won fare〕 is charged on the city buses here. ◉ ~요금〔운임〕 a flat rate; a uniform rate 〔fare〕. ~제도 a uniform system.

**균점**(均霑) ~하다 have 〔get〕 an equal share of profits.

**균제**(均齊) symmetry; balance(균형). ◉ ~미 beauty of proportion.

**균질**(均質) homogeneity. ¶ ~의 homogeneous / ~화하다 homogenize 《milk》. ◉ ~로(爐) a homogeneous reactor. ~유 homogenized milk. ~체 a homogeneous substance.

**균차**(均差) 『천문』 inequality; equation.

**균할**(均割) equal division 〔allotment〕. ~하다 divide 〔allot〕 equally.

**균형**(均衡) balance; equilibrium; equipoise. ¶ 수급의 ~ the balance of demand and supply / 세력〔힘〕의 ~ 《maintain》 the balance of power / ~잡힌 지역 개발 balanced regional development / ~을 잡다 balance; equilibrate / 몸의 ~을 잡다 balance *oneself* / ~이 잡혀 있다 be (well-)balanced; be in balance 〔equilibrium〕 / ~을 유지하다〔잃다〕 keep 〔lose〕 the balance / ~을 깨뜨리다 break 〔upset〕 the balance / 그는 몸의 ~을 잃고 넘어졌다 He overbalanced (himself) and fell down. / 물가가 오르지 않는 것은 최근 수요와 공급의 ~이 유지되어 있기 때문이다 It's because of the recent equilibrium of demand and supply that the prices are kept down. ◉ ~감 the sense of balance. ~발전 balanced development: 지역간의 ~발전 balanced development between regions. ~예산 a balanced budget. ~재정 balanced finance.

**귤**(橘) a mandarin (orange); a tangerine; an orange; a satsuma. ¶ 귤나무 an orange 〔a mandarin〕 tree / 귤밭 a tangerine orchard 〔plantation〕; an orange grove / 귤껍질 orange peel / 귤조각 a segment of a tangerine / 귤껍질을 벗기다 peel an orange.

**그**[1] 《사물》 that; the; it; 《사람》 that man 〔person〕; that woman; he; she. ¶ 그와 같은 경우에는 in a case like that / 그는 좋은 사람이다 He is a good man. / 그녀가 왔다 She is here.

**그**[2] [형용사적] that; the; those; 《전같은》 the 〔that〕 same; 《문제의》 《the book》 in question; that particular 《day, case》; [강조하여] the very 《day》; 《그것의》 its. ¶ 그 날 that 〔the〕 day / 그때 then; that time / 그 사람 that man; the woman / 그 근처에 about there / 그 당시에는 in those days; about that time / 그 때문에 for that reason / 그 모자를 주시오 Give me the hat. / 그 뜻을 그에게 전해 주시오 Tell him to that effect please.

**그간**(一間) = 그동안.

**그같이** like that; in that way; so; so much. ¶ 나는 ~ 아름다운 일출을 본 적이 없다 I have never seen so beautiful a sunrise.

**그건 그렇고** by the by(e) 〔way〕; apart 〔aside〕 from that; leaving that... (for the moment). ¶ ~ 누가 그걸하지요 Apart 〔Aside〕 from that, who will do it? / ~ 네가 사과하는 것이 좋겠다 You may well say so, you'd better apologize.

**그것** that (thing); it. ¶ ~은 좋다 That is good. / ~은 내 가방입니다, 이것이 당신 것입니다 That's my bag, this is yours. / ~을 가지고 가겠다 I will bring it with me. / ~봐 내 뭐라고 그랬니 I told you so! / ~만은 못 하겠다 I will do anything but that. / 「그밖에 다른 것은 없나」—「예, ~뿐입니다」 "Is there anything else?" —"No, That's it." / ~이 문제냐 Is that a problem? / ~이 현실이지 That's the way it is.

**그게** 《그것이》 that; it. ¶ ~ 문제다 That's the question [point].

**그곳** that place; there; 《상대방이 있는 곳》 your place. ¶ ~에 there; in that place / 나는 미국을 좋아한다. 왜냐하면 ~ 사람들이 친절하기 때문이다 I like America. Because the people there are friendly. / ~은 다들 별고 없으신지요 How are things going on in your place?

**그글피** four days hence [from now]; three days after tomorrow.

**그까지로** over [on] such a trifle [trifling thing]. ¶ ~ 걱정할 것 없다 Such a trifling thing is not worth worrying about.

**그까짓** so [such a] trifling [trivial, slight, little, small]. ¶ ~ 것을 누가 하겠소 Who would do that sort of thing? / ~ 것은 누구라도 할 수 있겠다 Everyone can do such a thing. / ~ 일로 걱정 마라 Don't worry yourself about such a trifle.

**그끄러께** three years ago [back 《구어》]; two years before last.

**그끄저께, 그끄제** three days ago [back 《구어》]; two days before yesterday. ¶ ~ 밤 three nights ago.

**그나마** even so; at that; and that. ¶ 조금 얘기 했을 뿐이야, ~ 작은 소리로 We spoke little and that in whispers. / 커피 한 잔에 3,000원이나 했는데, ~ 맛도 별것 아니었어 They charged 3,000 won for only a cup of coffee, and not a good one at that.

**그날** that day; the very (same) day (강조형). ¶ ~의 일 the day's work / ~그날 every day; daily; from day to day / ~따라 on that particular day / ~중으로 in the course of the day; before the day is over / ~그날 겨우 살아가다 scrape a living day by day / ~이 ~이다 Each day is just like every other day. / 나는 ~로 집에 돌아왔다 I returned home the same day.

**그냥** ① 《그대로》 (in) that way; (in) the same way as before; as it is [was]; still; with no change; with no let-up. ¶ ~ 두다 leave 《*a thing*》 as it is; leave [let] 《*a thing, a person*》 alone; let 《it》 stand [go]; leave 《*a thing*》 intact [untouched] / ~ 비가 오고 있다 It is still raining. *or* The rain doesn't let up. ② 《…않고》 (just) as one is; without doing anything; just. ¶ 밥 먹지 않고 ~ 학교에 가다 go to school without breakfast / 다음 번에 위반하면 ~ 두지 않겠다 You won't get away with it next time! *or* Such an offense cannot be over looked again. ③ 《줄곧》 all the time [way]; all along; continuously. ¶ ~ 울기만 하다 keep crying; do nothing but cry / ~ 서 있다 keep standing.

**그네** a swing; 《서커스의》 a trapeze. ¶ 그넷줄 the swing rope(s) / ~를 뛰다 have a swing; swing / ~를 뛰고 있다 be on a swing / ~에 올라타다 get on a swing / ~에 올라앉다 sit on [in] a swing / ~를 매다 put up a swing.

**그네(들)** those people; they. ¶ ~의 their / ~을[에게] them / ~의 것 theirs / ~는[은] 누구입니까 Who are those people?

**그녀**(—女) she. ¶ ~의[에게, 를] her / ~ 스스로 나를 만나러 왔다 She herself came to see me. / 그것은 ~ 것이지 내 것이 아니다 It's hers, not mine.

**그놈** that fellow [guy, chap]; he; that thing; it. ¶ ~ 잘 생겼다 The boy has a good look. / ~이 ~이다 They're all bastards!

**그느르다** look after; take care of; 「protect.

**그늘** ① 《응달》 (the) shade. ¶ ~에서 in the shade / ~에 두다 keep 《*a thing*》 in the shade / (나무 등이) ~을 짓다 give [provide, afford] shade 《from the warm sun》 / 나무 ~에서 쉬다 take a rest in the shade of a tree; rest under a tree / 얼굴에 ~이 지니, 왼쪽으로 조금만 움직이시오 《사진 따위를 찍을 때》 Your face is in shadow. Please move a little to the left. ② 《보호》 protection; care. ¶ 부모 ~에서 자라다 grow up under the protection [good care] of *one's* parents; grow up under *one's* parents' wings. ③ 《음지·배후》 obscurity. ¶ ~에서 behind the scenes; in 「the rear [back] 《of》 / 그는 평생을 ~에서 살았다 He lived in 「obscurity [the shadow] all his life.

**그늘지다** get [be] shaded [clouded];

be shady. ¶ 그늘진 shady / 그늘진 곳〔오솔길〕 a shady spot〔path〕/ 그늘진 얼굴《wear》a gloomy〔long〕face / 그녀의 얼굴은 근심으로 그늘져 있었다 Her face was clouded with anxiety.

**그닐거리다** ①《피부가》feel itchy〔ticklish, creepy, crawly〕; itch; tickle. ¶ 손바닥이 ~ *one's* palm is itchy. ②《마음이》feel uneasy〔nervous〕; be ill at ease.

**그다지** 《not》 much; 《not》 so〔very〕; 《not》 so〔that〕much; 《not》 particulary. ⇨ 그렇게, 그리 ①. ¶ ~ 비싸지〔좋지〕 않다 be not so expensive〔good〕/ ~ 심하게 굴지 마라 Don't be so severe with me. / ~ 큰 차이는 없다 There is no great difference. / 그녀의 병은 ~ 위중하지 않다 She is not so ill. / 나는 위스키를 ~ 좋아하지 않는다 I am not particulary fond of whisky. / 성공할 가망은 ~ 없다 There is little hope of his success. / 그것은 ~ 큰 건물이 아니다 It is not so big a building.

**그달** that month. ¶ ~ 초사흘에 on the third of that month.

**그대** thou; you. ¶ ~들 you; all of you; you people / ~ 자신을 알라 Know thyself. / 나는 ~가 몹시 그립다 I miss you terribly〔very much〕.

**그대로** ① 《있는 그대로》 as it is〔stands〕; intact; untouched; as things stand (there); 《하는 그대로》 like that; thus; that way. ¶ ~ 두다 leave 《*a thing*》 (just) as it is; leave〔let〕《*a thing*》 alone; leave 《*a thing*》 intact〔untouched〕/ 꼭 ~ 하다 do just like that / 나는 그것을 ~ 두는게 더 좋다 I like it better as it is. / 나는 들은 ~ 이야기했다 I told〔repeated〕the story just as I had heard it. / 꼼짝말고 ~ 있어라 Just stay where you are. *or* Just stay put. / 왔다가는 ~ 갔다 He came but just went away (without doing anything). / ~ 두면 큰일이 날지도 모르겠다 It might bring about grave consequences, if left alone. / 나는 지금 ~의 네가 좋다 I like you the way you are. ② 《곧》 thereupon; at once; immediately.

**그도그럴것이** because; for. ¶ 그녀의 발음은 훌륭했다. ~ 아나운서였으니까 Her pronunciation was excellent because she had been an announcer.

**그동안** this〔that〕while; the while; meanwhile. ¶ ~ 안녕하셨는지요 Have you been well all these days? / ~ 무엇을 하고 있었니 What were you up to during that time? / 그는 ~ 내리 침묵을 지켰다 He kept silent all the while.

**그뒤** ① 《그후》 after that; afterward(s); later (on); thereafter; subsequently. ¶ ~의 later; subsequent / ~ 그녀는 미국에 유학갔다 After that she went to America to study. ② 《이래》 since (then); ever since; from that time on. ¶ ~ 쭉 ever since / ~ 3년 동안 for the three ensuing years / ~ 어떻게 지냈어요 How have you been (getting along)? / ~ 그가 어떻게 되었는지 모르겠다 I don't know what has become of him since.

**그득** ⇨ 가득.

**그들** they. ¶ ~의 their / ~을〔에게〕 them / ~의 것 theirs / ~ 자신 themselves / 나쁜 쪽은 ~이다 It is they who are to blame.

**그들먹하다** (be) nearly〔almost〕full.

**그따위** a thing〔person〕of that sort; such; like that; 《of》 that kind〔sort〕. ¶ ~ 나쁜 짓 crimes of that sort / ~ 사기 that type〔form〕of swindling / ~ 소문에 신경쓰지 마라 Pay no attention to such a rumor. / ~ 이야기는 들어본 적이 없다 I have never heard「such a story〔a story like that〕. / ~ 것은 거저라도 싫다 I would not have such a thing as a gift.

**그때** (at) that time〔moment〕; then; 《on》 that occasion. ¶ ~의 교장 the then principal; the principal at that time / ~까지 till then; by that time / ~ 이후 since then / 바로 ~ just then; at the moment / ~ 마침 김군이 왔다 Mr. Kim came just at that moment. / ~까지는 일을 끝내겠습니다 I'll have finished the work by that time. / ~ 이후로는 그녀를 만난 적이 없다 I haven't seen her since then.

**그라비어** 〖인쇄〗 (photo)gravure. ¶ ~판으로 하다 photogravure. ◉ ~인쇄기 a gravure press. ~잉크 gravure ink.

**그라운드** a ground; a (playing〔sports〕) field; a playground (학교의); a stadium (경기장) (★ ground는 a playground, a cricket ground처럼 복합어로 쓰이며 단독으로는 쓰지 않는다). ¶ 야구 ~ a baseball ground; a ballpark / ~를 메운 관중 great crowds of spectators around the stadium. ◉ ~관리인 a groundskeeper 《미》〔groundsman 《영》〕. ~룰 a ground rule. ~매너 ground manners. ~스트로크 a ground stroke.

**그라인더** a grinder.

**그라탱** 〖요리〗 *gratin* (F.). ¶ 마카로니 ~

macaroni *au gratin.*

**그랑프리** the *grand prix* (F.); 《win》 the grand prize.

**그래**[1] ⇨ 그래서.

**그래**[2] ① 《친구·아랫사람에게》 yes; all right; O.K. ¶ 「너 안 가니」—「~, 안 가」 “Don't you go?”—“No, I don't”. (★ 부정문의 대답에서 Yes, No는 영어와 우리말이 거꾸로 됨). ② 《아·글쎄》 What?!; Well!! ¶ ~ 어쨌단 말이오 So what? *or* What is it to you? / ~ 그걸 어찌할 것이냐 Well, what are you going to do about it? / ~ 이게 무슨 꼴인가 Well, what is this mess? / ~ 어떻게 됐느냐 Then, what happened?

**그래도** but (still); and yet; none the less; nevertheless; still; for all that; notwithstanding. ¶ ~ 나는 그를 좋아한다 For all that, I like him none the less. / ~ 아직 믿을 수 없다 Still 〔Nevertheless〕, I can't believe it. / 악한 사람이지만 ~ 양심은 조금 있나 봐 Wicked man as he is, he seems to have just a bit of conscience. / 가능성은 거의 없었지만 ~ 그는 단념하지 않았다 There was little chance, (and) still he didn't give up.

**그래미상**(—賞) a Grammy (award).

**그래서** and; (and) then; (and) so; so that; therefore; for that reason; on that account 〔score〕. ¶ ~ 어찌 되었느냐 Then, what happened? / 어머니가 아프시다. ~ 내가 대신 왔다 My mother is ill, so I came in her place. / ~ 화가 났느냐 Are you angry with me on that score? / ~ 너는 뭐라고 했느냐 And then what did you say? / ~ 이렇게 말했지 Thereupon, I said to him like this. / ~ 그녀는 친구가 많다 That is why she has so many friends.

**그래스코트** a grass court.

**그래야** only if one does 〔says〕 that; only if it is that way; only 〔unless, if〕 so; then. ¶ ~ 사나이지〔내 아들이지〕 That's worthy of 「a men 〔my son〕. / 이렇게 하시오. ~ 잘 될 거요 Do it this way, and it'll work out well.

**그래프** a graph; a graphic chart; a diagram. ¶ 막대〔선〕 ~ a bar 〔line〕 chart / ~로 만들다 make a graph 《of》. ◉ ~대수학 graphic algebra. ~용지 graph 〔squared, section〕 paper.

**그래픽** a graphic (magazine); a pictorial magazine. ◉ ~디자이너 a graphic designer 〔artist〕. ~디자인 a graphic design. ~소프트웨어 software for graphics. ~아트 the graphic arts.

**그랜드** grand. ◉ ~슬램 a grand slam. ~오페라〔피아노〕 a grand opera 〔piano〕.

**그램** a gram(me) (생략 g). ◉ ~당량(當量) gram equivalent. ~분자〔원자〕 a gram molecule 〔atom〕. ~칼로리 a gram calorie.

**그러고 보니** ¶ ~ 아버지께 전화해야 할 일이 생각났어 That reminds me that I must phone my father.

**그러구러** somehow; somehow or other; 《어쩌다가》 by some chance (or other). ¶ 일이 ~ 다 됐다 The work got finished somehow or other. / ~ 나는 그녀와 사귀게 되었다 By some chance I got acquainted with her.

**그러그러하다** (be) middling; so-so; be neither good nor bad; be neither better nor worse; be about the same. ¶ 그의 시는 모두 ~ His poems are none too good, either. / 「요즈음 기분이 어때」—「그러그러해」 “How are you these days?” — “I feel only so-so.”

**그러께** the year before last. ¶ ~ 겨울에 in the winter before last.

**그러나** but; however; still; (and) yet; nevertheless. ¶ ~ 나중에 그는 그것을 반환하기로 결심했다 Later, however, he decided to return it. / 그는 나의 절친한 친구였다. ~ 나를 도우려하지 않았다 He was my close friend, yet he wouldn't help me. / 그들은 다 낚시질하러 갔다. ~ 나는 집에 있었다 They all went fishing, but I stayed at home. / ~ 어딘가 좀 이상한 점이 있다 There's something strange, though.

**그러나저러나** this (way) or that; anyway; anyhow; at any rate; in either case. ¶ ~ 그것은 확실히 중요한 일이다 At any rate, it's clearly an important matter. / ~ 너는 책임을 면할 수 없을 것이다 Well, anyway, you'll be blamed for it in one way or another.

**그러내다** rake out; scrape out. ¶ 난로에서 재를 ~ rake out the ashes from a stove.

**그러넣다** rake in; put into. ¶ 삼태기에 자갈을 ~ rake gravels into a straw basket / 음식을 입에 ~ shovel food into *one's* mouth; eat greedily.

**그러니까** so; therefore; consequently; for that reason; accordingly. ¶ ~ 자넨 낙제했단 말일세 That is why you have failed in the examination. / 그는 남의 말을 듣는 사람이 아니다. ~ 그를 설득하려는 것은 시간 낭비다 He is not a man to listen to others. It would therefore be a waste of time to reason with him.

**그러니저러니** this and that; one thing and 〔or〕 another. ¶ ～할 것 없이 without saying this or that; without question; without useless objection; with a good grace / 지금에 와서 ～ 해봐야 소용없다 It is too late now to raise any objection. / 그는 언제나 ～투덜댄다 He is always complaining of this and that.

**그러담다** rake 〔gather, scrape〕 up into. ¶ 낙엽을 가마니에 ～ rake up fallen leaves into a straw bag / 숯불을 화로에 ～ rake charcoal fire into a brazier.

**그러당기다** gather up and pull 〔draw, drag, tug〕. ¶ 머리채를 ～ pull 《*a person's*》 hair.

**그러들이다** rake in; collect. ¶ 판돈을 ～ rake in the money on a gambling table / 빚 준 돈을 ～ collect loans.

**그러루하다** be much 〔nearly〕 the same; be nearly 〔very much〕 alike; be much of muchness. ¶ 그 제안들은 내 보기엔 모두 ～ Those proposals are all much the same to me.

**그러면** 《그렇다면》 if so; in that case; then; if 〔when〕 it is like that; 《그렇게 되면》 if that happens; if you do that; in that case; then. ¶ 자 ～ 안녕히 들 계시오 Well, so long! / ～ 내일 오죠 Well then, I shall come tomorrow. / ～ 그것은 사실이 아니었던가 So it was not the truth? / ～ 나는 어찌 해야 하나 In that case, what shall I do? / ～ 곧 그에게 전화를 하지요 If so I will call him about it at once.

**그러면 그렇지** 《만족의 표시》 Well, all right!; That's the way!; Attaboy!; That's what I mean!; 《예상대로임》 (just) as 《*one*》 expected 〔thought〕; 《구어》 sure enough; I told you so!; I thought so! ¶ 거봐, ～, 벌써 부수어 버렸잖아 There, you have broken it! Didn't I tell you so? / ～ 그는 그곳에 있었다 Sure enough, he was there. / ～ 급행열차는 만원이어서 좌석을 구할 수 없었다 Just as I (had) feared, the express train was very crowded and I couldn't get a seat. / ～ 그것이 저절로 깨질 리가 있나 I see. It cannot break of itself.

**그러모으다** rake up 〔together〕; gather up; scrape up 〔together〕; collect. ¶ 낙엽을 ～ rake up fallen leaves / 그는 집을 사기 위해 돈을 그러모았다 He scraped up enough sum of money to buy a house.

**그러므로** since it is so; since *one* does or says; therefore; hence; so; for that reason; consequently; accordingly. ¶ 나는 생각한다. ～ 나는 존재한다 I think, therefore I am. / ～ 이번에는 그놈이 무슨 짓을 할지 모른다 So, there is no knowing what he will be up to next.

**그러안다** embrace; hug; hold 〔take〕 in *one's* arms; press to *one's* bosom; hug (to *one's* breast). ¶ 어린애를 ～ hold a baby in *one's* arms; hug a baby to *one's* breast / 소녀는 인형을 그러안았다 The girl hugged her doll.

**그러자** (just) then; and (just then); thereupon. ¶ 그는 문 앞에 섰다. ～ 문이 저절로 열렸다 He stood at the door. Then the door opened by itself.

**그러잖아도** even without this 〔that〕; even if it were not so; be it otherwise; what is more; even so. ¶ ～ 피곤한데 그는 한 시간이나 더 일을 하란다 I am already tired, and still he asks me to work one hour longer. / ～ 미운데 그가 돈까지 꾸어 달라고 했다 To make himself more hateful to me, he asked me to lend him some money. / ～ 바쁜데 또 다른 일을 하라니 어찌 된 일이야 I am busy enough now, I can't understand why you are asking me to do yet another work.

**그러잡다** grab 《at》; grasp; grip; seize; snatch; take hold of. ¶ 손을 ～ grasp 《*a person's*》 hand / 벼포기를 그러잡고 베다 grasp a sheaf of rice and cut it / 그는 내 멱살을 그러잡았다 He grabbed me by the collar.

**그러저러하다** be like that and like that; (be) such and such; so and so. ¶ 그러저러해서 for such and such reasons / 그러저러한 날에 on such and such a day.

**그러쥐다** hold; take hold of; grip; grasp; grab; seize; clench; clutch. ¶ 손잡이를 ～ hold a handle / 머리채를 ～ seize 《*a person's*》 hair / 확실한 증거를 ～ have 〔get〕 positive proof / 권력을 ～ take 〔assume〕 power / 물에 빠진 사람은 지푸라기라도 그러쥔다 A drowning man grasps at a straw.

**그러하다** (be) so; such. ¶ 그러한 such; of the sort 〔kind〕; like that / 그러하게 so; like that / 그러한 사람 such a person; a man of that kind / 그러한 까닭에 therefore; for that reason; such being the case / 그러한 경우엔 in such a case; in a case like that; on such an occasion / 세상이란 그러한 것이다 Such is the way of the world. / 그러한 태도로는 성공 못하네 You'll never get anywhere with that attitude. / 그러한 이름의 사람은 여기 없습니다 There is no one by that name here.

**그럭저럭** this way and that (way); one way or another; somehow (or other); by hook or crook; in the meantime; meanwhile; 《거의》 nearly; almost. ～하다 do somehow (or other); manage (to do) in some way. ¶ ～하는 동안에 in the meantime; meanwhile / ～ 살아간다 I manage to get along, one way or another. *or* I am getting along somehow. / ～ 일을 끝냈다 Somehow, I got the job done. / 하는 것 없이 ～ 하루가 지나갔다 The day has been wasted on this and that (getting nothing accomplished). / ～ 하는 동안에 날이 아주 어두워졌다 In the meantime it became completely dark. / 일을 ～ 해 가고 있다 I am managing to do the work somehow or other. / 여기 온 지도 ～ 5년이 된다 It is 〔It's been〕 nearly five years since I came here.

**그런** such; like that; that sort of. ⇨ 그러하다.

**그런고로**(一故一) for that reason; so (that); therefore; hence. ⇨ 그러므로.

**그런대로** 《그러한 대로》 (such) as it is 〔stands〕; 《그 나름대로》 in *its* own way; after *its* fashion; 《썩 좋지는 않지만》 rather; passably; tolerably; enough; 《그럭저럭》 somehow. ¶ ～ 괜찮은 rather nice / ～ 쓸만한 사나이 a good enough man in his own way / 그것을 지금 ～ 놔두는 것이 어떻겠느냐 What about leaving it as it is 〔stands〕? / 그의 이야기는 ～ 재미있다 His story is interesting in its own way. / 그는 연금으로 ～ 살아간다 He somehow manages to make a living on his pension.

**그런데** 《그러나》 but; however; and (yet); for all that; still; 《그건 그렇고》 well; by the bye; now; by the way; incidentally. ¶「그럼 돈을 모았겠네」—「～ 전혀 그렇지 않다」"Then you can save money." — "Far from it." / 인물은 좋아, ～ 키가 좀 작구나 She is nice=looking, but she is rather short in stature. / ～, 이 원고는 마감이 언제지 Incidentally, when is the deadline for this manuscript?

**그런양으로** in that manner; (in) that way; like that. ¶ ～ 처신하면 그는 인심을 잃을 것이다 If he continues to act that way, he will become unpopular.

**그런즉** therefore; so; accordingly; thereupon; then; consequently. ⇨ 그러므로.

**그럴듯하다** (be) plausible; specious; be very likely; (it) may well be. ¶ 그럴듯한 핑계 a specious plea / 그럴듯하게 들리다 sound plausible / 그럴듯하게 말하다 talk with much show of truth / 그럴듯한 거짓말을 하다 tell a plausible lie; tell a lie that sounds like truth / 그의 설명은 그럴듯하게 들렸으므로 모두가 그것을 믿었다 His explanation sounded so plausible (that) everyone believed it.

**그럴싸하다** ＝그럴듯하다.

**그럼** ① 《그러면》 if (that is) so; if that is the case; if that is true 〔right〕; then; well (then). ¶ ～ 가자 Well, then, let's go. / ～ 그가 잘못이다 If that is the case, he is to blame. / ～ 내일 또 전화하겠습니다 Well, (then,) I'll call again tomorrow. ② 《그렇지》 yes; indeed; that's true 〔right〕. ¶ ～ 그렇고말고 Yes, of course that is true. / ～ 그는 참말 큰 부자다 Yes, indeed. He is really a very rich man.

**그렁그렁** ① 《물이》 almost full; all watered up; 《눈물이》 tearful. ～하다 (be) almost full 〔tearful〕; be watered up; water up. ¶ 눈물이 ～한 눈 eyes suffused 〔filled〕 with tears; moist 〔tearful〕 eyes / 독에 물이 ～ 찼다 A jar is almost full of water. / 그녀의 눈에 눈물이 ～했다 Tears stood 〔gathered〕 in her eyes. / 그렇게 말했을 때 그녀는 눈물이 ～했다 The tears were in her eyes when she said so. ② 《국물이》 ～하다 (be) watery. ¶ 국이 ～하다 soup is watery. ③ 《뱃속이》 ～하다 feel bloated 〔waterlogged〕 from drinking too much water. ¶ 물을 많이 마셔 뱃속이 ～하다 *one's* stomach feels too full of water.

**그렁저렁** ＝그럭저럭.

**그렇게** so; so much; to that extent; 《부정과 함께》 《not》 very (much); 《not》 so (much, many); 《그런 식으로》 in that manner 〔way〕; like that. ¶ ～까지 so far 〔much〕; as much 〔far〕 as that; that 〔thus〕 much 〔far〕; such; to such an extent; to that extent / ～ 말은 하지만 You may be right in saying so, but.... / 그 문제는 ～ 어렵지 않다 The question is not so difficult. / 넌 ～ 그녀를 만나고 싶으냐 Are you so anxious to see her? / 누가 ~ 말했는지 말해봐 Do tell me who has said so. / 그럼 ~ 하기로 정하세 Well, then, let us fix it that way. / ~ 화내지 마라 Don't be so angry. / ~ 서두르지 않아도 돼 You need not 〔You don't have to〕 be in such a hurry. / ~ 해 준다면 고맙겠네 I should be much obliged if you would do so. / ~ 좋지도 않다 It's not very good. / 책이 ~ 많지도 않다 I don't have so many books. / ~ 생각지 않는다 I don't think so. / ~까지 안 해도 된다 You need not go that far. / ~까지 나를 생각해 주다니 How sweet of you to care so much for me! / ~ 말하다니 그 사람 미쳤음에 틀림없다 He must be mad to talk that way. / 술은 ~ 즐기지 않는다 I am not particularly fond of wine. / 일이 ~ 잘 되리라고는 전혀 생각 못 했다 I never thought it would work so well. / 상황이 ~ 악화된 줄은 몰랐다 I didn't realize the situation was that 〔quite so〕 bad. / 비록 말은 ~ 했지만 역시 걱정이 된다 Though I said positively, I feel anxious about it. / (일이란) ~ 되게 마련이지 That's the way it goes.

**그렇고 말고** Indeed (it is).; Of course.; Certainly.; So it is.; Quite (so).; That's right. ¶「우리는 이재민을 도와야 한다」—「~」"We must help the sufferers."—"Quite."

**그렇다** 《그러하다》 be that way; (be) right; so; true; 《대답》 That's right.; So it is.; You're right.; Yes; No(부정문에 대하여). ¶ ~하더라도 even so; and yet; for all that; still; nevertheless; be that as it may... / ~면 if (it is) so; then / 그런 까닭으로 such being the case / 그건 ~ 치고 be that as it may; you may well say so, but...; be the matter what it may / 그렇지 않아도 그는 가난한데 Poor enough as he is.... / 나 역시 그렇단 말이야 That's also the case with me. / 「영하 5도나 돼」—「어머 정말 그렇군요」"It's five degrees below zero."—"Why, so it is." / 「난 등산을 좋아해」—「나도 ~」"I like mountaineering."—"So do I." / 「자네 거기 안 갔지」—「예, 그렇습니다」"You didn't go there, did you?"—"No, I didn't." / 그렇지 않다 It 〔That〕 is not so. *or* You are wrong. / 꼭 그렇지도 않습니다 Not exactly. / 그렇습니까 Is that so 〔right〕? *or* Really? *or* Are you sure? / 「자네 훨씬 나아졌네그려」—「그렇습니까」"You're much better now."—"Am I?" / 「나는 그분을 못 만났습니다」—「그렇습니까」"I didn't see the man."—"Oh, you didn't." / 「한국은 정말로 경제적으로 부강해졌어. 오늘 아침 라디오에서 일부 제3세계 국가에게 경제 원조를 할지도 모른다고 하던데」—「~고 하더군」"Korea has really become economically prosperous. This morning, I heard on the radio that it might extend economic aid to some of the Third World countries."—"So they say."

**그렇다고해서** yet; for all that; even so. ¶ ~ 단념 할 수는 없다 Even so, I cannot give up. / ~ 안 갈 수는 없다 That doesn't mean I don't have to go.

**그렇다면** if (it is) so; then; in that case. ¶ ~ 내일 다시 전화해 주시오 If so, please call me tomorrow again. / ~ 이렇게 하자 In that case let's do it this way. / ~ 너 좋을 대로 하렴 Well then, do as you like!

**그렇듯(이)** = 그렇게.

**그렇지** ① 《그렇고 말고》 So it is.; Certainly.; Quite (so).; Indeed it is. ¶ 그도 ~만 That's all very well, but....; You are right in a way, but.... / ~, 그렇게 해야지 That's it. / 「너는 집에서 음악을 많이 듣느냐」—「~도 못 해요」"Do you listen to much music at home?"—"Not really." ② 《그러면 그렇지》 Well all right. ⇨ 그러면 그렇지.

**그렇지만** but; however. ⇨ 그러나.

**그렇지않으면** otherwise; if... not (so); or (else); else. ¶ 열심히 공부해라, ~ 낙제할 거야 Study hard, or (else) you'll fail. / 이르는 대로 해라 ~ 벌을 받을 게다 Do what you are told, otherwise you will be punished.

**그레고리력**(—曆) the Gregorian calendar.

**그레고리오** 《로마 교황》 Gregorio; Gregory. ◉ ~성가 the Gregorian chant.

**그레셤** 《영국 경제학자》 Sir Thomas Gresham (1519?-79). ◉ ~의 법칙 Gresham's law.

**그레이트브리튼** 《영국본토》 Great Britain.

**그레이프** 《포도》 a grape. ◉ ~주스 grape juice.

**그레이프프루트** 《미국 특산 과일》 a grapefruit; a pomelo.

**그레이하운드** 《개 종류》 a greyhound.

**그레인** 《중량의 단위》 a grain.

**그레코로만** 〖레슬링〗 the Greco-Roman style.

**그려** ① 《"…습니다" 뒤에서》 ¶ 참 이상한 질문도 다 하십니다~ Well, that's an odd question, I must say. / 저 분은 성미가 몹시 까다롭습니다~ You see, he is very hard to please. / 그렇게 많은

피난민들이 몰려들어 왔으니 시내의 식량 배급이 곤란하겠습니다~ With so many refugees pouring in, I realize it must be hard keeping the city supplied with food. ② 《"…네, …일세" 다음에》 ¶ 자네 말 잘 하네~ You are very eloquent indeed. / 홍형의 자제일세~ Why it's Hong's son! ③ 《친근한 명령》 ¶ 갑시다~, 가세~ Let's go. / 가게~ Go on!

**그로기** groggy. ¶ ~ 상태가 되다 become groggy; be done up.

**그로스** 《12다스》 a gross 《of buttons》.

**그로스톤** a gross ton.

**그로테스크** grotesque(ness). ~하다 (be) grotesque; bizarre. ¶ ~ 양식〔장식〕 the grotesque / ~한 물건〔사람〕 a grotesque / ~한 모습 a grotesque appearance.

**그루** ① 《나무의》 a stump; a stub; 《벼·보리의》 stubbles; 《세는 단위》 a plant; a tree. ¶ 나무 ~ the stump of a tree / 벼 ~ stubbles of rice plants / 한 ~의 소나무 one pine tree. ② 《농사의》 a crop; a sowing. ¶ 한 ~ 농사 a single crop / 두 ~ 농사 two crops a year / 둘째 ~ a second crop.

◉ ~갈이 double-cropping; a second crop; a second sowing 〔planting〕: ~갈이하다 raise two crops a year; plant 〔sow〕 as a second crop. ~밭 an aftercrop field; a field used again after a barley crop. ~벼 rice plants raised after harvesting the barley. ~빈대 bugs late for the season. ~콩 an aftercrop of beans. ~터기 《나무의》 a stump; 《벼 따위의》 stubbles. ~팥 an aftercrop of redbeans.

**그루되다** be stunted (in growth).

**그루뒤다** turn over the soil for a second crop; plow 〔plough 《영》〕 under the remains of an earlier crop.

**그루들이다** turn over the soil and sow for a second crop.

**그루박다** ① 《거꾸로》 throw 《*a thing*》 down; drop 《*a thing*》 headlong. ② 《연머리를》 make the top of a kite go down; turn a kite upside down (in midair). ③ 《압박》 oppress; suppress; coerce; exert pressure on 《*a person*》.

**그룹** a group; a 《study》 circle. ¶ 록〔팝〕 ~ a rock 〔pop〕 group / H~ H (business) Group / ~을 지어 in groups / ~에 참가하다 join the group / ~으로 나누다 divide into 《four》 groups; group 《into》 / ~을 만들다 form a group; group 《together》.

◉ ~학습 group study.

**그르다** ① 《옳지 못하다》 (be) wrong; blamable; improper; be in the wrong; be to blame; be at fault. ¶ 마음이 그른 사람 a bad 〔an evil, an ill-natured〕 person / 그른 짓 a wrong; an evil deed; a misdeed / 그르고 바른 것을 가리다 know right from wrong / 네가 글렀다 It is your fault. *or* You are to blame. *or* You are wrong. / 대답이 글렀다 The answer is wrong.

② 《나쁘다》 (be) bad; foul; ill; be not well. ¶ 맛이 ~ taste bad / 날씨가 ~ weather is foul / 건강이 ~ be in bad health.

③ 《가망이 없다》 (be) no good; hopeless; go wrong. ¶ 일이 글렀다 The matter is hopeless. *or* There is no hope for it. *or* Things have all gone wrong. / 그는 글렀다 He is no good. *or* He is a hopeless case. / 일이 되기는 글렀다 The plan will never come off. / 그 애 사람되기는 글렀다 That boy「will never 〔can never hope to〕 become a good man.

**그(르)렁거리다** 《소리가》 rattle; ruckle; 《고양이가》 purr; 《소리를》 make a rattling sound; make purr. ¶ 임종의 그르렁거리는 소리 the (death) rattle; rattling sound / 목이 그르렁거려 숨쉬기가 힘들다 have difficulty in breathing on account of rattling / 고양이가 목을 그르렁거린다 The cat is purring.

**그(르)렁그(르)렁** rattling (in *one's* throat); purring.

**그르치다** 《잘못하다》 mistake; make a mistake 〔an error〕; commit an error; err; 《망치다》 spoil; ruin; destroy; mar; mislead; 《실패하다》 fail. ¶ 계산을 ~ make an error in calculation; miscalculate / 방침을 ~ take a wrong course / 계획을 ~ spoil 〔ruin〕 a plan / 판단을 ~ err in judgment; misjudge / 건강을 ~ lose 〔ruin〕 *one's* health / 미관을 ~ spoil 〔mar〕 the beauty 《of the street》 / 신세를 ~ go to the bad; ruin *oneself* / 일생을 ~ make a failure of *one's* life; ruin *one's* life / 나는 상황 판단을 그르쳤다 I misjudged the situation.

**그릇**[1] ① 《용기》 a container; a vessel; a receptacle. ¶ 밥~ a rice bowl / 질~ an earthen vessel; earthenware [총칭] / 놋~ a brazen vessel / 물 한 ~ a cup 〔bowl〕 of water / 이것을 담아 갈 ~이 있습니까 Do you have anything to carry this in? ② 《기량》 caliber; calibre 《영》; capacity; ability. ¶ ~이

크다 be a man of large 〔high〕 caliber / ～이 작다 be a man of small 〔poor〕 caliber / 그는 그 일을 할 만한 ～이 못 된다 He is not up to it. *or* He is not equal to the task.

**그릇**[2] 《그르게·틀리게》 ¶ 아무를 ～ 보다 judge *a person* wrongly; misjudge *a person* / ～ 전하다 report wrongly; give false information; misinform / 아무의 말을 ～ 듣다 take *a person's* remarks in the wrong sense; misunderstand 「*a person's* remarks 〔what *a person* said〕 / 판단을 ～하다 judge wrong; misjudge / 일을 ～하다 go amiss (on a job); make a mistake in what *one* is doing.

**그릇되다** 《잘못되다》 go wrong 〔amiss, awry〕; become wrong; 《망쳐지다》 be spoiled 〔ruined〕; 《실패하다》 fail; come to nought; end in failure. ¶ 그릇된 mistaken; wrong; incorrect; erroneous / 그릇된 생각 a false 〔wrong〕 idea; a mistaken notion / 그릇된 행실 a misdeed; an evil doing / 그릇된 길 the wrong way; an evil course; an erroneous path / 계산이 ～ the calculation is wrong; the figures are wrong / 판단이 ～ a judgment is 〔proves to be〕 wrong / 계획이 ～ a plan goes wrong / 나는 그의 그릇된 생각을 버리게 했다 I cured him of his mistaken idea.

**그리** ① 《그렇게》 so; to that extent 〔degree〕; in that way. ¶ ～ 나쁘지도 않다 be not altogether bad / ～ 재미있는 영화는 아냐 It is not a very interesting film. / ～ 크지 않다 It's not so big. / ～ 생각하나 Do you think so? / ～ 성내지 마라 Don't be so angry. / ～ 알고 당분간 기다려라 Wait for some time keeping my words in mind. ② 《그 쪽》 that way; that direction; there; to that place. ¶ ～ 가겠다 I'll come there. / ～ 가려면 어느 길로 가야겠나 Which way shall I take to go there?

**그리고** and; and then; as well as; and also. ¶ 방을 먼저 치우고～ 공부를 시작했다 First he tidied up his room, and then he began studying. / 그는 연필 둘과 공책 둘, ～ 지우개 하나를 샀다 He bought two pencils, two notebooks and an eraser.

**그리니치** Greenwich. ◉ ～천문대 《과거의》 the Royal Greenwich Astronomical Observatory. ～표준시 Greenwich (Mean) Time (생략 G.M.T.).

**그리다**[1] 《그리워하다》 be homesick for; miss 《*a* friend》; long for 〔after〕; yearn for 〔after〕; pine for 〔after〕; feel a longing for. ¶ 애타게 ～ long 〔yearn〕 for; burn with passion for; be desperately in love with / 고향을 ～ be 〔feel〕 homesick; long 〔yearn〕 for *one's* home / 애인을 ～ miss *one's* sweetheart; long to see 〔yearn for〕 *one's* lover.

**그리다**[2] 《그림을》 draw (무채색); paint (채색); picture; sketch (약도); portray (인물화); 《작도》 describe (원 등을); construct (삼각형 등을); plot (out) (그래프를); 《묘사》 describe (말로); depict (그림으로); 《마음에》 imagine; picture 《*a thing*》 in *one's* mind. ¶ 원을 ～ draw 〔make〕 a circle / 그림을 ～ draw 〔paint〕 a picture / 마음에 ～ picture to *oneself;* imagine / 사회 생활을 ～ depict 〔describe〕 social life / 입술을 ～ rouge *one's* lips / 눈썹을 ～ pencil the eyebrows / 앞으로〔미래〕의 세계를 마음속에 ～ picture the future world to *oneself;* form a mental picture of the world to come / 당신 집의 위치를 약도로 그려 주시겠소 Will you draw 〔make〕 a rough map showing the location of your house?

**그리드** 〖전자〗 a grid. ◉ ～검파 grid detection. ～전류 a grid current.

**그리로** ⇨ 그리 ②.

**그리마** 〖동물〗 a house centipede.

**그리스**[1] 《윤활유》 grease. ¶ 자동차에 ～를 치다 grease a car.

**그리스**[2] Greece. ¶ ～의 Greek; Grecian; Hellenic. (★ Grecian은 건축·미술, 사람의 얼굴 모양 등에만 쓰임).
◉ ～공화국 the Hellenic Republic. ～문명 Greek 〔Hellenic〕 civilization; Hellenism. ～문자 the Greek alphabet. ～사람 a Greek; the Greeks [총칭]. ～신화〔철학, 문학〕 Greek mythology 〔philosophy, literature〕. ～어 Greek. ～정교회 the Greek 〔Eastern〕 Orthodox Church.

**그리스도** 《예수》 Christ; 《이명》 the Nazarene; the Messiah; the Savior; the Lord. ¶ 예수 ～ Jesus Christ.
◉ ～교 ＝기독교. ～재림 the Advent 〔Second Coming〕 of Christ: ～ 재림론자 an Adventist.

**그리움** yearning; longing; nostalgia. ¶ 고향에 대한 ～ nostalgia; homesickness / ～에 못 이기다 feel an irresistible yearning for 〔after〕 / 떨어져 있으면 ～이 한결 더한 법이다 Absence makes the heart grow fonder. / 그 당시를 돌이켜보면 내 마음은 ～으로 가득해

진다 Looking back to that time, I am filled with nostalgic sweetness.

**그리워하다** = 그리다[1]. ¶ 행복했던 옛날을 ~ look back to the happy past with nostalgia.

**그리저리** this way and that; such and so; in a hit-or-miss manner; by trial-and-error; (along) at random. ~하다 try this way and that; do in a hit-or-miss manner; do by trial-and-error; feel *one's* way along. ¶ ~ 말을 둘러대다 prevaricate; make random 〔temporary〕 excuses.

**그린** 《푸름》 green; 『골프』 the (putting) green. ¶ 그는 한 타로 ~에 올려 놓았다 He got to the green in one stroke. ◉ ~백 《미국 지폐》 a greenback. ~베레 《대원》 a Green Beret; [총칭] the Green Berets. ~벨트 a greenbelt: ~벨트지역 a greenbelt zone. ~피스 Greenpeace (국제 환경 보호 단체).

**그린란드** 《북대서양의》 Greenland.

**그릴** 《식당》 a grill (room).

**그림** 《회화》 a picture (일반적인 용어); a painting (채색화); a drawing (무채색화); a sketch (사생화·약도); an illustration (삽화) (★ 특히 페이지 일부에 넣는 삽화는 a cut, 전면적인 것은 a plate라고 함); a figure (도형); a diagram (설명도); a print (판화); a cut (잡지 따위의). ¶ 피카소의 ~ a (picture by) Picasso / ~의 떡 a prize beyond *one's* reach; an unattainable object; 《구어》 pie in the sky / 내 아버지의 ~ a picture of my father's (★ a picture of my father's는 「아버지가 가지고 있는 그림」과 「아버지가 그린 그림」의 두 가지 뜻이 있음. a picture of my father는 「아버지를 그린 그림」이며, my father's picture는 위의 세 가지 뜻 가운데 어느 것으로나 쓰임) / ~으로 그린 pictured; painted / ~을 넣은 illustrated; pictorial / ~ 같은 picturesque 《view》 / ~을 그리다 draw a picture; paint (a picture); make a picture 〔drawing, painting〕 《of》 / ~을 잘 그리다 draw 〔paint〕 well; be a good painter; be good at drawing 〔painting〕 / ~같이 아름답다 be as pretty as a picture / ~으로 나타내다〔설명하다〕 illustrate 「by a diagram 〔with a figure〕 / 이 ~은 누가 그린 것이지 Who painted this picture? *or* Who is this picture (painted) by?
◉ ~본 a model (drawing). ~붓 a (painting) brush; a paintbrush. ~설명 a caption. ~쇠 a rule(r); a measure. ~수수께끼 a pictorial 〔picture〕 puzzle. ~엽서 a picture 〔pictorial〕 postcard; a postcard. ~족자 a picture scroll. ~책 a picture book; an illustrated book. ~첩 a sketchbook. ~패 《카드의》 a face card.

**그림물감** colors; paints; 《유화용》 oils; 《수채화용》 watercolors. ¶ ~을 칠하다 paint; color / ~을 풀다 dissolve colors. ◉ ~상자 a paintbox. ~접시 a dish for mixing colors; 《손에 쥐는》 a palette.

**그림자** ① 《빛에 의한》 a shadow; a silhouette. ¶ 지면에 드리운 나무 ~ the shadow on the ground by the trees / ~를 드리우다 cast 〔throw〕 《its》 shadow 《on, over》; project a shadow / 불길한 어두운 ~를 드리우다 an ominous shadow looms 《across》 / 사람 ~가 장지문에 비치다 the shadow of a man falls on the paper sliding door / ~처럼 쫓아다니다 follow 《*a person*》 like a shadow; shadow 《*a person*》; tag at 《*a person's*》 heels / 저녁에는 ~가 길어진다 Shadows become longer in the evening.
② 《거울 따위에 비친》 a reflection; an image; a figure; a shadow. ¶ 거울에 비친 자기 ~ *one's* shadow 〔image〕 in a mirror / 호수에 비친 산의 ~ the mountain reflected 〔mirrored〕 in 〔on〕 the lake / ~가 비치다 mirror the image 〔reflection〕 《of》; reflect / 수면에 비친 자기 ~를 보다 look at *one's* image reflected on the water; look at *one's* shadow on the water.
③ 《자취》 a trace; a shadow; a clue (단서). ¶ 죽음의 ~ the shadow of death / ~도 볼 수 없다 be nowhere to be seen; be out of sight / 적이라곤 ~도 보이지 않았다 Not a shadow 〔vestige〕 of the enemy was to be seen. *or* There wasn't a single enemy to be seen. / 왠지 그는 요즘 ~도 얼씬 않는다 I don't know why but he never comes to see me these days. / 그녀의 얼굴에 실망의 ~가 스쳐 지나갔다 A shadow of disappointment passed over her face.

**그립다** (be) dear; sweet 《memories》; beloved; longed-for; fondly-remembered 《scenes》; be yearned after. ¶ 그리운 추억 happy 〔sweet, fond〕 memories; memories dear to *one* / 그리운 사람 a person dear to *one;* my beloved; a person whom I miss; a person that *one* 「think of 〔recalls〕 with affection / 그리운 고향 *one's* dear old home / 옛날이 그리워서 out of love for the good old days / 그리운 눈으로 바라보다 gaze fondly 《at》; fix *one's* eyes wistfully 《on》 / 옛날이 ~ I long for the good old days. / 자기 고향이 그립지 않은 사람은 없다 There is no one who doesn't yearn for 〔feel nostalgic about, miss〕 his hometown. / 이 사진을 보면 그리운 그녀의 모습이 떠오른다 Whenever I see this photo, I remember her beloved image.

**그만**[1] 《그만한》 so trifling; so little 〔small〕 as; to that (small) extent; such a tiny 〔little, small〕 《thing》. ¶ ~ 수고를 아끼느냐 Do you begrudge such a small favor? / ~ 것을 지지 못할까 Who can't carry that much on his back? / ~ 일에 낙심마라 Don't be disappointed about such a trifle. / ~ 일로 화내지 마라 Don't get angry over such a tiny little thing. / ~ 것을 갖고 끙끙 앓을 것 없네 Don't worry yourself over such a trifle.

**그만**[2] ① 《그 정도로》 that much and no more; to that extent only; no more than that; 《명령형》 Stop 《*do*ing》. ¶ ~ 울어라 Don't cry any more. / ~ 해 두는 것이 좋겠다 You had better not go further. / 이제 ~ 해라 Oh, (why don't you) lay off! *or* That's enough. / 농담 ~ 해라 Enough of your jokes! / 자랑 좀 ~ 해라 No more of your bragging. / ~ 먹어라 Stop eating. / ~ 놀려라 Lay off teasing. / 오늘은 ~ 해 두자 That is all for today. *or* So much for today. / 그러면 ~이다 Well, that is all 〔enough〕. *or* That is it. *or* Nothing more can be done.

② 《곧》 as soon as; no sooner than; immediately; directly; the moment 〔instant〕. ¶ 그는 나를 보더니 ~ 달아났다 He ran off the moment he saw me. / 그는 자리에 들자 ~ 잠이 들었다 As soon as he went to bed, he fell asleep. / 그 소식을 듣더니 ~ 그녀는 울음을 터뜨렸다 When she heard the news, she burst right out crying.

③ 《그만하고 …하다》 without doing anything further 〔more than that〕. ¶ ~ 가세 Let's just up and go.

④ 《까딱 잘못하여》 carelessly; by mistake 〔accident〕; unintentionally. ¶ ~ …하다 *do* by mistake; be careless enough to *do* / ~ 잊어버리고 말다 [사람이 주어] carelessly forget; [사물이 주어] just slip (from) *one's* mind 〔memory〕 / ~ 입 밖에 내다 blurt out 《a secret》; let 《the truth》 (slip) out; inadvertently talk about / 오늘 외출한다고 말하는 것을 ~ 잊었다 I (carelessly) forgot to say that I should go out today. / 그의 이름을 ~ 잊었다 His name escapes my memory. *or* His name has slipped my mind.

⑤ 《으뜸》 the best (in the world); the most; (the) tops. ⇨ 그만이다 ②.

**그만그만하다** be about the same; be much 〔nearly, almost〕 the same 《as》; (be) so-so; be much of a muchness; be (both) of a sort. ¶ 나이가 ~ be about the same age / 모두 ~ All of them are 「about the same 〔so-so〕. / 환자의 용태는 ~ The patient is much the same. / 영어 실력이 다 ~ All the students have about the same amount of English. / 이 점에서 두 사람은 ~ There is not much to choose between them in that respect. / 그들은 둘 다 ~ They are both of a sort.

**그만두다** ① 《중지하다》 quit; stop 《*do*ing, a fight》; leave off; cease 《*do*ing, to *do*》; discontinue 《*do*ing》; 《끝내다》 end; put an end to 《the work》; 《포기하다》 give up 《*do*ing, the work》; abandon 《the attempt》; 《취소하다》 call off 《a meeting》. ¶ 계획을 ~ lay aside 〔drop〕 a plan; give up a project 〔an idea〕 / 공부를 ~ give up *one's* studies; stop studying / 이야기를 ~ stop 〔leave off〕 talking / 거래를 ~ break off business connections 〔relations〕 《with》; close accounts 《with a bank》 / 싸움을 ~ give up a fight; quit (fighting) / 일을 ~ stop 〔quit〕 working; 《구어》 knock off (for the day) / 사업을 ~ quit *one's* business / 학교를 ~ leave 〔give up〕 school / 학교를 그만두게 하다 make 《*a person*》 leave 〔quit〕 school / 그녀는 집안 사정으로 학교를 그만두었다 She left 〔gave up〕 school for family reasons. / 그들은 그 연구를 그만두지 않았다 They continued 〔went on〕 with their study. / 이 정도로 진척된 일을 그만둔다는 것은 참으로 안타깝다 What a pity it is to discontinue a job that has got so far! / 오랫동안 연습을 그만두고 있다 I have been out of practice for a long time.

② 《폐지하다》 abolish; do away with. ¶ 형식적인 것은 모두 그만두자 Let us do away with all formalities. / 그런 관행은 그만두어져야 한다 Such practice should be done away with.

③ 《술·습관 따위를》 stop 《drinking》;

give up 《smoking》 (★ stop과 give up은 동명사를 목적어로 취함. 부정사를 사용하여 stop to drink로 하면 「술을 마시기 위해서 서다」의 뜻이 됨); break *oneself* of 《a habit》; 《삼가다》 refrain 〔abstain〕 from 《drinking》. ¶ 술을 ~ stop 〔give up〕 drinking / 나쁜 습관을 ~ abandon 〔leave off〕 *one's* bad habits.
④ 《사임하다》 resign 《*one's* post》; retire 《from office》; quit 〔throw up〕 《*one's* job》. ¶ 회사를 ~ leave (the job of) the company / 공무원 생활을 ~ leave 〔retire from〕 government service / 그는 교장직을 그만두었다 He resigned his post as headmaster.

**그만이다** ① 《그것뿐이다》 be the end 《of it》; be no more than that; 《상관없다》 do not mind 〔care, matter〕. ¶ 이제 ~ This is all I have. / 늦어도 ~ It doesn't matter if you are late.
② 《더할 나위 없다》 《최고》 (be) superb; the best; perfect; 《이상적》 (be) ideal; best fit 《for》; most suitable 《for》; 《탈잡을 데 없다》 (be) impeccable; unimpeachable. ¶ 낚시에 그만인 곳 a capital spot for fishing / 날씨가 ~ This is ideal weather. / 이건 맛이 ~ This tastes superb. / 그녀의 요리 솜씨는 ~ She is a perfect cook.
③ 《만족하다》 (be) satisfactory; 《족하다》 (be) enough; sufficient. ¶ 만 원만 있으면 ~ Ten thousand won 「will do 〔is enough〕. / 커피 한 잔이면 ~ Just a cup of coffee will suffice me.

**그만저만** to about that extent 〔degree〕; about so far 〔much〕; reasonably (much). **~하다** (be) so-so; ... or so; ... or thereabout; be not so bad; be neither good nor bad. ¶ 음식을 ~ 먹어라 eat reasonably 〔reasonable amount〕 / 그녀의 성적은 그만저만하다 Her grades are so-so. / 날도 저물었으니 이제 일을 ~ 끝내자 Darkness has got around and let's wind up our work now. / 「그 사람 병세는 어떻습니까」—「그저 ~합니다」 "How is he?"—"He is just so-so." / 그는 ~한 사람이 아니다 He is no ordinary man.

**그만큼** that much; so much; to that extent; in that degree. ¶ ~ 말했는데도 after all I have said; after all advice I gave / ~이나 돈이 있으면서도 for all *one's* riches; with all *one's* wealth / 나도 ~의 노력은 했다 I too have done that much effort. / ~이면 당장에는 충분하다 That's all I want for the moment. / ~ 충고를 해도 그는 듣지 않았다 All my advice was lost upon him. / 내 장서는 그것이 전부가 아니고 2층에 ~ 또 있다 These are not all the books I have, I have as many more upstairs. / 그는 ~ 공부를 했으니 시험에 떨어지는 일은 없을 것이다 Since he worked so hard, he can't fail the examination.

**그만하다** 《정도》 be in the same condition; be neither better nor worse; 《수량·정도》 be about 〔much〕 the same; be as much 〔many〕 as; be not less (than); be not more (than). ¶ 그의 병세는 그저 ~ His condition is getting neither better nor worse. / 사고가 그만하기 다행이다 It was fortunate for you that the accident wasn't so bad. / 그도 키가 꼭 ~ He is just about the same height. / 이것도 그만한 무게를 가지고 있다 This is as heavy as that. / 이것도 역시 그만한 날짜가 걸린다 This will take me as many days as that. / 내 모자의 크기도 꼭 ~ My hat is just as big as that. *or* My hat is of the same size with it. / 그만한 노력도 안 하고 어찌 성공하기를 바라느냐 How could you dream of a success without making that much of effort. / 그만한 일을 갖고 소란을 피우지 마라 Don't make a fuss about a minor thing like that.

**그맘때** about 〔around〕 that time; (at) that time of day 〔night, year〕. ¶ 사과는 ~가 제일 맛이 좋다 That is the time when apples taste most delicious. / ~의 만 원은 내게 큰 돈이었다 In those days ten thousand won was a big amount for me. / ~ 나도 무척 장난이 심했다 I was quite naughty when I was that age. / ~가 사내로서 한창 기운이 왕성한 때다 Men are most vigorous at that time of life. / 그는 어제도 바로 ~ 왔었다 He was here yesterday too at just about that time.

**그물** ① 《고기 잡는》 a net; netting [총칭]. ¶ ~을 뜨다 make 〔weave〕 a net; net / ~을 던지다 cast 〔throw〕 a net / ~을 치다 set 〔stretch〕 a net / ~을 당기다 draw a net (ashore); pull a net in; trawl a net (트롤어선에서) / ~로 고기를 잡다 net (a) fish; catch (a) fish in a net / ~에 걸리다 be caught in a net / ~에 든 고기 (a) fish caught in a net; (a) netted fish / 한 ~로 수천 마리의 정어리가 잡힌다 One haul of the net catches thousands of sardines. ② [비유적] ¶ 철도가 ~처럼 전국

에 퍼져 있다 A network of railroads covers the whole country. / 그는 정적이 쳐놓은 ~에 걸렸다 He found himself caught in the trap that had been laid by his politcal enemies.
◉ ~눈 the meshes of a net. ~바늘 a netting needle. ~선반 a baggage 〔luggage〕 rack. ~채 a netted ladle; a skimmer. ~침대 a hammock (of netting). ~코 =그물눈.

**그믐** the end 〔last day〕 of the month. ¶ 섣달 ~《on》 the last day of the year; 《on》 New Year's Eve / ~께 around the end of the month / 이 달 ~에 at the end of this month.
◉ ~날=그믐. ~(날)밤 the last night of the (lunar) month. ~사리 corbina caught around the end of the month. ~ 초승 the end of the month and the beginning of the following month. ~치 rain 〔snow〕 around the end of the lunar month. ~칠야 the dark night around the end of the (lunar) month.

**그밖** the rest; the others. ¶ ~의 other; 《덧붙여》 additional; further / ~에 besides; moreover; in addition; on top of that; further / ~의 여러 가지 것 many other things / ~의 것은 아무 것도 모른다 I know nothing else.

**그빨로** in *one's* usual nasty way.

**그뿐** only that (much); no more than that; that alone. ¶ 필요한 것은 ~이다 That is all I want. / 이야기는 ~이다 That's all there is to it.

**그사이, 그새** the while; the interval; meantime; the time that has elapsed; this while《since I saw you, since *a thing* happened, *etc.*》; so soon; before *one* knows it. ¶ ~에 in that time 〔interval〕; in the meantime; so soon / ~에 점심을 먹을 수 있다 We can take our lunch in that time. / ~에 그는 달아났다 In the meantime he ran away. / ~ 안녕하십니까 How have you been all this while?

**그스르다** ⇨ 그슬리다.

**그슬리다** 《표면을》 scorch; brown 《the meat》; singe (모발을); char (까맣게); burn; smoke (연기로). ¶ 돼지〔개〕를 불에 ~ singe a pig 〔dog〕 / 셔츠를 약간 ~ scorch *one's* shirt a little / 새까맣게 ~ char; burn to a cinder.

**그악스럽다** (be) excessive; undue; hard; harsh; fierce; ferocious; overeager; 《장난이 심하다》 (be) mischievous; 《부지런하다》 (be) industrious. ¶ 그악스러운 사람〔짐승〕 a fierce person 〔animal〕 / 그악스럽게 일하다 overwork *oneself;* work too hard / 그악스럽게 돈을 벌다 be all eagerness to make money; be engrossed in moneymaking / 아무를 그악스럽게 부리다 drive *a person* hard; sweat *a person.*

**그야** ① 《그것이야》 that; it. ¶ ~ 그렇지만 It may be so, but…. / ~ 물론이다 It is a matter of course. / ~ 그렇지 Oh, that is true. / ~ 그럴 수 있지 That is quite possible. / ~ 누가 모르나 Who wouldn't know that? ② 《그 사람이야》 he; she. ¶ ~ 돈이 많지 Him—he has lots of money.

**그야말로** ① 《참으로》 really; indeed; certainly. ¶ ~ 네가 잘못이다 Certainly you are wrong. *or* You are indeed to blame. / ~ 구사일생이었구나 You really had a narrow escape. / 불꽃놀이는 ~ 장관이었다 The display of fireworks was nothing short of spectacular. ② 《그 사람이야말로》 he himself. ¶ ~ 그 자리에 적임자이다 He is the very man for the job. ③ 《그것이야말로》 that is... indeed. ¶ ~ 안성맞춤이다 That is just the thing. / ~ 내가 원하던 것이다 That's the very thing I wanted. / ~ 힘든 일이다 That is indeed a difficult job.

**그어주다** share; apportion. ¶ 아무에게 한몫을 ~ give a share to *a person;* 《미구어》 cut *a person* in 《on》.

**그역시**(—亦是) that 〔it〕 also; that 〔it〕 too; 《사람》 he, too 〔also〕. ¶ ~ 사실이다 That also is true. / ~ 마음에 들지 않는다 I don't like it either. / ~ 피아노를 칠 줄 안다 He, too, can play the piano.

**그예** at last; at length; at long last; finally; ultimately; in the long run; in the last analysis. ¶ ~ 실패하고 말다 end in failure / 그는 ~ 술 때문에 죽고 말았다 Drink ended him. / ~ 시험에 합격하였다 He has passed the examinations at last. / ~ 빚을 받아냈다 I collected the debt at long last.

**그외**(—外) the rest; the others. ⇨ 그밖. ¶ ~에는 아무 말도 안 했나 Did he not say anything else?

**그윽이** in secret 〔private〕; in *one's* heart; inwardly; quietly. ¶ ~ 사모하다 love 〔admire〕 《*a person*》 in *one's* heart.

**그윽하다** ① 《장소가》 (be) quietly secluded; peacefully retired; calmly hidden; lonely; quiet. ¶ 골짜기의 그윽한 곳 the secluded 〔quiet〕 place of a valley. ②《생각·뜻이》(be) subtle and profound; mystic; deep; 《소리가》(be) dim and lonely. ¶ 절에서 울려오는 그윽한 종소리 the dim and lonely sound of a temple bell / 그의 그림에는 그윽한 아름다움이 있다 There is a mystic beauty in his painting. ③《정취가》(be) refined; tasteful; elegant; 《향기 등이》(be) sweet; fragrant. ¶ 장미의 그윽한 향기 a sweet scent [a faint fragrance] of roses.

**그을다** ①《연기에》get [become] sooty; be black with smoke; be soot-covered. ¶ 연기에 그을은 천장 a「smoke=stained [sooty] ceiling / 부엌 천장이 거멓게 그을었다 The ceiling of the kitchen has become sooty.
②《볕에》get a tan [suntan] (알맞게); get sunburned [sunburnt] (심하게). ¶ 햇볕에 그을은 얼굴 a sunburnt [sunbrowned] face / 바닷바람에 구릿빛으로 그을은 어부 a fisherman tanned leathery in the salt air / 알맞게[새까맣게] ～ be「well [heavily] tanned (with the sun); have a good [deep] tan《on *one's* back》/ 햇볕에 피부가 구릿빛으로 그을었다 His skin is bronzed by the sun.

**그을리다**《연기에》smoke; fume; fumigate; cover [stain] with soot; make (all) sooty; 《볕에》sunburn. ¶ 연기가 천장을 ～ smoke stains the ceiling with soot / 난로의 연기가 천장을 그을렸다 The stove smoked the ceiling.

**그을음** soot. ¶ ～이 앉다[끼다] be sooted; become sooty; have soot on it / ～을 쓸어내다 sweep away [wipe off] the soot.

**그이** that person; he; him; 《여자》she; her.

**그이들** those people; they; them.

**그저** ①《그대로 사뭇》still; without ceasing [stopping]; with no letup; with no halt. ¶ 비가 ～ 오고 있다 It keeps on raining. / ～ 책만 읽고 있다 He is still reading.
②《생각 없이》recklessly; wildly; aimlessly; intemperately; heedlessly; blindly; casually; 《하는 일 없이》without doing anything (in particular); 《아무것도 안 가지고》without bringing anything; 《까닭 없이》without (giving any) reason; unreasonably. ¶ ～ 자꾸 두드리다 hit wildly; beat《*a person*》blind / ～ 빚을 마구 지다 go into debt recklessly / 지나는 길에 ～ 들렀네 As I happened to come this way, I have just dropped in at your house. / ～ 농으로 한 말일세 I said it just for fun. / 그는 ～ 앉아만 있다 He is sitting down doing nothing.
③《보통으로》so-so; all right (but not terribly good). ¶ ～ 쓸 만하다 be just passable /「영화가 재미있었느냐」—「～ 그렇더라」"Was the movie interesting?"—"It was so-so." /「사업이 어떤가」—「～ 그래」"How is your business?"—"Just so-so [It is not quite satisfactory]."
④《단지》mere; slight; just; only. ¶ ～ 약간 just a little [bit] / ～ 재미로 just for fun / 그는 ～ 이름뿐인 총재이다 He is a president only in name.
⑤《제발》please; I beg of you. ¶ ～ 네가 참아라 Won't you be patient, please? / ～ 살려만 주시오 Please save me!
⑥《그것 봐》there! (just as I expected). ¶ 내 ～ 그럴 줄 알았어. 역시 찻잔을 깨뜨렸구나 There—I knew you'd do it, you have broken the cup.

**그저께** (the) day before yesterday. ¶ 그저껫밤 (the) night before last.

**그적거리다** scrawl; dash; scribble. ¶ 그적그적 scribblingly / 그녀는 엽서에 몇 자 그적거렸다 She scrawled a few words on a postcard.

**그전**(—前) before that; previous [prior] to that time; former times [days]; sometime before. ¶ ～에 ago; formerly; in former times; before; before that time; previous [prior] to that / ～같이 as before; as of old; as usual; as heretofore / ～에 돌아오너라 Come back before that time. / ～에는 여기에 집이 있었다 Formerly a house stood here. / 우리는 ～부터 아는 사이다 We've known each other for a long time. / 그는 ～에 빌려 갔던 책을 가져왔다 He has returned the book he borrowed sometime ago.

**그제야** only then; not... until; for the first time; only when; only after. ¶ 세 번 고함을 지르니 ～ 내다보았다 He did not look out of the window until I had shouted three times. *or* He looked out of the window only after I had shouted three times. / 사람은 건강을 잃게 되면 ～ 그 고마움을 알게 된다 People do not know the blessing [value] of health until they lose it. / 내 말을 듣고 ～ 자기가 잘못한 것을 그는 알았다 At my explanation he realized for the first time that he had made a mistake. *or* I had to explain it to him before he realized he had made a mistake.

**그중**(一中) ①《그것 중》among the rest 〔others〕; among them (all); of them (all); between them. ¶ 너도 ~의 한 사람이다 You are (one) of the number. ②《가장》the most; the best. ¶ ~ 좋다〔나쁘다〕be the best〔worst〕/ 나는 이 걸 ~좋아한다 I like this better than the others.

**그즈음** about that time; around then.

**그지없다** 《한이 없다》(be) endless; boundless; limitless; 《표현할 수 없다》(be) indescribable; inexpressible; be beyond expression〔description〕; be too… for words. ¶ 그지없는 기쁨 a limitless joy / 그지없이 넓은 평야 the boundless expanse of the plains / 그지없이 행복하다 be as happy as (happy) can be / 불쌍하기 ~ be too pitiful for words / 그지없이 기뻐하다 be delighted beyond measure; be only too pleased / 그지없이 유감이다 be most regrettable; nothing is more regrettable than 《this》/ 파도타기는 통쾌하기 ~ Surf riding is extremely thrilling. / 그 경치는 아름답기 ~ The view is beautiful beyond description.

**그쯤** ①《그 정도》that〔as〕much; that quantity〔degree〕; such a caliber. ¶ ~은 알고 있다 I know as〔that〕much. / ~은 문제가 아니다 To that extent〔If that's all〕, there is no problem. / ~이면 충분할 테죠 That will be enough. ②《장소》around there. ¶ 이것은 ~에다 놓아라 Put this somewhere around there.

**그치다** ① [자동사]《멎다》stop; cease; 《조용해지다》calm down; subside; 《끝나다》end; come to an end; be over; 《바람·소리 따위가》die down. ¶ 그칠 새 없이 ceaselessly; continuously; with no break〔letup〕/ 그칠 새 없는 걱정 ceaseless〔never-ending〕anxiety; constant worry / 비가 그쳤다 The rain has stopped. *or* It has stopped raining. (★ It has stopped to rain.은 불가함). / 바람이 그쳤다 The wind has died〔calmed〕down. / 소나기가 그쳤다 The shower has passed. / 비가 그치는 대로 밖으로 나가자 As soon as the rain is over, let's go out. / 우레와 같은 박수 소리가 한동안 그치지 않았다 The thunderous applause didn't die down for some time. / 그의 장광설이 언제 그칠지 알 수 없다 I cannot imagine when his long speech will come to an end. ② [타동사]《중단하다》stop《*do*ing》; cease from《*do*ing》; discontinue; leave off; drop; 《끝내다》end; put an end to; bring《*a matter*》to an end. ¶ 울음을 ~ stop crying / 일을 ~ stop working; end *one's* work / 이야기를 ~ stop〔cease, leave off〕talking / 그치지 않고 …하다 go on *do*ing; keep on *do*ing; continue to… / 내가 방에 들어가자 그들은 얘기를 뚝 그쳤다 On my entering the room, they suddenly ceased talking. / 나는 프랑스어 공부를 그친지 꽤 오래되었다 I stopped〔left off, gave up〕studying French quite a long time ago.

**그토록** so; so much〔many〕; to such an extent; so〔that〕far; 《부정》not very〔so〕. ¶ ~ 잘해 주시니 고맙습니다 Thank you for doing so much for me. / ~ 심한 병은 아니다 It is not a very serious illness. / ~ 그를 만나 보고 싶습니까 Are you so anxious to see him? *or* Do you want to see him that bad?《미》/ 정세가 ~ 나쁠 줄은 몰랐다 I didn't realize the situation was that〔quite so〕bad.

**그후**(一後) after that; thereafter; subsequently; 《이래》since (then); ever since (그후 내내); 《그때부터》from that time on. ¶ ~의 later; subsequent / ~에 later (on); at a later time / ~ 그녀 소식을 듣지 못했다 I have not heard anything about her since then. / ~ 그녀를 만나지 못했다 I have not seen her since that time. / ~ 그는 미국으로 유학을 갔다 After that he went to America to study. / ~ 쭉 그는 서울에 살고 있다 He has lived in Seoul「since then〔from that time on〕. / ~ 어떻게 지냈느냐 How have you been (getting along)? / ~ 며칠 지나서 그가 나를 찾아왔다 A few days later he called on me.

**극**(極) ①《지구·자기의》a pole. ¶ ~의 polar / 북〔남〕극 the north〔south〕pole / 양〔음〕극 the positive〔negative〕pole. ②《절정》the height; the zenith; 《최악의 상태》the bottom〔worst〕; 《극도·막다른 곳》the climax; the extreme; the extremity. ¶ 영화(榮華)의 극 the height of glory / 피로가 극에 이르다 be exhausted to the extreme; be utterly exhausted / 가난이 극에 이르다 be reduced to extreme poverty / 흥분은 극에 달했다 The excitement rose to a climax. / 그 나라의 경제는 번영의 극에 달해 있다 The economy of the country is at the height of its prosperity. ◉ 극궤도 a polar orbit. 극좌표 〖수학〗 polar coordinates. 극지방 the polar regions.

**극**(劇) a drama; a play (★ 예술의 한 부문으로서의 연극을 뜻할 때는 drama에 the가 붙는 경우가 많음. drama는 play보다 문어적임. 구어에서는 흔히 play가 쓰임). ¶ 극문학 dramatic literature / 극중 극 a play within a play / 극으로 꾸미다 dramatize 《a novel》; make a dramatic version of 《a story》/ 극을 공연하다 perform 〔stage〕 a play / 극에 출연하다 play a part in the play / 이 극은 아주 호평이었다 The play made a tremendous hit. *or* The play was very popular. ◉ 극영화 a narrative film. 극화(畫) a story comic.

**극값**(極—) 〖수학〗 extreme value.

**극광**(極光) an aurora; the polar lights. ¶ 북〔남〕~ aurora borealis 〔australis〕; the northern 〔southern〕 lights.

**극구**(極口) [부사적] exceedingly; very; in the extreme; to a high degree. ¶ ~ 변명하다 spare no pains to defend *oneself;* make every sort of excuses; go to extremes in excusing *oneself* / ~ 칭찬하다 speak highly of; be loud in 《*a person's*》 praise; praise 〔speak of〕 《*a person*》 in the highest possible terms; praise 《*a person*》 to the skies.

**극권**(極圈) the polar circles. ◉ 남〔북〕~ the Antarctic 〔Arctic〕 Circle.

**극기**(克己) self-restraint; self-control; self-denial (★ self-restraint〔-control〕은 「외부로부터의 자극이나 유혹을 무시하는 능력」, self-denial은 「자기 내부의 욕망을 억제하는 인내력」을 뜻함). ~하다 control 〔deny〕 *oneself;* exercise self-control 〔self-denial〕. ◉ ~심 a self-denying spirit; a spirit of self-denial: ~심이 없다 have no command over *oneself* / ~심이 있는 self-denying; stoical / ~심이 있는 사람 a stoic person; a man of self-restraint. ~주의 stoicism.

**극난**(極難) extreme difficulty. ~하다 (be) very difficult 〔hard〕.

**극단**(極端) an extreme; an extremity; an excess. ¶ ~의〔적인〕 extreme; excessive (과도한); radical (과격한) / ~적으로 extremely; to excess; too far / ~적인 수단 extremes; an extreme measure; radical steps / ~적 좌경파 the ultra-left / ~으로 흐르다 go to extremes 〔excess〕; run to an extreme; go too far / ~에서 ~으로 흐르다 go from one extreme to another / 그것은 ~적인 예다 That is an extreme case. / ~적으로 말하면 그는 인간 쓰레기다 To put it in an extreme way, he is the scum of the earth. / 젊은 사람들은 ~으로 흐르기 쉽다 Young people are apt to go to extremes. / 양 ~은 일치한다 Extremes meet. ◉ ~론 an extreme 〔a radical〕 view. ~주의 extremism; radicalism; ultraism: ~주의자 an extremist.

**극단**(劇團) a theatrical 〔dramatic〕 company; a troupe. ¶ 지방 순회 ~ a troupe on the road; a traveling troupe. ◉ ~원 a member of a dramatic company.

**극단**(劇壇) 《무대》 the stage; 《연극계》 the theatrical world. ¶ ~에 서다 come 〔go〕 on the stage / ~을 떠나다 leave 〔go off〕 the stage / ~ 출신이다 come from the legitimate stage.

**극대**(極大) ① 《지극히 큼》 the greatest; the largest. ② 〖수학〗 the maximum. ◉ 극대값 the maximum value.

**극대화**(極大化) maximization. ~하다 maximize. ¶ 우리는 이윤을 ~해야 한다 We must maximize profits.

**극도**(極度) the highest degree; the extreme; the utmost. ¶ ~의 utmost; extreme; maximum / ~로 extremely; in the extreme; to the utmost 〔highest degree〕 / ~에 달하다 reach 〔be carried to〕 an extreme; reach the utmost limit 《of》 / ~로 흥분하다 be extremely excited; be excited in the extreme / ~로 비관하다 be in extreme grief / ~로 불행하다 be at the bottom of Fortune's wheel / ~로 피곤하다 be exhausted to the extreme; be extremely tired / ~의 신경 쇠약에 걸리다 have a nervous breakdown of the worst kind / 요즘 도덕의 퇴폐는 ~에 이르렀다 In these days, the depravity of morals is at its worst.

**극독**(劇毒) a deadly 〔violent, terrible〕 poison.

**극동**(極東) the Far East. ¶ ~의 Far Eastern. ◉ ~공군 the Far East Air Force. ~문제 Far Eastern problems. ~위원회 《유엔의》 the Far Eastern Commission (생략 F.E.C.): ~ 자문 위원회 the Far Eastern Advisory Commission (생략 F.E.A.C.).

**극락**(極樂) ① 〖불교〗 (the Buddhist) paradise; the abode of the blessed; the home of the happy dead. ¶ 저 다락방에 비하면 이곳은 정말 ~이다 Compared with that attic, this is a real paradise. ② 《극히 안락함》 supreme

happiness; perfect bliss.
◉ ~(세)계 = 극락. ~왕생(往生): ~왕생하다 die a peaceful death. ~전(殿) the hall of Paradise. ~정토(淨土) the land of Perfect Bliss. ~조(鳥) a bird of paradise.

**극량**(極量) 《약의》 a maximum 〔fatal〕 dose. ¶ ~ 이상으로 수면제를 먹다 take an overdose of sleeping tablets.

**극력**(極力) [부사적] with all *one's* might; to the best of *one's* ability; to the utmost; as... as possible 〔as *one* can〕. ¶ ~ 힘쓰다 do 《it》 with all *one's* might; do *one's* best; make every effort 《to *do*》 / ~ 반대하다 oppose stubbornly 〔to the last〕.

**극렬**(極烈) severity; violence; intensity. ~하다 (be) severe; violent; intense; vehement. ¶ ~한 언사 vehement language.

**극론**(極論) an extreme 〔a radical〕 argument. ~하다 make an extreme argument; go so far as to say (that...). ¶ 매국노라고까지 ~하다 go so far as to brand 《*a person*》 as a traitor.

**극명하다**(克明—) [형용사적] 《분명하다》 (be) clear; distinct; plain; obvious; [동사적] 《똑똑히 밝힘》 make 《*a matter*》 clear 〔plain〕; bring 《*a matter*》 to light. ¶ 극명한 사실 an obvious fact / 문제를 극명하게 설명하다 explain a matter 「clearly 〔in detail〕.

**극미**(極微) ~하다 (be) infinitesimal; microscopic. ◉ ~량 an infinitesimal quantity.

**극복**(克服) conquest. ~하다 conquer; overcome; get over 《*something*》; surmount. ¶ ~하기 어려운 insuperable 《problem》; unsurmountable 《difficulty》 / 병을 ~하다 get over an illness / 온갖 어려움을 ~하다 overcome 〔surmount, weather〕 all difficulties / 그들은 재정상의 곤란을 잘 ~했다 They successfully tided over their financial difficulties. / 정부는 인플레를 ~했다 The government succeeded in beating inflation.

**극본**(劇本) the script of a play; the acting edition of a play; a playbook.

**극북**(極北) the extreme north; 《북극》 the North Pole.

**극비**(極秘) strict secrecy; 《극비사항》 a top secret. ¶ ~의 top-secret; highly-classified 《미》; strictly confidential / ~리에 「with utmost 〔under tightest〕 secrecy / ~에 부치다 keep 《*a matter*》 in absolute secrecy; guard 《*a matter*》 with great secrecy / 그에게 ~의 서한을 보냈다 I have sent him a top-secret letter. / 그 사건은 ~로 되어 있다 The affair is kept 「strictly confidential 〔in strict secrecy〕. *or* Strict secrecy is being preserved over the affair. / 의사(議事)는 ~리에 진행되었다 The proceedings were conducted in profound secrecy. ◉ ~서류〔문서〕 top-secret 〔highly classified〕 documents. ~정보 a 「highly confidential 〔top-secret〕 information.

**극빈**(極貧) extreme 〔dire〕 poverty; destitution. ~하다 (be) extremely poor; destitute. ◉ ~자 a destitute person; the destitute [총칭]; a pauper.

**극상**(極上) the best; the first rate; the highest quality. ¶ ~의 first-rate; of the finest quality; the best; the choicest / ~의 치즈 cheese of the highest quality. ◉ ~품 the best (of *its* kind); an article of the finest 〔highest〕 quality.

**극성**(極性) 『전기·화학』 polarity. ¶ ~의 polar / (…에) ~을 주다〔없애다〕 polarize 〔depolarize〕.

**극성**(極盛) ① 《세력이》 highly flourishing 〔thriving〕; being very prosperous. ② 《성질이》 being extreme. ~스럽다 (be) impatient; impetuous; overeager; mad; [서술적] get frantic; run to extremes; run high. ¶ ~스러운 사람 an impatient 〔impetuous〕 person / ~스러운 언동 impatient 〔intemperate〕 conduct / 자녀 교육에 ~스러운 어머니 a mother over-solicitous for her children's education / ~스럽게 일하다 work like mad; work furiously / 그는 직공들이 쓰러질 때까지 ~스럽게 일을 시켰다 He drove the workers unmercifully until they collapsed.

**극소**(極小) the smallest; 『수학』 the minimum. ¶ ~의 smallest; minimum; infinitesimal. ◉ ~값 『수학』 the minimum value. ~량 the minimum. ~수 the minimum number; a small minority.

**극시**(劇詩) a dramatic poem; dramatic 「poetry [총칭].

**극심하다**(極甚—) (be) extreme; excessive; intense; severe; terrible; heavy. ¶ 극심한 경쟁 a keen 〔tough〕 competition / 극심한 더위 an intense heat / 극심한 추위 a severe cold / 극심한 타격 devastating damage / 극심한 피해를 입다 suffer heavy losses / 재계의 불황이 요새처럼 극심한 때는 없었다 Never before has the financial world experienced such a heavy depression.

**극악**(極惡) atrocity; villainy. ～하다 (be) flagrant; most wicked (사악한); atrocious (잔악한); heinous (증오의); villainous (지독한). ¶ ～한 범죄 a heinous crime / 그의 ～무도한 행위는 용서할 수 없다 His flagrant misconduct is unpardonable. ◉ ～인 an utter villain; a scoundrel of the deepest dye; a fiend; a devil.

**극약**(劇藥) a powerful medicine [drug]; 「a poison (독약).

**극양**(極洋) the polar seas. ◉ ～어업 the polar-sea fishery.

**극언**(極言) severe [unreserved] criticism; unsparing words. ～하다 criticize《*a person*》severely; go so far as to say (that…); speak in unsparing words. ¶ ～하면 to put it「strongly [at its most extreme] / 반역자라고까지 ～하다 go so far as to brand《*a person*》as a traitor / ～하면 그는 배신자다 To put it strongly, he is a betrayer.

**극우**(極右) the extreme [far] right. ¶～의 extreme right-wing; ultrarightist. ◉ ～단체 an ultrarightist group [organization]. ～분자 an extreme rightist; extreme right-wing elements; ultraconservatives. ～사상 an ultrarightist ideology; ultraconservatism.

**극작**(劇作) playwriting; dramatic writing. ～하다 write a play. ◉ ～가 a playwriter; a playwright. ～법 (techniques of ) playwriting.

**극장**(劇場) a theater [theatre《영》]; a playhouse. ¶ 원형 ～ an amphitheater / 야외 ～ an open-air theater / 개봉 ～ a first-run theater. ◉ ～가 a theater district [quarter]. ～식당 a theater restaurant. ～안내인 a theater attendant; an usher. ～주(主) the proprietor of a theater. 국립～ the National Theater of Korea.

**극저온**(極低溫) an extremely low temperature. ◉ ～물리학 very low temperature physics.

**극적**(劇的) dramatic. ¶ ～인 장면[정경] a dramatic scene [sight] / ～으로 dramatically / ～인 생애 an eventful life / 그 사건의 ～인 재현 the dramatic representation of the event / ～ 효과를 노리다 aim at a dramatic effect / ～인 역전 홈런으로 승리를 거두다 win a game by a dramatic reversal home run / 두 사람은 ～으로 다시 만났다 The two met again most dramatically [in a most pathetic way].

**극점**(極點) 〖지리〗《남·북극점》 the South [North] Pole. ⇨ 극(極).

**극젱이** 〖농업〗 a kind of plow which is used for light plowing.

**극좌**(極左) the extreme left. ¶ ～의 extreme left-wing; ultraleftist. ◉ ～분자 an extreme leftist; extreme left-wing elements; an ultraleftist. ～사상 an ultraleftist ideology; extreme left-wing thought. ～파 the extreme left (wing, faction).

**극지**(極地) the polar regions. ◉ ～식물 an arctic plant. ～탐험 a polar exploration [expedition]. ～횡단비행 a transpolar flight.

**극진**(極盡) ～하다 (be) very kind [cordial]; (utterly) devoted; hearty. ¶ ～히 kindly; cordially; heartily; devotedly / ～한 대접 heartwarming hospitality / ～히 대접하다 treat《*a person*》with the utmost courtesy / ～히 사랑하다 love deeply.

**극초단파**(極超短波) microwave.

**극치**(極致) the acme; the zenith; the culmination; the perfection. ¶ 예술의 ～ the highest reach of art / 미의 ～ the ideal of beauty / ～에 이르다 attain [reach] the highest perfection / 번영의 ～에 이르다 reach the zenith of prosperity / 원숙의 ～에 이르다 reach the acme of maturity / 정사(情死)는 숭고한 사랑의 ～라고 주장하다 argue that a lovers' suicide is the sublime culmination of love.

**극터듬다** scramble *one's* way up; struggle up inch by inch.

**극통**(劇痛·極痛) an acute [intense] pain; a severe [sharp, keen] pain.

**극평**(劇評) drama [theater] criticism. ◉ ～가 a drama [theater] critic.

**극피동물**(棘皮動物) an echinoderm.

**극하다**(極—) go to extremes; run to an extreme. ¶ 사치를 ～ indulge in an extravagant life; live in extreme luxury / 포학을 ～ act with extreme violence; be most tyrannical / 참상을 ～ present a most miserable sight.

**극한**(極限)《한계》a limit; bounds;《극단》an extremity; 〖수학〗 a limit. ¶ 인내의 ～에 달하다 reach the limit of *one's* patience / ～을 넘지 않다[넘다] keep within [go beyond] bounds / 능력의 ～까지 노력하다 exert *oneself* to the utmost limit of *one's* ability. ◉ ～값 a limiting value. ～대립 an extreme confrontation. ～상황 an extreme situation: ～ 상황에 놓이다 be placed in an extreme situation; be pushed to the limit. ～투쟁 struggle to the extremes; fight to the end; resorting to the extremism.

**극한**(極寒) intense 〔severe〕 cold; extremely cold weather.

**극형**(極刑) 《사형》 capital punishment; 《최대한의 형》 the maximum penalty. ¶ ～에 처하다 condemn 〔put〕 《*a person*》 to death 〔capital punishment〕 / 반역죄로 ～의 판결을 받다 be sentenced to death on a charge of treason.

**극히**(極—) extremely; exceedingly; in the extreme; to a (high) degree; very; most. ¶ ～ 미묘한 most delicate / ～ 드물게 very rarely / ～ 겸손하다 be extremely modest; be modest to a degree / ～ 유감이다 be most regrettable / ～ 만족해하다 be altogether satisfied 《at》 / 그것은 ～ 중요한 문제이다 It is a problem of vital 〔extreme〕 importance.

**근**(根) ① 《부스럼의》 the core 〔nucleus〕 (of a boil). ② 《뿌리》 a root. ③ 〖수학〗 a root. ④ 〖불교〗 bases of sensation (*i.e.* eye, ear, nose, tongue, body and mind).

**근**(筋) a muscle; 《심줄》 a sinew; a tendon. ¶ 근운동 muscular movement 〔motion〕 / 후두근 a posterior head muscle / 근무력증 myasthenia.

**근**(斤) a *kŭn* (= 600g).

**근**(近) about; near(ly); almost. ¶ 근 만 원 about 10,000 won / 근 삼백리 nearly 300 *ri*.

**근간**(近刊) 《최근에 나온》 a recent publication; a recent edition; 《곧 나올》 a forthcoming book. ¶ ～의 《magazines》 just out; recently published; latest; 《곧 나올》 forthcoming; upcoming 《미》; in preparation. ◉ ～(도)서 a recent publication; books just out; 《곧 나올》 forthcoming books: ～(도)서 소개 a review of recent publications. ～(도서)목록 a catalog of recent publications. ～예고 an announcement 「of books in preparation 〔of forthcoming books〕.

**근간**(近間) = 요새.

**근간**(根幹) ① 《뿌리와 줄기》 the root and the trunk. ② 《근본》 the basis (*pl.* -ses); 《핵심》 the nucleus; 《기조》 the keynote. ¶ …을 ～으로 on the basis of / 한국 산업의 ～ the basis of Korean industry / 우리 나라 외교의 ～ the keynote of our diplomacy / 농업은 나라의 ～이다 Agriculture is the basis of a nation.

**근거**(根據) a basis (*pl.* -ses); ground(s); a foundation; 《전거》 authority. ～하다 be based 〔founded〕 《on, upon》. ¶ ～ 있는 well-grounded〔-founded〕 / ～ 없는 groundless; baseless; unfounded / 전혀 ～ 없는 주장 a totally unfounded allegation / ～ 있는 보도 information from a reliable source; an authentic report / 역사적 ～가 없다 be historically unsupported / 그 소문은 전혀 ～ 없는 것이다 The rumor is totally unfounded. / 그의 비난에는 확실한 ～가 없다 There is no solid foundation for his charges. / 그의 말은 사실에 ～를 두고 있다 His statement is 「based on fact 〔authenticated in fact〕. / 그의 소문은 나도 들었지만, ～도 없고 사실도 아니었다 I heard a rumor about him, but there was nothing to it. It wasn't true. ◉ ～지 a base (of operations).

**근거리**(近距離) a short distance; a close range. ¶ ～에 at close quarters 〔range〕 / ～에 있다 be a little way off; be a short distance away 《from, here》. ◉ ～열차 a local train. ～전화 a short-distance call.

**근검**(勤儉) diligence and frugality; thrift and industry. ～하다 (be) diligent and thrifty. ◉ ～저축 thrift and saving.

**근경**(近景) a short-〔close-〕range view 「《of》.

**근경**(根莖) 〖식물〗 a rhizome; a rootstock; a rootstalk.

**근계**(謹啓) 《개인에 대해》 Dear Sir; Dear Mr. 〔Miss, Mrs., Ms.〕 ...; 《회사 등에》 Dear Sirs; Gentlemen 《미》.

**근고**(近古) the early modern age. ◉ ～사 the history of the early modern age.

**근고**(謹告) ～하다 inform with respect; 「announce respectfully.

**근골**(筋骨) bones and sinews; 《체격》 physique; build; physical structure. ¶ ～이 억센 팔 a sinewy 〔brawny〕 arm / ～이 건장한 사람 a muscular 〔sturdy〕 man; a man of the physique 〔strong build〕.

**근교**(近郊) the suburbs; the outskirts; the environs; the suburban districts. ¶ ～의 suburban; neighboring / 서울 ～에 in the suburbs 〔on the outskirts〕 of Seoul / 서울 및 그 ～ Seoul and its environs. ◉ ～농업 agriculture in suburban areas. ～도시 neighboring towns; the towns around a large city. ～주택 지구 suburban residential area.

**근근**(近近) shortly; before long; in a few days; in the near future.

**근근이**(僅僅―) 《가까스로》 narrowly; barely; with (much) difficulty. ¶ ~ 피하다 〔모면하다〕 have a narrow escape; escape 《death》 「narrowly 〔by a hairsbreadth〕 / ~ 생계를 이어나가다 make a meager living; be eking out a scanty livelihood / ~ 시험에 패스하다 scrape through 〔barely pass〕 the examination.

**근기**(根氣) 《인내력》 patience; perseverance; 《지구력》 endurance; stamina(육체적); staying power (정신적); 《정력》 energy. ¶ ~ 있는 patient; persevering / ~ 있게 patiently; perseveringly; with perseverance / ~가 필요한 일 work that demands perseverance; a laborious task / ~가 다하다 run out of energy; find *one's* energy exhausted; be unable to carry on any longer / ~가 없다 lack patience / ~ 있게 기다리다 wait patiently.

**근년**(近年) (in) recent 〔late〕 years.

**근농**(勤農) farming diligently. ~하다 farm diligently. ◉ ~가 a diligent farmer.

**근대** 〖식물〗 a chard. ◉ ~국 chard 「soup.

**근대**(近代) the modern age 〔period〕; modern 〔recent〕 times. ¶ ~의 modern; late / ~적인 modernistic; up-to-date (최신식의) / 비~적인 unmodern / ~적인 건물 a modern building / 지금도 사회 곳곳에는 전~적인 관습이 남아 있다 Premodern customs persist everywhere in our society now.
◉ ~건축 modern architecture. ~과학 modern science. ~국가 a modern nation. ~극 a modern drama. ~문명 〔문학〕 modern civilization 〔literature〕. ~사 modern history. ~사상 modern ideas; modernism. ~생활 modern life. ~성 modernity. ~영어 modern English. ~음악 modern music. ~5종경기 〖스포츠〗 the modern pentathlon. ~인 a modern; [총칭] modern people. ~장비 modern equipment. ~화 modernization: ~화하다 modernize; be modernized / 완전히 ~화된 공장 a fully modernized factory / 한국은 지난 50년간 급속히 ~화되었다 Korea has rapidly modernized itself for the last fifty years.

**근동**(近東) 〖지리〗 the Near East. ¶ ~의 Near Eastern / 중~ the Middle and Near East. ◉ ~제국(諸國) the Near Eastern countries.

**근드적거리다** sway slightly. ⇨ 간드작거리다.

**근래**(近來) these days; recently; lately; (in) recent years. ¶ ~의 recent; late / ~에 없던 쾌거 the most spectacular undertaking in recent years / ~에 보기 드문 큰 인물 the greatest man in recent years / 그건 ~에 없던 일이다 It is an incident we have seldom heard of. / ~에 없던 큰 비가 왔다 We haven't had such a heavy rain for some time.

**근량**(斤兩) weight. ¶ ~을 속이다 give 「short weight.

**근력**(筋力) ① 《힘》 muscular strength 〔power〕. ¶ ~을 강화하는 운동 strength training; muscle-building. ② = 기력.

**근로**(勤勞) labor; work; service. ~하다 work (hard); labor. ¶ ~에 대한 보수 compensation for *one's* service 〔work〕.
◉ ~감독관 a labor supervisor. ~계층 the working 〔wage earning〕 class. ~기준법 the Labor Standard Law. ~대중 the working people 〔masses〕. ~봉사(대) (volunteer) labor service (corps): ~봉사하다 serve 《a community》 by contributing physical labor. ~소득 an earned income: ~소득세 the earned income tax / ~소득자 a wage earner / ~ 소득자의 세 부담을 가중시키다 raise 〔hike〕 the tax burden of wage earners. ~의욕 the will to work: 이런 싼 보수로는 ~의욕이 상실된다 This low salary takes away my will to work. ~자 a worker; a working person; working people [총칭]: ~자의 날 labor day / ~자의 복지 the welfare of workers / 여성 ~자 a working woman. ~조건 working 〔labor〕 conditions. ~포장(褒章) the Labor Medal.

**근린**(近隣) *one's* 〔the〕 neighborhood, the vicinity. ¶ ~ 여러 나라 neighboring countries.

**근면**(勤勉) hard work; diligence; industry; assiduity. ~하다 be diligent 〔industrious, hardworking, assiduous〕.

> (용법) **diligent** 특정한 일에 열심히 종사하는, **industrious** 습관적, 성격적으로 부지런히 일하는, **hardworking** 구어적 표현으로 일·공부 따위에 성의를 다해 노력하는, **assiduous** 격식을 갖춘 말로, 맡은 일에 주의를 기울여 근기 있게 노력한다는 뜻을 각각 나타낸다.

¶ ~하게 industriously; diligently / ~한 사람 a hard worker / ~한 국민 an industrious 〔a hardworking〕 people / ~한 정신 a hardworking spirit / ~하게 일하다 work hard 〔diligently〕 / ~

과 노력으로 그는 오늘날을 이룩하였다 By constant application and industry, he has made himself what he is. / ~은 성공의 어머니 《속담》 Diligence 〔Industry〕 is the mother of success.

**근모**(根毛) a root hair. =뿌리털.

**근무**(勤務) service; duty; work. ~하다 serve; do duty; work. ¶ N서(署) ~ 경찰 a policeman of 〔assigned to〕 the N police station / ~중에 (while) on duty / 시간 외 ~ overtime (work) / 야간 ~ night duty; a night shift / ~중이다 be on duty 〔at work〕 / ~를 게을리하다 neglect *one's* duties / 충실히 ~하다 serve faithfully; attend faithfully to *one's* work / ~를 쉬다 stay 〔be〕 away from work / 통역으로 ~하다 serve as an interpreter / 하루 8시간 ~하다 work 8 hours a day; work an 8-hour day / 나는 아침 8시부터 오후 4시까지 ~한다 I work from eight to four. / 그는 석유 회사에 ~하고 있다 He works for an oil company. / 나는 런던 지점 ~를 명받았다 I was assigned to work in the London branch office.
◉ ~능률 service efficiency. ~성적〔실적〕 work performance; *one's* service record. ~소집 service call. ~수당 duty allowance: 초과~수당 allowance for overtime work / 특별~수당 specific duty allowance / 해외~수당 a foreign service 〔an overseas〕 allowance. ~시간 office 〔working〕 hours; hours of duty: ~시간 후에 after (working) hours. ~연한 the term 〔period〕 of *one's* service. ~자 men in service 〔on duty〕. ~조건 working conditions 〔terms〕. ~지 수당 a service-area allowance. ~처 *one's* place of employment; *one's* office. ~평점서 an efficiency report. ~평정 the 《teacher's》 efficiency rating: ~평정서 an efficiency rating report. 8시간 ~제 the "portal-to-portal" 8-hour system.

**근묵자흑**(近墨者黑) He who touches pitch shall be defiled therewith. *or* You cannot keep bad company without being corrupted too.

**근방**(近方) the neighborhood; the vicinity. ⇨근처, 부근. ¶ 서울 ~ the suburbs of Seoul / 집 ~에 학교가 있다 There is a school in my neighborhood.

**근배**(謹拜) Yours truly 〔cordially, sincerely, respectfully〕.

**근본**(根本) 《근원》 the root; the source; the origin; the cause; 《기초》 the foundation; the basis; 《본질》 the essence. ¶ ~적(인) fundamental; basic; 《철저한》 drastic / ~적으로 fundamentally; 《철저히》 thoroughly; drastically / ~적인 세제 개혁 a drastic 〔radical, thorough〕 tax reform / 아무의 ~을 캐다 inquire into *a person's* past 〔precedents〕 / 사건을 ~적으로 조사하다 examine a matter to the last detail; make a thorough investigation of a matter 〔an affair〕 / 당분열의 ~원인은 수뇌부간의 세력 다툼에 있다 The split of the party has its origin in the struggle for power among its leaders. / 그 문제는 ~적으로 잘 해결되었다 The problem was settled completely. ◉ ~문제 a fundamental 〔root〕 problem. ~법칙 a fundamental law (기본법). ~원리 the fundamental 〔basic〕 principles. ~원인 the root cause 《of failure》. ~원리 the fundamental principle.

**근사**(近似) 《수치 따위가》 approximation. ◉ ~값 approximate quantity 〔value〕. ~계산 approximation; a rough calculation.

**근사하다**(近似—) ① 《거의 비슷하다》 be much 〔almost〕 the same 《as》; be closely akin 《to》; resemble closely; be almost similar 《to》. ¶ 그녀는 어머니와 성격이 ~ She bears a close resemblance to her mother in character. ② 《멋지다》 (be) fine; nice; wonderful; great; lovely; splendid. ¶ 근사한 미인 a striking 〔stunning〕 beauty / 근사한 스웨터 a lovely 〔nice〕 sweater / 참 근사한 아이디어로군 What a splendid idea! / 이것 참 근사하군 This is just great! *or* Oh, this is simply wonderful!

**근성**(根性) 《성질》 (a) nature; 《기질》 (a) temper; (a) disposition; 《정신·기백》 spirit; 《구어》 guts (기백). ¶ ~이 나쁜 ill-natured / ~이 썩어빠진 base; mean; despicable / 비뚤어진 ~ a crooked nature / 야비한 ~ a mean mind 〔spirit, disposition〕 / 상인 ~ a merchant spirit / 관리 ~ a bureaucratic nature / 그는 ~이 썩어 빠졌다 He is rotten-hearted. / 돈에 궁하면 거지 ~이 나오는 법이다 When a man is hard up for money, the beggar will come out. / 그에겐 ~이 있다〔없다〕 He has guts 〔no guts〕.

**근세**(近世) modern times. ⇨근대(近代). ◉ ~사(史) modern history.

**근소하다**(僅少—) (be) little; few; small; trifling. ¶ 근소한 수입 a small 〔meager〕 income / 근소한 차이 a slight difference; a narrow 〔slim〕 margin / 근소한 차로 이기다 win by a narrow margin / 그 법안은 50대 49라는 근소한 차로 통과되었다 The bill was passed by a narrow majority of 50 to 49.

**근속**(勤續) continuous service. ~하다 be in continuous service; serve long. ¶ 10년 ~ 사원 an office clerk with ten years of continuous service / 10년간 ~하다 keep *one's* seat for ten years; serve in《a company》for ten straight years / ~ 20년을 축하하다 celebrate the completion of《*a person's*》20 years' service. ◉ ~수당 a long-service allowance. ~연한 the length of *one's* service: ~연한에 따라 in proportion to the length of service. ~자 a person in long service. 장기~ 공무원 a public official on long-term service.

**근수**(斤數) the number of *kŭn*; the weight. ¶ ~를 속이다 give short weight / ~를 후하게 주다 give good weight.

**근수**(根數) 〖수학〗 a root; a radical.

**근시**(近視) short sight; 《근시안》 nearsightedness; shortsightedness; 〖의학〗 myopia. ¶ ~의 nearsighted; shortsighted / ~인 사람 a shortsighted person; a myope / ~용 안경 spectacles for shortsightedness / ~안적인 생각〔정책〕 a nearsighted view 〔policy〕 / 네 생각은 ~안적이다 You cannot see beyond your nose. ◉ 가성(假性)~ false nearsightedness; 〖의학〗 pseudomyopia.

**근신**(謹愼) 《언행을 삼가함》 behaving *oneself;* prudence; 《회개》 repentance; penitence 《from *one's* sins》. ~하다 be prudent (in speech and action); behave *oneself* (prudently); be on *one's* best behavior; repent 《of *one's* sins》. ¶ ~을 명하다 put 《*a person*》 on best behavior / 집에서 ~하도록 명받다 be ordered to confinement at home / 그는 지금 ~중이다 He is on his best behavior now.

**근실**(勤實) diligence and sincerity. ~하다 (be) diligent and sincere.

**근심** 《마음에 걸리는 것》 anxiety; uneasiness; apprehension; concern; 《불안》 misgivings; (a) fear; 《걱정》 worry; care; trouble. ~하다, ~스럽다 be anxious 〔concerned, solicitous〕 《about》; feel uneasy 《about》; be afraid 《of, that》; be troubled 〔worried〕 《about, that》; care; worry; fear.

> 용법 **anxiety** 무언가 좋지 않은 일이 장차 일어나지 않을까 염려하는 불안을 나타내는 말. **uneasiness** 불안·마음이 쓰여서 마음이 편치 않음을 나타내는 말. **apprehension** 미래에 대한 불안감. **concern** 무척 마음이 쓰이는 것을 뜻하나, anxiety보다는 부드러운 뜻. **misgivings** 미래의 일에 대한 의심·두려움·불신 등으로 생기는 초조한 마음. **fear** 현존하거나 예상되는 위험으로 야기되는 불유쾌하고 불안한 강력한 느낌. **worry** 걱정·애태움을 뜻하는 일상어로, 흔히 필요 없이하는 지나친 걱정을 뜻함. **care** 비교적 작은 걱정·근심을 나타내는 말로, 복수형으로 해서 걱정거리를 뜻함. **trouble** 귀찮고 성가신 일로 인한 걱정·근심을 뜻함.

¶ 돈에 관한 ~ financial troubles 〔worries〕; worries about money / ~으로 속을 썩이다 be worried sick / ~ 없이 살다 live 「at ease 〔free from care〕 / ~에 싸이다 be full of cares 〔worries〕; be beset with troubles / 아들의 건강을 ~하다 be anxious about *one's* son's health / 집안에 ~ 떠날 날이 없다 I always have one trouble or another at home. / 뭘 그리 ~하고 있는가 What are you worrying about? *or* What's the trouble 〔worry〕? / 그녀는 ~스러운 듯이 아들의 얼굴을 바라보았다 She looked at her son 「anxiously 〔with a worried look〕.

**근엄**(謹嚴) being dignified and serious; sobriety; sternness. ~하다 (be) dignified and serious; sober; stern. ¶ ~한 사람 a serious person; a man of stern morals / ~한 태도 a dignified mien / 아주 ~하다 be as grave as a judge 〔an owl〕.

**근염**(筋炎) 〖의학〗 myositis; inflammation of a muscle.

**근영**(近影) *one's* latest photograph. ¶ 저자 ~ the author's recent photograph.

**근원**(根源) the root; the source; the origin. ⇨ 근본. ¶ 모든 사회악의 ~ the root of all social evils / ~을 캐다 trace 《*a thing*》 to its origin; get at the root of 《*a thing*》 / ~을 …에 두다 originate 〔have its origin〕 in; take rise in / 분쟁의 ~을 없애다 eradicate the root of trouble; uproot 〔stamp out〕 the cause of trouble / 금전욕은 모든 악의 ~이다 Love of money is the root of all evil.

**근위대**(近衛隊) 《영》 the Royal Guards.

**근육**(筋肉) muscle(s); sinew(s). ¶ 손〔팔〕의 ~ a hand 〔an arm〕 muscle / ~의 muscular / ~이 잘 발달한 well-muscled; muscular; sinewy / 수영은 거의 모든 전신 ~을 움직이게 한다 Swimming brings nearly all the muscles of the body into active play.
◉ ~미 muscular beauty. ~보강제 a muscle enhancing drug. ~운동 a muscular movement. ~주사 an intramuscular injection. ~질 muscularity. ~통 a muscular ache. ~피로 muscular fatigue.

**근인**(近因) an immediate cause; a proximate cause.

**근일**(近日) recent days; one of these days; shortly; soon. ¶ ~중에 shortly; in a few days; at an early date / 이 영화는 ~ 개봉 예정이다 This film is to be released in a few days.

**근일점**(近日點) 〚천문〛 the perihelion.

**근자**(近者) these days; [부사적] recently; lately; of late.

**근작**(近作) *one's* latest work 〔product〕.

**근저**(近著) *one's* recent literary work.

**근저**(根柢) the root; the bottom; the foundation; the basis. ⇨ 근본. ¶ ~를 이루다 form the basis 《of》; be basic 《to》 / 이론을 ~부터 뒤집어 엎다 overturn a theory completely.

**근저당**(根抵當) fixed collateral.

**근절**(根絶) eradication; extermination. ~하다 eradicate; exterminate; root 〔stamp〕 out; wipe out; do away with. ¶ ~할 수 있는 eradicable / ~하기 어려운 악폐 ineradicable evils / 사회악을 ~하다 root 〔stamp〕 out social evils / 부정부패를 ~하다 exterminate irregularities and corruption.

**근점**(近點) 《가까운》 a near point; 《근지점》 the perigee; 《근일점》 the perihelion.

**근접**(近接) proximity; approach. ~하다 come 〔go〕 close 《to》; approach; draw near. ¶ ~한 neighboring; adjacent / ~한 마을 the neighboring villages / …에 ~해 있다 be 〔stand〕 close 〔adjacent〕 《to》; be near; be contiguous 《to, with》. ◉ ~관제 레이더 approach control radar (생략 ACR). ~지역 neighboring districts. ~표시기 〚철도〛 an approach indicator.

**근정**(謹呈) presentation; 《책을 출판사가 증정할 때》 A complimentary copy; 《책을 저자가 증정할 때》 With the author's compliments. ~하다 give; present 《*a thing* to *a person*》.

**근제**(謹製) 《제품에 붙여 쓸 때》 carefully produced 〔prepared〕 《by》. ~하다 make 〔produce〕 carefully.

**근조**(謹弔) offering 〔extending, tendering〕 *one's* condolence.

**근종**(筋腫) 〚의학〛 a myoma (*pl.* ~ta, ~s).

**근지럽다** ⇨ 간지럽다, 근질거리다.

**근지점**(近地點) 〚천문〛 the perigee; 《달의》 the lower apsis.

**근직**(謹直) conscientiousness. ~하다 (be) conscientious; scrupulous.

**근질거리다** ① 《몸이 가려워》 itch; feel itchy 〔creepy〕. ¶ 등이 ~ feel *one's* back itchy 〔creepy〕 / 코가 ~ *one's* nose tickles / 근질거리는 곳을 긁다 scratch an itchy place / 온몸이 ~ I itch all over. / 귀가 ~ My ear itches. ② 《마음이》 (have an) itch 《for action》; be impatient 〔irritated, nervous, itching〕 《for, to *do*》; ache 《to *do*》. ¶ 싸움을 하고 싶어 몸이 ~ have an itch for fighting; feel impatient to fight 〔attack〕 / 사실을 말하고 싶어 속이 ~ burn to tell the truth; can hardly wait to tell what happened / 그녀는 말대답이 하고 싶어 입이 근질거렸다 She was itching to talk back.

**근착**(近着) new 〔recent〕 arrival. ¶ ~의 recently received; just 〔recently〕 arrived / ~ 도서 recently arrived books. ◉ ~품 new 〔latest〕 arrivals.

**근채류**(根菜類) root crops; edible 〔esculent〕 roots; root vegetables.

**근처**(近處) the neighborhood. = 근방.

**근청**(謹聽) listening with attention. ~하다 listen to 《*a person*》 attentively 〔with attention〕.

**근치**(根治) a radical 〔complete〕 cure. ~하다 cure 《cancer》 completely 〔radically〕. ¶ ~하기 어렵다 be hard of radical cure / ~되다 be completely 〔radically〕 cured. ◉ ~약 an eradicative medicine.

**근친**(近親) a near 〔immediate〕 relation; a close relative; [집합적] kin. ¶ ~의 nearly related / 우리는 ~간이다 We are closely related to each other. ◉ ~결혼 intermarriage; consanguineous marriage. ~상간 《commit》 incest.

**근친**(覲親) a bride's (first) call at her parents' home. ~하다 make a bride's (first) call on her parents after her marriage.

**근태**(勤怠) diligence and indolence.

**근풀이**(斤—) 《근으로 팖》 selling by the pound; 《값을 따짐》 figuring out the cost of a pound. ~하다 figure out the cost of a pound; sell by the pound. 「Happy New Year.

**근하신년**(謹賀新年) (I wish you) A

**근해**(近海) 「the neighboring 〔home〕 waters; the adjoining 〔near〕 sea. ¶ ~의 coastal; coastwise / 부산 ~에서 in the sea near Busan / 한국 ~를 순항하다 cruise in Korean waters. ◉ ~어 a shorefish. ~어업 inshore 〔coast-wise〕 fishery 〔fishing〕. ~취항선 a coaster; a coastal liner. ~항로 a coastal line 〔route〕.

**근황**(近況) 《상황》 the recent 〔present〕 situation; 《안부》 how *one* is getting along. ¶ 우리 나라 대외 무역의 ~ the recent state of our foreign trade / ~을 알려 주십시오 Please let me know how you are getting along.

**글** ① 《학문》 learning; study; 《학식》 studies; scholarship; 《지식》 knowledge. ¶ 글이 있는〔없는〕 사람 a man of 〔without〕 learning / 글을 배우다 learn; study; pursue *one's* studies / 글을 좋아하다 love learning; be a great booklover / 글깨나 배웠다고 뽐내다 be proud of *one's* learning 〔scholarship〕 / 어깨너머 글도 쓸모가 있다 Picked=up knowledge is useful, too.
② 《문장》 a sentence; a piece of writing; a composition; an article; a style (문체). ¶ 좋은〔나쁜〕 글 good 〔bad〕 writing 〔style〕 / 글을 쓰다 write 《an essay, a composition》 / 글을 다듬다 polish 〔elaborate〕 *one's* style (of writing) / 글을 잘 쓰다 write well; write a good style / 감상을 글로 쓰다 put *one's* impression in writing.
③ 《글자》 a letter; a character. ¶ 글을 모르다 be unlettered 〔illiterate〕.

**글겅이** a currycomb. ◉ ~질 《빗질》 currying; 《착취》 exploiting the peasants: ~질하다 《빗질하다》 curry 《a horse》; 《착취하다》 exploit 《the peasants》.

**글구멍** a talent for learning. ¶ ~이 크다 have a great talent for learning.

**글귀**(一句) 《어구》 a phrase; a clause; 《인용절》 a passage; a line 《of a poem》. ¶ ~를 외다 memorize a passage.

**글그렁거리다** 《천식 따위로》 wheeze; 《고양이가》 purr; [서술적] make wheeze; make purr. ¶ 고양이가 목을 글그렁거리고 있다 The cat is purring.

**글동무** a schoolmate.

**글라디올러스** 〚식물〛 a gladiolus.

**글라스** ① 《잔》 a glass. ¶ ~를 서로 부딪치다 touch glasses / ~를 기울이다 drink wine 〔beer〕. ② =유리.

**글라이더** a glider. ¶ 패러~ a paraglider / 행~ a hang glider.

**글래머** glamour. ◉ ~걸 a glamour 〔well=stacked, busty〕 girl. 「수·포수).

**글러브** a (baseball) glove; a mitt (1루

**글러지다** 《잘못되어 가다》 go wrong 〔amiss, awry〕; 《잘못되다》 be spoiled 〔ruined〕; come to nothing; fail; end in failure; 《악화되다》 grow 〔get〕 worse; grow from bad to worse; deteriorate; decline (건강 따위가). ¶ 계획이 ~ a plan goes wrong 〔awry〕 / 정세는 점점 글러지고 있다 The situation is going from bad to worse. 「tamic acid.

**글루타민** 〚화학〛 glutamine. ◉ ~산 glu-

**글리세린** 〚화학〛 glycerin(e).

**글리코겐** 〚화학〛 glycogen.

**글발** ① 《글씨》 jottings; notes. ② 《글씨 모양》 the appearance of *one's* letters. ¶ ~이 고르다 The letters are even. ③ 《문맥》 coherence; the context. ¶ ~이 서다 be coherent.

**글방**(一房) a schoolroom; a private school for Chinese classics; a village school.

**글벗** a literary friend; a pen pal.

**글썽글썽** 《눈물이》 with tearful eyes. ~하다 tear blur *one's* eyes; be filled with tears; be about to cry. ¶ 눈물이 ~한 눈 tearful eyes; eyes filled with tears / 그녀 눈에는 눈물이 ~했다 Tears stood 〔formed〕 in her eyes.

**글쎄** 《불확실·주저·의심·비난》 well; now; there; ah; uh…. ¶ ~ 좀 기다려 봅시다 Well, let us wait for a while. / ~ 그 옷이 그에게 잘 맞을는지 Well, I wonder if the clothes suit him well. / ~ 모르겠어, 가야 할지 말아야 할지 Well, I am not quite sure about my going there. *or* Well, I don't know whether I shall go there or not.

**글쎄요** Well, let me see. ¶ 「몇 사람이나 됩니까」—「~ 한 500명쯤 되겠죠」 "How many people are there?"—"Well, I should say about five hundred."

**글씨** 《문자》 a letter; a character; 《필적》 a hand; handwriting. ¶ ~ 잘 쓰는 사람 a penman 〔calligrapher〕 / 굵은〔가는〕 ~ a heavy 〔slender〕 character / 알아보기 힘든 ~ a handwriting hard to read / ~를 잘 쓰다 write a good hand / ~를 휘갈겨 쓰다 write hastily; scribble; scrawl / 알아보기 쉬운〔어려운〕 ~로 쓰다 write in a legible 〔illegible〕 hand. ◉ ~본 a book of pen-

manship. ～체 a style of handwriting.
**글안**(契丹) 〖역사〗 ⇨ 거란(契丹).
**글월** ① = 글. ② = 편지. ③ = 문장.
**글자**(—字) a letter; a character; a written symbol; an ideograph. ¶ ～ 그대로 to the letter; literally / ～ 한 자 모르다 be unlettered; be illiterate; be an ignoramus.
**글재주** literary talent 〔ability, genius〕. ¶～가 있다 have a talent for writing.
**글제**(—題) the title 〔subject, theme〕 of an article 〔a composition, a poem〕. ¶ ～를 내다 give a subject 〔theme〕 / 자연이란 ～를 두고 글을 짓다 write a composition on "Nature"; take "Nature" for the subject of *one's* composition.
**글줄** a line 〔some lines〕 of writing.
**글짓기** composition.
**글쪽지** a card 〔slip〕 with writing on it.
**글체**(—體) (literary) style.
**글피** three days hence 〔from now〕; two days after tomorrow.
**글하다** engage in studies.
**긁다** ① 《손톱·연장 따위로》 scratch; scrape 《off, away, out》. ¶ 긁어 부스럼 내다 ask for trouble; invite trouble unnecessarily / 머리를 ～ scratch *one's* head / 가려운 데를 ～ scratch an itchy spot 〔place〕 / 구두의 흙을 ～ scrape the mud off *one's* shoes. ② 《그러모으다》 rake. ¶ 낙엽을 ～ rake (up) fallen leaves / 돈을 긁어 모으다 rake 〔scrape〕 together a sum of money. ③ 《남의 비위를》 offend; irritate; nag 《at》; tease; 《헐뜯다》 find fault with; carp 〔cavil〕 at. ¶ 아무를 ～ irritate *a person;* find fault with *a person;* nag 〔pick〕 at *a person* / 바가지를 긁어 남편을 못살게 굴다 nag *one's* husband to death. ④ 《남의 재물을》 exploit; squeeze 〔extort, wring〕 《money》 from 《*a person*》; bleed *a person* 《for money》. ¶ 돈을 몽땅 긁어내다 bleed *a person* white 〔dry〕 / 그들은 그로부터 많은 돈을 긁어냈다 They squeezed a lot of money from 〔out of〕 him.
**긁어당기다** rake 〔scrape〕 in. ¶ 판돈을 ～ rake in the money on the game table.
**긁어먹다** ① 《이·연장으로》 scrape 〔scratch〕 (out) and eat. ¶ 참외를 숟가락으로 ～ scrape out the meat of a melon (and eat it). ② 《재물을》 live on the money squeezed out of others; live by bleeding 〔exploiting〕 others; live off 《*a person*》. ¶ 가난한 사람의 것을 ～ live off poor people.
**긁어모으다** = 그러모으다.
**긁적거리다** scratch (and scratch) 《*one's* back》; scrape and scrape.
**긁적긁적** scratching and scratching; scraping and scraping.
**긁히다** ① 《살·표면 등이》 be scratched; be scraped. ¶ 나뭇가지에 얼굴이 ～ *one's* face is scratched by a twig / 가시에 손이 긁혔다 I had my hand scratched with the thorns. ② 《낙엽이》 be raked; rake. ¶ 낙엽이 잘 ～ fallen leaves rake up easily / 갈퀴가 잘 ～ a rake rakes well. ③ 《헐뜯기다》 be carped 〔caviled〕 at; be picked 〔nagged, griped〕 at; be found fault with. ④ 《재물 등을》 be exploited 〔bled, sweated〕; be squeezed out 〔fleeced〕 of *one's* money.
**금**[1] 《값》 the price; the value; the cost. ⇨ 금하다. ¶ 금이 비싸다〔싸다〕 the price is high 〔low〕 / 금이 오르다 the cost goes up 〔rises〕; it rises in price / 금이 내리다 the cost goes down; it falls 〔comes down, declines〕 in price / 금을 놓다 name 〔bid〕 a price; make an offer; set a price 《on》; appraise / 금이 나가다 cost much; be high in price; be dear 〔expensive〕.
**금**[2] ① 《줄》 a line; 《접은 자국》 a crease; a fold; 《주름》 a wrinkle. ¶ 금을 긋다 draw a line / 손금을 보다 read (the lines of ) 《*a person's*》 palm. ② 《균열》 a crack; a cleft; a cleavage; a fissure; chaps; cracks in *one's* skin. ¶ 벽에 생긴 금 a crack in the wall / 금이 간 찻잔 a cracked cup / 금(이) 가다 crack; be cracked; split. / 벽에 금이 갔다 The wall had a crack in it. / 컵이 뜨거운 물로 금이 갔다 The hot water has cracked the glass. / 근거 없는 중상으로 두 사람 사이에 금이 갔다 The groundless slander caused a split between them.
**금**(金) ① 《황금》 gold. ¶ 금의 gold; golden / 금을 입힌 gold-plated; gilded / 금을 입히다 plate 《*a thing*》 with gold / 금시계 a gold watch / 금귀걸이 golden earrings / 이에 금을 씌우다 crown a tooth with gold / 침묵은 금이다 Silence is golden. / 번쩍인다고 모두가 금은 아니다 《속담》 All is not gold that glitters. ② 《금속》 metals. ③ 《돈》 money. ¶ 일금 만원 (the sum of ) 10,000 won. ④ 《오행의》 Metal as one of the *ohaeng* 〔Five Elements〕. ⑤ ⇨

금요일.
**금-**(今) the present 《time》; this 《year》. ¶ 금월 this month; the present month / 금세기 this century; the present century.
**금가락지**(金—) a gold ring.
**금가루**(金—) gold dust.
**금강**(金剛) 《금강력》 the moral strength of the Mahāvairocana; adamantine might; Herculean strength. ◉ ~사(砂) 〖광물〗 emery (powder). ~석 〖광물〗 a diamond. ~역사 〖불교〗 a Deva king.
**금강산**(金剛山) Mt. Kŭmgang; the Diamond Mountains. ¶ ~도 식후경이라 《속담》 It takes a full stomach to appreciate even the best of scenery. *or* Bread is better than the song of the birds. 「off-limits area.
**금계**(禁界) the forbidden ground; an
**금계**(錦鷄) 〖조류〗 a golden pheasant.
**금계랍**(金鷄蠟) 〖약〗 quinine.
**금고**(金庫) ① 《돈·서류를 넣는》 a safe; a strongbox; a cash box; a coffer; a vault (은행의). ¶ 내화 ~ a fire-proof safe / 대여 ~ a safe-deposit 〔safety deposit〕 box / ~에 넣다 put 《the money》 away in a safe / ~를 잠그다 lock a safe. ② 《국고》 a cash office; a depository. ◉ ~털이 safebreaking; 《사람》 a safe-breaker; a safeblower.
**금고**(禁錮) 〖법〗 imprisonment; confinement. ¶ 10년의 ~에 처하다 sentence 《*a person*》 to 10 years' imprisonment / 5년의 ~형을 받다 be sentenced to 5 years' imprisonment. ◉ ~형 imprisonment.
**금공**(金工) 《공예》 metalworking; 《사람》 metalworker; a metalsmith.
**금과옥조**(金科玉條) most precious rules; a golden rule. ¶ ~로 삼다 adhere strictly 《to》; stick fast 《to》; recognize no other authority 《than》 / 너의 충고를 나는 ~로 삼겠다 I shall 「abide by 〔live up to〕 your advice faithfully.
**금관**(金冠) 《왕관》 a gold crown; 《이의》 a (gold) crown. ¶ 이에 ~을 씌우다 crown a tooth with gold.
**금관악기**(金管樂器) (a) brass.
**금광**(金鑛) 《광산》 a gold mine; 《광석》 gold ore. ¶ ~을 발견하다 discover 〔find〕 gold deposits.
**금괴**(金塊) a nugget 〔lump〕 of gold (미정련의); a gold bar (막대의); a gold ingot (정련된); gold bullion [총칭].
**금권**(金權) the power 〔influence〕 of money 〔wealth〕; financial influence. ¶ 요즈음은 ~ 만능의 세상이다 Money 「is everything 〔rules the world〕 nowadays. ◉ ~정치 plutocracy; timocracy; money politics: ~ 정치가 a plutocrat.
**금궤**(金櫃) a cashbox; a money chest; a strongbox (금고식의). 「quat.
**금귤**(金橘) 〖식물〗 a kumquat; a cum-
**금기**(禁忌) (a) taboo; tabooing; eschewal; 〖의학〗 contraindication. ~하다 taboo; eschew. ¶ 배합 ~ 약품 incompatible drugs.
**금나다**[1] 《값이》 be fixed 〔appraised, priced〕. ¶ 백 원에 ~ be priced 〔fixed〕 at 100 won.
**금나다**[2] 《줄이 생김》 crease; wrinkle; be creased 〔wrinkled, cracked (터지다)〕.
**금난초**(金蘭草) 〖식물〗 a helleborine.
**금남**(禁男) off-limits to men; forbidden to men; "Woman Only." ¶ ~의 집 a home off-limits to men; a home for women only.
**금납**(金納) cash payment; payment in money. ~하다 pay in money.
**금낭화**(錦囊花) 〖식물〗 a bleeding heart.
**금년**(今年) this year; the present 〔current〕 year. ¶ ~ 여름 this summer / ~ 중에 before the end of this year / ~은 윤년이다 This is a leap year.
**금년생**(今年生) a baby born this year; 〖식물〗 a plant new this year.
**금놓다** name 〔bid〕 a price; make an offer; set a price 《on》; appraise. ¶ 금 놓아 보시죠 Make an offer for it, please. *or* Try bidding.
**금니**(金—) a gold tooth. ¶ ~를 하다 have a gold tooth put in; have a tooth capped with gold. ◉ ~박이 a person with a gold tooth.
**금단**(禁斷) prohibition. ~하다 prohibit. ¶ ~의 열매 the forbidden fruit. ◉ ~증상 withdrawal symptoms: 담배를 끊은 지 몇일 만에 나는 ~증상에 시달리기 시작했다 A few days after giving up smoking, I started to suffer from withdrawal symptoms.
**금단추**(金—) 《놋쇠의》 a brass button; 《금의》 a gold button.
**금달맞이꽃** 〖식물〗 an evening primrose.
**금닿다** 《값이 알맞다》 be reasonable in price; 《값이 꽤 나가다》 have a considerable value 〔price〕.
**금덩이**(金—) a (gold) nugget. ⇨ 금괴.
**금도**(襟度) generosity; magnanimity; broad-mindedness. ¶ ~가 넓다 be broad-〔large-〕minded.
**금도금**(金鍍金) gilding; gold plating. ~

하다 gild; plate with gold. ¶ ～의 gilt; gold-plated; gold-filled.

**금돌**(金—) 〖광산〗 a gold-bearing rock; a orerock.

**금동불**(金銅佛) a gilt bronze image 「〔statue〕 of Buddha.

**금딱지**(金—) a gold case 《of a watch》; a gold lid. ◉ ～시계 a gold watch.

**금띠**(金—) a golden belt.

**금란지계**(金蘭之契) close friendship.

**금력**(金力) the power of wealth 〔money〕; the influence of money. ¶ ～으로 by employing 〔using〕 *one's* financial power; under 〔through〕 the influence of money / 그는 ～으로 좌우될 사람이 아니다 He is the last man to be influenced by money. ◉ ～가 a plutocrat. ～만능 mammonism; L. S. Deism (우스개); the almighty dollar principle. ～정치 plutocracy; timocracy.

**금렵**(禁獵) prohibition of hunting 〔shooting〕; a ban on hunting; "no hunting". ～하다 prohibit the hunting 〔shooting〕 《of 》; ban hunting. ¶ ～의 조수(鳥獸) forbidden game. ◉ ～구〔지〕 a (game, hunting) preserve; a (wildlife, bird) sanctuary: ～지를 범하다 violate a 《bird》 sanctuary / 이 숲은 ～지이다 These woods are preserved. ～기 a closed season.

**금령**(禁令) a prohibition 《against》; a ban 《on》; a prohibitory 〔an interdictory〕 decree. ⇨ 금지령. ¶ ～을 어기다 violate the prohibition 〔ban〕 / ～을 내리다 issue a ban 〔an embargo〕 / ～을 해제하다 lift the ban 《on》; remove the prohibition.

**금리**(金利) 《이율》 a rate of interest; money 〔interest〕 rate. ¶ 연(年) 6푼의 ～로 at an annual interest rate of 6 percent / ～를 올리다〔내리다〕 raise 〔lower〕 the rate of interest / ～가 높다〔낮다〕 Money is dear 〔cheap〕. ◉ ～생활자 a *rentier* (F.); a money-lender; a coupon clipper. ～인상〔인하〕 a rise 〔fall〕 in the rate of interest. ～자유화 the liberalization of interest rates. ～재조정 readjustment of bank interest rates. ～정책 interest adjustment policy; a bank-rate policy. ～특혜 preferential interest rates. ～하향조정 downward readjustment of bank interest rates.

**금맞추다** arrive at a price; set the price; arrange 〔adjust〕 the price 《of》.

**금맥**(金脈) 《광산의》 a vein of gold; 《돈줄》 a supplier of funds; (shady) sources of funds; a financial supporter. ¶ ～을 찾아내다 strike a gold vein.

**금메달**(金—) a gold medal. ¶ ～을 따다 win 〔be awarded〕 a gold medal.

**금명간**(今明間) today or tomorrow; in a couple of days.

**금모래**(金—) ① 《사금》 gold dust. ② 《금빛의》 golden sand(s). 「gold-braided.

**금몰**(金—) gold braid 〔lace〕. ¶ ～이 달린

**금문자**(金文字) 《금글자》 a gold 〔gilt〕 letter 〔character〕; gilt lettering. ¶ ～가 박힌 표지 a gold-lettered book cover.

**금물**(禁物) a prohibited thing; a taboo; prohibited 〔forbidden〕 goods; contraband; 《유해물》 an injurious 〔a harmful〕 thing; 《끊어야 할》 a thing (to be) abstained from; 《피해야 할》 a thing to be carefully avoided. ¶ ～의 forbidden; taboo(ed) / 환자에게 담배는 ～이다 Smoking is very bad for the patient. / 그녀 앞에서 그런 이야기는 ～이다 That topic is taboo in her presence.

**금박**(金箔) (a piece of ) gold leaf; gold foil; beaten gold; gilt. ¶ ～을 입히다 plate 《*a thing*》 with gold.

**금반지**(金斑指) a gold ring.

**금발**(金髮) golden 〔fair〕 hair; blonde (여자의); blond (남자의).

> **용법** **blond(e)**는 금발, 흰 피부, 푸른 눈을 가진 사람. 검은 또는 다갈색의 피부, 머리와 눈을 가진 사람은 brunet(te).

¶ ～의 golden-haired; blond(e) / 그녀는 ～이다 She is blonde. ◉ ～미인 a blonde beauty.

**금방**(今方) 《방금》 just 〔right〕 now; 《바로 전에》 (just) a moment ago; 《곧》 at once; in a moment; 《당장이라도》 every 〔at any〕 moment. ¶ 그녀는 ～ 나갔다 She went out just a minute ago. / 나는 ～ 죽는 줄 알았다 I scared every moment to be killed.

**금방**(金房) a goldsmith's shop.

**금방망이**(金—) 〖식물〗 a groundsel.

**금배**(金盃) a gold cup 〔goblet〕.

**금번**(今番) this time. = 이번.

**금법**(禁法) a ban; a prohibition law.

**금보다** 《평가하다》 make an appraisal 〔estimate, evaluation〕; 《값을 알아보다》 ask the price 《of an article》. ¶ 이 물건이 얼마나 가나 금보아 주시오 Please appraise this article. *or* Tell me what this is worth.

**금본위**(金本位) 〖경제〗 the gold standard; gold basis. ¶ ～를 폐지하다 suspend the gold standard; go off gold. ◉ ～국 a gold-using country. ～제도 the gold standard (system).

**금뵈다** ①《물건값을》get《*a person*》to ｢name his price 〔make an offer〕; make 〔let〕《*a person*》appraise. ② = 금맞추다.

**금분**(金粉) gold dust. ｢gilded Buddha.

**금불**(金佛) a gold statue of Buddha; a

**금불초**(金佛草)〖식물〗an elecampane.

**금붕어**(金―) a goldfish. ¶ ～ 어항 a goldfish basin 〔bowl〕.

**금붙이**(金―) things made of gold.

**금비**(金肥) (a) chemical 〔commercial〕 fertilizer.

**금비녀**(金―) a golden hairpin.

**금빛**(金―) golden color. ¶ ～이 찬란하다 glitter with golden colors. ｢King.

**금상**(今上)《임금의 옛 칭호》the present

**금상**(金像) a gold 〔gilded, gilt〕 statue.

**금상첨화**(錦上添花) "adding flowers to embroidery"; making still more beautiful. ～하다 add luster to what is already beautiful 〔brilliant〕; add something more to the beauty 〔honor〕《of》; give an added grace to what is already beautiful.

**금서**(禁書) a banned 〔forbidden〕 book.

**금석**(今昔) past and present. ◉ ～지감(之感) a sentimental mood caused by the contrast between the past and the present: ～지감을 금할 수 없다 be struck with the contrast between the present and past; be struck by the effects of time / ～지감을 주다 strike《*a person*》with the change of the times.

**금석**(金石) ①《쇠붙이와 돌》minerals and rocks. ②《굳음》being adamant 〔firm, unyielding〕. ¶ ～지교(之交) a firm friendship / ～지약(之約) a firm promise. ◉ ～문(자) an epigraph; an inscription engraved on stone or other durable material. ～학 epigraphy;《옛 광물학》mineralogy.

**금선**(金線) a line of gold thread; gold braid 〔stripes〕.

**금성**(金星)〖천문〗Venus; Hesperus; the daystar. ¶ ～의 태양면 통과 the transit of Venus over the sun's disc 〔disk〕.

**금성철벽**(金城鐵壁) a citadel; an impregnable fortress.

**금세**《금시에》in a moment 〔a flash, an instant〕; right away; at once; immediately; without delay; instantly; a moment ago; just (now). ¶ ～ 돌아오다 come back immediately / ～ 대답하다 answer right away 〔off〕 / ～ 가겠다 I'll go at once. ｢mundane world.

**금세**(今世)〖불교〗《이승》this world 〔life〕;

**금세공**(金細工) goldwork. ◉ ～장이 a goldsmith. ～점 a goldsmith's shop.

**금속**(金屬) (a) metal. ¶ 귀〔경〕～ precious 〔light〕 metal / ～의 metallic / ～제의 made of metal; metal / ～화하다 metallize; metallicize / 그 ～은 열에 녹는다 The metal melts with heat. /철은 유용한 ～이다 Iron is a useful metal.
◉ ～가공 metalworking: ～ 가공학 metallurgical technology. ～가구 metal furniture. ～공 a metal-worker. ～공업 the metalworking industry. ～공학 metal engineering. ～관 a metal tube. ～광물 metallic mineral. ～광산 metalliferous mines. ～광택 metallic luster: ～ 광택이 있다 have a metallic luster. ～성 metallicity: ～성의 metallic / ～성의 소리 a metallic sound 〔clang〕. ～세공 a metalwork: ～ 세공의 toreutic. ～악기 a brass instrument. ～염(塩) metallic salts. ～원소 metallic elements. ～정련 metal refinery: ～ 정련법 metal refining work. ～제품 metal goods; hardware. ～조직학 metallography. ～탐지기 a metal detector. ～티타늄 ferrotitanium. ～판(板) a metal (-lic) plate;《얇은》a latten; a web. ～판(版)〖인쇄〗a metallograph: ～판 인쇄(술) metallography. ～화폐 metallic currency.

**금쇠** a line-cutter; a tool used to make lines on board; a kind of burin.

**금수**(禁輸) an embargo (on the export 〔import〕). ～하다 forbid the export 〔import〕《of》. ¶ ～ 조치의 해제 the lifting of the trade embargo / 정부는 그 나라에 대한 무기 ～를 풀었다 The Government lifted the embargo on arms exports to that country.
◉ ～품 articles under an embargo; contraband (goods).

**금수**(禽獸) birds and beasts; a beast; a brute; dumb animals. ¶ ～와 같은 행위 conduct worthy of a beast; bestial 〔beastly〕 conduct / ～보다 못한 사람 a person worse than a brute / ～와 다를 바 없다 be no better than a beast; be on a level with brute.

**금수**(錦繡)《비단과 수》brocade and embroidery; embroidered brocade.
◉ ～강산 (a land of) picturesque rivers and mountains; a land of beautiful scenery.

**금수출**(金輸出) the export of gold.

◉ ～금지 a ban 〔an embargo〕 on gold export. ～해금(解禁) lifting 〔removing〕 the gold embargo.

**금슬**(琴瑟) ① 《거문고와 비파》 a Korean harp and a lute. ② ⇨ 금실(琴瑟).

**금시**(今時) nowadays; these days; the present time 〔moment〕. ¶ ～에 ＝금세 / ～ 변하다 change 《*one's* mind》 in a flash. ◉ ～발복 making a fortune overnight; "going from rags to riches"; sudden wealth 〔success〕. ～초견〔초문〕 seeing 〔hearing〕 《*something*》 for the first time: 이건 ～초문이다 This is news 〔a revelation〕 to me.

**금식**(禁食) a fast; fasting. ～하다 fast; observe a fast; go without food. ¶ 2일간 ～하다 fast for two days. ◉ ～요법 a starvation 〔fasting, hunger〕 cure. ～일 a fast day.

**금실**(金—) gold thread; spun gold. ¶ ～로 수놓다 embroider with gold thread.

**금실**(琴瑟) 《부부의》 conjugal harmony; connubial felicity. ¶ ～지락(之樂) the pleasures of married life; conjugal happiness / ～ 상화하다 live in conjugal harmony / ～이 좋다 have a happy married life; live happily together as man and wife.

**금싸라기**(金—) a thing of great value. ◉ ～땅 an exceedingly high-priced plot of land.

**금액**(金額) an amount 〔a sum〕 of money. ¶ 큰〔적은〕 ～ a large 〔small〕 amount of money / 상당한 ～ a good sum of money; a sizable amount of money / ～으로 치면 3백만 원에 달한다 amount 〔come up〕 to three million won / ～으로 쳐서 약 2백만 원 짜리이다 It is valued at about two million won.

**금야**(今夜) tonight. ⇨ 오늘밤.

**금어**(禁漁) prohibition of fishing; a ban on fishing; a fishing ban. ◉ ～구 an area closed to fishing; a no-fishing area 〔zone〕; 《바다의》 a marine preserve. ～기 a closed season 《for trout》; 《영》 a close season.

**금언**(金言) ① 《격언》 a golden saying; a maxim; an adage; an aphorism; an old saw. ¶ 옛 사람의 ～ wise sayings of the ancients. ② 《법어》 Buddha's remarks. ◉ ～집 collection of proverbs and maxims.

**금연**(禁煙) 《못 피우게 함》 prohibition of smoking; 《끊음》 giving up smoking; abstaining 〔refraining〕 from smoking; 《게시》 No smoking! *or* No smoking allowed (here). ～하다 stop 〔give up, 《미구어》 quit, abstain from〕 smoking (★ He stopped to smoke. 그는 멈춰 서서 담배를 피웠다). ¶ 의사는 나에게 ～을 권했다 My doctor advised me to quit 〔stop〕 smoking. / 「～」 표시가 들어와 있는 동안은 담배를 삼가해 주십시오 Please refrain from smoking while the 'No Smoking' signs are on. ◉ ～석 a nonsmoking seat. ～운동 an antismoking 〔antitobacco〕 campaign. ～차 a no-smoking car; 《열차의》 a nonsmoker. ～파이프 an antismoking cigarette holder.

**금요일**(金曜日) Friday (생략 Fri.).

**금욕**(禁慾) asceticism; abstinence; 《성욕의》 continence. ～하다 repress 〔control〕 *one's* passions 〔bodily desires〕; practice asceticism 〔continence〕. ¶ ～생활을 하다 lead an ascetic life. ◉ ～주의 asceticism: ～주의자 an ascetic.

**금월**(今月) this month. ＝이달.

**금융**(金融) finance; circulation of money; financing (융자); the money market. ¶ ～의 monetary; banking; financial / ～을 긴축하다 tighten the money market; tigthten credit / ～ 시장이 핍박〔원만〕하다 The money market is tight 〔easy〕. ◉ ～감독원 the Financial Supervisory Service. ～감독 위원회 the Financial Supervisory Commission. ～경색 money 〔monetary〕 stringency; a tight-money situation 〔market〕. ～계 the financial world; financial circles: ～계의 불황 stringency in the money market. ～공황 a financial crisis 〔panic〕: ～ 공황을 초래하다 cause a financial crisis 〔panic〕. ～기관 a financial agency 〔institution〕; a banking organ; banking 〔monetary〕 facilities: ～기관 예금 an interbank deposit. ～긴축 tight money: ～ 긴축으로 기업은 경영이 어려워졌다 The money squeeze on 〔Tight money for〕 businesses has put strong pressure on their management. ～단 a financial syndicate. ～범죄 banking crimes: ～ 범죄 가중 처벌법 a special additional punishment law for banking crimes. ～부조리 malpractices at banks; bank-related irregularities. ～사고 a banking incident. ～사기 a loan fraud. ～시장 the money market. ～업 financial 〔banking〕 business: ～업자 a financier; a moneylender; a moneyman 《미》; [총칭] the moneyed interests. ～완화 easy money. ～자본 financial 〔banking〕 capital. ～정책 a financial policy: ～ 긴축〔완화〕 정책 a tight=〔an easy-〕money policy. ～조작 money market management 〔manipulation〕. ～조직 a financial system. ～지원 financial support. ～채 a bank debenture. ～통제 monetary 〔financial〕 control. ～통합 the merger of monetary facilities. ～통화 운영위원회 the Monetary Board. ～특혜 《우선적인》 a preferential 〔privileged〕 loan; 《부정의》 an illegal loan. ～핍박 = 금융 경색. 제2 ～권 second financial circles; non-bank financial intermediaries.

**금융거래실명제**(金融去來實名制) (the) real-name financial transaction system; real-name accounting system.

**금융자유화**(金融自由化) financial liberalization.

**금은**(金銀) gold and silver. ◉ ～괴(塊) gold and silver ingots. ～ 방 a goldsmith's shop. ～ 복본위 제도 bimetallism; the gold and silver standard. ～보배〔보화〕 money and valuables; treasures: 건강은 ～ 보화 보다 귀중하다 Health is more precious than treasures. ～붙이 things made of gold and silver. ～세공 work in gold and silver; goldwork and silver-work.

**금의**(錦衣) clothes of silk brocade. ¶ ～옥식하다 live in clover; lead 〔have〕 an easy life / ～환향하다 return home loaded with honors; go 〔come〕 home in glory.

**금일**(今日) today. = 오늘. ¶ ～ 휴업 《게시》 「Closed today.

**금일봉**(金一封) an enclosure 〔a gift〕 of money. ¶ ～을 주다 grand 〔give〕 《*a person*》 a gift of money / ～을 받다 get a gift of money.

**금자**(金字) a gold 〔gilt〕 letter; illuminated characters.

**금자둥이**(金字—) a precious child.

**금자탑**(金字塔) a pyramid; 《업적》 a monumental achievement; a monument 《of learning》; a landmark 《in》. ¶ 출판계의 ～ a monumental publication / ～을 세우다 accomplish a monumental work 《in》.

**금작화**(金雀花) 〖식물〗 a common broom; 「a genista.

**금잔디**(金—) "golden" 〔beautiful autumnal〕 turf; Korean lawn grass. ◉ ～동산 soft golden hills.

**금잔화**(金盞花) 〖식물〗 a pot marigold; 「a yellow oxeye.

**금장**(禁葬) prohibition of burials 《in certain place(s)》. ～하다 prohibit burial.

**금장**(襟章) a collar badge 〔mark, ensign, bar〕.

**금장도**(金粧刀) a gold 〔gilded〕 pocketknife.

**금장식**(金粧飾) gold(en) decoration.

**금전**(金錢) 《돈》 money; cash; 《금화》 a gold coin. ¶ ～(상의) 문제 a money 〔pecuniary〕 matter; a question 〔matter〕 of money / ～의 노예 a slave of mammon / ～에 세심〔무관심〕하다 be exacting in 〔careless about〕 money matters / 아무 것이나 ～으로 평가하다 see everything in terms of money / 그들은 ～상의 문제로 크게 다퉜다 They had a big quarrel over the money. / 그는 ～적으로 치사스럽다 He is stingy with his money. / 나는 그녀와 아무런 ～상의 거래가 없다 I have never had any financial dealings with her.
◉ ～등록기 a cash register. ～신탁 money trust. ～채무 debt (to be paid in money). ～출납계 a cashier; a treasurer; a teller (은행의). ～출납부 a cashbook; an account book.

**금제**(禁制) (a) prohibition; (a) interdiction; (a) taboo; a ban. ～하다 prohibit; forbid; interdict; taboo; ban; place 《*a thing*》 under a ban; lay an embargo 《on》. ¶ ～의 prohibited; forbidden; contraband 《goods》 / 여인 ～의 《be》 closed to women / ～를 풀다 〔해제하다〕 remove a prohibition; lift a ban 〔an embargo〕 《on》 / ～되어 있다 be under a ban 〔an embargo〕.
◉ ～품 prohibited 〔banned〕 goods; 《무역상의》 contraband goods.

**금족**(禁足) ① 〖불교〗 prohibition against entrance. ② 《외출 금지》 confinement; detention. ¶ 5일간의 ～을 명하다 order 《*a person*》 to stay in one place 〔at home〕 for five days; place 《*a person*》 under five day's confinement. ◉ ～령 a prohibition 〔standstill〕 order.

**금종이**(金—) golden paper.

**금주**(今週) this week. ¶ ～중으로 within 〔during〕 this week; by the end of this week.

**금주**(禁酒) ① 《끊음》 (total) abstinence from drink; temperance(★ 정확히는 「절주」의 뜻이지만, 실제로는 「금주」의 뜻으로 쓰임). ～하다 give up 〔stop, 《미구어》 quit, abstain from〕 drinking; go dry (제도적으로). ¶ 지금 ～중이다 I am abstaining from drinking. / 의사는 나에게 ～를 명했다 The doctor ordered me to abstain from drinking. ② 《못 마시게 함》 prohibition 《of liquor》; "no drinking". ～하다 prohibit drinking.
◉ ～가 a total abstainer; a teetotaler. ～국 a country with prohibition 《of

liquor》. ～동맹 a temperance union 〔league〕. ～운동 a temperance movement; a dry campaign. ～주의 teetotalism; prohibitionism. ～주의자 a prohibitionist; a pussy-footer. ～회 a temperance society.

**금준비**(金準備) 〖경제〗 the gold reserve.

**금줄**[1](金—) ① 《시계 등의》 a gold chain 《on a watch》. ② 《계급장 등의》 a gold stripe. ③ 《금실》 gold thread.

**금줄**[2](金—) 《금맥》 a gold vein.

**금지**(禁止) (a) prohibition; (a) taboo; a ban; an embargo. ～하다 forbid 《*a thing, a person* to *do*》 (사적); prohibit 《*a person* from *do*ing》 (공적); ban (법적); put an embargo on 《*a thing*》. ¶ 발행 ～ suppression / 수출입 ～ an embargo; 〖법〗 injunction / 판매 ～ prohibition of sale / 상연 ～ a ban on performance / 핵실험 ～ 운동 the campaign for a nuclear test ban / ～를 해제하다 remove 〔withdraw〕 the prohibition; lift 〔remove〕 the ban 〔embargo〕 《on》 / 법률에 의해 ～되어 있다 be prohibited by law 《from *do*ing》 / 회의 참석을 ～당하다 be shut off from attending a conference / 이 대합실에서의 흡연은 ～ 되어 있다 Smoking in this waiting room is forbidden 〔prohibited〕. / 이 약품의 판매는 법률에 의해 ～되어 있다 The sale of this drug is 「under ban of the law 〔prohibited by law〕. / 주차 ～ 《게시》 No Parking. / 출입 ～ 《게시》 Keep out. *or* Off limits. / 통행 ～ 《게시》 No thoroughfare.
◉ ～법 prohibition law. ～조항 a forbidden clause. ～처분 prohibitive measure; prohibition.

**금지령**(禁止令) a prohibition order; a prohibitory 〔an interdictory〕 decree; an embargo; a ban. ¶ ～을 내리다〔풀다〕 issue 〔lift, remove〕 the ban 〔embargo〕.

**금지옥엽**(金枝玉葉) ① 《임금님의》 a person of royal birth. ② 《귀하게 자란》 precious sons and daughters. ¶ ～으로 자라다 be brought up like a prince 〔princess〕.

**금쳐놓다** foretell the result; tell the consequence in advance.

**금촉**(金鏃) a gold pen 〔nib〕.

**금추**(今秋) this 〔coming〕 autumn.

**금춘**(今春) this 〔coming〕 spring.

**금치다** 《값을》 name 〔offer, bid〕 *one's* price 《for》; appraise; set a price 《on》.

**금치산**(禁治産) 〖법〗 incompetency. ¶ ～선고를 받다 be declared incompetent. ◉ ～자 an incompetent.

**금침**(衾枕) quilt and pillow; bedclothes and a pillow; bedding.

**금테**(金—) a gold frame; gold rims; 《책》 a gilt edge. ◉ ～안경 《wear, be in》 gold-rimmed〔-framed〕 glasses 〔spectacles〕.

**금파리**(金—) 〖곤충〗 a green-bottle 〔blue-「bottle〕 fly; a blowfly.

**금품**(金品) money and other valuables 〔articles〕. ¶ ～으로 in money or in kind / ～을 주다 make a gift of money and other valuables / ～으로 매수하다 bribe 《*a person*》 with money and goods.

**금하**(今夏) this 〔coming〕 summer.

**금하다** 《값을 정하다》 agree 〔come to an agreement〕 on the price.

**금하다**(禁—) ① 《금지하다》 forbid 《*a person* to *do*》 (★ 구어에서는 forbid 대신 tell 〔order〕... not to를 씀); prohibit 〔stop, bar〕 《*a person* from *do*ing》; 《법령으로》 interdict; ban; put 〔place〕 《*a matter*》 under a ban; enjoin 《*a person* from》. ¶ 아무에게 육식을 ～ forbid *a person* to eat meat / 집에 출입을 ～ forbid 《*a person*》 to enter the house; close the door to 《*a person*》 / 마약 매매를 ～ prohibit the sale and purchase of narcotics / 미성년자의 흡연은 법률로 금하고 있다 The law prohibits minors from smoking.
② 《억제하다》 suppress; restrain; keep under 〔back〕; refrain 《from an urge》. ¶ 눈물을 금할 수 없다 cannot hold back *one's* tears / 동정을 금할 수 없다 cannot restrain *one's* sympathy / 웃음을 금할 수 없다 cannot help laughing.

**금형**(金型) a mold; a matrix; a cast.

**금혼**(禁婚) prohibition of marriage.

**금혼식**(金婚式) a golden wedding (anniversary). ¶ ～을 올리다 celebrate *one's* golden wedding (anniversary).

**금화**(金貨) a gold coin 〔piece〕; gold currency [총칭].

**금환**(金環) ① a gold ring. ② 〖천문〗 an annulus (*pl.* -li, -luses); 《태양의》 the corona. ◉ ～식(蝕) 〖천문〗 an annular 〔gold ring〕 eclipse (of the sun).

**금후**(今後) from now on; after this; hereafter; henceforth; in future. ¶ ～의 future; coming / ～ 3년에 (in) three years from now; three years hence / ～ 계속해서 from now on / ～ 3년은 여기서 살 생각이다 I will live here for the next three years from now. / ～의 계획은 이미 세워져 있느냐 Have you already made a future plan?

**급**(急) 《위급》 (a) danger; an emergency; a crisis (*pl.* -ses); 《긴급》 urgency. ⇨ 급하다. ¶ 초미지급 an urgent need / 이 일은 급을 요한다 This matter is pressing 〔urgent〕. / 급을 요함 《지시》 Urgent.

(-)**급**(級) ① 《등급》 a class; a grade; a rank. ¶ 1급품 first-class goods; an article of the highest quality / 헤비급 선수 a heavyweight / 5천 톤급의 배 a ship in the 5,000-ton class / 대사급 회담 a conference at the ambassadorial level; an ambassador-level talk / 백두급에서의 3연승 *one's* three consecutive victories in the *Paektu* class / 그의 노래는 프로급이다 His singing is 「at a 〔on the〕 professional level. ② 《학년》 a class; a grade; a form 《영》. ¶ 그녀는 나와 동급생이다 She is in the same class with me.

**급**-(急) steep 《slope》; urgent 《report》; sudden 《illness》; sharp 《attack》; swift 《current》; rapid 《stream》.

**급각도**(急角度) an acute 〔a sharp〕 angle 〔turn〕. ¶ ~로 《turn》 at an acute 〔a sharp〕 angle; 《bend》 sharply 〔in a sharp curve〕.

**급강하**(急降下) 〖항공〗 a steep dive 〔diving〕; a nose dive; 《온도의》 a sudden drop. ~하다 dive; 《온도가》 drop suddenly. ¶ 오늘 아침 기온이 ~했다 There was a sudden drop in the temperature this morning. ◉ ~폭격 dive bombing: ~ 폭격기 a dive bomber / ~ 폭격을 하다 dive-bomb.

**급거**(急遽) in haste; in a hurry; hurriedly. ¶ ~ 현장으로 달려가다 rush to the scene / ~ 집으로 돌아가다 hurry back home. 「급습.

**급격**(急擊) a sudden attack 〔raid〕. ⇨

**급격하다**(急激—) (be) sudden; abrupt; rapid; drastic (격렬한); radical (급진적인). ¶ 급격히 suddenly; abruptly; drastically; rapidly; radically / 밤이 되면 기온이 급격히 떨어진다 When night comes, temperature drops suddenly. / 지난 10년 사이에 전자 산업은 급격한 진보를 이룩했다 Electronic industry has made great 〔rapid〕 progress during the last decade. / 청소년의 자살이 급격히 증가하고 있다 The number of suicides of young people has increased rapidly.

**급경사**(急傾斜) a steep slope; 《치받이》 steep ascent; 《내리받이》 steep descent. ¶ ~의 steep; high-pitched 《roof》 / ~ 커브길 감속하시오 《게시》 Slow! Sharp curve steep hill.

**급경성**(急硬性) ¶ ~의 quick-hardening 《cement》.

**급고**(急告) an urgent notice. ~하다 notify urgently; give an urgent notice. ¶ ~—김군은 즉시 사무실로 출두할 것 Urgent—Mr. Kim is requested to report to the office immediately.

**급급하다**(汲汲—) be intent 〔bent〕 《on》; be engrossed 〔absorbed〕 《in》; be eager 《to please *one's* employer》; think only of. ¶ 돈벌이에 ~ be bent 〔intent〕 on making money / 책임 전가에 ~ be busy trying to shift the responsibility to others / 명리에 ~ be striving hard after fame and gain; be hungry 〔thirsty〕 for fame 〔reputation〕 / 너무 일에만 급급하는 것이 능사는 아니다 There is something else in life besides working so hard.

**급기야**(及其也) at last; finally; in the end; ultimately; after all. ¶ ~ 그는 바라던 대학에 합격했다 At last he was admitted to the university he wanted. / 그는 실패를 거듭했지만 ~ 성공을 거뒀다 He failed so many times, but finally succeeded. / 노름을 자꾸 하더니 ~ 재산을 탕진하고 말았다 He went on gambling until at last he lost all his fortune.

**급난**(急難) an imminent 〔impending〕 danger 〔calamity〕.

**급등**(急騰) a sudden 〔sharp〕 rise 《in prices》; a jump. ~하다 rise suddenly 〔sharply〕; jump 《to》; shoot up; skyrocket. ¶ 물가가 ~했다 Prices skyrocketed. / 쌀값이 ~하고 있다 Rice soars in price. / 선거에서 그의 승리를 예상하고 증권 시세는 ~하였다 The stock market zoomed in anticipation of his victory in the election.

**급락**(及落) success or failure 《in an examination》; the result of an examination. ¶ ~을 결정하다 decide the result of an examination / 그것으로 자네의 ~이 결정될 것이다 Your success will depend on it.

**급랭**(急冷) quick freezing; rapid cooling.

**급료**(給料) pay; wages (★ wages는 흔히 복수형); a salary; (a) remuneration; 《전체 급료》 a payroll.
¶ 높은〔낮은〕 ~ a high 〔low, small〕 salary; high 〔small〕 pay / ~가 좋다 [회사 등이 주어] pay well; pay good wages; [사람이 주어] be well paid / ~를 받다 get 〔receive〕 *one's* salary 《from》 / ~를 받고 일하다 work on

salary / 월 이백만 원의 ~를 받다 draw 〔get〕 a monthly salary of 2,000,000 won 《from a firm》 / 자네 ~는 얼마지 What is your salary? *or* How much 〔What〕 salary do you get 〔draw〕?

> 용법 **pay** 급료를 뜻하는 가장 일반적인 말. salary, wage 대신으로 두루 쓰임: The pay is good.(급료는 좋다). **wage(s)** 육체 노동·공원·임시고용인 등에게 지급되는 시간급·일급·주급 따위 급료: work at an hourly wage of 4,000 won(시간급 4,000원으로 일하다). **salary** 사무직·전문직·관리직 따위 정규 직자에 대해 지불되는 급료: get a moderate salary(보통 수준의 급료를 받다).

◉ ~생활자 a salaried employee 〔worker〕; a wage earner. ~일 a payday 《미》; a wage day 《영》. ~체불 delay in wage payment.

**급류**(急流) a rapid 〔swift, rushing〕 stream; a swift current; a torrent; rapids. ¶ ~에 휩쓸리다 be swept away by swift currents / ~를 타다 shoot the rapids 《on a raft》.

**급모**(急募) urgent invitation. ~하다 recruit 〔enlist〕 《personnel》 hurriedly. ¶ 사무 직원 ~ 《게시》 Office workers urgently wanted. *or* Urgent recruitment of office workers.

**급무**(急務) a pressing 〔crying〕 need; urgent 〔pressing〕 business. ¶ 이 문제의 해결이 지금 해야 할 ~이다 This problem requires immediate attention. / ~의 과제는 경제 재건이다 The first thing we must do is to reconstruct the economy. / 수출을 늘리는 것이 지금 우리 나라가 해야할 ~이다 It is urgently necessary for our country to increase its export.

**급박하다**(急迫―) (be) imminent; pressing; urgent. ¶ 급박해지다 become 〔grow〕 acute 〔critical, tense〕 / 아시아의 급박한 정세 an acute situation in Asia / 북한에서는 식량 문제가 ~ The food problem is acute in North Korea.

**급변**(急變) ① 《변고》 an emergency; an unforeseen occurrence; an accident. ¶ 버저가 ~을 알렸다 The buzzer sounded an emergency. ② 《빠른 변화》 a sudden 〔an unexpected〕 change. ~하다 change suddenly; undergo a sudden change; 《병세가》 take a sudden turn for the worse. ¶ ~하는 세계 정세 the rapidly changing world situation / 형세의 ~ a sudden turn of events / 일기가 ~하다 the weather suddenly changes.

**급병**(急病) a sudden (attack of) illness. ¶ ~의 경우에는 in case of sudden illness / ~에 걸리다 be suddenly taken ill; be seized with a sudden illness.

**급보**(急報) an urgent 〔hurried〕 message 〔report〕; 《화재의》 an alarm. ~하다 report in haste; send an urgent message 《to》; give the alarm 《for a fire》; report promptly; send an emergency call 《for》. ¶ ~에 접하다 receive the urgent news 《of》 / ~를 접하자 경찰대가 현장에 달려갔다 At the report a police squad was dispatched 〔rushed〕 to the scene.

**급부**(給付) 《지급》 (a) payment; provision; a benefit (급부금). ~하다 make a presentation 《of》; pay 《a benefit》; provide 《*a person* with an allowance》. ◉ ~금 a benefit. ~연한 a benefit year. ~제한 restriction on benefit.

**급비생**(給費生) a scholarship student.

**급사**(急死) (a) sudden 〔(an) untimely〕 death. ~하다 die suddenly; meet with an untimely death. ¶ 열병으로 ~하다 die suddenly of a fever.

**급사**(急使) an express messenger; a courier; dispatch rider.

**급사**(給仕) 《사무실의》 an office boy 〔girl〕; 《호텔의》 a bellboy; a page (boy); 《배의》 a cabin boy; 《식당의》 a waiter; a waitress.

**급사면**(急斜面) a steep 「hill 〔slope, decline〕.

**급살**(急煞) 『민속』 the most baleful influence; the worst fate. ¶ ~맞다 meet a sudden death; be suddenly struck down by evil influences / ~(을) 맞을 놈아 A plague on you!

**급상승**(急上昇) a sudden rise 《in prices》; 『항공』 a steep climb; a zoom; zooming. ~하다 rise suddenly 〔sharply〕; shoot up; climb steeply; zoom.

**급서**(急逝) ⇨ 급사(急死).

**급선무**(急先務) the most urgent business; a pressing need; an exigency; a priority matter; a matter demanding the most immediate attention. ¶ 당면한 ~ the pressing need of the hour.

**급선봉**(急先鋒) the vanguard; a forerunner; an active leader; a champion; a spearhead. ¶ …의 ~이 되다 be an active leader of 《the revolt》; be in the 「van 〔forefront〕 of 《the movement》.

**급설**(急設) rapid 〔hasty, hurried〕 installation. ～하다 hastily install 〔equip 《with》, provide, set up〕; lay 《a telephone》 speedily 〔without delay〕.

**급성**(急性) 〖의학〗 acute form of a disease. ¶ ～의 acute. ◉ ～맹장염 acute appendicitis. ～폐렴〔중독〕 acute pneumonia 〔poisoning〕.

**급성장**(急成長) a rapid growth. ～하다 grow rapidly; achieve a rapid growth. ¶ M회사는 지난 몇 해 동안에 ～을 해 왔다 The M company has achieved a rapid growth over the past few years. ◉ ～시장 the big emerging market.

**급소**(急所) ① 《몸의》 a vital part 〔spot〕; the vitals [총칭]. ¶ ～를 때리다 hit 《*a person*》 on a fatal spot / ～를 맞다 be hit in the vitals / (탄알 등이) ～를 벗어나다 miss the vital part 〔organ〕. ② 《아픈 데》 a sore 〔tender〕 spot; the quick; 《약점》 a weak 〔vulnerable〕 spot. ¶ ～를 찌르다 hit 《*a person*》 on a tender 〔sore, fatal〕 spot / ～를 쥐고 있다 have a hold over 《*a person*》. ③ 《요점》 the vital 〔key〕 point. ¶ ～를 찌르다 《질문·비판 등이》 strike 〔go〕 home; hit the mark / ～를 찌른〔벗어난〕 질문 a question (that is) to the point 〔beside the mark〕.

**급속**(急速) ～하다 (be) rapid; swift; fast; prompt; expeditious. ¶ ～히 swiftly; rapidly; promptly; expeditiously / ～한 성장 (a) rapid growth / ～한 해결 a prompt settlement / ～한 진보를 이루다 make rapid progress; advance by rapid strides / 문제를 ～히 처리하다 settle a matter in quick order. ◉ ～냉동 quick freezing: ～냉동 생선 quick-frozen fish.

**급송**(急送) speedy dispatch; sending by express 〔in haste〕. ～하다 dispatch 〔rush〕 《*a thing*》 to; send 《*a thing*》 by express 〔in haste〕.

**급수**(級數) ① 〖수학〗 《일련의 수》 a series; 《그 수의 증가 방식》 (a) progression. ¶ 산술〔기하〕 ～적으로 증가하다 grow in an arithmetical 〔a geometical〕 progression. ② ＝등급.

**급수**(給水) water supply 〔service〕; 《보일러 등의》 water feeding; 《물》 feed water. ～하다 supply 《a town》 with water. ¶ 시간 ～ restriction of water supply to fixed hours; rationing water according to a timetable / ～를 제한하다〔중지하다〕 restrict 〔turn off〕 the water supply / 배에 ～하다 water a ship / 이 근방은 ～ 사정이 좋다〔나쁘다〕 We have a good 〔bad〕 supply of water in this vicinity. ◉ ～계량기 a water meter. ～관 a water pipe; a water service line; a feed pipe (보일러의). ～난 water shortage. ～량 the amount of water supplied. ～설비 water supply facilities; waterworks. ～소 a water station 〔point〕. ～장 a water service point. ～전(栓) a water tap; a hydrant. ～제한 restriction(s) on water supply. ～차〔선〕 a water wagon 〔boat〕. ～탑 a water tower. ～탱크 a feed tank. ～펌프 a feed water pump.

**급습**(急襲) a surprise 〔sudden〕 attack; a raid. ～하다 make a surprise 〔sudden〕 attack 《on》; raid; storm. ¶ 현금 수송차를 ～하다 make a surprise attack on a security vehicle / 경찰의 ～을 받다 be raided by the police / 그들은 적을 ～했다 They made a surprise attack on the enemy.

**급식**(給食) (provision of) meals. ～하다 provide 〔supply〕 《the poor》 with meals; provide meals for 《*a person*》. ¶ 학교 ～ (provision of) school meals 〔lunch〕 / 학교 아동들에게 ～하다 provide lunch 〔meals〕 for school children. ◉ ～아동 children supplied 〔provided〕 with meals 〔lunch〕.

**급양**(給養) supplies such as food, clothing, bedding, and the like.

**급여**(給與) 《수당》 an allowance; 《물품》 supply; grant; 《급료》 pay; a salary; wages. ～하다 allow; grant; supply 《*a person* with *a thing*》. ¶ 현물 ～ an allowance in kind / 제복을 ～하다 supply 《*a person*》 (with) a uniform. ◉ ～소득 (an) earned 〔(a) wage〕 income: ～소득자 a salaried employee. ～수준 a pay 〔wage〕 level. ～체계 a pay 〔wage〕 structure 〔system〕.

**급용**(急用) urgent 〔pressing〕 business. ¶ ～으로 on urgent 〔pressing〕 business.

**급우**(級友) a classmate.

**급유**(給油) oil supply; 《연료의》 refueling; 《기계에》 oiling; lubrication. ～하다 fill 《a tank》; refill 《a car》 with gas; refuel 《an airplane》; oil 〔lubricate〕 《wheels》. ¶ 공중 ～ air-to-air refueling; midair 〔in-flight〕 refueling / 탱크에 가득 ～해 주시오 Fill it up, please. / 비행기는 김포에서 ～를 받고 비행을 계속했다 The plane refueled at Kimpo and flew on. / 비행기는 ～를 위해 홍콩에서 1시간 머물렀다 The aircraft made a refueling stop of about an hour at Hong Kong.

◉ ~기 a tanker plane. ~대 《차량의》 a vehicle refueling stand. ~선 a tanker (vessel). ~소 an oil depot; 《주유소》 a filling 〔gas 《미》, petrol 《영》〕 station. ~탱크 an oil tank.

**급전**(急電) an urgent telegram. ¶ ~을 치다 wire an urgent message; dispatch a radio message.

**급전**(急錢) urgently needed money; money for immediate use.

**급전**(急轉) a sudden change 〔turn〕. ~하다 change suddenly; take a sudden turn. ¶ 정세는 ~했다 There was a sudden change in the situation.

◉ ~직하 a sudden turn 《of affairs》; a spectacular change: ~직하로 suddenly; all at once; abruptly; 《구어》 all of a sudden / 형세는 ~직하로 변했다 The situation changed all of a sudden. / 다년간의 현안 문제가 ~직하로 해결되었다 A long-pending question has come to an immediate solution.

**급전**(給電) electric 〔power〕 supply. ~하다 supply electricity 〔electric power〕.

**급전환**(急轉換) a sudden change 〔turn〕; 《항공기의》 a reverse turn. ~하다 change 〔turn〕 suddenly. ¶ 평화 산업으로 ~하다 be switched over to peace industry / 정부는 경제 정책을 180도 ~시켰다 The government has made a rapid and complete about=face in its economic policy.

**급정거**(急停車) a sudden stop. ~하다 [사람이 주어] bring 《a car》 to a sudden stop; 《구어》 stamp 〔slam〕 on the brakes; [차가 주어] stop suddenly 〔short〕; come 〔be brought〕 to a sudden stop. 「⇨ 합격.

**급제**(及第) success in an examination.

**급조**(急造) hurried construction. ~하다 build 《a building》 in haste; construct hurriedly; 《구어》 run up 《a house》. ¶ ~의 hurriedly 〔hastily〕 built; improvised / 도시 주민을 위해 ~된 주택 계획 a crash housing program for urban residents. ◉ ~내각 a Cabinet formed in haste.

**급증**(急症) a sudden illness; an acute disease; an emergency case.

**급증**(急增) a rapid 〔sudden〕 increase. ~하다 increase rapidly 〔suddenly〕; jump. ¶ 교통 사고〔흉악 범죄〕의 ~ rapid increasing of traffic accidents 〔dreadful crimes〕.

**급진**(急進) 《진행》 rapid progress; 《과격》 radicalism. ~하다 speed up; push forward; rush. ¶ ~적인 radical; extreme / 그는 ~적인 사상의 소유자다 He has radical ideas. ◉ ~당 a radical 〔an extreme〕 party: ~ 당원 a radical; an extremist. ~분자 a radical element. ~사상 radical ideas. ~주의 radicalism. ~파 the radicals; the radicalists: ~개혁파 radical reformers.

**급커브**(急—) a sharp curve 〔turn〕. ¶ ~를 틀다 make a sharp 〔sudden〕 turn / 전방 ~ 《게시》 Sharp bend ahead.

**급탄**(給炭) supplying coal; coaling.

◉ ~소 a coaling station 〔depot〕. ~차 a stoker (car). ~항 a coaling port.

**급템포**(急—) quick tempo. ¶ ~의〔로〕 double-quick; double-time / 서양 문화를 ~로 흡수하다 absorb Western culture double-quick / 복구공사는 ~로 진척되었다 The restoration work progressed rapidly.

**급파**(急派) speedy dispatch. ~하다 dispatch (speedily); rush; expedite. ¶ 현장에 경찰대를 ~하다 rush a police force to the scene / 사고 현장에 구급차를 ~하다 dispatch an ambulance to the scene of the accident.

**급하다**(急—) ① 《일이》 (be) urgent; pressing; impending; imminent. ¶ 급한 일 urgent 〔pressing〕 business / 돈이 ~ be in urgent need of money / 일이 ~ the matter is pressing / 시간이 매우 급해졌다 We are pressed for time. / 돈이 급하게 필요했다 We were in immediate need of money.

② 《성미가》 (be) impatient; impetuous; hasty-tempered; hotheaded. ¶ 급한 성미 hotheadedness; impetuousness; impatience / 내 급한 성질은 고칠 수 없을 것 같다 I don't seem to be able to cure my impatience. / 「그 친구 참 성미도 급하군」—「다들 그러더군」 "He's very impatient, isn't he?"—"Everybody says so."

③ 《병이》 (be) sudden; serious; critical; be an emergency. ¶ 급한 병 a sudden 〔critical〕 illness / 급한 환자 an emergency case 〔patient〕.

④ 《경사가 가파르다》 (be) steep; precipitous; 《커브가》 (be) sharp. ¶ 급한 언덕〔언덕길〕 a steep hill 〔slope〕 / 급한 굽이〔커브〕 a sharp turn / 나는 길고 급한 돌계단을 올라갔다 I climbed a long steep flight of stone steps.

⑤ 《처지가》 be hard pressed; be hard put (to it) to *do;* be in a tight corner; be pushed to extremes.

**급행**(急行) ① 《급히 감》 a hurry; a rush. ～하다 hasten 《on *one's* way》; hurry 〔rush〕 《to》. ¶ 현장으로 ～하다 rush to the scene 《of the murder》. ② 《열차》 an express (train); 《특급》 (a) special 〔limited〕 express (train); 《초특급》 (a) superexpress (train). ¶ 8시 30분 발 목포행 ～ the 8:30 express for Mokp'o / ～을 타고 가다 take an express 《to》; travel 《to a place》 by express. ◉ ～버스 an express bus. ～열차 =급행 ②: ～열차 정차역 an express station. ～요금 express fare 〔charge〕.

**급환**(急患) an emergency case 〔patient〕; 《병》 a sudden illness 〔disease〕. ¶ ～에 걸리다 be suddenly taken ill; be seized with a sudden illness / (의사가) ～이 있어 왕진 중이다 be away on an emergency call.

**급히**(急—) hastily; in haste; in a hurry 〔rush〕; hurriedly; urgently; abruptly; quickly; immediately. ¶ ～ 걷다 walk hurriedly; go with speed; make the best of *one's* way / ～ 떠나다 leave in a great rush 〔hurry〕; make a hasty departure; hurry off 〔away〕; hustle off / ～ 몰다 drive in haste / ～ 멈추다 stop short / ～ 쓰다 write in haste / ～ 타다〔내리다〕 hurry on 〔off〕 / ～ 언덕을 내려오다 tear down the hill / 밥을 ～ 먹다 take a hasty meal; rush through *one's* meal / ～ 정거장까지 오너라 Hurry up to the station, please. / 그는 ～ 설명을 추가했다 He hastened to add an explanation. / 그들은 현장으로 ～ 달려갔다 They hurried 〔rushed〕 to the scene. / ～ 서두르는 통에 지갑을 두고 왔다 In my hurry I left my wallet behind me. / ～ 돌아오너라 Come back quickly. / ～ 먹는 밥에 목이 멘다 《속담》 Haste makes waste. *or* More haste, less speed.

**긋다**[1] ① 《줄 따위를》 draw; mark. ¶ 줄을 ～ draw a line / 땅에 줄을 ～ cut 〔dig〕 a line on ground / 획을 ～ draw a stroke 《of a character》. ② 《성냥을》 strike. ¶ 성냥을 ～ strike 〔light〕 a match. ③ 《장부에》 put 《*one's* name》 down; enter 《an item》 in 《a book》. ¶ 긋고 마시다 drink on credit 〔trust〕.

**긋다**[2] ① 《비가》 hold up; stop (falling). ② 《비를 피하다》 take 〔seek〕 shelter from the rain; take cover 《under a tree》 from a shower; get out of the rain. ¶ 처마 밑에서 비를 ～ shelter 〔take shelter〕 from rain under the eaves of a house / 가까운 다방으로 뛰어들어 비를 ～ run into a nearby coffee shop to shelter from the rain.

**긍긍하다**(兢兢—) be fearful; be in fear; be cautious; be in trepidation. ⇨ 전전긍긍.

**긍정**(肯定) affirmation; affirming. ～하다 affirm; agree; answer in the affirmative; answer "yes"; acknowledge. ¶ ～적(인) affirmative; positive / ～적인 대답〔태도〕 a positive answer 〔attitude〕 / ～도 부정도 하지 않다 make no comment either way; refuse to deny or confirm; say neither "yes" nor "no" / 인생을 ～적으로 보다 take a cheerful view of life / 증인은 사실을 ～했다 The witness affirmed the fact. ◉ ～명제 〖논리〗 an affirmative (proposition). ～문 an affirmative sentence. ～판단 〖논리〗 an affirmation.

**긍지**(矜持) pride; dignity; self-respect.

> 용법 **pride** 자기 자신 또는 자신의 지위·특성 따위에 대한 자랑스러움을 뜻하는 말. 때로는 「오만」이란 나쁜 뜻이 되는 경우도 있음. **dignity** 인격·지위 따위의 위엄·품위·무게 등을 나타내는 말. **self-respect** 타인에 의한 평가보다도 높게 자신을 평가하는 기분. 자존심을 나타냄.

¶ ～를 느끼다 feel proud; walk tall / ～를 지키다 maintain *one's* dignity; save *one's* honor 〔face〕 / ～를 손상시키다 hurt 《*a person's*》 pride / 그는 자기 일에 ～를 가지고 있다 He has 〔takes〕 pride in his work. / 우리는 흑, 백인 모두가 마음 속에 아무 두려움을 느끼지 않고, 인간의 존엄성에 대한 불가침의 권리를 확신하고 자신에 대한 ～를 느끼며 살아갈 수 있는 사회를 건설하겠습니다 We shall build the society in which both black and white will be able to walk tall, without any fear in their hearts, assured of their inalienable right to human dignity.

**긍휼**(矜恤) pity; commiseration; sympathy; compassion. ～하다 pity; have pity on; have compassion on. ¶ ～히 여기다 feel pity 《for》; have compassion 《on》.

**기**(己) 《천간의》 the 6th of the 10 Heaven's Stems.

**기**(忌) an anniversary of *one's* death; (a period of ) mourning. ¶ 7주기 the seventh anniversary of 《*a person's*》 death.

**기**(氣) ① 《기력·기운》 energy; spirit; vigor; vitality (활력); pep 《구어》;

stamina (근기); will-power (의지력). ¶ 기가 찬 사람 a man of spirit 〔vitality〕 / 기가 부족한 사람 a man of lacking in energy / 기가 나서 exultantly; energetically; triumphantly / 기가 왕성하다 be full of energy 〔vigor, vitality〕 / 기가 없다 be spiritless; do not have the energy to *do* / 기가 쇠약해지다 *one's* energy 〔will-power〕 fails *one;* lose *one's* vigor 〔spirit〕.
② 《온 힘》 all *one's* strength 〔energies, might〕. ¶ 기를 쓰다 exert *oneself* to the utmost; do *one's* utmost; make every effort / 기를 쓰고 달려들다 tackle with all *one's* might / 기를 쓰고 반대하다 be bent on opposing 《*a person*》 / 기를 쓰고 변명하다 try to apologize with heat; speak (up) for *oneself* one way or the other / 그는 성적을 올리려고 기를 쓰고 공부하고 있다 He is studying very hard to get good marks 〔grades〕.
③ 《아연》 breath; wind. ¶ 기가 막히다 be stifled; be at a loss (for words); be dumbfounded / 너의 바보짓에는 정말 기가 찬다 Your stupidity really shocks me.
④ 《정신력·의기》 spirit(s); heart; morale (사기). ¶ 기가 왕성하다 be in high spirits; be elated / 기가 죽다 lose heart 〔courage〕; get disheartened / 기가 꺾여 있다 be in low spirits; be depressed / 기를 꺾다 depress 《*a person's*》 spirits; shake 《*a person's*》 courage; cast a damp over 《*a person's*》 spirits / 기를 펴다 feel relaxed 〔easy, at ease〕 / 기를 돋우다 cheer 《*a person*》 up; encourage; heighten *one's* spirit / 기를 펴지 못하다 feel ill at ease; feel constrained; cower / 「무슨 일이냐, 기가 꺾여 있으니」—「또 엄청난 실수를 저질렀단 말이야」 "What's wrong with you? You look so depressed."—"I made a bad mistake again."
⑤ 〖철학〗 natural passion; the life force; *élan vital* (F.).
⑥ ill-advised bravery; blind valor. ⇨ 객기(客氣).
⑦ 《기미》 a feeling 《of》; a touch; a shade; a tinge; a hint; a symptom (징후). ¶ 불기가 없는 방 an unheated room / 익살 기가 있다 have a touch of humor; be tinged with humor / 감기 기로 누워 있다 be laid up with a touch of cold / 시장기를 느끼다 feel hungry / 불기가 없는 오두막에서 불이 났다 A fire broke out in the hut where there was no trace of any fire having been used.

**기**(記) an account; a narrative.

**기**(基) 〖화학〗 a radical; a group; 〖수학〗 a radix. ¶ 산기 an acid radical.

**기**(期) 《시기》 a time; an age (시대); 《기일》 a date; 《기간》 a term; a period; a session (회기); 《단계》 a stage; 《계절》 a season. ¶ 제1기의 결핵 tuberculosis in its first stage / 수렵기 the hunting season / 제1학기 the first term / 차기 국회에서 at the next session of the National Assembly.

**기**(旗) a flag; a banner 《문어》; a standard (군기); an ensign (함선기); a pennant (가늘고 긴 삼각기). ¶ 기의 행렬 a procession with flags flying / 연대기 the regimental standard 〔colors〕 / 기를 올리다 put up 〔hoist, raise〕 a flag / 기를 내리다 take down 〔lower, pull down〕 a flag / 기를 흔들다 wave a flag / 기를 펴다〔접다〕 unfurl 〔furl〕 a flag / 기를 흔들어 멈추다 flag down 《a train》 / 기가 바람에 펄럭이고 있다 A flag is waving 〔fluttering, flying, streaming〕 in the wind. / 일몰이 되어 기가 내려졌다 The flag was lowered at sunset.

**-기** [동사적 명사 구실] to do or be; that it does or is. ¶ 돕기 위해서 in order to help / 참가하기를 거절하다 refuse to participate / 쓰기(를) 시작하다 begin to write / 배가 고프기 시작하다 start to get hungry / 주기를 주저하다 hesitate to give it / 나가기(를) 싫어하다 hate to go out / 배우기(가) 쉽다 It is easy to learn.

**-기**(機) a machine. ¶ 세탁기〔자판기〕 a washing 〔vending〕 machine.

**기각**(棄却) rejection; turning down; 〖법〗 dismissal. ～하다 reject; turn down; dismiss 《a suit》; remand 《a case to a lower court》. ¶ 신청을 ～하다 reject 〔turn down〕 an application.

**기간**(基幹) a mainstay; a nucleus (*pl.* -clei); the main stem. ¶ ～의 hard=core; key. ◉ ～산업 key 〔basic〕 industries. ～시설 《사회의》 an infrastructure: ～ 시설 확장 작업 infrastructure expanding works. ～ 시설 투자 (an) infrastructure investment. ～요원 cadre members; key personnel.

**기간**(既刊) ¶ ～의 already 〔previously〕 published 〔issued〕. ◉ ～도서 a book already published: ～ 도서 목록 a list of books already published. ～호(號) back 〔previous〕 numbers.

**기간**(期間) a term; a period (of time). ¶ 짧은 ~ a short period / 전람회의 개최 ~ a period for an exhibition / 일정한 ~ 내에 within a definite 〔certain, given〕 period of time / ~을 연장하다 extend the period / 이 표의 유효 ~은 2개월이다 This ticket is valid for two months. / 원서의 접수 ~은 5일부터 10일까지이다 Applications are accepted from the 5th to the 10th.

**기갈**(飢渴) hunger and thirst; starvation. ¶ ~에 신음하다 suffer from 〔be pressed by〕 hunger and thirst / ~을 면하다 stave 〔keep〕 off (*one's*) hunger and thirst 《with an apple》 / ~이 감식이다 《속담》 Hunger is the best sauce.

**기갑**(機甲) ¶ ~부대 an armored corps 〔forces〕 / ~사단 an armored division.

**기강**(紀綱) fundamental principles 《of a government》; official 〔government〕 discipline; 《질서》 public order; law and order. ¶ ~의 문란 the deterioration of (official) discipline / ~을 바로잡다 tighten discipline 《among》; improve the moral fiber 《of》 / 공무원의 ~을 바로잡아야 한다 We must enforce strict official discipline among government employees.
◉ ~숙정 enforcement of official discipline. ~해이 relaxation of discipline; slack discipline.

**기개**(氣槪) spirit; backbone; mettle; pluck; guts 《구어》. ¶ ~가 있는 high=〔noble-〕spirited; of spirit; plucky; mettlesome; gutsy 《구어》 / ~ 있는 사람 a man of spirit 〔pluck〕; a high-spirited man / ~가 없다 have no spirit 〔backbone〕; be lacking in spirit / ~를 보이다 show *one's* mettle 〔pluck〕.

**기거**(起居) *one's* daily life. ¶ ~를 같이하다 live together (under the same roof) with 《*a person*》. ◉ ~동작 *one's* daily conduct and behavior.

**기겁** astonishment; being shocked 〔thunderstruck〕. ~하다 be startled; be frightened (out of *one's* wits). ¶ ~을 해서 그는 말도 할 수 없었다 He was too frightened 〔surprised〕 to speak.

**기결**(旣決) having already decided 〔settled, adjudged〕. ~하다 have already decided 〔settled〕. ¶ ~의 decided; settled; 《죄가》 convicted.
◉ ~사항 a matter settled 〔decided on〕. ~서류꽂이 an out-tray. ~수(囚) a convict; a convicted prisoner.

**기경**(起耕) ~하다 〖농업〗 bring 《land》 under cultivation; cultivate.

**기계**(奇計) a cunning plan; a clever scheme. ¶ ~를 꾸며 내다 map out a clever scheme / ~를 쓰다 resort to a cunning plan.

**기계**(器械) an instrument; an appliance; an apparatus (장치) (★ 복수형은 흔히 pieces of apparatus로 함). ¶ 의료~ medical instruments 〔appliances〕 / 그는 광학 ~를 취급한다 He deals in optical instruments. ◉ ~체조 apparatus gymnastics.

**기계**(機械) a machine; a gin; machinery [총칭]; 《장치》 a mechanism; works (시계 등의). ¶ 공작~ a machine tool / 인쇄〔정밀〕~ a printing 〔precision〕 machine / 복잡한 ~ an intricate piece of machinery; complex mechanism / 자동차 부품을 만드는 ~ a machine for producing car parts / ~와 같은 machinelike / ~처럼 정확히 like clockwork.
기계는: 이 ~는 잘 돌아가고 있다 This machine is working 〔running〕 well 〔beautifully〕. / 이 ~는 어딘가 고장이 난 것 같다 Something seems to be wrong with this machine. / 기계는 육체 노동을 많이 덜어준다 Machines save us a lot of manual labor.
기계로: ~로 만든 machine-made; made by machine / ~로 누빈 machine-sewn / ~로 짠 스웨터 a machine-knit sweater.
기계를: ~를 움직이다 《작동》 start a machine; set a machine in motion; 《조작·가동》 operate 〔run〕 a machine; 《취급·사용》 handle 〔work, use〕 a machine / ~를 설치〔설비〕하다 install a machine / ~를 조립하다 assemble a machine; put a machine together / ~를 분해하다〔뜯어내다〕 disassemble 〔dismantle〕 the machine / 서투른 사람이 ~를 조작하는 것은 매우 위험하다 It is very dangerous for unqualified people to operate machinery.
¶ 이것은 무슨 ~인가요 What is this machine for? / ~에 손대지 마시오 《게시》 Hands off the machinery. / 나는 이 새로운 ~ 조작에 익숙하지 않다 I'm not used to operating this new machine. / 이 공장은 금년에 새로운 ~를 설치해서 생산량을 증가시켰다 This factory installed new machines this year and increased its output.
◉ ~가공 machine work; machining. ~공 a mechanic. ~공구 a machine tool. ~공업 the machine industry. ~공장 a machine shop 〔factory, works〕.

~공학 mechanical engineering. ~과(科) a mechanical course; a course in mechanical engineering. ~과(課) a machinery section. ~기사〔기술자〕 a mechanical engineer; a mechanician. ~기술 mechanical 〔machine〕 technology. ~날염〔염색〕 machine printing 〔dyeing〕. ~능률〔효율〕 mechanical efficiency. ~력 mechanical power. ~론 mechanism: ~론적 우주관 〖철학〗 a mechanistic view of the universe. ~문명 machine 〔mechanized〕 civilization. ~번역 machine translation. ~부(속)품 a machine part: ~ 부속품상 a machine-parts supplier. ~설계 the design of a machine. ~수리공 a repairman; a machinist. ~시대 the machine age. ~실 a machine(ry) room; an engine room. ~어(語) a machine code 〔language〕. ~유(油) machine oil; lubrication oil. ~작용 mechanical action 〔work〕. ~장치 mechanism. ~제도(製圖) mechanical drawing. ~제작소 a machine shop. ~조립 assembling; fitting. ~조립공 a fitter of machinery. ~틀 machinery mount(ing); machine frame. ~학 mechanics.

**기계적**(機械的) mechanical; automatic. ¶ ~으로 mechanically; automatically; 《*do*》 by rote 〔rule〕 / ~인 대답 a mechanical 〔an automatic〕 answer / ~으로 암기하다 learn 《a passage》 by rote / 무슨 일이나 ~으로 하다 do everything mechanically 〔in a mechanical way〕 / ~인 일은 재미가 없다 I find mechanical work is uninteresting 〔monotonous〕. ◉ ~ 노동 mechanical labor. ~ 처리 mechanical processes.

**기계화**(機械化) mechanization. ~하다 mechanize; introduce machinery 《into》. ¶ 농촌의 ~ farm mechanization; mechanized farming. ◉ ~ 병기 mechanized arms. ~ 부대 a mechanized unit.

**기고**(起稿) drafting 《a manuscript》; 《초고》 a draft. ~하다 draft; frame a draft; begin to write; start writing.

**기고**(寄稿) (a) contribution 《of manuscripts》. ~하다 contribute 《an article》 to 《a newspaper》; write for 《a magazine》. ◉ ~가 a contributor.

**기고만장**(氣高萬丈) ① 《성남》 bursting with anger; blowing *one's* top. ~하다 become very angry; burst with anger; blow *one's* top. ② 《의기양양》 elation; high spirits. ~하다 (be) elated; be in high spirits; be 「big 〔puffed up〕 with pride. ¶ 그는 큰 성공을 거두어 ~해 있다 He is highly elated by his big success.

**기골**(氣骨) 《기와 골격》 body and spirit; 《기개》 spirit; mettle; pluck. ¶ ~이 장대한 사람 《골격이 큰》 a man of large and robust frame / ~이 없는 인물 《기개가 없는》 a backboneless 〔spineless〕 fellow; an invertebrate.

**기공**(技工) 《기술자》 a craftsman; 《기술》 a craft. ◉ ~사(士) 《치과의》 a dental technician.

**기공**(起工) 《착공》 the start 〔commencement〕 of (construction) work. ~하다 begin 〔start〕 the construction 《of a bridge》; set to work; 《토목의》 break ground 《for》; 《건축의》 lay the cornerstone 《of》; 《배의》 lay the keel 《of》. ¶ 작년 ~한 다리가 오늘 준공되었다 The construction of the bridge, which was begun last year, has been completed today. ◉ ~식 the ceremony of laying 「the cornerstone (건축의) 〔the keel (배의)〕; the ground-breaking ceremony (토목의).

**기공**(氣孔) a pore; a stoma (식물의); a stigma (곤충의).

**기관**(汽管) a steam pipe.

**기관**(汽罐) a (steam) boiler. ◉ ~사 a boiler man. ~실 a boiler room; a stokehold (배의).

**기관**(奇觀) a strange sight; a wonder; a wonderful sight; a singular 〔rare〕 spectacle. ¶ ~을 이루다 present a wonderful sight.

**기관**(氣管) 〖해부〗 the windpipe; the trachea (*pl.* ~s, -cheae). ¶ ~의 tracheal. ◉ ~절개(술) tracheotomy. ~지(支) the bronchus (*pl.* -chi [-kai]); a bronchial tube: ~지염 bronchitis / ~지 천식 bronchial asthma / ~지 카타르 bronchial catarrh / ~지 폐렴 bronchial pneumonia.

**기관**(器官) 〖동·식물〗 an organ. ¶ 몸의 여러 ~ the (individual) organs of the body / 생명 유지에 중요한 ~ a vital organ / 호흡〔소화〕 ~ the respiratory 〔digestive〕 organs. ◉ ~계통 an organ system. ~질환 an organic disease.

**기관**(機關) ① 〖기계〗 an engine; a machine. ¶ 전기〔증기, 디젤〕 ~ an electric 〔a steam, a diesel〕 engine / 내연 ~ an internal-combustion 〔IC〕 engine / 보조 ~ an auxiliary engine. ② 《수단·기구 따위》 means; an institution; a system; an organ. ¶ 정당의

～ the apparatus 〔organs〕 of the party / 심의～ a deliberative body 〔organ〕 / 보도～ the press; a news medium / 행정～ administrative machinery / 정부～ a government agency / 자치 ～ a self-government body / 국가의 최고 ～ the highest state body.
◉ ～고 『철도』 an engine shed 〔house〕. ～고장 malfunctioning of an engine; an engine trouble. ～단총 a submachine gun. ～사 an engine driver; a locomotive engineer: 2〔3〕등 ～사 the second 〔third〕 engineer. ～실 an engine room. ～원 a secret service man. ～장 《기관실 따위의》 the first 〔chief〕 engineer; 《행정 조직의》 the head 〔chief〕 of an administrative organ. ～차 a locomotive; an engine 《영》: 전기〔증기〕～차 an electric 〔a steam〕 locomotive. ～투자가 an institutional 〔corporate〕 investor.

**기관지**(機關紙〔誌〕) a bulletin; an organ. ¶ 정당〔조합〕의 ～ a party 〔union〕 organ / 정부 ～ a government organ 〔bulletin〕.

**기관총**(機關銃) a machine gun (생략 MG). ¶ ～수 a machine-gunner; an air gunner (비행기의) / ～을 마구 쏘(아대)다 rattle away 《at the enemy》 with a machine gun / ～ 소사(掃射)를 하다 sweep 〔rake〕 《the enemy position》 by machine-gun fire; machine=gun / ～이 타타타타 울렸다 'Rat-tat=tat' went a machine gun. ◉ ～진지 a machine-gun position 〔nest〕.

**기괴망측**(奇怪罔測) ～하다 (be) outrageous; scandalous; monstrous.

**기괴하다**(奇怪—) 《이상야릇하다》 (be) strange; mysterious; weird; 《괴이쩍다》 (be) outrageous; outlandish; monstrous. ¶ 기괴한 사건 a strange affair; a mystery / 기괴한 소문 a wild rumor / 매우 기괴하게도 funnily enough.

**기교**(技巧) art; craftsmanship; workmanship; a technical skill; technique; technics; 《책략》 (an) artifice; a trick; (a) finesse; 《예술의》 artistic excellence; mechanism. ¶ ～를 부리다 use art; use a trick; resort to artifice / 이 그림은 ～에 있어서 조금도 흠잡을 데가 없다 This picture leaves nothing to be desired in technique. / 이 가구는 ～적인 면에서 뛰어나다 This furniture excels in craftsmanship.
◉ ～가 a technician; an artist 〔a painter〕 of (great) skill. ～주의 《예술상의》 technicalism. ～파 technists.

**기구**(氣球) a balloon; an aerostat. ¶ ～를 띄우다 fly 〔send up〕 a balloon / ～를 타고 올라가다 go up 〔ascend〕 in a balloon / ～로 영국 해협을 횡단하다 cross the English Channel by balloon / ～에 바람이 찼다 The balloon filled out. ◉ ～위성 a balloon satellite.

**기구**(器具) 《가정용의》 a utensil; an appliance; a tool (공구); 《특정 목적의》 an implement; 《정밀·정확한》 an instrument; 《설비된 것》 fixtures; an apparatus. ¶ 조리～ cooking utensiles / 전기～ an electric appliance / 의료～ a medical instrument / 농～ a farm implement / 난방～ a heating apparatus.

**기구**(機構) 《구조》 (a) structure; framework; 《조직》 organization; 《짜임새》 a mechanism; machinery (운영의); 《제도》 a system. ¶ 사회 ～ the structure of society / 경제 ～ the economic structure / 유통 ～ a distribution system / 유엔의 복잡한 ～ the complex mechanism 〔machinery〕 of the United Nations / ～를 개편하다 reorganize 〔restructure〕 the system / ～를 만들다 provide machinery 《for》 / 우리 나라의 유통 ～는 미국의 그것보다 30년 뒤져 있다 The distribution fabric of our economy is behind that of the United States by thirty years. ◉ ～개혁 the reorganization of the system; a structural reform. 국제～ an international organization.

**기구하다**(崎嶇—) 《산길 따위가》 (be) steep; rugged; precipitous; 《팔자가》 (be) unlucky; unfortunate; ill-fated; checkered. ¶ 기구한 생애 a checkered 〔varied〕 career / 기구한 운명에 희롱되다 be the sport of adverse 〔strange〕 fortune; be the puppet of hapless fate / 기구한 팔자를 타고나다 be born under an unlucky star / 기구한 인생을 살다 lead a checkered life.

**기권**(棄權) 《권리의》 abandonment 〔renunciation〕 of *one's* rights; 《투표의》 abstention from voting; 《경기의》 absence; default. ～하다 renounce 〔abandon, waive, relinquish〕 *one's* right; abstain from voting; withdraw *one's* entry. ¶ ～을 막다 prevent abstention from voting / 유권자의 거의 반수가 ～했다 Nearly half of the voters abstained 〔stayed away〕. / 그녀는 수영 경기 도중에 ～했다 She dropped out of the swimming race. ◉ ～율 an abstention rate. ～자 a nonvoter; an abstainer; 《권리의》 a releasor. ～표 a blank ballot.

**기근**(氣根) 〖식물〗 an aerial root.

**기근**(飢饉) (a) famine; a crop failure (흉작); (a) shortage (부족); a dearth. ¶ ～의 해 a lean year / ～에 시달리다 suffer from a famine / ～으로 죽다 perish with 〔by〕 famine; die of famine / 그 지방에 ～이 들었다 A famine hit 〔visited〕 that district. / 그들의 눈앞에 ～이 다가왔다 Famine stared them in the face. / 그 지역에서는 3년에 걸친 ～으로 20만명 이상의 사람들이 굶어 죽었다고 한다 It is reported that up to two hundred thousand people have died of starvation in three years of famine in the region. ◉ ～구제기금 a famine-relief fund. ～지역 a famine-stricken district. 달러 ～ a severe dollar shortage. 대～ a great 〔severe〕 famine.

**기금**(基金) 《자금》 a fund; a foundation (재단); an endowment (기본 재산). ¶ 구제 ～ a relief fund / ～을 설립하다 establish a fund; set up a foundation / ～을 내다 donate a fund to 《a college》; endow 《a hospital》 / ～을 모집하다 collect 〔raise〕 a fund. ◉ ～모집(운동) (campaign for the) collection of a fund.

**기급하다**(氣急—) 《놀라다》 be aghast; be petrified with terror 〔fright〕; be astounded 〔shocked〕; be taken aback; 《소리치다》 cry out in surprise 〔astonishment〕. ¶ 개가 짓는 바람에 기급하여 달아나다 be frightened away by the barking of a dog / 그 폭발에 나는 기급했다 The explosion made me jump out of my skin. / 기급하게 놀란 승객들은 앞을 다투어 차창 밖으로 뛰어나왔다 The startled passengers struggled to leap out of the carriage windows. / 기급할 소리 다 듣겠군 I have never heard anything so outrageous.

**기기**(器機) machinery; equipment; an instrument. ¶ 오디오 ～ audio equipment / 정밀～ a precision instrument.

**기기묘묘**(奇奇妙妙) ～하다 《기이하다》 (be) wonderful and beautiful; marvelous; fabulous; 《기묘하다》 (be) very clever; ingenious; cunning; exquisite; extremely strange. ¶ ～한 사건 a very strange affair; a mysterious incident / ～한 소문 a bizarre rumor.

**-기까지** even; to; so far as 《to *do*》; to the extent of 《*do*ing》. ¶ 도둑질 하기까지에 이르다 go so far as to commit theft; go to the length of committing theft.

**기꺼워하다** ＝기뻐하다. ¶ 그 소식에 ～ be glad to hear the news.

**기꺼이** willingly; with pleasure; joyfully; with all *one's* heart; with a good grace. ¶ ～ …하다 be ready 〔willing〕 to *do;* be delighted to *do* / ～ 승낙하다 consent with pleasure / ～ 거들어 드리겠습니다 I am only too glad to help you. / 너의 말이라면 무엇이든 ～ 듣겠다 I'm ready to listen to anything that you tell me.

**기껏** ① 《힘껏》 to the utmost (of *one's* energy); to the best on *one's* ability; with all *one's* might; as hard as 「possible 〔*one* can〕. ¶ ～ 힘쓰다 put forth *one's* strength to the utmost; do *one's* best; do everything in *one's* power / ～ 모은 돈을 다 써버리다니 바보 같은 짓을 했다 I was foolish enough to spend the money I had saved at no small pains. ② ⇨ 기껏해야.

**기껏해야** at (the) most; at (the) best; at the utmost; at the ...-est. ¶ ～ 1마일 a mile at the (very) outside / ～ 한 시간에 10마일 걷는다 *one* walks 10 miles an hour at most; 10 miles is as much as *one* can walk in an hour / ～ 한주일밖에 묵지 못하겠다 I can stay for a week at the longest. / ～ 「C」밖에 못 받을 것이다 I'll get C at best. / 그녀는 ～ 20세다 I think she is twenty at most. / 그것은 ～ 1만원 정도일 것이다 It will cost ten thousand won at most.

**기낭**(氣囊) 《물고기의》 an air bladder; 《조류·식물의》 an air sac.

**기내**(機內) 《항공기의》 the inside of a plane; the cabin. ¶ ～에서 in 〔inside〕 a plane / ～용의 in-flight / ～에서 식사를 하다 have a meal on the plane / K 항공은 ～ 서비스가 좋다는 평판이다 K Airlines has a reputation for good in-flight service. / 기장이 ～ 방송을 통해 승객에게 비행 위치를 전했다 The captain announced the passengers where they were flying over the aircraft's public-address system. ◉ ～반입 수화물 a carry-on 〔hand-carry〕 baggage. ～방송 an in-flight announcement. ～서비스 in-flight 〔cabin〕 service. ～식 a meal served on the plane; an in-flight meal; airline food. ～영화 an in-flight movie.

**기네스북** The Guinness Book of Records.

**기녀**(妓女) ① 《관비》 an official *kisaeng.* ② ＝기생(妓生).

**기념**(紀念) commemoration; memory; 《기념품》 a remembrance. ～하다 commemorate; honor the memory of.
¶ ～의 commemorative; memorial / …의 ～으로 in memory 〔commemoration〕 of…; as a souvenir 〔token, keepsake〕 of… / 독립 선언 50주년을 ～하는 제전 a festival commemorating the 50th anniversary of the Declaration of Independence / 졸업 ～으로 식수하다 plant a tree to commemorate *one's* graduation / 결혼 ～으로 사진을 찍었다 We had our picture taken in memory of our wedding.
◉ ～관 a memorial hall. ～논문집 a Festschrift; essays (contributed) in celebration of 《the 5th anniversary of…》. ～물〔품〕 a souvenir; a remembrance; a momento; a keepsake. ～비 a monument; a cenotaph (고인을 위한): ～비적인 monumental. ～사 a commemorative address. ～사진 a souvenir picture 〔photo〕. ～스탬프〔우표〕 a commemorative stamp. ～수(樹) a memorial tree. ～식 a commemorative ceremony. ～일 a memorial 〔commemoration〕 day; an anniversary (연 1회의): 결혼 ～일 a wedding anniversary / 창립 ～일 a foundation day. ～출판 a commemorative publication. ～패(牌) a memorial tablet 〔plaque〕. ～행사 a commemorative event: 여러 가지 ～ 행사를 마련하다 prepare a variety of commemorative events. ～호 a commemoration number; a special number issued in memory of 《the late Prof. Kim》. ～회 a commemorative party 〔meeting〕; a memorial service.

**-기는** as for doing or being. ¶ …하기는 커녕 far from *do*ing 〔being〕; instead of *do*ing 〔being〕; on the contrary / 이 책을 읽기는 읽지만 뜻은 모른다 I do read this book (all right), but I don't understand what it is talking about. / 그것을 먹기는 먹었지만 맛은 없었다 I did eat it, but it had no flavor.

**기능**(技能) (technical) skill; ability (능력). ¶ 특수 ～ expert skill / ～이 있는 skilled; able / ～을 닦다 improve *one's* skill / ～이 뛰어나다 be highly skilled 《in》/ ～ 인력을 양성하다 foster skilled technicians / 그 일을 할만한 ～이 있다 be competent for the task.
◉ ～교육 technical education. ～상 a technique 〔technical〕 prize; a prize for skill. ～인〔자〕 a vocational technician. ～직 technical service: ～직 공무원 a technical official. 국제 ～ 올림픽 (대회) the International Vocational Training Competition (생략 IVTC); the International Skills Contest.

**기능**(機能) a function; a faculty. ¶ 소화 ～ digestive functions / ～적(으로) functional(ly) / ～을 하다 function; work / ～을 발휘하다 fulfill *one's* 〔*its*〕 function / 워드 프로세서의 ～을 설명하다 explain the functions of the word processor / ～이 정지되다 stop functioning / 이 책상은 매우 ～적이다 This desk is very functional. / 이 장치는 제대로 ～을 발휘하지 못했다 This system didn't function 〔work〕 adequately. / 인간에게는 언어 ～이 있다 Men have the faculty of speech.
◉ ～검사 a functional test. ～구조 functional structure. ～기관(器官) a functional organ. ～성 질환 a functional 〔dynamic〕 disease. ～심리학 functional psychology. ～장애 a functional disorder: ～ 장애를 일으키다 be functionally disordered. ～저하 malfunction. ～주의 functionalism. ～훈련 functional training.

**기니** 《서아프리카의 독립국》 Guinea.

**기니피그** 〖동물〗 a guinea pig; a cavy.

**기다** crawl; creep; go on 「all fours 〔*one's* hands and knees〕. (★ crawl은 뱀같이 발이 없는 동물에, creep는 곤충, 사람처럼 발 가진 동물이나 담쟁이 덩굴같은 식물에 씀). ¶ 기어가다 crawl about / 바위를 기어오르다 creep 〔crawl〕 up 〔over〕 the rock / 그들은 덤불 속을 기어서 전진했다 They crept along through the bushes. / 교통 정체로 차는 시속 5마일로 기어갔다 There was bad traffic congestion and the car crawled 〔crept〕 along at five miles an hour. / 기는 놈 위에 나는 놈 있다 《속담》 You cannot always outdo others. *or* There is always someone who does it 〔who knows it〕 a little bit better.

**기다랗다** (be) rather long; lengthy; 《연설 따위가》 long-winded 《lectures》. ¶ 기다란 장대 a long pole.

**기다리다** ① 《사람·때를》 wait 《for》; await; 《전화를 끊지 않고》 hold on.
¶ 사람을 ～ wait for a man / 기회를 ～ wait 〔watch〕 for an opportunity / 때를 ～ bide 〔wait〕 *one's* time; watch and wait / 잠자지〔외출하지〕 않고 ～ wait up 〔in〕 《for》/ 애타게 ～ wait impatiently for; be dying 〔pining〕 to

see 《*a person*》/ 차례를 ～ wait (for) *one's* turn / 오래 ～ have a long wait 《for》; be kept waiting for a long time / 기다림에 지치다 grow tired 〔get weary〕 of waiting / 나 기다리지 말고 먼저 식사해요 《남편이 아내에게》 Don't wait dinner for me. / 조금만 더 기다려 주십시오 Please wait a little longer. / 잠깐 기다려 주십시오, 연필과 종이를 준비하겠습니다 《전화에서》 Please hold on a minute while I get a pencil and paper. / 오래 기다리시게 해서 죄송합니다 I am awfully sorry to have kept you waiting so long. *or* Pardon me for keeping you waiting for a long time. / 세월은 사람을 기다리지 않는다 Time and tide wait for no man. / 벌써 세 시간이나 그를 기다리고 있다 I have been waiting for him these three hours.

> 용법 **wait** 흔히 자동사로 쓰여 wait for의 형식이 된다. 「기다리다」란 뜻의 가장 일상적인 말. 목적어로 「차례, 기회, 명령」 따위 뜻의 말이 와서 타동사로 쓰게 되면 전치사 for가 필요 없게 된다. **await**는 타동사로 전치사 불필요함. 딱딱한 뜻이어서 상용문에서 흔히 쓰인다.

② 《기대하다》 expect; anticipate; look forward to 《*something, do*ing》.

> 용법 **expect** 당연한 것으로 알고 「기다리다, 기대하다」란 뜻. 따라서 「그럼 내일 9시에 뵙겠습니다」 Well, I'll see 〔I look forward to seeing〕 you at 9 tomorrow.—이것을 I'll be expecting you ...로 말하면, 상대방에게 강요하는 기분이 들어 피하는 것이 좋다. **anticipate** 「wait for... with pleasure」란 뜻의 문어적 표현. **look forward to** 「wait for... with pleasure」의 뜻. to 다음에는 명사·대명사·동명사가 오며 동사 원형은 오지 않음.

¶ 이제나 저제나 하고 ～ look eagerly for; be on (the) tiptoe of expectation 《for》/ 기다렸다는 듯이 응하다 jump at 《an offer》/ 기다렸다는 듯이 …하다 seize the opportunity to *do;* lose no time in *do*ing / 기다리던 사람이 왔다 The expected man has come. / 기다리고 기다리던 날이 왔다 The long=awaited day has come. / 조속한 회답을 기다리겠습니다 I look forward to an early reply. / 우리는 즐거운 마음으로 휴가를 기다리고 있다 We are eagerly looking forward to the vacation.

**기다마하다** 《꽤 길다》 (be) very long. ¶ 기다마한 막대 a long pole.

**기단**(氣團) 〖기상〗 an air mass. ¶ 차가운 〔따뜻한〕 ～ a cold 〔warm〕 air mass.

**기담**(奇談) a strange story 〔tale〕.

**기대** 〖민속〗 ① 《무동을 따라다니는》 a woman who takes a child dancer around to perform. ② 《굿에서》 the person in charge of music for a shaman's exorcism rite.

**기대**(期待) expectation(s); hope(s); anticipation; expectancy; counting on. ～하다 expect; anticipate; hope for; look (forward) to 《*something, do*ing》; count on. ¶ 앞날이 ～되는 작가 a promising 〔hopeful〕 writer / …을 ～하고 in anticipation 〔expectation, hope〕 of...; in the hope 《that..., of *do*ing》/ ～에 반하여 「contrary to 〔against〕 *one's* expectations / ～에 부응하다 meet *one's* expectations; live 〔come〕 up to 《*a person's*》 expectations / ～에 어긋나다 fall short of *one's* expectations; run counter to *one's* expectations / ～를 걸다 put *one's* hopes 《in, on》; place 〔lay〕 *one's* hope 《on》/ ～에 미치지 못하다 be not up to the expectation 《of》/ 그의 기록은 ～ 밖으로 저조했다 His poor record was the last thing we expected. / 그 영화는 ～했던 만큼 좋지 못했다 The movie was not as good as we had expected. / 그에게 너무 ～를 걸어서는 안된다 You must not expect too much of him.

**기대다** ① 《몸을》 lean against 〔on〕; rest against; recline on. ¶ 몸을 벽에 ～ rest 〔lean〕 *one's* body against a wall / 난간에 ～ lean over the rail / 벽에 기대고 앉다 sit with *one's* back against the wall / 벽에 사다리를 기대어 놓다 lean a ladder up against the wall; place 〔rest〕 a ladder against the wall / 그녀는 안락의자에 등을 기대고 앉아 깊은 생각에 잠겨 있었다 She was leaning back in her armchair, lost in thought. ② 《의지하다》 rely 〔depend, count〕 on; turn 〔look〕 to 《*a person*》 for help; lean on. ¶ 친척에게 ～ lean 〔depend〕 on *one's* relatives 《for support》/ 친구의 원조에 ～ rely on the help of a friend / 남에게 기대지 마라 Don't depend 〔rely〕 on others.

**기도**(企圖) 《시도》 an attempt; try; 《계획》 a project; a design; 《음모》 a plot; an intrigue; 《사업 따위의》 an undertaking. ～하다 《시도하다》 attempt; try; 《계획하다》 plan; scheme; project; 《의도하다》 intend; have 《*something*》 in mind; purpose 《to make an attempt》; 《착수하다》 undertake. ¶ 아무를 살해하려는 ～ an attempt 〔a conspiracy〕 against *a person's* life / 자살을 ～하다 attempt suicide / 적의 ～를 분쇄하다 frustrate the enemy's attempt / 국왕을 살해하려는 ～가 발각 되었다 A plot to assassinate the king was uncovered 〔detected〕. / 우리 회사는 해외 진출을 ～하고 있다 Our company is planning to expand its business overseas.

**기도**(氣道) 〖해부〗 the respiratory tract.

**기도**(祈禱) a prayer; 《식사 전후의》 grace. ～하다 pray 《to》; say 〔offer〕 a prayer; say grace 《before 〔after〕 a meal》. ¶ 그는 어머니의 건강 회복을 위해 하느님께 ～했다 He prayed to God for her mother's recovery from illness. ◉ ～문 a prayer; the Lord's Prayer. ～사(師) a faith healer; a shaman; an exorcist. ～서 a prayer book; the Book of Common Prayer (영국의). ～원 a prayer house 〔retreat〕. ～자 a prayer; a supplicant. ～회(會) a prayer meeting.

**-기도하다** ① *do* 〔be〕 indeed. ¶ 춥기도 하다 be really cold / 참 단풍이 아름답기도 하다 My, the autumn leaves are so pretty! / 공부만 하기란 어렵기도 하다 It is pretty tough to do nothing but study all the time. / 그 학생은 부지런하기도 하다 He is really a hard-working student. ② *do* 〔be〕 both ... and .... ¶ 좋기도 하고 나쁘기도 하다 It has its good points and its bad points. / 배고프기도 하고 목마르기도 했다 I was hungry and thirsty.

**기독교**(基督教) Christianity; the Christian religion 〔faith〕. ¶ ～의 Christian. ◉ ～교회 a Christian church. ～국 a Christian country; Christendom (전체). ～도 a Christian. ～ 사회주의 Christian socialism. ～선교사 a Christian missionary. ～ 여자 청년회 the Young Women's Christian Association (생략 Y.W.C.A.). ～ 청년회 the Young Men's Christian Association (생략 Y.M.C.A).

**기동**(起動) ① 《몸의 움직임》 *one's* movement; (a) motion (동작). ～하다 move; stir. ¶ ～을 못하는 환자 a bedridden invalid / ～이 자유롭지 못하다 have difficulty in moving about / 너는 2,3 일이면 ～할 수 있을 것이다 You will be able to get up and walk in a few days. ② 《시동》 starting. ～하다 start. ◉ ～력 motive power. ～장치 a starter; a starting apparatus.

**기동**(機動) maneuvering; mobile; 〖군사〗 movement. ¶ ～성 mobility; maneuverability. ◉ ～경찰 mobile police forces. ～대 《경찰의》 the riot police; a riot squad (소규모의): ～대원 a riot policeman. ～력 mobile power. ～부대 a mechanized unit; 《특수 임무의》 a task force. ～연습 a maneuver: 야외 ～ 연습 a field maneuver. ～작전 mobile operations. ～전 mobile warfare; a war of movement. ～타격대 a special strike 〔task〕 force (ready to act).

**기동차**(汽動車) an internal-combustion car; a diesel railcar.

**기둥** ① 《건축물의》 a pillar; a column (원주); 《지주》 a support; a prop; a post; 《천막 등의》 a pole. ¶ 전화선용의 ～ a telephone pole / 가로등의 ～ a lamppost / 물～ a column of water / ～을 세우다 put 〔set〕 up a pillar / 방 한 가운데에 ～이 있어서 방해가 된다 There is a pillar right in the middle of the room which is in the way. ② 《중심이 되는 사람·물건》 a mainstay; a support; a pillar. ¶ 한 집안의 ～ the mainstay 〔pillar, support〕 of the family / ～으로 믿다〔의지하다〕 rely on 《*a person*》 as the mainstay 〔sole support〕 《of the family》. ◉ ～머리 〖건축〗 a capital; a cap (piece). ～목(木) logs suitable for pillars. ～뿌리 the base of a column.

**기둥서방**(一書房) a man who lives off a *kisaeng's* earnings; a fancy man; a gigolo.

**기드림**(旗一) a streamer; a pennant; a banderole.

**기득**(既得) ～하다 have already acquired 〔obtained〕. ¶ ～의 already acquired 〔obtained〕. ◉ ～권 vested rights 〔interests〕: ～권의 침해 infringement of 《*a person's*》 vested rights / ～권을 상실〔포기〕하다 lose 〔give up〕 *one's* vested rights.

**-기라도** ¶ 그를 만나 보기라도 했으면 좋겠소 I wish I could just see him!

**기라성**(綺羅星) glittering 〔bright〕 stars. ¶ ～ 같은 고관들 a galaxy of dignitaries / 외국 대사들이 ～처럼 늘어서 있다 There is a galaxy 〔an impressive array〕 of foreign ambassadors.

**기략**(機略) resources; tact. ¶ ～이 종횡무진한 사람 a resourceful man / ～이

풍부하다 be full of resources; be tactful 〔resourceful〕.

**기량**(技倆) skill; ability; talent; competence. ¶ ~을 (갈고) 닦다 cultivate *one's* ability; improve *one's* skill / ~을 보이다〔발휘하다〕 show 〔display〕 *one's* ability 〔skill〕 / 그녀는 ~은 충분하나 경험이 부족하다 She is capable enough, but lacks experience. / 그들의 ~은 서로 백중하다 They are equal to each other in skill.

**기량**(器量) ability; capacity; talent; caliber. ¶ ~이 있는 able / 그는 지도자가 될 만한 ~이 있다 He is talented 〔competent〕 enough to be a leader.

**기러기** a wild goose. ¶ ~떼가 V자형을 이루며 울면서 북쪽으로 날아갔다 A flock of wild geese honked their way north, flying in V shape. ◉ ~아빠 a only wild goose father (separated from his family staying abroad).

**기러기발** 《현악기의》 the bridge 《on a string instrument》.

**기력**(汽力) steam power. ¶ ~으로 움직이는 기계 a machine worked by steam. ◉ ~계 a steam-gauge 〔indicator〕.

**기력**(氣力) ① 《정신·육체의 힘》 energy; spirit; vigor; 《활력》 vitality; 《의지력》 will-power; 《용기》 pluck; mettle. ¶ ~이 왕성한 energetic; vigorous; full of vitality / ~이 다하다 exhaust *one's* energy 〔strength〕 / ~이 없다 be lacking in energy; be spiritless; do not have the energy to *do* / ~이 쇠하다 lose *one's* vigor 〔energy〕; become enervated / ~을 회복하다 recover *one's* spirits; recuperate *one's* 《used-up》 strength. ② 〖물리〗 air pressure.

**기로**(岐路) a forked 〔branch〕 road; a crossroad (십자로). ¶ 인생의 ~에 서다 stand 〔be〕 at「the crossroads of 〔a turning point in〕 *one's* life.

**-기로** ① 《…하는〔한〕 것으로》 for; by; with 〔as〕 《the *do*ing》. ¶ 경치가 좋기로 유명하다 be celebrated for *its* scenic beauty / 그는 글씨를 잘 쓰기로 유명하다 He is famous for his handwriting.
② 《이유》 as; since; because; given that; it(s) being the case that. ¶ 달이 밝기로 산책하기로 했다 Finding the moon bright, I decided to take a walk. / 그렇기로 어찌 가지 않을 수 있겠느냐 Just because of that, it doesn't mean I don't have to go. *or* Even so 〔For all that〕, I must go.
③ 《추정》 thinking 〔supposing〕 that. ¶ 비가 오겠기로 우산을 가지고 왔다 Thinking it might rain, I have brought my umbrella.
④ 《…다 하더라도》 even though 〔if〕; even given 〔admitted〕 that; it's true that… but…. ¶ 아무리 그가 걸음을 잘 걷기로 기차를 따를 수야 있나 Even though he walks fast how can he (=he can't) possibly beat a train? / 전등이 아무리 밝기로 햇빛만 할까 No matter how bright a lamp may be, how can it possibly rival the sun?
…기로 하다: decide to *do;* make up *one's* mind to *do;* arrange to *do;* promise 〔agree〕 to *do.* ¶ …하기로 하고 있다 have it arranged so that…; be so disposed as to / 내일 가기로 하자 Let's (decide or arrange to) go tomorrow. / 그는 내일 가기로 약속했다 He promised to go tomorrow. / 가급적 돈을 빌려 주지 않기로 했다 I don't lend money if I can possibly help it.

**-기로서니, -기로선들** 《강조형》 ¶ 그가 아무리 장사~ 그 바위를 들어올릴 수는 없다 No matter how strong he is, he can't lift the rock.

**기록**(記錄) 《적는 일》 recording; 《적은 것》 a record; 《문서》 a document; 《고〔공〕문서》 archives; 《의사록》 minutes; 《경기 등의》 a 《world》 record. ~하다 record 《a speech》; write down; put 《*a thing*》 on record; register. ¶ 정확한 ~ an accurate record / 공식 ~ an official record / 최고 ~ the best record / 인생 ~ human document / ~을 깨는 record-breaking / ~을 경신하다 better 〔renew〕 the record / 한국〔세계〕 신~을 수립하다 make 〔establish, set〕 a new Korean 〔world〕 record / ~에서 삭제하다 strike 《some words》 from 〔off〕 the record / ~에 남다 be recorded; be on record / ~에 남기다 put … on record; keep a record 《of》 / 그 살인 사건은 ~에 남아 있다 The murder case is on record. / 그녀는 높이뛰기의 세계 ~을 깼다 She has broken the world record for the high jump. / 온도계는 30℃를 ~했다 The thermometer registered 30℃. ◉ ~계원 recorder; a scorer (경기의). ~문학 documentary literature. ~보유자 a record holder. ~영화 a documentary film.

**기록적**(記錄的) ¶ ~인 record 《surpluses》; record-breaking 《summer temperatures》 / ~인 사건 an extraordinary occurrence; one for the book 《구어》 / ~인 짧은 시간에 in record time / ~인 저온 the record-low temperature / ～인 풍작이다 It is a record harvest. / ～인 엔고(円高)가 되었다 The yen rose to 「a record 〔an unprecedented〕 level. *or* The yen hit a record high.

**기뢰**(機雷) an underwater 〔a submarine〕 mine; a mine. ¶ ～를 부설하다 lay 〔place〕 mines 《in the sea》 / ～를 건드리다 strike 〔hit〕 a mine / ～ 방지 장치를 하다 provide 《a ship》 with an antimine device. ◉ ～부설선 a minelayer. ～원(原) a minefield. ～ 제거선 a minesweeper. 계류～ a moored mine. 음향〔촉각〕～ an acoustic 〔an antenna〕 mine.

**기류**(氣流) an air 〔an atmospheric〕 current 〔stream〕; a stream of air; an airflow (항공기 표면을 스치는). ¶ 상승〔하강〕～ the ascending 〔descending〕 air current / 난～ turbulence; a bump / 불안정한 ～ a treacherous air current / 상층〔하층〕～ the upper 〔lower〕 air current / ～를 타다 ride 〔soar on〕 an air current.

**기류**(寄留) temporary residence. ～하다 reside 〔live〕 temporarily 《at a place, with *a person*》. ◉ ～자 a temporary resident. ～지 a place of *one's* temporary residence.

**기르다** ① 《양육하다》 bring up; foster; nurse 《a baby》; raise; feed 《on milk》. ¶ 아기를 모유〔우유〕로 ～ feed 〔raise〕 a baby 「at the breast 〔on the bottle〕; breast-feed 〔bottle-feed〕 *one's* baby / 손수 돌보아 ～ bring up 《a child》「under *one's* own 〔with tender〕 care / 아이들을 성실한 인간으로 ～ bring up *one's* children to be truthful / 그는 다섯명의 고아들을 기르고 있다 He is fostering five orphans. / 어머니는 혼자서 아이 여덟명을 길렀다 Mother brought up eight children entirely by herself. / 낳은 정보다 기른 정 《속담》 The foster parent is dearer to one than the real parent.

② 《동·식물을》 raise; rear; 《사육》 breed; 《재배》 grow 《potatoes》; 《배양》 cultivate 《roses》. ¶ 곡식과 가축을 ～ raise crops and livestock / 우유 생산을 위해 소를 ～ breed cows for milk production / 그는 고양이를 두 마리 기른다 He keeps two cats.

③ 《머리 따위를》 (let *one's* hair) grow; cultivate. ¶ 머리를 길게 기른 사람 a person who has cultivated long hairs; a long-haired person / 콧수염을 ～ grow 〔wear〕 a moustache.

④ 《양성하다》 cultivate; foster; develop; build (up); train; educate. ¶ 국력을 ～ build up national power / 정신을 ～ cultivate 〔develop〕 *one's* mind / 체력을 ～ develop 〔build up〕 *one's* body 〔physical〕 strength / 담력〔도의심〕을 ～ cultivate courage 〔moral sense〕 / 상상력을 ～ foster *one's* imagination; feed *one's* fancy / 좋은 습관을 ～ form 〔cultivate〕 a good habit / 인재를 ～ foster men to be great / 그는 많은 제자를 길러냈다 He trained up many disciples.

> 용법 **bring up** 어린애를 성인이 되도록 돌보다란 의미로 「기르다, 양육하다」란 뜻. **foster** 양자로서 「기르다, 양육하다」. **nurse** 어린애, 환자 등을 건강해지도록 잘 「돌보다」란 원래의 뜻에서 확대되어, 사람·동식물의 어린 것을 「소중하게 기르다」란 뜻으로 쓰임. **raise** 특히 미국에서, 어린이·동물·식물을 「기르다, 양육하다, 사육하다, 재배하다」 등의 넓은 뜻으로 광범위하게 쓰이는 말. **rear**는 raise와 거의 같은 뜻으로 쓰이는 격식차린 말. **feed** 사람·동식물에게 「음식·먹이·비료 등을 주다」란 뜻에서 「기르다」란 개념이 된 것. **breed** 가축·물고기 등을 「번식시키다, 사육하다」란 뜻. **grow** 식물·과실수 등을 「재배하다」란 뜻.

⑤ 《버릇·병을》 make (even) worse; worsen; aggravate. ¶ 병을 ～ aggravate *one's* illness / 나쁜 버릇을 ～ form 〔pick up〕 a bad habit.

**기름** 《액체의》 oil; 《연료》 fuel; 《지방》 fat; lard (돼지기름); grease (기계유).

> 용법 **oil** 윤활유·식용유·연료 따위로 사용되는 광유·동식물유를 나타내는 총칭어. **grease** 고체가 아닌 동물의 기름·기계 윤활유·두발용 기름 따위. **fat** 동식물의 지방, 상온에서는 고체로 식용하는 것. **lard** 요리용의 정제된 돼지기름. **fuel** 「연료」로서의 기름. 휘발유·경유 등.

¶ 기계용의 ～ machine oil / 샐러드용 ～ salad oil / ～ 묻은〔투성이의〕 oily; oil=stained; stained with oil; smeared with oil / ～이 떨어지다 run out of oil / ～이 묻다 get 〔be〕 oily 〔oil=stained〕 / ～을 치다 oil 《a machine》 / ～을 짜다 press 〔squeeze〕 oil 《from》 / 머리에 ～을 바르다 grease *one's* hair / 생선을 ～에 튀기다 fry fish in oil / 이 기계에 ～을 쳐야 한다 This machine needs oiling. / 이 고기에는 ～이 많다

This meat has a lot of fat. / 그의 중재는 불에 ～을 붓는 꼴이었다 His intervention is like adding fuel to the fire. ◉ ～때 an oil 〔a grease〕 stain. ～띠 《해면의 유막》 an oil slick: 그 ～띠는 연안을 따라 60km나 되는 해면을 덮었다 The oil slick has spread 60km along the coastal waters. ～병 an oil bottle. ～복자 a measuring cup for oil. ～수송차〔선〕 an oil tanker. ～옷 greasy 〔oil-stained〕 clothes. ～종이 oilpaper. ～체 an oil strainer. ～탱크 an oil (storage) tank. ～통 an oilbarrel 〔can, vessel〕. ～틀 an oil press.

**기름기** fat 《of meat》; oiliness; greasiness. ¶ ～ 있는 oily; greasy / ～ 없는 oilless; lean / ～있는 음식 fatty 〔greasy, rich〕 food / ～없는 머리 unoiled hair / 나는 ～ 있는 요리가 좋다 I like fatty 〔greasy〕 dishes.

**기름먹이다** oil. ¶ 기름 먹인 종이 oilpaper; oiled paper / 기름 먹인 헝겊 oilcloth; oilskin / 종이에 ～ oil paper.

**기름지다** ① 《음식이》 (be) fat; oily; greasy; 《사람이》 (be) fatty; fattish. ¶ 기름진 국 fat soup / 기름진 음식 greasy 〔rich〕 food. ② 《땅이》 (be) rich; fertile; productive. ¶ 기름진 땅 rich soil; fertile land(s) / 메마른 땅을 기름지게 하다 make barren soil fertile.

**기름콩** a sprouting bean.

**기름하다** (be) longish; be somewhat long. ¶ 얼굴이 기름한 long-faced; with an oval 〔egg-shaped〕 face / 기름한 얼굴 a longish 〔a rather long〕 face / 스커트를 기름하게 하다 lengthen a skirt.

**기리다** praise; extol; give high praise to; pay tribute to. ¶ 기리는 말 a eulogy / 스승의 덕을 ～ praise *one's* teacher for his virtue 〔goodness〕.

**기린**(麒麟) ① 〖동물〗 a giraffe. ② 《상상의 동물》 a kylin; a fabulous and auspicious beast. ◉ ～아(兒) a (child) prodigy; a wonder child; a genius (천재). ～자리 〖천문〗 the Camelopard.

**기립**(起立) standing up; rising; 《구령》 Stand up!; Rise! On your feet! ～하다 stand up; rise 〔get〕 to *one's* feet. ◉ ～투표 a standing 〔rising〕 vote: ～투표에 부치다 put 《*a matter*》 to a standing vote; take a standing 〔rising〕 vote 《on a question》.

**기마**(騎馬) 《말타기》 horse riding; 《말》 a saddle horse. ◉ ～경찰관 a mounted policeman; the mounted police [총칭]. ～무사 a mounted warrior. ～민족 an equestrian 〔a nomadic〕 people. ～전 《play》 a mock cavalry battle. ～전령사 mounted orderly. ～행진 a cavalcade.

**기막히게**(氣—) breathtakingly; amazingly; wonderfully; stunningly; extremely; strikingly; 《구어》 awfully; terribly. ¶ ～ 잘하는 연기 a breathtaking performance / ～ 부자다 be fabulously wealthy / ～ 예쁘다 be stunningly beautiful / ～ 크다 be terribly 〔extremely〕 big / 그 산은 ～ 아름답다 The beauty of the mountain is breathtaking. / 그녀는 노래를 ～ 잘 불렀다 She sang wonderfully well.

**기막히다**(氣—) ① 《숨막히다》 stifle; suffocate; smother; choke; feel stifled 〔suffocated, smothered, choked〕; have *one's* breath taken away. ② 《놀랍다·어이없다》 (be) amazed; stunned; aghast; dumbfounded; flabbergasted; be at a loss for words; be left breathless. ¶ 기막힌 소식 stunning 〔amazing〕 news / 기막힌 일 a horrible 〔disgusting〕 thing 〔event〕 / 기막힌 사정 a reason 〔matter〕 hard to tell / 기가 막혀 말이 안 나오다 be (struck) dumb with amazement; be dumbfounded / 그같은 경험자가 그런 바보짓을 하다니 기가 막힌다 I should not have expected such folly from a man of his experience. / 네 어리석음에 기가 막힌다 Your stupidity really shocks me. / 자네까지 내가 거짓말을 한다니 기가 막히는군 I am simply aghast to hear that you think I am lying. ③ 《대단하다》 (be) breathtaking; amazing; astounding; stunning; baffling. ¶ 기막힌 미인 a stunning 〔breathtaking〕 beauty / 기막힌 부자 an amazingly rich man / 기막힌 재간 fantastic talent / 기막힌 생각 a splendid idea.

**기만**(欺瞞) deceit; deception; cheating; imposition. ～하다 deceive; cheat; impose 《upon》; hoodwink. ¶ ～적인 deceitful; false; fraudulent / 세상을 ～하다 deceive the world. ◉ ～성 deceitfulness. ～술 trickery. ～(정)책 a deceitful policy. ～행위 a fraudulent act.

**-기만** just *do*ing. ¶ 아기가 자기만 한다 The baby does nothing but sleep. / 그 두 사람은 서로 만나기만 하면 장사 얘기를 한다 Whenever those two meet it is always shop-talk.

**기말**(期末) the end of a term; a term end. ¶ ～에 at the end of the term; at the term end. ◉ ～결산 a term-end account. ～수당 a terminal allowance.

～시험 a term-end 〔final〕 examination. ～잔고 a final balance.

**기맥**(氣脈) 《서로 통함》 secret mutual understanding; communication. ¶ ～이〔을〕 통하다 have a secret 〔tacit〕 understanding 《with》; conspire 《with》; be in secret communication 《with》; be in collusion 《with the enemy》/ 두 사람은 ～이 서로 통한다 They understand each other's feeling very well. *or* They are in perfect sympathy with each other.

**기면**(嗜眠) lethargy. ¶ ～ 상태에 있다 be lethargic. ◉ ～성 뇌염 〖의학〗 encephalitis lethargica.

**기명**(記名) register; inscription; a signature. ～하다 sign 〔put down〕 *one's* name; register; inscribe. ¶ ～식의 registered; inscribed / ～ 날인하다 sign and seal 《a document》. ◉ ～주(권) a registered 〔an inscribed〕 stock. ～투표 an open 〔a signed〕 vote 〔ballot〕.

**기모**(起毛) 《직물의》 napping; nap raising. ～하다 nap; raise a nap 《on》; fluff. ¶ ～한 면 플란넬 napped 〔fluffy〕 cotton flannelette. ◉ ～기(機) a napping 〔nap-raising〕 machine.

**기묘**(己卯) 〖민속〗 the 16th binary term of the sexagenary cycle.

**기묘하다**(奇妙—) (be) strange; curious; queer; peculiar; odd. ¶ 기묘한 그림 a strange 〔curious〕 painting / 기묘한 버릇 a strange 〔an odd, a peculiar〕 habit / 기묘하게 생각하다 feel strange / 기묘하게도 strangely 〔oddly〕 enough; strange to say / 기묘한 짓을 하다 behave strangely 〔oddly, curiously〕.

**기문**(奇聞) strange 〔peculiar〕 news.

**기문**(氣門) a pore. ⇨ 기공(氣孔).

**기물**(器物) 《그릇》 a vessel; a receptacle; 《기구》 a utensil; 《가구》 furniture. ¶ ～ 파손 damage to property; property damage.

**기미** 《얼굴의》 freckles; a liver spot. ¶ ～가 끼다 freckle / ～ 낀 얼굴 a freckled face / 얼굴에 ～가 낀 소녀 a freckle-faced girl / 그녀의 얼굴은 ～투성이다 Her face is covered with freckles.

**기미**(己未) 〖민속〗 the 56th binary term of the sexagenary cycle.

**기미**(氣味) ① 《냄새와 맛》 smell and taste. ② 《마음과 취미》 *one's* disposition 〔temper, mind〕 and taste(s). ¶ ～ 상합하다 be congenial; be birds of a feather; be of a mind. ③ 〖한의〗 the efficacy of a medicinal herb.

**기미**(機微) 《낌새》 a touch 《of》; a smack; a shade; a tinge; a dash; an indication. ⇨ 낌새. ¶ 자만하는 듯한 ～가 엿보인다 show a touch of conceit / 최근 그녀의 시에는 우울한 ～가 감돈다 Her recent poetry has been tinged with melancholy.

**기민**(機敏) smartness; shrewdness; quickness; promptness; alertness. ～하다 《마음이》 (be) smart; shrewd; alert; 《동작이》 (be) quick; prompt. ¶ ～하게 quickly; promptly; alertly / ～한 상인 a shrewd man of business / ～한 동작 quick action 〔movement〕 / ～하게 기회를 포착하다 be prompt to seize an opportunity; snap at a chance / ～하게 행동하다 act smartly / ～한 조치가 필요하다 It is necessary to take prompt measures.

**기민**(饑民) the starving 〔hungry〕 populace; starved people; the famished.

**기밀**(氣密) airtight(ness). ¶ ～한 airtight. ◉ ～복 a pressurized suit. ～실 an airtight chamber; a pressure cabin (비행기의); a pressure hull (잠수함의). ～용기 an airtight container.

**기밀**(機密) 《상태》 secrecy; 《비밀 사항》 secret information; a secret. ¶ ～의 secret; confidential; classified 《미》/ 군사〔외교〕상의 ～ a military 〔diplomatic〕 secret / ～에 관한 일 confidential duties / ～로 해두다 keep 《*a matter*》 secret; keep 《*a matter*》 under wraps / ～을 누설하다 let 〔leak〕 out a secret / ～을 지키다 keep 〔guard〕 a secret; observe secrecy. ◉ ～누설 a leakage of 《military secrets》: 그는 국가 ～ 누설 죄로 어제 기소되었다 He was indicted yesterday on charges of leaking national secrets. ～비(費) secret (service) funds. ～사항 confidential matters: 그것은 ～사항이다 That is classified information. / 이것은 ～ 사항이므로 절대로 입밖에 내서는 안 된다 This is a secret matter; so don't tell anyone no matter what happens. ～서류〔문서〕 confidential 〔classified〕 documents 〔papers〕.

**기박하다**(奇薄—) (be) unlucky; ill-starred; ill-fated; unfortune. ¶ 기박한 팔자를 타고 나다 be born under an unlucky star / 팔자가 기박한 것을 한탄하다 grieve over *one's* ill 〔tough〕 luck / 그 여자는 한평생 팔자가 기박했다 She led an ill-fated life. *or* She was dogged by misfortune all her life.

**기반**(基盤) ① 《기초》 a base; a foundation; a basis. ¶ X를 ～으로(하고) with

X for a basis / …을 ~으로 하다 be based 〔founded〕 on / …의 ~을 이루다 form the basis 〔foundation〕 of… / 나라의 경제를 단단한 ~ 위에 올려놓다 put the nation's economy on a solid foundation / 가족은 사회의 ~을 이룬다 Families form the basis of society. / 그의 결론에는 과학적인 ~이 없다 His conclusion has no scientific basis. ② 《위치》 a footing; a foothold. ¶ ~을 굳히다 solidify *one's* footing / 사회에서의 착실한 ~을 확보하다 get 〔gain, obtain〕 a footing in society / 사내에서 그의 ~은 튼튼하다 His position in the company is secure. ③ 《선거에서의》 *one's* constituency 〔district〕; constituents (선거구민); *one's* sphere of influence (세력 범위). ¶ 선거 ~을 쌓다〔굳히다〕 nurse *one's* constituency; mend *one's* (political) fences 《미》. ◉ ~시설 an infrastructure: 3단계 ~시설 확장 계획 a three-stage infrastructure expansion program.

**기반**(羈絆) 《굴레》 fetters; shackles; bonds; ties; a yoke. ¶ 애정의 ~ bonds 〔ties〕 of affection; the yoke of love / ~을 벗어나다 free *oneself* from restraints; shake 〔cast, throw〕 off the yoke 《of》 / 인습의 ~을 끊다 break the bonds of convention / 그 나라는 외국의 ~을 벗어나 독립했다 The nation rid itself of the foreign yoke and became independent.

**기발하다**(奇拔—) (be) unconventional; extraordinary; novel; original; striking; fanciful. ¶ 기발한 디자인 a fantastic design / 기발한 착상 an original idea; a novel conception / 기발한 아이디어로 사람들을 깜짝 놀라게 하고 싶다 What I want is a novel idea that will set people back on their heels.

**기백**(氣魄) spirit; soul; vigor. ¶ ~이 있다〔없다〕 be full of 〔be lacking in〕 spirit / ~이 있는 full of vigor 〔vitality〕 / ~이 있는 사람 a man of spirit / 기술보다는 그들의 ~에 눌려 패했다 We were beaten not by their technique but by their spirit.

**기백**(幾百) hundreds. ¶ ~만 millions.

**기법**(技法) (a) technique. ¶ 영화의 ~ cinematic technique / ~상의 문제 technical problems / ~을 익히다 acquire 〔master〕 the technique 《of》 / 목각의 ~을 배우다 learn the craft of a woodcarver.

**기법**(記法) (a) notation.

**기벽**(奇癖) an eccentric 〔a strange〕 habit; an eccentricity.

**기별**(奇別·寄別) news; a letter; a report; a notice; information; tidings; (the) word. ~하다 inform 《*a person*》 of 《*a matter*》; let 《*a person*》 know; give information; send 〔bring〕 word 《to》; report 《*something* to *somebody*》. ¶ 미리 ~하다 give 《*a person*》 previous notice / ~하지 않다 leave 《*a person*》 uninformed 《about *something*》 / 그가 오면 ~해 주오 Please let me know if he comes. / 좀더 일찍 ~해 주었으면 좋았을 것을 You might have let me know earlier.

**기병**(起兵) raising an army. ~하다 raise an army; rise in arms.

**기병**(騎兵) a cavalry soldier; a cavalryman; a horseman; a trooper; cavalry [총칭]. ◉ ~대 the cavalry. 중〔경〕 ~대 heavy 〔light〕 cavalry.

**기보**(既報) a previous report; prior information. ~하다 have already reported 〔announced〕. ¶ ~한 바와 같이 as previously 〔already〕 reported 〔announced〕; as stated in a previous issue.

**기보**(棋譜) the record of the game of *paduk.*

**기보법**(記譜法) 〖음악〗 (music) notation.

**기복**(起伏) rise and fall; ups and downs; undulations. ~하다 rise and fall; roll; undulate. ¶ ~ 있는 평야〔지형〕 a rolling 〔an undulating〕 plain 〔land〕 / ~이 완만한 산 gently undulating hills / ~이 많은 생애 a life full of ups and downs; a colorful life / ~이 많은 길 a rugged road / 그는 감정의 ~이 크다 He is emotionally unstable. / 건설업은 ~이 심한 사업이다 Construction business is a boom-and-slump 〔a highly cyclical〕 industry.

**기본**(基本) 《기초》 a basis (*pl.* -ses); a foundation; 《기본적 사항》 a fundamentals; basics; 《기준》 a standard. ¶ ~적(으로) fundamental(ly); basic(-ally) / ~적 인권 fundamental human rights / 영어의 ~ the ABC's of English / 영어를 ~부터 공부하다 study English from the basics / 스포츠에는 ~이 가장 중요하다 Nothing is more important in sports than the basics. / 자네 이론에 몇가지 잘못은 있지만, ~적으로는 옳다 Though a few of your theories are not right, you are fundamentally correct. ◉ ~계획 a master 〔basic〕 plan. ~급(給) the basic wage 〔pay〕; the base pay (퇴직금 계산시). ~단위 a basic 〔standard〕 unit. ~방

침 a basic policy; a keynote. ～어휘 basic vocabulary. ～요금 a basic rate; 《택시 따위의》 the basic fare; 《사용료 따위》 the basic charge. ～운임 basic freight. ～원리 a basic 〔fundamental〕 principle. ～재산 permanent property; original property. ～조건 a basal 〔basic〕 condition. ～조약 a basic treaty.

**기부**(寄附) (a) contribution; (a) donation; (a) subscription. ～하다 donate; make a contribution 〔donation〕 《to, for》; subscribe 《to》; chip in 《구어》.

> **용법** **contribution** 가장 일반적인 말로, 단체나 조직에 내는 기부금. **donation** 특히 자선·종교상의 목적으로 내는 기부(금). **subscription** 취지에 찬동해서 정기적으로 내는 헌금의 뜻.

¶ ～를 요청하다 ask for a contribution; invite donations / 그는 적십자사에 큰 돈을 ～했다 He donated a large amount (of money) to the Red Cross. / 그는 수해 지역 사람들의 구제를 위해 백만원을 ～했다 He 「contributed 〔made a donation of〕 one million won to the relief of the people in the flood-stricken district.

◉ ～금 a contribution; a donation; a subscription; an endowment: ～금을 모금하다 collect 〔raise〕 contributions 《from》. ～자 a contributor; a donor; a subscriber. ～재산 an endowment. ～행위 an act of endowment 〔donation, contribution〕.

**기부**(基部) the base; the foundation; the basal part 《of a column》.

**기분**(氣分) (a) feeling; (a) sentiment; a mood; atmosphere (분위기). ¶ 유쾌〔불쾌, 우울〕한 ～(으로) (in) a pleasant 〔sulky, gloomy〕 mood / 차분한 ～ a quiet mood / ～ 나쁜 광경 a sickening sight / 울고 싶은 ～이다 I feel like crying. / 부자가 된 ～이다 I feel rich.

기분에: 그때 ～에 따라서 according to the mood of the moment / ～에 따라 움직이다 be swayed 〔influenced〕 by sentiment.

기분이: ～이 좋다 feel well 〔good, all right〕; be in a good humor 〔mood〕 / ～이 나쁘다 feel unwell 〔ill, bad, poorly, low〕; be in a bad temper; be in ill humor; feel rotten 《구어》/ 책 읽을 ～이 안 나다 don't feel like reading books; be in no mood for reading.

기분을: ～을 바꾸다 change *one's* mood / 잔치 ～을 내다〔깨다〕 create 〔destroy〕 a festive mood 〔an atmosphere of festivity〕 / 한 잔하고 ～을 내다 be gay over a glass of wine / ～을 돋우다 cheer 〔brighten〕 up / ～을 상하게 하다 hurt 《*a person's*》 feelings.

¶ 오늘은 ～이 별로 좋지 않다 I'm feeling low today. *or* I'm not feeling too well today. / 오늘은 자네 ～이 좋아 보이는데 You look fine 〔well〕 today. / 오늘은 ～이 어떠십니까(환자에게)」—「매우 좋습니다」 "How do you feel today ?"— "Much better, thanks." / 그는 ～나는 대로 일을 한다 He works as the mood takes him. / 자네의 ～은 잘 이해하네 I fully understand your feelings. *or* I can sympathize with you. /「어떤 음악을 가장 좋아하지」—「～에 따라 다르지」 "What do you like most about music ?"—"It depends on the mood I'm in." / 그는 행복한 ～에 잠겨 있었다 He was in a happy state of mind. / 「춤추러 갈까」—「미안해, 오늘밤은 외출할 ～이 안 나는데」 "Let's go dancing."— "I'm sorry, but I don't feel like going out tonight." ◉ ～파 a moody 〔temperamental〕 person; a man of moods.

**기분전환**(氣分轉換) (a) diversion; a change (of *one's* mood); a pastime; (a) recreation; refreshment. ～하다 refresh *oneself* 《with a song》; divert 〔recreate, amuse〕 *oneself;* take *one's* mind off *one's* troubles 〔worries〕. ¶ ～으로 《go to Onyang》 for a change; for recreation / ～으로 노래를 부르다 divert *oneself* by singing / 우리 ～으로 산책이나 하자 Let's take a walk for a change. / 음악을 듣는 것은 ～에 좋다 Listening to music is a good pastime 〔recreation〕. / ～을 위해 해변에 가다 go to the seaside to refresh *oneself* / 오늘밤 ～으로 외식이나 하자 What 〔How〕 about eating out this evening for a change ?

**기뻐하다** be glad 《of, about》; be pleased 〔delighted〕 《with, at, to *do*》; (take) delight 《in》; rejoice 《at, over》; congratulate *oneself* 《on》; be happy with. ¶ 성공을 ～ be pleased with *one's* success / 고향 소식을 듣고 ～ be delighted at the news from home / 뛸 듯이 ～ dance 〔jump〕 with 〔for〕 joy / 그의 양친은 그의 성공을 크게 기뻐하신다 His parents are very glad about his success.

**기쁘다** (be) glad; happy; pleased; delighted; joyous; 《즐겁다》 (be) delightful; pleasant; happy; joyful.

¶ 기쁘게 gladly; with joy; with pleasure / 기쁘게도 to *one's* delight 〔joy〕/ 너무 기뻐서 in the excess of joy / 기쁜 날 a happy day; a joyous occasion / 기쁜 소식 happy news 《of success》/ 기쁜 일 a happy event; a matter for joy 〔congratulation〕/ 기쁜 빛〔얼굴〕《with》 a happy 〔delightful〕 look / 기쁘게 하다 make 《*a person*》 happy; please; delight / 기뻐서 울다 cry 〔weep〕 for joy; cry with delight / 기뻐 날뛰다 leap 〔jump〕 for joy 《at the news》/ 시험에 합격하여 ~ be glad 〔happy〕 to have passed the examination / (얼굴에) 기쁜 빛을 띄다 look pleased 〔happy, *etc.*〕/ 기쁘기도 하고 슬프기도 하다 have mixed feelings of joy and sorrow / 이렇게 기쁜 일은 없다 Nothing gives us such a great pleasure as this. / 눈물이 나도록 기뻤다 I nearly wept for joy. / 그는 기뻐 어쩔 줄을 몰랐다 He was beside himself with joy. / 나는 가사를 도와서 어머니를 기쁘게 해 드렸다 I made my mother happy by helping her with the domestic chores.

**기쁨** joy; delight; gladness; 《환희》 rapture; 《만족》 pleasure; gratification; 《축의》 congratulation(s). ¶ ~에 겨워 in *one's* joy 〔delight〕/ 인생의 ~ joys of life / 독서의 ~ the pleasure of reading / 커다란 ~ great pleasure / ~을 금치 못하다 cannot 〔be unable to〕 contain *one's* joy / ~으로 가슴이 뛰다 *one's* heart beat with delight / ~의 눈물을 흘리다 shed tears of joy / ~을 말하다 express *one's* delight 《at》; express 〔offer〕 *one's* congratulations on 《*a person's* success》/ 그의 얼굴에는 ~이 넘쳐 있었다 His face beamed with joy. / ~이 그의 얼굴에 나타났다 His joy showed on his face.

**기사**(己巳) 〖민속〗 the 6th binary term of the sexagenary cycle.

**기사**(技師) an engineer; a technician; a technical expert. ¶ 건축~ a building engineer; an architect / 기계〔전기, 항공〕~ a mechanical 〔an electrical, an aeronautical〕 engineer.

**기사**(記事) 《서술》 (a) description; an account; 《신문의》 news; a news item 〔story〕; a report (보도); an article (논설). (★ news는 단수 취급. 하나 둘 셀 때에는 a piece of news, two pieces of news로 한다). ¶ 특종 ~ a scoop; 《미》 a beat / 특집 ~ a feature (story 〔article〕) / 기삿거리 a news item; a piece of news; a newsbreak; news matter / ~를 싣다 give 〔print〕 an account of 《a fire》; carry a story 〔news item〕 (in the paper) / ~를 쓰다 write an article 〔a report〕 《on》/ (신문이) ~를 작게 다루다 play down / ~를 삭제하다 erase a news item; 《일부를》 blue-pencil / 나는 정치 ~에 관심이 있다 I am interested in political news. / 무슨 재미있는 ~라도 나와 있습니까 Is there any interesting news in the paper? / 신문 ~를 그대로 믿을 수는 없다 You can't believe everything you read in the paper. / 그 잡지에 사건의 자세한 ~가 나와 있다 The magazine carries a full account of the event. ◉ ~게재 금지 a press ban; ban on the publication of news. ~체 a descriptive style. ~폭주 a congestion of news 〔reading matter〕.

**기사**(棋士) a (professional) *paduk* player; a Korean chess player (장기의).

**기사**(騎士) 《기수》 a rider; a horseman; 《중세의》 a knight. ◉ ~도 knighthood; chivalry: ~도 정신 (a spirit of) chivalry.

**기사회생**(起死回生) restoration from death; resuscitation; revival. ~하다 restore from death; resuscitate; revive. ¶ ~의 영약 a wonder 〔miracle〕 drug; a wonderful medicine capable of reviving the dead / ~의 비법을 강구하다 devise a means of pulling back from the brink of disaster / ~의 홈런을 치다 《야구에서》 hit a homer to pull the game out of the fire.

**기산**(起算) ~하다 reckon 〔count, compute〕 from 《a date》. ¶ 개통일에서 ~하여 한 달간 for a month counting from the opening day. ◉ ~일 the date from which a period of time is reckoned; the initial 〔base〕 date for reckoning 《a period of time》. ~점 a starting point for reckoning.

**기상**(奇想) a fantastic idea; a fanciful notion; a conceit. ¶ ~천외의 fantastic; totally unexpected; amazing / ~천외한 생각이로다 It is a most unexpected 〔original〕 idea. ◉ ~곡 a capriccio.

**기상**(起床) getting up from bed; rising. ~하다 get out of bed; get up; rise (from *one's* bed). ¶ 우리는 아침 5시에 ~한다 We get up at five in the morning. ◉ ~나팔 the reveille; the morning bugle: ~나팔을 불다 sound 〔blow〕 the reveille. ~벨 a bell for rising. ~시간 the rising hour.

**기상**[1](氣象) atmospheric phenomena; weather; weather conditions. ¶ ～의 변화 a change in the weather 〔in weather condition〕/ ～을 관측하다 make meteorological observations.
◉ ～개황 general weather conditions. ～경보 a weather alarm. ～관제 the meteorological 〔met〕 control (공항 따위의). ～관측 weather 〔meteorological〕 observation: ～관측 로켓 a meteorological rocket / ～관측선 a weather ship / ～관측소 a meteorological station 〔observatory〕; a 〔local〕 weather bureau 〔station〕. ～구(區) a meteorological area. ～대 a meteorological observatory: ～대원 a weatherman. ～데이터 weather 〔meteorological〕 data. ～도 a weather chart 〔map〕. ～레이더 a weather radar. ～사진 a weather picture 《from a satellite》. ～위성 a meteorological 〔weather〕 satellite. ～이변 an unusual 〔abnormal〕 change of weather. ～재해 a weather disaster. ～정보 weather 〔meteorological〕 information. ～주의보 a weather warning 〔advisory 《미》〕. ～청 the Meteorological Administration: ～청장 the administrator of Meteorological Administration. ～통계 meteorological statistics. ～통보 a weather report: ～통보관 a weathercaster; 《구어》 a weatherman. ～특보 a special weather report. ～학 meteorology: ～학자 a meteorologist; a weather expert. ～현상 meteorological phenomena.

**기상**[2](氣象〔像〕) spirit; temperament; nature; temper. ¶ 씩씩한 ～ a manly 〔valiant〕 spirit / 독립〔진취〕의 ～ an independent 〔enterprising〕 spirit.

**기상**(機上) ¶ ～에 오르다 get on (board) a plane; board an airplane; enplane / ～에서 내려다보다 look down from an airplane; get 〔take〕 a bird's-eye view 《of a city》 from an aircraft.

**기색**(氣色) 《안색》 looks; countenance; appearance; 《감정》 mood; humor; feeling; 《기미》 a sign; an indication. ¶ 조금도 두려워하는 ～없이 without showing the slightest sign of fear / ～이 좋지 않다 look bad; be out of sorts / ～을 조금도 나타내지 않다 never betray in *one's* looks / ～을 살피다 study 〔read〕 *a person's* face 〔expression〕; try to gauge 〔judge〕 *a person's* feelings 〔state of mind〕 (from *his* expression) / …한 ～을 보이지 않다 show no sign of 《fear, joy, anger》/ 비가 올 ～이 없다 There is no sign of the rain. / 그는 아내의 ～을 살피면서 외박한 핑계를 댔다 He made excuses for having stayed out for the night, while watching to see how his wife is reacting.

**기생**(妓生) a *kisaeng.* ¶ ～집 a *kisaeng's* 「house.

**기생**(寄生) parasitism. ～하다 be parasitic 《on》; be a parasite 《to, on》; live upon; sponge on. ¶ 공동 사회에 ～하는 골치아픈 사람들 annoying hangers-on of our community / 벌레가 그 나무에 ～하고 있다 Insects live 〔are parasitic〕 on the tree.
◉ ～계급 a parasitic class. ～근 a parasitic root. ～동물 a parasite; a parasitic animal. ～물 parasites. ～식물 a parasitic plant. ～화산 a parasite volcano; a new volcanic hump.

**기생식물**(氣生植物) 〖식물〗 an aerial plant; an aerophyte.

**기생충**(寄生蟲) a parasite; a parasitic insect 〔worm〕. ¶ 사회의～ a parasite on the community / 장내(腸內) ～ an intestinal worm; a helminth / ～이 끓다 [숙주가 주어] get (parasitic) worms.
◉ ～구충제(劑) a parasiticide; a helminthic. ～병 helminthiasis; a verminous disease. ～학 parasitology; helminthology.

**기서**(奇書) a strange 〔rare〕 book.

**기선**(汽船) a steamship (생략 S.S); a steamboat (하천·연안용); a steamer; 《정기선》 a liner. ¶ ～을 타다 take 〔go on board〕 a steamer; board a steamship / ～으로 가다 go by steamer.
◉～회사 a steamship company.

**기선**(基線) 〖측량〗 the base line.

**기선**(機先) forestalling; getting ahead of 《*a person*》; taking the initiative. ¶ ～을 제압하다〔잡다〕 forestall 《*one's* rival (company), *a person's* attempt》; get a head 〔the start〕 of 《*a person*》; get 〔have〕 the jump on 《*a person*》; take the initiative 《in *do*ing》; steal a march upon 《another》/ 우리는 적의 ～을 제압했다 We 「got a head start 〔stole a march〕 on the enemy.

**기설**(旣設) ¶ ～의 established; existing. ¶ ～경기장 an existing stadium.

**기성**(奇聲) a peculiar 〔queer〕 voice. ¶ ～을 발하다 raise a queer voice.

**기성**(旣成) ¶ ～의 《이미 이룬》 existing; established; accomplished; completed; 《이미 만든》 ready-made.
◉ ～개념 a preconceived 〔ready-made〕 idea; a stereotype: ～ 개념을 버리다

get rid of *one's* stereotype / 너는 ～ 개념에 너무 사로잡혀 있다 You adhere too much to your stereotype. ～도덕 the established moral principles; positive morality. ～문단 existing literary circles. ～복 ready-made clothes 〔suit〕; a ready-made; a ready-to-wear (suit); hand-me-downs 《미》; 《싸구려의》 reach-me-downs 《영》; slops: ～복점 a ready-made shop; a slopshop. ～세대 the older generation. ～작가 an established 〔a well-known〕 writer. ～정당 the existing 〔established〕 political parties. ～품 ready-made goods 〔articles〕. ～화 ready-made shoes.

**기성**(期成) resolution to carry out 《a plan》. ◉ ～회 an association for the realization 《of a plan》; 《학교의》 a school supporting association: ～회비 dues for school supporting association.

**기성**(棋聖) a great master of *baduk*.

**기세**(氣勢) spirit; enthusiasm; vigor; ardor. ¶ ～좋게 vigorously; with vigor 〔spirit〕; in high spirits; with great force / 맹렬한 ～로 with great 〔violent〕 force; 《구어》 like a hundred 〔thousand, ton〕 of bricks; like forty 《미》 / ～가 오르다 be in high 〔good〕 spirits; be in good 〔great〕 form; be elated / ～를 올리다 arouse 〔excite〕 *one's* enthusiasm; drum up opposition 《to》 / ～를 꺾다 dispirit; discourage 《*a person*》; dampen 《*a person's*》 enthusiasm 〔ardor〕; put 〔cast〕 a damper on 《*one's* spirit》; chill 《*one's* morale》; throw a cold blanket 《over》 / ～를 돋우어 주다 give moral support to; encourage; cheer; inspirit 《*a person* to *do*》 / ～를 보이다〔부리다〕 show *one's* nerve 〔spirit〕; poise *oneself* 《to *do*》; make a demonstration / ～가 증가되다 gain 〔gather〕 strength; be fanned 《by》 / 성공 소식을 듣고 크게 ～가 올라갔다 The news of success put us in high spirits. / 그는 맹렬한 ～로 상대에게 대들었다 He rush.ed toward the opponent in full vigor.

**기소**(起訴) 《검사의》 prosecution; indictment. ～하다 《검사가》 prosecute 〔indict〕 《*a person* for a crime》; charge 《*a person* with a crime》; bring in an indictment 《against》. ¶ ～되어 있다 be under indictment / 수회〔마약 밀수〕로 ～되다 be prosecuted for taking bribes 〔smuggling drugs〕 / 살인죄로 ～되다 be indicted for murder / 적국을 위해 간첩 활동을 한 행위로 ～된 피고에게 사형을 선고하다 sentence the accused indicted for having conducted espionage activities for the enemy, to death / 그 사건은 ～되지 않았다 The case was dropped. / 그는 탈세로 ～되었다 He was indicted on charges of tax evasion. ◉ ～기각 dismissal of indictment. ～자 an indictor; a prosecutor. ～장 a bill of indictment; an 〔a written〕 indictment. 불～ 처분 a disposition not to institute a public action.

**기소유예**(起訴猶豫) 〖법〗 suspension of indictment. ～하다 dispense with a public action; suspend 〔shelve〕 an indictment; leave a charge on the file. ¶ ～가 되다 have *one's* indictment suspended.

**기송관**(氣送管) a pneumatic 〔dispatch〕 tube.

**기수**(汽水) brackish water.

**기수**(奇數) ＝홀수.

**기수**(基數) 〖수학〗 《서수에 대응한》 a cardinal number; 《1에서 9까지의》 a fundamental number.

**기수**(機首) the nose of an airplane. ¶ ～를 남쪽으로 돌리다 turn south(-ward); head for the south / 비행기는 ～를 올렸다〔내렸다〕 The plane nosed up 〔down〕. *or* The plane pulled up 〔lowered〕 the nose.

**기수**(旗手) a standard-〔color-〕bearer; a flag-bearer (올림픽 등의). ¶ 평화와 협력의 새로운 ～ a new standard-bearer for peace and cooperation 《in the world》.

**기수**(騎手) a rider; a horseman; a jockey (경마의).

**기수범**(旣遂犯) a consummated crime; a crime that has already been committed.

**기수법**(記數法) (a system of) numerical notation. ¶ 십진 ～ decimal notation.

**기숙**(寄宿) lodging; 《식사 포함》 boarding. ～하다 lodge 〔board, room 《미》〕 《at *a person's* house, with *a person*》. ◉ ～비 boarding expenses. ～사 a boardinghouse; a dormitory; 《구어》 dorm: ～사 생활을 하다 live in a dormitory / 학교 ～사에 들다 board in the school / ～사 사감 a dormitory superintendent; a warden; 《영》 housemaster. ～생 a boarding student; a boarder. ～학교 a boarding school.

**기술**(技術) (an) art; (a) skill; craft; (a) technique; technology; technics (학문); 《학과》 manual training.

> **용법** **technique** 기계·예술·과학 등의 작업에서 일반적으로 널리 쓰이는 전문적인 기술. **skill** 연습에 의해 얻어지는 정교한 특수 기능. **art** 기술상의 재주와 솜씨. **craft** 직업적인 특수 기술·솜씨. **technology** 과학·공업상의 기술.

¶ ～상의 technical / ～적으로 technically / ～상의 어려움 a technical difficulty / 건축 ～ the art of building / 최신～ the latest technique / 첨단～ high technology / 고도의～ high 〔advanced, sophisticated〕 technology / ～의 진보 technological 〔technical〕 advance 〔improvement(s)〕 / 외국 ～의 도입 introduction 〔importation〕 of foreign techniques / ～적인 지도 technical guidance / 새로운 ～의 개발 development of new technology / ～이 늘다 improve in *one's* skill; become proficient 〔attain proficiency〕 in *one's* art / 외국 ～을 도입하다 import 〔introduce〕「technological know-how from overseas 〔foreign techniques〕 / 그는 심장 수술에 새로운 ～을 개발했다 He developed a new technique for heart surgery. / 비행기 조종에는 고도의 ～이 요구된다 High-level skills are necessary to fly a plane. / 교섭은 약간의～적인 문제로 정체되어 있다 The negotiations have reached a deadlock on a few technicalities 〔technical points〕. / 「이 계획은 실현 가능합니까」—「～적으로는 문제가 없다고 생각합니다」 "Is this plan really feasible ?"—"I don't think there are any technical problems." ◉ ～개발 technical development. ～격차 disparity in technique; a technological gap. ～도입 the introduction of technology: ～ 도입으로 상품의 질을 높이기 위한 노력을 꾸준히 하다 make strenuous efforts to upgrade the quality of products through the introduction of technology. ～료 a technical fee. ～산업도시 《첨단기술을 활용한》 a technopolis. ～원조 a technical assistance 〔aids〕. ～이전 a technology transfer: ～ 이전 문제 a technology transfer issue. ～인력 《secure》 skilled technical hands; (highly) skilled technical manpower: 될 수 있는 대로 많은 ～ 인력을 양성하다 foster as much excellent skilled manpower as possible. ～자 a technician; a technologist; a technical expert; 《기사》 an engineer. ～정보 (technical) know-how; expertise. ～제휴〔협력〕 (an agreement for) technical cooperation; 《구어》《join in》 a technical tie-up. ～진흥심의회 the National Deliberation Council for Technology Promotion. ～집약산업 a technology-intensive industry. ～축적 the accumulation of technology 〔industrial know-how〕. ～혁신 technological innovation. 핵심～ core technology.

**기술**(奇術) jugglery; a feat of skill; sleight of hand; conjuring tricks; magic. ¶ ～을 부리다 juggle; perform sleight-of-hand 〔magic〕 tricks; play conjuring tricks. ◉ ～사 a juggler; a conjurer; a magician.

**기술**(記述) (a) description; an account. ～하다 describe; give an account of; make 〔give〕 a description of. ¶ ～적인 descriptive / ～적 과학 the descriptive science / ～되어 있다 be descriptive of. ◉ ～문법 descriptive grammar. ～언어학 descriptive linguistics. ～통계학 descriptive statistics.

**기술**(旣述) the foregoing. ¶ ～의 《items》 mentioned 〔described, explained〕 previously / ～한 바와 같이 as mentioned previously 〔above〕.

**기스락** the very edge (of eaves).

**기스면** 〔< 鷄絲麵 (中)〕 fine noodles served in the chicken soup.

**기슭** 《산의》 the foot; the base; 《강의》 the side; the bank; the brink. ¶ 강～ the side 〔brink〕 of a river / 산～ 《camp at》 the foot of a mountain / 언덕 ～에 있는 집 a house at the base 〔foot〕 of a hill.

**기습**(奇習) a strange 〔unusual〕 custom 〔habit〕.

**기습**(奇襲) a raid; a surprise 〔sudden, sneak 《구어》〕 attack. ～하다 raid 〔make a surprise attack〕 《on》; take 《the enemy》 by surprise. ¶ 배후에서 ～을 시도하다 attempt a surprise attack from behind / ～으로 요새를 탈취하다 take a fortress by surprise. ◉ ～부대 a surprise party; shock troops; 《영》 commandos. ～전 a surprise attack; guerrilla warfare.

**기승**(氣勝) an unyielding spirit; strong-mindedness; spiritedness. ～하다, ～스럽다 (be) unyielding; strong-minded; spirited. ¶ ～스러운 여자 a woman of spirit; a strong-minded woman / ～(을) 부리다 do not give in; refuse to yield; be obstinate 〔stubborn〕 / 늦더위가 올해는 유달리 ～을 부린다 The heat of late summer is unprecedently severe this year.

**기승전결**(起承轉結) 〖문학〗 part organization of Chinese poetry; the four steps in composition (*i.e.* introduction, development, turn and conclusion). ¶ ~을 갖춘 글 a well organized passage / ~을 염두에 두며 글을 써라 Keep coherence in mind when you write your composition.

**기식음**(氣息音) 〖음성〗 an aspirate; an aspirated sound.

**기식**(寄食) boarding (and lodging); 《공짜로》 freeloading 《미구어》; sponging on. ~하다 board 〔be a boarder〕 《at *a person's* house》; 《공짜로》 live off 〔sponge on〕 *a person;* freeload 《on》; be a parasite 《on, to》. ¶ 나는 숙부댁에서 ~한다 I lodge with my uncle. *or* 《공짜로》 I sponge on my uncle. *or* I live with my uncle at his expense. ◉ ~자 《공짜의》 a sponger; a hanger-on; a parasite; a freeloader 《미구어》.

**기신거리다** idle about; move limply 〔listlessly〕; stir languidly; shuffle around. ¶ 그 취객은 기신거리며 길을 걸어갔다 The drunkard staggered along the road.

**기신기신** idly; listlessly; shuffling; moving vacantly.

**기신없다**(氣神一) be unenergetic in body and unsound in mind.

**기신호**(旗信號) flag signaling 〔semaphore〕; 《속어》 flag-wagging. ¶ ~를 하다 signal with flags.

**기실**(其實) 《그 사실·실상》 the truth 《is that...》; the reality; 《사실상으로》 really; in reality 〔fact〕; to tell the truth; as a matter of fact. ¶ 큰소리는 치지만 ~ 그는 아무 것도 모른다 He talks big, but in reality he knows nothing.

**기실**(氣室) an air chamber.

**기쓰다**(氣一) 《있는 힘을 다 내다》 strain *oneself;* try too hard; do *one's* best; do everything in *one's* power; 《기가 나다》 be 〔get〕 excited 《over》; get heated 《about》; be out 《to *do*》. ¶ 기쓰고 일하다 work as hard as *one* can; work with all *one's* strength 〔might〕 / 기쓰고 변명하다 defend *oneself* with heat 〔vehemently〕.

**기아**(棄兒) 《아이》 a foundling; an abandoned child; a deserted child; 《버리기》 abandoning a child. ~하다 abandon 〔desert〕 a child.

**기아**(飢餓·饑餓) hunger; starvation. ¶ ~를 면하다 keep the wolf from the door / ~에 직면하다, ~선상에 있다 be starving; be on 〔live at〕 the verge 〔brink〕 of starvation; face 〔be threatened with〕 starvation. ◉ ~수출 hunger export. ~임금 starvation wages. ~행진 a hunger march.

**기악**(器樂) 〖음악〗 instrumental music. ◉ ~곡 an instrumental piece 〔work〕. ~부 instrumental parts. ~연주가 an instrumentalist; an instrumental musician. ~편성법 instrumentation.

**기안**(起案) drafting 《a document》. ~하다 draft; draw up 《a plan》; prepare 〔make out〕 a draft; plan 《for》. ¶ 그가 그 법안을 ~했다 He made a draft of the bill. ◉ ~자 a drafter; a draftsman.

**기암**(奇岩) a strangely shaped rock; rocks of strange shape. ◉ ~괴석 fantastically-shaped rocks.

**기압**(氣壓) air 〔atmospheric, barometric〕 pressure. ¶ 고〔저〕~ high 〔low〕 (atmospheric) pressure / 절대 ~ absolute atmosphere / ~ 관계로 affected by atmospheric pressure / 어제의 ~은 980 헥토파스칼이었다 The barometer registered 980 hpa 〔hectopascals〕 yesterday. ◉ ~계 a barometer. ~골 a trough of low pressure; a low pressure trough. ~배치 the distribution of atmospheric pressure.

**기약**(期約) pledge; promise; appointment; engagement. ~하다 pledge; promise. ¶ 두 사람은 재회를 ~하고 헤어졌다 The two parted, pledging to meet again. / ~한 시간에 그 장소에 갔다 I went to the place at the appointed time.

**기어** (a) gear. ¶ 4단 ~의 차 a car with four gears / ~를 넣다 put 《the car》 in gear; thrust the gear lever / ~를 2단〔후진〕으로 넣다 put 《the car》 in second 〔reverse〕 (gear); get into second 〔reverse〕 (gear) / 기어를 3단〔상단〕으로 바꾸다 change (up) into third 〔top〕 gear / ~를 바꾸다 change 〔shift 《미》〕 gear(s) / 자동차는 ~를 넣지 않으면 움직이지 않는다 A car cannot go unless it is in gear.

**기어가다** crawl 〔creep〕 on 〔along〕; crawl on hands and knees; go on all fours. ¶ 차들은 시속 10마일로 기어가듯이 나아갔다 The cars crawled 〔crept〕 along at ten miles an hour.

**기어나오다** crawl 〔creep〕 out. ¶ 토끼가 구멍에서 기어나왔다 A rabbit crept out of its burrow. / 봄이 되면 벌레가 기어나온다 Worms creep out in spring.

**기어다니다** crawl 〔creep〕 about. ¶ 아기는 방 안을 기어다니고 있었다 The baby was crawling about the room.

**기어들다** crawl 〔creep〕 in 〔into〕. ¶ 그는 울타리 밑으로 기어들었다 He crawled in through the hedge. / 그녀는 기어들어가는 목소리로 말했다 She spoke in a faint 〔scarcely audible〕 voice.

**기어오다** crawl 〔creep〕 up to; come crawlingly 〔creepingly〕. ¶ 아기는 내가 가진 장난감을 잡으려고 방바닥을 기어왔다 The baby crawled across the floor to reach the toy in my hand.

**기어오르다** crawl 〔creep〕 up; clamber up; climb up. ¶ 줄사다리를 ～ climb up a rope ladder / 성벽을 ～ clamber up the fort wall / 그는 더 높은 나뭇가지로 기어올랐다 He climbed up onto a higher branch of the tree.

**기어이**(期於―) 《꼭》 without fail; for sure; certainly; by all means; at any cost 〔price, risk〕; 《드디어》 at (long) last; at length. ¶ ～ 약속을 지켜야 한다 Never fail to keep a promise. *or* By all means, you must keep your promise. / 그는 ～ 성공하고야 말 것이다 He is sure to succeed in the end. / 그는 ～ 떠나려 한다 He wants to leave for sure. / 이번에는 ～ 성공해 보이겠다 I give you my word that I shall make it a success this time. / 그는 ～ 그 문제를 풀었다 He solved the problem at last.

**기어코**(期於―) = 기어이.

**기억**(記憶) (a) memory; remembrance; (a) recollection. ～하다 remember; recall; recollect; bear 〔keep〕 《*a matter*》 in mind; 《외다》 learn 〔get〕 《*a matter*》 by heart; memorize; commit 《*a matter*》 to memory; 〖컴퓨터〗 store 《information》.

¶ 희미한 ～ a vague recollection; dim memories / ～할 만한 날 a memorable day; a day to be remembered / 내 ～에 의하면 as I recall; to the best of my recollection; as far as I can remember / 내 ～이 틀림 없다면 if I remember rightly 〔correctly〕; if (my) memory serves me right / 잘 ～해 두다 fix firmly 〔indelibly〕 in *one's* memory; bear firmly in mind / ～에 남다 remain 〔be, live〕 in *one's* memory; still have a memory 《of》 / ～에 새롭다 be fresh in *one's* memory / ～을 불러일으키다 call 《*a thing*》 to mind; recall 〔bring back〕 to *one's* mind; evoke memories 《of the past》 / ～을 더듬다 trace back in memory / ～을 새롭게 하다 refresh *one's* memory / ～을 상실〔회복〕하다 lose 〔recover〕 *one's* memory / 잘 ～해 두시오 Bear it firmly in mind. / 이 읍에서는 이미 그 일을 ～하고 있는 사람은 아무도 없다 It is no longer remembered by anyone now living in this town. / 전에〔어디선가〕 그를 한번 만난 것을 ～하고 있다 I remember seeing him once before 〔somewhere〕. (★ remember 뒤에 부정사가 올 때가 있으나 이 경우는 뜻이 다름: I remember to write him every week. 「나는 매주 잊지 않고 그에게 편지를 쓴다」).

◉ ～광고 remembrance advertising (★ 장기간에 걸쳐 제품·광고주의 이름 등이 구입자 눈에 접하도록 하는 광고. 캘린더·볼펜 따위). ～법 a mnemonic system. ～상실 loss of memory: ～상실증 amnesia. ～소자 〖컴퓨터〗 a storage cell 〔element〕. ～술 the art of memorizing; mnemonics. ～용량 〖컴퓨터〗 memory 〔storage〕 capacity: ～용량이 3.2기가바이트이다 have 3.2 gigabytes of memory. ～장애 defects of memory. ～장치 〖컴퓨터〗 a memory (unit); a storage (unit): 대용량 ～장치 large capacity storage (unit) / 전자 ～장치 an electronic memory machine; a ticketer / 주～장치 a main storage (unit); a main memory (unit). ～중추 a memory center. ～착오 a lapse of memory.

**기억력**(記憶力) memory; power of remembering. ¶ ～의 감퇴 failure of *one's* memory / ～이 좋다〔나쁘다〕 have a good 〔bad, poor〕 memory / ～을 잃다 lose *one's* memory / ～이 감퇴하다 *one's* memory fails 〔falters, gives out〕 / 나이를 먹게 되면 ～이 점점 감퇴한다 As one gets older his memory becomes poorer 〔weaker〕.

**기언**(奇言) strange words; a strange 〔peculiar〕 remark; a bit of sophistry.

**기엄기엄** crawling 《along》; creeping 《up, down, about》; on hands and knees; on all fours. ¶ ～ 산에 올라가다 climb up a hill on hands and knees.

**기업**(企業) an 〔a business〕 enterprise; an undertaking; 《회사·기업체》 a company; a corporation. ¶ 개인〔민간〕 ～ a private enterprise / 국영 ～ a government 〔state〕 enterprise / 공공 ～ public enterprise / 한국의 해외 ～ Korea's overseas enterprises / 대～ a large(-scale) 〔major〕 enterprise; a large corporation 〔company〕; a big firm 〔business〕 / ～계열 a corporate group / 부실 ～(체) an improperly-run 〔insolvent〕 enterprise / ～내 종합 통신 시스

템 in-house total communication system / ～의 자기 자본 비율 the owned capital ratio 〔share〕 of companies to their total capital / ～을 일으키다 plan 〔embark in〕 an enterprise / ～의 균형 발전을 모색하다 seek balanced development between enterprises / ～은 망해도 기업인은 산다 A businessman can survive although his company has gone bankrupt. / 인플레로～ 경영이 어려워졌다 Business has encountered financial difficulties because of inflation.
◉ ～가 an enterpriser; a man of enterprise; an entrepreneur. ～간 신용 inter-business credit; mutual credit. ～공개 a corporation's public offering 〔sale〕 of stocks 〔shares〕; going public: ～공개를 권장하다 encourage 《a corporation》 to go public. ～공채(公債) an industrial loan. ～광고 a corporate advertisement. ～금융 business 〔corporate〕 finance. ～농 commercialized 〔market〕 farming. ～부조리 irregularities among 〔in〕 business. ～비밀 an industrial 〔a company〕 secret. ～연금 a company pension. ～연합 a cartel. ～열 enthusiasm for business enterprise; industrial fever. ～윤리 《establish sound》 business ethics; the ethics of enterprise. ～은행 Industrial Bank of Korea. ～이미지 a corporate image. ～인＝～가: ～인으로서 요구되는 최소한의 윤리 the minimum ethics required for enterprisers. ～정비〔재조정, 재편성〕 industrial readjustment; business reorganization 〔restructuring〕. ～진단 management consulting. ～집중 business concentration. ～체질개선 improvement of industrial structure. ～합동 a trust; a combine; a cartel. ～합리화 rationalization of enterprises. ～합병 (an) amalgamation; (a) merger. ～형태 a form 〔type〕 of enterprise. ～화 industrialization; commercialization: ～화하다 industrialize; produce 《goods》 on a commercial basis.

**기업**(起業) starting a business; promotion 《of an enterprise, undertaking》. ～하다 start 〔initiate〕 a business 〔an undertaking〕; promote; 〔organize〕 《an enterprise》. ◉ ～비 initial expenses.

**-기에** ① 《…하는 데》 for; to *do;* with; for 〔in, of〕 *do*ing. ¶ 일하기에 바쁘다 be busy with *one's* work / 준비하기에 간단하다 be simple to prepare / 기다리기에 지치다 get tired of waiting 《for》. ② 《…(하)기 때문에》 as; because. ¶ 책이 싸기에 한 권을 샀다 As the book was cheap, I bought a copy. / 그가 초청하기에 가보았다 As he had invited me, I went to see him. / 날이 하도 좋기에 산책 나갔었다 As it was such a lovely day, I went out for a walk. ③ ＝-관데.

**-기에는** ¶ 내가 보기에는 the way I see it; 《내 생각에는》 in my opinion / 다른 사람들이 보기에는 the way others look at it.

**-기에망정이지** it is fortunate that…; fortunately… otherwise; or (else); if not so. ¶ 그가 가만히 있었기에망정이지 싸움이 될 뻔했다 If he had not kept quiet, they would have quarreled. / 돈이 없었기에망정이지 도둑에게 다 빼앗겼을 게다 It was good that I had no money with me, otherwise I would have been robbed of it by the thief.

**기여**(寄與) (a) contribution; services. ⇨ 공헌. ～하다 contribute 《to》; do (a lot) for 《national welfare》; help 《*a person*》「(to) do 〔out〕; render services 《to》; go a long way 〔go far〕 toward 《solving the problem》. ¶ 대외무역에 크게 ～하다 render great services to foreign trade / 동아시아는 물론 한반도 평화와 안정 유지에 ～하다 contribute to the maintenance of peace and stability on the Korean peninsula as well as in the East Asia / 그것은 인구 문제 해결에 크게 ～할 것이다 That will do much for solving the population problem. ◉ ～입학 허가제 《대학의》 an "admission via donation" system; a system to grant admission to college aspirants in exchange for financial contributions to the school foundation.

**기역** *kiyŏk;* the name of the first letter of the Korean alphabet 《ㄱ》. ¶ (낫 놓고) ～자도 모른다 do not know A from B; be utterly illiterate.

**기역니은순**(—順) ⇨ 가나다순(—順).

**기역시**(其亦是) (that is) also; too; as well; likewise; again; 《부정》 neither…. ¶ ～ 좋다 That is also good. / ～ 곤란한 문제다 That is again a difficult question. *or* That is another tough problem.

**기연**(奇緣) a strange turn of fate; an irony 〔a twist〕 of fate; a curious coincidence. ¶ ～으로 만나게 된 사이

〔관계〕 a relationship formed due to a strange turn of fate / 자넬 여기서 만나다니 참으로 ～이로군 What a coincidence meeting you here!

**기연**(機緣) ① 《기회》 a chance; an opportunity; occasion. ¶ 이를 ～으로 삼아 taking this opportunity. ② 〖불교〗 affinity.

**기연가미연가하다**(其然—未然—) (be) vague; indistinct; inarticulate; be uncertain (whether... or not). ¶ 이 말의 뜻이 ～ I don't exactly understand the meaning of this word.

**기염**(氣焰) high spirits; enthusiasm. ¶ ～을 토하다 talk big; speak with great vehemence; argue heatedly 《for, against》.

**기영**(機影) the sight of an airplane.

**기예**(氣銳) ¶ ～의 spirited; energetic / 신진 ～의 작곡가 a young and energetic 〔an up-and-coming〕 composer.

**기예**(技藝) arts and crafts; 《공예》 handicrafts. ◉ ～가 an artist. ～학교 a crafts 〔handicrafts〕 school.

**기온**(氣溫) an air 〔atmospheric〕 temperature. ¶ (연)평균 ～ the average temperature (for the year) / ～의 변화 a change of 〔in〕 temperature / ～의 급상승〔급강하〕 a sudden rise 〔fall, drop〕 in temperature / ～이 섭씨 20도로 올라갔다〔내려갔다〕 The temperature rose 〔dropped, went down〕 to 20℃. ◉ ～파(波) 〖기상〗 temperature waves.

**기와** a (roofing) tile. ¶ ～를 이다 tile the roof; roof 《a house》 with tiles / ～를 굽다 make 〔bake〕 tiles / ～ 한 장 아껴서 대들보 썩힌다 《속담》 Penny wise, (and) pound foolish. ◉ ～공장 a tilery. ～장이 《만드는 사람》 a tilemaker; a tiler; 《이는 사람》 a tile layer. ～지붕 a tiled roof. ～집 a tile-roofed house; a house with a tile roof. 기왓가마 a tile-kiln. 기왓고랑 a furrow in a tiled roof.

**기왕**(旣往) the past; bygones; the bygone days. ⇨ 이왕(已往). ¶ ～에 since it is done; since it has already happened / ～이면 if it is done; if it has already happened; 《선택》 if I must take 〔choose〕 / ～지사는 불문에 부치자 Let bygones be bygones. / ～ 경기에 참가하려면 최선을 다해라 Do your best, if you are to take part in a game at all. ◉ ～증 〖의학〗 《병》 a disease which *one* had in the past; *one's* past illness; 《병력》 the medical history (of a patient).

**기왕**(棋王) the best player of *paduk*.

**기외**(其外) besides that; others; the rest. ¶ ～의 other.

**기용**(起用) ① appointment. ⇨ 등용, 발탁. ～하다 appoint *a person* 《to a position of responsibility》; promote *a person* 《to a higher rank》. ¶ 대타자로 ～하다 lift 《a player》 for a pinch hitter / (야구에서) 그를 선발로 ～하다 give him a starting job 〔assignment〕 / 그는 판매 부장으로 ～되었다 He was appointed to the post of sales director. / 그녀는 새로운 자리에 ～될 것 같다 She is likely to be appointed to the new position. / 이 중대한 시점에서 정말로 신인을 ～하려는 것일까 Are they really going to appoint a newcomer to take over 《the job》 at this important point? ② 《재임용》 reappointment; reemployment. ～하다 《다시 임용하다》 reappoint; reemploy.

**기우**(杞憂) baseless 〔needless〕 anxiety; imaginary 〔unfounded〕 fears; a bugbear; groundless apprehensions. ¶ ～를 품다 entertain groundless fears 〔apprehensions〕; trouble *oneself* unnecessarily / ～일지 모르겠으나 I may be worrying unduly, but... / 네 걱정은 한낱 ～에 불과하다 Your fears are utterly groundless.

**기우**(奇遇) a chance 〔an unexpected〕 meeting; a fortuitous meeting. ～하다 meet by chance; meet unexpectedly.

**기우**(祈雨) prayer for rain. ～하다 pray for rain; offer prayers for rain. ◉ ～단 an altar where prayers are offered for rain. ～제 「a traditional Korean rite 〔a shamanist service〕 to pray for rain.

**기우듬하다** (be) somewhat slanted 〔sloping, tipped, leaning〕; be sort of oblique; be slightly askew. ¶ 기우듬한 기둥 a slanting pillar / 왼쪽으로 ～ have a tilt to the left / 책상이 한쪽으로 ～ The desk is tilted on one side.

**기우듬히** in a somewhat slanted way; slightly askew; at a tilt; on a slant.

**기우뚱거리다** ① [자동사] totter; shake; waver; sway 〔rock〕 from side to side; 《불안정하다》 be shaky 〔unsteady〕. ¶ 기우뚱거리는 의자 an unsteady 〔a rickety〕 chair / 배가 몹시 ～ a boat is rocking heavily / 버스가 ～ a bus is swaying 〔joggling〕 / 기우뚱거리며 걷다 walk along swaying *one's* body / 집이 갑자기 기우뚱거렸다 I suddenly felt the house shake.

② [타동사] 《흔들다》 move 《*a thing*》 from side to side; shake; rock; sway; tilt. ¶ 목을 ~ tilt 〔cock〕 *one's* head from one side to the other / 몸을 ~ sway *one's* body / 지진으로 집들이 기우뚱거렸다 The earthquake rocked the houses.

**기우뚱기우뚱** rocking 〔swaying〕 from side to side; tilting repeatedly; cocking 《*one's* head》 from one side to the other. ¶ ~ 걷다 walk swaying *one's* body from side to side.

**기운** ① 《체력》 (physical) strength; energy; might; stamina (내구력). ¶ ~이 센 strong; powerful; mighty / ~을 다해서 with all *one's* might / ~이 좋다 be strong 〔mighty〕; have great physical strength / ~이 없다 be weak 〔feeble〕; do not have much strength / ~이 나다〔빠지다〕 gain 〔lose (all) *one's*〕 strength / ~을 회복하다 recover *one's* strength / ~을 기르다 build up 〔develop〕 *one's* physical strength / 그는 요즘 ~이 쇠퇴해짐을 느낀다 He feels his strength 〔power〕 falling these days. / 그녀는 매우 쇠약해서 걸을 ~도 없다 She is so weak that she has not got the strength to walk.

② 《원기·생기》 vigor; energy; vitality; spirits; 《미구어》 pep. ¶ ~이 있는 high-spirited; vigorous; spry; lively; energetic; healthy (건강한) / ~이 정정한 노인 a spry old man / ~이 없다 be in low spirits; be lifeless 〔weak〕 / ~이 나다〔을 내다〕 cheer up; pick up; be refreshed / ~이 넘치다 be in good 〔high〕 spirits; be full of vigor / ~을 회복하다 recover *one's* spirits / 그녀는 꽤 ~이 있어 보였다 She seemed to be quite healthy 〔in good spirits〕. / 그녀를 만나게 되면 자네도 ~이 날 것이다 You will cheer up if you see her. / 물을 한 잔 마시니 ~이 났다 A glass of water 「picked me up 〔refreshed me〕. / 나는 어머님의 다정한 말에 ~이 났다 I was encouraged by my mother's kind words. / 한 잔 하면 ~이 날게다 A glass of wine will 「give you a lift 〔pep you up 《구어》〕. / 너무 피곤해서 말할 ~도 없었다 I was too tired to speak.

③ 《기미·징후》 a sign; an indication; a touch 《of》; a tinge; 《흔적》 a trace; 《약·술 따위의》 an effect; efficacy. ¶ 봄 ~ the signs of spring / 독한 ~ poisonous character; virulence (독성) / 감기 ~이 있다 have a touch of cold / 술~이 있다 be under the influence of liquor / 붉은 ~이 돌다 be tinged with red / 따뜻한 ~이 있다 《a room》 show signs of warmth (from the fire) / 약~이 곧 퍼졌다 The medicine quickly took effect. *or* The medicine worked almost at once.

④ 《천지만물의》 anima; the universal spirit thought to underlie the living things and to be manifested in negative 〔"dark (=음)"〕 and positive 〔"bright (=양)"〕 aspects.

**기운**(氣運) 《경향·형편》 a tendency; a trend. ¶ …의 ~이 고조되다 show a strong tendency to *do* / 두 나라 사이에는 화해의 ~이 증대되고 있다 There is a growing tendency toward peace between two countries.

**기운**(氣韻) 《멋》 atmosphere 《in art, literature》; elegance; tone; grace. ¶ ~이 넘치는 그림 a picture full of grace.

**기운**(機運) 《운수》 luck; fortune; 《기회》 an opportunity; a chance; the time. ¶ ~이 무르익기를 기다리다 await 〔wait for〕 a ripe opportunity; bide *one's* time / 개혁의 ~이 마침내 무르익었다 At last the time is ripe for a reform.

**기울** the inner chaff of grain; 《wheat》 bran.

**기울다** ① [경사지다] 《선·면 따위가》 lean 《to, toward》; incline 《to, toward》; tilt; slant; have a tilt 《to the right》; slope (완만히 밑으로); 《배가》 list (옆으로); 《차·비행기가》 bank. ¶ 기운 지붕 a slanted 〔sloped〕 roof / 40°로 기울어 있다 be inclined at forty degrees / 오두막이 오른쪽으로 기울어 있다 The hut leans 〔tilts〕 to the right. / 벽의 그림이 조금 기울어져 있다 The picture on the wall is slanted a little. / 탑은 동쪽으로 약간 기울어 있다 The tower leans somewhat toward the east. / 비행기는 조금 기울면서 우로 회전했다 The aircraft turned to the right, banking slightly. / 배는 좌현으로 기울기 시작했다 The ship began to list to port. / 차는 커브를 돌 때 크게 기울었다 The car banked as it turned. / 그녀의 글씨는 왼쪽으로 기울어져 있다 Her handwriting inclines to the left.

② 《해·달이》 decline; go down; sink. ¶ 해가 서산 너머로 기울고 있다 The sun is going down behind the western mountains.

③ 《경향을 띠다》 lean 《toward》; be inclined 《to》; incline 《to, toward》; tend 《to》; be disposed 《to》. ¶ 그는 나

의 의견에 기울고 있다 He leans 〔inclines〕 toward my opinion. / 그는 정치적으로 우파에 기울어 있다 He is politically inclined 〔tended〕 to the right. / 나는 그것에 동의하는 쪽으로 기울어 있다 I'm inclined 「to agree 〔toward agreeing〕 to it.
④ 《쇠퇴하다》 decline; wane; sink. ¶ 기울어가는 운 a declining fortune / 가산이 ～ *one's* family fortune is declining / 그의 운도 이제 기울고 있다 His fortune is 「waning 〔on the wane〕. / 그 나라는 국력이 기울었다 The country waned in influence.

**기울어지다** ⇨ 기울다. ¶ 어머니의 마음은 결혼을 승낙하는 쪽으로 기울어졌다 The mother was inclined to consent to the marriage.

**기울이다** ① 《경사지게 하다》 incline; lean; tilt; 《기구 따위를》 tip; slant. ¶ 몸을 ～ bend 〔lean〕 *one's* body / 고개를 한 쪽으로 ～ cock 〔tilt〕 *one's* head to one side / 테이블을 ～ tip 〔tilt〕 the table / 술잔을 ～ have a drink; have a glass of liquor / 앞으로〔뒤로〕 의자를 ～ tilt a chair forward 〔backward〕 / 통을 ～ tilt 〔tip〕 a barrel.
② 《마음·주의를 경주하다》 devote *oneself* 〔all *one's* energies〕 to 《*something*》; concentrate (*one's* attention) on 《*something*》. ¶ 귀를 ～ listen to 《*a person*, what *a person* says》; bend *one's* ear 《to *a person*》 / 마음을 기울여 공부하다 keep *one's* mind on *one's* studies; devote *oneself* to *one's* studies / 연구에 온 정력을 ～ devote all *one's* strength 〔energies〕 to *one's* research / (…에게) 애정을 ～ fix 〔set〕 *one's* heart 《on》; be deeply attached 《to》.

**기웃거리다** 《고개를》 crane and crane (*one's* neck) to see; successively crane 〔stretch〕 *one's* neck to see; 《엿보다》 peep 〔peek, look〕 《into a room, out of the window, through a hole》; snoop around. ¶ 기웃거리는 사람 a snooper; a peeping Tom; a voyeur / 가게를 ～ show *one's* nose in a shop; look in at a store / 누가 있나 방을 ～ peek into a room to see 「who is there 〔if someone is there〕 / 이방 저방 ～ peek 〔snoop〕 around this room and that / 수상한 사나이가 문에서 안을 기웃거렸다 A suspicious-looking fellow peeped in at the door.

**기웃하다**[1] [형용사] ＝기우듬하다.

**기웃하다**[2] [타동사] tip 〔tilt, slant, incline〕 《*a thing*》 a bit; put 《*a thing*》 a bit askew; place 《*a thing*》 a little out of line 〔off center〕; fix 《*a thing*》 at a slight angle.

**기원**(技員) an assistant engineer 〔technician〕.

**기원**(祈願) (a) supplication; (a) prayer; a petition. ～하다 pray 《for peace》; supplicate; petition. ¶ 병의 회복을 ～하다 pray for 《*a person's*》 recovery / 간곡히 ～하다 offer (up) a fervent prayer 《for the safety of *one's* son》 / 내 ～이 이루어졌다 My prayer was answered. ◉ ～문 〖문법〗 an optative sentence. ～법 〖문법〗 the optative (mood). ～자 a supplicant; a prayer.

**기원**(紀元) an era; an epoch. ¶ ～전 80년에 in 80 B.C. (★ B.C.는 Before Christ의 생략형) / 서력～ 1945년에 in the year 1945 of the Christian era; in 1945 A.D. (★ A.D.는 Anno Domini의 생략형) / 신～을 이루다 mark a new epoch 《in》 / 하나의 ～을 이루는 사건 an epoch-making event.

**기원**(起源) the origin; the source; the beginning; the rise; the genesis. ～하다 have its origin 〔roots〕 《in》; originate 《in》; take its rise 《in》; derive its origin 《from》; be traceable 《to》. ¶ 종의 ～ 《책이름》 *The Origin of Species* / 문명의 ～ the origin of civilization / ～을 더듬다〔조사하다〕 trace 《a custom》 to *its* origin 〔source〕 / 그 ～은 확실하지 않다 Its origin is unknown. *or* It is of unknown 〔uncertain〕 origin. / 의회의 ～은 이보다 훨씬 이전으로 거슬러 올라간다 The origin of parliaments goes back far beyond this. / 이 건축 양식은 중국이 ～이다 This style of architecture has its origin in China.

**기원**(棋院) a *baduk* club(house).

**기유**(己酉) 〖민속〗 the 46th binary term of the sexagenary cycle.

**기율**(紀律) order; discipline. ¶ 엄격한 ～ rigid discipline / ～이 문란하다 Discipline is lax 〔loose, slack〕.

**기음**(基音) 〖음악〗 a keynote.

**기음**(氣音) 〖음성〗 an aspirate; an aspirated sound.

**기음문자**(記音文字) phonetic letters.

**기이하다**(奇異―) (be) strange; odd; queer; singular; curious. ¶ 기이한 소문 a strange rumor / 기이한 현상 a weird 〔strange〕 phenomenon / 기이하게도 strangely enough; strange to say / 기이하게 생각하다 feel 《*a thing*》 strange / 사람들은 우리를 기이한 눈으로 보았다 People gave us queer looks. /

참으로 기이한 인연이로군 What a curious coincidence!

**기인**(奇人) an eccentric (person); a strange 〔an odd〕 fellow. ¶ 그는 ~이다 He is quite a character. *or* 《구어》 He is a queer fish.

**기인**(起因) ~하다 be caused 《by》; be due 《to》; have its origin 《in》; originate 《in》; arise 〔result, spring〕 《from》; 《미》 stem 《from》. ¶ 이 병은 대개의 경우 과로에 ~한다 This disease is, in most cases, caused by overwork. / 청소년 비행의 대부분은 가정환경에 ~한다 Most cases of juvenile delinquency have their roots in family conditions.

**기인**(基因) (fundamental) cause; (basic) 「origin.

**기일**(忌日) the anniversary of 《*a person's*》 death; the deathday 《of *a person*》. ¶ 11월 10일은 선친의 ~입니다 November 10 「falls on 〔is〕 my father's deathday.

**기일**(期日) a (fixed) date; an appointed day; 《기한》 a due date; a term; a time limit. ¶ 납부 ~이 지난 가스 요금 청구서 an overdue gas bill / ~까지는 by the appointed time 〔day〕 / ~을 지키다 keep to the 「appointed day 〔schedule〕; keep to 〔comply with〕 the deadline 《for》 / ~을 잘못 알다 make a mistake about the date.

**기입**(記入) (an) entry; 《서식의》 filling up 〔in〕. ~하다 enter; make an entry 《in a ledger》; 《서식에》 fill in; write in. ¶ 용지에 ~하다 fill in 〔out 《미》〕 a blank 〔form〕 / 이름을 ~하다 enter 〔write〕 *one's* name; register (*one's* name) / 일기에 ~하다 write 〔record, make an entry〕 《*a matter*》 in a diary / 장부에 ~하다 enter in a book; make an entry in a book / 원장(元帳)에 금액을 ~하다 enter a sum in a ledger / 이 항목들을 ~하여 주십시오 Just enter these items. / 해답은 소정의 용지에 ~하시오 Fill 〔Write〕 your answers on the prescribed forms.

◉ ~누락 an omission. ~장 〖부기〗 an entry book. ~필 《표시》 Entered.

**기자**(記者) 《보도관계자》 a journalist; 《신문기자》 a newspaperman; a newsperson; a pressman 《영》; a reporter 《취재기자》; a correspondent (특파원); an editor (편집자); a writer (집필자). ¶ 수습~ a junior reporter; 《속어》 a cub reporter / 스포츠 ~ a sports writer / 여~ a newspaperwoman; a woman 〔lady〕 reporter / ~ 노릇을 하고 있다 be (engaged) on the staff of a newspaper; hold a reporter's job on a 《local》 paper / 그녀는 워싱턴 포스트의 ~이다 She is a reporter for the Washington Post. / 그는 타임지의 편집~이다 He is the editorial staff of the Time (magazine). / 그는 M신문의 편집 ~이다 He holds a desk position of the M newspaper.

◉ ~교류 the exchange of resident journalists. ~단 a press corps. ~석 《회의장·경기장의》 a press box; 《의회 따위의》 a press gallery. ~증 a press card. ~클럽 a press 〔journalists'〕 club: 서울외신 ~클럽 The Seoul Foreign Correspondents' Club. 한국~협회 The Journalists Association of Korea.

**기자감식**(飢者甘食) Nothing comes amiss to a hungry man.

**기자력**(起磁力) magnetomotive force.

**기자회견**(記者會見) a press interview; a news 〔press〕 conference. ~하다 have 〔hold, call〕 a press conference; meet the press. ¶ 즉석~ an impromptu conference with newsmen / 텔레비전 ~ a televised press 〔news〕 conference / ~을 요청하다 seek 〔request〕 a press interview 《with the President》 / 대통령은 ~을 했다 The President met the press.

**기장**[1] 〖식물〗 (Chinese) millet.

**기장**[2] 《옷의 길이》 the length of a suit; the dress length. ¶ 이 오버코트의 ~은 내게 너무 짧다〔길다〕 This overcoat is too short 〔long〕 for me.

**기장**(記章) a medal; a badge. ¶ 종군 ~ a war 〔service〕 medal / 제복에 ~을 달다 wear a badge on *one's* uniform.

**기장**(機長) a (senior) pilot; the captain 《of the crew》.

**기장**(記帳) register; (an) entry. ~하다 register; enter (up) 《the sum in the account book》; make an entry 《of》.

**기재**(奇才) an extraordinary talent; remarkable talent; unusual ability; 《사람》 a genius; a prodigy; an outstandingly talented person.

**기재**(記載) recording; mention; 《장부에》 entry. ~하다 mention; record; 《장부에》 enter; 《신문·잡지에》 print; carry. ¶ 일련 번호를 ~한 꼬리표 labels bearing serial numbers / 별항 ~와 같이 as stated 「elsewhere 〔in a separate paragraph〕 / 장부에 ~하다 make an entry of 《it》 in an account book / 이 문제에 관해선 아무런 ~도 없다 There is no mention of this matter. / 그것은

국제연합 헌장에 ~되어 있다 It is stated [mentioned] in the U.N. Charter. ◉ ~누락 an omission. ~사항 mentioned items; (the) items mentioned: 장부의 ~사항은 모두 정확해야 한다 All the entries in the book should be correct.

**기재**(器材) 《기구와 재료》 instruments and materials. ¶ 실험용 ~ instruments and materials for experiments.

**기재**(機材) 《기계와 재료》 machinery and materials.

**기저**(基底) a foundation; a base; a basis (*pl.* bases). ⇨ 기반. ¶ ~의 basal.

**기저귀** a diaper; a nappy 《영》; a (baby's) napkin. ¶ 종이 ~ a paper [disposable] diaper / 젖은 ~ a wet [soiled] diaper [napkin] / 아기의 ~를 갈다 change the baby's diaper; change the baby / 아기에게 ~를 채우다 diaper [put a diaper on] a baby.

**기적**(汽笛) a (steam) whistle; a siren 《미》; a hooter 《영》. ¶ ~소리와 함께 with the sound of the steam whistle / ~을 울리다 give [blow, sound] a whistle / ~이 울린다 The whistle is blowing. *or* There goes the whistle.

**기적**(奇蹟) a miracle; a wonder. ¶ ~적인 miraculous / ~적으로 miraculously / 한강의 ~ the miracle on the Han River / ~이 일어나지 않는 한 as long as no miracle comes up / ~을 행하다 work [perform, do] miracles; work [do] wonders / ~적으로 죽음을 면하다 escape death by a miracle / 때때로 ~은 일어난다 Miracles do occur from time to time. / ~ 없이는 환자가 살기 힘들 것이다 Nothing short of a miracle will save the patient. / 그 미래학자는 한국을 「아시아의 ~」이라고 말했다 The futurist called South Korea the "miracle of Asia." ◉ ~극 a miracle play; 《그리스도의》 a mystery play.

**기전기**(起電機) 〖물리〗 an electric motor.

**기전력**(起電力) 〖물리〗 electromotive force (생략 E.M.F., e.m.f.).

**기절**(氣絶) 《까무러침》 fainting; a faint; a swoon. ~하다 faint; get stunned; 《의식을 잃다》 lose *one's* senses; lose consciousness; black out (일시적 의식 불명). ¶ ~하여 in a (dead) faint / ~할 듯이 놀라다 be frightened out of *one's* senses [wits] / ~해서 쓰러지다 fall down in a faint / 때려서 ~시키다 knock 《*a person*》 unconscious [out, senseless] / 그녀는 공포로 ~했다 She fainted (away) with horror.

**기절초풍하다**(氣絶一風一) be thunderstruck; be frightened to death; be frightened out of *one's* wits; get the fright of *one's* life; (nearly) jump out of *one's* skin.

**기점**(起點) 《거리측정의》 the starting [base] point; 《철도의》 the railhead. ¶ …을 ~으로 하다 start from… / 학교를 ~으로 하여 거리를 측정하다 measure the distance with the school as its starting point / 이 철도의 ~은 부산이다 This railroad line starts from Pusan.

**기점**(基點) a cardinal [reference] point. ¶ 방위(方位) ~ the cardinal points of the compass.

**기정**(既定) ¶ ~의 established; fixed; prearranged; predetermined / ~사실 an established fact; *fait accompli* 《프》/ 여러분은 ~방침에 따라 행동해 주기 바란다 Everybody is required to act according to the prearranged plan [program]. ◉ ~세입 established revenue. ~세출 established expenditure. ~예산 the established budget.

**기제**(忌祭) a memorial service held on the anniversary of 《*a person's*》 death.

**기조**(基調) the keynote; the basis; the underlying tone. ¶ 경제 ~ the basic economic conditions 《of Korea》/ …에 ~를 두고 있다 be based on…; stand on the basis of… / …의 ~를 이루다 form the keynote of… / 그의 연설 ~는 기독교적 사랑이었다 The keynote of his speech was Christian love. / 이것이 양국 관계의 ~가 되었다 This set the tone for the relations between the two countries. ◉ ~연설 《make, deliver》 a keynote speech [address]: ~연설자 a keynote speaker.

**기존**(既存) ¶ ~의 existing; established. ◉ ~시설 the existing facilities.

**기종**(氣腫) 〖의학〗 emphysema. ¶ ~의 emphysematous; emphysemic / 폐~ pulmonary emphysema.

**기종**(機種) 《비행기의》 kinds [types] of airplane(s); 《기계의》 kinds [types] of machine(s).

**기준**(基準) 《표준》 a standard; 《기초》 a basis; 《척도》 a yardstick; 《판단·비판의》 a criterion (*pl.* -ria). ¶ 안전~ 《meet》 safety standards / ~의 standard 《wage》; basic / ~ 미달의 below standard / ~에 달한 up to (the) standard / ~에 맞추다 standardize / ~을 올리다 raise the standards 《of living》/ 대학의 입학 ~을 정하다 set [establish] standards for admission to college / …을 ～으로 해서 정하다 set 〔fix〕《price》 on the basis of… / 그녀는 합격 ～에 미달했다 She has failed to get the passing mark in the exam. / 인기는 성공을 가늠하는 ～이 아니다 Popularity is not a criterion of success.

◉ ～가격 a standard price. ～기간《물가 통계 등의》 the base period. ～량 a norm; standard amount. ～선《측량의》 a baseline; a datum line. ～시가 the standard value《of real estate》. ～시세《외환의》 the central rate. ～연도 the basic「period 〔year〕. ～임금 standard wages. ～점《측량》 a「reference 〔datum〕 point; a reference mark (좌표의). ～지가 the standard land price.

**기중**(忌中) 《be in》 mourning《for》. ¶ ～《게시》 In Mourning.

**기중기**(起重機) a crane; a derrick(선박의). ¶ 고정식 ～ a stationary crane / 운반식 ～ a portable crane / 이동 ～ a traveling crane / ～로 들어올리다 lift 〔hoist〕《*a thing*》 with a crane.

◉ ～선 a floating crane.

**기증**(寄贈) donation; presentation; contribution (기부). ～하다 donate; present; contribute; make a donation of《a sum of money to》. ¶ 그는 장서를 모교에 ～했다 He has「donated 〔presented〕 his library to his school.

◉ ～본〔도서〕 a「complimentary 〔presentation〕 copy; a giftbook. ～자 a contributor; a donor; a giver. ～품 a gift; a present; a donation.

**기지**(基地) 〖군사〗 a base; 《터전》 a site. ¶ 군사〔미사일, 주둔, 연료 보급〕 ～ a「military 〔missile, garrison, fueling〕 base / 관측 ～ an observation base / 중계 ～ a relay base / 작전 ～ a base of operations / 공군〔해군〕 ～「an air (force) 〔a naval〕 base / ～를 폐쇄하다 shut down《U.S.》 bases《on Korean soil》. ◉ ～국 a base station. ～촌 a military campside town.

**기지**(旣知) ¶ ～의 (already-)known; established / ～의 사실 an already= known fact; an established fact.

◉ ～수 〖수학〗 a known「number 〔quantity〕.

**기지**(機智) wit; resource. ⇨ 재치. ¶ ～있는 witty; resourceful; tactful / ～가 있는 사람 a witty man; a man of wit / ～의 번득임 a flash of wit / ～가 있다〔없다〕 have a「quick 〔dull〕 wit(s); be quick-〔dull-〕witted / ～가 넘치다 be witty; be full of「resources 〔wit〕 / 그의 이야기는 ～가 번득였다 His speech sparkled with wit.

**기지개** a stretch; stretching *oneself* (to relieve fatigue). ～하다, ～켜다 stretch (*oneself*); take a good stretch; stretch; *one's* body with raised hands.

**기직** a straw-and-rush mat; 《spread》 a「coarse 〔rough〕 straw mat.

**기진**(氣盡) exhaustion. ～하다 be exhausted; be「worn 〔tired〕 out.

◉ ～맥진 complete 〔utter〕 exhaustion: ～맥진하다 be「dead 〔quite〕 tired; get dog-tired《구어》/ 그는 무거운 짐을 운반하느라 ～맥진했다 He was quite exhausted from carrying heavy luggage.

**기질**(氣質) (a) disposition; temperament; nature; a temper; a cast of mind. ¶ 강한〔온순한〕 ～ a「strong 〔mild〕 disposition / 예술가 ～ an artistic temperament / 지기 싫어하는 ～ an unyielding nature / 유쾌하고 사교적인 ～ a cheerful and sociable temper / 학자 ～의 사람 a man of scholarly turn of mind / 격한 ～의 사람 a man of a fiery temperament / ～에 맞지 않다 go against *one's* grain / 아버지의 ～을 물려받다 inherit *one's* father's disposition / 그는 어떤 ～의 사람인가요 What sort of (a) man is he? / 그는 신경질적인 ～을 가진 사람이다 He is of a nervous disposition.

**기질**(基質) 〖의학〗 a stroma (*pl.* -mata); 〖생화학〗 a substrate. ¶ 암의 ～ a cancer stroma.

**기차**(汽車) 《열차》 a (railroad) train; 《객차》 a railroad「car 〔coach〕《미》; a railway carriage《영》. ¶ ～로 by train; by rail 〔railroad〕 / 내려가는〔올라가는〕 ～「a down 〔an up〕 train / 부산행 ～ a train for Pusan / ～를 타다 take 〔catch, ride in, ride on〕 a train; board a train / ～에서 내리다 get off the train; leave the train / ～로 가다 go 〔travel〕 by train / ～를 놓치다 miss a train / ～를 대구에서 바꿔 타다 change trains at Daegu / ～가 제시간에 오다 a train arrives「on time 〔on schedule〕 / ～가 제시간보다 늦게 오다 a train arrives late; a train is behind (time) / 오후 5시 10분발 서울행 ～로 집에 돌아가다 go home on the「5:10 〔five-ten〕 p.m. train for Seoul / ～ 주의《게시》 Look out for the cars.《미》 *or* Beware of the trains《영》.

◉ ～시간표 a railroad schedule《미》; a railway timetable《영》. ～여행 a train journey; a railroad trip. ～요금 train

〔railroad〕 fares. 기찻길 a (railroad) track《미》; a railway line《영》.

**기차다**(氣―) 《어이없다》 be dumbfounded 〔flabbergasted, nonplused, stunned〕《at, by》; be (greatly) amazed《at》; be shocked《at, by》; 《놀랍다》 be wonderful. ¶ 기차게 wonderfully; awfully; terribly / 기찬 솜씨 remarkable 〔exceptional〕 ability; great skill / 기찬 미인 a stunning beauty / 기차게 맛있다 be so delicious; be very palatable 〔tasty〕 / 원 참 기(가) 차서 Well, I never! *or* Words fail me! / 그녀의 뻔뻔스러움에 기가 찼다 I was amazed at 〔by〕 her impudence. / 우리는 기가 차서 서로 얼굴만 쳐다 보았다 We looked at each other in amazement.

**기차표**(汽車票) a (railroad) ticket. ¶ ～를 끊다 buy a ticket. ◉ ～매표소 a ticket 〔booking《영》〕 office. ～매표인 a ticket agent《미》; a booking clerk《영》. 왕복～ a round-trip ticket《미》; a return ticket《영》; 편도～ a one-way ticket《미》; a single ticket《영》.

**기착**(寄着) stopover; stop-off. ～하다 stop over《at Sydney》; make a (brief) stop《at... for refueling》.
◉ ～지 a stopover; a place of call.

**기채**(起債) flotation of a loan; issue 〔issuance〕 of bonds; capital 〔debt〕 issue. ～하다 float 〔raise〕 a loan; issue bonds. ¶ 고속 철도를 놓기 위해 ～가 행해졌다 Bonds have been issued to finance the high-speed railroad construction. ◉ ～시장 the capital 〔bond〕 market; the bond (flotation) market.

**기척** 《징후》 a sign; an indication. ¶ 옆방에 사람 ～이 있다 I felt the presence of some person in the next room. / 누군가 다가오는 ～이 있었다 I sensed someone approaching. / 그 집에는 사람 ～이 전혀 없었다 There was no sign of anyone at the house. / 그러한 ～은 전혀 없다 There are no such indications at all.

**기체**(氣體) 〖물리〗 (a body of) gas; vapor (증기); a gaseous body. ¶ ～의 gaseous; aerial (공기의); vaporous (증기의) / ～의 분자 a gas molecule / ～로 되다 become 〔turn into〕 a gas / 공기는 여러 가지 ～로 구성되어 있다 Air is composed of various gases. ◉ ～역학 gas dynamics; aeromechanics. ～연료 gaseous fuel. ～온도계 a gas thermometer.

**기체**(機體) 〖항공〗 the airframe; 《동체》 the body; the fuselage. ¶ ～의 반환을 요구하다 ask for the return of the aircraft 〔plane〕 / ～가 대파됐다 The airplane was greatly damaged.

**기체화**(氣體化) vaporization; gasification; aerification. ～하다 vaporize; gasify; aerify. 「teemed health.

**기체후**(氣體候) 《편지에서》 (your) es-

**기초**(起草) drafting. ～하다 draft《a bill》; draw up《a plan》; make a draft《of》. ¶ 국회에 제출할 법안을 ～하다 draft a bill to present to the National Assembly / 그는 그 평화 조약을 ～했다 He made a draft of the peace treaty. ◉ ～위원 a member of the drafting committee. ～위원회 a drafting committee. ～자 a drafter.

**기초**(基礎) the basis; the base; the foundation; the groundwork; the footing; the substructure.

> **용법** **basis** 의견·판단 따위의 추상적인 사항에 대한 기초를 나타내는 말로 「근거·원리」란 뜻. **base** 구체적인 사물의 기초를 나타내는 말로 「기초·토대」란 뜻. **foundation** 특히 확고한 base 또는 basis. **groundwork** basis, foundation과 비슷한 단어로 정신적·추상적인 것의 기초를 나타내는 말: Primary education forms the groundwork for building up one's character. (초등 교육은 인격 형성의 토대를 이룬다). **footing** 「발판」, 「집단 내에서의 확실한 지위·지반」이란 개념에서 기념비·벽 따위의 「토대·기초」, 사물의 확고한 「기반, 기초」란 뜻으로 쓰이게 됨: 견실한 기초 위에 사업을 올려 놓다 put business on a sound footing. **substructure** 「하부구조·토대」란 개념에서의 「기초」란 뜻.

¶ 영문법의 ～ the elements of English grammar / …을 ～로 하여 on the basis of... / ～가 없는 groundless; baseless / …에 ～를 두다 be based on... / …의 ～를 튼튼히 하다〔굳히다〕 consolidate 〔solidify〕 the foundation《of, for》; make the foundation secure / ～부터 배우다 learn《English》 from the beginning / 이 건물은 ～가 튼튼하다 The building has a firm 「base 〔foundation〕. / 그녀는 근대 언어학의 ～를 쌓았다 She laid the foundation 〔basis, groundwork〕 for modern linguistics. / 「그 계획은 어떻게 진행되고 있느냐」— 「～적인 자료를 모으고 있는 단계이다」

"How's that project coming along?" —"I'm in the process of getting the basic materials together."
◉ ～공사 foundation work: ～공사를 하다 lay the foundation《of》; level the ground; [비유적] pave the way 《for》. ～공제(控除) basic exemption; basic deduction《from the taxable income》. ～과목 fundamental studies; primary subjects《of study》. ～과학 (a) basic science. ～대사(代謝)〖생리〗 basal metabolism. ～산업 a basic 〔key〕 industry. ～영어강좌 lectures in English for beginners; elementary lessons in English. ～의학 the basic medical sciences. ～지식 a《good》 grounding《in》; a basic 〔a fundamental, an elementary〕 knowledge: 너는 영문법에 대한 ～지식이 부족하다 You lack a basic knowledge of English grammar. ～체온〖생리〗 the basal body temperature (생략 BBT). ～학과 primary subjects《of study》. ～훈련 a basic training.

**기초시계**(記秒時計) a stopwatch. ⇨ 스톱워치.

**기총**(機銃) a machine gun. ◉ ～소사(掃射) machine-gunning; strafing: ～소사하다 machine-gun; strafe.

**기축**(己丑)〖민속〗 the 26th binary term of the sexagenary cycle.

**기축**(機軸) ①《중추》 an axis; an axle. ②《고안》 a device; a contrivance. ¶ 신～ a new device. ③《체재》 the scheme 〔structure〕 of a composition.

**기축**(基軸) a standard; yardstick; a criterion. ◉ ～통화〖경제〗 a key currency.

**기치**(旗幟) ①《깃발》 a flag; a banner; a pennant; an ensign; an emblem; 《내건 목표》 a slogan; a motto. ¶ 그들은 자유의 ～ 아래 결속되어 있다 They are united under the banner 〔flag〕 of freedom. ②《태도》 *one's* attitude; *one's* position; *one's* stand. ¶ ～를 선명히 하다 define *one's* attitude; clarify *one's* position; show *one's* hand.

**기침** a cough; coughing;《헛기침》 clearing the throat;〖의학〗 a tussis. ～하다 cough; have a cough;《헛기침하다》 clear *one's* throat; give a cough; hem; harrumph (위엄있게). ¶ 마른 ～ a dry cough; a hacking cough (계속되는) / ～으로 고생하다 suffer from 〔be troubled with〕 a cough / ～이 멎다 get over 〔get rid of〕 *one's* cough / ～을 멎게 하다 stifle 〔suppress〕 a cough; relieve a cough (약으로) / 심하게 ～하다 cough violently; cough *one's*「lungs out 〔head off〕/ 그 아이는 ～을 심하게 했다 The child had a bad cough. / 아직 ～을 조금 한다 I still have a slight cough. / 그는 갑자기 연달아 ～이 나서 말을 할 수 없었다 He could not speak because of a fit of coughing. / 선생님은 ～으로 학생들을 조용하게 만들었다 The teacher coughed to silence his students.
◉ ～약 a cough medicine 〔syrup〕; a remedy 〔cure〕 for cough.

**기타**(其他) the others; the rest;《등등》 and others; et cetera (생략 etc.); and so forth; and the like; and what not. ⇨ 그외. ¶ ～ 다수… and many others / 우리는 사랑, 인생, 죽음과 ～ 문제에 대해 이야기 했다 We talked about love, life, death, and so forth 〔on〕. / 다섯명은 교실에서 공부하고 ～ 학생들은 밖에서 놀고 있었다 Five pupils were studying in the classroom while「the others 〔the other pupils, the rest〕 were playing outside. (★ the가 없는 other pupils는「다른 학생」이란 뜻. 또 the rest pupils 라는 표현은 쓰지 않음).

**기타** a guitar. ¶ ～를 치다 play 〔strum〕 (on) the guitar. ◉ ～연주가 a guitarist. 클래식～ a classical guitar.

**기탁**(寄託) deposition;〖법〗 bailment. ～하다 deposit《*a thing* with *a person*》; entrust《*a person* with *a thing*》; commit《*a thing*》 to the care《of *a person*》. ◉ ～금 trust money; money consigned. ～물 a deposit; a trust; a thing entrusted. ～자 a truster; a depositor;〖법〗 a bailor. ～증서 a deposit certificate.

**기탄**(忌憚) scruple(s); reserve. ¶ ～없는 frank; outspoken; candid; unreserved / ～없이 without reserve; frankly; candidly; boldly; outspokenly / ～없이 의견을 말하다 give *one's* frank opinion; speak out *one's* thought / ～없이 말하면 자네는 학자가 아니다「To be frank (with you) 〔Frankly speaking〕, you are not a scholar. / 이에 대해 자네의 ～없는 의견을 듣고 싶네 Let me hear your candid opinion about this.

**기통**(汽筒·氣筒)〖기계〗 a (gas, steam) cylinder. ¶ 6 ～ 자동차〔엔진〕 a six=cylinder(ed) motorcar 〔engine〕.

**기특하다**(奇特—) (be) admirable; commendable; laudable; praise-worthy. ¶ 기특한 행동 a commendable deed /

기특한 마음씨 a laudable intention / 기특하게도 in an admirable manner; what is praiseworthy…; admirably; like a good boy 〔girl〕/ 그의 정직함이 기특해서 in reward of his honesty / 그것 참 기특한 일이다 That is highly commendable. / 그는 기특하게도 열심히 공부한다 He studies hard like a good boy. / 불평 한마디 안하다니 정말 그녀는 기특하군 How admirable of her not to complain at all.

**기틀** the crux 《of *a matter*》; the key 〔pivotal〕 point; 《계기》 a (most appropriate) moment; an opportunity; a chance; 《토대·기초》 a base; a basis (*pl.* bases); a foundation. ¶ 성공의 ~을 마련하다 「lay the groundwork 〔pave the way〕 for *one's* success / 장래 생활의 ~을 다지다 establish the base for *one's* future life / 과거의 불행했던 대결의 시대를 민족 화합의 시대로 전환하는 ~을 다지다 lay a firm foundation for turning the unhappy past of confrontation into the era of national harmony.

**기펴다**(氣—) feel 〔be〕 relaxed; be relieved; feel at 「rest 〔ease〕; feel easy 《about》; keep 〔stay〕 loose 《미구어》; be carefree. ¶ 기를 못 펴다 feel ill at ease; feel constrained 〔oppressed〕 / 기펴고 살다 have 〔lead〕 a (happy and) carefree life / 이제 시험이 끝났으니 기펴도 된다 You may feel relaxed since the examination is over.

**기포**(氣泡) a 〔an air〕 bubble; a blowhole (주물의). ◉ ~유리 foam glass. ~콘크리트 aerated concrete.

**기포**(氣胞) 《물고기의》 a fish sound; a swimming bladder; 《식물의》 an air vesicle; a bladder. ◉ ~음 a vesicular murmur.

**기포제**(起泡劑) a foaming.

**기폭**(起爆) ignition. ◉ ~장치 a triggering device 《for nuclear blast》; a detonator. ~제 priming (powder); a detonator: 혁명의 ~제가 되다 [사물이 주어] trigger a revolution.

**기품**(氣品) nobility; grace; elegance; refinement; dignity. ¶ ~이 있는 dignified; graceful; elegant; refined / 그에겐 어딘지 모르게 ~이 있다 There is something noble and dignified about him. / 그녀에겐 ~이 없다 She has no elegance. *or* She is lacking in grace.

**기품**(氣稟) natural endowment; disposition; predisposition.

**기풍**(氣風) 《개인의》 character; (a) disposition; temper; 《단체의》 morale; tone; 《사회의》 ethos; 《정신》 spirit; 《특성》 traits. ¶ 국민의 ~ the traits 〔tone, spirit, ethos〕 of a nation / 진취적인 ~ an enterprising spirit / 그 지역의 보수적인 ~ the conservative traits of the locality / ~을 진작하다 arouse 〔enhance〕 the national spirit / 그 대학에는 아직 옛날의 ~과 전통이 좀 남아있다 The college retains some of its tone and tradition. / 나는 그 회사의 창조적인 ~이 마음에 든다 I like the creative spirit of the company.

**기피**(忌避) 《징병의》 evasion; shirking; 《법률상의》 a challenge. ~하다 evade; shirk; avoid; shun; challenge 《the judge》. ¶ 징병을 ~하다 evade 〔shirk〕 military service; 《구어》 dodge the draft / 책임을 ~하다 shirk *one's* responsibility / 심판부를 ~하다 challenge the judges 《of the court》 / 증인을 ~하다 except against a witness. ◉ ~자 an evader; a shirker. 병역~ an evasion of military service; draft dodging. 재판관~ challenge to judges.

**기필코**(期必—) 《꼭》 assuredly; surely; certainly (★ surely는 주관적·희망적 판단을, certainly는 객관적 증거나 사실을 근거로 한다는 뜻이 내포됨); 《틀림없이》 without fail; undoubtedly; 《무슨 일이 있어도》 by all means; at any cost; at all costs; whatever may happen; under 〔in〕 any circumstances. ¶ ~ 해야 할 일 a thing that has to be done; a must / 그는 ~ 성공할 것이다 He is sure 〔certain〕 to succeed. *or* He will surely succeed. *or* He will succeed without fail. / 나는 ~ 그것을 해 낼 것이다 I will carry it out at any cost 〔no matter what〕.

**기하**(幾何) 『수학』 geometry. ¶ ~학적(으로) geometrical(ly) / ~학적 모양의 벽지 wallpaper with a geometrical pattern 〔geometric design〕. ◉ ~공리 a geometrical axiom. ~평균 a geometric mean. ~학자 geometrician. 구면~학 spherical geometry.

**기하급수**(幾何級數) a geometrical series 〔progression〕. ¶ ~적으로 증가하다 《population》 increase in (a) geometric progression; increase geometrically.

**기하다**(忌—) 《싫어하다》 loathe; detest; abhor; dislike; 《피하다》 shun; avoid; 《금지하다》 taboo.

**기하다**(期—) ① 《날짜·기한 등을》 fix the date; set a term 〔time limit, deadline〕 《for》. ¶ 이 달 말을 기해 납부하다

pay 《*one's* tuition》 at the end of this month / 다음달 1일을 기해 우리 모임을 갖기로 했다 The date of our meeting is fixed for the first of next month.
② 《기약하다》 pledge 《*oneself* to *do*》; vow; 《약속하다》 promise. ¶ 둘은 재회를 기하고 헤어졌다 The two parted, pledging to meet again.
③ 《목표로 삼다》 aim at 《*something* to *do*》; have 《*a thing*》 as an object; 《결심하다》 determine; resolve. ¶ 만전을 ~ aim at perfection / 필승을 ~ resolve to win 《the contest》.

**기한**(飢寒) hunger and cold. ¶ ~에 떨다 suffer from hunger and cold / ~으로 죽다 die from exposure and starvation.

**기한**(期限) 《기간》 a term; a period (of time); 《마감》 a time limit; a deadline. ¶ 일정한 ~ 내에 within a definite 〔certain, fixed〕 period of time / ~부로 with a 《one-year》 time limit 〔deadline〕 / ~이 끝났을〔만료되었을〕 때 when the term expires 〔runs out〕; on 〔at〕 the expiration 〔expiry〕 《of the lease》; at 〔on〕 maturity / ~을 정하다 set 〔fix〕 a 「time limit 〔deadline〕 《for》; set 〔fix〕 a term 《to》 / ~을 연장하다 extend a 「time limit 〔deadline〕 / 너의 지불 ~은 내일이다 Your payment is due tomorrow. / 지불 ~을 2개월 연장했다 We have extended the term of payment by two month. / 이 어음은 ~이 지났다 This bill is overdue. / 이 일에는 완성 ~이 없다 There is no time limit for completing this job. / ~ 전에 이 일을 끝내도록 하자 Let's get this job done before the deadline. / 「리포트 제출 ~은 언제지」—「다음 달 말이야」 "When is the deadline for the report ?" —"It's at the end of next month." / 이 계약의 ~은 1년이다 The contract holds 〔is〕 good for one year. / 나는 이 아파트를 2년 ~으로 빌렸다 I rented this apartment for a period of two years. ◉ ~경과 어음〔수표〕 an overdue bill 〔check〕. ~만료 the expiration 〔termination〕 of a term: ~만료일 the due date. ~부 채용 temporary employment. ~연장 extension of a deadline. 예정~ the target date. 유효~ the term of validity.

**기함**(旗艦) a flagship.

**기합**(氣合) ① 《정신 집중》 concentration of spirit; 《기세·투지》 vigor of spirit; fight; 《지르는 소리》 a yell; a shout; a cry. ¶ ~을 넣다 《소리치다》 yell 〔shout〕 at 《*a person*》; 《독려하다》 spur 〔urge〕 on 《*a person*》 to *do;* encourage 《*a person*》 to *do* / ~과 함께 검을 내리치다 bring down *one's* sword with a yell / ~을 지르면서 상대에게 달겨들다 charge at the opponent with a cry.
② 《군·학교 등에서의 벌》 disciplinary punishment; reprimand. ¶ ~을 주다 discipline 〔chastise, punish〕 《on a group》. ◉ ~술 the art of hypnotizing by *one's* willpower.

**기항**(寄港) a call 〔stop〕 at a port. ~하다 call 〔stop, touch〕 《at》; put in 《at》; make a call 《at》. ¶ 배는 도중에 여기저기 ~했다 The vessel called at many ports on her route. / 그들은 유럽의 거의 모든 항구에 ~했다 They touched at every port in Europe. ◉ ~지 a port of call.

**기해**(己亥) 〚민속〛 the 36th binary term of the sexagenary cycle.

**기행**(奇行) eccentric conduct 〔behavior〕; an eccentricity. ¶ 그는 여러가지 ~으로 유명하다 He is well-known for his eccentricities.

**기행**(紀行) an account of a trip 〔journey〕; a traveler's journal; a record of *one's* travels. ◉ ~문 an account of *one's* journey 《in America》; a travel piece. ~작가 a travel writer.

**기형**(畸形·奇型) (a) malformation; (a) deformity. ¶ ~적(인) malformed; deformed; abnormal / 선천성 ~ a congenital malformation. ◉ ~아 a deformed 〔malformed〕 child. ~족(足) a club foot.

**기호**(記號) a sign; a mark; a symbol. ¶ 발음 ~ a phonetic sign / 음 ~〚음악〛 a clef / 화학~ a chemical symbol / ~를 달다 mark / 플러스 ~를 하다 mark with a plus sign / 언어는 생각을 나타내는 ~이다 Words are the signs of ideas. ◉ ~논리학 mathematical 〔symbolic〕 logic. ~론 semiotics. ~화 symbolization. ~학 semiology.

**기호**(嗜好) (a) taste; (a) liking 《for》; a fancy 《to, for》; *one's* likes and dislikes; a preference 《for》. ~하다 have a taste 〔liking, fancy〕 《for》; like. ¶ ~에 따라 according to *one's* liking 〔preference〕 / ~에 맞다 be to *one's* taste 〔liking〕; suit *one's* taste / ~는 사람마다 다르다 Tastes differ. / 그것은 그녀 ~에 가장 잘 맞는다 That suits her taste best. / 이 포도주는 내 ~에 안 맞는다 This wine is not to my taste 〔liking〕. ◉ ~품 《식품》 *one's* favorite food; 《술·커피 따위》 a table luxury; luxury grocery items; 《사치성의》 an article of luxury.

**기혼**(旣婚) ¶ ~의 married. ◉ ~자 a married person: 그는 ~자다 He is already married.

**기화**(奇貨) ① 《진품》 a rare treasure; a rarity; a curiosity. ② 《좋은 기회》 a rare 〔good〕 opportunity. ¶ …을 ~로 삼아 taking advantage 《of》; availing *oneself* 《of》 / …을 ~로 삼다 take 〔make〕 advantage of…; presume on / 상대가 약한 것을 ~로 삼다 take (mean) advantage of a weaker opponent / 사람이 좋은 것을 ~로 삼다 presume on 《*a person's*》 good nature / 우리의 무지를 ~로 삼아 그는 싸구려 물건을 우리에게 팔았다 Taking advantage of our ignorance, he palmed inferior goods off on us.

**기화**(氣化) evaporation; vaporization; gasification. ~하다 evaporate; vaporize; gasify. ◉ ~기 a vaporizer; an evaporator; 《내연기관의》 a carburetor. ~열 〖물리〗 evaporation heat; heat of vaporization. ~점 〖물리〗 the evaporation point. ~폭탄 a fuel-air explosive bomb.

**기회**(機會) an opportunity; a chance; an occasion (우발적인).

> 용법 **opportunity** 야심·목적 따위를 이루는 데 알맞은 기회. **chance** 우연히 운좋게 만난 기회로서, 「호기·시기」란 뜻을 함유. **occasion** 어떤 계기 따위를 만드는 데 시기 적절한 기회.

¶ 교육〔취업〕의 ~ an opportunity for education 〔employment〕; an education 〔a job〕 opportunity / 절호의 ~ a golden opportunity / 다시없는 ~ a rare opportunity / 일생에 한 번 있는 ~ the chance of lifetime / 천재일우의 ~ one in a thousand chances / ~있을 때마다 at every opportunity; whenever the opportunity arises 〔presents itself〕 / 다음 ~로 돌리다 reserve it for another occasion.

기회가: ~가 있으면 when occasion comes; if occasion offers; (if ) given a chance / ~가 오는 대로 at any opportunity available; as soon as opportunity offers / ~가 있다〔생기다〕 have 〔get〕 a chance 〔an opportunity〕 / ~가 없다 have no chance 〔opportunity〕 《to see her》 / ~가 있는 대로 at the first 〔earliest〕 opportunity; on the first occasion.

기회에: 이 ~에 on this occasion / 가능한한 빠른 ~에 on the first possible occasion / 다른〔다음〕 ~에 《let's make it》 some other time; on another occasion; some time later.

기회를: ~를 기다리다〔노리다〕 wait 〔watch for〕 a 〔*one's*〕 chance 《to *do*》 / ~를 얻다 get a chance; find 〔have〕 an opportunity / ~를 만들다〔놓치다〕 make 〔miss, lose〕 a chance 〔an opportunity〕 / ~를 잡다 seize 〔catch〕 an opportunity 〔occasion〕 / ~를 주다 afford 〔give, allow〕 an opportunity 《of》 / ~를 이용하다 take advantage 〔avail *oneself*〕 of an opportunity; make use of an opportunity / 비용이 싸게 드는 패키지 투어의 ~를 놓칠세라 달려들다 jump at the chance of a cheap package tour.

¶ 지금이 절호의 ~다 Now is 「the 〔your, my, our〕 time 《to *do*》. / 한 번 놓친 ~는 다시 오지 않는다 An opportunity once lost is lost forever. / ~가 있으면 또 오겠습니다 When I have chance I'll come here again. / 그녀와 이야기할 ~가 많지 않다 I don't have many occasions to talk to her. / 이 건은 다음 ~에 해결하도록 합시다 We shall leave the solution of this problem until the next time. / 이 ~를 빌려 여러분께 감사의 말씀을 드리고자 합니다 I'd like to take this opportunity 〔occasion〕 to thank you all 《for the kindness you showed me during my stay in New York》. / 이것은 영어 회화를 연습할 좋은 ~이다 This is a good chance for me to practice speaking English. / 내게 이런 ~는 두 번 다시 오지 않을 것이다 No better chance 〔opportunity〕 will ever come to me. *or* I'll never have such a golden opportunity again. / 낸시를 만날 ~가 있으면 내 안부를 전해다오 Say hello to Nancy for me if you have 〔get〕 a chance to see her. / 「여기 자주 오니」—「~ 있을 때마다 와」 "Do you come here often?"—"Every chance I get."

◉ ~균등 equality of opportunity; equal opportunity: ~균등주의 the principle of equal opportunity. ~주의 opportunism; timeserving: ~주의자 an opportunist.

**기획**(企劃) planning; (making) a plan; a project. ~하다 make 〔form〕 a plan; draw up a project; plan. ¶ ~중에 있다 be in the planning stage / ~을 세

우다 lay 〔work out〕 a plan 〔scheme〕. ◉ ～과 the planning section. ～관리실 the Planning and Management Office: ～관리실장 director for planning and management. ～력 planning ability. ～부 a planning department. ～성 the ability to make plans. ～예산처 the Ministry of Planning and Budget. ～위원회 a planning committee. ～조정실 the Office of Planning and Coordination.

**기후**(氣候) climate; weather (날씨); a season (계절).

> **용법** **climate** 특정 지역의 장기간에 걸친 평균적 기후 : an antarctic climate (남극의 기후). **weather** 특정의 때·장소에 따라 일어나는 하늘의 변동 상태 즉 날씨를 뜻하는 말, 단순히 날씨만을 나타낼 때는 the를 붙이나 형용사를 수반할 때는 관사가 붙지 않는다: changeable summer weather (자주 변하는 여름의 기후). **season** 「계절」을 뜻하는 말: at all seasons (4계절을 통해서).

¶ 온화한〔해양성, 대륙성〕 ～ a mild 〔an oceanic, a continental〕 climate / 불순한 ～ unseasonable weather / 열대성 ～ a tropical climate / 변덕스러운 ～ unpredictable weather / ～의 변화 a climatic change / 해양성 ～의 영향을 받다 be subject to oceanic climate / 금년은 ～가 불순해서 장마철에도 가물었다 We had unseasonably dry weather during the rainy season this year. / 이곳의 ～는 온화해서 건강에 좋다 The climate here is mild and healthy. / 그곳은 ～의 변화가 심하다 The place is subject to extreme 〔violent〕 climate change. ◉ ～요법 climate treatment. ～조건 climatic conditions. ～학 climatology. ～학자 a climatologist.

**기휘**(忌諱) avoiding things; superstitious avoidance. ～하다 avoid; shun.

**기흉요법**(氣胸療法) 〖의학〗 a pneumothorax 〔chest-airing〕 treatment.

**긴급**(緊急) urgency; emergency. ～하다 (be) urgent; pressing; crying; imminent. ¶ ～한 수요〔필요〕 an urgent 〔a pressing, a crying《구어》〕 need 《for》/ 의회에 ～ 상정하다 lay an urgent bill before the Assembly / ～ 시에는 나에게 전화를 주십시오 Call me up in an emergency. / 그것은 매우 ～을 요하는 사항이다 It is a matter of great urgency. / 그녀는 ～한 용무로 홍콩에 날아갔다 She flew to Hongkong on urgent 〔pressing〕 business. / 나는 ～히 돈이 필요하다 I'm in urgent need of money. *or* I need money very badly. ◉ ～관세 emergency tariff. ～구속 (an) arrest without (a) warrant: ～구속되다 be arrested on the spot. ～대통령령 an emergency presidential decree. ～동의 an emergency resolution; an urgent motion: ～동의하다 put an urgent motion. ～명령 an emergency order. ～문제 a pressing problem. ～발진〔출격〕《비행기의》 scrambling; a scramble. ～사태 a state of emergency: ～사태를 선언하다 declare 〔proclaim〕 a state of emergency. ～수입제한조치 an emergency import relief 《against》; a safeguard 〔curb〕 on imports. ～용 직통 전화(선) the hot line. ～조정 an emergency adjustment. ～조치〔대책〕《take, issue》 emergency measures; 《devise》 urgent countermeasures. ～피난 emergency evacuation: 홍수 위험이 닥쳐 주민들은 학교로 ～ 피난했다 The residents took refuge in the school as the danger of flooding was imminent. ～회의 《hold》 an urgent 〔emergency〕 conference.

**긴대답**(一對答) a drawled reply. ～하다 make a drawled 〔long-drawn〕 reply.

**긴말** a long (boring) talk; a yarn. ～하다 give 〔tell〕 a long boring 〔tedious〕 talk; spin a yarn. ¶ ～하지 않겠다 I'll not bother you with a long talk. *or* I shall not enlarge upon the subject.

**긴맛** 〖조개류〗 a razor shell 〔clam〕.

**긴밀**(緊密) ～하다 (be) close; intimate. ¶ ～히 협력하여 in close cooperation 《with》/ ～한 연락을 취하고 있다 be in close touch 〔contact〕 《with》/ 두 사람은 서로 ～한 관계에 있다 They have a close connection with each other. / 그들은 ～한 협력〔제휴〕하에 일했다 They worked in close cooperation.

**긴박**(緊迫) tension; strain. ～하다 (be) tense; acute; strained. ¶ ～한 국제 관계 a tense international relationship / ～한 정세〔공기〕 a tense 〔an acute〕 situation 〔atmosphere〕/ ～해지다 grow strained; become acute 〔tense〕/ 양국 관계는 영토 문제로 ～해졌다 Relations between the two nations have become 「very tense 〔troubled〕 because of territorial problems. / ～한 국제 관계가 좀 완화되었다 International tension has become less acute.

**긴병**(一病) a protracted 〔lengthy〕 disease; a lingering illness. ¶ ～을 앓다 suffer from a long [chronic] illness; be ill in bed for a long time / ～에 효자 없다《속담》Enthusiasm is short-lived. *or* A protracted illness wears out filial devotion.

**긴사설**(一辭說) a 「long [tedious] speech; a long-winded talk. ¶ ～을 늘어놓다 give a long tedious talk《to》.

**긴요**(緊要) ～하다 (be) vital; important; essential《to》; indispensable《to》; be of vital importance. ¶ ～도를 더하다 gain urgency / 이 계획을 이루기 위해서는 우리들의 협력이 ～하다 Our cooperation is vital to the success of the scheme.

**긴장**(緊張) strain; tension; tenseness. ～하다 get [become] tense; be strained; get nervous; be on edge.

> (용법) **strain** 심신에 대한 중압감이나 과로 등에 의한 긴장 상태. **tension** 정신적인 긴장. 불안감, 대인 관계, 정세 따위로 인한 긴장 상태도 뜻함. 후자의 뜻일 때는 종종 복수형을 씀.

¶ ～된[한] strained; tense / ～된 분위기 a tense atmosphere / 국제간의 ～ international tension / 두 나라 사이의 ～ the tension(s) [strained relations] between the two countries / ～을 완화하다 relieve [ease] the tension《of》/ ～이 풀려 있다 lack seriousness / 극도의 ～속에서 살다 live [make a living] under extreme tension / 근육을 ～시키다 tense *one's* muscles / 음악을 들으면 ～이 풀린다 Music 「makes me relax [relieves me]. / 그의 농담으로 실내의 ～이 풀렸다 His joke eased [relieved] the tension in the room. / 증인은 매우 ～되어 있었다 The witness was 「very nervous [under extreme tension]. / 노사간의 ～이 고조되고 있다 Tension is 「building up [mounting] between labor and management. / 그녀는 ～된 얼굴로 상사의 이야기를 듣고 있었다 She was listening to his superior with a tense look. / 회의는 ～된 분위기였다 There was a tense atmosphere in the meeting. / 대일 관계는 매우 ～되어 있었다 Relation with Japan were very strained. / 마사지는 근육의 ～을 푸는데 도움이 된다 Massage helps relieve the tension in *one's* muscles. ◉ ～감: 그 도시 어디에나 ～감이 감돌았다 A tense atmosphere could be felt everywhere in the town. ～도 the level of tension. ～력 tensible force. ～병 〖의학〗 catatonia. ～상태 a state of tension: ～ 상태로《live》in strain.

**긴장완화**(緊張緩和) détente. ¶ 국제간의 ～ détente; the easing [relief] of international tensions / 한반도의 ～ the easing of tensions on the Korean Peninsula / 그는 세계의 ～를 위해 정상회담을 제안했다 He suggested a summit meeting for the alleviation of world tension.

**긴지름** 〖수학〗 the major axis [diameter].

**긴축**(緊縮) (strict) economy; austerity; 《삭감》curtailment; retrenchment; 《통화의》deflation. ～하다 economize; 《삭감하다》cut down; curtail; retrench. ¶ 재정의 ～ retrenchment in finance. ◉ ～경영 belt-tightening management. ～계획 an austerity plan. ～생활 an austere life: ～생활을 하다 lead an austere life. ～예산 an austerity [a retrenchment] budget: ～예산을 짜다 formulate an austerity budget. ～재정 a reduced budget: 금년 말까지는 ～재정으로 버텨나가자 Let's tighten our purse strings until the end of this year. ～정책《adopt》a retrenchment [curtailment] policy; a belt-tightening policy; a policy of austerity.

**긴치마** a maxi(skirt)《미》; a long skirt.

**긴팔원숭이** 〖동물〗 a long-armed ape; a gibbon.

**긴하다**(緊—) ① 《긴요하다》(be) important; vital; essential《to》; indispensable《to》; 《필요하다》(be) necessary《to》; useful; 《간절하다》(be) earnest; ardent. ¶ 긴한 때《in》time [hour] of need / 긴한 물건 a useful object (to have around) / 긴한 사람 an indispensable person / 긴한 일 the most important [vital] matter / 긴한 청 an earnest entreaty / 돈을 빌려주어 긴하게 썼다 Thank you for the money you lent me—it was a great help to me. / 긴한 부탁이 있어 왔네 I have come with an ardent [earnest] favor to ask of you. / 긴한 때 친구가 참된 친구이다《속담》A friend in need is a friend indeed. ② 《긴밀하다》(be) close《to》; be on good [close] terms《with》. ¶ 나는 저 유명한 소설가와 긴한 사이이다 I am very close to that famous novelist.

**긷다** draw; pump. ¶ 두레박으로 우물에서 물을 ～ draw water from a well with a bucket.

**길**[1] ① 《도로》 a way; a road; a street (거리); an avenue (가로수길); 《간선도

로》 a highway; 《소로》 a path; a lane; a pass; 《통로》 a passage. ¶ 지름길 a shorter way; a short cut / 산길 a mountain pass / 시골길 a country lane / 에움길 a roundabout way / 길을 잃다 lose *one's* way; get lost 《in the woods》 / 길을 묻다 ask 《*a person*》 *one's* 〔the〕 way 《to the station》; ask 《*a person*》「for direction 〔how to get〕 《to》 / 길을 가르쳐 주다 tell 《*a person*》 the way 《to》; direct 《*a person*》 《to a place》; show 《*a person*》 the way 《to》 / (남의) 길을 막다 stand in 《*a person's*》 way; bar the way; block 《*a person's*》 passage / 길이 막히다 the road is blocked / 길을 비켜주다〔양보하다〕 make way 《for》; give way 《to》 / 길을 잘못 들다 be on 〔take, go〕 the wrong way / 길을 만들다 build a road / 새로운 길을 내다 make 〔cut (out)〕 a road 〔way〕 through 《forest》 / (장애물을) 길에서 치우다 clear the way 《for》; keep the passage open / 시청으로 가는 길을 가르쳐 주십시오 Please tell me the way to the City Hall. / 이 길을 곧장 가시오 Go straight on along this street. / 이 길로 가면 그 호텔이 나옵니다 This road leads 〔goes〕 to the hotel. / 아무래도 길을 잘못 든 것 같다 I seem to have taken the wrong way. / 동물원에 가려는 데 이 길이 맞습니까 Is this the right way to the zoo? / 길을 묻지 않고도 그녀의 집을 쉽게 찾을 수 있었다 I was able to find her house easily without asking the way. / 길을 묻고 물어서 여기까지 왔다 I got here inquiring along the way. / 길은 눈이 녹아서 질척거렸다 The road was slushy with melting snow. / 학교에서 오는 길에 낸시를 만났다 I ran into Nancy on my way (home) from school. / 학교에 가는 길에 우체국이 있다 There is a post office on the road I take to school. / 길을 비키시오 Get out of my way. / 그는 파멸의 길을 걷고 있었다 He was on the way 〔road〕 to ruin.

② 《가야 할》 a way; journey; 《거리》 distance. ¶ 하룻길 a day's distance / 길을 떠나다 start 〔set out〕 on a journey / 길을 재촉하다 make the best of *one's* way; hurry along 〔on〕 *one's* way / 40킬로미터가 되는 길을 가다 cover 〔go, walk〕 a distance of 40 kilometers / 이 문제 해결의 길은 아직도 멀다 There is still a long way to go toward solution of this problem.

③ 《진로》 a course; a way; 《경로》 a route; a channel. ¶ 성공으로 가는 길 the way 〔road〕 to success / 취해야 할 길 the course「to take 〔to be taken〕; the course「to follow 〔to be followed〕 / 성공과 번영에 이르는 길 a road 〔an avenue〕 to success and prosperity / 산정에 이르는 새로운 길 a new route to the top of the mountain / 대화〔통신〕의 길을 열어 놓다 keep the channels of dialogue 〔communication〕 / 선인의 길을 따르다 follow in a forerunner's path / 후진을 위해 길을 열어 주다 make way for younger generation / 길을 잘못 선택하다 《직업의》 make the wrong choice of *one's* job; 《판단을》 make the wrong decision / 취해야 할 다른 길이 없었다 I had 〔There was〕 no other way 〔choice〕 about it. / 그 길이 취해야 할 바른 길이다 That's the proper course to take.

④ 《수단》 a means; 《방법》 a way. ¶ 생활의 길 a means of living / 학자가 되는 길은 열심히 공부하는 것 이외는 없다 The only way to become a scholar is to study with all your might.

⑤ 《올바른 길》 a way 《of behaving, of life》; a path (of duty); a duty; 《도의》 a moral principle 〔doctrine〕; 《가르침》 teachings; 《진실》 truth; the true way; 《구어》 the straight and narrow. ¶ 세속의 길 the way(s) of the world / 사람의 길 *one's* path of duty / 공맹(孔孟)의 길 the teachings of Confucius and Mencius / (옳은) 길에서 벗어나다 stray from the path of virtue 〔righteousness, duty〕 / 옳은 길을 찾다 seek after truth / 길을 잘못 들게 하다 lead 《*a person*》 astray / 스님은 우리에게 사람의 바른 길을 설교하셨다 The Buddhist priest preached the right way of life to us.

⑥ 《전문분야·영역》 a line (of business); a profession; a speciality. ¶ 그는 그 길의 전문가이다 He is an expert in the line.

**길**[2] ⇨ 길들다, 길들이다.

**길**[3] 《품질·등급》 a grade; a class. ¶ 상길 the best quality; top grade 〔first-class, first-rate〕 merchandise / 윗길 a superior 〔choice〕 product; a better-grade article / 아랫길 an inferior article; an article of lower grade / 그 물건은 윗길〔아랫길〕이다 The goods are of good 〔inferior〕 quality.

**길**[4] 《책의 질(帙)》 a set of volumes. ¶ 논어 한 길 a set of the (Confucian) Analects.

**길**[5] 《옷의》 the large section(s) of cloth forming the body of a Korean coat or jacket.

**길**[6] ① 《길이 단위》 a *gil;* a measure of length; either 10 or 8 *ja* (=11′9″ or 9′5″). ② 《사람의 키》 the height of a man; 《깊이》 a fathom (= about 6 *ja*). ¶ 열 길 되는 나무 a tree 60 *ja* high / 다섯 길 되는 물 water 5 fathoms deep / 열 길 물 속은 알아도 한 길 사람 속은 모른다 《속담》 It is hard to fathom the real minds and intentions of men.

**길가** 《at, by, on》 the roadside; 《by, on》 the wayside. ¶ ~의 wayside; roadside / ~에 버려진 자전거 a bicycle discarded at the roadside / 그들은 ~에 서서 이야기를 하고 있었다 They stood chatting by the roadside.

**길거리** a road; a (downtown) street; a thoroughfare; an avenue. ¶ ~를 쏘다니다 roam about the streets / ~에 가게를 내다 open a store on a (downtown) street / ~에서 노는 것은 위험하다 It is dangerous to play in 〔on 《영》〕 the street. / 이 창문은 ~에 면해 있다 This window faces the street.

**길길이** ① 《높이 쌓인 꼴》 《pile up》 high; to a great height. ¶ 책이 ~ 쌓여 있다 Books are piled up high. / 나무가 ~ 자라다 Trees are growing tall. ② 《성이 나서 높이 뛰는 모양》 ¶ 성이 나서 ~ 뛰다 get hopping mad; 《구어》 hit the ceiling.

**길꾼** a skilled gambler.

**길나다** 《버릇·습관이 되다》 get used to 《*a thing, doing*》; grow 〔be〕 accustomed to 《*a thing, doing*》; 《사용해서 길이 들다》 be broken in; be well-used; 《윤이 나다》 become glossy 〔shinny〕. ¶ 더위에 ~ get 〔become〕 used 〔accustomed〕 to the heat 《of Seoul》 / 새로운 환경에 ~ be acclimated to *one's* new environment / 이 구두는 길나는 데 꽤 시간이 걸렸다 It took quite some time before these shoes were broken in.

**길년**(吉年) an auspicious year.

**길눈** 《방향감각》 *one's* sense of direction. ¶ ~이 밝다〔어둡다〕 have a good 〔poor〕 sense of direction.

**길다** ① 《공간적》 (be) long. ¶ 긴 막대 a long pole / 길게 하다 make 《*a thing*》 longer; lengthen 《a skirt》 / 다리를 길게 뻗다 stretch out *one's* legs at full length / 소매가 2인치 ~ The sleeves are two inches too long. / 그 기사는 좀 ~ The articles are a bit too lengthy. / 그녀는 머리가 ~ She has long hair. / 길고 짧은 것은 대봐야 안다 《속담》 A real test will prove who is stronger 〔better〕 at doing something.
② 《시간적》 (be) long; lengthy. ¶ 긴 세월 long years / 긴 장마 a long rainy season / 길어지다 get 〔become, grow〕 longer; be lengthened / 긴 안목으로 보다 take the long(-term) 〔a long-range〕 view 《of》 / 긴 세월이 걸리다 It takes a long time 《to master English》. / 그는 앞날이 길지 못하다 He will not last long. *or* His days are numbered. / 인생은 짧고 예술은 ~ Life is short, art is long. / 사람은 길게 두고 봐야 안다 It takes a long time to understand a person. / 얘기가 길어졌다 Our talk took time. / 그렇게 하루가 긴 적은 없었다 I have never put in such a long day in my life. / 길어야 3일 걸린다 It will take three days at (the) longest. / 밤이 조금씩 길어진다 The nights grow longer little by little.

**길동무** a fellow traveler; a traveling 〔road〕 companion. ~하다 go 〔travel〕 with 《*a person*》 as a companion; keep 《*a person*》 company. ¶ ~가 되다 (happen to) travel together 《with》; fall into company 《with》.

**길둥글다** (be) long and round 《like a log》.

**길드** a guild. ◉ ~사회주의 guild socialism. ~상인 a guild merchant.

**길들다** ① 《윤나다》 get 〔take, show〕 a polish 〔shine, gloss, luster〕; get glossy 〔lustrous〕. ¶ 노상 닦아서 마루가 길들었다 The floor has a shine from constant polishing. ② 《동물이》 become 〔grow〕 tame; become 〔get〕 domesticated; get housebroken 〔trained〕. ¶ 길든 고양이 a tame 〔housebroken〕 cat / 길들지 않은 undomesticated; untamed; unbroken; wild / 길들지 않은 새 a wild bird. ③ 《익숙해지다》 become 〔get〕 used 〔accustomed〕 to; get familiar with; get inured 《to hardships》; grow experienced 《in teaching》; become skillful 〔good〕 at. ¶ 5년 이상이나 길든 공구 the tools *one* has become used to over five years / 길든 펜을 잃었다 I have lost the pen familiar to me.

**길들이다** ① 《윤나게》 give a polish 〔shine, gloss, luster〕 to. ¶ 가구를 문질러 ~ give a polish to furniture by rubbing it. ② 《동물을》 tame; domesticate; train; break (in); housebreak. ¶ 야수를 길들이는 사람 a trainer of wild animals / 원숭이를 ~ domesticate

〔train〕 a monkey / 말을 ～ break (in) a horse. ③《익숙해지게》 make 《*a person*》 used 〔accustomed〕 to; inure; make 《*a person*》 skillful 〔good〕 at; acclimate. ¶ 상부 명령에 복종하도록 길들여진 국민 a people accustomed 〔conditioned〕 to accepting orders from above / 몸을 추위에 ～ accustom 〔inure〕 *oneself* to the cold.

**길라잡이** a guide.

**길례**(吉禮) 《경사스런 예식》 a happy ceremony; an auspicious 〔congratulatory〕 ceremony.

**길로틴** a guillotine. ⇨ 단두대.

**길리다** 《남에게》 be brought up; be reared 〔raised, nursed, fostered〕; be cultivated (식물). ⇨ 기르다. ¶ 큰어머니 손에 ～ be brought up by an aunt / 유모 손에 ～ be fed by a wet nurse.

**길마** a packsaddle. ～ 지우다〔짓다〕 put a packsaddle on; fix a packsaddle; saddle up. ¶ 두～보기를 하다 《기회주의적 태도》 wait and see; sit on the fence; see how the wind blows.
◉ ～상처 saddle burn(s).

**길모퉁이** 《at, on》 a street corner.

**길목** ①《길모퉁이》 a corner (at a junction of roads); a street corner; a turn; a turning. ¶ ～에 있는 가게 a corner store / ～을 돌아서 셋째집 the third house round the corner / ～에 가게를 내다 open a shop on a street corner / ～을 돌다 turn 〔go around〕 the corner (of a street) / 모든 ～은 기계화 부대가 봉쇄하고 있다 All the street corners are blocked by the mechanized unit. ②《중요한 어귀》 an important 〔a key〕 position (on the road); the main 〔a strategic〕 point. ¶ ～을 지키다 fortify the points of strategic importance / ～에 군인들이 배치되었다 Soldiers were posted at important places. 「good omen.

**길몽**(吉夢) a lucky dream; a dream of

**길바닥** the roadbed; the road surface. ¶ ～에 쓰러지다 fall down on the road.

**길벗** a fellow traveler. ⇨ 길동무.

**길보**(吉報) good news; glad tidings. ¶ 너에게 ～를 가져왔다 I have some (very) good news for you.

**길사**(吉事) an auspicious event; 《혼례》 a wedding (ceremony).

**길상**(吉相) 《좋은 상》 a lucky face; a lucky physiognomy. 「auspices.

**길상**(吉祥) a lucky 〔good〕 omen; good

**길섶** the edge of a road; the roadside.

**길손** a traveler; a wayfarer.

**길쌈** weaving 《by hand》. ～하다 make cloth; (hand-)weave; weave by hand.

**길안내**(—案內) showing the way; guidance of the road; 《사람》 a guide. ～하다 show 《*a person*》 the way 《to》; guide 〔direct〕 《*a person* to *a place*》; act as a guide. 「(good) luck.

**길운**(吉運) (a stroke of) good fortune;

**길이**[1] 《긴 정도》 length. ¶ 방의 ～ the length of a room / 3백 미터 ～의 다리 a bridge 300 meters long / 각각 석자 ～로 자르다 cut 《*a thing*》 down to three *cha* each / ～가 얼마입니까 How long is it? *or* What is its length? / ～가 다섯 자입니다 It is five *cha* long. / ～가 모두 비슷비슷하다 They are all about the same length.

**길이**[2] 《오래도록》 long; for a long time; 《영원히》 forever (and ever); for good (and all). ¶ ～길이 for a long long time / ～ 보존하다 preserve 〔cherish〕 《*a thing*》 for good / 이름을 ～ 남기다 immortalize *one's* fame 〔name〕.

**길일**(吉日) a lucky 〔a propitious, an auspicious〕 day. ¶ ～을 택하다 choose a lucky day.

**길잡이** a guidepost; a signpost; a fingerpost; a waypost; 《초심자》 a guide 《to》; a handbook. ¶ 산의 갈림길에 있는 ～ the signpost at the fork in the mountain path / 영문학의 ～ a guide to English literature / ～가 되다 serve as a guide to 《the beginners》/ 성서는 나의 인생의 ～였다 The Bible was my guide in life.

**길조**(吉兆) a good 〔lucky〕 omen; a propitious 〔favorable〕 sign. ¶ ～가 보이다 be of good omen; augur well 《for》. 「creepers.

**길짐승** a creeping animal; a creeper;

**길쭉길쭉** ～하다 (be) severally longish; be all rather long; (such that) each is on the long side. ¶ 대를 ～ 자르다 cut a piece of bamboo in long sections.

**길쭉스름하다** (be) appropriately longish; be nicely on the long side.

**길쭉이** somewhat long. ¶ 좀 ～ 썰다 cut 《a bamboo》 a little longer / 그것을 조금 ～ 만들어 주시오 Please make it a little longer.

**길쭉하다** (be) longish; somewhat long; rather long; be on the long side. ¶ 길쭉한 지팡이 a longish stick / 얼굴이 ～ have a longish face.

**길쯔막하다** be about longish enough;

be quite longish (enough).

**길쯤하다** (be) quite longish; be quite on the long side.

**길차다** 《우거지다》 [장소가 주어] be overgrown [densely covered] 《with》; [초목이 주어] be rank [rampant]; 《가늘고 길다》 slender; slim.

**길품** 《남의 갈 길을 대신 가고 삯을 받는 일》 running [going on] errand 《for *a person*》 to receive a reward [tip]. ¶ ～을 팔다 run [go on] errands for a reward [tip].

**길하다**(吉—) (be) lucky; fortunate; auspicious; propitious; good.

**길항**(拮抗) rivalry; contention; competition. ～하다 compete [vie, contend] 《with》. ◉ ～근 〖해부〗 an antagonist. ～작용 〖생물〗 antagonism.

**길흉**(吉凶) good and [or] bad luck; lights and shadows; ups and downs; fortune. ¶ ～을 점치다 tell 《*a person's*》 fortune.

**김**[1] 《해태》 laver; seaweed (★ seaweed는 본래 「해초」의 뜻이나, 일반적으로 「김」의 뜻으로 쓰임). ¶ 맛김 toasted and seasoned laver [seaweed] / 마른 김 dried laver [seaweed] / 김을 재다[굽다] season [toast] laver. ◉ 김밥 rice rolled in dried laver with ingredients in the center. 김양식 laver farming: 김양식을 하다 cultivate [grow] laver. 김양식장 a laver farm.

**김**[2] ① 《증기》 steam; vapor. ¶ ～이 나는 요리 a steaming dish / 김이 서린 거울 a steamy mirror / 김이 나다 steam; give off [send up] steam / 김이 무럭무럭 나다 be steaming hot / 김을 쐬다 expose 《*a thing*》 to steam; give 《*a thing*》 a good steaming / 창문에 김이 서려 있다 The window are fogged up. ② 《입·코의》 breath. ⇨입김·콧김. ¶ 냄새 나는 입김 bad [foul] breath. ③ 《맛》 taste; 《풍미》 flavor; savor; 《냄새》 (a) smell; (a) scent; an aroma. ⇨김빠지다. ¶ 뜨거운 커피의 구수한 김냄새 the aroma of hot coffee / 김새게 하는 사람[것] [비유적] a kill-joy; a wet blanket / 김이 새다 [비유적] lose [kill] *one's* interest 《in》; *one's* enthusiasm dies down; spoil *one's* fun [pleasure] / 이 위스키는 김이 빠져 있다 This whisky tastes insipid. / 「정말 그녀는 김새게 하는구나」하고 아이들은 투덜거렸다 "What a kill-joy she is!" the children grumbled.

**김**[3] 《기회·계기》 an occasion; an opportunity; a chance. ¶ …하는 김에 while *one* is at *it;* taking [availing *oneself* of] this opportunity / 여기 온 김에 on *one's* way here / 술김에 under the influence of alcohol / 홧김에 in a fit of anger [passion] / 물건 사러 가는 김에 편지를 부쳤다 I mailed the letter when I went shopping. / 청소하는 김에 내 방도 치워주겠느냐 Could you clean my room, while you are doing yours?

**김**[4] 〖농업〗 weeding. ¶ 김매다 weed 《a field》; remove weeds 《from a paddy field》 / 김매는 사람 a weeder / 김매는 기계 a weeder; a weeding fork.

**김빠지다** 《맥주 따위가》 go flat; 《차·커피 따위가》 lose *its* flavor [taste]; 《사물이》 go [get, become] stale [insipid, dull]. ¶ 김빠진 강의 a dull [flat] lecture / 김빠진 맥주 vapid [flat] beer / 김빠진 대화 an inanimate conversation; a wishy-washy talk / 김빠진 농담 a flat joke / 김빠진 대답을 하다 answer vaguely; make [give] an equivocal answer; do not respond definitely 《to a request》.

**김장** 《담근 것》 kimchi prepared for the winter; 《담그기》 kimchi-making [preparing kimchi] for the winter. ～하다 make [prepare] kimchi for the winter. ◉ ～감 vegetables for kimchi. ～거리 kimchi stuff; vegetables and seasoning materials for kimchi. ～독 a kimchi [pickle] jar [pot]. ～때, ～철 the kimchi-making season; the time for preparing kimchi for the winter. ～밭 field of kimchi makings; a truck farm for kimchi.

**김치** kimchi; a spicy pickled [fermented] vegetables [Korean cabbages, radishes, cucumbers, *etc.*] seasoned with garlic, red pepper, ginger, and sometimes fish that is the national dish of Korea. ¶ 익은[덜 익은, 신] ～ mellow [rare, sour] kimchi / ～를 담그다 prepare [make] kimchi / 무[배추, 오이] ～ radish [Korean cabbage, cucumber] kimchi / 보쌈～ wrapped [bundle] kimchi. ◉ ～찌개 kimchi stew; pork stew with kimchi. 김칫국 kimchi juice: 김칫국부터 마시다 [비유적] count *one's* chickens before they are hatched; sell the skin before *one* has killed the bear.

**깁** silk gauze; silk.

**깁다** patch; mend; stitch; darn. ¶ 기운 옷 patched clothes / 누덕누덕 기운 양말 socks darned over and over again; socks full of patches / 옷을 ~ patch up clothes / 신을 ~ mend *one's* shoes / 터진 데를 ~ stitch up a tear.

**깁스** [< *Gips* (G.)] a (plaster) cast. ¶ ~를 하다 wear a (plaster) cast.

**깃**[1] ① 《날개털》 feathers; plumes; [집합적] plumage. ¶ 새가 깃을 다듬다 birds preen their feathers; birds plume themselves / 깃이 빠지다 feathers come off; (birds) shed feathers / 깃을 갈다 molt / 깃털을 뽑다 pluck feathers 《from a fowl》/ 깃으로 장식하다 decorate with a feather / 닭이 깃을 곤두세웠다 The chicken ruffled up feathers. ② 《화살의》 a feather (of an arrow). ¶ 화살에 깃을 달다 feather an arrow.

**깃**[2] 《짚·마른풀》 litter; horse bedding. ¶ 깃을 깔다 litter 《a stall》 down; spread 《a sty》 with straw.

**깃**[3] 《부싯깃》 tinder; touchwood.

**깃**[4] ① 《옷의》 coat lapels; a coat collar. ¶ 깃을 달다 sew a collar on a coat / 깃을 세우다 turn *one's* collar up. ② 《이불깃》 the upper strip on the outside of a quilt.

**깃대**(旗—) a flagpole; a flagstaff.

**깃들다** ⇨ 깃들이다.

**깃들이다** 《새가》 nest; build 〔put up〕 a nest; roost; [비유적] lodge; dwell. ¶ 건전한 신체에 건전한 정신이 깃들인다 A sound mind (dwells) in a sound body.

**깃발**(旗—) ① 《기》 a flag; a banner; a pennant; 《기에 매단 긴 오리》 ribbons attached to the corners of a flag. ¶ ~을 흔들다 wave a flag / ~을 올리다 hoist 〔raise, lift, fly out〕 a flag / ~을 내리다 take down a flag / ~이 휘날리다 a banner is streaming 〔waving, fluttering〕 / ~이 바람에 펄럭이다 A flag is fluttering in the wind.
② 《구호》 a slogan; a motto. ¶ 민주주의의 ~을 내걸고 with "Democracy" as the slogan; under the slogan 〔watchword〕 of "Democracy".

**깃옷** a raw-cotton garment worn for the first three months of mourning *one's* parents.

**깃이불** a feather quilt.

**깃저고리** clothes with no collar.

**깃주다** (spread) litter. ⇨ 깃[2].

**깃털** feathers; plumes. ⇨ 깃[1].

**깃펜** a quill pen.

**깊다** ① 《물·산 따위가》 (be) deep. ¶ 한없이 깊은 bottomless; fathomless / 깊은 곳 a depth; a deep place / 깊은 동굴 〔구멍〕 a deep cave 〔hole〕 / 깊은 바다 the deep sea / 깊은 산 속 the depths of a mountain / 깊은 산골짜기 a deep valley / 빠질라 깊은 데 들어가지 마라 Keep within 〔in〕 your depth or you may drown. / 잔잔한 물이 ~ Still waters run deep. / 이 호수에선 이 곳이 가장 ~ The lake is deepest here.
② 《학문·뜻이》 (be) deep; profound. ¶ 깊은 학문 deep learning; profound erudition / 깊은 뜻 a deep 〔profound〕 meaning / 깊은 생각 a deep thought 〔idea〕 / 깊은 종교 사상 profound religious thought / 깊은 연구 profound studies / 그는 깊은 통찰력의 소유자이다 He is a man of deep insight. / 그는 한국의 고전문학에 조예가 ~ He has a profound 〔deep〕 knowledge of Korean classical literature.
③ 《잠이》 (be) deep; heavy; sound. ¶ 깊은 잠 a deep 〔heavy, sound〕 sleep / 깊은 잠이 들다 fall into a deep 〔sound〕 sleep.
④ 《밤이》 (be) late. ¶ 깊은 밤 midnight; the dead of night / 밤이 깊어지다 grow late; be getting far into the night.
⑤ 《계절이》 (be) far advanced. ¶ 가을이 깊어 가고 있다 Autumn is getting far advanced 〔well on〕.
⑥ 《정분이》 (be) intimate; close; familiar (★ 이성간에 단지 친구인 경우는 intimate 대신 close를 쓰는 것이 좋음). ¶ 깊은 우정 close 〔deep〕 friendship / 깊은 관계 a close connection 〔relation〕 / 남녀간의 깊은 사이 an intimate relationship / 그녀와 너무 깊이 교제하지 않는 것이 좋겠다 If I were you, I wouldn't have too much to do with her. / 두 사람은 깊은 사이였다 The two were deeply in love with each other. *or* They were far more than mere friends.
⑦ 《상처가》 (be) serious. ¶ 깊은 상처 a severe 〔bad〕 wound; a serious 〔mortal〕 wound; a gash / 깊은 상처를 입다 sustain 〔receive〕 a severe wound; be mortally wounded.
⑧ 《정도를 나타내는 관용적 표현》 (be) deep; profound. ¶ 깊은 슬픔 〔애정〕 deep sorrow 〔affection〕 / 깊은 흥미 a deep interest / 깊은 감명을 주다 make a profound impression 《on》/ 깊은 사색에 잠기다 be deep in thought / 그들은 백인에 대해 깊은 증오심을 갖고 있었다 They had a deep-seated hatred for the whites.

**깊드리** a low-set ricefield.

**깊숙이** deep; far. ¶ 골짜기 ~ 들어앉은 집 a house set deep in a valley / 장 속에 ~ 넣다 put deep into a chest / 모자를 ~ 눌러쓰다 pull 〔draw down, slouch〕 *one's* hat over *one's* eyes; jam *one's* hat on / 구석에 ~ 들어앉다 take a seat far in the corner / 그의 집은 길에서 ~ 들어간 곳에 있다 His house stands a far back from the road.

**깊숙하다** (be) deep; retired; recessed; secluded; be set in; be set back. ¶ 깊숙한 시골 a secluded village / 깊숙한 곳 a recess; a secluded place; a nook / 숲 속의 가장 깊숙한 곳 the most secluded part of a forest / 빌딩 내의 가장 깊숙한 방 the innermost room of the building.

**깊어지다** 《깊이가》 deepen; become 〔get〕 deeper; 《때가》 be advanced; be well on; ripen; 《관계가》 grow intimate 《with》; become deeper 〔closer〕; 《강해지다》 become intense 〔strong〕. ¶ 밤이 깊어질 때까지 far into the night; into the depth of night / 그녀와의 사이가 ~ become deeply in love with her / 가을은 이제 깊어졌다 Autumn is far advanced now. / 그들의 사랑은 날이 갈수록 깊어졌다 Their love deepened day by day.

**깊이** ① [명사적] depth. ¶ 애정〔연못〕의 ~ the depth of affection 〔a pond〕/ ~가 다섯자다 be five *cha* deep; be five *cha* in depth / 발목까지 오는 ~일 뿐이다 be only ankle-deep / ~가 있다 be deep; be profound / ~가 없다 be shallow; be superficial / ~을 재다 measure the depth 《of a lake》; sound 《the sea》.
② [부사적] deep(ly); profoundly; 《철저히》 thoroughly; 《강하게》 intensely; 《마음으로부터》 heartily. ¶ ~ 파다 dig deep / ~ 연구하다 study 〔dig 《구어》〕 deep into a subject / ~ 사귀다 establish a close friendship with; be on intimate terms with / ~ 잠들다 fall fast asleep / ~ 사랑하다 love deeply 〔dearly, intensely〕/ ~ 빠져 들다 be taken up too much 《with gambling》/ 숨을 ~ 들이마시다 breathe in deeply; draw a deep breath / ~ 뿌리박히다 be deep-rooted / 너는 그 문제를 ~ 생각해야 한다 You should 「think of 〔ponder over〕 the problem deeply. / 당신에게 ~ 감사드립니다 I thank you from the bottom of my heart.

**까까머리** a head shaved bald; a shaven 〔close-cropped〕 head.

**까까중** (a Buddhist monk with) a head shaved bald; a shaven head.

**까뀌** a hatchet; a hand-ax.

**까끄라기** an awn; a beard; an arista (*pl.* -tae).

**까놓다** 《껍질을》 ⇨ 까다[2] ①; 《겉이 보이게 뒤집다》 turn 〔place〕 《*a thing*》 face up. 《털어놓다》 speak *one's* mind 《to》; speak 「frankly 〔without reserve, outright〕; lay *one's* heart bare; open 〔unlock〕 *one's* mind 〔heart〕; unbosom *oneself* 《to》. ¶ 탁자 위에 카드를 ~ place the cards face up on the table / 까놓고 말하면 to be frank with you / 까놓고 말해라 Speak your mind./ 나는 그에게 까놓고 이야기하였다 I gave him my honest opinion. / 까놓고 말하면 이 장사는 끝장이 났다 To tell you the truth, this business is finished 〔ruined〕.

**까다**[1] 《셈에서 빼다》 take away 〔off〕; deduct; subtract. ¶ 급료에서 ~ deduct 《a sum》 from 《*a person's*》 pay; take 《a sum》 off 《*a person's*》 salary.

**까다**[2] ① 《껍질을》 peel (손으로); pare (칼로); shell 〔hull〕 《peas》; crack 《a nut》; husk 《Indian corn》. ¶ 귤을 ~ peel an orange / 사과 껍질을 ~ pare 《an apple》/ 삶은 달걀을 ~ shell a boiled egg / 우선 감자 껍질을 까주세요 First pare 〔peel〕 the potatoes. (★ peel은 「손으로」, pare는 「칼로」 벗기는 것을 뜻하나 pare 대신 peel을 쓰는 경우도 많음).
② 《부화하다》 hatch 《eggs》; sit on 《eggs》. ¶ 갓 깐 새새끼 a nestling; a hatching / 암탉이 병아리를 깐다 A hen hatches chickens.
③ 《살갗을》 abrade; graze; bark 《*one's* skin》; skin 《*one's* knee》. ¶ 팔꿈치를 ~ have *one's* elbow skinned 〔barked〕.
④ 《치다·때리다》 strike; beat; hit; knock; 《차다》 kick 《at》; hack (축구에서). ¶ 정강이를 ~ kick 《*a person*》 in the 《left》 shin.
⑤ 《비난·공격하다》 slander; speak ill of; censure; accuse; take 〔call〕 《*a person*》 to task 《*for something*》; write down (글로). ¶ 서로 상대를 ~ slander each other / 그들은 대통령을 거짓말쟁이라고 깠다 They accused the President of being a liar.
⑥ [비유적] 《말만 앞세우다》 talk glibly; be a glib talker; be fair-spoken 〔honey-tongued〕. ¶ 그는 입만 까졌다 He never means what he says. *or* He is all talk and no action.

**까다롭다** ① 《어렵다》 (be) difficult;

hard; 《성가시다》 (be) troublesome; vexing; delicate (미묘함); 《복잡하다》 (be) complicated; intricate; involved; tricky. ¶ 까다로운 문제 a hard 〔tough〕 question; a troublesome 〔delicate, vexing, touchy〕 question.
② 《규칙 등이》 (be) strict; stringent. ¶ 까다로운 규칙 a strict 〔stringent〕 rule / 이 학교는 규칙이 ~ Strict rules are enforced in this school.
③ 《성미가》 (be) hard to please 〔handle〕; hypercritical; harsh; stern; 《음식·기호가》 (be) particular 《about》; fastidious 〔overnice〕 《about》. ¶ 까다로운 사람 a difficult person; a man hard to please; a fussy 〔fastidious〕 person; a hard disciplinarian (규칙에) / 까다로운 상사 a superior hard to be contented / 까다로운 선생 a strict 〔an exacting〕 teacher / 자식들에게 ~ be strict with *one's* children / 음식에 ~ be particular about food / 옷에 ~ be fastidious about clothes / 취미가 매우 까다로운 사람이다 be a man of very difficult tastes.

**까닭** ① 《이유·원인》 reason; cause; 《근거》 ground; score; account; occasion; a justification; 《구실》 an excuse; 《동기》 a motive. ¶ ~없이 without any reason; without cause; without provocation; groundlessly; 《부당하게》 unreasonably; without justification; causelessly / ~이 있어 for a certain reason / ~ 모를 일 a strange 〔mysterious, unexplainable〕 thing; a mystery; a nonsensical thing / 그 ~을 묻다 demand 〔inquire〕 the reason.
까닭으로: 영문 모를 ~으로 for some unknown reason; for no reason that could be discovered / 무슨 ~으로 why; for what reason; on what ground / 어떤 ~으로 for reasons not specified; because of; by reason of (that); on account of; for; on the grounds (that); for certain unexplained 〔undisclosed〕 reasons / 이런 저런 ~으로 for some reason or other.
¶ ~은 이러하다 The reason is that... / 그것엔 ~이 있다 I have (a) reason for it. / 주의하지 않는 ~에 그런 일이 생긴다 Things like that happen through carelessness. / 무슨 ~에 사직했나요 What was your reason for resigning? *or* How come you left your company? / 거기엔 무슨 ~이 있음에 틀림없다 There must be some reason for it. / 무슨 영문인지 통 ~을 모르겠다 There is neither rhyme nor reason about 〔in〕 it. / 내가 사과해야 할 ~이 없다 Why should I apologize? / 그렇게 한 정당한 ~이 있었다 I had good reason to do so. *or* I did so with good reason. / ~을 알겠다 That accounts for it. / 그가 알 ~이 없다 How can he know it?
② 《사정·곡절》 circumstances; the matter; the case. ¶ 그를 알게 된 ~을 말씀드리지요 I'll tell you how I came to know him. / 그 사람이 오지를 않으니 무슨 ~이냐 What's the matter with him that he doesn't come?

**까대기** a makeshift side shed; a lean-to.

**까뒤집다** turn 《a sock》 inside out.

**까딱** (by) budging; (in) making a slight movement of; nodding; bobbing (the head). ~하다, ~이다 budge; move slightly; nod; bob (the head). ¶ ~ 실수하다 make an inadvertent mistake; slip up; make a bobble / ~도 않다 remain unmoved 〔unperturbed〕; do not turn a hair; keep cool 〔calm〕; stand firm 《against》; do not budge an inch / ~도 않고 without flinching; undaunted(ly) / ~하면 넘어간다 It will topple over at the slightest movement 〔touch〕. / 그는 손가락 하나 ~하지 않는다 He doesn't lift a finger. / 그녀는 무슨 일에도 ~하지 않는다 Nothing flinches her. *or* Nothing makes her wince.

**까딱거리다** 《…을》 budge and budge; make a slight movement of 《*something*》 again and again; bob and bob (the head); 《…이》 sway back and forth; bob; nod. ¶ 고개를 몇 번 ~ nod *one's* head several times.

**까딱까딱** (by) budging and budging; (in) making a slight movement again and again; nodding and nodding; bobbing and bobbing (the head).

**까딱수**(—手) a risky measure; relying on luck 〔chance〕; a daring maneuver a venture; a wild 〔a rash, a chance, an off-chance〕 move; an off-chance; a shot in the dark; a long shot; a mean device. ¶ ~로 아무를 속이려 하다 take a chance *one* can deceive *a person* / ~(를) 쓰다 resort to a wild 〔risky, rash〕 move; take a chance; take an off-chance; run a risk; take a long shot; take a shot in the dark; venture; dare / ~에 넘어가다 play into the hands of 《an opponent》; fall into a trap 〔snare〕.

**까딱없다** ①《사물이》 stand firm as a rock; (be) safe and sound; intact; undamaged; unimpaired. ¶ 그 집은 그 바람에도 ~ In spite of the wind, the house remains firm as a rock. / 맹렬한 불길에도 금고는 까딱없었다 The safe remained intact in spite of the raging flames. / 우리 회사는 최근의 경제 불황에도 까딱없다 Our firm is quite unaffected by the recent economic panic. / 그쯤 손해로는 회사는 ~ Such a small loss does not make any difference to the company. ②《마음·인품이》 remain calm 〔unperturbed, cool〕; take《*something*》 coolly《without batting an eye》; do not turn a hair; do not flinch; be not daunted at all. ¶ 그는 그 소식을 듣고도 까딱없었다 He remained cool as a cucumber when he heard the news.

**까라지다**《몸이》 get languid; go limp; be dead tired;《목소리가》 become 〔get〕 hoarse 〔husky〕; grow feeble.

**까르르** ¶ ~ 웃다 burst out laughing; burst into laughter / 여학생들이 모두 일제히 ~ 웃어댔다 Every schoolgirl burst out laughing 〔into laughter〕.

**까르륵** with a squall 〔bawl〕. ~하다, ~거리다《젖먹이가》 cry wildly 〔frantically〕.

**까마귀** 〖조류〗 a crow; a raven (큰). ¶ ~떼 a flock of crows / ~가 울다 a crow 〔raven〕 caws 〔croaks〕 / ~ 고기를 먹었나 Why are you so forgetful? / ~ 날자 배 떨어진다《속담》 It is just a coincidence that two events have happened at the same time.

**까마말쑥하다** (be) black 〔dark〕 and neat.

**까마반드르하다** (be) dark and sleek.

**까마(아)득하다** be far off 〔away〕; be in the distance; (be) remote. ¶ 까마(아)득한 옛날에 a long, long time ago; in the remotest past; in the old far-off days / 까마(아)득한 옛날을 생각하다 think of 〔look back on〕 the days long past / 일이 완성되려면 아직 ~ The work is still far from being completed. / 그곳까지 가려면 아직 ~ It is a long way yet to the place. 「a morel.

**까마종이** 〖식물〗 a (black) nightshade;

**까막거리다**《등불 따위가》 flicker; waver; 《눈을》 blink; wink《*one's* eyes》.

**까막까치** crow(s) and magpie(s).

**까막눈** the eye of an ignoramus. ◉ ~이 an ignoramus; an unlettered person; an illiterate.

**까막잡기**《술래잡기》 blindman's buff.

**까맣다** ①《빛깔이》 (be) jet-〔coal-, deep-〕black; inky; be as black as coal. ¶ 까만 머리 jet-black 〔raven〕 hair / 까맣게 더럽혀진《clothes》 stained black as coal / 까맣게 타다 be scorched 〔burned〕 black; be charred. ②《기억이 없다·모르다》 (be) completely forgotten; utterly ignorant. ¶ 그 일을 까맣게 잊고 있었다 I had clean forgotten the matter.

**까매지다** get dark; darken; become 〔turn〕 black; blacken; tan (in the sun); be sunburnt. ¶ 햇볕에 까매진 얼굴 a sunburnt 〔suntanned, sunbrowned〕 face / 볕에 까매지지 않도록 하다 keep *oneself* from getting sunburnt.

**까먹다** ①《껍데기를》 peel 〔break, crack, shell〕 and eat. ¶ 굴을 ~ shuck 〔shell〕 an oyster and eat it. ②《돈을》 spend all *one's* money《on》; use up; go 〔run〕 through. ¶ 그는 밑천을 다 까먹었다 He wasted all the money he had. / 그 애는 오전에 벌써 천 원이나 까먹었다 He has eaten up 1,000 won worth of sweets already this morning. ③《잊다》 forget《to deliver a message, to fulfill a request》; fail to keep in mind. ¶ 약속을 ~ 「forget to fulfill 〔neglect〕 *one's* promise.

**까무러지다** faint (away); become 〔go, feel〕 faint; black out;《*one's* mind》 become hazy 〔dulled〕.

**까무러치다** faint; swoon; lose *one's* senses. ¶ 놀라서 ~ faint with surprise / 때려서 까무러치게 하다 knock 《*a person*》 unconscious 〔out, senseless〕 / 까무러칠 듯이 놀라다 be frightened out of *one's* senses 〔wits〕 / 까무러쳐 쓰러지다 fall senseless 〔unconscious〕.

**까무스름하다** ⇨ 거무스름하다.

**까무잡잡하다** (be) darkish; swarthy; dark-skinned; have a dark complexion. ¶ 얼굴이 까무잡잡한 사내 a dark-skinned 〔swarthy〕 man; a dark-complexioned man.

**까물거리다** ⇨ 가물거리다.

**까뭉개다** cut through《a mountain》; level (down)《a hill》. ¶ 언덕을 까뭉개서 주택지를 개발하다 level down the hill and develop a residential area.

**까바치다** tell 〔squeal〕《on *a person*》; tell 〔carry〕 tales《about, against, upon *a person*》; inform《*a person* against another》; confide《a secret to another》. ¶ 그를 까바치지 마라

Don't tell on him. / 엄마한테 까바칠테야 I am going to tell mother on you.

**까발리다** ① 《속에 든 것을》 pop 〔peel, shuck, shell〕 《*something*》 out. ¶ 《콩 등의》 깍지를 ~ shell 〔peel〕 《peas》. ② 《폭로하다》 expose; disclose; lay bare; bring to light. ¶ 비밀을 ~ disclose a secret / 사기꾼의 정체를 ~ expose an impostor.

**까부르다** winnow 《chaff from grain》. ¶ 키로 ~ winnow away 〔out〕 《the chaff from grain》.

**까불거리다** ⇨까불다.

**까불까불** 《위아래로》 moving up and down lightly; 《경망스럽게》 frivolously.

**까불다** ① 《배가》 toss; pitch and toss; heave; 《차 따위가》 jolt; 《불꽃 등이》 flicker. ¶ 배가 물결에 몹시 까분다 The ship is pitching and tossing in the heavy sea. ② 《행동을》 behave frivolously; act carelessly 〔boisterously〕; be roguish 〔rash〕. ¶ 까불지 말고 좀 가만히 앉아 있거라 Just sit down, and don't be so boisterous 〔frivolous〕. ③ ⇨까부르다.

**까불리다**[1] 《재물을》 squander; waste. ¶ 가진 돈을 모두 ~ waste all the money *one* has / 술로 재산을 ~ drink away *one's* fortune.

**까불리다**[2] 《곡식을》 make 〔let〕 《*a person*》 winnow; 《곡식이》 get 〔be〕 winnowed.

**까불이** 《까부는 사람》 a flippant 〔frivolous〕 person; a harum-scarum; a flibbertigibbet (특히 여자); 《까부는 아이》 a sportive 〔jocose, playful〕 boy.

**까붐질** winnowing; fanning. ~하다 do (the) winnowing.

**까슬까슬하다** 《성질이》 (be) hard-grained; particular; choosy; intractable; 《촉감이》 (be) rough (to the touch 〔feel〕); rugged; sandy. ¶ 성격이 까슬까슬한 노부인 a difficult old lady / 까슬까슬한 촉감〔옷감〕 rough 〔sandy〕 feel 〔texture〕 / 그녀의 손은 터서 ~ Her hands are chapped and rough.

**까지** ① 《시간》 till; until; to; up 〔down〕 to; into; by.
¶ 지금~ till now; so far; up to the present / 아침부터 밤~ from morning till night / 수요일에서 금요일~ from Wednesday till 〔through 《미》〕 Friday / 고대에서 현대~ from ancient times down to the present / 칠십~ 살다 live to be seventy / 기차가 떠나기~ 10분 있다 We have ten minutes before the train leaves. / 외출 시간은 밤 10시 ~다 The hours (allowed out) are till 10 p.m. / 7시 ~는 그곳에 도착하겠습니다 I'll be there by 7 o'clock. / 연말~는 그것을 마칠 수 있습니까 Can you finish it by the end of this year? / 나는 어제 밤늦게~ 책을 읽고 있었다 I was reading a book (till) late last night. / 비가 멈출 때~ 기다리자 Let's wait till 〔until〕 the rain stops. / 영업시간은 오전 9시부터 오후 5시~이다 Our business hours are from 9 a.m. to 5 p.m. / 그녀는 매일 밤늦게~ 일한다 She works far into the night every day. / 입학 원서는 1월 15일 ~ 제출할 것 Applications for admission should be presented not later than the 15th of January. / 오늘에 이르기~ 그 사건의 진상은 수수께끼에 싸여 있다 Up to the present-day the real fact of the case has been cloaked in mystery. / 이번 전쟁이 언제 ~ 갈는지 아무도 모른다 No one knows 〔God knows〕 how long this war is going to last.

> 용법 **till**, **until** 둘 다 거의 같은 뜻으로, 전치사·접속사로 쓰임. till은 구어적인 일상어 중에서, until은 격식을 차린 문체에서 흔히 쓰임. until은 글머리에 나오는 경우가 많음. **to**는 기간이 끝나는 시점을, **up to**는 「…에 이르기까지」란 뜻이 함축되어 있고, **into**는 「…시각이 될 때 까지」, **by**는 어느 때까지 동작이 끝나는「기한」을 나타냄.

② 《장소》 as far as; (all the way) to; up to. ¶ 여기서 거기~ from here to there / 서울~ 가다 go as far as Seoul / 어디~ 가십니까 How far do you go? / 서울역~ 부탁드립니다 《택시에서》 Can you take me to Seoul Station? / 부산~ 차표 두 장 주세요 Two tickets to Pusan, please. / 역~ 걸으면 10분 정도 걸린다 It takes ten minutes or so to walk to the station.
③ 《정도·범위·강조》 even; so 〔as〕 far as; (by) up to; to the extent of; to the limit. ¶ 도둑질~ 하다 go so 〔as〕 far as to commit theft; go to the length(s) of committing theft / 밤이 되자 비~ 오기 시작했다 Furthermore, it began to rain at night. / 친구들 뿐만아니라 아내 ~도 나를 비난했다 Not only (did) my friends (blame me), but my wife blamed me too. / 형~ 그를 나무란다 Even his brother blames him. / 자기의 제일 가까운 친구~도 안

찾아보고 떠났단다 You see, he didn't even say goodbye to his best friend! / 물은 내 무릎~ 차 올랐다 The water came up to my knees. / 비에다 바람~ 분다 It is raining and the wind is blowing as well. / 나는 회사에서 100만 원~는 빌릴 수 있다 I can get a loan of money to the extent of 1,000,000 won from my company. / 오늘은 여기 ~ 한다 《학과 종료시》 So much for today. *or* That's all for today. / 너의 말을 어느 정도~는 이해할 수 있다 I can understand what you say to a certain extent. / 그녀는 작은 소리로 20~ 셌다 She counted (up) to twenty under her breath. / 그녀는 나에게 선물~ 주었다 She even gave me a gift. / 그것은 말할 것~도 없다 That goes without saying.

**까지가** ¶ 사실은 학위를 받기~ 문제다 Actually the problem is how to get by untill he receives his degree.

**까지다**[1] ① 《살갗이》 be grazed 〔abraded, skinned〕; 《껍질이》 peel (off). ¶ 팔꿈치가 ~ get *one's* elbow grazed (abraded, skinned). ② 《몸이 여위다》 get 〔become〕 thin 〔haggard〕; lose flesh; 《재산이》 get fewer 〔less, smaller〕; lessen.

**까지다**[2] 《지나치게 약다》 (be) sly; cunning; crafty; wily; 《닳고 닳았다》 (be) world-wise; experienced in worldly affairs. ¶ 까진 녀석 an old fox.

**까지로** ¶ 네 시~ 정해두자 Let's decide to have it by 〔until〕 4 o'clock.

**까지르다** wander 〔roam〕 about; wander from place to place. ⇨ 싸다니다.

**-까짓** 《…만한 정도의》 such as 〔like〕; any such; 《하찮은》 so trifling. ¶ 이까짓 this kind of… / 그까짓 that kind of… / 제까짓 …such as him 〔her, they〕; …such as *oneself* / 네까짓 놈이 알 수 있겠느냐 Such as you wouldn't understand. / 그까짓 일로 울지 마라 Don't cry over such a trifle.

**까짜올리다** 《추어 올리며 놀리다》 tease 《*a person*》 with praise.

**까치** 〖조류〗 a magpie. ◉ ~걸음 a hopping 〔bounding〕 walk: ~걸음으로 in 〔with〕 a bound; in a single leap. ~두루마기〔저고리〕 multicolored outer coat 〔jacket〕 worn by children on New Year's Eve. ~설날 New Year's Eve. ~설빔 children's gala dress for New Year's Eve.

**까치눈** a crack 〔chap〕 in the bend of a toe.

**까치발** 〖건축〗 a bracket; a cross-arm; a strut.

**까치선**(—扇) a 4-color fan used by ladies.

**까치콩** 〖식물〗 an Egyptian kidney bean.

**까칠하다** (be) haggard; worn-out; gaunt; look emaciated 〔undernourished, thin〕. ¶ 까칠한 얼굴 a haggard face. / 열병으로 까칠해지다 be consumed with fever / 병후라 까칠해 보이다 look thin after an illness / 근심으로 볼품없이 까칠해지다 be worn almost to a shadow with anxiety / 그녀는 과로로 몹시 까칠했다 She was worn out with overwork.

**까탈** 《방해》 (a) disturbance; trouble; 《장애·장해》 an obstacle; a hindrance; a hitch; a stumbling block; 《트집》 a false charge. ~부리다 raise problems; make trouble; cause hindrances; throw an obstacle in 《*a person's*》 path; find 〔raise〕 objections. ~스럽다 (be) troublesome; have a lot of trouble in controlling 《*a thing, a person*》; be put out 《with》; be complicated. ~지다 run into problems 〔obstacles, hindrances, objections〕. ¶ ~을 잡다 make a false charge / 일을 끝내기까지 여러 가지 ~지는 일이 있을지 모른다 You may run into all sorts of obstacles before you finish the job.

**까투리** a pheasant hen.

**까팡이** broken pieces of unglazed pottery.

**까풀** the outer layer of the skin; a film. ¶ ~(이) 지다 get a skin 〔film〕 on 《it》 / 눈~이 지다 get wrinkles on *one's* eyelid / 그도 한 ~ 벗기면 사기꾼이다 Under a thin veneer he is a swindler.

**깍깍** Caw! Caw! ~하다, ~거리다 keep cawing.

**깍두기** cubed radish kimchi.

**깍둑거리다** cut 〔chop〕 《a cucumber》 to pieces 〔into chunks〕 unevenly.

**깍듯이** politely; civilly; courteously; respectfully. ¶ ~ 인사하다 greet 《*a person*》 politely; make a low bow.

**깍듯하다** 《공손하다》 (be) polite; civil; courteous; respectful. ¶ 인사가 깍듯한 사람 a courteous man; a man of polite greetings / 인사가 ~ be polite in *one's* greetings / 말씨가 ~ use polite language; speak politely.

**깍쟁이** 《인색한 사람》 a stingy person; a closefisted fellow; 《미》 a cheap fellow; 《미구어》 a tightwad; 《구어》 a cheapskate; a niggard; a sharp customer; 《애칭어로서》 a cute boy 〔girl〕; 《약삭빠른 사람》 a tricky person; a cunning 〔shrewd, calculating〕 fellow.

¶ 서울 ~ the shrewd Seoulite; a city slicker / 불~ a real stinker / ~야! You stinker! / 그렇게 ~ 노릇하지 마라 Don't be such a stinker.

**깍정이** ①《도토리의》 an acorn cup; a cupule. ②《어린 땅꾼》 a young snake-catcher.

**깍지** ①《껍질》 a pod; a hull; a shell; a husk. ②《활 쏠 때의》 a horn ring for the thumb (in archery). ¶ ~(를) 떼다 let an arrow fly / ~(를) 끼다 put the archer's ring on.

**깍지끼다** 《손가락으로》 interlace *one's* fingers; knot *one's* fingers together.

**깍짓손** the hand that wears the archer's ring; the hand that draws the bow.

**깎낫** a sickle whittling the wood into a club.

**깎다** ①《머리를》 cut; clip; crop (짧게); trim (다듬다). ¶ 머리를 짧게 ~ cut *one's* hair short 〔close〕; crop *one's* hair short / (남에게) 머리를 깎게 하다 have *one's* hair cut 〔trimmed〕; get 〔have〕 a haircut / 머리 좀 깎아 주시오 I want to have my hair cut. *or* I want a haircut. / 자네 머리를 깎아야겠군 I think you need a haircut.
②《풀·잔디를》 mow; trim; cut (풀을); 《손톱 따위를》 cut; pare; trim. ¶ 잔디를 ~ mow the lawn / 풀을 ~ cut 〔mow〕 grass / 손톱을 ~ trim 〔cut, pare〕 *one's* nails / 나는 1주일에 한 번 잔디를 깎는다 I mow the lawn once a week. / 오늘 잔디를 깎아야 한다 I need my lawn yard be mowed today.
③《양털 따위를》 shear 《a sheep》; fleece 《the sheep》; clip off 《the wool》; 《수염을》 shave *oneself* (자신이); have a shave; get a shave (남이). ¶ 양털을 ~ shear wool from a sheep / 천의 보풀을 ~ shear cloth.
④《연필·목재 따위를》 shave 《wood》; plane 《a plank》; sharpen 《a pencil》; whittle; chip. ¶ 판자를 ~ plane a piece of board 〔plank〕.
⑤《벗기다》 pare; peel. ¶ 배〔사과〕를 ~ peel a pear 〔an apple〕.
⑥《삭감하다》 cut down; curtail; reduce; retrench; slash. ¶ 비용을 ~ curtail 〔cut down, reduce〕 the expenses / 예산을 ~ reduce 〔cut down〕 the budget / 월급을 십만원 ~ cut down 《*a person's*》 salary by 100,000 won / 시장은 하는 수 없이 예산의 20%를 깎았다 The mayor was forced to slash 〔cut down, reduce〕 the budget by twenty percent.
⑦《값을》 beat down 《the price》; haggle 〔bargain〕 over 《the price》; 《구어》 knock 《the price》 down; bargain. ¶ 값을 2천원으로 ~ beat down the price to 2,000 won / 1할 깎아 주다 take off ten per cent / 값을 몹시 깎아 내리다 drive a hard bargain 《with a merchant》 / 좀 더 깎아 주시오 Come down a little more, please. / 좀 깎아 주시지 않겠습니까 Can't you make it cheaper? / 3천원 깎아 드리죠 I'll take 3,000 won off the price. / 한푼도 깎을 수 없소 I won't take off a cent. / 값을 그렇게 깎아서야 되겠습니까 Don't bid so low. / 값은 깎지 마십시오 We do not bargain; our prices are fixed. / 나는 그 옷을 2만원까지 깎았다 I bargained the clothes to twenty thousand won. / 그들과 잘 흥정하면 값을 깎아줄지도 모른다 If you bargain with them, they might reduce the price.
⑧《낯·체면을》 make 《*a person*》 lose face; disgrace 《*a person*》; bring disgrace upon 《*a person*》; stain 《*a person's*》 honor; dishonor; blemish; run 《*a person*》 down. ¶ 깎아 내리다 《중상하다》 speak slightingly 〔ill, evil〕 of 《*a person*》; run down 《a work》 / 못된 짓으로 아비의 낯을 ~ disgrace *one's* father by misbehavior 《of》 / 남의 업적을 깎아내리다 belittle 〔depreciate〕 another's achievement.

**깎아지르다** rise 〔tower up〕 steeply.

**깎아지른 듯하다** (be) very steep; precipitous. ¶ 깎아지른 듯한 절벽 a precipitous cliff.

**깎은** smart; handsome; smartly dressed. ● ~새서방〔서방님〕 a smartly dressed young man. ~선비 a handsome 〔fine-looking〕 gentleman.

**깎음질** cutting; shaving; whittling; planing (대패로). ~하다 cut 〔shave, whittle〕 《wood》; plane 《a board》.

**깎이** a 《pencil》 sharpener; a 《nail》 clipper.

**깎이다** ①《깎게 하다》 make 〔have〕 《*a person*》 trim; get 《*a person*》 to cut 〔mow, peel, pare〕. ¶ 머리를 ~ have *one's* hair cut 〔trimmed〕 / 뜰의 풀을 ~ get the grass cut; have the lawn mowed.
②《깎여지다》 be trimmed; be cut (back, down); be mowed; be peeled; be pared. ¶ 풀이 ~ the grass is cut; the lawn is mowed / 연필이 잘 ~ a pencil sharpens nicely.
③《값·예산·봉급 따위가》 be reduced;

be slashed; be bargained 〔beat〕 down. ¶ 값이 3할 ～ a price is reduced thirty percent / 예산이 ～ a budget is cut down / 영업 부진으로 그는 봉급이 대폭 깎였다 His salary was slashed as business became dull.
④ 《낯·체면이》 be disgraced; be put to shame; lose *one's* face 〔honor〕; disgrace *oneself.* ¶ 그런 낯깍이는 말을 하지 마라 Don't say that. It is beneath your dignity. / 그 말 한 마디에 낯이 많이 깎였다 Because of that single remark he has lost a great deal of face. / 네 덕분에 낯이 깎이지 않고 체면을 유지할 수 있었다 Your help has saved my honor. *or* Your help has allowed me to save my face.

**깐** 《가늠·속셈》 estimation; account; a thought; something in *one's* mind. ¶ 제 깐에는 in *one's* thought 〔estimation〕; by *one's* account / 그녀는 제 깐에는 미인이라고 생각한다 She fancies herself beautiful. / 그는 제 깐에는 일이 잘 될거라고 생각했던 모양이다 He seems to have thought in his own mind that all would go well. *or* He seems to have had an idea that all would go well.

**깐깐오월**(一五月) the "sticky" 〔tedious〕 fifth month of the lunar calendar.

**깐깐하다** 《검질기다》 be a stickler; (be) persistent; obstinate; tenacious; 《꼬치꼬치 캐묻다》 inquisitive; 《꼼꼼하다》 (be) cautious; scrupulous; meticulous; exact; 《까다롭다》 (be) particular; fastidious. ¶ 성질이 깐깐한 사람 a man of hard-grained character; a particular person / 깐깐하게 질문하다 pester 〔plague〕 《*a person*》 with questions / 왜 그렇게 깐깐하게 굽니까 Don't be so tenacious. / 참 깐깐한 녀석이로군 What a pest!

**깐깐히** 《집요하게》 persistently; tenaciously; 《세심하게》 meticulously; closely; scrupulously. ¶ ～ 조사하다 examine 《*a thing*》 closely / 일을 ～ 하다 do *one's* work with scrupulous care.

**깐작거리다** ① 《달라붙다》 stick 《to》; adhere 《to》; cling 《to》. ② 《성질·행동이》 stick 《to》; be tenacious; persist 《in》; be persistent; get on 《*a person's*》 nerves; irritate by being persistent.

**깐작깐작** 《끈적끈적하게》 stickily; adhesively; glutinously; 《깐질기게》 tenaciously; persistently; importunately (귀찮게). ～하다 = 깐작거리다.

**깐지다** tenacious; pertinacious; persistent.

**깐질기다** (be) strong and sticky; strongly adhesive.

**깔개** 《방석》 a cushion; 《돗자리류》 matting; 《융단》 a carpet; a rug (부분적인); 《물건 밑에 까는》 an underlay; a floorcloth (★ linoleum, oilcloth 따위). ¶ 마루에 ～를 깔다 spread a rug 〔lay a carpet〕 on the floor.

**깔기다** 《오줌·똥을》 relieve 〔ease〕 nature indiscriminately; discharge 《excrements》 where *one* happens to be. ¶ 길가에다 오줌을 ～ urinate 〔relieve *oneself*〕 in the street; 《비어》 piss in the street.

**깔깔** laughing loudly; screaming with laughter. ～거리다 laugh loudly; guffaw. ¶ ～ 웃다 scream with laughter; laugh aloud; burst into a roar of laughter.

**깔깔하다** ① 《감촉이》 (be) rough; sandy; coarse. ¶ 깔깔한 촉감〔감촉〕 a rough 〔sandy〕 feel 〔texture〕 / 혓바닥이 ～ My tongue is rough. ② 《마음이》 (be) clean and pure; honest.

**깔끄럽다** ⇨ 껄끄럽다.

**깔끔거리다** ⇨ 껄끔거리다.

**깔끔하다** 《외양·태도가》 (be) smart; neat and tidy; sleek and clean; 《성격이》 (be) cleanly; neat and tidy; sharp. ¶ 깔끔한 사람 a person fond of cleaniness / 깔끔한 성격 a sharp temper / 옷맵시가 ～ be neatly dressed / 그는 깔끔한 사람이다 He is habitually clean 〔neat〕 and tidy.

**깔다** ① 《자리·담요·돗자리 등을》 spread (out); lay (out); cover 《the floor with carpet》; 《돌 등을》 pave 《a path with flagstones》; gravel(자갈을). ¶ 자리를 ～ make a bed; lay out bedding / 마루에 매트를 ～ lay a mat on a floor / 방석을 깔고 앉다 place a cushion and sit on it; sit *oneself* on a cushion / 길에 자갈을 ～ pave a road with gravel; gravel a road / 철로를 ～ lay a (railroad) track / 우리는 멍석 위에 담요를 깔고 그 위에 앉았다 We spread a blanket over the mats and sat on it. / 길에는 돌이 깔려 있다 The road is paved with stones.
② 《사람을 깔고 앉다》 get 《*a person*》 under 〔down〕; hold 〔pin〕 《*a person*》 down. ¶ 남편을 깔고 뭉개다 dominate *one's* husband; keep *one's* husband under *one's* thumb.
③ 《돈·곡식·상품 따위를》 lend out money 〔grain〕 widely. ¶ 빚을 여기저기

깔아놓다 lend *one's* money out near and far.
④《눈을》 cast 〔drop〕 *one's* eyes down.

**깔딱** 《삼키는 소리》 with a gulp; 《숨이》 with gasps. ¶ 숨이 ～ 넘어가다 gasp *one's* life away.

**깔딱거리다** 《삼킬 때》 gulp and gulp; gulp repeatedly; gulp away; keep gulping; 《숨이》 gasp for breath.

**깔딱하다** 《*one's* eyes》 be drawn 〔sunken deep〕 with fatigue 〔hunger〕.

**깔때기** a funnel. ¶ ～꼴의 funnel-shaped / ～ 모양의 통 a funnel tube.

**깔리다** ①《널리》 be spread; be covered; 《흩어지다》 be scattered 〔strewn〕 《with》; be dispersed; 《밑에》 be laid; 《내리덮친 것에》 be buried 〔pressed, pinned, held, caught〕 under 《a fallen tree》. ¶ 낙엽이 깔린 작은 길 a path covered with fallen leaves / 벚꽃이 깔린 뜰 a garden strewn with cherry blossoms / 떨어진 바위에 깔려 죽다 be crushed to death under the fallen rocks / 마루에는 융단이 깔려 있다 The floor is laid 〔covered〕 with a carpet. / 구름이 낮게 깔려 있다 Clouds are hanging low.
②《돈·곡식이》 be lent out widely.
③《남에게》 be held 〔pinned〕 down 《by》.

**깔밋하다** (be) simple and neat; attractive; tidy.

**깔보다** 《얕보다》 make light of 《*a person*》; think 〔make〕 little of 《*a person*》; take 《*a person, a thing*》 lightly; do not pay much attention 《to》; 《과소평가하다》 underrate; belittle; play down; 《멸시하다》 despise; look down on; hold 《*a person*》 in contempt.
¶ 깔볼 수 없는 적 a formidable enemy; a no mean adversary / 남의 능력을 ～ underrate another's ability / 사람을 깔보는 버릇이 있다 have a habit of looking down upon people / 나를 그렇게 깔보지 마오 Don't look down on me so. *or* Don't think 〔make〕 little of me. / 그것은 나를 깔보고 하는 말이다 You slight me by saying that. / 어린 애라고 깔보아서는 안 된다 Don't make light of him because he is a child. / 그런 짓을 하면 남에게 깔보인다 That will lower you in public estimation.

**깔색**(—色) 《물건의 빛깔》 a tone 〔shade〕 of color; 《윤기》 sheen; luster; 《품질》 quality. ¶ ～이 좋다〔나쁘다〕 have a fine 〔bad〕 tone of color.

**깔아뭉개다** ①《눌러서》 press down; 《앉아서》 sit (up) on 《*a thing*》 (and crush it). ②《안건 따위를》 shelve; kill; pigeonhole; put 〔lay, cast〕 on the shelf. ¶ 법안을 ～ pigeonhole; 《미》 lay a bill on the table / 부장은 내 개선안을 깔아뭉갰다 Our department chief quashed my proposal for improvements.

**깔짝거리다** crunch; grate; scratch; 《펜촉 등으로》 make a scratching sound; 《쥐가》 gnaw 《at》.

**깔짝깔짝하다** crunch; grate. ⇨ 깔짝거리다.

**깔쭉거리다** feel 〔be〕 rough (to the touch); be sandy.

**깔쭉깔쭉** rough (to the touch). ～하다 (be) rough; notched; jagged; milled. ¶ ～하게 하다 notch; jag; make notches; mill (동전).

**깔쭉이** a milled silver coin.

**깔치** 《비어》 a gal; a girl friend.

**깜깜하다** 《어둡다》 (be) very dark; pitch=black; pitch-dark; be as dark as pitch; 《모르다》 (be) ignorant; unlearned; blank; be unfamiliar with 《the law》. ¶ 깜깜한 어둠 dead darkness / 깜깜한 밤 a jet-black 〔pitch=dark〕 night / 깜깜한 속에서 in utter darkness / 나는 한학에는 전혀 ～ I am utterly ignorant of the Chinese classics. / 그런 일에는 아주〔전혀〕 깜깜이다 I know nothing about matters of that kind.

**깜둥이** ⇨ 검둥이.

**깜박** ①《눈을》 with a wink; with a blink 〔blinking〕. ¶ 눈을 ～이다 blink *one's* eyes / 눈도 깜박이지 않고 보다 stare 〔gaze〕 at 《*a thing*》 without blinking; look unblinkingly 《at》.
②《불·빛이》 with a twinkle 〔flash〕. ～하다 flicker; twinkle; blink; dim for the moment. ¶ 촛불이 바람에 ～대다 a candle flickers in the wind / 별이 ～이다 a star twinkles.
③《정신이》 carelessly (부주의해서); in spite of *oneself* (자기도 모르게); absent=mindedly (멍해서); 《잠시동안》 for a moment 〔a while〕; in a flash; 《순간적으로》 momentarily; suddenly. ¶ 편지 부치는 것을 ～ 잊다 carelessly forget to mail a letter / ～해서 비밀을 말하다 let out a secret; blurt out a secret / ～하는 사이에 in a moment 〔minute〕; in the twinkling of an eye / ～ 잠들다 fall asleep suddenly / ～ 그녀의 이름을 잊다 forget her name for the moment / ～하는 사이에 기차를 놓쳤다 I missed the train by one minute. / ～해서 택시에 우산을 놓고 내렸다 I absent-mindedly left my

umbrella in the taxi. / 일주일이 ～ 지나갔다 The week has passed in a flash. ④《완전히》 completely; entirely; utterly; quite. ¶ ～ 속다 be taken in unawares; be swindled before 《*a person*》 knows it.

**깜박거리다** 《별이》 twinkle; 《불이》 flicker; waver; 《눈을》 blink and blink 《*one's* eyes》. ¶ 눈을 ～ blink *one's* eyes / 별이 ～ a star twinkles / 불이 ～ a fire flickers / 정신이 ～ *one's* mind keeps ⌈giving way 〔dimming, blacking out〕/ 어둠 속에서 남폿불이 깜박거리고 있다 The lamp is flickering in the dark.

**깜박깜박** with many a wink; with repeated blinking 〔flickering〕; closing *one's* eyes again and again. ¶ ～ 졸다 nod in a doze; nod off.

**깜박불** twinkling 〔flickering〕 light.

**깜박이** ⇨ 점멸등.

**깜부기** ①《병걸린 이삭》 a smutted 〔blighted〕 ear of barely 〔grain〕; a smut ball. ②《숯》 charcoal from the burnt remains of firewood. ¶ ～불 a dying 〔low〕 fire; embers.

**깜작깜작** 《까만 점이》 with black spots here and there; dotted sparsely. ～하다 be sparsely dotted; have black spots (on it) here and there.

**깜작이다** ＝ 깜박거리다.

**깜짝** 《놀람》 with surprise 〔astonishment〕; with a start. ¶ ～ 놀랄 만한 비싼 가격 the surprisingly high price / ～ 놀랄 속도로 with amazing speed / ～ 놀라다 be surprised 〔astonished〕《at, that》; be startled 《at》; take fright 《at》; be taken aback; be amazed (당혹하다); be shocked (충격을 받다) / ～ 놀라게 하다 surprise; astonish; startle; frighten; knock *one's* hat off / ～ 놀라서 눈을 뜨다 wake up in surprise; awake with a start / ～ 놀라서 기절하다 faint from fright / 세상을 ～ 놀라게 하다 startle the world; cause the public to gasp with surprise / 아이구 ～이야 What a startle you gave me! / 자네를 ～ 놀래 줄 일이 있네 I have a surprise for you. / 그 소식을 듣고 ～ 놀랐다 I was surprised ⌈to hear 〔at, by〕 the news. *or* The news surprised me. / 그녀의 갑작스런 죽음에 모두가 ～ 놀랐다 Everyone was shocked by her sudden death. / 그의 대담한 발언에 ～ 놀랐다 I was astonished by his bold remarks.

**깜짝거리다**[1] 《놀라다》 repeatedly start up with surprise; jump with a start again and again.

**깜짝거리다**[2] 《눈을》 blink and blink (*one's* eyes); keep blinking.

**깜짝깜짝** 《놀람》 with (repeated) start.

**깜찍이** exceedingly; surprisingly 《clever, small, *etc.*》; shrewdly; craftily; precociously. ¶ ～ 굴다 behave shrewdly; play the fox.

**깜찍하다** ①《사람이》 (be) precocious; be (too) clever for *one's* age; (be) overly shrewd 〔smart〕; crafty. ¶ 깜찍한 놈 a foxy fellow / 깜찍한 아이 a precocious child / 깜찍한 소리를 하다 say cheeky things / 깜찍해지다 become cheeky 〔saucy〕/ 너무 깜찍하게 굴지 말라 Don't play the fox. *or* You are being too smart.
②《물건이》 (be) small and cute; saucy; (be) surprisingly 〔cleverly〕 small. ¶ 깜찍한 모자 a saucy little hat.

**깝살리다** ① 《안 만남》 say "not at home" to 《a caller》; refuse to see; close the door to. ②《탕진하다》 squander 《*one's* fortune》. ③《기회를 놓치다》 miss 〔lose, overlook〕 an 〔*one's*〕 opportunity.

**깝신거리다** behave frivolously 〔giddily〕.

**깝신깝신** frivolously; lightly; giddily.

**깝죽거리다** behave flippantly; act lightly.

**깡** 〖광산〗《뇌관》 a percussion cap.

**깡그리** (one and) all; entirely; without exception; wholly. ¶ ～ 가져가다 take everything away / ～ 잊어버리다 entirely forget / ～ 끝내다 finish 《*something*》 up completely / 땅을 ～ 팔아버리다 sell all *one's* estate; make a clean sweep of *one's* estate / 소지품을 ～ 도둑맞았다 My personal effects were stolen to the last particle.

**깡그리다** complete 〔finish〕《*a thing*》; bring 《*a matter*》 to a finish; round off 〔out〕.

**깡깡이** 《해금》 a Korean musical instrument somewhat like a violin; a two-stringed fiddle.

**깡똥하다** (be) unbecomingly short.

**깡마르다** (be) lean; haggard; skinny. ¶ 깡마른 사람 a skinny person; a living skeleton.

**깡총깡총** ¶ ～ 뛰다 hop; skip; jump up and down / ～ 뛰어다니다 romp; frisk.

**깡통** a can 《미》; a tin 《영》. ¶ 빈 ～ an empty can / ～ 맥주 a canned beer / ～을 따다 open a can 〔tin〕/ ～을 차

다 《거지가 되다》 be reduced to begging; go broke (파산하다). ◉ ~따개 a can 〔《영》 tin〕 opener.

**깡패** (一牌) 《불량배》 a hoodlum 《미》; a hooligan; a rough; a hood 《미속어》; a ruffian; 《폭력배》 a gangster; a racketeer; a mobster 《미속어》; 《폭력단》 a gang. ¶ ~집단간의 싸움 gang war / ~ 생활에서 손을 씻다 make a clean break with the gang 〔mob〕; quit the life of a gangster. ◉ ~기질 hooliganism; hoodlumism.

**깨** 『식물』 《참깨》 sesame; a gingili (plant); 《들깨》 green perilla. ¶ 검은 ~ black sesame.

**깨갱** 《강아지의 울음소리》 yelp; yap, yap. ~거리다 yelp; yap; whine (끙끙거리다). ¶ 강아지가 ~거렸다 The puppy cried, "yap, yap, yap."

**깨끔스럽다** (be) neat and clean; comely; trim. ¶ 깨끔스러운 얼굴 a fair countenance; a nice face / 깨끔스러운 여자 a comely woman.

**깨끔찮다** (be) untidy; be not clean; be a mess; (be) messy; unkempt.

**깨끔하다** = 깨끔스럽다.

**깨끗이** ① 《청결히》 clean; cleanly; 《단정히》 tidily; neatly. ¶ ~ 하다 clean; cleanse; make 〔keep〕 《*a thing*》 clean; 《정돈하다》 make 《*a thing*》 tidy; tidy up; put 《*a thing*》 in order / ~ 훔치다〔닦다〕 wipe 《*a thing*》 clean / ~쓰다 write neatly; make a fair copy 《of》 / 손을 ~ 씻다 wash 〔cleanse〕 *one's* hands / 방을 ~치우다 《청소해서》 clean a room (up); sweep a room clean; 《정돈해서》 put a room in good order; straighten a room / ~ 면도하다 shave *oneself* clean / 식탁을 ~ 치우다 clear the table / 부엌을 ~해라 Clean 〔Tidy〕 up the kitchen. / 그녀는 죄를 ~ 씻었다 She was cleansed of her sin. / 손은 항상 ~해라 Always keep your hands clean.
② 《결백·순수하게》 clean(ly); innocently; honorably (훌륭히). ¶ ~ 살다 live a clean life; live an honest 〔a pure〕 life; lead an immaculate life / ~ 교제하다 have 〔make〕 a real friendship 《with》; 《남녀간의》 be in platonic love 《with》.
③ 《모두·완전히》 entirely; completely; all; thoroughly; clean. ¶ ~ 잊다 forget all about 《*something*》; 《구어》 clean forget 《*something*》 / 빚을 ~ 갚다 clear 〔pay off〕 *one's* debts / 셈을 ~ 치르다 settle the accounts completely / ~ 손을 떼다 make a clean break 《with》; break completely 《with》; sever all ties 《with》 / 병이 ~ 낫다 a (medical) trouble clears up 〔goes away〕; recover completely from an ailment / 과거는 ~ 잊어라 Forget all about the past. / 그는 요리를 ~다 먹었다 He ate up the dish clean.
④ 《공정·정당히》 fairly (and squarely); justly; openly; clean. ¶ ~ 싸우고 ~ 지다 Play fair and be a good loser. / 거래는 ~ 행해졌다 The transaction went on fairly.
⑤ 《미련없이》 without (any) regret; with no lingering attachment. ¶ 우리는 그 계획을 ~ 단념했다 We gave up the plan without any regret. / 나는 그녀를 아직 ~ 잊지 못하고 있다 I still have a lingering attachment for her.
⑥ 《관용적 표현》 ¶ ~ 사죄하다 have the grace to apologize / ~ 자백하다 make a manly confession; make a clean breast 《of》.

**깨끗잖다** ① 《더럽다》 be not clean 〔neat, tidy〕; (be) untidy; dirty; soiled. ¶ 깨끗잖은 방 a dirty room; an untidy room / 깨끗잖은 사람 a dirty 〔slovenly〕 man; a slob / 깨끗잖은 여자 a loose woman; a slut. ② 《몸이》 be not well; be out of sorts; (be) sick. ¶ 몸이 ~ feel ill 〔sick〕; be in a bad way 《구어》; be in bad 〔poor〕 health.

**깨끗하다** ① 《말쑥하다》 (be) trim; neat; tidy. ¶ 방을 깨끗하게 정돈하다 put the room in good order / 그녀는 언제나 옷차림이 ~ She is always neatly dressed. / 정원은 깨끗하게 손질이 잘 된 것같이 보였다 The garden looked neat and tidy.
② 《맑다·정결하다》 (be) pure; clear; clean. ¶ 깨끗한 공기 clear 〔fresh〕 air / 깨끗한 물 clear water; unpolluted water (오염되지 않은) / 깨끗한 옷 clean clothes; a clean suit / 깨끗하게 하다 purify; cleanse; make clean.
③ 《순수·결백하다》 (be) pure; clean; innocent; noble (고상); chaste (순결); 《공명 정대하다》 (be) fair; clean. ¶ 깨끗한 마음 a pure heart 〔soul〕 / 깨끗한 생활 a clean life; an honest life / 깨끗한 일생 a career with a clean record / 깨끗한 사랑 《남녀의》 platonic 〔pure〕 love / 깨끗한 여자 a chaste woman / 깨끗한 사람 a man of integrity; a man of pure heart; a clean-handed man / 깨끗한 한 표(票)〔선거〕 a clean vote 〔election〕 / 깨끗한 승부 a fine 〔fair〕

play / 깨끗한 정치 clean politics / 깨끗한 투표 corruption-free balloting / 마음이 깨끗한 사람은 복이 있다 Blessed are the pure in heart.
④《병에서 회복되다》 get well; recover from illness; be restored to health. ¶ 이 약 한 봉이면 심신이 깨끗해집니다 A dose of this will refresh you in mind and body.

**깨끼** 《깨끼옷》 *kkaekki* clothes, an early summer outfit for ladies which has ｢silk gauze 〔gossamer〕 lining, hemmed with elaborate seams. ¶ ~저고리 a *kkaekki* jacket (for a lady).

**-깨나** 《어느 정도의》 a certain 〔considerable〕 amount 〔sum, degree〕 of. ¶ 돈깨나 있다 have a sizable 〔considerable〕 sum of money / 수입깨나 있다 have a decent 〔respectable〕 income / 영어깨나 하다 speak English rather well / 주먹깨나 쓴다고 덤비지 마라 Don't come at me just because you can use your fists.

**깨나다** ⇨ 깨어나다.

**깨다**[1] ①《조각나게 부수다》 break; smash; shatter; crush. ¶ 접시를 산산조각으로 ~ break a dish into pieces; smash a dish / 유리창을 ~ smash a windowpane; break 〔shatter〕 a window / 얼음을 잘게 ~ break 〔smash, crush〕 ice to pieces / 그녀는 커피잔을 마루에 떨어뜨려 깼다 She dropped a coffee cup on the floor and broke it. / 도둑이 창문 유리를 깨고 침입했다 The robber broke the glass and climbed in through the window.
②《침묵·분위기·조화 따위를》 break; disturb; spoil. ¶ 무거운 침묵을 ~ break the heavy 〔oppressive〕 silence / 조화를 ~ spoil 〔disturb〕 the harmony / 흥을 ~ spoil *one's* pleasure 〔fun〕 / 행복을 ~ disturb *one's* happiness / 평화를 ~ break the peace / 한 발의 총성이 그 주변의 정적을 깼다 A shot broke 〔pierced〕 the quiet of the place.
③《위반하다》 break; violate; 《갱신하다》 break 《a record》. ¶ 계약〔협정〕을 ~ break a contract 〔an agreement〕 / 올림픽 기록을 ~ break 〔beat〕 the Olympic record / 혼담을 ~ break up marriage talks / 그녀는 약속을 깼다 She broke her promise. / 이 기록은 당분간 깨질 것 같지 않다 No one will break this record for some time. / 이 기록은 아직 깨지지 않았다 This record still hasn't been broken.

**깨다**[2] ①《잠에서》 wake (up); (come) awake; be awaken 〔be roused〕 from sleep 《by a noise》. ¶ 꿈에서 ~ come out of a dream / 나는 쉬이 잠에서 깬다 I am a light sleeper. / 오늘 아침에는 5시경에 깼다 I woke up (at) about five this morning.
②《환상·미몽 따위에서》 come to *one's* senses; be disillusioned; be undeceived. ¶ 나는 실패를 통해 꿈에서 깼다 My failure brought me to my senses. / 그는 아직도 환상에서 깨어나지 못하고 있다 He has not awakened from the illusion yet. *or* He hasn't come to his senses yet.
③ 《술에서》 sober up 〔down〕; get 〔become〕 sober. ¶ 그가 술이 깰 때까지 기다리자 Let's wait till he becomes sober. / 깜짝 놀라 취기가 깼다 With a surprise, I sobered up drunkenness.
④《지적(知的)으로》 be awakened; be enlightened; open *one's* eyes; get to know better. ¶ 신교육을 받아 사람들이 깼다 The people have been enlightened by new education.

**깨다**[3] ①《잠을》 awake; wake up; (a)rouse 《*a person*》 from sleep. ¶ 나는 그 소리에 잠을 깼다 I was awakened by the sound.
②《술기운을》 make 《*a person*》 sober; sober 《*a person*》 up; get rid of the effects of wine / 집에 데려가기 전에 그를 취기에서 깨게 하려고 했다 We tried to sober him up before taking him home.
③《환상 따위를》 disillusion; awaken. ¶ 그의 말이 환상에서 나를 깨게 했다 His remarks ｢awakened me from a dream 〔brought me to my senses〕.

**깨다**[4] ①《부화되다》 be hatched. ¶ 갓 깬 《chickens》 just hatched. ②《부화시키다》 (make) hatch; hatch (out) 《an egg》; sit on 《eggs》 (새가). ¶ 알이 깨는 데는 3주일이 걸린다 It takes three weeks for eggs to hatch.

**깨닫다** ①《인식·이해하다》 see; realize; perceive; understand; 《알아채다》 become aware 〔conscious〕 of 《*a thing*》; find; sense; get wind of 《*a thing*》; notice. ¶ 뜻을 ~ understand 〔grasp〕 the meaning / 자기 입장을 ~ realize *one's* own situation / 잘못을 ~ find out *one's* mistake; be convinced of *one's* error / 진리를 ~ perceive a truth / 의무를 ~ awaken to *one's* duty / 닥쳐오는 위험을 ~ sense an approaching danger / 깨닫게 하다 make 《*a person*》 realize 《*a thing*》; open 《*a person's*》 eyes 《to *a thing*》 / 상황의 중대성을 ~

realize 〔become aware of〕 the seriousness of the situation / 내가 실수하였음을 즉시 깨달았다 I saw at once that I had made a mistake. / 그녀는 위험에 처해 있다는 것을 분명히 깨달았다 She certainly realized that she was in danger.
② 《깨달음을 얻다》 be spiritually awakened; attain spiritual enlightenment; be enlightened. ¶ 완전히 ~ attain complete enlightenment.

**깨드득** with a smashing sound. ~하다 sound smashed.

**깨떡** sesame-coated rice cake.

**깨뜨리다** ⇨ 깨다[1].

**깨물다** bite; gnaw. ¶ 개에게 다리를 깨물렸다 I was bitten in the leg by a dog. / 분할 때 우리들은 입술을 깨문다 When we are vexed, we bite our lip.

**깨소금** powdered sesame mixed with salt.

**깨알** a grain of sesame; sesame seed. ¶ ~ 같다 be tiny (as a grain of sesame) / ~ 같은 글씨 fine 〔small〕 characters 〔letters〕 / ~같이 글씨를 쓰다 write closely / 동정심이라곤 ~만큼도 없다 He has not a grain 〔an ounce〕 of sympathy.

**깨어나다** ① 《잠에서》 ⇨ 깨다[2] ①. ② 《환상에서》 ⇨ 깨다[2] ②. ③ 《술에서》 ⇨ 깨다[2] ③. ④ 《의식이》 recover 〔regain〕 consciousness 〔*one's* senses〕; come to *one's* senses; 《소생하다》 come to life; be resuscitated; be restored to life. ¶ 깨어나게 하다 bring 《*a person*》 (back) to life 〔*his* senses〕; raise 《*a person*》 from the dead; revive; resuscitate / 기절했다가 ~ regain *one's* consciousness after a fainting spell / 마취에서 ~ come out from under the anesthesia / 인공호흡으로 그녀는 겨우 깨어났다 Artificial respiration took effect and she soon revived.

**깨우다** ① 《남을》 wake (up); awake; rouse 〔arouse〕 《*a person*》 from sleep. ¶ 문을 두드려〔벨을 울려〕 ~ tap 〔ring〕 up 《*a person*》 / 내일 아침 6시에 깨워주시오 Please call me 〔get me up, wake me〕 at six tomorrow morning. / 몇 시에 깨워드릴까요 When shall I wake 〔call〕 you? / 나는 낸시를 깨웠다 I woke 〔got〕 Nancy up. *or* I woke up Nancy. ② 《미몽 등에서》 disillusion 《*a person*》; awaken; bring 《*a person*》 to *his* senses; 《술에서》 sober 《*a person*》 up; make 《*a person*》 sober. ¶ 무지(無知)에서 ~ awaken 《*a person*》 from ignorance / 술에서 깨우려고 그에게 커피를 한 잔 주다 give him a cup of coffee to sober him up.

**깨우치다** make 《*a person*》 realize 《*a matter*》; bring 《*a person*》 to reason; open 《*a person's*》 eyes 《to *a thing*》; reason with 《*a person*》 《about, on》. ¶ 사리를 ~ reason with 《*a person*》 on the right and wrong of a matter / 잘못을 ~ make 《*a person*》 realize *his* mistake; reason with 《*a person*》 on *his* fault / 그가 틀렸다는 것을 깨우쳐 주십시오 Convince him of his error.

**깨죽**(一粥) sesame porridge; porridge made of ground sesame and rice.

**깨죽거리다** ① 《투덜거리다》 grumble 《at, over, about》; complain 《of, about》. ¶ 그는 늘 깨죽거리기만 한다 He is always grumbling. ② 《음식을》 trifle with *one's* food; eat 〔pick at〕 *one's* food as if *one* doesn't like it.

**깨지다** ① 《물건이》 break; get 〔be〕 broken; get 〔be〕 smashed; come to pieces (산산이); crack (금이 가다). ¶ 깨지기 쉬운 easily breaking; easy to break; fragile; frail; delicate; brittle / 깨진 냄비 a broken pan / 산산이 ~ be broken to fragments 〔pieces〕; be smashed into pieces / 깨지지 않도록 하다 keep 〔prevent〕 《*something*》 from breaking / 깨지지 않도록 다루다 handle 《an article》 with care / 깨지는 물건—취급 주의 《게시》 Fragile—Handle with care. ② 《계획 따위가》 fall through; miscarry; 《교섭 따위가》 be broken off; come to 〔end in〕 a rupture. ¶ 균형이 ~ the balance is upset 〔destroyed〕 / 협상〔혼담〕이 깨졌다 The negotiations 〔engagement, match〕 were broken off. ③ 《분위기 등이》 become chilled; be spoiled. ¶ 흥이 ~ *one's* fun is spoiled 《by》; *one's* enthusiasm is dampened 《by》.

**깨지락-** ⇨ 께지럭-.

**깨치다** ① 《깨닫다》 understand; comprehend; realize; find; perceive. ¶ 글뜻을 ~ understand the meaning of a sentence / 진리를 ~ perceive a truth. ② = 깨뜨리다.

**깩** with shriek 〔scream, screech〕; Eek!; Yipe!; Yelp! ~하다 shriek; screech; scream; shout out. ¶ 깩깩 소리 지르다 shriek and screech; scream.

**깩깩거리다** give 〔utter〕 a shriek 〔scream〕; shout and shout.

**깩소리** even one word of protest or complaint; a peep 《of protest》. ⇨ 끽

소리. ¶ ~ 못 하다 cannot let out a peep (of protest).
**깰깩거리다** make choking sounds.
**깰깰거리다** giggle; titter; 《미》 snicker. ¶ 무엇을 가지고 깰깰거리느냐 What are you giggling 〔snickering〕 about?
**깻묵** sesame dregs; oil cake. ¶ 콩~ bean cake.
**깻잎** a sesame leaf.
**깽** with a moan 〔whimper〕. ~하다 make a moan 〔whimper〕.
**깽깽** with groans 〔moans〕; 《강아지 울음소리》 yap, yap. ~하다, ~거리다 groan, moan; whimper; 《강아지가》 cry "yap, yap." ¶ 강아지가 ~거렸다 The puppy cried, "Yap, yap, yap."
**깽깽이풀** 〖식물〗 a kind of barberry shrub.
**꺄룩거리다** ⇨ 끼룩거리다 ②.
**꺅** ⇨ 깩.
**꺅도요** 〖조류〗 a (common) snipe.
**꺼꾸러-** ⇨ 거꾸러-.
**꺼끄러기** a beard; an awn; an arista.
**꺼끙그리다** hull grain lightly in a mill.
**꺼내다** ① 《손으로》 take 〔bring, get, pull, draw〕 out; carry out 〔away〕; 《화재 때에》 save; rescue. ¶ 주머니에서 …을 ~ take 〔draw〕 《*a thing*》 out of *one's* pocket / 방에서 가구를 ~ carry furniture out of a room / 궤에서 돈을 ~ take out some money from a box; take some money out of a box / 호주머니를 뒤져 동전을 ~ fish a coin out of the pocket / 화재시에는 이 상자를 먼저 꺼내야 한다 In case of fire we must be sure to save this box. ② 《말·문제를》 put forward; bring forward; introduce; drag out. ¶ 말을 ~ begin to speak; introduce 〔broach〕 a subject 〔topic〕; start talking; draw out conversation / 어려운 문제를 ~ bring up a difficult problem / 인원 삭감의 말을 ~ broach the subject of personnel cut 〔reduction〕 / 언제 이 이야기를 꺼내느냐가 문제이다 The problem is when to broach the subject.
**꺼당기다** pull; draw; haul; drag; tug (세게). ¶ 팔을 ~ pull 《*a person*》 by the arm / 밧줄을 ~ pull (at 〔on〕) a rope / 세게 ~ jerk; give 《*something*》 a jerk 〔a strong pull〕.
**꺼덕꺼덕** ¶ ~ 마른 damp-dry; damp=dried / 옷이 ~ 말랐다 The clothes are damp-dry.
**꺼두르다** 《움켜쥐고 휘두르다》 grab and pull about; drag 〔shake〕 《a woman by the hair》.
**꺼둘리다** get grabbed and pulled about; get dragged.
**꺼드럭-** ⇨ 거드럭-.
**꺼들다** take up; pick up; hold up. ¶ 치맛자락을 ~ hold 〔tuck〕 up (the edge of) *one's* skirt / 책상 한 귀퉁이를 ~ hold up a corner of the table.
**꺼들먹-** = 거드럭-.
**꺼들이다** take 〔bring〕 in; pull 〔draw〕 in. ¶ 나무를 광에 ~ take firewood into a storeroom / 아무를 집에 ~ take *a person* into *one's* house.
**꺼떡-** = 거드럭-.
**꺼뜨리다** put out a fire 〔light〕 by mistake; let a fire 〔light〕 go out. ¶ 연탄불을 꺼뜨리지 않다 keep briquet fire alive.
**꺼리다** ① 《싫어서 피하다》 be shy 〔afraid〕 《of *do*ing》; have scruples about 《*do*ing》; shun 〔avoid〕 《meeting other people》; 《주저하다》 hesitate 《to *do*》; be diffident 《about *do*ing》; 《싫어하다》 have a dislike 《to, for》; 《삼가하다》 abstain 〔refrain〕 《from *do*ing》. ¶ 남이 알까봐 꺼리는 사항 a confidential matter / 꺼리지 않고 without reserve 〔scruple, hesitation〕; openly; in public / 남이 어떻게 생각할까를 ~ be afraid of what others may think / 낯선 사람을 ~ be diffident to strangers / 사진 찍기를 ~ be shy of cameras; be camera-shy / 남들 앞에서 안 꺼리고 키스하다 kiss each other openly in public / 남의 눈을 꺼려 집안에만 있다 stay indoors for fear of being seen by others / 꺼리지 않고 자기 의견을 말하다 express 〔speak out〕 *one's* opinion (frankly) / 너에겐 세상에 꺼릴 것이 하나도 없다 You can look the world in the face. ② 《터부시하다》 taboo; be under (a) taboo.
**꺼림(칙)하다** feel leery 《about *do*ing》; feel uneasy; feel uncomfortable 《about》; 《양심에》 have pricks of conscience. ¶ 꺼림칙한 일 something *one* feels leery about doing / 이 음식은 먹기에 꺼림칙하다 I am a bit leery about eating this food.
**꺼머멀쑥하다** ⇨ 까마말쑥하다.
**꺼머번드르하다, 꺼머번지르하다** (be) dark and sleek; have black luster 〔gloss, sheen〕.
**꺼멓다** ⇨ 거멓다.
**꺼벙하다** (be) big but shaky; bulky and clumsy.
**꺼병이** ① 《새끼꿩》 a young 〔chick〕 pheasant. ② 《사람》 an unsightly person.
**꺼오다** pull 〔draw〕 《*a thing, a person*》 near 〔toward, close〕 to 《*one*》.
**꺼지다** ① 《불이》 go out; die out; 《전등

이》 go off 〔out〕; 《화재가》 be put out; be got under (control); be extinguished. ¶ 꺼져가는 불 a dying fire / 불이 ~ a fire goes out 〔is put out〕; a light fails / 촛불이 바람에 꺼졌다 The candle was blown out by the wind. / (전기)불이 꺼졌다 The light has gone out 〔off〕.
② 《지반이》 sink; subside; cave 〔fall〕 in; 《마루 따위가》 give in; 《배·눈이》 become empty 〔hollow〕; 《얼음이》 break; crack. ¶ 발 밑 땅이 ~ ground caves in under *one's* feet / 배가 ~ *one's* stomach becomes empty / 눈이 ~ *one's* eyes become hollow / 얼음이 꺼졌다 The ice cracked. / 도로의 지반이 약 20cm나 꺼졌다 The road subsided up to a depth of about 20 centimeters. / 무거운 상자 때문에 마루가 꺼졌다 The floor gave in under the weight of the heavy boxes.
③ 《사라지다》 vanish; disappear; go out of sight; fade away. ¶ 여기서 꺼져 Go away! *or* Get out of here.

**꺼칠하다** (be) worn-out 〔haggard〕; lack a sleek well-fed look; look emaciated 〔undernourished, thin, skinny〕; look worn-out 〔tired, washedout〕. ¶ 꺼칠한 얼굴 a haggard face / 병 치레로 ~ look worn-out 〔thin〕 after an illness / 그는 앓아서 꺼칠해졌다 The disease has made him lose flesh.

**꺼칫거리다** feel rough; be rough to the touch 〔feel〕; be prickly.

**꺼펑이** a covering; a cover; a hood.

**꺼풀** ⇨ 까풀.

**꺽** with a burp 〔belch〕.

**꺽다리** a very tall fellow; a lanky 〔gangling〕 person; a long-legged person.

**꺽두기** ① 《나막신》 wooden shoes. ② 《가죽신》 oiled leather shoes.

**꺽둑거리다** cut in uneven slices.

**꺽둑꺽둑** cutting in uneven slices; chop! chop! ¶ 무를 ~ 썰다 cut radish in uneven bits.

**꺽저기** 〖어류〗 a variety of perch.

**꺽죽거리다** behave brashly; push 〔shove〕 *oneself* forward; show cheek; get fresh; be brash 〔forward, fresh, pushy, cheeky〕. ¶ 꺽죽거리는 젊은이 a forward youth.

**꺽지다** (be) bold; dauntless; brave; 〔resolute.

**꺽짓손** means 〔measures〕 that are bold and compelling; an unshakable measure. ¶ ~ 세다 have the means to be bold and decisive; be indomitable; be unshakable.

**꺾꽂이** a cutting; 《방법》 cuttage. ~하다 plant 〔make〕 a cutting. ¶ 이 나무는 ~가 가능합니까 Can this tree be grown from a cutting? ◉ ~묘(苗) a sapling grown up from a cutting; 《삽수》 a cutting; a set.

**꺾다** ① 《부러뜨리다》 break off 《*a thing*》; snap 《*a thing*》 (in two). ¶ 나뭇가지를 ~ break a branch 〔(from a tree)〕 / 꽃을 ~ pick 〔pluck〕 a flower / 막대를 둘로 ~ snap a stick in two / 가지를 꺾지 마시오 《게시》 Do not break off branches.
② 《방향을》 make a (right-angled) turn; change (*one's*) course (at right angle). ¶ 핸들을 좌〔우〕로 ~ cut to the left 〔right〕 《미》; turn the wheel to the left 〔right〕 / 트럭은 방향을 급히 오른쪽으로 꺾었다 The truck turned sharp right.
③ 《마음을 굽히다》 give in 〔yield〕 《to *a person's* opinion》. ¶ 소년은 고집을 꺾고 어머니 말씀을 따랐다 The boy gave in to his mother.
④ 《접다》 fold 《*a thing*》 over; double 《*a thing*》; turn 《*a thing*》 down. ¶ 옷깃을 ~ turn a collar down / 꺾어 접다 fold twice; fold in two.
⑤ 《기세·사기 등을》 discourage; dishearten; dispirit; break (down); crush; depress; damp(en); 《계획·노력·희망 등을》 baffle 〔frustrate〕 《*a person's* plans 〔hopes〕》. ¶ 기를 ~ [원인이 주어] break 《*a person's*》 spirits; depress 〔dampen〕 《*a person's*》 spirits / 적의 사기를 ~ depress 〔break down〕 the enemy's morale / 초장에 아무의 콧대를 ~ baffle 《*a person*》 at the start / 적의 예봉을 ~ break the brunt of the enemy / 열의를 ~ cast a damper on 《*a person's*》 enthusiasm; damp 《*a person's*》 ardor / 강자를 꺾고 약자를 돕다 help 〔side with〕 the weak and crush the strong / 그 실패는 그의 열의를 꺾었다 The failure damped his enthusiasm.
⑥ 《지게 하다》 beat; defeat; 《구어》 get the better of.... ¶ 상대를 꺾고 결승에 진출하다 go into the finals by defeating the opponent / 그들은 우리 팀을 3점차로 꺾었다 They beat our team by three points.
⑦ 《가로막다》 interrupt 《*a person*》. ¶ 남의 말허리를 ~ interrupt 《*a person*》 (while he is speaking); cut 《*a person*》 short 〔off〕.

**꺾쇠** a ㄷ-shaped hook; a cramp (iron);

a clam. ¶ ~를 박다 fix a ㄷ-shaped hook / ~로 단단히 고정시키다 make 《*things*》 fast with cramps; fasten 〔hold〕《*things*》 with cramps.

**꺾쇠묶음** 〖인쇄〗 (square) brackets.

**꺾어지다** [자동사] ① 《부러지다》 break; snap (딱하고); give way (무게로). ¶ 두 동강으로 ~ break in two / 이 작대기는 좀처럼 꺾어지지 않는다 This stick won't break. / 가지가 눈의 무게로 꺾어졌다 The branch gave way under the weight of the snow. / 강풍으로 나뭇가지가 뚝하고 꺾어졌다 The branch snapped in the strong wind. / 너무 구부리지 마라. 꺾어질라 Don't bend it too far, or it will break.
② 《접히다》 fold 《in two》. ⇨ 꺾이다 ②.
③ 《방향이》 turn. ¶ 강은 다리 있는 곳에서 남쪽으로 꺾어진다 The river turns south at the bridge.

**꺾이다** ① 《부러지다》 be broken. ⇨ 꺾어지다 ①. ¶ 세 동강으로 ~ be broken in three / 좀처럼 꺾이지 않는 막대기 a tough stick.
② 《접히다》 be folded 《in three》; be doubled (둘로). ¶ 책귀가 ~ make a dog's ear (at the corner of a page).
③ 《방향이》 turn; go round; round; 《굽어지다》 be bent; be crooked; bend; curve. ¶ 강은 오른쪽으로 꺾인다 The river turns to the right. / 도로는 거기서 왼쪽으로 꺾여 있다 The road made a turn to the left there.
④ 《기세·사기 등이》 be discouraged 〔disheartened〕; be depressed 〔dispirited〕; lose heart 〔courage〕; break 〔down〕; be broken in spirit. ¶ 그는 의기가 꺾였다 His enthusiasm was dampened 〔weakened〕. *or* His ardor was cooled 〔chilled〕. / 그의 용기는 어떤 일에도 꺾이지 않는다 His courage will never be shaken by anything. / 한 번의 작은 실수로 기가 꺾여서는 안 된다 You should not be discouraged by one little failure.
⑤ 《굴하다》 yield 〔submit, bow〕 《to》; give in 《to》; 《기가 죽다》 be daunted 《by》. ¶ 압력에 ~ yield under pressure / 돈에 ~ bow to money / 역경에도 꺾이지 않다 bear up well under difficult 〔adverse〕 circumstances / 그는 한 번 실수 따위로 꺾일 사람이 아니다 He is not a man to be daunted by a single failure.
⑥ 《패하다》 be beaten; be defeated.

**꺾임새** the fold; the way it is folded back 〔turned down〕.

**껄껄** ¶ ~ 웃다 laugh loudly; burst into (a roar of) laughter.

**껄껄거리다** guffaw and guffaw; keep laughing loudly; roar with laughter.

**껄껄하다** (be) rough; coarse; be rough to the touch 〔feel〕. ¶ 껄껄한 살결 rough skin / 껄껄한 천 coarse fabric / 혀가 ~ the tongue is rough; have a rough tongue.

**껄끄럽다** ① 《거칠다》 (be) rough; itchy; coarse; 《따끔거리다》 (be) prickly; be bristly to the touch. ¶ 껄끄러운 털실 내복 itchy woolen underwear / 껄끄러운 감촉 a rough 〔sandy〕 feel 〔texture〕.
② 《성질이》 (be) rough-natured; be hard「to deal with 〔to please〕.

**껄끄렁베** hemp cloth of a rough texture.

**껄끄렁벼** rice grains with lots of bits of awns in them; husky rice grains.

**껄끔거리다** prick; prickle; tickle.

**껄떡이** a covetous 〔greedy〕 person.

**껄떡하다** 《*one's* eyes》 be sunken with fatigue 〔hunger〕. ¶ 그는 피로해서 눈이 껄떡했다 His eyes were deeply sunk with fatigue.

**껄렁껄렁하다** be no good; (be) poor; worthless; good-for-nothing; trashy. ¶ 껄렁껄렁한 물건 poor 〔wretched〕 stuff; mere trash / 껄렁껄렁한 사내 a good-for-nothing fellow.

**껄렁이** a good-for-nothing 〔silly〕 fellow; a shiftless character.

**껄렁패** good-for-nothing crews; hooligans; scamps.

**껄머리** a big false-hair chignon worn by the bride at a wedding.

**껄쭉거리다** feel rough (to the touch).

**껌** chewing gum. ¶ 풍선껌 bubble gum / 껌을 씹다 chew gum.

**껌껌하다** ① 《어둡다》 (be) very dark; pitch-black. ② 《마음이》 (be) black; deep; wicked; evil-〔black-〕hearted.

**껍죽거리다** behave haughtily; put on 〔give *oneself*〕 airs; be too forward; assume an air of importance. ¶ 껍죽거리는 관리 a pompous 〔haughty, pretentious〕 official.

**껍데기** 《딱딱한 표피. 각(殼)》 a shell (조개·열매의); a (nut)shell (견과의). ¶ 굴 ~ an oyster shell / 달걀 ~ an eggshell / 밤 ~ a chestnut shell. ¶ ~를 벗기다 / take the shell off; shell; [비유적] take all 《*a person's*》 money 〔possessions〕.

**껍질** 《딱딱하지 않은 표피》 skin; 《나무의》 bark; 《과일의》 (a) rind (두꺼운 것); peel; 《곡식의》 husk; hull; chaff. ¶ 오

렌지 ~ orange peel / 나무 ~ the bark of a tree / 빵 ~ the crust of bread / 사과 ~ the skin of an apple / 수박 ~ the rind of a watermelon / 양파 ~ the coats of an onion / 옥수수 ~ the husk of corn / 토마토〔바나나〕~ tomato 〔banana〕 skin / ~째 구운 감자 a jacket potato; a potato in its jacket / ~을 벗기다 skin 《onions》; peel 《a banana》; pare 《an apple》; husk; shuck / 귤 ~을 벗기다 peel a tangerine / 나무 ~을 벗기다 take the bark off a tree; bark a tree / ~째 먹다 eat 《an apple》 skin and all; eat 《sweet potatoes》 with the skin on.

**-껏** ① 《있는 대로》 to the full extent of; to the utmost of 《capability, capacity》. ¶ 힘껏 일하다 work to the utmost of *one's* power; work as hard as *one* can / 정성껏 대접하다 entertain 《*a person*》 with all *one's* heart / 양껏 먹다 eat *one's* fill; eat as much as *one* can / 욕심껏 먹다 eat greedily / 마음껏 울다 cry *one's* heart out / 재간껏 하다 do *one's* best. ② 《까지》 《right》 up to (now). ¶ 여태껏 한 것이 이것뿐이다 This is all I have done up to now. / 그 애가 여태껏 울고 있다 The boy is still crying. / 그는 여태껏 오지 않았다 He has not come as yet.

**껑거리** a crupper (made of a crossbar and two strings). ◉ ~끈 hip-strap strings; a crupper. ~막대 the crossbar of a hip strap.

**껑짜치다** 《면목없다》 (be) ashamed (of *oneself*); 《어색하다》 (be) embarrassed; feel awkward.

**껑충** with a jump 〔leap〕; lightly. ¶ 담을 ~ 뛰어넘다 hop 〔jump clean over〕 the fence.

**껑충거리다** walk with leaping 〔bouncing〕 strides.

**껑충하다** (be) tall and slender; lanky. ¶ 키가 껑충한 사람 a man with a tall, trim form / 껑충이 a lanky and fickle man / 두루미는 다리가 ~ A crane has long, slender legs.

**께**[1] 《에게》 to 〔for〕 《*a person*》. ¶ 어머님께 온 편지 a letter for my mother / 하느님께 기도 드리다 pray to God / 한 선생님께 드림 To 〔Presented to〕 Mr. Han (with compliments). / 아버님께 책을 드렸다 I gave the book to my father.

**께**[2] ① 《경(頃)》 about; around; towards 《a time》. ¶ 보름께 about 〔towards〕 the middle of the month / 그믐께 about 〔towards, near〕 the end of the month / 정오께 around noontime; towards noon. ② 《장소》 around; in the vicinity 〔neighborhood〕 of; near 《a place》. ¶ 남대문께 near the South Gate; in the vicinity of Namdaemun / 종로 네거리께 around 〔in the neighborhood of〕 Chongno crossing.

**께끄름하다** [사람이 주어] feel a bit unpleasant; feel uneasy 〔anxious, uncomfortable〕 《about》; [사물이 주어] weigh on *one's* mind; lie at *one's* heart; be not quite happy 《about》. ¶ 양심상 ~ have an uneasy conscience / 뒷맛이 께끄름한 좋지 않은 꿈 a bad dream remembered with discomfort / 좋지 않은 시험 결과가 께끄름해서 잠이 오지 않았다 The poor result of the examination weighed so heavily on my mind that I couldn't get to sleep.

**께끼다** ① 《절구질할 때》 put overflowing grain back into the mortar. ② 《노래·말할 때》 chime in with 《*a person's* remark or song》.

**께느른하다** (be) languid; weary; listless; dull; feel languor. ¶ 께느른한 여름날 오후 a languid summer afternoon / 먼 길을 걸었더니 몸이 ~ I am quite exhausted after the long walk. / 날씨가 더워 ~ The warm weather makes me feel listless.

**께서** from 《*a person*》. ¶ 아버지~ 주신 돈 the money that I got from father.

**께죽거리다** ① 《투덜대다》 grumble about 〔at〕 《*something*》; growl 《at》. ② 《음식을》 chew 《food》 over and over again without appetite; chew dryly at 《*one's* food》; pick at *one's* food. ¶ 께죽거리지 말고 빨리 먹어라 Stop picking 〔poking, dawdling〕 at your food —eat it up!

**께지럭거리다** go at 〔do〕 《*a thing*》 half-heartedly 〔listlessly, unenthusiastically, with little interest〕.

**꼑꼑** yelling. ~하다 yell; yelp. ¶ ~거리다 shout 《at *a person*》; yell out.

**껴들다** 《두 팔로》 lift 〔take, raise〕 《*a thing*》 in *one's* arms; 《두 가지를》 hold both at once. ¶ 무거운 가방을 ~ lift 〔raise〕 a heavy bag in *one's* arms.

**껴안다** ① 《포옹》 hold 〔take〕 《a baby》 in *one's* arms; hug; embrace. ¶ 어깨를 ~ take 〔hold〕 《*a person*》 round the shoulders / 목을 ~ throw *one's* arms around 《*a person's*》 neck / 껴안고 있다 have 〔carry〕 《a baby》 in *one's* arms / 연인들은 서로 꼭 껴안았다 The lovers hugged 〔embraced〕 each other tightly. / 두 사람은 서로 껴안고 울었다 The two threw themselves into each other's arms and wept. ② 《일을》 take a lot of tasks upon *oneself*.

**껴입다** put more 《clothes》 on top of what *one* is wearing; warm *oneself* with thick clothes; dress (*oneself*) warmly; wrap up well [warmly]. ¶ 내의를 두 장 ~ wear [put on] two undershirts one over the other.

**꼬기꼬기** ~하다 (be) crumpled; wrinkled; rumpled; mussed (up). ¶ ~ 구긴 시트 rumpled sheets / 종이를 ~ 뭉치다 crumple a piece of paper into a ball / 그는 그 편지를 ~ 구겨서 휴지통에 넣었다 He crumpled (up) the letter (into a ball) and put it in the wastebasket.

**꼬꼬댁** cackling (of a hen after laying an egg). ~거리다 cackle. ¶ ~ 소리 (the) cackle; the sound of cackling.

**꼬끼오** cock-a-doodle-doo; the crow (of a cock). ~하다 《roosters》 cry cock-a-doodle-doo; crow.

**꼬느다** ① 《치켜들다》 lift up 《*a heavy thing*》 and take aim with *one's* stretched arms 《at》. ② 《벼르다》 wait [watch for] a chance 《to *do*》; 《이럴까 저럴까 생각하다》 nurse [toy with] an idea. ¶ 꼬느기만 해서 소용이 있느냐 What's the use of just nursing your plans?

**꼬다** ① 《끈을》 twist (together); twine. ¶ 새끼를 ~ twist [make] a rope / 노끈을 ~ twist strands into a cord [rope, string] / 지노를 ~ twist paper into a string. ② 《몸을》 twist *oneself*; writhe 《in pain》. ¶ 사지를 ~ twist *one's* limbs / 다리를 꼬고 앉다 sit with *one's* legs crossed. ③ ⇨ 비꼬다.

**꼬드기다** ① 《연줄을》 tug at a kite line (to get the kite to rise in the air). ② 《부추기다》 stir up; incite; instigate; urge; set [spur, egg] on. ¶ 꼬드겨(서) …하게 하다 set [needle, tempt] 《*a person*》 to 《*do*》; incite [instigate] 《*a person*》 to 《*do*》; cajole [wheedle] 《*a person*》 in 《*doing*》 / 꼬드겨서 죄를 짓게 하다 abet 《*a person*》 in a crime / 근로자들을 꼬드겨 파업을 일으키려 하다 try to incite the workers to go on strike / 그는 친구들을 꼬드겨서 그 소년을 괴롭혔다 He egged his friends on to bully the boy.

**꼬들꼬들하다** hard. ¶ 꼬들꼬들한 밥 hard boiled rice / 밥이 좀 ~ The rice is boiled rather hard.

**꼬락서니** = 꼴[1]. ¶ ~ 좀 봐라 How dirty you are! *or* What a wretched state you are in!

**꼬리** ① 《동물의》 a tail; a scut (토끼·사슴 등의); a brush (여우 등의); a train (공작 등의). ¶ ~가 긴[짧은] long-[short=] tailed 《monkeys》 / ~가 길다[짧다] have a long [short] tail / 강아지가 ~를 치며 나를 따라왔다 A puppy followed me wagging its tail. / 개가 ~를 사리고 달아났다 A dog run away [off] with its tail between its legs.

② 《유성·혜성 따위의》 a tail; a trail 《of a comet》; 《무·배추의 뿌리》 the end 《of a raddish》. ¶ 제트기가 길게 ~를 남겼다 The jet left a long tail behind it.

③ [비유적 표현] ¶ 말~를 잡다 take up 《*a person*》 on a slip of the tongue; trip 《*a person*》 up with *his* own words; cavil at 《*a person's*》 words / 용의자의 ~를 잡다 find the trace of a culprit / ~를 치다 《유혹하다》 tempt; entice; allure; 《여자가 아양떨다》 flirt 《with》; play the coquette 《with》; act seductively [coquettishly] / ~가 잡히다 [사물이 주어] give a clue 《to the police》; [사람이 주어] be traced [tracked]; be found out [caught] in wrongdoing / 그것이 ~가 잡혀 그는 체포되었다 That supplied a clue which led to his arrest. / 사건들이 ~를 물고 일어났다 Several incidents happened one after another. *or* One incident followed on the heels of another. / 버스, 택시 및 승용차들이 ~를 물고 달린다 Buses, taxis and cars run bumper to bumper. / ~가 길면 밟힌다 《속담》 Repeated misbehavior eventually catches up with *one*.

◉ ~곰탕 oxtail soup (and rice). ~깃 tail feathers. ~날개 《비행기의》 the tail assembly 《of an aircraft》. ~지느러미 a caudal fin.

**꼬리보** 『건축』 a beam bent at one end so as to touch a purlin(e).

**꼬리표**(一票) a (shipping) tag; a (tie=on) label. ¶ ~를 달다 put a label on; fasten [attach, fix 《미》] a label [tag] to 《*one's* baggage》; tag [label] 《*one's* baggage》 / 서울행 ~가 달려 있다 be labeled for Seoul.

**꼬마** 《사람》 a tiny person; a midget; 《키 작은 사람》 a short man; 《아이》 a (little) kid; 《애칭으로》 a shorty [shortie] 《속어》; 《물건》 a tiny thing; a midget one. ◉ ～둥이 a small child; a little darling; a midget; a shorty. ～자동차 a midget car; a minicar. ～전구 a midget lamp.

**꼬박**[1] 《내내》 straight 〔all〕 through; without a break; continuously; 《뜬눈으로》 without sleeping a wink; 《온》 full; fully; whole. ¶ ～사흘 동안 for three full days; for three straight 〔successive〕 days / ～ 하룻밤을 새우다 sit 〔stay〕 up all night / ～ 이틀간이나 눈이 내리고 있다 It has been snowing for two days without a break 〔stop〕. / 사장은 ～ 세 시간 동안 이야기를 했다 The president spoke for three hours at a stretch. / 이 문제를 푸는 데 ～ 사흘이나 걸렸다 I spent three full days to solve this problem.

**꼬박**[2] ⇨ 꾸벅.

**꼬박꼬박** ① ⇨ 꾸벅꾸벅. ② 《순종》 humbly obeying; 《어김없이》 regularly; 《성실히》 faithfully. ¶ 어른의 말을 ～ 잘 듣다 readily obey *one's* elders; be very obedient to *one's* superiors / 세금을 ～ 내다 pay *one's* taxes regularly / 가계부를 ～ 적다 keep household accounts every day.

**꼬박이** ＝ 꼬박[1].

**꼬부라뜨리다** bend; hook; curve; twist (비틀어서). ¶ 철사 끝을 ～ bend the end of the wire.

**꼬부라지다** ① 《몸·도로·나무 따위가》 bend; curve; be bent; be crooked; wind; turn. ¶ 꼬불꼬불 꼬부라진 길 a winding path / 꼬부라진 소나무 a crooked pine / 철사가 ～ a wire is bent / 늙어 허리가 ～ be bent 〔stooped〕 with age / 길이 오른쪽으로 ～ a road turns to the right. ② 《혀가》 be tongue-tied; be unable to speak distinctly; have an impediment in *one's* speech; *one's* speech is slurred (술이 취해서). ¶ 혀 꼬부라진 소리로 말하다 speak thickly 〔inarticulately〕.

**꼬부랑글자**(一字) 《졸필》 a poor handwriting; "hen tracks 〔scratches〕"; 《서양 글자》 the Roman 〔Latin〕 alphabet.

**꼬부랑꼬부랑** being bent here and there; winding now and then; meanderingly. ～하다 be bent here and there; (be) winding; meandering; sinuous; serpentine. ¶ ～한 길 a winding 〔meandering〕 path 〔road〕 / 그 ～한 길이 산마루까지 이어져 있다 The winding road leads to the top of the hill.

**꼬부랑늙은이** a bent 〔stooped〕 old person.

**꼬부랑하다** (be) bent; crooked. ¶ 나뭇가지가 ～ a bough is crooked / 그녀는 늙어서 허리가 ～ She is bent 〔bowed〕 with age. *or* She stoops from age.

**꼬부리다** bend; curve; 《갈고리 모양으로》 crook; hook. ¶ 철사를 ～ bend a wire / 허리를 ～ bend *oneself* 〔*one's* back〕; bend over / 손가락을 ～ hook 〔crook〕 *one's* finger.

**꼬부장하다** ① 《물체가》 (be) gently bent 〔curved〕. ¶ 꼬부장한 나뭇가지 a gently bent bough / 허리가 ～ be slight bent (at the waist) / 그 길은 꼬부장하게 굽어 있다 The road bends in a wide curve. ② 《마음이》 (be) crooked; perverse; warped; twisted. ¶ 그는 근성〔성격〕이 ～ He has a crook in his character. *or* His character is warped 〔twisted〕.

**꼬불거리다** wind; meander; zigzag. ¶ 길이 여기서부터 꼬불거리기 시작한다 The road begins to zigzag from here.

**꼬불꼬불** winding; zigzag. ～하다 (be) winding; meandering; zigzag. ¶ ～한 길 a winding path / ～한 골목길 meandering back alleys / 길은 가파른 비탈에 ～ 나 있었다 The path zigzagged up the steep slope.

**꼬불탕하다** (be) winding; meandering; zigzag.

**꼬이다** ① 《로프·호스·끈 따위가》 be 〔get〕 twisted 〔kinked〕; 《얽히다》 get 〔be〕 entangled 〔snarled〕. ¶ 실이 ～ strings are twisted; thread gets entangled 〔snarled up〕 / 이 호스는 잘 꼬인다 This hosepipe kinks easily. / 좌석 벨트를 맬 때는 꼬이지 않도록 하여라 When you fasten your seat belt, make sure it isn't twisted. ② 《일이》 go wrong 〔amiss〕; get complicated; be in a tangle; 《미》 be snarled (up). ¶ 계획을 꼬이게 하다 throw the plan into disorders / 일이 ～ a matter goes amiss 〔goes wrong〕; something gets all fouled up / 사업이 꼬여서 고생하다 suffer from the unsatisfactory state of *one's* business / 그는 언제나 단순한 문제를 꼬이게 한다 He always snarls up a simple problem. ③ 《마음이》 become crooked 〔distorted, peevish, perverse〕; get cranky. ¶ 속이 ～ get cranky; grow peevish / 성격이 꼬여 있다 have a crook in *one's* character.

**꼬장꼬장하다** ① 《가는 물건이》 (be) straight and stiff. ② 《노인이》 (be) straight and strong; hale and hearty; carry *one's* frame upright. ¶ 할아버지는 여든이시지만 아직 꼬장꼬장하

시다 My grandfather is hale and hearty though he is eighty years old. ③《성미가》(be) upright; unbending; incorruptible; staunch. ¶성미가 꼬장꼬장한 사람 a man of upright character.

**꼬집다** ①《살을》pinch; give a pinch; nip《*a person's* arm》. ¶세게 ~ give 《*a person*》a sharp pinch《on the arm》/ 꼬집어 멍들게 하다 pinch《*a person*》black and blue / 꿈이 아닌가 하고 자기 몸을 꼬집어 보다 pinch *oneself* to see if it is real. ②《비꼬다》make cutting〔sarcastic, insinuating〕remarks about《*a thing*》; talk cynically《about》; have〔take〕a dig at《*a person*》about《*a thing*》. ¶아픈 데를 ~ touch《*a person*》on a sore spot; find〔hit〕《*a person's*》Achilles heel / 꼬집어 말하다 say sarcastic〔spiteful〕things《about》/ 결점을 꼬집어 내다 find fault with《*a person*》; pick〔point〕out《*a person's*》flaws.

**꼬창모** 〖농업〗rice plants set out with a dibble〔stick〕.

**꼬챙이** a skewer; a spit (굵은 것); a (pointed) stick; a dibble (농업용). ¶~에 꿰다 skewer《meat》; spit《chicken》/ ~로 찌르다 prod〔thrust at, poke〕with a stick / 생선을〔고기를〕~에 꿰어 굽다 roast〔grill〕fish〔meat〕on skewers.

**꼬치** ①＝꼬챙이. ②《꿴 음식》skewered stuff; food on a skewer.
◉ ~안주 a skewered tidbit〔side dish〕taken with alcholic drinks.

**꼬치꼬치** ①《여윔》becoming extremely thin; wasting away. ¶~ 마르다 be very thin〔skiny〕; be much emaciated; be worn〔reduced〕to a shadow〔skeleton〕; be skin and bone(s). ②《따짐》inquisitively. ¶~ 캐묻다 inquire of《*a person*》about every detail of《*a matter*》; question to the minutest details; catechize《*a person*》to the last detail about《*a matter*》/ 형사는 그녀에게 그때 상황에 대해서 ~ 물었다 The detective made her describe the situation down to the smallest detail.

**꼬치백반**(―白飯) rice with a skewered dish.

**꼬투리** ①《깍지》a pod; a shell; a husk; a legume (*pl.* -gumina). ¶(콩의) ~를 까다 shell〔pod〕peas. ②《담배 꽁초》a cigarette butt〔end〕; a half-smoked cigarette〔cigar〕. ③《근본·원인·이유》origin《of *an affair*》(근본); cause (원인); reason (이유). ¶아무 ~도 없이 without any reason; without cause; causelessly / 의심을 사는 ~가 되다 offer a cause to invite suspicion / 도대체 무엇이 ~가 되어 싸웠는가 What on earth was the bone of contention?

**꼭** ①《틀림없이》certainly; surely; 《어김없이》without fail; for sure; 《무슨 수를 써서라도》by all means; at any cost. ⇨ 반드시. ¶꼭 해야 할 일 a thing that has to be done; a must / 꼭 필요하다 want〔need〕《*a thing*》badly / 꼭 해라 Do it without fail. *or* By all means, do so. / 꼭 가겠다 I'll come for sure〔in any event〕. *or* I will not fail to come. / 꼭 오너라 You must come! *or* Do〔Be sure to〕come. / 그 영화는 놓치지 말고 꼭 보아라 You mustn't miss that picture. / 꼭 해 볼 생각이다 I will try whatever happens. / 아무리 비싸도 그 고급 차를 꼭 사겠다 I will get that classic car at any〔all〕cost.
②《틈새 없이·밀착되게》close(ly); tight(-ly). ¶몸에 꼭 끼는 스커트 a close-〔tight-〕fitting skirt / 문을 꼭 닫다 close the door tight(ly) / 서로 꼭 붙어 앉다 sit close together / 꼭 껴안다 embrace〔hug〕《*a person*》closely / 벽에 몸을 꼭 붙이고 있다 keep up against the wall / 이 셔츠는 몸에 너무 꼭 낀다 This shirt is too tight. / 구두가 꼭 끼어 뒤꿈치가 아프다 The shoe pinches me at the heel.
③《정확히·딱》exactly; rightly; just; perfectly. ¶꼭 한 시간 just〔exactly〕an hour / 꼭 2마일 exactly two miles / 꼭 사흘 three days to the hour / 꼭 같은 시간에 at exactly the same time / 꼭 맞다《옷 따위가》fit《*a person*》perfectly; fit「to a T〔to a nicety〕(★ to a T는 to a title의 약자로 perfectly의 뜻); 《계산 따위가》be perfectly correct; [일반적으로] fit right in《with》/ 꼭 들어맞는 말 an apt remark; the right word《for》/ 꼭 맞는 상의 a well-fitting coat / (옷·신발이) 꼭 맞지 않는다 do not fit well; be a poor fit / 이 상의는 너에게 꼭 맞는다 This coat fits you well. / 네 짐작이 꼭 들어 맞았다 You've guessed right. *or* You hit the nail on the head.
④《단단히》firmly; tight(ly); fast; securely. ¶꼭 매다 tie up〔fasten〕《*a thing*》tightly / 꼭 쥐다 grasp firmly; take a firm grasp of《*a person's*

hand》/ 마개를 꼭 닫다 close a cap tightly / 이 밧줄을 꼭 잡고 있어라 Keep holding this rope fast 〔tight〕. / 그는 신문지를 끈으로 꼭 묶었다 He bound the newspaper tightly with a string. / 난간을 꼭 잡아라 Hold on fast 〔tight〕 to the handrail.
⑤ 《똑 닮은 모양》《look》 exactly 〔just〕 like; like as two peas; 《마치》 as if 〔though〕; much 〔nearly〕 as. ¶ 꼭 같다 be just 〔exactly〕 like 《*a person*》; be a look-alike for 《*a person*》/ 박 대통령과 꼭 닮은 President Park's look=alike; Mr. Look-Like President Park / 꼭 죽은 사람 같다 look as if dead; be more dead than alive / 꼭 미친 사람 같다 look as if *one* were mad / 그는 하는 짓이 꼭 버릇없는 애 같다 He behaves just like a spoiled child. / 그 그림은 실물과 꼭 같다 The picture is true to life 〔nature〕. / 그 두 소년은 정말로 꼭 닮았다 There is a great resemblance between those two boys. *or* The two boys are exactly 〔just〕 like two peas.

**꼭꼭**[1] ① 《어김없이》 without fail; for sure; regularly; precisely; exactly; punctually (시간을). ¶ 집세를 ～ 지급하다 be regular 〔punctual〕 in paying *one's* rent / 시간을 ～ 지키다 keep a careful eye on *one's* time; be punctual / 약속을 ～ 지키다 keep *one's* promise scrupulously; never fail to keep *one's* promise / 명령을 ～ 실행하다 carry out orders punctiliously; never fail to obey an order. ② 《단단히》 tight(ly); fast; firmly; 《충분히》 fully; thoroughly; well, sufficiently. ¶ ～ 묶다 tie (up) 〔fasten〕 《*a thing*》 tightly; tie 〔fasten〕 tight / 음식을 ～ 씹어 먹다 chew *one's* food well 〔fully〕. ③ 《꽉·잔뜩》 with no room 〔not an inch〕 to spare; to the full. ¶ 작은 가방에 옷을 ～ 쑤셔 넣다 squeeze clothes into a small bag; cram clothes into a small bag / ～ 채워져 있다 be crammed full 〔cramfull, chockfull〕 《of》; be closely packed 《with》.

**꼭꼭**[2] 《암탉이》 cluck-cluck. ～하다〔거리다〕 cluck; chuck; cackle (알을 낳았을 때).

**꼭대기** ① 《위》 the top; the summit (산의); the crown (머리의). ¶ 산～ a mountaintop; the crest of a mountain / 나무 ～ the top of a tree; a treetop / 머리 ～ the top of the head; the crown of *one's* head / 백두산 ～에 는 연중 눈이 싸여 있다 Mt. Baekdu is crowned with snow the whole year round. ② 《우두머리》 the head; a chief; a leader; a boss. ¶ 사람들의 ～에 서다 become 〔be looked up to as〕 a leader; lead others.

**꼭두각시** a puppet; a marionette; [비유적] a tool; a cat's-paw 《of》. ¶ ～처럼 as if *one* were on wires / 남의 ～ 노릇을 하다 act as another's tool 〔cat's=paw〕. ◉ ～놀음 a puppet show 〔play〕; puppetry; a puppet drama 〔acting〕.

**꼭두새벽** early morning; the peep of dawn 〔day〕. ¶ ～에 《get up》 quite early in the morning; before dawn 〔daybreak〕/ 이런 ～에 전화를 걸어 미안합니다 I'm sorry to call you this early in the morning.

**꼭두서니** 『식물』 a madder; 《빛깔》 madder (red).

**꼭뒤** 《뒤통수》 the back of the head; the occiput; 《활의》 a (bow) nock.

**꼭뒤누르다** suppress; have 《*a person*》 under perfect control 〔under *a person's* thumb〕.

**꼭뒤눌리다** be suppressed; be under perfect control; be under *a person's* thumb; be dominated. ¶ 아무한테 ～ be dominated by *a person*.

**꼭뒤잡이하다** grasp 《*a person*》 by the back of the neck. ¶ 서로 ～ grapple with each other (grasping the back of the neck).

**꼭뒤지르다** 《선수치다》 forestall 《*one's* rival, *a person's* attempt》; get the 「start 〔better〕 of 《*a person*》; outwit 《*a person*》; get ahead of 《*a person*》; beat 《*a person*》 to the draw.

**꼭뒤질리다** be forestalled; get beaten to 《*a thing*》. ¶ 그 골동품을 사려다 다른 사람한테 꼭뒤질렸다 I was going to buy the curio but I got beaten to it 〔someone bought it ahead of me〕.

**꼭지** ① 《식물의》 a stem; a stalk; a peduncle (꽃의). ¶ ～가 떨어지다 fruit falls 〔drops〕; [비유적] mature; become independent; get where *one* can stand on *one's* own feet. ② 《손잡이》 a knob; 《수도·가스의》 a cock; a faucet 《미》; a tap 《영》. ¶ 수도 ～를 틀다〔잠그다〕 turn the water on 〔off〕; turn on 〔off〕 the water / 냄비 뚜껑의 ～가 떨어졌다 The knob has come off the pot lid. ③ 《연의》 a decorative strip pasted near the top of a kite. ④ 《두목》 the leader 〔boss〕 《of a band of vagrants or pickpockets》; a ringleader. ⑤ 《도리깨의》 the pivot of a flail. ⑥ 《묶음》 a bunch; a bundle. ¶ 미역 세 ~ three bunches 〔bundles〕 of (brown) seaweeds.

◉ ~각 〚수학〛 vertical angles. ~점 〚기하〛 the apex (*pl.* ~es, apices); the vertex (*pl.* ~es, vertices): 삼각형의 ~점 the apex 〔vertex〕 of a triangle.

**꼰질꼰질하다** (be) overmeticulous; too fussy 〔fastidious〕.

**꼴**[1] 《모양》 a shape; a form; 《모습》 a figure; (an) appearance (외관); 《상태》 a state 《of things》; a condition; circumstance; 《광경》 a sight; a scene. ¶ 네모꼴의 건물 a square building / 달걀꼴의 얼굴 an egg-shaped 〔an oval (=shaped)〕 face / 꼴이 말이 아니다 be out of shape; look miserable; be in bad shape / 꼴이 초라하다 look shabby; be shabbily dressed / 자네 이게 무슨 꼴인가 What a wretched state you are in! *or* How miserable you look! / 자넨 꼴도 보기 싫네 I hate the very sight of you. / 꼴 좋다 It serves you 〔him〕 right! / 이런 꼴로 실례합니다 Pardon me for being in this dress. / 그런 꼴로 나가면 사람들이 웃겠다 If you go out 「in that outfit 〔dressed like that〕, people will laugh at you.

**꼴**[2] 《풀》 fodder; forage; hay; grass. ¶ 꼴을 먹이다 feed 〔fodder〕 《an ox》 / 꼴을 베다 mow grass.

**-꼴** 《비율》 (priced) at the rate of... each; per unit. ¶ 한 다발에 천원꼴이다 The price is (at the rate of) 1,000 won per bunch. / 하루 평균 만원꼴이 된다 It will work out at ten thousand won per day.

**꼴간**(一間) a barn; 《다락방》 a hayloft.

**꼴깍** ⇨ 꿀꺽.

**꼴꾼** a fodder 〔grass〕 mower.

**꼴뚜기** 〚동물〛 a small kind of octopus (*pl.* -puses, -pi). ¶ ~ 같은 octopal.

◉ ~장수 an octopus peddler; [비유적] a businessman who has gone broke. ~젓 pickled octopus. ~질 a gesture of insult (made by pointing *one's* middlefinger at 《*a person*》).

**꼴리다** ① 《성기가》 stand erect; become stiff 〔rigid〕. ¶ 음경이 ~ get 〔have〕 an erection. ② 《배알이》 *one's* temper flares up. ¶ 배알이 ~ be offended 〔provoked〕 《at, by》; feel vexed 〔annoyed〕 《at, with》.

**꼴머슴** a farm chore-boy.

**꼴보다** examine 《*a person's*》 face 〔appearance〕; look 《*things, a person*》 over; see how things stand; see how a situation is. ¶ 꼴(을) 보아서는 재간이 있을 것 같지 않다 Judging 〔To judge〕 from his appearance, he doesn't seem to have any talent at all. / 꼴보니 일이 잘 되긴 틀렸다 Judging from the present state of affairs, the plan will come to no good.

**꼴불견**(一不見) unsightliness; unseemliness; unpresentableness. ¶ ~이다 be unsightly 〔unseemly〕; be unbecoming 〔indecent〕. ⇨ 꼴사납다.

**꼴사납다** 《보기 흉하다》 (be) unsightly; unseemly; ugly; 《초라하다》 shabby; disreputable; 《창피하다》 disgraceful; shameful; 《역겹다》 disgusting; 《천하다》 despicable; indecent; 《어울리지 않다》 unbecoming. ¶ 꼴사나운 놈 a disgusting 〔despicable〕 fellow / 꼴사나운 광경 an ugly scene / 꼴 사납게 굴다 behave in 「a disgraceful 〔an unseemly〕 fashion; behave badly / 꼴사나운 복장을 하고 있다 be shabbily 〔indecently〕 dressed / 돈갖고 싸우는 것은 ~ It is really vulgar to fight over money. / 이런 꼴사나운 모습을 보시게 해서 부끄럽습니다 I am ashamed to have you witness such a disgraceful sight.

**꼴짝거리다** squish and squish; sniffle and sniffle. ¶ 국을 ~ slurp *one's* soup.

**꼴짝꼴짝** squashing (and squashing); sniffling (and sniffling). ¶ ~ 울다 sniffle; sob.

**꼴찌** the bottom; the last; the tail end; the tail-ender (최하위자). ¶ 행렬의 ~ the tail end of a procession / ~로 오다 be the last to come / ~에서 둘째이다 be second from the bottom of the list; be the last but one / ~로 졸업하다 graduate last on the list / 그녀는 경주에서 ~로 들어왔다 She 「came in 〔finished〕 last in the race. / 그녀는 반에서 ~이다 She is at the bottom of her class.

**꼼꼼쟁이** a meticulous person; a stickler for details.

**꼼꼼하다** (be) very careful; meticulous; scrupulous; detailed; close. ¶ 꼼꼼한 교정원 a scrupulous proofreader / 꼼꼼한 일꾼 a careful worker / 꼼꼼히 carefully; meticulously; scrupulously; in detail; elaborately / 일을 꼼꼼히 하다 do *one's* work carefully / 꼼꼼하게 검사하다 examine 《*a matter*》 closely; make a close investigation 《into》.

**꼼바르다** 《도량이》 (be) narrow-minded and stingy.

**꼼바리** a narrow-minded tightwad 〔skinflint〕; a niggard.

**꼼짝** budging; stirring. ～하다 budge; stir; move; make a move. ¶ ～(도) 할 수 없다 cannot move at all; cannot stir an inch; have no elbowroom / ～도 안 하다 do not budge 〔stir〕 an inch; 《끄떡도 않다》 do not turn a unmoved / ～ 말고 거기 있거라 Stay put there! *or* Hold it (right) there! / ～마라, 움직이면 죽는다〔쏘겠다〕 Freeze! One move and「you are a dead man 〔I will shoot〕. / 바위가 ～ 않는다 The rock won't budge an inch. / 그는 한 동안 ～ 않고 앉아 있었다 He sat motionless for a while. / 그는 ～ 않고 집에 들어박혀 있다 He shuts himself in his home and never stirs (outside). / 그는 손가락 하나 ～ 않는다 He does not stir a finger.

**꼼짝거리다** 《…이》 budge and budge; stir 《about》; move 《about》; fidget 《about》; wiggle; wriggle; 《…을》 keep budging 《it》; move 《it》. ¶ 꼼짝거리지 말고 좀 가만 있거라 Be still and don't keep fidgeting!

**꼼짝못하다** ① 《몸을》 cannot move 〔budge, stir〕 an inch; be stuck 〔tied up〕 《in traffic》; be held up; 《곤경에 처해서》 be helpless; be in a fix 〔quandary〕; be at a loss; be in a dilemma. ¶ 허리가 아파 꼼짝 못하겠다 I cannot budge for the pain in my back. / 그들은 자금 부족으로 꼼짝 못할 지경이다 They find themselves stuck for want of funds. / 내 차는 교통 정체로 꼼짝 못했다 My car was「stuck 〔tied up〕 in a traffic jam. ② 《무서워서》 be cowed; cower 〔quail〕 《before, at》; shrink. ¶ 무서워서 ～ quail 〔shrink〕 with fear / 그는 주인 앞에선 언제나 꼼짝 못한다 He is always cowed in the presence of his master. / 그는 마누라한테 꼼짝 못한다 He is henpecked by his wife. / 그 말 한마디에 그는 꼼짝을 못했다 He was silenced 〔brought up short〕 by that one word.

**꼼짝없이** 《별 수 없이》 helplessly; with no way out; without recourse; 《강요되어》 under compulsion; 《움직이지 않고》 without moving 〔the slightest stir〕. ¶ ～ 굶고 있다 be starving helplessly / ～ (붙)잡히다 be held 〔arrested〕 with no way out 〔without recourse〕 / ～ 죽게 되다 face the unescapable death / 날씨가 나빴기 때문에 우리는 ～ 집에 있었다 The bad weather compelled us to stay indoors.「person.

**꼽꼽쟁이** an ungenerous and stingy

**꼽꼽하다** be a bit moist.

**꼽다** 《세다》 count (on *one's* fingers); 《지목하다》 rank 〔be reckoned〕 《among》. ¶ 날짜를 ～ count 〔reckon〕 the days / 손꼽아 기다리다 look forward 《to》; wait eagerly for / 이 마을에서 부자로는 그를 첫째로 꼽는다 He is one of the richest men in the town. / 그녀는 세계에서 다섯손가락 안에 꼽히는 훌륭한 피아니스트이다 She is among the five best pianists in the world. / 그와 같은 사람은 손에 꼽을 정도밖에 없다 Such a man is very rare. *or* The like of him you can count on the fingers of one hand.

**꼽재기** ① 《때·먼지 따위 더러운 것》 dirt; filth; foul matter; muck; grime; discharge (배설물). ¶ 눈～ the discharge from the eyes; eye mucus; gum. ② 《미미한 것》 anything small; a bit; a whit; a mite; a trifle. ¶ ～ 같은 놈 a small and despicable fellow / 양심이라곤 ～만큼도 없다 have not a glimmer of conscience / 그들에겐 일에 대한 열의가 ～만큼도 없다 They don't have an ounce of enthusiasm for their work. / ～만도 못한 녀석들이니 상관 말게 Don't mind what they say, for they are fellows quite beneath notice.

**꼽추** ＝곱사등이. ◉ ～춤 a comic dance with a pillow on *one's* back.

**꼿꼿이** ① 《사물이》 straight; upright; erect. ¶ ～ 서다 stand upright 〔erect, straight〕 / 몸을 ～ 세워라 Hold yourself straight. ② 《언행을》 honestly; straightforward(ly); forthright; upright; firmly. ¶ ～ 대답하다 answer forthright; give a straight answer; answer firmly / ～ 살다 live upright 〔honestly〕. ③ 《빳빳이》 hard; stiff(ly). ¶ ～ 굳다 stiffen; get stiff 〔rigid〕.

**꼿꼿하다** ① 《곧다》 (be) straight; upright; erect. ¶ 꼿꼿한 나무 a straight tree / 꼿꼿한 자세 straight posture / 그의 머리는 백발이었지만 아직 허리는 꼿꼿했다 Though his hair was white, he still stood erect. ② 《언행이》 (be) honest; upright; straight; straightforward; firm; steady; strong. ¶ 성질이 꼿꼿한 사람 a man of straightforward disposition / 언행이 ～ be upright in *one's* conduct / 의지가 ～ have a strong 〔an iron〕 will; be strong-willed. ③ 《굳다》 (be) hard; stiff. ¶ 꼿꼿한 시체 a stiff corpse 〔body〕 / 꼿꼿해지다 《a body》 stiffen; get stiff 〔rigid〕.

**꽁꽁** ① 《얼어붙음》 frozen hard. ¶ 땅이

～ 얼었다 The ground is frozen hard. / 추워서 몸이 ～ 얼었다 I am almost frozen with cold. *or* I am chilled to the bone. ② 《숨음》 hiding *oneself* "good"; getting well hidden. ¶ ～ 숨어라 Hide yourself good! *or* Get well hidden!

**꽁무니** the lower end of the backbone; the behind; the backside; the rear end; 《궁둥이》 the buttocks. ¶ ～ 바람이 세다 move briskly 〔forcefully〕 / ～(를) 빼다 shrink 〔recoil, flinch〕 《from》; hang back; hesitate 《at, before》; balk 《at》; chicken out 《of》; back down; 《달아나다》 turn tail; run away 〔off〕 / ～가 빠지게 달아나다 take to *one's* heels; turn tail and run away / 여자 ～를 따라다니다 dangle after 〔hang about〕 a girl; chase 〔run〕 after a woman / 그는 막판에 가서는 언제나 ～를 뺀다 He always draws 〔pulls〕 back at the last moment. / 그들이 맞고소를 하겠다고 위협하는 바람에 그는 ～를 뺐다 He chickened out when they threatened a countersuit. ◉ ～뼈 『해부』 the coccyx; the tailbone.

**꽁보리밥** boiled barley.

**꽁생원**(―生員) a narrow-minded 〔illiberal〕 man.

**꽁지** a tail; a train (공작 등의). ◉ ～깃 a tail feather. ～머리 a piece of wood with a drumstick end.

**꽁지벌레** 『곤충』 a maggot.

**꽁초** a cigarette butt 〔end, stub〕; 《엽권련의》 a cigar stub. ¶ ～를 버리다 throw away a cigarette butt.

**꽁치** 『어류』 a saury; a mackerel pike. ◉ ～아재비 a billfish.

**꽁하다** 《성질이》 (be) reserved and unsociable; reticent and unadaptable; introvert and narrow-minded; 《기분이》 (be) moody and silent; sullen; be in a bad humor. ¶ 꽁한 성질 introvert nature / 꽁하게 생각하다 bear 《*a person*》 ill will; have 〔harbor〕 a grudge against 《*a person*》; hold 《*something*》 against 《*a person*》 / 그는 내 말에 대해서 아직 꽁하고 있다 He still bears me a grudge over my words.

**꽂다** ① 《끼워 넣다》 insert; put in 〔into〕; inset; 《박거나 찔러넣다》 stick in 〔into〕; put into 〔in〕; drive 〔wedge, fix〕 in; pin up (핀으로). ¶ 열쇠를 자물쇠 구멍에 ～ put 〔insert, fit〕 a key into a lock / 플러그를 콘센트에 ～ put 〔insert〕 a plug into a outlet; plug a cord in the outlet / 꽃을 화병에 ～ put 〔stick〕 flowers in a vase / 머리에 비녀를 ～ wear 〔stick〕 an ornamental pin in *one's* hair / 땅에 말뚝을 ～ fix 〔set, drive〕 a stake into the ground / 책을 서가에 ～ put 〔set〕 a book on a shelf / 핀으로 벽에 사진을 ～ pin up *one's* picture on the wall / 편지를 책갈피에 ～ put 〔lay〕 a letter between the page of a book. ② 《가로지르다》 put 《a bar》 across. ¶ 문에 빗장을 ～ bar 〔bolt〕 the gate. ③ 《거꾸로 박히게 하다》 ¶ 짐을 메어 ～ throw 〔hurl〕 the load head down.

**꽂을대** 《장전용의》 a ramrod; 《총포 청소용의》 a cleaning rod; a gunstick.

**-꽂이** a thing which is inserted or in which something is inserted.

**꽂히다** 《끼이다》 get 〔be〕 inserted; be put in; 《찔리다》 stick; be stuck 〔pinned〕; be stabbed 〔pierced〕; 《박히다》 be driven 〔fixed〕 in; 《걸리다》 be bolted; 《맞히다》 (be) hit. ¶ 핀에 꽂힌 나비 표본 a specimen of butterfly pinned up 《on the board》 / 칼이 땅에 꽂혔다 The knife stuck in the ground. / 던진 칼이 벽에 꽂혔다 The thrown knife pierced the wall. / 화살이 과녁 중앙에 꽂혔다 The arrow hit the target right in the center. / 그녀는 가슴에 칼이 꽂힌 채 죽어 있었다 She was found dead with a dagger stuck in her chest. / 내 차 타이어에 못이 꽂혔다 A nail pierced the tire of my car.

**꽃** ① 《식물의》 a flower; a blossom; a bloom (★ flower는 일반적으로 모든 꽃을 가리키나, 협의로는 관상용 꽃을 뜻함. blossom은 흔히 과수의 꽃을 뜻하며, 대개 복수형으로 쓰임. bloom은 과수, 관상용 구별없이 꽃이 피어 있는 상태를 가리킴).

¶ 겹꽃 a double flower / 나라 꽃 the national flower / 활짝 핀 꽃 a full-blown flower / 꽃 한송이 a flower / 시든꽃 withered 〔faded〕 flower / 꽃 파는 아가씨 a flower girl / 일찍〔늦게〕 피는 꽃 an early 〔a late〕 flower / 꽃의 floral / 꽃이 피는 초목 a flowering 〔blossoming〕 plant / 꽃이 피어 있는 나무 a tree in flower / 꽃을 심다 plant flowers / 꽃에 물을 주다 water flowers / 꽃을 가꾸다 grow 〔raise〕 flowers / 꽃을 자르다 cut a flower / 화병에 꽃을 꽂다 put flowers in a vase / 현관에 꽃을 장식하다 arrange flowers in the hall / 들꽃을 따다 pick 〔gather〕 wild flowers / 이 꽃은 봄에 핀다 This flower 「comes out 〔blooms〕 in spring. / 자두꽃이 피어 있다 The plum blossoms are out. / 공원의 벚꽃은 지금

활짝 피어 있다 The cherry trees in the park are now in full bloom. / 꽃이 모두 시들었다 The flowers have all withered 〔drooped〕. / 살구꽃이 모두 졌다 The apricot blossoms are all 「gone 〔over〕. / 꽃은 져서 열매를 맺는다 Flowers develop into fruit. / 꽃을 따지 〔꺾지〕 마시오 《게시》 Don't pick flowers. / 꽃도 한때 사람도 한때 Roses and maidens soon lose their bloom. *or* All that's fair must fade.

② [비유적] 《정화》 the flower; the essence; 《호시절》 the best days 〔time〕. ¶ 기사도의 꽃 the flower of chivalry / 젊음은 인생의 꽃이다 Youth is the essence 〔flower〕 of life. *or* Youth is a treasure. / 꽃필 날이 있겠지 Let's hope for the best days. / 우리는 그 일로 이야기 꽃을 피웠다 We talked a lot about it. *or* We had a long and animated chat over the topic.

③ [비유적] 《미인》 a beauty; a beautiful woman. ¶ 사교계의 꽃 a society beauty; the belle of the society / 직장의 꽃 a beauty in the office.

◉ ~가게 a flower shop; a florist's; 《노점》 a flower stall: ~가게 주인 a florist; a flower person.

**꽃가루** 『식물』 pollen; anther dust.
◉ ~주머니 a pollen sac. 꽃가룻병 『의학』 pollinosis.

**꽃가지** a spray 〔sprig〕 of flowers. ¶ 라일락 ~ a sprig of lilac flowers.

**꽃게** 『동물』 a blue crab.

**꽃구경** flower viewing. ¶ ~ 가다 go to see the flowers 《at》; go (out) flower viewing.

**꽃꼭지** 『식물』 = 꽃자루.

**꽃꽂이** flower 〔floral〕 arrangement. ~하다 arrange 〔set〕 flowers. ¶ ~한 꽃 arranged flowers / ~를 배우다 take lessons in flower arrangement.

**꽃나무** a flowering plant; a flower tree.

**꽃놀이** a picnic for viewing flowers. ~하다 enjoy a flower-viewing picnic. ¶ ~ 가다 go on an outing to see the flowers / 비 때문에 ~를 완전히 망쳤다 The rain has entirely spoilt the flower-viewing picnic.

**꽃눈** 『식물』 a flower bud.

**꽃다발** a bouquet; a bunch of flowers. ¶ 그녀에게 장미 ~을 바치다〔선물하다〕 present a bunch of roses to her; present her a bunch of roses.

**꽃다지** ① 《첫 열매》 the first fruits 《of cucumber, eggplant, etc.》. ② 『식물』 a whitlow grass.

**꽃답다** be lovely 〔pretty〕 as a flower; (be) lovely; flowery; pretty; beautiful. ¶ 꽃다운 청춘 the bloom 〔charm, glow〕 of *one's* youth; the prime of life / 꽃다운 처녀 a beautiful young girl.

**꽃대** 『식물』 a flower stalk; a floral axis.

**꽃덮이** 『식물』 a floral envelope, the perianth.

**꽃돗자리** a mat embroidered with a floral design; a fancy mat.

**꽃동산** a flowery hill; a flower garden.

**꽃말** flower 〔floral〕 language; the language of flowers. ¶ 장미의 ~은 순애를 뜻한다 A rose means pure love in the language of flowers.

**꽃망울** a (flower) bud. ¶ ~이 서다 bud; have 〔bear〕 buds; put forth 〔out〕 buds / ~이 커지다 a bud swells.

**꽃맞이** 《꽃필 때 하는 굿》 a shamanistic ceremony to welcome the new blossoms.

**꽃맺이** just-sprouted fruit.

**꽃무늬** a floral 〔flower〕 pattern. ¶ ~를 수놓은 치마 a skirt embroidered with a floral pattern.

**꽃물** thick beef soup.

**꽃바구니** a flower basket.

**꽃받침** 『식물』 a calyx. ◉ ~조각 a sepal.

**꽃방**(一房) 《조화를 파는》 an artificial 〔imitation〕 flower shop. ⇨ 꽃집.

**꽃방석**(一方席) a cushion embroidered with a floral design; a fancy cushion.

**꽃밭** a flower garden; a flower bed; a field of flowers.

**꽃병**(一瓶) a (flower) vase. ¶ 장미를 ~에 꽂다 put roses in a vase.
◉ ~받침 a doily.

**꽃봉오리** a (flower) bud; a button; 《청춘》 the youth. ¶ 부풀어오른 ~ a swollen 〔fat〕 bud / ~ 같은 처녀 a young maiden; a budding beauty / ~가 맺히다 bear 〔have〕 buds; put forth 〔put out〕 buds / ~가 피다 a bud 「develops into a flower 〔bursts into blossom〕 / ~를 따다 pluck a flower in the bud / ~는 크게 부풀어 막 벌어지려고 한다 The buds are swollen to bursting.

**꽃부리** 『식물』 the corolla 《of a flower》. ¶ ~가 있는 corollate.

**꽃불** ① 《화염》 a blazing 〔flaming〕 fire. ② 《불꽃놀이의》 fireworks. ¶ ~을 올리다 display 〔set off〕 fireworks.

**꽃상추** 『식물』 an endive; an escarole.

**꽃샘(추위)** a cold snap in the flower(-ing) season; a spring cold. ~하다 get cold or windy in the flower season.

**꽃송이** a blossom; a flower. ¶ 국화 ~ a flower of a chrysanthemum.

**꽃수레** a car decorated with flowers;

a decorated 〔flower-bedecked〕 car; a float (in a parade). ¶ ~의 행렬이 거리를 행진했다 A procession of decorated floats paraded the streets.

**꽃술** 〖식물〗《전체》 the pistils and stamens (of a flower); 《암술》 a pistil; 《수술》 a stamen.

**꽃시계**(一時計) a flower clock.

**꽃식물**(一植物) a flowering plant.

**꽃쌈** 《따모으기》 a flower-gathering game. ~하다 play a flower-gathering game.

**꽃잎** a petal; 《구어》 a floral leaf. ¶ ~ 넷 있는 tetrapetalous; 4-petaled / ~ 열 있는 decapetalous; 10-petaled / ~ 없는 apetalous; petalless / 장미 ~ a rose leaf.

**꽃자동차**(一自動車) a flower-bedecked automobile; a floral car. ⇨ 꽃수레.

**꽃자루** 〖식물〗《화경》 a flower stalk; a footstalk; a peduncle. ¶ ~의 peduncular.

**꽃자리** a mat with flower patterns on it.

**꽃전**(一煎) 《꽃 모양의》 a griddle cake made in flower pattern; 《꽃잎을 넣은》 a griddle cake decorated with flower petals (on it).

**꽃전차**(一電車) a streetcar float; a floral car.

**꽃줄기** a flower stalk; a scape.

**꽃집** a flower shop; a florist's. ¶ ~ 주인 a florist.

**꽃차례** 〖식물〗 inflorescence; anthotaxy. ¶ 유한〔무한〕 ~ a definite 〔an indefinite〕 inflorescence.

**꽃창포**(一菖蒲) 〖식물〗 an iris.

**꽃철** the blossom 〔flower〕 season.

**꽃턱** the torus.

**꽈르르** gurgling; with a gurgle. ¶ 물이 병에서 ~ 쏟아져 나오다 water gurgles out of a bottle.

**꽈리** ① 〖식물〗 a ground 〔bladder〕 cherry; a Chinese lantern plant; 《입에 넣어 부는》 a mouth clacker. ¶ ~를 불다 blow (on an empty) ground cherry. ② 〖의학〗《피부의》 a blister.

**꽉** ① 《단단히》 tight; hard; firm(ly); fast; secure. ¶ 꽉 묶다 tie fast 〔firmly〕 / 꽉 붙들다 cling to 《*a thing*》; hold 〔hang〕 on fast to 《*a thing*》; take a firm hold of / 문을 꽉 잠그다 shut a door fast; lock a door tight / 손을 꽉 붙잡다 grasp 《*a person's*》 hand hard / 꽉 잡고 있어라 Hold it firmly. / 나를 꽉 잡아라 Hold on to me tight. ② 《빽빽이》 compact(ly); squeezed in; 《가득히》 full; chock-full. ¶ 책이 꽉 찬 서가 a shelf closely packed 〔lined〕 with books / 꽉 채우다 fill up full; fill to capacity / 여행 가방에 물건을 꽉 채워 넣다 squeeze things into a suitcase / 꽉 차다 be full; be chock-full; be squeezed in (like sardines); be packed full 〔solid〕. ③ 《굳이 참고》 patiently. ¶ 눈물을 꽉 참다 gulp down a sob; fight back *one's* tears.

**꽉꽉** ① 《단단히》 tying up 《*a thing*》 several times; much more tightly 〔firmly〕; fast. ¶ 짐을 ~ 동여매다 tie a load several times around with tight ropes / 문이 모두 ~ 닫혀 있다 All the doors are shut fast 〔are closed tight, are secured〕. ② 《가득히》 packing 〔squeezing〕 closely 〔tightly, compactly, fully〕. ¶ 밥을 ~ 눌러담다 stuff 《a bowl》 full of rice / 방이 모두 사람으로 ~ 들어찼다 All the rooms are crowded 〔packed, jammed〕 with people. / 창고마다 곡식이 ~ 차 있다 The storehouses were all bursting with grain.

**꽐꽐** gurgling; gushing; with the gurgle; with a gush. ~하다, ~거리다 gurgle 〔gush〕 out. ¶ ~ 뿜어나오는 석유 a gush of oil / 포도주가 병에서 ~ 흘러 나왔다 The wine gurgled out of the bottle.

**꽝**[1] 《제비뽑기 등의》 a blank. ¶ 꽝이 나오다, 꽝을 뽑다 draw a blank 《in a lottery》.

**꽝**[2] with a bang 〔boom, whomp〕; with a thump 〔thud, bump, crash〕. ~하다 bang; boom; thump; thud; bump; crash. ¶ 대포를 꽝하고 쏘다 boom a gun; shoot a cannon off "boom!" / 문을 꽝 닫다 bang a door (shut) / 꽝 떨어지다 fall down with a thump 〔bump, boom, bang〕 / 꽝 넘어지다 fall over with a thump; fall off with a thud 〔crash〕 / 꽝하고 폭발하다 go off with a bang.

**꽝꽝** 《폭발음》 Bang-bang!; Boom-boom!; Whomp-whomp!; banging 〔booming〕 repeatedly. ~하다, ~거리다 go bang-bang 〔boom-boom, whomp-whomp〕!; bang and bang; boom and boom. ¶ 대포를 ~ 쏘다 boom an artillery gun repeatedly / 총을 ~ 쏘다 go bang-bang with a gun 〔rifle〕.

**꽝꽝나무** 〖식물〗 an ilex; a holm-oak.

**꽤** ① 《제법》 quite; fairly; pretty; considerably; rather; a good deal 《of》; 《구어》 good bit 《taller》. ¶ 꽤 큰 집 「rather a 〔a rather〕 large house; a pretty big house / 꽤 오래 전에 「quite a long 〔a while〕 ago / 꽤 힘들다 be pretty hard / 꽤 잘 읽다 read quite well / 꽤 크다 be fairly large / 꽤 여러 날 걸리다 take a good many days / 아직 꽤 시간이 있다 We have plenty of time yet. / 그는 꽤 알려진 인물이다 He is quite a man. *or* He is (a) somebody 《in his circle》. (★ 이 somebody는 someone으로 바꿀 수 없음) / 작년엔 비가 꽤 왔다 We had a good deal of rain last year. / 그는 나이를 꽤 먹었다 He is well on in years. / 한국은 과학이 꽤 발달했다 Korea has remarkably progressed in science. / 그는 영어 회화를 꽤 잘한다 He speaks English pretty well.

② 《비교적》 comparatively; relatively. ¶ 꽤 좋다 be comparatively good; (be) not so 〔too〕 bad / 「이 포도주 맛이 어떠세요」—「꽤 좋은데」 "How do you like this wine?"—"Not so bad."

**꽥** with a shout 〔yell, scream, quack〕. ∼하다 shout; scream; raise a shout; give a yell; go "quack!" ¶ 꽥 소리 a shout; a yell; a quack / 꽥 소리지르다 give a shout 〔yell〕; let out a quack; cry 〔call out〕 loudly / 성이 나서 꽥하다 shout with anger / 놀라서 꽥하다 yell with surprise.

**꽥꽥** shouting and shouting; quacking. ∼하다, ∼거리다 shout and shout; yell and yell; 《새 따위가》 quack(오리가); gaggle(거위가). ¶ ∼ 소리지르다 shout and shout; rant to right and left / 귀머거리가 아니니 ∼거리지 마시오 I'm not deaf—don't shout.

**꽹** Bong!; Boom!; Clang!

**꽹과리** a (small) gong. ¶ ∼를 치다 beat 〔sound, ring〕 a gong.

**꽹나무** 〖식물〗 the Korean cranberry plant; *Vaccinium Koreanum* (학명).

**꾀** 《슬기》 wise counsel; wit(s); resource; resourcefulness; 《계략》 a trick; a wile; a ruse; an artifice; a trap; 《계책》 a device; contrivances.
¶ 나쁜 꾀 cunning; craft / 꾀(가) 있는 사람 a man of resource / 꾀(가) 많다 be resourceful 〔witty〕; be tricky; be full of tricks; be artful 〔wily, clever〕 / 꾀(가) 없다 be brainless; be harebrained; be tactless / …할 만한 꾀가 없다 have no sense to *do* / 아무를 꾀로 속여 넘기다 outwit *a person;* trick *a person* into 〔out of〕 《*a thing*》 / 꾀가 모자라다 be on the dull side / 꾀가 늘다 grow wise 〔intelligent〕 / 꾀를 빌리다 ask 《*a person*》 for advice 〔counsel〕; pick 《*a person's*》 brain / 꾀를 쓰다 use 〔work〕 *one's* wits / 꾀를 짜내다 cudgel 〔rack, beat〕 *one's* brains / 꾀가 다하다 come to the end of *one's* wits 〔resource〕 / 일에 꾀가 나다 get 〔grow〕 tired 〔weary〕 of a task; get sick of a task / 제 꾀에 제가 넘어가다 be outwitted by *one's* own cleverness; outwit *oneself;* overreach *oneself;* fall for *one's* own trick 〔scheme, game〕 / 그들은 그의 꾀에 넘어갔다 They fell a victim to his schemes.

**꾀까다롭다** ⇨ 괴까다롭다.

**꾀꼬리** 〖조류〗 a bush warbler; an oriole. ¶ ∼ 같은 목소리 a sweet 〔beautiful〕 voice.

**꾀꼴꾀꼴** warbling and warbling; singing away (of an oriole). ∼하다 《an oriole》 warbles away; trill; sing.

**꾀꾀** ¶ 얼굴이 ∼ 마르다 *one's* face is drawn and haggard / 병으로 몸이 ∼ 마르다 become worn out from illness; be pulled down by *one's* illness / ∼ 말랐다 be worn to a shadow; be a mere shadow of *one's* former self.

**꾀꾀로** 《틈틈이》 taking advantage of odd moments; 《살짝》 quietly; stealthily.

**꾀다**[1] 《벌레 따위가》 swarm; gather; flock; collect; 《사람이》 gather; crowd. ¶ 음식에 파리가 ∼ food is swarmed with flies / 파리가 꾀지 않도록 하다 keep flies away from 《the food》; do not let flies collect on 《the food》 / 설탕에 개미가 새까맣게 꾀어 있다 Ants are swarming upon the sugar. / 구경꾼이 그 가게 앞에 꾀었다 Crowds of curious people gathered in front of the store.

**꾀다**[2] 《유혹하다》 tempt; allure; lure; entice; seduce. ¶ 꾀어 내다 tempt 〔coax〕 《*a person*》 away 〔out〕 / 꾀어서 나쁜 짓을 하게 하다 tempt 《*a person*》 into evil doing / 적을 위험한 곳으로 꾀어 들이다 lure the enemy into a dangerous position / 아무를 돈으로 ∼ lure *a person* with money / 여자를 ∼ seduce a girl 《with all kinds of sweet talk》.

**꾀다**[3] ⇨ 꼬이다.

**꾀바르다** (be) crafty; be clever 《at getting out of hard work》.

**꾀배** a pretended stomachache. ¶ ∼(를) 앓다 pretend to have a stomachache.

**꾀병**(—病) pretended 〔faked, feigned〕 illness; malingering. ∼하다 malinger; feign 〔fake, sham〕 illness. ¶ ∼을 앓다 feign 〔fake, sham〕 illness; pretend to be sick; malinger.

**꾀보** a tricky 〔wily〕 person; a person

full of wiles [schemes, stratagems]; a resourceful man; a person of resource.

**꾀부리다** 《구실을 붙여서》 evade [shirk] 《*one's* duty》 with a phoney excuse; 《몸을 아끼다》 spare *oneself;* be sparing of 《*oneself*》. ¶ 일에 꾀 부리지 않다 labor without stint; work without sparing *oneself;* spare no pains / 어려운 일에 ~ be sly on the difficult problem / 그는 꾀부리지 않고 일한다 He is a willing worker. / 이리저리 꾀만 부리고 책임을 다하지 않는다 He shirks his responsibilities with all sorts of excuses.

**꾀쓰다** ① 《지략을》 use a trick; use *one's* brains; play tricks 《on》; resort to wiles [a ruse]; devise a scheme; exercise [use, work] *one's* wits; maneuver. ¶ 꾀(를) 써서 적을 물리치다 employ a stratagem to repulse the enemy. ② =꾀부리다.

**꾀어내다** lure [decoy] 《*a person*》 out; entice away. ¶ 그들은 그 딸을 집에서 꾀어내려고 했다 They tried to entice the daughter away from home [her house]. 「《a place》.

**꾀어들이다** decoy [lure] 《*a person*》 into

**꾀음꾀음** tempting 《*a person*》 with fine words. ~하다 tempt; lure; seduce.

**꾀이다** be lured [enticed, tempted, beguiled]; get seduced; get led astray. ¶ 아무한테 ~ be led astray by *a person* / 그는 나쁜 친구들에게 꾀어서 나쁜 길로 들어섰다 He was tempted [enticed] into wrong ways by the bad company.

**꾀잠** sham [pretended, feigned] sleep; make-believe sleep. ¶ ~(을) 자다 pretend to be asleep; play possum; feign [sham] sleep.

**꾀죄(죄)하다** (be) shabby; poor-looking; dirty; seedy; 《구어》 scruffy; untidy. ¶ 꾀죄(죄)한 옷 scruffy clothes / 꾀죄(죄)한 주제[사람] a seedy appearance [person] / 꾀죄(죄)한 옷차림을 하고 있다 be poorly attired; be miserably clad; be ill-clad; be down at heel.

**꾀피우다** =꾀부리다.

**꾀하다** 《계획·획책하다》 plan; scheme; design; devise 《a scheme》; 《나쁜 짓을》 plot; conspire; 《시도하다》 attempt; 《노력하다》 strive [labor] for; try to; 《의도하다》 intend; contemplate.
¶ 사전에 꾀한 일 a put-up job; a got=up affair / 모반을 ~ conspire to rise in revolt / 승리를 ~ plan (to win) a victory / 공익을 ~ promote [work for] the public good / 사리(私利)를 ~ look to [after] *one's* own interests; try to feather *one's* own nest / 그녀는 자살을 꾀했으나 실패했다 She attempted suicide but failed. *or* She failed in an attempt to kill herself. / 그들은 정부 전복을 꾀했다 They plotted to overthrow the government. / 외국에 가기 전에 일의 완성을 꾀하고 있다 I intend to finish this work before I go abroad. / 그는 작은 배로 태평양 횡단을 꾀했다 He planned to cross the Pacific Ocean in a small boat.

**꾐** (a) temptation; (an) allurement; (an) enticement; seduction. ¶ 꾐질 tempting; seducing / 꾐에 빠지다[넘어가다] fall into [yield to] temptation; fall victim to 《*a person's*》 temptation / 꾐을 당하다 be tempted [lured, enticed, seduced]; be led astray / 친구들의 꾐에 빠져 그는 노름을 하게 되었다 His friends tempted him into gambling. / 그녀는 꾐에 넘어가서 모조품을 샀다 She was seduced into buying imitations.

**꾸다**[1] 《꿈을》 dream. ¶ 좋은 꿈을 ~ dream [have] a good dream / 꿈을 꾸고 있는지 생시인지 모르다 doubt the evidence of *one's* senses; be unable to believe *one's* eyes / 꿈도 꾸지 않고 잠들었다 I sank into dreamless sleep. / 어젯밤에는 재미있는[나쁜] 꿈을 꾸었다 I had a funny [bad] dream last night. / 마치 꿈을 꾸는 기분이었다 I felt as if I were in a dream.

**꾸다**[2] 《빌어 쓰다》 borrow; 《돈을》 make a loan. ¶ 돈을 ~ borrow money 《from *a person*》 / 여기저기서 꾸어 들이다 borrow 《money》 from many people / 만원을 ~ have a loan of 10,000 won / 돈을 꾸러 오다 come for a loan 《of 2,000 won》 / 토지를 저당잡히고 돈을 ~ raise [borrow] money on *one's* estate / 돈 좀 꾸어 주시지 않겠습니까 May I trouble you for some money? / 교실에서 그녀는 꾸어다 놓은 보릿자루 같다 In the classroom she is tongue-tied.

**꾸드러지다** ⇨ 구드러지다.

**꾸들꾸들** somewhat dry and hard. ~하다 (be) dry and hard. ¶ 떡이 ~하다 The cake has become dry and hard.

**-꾸러기** a person who overdoes 《*something*》; an overindulger; a glutton for…. ¶ 장난꾸러기 a naughty child; a mischievous child; a mischief; 《구어》 a little monkey.

**꾸러미** ①《뭉쳐 싼 것》 a bundle (in a wrapper); a bunch. ¶ 옷 ~ a bundle of clothes / 열쇠 ~ a bunch of keys (on a ring) / 책 ~ a package of books / ~를 만들다 make a bundle 〔parcel, package, packet〕; bundle 《clothes》; pack 《good》 / ~를 풀다 unpack; undo a package 〔bundle〕. ②《짚으로 만든》 a straw wrapper. ¶ 달걀 한 ~ ten eggs in a straw wrapper.

**꾸르륵** ①《뱃속이》 with a rumble; with a growl; with a gurgle. ~하다 give a growl; make a rumble; gurgle. ¶ 배가 고파서 뱃속에서 ~ 소리가 났다 My stomach rumbled 〔growled〕 with hunger. ②《닭이》 with a cackle. ~하다 (let out a) cackle. ③《물이》 with a gurgle. ~하다 gurgle. ¶ ~ 솟아나오다 gurgle up; well up with gurgles.

**꾸리**[1] 《실뭉치》 a spool; a bobbin. ¶ 실 두 ~ two spools of thread.

**꾸리**[2] 《쇠고기의》 beef from the back of the front leg; foreshank.

**꾸리다** ①《짐을》 wrap up; do up 《a parcel》; tie up; pack (up); bundle. ¶ 짐을 ~ pack (up); package; pack up *one's* things 〔belongings〕 / 이삿짐을 ~ pack up household goods to be moved / 짐을 꾸리고 떠나다 pack up and leave / 그는 트렁크에 소지품을 꾸렸다 He packed the trunk with his belongings. / 짐은 다 꾸렸습니까 Have you finished packing?
②《일을》 manage; keep 《*a thing*》 running 〔going〕; maintain; cover. ¶ 살림을 ~ manage a household / 그럭저럭 살림을 꾸려 가다 manage to keep a house going; run a household / 94만원으로 살림을 ~ cover *one's* household expenses with 940,000 won / 사업을 ~ manage a business; manage to keep a business going.
③《매만져 꾸미다》 touch up (the external appearance); decorate; tidy 〔do〕 up 《a room》; adjust. ¶ 매무새를 ~ adjust *oneself* 〔*one's* dress〕 / 여장을 ~ outfit 〔equip〕 *oneself* for journey.

**꾸며내다** 《거짓말 등을》 fabricate; concoct; invent; make 〔cook 《구어》, trump〕 up. ¶ 꾸며낸 이야기 a made-up 〔cooked-up, trumped-up〕 story; a fiction / 그 이야기는 순전히 꾸며낸 것이다 The story is a pure 〔complete〕 fabrication.

**꾸며대다** 《말을》 make an excuse 《for》; gloss over 〔cover up〕 《*one's* fault》; explain away. ¶ 그는 자기 잘못을 그럴듯하게 꾸며대려고 했다 He tried to gloss over his mistakes.

**꾸물거리다** ①《꿈틀대다》 wriggle; wiggle. ¶ 벌레가 ~ worms wriggle / 아파서 ~ writhe in agony. ② = 구무럭거리다.

**꾸물꾸물** 《꿈틀댐》 wiggling; wriggling; 《느릿느릿》 slowly; tardily; lingeringly.

**꾸미** beef shreds 《for soup, *etc.*》.

**꾸미개** a decorative edging band; a frill; an edging.

**꾸미다** ①《마무르다》 finish up; 《기계 따위를》 fix up; put 〔piece〕 together.
②《치장하다》 decorate; ornament; adorn; deck; 《화장하다》 make (*oneself*) up; put on make-up. ¶ 식탁을 꽃으로 ~ decorate the table with flowers / 보석으로 몸을 ~ adorn 〔dress〕 *oneself* with jewels / 방을 그림들로 ~ decorate a room with pictures / 얼굴을 곱게 ~ make up *one's* face beautifully / 왕관은 다이아몬드로 아름답게 꾸며져 있다 The crown is finely ornamented with diamonds. / 그 거리는 제등과 꽃으로 아름답게 꾸며져 있었다 The street was 「decked out 〔decorated〕 with lanterns and flowers.
③《문장·말을》 embellish; garnish. ¶ 문장을 ~ embellish 〔garnish〕 *one's* style / 말을 ~ use fine language; use fair words.
④《거짓 태도를 취하다》 affect; pretend; feign; make a show; 《가장하다》 disguise *oneself;* take on the guise 《of》. ¶ 꾸민 태도 an affected attitude 〔manner〕 / 허울만 꾸미는 사람 a showy 〔an ostentatious〕 person / 짐짓 덕이 있는 체 ~ pretend to be a virtuous man / 그는 부자가 아니다. 다만 그렇게 보이도록 꾸미고 있을 뿐이다 He's not a rich man. He's just pretending 〔feigning〕.
⑤《조작하다》 make up; invent; devise; fabricate; manufacture. ¶ 꾸민 이야기 a made-up 〔cooked-up〕 story; a fiction / 꾸며낸 일 a fabrication; an invention / 사전에 꾸민 일 a deliberate 〔put-up〕 job / 말을 ~ make up 〔fabricate, cook up 《구어》〕 a story; tell a lie / 알리바이를 ~ fake an alibi / 엉터리 보고서를 ~ make up a false report / 그는 결석을 해명하기 위해 없는 이야기를 꾸몄다 He cooked up a story to explain his absence. / 그의 증언은 순전히 꾸민 이야기였다 His testimony was a complete fiction.
⑥《꾀하다》 plot; scheme; plan; be up to; conspire; design; devise. ¶ 왕에 대한 음모를 ~ plot 〔conspire〕

against the king / 정부 전복의 음모를 ~ plot 〔conspire〕 to overthrow the government; plot 〔scheme〕 the over-throwing of the government / 그는 무언가 못된 짓을 꾸미고 있다 He is up to something. / 그 다툼은 미리 꾸민 짓이었다 The quarrel was a put-up job.
⑦ 《조직하다》 form; organize; set up; 《구성하다》 make; build; compose. ¶ 새 내각을 ~ form 〔organize〕 a new cabinet / 공원을 ~ lay out a park / 둘이서 함께 행복한 가정을 꾸미기 바란다 I hope you'll make a happy home together.
⑧ 《작성하다》 draw up; make out; prepare 《a deed》; write out. ¶ 연극으로 ~ dramatize 《a story》 / 서류를 두 통 ~ make out 《a contract》 in duplicate / 증서를〔유언장을〕 ~ draw up a deed 〔*one's* testament〕 / 서류를 ~ draw up 〔make out, write out〕 a document / 삼개월간 조사한 후에 위원회는 보고서를 꾸몄다 After three months' investigation, the committee produced 〔drew up〕 a report.

**꾸민잠**(—簪) a decorated hairpin.

**꾸민족두리** a woman's jeweled head-piece.

**꾸밈** 《장식》 a decoration; an ornament; 《태도·마음의》 affectation; show; ostentation; 《의상의》 trimmings. ¶ ~ 없는 《사람·말이》 unaffected; plain; natural; artless; 《물건이》 simple; plain; unadorned / ~없이 말하다 say plainly; speak in plain words / 그녀는 ~없기 때문에 이야기하기가 즐겁다 Since she is not pretentious, I enjoy talk-ing to her.

**꾸밈새** ① 《모양》 a shape; a form; 《모양새》 the way *one* fixes up 〔finishes up〕. ¶ ~가 좋은 shapely; well-formed 〔=shaped〕 / ~가 훌륭하다 be nicely made / ~가 서투르다 be poorly con-structed; be a poor make. ② 《치레》 the way *one* decorates 〔adorns, embellishes〕. ¶ ~가 예쁘다〔흉하다〕 be nicely 〔poorly, clumsily〕 decorated 〔made〕 / 실내의 ~가 훌륭하게 되었다 The room was decorated splendidly.

**꾸벅** ~하다 《졸다》 doze; nod; fall into a doze; snooze; 《절하다》 bow; make a bow. ¶ 책을 읽다가 ~ 졸다 nod 〔doze〕 over a book / 그녀는 나에게 ~하고 인사했다 She made a slight bow to me. *or* She greeted me with a slight bow 〔nod〕.

**꾸벅거리다** 《졸려서》 doze off; fall into a doze; feel drowsy. ¶ 꾸벅거리면서도 열차가 출발하는 것을 알았다 Half asleep, I felt the train start moving.

**꾸벅꾸벅** ① 《인사로》 ¶ ~ 절하다 make repeated bows. ② 《조는 모양》 ¶ ~ 졸다 nod in a doze; doze off / ~ 졸면서 일하다 nod 〔doze〕 over *one's* work / 할머니는 뜨개질하다가 ~ 졸기 시작했다 My grandmother was nodding over her knitting.

**꾸역꾸역** crowding; swarming. ¶ ~ 모여들다 crowd in; swarm about; rush on 《*a place*》 / 관객은 경기장으로 ~ 들어왔다 Spectators crowded into the stadium.

**꾸이다** 《꿈이》 be dreamed 〔dreamt〕.

**꾸준하다** (be) steady; constant; persis-tent; unremitting; unflagging; untir-ing. ¶ 꾸준한 노력 steady 〔persistent, unremitting; untiring〕 effort(s) / 꾸준한 우정 a constant friendship / 꾸준한 속도 a steady pace / 꾸준한 성격 a stable 〔steady〕 character / 그녀는 꾸준한 노력으로 그 시험에 합격했다 She succeeded in the examination through her untiring effort.

**꾸준히** 《쉬지않고》 steadily; constantly; 《끈기있게》 untiringly; persistently; unremittingly. ¶ ~ 공부하다 study 〔work〕 steadily / 그들은 매일 ~ 고된 훈련을 했다 They trained hard and tirelessly everyday.

**꾸중** = 꾸지람.

**꾸지나무** 〖식물〗 a paper mulberry; a tapa.

**꾸지람** (a) scolding; a reprimand; a rebuke; (a) reproof; (a) reproach; a telling-off. ~하다 = 꾸짖다. ¶ ~ 듣다 be scolded 《about *a matter*》; have a scolding; get reprimanded; catch 〔get〕 it 《from dad》 / 자주 ~을 듣다 be often reproved by 《*a person* for》 / 들키면 ~ 듣는다 If you are found out, you will catch it. / 그는 나태하다고 아버지한테 ~을 들었다 He was scolded by his father for his negligence.

**꾸짖다** scold; rebuke; reprove 《*a person* for *his* carelessness》; reproach 《*a person* with *his* folly》; chide; give 《*a person*》 a scolding; give 《*a person*》 a telling off; dress 《*a person*》 down 《구어》; 《나무라다》 find fault with; give a lecture 《to》 (잔소리).
¶ 가볍게〔호되게〕 ~ scold mildly 〔severely〕; give 《*a person*》 a mild 〔sharp, severe〕 scolding / 아무의 부주의를 ~ chide 〔reprove〕 *a person* for *his* carelessness / 그는 다른 사람들 앞

에서 나를 꾸짖었다 He took me to task in front of others. / 아이를 그렇게 어하지 말고, 가끔 꾸짖어라 Do not indulge your child so much, but scold sometimes.

> **용법** **scold** 「꾸짖다」를 뜻하는 가장 일반적인 말. 선생·부모 등이 아이가 잘못한 것을 꾸짖을 때 흔히 쓰임. **rebuke** 심하게 잘못을 꾸짖을 때 쓰이는 표현. **reprove** 온건하게 호의적으로 「꾸짖다」의 뜻. **reproach** 잘못에 대해서 화를 내지 않고 실망을 표현하면서 「비난·나무라다」의 뜻. **chide** 문어적인 표현.

**꾹** ⇨ 꼭 ②. ¶ 꾹 참다 stand firm 〔resolute〕; suffer patiently; stand up bravely; bite the bullet.

**꾹꾹** ⇨ 꼭꼭[1] ②, ③.

**-꾼** a man occupied with...; a doer of...; a person engaged in...; a person noted 〔notorious〕 for.... ¶ 씨름꾼 a wrestler / 장사꾼 a trader 〔dealer〕.

**꿀** 《벌꿀》 honey; 《꽃의》 nectar. ¶ 꿀떡 honey cake / 꿀 있는 꽃 a nectar-bearing flower / (벌이) 꿀을 빨다 《a bee》 suck nectar from a flower / 꿀먹은 벙어리 a person who would not open his mouth to another about something kept in his heart / 꿀같이 달다 be sweet as honey.

**꿀꺽** ① 《삼킴》 gulping down. ∼하다 gulp; make a gulping sound. ¶ 한 모금에 ∼ 들이마시다 gulp down at a draft 〔with one breath〕; "chug-a-lug"; swallow 〔drink〕 (down) at a gulp. ② 《누름》 repressing 〔holding back〕 *one's* anger. ¶ 분(憤)을 ∼ 참다 gulp down *one's* resentment.

**꿀꺽꿀꺽** gulping; gulpingly. ¶ ∼ 들이마시다 drink 《water》 in big swallows 〔gulps〕; gulp 《*one's* beer》 down.

**꿀꿀** 《돼지가》 Oink-oink!; the snort of a pig. ∼하다, ∼거리다 snort; grunt; go oink-oink!

**꿀꿀이** [비유적] a greedy person; a pig.

**꿀떡**[1] 《삼키는 모양》 swallowing eagerly; gulping hungrily. ∼하다 swallow 〔gulp〕 《*a thing*》 down; quaff. ¶ ∼ 한입에 삼키다 swallow 〔drain〕 at one 〔a〕 gulp / 침을 ∼ 삼키다 swallow *one's* saliva; 《군침을》 make *one's* mouth waters; 《초조·긴장해서》 be intensely anxious; catch 〔hold〕 *one's* breath.

**꿀떡**[2] honeyed rice cake; rice cake covered with honey.

**꿀떡거리다** swallow; gulp away; make a gulping sound.

**꿀렁** ① 《그릇 안의 액체가》 with a splash 〔slop, slosh〕 inside. ∼하다 slosh 〔slop〕 about inside; tumble 《in a vessel》. ② 《옷 따위가》 puffily; baggily. ∼하다 (be) loose; puffy; baggy 《trousers》. ¶ 바지 무릎이 ∼하다 The trousers are baggy at the knees.

**꿀리다** ① 《구겨지다》 get 〔be〕 wrinkled 〔crumpled〕; become rumpled 〔creased〕. ¶ 꿀리게 하다 crumple; rumple; wrinkle; crush / 옷이 ∼ *one's* clothes are wrinkled 〔creased〕.
② 《옹색해지다》 be hard up 《for money》; be badly off; be in straitened circumstance; grow 〔become〕 poor; be 〔come, run〕 short of. ¶ 살림이 ∼ find it difficult to make a living; be badly 〔ill〕 off; be busy making ends meet.
③ 《마음이 켕기다》 be ill at ease; be 〔get, become〕 self-conscious; feel the pricks of 《conscience》; feel ashamed 《of, to *do*》. ¶ 양심에 꿀리는 데가 있다 have a guilty conscience; have scruples about 《*do*ing》.
④ 《힘·능력 등에서 남에게 눌리다》 feel inferior 《to *a person*》; feel small 〔timid〕 《in *a person's* presence》; be overwhelmed. ¶ 적에게 ∼ be overwhelmed by the enemy / 그의 위엄에 ∼ feel small in the presence of his dignified appearance / 말에 ∼ be cornered in an argument; be at a loss what to say in an argument / 누구에게도 꿀리지 않다 yield 〔be second〕 to none; prove *oneself* equal to anyone.

**꿀물** honeyed water.

**꿀벌** a (honey)bee. ¶ ∼을 치다 keep bees. ◉ ∼통 a beehive.

**꿀찌럭** with a splatter 〔splash, plop〕. ∼하다 make a splatter 〔splash〕.

**꿇다** 《무릎을》 bend (*one's* knees); kneel down; fall 〔go down, drop〕 on *one's* knees. ¶ 무릎꿇고 앉다〔절하다〕 sit 〔kowtow〕 on *one's* knees / 무릎꿇고 애원하다 implore 《*a person*》 on *one's* (bended) knees / 무릎꿇고 기도하다 kneel down in prayer / 그녀는 무릎꿇고 신에게 기도했다 She went down on her knees to pray to God.

**꿇리다** ① 《무릎을》 make 《*a person*》 kneel down; bring 《*a person*》 to his knees. ② 《억누르다》 press down; oppress; overwhelm; 《복종시키다》 make 《*a person*》 obey; subordinate; force to yield.

**꿇(어)앉다** sit on *one's* knees.

**꿈** 《수면중의》 a dream; a nightmare (악몽); 《희망·이상》 a dream; a vision; 《야심》 an ambition; 《환상》 an illusion; visions; 《망상》 a delusion.
¶ 꿈이 없는 dreamless / 참꿈 a true dream; a dream that comes true / 개꿈 a false dream; a dream that does not come true / 좋은 꿈 a good 〔happy〕 dream; a dream that bodes good luck / 불길한 꿈 an evil dream; a dream that bodes ill luck / 무서운 꿈 a terrible dream; a nightmare / 허황된 꿈 a pipe dream / 꿈점 divination by means of dreams; oneiromancy / 꿈의 계시 a revelation in a dream / 꿈의 분석 (a) dream analysis / 젊은 시절의 낭만적인 꿈 the romantic vision of youth / 꿈이 아닌가 하고 의심하다 wonder if it is only a dream / 꿈이 아닌가 하고 몸을 꼬집어 보다 pinch *oneself* to make sure that *one* is not dreaming 〔that *one* is awake〕 / 꿈에서 깨다 awake from sleep 〔a dream〕; 《허황된 것에서》 wake from *one's* reverie / 꿈에도 생시에도 잊지 못하다 can never forget 〔get 《it》 off *one's* mind〕 asleep or awake / 꿈속을 헤매는 것 같다 feel as if in a dream.
꿈을: 꿈을 꾸다 dream 《a good dream》; have a dream / 꿈을 가지다 have 〔cherish〕 a dream / 꿈을 풀다 interpret a dream / 오랜 꿈을 실현하다 realize *one's* long-cherished dream 〔vision〕 / 나는 시험에 합격한 꿈을 꾸었다 I dreamed 〔had a dream〕 that I passed the exam. / 그녀는 새처럼 자유롭게 하늘을 나는 꿈을 꾸었다 She dreamed that she was flying like a bird. / 새 시장은 그의 도시에 대한 꿈을 가지고 있다 The new mayor has a dream for his town. / 너는 어떤 꿈을 가지고 있느냐 What dreams do you have for the future? / 그는 매우 비현실적이다. 항상 허황된 꿈을 좇고 있으니 말이야 He is so unrealistic. He's always chasing rainbows. / 소년들이여, 꿈을 가져라 Boys, be ambitious! / 마치 꿈을 꾸고 있는것 같은 기분이다 I feel as if I were dreaming 〔in dream〕.
꿈에: 꿈에 나타나다 appear in *one's* dream; come to *one* in sleep 〔in a dream〕/ 꿈에 서방맞은 격 not entirely satisfactory; leave something to be desired / 돌아가신 어머니를 꿈에 보았다 I saw my dead mother in my dream. / 어젯밤에 무서운 꿈에 시달렸다 Last night I was disturbed by a terrible dream. / 인생은 한갓 꿈에 지나지 않는다 Life is but a dream.
¶ 하루하루가 꿈처럼 지나갔다 Every day passed like a dream. / 나는 미래에 대한 큰 꿈이 있다 I have a great vision for the future. / 나는 꿈도 희망도 없다 I have neither dream nor hope. / 꿈이 맞았다〔맞지 않았다〕 The dream 「came true 〔turned out false〕. / 이곳에서 너를 만나리라고는 꿈에도 생각지 못했다 I never 〔little〕 dreamed of meeting you here. / 그녀가 1등을 하리라고는 꿈에도 생각 못했다 I never dreamed that she would win the first prize. / 나의 꿈은 우주비행사가 되는 것이다 My dream is to be an astronaut. / 대통령이 되겠다는 그의 꿈이 실현되었다 His dream of becoming President has come true. / 인생은 현실이지 꿈이 아니다 Life is 「a reality 〔real〕 and not a dream. / 모국으로 돌아가려는 그녀의 꿈은 덧없이 무산되었다〔산산히 깨졌다〕 Her dream of going back home has been dashed 〔shattered〕.

**꿈같다** be like a dream; (be) dreamlike; (be) dreamy; visionary; illusory; chimerical. ¶ 꿈같은 이야기 a dreamlike story; a story too good to be true / 꿈같은 「세상 an illusory 〔a chimerical〕 world / 꿈같이 like a dream / 일생을 꿈같이 보내다 dream away *one's* life / 모든 것이 ~ Everything seems like a dream.

**꿈결** (the midst of) a dream; a dreamy 〔an ecstatic〕 state; a trance. ¶ ~에 듣다 listen half asleep; hear to 《*a thing*》 dreamily / ~ 같다 be like a dream; be dreamlike; be as if in a dream / ~에 「불이야」 하는 외침을 들었다 Half asleep and half awake, I heard the cry, "Fire!"

**꿈꾸다** ① 《자면서》 dream 《of, about》; have a dream 《about》. ¶ 꿈꾸는 듯한 표정 a dreamy expression / 고향을 ~ dream of home / 꿈(을) 꾸는 것 같다 be like being in a dream; be unable to believe *one's* eyes. ② 《바라다》 dream; desire; wish; fancy; have an ambition 《to...》. ¶ 큰 정치가를 ~ 「dream of 〔fancy *oneself*〕 becoming a great statesman.

**꿈나라** the 〔a〕 dreamland; the land of dreams. ¶ ~로 가다 go to the dreamland; 《잠들다》 fall asleep / ~를 헤매는 기분이다 feel as if in a dream.

**꿈땜** a bad luck deemed to offset the

bad dream. ～하다 escape a bad luck by a lesser sacrifice after having an evil dream.

**꿈자리** the happenings 〔portents〕 in a dream; dreams; portents. ¶ ～가 사납다 《a dream》 be of bad omen / ～ 사나운 꿈을 꾸다 have a bad dream; have a dream of ill omen.

**꿈쩍없다** 《동요·움직이지 않다》 (be) firm; immovable; remain unmoved; do not stir 〔budge〕 an inch.

**꿈틀-** ⇨ 굼틀-.

**꼽꼽하다** 《축축하다》 be a bit damp; 「(be) dampish.

**꿋꿋이** strongly; firm(ly); unyieldingly. ¶ ～ 서다 stand firm / ～ 역경을 견뎌내다 endure adversity firmly.

**꿋꿋하다** (be) strong; hard; firm; indefatigable; determined; inflexible; unyielding. ¶ 꿋꿋한 의지 a strong 〔an iron〕 will / 꿋꿋한 마음 a firm 〔determined〕 mind; an unyielding mind.

**꿍꽝** 《북 따위의》 rattling and booming; 《포·총 따위의》 popping 〔crackling〕 and booming 〔roaring〕. ～하다, ～거리다 《북 따위가》 be rattling and booming; make 《a drum》 rattle and boom; 《총포 따위가》 be popping 〔crackling〕 and booming 〔roaring〕; make 《a gun》 pop and boom. ¶ 북을 ～거리다 beat 〔sound〕 a drum continuously / 대포를 ～거리다 fire a (artillery) gun in succession / 아이들은 2층에서 꿍꽝거려 욕을 먹었다 The children were scolded for making too much noise upstairs.

**꿍꿍** 《앓는 소리》 groaning; moaning 《with pain》. ～하다, ～거리다 groan; moan. ¶ ～ 앓다 《병으로》 moan with *one's* ailment; 《걱정하다》 worry (*oneself*) 《about, over》; brood 《over》; fret 《about》 / 아파서 꿍꿍거리다 be groaning with pain / 무슨 일로 ～ 앓고 있는 거야 What's your worry 〔trouble〕? *or* What are you worried about? / 성적이 나빴다고 너무 꿍꿍 앓지 마라 Don't let your bad grades bother 〔worry〕 you too much!

**꿍꿍이셈, 꿍꿍이속** a secret scheme of *one's* own; a secret design; an underhand scheme; an underlying motive. ¶ ～이 있다 have a plot in mind; have a secret design / 틀림없이 ～이 있다 There must be something secret behind the scene. / 무슨 ～인지 도무지 모르겠다 I cannot quite see his motive 〔idea〕.

**꿍하다** ⇨ 꽁하다.

**꿩** 〖조류〗 a pheasant. ¶ 꿩사냥 pheasant hunting / 꿩잡이 a pheasant hunter / 한 쌍의 꿩 a brace of pheasants.

**꿩의다리** 〖식물〗 a feather columbine.

**꿩의비름** 〖식물〗 a blush stonecrop.

**꿰다** ① 《구멍에》 thread; pass 〔run〕 《*a thing*》 through. ¶ 바늘에 실을 ～ thread a needle; run a thread through a needle / 구슬을 ～ thread beads. ② 《꿰어 꽂다》 pierce; spit; skewer. ¶ 칼끝으로 ～ spit 《*a thing*》 with a point of knife / 꼬챙이에 꿰어 굽다 broil 《a fish》 on a skewer. ③ 《옷·신을》 put 〔throw〕 on; slip 〔kick〕 *one's* feet into. ¶ 소매에 팔을 ～ slip 〔put〕 *one's* arm into the sleeve.

**꿰들다** ① 《꿰어 들다》 spear 〔pierce〕 《*a thing*》 and hold it up. ¶ 물고기를 창끝에 ～ hold up a fish on the end of a spear. ② 《드러내다》 disclose; expose; reveal.

**꿰뚫다** ① 《관통하다》 pierce; penetrate; cut 〔run〕 through; perforate. ¶ 총알이 가슴을 ～ a bullet pierces the chest; a bullet shoots 〔goes〕 through the chest / 적진을 ～ pierce the enemy's lines; penetrate the enemy's lines / 탄알이 담벼락을 ～ a bullet penetrates the wall / 그 강은 시내를 꿰뚫고 흐른다 The river runs through the city. ② 《꿰뚫어 보다》 《남의 속을》 see into 〔through〕 《*a person,* a plot》; see 〔penetrate, have an insight〕 into 《*a person's* heart》. ¶ 거짓말을 꿰뚫어 보다 see through 《*a person's*》 lies / 그에게는 인간성〔미래의 일〕을 꿰뚫어 보는 통찰력이 있다 He has an insight into character 〔things to come〕.

**꿰뜨리다** puncture; break; burst; wear out 〔down〕. ¶ 공을 ～ burst a ball / 신을 ～ wear *one's* shoes out / 옷을 ～ tear 〔wear out〕 *one's* clothes.

**꿰매다** 《바늘로》 sew; stitch; 《조각을 대어》 patch; put a patch on; darn; 《수선하다》 mend. ¶ 터진 데를 ～ sew up a rip / 상처를 세 바늘 ～ put three stitches in the wound; close a wound with three stitches / 옷을 ～ sew 〔patch〕 a dress / 양말을 ～ darn (a hole) in a sock / 듬성듬성〔촘촘히〕 ～ take long 〔short〕 stitches / 손으로〔재봉틀로〕 ～ sew 《clothes》 「by hand 〔with a machine〕 / 꿰맨 곳을 풀다 undo a place once sewed.

**꿰미** ① 《끈》 a string 〔thin cord〕 《for skewering 「coins 〔fish, persimmons, mushrooms, *etc.*]》. ② 《꿴 것》 things on a string《such as coins, fish, persimmons》. ¶ 돈〔생선〕 한 ~ a string of coins〔fish〕.

**꿰지다** 《으깨지다》 be crushed〔smashed〕; 《부서지다》 be broken; break; go to pieces; 《찢어지다》 be〔get〕 torn; be ripped〔rent〕(up); 《터지다》 burst〔split〕 upon; 《미어지다》 wear〔be worn〕 out. ¶ 토마토는 잘 꿰진다 Tomatoes crush easily. / 이 옷감은 잘 꿰지지 않는다 This cloth material doesn't wear out easily. / 종이 봉지가 꿰졌다 The paper bag is broken〔split〕.

**꿰찌르다** pierce; stab; thrust〔put〕 through; stick (바늘 따위로). ¶ 단도로 ~ stab 《*a person*》 with a dagger; thrust〔run〕 a dagger into 《*a person's* chest》 / 바늘로 ~ stick〔put〕 a pin into 《*a thing*》 / 창으로 아무의 옆구리를 ~ pierce *a person's* side with a spear〔lance〕.

**꿰차다** ① 《허리춤에 차다》 hang〔suspend〕 《*a thing*》 at *one's* side; sling 《*a thing*》 around *one's* waist. ¶ 주머니를 꿰차고 거리를 활보하다 stride along the street with a bag dangling from the belt. ② 《제것으로 하다》 make 《*a thing*》 *one's* own; get 《*a thing*》 into *one's* hand; latch on to 《구어》; take〔get〕 possession 《of》.

**꽥** shouting; yelling. ~하다 shout〔yell, bark, roar〕 《at》. ¶ 꽥하는 소리 a shout; a yell / 화가 나서 그녀에게 꽥 소리질렀다 I shouted at her in anger.

**꽥꽥거리다** ① rant and rave. ⇨ 꽥하다. ¶ 사소한 일로 ~ roar〔thunder〕 at trifles / 화가 나서 ~ roar at 《*a person*》 in anger; roar with anger. ② 《토하려고 하다》 retch; feel sick; be sick at stomach. ③ 《오리가》 quack; 《거위가》 gaggle.

**뀌다** 《방귀를》 break wind; pass gas; 《속어》 fart. ¶ 고구마를 먹으면 방귀를 뀌게 된다 Sweet potatoes will make you break wind.

**끄나풀** ① 《끈》 a piece of string; a (bit of) cord. ¶ ~로 잡아매다 fasten〔tie〕 with a string / ~을 풀다 untie the strings / ~이 풀어졌다 The strings come untied. ② 《앞잡이》 a tool; a cat's-paw; an agent; a pawn. ¶ 경찰 ~ a police agent; a pawn of the police / ~ 노릇하다 work〔act〕 as an agent; be a tool〔cat's-paw〕 / ~로 부리다 make a cat's-paw〔a tool〕 of 《*a person*》; use 《*a person*》 as a tool / 그는 FBI의 ~이다 He is being used as a tool by the FBI.

**끄느름하다** ① 《날씨가》 (be) cloudy; overcast; gloomy. ¶ 오늘은 날씨가 ~ It's gloomy today. ② 《불기운이》 (be) low heat. ¶ 끄느름한 불에 고다 cook 《meat》 for a long time over (a) low heat.

**끄다** ① 《불을》 put 《the fire》 out; extinguish. ¶ 밟아서〔두들겨서, 불어서〕 ~ trample〔beat, blow〕 out 《the flames》 / 모래로 불을 ~ quench a fire with sand / 담요를 덮어 불을 ~ smother the fire with a blanket / 비벼(서) ~ rub〔crush〕 out 《the fire》 / 소방대원이 불을 껐다 The firemen「put out〔extinguished〕 the fire.

② 《전등·가스를》 switch off 《an electric light》; turn off 《the gas》; 《엔진 따위를》 stop. ¶ TV〔가스〕를 ~ switch〔turn〕 off the television〔gas〕 / 컴퓨터를 ~ turn off〔shut down〕 the computer / 엔진을 ~ stop an engine / 자기 전에 반드시 전등을 꺼라 Don't forget to turn〔switch〕 off the light before you go to bed.

③ 《깨뜨리다》 break; crush; loosen. ¶ 흙덩어리를 ~ break a clod of earth; crush a bit〔lump〕 of clay / 얼음을 ~ break〔smash〕 ice.

④ 《빚을》 pay back; repay. ¶ 빚을 꺼 나가다 clear〔pay〕 off *one's* debt.

**끄덕이다** nod (*one's* head) 《to, at》; bow *one's* head in assent; agree 《to》. ¶ 가볍게 ~ give a slight nod / 끄덕여 승낙하다 nod approval; nod *one's* agreement / 두 사람은 서로 머리를 끄덕이며 이야기 했다 They were talking to each other with nodding.

**끄덩이** ① 《머리털·실의》 the end of「a tangle of hair〔a bunch of thread〕. ¶ 머리~를 그러잡다 seize〔grab〕 《*a person's*》 hair; seize 《*a person*》 by the hair / 머리~를 잡고 꺼두르다 drag 《a woman》 by the hair / 실 ~를 잡아당기다 pull out a thread from a bunch. ② 《일의》 a clue (단서).

**끄떡** ① nodding; with a nod. ⇨ 끄덕이다. ¶ (머리를) ~하고 인사하다 nod (a greeting) to 《*a person*》. ② 《미동》 a stir; a slight movement. ¶ ~도 않다 do not move〔budge, stir〕 an inch; stand as firm as a rock.

**끄떡없다** 《탈없다》 (be) safe (and) sound; all right; 《물·불 따위에》 (be) proof 《against》; 《태연하다》 (be) unmoved; unflinching; do not yield. ¶ 좀 다치기

는 했지만 이 정도는 ～ I hurt a little myself, but it's nothing. / 그는 위협을 당해도 끄떡없었다 He 「was unmoved 〔didn't flinch〕 even when threatened.

**끄르다** 《맨 것을》 undo 《buttons》; untie 《a bundle》; loose; loosen; unloose; unfasten; unlace; unpack. ¶ 단추를 ～ undo a button / 여행 가방을 ～ unpack a trunk / 맨 것을 ～ unfasten 〔loosen〕 《*a thing*》 tied up / 구두끈을 ～ unlace *one's* shoes / 매듭을 ～ undo a knot; unknot.

**끄르륵** with a burp 〔belch〕. ～하다 burp; belch; give a burp 〔belch〕.

**끄르륵거리다** keep burping; belch; eruct; eructate.

**끄무러지다** 《날씨가》 get cloudy; become cloudy 〔overcast〕; become covered with clouds. ¶ 끄무러진 날씨 cloudy weather; a cloudy day.

**끄무레하다** 《날씨가》 (be) cloudy; be clouded over; (be) overcast; dull. ¶ 끄무레한 날씨 cloudy weather.

**끄물거리다** 《날씨가》 get cloudy 「from time to time 〔off and on〕; be clear and cloudy at intervals. ¶ 끄물거리는 날씨 a partly cloudy day; unsettled weather / 매년 이맘때쯤이면 날씨가 끄물거린다 The weather is unsettled 〔changeable, variable〕 at this time of (the) year.

**끄집다** take; hold and pull; draw. ¶ 여럿 중에서 하나를 ～ take one among many / 난롯가로 의자를 끄집어 오다 draw a chair up to the fireplace.

**끄집어내다** ① 《속의 것을 밖으로》 take 〔bring, get〕 《*a thing*》 out; pull 〔draw〕 《*a thing*》 out; produce 《from》; fish out (더듬어); pick up (골라서); drag out (끌어서). ¶ 가방에서 책을 ～ take out a book from *one's* bag; take a book out of *one's* bag / 외양간에서 소를 ～ lead a cow out of a cowshed / 그 자료에서 결론을 ～ draw a conclusion from the data / 그녀는 마음에 드는 옷을 한 벌 끄집어냈다 She picked out one dress that she liked. / 그로부터 그 문제에 관한 정보를 끄집어냈다 I coaxed the information about 〔on〕 the matter out of him. ② 《이야기 따위를》 bring 《a topic》 into the conversation; bring up 《an interesting subject》; propose 《the subject for discuss》; introduce. ¶ 사업 이야기를 ～ bring business matter into conversation / 돈 문제를 ～ lead up to the question of money / 그는 교육 문제에 관한 이야기를 끄집어냈다 He introduced the problem of education into conversation.

**끄집어내리다** pull 〔drag, draw〕 down; 《기 따위를》 take 〔haul〕 down. ¶ 셔터를 ～ pull down a shutter.

**끄집어당기다** pull; draw; drag. ¶ 귀를 ～ pull 《*a person's*》 ear / 소매를 ～ pull 《*a person*》 by the sleeve / 머리를 ～ pull 《*a person's*》 hair.

**끄집어들이다** draw 〔pull〕 in 〔into〕; lead 〔take〕 《*a person*》 into. ⇨ 끌어들이다.

**끄집어올리다** pull 〔draw〕 up. ⇨ 끌어올리다.

**끄트러기** a broken piece; a scrap; a chip; a fragment; odds and ends. ¶ 나무 ～ odd pieces of wood / 천 ～ odds and ends 〔scraps〕 of cloth.

**끄트머리** ① 《맨 끝 부분》 an end; a tip; the tail end. ¶ 맨 ～에 서다 stand at the tail end / 로프의 ～를 잡아라 Get hold of the end of the rope. ② 《실마리》 a clue. ¶ 그 수수께끼를 풀만한 무슨 ～라도 잡았느냐 Do you have any clue to the mystery? ③ 《관용적 표현》 ¶ ～에서 두번째 the last but one; second from the bottom of the list / ～로 졸업하다 graduate last on the list.

**끈** ① 《묶는 줄》 (a) string; (a) cord; 《꼰 것》 braid; a lace; 《띠 모양의》 a band; a ribbon; 《주머니의》 a drawstring. ¶ 가죽 끈 a (leather) strap; a thong / 끈을 매다〔풀다〕 tie 〔untie〕 the strings / 끈으로 매다〔묶다〕 tie (up) with (a) string / 구두끈을 매다〔풀다〕 lace 〔unlace〕 *one's* shoes / 구두끈이 풀렸다 My (shoe)laces came untied 〔loose〕. ② 《연줄》 ties; connections; a pull 《구어》. ¶ 끈이 좋다 be well-connected; have a strong 〔good〕 pull / 끈을 찾다 hunt up connections / 그 회사에 매달릴 만한 ～이 없느냐 Don't you have any 「good connections 〔particular pull〕 in that company?

**끈기**(一氣) ① 《참을성 있는 기질》 patience; perseverance; persistence; endurance; tenacity; stick-to-itiveness 《미구어》. ¶ ～ 있다 be patient 〔persevering, untiring〕; have tenacity of purpose / ～ 있게 patiently; with perseverance 〔patience〕; untiringly / ～를 잃다 lose stamina 〔staying power〕 / ～가 다하다 run out of energy; be unable to carry on any longer / 그는 ～가 없다 He lacks tenacity of purpose. *or* He has not the gift of sticking-to-it. / 그는 한 가

지 일에 끝까지 파고드는 ~가 없다 He is not steady enough to stick to one job.
②《끈끈한 기운》stickiness; viscosity; glutinosity; adhesiveness. ¶ ~ 있는 풀 sticky paste / ~ 있는 쌀 glutinous rice / 이 쌀은 ~가 많다 The rice is rich in gluten.

**끈끈이** birdlime; lime. ¶ ~로 새를 잡다 catch a bird with birdlime.

**끈끈이주걱** 〖식물〗 a dew grass; a (round-leaved) sundew; a sundew plant.

**끈끈하다** ①《끈적끈적하다》(be) sticky; gluey; viscous; glutinous; gooey《구어》. ¶ 끈끈한 풀 sticky 〔gluey〕 paste 셔츠가 땀으로 ~ *one's* shirt is sticky with sweat / 마르지 않은 페인트는 ~ The wet paint is sticky. ②《성질이》 be a stickler; (be) persistent; tenacious; dogged. ¶ 성질이 끈끈한 사람 a stickler; a man of great tenacity.

**끈덕지다** (be) persistent; tenacious; pertinacious. ¶ 끈덕지게 tenaciously; persistently; with persistence 〔tenacity〕 / 끈덕지게 여자를 따라다니다 dangle after a girl with the grimmest tenacity.

**끈 떨어지다** 《끈이》 a string breaks; 《의지하던 것에서》 lose *one's* means of livelihood; become helpless. ¶ 끈 떨어진 뒤웅박《속담》a fish out of water.

**끈목** a braid; a plaited cord.

**끈 붙다** 《살길이 생기다》 get a means of livelihood. 「means of livelihood.

**끈 붙이다** provide 《*a person*》 with a

**끈적거리다** 《들러붙다》 stick 〔adhere〕 《to》; [서술적] (be) sticky; adhesive; gummy; glutinous. ¶ 내의가 땀으로~ My undershirt is sticky with sweat. / 무언가 끈적거리는 것이 손에 만져졌다 I happened to touch something sticky.

**끈적끈적** ①《물체가》~하다 (be) sticky; adhesive; gummy; gooey《구어》. ¶~한 테이프 a sticky tape / 그의 손가락은 풀이 묻어 ~하다 His fingers are sticky with glue. ②《사람이》~하다 (be) tenacious; persistent.

**끈질기다** (be) tenacious; persevering; stick-to-itive《미구어》; 《집요하다》(be) persistent; insistent; stubborn. ¶ 끈질긴 사람 a persevering 〔patient, persistent〕 person / 끈질긴 병 a stubborn 〔lingering〕 illness / 끈질긴 노력을 하다 make persistent 〔steady〕 efforts / 끈질기게 저항하다 meet with stubborn 〔tenacious〕 resistance / 끈질기게 따라다니다 hang around 《*a person*》 with annoying persistence / 끈질기게 조르다 ask 《*a person*》 importunately for 《money》 / 그녀는 끈질기게 그 일을 성취해 냈다 She carried through the work tenaciously. / 그는 끈질긴 데가 있다 He has a tenacity in him. / 참 끈질긴 녀석이로군 What a pest! *or* What a bore he is!

**끊기다** = 끊어지다.

**끊다** ①《자르다》cut (off); sever; break; snap; disconnect (연결 부분을). ¶ 철사를 ~ cut 〔break〕 a steel wire / 밧줄을 두 가닥으로 ~ cut 〔sever〕 a rope in two / 실을 ~ snap a string / 이 부분을 끊어 버리자 Let's cut this section off. / 요금 체납으로 전화국에서 전화를 끊었다 The telephone office disconnected my telephone because I didn't pay the bill.
②《옷감·차표 따위를 사다》buy; 《개찰하다》clip 〔punch〕 《a ticket》. ¶ 표를 끊는 사람들의 늘어선 줄 a ticket line / 옷감을~ buy a piece of cloth / 부산행 차표를 ~ buy 〔get〕 a ticket for Pusan.
③《전기 따위를》turn 〔switch〕 off; 《통화를》hang up; ring off 《영》; 《언동·흐름·움직임 따위를》cut 〔shut〕 off; stop; interrupt; intercept. ¶ 수도를 ~ cut off water supply / 가스를 ~ turn off gas / 전류를 ~ switch off the electric current / 회로를~ kill a circuit / 적의 퇴로를~「cut off 〔intercept〕 the enemy's retreat / 그는 갑자기 말을 끊고 침묵했다 He「suddenly stopped talking 〔broke off abruptly〕 and became silent. / 전화를 끊지 마세요 Please hold 〔hang〕 on. *or* Hold the line, please. / 그는 화가 나서 내가 말하는 중에 전화를 끊었다 He hung up on me in anger. / 그럼, 이제 전화를 끊겠습니다 I'll hang up now. *or* I'll get off the line.
④《인연·관계를》break off relation 《with *a person*》; cut 〔sever〕 connection 《with》; cut off 《communication》; break (off) with 《*a person*》; be through 《with》. ¶ 끊을래야 끊을 수 없는 관계에 있다 be closely 〔inseparably〕 bound up 《with》 / 아무하고 관계를 ~ sever connections 〔relations〕 with *a person* / 발길을 ~ stop visiting; keep *oneself* away from; cease to visit / 외교 관계를 ~ break off 〔sever〕 all diplomatic relations / 나는 그녀와 교제를 끊었다 I ended 〔terminated〕 my friendship with her. *or* I have

broken off with her. / 나는 그 회사와 완전히 손을 끊었다 I broke off all relations with the firm. / 그의 부친은 그와 부자관계를 끊었다 His father has「cut him off 〔disowned him〕.

⑤《술·담배 따위를》stop; give up (★ stop, give up은 모두 동명사를 목적어로 취함. 부정사를 써서 stop to drink로 하면「술 마시기 위해 멈춰 서다」의 뜻이 됨); quit; abstain from. ¶ 담배를 ～ give up 〔quit〕 smoking / 술을 ～ stop 〔give up〕 drinking; abstain from liquor / 나는 담배를 끊기로 결심했다 I have made up my mind to give up smoking.

⑥《목숨을》take《*a person's, one's* own》life; kill. ¶ 그는 스스로 목숨을 끊었다 He killed himself. *or* He committed suicide.

⑦《수표·어음을》draw; issue. ¶ 전표를 ～ issue an invoice / (백만원짜리) 수표를 ～ issue 〔make out〕 a check (for one million won).

⑧《문장·말을》punctuate《a sentence》; mark off《by a comma》. ¶ 한 구절씩 끊어 읽다 read《a text》with pauses between phrases / 한 마디씩 신중히 끊어서 말하다 talk carefully, spacing *one's* words.

**끊어뜨리다** ①《줄 따위를》cut off; sever;《관계 따위를》break off; sever. ¶ 저희 회사와의 관계를 끊어뜨리지 않으시기를 바랍니다 Please don't「break off 〔sever〕 ties with our company.

②《공급 따위를》run out 〔short〕《of》; exhaust the supply《of》. ¶ 원료의 공급을 끊어뜨렸다 Our supply of raw materials has been exhausted.

**끊어맡다** take on《a job》as subcontractor; be a subcontractor《on a construction work》. ¶ 끊어맡은 일 a piece work; a subcontracted work.

**끊어주다** pay《*a person*》off 〔out〕; square accounts with《*a person*》.

**끊어지다** ①《줄 따위가》break; snap; be cut 〔rent〕; come apart;《무너지다》collapse; give way; break down. ¶ 실이 ～ a string breaks 〔snaps〕 / 백열전구가 ～ a light bulb is burnt out / 전선이 ～ an electric wire is down / 퓨즈가 끊어졌다 The fuse is gone. / 홍수로 제방이 끊어졌다 The bank「broke down 〔collapsed〕 under the flood.

②《관계가》break (off) with《*a person*》; come to an end; be cut 〔severed〕;「be through 〔have, done〕 with《*a person*》. ¶ 인연이 ～ be separated; be divorced (부부의); be finished with each other / 나와 그녀의 관계는 끊어졌다 My relation with her was finished. / 그녀와 연락이 끊어졌다 I have lost contact with her.

③《소식·통신·연결 등이》be stopped; be cut off; be interrupted 〔suspended, discontinued〕; cease; come to an end. ¶ 교통이 ～ traffic 〔transportation〕 is stopped 〔interrupted〕 / 여객기와 통신이 끊어졌다 Communication with the passenger plane was cut off. / 그의 소식은 3년이나 끊어져 있다 I haven't heard from him for three years. / 그 화가의 가계는 그에게서 끊어졌다 The painter's family line died out with him. / 통화 중에 전화가 끊어졌다 We were cut off in the middle of our telephone conversation.

④《물자의 공급·자금의 흐름 등이》run out《of》; be out 〔short〕 of; be out of stock; be cut off. ¶ 물의 공급이 ～ the supply of water runs out / 물자의 공급이 ～ Our supplies run out. / 자금의 흐름이 ～ We are running out of money. / 만일 석유의 수입이 끊어지면 한국 경제는 큰 타격을 받을 것이다 If the import of oil should be cut off, it would give a severe blow to the Korean economy.

⑤《숨·생명이》expire; die. ¶ 목숨이 ～ die; breathe *one's* last; gasp *one's* life away / 그는 그렇게 말하고 숨이 끊어졌다 So saying, he breathed his last. / 숨이 끊어질 듯하다 I am short 〔out〕 of breath.

**끊이다** ⇨ 끊어지다. ¶ 그녀에겐 걱정거리가 끊이지 않는다 She always has something worrying her. *or* There is no end to her worries. / 끊이지 않고 비가 계속 내렸다 It rained without a break.

**끊임없다** (be) ceaseless; incessant; constant; continual; continuous. ¶ 끊임없는 노력 ceaseless 〔constant〕 efforts / 끊임없는 발전 continuous development / 끊임없는 열성 unremitting zeal / 우리 사무실 앞에는 차의 흐름이 ～ There is a constant stream of cars in front of our office.

**끊임없이** constantly; incessantly; always (항상); without「a break 〔interruption, cease〕; continually; continuously (★ continually는 단속적으로「몇 번이고」의 뜻이고, continuously는「쭉 계속해서」의 뜻). ¶ ～ 노력하다 make constant 〔ceaseless〕 efforts / ～ 지껄이다 talk without a pause; have no end of talk; chatter ceaselessly / ~ 불평을 늘어놓다 complain「incessantly 〔all the time〕/ ~ 감시하다 keep a constant watch 《over》/ ~ 두리번거리다 look around ceaselessly / ~ 전화가 걸려 오다 have telephone calls almost without a break / 풍향은 ~ 변화한다 The direction of the wind shifts constantly.

**끌** a chisel. ¶ 끌로 파다 chisel; cut「with a chisel.

**끌꺽끌꺽하다** keep belching.

**끌끌** ① 《혀 차는 소리》 clicking *one's* tongue; going tut-tut! 〔tsk-tsk!〕. ¶ 혀를 ~ 차다 tut; go tut-tut 〔tsk-tsk〕. ② 《트림 소리》 belching; burping.

**끌끌하다** 《마음이》 (be) clean and pure; honest; good-intentioned.

**끌끔하다** (be) dashing; smart; sleek and clean.

**끌다** ① 《질질》 drag (무거운 것을); trail (옷소매나 가벼운 것을). ¶ 스커트 자락을 질질 끌며 걷다 walk with *one's* skirt trailing / 발을 질질 끌며 걷다 drag *oneself* along; shuffle *one's* feet along / 피로한 다리를 질질 ~ drag *one's* weary feet / 그녀는 옷자락을 마루에 끌면서 걸었다 She trailed her dress along the floor. / 나는 도둑을 경찰서로 끌고 갔다 I dragged the burglar to the police station.
② 《잡아당기다》 pull; draw; tug (강한 힘으로); haul (무거운 것을 밧줄 따위로); tow (밧줄·쇠사슬로). ¶ 소매를 ~ pull 《*a person*》 by the sleeve; tug 〔pull〕 《*a person's*》 sleeve / 부서진 자동차를 ~ tow a wrecked car / 짐수레를 ~ pull 〔draw〕 a cart / 통나무를 ~ haul logs / 밧줄을 힘껏 잡아 ~ pull 〔tug at〕 a rope as hard as *one* can.
③ 《동정·주의·인기 따위를》 attract; catch 《*a person's*》 attention; win; draw; arrest. ¶ 사람을 끄는 힘 personal attraction 〔magnetism〕/ 남의 동정을 ~ draw 〔win〕「the sympathy of other people 〔*a person's* sympathy〕/ 그녀 손가락의 보석 반지는 사람들의 눈을 끌었다 The jewel ring on her finger attracted the attention of people. / 왠지 그녀에게 마음이 끌린다 I feel somehow drawn 〔attracted〕 to her. / 그의 연설은 사람을 끄는 힘이 있다 His speech is magnetic.
④ 《일·시간·기일 등을》 prolong; extend; put off; delay; postpone; drag out 〔on〕; linger (on); take a long time. ¶ 오래 끌어온 협상 long-pending 〔drawn-out〕 negotiations / 시간을 끌려는 술책〔전술〕 《adopt》 delaying measures 〔tactics〕/ 대답을 질질 ~ delay giving an answer / 마지막까지 ~ put off to 〔till〕 the last moment / 전투는 오래 끌었다 The battle dragged on. / 그녀의 병은 오래 끌었다 She was long in recovering from her illness. *or* Her illness lingered on. / 그들의 회의는 꽤 오래 끌었다 Their meeting was much prolonged. / 최종기한을 더 이상 끌 수는 없다 We cannot extend the deadline. / 재판이〔교섭이〕 오래 끌었다 The「trial 〔negotiations〕 dragged「on 〔along〕. / 그들은 지불을 차일피일 끌려고 한다 They are trying to「put off the payment from day to day.
⑤ 《시설하다》 lay on 《gas, water》; install 《a telephone》. ¶ 수돗물을 ~ have water supplied / 전화를 ~ have a telephone installed / 파이프로 물을 ~ pipe water to 《a place》/ 강물을 ~ draw water off a river 《into》.
⑥ 《이끌다》 lead; 《손님을》 tout; entice. ¶ 말을 ~ lead a horse / 호텔 여리꾼이 자기네 호텔로 손님을 ~ Hotel employees entice people to their hotels.

**끌러지다** get 〔come〕 loose; be loosened; get untied 〔undone〕. ¶ 구두끈이 ~ *one's* shoestrings come untied / 허리띠가 ~ *one's* belt comes loose.

**끌리다** ① 《질질》 be dragged 〔trailed, draggled〕; drag; draggle; trail. ¶ 치마가 ~ *one's* skirt trails 〔drags〕 《on the floor》/ 신이 ~ *one's* shoes drag (on the ground) / 나는 그 곳에 끌려갔다 I was dragged to the place.
② 《당겨지다》 be pulled 〔drawn〕; be tugged 〔hauled〕; 《끌려가다》 be taken 《to the police》. ¶ 어선이 해변으로 끌려왔다 A fishing boat was tugged to shore.
③ 《마음이》 be attracted 〔charmed, fascinated〕 《by》; be drawn 〔moved〕 《by》; be touched 《with emotion》; 《꾐에》 be enticed 〔tempted〕. ¶ 부모 자식의 정에 ~ be drawn by the ties of parent and child / 인정에 ~ be touched with humanity / 이야기에 끌려들다 be drawn into the conversation / 친구 말에 끌리어 나쁜 짓을 하다 be enticed by a companion to do something wrong / 나는 그녀의 아름다운 목소리에 끌렸다 I was fascinated by her beautiful voice.
④ 《말려들다》 get intangled 《in》; be involved 《in》; be drawn 〔dragged〕 《into》. ¶ 논쟁에 끌려들다 be dragged

into a debate.
⑤《지체·지연》 be delayed; be prolonged [protracted]; be retarded; drag on; be set back (in time).

**끌밋하다** (be) simple and neat; attractive.

**끌밥** sawdust from chiseling; chisel-「dust.

**끌방망이** a chisel hammer.

**끌어내다** take drag [pull] 《*a thing*》 out 《of the house》; take [get] 《*a thing*》 out; tug out. ¶ 의자를 방에서 ~ take [get] a chair out of a room / 집에서 아무를 ~ pull [drag] *a person* out of the house / 진구렁에 빠진 차를 ~ tug a car out of the mire.

**끌어내리다** pull [drag, draw] down; take [bring] down. ¶ 셔터를 ~ pull down a shutter / 연단에서 연사를 ~ drag down a speaker from the platform / 아무를 권좌에서 ~ drag *a person* down from a position of power.

**끌어넣다** 《잡아당기다》 draw [pull, drag] in [into]; 《이끌다》 lead 《*a person*》 in [into]; 《데려오다》 take 《*a person*》 into 《a room》; 《자기편으로》 get [win, gain] 《*a person*》 over 《to *one's* side》; tempt [entice] 《*a person*》 in [into]. ¶ 소를 외양간에 ~ take [bring] a cow into a barn / 아무를 음모에 ~ tempt *a person* into an intrigue / 아무를 자기 당에 ~ win *a person* over to *one's* political party / 영국을 전쟁에 ~ drag England into a war / 그들은 그녀를 자기 편에 끌어 넣으려고 야단이다 They are trying very hard to win her over to their side.

**끌어당기다** 《가까이》 pull [draw] 《*a thing*》 near [toward, close to] *one;* 《손님 따위를》 draw; attract. ¶ 의자를 난로가로 ~ draw *one's* chair up to the fire / 밧줄을 내 앞으로 ~ draw [pull] a rope toward me / 소매를 ~ pull 《*a person*》 by the sleeve.

**끌어대다** ① 《돈을》 borrow money 《from》; raise a loan 《from》. ¶ 집을 사려고 돈을 ~ borrow money to buy a house / 토지를 저당잡혀 돈을 ~ raise money on *one's* land / 자금을 끌어댈 수 없다 can't manage to raise the funds 《for》 / 사장은 돈을 끌어대느라 바쁘다 The president is busy「financing [raising funds]. ② 《인용하다》 quote; cite. ¶ 전례를 ~ cite precedents.

**끌어들이다** draw [drag] in(to). ⇨ 끌어「넣다.

**끌어매다** tie; fasten; sew [stitch] up. ¶ 짐을 끈으로 ~ tie up a bundle with a rope / 소를 말뚝에 ~ tie a cow to a post.

**끌어안다** draw 《*a person*》「to *one's* breast [closer to *oneself*]; snuggle 《a child》 to *one's* arms; 《껴안다》 hug; embrace; hold [press] 《*a person*》 to *one's* bosom. ¶ 어린애를 ~ hug a child / 서로 ~ embrace each other; fall into each other's arms / 어머니는 아기를 꼭 끌어안았다 The mother pressed her baby to her breast.

**끌어올리다** 《당겨올리다》 pull [draw] up; 《난파선을》 salvage; refloat; 《승진시키다》 promote 《*a person*》 to a higher position; 《값을 올리다》 increase; raise. ¶ 펌프로 물을 ~ pump up water / 가라앉은 배를 ~ salvage [pull up] a sunken vessel / 석유가격을 15퍼센트 ~ raise the price of oil by 15% / 배를 해변으로 ~ haul the boat up on the beach / 그물을 끌어올리니 많은 물고기가 가득 잡혀 있었다 When we「pulled up [landed] the net, there were many fish caught in it.

**끌채** a shaft; a thill.

**끌탕** affliction; anguish; agony; worry. ~하다 be troubled [afflicted] 《with》; be worried 《about》; worry (*oneself*) 《about, over》.

**끓는점**(―點) 『물리·화학』 the boiling point. ¶ ~에 달하다 reach a boil; come to the boil.

**끓다** ① 《물이》 boil; seethe; 《피가》 (be) stiring; thrilling; tingling. ¶ 끓는[끓은] 물 boiling [boiled] water / 피가 끓는 이야기 an exciting [a stiring, a thrilling] story / 끓기 시작하다 come to a boil / 냄비가 끓어 넘치다 the pot is boiling over / 물이 펄펄 끓고 있다 The water is boiling briskly. / 물은 섭씨 100도에서 끓는다 Water boils at 100°C. / 결승에서 승리했을 때는 흥분으로 피가 끓는 기분이었다 Every drop of my blood tingled with excitement when we won the final match.
② 《뜨거워지다》 become very [boiling] hot; grow hot. ¶ 온돌방이 절절 ~ The *ondol* floor is boiling hot.
③ 《속이》 fret; fume; become irritated. ¶ 노여움으로 속이 부글부글 ~ fret and fume; seethe [boil] with anger; be convulsed with anger.
④ 《뱃속이》 rumble. ¶ 배가 ~ *one's* stomach rumbles.
⑤ 《가래가》 accumulate. ¶ 가래가 ~ phlegm accumulates in *one's* throat.

**끓어오르다** boil 〔seethe〕 up. ¶ 물은 이내 끓어올랐다 Water soon boiled up. / 분노로 피가 끓어올랐다 My blood boiled with indignation.

**끓이다** ① 《끓게 하다》 boil; heat; make 《it》 hot. ¶ 물을 ~ boil water / 우유를 ~ scald milk / 차를 ~ make tea / 목욕물을 ~ heat the bath; get the bath ready / 물을 끓여 두다 keep the water boiling. ② 《익히다》 cook. ¶ 밥을 ~ cook 〔boil〕 rice / 국을 ~ make soup. ③ 《속태우다》 worry; trouble; bother; be 〔feel〕 nervous 《about》. ¶ 그런 일로 속을 끓일 필요는 없다 It's useless to worry 〔fret〕 about such a thing.

**끔벅** ① 《불·빛 따위가》 flickering. ~하다 flicker; waver; dim for a moment. ⇨ 깜박. ¶ 촛불이 바람에 ~하다 a candle flickers in the breeze (for a moment). ② 《눈을》 winking; blinking. ~하다 wink; blink; give a wink. ¶ 눈을 ~하다 wink 〔blink〕 *one's* eyes / 알았다는 듯이 눈을 ~하다 give a knowing wink.

**끔벅거리다** 《불·빛이》 flicker; twinkle; waver; 《눈을》 blink; wink. ¶ 끔벅거리는 등불 a flickering light / 눈을 ~ wink 〔blink〕 *one's* eyes / 한쪽 눈을 ~ bat *one's* eye.

**끔벅끔벅** (with) blinking 〔flickering, wavering〕. ¶ ~ 졸다 doze off; drop 〔nod〕 off to sleep; fall into a doze.

**끔벅이다** =끔벅거리다. ¶ 먼데서 불빛이 끔벅이는 것을 보았다 I saw a blink of light in the distance.

**끔찍스럽다** (be) horrible; appalling; ghastly; gruesome. ⇨ 끔찍하다. ¶ 끔찍스러운 살인 현장 horrific 〔gruesome〕 murder scene / 생각만 하여도 ~ The mere thought of it makes me shudder. / 자동차 사고로 사람이 다쳤는데 끔찍스러워 못 보겠더라 A man was injured by a car accident—it was an appalling sight.

**끔찍이** 《지독히》 terribly; awfully; horribly; 《대단히·매우》 very (much); greatly; extremely; exceedingly; 《극진히》 kindly; cordially; heartily; devotedly; wholeheartedly. ¶ ~ 크다 be awfully big / 딸을 ~ 사랑하다 love *one's* daughter very much / 나는 ~ 운이 좋았다 I was terribly lucky.

**끔찍하다** ① 《놀랍다》 (be) awful; terrible; frightful; horrible; grim; gruesome; appalling. ¶ 끔찍한 죽음 a horrible death / 끔찍하게 죽다 meet a terrible death / 끔찍하게 무겁다 be terribly heavy / 끔직한 짓을 하다 do a cruel thing; commit cruelties 〔atrocities〕 / 사고 현장은 끔찍했다 The scene of the accident was extremely horrible. ② 《극진하다》 (be) terribly kind; awfully thoughtful 〔considerate〕; very courteous. ¶ 끔찍한 사랑 ardent love / 아무를 정성드려 끔찍하게 대하다 give *a person* a hearty welcome; receive *a person* cordially.

**끗수**(一數) score; grade points; 《낱장의》 pips. ¶ ~가 높은 패를 잡다 get a higher number of pips / 내 ~는 7이다 My point is seven.

**끙끙** ~거리다 《고통 따위로》 groan; moan; 《투덜거리다》 grumble; 《힘을 내다》 strain *oneself;* 《걱정하다》 worry *oneself* 《about, over》; brood 〔grieve〕 《over》; 《힘들어서》 toil 《at, along》. ¶ 아파서 ~거리다 groan with pain / 변기에 앉아 ~거리다 strain at stool / 가파른 언덕을 ~거리며 오르다 toil 〔make *one's* way〕 up a steep hill / 그런 사소한 일로 ~거리지 말게 Don't brood over such trifles. / 무슨 일로 ~거리고 있느냐 What are you worried about? / 부상병은 심한 고통으로 ~거리며 누워 있었다 The wounded soldiers lay groaning in great pain.

**끝** ① 《끄트머리》 a point 《of a pencil》; the nib 《of a penholder》; the tip 《of a finger》; the end 《of a stick》. ¶ 혀끝 the tip of a tongue / 코끝 the end 〔tip〕 of a nose / 이 끝에서 저 끝까지 from this end to the other end / 머리끝에서 발끝까지 from head to toe / 끝이 둥긋〔뾰족〕하다 be rounded 〔pointed, sharp〕 at the end / 끝이 점점 가늘어지다 taper (to a point) / 꼬리 끝이 술처럼 되어 있다 The tail ends in a tuft.
② 《맨 나중》 an end; a close; an ending (이야기 따위의); a finish; conclusion(결말); 《기한의》 expiration; expiry; 《최후》 the last. ¶ 끝의 last; final; concluding; terminal / 끝에서 두 번째 next to the last; last but one / 행렬의 끝 the tail end of a procession / 끝날 무렵에 toward the end 〔close〕 《of》 / 끝에 가서 in the end; finally; at last / 끝이 가까이 오다 draw to a close / 끝을 내다 bring 《*a thing*》 to an end 〔a close〕; finish / 끝까지 싸우다 fight to the 「finish 〔last〕; fight it out / 끝까지 저항하다 resist to the bitter end / 이야기를 끝까지 듣다 hear 《*a person*》 out; let 《*a person*》 finish his story / 끝까지 보다 sit through

〔out〕《a play》/ 오늘은 이것으로 끝내자 Let's call it a day. *or* So much for today. *or* That's all for today. / 무슨 일이나 끝이 있는 법이다 All things have an end. / 그녀는 연설 끝에 이런 말을 했다 She ended her speech with these words. / 끝으로 이 말을 하고 싶다 In conclusion, I'd like to say this. / 즐거운 여행도 이제 끝났다 Our pleasant trip has come to a close. / 그녀는 처음부터 끝까지 거기 서 있었다 She stood there from beginning to end. / 끝이 좋아야 모든 것이 좋다 《속담》 All's well that ends well.

③ 《한도》 a limit; limits; bounds; an end. ¶ 사람의 욕망에는 끝이 없다 Human desire knows no limits. / 인간의 진보에는 끝이 없다 There is no limit 〔end〕 to human progress.

④ 《마지막에 이른 결과》 the end; 《as the 〔a〕》 result; outcome 《of a matter》. ¶ 다년간의 노력 끝에 after many years' effort / 수술 끝이 좋지 않았다 The surgical operation resulted in failure. / 일이 어떻게 되어갈지 끝을 기다려 보는게 좋겠다 We'd better wait and see how things will turn out.

**끝갈망** 《뒷수습》 setting 《*a matter*》 right; settlement; after-adjustment. ~하다 set 《*a matter*》 right; settle; sort 《*things*》 out; wind up 《*one's* affairs》; deal with the aftermath. ¶ 도산된 회사의 ~을 하다 wind up the affairs of a bankrupt company.

**끝끝내** to 〔till〕 the very end; to the last; to a finish; to the bitter end. ¶ ~ 돈을 갚지 않다 don't pay the money to the last / ~ 버텨내다 persist to the bitter end / ~ 자기 주장을 굽히지 않다 stick to *one's* opinion / 그는 ~ 그것을 반대했다 He opposed it stubbornly.

**끝나다** ① 《토의·시일이》 end; come to an end 〔a close〕; finish (일이); close (회의가); be over; terminate; 《기한이》 expire; run out; 《완료되다》 be finished 〔completed done〕.

¶ 이 달이 끝나기 전에 before the month is out / 기한이 끝났을 때 when the term expires 〔runs out〕/ 전쟁이 끝났다 The war ended 〔came to an end〕. / 수업은 3시에 끝난다 School is over at three o'clock. / 회의는 오후 4시에 끝났다 The meeting closed 〔ended〕 at 4:00 p.m. / 일은 아직 끝나지 않았다 I haven't finished 〔completed〕 the work yet. / 건설 공사가 끝났다 The construction work has been finished 〔completed〕. / 시험이 모두 끝났다 The examinations are all over. / 여름 방학이 끝나가고 있다 The summer vacation is coming to an end. / 이 조약은 2,000년에 끝난다 This treaty expires in 2,000. / 연주가 끝나자 우레와 같은 박수 갈채가 터져나왔다 Thunderous applause arose the moment the performance was over. / 영화가 끝났을 때 모든 사람이 울고 있었다 Everyone was crying at the end of the movie. / 초고층 빌딩 공사는 5월에 끝날 예정이다 The skyscraper is to be completed in May. / 동창회는 교가 합창으로 끝났다 The alumni meeting was rounded off by everyone singing the school song together.

② 《결국 …이 되다》 end 〔result〕 in; end up. ¶ 실패로 ~ end (up) in failure / 유야무야로 ~ end up undecided; remain unsolved / 그의 시도는 헛수고로 끝났다 Everything he did came to nothing. / 시합은 무승부로 끝났다 The game ended 〔resulted〕 in a tie.

**끝내** ① ⇨ 끝끝내. ② 《결국에는》 at last; after all; finally; in the end. ¶ 온갖 장애를 극복하고 그녀는 ~ 그 일을 완성했다 In spite of every obstacle, she has 「at last 〔finally〕 accomplished the job. / 나는 그녀를 2시간이나 기다렸으나 ~ 나타나지 않았다 I waited for two hours, but she didn't appear after all.

**끝내기** 〖바둑〗 the end game; the last stages of a game.

**끝내다** finish 《*doing*, *a thing*》; end; be 〔get〕 through with 《*one's* task》; get 《*a thing*》 over 《with》; 《완결·수행하다》 conclude; complete (완벽히); accomplish; 《졸업하다》 graduate 《from》.

¶ 수속을 모두 ~ go through all the procedures / 용무를 ~ get *one's* job done / 대학 과정을 ~ complete 〔pass through〕 *one's* university course / 하루의 일을 끝내고 귀가하다 go home after a day's work / 숙제를 끝냈느냐 Are you done with your homework? / 숙제를 빨리 끝내라 Finish your homework quickly. / 모임을 끝낸 것은 밤 12시가 지나서였다 It was after the midnight by the time the meeting 「ended 〔was over〕. / 오늘 중에 그 일을 모두 끝내야 한다 I have to 「finish 〔get through (with)〕 all the work today. / 그는 감사하다는 말로 연설을 끝냈다 He ended (up) 〔closed〕 his speech by expressing his thanks. / 우리는 6개월

에 걸친 교섭을 끝냈다 We've wrapped up six months of negotiations.

**끝닿다** reach the end 〔bottom, top〕; touch bottom. ¶ 끝닿은 데를 모르다 be boundless 〔endless〕.

**끝돈** the remainder (to be paid); the unpaid balance. ¶ ～을 치르다 pay the remainder 〔balance〕.

**끝동** a cuff. ¶ ～을 달다 sew a cuff on a sleeve.

**끝마감** 《끝내기》 a finish; an end; a close; conclusion (종결); 《기일 등의》 closing; closure. ～하다 finish; close; come 〔be brought〕 to an end 〔a close〕; be concluded. ¶ 일을 ～하다 finish with 〔wind up〕 *one's* work / 신청의 ～은 3월 말이다 The closing date for applications is the end of March. / 도안 모집의 ～은 오는 4월 5일이다 Competitors are requested to send in their designs not later than April 5th of this month.

**끝마무리** = 마무리.

**끝마치다** finish up 《a job》. ⇨ 끝내다.

**끝막다** finish; complete; conclude; terminate; close; put an end to; bring 〔draw〕 to a close. ⇨ 끝마감하다.

**끝맺다** 《일 따위를》 settle 《*a matter*》; bring 《*a matter*》 to a conclusion; finish; complete; 《말 따위를》 conclude 《*one's* statement》; close; end up 《*one's* speech》. ¶ …이라고 말하여 이야기를 ～ conclude by saying that…; conclude with the remark that…. / 그는 여러 가지 일을 시작은 하지만 아무것도 끝맺지 못한다 He starts many things, but finishes nothing.

**끝머리** the end; the close. ⇨ 끄트머리. ¶ ～의 번호 the final number / 보고서 ～에 at the end of the report / 편지 ～에 감사의 말을 첨가했다 I added a word of thanks at the end of letter.

**끝물** the last 《farm》 products of the season. ¶ ～ 수박 late watermelons.

**끝수**(一數) 〖수학〗 a fraction; an odd sum(금액). ¶ ～를 버리다 omit 〔round off〕 fractions / ～를 올리다 raise to a unit; reckon 《0.5 and over》 as a unit.

**끝없다** 《한이 없다》 (be) endless; limitless; boundless (넓이가); 《시간이》 everlasting; eternal. ¶ 끝없이 endlessly; without end 〔limit〕; eternally / 끝없는 대양 the boundless (expanse of the) ocean / 끝없이 넓은 하늘 the unlimited expanse of the sky / 끝없는 논쟁〔연설〕 an endless 〔everlasting〕 argument 〔speech〕 / 그들의 논쟁은 끝없이 이어지는 것 같았다 Their argument seemed to go on without end. / 인간의 진보는 ～ There is no limit to human progress.

**끝으로** ① 《결론적으로》 lastly; finally; at 〔in〕 the end 〔conclusion〕. ¶ ～ 한마디 더 하겠다 In conclusion, there is one thing more I will tell you. ② 《순서·차례에서》 at the (tail) end. ¶ ～ 둘째 the last but one.

**끝일** ① 《맨 나중의》 the final job 〔affair〕. ② 《뒷정리》 the windup of an affair.

**끝장** 《마지막》 an end; a finish; a close; a conclusion; 《낙착》 a settlement; fixing (up); 《결과》 the result; the outcome. ¶ 싸움의 ～ the end 〔outcome〕 of a quarrel / ～을 보다 see the end 〔conclusion〕 of; be finished / ～이 나다 come to an end 〔a conclusion〕; be settled / 토론이 ～나다 a discussion is ended 〔wound up, fixed up〕 / 그도 이젠 ～이다 It's all over for him. *or* The game is up for him. / 이 문제를 어서 ～내자 Let's settle this problem quickly. / 이 전쟁은 어떻게 ～날 것인가 How will the war end 〔result〕? *or* What will be the consequence of this war?

**끝장내다** end 〔finish, conclude, terminate〕 《it》; bring 《*a thing*》 to a conclusion 〔an end〕; wind 《*a thing*》 up; put an end to 《*a thing*》; settle 《*a matter*》; fix 《*a matter*》 up. ¶ 일을 ～ finish *one's* work / 싸움을 ～ put an end to a quarrel; settle a quarrel.

**끝판** ① 《마지막》 the last part 〔job, game, *etc.*〕; the end; the close; the conclusion; the finish; the windup. ¶ 일의 ～ the last part of *one's* work; the end of the work / 토론 ～에 가서 싸움이 벌어졌다 A quarrel was started at the end of the discussion. ② 《승부에서의》 the last round 《of a game》. ¶ ～에 지다 lose a game in the last round.

**끼** ⇨ 끼니. ¶ 하루에 세 끼를 먹다 have 〔take〕 three meals a day; eat three times a day / 한 끼에 달걀 세 개를 먹다 eat three eggs at a meal.

**끼끗하다** (be) fresh and neat 〔smart〕; neat and tidy; clear-〔clean-〕cut. ¶ 옷차림이 ～ be smartly 〔neatly〕 dressed / 끼끗하게 차려 입다 dress *oneself* neat and tidy / 끼끗하게 생기다 have clean-cut features.

**끼니** a meal; daily meals; (three) regular meals (a day). ¶ ～때 mealtime / ～마다 at every meals / ～를 거르다 miss 〔skip, do not take〕 a meal / ～를 준비하다 prepare a meal / ～도 잇기가 어렵다 be unable to earn *one's* daily bread; be badly pressed for living / 우리는 ～도 제대로 이어갈 수 없는 형편이었다 We were so hard pressed that we couldn't buy enough to eat.

**끼다¹** ① 《안개·연기 등이》 hang over; envelop; shroud; cloud up 〔over〕 (구름이); fog up (안개가); be veiled 〔wrapped〕. ¶ 산 봉우리에 자욱이 낀 구름 clouds hanging over the mountain peaks / 아침 안개가 낀 촌락들 villages veiled 〔wrapped〕 in a morning mist / 연기가 자욱이 ～ be enveloped 〔wreathed〕 in smoke / 골짜기에는 아침 안개가 잔뜩 끼어 있었다 The valley was veiled 〔blanketed〕 in morning mist. / 실내에는 담배 연기가 자욱이 끼어 있었다 The room was heavy with cigarette smoke. / 하늘에는 구름이 잔뜩 끼었다 The sky clouded over.
② 《때가》 get 〔become〕 dirty 〔filthy〕; be 〔get, become〕 soiled; be stained (얼룩지다); 《먼지가》 become dusty; be covered with dust; gather; 《이끼 따위가》 gather 《moss》; be mossed 〔mossy〕. ¶ 때가 낀 옷 soiled 〔dirty〕 clothes; 《세탁물》 washing; the laundry / 때가 낀 손 a hand soiled 〔smudged〕 with dirt / 이끼가 낀 바위 a rock covered with moss / 눈에 눈꼽이 ～ *one's* eyes are gummy / 선반에 먼지가 잔뜩 끼어 있다 Dust is covered thick on the shelf. / 검댕이 끼지 않도록 해라 Keep clean off soot! / 흰 양말은 때가 잘 낀다 White socks soil easily. / 구르는 돌에는 이끼가 끼지 않는다 《속담》 A rolling stone gathers no moss.

**끼다²** 《틈에》 be caught in; get jammed in; 《사이에》 lie 〔get〕 between; be sandwiched between; 《참가하다》 join (in); take part in; participate (in); 《가담하다》 be involved in; be a party to 《*a matter*》; be a hand in 《*doing*》. ¶ 손가락이 문틈에 ～ get *one's* finger caught in a door / 두 사람 사이에 끼게 되다 be sandwiched between the two / 음모에 ～ be a party to a conspiracy / 두 이해 당사자 사이에 끼어 난처한 입장에 있다 I am in an awkward position, caught between the two interested parties.

**끼다³** ① 《삽입하다》 insert; 《박아넣다》 put 〔get, fit, fix〕 《*a thing*》 in 〔into〕; 《사이에 끼우다》 put 〔hold〕 《*a thing*》 between 《*one's* knees》. ¶ 문틀에 유리를 ～ put a pane of glass in the door frame / 책장 사이에 연필을〔서표를〕 ～ put a pencil 〔a marker〕 between the leaves of a book.
② 《장갑·반지 등을》 put 《a ring》 on; wear 《a diamond ring》; pull 〔draw〕 on 《*one's* gloves》; 《팔을》 fold *one's* arms (자기의); put *one's* arm through another's; link arms with 《*a person*》. ¶ 그녀는 다이아몬드 반지를 끼고 있다 She has 〔wears〕 a diamond ring on her finger. / 그는 팔짱을 끼고 곰곰히 생각했다 He thought it over with folded arms. / 그는 그녀와 팔짱을 끼고 걸었다 He walked arm in arm with her.
③ 《채우다》 ¶ 옷의 단추를〔훅을〕 ～ button 〔hook〕 (up) a dress.
④ 《품속·팔에》 hold 〔carry〕 《*a thing*》 in 〔under〕 *one's* arms; 《껴안다》 hug; embrace. ¶ 책을 옆에 ～ hold a book under *one's* arm / 어린애를 끼고 자다 sleep holding a baby in *one's* arm.
⑤ 《…을 따라》 skirt 《a shore》. ¶ …을 끼고 along; parallel to; alongside with / 강을 끼고 가다 go along a river / 바닷가를 끼고 초가집들이 있었다 There were thatch-roofed houses along the seashore.
⑥ 《배경이 있다》 be backed (up) by; be patronized by; have 《*a person*》 「behind *one* 〔at *one's* back〕. ¶ 권력자를 끼고 있다 have an influencial person at *one's* back / 고관의 권력을 끼고 횡포를 일삼다 carry matters with high hand under the backing 〔pull〕 of the high ranking official.

**끼뜨리다** throw 《water》 away; sprinkle 《water》 around.

**끼루룩** honking. ～하다 honk; make a honk. ¶ 기러기가 ～거렸다 Wild geese were honking.

**끼룩거리다** ① 《기러기가》 honk. ② 《목을 빼다》 make a long neck; crane 〔stretch〕 *one's* neck 《to see *something*》.

**-끼리** 《한 패를 짓는다는 뜻의 접미사》 ¶ 남자끼리의 공감 fellow-feeling between men / 가족끼리의 모임 a family gathering / 우리들끼리의 이야기지만 between 「ourselves 〔you and me〕 / 우리끼리 가자 Let's go by ourselves. / 버스끼리 충돌하다 two buses run into each other / 나는 지난 주, 친한 사람끼

리 여행을 갔다 I went on a trip with some close friends last week.

**끼리끼리** group by group; in separate groups; only the same species. ¶ ~ 돌아다니다 walk around in (separate) groups / ~ 해먹다 each group looks to its own interests / 사람들은 ~ 모인다 Birds of a feather flock together 《속담》.

**끼어들다** wedge 〔squeeze, thrust〕 *oneself* in 〔into〕; force *one's* way in 〔into〕; intrude *oneself* into 《a meeting》; break 〔cut〕 into 《a conversation》; 《줄 따위에》 cut into 《the line》; cut 〔push〕 in front of 《*others*》; jump the line 〔queue 《영》〕. ¶ 만원 버스에 억지로 ~ squeeze *oneself* 〔push *one's* way〕 into a crowded bus / 남 이야기에 끼어드는 법이 아니다 You shouldn't cut 〔break〕 in other people's conversations. *or* You shouldn't 「cut in 〔break in〕 when other people are talking. / 줄 서 있는 내 앞에 그가 끼어들었다 He cut (in) in front of me in line. / 속도를 낸 차가 끼어드는 판에 자칫했으면 사고가 날 뻔했다 A speeding car cut in and nearly caused an accident. / 나는 그들의 한패로 끼어들었다 I thrust myself 「on them 〔into their company〕.

**끼얹다** put 〔throw, splash〕 《water》 on 〔over〕 《*a person*》; shower 〔sprinkle〕 《water》 《on, over》. ¶ 물을 ~ splash water on 《*a person*》.

**끼우다** 《삽입하다》 insert; put in 〔into〕; thrust in; 《맞추어 넣다》 set in; fit; mount (보석 등을). ⇨ 끼다[3]. ¶ 열쇠를 자물쇠에 ~ put 〔insert〕 the key into the lock / 플러그를 콘센트에 ~ put 〔insert〕 a plug into the outlet; plug in / 금관에 보석을 ~ mount jewels in a gold crown / 신문지 사이에 광고를 ~ insert a bill in a newspaper / 펜에 펜촉을 끼우다 fit a pen with a nib / 이 반지에는 다이아몬드가 끼워져 있다 A diamond is set in this ring.

**끼워팔기** a tie-in 〔combination〕 sale.

**끼이다** ① 《사이에》 get between; be caught in; get jammed 〔hemmed〕 in; be sandwiched between; 《맞다》 fit (in(to)); be fit for. ⇨ 끼다[2, 3]. ¶ 잇새에 ~ get in between the teeth / 잇새에 끼인 것을 빼다 remove matter lodged between the teeth / 이 미닫이는 잘 끼이지 않는다 This sliding door will not fit 〔go〕 in.

② 《양자 사이에》 lie 〔get〕 between. ⇨ 끼다[2]. ¶ 나는 두사람 사이에 꽉 끼어서 버스에서 나올 수 없었다 I was so tightly wedged between two other passengers that I couldn't get off the bus.

③ 《축·대열에》 be reckoned 〔numbered, ranked〕 among; rank with 〔among〕. ⇨ 끼다[2, 3]. ¶ 열강에 ~ be ranked as a Power / 축에 끼이지 못하다 be insignificant; count for nothing; be of no account.

④ 《옷·구두 등이》 be tight 〔close〕. ¶ 꽉 끼이는 바지 tight trousers / 이 구두는 너무 꽉 끼인다 These shoes are too tight. *or* These shoes pinch. / 겨드랑이가 좀 끼이는 느낌이다 I feel a little tight under the arms. / 장갑이 너무 끼이는 느낌이다 My gloves feel tight.

**끼인각**(一角) 〖수학〗 an included 〔a contained〕 angle.

**끼적거리다** scribble; scratch; scrawl; dash. ¶ 편지를 몇 줄 ~ scribble 〔scratch〕 a few lines of a letter; write in haste; dash off a letter / 글씨를 ~ scribble some characters.

**끼치다**[1] 《소름이》 have 〔get, feel〕 gooseflesh; feel *one's* hair stand on end. ¶ 그 광경을 보고 소름이 끼쳤다 The sight gave me gooseflesh. / 그 일을 생각하니 온 몸에 소름이 끼쳤다 I got gooseflesh all over me when I thought of it. / 나는 뱀을 봐도 소름이 끼친다 I get goosebumps when I see snakes. / 그 이야기는 소름 끼치는 것이었다 The story made my hair stand on end. *or* It was a hair-raising story.

**끼치다**[2] ① 《폐·괴로움·불편 등을》 cause; give; do. ¶ 남에게 해를 ~ do 〔cause〕 harm to others / 부모에게 많은 괴로움을 ~ give *one's* parents a lot of trouble / 걱정을 ~ cause anxiety to 《*a person*》; give 《*a person*》 trouble; trouble 《*a person*》 / 불편을 ~ cause 《*a person*》 inconvenience / 많은 번거로움을 끼쳐 죄송합니다 I am sorry to 「give you 〔put you to〕 so much trouble. / 그녀는 남에게 폐를 끼치면서도 태연하다 She thinks nothing of giving trouble to others.

② 《영향을 미치다》 exert 〔exercise〕 《influence on》; 《뒤에 남기다》 hand down; leave behind; bequeath. ¶ 영향을〔감화를〕 ~ exert 〔exercise〕 *one's* 〔an〕 influence 《*a person*》; have an effect on 《*a person*》; influence / 후세에 누명을 끼치다 leave a bad reputation 〔name〕 to posterity / 그의 충고

는 소년들에게 좋은 영향을 끼쳤다 His advice exerted a favorable influence upon the boys.
③ 《셈 따위를》 leave part of *one's* debt unpaid. ¶ 아들에게 빚을 끼치고 죽다 die leaving debts for *one's* son.

**끽끽거리다** keep 〔give, utter〕 chocked screams 〔shrieks〕.

**끽소리** a yell of protest; a squawk of complaint. ¶ ～ 못하다 can't say even *a thing;* be (utterly) silenced; be completely nonpulsed 〔beaten〕 / ～ 못하게 하다 silence 《*a person*》; put 《*a person*》 to silence; leave 《*a person*》 speechless 〔wordless〕 / 나는 ～도 못했다 I was left without a word to say. *or* I couldn't utter a word in reply. *or* I was completely beaten 〔defeated〕. / 그의 통렬한 비판에 나는 ～도 못했다 His scathing comments 「silenced me 〔put me to silence〕.

**끽연**(喫煙) smoking. ～하다 smoke (tobacco); have a smoke. ◉ ～실 a smoking room. ～장소 a smoking area 〔corner〕.

**끽해야** all 〔the most, the worst〕 you can do is…; at the utmost; at (the) best. ⇨ 기껏해야. ¶ ～ 1마일 a mile at the (very) outside / ～ 10일 ten days at the longest / ～ 5천원 정도겠지 It will cost 5,000 won at (the) most. / ～ 선생한테 고자질밖에 더 하겠니 All you can do is to tell the teacher (on me).

**낄낄** giggling; snickering. ～하다, ～거리다 giggle; titter; snicker; chuckle; laugh up 〔in〕 *one's* sleeve. ¶ 무엇을 ～거리고 있느냐 난 하나도 우습지 않군 그래. What are you giggling 〔snickering〕 about? I don't see anything funny.

**낌새** 《일이 되어가는 형편》 the course 〔turn〕 《of events》; the development 〔progress〕 《of an affair》; 《기미(機微)·낌새》 secrets; subtleties; inner workings; the delicate turn 《of a situation》; 《모양·징후》 a sign; a look; an indication.
¶ ～를 보다 《되어가는 형편을》 watch the development 〔course〕 of events; see which way the wind blows; 《기미를》 sound 〔probe, feel〕 the secrets 《of an affair》; observe 〔watch〕 the delicate turn 《of a situation》 / (…의) ～를 보이다 show 〔give〕 an indication 〔a sign〕 of 《recession》 / (…의) ～를 보이지 않다 reveal no secrets; do not show the slightest sign 〔hint〕 of / ～를 채다 sense 〔smell〕 《danger》; sense the secrets 《of an affair》; sense the delicate turn 《of a situation》; be 〔become〕 aware of; suspect / 어렴풋이 ～는 챘다 I've been vaguely conscious of it. / 정국이 달라질 ～는 보이지 않는다 I can't see any sign that there will be a change in the political situation. / 그들이 ～를 채지 않게 주의하여라 Be careful not to excite their suspicion. / 우리가 무엇을 하고 있는지 그도 이젠 ～를 챈 모양이다 He seems to have caught on to what we are up to.

**낑낑** groaning (and grunting); moaning. ～하다, ～거리다 groan (and groan); groan away; moan. ¶ ～거리며 with a great deal of grunting and groaning / 무거운 짐을 지고 ～거리다 groan under the load of heavy burden.

**낑하다** make a groan. ¶ 낑하고 힘쓰다 put forth *one's* strength with a groan.

ㄴ

**-ㄴ가** ① 《의문》 is it 〔he, she〕?; isn't it 〔he, she〕?; aren't you 〔they〕?; if 〔whether〕... or .... ¶ 누군가요 Who is it ? / 자네는 학생인가 Are you a student ? / 자네 김 군 아닌가 Oh, you are Mr. Kim, aren't you ? / 그것이 개인가 아닌가 확인해 보자 Let's see if it is a dog or not.

② 《추측》 it seems that...; it seems to be. ¶ 아마 김 선생인가 보다 It seems to be Mr. Kim. / 밖이 추운가 보다 It seems cold outside. / 고양이가 뭔가 마시고 싶은가 보다 The cat seems to want something to drink.

③ 《막연한 사람·시간·장소》 someone; sometime; somewhere. ¶ 누군가 다른 사람이 그것을 가져갔다 Someone else has taken it. / 나는 3월 언젠가 그녀를 만났다 I met her sometime in March. / 어딘가에 우산을 놓고 왔다 I have left my umbrella somewhere.

**-ㄴ 끝에** 《…한 결과》 as a 〔the〕 result of...; after 《*do*ing》. ¶ 많이 생각한 끝에 after much thinking / 그녀는 악전고투 끝에 선거전에서 승리했다 She won the election as a result of the hard=fought campaign.

**-ㄴ다느냐** 《의문》 ¶ 그녀가 언제 간다느냐 When do you think she will go ? *or* When is she supposed to go ?

**-ㄴ다니** 《상황》 ¶ 공부를 잘 한다니 기쁘다 I am delighted to hear that you are a good student.

**-ㄴ대서** 《-ㄴ다고 해서》 ¶ 증기선은 증기로 간대서 그렇게 부른다 A steamer is so called because it is run by steam.

**-ㄴ대서야** 《-ㄴ다고 하여서야》 ¶ 아직도 컴퓨터를 모른대서야 말이 되나 It is absurd for you to say that you do not know about computers yet.

**-ㄴ대야** 《-ㄴ다고 하여도》 even if. ¶ 그가 아무리 빨리 걸어간대야 한 시간에 30킬로미터는 못 가겠지 No matter how fast he walks he won't be able to walk 30 kilometers an hour. / 그 녀석이 먹는대야 얼마나 먹겠니, 내버려 둬라 Let him eat as much as he likes, he can't eat much anyway.

**-ㄴ들** 《비록 …한다 할지라도》 granted that; even though. ¶ 그가 간다 한들 아주 가랴 Even though he leaves, he won't be going away for good. / 내가 힘이 약하다 한들, 너보다야 약하랴 I may be weak, but I am sure I'm no weaker than you. / 그가 칭찬을 많이 받은들 무슨 소용이 있으랴 So he received much praise — what good is it ?

**-ㄴ바** 《…하고 보니까》 since; when. ¶ 그의 말을 들어본바 사실과 틀림이 없다 According to what he says, it is true to the fact.

**-ㄴ 바에** 《…한 김에》 ¶ 이왕 온 바에 만나 보고 가겠다 As long as I am here, I might as well see him before I leave.

**-ㄴ즉** ¶ 그런즉 if so; then; if that is the case / 그런즉 내가 어떻게 하면 좋겠느냐 Well then, what would you like me to do ? / 경치인즉 금강산이 한국에서 제일이지 As far as scenic beauty goes, Mt. Kŭmgang is the best in Korea. / 알아본즉 그것은 허보였다 On inquiry, the report proved false. / 그의 말을 들어 본즉 그럴듯하다 As I heard him say so, it seems quite plausible.

**-ㄴ지** 《막연한 의문》 ¶ 뭔지 빨갛게 보이는 것 something that looks red / 송 씨인지 하는 사람 a (certain) Mr. Song; a man named Song or something / 왠지 모르겠으나 저 녀석은 싫다 I don't know why, but I dislike him. / 뭐가 뭔지 모르겠다 I don't know what's what.

**나**[1] ① 《자신》 I; myself. ⇨ 우리[2]. ¶ 나의 my / 나의 것 mine / 나를, 나에게 me / 나는 한국인이다 I am (a) Korean. (★ 국적을 말할 때는 관사 a를 안 붙이는 것이 일반적) / 그녀는 나보다 빨리 달린다 She runs faster than I 〔me 《구어》〕. / 그 접시를 깬 것은 나다 It is I that broke the dish. (★ 강조형일 때는 me가 아니라 I를 쓰는 것이 일반적) / 이것은 나의 책이다 This is my book. / 저 차는 나의 것이다 That car is mine. / 그는 나에게 꽃을 주었다 He gave me the flowers. *or* He gave the flowers to me. / 나 자신이 그것을 했다 I did it myself. / 나 혼자서는 그 상자를 들어올릴 수 없다 I can't lift the box by myself. / 나로서

는 너의 계획에 반대하지 않는다 As for me 〔For my part〕, I am not against your plan. /「나는 사과를 좋아한다」—「나도 그래」 "I like apples." — "So do I." *or* "Me, too." 《구어》.
② 《개인》 ¶ 나의 일 a private affair; a personal matter / 이것은 나 개인의 일이므로 여러분께 폐를 끼치고 싶지 않다 This is my private affair and I don't want to worry all of you.

**나**[2] 〖음악〗 B. ¶ ~장조〔단조〕 B major 〔(minor〕.

**-나** ① 《의문 어미》 ¶ 춥나 Is it cold? / 먹었나 Did you eat? / 가겠나 Will you go? ② 《동작·상태를 가려 말할 때》 and; or; whether… or. ¶ 크나 작으나 가리지 않고 regardless of whether it is big or small / 너나 나나 both you and I / 그들이 거기 있나 없나 가 보시오 Go and see if they're there or not. / 보나 마나 마찬가지다 There is no difference whether I see it or not. ③ 《앞뒤 상반된 말을 할 때》 but; though. ¶ 가난하나 정직하다 be poor but honest / 나이는 젊으나 재능은 대단하다 Though (he is) young, he has great ability.

**나가다** ① 《밖으로》 go out; get 〔step〕 out 《of》; leave (떠나다); find *one's* way out 《of the cave》. ¶ 방에서 ~ go out of a room / 살그머니 ~ go away stealthily; make *oneself* scarce 《구어》 / 그는 뒷문을 통해 밖으로 나갔다 He went out by the back door. / 뜰에 나가 신선한 공기를 마셨다 We went out into the garden for a breath of fresh air. / 그녀는 오늘 아침 7시에 집을 나갔다 She left at seven in this morning. /밖에 나갈 기분이 안 났다 I didn't feel like going outdoors. / 흰 선 밖으로 나가지 마시오 Keep within the white line. / 여기서 나가라 Get out of here! *or* Be off with you! / 어머니는 쇼핑하러 나가셨다 Mother is out shopping.
② 《퇴거하다》 move out; leave; quit; 「go away 〔withdraw, depart〕 《from》. ¶ 나갈 것을 명하다 order 《*a person*》 out of 《a place》; order 《*a person*》 to quit 《a place》 / 그들은 내달 이 집에서 나간다 They will move out of this house next month.
③ 《근무하다》 work 《in》; serve 《in》; be in service. ¶ 관청에 ~ be in the service of the government / 은행에 ~ work at 〔in〕 a bank / 출판사에 ~ work for a publishing company (★ for는 고용 관계를 강조) / 학교에 ~ be teaching 〔working〕 in a school / 회사에 ~ be employed in a company / 그는 어디에 나가지요 Where does he work? / 지금 (아무데도) 나가는 데가 없다 I am now out of work 〔job〕.
④ 《출근·출석하다》 attend 《a meeting》; be present at; appear in 《a party》. ¶ 회사에 ~ go to the office / 법정에 ~ appear in court / 어제는 학교에 나가지 않았다 I did not 「attend 〔go to〕 school yesterday. / 금주 토요일에 회사에 나가겠다 I will be at the office this Saturday.
⑤ 《참가·출장하다》 join; take part 《in》; enter 〔go in for〕 《a beauty contest》; participate 《in》. ¶ 올림픽 경기에 ~ take part in the Olympic Games / 100미터 경주에 나가기로 하다 decide to 「take part in the 100-meter race / 그녀는 테니스 결승 전에 나갔다 She was in the tennis final.
⑥ 《진출하다》 advance 《into》; go 〔launch〕 《into》; enter 《into》; find *one's* way 《into》. ¶ 학교를 졸업하고 사회에 ~ go forth into the world after finishing *one's* schooling / 정계〔영화계〕에 ~ go into politics 〔the movies〕 / 해외 시장으로 ~ make inroads into foreign markets / 한국의 자동차 산업은 해외 각지로 퍼져 나가고 있다 The car industry of Korea is 「branching out 〔making its way〕 into various foreign countries.
⑦ 《출마하다》 run 〔stand〕 《for》. ¶ 대통령 후보로 ~ run for the Presidency / 그는 시장 선거에 나가기로 했다 He decided to run for mayor.
⑧ 《팔리다》 sell; be sold. ⇨ 팔다, 팔리다. ¶ 가장 잘 나가는 책 the top 〔best〕 seller / 잘 안 나가는 물건 a poor 〔bad〕 sell 〔seller〕; a drag in the market / 어머니날에는 카네이션이 잘 나간다 Carnations sell well on Mother's Day. / 이 신문이 제일 많이 나간다 This newspaper has the largest circulation.
⑨ 《전기 따위가》 be 〔go〕 out; blow out; fail; be cut off. ¶ 퓨즈가 나갔다 The fuse was gone 〔blown〕. / 전기가 예고 없이 나갔다 The electricity was cut off without warning.
⑩ 《닳음·해짐》 wear; wear 〔be worn〕 out; get 〔become〕 threadbare; be 〔get〕 torn (터지다). ¶ 그의 구두 뒤축이 나갔다 The heels of his shoes were worn out. / 바지의 무릎이 나갔다 My trousers were worn out at the knees.
⑪ 《정신이》 go out of *one's* mind; be abstracted 〔absentminded〕; forget *oneself;* be stupefied (놀라서); 《돌다》

go mad; become insane. ¶ 정신 나간 소리 그만둬 Don't talk nonsense!
⑫ 《비용이》 be spent; be paid out. ⇨ 나다, 들다. ¶ 돈이 다 나갔다 We have no money left. *or* Money is all out. / 나가기만 하고 통 수입은 없다 All outgo and no income. / 생각보다 비용이 많이 나갔다 My expenses were greater than I (had) expected.
⑬ 《조수가》 ebb; flow back. ¶ 조수가 나가는 중이다 The tide is ebbing 〔going out〕. ⇨ 빠지다[1] ④.
⑭ 《가치·무게가》 cost; be worth; weigh. ¶ 2만원 나가는 물건 an article worth twenty thousand won / 이것은 무게가 30파운드 나간다 This weighs thirty pounds. / 그것들은 하나에 1,000원 나간다 They cost one thousand won a piece.
⑮ 《요리가》 be served. ¶ 이제 커피가 나갑니다 There is coffee coming.
⑯ 《기타》 ¶ 이 신문은 1주에 두 번 나간다 This gazette will 「come out 〔be issued〕 twice a week. / 이 길로 가면 어디로 나갑니까 Where does this road 「go 〔lead〕 to? / 지난번에는 (진도가) 어디까지 나갔지요 How far did we get 《in the textbook》 in our last class?

**나가동그라지다, 나가둥그러지다** fall over 〔down〕; tumble down; fall head over heels (and rolls). ¶ 그는 빙판길에서 미끄러져 뒤로 나가동그라졌다 He slipped on the frozen path and fell on his back.

**나가떨어지다** ① 《넘어지다》 fall backward; fall flat on *one's* back; 《맞아서》 be knocked down; 《멀리》 be thrown off. ¶ 큰대자로 ~ fall full length 《on the ground》 / 한방에 ~ be knocked down at a single blow.
② 《녹초가 되다》 be worn 〔fagged〕 out; get tired out; be dead tired; be done up; 《술에 취해》 drink *oneself* down; be 〔get〕 dead drunk; pass out. ¶ 술에 나가떨어져 잠들다 drink *oneself* to sleep / 몇 잔 술에 ~ pass out with a few glasses of wine / 그녀는 너무 피곤해서 침대에 나가떨어졌다 She dropped on the bed, utterly worn out.

**나가자빠지다** ① = 나가떨어지다. ② 《불이행하다》 back out; fall down on 〔fail to fulfill〕 a promise 〔an obligation〕; draw 〔pull〕 back *oneself* 《at, from》; 《떼어먹음》 do not pay 《*one's* debt》; fail to pay; evade payment; bilk 《*a person*》 out of debt; cheat 《*a person*》 of a loan. ¶ 빚을 안 갚고 ~ welsh on a debt; do not pay *one's* debt / 계약을 해놓고 ~ back out of a contract; draw back from a contract / 마지막 순간에 그는 항상 나가자빠진다 He always draws 〔pulls〕 back at the last moment.

**나귀** a donkey; an ass.

**나그네** 《여행자》 a traveler; a wayfarer; a tourist; 《객지에 있는 사람》 a person away from home; a stranger; 《방랑객》 a vagabond; a wanderer; 《손》 a visitor; a guest. ¶ 정처 없는 ~ an aimless wanderer 〔vagabond〕 / ~생활을 하다 lead a wayfaring life. ◉ ~새 a bird of passage; a migratory (bird).

**나그넷길** a journey: 나그넷길을 떠나다 start 〔set out〕 on a journey.

**나근거리다** bend; be flexible; sway; swing; flicker (불꽃 따위가). ¶ 바람에 나근거리는 촛불 the candle light flickering in the wind.

**나근나근** bending; flexing; swaying.

**나긋나긋하다** ① 《음식이》 (be) tender. ¶ 고기가 나긋나긋하고 맛있다 The meat is tender and tasty. ② 《살결이》 (be) soft. ¶ 나긋나긋한 손 a soft and smooth hand / 살결이 ~ have soft skin. ③ 《언행이》 (be) mild; gentle; amiable. ¶ 나긋나긋한 성질 a mild 〔an amiable〕 disposition.

**나깨** 《메밀 속껍질》 inner husk of buckwheat. ◉ ~떡 a coarse cake made with buckwheat husks.

**나나니(벌)** 〖곤충〗 a digger wasp; a mud 「dauber.

**나날이** day after 〔by〕 day; every day; from day to day; daily. ¶ ~ 따뜻해진다 It is getting 〔growing〕 warmer day by day 〔from day to day〕. / 정세는 ~ 악화되어 갔다 The situation grew worse with each passing day.

**나녀**(裸女) a nude 〔naked〕 woman.

**나누기** dividing. ~하다 divide. ¶ 6 ~ 2는 3이다 6 divided by 2 is 〔gives, equals〕 3.

**나누다** ① 《분할하다》 divide 《into》; part; sever 《into》; split (up). ¶ 나눌 수 없는 indivisible; inseparable / 둘로 ~ divide 〔cut〕 《*a thing*》 in(to) two / 나는 자동차 대금을 다섯번에 나누어서 지불했다 I paid for the car in five installments. / 선생님은 아이들을 세 그룹으로 나누었다 The teacher split the children (up) into three groups. / 44를 5로 나누면 8이 되고 4가 남는다 Five into forty-four is eight, remainder four.
② 《분배하다》 divide 《to, among》; dis-

tribute 《among》; allot 《to》; share 《*something* with *somebody*》; deal (out) 《cards》. ¶ 음식을 나누어 먹다 share food with 《*a person*》 / 이익을 동업자와 ~ share the profit with a partner / 아이들에게 과자를 나누어 주다 divide 〔distribute〕 the cakes among the children / 나는 자식들에게 재산을 나눠 주었다 I distributed my possessions among my children. / 비용은 우리 둘〔셋〕이서 나누어 내자 Let's split the cost「between us 〔among us three〕. / 그들은 둘이서〔셋이서〕 그 돈을 나누었다 They divided 〔shared〕 the money「between them 〔among the three〕.
③ 《구분하다》 classify (유별); sort (out). ¶ 선인과 악인을 ~ sort out the good men from the bad / 그것은 여러 항목으로 나눌 수 있다 It can be classified into many items.
④ 《함께하다》 share 《*something*》 with; drink 〔eat〕 together (합석하여). ¶ 점심을 ~ have lunch together / 기쁨〔슬픔〕을 ~ share *one's* joy 〔sorrow〕 / 술을 나누며 이야기하다 have a chat (with each other) over wine glasses / 그는 술 한 병을 친구와 나누어 마셨다 He shared a bottle of wine with his friend.

**나누이다** get divided; be separated; be split up. ¶ 세 몫으로 ~ be split into three portions.

**나눗셈** (a) division. ~하다 divide. ¶ ~을 풀다 do 〔work on〕 an exercise in division.

**나눠다** ⇨ 나누이다.

**나닐다** fly 〔flutter, flit〕 about. ¶ 꽃에서 꽃으로 나니는 나비 butterflies flitting about from flower to flower.

**나다**[1] ① 《태어나다》 be born; come into the world; come into being 〔existence〕. ¶ 내가 난 고장 my birthplace / 내가 나서 지금까지 ever since my birth; in all my born days / 그는 서울에서 나서 자랐다 He was born and raised in Seoul.
② 《자라다》 grow; 《돋아나다》 sprout; bud (out); come out. ¶ 풀이 난 땅 grass-grown ground / 깃털이 ~ a bird grows feathers / 싹이 ~ The buds are showing 〔sprouting〕. / 풀이 나기 시작한다 Grass is coming out. / 정원에 잡초가 무성하게 나 있다 The garden is overgrown with weeds. / 아기가 이가 났다 The baby has cut its teeth.
③ (***a***) 《발생·일어나다》 happen; occur; take place; break out (전쟁·화재 따위가); arise; have.

> **용법** **happen** 우연히「나다, 일어나다」란 뜻. 가장 일반적으로 쓰이는 말. **occur** happen보다 격식 차린 말. 특정한 일이 특정한 때에 일어남을 뜻함. **take place** 예정된 일이 일어난다는 뜻. **break out** 전쟁·화재 등이 갑자기 일어난다는 뜻. **arise** 원인이 있어, 그 결과로 문제·사건이 일어난다는 뜻. **have** 영어에서 가장 다양한 뜻으로 쓰이는 말의 하나. 여기서는「경험하다, 당하다, 겪다」등의 뜻에서 →「나다」로 된 말.

¶ 불이 ~ a fire breaks out / 연기가 ~ have smoke; be smoky / 홍수가 ~ have a flood / 난리가 ~ a war breaks out / 고장이 ~ have a breakdown; get out of order / 사건이〔사고가〕 ~ have an incident 〔accident〕 / 탈이 ~ run into a hitch; get ill (병나다) / 야단이 ~ have trouble 〔a fuss〕 / 나는 전쟁이 난 해에 태어났다 I was born in the year (when) the war broke out. / 비행기가 이륙했을 때 사고가 났다 The accident occured when the plane took off. (***b***) 《생기다》 produce 《good results》; make 〔get〕 《a profit》; yield 《profit》; generate 《heat》; cause 《damage》; come 《out of, from》; accrue 《from》. ¶ 토지에서 나는 이익 profits accruing from lands / 그의 이마에 여드름이 났다 Pimples came 〔broke〕 out on his forehead. /그것을 팔면 이익이 얼마나 나느냐 What 〔How much〕 profit will you make if you sell it ? /거기서 5백만원의 이익이 났다 It made a profit of five million won.
④ 《소리가》 sound; come out 〔forth〕; make a sound 〔noise〕. ¶ 높은 소리가 ~ sound loud / 문 두드리는 소리가 난다 There is a knock at the door. / 그 종은 금이 간 소리가 난다 The bell sounds cracked.
⑤ 《병·증상 따위가》 become; fall; get; have. ¶ 구역질이 ~ feel like vomiting; suffer from nausea; feel sick / 심하게 기침이 나서 혼이 났다 I was troubled with 〔by〕 a bad cough. / 나는 고열이 났다 I had a high fever. / 그는 과로해서 병이 났다 He got sick from 〔because of, through〕 overwork. *or* Overwork made him sick.
⑥ 《명성·소문 따위가》 acquire; get abroad; circulate 《among》. ¶ 이름이 ~ acquire fame 〔a name〕; come to fame; win a fame / …하다는 소문이 ~ a rumor is abroad 〔current, in cir-

culation] about…; a rumor has it that…; a word goes out that….
⑦ (***a***) 《흥미·능률이》 grow to be; get. ¶ 재미가[흥이] ~ be [grow] interesting / 열성이 ~ get enthusiastic / 능률이 ~ be efficient; improve efficiency. (***b***) 《기분·생각이》 occur; come [flush] across [into] *one's* mind. ¶ 성이[화가] ~ get [become] angry / 심술이 ~ get cross / 생각[기억](이) ~ occur to *one;* come into *one's* mind; *one* remembers / 싫증이 ~ become sick [tired, weary] 《of》; lose interest 《in》; 《음식에》 be fed up 《with》 / …할 마음이 ~ be [feel] inclined 《to *do*》; feel like 《*do*ing》 / 오늘은 더워서 능률이 나지 않는다 It's so hot that I can't do much work today.
⑧ 《흘러나오다》 come out; gush out [forth]; flow [run] out. ¶ 콧물이 ~ *one's* nose runs / 땀이 ~ sweat / 너 코피가 나는 구나 Your nose is bleeding. *or* You are bleeding at the nose. / 그녀의 눈에서 눈물이 났다 Tears flowed [ran] from her eyes. *or* Her eyes ran with tears.
⑨ 《생산되다》 be produced; be yielded; be raised [grown]; be found. ¶ 대구에서 사과가 난다 Apples are grown in Taegu. / 한국에서 홍삼이 난다 Red ginseng is produced in Korea. / 이 광산에서 금이 난다 Gold is found in this mine. / 이 산에서 우라늄이 난다 They get uranium out of this mountain. / 포도가 나기 시작한다 Grapes are now getting in season.
⑩ (***a***) 《티가》 have an air [a look, a style]; look like. ¶ 시골 티가 ~ look rustic; have a rural appearance / 학자 티가 ~ have a smack of the pedant / 그는 장사꾼 티가 난다 He looks like a merchant. (***b***) 《맛·냄새가》 smell; taste. ¶ 매운맛이 ~ have a hot [biting] taste; be hot to the taste / 신맛이 ~ taste sour / 장미꽃 향기가 ~ have scents [a scent] of a rose / 라일락은 좋은 냄새가 난다 The lilacs smell sweet. / 이것은 단맛이 난다 This tastes sweet.
⑪ 《신문 등에》 appear [come out] 《in》; go into 《a newspaper》. ¶ 그 뉴스는 신문마다 났다 The news is in every newspaper. *or* Every newspaper carries the news.
⑫ 《늘다》 gain 《in》; gather. ¶ 속력이 ~ gain in velocity; gather speed / 힘이 ~ gain strength; cheer up; take heart (기운이) / 당신 덕분에 용기가 났다 You encouraged me.
⑬ 《결과 따위》 be forthcoming; 《결과로서》 come out as a result; turn out (to be); turn up (as). ¶ 결말이 ~ be settled; come [be brought] to a conclusion [an end] / 성과[효과]가 ~ have an effect / 약효가 ~ tell [act, work] 《on》; have an effect 《on》 / 좋은 결과가 ~ turn out well / 결딴~ be spoilt [ruined] / 동이 ~ become scarce; run short 《of》 / 승부가 날 때까지 싸워라 Fight it out. / 학원 분쟁은 결말이 나지 않았다 The campus dispute has not been settled yet.
⑭ 《잘생기다》 be handsome; be good=looking; 《탁월하다》 be great; be extraordinary. ¶ 난 사람 an extraordinary character; a bigwig 《속어》 / 못~ be ugly / 난 체하다 be self-important[-conceited]; put on airs / 그렇게 난 체하지 마라 You don't need to put on such airs.
⑮ 《눈 밖에》 leave; go [get] out. ¶ 눈 밖에 ~ get out of 《*a person's*》 favor; be in bad with 《*a person*》 / 그는 사장의 눈 밖에 났다 He is out of favor with his boss.
⑯ 《나오다》 appear 《on the market》; come on 《to the market》.
⑰ (***a***) 《뚫리다》 be made; be open(ed). ¶ 구멍이 ~ A hole is made [opened]. / 새 길이 났다 A new road is open(ed). (***b***) 《비다》 open up; be vacated; become vacant. ¶ 자리가 ~ a place [job, seat] opens up / 방이 ~ a room is available / 빈 집이 ~ a house is vacant (for rent) / 교사 자리가 하나 나 있다 「There is [We have] an opening on the teaching staff. (***c***) 《방향으로》 open on. ¶ 창문이 거리 쪽으로 나 있다 A window opens on the street.
⑱ 《계절을 지내다》 go [get] through; pass 《a season》. ¶ 봄을 ~ see spring through / 그는 해안 별장에서 겨울을 난다 He winters at a seaside villa.
⑲ 《되다》 ¶ 탄로~ get discovered [revealed, exposed].
⑳ 《흠 따위가 생기다》 flaw; crack. ¶ 흠집이 ~ get cracked; have a flaw.
㉑ 《나이 먹다》 ¶ 아홉 살 난 아이 a child of nine.
㉒ 《시간·여가 따위가》 ¶ 틈이 ~ have a time to spare / 손이 ~ be at leisure; have no work to do.

**나다**[2] ① 《계속》 keep [go on] 《*do*ing》. ¶ 차차 자라나면 알게 돼 If you grow older, you will come to understand it. ② 《「…고 나다」로 완료의 뜻》 have just finished 《*doing*》; come from 《*doing*》. ¶ 한잠 자고 나니 한결 상쾌하다 I have had a nap and now I feel much refreshed. / 하고 싶은 말을 하고 나니 속이 후련하다 Now that I have had my say, I feel the easier for it.

**나다니다** 《외출》 go out; go 〔move〕 about; gad 〔wander〕 about. ¶ 잘 나다니는 사람 a regular gadabout / 밤낮 ~ be always on the gad; be quite a gadabout / 그녀는 잘 나다닌다 She is a regular gadabout.

**나달** 《사오일》 four or five days; about 〔around〕 four days; several days. ¶ 이 일을 하려면 한 ~ 걸리겠다 This work will take me several days.

**나도범의귀** 『식물』 bishop's-cap.

**나돌다** ① 《나다니다》 wander about (outdoors); 《말·소문이 돌다》 (a rumor) get around; be rumored; 《떠돌다》 float about. ¶ 그 장관이 곧 사임하리라는 소문이 나돌고 있다 Rumor has it 〔There is a rumor〕 that the minister will soon resign. / 만원권 위조 지폐가 부산에 나돌고 있다 Fake ten-thousand-won bills are floating around in Busan.
② 《시장에》 arrive 〔appear〕 on the market; 《과일·생선 등이》 be in season. ¶ 송이 버섯이 나돌기 시작했다 *Song-i* mushrooms started appearing on the market.

**나동그라지다** ⇨ 나가동그라지다.

**나뒹굴다** tumble all about; be spread all over.

**나들이** 《가까운 외출》 going out; an outing; a short visit. ~하다 go out; go on a visit. ¶ ~ 가다〔오다〕 go 〔come〕 on a visit / 우리 며느리가 친정에 ~갔다 My daughter-in-law has gone to her parental home.
◉ ~옷 *one's* best clothes (for outings 〔visits〕); *one's* Sunday best; outdoor clothes; a gala dress.

**나라** ① a state; a nation; 《국토》 a country; a land; soil; 《국적》 *one's* nationality; 《고국》 *one's* country.

> **용법** **state** 주권·정부가 있는 나라. **nation** 민족·인종적 관념이 강한 말로 정치적 통일·독립의 개념이 함유된 말. **country** 지리적 관념이 강한 말로, 「국가가 존재하고 있는 땅」이란 뜻이 강함. **land, soil** country의 문어적 표현.

¶ ~의 national / ~의 일 affairs of state / 조용한 아침의 ~ the land of morning calm (한국을 뜻함) / ~를 사랑하는 마음 *one's* love for *one's* country / 세계의 여러 ~들 the countries of the world / 극한(極寒)의 ~ a very cold land / 미지의 ~로 들어가다 go into a strange land / ~를 세우다 found 〔build up〕 a nation / ~를 위하여 목숨을 던지다 lay down *one's* life for *one's* country; die for *one's* country / ~를 다스리다 govern a nation 〔country〕 / 다른 ~를 침범하다 violate the territory of another country; invade another country / 농업은 ~의 근본이다 Agriculture is the foundation of the nation. / 어느 ~ 사람이십니까 What is your nationality? / 그는 평생 ~에 헌신했다 He devoted himself to his country throughout his life. / 대통령은 동남 아시아의 ~들을 방문했다 The President visited Southeast Asian countries. / 그 뉴스는 온 ~에 퍼졌다 The news spread all over the country. / 러시아는 여러 민족으로 이루어진 ~다 Russia is a nation of many different races.
② 《특수한 세계》 a world; a realm. ¶ 꿈~ a dreamland / 달~ the lunar world; the moon / 별~ the starry world / 동화 ~ (a) fairyland.
◉ ~님 《임금》 the king; the monarch; the sovereign; the ruler. ~사랑 *one's* love for *one's* country; patriotism.

**나락**(奈落) 《지옥》 hell; Hades; 《심연》 the abyss; the bottomless pit. ¶ ~에 떨어지다 fall into the bottomless pit.

**나란하다** (be) even; uniform; equal; be in a line; be lined up; (be) parallel 《to, with》(평행하다). ¶ 대열이 ~ The row 《of troops》 is lined up. / 선 A와 선 B는 ~ Line A is parallel to 〔with〕 line B.

**나란히** 《줄지어》 in line 〔row〕; side by side; 《가지런히》 evenly; uniformly; in order. ¶ 철로와 ~ 뻗은 길 a road running parallel with the railway / ~ 앉다 sit side by side with 《*a person*》 / 높이를 ~하다 make them all of uniform height / (한 줄로) ~ 서다 stand in a row; form a line; line up; be drawn up in line / 두 줄로 ~ 서다 stand in 〔form〕 two lines / 어깨를 ~하고 가다 go shoulder to shoulder 〔side by side〕 / 우로〔좌로〕 ~ 서다 dress to 〔by〕 the right 〔left〕 / 우로 ~ 《구령》 Right, dress! / 영어 성적에서 그들은 어깨를 ~한다 They are of equal

achievement in English.
◉ ~꼴 a parallelogram.

**나래**[1] 《농기구》 a soil leveler. ◉ ~꾼 a soil-leveler operator. ~질 leveling soil with a soil-leveler: ~질하다 level (soil) with a soil-leveler.

**나래**[2] 《노》 an oar; a pair of oars.

**나루** ① 《나루터》 a ferry (crossing); a ferry point. ¶ ~를 건너다 ferry over; cross a river by ferry. ② ⇨나룻배.
◉ ~질 ferrying; operating a ferry: ~질하다 ferry. ~터 a ferry (point, crossing). ~(터)지기 a ferryman; a ferry (point) guard. ~턱 a ferry (mooring): ~턱에 배를 대다 draw a boat up to the ferry. 나룻가 the vicinity 〔side〕 of the ferry. 나룻목 《물목》 a ferry narrows. 나룻삯 ferriage.

**나룻** 《구레나룻》 whiskers; 《턱수염》 a beard; 《콧수염》 a mustache. ¶ ~이 석 자라도 먹어야 샌님 《속담》 Even a gentleman has to eat. *or* Long beards alone cannot make a gentleman.

**나룻배** a ferryboat; a ferry. ¶ ~로 건너다 cross 《a river》 by ferry; ferry across 《a lake》 / ~를 타다 take a ferryboat. / 강 건너로 사람들을 ~로 날라다 주다 ferry people to the other side of the river. ◉ ~사공 a ferrymaster; a ferryman. ~삯 ferriage.

**나르다** 《운반하다》 carry; 《수송》 transport 《goods》; convey; 《바람·물 따위가》 waft. ¶ 손으로〔수레로〕 짐을 ~ carry luggage by hand 〔cart〕 / 2층으로~ get 《*a thing*》 upstairs / 물품을 트럭으로 ~ transport goods by truck / 이 짐은 너무 무거워서 혼자서는 나를 수 없다 This baggage is too heavy for me to carry alone.

**나르시시즘** narcissism.

**나른하다** ① 《피곤하다》 (be) tired; languid; heavy; weary; be all in. ¶ 나른한 날씨 slack 〔sweltering〕 weather / 오늘은 몸이 ~ I feel tired today. / 더워서 몸이 ~ The heat makes me feel languid. / 길을 많이 걸었더니 몸이 ~ I am all in after the long walk. / 나른해서 일하기 싫다 I feel too lazy to work. ② 《연약하다》 (be) feeble; delicate.

**나름** depending on .... ¶ 능력 ~으로 according to *one's* ability / 그것은 사람 ~이다 That depends on the person. / 값은 품질 ~이다 The price varies with the quality. / 성공은 네 실력 ~이다 Success is up to your ability. / 네 인생은 네 하기 ~이다 Your life is what you make it.

**나리**[1] 〖식물〗 a lily. ¶ 참~ a tiger lily / 흰 ~ a white lily; a Madonna lily; an Annunciation lily / ~꽃 a lily flower.

**나리**[2] 《존칭》 your honor; sir. ¶ 시장 ~ His 〔Your〕 Honor the Mayor 《미》.

**-나마** 《…라도》 though; however; if only; 《…마저》 even. ¶ 그 집은 작으나마 아담하다 The house may be small, but it is nice. / 그만한 비나마 와주니 다행이다 Even that much of rain is of great help.

**나막신** (wooden) clogs; pattens; sabots. ¶ ~을 신다 wear 〔put on〕 clogs. ◉ ~끈 a clog thong.

**나맥**(裸麥) rye. =쌀보리.

**나머지** ① 《남은 것》 the remainder; the remnant(s); the remainings; the rest; what is left; leftovers; surplus (잉여); the balance (잔금). ¶ ~의 remaining; residuary / ~ 반 the other half / ~ 사람들 the rest of the people / ~ 상품 unsold stock; stock left over / ~ 재산 the residuary estate 〔property〕 / ~ 일은 내일 하도록 하자 Let's do the remaining work tomorrow. / ~ 여섯개는 어떻게 할까 What shall we do with the odd six? / ~ 돈이 얼마나 되느냐 How much money have you left? / 식사의 ~는 개에게 주어라 Give the leftovers 〔remains of a meal〕 to the dog. / 빚 갚고 난 ~로 집을 샀다 I have paid off the debt and bought a house with what was left.
② 《…한 끝에, 너무 …하여》 (as) a result of; (from) an excess of; driven by. ¶ 미워한 ~ out of hatred / 사랑한〔기쁜〕 ~ from an excess of love 〔joy〕 / 슬픈 ~ in a passion of grief / 분한 ~ out of vexation 〔chagrin, mortification〕 / 당황한 ~ all in a fluster / 질투한 ~ 그녀는 남편을 죽였다 Driven by jealousy, she killed her husband.

**나무** ① 《수목》 a tree; a plant; 《관목》 a shrub; bush (덤불). ¶ ~가 우거진 산 a (thickly) wooded hill; a hill covered with trees / ~가 없는 산 a treeless mountain; a bald hill / ~ 밑에서〔그늘에서〕 쉬다 rest under 〔in the shade of〕 a tree / ~에 물을 주다 water a plant / ~를 심다 plant a tree / ~를 가꾸다 look after the plants / ~를 베다 cut down a tree / ~를 다듬다 trim a tree / ~에 올라가다 climb a tree / ~를 꺾지 마시오 《게시》 Please do not damage the trees. / ~를 보되 숲을 보지 못한다 《속담》 You cannot 〔are unable to〕 see the wood for the trees. *or* We see trees but fail to see

them together as a forest.
② 《재목》 wood; timber; lumber 《미》. ¶ ～로 된 책상 a wooden desk / ～로 만들다 make 《*a thing*》 of wood.
③ 《땔나무》 firewood. ¶ ～하러 가다 go to gather firewood.
◉ ～거울 《무용지물》 a good-for-nothing (fellow). ～공이 a wooden pestle. ～그루터기 the stump (of a tree). ～깽이 a piece of a wood; a splinter. ～껍질 the bark of a tree. ～꾼 a woodman; a woodcutter; lumber jack 《미, 캐》. ～딸기 〖식물〗 a raspberry. ～때기 a chip 〔piece〕 of wood; a stick; a board; a lath. ～막대기 a stick; a rod; a pole; a club. ～못 a wooden nail 〔peg〕. ～발바리 〖조류〗 the common treecreeper. ～배 a wooden boat 〔ship〕. ～뿌리 the root of a tree 〔plant〕. ～상자 a wooden box. ～장수 a firewood seller; a fuel dealer. ～좀 〖곤충〗 a (wood) borer. ～줄기 the trunk of a tree. ～진디 〖곤충〗 a wood louse. ～토막 a block (큰); a chip of wood (작은). ～판자 a board. ～판장 (板牆) wooden wall; a board fence. 나뭇가지 《줄기에서 나는》 a branch (of a tree); 《큰》 a bough; 《작은》 a twig; a sprig. 나뭇간 a woodshed. 나뭇개비 a piece of wood; a splinter. 나뭇결 the grain (of wood): 나뭇결이 곱다 〔거칠다〕 be fine-grained 〔coarse-grained〕. 나뭇고갱이 the pith 〔heart〕 (of wood). 나뭇길 a woodman's path. 나뭇단 a fagot; a bundle of firewood. 나뭇더미 a woodpile. 나뭇동 a large bundle of wood. 나뭇등걸 a stump. 나뭇바리 a load of wood. 나뭇잎 a leaf (*pl.* leaves); leafage 〔foliage〕 [총칭]. 나뭇조각 a splinter; a piece 〔chip, block〕 of wood; 《큰》 a chunk (of wood) 《미》. 나뭇진 sap of a tree; resin.

**나무늘보** 〖동물〗 a sloth.

**나무라다** scold; rebuke; reprove; reproach; give 《*a person*》 a scolding 〔talking-to〕; chide; lecture; 《구어》 tell off; dress down.
¶ 설교하듯 길게 ～ give 《*a person*》 a lecture 〔lesson〕 / 부드럽게 〔엄하게〕 ～ scold mildly 〔severely〕; give 《*a person*》 a mild 〔severe, sharp〕 scolding / 경솔한 행동을 ～ reprove 《*a person*》 for *his* careless manners / 어머니는 방을 청소하지 않는다고 나를 나무라셨다 My mother scolded me for not cleaning up my room. / 그는 품행이 단정치 못하다고 부하들을 엄히 나무랐다 He sternly rebuked his men for their misconduct. / 어머니의 요리 솜씨는 나무랄 데가 없다 My mother is a perfect cook. / 그녀의 성격은 나무랄 데가 없다 Her character is without blemish. / 서투른 목수가 연장을 나무란다 《속담》 A bad 〔poor〕 carpenter quarrels with his tools.

> 용법 **scold** 「나무라다」란 뜻의 가장 일반적인 말. 「상당히 엄하게 나무라다」는 뜻이 내포됨. **rebuke** 「잘못을 추궁하며 나무라다」는 뜻으로 흔히 공식적인 비난을 말함. **reprove** 온건하게 호의적으로 「나무라다」란 뜻. **reproach** 잘못·실수 따위를 불쾌히 여기며 「비난하다」라는 뜻. **chide** 화가 나서 「나무라다」라는 문어적인 표현. **lecture** 설교하듯 길게 「나무라다」라는 뜻.

**나무람** a scolding; a reproof; a reproach; a rebuke; 《질책·비난》 a reprimand; a blame; a censure. ¶ 그는 불려가서 ～을 들었다 He was summoned to receive a reproof.

**나무아미타불** (南無阿彌陀佛) 《구원을 빌 때》 Save us, merciful Buddha!; 《명복을 빌 때》 May his soul rest in peace!

**나문재** 〖식물〗 a sea-blite.

**나물** ① 《먹는 풀》 herbs; a potherb; greens; wild vegetables; salad makings. ～하다 pick herbs; gather greens. ¶ 산에 ～하러 가다 go to pick herbs in the mountains.
② 《무친 것》 cooked potherbs; seasoned greens 〔vegetables〕; herb salad. ¶ 시금치～ boiled spinach seasoned with soy sauce / ～을 무치다 cook greens; prepare herbs 〔greens〕 for eating / ～ 먹고 물 마시고 팔을 베고 눕다 lead a simple and leisurely life.
◉ ～국 soup with greens in it; vegetable soup.

**나박김치** watery kimchi (made of radish sliced squarely).

**나발** (喇叭) ⇨ 나팔. ¶ ～을 불다 brag; boast; talk big / 규칙이고 ～이고 필요없어 Regulations be hanged!

**나발대** ① 《나발의 몸채》 the tube of a bugle. ② 《돼지의 부리》 the snout (of a pig).

**나방** 〖곤충〗 a moth.

**나변** (那邊) ① ＝ 거기. ② 《어디》 where. ¶ 그 이유가 ～에 있는가 Where is the reason? / 그의 진의가 ～에 있는지 알 수 없다 I cannot understand what he really means.

**나볏하다** (be) nice and neat.

**나병**(癩病) 〖의학〗 leprosy; Hansen's disease. ¶ ~에 걸렸다 be leprous.
◉ ~균 Hansen's bacilli. ~원 a leprosarium; a leper's home. ~환자 a leper; a leprous patient: ~환자 수용소 a leper colony.

**-나보다** seem; it seems that…; I think that…. ¶ 아무래도 실패하나보다 I shall fail in all probability. / 누가 왔나보다 I think someone's here. / 눈이 오려나 보다 It looks like snow. / 그는 오지 않으려나 보다 He seems not to be coming.

**나부**(裸婦) 《paint》 a woman in the nude; a nude woman.

**나부끼다** flutter; flap; wave; stream; fly. ¶ 바람에 ~ 《a flag》 flutter 〔wave, flap〕 in the wind / 온 거리에 깃발이 나부끼고 있었다 Flags were flying all over the streets.

**나부대다** 《몸을》 move restlessly; keep budging nervously; fidget 《about》; 《입을》 talk glib and flippant; gabble away 〔on〕.

**나부대대하다** have a round flat little face.

**나부랭이** ① 《조각》 pieces; slips; strips; bits; odd pieces. ¶ 종이 ~ pieces 〔scraps, slips, strips〕 of paper / 헝겊 ~ pieces 〔scraps, strips〕 of cloth.
② 《사람》 a fag end. ¶ ~의 petty; minor / 귀족 ~ a fag end of nobility / 관리~ a petty 〔minor〕 official / 대단치는 않아도 나는 화가 ~는 된다고 여긴다 I regard myself as a painter, if not much of one.

**나부시** 《coming down》 lightly; gently; softly; 《다소곳이》 politely. ¶ ~ 절하다 bow with a gentle sweep; make a polite bow / 새가 나뭇가지에 ~ 내려앉았다 A bird 「sat lightly 〔alighted gently〕 on a branch.

**나부죽하다** ⇨ 너부죽하다.

**나불거리다** ① 《나붓거리다》 flutter; flap; flit. ¶ 선풍기가 돌 때 달린 리본이 나불거린다 The ribbons attached to the electric fan flutter when it is in motion. ② 《입을》 wag *one's* tongue; chatter; rattle; prattle; talk away; be talkative. ¶ 쓸데 없는 말을 ~ talk nonsense / 혼자서 ~ do all the talking / 무슨 일이 있어도 나불거리지 마라 Don't speak under any circumstances! / 잘도 나불거리는군 How your tongue runs!

**나불나불** 《나풀거림》 fluttering 〔flapping〕 away; 《입을 놀림》 wagging away; wagging *one's* tongue; rattling; chattering.

**나붓거리다** keep fluttering 〔flapping, blowing〕. ⇨ 나부끼다.

**나붓나붓** fluttering 〔flapping, blowing〕 away.

**나붙다** appear 《on》; be stuck 〔posted up〕 《on》. ¶ 벽에 여러 가지 포스터가 나붙어 있다 A lot of posters are posted on the wall.

**나비**[1] 〖곤충〗 a butterfly. ¶ 고산 ~ an alpine butterfly / ~ 모양의 butterfly-shaped / ~를 채집하다 collect butterflies / ~처럼 날다 fly like a butterfly / ~가 이꽃 저꽃 날아다닌다 Butterflies are fluttering from flower to flower. / ~가 꽃을찾지 어디 꽃이 나비를 찾는가 Men court women, not women men.
◉ ~넥타이 a bow tie. ~매듭 《make》 a bowknot. ~잠 a baby's way of sleeping with outstretched arms. ~잠(簪) a butterfly-shaped hairpin. ~장 〖건축〗 the tenon of a dovetail joint: ~장 붙임 dovetailing; joining with mortise and tenon. ~춤 a butterfly dance.

**나비**[2] 《고양이》 a cat; 《애칭》 a puss(y); a kitty; a kitten (새끼고양이). ¶ ~가 야옹거리다 A cat is meawing 〔miaowing, mewing〕. / ~가 가르릉 거리다 A cat purrs.

**나비**[3] 《폭》 width 《of cloth》. ⇨ 너비.

**나비가오리** 〖어류〗 a (sting)ray.

**나빠지다** grow 〔get〕 worse; go 〔turn〕 bad; 《점점 더》 grow from bad to worse; 《품질 등이》 spoil; become deteriorated. ¶ 나빠지게 하다 make 《*something*》 worse; 《질을》 deteriorate / 그들 사이가 나빠졌다 Their relation 「has gone sour 〔has got worse〕. / 사태는 더한층 나빠졌다 Things went from bad to worse. / 환자의 병세가 갑자기 나빠졌다 The patient suddenly took a turn for the worse. / 그는 살림이 전보다 나빠졌다 He became worse off than before. / 우리나라의 경제 상태는 점점 나빠지고 있다 The economic situation in our country is getting increasingly worse.

**나쁘게** 《좋지 않게》 badly; ill. ⇨ 나뻬.
¶ 남을 ~ 말하다 speak ill of others; talk against 《*a person*》 / ~ 생각하다 think ill 〔harshly〕 of 《*a person*》 / 그를 ~ 말하는 사람은 하나도 없다 There are none who talk against him. / 내가 안 간다고 ~ 생각지 말게 Please don't think ill 〔badly〕 of me because I'm not coming. / 사물을 ~ 보지 마라 Don't look on the dark side of things.

**나쁘다** ① 《좋지 않다》 (be) bad; wrong; evil; ill; foul; 《마음이》 (be) wicked;

malicious; ill-natured; 《도덕상》 (be) immoral; sinful. ¶ 나쁜 짓 《악행》 a wrong; an evil deed; a misdeed; 《범죄》 a crime; a sin (죄악) / 나쁜 사람 a bad 〔an evil, a wicked〕 person / 나쁜 짓을 하다 do 《*something*》 wrong; commit a crime 〔sin〕 / 그녀는 마음씨가 나쁜 여자다 She is an ill-natured woman. / 인간은 나쁜 짓을 쉬이 배운다 Man takes to vice easily. / 약한 자를 못살게 구는 것은 ～ It is wrong 〔bad〕 to bully the weak. / 약속을 어기는 일은 ～ It is not good to break your promise. / 나쁜 사람과 사귀지 마라 You should keep away from bad company. / 나는 나쁜 짓을 하지 않았다 I did nothing wrong.
② 《잘못하다》 (be) wrong 〔blamable〕; be in the wrong; be to blame. ¶ 그것은 내가 나빴다 It's my fault. *or* I am to blame for it. / 자네에게 그런 무리한 일을 시킨 내가 나빴다 It was wrong of me to force such a task on you. / 자네에겐 아무런 나쁜 점이 없네 There is nothing wrong with you. / 그녀는 자기가 나빴다는 것을 인정했다 She acknowledged that she was in the wrong. / 그에게 책임을 미는 것은 ～ You are wrong to put the blame on him.
③ 《해롭다》 (be) bad; harmful; injurious. ¶ 눈에 ～ be bad for the eyes / 흡연은 건강에 ～ Smoking is bad for your health. / 과로는 몸에 ～ Overwork is injurious to health. / 해보는 것도 나쁘지 않다 There's no harm in trying. / 이런 날씨는 농작물에 나쁘다 The weather is bad for the crops.
④ 《신체·몸이》 (be) ill; be sick 〔unwell〕. ¶ 위가 ～ have 〔suffer from〕 stomach trouble / 안색이 ～ look pale / 몸의 상태가 ～ feel ill 〔unwell, out of sorts〕 / 그는 간장이 ～ He has a bad liver. / 그녀는 심장이 ～ She has heart trouble. *or* She has a weak heart. / 나는 눈이 좀 ～ I have something wrong with my eyes. / 선수는 연습 부족으로 몸의 컨디션이 나빴다 The athlete was stale from lack of exercise.
⑤ 《품질이》 (be) bad; poor; inferior; coarse (조제의); be of low grade. ¶ 질이 나쁜 포도주 wine of poor 〔bad〕 quality / 이 상품은 품질이 ～ This product is of poor 〔inferior〕 quality. / 싼 것이라고 꼭 나쁜 것은 아니다 Cheap things are not always bad.
⑥ 《머리·기억력이》 (be) poor; weak; feeble. ¶ 머리가 ～ be weak-headed 〔dull, stupid〕; have a dull head; be slow of learning / 나는 기억력이 ～ I have a poor 〔bad〕 memory.
⑦ 《날씨가》 (be) bad; foul; nasty. ¶ 나쁜 날씨 foul 〔bad〕 weather / 오늘은 날씨가 ～ The weather is bad today.
⑧ 《도로가》 (be) muddy (질다); bad; rough (울퉁불퉁하다). ¶ 길이 몹시 ～ The road is very rough. / 그 나라는 도로가 나쁘기로 유명하다 That country is notorious for its bad roads.
⑨ 《불쾌·불편·불운하다》 (be) bad; unlucky; ominous. ¶ 나쁜 징조 a bad omen / 자네에게 나쁜 소식이 있네 I have bad 〔sad〕 news for you. / 오늘은 일진이 나쁜가 봐 It seems this is an evil 〔a bad〕 day. / 칭찬을 받고 기분이 나쁠 사람은 없다 No one feels displeased when he is praised. / 그것은 기분 나쁜 소리로 들린다 That doesn't sound nice. / 오늘 나는 운이 나빴다 I was unlucky today.
⑩ 《비정상이다·고장나다》 (be) wrong; bad; be out of order. ¶ 엔진의 어딘가가 ～ Something is wrong with the engine. / 이 진공 청소기는 작동 상태가 ～ This vacuum cleaner does not work well. / 그 나라의 식량 사정은 매우 ～ The food situation in the country is very bad. / 이 부근은 치안 상태가 ～ This area is not safe.
⑪ 《평판이》 (be) bad; ill; unsavory. ¶ 그녀는 이웃의 평판이 ～ She has 「a bad 〔an unsavory〕 reputation in her neighborhood. / 그는 학급에서 평판이 ～ He is unpopular in his class.
⑫ 《모자라다》 (be) deficient; insufficient; inadequate; unsatisfactory; be not enough. ¶ 그렇게 먹고도 아직 나쁘냐 You really ate much. And are you not filled 〔satisfied〕 yet? / 식사는 좀 나쁜듯이 먹어야 탈이 없다 Feed by measure and defy the physician.

**나삐** 《나쁘게》 badly; ill; 《부족하게》 insufficiently; unsatisfactorily; not enough. ¶ 남을 ～ 말하다 speak ill of others; say bad things about 《*a person*》; speak badly about 《*a person*》 / 조반을 좀 ～ 먹다 do not have enough breakfast / ～ 보다 think meanly of / ～ 여기다 think ill of 《*a person*》; take 《it》 amiss 〔ill〕 / 내 말을 그렇게 ～들을 것은 없다 There is no reason for you to take my words so ill. / 악의로한 말이 아니니 그리 ～ 여기질랑 마시오 Don't take my remarks so ill since I didn't make them out of spite.

**나사** 《미국 국립 항공 우주국》 NASA.

[<the *N*ational *A*eronautics and *S*pace *A*dministration]

**나사**(螺絲) 《나사못》 a screw. ¶ 십자 ~ a phillips(-head) screw; a cross head screw / 일자 ~ a slotted head screw / 수〔암〕~ a male 〔female〕 screw / ~를 죄다 drive a screw in 〔home〕; tighten a screw / ~를 늦추다〔풀다〕 loosen 〔slacken〕 a screw / ~를 빼다 unscrew 《a plate》; take a screw off 《a board》 / ~로 고정시키다 screw 《*a thing*》 down 〔up〕 / ~를 돌리다 turn a screw / ~가 헐거워졌다 The screw is loose. / 저 친구 머리의 ~가 좀 빠졌군 [비유적] There is something loose about his brainwork. ◉ ~대가리 a screwhead; the head of a screw. ~돌리개 《remove a screw with》 a screwdriver. ~송곳 an auger; a gimlet. 나삿니 a screw thread; the thread (of a screw).

**나사**(羅紗) woolen cloth. ¶ 능직 ~ twilled cloth; twill; tweed / 체크 무늬 ~ plaid (cloth); tartan. ◉ ~상인〔점〕 a woolen draper; a woolen dealer.

**나상**(裸像) a nude figure 〔statue〕.

**나서다** ① 《나타나다》 come out 〔forth〕; appear; make an appearance; present *oneself.* ¶ 무대에 ~ appear on the stage; make a stage appearance / (사람이) 표면에 ~ be 〔appear〕 in the limelight; show *oneself* in the public eye / 남 앞에 나서기를 싫어하다 avoid 〔shun〕 company 〔the public〕; be not sociable / 남 앞에 나서지 못하다 be not fit to be seen; be not presentable.
② 《앞으로》 come 〔step〕 forward. ¶ 한 발 앞으로 ~ take 〔make〕 a step forward / 선두에 ~ take 〔gain〕 the lead; get ahead of 《others》 / 줄에서 나서지 마시오 Don't get 〔step〕 out of line.
③ 《떠나다》 leave; go out; get out 《of》; start (off); set off 〔out〕. ¶ 집을 ~ leave home; leave *one's* house / 교문을 ~ get out of the campus; leave school; graduate from school (졸업하다) / 여행길에 ~ start 〔set out〕 on a journey 〔tour〕; go 〔leave〕 on a trip / 그는 고등학교를 나서자마자 일했다 He started working as soon as he finished high school.
④ 《진출하다》 go 〔launch〕 《into》; enter upon; get started; find *one's* way 《into》. ¶ 정계〔실업계〕에 ~ go into politics 〔business〕 / 세상에 ~ make *one's* start in the world; sally forth into life / 사회 개혁에 ~ set out to reform the society / 그는 정계에 나설 계획이다 He is planning to launch into politics.
⑤ 《출마하다》 run 〔stand〕 for 《the Congress》; come 〔put *oneself*〕 forward 《as a candidate》; go in person (스스로). ¶ …의 후보로 ~ stand 〔run〕 as a candidate for... / 대통령 후보로 ~ run for President / 그는 다가오는 지사 선거에 나서기로 했다 He decided to run for the coming gubernatorial election.
⑥ 《어떤 장소에 이르다》 lead to; find *oneself* 《at, in》; come upon 〔to〕; run 《into》; lead to. ¶ 이 길로 가면 큰 길로 나서게 된다 This path leads 〔goes〕 to the main road. / 이 모퉁이를 돌면 우체국이 나섭니다 Turn the corner, and you will find yourself at the post office.
⑦ 《간섭·참견하다》 interfere 《in *a matter,* with *a person*》; meddle 《in, with》; put 〔poke, thrust〕 *one's* nose 《into》; poke 《into》; obtrude; intrude; be forward. ¶ 나서기 좋아하는 interfering 《neighbor》; 《people》 in the habit of interfering in the other people's affairs; meddlesome / 남의 일에 나서기를 싫어하다 be unobtrusive 〔unassuming〕; keep *one's* place / 중뿔나게 ~ butt in on 〔intrude *oneself* into〕 《another's affairs》; make an uncalled-for remark (말간섭) / 자기와 상관 없는 일에 ~ intrude where *one* is not wanted / 남의 일에 나서지 말게 You should keep your nose out of other people's affairs. / 네가 나설 자리가 아니야 This is none of your business.
⑧ 《일자리 등이》 turn up; be found; 《희망자 등이》 apply 〔volunteer〕 《for》; present 《for》. ¶ 운좋게 일자리가 ~ be lucky enough to find a job 〔position〕 / 딸에게 좋은 혼처가 나섰다 A good offer of marriage has come up for my daughter.

**나선**(螺旋) a spiral; a helix (*pl.* ~es, helices); a screw (나사). ¶ ~형〔상〕의 spiral; helical; screw-shaped / ~형을 그리며 치솟다 climb in a spiral. ◉ ~강하〔하강〕 a spiral dive 〔descent〕. ~계단 a spiral staircase. ~균 a spirillum (*pl.* -rilla). ~상승 a spiral climb. ~성운 『천문』 a spiral nebula. ~운동 screw motion. ~장치 a screw (device). ~제동기 a screw brake. ~체 a helicoid; a screw. ~추진기 a screw propeller. ~펌프 a screw pump.

**나스닥** 『증권』 National Association of Securities Dealers Automated Quotations(생략 NASDAQ)(투자자에게 점두거래되는 증권류의 가격 등을 알리는 전미

(全美) 증권업협회의 온라인 서비스).

**나스르르하다** (be) fluffy; plushy; downy; woolly; shaggy. ¶ 털이 나스르르한 개 a shaggy dog / 털이 나스르르한 담요 a woolly blanket.

**나아가다** ① 《전진하다》 go 〔step, move〕 forward 〔ahead〕; make *one's* way 《to》; advance; proceed.

> **용법** **make one's way**는 「나아가다」란 일반적인 개념이나, make 대신 다른 동사를 붙여 「나아가는」 다양한 방법·형태를 나타낼 수 있다. elbow *one's* way (팔꿈치로 헤치며 나아가다) / feel *one's* way (손으로 더듬으며 나아가다) / push *one's* way (밀어제치며 나아가다).

¶ 3보 앞으로 ~ take three steps forward / 준결승에 ~ go to the semifinals; get 〔win *one's* way〕 into the semifinals / 그들은 하루에 40km 나아갔다 They made 〔advanced〕 forty kilometers in a day. / 실험은 계획대로 나아가고 있다 The experiment is proceeding as planned. / 그녀는 무대 중앙으로 나아갔다 She moved toward the center of the stage. / 이것이 장차 한국이 나아갈 길이다 This is the course Korea should take 〔follow〕 in the future. / 빛은 소리보다 훨씬 빠르게 나아간다 Light travels much faster than sound.
② 《진척·진보하다》 advance; improve; make progress 〔headway〕; get on with. ¶ 이대로 나아가면 at the present rate of progress / 시대와 함께 ~ keep up with 〔keep abreast of〕 the times / 시대보다 앞서 ~ get 〔go〕 ahead of the times; be ahead of *one's* times / 이 일은 예정보다 빨리 나아가고 있다 The work is going ahead of schedule. / 「지난 시간에는 어디까지 나아갔습니까」—「20페이지 제10행째까지 입니다」 "How far did we get in our last lesson?"—"We got to page twenty, line eight." / 자, 다음 주제로 나아갑시다 Let's go on to the next topic now.
③ 《지위·단계 따위가》 be moved up 《to a higher grade》; be advanced. ¶ 대학으로 ~ go on to college / 결승까지 ~ advance to the finals.

**나아지다** 《좋아지다》 get 〔become〕 better; improve; be improved; 《병세가》 take a turn for the better; recover (from *one's* illness). ¶ 건강이 ~ get better and better; enjoy better health / 솜씨가 ~ become more skillful; get better at / 학교 성적이 ~ show a better school record / 지내기가 ~ get better off; be in easier circumstances / 그는 영어 회화 실력이 훨씬 나아졌다 He made a good progress in English conversation. / 식량 사정이 나아졌다 The food situation has greatly improved. / 환자는 병세가 나아지고 있다 The patient is taking a turn for the better. / 대미 수출은 점차적으로 나아지리라 생각된다 Exports to the U.S. are expected to pick up by degrees.

**나약**(懦弱) feebleness; feeble-mindedness; spiritless; timidness; 《우유 부단》 effeminacy; irresolution. ~하다 《몸이》 (be) weak; faint-hearted; weak-spirited; timid; effeminate; feeble-minded; irresolute. ¶ ~한 국민 a soft and spiritless people / ~해지다 become effeminate / ~함을 보이다 show a weak attitude 《to, toward》 / 그는 ~한 사내다 He is a faint-hearted man.

**나열**(羅列) (an) enumeration. ~하다 enumerate; arrange 《*things*》 in a row; cite 《one example after another》. ¶ 통계 숫자를 ~하다 marshal statistical figures; give a wealth of statistics / 그것은 무의미한 문자 ~에 불과하다 It is nothing but a meaningless list of letters 〔characters〕.

**나오다** ① 《밖으로》 come 〔go, get〕 out; take *one's* way out; step out (잠시). ¶ 집에서 ~ get out of the house; leave home / 뜰로 ~ come out into the garden / 방에서 ~ get out of a room / 물에서 ~ come 〔emerge〕 out of the water / 차에서 ~ step out of a car / 밖에 나오지 않다 keep to *one's* house / 지하철역을 나와서 그녀는 신문팔이에게 길을 물었다 Outside the subway station, she asked a newspaper seller the way.
② (a) 《모습이 나타나다》 appear; show *oneself;* emerge 《from, out of, on》; make *one's* appearance; turn 〔show〕 up; come forward; present itself; rise (해·달 등이). ¶ 무대에 ~ appear on the stage / 법정에 ~ appear in court / 공중〔청중〕 앞에 ~ appear in public 〔before the audience〕 / 존 웨인이 나오는 서부극 a Western with John Wayne / 별이 ~ the stars appear in the sky / 달이 나왔다 The moon has risen 〔come up〕. / 그 시대엔 많은 영웅이 나왔다 The age was productive of many heroes. / 그는 내주 월요일에 텔레비전에 나온다 He will appear on TV next Monday.
(b) 《출근·참석하다》 be present at 《a ceremony》; attend 《a meeting》; 《참가

하다》 join; take part in 《a quiz show》; participate 《in》; enter 〔go in for〕 《a beauty contest》. ¶ 전원이 다 ～ be all present 〔out〕 / 파티에 ～ attend 〔be present at〕 a party / 시합에 ～ take part in the game / 그는 회의에 안 나와 있다 He is not present at the meeting. / 왜 안 나왔나 Why did you absent yourself? / 이번 일요일에는 회사에 나와야 한다 I'll have to go to「work 〔the office〕 next Sunday.

(***c***) 《드러나다》 show *itself;* be revealed 〔exposed〕; assert 〔reveal, betray〕 *itself;* peep out. ¶ 나쁜 버릇이 ～ *one's* bad habit peeps 〔crops〕 out / 평소의 고집이 ～ *one's* usual stubbornness asserts itself; show *one's* customary obstinacy.

(***d***) 《시장에》 appear on the market; hit 〔come out to〕 the market. ¶ 사과가 시장에 ～ apples「appear 〔are out〕 on the market.

(***e***) 《출몰하다》 haunt. ¶ 유령이 나오는 집 a haunted house / 유령이 ～ a ghost walks 〔haunts〕 the place / 저 집에는 유령이 나온다고 한다 They say that house is haunted.

③ 《말이》 be said 〔spoken, uttered〕. ¶ 욕설이 ～ abusive language is spoken / 볼멘 소리가 ～ angry words are spoken 〔uttered〕 / 사투리가 나왔다 His provincial dialect「came out 〔showed itself〕. / 우리는 어이가 없어 말이 안 나왔다 We were so amazed 〔astonished〕 that we couldn't speak. *or* We were struck dumb with amazement.

④ 《없어진 것이》 turn up; be found; be restored 《to》; get 《*a thing*》 back. ¶ 잃어버린 책이 나왔다 The book which was lost has been found. / 잃어버렸다고 생각했던 시계가 서랍에서 나왔다 The watch I thought I had lost turned up in the drawer.

⑤ 《음식이》 be brought 〔served〕; be given as a treat. ¶ 술과 밥이 나왔다 We were treated with wine and food. *or* Wine and food were set before us. / 회합이 끝나고 다과가 나왔다 Fruits and cakes were served after the meeting.

⑥ 《물 따위가》 flow 〔stream〕 out; come out; gush out (솟아나오다); 《피가》 bleed; 《땀이》 perspire; sweat; 《재채기가》 sneeze; 《배어나오다》 ooze (out); exude. ¶ 샘이 ～ a spring 〔fountain〕 flows / 눈물이 ～ tears flow 〔fall〕; tears come to *one's* eyes / 침이 ～ salivate; water / 콧물이 ～ *one's* nose runs / 재채기가 자꾸 나온다 have a fit of sneezing / 땀이 많이 ～ sweat a lot 《after running》 / 그는 코에서 피가 나오고 있었다 He was bleeding from the nose. *or* His nose was bleeding. / 수도 꼭지를 틀었으나 물이 나오지 않았다 I turned on the faucet but no water came out.

⑦ 《발행하다》 be published 〔issued, brought out〕; come out; be given to the world. ¶ 책이 방금 나왔다 The book has just been published. / 다음 호가 곧 나온다 The next number will be out soon. / 곧 새 우표가 나온다 A new stamp will be issued shortly. / 책이 언제 나오나 When will the book come out? / 그의 책은 내년 봄에 나온다 His book will come out next spring.

⑧ 《책·신문에 나다》 appear 〔come out, be reported〕 《in》; be found; go into 《a newspaper》. ¶ 사전에 나와 있다 be given 〔found〕 in a dictionary / 네 얘기가 신문에 나와 있다 There is something about you in the paper. / 어느 신문에 나왔나요 What paper did it come out in? / 그 섬은 지도에 안 나와 있다 The island is not on the map.

⑨ 《몸담았던 곳을》 (***a***) 《졸업하다》 graduate 《from, at 《영》》; be graduated; finish. ⇨ 졸업. ¶ 대학을 갓 나온 여성 a woman fresh from college / 그는 작년에 고등학교를 나왔다 He finished 〔graduated from〕 high school last year. / 「윤 선생님은 어느 대학을 나오셨나」—「K 대라더군요」 "What university did Mr. Yun graduate from?"—"I hear that he「graduated from 〔is a graduate of〕 K University."

(***b***) 《그만두다》 resign 《*one's* post》; throw up a situation; leave 《*one's* place》; quit 《*one's* job》. ¶ 그는 회사에서 나왔다 He left (the service of) the company.

(***c***) 《풀려나오다》 be released. ¶ 그는 특사로 교도소에서 나왔다 He was released from prison on a special pardon.

⑩ 《앞으로 나서다》 come 〔step〕 forward; 《진출하다》 enter 〔launch, go〕 into; advance. ¶ 3보 앞으로 ～ take 〔make〕 three steps forward / 결승에 ～ advance to the finals / 그는 정계에 나오려고 한다 He is planning to launch 〔enter〕 into politics.

⑪ 《출마하다》 run 〔stand 《영》〕 for 《President》; come 〔put *oneself*〕 forward at a candidate 《for》. ¶ 그녀는 국회의원 선거에 나올 것 같다 It seems that she is planning to run for the National Assembly.

⑫ 《산출·배출되다》 be produced 〔raised〕; be found; produce. ¶ 이 광산에서 구리가 나온다 This mine produces copper. / 옛날에는 이 산에서 금이 나왔었다 Gold used to be found on this mountain. / 그 나라에서는 위대한 과학자가 많이 나왔다 The country has produced many great scientists. / 포도가 나오기 시작했다 Grapes are now getting in season.
⑬ 《발생하다》 start; originate 《in》; occur; 《유래하다》 come of 〔from〕; stem from; be derived from. ¶ 이 근처에서 콜레라 환자가 나왔다 A case of cholera has occurred in this neighbor. / 이 단어는 라틴어에서 나왔다 This word is derived 「from Latin 〔of Latin origin〕. / 그 사고로 많은 부상자가 나왔다 A lot of people were injured in the accident. / 그의 말은 그의 무지에서 나왔다 His remarks stemmed from his ignorance / 그 말이 누구한테서 나왔느냐 Who started 〔first told〕 the story? / 이 보도는 확실한 소식통에서 나왔다 The report came from a reliable source. / 그가 하는 일은 만사 자기 중심에서 나온다 He does everything from 〔out of〕 a self-centered motive.
⑭ 《내밀다》 project; stick 〔jut〕 out; protrude. ¶ 이마가 ~ have a prominent forehead / 못대가리가 나와 있으니 쳐서 박아라 Hit the nail on the head, as it is out. / 그는 요즘 배가 나오기 시작한다 He is starting to get a potbelly.
⑮ 《태도를 취하다》 assume 《an attitude》; take 《a move》. ¶ 대담하게 ~ put 〔show〕 a bold front / 고압적인 태도로 ~ act 〔speak〕 high-handedly; carry 《*a matter*》 with a high hand; take the high hand 《with *a person*》 / 그가 어떻게 나오나 두고 보자 Let's wait and see what move he will take.
⑯ 《지불되다》 be paid 〔given〕; 《제공되다》 be provided 〔furnished, supplied〕 《*a person* with *something*》; 《허가되다》 be granted 〔authorized, permitted〕; 《면허를 얻다》 be licensed; get a license. ¶ …하는 허가가 ~ be authorized to *do* / 여권이 ~ have 〔get〕 *one's* passport 「issued 〔visaed (비자가)〕 / 운전 면허가 ~ obtain 〔get〕 a driving license / 월급은 20일에 나온다 We are paid on the 20th every month. *or* Our monthly salary is given on the 20th. / 학생들에게 교과서가 나왔다 Textbooks were supplied 〔furnished〕 to 〔for〕 pupils.
⑰ 《결과로서》 come out 《as a result》; work out. ¶ 10을 5로 나누면 2가 나온다 Ten divided by five gives two. / 이 문제는 답이 안 나온다 It is impossible to solve the problem.
⑱ 《길이》 lead to; come to. ¶ 이 길을 따라가면 바다가 나온다 This way leads 〔goes〕 to the sea. / 곧 호수가 나왔다 Soon I came to a lake.
⑲ 《싹이》 shoot out; sprout; bud. ¶ 나무의 싹이 나오기 시작했다 The trees have begun to bud.
⑳ 《문제가》 be given. ¶ 시험에 열 문제가 나왔다 Ten questions were given in the examination.
㉑ 《기타 관용적 표현》 ¶ 이 사진은 잘 안 나왔다 This photo is 「badly 〔not well〕 taken. / 이 사진에 너는 참 잘 나왔다 You came out well in this photo. / 이 달에도 적자가 나올 것 같다 I'm afraid we seem to be in the red this month. / 그 회의에서는 아무에게서도 좋은 아이디어가 나오지 않았다 Nobody came up with a good idea at the meeting. / 전화가 나왔습니다 — 응답해 주세요 《교환수의 말》 You are connected. — Answer the phone right away, please.

**나왕** (羅王) 〖식물〗 a lauan; lauan (재목).

**나위** 《여지·이유·필요》 ¶ 더할 ~ 없이 좋은 perfect (완벽한); completely satisfactory (만족스러운); ideal (이상적인); impeccable (나무랄데 없는); 《매우 좋은》 very fine; the very best; best fit 《for》 (알맞은) / …은 말할 ~도 없다 It goes without saying that…; It is needless to say that… / 지금은 공부하기에 더할 ~없는 계절이다 This is 「an ideal 〔the best〕 season for study. / 나의 컨디션은 더할 ~없다 I'm in the best of 「health 〔condition〕. *or* I've never felt better. / 날씨는 더할 ~ 없었다 The weather was perfect. *or* The weather couldn't have been better. / 품질에 관해서는 더할~ 없다 There is nothing to complain of as far as the quality is concerned. / 이 방이라면 나에게 더할 ~없다 This room will suit me perfectly. / 이것은 더할 ~없다 This leaves nothing 「to be desired 〔to wish for〕. / 그들은 더할 ~ 없이 행복하다 They are as happy as can be. / 그녀는 아내로서 더할 ~ 없다 She is a perfect wife. *or* She is all that can be desired as a wife. / 말할 ~도 없이 네가 잘못이다 Needless to say, you are wrong. / 차는 말할 ~도 없고, 자전거를 살 형편도 안된다네 I can't afford a bicycle to say nothing of a car.

**나이** age; years.
¶ ～에 상관 없이 with no age limit / 이〔그〕 ～에 at my〔his〕age / ～는 젊어도 though young (in years) / ～를 숨기다 represent *oneself* as younger〔older〕than *one* really is / ～가 지긋하다 be well up in years / ～를 먹다 grow older; age; go on years; 《늙다》 get〔grow, become〕old; advance in age〔years〕/ ～만큼 보이다 look *one's* age / ～만큼 안 보이다 do not look *one's* age / 나잇값을 해라 Act as you should at your age. *or* Act your (own) age. / 이제 그만한 것은 알만한 ～다 You are old enough to know better. / 너는 ～에 비해 젊어〔늙어〕 보인다 You look young〔old〕for your age. / 「～가 몇 살이지」―「18세입니다」 "May I ask your age?" *or* "How old are you?" *or* "What's your age?"―"(I'm) eighteen." / 그는 나보다 ～가 두 살 아래〔위〕다 He is my junior〔senior〕by two years. / 우리는 ～가 같다 We are (of) the same age. / 여자의 ～는 알 수가 없다 I can't tell a woman's age. / 그녀는 ～가 30정도로 보인다 She looks〔appears to be〕about thirty. / 너는 아직 결혼할 ～가 아니다 You are too young to marry. / 60이라는 ～에 비해 젊어 보이십니다 You look younger than your 60 years. / 나는 ～는 먹었어도 마음은 젊다네 I am old but young at heart. / 나는 ～가 들면서 백발이 늘었다 As I grew older, much of my hair turned gray. / 그는 ～ 탓으로 허리가 구부정하다 He stoops a little with age. / 그도 ～가 ～인만큼 어쩔 수 없다 It can't be helped, considering his age. / ～탓인지 요즘은 잊기를 잘 한다 I have grown extremely forgetful lately「due to〔because of〕my age. / ～에는 장사가 없다 Age will tell. *or* You can't fight the years. *or* You cannot escape the effect of (old) age. / 그녀는 ～를 헛먹지 않았다 She hasn't put on years「in vain〔for nothing〕. / ～ 탓인지 눈이 침침해졌다 My sight has become poor from age. / ～순으로 명단을 만들어라 Arrange the list of names according to age. / ～ 차이는 문제가 안 된다 The difference in our age doesn't matter. / 자네 아직 여자에게 눈길이 안 갈 정도의 ～도 아닌데 You aren't past looking at a woman, are you?
◉ ～배기 a person older than he looks. 나잇살 age; years: 나잇살이나 들어가지고 being old enough to be more prudent.

**나이로비** 《케냐의 수도》 Nairobi.

**나이아가라폭포**(―瀑布) Niagara Falls.

**나이지리아** 《아프리카의 공화국》 (the Federal Republic of) Nigeria. ¶ ～의 Nigerian. ◉ ～사람 a Nigerian.

**나이터** 〖스포츠〗 a night game.

**나이테** 《나무의》 an annual「a growth〕ring.

**나이트**[1] a knight. ◉ ～작위 knighthood: ～ 작위를 받다 receive a knighthood.

**나이트**[2] night. ◉ ～가운 a nightgown; a night-robe. ～게임 a night game. ～드레스 a nightdress. ～캡 a nightcap. ～클럽 a nightclub; 《미구어》 a night spot.

**나이팅게일** 〖조류〗 a nightingale.

**나이프** a knife. ⇨칼[1]. ◉ ～스위치 〖전기〗 a knife switch. 잭～ a jackknife.

**나인**(内人) 〖역사〗 a lady attendant in the palace; a court lady; a maid of honor.

**나일강**(―江) the Nile. ¶ 청〔백〕～ the Blue「〔White〕Nile.

**나일론** nylon. ◉ ～양말 nylon stockings〔socks〕; 《a pair of》 nylons (여성용). ～제품 nylon goods; nylons.

**나잇값** behavior「appropriate to〔befitting〕*one's* age. ¶ ～도 못 하다 be thoughtless〔unsuitable〕for *one's* age; be unworthy of *one's* years; be unbecoming to *one's* age / ～ 좀 하시오 Be〔Act〕your age! *or* You should「know better〔be wiser〕at your age.

**나전**(螺鈿) mother-of-pearl; nacre.
◉ ～세공 mother-of-pearl work. ～칠기 lacquerware〔lacquerwork〕inlaid with mother-of-pearl.

**나절** the period of about half the daylight hours. ¶ 아침 ～ 《in》 the「morning〔forenoon〕; morning hours / 저녁 ～ 《in》 the「evening〔late afternoon〕; evening hours / 반～ a fourth of the day / 방을 치우는 데 거의 한～이나 걸렸다 I spent almost half a day in putting the room in order.

**나조**(―調) 〖음악〗 B. ◉ 나장조〔단조〕 《a symphony》 B major〔minor〕.

**나졸**(邏卒) 〖역사〗 a patrol(man).

**나중** 《다음》 next〔a latter〕time; 《장래》 the future; 《결과》 a consequence; 《나머지》 the rest; the others; 《마지막》 an end; the last; 《다음의 것》 the latter. ⇨뒤, 끝.
¶ ～의 《이후·다음의》 later; subsequent; following; 《앞으로의》 future; coming; 《마지막의》 last; final / ～에 later (on); after; afterward(s); subsequently; in (the) future; some time later; 《마지막에》 at the end; finally; 《뒤에》 behind /

맨 ~ 열차 the last train / ~의 세대 future generation / ~ 세상 life to come / 맨 ~까지 till the end; to the last / ~ 생각을 하다 think of the future / ~까지 다 듣다 hear 《*a person*》 out; let 《*a person*》 finish his story / 그는 ~에 왔다 He came later. / 그녀는 맨 ~에 왔다 She was the (very) last to come. / ~에는 어떻게 되든 내 알 바 아니다 I don't care about the consequences. / ~(의 일)은 내게 맡겨라 You can leave the rest to me (now). / 그 진상은 ~에야 밝혀졌다 The truth was revealed later. / ~에 찾아뵈도 괜찮겠습니까 May I call on you later? / 위스키와 맥주 중 어느 것을 마시겠냐고 하면, 나는 ~ 것을 택하겠다 If offered whisky or beer, I'd choose the latter. / 그 일에 관해서는 ~에 자세히 이야기 하겠다 I'm going to tell you about it in detail later. / 그는 ~ 일은 생각할 줄 모른다 He is not a man to think about the future. / 누가 맨 ~에 사무실을 나왔지? Who was the last to leave the office? / ~에 전화할께 I'll call 〔phone〕 you later (on). / 그것은 ~으로 미룹시다 Let's put it off till some other time. / ~에 가겠다 I'll come later (on). / ~에 뵙겠습니다 《I will》 See you later. *or* I'll be with you later. / 너는 ~에 가서 후회할 게다 You will repent for it later 〔in future〕. / ~에는 별소리를 다 듣겠다 I never expected to hear such nonsense from you. / ~에야 될 대로 되라지 I don't give a damn what becomes of it! *or* After me the deluge! / 「지금 지불해야 합니까」—「~에 내셔도 됩니다」 "Should I pay you now?"—"Later will be all right." / ~난 뿔이 우뚝하다 《속담》 The person who was behind (unexpectedly) overtook the one ahead. *or* The younger generation is better prepared.

**나지리 보다** look down (up)on 《*a person*》; despise. ⇨경멸, 멸시. ¶ 사람을 그리 나지리 보지 마라 Don't look down upon people so.

**나지막이** somewhat 〔rather〕 low; somewhat 〔rather〕 soft. ⇨나직이.

**나지막하다** 《사물의 위치·높이 등이》 (be) lowish; low; somewhat 〔rather〕 low; 《목소리 따위가》 (be) low; low-pitched 〔=toned〕; somewhat 〔rather〕 soft. ¶ 나지막한 목소리로 in a low 〔soft, subdued〕 voice; in an undertone; in whispers; under *one's* breath; in a low key (저음으로) / 나지막한 집 a low-built house.

**나직이** (somewhat) low. ¶ (…을) ~ 하다 lower; bring 《*a thing*》 down; drop (목소리를) / 집을 ~ 짓다 build a house low / ~ 노래하다 sing softly; sing in a low voice / ~ 말하다 speak in a low 〔subdued〕 voice; speak low; speak in whispers / 비구름이 ~ 깔려있다 Rain clouds are hanging low in the sky. / TV 소리를 좀 ~ 해라 Turn down the TV, please.

**나직하다** 《위치·높이가》 (be) low; 《목소리가》 (be) low; soft; be in an undertone. ¶ 나직한 산 a low hill / 나직한 목소리 《speak in》 a low 〔soft〕 voice; an undertone / 가뭄으로 강의 수위가 ~ The river is low because of the drought. / 이 방은 천장이 ~ This room has a low ceiling.

**나체**(裸體) a naked body; a nude (미술품 등); nakedness; nudity. ¶ ~의 naked; nude / ~가 되다 take off *one's* clothes; undress *oneself;* become naked / ~로 만들다 undress 《*a person*》; strip 《*a person*》「naked 〔of *his* clothes〕/ ~로 포즈를 취하다 pose 「nude 〔in the nude〕/ ~로 수영하다 swim in the nude / 나는 그녀의 ~ 사진을 찍었다 I photographed her in the nude. / 화재가 났을 때 그녀는 완전한 ~였다 She had nothing on when the fire started.

◉ ~미 the beauty of the nude. ~미인 a nude beauty. ~상 a nude statue 〔figure〕. ~주의 nudism. ~주의자 a nudist: ~주의자 부락 a nudist colony 〔camp〕. ~행렬 a nude parade. ~화 a nude (picture): ~화를 그리다 paint 《a woman》 in the nude. 반~ seminudity. 완전~ a stark naked body; complete nudity; starknakedness.

**나치(스)** 《개인》 a Nazi; Nazis [총칭]. ¶ ~의 Nazi. ◉ ~당원 a Nazi (party member). ~화 Nazification: ~화하다 Nazify. 나치즘 Nazism.

**나침**(羅針) a compass needle. ◉ ~반 a (mariner's) compass: 항공 ~반 an aero compass / 삼각 ~반 a triangular compass / 회전 ~반 a gyrocompass. ~방위 a compass bearing.

**나타나다** ① 《눈에 보이다》 appear; present 〔show〕 *oneself;* turn 〔show〕 up; emerge; make *one's* appearance; 《시야에 들어오다》 come 「in sight 〔into view〕; 《모습이 나오다》 come out. ¶ 불쑥 ~ make an abrupt appearance / 그는 파티에 늦게 나타났다 He 「turned up 〔appeared, showed up〕 late for the party. / 달이 구름 사이에서 나타났다 The moon came out from behind the clouds. / 그는 곧 나타날거야 He'll show up soon. / 그녀는 약속 시간에 나타나지 않았다 She did not show 〔turn〕 up at the appointed time. / 수평선 상에 섬이 어렴풋이 나타났다 An island came in sight faintly on the horizon. / 다음에는 언제 핼리 혜성이 나타나지 When will Halley's comet 「appear 〔come around〕 next time? / 말세에는 영웅이 나타난다 Turbulent ages produce heroes. / 때마침 경관이 현장에 나타났다 A policeman made a timely appearance on the scene. / 안개 속에서 갑자기 배가 나타났다 A boat suddenly appeared out of the mist. *or* A boat 「burst 〔suddenly came〕 into view through the mist.

② 《겉으로 드러나다》 show 〔display, assert〕 *itself;* be expressed 〔described〕; be revealed 〔exposed〕. ¶ 그 정경이 글에 잘 나타나 있다 The scene was well written (up). / 그 행동에 그의 성격이 잘 나타나 있다 What he did shows the sort of person he is. / 그녀의 얼굴에는 피로한 기색이 나타나 있었다 Fatigue was written on her face. / 현대 생활의 갖가지 스트레스는 몸의 병으로 나타난다 The various stresses of modern life find their expression in physical illness. / 그의 얼굴에 고민의 빛이 나타나 있다 Agony shows itself in his face. / 술을 마시면 그 사람의 본성이 나타난다 One's true self is revealed when he drinks. *or* Liquor reveals one's true self.

③ 《발견되다》 be found (out); be discovered. ¶ 범행의 결정적 증거가 될 흉기가 아직 나타나지 않았다 They still have not discovered the weapon which would be decisive evidence for the crime. / 잃었던 물건이 ~ a lost article turns up.

④ 《효과 등이》 have an effect 《on》; 《사실 등이》 come to light; take 〔produce〕 effect; work. ¶ 효과가 즉각 ~ have an instant 〔immediate〕 effect 《on》 / 약효가 곧 나타났다 The medicine worked almost at once. *or* The medicine quickly took effect. / 몇 가지 사실들이 나타났다 A few facts have 「come 〔been brought〕 to light.

⑤ 《기재되다》 be mentioned 〔recorded, shown〕; appear. ¶ 미국 문헌에 나타난 한국 Korea mentioned in American literature / 그 작은 산촌은 지도에 나타나 있지 않다 The little mountain village is not shown on the map.

**나타내다** ① 《모습을》 appear; show 〔turn〕 up. ⇨ 나타나다; 《감정·성격 따위를》 show; display; indicate; manifest; 《숨겨진·가려진 것 등을》 betray; expose; reveal; disclose; 《증명하다》 prove. ¶ 불쑥 모습을 ~ appear 〔show up〕 unexpectedly / 감정을 ~ manifest *one's* feeling (의식해서); betray *one's* feeling (무의식으로) / 노여움을 ~ show 〔betray〕 *one's* anger / 자기의 무지를 ~ expose *one's* ignorance / 정체를 ~ show *one's* true nature 〔colors〕; betray *oneself* / 이 사건은 그의 어리석음을 나타낸다 This incident proves his stupidity. / 그는 그 회의에 모습을 나타내지 않았다 He didn't turn up at the meeting. / 그녀의 태도는 불만을 나타내고 있다 Her attitude shows her dissatisfaction.

② 《두각·재능 따위를》 distinguish *oneself;* cut 〔make〕 a conspicuous 〔brilliant〕 figure 《in》; show 〔display〕 《*one's* ability》; give full play to 《*one's* talent》. ¶ 음악에서 그녀는 단연 두각을 나타냈다 She distinguished herself in music. / 그는 학계에서 두각을 나타낼 것이다 He will cut a conspicuous figure in the scholary world. / 그런 일이라면 그도 그의 재능을 충분히 나타낼 수 있을 것이다 In that work, he will be able to show his ability. / 그는 냉정과 용감성으로 유능한 지휘관으로서의 두각을 나타냈다 He distinguished himself as an able commander by his coolness and bravery.

③ 《표현하다》 express; give expression 《to》; show; describe (묘사). ¶ 말로 나타낼 수 없는 만족감 an inexpressible 〔undescribable〕 sense of satisfaction; a sense of satisfaction beyond expression 〔description〕 / 생각을 말로 ~ put *one's* thoughts into words; express *one's* thoughts in words / 나는 내 기분을 말로 잘 나타낼 수 없었다 I could not express my feelings in words. / 그 일몰은 필설로 나타낼 수 없을 정도로 아름다웠다 The beauty of sunset was beyond all description. / 그는 감정을 겉으로 나타내지 않는다 He does not show his emotions. / 그는 그의 깊은 슬픔을 이 그림에서 나타내고 있다 In this painting he expresses his deep sorrow.

④ 《의미·상징하다》 represent; stand for; symbolize. ¶ 기호로 ~ represent by signs / 이 그림은 무엇을 나타내느냐 What does this picture represent? /

비둘기는 평화를 나타낸다 The dove symbolizes peace. / 노랑은 사랑과 평화를 나타낸다 Yellow symbolizes love and peace. / 이 머리글자는 무엇을 나타냅니까 What do these initials stand for?

**나태**(懶怠) laziness; sloth; idleness; indolence. ～하다 (be) lazy; slothful; idle; indolent.

> (용법) **lazy** 부지런히 일하는 것을 싫어한다는 뜻으로, 비난의 뜻이 내포되어 있는 말. **slothful** 「태만·게으름을 피우는」이란 뜻의 문어적인 말. **idle** 활동·일을 하지 않고 있는 상태를 뜻하는 말로, 비난의 뜻이 내포되지 않는 경우도 많음. **indolent** 힘들여 일하는 것을 싫어하는, 게으른 성질을 뜻하는 말.

¶ ～한 사람 a lazy 〔an idle〕 man; an idler; a sluggard / ～한 생활 《lead》 a lazy 〔an idle〕 life. ◉ ～벽(癖) 《form》 an idle 〔indolent〕 habit. ～심 a lazy mind; a disinclination to work.

**나토** 《북대서양 조약기구》 (the) NATO [néitou]. [<*N*orth *A*tlantic *T*reaty *O*rganization]

**나트륨** 〖화학〗 sodium; natrium (기호 Na) (★ 영·미에서는 현재 sodium이 일반적).

**나팔**(喇叭) a trumpet (관악기); a bugle (군대용). ¶ ～ 소리 a trumpet call; a bugle note / ～ 모양의 trumpet-shaped / ～을 불다 blow 〔sound〕 a bugle 〔trumpet〕 / 진군〔돌격, 퇴각〕 ～을 불다 sound the advance 〔charge, retreat〕 / ～ 소리가 울려퍼졌다 A bugle call rang out. *or* A bugle was sounded.
◉ ～관 〖해부〗 the Fallopian tubes; the oviduct: ～관염 〖의학〗 salpingitis / ～관 폐쇄 a blockage in a Fallopian tube. ～꽃 a morning glory. ～바지 sailor pants; bell-bottom trousers. ～벌레 〖동물〗 a stentor; a kind of trumpet-shaped ciliate. ～수 a bugler; a trumpeter; a trumpet player.

**나팔거리다** flutter. ⇨ 너풀거리다.

**나팔불다**(喇叭―) 《나팔을》 blow 〔sound〕 a bugle 〔trumpet〕; 《술 따위를》 drink 《beer》 (straight) from the bottle; take a swig; 《허풍떨다》 brag; talk big; boast; 《말을 퍼뜨리다》 make 《*a matter*》 known; spread 《the news》; set 《a rumor》 afloat. ¶ 그녀는 김 씨가 도둑이라고 나팔불고 다녔다 She was telling everybody that Mr. Kim was a thief.

**나포**(拿捕) capture; seizure. ～하다 capture; seize; make a prize of 《a fishing boat》. ¶ 3척의 어선이 외국 경비선에 ～되었다 Three fishing boats were captured 〔seized〕 by a foreign (coastal) patrol boat. ◉ ～선박 a captured ship; a prize. 불법～ illegal seizure.

**나폴레옹** Napoleon. ◉ ～법전 the Napoleonic Code. ～1세 Napoleon I, Bonaparte (1769-1821). ～전쟁 《서양사》 the Napoleonic wars.

**나풀거리다** flutter lightly; flap gently.

**나풀거리다** flutter 〔flap〕 roughly.

**나프타**[1] 〖화학〗 naphtha.

**나프타**[2] 《북미 자유 무역 협정》 (the) NAFTA. [<the *N*orth *A*merican *F*ree *T*rade *A*greement]

**나프탈렌** 〖화학〗 naphthalene.

**나한**(羅漢) 〖불교〗 a disciple of Buddha. ¶ 5백 ～ the five hundred Buddha's disciples who attained Nirvana / ～에도 모래 먹는 나한이 있다 《속담》 High position is no guarantee against hardship.

**나화**(裸花) 〖식물〗 《무피화》 an achlamydeous flower.

**나흗날** the fourth day of the month.

**나흘** 《4일간》 four days; 《나흗날》 the fourth day of the month.

**낙**(樂) 《즐거움》 pleasure; joy; delight; enjoyment; 《오락》 (an) amusement; a diversion (기분전환의); 《위안》 comfort; 《취미》 a hobby; 《기대》 hope. ¶ 인생의 낙 the joy 〔pleasure, enjoyment〕 of life / 노후의 낙 pleasures 〔enjoyments, delights〕 of *one's* old age / 낙 없는 사람 a man of few pleasures / 낙이 많은 사람 a person who has a lot of things to enjoy / 낙으로 …하다 《write》 for pleasure; 《travel》 by way of amusement; 《play chess》 as a hobby 〔pastime〕 / …을 낙으로 삼고 기다리다 look forward to 《*do*ing》 with pleasure; wait in anticipation of… / …을 낙으로 삼다 delight in 《dancing》; take pleasure 〔delight〕 in 《fishing》 / 그에게는 음악을 듣는 것이 큰 낙이다 Listening to music is a great pleasure to him. / 독서하는 것 외에 그에겐 낙이 별로 없었다 Besides reading, there were very few things in which he took pleasure. *or* He had few diversions apart from reading. / 조부께서는 정원 가꾸기를 낙으로 삼고 계시다 My grandfather takes pleasure in 〔enjoys〕 gardening. / 저 사람은 무슨 낙으로 살아갈까 What does he live for, I wonder? / 애들 자라는 것을 보는 것이 그의 유일한 낙이다 His sole pleasure is to see his children growing up.

**낙과**(落果) the falling of fruits; fallen fruit (떨어진 과실). ～하다 a fruit falls.

**낙관**(落款) a writer's 〔painter's〕 signature and seal. ～하다 sign and seal; affix *one's* signature and seal. ¶ ～이 없는 그림 an unsigned painting / 이 그림에는 유명한 화가의 ～이 있다 This picture bears the signature of a famous painter.

**낙관**(樂觀) optimism; an optimistic 〔a rosy, a hopeful〕 view. ～하다 take an optimistic view 《of 》; be optimistic 《about the future》; assume an optimistic attitude 《toward》; look on the bright 〔sunny〕 side of things; take things easily. ¶ ～을 불허하다 be far from reassuring; do not warrant any optimism; give no grounds for optimism / (성공을) 너무 ～하지 마라 Don't paint too rosy a picture of things. *or* Don't be too sure of success. / 사태는 아직 ～을 불허한다 The situation is still too serious for comfort. / 너무 ～하면 나중에 후회하게 될지도 모른다 If you are too optimistic, you may regret it later. ◉ ～론〔주의〕 optimism: ～론자〔주의자〕 an optimist.

**낙관적**(樂觀的) (be) optimistic; rosy; hopeful; sanguine. ¶ ～인 생각 an optimistic idea / ～으로 생각하다 see things in a rosy light; take a rosy-colored view of things / 지나치게 ～이다 be too optimistic; paint too rosy a picture of things / 그는 취직에 대하여 ～이었다 He was optimistic about his chances of getting a job. / ～인 분위기가 강했다 Optimism was high.

**낙길**(落—) a missing 〔lacking〕 volume.

**낙농**(酪農) dairy farming. ¶ 그는 ～에 종사하고 있다 He runs a dairy farm. *or* He is engaged in dairy farming. ◉ ～가 a dairy farmer; a dairyman. ～가공 합작공장 a dairy processing joint venture plant. ～업 dairy farming. ～장 a dairy farm. ～제품 dairy products.

**낙담**(落膽) 《실의》 discouragement; disappointment; despondency. ～하다 be discouraged; be disappointed; get disheartened 〔downhearted〕; lose heart 〔courage〕. ¶ ～시키다 discourage; dishearten; disappoint / 그녀는 그 소식을 듣고 크게 ～했다 She was very 〔greatly〕 disappointed at the news. / 그 실패는 그를 ～케 했다 The failure discouraged him. *or* He was discouraged by the failure.

**낙도**(落島) a remote 〔distant〕 island; an isolated island; an out-island. ◉ ～주민 remote-islanders.

**낙락장송**(落落長松) a pine tree with trailing branches; a tall and exuberant pine tree.

**낙뢰**(落雷) the falling of a thunderbolt. ～하다 a thunderbolt falls; lightning strikes; [장소 등이 주어] be struck by lightning. ¶ ～로 인한 피해 lightning damage / 그는 ～에 맞아 죽었다 The lightning struck him dead.

**낙루하다**(落淚—) [사람이 주어] shed 〔drop〕 tears; weep. ¶ 그 이야기를 듣고 그는 슬픔에 겨워 낙루했다 Hearing the story he shed tears of sorrow.

**낙마**(落馬) a fall from *one's* horse. ～하다 fall 〔be thrown〕 off *one's* horse; have a fall from *one's* horse. ¶ 그는 경마 중에 ～하였다 He fell 〔was thrown〕 off his horse in the race.

**낙망**(落望) disappointment. ⇨ 낙담, 실망. ¶ ～하지 마라 Don't be discouraged. *or* Keep your heart up!

**낙반**(落磐) a cave-in; a roof-fall. ¶ 광산에서 ～이 일어나 광부 2명이 다쳤다 The mine roof caved in and two miners were injured. ◉ ～사고 a roof-fall 〔cave-in〕 accident.

**낙방**(落榜) failure in an examination. ～하다 fail 《an examination》; 《미구어》 flunk 《an exam》; be 〔get〕 flunked. ¶ ～시키다 fail 〔flunk〕 《a student》 / 그는 화학 시험에 ～했다 He failed 〔flunked〕 chemistry. / 그는 판매원으로는 ～이다 He's「a failure 〔getting nowhere〕 as a salesman. ◉ ～생 a failed 〔flunked 《미》〕 student; a failure.

**낙법**(落法) 《유도 등에서》 a defensive fall; a break-fall. ¶ 전방〔후방〕 ～ the「forward rolling 〔backward〕 break-fall.

**낙산**(酪酸) 〖화학〗 butyric acid. ◉ ～염「butyrate.

**낙상**(落傷) a hurt 〔an injury〕 from a fall. ～하다 get hurt from a fall; fall and hurt *oneself.* ¶ 항우(項羽)도 ～할 적이 있다 《속담》 The best horse sometimes stumbles.

**낙서**(落書) 《장난으로 씀》 a scribble; scribbling; a scrawl; a doodle; doodling; graffiti (특히 공공 장소의). ～하다 do 〔write〕 graffiti 《on the wall》; scribble 《on the door》; doodle 《in *one's* notebook》. ¶ 벽의 ～를 지우다 clean the graffiti off the wall / 정거장의 벽에는 ～투성이었다 The station wall was covered with graffiti. / ～ 금지

《게시》 No Graffiti. *or* No scribbling.

**낙석**(落石) 《암석》 a falling 〔fallen〕 rock; 《사고》 a fall of rocks; a rockslide. ¶ ～으로 그 도로가 봉쇄됐다 A fall of rocks blocked the road. / 위험: ～ 주의 《게시》 Danger: falling rocks. *or* Watch (out) for falling rock(s).
◉ ～사고 a rockslide accident.

**낙선**(落選) 《선거의》 defeat 〔failure〕 in an election; 《응모 작품 등의》 rejection. ～하다 《선거에서》 lose 〔fail in〕 an election; be defeated in an election; 《출품 등에서》 be rejected. ¶ 3표차로 ～하다 miss winning the election by three votes / 그는 총선에서 ～했다 He was defeated 〔unsuccessful〕 in the general election. / 당 간부는 모조리 ～했다 All the officers of the party failed to get elected. / 그가 출품한 유화는 ～되었다 His oil painting was 「rejected 〔not accepted〕. / 현상 소설에 응모했으나 ～되었다 I entered for the prize novel contest, but failed to win anything.
◉ ～자 an unsuccessful candidate. ～작 a rejected 〔an unaccepted〕 work.

**낙성**(落成) completion. ⇨ 준공. ～하다 be completed 〔finished〕. ¶ 도서관 ～축하회 a ceremony to celebrate the completion of a library / 새 체육관이 ～되었다 The new gymnasium has been completed 〔finished〕. ◉ ～식 a completion 〔an inauguration〕 ceremony: 새 사옥의 ～식이 월요일에 있었다 The completion of the new office building was celebrated on Monday.

**낙성**(落城) the fall of a castle. ～하다 the castle falls 《to the enemy》.

**낙숫물**(落水—) raindrops from the eaves; eavesdrips. ¶ ～ 홈통 a gutter (가로의); 《세로의》 a downspout 《미》; a downpipe 《영》 / ～이 떨어지고 있다 Rain is dripping from the eaves.
◉ ～ 소리 pattering of eavesdrips.

**낙승**(樂勝) an easy victory 〔win〕; 《구어》 a walkaway; a walkover. ～하다 gain 〔win〕 an easy victory 《over》; win 《a game》 hands down. ¶ 우리 팀은 B팀에 ～했다 Our team won an easy victory over B team. / 이번 선거에서는 K씨가 P씨에게 ～하리라고 본다 I'm sure Mr. K will beat Mr. P easily in the election that's coming up.

**낙심**(落心) disappointment; discouragement; loss of heart. ⇨ 낙담, 실망. ¶ ～ 천만이다 be much disappointed 〔discouraged〕 / 여보게 ～ 말게 Don't lose your heart, old fellow! / 우리 계획이 실패했다는 말을 듣고 ～했다 My spirits sank when I heard of the failure of our plan.

**낙양**(落陽) the setting sun.

**낙엽**(落葉) 《떨어진 잎》 fallen 〔dead〕 leaves; 《떨어짐》 the falling of leaves. ¶ ～이 지다 《the trees》 cast 〔shed〕 《their》 leaves; 《leaves》 fall / ～을 긁어모으다 rake up fallen leaves / ～을 밟으면서 산책했다 I took a walk over the fallen leaves. / 공원의 나무들은 모두 ～이 졌다 All the trees in the park have shed their leaves. *or* The leaves are gone from all the trees in the park. ◉ ～기 defoliation. ～색 russet; foliage brown. ～송 a larch. ～수 a deciduous tree.

**낙오**(落伍) 《대열에서의》 falling behind; dropping 〔falling〕 out of the ranks 〔line〕; straggling; 《시대·사회에서의》 being out of step with the times. ～하다 drop 〔fall〕 out; drop 〔fall, lag, be left〕 behind 《the others》; 《대열에서》 fall out of the ranks; straggle; be out of step with the times. ¶ 행군중에 ～되다 fall out while on the march / 그는 경쟁에서 ～했다 He dropped out of the competition.

**낙오자**(落伍者) a dropout; a straggler; a (social) failure (인생의). ¶ 인생의 ～가 되다 make a failure of *one's* life / 그 행군에서 많은 ～가 생겼다 Many soldiers dropped out during the march. / 그는 인생의 ～였다 He was a failure 〔loser〕 in life.

**낙원**(樂園) a paradise; Eden. ¶ 지상의 ～ an earthly paradise; heaven 〔a paradise〕 on earth / 어린이의 ～ a paradise for children / 그 섬은 새들의 ～이다 The island is a paradise for birds.

**낙인**(烙印) a brand; a stigma. ¶ ～을 찍다 put a brand 《on》; [비유적] brand 《*a person* as a liar》; stigmatize / ～이 찍히다 be branded 〔stigmatized〕 / 그는 사기꾼으로 ～이 찍혔다 He was branded as a swindler.

**낙일**(落日) the setting 〔declining〕 sun; 「sunset.

**낙자**(落字) a missing word; an omission.

**낙장**(落張) 《제본에서》 a missing page 「〔leaf〕.

**낙장거리** 《벌떡 자빠짐》 falling flat 〔outstretched〕 on *one's* back. ～하다 fall 〔be thrown〕 flat 〔outstretched〕 on *one's* back; fall backward.

**낙제**(落第) failure (in an examination); rejection. ⇨ 낙방, 유급(留級). ～하다 fail 《an examination》; 《미》 flunk 《an exam》; 《영구어》 be 〔get〕 ploughed; 《유급》 repeat the same class; 《검사에서》 be rejected. ¶ ~시키다 fail 〔flunk〕 《a student》 / 두 과목에 ~하다 fail 〔flunk〕 two sub-jects / 거의 전학급 학생이 대수에서 ~했다 Nearly the whole class flunked 〔fizzled〕 in algebra. / 그는 뛰어난 학자이긴 하지만 남편으로서는 ~다 Although he's a good scholar, he's a failure as a husband.

◉ ~생 a failure; a failed 〔plucked 《영》〕 student; 《미》 a repeater (유급생). ~점 a failing mark 〔grade〕.

**낙조**(落照) the glow of the setting sun; the setting 〔declining〕 sun.

**낙지** 『동물』 an octopus. ◉ ~볶음 pan-broiled octopus (seasoned with red pepper).

**낙진**(落塵) (nuclear) fallout; the fall of ash 〔dust〕; the lethal ash 〔dust〕 (죽음의 재). ◉ 방사성~ (radioactive) fallout; a silent killer 《구어》.

**낙차**(落差) 『물리』 a head; the difference in elevation 《between》; 《차이》 (a) difference; a gap. ¶ ~ 20피트의 물, 20-feet head of water / 이 폭포의 ~는 50미터이다 This waterfall is 50 meters high. ◉ 수압~ a pressure head. 유효~ an effective head.

**낙착**(落着) 《결말》 a settlement. ~하다, 되다 be (finally) settled; reach 〔come to〕 a (final) settlement. ¶ 그 사건은 예정대로 잘 ~되었다 The incident was brought to a happy end as scheduled 〔planned〕. *or* The case was settled satisfactorily as scheduled 〔planned〕.

**낙찰**(落札) a successful bid. ~하다 *one's* tender 《for the construction》 is accepted 〔successful〕; [사람이 주어] make a successful bid 《for》; [사물이 주어] be knocked down to 《*a person*》; 《주어지다》 be awarded 《to》. ¶ 그 그림은 나에게 ~되었다 The picture was knocked down to me. / 그 공사는 그에게 ~되었다 The construction was awarded to him. / 교량 건설 공사는 우리 회사가 ~했다 Our company won the contract for building the bridge.

◉ ~가격 a highest 〔lowest〕 bid price; the contract price. ~물 an object knocked down. ~인〔자〕 a successful bidder.

**낙천**(樂天) optimism. ¶ ~적(인) optimistic; sanguine; cheerful; easygoing; hopeful / 그는 ~적인 인생관을 가지고 있다 He has an optimistic view of life. / 그는 만사에 ~적이다 He is optimistic about everything. *or* He takes things easy. ◉ ~가 an optimist. ~주의 optimism: ~주의자 an optimist.

**낙천**(落薦) a failure in an application 《for nomination》. ~하다 fail in *one's* application 《for nomination》. ◉ ~자 an unsuccessful applicant 〔candidate〕; a person who failed in his application 《for nomination》.

**낙타**(駱駝) 『동물』 a camel. ¶ 단봉〔쌍봉〕 ~ an Arabian 〔a Bactrian, two-humped〕 camel / ~의 털 camel('s) hair / ~의 혹 a (camel's) hump.

**낙태**(落胎) 『의학』 (an) abortion; aborticide. ~하다 abort; have an abortion; commit feticide. ¶ ~시키다 cause 〔induce〕 abortion.

◉ ~수술 a surgical abortion: ~ 수술을 하다 perform a criminal operation 《on》. ~아 an abortive offspring. ~약 an abortive drug 〔medicine〕; an aborticide. ~죄 criminal 〔illegal〕 abortion; aborticide; feticide. 인공~ an induced 〔artificial〕 abortion.

**낙토**(樂土) (a) paradise; Heaven.

**낙하**(落下) a fall; falling. ~하다 fall; come down; drop; descend. ¶ ~의 법칙 the law of falling / 운석의 ~ the fall of a meteorite (on the earth) / 수직으로 ~하다 fall plumb down / 큰 바위가 선로상에 ~했다 A big rock fell 〔dropped〕 on the rail. ◉ ~지점 《미사일 등의》 an impact point. 나선~ a spiral; a corkscrew descent.

**낙하산**(落下傘) a parachute; a chute. ¶ ~으로 내리다 parachute (down); descend by parachute; come down in a parachute; bail out (비상 탈출) / ~을 펴다 release the chute / ~으로 뛰어내리려면 용기가 필요하다 You need courage to make a parachute jump. / 우리는 추락하는 비행기에서 ~으로 탈출했다 We bailed out of the falling plane.

◉ ~병 a parachutist; a paratrooper. ~부대 a parachute troop 〔unit〕; paratroopers. ~식 융자 [비유적] a loan given 〔made〕 through political influence. ~식 인사 [비유적] high-handed personnel administration. ~투하 a paradrop; an airdrop. 보조~ a pilot 〔an auxiliary〕 parachute.

**낙향**(落鄕) rustication. ~하다 rusticate; move to 〔retire into〕 the country; go into the provinces. ¶ 그는 서울을 떠나 시골로 ~했다 He left Seoul to retire into the country.

**낙형**(烙刑) branding《a criminal》 as punishment.

**낙화**(落花)《꽃이 짐》the falling of blossoms〔flowers〕;《꽃》fallen〔falling〕blossoms. ～하다 flowers〔blossoms〕fall〔scatter〕. ¶～유수 fallen blossoms on running water / ～ 유수의 정 [비유적] mutual love〔attachment〕between man and woman / ～난상지(難上枝) What is done cannot be undone.

**낙화**(烙畫) a poker engraving; poker work; pyrography.

**낙후**(落後) falling behind. ～하다 drop〔fall〕out; fall〔drop, lag, be left〕behind《the others》; be in arrear《of the times》. ¶～된 lagging behind; backward《country》/ 그 나라는 문화가 ～되어 있다 The country is backward in civilization.

**낚다** ①《고기를》fish《trout》; angle for《fish》; catch《a fish》. ¶배를 타고 고기를 ～ fish from a boat / 지렁이 미끼로 고기를 ～ fish with the bait of an earthworm / 나는 대어를 낚았다 I have hooked a big fish. / 이 강은 고기가 잘 낚인다 The fishing is good in this river. *or* The fish bite well in this river. ②《이성을 꾀다》lure; entice; take in; attract; tempt. ¶여자를 ～ entice a woman / 그녀의 달콤한 말에 낚이다 be lured by her honeyed word / 그녀는 사내를 잘 낚는다 She has a way of drawing men to her.
③《이름을》¶돈으로 명예를 ～ angle for fame by money.

**낚시**《낚싯바늘》a (fish)hook;《낚시질》fishing; angling. ¶강〔바다〕～ river〔sea〕fishing / 밤～ night fishing / 둔치～ rock fishing / (해안에서) 던질～ surf fishing / ～하러 가다 go fishing〔angling〕《in a river》/ 하루 ～를 즐기다 have〔enjoy〕a good day's fishing / ～를 드리우다 drop〔cast〕a line《in》/ ～에 미끼를 달다 bait a hook; put a bait on a fishhook / 물고기가 ～를 물다 a fish bites / 물고기가 ～에 걸렸다 A fish is hooked. / 그는 ～ 도사다 He is a good〔an expert〕angler. / 이 강은 ～하기에 아주 좋은 곳이다 This river has〔provides, affords〕good fishing.
◉ ～꾼 a fisherman; an angler. ～도구 fishing tackle〔gear〕. ～찌 a float; a cork; a bob; a quill: ～찌가 까딱거리고 있다 A float is bobbing up and down. ～친구 a fishing companion; a fellow-angler. ～터 a fishing place〔spot〕. ～회 a fishing〔an angling, an angler's〕club. 낚싯거루 a fishing boat〔skiff〕. 낚싯대 a fishing〔an angling〕rod. 낚싯바구니 an angler's basket; a creel. 낚싯바늘 a fishhook. 낚싯밥 a bait: 낚싯바늘에 낚싯밥을 달다 fix a bait on the hook. 낚싯배 a fisherman's〔an angler's〕boat. 낚싯봉 a sink(er); a bullet; a plumb; a weight: 낚싯줄에 낚싯봉을 달다 weigh a line. 낚싯줄 a (fishing) line; a fishline.

**낚아채다**《잡아채다》snatch (away)《from, off》; wrest《from》; tear (off, away)《*a thing*》from《*a person*》. ¶그는 내게서 편지를 낚아챘다 He snatched the letter (away) from me.

**난**(亂)《전란》a war;《반란》a rebellion; a revolt; an insurrection; a riot. ¶난을 일으키다 raise a war; start a rebellion; rise in revolt / 난을 평정하다 suppress a rebellion; quell a revolt.

**난**(難) ① [접미어]《곤란》hardship; difficulty; trouble;《부족》shortage. ¶교통난 traffic congestion jam / 식량난 a shortage of food / 주택난 a housing shortage / 취업난 (a) job shortage. ② [접두어] difficult; hard; tough; troublesome. ¶난문제 a difficult〔tough, hard〕problem / 난이도(難易度) the degree of difficulty.

**난**(蘭) ⇨ 난초. ◉ 동양난 an Oriental orchid: 동양난 재배가 an orchidist.

**난**(欄)《신문 따위의》a column; a section; a page;《기입란》a blank; a column;《여백》a space. ＝란. ¶스포츠난 the sports column〔page, section〕/ 난에 기입하다 fill up the blank on the sheet〔page〕/ 이 난에는 기입하지 말 것 Do not write in this space.

**난간**(欄干) a railing; a handrail; a guardrail. a parapet《발코니·교량 따위의》; a balustrade; a banister. ¶다리 ～ a bridge railing / ～에 기대다 lean over〔upon〕the balustrade / ～을 만들다 provide with a railing.

**난감하다**(難堪—)《견디기 어렵다》(be) unbearable; intolerable; be hard to stand〔bear〕;《힘겹다》be unable to cope with; be beyond *one's* capacity〔power〕;《당혹하다》be quite at a loss; be greatly perplexed; be in a bad〔pretty〕fix; be at *one's* wits' end. ¶IMF시대에 살아나갈 일이 ～ It is intolerable to live through an IMF era. / 이 과업은 내게 난감한 일이다 This task is beyond my capacity. *or* I'm not equal to this task. / 무어라고 대답

을 해야 할 지 매우 난감했다 I was completely「at a loss〔lost〕for a suitable answer.

**난거지 든부자**(一富者) a person who puts up a front of poverty but is really rich.

**난경**(難境) a predicament; a difficult situation; adverse circumstances; a fix《구어》. ¶ ~에 처하다 be in a fix; be in trouble〔difficulties〕/ ~에 빠지다 get into trouble / ~에서 벗어나다 get out of difficulty〔trouble〕.

**난공불락**(難攻不落) impregnability. ¶ ~의 요새 an impregnable fortress / 그 요새는 ~처럼 보였다 The fortress seemed impregnable. / 그녀는 ~이다 [비유적] It is impossible to win her heart.

**난공사**(難工事) a difficult construction〔building〕work. ¶ 많은 기술상의 어려움이 있는 ~ a hard construction work with great engineering difficulties.

**난관**(卵管)〖해부〗an oviduct; a fallopian tube. ◉ ~절제술 a salpingectomy. ~파열 (a) tubal rupture.

**난관**(難關)《장애》a〔an insurmountable〕barrier; an obstacle;《곤란》a difficulty;《난국》a difficult situation; a deadlock (교착). ¶~에 봉착하다 come to a deadlock (교섭 등에서); be faced with an obstacle; meet with a difficulty / ~을 극복하다〔돌파하다〕get over〔overcome, surmount〕a difficulty / 이 ~을 잘 넘기면 우리 일은 쉬워진다 Once over this obstacle, our work will be easier. / 양국의 교섭은 어획량 할당에서 ~에 부딪쳤다 The two countries reached a deadlock over the catch quota. / 인생길에는 넘어야 할 ~이 많다 You will have a lot of hurdles to get over in the course of your life.

**난국**(難局) a difficult〔grave〕situation〔position〕;《위기》a crisis;《곤란》a difficulty; difficulties (재정적인);《교착상태》a deadlock. ⇨ 난관.
¶~에 처해 있다 be in「a difficult situation〔a fix〕; find *oneself* in a fix〔tight place〕/ ~에 대처하다 deal〔cope〕with the difficult situation / ~을 극복하다〔타개하다〕get over the difficulty〔crisis〕; weather a storm / ~을 수습하다 save a difficult situation / 그는 어떤 ~에도 대처할 수 있는 사나이다 He knows how to cope with any difficult situation. / 우리는 어떤 ~에도 대처할 각오가 되어 있다 We are fully prepared to deal with any difficult situation. / 그들은 ~ 타개책을 찾고자 머리를 짰다 They cudgeled their brains to find a way out of the crisis. / 교섭은 지금 ~에 직면해 있다 The negotiations are now at a deadlock. / 그의 제안이 ~을 타개했다 His suggestion broke the deadlock.

**난군**(亂軍) a lawless〔disorderly〕army; rampaging troops.

**난기류**(亂氣流)〖기상〗(air) turbulence;「turbulent air.

**난다긴다하다**《뛰어나다》be better than《anybody else》; surpass《others in skill》; be excellent;《다재다능하다》be versatile;《민첩하다》be incomparably deft. ¶ 난다긴다하는 사람 a man of great ability〔talent〕; an expert.

**난대**(暖帶)〖지리〗the subtropical zone; the subtropics. ¶ ~성의 subtropical《plants, animals》. ◉ ~림 a subtropical forest.

**난데없다**《뜻밖이다》(be) unexpected; unforeseen; unlooked-for;《갑작스럽다》sudden; abrupt; be (a bolt) out of the blue;《엉뚱하다》(be) unusual; wild; extravagant; unreasonable. ¶ 난데없는 생각 a wild idea / 난데없는 요구 an extravagant demand / 난데없는 방문객 an unexpected visitor / 난데없이 unexpectedly; suddenly / 난데없이 나타나다 make an abrupt appearance; appear「unexpectedly〔out of the blue〕/ 그의 난데없는 방문에 당황했다 I was puzzled by his unexpected〔surprise〕visit.

**난도질**(亂刀—) mangling; hacking; wild cuts〔stabs〕;《고기 따위의》mincing; chopping; hashing. ~하다 hack〔chop, cut〕《*a thing*》to pieces; mangle; mince; hash. ¶ ~을 당한 시체 a mangled body.

**난동**(暖冬) a warm〔mild〕winter. ¶ 이상~ an abnormally warm winter.

**난동**(亂動)《난폭한 행동》outrageous〔violent〕behavior;《소란》a disturbance; a commotion;《폭동》a riot; an uprising. ¶ ~을 부리다 make〔raise, cause〕a disturbance; stir up troubles; run〔raise a〕riot; do violence / ~을 진압하다 quiet〔suppress〕a disturbance; suppress〔put down〕a riot / 취객이 술집에서 ~을 부렸다 A drunk ran amuck in the bar.

**난딱**《손쉽게》easily; with ease; without any trouble〔difficulty〕; readily; lightly;《신속히》promptly; instantly; at once. ¶ 일을 ~ 해치우다 knock off the task《구어》/ 큰 돌을 ~ 들어올리다 lift up a huge rock easily / 그는 밥 한 그릇을 ~ 먹어 치웠다 He downed a bowl of rice just like that.

**난로**(煖爐) a stove; a heater; 《벽난로》 a fireplace. ¶ ～를 쬐다 warm *oneself* at a stove / ～를 피우다〔때다〕 make a fire in the stove; light a stove / 《전기·가스 따위의》 ～를 켜다〔끄다〕 turn on 〔off〕 a heater.

**난류**(暖流) a warm current.

**난류**(亂流) 〖물리〗 a turbulent flow; 〖기상〗 turbulence; turbulency.

**난리**(亂離) 《소동》 an uproar; a disturbance; commotion; 《전쟁》 a war; 《반란》 a revolt; a rebellion; a riot (폭동); an uprising (봉기); 《혼란》 confusion. ¶ ～가 나다 a war breaks out; have a war (전쟁이); have a disturbance 〔an uproar〕 (소란이) / ～를 일으키다 raise a war; start a rebellion; rise in revolt / ～를 가라앉히다 suppress a rebellion; put down a revolt / 물 ～가 나다 《홍수》 suffer from a flood; 《물기근》 suffer from water famine / 큰 ～가 났다 A serious riot broke out. / 그 소식을 듣고 온 집안에 ～가 났다 The news threw the whole house into utter confusion.

**난립**(亂立) ① 《무질서하게 들어섬》 ¶ 높은 빌딩이 ～해 있다 be crowded with every sort of tall building / 이 지역에는 주유소가 서로 경쟁하며 ～해 있다 There are too many gas stations competing with one another in this district. ② 《너무 많은 입후보자》 ¶ 후보자의 ～을 막다 check random candidacy / 그 선거구는 입후보자가 ～해 있다 The constituency is flooded with candidates.

**난마**(亂麻) 《삼》 tangled hemp fiber; [비유적] chaos; confusion; disorder; a mixup; a state of anarchy. ¶ ～와 같다 be in a chaotic state / 쾌도로 ～를 자르다 cut the Gordian knot; act decisively to solve a complicated problem / 그 나라의 정국은 ～처럼 얽혀 있다 The political situation of the country is chaotic.

**난막**(卵膜) 〖동물〗 an egg membrane.

**난만**(爛漫) glory (of flowers); being in full bloom. ～하다 be in splendor; be in full bloom. ¶ 백화가 ～하다 All sorts of flowers are at their best.

**난망**(難忘) unforgettable(ness). ¶ 당신의 은혜는 백골～입니다 I shall never forget 「your kindness 〔what you have done for me〕. *or* Your kindness will live in my memory for ever.

**난맥**(亂脈) confusion; disorder; chaos. ¶ ～에 빠지다 fall 〔be thrown〕 into disorder; be in a chaotic state / 정부의 경제 시책은 ～상을 드러내고 있다 The government's economic policy is in utter disorder.

**난무**(亂舞) 《춤》 a boisterous dance; 《날뜀》 prevailing (over); being rampant. ～하다 dance boisterously 〔wildly〕; prevail (over); be rampant. ¶ 폭력배가 ～하는 거리 a gangster-ridden street / 그 소식에 우리는 광희 ～했다 We danced wildly for joy at the news. / 이 도시에는 폭력이 ～하고 있다 Violence is rampant in this city.

**난문제**(難問題) a difficult 〔hard, tough, knotty〕 problem 〔question〕; a poser; 《구어》 a hard nut to crack. ¶ ～를 내다 put a hard question to 《*a person*》; set a poser for 《*a person*》 / ～를 풀다 solve 〔work out〕 a hard problem / ～와 씨름하다 tackle a tough problem / ～에 부닥치다 meet a hard problem / 처리해야 할 ～가 산적해 있다 There is a whole stack of difficult problems that we must deal with.

**난민**(亂民) riotous people; a mob; insurgents.

**난민**(難民) 《이재민》 sufferers; 《flood, war》 victims; 《빈민》 the destitute; 《피난민》 refugees; displaced persons (전쟁으로 조국에서 쫓겨난). ¶ 경제 ～ an economic refugee / 팔레스타인 ～ the displaced Palestinians / 전화(戰禍)를 피해 도망친 ～의 무리 a flood of refugees fleeing (from) the disasters of war. ◉ ～구제 refugee relief; the relief of the destitute 〔sufferers〕. ～구제법 《유엔의》 the Displaced Persons Act. ～수용소 a refugee camp. ～정착사업 a refugee resettlement project; a resettlement project for needy families. ～조약 the Convention Relating to the Status of Refugees. ～촌 a shanty quarter; a ghetto.

**난바다** the far-off sea; the offing; the open sea (공해). ¶ ～에 있는 섬 an off-lying island / 4마일 밖 ～에서 four miles off the shore / ～에 나가다 put out to the open sea.

**난반사**(亂反射) 〖물리〗 diffused reflection.

**난발**(亂發) ① 《총포의》 random 〔reckless〕 firing. ～하다 shoot 〔fire〕 at random. ② ＝남발(濫發).

**난발**(亂髮) disheveled 〔unkempt〕 hair.

**난방**(煖房) 《데움》 heating 《a room》; 《방》 a heated 〔warm〕 room. ¶ ～용 기름 heating oil / ～용 기구 a heating apparatus; a heater / 증기〔온풍〕 ～ steam 〔hot-air〕 heating / 온수 ～ hot

water heating / 중앙〔집중〕 ~ central heating / 지역 ~ district heating / ~으로 방은 곧 따뜻해졌다 The room was soon warmed up by the heater. / 이 건물은 ~이 되어 있지 않다 There is no heat in this building. / 우리는 ~용 석유 난로를 사용한다 We use oil heaters for heating. / 냉난방 완비 《게시》 All room (are) Air-Conditioned.
◉ ~비 heating expenses. ~장비〔시설〕 heating equipment 〔facilities〕. ~장치 a heating system 〔apparatus〕; a heater; a radiator (복사식의): ~ 장치를 하다 install a heater 《in a room》 / ~ 장치를 켜다〔끄다〕 turn heating 〔a heater〕 on 〔off〕. 한국 지역 ~ 공사 Korea District Heating Corporation (생략 KDHC).

**난백**(卵白) 〖동물〗 the white (of an egg).

**난번**(—番) 《비번》 off duty; the off(-duty) shift. ¶ ~이다 be off duty; be off.

**난봉** dissipation; prodigality; debauchery; fast living; a dissipated life. ¶ ~나다 take to fast living / ~부리다〔피우다〕 lead a dissipated life; indulge in 「dissipation 〔fast living〕 / ~으로 패가망신하다 be ruined by dissipation / 그는 젊었을 때 ~을 진탕 피웠다 He drained the cup of pleasure to the dregs when he was young. *or* He sowed his wildest oats.
◉ ~꾼 a libertine; a debauchee; a fast liver; a loose fish 《구어》.

**난부자 든거지**(—富者—) a person who puts up a front of wealth but is really poor.

**난비**(亂飛) ~하다 flutter 〔fly, flit〕 about; fly past each other.

**난사**(難事) a difficult thing 〔matter〕; a difficulty; a hard task; a tough job. ¶ ~중의 난사 the most difficult of all things; the hardest thing to do.

**난사**(亂射) random firing 〔shooting〕. ~하다 fire blindly; shoot at random. ¶ 적은 기관총을 ~했다 The enemy fired machine guns 「blindly 〔at random〕.

**난사람** an outstanding 〔a distinguished〕 person 〔figure〕; a person of extraordinary ability; a man of high caliber. ¶ 세계적으로 ~ a world figure; a person of world-wide fame.

**난산**(難産) ① 《분만의》 a hard 〔difficult〕 labor 〔delivery〕. ~하다 have a hard 〔difficult〕 labor; have a hard time in labor; be delivered of a child with difficulty. ¶ 그녀는 ~을 했다 She had a hard labor 〔difficult delivery〕.
② 《문제의》 ~하다 bring forth with difficulty. ¶ 새 내각의 구성은 ~이었다 The new cabinet was formed with much difficulty.

**난삽**(難澁) hardship(s); difficulties. ~하다 (be) troublesome; hard; difficult; toilsome. ¶ ~한 글 a difficult passage; an article hard to understand / ~한 문제 a problem that is fairly difficult to deal with.

**난색**(難色) 《비난·불찬성》 disapproval; 《내키지 않음》 unwillingness; reluctance. ¶ ~을 보이다 show 〔express〕 disapproval 《of》; be opposed 《to a plan》; hesitate 《to *do*》; jib at 《*do*ing》 / 그의 입각에 ~을 보이다 disapprove of his entry into the Cabinet / 그는 우리들의 제의에 ~을 보였다 He was reluctant to accept our offer. (★ 마지못해 받아들였음을 함축함).

**난생**(卵生) 〖생물〗 oviparity; oviparousness. ~하다 bear 《offspring》 by egg; be oviparous. ¶ 물고기는 ~이다 Fish are produced from eggs. ◉ ~동물 an oviparous animal.

**난생처음**(—生—) (for) the first time in *one's* life. ¶ ~ 당하는 일 an experience met for the first time in *one's* life / 그는 ~ 바다를 보았다 He saw the sea for the first time in his life.

**난생후**(—生後) after *one's* birth; (ever) since *one's* birth.

**난세**(亂世) troubled times; a turbulent period 〔age〕; a state of anarchy (무정부 상태). ¶ ~의 영웅 a hero in a turbulent age.

**난세포**(卵細胞) 〖생물〗 an ovum; an egg 「cell.

**난센스** nonsense. ¶ 그건 완전히 ~다 That's absolute nonsense. *or* That's utterly nonsensical !

**난소**(卵巢) 〖해부〗 the ovary; the ovarium (*pl.* -ria). ¶ ~의 ovarian.
◉ ~내 임신 ovarian pregnancy. ~선(腺) a nidamental gland. ~염 〖의학〗 ovaritis. ~적출 〖의학〗 removal of the ovary. ~절제술 ovariotomy. ~호르몬 ovarian hormones.

**난숙**(爛熟) 《과일의》 overripeness; 《사물의》 full development; full maturity. ~하다 get 〔be〕 overripe; be over=mature; be fully matured; attain full maturity. ¶ ~기(期) the age of matured culture / ~한 overripe; fully=matured; highly developed / ~기에 at the apex of 《Greek civilization》 / 그 소설은 그의 ~기에 집필된 것이다 The novel was written when his literary skill was at its full maturity. / 그 당시 한국은 문화의 ~기를 맞이했다 Korea's culture reached maturity then.

**난시**(亂視) 〖의학〗 astigmatism; distorted vision. ¶ ~의 astigmatic / ~인 사람 an astigmatic person / 그는 ~다 He is astigmatic. ◉ ~안 astigmatic eyes. ~용 안경 astigmatic glasses 〔lenses〕. ~측정 astigmometry. ~측정기 an astigmometer.

**난외**(欄外) the margin 《of a page》; 《신문의》 a marginal column. ¶ ~의 marginal / ~(의) 여백 marginal space / ~에 …을 써넣다 write… down in the margin / ~의 주석도 훑어 보았다 I also looked through the 「marginal notes 〔notes in the margin〕. / ~에는 기재하지 마시오 Please do not write in the margin. ◉ ~기사 stop-press news. ~표제〔제목〕 《사전의》 a catchword; 《일반 도서의》 a running title 〔head〕.

**난운**(亂雲) 〖기상〗 a nimbus (*pl.* -bi, ~es); a rain cloud.

**난이**(難易) (relative) difficulty; hardness or ease. ¶ 보수는 일의 ~에 달려 있다 The remuneration is according to the difficulty of the job. *or* The pay depends on how hard your job is. ◉ ~도 the degree of difficulty 《of the test》: 문제의 ~도를 비교하다 weigh the relative difficulty of the questions.

**난입**(亂入) intrusion. ~하다 intrude 〔rush〕 《into》; break 〔burst〕 into; force *one's* way into. ¶ 시위대는 앞을 다투어 회의장에 ~했다 Demonstrators struggled to rush into the hall. ◉ ~자 an intruder; a trespasser.

**난자**(卵子) an ovum (*pl.* ova); an egg cell; an ovule (식물의).

**난자**(亂刺) ruthless 〔wild〕 stabbing. ~하다 stab 《*a person*》 wildly. ¶ 단도로 ~하다 stab 《*a person*》 all over with a dagger.

**난자완스** 《중국요리》 beef balls in brown 「sauce.

**난잡**(亂雜) ① 《혼잡·무질서》 disorder; confusion; 《조촐하지 못함》 untidiness; disarray. ~하다 (be) disorderly; confused; untidy; be in confusion 〔disorder〕; be at sixes and sevens. ¶ ~한 옷차림 untidy dress / ~하게 마구 쌓아놓다 pile 《books》 up in a disorderly fashion / 이 방은 ~하기 짝이 없다 This room is in a terrible mess 〔clutter〕. ② 《언행의》 indecency; slovenliness; obscenity. ~하다 (be) indecent; obscene; lewd; loose; wanton. ¶ ~한 여자 a slut; a wanton hussy / 품행이 ~한 학생 a student loose in morals / 그 주간지에는 ~한 기사가 가득하다 The weekly magazine carries a lot of obscene 〔indecent〕 articles.

**난장판**(亂場―) a scene of confusion and disorder; a chaotic scene; a tumult; a turmoil; a mess. ¶ ~을 이루다〔이 되다〕 be thrown into confusion 〔disarray〕; be in a turmoil / 회의가 ~이 되었다 The meeting 「fell 〔was thrown〕 into disorder. / 그 소식으로 온 집안은 ~이 되었다 The news threw the whole house into the utter confusion. / 장내는 ~이었다 There was a great fuss in the hall.

**난쟁이** a midget; a pigmy; a dwarf (기형의).

**난전**(亂戰) confused fighting; a dogfight; a scuffle; a melee; 《거친 경기》 a confused game with a lot of points scored on both sides. ¶ 싸움은 서로가 뒤섞이는 ~이었다 The fight between the two sides was 「chaotic 〔confused〕. / 경기는 ~이었다 The game was rather a confused one.

**난점**(難點) 《어려운 점》 a 「difficult 〔knotty〕 point; a crux of a matter; a drawback (결점). ¶ 이 계획의 유일한 ~은 과다한 경비가 드는 것이다 The only drawback 〔knotty problem〕 to this project is that it will cost too much.

**난제**(難題) 《어려운 문제》 a difficult 〔knotty〕 subject 〔problem〕; a puzzling 〔baffling〕 question; a crux; 《무리한 제안》 unreasonable terms; an unjust 〔unfair〕 proposal. ¶ 우리는 풀어야 할 ~를 안고 있다 We have a difficult problem to solve. / 환경보호는 오늘날 해결해야 할 ~중의 하나다 Environmental protection is one of the most difficult problems to be settled 〔solved〕 nowadays.

**난조**(亂調) 《음악의》 discord; ragtime tune; 《혼란》 disorder; confusion; 《맥박의》 irregularity; 《주식 시세 등의》 violent fluctuations. ¶ ~를 보이다 《투수가》 lose control / ~를 이루다 be thrown into disorder 〔confusion〕; be out of tune / 주가가 ~를 보이고 있다 Stock prices are fluctuating violently.

**난중**(亂中) the midst of turmoil 〔commotion〕; time of war. ¶ ~에 during a war 〔revolt〕; in the midst of turmoil. ◉ ~일기 《책이름》 *A War Diary.*

**난중지난**(難中之難) the most difficult of all things; the hardest things to *do.*

**난증**(難症) an incurable case; a malignant 〔serious〕 disease.

**난처하다**(難處—) (be) perplexed 〔puzzled, embarrassed, troubled〕; be at a loss; be at *one's* wits' end; be in a fix 〔dilemma〕; be 〔put〕 in a difficult position. ¶ 난처한 얼굴 a perplexed 〔an embarrassed〕 look / 난처한 입장 an awkward 〔a difficult〕 situation / 난처한 표정으로 with a perplexed 〔bewildered〕 look 〔air〕 / 난처해서 in perplexity / 난처하게 하다 puzzle; perplex; embarrass / 어찌하면 좋을지 나는 난처했다 I was 「puzzled 〔at a loss〕 as to what to do. / 뭐라고 대답해야 할 지 그는 아주 난처했다 He was completely at a loss for a suitable answer. / 그녀의 얼굴에는 난처한 빛이 역력했다 Her face expressed a perplexity. / 너를 난처하게 할 생각은 아니었다 I didn't mean to put you on the spot.

**난청**(難聽) difficulty in hearing. ¶ ~의 hard of hearing / 그는 가벼운 ~이다 He is slightly hard of hearing. / 이곳은 ~자를 위한 학교이다 This school is for the 「hard of hearing 〔hearing impaired〕. / 이 부근은 TV ~구역이다 TV programs are hard to pick up in this area. ◉ ~자 a person who is hard of hearing. ~지역 《라디오·TV의》 a poor reception area; a fringe area (where reception is poor); a blanket area (라디오의).

**난초**(蘭草) 『식물』 an orchid; an orchis.

**난층운**(亂層雲) 『기상』 nimbostratus.

**난치**(難治) 《의료의》 incurableness; inveteracy. ¶ ~의 hard to cure; almost incurable; fatal; 《통치의》 hard to govern / ~병 an obstinate disease.

**난침모**(—針母) a non-resident 〔living=out, visiting〕 seamstress.

**난타**(亂打) pummeling; repeated knocking 〔blows〕; random blows. ~하다 strike 《a firebell》 wildly 〔madly〕; hit 〔beat〕 《*a person*》 repeatedly; give 《*a person*》 pummeling; 《야구에서》 slug. ¶ 투수의 공을 ~하다 hit a pitcher all over the field. ◉ ~전 『권투·야구』 a slugfest 《미구어》.

**난투**(亂鬪) a confused 〔free〕 fight; a scuffle; a scrimmage; a rough-and=tumble; a free-for-all. ~하다 have a free 〔confused〕 fight; grapple 〔scuffle〕 《with》. ¶ ~ 국회 a roughhouse session of the National Assembly / ~를 벌이다 come to fisticuffs 〔scuffles, blows〕 / 서로가 뒤섞여 싸우는 ~가 시작되었다 A free fight developed 〔entered〕 between the two sides 〔teams〕.

◉ ~극〔장면〕 a scene of violence and confusion; 《영화·연극의》 a fight scene.

**난파**(暖波) a current of warm air.

**난파**(難破) a shipwreck. ~하다 be wrecked. ¶ 암초에 걸려 ~하다 be wrecked on the hidden reef. ◉ ~선 a wrecked ship; a ship in distress: ~선 구조 salvage / ~선 구조선 a wrecker. ~신호 a signal of distress; a May-day (call): 배는 ~신호를 보냈다 The ship signaled its distress. ~화물 wreckage.

**난폭**(亂暴) 《폭력》 violence; an outrage; 《거침》 roughness; 《무례》 rudeness; 《무모》 recklessness. ~하다 (be) violent; rude; rough; rowdy. ¶ ~하게 violently; rudely; roughly; recklessly / ~하게 행동하다 behave rudely 〔outrageously, recklessly〕; be rude 《to》 / ~한 짓을 하다 act 〔get〕 rough 《with *a person*》; do 〔use〕 violence 《to, toward》; commit an outrage 《on》; resort to violence / ~하게 다루다 handle 《*a thing, a person*》 roughly; manhandle 《*a person*》 / ~한 말을 쓰다 use violent 〔bad〕 language / 차를 ~하게 운전하지 마라 Don't drive your car recklessly. / 그는 ~하게 문을 닫았다 He shut the door violently. *or* He slammed door. / 그렇게 ~하게 다루면 부서진다 It may break with such rough handling. / 앞으로는 절대로 ~하게 굴지 않겠다 I will never 「play rough 〔resort to violence〕 from now on. ◉ ~운전 reckless driving. ~운전자 a reckless driver. ~자 a wild 〔rowdy〕 fellow; a roughneck 《미》. ~차량신고함 a Report Box 〔Booth〕 for Reckless Driving.

**난필**(亂筆) hasty 〔slipshod〕 handwriting; (a) scribble; (a) scrawl. ¶ ~을 용서하십시오 Please excuse my bad handwriting. *or* Please excuse this scribbled 〔hastily written〕 note.

**난하다**(亂—) (be) loud; gaudy; showy; garish. ¶ 난한 색 a loud color / 빛깔이 난한 넥타이 a loud 〔gaudy〕 necktie / 옷차림이 ~ be gaily 〔loudly〕 dressed; be dressed in loud colors / 그녀의 치마 무늬는 좀 ~ The pattern of her skirt is a bit too garish 〔flashy〕.

**난항**(難航) ① 《배의》 a difficult 〔stormy, rough〕 voyage; 《비행기의》 a difficult 〔rough〕 flight. ~하다 have a rough passage. ② 《일·교섭 따위의》 ~하다 make slow progress; face 〔have〕 hard 〔rough〕 going; meet with difficulty. ¶ 노사 교섭은 ~이다 The labor-management negotiation faces rough going. / 새로운 조각은 ~을 거듭하고 있다 Difficulties are being experienced in the formation of the new Cabinet. / 두 나라 사이의 분쟁 조정은 ~하고 있다 The mediation of the dispute between the two countries is making slow progress.

**난해**(難解) ~하다 be hard 〔difficult〕 to understand 〔solve〕; be knotty. ¶ ~한 이론 an abstruse theory / ~한 글 a difficult passage; an article hard to understand / 이것은 ~한 문제다 This is a difficult problem to solve.

**난행**(亂行) 《난폭한 행동》 violent 〔reckless, outrageous〕 behavior 〔conduct〕; 《추행》 immoral conduct; misconduct; debauchery (방탕). ¶ ~하다 live a debauched life; live a life of immorality; do violence 《to》.

**난행**(難行) 《고행》 penance; religious austerities. ⇨ 고행. ~하다 do penance; practice religious austerities; go through all sorts of hardships.

**난형**(卵形) an egg shape; ovalness. ¶ ~의 ovate; egg-shaped; oval.

**난형난제**(難兄難弟) ¶ ~다 be hard to tell who 〔which〕 is better; be almost equal; be nearly alike / 두 사람의 재능은 ~다 The two are nearly equal in their talent.

**난혼**(亂婚) promiscuous sexual relations; (sexual) promiscuity.

**난황**(卵黃) (an) egg yolk; the yolk 〔yellow〕 of an egg.
◉ ~막(膜) a vitelline membrane. ~분(粉) yolk powder. ~소(素) vitellin.

**낟가리** a stack of grain stalks; an unhusked rice stack.

**낟알** ① 《곡식의》 a grain. ② = 쌀알.

**날**[1] ① 《하루》 a day; 《시일》 time; 《일진》 the kind of day. ¶ 어느 날 one day / 좋은 날 a happy day; 《길일》 a red-letter day; a lucky 〔an auspicious〕 day / 날로 《나날이》 day by 〔after〕 day / 날이 감에 따라 as days go by; as the days roll on; as time passes / 날마다 every 〔each〕 day; daily; from day to day; day after day.
날을: 날을 보내다 pass 〔spend〕 *one's* time / 날을 보다 cast a horoscope to see if the day is auspicious / 혼인날을 잡다 choose a day for *one's* wedding.
날이: 날이 가다 days go by; time passes / 날이 밝다〔새다〕 the day dawns; morning breaks / 날이 저물다 It grows dark. *or* The sun sets. *or* Night falls. / 날이 길어진다 The days are getting longer. / 날이 좋다〔나쁘다〕 The day is lucky 〔unlucky〕.
¶ 겨울철에는 날이 짧다 The days are short in winter. / 시험볼 날이 며칠 안 남았다 We have but a few days left before the examination. / 나는 미국에서 보낸 즐거웠던 날들이 생각났다 I thought (of) the happy days I had when I was in America. / 날이 지남에 따라 그의 분노도 가라앉았다 As (the) days went by his anger cooled off.
② 《날씨》 the weather. ¶ 좋은 날 a fine 〔clear, nice〕 day / 궂은 날 a foul 〔bad, rainy〕 day / 날이 좋든 나쁘든 rain or shine; whatever the weather / 날이 든다 It clears (up). / 오늘은 날이 좋다〔나쁘다〕 We have fine 〔bad〕 weather today. / 날이 더워진다 It is getting warmer. / 날이 좋으면 내일 떠나겠다 I will start tomorrow if it is fine. / 햇살이 강한 날에는 선글라스를 낀다 I wear sunglasses on sunny days. / 등산하기 아주 좋은 날이다 It is a perfect day for mountain climbing.
③ 《날짜》 a day of the week 〔month〕; a date. ¶ 초하룻날 the first (day) of the month / 날을 정하다〔잡다〕 fix 〔set〕 the date / 출발하는 날을 정하다 fix the date of departure / 날을 물리다 put off; postpone / 오늘이 며칠날인가 What day of the month is it today? *or* What's the date today? / 혼인날이 정해졌다 The date has been set 〔fixed〕 for our wedding.
④ 《경우》 a case; an occasion; a time 〔moment〕; 《때·시기》 time; *one's* days. ¶ 젊은 날의 어머니 my mother in her young days / 성공하는 날에는 when *one* succeeds / 완성하는 날에는 on the completion of the work / 실패하는 날에는 내가 책임을 져야 한다 If I fail, I have to bear 〔take〕 the responsibility. / 비가 오는 날은 파티는 실내에서 열리게 된다 If it rains 〔In case of rain〕, the party will be held indoors. / 젊은 날의 기억은 잊혀지지 않는다 We cannot forget the 《memories of our》 younger days. / 세상에서 전쟁이 없어지는 날이 곧 올 것이다 The day will soon come when there will be no war in the world.

**날**[2] 《날붙이의》 a blade; an edge. ¶ 칼날 the blade of a knife 〔sword〕 / 날이 예리하다〔무디다〕 have a sharp 〔blunt〕 edge / (…의) 날을 세우다 put an edge on; sharpen; whet / 그것을 칼로 자르려

다간 날이 상한다 If you try to cut it with the knife, the edge will be nicked.

**날**[3] 《세로실》 warp; a warp thread 〔yarn〕. ¶ 베틀의 날 the warp on a loom / 날과 씨 warp and woof 〔weft〕.

**날-** 《자연 그대로의》 raw 《meat》; uncooked 《cabbage》; 《가공하지 않은》 crude 《rubber》; raw 《hide》; 《익지 않은》 green 〔unripe〕 《persimmons》. ¶ 날달걀 a raw egg / 날된장 unmatured 〔unmellowed〕 soybean paste / 날로 먹다 eat 《fish》 raw / 고기를 날로 먹는 것을 좋아하는 사람들도 있다 Some people like to eat raw meat.

**날강도**(一強盜) a barefaced robber; a racketeer. ¶ 그것은 ～짓이다 It would be sheer robbery to do so.

**날강목치다** 〘광산〙 dig in vain; mine for nought; make vain effort.

**날개** a wing; 《기계의》 fan; 《추진기의》 a blade; 《풍차의》 a flier. ¶ 비행기의 오른쪽 ～ the right wing of an airplane / ～치는 소리 the flapping of wings / ～가 있는〔달린〕 winged 《angels》 / ～를 펼치다〔치다, 접다〕 spread 〔flap, fold〕 its wings / ～가 돋다 grow wings / ～를 자르다 clip 《a chicken's》 wings / ～를 치며 날아가다 fly with a flap of its wings / ～를 펴다 spread its wings; 《재능을 발휘하다》 give full play to *one's* ability 〔talent〕 / ～ 돋친 듯 팔리다 sell like hot cakes / 그 독수리는 ～길이가 약 2미터나 된다 The eagle has a wingspan of about two meters.
◉ ～개미 a winged ant. ～길이 《한쪽의》 wing length; 《양쪽을 합친》 wingspan; wingspread. 날갯죽지 the (shoulder=) joint of a wing: 날갯죽지가 늘어지다 have drooping wings.

**날것** raw 〔uncooked〕 food; green 〔unripe〕 fruit. ¶ ～으로 먹다 eat 《fish》 raw 〔fresh〕.

**날고치** a raw 〔an unboiled〕 cocoon.

**날공전**(一工錢) daily wages.

**날귀** 《대패·끌의》 the two corners of a blade on a plane 〔chisel〕.

**날기와** an unbaked tile.

**날김치** freshly prepared kimchi; unfermented 〔raw〕 kimchi.

**날다**[1] ① 《공중을》 fly 《in the sky》; soar (하늘 높이); flit (나비 따위가); flutter (펄럭펄럭); be blown off (바람에 날려). ¶ 나는 새 a bird flying in the air 〔sky〕 / 높게〔낮게〕 ～ fly high 〔low〕 / 날아가다 fly away; take wing / 날아다니다 fly about; flutter 〔flit〕 about / 갈매기가 벼랑 위로 날아 올라갔다 The seagull soared above the cliff. / 우리 비행기는 알프스 상공을 날았다 Our plane flew over the Alps. / 비행기는 5,000피트 고도로 날고 있었다 The plane was flying at the altitude of 5,000 feet. / 바람에 모자가 날려 시궁창에 빠졌다 The wind blew off my hat into the gutter. / 나는 새도 깃을 쳐야 날아간다 《속담》 One can't attain one's object without preparing oneself for it.
② 《빨리 가다》 fly 〔run, rush〕 to; go very fast. ¶ 나는 듯이 달려가다 run with flying feet; run like the wind / 기별을 듣고 날 듯이 집으로 달려왔다 At the news I flew home like the wind.
③ 《달아나다》 run away 《from, to》; flee; get away; make off 《with》; obscond 《from, with》. ¶ 그는 그 돈을 갖고 날아버렸다 He absconded 〔make away〕 with the money.

**날다**[2] ① 《색이 바래다》 fade; discolor; lose color. ¶ 색이 날지 않는 천 cloth of fast colors / 색이 난 청바지 a pair of faded jeans / 색이 잘 나는〔날지 않는〕 색깔 fugitive 〔fast〕 colors / 햇볕으로 커튼의 색이 날았다 The sun faded the curtains. *or* The curtains were discolored by the sun. / 이 천은 색이 날지 않는다 This materials won't fade 〔discolor〕. / 햇볕을 쬔 데는 색이 날았다 The part exposed to the sunlight has discolored. ② 《냄새가》 vanish; go away; lose odor; evaporate (알코올 따위). ¶ 향내가 날아 버렸다 Perfume lost its fragrance.

**날다람쥐** 〘동물〙 a flying squirrel.

**날도**(一度) 《경도》 degree of longitude. ¶ ～와 씨도 longitude and latitude.

**날도둑놈** a barefaced swindler 〔crook〕; a shameless scoundrel.

**날들다** become clear; 《it》 clear up. ¶ 날이 들기 시작한다 It is clearing up. / 날들 것 같다 It is going to be fine.

**날뛰다** ① 《껑충껑충 뛰다》 jump 〔leap, bounce〕 up; jump 〔skip, ramp〕 about. ¶ 기뻐 ～ jump 〔leap〕 for joy / 지금은 좋아서 날뛸 때가 아니다 This is no hour dancing with joy. ② 《거칠게 행동하다》 act violently; rush 〔run〕 about wildly; rage about. ¶ 날뛰기 시작하다 start acting violently; go on a rampage; go unruly; get riotous (많은 사람이) / 미친듯이 ～ rush about in a frenzy 〔rage〕 / 말이 갑자기 날뛰기 시작했다 The horse suddenly turned restive.

**날라리** 〘악기〙 a shawm; a Chinese clarinet.

**날래다** (be) quick; fast; swift; speedy; agile; nimble. ¶ 날랜 동작 a swift 〔quick〕 motion / 날랜 말 a speedy horse / 걸음이 ~ be quick on *one's* feet; be a fast walker / 날래게 행동하다 act smartly / 그 애는 참 ~ The child is quick in his motion.

**날려보내다** ① 《놓아주다》 let 《a kite》 fly away; set 《a bird》 free; 《바람에》 blow off 〔away〕. ¶ 기구를 ~ send a balloon fly away / 바람에 모자를 날려보냈다 I had my hat blown off. ② 《탕진하다》 squander; dissipate 《a fortune》; run 〔go〕 through 《money》; play fast and loose with 《*one's* fortune》; waste. ¶ 그는 순식간에 돈을 다 날려보냈다 He went through all his money almost in no time.

**날렵하다** 《동작이》 (be) quick; alert; nimble; agile; 《성질이》 (be) quick-witted; smart; sharp. ¶ 날렵하게 quickly; nimbly; with agility; smartly / 동작이 ~ be nimble in *one's* movement / 날렵하게 일을 해내다 carry through a job smartly.

**날름** ① 《혀를》 ¶ 혀를 ~ 내밀다 put 〔stick, thrust〕 *one's* tongue out. ② 《잽싸게》 quickly; swiftly; with a quick snatch; with a dart. ¶ 책상 위의 책을 ~ 가져가다 snatch a book off the desk / ~ 먹어치우다 eat up 《*one's* lunch》 in a flash; make short work of 《*one's* ice cream》.

**날름거리다** ① 《혀 따위를》 let 《a tongue》 dart in and out; 《손을》 take *one's* hand in and out quickly. ¶ 개구리를 보자, 뱀이 혀를 날름거렸다 On seeing a frog, the snake began to dart its tongue in and out. ② 《탐내다》 covet; be greedy 《after》; have an eye for; have a desire 《for, to do》.

**날름날름** darting 〔taking〕 in and out repeatedly.

**날름쇠** 《무자위의》 a valve; 《총의》 a tumbler; a cock; 《자물쇠의》 a tumbler; a tongue.

**날리다**[1] ① 《공중으로》 fly; let 〔make〕 fly; blow off (바람이). ¶ 연을〔새를〕 ~ fly a kite 〔bird〕 / 공을 ~ send a ball flying / 모형 비행기를 ~ fly a model plane / 먼지를 ~ blow off the dust / 센터를 넘어가는 2루타를 ~ send a two-base hit over the center. ② 《이름을》 become famous; win fame; distinguish *oneself;* be 「well-known 〔widly known〕; be popular 〔famous〕. ¶ 이름을 날리는 화가 a painter rising in popularity / 전세계에 이름을 ~ be known all over the world; win 〔achieve〕 global fame. ③ 《재산을 없애다》 lose; waste; ruin *oneself;* dissipate 〔squander〕 《a fortune》. ¶ 도박으로 재산을 ~ lose a fortune in gambling; gamble 〔play〕 away *one's* fortune / 하찮은 일로 돈을 ~ waste money for useless purpose / 갑작스런 경제 불황으로 지금까지 축적해온 이익을 모두 날렸다 The sudden business depression has blown away all the profits hitherto accumulated. ④ 《일을 대충하다》 scamp 《*one's* work》; do 《a job》 hastily 〔carelessly, sloppily〕; do slipshod 〔slapdash〕 《job》; do 《*one's* job》 in a half-hearted way. ¶ 일을 날리지 마라 Don't be so slipshod in your work. / 저 목수는 절대로 일을 날리지 않는다 That carpenter never scamps his work.

**날리다**[2] 《펄럭이다》 wave; flutter 〔flap, fly〕 《in the wind》. ¶ 깃발이 바람에 날리고 있다 A flag is flapping in the wind.

**날림** 《날림일》 a slipshod job; a patch-work job; sloppy 〔rush and hurried〕 work; a job just thrown together. ¶ ~으로 일하다 skimp 〔scamp〕 *one's* work; do *one's* work in a rough-and-ready way / 그것은 주문 날짜에 맞추기 위한 ~작업이었다 It was a slipshod job, done to order in a hurry. / 「그 사람들 다리 보수 작업은 잘 했나」—「아니, 날림으로 했어」 "Did they keep the bridge in good repair?"—"No, they didn't. They just gave it a lick and a promise." ◉ ~글씨 sloppy handwriting. ~공사 「rough-and-hurried 〔slipshod, jerry-built〕 construction. ~집 a jerry-built house. ~치 a slipshod thing; a slipshod piece of work.

**날망제** 〖민속〗 an unexorcised soul; a wandering ghost.

**날목**(一木) 《생나무》 unseasoned wood 〔timber〕.

**날물** 《나가는 물》 outflowing water; 《썰물》 low water; an ebb tide.

**날밑** the guard 《on a sword》; a sword guard.

**날바닥** the bare floor 〔ground〕.

**날바람잡다** gad 〔roam〕 about.

**날반죽** cold-water dough; kneading with cold water. ~하다 knead with cold water.

**날밤**[1] ¶ ~ 새우다 stay up all night; kill the night.

**날밤**[2] 《생률》 a raw 〔an unroasted〕 chestnut. ¶ ~을 까다 pare a raw chestnut.

**날벌레** a winged insect.

**날벼락** a bolt from 〔out of〕 the blue;

《야단》《get》 an unreasonable scolding; 《재앙》《meet》 an undeserved misfortune; a sudden calamity. ¶ 이번 부산 지점으로의 전근 명령은 그에게는 ~이었다 The recent order of transfer to the Pusan branch came to him as a bolt from the blue.

**날변**(一邊) daily interest; interest per day. ¶ ~의 고리 대금 money lent at high daily interest.

**날불한당**(一不汗黨) a barefaced swindlers 〔crooks〕; shameless scoundrels.

**날붙이** an edged tool; cutlery [총칭].

**날사이** 《지난 며칠》《for》 the past several days.

**날삯** daily wages. ◉ ~꾼 a day laborer.

**날샐녘** dawn; daybreak; the early hours of the morning. ¶ 우리는 ~에 출발했다 We set out at dawn 〔daybreak, the crack 〔peep〕 of dawn〕.

**날서다** become sharp 〔keen〕; be sharpened; take an edge. ¶ 날선 칼 a sharp 〔keen〕 knife.

**날세우다** sharpen 〔whet〕《a knife》; put an edge on 《a knife》; give an edge to.

**날수**(一數) ① 《날의 수효》(the number of) days. ¶ 출발까지는 아직 ~가 있다 I still have 〔There are still〕 a number of days before I start. ② 《날성수》 the luck 〔fortune〕 of a particular day. ¶ ~를 보다 tell 〔read〕 *one's* fortune for the day / ~가 좋다〔나쁘다〕 have a lucky 〔an unlucky〕 day.

**날숨** 《내쉬는 숨》 (an) exhalation. ¶ ~과 들숨 exhalation and inhalation / ~쉬다 exhale; breathe out.

**날실** 《경사(經絲)》 the warp threads; 《삶지 않은 실》 raw 〔untreated〕 thread.

**날쌔다** 《동작이》 (be) quick; prompt; swift; agile; nimble. ¶ 동작이 ~ be quick 〔agile〕 in *one's* movement / 날쌔게 낚싯줄을 감아올리다 wind up the fishing line quickly / 소매치기는 날쌔게 모습을 감췄다 The pickpocket disappeared in a flash.

**날씨** 《일기》 the look of the sky; the weather; weather conditions. ¶ 좋은 ~ fine 〔good, favorable〕 weather / 궂은 ~ foul 〔bad, unpleasant〕 weather / 음산한 ~ gloomy 〔dismal〕 weather / 변덕스러운 ~ changeable 〔unsettled〕 weather / 험한 ~ stormy 〔rough〕 weather / 지금 ~같아서는 judging from the look of the sky / ~가 좋으면 if it is fine; weather permitting / ~가 좋건 나쁘건 rain or shine; whatever the weather; in all weathers / ~가 변덕스럽다 the weather is changeable / ~를 예보하다 forecast the weather; make a weather forecast / 오늘 저녁은 ~가 어떨가 I wonder how the weather will be this evening. / ~가 좋아질 것 같다 The weather is likely to 「clear up 〔improve〕. / ~가 좋지 않을 것 같다 The weather is threatening. / ~가 좋아지는 대로 출발한다 We will start as soon as it clears up. / ~ 참 좋군요 Nice day today, isn't it? / 아주 고약한 ~로군요 It is nasty 〔wretched〕 weather, isn't it? / 오늘은 겨울 ~ 같군요. It is winter weather today, isn't it?

**날씬하다** 《가느다란》 (be) slender; slim; svelte; 《낭창낭창한》 supple; lithe. ¶ 날씬한 여자 a slim 〔slender〕 woman / 날씬한 허리 a supple 〔slim, slender〕 waist / 그녀는 몸매가 ~ She is trim and slender in figure.

**날아가다** ① 《공중을》 fly away 〔off〕; wing off; take wing; rise in the air. ¶ 날아가는 새를 잡다 catch a bird on the wing / (사냥에서) 새를 날아가게 쫓다 start 〔flush up〕 a bird / 기러기떼가 북녘 하늘로 날아갔다 A flock of wild geese flew away into the northern sky. ② 《없어지다》 be gone; go away; vanish. ¶ 모든 희망이 날아갔다 All hope has 「vanished 〔gone〕. / 돈이 어느새 다 날아갔다 My money is all gone already. ③ 《파면되다》 ¶ 모가지가 ~ be fired 《from a job》; be dismissed 〔discharged, sacked 《구어》〕; get the sack 《영구어》; be laid off (일시적으로).

**날아다니다** 《공중을》 fly about; flutter about (펄럭펄럭). ¶ 나비가 정원을 ~ Butterflies flutter about the garden. / 그는 비행기로 전국을 날아다녔다 He flew all over the country in the plane.

**날아들다** ① 《새·파리 따위가》 fly in 〔into〕. ¶ 참새가 방안으로 날아들었다 A sparrow flew into the room. ② 《소식·정보 따위가》 get; have; come in 〔by〕. ¶ 새로운 정보가 날아들었다 A new piece of information came in. / 모르는 사람으로부터 이상한 편지가 날아들었다 I got a strange letter from whom I did not know.

**날염**(捺染) (textile) printing. ~하다 print. ¶ ~한 천 printed cloth 〔cotton〕; 《미》 calico. ◉ ~기(機) a printing machine.

**날인**(捺印) affixing a seal. ~하다 seal; put *one's* seal on; affix *one's* seal to 《a paper》. ¶ 기명 ~하다 write *one's* name and verify it by affixing *one's* seal / 그들은 조약에 서명 ~했다 They signed and sealed the treaty.

**날조**(捏造) (a) fabrication; (an) invention; (a) concoction; a frame-up 《미》. ~하다 fabricate; forge; invent; make 〔frame 《구어》, cook 《구어》〕 up 《a story》; fake. ¶ 이야기를 ~하다 invent a false story / 문서를 ~하다 forge 〔fabricate〕 the document / 그의 증언은 모두 ~된 것이었다 His whole testimony had been faked 〔concocted〕. / 그 보도는 신문이 ~한 것이다 The report is an invention of the newspapers.
◉ ~기사 a fabrication; a fabricated report. ~자 a fabricator.

**날줄** 《경선(經線)》 a line of longitude; a meridian.

**날짐승** birds; fowls; the feathered tribe; 「bird life.

**날짜**[1] ① 《일부》 a date; dating; 《정해진 날》 the 《fixed》 date; the appointed day. ¶ ~가 없는 편지 an undated letter / 3월 3일 ~의 편지 a letter dated 〔of〕 March 3rd / ~를 당기다 move up 〔advance〕 the date / ~를 쓰다 date 《a letter》; put a date to 《a document》 / ~를 정하다 fix 〔decide〕 the date; name the day; make 〔set〕 a date / ~가 잘못되다 be wrongly dated / 그들의 결혼 ~는 미정이다 The date has not yet been fixed for their wedding. / 그 편지는 6월 20일 ~였다 The letter was dated Jun. 20. / 이 영수증에는 ~가 없다 This receipt has no date on it. ② 《일수》 the number of days. ¶ ~가 꽤 걸리다 take 「a great number of days 〔a long time〕 / 그 일에는 ~가 얼마나 걸립니까 How long 〔many days〕 will it take to finish the work?
◉ ~변경선 the (international) date line. 계약〔약속〕~ the date of a contract 〔an appointment〕.

**날짜**[2] ① 《날것》 raw stuff; uncooked food (음식); unripe fruit (과일). ⇨ 날것. ② 《무경험자》 an inexperienced person; a novice; an amature; 《풋내기》 a greenhorn; a green youth.

**날짝지근하다** ⇨ 늘쩍지근하다.

**날치** 〖어류〗 a flying fish.

**날치기** 《행위》 swiping; filching; snatching; pilfering; 《사람》 a petty thief 〔pilferer〕; a snatcher. ~하다 swipe 《구어》; filch; pinch 《구어》; lift 《구어》; snatch 《a woman's handbag》; rip off 《a bicycle》. ¶ ~를 당하다 have 《*a thing*》 snatched / 의안을 ~로 통과시키다 [비유적] rush a bill through the Assembly by surprise / 오토바이를 탄 사내가 그녀의 핸드백을 ~해서 달아났다 A man on a motorcycle snatched her handbag and ran away.
◉ ~꾼 a snatcher. ~통과 《법률안의》 the unilateral passage of a bill in lightning action; (a) snap passage 《of a bill》.

**날카롭다** ① 《칼 따위가》 (be) pointed; sharp; keen. ¶ 날카로운 칼 a sharp knife / 날카롭게 하다〔갈다〕 sharpen / 이 칼의 날은 매우 ~ This knife has a very sharp edge.
② 《두뇌 따위가》 (be) smart; sharp; shrewd; quick; 《감각·판단력·통증 따위가》 acute; piercing; keen. ¶ 날카로운 관찰 keen 〔acute〕 observation / 머리가 날카로운 남자 a quick-witted man; a man of keen intelligence / 청각〔후각〕이 ~ have 「acute hearing 〔a keen sense of smell〕 / 무릎에 날카로운 통증을 느꼈다 I felt 「a sharp 〔an acute〕 pain in my knee. / 형사는 날카로운 눈매를 하고 있었다 The detective had a sharp 〔piercing〕 look in his eyes. / 그 아가씨는 음감이 ~ The girl has a keen sense of music. / 그는 정말로 날카로운 사내다 He is as sharp as a needle 〔razor〕.
③ 《비판·공격 따위가》 stinging 〔caustic, pungent〕 《sarcasm》; biting 〔cutting〕 《criticism》; poignant 《satire》. ¶ 날카롭게 공격하다 make fierce 〔hot〕 attack 《on》; 《입으로》 make cutting remarks 《about》 / 그 학생은 선생님에게 날카로운 질문을 했다 The student asked the teacher a sharp question. / 그는 날카로운 어조로 내게 달려들었다 He closed in on me in a cutting tone.

**날탕** 《사람》 a person with no means.

**날틀** 《베틀의》 a (10-holed) warp-adjuster for a loom.

**날품** daily employment; work done on a daily wage basis. ¶ 나는 ~으로 일한다 I work by the day. ◉ ~삯 daily wages. ~팔이 《일》 day labor; 《사람》 a day laborer; a day man.

**낡다** 《오래되다》 (be) old; aged; antiquated; 《써서》 (be) worn-out; 《시대에 뒤지다》 (be) old-fashioned; outmoded; outdated; out of date; 《진부하다》 (be) hackneyed; stale; timeworn. ¶ 낡은 관습 an obsolete; a worm-eaten 〔an obsolete〕 custom / 낡은 소파〔모자〕 a worn-out sofa 〔hat〕 / 낡은 차 a used 〔beat-up〕 car / 낡은 표현 hackneyed phrase; threadbare expressions / 낡은 학설 an outdated 〔a worn-out〕 theory / 그것은 낡은 수법이다 That's an old trick. / 그것은 낡은 생각이다 That's a moss-grown 〔an old-fashioned, an outdated〕 idea. / 이것은 낡은 건물이다 This is an antiquated building.

**남** ① 《타인》 another person; others; other people; 《친척 아닌 사람》 an unrelated person; 《모르는 사람》 a stranger; 《국외자》 an outsider; a third party. ¶ 남의 일 another person's 〔other people's〕 affair / 남모르는 슬픔 a hidden sorrow / 남의 집 other people's house / 생판 모르는 남 an utter stranger / 남들이 하는 대로 따라하다 act according to others 〔custom〕; follow the world / 남의 눈을 끌다 attract people's attention; be conspicuous; be eye-catching / 남의 눈에 띄다 be in the public eye; be open for all to see / 남의 눈에 띄지 않다 escape notice 〔observation〕 / 남의 눈을 피하다 shun the public eye; avoid 「public notice 〔the eyes of others〕; keep *oneself* from being seen / 남의 눈을 피해서 만나다 have a secret meeting 《with》 / 남의 일같지 않다 feel as if it were *one's* own; sympathize deeply with *a person* / 남의 말에 신경쓰지 마라 Never mind what people 〔others〕 say. / 남들 앞에서 그런 말을 하지 마라 Don't ever say such a thing 「in front of 〔in the presence of〕 other people. / 나도 남들처럼 잘 살고 싶다 I also want to make a decent living like other people. / 나는 남들 앞에서는 말을 못한다 I cannot speak in public. / 이 집을 남의 손에 넘기는 일은 절대로 하지 않겠다 I shall never let this house fall into strange hands. / 그는 남이라고 여길 수 없을 정도로 친절했다 He was kinder to me than I could ever have expected from a stranger. / 먼 친척보다는 가까운 남이 낫다 A good neighbor is better than a brother far off. / 그가 촌수는 멀지만 아주 남은 아니다 Though distant, he is still my relative. / 본인보다는 남이 시비곡직을 더 잘 안다 The outsider sees best 〔most〕 of the game.
② 《나》 me; I. ¶ ～의 애타는 마음을 몰라주는 여자 the girl 「unaware of 〔indifferent to〕 my pining heart / 너 어째서 남의 책을 가져 갔느냐 Why did you take my book?

**남**(男) ① 《남자》 a man; 《남성》 a male; the male sex. ¶ 《서류 등에서》 성별: 남 SEX: *male.* ② 《아들》 a son. ¶ 2남 1녀가 있다 I have two sons and a daughter.

**남**(南) (the) south. ¶ 남의 south; southern / 남으로 to the south; southward / 남으로 가다 go south 〔southward〕 / 남을 향하다 face 〔look toward〕 the south. ⇨ 남쪽.

**남**(藍) 《쪽》 indigo; 《남빛》 indigo (blue); deep blue. ¶ 남의 indigo / 남으로 물들이다 dye 《a cloth》 deep blue.

**남-**(男) masculine; male. ¶ 남동생 *one's* younger brother / 남장 male attire.

**남가일몽**(南柯一夢) a vain dream; an empty 〔idle〕 dream.

**남경**(男莖) the penis.

**남계**(男系) the male line; the spear side. ¶ ～의 on the male line; on the father's 〔spear〕 side. ◉ ～상속 succession in the male line. ～친척 an agnate; an agnate relative.

**남구**(南歐) 《남유럽》 Southern Europe.

**남국**(南國) a southern country; the South (남부지방).

**남극**(南極) the South 〔Antarctic〕 Pole; 《자석의》 the south pole. ◉ ～관측〔탐험〕 Antarctic exploration: ～관측탐험대 an Antarctic expedition (team). ～광 the southern lights; an aurora australis. ～권 the Antarctic Circle. ～대(帶) the Antarctic Zone. ～대륙 the Antarctic Continent; Antarctica. ～성(星) the south pole star. ～점 the South 〔Antarctic〕 Pole. ～조약 the Antarctic Treaty. ～해〔양〕 the Antarctic Ocean 〔Sea〕. ～해양 생물자원 보존 협약 the Convention on the Conservation of Antarctic Marine Living Resources (생략 CCAMLR).

**남근**(男根) the penis. ◉ ～숭배 phallicism; phallic worship.

**남기다** ① 《사람·물건을 뒤에》 leave 《behind》; 《이름을》 hand down; 《유산을》 bequeath 《a fortune to》. ¶ 뒤에 남겨진 유족 the bereaved family / 어머니가 내게 남겨주신 반지 the ring handed down to me from my mother / 좋은 인상을 ～ leave a favorable impression 《upon》 / 아내를〔빚을〕 남기고 죽다 leave 「one's wife 〔a debt〕 behind (*one*) / 그에게 쪽지를 ～ leave a note for him; leave him a note / 이름을 후세에 ～ leave 〔hand down〕 *one's* name to posterity / 그녀는 아들에게 큰 재산을 남겼다 She left a large fortune to her son. *or* She left her son a large fortune. / 그는 아내와 두 아이를 집에 남기고 행방불명이 되었다 He disappeared leaving his wife and two children home. / 나만 남겨 놓고 모두 놀러 나갔다 They went

out to play leaving me all alone.
② 《이익을》 gain; make 〔get, realize〕 a profit. ¶ 거래에서 많이 ~ make 〔gain〕 a large profit on a deal / 별로 크게 못 ~ realize just a bare profit / 1할을 남겨 팔다 sell at a 10% profit / 양복 한 벌에 약 5만원 남긴다 They make a profit of about 50,000 won on a suit.
③ 《…하지 않고 내버려 두다》 leave 《*a thing*》 undone; 《절약해서》 save; 《예비로》 set aside; reserve. ¶ 용돈을 ~ save something from *one's* pocket money / 일을 하다 말고 ~ leave *one's* work unfinished 〔half-done〕 / 한푼도 안 남기고 쓰다 spend *one's* money to the last cent; spend all *one's* money / 밥을 ~ leave rice in *one's* bowl / 여행을 위해 얼마간의 돈을 ~ put 〔set〕 some money aside for a trip / 케이크를 좀 남겨줘 Leave some cake for me.

**남김없이** all; wholly; entirely; without exception. ¶ 한 사람〔방울〕도 ~ to the last man 〔drop〕 / 그는 ~ 다 먹었다 He ate it all up. / 자네가 알고 있는 것을 ~ 말해다오 Tell me all you know about it.

**남남동**(南南東) the south-southeast (생략 SSE).

**남남북녀**(南男北女) Manly persons are found in the south and womanly beauties in the north.

**남남서**(南南西) the south-southwest (생략 SSW).

**남녀**(男女) man and woman; male and female; both (the) sexes.
¶ ~관계 a man-woman relationship; relations between the sexes / ~의 역할 sex roles; male and female roles / ~간의 격차 a gender gap (가치관 따위의); a disparity between the sexes (임금·기회 등의) / 소득의 ~간 격차 the disparity of earnings between the sexes / ~를 불문하고 regardless 〔without distinction〕 of sex / ~ 7세 부동석 A boy and a girl should not sit together after they have reached the age of seven. / 20명의 ~가 그 사고로 부상을 입었다 Twenty men and women were injured in the accident. / 그 방은 젊은 ~로 가득 차 있었다 The room was full of young men and women.
◉ ~고용 기회 균등법 the Equal Employment Opportunity Law. ~공용: ~공용의 unisex 《clothes, toilet》 / 이 우산은 ~공용이다 This umbrella can be used by both men and women. ~공학 coeducation: ~공학 학교 a coeducational 〔co-ed〕 school / ~공학제 the coeducational method 〔system〕. ~ 노소 people of all ages and both sexes; men and women of all ages: ~노소를 불문하고 without distinction of age or sex. ~동(등)권 equal rights for men and women. ~유별 distinction between the sexes. ~차별 sex discrimination; sexism: ~차별주의자 a sexist; a male chauvinist (남성우월주의자). ~평등 sexual equality.

**남녘**(南—) the south. ⇨ 남쪽.

**남다** ① 《…하고 남다》 be left over 〔behind〕; 《뒤에 남다》 remain; stay; stop. ¶ (…하고) 남은 돈 the money left over / 남은 것 remnants; leftovers; leavings; what was left of 《yesterday's evening meal》; unsold stock (팔다남은) / 먹고 남은 케이크 leftover cakes / 먹고 남은 것으로 요리를 만들다 prepare a dish from leftovers / 졸업후 대학에 ~ remain 〔stay on〕 at the college after graduation / 늦게까지 회사에 ~ remain 〔stay〕 late at the office / 남은 일은 내일 하도록 합시다 Let's do the remaining work tomorrow. / 그는 서울로 막벌이하러 떠났지만 처자식은 집에 남았다 He left for Seoul to find temporary work, while his wife and children remained at home. / 10에서 6을 빼면 4가 남는다 Six from ten leaves four. / 25를 6으로 나누면 4가 되고 1이 남는다 Six into twenty-five goes four times and one over. / 비용을 지불하고 나니 50달러밖에 남지 않았다 After expenses, I only had 50 dollars left over. / 금년도 며칠 남지 않았다 The year is drawing to a close. *or* Now there's only a few days left before the year end. / 돈은 남아있지 않다 There is 〔I have〕 no money left.
② 《잔존하다》 remain; linger; 《살아남다》 be left alive; survive; 《전래되다》 be handed down. ¶ 최후까지 살아~ survive to the last / 젊었을 때 받은 강한 인상처럼 기억에 오래 남는 것은 없다 Nothing remains longer in our memory than strong impressions that we received in early youth. / 아마 이 사건은 오래 내 기억에 남을 것이다 Perhaps this event will linger long in my memory. / 그 향기는 한동안 남아 있었다 The fragrance hung around for a while. / 그 관습은 그 지방에 아직도 남아 있다 The custom still survives 〔lingers on, remains〕 in the countryside.
③ 《이익이》 《a business》 yield a profit; 《*a person*》 make 〔gain, get〕 a profit 《on, out of, from》; earn. ¶ 남는 장사

a profitable 〔lucrative, paying〕 business / 남지 않는 장사 an unprofitable business; a business that does not pay / 그것을 천만 원에 팔면 이익이 얼마 남느냐 What profit will you make if you sell it for ten million won?

**남다르다** (be) uncommon; unusual; out of the ordinary; above (the) average; extraordinary; singular. ¶ 남다른 미모의 여성 a woman of singular beauty / 그녀는 기억력이 ~ She has an extraordinary memory. / 그는 어딘지 남다른 데가 있다 He has something out of the common.

**남단**(南端) the southern extremity 〔end, tip, rim〕. ¶ 부산은 한반도 ~에 있다 Pusan is on the southern tip of the Korean peninsula.

**남달리** unusually; more than others; uncommonly; exceptionally; in a different way from others; uniquely. ¶ ~ 노력하다 work harder than others / ~ 손재주가 뛰어나다 be extraordinarily skillful with *one's* hands / ~ 고집이 세다 be unique in *one's* stubbornness / 그는 ~ 운동신경이 민감하다 He is exceptionally quick in his movements. / 그는 ~ 키가 크다 He is unusually tall.

**남대문**(南大門) *Namdaemun;* the South Gate 《of Seoul》.

**남대서양**(南大西洋) the South Atlantic 「(Ocean).

**남독**(濫讀) random 〔unsystematic, desultory〕 reading. ~하다 read at random 〔without system〕. ¶ 젊었을 때 나는 소설을 ~했다 I read novels at random when young. ◉ ~가 an omnivorous 〔a voracious and indiscriminate〕 reader.

**남동**(南東) (the) southeast (생략 SE). ⇨ 동남(東南). ¶ ~풍 a southeastern wind.

**남동생**(男同生) a (*one's*) younger broth- 「er; *one's* little brother.

**남루**(襤褸) 《누더기》 a rag; a shred; 《헌옷》 ragged 〔tattered〕 clothes; rags; tatters. ~하다 (be) tattered; shabby; threadbare; ragged; be in rags. ¶ ~한 옷을 입은 사람 a person in rags.

**남만**(南蠻) southern barbarians. ◉ ~북적(北狄) southern and northern barbarians.

**남매**(男妹) brother and sister. ¶ 삼~ a brother-and-sister threesome / 그들은 ~간이다 They are brother and sister.

**남모르다** (be) unknown to other people; secret; hidden; inward (내심의). ¶ 남모르는 고생 hardships unknown to others / 남모르는 고민 《have》 a difficulty that nobody is aware of; inward trouble / 남모르는 슬픔 a hidden sorrow / 남모르게 울다 weep secretly 〔in secret, inwardly〕 / 그녀는 남모르는 고생을 해왔다 She has suffered hardship unknown to others.

**남미**(南美) ⇨ 남아메리카.

**남미동**(南微東) south by east (생략 SbE).

**남미서**(南微西) south by west (생략 SbW).

**남바위** a (winter) hood hemmed with 「fur.

**남반구**(南半球) the Southern Hemisphere.

**남발**(濫發) an excessive issue; an overissue. ~하다 overissue; issue 《notes》 recklessly 〔excessively〕. ¶ 어음〔지폐〕의 ~ an overissue of bills 〔bank notes〕.

**남방**(南方) the south. ¶ ~의 south; southern / ~에〔으로〕 south; southward; 《far》 to the south 《of》 / ~으로 항해하다 sail south 〔southward〕. ◉ ~셔츠 an aloha shirt: ~셔츠를 입은 사내 a man in aloha shirt.

**남벌**(濫伐) reckless 〔indiscriminate〕 deforestation. ~하다 cut down 〔fell〕 trees at random; deforest recklessly 〔indiscriminately〕.

**남복**(男服) men's clothes 〔wear〕; 《여자의 남장》 male attire; clothes in which a woman disguises herself as a man. ~하다 = 남장하다.

**남부**(南部) the south(ern) part 〔district〕; 《한 나라의》 the South. ¶ ~ 사람 《미국의》 a Southerner / ~의 주들 《미국의》 the Southern States / 시 ~에 있는 호수 a lake (located) in the south of the city. ◉ ~순환도로 the southern circular highway (around the city).

**남부끄럽다** be 〔feel〕 ashamed 《of》; (be) shameful; disgraceful. ¶ 남부끄러운 짓 a disgraceful 〔shameful〕 act / 남부끄러운 줄도 모르고 unshamedly; brazenly; unabashedly / 남부끄럽지 않은 decent; worthy; honorable / 남부끄럽지 않은 살림 a decent living / 남부끄럽지 않게 차려 입다 be decently dressed / 남부끄러운 일을 당하다 be put to shame; be disgraced / 남부끄럽지 않다 have nothing to be ashamed 《of》 / 남부끄러워 그런 말은 못하겠다 I am ashamed to say such a thing. / 그런 짓을 하고도 남부끄럽지 않느냐 Aren't you ashamed of what you have done?

**남부럽다** be 〔feel〕 enviable; be envious of others. ¶ 남부럽지 않게 살고 있다 be well off; be well-to-do; make a decent living.

**남부여대**(男負女戴) ~하다 set out on a wandering life; become poor wanderers 〔refugees〕.

**남북**(南北) north and south; 《남북한》 the South and North of Korea; South and North Korea; Seoul and Pyŏngyang. ¶ ~ 문제 《빈국과 부국간의》 the North-South problems; the problem of disparity in income levels between developed and developing countries; 《한국의》 the North-South problem of Korea; the inter-Korean problems / ~ 관계의 실질적인 진전 substantial progress in the inter-Korean relations / ~으로 흐르는 강 a river running from north to south / ~으로 뻗은 고속도로 a north-south highway / ~에 걸쳐 있다 lie from north to south; extend north and south / 어제 정부는 ~무역은 국내에서 행해지는 것이기 때문에 WTO의 규정에 영향을 받지 않는다고 말했다 The government said yesterday that inter-Korean trade is not affected by the regulations of the WTO because it takes place within the nation.

◉ ~경제교류 (the) North-South economic exchanges; 《한국의》 (the) inter-Korean economic exchanges. ~고위급 회담 the inter-Korean high-level talks. ~공동성명 the joint communique of 4 July 1972 between the South and North Korea. ~교류 exchanges between north and south Korea. ~교차승인 a cross recognition of south and north Korea. ~대결 《한국의》 the rivalry 〔confrontation〕 between two Koreas. ~대화 《한국의》 inter-Korean dialogue 〔talks〕. ~분단 《한국의》 the division of Korea (into north and south). ~상호 핵사찰 inter-Korean mutual nuclear inspections. ~아메리카 North and South America; both Americas. ~연락 사무소 the South-North Liaison Office. ~적십자 회담 the South-North Red Cross talks 〔conference〕. ~정상 회담 the South-North Korean summit talks; the inter-Korean summit talks. ~전쟁 《미국의》 the Civil War. ~조절위원회 the South-North Coordinating Committee(생략 SNCC). ~체육회담 the sports meeting between south and north Korea; the inter-Korean sports talks. ~통일 the reunification of North and South (Korea); the national reunification. ~합의서 the inter-Korean accords. ~협력 (the) North-South cooperation. ~협상 (the) North-South negotiations.

**남북한**(南北韓) the South and the North of Korea; south and north Koreas; Seoul and Pyŏngyang. ¶ ~ 직통 전화 a South-North 〔Seoul-Pyŏngyang〕 hot line.

**남빙양**(南氷洋) the Antarctic Ocean 〔Sea〕.

**남빛**(藍—) indigo (blue); deep blue.

**남사당**(男寺黨) 〖민속〗 a wayfaring male entertainer. ◉ ~패 a troupe of strolling entertainers 〔actors, players〕.

**남산골 샌님**(南山—) a penniless 〔poor〕 scholar.

**남상**(男相) a woman's face having masculine features; an unwomanly face. ¶ ~지르다 have an unwomanly face.

**남새** vegetables. ¶ 뒤뜰에 ~를 가꾸다 grow vegetables in the backyard. ◉ ~밭 a vegetable garden 〔patch〕.

**남색**(男色) sodomy; pederasty; 《비어》 buggery. ◉ ~가 a sodomite; a pederast.

**남색**(藍色) ① 《남빛》 indigo (blue); deep blue. ¶ ~물을 들이다 dye 《a cloth》 deep blue. ② 《남색짜리》 a married woman around twenty.

**남생이** 〖동물〗 a Korean terrapin.

**남서**(南西) the southwest (생략 SW).

**남선북마**(南船北馬) constant traveling; restless wandering; being on the move.

**남성**(男性) the male (sex); a man; 〖문법〗 the masculine gender. ¶ ~의 male / ~적인 manly; masculine / 그에겐 ~적인 데가 없다 He lacks manliness. / ~은 여성보다 육체적으로 강하다 Man is physically stronger than woman.

◉ ~미 manly 〔masculine〕 beauty. ~복 men's clothes; men's wear. ~호르몬 male (sex) hormone; androgen. ~화 virilism. ~화장품 men's toiletries.

**남성**(男聲) a male voice. ◉ ~4중창 a male quartet. ~합창 a male chorus; a male-voice choir: ~합창곡 a chorus for male voices.

**남실–** ⇨ 넘실–.

**남십자성**(南十字星) 〖천문〗 the Southern Cross; Crux.

**남아**(男兒) ① 《대장부》 a manly man. ¶ ~답게 like a man; in a manly manner / ~일언 중천금 A man's word is as good as a bond. *or* A man never goes back on his word. / 그는 진짜 한국 ~다 He is a true 〔real〕 Korean man. ② 《아이》 a boy; a son.

◉ ~선호사상 a notion of preferring a son to a daughter.

**남아**(南阿) South Africa.

**남아돌다** [사물이 주어] be more than enough; be superabundant; be in excess; [사람이 주어] have more than enough; have too many 〔much〕. ¶ 쌀이 ~ have enough rice to spare / 정력이 ~ have an excess of energy / 그에겐 남아돌 정도로 돈이 많다 He has more money than he can spend.

**남아메리카**(南—) South America. ¶ ~의 South American. ◉ ~대륙 South American Continent.

**남아프리카**(南—) (the Republic of) South Africa. ¶ ~의 South African. ◉ ~사람 a South African.

**남양**(南洋) the South Seas. ◉ ~군도 the South Sea Islands.

**남여**(籃輿) 《가마》 an open palanquin; a sedan chair.

**남용**(濫用) (an) abuse 〔(a) misuse〕 《of *one's* power》; overuse; improper 〔unlawful〕 use. ~하다 abuse 《*one's* authority》; misuse; overuse; make (an) improper use of; use improperly. ¶ 권리〔권력〕의 ~ an abuse of *one's* rights 〔power〕 / 마약 ~ drug abuse / 직권 ~ 죄 『법률』 oppression / 직권을 ~하다 abuse *one's* official authority / 공금을 ~하다 misappropriate public money / 아무리 좋은 약이라 해도 ~은 위험하다 The thoughtless use of medicine is very dangerous no matter how good the medicine is.

**남우**(男優) an actor. ¶ 주연 ~ a featured player 〔actor〕 / 오스카상 수상 ~ an Oscar actor.

**남우세** being a laughingstock; the butt of ridicule. ~하다 be a laughingstock; be the butt of ridicule. ~스럽다 (be) ridiculous; indecent; disgraceful; disreputable. ¶ ~스런 짓 하지 마라 Don't disgrace yourself.

**남위**(南緯) the south latitude (생략 S.lat.). ¶ ~ 15도 40분에 at 〔in〕 lat. 15°40′S. (★ at 〔in〕 fifteen degrees forty minutes of south latitude로 읽음) / 폭발로 인해 그 배는 ~ 20도 40분, 동경 160도 지점에서 침몰했다 The boat was sunk by an explosion at lat. 20°40′ S. and Long. 160°E. ◉ ~선 a line of south latitude.

**남유럽**(南—) Southern Europe.

**-남은** odd. ¶ 여남은 ten odd.

**남의눈** public notice 〔attention〕. ⇨남①. ¶ ~을 끄는 attractive; attracting; striking / ~을 꺼리는 사랑 secret love / ~에 띄지 않는 곳 a secret 〔private〕 place / ~을 끌다 attract (public) attention / ~을 피하다 avoid the eyes of others; shun the public eye / ~에 띄지 않다 escape notice 〔observation〕; slip from the sight of the world / 이곳에는 ~이 너무 많다 There are too many eyes around here. / 이제 부부가 되었으니 ~을 꺼릴 것 없다 As you are husband and wife now, you need not be afraid of what others may say.

**남의달** 《해산할 다음달》 the month following the estimated month of childbirth. ¶ ~ 잡다 be a month late in childbirth.

**남의집살다** work 〔be employed〕 as a domestic servant of a household. ¶ 식모로 ~ work as a kitchenmaid for a family.

**남자**(男子) a man (*pl.* men); a male (sex); a fellow (녀석); 《미구어》 a guy; 《영구어》 a chap. ¶ 잘생긴 ~ a handsome man / 재미있는 ~ an amusing fellow; a funny guy / ~선생 a man teacher / ~학생〔점원〕 a male student 〔clerk〕 / ~아기 a baby boy / ~가 반할 만한 남자 a man's man / ~다운 manly; masculine / ~답지 못한 unmanly; effeminate / ~ 같은 mannish 《woman》 / ~들만의 세계 the man-only world / ~옷〔시계〕 men's wear 〔watch〕 / ~들만의 파티 a stag party / ~답게 행동하다 behave 〔act〕 like a man / 그는 말이 없는 ~다운 소년이다 He is a silent, manly boy. / 이전에 저 ~를 본 적이 있다 I have seen that guy. / 저 ~는 누구지 Who is that guy 〔fellow〕? / 그는 대단한 ~다 He is quite a man. / 그는 ~ 중의 남자다 He is a man among men. / 그는 ~답지 못한 녀석이다 He's not much of a man. / ~는 배짱 여자는 절개 In a man courage, in a woman chastity. / ~가 아니냐, 울지마라 Be a man, don't cry! / 이것은 ~와 남자간의 약속이다 This is a promise between man and man. / 그는 40세 한창 나이의 ~다 He is 40 years old in the prime of manhood. ◉ ~친구 a boyfriend; a man friend. ~학교 a boy's school.

**남작**(男爵) a baron. ¶ ~에 서작되다 be created a baron / 윌리엄 ~ Baron William; Lord William 《영》. ◉ ~부인 a baroness: 헌트 ~부인 Lady Hunt 《영》; Baroness Hunt.

**남작**(濫作) excessive production; overproduction. ~하다 produce too much 〔an excess〕; 《작가 따위가》 write a large number of stories at a reckless speed; churn out one book after another.

**남장**(男裝) male attire; men's clothes. ~하다 disguise *oneself* as a man; be dressed like a man; be in men's clothes. ¶ ~ 미인 a pretty 〔beautiful〕 woman in male attire / 그녀는 자주 ~을 한다 She often wears men's clothes.

**남정**(男丁) a man above the age of fifteen; an adult; a grown-up. ◉ ~네 《남자들》 the menfolk(s); 《남편들》 the husbands.

**남존여비**(男尊女卑) predominance of men over women; (the) domination of men over women; (the) subjection of women. ¶ ~의 사회 a male-dominated society / 한국에는 아직도 ~의 관습이 남아 있다 The custom of treating women as inferior to men still remains in Korea.

**남종**(男—) a manservant; a male servant.

**남중국해**(南中國海) the South China Sea.

**남진**(南進) southward advance. ~하다 march 〔advance〕 southward. ◉ ~정책 the southward expansion policy.

**남짓** 「a little 〔some〕 above 〔over, more than, upward of〕; 《three》 odd 《years》. ¶ 서 말 ~ a little over 〔more than〕 three *mal* / 4년 ~ some more than four years; a little upward of four years / 4달러 ~ four dollars and some odd cents.

**남짓하다** be a 「bit 〔little〕 over 〔above, more than〕; be upward of. ¶ 30명 ~ be a bit more than thirty people; be thirty strong / 두 말 ~ be a bit more than two *mal* / 나는 2시간 남짓하게 기다렸으나 그녀는 오지 않았다 I waited for a little over two hours, but she didn't 「come 〔appear, turn up〕.

**남쪽** the south. ¶ ~의 southern; south / ~ 나라 a southern country / ~에 south; southward; to the south 《of》 / ~을 바라보다 face 〔look toward〕 the south / ~으로 가다 go south 〔southward〕 / ~으로 떠나다 leave for the south / ~이 바다에 면하다 face the sea on the south / 오산은 수원 ~에 있다 Osan is to the south of Suwŏn. / 그 도시는 서울에서 ~으로 약 40km 떨어진 곳에 있다 The city is located about 40km south of Seoul.

**남창**(男唱) 《노래》 a song sung by a woman in male voice; 《사람》 a woman singing the man's part.

**남창**(男娼) a male prostitute.

**남첩**(男妾) a paramour; a keptman; a gigolo. ¶ 돈 많은 과부의 젊은 ~ a rich widow's 「pet 〔darling, young lover〕.

**남침**(南侵) the invasion of the South Korea 《by the North Korean forces》. ~하다 invade the south.

**남탕**(男湯) the men's bathroom 《of a public bath》.

**남태평양**(南太平洋) the South Pacific.

**남파**(南派) ~하다 send 《a spy》 into the south. ¶ 무장 공작원의 ~ sending of armed commandos into the south. ◉ ~간첩 an espionage agent sent by the north to the south.

**남편**(男便) a husband; 《구어》 *one's* old man. ¶ ~ 있는〔없는〕 여자 a married 〔a single, an unmarried〕 woman / ~에게 충실하다 be faithful to *one's* husband / ~을 깔고 뭉개다 dominate *one's* husband; keep *one's* husband under *one's* thumb / ~을 섬기다 be attentive 〔devoted〕 to *one's* husband / ~을 얻다 get married; get a husband / ~을 잃다 lose *one's* husband; be widowed / ~ 얼굴에 먹칠을 하다 bring disgrace upon *one's* husband / 그는 내게 이상적인 ~입니다 He is an ideal husband for me.

**남포**[1] 《램프》 a lamp. ¶ 석유 ~ an oil lamp / ~를 켜다〔끄다〕 light 〔put out〕 a lamp. ◉ ~갓 a lamp shade. ~등피 a lamp chimney. ~심지 a lamp wick. 안전~ a safety 〔miner's〕 lamp. 남폿불 lamplight; a lamp: 남폿불을 돋우다〔낮추다〕 turn up 〔down〕 a lamp.

**남포**[2] 《화약》 dynamite. ¶ ~질하다 blast with dynamite.

**남풍**(南風) a south 〔southerly〕 wind. ¶ ~이 분다 The wind blows southerly 〔from the south〕.

**남하**(南下) southward advance. ~하다 go 〔advance〕 south 〔southward〕. ¶ 자유를 찾아 ~하다 come to the south seeking for freedom / 연대는 ~를 계속했다 The regiment kept moving south. / 일행은 반도를 ~했다 The party went southward the peninsula.

**남학생**(男學生) a male pupil; a schoolboy; a boy student.

**남한**(南韓) South Korea. ¶ ~의 South Korean. ⇨ 한국(韓國).

**남해**(南海) the southern sea; 《한국의》 the South Sea. ¶ ~에는 크고 작은 섬이 많다 There are many islands large and small in the South Sea.

**남해안**(南海岸) the south coast.

**남행**(南行) going south; southing. ~하다 go south 〔southward〕; go down to the south. ◉ ～열차 a south-bound train.

**남향**(南向) a southern exposure 〔aspect〕; looking toward south; facing the south. ～하다 face the south; look south; be exposed to the south. ◉ ～방〔집〕 a room 〔house〕 facing 〔looking〕 (toward the) south. ～판 a site facing south.

**남회귀선**(南回歸線) the Tropic of Capricorn.

**남획**(濫獲) excessive 〔reckless, indiscriminate〕 fishing 〔hunting〕. ～하다 fish 〔hunt〕 recklessly 〔excessively, indiscriminately〕; overfish; overhunt. ¶ 근해에서는 고기가 ～되었다 The coastal waters have been overfished.

**납** 〖화학〗 lead (기호 Pb). ¶ 납 같은 leaden / 납 색깔의 lead-colored; leaden 《skies》. ◉ 납중독 lead poisoning.

**납**(蠟) wax; white 〔refined〕 wax. ¶ 마루에 납칠을 하다 wax the floor. ◉ 납세공 waxwork. 납인형 a wax doll. 납지(紙) wax(ed) paper.

**납**(鑞) 《땜납》 solder.

**납거미** 〖동물〗 a flat-shaped spider of the *Urocteidae*.

**납골**(納骨) laying 《*a person's*》 ashes to rest. ～하다 lay 〔place〕 《*a person's*》 ashes to rest. ◉ ～당 a charnel (house); an ossuary.

**납금**(納金) 《지불》 payment of money; money due (지불할 돈); money paid (지불한 돈). ～하다 pay 《money》. ¶ 만기일까지 반드시 ～할 것 Be sure to complete the payment by the due date.

**납기**(納期) 《금전의》 the date 〔time〕 of payment; 《물품의》 the appointed date of delivery; 《세금의》 the date of tax payment. ¶ 종업원들은 ～ 내에 납품하려고 열심히 일했다 The employees worked hard so that they could deliver the goods by the appointed date.

**납길**(納吉) ～하다 notify the bride's family of the date set for the wedding.

**납대대하다** (be) flattish. ¶ 납대대한 얼굴 a flat face.

**납덩이** a slug 〔lump〕 of lead; a lead ingot. ¶ ～처럼 무거운 팔다리 leaden limbs / ～ 같다 《얼굴이 창백하다》 be pale; be white as a sheet; 《몸이 무겁다》 be 〔feel〕 as heavy as lead; be sluggish / 아침에 잠을 깨니 팔다리가 ～처럼 무거웠다 In the morning I woke up feeling that my limbs were as heavy as lead.

**납득**(納得) 《이해》 understanding; 《승낙》 consent; assent; compliance. ～하다 《이해하다》 understand; be convinced 《of, that...》; accept 《that...》; be persuaded; 《승낙하다》 agree 《to》; consent 〔assent〕 《to》; comply 《with》. ¶ ～하기 어려운 unconvincing; hard to understand / ～시키다 make 《*a person*》 consent 《to》; convince 《*a person*》 of; persuade 《*a person*》 to *do* 〔into *do*ing〕; win 《*a person*》 over; satisfy *oneself* 《of, that...》 / 너의 그런 설명으로는 ～이 안 간다 That explanation of yours does not go down with me. / 그녀는 그에게 그의 잘못을 ～시켰다 She convinced him of his error. / 내가 ～할 수 있도록 설명해 주시오 Please explain (it) to my satisfaction. / 충분히 ～이 갈 때까지 선생님께 질문해라 Ask the teacher questions again and again till you understand well. / 내 설명으로 완전히 ～이 되었습니까 Are you completely satisfied with my explanation? / 소액의 보상으로는 그들이 ～하지 않을 게다 They won't be satisfied with a small amount of compensation.

**납땜** soldering. ～하다 solder 《a leaky pot》. ¶ ～한 soldered 《kettle》. ◉ ～인두 a soldering iron.

**납량**(納涼) enjoying the cool air; cooling *oneself*. ¶ ～하러 나가다 go out to enjoy the evening cool. ◉ ～객 people out to enjoy the cool breezes of the evening. ～음악회 a summer-evening concert. ～특집 프로 a special summer evening program.

**납본**(納本) 《행위》 presentation of a specimen copy; 《책》 a specimen copy. ～하다 present a specimen copy 《to the authorities, for censorship》.

**납부**(納付) 《세금 따위의》 payment; 《물품의》 delivery. ～하다 pay 《taxes》; deliver 〔supply〕 《goods》. ¶ 분할 ～ divided payments; payment on an installment basis / 1학기 수업료를 ～하다 pay the tuition fees for the first semester. ◉ ～기한 the deadline for payment. ～금 《납부할》 money due; 《납부한》 money paid. ～서 a statement of payment 〔delivery〕. ～액 the amount of payment. ～자 a payer.

**납북**(拉北) ～하다 kidnap 〔abduct〕 《*a person*》 to the north; hijack 《an airplane》 to the north. ◉ ～어선〔어부, 인사〕 a fishing boat 〔a fisherman, a person〕 kidnapped to North Korea.

**납석**(蠟石) 〖광물〗 agalmatolite; pagodite.

**납세**(納稅) payment of taxes. ～하다 pay *one's* taxes. ¶ ～의 의무 a legal obligation to pay (*one's*) taxes; liability to pay taxes / ～ 이의 신청 권리 the

rights of a tax payer to protest the assessment / 국민은 ～의 의무를 진다 The people are liable to taxation.
◉ ～고지서 a tax notice 〔paper〕. ～기일 the tax due date; the date on which taxes are due (for payment). ～기한 the time limit for tax payment. ～신고 《make *one's*》 income tax declaration 〔returns〕: ～ 신고서 tax forms. ～액 the amount 「of *one's* taxes 〔of taxes that *one* has to pay〕. ～연체이자 interest on a delinquent tax. ～자 a taxpayer: 자진 신고 ～자 a self-assessed taxpayer. ～자격 tax payment requirements; the qualifications of a taxpayer. ～자진 신고제 the voluntary tax returns filing system. ～증지 a tax-payment stamp; a revenue stamp. ～지(地) the place of tax payment. ～필 duty paid: ～미필 duty 「in arrear 〔unpaid〕 / ～필증 a tax clearance.

**납시다** 《the king》 deign to come out; 「appear.

**납신거리다** 《재잘거리다》 chatter; patter; prattle; talk glib and flippant; 《굽실거리다》 kowtow 《to》; cringe 《to》. ¶ 입을 ～ wag *one's* tongue / 무엇을 그리 납신거리느냐 What are you prattling on so excitedly about? / 그는 늘 지점장에게 납신거린다 He is always kowtowing to the office manager.

**납입**(納入) payment 《of a tax, fee, *etc.*》; delivery 《of goods》. ～하다 pay 《a tax》; deliver 《goods》; make a delivery. ¶ 일부 ～ partial payment / 은행에 돈을 ～하다 pay money into a bank / 주금(株金) 전액을 ～하다 pay up shares.
◉ ～금 the sum of money (to be) paid; subscription. ～액 the amount paid-up. ～자본 paid-up 〔paid-in〕 capital. ～최고(催告) a call. ～품 supplies; goods for supply.

**납작-** ⇨ 넓적-.

**납작보리** flattened barley; rolled barley 「(사료용).

**납작코** a flat nose; a snub nose; 《사람》 a flat-nosed person.

**납작하다** ① 《판판하고 얇다》 (be) flat; low (낮은); thin (얇은); 《평탄하다》 (be) level; even. ¶ 납작한 얼굴 a flat face / 납작한 집 a low house / 납작하게 flatly / 가슴이 납작한 여자 a flat-chested woman / 납작하게 하다 flatten; level / 납작해지다 become flat 〔thin〕; be flattened 〔crushed〕 / 모자를 깔고 앉아 납작하게 하다 sit on a hat and crush 〔flatten〕 it / 깡통이 납작하게 찌부러졌다 The empty can got crushed flat. / 승용차가 대형트럭과 충돌하여 납작해졌다 A car was squashed flat by a big truck. *or* A car collided with a big truck and was left as flat as a pancake.
② [비유적] ¶ (아무의) 코를 납작하게 하다 humble 《*a person's*》 pride; take 〔bring, let〕 《*a person*》 down a peg (or two); 《구어》 cut 《*a person*》 down to size / 그와의 토론에서 나는 코가 납작해졌다 In the argument with him, I was beaten hand down.

**납줄개** 〖어류〗 a bitterling.

**납지**(鑞紙) tin foil; lead foil.

**납질**(蠟質) waxy substance.

**납채**(納采) 《납폐》 sending wedding presents from the bridegroom's house to the bride's house.

**납치**(拉致) 《사람의》 taking 《*a person*》 away forcibly; 《사람 외의》 a (plane) hijacking. ⇨ 유괴. ～하다 《사람을》 take 《*a person*》 away forcibly; 《비행기 따위를》 hijack 《an airplane》. ¶ ～된 여객기의 승객들 passengers from 〔on〕 the hijacked airbus / 그는 범죄 용의자에게 ～되었다 He was taken away forcibly by a criminal suspect. ◉ ～범 《비행기의》 a hijacker; a skyjacker.

**납폐**(納幣) sending blue and red silks to the bride's house.

**납품**(納品) 《일》 delivery of goods; 《물품》 delivered goods. ～하다 deliver 《goods to》; supply 《the government with goods》. ¶ 이것은 K상사에 ～할 상품이다 This goods goes to K firm. ◉ ～서 a statement of delivery. ～업자 a supplier.

**납회**(納會) 《모임의》 the last meeting of the year; 《거래소의》 the last session of the year.

**낫** a sickle; a scythe (자루가 긴). ¶ 낫으로 풀을 베다 mow grass with a sickle / 낫놓고 기역자도 모른다 be illiterate 〔unlettered〕; do not know A from B.

**낫낫하다** (be) tender; soft.

**낫다**[1] 《더 좋다》 be better 《than》; be superior 〔excellent, preferable〕 《to》; [자동사로] outdo; surpass; excel 《in》. ¶ 나아지다 become better; be improved / 누구보다도 ～ surpass 〔be superior to〕 all / 나으면 나았지 못하지 않다 be not at all inferior to 《*a person*》; can favorably compare with; be as good as / 오히려 이것이 ～ This is rather preferable. / 그는 영어에서 남보다 ～ He excels 〔outdoes〕 the others in English. / 그것보다 이것이 훨씬 ～ This (one) is much [far] better than that. / 건강이 재산보다 ~ Health is above wealth. / 그는 나보다 나은 월급을 받는다 He gets a better salary than I do. / 무어라도 있는 것이 없는 것보다 ~ Something is better than nothing. / 늦더라도 안 하느니보다는 ~ Better late than never. / 내 집보다 더 나은 곳은 없다 There's no place like home. / 이 차는 연료 절약이란 면에서는 다른 어떤 차보다 ~ This car beats all others in fuel economy.

**낫다²** 《병 따위가》 get well [better]; recover from 《illness》; be restored 《to health》; be cured of 《a disease》; get over (회복하다); 《상처가》 heal (up); be healed. ¶ 낫지 않는 병 an incurable disease / 잘 낫지 않는 피부병 a stubborn skin disease / 저절로 ~ get well of itself; heal of itself / 상처는 아직 낫지 않았다 The wound is not yet healed. / 어머니는 곧 병이 나을 것이다 Mother will soon recover from her illness. *or* Mother will 「get well [be all right] soon. / 그는 폐렴이 나아지고 있다 He is recovering from pneumonia. / 감기가 낫는데 꽤 오래 걸렸다 It took me a long time to get over [shake off] my cold. / 이 약으로 병이 나았다 This medicine cured me. / 하루만 늦었어도 나을 수 없었다고 의사가 말했다 The doctor said that another day's delay would have made a cure hopeless.

**낫살** a mature age; an advanced age. ¶ ~깨나 먹은 사람 a man well up in years / 자네, ~깨나 먹은 사람이 꼴불견일세 Be [Act] your age! *or* You ought to know better at your age.

**낫잡다** ① 《넉넉하게 치다》 estimate [rate] high. ¶ 낫잡아 at the (very) outside; at most / 값을 시세보다 ~ rate the cost higher than the current price / 낫잡아 만 원밖에 하지 않을 것이다 It won't cost more than 10,000 won at the highest. ② 《여유를 두다》 leave a margin; give ample measure 《to》. ¶ 여비를 낫잡아 계산하다 allow *oneself* an ample margin for travel expenses.

**낫질** using [wielding] a scythe. ~하다 scythe; use [wield] a scythe.

**낫표**(—標) Korean quotation marks 《「」》; corner brackets.

**낭군**(郎君) 《my》 dear husband.

**낭독**(朗讀) (a) reading aloud; 《암송》 (a) recitation. ~하다 read aloud; recite. ¶ 시를 ~하다 read a poem aloud; recite a poem. ◉ ~법 elocution. ~연설 a set [reading] speech: ~ 연설을 하다 speak from *one's* notes. ~자 a reader; a reciter. ~회 《give》 a public reading [a recitation] 《of Hamlet》.

**낭떠러지** a cliff; a precipice; a bluff (바닷가의). ¶ ~가 많은 cliffy / 깎아지른 ~ sharp cut cliff / ~ 끝에 서다 stand on the edge of a precipice [cliff] / ~에서 떨어지다 fall over [down] a precipice / ~를 기어 오르다 climb up a cliff; go over a precipice / 그 차는 ~에서 추락했다 The car fell over a precipice.

**낭랑하다**(朗朗—) (be) ringing; clear; sonorous; resonant. ¶ 낭랑한 목소리로 in a 「clear [ringing, resonant] voice / 낭랑하게 한 편의 시를 읽다 read a poem in a clear, resonant voice.

**낭만**(浪漫) (being) romantic. ¶ ~적(인) romantic / ~적인 생각에 잠기다 indulge in romantic dreaming [thoughts] / 이 카페에는 ~적인 분위기가 있다 This café has a romantic atmosphere. ◉ ~주의 romanticism: ~주의자 a romanticist / ~주의 문학 Romantic literature. ~파 the romantic school; the Romantics. 신~주의 neoromanticism.

**낭보**(朗報) good news; glad tidings.

**낭비**(浪費) (a) waste 《of time and energy》; extravagance. ~하다 waste 《*one's* money on trifles》; throw [fritter] 《*one's* money》 away; dissipate 《*one's* savings》; squander 《on》. ¶ ~적인 wasteful; extravagant / ~를 줄이다[피하다, 없애다] reduce [avoid, eliminate] waste / 그의 노력도 결국 시간 ~로 끝났다 His efforts 「resulted in [ended up as] a waste of his time. / ~하지 말고 저금해라 Don't waste your money. Save it. / 우리는 기름을 ~하고 있지 않은가 Aren't we wasteful with oil? / 그는 물쓰듯 돈을 ~했다 He made ducks and drakes of his money. ◉ ~벽 wasteful habits: ~벽이 있다 have [be in] the habit of wasting money 《on luxury》. ~자 a waster; a spendthrift; an extravagant [thriftless] person.

**낭설**(浪說) a groundless [wild] rumor; an unfounded [a groundless] report. ¶ ~이 퍼지다 a rumor is abroad [current] / ~을 퍼뜨리다 set a false rumor afloat / ~을 믿다 take rumor as it is.

**낭송**(朗誦) recitation; reading. ~하다 read aloud; recite. ¶ 각본 ~ reading a play; 《배우의》 rehearsal.

**낭자**(娘子) a maiden; a virgin; a girl; a young woman.

**낭자**(狼藉) ① 《흩어져 어지러움》 disorder;

confusion. ～하다 be in wild disorder; be in great confusion; be scattered all over. ¶ 유혈이 ～하다 be covered with blood. ② 《소문 등이 파다함》 circulation 《of a scandal》; propagation. ～하다 be widely rumored; be gossiped about.

**낭종**(囊腫) 『의학』 a cystoma (*pl.* ～s, -mata); a cystic tumor. ¶ 난소～ an ovarian cystoma.

**낭중**(囊中) the inside of a purse 〔pocket〕. ¶ ～ 무일푼이다 be penniless; do not have a penny to bless *oneself.* ◉ ～취물 an easy task.

**낭창낭창** ～하다 (be) pliant; flexible; supple. ¶ ～한 대나무 pliant bamboo / ～한 나뭇가지 a flexible twig; a switch.

**낭패**(狼狽) 《딱한 처지》 a difficult situation; a dilemma; a fix 《구어》; difficulties; 《당혹스러움》 perplexity; embarrassment. ～하다 be in a difficult situation 〔position〕; be in trouble 〔a dilemma, a fix〕; be perplexed 〔embarrassed〕. ¶ ～를 보다〔당하다〕 get into 「a difficult situation 〔trouble, hot water 《구어》〕 / 무어라고 대답해야 할지 ～다 I'm completely 「at a loss 〔perplexed〕 for a suitable reply. / 이거 ～로구나 What an embarrassing 〔awkward〕 case this is! *or* Good heavens! / 차가 고장나서 ～다 We are in a fix. Our car has broken down. / 머리털이 자꾸 빠져 ～다 I am troubled with falling hair. / 정부를 ～케 하는 폭로기사가 계속되고 있다 There has been a series of revelations that has embarrassed the Government. / 그녀는 ～스런 얼굴로 서 있었다 She was standing with a perplexed look on her face.

**낮** 《주간》 day; the daytime; 《정오》 noon; midday; noontime. ¶ 낮일 day work / 대낮, 한낮 midday; high noon / 낮에 by day; in the daytime; during the day (time) / 달이 낮같이 밝다 The moon is as bright as day. / 그는 낮에는 일하고 밤에는 학교에 다닌다 He works by day and attends school by night. / 그는 밤낮없이 일을 계속했다 He went on working 「night and day 〔day and night, around the clock〕. / 그 거리는 낮에도 어둡다 The street is dark even in the daytime. / 낮말은 새가 듣고 밤말은 쥐가 듣는다 《속담》 Walls 〔Pitchers〕 have ears.

**낮거리** sex in broad daylight; daytime intercourse.

**낮결** the first half of the afternoon; 「early afternoon.

**낮다** ① 《높이가》 (be) low; 《코 따위가》 (be) flat. ¶ 낮은 언덕 a low hill / 낮은 코 a flat nose / 물은 낮은 데로 흐른다 Water finds its level. ② 《목소리가》 (be) low. ¶ 낮은 음 a low-pitched sound; bass / 낮은 목소리로 in whispers; in a low 〔soft〕 voice; in an undertone; in a low key (저음). ③ 《신분·지위가》 (be) low 《status》; humble 《origins》; mean. ¶ 신분이 ～ 《지위가》 have low status; be low in social standing; 《태생이》 come from a humble background; have 〔be of〕 humble origins; be of low birth / 소령은 대령보다 계급이 ～ A major is below a colonel. / 그는 능력이 많은데도 지위가 아직 ～ He still holds a minor position even though he has a lot of ability. ④ 《능력·수준이》 (be) low. ¶ 그들의 생활 수준은 ～ Their standard of living is low. / 이 대학은 수준이 ～ This university is of a low level. ⑤ 《정도·수치·가격 등이》 (be) low; small. ¶ 낮은 수입으로 살다 live on a small 〔low〕 income / 나는 혈압이 ～ I have low blood pressure. / 오늘은 온도가 ～ The temperature is low today. / 현재의 토지 가격은 작년 이맘때 가격에 비해 ～ The current value of land is low compared with this time last year.

**낮도깨비** ① 《도깨비》 a goblin that plays (evil) tricks on people in broad daylight. ② 《사람》 a shameless bastard.

**낮도둑** 《도둑》 a noonday 〔sneak〕 thief; 《염치 없는 사람》 a shameless hog; a greedy 〔grasping〕 person.

**낮번**(一番) the day shift. ¶ ～을 들다 take the day shift.

**낮은말** ① ＝낮춤말. ② 《천한 말》 a vulgar word; a vulgarism. ③ 《속삭임》 a whisper; murmuring.

**낮은음자리표** 『음악』 the bass 〔F〕 clef.

**낮잠** a nap; an afternoon nap; a siesta. ¶ ～을 자다 take a nap 〔siesta〕.

**낮잡다** underestimate; underrate; estimate 〔evaluate, appraise, rate〕 low. ¶ 낮잡은 숫자〔액수〕 a conservative figure 〔amount〕 / 아주 낮잡아도 at the lowest estimate; on a conservative basis (of appraisement) / 집값을 ～ rate the price of a house low / 그들의 능력을 낮잡아 보지 마라 Don't underestimate their ability. / 아주 낮잡아도 비용이 3백 달러는 들 것이다 At the lowest 〔a safe, a moderate〕 estimate, the expense will be $300.

**낮차**(一車) 《열차》 a day train 〔coach〕.

**낮참** 《음식》 eating between meals (usually for day laborers); 《쉬는 시간》 a recess 〔break〕 after eating between meals. ¶ ~을 먹다 eat 〔have a snack〕 between meals.

**낮추다** ① 《높이·값·소리 따위를》 lower; bring 〔let〕 down; make low; drop; reduce. ¶ 값을 ~ lower 〔bring down, reduce〕 the price / 허리를 ~ bend down; stoop / 소리를 ~ turn 〔tone, tune〕 down 《the radio》 / 출산율을 ~ lower the birthrate / 비행기의 기수를 ~ lower 〔drop〕 the nose of a plane / 온도를 ~ reduce 〔lower〕 the temperature / 속도를 ~ slow down 〔reduce〕 speed / 목소리를 ~ lower *one's* voice / 목소리를 낮추어 말하다 speak in a low 〔subdued〕 voice; speak low / 「이득 없는 가격 낮추기 경쟁이 끝나지 않을 것 같다」—「그건 마치 자신의 목을 자신이 죄는 격이지」 "The ugly war of price reductions just won't quit."—"That's just like cutting your own throat."
② 《인기·품질 등을》 lower; degrade; debase; 《계급을》 reduce 《a soldier》 to a lower rank; demote 《to》. ¶ 환경 기준을 ~ lower the environmental standards 《for sulfurous acid gas》 / 상품의 품질을 ~ lower 〔debase, deteriorate〕 the quality of goods / 강의의 정도를 ~ make *one's* lecture easier to follow / 거듭되는 실언으로 인기도를 ~ lower 〔injure〕 *one's* popularity by *his* continued slips of the tongue.
③ 《말을》 drop *one's* honorifics in talking; speak in familiar 〔plain〕 terms. ¶ 말씀 낮추시지요 Please drop honorifics. *or* Your words sound too polite to me.

**낮추보다** look down (up)on; despise; belittle; think lightly 〔meanly〕 of 《*a person*》; hold 《*a person*》 in contempt. ¶ 남을 낮춰보는 듯한 행동은 삼가해야 한다 You should refrain from acting as if you were looking down on others. *or* You must stop taking on a condescending air.

**낮춤말** 《낮은 말》 intimate 〔friendly〕 speech 〔terms〕; 《겸손어》 humble 〔modest〕 words.

**낯** ① 《얼굴》 a face; a visage 《문어》; 《이목구비》 *one's* looks 〔features〕; 《표정》 a look; *one's* countenance. ⇨ 얼굴. ¶ 낯을 대하다 face each other / 낯을 찡그리다 make a 「wry face 〔grimace〕; frown / 낯이 익다 *a person's* face is familiar / 낯을 익히다 become acquainted 〔familiar〕 with 《*a person*》 / 좋은 낯을 하다 look satisfied 〔pleased〕; have a smile on *one's* face / 좋지 않은 낯을 하다 look displeased 〔dissatisfied〕 / 그는 웃는〔환한〕 낯으로 들어왔다 He came in with 「a smile (on his face) 〔a beaming face〕.
② 《체면》 face; honor; (a) reputation; prestige; dignity (위엄). ¶ 낯을 세우다 〔유지하다〕 save *one's* face 〔honor, dignity〕 / 낯을 깎이다 disgrace *oneself;* lose face 〔honor, reputation〕; be put out of countenance / 아무의 낯을 깎다 injure 〔impair〕 《*a person's*》 honor; put 《*a person*》 to shame / 당신을 뵐 낯이 없습니다 I'm really ashamed of myself to see you. / 내 낯을 봐서 그 애를 용서해 주시오 Please forgive the boy 「for my sake 〔just to save my face〕. / 무슨 낯으로 또 돈을 꾸어 달라느냐 Where do you get the gall to ask me to lend you money again? / 내 무슨 낯으로 그들을 대할 수 있겠느냐 How can I ever have the face to see them?

**낯가리다** ① 《어린아이가》 be afraid 〔shy〕 of strangers; be timid 《with》; be bashful in front of strangers. ¶ 낯가려 울다 cry at the sight of a stranger / 이 애는 낯가리지 않아요 This baby takes to strangers. ② 《얼굴을 가리다》 cover 〔hide, bury〕 *one's* face. ¶ 양손〔수건〕으로 ~ bury 〔cover〕 *one's* face 「in *one's* hands 〔with *one's* handkerchief〕.

**낯가죽** 《얼굴의 껍질》 the skin of the face; 《체면에 관계되는 감각》 sense of honor 〔shame〕. ¶ ~이 두껍다 have lots of nerve (in *one*); be 「thick-skinned 〔brazen-faced〕 / 그 녀석 ~이 두껍기도 하다 What a brazen-faced fellow he is! *or* What (a) nerve (he's got)!

**낯간지럽다** (be) embarrassed; ashamed; abashed; conscience-stricken; feel shy 〔embarrassed〕. ¶ 지나친 칭찬에 ~ be 「embarrassed 〔made to feel self-conscious〕 by an excess of praise / 낯간지러워서 그런 말은 못하겠다 I am ashamed to say such a thing.

**낯나다** gain 〔win, save〕 *one's* honor 〔face〕; get credit; reflect credit on 《*a person*》. ¶ 양쪽이 다 낯나는 분쟁의 해결책 a face-saving solution to the dispute / 그렇게 하면 나도 낯난다 That would save face for me.

**낯내다** 《자신을》 act so as to gain the respect of others; do honor to *oneself;* do *oneself* proud; reflect credit on *oneself;* 《남을》 show deference 《to》;

save 《*a person's*》 face. ¶ 세상에 낯내느라고 기부하는 사람도 없지 않다 Some people donate their money just to reflect credit on themselves. / 너, 이 조그만 것을 주고 낯내려 드는구나 You are doing yourself proud by giving me this small present, aren't you?

**낯두껍다** (be) thick-skinned; shameless; brazen-faced; impudent; cheeky 《구어》. ¶ 낯두껍게도 …하다 have the impudence 〔nerve〕 to 《*do*》; be shameless 〔impudent〕 enough to 《*do*》 / 그는 낯두껍게도 돈을 빌리러 왔다 He had the crust to ask for a loan.

**낯바닥** a face; a phiz 《영속어》; a mug 《속어》; a pan 《미속어》.

**낯부끄럽다** (be) ashamed; shameful; disgraceful. ¶ 낯부끄러운 짓 a shameful conduct 〔behavior〕.

**낯붉히다** blush 《at, for》; flush 《with》; turn red. ¶ 화가 나서 ~ flush 〔redden〕 with anger / 부끄러워 ~ blush for shame / 여간해서 낯붉히지 않다 be slow to get angry / 낯붉히게 하다 put 《*a person*》 to shame 〔the blush〕.

**낯빛** a 〔*one's*〕 complexion; face color.

**낯설다** (be) unfamiliar; strange; unknown. ¶ 낯선 얼굴 an unfamiliar face / 낯선 곳 a strange place / 낯선 광경 an unfamiliar 〔a new〕 scene / 낯선 땅에서 일하다 work in a strange 〔an unfamiliar〕 land / 거리에서 낯선 사람이 내게 인사를 했다 A stranger greeted me on the street.

**낯알다** know the face of 《*a person*》; know 《*a person*》 by sight. ¶ 그들은 모두가 낯아는 사람들이었다 I knew them all by sight.

**낯없다** 《면목없다》 be ashamed 《of *oneself*》; have no face 《to》; do not have the face 〔courage〕 to. ¶ 정말 뵐 낯 없습니다 I'm really ashamed of myself. / 돈을 갚지 못해 볼 낯 없네 I am ashamed to see 〔face〕 you because I couldn't pay my debt to you.

**낯익다** (be) familiar; be well-known. ¶ 낯익은 사람 an acquaintance / 낯익은 얼굴 a familiar face / 낯은 익으나 이름은 모르겠다 I recognize him but don't know his name. / 그 사람은 낯익은 얼굴인데 I fancy I have seen him somewhere before. *or* I remember seeing him once.

**낯익히다** get 《*a person*》 familiar with *oneself*.

**낯짝** =낯바닥. ¶ 무슨 ~으로 부탁을 하러 왔느냐 How cheeky you are to come to ask me a favor!

**낱** a piece; an item; each piece; a unit.

**낱개** a piece; each piece. ¶ ~로 파는 loose 《flowers, pencils》 / ~로 5,000원 five thousand won apiece 〔each〕 / ~로 팔다 sell by the piece / 비누를 ~로 팔다 sell soap by the cake 〔bar〕 / 연필을 ~로 팔다〔사다〕 sell 〔buy〕 pencils loose 〔in loose pieces〕.

**낱개비** each split piece 《of firewood》; a piece 《of cigarette》; a stick 《of match》.

**낱낱이** ① 《하나하나》 one by one; individually; separately; piece by piece. ¶ 물건을 ~ 세다 count articles one by one / ~ 예를 들다 give separate examples (for each) / ~ 이름을 들다 mention 〔single out〕 each by name. ② 《모두》 everything; everyone; each and every one; all; without omission 〔exception〕; entirely. ¶ 친구를 ~ 찾아보다 pay a visit to each and every friend / 나는 그것에 관하여 ~ 그에게 말했다 I told him all about it. ③ 《자세히》 in detail; in full; fully. ¶ ~ 캐묻다 ask questions in detail / ~ 설명하다 explain 《*a thing*》 in detail; give full explanation / ~ 보고하다 make a detailed report 《of》.

**낱단** a bunch; a bundle. ¶ 무는 ~으로 판다 Radish is sold by the bundle.

**낱돈** odd money; small change.

**낱뜨기** merchandise sold by the piece.

**낱말** a word; a vocabulary. ⇨단어.

**낱알** a grain 《of rice》.

**낱장**(―帳) a sheet 〔piece〕 《of paper》; a copy 《of photograph》; a leaf 《of a book》.

**낳다** ① 《출산하다》 bear 《a child》; have 《a baby》; give birth to 《a baby》; be delivered of 《a baby》; 《동물이》 have 《kittens, puppies》; breed; 《산란하다》 lay 《eggs》; spawn (물고기가). ¶ 갓 낳은 알 a new-laid egg / 그녀는 어제 아들을 낳았다 She had a baby boy yesterday. / 그녀는 아이를 다섯 낳았다 She has had five children. / 고양이는 1년에 몇번 새끼를 낳느냐 How many times does a cat breed in a year?
② 《발생·산출하다》 produce; bring forth; give rise to; yield 〔bear〕 《interest at 10 percent》. ¶ 좋은 결과를 ~ produce good results / 그는 한국이 낳은 가장 훌륭한 과학자이다 He is the greatest scientist that Korea has ever produced. / 돈이 돈을 ~ Money begets money. / 그 뉴스는 갖가지 억측을 낳았다 The news has given rise to all sorts of specu-

lation. / 그 투자는 많은 이익을 낳았다 The investment returned much profit. / 소문이 소문을 낳는다 One rumor begets another.

**내**[1] smoke; fume. = 연기(煙氣).

**내**[2] 《냄새》 (a) smell; an odor; (a) scent. ⇨ 냄새. ¶ 땀내 a smell of sweat / 입내 (a) bad breath / 뭔가 타는 내가 나다 smell something burning.

**내**[3] 《시내》 a stream; a streamlet; a brook; a brooklet; a rivulet. ¶ 내를 건너다 go across a stream / 내를 따라 가다 go along a stream.

**내**[4] ① 《나》 I. ¶ 내가 가겠다 I will go. / 내 그런 것은 처음 보았다 I have never seen such a thing before. ② 《나의》 my. ¶ 내 책 my book / 내 것 mine / 내 것 네 것을 혼동하다 get confused as to what is his and what isn't / 이것이 당신 질문에 대한 내 대답이다 Here are my replies to your questions. / 그 빨간 코트는 내것이다 The red coat is mine. / 이것은 내 일이므로 여러분께 염려를 끼치고 싶지 않다 This is my private affair and I don't want to worry all of you.

**내-**(來) 《오는》 coming; to come; forthcoming; next. ¶ 내주 next week / 내주 월요일 next Monday; 《on》 Monday next / 내년 여름 next year summer.

**내-**(耐—) -proof. ¶ 내알칼리의 alkali=proof / 내화성의 fireproof.

**-내**(內) within. ¶ 기한 〔범위〕 내 within the「period 〔limit, range〕 《of》.

**-내** 《내내》 throughout; all through. ¶ 봄내 비가 오고 있다 It rains throughout the spring. / 일년내 꽃을 볼 수 있다 You can see flowers all the year round. / 바람이 아침내 분다 The wind has been blowing all morning long.

**내가다** take 〔bring, carry〕 out 〔away〕; remove. ¶ 책상을 방에서 ~ take 〔carry〕 a desk out of the room / 의자를 정원으로 ~ take the chairs to the garden.

**내각**(內角) 〖수학〗 an interior 〔internal〕 angle; 〖야구〗 the inside (corner). ¶ ~을 찌르다 pitch a ball inside.

**내각**(內閣) a cabinet; the Ministry 《영》; the government (정부); the administration 《미》. ¶ 현~ the present Cabinet / 김~ the Kim Cabinet / 거국〔초당파〕 ~ an all-nation 〔a suprapartisan, a non-party〕 Cabinet / 약체〔연립〕 ~ an effete 〔a coalition〕 Cabinet / 야당 ~ a shadow Cabinet / ~의 경질 a cabinet 〔ministerial〕 change / ~의 면모 the personnel 〔lineup〕 of the Cabinet / ~을 조직하다 form 〔organize〕 a Cabinet / ~을 개편하다 reshuffle the Cabinet / ~에 끼다 hold 〔occupy〕 a post in the Cabinet; join the Cabinet (입각하다) / 국민들은 새로운 ~에 큰 기대를 걸고 있다 The people have high hopes for the new government. / 그는 새 ~의 장관으로 임명될 것이다 He will be appointed a minister in the new Cabinet. / 1년에 두 번 ~이 바뀌었다 The Cabinet changed twice in one year. ◉ ~개편 a reshuffle of the Cabinet. ~불신임 결의 a nonconfidence vote in the Cabinet. ~수반 the Premier; the Prime Minister. ~ 지지율 the cabinet's pull ratings. ~책임제 the parliamentary cabinet system: ~책임제 정부 a cabinet-responsible government. ~총사퇴 a general resignation of the Cabinet.

> **참고** **우리 나라 내각의 장**(長)
> 국무총리 the Prime Minister / 재정경제부장관 the Minister of Finance & Economy / 통일부장관 the Minister of Unification / 외교통상부장관 the Minister of Foreign Affairs & Trade / 행정자치부장관 the Minister of Government Administration & Home Affairs / 법무부장관 the Minister of Justice / 국방부장관 the Minister of National Defense / 교육인적자원부장관 the Minister of Education and Human Resources Development / 문화관광부장관 the Minister of Culture & Tourism / 농림부장관 the Minister of Agriculture & Forestry / 산업자원부장관 the Minister of Commerce, Industry & Energy / 정보통신부장관 the Minister of Information & Communication / 환경부장관 the Minister of Environment / 보건복지부장관 the Minister of Health & Welfare / 노동부장관 the Minister of Labor / 건설교통부장관 the Minister of Construction & Transportation / 해양수산부장관 the Minister of Maritime Affairs & Fisheries / 과학기술부장관 the Minister of Science & Technology / 여성부장관 the Minister of Gender Equaliy.

**내갈기다** 《힘껏 때리다》 thrash; wallop 〔strike, slap〕 《*a person*》 on 《the cheek》; sock 《*a person*》 on 《the jaw》; 《후려치다》 hit; 《글씨를》 dash off; scribble; scrawl. ¶ 두서너 줄 내갈겨 쓰다 scrawl 〔scribble〕 a few lines 《on》.

**내강**(內剛) strong-mindedness; a strong will; inner strength. ¶ 그는 외유 ~한 사람이다 He looks gentle but is tough inside.

**내객**(來客) a caller; a visitor; a guest; [집합적] company. ¶ 오후에 ~이 있다 I am going to have a visitor this afternoon. / 사장님은 ~과 면담중이시다 The president is meeting a visitor.

**내걸다** ① 《밖에》 hang out 《a sign》; fly 〔hoist, put up〕 《a flag》. ¶ 문패를 대문에 ~ put up *one's* nameplate on the main door / 상점 주인은 큰 세일 간판을 내걸었다 The shopkeeper put up 〔hang out〕 a large "for sale" sign. / 국기가 돛대 꼭대기에 내걸려 있었다 The national flag was flying from the top of the mast. (★ 상태를 나타낼 경우는 hoist, put up 등은 쓸 수 없음).
② 《목숨을》 stake; risk (*one's* life). ¶ 그는 목숨을 내걸고 해저로 잠수했다 He dived to the bottom of the sea at (the) risk of his life.
③ 《주장을》 hold up; advocate. ¶ 이상을 ~ hold up an ideal.

**내경**(內徑) the inside 〔internal〕 diameter. ◉ ~측정기 a calibrator; an internal caliper.

**내계**(內界) the inner world; the mind.

**내공**(內攻) 〖의학〗 retrocession. ~하다 retrocede; strike inward. ¶ ~성 질환 a retrocessive 〔retrocedent〕 disease.

**내공**(來貢) 《공물을》 ~하다 come to pay a tribute.

**내공**(耐空) 〖항공〗 endurance in flying 〔flight〕. ~하다 stay up (in the air); make an endurance flight. ◉ ~성(性) airworthiness: ~성이 있는 air worthy.

**내과**(內科) 《내과학》 internal medicine; 《병원의》 the internal department. ¶ ~ 치료를 받다 be treated by an internist; be internally treated.
◉ ~과장 the director of the internal department. ~병동 a medical ward. ~병원 a hospital (for internal diseases). ~의(醫) an internist; a physician. ~질환 an internal disease. ~치료 internal treatment. ~환자 a medical case.

**내과피**(內果皮) 〖식물〗 an endocarp. = 속「열매껍질.

**내관**(內官) = 내시(內侍).

**내관**(內棺) an inner coffin.

**내관**(內觀) 〖불교〗 inward looking; 〖심리〗 introspection. ~하다 introspect; look inward. ¶ ~적 작가 an introspective writer.

**내구**(來寇) an invasion.

**내구**(耐久) endurance; durability. ◉ ~경쟁 an endurance contest. ~력〔성〕 《사물의》 durability; persistence; 《사람의》 power of endurance; staying power; perseverance; stamina: ~력이 있는 durable; enduring; lasting; persistent / ~력이 꽤 있다〔별로 없다〕 have considerable 〔not much〕 endurance 〔durability〕 / 그에게는 ~력이 없다 He has no endurance in him. ~비행 〖항공〗 an endurance 〔a sustenance〕 flight. ~소비재 durable consumer goods; consumer durables. ~시험 an endurance test: ~시험을 하다 test 《*something*》 for endurance; do an endurance test. ~재 durables; durable goods: 비~재 nondurables.

**내국**(內國) home; the home country. ¶ ~의 home; domestic; internal / ~제의 of home make; home-made / ~산의 home-grown 《rice》.
◉ ~공채 internal 〔domestic〕 loans. ~근무 home service. ~무역 home 〔inland, domestic〕 trade. ~법 national law. ~세 an internal 〔inland〕 tax 〔duty〕: ~세 수입 inland revenue. ~시장 the home 〔domestic〕 market. ~우편 domestic mail. ~인 a native. ~항로 a domestic line; a coastwise service. ~환 domestic 〔inland〕 exchange: ~환어음 an inland bill of exchange.

**내굽다** 《it》 bend out; be bent out. ¶ 팔이 들이굽지 내굽나 《속담》 Blood will tell. *or* Blood is thicker than water.

**내규**(內規) 《회사 등의》 bylaws 《미》; 《단체 내의》 private rules 〔regulations〕. ¶ ~를 위반하다 violate the bylaw / …라는 ~가 있다 It is provided in the bylaws that…. / 이것은 회사 ~에 정해져 있다 This is「laid down 〔provided〕 in the bylaws 〔rules〕 of the company.

**내근**(內勤) indoor 〔inside〕 service; office 〔desk〕 work. ~하다 work inside 〔in the office〕. ◉ ~경찰관 a policeman on inside duty. ~사원 an office employee; a desk 〔an indoor〕 worker.

**내기** a bet; a wager; betting; gambling. ~하다 make a bet 《on》; lay a wager 《on》; gamble 《at cards》. ¶ 만원〔점심〕 ~ a bet of ten thousand won 〔lunch〕 / ~하는 사람 a better; a layer; a backer (경마 등에) / 큰〔작은〕 ~에 이기다〔지다〕 win 〔lose〕 a big 〔small〕 bet 〔wager〕 / ~에 응하다 take 〔accept〕 a bet 〔wager〕 / ~ 장기를 두다 play chess for money / 아버지의 유산을 ~로 다 잃다 gamble away all the property left by *one's* father / 축구 시합에 나는

그녀와 만원 ～를 했다 I made a bet of 10,000 won with her on the football game. *or* I bet her 10,000 won on the football game. /「우리 ～하자」—「넌 ～를 좋아하는군. 난 ～ 따윈 하지 않아」 "Let's make a bet."—"You like gambling, don't you? I never bet." ◉ ～돈 a bet; stakes; a wager.

**-내기** a person from...; a man just out of.... ¶ 서울내기 a person from 〔born in〕 Seoul; a (native) Seoulite / 풋내기 an inexperienced person; a green hand.

**내기성**(耐氣性) ¶ ～의 airproof.

**내남없이** every one of us; without any exception to us all; everybody alike 〔equally〕. ¶ ～ 다 여행을 떠난 것은 아니다 Not all 〔every one〕 of us went on the trip. / 그것은 ～ 다 아는 사실이다 It is a fact known to everybody.

**내내** from beginning to end; from start to finish; all the time 〔while〕; all the way; throughout. ¶ 1년 ～ throughout the year; all the year round / ～ 선두를 달리다 lead the race from start to finish / 서울까지 ～걷다 walk all the way to Seoul / 대전에서부터 ～ 서서 와야만 했다 《차에서》 I was kept standing all the way from Taejŏn. / 그 애는 ～ 말썽이다 That boy is troublesome as ever. / 그는 3년 동안 ～ 수석이었다 He has been at the top of his class for the whole three-year period.

**내내년**(來來年) the year after next.

**내내월**(來來月) the month after next.

**내년**(來年) next year; the coming year. ¶ ～ 봄〔3월〕 next spring 〔March〕 / 너는 ～ 오늘〔이맘때쯤〕 그녀를 만날 수 있을 것이다 You'll be able to meet her「on this day 〔about this time〕 next year.

**내놓다** ① 《밖으로》 put 〔take〕 out; bring out. ¶ 책상을 밖으로 ～ take a desk out / 주머니에서 지갑을 ～ take *one's* purse out of *one's* pocket / 창문 밖으로 머리를 ～ put 〔stick〕 *one's* head out of the window.

② 《가둔 것을》 let loose 《a dog》; set 《a bird》 free 《from》; let go 《of》; release. ¶ 소를 목장에 ～ put 〔send, turn〕 cattle out to grass 〔graze〕 / 개를 내놓아 기르다 leave 〔let〕 *one's* dog loose (in the house) / 죄수를 감옥에서 ～ let a prisoner out of jail.

③ 《드러내다》 expose; bare; show. ¶ 다리를〔가슴을〕 ～ bare *one's* legs 〔chest〕 / 사람들 앞에서 살을 그렇게 내놓지 마라 You shouldn't expose your body in public like that. / 아이가 배를 내놓고 자고 있다 The child is sleeping with its belly uncovered.

④ 《진열하다》 exhibit; place 《*a thing*》 on display; 《팔려고》 lay 《articles》 out for sale; put up 《the house》 for sale. ¶ 팔려고 내놓은 집 a house for 〔on〕 sale / 그림을 전람회에 ～ exhibit a picture at a show / 새 옷을 쇼윈도에 ～ display new dresses 《in the show window》.

⑤ 《책 따위를》 publish; issue; 《제품 따위를》 put 〔bring〕 out. ¶ 좋은 책을 ～ publish a good book / 우리는 연말까지 몇가지 신제품을 시장에 내놓을 것이다 We are going to put out a number of new products on the market by the end of the year.

⑥ 《제시·제출하다》 present; show; send in 《a written application》; bring forward. ⇨ 내다[2] ⑥. ¶ 검문소에 운전면허증을 ～ present 〔show〕 *one's* driver's license at a checkpoint / 동의안을 ～ bring forward a motion / 그는 명함을 내놓고 방문 목적을 설명했다 He presented his card and explained the purpose of his visit.

⑦ 《돈을》 pay; give; furnish; contribute (기부); invest (투자). ¶ 교회 짓는데 돈을 ～ contribute money for building a church / 사업에 돈을 ～ invest money in an enterprise / 사업에 필요한 돈을 ～ furnish the necessary funds to an enterprise.

⑧ 《음식을》 offer; serve; set 〔put, lay〕 out. ¶ 손님에게 차를 ～ serve tea to the guest; offer a guest a cup of tea / 손님 앞에 갖가지 요리를 ～ set 〔lay〕 out various dishes before a guest.

⑨ 《제외하다》 exclude; except; leave out. ¶ 그를 내놓고는 아무도 회의에 참석지 않았다 None of the members attended the meeting except him. / 너를 내놓고는 의지할 사람이 없다 I have no one but you to turn for help. / 나를 내놓고 출석자는 다섯명이었다 There were five present, excluding myself.

⑩ 《포기하다》 give 〔throw〕 up; abandon; renounce; 《희생을 무릅쓰다》 sacrifice; lay down 《*one's* life》 《for》. ¶ 권리를 ～ give up 〔relinquish〕 *one's* right to 《*a thing*》 / 상속권을 ～ renounce the right of succession / 직장을 ～ walk off 〔throw up〕 the job / 목숨을 내놓고 물에 빠진 아이를 구하다 save a drowning child at the risk 〔sacrifice〕 of *one's* life / 연구를 위해 기꺼이 전재산을 내놓겠다 I'm willing to give up all I have for the sake of research.

**내다**[1] 《연기가》 《it》 smoke; become smoky. ¶ 불이 ~ a fire smokes / 난로가 ~ a stove smokes.

**내다**[2] ① 《밖으로》 take 〔bring〕 out. ② (***a***) 《배출하다》 produce; turn out. ¶ 졸업생을 ~ turn out graduates / 우리 학교는 정계에 많은 지도자를 냈다 Our school has produced 〔turned out〕 a large number of political leaders. (***b***) 《낳다》 produce 《results》; yield 《profit》; generate 《heat》; 《발생시키다》 cause; bring about; lead to; give rise to. ¶ 불을 ~ start 〔cause〕 a fire / 그는 귀가 중에 사고를 냈다 He caused an accident on his way home. / 그 사고는 10명의 사망자를 냈다 The accident resulted in ten dead. / 그는 어디를 가나 말썽을 내기로 유명하다 He is known for getting into troubles wherever he goes. / 불을 내지 않도록 조심하자 Let's all be careful not to start any fires. / 이 달에는 적자를 낼 것 같다 It looks like we are in the red this month.
③ 《힘·용기 따위를》 put 〔call〕 forth; pluck 〔summon〕 up; 《능력 따위를》 display; show. ¶ 힘을 ~ put forth all *one's* strength / 기운을 ~ cheer up; brace *oneself* up / 능력을 최대로 ~ display *one's* ability to the full / 기운을 내라 Cheer up! / 용기를 내라 Pluck 〔Screw〕 up courage!
④ 《이름을》 become famous; make *one's* name; 《티를》 put on an air 《of》; 《감정·기분을》 express; show; display. ¶ 세상에 이름을 ~ make *one's* name known to the public; make *oneself* famous / 선배 티를 ~ make much of *one's* seniority; assume an air of seniority / 두려움을 겉으로 내지 않다 display no fear / 화를 ~ show *one's* anger; get angry.
⑤ 《발표·발행하다》 publish; issue; bring 〔put〕 out; 《게재하다》 carry; print. ¶ 소설을 잡지에 ~ publish a story in a magazine / 명령을 ~ give 〔issue〕 an order / 신문에 광고를 ~ put 〔place〕 an advertisement in a newspaper / 여권을〔비자를, 증명서를〕 ~ issue a passport 〔visa, certificate〕/ 그녀는 회고록을 냈다 She published her memoirs. / 그는 잡지에 수필을 냈다 He wrote an essay for a magazine. / 교육부 장관이 성명을 냈다 The Education Minister issued a statement.
⑥ 《발송하다》 send; mail; post; 《제출하다》 hand 〔give, send〕 in; submit; 《제시하다》 show; present. ⇨ 내놓다 ⑥. ¶ 편지를 ~ 《쓰다》 write a letter to 《*a person*》; 《투함하다》 mail 〔post〕 a letter / 원서를 ~「send in 〔file〕 an application / 초대장을 ~ send out an invitation / 개찰구에서 차표를 ~ show *one's* ticket at the wicket / 그는 사표를 냈다 He handed in his resignation. / 그는 곧 필요한 서류들을 냈다 He submitted the necessary papers at once. / 시간이 다 됐습니다. 모두 답안지를 내세요 Time's up. All hand in your papers, please.
⑦ 《발설하다》 set forth; put forward; start 《a rumor》. ¶ 소문을 ~ start 〔spread〕 a rumor afloat / 비밀을 입밖에 ~ let out 〔divulge, reveal〕 a secret / 그 일은 한 마디도 입 밖에 내지 않았다 I said nothing about the matter.
⑧ 《얻다》 take out; get; obtain. ¶ 허가를 ~ take out 〔get〕 a license / 빚을 ~ get 〔take out〕 a loan.
⑨ 《장소·자리·시간 등을》 set up; make; fix; arrange 《for》; 《구멍·도로 등을》 make; bore; open (up). ¶ 시간을 ~ make 〔find, arrange〕 time for 《*something*》 / 책상이 들어갈 자리를 ~ make room for a desk / 앉을 자리를 ~ make 〔arrange〕 a seat; leave room for 《*a person*》 to sit / 본채에 방을 하나 더 ~ add 〔attach〕 a room to *one's* main building / 구멍을 ~ make 〔start〕 a hole 《in》 / 길을 ~ break 〔build, open up〕 a road / 창문을 ~ put in a window / 틈을 내서 같이 가도록 하겠다 I will manage to accompany you.
⑩ 《팔다》 sell. ¶ 곡식을 ~ sell grain; put grain on sale 〔on the market〕.
⑪ 《지불하다》 pay (out); defray 《expenses》; 《자금·기부금 따위를》 ⇨ 내놓다 ⑦. ¶ 물건 값을 ~ pay for an article / 세금을 ~ pay *one's* taxes / 집세를 잘 안 ~ neglect to pay *one's* rent / 식사대는 카드로 냈다 I paid for our meal by credit card. / 새 차를 사려면 매월 30만 원씩 돈을 내야 한다 I'll have to pay out 300,000 won a month to get a new car. / 비용을 각자가 냈다 Each paid his share in the expenses.
⑫ 《턱을》 treat 《*a person*》 to 《a steak》; stand 〔buy〕 《*a person*》 《a dinner》; give 《*a person*》 《beer》 as a treat; 《음식을》 ⇨ 내놓다 ⑧. ¶ 그녀는 나에게 맥주 한 잔을 냈다 She treated me to a glass of beer. / 이것은 내가 내는 거다 This is「on me 〔my treat〕. / 점심값은 제가 내겠습니다 Let me buy your

lunch for you. / 내가 낼테니 한 잔 더 하게 Have another drink on me.
⑬ 《비우다》 empty; clear. ¶ 병을 ~ empty a bottle / 방을 ~ clear 〔vacant〕 a room.
⑭ 《뽑다》 put forward; select; appoint; offer. ¶ 후보자를 ~ select a candidate / 대표자를 ~ offer 〔put forward〕 a representative.
⑮ 《모를》 transplant. ¶ 모를 ~ set out 〔transplant〕 rice plants.
⑯ 《소리를》 let out; utter; make. ¶ 큰 소리를 ~ cry out; give a loud cry / 이상한 소리를 ~ make a strange noise / 소리를 내지 마라 Don't make a sound. *or* Keep quiet.
⑰ 《가게·살림을》 open; start; set up; run; keep. ¶ 새로 가게를 ~ set up 〔start, open〕 a shop / 살림을 ~ set up *one's* own home / 이번에 이 근처에 가게를 냈다 We have just opened a store near here.
⑱ 《속력을》 speed up; increase speed; gain 〔gather, put on, pick up〕 speed. ¶ 전속력을 ~ put on full speed / 열차는 서서히 속력을 냈다 The train gradually increased 〔gathered〕 speed. / 이 차는 최고 시속 150km의 속도를 낸다 This car has a maximum speed of 150 kilometers an hour.
⑲ 《빛·열·향기 따위를》 emanate; give out 〔off〕; 《먼지를》 raise. ¶ 먼지를 ~ raise a dust / 빛을 ~ emit 〔give out〕 light / 좋은 냄새를 ~ emit 〔give off, give out〕 a sweet fragrance.
⑳ 《운행하다》 run; put. ¶ 배를 ~ put out a boat / 임시 열차를 ~ run a special train.
㉑ 《부과하다》 set 〔give〕 《a question》. ¶ 저 선생님은 일년 내내 많은 숙제를 낸다 The teacher gives us a lot of homework all the year round. / 어떤 문제를 내시겠습니까 What kind of question are you going to set us?

**내다**[3] [조동사] do all the way (to the very end or thoroughly). ¶ 모든 고생을 견뎌 ~ endure all hardships (to the last) / 지갑을 끄집어 ~ draw *one's* purse 《from *one's* pocket》 / 일을 해~ carry out the work through.

**내다보다** ① 《밖을》 look out 《of, over, on》; see from within. ¶ 거리를 ~ look out on the street / 창 밖을 ~ look out (of) the window / 바다를 ~ look out over the sea. ② 《앞일을》 look ahead at; foresee; forecast; expect; anticipate; predict. ¶ 장래를 내다보고 with an eye to the future / …을 내다보고 in expectation 〔anticipation〕 of 《war, a rise in price》 / 그는 불경기를 내다보고 사업을 축소했다 He reduced his business in expectation of depression. / 항상 '10년 앞을 내다본다'는 경영 방침이 이제야 열매를 맺고 있다 Our business philosophy of always looking ten years ahead is bearing fruit now.

**내다보이다** ① 《밖이》 be 〔can be〕 seen from within; be seen out of; show through. ¶ 창으로 바다가 내다보인다 The sea can be seen through the window. / 창에서 거리가 내다보인다 The street is seen from the window. *or* The windows overlook the street. / 창문에서 내다보이는 경치가 좋다 The window commands a fine view.
② 《안이》 be seen 〔be visible〕 from without. ¶ 환히 ~ be seen through clearly; be patently transparent.
③ 《예상되다》 be foreseen; be anticipated; be foretold. ¶ 많은 어려움이 있을 것이 내다보인다 It is anticipated that there will be much difficulties. / 네 장래가 훤히 내다보인다 It is easy to see what will become of you.

**내닫다** dash 〔dart〕 off; start running; run 〔dash, rush〕 out. ¶ 거리로 ~ rush out into the street.

**내달**(來―) next 〔the coming〕 month; the month ahead; proximo. ¶ ~의 오늘 (on) this day (next) month / ~ 1일은 월요일이다 The first day of next month is Monday.

**내담**(來談) ~하다 visit for a talk; come to talk 《about *something*》. ¶ 내일 ~을 바랍니다 Please come and see me tomorrow. *or* I beg you to call on me tomorrow. / 본인 직접 ~ 요망 《광고》 Apply in person. *or* Personal application (is) requested.

**내대다** 《반항하다》 oppose; disobey; defy; put 〔set〕 *oneself* against; 《말대꾸하다》 talk back; retort. ¶ 윗사람에게 ~ disobey 〔defy〕 *one's* elders; set *oneself* against *one's* superiors.

**내던지다** ① 《던지다》 throw 〔cast, fling〕 《garbage》 away; throw 〔cast〕 《an empty can》 out 《of the window》; throw 〔fling〕 《a book》 down 《on the floor》. ¶ 화가 나서 화병을 벽에다 ~ dash a vase against the wall in anger / 담배꽁초를 내던지지 마라 Don't throw away your cigarette butts.
② 《중도에서 포기하다》 abandon; give 〔throw〕 up. ¶ 일〔직장〕을 ~ give

〔throw〕 up *one's* job / 시작한 일을 중도에서 내던지지 마라 Don't quit what you set out to do before you finish it. / 그녀는 하던 뜨개질을 내던지고 외출했다 She left off her knitting and went out. / 그는 왕위를 내던지고 그녀와 결혼했다 He gave up the throne to marry her.

③《목숨·직업·기회 따위를》throw away; give 〔throw〕 up; lay down; sacrifice. ⇨ 내놓다 ⑩. ¶ 목숨을 내던지고 at the cost 〔sacrifice〕 of *one's* life / 장관의 지위를 ～ give up 〔resign〕 *one's* position as (a) minister / 그는 모든 것을 내던지고 그 일에 전념했다 He sacrificed everything to devote himself to the job.

**내도**(來到) arrival; incoming. ～하다 arrive《at》; come《to》. 「endotoxic.

**내독소**(內毒素) 〖의학〗 endotoxin. ¶ ～의

**내돋다** rise to the surface; come out; 《싹이》 sprout; spring up; put forth shoots. ¶ 여드름이 ～ pimples come out《on *one's* face》/ 나뭇잎이 ～ leaves sprout.

**내돌리다** hand 〔pass〕《*a thing*》 around indiscriminately; pass《*a thing*》 from hand to hand.

**내동댕이치다** = 내던지다.

**내두르다** ①《휘두르다》swing 〔wave〕《*a thing*》 about; fling《*a thing*》 around; brandish; wield《a club, a sword》; flourish. ¶ 우산을 내두르면 위험하다 It's dangerous to swing an umbrella. / 그는 몽둥이를 내두르며 상대를 위협했다 He threatened his opponent flourishing a stick. / 그는 칼을 내두르며 적을 향해 돌진했다 He rushed at the enemy brandishing his sword.

②《남을》lead《*a person*》 by the nose; have《*a person*》 under *one's* thumb 〔control〕. ¶ 아무를 마음대로 ～ do with《*a person*》 as *one* pleases; lead《*a person*》 by the nose.

**내둘리다** ①《남에게 쥐다》be pushed around《by》; be led by the nose; be at the mercy of《*a person*》. ¶ 아무한테 ～ be at *a person's* beck and call; be under *a person's* thumb 〔control〕.

②《어지럽다》get dizzy; be 〔feel〕 dizzy.

**내디디다** step forward; advance; take a step forward; enter upon《a new career》. ¶ 한 걸음 앞으로 ～ take a step forward / 해결을 향해 한 걸음 ～ take a step toward solution / 인생의 첫 걸음을 잘못 ～ make a wrong start in life / 그 개발도상국은 근대화의 첫발을 내딛었다 The developing country embarked on the road to modernization.

**내뚫다** pierce; penetrate; bore 〔punch〕 through; cut 〔go, pass〕 through; 《탄알이》 shoot through. ¶ 산에 터널을 ～ cut a tunnel through a mountain / 판자에 구멍을 ～ bore a hole through a board.

**내뜨리다** throw away; cast away; fling; hurl; toss. ¶ 그릇을 마루에 ～ fling a dish on the floor.

**내락**(內諾) an informal 〔a private〕 agreement 〔consent〕. ～하다 give an informal 〔a private〕 consent. ¶ ～을 얻다 obtain《*a person's*》 informal consent / 나는 그 사람과의 결혼에 대해서 아버지의 ～을 받아두었다 I have my father's private consent to marry him.

**내란**(內亂) (a) civil war; civil strife; internal disturbances; 《반란》 (a) rebellion. ¶ ～을 일으키다 raise a rebellion / ～을 선동하다 incite rebellion / ～이 일어났다 A civil war broke out. / 그들은 ～을 진압하려고 애쓰고 있다 They are trying hard to suppress the rebellion. ◉ ～음모 conspiracy of a rebellion. ～죄 high treason; an offense against the safety of a state.

**내레이션** narration. 「(여자).

**내레이터** a narrator (남자); a narratress

**내려가다** ①《낮은 곳으로》go 〔come, get, step〕 down; descend; 《도시에서 시골로》 go down. ¶ 서둘러 산을 ～ go down 〔climb down, descend〕 a mountain in a hurry; hurry down a mountain / 계단을 뛰어 ～ run down the stairs / 강을 보트로 1km ～ go one kilometer down the river by boat / 외딴 시골로 ～ go down to the remotest country.

②《물가 따위가》go 〔come〕 down; fall; drop. ¶ 가격이〔가치가〕 ～ the price 〔value〕《of *something*》 go down 〔fall〕; [사물이 주어] go down 〔fall〕 in price 〔value〕 / 땅값이 꾸준히 내려가고 있다 The price of land has been 「going down 〔coming down, falling, dropping〕 steadily. *or* There has been a steady fall 〔drop〕 in the price of land. / 원화에 대한 달러 가치가 내려갔다 The value of the US dollar went down against the (Korean) won.

③《고도·온도 따위가》go 〔come〕 down; fall; drop. ¶ 열이 내리기 시작했다 My fever began to go down. / 기온이 영하 3도로 내려갔다 The temperature 「went down 〔fell, dropped〕 to three degrees below zero.

④《지위·순위 따위가》come 〔go〕 down;

drop; fall; be demoted 《to》; be degraded 《from》. ¶ 지위가 아래로 ~ be demoted to a lower rank / 나의 학교 성적이 내려갔다 My school record got worse. / 지난 시험에서 나의 등수는 5등이나 내려갔다 I dropped 〔went down〕 five places in class after the last examination. / 그 배우의 인기가 요즘 내려갔다 The actor's popularity has fallen 〔gone down〕 recently. ⑤ 《소화되다》 digest. ¶ 잘 ~ 〔안 ~〕 digest well 〔poorly〕 / 빨리 ~ be quick of digestion / 점심 먹은 것이 잘 안 ~「다. get *one's* lunch ill digested.

**내려긋다** draw 《a line》 down. ⇨ 내리긋다

**내려놓다** take 〔bring, put〕 down; lower; 《짐을》 unload; discharge (뱃짐 등을). ¶ 불에서 냄비를 ~ take a pot「off 〔from over〕 the fire; take 〔remove〕 a pot from the stove 〔heat〕 / 선반에서 꽃병을 ~ take 〔reach〕 a vase down from the shelf (★ reach를 쓰면「팔을 뻗쳐서」 내리다란 뜻) / 보트를 ~ lower a boat; get a boat on the water / 트럭에서 짐을 ~ unload cargos from the truck.

**내려다보다** ① 《아래를》 look down; overlook; take a bird's-eye view of. ¶ 창문에서 거리를 ~ look down the street from the window / 우리 학교는 바다를 내려다보는 언덕 위에 있다 Our school stands on a hill,「looking down 〔overlooking〕 the sea. / 헬리콥터로 서울 상공을 고공 비행하니, 전 시내를 내려다볼 수 있었다 Flying high over Seoul in a helicopter I had a bird's-eye view of the whole city. ② 《얕보다》 look down upon 《*a person*》; despise; hold 《*a person*》 in contempt. ¶ 남을 내려다보는 듯한 태도를 삼가해라 You should refrain from acting as if you were looking down on others.

**내려디디다** step on; tread on.

**내려뜨리다** drop; let 《*a thing*》 fall 〔slip〕; throw 《*a thing*》 down. ¶ 찻종을 ~ drop a cup; let a cup slip.

**내려서다** come down on *one's* feet; go down to 〔into〕 《the ground, the garden》; step down 《from》.

**내려앉다** ① 《자리를》 come down to a lower seat; take a lower seat; be reduced to a lower rank (지위가). ¶ 의자에서 마루로 ~ get up from *one's* chair and sit on the floor / 그는 이사에서 부장으로 내려앉았다 He was demoted to department chief from director. ② 《무너져 내리다》 fall down 〔in〕; collapse; tumble down; crumble; give way; 《침하하다》 sink; subside. ¶ 홍수로 다리가 내려앉았다 The bridge collapsed in the flood. / 격렬한 지진으로 지붕이 내려앉았다 The roof fell in because of severe earthquake. / 많은 사람들의 무게로 마루가 내려앉았다 The floor gave way under the weight of the crowd. / 도로의 지반이 약 6cm 내려앉았다 The road subsided 〔sank〕 about six centimeters.

**내려오다** ① 《위에서》 come 〔go, get〕 down; descend; 《명령 따위가》 be given 〔issued〕. ¶ 아래층으로 ~ go 〔come〕 downstairs / 어둡기 전에 산에서 ~「come down 〔descend〕 the mountain before dark / 사령부에서 철수 명령이 내려왔다 An order of withdrawal was given 〔issued〕 us from the command. ② 《전래되다》 be handed down 《to》; descend 《from father to son》. ¶ 가보로 전해 내려오는 칼 a sword handed down as an heirloom / …라고 전하여 ~ tradition says…; there is a tradition that…. / 그것은 그의 선조 대대로 물려 내려온 비법이었다 It was a secret recipe that had come down in his family. ③ 《탈것에서》 ⇨ 내리다[1] ②.

**내려찍다** cut with a downward blow. ¶ 내려찍어 두 쪽을 내다 cleave 〔cut〕 《*a thing*》 in two.

**내려치다** bring 《a stick》 down 《on *a person's* head》; give a down blow; 《세차게 치다》 hit 〔strike〕 hard. ¶ 책상을 주먹으로 ~ hit the table hard with *one's* fist / 땅에 말뚝을 내려쳐 박다 drive a stake into the ground.

**내력**(來歷) 《경력》 *one's* personal history; *one's* career 〔record〕; 《기원》 an origin; 《유래》 the history. ¶ ~ 있는 건물 a historic 〔legend-rich〕 building / ~을 캐다 inquire into the origin 《of》; trace 《*a thing*》 to its origin / 그는 대체 어떤 ~을 가진 사람이냐 I'd like to know something about his past career.

**내륙**(內陸) an inland; the interior of a country. ¶ 뉴욕에서 400km ~에 400 km inland 〔upcountry〕 from New York. ◉ ~국 a landlocked country; a country without a coastline. ~기후 a continental climate; an inland climate. ~수운 inland water transportation. ~운수 inland transport. ~지방 inland provinces.

**내리** ① 《아래로》 down(ward); off. ¶ 지붕에서 ~ 떨어지다 fall off the roof / 비가 ~ 쏟아지다 rain pours down.

② 《처음부터 끝까지》 from beginning to end; throughout; straight 〔all〕 through; consecutively; continually; without a break 〔stop〕. ¶ ~ 닷새동안 for five consecutive 〔straight〕 days; for five days running 〔at a stretch〕 / ~ 이기다 gain 〔win〕 consecutive victories / 비가 사흘 ~ 왔다 It has rained continuously for three days. / 그는 휴가 중 ~ 공부만 했다 He kept studying all through the vacation.

**내리긋다** draw a vertical 〔longitudinal〕 line.

**내리깎다** 《값을》 knock 〔beat〕 down the price; drive a hard bargain. ¶ 책값을 단 천 원으로 ~ beat the price of a book down to as low as one thousand won.

**내리깔다** 《눈을》 lower 〔drop, cast down〕 *one's* eyes. ¶ 눈을 얌전하게 내리깔고 with modestly downcast eyes.

**내리누르다** ① 《위에서》 press 〔hold, keep〕 down. ¶ 끓어오르는 노여움을 ~ control 〔restrain; keep down〕 *one's* surge of anger / 공기 탱크의 뚜껑이 날아가지 않도록 두 손으로 ~ hold 〔press〕 the air-tank's cover down with *one's* hands to keep it from blowing away. ② 《압박하다》 press; oppress; put pressure on; 《강요하다》 force; compel; urge. ¶ 복종하도록 ~ compel 《*a person*》 to obey / 억지로 내리눌려서 그 일을 떠맡았다 I was coerced to undertake the job.

**내리다**[1] [자동사] ① 《높은 데서》 come down; fall; drop. ¶ 방금 내린 눈 new=fallen snow / 비가 ~ it rains / 막이 ~ the curtain falls / 비가 부슬부슬 내리기 시작했다 It began to sprinkle with rain. / 서리가 내렸다 We had frost. ② 《탈것에서》 get off; get out (of); leave 《the bus》; alight 《from a plane》. ¶ 택시에서 ~ get out of a taxi / 기차에서 ~ get 〔step〕 off a train / 나는 역 앞에서 버스를 내렸다 I got off the bus in front of the station. / 그녀는 말에서 내렸다 She「got off 〔dismounted from〕 her horse. / 다음 정류장에서 내립니다 I'm getting off at the next stop. ③ 《비행기 따위가》 land. ¶ (비행기가) 공항에 내리다 land on an airport. ④ 《물가 따위가》 go 〔come〕 down; fall; drop; decline. ¶ 물가가 ~ prices「go down 〔are on the decline〕. ⑤ 《열·기온·고도 등이》 fall; drop; go down; subside. ¶ 온도가 갑자기 내렸다 There was a sharp drop in temperature. ⑥ 《먹은 것이》 ⇨ 내려가다 ⑤. ⑦ 《살이 빠지다》 become lean 〔thin〕; lose flesh; lose weight (체중이); 《부기 따위가》 go down. ¶ 살이 ~ get thin; become leaner 〔thinner〕 / 부기가 ~ the swelling goes down. ⑧ 《신들리다》 be possessed 〔inspired〕 by. ¶ 신령이 ~ be possessed 〔inspired〕 by a spirit. ⑨ 《뿌리가》 take 〔strike〕 《root into the soil》. ¶ 뿌리가 깊게 ~ spread deep root / 그 식물은 건조한 땅에서는 뿌리가 내리지 않는다 The plant will not root in arid soil. / 이 나라에서는 아직 민주주의가 뿌리내리지 못했다 Democracy hasn't really taken root in this country yet. ⑩ 《판단·결정 등이》 be decided 〔settled, determined〕; 《명령 등이》 be given 〔issued〕. ¶ 허가가 ~ be granted permission / 전진 명령이 내렸다 We were ordered to march forward.

**내리다**[2] [타동사] ① 《높은 곳에서 낮은 곳으로》 take 〔get, bring, put〕 down; lower; 《커튼 따위를》 pull down; drop; 《짐 따위를》 unload; discharge. ⇨ 내려놓다. ¶ 돛을 ~ lower the sails / 기를 ~ lower 〔hall down〕 a flag / 커튼을 ~ drop 〔pull down, let down〕 a curtain / 상점의 셔터를 ~ pull 〔roll〕 down the shutters of a store / 창문의 블라인드를 ~ pull 〔draw〕 down the blinds of a window / 상점의 간판을 ~ take down 〔remove〕 the shop sign / 아무의 어깨에서 짐을 내려주다 take a load off *a person's* shoulder / 선반에서 가방을 좀 내려주세요 Please bring down the suitcase from the shelf. ② 《값을》 lower; drop; bring down; reduce; cut down. ¶ 값을 ~ lower 〔bring down〕 the price / 임금을 10만 원 ~ cut wages (down) by hundred thousand won / 작년 선으로 값을 ~ reduce prices to last year's levels. ③ 《지위·위치·품질·소리 등을》 demote; reduce; degrade; lower. ¶ 아무의 지위를 ~ demote *a person* to a lower rank / 상품의 질을~ lower 〔debase〕 the quality of goods / 강의의 수준을 ~ make *one's* lecture easier to follow / TV의 음량을 ~ lower 〔turn down〕 the volume of the television / 노래의 음정을 한 음 ~ lower the key of a song / 목소리를 ~ lower *one's* voice. ④ 《승객 등을》 set 《a passenger》 down; let 《a passenger》 off; drop; help 《*a person*》 off 《a car》. ¶ 버스에서 노부인

을 내려주다 help 〔hand〕 an old woman down 「out of 〔from〕 the bus / 어디서 내려드릴까요 Where would you like to be dropped off? / 다음 정거장에서 내려주세요 Please drop me 〔Let me off〕 at the next stop.
⑤ 《허가·상금 등을》 grant 〔allow〕 《*a person's* request》; give 《*one's* approval》; confer 《a prize, an award》; 《명령·판결 등을》 give; issue 《orders》; 《결론·판단 등을》 make 《a decision》; draw 《a conclusion》. ¶ 사건의 판결을 ～ deliver 〔give, render〕 a judgment on a case / 그 건에 대해 조급한 결론을 내리는 것은 피해야 한다 You ought to avoid a hasty conclusion on the matter. / 누가 이런 지시를 내렸느냐 Who has given 〔issued〕 these instructions?

**내리닫다** run down; rush downward.

**내리닫이**[1] 《어린이 옷》 children's overalls with a slit in the seat.

**내리닫이**[2] 《창문》 a sash window; a vertically sliding window.

**내리뜨다** lower 〔drop, cast down〕 *one's* eyes. ¶ 그녀는 눈을 내리뜨고 서서 두어 번 나를 훔쳐 보았다 She stole a glance or two at me while standing with lowered eyes.

**내리막** ① 《길의》 a downward slope; a downhill (road); a descent. ¶ ～이 되다 slope 〔go〕 down; go 〔run〕 downhill / 도로는 ～이 되어 있었다 The road sloped 「down 〔downwards〕. / 앞에 가파른 ～길 있음 《게시》 Sharp drop in road level ahead. ② 《쇠퇴》 (a) decline; an ebb; the wane. ¶ 인생의 ～ the downhill of life; the afternoon of life / ～이 되다 decline; wane; be on the wane 〔ebb〕; be in decline / 그의 인기는 이미 ～이다 His popularity is already in decline. / 사업이 ～(길)에 접어들었다 Business has begun to change for the worse. / 더위도 이제 ～이다 The heat is on the decline.

**내리매기다** number down(ward).

**내리밀다** push 〔shove〕 down 〔off〕.

**내리받이** a downward slope; a descent; a downhill. ⇨내리막.

**내리사랑** parental love toward youngsters; love from older toward younger members of a family.

**내리지르다** ① 《물·바람이》 flow 〔blow〕 down forcefully. ② 《주먹·발로》 kick 〔knock〕 down(ward). ③ 《잠그다》 bolt 〔lock〕 down 《a gate》.

**내리질리다** get kicked 〔knocked〕 downward.

**내리쬐다** 《햇볕이》 shine 〔blaze, beat〕 down 《on》. ¶ 따갑게 내리쬐는 햇볕〔태양〕 《under》 a burning 〔scorching〕 sun / 지붕에 햇볕이 내리쬐고 있다 The sun is blazing down on the roofs. / 햇볕이 쨍쨍 내리쬐고 있다 The sun is pouring down its full strength from the sky. *or* The sun is beating down unsparingly.

**내리치다** strike down; give a downright blow.

**내리키다** pull down; lower; drop; take down. ¶ 허리춤을 ～ lower *one's* belt.

**내리퍼붓다** 《눈·비 따위가》 pour down; rain 〔snow〕 hard 〔incessantly〕. ¶ 비가 내리퍼부었다 It rained in torrents. *or* The rain poured down.

**내리훑다** thresh down.

**내릴톱** 《세로로 켜는》 a ripsaw.

**내림**[1] 《유전》 inheritance; heredity; (hereditary) transmission. ¶ 책을 좋아하는 것은 우리 집안의 ～이다 A love of books is in my blood.

**내림**[2] 〖건축〗 a frontage; a width. ¶ 세 칸 ～의 with a frontage of 3 *kan*.

**내림**[3] 〖음악〗 flat. ¶ ～바장조〔단조〕 《in》 F flat major 〔minor〕.

**내림**(來臨) an esteemed visit; an honored call; deigning to come. ～하다 deign to come; honor with a visit.

**내림굿** 〖민속〗 a shaman's invocation rite.

**내림대** 〖민속〗 a wand 〔rod〕 used by a shaman to be possessed by a spirit.

**내림새** 〖건축〗 《암키와》 concave tiles at the edge of eaves.

**내림세**(—勢) a downward 〔falling, declining〕 tendency; a downtrend; a weakness. ¶ ～를 보이다 show a downtrend 〔downward tendency〕 / 마침내 물가는 ～가 되었다 At last prices have shown a downward 〔falling〕 trend.

**내림차**(—次) 〖수학〗 a descending series.

**내립떠보다** glare down 《at》.

**내막**(內幕) 《내부 사실》 the inside story; the inside facts; 《내부 정보》 inside information; 《구어》 the lowdown 《on》; 《실정》 actual conditions; 《비밀》 a secret. ¶ ～을 아는 사람 《구어》 an insider / ～을 살피다 peep behind the scenes / ～을 폭로하다 expose a secret 《of》 / ～을 알고 있다 be familiar with the inside story; have inside knowledge of / ～을 알리다 give 《*a person*》 inside information 《on》 / 그는 겉으로는 큰소리치지만 ～을 알고 보면 고생하는 것 같다 He seems to be straitened in real circumstances though he poses big outside. / 그는 정계의 ～을 알고 있었

다 He knew what was going on behind the scenes in the political world. ◉ ~이야기 an inside story 〔report, account〕《of》; a behind-the-scenes story.

**내막**(內膜) 〖해부〗 lining membrane.

**내맡기다** 《일임하다》 leave 〔put〕《*a thing*》 in 《*a person's*》 hands; leave 《*a person*》 with 《*a matter*》; entrust 《*a matter*》 to 《*a person*》; entrust 〔charge〕《*a person*》 with 《a task》; 《방임하다》 let 《*a person*》 *do;* let 《*a matter*》 take *its* own course. ¶ 환자를 의사에게 ~ leave a patient to the doctor's care / 재산관리를 그에게 ~ leave 〔put〕 *one's* property in 〔under〕 his charge / 일체를 운에 ~ leave everything to chance / 격정에 몸을 ~ give *oneself* up to *one's* passions / 자녀의 교육을 선생님에게만 내맡겨서는 안된다 We should not leave our children's education to the teacher alone. / 저 사람에게 이 일을 내맡길 수는 없다 This work must not be entrusted to him. *or* I cannot entrust the work to him.

**내면**(內面) the inside; the interior. ¶ ~적(인) internal / ~적으로 internally / ~적인 갈등의 이면에는 behind the inner conflict / 사람은 외면이 아니라 ~에 의해 평가되어야 한다 A man should be valued by what he is, not by what he looks.
◉ ~고찰 introspection. ~관찰 an inside view. ~묘사 (an) inner description; 《소설·연극 등에서》 (a) description of the workings of 《a character's》 mind. ~생활 *one's* inner life. ~세계 the inner world. ~화 internalization; interiorization.

**내명**(內命) informal 〔secret〕 orders 〔instructions〕. ¶ ~을 받다 receive secret instructions.

**내명년**(來明年) the year after next.

**내몰다** ① 《밖으로 내쫓다》 turn 〔drive, force, put, get〕 out 《*a person* from *a place*》; expel; 《직위에서》 oust 《from》; fire (해고하다). ¶ 직위에서 ~ oust 《*a person*》 from a position / 방 밖으로 ~ drive 〔force〕 《*a person*》 out of the room / 세든 사람을 ~ drive out *one's* tenant from the house / 국토에서 적을 ~ expel the enemy from the country; drive the enemy out of the country. ② 《냅다 몰다》 drive 《a car》 fast; speed up. ¶ 우리는 고속도로에서 차를 내몰았다 We drove down the superhighway at full speed.

**내몰리다** be driven 〔forced〕 out 〔away〕. ¶ 집세를 내지 못해서 아파트에서 내몰렸다 I was thrown out of my apartment for not paying my rent.

**내몽고**(內蒙古) Inner Mongolia.

**내무**(內務) home 〔internal, domestic〕 affairs. ◉ ~반 〖군사〗 (living) quarters; barracks. ~부 《미》 the Department of Interior; 《영》 the Home Office. ~부 장관 《미》 the Secretary of the Interior; 《영》 the Home Secretary. ~사열 an inspection of the soldier's living quarters.

**내밀**(內密) a secret; privacy; secrecy. ~하다 (be) secret; private; confidential; 《비공식의》 (be) informal; unofficial. ¶ ~한 이야기 a confidential talk / ~히 secretly; privately; in secret; confidentially / ~히 조사하다 make confidential inquiries / ~한 이야기를 하다 have a talk privately 《with》; talk secretly together.

**내밀다** ① [자동사] stick 〔jut〕 out; project; protrude. ¶ 내민 이마 a projecting 〔protruding〕 forehead / 배가 ~ have a big paunch; be paunchy; be thick in the middle / 곶이 바다 가운데로 쑥 내밀려 있다 A cape juts out into the sea. / 큰 바위가 길 위로 쑥 내밀고 있다 A huge rock「sticks out 〔juts out, projects〕 over the path.
② [타동사] 《안에서 밖으로》 thrust 〔stick〕 out; stretch 〔hold〕 out 《*one's* hand》; throw out; 《남에게 미루다》 leave 《*a matter*》 to 《*a person*》; thrust 《*a matter*》 before 《*a person*》; shift 《on》; 《서류 등을》 thrust out; tender; 《얼굴을》 show *one's* face; appear 《in public》; attend 《a meeting》. ¶ 손을 (불쑥) ~ thrust 〔stretch〕 out *one's* hand / 사표를 ~ thrust out a letter of resignation / 구원의 손길을 ~ extend a helping hand 《to》; give aid 《to》 / 일거리를 남에게 ~ thrust work before *a person;* shift *one's* work on another / 그는 가슴을 내밀고 걷는다 He walks with his chest out. / 창밖으로 머리를 내밀지 마시오 Don't stick 〔poke〕 your head out of the 《train》 window.

**내밀리다** be thrust 〔pushed, thrown〕 out.

**내밀힘** 《자신있게 내세우는 기세》 pushing 〔driving〕 force 〔strength〕; drive; push 《구어》; aggressiveness; 《배짱》 self-confidence; boldness. ¶ ~이 있는 외판원 an aggressive 〔a pushing, a pushy〕 salesman / 장사에는 ~이 가장 중요하다

Push is everything in business.

**내박차다** ①《발길로 차다》 kick out hard. ②《거절하다》 reject flatly.

**내발뺌하다** excuse *oneself*《for》; clear *oneself*《of a charge》.

**내방**(來訪) a visit; a call. ～하다 visit; call on《*a person*》; call at《*a person's* house》. ¶ 한국을 ～중인 미국인 실업가들 the American businessmen now on a visit to Korea / ～을 받다 have a visit from《*a person*》/ 내주의 ～을 기다리고 있습니다 I am expecting 〔looking forward to seeing〕 you next week. ◉ ～자 a visitor; a caller: ～자 명부 a visitors' book; a guest book.

**내배다** ooze 〔seep〕 out; soak through. ¶ 땀이 내배어 얼룩진 셔츠 a sweat-stained shirt; a shirt stained with sweat / 붕대에 피가 내배었다 Blood came oozing through his bandage. *or* Blood oozed out of the bandage.

**내뱉다** 《침을》 spit (out); expectorate; spew (out); 《말을》 spit 〔rap〕 out; spit 《*one's* words》 at; say 《*something*》 over *one's* shoulder; make a parting remark 〔shot〕. ¶ 아무의 얼굴에 침을 ～ spit in *a person's* face / 마음 속의 울분을 ～ spew out all *one's* grudges 《against *a person*》; give vent to *one's* pent-up feelings / 그렇게 내뱉고 그는 방을 뛰쳐나갔다 Flinging this (remark) over his shoulder, he stormed out of the room. /「마음대로 해. 난 모른다.」라고 그는 내뱉듯이 말했다 He spat 〔rapped〕 out, "Do it your own way. I don't care."

**내버려두다** 《방치하다》 leave 《*a thing*》 as it is 〔stands〕; let 《*a thing*》 take its own course; neglect; lay aside; 《간섭 않다》 let 〔leave〕 《*a person*》 alone; 《묵과하다》 overlook; pass over 《*a matter*》; turn a blind eye to. ¶ 일을 하지 않고 ～ leave *one's* work undone / 병을 치료하지 않고 ～ let *one's* disease go untreated / 울게 ～ leave 《*a person*》 alone and let *him* cry / 제마음대로 하게 ～ let 《*a person*》 do what *he* wants / 자네, 그 일을 그대로 내버려둬서는 안 되네 You must not leave the matter as it is. / 그 소녀가 학대 당하는 것을 못본 체 내버려 둘 수는 없다 I can't stand by and let the girl be ill-treated. / 내버려두게나. 시간이 해결할 걸세 Leave it alone, time will take care of it. / 그것을 그냥 내버려둘 수는 없다 I can't leave it alone. *or* I can't pass it over in silence.

**내버리다** throw 〔cast, fling〕 《*a thing*》 away; dump; discard; get rid of…; 《구어》 junk 《an old TV set》. ¶ 낡은 코트를 ～ throw away an old coat; 「get rid of 〔discard〕 an old coat / 서류를 휴지통에 ～ throw papers in a waste basket / 그건 돈을 거저 내버리는 것과 같은 것이다 It is mere waste of money.

**내벽**(內壁) an inner 〔inside〕 wall.

**내보내다** ①《밖으로》 put 〔let, turn〕 out; let go out; push out (밀어서); 《파견·출발시키다》 put out; send out; 《석방하다》 release; free. ¶ 고양이를 방에서 ～ let a cat out of the room / 소를 들로 ～ turn the cattle out to the fields / 졸업생을 사회로 ～ turn 〔send〕 out graduates into the world / 축구팀을 경기에 ～ put a soccer team into the field / 밤에는 아이들을 밖으로 내보내지 마라 Don't allow the children to go out at night. / 심한 폭풍으로 배를 내보낼 수 없다 It is too stormy to put out a boat. ②《내쫓다》 turn 〔drive, force, put〕 out; expel; oust 《from》; 《해고하다》 fire; dismiss; discharge; lay 《*a person*》 off (일시적으로). ¶ 파리를 방 밖으로 ～ drive 〔get〕 flies out of the room / 가정부를 ～ dismiss 〔fire〕 a housemaid / 세입자를 ～ put a tenant out of the house; evict 〔eject〕 a tenant from the house / 스스로 나가지 않으면 내가 내보내겠다 If you won't go yourself, I shall turn 〔rush〕 you out.

**내복**(內服) ①《속옷》 underwear; underclothes; 《여성용》 lingerie; undies 《구어》. ②《약의》 internal use. ～하다 use 〔apply〕 internally. ¶ 약을 하루 3번 ～하다 take 《medicine》 three times a day. ◉ ～약 internal medicine; medicine for internal use.

**내부**(內部) the inside; the interior; the inner part. ¶ 집의 ～ the inside 〔interior〕 of a house / 신체 ～ the inner parts of the body / ～ 사람 a person on the inside; an insider / ～의 internal; inner; interior / ～ 사정에 밝다 have a good inside knowledge 《of》; be well up in the internal affairs 《of》 / 신체 ～에 상처를 입다 receive an internal injury; be hurt internally / 그 집은 ～를 새로 페인트칠 했다 The house had been repainted inside. / ～에서 보니 동굴은 더 커 보인다 Seen from within, the cave looks larger. / 도난은 ～ 사정에 밝은 자의 범행 같다 The theft seems to be an inside job. / 건물 ~가 몽땅 타버렸다 The inside of the building was burned out.

◉ ~감사 internal audit. ~고발 an insider's accusation; whistle-blowing from the inside: ~ 고발자 a whistle-blower. ~구조 《물체의》 (an) inner 〔internal, interior〕 structure; 《동물체의》 internal anatomy. ~기억장치 〖컴퓨터〗 internal memory; internal storage. ~분열〔분쟁〕 an internal disunion 〔struggle〕. ~설명도 《기계 따위의》 a cutaway drawing. ~요인 internal factor. ~유보 internal reserves. ~자 거래 insider's trading. ~저항 〖물리〗 internal resistance. ~정보 〖컴퓨터〗 internal information. ~조직 internal organization. ~질환 an internal disease.

**내부딪다** ① 《부딪다》 strike; hit; knock; bump. ② 《충돌》 run against 〔into〕; collide with; crash into 〔against〕.

**내부딪히다** get struck 〔hit, bumped〕.

**내분**(內紛) (an) internal trouble 〔conflict〕; internal strife; domestic discord. ¶ 정당의 ~ internal troubles 〔strife〕 in a political party; (an) intraparty conflict / ~을 일으키다 give rise to an internal trouble / ~에 시달리다 suffer from internal troubles / ~에 휘말리다 get involved in internal trouble / ~으로 분열되다 be torn by internal 〔factional〕 strife.

**내분비**(內分泌) 〖생리〗 internal secretion. ◉ ~선 an endocrine gland; a ductless gland. ~성 질환 endocrine disorders. ~액 an internal 〔endocrine〕 secretion. ~작용 endocrine function. ~학 endocrinology.

**내불다** ① [타동사] blow 〔breathe〕 out 〔forth〕. ¶ 입김을 내불어 더운 우유를 식히다 blow on hot milk to cool it / 입김을 내불어 손을 녹이다 blow on *one's* fingers to warm them. ② [자동사] blow away 《from, toward》. ¶ 바람이 바다 쪽으로 ~ the wind blows away toward the sea.

**내비치다** ¶ 내비치는 clear; transparent / 내비치는 옷감 see-through cloth / 사임할 뜻을 ~ hint at *one's* resignation.

**내빈**(來賓) a guest; a visitor. ¶ 그녀는 ~ 접대로 바쁘다 She is busy entertaining visitors. ◉ ~명부 a guest book; a visitors' register. ~석 the visitors' seats 〔gallery〕; 《게시》 For guests. ~실 a reception room.

**내빼다** flee; run away. ¶ 이런 때는 내빼는 것이 장땡이다 The wisest thing to do in this case is to run away.

**내뻗다** put forth 〔out〕; spread out. ¶ 등덩굴이 ~ a wisteria puts out its vine.

**내뿜다** 《물·피 따위가》 spout (out); spurt 〔gush〕 out; 《증기·가스 따위가》 blow out 〔up〕; emit; 《연기·불꽃 따위가》 belch out; shoot up; send out (연기를). ¶ 화산이 불을 ~ a volcano belches fire / 분수가 물을 ~ a fountain spouts water / 상처에서 피가 내뿜었다 Blood spurted from the wound. *or* The wound spouted blood. / 석유가 지면위로 내뿜고 있었다 Oil was gushing up out of the ground. / 갈라진 바위 틈에서 증기가 내뿜고 있었다 Steam was belching out from cracks in the rocks.

**내사**(內査) a secret investigation; a private inquiry; an internal probe. ~하다 make secret inquiries into 《*a matter*》; investigate secretly; make an internal probe (of). ¶ 지금 ~중이다 A secret investigation is proceeding.

**내사**(來社) a visit to a company 〔an office〕. ~하다 visit a company 〔an office〕. ¶ 내일 ~하여 주십시오 Please come to our office tomorrow.

**내상**(內相) ① 《내무장관》 the Home Minister. ② 《남의 부인》 your 〔his〕 esteemed wife.

**내상**(內喪) mourning for *one's* wife.

**내색**(一色) the facial expression of *one's* feelings 〔emotion〕; a revealing look. ~하다 betray *one's* emotions; let *one's* face show *one's* thoughts. ¶ 아무 ~도 하지 않다 do not show any emotion (in *one's* look) / 그는 불평 따위를 전혀 ~하지 않았다 He did not betray his dissatisfaction either in his look or in his manner.

**내생**(內生) 〖생물〗 endogeny. ¶ ~적인 endogenous. ◉ ~식물 an endogen.

**내생**(來生) 〖불교〗 (the) afterlife; the life after death. ⇨ 내세.

**내선**(內線) 《전기의》 interior 〔indoor〕 wiring; 《전화의》 an extension. ¶ ~203번 부탁합니다 Give me extension 203, please. ◉ ~번호 an extension number. ~전화 an interphone.

**내성**(內省) 《내관》 introspection; 《반성》 reflection; self-examination. ~하다 introspect; reflect on *oneself;* turn *one's* thoughts inward. ¶ ~적 introspective; reflective / ~적 성격 an introspective nature / ~적인 사람 a reserved man.

**내성**(耐性) 〖의학〗 (a) tolerance 《to radioactivity》. ¶ ~이 있다 be tolerant 《of, to》/ …에 대해 ～이 생기다 develop 〔acquire, build up〕 resistance to《insecticides》. ◉ ～균 (drug-)resistant bacteria: 항생물질 ～균 antibiotic-resistant bacteria.

**내세**(來世) (the) afterlife; the future life 〔existence〕; the life 〔world〕 to come; the next 〔other〕 world; the world beyond. ⇨ 내생(來生). ¶ 현세와 ～ this world and the next / ～를 믿다 believe in 「the world beyond 〔the life after death〕 / 많은 젊은이들은 ～를 믿지 않는다 Many young people don't believe in the life after death. ◉ ～신앙 belief in 「the hereafter 〔the life after death〕.

**내세우다** ① 《대표·후보 등을》 put up; support; make 〔have〕《*a person*》 stand for; make 〔let, have〕《*a person*》 represent. ¶ 우두머리로 ～ place 《*a person*》 at the head / 후보자로 ～ put up 《five》 candidates 《in the coming election》; have 《*a person*》 stand for 《the Assembly》/ 아무를 회사 대표로 ～ have *a person* represent the company; present *a person* as the company's representative.
② 《권리·주장·조건·학식 등을》「insist on 〔assert〕《*one's* right》; 「set forth 〔advance〕《a new theory》; claim; advocate; urge; impose 〔attach〕 conditions 《on, to》; display 《*one's* learning》. ¶ 군축의 필요성을 ～ urge 〔preach〕 the necessity of arms reduction / 개선된 근로 조건을 ～ urge 〔insist on〕 the improved working conditions / 인도주의를 ～ claim to stand for humanitarian principles; advocate the cause of humanitarianism / 그들이 내세운 권리는 기각되었다 The assertion of their rights were ignored. / 그에게는 내세울 만한 재주가 없다 He has no talent to speak of.

**내셔널 리그** 《미국 야구의》 the National League.

**내셔널리스트** a nationalist.

**내셔널리즘** nationalism.

**내소박**(內疏薄) ～하다 mistreat 〔abuse, ill-treat〕 *one's* husband. ¶ ～당하다 be treated coldly by *one's* wife.

**내솟다** spring 〔surge, spurt〕 up 〔out〕.

**내수**(內需) domestic demand; home consumption. ¶ ～의 증가〔확대〕「an increase in 〔expansion of〕 domestic demand / 정부는 ～ 확대책을 취하도록 압력을 받고 있다 The government has been pressured to take measures to expand domestic demand 〔consumption〕. ◉ ～산업 an industry for domestic demand. ～용 원자재 raw materials for domestic demand.

**내수**(耐水) ¶ ～의 waterproof; water-tight; impervious to water; water=resistant (완전 방수가 아닌); water=repellent (물을 튕기는). ◉ ～성 water-proofing; water-resisting qualities.

**내수면**(內水面) inland waters. ◉ ～어업 fresh-water fishery.

**내숭** wickedness; trickiness; underhandedness. ～하다, ～스럽다 (be) wicked; under-handed; sneaky; tricky. ¶ ～스런 사람 a tricky 〔sneaky〕 fellow / ～스러운 웃음 an insidious smile.

**내쉬다** exhale; breathe out. ¶ 숨을 천천히 ～ breathe out slowly.

**내습**(來襲) 《공격》 a raid 〔an attack〕 《on our position》; 《침입》 an invasion; an incursion. ～하다 attack; invade; raid; make an incursion into 《our territory》. ¶ 적군의 ～에 대비하다 provide against the enemy's invasion / 적의 ～을 물리칠 수 있도록 방어를 강화했다 We tightened our defense to fight to repulse the enemy attack.

**내습**(耐濕) ¶ ～의 dampproof; moisture=resistant; moisture-proof / 이 벽지는 ～성이 탁월하다 This wallpaper resists dampness very well.

**내시**(內示) an unofficial 〔informal〕 announcement. ～하다 announce unofficially.

**내시**(內侍) a eunuch.

**내시경**(內視鏡) 〖의학〗 an endoscope. ◉ ～ 검사(법) endoscopy.

**내신**(內申) a confidential report. ～하다 report confidentially 《to》. ◉ ～서 《학교의》 a school report 《on students' grades and conduct》; school recommendations. ～성적 the academic reports (from high schools to universities); the high school records.

**내신**(來信) a letter received.

**내실**(內室) 《안방》 the main room; women's quarters; 《남의 아내》 your 〔his〕 wife.

**내실**(內實) substance; substantiality. ¶ ～있는 생활 a full 〔fulfilling〕 life / ～을 기하다 insure substantiality / ～화하다 make 《*something*》 substantial 〔solid〕/ 규모의 확대보다는 ～을 기하는 것이 더 중요하다 It is more important to enrich the substance than to enlarge the size.

**내심**(內心) 《마음 속》 *one's* inmost heart; 《진의》 *one's* real intention; *one's* mind; 〖수학〗 the inner center. ¶ ～으로(는)

at heart; in *one's* heart; inwardly; secretly / ～ 기뻐하다 be delighted at heart; be inwardly pleased / ～ 걱정하다 be secretly worried 《about》/ ～ 후회하다 repent 「at heart 〔inwardly〕/ ～으로는 …하고 싶어하다 have a secret desire to *do* / 그는 ～ 겁을 먹고 있었다 At heart he was scared. / 정치가는 결코 ～을 털어놓지 않는다 Politicians never tell us their inner thoughts. *or* Politicians never tell us what they are really thinking in their hearts.

**내앉다** sit forward.

**내앉히다** let 〔have〕《*a person*》 sit forward; let 《*a person*》 come out and occupy a seat.

**내압**(內壓) 『물리』 internal pressure.

**내압**(耐壓) resisting pressure. ¶ ～(성)의 pressure-resistant. ◉ ～력 capacity to resist pressure. ～복 《비행용》 a flying skin.

**내야**(內野) 『야구』 the infield; the diamond. ◉ ～석 the infield stands 〔bleachers〕. ～수 an infielder. ～안타 〔플라이〕 an infield hit 〔fly〕.

**내약**(內約) a private 〔secret〕 contract 〔agreement〕; 《묵계》 a tacit understanding. ～하다 make a private agreement 〔contract〕; have a tacit understanding 《with》.

**내역**(內譯) a breakdown; items; details. ⇨ 명세. ¶ 여행 비용의 ～ a breakdown of traveling expenses / ～을 밝히다 itemize 《a bill》; give 《*a person*》 breakdown; state the items 《of an account》/ 지출 ～을 알고 싶은데요 Give me the details of the expenses. ◉ ～서 an itemized statement.

**내연**(內緣) ¶ ～의 처 a common-law wife; a wife not legally married / ～의 부부로서 살다 live together without being legally married. ◉ ～관계 a common-law marriage: ～관계를 맺다 make 〔contract〕 a common-law 〔*de facto*〕 marriage 《with》.

**내연**(內燃) internal combustion. ◉ ～기관 an internal-combustion engine.

**내열**(耐熱) ¶ ～의 heatproof; heat-resisting〔-resistant〕/ …보다 ～성이 강하다 have greater heat-resistance than…. ◉ ～복 a heatproof suit. ～시험 a heat-resistance test. ～유리 heat-resistant glass; Pyrex (상표명).

**내오다** take 〔bring, carry〕 out. ¶ 의자를 뜰로 ～ bring a chair out into the garden.

**내왕**(來往) 《통행》 comings and goings; come-and-go; traffic; 《교제》 association. ～하다 come and go; 《교제하다》 associate 《with》; be on visiting terms 《with》. ¶ 차(량)의 ～ vehicular traffic / ～하지 않다 do not associate 《with》; 《절교하다》 part company 《with》/ ～이 많다〔적다〕 the traffic is heavy 〔light〕/ 거리에 사람 ～이 많다 Lots of people come and go on the street. / 지금도 우리는 서로 자주 ～합니다 We often see each other even now.

**내외**[1](內外) ① 《안과 밖》 the inside and outside. ¶ ～의 internal and external; home 〔domestic〕 and foreign 《affairs》/ ～에(서) in and out; inside and outside; within and without; 《국내와 외국에서》 《be well known》 at home and abroad / ～의 정세 the internal and external state of affairs / ～다사한 해 an eventful year both at home and abroad / 그는 ～사정에 정통하다 He is well versed in domestic and foreign affairs. ② 《부부》 man 〔husband〕 and wife (★ 뜻이 서로 관련된 두 개의 명사가 and로 결합되면 관사가 생략됨); a (married) couple. ¶ ～ 금실이 좋다 The couple are happy together. ③ 《약》 around; about; some; or so. ¶ 일주간 ～ a week or so; about a week / 5백원 ～ 500 won or so; around ₩500 / 비용은 2만원 ～일 것이다 The outlay will be about twenty thousand won. ◉ ～간 《부부간》 relationship between man and wife. ～동포 *one's* countrymen both at home and abroad. ～분 you and your esteemed wife 〔husband〕. ～정책 domestic and foreign policy. ～종(從) 《내종》 a cousin by a paternal aunt; 《외종》 a cousin by a maternal uncle. ～채(債) domestic and foreign bonds.

**내외**[2](內外) 《남녀간의》 keeping some distance from 〔avoiding society with〕 the opposite sex. ～하다 《the sexes》 keep their distance (from each other); avoid society with the opposite sex.

**내용**(內用) ① 《가용》 home expenditure. ② ＝ 내복(內服) ②.

**내용**(內容) 《속에 든》 content(s); 《실질》 substance; subject matter; 《의미》 meaning; import; depth (깊이). ¶ 형식과 ～ form and substance 〔matter〕/ 책(의) ～ the contents of a book / 편지(의) ～ the text of a letter / 이야기(의) ～ what 《*a person*》 said; the import 〔gist〕 of the story / 사건(의) ～ the details of a case / ～이 충실한 강

의〔책〕 a substantial lecture 〔book〕/ ～이 풍부〔빈약〕하다 be rich 〔poor〕 in contents / ～은 좋지만 문체가 싫다 The substance is good, but the style is repellent. / 회담의 ～은 극비에 붙여졌다 The nature of the conference is kept a strict secret. / 이 가요는 ～과 음악의 형식이 잘 맞지 않는 것 같다 I'm afraid the lyrics of this folksong and its tune don't go together very well. ◉ ～견본 《책의》 specimen 〔sample〕 pages. ～목록 a table of contents. ～분석 content analysis. ～증명 certification of contents: ～증명 우편 contents-certified mail.

**내용연수**(耐用年數) durable years; the life 《of a machine》. ¶ 이 냉장고의 ～는 10년 가량이다 This refrigerator will last about ten years. *or* The life of this refrigerator is about ten years.

**내우**(內憂) internal 〔domestic〕 trouble(s). ◉ ～외환 domestic troubles and external threats; troubles both at home and abroad: ～외환이 겹치다 be beset with troubles both at home and abroad.

**내원**(來援) coming to help; offering help 〔aid, assistance〕. ～하다 come to help 〔aid, assist〕. ¶ ～을 요청하다 ask 《*a person*》 to come and help.

**내월**(來月) next 〔the coming〕 month; proximo (생략 prox.). ¶ ～ 초하룻날 《on》 the first of next month; 《on》 the 1st prox. / ～의 오늘 this day (next) month; a month from today / ～ 10일에 상경하겠다 I'll come (up) to Seoul on the tenth of next month.

**내응**(內應) 《내통》 a secret communication. ⇨ 내통(內通) ①. 「⇨ 속옷.

**내의**(內衣) underwear; underclothes.

**내의**(內意) 《의중》 *one's* (secret) intention; 《견해》 *one's* private 〔personal〕 opinion.

**내의**(來意) the purpose of *one's* visit. ¶ ～를 알리다〔전하다〕 tell what *one* has come for.

**내이**(內耳) 〖해부〗 the inner ear. ◉ ～염 the inflammation of the inner ear.

**내인**(內因) an internal cause. ¶ ～성 질환 an endogenous disease.

**내일**(來日) tomorrow. ¶ ～ 아침〔저녁, 밤〕 tomorrow morning 〔evening, night〕/ ～의 한국 《talk of》 Korea's tomorrow / ～에 대비하다 provide for the future / ～ 보세 See you tomorrow. / 오늘 할 수 있는 일을 ～로 미루지 마라 《속담》 Never put off till tomorrow what you can do today.

**내입**(內入) ① 《돈의 부분 납입》 partial payment; payment on account. ～하다 pay on account 〔as part, in part settlement〕. ② 《궁중에》 delivery of goods to the Royal Court. ～하다 supply the Royal Court with goods. ◉ ～금 money paid on account; partial payment.

**내자**(內子) 《자기 아내》 my wife.

**내자**(內資) domestic 〔local, home〕 capital 〔fund〕. ¶ ～를 동원하다 mobilize domestic capital / ～ 100만 달러와 외국 차관 200만 달러로 회사를 설립하다 establish a company with an aggregate capital of one million dollars of domestic fund and two million dollars of foreign loan.

**내장**(內粧) interior decoration 〔furnishings〕; 《자동차의》 trim; upholstery. ¶ 집의 ～ 《decorate》 the interior of a house. ◉ ～공사 interior finishing.

**내장**(內障) 〖의학〗 cataract (백내장); amaurosis (흑내장); glaucoma (녹내장).

**내장**(內藏) ～하다 have 《*a thing*》 built-in. ¶ 자동 셔터가 ～된 카메라 a camera with a built-in self-timer.

**내장**(內臟) the internal organs; the viscera; the entrails; 《장》 the intestines; the bowels. ◉ ～신경 a splanchnic nerve. ～외과 internal surgery. ～질환 an internal disease 〔disorder〕. ～파열 a visceral cleft. ～학 splanchnology. ～해부 splanchnotomy.

**내재**(內在) 〖철학〗 immanence. ～하다 be immanent 〔inherent〕 《in》. ¶ ～적 immanent; inherent / 신의 ～ the divine immanence / 사물의 ～적 가치 the intrinsic 〔inherent〕 value of a thing.

**내재율**(內在律) 《시의》 (inner) rhythm 〔cadence〕 《of free verse》.

**내적**(內的) internal; inner; intrinsic; mental. ◉ ～가치 intrinsic value. ～경험 inner experiences. ～생활 《enrich》 *one's* inner life. ～요인 an internal cause.

**내전**(內殿) 《왕비》 a queen; 《궁의 안채》 the inner palace; the king's residence.

**내전**(內戰) a civil 〔an internal〕 war; domestic 〔internal〕 warfare.

**내전**(來電) an incoming telegram. ¶ 뉴욕으로부터의 ～에 의하면 according to a telegram 〔dispatch〕 from New York.

**내전보살**(內殿菩薩) 《행위》 feigned ignorance; 《사람》 a person who feign ignorance 《about》.

**내접**(內接) ～하다 touch internally. ¶ ～

시키다 〖수학〗 inscribe. ◉ ～다각형 an inpolygon. ～원 an inscribed circle.

**내젓다** 《손을》 wag; wave; swing (팔을); 《배를》 row out 《a boat》. ¶ 고개를 ～ shake *one's* head / 그는 손을 내저어 아무 염려 말라는 시늉을 했다 He indicated with a wave of the hand that there was nothing to worry about.

**내정**(內定) (an) unofficial 〔informal〕 decision. ～하다 decide informally 〔unofficially〕. ¶ ～되다 be informally arranged 〔decided〕 / 그는 차기 사장으로 ～되어 있다 He has been informally designated as next president.
◉ ～가격 《입찰의》 a reserved price.

**내정**(內政) domestic 〔home〕 administration; internal affairs. ¶ ～에 간섭하다 interfere 〔intervene〕 in the domestic 〔internal〕 affairs 《of a nation》. ◉ ～간섭 interference in the domestic 〔internal〕 affairs 《of other nations》. ～불간섭 nonintervention.

**내정**(內庭) 《안뜰》 an inner yard; a courtyard.

**내정**(內情) 《속사정》 (the) internal conditions; (the) inside affairs; 《실정》 the real state of affairs. ¶ ～에 밝은 사람 an insider (소식통) / ～에 밝다 be 「familiar with 〔well up in〕 the inside affairs 《of *a matter*》; have a good inside knowledge 《of 》 / ～을 탐지하다 inquire into the real state.

**내조**(內助) *one's* wife's help 〔aid, assistance〕. ～하다 help *one's* husband. ¶ ～의 덕〔공〕으로 「through the assistance 〔thanks to the support〕 of *one's* wife / 그의 성공은 부인의 ～에 힘입은 바 크다 He owes much of his success to his wife 〔helpmate〕. ◉ ～자 a helpmate; a helpful partner; 《아내》 a wife.

**내조**(來朝) 《외국 사신이 옴》 the arrival 〔visit〕 of foreign envoy. ～하다 《a foreign envoy》 arrive in this country; visit 〔come to〕 Korea.

**내종**(內從) 《고종 사촌》 a cousin by a paternal aunt.

**내주**(來週) next week; the coming week. ¶ ～ 오늘 today 〔this day〕 week; a week (from) today / ～토요일에 여기서 만납시다 Let's meet here 「next Saturday 〔on Saturday next〕.

**내주다** ① (***a***) 《꺼내어 주다》 give 《*a thing*》 out 《of a place》; 《물건·돈 등을》 hand 〔turn〕 over; give (away); deliver; pay. ¶ 지갑에서 돈을 내주다 give money out of *one's* purse / 월급을 ～ pay 《*a person's*》 salary / 가난한 사람들에게 쌀을 ～ hand out 〔give away〕 *one's* rice to the poor. (***b***) 《교부·허가하다》 grant; issue; deliver; 《차려주다》 set 《*a person*》 up. ¶ 여권을 ～ issue 〔furnish 《*a person*》 with〕 a passport / 가게를 ～ set 《*a person*》 up in business.
② (***a***) 《자리·길을》 give; offer; yield. ¶ 자리를 ～ make room 《for *a person*》; give 〔offer〕 a seat / 길을 ～ make way 《for *a person*》; give the road 《to *a person*》 / 버스에서 노인에게 자리를 내주었다 I gave my seat to an old man in the bus. (***b***) 《실권 등을》 hand 〔turn〕 over; transfer; surrender. ¶ 권리를 ～ transfer *one's* right to 《another》 / 정권을 ～ hand over the reins of power / 성을 ～ surrender a castle / 왕위를 ～ turn the throne over 《to》.

**내주장**(內主張) petticoat government. ～하다 exercise petticoat government; tie 《*one's* husband》 to *one's* apron strings; henpeck 《*one's* husband》. ¶ 그 집은 ～이다 The wife is the ruler 〔boss〕 in that house.

**내지**(內地) 《안쪽 지방》 the interior 《of a country》; inland; 《오지》 hinterland; back country; 《본토》 a mainland. ¶ ～의 inland; interior; home; domestic / 중국 ～를 여행하다 travel in the interior of China.

**내지**(乃至) ① 《…부터 …까지》 from 《ten》 to 《fifteen》; between 《ten》 and 《fifteen》. ¶ 700원 ～ 천원 (anywhere from) ₩700 to ₩1,000; between 700 and 1,000 won / 비용은 5만원 ～ 6만원일 것이다 The outlay will be between fifty thousand and sixty thousand won. / 그것은 1주일 ～ 2주일이면 당신에게 도착할 것이다 It will reach you in one or two weeks. ② 《또는》 or; and; and/or. ¶갑 ～ 을 A or B / 20 ～ 그 이상〔이하〕 twenty or more 〔under〕.

**내직**(內職) 《부녀의》 a job 〔work〕 for housewives; 《부업》 a side job 〔work〕; a sideline (겸업); 《가내 노동》 piecework done at home. ～하다 do a side job; work part-time. ¶ 아내는 ～으로 영어를 가르친다 My wife is teaching English on the side.

**내진**(內診) 《부인과의》 an internal examination. ～하다 make an internal examination 《of 》.

**내진**(來診) ¶ ～을 청하다 send for 〔call in〕 a doctor.

**내진**(耐震) ¶ ～의 earthquake-proof 《buildings》; (earth)quake-resistant / 이 건물은 ～건축이다 This is an earthquake-proof building. ◉ ～구조 earthquake-resistant construction. ～설계

an earthquake-resistant design.

**내집단**(內集團) 〖사회〗 an in-group.

**내쫓기다** ① 《쫓겨나다》 be 〔get〕 thrown 〔driven, turned〕 out; be forced out; be ousted 《from a party》; be expelled 《from school》. ¶ 집 밖으로 ～ be turned out of the house / 시집에서 ～ be forced 〔driven〕 out from *one's* husband's house; be compelled to leave *one's* husband's house. ② 《해고되다》 be dismissed 〔discharged, fired, sacked〕; be laid off (일시적). ¶ 회사에서 ～ be fired 〔sacked〕 by the company.

**내쫓다** ① 《밖으로》 drive 〔put, send, force, get, throw〕 out 《*a person* from a place》; expel; 《세든 사람을》 eject 〔evict〕 《a tenant》 from 《the house》. ¶ 아무를 밖으로 ～ turn *a person* out; show 〔give〕 *a person* the door 〔gate〕 / 학생을 학교에서 ～ expel a student from school; throw a student out of school / 네발로 안 나가면 내쫓을 테다 If you won't go yourself, I shall turn you out. ② 《해고하다》 dismiss; fire; discharge; sack 《구어》; 《지위 등에서》 oust. ¶ 종업원을 ～ dismiss an employee / 직장에서 경쟁 상대를 ～ oust a rival from office.

**내차다** kick hard; give 《*a person*》 a hard kick 《on the shin》.

**내채**(內債) an internal 〔a domestic〕 loan. ¶ ～를 발행〔모집〕하다 raise 〔float〕 a domestic loan.

**내처** 《끝까지》 throughout; to the very end; 《중단없이》 without a pause 〔break〕; continuously; 《단숨에》 at a breath; at a stretch; at a heat 〔dash〕; straight. ¶ 길을 ～ 가다 go on *one's* way without a pause / 일을 ～ 끝마치다 finish *one's* work at one stretch / 올라가는 참에 ～ 정상까지 오르다 go on and climb straight up to the top of a hill / 우리는 6시간 ～ 일했다 We worked for six hours running 〔at a stretch〕. / ～ 자버렸다 I kept on sleeping.

**내출혈**(內出血) 〖의학〗 internal hemorrhage 〔bleeding〕. ～하다 bleed internally; have an internal hemorrhage.

**내치**(內治) ① 《병의》 cure by internal treatment 〔medicine〕. ～하다 cure by internal medicine. ② 《국내 정치》 home 〔internal, domestic〕 administration. ～하다 administer the affairs of state.

**내치다** ① 《버리다》 throw away; cast away; abandon; desert. ② 《쫓아내다》 drive away; send away; expel.

**내치락들이치락하다** ① 《변덕스럽다》 change *one's* mind constantly; be fickle; be capricious; be full of whims; blow hot and cold. ② 《병세가》 change constantly; get better one day and worse the next; be uncertain; have 《its》 ups and downs. ¶ 환자의 병세는 내치락들이치락 한다 The condition of the patient neither improved nor got worse. *or* The patient is better one minute 〔day〕 and worse the next.

**내친걸음** having set about *do*ing 《*a thing*》. ¶ ～에 while *one* is at it; on *one's* way 《to》 / ～이다 We are in for it. *or* The die is cast. / ～에 부서진 창문도 수리하겠다 I'll fix the broken window when I have chance. / ～에 묻겠는데 그는 이혼했느냐 While we're at it, do you know if he is divorced? / 이왕 ～이니 지금에 와서 어찌 하겠나 I have gone too far to retreat 〔go back〕.

**내키다**[1] 《마음이》 feel like 《*do*ing》; have a mind 《to》; be 〔feel〕 inclined 《to *do*》; be in the mood 《to *do*》; have an inclination 《for》. ¶ 내키지 않는 일 a job *one* would prefer not to do / 마음만 내키면 when the fancy 〔mood, urge〕 takes *one;* when (*one* is) in the mood 〔humor〕 《to *do,* for *do*ing》 / 마음 내키는 대로 as *one's* 〔the〕 fancy takes *one;* as *one's* whim dictates / 마음이 썩 ～ have a great mind 《to *do*》 / 마음이 내키지 않다 have no mind 〔inclination〕 《to *do*》; be unwilling 〔reluctant〕 《to *do*》; be in no mood 《to *do*》 / 나는 그 사람과 결혼할 마음이 내키지 않는다 I can't bring myself to marry him. / 오늘 밤에는 저녁 준비할 마음이 내키지 않는다 I'm in no mood to cook dinner tonight. / 마음이 내키거든 전화하렴 Please call me up whenever you feel like it. / 오늘은 일할 마음이 안 내킨다 I am in no humor for work today.

**내키다**[2] 《물려 내다》 make 〔leave〕 room for; remove farther; set farther ahead.

**내탄**(耐彈) endurance against bullets; bulletproof.

**내탐**(內探) a private inquiry; a secret investigation. ～하다 make private 〔secret〕 inquiries 《into》; investigate 《a case》 secretly.

**내탕금**(內帑金) money in the personal possession of the king; 《영》 a privy 〔private〕 purse.

**내통**(內通) ① 《내응》 secret communication; collusion; 《배신》 betrayal; treason. ～하다 communicate secretly 《with the enemy》; hold [be in] secret communication 《with the enemy》; be in collusion 《with an outsider》. ¶ 그는 적과 ~했다 He secretly communicated with the enemy. ② 《남녀의》 adultery; illicit intercourse; misconduct. ~하다 commit adultery 《with》; misconduct *oneself* 《with》; fornicate. ◉ ~자 《배반자》 a betrayer; 《사통자》 a fornicator.

**내팽개치다** throw 《*a thing*》 out; toss 《*a thing*》 away; fling [cast] off; 《내버려두다》 lay aside 《*one's* work》. ¶ 지위도 체면도 ~ cast [throw] both position and reputation to the winds / 홧김에 그녀는 잿떨이를 방바닥에 내팽개쳤다 In a fit of anger she threw an ashtray on the floor.

**내포**(內包) 〚논리〛 connotation. ~하다 connote; involve. ¶ 그것은 여러가지 문제를 ~하고 있다 It involves various problems.

**내폭**(耐爆) ¶ ~성의 antiknock. ◉ ~성 휘발유 antiknock gasoline. ~제 (an) antiknock.

**내풀로** 《내 마음대로》 of *one's* own accord; voluntarily; on *one's* own (initiative).

**내피**(內皮) the inside skin; 《식물의》 the endodermis; 《동물의》 the endothelium (*pl.* -lia).

**내핍**(耐乏) austerity. ~하다 tighten *one's* belt; practice austerities.
◉ ~생활 a life of austerity; belt-tightening: ~ 생활을 하다 「put up with [bear] a hard life; lead a life of austerity; tighten *one's* belt / 국민에게 더한층의 ~생활을 촉구하다 urge more austerity for the people; impose greater austerity on the people. ~정책 a belt-tightening policy.

**내한**(來韓) a visit to Korea; arrival in Korea. ~하다 visit [come to] Korea; arrive in Korea [this country]. ¶ ~중인 버드 박사 Dr. Bird now in [visiting] Korea.

**내한**(耐寒) enduring the cold. ~하다 endure the cold; be cold-proof. ¶ ~의 cold-proof; proof against the cold.
◉ ~설비[장치, 준비] winterization: ~설비를 하다 winterize. ~성(性): ~성의 cold-resistant[-resisting, -tolerant] 《plants》; (winter-)hardy 《grasses》 / 반~성의 half-hardy. ~성 식물 a hardy plant. ~시험 a cold endurance [resistance] test. ~행군 a cold-weather endurance march. ~훈련 training 「in the cold season [for endurance in low temperature].

**내항**(內航) coastal service. ◉ ~로 a coasting line [route]. ~선 a coaster. ~해운업 coastal shipping.

**내항**(內港) the inner harbor.

**내항**(內項) 〚수학〛 internal terms.

**내항**(來航) a visit to 《Korea》. ~하다 《a ship》 come on a visit. ¶ 영국 함대의 ~ a visit of the British fleet 《to Korea》.

**내항성**(耐航性) 《배의》 seaworthiness; 《항공기의》 air worthiness. ¶ ~ 있는 seaworthy; airworthy.

**내해**(內海) an inland sea.

**내향**(內向) 〚심리〛 introversion. ~하다 turn in upon *oneself*. ¶ ~적인[성의] introvert / ~적인 사람 an introvert / 그녀는 ~적이다 She is introverted [an introvert]. ◉ ~성 introversion.

**내홍**(內訌) an internal strife [trouble]; domestic discord. ⇨ 내분(內紛).

**내화**(內貨) local currency [money].

**내화**(耐火) fire resistance; fireproofing. ¶ ~의 fireproof; fire-resistant.
◉ ~건축 a fireproof [fire-resistant] building: ~건축 재료 fire-resistant building materials. ~구조 fire=resisting [fireproof] construction. ~금고 a fireproof safe. ~도 refractoriness. ~력 fire-resisting qualities. ~벽돌 a firebrick. ~석재 firestone. ~성 refractory: ~성이 있다 be able to resist fire / ~성이 강하다 have great resistance to fire. ~장치 a fireproof installation; fireproofing: ~ 장치를 하다 equip with fireproof materials; fireproof. ~재(材) fireproof [refractory] material; refractories. ~ 점토 fireclay.

**내환**(內患) 《아내의 병》 *one's* wife's illness; 《내우》 domestic [internal] troubles.
◉ 외우~ troubles 「both at home and abroad [from within and without]; domestic troubles and external threats.

**내후년**(來後年) the year after next.

**냄비** a pan (얕은); a pot (깊은); [총칭] pots and pans. ¶ 스튜 ~ a stew pot [pan]; a saucepan / ~를 불에 올려놓다 put a pan over the fire / ~에 끓이다 boil 《fish》 in a pot (over the fire).
◉ ~국수 noodles served hot in a pot. ~뚜껑 a pot lid. ~손잡이 a pot bail. ~요리 a dish served hot in a pot; pot cooking.

**냄새** ① [일반적] (a) smell; (an) odor; (a) scent; 《향기》 perfume; aroma; fragrance; 《악취》 reek; stench; stink.

> **용법** **smell** 좋고 나쁜 것을 가리지 않고「냄새」를 뜻하는 가장 일반적인 말. **perfume** 향수와 같은 냄새. **fragrance** 꽃에서 나는 향긋한 냄새. **scent** 희미한 좋은 냄새. **aroma** 식욕을 돋우는 좋은 냄새. **odor** 화학적 특성을 나타내는 강렬한 냄새. **stink**, **stench**, **reek** 역겨운 나쁜 냄새.

¶ 좋은〔나쁜, 강한〕 ~ a good 〔a bad, a strong〕 smell / 요리~ a cooking smell; the smell of cooking / 장미꽃의 향긋한 ~ a scent 〔a faint fragrance〕 of roses / 커피의 향긋한 ~ the aroma of coffee / ~가 좋은 꽃들 fragrant 〔sweet-smelling〕 flowers / 상한 고기의 ~ the stink 〔unpleasant smell, vile odor〕 of rotten meat / 좋은 ~가 나는 sweet-smelling; fragrant; aromatic / 고약한〔나쁜〕 ~가 나는 foul-smelling; smelly / …한 ~가 나다 smell 〔have a smell〕 of 《fish》; stink of 《oil》; reek of 《garlic》 / …같은 ~가 나다 smell like 《bananas》 / ~를 맡다 smell 《this flower》 / ~를 피우다 emit 〔give out, send forth〕 a smell; 《나쁜 냄새를》 stink; reek / 나쁜 ~를 제거하다「get rid of 〔remove〕 an unpleasant odor 《from》; deodorize / ~가 풍기다 a smell hangs in the air; an odor fills the air / 땀~가 나다 reek with sweat / 이것은 ~가 좋다 This smells nice. / 쓰레기는 고약한 ~가 난다 Garbage stinks. / 그는 술~만 맡아도 취한다 He gets drunk on the smell of liquor. / 그에게선 술~가 난다 His breath smells of alcohol. / 그의 방은 담배 ~가 배어 있었다 His room was impregnated 〔soaked〕 with the scent of tobacco. / 가스〔무엇이 타는〕~가 난다 I smell gas 〔something burning〕. / 감기가 들어서 ~를 못 맡는다 I can't smell because I have a cold. / 그녀는 언제나 진한 향수 ~를 풍긴다 She is always giving off a strong smell of perfume. / 마시거나 ~맡지 마시오 《게시》 Do not drink or breathe on this product.

② 《낌새·느낌》 ¶ ~를 맡다 smell out 〔get wind of〕 《a scandal》; get scent of 《a plot》 / 범죄 ~가 나다 It has a sign 〔feeling〕 of a foul play 〔crime〕. / 그의 이야기는 수상한 ~가 난다 His story smells fishy 〔of something tricky〕.

**냅다**[1] 《연기가》 smart; sting. ¶ 연기가 ~ Smoke stings. / 아이, 내워 Oh, how smoky!

**냅다**[2] 《빠르고 세차게》 with force 〔all *one's* strength〕; violently; hard. ¶ ~ 달아나다 run for *one's* life / ~ 메치다 throw down hard / ~ 차다 kick hard.

**냅킨** a (table) napkin; 《영》 a serviette. ¶ 종이 ~ a paper napkin / ~을 무릎 위에 펴다 lay 〔spread〕 *one's* 〔a〕 napkin across 〔over〕 *one's* lap.

**냇가** a streamside; the bank of a stream 〔creek〕; a riverside. 「smell.

**냇내** the smell of smoke; a smoky

**냇물** (water of ) a stream. ¶ ~을 마시다 〔긷다〕 drink 〔draw〕 water from a stream / ~을 걸어서 건너다 wade across a stream.

**냇버들** 〖식물〗 a purple willow.

**냉**(冷) 〖한의〗 ① 《배의》 a chill stomach; a stomach chill. ② 《몸의》 a chill; a body chill. ③ 《대하증》 leucorrhea; whites; a discharge from the womb.

**냉-**(冷) cold; iced; chill(ed). ¶ 냉수 cold water / 냉맥주 cooled beer.

**냉가슴**(冷—) a hidden 〔secret〕 worry; inward 〔inner〕 trouble; spiritual agony (unknown to others). ¶ 그녀는 ~을 앓았다 She had「inner troubles 〔hardships unknown to others〕.

**냉각**(冷却) cooling; refrigeration. ~하다 cool; refrigerate; take the heat out of 《*a thing*》; cool down 〔off〕 《an engine》. ¶ 이 변화는 양국간의 관계가 ~됨으로써 생겼다 This change has been brought about by a cooling off in the relations between the two countries.
◉ ~기(器) a refrigerator; a cooler; 《엔진의》 a radiator. ~수 cooling water; (a) coolant(엔진·원자로의). ~장치 a cooling device 〔apparatus〕. ~제 a refrigerant. ~효과 a cooling effect.

**냉각기간**(冷却期間) a cooling-off period. ¶ 약간의 ~을 두고 난 다음에 토의하는 것이 좋겠다 Give yourself a bit of a cooling-off period before you discuss it (with him). / 긴 ~ 후에 그는 아내와 화해했다 After a long cooling-off period he was reconciled with his wife.

**냉간**(冷間) ◉ ~가공 cold working. ~압연 cold-rolling: ~ 압연 공장 a cold-rolling mill. ~압접법 cold pressure welding.

**냉국**(冷—) soup prepared cold.

**냉기**(冷氣) 《찬 공기》 cool air; 《추위》 a cold wave; cold weather; 《찬 기운》 cold; chill. ¶ ~를 느끼다 feel chilly / 아침의 ~를 느끼다 feel the morning chill.

**냉난방**(冷暖房) air conditioning. ¶ ~완비 《게시》 Air-conditioned. ◉ ~장치

an air conditioner.

**냉담**(冷淡) coldness; coolness; 《냉정》 cold-heartedness; 《무관심》 indifference. ~하다 (be) cold; cool; cold-hearted; indifferent (무관심). ¶ ~하게 coolly; coldly; cold-heartedly; indifferently / ~한 관리 a cold-hearted public official / ~하게 대하다 treat 《*a person*》 coldly; show 〔turn〕 the cold shoulder to 《*a person*》; give 《*a person*》 a cold reception / ~해지다 grow 〔become〕 cold 《to, toward》; lose *one's* enthusiasm 《for》 / 그녀는 그의 ~한 대접에 분개했다 She went mad at his cold-hearted treatment. / 나는 그녀에게 데이트를 신청했으나 ~하게 거절당했다 When I asked her for a date, I was refused coldly. / 그녀는 나에게 ~하게 굴었다 She behaved coldly toward me. *or* She gave me the cold shoulder.

**냉대**(冷待) a cold treatment 〔reception〕; inhospitality. ~하다 treat 〔receive〕 《*a person*》 coldly; give 《*a person*》 a cold reception; give 〔show〕 《*a person*》 the cold shoulder. ¶ 나는 그들에게서 ~받았다 I received a cold treatment from them. / 그는 회사에서 ~받고 있다 He is left out in the cold in the company.

**냉동**(冷凍) freezing; refrigeration. ~하다 freeze; refrigerate. ¶ 급속 ~하다 freeze 《food》 quickly; quick-freeze; deep-freeze / 이 생선은 상하기 쉬우니 바로 ~해야 한다 You must freeze these fish at once, as they are perishable. / 생선은 ~되어 이곳으로 운반된다 The fish is frozen 〔refrigerated〕 and brought here. ◉ ~건조 freeze-drying; 〖생화학〗 lyophilization: ~건조하다 freeze-dry; lyophilize / ~ 건조기 a freeze-dryer. ~고 a (deep) freezer. ~기 a freezing machine; a refrigerator. ~보존: ~보존하다 keep 《*a thing*》 in a freezer. ~선 a refrigerator boat. ~식품 frozen 〔deep-frozen〕 food. ~실〔칸〕 《냉장고의》 a freezing compartment; a freezer. ~어〔야채, 육〕 frozen fish 〔vegetables, meat〕. ~업 the cold-storage business. ~제 a refrigerant. ~차 a refrigerator car 〔van 《영》〕; a freezer (car). ~창고 a cold store. ~ 컨테이너 a reefer container.

**냉랭하다**(冷冷―) 《춥다》 (be) very cold; chilly; icy; freezing; 《냉정하다》 (be) cold; cool; cold-hearted; cold-blooded. ¶ 냉랭하게 coldly; coolly / 냉랭한 태도 a cool attitude; a distant air / 방바닥이 ~ The floor is cold.

**냉면**(冷麵) *naengmyeon,* cold buckwheat vermicelli 〔noodles〕.

**냉방**(冷房) 《찬 방》 a cold 〔an unheated〕 room; 《온도 조절》 air conditioning. ~하다 air-condition 《a room》; air-cool. ¶ ~이 지나치게 되어 있어요. 좀 낮춰 주시오 The air conditioning is on a bit too high. Please turn it down. / 그녀의 방은 알맞게 ~되어 있었다 Her room was comfortably air-conditioned. / ~완비 《게시》 Air-conditioned. / ~중―문을 닫으시오 Air conditioning is operating. Close the door, please. ◉ ~병 《be sick with》 air-conditioningitis. ~장치 air-conditioning; an air-conditioner; an air-cooler: ~ 장치가 돼 있는 건물 an air-conditioned building / ~ 장치를 하다 air-condition / ~ 장치가 되어 있다 be air-conditioned; be equipped with an air-conditioner. ~차 an air-conditioned car.

**냉소**(冷笑) a cold 〔sardonic〕 smile; a sneer; a jeer. ~하다 sneer 〔mock, scoff, jeer〕 《at *a person*》; smile derisively 〔mockingly〕 《at》. ¶ ~적 sneering; mocking; sardonic; sarcastic / 입가에 ~를 띄우고 with a cold smile on *one's* lips / ~를 금할 수 없다 cannot repress a cold smile / 그는 나의 시도를 ~했다 He sneered at my attempt.

**냉수**(冷水) cold water. ¶ ~ 먹고 이쑤시기 pretending to have eaten *one's* fill; showing off; putting on a big act / ~ 한 잔 주시오 Please give me a glass of cold water. / ~ 먹고 된 똥 누다 make something from nothing / ~도 잠깐 요기는 된다 Anything is better than nothing. ◉ ~마찰 cold-water rubbing: ~ 마찰하다 rub *oneself* with a cold wet towel; have a rubdown with a (cold) wet towel. ~욕 cold-water bathing; a cold bath: ~욕하다 take a cold bath; bathe in cold water.

**냉습**(冷濕) ① 《차고 누짐》 ~하다 (be) cold and humid 〔damp〕. ¶ ~한 기후 a cold and damp climate. ② 〖한의〗 a disease caused by cold and dampness.

**냉안시하다**(冷眼視―) look with coldness 「〔indifference〕 《at》.

**냉엄**(冷嚴) ~하다 (be) grim; stern; strict; stark. ¶ ~한 사실 《face》 a cold (hard) fact / 우리는 경제 상태의 ~한 현실을 모른다 We don't know the 「grim realities 〔hard fact〕 of the economic situation.

**냉온**(冷溫) cold and warmth. ◉ ~탕 a cold bath and a hot bath. 「놓은〕.

**냉육**(冷肉) cold meat; cold cuts (썰어

**냉이** 『식물』 a shepherd's purse; a mother's-heart; a pickpurse.

**냉장**(冷藏) cold storage; refrigeration. ～하다 keep 《*a thing*》 in cold storage; refrigerate; keep 《food》 cold. ◉ ～고 a refrigerator; 《미》 an icebox: 전기～고 an electric refrigerator / ～고에 넣다 put 《food》 in an icebox. ～법 refrigeration. ～선 a cold storage ship. ～실 a cold room; a cool chamber. ～업 the cold-storage business. ～차 a refrigerator 〔refrigerated〕 car; 《미구어》 a reefer; a chill car 《미》. ～창고 a cold store. ～회사 a cold-storage company.

**냉전**(冷戰) 《미·구소련간의》 the Cold War; [일반적] a cold war. ¶ ～을 완화하다 ease 〔alleviate〕 cold war tensions / 판문점은 ～의 상징적 유적의 하나이다 The (truce village of) P'anmunjŏm is one of the symbolic remains of the Cold War. / 저 부부는 지금 ～ 상태에 있다 That couple is hardly speaking to each other right now. ◉ ～외교〔전략〕 cold war diplomacy 〔strategy〕.

**냉정**(冷靜) calmness; coolness; composure; presence of mind. ～하다 (be) calm; cool; composed; self-possessed; cool-headed; serene. ¶ ～한 사람 a cool-headed person / ～한 태도 a calm attitude / ～히 calmly; coolly; composedly / ～을 잃다 lose *one's* presence of mind; be 〔get〕 excited; lose *one's* temper / ～을 되찾다 regain *one's* composure / 사물을 ～히 생각하다 take things coolly / 그는 ～한 판단력을 갖고 있다 He has a cool judgment. / 그녀는 언제나 ～함을 잃지 않는다 She always keeps a cool head. / 그렇게 흥분하지 말고 좀 ～해져라 Don't be so excited, calm yourself. / 그는 위험에 직면해도 ～하다 He「is cool 〔keeps his head〕 in the face of danger. / 아무도 이런 슬픔을 당하고 ～할 수는 없다 No mind could face such a grief with composure.

**냉차**(冷茶) iced tea.

**냉채**(冷菜) a cold (vegetable) dish dressed with various seasonings. ¶ 닭고기 ～ cold shredded-chicken and vegetables with various seasonings.

**냉천**(冷泉) a cold (mineral) spring.

**냉철**(冷徹) cool-headedness. ～하다 (be) cool-headed; 《현실적인》 hardheaded 《businessman》; realistic; 《구어》 hard-boiled 《newspapermen》. ¶ ～한 두뇌 a cool head / ～한 눈으로 현실을 바라봐야만 한다 We must look dispassionately at the realities.

**냉큼** 《곧·당장》 at once; immediately; right away 〔off〕; on the spot; 《재빨리》 quickly; promptly; without delay. ¶ ～ 다녀오다 (go and) come back right away / ～ 대답하다 answer promptly 〔readily〕 / ～ 말해라 Tell me quick. *or* Spit it out!

**냉평**(冷評) sarcastic criticism; a sneer. ～하다 make sarcastic remarks 《on》.

**냉풍**(冷風) a cold 〔chilly〕 wind.

**냉하다**(冷—) (be) cold; chilly. ¶ 냉한 기후 a cold climate / 냉한 음식 cold food.

**냉한**(冷汗) a cold sweat.

**냉해**(冷害) cold-weather damage. ¶ ～를 입다 suffer damage「due to 〔from〕 cold weather.

**냉혈**(冷血) ① 『동물』 cold-bloodedness. ② 《사람》 cold-heartedness; heartlessness. ◉ ～동물 a cold-blooded 〔hematocryal〕 animal. ～한(漢) a cold-hearted 〔heartless〕 fellow: 그는 ～한이야 He is a cold-hearted guy. *or* His heart is a stone.

**냉혹**(冷酷) cruelty; heartlessness. ～하다 (be) cruel; heartless; cold-hearted. ¶ ～하게 cruelly; mercilessly / 몹시 ～하다 be as cold as stone; have a heart of stone / 그는 ～한 사람이다 He is a heartless 〔an unfeeling〕 fellow.

**-냐** 《의문》 who; what; when; how, *etc.* ¶ 너 몇 살이냐 How old are you? / 저 책을 읽었느냐 Did you read that book?

**냠냠** Yum-yum! ～거리다 smack *one's* lips; go yum-yum. ～하다 《먹고 싶어》 want 〔wish, desire〕 to eat.

**냥**(兩) ① 《옛날 돈의 단위》 a *nyang;* a tael. ¶ 한 냥 one *nyang;* an old Korean dime / 엽전 열닷 냥 fifteen copper *nyang.* ② 《중량》 a *nyang*(= 37.5g). ¶ 한냥쭝 one *nyang* of weight.

**너**[1] 《2인칭》 you; 《고어》 thou. ¶ 너의 your; 《고어》 thy / 너에게 (to) you; 《고어》 thee / 너를 you; 《고어》 thee / 너 자신을 알라 Know yourself 〔thyself〕. / 너는 내가 믿는 유일한 친구다 You are the only friend I trust. / 나를 내버려 두게. 너는 너. 나는 나니까 Just leave me alone. You're you. I'm me.

**너**[2] 《넷》 four. ¶ 쌀 너 말 four *mal* of rice.

**너구리** 『동물』 a raccoon (dog).

**너그러이** generously; liberally; magnanimously; tolerantly; leniently; indulgently. ¶ ～ 용서하다 forgive generously / ～ 대하다 treat 〔receive〕 《*a person*》 with generosity 〔with open arms〕; deal leniently with 《*a person*》.

**너그럽다** (be) broad-minded; generous; liberal; magnanimous; tolerant; lenient; indulgent. ¶ 너그러운 사람 a generous person / 너그러운 생각 a liberal mind / 너그러운 태도 a generous attitude / 너그러운 처분을 바라다 plead for leniency / 그 사회는 성에 대해서 ～ That society is permissive regarding sex.

**너글너글하다** (be) broad-minded; big=hearted; generous; magnanimous. ¶ 성질이 ～ be of a generous nature.

**너나들이** a first-name basis; a close fellowship. ～하다 be on a first-name basis; be on intimate terms. ¶ 우리는 ～하는 사이다 We are on a first-name basis.

**너나없다** there is no difference between you and me; all of us are the same. ¶ 너나없이 irrespective of persons / 우리는 너나없이 가난하고 배고프다 All of us are 〔We are all〕 poor and hungry. / 우리는 너나없이 모두 같은 운명에 처해 있다 We are all in the same boat. / 마을 사람들은 너나없이 그것을 다 알고 있다 Everybody in the village knows it.

**너더댓** about four or five. ¶ ～새 about 4 or 5 days.

**너더분하다** ① 《지저분하다》 (be) untidy; disorderly; disheveled (복장·머리 등이); [서술적] be in disorder 〔disarray〕; be in untidy state; be in a mess 〔shambles〕. ¶ 너더분한 방 a room in a mess; an untidy room / 책을 너더분하게 쌓아 놓다 pile up books in disorder. ② 《장황하다》 (be) long and boring; tedious; long-winded.

**너덕너덕** in tatters 〔pieces, rags〕; in shreds 〔ribbons〕; full of patches. ¶ 옷이 ～ 떨어지다 *one's* clothes are in tatters 〔shreds〕 / 옷을 ～ 깁다 patch up *one's* clothes all over.

**너덜거리다** ① 《가닥이》 flutter; flap; be in tatters. ¶ 찢어진 옷소매가 팔을 움직일 때마다 너덜거린다 The torn sleeve of my coat is fluttering as I move my arm. ② 《언행이》 talk 〔behave〕 indiscriminately; get uppish; talk irresponsibly.

**너덜너덜** 《가닥이》 in tatters 〔shreds〕; 《언행이》 forwardly; uppishly. ¶ ～한 tattered; ragged / ～해진 구두 worn-out shoes / ～ 닳아 해어지다 《옷 따위가》 be worn to a thread (해져서); be torn to shreds (찢어져서) / 사전은 ～ 해지도록 써라 Use your dictionary so frequently that it falls apart.

**너덧** about four. ¶ ～ 사람 four or five people.

**너도나도** both of us; we. ¶ ～ 불조심 Let's take precautions against fire.

**너도밤나무** 〖식물〗 a beech.

**너럭바위** a broad and flat rock.

**너르다** (be) wide; spacious; roomy; vast; open. ¶ 너른 공간〔벌판〕 an open space 〔field〕 / 너른 집 a spacious house / 그는 이 너른 세상에 몸 붙일 곳도 없다 He is a forsaken man in this wide world.

**너름새** managerial ability 〔capacity, talent〕; resourcefulness.

**너머** beyond; across; over; the other side. ¶ 재 ～ 마을 a village beyond 〔across〕 the hill / 강 ～에 《live》 across the river 《from》; on the opposite 〔other〕 side of the river / 창 ～(로) through a window / 지붕 ～로 보이는 달 the moon seen over the roof of a house / 울타리〔안경〕 ～로 보다 look over 「the fence 〔*one's* glasses〕 / 담 ～로 엿듣다 overhear what is said on the other side of the wall.

**너무** too (much); ever so much; 《과도하게 …해서》 so … that …; such … that …; too … to …. (★ so … that의 so 다음에는 「형용사, 부사」가, such … that의 such 다음에는 「명사」가, too … to의 too 다음에는 「형용사·부사」가 옴에 주의). ¶ ～ 젊다〔크다〕 be too young 〔large, big〕 / ～ 먹다 eat too much; overeat / 일을 ～ 하다 work too much 〔hard〕; overwork *oneself* / 나를 ～ 믿지 말게 Don't expect too much of me. / 그놈은 세상을 ～ 몰라 How little he knows the world! / 그는 ～ 온순해서 탈이야 He is gentle to a fault. / ～ 확신하지 마라 Don't be too sure of it. / 이 책은 ～ 어려워서 모르겠다 This book is too difficult for me (to read). / 나는 ～나 무서워서 말 한 마디 할 수 없었다 I was so terrified that I could not say a word.

**너무하다** (be) unreasonable; (too) bad; too much 〔hard〕. ¶ 그것은 ～ 《공정치 않다》 That isn't fair. *or* 《지나치다》 You are going too far. / 그런 말을 하다니 자네도 너무하군 It is too cruel of you to say such a thing.

**너벅선**(一船) a flat-bottomed boat.

**너부데데하다** have an unpleasantly flat face.

**너부시** 《coming》 down lightly 〔gently, softly〕. ¶ ～ 절하다 bow with a gentle sweep; kneel down and bow politely.

**너부죽하다** (be) somewhat flat and broad. ¶ 너부죽한 얼굴 a flat face / 너부죽이 flat; pronely / 너부죽이 엎드리다 lay *oneself* flat.

**너비** width; breadth. ¶ 넉 자 ～ 《cloth》

four feet wide / ~가 넓은 wide; broad / ~가 좁은 narrow / ~를 넓히다 widen; broaden / 이 도로는 ~가 넓다〔좁다〕 This road is broad〔narrow〕. / 그것은 길이 20미터, ~ 15미터이다 It is 20 meters long by 15 wide. / 이 강의 ~는 얼마냐 How wide is this river? / ~가 20미터이다 It is twenty meters wide 〔in width, across〕.

**너새** ① 〖조류〗 a great bustard. ② 〖건축〗 a hip. ¶ ~ 지붕 a hip(ped) roof.

**너설** a jag 《of rock》; a rock-ribbed 〔rocky, craggy〕 spot.

**너스래미** loose ends 〔strips〕. ¶ 멍석 ~ loose ends of a straw mat.

**너스레** ① 《걸쳐놓은 것》 a frame of crisscross 〔twigs, sticks〕. ¶ ~를 놓다 set up crosspieces; cover 《a hollow》 with crosspieces 〔twigs〕. ② 《허튼 소리》 a sly jest 〔remark〕; an idle talk; nonsense. ¶ ~ 떨다, ~ 놓다 make a sly jest 〔remark〕; talk nonsense 〔rubbish〕.

**너울**[1] 《여자가 머리에 쓰는》 a long black veil (for women); a lady's veil. ¶ ~을 쓰다 veil *one's* face / ~ 쓴 거지 a beggar who can't afford to be a gentleman.

**너울**[2] 《큰 파도》 a big wave; a billow; raging waves; rough waters; a heavy sea. ¶ (배가) ~에 들까불리다 be tossed about by heavy seas.

**너울가지** 《붙임성》 sociability; affability; companionability. ¶ ~가 좋다 be sociable 〔amicable〕.

**너울거리다** 《물결이》 surge; roll; swell; billow; undulate; 《나뭇잎 등이》 swing; flutter; sway; waver. ¶ 파도가 너울거리는 바다 the billowing 〔heaving〕 sea / (나뭇잎 따위가) 바람에 ~ tremble 〔rustle〕 in the breeze; be swayed by the wind; sway to the wind.

**너울너울** wavingly; undulatingly; waveringly; swayingly. ¶ ~ 춤을 추다 dance with swaying arms / 나비가 이 꽃 저 꽃으로 ~ 춤추며 다닌다 A butterfly is fluttering from flower to flower.

**너울지다** 《물결이》 be rough in the distance.

**너저분하다** (be) shabby and untidy; disorderly; [서술적] be in disorder 〔confusion〕. ¶ 너저분한 방 a (shabby and) untidy room / 행락객이 버린 너저분한 쓰레기 dirty leavings littered by picnickers / 책을 너저분하게 어질러 놓다 leave books in a jumble 〔mess〕.

**너절하다** ① 《허름하다》 (be) shabby; poor-looking; miserable; seedy; unpresentable. ¶ 너절한 옷 shabby clothes / 너절한 집 a poor 〔shabby〕 house / 너절한 환경 shabby surroundings / 그녀는 너절한 옷차림이었다 She was shabbily 〔poorly〕 dressed.
② 《변변치 않다》 (be) worthless; valueless; poor; shabby; 《하찮다》 (be) trifling; trivial; petty; paltry. ¶ 너절한 녀석 a worthless fellow; a good-for-nothing (fellow) / 너절한 일〔것〕 a trivial 〔trifling〕 thing / 너절한 책 a valueless book / 너절하게 굴다 act in a shabby sort of way / 너절한 소리를 하다 talk nonsense 〔rubbish〕.
③ 《품격이》 (be) low; vulgar; mean; shabby. ¶ 너절한 농담 a「vulgar 〔low, nasty〕 joke / 너절한 생각 a mean thought 〔idea〕 / 너절한 친구들과 사귀다 keep low company.

**너즈러지다** 《낙엽 따위가》 lie scattered all over.

**너클볼** 〖야구〗 a knuckle ball.

**너털거리다** ⇨ 너덜거리다.

**너털웃음** loud 〔hearty, boisterous〕 laughter; a horselaugh; a guffaw; a belly laugh. ¶ ~을 웃다 laugh loudly 〔heartily, boisterously〕; guffaw.

**너트** 〖기계〗 a nut. ¶ 볼트를 ~로 죄다 fix 〔attach〕 a bolt with a nut.

**너풀거리다** flutter; flap; wave; sway 《in the wind》. ¶ 그녀의 모자 리본이 바람에 너풀거린다 The ribbons on her hat are fluttering in the wind. / 깃발이 바람에 너풀거린다 The flag is flapping in the wind.

**너희(들)** you (all); you people; you folks.

**넉** four. ¶ 넉 달 four months.

**넉가래** a wooden 〔snow〕 shovel. ◉ ~질 shoveling with a wooden shovel: ~질하다 shovel with a wooden shovel.

**넉걷이** raking the vines out of a garden 〔field〕. ~하다 do the vine raking.

**-넉넉** ... odd; ... strong; more than 《two years》. ¶ 30명 ~ thirty (people) strong / 30년 ~ thirty odd years.

**넉넉잡다** estimate 〔calculate〕 sufficiently 〔highly〕. ¶ 아무리 넉넉잡아도 at the highest estimate / 넉넉잡아 1주일 a week at (the) most /「25명분 요리를 위해 닭 가슴살이 몇 개 필요하죠」—「넉넉잡고 40개쯤이면 될 거예요」 "How many chicken breasts do I need for 25 people?"—"I'd say about 40, to be on the safe side."

**넉넉하다** ① 《충분하다》 (be) enough; sufficient; ample; plenty of; full; adequate.
¶ 5명이 한 달 살기에 넉넉한 식량 suffi-

cient food for five people to live a month / 돈이 ~ have enough money; have money enough (★ enough를 money 앞에 놓는 것이 더 뜻이 강함) / 시간이 ~ have enough 〔ample〕 time; have plenty of time / 치수가 ~ have ample measure / 세 사람이면 넉넉할 게다 Three men will be enough. / 그의 월급은 가족을 부양하기에 ~ His salary is adequate to support his family.

> 용법 모두 「넉넉하다」란 뜻으로 쓰일 수 있는 말이나, 그 차이는 다음과 같다. **enough** 주로 양이 「필요·희망 따위를 충족시킬 만큼」, **sufficient** 정도·양 따위가 「필요를 충족시킬 만큼」이란 미묘한 뜻의 차이가 있으나 거의 같은 뜻으로 쓰임. sufficient가 enough보다는 더 격식차린 말. **ample**, **plenty of**, **full** 모두 필요한 수량보다 「남을 정도로 많은」이란 뜻. **adequate** 양·질 따위가 「목적에 상응되는 만큼」의 뜻.

② 《살림이》 (be) rich; wealthy; well=to-do. ¶ 넉넉한 집 〔가정〕 a well-to-do family.

③ 《도량이》 (be) broad-〔big-〕minded; 《관대하다》 generous; liberal; big.

**넉넉히** 《충분히》 sufficiently; enough; well; fully; 《풍부히》 amply; plentifully; 《부유하게》 wealthily; richly. ¶ ~ 살다 live comfortably; be well-off / 옷을 ~ 짓다 cut clothes full; give a loose 〔an ample〕 fit / ~ 먹다 eat *one's* fill / 역까지 3마일은 ~ 된다 It is a good 〔full〕 three miles to the station. / 그 일을 끝낼 수 있는 시간은 ~ 있다 We have time enough to complete the work.

**넉살** impudence; shamelessness; brazen(-faced)ness; cheekiness; audacity; nerve; cheek. ~스럽다, ~좋다 (be) impudent; shameless; brazen(-faced); cheeky 《구어》; nervy 《미구어》; pushy. ¶ ~ 부리다 behave impudently; act brazenly 〔with cheek〕 / ~좋게도 …하다 have the 「impudence 〔cheek, nerve〕 to *do;* be shameless 〔impudent〕 enough to *do* / 그는 참 ~좋은 친구야 What nerve he has got! *or* What a shameless 〔cheeky〕 fellow he is!

**넋** ① 《영혼》 a soul; a spirit; the ghost 《of a dead person》. ¶ 죽은 자의 넋 the departed spirit 〔soul〕 《of *a person*》 / …의 넋을 달래다 propitiate 〔appease〕 the souls of… / 넋은 죽지 않는다 The soul 〔spirit〕 never dies. / 죽으면 넋이 몸 밖으로 빠져나가는 것일까 Does the soul leave the body at death?

② 《기력·생명력》 life; *one's* spirit. ¶ 넋이 없는 soulless; lifeless (생기없는) / 넋을 빼앗다 captivate; fascinate; charm; bewitch / 넋이 없다 be absent-minded / 넋을 잃다 lose *one's* senses; become 〔get〕 absent-minded; forget *oneself* / 그는 그녀의 아름다움에 넋을 빼앗기고 있다 He is 「fascinated 〔charmed〕 with her beauty. / 그는 그 광경에 넋을 잃고 바라보았다 He was captivated by the scene and gazed at 〔upon〕 it.

**넋두리** ① 《무당의》 utterances of a shaman given as those of a deceased spirit. ~하다 《a shaman》 speak in behalf of a deceased spirit.

② 《주절거림》 silly talk; gibberish; nonsense; 《푸념》 a complaint; a grumble; a murmur. ~하다 talk gibberish 〔nonsense〕; complain 《of, about》; grumble 《at, about, over》. ¶ 늙은이의 ~ the tedious silly talk of the age / 그것에 관해 ~를 늘어놓지 마라 Don't grumble 〔complain〕 about it.

**넌더리** 《지긋지긋함》 an aversion; a dislike; a disgust; a hatred; a repugnance. ~나다 be 〔get〕 sick (and tired) 《of》; become 〔feel, be〕 disgusted 《with》; get 〔become〕 tired of (★ get tired with면 「…에〔으로〕 지치다」의 뜻); get sick 〔weary〕 (to death) 《of》; have had enough 《of》; 《구어》 be fed up 《with》. ¶ ~나게 하다 make 《*a person*》 sick 〔fed up〕; bore 〔weary〕 《*a person*》 with 《lengthy talk》 / 그 생각만 해도 ~난다 The bare idea makes me sick. / 그의 이야기는 이제 ~난다 I am now sick of his talk. / 그의 지루한 강의에는 ~가 난다 His tedious lecture bored 「me stiff 〔the life out of me〕.

**넌더리대다** behave disgustfully 〔revoltingly, repugnantly〕.

**넌덕** witty remarks with Homeric laughter. ¶ ~ 부리다 make a Homeric laughter with witty remarks.

**넌덜머리** ⇨ 넌더리.

**넌지시** secretly; indirectly; casually; in a casual way 〔manner〕; allusively; implicitly. ¶ ~ 말하다 hint 《at》; drop a hint; allude 《to》; insinuate 《that …》 / 아무를 ~ 떠보다 sound *a person* 《about *a thing*》 / 아무를 ~ 놀리다 make fun of *a person* indirectly / ~ 추파를 건네다 make eyes at 《*a person*》 secretly / 그는 그 문제에 대해서 ~ 언급했다 He made a distant allusion to the question. / 그녀는 ~ 내가 있는 쪽을 보

앖다 She gave a casual glance in my direction.

**널** ①《널빤지》 a board; a plank. ¶ ~을 깔다 board 《over》; lay boards 《on》. ②《관》 a coffin; 《미》 a casket. ¶ 죽은 사람을 널에 넣다 lay a dead person in a coffin; coffin. ③《널뛰기의》 a seesaw board; a teeter-totter.

**널감** ①《재료》 material for a coffin. ② [비유적] 《사람》 a person ready for the coffin; an old person.

**널기와집** a shingle-roofed house 〔cottage〕.

**널다** 《볕·바람에》 spread 《grains》 out; hang 《*a thing*》 out (to dry); 《말리다》 dry; air. ¶ 멍석에 벼를 ~ spread rough rice out on a straw mat / 빨랫줄에 옷을 ~ hang clothes out on the laundry line / 이부자리를〔옷을〕 내 ~ air bedding 〔clothes〕.

**널다리** a wooden footbridge.

**널따랗다** (be) rather wide 〔broad〕; open; spacious; roomy; extensive. ¶ 널따란 어깨 broad shoulders / 널따란 거리 a wide 〔broad〕 street / 널따란 들판 an open field / 널따란 뜰〔방〕 a spacious garden 〔room〕.

**널뛰기** seesaw; seesawing; teeter-totter(ing). ~하다 = 널뛰다.

**널뛰다** seesaw; teeter-totter; play (at) seesaw 〔teeter-totter〕.

**널리** ①《광범하게》 widely; broadly; far and wide; extensively; 《일반적으로》 generally; universally; at large. ¶ ~ 광고하다 advertise extensively / ~ 알려지다 be widely known / ~ 교제하다 have a large circle of acquaintance / ~ 여행하다 travel far and wide / ~ 읽히다 have 〔obtain〕 a wide circulation / ~ 배포하다 distribute widely 《among》 / 고전(古典)을 ~ 섭렵하다 read widely in the classics / ~ 사용되다 be widely used 《in school》 / 이들 식물은 ~ 분포되어 있다 These plants are widely 〔extensively〕 distributed. / 그것은 ~ 알려진 바이다 It is a matter of common knowledge.
②《너그럽게》 generously; liberally. ¶ 아무의 잘못을 ~ 용서하다 be generous enough to pardon *a person's* mistake.

**널리다**[1] 《널려 있다》 be spread 《over, around》; be scattered 《over, around》. ¶ 낙엽이 뜰에 널려 있다 Fallen leaves are spread all over the garden. / 휴지가 온 방안에 널려 있다 Wastepaper is scattered all over the room.

**널리다**[2] = 넓히다.

**널마루** a wooden 〔boarding〕 floor.

**널문**(一門) a wooden gate 〔door〕.

**널반자** a wooden 〔boarding〕 ceiling.

**널방석**(一方席) a large straw mat (to spread grains out on); a drying 〔an airing〕 mat.

**널브러지다** spread (out); scatter (widely).

**널빤지** a board; a plank (두꺼운). ¶ 두치 ~ a two-*chi* board; a board two *chi* thick / ~를 입힌 벽 walls lined with boards / ~로 울타리를 치다 fence 《a house》 with boards.

**널어놓다** spread out; 《걸어서》 hang out (*a thing* to air or dry it). ¶ 고추를 ~ spread hot peppers out 《on the sunny ground》.

**널음새** 《말솜씨》 *one's* ability 〔capacity〕 to speak 〔talk〕; 《일솜씨》 capacity of handling a matter.

**널장** a plank; a board.

**널조각** a piece of board.

**널찍널찍하다** (be) all rather wide; quite wide. ¶ 널찍널찍하게 자리를 잡다 take 〔occupy〕 ample space 《to sit down》.

**널찍이** rather widely; extensively; amply; fully. ¶ 자리를 ~ 잡고 있다 take ample space to sit down / 구멍을 ~ 파다 dig a hole big enough.

**널찍하다** = 널따랗다.

**널판때기, 널판자**(一板子) a big 〔long, broad and thick〕 piece of board.

**널판장**(一板牆) a board fence.

**널평상**(一平床) a movable square wooden floor 《for outdoor use》.

**넓다** ①《폭·넓이 따위가》 (be) wide; broad; large; extensive; spacious; vast; roomy.

> (용법) **wide**와 **broad**—wide와 broad는 거의 같은 뜻으로 쓰이지만, 함축된 뜻의 차이를 들면 wide는 한 끝에서 한 끝까지의 폭의 넓이에 중점을 두고, broad는 넓이·폭 따위에 대하여 표면상으로 본 넓이의 느낌을 강조함: a wide road / a wide piece of ribbon / a broad valley / broad shoulders.

¶ 넓은 거리 a broad street / 넓은 세계 the wide world / 넓은 방 a large 〔spacious〕 room / 넓은 사막 an expanse of desert / 넓은 이마 a broad 〔high〕 forehead / 넓은 집 a spacious 〔roomy〕 house / 넓은 조망 a wide view / 그 강은 어귀가 ~ The river is wide-mouthed. / 그 대학 교정은 ~ The college has a large campus.
②《범위가》 (be) broad; wide; extensive. ¶ 넓은 경험 wide experience / 견

문이 넓은 사람 a well-informed person / 시야가 넓은 사람 a man of broad outlook / 넓은 의미로 in a broad sense / 교제 범위가 ~ have a large circle of acquaintance(s); have many friends / 그는 그 문제에 관해 넓은 지식을 갖고 있다 He has an extensive 〔a wide, a broad〕 knowledge on the subject. / 그는 사업의 폭이 ~ He does his business on a large scale 〔extensively〕.
③ 《마음이》 (be) generous; liberal; broad-minded; big-hearted. ¶ 마음이 넓은 사람 a generous 〔broad-minded〕 man.

**넓데데하다** (be) unpleasantly flattish. ¶ 넓데데한 얼굴 a flat (ugly) face.

**넓둥글다** (be) flat and round.

**넓어지다** widen; broaden; become wider 〔broader〕. ¶ 끝으로 가면서 점점 ~ widen 〔become wider〕 toward the end / 강어귀에서 ~《the river》 widen at its mouth.

**넓이** ① 《폭》 width; breadth. ¶ 다섯 자 ~ a width of 5 feet; 5 feet wide / ~가 넓다〔좁다〕 be wide 〔narrow〕 / ~가 다섯 자다 be five feet broad 〔wide, in breadth〕. ② 《면적》 (an) area; dimensions; (an) extent. ¶ 정원의 ~ the area of the garden / ~가 백 평방미터이다 cover an area 〔a space〕 of 100 square meters.

**넓이뛰기** ⇨ 멀리뛰기.

**넓적넓적** 《넓적하게》 all flat; so that all are flat. ¶ 떡을 ~ 썰다 cut a rice cake into flat pieces.

**넓적다리** a thigh. ¶ ~를 드러내다 show 〔expose, bare〕 *one's* thighs. ◉ ~뼈 a thighbone.

**넓적부리** 〖조류〗 a spoonbill; a shoveler; shovelbill. ◉ ~ 도요 〖조류〗 a spoon-billed sandpiper.

**넓적스름하다** (be) rather flat. ¶ 넓적스름한 얼굴 a flattish face.

**넓적이** ① 《사람》 a person with a flat face. ② 《넓게》 flat; flatwise. ¶ 떡을 ~ 썰다 cut the rice cake into flat pieces.

**넓적하다** (be) broad and flat. ⇨ 납작하다.

**넓히다** 《폭을》 widen; broaden; 《확대하다》 extend; enlarge; expand; spread. ¶ 경험을 ~ enlarge *one's* experience / 길을 ~ widen 〔broaden〕 a road / 옷 품을 ~ make a coat wider 〔fuller〕; let a coat out / 판도를 ~ extend the territory / 시야를 ~ broaden *one's* outlook / 운동장을 ~ enlarge the playground / 과학 지식의 영역을 ~ enlarge 〔extend〕 the boundaries of scientific knowledge / 그들은 해마다 그들의 사업을 넓히고 있다 They are enlarging 〔expanding〕 their business every year.

**넘겨다보다** ① 《탐내다》 covet; look on with envy. ¶ 남의 재산을〔아내를〕 ~ covet another's property 〔wife〕. ② = 넘어다보다.

**넘겨쓰다** take 〔bear〕 the blame for 《the accident》 upon *oneself.* ¶ 남의 죄를 ~ take another man's fault upon *oneself* / 남의 부채를 ~ shoulder *another's* 〔somebody else's〕 debts.

**넘겨씌우다** 《죄·책임 등을》 put 〔lay〕 《*one's* guilt》 on 《*a person*》; lay 《the blame》 at 《*a person's*》 door; lay 〔put〕 《the responsibility》 on 《*a person*》. ¶ 친구에게 잘못을 ~ shuffle off *one's* fault onto *one's* friend's shoulder / 실패의 책임을 하급자에게 넘겨씌워서는 안 된다 Don't lay the responsibility for a failure on your subordinates.

**넘겨잡다** make a random guess; hazard a conjecture 〔guess〕. ¶ 아무의 생각을 ~ guess *a person's* intention / 잘못〔바로〕 ~ guess wrong 〔right〕 / 넘겨잡아 대답하다 answer at random; take a shot 〔stab〕 at the answer / 사물을 넘겨잡고 이야기해서는 안된다 You must not tell about things by 〔at〕 a guess.

**넘겨주다** = 넘기다 ①, ③, ⑦.

**넘겨짚다** ⇨ 넘겨잡다. ¶ 넘겨짚은 것이 들어맞다 make a lucky shot 〔guess〕 《at the answer》 / 내가 그런 짓을 했다고 넘겨짚지 마라 Don't run away with the idea that I did such a thing.

**넘고처지다** be good for neither one thing nor the other; be not adequate 〔suitable〕. ¶ 넘고처지는 결혼은 화목하지 않다 A ill-matched marriage will not do well. / 취직자리는 몇 군데 있으나 내게는 모두 넘고처진다 There are several positions, but none of them is quite suitable for me.

**넘기다** ① 《너머로》 pass 《*a thing*》 over; pass 〔go〕 over. ¶ 담 너머로 ~ pass 《*something*》 over a wall.
② 《기한·정원을》 pass; exceed. ¶ 출원 기한을 ~ pass 〔miss〕 the deadline for applications / 빚 갚을 기한을 ~ fail to pay a debt by a fixed date; be overdue.
③ 《양도하다》 transfer; make over; turn over; pass on; deliver up; give up. ¶ 권리를 남에게 ~ transfer *one's* rights to another / 책임을 남에게 ~ shift 〔shuffle〕 the responsibility on to another / 재산을 아들에게 ~ make over 〔pass on〕 *one's* property to *one's*

son / 채권을 아무에게 ~ turn *one's* claim over to *a person* / 농장을 채권자에게 넘겨주다 assign 〔turn over〕 *one's* farm to a creditor.
④ 《젖히다》 turn over; put one across 〔on top of〕 the other. ¶ 책장을 ~ turn over the leaves 《of a book》; turn 〔leaf〕 the pages 《of》.
⑤ 《쓰러뜨리다》 throw down; trip. ¶ 다리를 걸어 아무를 ~ trip up with *one's* foot / 나무를 잘라 ~ cut a tree down.
⑥ 《거르다》 skip; omit; overlook; forget. ¶ 책 첫머리를 넘기고 읽다 skip the first part of a book.
⑦ 《인도하다》 hand 〔turn〕 over; make over; 《포로·범인을》 hand over; surrender; give 《a thief》 in charge (경찰 등에). ¶ 도둑을 경찰에 ~ hand 〔turn〕 over a thief to the police.
⑧ 《세월·계절을 보내다》 pass (through). ¶ 해를 ~ pass 〔ring out〕 the old year; enter a new year / 겨울을 ~ pass the winter / 이 사과는 겨울을 넘길 수 있을까 Will these apples keep over the winter ?
⑨ 《이월하다》 carry over 〔forward〕. ¶ 잔액을 다음 회계 연도로 ~ carry the balance over to the following fiscal year / 이 토의는 다음 모임으로 넘기겠습니다 We will carry this discussion over into the next meeting.
⑩ 《고비를 모면하다》 pass 〔go〕 through; tide over; turn the corner; weather. ¶ 난관을 ~ surmount a difficulty / 위기를 ~ get 〔pass〕 through a crisis; tide over a crisis / 재정 위기를 ~ weather a financial crisis / 우리나라는 경제 위기를 그럭저럭 넘겼다 Our country managed to weather its economic crisis.
⑪ 《돌리다》 transmit; transfer; refer 《to》. ¶ 사건을 다른 관청으로 ~ refer a matter to another office / 신규 사업의 감독권은 본사에서 지사로 넘겨졌다 The control of the new business was transferred from the head office to a branch.

**넘나다** behave out of keeping with *one's* station; be too forward.

**넘나들다** haunt; visit often; frequent. ¶ 권문의 문턱이 닳도록 ~ frequent the house of an influential person.

**넘노닐다** stroll around 〔to and fro〕.

**넘늘다** indulge *one's* humor without losing *one's* dignity.

**넘다** ① 《초과하다》 exceed; be over 〔above〕; go beyond; be more than; be in excess 《of》. ¶ 중량 제한을 ~ exceed the weight limit / 자기 권한의 한계를 ~ exceed 〔go beyond〕 *one's* authority / 나이 50세가 ~ be more than fifty years old; be over fifty / 그것은 우리들의 상상을 넘는 것이었다 It was far beyond our imagination. / 응모자는 모집 인원을 넘었다 There were more applicants than required. / 제한된 시간이 넘었으니 질문을 끝내주시오 You must finish your question because you have already exceeded the time limit.
② 《넘어가다》 go 「over 〔across, beyond〕; pass; cross. ¶ 국경〔산〕을 ~ cross 「the border 〔a mountain〕 《by car》 / 걸어서 들과 산을 ~ walk across the fields and over the hills / 담을 ~ go 〔jump〕 over a wall / 단번에 울타리를 ~ clear the hedge at one bound / 고개 둘을 넘으니 마을의 불빛이 보였다 I went over two hills before I saw the lights of the village. / 공은 좌익수의 머리 위를 넘었다 The ball sailed over the left fielder's head. / 「여기가 어디지」—「지금 오하이오주와 펜실베이니아주의 경계를 막 넘었다」 "Where are we ?" —"We've just crossed the border between Ohio and Pennsylvania."
③ 《때·시한 따위가》 be past 〔over〕; pass (away); fall due; run out; expire; be out. ¶ 2개월을 넘지 않는 기한 내에 not later than two months 《from the date》 / 낮 12시가 넘었다 It is now past noon. / 계약 기한이 넘었다 The contract has 「run out 〔expired〕.
④ 《범람하다》 overflow; run 〔flow〕 over. ¶ 폭우로 강물이 둑을 넘었다 The heavy rain caused the river to overflow its banks.
⑤ 《극복하다》 overcome 〔surmount〕 《obstacles》; tide 〔get〕 over 《difficulties》; weather 《a crisis》. ⇨ 넘기다 ⑩. ¶ 그녀는 불굴의 정신으로 이들 장애를 넘었다 Her indefatigable spirit carried her over these obstacles.

**넘버** ① 《수·번호》 a number. ② 《번호판》 a license 〔number〕 plate. ¶ ~ 1-2345의 택시 a taxi with the license number 1-2345 / 외교관 ~의 차 a car with a diplomatic plate. ◉ ~원 number one; an ace: ~원 골퍼 the 「top 〔No. 1〕 golfer; an ace golfer

**넘버링(머신)** 《기구》 a numbering machine.

**넘보다** look down on 《*a person*》; hold 《*a person*》 cheap 〔in contempt〕; make light of 《*a person*》; do not think much of; underestimate; belittle. ¶ 사

람을 넘보는 태도로 with a superior 〔condescending〕 air / 상대 팀을 넘보아서 그들은 시합에 졌다 Since they underestimated their opponents, they lost the game.

**넘성거리다** 《탐이 나서》 stretch 〔crane〕 *one's* neck avidly; cast greedy eyes 《on》. ¶ 남의 재산을 ~ be eager to swindle *a person* out of *his* possessions; covet *another's* property.

**넘실거리다** ① =넘성거리다. ② 《물결이》 swell; undulate; surge; roll. ¶ 파도가 ~ The waves are swelling 〔rolling〕.

**넘실넘실** ① 《넘성거림》 stretching 〔craning〕 *one's* neck avidly; rubbernecking. ② =너울너울.

**넘어가다**[1] ① 《쓰러지다》 fall (down); tumble 〔come〕 down; collapse. ⇨넘어지다, 쓰러지다. ¶ 앞으로〔뒤로〕 ~ fall forward 〔backward〕 / 넘어가려는 순간에 있다 be on the point of falling; be on the verge 〔brink〕 of collapse / 폭풍으로 정원의 나무가 넘어갔다 The trees in the garden fell down in the storm.
② 《망하다》 be ruined; go to ruin; 《붕괴하다》 fall; collapse; be overthrown; 《파산하다》 go 〔become〕 bankrupt. ¶ 노동당은 경제 정책의 실패로 넘어갔다 The Labour Party fell (from power) 〔collapsed〕 because of its mistaken economic policy. / 불경기로 많은 중소기업이 넘어갔다 Because of depression a lot of minor enterprises have 「become bankrupt 〔failed〕.
③ 《때·시한이》 pass; expire; be over; be overdue. ¶ 계약 날짜가 ~ the date of a contract 「expires 〔is over〕 / 기한이 ~ the term expires 〔runs out〕; pass a fixed term; be overdue / 집세 낼 기한이 ~ the rent is overdue.
④ 《해·달이》 sink; set; go down. ¶ 해가 넘어가기 전에 before dark 〔dusk〕 / 해가 ~ the sun sets 〔sinks〕 / 해가 서산으로 넘어갔다 The sun has sunk behind the western mountains.
⑤ (a) 《남의 손으로》 pass 〔fall〕 into *another's* hands 〔possession〕; change hands; be transferred. ¶ 토지는 그 회사로 넘어갔다 The land passed into the possession 〔hands〕 of the firm. / 그 그림은 그 이후 이 사람 저 사람 손으로 넘어갔다 The picture has changed hands many times since then. (b) 《차례·주제 등이》 pass 《into, to》; come 〔fall〕 《to》; drift. ¶ 화제가 딴 데로 ~ drift from one subject to another / 그럼 다음 장으로 넘어갑시다 Well, let's come to the next chapter.
⑥ 《속다》 be cheated 〔deceived〕 《by *a person*》; get 〔be〕 taken in 《by》; 《빠지다》 give in 〔yield, succumb〕 to 《temptation》; be led into; be blinded by 《money》. ¶ 계략에 ~ play into 《*a person's*》 hands; fall into a trap 《set by *a person*》 / 그런 수작에는 안 넘어간다 I won't be taken in by that trick. *or* That trick won't work with me. / 그녀는 그 사내에게 넘어가 결혼을 했다 She was tricked into marrying that man. / 그녀는 누구에게나 쉬이 넘어갈 사람이다 She is an easy mark.
⑦ 《음식이》 go down *one's* throat; be swallowed; be taken down. ¶ 그는 약조차 목에 걸려 넘어가지 않았다 Even medicine wouldn't go down his throat. *or* He couldn't even get his medicine down.
⑧ 《젖혀지다》 be turned over. ¶ 책장이 바람에 넘어갔다 A leaf of the book was turned over by the wind.

**넘어가다**[2] 《고개·담 등을》 cross; pass; go over 〔beyond〕. ⇨넘다 ②.

**넘어다보다** look 〔peep〕 over 〔across〕; see over 《*something*》. ¶ 담너머로 ~ look 〔peep〕 over a wall.

**넘어뜨리다** ① 《쓰러뜨리다》 knock 〔push, throw, bring, tip〕 《*a thing*》 down; blow 《*a thing*》 down (바람 등이); cut 《a tree》 down; fell (베어넘기다); 《허물다》 pull down; demolish. ¶ 집을 ~ pull down 〔demolish, wreck〕 a house / 그는 강한 펀치로 상대를 넘어뜨렸다 He knocked down his opponent with powerful punches. / 그녀는 실수로 방안의 스탠드를 넘어뜨렸다 She accidentally tipped over the room lamp. ② 《지우다》 beat; defeat; 《전복시키다》 overthrow; topple. ¶ 우리는 마침내 상대 팀을 넘어뜨렸다 We finally beat the opposing team. / 그들은 부패한 정권을 넘어뜨렸다 They overthrew the corrupt government.

**넘어서다** pass 〔get, go〕 over; cross. ¶ 산을 ~ go 「over 〔across〕 a mountain / 어려운 고비를 ~ get over the 「hump 〔hard period〕 / 60 고개를 ~ have turned sixty; be over sixty.

**넘어오다** ① 《넘어서 이쪽으로》 come over 〔across〕; 《쓰러져서》 come down; topple 〔fall〕 over (this way). ¶ 국경을 ~ come over 〔across〕 the border (line) 《to》 / 산을 ~ come over a mountain / 정원 쪽으로 넘어올 것 같은 담 a wall likely to 「topple over 〔collapse〕

toward the garden.
② 《옮겨오다》 come into; be transferred; be made 〔turned〕 over; be passed on. ¶ 내 손으로 ~ come into my hand 〔possession〕 / 상속권이 아버지한테서 아들에게로 넘어왔다 The right of inheritance is transferred from father to his son.
③ 《이월하다》 be carried over. ¶ 차감 잔액이 금년도로 ~ a balance is carried over to the present year.
④ 《토하다》 throw 〔bring, fetch〕 up 《food》; vomit; puke 《구어》. ¶ 먹은 것이 넘어올 것 같다 feel sick 〔nausea〕; feel like vomiting; feel queasy 《미》.
⑤ 《투항하다》 come over; surrender. ¶ 자유 진영으로 ~ come over to the free world 《from》.

**넘어지다** ① 《쓰러지다》 fall (down 〔over〕); tumble 〔topple〕 down; be off *one's* feet. ¶ 돌부리에 걸려 ~ fall 〔tumble, trip〕 over a stone / 앞으로 〔뒤로〕 ~ fall forward 〔backward〕 / 벌렁 ~ fall flat on the back / 쿵하고 ~ fall with a thud; fall like a log / 넘어진 사람을 일으켜 주다 help 《*a person*》 up (to *his* feet) / 그녀는 인파에 밀려 넘어졌다 She was pushed down by the crowd. ② 《도산하다》 go 〔become〕 bankrupt; go into bankruptcy; go under 〔broke〕. ¶ 작년에 이 도시만 해도 20여개 기업이 넘어졌다 Last year there were more than twenty firms that went bankrupt in this city alone.

**넘치다** ① 《물·기운 등이》 overflow; flow 〔run〕 over; brim over 《with》; flood. ¶ 생동감이 넘치는 그림 a picture instinct with life / 강물이 ~ a river overflows 〔floods〕 its banks / 감사의 마음이 ~ be overwhelmed with gratitude / 넘칠 듯이 가득하다 be full to the brim; be brimful / 기운이 ~ be full 〔brimful〕 of vigor; be in high spirits / 애교가 철철 ~ be full of charms; be all smiles / 잔에 넘칠 정도로 술을 따르다 fill a wine cup to overflowing / 기쁨에 넘쳐 울다 weep overwhelmed with joy / 그녀의 눈에는 눈물이 가득 넘쳐 있었다 Her eyes were filled with tears.
② 《지나치다》 exceed; be more than 〔above, over〕; be beyond 《*one's* power》; 《정도를》 go too far 〔to excess〕. ¶ 분에 넘치는 칭찬 excessive 〔undeserved〕 praise / 분수에 넘치게 살다 live beyond *one's* means / 집이 분에 ~ the house is too good 《for *a person*》 / 힘에 ~ be beyond *one's* power 〔ability〕 / 그에게는 분에 넘치는 영광이다 The honor is more than he deserves.

**넙데데하다** ⇨ 너부데데하다.

**넙적** ① 《입을》 ¶ 입을 ~ 벌리다 open *one's* mouth wide. ② 《몸을》 ¶ ~ 엎드리다 lay down flat 《on the ground》.

**넙치** 〖어류〗 a flatfish; a (left-eyed) flounder. ◉ ~눈이 a cross-eyed person.

**넛손자**(—孫子) a grandson of *one's* sister; a grandnephew on *one's* sister's side.

**넛할머니** *one's* father's maternal aunt; a great-aunt on *one's* father's maternal side.

**넛할아버지** *one's* father's maternal uncle; a great-uncle on *one's* father's maternal side.

**넝마** 《천》 an old piece of cloth; a rag; a shred; 《옷》 ragged 〔tattered〕 clothes; rags; tatters. ◉ ~장수 a rag dealer; a ragman. ~전 a rag store. ~주이 a ragpicker; a ragman.

**넣다** ① 《속에》 put 〔take〕 《*a thing*》 in 〔into〕; let 《*a person*》 in 〔into〕 《the room》; pack (채워넣다); pour (붓다). ¶ 공에 바람을 ~ pump 〔blow〕 air into a ball / 돈을 주머니에 ~ put money into *one's* pocket / 필름을 카메라에 ~ load (a roll of ) film into a camera / 안약을 눈에 ~ drop a lotion into the eye / 주전자에 물을 ~ pour water into a pot / 차고에 차를 ~ run a car into a garage / 커피에 우유를 ~ put milk into coffee / 타이어에 바람을 ~ pump up the tires / 호주머니에 손을 ~ put *one's* hand(s) in(to) *one's* pocket(s) / 아무를 뒷문으로 넣어주다 let *a person* into 《the house》 by the back door / 그녀는 옷을 여행 가방에 (채워) 넣었다 She packed her clothes in the suitcase. / 돈은 금고에 넣어 두어라 Keep the money in the safe. / 홍차에 밀크를 넣으십니까 Do you take milk in your tea ?
② 《끼워넣다》 set 〔fit〕 《*a thing*》 in 〔into〕; insert; stuff (채워넣다). ¶ 반지에 보석을 ~ set a jewel in a ring; set a ring with a jewel / 옷에 솜을 ~ stuff 〔wad〕 clothes with cotton wool / 책갈피에 서표를 ~ slip 〔put〕 a bookmark between the pages 〔leaves〕 / 계약서에 반드시 이 조항을 넣어주시오 We demand that this clause be inserted in the contract.
③ (a) 《수용하다》 take in 《a patient》; admit 《200 students》; 《수감하다》 commit 《a criminal to prison》; accom-

modate《300 guests》; hold《so many people》;《보내다》send《*one's* son》to《college》. ¶ 이 강당에는 5백 명을 넣을 수 있다 This hall seats〔can hold〕500 people. / 저 피아노가 이 방에 넣기에는 너무 크다 The piano is too large for this room. (***b***)《단체 등에》admit〔receive, accept〕《*a person*》in(to); grant《*a person*》to membership. ¶ 회원에 넣어주지 않다 exclude《*a person*》from membership / 그녀를 우리 클럽의 회원으로 넣었다 We received〔accepted〕her as a member of our club.
④《입금하다》deposit《money in a bank》; place《money》on deposit;《납입하다》pay《money》. ¶ 돈을 은행에 ∼ put〔deposit〕money in a bank / 내 은행 계좌에 10만원을 넣어야 한다 Hundred thousand won should be deposited in my bank account.
⑤《손에 넣다》get; obtain; come by; get〔come〕at. ¶ 진귀한 책을 손에 ∼ get a rare book / 자금을 손에 ∼ get funds《from *a person*》.
⑥《포함시키다》include; count in〔among〕. ¶ 이자를 넣어〔넣지 않고〕8만원 eighty thousand won, inclusive〔exclusive〕of interest / 그 사실을 고려에 넣는 것이 좋겠다 You had better take the fact into account. / 합격자는 나까지 넣어 10명이다 Ten applicants passed the examination, including myself among the number.
⑦《중간에》put《*a person*》between《two parties》; make《*a person*》a mediator. ¶ 중개자를 넣어 교섭하다 negotiate through an intermediary / 통역을 넣어서 바이어와 이야기하다 talk with a buyer through an interpreter.
⑧《기타》¶ 스위치를 ∼ switch〔turn〕《the light》on / 전화를 ∼ phone《*a person*》; put in a call to《*a person*》/ 도서관에 신간을 10권 ∼ supply ten new books to the library.

**네**[1] ①《너》you. ¶ 네가 잘못했다 You are to blame. / 네 이놈 You bastard〔swine〕! / 네가 관여할 바 아니다 That's no business of yours. *or* It is none of your business. ②《너의》your. ¶ 네 집이 어디냐 Where is your home? / 이건 네 장갑이냐 Are these your gloves?

**네**[2]《넷》four. ¶ 네 사람 four people / 네 식구 a family of four.

**네**[3] ①《긍정의 답》yes; certainly; all right; very well;《부정의 답》no;《출석의 답》here, (present) sir! ¶「당신은 외국인이신가요」—「네, 그렇습니다」"Are you a foreigner?"—"Yes, I am." /「너 헤엄 못 치니」—「네, 못쳐요」"Can't you swim?"—"No, I can't." /《출석부를때》「김남수」—「네」"Namsu Kim (present)?"—"Yes(, sir). *or* Here(, sir)." ②《의문》eh?; what? ¶ 네 뭐라구요 What? *or* What did you say?

**-네** ¶ 우리네 we all / 당신네 you all / 그네 they / 삼봉이네 Sambong's family.

**네거** [<negative]【사진】a (photographic) negative. ◉ ∼필름 negative film.

**네거리** a crossroads; a crossing; an intersection. ¶ 종로 ∼ Jongno square〔crossing〕/ ∼에 가게를 내다 set up a store at the crossroads / ∼에서 왼쪽으로 돌다 take〔turn〕the crossroads to the left.

**네거티브** (a) negative.

**네것** your thing; yours. ¶ ∼이 내것보다 좋다 Yours is better than mine.

**네글리제** a negligee; *négligé* (F.).

**네까짓** ¶ ∼것 the likes of you; a person like you / ∼놈 such a fellow as you / ∼것한테 지겠느냐 I shall never be beaten by a fellow like you. / ∼놈한테는 속아넘어가지 않는다 I will not be cheated by the likes of you.

**네눈(박)이** a dog with a white spot above each eye.

**네다리** four legs. ¶ ∼를 뻗고 자다 sleep with *one's* limbs outstretched; sleep with ease.

**네다섯** four or five. ¶ ∼개 four or five pieces.

**네댓** about four or five. ¶ ∼새〔사람〕about four or five days〔persons〕.

**네덜란드** (the Kingdom of) the Netherlands; Holland. ¶ ∼의 Dutch. ◉ ∼말 Dutch. ∼사람 a Dutchman; the Dutch [총칭].

**네모**《사각형》a quadrilateral; a four-sided figure;《정사각형》a square. ¶ ∼진〔난〕square; quadrilateral; four-square; four-sided / ∼난 탁자 a square table / ∼나다, ∼지다 be square; be tetragonal; be quadrilateral / ∼로 자르다 cut《a sheet of paper》square. ◉ ∼꼴 a square; a tetragon; a quadrangle; a quadrilateral.

**네미**《송아지 부를 때》Here calf!;《욕》Son of a bitch!;《너의 어미》your mother.

**네바다**《미국의 주》Nevada (생략 Nev.);《속칭》the Silver State. ¶ ∼(사람)의 Nevadan. ◉ ∼사람 a Nevadan.

**네발** four feet. ¶ ∼ 달린 four-footed; quadruped / ∼ 타다 be allergic to (four-legged) meat / ∼로 기다 crawl〔go〕on all fours. ◉ ∼짐승 a four=

footed〔-legged〕 animal; a quadruped.

**네브래스카** 《미국의 주》 Nebraska (생략 Neb., Nebr.). ◉ ~사람 a Nebraskan.

**네쌍둥이**(―雙―) quadruplets.

**네안데르탈** Neanderthal. ◉ ~인 〖고고학〗 the Neanderthal man.

**네오-** 《신, …근대의》 neo-. ◉ 네오나치즘 neo-Nazism. 네오로맨티시즘 neo-romanticism. 네오리얼리즘 neorealism. 네오마이신 neomycin. 네오클래시시즘 neoclassicism.

**네오디뮴** 〖화학〗 neodymium (기호 Nd).

**네온** 〖화학〗 neon (기호 Ne). ¶ ~빛이 밝은 거리 a neon-lit street. ◉ ~등 a neon lamp〔light〕. ~사인 a neon sign.

**네이블** 〖식물〗 a navel (orange).

**네이비블루** dark blue; navy blue.

**네이팜** 〖화학〗 napalm. ◉ ~(폭)탄 a napalm bomb.

**네임** a name. ¶ ~밸류가 있는 가수 a well-known singer; a singer with an established reputation. ◉ ~플레이트 a nameplate.

**네커치프** a neckerchief.

**네크라인** a neckline. ¶ 깊이 팬 ~ a low-cut neckline.

**네크리스** a necklace.

**네트** 《그물》 a net; 《공이 네트에 닿음》 a net. ¶ (테니스) ~를 치다 put up a (tennis) net / 공을 ~에 맞히다 net the ball / ~ 플레이를 하다 play close to the net / ~터치를 하다 touch the net. ◉ ~볼 a net ball; a let.

**네트워크** a 《TV, radio》 network. ¶ 전국 TV ~로 on a national television network.

**네티즌** 〖컴퓨터〗 a netizen; a user of the internet(인터넷 사용자). [< *net*work+cit*izen*]

**네팔** Nepal. ¶ ~의 Nepalese; Nepali. ◉ ~사람 a Nepalese; a Nepali.

**네활개** four limbs (stretched out). ¶ ~치다 strut; swagger; [비유적] act with nothing to fear; behave triumphantly / ~치며 swaggeringly / ~치며 다니다 strut〔swagger〕 about a street / ~를 뻗다 stretch *one's* arms and legs / ~를 뻗고 자다 sleep at full length; sleep spread-eagled.

**넥타이** a tie; a necktie. ¶ 나비 ~ a bow (tie) / ~를 하다〔매다〕 put on a necktie; tie〔wear〕 a necktie / ~를 풀다 untie a necktie / ~가 비뚤어졌어요 Your tie is crooked. ◉ ~핀 a tiepin; a tie clip〔clasp〕; a stickpin 《미》.

**넨장(맞을)** [감탄사] Damn!; Damn it!; Damn him! (주저할 때); Damn you!; Hang it!; [형용사적] damned; damnable; wretched; cursed; accursed; deuced. ¶ 넨장맞을 녀석 a cursed〔damnable, damned〕 fellow / 넨장맞을 놈 같으니 Damn you! *or* God damn you! / 넨장, 덥기도 하다 How damned hot it is!

**넵투늄** 〖화학〗 neptunium (기호 Np).

**넵튠** 〖로神〗 Neptune.

**넷** four. ¶ 넷으로 가르다 quarter; cut 《*a thing*》 into four equal parts; divide 《*a thing*》 into quarters.

**넷째** the fourth; No. 4; the fourth place. ¶ ~의 fourth / ~로 fourthly.

**녀석** ① [경멸적] a fellow; a guy; a chap. ¶ 나쁜 ~ a bad guy / 경칠 ~ a cursed fellow / 별난 ~ a queer guy / 불쌍한 ~ a poor wretch / 운좋은 ~ a lucky guy / 저 ~은 질색이다 I hate that fellow. / 참 바보 ~이로군 What a stupid guy! ② 《귀엽게》 a little rascal; a nice chap; a good boy. ¶ 귀여운 ~ a sweet little rascal of a boy / 요~ You young rascal!

**년** ① [경멸적] a woman; a girl; a wench. ¶ 망할 년 a damned wench / 미친 년 a crazy woman〔bitch〕/ 이년 You wretched woman! ② 《귀엽게》 a little wench; a little girl. ¶ 귀여운 년 a sweet little wench of a girl.

**년**(年) a year. ¶ 3년 3개월, 3 years and 3 months / 1984년에 in (the year) 1984 / 2년에 한 번 once in two years; biennial / 1년은 열두 달이다 There are twelve months in a year.

**-년제**(年祭) an anniversary. ¶ 10~ the tenth anniversary / 100~ the centenary; 《주로 미》 the centennial / 1000~ the millenary; the millennial / 미국 건국 200~ the Bicentennial of the founding of the U.S. / 우리 학교는 내년에 백~를 거행한다 Our school will celebrate its centennial anniversary next year.

**녘** ① 《방향》 《in》 the direction of; toward(s); 《장소·지역》 《in》 the area of…. ¶ 북녘 the north; the northern district〔region, part〕; up north / 아랫녘 a place in the lower part 《of》; a place down from here / 윗녘 a place in the upper part 《of》; a place up from here. ② 《무렵》 toward 《미》; towards 《영》; about 《영》; around 《미》. ¶ 새벽녘에 around〔at〕dawn; toward dawn / 해질 녘에 toward evening; at nightfall〔sunset〕.

**노**[1] 《노끈》 a string; a paper string (지노). ¶ 삼노 a hemp cord / ~를 꼬다

twist a string.

**노**[2] always. ⇨ 노상.

**노**(櫓) an oar; a paddle; a scull. ¶ 한〔두〕쌍의 노 「a pair 〔four〕 of oars / 노를 젓다 pull an oar; row 《a boat》; paddle 《a canoe》 / 노를 저어 나아가다 oar *one's* way.

**노**(爐) 《화덕》 a hearth; a fireplace; 《용광로》 a furnace; a kiln.

**노-**(老) old; aged. ¶ 노신사 an old gentleman / 노대국 a great country that has grown old.

**노가다** 《막노무자》 a construction laborer; a navvy 《영》. ¶ ~패 a construction crew.

**노가리**[1] broadcast sowing. ~하다 sow 「seed broadcast.

**노가리**[2] 〚어류〛 a little 〔young〕 pollack.

**노각**(老—) a yellowish overripe cucumber.

**노간주** 〚식물〛 a juniper. ◉ ~나무 a ju- 「niper tree.

**노게임** 〚야구〛 ¶ 비 때문에 시합은 ~이 되었다 The game was rained out.

**노경**(老境) old 〔advanced〕 age; *one's* declining years. ¶ ~에 들다 be in *one's* 「old age 〔declining years〕; be advanced in life 〔age〕.

**노고**(勞苦) 《고생》 labor; 《고통》 pains; toil; trouble. ¶ ~의 성과 the result of *one's* labor / ~를 아끼지 않다 spare no pains / ~를 치하하다 reward 〔praise〕 《*a person*》 for *his* labor; thank 《*a person*》 for *his* trouble / ~에 보답하다 remunerate 《*a person*》 for *his* labor.

**노고지리** 〚조류〛 a skylark.

**노곤하다**(勞困—) (be) languid; heavy; weary. ⇨ 나른하다.

**노골적**(露骨的) ① 《숨기지 않은》 naked; undisguised; 《거리낌없는》 broad; outspoken; 《솔직한》 frank; open; plain; 《단도직입적인》 blunt; direct. ¶ ~인 사람 an outspoken person / ~으로 plainly; openly; frankly; outspokenly; candidly; straightforwardly; downright; flatly / ~으로 말하면 to be plain 〔frank〕 with you; frankly speaking; in plain words 〔terms〕 / ~으로 말하다 speak plainly; call a spade a spade / 그는 ~으로 불쾌한 표정을 지었다 He showed his disgust plainly 〔openly〕. / 그는 ~으로 말하는 성질이다 He is an outspoken man. *or* He is not a man to mince his words. / ~으로 말해서 그는 도둑놈이다 The bald truth is that he is a thief. / 그 나라는 강대국의 ~인 내정 간섭에 항의했다 The country protested against the undisguised interference of the superpower in its domestic policies. ② 《음란한》 broad 《joke》; lewd; indecent; 《도발적》 suggestive. ¶ ~인 말 a broad story / ~인 책〔그림〕 indecent books 〔pictures〕 / 저 그림은 너무 ~이다 That picture is too suggestive. / 그의 농담은 점잖은 사람들에게는 지나치게 ~이다 His jokes are too lewd 〔broad〕 for refined people.

**노구**(老軀) old bones; old and weak limbs; an advanced age. ¶ ~를 이끌고〔돌보지 않고〕 조난 구조에 임하다 go to offer help in the accident in spite of *one's* advanced 〔old〕 age.

**노구솥** a brass 〔copper〕 kettle.

**노그라지다** ① 《지치다》 be exhausted 〔worn out〕; be dog-tired; be dead tired. ¶ 노그라져 잠들다 fall asleep dog-tired. ② 《마음이 쏠리다》 be infatuated with 《a woman》; be crazy about; be 〔get〕 stuck on 〔after〕 《미구어》. ¶ 그는 그녀한테 아주 노그라졌다 He is crazy about that girl.

**노그름하다** (be) rather soft; tender.

**노글노글하다** (be) soft; tender; pliant. ¶ 노글노글한 가죽 soft leather / 노글노글한 성격 a pliant nature / 갖풀을 노글노글하게 끓이다 boil the glue soft.

**노긋노긋하다** 《물체가》 (be) quite 〔all〕 supple; elastic; soft and flexible; 《성질이》 (be) mild; gentle; obedient. ¶ 노긋노긋한 가죽 끈 soft leather strings / 말 잘 듣는 노긋노긋한 아이 an obedient child.

**노긋하다** 《물체가》 (be) supple; elastic and soft; 《성질이》 (be) mild; gentle.

**노기**(老妓) an old *kisaeng*.

**노기**(怒氣) anger; indignation; an angry mood. ¶ ~를 띠고 in anger; angrily; 《말에》 in an angry tone; in a huff / ~ 등등하다 be in a black rage; be furious / ~ 충천하다 boil with rage / 얼굴에 ~를 띠고 있다 look black 〔red〕 with anger; take on an angry look.

**노깃**(櫓—) a paddle 〔an oar〕 blade; the blade of an oar 〔a paddle〕.

**노끈** a string; a small cord. ¶ 삼으로 ~을 꼬다 twist hemp into a cord / ~으로 묶다 tie 《a parcel》 with a string / 그녀는 그 꾸러미를 ~으로 묶었다 She bound the package with a piece of string.

**노나무** 〚식물〛 a catalpa tree; an Indian 「bean.

**노년**(老年) old 〔advanced〕 age; declining years. ¶ ~에 이르러 in *one's* 「old age 〔later years〕. ◉ ~기 old age; senescence: ~기에 접어들다 arrive at senescence; become senescent.

**노농**(勞農) 《노동자와 농민》 laborers and farmers. ◉ ～적위대 《북한의》 the Workers and Farmers Red Guards. ～제휴 collaboration of peasants and laborers.

**노느다** 《분배하다》 distribute 〔divide (up)〕 《among》; share; portion (out). ¶ 이익을 두 사람이 ～ divide the gain between the two / 이익을 반반씩 ～ split the profit half-and-half 〔fifty=fifty〕 / 음식을 노나 먹다 share food with others / 재산을 세 자식에게 균등하게 ～ divide *one's* property equally among *one's* three children.

**노느매기** sharing; distribution; allotment.

**노는계집** a prostitute; a harlot.

**노닐다** stroll; ramble; wander; loiter; linger; saunter about 〔along, around〕. ¶ 호수 위에서 노니는 백조들 swans swimming leisurely on the lake.

**노다지** ① 《광맥》 a bonanza; a rich vein. ¶ ～를 발견하다 strike a bonanza. ② 《횡재》 a bonanza; a fortune. ¶ ～를 만나다 strike a bonanza; hit the jackpot. ③ 《노상》 always; any time; all the time. ¶ ～ 웃고 있다 be always smiling. ◉ ～판 a mine where gold is found in nuggets; a bonanza.

**노닥거리다** keep talking 〔chatting, joking〕 playfully; be bantering away.

**노닥다리**(老—) an old person; an oldster 《미》.

**노닥이다** talk 〔chat, joke〕 playfully; wag *one's* tongue humorously; banter.

**노대**(露臺) 《건물의》 a balcony; 《공연장의》 an open-air platform 〔stage〕.

**노대가**(老大家) an old master; a veteran 〔venerable〕 authority 《on》. ¶ 서예의 ～ an old master of calligraphy / 국문학의 ～ a veteran authority on Korean literature / 문단의 ～들 leading figures in literary circles.

**노대국**(老大國) a great country that has grown old; a once powerful nation now in its decline.

**노도**(怒濤) raging billows; angry 〔furious, turbulent, roaring〕 waves. ¶ ～처럼 밀려오는 군중 surging crowds / ～를 헤치고 나아가다 advance in the face of high seas / 적이 ～처럼 밀려 왔다 The enemy surged upon us.

**노독**(路毒) the fatigue 〔strain〕 of traveling. ¶ ～을 풀다 take a good rest after a tiring journey.

**노동**(勞動) labo(u)r; work; toil. ⇨ 근로. ～하다 labor; work; toil. ¶ 하루 8시간 ～ 《work》 an eight-hour day / 주 5일〔40시간〕 ～ a 5-day 〔40-hour〕 (working) week / ～으로 생활하다〔돈을 벌다〕 live 〔earn money〕 by 「labor 〔the sweat of *one's* brow〕. ◉ ～가치설 the labor value theory. ～경제(학) labor economy 〔economics〕: ～ 경제학자 a labor economist. ～계약 a work 〔labor〕 contract. ～권 the right to labor 〔work〕. ～귀족 a labor aristocrat; an aristocracy of labor. ～규약 a union constitution 《미》; constitution of a trade union 《영》. ～능률 labor efficiency. ～당 the Labour Party (영국의): ～ 당원 a Labourite. ～력 labor power 〔force〕; manpower: ～력 부족 a shortage of labor; a labor shortage 〔famine〕 / 값싸고 풍부한 ～력 cheap and plentiful labor. ～문제 a labor problem 〔question〕. ～법(규) labor laws; industrial laws 《영》. ～부 the Ministry of Labor; the Labor Ministry: ～부 장관 the Minister of Labor. ～삼권 labor's three primary 〔major〕 rights. ～생산성 labor productivity. ～수요 demand for labor. ～시간 working hours; hours of labor; the workday: ～ 시간을 단축〔연장〕하다 shorten 〔lengthen〕 working hours. ～시장 the labor market: ～시장정보 labor market information. ～운동 a labor movement: ～운동가 a labor agitator / ～ 운동 지도자 a labor leader. ～원가 labor cost. ～위원회 a labor relations board 〔commission〕. ～이동률〔회전율〕 labor turnover (rate). ～인구 labor force; the working population. ～임금 wages; pay: ～임금을 인상〔인하〕하다 raise 〔reduce〕 wages. ～재해 a labor accident: ～재해법 a workmen's compensation law. ～쟁의〔분쟁〕 a labor dispute 〔strife〕; 《파업》 a strike; a walkout: 긴급 ～쟁의 조정권 an emergency mediation power against labor disputes. ～절 Labor Day; May Day 《미》 (★ 유럽에서는 5월 1일, 미국과 캐나다에서는 9월의 첫째 월요일). ～정책 (a) labor policy. ～조건 working 〔labor〕 conditions. ～조정법 the Labor Mediation Law: ～ 관계 조정법 the Labor Relations Adjustment Act. ～집약 산업 labor-intensive industries. ～집약성 labor intensity. ～행정 labor administration. ～협약 a labor agreement. ～환경 labor environment. ～회관 the Labor Hall. 무～ 무임금 규칙 a 'no=work-no-pay' rule 〔policy〕: 그 회사는 파업 중인 종업원들에게 무～ 무임금 규칙

을 적용하겠다고 말했다 The company said that it will enforce a 'no-work= no-pay' policy for the employees participating in a strike. 시간외~ overtime work. 2교대제 ~ two-shift system; work in two shifts.

**노동자**(勞動者) a worker; a laborer; a workman; a workingman; a wage earner; working people; labor [총칭].

> (용법) **worker** 「근로자」를 뜻하는 가장 일반적인 말로, 육체·두뇌를 불문하고 일하여 생계를 유지하는 사람. **laborer** 숙련보다는 체력을 이용하는 육체 노동자. **workman** 일정한 숙련과 체력을 요하는 작업에 종사하는 사람. **workingman** 목공·석공·배관 작업 등에서 시간급·일급·주급으로 일하는 육체 노동자.

¶ ~측과 사용자측 labor and management 《미》/ ~ 처우를 개선하다 better 〔ameliorate〕 labor conditions / ~를 착취하다 sweat 〔exploit〕 laborers / 그들은 ~의 권리를 지키기 위해 파업했다 They went on a strike in order to protect the rights of the workers. ◉ ~계급 the laboring 〔working〕 class(-es). ~보호 protection of laborers. ~수용소 a labor camp. ~재해 보상 compensation for workmen's accident. ~합숙소 a labor boarding house. 계절〔일용〕~ a seasonal 〔day〕 laborer. 숙련~ a skilled laborer: 미숙련 ~ an unskilled laborer. 육체〔근육〕~ a manual 〔mascular〕 worker. 정신〔두뇌〕~ a mental 〔brain〕 worker. 자유~ a casual laborer.

**노동조합**(勞動組合) a labor union 《미》; a trade(s) union 《영》. ¶ ~의 운영 management 〔operation〕 of a trade 〔labor〕 union / ~을 조직하다 organize a union; unionize 《employees》. ◉ ~간부 a union leader. ~법 the Trade 〔Labor〕 Union Act. ~원 a union man; a member of a labor union; a unionist. ~주의 unionism. ~협의회 a council of trade 〔labor〕 unions. 전국민주~총연맹 the Korea Confederation of Trade Union (한국의). 한국 ~총연맹 the Federation of Korea Trade Union (생략 F.K.T.U.).

**노두**(露頭) 〖광산〗 the beginning of an ore vein in a mine; an outcrop; a basset.

**노둔**(魯鈍) stupidity; dullness; thickheadedness. ~하다 (be) stupid; dull; thickheaded.

**노드리듯하다** 《비가》 rain heavily 〔in torrents〕.

**노랑** yellow; 《물감》 yellow dyes. ◉ ~감투 《우스개》 a mourner's cap. ~나비 〖곤충〗 a sulfur butterfly. ~머리 a yellow head; yellow hair. ~참외 a yellow melon. ~퉁이 a person with an unusually yellow complexion.

**노랑이** ① 《노란 것》 a yellow thing 〔stuff〕; a yellow one. ② 《개》 a yellow dog. ③ 《구두쇠》 a miser; a cheapskate 《구어》; a stingy 〔close-fisted〕 person; a tightwad 《구어》. ¶ ~다 be stingy with *one's* money / 그는 지독한 ~라서 한푼도 기부하지 않을 게다 Because he is terribly stingy, he won't contribute any money.

**노랗다** ① 《색이》 (be) quite yellow; be a golden yellow. ¶ 노란 저고리〔셔츠〕 a yellow coat 〔shirt〕 / 얼굴이 ~ *one's* complexion is yellow; look poor. ② 《가능성 등이》 ¶ 그녀는 싹수가 ~ There is a very slim chance before her. *or* She shows no promise of success.

**노래** 《가요》 a song; a chant (성가); a ballad (민요); 《시가》 a poem; 《노래부르기》 singing. ~하다 sing 《a song》; hum 《a tune》; chant 《a hymn》; recite 《a poem》. ¶ 가을을 ~한 시 a poem sung about autumn / ~를 좋아하다 love songs 〔poetry〕 / ~하며 일하다 sing at *one's* work / ~를 불러 아기를 잠재우다 sing a baby to sleep / 피아노에 맞춰 ~하다 sing to a piano (accompaniment) / 그녀는 ~를 잘한다 She is a good singer. *or* She sings well. / 어떤 종류의 ~를 좋아하십니까 What kind of songs do you like? / 이 ~가 지금 한창 유행이다 This song is very popular now. ◉ ~자랑 an amateurs' singing contest. 노랫가락 《무당의》 a kind of song formerly sung by shamans; 《속요》 a popular 〔folk〕 song; a ballad. 노랫소리 singing; a singing voice: 새벽을 알리는 새의 노랫소리 the song of birds that ushers in the dawn.

**노래기** 〖동물〗 a milliped(e); a wireworm; a myriapod.

**노래방** a *Noraebang,* the Korean commercial singing establishment (where *one* can sing a song to musical accompaniment, while reading the lyrics on a video monitor).

**노래지다** turn 〔become〕 yellow; yellow.

**노략질**(擄掠—) plunder; pillage; looting; despoilment. ~하다 plunder; pillage; despoil; loot; seize as booty. ¶ 정복한

도시를 ~하다 loot a conquered city / 해적들이 연안 도시들을 ~했다 Pirates pillaged the towns along the coast.

**노려보다** glare [scowl] 《at》; stare hard 《at》; look sharply [daggers, angrily] 《at》. ¶ 서로 ~ glare at each other; 《반목하다》 be at odds with each other; be at daggers drawn / 당혹스럽게 ~ stare 《*a person*》 down [out of countenance] / 그는 화가 나서 나를 한참 노려봤다 He stared at me in anger for a while. / 그가 무서운 눈으로 노려보아서 나는 움츠러들었다 He glared at me so fiercely (that) I was scared.

**노력**(努力) (an) effort; (an) endeavor; (an) exertion; a struggle. ~하다 endeavor; do *one's* best; make efforts [an effort]; exert *oneself;* strive for.

> **용법** **effort** 특정 목적을 달성하기 위한 노력. 가장 일반적인 말: 그녀는 그 수수께끼를 풀려고 노력했지만[애썼지만] 실패했다 Her efforts at clearing up the mystery failed. **endeavor** effort 보다 격식차린 말. 어렵지만 가치있는 목적을 위해 어떤 기간 동안 계속되는 노력: 평화적 해결을 위해 노력[진력]하겠다 We will make every endeavor for its peaceful settlement. **exertion** effort보다 더 강력한 노력. 특히 정력적인 육체적 노력을 뜻함: 그는 아무 노력[수고]도 하지 않고 그것을 손에 넣었다 He got it without any exertion. **struggle** 적극적으로 경주되는 필사의 노력: 그는 모든 장애를 극복하려고 남다른 노력을 했다 He had a hard struggle to overcome all obstacles.

¶ 부단한[필사적인] ~《make》 constant [desperate] efforts / 헛된 ~ fruitless [futile, vain, wasted] effort / ~의 결과[보람] the result [fruit] of *one's* efforts / 피눈물 나는 ~ blood-and-tears endeavor / ~한 덕택으로 thanks to *one's* efforts / 좀 더 ~하면 with a little more effort / 꾸준히 ~하다 persevere in *one's* efforts / …에 ~을 집중하다 concentrate *one's* effort on... / …을 얻고자 ~하다 strive [labor] for... / ~을 아끼지 않다 spare no effort [pains] 《to *do*》 / ~한 보람이 있었다 My efforts were rewarded. / 그의 승리는 부단한 ~의 결과였다 His victory was the result of his constant 「efforts [exertions, endeavors]. / ~한 보람도 없이 실패했다 In spite of my 「efforts [hard work], I failed. / 그는 목표 달성을 위해 ~했다 He strained to reach his goal. / 그녀의 모든 ~이 수포로 끝났다 All her efforts ended in vain. / 우리는 그를 돕기 위해 온갖 ~을 다 했다 We made every (possible) effort to help him. / 그 계획에 많은 ~이 기울여졌다 A great deal of effort 「went [was put] into the project. / 그는 사업을 성공시키기 위해 ~하고 있다 He is trying hard to make his business a success. / ~없이는 아무것도 얻을 수 없다 Nothing can be got without efforts.
◉ ~가 a hard worker; a hard-working [an industrious] person; a man of industry.

**노력**(勞力) 《노동력》 labor; 《수고》 labor; trouble; pains; effort. ¶ ~의 부족 a shortage of labor / ~을 제공하다 offer *one's* labor / ~을 아끼다 be sparing of *oneself;* be stingy of labor / ~을 덜다 save labor [*one's* trouble] / 이 일은 들인 ~에 비해 결과가 신통치 않다 This work is not rewarded enough, considering the labor involved.

**노련**(老鍊) ~하다 (be) experienced; veteran; expert; skilled. ¶ ~한 솜씨 masterly skill [dexterity] / ~한 의사 an experienced [a veteran] doctor / ~한 선수 a veteran player / ~한 목수 a skilled carpenter / ~한 선원 an old sailor / 그는 등산에 ~하다 He is an old hand at mountaineering.
◉ ~가 an expert; a veteran; an old hand; a man of experience; a master hand.

**노령**(老齡) old age; advanced years. ¶ ~에 이르다 attain an advanced age; reach a great age; grow old / 어느새 ~에 이르렀다 I am getting old now without knowing it. ◉ ~연금 an old-age pension: ~연금 수령자 an old-age pensioner. ~화 사회 an aging society.

**노루** 『동물』 a roe deer; 《수노루》 a roebuck. ◉ ~잠 a short and wakeful sleep; unsound slumber; a cat nap.

**노루발** 《쟁기의》 the two triangular pieces under the metal handle of a plow-blade. ◉ ~장도리 a claw hammer.

**노르께하다** be tinged [stained] with 「yellow.

**노르딕종목**(一種目) 『스키』 a Nordic event.

**노르마** [< *norma* (Russ.)] a norm; a work [production] quota. ¶ ~를 정하다 set a quota 《for *a person*》 / ~를 완수하다 fulfill *one's* (working) norm [quota]; finish the work assigned to *one.* ◉ 생산~ a production norm.

**노르만** ¶ ~인 a Norman; the Normans [총칭] / ~인의 정복 〖역사〗 the Norman Conquest.

**노르무레하다** be a little yellowish.

**노르스름하다** (be) yellowish; be somewhat yellow.

**노르웨이** (the Kingdom of) Norway. ¶ ~의 Norwegian. ◉ ~말 Norwegian; 《고대의》 Old Norse. ~사람 a Norwegian.

**노른자(위)** the yolk 〔yellow〕 (of an egg); 《알짜배기》 the pith; the cream; the best. ¶ ~가 두 개 있는 달걀 a double=yolked egg.

**노름** gambling; gaming; gambling game. ⇨ 도박. ~(질)하다 gamble; bet; wager; play for stakes 〔money〕. ¶ ~을 크게 하다 play for heavy 〔high〕 stakes; gamble heavily / ~으로 패가망신하다 gamble *oneself* out of house and home / ~에서 돈을 잃다[따다] lose 〔gain〕 *one's* money in gambling / 그는 ~으로 전재산을 탕진했다 He gambled all his fortune away. ◉ ~꾼 a gambler. ~돈 a bet; 《판돈》 wager; stakes. ~방 a gambling room. ~빚 a gambling debt. ~패 a gang of gamblers.

**노름판** a gambling place 〔house〕; a gambler's den; 《도박장》 a casino. ¶ ~을 벌이다 open a gambling house 〔den〕; start gambling; gamble / 경찰이 ~을 덮쳤다 The police made a raid on the gambling place.

**노릇** 《일》 a job; work; 《기능》 function; 《직분》 duty; an office; 《역할》 a part; a role; 《직업》 an occupation. ¶ 선생~ a teaching job; teaching / 중매쟁이 ~을 하다 act as go-between.

**노릇노릇** yellowish; yellow here and there; spotted with yellow. ~하다 (be) yellowish; be spotted 〔dappled〕 yellow. ¶ 벼가 ~ 익어간다 Rice is ripening yellow.

**노리개** ① 《패물》 a pendent trinket worn by ladies. ② 《장난감》 a plaything; a toy; 《농락물》 a sport; a trifle ¶ 여자를 사내 ~로 생각하다 regard women as the plaything of men / (여자가) 사내의 ~가 되다 be made a man's plaything; be trifled with by a man; fall a prey to a man's lust. ◉ ~젖꼭지 a pacifier 《미》; a dummy 《영》; a comforter 《영》; a teething ring. ~첩 a young and beautiful concubine.

**노리다**[1] ① 《냄새가》 stink; (be) rank; foul-smelling; fetid; offensive; smell like burning hair (털 따위); smell like a skunk (동물 냄새). ② 《다랍다》 (be) stingy; miserly; niggardly.

**노리다**[2] ① 《노려보다》 glare 〔scowl〕 《at》; stare fiercely 《at》. ¶ 무서운 눈으로 ~ look with glaring eyes; glare fiercely 《at》; look daggers 《at》. ② 《목표·기회 등을》 aim 《at》; have 〔fix, keep〕 an eye 《on》; watch for 《a chance》; be after. ¶ …을 노리고 with the aim of…; with the eye on… / 목숨을 ~ seek 《*a person's*》 life; seek to kill 《*a person*》 / 방심한 순간을 ~ watch for a moment when 《*a person*》 is off *his* guard / 상대방 머리에 일격을 가하려고 ~ aim a blow at the opponent's head / 재산을 ~ have an eye upon 《*a person's*》 property / 효과를 ~ calculate upon 〔be out for〕 an effect / 그는 사장자리를 노리고 있다 He is going after the presidency. / 그는 도망칠 기회를 노리고 있다 He is watching for a chance to escape. / 그는 그녀의 유산을 노리고 결혼했다 He married her for her fortune.

**노리쇠** 《총의》 a breechblock.

**노리착지근하다, 노리치근하다** ⇨ 노릿하다.

**노린내** the smell of burning fat 〔hair〕 (털 따위); the smell of a skunk (동물의); a stench; a fetid 〔stinking〕 smell. ¶ 어디서 털이 타는 ~가 났다 There was a smell of burning hair somewhere.

**노릿하다** be somewhat fetid 〔stinking〕.

**노망**(老妄) senility; dotage; second childhood; 《질환으로서》 senile dementia 〔psychosis〕. ~하다 be in *one's* dotage 〔second childhood〕; fall into *one's* dotage; become 〔get〕 senile. ⇨ 망령(妄靈). ¶ ~든 노인 a dotard; an old man in his dotage / ~부리다 dote; behave childishly 〔foolishly〕; behave like a dotard / 할아버지는 ~드셨다 My grandfather has become senile. / 내가 요즘 건망증이 아주 심한데, 혹시 ~이 드는 것 아닐까 I'm so forgetful lately, perhaps I'm getting a little senile.

**노면**(路面) the road surface. ¶ ~을 재포장하다 resurface the road / ~결빙주의 《게시》 Beware of Icy Roads. ◉ ~교통 surface traffic. ~전차 a streetcar 《미》; a tramcar 《영》. ~포장 road-surfacing; paving the road.

**노모**(老母) *one's* old 〔aged〕 mother.

**노무**(勞務) labor; work; service. ¶ ~를 제공하다 offer 〔render〕 *one's* service. ◉ ~과 the labor section. ~관리 labor 〔personnel〕 management. ~기본계약

a master labor contract. ~동원 mobilization of labor. ~비 labor expenses 〔cost〕. ~자 a workman; a laborer; a worker: ~자 모집 labor recruitment.

**노박이로** 《줄곧》 always; steadily; in succession; without a break; 《붙박이로》 steadfastly; fixedly.

**노박히다** shut *oneself* up; be fastened 〔stuck〕 《to, with》; be steady 〔firm, stuck〕.

**노반**(路盤) a roadbed.

**노발대발**(怒發大發) a big blowup; wild rage. ~하다 be furious 〔enraged〕; be in a towering rage.

**노방**(路傍) the roadside; the wayside. ◉ ~초 grass at 〔by〕 the roadside.

**노벨** 《스웨덴의 화학자》 Alfred Bernhard Nobel(1833-96). ◉ ~상 a Nobel prize 《for medicine》: ~상 수상자 a Nobel prize winner; a Nobelist. ~평화〔문학〕상 a Nobel prize for peace 〔literature〕.

**노변**(路邊) the roadside; the wayside.

**노변**(爐邊) the fireside. ¶ ~에서 by the hearth 〔fireside〕. ◉ ~잡담 a fireside chat.

**노병**(老兵) an old soldier; a war veteran. ¶ ~은 죽지 않고 사라질 뿐이다 Old soldiers never die; they just fade away.

**노복**(奴僕) a male servant.

**노부**(老父) *one's* old 〔aged〕 father.

**노부모**(老父母) *one's* aged 〔old〕 parents.

**노비**(奴婢) 《남종과 여종》 male and female servants 〔slaves〕.

**노비**(路費) traveling expenses. = 노자(路資).

**노사**(勞使) capital and labor; labor and management. ¶ ~의 주장에는 아직 큰 차이가 있다 There is still a great difference between the claims of the labor and management sides. / ~양측은 어젯밤 임금 인상에 대하여 합의에 이르렀다 An agreement was reached by labor and management over the pay increase last night.
◉ ~간담회 a round-table conference between labor and management. ~관계 the relations between labor and capital; labor-management relations: ~관계법 the Labor-Management Relations Act 《미》 / 건전한 ~관계 a sound labor-management relation. ~교섭 negotiations between labor and management. ~분규〔분쟁〕 a labor-management dispute; a conflict between labor and capital; an industrial strife: ~분규 조정 위원회 a labor dispute mediations committee. ~불이(不二) the amicable labor-management relations. ~정(政) labor, management and government: ~정 위원회 the Korean Tripartite Committee, the official dialogue channel between labor, government and business. ~협의(제) a joint labor-management conference (system). ~협조 cooperation of capital and labor; labor=management cooperation.

**노산**(老産) delivery in *one's* old age. ~하다 deliver a child in *one's* old age.

**노상** always; all the time; usually (일상); habitually (습관적으로). ¶ ~ 앉는 자리 *one's* usual seat / ~하는 식으로 in *one's* usual way / ~ 책만 읽다 always read books / 토요일 밤에 우리는 ~ 외출한다 We usually go out on Saturday nights. / 저 녀석은 ~ 불평만 늘어놓는다 That fellow is grumbling all the time.

**노상**(路上) ¶ ~에서 on 〔in〕 the road 〔street〕 (★ on은 《미》, in은 《영》) / ~에서 노는 것은 위험하다 It's dangerous to play on the road.
◉ ~강도 《짓》 highway robbery; (a) holdup; 《사람》 a footpad; a highwayman; a holdup (man) 《구어》: ~강도를 만나다 fall in with footpads / ~강도짓을 하다 rob wayfarers; hold up 《미》. ~사고 an accident on the road; a road accident. ~시험 《자동차의》 a road test. ~주차 street parking: ~주차하다 park *one's* car on the street.

**노새** 〖동물〗 a mule.

**노색**(怒色) flush of anger; an angry face 〔look〕.

**노선**(路線) 《교통기관의》 a route; a line; 《기본 방침》 a line. ¶ 버스〔항공〕 ~ a bus 〔an air〕 route 〔line〕 / 버스〔철도〕의 적자 ~ a deficit-ridden bus 〔railroad〕 route 〔line〕 / 버스 ~의 재조정 readjustment of bus routes / 정치 ~ *one's* political line; a party line (정당의) / … ~을 따라 in line 〔alignment〕 with 《U.S. foreign policy》 / 강경 ~을 취하다 take a hard 〔tough〕 line / 수정주의 ~을 따르다 follow the revisionist line / 당의 ~을 따르다〔변경하다〕 follow 〔change〕 the party line / 독자적인 ~을 밟다 take *one's* own line. ◉ ~버스 a route bus; a bus on a regular route.

**노성**(怒聲) an angry 〔excited〕 voice. ¶ ~을 지르다 give 〔yell, shout〕 an angry voice.

**노소**(老少) the old and the young; age and youth. ¶ 남녀~ people of all ages and both sexes / ~를 막론하고 regardless of the old and the young; without distinction of age.

**노송**(老松) an old pine tree.

**노쇠**(老衰) infirmity of old age; senility; decrepitude; anility. ∼하다 be old and infirm; grow senile. ¶ ∼한 old and infirm; senile; decrepit / ∼하여 죽다 die of old age / 어머니도 이젠 ∼하셨다 My mother is quite infirm due to age. *or* My mother is well stricken in years. ◉ ∼기 senescence.

**노숙**(老熟) = 노련(老鍊). ¶ ∼한 경지에 이르다 attain (a stage of perfect) maturity.

**노숙**(露宿) sleeping outdoors; camping (out). ∼하다 sleep 〔pass the night〕 in the open air; camp out; have a night out. ◉ ∼자 street people.

**노스다코타** 《미국의 주》 North Dakota (생략 N. Dak., N.D.).

**노스캐롤라이나** 《미국의 주》 North Carolina(생략 N.C.).

**노스탤지어** nostalgia 《for》; homesickness. ⇨향수.

**노승**(老僧) an old 〔aged〕 (Buddhist) priest.

**노심초사**(勞心焦思) exertion of the mind; anxiety; worry. ∼하다 exert *one's* mind; worry (*oneself*) 《about》; be anxious 《about》. ¶ ∼하게 하다 [사물이 주어] worry 《*a person*》; keep 〔have〕 《*a person*》 in (a state of) suspension.

**노아** 〖성서〗 Noah. ¶ ∼의 방주 Noah's ark / ∼의 홍수 Noah's flood; the Deluge.

**노아웃** 〖야구〗 no out. ¶ ∼에 만루이다 The bases are loaded 〔full〕 with no outs 〔nobody out〕.

**노안**(老眼) the eyesight of the aged; farsightedness 〔longsightedness〕 due to old age; 〖의학〗 presbyopia. ¶ ∼인 사람 a presbyopic 〔farsighted〕 person / ∼이 되다 *one's* eyes get dim with age. ◉ ∼경(鏡) spectacles for the old; convex glasses; reading glasses.

**노약(자)**(老弱(者)) the old and the weak.

**노어**(露語) Russian.

**노여움** anger; indignation; rage; fury; wrath. ⇨분노.

> **용법** **anger** 일시적인 노여움을 나타내는 가장 일반적인 말. **indignation** 부당한 취급이나 부정에 대한 노여움. **rage** 격렬한 노여움. **fury** rage보다 강렬한 노여움으로 광기에 가깝고 파괴적인 요소를 포함. **wrath** 문어적인 말로서 복수나 처벌을 바라는 격한 노여움.

¶ ∼을 사다 arouse 〔excite〕 《*a person's*》 anger; incur 《*a person's*》 anger 〔wrath〕; offend 《*a person*》 / ∼을 가라앉히다 calm 〔quell, appease〕 *one's* anger / ∼을 억누르다 restrain 〔hold in, contain〕 *one's* anger; keep *one's* temper / ∼을 터뜨리다 explode with 〔in〕 anger; blow *one's* top 《속어》 / ∼을 …에게 터뜨리다 vent 〔wreak〕 *one's* anger 《on *a person*》; take it out 《on》 《구어》 / ∼을 억누를 수 없게 되다 give way to (*one's*) anger 〔rage〕 / ∼이 치밀어 올랐다 Anger welled up in my heart. / 나는 가까스로 ∼을 참았다 I managed to control my anger. / 그녀는 ∼에 불타 있었다 She was filled 〔burning〕 with anger. / 그는 격렬한 ∼으로 말도 할 수 없었다 He couldn't speak because he was furious. / 그는 ∼으로 제정신이 아니었다 He was beside himself with rage.

**노여워하다** get angry 《with *a person*, at 〔about〕 *a thing*》; be offended 《at》; be angry 〔mad〕 《with, at》; feel hurt 《at》; be displeased 《at》. ¶ 그녀는 하찮은 일에도 곧잘 노여워한다 She easily 「gets angry 〔loses her temper〕 over trifles. / 그는 매우 노여워하고 있다 He is 「red 〔hot〕 with anger. / 그녀의 말에 너무 노여워하지 마시오 Please don't be offended by her remark.

**노역**(勞役) hard 〔exhausting〕 work; labor; toil. ∼하다 labor; do hard work. ¶ 강제 ∼에 끌려나가다 be hunted 〔conscripted〕 for forced labor. ◉ ∼장 《죄수 등의》 the forced-labor workplace.

**노엽다** be displeased 《at》; (be) offended; ill-humored; indignant; feel displeasure over; feel hurt. ¶ 노여운 빛을 나타내다 betray *one's* anger / 그의 말이 나는 ∼ I am offended by his remark. *or* I am indignant at his remark. / 자네를 노엽게 할 생각은 없었네 I did not mean to offend you.

**노예**(奴隷) a slave. ¶ ∼와 같은 slavish; servile / 사랑의 ∼ slaves of love / 생활의 ∼ slaves for living / 습관의 ∼ a slave of habit / ∼로 팔리다 be sold into slavery / ∼처럼 일하다 work like a slave / ∼화하다 enslave 《*a person*》 / 사장은 우리를 ∼처럼 부렸다 The boss made slaves of us. / 그들은 ∼나 다름없다 They are no better than slaves. / 금전의 ∼가 되어서는 안된다 You must not become a slave to money. ◉ ∼근성 a servile spirit. ∼노동 slave labor. ∼매매 slave trade. ∼상인 a slaver; a slave dealer. ∼생활 slavery; bondage. ∼제도 slavery. ∼폐지론 abolitionism; antislavery: ∼ 폐지론자 an abolitionist. ∼폐지 운동 an antislavery movement. ～해방 the emancipation of slaves: ～해방 선언 〖역사〗 the Emancipation Proclamation.

**노옹**(老翁) an elderly gentleman; an aged man.

**노유**(老幼) the young and the old; old people and children. ¶ ～를 막론하고 irrespective of age.

**노을** a glow in the sky; a red sky. ¶ ～진 하늘 the sky aglow with the rising 〔setting〕 sun / 서쪽 하늘에 저녁 ～이 붉게 타오르고 있다 The western skies are lit up with the glow of the setting sun.

**노이로제** [<*Neurose*(G.)] (a) neurosis (*pl.* -ses); (a) nervous breakdown. ¶ ～의〔에 걸린〕 neurotic / ～에 걸리다 have a nervous breakdown; become neurotic / ～에 시달리다 suffer from neurotic / 그녀는 입학 시험 때문에 약간의 ～증세가 있다 She is slightly neurotic due to the entrance examination. ◉ ～환자 a neurotic.

**노익장**(老益壯) a vigorous old age. ¶ ～을 누리다 enjoy a green old age; be hale and hearty.

**노인**(老人) an old 〔aged〕 person; an oldster 《미》; [총칭] the aged 〔old〕 (★ 고령자); the elderly (★ 중년을 지난 60세 정도의 노인); old people; a senior citizen (★ 65세 이상의 연금 생활자). ¶ ～을 공경하다 respect 〔revere〕 the old 〔aged〕 / ～을 돌보다 look after 〔take good care of〕 *one's* old folks; tend the aged / 마치 ～같은 소리를 하다 talk as if *one* were quite old / ～에게 친절해라 Be kind to the elderly.
◉ ～병 the disease of the aged; the infirmities of age: ～병 전문 병원 a geriatrics hospital / ～병 전문의(醫) a geriatrician. ～(병)학 gerontology; geriatrics; geriatric medicine. ～복지 old people's welfare; welfare for the aged 〔elderly people〕: ～복지법 the welfare law for the aged. ～성 질환 ⇨ 노인병. ～성 치매증 senile dementia; Alzheimer's disease. ～연금 old-age pensions. ～우대증 《미》 the Golden Age Passport. ～의료보험 《미》 Medicare. ～의학 geriatrics. ～차별 ageism. ～회 a 〔the〕 club for senior citizens 〔elderly people〕: 대한～회 the Korean Senior Citizens Association.

**노임**(勞賃) pay; wages (★ 보통 복수형). ⇨ 임금. ¶ ～을 지급하다〔받다〕 pay 〔receive〕 wages / 싼〔비싼〕 ～을 받고 일하다 work for low 〔high〕 wages / ～을 올리다〔내리다〕 increase 〔cut〕 *a person's* wages / 그의 회사는 ～이 높다〔낮다〕 His company pays high 〔low〕 wages.
◉ ～격차 wage differential. ～인상〔인하〕 a wage increase 〔decrease〕. ～투쟁 a wage struggle. 기본～ basic wages. 실질〔명목〕～ real 〔nominal〕 wages. 최저〔최고〕～ minimum 〔maximum〕 wages.

**노자**(老子) 《중국의 철학자》 Lao-tzu (604?-531? B.C.). ¶ ～의 사상 《도교》 Taoism.

**노자**(路資) traveling expenses. ⇨ 여비.

**노작**(勞作) 《일》 a hard work; a job involving much labor; 《작품》 the product of hard work. ¶ 다년간의 ～ the product 〔fruit〕 of *one's* many years' labor; a piece of work completed after many years' labor.

**노장**(老將) a veteran general; an old general.

**노장**(老壯) the old and the middle aged.

**노적**(露積) stacked grain. ◉ ～가리 a stack 〔rick〕 of grain; a grain stack.

**노점**(露店) a street stall; a roadside stand; a booth. ¶ ～을 벌이다 open 〔keep〕 a street stall / ～이 일제히 철거되었다 All the street stalls were pulled down simultaneously.
◉ ～가(街) open-air stall quarters. ～상인 a stall 〔booth〕 keeper; a street vendor. 「슬점.

**노점**(露點) 〖물리〗 the dew point. ＝이

**노정**(路程) 《이수(里數)》 mileage; (a) distance; 《여정》 an itinerary; a route; a course. ¶ 50 마일의 ～ a distance of 50 miles; a fifty miles' journey.
◉ ～계 a measuring wheel; a pedometer. ～기(記) a traveler's guide; an itinerary. ～표 a table of itinerary.

**노정**(露呈) disclosure; exposure; revelation. ～하다 expose; disclose; reveal.

**노조**(勞組) ⇨ 노동 조합.

**노질**(櫓—) pulling an oar; rowing; paddling; sculling. ～하다 pull an oar; row 《a boat》; paddle; scull.

**노처녀**(老處女) an old maid; a spinster (★ old miss는 우리 나라식 영어임). ¶ ～같은 spinsterish / ～더러 시집가라 한다 make a superfluous remark.

**노천**(露天) the open air; the open. ¶ ～에서 in the open (air); out of doors; outdoors. ◉ ～광(鑛) a strip mine. ～교실 an open-air schoolroom 〔class〕. ～극장 an open-air theater. ～상인 a pitchman. ～수업 open-air classes. ～시장 an open-air 〔outdoor〕 market. ～

온천 an open-air 〔outdoor〕 hot spring.

**노천굴**(露天掘) strip 〔opencut, opencast《영》〕《coal》 mining. ◉ ～탄광 an open(-pit) coal mine.

**노총각**(老總角) an old bachelor.

**노출**(露出) (an) exposure;《광맥의》 outcrop《of a vein of coal》. ～하다 expose; bare《*one's* chest》; crop out (광상 따위가). ¶ ～된 exposed; bare; naked / 잠재의식의 ～ the outcrop of the subconscious / 100분의 1초의 ～ an exposure of 1 / 100 second / 위험에 몸을 ～시키다 expose *oneself* to danger / 필름을 ～시키다 expose a film to light / 사람들 앞에서 그렇게 몸을 ～해서는 안된다 You shouldn't expose your body in public like that.
◉ ～계 an actinometer; a photometer; an exposure meter: ～계 내장(內藏) 카메라 a camera with a built-in exposure meter. ～과다〔부족〕〖사진〗 overexposure 〔underexposure〕: ～ 과다증〖의학〗 a mania for indecent overexposure; an exposure mania; exhibitionism. ～광맥 an exposed deposit. ～시간〖사진〗 the time of exposure. ～증 exhibitionism: ～증 환자 an exhibitionist / 국부 ～증 a mania 〔maniac〕 for indecent exposure; an exposure mania.

**노친**(老親) *one's* old 〔aged〕 parents.

**노카운트** no count. ¶ ～가 되다 be called no count.

**노커** a (door-)knocker.

**노커트**《영화에서》¶ ～ 영화 an uncut 〔uncensored〕 movie 〔film〕.

**노코멘트** no comment. ¶ 그 문제에 관해선 ～다 I don't want to make any comment on the matter.

**노크** a knock; knocking. ¶ 문을 ～하다 knock on 〔at〕 the door / 문을 ～했지만 대답이 없었다 There was no answer to my knock. *or* No one answered the door.

**노킹**《내연 기관의》 knocking. ◉ ～방지제 an antiknock.

**노타이셔츠** an openneck(ed) shirt.

**노트**[1]《배의 속도 단위》 a knot. ¶ 이 배는 30～를 낼 수 있다 This ship can make 〔do〕 30 knots.

**노트**[2]《필기·주석》 a note;《공책》 a notebook. ～하다 take notes of《a lecture》; note 〔write, put, jot〕 down. ¶ 그는 선생님의 말을 일일이 ～했다 He noted down every word the teacher said.

**노트북** a notebook. ◉ ～ 컴퓨터 a notebook computer.

**노티**(老—) signs of (old-)age; looking old. ¶ 나이에 비해 ～가 난다 look older than *one's* age; look old for *one's* age.

**노파**(老婆) an old woman; a beldam.
◉ ～심 excessive solicitude; useless 〔unnecessary〕 anxiety: ～심에서 충고하다 give《*a person*》 advice though《it》 may not be necessary / 나는 ～심에서 이렇게 말하는 거다 I say this「for your own good 〔out of kindness〕.

**노폐물**(老廢物) wastes; waste matter. ¶ 체내의 ～ body wastes.

**노폭**(路幅) the width of a street.

**노하다**(怒—) become 〔get, grow〕 angry《with *a person*, at *a matter*》; be angered 〔offended, enraged, furious〕; be stirred to anger; get mad; lose *one's* temper. ¶ 노해서 in anger / 툭하면 ～ anger easily / 하찮은 일에 ～ fall 〔get〕 into a passion at trifles / 그는 그녀의 말을 듣고 노했다 He got「angry 〔into a temper〕 at what she said.

**노하우**《기술적 지식》 know-how. ¶ 원폭 제조의 ～ the know-how of the making of the atomic bomb / 상거래의 ～ business know-how.

**노형**(老兄) you.

**노호**(怒號) a roar (of anger); a bellow. ～하다 roar (in anger); bellow; howl (with rage). ¶ 군중의 ～ the roar of the crowd.

**노화**(老化) ag(e)ing; senility; growing old. ～하다 age. ¶ 남성이 여성보다 더 빨리 ～한다 Men age more rapidly than women. / ～를 방지하기 위해 머리 쓰는 일에 종사하고 있다 I am engaged in brainwork to stave off senility.
◉ ～현상《develop》 the phenomena of ag(e)ing; the symptoms of senility.

**노환**(老患) the infirmities 〔diseases〕 of old age; senile infirmity. ¶ ～으로 죽다 die of「old age 〔senile infirmity〕.

**노회하다**(老獪—) (be) crafty; cunning; foxy. ¶ 노회한 사람 an old 〔a cunning〕 fox; a sly old dog.

**노획**(鹵獲) capture; seizure; plunder. ～하다 capture; seize; plunder. ¶ 적군에게서 노획한 총기 guns captured from the enemy. ◉ ～물〔품〕 booty; spoil(s); a prize; [총칭] booty; plunder.

**노후**(老朽) decrepitude; superannuation; senescence. ～하다 (be) superannuated; old and decrepit; time-worn; worn-out. ¶ 황폐한 ～ 건물 a run=down old building / 이 집은 오래 사용하여 ～했다 This house became decrepit by long usage. ◉ ～선(船) an overage 〔a superannuated〕 ship; a hulk. ～시설〔설비〕 outworn 〔superannuated, ageing〕 equipment. ～차량 a superannuated 〔decrepit〕 car. ～화 deterioration: ～화하다 become too old for use 〔work〕; get time-worn; become superannuated.

**노후**(老後) *one's* declining years; 《in》 *one's* old age. ¶ ～의 낙 consolations of *one's* old age / ～ 보장 security 〔insurance〕 for the aged / ～에 대비하다 provide for 〔against〕 *one's* old age / ～를 조용하고 평온하게 지내다 spend *one's* 「last days 〔remaining years〕 in peace and quiet / ～를 잊혀져서 지내다 live the rest of *one's* life in obscurity / ～를 시골에서 보내다 spend *one's* declining years in the country.

**녹**(祿) 《녹봉》 a stipend; a salary. ¶ 녹을 먹다 receive a stipend / 하는 일없이 녹을 먹다 receive a stipend without rendering any service.

**녹**(綠) 《쇠의》 rust. ⇨ 녹슬다. ¶ 녹을 방지하는 rustproof / 녹을 벗기다 take off 〔remove〕 the rust; get the rust off; derust / 녹을 문질러 벗기다 rub off the rust / 녹을 방지하다 prevent rust(ing); keep from rusting / 쇠붙이에는 녹이 잔뜩 슬어 있었다 Rust had eaten deeply into the metal parts. ◉ 녹방지제 a rust preventive; an antirust compound; an anticorrosive.

**녹각**(鹿角) a deer's horn; an antler.

**녹나무** 〖식물〗 a camphor tree.

**녹내장**(綠內障) 〖의학〗 glaucoma.

**녹는점**(—點) 〖물리〗 a melting 〔fusing〕 point; the point of fusion.

**녹다** ① (*a*) 《고체가》 melt; thaw (눈 따위가); run (버터·양초 등이). ¶ 열에 ～ melt with 〔yield to〕 heat / 녹아서 물이 되다 melt into water / 눈이 햇볕에 녹았다 The snow has melted 〔thawed〕 in the sun. / 보도의 얼음이 모두 녹았다 The ice has melted off the sidewalks. (*b*) 《쇠붙이 등이》 melt; fuse. ¶ 잘 〔안〕～ be fusible 〔infusible〕; be meltable 〔unmeltable〕 / 불에 ～ melt in the fire; be fused by the fire / 녹아서 섞이다 melt into each other / 그 금속은 열에 녹는다 The metal melts with heat. / 은은 섭씨 900도에서 녹는다 Silver melts at nine hundred degrees C. (*c*) 《용해되다》 dissolve. ¶ 잘 ～ be soluble / 녹지 않다 be insoluble 《in water》 / 소금은 물에 녹는다 Salt dissolves in water. / 이 세제는 물에 잘 녹지 않는다 This cleanser 〔detergent〕 doesn't dissolve easily in water.
② 《따뜻해지다》 warm up; be warmed; get warm. ¶ 손이 ～ *one's* hands warm up / 몸이 ～ *one* gets warm / 몸이 차차 녹아 온다 I'm gradually thawing.
③ 《주색잡기에》 get ruined by dissipation; be dissipated. ¶ 술에 녹아 떨어지다 get dead drunk / 주색에 ～ ruin *one's* health with dissipation.
④ 《혼나다》 have a hard 〔bad〕 time (of it); have a hell of a time; have bitter experiences; be done 《in》; be broke 〔ruined, exhausted〕. ¶ 그는 과로로 녹아 떨어졌다 He was quite exhausted with overwork. / 그는 주먹 한 대에 녹아 떨어졌다 He was knocked out by only one punch.
⑤ 《반하다》 be enraptured 〔captivated〕 《by》; be madly in love 《with》; be stuck 《on》; be crazy 《about》; be gone on 《a girl》. ¶ 그는 그녀에게 녹았다 He is stuck on her. / 나는 그녀의 매력에 녹아 떨어졌다 I am stuck by her charms.

**녹다운** a knockdown. ¶ ～시키다 knock 《*a person*》 down; put 《*a person*》 on the canvas; floor 《미》 / ～된 후 카운트 9 만에 일어나다 survive a nine-count knockdown.

**녹두**(綠豆) 〖식물〗 mung beans; green gram. ◉ ～묵 mung bean jelly. ～죽 mung bean porridge 〔gruel〕.

**녹로**(轆轤) a potter's wheel (도자기의); a (turning) lathe (선반). ◉ ～꾼〔공(工)〕 a turner. ～세공 turnery.

**녹록하다**(碌碌—) be poor 《in》; (be) worthless; good-for-nothing; trifling; trivial. ¶ 녹록찮은 적 a formidable enemy.

**녹림**(綠林) ① 《숲》 a green forest. ② 《도둑의 소굴》 a den of bandits. ◉ ～당 robbers; brigandage. ～호객(豪客) a bandit; a robber; a brigand.

**녹말**(綠末) starch; 〖화학〗 dextrin. ◉ ～당화 효소 diastase. ～질 starchiness.

**녹물**(綠—) 《얼룩》 rust stain; 《빛깔》 rust (color); reddish brown.

**녹변**(綠便) green stools.

**녹봉**(祿俸) a stipend; a salary. = 녹(祿).

**녹비**(鹿—) deerskin; buckskin 《gloves》. ¶ ～에 가로왈자 be easily swayed by others.

**녹비**(綠肥) green manure. ◉ ～작물 a green manure crop.

**녹색**(綠色) a green color; green; verdure (초목의). ¶ ～의 green; verdant / ～의 언덕 a green hill. ◉ ～신고 a green return; a green paper report 《on business income》: ～ 신고업체 a green return corporation / ~ 신고제 a green return 〔green tax report(ing)〕 system. ~혁명 green revolution: 곡물생산량을 증대시키기 위한 ~ 혁명을 이룩하다 achieve a green revolution so as to boost the nation's grain productions.

**녹슬다**(綠—) ① 《쇠붙이가》 get 〔go〕 rusty; gather 〔form〕 rust; rust; be rusted. ¶ 녹슬기 쉽다 rust easily; be apt 〔easy〕 to rust / 녹슨 칼 a rusty 〔rusted〕 knife / 사용하지 않아 ~ rust from disuse / 속속들이 ~ be rusted through 〔to the core〕 / 수분은 쇠붙이를 녹슬게 한다 Water rusts iron. ② 《능력·두뇌가》 become blunt 〔dull〕; weaken; be rusty. ¶ 게으름을 피우면 능력이 녹슨다 You'll just rust away in idleness. / 너의 재능을 녹슬게 하지 마라 Don't let your talents become rusted.

**녹신녹신하다** (be) very soft and flexible; quite pliant; very elastic.

**녹신하다** (be) soft and flexible; elastic; pliant. ¶ 녹신한 가죽 soft leather.

**녹아웃** 『권투』 a knockout (생략 K.O.); a kayo 《미속어》. ¶ ~시키다 『권투』 knock out; kayo; count out / ~되다 be knocked out; be kayoed 《미속어》.

**녹야**(綠野) a green field; 《초원》 a grassland.

**녹엽**(綠葉) green leaves; verdant leafage.

**녹용**(鹿茸) the young antlers of the deer; deer 〔stag〕 antlers. ◉ ~밀수 smugging of deer antlers.

**녹음**(綠陰) the shade of trees; a shady nook. ¶ ~에서 in the shade of trees; in a shady nook. ◉ ~기 the season of thick foliage. ~방초(芳草) green shades and fragrant plants.

**녹음**(錄音) (sound) recording; (electrical) transcription. ~하다 record 《a speech, music》; transcribe 《a program》. ¶ 테이프에 ~한 audio-taped / 테이프에 ~하다 record 《music》 on (a) tape; tape 《a speech》. ◉ ~기 a (tape) recorder; a recording machine 〔instrument〕: 노래를 ~기에 녹음하다 pour *one's* songs into the recording instrument. ~기사 a recording engineer; a recordist; a sound mixer. ~실 a recording room. ~연설 a transcribed speech. ~ 장치 recording equipment. ~재생 playback. ~테이프 a recording tape; a magnetic recording tape.

**녹음방송**(錄音放送) 《라디오》 transcription (broadcast); broadcasting by electrical transcription. ~하다 broadcast 《a program》 by electrical transcription.

**녹이다** ① (a) 《고체를》 melt; dissolve (고체를 액체 속에서); liquefy (액화시키다); 《얼음을》 thaw. ¶ 버터를〔밀납을〕 ~ melt butter 〔wax〕 / 눈을 ~ thaw 〔melt〕 snow / 소금〔설탕〕을 물에 ~ dissolve salt 〔sugar〕 in water. (b) 《금속을》 melt (up, down); fuse; smelt. ¶ 광석을 ~ smelt ore / 쇠를 ~ melt 〔fuse〕 iron. ② 《몸을》 make 《it》 warm; warm 《it》 (up); warm *oneself*. ¶ 손을 ~ warm *one's* hands 《over the fire》 / 몸을 ~ make *oneself* warm; take warmth; warm *oneself* up / 떠나기 전에 이리와 몸 좀 녹이시오 Come in and get yourself warm before you leave. ③ 《망치다》 ruin; blast; play havoc 〔the devil〕 with it. ¶ 주색은 젊은 사람을 녹인다 Woman and drink play havoc with young men. ④ 《매혹시키다》 enchant; charm; bewitch; captivate; fascinate. ¶ 살살 녹이는 눈길 《cast》 a killing glance / 남자를 ~ captivate 〔fascinate〕 a man / 그녀의 미소는 뭇 남자의 마음을 녹였다 Her smile captivated every man. ⑤ 《탕진하다》 waste 《on, over》; throw away; squander 《away》. ¶ 그는 도박으로 재산을 녹여 없앴다 He gambled away his fortune. *or* He threw away a fortune in gambling.

**녹즙**(綠汁) green vegetable juice. ◉ ~기 a juicer for green vegetable juice.

**녹지**(綠地) a green tract of land. ¶ ~화하다 afforest / 그 도시 교외에는 광대한 ~가 펼쳐져 있다 There are vast tracts of green land outside the city. ◉ ~계획 a plan for afforestation. ~대(帶) a green belt 〔zone〕 (도시 주변의); the green areas; a tree lawn (보도와 차도 사이의).

**녹진녹진하다** (be) all soft and sticky. ¶ 갖풀을 가열하면 녹진녹진해진다 Glue gets all soft and sticky when it is heated.

**녹진하다** (be) soft and sticky.

**녹차**(綠茶) green tea.

**녹채**(鹿砦) 《방어용 울타리》 an abatis; an entanglement.

**녹청**(綠靑) green rust, verdigris.

**녹초** ① 《낡아 결딴난 상태》 ¶ ~가 된 all 「tattered 〔out of shape〕; tattery; ragged. ② 《기진맥진함》 utter exhaustion; dog-tiredness 《구어》. ¶ ~가 되다 be worn 〔tired〕 out; be utterly exhausted; be worn to a frazzle; be dog-tired; be reduced to pulp / ~가

되게 두들겨 패다 beat《*a person*》 to a pulp / 나는 과로로 ~가 되었다 I was exhausted 〔dead tired〕 with overwork. / 그는 등산 도중에 ~가 되었다 He collapsed halfway up the mountain.

**녹초**(綠草) green grass.

**녹턴** 〖음악〗 a nocturn(e).

**녹화**(綠化) tree planting; afforestation. ~하다 plant trees《in an area》; plant《an area》 with trees. ◉ ~계획 a plan for afforestation. ~운동 a tree-planting campaign 〔drive〕.

**녹화**(錄畫) video tape recording (생략 VTR). ~하다 record《a scene》 on video tape. ¶ 드라마를 비디오에 ~하다 record a drama on video tape; videotape a drama. ◉ ~방송 a filmed TV broadcast: ~방송을 하다 broadcast a program recorded on video tape. ~실 telerecording room.

**논** a rice 〔paddy〕 field; a rice paddy. ¶ 비옥한〔척박한〕 논 a rice field of rich 〔poor〕 soil / 논을 갈다 till 〔plow〕 a rice field / 논에 물을 대다 irrigate 〔flood〕 a rice field / 논을 매다 weed a rice paddy / 논농사를 짓다 cultivate 〔crop〕 a rice field / 논에 모를 심다 plant 「rice 〔rice-seedlings〕 in the rice paddy.

**논**(論) 《논설》 an essay; a treatise; 《평론》 (a) comment; (a) criticism; a leading article; 《이론》 a theory; 《의견》 an opinion; 《문제》 a question; a problem; 《논의》 (an) argument; (a) discussion; (a) debate; (a) controversy.

**논-** non-. ¶ 논픽션 nonfiction / 논스톱 nonstop.

**논갈이** plowing a rice field. ~하다 plow 〔till〕 a rice field.

**논객**(論客) a controversialist; a disputant; a polemic (신학의). ¶ 자기 주장에 강경한 ~ a stubborn controversialist.

**논거**(論據) the grounds 〔basis〕 of an argument; 《전거》 data. ¶ ~가 확실하다《*one's* argument》 be well grounded; be sound / …의 ~가 되다 supply arguments for... / 너의 ~는 빈약하다〔잘못되어 있다〕 You are arguing on tenuous 〔false〕 grounds. / 그의 제안을 인정하는 ~는 무엇인가 What are the arguments for accepting his proposal?

**논고**(論考·論攷) a study 《on 〔in〕 English literature》.

**논고**(論告) 〖법〗 the prosecutor's final 〔concluding〕 address; (a) prosecution. ~하다 《the prosecutor》 address the court; prosecute. ¶ 준엄한 ~ a scathing address / ~를 개시하다 open the arguments 《on a case》 / 검사가 ~했다 The prosecutor addressed the court.

**논공**(論功) estimating the merits; weighing *a person's* merit. ~하다 weigh *a person's* merit; estimate the merits.

**논공행상**(論功行賞) the 「grant of honors 〔distribution of rewards〕 according to the merits 《of》; the official recognition of distinguished services. ~하다 award rewards according to 《each *person's*》 merits; confer 〔distribute〕 honors 〔rewards, *etc.*〕. ¶ ~은 공정하지 못했다 The honors were not justly distributed.

**논구하다**(論究—) discuss 《*a matter*》 thoroughly; give a full discussion.

**논급**(論及) reference; mention. ⇨ 언급. ~하다 refer to; enter into; touch on 〔upon〕 (짧게); make reference to; talk about.

**논길** a paddy path.

**논농사**(—農事) rice farming; rice cultivation 〔culture〕. ¶ ~를 짓다 do rice farming; cultivate a paddy field.

**논다니** 《창녀》 a prostitute; a courtesan.

**논단**(論壇) ① 《토론 장소》 a (public) platform; a forum; a rostrum. ② 《평론계》 the world of public criticism; the circle of critics 〔publicists〕. ¶ ~의 거물 a great critic; an eminent publicist / 그 문제는 ~을 떠들썩하게 했다 The question evoked much controversy among the critical circles.

**논단**(論斷) ~하다 conclude 《that...》; pass a verdict 《on *a matter*》.

**논담**(論談) discussion; discourse; debate; 《논쟁》 dispute; controversy.

**논도랑** a ditch 〔waterway〕 of a rice field.

**논두렁** a ridge between rice 「fields 〔paddies〕. ◉ ~길 a 〔ridgeway〕 between rice fields.

**논둑** the bank around a rice field.

**논란**(論難) (adverse) criticism; denunciation; (a) censure; a charge. ~하다 criticize; censure; denounce; attack. ¶ 현행의 세금 제도를 ~하다 denounce the present taxation system.

**논리**(論理) logic. ¶ ~적인 logical / 비~적인 illogical / ~적 추리 logical reasoning / ~적 사고 logical thinking / ~적 필연성 logical necessity / 광고〔정치〕의 ~ the logic behind advertising 〔politics〕 / ~를 무시하고 regardless of logic / ~상, ~적으로 logically; from a logical point of view / ~가 분명하다 be perfectly logical / 문제를 ~적으로

생각해야 한다 You should consider the problem logically. / 너의 의견에는 ~의 비약이 있다 There is a leap of logic in your opinion. / 그의 의론은 ~ 정연하다 His argument is perfectly logical.
◉ ~성 logicality. ~학 logic: ~학자 a logician / 귀납 ~학 inductive logic / 기호 ~학 symbolic logic / 순수 ~학 pure logic / 연역 ~학 deductive logic / 형식 ~학 formal logic.

**논마지기** a small plot 〔a patch〕 of paddy land. ¶ 그는 ~나 가지고 있다네 He is something of a landowner.

**논매기** the weeding of rice paddy.

**논문**(論文) [일반적] a treatise; an essay; 《연구상의》 a thesis (*pl.* theses); a dissertation; 《학회 등의》 a paper; 《전문적인》 a monograph; 《신문 등의》 an article. ¶ 미국 문학에 관한 ~ a paper 〔theme, treatise〕 on American literature / ~을 심사하다 examine 《*a person's*》 paper 《on》 / ~을 쓰다 write a paper 〔thesis〕 《on》 / ~을 제출하다 submit 〔present〕 a thesis 《to》 / ~을 제출하여 박사 학위를 받다 obtain a doctorate by presenting a thesis.
◉ ~시험 a thesis examination; an essay test. ~심사 examination of theses. ~지도 교수 a thesis director. ~집 a collection of learned papers. 과제~ 《기말 시험의 일부》 a term paper. 박사~ a doctoral dissertation; a treatise for doctor's degree. 졸업~ a graduation thesis.

**논문서**(一文書) the title deed of a paddy field.

**논박**(論駁) (a) refutation; confutation. ~하다 refute; confute; argue against. ¶ 나는 그와 견해를 달리했지만 ~할 수가 없었다 I disagreed with his views, but I couldn't refute them.

**논밭** paddy fields and dry fields; fields; a farm.

**논배미** a strip 〔patch, section〕 of rice paddy; a plot.

**논법**(論法) reasoning; logic; argument. ¶ 그의 ~은 이치에 안 맞는다 His logic is absurd. / 그것 참 묘한 ~이로군 That's strange logic, isn't it? / 그의 ~은 언제나 똑같다 He always uses the same logic. / 너의 ~에는 따를 수 없다 I can't follow your argument. / 그는 그의 특유의 ~으로 모두를 어리둥절케 하였다 His peculiar line of argument 〔reasoning〕 mystified everybody. ◉ 삼단~ a syllogism.

**논변**(論辯) an argument. ⇨ 변론.

**논봉**(論鋒) the force of an argument; a wordy attack. ¶ ~이 예리하다 make a keen 〔an incisive〕 argument.

**논설**(論說) 《논문》 an essay; a discourse; a dissertation; 《논평》 a comment; 《잡지 등의》 an article; 《사설》 an editorial 《미》; a leading article; a leader 《영》. ¶ 청소년 범죄에 관한 ~ an editorial on juvenile crimes / 사건을 ~로 다루다 devote an editorial to a matter; editorialize on a topic 《미》.
◉ ~란 the editorial column. ~위원 an editorial writer; an editorialist 《미》; a leader writer 《영》. ~주간 an editor-in-chief.

**논술**(論述) a statement. ~하다 state; set forth. ◉ ~고사, ~식 테스트 an essay-type test 〔examination〕; an essay writing examination.

**논어**(論語) 《공자의》 the Analects 〔Discourses〕 of Confucius.

**논외**(論外) irrelevancy to the subject 〔issue〕. ¶ ~의 문제다 be beside 〔aside from〕 the point 〔question〕; be outside the question; 《문제가 안 되는》 be out of the question.

**논의**(論議) (an) argument; (a) discussion; (a) debate. ~하다 discuss 《*a matter*》; debate 《on, about》; argue 《about》. ¶ 정치상의 ~ a political discussion / ~ 중이다 be under discussion 〔debate〕 / 열띤 ~를 벌이다 develop heated discussions / 이 문제에 대해서는 활발한 ~가 있었다 There was a lively discussion on this subject.

**논자**(論者) 《토론자》 a debater; a disputant; 《필자》 the (present) writer; 《주창자》 an advocator.

**논쟁**(論爭) 《토론》 (a) dispute; (a) controversy; 《주장》 a polemic; (an) argument. ~하다 argue 〔dispute〕 《against, with》; have 〔engage in〕 a controversy 《with》; take issue 《with *a person* on》. ¶ 법률상의 ~ a dispute over a point of law / 열띤 ~ a heated controversy / ~에 가담하다 join in a dispute / ~ 중이다 be in a controversy 《with》 / ~의 여지가 있다 be debatable; be open to argument / ~의 여지가 없다 be indisputable 〔incontestable〕; be beyond controversy / 어떤 문제에 관해 아무와 ~을 벌이다 argue about a subject with *a person* / 그 학설에 관해 ~이 끊이지 않다 There is constant controversy concerning the theory.
◉ ~자 a disputant; a controversialist; a debater. ~점 a point of dispute.

**논전**(論戰) a battle of words; wordy warfare; an argument; a controversy.

~하다 fight with words; have wordy warfare; engage in a battle of words.

**논점**(論點) a (disputed, moot) point; the point at issue〔in question〕. ¶ ~을 벗어나다 be beside〔off〕the point / ~을 분명히 하다 make *one's* point clear / 그의 논문은 ~을 파악하기가 어렵다 It is hard to grasp the point of his essay.

**논제**(論題) the subject〔theme, text〕of *one's* argument〔article, lecture〕; a topic for discussion. ¶ ~에서 벗어나다 stray〔digress〕from *one's* theme〔text〕/ ~에서 벗어나지 않다 keep〔stick〕to *one's* theme〔text〕.

**논조**(論調) the tone〔tenor, drift〕of an argument. ¶ 신문의 ~ the tone of the press / 이 문제에 관한 신문 ~는 모두 같다 The press comments on this question are the same in tenor. / 신문의 ~는 새로운 정책에 비판적이다 The tone of press comments is critical about the new policy.

**논죄**(論罪) ruling; finding; a debate in the process of finding〔proving〕guilt. ~하다 rule; find; pass judgment on.

**논증**(論證) (a) demonstration; proof. ~하다 demonstrate; prove; produce〔adduce〕proof〔evidence〕to support《*one's* statement》. ¶ ~적(으로) demonstrative(ly). ◉ ~자 a demonstrator.

**논지**(論旨) the point〔gist〕of an argument. ¶ ~를 분명히 하다 make *one's* point (of argument) clear / 그의 논문의 ~를 이해할 수 없다 I cannot make out what he is aiming at in his paper.

**논진**(論陣) ¶ ~을 펴다 set〔put〕out〔forth〕an argument《for, against》; make out a case《for, against》.

**논파**(論破) confutation; refutation. ~하다 confute; refute; outdebate. ¶ 나는 그의 이론을 ~하였다 I refuted his theory.

**논평**(論評) (a) criticism; a comment; a review. ~하다 criticize; review; comment《on》. ¶ 이 문제에 관한 신문의 ~ newspaper〔press〕comments on this subject / 남의 작품에 ~을 가하다 make a review of another's work / ~을 삼가하다〔피하다〕reserve〔eschew〕comment《on》.

**논픽션** nonfiction. ◉ ~작가 a nonfiction writer.

**논하다**(論―) ① 《의론하다》 argue《on, about》; discuss《*a matter*》; dispute《on, about》; debate《on》; reason《that…》; 《평론하다》 comment《on》. ¶ 시사를 ~ comment on current topics / 철학을 ~ talk〔debate〕philosophy《with *a person*》/ 정치를 ~ discuss politics (★「정치에 대한 논의」는 a discussion on politics가 되지만, 동사 용법에서는 on을 쓰지 않음) / 그것은 논할 여지도 없이 명백하다 It is too obvious to require any argument. / 기본적 인권이 존중되어야 함은 논할 필요도 없다「It goes without saying that〔Needless to say,〕fundamental human rights should be respected. ② 《다루다》 treat of; deal with. ¶ 유전자 공학의 위험성을 논한 책 a book concerned〔dealing〕with the hazards of genetic engineering / 노동 문제를 ~ treat of〔deal with〕the labor question. ③ 《문제로 삼다》 consider; take into account. ¶ 논할 거리도 못 되다 be not worth consideration; be beneath criticism / 이 책은 논할 가치가 없다 This book is beneath criticism.

**놀**[1] 《하늘의》 a red sky; a glow in the sky. ⇨ 노을.

**놀**[2] 《큰 물결》 billows; a heavy〔high〕sea; wild waves; raging waters. ¶ 놀(이) 치다 have a heavy sea; The waves are high. *or* The sea is rough.

**놀다**[1] ① (***a***) 《유희·장난하다》 play (at) (★ at 없는 것이 구어적. 특히 실외 경기의 경우 at는 거의 붙지 않음); frolic; gambol. ¶ 소꿉질을 하며 ~ play (at) house; play at housekeeping / 숨바꼭질을 하며 ~ play hide-and-seek / 카드놀이를 하며 ~ play cards / 장난감을 가지고 ~ play with a toy / 재미나게 ~ have a good〔nice〕time; have fun / 뛰어다니며 ~ play jumping〔romping〕about / 놀며 시간을 보내다 play away *one's* time / 노는 데에 정신이 팔리다 be given to play / 놀러 나가다《어린이가》go out to play / 고양이가 공을 가지고 놀고 있다 The cat is playing〔sporting〕with a ball. (***b***) 《즐기다, 기분 전환하다》 amuse〔divert, disport〕*oneself;* enjoy *oneself.* ¶ 놀기 좋아하는 fun-〔amusement-〕loving; pleasure-seeking / 그림책을 보며 ~ amuse *oneself* with picture books / 노래하며 ~ divert *oneself* in singing / 놀러 나가다 go for an outing / 시골로 놀러가다 go into the country for pleasure / 이번 일요일엔 수원에 놀러 간다 We are going on an excursion to Suwŏn next Sunday. / 볼일도 볼겸 놀러 왔다 I've come partly on business and partly for pleasure. / 오늘 저녁에 놀러 오지 않겠소 How would you like to come and spend the evening with me?

② 《유흥에 빠지다》 make merry; have

a spree; go on a spree; take *one's* pleasure; 《방탕하다》 lead a dissipated life; indulge in dissipation 〔fast living〕. ¶ 진탕 ～ have an all-out fling with 《*a kisaeng*》 / 놀러 다니다 spend *one's* time in pleasure 《on the town》; gad 〔gallivant〕 about; be out for a lark / 놀기 좋아하는 사람이다 be a pleasure-seeker / 오늘 저녁 한잔 마시며 놀자 Let's have a spree tonight. / 그는 독신일 때 많이 놀았다 He spent a lot of time and money on pleasure when he was single.

③ 《일하지 않다》 take *one's* ease; be idle; loaf 〔idle〕 《*one's* time》 away; live in idle life. ¶ 노는 사람 an idler; a loafer / 노는 시간 playtime; 《학교의》 a recess; a break / 노는 날 a holiday; an off day / 하루 (쉬며) ～ take a holiday; take a day off / 놀며 지내다 live in idleness; spend idle hours; lead a lazy life / 나는 놀고 지낼 형편이 아니다 I cannot afford to be idle. / 재산이 많아도 놀면 바닥이 난다 Idleness will eat away a mountain of wealth.

④ 《실직하다》 be out of work; be jobless 〔unemployed〕; have no job 〔work〕 to do. ¶ 나는 회사가 파산된 다음에 계속 놀고 있다 I have been out of work since my company went bankrupt.

⑤ 《사용치 않고》 lie 〔stand〕 idle; be not in use; be out of operation. ¶ 노는 기계 a machine not in use / 노는 자본 unemployed 〔idle〕 capital; idle 〔sleeping〕 funds / 노는 땅 land lying idle / 그에겐 은행에 쓰지 않고 놀고 있는 돈이 많다 He has a lot of money lying idle in the bank. / 이 공장에는 놀고 있는 기계가 한 대도 없다 In this factory there is not a machine that is not in use.

⑥ 《헐거워지다》 totter; shake; give; become 〔get〕 shaky 〔loose, unstable〕; loosen. ¶ 바위가 ～ a rock shakes 〔gives〕 / 나사못이 ～ a screw is loose.

⑦ 《멋대로》 behave as *one* likes 〔pleases〕; act 〔take〕 *one's* own way 〔course〕. ¶ 멋대로 놀게 하다 allow 《*a person*》 to go 〔have〕 ***his*** (own) way; give 《*a person*》 a free hand.

⑧ 《움직이다》 move; be in motion; stir. ¶ 어항에서 금붕어가 놀고 있다 Some goldfishes are swimming in the fishbowl. / 태아가 놀기 시작한다 The child in the womb begins to move.

**놀다**[2] 《던지다》 throw; cast; play; shoot 《dice》. ¶ 윷을 ～ throw *yut* sticks; play *yut*.

**놀라다** ① 《경악하다》 be surprised 〔astonished, amazed〕 《at, to see》; be startled; be taken aback; be shocked (섬뜩하다); get a start 〔turn〕. ¶ 깜짝 놀랄만한 surprising; startling; astonishing; amazing / 놀랍게도 to *one's* surprise 〔astonishment〕 / 놀란 빛을 안 보이다 exhibit 〔show〕 no surprise / 총소리에 ～ be startled at the sound of a gun / …을 보고〔듣고〕 ～ be surprised at the sight 〔news〕 of / 놀라서 소리치다 cry out in surprise 〔astonishment〕 / 놀라서 말이 안 나오다 be struck dumb; be speechless with surprise / 놀라서 눈이 휘둥그래지다 open *one's* eyes wide in surprise / 정말 놀랐다 I was scared to death. / 놀랄 것까지는 없다 This is hardly a matter for surprise.

② 《질리다》 be frightened 〔alarmed, terrified, horror-struck〕. ¶ 놀라서 in *one's* fright; with alarm / 화재 경보에 ～ be alarmed by a fire alarm / 천둥에 ～ be frightened by the thunder / 놀라서 기절〔실신〕하다 faint from fright; be frightened 〔terrified〕 out of *one's* senses / 놀라 달아나다 run away horror-struck; be frightened away / 놀라서 병이 나다 be ill with 〔from〕 fright / 놀라서 허둥대다 be frightened out of *one's* wits 《by, at》 / 개가 갑자기 짖어 놀랐다 The sudden barking of a dog frightened 〔startled〕 me.

③ 《경탄하다》 be amazed 《at》; wonder 〔marvel〕 《at》; admire. ¶ 새롭고 놀랄 만한 과학적 발견 a new and wonderful scientific discovery / 아무의 무식에 ～ be amazed at *a person's* ignorance / 아무의 비상한 재간에 ～ marvel at the extraordinary talent of *a person* / 그의 문학적 재능은 놀랄 만하다 His literary talent well deserves admiration.

**놀라움** 《경악》 surprise; astonishment; 《질림》 fright; horror; terror; 《경탄》 marvel; amazement; wonder. ¶ ～에 눈을 크게 뜨다 stare in wonder 《at》 / ～이 얼굴에 보이다 show *one's* surprise; look surprised / 그것을 들었을 때 그 사람 부모의 ～은 어떠했을까 How surprised his parents were when they heard it!

**놀란가슴** a startled 〔frightened〕 mind. ¶ 자라 보고 ～ 소댕 보고 놀란다 《속담》 "Once bit(ten), twice shy." *or* A burnt child dreads the fire.

**놀랍다** ①《놀랄 만하다》(be) amazing; surprising. ¶ 놀랍게도 to *one's* surprise 〔astonishment, shock, dismay〕. ②《경탄할 만하다》(be) wonderful; remarkable; marvelous; admirable; astonishing; astounding; amazing; fantastic; fabulous. ¶ 놀라운 사건 a remarkable incident; an eye-opener《미》/ 놀라운 사람 a wonderful man / 놀라운 재간〔솜씨〕 amazing talent 〔skill〕/ 놀라운 기억력 a remarkable 〔an astonishing〕 memory / …은 놀라운 일이 못 된다 It is no wonder that…. / 이 약의 효험이 ~ This drug works wonders. / 놀랍게도 그는 그 일을 하룻밤 사이에 해치웠다 The marvel is that he accomplished the task in a single night.

**놀래다** 《놀라게 하다》 surprise; astonish; amaze; startle; 《충격을 주다》 shock; give 《*a person*》 a start; 《겁나게 하다》 frighten; terrify; scare. ¶ 세상을 ~ startle the world / 아무를 (깜짝) ~ knock the breath out of *a person;* take *a person's* breath away / 자네 나를 놀래는군 You amaze me! / 그녀의 돌연한 죽음이 나를 놀랬다 I was shocked by her sudden death. / 갑작스런 소음이 우리를 놀랬다 We were frightened 〔scared〕 at a sudden noise. / 너를 놀래 줄 일이 있다 I have a surprise for you. / 놀래 드려 죄송합니다 I am sorry for alarming you.

**놀리다** ①《놀게 하다》 let 〔have, make〕 《*someone*》 play. ¶ 어린애들을 집안에서 ~ let 〔have〕 the children play indoors / 아이를 밖에 데리고 나가 ~ take a child out for play.
②《방치·쉬게 하다》 have 〔leave〕 《*a person, a thing*》 idle; leave 《*a thing*》 unused. ¶ 땅을 ~ keep a land idle / 공장을 ~ leave a factory idle 〔unused〕/ 돈을 ~ have *one's* money lying idle / 아무를 한동안 ~ leave *a person* idle for a while; give *a person* some days off / 나는 너를 놀려 둘 처지가 못 된다 I cannot (afford to) have you idle.
③《조롱하다》 tease; make fun of 《*a person*》; play a joke on 《*a person*》; banter; poke fun at; 《구어》 kid. ¶ 고양이를 ~ tease a cat / 여자를 ~ chaff with a woman / 그들은 내 시골 말투를 놀렸다 They made fun of my provincial accent. / 너 나를 놀리는 거지 You must be kidding me. / 사람을 놀리는 것도 분수가 있지 There is a limit in befooling one. / 그는 내 요리를 칭찬했지만, 실은 놀리고 있었다 He praised my cooking, but he was pulling my leg. / 놀리지 마라. 나는 진지하니까 Don't make fun of me. I'm serious. *or* Don't be kidding. I'm serious.
④《조종하다》 manipulate; handle; manage; twist 《*a person*》 round *one's* little finger. ¶ 인형을 ~ manipulate 〔work〕 a puppet / 아무를 제 마음대로 ~ pull the wires 〔strings〕 of *a person* / 뒤에서 ~ pull the strings 〔wires〕 (behind the scenes).
⑤《움직이다》 move; set 〔put〕 in motion; operate 《a machine》. ¶ 손발을 ~ move 〔work〕 *one's* arms and legs / 입을 ~ move *one's* lips; talk; chatter / 입 좀 작작 놀려라 Don't talk rubbish. *or* Stop your nonsense.
⑥ 《돈놀이》 lend out money; loan; lend money at interest. ¶ 5푼 이자로 돈을 ~ lend money at five percent interest.

**놀림** banter; teasing; kidding; ridicule. ¶ 반~조로 (half) in fun; half teasingly; banteringly.
◉ ~감, ~가마리, ~거리 a laughingstock; a butt of ridicule: ~거리가 되다 become a laughingstock 〔a butt of ridicule〕/ 그는 그의 학급의 ~거리가 되었다 He made himself the laughingstock of his class. *or* He was laughed at by everyone in his class.

**놀부심사**(一心思) wickedness; ill-naturedness; cross-grainedness.

**놀아나다** ①《바람을 피우다》 lead a dissipated life; become a playboy; indulge in dissipation 〔fast living〕. ¶ 놀아난 계집 a dissipated 〔loose〕 woman / 얌전하던 그가 놀아나기 시작했다 He used to be so well-behaved but now he has started on the life of a playboy. ②《남의 장단에》 play into another's hands. ¶ 아무의 장단에 ~ dance to 〔after〕 *a person's* tune 〔pipe〕; move at *a person's* beck.

**놀아먹다** 《놀고 먹다》 lead an idle life; idle *one's* time away; 《방탕하게 살다》 lead a dissipated life.

**놀음** play; merrymaking; a spree; a good time; fun; (good) sport. ~하다 play; make merry; go on a spree; have fun 〔a good time〕. ◉ ~판 the scene of a spree; merrymaking.

**놀음차** a tip; a gratuity; gratuities given entertainers at a party.

**놀이** ①《유희》 play. ~하다 play. ¶ 술래잡기 ~를 하다 play tag; play hide=

and-seek 《*with*》. ② 《행락》 an outing; a junket; a picnic; a pleasure trip; holiday-making; an excursion. ～하다 picnic; make an excursion 《to》. ¶ 단풍～를 가다 go maple-viewing. ③ 《오락》 a game. ～하다 play 〔have〕 (a game). ¶ ～ 기분으로 하다 do 《*something*》 (partly) for pleasure 〔fun, diversion〕 / 은행 ～를 하다 play at banks. ◉ ～터 an outing place; a pleasure resort. 놀잇배 a pleasure boat.

**놀이꾼** a merrymaker; a junketer; a person on 〔a member of〕 an outing; a picnicker; a holidayer; an excursionist.

**놀치다** big waves rise 〔billow up〕 roughly; the water grows rough. ¶ 놀치는 바다 raging waves; rough waters.

**놈** ① a fellow; a chap 《영》; a guy; a fish.

> **용법** **fellow** 통상 앞에 형용사를 수반하여 친밀·경멸의 감정을 나타내어 「…한 놈〔녀석〕」의 뜻이 됨: a good 〔poor〕 fellow (좋은〔가엾은〕 놈). **chap** fellow와 같은 쓰임새와 뜻을 가짐. 주로 《영》에서 boy, man, fellow 대신으로 쓰임: a nice chap (좋은 놈). **guy** 《미구어》로 fellow와 같은 쓰임새와 뜻을 가진 말: A nice guy, but a slow learner. (좋은 놈이지만 머리가 둔하다). **fish** 앞에 형용사를 수반하며 「…한 놈」이란 경멸적인 뜻으로 쓰임: a cool fish (뻔뻔스런 놈), a queer fish (괴상한 놈). 이 밖에도 나쁜 뜻의 형용사를 수반하여 「…한 놈」이란 의미를 나타내는 낱말에는 an unsavory *character* (고약한 놈) / a bad *egg* (나쁜 놈) / a dirty *bastard* (더러운 놈) / a poor *wretch* (불쌍한 놈) 등이 있다.

¶ 참으로 바보스런 놈이군 What a stupid guy 〔fellow〕! / 놈은 아직 그것을 모른다 He still doesn't know it. / 난 저런 놈이 질색이다 I hate that fellow. ② 《동물·물건》 a thing; one; a damn thing 〔one〕. ¶ 암놈 a female one / 그 놈의 말 that damn horse / 저 흰 놈을 주시오 Give me that white one.

**놈팡이** ① ⇨ 놈 ①. ② 《실업자·건달》 a jobless person; a bum; a loafer; 《여자의 남자》 a girl's boyfriend; a gigolo.

**놋** brass. ◉ 놋그릇 brass tableware; brassware. 놋대야 a brass basin. 놋대접 a brass bowl. 놋요강 a brass chamber pot. 놋점 a brassware shop.

**놋쇠** brass. ⇨ 놋. ¶ ～로 만든 brazen. ◉ ～세공 brass-work: ～ 세공인 a brass-smith.

**놋좆**(櫓—) a rowlock; an oarlock; an oar pivot; a thole(pin).

**농**(弄) ① 《장난》 sport; fun. ¶ 농으로 for fun; out of fun; in sport / 농을 좋아하다 be fond of fun / 농으로 한 말이니 성낼 것 없다 Don't get angry.—I said it just for fun. ② ⇨ 농담.

**농**(膿) pus; purulent matter. ⇨ 고름[1].

**농**(籠) ① 《버들채 함》 a wicker basket; (wicker) trunk 〔suitcase〕. ② ＝ 장롱.

**농가**(農家) 《집》 a farmhouse; 《가정》 a farm household; a farm family. ¶ 그는 ～에서 자랐다 He was brought up on a farm. / ～는 지금이 가장 바쁜 시기다 This is the busiest season for farmers. ◉ ～보조금 farm subsidies. ～ 소득원 개발 촉진법 the Rural Household Income Promotion Law. ～월령가(月令歌) "*Nongga Wollyong-ga*", the Farmers Song of the Seasons.

**농간**(弄奸) a trick; wiles; a sly artifice; a wicked design. ¶ ～을 부리다 play tricks; carry out a wicked design / 쉽사리 아무의 ～에 넘어가다 fall an easy victim to *a person's* trick / 아무래도 무슨 ～이 있다 I suspect some tricks. / 그 정치가는 당선을 위해 온갖 ～을 다 부렸다 The politician used all his wiles to win the election.

**농갈색**(濃褐色) deep 〔dark〕 brown. ¶ ～의 deep 〔dark〕 brown.

**농게**(籠—) 〖동물〗 a sand crab.

**농경**(農耕) agriculture; farming; tillage. ¶ ～의 agricultural; farming / ～용 트랙터 an agricultural tractor. ◉ ～민족 an agricultural people 〔tribe〕. ～법 agricultural techniques. ～사회 an agrarian society. ～시대 the Agricultural Age. ～지 farmland.

**농공상**(農工商) 《일》 agriculture, industry and commerce; 《사람》 farmers, manufacturers and tradesmen.

**농과**(農科) the agricultural department (학부); an agricultural course (과정). ¶ ～를 수료하다 complete a course in agriculture. ◉ ～대학 a college of agriculture.

**농구**(農具) farm 〔agricultural〕 implements 〔appliances〕; farming tools.

**농구**(籠球) basketball. ◉ ～공 a basketball. ～선수 a basketball player; a cager 《미속어》. ～코트 a basketball court. ～화 basketball shoes. 대한 ～협회 the Korea Amateur Basketball Association.

**농군**(農軍) a farm laborer; a peasant;

a farmer; [총칭] the peasantry.

**농기**(農期) the farming season.

**농기계**(農機械) farming machines.

**농기구**(農器具) = 농구(農具).

**농노**(農奴) a serf; serfdom (신분).
◉ ～해방 the emancipation of serfs.

**농단**(壟斷) monopolization; assumption of an exclusive privilege 〔right〕. ～하다 monopolize. ¶ 이익을 ～하다 monopolize the profit.

**농담**(弄談) 《우스갯소리》 a joke; a jest; a wisecrack (재치 있는); 《놀리다》 chaff; banter; 《장난》 a prank; a trick. ～하다 joke; crack 〔make〕 a joke; jest; banter; poke fun 《at》.
¶ ～으로 as 〔for〕 a joke; for fun; out of fun; in 〔for〕 sport / ～조로 jestingly; playfully; jokingly; in jest / 반 ～으로 half in jest 〔joke〕 / ～은 그만하고 joking 〔jesting〕 apart; jokes aside; to be serious / ～으로 돌리다 take 〔treat〕 《*something*》 as a joke / ～을 주고받다 exchange pleasantries / ～을 건네다 make a joke 《at》; poke fun 《at》; pass a pleasantry 《to》 / ～을 곧이듣다 take a joke seriously / ～은 집어치워 Stop joking! *or* None of your jokes! *or* Quit your kidding! / ～이 아니다 It is no joke. *or* I mean what I say. *or* It's no joking matter. / ～이실 테죠 You must be joking! *or* You don't mean it, do you! / 그저 ～으로 말했을 뿐일세 I said so only in fun. *or* I meant it for a joke. / 그는 재치있게 ～을 받아넘긴다 He knows how to take a joke. / ～이 진담이 된다 What was said as a joke comes true. / ～이 지나치다 You carry your joke too far. / ～ 속에 진담이 있다 Many a true word is spoken in jest.

**농담**(濃淡) light and shade; shading; relative lightness or darkness. ¶ 색의 ～ shades of color / ～을 나타내다 shade 《a painting》. ◉ ～도(度) (the) depth (of color). ～법 shading; chiaroscuro.

**농도**(濃度) density; thickness; 〖화학〗 concentration; 〖사진〗 intensity. ¶ 바닷물의 염분 ～ the concentration of salt in sea water / 빛깔의 ～ the depth 〔strength〕 of color / 차〔커피〕의 ～ the strength of tea 〔coffee〕. ◉ ～계 〖사진〗 a densitometer.

**농들다**(膿―) maturate; form pus; suppurate.

**농땡이** 《사람》 an idle 〔a lazy〕 fellow; a lazybones; a sluggard; 《행위》 idleness; laziness. ¶ ～부리다 be idle 〔lazy〕; idle away *one's* time; be neglectful of 《*one's* duty》; slow down / ～부리지 말고 열심히 일해라 Don't be lazy! Work harder! / 너무 바빠서 ～ 칠 시간이 없다 I'm too busy to be idle.

**농락**(籠絡) trifling; toying. ～하다 trifle 〔sport, toy〕 《with》; make sport 〔a fool〕 of 《*a person*》; play fast and loose with 《*a person*》. ¶ 정조를 ～하다 trifle with a woman's virtue / 돈으로 ～하다 entice 《*a person*》 with money / 남의 감정을 ～하다 play on 《*a person's*》 feeling / 남자에게 ～당하다 fall a prey to a man's lust.

**농림**(農林) agriculture and forestry.
◉ ～부〔부 장관〕 the Ministry 〔Minister〕 of Agriculture and Forestry: ～부 차관 the Vice Minister of Agriculture and Forestry. ～사업 agricultural and forestry industries. ～정책 a policy toward agriculture and forestry. ～학교 an agriculture and forestry school. ～행정 administration of agriculture and forestry.

**농마**(農馬) a plow horse.

**농막**(農幕) a farm(er's) hut.

**농무**(農務) 《농사일》 agricultural affairs; farming; 《행정》 agricultural administration. ◉ ～부 《미》 the Department of Agriculture. ～장관 the Secretary of Agriculture.

**농무**(濃霧) a dense 〔thick, heavy〕 fog. ¶ ～로 교통이 마비되었다 The traffic was paralyzed by heavy fog. ◉ ～주의보 a dense fog warning. ～경적 a fog horn.

**농민**(農民) a farmer; a peasant; a farm hand; [총칭] the farming population; the peasantry.

> (용법) **farmer** 본래는 「농장을 경영하는 사람」의 뜻이었으나, 현재 미국에서는 「일반 농민」을 지칭하는 데도 쓰인다. **peasant** 「소작농」의 뜻으로 현재 미국에서는 쓰지 않는 말. 옛날의 농민이나 발전도상국의 가난한 농민을 말한다. **farm hand** 농장 경영자인 farmer에 의해 고용되어 일하는 농장 노동자.

◉ ～문학 peasant 〔agrarian〕 literature. ～사회 a farming 〔rural〕 community. ～생활 peasant life. ～운동 an agrarian 〔a peasant〕 movement.

**농번기**(農繁期) the (busy) farming season; the farmers' busy season.
◉ ～휴가 《학교의》 the school holidays in the (busy) farming season; 《군대

의》 a leave in the (busy) farming season. 「(methods).

**농법**(農法) agricultural techniques

**농병**(農兵) agrarian soldiers. 「chick.

**농병아리** 〖조류〗 a (little) grebe; a dab-

**농본주의**(農本主義) physiocracy; the principle of basing a country's economy on agriculture; the belief that agriculture forms the basis of the nation's economic and social life. ◉ ~자 a physiocrat.

**농부**(農夫) 《자작농》 a farmer; 《품팔이》 a farm hand; a farm laborer.

**농사**(農事) farming; farm work; agricultural affairs; husbandry. ~짓다 engage in farming; do 「farming (farm work). ◉ ~꾼 a farmer. ~시험장 an agricultural experiment station. ~일 farm work. ~철 the farming season.

**농산물**(農産物) farm (agricultural) products; farm produce; the crops. ¶ ~이 많다 be rich in farm produts. ◉ ~가격 farm prices: ~가격 유지 제도 a system for shoring up farm prices / ~가격 지지 제도 the farm-price-support system. ~전시회 an agricultural products exhibition.

**농성**(籠城) ① 《성안에서》 holding a castle. ~하다 be besieged; hold a castle; be shut up. ¶ ~군 a besieged army. ② 《투쟁의 방법》 a sit-in; a sit-down 《strike》. ~하다 go on a stay-in (sit-in) 《demonstration》. ¶ ~투쟁을 하다 go on (resort to) a stay-in strike; stage a sit-in demonstration.

**농수산**(農水産) agriculture and fisheries. ◉ ~물 agricultural and marine products; agro-fishery products (goods); agro-marine items: ~물의 가격 안정 the price stabilization of agricultural and fisheries products / ~물 수출전시관 the agro-fishery products export pavilion / ~물 유통 공사 the Agricultural and Fishery Marketing Corporation (생략 AFMC) / ~물 종합 도매시장 a wholesale market dealing in agro-fisheries products.

**농아**(聾啞) deafness and dumbness; 《사람》 a deaf-and-dumb person; a deaf-mute. ◉ ~교육 education of the deaf and dumb. ~학교 a school for the deaf and dumb.

**농악**(農樂) instrumental music of peasants; a farm music. ◉ ~대 a farmer's folk band.

**농액**(濃液) a thick (ropy) liquid; 《농축 용액》 a concentrated solution.

**농약**(農藥) agricultural chemicals (insecticide). ¶ ~을 뿌리다 spray (dust) 《vegetables》 with agricultural chemicals / 인체에 해롭지 않은 ~을 개발하다 develop agricultural chemicals that do not cause damage to the human body. ◉ ~분무기 an agricultural chemicals (insecticide) sprayer. ~살포 《비행기에서의》 crop(-)dusting (spraying). ~살포기 a crop duster. ~중독 poisoning by agricultural chemicals; parathion poisoning (파라티온의).

**농양**(膿瘍) 〖의학〗 an abscess.

**농어** 〖어류〗 a sea bass; a perch.

**농어민**(農漁民) farmers and fishermen. ¶ ~소득 증대 사업 a project to increase the income of farmers and fishermen.

**농어촌**(農漁村) farming and fishing villages (communities). ◉ ~개발 공사 the Agriculture and Fishery Development Corporation (생략 A.F.D.C.). ~학생 특별 전형제 《학교 입학의》 a special admission program for children of farmers and fisheries. ~후계자 the future leaders for farming and (or) fishing communities.

**농업**(農業) agriculture; farming; agricultural (farming) industry. ¶ 집약(조방) ~ intensive (extensive) agriculture / 집단 ~ collective farming / ~의 agricultural; farming / ~에 종사하다 engage in agriculture (farming); be a farmer; follow (hold) the plow / ~용 기계 a farm machine; agricultural (farm) machinery / ~ 보조금 agricultural subsidies. ◉ ~개혁 agrarian reforms. ~경영법 agronomics. ~경제 agricultural economy: ~경제학(과) (the department of) agricultural economics. ~ 고등학교 an agricultural high school. ~공동경영 cooperative management of agriculture. ~공학 agricultural engineering. ~관련산업 agribusiness. ~교육 agricultural education. ~국 an agricultural (a farming) country. ~기계화 mechanization of farming. ~기상학 agrometeorology. ~기술 agricultural technology; farming techniques: ~기술 교류 센터 the Agricultural Technology Cooperation Center (생략 ATCC). ~기술자 a agrotechnician. ~기후학 agroclimatology. ~노동자 a farm worker (laborer); a farmhand. ~생물학 agrobiology. ~생산 agricultural (farm) production (output). ~생산성 《increase》 agricultural productivity. ~시험장 an agricultural experiment station. ~용수 agricultural water: ~용수 개발계획 an agricultural water resources development project. ~인구 the farming 〔agricultural〕 population. ~정책 an agricultural 〔a farm〕 policy. ~학교 an agricultural school. ~혁명 an agricultural revolution. ~ 협동 조합 an agricultural cooperative (association); a farmer's cooperative: ~ 협동 조합 중앙회 the National Agricultural Cooperative Federation (생략 NACF).

**농예**(農藝) ① 《기술》 agricultural technology; husbandry. ② 《농업과 원예》 farming and gardening; agriculture and horticulture. ◉ ~화학 agricultural chemistry.

**농우**(農牛) a plow ox.

**농원**(農園) a farm; a plantation. ⇨ 농장.

**농익다**(濃—) get overripe.

**농자천하지대본**(農者天下之大本) Agriculture is 「the foundation of a nation 〔the basis of national existence〕.

**농작**(農作) cultivation of land; tillage of the soil; farming. ~하다 till. ◉ ~물 the crops; farm produce 〔products〕: ~물을 해치다 injure the crops; do damage to the crops / 올해는 ~물이 잘되었다 The harvest has turned out well this year.

**농장**(農場) a farm; 《대규모의》 a plantation (목화·커피 등의); 《목장》 a ranch. ¶ 집단〔실험〕 ~ a collective 〔an experimental〕 farm / ~에서 일하다 work on a farm / ~을 경영하다 run a farm. ◉ ~경영 farm management. ~관리인 a farm bailiff. ~노동자 a farm worker 〔laborer〕; a farmhand. ~인도가격 a price ex farm. ~주 a farmer; the proprietor of a farm 〔plantation〕.

**농정**(農政) farm policy; agricultural administration.

**농지**(農地) farmland; agricultural 〔farming〕 land. ◉ ~개량 improvement of farmland. ~개발 development of farmland. ~개혁 an agrarian 〔agricultural land〕 reform. ~법 the Farm Land Law. ~세 farmland tax. ~소유 상한 the ceiling on the ownership of farmland; the limit of farmland ownership.

**농지거리**(弄—) joking; bantering; jesting; poking fun. ~하다 joke; banter; jest; poke fun 《at》; pass pleasantries 《with》.

**농촌**(農村) a farm(ing) 〔an agricultural〕 village; 《사회》 a rural community; 《지역》 a rural 〔an agricultural〕 district. ¶ ~의 rural; agricultural; agrarian / ~의 전화(電化) electrification of agricultural villages / ~의 피폐 the impoverishment of rural communities. ◉ ~개선 운동 a movement to uplift the rural society. ~경제 rural economy: 한국 ~ 경제 연구원 the Korea Rural Economics Institute (생략 KREI). ~계몽 enlightenment of the farmers. ~고리채 farmer's usurious credit. ~문제 an agrarian problem. ~봉사 활동 the voluntary activities for rural communities: 학생들의 ~ 봉사 활동 students' voluntary service for rural communities 《during the summer vacation》. ~사회학 rural sociology. ~생활 farm life; life in rural communities. ~인구 the rural population. ~일손 지원 센터 the support center for helping hands to farmers. ~지대 a farm area; a rural district. ~진흥 development 〔advancement〕 of an agricultural community: ~ 진흥청 the Rural Development Administration. ~청년 farm youth(s).

**농축**(濃縮) enrichment; concentration; 〚약〛 incrassation. ~하다 concentrate; enrich; condense. ¶ ~ 맥주는 온 세상 양조업자들의 꿈이다 Beer concentrate is the dream of brewers all over the world. ◉ ~공장 an enrichment plant. ~오렌지 주스 orange juice concentrate; concentrated orange juice. ~우라늄 enriched uranium. ~우유 condensed milk.

**농축산**(農畜産) agriculture and stockbreeding; agro-livestock. ◉ ~물 agricultural and stockbreeding products; agro-livestock products.

**농축수산물**(農畜水産物) farm-livestock-fisheries products.

**농탕치다**(弄蕩—) flirt 〔dally, coquet, fondle, sport〕 with 《*a person*》; be jolly with 《a girl》; bill and coo (애인끼리).

**농토**(農土) farmland; agricultural 〔farming〕 land; cropland. ¶ 메마른 ~ a barren 〔sterile〕 land. ◉ ~확장 expansion of farmland.

**농하다**(弄—) ① 《실없는 장난》 play a prank 〔practical joke, trick〕 《on》. ② 《궤변 따위》 talk nonsense 〔rot, rubbish〕. ¶ 궤변을 ~ quibble; use sophistry; chop logic 《with *a person*》.

**농학**(農學) (the science of) agriculture. ¶ ~의 agricultural. ◉ ~과〔부〕 an agricultural department. ~사〔석사, 박사〕《사람》 a bachelor 〔master, doctor〕 of agriculture; 《학위》 Bachelor 〔Master, Doctor〕 of Agriculture (생략 B. 〔M., D.〕 Agr.). ~자 an agricultur(al)ist.

**농한기**(農閑期) the farmer's slack 〔leisure〕 season; the off-season 〔quiet season〕 for farmers.

**농혈증**(膿血症) 〖의학〗 pyemia; pyohemia.

**농협**(農協) ⇨ 농업 협동 조합.

**농화**(濃化) thickening; concentration. ~하다 thicken; concentrate. ◉ ~유(油) thickened oil. ~제(劑) thickener.

**농후**(濃厚) thickness; density. ~하다 (be) thick; dense; heavy; rich. ¶ ~한 색채 a rich 〔deep〕 color / ~해지다 thicken; deepen; get 〔become〕 dense 〔denser〕; condense / 전쟁이 일어날 기미가 ~하다 There is 「a strong possibility 〔a real danger〕 of war. / 그는 수뢰 혐의가 ~하다 He is strongly suspected of bribery. ◉ ~비료〔사료〕 concentrated fertilizer 〔fodder, feed〕.

**높낮이** 《고저》 high and low; 《음성의》 pitch; 《기복》 unevenness. ⇨ 고저.

**높다** ① 《높이가》 (be) high; tall; lofty; exalted; elevated. ¶ 높은 산 a high 〔lofty〕 mountain / 높은 건물 a tall 〔high〕 building / 아주 ~ be sky-high / 파도가 ~ The waves are high. / 에베레스트는 세계에서 가장 높은 산이다 Mt. Everest is the highest mountain in the world. / 그녀의 코는 꽤 ~ She has a 「long 〔prominent〕 nose.

② 《지위·신분·이상 등이》 (be) high; lofty; noble. ¶ 높은 지위 a high position 〔rank〕 / 신분이 높은 사람 《지위가》 a person of high position 〔status〕 《태생이》 a person of high 〔noble〕 birth / 높은 이상 a lofty ideal / 그녀의 숙부는 사회적 지위가 ~ Her uncle has 〔holds〕 a high social position. / 그의 뜻은 너무 ~ He sets his sights too high. *or* He aims too high.

③ 《물가가》 (be) dear; high; expensive; costly. ¶ 높은 생활비 a high cost of living / 서울의 식료품 가격은 뉴욕의 두 배 가까이나 ~ The price of food in Seoul is nearly twice as high as that in New York.

④ 《소리가》 (be) high-pitched; loud. ¶ 높은 음성 a high-pitched voice; a high voice / 높은 소리로 in a loud voice / 좀 소리를 높여 말하시오 Speak aloud, please. *or* Louder, please!

⑤ 《수치·율이》 (be) high. ¶ 높은 비율 a high rate / 도수(가) 높은 안경 strong 〔thick〕 glasses / 높은 이자로 at a high interest / 온도가 ~ the temperature is high / 열이 ~ have a high fever / 내 혈압은 정상보다 훨씬 ~ My blood pressure is far higher than normal.

⑥《명성이》 (be) high; 《평판 등이》 (be) widely known. ¶ 명성이 높은 well-known; famous / 악명이 높은 notorious; infamous; scandalous / 그녀의 그림은 프랑스에서 평판이 높은 것 같다 Her pictures seem to be held in high esteem in France.

⑦ 《수준이》 ¶ 높은 과학 기술 a high level of technology / 당신은 그림에 관해 눈이 높으시군요 You have an appreciative 〔a sharp〕 eye for good paintings. / 이 문제는 내게는 수준이 좀 ~ This question is a little too difficult for me.

**높다랗다** (be) rather high; lofty; towering. ¶ 현기증이 날 정도의 높이 a dizzy height.

**높아지다** rise; be raised; be elevated; become higher; swell; up 《속어》; increase (증가); 《위험 등이》 build (up). ¶ 감정이 ~ become excited / 명성이 ~ rise in fame / 물가가 ~ rise in price; prices go up / 열이 ~ *one's* temperature rises 〔goes up〕 / 지위가 ~ rise 〔be advanced〕 in position; rise 〔be raised〕 to a higher position / 그런 일로 속을 썩이면 혈압이 높아진다 A lot of worrying like that will send your blood pressure up.

**높은음자리표** 〖음악〗 a G clef; a treble 〔violin〕 clef.

**높이**[1] ① 《높은 정도》 height; altitude (고도). ¶ ~가 다섯 자다 have a height of 5 *cha;* be five *cha* high / 8천 피트의 ~를 날다 fly at a height 〔an altitude〕 of 8,000 feet / 그 ~에서는 공기가 희박해진다 The air grows thin in that altitude. ② 《소리》 pitch (음정); tone (가락); loudness (음량). ¶ 곡조의 ~ the pitch of a tone 〔tune〕 / 음성의 ~ the height 〔loudness〕 of a voice.

**높이**[2] 〔부사〕 ① 〔일반적〕 high; highly; aloft (드높이). ¶ 하늘 ~ (날다) (fly) high up in the air 〔sky〕 / ~ 뛰다 jump high / 건초를 ~ 쌓다 「heap up 〔stack〕 hay high / 손을 ~ 들다 raise *one's* hand high / ~ 평가하다 rate 〔appraise〕 high; value highly; esteem (존중) / 뜻을 ~ 갖다 aim high. ② 《소리를》 in a high pitch; loud; loudly; in a loud voice. ¶ 소리 ~ 노래하다 sing in a loud 〔high〕 voice.

**높이다** ① 《높이를》 make high 〔higher〕; heighten; elevate; raise. ¶ 담을 ～ make a wall higher; raise a wall / 둑을 ～ build a bank higher; raise a bank. ② 《정도를》 raise; lift; promote; heighten 《an effect》; elevate 《*one's* ideal》; improve 《the quality》; enhance 《the value》; ennoble (품격); boost (전압). ¶ 사기를 ～ raise 〔boost〕 morale / 언성을 ～ raise *one's* voice 《in anger》/ 정도를〔수준을〕 ～ raise 〔lift〕 the level 〔standard〕 / 가치를 ～ enhance 〔increase, heighten〕 the value 《of》/ 지위를 ～ promote in rank; raise 〔elevate〕 《*a person's*》 position / 비율을 ～ raise the rate / 품질을 ～ raise 〔improve〕 the quality / 품격을 ～ elevate *one's* character / 교양을 ～ cultivate 《*oneself*》. ③ 《공경·존중하다》 respect; revere; venerate; honor; do honor 《to》. ¶ 아무를 신으로 ～ deify *a person* / 말을 ～ use honorifics; speak to 《*a person*》 in honorifics.

**높이뛰기** the (running) high jump.

**높임말** an honorific (term). ⇨ 경어(敬語).

**높직이** rather 〔slightly〕 high; rather 「〔somewhat〕 loud.

**높직하다** (be) rather high; slightly elevated; rather loud (목소리가).

**놓다**[1] ① (***a***) 《두다》 put 《down》; place; lay (옆으로); set (세워서). ¶ 책상 위에 꽃병을 ～ put a vase on the desk / 상자를 내려～ put the box down / 식탁 위에 접시를 조심스레 ～ place the dishes carefully on the table / 책상 위에 스탠드를 ～ set the lamp on the desk / 달걀을 살그머니 식탁 위에 놓다 lay the eggs gently on the table / 어디에 놓을까요 Where shall I put it? / 다 쓴 다음에 제자리에 놓으시오 Put it back where it was when you are through. (***b***) 《하던 것에서 손을》 lay 〔put〕 down; down. ¶ 붓을 ～ put 〔lay〕 down *one's* pen; stop writing; close 《*one's* letter》. ② 《남겨두다》 leave (behind). ¶ 놓고 오다〔가다〕 leave 《*a thing*》 behind (*one*); leave 《*a thing*》 for 《*a person*》/ 명함을 놓고 가다 leave *one's* card / 그가 너에게 쪽지를 놓고 갔다 He left a note for you. / 장갑을 어디다 놓고 왔을까 Where have I left my gloves? ③ 《방치하다》 leave; let; keep (어떤 상태로). ⇨ 놓아두다. ④ 《잡은 것을》 let 《it》 go 〔off, loose〕; let go 《of》; release. ⇨ 놓아주다. ¶ (잡았던) 손을 ～ take *one's* hand off; let go *one's* hold 《of, on》; release *one's* hold 《of》/ 로프를 놓지마라 Don't let go of the rope. / 잡은 가지에서 손을 ～ let go *one's* grip on a branch / (차의) 핸들을 ～ take *one's* hands off the wheel / 내 팔을 놓아라 Let go of my arm. *or* Take your hand(s) off my arm. ⑤ 《마음을》 ease; set *one's* mind at ease. ¶ 마음을 ～ feel easy; feel at ease; set *one's* mind at rest; 《방심하다》 be inattentive; relax *one's* attention 〔guard〕 / 한시름 ～ feel relieved 〔reassured〕; stop worrying 《about》. ⑥ 《불을》 set fire to 《a shed》; set 《a house》 on fire. ¶ 집에 불을 ～ set fire to a house. ⑦ 《발사하다》 fire; shoot; discharge. ¶ 총을 (한 방) ～ fire a gun; fire 〔let off〕 one shot. ⑧ 《중간에 사람을》 put in 《as an intermediary》; send 《*a person*》. ¶ 사람을 놓아 교섭하다 negotiate through a third party / 사람을 놓아 수소문하다 get information through an agent; send a person for information. ⑨ 《기르다》 keep 《a dog》; raise 《sheep》; rear 《silkworms》. ⇨ 기르다. ⑩ 《심다·가꾸다》 sow; plant; grow; cultivate. ¶ 참외를 ～ sow melon seeds; grow melon. ⑪ 《덫을》 set 〔lay〕 《a trap》. ¶ 덫을 ～ trap; lay 〔set〕 a trap 〔snare〕 《for》. ⑫ 《주사·침을》 apply acupuncture; syringe. ¶ 주사를 ～ inject; give 〔apply〕 an injection / 침을 ～ needle; apply acupuncture 《on》. ⑬ 《무늬·수를》 adorn with. ¶ 무늬를 ～ provide 〔decorate with〕 a pattern / 수를 ～ embroider; do embroidery. ⑭ 《셈을》 calculate; reckon; figure; compute; estimate. ¶ 주판을 ～ count 〔reckon〕 on the abacus / 비용을 놓아보다 estimate the expense. ⑮ 《값을》 bid; name; offer (a price). ¶ 값을 ～ bid 〔name〕 a price / 이 피아노 값을 얼마에 놓으시겠습니까 How much will you offer for this piano? ⑯ (***a***) 《돈·빚을》 lend; loan (at interest) 《미》. ¶ 돈을 4푼 이자로 ～ lend money at four percent interest. (***b***) 《세를》 lease; hire; let; rent. ¶ 땅을 세 ～ put out land to lease / 방을 세～ rent a room. ⑰ 《속력을》 put on (speed); increase (the speed). ¶ 속력을 ～ increase 〔gather〕 speed; speed up / 시속 120km의 속도를 놓고 차를 달렸다 I drove at (a speed of) 120 kilometers an hour. ⑱ 《설비·가설하다》 install 《a tele-

phone》; lay on 《water》; 《다리를》 build 〔throw, construct〕 《a bridge》 across 〔over〕 《a river》. ¶ 수도를 ～ have water pipes laid; have water supplied / 철도를 ～ lay down a railroad 〔railway 《영》〕.
⑲ 《기타》 ¶ 석 점을 ～ 《바둑에서》 accept a three-stone handicap / 엄포를 ～ threaten; make a threat / 말을 ～ relax *one's* honorifics; talk plainly / 훼방을 ～ disturb 〔hinder, impede〕 《*a person*》 in 《*his* work》 / 퇴짜를 ～ give 〔show, turn〕 the cold shoulder to 《*a person*》; turn down.

**놓다**[2] [조동사] ① 《…해 두다》 ¶ 창문을 열어〔닫아〕 ～ keep the window(s) open 〔shut〕 / 논을 갈아 놓고 비를 기다린다 We have finished plowing the paddy field and are waiting for rain. / 표를 미리 사 놓으셔요 Buy the ticket in advance (now). ② 《…한 상태》 ¶ 매우 위태로운 상황에 놓여 있는 지구 the earth placed in a critical situation / 길이 너무 질어 놓아서 걸어 가기가 힘들다 The road is so sloppy that it is very hard to walk on.

**놓아두다** ① 《어떤 자리에》 lay; put; leave (behind). ¶ 책을 마루 위에 ～ lay 〔leave〕 a book on the floor / 과자를 먹지 않고 ～ leave cake uneaten / 자동차를 길에 ～ leave *one's* car on the road / 나를 놓아두고 떠나지 마세요 Don't leave me behind. / 담뱃대를 책상 위에 놓아두고 왔다 I left my pipe on the table at home. / 그대로 (가만) 놓아두시오 Leave it as it is. ② 《가만두다》 leave 〔let〕 alone; let (it) be. ¶ 어린애를 제 마음대로 놀게 ～ leave a child alone and let him play / 시계를 만지지 말고 놓아두게 Leave the watch alone. / 제 마음대로 하게 그를 놓아두어라 Let him have his own way. ③ 《제쳐놓다》 lay 〔put〕 aside. ¶ 비상용으로 식량을 좀 따로 놓아두어라 Put aside part of your foods for emergency need.

**놓아먹다** be badly brought up; be ill=bred. ¶ 놓아먹은 자식 a wild 〔an ill=bred〕 boy.

**놓아먹이다** 《방목》 graze; pasture; put 《cattle》 to grass; give 《a dog》 free run of 《*one's* house》; keep 《a pig》 loose. ¶ 놓아먹인 말 [비유적] a wild guy; a man of nature; a "nature boy" / 놓아먹이는 닭 yard fowls; fowls ranging freely / 소를 ～ pasture cattle.

**놓아주다** free; set free; set at large; let 〔cast〕 loose; unloose; release; liberate; set at liberty. ¶ 새를 ～ set a bird free / 죄수를 ～ set a prisoner free; release a prisoner; give a prisoner his freedom / 잡았던 물고기를 ～ put the fish back (into the water).

**놓이다** ① 《물건이》 be put 〔placed, laid, set〕. ¶ 책상 위에 놓인 꽃병 a flower vase set on the table / 식탁에 놓여 있다 be set 〔placed〕 on the table. ② 《마음이》 feel 〔be〕 relieved; feel at ease; be relaxed. ¶ 마음이 ～ 《*one's* mind》 be set at ease; [사람이 주어] feel at ease; be relieved / 마음이 놓일 때가 없다 have no moment of ease.

**놓치다** miss; lose; fail to catch; drop; miss *one's* hold 《of》; let 《prisoner》 escape 〔get away〕; be given the slip 《of》; let 《an opportunity》 slip. ¶ 그릇을 ～ drop a dish; let a dish fall / 공을 ～ miss a ball; fail to catch a ball / 물고기를 ～ lose a fish; let a fish get away / 기차를 ～ miss *one's* train / 기회를 ～ miss an opportunity; let a chance go / 이 좋은 기회를 놓치지 마라 Don't miss this golden opportunity. / 나는 한마디도 놓치지 않으려고 주의해서 들었다 I listened attentively so as not to miss a single word. / 경찰관은 강도를 놓치고 말았다 The policeman lost track of the robber. / 놓친 물고기는 커 보이게 마련이다 The fish that got away is always big. / 자넨 그와 가까워질 수 있는 좋은 기회를 놓쳤다 You missed a good chance to get acquainted with him.

**뇌**(腦) a brain; 《지력·두뇌》 brains. ¶ 뇌의 cerebral / 뇌의 작용 cerebration; mental activity / 뇌를 쓰다 use 〔tax〕 *one's* brains; 《너무 쓰다》 overtax 〔rack〕 *one's* brains / 뇌 쓰는 일 brain 〔mental〕 work / 뇌의 손상을 입다 suffer brain damage / 지나친 공부로 뇌를 상하게 하다 damage *one's* brain by studying too much / 그녀는 뇌에 이상이 있다 She has some brain trouble. / 때로는 뇌도 쉬게 해야 한다 You must give your brains a rest at times.
◉ 뇌경색 (a) cerebral infarction. 뇌매독 syphilis of the brain. 뇌세포 a brain cell. 뇌수종 hydrocephalus; water on the brain. 뇌외과 brain 〔cerebral〕 surgery. 뇌좌상(挫傷) (a) brain 〔cerebral〕 contusion.

**뇌간**(腦幹) 〖해부〗 the brainstem.

**뇌격**(雷擊) 〖군사〗 attacking with torpedoes; a torpedo attack. ～하다 attack with torpedoes; torpedo. ◉ ～기(機)

a torpedo plane 〔bomber〕. ～전 torpedo warfare.

**뇌관**(雷管) a percussion 〔detonation〕 cap; a detonator. ◉ ～장치 a percussion lock. ～화약 percussion-powder.

**뇌까리다** repeat 〔reiterate〕 another's unpleasant remarks; harp on 《faults》.

**뇌다** ① 《가루를》 sift (through a finer-meshed sieve). ② 《같은 말을》 repeat; reiterate. ¶ 한 말을 뇌고 또 ～ say 《*a matter*》 over and over again; repeat *oneself;* harp on the same string.

**뇌동**(雷同) blind following; going with the stream. ⇨ 부화뇌동(附和雷同).

**뇌동맥경화**(腦動脈硬化) 〚의학〛 cerebral arteriosclerosis.

**뇌랗다** be sickly yellow.

**뇌리**(腦裡) 《in》 the brain; *one's* mind; *one's* memory. ¶ ～에 그리다 picture 《*something*》 in *one's* mind; imagine / ～에서 사라지지 않다 linger in *one's* mind; haunt *one's* memory; be always 〔ever〕 present in *one's* mind / ～에 떠오르다 come across *one's* mind; occur to *one* / ～에 새겨지다 be stamped 〔impressed〕 on *one's* memory.

**뇌막**(腦膜) 〚의학〛 (cerebral) meninges. ◉ ～염 meningitis; brain fever.

**뇌명**(雷鳴) a roll 〔peal, clap〕 of thunder; a thunderclap; the rumbling of thunder; 《천둥》 thunder.

**뇌문**(雷文·雷紋) 〚건축〛 a fret; a meander. ◉ ～세공 fretwork; fretting.

**뇌물**(賂物) a bribe; 《속어》 grease; palm oil; the golden 〔silver〕 key; 《입막음을 위한》 silence 〔hush〕 money. ¶ ～이 통하는 corruptible; bribable / ～이 안 통하는 incorruptible; unbribable / ～을 먹다 be bribed 《by》; receive 〔accept, take〕 a bribe / ～을 주다 offer 〔give〕 a bribe 《to》; bribe 《*a person*》; grease the hand 〔palm〕 of 《*a person*》 / ～로 매수하다 buy off 《*a person*》 / ～을 써서 잘 해내다 buy *one's* way out / ～로 비밀을 지키게 하다 bribe 《*a person*》 into secrecy / ～의 효과가 있었다 The bribe has worked. / 그는 나에게 ～을 주어 비밀 문서를 제공케 했다 He bribed me 「to give 〔into giving〕 him the secret documents. ◉ ～사건 a bribery 〔graft 《미》〕 case. ～수뢰 ⇨ 수회(收賄). ～증여자 a briber.

**뇌병**(腦病) a brain disease 〔affliction〕.

**뇌병원**(腦病院) =정신 병원(精神病院).

**뇌빈혈**(腦貧血) 〚의학〛 cerebral an(a)emia; anemia of the brain. ¶ ～을 일으키다 have an attack of cerebral anemia / 가끔 ～을 일으키다 be given to frequent fainting spells.

**뇌사**(腦死) brain death; cerebral death. ¶ ～상태의 brain-dead / ～환자로부터 심장이나 다른 장기를 이식하는 데 관한 가이드라인 guidelines on the transplantation of the heart and other organs from brain-dead patients / 의사는 그의 ～를 선언했다 The doctor pronounced him brain death. / ～문제에 관해서는 많은 논쟁이 있다 There are many controversies surrounding the issue of brain death.

◉ ～자 brain-dead people: ～자로부터의 장기 이식을 합법화하는 특별 법안 a special bill to legalize the transplant of human organs from the brain-dead people.

**뇌색전증**(腦塞栓症) 〚의학〛 cerebral embolism.

**뇌성**(雷聲) a peal 〔roll, roar〕 of thunder. ◉ ～대명(大名) worldwide fame; a name heard round the world. ～벽력 《have》 thunder and lightning.

**뇌성**(腦性) 〚의학〛 ¶ ～마비 cerebral palsy / ～마비의 spastic 《children》 / ～소아마비 cerebral infantile paralysis.

**뇌쇄**(惱殺) ～하다 charm; bewitch; fascinate; enchant; captivate. ¶ ～시키는 웃음 a smile that wins 《*a person's*》 heart away / 사람을 ～시킬 듯한 매력 (an) irresistible charm / 남자를 ～시키는 여자 a fascinating woman; an "it" girl / ～적인 눈초리로 보다 throw 〔cast〕 seductive glances 《at》; 《구어》 give 《*a person*》 the (glad) eye.

**뇌수**(腦髓) 〚해부〛 the brain; the encephalon (*pl.* -la).

**뇌수술**(腦手術) brain surgery; a surgical operation on the brain. ～하다 perform an operation on the brain.

**뇌신경**(腦神經) 〚해부〛 a cranial 〔cerebral〕 nerve. ◉ ～세포 a brain cell. ～쇠약 nervous debility 〔prostration〕. ～외과(外科) neurosurgery; 《병원의》 the department of neurosurgery: ～외과의 a neurosurgeon. ～절(節) a cerebral ganglion.

**뇌실**(腦室) 〚해부〛 a ventricle of the brain; a cerebral ventricle.

**뇌연화증**(腦軟化症) 〚의학〛 softening of the brain; encephalomalacia.

**뇌염**(腦炎) 〚의학〛 brain inflammation; encephalitis; cerebritis; phrenitis. ¶ ～의 발생 an outbreak of encephalitis / ～에 걸리다 be stricken by encephalitis. ◉ ～경보 《issue》 a warning against the outbreak of (Japanese) encephalitis. ～모기 a culex mosquito; an encephalitis-bearing mosquito. ～증세 symptoms of encephalitis. ～환자 an encephalitis patient: ～환자로 확인되다 be confirmed an encephalitis patient.

**뇌우**(雷雨) 《be overtaken by》 a thunderstorm; a thundershower.

**뇌운**(雷雲) a thundercloud.

**뇌일혈**(腦溢血) 〖의학〗 cerebral h(a)emorrhage; an apoplectic stroke; (a stroke of) apoplexy; a stroke. ¶ ～을 일으키다 have a fit of apoplexy; be stricken with a cerebral hemorrhage / ～로 죽다 die of apoplexy.

**뇌장**(腦漿) 〖해부〗 the fluid in the brain.

**뇌장애**(腦障礙) a brain injury; brain trouble. ¶ ～를 일으키다 suffer from brain trouble; suffer injuries in the brain; get 〔be〕 injured in the brain.

**뇌전**(雷電) thunder and lightning; thunderbolts.

**뇌조**(雷鳥) 〖조류〗 a ptarmigan; a snow grouse.

**뇌졸중**(腦卒中) 〖의학〗 a stroke; cerebral apoplexy.

**뇌종양**(腦腫瘍) 〖의학〗 a brain tumor.

**뇌증**(腦症) brain trouble 〔fever〕. ¶ ～을 일으키다 suffer from brain trouble; get brain fever.

**뇌진탕**(腦震蕩) 〖의학〗 concussion of the brain; cerebral concussion. ¶ ～을 일으키다 have concussion of the brain / 그 권투 선수는 머리를 강타당해 ～을 일으켰다 The boxer received a blow to the head and suffered concussion.

**뇌척수**(腦脊髓) 〖해부〗 the brain and spinal chord. ◉ ～액(液) cerebrospinal fluid. ～염 〖의학〗 encephalomyelitis; myeloencephalitis.

**뇌척수막**(腦脊髓膜) 〖해부〗 meninges. ◉ ～염(炎) 〖의학〗 cerebrospinal meningitis 〔fever〕; brain fever.

**뇌출혈**(腦出血) 〖의학〗 cerebral h(a)emorrhage.

**뇌충혈**(腦充血) 〖의학〗 congestion of the brain; cerebral hyperemia.

**뇌파**(腦波) 〖생리〗 brain waves. ¶ ～를 기록하다 take electroencephalogram readings. ◉ ～검사 a brain wave test. ～계(計) an electroencephalograph. ～도(圖) an electroencephalogram. ～형 a brainwave pattern.

**뇌하다** (be) low and dirty; mean and foul.

**뇌하수체**(腦下垂體) 〖해부〗 a pituitary gland 〔body〕; a hypophysis. ¶ ～의 이식 transplanting of the pituitary gland. ◉ ～호르몬 pituitary hormone.

**뇌혈전**(腦血栓) cerebral thrombosis.

**뇌홍**(雷汞) fulminating mercury; mercury fulminate.

**뇟보** a low-down person; a mean bastard.

**누**(累) trouble; an evil influence 〔effect〕; implication; involvement. ¶ 남에게 누를 끼치다 bring 〔cause〕 trouble to 〔upon〕 others; implicate 〔involve〕 others in trouble; have a harmful 〔a damaging, an unfavorable〕 effect on *a person* / 남에게 누를 끼치지 않도록 해라 You must not make yourself a nuisance to others. / 그렇게 하면 자기 자신뿐만 아니라 남에게도 ～를 끼치게 된다 That would bring trouble on others as well as yourself.

**누**(樓) a tower; a turret; a lookout (성(城)의); a belvedere (망루). ¶ 누에 오르다 go up a tower.

**누** 〖동물〗 a gnu.

**누가** 〖성서〗 Luke. ◉ ～복음 (the Gospel of) Luke.

**누가**(累加) acceleration; cumulative rise; progressive increase. ～하다 accelerate; increase progressively.

**누각**(樓閣) a many-storied building.

**누감**(累減) degression. ◉ ～세〔과세〕 degressive tax 〔taxation〕.

**누계**(累計) the (cumulative) total; the sum 〔grand, full〕 total; the total amount 〔sum〕; the aggregate. ～하다 total. ¶ 어제 현재로 ～ 100만원이 된다 The aggregate (amount) comes to one million won as of yesterday. / 올해 교통 사고 사망자의 ～는 1만명에 이르렀다 The death toll of traffic accidents this year has already reached ten thousand.

**누관**(淚管) 〖해부〗 the tear 〔lachrymal〕 duct.

**누구** ① 《특정인을 가리키는 경우》 who (주격); whose (소유격); whom (목적격). ¶ 누가 그러더냐 Who told you? / 도대체 누가 그러더냐 Whoever (the devil) told you? / ～를 만났는가 Who 〔Whom〕 did you see? (★ 구어에서는 보통 who를 씀. 단, 전치사 다음에는 whom) / ～에게 줘야 할지 모르겠다 I don't know to whom to give it. / ～시라고 여쭐까요 What name shall I say? / ～십니까 May I have your name, please? *or* 《전화에서》 Who's speaking 〔calling〕, please? / 아니라고 누가 말할 수 있어 Who knows if it may be so? / 누군가 했더니 아버지였다 It was no other than my father. / ～를 데리고 가셨습니까 Whom 〔Who〕 did you take with you? / 깜깜한 어둠 속에서 나는 누가 누군지 분간할 수가 없었다 I couldn't tell them apart in the total darkness.

②《불특정인을 가리키는 경우》[긍정문] somebody; someone; [부정문·의문문] anybody; anyone. ¶ ～ 딴 사람 somebody else / ～ 적당한 사람 some suitable person / ～든〔라도〕, ～도《무차별적인 긍정》anybody; anyone; whoever; 《부정》no one; nobody; none / 누가 보더라도 to any eye / 영어만은 ～에게도 뒤지지 않다 be second to none in English / 누군가 찾아왔나 보다 Somebody is at the door. / 누가 그러는데 그는 벌써 떠났다더라 Somebody told me that he had left already. / ～도 그 곳에 가지 않았다 Nobody went there. (★ 위의 문장을 Anybody did not go there. 라고는 하지 않음). / 아직 ～에게도 말 안 했다 I haven't told it to anybody. / ～든 그 책을 찾으면 돌려주시오 If anybody should find the book, please return it to me. / ～나 그것을 알고 있다 Everybody knows that. / ～든 네가 좋아하는 사람에게 그것을 줘도 좋다 You may give it to anyone you like. / ～라도 결점이 없는 사람은 없다 No one is free from faults. ③ [양보절에서] whoever; whosever; whomever. ¶ ～라도 이 법률을 위반한 자는 처벌받는다 Whoever breaks this law shall be punished. / 누가 뭐라 하든 그것은 거짓이다 Whoever said so, it is false.

④《비꼬는 투》I; me; someone. ¶ 누가 안대 How should I know? / ～를 놀리는 거냐 Are you kidding me? / 누가 할 말을 네가 하는구나 You are saying what I should say. *or* It's me that should be saying that. / 그러면 누가 무서워할 줄 아느냐 Do you think I will be afraid if you do that? / ～는 밤에 자다가 오줌 쌌대요 "Someone I know" wet his bed last night!

**누구누구** just who and who; who all. ¶ ～할 것 없이 every last man; everybody; each and all; without distinction of person / ～ 왔나 Who all is here? / ～ 할 것 없이 다 나쁘다 You are all to blame, every last one of you. / 올 사람이 ～인지 알려 주십시오 Tell me the names of those who are coming.

**누군** 《누구는》 as for anyone 〔everyone〕. ¶ ～ 모르나 Who doesn't know that?

**누군들** whoever it may be; anyone; everyone; even I 〔me〕.

**누군지** someone or other; so-and-so; who it is. ¶ ～ 왔었다 Someone came (while you were away). / ～ 몰라 I don't know who it is.

**누굴** 《누구를》 who(m); someone. ¶ ～ 말하는 것이냐 Who(m) are you talking about? / ～ 보냈느냐 Whom did you send? *or* Did you send someone?

**누그러뜨리다** soften; ease; mellow; moderate; 《고통 등을》 relieve; lessen; alleviate; mitigate; 《감정을》 calm; appease; mollify. ¶ 노여움을 ～ appease 〔calm〕 《*a person's*》 anger / 고통을 ～ ease 〔allay〕 pain / 표정을 ～ soften 〔moderate〕 *one's* expression / 나는 목소리를 누그러뜨려 가면서 그를 설득했다 I lowered my voice and talked him into it. / 온갖 수를 썼지만 그의 노여움을 누그러뜨릴 수 없었다 Nothing could appease 〔pacify, abate〕 his rage.

**누그러지다** ① 《날씨가》 get milder 〔warmer, better〕; become less severe; ease up; 《바람 등이》 abate; subside; lull; go down. ¶ 추위가 ～ the cold weather eases up / 소나기가 오고나서 더위가 좀 누그러진 듯하다 It seems a little cooler after that shower.

②《시세가》 get lower; decline; be on the decline. ¶ 물가가 ～ prices become lower; prices are on the decline.

③ 《감정·태도 따위가》 soften; become conciliatory; grow calmer; be mollified; be pacified 〔softened〕; cool 〔calm〕 down. ¶ 누그러진 성미 placid 〔calm〕 temper / 태도가 ～ go soft; weaken in *one's* attitude; *one's* attitude becomes conciliatory; relent 《toward *a person*》/ 노여움이 ～ *one's* temper cools / 마음이 ～ *one's* spirit softens / 친절한 그의 말에 그녀의 마음도 누그러졌다 His kind words melted her heart.

④《아픔 등이》 be mitigated; be alleviated 〔allayed〕.

⑤《딱딱한 것이》 become soft 〔tender, pliant〕. ¶ 사탕이 ～ candy becomes 〔goes〕 soft / 가죽이 ～ leather becomes 〔gets〕 soft.

**누긋하다** ① ⇨ 노긋하다. ②《성질이》 (be) placid; calm; unruffled; easy(-going); carefree; unhurried. ¶ 누긋한 성질 a placid temper; an easygoing disposition.

**누기**(漏氣) dampness; wetness; moisture; humidity.

**누기차다**(漏氣―) (be) damp; moist; humid; wet; soppy; sticky. ¶ 누기찬 방 a damp room / 누기찬 바람 damp 〔humid〕 air.

**누기치다**(漏氣―) become damp 〔humid, moist, wet, soppy〕. ¶ 방에 ～ a room becomes damp.

**누나** 《a boy's》 older 〔elder〕 sister. ¶ 너의 ～ your sister.

**누년**(屢年) successive years; several 〔some〕 years; 《for》 a series of years; 《over》 a period of years. ◉ ～통계 annual statistics 〔figures〕.

**누누이**(屢屢—) often; frequently; repeatedly; time and again; a number of times; on several occasions. ¶ 공부 열심히 하라고 ～ 이르다 tell 《a student》 time and again to study hard.

**누다** discharge; evacuate; let out. ¶ 똥을 ～ defecate; evacuate; do *one's* business; go to stool; relieve 〔ease〕 nature; shit 《비어》/ 오줌을 ～ urinate; pass water; take 〔have, do〕 a leak; piss 《비어》.

**누대**(屢代) successive generations; 《over》 a number 〔series〕 of generations. ¶ ～에 걸쳐 내려오는 가보 a family heirloom.

**누더기** tattered 〔patched〕 clothes; rags; tatters. ¶ ～를 걸치다 be (clad) in tatters 〔rags〕/ ～를 걸친 사람 a person in rags / ～가 되다 be worn to rags.

**누덕누덕** to 〔in〕 tatters; in 〔with〕 patches. ¶ 옷을 ～ 깁다 patch and repatch *one's* clothes.

**누되다**(累—) (be) harassing. ⇨ 누(累).

**누두**(漏斗) a funnel. ＝깔때기.

**누드** (the) nude. ◉ ～댄서 a stripper; a striptease artiste. ～모델 a nude model. ～사진 a nude photo 〔picture〕: ～사진을 찍다 take a nude picture. ～쇼 a nude show; a strip show; striptease.

**누락**(漏落) an omission; an oversight. ～하다 《…을》 be missing; omit; leave out; 《…이》 be 「omitted 〔left out〕. ¶ 몇 마디 ～하다 miss out several words / 그들은 내 이름을 명단에서 ～시켰다 They dropped 〔omitted〕 my name from the list.

**누란**(累卵) a hazardous 〔perilous〕 matter; imminent danger. ¶ ～의 위기에 처하다 be in imminent danger 〔peril〕; be threatened with ruin.

**누렁** yellow; yellow dyes. ◉ ～물 yellow water; dirty water.

**누렇다** (be) quite yellow; be golden yellow. ¶ 보리가 누렇게 익다 the barley is ripe and golden.

**누룩** yeast; leaven; malt. ◉ ～곰팡이 leaven; an aspergillus (*pl.* -gilli). ～밀 malt made of glutinous rice.

**누룽지** scorched rice from the bottom of the pot.

**누르께하다** be tinged 〔stained〕 with yellow. ¶ 누르께한 얼굴 a sallow face.

**누르다**[1] 《빛이》 (be) yellow; golden; yellowish brown; tan. ¶ 누른 빛 a yellow 〔golden〕 color / 누른 잎 a yellow leaf.

**누르다**[2] ① (***a***) 《내리밀다》 press; press 〔push〕 down; depress 《a lever》. ¶ 초인종을 ～ press the bell button; press 〔push〕 the doorbell / 책으로 ～ keep 《papers》 down with a book / 발로 내리 ～ step on; tread on; trample on / 돌을 얹어 ～ press 《*a thing*》 under a stone / 국수를 ～ make noodles; squeeze out noodles. (***b***) 《도장을》 stamp; seal; impress 《a mark》. ¶ 서류에 승인하는 도장을 ～ stamp the papers with seals of approval.
② 《억압·진압하다》 suppress; oppress; put down; 《억제·저지하다》 control; govern; check. ¶ 백성을 ～ oppress the people / 반란을 ～ suppress 〔put down〕 a revolt; bring a riot under control / 물가의 상승을 5%이하로 ～ prevent prices from rising more than five percent / 그는 아내에게 눌려 지낸다 He is under the thumb of his wife.
③ 《감정 따위를》 restrain; (get under) control. ¶ 감정을 ～ stifle 〔suppress〕 *one's* emotions; get hold of *one's* feelings / 욕심을 ～ suppress 〔repress〕 a desire / 노염을 ～ master 〔control, swallow〕 *one's* anger; keep 〔gulp〕 down *one's* anger / 자존심을 ～ pocket *one's* pride; put *one's* pride in *one's* pocket.
④ 《상대방을》 beat 《a team, *a person*》; 《야구에서》 hold 《the opposing team》 almost scoreless. ¶ 4번 타자를 ～ put out 〔retire〕 the clean-up man / 그는 상대팀을 2안타로 눌렀다 He held 〔limited〕 the opposing team to two hits.
⑤ 《압도하다》 overwhelm; surpass; exceed. ¶ 품질에 있어서 단연 모든 것을 ～ lead the world in quality.

**누르락붉으락** 「turning red and blue 〔changing countenance〕 with anger; flaring up. 「yellow.

**누르스름하다** (be) yellowish; be a bit

**누르퉁퉁하다** (be) sallow; sallowish; pale-yellow. ¶ 누르퉁퉁한 얼굴 a sallow complexion.

**누름단추** a push 〔press〕 button; a bell button (초인종의). ¶ ～의 push-button / ～방식 a push-button system / ～식 전화기 a push-button telephone.

**누름돌** a (stone) weight. ¶ ～을 얹다 place 〔put〕 a stone as a weight on 《*something*》. 「kebab.

**누름적**(—炙) a kind of egg-coated shish

**누리**[1] 《세상》 the world; this world. ¶ 온

～에 in all 〔all over〕 the world.

**누리**[2] 〖곤충〗 a desert locust.

**누리**[3] 《우박》 hail; snow pellets.

**누리다**[1] 《냄새가》 (be) stenchy; foul-smelling; [서술적] smell of fat 〔beasts〕; have a burnt smell 〔taste〕; smell. ¶ 국이 ～ the soup smells of fat.

**누리다**[2] 《향유하다》 enjoy; be blessed with. ¶ 행복〔건강〕을 ～ enjoy happiness 〔good health〕 / 명예를 ～ enjoy honors / 장수를 ～ enjoy longevity / 전시민이 고루 혜택을 누릴 수 있도록 하다 enable all citizens to receive equal benefits.

**누린내** the smell of fat 〔beasts〕 (짐승의); a burnt smell (타는 내). ¶ 어디서 ～가 난다 I can smell something burning.

**누명**(陋名) a false 〔an unjust〕 charge 〔accusation〕; groundless 〔unfounded〕 suspicion. ¶ ～을 쓰다 be falsely 〔wrongly, unjustly〕 accused 《of stealing》; be falsely charged 《with murder》; be unjustly suspected 《of a guilt》 / ～을 씌우다 accuse 《*a person* of theft》 falsely 〔unjustly〕; make 〔bring〕 a false charge 《of espionage》 against 《*a person*》; charge 《*a person*》 unjustly 《with bribery》 / ～을 벗다 clear *oneself* of the charge of 《being a traitor》; remove the disgrace that has (been) attached to *one's* name.

**누범**(累犯) repeated offenses. ◉ ～자 a repeated 〔habitual〕 offender.

**누벨바그** [< *nouvelle vague* (F.)] the new wave 《movement》.

**누비** quilting; quilted work. ◉ ～옷 quilted clothes. ～이불 a quilt. ～질 quilting: ～질하다 quilt; do quilting. ～포대기 a baby quilt.

**누비다** ① 《바느질》 quilt. ¶ 이불을 ～ quilt; make a quilt. ② 《찡그리다》 ¶ 이마를 ～ knit *one's* brow; frown. ③ 《헤집다》 thread; weave. ¶ 군중 속을 누비며 건다 thread *one's* way through the crowd / 오솔길이 숲 속을 누비듯 뚫려 있다 A path weaves through the forest.

**누산기**(累算器) 〖컴퓨터〗 an accumulator.

**누선**(淚腺) 〖해부〗 lachrymal glands.

**누설**(漏泄) leakage; a leak; (a) disclosure; divulgence. ～하다 leak (out); get out; reveal; disclose. ¶ 군사기밀의 ～ a leakage of military secrets / 기밀〔비밀〕을 ～하다 let out 〔leak〕 a secret; betray 〔reveal, divulge, break〕 a secret / ～되다 leak (out); be 「divulged 〔disclosed, revealed〕 / 국가 기밀이 ～되었다 A secret of the nation has leaked out. / 시험 문제가 ～되어 대혼란이 일어났다 The leakage of some examination questions led to a grave complication. ◉ ～전류 〖전기〗 a leakage current.

**누속**(陋俗) sordid customs; low practices.

**누손**(漏損) 〖상업〗 leakage; ullage; 〖전기〗 a leakage (loss).

**누수**(漏水) (a) leakage of water; a water leak; 《물》 leaking water. ～하다 《it》 leak water; spring a leak. ¶ ～를 막지 않으면 안 된다 We must stop a leak of water. / 이 수도관에서 ～되고 있다 This pipe is leaking water. *or* Water is leaking from this pipe. ◉ ～검출기 a hydrostat.

**누습**(陋習) an evil practice; a bad custom. ¶ ～을 타파하다 do away with an evil custom.

**누심**(壘審) 〖야구〗 a base 〔field〕 umpire. ¶ 1루심 the umpire at first base.

**누에** a silkworm. ¶ ～를 치다 rear 〔raise, breed〕 silkworms / ～를 올리다 put silkworms on mulberry leaves to feed / ～가 오른다 Silkworms begin spinning. ◉ ～고치 a cocoon. ～나방 a silkworm moth. ～농사〔치기〕 sericulture; raising silkworms; silkworm breeding. ～씨 silkworm eggs; a strain 〔a breed〕 of silkworms.

**누옥**(陋屋) ① 《누추한 집》 a humble house; a wretched hut. ② 《자기 집》 my house.

**누운단** the lower hem of an upper garment.

**누운변**(一邊) interest paid back at the same time with the principal.

**누울외**(一椳) horizontal 〔lateral, cross〕 laths.

**누워먹다** eat the bread of idleness.

**누이** a boy's sister. ¶ 손위〔손아래〕 ～ *one's* older 〔younger, little〕 sister. ◉ ～동생 *one's* younger sister.

**누이다**[1] 《대소변을》 make 〔have, let〕 《*a person*》 defecate 〔urinate〕.

**누이다**[2] 《피륙을》 《cloth》 get washed in limewater.

**누적**(累積) accumulation; cumulation. ～하다 accumulate; cumulate; increase cumulatively. ¶ ～되는 cumulative / ～된 서류 accumulated papers 《on the table》 / ～된 사회악 accumulated public evils. ◉ ～적자 a cumulative deficit: ～적자가 5억원에 이르렀다 The cumulative deficit has reached 500 million won.

**누전**(漏電) 〖전기〗 (a) leakage of electricity; an electric leak; 《단락》 a short

circuit. ～하다 《electricity》 leak; short-circuit. ¶ ～에 의한 화재 a fire caused by a short circuit / ～을 일으키다 cause a 「short (circuit) 〔leak of electricity〕 / 화재의 원인은 ～이었다 The fire was caused by a short circuit. / 전기가 ～되고 있다 Electricity is leaking. / ～으로 퓨즈가 끊어졌다 The fuse has blown because of a short circuit.
◉ ～계(計) a ground 〔leakage〕 detector; a leakage indicator.

**누정**(漏精) 〖의학〗 involuntary emission of semen; spermatorrh(o)ea.

**누증**(累增) cumulative rise 〔increase〕; progressive increase. ～하다 cumulate; increase progressively 〔cumulatively〕.

**누지**(陋地) 《누추한 곳》 a sordid 〔humble〕 place; 《자기가 있는 곳》 my place; here; this place.

**누지다** (be) damp; wettish; moist. ¶ 누진 방 a moist 〔wettish〕 room.

**누진**(累進) successive 〔gradual〕 promotion; gradual advance. ～하다 advance 〔rise〕 step by step; be promoted from one position to another; get a steady rise. ¶ ～적으로 과세하다 impose taxes on a graduated 〔progressive〕 scale. ◉ ～과세 progressive 〔graduated〕 taxation. ～세 progressive taxes: ～소득세 progressive income taxes. ～세율 progressive tax rate.

**누차**(屢次) many times; repeatedly; over and over; time after time; time and (time) again. ¶ ～ 말하다 speak repeatedly / ～ 해보다 try again and again / ～ 충고했는데도 그는 기어이 억지를 부린다 He will have his own way though I have often advised him against it.

**누추**(陋醜) ～하다 (be) filthy; dirty; shabby; humble. ¶ ～한 집 a humble 〔filthy〕 house / ～한 집이지만 humble as our house is / 옷이 ～하다 be shabbily dressed / ～한 곳이지만 잘 오셨습니다 I'm delighted to welcome you under my humble roof 《문어》.

**누출**(漏出) leakage; escape. ～하다 leak; escape. ¶ 가스～ an escape of gas; a gas leak / 가스가 관에서 ～하고 있다 The gas is leaking from the pipe.

**누치** 〖어류〗 a cornet fish.

**누타**(壘打) 〖야구〗 a base hit. ¶ 2루타를 치다 make a two-base hit.

**눅눅하다** (be) humid; damp; wet; moist. ¶ 눅눅한 옷 wet clothes / 눅눅한 담배 damp tobacco / 눅눅한 빵 soggy bread / 눅눅해지다 get 〔become〕 damp 〔moist, wet〕; dampen; moisten / 이 셔츠는 눅눅하니까 햇볕에 말려라 This shirt is damp. Dry it in the sun.

**눅느즈러지다** become flabby; go limp.

**눅다** ① 《반죽 등이》 (be) soft; loose; ductile. ¶ 반죽이 ～ the dough is soft / 쇠가 ～ the iron is ductile. ② 《습기로》 (be) damp; wet; moist; become soft and damp. ¶ 담배가 ～ The tobacco is damp. ③ 《성질이》 (be) placid. ¶ 성질이 눅은 사람 a man of placid temper. ④ 《날씨가》 become milder; warm up. ¶ 날씨가 눅었다 The weather has become milder. ⑤ 《값이》 be lowered in price; (be) cheap. ¶ 눅은 변으로 at low interest; at a low rate of interest.

**눅이다** ① 《굳은 것을》 soften; make tender; loosen (up). ¶ 반죽을 ～ soften the dough. ② 《마음을》 soften; mollify; pacify; appease. ¶ 표정을 ～ soften *one's* expression / 아무의 마음을 ～ soften *a person's* heart; appease *a person* / 진통제로 고통을 눅였다 I took some painkillers to relieve the pain. ③ 《적시다》 wet; damp; moisten. ¶ 다림질을 하기 전에 옷을 ～ damp 〔sprinkle〕 clothes prior to ironing.

**눅지다** 《날씨가》 become less severe; decreases in severity; ease up. ¶ 날씨가 눅졌다 The cold has decreased in severity.

**눈**[1] ① [일반적] an eye. (★ 보통은 두 눈을 뜻하며 복수형으로 쓰이는 경우가 많음). ¶ 눈의 ocular; optic(al) / 눈의 피로 eyestrain / 눈 은행 an eye bank / 큰 〔작은〕 눈 large 〔small〕 eyes / 가느다란 눈 narrow eyes; slit eyes / 날카로운 눈 sharp 〔alert〕 eyes / 눈물 어린 눈 tearful eyes / 멍청한 눈 dull 〔fishy〕 eyes / 번쩍이는 눈 sparkling eyes / 빛나는 눈 bright eyes / 움푹 들어간 눈 sunken 〔deep-set〕 eyes / 퉁방울눈 goggle eyes / 부리부리한 눈 big bright eyes / 치켜 올라간 눈 peaked 〔slant〕 eyes / 졸린 눈 sleepy 〔heavy〕 eyes / 눈 깜짝할 사이에 in an instant; in the twinkling of an eye / 눈가리고 아웅하다 try to deceive by a transparent guile; bury *one's* head ostrich-like in the sand.
눈이: 눈이 아프다 have an eye disease; have sore eyes / 눈이 휘둥그레지다 stare in wonder; stare wide-eyed 《at》; be pop-eyed / 눈이 닮다 bear a resemblance in the cast of the eyes / 눈이 핑핑 돌다 be 〔feel〕 dizzy; get giddy.
눈에: 눈에 해롭다 be injurious to the eyes / 눈에는 눈으로 an eye for an eye / 눈에 티가 들다 「have a mote 〔get

*a thing*] in *one's* eyes / 눈에서 번쩍 불이 나다 see stars / 눈에 쌍심지를 켜다 anger shows in *one's* eyes / 내 눈에 흙이 들어가기 전에는 while [as long as] I live; so long as I am alive.
눈으로: 눈으로 알리다 wink at 《*a person*》; make a sign with the eye; give 《*a person*》 the eye / 눈으로 인사하다 (greet with a) nod; thank with *one's* eyes / 눈으로 말하다 give a significant look; wink at.
눈을: 눈을 뜨다[감다] open [close, shut] *one's* eyes / 눈을 크게 뜨고 with *one's* eyes wide open / 눈을 내리깔고 with *one's* eyes cast down; with downcast eyes / 눈을 똑바로 뜨고 with *one's* eyes set / 눈을 가리다 blindfold; bandage *one's* eyes / 눈을 치켜 뜨다 raise [lift] *one's* eyes; look up / 눈을 붙이다 sleep; go [get] to sleep / 눈을 깜짝이다 blink *one's* eyes / 놀라서 눈을 껌뻑이다 blink in surprise; goggle in astonishment / 눈을 끔적하다 wink *one's* eyes / 눈을 부라리다[부릅뜨다] glare 《at》/ 눈을 비비다 rub *one's* eyes / 눈을 속이다 deceive 《*a person*》 eye; pull [draw] the wool over 《*a person's*》 eyes / 눈을 앓다 have trouble with *one's* eyes.
¶ 내 눈을 믿을 수가 없다 I can't believe my eyes. / 그녀는 눈을 감고 앉아 있었다 She sat with her eyes closed. / 그는 오른쪽 눈이 안 보인다 He is blind in the right eye. / 네 눈이 충혈되어 있다 Your eyes are bloodshot. / 옆 사람의 담배 연기로 눈이 따갑다 My eyes smart from my neighbor's cigarette smoke. / 제 눈에 안경이다 《속담》 Beauty lies [is] in the eye of the beholder. / 아버지는 그녀를 눈에 넣어도 아파하지 않을 정도로 귀여워하신다 She is the apple of her father's eye. / 눈에 먼지가 들어갔다 I've got a speck of dust in my eye.
② 《표정》 a look; a gaze; an eye. ¶ 무언가 말하려는 눈 talking [eloquent] eyes / 무시무시한 눈 threatening [menacing] eyes / 꿈꾸는 듯한 눈 dreamy eyes; a faraway look / 성난 눈으로 with an angry look in the eye / 시기하는 눈으로 보다 see with a jealous eye; look on with jealousy / 의심하는 눈으로 보다 regard with suspicion / 경멸의 눈으로 보다 gaze in contempt 《upon *a person*》/ 눈도 입 못지 않게 말을 한다 Eyes are as eloquent as the tongue. / 당신의 눈을 보니까 내 말에 찬성하지 않는다고 쓰여 있었어요 Your eyes told me that you would not agree with me.
③ 《시력》 sight; eyesight; vision; 《시선》 eyes. ¶ 눈의 착각 an optical illusion / 밤눈이 밝다 have the eyes of a cat / 밤눈이 어둡다 suffer from night blindness.
눈이: 눈이 닿는 데까지 as far as the eye can see / 눈이 밝다[좋다] have good eyes [eyesight]; have a good sight / 눈이 어둡다[나쁘다] have bad eyes [defective vision]; have a poor sight / 눈이 어두워지다 《현혹되다》 be dazzled [blinded] / 눈이 멀다 be [become] blind; lose *one's* (eye)sight / 눈이 빠르다 be quick-eyed; be sharp-sighted.
눈에: 눈에 나쁘다 be bad for the eyes / 눈에 안 보이다 be invisible / 눈에 보이다 come in sight; come into view; [사람이 주어] catch sight of; happen to see / 눈에 띄다 be conspicuous / 눈에 띄지 않다 be inconspicuous / 눈에 띄게 conspicuously; perceptibly; remarkably.
¶ 어두운 곳에서 책을 읽는 것은 눈에 나쁘다 Reading in a poor light is bad for the eyes. / 최근에 눈이 나빠졌다 My eyesight has become poor recently. / 수술 후 어머니는 눈에 띄게 차도가 있었다 After my mother had the operation, she recovered her health very quickly. / 눈은 마음의 창이다 The eye is the window of the soul. / 그의 집은 눈에 띄기 쉽다 His house is quite easy to find. / 그의 열성은 교수의 눈에 띄었다 His enthusiasm caught the attention of the professor.
④ 《마음의》 eyes. ¶ (…의) 눈에 들다 be in favor; be in good 《with》; find favor with 《*one's* superior》/ 눈에 드는 사람 a man after *one's* fancy / (…의) 눈 밖에 나다 be out of favor; be in bad 《with》/ 눈을 즐겁게 하다 feast *one's* eyes 《upon》; delight *one's* eyes / 욕심에 눈이 어두워지다 be blinded 「with avarice [by greed] / 눈에 거슬리다 become an eyesore; obstruct [spoil] the view; offend the eye [sight] / 눈에 선하다 be vivid to *one's* eyes / 눈에 차다 be satisfactory / 눈에 밟히다 be haunted by the image of 《*a person*》/ 생일 선물을 받고 좋아할 손녀의 얼굴이 눈에 떠오른다 I can just see how happy my granddaughter will be to have a birthday present.
⑤ 《주의·눈길》 notice; attention; watch; observation; *one's* eyes. ¶ 눈에 안 띄는 장소 a secret corner; a backseat / 눈

감으면 코 베어 먹을 세상 a dog-eat-dog world / 눈을 떼다 look aside 〔away〕; take *one's* eyes off / 눈을 떼지 않다 keep 〔fix〕 *one's* eyes 《upon》; have an eye on / 아무의 눈을 끌다 attract 〔draw〕 *a person's* attention 〔notice〕; be striking; catch 〔strike〕 *a person's* eye; be attractive / 눈을 돌리다 turn *one's* attention to; turn *one's* eyes away 《from》/ 한눈을 팔다 give no heed 〔regard〕 to; pay no attention to / 남의 눈을 개의치 않다 be indifferent to *another's* observation / 남의 눈을 피하다 avoid *a person's* eyes / 모든 눈이 나에게로 쏠렸다 All eyes were focused on me. / 도둑은 경찰이 잠깐 눈을 떼는 사이에 도망쳤다 The thief ran away while the policeman looked aside for a moment. / 나는 저 개구쟁이들에게서 눈을 뗄 수가 없다 I cannot take my eyes off those naughty children. / 이제 아시아 여러 나라의 경제 상태에 눈을 돌려 봅시다 Now let us turn our eyes to the economic conditions of Asian countries.

⑥ 《안식》 an eye; insight; judgment. ¶ 전문가의 눈 a professional eye; an expert's eye / 골동품을 보는 눈이 있다 have an eye for curios; be a connoisseur of curios / 눈이 높다 aim high; be discerning; have an (expert) eye 《for》; be a good judge 《of》/ 그는 사람을 보는 눈이 있다 He 「is a good judge of 〔has an eye for〕 character. / 내 눈이 틀림없다 I have an unerring eye.

⑦ 《관점》 *one's* eye; a point of view; a viewpoint. ¶ 내 눈으로 보아서는 in my eyes; so far as I see; from where I sit 〔stand〕/ 서양 사람의 눈으로 보면 from a Western point of view / 법률의 눈으로 보면 in the eye of the law / 공평한 눈으로 보다 look up on 《*a person, a matter*》 with an impartial eye / 그의 눈은 옳았다 He was right in his judgment. / 그의 눈으로 보면 우리는 어린애다 We are babies in his eyes. / 이 사건을 공평한 눈으로 보면 그는 무죄다 If we look upon this case with an impartial eye, he is not guilty.

⑧ 《자각》 awakening. ¶ 눈을 뜨다 come to *one's* senses; awake from an illusion / 죄의식에 눈을 뜨다 be awakened to a sense of sin.

⑨ 《기타》 ¶ 서로 눈이 맞다 fall in love with each other / 눈 딱 감고 with (a determined) effort; without hesitation / 눈을 감다 [비유적] shut *one's* eyes 《to》; wink 〔connive〕 at; 《죽다》 die; breathe *one's* last / 눈에 새롭다 be new 〔novel, fresh, original〕.

**눈**[2] ① 《꽃눈·잎눈》 a bud; a germ (씨눈); a sprout (돋아나온). ¶ 감자(의) 눈 an eye of a potato / 눈이 트다 ⇨ 눈트다. ② 《눈금》 graduation; scale-notches. ¶ 저울눈이 모자라다 be of short weight / 저울눈을 속이다 give short weight.

**눈**[3] 《그물 따위의》 a mesh. ¶ 그물눈 the meshes of a net / 눈이 고운 체 a sieve of fine meshes.

**눈**[4] 《내리는》 snow; 《강설》 a snowfall. ¶ 많은 눈 a heavy snow; a heavy snowfall / 함박눈 big flakes of snow / 싸락눈 powdery snow / 진눈 wet snow; sleet; snow mixed with rain / 눈의 결정 a snow crystal / 눈이 많은 지방 a snowy district / 표면이 언 눈 crusted 〔ice-encrusted〕 snow / 눈이 쌓이다 snow lies 〔piles up, heaps〕/ 눈이 내리다 it snows; snow falls; we have a snow / 눈이 녹다 snow melts 〔disappears〕/ 눈에 싸이다〔덮이다〕 be covered 〔laden, blanketed〕 with snow; be under the snow; be snowed under / 눈에 갇히다 be snowbound; be snowed in / 눈에 묻히다 be buried under 〔in〕 the snow; be snowed under / 눈을 맞다 get snowed on; be exposed to snow / 눈을 치우다 sweep 〔shovel, rake〕 away snow; clear away 〔off〕 snow; clear 《the street》 of snow / 눈이 올 것 같은 날씨다 It threatens to 〔looks like〕 snow. *or* There are signs of snow. / 눈이 펑펑 쏟아진다 It snows hard and fast. / 눈이 다섯 자 왔다 We have had a snowfall of five feet. / 이 곳에서는 3월에 눈이 녹는다 The snow thaws in March here. / 오늘 아침에는 눈으로 모든 교통이 마비되었다 The snow tied up all traffic this morning.

**눈가** the eye rims. ¶ ~의 주름 the lines 〔wrinkles〕 at the corners of *one's* eyes; crow's-feet.

**눈가리개** 《말의》 blinkers; blinders; 《사람의》 an eye bandage; an eye patch. ¶ ~를 하다 blindfold 《*a person*》/ ~를 풀다 unblindfold / ~를 하고 끌려가다 be taken away blindfold.

**눈가림** hoodwinking; (a) deception; make-believe. ~하다 hoodwink; deceive; pull the wool over *one's* eyes. ¶ ~의 make-believe; sham; false / 어물어물 ~해서 넘기다 shuffle along 〔through〕/

～으로 일하다 scamp 〔fudge〕 *one's* work / 이 일은 ～으로 넘어가지 못한다 You're not going to get away with anything on this job.

**눈가죽** (the skin of ) an eyelid. ¶ ～이 두껍다 have thick eyelids.

**눈감다** ① 《눈을》 shut 〔close〕 *one's* eyes; 《죽다》 die; breathe *one's* last. ¶ 편안히 눈을 감다 die in peace / 서울은 눈감으면 코 베어갈 곳이다 Sharp practices prevail in Seoul. / 저 녀석은 눈 감으면 코베어 갈 놈이다 He is a 「sharp shooter 〔very shrewd man〕. / 그는 어린애들 때문에 편히 눈감지 못할 게다 He can hardly pass away, thinking he is leaving behind such young children. ② 《못본체하다》 turn a blind eye 《to》. ⇨ 눈감아 주다.

**눈감아주다** shut 〔close〕 *one's* eyes 《to》; wink at 《a fault》; connive 《at》; overlook; turn a blind eye 《to》; let 《*a matter*》 pass 〔go〕. ¶ 잘못을 ～ overlook 《*a person's*》 fault / 아무의 부정 행위를 ～ connive at *a person's* dishonesty / 불쌍해서 이번만 눈감아 준다 For pity's sake I will let the matter pass for this once. / 이번만은 자네 행동을 눈감아 주겠다 I will overlook your behavior this time. / 나는 커닝을 눈감아주는 선생님이 계실 것이라고는 생각지 않는다 I don't believe that some teachers turn a blind eye to cheating in examinations.

**눈거칠다** be hateful to see; be offensive to *one's* eyes; be unsightly.

**눈겨룸** a staring-out〔-down〕 game. ⇨ 눈싸움[2].

**눈결** 《see》 in passing; 《at》 a glimpse; out of the corner of *one's* eye. ¶ ～에 언뜻 보다 get 〔catch〕 a glimpse of.

**눈곱** ① 《눈의》 discharge from the eyes; eye mucus; matter 〔gum〕 (in the corner of the eye); 《구어》 sleep (아침의). ¶ ～이 낀 눈 eyes blurred with mucus / ～이 끼다 be bleary-eyed; *one's* eyes are gummy 〔mattery〕. ② [비유적] a bit; a very tiny object; a small quantity. ¶ ～만하다 be very small 〔tiny〕 / 과자를 ～만큼 주다 give a wee bit of cake / …라곤 ～만큼도 없다 not have an ounce of 《conscience in him》; there is not a grain of 《truth in what he says》.

**눈구덩이** a pit in heaped snow. ¶ ～에 빠지다 slip 〔tumble〕 in the snow.

**눈구멍** 〖해부〗 the eye socket; the orbit of the eye.

**눈구석** the inner corner of an eye.

**눈금** ① 《자·저울 따위의》 a scale 《on a beam balance》; the divisions 《of a scale》; 《온도계 따위의》 graduations. ¶ ～을 매기다 graduate; mark 《*a thing*》 with degrees; put a graded scale 《on》. ¶ 이 자는 센티미터로 ～이 새겨져 있다 This ruler is graduated 〔calibrated, marked off〕 in centimeters. ② 《눈짐작의》 a line drawn by eyesight.

**눈기이다** 《피하다》 avoid the eyes of others; shun 〔avoid〕 public notice; 《속이다》 hoodwink; deceive; pull 〔draw〕 the wool over *one's* eyes.

**눈길**[1] 《시선》 *one's* eyes 〔gaze〕; a glance; a look. ¶ ～을 끌다 draw 〔attract〕 《*a person's*, public》 attention / ～을 주다 〔보내다〕 look 《at》; turn *one's* eyes 〔gaze〕 《on》 / ～을 딴 데로 돌리다 avert 〔turn〕 *one's* eyes 《from, off》; look away 《from》 / ～을 모으다 attract public gaze / ～을 피하다 avoid 《*a person's*》 eyes / 우리는 ～이 마주쳤다 Our eyes met. / 모든 이의 ～이 내게로 쏠렸다 All eyes were turned 〔fixed〕 on me.

**눈길**[2] 《눈 덮인 길》 a snowy 〔snow-covered〕 road.

**눈까풀** ⇨ 눈꺼풀.

**눈깔** 《눈》 an eye. ◉ ～사탕 (a) candy; taffies; 《영》 toffees.

**눈깜작이, 눈깜짝이** a blinkard.

**눈꺼지다** *one's* eyes shrink 〔droop〕; *one's* eyes become hollow. ¶ 그녀는 아파서인지 눈이 꺼져 보였다 Her eyes seemed to have sunk into her face because of illness.

**눈꺼풀** an eyelid. ¶ 윗〔아랫〕～ the upper 〔lower〕 eyelid / 그의 ～이 실룩거렸다 His eyelids twitched.

**눈꼬리** ① the corner 〔tail〕 of *one's* eyes. ¶ ～의 주름 the lines 〔wrinkles〕 at the corners of *one's* eyes; crow's feet / ～가 올라가〔내려가〕 있다 have upward 〔downward〕 slanting eyes; have almond eyes. ② ＝눈초리 ①.

**눈꼴사납다** 《아니꼽다》 be offensive (to the eye); be hateful to see; 《꼴사납다》 (be) unsightly; be an eyesore. ¶ 그의 거드럭거리는 품이 몹시 ～ I hate to see him swaggering. / 술취한 여자는 정말 ～ What could be more unsightly than a woman in wine?

**눈꼴시다, 눈꼴틀리다** hate to see; be sick of. ¶ 태부리는 것이 눈꼴시다 hate to see 《*a person*》 putting on airs / 그가 사장한테 아첨하는 꼴이란 눈꼴시어 볼 수가 없다 I am sick of seeing him licking at his boss's heels.

**눈높다** ① 《안식이 높다》 (be) appreciative 《of》; be a good judge 《of》; be a connoisseur; have an eye 〔a keen eye〕 《for》. ¶ 골동품에 대한 눈이 높다 have an eye for curios. ② 《까다롭다》 aim high; be desirous of things beyond *one's* means. ¶ 그녀는 눈이 높아 웬만한 사람과는 결혼하지 않으려 한다 She aims high and won't marry a nobody.

**눈다랑어** 〖어류〗 a kind of tuna.

**눈대중** eye measurement; a rough estimate. ~하다 measure 「with *one's* eye 〔at a guess〕; go by rule of thumb. ¶ ~으로 at a rough estimate; at a guess / 소금의 양을 ~하다 guess the weight of salt / 그 나무의 높이는 ~으로 약 8미터가 된다 The tree is about eight meters tall by eye measurement.

**눈덩이** a snowball. ¶ ~처럼 커지다〔불어나다〕 snowball; increase 〔grow〕 at a rapidly accelerating rate.

**눈독** eyeing; having 〔keeping〕 *one's* eyes 《on》. ¶ ~들이다 have 〔keep〕 *one's* eyes 《on》; fix on 《*a person*》 as *one's* choice; mark 《*a thing, a person*》 out 〔down〕 / 재산에 ~을 들이다 have an eye on 《*a person's*》 property / 코트를 사게되면 저것으로 하겠다고 ~을 들이고 있다 I'll turn to that if I buy a coat. / 형사는 처음부터 그 여자를 유괴범이라고 ~을 들이고 있었다 From the beginning the detective marked the woman down as the kidnapper.

**눈동자**(一瞳子) the pupil (of the eye). ¶ 귀엽게 생긴 둥글고 검은 ~ lovely round black eyes.

**눈두덩** (the protuberant part of) the upper eyelid. ¶ ~이 붓다 have swollen eyes.

**눈딱부리** a bug-eyed person; a pop eye.

**눈딱지** sinister eyes; a sinister look.

**눈뜨다** ① 《감은 눈을》 open *one's* eyes; awake; wake (up). ¶ 눈뜨고 볼 수 없는 hideous; repulsive; shocking; too shocking 〔pitiful〕 to look at / 빗소리에 ~ wake up to the noise of the rainfall. ② 《자각하다》 come to *one's* senses; wake up 〔be awakend〕 《to》; become aware 《of》. ¶ 성(性)에 ~ be aware of *one's* sexual feelings / 진실에 ~ open *one's* eyes to the truth / 생의 냉엄한 현실에 ~ have *one's* eyes opened to the stern realities of life / 스스로의 가치에 ~ become conscious of *one's* own value.

**눈뜬장님** 《장님》 a blind person; 《문맹자》 an illiterate; an ignoramus. ¶ ~ 노릇하다 play 〔be〕 a blind fool / 그는 ~이다 He is an illiterate.

**눈망울** an eyeball. ¶ ~을 굴리다 roll 「*one's* eyes.

**눈맞다** fall in love with each other. ¶ 둘은 눈이 맞아 달아났다 They fell in love with each other and ran away together.

**눈맞추다** ① 《마주보다》 look at each other; exchange glances. ② 《남녀가》 make eyes at each other; make silent love to each other.

**눈매**, **눈맵시** a look; eyes; an expression (in *one's* eyes). ¶ 귀여운 ~ charming eyes / ~가 쌀쌀맞은 사람 a cold-eyed person / ~가 곱다 have lovely eyes / ~가 시원하다 have a bright 〔clear〕 pair of eyes / ~가 좋지 않다 have an unpleasant look to *one's* eyes / 그녀는 나를 의미있는 ~로 바라보았다 She gave me a meaningful look.

**눈멀다** lose *one's* sight; become 〔go〕 blind; 《현혹되다》 be blind; be dazzled 〔blinded〕. ¶ 눈먼 사람 a blind man / 눈먼 사랑 blind love / 돈에 눈이 멀다 be lured by money; be blinded by the lure of money / 사랑에 눈이 멀다 be blind in the matter of love / 욕심에 눈 먼 그는 투기로 결국 재산을 다 날리고 말았다 Blinded by greed, he ended up by losing his fortune in speculation.

**눈물**[1] ① [일반적] a tear (★ 복수형으로 쓰이는 경우가 많음). ¶ ~ 자국 tear-stains / 뜨거운 ~ hot 〔burning, scalding〕 tears / 피~ bitter tears / 피도 ~도 없는 cold-blooded / 뉘우침의 ~ tears of remorse / 거짓 ~ 《shed》 crocodile tears / ~ 바다가 되다 be turned into a sea of tears / ~의 이별 tearful parting / ~의 이별을 하다 part 《from *a person*》 in tears; take tearful leave 《of》 / ~로 세월을 보내다 lead a sorrowful life; pass *one's* days in tears.

눈물에: ~에 젖은 눈 moisted eyes / ~에 젖은 얼굴 a tear-stained face / ~에 젖다 be drenched with tears / 여자의 ~에 약하다 have a weakness for women's tears.

눈물을: ~을 흘리다 shed 〔drop〕 tears / 비분의 ~을 흘리다 shed tears of rage / ~을 흘리며 in tears; tearfully; weeping / ~을 머금다 《고이다》 tears stand 〔gather〕 in *one's* eyes; *one's* eyes are full of tears / ~을머금고 with deep regret / ~을 거두다 stop weeping; hold *one's* tears / ~을 씻다 wipe *one's* tears

away; dry *one's* eyes / ~을 참다 repress *one's* tears; keep 〔hold〕 back *one's* tears / ~을 삼키다 gulp down 〔choke back〕 *one's* tears; repress *one's* tears / ~을 자아내다 provoke tears; bring tears to *one's* eyes; draw tears from 《*a person*》; move 《*a person*》 to tears.
눈물이: ~이 나오다 tears well up in *one's* eyes; tears come to *one's* eyes / ~이 나오려고 하다 be near tears / ~이 어리다 be suffused with tears / ~이 떨어지다 tears fall 〔flow〕 / ~이 뚝뚝 떨어지다 tears fall in drops / ~이 쏟아지다 *one's* tears gush 〔run〕 out / ~이 비오듯하다 shed a shower of tears / ~이 글썽글썽하다 tears stand in *one's* eyes; *one's* eyes are full of tears / ~이 글썽글썽하여 with tearful eyes; with tears in *one's* eyes / ~이 나와 참을 수가 없다 cannot keep back *one's* tears.
¶ 그 생각만 해도 ~이 나온다 Just thinking of it brings tears to my eyes. / 그들은 ~을 흘리면서 그 노래를 듣고 있었다 They were listening to the song with tears in their eyes. / 그 소식에 그녀는 ~을 흘리며 주저앉았다 She collapsed in tears at the news. /연기 때문에 ~이 나왔다 The smoke made my eyes water. / 그녀는 하루 종일 ~만 흘렸다 She did nothing but weep all day. /나는 굶주림에 시달리는 어린 아이들을 보자 ~이 저절로 나왔다 I was moved to tears when I saw small children suffering from hunger.
② 《인정》 tender heart; sympathy. ¶ ~있는 사람 a sympathetic person; a person of tender heart / ~ 없는 사람 a "tearless" 〔heartless〕 person; a cold-blooded person / ~ 없이는 그 말을 들을 수가 없다 We cannot hear it with dry eyes 〔without tears〕.
**눈물**[2] 《녹은 눈》 snowmelt; melted snow; meltwater. ¶ ~로 강물이 불어났다 The river has risen with thawing 〔melting〕 snow.
**눈물겹다** (be) pathetic; tearful; teary. ¶ 눈물겨운 이야기〔광경〕 a pathetic story 〔scene〕 / 나는 그의 눈물겨운 노력에 감동을 받았다 I was impressed by his pathetically sincere efforts.
**눈물샘** 〖해부〗 a lachrymal gland.
**눈물지다** shed 〔drop〕 bitter tears.
**눈물짓다** be in tears; be moved to tears. ¶ 그녀는 눈물지으며 그것을 내게 이야기했다 She told me about it with tears (in her eyes).
**눈바람**[1] 《눈과 바람》 snow and wind.
**눈바람**[2] 《설풍》 a snow-chilled wind; a wind blowing over the snow; an icy wind; 《눈보라》 a snowstorm.
**눈발** streaks of snow; snowflakes. ¶ 굵은 ~ big flakes of snow / ~이 서다 It looks like snow. *or* It is threatening to snow.
**눈밭** snow-covered ground.
**눈병**(—病) 〖의학〗 eye trouble; an eye disease; sore eyes. ¶ ~나다 have eye trouble; be afflicted with an eye disease.
**눈보라** a snowstorm; a snowdrift; driving snow; a blizzard (심한). ¶ ~치다 have a snowstorm; snow drifts hard / ~를 만나다 be overtaken by a snowstorm / 열차는 ~에 갇혀 꼼짝 못했다 The train was brought to a standstill by the blizzard.
**눈부라리다** make *one's* eyes glare. ¶ 눈을 부라리고 노려보다 glare at 《*a person*》 with angry eyes.
**눈부시다** ① 《빛이》 (be) dazzling (to the eye); glaring; blinding. ¶ 눈부신 태양 the glaring sun / 눈부신 불빛 a glaring light / 눈(이) 부시게 흰 〔아름다운〕 dazzlingly white 〔beautiful〕 / 다이아몬드는 눈부시게 빛났다 The diamond sparkled with dazzling brilliance.
② 《업적 따위가》 (be) brilliant; splendid; striking; remarkable; conspicuous; wonderful; marvelous. ¶ 눈부신 업적 striking achievements / 눈부신 활약 remarkable activities / 눈부신 활약을 하다 「perform brilliant exploits 〔distinguish *oneself*〕 《in a battle》; play a conspicuous role 《in》 / 현대 과학은 눈부신 발달을 했다 Modern science has made startling progress.
**눈비음** dressing up for other's eyes. ~하다 dress up for other's eyes.
**눈빛** 《눈의 색》 the color of *one's* eyes; 《눈의 기색》 a look 〔the expression〕 in *one's* eyes. ¶ 호소하는 듯한 ~ a look of appeal / ~이 날카로운 남자 a man with a sharp look / 그 애가 거짓말을 하고 있다는 것을 ~으로 알 수 있다 I can see from his look that the boy is lying.
**눈사람** 《make》 a snowman.
**눈사태**(—沙汰) an avalanche; a snowslide. ¶ ~로 목숨을 잃은 등산가가 많다 Many mountain climbers were killed in the avalanche. ◉ ~방지 설비 《선로변의》 a snowshed.
**눈살** the furrow 〔wrinkles〕 between *one's* eyebrows. ¶ ~을 찌푸리고 with knitted brows; with a frown / ~을 찌

푸리다 knit *one's* brows 〔eyebrows〕; frown / 그녀는 ~을 찌푸리며 약을 먹었다 She made a face when she took the medicine.

**눈석이** snowmelt; meltwater.

**눈석임** a thaw; thawing (of snow). ~하다 thaw. ◉ 눈석잇길 a slushy 〔slush-filled〕 road.

**눈설다** (be) strange; unfamiliar (to *one's* eyes); new. ¶ 눈선 광경 an unfamiliar scenery.

**눈속이다** hoodwink 《*a person*》; take 《*a person*》 in; pull the wool over 《*a person's*》 eyes; cheat 〔deceive〕 《*a person*》. ¶ 감시의 눈을 속이다 elude vigilance / 세관원의 눈을 속이다 cheat a customs officer.

**눈속임** cheating; deceiving; hoodwinking; camouflage. ~하다 =눈속이다. ¶ 나는 눈속임을 당해서 가짜 보석을 샀다 I was hoodwinked into buying fake jewels.

**눈송이** a snowflake; a flake of snow. ¶ ~가 드문드문 내렸다 The flakes of snow fell sparsely.

**눈시울** the edge of the eyelid. ¶ ~이 뜨거워지다 be moved to tears; be touched 《by》 / 나는 ~이 뜨거워졌다 The tears were ready to well up in my eyes. *or* I was completely moved to tears. 「snow boots.

**눈신** 《설피》 《a pair of》 snowshoes;

**눈싸움**[1] snowballing; a game of snowballs; a snow(ball) fight. ~하다 play snowballs; have a snow(ball) fight.

**눈싸움**[2] 《눈겨룸》 a staring-out〔-down〕 game; an out-staring game.

**눈썰미** a quick eye for learning things. ¶ ~가 있다〔없다〕 have a quick 〔dull〕 eye for learning things.

**눈썹** eyebrows; brows. ¶ 반달 같은 ~ arched eyebrows / 짙은 ~ thick 〔bushy〕 eyebrows / 보기 좋은 ~ shapely eyebrows / ~을 밀다 shed 〔shave off〕 *one's* eyebrows / ~을 찌푸리다 frown; knit *one's* brows / 그는 그 광경을 보고서도 ~하나 까딱 안했다 He didn't even 「raise an eyebrow 〔bat an eyelid〕 at the sight. / 그녀는 ~을 그리고 립스틱을 발랐다 She penciled her eyebrows and put on lipstick. ◉ ~연필 an eyebrow pencil.

**눈씨** the force of *one's* stare; the power of *one's* eyes. ¶ ~가 맵다 be sharp=eyed; have keen 〔piercing〕 eyesight.

**눈알** an eyeball. ¶ ~이 툭 불거진 금붕어 a goldfish with bulging eyes / ~을 굴리다 roll 〔goggle〕 *one's* eyes / 그는 놀라서 ~이 튀어나올 지경이었다 His eyes almost popped out in surprise.

**눈앞** ① (***a***) 《면전》 ¶ ~에 before *one's* eyes; under *one's* (very) eyes 〔nose〕; in front of *one;* in the presence 《of *a person*》 / ~에 펼쳐지다 open 〔spread〕 out before 《*one, one's* eyes》; unfold itself out before 《*one, one's* eyes》 / 바로 내 ~에서 물건을 훔치다 steal a thing in my presence 〔under my very eyes〕 / 바로 ~에 우체국이 있다 There is a post office before us. / 교통사고가 그녀 (바로) ~에서 일어났다 A traffic accident occurred before her (very) eyes. (***b***) 《현재·당장》 ¶ ~의 immediate; at hand; direct / ~의 이익 an immediate profit / ~의 일만 생각하다 think only of the present 〔the immediate future〕; take a short view of things / ~의 이익만 노려서는 안 된다 You should not 「take a short-sighted policy 〔see immediate gains〕. ② 《가까운 장래》 ¶ ~에 닥치다 be near at hand; be imminent / 시험이 ~에 다가왔다 The examination is close at hand 〔is just ahead〕. / 그는 입시를 ~에 두고 열심히 공부하고 있다 He is studying hard just before the entrance examination. 「eyes.

**눈어리다** have dim 〔blurred, bleary〕

**눈어림** eye measure(ment). ⇨ 눈대중.

**눈엣가시** 《비유적》 a thorn in *one's* side; a pain in the neck; an eyesore. ¶ ~로 여기다 regard 《*a person*》 「as an eyesore 〔with hatred〕; treat 《*a person*》 like an enemy / 그녀는 왜 나를 ~처럼 여기는 것일까 Why does she always treat me like an enemy? *or* I wonder why she hates me.

**눈여겨보다** observe 〔watch, look at〕 carefully; have 〔take〕 a good 〔careful〕 look 《at》. ¶ 행동을 ~ observe 《*a person's*》 behavior carefully / 눈여겨보지 않으면 그 차이를 알아볼 수 없다 To the casual view there is almost no difference between them.

**눈요기**(―療飢) a feast for the eyes. ~하다 feast *one's* eyes 《on》. ¶ ~가 되다 be a feast 〔joy〕 to the eyes / 그녀의 춤은 ~가 되었다 Her dancing was a delight to watch.

**눈웃음** a smile with *one's* eyes; a smile in *one's* eyes. ¶ ~(을) 치다 smile with *one's* eyes; cast sheep's eyes 《at》.

**눈익다** (be) familiar (to *one's* eyes); become 〔get〕 used to seeing 《*a thing*》.

¶ 눈익은 얼굴〔광경〕 a familiar face 〔sight〕/ 눈에 익어 아무렇지도 않다 be hardened to the sight / 그 쌍둥이는 눈 익지 않으면 구별하기 어렵다 The twins are hardly distinguishable to the untrained eye.

**눈인사**(—人事) greeting with *one's* eyes. ~하다 nod 《to》; give 《*a person*》 a nod; greet with *one's* eyes. ¶ 서로 ~하다 exchange nods.

**눈자위** the rim of the eye. ¶ ~가 꺼졌다 《죽다》 "*one's* eyes have sunken"; be dead.

**눈접**(—接) 〖식물〗 bud grafting; budding; inlay. ~하다 graft a bud 《in, on》; bud; inlay. ¶ ~용 가지 a bud stick.

**눈정기**(—精氣) the keenness of *one's* eyes; the glitter of *one's* eyes. ¶~가 있다 be keen-eyed; have keen eyes.

**눈주다** give 《*a person*》 the eye; wink at; glance a message; eye 《*a person*》 meaningfully.

**눈짐작** = 눈대중.

**눈짓** a wink; winking. ~하다 wink at 《*a person*》; signal 〔make a sign with *one's* eyes〕; give an eye-signal; eye 《*a person*》 meaningly. ¶ 서로 ~하다 exchange glances 〔significant looks〕/ ~으로 알리다 make a sign with *one's* eye / 그녀가 ~하자 하인은 슬쩍 방을 나갔다 At a sign from her eyes the servant glided out of the room.

**눈초리** ① 《눈꼬리》 ⇨눈꼬리. ② 《눈매》 a look. ¶ 매서운 ~ a dreadful look / 의심하는 ~로 보다 view 《*something*》 with suspicious eyes; eye 〔regard, look on〕 《*something*》 with suspicion / 성난 ~로 보다 give an angry look 《to》/ 그는 무서운 ~로 나를 노려보았다 He glared at me with a fierce look.

**눈총** a glare; a sharp look; looking daggers 《at》. ¶ ~ 맞는 사람 an object of hatred; a hated person / ~(을) 맞다 be glared at; be hated 〔detested〕 《by》/ 뭇사람의 ~을 맞다 become a common object of hatred / 그런 짓을 하면 남의 ~을 맞을 뿐이다 To do so is to court hatred.

**눈총기**(—聰氣) eyesight; power of observation. ¶ ~가 좋다 have acute observation; have sharp 〔keen〕 eyes for...; be quick at learning.

**눈치** ① 《센스》 tact; sense; quick-wittedness. ¶ ~가 있다 be tactful; have the sense (enough) to *do* / ~가 없다 be tactless; lack the sense to *do* / ~가 빠르다〔무디다〕 be quick-witted 〔slow-witted〕; have quick 〔slow〕 wits / ~있게 …하다 have the good sense to *do;* be sensible enough to *do* / ~없게 굴어서 미안합니다 I'm sorry to be so slow to catch on. / 그는 정말 ~없는 녀석이다 He is terribly slow to see 「what's required 〔what he ought to do〕. /「어떻게 알아냈습니까」—「~지요」 "How did you make it out?"—"It was a hunch."

② 《마음의 기미》 *one's* mind 〔intention, inclination〕; *one's* mental attitude toward 《*a person*》; 《기색》 an expression; a sign; a hint; an indication. ¶ ~ 코치 다 알다 be well aware of the situation; know quite well how the wind blows / ~ 코치도 모르다 be blind to the whole situation; do not know how the wind blows / 좋아하는〔좋아하지 않는〕 ~를 보이다 give 〔show〕 signs of pleasure 〔displeasure〕/ 찬성하지 않는 ~를 보이다 hint *one's* disapproval / 싫어하는 ~ 하나 안 보이고 without showing the least sign of reluctance / ~를 살피다 read 〔study〕 《another's》 face / 그의 ~가 좀 이상하다 He is somewhat strange in his manners.

◉ ~놀음 adaptation of shy attitude and thinking much of what others say or think about them. ~작전 《입시 때의》 the wait-and-see 〔fence=sitting〕 policy in choice of university 《of an applicant》. 눈칫밥 food given unwillingly: 눈칫밥 먹다 eat 《another's》 salt.

**눈치레** (a) mere show; showy appearance; 《겉치레》 putting on a good front; make-believe. ~하다 dress up to appeal to the eye; make a show of; put on a good front. ¶ ~로 for show; for appearance sake.

**눈치보다** ① 《살피다》 read 〔study〕 《*a person's*》 expression; probe 《*a person's*》 motives; grasp a situation; see how the wind blows. ¶ 성내지 않았나 ~ study 《*a person's*》 face to see if *he* is angry / 눈치보아 가며 행동하다 act according to the situation / 어머니의 눈치를 보며 시험지를 내놓았다 I handed my mother the test paper, studying her face secretly. ② 《어려워하다》 feel constraint 〔uneasy〕 《in *a person's* presence》; have a regard for 《*a person's*》 feelings. ¶ 눈치보지 말고 얼마든지 오래 있어라 Make yourself at home and stay as long as you like.

**눈치채다** become aware of 《*a person's* intention, motive, design, *etc.*》; get a hint 《of》; scent; sense; get wind 〔scent〕 of; have an inkling 《of》. ¶ 눈치채이다 excite 〔arouse〕 《*a person's*》 suspicion; be smelled out / 눈치 안 채이고 without exciting suspicion; without being noticed; secretly; in secret / (일이) 눈치 안 채이고 넘어가다 pass unnoticed / 눈치 안 채이게 들어가다〔나오다〕 slip in 〔out〕; steal in 〔out〕; sneak in 〔out〕 / 주인은 마침내 두 사람 사이를 눈치챘다 The secret love between the two came to the knowledge of their master at last. / 그는 위험을 눈치채고, 바로 그 자리를 떠났다 He sensed (the) danger, and left the place at once. / 네가 나를 미워하는 것을 눈치챈 지 오래다 I have been aware of your hatred for some time.

**눈코** the eyes and the nose. ¶ ~ 뜰 새 없다 be very busy; have no time 〔leisure〕 / ~ 뜰 새 없이 지내다 live in a whirl 《of business》 / 나는 지금 ~ 뜰 새 없이 바쁘다 I'm terribly busy now. *or* I'm having a hectic time of it.

**눈트다** 《식물이》 bud (out); come into bud. ¶ 초목이 눈틀 무렵 when trees and grasses bud; when new buds begin to appear.

**눈허리시다** 《우습다》 (be) funny; side-splitting; 《아니꼽다》 (be) disgusting; revolting; sickening 《with》.

**눈흘기다** glare 〔stare〕 at; look sharply at; look daggers 《at》.

**눋다** get scorched 〔burned〕; burn; scorch; singe. ¶ 눌은 밥 scorched rice / 밥이 ~ rice gets scorched / 눋지 않도록 계속 휘저어라 Stir it constantly to prevent burning.

**눌러** ① 《계속하여》 repeatedly; continuously; 《내리》 straight; in a row; running. ¶ ~ 앉다 continue to stay; stay on (and on); 《유임하다》 remain in the same position; remain in power 〔office〕 / 내가 이곳에 ~ 살게 된지 벌써 2년이 된다 It has already been two years since I settled here.
② 《너그러이》 generously; tolerantly; leniently; kindly; gracefully. ¶ ~ 용서하다 forgive generously.

**눌러듣다** take 《*a person's* remark》 with kindly tolerance 〔with good grace〕. ¶ 무심코 한 말이니 눌러들어 주십시오 Please forgive me for my slip of the tongue.

**눌러보다** treat 「with generosity 〔kindly, with good grace〕. ¶ 철없는 애니 눌러보아 주십시오 Kindly forgive him, since he is just a boy with little sense.

**눌리다**[1] 《눋게 하다》 scorch; burn; singe. ¶ 옷을 불에 ~ scorch *one's* clothes in front of the fire / 밥을 ~ burn 〔overcook〕 rice.

**눌리다**[2] ① 《누름을 당하다》 be pressed down; be held down. ¶ 납작하게 ~ be pressed flat / 눌려 죽다 be crushed to death. ② 《압도되다》 be suppressed; be oppressed; be put down 〔repressed, overpowered, surpassed〕. ¶ 다수에 ~ be overwhelmed by the superior number / 마누라에 ~ be henpecked; be tied to *one's* wife's apron strings / 토론에서 ~ be overpowered 〔overwhelmed〕 by the argument 〔eloquence〕 / 적의 수에 ~ be overpowered by the enemy's numbers / 작은 가게는 큰 가게에 눌려서 장사가 잘 안된다 Little shops are jostled out of trade by big ones.

**눌변**(訥辯) being poor 〔clumsy〕 in speaking; being awkward in speech. ¶ ~이다 be a poor 〔an awkward〕 speaker; be ineloquent. ◉ ~가 a poor speaker.

**눌어붙다** ① 《타서》 get scorched and sticks 《to》. ¶ 밥이 솥에 ~ rice gets scorched and sticks to the bottom of the pot. ② 《한 곳에》 stay on; stay (too) long; overstay (*one's* time); 《한자리에》 remain in the same position; settle down. ¶ 눌어붙어 남의 눈총을 받다 outstay 〔wear out〕 *one's* welcome / 시골에 눌어붙어 살다 settle down in the country / 한 자리에 눌어붙어 움직이지 않다 squat down in one place and don't move; stay on in the same place; remain in the same position.

**눌은밥** scorched 〔burned〕 rice (at the bottom of a pot).

**눕다** lie down; lay *oneself* down; stretch *oneself*. ¶ 자리에 ~ lie in *one's* bed / 풀밭 위에 ~ lie 〔throw〕 *oneself* down on the grass / 몸을 죽 펴고 ~ lie at full length 《on the bed》 / 몸져 ~ lie sick in bed; be ill in bed / 누워 자다 lie down to sleep / 당분간 누워 있어야 해요 You ought to be in bed for the present. / 누워서 떡먹기다 《속담》 Nothing could be easier. *or* That's a piece of cake. *or* It's as easy as pie. / 누워 침뱉기다 《속담》 If you spit into the wind, you'll just get it back in your face. /그런 짓은 누워 침뱉기나 마찬가지다 If you do that, you're simply making a rod for your own back.

**눕히다** lay down; make 〔have〕 《*a per-*

*son*》 lie down. ¶ 자리에 ~ put 《a child》 to bed / 재목을 눕혀 놓다 lay the lumber down on the ground / (한 주먹에) 때려 ~ knock 《*a person*》 down; floor 《*a person*》 with a blow.

**눙치다** appease 〔soothe〕 with nice words. ¶ 슬쩍 눙쳐 노염을 풀게 하다 soothe 〔calm〕 down an angry man.

**뉘**[1] 《쌀에 섞인》 unhulled 〔rough〕 rice; rice in the husk.

**뉘**[2] 《자손의》 blessings from offspring. ¶ 뉘(를) 보다 「enjoy the attention of 〔be cared for by〕 *one's* children and grandchildren.

**뉘**[3] 《누구》 who; 《누구의》 whose. ¶ 당신은 뉘시오 Who are you? / 뉘 집에 죽이 끓는지 밥이 끓는지 아나 《속담》 There is no knowing who is rich and who is poor.

**뉘다** ⇨ 누이다[1,2].

**뉘렇다** (be) sallow; sickly yellow.

**뉘반지기** rice containing many grains of unhulled rice.

**뉘앙스** nuance; a (delicate) shade of meaning. ¶ 시적 표현의 미묘한 ~ a delicate 〔subtle〕 nuance of poetic expression / 그 말에는 미묘한 ~의 차이가 있다 The word has a delicate shade of difference in meaning.

**뉘엿거리다** ① 《해가》 be ready to set. ¶ 해가 서산에 뉘엿거린다 The sun hangs on the western hill ready to set. ② 《속이》 feel nauseated; feel sick. ¶ 속이 ~ feel nausea; feel sick to *one's* stomach / 그 치즈 때문에 속이 뉘엿거린다 The cheese sickens me.

**뉘엿뉘엿** ① 《해가》 ready to set. ② 《속이》 nauseating; sickening.

**뉘우쁘다** (be) regretful; penitent.

**뉘우치다** repent 《of *one's* past error》; regret; be sorry 《for》; be penitent 《for》; feel remorse 《for》. ¶ 뉘우치는 빛도 없이 without any contrition 〔repentance〕 / 죄를 ~ repent *one's* sin / 잘못을 ~ regret *one's* mistake / 뉘우칠 일은 없다 have no regrets; have nothing to repent of / 자기가 한 짓을 ~ regret *one's* act; be sorry for what *one* has done / 중도 퇴학한 것을 ~ I am sorry I left school halfway. / 그는 뉘우치는 빛이 조금도 없다 He makes no sign of repentance. / 이제 와서 뉘우쳐도 소용 없다 It is no use repenting now. *or* It is no use crying over spilt milk. / 그는 자기의 어리석은 짓에 대하여 뉘우침의 눈물을 흘렸다 He shed tears of remorse for his folly.

**뉴기니** 《오세아니아의 섬》 New Guinea. ◉ ~사람 a New Guinean.

**뉴딜정책**(一政策) 《1930년대 미국의 경기 회복 정책》 the New Deal.

**뉴라운드** 〖경제〗 the New Round.

**뉴런** 〖해부〗 《신경 단위》 a neuron(e). ¶ ~의 neuronal; neuronic.

**뉴룩** 《최신 유행형》 a new look. ¶ ~의 모자 a new-look hat / 이 옷이 금년의 ~이다 This dress is the latest fashion for this year.

**뉴멕시코** 《미국의 주》 New Mexico (생략 N.M.). ◉ ~사람 a New Mexican.

**뉴미디어** new media.

**뉴스** news (★ 단수 취급. 「한 가지 뉴스」의 경우는 a piece of news라고 함); 《방송의》 news events. ¶ 해외〔국내〕 ~ foreign 〔home, domestic〕 news / 스폿 ~ spot news / 전광판 ~ news on the sky sign / 십대 ~ ten big items of news / 요약된 짤막한 ~ news in brief / 좋은〔나쁜〕 ~ good 〔bad〕 news / ~의 출처 a news source / …에 관한 최신 ~ the latest news on... / ~(거리)가 되다 make 〔become〕 news / 방금 들어온 ~에 의하면 according to the latest news 《from Washington》 / 오늘 신문에 그 사고의 ~가 실려 있다 There's some news about the accident in today's paper. / 아폴로 11호가 달에 착륙에 성공했다는 ~가 들어왔다 A report came in that Apollo 11 succeeded in landing on the moon. / 오늘은 특별히 중요한 ~가 없다 There's no big news in particular today. / TV〔라디오〕로 7시 ~를 보았다 〔들었다〕 I watched 〔listened to〕 the seven o'clock news on TV 〔the radio〕. ◉ ~가치 news value: ~ 가치 있는 사건 a newsworthy event. ~방송 newscasting; 《1회의》 a news broadcast; a newscast. ~속보 a news flash. ~쇼 사회자 the host of news show. ~시간 《라디오·TV의》 the news (hour). ~영화 a newsreel; a news film 〔picture〕: ~영화관 a news theater. ~카메라맨 a news photographer. ~캐스터 a newscaster; 《종합 사회자》 an anchor(man); an anchorperson. ~해설 《radio, TV》 news commentary: ~ 해설자 a news commentator 〔analyst〕.

**뉴올리언스** 《미국의 항구》 New Orleans.

**뉴욕** ① 《미국의 주》 New York (생략 N.Y.). ② 《시》 New York (City). ◉ ~사람 a New Yorker.

**뉴잉글랜드** 《미국 북동부의 여러 주》 New England. ◉ ~사람 a New Englander.

**뉴저지** 《미국의 주》 New Jersey (생략 N.J.). ◉ ~사람 a New Jerseyite.

**뉴질랜드** New Zealand (생략 N.Z.). ◉ ~사람 a New Zealander.

**뉴캐슬병**(—病)《가금의》 Newcastle disease.

**뉴턴** ①《영국의 물리학자·수학자》 Isaac Newton (1642-1727). ¶ ~ 물리학 Newtonian physics / ~의 만유인력의 법칙 Newton's law of (universal) gravitation / ~의 운동 법칙 Newton's law of motion. ②〖물리〗《힘의 단위》 a newton (생략 N).

**뉴트론**〖물리〗《중성자》 a neutron.

**뉴펀들랜드**《캐나다의 섬》 Newfoundland (생략 N.F.). ◉ ~개 a Newfoundland (dog).

**뉴페이스**《신인》 a new face 〔star〕; a new name《among the actors》.

**뉴햄프셔**《미국의 주》 New Hampshire (생략 N.H.). ◉ ~사람 a New Hampshireman.

**느글거리다** feel nausea; feel sick 〔queasy〕; have a sick stomach. ¶ 속이 ~ feel nausea 〔sick〕; be sick at the stomach / 보기만 해도 느글거린다 The mere sight of it makes me sick.

**느긋하다** be greatly pleased 〔satisfied, contented, gratified〕《with》; be relaxed 〔relieved〕. ¶ 느긋한 기분 a contented feeling / 느긋한 생활을 하다 live in contentment; live a satisfied life / 저녁을 잘 먹고 나니 ~ After such a good dinner, I feel relaxed. / 일과 후의 커피 한 잔은 기분을 느긋하게 해준다 A cup of coffee after work relaxes me. / 한 3년 먹을 것을 벌어 놓으니 마음이 ~ I am sitting easy now that I have earned enough money to keep me going for three years.

**느끼다** ①《지각하다》 feel; be aware 〔conscious〕《of》; sense; realize (실감하다); appreciate (고맙게). ¶ 추위〔더위〕를 ~ feel the cold 〔heat〕/ 아픔을 ~ feel a pain《in *one's* chest》/ 어려움을 ~ find 〔have〕 difficulty《in *do*ing》; find it difficult《to *do*》/ 기쁨을 ~ feel 〔experience, know〕 joy / 배고픔을 ~ feel hunger / 불편을 ~ experience 〔suffer〕 inconvenience; find it inconvenient《to *do*》/ 슬픔을 ~ feel 〔undergo〕 sorrow / 의분을 ~ feel righteous indignation / 필요를 절실히 ~ see 〔feel〕 keenly the necessity《of》/ 팔에 무엇이 닿는 것을 ~ feel a touch on *one's* arm / 느끼지 않다 be insensitive《to pains》; be dead《to all sense of shame》/ 다리에 갑작스러운 통증을 느꼈다 I felt a sudden pain in my leg. / 그때처럼 나의 무지를 절실하게 느낀 적은 없었다 Never had I realized my ignorance more keenly than I did then. / 고된 일이 끝난 뒤의 휴일은 참 좋은 것이라고 그는 느꼈다 He appreciated a holiday after hard work. / 나는 갑자기 위험을 느꼈다 I suddenly sensed danger. / 그녀는 미행당하고 있음을 느꼈다 She was aware of being followed. *or* She was conscious that she was being followed.
②《감동하다》 be impressed《by, with》; be moved 〔touched〕《by》. ¶ 깊이 느끼게 하다 touch《*a person*》 to the heart; impress 〔move〕《*a person*》 profoundly / 세상의 덧없음을 ~ realize the uncertainty of life《with》/ 나는 그 시를 읽고 깊은 감동을 느꼈다 I am deeply touched by the poem. / 그는 느낀 바 있어 술을 끊었다 He gave up drinking for reasons of his own. / 나는 친구들의 친절에 고마움을 느끼고 있다 I am grateful to my friends for their kindness.
③《흐느끼다》 be overwhelmed with grief; sob. ¶ 느껴 울다가 잠들다 sob *oneself* to sleep.

**느끼하다**《맛이》 (be) greasy 〔fatty, oily〕; be too rich;《속이》 (be) sick to the stomach. ¶느끼한 국 greasy 〔fatty〕 soup / 기름진 음식을 먹었더니 속이 ~ I feel sick after having fatty 〔rich〕 food.

**느낌** ①《감각》 feeling; a sense;《촉감》 a 〔the〕 touch;《감촉》 a 〔the〕 feel. ¶ 아픈 ~ a sense of pain / ~이 들다 feel; have the feel of《*something*》/ …하고 싶은 ~이 들다 feel like《*do*ing》/ 무언가 이상한 ~이 들었다 Somehow I felt strange. / 이 천은 까칠까칠한〔매끈매끈한〕 ~이 난다 This cloth feels rough 〔smooth〕. *or* This cloth is rough 〔smooth〕 to the touch. / 추위로 손가락 끝의 ~이 없어졌다 My fingertips became numb with cold. / 누군가가 커튼 뒤에 있는 것 같은 ~이 들었다 I had a feeling that somebody was behind the curtain.
②《인상》 an impression; a feeling (예감·기분); an effect (그림 따위의). ¶~이 좋은 사람 a pleasant 〔an agreeable, a nice〕 person / ~이 나쁜 사람 an unpleasant 〔a disagreeable〕 person / 밝은 ~을 주는 그림 a cheerful picture / 좋은〔나쁜〕 ~을 주다 make 〔produce〕 a favorable 〔an unfavorable〕 impression on《*a person*》; impress《*a person*》 favorably 〔unfavorably〕/ …한 ~을 주다 impress 〔strike, affect〕《*a person*》 as《strange》; give an impression

《of》/ 이 그림은 전체적인 ~이 좋다 The general effect of this picture appeals to me. / 아무래도 길을 잘못 든 ~이 든다 I 「have 〔am under〕 the impression that we've taken the wrong road. / 그를 만나본 ~이 어떠했지 How did he impress you when you met him? / 내 ~으로 그는 오고 싶어하지 않는 것 같다 It is my impression that he's unwilling to come. ◉ ~표 〖문법〗 an exclamation mark 〔point〕.

**-느냐** what; why; how, *etc.* ¶ 어디로 가느냐 Where are you going? / 무엇을 하고 있느냐 What are you doing?

**느닷없다** (be) abrupt; sudden; unexpected. ¶ 느닷없는 방문 a surprise visit 《from *a person*》/ 느닷없는 말 an abrupt 〔unexpected〕 remark / 느닷없는 짓 unexpected and improper behavior; strange behavior / 느닷없는 물음에 나는 매우 당황했다 I was completely nonplused by his unexpected question.

**느닷없이** 《갑자기》 abruptly; suddenly; all of a sudden; 《뜻밖에》 unexpectedly; 《예고없이》 without notice 〔warning〕. ¶ ~ 치르는 시험 a pop test / ~ 나타나다 appear unexpectedly / ~ 덤벼들다 make a sudden spring 《at *a person*》/ ~ 치다 hit 《*a person*》 suddenly; hit 《*a person*》 without warning / ~ 해고하다 dismiss 《*a person*》 without notice / 나는 그녀가 ~ 방문하는 바람에 당황했다 I was puzzled by her 「unexpected 〔surprise〕 visit.

**-느라고** ① 《이유》 what with 《*do*ing》; as a result of 《*do*ing》. ¶ 공부하느라고 잠잘 시간이 없다 What with studying I have no time to sleep. / 점심 먹느라고 늦었다 Lunch made me late. ② 《의도》 with the idea to 《*do*》; with the intention of 《*do*ing》. ¶ …느라고 애를 쓰다 make an effort to *do* / 어머니는 쿠키 만드시느라고 분주하시다 Mother is busy (in) making cookies (★ in이 없는 꼴이 구어적).

**-느라니** ¶ 혼자 있느라니 쓸쓸하다 I feel lonesome all by myself.

**-느라면** ¶ 그러느라면 meanwhile / 사느라면 별일 다 당하는 법이다 You have to put up with a lot of things to stay alive.

**느럭느럭** slowly; sluggishly; leisurely; idly. ¶ ~ 움직이다 move sluggishly.

**느루** (stretched out) over a long period of time; so that 《it》 lasts. ¶ ~먹다 eat 《it》 sparingly; make 《it》 last.

**느릅나무** 〖식물〗 an elm (tree).

**느리광이** a sluggard; an idler.

**느리다** ① 《동작이》 (be) slow; tardy; sluggish. ¶ 느린 열차 a slow train / 동작이 ~ move slowly; be slow moving / 일(손)이 ~ be slow in 〔at〕 *one's* work; be a slow worker / 걸음이 ~ be slow-footed; be a slow walker / 말이 ~ talk slowly / 머리 회전이 ~ be slow-witted; be dull / 그는 계산이 ~ He is slow at figures. / 그는 느리기는 하지만 꾸준히 발전하고 있다 He is making slow but steady progress. / 그는 굼벵이처럼 ~ He is as slow as a snail. ② 《성기다》 (be) loose; slack. ¶ 올이 느린 천 a fabric of loose texture.

**느림** 《장식술》 a tassel.

**느릿느릿** ① 《더디게》 slowly; sluggishly. ~하다 (be) sluggish; slow-moving. ¶ ~ 걷다 walk slowly / ~ 나아가다 proceed at a slow 〔snail's〕 pace; make *one's* way with slow steps / 교통이 혼잡해서 굼벵이처럼 ~ 운전할 수밖에 없었다 I had to slow to a crawl because of heavy traffic. ② 《성기게》 loose(ly); slack. ~하다 be all loose 〔slack〕.

**느물거리다** talk 〔behave〕 brazenly 〔insidiously〕; act craftily 〔trickily〕.

**느물느물** trickily; insidiously.

**느슨하다** ① 《헐겁다》 (be) loose; slack; lax; be not tight (마개 따위가); 《복장 따위가》 (be) untidy. ¶ 느슨한 매듭 a loose knot / 느슨한 밧줄 a slack rope / 느슨하게 loosely / 느슨히 매다〔묶다〕 string 〔tie〕 loosely / 느슨해지다 loosen; become 〔get〕 loose 〔slack〕 / 복장이 ~ be untidily dressed. ② 《마음이》 (be) relaxed; loose; slack; easygoing. ¶ 《성격이》 느슨한 사람 an easygoing person; a slovenly fellow / 느슨해지다 become 〔get〕 remiss 〔loose〕; relax; slack(en) off; 《경계가》 be careless; be off *one's* guard / 시합이 끝나자 마음이 느슨해졌다 I found myself very relaxed after the game was over. / 경계심이 느슨한 탓에 소매치기를 당했다 I had my pocket picked because I was off my guard. / 대부분의 과오는 마음이 느슨해진 때문이었다 Most of the errors came from being careless.

**느즈러지다** ① 《이완되다》 loosen; slacken; become 〔get, come〕 loose; be loosened. ¶ 느즈러진 밧줄 slack rope / 느즈러진 피부 flabby skin / 허리띠가 ~ *one's* belt loosens 〔becomes loose〕 / 매듭이 ~ a knot becomes 〔gets〕 loose. ② 《기한이》 be put off 〔over〕; be postponed 〔prolonged〕. ③ 《마음이》 《*one's* mind》 relax; become 〔get〕 remiss 〔loose〕.

**느지감치** rather late; later (than usual). ¶ 아침 ～ 일어나다 get up rather late in the morning / 저녁 ～ 도착하다 arrive a bit late in the evening.

**느지막이** = 느직이.

**느지막하다** be rather late.

**느직이** ①《좀 늦게》 rather late; rather slow. ¶ 저녁 ～ 귀가하다 come home rather late in the evening. ②《느슨히》 rather slack 〔loose〕. ¶ ～ 매다 tie rather loose.

**느직하다** ①《시간이》 be rather late; somewhat 〔a little〕 late; 《행동이》 be rather slow. ¶ 느직한 아침식사 a late 〔latish〕 breakfast. ②《느슨하다》 be rather slack; a little loose.

**느타리** 『식물』《버섯》 an agaric.

**느티나무** 『식물』 a zelkova tree.

**느헤미야기**(一記) 『성서』 (The Book of) Nehemiah (생략 Neh.).

**늑간**(肋間) [형용사적] 『해부』 intercostal; between the ribs. ◉ ～근 intercostal muscle. ～신경 the intercostal nerve: ～신경통 『의학』 intercostal neuralgia.

**늑골**(肋骨) 『해부』 a rib; the ribs [총칭].

**늑대** a wolf (*pl.* wolves). ¶ ～의〔같은〕 wolfish / ～의 무리 a pack of wolves / ～ 울음소리 a wolf's cry 〔howl〕.

**늑막**(肋膜) 『해부』 the pleura (*pl.* -rae). ¶ ～의 pleural. ◉ ～염 『의학』 pleurisy: 건성〔습성〕 ～염 dry 〔wet〕 pleurisy.

**늑연골**(肋軟骨) 『해부』 a costal cartilage.

**늑장부리다** dawdle 《over》; dally away; linger; tarry; be slow(-moving); slow up 〔down〕 《work》; be tardy 《in *doing something*》. ¶ 늑장부리며 일하다 linger over *one's* work / ～가 기회를 놓치다 dally away *one's* opportunity / 늑장부리지 말고 빨리 다녀오너라 Come back without delay. *or* Don't linger along the way.

**늑재**(肋材) 『조선』 a frame (timber); a rib; futtocks.

**-는** [조사] ¶ 나는 가지 않는다 (As for me,) I won't go. / 그는 의사다 He is a doctor. / 국화는 지금 한창이다 The chrysanthemums are at their best.

**-는** [어미] -ing (★ 현재를 나타내는 시제). ¶ 나는 새 a flying bird / 오르는 물가 rising prices / 그가 읽고 있는 신문 the newspaper that he is reading.

**-는가** [종결어미] ¶ 무얼 하는가 What are you doing? / 자네 어디를 갔다 오는가 Where have you been?

**-는가 보다** ¶ 비가 오는〔왔는〕가 보다 It seems 「to be raining 〔to have rained〕. / 오늘 학교에 오지 않은 것을 보니 그는 병이 났는가 보다 I guess he is sick since he is absent from school today.

**-는가 하면** ¶ 새들이 머리 위에서 지저귀는가 하면 다람쥐들이 발 밑을 스쳐가기도 한다 Not only are there birds chirping overhead but also squirrels darting underfoot.

**-는 대로** ① ¶ 될〔할〕 수 있는 대로 to the extent possible; as much 〔nearly〕 as possible / 내가 하는 대로 하지 말고 당신 마음대로 하십시오 Don't do just as I do, do as you like. ②《즉시로》 as soon as. ¶ 여권이 나오는 대로 as soon as my passport is issued / 도착하는 대로 as soon as *one* arrives; on *one's* arrival / 그가 돌아오는 대로 곧 말씀 전하겠습니다 As soon as he comes back I'll give him your message.

**-는데** ① [연결어미] ¶ 우리 동네에 한 사람이 있는데 재간이 비상하다 There is a man in our village who is extraordinary talented. / 김 선생에게 편지를 쓰는데 무슨 부탁할 말씀이 없으십니까 I'm writing to Mr. Kim.—Is there anything you want me to tell him? / 사기는 사겠는데 지금은 돈이 없다 I'm going to buy it all right, but I have no money with me now.

② [종결어미] ¶ 잘하는데 You're doing well! / 참 맛있는데요 How tasty it is! / 그 아이 잘 생겼는데 What a handsome child (he is)!

**-는데도** ¶ 우리는 비가 오는데도 외출했다 We went out in spite of the rain. / 그는 50이 넘었는데도 황소처럼 일을 한다 Though past fifty, he works like an ox.

**는적거리다** (be) flabby 〔pulpy, squashy〕 「《from rot》.

**는적는적** pulpily; squashily; flabbily.

**-는 족족** every 〔each〕 occasion that it happens; whatever time (that); whenever; every 〔each〕 time (that); as often as. ¶ 낳는 족족 아들이다 give birth to sons every time / 보는 족족 체포해라 Arrest every one you see.

**-는지** ① [연결어미] ¶ 그가 잠자는지도 모른다 Maybe he's sleeping. / 몇 사람이나 가는지 아세요 Do you know how many people are going? ② [종결어미] ¶ 그녀는 지금 어떻게 지내고 있는지 How is she getting along, I wonder? / 도대체 언제쯤이라야 다 되는지 It pains me to think when it will be ready.

**는지렁이** sticky 〔viscous〕 liquid; mucilage; slime. ¶ 달팽이의 ～ the slimy trail of a snail.

**늗질거리다** be 〔feel〕 squashy 〔pulpy, flabby, soft and mushy〕.

**는커녕** [조사] anything but; far from; not at all. ⇨커녕. ¶ 그렇기는커녕 far from it; on the contrary / 실망하기는커녕 far from being disappointed / 위스키는커녕 맥주도 못한다 He does not drink beer, to say nothing of whisky.

**늘** 《항상》 always; usually; all the time (언제나); 《습관적으로》 habitually. ¶ 늘 그러하듯이 as usual; in *one's* usual way / 늘 …하곤 하다 be in the habit of *do*ing; make it a rule to *do* / 늘 아프다〔바쁘다〕 be always ill 〔busy〕 / 그는 늘 지각한다 He always comes late. / 저 녀석은 늘 불평만 한다 That fellow is grumbling all the time. / 우리는 토요일 밤에는 늘 외출합니다 We usually go out on Saturday nights. / 그에게 전화를 할 때마다 늘 통화중이다 Whenever 〔Every time〕 I call him, the line is busy. / 그는 부모에게 늘 걱정만 끼친다 He is a constant source of anxiety to his parents.

> 참고 「빈도」를 나타내는 부사
> (1) 문장 안에서 always, usually의 위치는 대개의 경우 일반 동사의 앞, 조동사·be동사의 뒤에 놓인다.
> (2) 빈도를 나타내는 부사의 그 정도를 백분율로 나타내 보면, 대체로 다음과 같다 always, all the time—(100%); usually—(80%); often, not always—(60%); sometimes—(50%); occasionally, not often—(40%); rarely, seldom—(25%); never—(0%).

**늘그막** *one's* old 〔advanced〕 age; *one's* later 〔declining〕 years. ¶ ～에 이르러 in *one's* old age; in *one's* declining years; when (*one* is) old / ～에 고생하다 have a hard time late in *one's* life / ～에 호강하다 live in luxury in *one's* old age / ～에 아들을 얻다 have a son in *one's* old age.

**늘다** ① 《수·양이》 increase; 《힘·무게 따위가》 gain; 《강물 따위가》 rise; swell; 《인구·이자 따위가》 augment. ¶ 수가〔양이〕 ～ increase 〔grow〕 in number(s) 〔volume〕 / 경험이 ～ gain experience / 체중이 (2킬로) ～ gain (two kilograms) in weight / 늘지 않도록 하다 keep 《the population》 from increasing; check the (further) increase 《of》; be careful not to gain 《weight》 / 세간의 신용이 ～ public confidence 《in the company》 increases 〔rises〕 / 인기가 ～ gain in popularity / 호우로 강물이 늘었다 The river swelled because of the heavy rain. / 이 도시의 인구는 최근 급속히 늘었다 The population of this city has increased rapidly in recent years. / 차량의 수가 계속 늘고 있다 The number of the cars 「goes on increasing 〔is on the increase〕. / 매출이 지난 2년간 두〔세〕배로 늘었다 Sales have doubled 〔tripled〕 in the last two years. / 수출이 작년보다 30% 늘었다 The export increased by 30 percent over last year. / 「자네 요즘 체중이 는 것 같은데」—「그래, 2킬로나 늘었어」 "You've gained weight lately, haven't you?"—"Yes, I've gained as much as two kilograms." ② 《번식하다》 breed; propagate; multiply. ⇨번식. ¶ 바퀴벌레의 수가 급격히 늘었다 Cockroaches multiplied rapidly. ③ 《솜씨·실력 따위가》 advance; make progress 《in》; improve 《in》; get better 《at》; get 〔become〕 good 《at》. ¶ 재간이 ～ improve in skill / 영어 실력이 ～ make progress in English; improve *oneself* in English / 그녀의 테니스 솜씨가 급격히 늘었다 She quickly became good 「at 〔in playing〕 tennis.

**늘리다** ① 《수·양을》 increase; add 《to》; augment; multiply; raise (증액하다). ¶ 재산을 ～ increase *one's* fortune; add to *one's* wealth; become richer / 인원을 ～ increase the personnel 〔number of persons〕 《from five to ten》; add to the staff; get more people to work / 저금을 ～ add to *one's* saving / 지지자를 ～ gain supporters / 차입금을 더 ～ get more deeply in debt / 경찰은 순찰차를 늘렸다 The police increased the number of their patrol cars. / 지식을 늘리기 위해 책을 더 많이 읽어야 한다 I have to read more to 「add to 〔enrich〕 my knowledge. ② 《확장하다》 enlarge; expand; extend; widen. ¶ 집을 ～ extend a house; build an annex 〔extension〕 to the house / 사업을 ～ extend *one's* business / 운동장을 ～ enlarge the playground / 강폭을 ～ widen a river / 길을 ～ widen the road.

**늘보** a sluggard; a slowpoke 《미구어》.

**늘비하다** be 〔stand〕 in a row 〔line〕; be arrayed 〔displayed〕; be lined up. ¶ 연도에는 선물 가게가 늘비했다 The street was lined with souvenir stores. / 자동차가 늘비하게 늘어서 있다 There is an array of motorcars. / 온갖 종류의 술병들이 진열창 안에 늘비했다 All sorts of wine bottles were displayed in the show window.

**늘썽늘썽** (all) coarsely; loosely.

**늘썽하다** (be) loose; rough; coarse (거친). ¶ 늘썽한 천 loose-woven cloth; (a) fabric with a loose weave / 늘썽한 그물 a large-mesh(ed) net; a net with large meshes / 늘썽하게 짜다 knit with large stitches.

**늘씬하다** ① 《키가》 (be) tall and slender; slim; graceful; svelte. ¶ 그 패션 모델은 몸매가 매우 늘씬했다 The fashion model had a very 「slim 〔slender〕 figure. ② 《힘없이 늘어지다》 [서술적] be exhausted; be fagged 〔worn〕 out; be reduced to pulp. ¶ 늘씬하게 severely; hard; soundly / 늘씬하게 때려주다 beat 《*a person*》 soundly 〔to a pulp〕; pommel 〔beat〕 《*a person*》 to a jelly 〔mummy〕 / 늘씬하게 얻어맞다 be struck hard; be pommeled to a jelly.

**늘어가다** ① 《수량이》 be on the increase; be increasing 〔swelling〕; go on increasing; 《금액이》 go 〔run〕 up 《to a large sum》. ¶ 빚이 늘어간다 My debts go on increasing. / 지출이 늘어간다 The expenditure is swelling. / 청소년 범죄가 늘어간다 Juvenile delinquency keeps 〔goes〕 on increasing. / 교통 사고로 인한 사망자의 수가 해마다 늘어가고 있다 The number of deaths by traffic accidents 「is increasing 〔is on the increase〕 every year. ② 《솜씨·실력 따위가》 be in progress; be progressing 〔advancing, improving〕. ¶ 너의 피아노 솜씨가 급속히 늘어가고 있다 You are making rapid progress at the piano.

**늘어나다** lengthen; grow longer; stretch; extend; expand. ¶ 늘어나는 (성질이 있는) extensible; expansible / 고무줄이 ~ a rubber band stretches / 늘어났다 줄어들었다하다 be elastic 〔flexible, adaptable〕 / 열을 받으면 대개의 금속은 부피가 늘어난다 Heat expands most metals.

**늘어놓다** ① 《벌여놓다》 arrange; array; display; place 《*things*》 in order; spread out. ¶ 책을 한 줄로 ~ arrange books in a row / 상품을 진열창에 ~ display goods in a show window / 상품을 노상에 ~ spread goods out on the street / 크기의 순으로 ~ range 〔arrange〕 things by size / 의자를 한 줄에 다섯 개씩 늘어놓았다 We arranged five chairs in every row. ② 《어지르다》 scatter about; put in disorder; leave 《*things*》 lying about. ¶ 옷을 방에 ~ leave *one's* clothes lying about in the room / 방에 종이쪽들을 ~ litter a room with scraps of paper. ③ 《사업을》 extend; expand. ¶ 장사를 크게 ~ extend *one's* business. ④ 《말을》 mention; enumerate; dwell on. ¶ 불평을 ~ make 〔voice〕 a series of complaints / 아무의 결점을 ~ enumerate 〔name〕 *a person's* faults one by one / 허튼 수작을 ~ talk a lot of nonsense / 그는 지루한 이야기를 길게 늘어놓았다 He dwelt on the uninteresting story. / 그는 그 계획의 장점을 조목조목 늘어놓았다 He itemized the good points of the plan.

**늘어뜨리다** hang (down); suspend; droop; dangle; let 《*one's* hair》 down; sling; [사물이 주어] trail. ¶ 팔을 축 늘어뜨리고 with arms dangling / 꼬리를 ~ droop it's tail / 커튼을 ~ hang down a curtain 《over, on》 / 시곗줄을 ~ dangle the chain of a watch / 머리를 ~ droop *one's* head / 치맛 자락을 ~ let down *one's* skirt; trail *one's* skirt / 줄을 지붕에서 ~ hang down 〔suspend〕 a rope from the roof / 소녀는 발을 (대롱대롱) 늘어뜨리고 의자에 앉았다 The girl sat on a chair with her feet dangling. / 그녀가 머리를 늘어뜨리면 허리까지 죽 내려온다 When she lets her hair down, it reaches all the way down to her waist.

**늘어서다** stand in a row; form a line; line up; be drawn up; make a queue. ¶ 두 줄로 ~ form 〔stand in〕 two rows / 군인들이 길가에 ~ soldiers line up along the road / 배급을 타려고 죽 ~ make a queue waiting for the ration / 우리는 가게가 늘어선 좁은 거리로 들어섰다 We entered a narrow street lined with shops. / 많은 젊은이들이 음악회의 표를 사려고 늘어서 있었다 A lot of young people were lining 〔queuing〕 up to buy tickets for the concert.

**늘어앉다** sit in a row; sit in line; sit around. ¶ 많은 사람이 방에 죽 늘어앉아 있다 Many people are sitting around in the room.

**늘어지다** ① 《처지다》 hang down 《from》; dangle; droop; be suspended. ¶ 귀가 늘어진 개 a flap-〔lop-〕eared dog; a dog with drooping ears / 축 늘어진 버들 a drooping willow / 가슴까지 늘어진 흰 수염 a long white beard that comes down to *one's* chest. ② 《길어지다》 get 〔become〕 longer; lengthen; extend; 《퍼지다》 spread; stretch. ¶ 늘어지게 기지개를 켜다 stretch

*oneself* / 고무는 잘 늘어진다 Rubber is very elastic.
③ 《지쳐서》 be tired out; be exhausted; collapse; get 〔go〕 groggy; be all in 《구어》; 《의식을 잃다》 lose consciousness; pass out. ¶ 그는 한 방에 축 늘어졌다 He was knocked out cold with one blow. / 그는 과로로 축 늘어졌다 He has been exhausted 〔utterly tired out〕 from overwork.
④ 《시간이》 be prolonged 〔extended〕 (연장); be postponed; be put off (연기). ¶ 기간이 늘어졌다 The term has been prolonged.
⑤ 《팔자가》 live 「in comfort 〔at *one's* ease〕; be comfortably 〔well〕 off. ¶ 그는 지금 아주 팔자가 늘어졌다 He is now quite at his ease. *or* He is free from care 〔worry〕.
⑥ 《잠을》 ¶ 늘어지게 자다 sleep *oneself* out; sleep as long as *one* likes.

**늘이다** ① 《길게하다》 lengthen; make 《*something*》 longer; stretch; extend. ¶ 고무줄을 ~ stretch a rubber band / 6미터 ~ lengthen 《a rope》 (by) six meters; make 《a rope》 six meters longer / 기한을 ~ extend the term 《from... to...》 / 수명을 ~ prolong 〔lengthen〕 *one's* life. ② 《드리우다》 hang 《it》; let 《it》 hang down; droop. ¶ 대발을 ~ hang a bamboo screen / 목을 늘이어 칼을 받다 let *one's* neck droop under the sword.

**늘임새** 《말투의》 drawl; dragging *one's* 「words out.

**늘임표** 〖음악〗 a fermata; a length mark.

**늘쩍지근하다** 《몸이》 (be) languid; weary; dull; heavy; feel lazy. ⇨ 나른하다 ¶ 온몸이 ~ feel languid all over / 날씨가 더워서 몸이 ~ The warm weather makes me feel languid.

**늘쩡거리다** 《행동이》 be lazy 〔tardy, slow〕 in doing 《*something*》; be slow-moving; idle about. ¶ 일을 ~ be lazy in doing *one's* work.

**늘컹거리다** be all soft and doughy; be pulpy 〔flabby, squashy〕. ¶ 늘컹거리는 것을 밟다 step upon something squashy 〔flabby〕. 「squashily.

**늘컹늘컹** softly; pulpily; flabbily;

**늙다** age; grow 〔get, become〕 old; grow older; advance in years. ¶ 나이보다 늙어 보이다 look much older than *one's* age; look old for *one's* age / 나날이 늙어 가다 be getting old day by day / 그녀는 앓고 나서 갑자기 늙었다 She has aged rapidly since her illness. / 그는 요 몇 해 사이에 눈에 띄게 늙었다 He has aged visibly for these years. / 자네 갑자기 늙었구먼 그려 You're aged suddenly, aren't you? / 그는 늙었지만 아직 정정하다 He is old in years but still hale and hearty. / 그녀는 좀처럼 늙지 않는 것 같다 She doesn't seem to age.

**늙다리** 《경멸》 ① 《늙은 짐승》 an old animal. ¶ ~ 소 an old ox. ② 《늙은이》 a dotard; a silly old man; an old crock. ¶ ~ 할멈 a withered old woman; a hag.

**늙수그레하다** (be) fairly old; oldish.

**늙어빠지다** (be) very old; be old as (old) can be; [서술적] go senile; get 〔become〕 decrepit. ¶ 늙어빠진 노인 a decrepit old man.

**늙은이** an old 〔aged〕 person; an oldster 《미》; [총칭] the aged 〔old〕. ¶ ~ 같은 말을 하다 use an old man's speech; talk as if *one* were quite old.

**늙정이** an 〔a silly〕 old person.

**늙히다** make 《*a person*》 old; let 《*a person*》 get old. ¶ 처녀로 ~ let 《a girl》 become an old maid.

**늠름하다**(凜凜—) (be) gallant; valiant; high-spirited; manly; imposing; awe-inspiring. ¶ 늠름한 기상 a manly 〔spirited〕 mien / 늠름한 태도 a gallant 〔a manly, an imposing〕 attitude / 늠름한 데가 있다 have a manly 〔commanding〕 looks. 「eye 《at》.

**늠실거리다** leer 〔squint〕 《at》; leer *one's*

**능**(陵) a royal tomb; a mausoleum.

**능**(稜) 〖수학〗 an angle; an edge.

**능가하다**(凌駕—) surpass; exceed; excel; override; outdistance; outstrip; outrival; outdo; stand high 《above》; be superior 《to》. ¶ …에서 타를 ~ excel the rest in... / 수에 있어서 적을 ~ outnumber the enemy; surpass the enemy in numerical strength / 훨씬 ~ far surpass; be far superior to 《others》 / 이 점에 있어 그를 능가할 자는 아무도 없다 He 「has no rival 〔stands unrivaled〕 in this respect. / 그는 기량에서 아버지를 능가했다 He surpassed his father in skill. / 품질면에서 외제를 능가하는 국산품이 많다 There are many kinds of Korean goods which are better in quality than those of foreign make.

**능갈치다** ① 《교활하다》 (be) sly; crafty; cunning; snaky; wily. ② 《뻔뻔하다》 (be) impudent; cheeky. ⇨ 능청스럽다.

**능구렁이** ① 〖동물〗 a yellow-spotted serpent. ② 《사람》 an insidious person; a wily 〔crafty〕 person; an old fox; a sly dog. ¶ 저 ～가 이번에는 무엇을 꾸미고 있는지 모르겠다 I wonder what the sly old fox is up to this time.

**능글맞다** (be) sly; sneaky; cunning; insidious. ¶ 능글맞은 미소 an insidious smile / 능글맞은 녀석 a sly 〔sneaky〕 guy.

**능금** a crab apple. ◉ ～나무 a crab=apple tree. ～산 malic acid.

**능놀다** 《쉬엄쉬엄하다》 do 《it》 slowly; idle about; be tardy; be slow-going.

**능동**(能動) 《자발적》 spontaneousness; voluntariness; 《활동적》 activeness; activity. ¶ ～적인 태도 an active 〔a positive〕 manner / ～적으로 spontaneously; actively; voluntarily / 이 문제에는 능동적으로 대처해야 한다 You should take the initiative in this matter. ◉ ～태 〖문법〗 the active voice.

**능란하다**(能爛—) (be) dexterous 《in, at》; deft; expert; good 《at》; skillful 《in》; adroit; clever 《at》; proficient 《in》. ¶ 능란하게 well; skillfully; adroitly; dexterously; tactfully / 글씨가 ～ be a ready writer; wield a facile pen / 말솜씨가 ～ have an oily tongue; say nice things 《about》 / 사람을 능란하게 다루다 be tactful with people; be dexterous in handling men / 공구 사용이 ～ be skillful with tools / 그는 프랑스어를 매우 능란하게 말한다 He speaks French very well. / 그녀는 댄스에 ～ She is a good dancer. *or* She dances well.

**능력**(能力) ability (성취의); capacity (잠재적); capability (실제적); faculty (지적); competency (적성); power(s).

> 용법 **ability** 어떤 일을 훌륭하게 해낼 수 있는 육체적·정신적 능력을 나타내는 가장 일반적인 말. **capacity** 사람·사물 따위의 잠재적인 가능성을 포함한 능력, 어떤 일을 해내거나 어떤 상태를 이해하고 받아들일 수 있는 능력. **faculty** 선천적, 후천적인 특수한 능력으로 그것을 행사하는 데 특별한 노력을 요하지 않는 지적 능력. **capability** 어떤 특정한 일을 행하는 데 알맞은 실제적인 능력.

¶ 타고난 ～ natural ability 〔talent〕 / 보행 ～ ability to walk / 영어 독해〔작문, 회화〕 ～ reading 〔writing, speaking〕 ability in English / ～에 따라 according to *one's* ability / ～이 있는 able; capable; competent / …할 ～이 있다〔없다〕 be able 〔unable〕 to 《*do*》; be capable 〔incapable〕 of 《*doing*》; be competent 〔incompetent〕 for 《a work》 / ～을 기르다 develop *one's* abilities 〔faculties〕 / ～을 발휘하다 display 〔show〕 *one's* ability / ～을 활용하다 make full use of *one's* ability / 이 일은 나의 ～ 이상의 것이다 This work is beyond me. / 그에게는 그 일을 할 ～이 없다 He is not capable of doing for that job. / 그 경기장은 3만 명의 수용 ～이 있다 That stadium has a capacity of 30,000. *or* That stadium has a seating capacity of 30,000. / 교사는 학생의 ～을 길러주어야 한다 Teachers should help their students (to) develop their abilities. / 컴퓨터에는 다량의 정보를 일시에 처리할 수 있는 ～이 있다 A computer has the ability to process a large quantity of information at a time. ◉ ～ 개발 man-power development. ～급 payment based on ability; efficiency wages. ～상실자 a person with a disability; a person adjudged incompetent. ～자 a person of full capacity; a capable person. ～테스트 a competence test. 생산～ productivity; productive capacity: 이 공장은 월5만 대의 TV생산 ～이 있다 This factory has a productive capacity of fifty thousand TV sets a month. 잠재적 ～ potential 〔dormant, latent〕 capacity. 지적 ～ intellectual capacity 〔faculty〕.

**능률**(能率) efficiency. ¶ ～적인 efficient / 비～적인 inefficient / ～을 올리다 increase 〔improve, enhance, develop〕 efficiency / ～을 저하시키다 diminish 〔lower, decrease〕 efficiency / 몇 갑절 ～을 올리다 multiply efficiency several fold / 최소 노력으로 최대 ～을 올리다 get maximum efficiency with minimum effort / 더 ～ 있게 해라 Do it more efficiently. / 이 도구를 사용하면 일의 ～이 오른다 The use of this tool is sure to increase the efficiency of your work. / 인원수는 많은데도 일의 ～은 오르지 않았다 In spite of the large number of workers, efficiency did not rise. ◉ ～곡선 an efficiency curve. ～급 efficiency wages. ～승급제도 the salary raise system based on efficiency. ～시험 an efficiency test. ～저하 lowering 〔diminution〕 of efficiency; reduced 〔low〕 efficiency. ～주의 the gospel of efficiency. ～증진 increase 〔improvement, enhancement〕 of efficiency. ～화 the promotion of efficiency: 생산의 ～화 streamlining production / 사업을 ～화하다 streamline the business. 작업～ efficiency of work. 행정～ administrative efficiency; efficient administration.

**능변**(能辯) ①《말》 eloquence; fluency; oratory. ②《사람》 an eloquent speaker; an orator. ¶ ～의 eloquent; fluent / 타고난 ～ unstudied eloquence / ～이다 have a fluent 〔well-oiled〕 tongue. ◉ ～가 = 능변 ②.

**능사**(能事) 《적당한 일》 proper and suitable work; 《잘하는 일》 a job that *one* can handle competently and easily; *one's* work; *one's* line 《of business》; (something within) *one's* competency. ¶ ～로 하다〔삼다〕 consider it *one's* job; make it *one's* business 《to *do*》/ 돈을 버는 것만이 장사꾼의 ～는 아니다 Money-making is not the only business of merchants. / 먹고 마시는 것만이 인생의 ～가 아니다 There is something in life besides eating and drinking.

**능선**(稜線) a ridge (line). ¶ ～을 따라 내려오다 come down along the ridge / ～에 포진하다 take up 〔occupy〕 a position on the ridge of the mountain.

**능소능대하다**(能小能大—) be good 〔skillful〕 at everything; (be) versatile; many-talented.

**능수**(能手) ①《솜씨》 ability; capacity; capability; talent. ②《사람》 an expert 《in》; a good 〔master〕 hand 《at *something*》; an able 〔a skillful〕 man; a veteran. ¶ 그 방면의 ～다 be a master-hand in *one's* speciality; be a veteran in the line. ◉ ～꾼 = 능수 ②.

**능수버들** 〖식물〗 a weeping willow.

**능숙**(能熟) 《솜씨》 skill(fulness); proficiency; expertness; adeptness. ～하다 (be) good 《at》; skilled; skillful; dexterous 《in, at》; experienced; proficient 《in》; expert. ¶ ～해지다 become 〔get〕 good 《at》; acquire 〔attain〕 skill 《in》; become proficient 〔skillful〕 《in》/ 영어에 ～하다 be 「proficient 〔strong〕 in 〔good at〕 English / 글씨를 ～하게 쓰다 write a good hand; be a good hand at penmanship / 그는 불어를 ～하게 말한다 He speaks good French. *or* He speaks French fluently.

**능욕**(凌辱) ①《모욕》 (an) insult; offense; an affront; (an) indignity. ～하다 insult; offend; affront; treat 《*a person*》 with indignity. ¶ ～을 받다 be insulted; be subjected to insult; be humiliated; be put to shame / ～을 참다 pocket 〔swallow, put up with〕 an insult / 아무를 ～하다 fling 〔hurl〕 an insult at *a person*. ②《폭행》 outrage; violation; rape (죄). ～하다 rape; assault; outrage; violate. ¶ ～을 당하다 be violated 〔raped〕/ 한 여자를 ～하다 deflower; commit an outrage on 〔upon〕 a woman.

**능지기**(陵—) the caretaker of a royal tomb.

**능지처참**(陵遲處斬) hacking a criminal into pieces. ～하다 hack 《a criminal》 into pieces.

**능직**(綾織) twill; cloth with a pattern of diagonal stripes.

**능철광**(菱鐵鑛) 〖광물〗 siderite; spathic iron.

**능청** dissimulation; a put-on innocent look; feigned innocence; false pretences. ¶ ～부리다〔떨다〕 pretend not to know; play (the) innocent; feign ignorance; disemble / 모르는 척 ～부리며 내게 묻지 마라 Don't ask me as if you didn't know. / ～떨지 마라 Don't play 〔look〕 innocent. / 그는 ～을 떨고 있다 He is only feigning ignorance. ◉ ～이 a person who 「pretends not to know 〔plays innocent〕.

**능청거리다** 《흔들리다》 sway; swing; 《탄력이 있다》 be elastic. ¶ 능청거리는 지팡이 an elastic cane / 바람에 가지가 능청거린다 The branches are swaying in the wind.

**능청능청** swinging(ly); swaying(ly).

**능청스럽다** (be) sly; wily; artful; deceitful; hypocritical. ¶ 능청스러운 웃음 sly 〔hypocritical〕 laughter / 능청스러운 짓 sly behavior; a hypocritical act / 능청스러운 사람 an old fox; a sly dog.

**능통**(能通) a full knowledge; mastery; proficiency. ～하다 have a thorough knowledge 《of》; (be) well versed 《in》; be well acquainted 《with》; be at home 《in, at》. ¶ 영어에 ～하다 be 「well versed 〔well up〕 in English; have a good command in English / 사무에 ～하다 be proficient in office work / 외교 문제에 ～하다 be thoroughly acquainted with the questions of diplomacy.

**능필**(能筆) good handwriting; skillful penmanship; 《사람》 a good pen(man); a skilled calligrapher.

**능하다**(能—) (be) able; capable; good 《at》; proficient; skillful; adept; be (an) expert 《in》; be at home 《in》. ¶ 처세에 능한 사람 a worldly-wise person / 문장에 ～ be a clever writer / 글씨에 ～ be a good hand in writing / 프랑스어에 ～ be good at French / 만사에 ～ be 「skillful in 〔good at〕 everything; be a master of all trades / 그녀는 수

영에 ~ She is good at swimming.
**능형**(菱形) 〖수학〗 = 마름모(꼴). ◉ ~무늬 a diaper pattern.
**능히**(能—) freely; 《쉽게》 easily; without difficulty; 《유능하게》 ably; capably; competently; 《잘》 well; nicely. ¶ ~ 할〔해낼〕 수 있다 be easily able to *do;* be competent to *do;* be competent in〔at〕 *do*ing / ~ …도 서슴지 않다 stick at nothing; make no scruple「to *do*〔of *do*ing〕; be capable of《any crime》/ 그는 어떤 일도 ~ 해낼 수 있는 사람이다 He is a man capable of doing anything. / 그는 ~ 그런 못된 짓을 할 수 있는 거친 녀석이다 He is rude enough to do such a mean thing.
**늦-** late; belated. ¶ 늦가을 late autumn / 늦곡식 late crop.
**늦겨울** late winter; the latter part of winter.
**늦다**[1] ① 《시간·시기적으로》 (be) late. ¶ 밤늦게 late at night; at a late hour / 밤이 늦기 전에 before it's too late / 밤늦게까지 앉아 있다 sit up late at night; stay up till late / 늦게 돌아오다 come back 《home》 late; be late (in) coming back / 늦게 아들을 얻다 have a son late in *one's* life / 아침 늦게까지 자다 sleep late in the morning / 늦어서 죄송합니다 Excuse me for (my) being late. / 그는 밤늦게 여기 도착했다 He got here late at night. (★ late를 lately「최근에」와 혼동하지 말 것) / 이렇게 늦은 밤에 어디 가느냐 Where are you going「this late〔at this time of night〕? / 일을 바로잡기에는 너무 늦었다 It is too late to mend matters now. / 금년은 봄이 (오는 것이) ~ Spring is late in coming this year. / 그를 찾아가기에는 시간이 너무 ~ It is too late to call on him. / 늦더라도 안하느니보다는 낫다 《속담》 Better late than never.
② 《더디다》 (be) slow; tardy; be behind. ¶ 진보가 ~ make slow progress; its progress is slow / 머리 회전이 ~ be slow-witted; be dull / 서울에 비하면 이곳은 유행이 반년이나 ~ Fashions here are half a year behind Seoul. / 생산이 예정보다 늦고 있다 Production is running behind schedule.
③ 《느슨하다》 (be) loose; slack. ⇨ 느슨하다.
**늦다**[2] 《정해진 시간에》 be late 《for》; 《시계가》 lose; go〔be〕 slow. ¶ 학교 시간에 ~ be late for school / 약속 시간에 2시간 ~ be two hours late for *one's* engagement / 기차가 5분 늦었다 The train is five minutes late. / 이 시계는 하루에 10분 늦는다 This clock loses ten minutes a day.
**늦더위** late (summer) heat; the lingering summer heat. ¶ 올해는 ~가 심하다 The heat of late summer is severe this year.
**늦되다** grow〔ripen, mature〕 late; be slow to mature. ¶ 늦된 아이 a retarded child / 늦되는 과일 late fruit / 벼가 금년은 늦된다 Rice ripens late this year.
**늦둥이** ① 《늦게 난》 a child *one* had late in *one's* life. ② 《늦된》 a retarded child.
**늦바람** ① 《바람》 an evening breeze; a wind blowing late in the evening. ¶ 서늘한 ~ a cool evening breeze.
② 《늦난봉》 dissipation in *one's* later years; going wild late in *one's* life. ¶ ~ 나다 start to lead a dissipated living late in *one's* life; take to〔indulge in〕 fast living in *one's* later years.
**늦배** offsprings born or hatched late. ◉ ~돼지 a litter of pigs born late. ~병아리 late-hatched chickens.
**늦벼** a kind of late-ripening rice; late rice.
**늦복**(—福) good fortune late in *one's* life; happiness in *one's* later days.
**늦봄** late spring.
**늦새끼** offspring born of an old animal; 《늦배의》 a late litter.
**늦서리** late frost.
**늦심기** planting late; late planting.
**늦어도** at (the) latest; at the farthest. ¶ ~ 3월 5일까지는 by〔not later than〕 March 5th / ~ 아침 식사 때까지는 돌아올 생각이다 I hope to return by breakfast at the latest. / ~ 2시까지는 그 일을 끝내 주시오 Finish the job〔work〕 by two o'clock at the latest.
**늦어지다** be delayed; be behind time〔schedule〕; be backward in (남보다). ¶ 도중에서 ~ be delayed on the way / 일이 ~ be behind in〔with〕 *one's* work.
**늦여름** late summer. ¶ ~에 late in summer.
**늦잠** oversleeping; sleeping late in the morning. ¶ ~ 자다 rise〔get up〕 late; sleep late (in the morning); stay in bed (till) late / 여느 때보다 ~ 자다 get up later than usual / 오늘 아침에는 ~을 자서 아침도 못 먹고 집을 나섰다 I overslept this morning and left home without breakfast.
◉ ~쟁이, ~꾸러기 a slugabed; a late riser; a sleepyhead (특히 어린이).
**늦잡죄다** exercise belated supervision

〔control〕.

**늦장마** a late rainy spell 〔season〕; a long rain in late summer. ¶ 올 여름에는 ~가 들었다 We have a late rainy spell this summer.

**늦추** ① 《늦게》 late. ② 《느슨히》 loosely; slack. ¶ 허리띠를 ~ 매다 tie *one's* belt loosely.

**늦추다** ① 《죈 것을》 loosen; slack(en); make loose; unfasten (풀다). ¶ 밧줄을 ~ slacken the rope; make a rope loose / 나사를 ~ loosen the screw / 허리띠를 ~ loosen *one's* belt / 고삐를 ~ slacken the reins / 넥타이를 ~ loosen *one's* tie / 잡은 손을 ~ loosen *one's* hold 〔grasp〕.
② 《속도를》 slow down; make slow; slack(en); reduce. ¶ 보조를 ~ slacken *one's* pace / 자동차가 다리 위에서 속도를 늦추었다 The car slowed up over the bridge. / 열차는 속도를 늦추고 멈췄다 The train slowed down and stopped.
③ 《날짜·시간을 연기하다》 postpone; put off; 《연장하다》 extend; defer; prolong. ¶ 기한을 ~ extend the term 《from... to...》 / 마감날짜를 이틀 ~ put the deadline off two days / 배의 출발을 ~ delay 〔postpone〕 the departure of the ship / 우리는 체류를 3일 늦추었다 We prolonged 〔extended〕 our stay for three days. / 지불을 늦추어 주십시오 Please let me defer the payment.
④ 《긴장·규제 따위를》 ease (up); relax; loosen; reduce. ¶ 경계를 ~ relax 〔be off〕 *one's* guard / 긴장을 ~ reduce the tension / 규율을 ~ loosen discipline / 정부는 무역에 대한 규제를 늦추었다 The government eased the restrictions on foreign trade.

**늦추위** (a) late cold 〔chill〕; the cold of late winter. ¶ ~가 매섭다 The cold of late winter is severe.

**늪** a swamp; a marsh; a bog.

**-니** ① [의문어미] is it?; does it? ¶ 먹니〔먹었니, 먹겠니〕 Do(es) 〔Did, Will〕 you 〔he〕 eat? / 가니〔갔니, 가겠니〕 Do(es) 〔Did, Will〕 you 〔he〕 go? / 좋니 Is it good?
② 《사유·사실》 since; because; as; for. ¶ 아무 말도 없는 것을 보니 그는 아직 그것에 관해 모르는 것 같다 Since he said nothing, it seems that he doesn't know about it yet.
③ [연결어미] and; or; and so forth. ¶ 사과니 배니 감이니 apples, pears, persimmons and so forth / 세상 사람들이 나에 관해서 이러니 저러니 한다 People say one thing or another of me.

**-니까** ① 《강조》 so, thus, I tell you; I say. ¶ 괜찮다니까 You needn't do it, I tell you. / 싫다니까 I tell you I don't like it.
② 《이유》 now that; since; because. ¶ 오늘은 토요일이니까 평소보다 일찍 돌아오겠다 I'll be back home earlier than usual because it is Saturday today.

**니스** varnish. ¶ ~를 칠하다 varnish (over) 《the surface》; apply varnish to 《the surface》. ◉ ~칠 varnishing.

**니제르** 《아프리카 서부의 공화국》 (the Republic of) Niger.

**니카라과** 《중미의 공화국》 (the Republic of ) Nicaragua.
◉ ~사람 a Nicaraguan.

**니켈** nickel (기호 Ni). ◉ ~시계 a nickel(-cased) watch. ~화(華) annabergite.

**니켈도금**(一鍍金) nickel plating. ¶ ~한 nickel-plated / ~을 하다 nickel-plate.

**니코틴** nicotine. ¶ ~이 없는 담배 denicotinized 〔nicotineless〕 cigarettes / ~을 제거하다 denicotinize; remove nicotine 《from》.
◉ ~산 nicotinic acid. ~중독 nicotinism; nicotine poisoning: ~ 중독에 걸리다 become addicted to nicotine.

**니크롬선**(一線) Nichrome wire.

**니트** ¶ ~의 knit 《suit》; knitted 《garment》. ◉ ~웨어 knitwear.

**니트로** 〖化〗 nitro(-). ◉ ~글리세린 nitroglycerine. ~기 a nitro group. ~벤젠 nitrobenzene. ~셀룰로오스 nitrocellulose; cellulose nitrate (질산 섬유소). ~화 nitrification: ~화하다 nitrify.

**니힐** nihil. ◉ 니힐리스트 《허무주의자》 a nihilist. 니힐리즘 〖철학〗 《허무주의》 nihilism.

**닉네임** a nickname. = 별명.

**닉슨** 《미국의 정치가》 Richard M. Nixon (1913-94). ◉ ~독트린 the Nixon Doctrine.

**-님** ① 《이름·직위명 앞에서》 Mr.; Esq. (★ Esquire의 간략형. 주로 영국에서 이름 뒤에 붙여 씀. 미국에서는 보통 변호사 등의 경칭으로밖에 쓰지 않음); 《미혼 여성》 Miss (*pl.* Misses); 《기혼 여성》 Mrs. (*pl.* Mmes.). ¶ 김소월님 Mr. Kim So-wŏl; Kim So-wŏl, Esq. / 사장님 Mr. President; Madam President (여사장).
② 《존경의 대상이 되는 명사 앞에》 esteemed; honorable; respected. ¶ 주인님 my honorable master; sir! / 선생님 my respected teacher; sir! / 신부님 Reverend Father; Father! / 임금님

Your Majesty; His Majesty.

**님비** (a) NIMBY. [<*N*ot-*I*n-*M*y-*B*ack=*Y*ard] ¶ ～ 현상 the NIMBY phenomena / 지방 자치 제도가 출범하자, 쓰레기 소각장 건설과 그린 벨트 지역 내의 상업적 개발을 둘러싸고 ～ 및 핌비 분쟁이 터져나왔다 Since the autonomous local government system set sail, not-in=my-back-yard (NIMBY) and please=in-my-back-yard (PIMBY) clashes have broken out over construction of incinerators and commercial development in the Green Belt zones.

**님프** 〖신화〗《요정》 a nymph.

**닢** ¶ 가마니 두 닢 two straw bags / 동전 한 닢 a piece of copper.

**다**[1] 〖음악〗 do. ¶ 다음〔조〕 C / 다장조〔단조〕 C major 〔minor〕.

**다**[2] ① 《모두》 (***a***) 《모든 사람》 all; everybody; everyone. ¶ 두 사람 다 both together / 아이들은 다 all the children / 다 같이 가자 Let's go all together. *or* Let's all go together. / 모두 다 왔다 All (of us, of them) have come. *or* All are here. / 나는 그들을 다 안다 I know all of them. / 이 동네 사람들은 다 차를 가지고 있다 Everybody in this town has a car. / 우리가 다 여행을 간 것은 아니다 Not all of us went on the trip. / 학생들은 다 출석했다 All of the students are present. (***b***) 《모든 것》 all; everything. ¶ 다 내 잘못이다 It's all my fault. / 일을 다 했다 I am all done. / 일이 다 틀렸다 All is over. *or* Everything went wrong for us. / 하나도 남기지 않고 다 가져갔다 They have taken it all away and left nothing. / 그의 이야기를 다 믿을 수는 없다 We cannot believe every part of his story. / 그 일은 내가 다 알고 있다 I have heard all about it. / 그는 케이크를 다 먹었다 He ate all the cake. / 내 주위가 다 조용했다 All was silent around me. / 돈을 다 도둑 맞았다 All of the money was stolen. / 반짝인다고 다 금은 아니다 《격언》 All that glitters is not gold. (★ all이 부정 대명사로서 「모든 사람들」이란 뜻일 때는 복수, 「모든 것」이란 뜻일 때는 단수 취급).
② 《거의》 almost; nearly; all but. ¶ 거의 다 almost all / 다 죽어가다 be almost to die 〔dying〕 / 몇 사람을 제외하고 다 그 파티에 참석했다 All but a few were present at the party. / 건물은 거의 다 완성되었다 The building is almost 〔nearly〕 finished. / 그는 한밤중이 다 되어 집에 돌아왔다 He came home at almost midnight.
③ 《감탄·조소》 all; completely; quite; indeed; on top of everything (else). ¶ 별 일 다 봤다 Now I've seen everything! / 별꼴 다 보겠네 What a shame! *or* Shame on you! / 별말씀 다 하십니다 Don't mention it. *or* Not at all. / 그 주제에 양복을 다 입었네 Well isn't he all dressed up!
④ 《고작》 as much as *one* can 《*do*》; at (the) most. ¶ 간신히 자식들을 먹여 살리는 것이 다다 I can just barely manage to feed my children. / 그의 지혜도 그것이 다다 That's the extent of his wisdom.

**-다** be. ¶ 높다 be high / 비싸다 be expensive / 그녀는 아름답다 She is beautiful. / 그는 의사다 He is a doctor.

**다가** ① [부사적 조사] 《장소·대상》 ¶ 그것을 어디～ 둘까 Where shall I put it? / 누구한테～ 그것을 맡겼느냐 Who 〔Whom〕 did you entrust with it? ② [강조하는 보조사] ¶ 벽돌로～ 지은 집 a house built of brick / 그는 외과의사인데～ 저명한 작가이기도 하다 Besides being a surgeon, he is a famous writer.

**-다가** [어미] 《동작의 이행》 ¶ 책을 읽다가 잠들었다 I fell asleep while reading. / 집에 오다가 그녀를 만났다 I met her on my way home.

**다가**(多價) 〖화학〗 polyvalence. ¶ ～의 polyvalent; multivalent.

**다가가다** go 〔come, get〕 near; approach; step up to. ¶ 등 뒤로 몰래 ～ steal up behind 《*a person*》 / 다가가서 보다 see 《a picture》 (from) close at hand; take a near(er) view of 《a picture》 / 아이를 불에 다가가지 않도록 하다 keep a child away from the fire.

**다가놓다** put 〔place, lay〕 《*a thing*》 closer; bring 《*a thing*》 near 《to》; draw (up) 《*a thing*》 nearer. ¶ 책을 ～ put a book closer 《to *one*》 / 난롯가에 의자를 ～ draw a chair up to the fire / 그는 내 옆에 제 의자를 다가놓았다 He placed 〔drew up〕 his chair next to mine.

**-다가는** ¶ 실수했다가는 큰일 난다 A miss, and all is up 〔over〕. / 무슨 수를 쓰지 않고 일을 그대로 그렇게 놔두었다가는 큰일 난다 If you leave things like that (and do nothing about it) you'll be in a fix.

**-다가도** ¶ 우리 아이는 대체로 혼자 잘 놀다가도 손님이 오기만 하면 운다 Ordinarily my baby plays nicely by himself, but just let a visitor appear, and he starts to cry.

**다가붙다** stick nearer 《to》.

**다가서다** step 〔come〕 up to; approach closer; come 〔go〕 nearer. ¶ 나에게 바싹 다가서라 Come close to me. / 안으로 다가서 주세요 《버스 등에서》 Move on, please.

**다가앉다** sit closer; take *one's* seat closer. ¶ 좀 다가앉아 주세요 Please sit up a little closer. / 자리가 없으니 서로 서로 다가앉아 주십시오 Sit close to each other, please, as there is very little room left. / 얘기 좀 하게 다가앉아라 Sit a little closer, so we can have a talk.

**-다가야** and (only) then; only when. ¶ 그와 한참 이야기하다가야 비로소 그의 이름이 생각났다 It was only after I had conversed with him a good long while that I remembered his name. / 한참 걸어가다가야 길을 잘못 든 것을 알았다 It was only after I had walked a good long distance that I realized I had taken the wrong way.

**다가오다** 《접근하다》 come 〔get〕 near; come 〔walk, step〕 up 《to》; approach; 《시간적으로》 draw 〔come〕 near; draw close 《to》. ¶ 다가오는 next; (forth=) coming / 다가올 선거 the forthcoming election / 점점 ～ get nearer 《to *a place*》 / 불 곁으로 ～ come up to the fire / (배가) 육지로 ～ approach land; close with the land; draw toward the shore / 종말이 ～ draw to a close / 크리스마스가 다가온다 Christmas is drawing near. / 시험이 다가왔다 The examination is close at hand 〔is drawing on〕. / 낯선 사람이 다가왔다 A stranger walked up to me. / 새해가 다가왔다 The New Year is just around the corner. 《미》

**다각**(多角) many-sidedness. ⇨ 다각적. ◉ ～경영 (a) diversification; many=sided 〔diversified〕 business operation; multiple 〔diversified〕 management 〔operation〕: 그는 사업의 ～경영을 시작했다 He started diversified business operations. ～농업 diversified farming. ～무역〔외교〕 multilateral trade 〔diplomacy〕.

**다각적**(多角的) many-sided; diversified; multilateral; multiple. ¶ ～으로 from different angles; from various points of view / ～인 투자 diversified investment / ～인 취미 many-sided interests 〔tastes〕 / ～인 관점에서 생각하다 consider 《*something*》 from different 「angles 〔points of view〕. ◉ ～ 결제(決濟) a multilateral settlement; multilateral payments. ～ 핵전력(核戰力) multilateral (nuclear) force.

**다각형**(多角形) 〖수학〗 a polygon. ¶ ～의 polygonal.

**다각화**(多角化) diversification. ～하다 diversify; branch out. ¶ 제품의 ～가 필요하다 need to diversify products 《so as to...》 / 농가 소득 증대를 위해 영농 ～가 필요하다 To boost farmers' income, farming should be diversified.

**다갈색**(茶褐色) brown color; liver brown. ¶ ～의 brown; liver-colored.

**다감**(多感) sensibility; susceptibility; sentimentality. ～하다 《민감하다》 (be) sensitive; susceptible; 《감상적이다》 (be) sentimental; 《다정다감하다》 (be) passionate; 《감동받기 쉽다》 (be) emotional; 《감수성이 강하다》 impressionable. ¶ ～한 젊은이 emotional young people; a sensitive youth / ～한 소녀기에 in *one's* impressionable girlhood / 다정～한 여인 a sentimental woman / ～한 성질이다 be of a sentimental 〔emotional〕 nature / 그녀는 한때 다정～한 소녀였다 She was once a passionate and emotional girl.

**다공**(多孔) ¶ ～의 porous. ◉ ～성 porosity. ～체 〖동물〗 a madreporite.

**다과**(多寡) (the more or less of) the quantity 〔number, amount〕 of something. ¶ 금액의 ～에 관계없이 regardless of the amount involved / 신청자의 ～에 따라 according to the number of applicants / 팁의 ～에 따라 대우를 달리하다 treat 《guests》 differently according to the amount of tips / 손해의 ～에 따라 보상금이 지급되었다 The reparations were paid in proportion to the damage suffered.

**다과**(茶菓) tea and cookies 〔cake〕; (light) refreshments. ¶ ～를 대접하다 〔들다〕 serve 〔partake of〕 light refreshments / 우리는 ～ 대접을 받았다 We were entertained with refreshments. ◉ ～회 a tea party: ～회에 초대하다 ask 《*a person*》 to come in to tea 〔a tea party〕 / ～회에 초대받다 be invited to tea.

**다구**(茶具) tea-things; tea utensils; 《한 벌의》 a tea service 〔set〕. ¶ ～ 한 벌 a set of tea-things.

**다국적**(多國籍) ¶ ～의 multinational. ◉ ～군 a multinational force. ～ 기업 a multinational corporation 〔company, enterprise].

**다그다** 《옮기다》 bring 〔draw〕 《*a thing*》 near; 《시간·날짜 등을》 advance; set ahead 《up》; move 〔carry〕 up. ⇨ 당기다. ¶ 의자를 난롯가로 ~ draw 〔move〕 *one's* chair near the fire / 기일을 ~ advance 〔move up〕 the date 《from... to...》 / 이틀을 ~ shift two days ahead; advance 〔move up〕 《the date》 by two days / 결혼 날짜를 ~ set ahead 〔advance〕 the date of wedding.

**다그치다** ① = 다그다. ② 《몰아치다》 urge 〔goad〕 on; press 《for》; impel; spur on. ¶ 다그쳐 묻다 press 《*a person*》 (hard) for an answer; ply 《*a person*》 with questions / 마부는 말을 다그쳐 몰았다 The driver urged his horse on.

**다극**(多極) ¶ ~의 multipolar / ~화된 세계 the multipolarized world / 정치의 ~화 the multipolarized politics. ◉ ~주의 polycentrism.

**다급하다** (be) extremely urgent; pressing; imminent; impending. ¶ 다급한 문제 a pressing 〔an urgent〕 question / 다급한 볼일로 on urgent 〔pressing〕 business / 우리는 시간이 ~ We are pressed for time.

**다기**(多岐) many branches 《of》; 《다방면》 many divergences 〔divisions〕.

**다기지다**(多氣―) (be) plucky; gritty; bold; brave; courageous; daring; have plenty of guts. ¶ 다기지게 bravely; boldly; courageously / 다기진 행동 a daring act 〔deed〕 / 다기진 사람 a man of steady nerve 〔iron nerves〕; a daring man / 그는 키는 작아도 아주 다기진 사람이다 Though small in stature, he is a man of stoic courage 〔with plenty of guts〕.

**다기차다**(多氣―) = 다기지다(多氣―).

**다난**(多難) many difficulties; lots of trouble. ~하다 be full of troubles 〔difficulties〕. ¶ ~한 해 a tumultuous year / 이 ~한 시대에 in these difficult times / 국가 ~한 때(에) (in) a national crisis / 우리의 전도는 ~하다 Our future is full of difficulties. *or* We have many difficulties ahead of us.

**다녀가다** drop in 《on *a person*, at *a person's* house》 and then go on; come round to see 《*a person*》 and then go on; look 《*a person*》 up; call at 《a house》; stop at 〔in〕 《*a place*》. ¶ 상경하시거든 다녀가시오 Look me up when you are in Seoul./어제 남군이 다녀갔다 Mr. Nam came to see me yesterday.

**다녀오다** drop in 《on *a person*》 and then come back; go round to see 《*a person*》 and then return; get 〔come〕 back 《from visiting》. ¶ 학교에 ~ come home from school / 곧 다녀와야 한다 You have to come back without delay. / 곧 다녀올게 I shan't be long. / 수원에 좀 다녀오겠다 I'm going to run down to Suwŏn. / 저녁때까지 다녀오기는 어려울걸 It will be difficult for us to be back before evening. /「어딜 다녀왔니」—「인천에 다녀왔다」 "Where have you been?"—"I have been to Inch'ŏn." / 다녀왔습니다 《인사말》 Hello, here I am! / 어머니, 다녀왔습니다 I'm home 〔back〕, mom. / 잘 다녀오세요 Have a nice day.

**다년간**(多年間) many years; [부사적] for (many) years; for a long time; through the years. ¶ ~에 걸쳐 for (many) years; for a number of years / ~의 노력 (*one's*) years of labor 〔efforts〕 / ~ 사귄 친구 a friend of many years' 〔long〕 standing; a long-time friend / ~의 연구 (*one's*) long years of research 〔study〕 / ~의 관습 customs of long standing / ~에 걸친 전쟁 a war of long duration / ~ 품었던 소망을 이루다 realize a long-cherished desire / 그의 ~의 노고에 보답하고 싶다 I wish to reward him for his many years' services.

**다년생**(多年生) 『식물』 perennation. ◉ ~ 식물〔초본〕 a perennial plant 〔herb〕.

**다뇨증**(多尿症) 『의학』 polyuria. ¶ ~의 polyuric.

**-다는** 《…다고 하는》 ¶ 만병에 좋다는 약수 a mineral water what is called a cure-all / 열심히 해야 한다는 것을 깨달았다 I realized that I must do it with enthusiasm. / 자네가 곧 미국으로 떠난다는 소문을 들었네 I heard (rumors) that you are leaving for America soon.

**다능**(多能) versatility; many-sidedness; many accomplishments. ⇨ 다재(多才). ~하다(be) versatile; multiple-skilled; many-sided; accomplished. ¶ (다재) ~한 사람 a man of great versatility; a many sided person.

**-다니** 《의외》 how 〔why〕 should...; 《유감》 I am sorry that...; It is a pity that.... ¶ 자네를 여기서 만나다니 (참 뜻밖일세) This is the last place where I expected to meet you. *or* I little dreamed of meeting you here. / 그런

정직한 사람을 내쫓으려 하다니 (기막히군) The idea of kicking out such an honest fellow! / 그 사람이 실패하다니 정말 안됐다 It is a great pity that he should have failed. / 그런 짓을 하다니 너는 바보다 It is very silly of you to do such a thing. / 사태가 이 지경이 되다니 유감 천만이다 It is a great pity that things should have come to this pass.

**다니다** ① 《왕래하다》 come and go; go about 〔around〕; walk about 〔around〕; go to and from 《a place》; go to 《a place》 and back; 《배가》 ply 《between, from… to…》; 《차 따위가》 run 《between》; be opened to traffic (개통). ¶ 자주 다니는 길 a familiar road / 미국 다니는 배 a ship on the American line 〔run〕 / 서울·대전간을 다니는 직행버스 a nonstop bus which runs between Seoul and Taejŏn / 목포·제주간을 다니는 배 a ship plying between Mokp'o and Cheju / 들고 ~ carry about / 한국에서는 차가 우측으로 다닌다 Cars keep to the right in Korea. / 거리에는 다니는 사람이 많다 Many people are coming and going in the street. / ~가 그 책을 보거든 사다 주시오 If you happen to find the book while walking around, please get it for me. / 지금은 그 지방에 기차가 다닌다 A railroad is now open to that locality. / 나는 1개월간 병원에 다녀야 한다 I have to keep going to the hospital for one month.
② 《들르다》 drop in; stop at; call at. ⇨ 다녀가다, 다녀오다.
③ 《통근·통학하다》 attend 《school, church》; go to 《school, work》; commute 《to work》; work 《in, at》. ¶ 관청에 ~ be in the service of a government agency / 대학에 ~ attend a college / 학교에 ~ attend 〔go to〕 school / 회사에 ~ work for a company / 그는 지하철〔버스〕로 회사에 다닌다 He commutes to the office by subway 〔bus〕. / 나는 자전거로 학교에 다닌다 I go 〔commute〕 to school by bicycle. / 그들은 매일 아침 걸어서 공장에 다닌다 They walk to the factory every morning.
④ 《드나들다》 go to 〔visit〕 《a place》 frequently; frequent 《a place》; hang out at. ¶ 그는 뻔질나게 이웃 동네 술집에 다녔다 He frequented 〔went frequently to〕 a bar in the next town. / 나는 한국사를 연구하기 위해 자주 도서관에 다녔다 I often went to the library to study Korean history.
⑤ 《직무·취미로》 ¶ 출장을 ~ go on a round of business trips / 학교 시찰을 ~ make a round of schools for inspection.

**다니엘** 〖성서〗 Daniel. ◉ ~서 (The Book of) Daniel.

**다다르다** come 《to》; arrive 《at, in, on》; reach; get to 〔at〕; come up to; gain; attain. ¶ 목적지에 ~ arrive at 〔reach, come to〕 *one's* destination; come to the end of *one's* journey / 산정에 ~ get to the mountain peak; arrive at the top of the mountain / 표준에 ~ come up to the standard / 같은 결론에 ~ arrive at 〔come to, reach〕 the same conclusion / 적군이 성문에 다다랐다 The enemy has reached the gate of the castle.

**다다미** a Japanese floor mat; *tatami*. ◉ 다다밋방 a room with *tatami* floor.

**다다이즘** Dadaism; Dada (★ 1차 대전 후에 일어난 유럽의 예술 운동).

**다다익선**(多多益善) The more, the better.

**다닥다닥** 《밀집》 in clusters. ~하다 (be) clustered; thick; crowded; congested. ¶ 꽃이 ~ 붙어 있다 Flowers are in thick clusters. / 사과가 ~ 달려 있다 Apples hang in clusters. *or* The apple tree is heavy with fruit. / 집들이 ~ 붙어 있다 Houses lie huddled together. *or* Houses stand roof to roof.

**다단**(多段) ¶ ~식 로켓 a multistage rocket.

**다단하다**(多端—) (be) complicated; eventful; busy. ⇨ 다사(多事).

**다달의** monthly. ¶ ~ 수입 monthly income / ~ 집세 a monthly rent.

**다달이** every 〔each〕 month; monthly; per month; a month. ¶ ~ 두 번씩 twice a month / 돈을 ~ 붓다 pay by the month / ~ 지급받다 be paid monthly / 이자를 ~ 지급하다 pay interest every month.

**다대** 《헝겊 조각》 a patch. ¶ ~를 대다 patch (up) 《a cloth》; put 〔add〕 a patch on 《a coat》.

**다대기** seasoned red-pepper paste 〔sauce〕.

**다대하다**(多大—) (be) great; considerable; a great deal of; heavy; serious. ¶ 다대한 이익을 얻다 gain a large 〔considerable〕 profit / 다대한 손해를 보다 suffer a heavy 〔serious〕 loss; sustain a severe loss / 다대한 피해를 입다 be seriously damaged; suffer a great deal of damage; be hard hit / 다대한 영향을 받다 be seriously affected; be greatly influenced / 다대한 원조를 받다 receive a great deal of assistance / 다대한 공적으로 표창을 받다 win commendation for *one's* great services 《to》.

**다도**(茶道) the tea ceremony.

**다도해**(多島海) an archipelago.

**다독**(多讀) wide 〔extensive〕 reading. ～하다 read widely 〔extensively〕.
◉ ～가 an extensive reader; a well-read person: 그는 ～가다 He is very well read. ～주의 the principle of extensive reading.

**다독거리다** ① 《물건을》 gather 《*things*》 up and press into order. ② 《사람을》 pat 《*a person* on the shoulder》. ¶ 그는 나의 등을 다독거렸다 He patted me on the back.

**다되다** ① 《떨어지다》 be exhausted; run out; be used up; be out. ¶ 다돼가다 run short 〔low〕; there is little left 《of》 / 전지가 다됐다 The battery has run down. / 휘발유가 다되어간다 The gas is running short. ② 《시한이》 expire; run out; fall 〔become〕 due. ¶ 다돼가다 draw to an end 〔a close〕 / 임대 기한이 ～ fall out of lease / 시간이 다 되었다 The time is up. / 그들의 계약은 이 달 말로 기한이 다된다 Their contract is to run out at the end of this month.

**다듬다** ① 《매만지다》 put 《*things*》 in order; make 《*a thing*》 tidy 〔neat〕; adjust 《*one's* dress》; fix (up); trim 〔spruce〕 up; embellish 《*one's* writing》. ¶ 잘 다듬은 머리 well-groomed hair / 머리를 ～ fix 〔arrange〕 *one's* hair / 옷매무새를 ～ straighten *one's* clothes 〔dress〕; tidy *oneself* (up) / 얼굴을 ～ do 〔pretty up, freshen up〕 *one's* face.
② 《푸성귀·나무·돌 따위를》 trim (off); prune (away, off, down); face; clean. ¶ 나뭇가지를 ～ trim the branches off a tree / 무〔배추〕를 ～ clean a radish 〔cabbage〕 / 널빤지를 ～ plane a piece of board smoothly / 돌을 ～ trim 〔face〕 a stone smoothly.
③ 《땅바닥을》 make even; level (off, out); smooth (off). ¶ 길을 ～ level 〔smooth〕 a road / 롤러로 땅을 ～ smooth 《a field》 with a roller; roll a ground.
④ 《깃털을》 plume; preen. ¶ 새가 깃을 다듬는다 Birds plume themselves 〔their feathers〕.
⑤ 《피륙을》 smooth 《cloth》 by pounding with round clubs; full 《cloth》. ¶ 빨래를 ～ smooth laundered clothes.
⑥ 《마무리하다》 give the final 〔finishing〕 touches to; finish up 〔off〕; do up. ¶ 조각을 ～ put the final touches on a piece of sculpture 〔carving〕.

**다듬이** ① 《다듬잇감》 cloth to be fulled 〔smoothed by pounding〕. ② ⇨ 다듬이질. ◉ 다듬잇돌 a block (of stone) for pounding cloth; a fulling block of stone. 다듬잇방망이 round clubs for pounding cloth.

**다듬이질** fulling 《cloth》. ～하다 full 《cloth》. ¶ ～ 소리 the sound of fulling 〔beating〕 cloth.

**다듬질** ① 《작품 따위의》 finish; finishing touches. ～하다 give the final touches to; finish (up); do 〔touch〕 up. ② ⇨ 다듬이질.

**다디달다** (be) very sweet.

**다라지다** (be) plucky; spunky; fearless; daring; bold. ¶ 그는 몸집은 작으나 매우 다라진 사람이다 He may be small but he sure has spunk.

**다락** an upper story; a loft over a kitchen.
◉ ～방 a garret; an attic; a loft (창고용). ～집 a two-storied〔-storeyed 《영》〕 house; a tower; a turret.

**다락같다** 《값이》 (be) very high 〔expensive〕. ¶ 물가가 ～ The prices are very high. / 물가가 다락같이 오르고 있다 The prices are skyrocketing. *or* The prices are going up 〔soaring〕 rapidly.

**다람쥐** 〖동물〗 a squirrel; a chipmunk. ¶ ～ 쳇바퀴 돌 듯하다 go round and round; repeat the same thing forever.

**다랍다** ① 《인색하다》 (be) stingy; niggardly; miserly; pinchpenny; close-fisted. ¶ 다라운 사람 a miser; a stingy person / 돈 쓰는 게 ～ spend money sparingly / 먹을 것에 다랍게 굴다 be mean about food / 돈에 다랍게 굴지 않다 be free 〔generous〕 with *one's* money; be liberal of 〔with〕 *one's* money. ② ⇨ 더럽다.

**다랑어** 〖어류〗 a tuna; a tunny. ¶ ～ 통조림 canned 〔tinned 《영》〕 tuna.

**다래** ① 《다래나무 열매》 fruit of the *Actinidia arguta*. ② 《목화의》 a cotton boll.

**다래끼** ① 《바구니》 a basket with a small opening. ② 《눈병》 a sty(e) 《in the eye》; a hordeolum(*pl.* -la). ¶ 눈에 ～가 나다 get 〔have〕 a sty in *one's* eye.

**다래다래** dangling in clusters. ～하다

dangle 〔grow〕 in clusters.

**다량**(多量) a large 〔great〕 quantity; a vast 〔great〕 amount 《of》. ¶ ∼의 a large 〔great〕 quantity of; plenty of; a great volume 〔deal〕 of; (very) much; abundant / ∼으로 in quantity 〔large quantities〕; in plenty 〔abundance〕 / ∼의 물 much 〔a great quantity of〕 water / ∼의 출혈 copious 〔profuse〕 bleeding / ∼의 수면제를 먹다 take a large dose of sleeping pills / 비타민 B를 ∼으로 함유하다 be rich 〔high〕 in vitamin B / ∼의 방사능이 검출되다 A large quantity of radioactivity was detected. / 한국은 ∼의 원유를 수입해야 한다 Korea has to import 「crude oil in large quantities 〔large quantities of crude oil〕. ◉ ∼생산 mass 〔quantity〕 production.

**다루다** ① 《처리·취급하다》 handle; treat; manage 《an affair》; deal with 《a problem》; carry on 〔handle, conduct〕 《business》; manage 《affairs》. ¶ 다루기 쉬운〔어려운〕 easy 〔hard〕 to deal with; manageable 〔unmanageable〕/ 사회 문제를 다룬 소설 a novel dealing with social problems / 다루기 어려운 문제 a matter hard to deal with; a delicate matter (미묘한 문제) / 문제를 가볍게〔신중히〕 ∼ deal with 〔handle〕 a matter lightly 〔carefully〕/ 그의 연설이 신문에 크게 다루어졌다 His speech got a big write-up in the newspapers./ 이 책은 문제를 실제적인 면에서 다루고 있다 This book deals with the problem from a practical angle. / 그것은 매우 까다로운 문제여서 신중히 다루어야 한다 It's a very delicate matter, which needs to be deal with carefully.

② 《사람을》 treat; deal with; handle. ¶ 다루기 힘든 사람 a difficult man to deal with; an awkward 〔ugly〕 customer (까다로운 고객) / 부하를 공평히 ∼ deal justly 〔fair〕 with *one's* men / 아무를 함부로 ∼ handle *a person* roughly / 어린애처럼 ∼ treat 《*a person*》 「like 〔as if *he* were〕 a child / 사람을 잘 ∼ have tact in treating 〔dealing with〕 people; manage 〔deal with〕 people skillfully.

③ 《손으로》 handle; manipulate; work 〔operate〕 《a machine》. ¶ 조심해서 ∼ handle with care / 거칠게 ∼ handle 《*a thing*》 roughly; give 《*a thing*》 rough handling / 이 기계는 다루기가 쉽다〔어렵다〕 This machine is easy 〔hard〕 to handle 〔operate〕. / 깨지는 물건은 조심히 다루어라 Handle the fragile articles carefully. / 이 기계를 다룰 줄 아십니까 Do you know how to handle 〔operate〕 this machine?

④ 《매매하다》 deal in 《goods》. ¶ 저희 회사는 목재를 다룹니다 Our firm 「deals in 〔handles〕 lumber. / 저희는 그런 상품을 다루지 않습니다 We don't deal in that line of goods. / 이 상점에서는 주류를 다루고 있지 않습니다 We don't 「carry 〔sell, deal in〕 liquor.

**다르다** ① 《상이하다》 (be) different 《from》; unlike; dissimilar 《to》; vary 〔differ〕 《from》. ¶ 전혀 ∼ be completely 〔entirely〕 different 《from》; differ entirely 《from》/ 조금도 다르지 않다 be quite the same; be exactly alike / 성격이 ∼ be dissimilar in character / 의견이 ∼ differ 《from *a person*》 in opinion; have a different opinion; be divided 〔vary〕 in opinion / 크기가 ∼ be different 〔vary〕 in size / 취미가 ∼ differ in *one's* taste 〔likes and dislikes〕/ 뜻이 ∼ have a different meaning; be different in meaning / 이것과 저것은 ∼ This and that are different (from each other). / 관습은 나라에 따라 ∼ Customs differ from country to country. / 유행은 시대에 따라 ∼ Fashion varies with the times. / 값은 계절에 따라 ∼ Prices vary with the seasons. / 품질에 따라 값이 ∼ Prices vary according to the quality. / 참석자들 사이에 의견이 크게 달랐다 Opinions varied greatly among the people present. / 내 생각은 ∼ I don't share that opinion. *or* I don't think 「so 〔that way〕. / 천재는 역시 다른 데가 있다 There is something extraordinary about 〔in〕 a genius. / 내가 생각했던 바와는 아주 ∼ It is quite different from what I expected. / 어떤 점이 다른가 What's the distinction 〔difference〕 between them? / 이 번역문은 원문과 다소 다른 데가 있다 The translation varies from the original in some points. / 그렇다면 이야기는 전혀 ∼ If that is so, the case is quite different. / 너는 거지나 다를 바 없다 You are little better than a beggar. (★ little better than은 「…와 한가지」란 뜻).

② 《별개이다》 (be) another; be not the same. ⇨ 딴[2]. ¶ 다른 책 another book; other books / 그는 다른 사람이다 He is another man. / 그것은 전혀 다른 문제다 That's quite another pair of shoes. / 그는 젊었을 때와는 ∼ He is

not what he was in his youth. *or* He is quite another man now. / 다른 호텔로 옮기는 편이 낫겠다 We had better move to some other hotel. / 다른 사람에게 말하면 안 된다 Don't tell anybody.
③ 《불일치하다》 be not in accordance 《with》; be contrary 《to》; disagree 《with》; run counter 《to》; be not in keeping with. ¶ 말과 속셈이 ~ say one thing and mean another / 그것은 약속과 ~ It is not in keeping with the agreement. *or* It does not accord with his promise. / 이건 견본과 ~ It does not come up to the sample. *or* It is not the same as the sample. / 사본이 원본과 ~ The copy does not correspond with the original. / 네 설명은 그의 설명과는 ~ Your explanation doesn't agree with his. / 그의 이야기는 사실과 ~ His story is not consistant with the facts. / 나의 생활 방식은 그들과는 ~ My lifestyle disagree with theirs. / 그는 말과 행동이 ~ He says one thing and does another.

**다름아니다** be nothing but; be no more than. ¶ 다름아니고, 다름아니라 (for) no other reason (than); (for) nothing but; just / 다름아닌 당신이니까 since it is you of all people / 다름아닌 자네의 부탁이니 최선을 다해 보겠네 Since the request comes from you and none other, I will try my best. / 그가 그렇게 말하는 것은 다름아니라 자기가 옳다는 것이다 He is saying so just to show that he was right. / 내가 여기 온 것은 다름아니라 자네를 보러 온 것일세 I came here for nothing else but to see you. / 그는 다름아닌 학장 그 분이었다 He was「no other person 〔no less a person〕 than the president.

**다름없다** [서술적] be the same; be not different 《from》; be similar 《to》; be alike; be as much 〔large, small〕 as; 《변함없다》 (be) constant; never=changing; unwavering; steady. ¶ 전과 다름없는 우정〔사랑〕 steady 〔constant〕 friendship 〔love〕; unchanging friendship 〔love〕 / 별 ~ be much the same; there is not much difference / …이나 ~ be not different from; be just all the same as / 사정은 이전과 ~ The situation is unchanged. / 가난하기는 옛날과 ~ We are just as poor as we used to be. / 이 시계는 신품이나 ~ This watch is as good as a new one. / 그 두 사람은 부부나 ~ They are practically man and wife. / 이건 협박이나 ~ This practically amounts to a threat. / 그는 죽은 거나 ~ He is「as good as 〔virtually〕 dead. / 이것은 나에겐 사형 선고나 ~ This is「as much as 〔tantamount to〕 a death sentence to me. / 승부는 결판난 거나 ~ The game is practically over. / 그런 놈한테 돈을 주는 것은 돈을 버리는 거나 ~ You might as well throw money away as give it to such a fellow. / 그가 완쾌된 건 기적이나 ~ His recovery is little short of a miracle.

**다름없이** similarly; likewise; alike; equally; in like manner; in the same way 〔manner〕 《as》. ¶ 전과 ~ as before; as usual; as always; (as...) as ever / 전과 ~ 아름답다 be as beautiful as ever / 제 자식이나 ~ 사랑하다 love 《a child》 like *one's* own.

**다리**[1] ① 《사람·동물의》 a leg; a (walking) limb; 《낙지 등의》 arms; tentacles. ¶ ~ 운동 〖체조〗 leg exercises.
다리가: ~가 굵은 heavy-legged; thick=legged / ~가 가는 slender-legged / ~가 굵은〔가는〕 여자 a heavy-legged 〔slender-legged〕 woman; a woman with plump 〔slender〕 legs / ~가 짧은 short-legged / ~가 길다〔짧다〕 have long 〔short〕 legs; be long-legged 〔short-legged〕 / ~가 부러지다 break *one's* legs / ~가 튼튼해지다 get stronger in *one's* legs / (지쳐서) ~가 말을 안 듣다 be worked off *one's* legs.
다리를: ~를 구부리다 bend *one's* legs / ~를 꼬다 cross *one's* legs / 꼰 ~를 풀다 uncross 〔unwind〕 *one's* legs / ~를 다치다 get *one's* leg hurt; injure *one's* leg / ~를 오므리다 draw in *one's* legs / ~를 뻗다 stretch out *one's* legs / ~를 뻗고 자다 sleep stretching *one's* legs; sleep carefree / ~를 뻗고 앉다 sit at ease / ~를 자르다 cut off 〔amputate〕 *one's* leg / ~를 질질 끌며 걷다 drag *one's* weary feet; trudge 《along》.
¶ 그는 ~가 부자유스럽다 He has lost the use of his legs. / ~를 쭉 뻗어 보시오 Try to stretch out your legs to their full extent. / 나는 ~가 뻣뻣해지도록 걸었다 I walked till my legs got stiff. / ~의 감각이 없어지다 I have no feeling in my legs. *or* My legs are asleep.
② 《물건의》 a leg; a leg piece. ¶ ~가 셋 달린 테이블 a three-legged table / 안경 ~ the bows 〔sidepieces〕 of a pair of glasses. ◉ ~ 보호대(帶) leg=

guards. ～뼈 a leg bone. ～살 the inner thighs. ～통 the girth of the leg: ～통이 굵다 have thick 〔fat〕 leg. ～품 expenditure of leg energy; walking: 공연히 ～품만 들이다 use *one's* legs in vain / ～품을 팔다 walk a great distance; 《심부름》 go on a paid errand. ～ 훅치기 〖씨름〗 a double right= leg hook. 다릿심 leg strength.

**다리**[2] 《교량》 a bridge. ¶ 돌～ a stone bridge / ～의 난간〔교각〕 a bridge rail 〔post〕 / (판문점의) 돌아오지 않는 ～ the Bridge of No Return / ～를 놓다 build 〔throw, construct〕 a bridge across 〔over〕 《a river》; span 《a river》 with a bridge; 《두 사람 사이에》 mediate 〔intermediate〕 《between》; act as an intermediary 〔a go-between〕; bridge / ～를 건너다 cross 〔go across〕 a bridge; cross a river by a bridge / 이 강에는 ～가 둘 있다 There are two bridges across this river. *or* Two bridges span this river. / 이 ～는 1986년에 개통됐다 This bridge was opened in 1986. / 그 다리는 지난번 홍수로 떠내려 갔다 The bridge was carried 〔washed, swept〕 away by the last flood. ◉ 다릿목 the path 〔approach〕 to a bridge: 다릿목을 지키다 keep watch at the foot of a bridge.

**다리**[3] 《머리의》 《a tress of》 false 〔artificial〕 hair; a "switch". ¶ ～를 넣다 put on a lock of artificial hair. ◉ ～꼭지 a bunch 〔clump〕 of false hair.

**다리다** iron (out); press. ¶ 다린 바지 ironed 〔pressed〕 trousers / 옷을 ～ iron clothes / 대충 ～ run over 《the clothes》 with an iron / 이건 다려야겠다 This needs ironing. / 바지 좀 다려 주시오 I want to have my trousers pressed.

**다리미** an iron; a flatiron. ¶ 전기 ～ an electric iron / ～로 주름을 펴다 smooth the winkles with an iron. ◉ ～판 an ironing board 〔stand〕.

**다리쇠** a trivet; a tripod; a spider.

**다림** 《수직의》 plumbing; 《수평의》 leveling. ◉ ～줄 a plumb line. ～추(錘) a plumb (weight); a plummet. ～판(板) a (carpenter's) level; a plumb rule.

**다림보다** ① 《겨냥대고》 plumb 《for depth》; level. ② 《살핌》 watch carefully; keep an eye on; keep alert to *one's* own interests (이해 관계를).

**다림질** ironing. ～하다 do the ironing; iron; press. ⇨ 다리다.

**다릿돌** stepping stones (징검다리).

**다마스쿠스** 《시리아의 수도》 Damascus.

**다만** ① 《오직》 only; just; merely; simply; solely; alone; nothing but. ¶ ～ 한번 only 〔but〕 once / ～ …하기만 하면 된다 have only to *do;* only have 〔need〕 to *do;* need only *do* / ～ 울기만 하다 do nothing but cry / 그건 ～ 소문에 불과하다 It is merely a rumor. / 어학에 숙달하는 길은 ～ 연습뿐이다 Practice is the only way of mastering a language. / 나는 ～ 그가 오라고 해서 왔을 뿐이다 I came just because he told me to (come). / 나는 ～ 내 의무를 다했을 뿐이다 I have done nothing but my duty. / ～ 조금 틀렸을 따름입니다 You made only 〔just〕 a few mistakes. (★ only, just, merely의 위치는 written English에서는 모호함을 피하기 위해 그 수식하는 어구 앞에 놓음: I want only three. 그러나 spoken English에서는 sentence stress, intonation, rhythm 등이 고려되기 때문에, I only want three.라고도 함). ② 《그러나》 [접속부사] but; however; only; provided that; on condition that. ¶ ～…은 차한에 부재한다 Provided that the same shall not apply to…. / 그것은 좋은 옷이나 ～ 색깔이 좀 어둡다 That is a nice clothes, but the color is a bit too dark. / 가도 좋으나 ～ 최악의 경우에 대비해야 한다 It is all right for you to go but you must prepare for the worst. / 할인해드립니다만 ～ 선불하는 조건입니다 I'll give you a discount on condition that you pay in advance. / 일이 싫다는 것이 아니라, ～ 시간이 없다는 것이다 Not that I dislike the job, but that I have no time.

**다망**(多忙) pressure 〔stress, press〕 of work 〔business〕; busyness. ～하다 (be) busy; be busily engaged 《in》; have a lot 〔a great deal〕 of work; have very many things to do; be pressed by business 〔work〕. ¶ ～한 일주일 a busy 〔rush〕 week / 공무 ～하여 by 〔on account of〕 stress 〔pressure〕 of official business / (공사) ～하신 중에도 불구하고 despite the claims of a busy life / ～한 생활을 하다 lead a busy life.

**다면**(多面) many sides; many faces 〔phases〕. ¶ ～적인 many-sided; versatile; multilateral. ◉ ～각(角) a polyhedral angle. ～체(體) a polyhedron: 정～체 a regular polyhedron.

**다모**(多毛) ¶ ～의 hairy; hirsute. ◉ ～류 〖동물〗 *Polychaeta.* ～증(症) 〖의학〗 hirsutism; hirsuties.

**다모작**(多毛作) 〖농업〗 multiple cropping.
**다목** 〖식물〗 a redbud; a Judas tree 《영》; 《목재》 sappanwood; Brazil wood.
**다목장어**(多目長魚) 〖어류〗 a brook lamprey.
**다목적**(多目的) multipurpose. ◉ ～댐 a multipurpose dam. ～ 차량 a multi=purposed vehicle(생략 MPV).
**다문**(多聞) being widely informed; extensive knowledge. ◉ ～박식(博識) wide information and extensive 〔encyclopedic〕 knowledge: ～ 박식한 사람 a person of various information and wide knowledge; an erudite.
**다물다** shut; close. ¶ 입을 꼭 다물고 with *one's* lips firmly 〔tightly〕 closed / 입을 ～ shut 〔close〕 *one's* mouth; keep *one's* lips tight; shut up; keep silent; hold *one's* tongue / 그는 입을 꼭 다물고 말을 하지 않았다 He refused to tell, shutting his mouth tight. *or* He kept mum about it.
**다민족국가**(多民族國家) a multiracial nation 〔country〕.
**다박나룻** a bushy 〔shaggy〕 beard; unkempt whiskers. ¶ ～이 나다 have a shaggy growth of beard.
**다반사**(茶飯事) ⇨ 항다반사.
**다발** a bundle; a bunch; a sheaf (*pl.* sheaves) (곡식·서류 따위의); a fagot (장작 따위의); a coil (새끼 따위). (★ bundle은 운반·저장하기 위하여 여러 가지를 느슨하게 다발지어 묶은 것, bunch는 같은 종류의 여러 개를 가지런히 다발지어 묶은 것). ¶ 꽃～ a bunch of flowers; a bouquet (F.) / 건초 ～ a bundle of hay / 장작 한 ～ a fagot 〔bundle〕 of firewood / 한 ～에 5천원 five thousands won a bundle / ～을 짓다 bundle; make 〔tie〕 up 《things》 into a bundle; pack into a bundle / ～로 팔다 sell by the bunch 〔bundle〕.
**다발**(多發) frequent occurrence. ¶ 교통사고 ～ 지점 an accident black spot; a black spot for traffic accidents.
**다발성**(多發性) ◉ ～경화증 〖의학〗 multiple sclerosis. ～신경염 〖의학〗 polyneuritis.
**다방**(茶房) a tea 〔coffee〕 house; a tearoom; a coffee shop (호텔 따위의).

> 참고 미국의 **tearoom**
> 미국에는 우리 나라 식의 다방이 없다. 흔히 tearoom 또는 teashop이라고 하는 곳은 일종의 작은 레스토랑으로 커피·홍차·가벼운 식사 등을 제공한다. 호텔이나 번화가에 있는 coffee house나 coffee shop은 좀 고급스런 tearoom이라 할 수 있다.

◉ ～레지 a tea house waitress. ～마담 a tearoom manageress.
**다방면**(多方面) 《방면》 many quarters; 《방향》 many directions; 《문제》 different subjects; 《취미》 many-sidedness; 《재능》 versatility. ¶ ～의 many-sided; various; varied; manifold; versatile / ～으로 in many 〔various〕 fields / ～에 걸친 학식 multifarious learning / ～으로 친구를 사귀다 have a wide circle of acquaintances / 그는 ～에 취미를 가진 사람이다 He is a man of catholic taste. *or* He has many-sided interests.
**다변**(多邊) many-sidedness. ¶ ～적 multilateral. ◉ ～무역〔외교〕 multilateral trade 〔diplomacy〕. ～형(形) a polygon: ～형의 polygonal.
**다변**(多辯) talkativeness; loquaciousness; garrulity; volubility. ¶ ～의 talkative; loquacious; garrulous; voluble. ◉ ～가 a great talker; a chatterbox; a garrulous person.
**다변화**(多邊化) diversification. ～하다 diversify; be diversified. ¶ 외교의 ～ diversified approach in diplomacy / 수출 시장의 ～ the diversification of export markets.
**다병**(多病) sickliness. ～하다 (be) sickly; fragile; weak; be of delicate health; be prone to illness. ¶ ～한 사람 a sickly person / 재자(才子)～이라 Men of talent are often delicate.
**다보록하다** (be) all tufty. ⇨ 더부룩하다.
**다보탑**(多寶塔) the *Tabot'ap*; the Pagoda of Many-treasured Buddha.
**다복**(多福) being favored with good luck 〔fortune〕; great happiness 〔fortune〕. ～하다 (be) blessed; lucky; happy; be blessed with good luck. ¶ ～한 생활을 하다 live a happy and blessed life.
**다복솔** a bushy young pine tree.
**다부닐다** come together in a friendly way; fraternize; socialize; get together.
**다부일처** (多夫一妻) polyandry.
**다부지다** ① 《과단성》 (be) staunch; firm; determined; stout-hearted; indefatigable; 《몸이》 (be) sturdy; stout; massive. ¶ 다부진 사람 a stout-hearted person; a person of staunch character / 다부지게 생긴 사람 a solidly=built person / 다부지게 일하다 work hard 〔indefatigably〕 / 그는 키는 작아도 사람이 ～ Though small in stature, he is a man of firm character. ② 《힘들다》 (be) hard; trying; tough. ¶ 다부진 일 a tough job; hard work.

**다북쑥** wormwood; mugwort. = 쑥[1].

**다분히**(多分—) much; largely; to a large 〔great〕 extent; greatly. ¶ 그럴 염려가 ~ 있다 That is very much to be feared. / 그에겐 속단하는 경향이 ~ 있다 He has a marked tendency to form a hasty conclusion. / 그는 시인의 소질이 ~ 있다 He has very much of the poet in him. / 그런 종류의 사고가 재발할 가능성이 ~ 있다 There is a very strong possibility that an accident of that type will occur again.

**다불다불** in tufts. ~하다 (be) tufty; fringy. ¶ ~ 늘어진 머리 tufty 〔abundant, flowing〕 hair 〔tresses (여성의)〕.

**다붓다붓** close(ly); dense(ly); at short intervals.

**다붓하다** (be) close; dense; be at short intervals. ¶ 다붓이 closely; densely.

**다붙다** close in together; come (close) together.

**다붙이다** bring 《them》 close together.

**다비**(茶毘) 〖불교〗 cremation; burning 《the body》 to ashes. ~하다 cremate 《the remains》; reduce 《the body》 to ashes. ◉ ~소(所) a crematory; a crematorium (*pl.* ~s, -ria). ~식 a cremation rite.

**다뿍** (to the) full; overflowingly; brimfully.

**-다뿐** 《강조어구》 ¶ 가라면 가다뿐이겠느냐 Do you think I would not go if you tell me to go? / 「나와 함께 가겠느냐」—「가다뿐이겠나」 "Will you go with me?" —"Sure!" *or* "Of course, I'll go."

**다사**(多事) ① 《일이 많음》 pressure of work; busyness; bustling; eventfulness. ~하다 (be) busy; eventful. ② 《간섭을 좋아함》 meddlesomeness; nosiness. ~스럽다 (be) meddlesome; nosy; officious. ¶ ~스러운 사람 a busybody; a meddler.

◉ ~다난(多難) eventfulness: ~다난하다 be eventful / ~다난한 한 해 an eventful year; a year big with events / 이런 ~다난한 시기에 in these eventful and critical times / 그의 생애는 ~ 다난했다 He has had an eventful life. / 지난해는 내외(內外)로 ~다난한 한 해였다 Last year was a very eventful one both at home and abroad. / 지난 2년 동안 우리는 참으로 ~다난했다 We have encountered one difficulty 〔obstacle, hardship〕 after another these last two years.

**다사제제**(多士濟濟) a galaxy 〔number〕 of brilliant talents. ¶ 우리 회사는 ~를 거느리고 있다 Our company has a large number of talented men and women.

**다산**(多産) bearing many young; fecundity; prolificacy; productivity (물품의). ~하다 bear many young; be fecund. ¶ ~하는 fecund; prolific; productive; 《한번에》 multiparous. ◉ ~부(婦) a prolific woman.

**다상**(多相) 〖전기〗 multiphase; polyphase. ◉ ~ 전동기〔발전기〕 a polyphase motor 〔dynamo〕.

**다색**(多色) several colors. ¶ ~의 polychromatic; versicolor(ed); multicolored. ◉ ~인쇄 multicolor printing. ~장식 polychromy. ~화 a polychrome.

**다색**(茶色) light brown; 《충충한 갈색》 drab. ¶ ~의 light-brown; brownish.

**다선의원**(多選議員) an assemblyman 〔a representative, a congressman〕 elected for many terms.

**다섯** five. ¶ ~배(의) five times; fivefold; quintuple / 우리 ~이 같이 간다 Five of us will be going together. ◉ ~쌍둥이 quintuplets; quins 《영구어》; quints 《미구어》.

**다섯째** fifth. ¶ ~ 사람 the fifth person / 이번 시험에서 그는 ~가 되었다 On the last test he came out fifth.

**다성(부)음악**(多聲(部)音樂) polyphony.

**다세대주택**(多世帶住宅) a multiplex house.

**다소**(多少) ① [수량] 《수》 the number; 《양》 the quantity; 《액》 the amount. ¶ ~를 불문하고 regardless of the amount; large or small / ~에 따라(서) according to the number 〔quantity, amount〕 of / 수입의 ~에 따라 세금을 매기다 tax 《*a person*》 according to the amount of *his* income / 양의 ~는 문제가 아니다 The quantity doesn't matter. / 신청자의 ~에 따라 할인 요금이 바뀝니다 According to the number of applicants, the reduced fare is subject to change. / ~를 불문하고 주문에 응합니다 All orders, large or small, will be accepted. ② 《얼마간》 a few; a little; a bit; some; somewhat; more or less; 《어느 정도》 to some degree 〔extent〕. ¶ 돈을 ~ 보내다 send some money / 영어를 ~ 하다 speak English a little; have some knowledge of English / ~ 춥다 be a bit cold / ~ 피로하다 be a little 〔be kind of〕 tired / 그는 ~ 건방진 데가 있다 He is fresh in a way. / 거기엔 ~ 의심스러운 점이 있다 There is something doubtful about it. / 그 일에는 그도 ~ 책임이 있다 He is also more-or-less responsible for that matter. / 아직 ～의 희망이 있다 There is yet some hope. / 그는 ～ 이기적인 데가 있다 He is a bit selfish. / 그의 말을 ～ 이해할 수 있을 것 같다 I seem to understand him to a certain extent. / 그는 ～ 초조한 듯했다 He looked somewhat impatient.

**다소곳이** quietly; gently; obediently. ¶ ～ 머리를 숙이다 drop 〔lower〕 *one's* head modestly / ～ 하라는 대로 하다 obey 《*a person*》 quietly / ～ 남의 말을 듣다 listen to another's advice (with *one's* head drooped).

**다소곳하다** ① 《고개를 숙이고 말이 없다》 be modest and quiet with lowered head. ② 《온순하다》 (be) modest; quiet; gentle; obedient. ¶ 다소곳한 태도 an obedient attitude.

**-다손 치더라도** (even) though; (even) if; no matter 《who, what, when, which》; granting 〔granted〕 that. ¶ 그렇다손 치더라도 even if it were so; granting that it is so / 아무리 돈이 많다손 치더라도 however 〔no matter how〕 rich *one* may be / 그가 그렇게 말했다손 치더라도 granted that he did say so / 돈은 없다손 치더라도 기마저 꺾이랴 I may be penniless, but is that any reason to lose heart!

**다수**(多數) ① 《수》 a large 〔great〕 number; 《대부분》 the greater part. ¶ ～의 a great many; a large number of 《people》; a lot of; numerous / 학생의 ～ the 「greater part 〔most〕 of the students / ～의 힘을 믿다 trust to 〔rely on〕 numbers / ～를 위해서 소수를 희생하다 sacrifice the few to the many / 최대 ～의 최대 행복 the greatest happiness of the greatest number / 그들은 ～를 믿고 횡포를 부렸다 They acted high-handedly by force of numbers. / 이 숲에는 ～의 사슴들이 서식하고 있다 A large number of deer inhabit this forest. *or* Deer are found in great numbers in this forest.

② 《과반수》 (a) majority 《of》. ¶ ～의 횡포 tyranny of the majority / 압도적인 ～ an overwhelming majority / 국민의 ～ the 「majority 〔large mass〕 of the people / 절대 ～로 with an absolute majority / 3분의 2의 ～를 요하다 require a two-thirds majority / ～를 차지하다 get 〔obtain〕 a majority / ～를 차지하고 있다 have 〔hold〕 a majority 《in》 / ～의 의견에 따르다 agree to the views of the majority / 그는 100대 20의 ～로 당선되었다 He was elected by a majority of 100 against 20.

◉ ～당〔파〕 a majority party; the majority: ～당의 당수 the Majority Leader. ～ 대표제 the majority representation system. ～안〔의견〕 a majority proposal 〔opinion〕. ～표 a plurality: ～표를 획득하다 poll a plurality.

**다수결**(多數決) (a) decision by majority; a majority vote 〔rule〕. ¶ ～의 원칙 majority rule / ～로 정하다 decide by majority; determine by a majority of votes / ～에 따르다 abide by the decision of the majority / 의회 제도는 ～의 원칙을 채용한다 The parliamentary system uses the principle of decision by majority. / 그 의안은 ～로 통과되었다 The bill was passed by a majority decision.

**다수확**(多收穫) a bumper crop. ¶ ～의 high-yield(ing). ◉ ～품종 the high=yield varieties (of grains).

**다스** a dozen (*pl.* ～(s)) (생략 doz., dz.). ¶ 연필 한 ～ a dozen pencils / 맥주 두 ～ two dozen bottles of beer / 열 ～ a small gross / 반 ～ half a dozen / 여러 ～의 (many) dozens of... / ～로 팔다 sell 《*things*》 by the dozen / 몇 ～나 필요하십니까 How many dozen do you want? / 그걸두 ～만 주시오 I will take two dozen of them.

**다스리다** ① (*a*) 《통치하다》 rule (over) (권력으로); reign (over) (군림하여); govern (조직을 통하여). ¶ 나라를 ～ rule over 〔govern〕 a country / 백성을 ～ rule 〔reign〕 over a people / 그 당시에는 누가 그 나라를 다스렸느냐 Who ruled (over) the country in those days? (*b*) 《관리하다》 manage; arrange; regulate; administer. ¶ 나랏일을 ～ manage a state; administer the affairs of a state / 집안을 ～ manage 〔order, regulate〕 *one's* household.
② 《통제하다》 control; keep under control; regulate 《rivers》. ¶ 물을 ～ control floods; take flood-control 〔river conservancy〕 measures.
③ 《평정하다》 pacify; quell; subdue; repress. ¶ 난을 ～ subdue a rebellion / 폭도를 ～ suppress 〔put down〕 the rioters.
④ 《병을》 cure; heal. ¶ 다스릴 수 없는 병 an incurable disease / 병을 ～ cure a disease.
⑤ 《죄를》 punish. ¶ 죄를〔죄인을〕 ～ punish a crime 〔criminal〕.

**다습**(多濕) high humidity; much moisture. ～하다 (be) damp; dampish; humid. ¶ 고온 ～의 hot and humid; high temperature and high humidity / ～한 기후 dampish weather.

**다시** ① 《또》 again; over again; for the second time; once more; once again. ¶ ～ 한 번 once more 〔again〕; a second time / ～ 하다 do over again 〔once more〕; try again / ～ 보다 look at 《it》 again 〔twice〕; have another look 《at》; 《전보다 좋게 보다》 think better of; come to have a better opinion of / ～ 읽다 read 《a passage》 (all over) again / ～ 한 번 해보다 make a second attempt / ～ 한 번 생각해 보다 come to think of it / 세 번 ～ 쓰다 rewrite thrice (again) / ～ 일을 시작하다 begin *one's* work again; resume *one's* work; be back at work / ～ 보자 I will see you again. / ～ 한 번 말해 보시오 Now say it once more. *or* Just restate once more. / 그는 고향을 떠난 뒤 ～ 돌아오지 않았다 He left his hometown 「for good 〔never to return〕. ② 《거듭》 repeatedly; again and again. ¶ ～ 자꾸 뇌다 repeat unendingly / 이런 실책은 두 번 ～ 되풀이 않겠다고 맹세한다 I swear that I shall never repeat the same error. / ～는 안 그럴게요 《부모에게》 I'll be good! ③ 《새로이》 anew; afresh; 《do》 over again. ¶ ～ 시작하다 begin anew; start afresh; start all over again / 집을 ～ 꾸미다 remodel 〔redecorate〕 a house / 책을 ～ 꾸미다 reedit a book; make a book over / 기와를 ～ 이어야겠다 We must have our roof retiled.

**다시금** ⇨ 다시.

**다시다** ¶ 입맛을 ～ smack *one's* lips; smack appreciative lips 《over a dish》; enjoy 《*one's* favorite dish》 / 입맛을 다시며 먹다 eat with great gusto 〔relish〕.

**다시마** 〖식물〗 a (sea) tangle(weed); kelp.

**다시없다** ① 《견줄 곳 없다》 (be) unique; unparalleled; unequaled; matchless; without peer. ¶ 다시없는 물건 a unique article; the only one of its kind / 그렇게 착한 사람은 ～ He is the best man I have ever seen. / 이렇게 좋은 사전은 다시없을 것이다 This dictionary has no equal. / 이렇게 경치 좋은 곳은 다시없을 게다 The place has no equal for scenic beauty. ② 《두 번 없다》 be never to happen again; will not be repeated; be for one time only. ¶ 그건 다시없는 기회다 That's a golden opportunity. / 이런 기회는 ～ We shall never have such a good opportunity again.

**-다시피** 《…는 바와 같이》 as; like; 《같은 정도로》 almost; nearly; practically; all but. ¶ 보시다시피 as you see; as you can see / 아시다시피 as you know; as you must realize / 보시다시피 나는 돈이 없습니다 As you can see, I have no money. / 누구나 다 알다시피 뉴욕은 미국 제일의 도시다 New York, as everybody knows, is the largest city in the United States. / 그들은 여기서 살다시피 한다 They practically live here. / 함대는 거의 전멸하다시피 했다 The fleet was all but annihilated. / 그는 술집에서 살다시피 한다 He spends most of his time at the bar.

**다식**(多食) eating much; heavy eating. ～하다 eat much; overeat; eat to excess. ◉ ～증 〖의학〗 polyphagia; bulimia.

**다신교**(多神教) polytheism. ◉ ～도 a polytheist.

**다실**(茶室) a teahouse. ⇨ 다방.

**다액**(多額) a large sum 〔amount〕. ¶ ～의 a large sum 〔amount〕 of 《money》; large 《fund》; considerable 《expenses》; heavy 《loss of money》 / ～의 비용 a huge cost / ～의 자본〔자금〕 large capital 〔funds〕. ◉ ～ 납세자 a high 〔an upper-bracket〕 taxpayer.

**다양**(多樣) variety; diversity. ～하다 (be) various; diverse; multifarious. ¶ ～한 직업의 사람들 men of diverse occupations / 그는 취미가 ～하다 He has many-sided interests. *or* He is a man of catholic taste. / 최근에는 ～한 잡지가 출판되고 있다 A great variety of magazines are published these days. ◉ ～성 diversity; variety; multiplicity.

**다양화**(多樣化) diversification. ～하다 diversify. ¶ 시장 확대를 위해 최근 제품의 ～를 기했다 We have recently diversified (the range of) our products so as to extend our market. / 새로운 수요에 호응하기 위해서는 제품의 ～가 필요하다 We need to diversify our products so as to meet new demands.

**다언**(多言) ① 《말 많음》 loquacity; garrulity; volubility; verbosity. ② 《여러 말》 many words. ¶ …에 대해서는 ～을 요하지 않는다 There is no need to dwell 〔of dwelling〕 upon 《the subject》.

**다염기산**(多塩基酸) 〖화학〗 polybasic acid.

**다오** ① 《물건을》 give me; let me have.

¶ 종이 한 장만 ~ Give me a piece of paper. ② 《…해다오》 ¶ 이 편지를 부쳐 ~ Have this letter posted. *or* Post this letter (for me). / 돈 좀 빌려 ~ Lend me some money. / 외투 좀 벗겨 ~ Help me off with my overcoat, if you please. / 그 얘기 좀 해 ~ Let me hear the story. *or* Tell me the story.

**다용**(多用) spending much; using much. ~하다 spend lavishly; use much.

**다용도**(多用途) ⇨ 다목적(多目的). ¶ ~의 multipurpose; all-purpose / ~로 쓰이다 be of wide 〔extensive〕 use / 이 상자는 ~로 쓸 수 있다 This box can be used 「for various purposes 〔in many ways〕. ◉ ~실 a multipurpose room.

**다우존스** ◉ ~ 산식(算式) the Dow-Jones formula. ~ 평균 주가 the Dow-Jones average price (of stocks); the average price computed under the Dow-Jones formula.

**다운** 〖권투〗 a knockdown. ¶ ~시키다 knock down; floor / ~되다 be knocked down; be floored / ~됐다가 일어나다 climb off the canvas.

**다운사이징** 《규모의 축소》 downsizing.

**다원**(多元) pluralism. ¶ ~적인 plural; pluralistic / ~적 국가론 pluralistic conception of the State / ~화 현상 polycentrism / 석유 수입원(輸入源)을 ~화하다 diversify oil purchase sources. ◉ ~론 pluralism: ~론자 a pluralist. ~묘사 descriptions from different viewpoints. ~방송 broadcasting from multiple origination; a networked broadcast. ~ 방정식 〖수학〗 a plural equation.

**다원**(茶園) a tea plantation 〔garden〕.

**다원발생**(多原發生) 〖생물〗 polygenesis; polyphylesis.

**다원자**(多原子) ¶ ~의 polyatomic. ◉ ~ 분자 a polyatomic molecule.

**다윈** 《영국의 박물학자》 Charles Robert Darwin (1809-82).

**다육**(多肉) 〖식물〗 fleshiness. ¶ ~질의 fleshy; pulpy. ◉ ~과(果) a drupaceous 〔fleshy, pulpy〕 fruit; a drupe. ~식물 a fleshy plant.

**다음** the next; the second; 《계속》 the sequel 《of a story》; [형용사적] next; following; coming; ensuing; 《인접한》 adjoining; adjacent; 《둘째》 second; the rest. ¶ ~ 방 the next 〔adjoining〕 room / ~사람 the next 〔following〕 person / ~주 next 〔the coming〕 week / ~ 정거장 the next station / ~ 대통령 the next term's 〔the future〕 president / ~부터는 from now on / ~에 next; secondly; in the second place; next time 〔occasion〕; in the following / ~으로 next to; in the second place; secondly / 그 ~으로 가장 좋은 것 the next best thing / (그리고 나서) ~ 수개월 동안(에) during the ensuing months / ~과 같다 it is 〔runs〕 as follows / 다음 기회로 미루다〔돌리다〕 hold 《it》 over till next time; postpone 《it》 to 〔till〕 next time / ~은 What (comes) next? / ~으로는 돈을 아껴 써야 한다 Secondly, you must be frugal of your money. / 너는 ~에 데리고 가마 I'll take you next time. / 그 기사는 ~과 같다 The article is as follows. / ~ 질문에 대답하시오 Answer the following questions. / ~에는 주의해라 Be (more) careful next time. / B씨 ~에는 누가 국무총리가 될까 Who will succeed Mr. B as Premier? / 그 ~은 말할 필요가 없다 You need not go any further. *or* We know the rest. / 그 ~을 얘기하게 Go on. *or* Proceed with your story.

**다음가다** rank next 〔second〕 to; be second 〔next〕 to; be in second place. ¶ 뉴욕 다음가는 대도시 the greatest city next to New York / 영어 다음가는 중요한 외국어 the most important foreign language after English / 인구에 있어서 부산은 서울 다음가는 대도시이다 Busan is the next 〔second〕 largest city to Seoul in population. / 그의 다음가는 선수는 남군이다 Mr. Nam is the champion who is second to him.

**다음날** 《이튿날》 the next 〔following〕 day; 《훗날》 someday; sometime later; another time. ¶ 도착한 ~ the day after 〔following〕 *one's* arrival / ~ 아침 (일찍) (early) the next morning / ~ 떠나다 leave the next day / ~ 다시 보자 I will see you someday again. / 그것은 ~로 미루자 Let's leave that for another time.

**다음다음** next but one; the one after the next. ¶ ~날 the day after next; the next day but one; two days later 〔after〕 / ~ 정거장 the station after next; the next but one station / ~ 일요일에 시간이 있느냐 Will you be free (on) the Sunday after next?

**다음달** the next 〔following〕 month; *proximo* (생략 *prox.*). ¶ ~ 초사흗날(에) (on) the third of next month; (on) the 3rd *prox.* / ~로 이월하다 carry 《the account》 forward to the next month.

**다음절**(多音節) a polysyllable. ◉ ～어 a polysyllabic word.

**다음해** the next〔following〕year. ¶ 불이 난 ～ the year after the fire / ～ 계획표 a schedule for the next〔coming〕year / ～ 3월에 in March next year / 계정을 ～로 이월하다 carry the account forward into next year's.

**다음호**(一號) the next number〔issue〕. ¶ ～에 계속 To be continued (in our next issue). / ～에 완결 To be concluded (in our next).

**다의**(多義) many〔various, diverse〕meanings; polysemy. ¶ ～의 《a word》 of many meanings; equivocal; ambiguous; multivocal. ◉ ～어 a word of many meanings; an equivocal〔ambiguous〕word.

**다이내믹하다** (be) dynamic; powerful. ¶ 저 단거리 선수는 다이내믹한 주법으로 달린다 That sprinter has a dynamic〔powerful〕way of running.

**다이너마이트** dynamite. ¶ ～로 폭파하다 blow up〔shatter〕《a rock》 with dynamite; dynamite《a rock》.

**다이닝 키친** an eat-in kitchen 《미》; a kitchen-(cum-)dining room; a breakfast-kitchen 《영》.

**다이렉트 메일** direct mail (생략 DM). ◉ ～ 광고 direct-mail advertising.

**다이빙** diving; 《1회의》 a dive. ～하다 dive; make〔do〕a dive 《into the water》. ¶ ～을 잘 하다 be a good diver; be good at diving. ◉ ～경기 a diving event; a fancy dive; fancy diving. ～대 a diving〔spring〕board. 공중 회전 ～ somersault diving. 스프링보드 ～ springboard diving. 플랫폼 ～ platform diving.

**다이아몬드** 〖광물〗 a diamond. ¶ ～반지 a diamond ring; a ring set with diamonds / ～를 깎다〔연마하다〕 cut〔polish〕a diamond. ◉ ～바늘 《전축의》 a diamond stylus. ～혼식 a diamond wedding anniversary.

**다이어그램** ① 《도표》 a diagram. ② 《열차의》 a (railroad) schedule〔timetable〕(운행표). ¶ ～을 개정하다 revise the time(table).

**다이어트** a diet. ¶ ～를 시작하다 go on a diet / 그들은 ～ 중이다 They are on a (slimming) diet. / 의사는 그녀에게 ～를 하도록 했다 The doctor put her on a diet. ◉ ～식품 diet〔low calorie〕food.

**다이얼** a dial. ¶ 전화〔라디오〕 ～ the dial on the telephone〔radio〕/ ～을 돌리다 turn a dial; dial / ～을 돌려 119번을 부르다 dial 119.

**다이오드** 〖전자공학〗 a diode.

**다이옥신** 〖화학〗 《제초제 등에 포함된 발암물질》 dioxin. ¶ ～에 오염된 식품 dioxin-tainted food.

**다이제스트** a digest; an abridgment. ◉ ～판: ～판으로 읽다 read *something* in an abridged version / ～판으로 편집하다 edit 《a long TV drama》 into a digest.

**다인** 〖물리〗 《힘 단위》 a dyne.

**다작**(多作) abundant production; prolificacy in writing. ～하다 produce〔write〕abundantly; be prolific (in writing). ◉ ～가 a prolific writer〔author〕.

**다잡다** ① 《사람을》 exercise close supervision 《over》; tighten the control 《of》; keep a close check 《on》; drive; urge; press. ¶ 학생들을 ～ tighten the control of students / 부하들을 다잡아 일을 속히 끝내다 urge *one's* men to finish the work. ② 《일을》 concentrate on 《a job》; stick close to 《*one's* work》; manage 《a job》. ③ 《마음을》 reform 《*one's* attitude》; brace *oneself* (up); brace (up) *one's* spirits; gird (up) *one's* loins.

**다잡이** (exercising) strict supervision〔control〕; tightening. ～하다 = 다잡다.

**다재**(多才) versatile talents; versatility. ～하다 (be) many-talented; versatile; have many talents. ¶ ～다능한 사람 a man of varied attainments; a many-talented person.

**다정**(多情) ① 《정이 많음》 humaneness; kindness; cordiality; warm-〔tender-〕heartedness. ～하다 (be) humane; kind; affectionate; cordial (충심으로부터의); warm-hearted; tender-hearted (다감한). ¶ ～히 warmly; tenderly; kindly; affectionately; sympathetically / ～한 사람 a warm-hearted man; a man of heart〔humane character〕/ 그는 ～하게 내 손을 잡았다 He clasped my hand warmly. ② 《친밀함》 a close friendship. ～하다 (be) intimate; familiar; close; friendly; chummy (사이가 좋은). ¶ ～하게 intimately; familiarly; on good terms / ～한 친구 a close〔bosom, great〕friend; a buddy 《미구어》/ ～하게 지내다, ～한 사이다 be on good〔friendly〕terms 《with》/ …와 ～한 사이가 되다 become〔get〕friendly〔familiar, intimate〕《with》/ 두 사람은 아주 ～한 사이다 They are hand and glove with each other.

**다정다감**(多情多感) sentimentality. ～하다 (be) sentimental (감상적인); emotional; passionate (정열적인). ¶ ～한 사람 a man of sentiment 〔feeling〕.

**다정다한**(多情多恨) sensibilities; susceptibilities; tears and regrets. ～하다 (be) sensible 〔susceptible〕; be full of tears and regrets. ¶ ～한 일생을 보내다 lead a life full of tears and regrets.

**다정불심**(多情佛心) warm-〔tender-〕heartedness; kindheartedness; compassion.

**다조지다** supervise closely; keep close rein on; press; urge.

**다족류**(多足類) 『동물』 ⇨ 다지류(多肢類).

**다종다양**(多種多樣) variety; multifariousness. ¶ 그녀는 ～한 벽지의 샘플을 보여 주었다 She showed us a large 〔wide〕 variety of wallpaper samples from which to choose. / 여자가 남자를 선택하는 이유는 ～하다 Women choose men for various kinds of reasons.

**다죄다** tighten 〔stiffen〕 《*a thing*》 up hard; 《마음을》 brace (up) *oneself*.

**다중**(多重) ¶ ～의 multiplex.
◉ ～매체 multimedia. ～방송 multiplex broadcasting; a multiplex broadcast (1회의). ～방식 a multiplex system: ～ 방식으로 송신하다 multiplex. ～인격 a multiple character. ～처리 『컴퓨터』 multiprocessing. ～충돌 a pile-up. 문자 ～방송 teletext broadcast(ing). 음성 ～방송 (sound) multiplex broadcast(-ing).

**다지다** ① 《단단히》 harden (by pounding); make hard (by stamping); 《기반 등을》 lay the foundation 《for》; pave the way 《for》. ¶ 땅을 ～ harden the ground / 흙을 ～ harden earth 〔clay〕 / 나라의 기틀을 ～ lay down a solid national foundation / 젊었을 때 학문의 기반을 다져 놓아야 한다 You should lay the foundation in learning when young.
② 《다잡다》 emphasize; underscore; make sure (of 〔that…〕); press 《*a person*》 for a definite answer 〔promise〕; keep after 《*a person*》. ¶ 나는 그에게 다섯시까지 와야 한다고 다졌다 I kept after him to come by five o'clock. / 내달에는 빚을 갚겠느냐고 다져서 물었다 I pressed him for a definite answer whether he would pay the debt next month.
③ 《마음을 가다듬다》 brace (up) *oneself;* pull *oneself* together. ¶ 그는 마음을 다져먹고 시험장 안으로 들어섰다 He braced himself 〔pulled himself together〕 and entered the examination room.
④ 《고기·양념을》 mince; hash; chop fine; chop up. ¶ 다진 고기 minced 〔ground〕 meat / 고기를 ～ mince meat / 마늘을 ～ chop garlic up fine.
⑤ 《잠자게》 press 《seasoned food》 with 《a stone》.

**다지류**(多肢類) 『동물』 ¶ ～의 multiped(e).
◉ ～동물 a myriapod.

**다지르다** press for a definite answer; make sure that….

**다질리다** get pressed for a definite answer; be assured; be ascertained.

**다짐** 《확약》 a firm 〔definite〕 promise; an assurance; a pledge. ～하다 make a definite promise; promise definitely 〔positively〕; give 《*a person*》 *one's* word 《to *do*》; commit *oneself* 《to *do*》; give *one's* word; make sure. ¶ 그는 내달까지는 빚을 갚겠다고 ～했다 He gave his word that he would pay the debt by next month. / 나는 그것을 어느 누구에게도 말하지 않겠다고 ～한다 I give you my word (of honor) that I won't tell it to anyone else.

**다짐받다** make 《*a person*》 pledge 〔promise〕; get an assurance from 《*a person*》; put 《*a person*》 on his oath. ¶ 다시는 죄를 짓지 않겠다는 다짐을 받고 그를 놓아 주었다 I set him free on his oath that he would never commit a crime again. / 갚겠다는 다짐받고 그에게 빌려준 돈인데 갚을는지 모르겠다 I don't know whether he will pay back the money I lent him on the promise that he would pay it back.

**다짜고짜(로)** 《예고 없이》 without (the slightest) notice 〔warning〕; 《느닷없이》 unexpectedly; abruptly; suddenly; 《까닭 없이》 without rhyme or reason. ¶ ～ 사람을 치다 hit *a person* abruptly / ～ 집을 비워달라고 하다 order 《*a person*》 out of the house without notice / ～ 아무를 체포하다 arrest *a person* without giving any reason.

**다채롭다**(多彩―) 《색채가》 (be) colorful; multicolored; variegated; varicolored; 《다양한》 (be) various; miscellaneous; multifarious. ¶ 다채로운 행사 a variety of festivities; all manner of events / 다채로운 경력 a colorful career / 가을에는 다채로운 학교 행사가 있다 We have a number of school events in autumn.

**다치다** ① 《부상하다》 be injured; get 〔be〕 hurt; hurt *oneself;* get 〔be〕 wounded; get a wound.

> **용법** 동사 「다치다」의 대표적인 명사꼴은 injury, hurt, wound라 할 수 있는데, 그 뜻의 차이는 대략 다음과 같다.
> **injury** 주로 사고로 인한 부상을 나타내는 일반적인 말: (그는 손과 발 여러 곳을 심하게 다쳤다) He got several serious injuries to the legs and arms.
> **hurt** injury 보다 구어적인 표현. injury, wound의 두 가지 뜻으로 다 쓰임. 정신적인 상처를 뜻하기도 함: (나는 그녀의 감정을 다치게 할 생각이 없었다) I didn't intend to hurt her feelings.
> **wound** 주로 무기에 의해 의식적으로 가해진 부상을 뜻하는 말로, 전쟁 등에서 다친 상처를 뜻함: (포탄 파편에 의한 머리의 부상) the wound in the head with a shell splinter.

¶ 다친 다리 an injured leg / 몹시 ～ be badly hurt 〔wounded〕 《on the head》; be seriously injured / 조금 ～ get a slight injury / 다리를 ～ get hurt in the leg / 차량 사고로 ～ be injured in an auto accident / 다치게 하다 do 《*a person*》 an injury; inflict 「an injury 〔a wound〕 on 《*a person*》; injure; hurt / 다치지 않도록 조심해라 Be careful not to get hurt. / 그는 넘어져서 무릎을 다쳤다 His knee was hurted by his fall. ② 《손상》 be injured; be damaged; be spoiled.

**-다 치더라도** even though. ⇨-다손 치더라도.

**다큐멘터리** a documentary. ¶ 내가 곧잘 보는 것은 뉴스 방송과 ～ 프로그램이다 My favorite programs are newscasts and documentaries. ◉ ～드라마 a documentary drama. ～영화 a documentary (film).

**다크호스** 《뜻밖의 결과를 가져오는 경주마·사람》 a dark horse.

**다투다** ① (***a***) 《말다툼하다》 quarrel 〔have a quarrel〕 《with *a person* over 〔about〕 *a matter*》; row; squabble; brawl; wrangle; have words with. ¶사소한 일로 ～ quarrel over a trivial matter / 그녀는 애들 문제로 남편과 다투었다 She quarrelled with her husband about their children. (***b***) 《논쟁》 dispute; argue; have 「a dispute 〔an argument〕; engage in a controversy. ¶ 다툴 여지가 없는 indisputable 《facts》; incontrovertible / 법정에서 ～ go to law 《with, against》; contest 《the point》 at law / 정부의 외교 정책에 관해 그들과 ～ dispute with them over the foreign policy of the government / 새로운 학설을 놓고 ～ debate a new theory; argue (for) a new theory / …한 사실을 다툴 여지가 없다 There is no denying the fact that…. (***c***) 《불화》 be at variance 〔discord〕 《with》; be in conflict with; be at odds. ¶ 다투게 하다 set 《*a person*》 at variance 〔odds〕 《with another》. ② 《겨루다》 compete 〔vie〕 《with *a person* for *something*》; contend 《with 〔against〕 others for a prize》; contest 《with 〔against〕 *a person* for *something*》; struggle 《for suprimacy》. ¶ 권력을〔수위를, 우승을〕 ～ vie for power 〔first place, dominance〕 / 일등상을 타려고 서로 ～ compete against each other for the first prize / 다투어 …하다 vie in *do*ing / 앞을 다투어 …하다 try to be the first to *do;* try to get ahead of other people in *do*ing / 저마다 좋은 자리를 차지하려고 ～ all scramble for better seats / 먼저 들어가려고 앞을 ～ try to be the first to enter / 그들은 앞을 다투어 달아났다 They ran away, everyone for himself.
③ 《시간·공간을 위해》 ¶ 지금은 1분 1초를 다투는 때다 We haven't a moment to lose. / 이것은 촌각을 다투는 문제이다 The problem does not admit of a moment's delay. / 한 치의 땅을 다투는 국지전(局地戰) a local war that shall not give up even an inch of land 〔territory〕.

**다툼** ① 《말다툼》 a quarrel; a wrangle; a squabble; 《논쟁》 a dispute 《on, over》; an argument; a controversy. ¶ 말～ a quarrel; an altercation / 법정에서의 ～ a judical dispute; gowned warfare / 학문상의 ～ an academic controversy. ② 《경쟁》 a competition; a contest; a contention; a struggle. ¶ 자리～ the competition for a position / 공명 ～ a contention 〔struggle〕 for honors / 세력〔정권〕 ～을 하다 vie 〔struggle〕 for influence 〔political power〕.

**다툼질** quarrelling; squabbling; 《논쟁》 controverting; arguing; disputing. ～하다 = 다투다.

**다트** 《화살 던지기》 dart(s); 《양재》 a dart.

**다하다**[1] 《떨어지다》 run 〔give〕 out; be exhausted; be 「used up 〔consumed, spent, gone〕; 《끝나다》 end; come to an end; terminate; be out 〔up〕. ¶ 식량이 ～ run out of food 〔provisions〕; the food is all gone / 수단이 ～ exhaust 〔be at the end of〕 *one's* resources; have tried everything that *one* can think of / 시간이 ～ time is up / 힘이

~ *one's* energy is exhausted / 목숨이 다할 때까지 싸우다 fight as long 《against the enemy》 as *one* lives.

**다하다**[2] ① 《끝내다》 finish; go through; be through 《with》. ¶ 일을 ~ finish *one's* work; get 〔be〕 through with *one's* work; get *one's* work done / 이야기를 ~ finish *one's* talk; be through with *one's* story.
② 《다 들이다》 exhaust; use up; run out of. ¶ 전력을 다하여 with all *one's* might; with *one's* whole heart; to the best of *one's* ability / 전력을 ~ exert all *one's* powers; make an all-out effort; make every possible effort; exert *oneself* to the utmost / 최선을 ~ do *one's* best 〔utmost〕; do everything in *one's* power / 온갖 수단을 ~ exhaust 〔try〕 every means in *one's* power; try everything; leave 「no stone unturned 〔no means untried〕 / 온갖 횡포를 ~ do everything in a high-handed manner / 효도를 ~ serve *one's* parents with devotion / 조국에 충성을 ~ be loyal to *one's* country; render devoted service to *one's* country / 의사는 온갖 가능한 방법을 다하여 그녀의 목숨을 구하려고 했다 The doctor tried every possible method to save her life.
③ 《책임 등을》 do; perform; discharge; fulfill; accomplish; carry out. ¶ 의무를 ~ do 〔perform〕 *one's* duty / 사명을 ~ accomplish *one's* mission / 책임을 ~ fulfill *one's* responsibility.

**다한증**(多汗症) 〖의학〗 excessive sweating; hyper(h)idrosis.

**다항선택법**(多項選擇法) a multiple choice 「method.

**다항식**(多項式) 〖수학〗 a polynomial 〔multinomial〕 expression; a polynomial.

**다행**(多幸) good fortune 〔luck〕. ~스럽다, ~하다 (be) lucky; fortunate; happy; blessed. ¶ ~히 fortunately; luckily; by good fortune 〔luck〕; by a happy chance / 불행중 ~ a bright spot in the misfortune / ~히(도) …하다 be lucky enough to *do;* have the good fortune 〔luck〕 to 《see her》 / ~히(도) 거기서 그를 만났다 I was lucky enough to meet him there. / ~히 다친 사람은 없었다 Fortunately no one was injured. / ~히 그는 집에 있었다 By good luck, I found him at home. / 날씨가 좋아서 ~이었다 We were fortunate in having good weather. / 이것으로 도움이 된다면 ~이겠습니다 I hope this will be of help to you. / ~히도 나의 시도는 성공했다 I was fortunate enough to succeed in my attempt. / 이것은 우리 나라를 위해 참으로 ~한 일이다 This is very fortunate for our country.

**다혈**(多血) sanguineness; full-bloodedness. ¶ 그는 ~질에다가 너무나 낙관적이다 He is sanguine and too optimistic. ◉ ~증 〖의학〗 plethora; repletion: ~증의 plethoric. ~질 a sanguine 〔hot〕 temperament: ~질의 full-blooded; sanguine; plethoric. ~한(漢) a hot-blooded fellow; a man of sanguine temperament; a hothead.

**다홍**(一紅) deep red; crimson. ◉ ~실 deep red 〔crimson〕 thread 〔yarn〕. ~치마 a red skirt.

**닥나무** 〖식물〗 a paper mulberry (tree).

**닥다그르르** ⇨딱다그르르.

**닥뜨리다** be faced with; be confronted with 〔by〕; be brought face to face with; encounter; face; meet with. ¶ 난관에 ~ face 〔meet with〕 a difficulty; encounter a difficult situation.

**닥치는대로** at random; haphazardly; randomly; in a desultory way; desultorily. ¶ ~ 무엇이나 whatever 〔anything that〕 comes 「handy 〔along, *one's* way, to *one's* hand〕 / ~ 먹다 eat anything *one* can put 〔get〕 *one's* hands on / ~ 읽다 read whatever *one* can lay hands on; read desultorily.

**닥치다** 《다가오다》 draw near; come round; approach; be near 〔close〕 at hand; 《임박하다》 impend; be impending; be imminent. ¶ 눈앞에 닥친 위험 「an impending 〔a pressing〕 danger / 곤란이 ~ difficulties arise / 위험이 그녀에게 닥쳐왔다 Danger threatened her. / 죽음이 그에게 닥쳐왔다 Death stared him in the face. / 파산이 눈 앞에 닥쳤다 We were on the verge of bankruptcy. / 약속 날짜가 닥쳐왔다 The appointed day is now close at hand. / 전혀 뜻하지 않은 재난이 그에게 닥쳤다 Quite an unforeseen disaster suddenly befell him.

**닥터** a doctor; a doc 《구어》. ¶ ~ 김 Dr. 「Kim.

**닦다** ① 《윤내다》 polish; give 《*a thing*》 a polish 〔a rub-up〕; rub up 《silver spoon》; burnish 《metal》; shine 《*one's* shoes》; grind (렌즈를). ¶ 구두를 닦게 하다 have *one's* shoes shined / 구두를 번쩍번쩍하게 ~ put a good shine on *one's* shoes / 구두 좀 닦을 수 있을까요 Can I have my shoes polished?
② 《물로 씻다》 clean; wash; brush; 《훔

침》 wipe; mop (up); 《물기를》 dry 《a dish》 with 《a cloth》. ¶ 걸레로 ~ wipe 〔scrub〕 《the floor》 with a floorcloth / 눈물을 ~ dry *one's* eyes; wipe away the tears / 물로 ~ wash in water / 이를 ~ brush 〔clean〕 *one's* teeth / 자동차를 ~ wash a car / 창문을 ~ clean a window / 수건으로 얼굴을 ~ wipe 〔dry〕 *one's* face with a towel / 이마의 땀을 ~ wipe the sweat off the brow / 엎지른 물을 ~ mop up spilt water / 닦고 조이고 기름치자 《게시》 Clean, tighten, and lubricate.

③ 《길·터를》 improve; level. ¶ 길을 ~ improve a road / 터를 ~ level 〔smooth〕 the ground / 운동장을 ~ level a playground.

④ 《솜씨·기술 등을》 improve; cultivate; polish; 《연습을 거듭하여》 practice; train. ¶ 기술을 ~ improve *one's* skill; practice an art / 덕을 ~ cultivate 〔improve upon〕 *one's* virtue / 무예를 ~ practice 〔train *oneself* in〕 military arts / 학업을 ~ pursue *one's* studies.

⑤ 《기반·토대를》 prepare the ground 《for》; pave the way 《for》; solidify *one's* footing. ¶ 선거 기반을 ~ nurse *one's* constituency; mend *one's* (political) fences 《미》.

**닦달질** 《닦아세움》 a scolding; (a) rebuke; a reproach; taking to task; a telling-off. ~하다 = 닦아세우다.

**닦아세우다** scold; rebuke; reproach; give 《*a person*》 a good talking-to; take 〔bring〕 《*a person*》 to task; give 《*a person*》 a telling-off. ¶ 잘못했다고 ~ take 《*a person*》 to task for *his* mistake / 지각했기에 그를 한참 닦아세웠다 I gave him a good talking-to for being late.

**닦음질** polishing; cleaning; washing; brushing; burnishing; scrubbing. ~하다 clean; wash; brush; scrub.

**닦이다** ① 《윤이 나도록》 be polished 〔burnished, shined, rubbed up〕. ¶ 이 쟁반은 잘 닦였다 This tray is well polished. ② 《깨끗이》 be cleaned 〔washed, brushed, scrubbed〕; 《훔쳐지다》 be wiped; be mopped. ③ 《홀닦이다》 be scolded; be rebuked; be given a good talking-to. ¶ 호되게 ~ have 〔be given〕 a good scolding.

**단** 《묶음》 a bundle 《of straw》; a bunch; a sheaf 《of wheat, of papers》; a load (짐); a fagot (장작). ⇨다발. ¶ 장작단 a bundle 〔load〕 of firewood / 짚단 a bundle of straw / 장작 한 단 a bundle of firewood / 시금치 두 단 two bunches of spinach / 단을 짓다 「tie up in 〔make up〕 a bundle; sheave (곡물 등) / 단으로 팔다 sell by the bunch.

**단**(段) ① 《지적의 단위》 a *tan* (= about 0.245 acres). ¶ 단당 수확량 production per *tan*.

② 《인쇄물의》 a column. ¶ 2단 조판 the double column setting / 4단(짜리) 광고 a four-column advertisement / 이 지면은 3단으로 되어 있다 There are three columns on this page.

③ 《등급》 a *tan;* a grade 《of black belt》; a class; a rank. ¶ 유단자 a grade 〔rank〕 holder / 바둑 3단 《사람》 a third grader in *paduk* / 단이 다르다 be not in the same class 《as》; stand on different levels / 단이 올라가다 be promoted to a higher rank 〔*tan*〕 / 그녀는 태권도 3단이다 She holds a third degree black belt in t'aekwondo. *or* She is a third *tan* at t'aekwondo.

④ 《계단·층계 등의》 a step 《of the stairs》; a stair; a flight 《of stairs》; a rung 《of a ladder》. ¶ 열두 단의 층계 a flight of twelve steps / 위에서 두번째 단 the next to the top stair / 한 번에 두 단씩 계단을 오르다 go up the steps two at a time.

⑤ 《침대·로켓 등의》 ¶ (열차의) 침대 상〔하〕단 the upper 〔lower〕 berth / (로켓의) 제1단 the first stage (of a rocket).

**단**(壇) ① 《높게 가설한 자리》 a platform; a raised floor; a stage (무대); a rostrum (연단); a podium (오케스트라의 지휘대); a dais (연단); an altar (제단). ¶ 설교단 a pulpit / 단에 오르다 take 〔stand on〕 the platform / 그는 우레와 같은 박수를 받으며 단에 올랐다 He took the rostrum amid a thunderous clapping of hands. ② 《…계》 a world; circles. ¶ 문단 the literary world; literary circles.

**단**(斷) a decision; a resolution; a judgment. ¶ 단을 내리다 give *one's* 〔make a〕 (final) decision / 지금이 바로 단을 내릴 때다 Now is the time for a prompt decision.

**단**(單) only (one); single; merely. ¶ 단 하나의 only; sole; single / 단 하나도 not a single one / 단 한 번 only once / 단 혼자서 (all) alone; solely; by *oneself* / 단 3년 동안에 in three short years / 단 한 번도 …않다 never once; not even once / 승객은 단 한 사람이었

다 There was the only passenger. / 나는 지난 해 단 하루도 결석한 일이 없다 I have never missed a day in the last year.

**단**(但) = 다만②.

**-단**(團) 《단체》 a body; a group 《of boys》; a party; a corps (집단); a team (경기의); a troupe (극단); a band (악단); a gang (폭력의). ¶ 관광단 a tourist party / 기자단 the press group; a party of reporters / 재일 동포 모국 방문단 a home-visiting group of Korean residents in Japan.

**단가**(短歌) 《짧은 노래》 a kind of song with short quick notes; 《시조》 a kind of short poem.

**단가**(單價) a unit cost 〔price〕. ¶ 생산 ~ the unit cost of production; the cost per unit of production / ~ 80원으로 at eighty won apiece 〔each〕 / 나는 이것들을 ~ 천 원씩에 샀다 I bought these at 1,000 won apiece.

**단가**(團歌) the official song of 「a body 〔a party, an association〕.

**단가**(檀家) 〖불교〗 a supporter of a Buddhist temple; a parishioner.

**단가살이**(單家—) the household of a small family; the life of a small family. ~하다 have a small family.

**단감** a sweet persimmon.

**단강**(鍛鋼) forged steel.

**단거리**[1] ① 《재료》 the only material *one* has available. ② = 단벌.

**단거리**[2] 《단으로 묶은》 firewood in bundles 〔fagots〕; 《단으로 파는》 firewood sold by the bundle 〔fagot〕.

**단거리**(短距離) a short distance; a short 〔close〕 range (사격의). ¶ ~에서 at 「a short distance 〔close range〕.
◉ ~경영(競泳) a short-distance swimming race. ~경주 a short-distance race; a sprint (race); a dash. ~선수 a sprinter. ~수송 short-haul transportation. ~이착륙 a short take-off and landing (생략 STOL): ~ 이착륙기 a STOL plane. ~ 탄도〔공격〕미사일 a short-range ballistic 〔attack〕 missile (생략 SRBM 〔SRAM〕). ~폭격기 a close-range bomber.

**단검**(短劍) a short 〔small〕 sword; 《비수》 a dagger; a dirk; a stiletto. ◉ ~표 〖인쇄〗 a dagger; an obelus (†).

**단것** sweet things; sweets; a sweet. ¶ ~을 좋아하다 have a weakness for sweets; have a sweet tooth.

**단견**(短見) ① 《좁은 소견》 《take》 a short-sighted view; 《have》 a narrow-minded viewpoint 〔point of view〕; a myopic outlook. ② 《자기의》 my humble opinion; my personal views.

**단결**(團結) solidarity; unity; union. ~하다 unite; stand together. ¶ ~된 united; solid / ~하여 in union; in a body; solidly / ~하여 일하다 work 「with perfect unity 〔in a body〕 / ~하여 …에 대항하다 be united 〔banded together〕 against… / 굳게 ~돼 있다 be closely banded together; be strongly united / ~하여 난국에 대처하다 unite (together) to deal with the difficulties / ~은 힘이다 Union is strength. / 폭력 행위에 대하여 ~해서 싸우자 Let's fight in a body against violence.
◉ ~권 《근로자의》 the right of organization 〔unity〕. ~력 the power of unity. ~심 cooperative spirit; (an) *esprit de corps* (F.); the spirit of unity.

**단결에** at a breath 〔stroke〕; 《기회 있을 때에》 while there is 「a chance 〔an opportunity〕; before the chance slips away; without missing the chance. ⇨ 단숨에. ¶ 일을 ~ 해치우다 finish *one's* work at a breath 〔stroke〕.

**단결합**(單結合) 〖화학〗 a single bond.

**단경**(短徑) 〖수학〗 the minor axis.

**단경**(斷經) 〖한의〗 menopause. ~하다 go through menopause; *one's* menstruation ceases.

**단경기**(端境期) a between season; an off-crop 〔a preharvest〕 season.

**단계**(段階) ① 《과정의 한 시기》 a stage; a step; 《국면》 a phase. ¶ 예비적 ~ preliminary stage(s) / ~적으로 by 〔in〕 stages / 현 ~에 있어서 at this stage 《of》 / ~를 설정하다 establish grades; grade / ~를 밟아 나아가다 proceed step by step / 초기 ~에 있다 be at an early stage; be in its early stages / 출판 ~에 이르다 be ripe for publication / 세 ~를 거치다 pass through three phases 〔stages〕 / 조사 결과는 아직 발표할 ~가 아니다 The result of the investigation is not yet ready for disclosure. / 그 계획은 아직 실험 ~에 있다 The project is still in an experimental stage. / 교섭은 최종 ~에 이르렀다 The negotiations reached their final stage. / 전쟁은 이제 최종 ~에 접어들었다 The war now entered on its last phase.
② 《등급》 a rank; a grade; a level; a gradation. ¶ 학생을 4~로 평가하다 evaluate students according to the four-grade system / 이 물건들은 A에서 E까지의 ~가 있다 These articles are graded 〔ranked〕 from A to E.

◉ ～적: ～적인 phased《withdrawals of troops》/ ～적 해소〔폐지〕a phase-out《of the old system》/ ～적 도입 a phase-in《of the new policy》/ 당국은 그 제도를 ～적으로 도입〔폐지〕할 예정이다 The authorities intend to phase the system in〔out〕.

**단골**[1]《집》*one's* favorite〔accustomed〕store〔bar〕; a customary〔regular〕establishment;《손님》a (regular) customer; a client; [총칭] custom. ¶ 오랜 ～ a customer of long standing; an old customer / ～ 술집 a drink-shop *one* goes to regularly / ～ 식당 *one's* favorite〔accustomed〕restaurant / ～로 사다 buy usually; be accustomed to buy / ～이 되다 become a regular customer《of》; give *one's* custom to / ～을 얻다〔잃다〕gain〔lose〕*one's* custom / ～(손님)이 많다 have a large connection〔custom〕; enjoy a large patronage / 저 상점의 ～ 손님들은 돈 많은 부인들이다 That store is patronized by wealthy ladies.

**단골**[2]〖건축〗a half-sized tile (기와).

**단공**(鍛工) a metalworker; a hammer-smith.

**단과대학**(單科大學) a college.

**단광**(單光)〖물리〗monochromatic light. ◉ ～색 a monochrome; a single hue.

**단교**(斷交) breaking〔severing〕relations; (a) rupture. ～하다 break off〔sever〕relations《with》. ¶ 양국간의 경제 ～ a rupture of economic relations between two countries / 두 나라는 ～하였다〔상태에 있다〕The two nations have severed diplomatic relations.

**단교경주**(斷郊競走) a cross-country race〔run〕.

**단구**(短句) a (short) phrase.

**단구**(短軀) short stature〔build〕. ¶ ～이다 be short of stature; be of short stature.

**단구**(段丘)〖지리〗a terrace; a bench. ¶ 해안〔하안〕～ a marine〔river〕terrace.

**단군**(檀君) *Tangun,* the founding father of the Korean nation. ◉ ～기원＝단기(檀紀). ～성전(聖殿) a *Tangun* shrine. ～신화 *Tangun* mythology. ～조선 Korea in the reign of *Tangun; Tangun Choson.*

**단권(책)**(單卷(冊)) (a work in) one volume; a one-volume edition.

**단궤**(單軌) a single rail; a monorail. ◉ ～철도 a monorail.

**단근**(單根) ①〖화학〗a simple radical. ②〖식물〗a simple root.

**단근질** torturing with a red-hot iron. ～하다 torture《a criminal》with a red-hot iron.

**단금지교**(斷金之交) close friendship; a Damon-and-Pythias friendship. ¶ ～를 맺다 swear eternal friendship.

**단급**(單級) a single class. ◉ ～학교 a one-〔single-〕class school.

**단기**(單記) (a) single entry. ◉ ～무기명 투표 a secret vote〔ballot〕with single entry. ～투표 single voting: ～투표제 a single ballot〔vote〕system.

**단기**(單機) a single〔lone〕plane.

**단기**(單騎) a single horseman〔rider〕. ¶ ～로 적진에 뛰어들다 rush alone on horseback into the enemy's ranks.

**단기**(短期) a short term〔time, period〕. ¶ ～의 brief; short(-term); short-dated (어음 등); of short duration / ～ 집중 강좌〔강습〕a short, intensive course / 우리 회사는 은행에 ～ 대부를 신청했다 Our company asked the bank for a short-term loan.

◉ ～간《in, for》a short period; a short space of time: 지연된 시간을 ～간 내에 만회해야 한다 We have to make up for the lost time in a short period. ～거래 short-term transaction. ～계약 a short-term contract. ～공채〔사채〕a short(-term)「public bond〔debenture〕. ～과정 a short(-term) course《in French》: 나는 영어 회화를 배우기 위해 ～ 과정을 찾고 있다 I'm looking for a short course to learn English conversation. ～대부 a short(-term) loan. ～보험 short-period insurance. ～복무 a short service. ～시장 a short-term market. ～시효 short-period prescription. ～어음 a short(-dated) bill. ～유학 a short period of study abroad. ～융자 a short-term loan; a call loan (요구불의). ～자본 short-term capital. ～재정증권 a treasury bill (생략 T.Bi.) ～전 a short war. ～채(권)(債(券)) a short-term bond. ～체류〔체재〕a short stay;《여행 경유지에서의》a stopover. ～흥행 a short run.

**단기**(團旗) an association banner; a party flag.

**단기**(檀紀) the *Tangun* era. ¶ 서기 1985년은 ～ 4318년이다 The year 1985 in the Christian era falls on 4318 in the *Tangun* era.

**단김에** at a breath. ＝단결에. ¶ 쇠뿔도 ～ 빼랬다《속담》Make hay while the sun shines. *or* Strike the iron while it is hot.

**단꿈** a sweet〔happy〕dream. ¶ ～을 꾸

다 dream 〔have〕 a sweet dream.

**단나무** bundled firewood; 《단으로 파는》 firewood sold by the bundle.

**단내** 《탄내》 a scorched 〔burnt〕 smell; 《코에서 나는》 a stuffy smell from *one's* nostril. ¶ ~가 난다 I smell something burning. / 그 과자는 ~가 난다 The cake tastes scorched.

**단념**(斷念) abandonment; relinquishment; resignation. ~하다 give up (an idea of *do*ing); abandon; relinquish 《*one's* right》; resign *oneself* 《to》. ¶ 죽은 것으로 ~하다 give 《*a person*》 up for dead / 없어진 것으로 ~하다 give 《*a thing*》 up for lost / 출세를 ~하다 give up hope of success in life / 해외로 가는 것을 ~하다 give up the idea of going abroad / 어쩔 수 없다고 ~하다 abide by 〔resign *oneself* to〕 the inevitable / 어떤 일이 있어도 이것은 ~ 않는다 Nothing can make me give this up. / 그는 아직도 그녀를 ~ 못 하고 있다 He still retains a lingering love for the girl. / 그는 가정 형편 때문에 진학을 ~했다 He waived 〔gave up〕 the idea of entering a college for family reasons. / 자금 부족 때문에 그 계획을 ~했다 I gave up the plan for want of money. / 나는 여동생이 혼자 여행하는 것을 ~시켰다 I dissuaded my sister from traveling alone.

**단단하다** ① 《굳다》 (be) hard; solid. ¶ 단단한 돌 a hard stone / 단단해지다 harden; get 〔become〕 hard / 쇠같이 〔돌처럼〕 ~ be as hard as iron 〔a rock〕 / 단단한 땅에 물이 괸다 《속담》 Only a frugal man can save money. ② (***a***) 《군세다·튼튼하다》 (be) strong; solid; firm; fast; secure; steady; sound. ¶ 단단한 결심 a firm 〔a determined, an unshakable〕 resolution / 단단한 약속 《make》 a solemn promise / 단단한 건물 a solid building / 단단한 기초 a solid foundation / 단단한 사람 a strong person; a man of solid build / 단단한 회사 a sound business firm / 몸이 ~ be robust / 이 집은 지반이 ~ This house stands on firm ground. / 적의 방어는 매우 ~ The defense of the enemy is very strong. / 그는 영어 기초가 ~ He has a good grounding in English. (***b***) 《맨 것·박인 것이》 (be) tight; close. ¶ 단단히 매다 tie tightly 〔fast〕.

**단단히** ① 《굳게》 hard; solidly. ¶ 땅을 ~ 다지다 stamp 〔tramp〕 the earth down hard / 거리의 눈이 ~ 얼었다 The snow of the street has been frozen hard. ② 《꽉》 tight(ly); firmly; fast; securely. ¶ ~ 매다 tie fast 〔firmly〕 / ~ 붙들다 cling fast to 《*a thing*》; hold 〔hang〕 on tight to 《*a thing*》; take a firm hold of / 짐을 ~ 싸다 pack a bundle tight / 손발을 ~ 묶다 bind hand and foot tightly / 문단속을 ~ 하다 fasten the doors securely; fasten up every door. ③ 《굳세게·튼튼하게》 firmly; strongly; solidly; stably; steadily. ¶ ~ 결심하다 make a firm resolution; be firmly resolved 〔determined〕 / ~ 약속하다 make 〔give〕 a solemn 〔firm〕 promise / 집을 ~ 짓다 build a house solidly / 기초를 ~ 닦다 make a solid foundation; establish a firm ground; do good spadework / 그는 마음을 ~ 먹었다 He steeled his heart. ④ 《엄중히》 strictly; rigidly; rigorously. ¶ …하는 것을 ~ 금하다 strictly prohibit 《*a person* from *do*ing, *a person's do*ing》; strictly forbid 《*a person*》 to *do*. ⑤ 《크게》 greatly; severely. ¶ ~ 꾸지람을 듣다 be severely scolded / ~ 재미(를) 보다 have great fun; have a very good time; make a sizable profit (이득을) / ~ 혼내줄 테다 I will let him have it.

**단당류**(單糖類) 〚화학〛 a monosaccharide.

**단대목**(單—) the high tide 《of》; an important opportunity 〔position〕.

**단도**(短刀) a short sword; 《비수》 a dagger; a poniard; a stiletto (양날의). ¶ ~를 품고 with a dagger in *one's* bosom / ~를 들고 (with a) dagger in hand / ~로 찌르다 stab 《*a person*》 with a dagger.

**단도직입**(單刀直入) coming straight to the point; straightforwardness. ¶ ~적인 point-blank; direct / ~적으로 straightforwardly; directly; point-blank; without preamble / ~적으로 말하다 speak in a downright way / ~으로 말해라 Come 「straight 〔right〕 to the point. / 그는 내게 ~적으로 질문을 했다 He asked me a point-blank question.

**단독**(丹毒) 〚의학〛 erysipelas; St. Anthony's fire; the rose. ¶ ~성의 erysipelatous.

**단독**(單獨) singleness; independence; separateness; exclusiveness. ¶ ~의 《독립된》 independent; 《개개의》 individual; separate; 《혼자》 single; sole; solo; 《혼자 힘의》 single-handed; unas-

sisted / ~으로《독립으로》independently; 《각자》individually; separately; 《혼자서》singly; alone; by *oneself;* 《혼자 힘으로》single-handed(ly) / ~으로 일을 하다 act single-handed 〔by *oneself*〕/ 그는 ~으로 그 산 등정에 성공했다 He succeeded in climbing the mountain「alone 〔by himself〕. / 이번 여행 중에는 ~ 행동은 삼가라 Don't act independently during this trip. / 여당은 그 안건을 ~ 심의했다 The ruling party discussed the bill on its own.
◉ ~강화《conclude》a separate peace (treaty). ~개념 an independent conception. ~경제 independent economy. ~기관 an exclusive organization. ~내각 a one-party 〔single-party〕 cabinet. ~범《범인》a sole offender; a lone wolf; 《범죄》a one-man crime; a single-handed offence. ~보험 simple insurance. ~비행《make》a solo flight. ~운영 unilateral operation《of the National Assembly》. ~재판 trial by a single judge. ~제《재판의》the single-judge system. ~책임 sole responsibility. ~판사 a single judge. ~해손(海損) particular average (생략 P.A.). ~행동 〖법〗《take》(an) independent action. ~행위 〖법〗an individual act 〖법〗a unlateral act. ~회견《have》an exclusive interview《with》.

**단돈** a small amount of money. ¶ ~ 백 원도 없다 haven't even got a hundred won.

**단두대**(斷頭臺) a guillotine; a scaffold; a block. ¶ ~에 오르다 go to the guillotine / ~의 이슬로 사라지다 be guillotined; die on the block.

**단둘** only two persons. ¶ 방엔 ~밖에 없다 There are only two persons in the room. / 그들은 항상 ~이서 낚시하러 간다 The two of them always go fishing together.

**단락**(段落)《문장의》(the end of) a paragraph; 《일·사건 등의》an end; a close; conclusion; settlement. ⇨ 일단락(一段落). ¶ ~을 짓다 bring《*a matter*》to conclusion / 이 ~은 너무 길어서 이해하기 어렵다 This paragraph is too long to follow.

**단락**(短絡) 〖전기〗a short (circuit). ~하다 short-circuit; short. ¶ 이 회로는 ~되었다 This circuit is affected with a short. *or* This is short-circuited.

**단란**(團欒) a happy (family, home) circle. ~하다 (be) harmonious; happy; sit in a happy circle and chat happily; enjoy each other's 〔one another's〕 company. ¶ ~한 가정 a happy home / 온 식구가 저녁식사를 함께 하며 ~한 한때를 보냈다 All the members of the family sat down to dinner and had a pleasant evening.

**단량체**(單量體) = 단위체.

**단련**(鍛鍊) ①《쇠붙이의》temper(ing); forging. ~하다 temper《iron》; forge. ②《심신의》training; discipline; drill(ing). ~하다 train; discipline; drill. ¶ 정신의 ~ mental training / 몸을 ~하다 train *oneself;* strengthen *one's* body; build up *one's* constitution / 심신을 ~하다 train *one's* body and mind / 역경에 ~되다 be schooled in adversity / 추위에 몸을 ~하다 harden *oneself* to the cold / 신체를 ~하면 극한에도 견딜 수가 있다 The human body can be so trained that it can stand extreme cold.

**단리**(單利) 〖경제〗simple interest. ¶ ~로 계산하다 calculate at simple interest / ~로 돈을 맡기다 deposit *one's* money at simple interest. ◉ ~법 the method of simple interest. ~표 a simple interest table.

**단막**(單幕) one act. ◉ ~극〔물〕a one-act drama 〔play〕. 「(unit).

**단말기**(端末機) 〖컴퓨터〗 a terminal

**단말마**(斷末魔) ①《죽을 때》*one's* last moments 〔gasp, breath〕; the 〔*one's*〕 hour of death. ②《죽을 때의 고통》death agonies 〔throes〕 (★ 복수형으로 쓰임). ¶ ~의 외침 a death cry / ~의 고통으로 몸부림치다 writhe in *one's* death agonies.

**단맛** a sweet taste; sweetness. ¶ ~이 나는 포도주 sweet wine / ~이 있다〔나다〕 have a sweet taste; be 〔taste〕 sweet / ~이 들다 be sweetened / 이 케이크는 ~이 모자란다 This cake needs more sugar.

**단면**(斷面) a section (★ 비유적으로 많이 쓰임). ¶ ~의 sectional / 수평〔수직, 종, 횡〕~ a horizontal 〔vertical, longitudinal, cross〕 section / 사회생활의 한 ~ a phase of social life / 이 사건은 현대 사회의 어두운 ~을 나타내고 있다 The incident reveals the dark side of modern society.
◉ ~도 a cross section《of》; a sectioned drawing 〔diagram〕: 부분 ~도 a partial cross section / ~도로 나타내다 show《*a thing*》in section. ~저항 profile drag.

**단명**(短命) a short life; a brief span of

life. ～하다 (be) short-lived; ephemeral; have a short life. ¶ ～한 집안 a short-lived family / 재사(才士) ～ Men of talent die young. / 슈베르트는 ～했다 Schubert died young.

**단명수**(單名數) 〖수학〗 a simple denominate number. 「monophthong.

**단모음**(單母音) a single vowel; a

**단모음**(短母音) a short vowel.

**단무지** pickled radish.

**단문**(短文) ① 《글》 a short sentence 〔composition, piece〕. ¶ 다음 어구를 써서 ～을 지어라 Make short sentences using each of the following phrases. ② = 천학(淺學).

**단문**(單文) 〖문법〗 a simple sentence.

**단물** ① 《담수》 fresh 〔sweet〕 water. ¶ ～고기 freshwater fish. ② 《맛이 단》 sweet water 〔juice〕. ③ 《알속》 the cream; the lion's share. ¶ ～을 빨아먹다 get all the profit 《out of》; take the lion's shares; skim the cream off. ④ 《연수(軟水)》 soft water.

**단물나다** wear out 〔through〕; be worn threadbare. ¶ 단물난 옷 threadbare clothes.

**단박(에)** at once; immediately; quickly; instantly; promptly; in an instant. ¶ 일을 ～ 해치우다 finish up *one's* work in a jiffy / ～ 승부를 내도록 하자 Let's fight (it out) on the spot.

**단발**(單發) ① 《한 발》 a (single) shot. ¶ ～에 with a single shot / 사냥꾼은 ～에 꿩을 잡았다 The hunter killed a pheasant with 「a single shot 〔his first shot〕. ② 《발동기》 a single engine. ③ 〖야구〗 only one hit. ¶ 마지막 회의 공격도 ～로 끝났다 The batting of the last inning was held down only with one hit.
◉ ～기 a single-engined plane. ～총 a single loader; a single-shot rifle.

**단발**(短髮) short 〔cropped〕 hair; crop.

**단발**(斷髮) bobbed hair; a bob. ～하다 bob *one's* hair; get 〔have, wear〕 *one's* hair bobbed. ¶ ～ 머리 소녀 a bobbed girl. ◉ ～령 the ordinance prohibiting topknots. ～미인 a pretty girl with bobbed hair.

**단방**(單放) ① 《한 방》 a (single) shot. ¶ ～에 잡다 kill 《a bird》 with a single shot. ② = 단번(單番).
◉ ～치기 a single try; a single effort; doing 《*a thing*》 「at a single stroke 〔in a single effort〕: ～치기로 at a single stroke; in a single effort; at one try.

**단배** a strong 〔good, lively〕 appetite. ¶ ～ 곯리다, ～ 주리다 go hungry in spite of a good appetite; be underfed.

**단백**(蛋白) 《난백》 albumen. ◉ ～뇨증 〖병리〗 albuminuria. ～석(石) 〖광물〗 opal: ～석의 opaline.

**단백질**(蛋白質) 〖생화〗 protein; albumin; albuminous substance. ¶ ～의 protein(ic); albuminous; albuminoid / 동물성〔식물성〕 ～ (an) animal 〔(a) vegetable〕 protein / ～원(源) a source of protein(s); a protein source / ～이 풍부하다 be rich in albuminous substances / ～이 풍부한〔적은〕 식품 high=〔low-〕protein foods; protein-rich 〔=poor〕 foods / 고급 ～을 함유한 식품 high-quality protein foods / 그의 오줌에서 다량의 ～이 검출되었다 A large quantity of albumin was found in his urine.

**단번**(單番) a single time; just once. ¶ ～에 at a 〔single〕 stroke; at one coup; at one try 〔effort〕; all at once / ～에 때려눕히다 knock 《*a person*》 down with a single blow / ～에 결정짓다 decide 《*a matter*》 by one effort / ～에 알아맞히다 guess right at once / 그는 운전 면허 시험에 ～에 합격했다 He succeeded in the driving test at his first attempt.

**단벌**(單一) a single one; the only one; 《옷》 *one's* only suit; the only clothes *one* has. ¶ ～나들이옷 *one's* sole Sunday best / ～ 신사 a poor gentleman in his only suit. 「tion).

**단복**(團服) a uniform (of an associa-

**단본위**(單本位) 〖경제〗 single standard 〔base〕. ◉ ～제 monometallism; the single metallic monetary standard. ～화폐 a monometallic currency.

**단봇짐** a handy bundle.

**단봉낙타**(單峰駱駝) 〖동물〗 an Arabian 〔an one-humped〕 camel.

**단분수**(單分數) 〖수학〗 a simple fraction.

**단비** a welcome 〔timely, seasonable〕 rain; a refreshing 〔long-awaited〕 rain. ¶ 주말 동안 전국에～가 내렸다 A welcome rain fell across the nation during the weekend.

**단비**(單比) 〖수학〗 simple ratio. 「tion.

**단비례**(單比例) 〖수학〗 simple propor-

**단사**(單絲) = 홑실.

**단사**(丹砂) 〖광물〗 cinnabar.

**단산**(斷産) natural cessation of childbearing. ～하다 stop childbearing; pass the age of bearing. ¶ 마흔살에 ～하다 stop her childbirth at the age

of forty.
**단산꽃차례**(團繖―), **단산화서**(團繖花序) 〖식물〗 a monochasium(*pl.* -sia).
**단삼**(丹蔘) 〖식물〗 a kind of sage plant.
**단상**(單相) 〖전기〗 a single phase. ◉ ～교류 single-phase current.
**단상**(壇上) 《on》 the platform. ¶ ～에 서다 stand on the platform; take the platform / 의정 ～에 서다 become a member of the National Assembly.
**단상**(斷想) a fragmentary 〔stray, random〕 thought.
**단색**(單色) a single color; monochrome. ¶ ～의 one-color 《light》; unicolor(ed); monochromatic / 파랑 ～의 바다 그림 a blue monochrome seascape / ～으로 그리다 paint in one 〔a single〕 color. ◉ ～광(光) monochromatic 〔one=color〕 light. ～화 a monochrome; a monochromatic painting. ～화법 monochromy.
**단서**(但書) a proviso (*pl.* ～(e)s); a provisory 〔conditional, saving〕 clause. ¶ ～가 붙은 conditional / …라는 ～를 붙이다 add the proviso that... / 그 제안은 ～를 붙이고 통과됐다 The proposal was passed with a proviso.
**단서**(端緖) 《처음》 the beginning; the start; the commencement; the first step (제일보); 《실마리》 a clue; a key; 《범인 등의》 a scent; a track. ¶ 문제 해결의 ～ the first step toward the solution of a question; a clue for solving a problem / 범인 수사의 ～ a clue for tracking the culprit down / …을 ～로 하다 have *its* origin in...; originate in 《with》...; date from... / ～를 잡다〔얻다〕 have 〔get, gain, find〕 a clue 《to, for》; get on the track 《of》 / ～를 놓치다 lose a 〔the〕 clue 《to》 / ～를 찾다 look for clues / 그녀는 문제 해결의 ～를 찾아냈다 She found 〔got〕 a clue that led to the solution of the problem. / 아직 문제 해결의 ～가 잡히지 않았다 Not a clue has yet been found which might lead to a solution of the problem. / 지문이 범인 체포의 ～가 되었다 The fingerprints gave a clue that led to the arrest of the culprit. / 전당잡힌 시계가 경찰의 ～가 되었다 The watch he pawned put the police on the scent.
**단선**(單線) ① 《외줄》 a single line. ② 《궤도》 a single track. ¶ 경춘선은 ～이었다 The Seoul-Ch'unch'ŏn Line was a single-track railroad.
◉ ～운행 single-track operation; one=way traffic: 현재 그 구간은 ～ 운행을 하고 있다 Trains are being run on a single track in that section. ～철도 a single-track railroad 〔railway〕.
**단선**(團扇) a round fan.
**단선**(斷線) disconnection; the snapping 〔breaking (down)〕 of a wire. ～되다 [선이 주어] break (down); be disconnected; snap; come down. ¶ ～으로 on account of broken wires / 폭설로 각처에서 전선이 ～되었다 The heavy snowfall caused the breaking down of power lines in several places.
**단성**(丹誠) *one's* true heart; sincerity; devotion.
**단성**(單性) 〖생물〗 one sex; unisexuality. ◉ ～생식 unisexual reproduction; parthenogenesis. ～잡종 a monohybrid. ～화 a unisexual flower.
**단세**(單稅) a single tax. ◉ ～주의 single-taxism.
**단세포**(單細胞) ① 〖생물〗 one cell; a single cell. ¶ ～의 single-〔one-〕celled; unicellular 《microorganisms》. ② 《단순》 ¶ (생각이) ～적인 simple-minded / ～적인 사고 방식 a simple-〔one-track=〕 minded way of thinking / 그의 사고 방식은 매우 ～적이다 His way of thinking is contemptibly simple. ◉ ～생물 a monad. ～식물〔동물〕 a unicellular plant 〔animal〕.
**단소**(短小) ～하다 (be) small and short.
**단소**(短簫) a small-notched bamboo vertical flute. ¶ ～를 불다 play 《a tune》 on the flute.
**단속**(團束) 《규제》 control (권력을 수반하는); regulation (규칙에 의거한); a crackdown 《on drunken driving》; 《감독》 supervision; surveillance. ～하다 control; regulate; manage; supervise; oversee; keep control over; maintain discipline; keep 《the school》 in order; crack down on 《gamblers》. ¶ 주차위반 일제 ～ a crackdown on illegal parking / ～의 강화 rigid enforcement of regulations / ～의 대상 a subject of control / ～ 소홀로 견책받다 be reprimanded for lack of supervision / 엄중히 ～하다 maintain 〔exercise〕 strict control 《over》; keep strict order; control strictly / ～이 잘 되어 있다 be well supervised 〔controlled〕; be in good order / ～을 할 수 없게 되다 lose control over; be unable to maintain discipline among; [단속을 받는 쪽이 주어] get beyond control 〔out of hand〕 / 학생을 ～하다 keep

students under control / 폭력 행위를 ~하다 keep control over terrorist(ic) activities / 전국 경찰에 비행 청소년의 철저 ~을 지시하다 direct the police across the nation to crack down on juvenile delinquents / 교통 ~을 더 엄하게 해야 한다 Severe traffic regulations should be enforced. / 많은 경찰관이 교통 ~을 하고 있다 There are a lot of policemen directing traffic. / 2킬로미터 앞 지점에서 속도 위반을 ~하고 있다 There's a speed trap two kilometers ahead. / 당국은 과잉 ~을 했다 The authorities enforced too rigid a control.
◉ ~법〔규칙〕 control law; regulations; rules: 음식점 ~ 규칙 the law regulating restaurants / 마약 ~법 the Narcotic Control Law / 폭력 행위 ~법 the Terroristic Activity Control Law. ~자 a controller; a regulator; supervisor; an overseer. 집중~ intensive control.

**단속**(斷續) intermittence. ~하다 intermit; be intermittent; come off and on. ¶ ~적(인) intermittent; snatchy; fitful; sporadic / ~적으로 intermittently; fitfully; by snatches; at intervals; on and off / 비가 ~적으로 오고 있다 The rain falls intermittently 〔off and on〕. ◉ ~기(器) 〖전기〗 an interrupter; a rheotome.

**단속곳**(單—) an underskirt 〔under= petticoat〕.

**단손**(單—) ① 《혼잣손》 a lone hand. ¶ ~으로 single-handedly; without help. ② 《일격》 one stroke 〔coup〕. ⇨ 단번.

**단솥** a heated iron pot.

**단수**(單數) ① 〖문법〗 the singular number. ¶ ~의 singular / 3인칭 ~ the third person singular / ~로 쓰이다 use 《a word》 in the singular / 이 낱말은 ~이다 This word is in the singular. ② 《홀수》 a unit. ⇨ 끝수.

**단수**(端數) an odd sum; a fraction; odds.

**단수**(斷水) suspension of water supply. ~하다 stop the supply of water; cut off (the) water. ¶ 시(市) 전역에 걸친 ~ the failure of water supply over the whole city / 수도관 공사로 인해 다음 지역은 내일 오전 9시부터 12시까지 ~된다 Owing to repair work on the service pipe, water supply will be cut off from 9 a.m. to 12 noon in the following areas. ◉ ~구역 an area where the water supply is cut off.

**단수로**(短水路) 〖수영〗 a short course; a 25-meter course. ◉ ~ 기록 a short= course record.

**단순**(單純) simplicity. ~하다 (be) simple; plain; 《생각이》 simple-minded. ¶ ~히 simply / ~한 생활 《live》 a simple life / 머리가 ~하다 be simple= minded / ~하게 생각하다 take 《*things*》 simple and easy / 그는 ~한 사람이다 He is a simple 〔simple-minded〕 person. / 사태를 ~하게 생각하지 마라 Don't take the situation simply and easily.
◉ ~개념 a simple concept. ~골절 a simple fracture. ~기계 a simple machine. ~림(林) a pure forest. ~(온)천((溫)泉) a simple spring. ~점유 〖법〗 naked possession. ~평균 a simple average. ~평균 주가 the arithmetic stock price average.

**단순화**(單純化) simplification. ~하다 simplify. ¶ 지나친 ~ oversimplification / 생활〔방법〕을 ~하다 simplify 「*one's* life 〔the method〕.

**단순호치**(丹脣皓齒) 《입술과 이》 red lips and white teeth; 《용모》 a lovely face; 《미인》 a beauty.

**단술** a sweet drink prepared with rice and malt.

**단숨에** at a breath; in one breath; at a 〔one〕 stretch 〔stroke〕. ¶ ~ 마시다 drink 《*one's* wine》 down 〔up〕 in a single draft 〔gulp〕 / 일을 ~ 해치우다 finish up *one's* work in a jiffy; finish a job 「at a 〔one〕 sitting 〔at one go 《구어》〕 / ~ 30리를 가다 walk 30 *ri* 「at a stretch 〔without rest〕 / 책 한 권을 ~ 읽다 read a book through at a sitting / ~ 편지를 쓰다 dash off a letter / ~ 학교까지 달려가다 rush to school without stopping for breath / ~ 언덕을 뛰어 올라가다 run up a hill at a dash; run right up to a hill.

**단시**(短詩) a short poem 〔verse〕. ◉ ~작가 a writer of short verses.

**단시간**(短時間) a short time. ¶ ~에 in 「a short time 〔a few hours〕 / 서울에서 동경까지 ~에 비행하다 fly from Seoul to Tokyo in a short time.

**단시일**(短時日) a short period of time. ¶ ~에 in a short (period of ) time; in a few days / 사회 개혁은 ~에 이루어지는 것이 아니다 Social reform is not to be effected in a day. / 러시아의 경제 개혁은 ~에는 이루어지지 않을 것이다 The Russian economic reforms won't take a short time to take effect.

**단식**(單式) simple system; 〖부기〗 single entry system; bookkeeping by single entry; 〖수학〗 a simple expression;

《테니스·탁구의》 a singles. ¶ ～의 simple; single / 여자 ～ 준결승 a women's singles semifinal (match).
◉ ～경기《테니스·탁구의》a single game; a singles. ～부기 single-entry bookkeeping. ～투표 single voting. ～화산 a simple volcano.

**단식**(斷食) a fast; fasting. ～하다 fast 《for 3 days》; observe a fast. ¶ 24시간의 ～ a 24-hour fast / ～을 중지하다 break (*one's*) fast / 그녀는 4일간 ～했다 She fasted for four days.
◉ ～법 a fasting method. ～요법 a fasting 〔starvation, hunger〕 cure; a fasting treatment. ～일 a fast day. ～투쟁 《go on》 a hunger strike.

**단신**(單身) a single person; [부사적] (all) alone; single-handed; by *oneself;* unaccompanied; unattended. ¶ ～ 상경하다 come up to Seoul all alone 〔unaccompanied〕 / ～ 적지에 잠입하다 penetrate single-handed into the enemy's territory / 그는 ～ 요트로 태평양을 횡단했다 He sailed across the Pacific in a yacht by himself. / 그는 부산으로 ～ 부임했다 He left for his new post in Pusan 「alone 〔without his family, by himself〕.
◉～총 a single-barreled gun.

**단신**(短身) short 〔small〕 stature.

**단신**(短信) a short 〔brief〕 letter; a note; a brief message; brief news.

**단심**(丹心) *one's* true heart; single-heartedness; devotion.

**단심제**(單審制) 『법』 the single-trial system.

**단아**(端雅) elegance; grace; refinement. ～하다 (be) elegant; graceful; refined (세련된). (★ elegant와 graceful는 품위가 있고 우아하다는 뜻이지만, elegant는 인공적인, graceful은 자연적으로 갖추어진 우아함을 각각 강조함). ¶ 용모 ～한 사람 a man of regular features 〔good looks〕 / 옷차림이 ～하다 be dressed 「in good taste 〔in tasteful style〕.

**단안**(單眼) 『동물』 a stemma; an ocellus. ＝홑눈. ◉ ～현미경 a monocular microscope.

**단안**(斷案) 《결정》 a decision; 《결론》 a conclusion; 《최후의》 a final judgment 〔verdict〕. ¶ ～을 내리다 make a (final) decision; form a conclusion 〔judgment〕 / 최후의 ～을 내리다 say the last word 《on a subject》; give a final verdict.

**단안경**(單眼鏡) a monocle. ¶ ～을 낀 monocled.

**단애**(斷崖) a precipice; 《특히 해안 등의》 a cliff; a bluff. ⇨ 벼랑.

**단어**(單語) a word; a vocabulary (어휘). ¶ 기본 ～ basic words / 중요 ～ most frequently used words / 알고 있는 ～의 수 *one's* vocabulary / ～ 실력을 늘리다 build up *one's* word power / ～를 많이 알고 있다 have a large 〔rich〕 vocabulary. ◉ ～놀이 a word game. ～집 a collection of 《everyday》 words; a wordbook.

**단언**(斷言) (a) declaration; (an) assertion; (an) affirmation; a positive 〔definite〕 statement. ～하다 affirm; assert; declare; state definitely 〔positively〕; make an assertion.

> 용법 **affirm** 확신을 갖고 단언하다. **assert** 확신은 있지만 객관적 증거가 없이 단언하다. **declare** 정식으로 또는 반대를 무릅쓰고 공공연히 단언하다.

¶ ～할 수는 없지만 I cannot say positively 〔for certain〕, but…. / 그런 일이 일어날 것이라고 ～하다 assert that such a thing will happen / ～하기를 꺼리다 hesitate to say positively; refrain from asserting; fear to affirm / 그가 위선자임을 나는 ～한다 I have no hesitation in saying that he is a hypocrite. / 그 점은 ～할 수 없다 I am not positive about the point. / 그가 거기 있었다고는 ～할 수 없다 I cannot affirm that he was there.

**단역**(端役) 《역》 a minor 〔small〕 part 〔role〕; a bit part 《미구어》; 《대사 없는》 a walk-on (part); 《배우》 a bit player; an extra; a super. ¶ ～을 하다 play a minor part; be a bit player.

**단연**(斷煙) giving up smoking; abstention from tobacco. ～하다 give up 〔stop, quit〕 smoking. ⇨ 금연.

**단연(코)**(斷然—) ① 《단호히》 resolutely; decisively(결정적으로); without hesitation (망설임 없이); firmly (굳게); absolutely (절대적으로); 《확실히》 positively; decidedly; definitely. ¶ ～ 거절하다 refuse 「without hesitation 〔positively, flatly〕; give a flat 〔point-blank〕 refusal / ～ 부정하다 deny 《*a thing*》 emphatically / ～ 배격하다 reject positively / ～ 새롭다 be absolutely new / ～ 유리하다 have a decided advantage / 그 조처에는 ～ 반대다 I am decidedly opposed to the measure.
② 《훨씬》 by far 《the best》; far and away 《better》. ¶ 이것이 ～ 좋다 This is by far the best. / 나보다 그녀가 ～ 한 수 위다 She is far more skillful

than「me〔I am〕. / 스케이트와 스키는 ~ 인기있는 겨울 스포츠이다 Skating and skiing are by far the most popular winter sports.

**단열**(斷熱)〖물리〗insulation. ~하다 insulate. ¶ 불완전한 ~ inadequate insulation / 이 벽은 ~이 필요하다 This wall requires insulation. ◉ ~과정〖물리〗an adiabatic process. ~도 an adiabatic chart〔diagram〕. ~재 a heat insulator; (heat) insulating material; an insulator; insulation. ~효과 adiabatic effect.

**단엽**(單葉)〖식물〗a simple leaf. ◉ ~(비행)기 a monoplane. ~식물 a unifoliate plant.

**단오**(端午)〖민속〗the *Dano* Festival (on the fifth day of the fifth lunar month).

**단원**(單元)《학습 단위》a unit. ¶ 이 교과서는 10~으로 되어 있다 This textbook is composed of ten units. ◉ ~제도 the unit〔credit《미》〕system.

**단원**(團員) a member of「a party〔an association, a group, *etc.*〕.

**단원제**(單院制) the unicameral〔single-chamber〕system. ¶ (240석의) ~ 의회 a (240-seat) unicameral legislature.

**단위**(單位) a unit; a denomination (화폐의). ¶ 기본 ~ a standard unit / ~를 100으로 한 expressed in terms of hundred / 계산〔매매, 무게, 부피〕의 ~ the unit of calculation〔trading, weight, volume〕/ 사회의 기본 구성 ~로서의 가족 a family as the basic unit of society / 이 표의 ~는 10,000이다 The numbers in this table is shown in units of ten thousand. / 미터는 길이의 ~다 The meter is a unit of length. / 이 계산은 ~가 잘못되어 있다 This is calculated on the wrong units. / 인구는 천 ~로 표시되어 있다 The population is shown in thousands. / 주식은 보통 1,000주 ~로 매매된다 Usually, stocks are bought and sold in blocks of a thousand. / 한국의 화폐 ~는 원이다 The monetary unit of Korea is the won.
◉ ~ (노동)조합 a local (labor) union. ~면적 the unit area: ~면적 당 per unit area. ~원(圓)〖수학〗a unit circle. ~질량 the unit mass. ~행렬〖수학〗a unit matrix.

**단위생식**(單爲生殖)〖생물〗parthenogenesis;〖식물〗apogamy.

**단위체**(單位體)〖화학〗a monomer. ¶ ~의 monomeric.

**단음**(短音)〖음성〗a short sound. ◉ ~기호 a breve(모음 위에 붙이는 ˘표).

**단음**(單音)〖물리〗《최소단위의 음》a single sound;〖음악〗a monotone; a simple tone;〖언어〗a phone. ◉ ~하모니카 a monotone harmonica.

**단음**(斷音)〖음성〗stops;〖음악〗a staccato. ◉ ~기호 a staccato mark. ~장치 a damper (피아노의).

**단음계**(短音階)〖음악〗a minor (scale); the minor mode. ¶ 선율적〔화성적〕~ the melodic〔harmonic〕minor scale.

**단음절**(單音節) monosyllable. ¶ ~의 monosyllabic. ◉ ~어 a monosyllable; a monosyllabic word.

**단음정**(短音程)〖음악〗a minor interval.

**단일**(單一) singleness. ~하다 (be) single; sole. ¶ 암은 ~세포로 시작된다 Cancer begins as a single cell. / 미국은 ~ 민족의 나라가 아니다 The U.S.A. is not a single-race nation.
◉ ~경작 monoculture. ~국가 a unitary state. ~기계 a machine unit. ~기판 컴퓨터〖컴퓨터〗a single-〔one-〕board computer. ~단계 오류수정〖컴퓨터〗single step debugging. ~민족 국가 a racially homogeneous nation. ~변동 환율제 the unitary fluctuation〔floating〕foreign exchange system. ~세율 single tariff; single-line tariff. ~신교(神教) henotheism; monotheism. ~오류〖컴퓨터〗a single error. ~팀《form》a single《inter-Korean》team: 남북한 ~팀 a single South-North team. ~호봉 single pay(roll): ~ 호봉제 the single payroll〔pay scale〕system. ~화 simplification; unification: ~화하다 simplify; unify. ~환율 a single exchange rate. ~후보 a single〔sole〕candidate.

**단임제**(單任制) the single-term system《for》. ¶ 대통령 ~ the single-term system for the presidency.

**단자**(單子) ①《부조 등의》a list of gifts〔presents〕. ②〖철학〗a monad. ◉ ~론 monadism; monadology.

**단자**(單字) ①〖글자〗characters representing a word. ②=단어(單語).

**단자**(短資) a short-term〔-dated〕loan; a call loan. ◉ ~거래 call loan transaction. ~시장 a call market. ~회사 a short-term financing company.

**단자**(端子)〖전기〗a terminal. ◉ ~판(板) a terminal plate〔board〕.

**단자엽**(單子葉)〖식물〗= 외떡잎. ◉ ~식물 a monocotyledonous plant.

**단작**(單作) a single crop; single culture. ◉ ～농업 single-crop farming. ～지대 a one-crop area.

**단작스럽다** (be) dirty; mean; stingy. ¶ 그녀는 단작스럽게 버터를 아낀다 She is so stingy with the butter.

**단잠** a sweet 〔sound, deep, good〕 sleep. ¶ ～을 깨다 wake up from a sound sleep / ～을 자다 sleep well 〔soundly〕; have a sound sleep / ～이 들다 fall into a sound 〔deep〕 sleep / ～을 자고 있다 be「fast 〔sound〕 asleep.

**단장**(丹粧) ① 《화장》 (a) toilet; (a) make-up; dressing (옷치장). ～하다 《화장하다》 make up; put on makeup; 《옷치장하다》 dress 〔attire〕 *oneself;* smarten *oneself* up; deck *oneself* up 〔out〕. ¶ 곱게 ～하고 나서다 go out beautifully dressed up. ② 《꾸밈》 decoration; painting (칠). ～하다 decorate; adorn; paint (칠하여). ¶ 새로 ～한 newly finished 〔repainted〕 / 새로 ～한 예배당 the refurbished chapel / 새로 ～하다 give a new look 《to》; newly decorate.

**단장**(短杖) a cane; a (walking) stick. ¶ ～을 짚고 걷다 walk with a cane 〔stick〕.

**단장**(團長) the head 《of a group》; the leader 《of a party》. ¶ 보이스카우트 ～ a scout master; a chiefscout / 김 박사를 ～으로 하는 교육 사절단 an educational mission headed by Dr. Kim.

**단장**(斷腸) heartbreak. ¶ ～의 능선 the Heartbreak Ridge / ～의 설움 heart-breaking 〔heartrending〕 grief / ～의 비애를 느끼다 feel as if *one's* heart would break; feel *one's* heart rent 〔torn to pieces〕.

**단적**(端的) ¶ ～인 direct; straightforward; point-blank; frank; plain / ～으로 directly; frankly; point-blank; plainly / ～으로 말하다 speak frankly 〔plainly〕; talk straight; go right to the point / ～으로 묻다 ask 《*a person*》 point-blank / ～으로 말해서 그는 불성실하다 Frankly speaking 〔To be frank (with you)〕, he is insincere.

**단전**(丹田) the lower abdomen; the hypogastric center. ¶ ～의〔에〕 under the navel / ～에 힘을 주다 strain the lower abdomen; concentrate *one's* whole strength in the hypogastric center. ◉ ～호흡 hypogastric breathing.

**단전**(斷電) 《정전》 power failure; 《공급중단》 suspension of power supply. ～하다 cut off electricity. ¶ ～되다 the power supply 〔the electricity〕 is cut off / 예고 없이 ～되었다 The electricity was cut off without warning.

**단절**(斷切·斷折) cutting; severance. ⇨ 절단.

**단절**(斷絶) ① 《종식》 extinction. ～하다 become extinct; cease to exist. ¶ 가문이 ～되었다 The family line has died out. ② 《중절》 discontinuation; severance(분리); (a) rupture(결렬). ～하다 sever; cut 〔break〕 off. ¶ ～의 시대 an age of discontinuity / 세대 간의 ～ a generation gap; the lack of communication between the young and the old generation / ～되다 be broken 〔cut〕 off; come to a rupture / 외교 관계〔국교〕를 ～하다 break off diplomatic relations 《with》. ◉ ～감 a sense of estrangement 〔alienation〕. 국교～ severance 〔rupture〕 of diplomatic relations: 양국간의 국교가 ～되었다 Diplomatic relations between the two countries were broken off.

**단점**(短點) a fault; a shortcoming; a defect; a weak point; a weakness. ⇨ 결점. ¶ ～을 보완하다 make up for *one's* shortcomings / ～을 고치다 remedy *one's* defects / 자기의 ～을 깨닫다 be aware 〔conscious〕 of *one's* own weakness / 장점으로 ～을 보완하다 set off *one's* merits against *one's* faults / 성마른 것이 그의 ～이다 A hot temper is his weak point. / 너의 계획에는 장점도 있고 ～도 있다 Your plan has「both strong and weak 〔good and bad〕 points. *or* There are both advantages and disadvantages in your plan.

**단접**(鍛接) welding. ～하다 weld.

**단정**(端正) decency; neatness. ～하다 (be) decent; tidy; proper; seemly; decorous; neat; clean-cut (용모가). ¶ ～한 얼굴 《have》 a well-featured 〔handsome, clear-cut〕 face / ～히 properly; neatly; tidily; smartly / 옷차림이 ～한 사람 a well-groomed 〔neatly-dressed〕 person / 품행이 ～한 사람 a man of upright 〔good moral〕 character / 품행이 ～하다 be of upright conduct; behave *oneself* decently / ～히 앉다 sit up square / 옷차림을 ～히 하다 tidy *oneself* up; straighten *one's* clothes 〔dress〕 / 옷차림이 ～치 못하다 be slovenly 〔untidily〕 dressed.

**단정**(斷定) a conclusion; a decision (결정). ～하다 conclude; come to 〔arrive at〕 a conclusion; make up *one's* mind 《that...》. ¶ ～적인 언사 a conclusive remark / 성급히 ～해서는 안 된다 You must not jump to a conclusion. / 이런 사정으로 미루어 그가 익사한 것으로 ~했다 From these circumstances, I concluded him to have been drowned.

**단조**(短調) 〖음악〗 a minor (key). ¶ ~로 in a minor key / 마~의 소나타 a sonata in E minor.

**단조롭다**(單調—) (be) monotonous; dull; flat; humdrum; monotonic. ¶ 단조로이 monotonously; in a monotone / 단조로운 빛깔 a dull 〔flat〕 color / 단조로운 경치 a scene lacking variety / 단조로운 연설 a dull speech; a drone / 단조로운 생활을 하다 lead a monotonous 〔dull〕 life; live a humdrum 〔treadmill〕 existence / 단조로움을 깨뜨리다 break the monotony / 일이 단조로워서 싫증났다 I am really bored by the monotonous work.

**단종**(斷種) sterilization; 《거세》 castration. ~하다 sterilize 《*a person*》; castrate. ◉ ~수술 〖의학〗 a sterilization operation.

**단좌**(單坐) a single seat. ◉ ~(비행)기 a single-seated plane.

**단좌**(端坐) ~하다 sit straight 〔upright〕; sit up straight (고쳐 앉다).

**단죄**(斷罪) conviction; condemnation. ~하다 convict; condemn; punish; find 《*a person*》 guilty. ¶ ~되다 be convicted 《of a crime》; be condemned 《to death》; be executed / 그를 ~해야 한다 He is to be executed. / 그는 살인범으로 ~되었다 He was 「convicted of 〔condemned for〕 murder.

**단주**(端株) 〖증권〗 an odd lot.

**단주**(斷酒) (total) abstinence from alcohol. ~하다 stop 〔give up, quit〕 drinking; abstain from liquor; leave off alcohol. ⇨금주(禁酒).

**단지** a jar; a pot; a crock. ¶ 꿀~ a honey jar / 된장 한 ~ a potful of soybean paste.

**단지**(但只) only; merely; simply; solely; alone; just. ⇨다만. ¶ ~ 혼자서 (all) alone; by *oneself* / ~ …하기만 하면 된다 all *one* has to do is (to) *do;* have only to *do* / ~ 너를 위해 그리 하였다 I did it 「only 〔just〕 for your sake. / 그것은 ~ 돈의 문제일 뿐이다 It is merely a question of money. / 그는 ~ 친절할 뿐 아니라 정직하기도 하다 He is not only kind but (also) honest.

**단지**(團地) 《주택의》 a housing development 〔estate 《영》〕; a housing complex; a housing project (저소득층을 위한). ¶ 아파트 ~ an apartment complex / 주택 ~ a collective housing area.

**단지**(斷指) ~하다 cut off *one's* finger.

**단지증**(短肢症) 〖의학〗 phocomelia; phokomelia. ¶ ~의 phocomelic.

**단짝** an inseparable 〔a bosom, a great〕 friend 〔comrade, buddy 《구어》〕; a shadow; 《구어》 a chum; a side-kick.

**단참에**(單站—) at a breath. = 단숨에.

**단채**(單彩) monochrome. ¶ ~의 monochromatic / ~로 그리다 paint 〔draw〕 in monochrome. ◉ ~화 a monochrome; a painting in monochrome: ~화가 a monochromist.

**단처**(短處) a fault; a shortcoming; a defect. ⇨단점(短點).

**단철**(鍛鐵) 《벼리기》 tempering iron; 《무쇠와 대조하여》 malleable cast iron.

**단청**(丹青) 《그림》 a picture of many colors and designs; 《색·칠》 various colors; colorful painting. ~하다 paint colorfully 〔in various colors〕. ¶ ~의 묘(妙) the exquisite beauty of the painting. ◉ ~공사 a painting work.

**단체**(單體) 〖화학〗 a simple substance.

**단체**(團體) ① 《집단》 a party; a company; a group; a body; a corps (*pl.* corps). ¶ 20명의 ~ a party of twenty / 정치적 압력 ~ pressure groups in politics / ~를 만들다 make up a party 〔body〕 / ~로 관람하다 go to 《a theater》 in a party 〔group〕 / ~로 신청하다 apply in a body 《for》 / 50명 이상의 ~에는 운임을〔입장료를〕 20% 할인해 준다 Twenty percent reduction of 「fares 〔admission fees〕 is allowed for a party of not less than 50. / 우리들은 20명이 ~로 서울 구경을 갔다 Twenty of us made up a party and went to Seoul for sightseeing.

② 《조직체》 an organization; a corporation; an association. ¶ ~를 조직하다 form an organization.

◉ ~경기 a team race 〔game, event〕; team competition. ~관념 a sense of community life. ~관람 a group viewing. ~교섭(권) collective bargaining (right): ~ 교섭을 하다 bargain collectively 《with》. ~보험 collective insurance; 《생명 보험》 group (life) insurance. ~생활 group 〔corporate〕 life. ~손님 group travelers 〔customers〕; a party of tourists. ~여행 a group tour: ~ 여행객 group travelers; a party of tourists 〔travelers〕 / ~ 여행을 하다 make a group tour; travel in a party. ~운동 a collective 〔mass〕 movement. ~전 the 《men's》 team event. ~정신 *esprit de corps* (F.); a team 〔group〕 spirit. ~할인 a group discount 〔rate, reduction〕. ~행동 a collective action: ~ 행동을 취하다 act as a group; act together; take a collective action. ~협약 a collective agreement. ~활동 group activity. ~훈련 mass training.

**단총**(短銃) a short-barreled gun; 《권총》 a pistol; a revolver; a handgun. ¶ 기관~ a submachine gun.

**단추** ①《옷의》 a button; a stud (장식의). ¶ 자개〔장식〕 ~ a shell 〔fancy〕 button / 호박~ an amber stud / ~ 3개 달린 양복 저고리 a three-button jacket / ~를 달다 put on a button; sew a button 《on a coat》; fix a button / ~를 채우다 fasten a button; button (up) / ~를 끄르다 unfasten 〔undo〕 a button; unbutton / ~가 떨어지다 a button comes off 〔is torn out〕 / ~를 떼다 take off a button / 바지 ~가 열려 있군요 《완곡하게》 Your stable door is open. / 누이가 떨어진 ~를 달아주었다 My sister sewed on the button that had come off. / 이 드레스는 등쪽에서 ~를 채우게 되어 있다 This dress buttons at the back. ②《기계의》 a button. ¶ 누름~ a push button / 나는 비상 ~를 눌러서 구조를 청했다 I pressed 〔pushed〕 the emergency button for help. / 다음 전쟁이 일어난다면 아마 ~ 누르기 전쟁이 될 것이다 The next war would be a push-button war.
◉ 단춧구멍 《make》 a buttonhole.

**단축**(短軸) 〖수학〗 the minor axis.

**단축**(短縮) shortening; reduction; curtailment (감축); 《표현 따위의》 (a) condensation; 〖문법〗《어·구의》 (a) contraction. ~하다 shorten; reduce; cut (down); curtail. ¶ 학년을 ~하다 shorten the school years / 노동 시간을 30분 ~하다 reduce the working hours by thirty minutes / 노동 시간의 ~을 요구하다 demand 〔clamor for〕 shorter working hours / 거리를 5마일 ~하다 cut the distance by 5 miles / 겨울방학을 열흘로 ~하다 shorten 〔cut down〕 the winter vacation to ten days / 비행기는 세계의 거리를 ~했다 Airplanes have made the world smaller. / 일상 회화에서는 "I will"을 흔히 "I'll"로 ~한다 In everyday speech, "I will" is often shortened to "I'll". / 그는 400미터 경주에서 세계 기록을 0.4초 ~했다 He took four-tenths of a second off the world record in the 400-meter dash.
◉ ~다이얼 speed 〔simplified, shortened〕 dialing. ~수업 shortened school hours: 오늘은 30분 ~수업을 한다 Our class today will be shortened by 30 minutes. ~형 〖문법〗 a contracted 〔shortened〕 form; a contraction.

**단출하다** ①《식구가》 (be) neat-sized; small. ¶ 단출한 식구 a small family / 우리는 식구가 매우 ~ Our family is small. *or* I have a small family. ②《간편》 (be) simple; handy; convenient. ¶ 단출한 보따리 a handy bundle; a light pack / 단출한 살림 a simple menage 〔household〕.

**단층**(單層) a single story; one-story.
◉ ~집 a one-storied house.

**단층**(斷層) 〖지질〗 a 〔an earth〕 fault; a dislocation; 《사고 방식 등의》 a gap 《between》. ◉ ~면 a fault plane. ~사진 〖의학〗 a tomogram. ~산맥 fault mountains. ~선 〖지질〗 a fault line. ~작용 faulting. ~지진 a dislocation earthquake. ~지형 fault topography. ~촬영 〖의학〗 tomography: ~촬영의 tomographic / ~촬영 장치 a tomograph.

**단침**(短針) 《시계의》 the hour 〔short〕 hand.

**단칭**(單稱) ¶ ~의 singular. ◉ ~명사 a singular term. ~명제 a singular proposition.

**단칸**(單—) a single room; an 6-foot square room. ◉ ~마루 an 6-foot square floor. ~방 an 6-foot square room. ~살림 living in a single room; a single-room household.

**단칼에**(單—) 《cut》 with a single stroke of *one's* sword 〔knife〕.

**단타**(單打) 〖야구〗 a single (hit); a base hit. ¶ ~를 치다 single 《to left field》; make a one-base hit.

**단타**(短打) 〖야구〗 a short-distance hit.

**단파**(短波) 〖물리〗 a shortwave. ¶ ~로 송신하다 shortwave 《a message》; transmit 《a message》 on shortwave.
◉ ~무전 shortwave radio: ~ 무전기 a shortwave radio set. ~방송 shortwave broadcasting: ~ 방송을 듣다 listen to the shortwave broadcast 《from London》. ~ 송신기〔수신기〕 a shortwave transmitter 〔receiver〕.

**단판**(單—) a single round. ¶ ~에 in a single round; 《곧장》 right (away); at once (즉시) / 나는 ~에 그에게로 갔다 I went right at him.
◉ ~승부 a single game (of *paduk*); 《레슬링 등에서》 a single-throw 〔one=

throw] bout [match]; 《골프 등에서》 a sudden-death match. ~씨름 single-round *ssirum* [wrestling].

**단판**(單瓣) a single valve. ¶ ~의 『동물』 univalve; 『식물』 one-petaled 《flower》.

**단팥죽**(─粥) sweet red-bean porridge (with rice cake).

**단편**(短篇) 《소설》 a short piece [story]; a sketch; 《영화》 a short film.
◉ ~소설 a short novel [story]: ~ 소설가 a (short) story writer / ~ 소설 선집 a selection of short stories. ~영화 a short film; a briefie 《미속어》. ~집 a collection of short stories; collected short stories 《of O. Henry》.

**단편**(斷片) a fragment; a scrap; a piece; a fraction; odds (and ends). ¶ ~적(인) fragmentary 《report》; scrappy; piecemeal / ~적으로 in fragments; fragmentarily; piece by piece / ~적(인) 지식 fragmentary knowledge; scraps of information / ~적인 소식밖에 못 듣는다 Only fragmentary news comes to us. / ~적 지식이나 얻으려 하지 말고 조직적인 독서를 해라 Instead of gathering bits of information you should read systematically.

**단평**(短評) a short criticism; a brief [short] comment [remark]. ¶ ~을 하다 make a short [brief] comment 《on》; comment briefly 《on》 / 선생님은 우리 리포트에 각각 ~을 적어서 돌려주셨다 Our teacher 「handed back [returned] our papers with a few remarks on each. ◉ 시사~ a brief comment on current events.

**단풍**(丹楓) 《나무》 a maple (tree); 《나뭇잎》 red [scarlet-tinged, yellow] leaves; 《추색》 autumn [autumnal] tints [colors]. ¶ ~이 들다 turn red [yellow]; be tinged with red; put on autumnal tints / ~이 한창이다 The scarlet autumn leaves are at their best. / 설악산은 가을 ~으로 유명하다 Mt. Sŏrak is noted for the glorious tints of its autumn foliage.
◉ ~놀이 an excursion for viewing scarlet autumn leaves: ~놀이 가다 go to see the colored autumn leaves. ~잎 maple [autumn] leaves.

**단합**(團合) = 단결(團結). ◉ ~ 대회 a rally to strengthen the unity.

**단항식**(單項式) 『수학』 a monomial (expression).

**단핵**(單核) ◉ ~(구)증 《백혈구 증가증》 『의학』 mononucleosis: 전염성 ~증 『의학』 infectious mononucleosis.

**단행**(斷行) resolute enforcement; decisive action; execution; carrying out. ~하다 carry out 《one's plan》 (resolutely); carry 《a plan》 into effect; act up to 《*one's* convictions》. ¶ 내각 개편을 ~하다 carry out the reshuffle of the cabinet / 소신을 ~하다 act according to *one's* convictions / 반대가 있어도 그 개혁은 ~되어야 한다 We must 「carry through [execute] the reform resolutely in spite of opposition. / 다국적군은 적 표적에 대한 공습을 ~했다 The multinational force carried out an air raid on enemy targets.

**단행범**(單行犯) 『법』 a single offense.

**단행법**(單行法) 『법』 a special law.

**단행본**(單行本) a book; a separate volume. ¶ ~으로 내다 publish 《*one's* essays》 in book form.

**단호하다**(斷乎─) (be) firm; determined; resolute; decisive; drastic (과감한). ¶ 단호한 언사 a stiff way of speaking; cut and dried expressions / 단호한 태도를 취하다 assume [take] a firm attitude [stand] / 정부는 이런 종류의 테러리즘에 대해 단호한 조치를 취할 것으로 기대된다 The government is expected to take decisive [drastic] measures against this kind of terrorism.

**단호히**(斷乎─) firmly; resolutely; decisively; positively; in a determined manner; flatly (특히 부정문에). ¶ ~ 거절하다 give 《*a person*》 a flat refusal / ~ 부정하다 deny 《*a thing*》 emphatically / ~ 주장을 굽히지 않다 stick to *one's* opinion and will not yield / 나는 그 법안에 ~ 반대한다 I'm firmly resolved to oppose the bill.

**단화**(短靴) 《a pair of》 shoes.

**닫다**[1] 《달리다》 run; rush; dash; dart; 《말이》 canter; gallop. ⇨ 달리다[5].

**닫다**[2] ① 《열린 것을》 shut; close. ¶ 문을 ~ shut [close] a door / 문을 탁[꽝] ~ slam [bang] a door; shut a door with a bang / 서랍을 ~ shut [close, pull in] a drawer / 수문을 ~ shut up [close] a sluice / 창문을 꼭 ~ shut the window tight(ly); pull the window tight shut / 닫아두다 keep 《the door》 shut / 출입시 문을 닫아주시오 Shut the door after [behind] you.
② 《폐업하다》 close [give up] *one's* business (장사를); give up *one's* practice (의사·변호사가); close down (가게를). ¶ 가게를 ~ close down *one's* store; shut [close] up *one's* shop / 가까이에 수퍼마켓이 생겨 많은 소매점이 문

을 닫아야 했다 Because a supermarket opened in the neighborhood, many retail stores had to close.

**닫아걸다** fasten 《a door》; lock (up); bolt; latch. ¶ 문을 안으로〔밖으로〕 ~ fasten a door from within 〔without〕/ 방문을 닫아걸고 나오지 않다 lock *oneself* up in *one's* room / 그는 가게문을 닫아걸고 귀가했다 He locked up the shop and went home.

**닫치다** shut (up); close (up). ¶ 문을 ~ shut the door tight; make the door fast / 쾅 ~ slam; bang 《the door》; shut the door with a bang.

**닫히다** get closed; be shut; shut; close. ¶ 닫힌 회로 closed circuit / 문이 ~ a door is shut 〔closed〕/ 저절로 ~ shut of itself / 문이 좀처럼 닫히지 않는다 The door won't shut at all. / 가게는 닫혀 있었다 The store was closed 〔shut〕. / 바람에 문이 쾅 닫혔다 The wind slammed the door shut.

**달**[1] ① 《하늘의》 the moon. ¶ 그믐달 a waning moon; a crescent (moon) / 맑은〔밝은〕 달 a clear moon / 보름달 a full moon / 반달 a half moon / 초승달 a waxing moon; a crescent (moon) / 달 로켓 a moon rocket / 달빛 moonlight / 달 착륙 (a) lunar landing / 달 착륙선 a lunar module (생략 LM) / 달 탐험〔탐색〕 a moon 〔lunar〕 expedition 〔probe〕/ 달 탐험 계획 《U.S》 lunar program / 달의 표면〔궤도〕 the lunar surface 〔orbit〕/ 달의 뒷면 the other 〔dark, hidden〕 side of the moon / 달의 여신 《로마 신화》 Diana; 《그리스 신화》 Artemis / 달이 밝다 the moon shines bright / 달은 차고 이지러진다 The moon waxes and wanes. / 달이 떴다 The moon rose 〔came up〕. / 달이 졌다 The moon set 〔went down〕. / 달이 참 밝네요 What a bright moon we have tonight! / 달도 차면 기운다 《속담》 "What goes up must come down." *or* Every flow has its ebb.
② 《달력의》 a month. ¶ 지난〔다음〕 달 last 〔next〕 month / 윤달 an intercalary month / 큰〔작은〕 달 an odd 〔even〕 month (★ even은 「짝수의」, odd는 「홀수의」란 뜻) / 한 달에 한 번 once a month; monthly / 한 달 두 번의 semimonthly; fortnightly / 달마다의 every month; monthly / 이달 초사흘에 on the third of this month / 우리는 한 달에 한 번 모인다 We meet once a month. / 그는 아르바이트를 해서 한 달에 10만원쯤 번다 He earns 〔makes〕 about 100,000 won a month by working part-time.
③ 《임신의》 ¶ 달이 차다 be in her ninth month of pregnancy; have gone her full time / 달이 차 감에 따라 as pregnancy advances / 달이 차지 않은 아이 a premature infant; a prematurely=born baby / 그녀는 임신 여섯 달이다 She is six months pregnant.

**달**[2] 〖식물〗 a kind of wild reed.

**달**[3] 《연의》 a kite-frame; a kite-stick.

**달가닥** with a rattle 〔clatter〕.

**달가닥거리다** rattle; clatter. ¶ 달가닥거리는 접시 소리 the clatter of plates and dishes / 바람에 창문이 달가닥거리고 있다 The window is rattling in the wind. / 수레가 달가닥거리며 지나간다 A wagon is clattering along the road.

**달가닥달가닥** rattling; clattering; with a rattle 〔clatter〕.

**달가당** with a clang 〔clink, bang〕. ¶ 문이 ~ 잠겼다 The door was shut with bang.

**달가당거리다** clink; clang; rattle. ¶ 문고리가 달가당거리고 있다 The iron door=ring is clanging.

**달갑다** (be) satisfactory; desirable. ¶ 달갑지 않은 손님 an unwelcome guest / 달갑잖은 친절이다 It is misplaced kindness. *or* It is an unwelcome favor. / 그것은 달갑지 않은 이야기였다 That was not much of a good thing.

**달개** 〖건축〗 a penthouse; a lean-to (shed). ◉ ~집 a penthouse.

**달걀** an egg. ¶ 갓낳은 ~ a new(ly)-laid egg; a fresh egg / 생〔날〕~ a raw egg / 곯은 ~ a rotten 〔an addled〕 egg / 삶은 ~ a boiled egg / 반숙한〔완숙한〕 ~ a soft-boiled 〔hard-boiled〕 egg / ~ 껍질 an eggshell / ~ 모양의 egg-shaped; oval / ~을 깨다 break 〔open〕 an egg / ~을 낳다 lay an egg / ~을 품다 sit on an egg; brood / ~을 부치다 fry an egg / ~을 까다 hatch an egg / 그 닭은 ~을 잘 낳는다 The hen is a good layer. / ~로 백운대 치기 《속담》 It is like sweeping the sea with a broom.

**달게굴다** badger; importune 〔tease, press, ask〕 《*a person* for *a thing*, *a person* to *do*》; clamor for.

**달게받다** submit to; put up with; tolerate; endure; be resigned to 《*one's* fate》. ⇨ 감수(甘受). ¶ 비난을 ~ submit to reproach / 가혹한 운명을 ~ accept *one's* bitter fate without complaining.

**달견**(達見) an excellent view 〔opinion〕; a capital 〔fine, brilliant〕 idea; a far=sighted view; clear-sightedness.

**달곰새금하다** (be) somewhat sweet and sour; sour-sweet.

**달곰쌉쌀하다** (be) somewhat sweet and bitter; bitter-sweet.

**달관**(達觀) ~하다 《멀리 내다보다》 take a far-sighted [long] view 《of》; have a broad outlook; 《세속을 벗어나다》 take a philosophical view; regard [consider] 《*a matter*》 philosophically. ¶ 장래를 ~하다 take a far-sighted view; see far into the future / 그는 인생을 ~하고 있다 He takes a philosophical view of life.

**달구** a (ground) rammer. ◉ ~질 pounding [ramming, beating down] earth: ~질하다 pound [ram, beat down] earth with a rammer; harden the ground.

**달구다** make hot; heat. ¶ 쇠붙이를 ~ heat a piece of iron / 부젓가락을 ~ heat tongs / 프라이팬을 ~ heat up a frying pan.

**달구지** a cart; a wagon. ¶ 소~ an oxcart / ~로 나르다 cart; carry in a cart / ~를 끌다 draw a cart / ~에 싣다 load a cart [wagon] 《with goods》.

**달궁이** 〖어류〗 a gurnard.

**달그락** with a clatter. ⇨ 달가닥.

**달나라** the lunar world; the moon. ¶ ~로 로켓을 발사하다 shoot a rocket at [to, toward] the moon. ◉ ~여행 a journey [flight] to the moon; a lunar flight [journey].

**달다**[1] ① 《매달다》 hang (up); suspend; dangle; 《내달다》 put up; hang out. ¶ 간판을 ~ put up [hang out] a sign(board) / 기를 ~ hoist a flag / 천장에 램프를 ~ hang a lamp from the ceiling / 문패를 ~ put up a name plate / 처마끝에 풍경을 ~ hang a wind-bell at the edge of an eave / 창문에 커튼을 ~ hang curtains on a window.

② 《붙이다》 attach [affix, fix, fasten] 《A to B》; set [put] 《A on B》; stick 《*a thing*》 《on, to》; 《꿰매붙이다》 stich [sew] 《a button》 on 《coat》; 《몸에》 wear; put on; have on. ¶ 소포에 꼬리표를 ~ attach a tag on a package / 문에 초인종을 ~ fix a bell on the door / 모자에 장식깃을 ~ stick a feather in a hat / 기관차에 객차를 ~ attach [couple] a passenger train to an engine / 가슴에 훈장을 ~ wear a decoration on *one's* chest / 소장 계급장을 달아 주다 pin the insignia of major general 《on the shoulders of *a person*》.

③ 《설비하다》 fit (up); set [put] up; furnish; install; lay on. ¶ 선반을 ~ make [put up] a shelf; fix a shelf 《to》 / 전화를 ~ have a telephone installed / 집에 전등을 ~ furnish [fit up] a house with electric lights.

④ 《기입하다》 enter 《an item》 in 《a book》; put down 《an item》 on 《a bill》; 《외상을》 charge 《the bill》 to 《*a person's* account》; put 《the purchases》 down 《on *a person's* bill》; 《첨가하다》 add [annex, append] 《A to B》. ¶ 단서를 ~ annex a proviso 《to a deed》 / 책에 주(註)를 ~ add [append] notes to a book; annotate a book / 장부를 ~ keep books [accounts] / 장부에 ~ enter 《an item》 in a book; put down 《an item on a bill》 / 계산은 외상으로 달아두시오 Please charge the bill to my account. *or* Put it on my bill, please. / 내 앞으로 기부금 10,000원을 달아 두시오 Put me down for ten thousand won donation / 한자에 한글로 토를 ~ show the reading of a Chinese character by writing *Hangul* at its side.

⑤ 《값을》 set. ¶ 물건에 값을 ~ set [put] a price (tag) on an article.

⑥ 《신랑을》 put 《a bridegroom》 on a mock trial; subject 《a bridegroom》 to a mock kangaroo court.

**달다**[2] 《무게를》 weigh; measure. ¶ 무게를 ~ weigh; measure the weight / 저울로 ~ weigh 《*a thing*》 in the balance [on the scales] / 달아서 팔다 sell 《*a thing*》 by weight / 체중을 ~ weigh *oneself* [*a person*].

**달다**[3] ① 《졸아들다》 be boiled down [dry]; boil down.

② (***a***) 《뜨거워지다》 become red-hot [very hot]; glow; heat. ¶ 벌겋게 단 부젓가락 red-hot tongs / 쇠가 ~ iron is heated / 방이 ~ a room is very warm. (***b***) 《화끈해지다》 feel hot [warm]; burn; flush. ¶ 화끈 단 얼굴로 with a flushed face / 부끄러워 얼굴이 ~ *one's* face burns with shame / 열이 있어 몸이 ~ be burning up with fever; feel feverish / 술을 마시니 얼굴이 달아오른다 My cheeks are flushed with wine.

③ 《마음·몸이》 fret; be impatient; be irritated; grow impatient; be eager [anxious] to; be burning to; be on fire to. ¶ 돈을 못 써 몸이 ~ the money is burning a hole in *one's* pocket / 돈

을 벌려고 몸이 달아 돌아다니다 be running about eager to make money / 애인이 보고 싶어 몸이 ~ be anxious to see *one's* sweetheart.

**달다**[4] ① 《맛이》 (be) sweet; sugary; sweet-flavored. ¶ 단 것 sweet things; 《과자》 sweets; a sweet / 맛이 ~ have a sweet taste; it is sweet; taste sweet / 달게 하다 sweeten; sugar / 단 것을 좋아하다 be fond of sweets; have a sweet tooth / 그는 단맛 쓴맛 다 본 사람이다 He has tasted the sweets and bitters of life. / 달면 삼키고 쓰면 뱉는다 Utilize *a person* when his service is needed, and keep him at a distance when he is no longer wanted. ② 《맛있게 먹다》 have a good 〔keen〕 appetite; (be) pleasant; tasty; sweet; nice. ¶ 달게 with good appetite; with grace / 음식을 달게 먹다 have a sweet tooth; eat food with a good appetite / 참 달게 먹었습니다 I made a good dinner of it.

**달달**[1] ① 《콩 따위를》 stirringly; thoroughly. ¶ 콩을 ~ 볶다 roast beans stirring them; stir roast beans; roast beans thoroughly. ② 《들볶다》 《tormenting》 to the extreme. ⇨ 들볶다. ¶ ~ 볶다 torment 《*a person*》 to the extreme; make it too hot 《for *a person*》. ③ 《뒤지다》 ransacking; rummaging. ¶ 서랍을 ~ 뒤지다 「poke around 〔rummage〕 in a drawer.

**달달**[2] ⇨ 덜덜[1,2].

**달뜨다** grow restless; be fickle. ⇨ 들뜨다.

**달라다** ask 《for》; beg; request; appeal; call upon 《*a person*》 to 《*do*》; plead 《for》; solicit 《for》. ¶ 해 달라는 대로 at 《*a person's*》 request; as requested / 도와 ~ ask 〔call〕 for help; appeal for aid / 돈을 꾸어 ~ ask 《*a person*》 to lend money / 밥을 ~ ask 〔beg〕 for food / 하룻밤 재워 ~ ask for a night's lodging / 그에게 있어 달라야겠다 I will have him stay.

**달라붙다** stick 〔cling, adhere〕 《to》; hold 〔hang〕 on to; keep 〔stand〕 close 《to》 (바싹). ⇨ 들러붙다. ¶ 착 ~ stick fast 《to》 / 일에 ~ stick at a job 〔*one's* work〕 / 벽에 착 ~ stand close to the wall; hug the wall 《미속어》 / 여자에게 성가시게 ~ hang around 〔about〕 a girl 〔woman〕 importunately.

**달라이 라마** the Dalai 〔Grand〕 Lama.

**달라지다** 《변화하다》 become different; change; undergo a change; alter; be altered; vary; 《…으로》 change 〔turn〕 《into》; be turned 〔transformed〕 《into》. ¶ 마음이 ~ change *one's* mind / 이야기가 ~ 「change the 〔pass to another〕 subject of conversation / 달라지지 않다 be 〔remain〕 unchanged; be the same (as before); be constant 《in *one's* opinion》 / 시대와 함께 풍속과 습관도 달라진다 Manners and customs become different with the times. / 정세는 달라진 것이 없다 The situation continues to be unchanged. / 그녀는 결혼 후 많이 달라졌다 She has changed a lot since she got married. / 지난 10년간 서울은 많이 달라졌다 Seoul has undergone a lot of changes over the last ten years. / 그녀의 기분은 매일 달라진다 Her mood varies from day to day. / 5월 1일부터 규칙이 달라진다 The new regulations will come into force on and after May 1st.

**달랑** ① 《홀로》 alone; lonely; solitarily. ¶ ~ 혼자만 남다 be left 「alone 〔to *oneself*〕 / 그 노인은 벤치에 ~ 혼자 앉아 있었다 The old man was sitting on the bench 「alone 〔by himself〕. ② 《가슴이 뜨금하는 모양》. ~하다 be startled; get a start; be shocked; feel a shock. ¶ 그 소식에 가슴이 ~했다 I was startled by the news. *or* The news gave me a shock.

**달랑거리다** ① 《방울이》 ring; jingle; tinkle. ¶ 방울이 ~ bell rings 〔tinkles〕; bells jingle. ② ⇨ 덜렁거리다②.

**달랑달랑** ① 《방울이》 ringing; tinkling; jingling. ② 《까불어 댐》 frivolously; restlessly.

**달랑달랑하다** ① = 달랑거리다. ② 《돈 따위가》 be about to run out; run short 〔low〕; get low.

**달래** 『식물』 a wild rocambole.

**달래다** ① 《좋은 말로》 soothe; calm (down); pacify; appease (요구 조건 따위를 받아들여); stroke 《*a person*》 down; 《비위를 맞추어》 fondle; dandle; nurse; try to please 《a baby》; 《살살 꾀어》 coax; humor; cajole; wheedle. ¶ 달래기 쉬운 appeasable; placable; mitigable / 달래기 어려운 inappeasable; implacable; immitigable / 을렀다 달랬다 하여 by threats and by entreaties / 달래어 …하게 하다 cajole 〔wheedle〕 《*a person*》 into 《*doing*》 〔to 《*do*》〕 / 우는 애를 ~ soothe 〔still〕 a crying child / 아이를 달래어 약을 먹이다 coax a child to take a medicine / 젖먹이를 달래어 잠재우다 lull a baby to sleep / 가까스로 달래어 집으로 돌려보냈다 I had great difficulty in persuading him to return home. / 나는 아내의 노여움을 달래려고 했다 I tried to appease my wife's anger.

② 《마음을 딴 데로》 divert 〔distract〕 《*one's* mind》; beguile 《the time》. ¶ 슬픔을 ~ divert *one's* mind from sorrow / 술로 시름을 ~ drown *one's* grief in drink / 무료함을 달래기 위해 쇼핑하다 go shopping to kill time 〔to relieve tedium〕 / 그들은 즐거운 대화로 긴 여행의 지루함을 달랬다 They beguiled their long journey with pleasant conversation.

**달러** a dollar (기호 $); a buck 《미구어》. ¶ 1 ~ 은화 a one-dollar silver coin / 5 ~ 지폐 a five-dollar bill 〔note〕; a fiver 《구어》 / 5 ~ 금화 a half eagle / 10 ~ 지폐 a ten-dollar bill 〔note〕; a sawbuck 《구어》 / 10 ~ 금화 an eagle / 20 ~ 금화 a double eagle / ~로 지급하다 pay in dollars / ~를 벌다 earn dollars / ~를 크게 벌어들이는 상품 a big dollar earner 〔winner〕.

◉ ~박스 a source of big profits; a moneymaker; a milch cow; a gold mine; 《돈줄》 *one's* patron 〔financial backer〕: ~박스 스타 a star with a high box-office value. ~매입 dollar buying 〔purchase〕. ~방위 the defense of the dollar. ~부족 a dollar shortage 〔deficit〕; a dollar gap. ~시세 the exchange rates of the dollar: 높은〔낮은〕 ~ 시세 a high 〔low〕 dollar rate. ~외교 dollar diplomacy. ~위기 a dollar crisis. ~자금 dollar funds. ~지역 the dollar area.

**달려가다** run 〔rush (돌진하듯), dash (급히), hasten (서둘러), hurry (허둥대며)〕 《to the spot》. ¶ 학교에 ~ run to school / 말이 ~ a horse is running along / 의사한테 ~ run to the doctor's; run for the doctor / 현장으로 ~ rush to the scene 《of》 / 그들은 그녀를 도우러 달려갔다 They ran to her aid.

**달려나가다** run 〔rush〕 out; run 〔scamper〕 off. ¶ 밖으로 ~ run 〔rush〕 outdoors; dash out 《into the street》.

**달려들다** 《별안간》 pounce 〔spring, jump〕 (up)on; spring 〔fly, jump, leap〕 at; rush at (일제히); 《일에》 grapple with. ¶ 개가 사람에게 ~ a dog jumps 〔leaps〕 at a person / 고양이가 쥐한테 ~ a cat pounces on a rat / 주먹으로 때리려고 ~ go at 《*a person*》 with *one's* fists / 전원이 달려들어 with combined 〔concerted, united〕 efforts / 세 사람이 그 일에 달려들어 하루만에 끝냈다 The three men grappled with the work, and finished it up in a day. / 경찰관들은 권총을 가진 남자에게 일제히 달려들었다 All at once the police rushed (at) 〔hurled themselves at〕 the man with the pistol.

**달려오다** run here; come running 〔rushing, on the run〕; hasten 〔hurry, rush〕 to 《a place》. ¶ 사람이 ~ a person comes running / 말이 ~ a horse gallops over.

**달력**(一曆) a calendar; an almanac (책력). ¶ 걸어 놓는 ~ a hanging calendar / 매일 들쳐보는 ~ a block-calendar / 매일 찢어내는 ~ a daily pad calendar / ~을 넘겨보다 consult 〔refer to〕 the calendar / ~으로는 봄이지만 아직 춥다 It is spring according to the calendar, but it is still cold.

**달리** 《다르게》 differently; dissimilarly (같지 않게); variously (여러 가지로); distinctively (특수하게); in a different way; in another way; in some other way; 《따로》 apart; separately; 《그밖에》 extra; additionally; in addition; besides; 《특별히》 especially; particularly; in particular. ¶ 글 뜻을 ~ 해석하다 construe the meaning of a sentence differently / 문제를 ~ 취급하다 treat a problem in another way / ~ 물어 볼 사람이 없다 haven't any other person to ask / 이것과 저것은 ~ 논해야 한다 This must be discussed separately from that. / ~ 방법이 없다 There is no alternative 〔choice〕 left. *or* There is no other way. / ~ 설명할 도리가 없다 I can't explain it any other way. / 오늘 오후에는 ~ 용무가 없다 I have nothing particular to do this afternoon. / 오늘은 ~ 이렇다 할 뉴스가 없다 There is no particular news today.

**달리기** a run; 《경주》 a race; a footrace. ¶ ~선수 a runner; a racer; a sprinter(단거리) / ~를 하다 run 〔have, do〕 a race 《with》; race 《with》 / 백미터 ~ the 100-meter race 〔dash〕.

**달리다**[1] ① 《매달리다》 hang down 《from》; dangle 《from》; suspend. ¶ 허공에 ~ hang in the (mid)air / 사과가 가지에 ~ apples dangle from branches / 나뭇가지에 뭔가 달려 있다 Something is hanging (down) 〔dangling〕 from a branch of the tree. / 처마에 고드름이 달려 있다 Icicles hang from the eaves.

②《좌우되다》 depend 《(up)on》; hang 《on》; turn 《(up)on》; rest 〔lie〕 《with》; hinge 《on》. ¶ 경우에 ~ depend upon the situation / 대답에 ~ turn 〔hang〕 on the answer / 사람에 ~ depend upon the person / 결정은 너에게 달려 있다 Decision rests with you. / 수확은 날씨에 달려 있다 Crops are dependent upon weather. / 계약의 수락 여부는 조건 여하에 달려 있다 The acceptance of the contract hinges upon what the terms are. / 만사는 저쪽에서 나오는 태도 여하에 달려 있다 Everything depends on what move they will make.

③ 《우수리가》 be tacked on 《to a round sum》. ¶ 값이 만원하고 귀가 달린다 The price is a little more than ten thousand won.

**달리다**[2] ① (***a***) 《붙어 있다》 be attached 〔affixed, appended, fixed, tagged〕; be joined 〔coupled〕. ¶ 큰 거울이 달린 화장대 a dressing table with a large mirror / 꼬리표가 달린 트렁크 a trunk with a tag attached 〔fixed〕 / 이 열차에는 식당차가 달려 있다 There is a dining car attached to this train. (***b***) 《시설되다》 be installed; be fitted (up); be set 〔put〕 up. ¶ 전등이 ~ an electric lamp is fixed; be furnished 〔fitted up〕 with electric lights / 전화가 달려 있다 A telephone is installed. *or* The telephone service is operated.

② 《첨가되다》 be added 〔annexed, affixed, appended〕; be given 〔put entered〕. ¶ 책에 주가 ~ notes are added 〔appended〕 to a book / 이 책에는 색인이 달려 있지 않다 This book has no index.

**달리다**[3] ① 《느른하다》 sag; feel languid 〔tired〕; become droopy. ¶ 몸이 ~ *one's* body sags; be tired. ② 《눈이》 sag; droop; be drawn. ¶ 잠을 자지 못해서 눈이 ~ *one's* eyes feel heavy 〔are drawn〕 from lack of sleep.

**달리다**[4] ① 《부족하다》 [사물이 주어] be insufficient; be in short supply [사람이 주어] do not have enough 《of》; run 〔come, be, fall〕 short 《of 》; run low 《on》; lack; be shy 《of 》; want; be in want 〔need〕 of. ¶ 돈이 ~ run short of money; be shy of money / 식수가 ~ run short of drinking water / 일손이 ~ be short of hands 〔workers〕; be shorthanded / 식량이 ~ be 〔run〕 short of provisions / 근량이 좀 달린다 The weight is a bit short. / 돈이 좀 달리겠는데 I'm afraid this money will not go so far.

② 《부치다》 be not enough; be not up to; be not equal to; be beyond 《*one, one's* power》; be no match 〔equal〕 for; be deficient. ¶ 재능이 ~ be poor 〔wanting〕 in ability / 수학 실력이 ~ be deficient 〔poor〕 in mathematics / 힘이 ~ be not strong enough.

**달리다**[5] ① 《질주하다》 run; rush; hurry; dash; dart. ¶ 사람이 ~ a person runs / 말이 ~ a horse runs 〔canters, gallops〕(★ 말의 속도는 walk, amble, trot, canter, gallop의 차례로 빨라짐.) / 전속력으로 ~ run 〔dash〕 at full 〔top〕 speed / 달려가다 go running; go at a run; run 《to》; rush 《for》 / 달려 들어오다〔내려가다, 올라가다〕 rush in 〔down, up〕 / 달려 돌아오다 run back; come home running / 달려 지나가다 run past 《a house》 / 너무 달려 지치다 overrun *oneself* / 갑자기 ~ break into a run; dart forth / 시속 40마일로 ~ make 〔run〕 forty miles an hour / 달리는 차에서 뛰어내리다 jump off 〔out of 〕 a moving car / 배는 시속 20노트의 속력으로 달리고 있다 The ship is making twenty knots an hour. / 기차를 놓치지 않으려고 급히 달렸다 I had a hard run to catch the train.

② 《몰다》 run 《it》; drive 《a car》; urge 《a horse》 on. ¶ 말을 ~ gallop a horse / 자동차를 ~ drive a car.

**달리아** 〖식물〗 a dahlia.

**달리하다** differ 《from》; be different 《from》; vary; be unlike. ¶ 대우를 ~ treat 《*a person*》 differently 《from others》 / 관점을 ~ view things from a different angle / 달리하는 different / 나는 그 문제에 관해 너와 의견을 달리한다 I differ with 〔from〕 you on that question. / 소포들은 각각 무게를 달리한다 Each parcel varies in weight.

**달마**(達磨) 〖불교〗 Dharma.

**달마다** every month; monthly; *per mensem* (L.)

**달맞이** 〖민속〗 welcoming 〔viewing〕 the first full moon. ~하다 welcome 〔view〕 the first full moon.

**달맞이꽃** 〖식물〗 an evening primrose.

**달무리** a halo 〔ring〕 (a)round the moon. ¶ ~가 졌다 The moon has a ring around it.

**달밤** a moonlight 〔moonlit〕 night. ¶ ~의 moonlit; moonshiny / ~에 산책하다 stroll in the moonlight; walk under 〔in〕 the moonlight / 밝은 ~이다 It is (a) bright moonlight (night).

**달변**(—邊) 《이자》 a monthly interest.
**달변**(達辯) fluency; eloquence; 《have》 a fluent tongue. ¶ ～의 eloquent; fluent / 그는 ～이지만, 곧잘 실언을 한다 He is a fluent speaker to be sure, but he often makes inappropriate remarks. ◉ ～가 a ready tongue; a fluent speaker; an eloquent tongue; a good talker 〔orator〕.
**달빛** moonlight; moonshine; a moonbeam. ¶ ～이 비친 뜰 a moonlit garden / ～이 밝다 the moonlight is bright / ～을 받다 be bathed in 〔be flooded by〕 the moonlight / ～에 책을 읽다 read by moonlight / 커튼을 열어 젖히자 ～이 흘러들었다 When the curtain was opened, the moonlight streamed into the room.
**달삯** monthly wage(s).
**달성**(達成) achievement; attainment; accomplishment. ～하다 achieve 《a purpose》; attain 《*one's* object》; accomplish; realize; carry through 〔out〕.

> **용법** **achieve** 장애·어려움 따위를 극복하여 목적·희망 등을 달성한다는 뜻. **attain** 노력해서 힘들게 목표에 도달한다는 뜻. **accomplish** 특정한 계획·사명 따위를 노력과 인내로써 성취한다는 뜻.

¶ 목적을 ～하다 attain *one's* object 〔purpose〕; accomplish 〔achieve〕 《*one's* purpose》 / 그 목표는 ～하기 힘들다 The object is beyond attainment. / 이렇게 해서 이 위업은 ～되었다 That was how this great work was achieved 〔accomplished〕.
**달싹하다** 《움직이다》 budge; move slightly. ¶ 달싹하지도 않다 do not budge 〔stir, move〕 an inch.
**달아나다** ① 《빨리 가다》 speed; scurry 《away, off》; run off 〔away〕; fly off 〔away〕 (새가); run fast. ¶ 차는 쏜살같이 달아났다 The car sped away.
② 《도망가다》 run away 〔off〕; get away; escape; take to *one's* heels; make *one's* escape 〔getaway〕; flee; take (to) flight; break out 〔loose〕 (가축 등이); fly away (새가). ¶ 간수의 눈을 피해 ～ slip *one's* guard / 애인과 눈이 맞아 ～ elope 〔run away〕 with a sweetheart / 돈을 갖고 ～ abscond with the money / 몰래〔가만히〕 ～ slip off; sneak 〔steal〕 away / 밤을 타 ～ run away under cover of night / 빚을 진 채 ～ run out on *one's* debts; give *one's* creditors the slip / 허둥지둥 ～ run away with the tail between the legs; beat a hasty retreat / 숲속으로 ～ flee into the woods / 오금아 날 살려라 하고 ～ run away for *one's* (dear) life; betake *oneself* to flight 〔*one's* heel〕 / 자동차로 ～ make *one's* escape in a car / 무사히 ～ make good *one's* escape; be safe from pursuit / 미처 못 ～ fail to (effect *one's*) escape / 전속력으로 ～ run away at top speed / 경관을 보더니 그는 달아났다 At the sight of the police, he took to his heels. / 곰이 우리에서 달아났다 The bear has 「got(ten) out of 〔broken loose from〕 its pen. / 새가 새장에서 달아났다 The bird flew out of its cage.
③ 《잠·입맛 따위가》 lose *one's* appetite; be sleepless; vanish. ¶ 졸음이 달아나게 커피를 마셨다 I had a cup of coffee to shake off (my) drowsiness. / 나는 요즘 입맛이 달아났다 I have no appetite in these days.
**달아매다** ① hang (up); suspend; sling. ¶ 그네를 ～ put up a swing / 해먹을 ～ sling 〔swing〕 a hammock. ② 《붙들어 매다》 bind 《*a person*》 to 《a stake》; tie; fasten. ¶ 돛을 돛대에 ～ fasten sails to the mast.
**달아보다** ① 《무게를》 check the weight of; weigh 《*a thing*》. ¶ 짐을 ～ weigh a bundle; check the weight of a bundle. ② 《사람을》 size up; evaluate 《*a person's* ability》. ¶ 아무를 ～ size *a person* up / 아무의 역량을 ～ size up *a person's* ability.
**달아오르다** ① 《쇠가》 get very hot; become red-hot; glow. ② 《몸이》 feel hot; burn; flush; ¶ 얼굴이 달아올라 화끈거리다 *one's* cheeks burn 《with shame》.
**달음(박)질** running. ～하다 run; rush; 「dash; dart.
**달이다** boil down; decoct; infuse; brew up. ¶ 약을 ～ prepare 〔make〕 a decoction of; decoct herbs; boil down medical herb / 차를 ～ draw 〔brew〕 tea.
**달인**(達人) ① 《학문·기예의》 an expert; a (past) master; a master-hand; an adept. ¶ …에 있어서 ～이다 be a master of...; be at home in...; be clever at.... ② 《달관자》 a far-sighted person; a man of wisdom; a philosopher; a mastermind. 「sweet.
**달짝지근하다** (be) rather 〔pleasantly〕
**달창나다** ① 《해지다》 wear out 〔through〕; be worn out; become threadbare (옷 따위가). ¶ 구두가 ～

*one's* shoes are worn out. ②《바닥나다》 run out; be exhausted; be used up; be all gone. ¶ 그들은 식량이 달창났다 They ran out of food supplies.

**달치다** ①《달다》 get too hot. ②《바싹 조리다》 boil 《*something*》 down; boil 《salt》 dry; condense 《milk》.

**달카닥-, 달칵-** ⇨ 덜커덕-.

**달콤하다** ①《맛이》 (be) sweetish; sweet (flavored); nicely sweet. ¶ 맛이 ~ taste sweet; have a sweet flavor / 사랑의 달콤한 맛 the manna 〔charm〕 of love. ②《말·장면 등이》 (be) honeyed; sugary; sweet; flattering; smooth; oily; well-oiled. ¶ 달콤한 말 honeyed 〔fine〕 words; sweet talk; soft soap (아첨); flattery (치렛말) / 달콤한 장면 a sugary scene 《in a film》 / 달콤한 말을 하다 say sweet things / 달콤한 말로 속이다 deceive 《*a person*》 with sweet words / 달콤한 말에 넘어가다 be caught by 《*a person's*》 sweet talk; be soft=soaped.

**달팽이** 〖동물〗 a snail. ¶ ~ 눈이 되다 shrink 《with fear》. ◉ ~ 걸음 a snail's gallop 〔pace〕. ~ 껍질 a snail shell. 식용 ~ an edible 〔a Roman〕 snail.

**달포** about a month; a month odd. ¶ 그가 떠난 지 한 ~된다 It is about a month since he left.

**달품** work paid for by the month.

**달필**(達筆) 《솜씨》 good handwriting; a ready 〔facile〕 pen; a skillful hand; 《글씨》 skillful penmanship. ¶ ~로 쓰여 있다 be written 「in a good hand 〔with a facile pen〕 / 그는 ~이다 He writes a good hand. ◉ ~가 a man with a ready pen; a good penman.

**달하다**(達一) ①《도달하다》 reach; gain; attain; come up to; arrive at 〔in, on〕; get to 〔at〕. ¶ 기준에 ~ come up to the standard / 표준에 달하지 못하다 《상품 따위가》 fall short of the mark 〔standard〕 / 성년에 ~ attain 〔reach〕 *one's* majority; come of age / 전쟁 전 수준에 ~ reach the prewar level / 절정에 ~ come to the climax / 완전한 경지에 ~ attain (to a state of) perfection / 프로 수준에 ~ reach the professional level / 그녀의 작업 능률은 기준에 달하지 못한다 The efficiency of her work isn't up to standard.
②《수량에》 amount (up) to; come (up) to; reach; mount 〔run〕 up to; work out at. ¶ 지원자가 천명에 ~ the number of applicants mounts up to one thousand / 재산이 수십 억에 ~ *one's* fortune amounts to several billions / 천문학적 숫자에 ~ run into astronomical figures / 참석자는 다 합해서 50명에 달했다 The attendants numbered fifty in all. / 총액이 1만 달러에 달할 것이다 The money collected will aggregate to 10,000 dollars. / 손실은 3,000만 원 이상에 달한다 The loss is estimated to reach upward of thirty million won.
③《이루다》 attain; gain; accomplish; achieve; realize. ¶ 목적을 ~ achieve 〔accomplish, realize〕 *one's* purpose; reach 〔attain〕 *one's* goal.

**닭** 《암탉》 a hen; 《수탉》 a cock; a rooster 《미》; 《병아리》 a chick; 《거세한 육용》 a capon; 《산란용》 a layer; a laying hen; [총칭] 《미》 chickens; 《영》 fowl. ¶ 싸움닭 a gamecock; a fighting cock / 놓아기르는 닭 yard fowls / 알을 잘〔안〕 낳는 닭 a good 〔bad〕 layer / 닭이 먼저냐 달걀이 먼저냐 하는 문제 the question of which came first, the chicken or the egg; a chicken-or-egg question / 닭을 치다 keep 〔raise〕 chickens / 닭이 울다 a rooster crows / 닭 소 보듯 소 닭 보듯 look at each other 「in silence 〔indifferently〕 / 닭 잡아먹고 오리발 내놓기 trying to throw 《*a person*》 off the track of *one's* misdeed / 닭 쫓던 개 지붕 쳐다보듯 be frustrated in *one's* attempt.

**닭고기** chicken (meat); fowl. ◉ ~ 고추볶음 sautéed diced chicken with red pepper. ~ 마늘볶음 sautéed chicken in garlic sauce. ~ 야채볶음 sautéed chicken and vegetables.

**닭고집**(一固執) a stubborn 〔an obstinate, a stiff-necked〕 fellow.

**닭구이** (a) barbecued chicken.

**닭똥집** 《닭의 모래주머니》 a gizzard.

**닭백숙**(一白熟) (a) boiled chicken.

**닭살** gooseflesh; goose bumps 〔pimples〕. ¶ 그 일을 생각하면 온몸에 ~이 돋는다 I get 〔have, feel〕 gooseflesh all over (me) when I think of it.

**닭싸움** cockfighting; a cockfight.

**닭(의)어리** a chicken coop.

**닭(의)장**(一藏) a hencoop; a henhouse. ¶ ~에 넣다 house chickens 〔fowls〕.

**닭의장풀**(一藏一) 〖식물〗 a spiderwort; a dayflower.

**닭찜** a stewed chicken.

**닭튀김** fried chicken.

**닮다** be 〔look〕 like 《another》; be alike; resemble; take after; be similar 《to》; have a likeness 《to》; be the very image of. ¶ 꼭 ~ be as like as two peas; be the exact counterpart of; be the spit of / 다소 닮은 데가 있다 bear some resemblance 《to》; have some similarities 《between》 / 닮은 점이 많다 have many points of likeness 《to》 / 닮지 않다 bear no resemblance 《to》; look different / 전혀 닮은 데가 없다 do not bear the slightest resemblance 《to》; be quite unlike 〔different from〕 《another》 / 부자가 꼭 ~ the son is the spitting image of his father; the father and son are just 〔quite, exactly〕 alike (★ alike는 명사 앞에서는 쓰지 않음. 또 very alike라는 표현은 없음: They look *much alike.*) / 형제가 꼭 ~ the brothers are as like as two peas / 하는 짓이 아버지를 ~ take after *one's* father in behavior / 그의 얼굴은 원숭이를 닮았다 His face is like a monkey's. / 그들은 성격이 닮았다 They are much alike in character. / 난 아버지보다 어머니를 더 닮았다 I take after mother more than father. / 부부는 서로 닮는다 Like husband, like wife.

**닮은꼴** 〖기하〗 a similar 〔like〕 figure.

**닳다** ① 《해지다》 wear 〔be worn〕 out 〔off〕; 《옷이》 get 〔become〕 threadbare. ¶ 닳아 빠진 worn-out; threadbare; frayed / 닳아 빠진 구두 a pair of worn-out shoes / 구두 뒤축이 ~ the heels of *one's* shoes wear down; *one's* shoes wear down at the heels / 닳아서 얇아지다 wear thin / 닳아서 너덜너덜해지다 be worn to rags / 입이 닳도록 말하다 tell *a person* over and over again / 치맛〔옷〕자락이 다 닳았다 The skirts are quite worn out.
② 《졸아들다》 be 〔get〕 boiled dry; boil down. ¶ 국이 다 닳았다 The soup boiled down to nothing.
③ 《세파에》 become sophisticated; lose *one's* simplicity. ¶ 닳고 닳은 사람 a sophisticated person; 《여자》 a saucy 〔debased〕 jade; a hussy / 닳고 ~ become oversophisticated; be too much a man of the world.
④ 《피부가》 flush; be flushed. ¶ 볼이 추위로 ~ *one's* cheeks flush with cold.

**닳리다** ① 《해뜨리다》 wear away 〔down〕; rub off 〔down〕; abrade. ¶ 구두 뒤축을 ~ wear down the heels of *one's* shoes; wear down *one's* shoes at the heel / 연필을 ~ wear down the lead of a pencil. ② 《액체를》 boil dry; boil away; boil off. ¶ 약을 다 ~ let a herb brew boil down / 국물을 ~ boil the soup away. ③ 《피부를》 make 《*one's* cheeks》 flush.

**담**[1] 《집의》 a wall; a fence (울타리). ¶ 담을 두르다 wall in 《a garden》; surround 《a house》 with a wall / 담을 두른 집 a wall-in house / 담을 타고 넘다 climb 〔jump〕 over a wall / 담 너머로 보다 look over a wall.

**담**[2] 《머리털 결》 ease of combing. ¶ 담이 좋다 comb nicely.

**담**(痰) ① 《가래》 phlegm; sputum (*pl.* -ta, ~s). ¶ 피가 섞인 담 bloody phlegm / 담을 뱉다 spit (out); expectorate phlegm; cough out 〔bring up〕 phlegm / 담이 생기다 raise phlegm; have phlegm / 담이 목에 걸리다 *one's* throat is choked with phlegm. ② 《담병》 congestion. ¶ 가슴에 담이 들다 suffer from a chest congestion.
◉ 담약 an expectorant (medicine).

**담**(膽) ① 《쓸개》 gall(bladder). ② 《담력》 spirit; courage; pluck; nerve; 《구어》 guts. ¶ 담이 크다 be bold 〔courageous, daring, plucky, fearless〕 / 담이 작다 be cowardly; be chicken (=hearted) / 그녀의 담을 시험하다 test the strength of her nerve.

**-담**(談) a talk; a story; a tale. ¶ 모험담 a tale of an adventure / 성공담 a success story.

**담갈색**(淡褐色) light brown (color).

**담그다** ① 《물에》 soak 〔dip, steep〕 《in》; souse 《in(to)》; immerse 《in》. ¶ 물에 ~ soak 〔put〕 in water; give 《leather》 a soaking in water / 더운 물에 발을 담가라 Dip your feet in the hot water.
② 《김치 따위를》 prepare 〔make〕 《kimchi》; 《절이다》 pickle 〔salt〕 《vegetables》; preserve in 〔with〕 《salt》. ¶ 젓갈을 ~ preserve fish in salt / 과일을 설탕에 ~ preserve fruit in sugar.
③ 《술·장 등을》 brew; ferment. ¶ 술을 ~ brew 〔make〕 rice wine / 콩으로 간장을 담근다 Soybean is made into soy.

**담금질** 〖야금〗 quenching; tempering. ~하다 harden; quench; temper.

**담기다** ① 《그릇에》 be filled; be put in; hold; 《음식이》 be dished up; be served; be filled; 《병에》 be bottled. ¶ 그릇에 물이 담겨 있다 The bowl has water in it. / 그 그릇엔 물이 많이 담긴다 The bowl holds a lot (of) water. ② 《포함되다》 be put into; be included 〔comprised〕 in. ¶ 이 몇 마디 말에 담긴 내용 the matter comprised in these few words / 그 말에 무슨 뜻이 담겨 있느냐 What is implied by the word?

**담낭**(膽囊) 〖해부〗 the gallbladder; the

gall. ◉ ～관 the cystic duct. ～염 〖의학〗 cholecystitis. ～절개술 cholecystectomy.

**담녹색**(淡綠色) light green. ¶ ～의 light-green.

**담다** ① 《그릇에》 fill; put in; 《음식을》 fill; serve; help; dish up 〔out〕; 《병에》 bottle. ¶ 물을 ～ contain water; be filled with water / 그릇에 물〔밥〕을 ～ fill a bowl with water 〔rice〕 / 바구니에 과일을 ～ put fruit in a basket / 음식을 접시에 ～ serve food on a plate 〔in a dish〕; dish up the dinner. ② 《입에》 use; employ 《bad language》; speak 《foul, ill》; say 《*a thing* abusive》; have 《a word of abuse》 on *one's* lips. ¶ 입에 담지 못할 욕 abusive 〔very foul〕 language; scurrilous 〔uncivil〕 language / 그런 말은 입에 담지도 마라 Keep a civil tongue in your head! ③ 《포함시키다》 put into; incorporate 《in》; include; comprehend. ¶ 정성을 담은 선물 a gift from 《*a person*》 with *his* best wishes / 자기 생각을 그 계획에 ～ incorporate *one's* idea in the plan / 그녀의 한 마디 한 마디에는 진실이 담겨 있었다 Her sincerity shone through in every word she spoke.

**담담하다**(淡淡—) ① 《물이》 (be) clear; 《달빛이》 (be) bright; 《색이》 (be) plain; light. ¶ 담담한 색깔 a plain color / 밤하늘에 달빛이 ～ A bright moon shines in the sky. ② 《맛이》 (be) flat; plain; light. ¶ 담담한 맛 plain 〔light〕 taste. ③ 《심경이》 (be) unconcerned; indifferent (무관심한); disinterested (사심 없는); calm (냉정한); serene (차분한); tranquil (조용한). ¶ 담담히 calmly; dispassionately / 담담한 심경 a serene state of mind / 담담한 태도로 임하다 assume a disinterested attitude 《toward》 / 담담한 어조로 말하다 talk in a quiet tone.

**담당**(擔當) charge. ～하다 take 〔have〕 charge of; be in charge of; take *something* under *one's* charge. ¶ 이 과목의 ～ 교수 the professor who teaches the subject / (…을) ～시키다 put 〔place〕 《*a person*》 in charge of; assign 《a work》 to 《*a person*》 / 사건을 ～하다 take charge of the affair / 그는 3학년을 ～하고 있다 He is in charge of a 3rd-year class. / 그 기자는 가정란을 ～하고 있다 The reporter writes a family column. / 나는 수학을 ～하고 있다 I teach mathematics. / 남 박사가 이 병실의 ～ 의사다 Dr. Nam is in charge of this ward. / 「누가 그 사건을 ～하게 됩니까」—「김 경감이십니다」 "Who will take charge of the case?"—"Inspector Kim."
◉ ～검사 the prosecutor in charge. ～구역 the section under *one's* charge; 《경찰 등의》 *one's* round; *one's* beat; 《배달의》 *one's* walk: ～ 구역을 돌다 make 〔go〕 *one's* rounds. ～기자 a reporter assigned; an assignment man. ～업무〔사무〕 the business under *one's* charge; the business for which *one* is responsible. ～자 a person in charge 《of the Export Dept.》. ～책임자 the responsible person in charge 《of the affair》.

**담대하다**(膽大—) ⇨ 대담(大膽).

**담략**(膽略) courage and resourcefulness. ¶ ～이 있다 be courageous and resourceful.

**담력**(膽力) pluck; courage; nerve; grit; 《구어》 guts. ¶ ～이 있는 brave; bold daring; plucky; courageous / ～이 없는 timid; cowardly; chicken-hearted; white-livered / ～ 있는 사람 a man of nerve; a man with plenty of guts; a daring man / ～을 기르다 cultivate 〔foster, train〕 courage / ～을 시험하다 put 《*a person's*》 courage to the test / ～을 (가다듬어) 모으다 muster 〔pluck〕 up *one's* courage; brace *oneself* / 나는 그것을 해볼만한 ～이 없다 I haven't the nerve to try it. / 나는 그녀의 ～에 놀랐다 I was surprised at her daring 〔pluck〕.

**담론**(談論) (a) (lively) conversation; discourse; discussion; argument. ～하다 discourse; discuss; argue.

**담박하다**(澹泊·淡泊—) ① 《맛·빛깔이》 (be) light; plain; simple. ¶ 담박한 색 a light color / 담박한 음식 light 〔plain〕 food; a simple diet. ② 《마음이》 (be) indifferent 《to》; 《솔직하다》 (be) frank; unselfish; ingenuous; outspoken; candid; open-hearted. ¶ 담박한 사람 a man of frank disposition / 금전에 ～ be indifferent about money; do not care much for money.

**담배** tobacco; 〖식물〗 a tobacco; 《궐련》 a cigarette; 《엽궐련》 a cigar; 《잎담배》 leaf tobacco; 《살담배》 cut 〔pipe〕 tobacco; 《씹는》 chewing tobacco; 《코담배》 snuff. ¶ ～ 한 개비 a cigarette / ～ 한 갑 a pack of cigarettes / ～ (10 갑들이) 한 포 a carton of cigarettes / ～ 한 대 a fill of tobacco / ～ 연기 tobacco 〔cigarette〕 smoke / 불꺼진 ～ a dead cigarette / ～ 연기를 둥글게 내

뿜다 blow 〔puff (out)〕 a smoke ring 〔make smoke rings〕 into the air.
담배에: ～에 취하다 smoke *oneself* sick / ～에 불을 붙이다 light a cigarette.
담배를: ～를 물고 with a cigarette in 〔between〕 *one's* lips / ～를 권하다 offer 《*a person*》 a smoke / ～를 끊다 give up 〔quit〕 smoking / ～를 피우지 않는 사람 a non-smoker / ～를 말다 roll (tobacco into) a cigarette / ～를 한 대 피우다 have a smoke; smoke a pipe / ～를 많이 피우다 smoke heavily 〔hard〕 / ～를 깊이 빨아들이다 draw deeply on *one's* cigarette / ～를 몇 모금 빨다 take several pulls on 〔from〕 *one's* cigarette / ～를 뻐끔뻐끔 빨다 puff at *one's* pipe 〔cigarette〕; smoke 〔puff〕 away / ～를 너무 피우다 smoke to excess 〔too much〕 / 줄 ～를 피우다 chain=smoke / 줄 ～를 피우는 사람 a chain smoker; 《골초》 a heavy smoker / ～를 비벼 끄다 crush 〔stub〕 *one's* cigarette out / 호기심으로 ～를 시작하다 start smoking out of curiosity.
¶ 이 ～는 순하다〔독하다〕 This tobacco is mild 〔strong〕. / ～ 피워도 괜찮습니까 Do you mind if I smoke 〔light (up)〕? / ～를 삼가주십시오 《게시》 Kindly 〔Please〕 refrain from smoking.
◉ ～가게 《미》 a cigar store; 《영》 a tobacconist's (shop). ～꼬투리 《줄기》 the unusable refuse of tobacco leaves. ～꽁초 a cigarette butt 〔stub〕; a snipe 《미속어》; 《여송연의》 a cigar end: ～ 꽁초 버리는 곳 《게시》 Cigarette butts here. / ～꽁초를 버리지 마시오 Don't throw away cigarette butts. ～물부리 《담배의》 a cigarette holder; 《담뱃대의》 the mouthpiece of a pipe. ～밭 tobacco plantation. ～설대 a pipestem. ～쌈지 a tobacco pouch. ～자동 판매기 a cigarette-vending machine. ～장수 a tobacconist. 담뱃갑 a cigarette case; a tobacco box. 담뱃값 cigarette money; 《생기는 푼돈》 a small amount of money; a tip: 담뱃값도 없다 be hard up for money (궁하다) / 담뱃값으로 만원을 주다 [비유적] tip 《*a person*》 10,000 won. 담뱃재 tobacco 〔cigarette〕 ashes: 담뱃재를 털다 flick the ashes from a cigarette. 담뱃진 nicotine; tobacco tar(s): (파이프에) 담뱃진이 끼다 be choked with nicotine. 한국 ～ 인삼 공사 (the) Korea Tobacco and Ginseng Corp. (생략 KT & G).

**담뱃대** a (tobacco, smoking) pipe. ¶ ～를 물다 have a pipe in *one's* mouth / ～를 입에 물고 with a pipe in *one's* mouth; pipe in mouth / ～를 털다 knock the ashes off 〔from〕 *one's* pipe / ～에 불을 붙이다〔담배를 담다〕 light 〔fill〕 *one's* pipe.

**담뱃불** a light for *one's* pipe 〔cigarette〕; the light of a cigarette 〔pipe〕. ¶ ～을 붙이다 light (up) a cigarette; light *one's* pipe / ～을 끄다 put 〔snuff〕 out *one's* cigarette / ～을 빌리다 borrow a light for *one's* cigarette / ～ 좀 얻읍시다 Let me have a light, please.

**담벼락** 《담》 the surface of a wall; 《사람》 a person as unresponsive as a wall; a person of slow understanding; a blockhead. ¶ ～하고 말하는 셈이다 You might as well speak to a stone wall as talk to him.

**담보**(擔保) security; mortgage; 《담보물》 a security; a mortgage; a guarantee; a surety. ¶ ～ 없이, 무～로 without security; unsecured / ～로 넣다 give 〔offer〕 《*a thing*》 in 〔as〕 security 《for》; mortgage; 「take out 〔raise〕 a mortgage on 《*one's* property》; put 〔lay〕 《*a thing*》 in pledge / ～를 잡다 take security; secure *oneself* from loan / …을 ～로 잡고 있다 hold a mortgage on 《the house》 / …을 ～로 돈을 빌리다 borrow money on (the) security of 《*a thing*》 / 충분한 ～를 잡고 돈을 빌려 주다 lend money on good 〔ample〕 security / 나의 집은 1000만원 ～로 잡혀 있다 There is a mortgage of ten million won on my house. *or* My house is mortgaged for ten million won. / 무엇을 ～로 하시겠습니까 What security can you offer 〔put up〕 for it?
◉ ～권 security interest; mortgage rights: ～권자 a mortgagee. ～금 a margin. ～대출 a secured loan; a loan on security: ～ 대출금 a secured 〔covered〕 loan; a loan secured 《on the land》. ～물 a security; (a) collateral (근저당). ～물권 real rights granted by way of security; collateral security. ～변경 change of securities. ～부사채 secured bonds; a secured debenture. ～부 채권 a mortgage bond. ～인 a guarantor; a voucher. ～증서 a warranty deed. ～책임 responsibility for security 〔mortgage〕.

**담불**[1] 《마소의》 a ten-year-old 《ox, horse》.

**담불**[2] 《곡식의》 a stack 〔rick〕 of grain;

a pile 〔heap〕 of corn 〔cereals〕.

**담비** 〖동물〗 a marten; a sable. ◉ ∼가죽 marten; sable. 검은∼ a sable. 흰∼ an ermine.

**담뿍** much; in plenty.

**담색**(淡色) a light color.

**담석**(膽石) a gallstone; 〖의학〗 a cholelith. ◉ ∼증 cholelithiasis.

**담세**(擔稅) bearing tax. ∼하다 bear tax. ◉ ∼능력 tax-bearing capacity; tax-paying ability. ∼자 a tax-bearer; a taxpayer.

**담소**(談笑) a pleasant chat; chatting; a friendly talk. ∼하다 chat 《with》; have a pleasant chat 《with》; talk cheerfully 《with》. ¶ 문제는 ∼하는 사이에 해결되었다 The question was settled by friendly talk.

**담소하다**(膽小―) (be) timid; fainthearted; chicken-hearted; white-livered. ¶ 그는 담소해서 회의에서 발언을 거의 못한다 He is timid and hardly expresses his opinions in a meeting.

**담수**(淡水) fresh water. ◉ ∼어〔호〕 a freshwater fish 〔lake〕.

**담수**(湛水) contained 〔containing〕 water. ∼하다 contain water; be filled with water.

**담쌓다** ① 《담 두르다》 build 〔set up〕 a wall; surround 《a house》 with a wall. ② 《관계를 끊다》 sever *one's* connections 〔relations〕 with; break off 《with *a person*》; be through 《with》. ¶ 이제 그와는 담을 쌓았다 I'm through with him now.

**담요**(毯―) a blanket; a rug. ¶ ∼로 몸을 싸다 wrap *oneself* 〔be wrapped〕 up in a blanket.

**담임**(擔任) 《담당》 charge; 《선생》 a teacher in charge 《of a class》. ∼하다 take 〔have, be in〕 charge of; take 《a class》 under *one's* charge. ¶ ∼을 맡기다 put 〔place〕 《*a person*》 in charge of 《a class》 / 금년 우리 반 ∼ 선생은 어느 분이냐 Who is in charge of our class this year? / 나는 3학년 ∼이다 I have 〔am in〕 charge of the third-year class. ◉ ∼선생 a class 〔homeroom 《미》〕 teacher; a teacher in charge 《of a class》. ∼학급 the class under 〔in〕 *one's* charge.

**담자색**(淡紫色) light purple.

**담쟁이** 〖식물〗 ivy. ¶ ∼가 덮인 벽 an ivy-covered wall / ∼가 덮인 오두막 an ivy-mantled cottage / 벽에 ∼가 뻗게 두다 let ivy creep on the wall.
◉ ∼덩굴 ＝ 담쟁이.

**담즙**(膽汁) bile; gall; choler. ¶ ∼의 bilious; biliary. ◉ ∼병 biliousness. ∼산 bile acid. ∼질 bilious 〔choleric〕 temperament.

**담차다**(膽―) be full of courage 〔pluck〕; (be) bold; daring; plucky. ¶ 담찬 사람 a bold man / 담찬 계획 a bold 〔daring〕 plan 〔attempt〕.

**담채**(淡彩) thin 〔light〕 coloring. ¶ ∼의 light-colored / ∼를 하다 apply light coloring 《to》.

**담청색**(淡靑色) light 〔pale〕 blue. ¶ ∼의 light-〔pale-〕blue.

**담틀** a frame used in building a mud wall.

**담판**(談判) (a) negotiation; bargaining; a parley (외교상); talks (회담). ∼하다 negotiate 〔bargain〕 《with》; parley 《with》; have talks with. ¶ ∼의 결렬 a rupture of negotiations / ∼을 개시하다 open 〔enter into〕 negotiations / ∼중이다 be under negotiation / ∼이 매듭지어지다 come to terms 〔an agreement〕 《with》 / ∼이 결렬되었다 The negotiations broke down. / 그들은 임금 인상건으로 회사측과 직접 ∼했다 They had direct negotiations with the company for a pay raise.

**담합**(談合) ① 《의논》 (a) consultation; (a) conference. ∼하다 hold consultations 〔talks, a conference〕 《with the EU on trade issues》; confer 《with *a person* on *a matter*》. ② 《입찰 가격 사전 모의》 (illegal) collusion 《between contractors》; an illegal 〔improper〕 agreement 《to fix prices》; 《구어》 bid rigging. ∼하다 conspire 〔collude〕 to fix prices before tendering; 《구어》 (get together and) rig the bids 《for a construction contract》.
◉ ∼입찰: ∼입찰을 하다 put in 〔make〕 a rigged bid 〔collusive tender〕 《for the contract》.

**담해**(痰咳) 《가래와 기침》 cough and phlegm; 《가래 섞인 기침》 a moist cough.

**담홍색**(淡紅色) pink; rose pink; pale rose-color; salmon-red〔-pink〕.

**담화**(談話) ① 《이야기》 (a) talk; (a) conversation. ∼하다 talk 〔converse, speak〕 《with》; have a talk 〔conversation, chat〕 《with》. ¶ ∼형식으로 발표하다 publish 〔announce〕 in the form of an informal talk. ② 《의견》 a comment; a remark. ¶ 국무총리는 이재민 구제를 위해 정부가 최선의 노력을 다할 것이라는 ∼를 발표했다 The Prime Minister published a comment to the effect that the government would

〔will〕 do its best to aid the disaster victims. ◉ ～체 a conversational 〔colloquial〕 style. 「citrine.

**담황색**(淡黃色) light 〔lemon〕 yellow;

**답**(答) an answer; a reply; 《응답》 a rejoinder; a response; 《해답》 an answer; a solution. ⇨ 답하다. ¶ 답을 내다 get 〔work out〕 a solution 〔an answer〕; find an answer 《to the question》 / 답을 틀리게 내다 answer wrong / 내 답이 옳으냐 Is my answer correct? / 그것으로는 답이 될 수 없다 That is not quite the answer. / 문의한 데 대한 답은 얻어냈느냐 Have you received a reply to your inquiry? / 전화로 아무리 불러도 답이 없었다 There was no response to my repeated calls. 「fields; rice.

**답곡**(畓穀) grain from the paddy

**-답다** be like; be worth being; be worthy of the name; be becoming to; be as may 〔might〕; be expected; be every bit a ...; -ly; -like (★ -like는 대부분의 명사에 붙어서 「…다운」「…같은」의 뜻을 가진 형용사를 만듦: gentlemanlike). ¶ …다운 like; becoming; worthy of / 남자〔여자〕다운 manly 〔womanly, ladylike〕 / 신사다운 gentlemanlike / 사내답게 like a man / 글다운 글 an essay worthy of the name / 꽃답다 be flowerlike; be lovely as a flower / 남자답다 be manly; be every inch a man / 여자답다 be womanly / 신사답게 행동하다 behave like a gentleman / 그에게는 예술가다운 데가 있다 He has something of the artist in him. / 그에게는 학자다운 데가 조금도 없다 There is nothing of the scholar about him. / 그는 시인다운 시인이다 He is a poet worthy of the name. / 대학다운 대학이 적다 There are few universities worthy of the name. / 그는 사내답게 싸웠다 He fought the way a man should. / 학생이면 학생답게 굴어라 If you are a student, behave like one. / 요즘 아이들은 아이답지가 않다 These days most children are not very childlike.

**답답하다**(畓畓—) ① 《가슴이》 feel heavy 《in the chest》; 《*one's* chest》 feel tight; have a tightness 《in *one's* chest》; 《숨이》 have difficulty (in) breathing; breathe with difficulty; 《날씨 등이》 (be) gloomy; depressing. ¶ 답답한 날씨 gloomy 〔sullen〕 sky / 답답한 더위 oppressive 〔suffocating〕 heat / 답답한 분위기 an oppressive atmosphere; an atmosphere of heavy strain / 걱정으로 그는 가슴이 답답했다 Cares weighed heavily upon him.
② 《갑갑하다》 《장소가》 (be) stifling; suffocating; choking; stuffy; close. ¶ 답답한 방 a stuffy 〔close〕 room / 답답한 집 a narrow and close house / 극장은 초만원이어서 답답했다 The theater was overcrowded and stuffy 〔stifling〕. / 답답하니 방문 좀 열어 놓자 The room is stuffy — we had better open the window.
③ 《사람됨이》 (be) hidebound; strait=laced; lack versatility 〔adaptability〕; have no resources; 《언동이》 (be) irritable; clumsy; awkward; feel 〔be〕 impatient 《at》. ¶ 답답한 사고 방식 a narrow 〔rigid〕 view of things / 답답한 사람 an unadaptable 〔illiberal〕 man; a man of no resources / 말을 답답하게 하다 drawl; speak with a drawl / 그가 망설이는 것이 답답했다 I was impatient at his irresolution. / 그가 얼마나 꾸물대는지 몹시 답답했다 I was most impatient at his slowness.
④ 《소식이 없어》 feel anxious 〔uneasy〕 《about》; worry 〔be concerned〕 《about》. ¶ 집에서 소식이 없어 ～ There are no letters from home so I am concerned about my family.

**답례**(答禮) 《인사》 a return salute 〔call〕; a return present (선물에 대한). ～하다 return a 「salute 〔call〕; salute in return; send a present in return; 《특히 국가 원수가》 take 〔answer〕 the salute. ¶ ～로 in acknowledgment of; in return for; to return the courtesy of / ～로 그를 방문했다 I called on him by way of returning the compliment. / ～로 무엇을 선물할까 What shall I give him in return for his present?
◉ ～물〔품〕 a return present. ～방문 a return visit 〔call〕. ～사절 an envoy for returning courtesies; an envoy of gratitude.

**답변**(答辯) 《대답》 a reply; an answer; an explanation (변명); 《피고의》 a defense. ～하다 reply; answer; make a reply; give an answer; 《변호하다》 defend 〔explain〕 *oneself;* speak in defense 《of》. ¶ …에 대한 ～으로 in answer to... / ～을 요구하다 demand an explanation 《from *a person*》; call 《*a person*》 to account / 질문에 ～하다 answer 〔reply to〕 《*a person's*》 question / ～을 보류하다 reserve *one's* answer 《to》 / ～에 궁하다 be at a loss for an answer 〔explanation〕 / ～을 잘하다 be clever in reply / 그는 ～을 하지 못했다

He had no answer for that. / 어떻게 ～해야 좋을지 모르겠다 I don't know what to say to that. / 뭐라 ～하겠는가 What have you to say to that? *or* What reply have you for that? / 그 질문에 대해 ～할 처지가 못 됩니다 I am not in a position to answer that question. ◉ ～서 a written answer 〔reply, refutation〕; a defense (피고인의). ～자 an answerer; a pleader.

**답보**(踏步) step(ping); stamping; a tread; marking time; 《정체》 a stalemate; a standstill. ～하다 step; stamp; mark time; 《정체하다》 make no progress 〔headway〕; be at a standstill. ¶ ～ 상태에 있다 be at a standstill; be in a stalemate / 경기(景氣)는 앞으로 ～ 상태에 빠지게 될지 모르겠다 I'm afraid the market will be at a standstill in the future.

**답사**(答辭) an address in reply; a (formal) reply. ～하다 (make an) address in reply; make a formal reply 《to》. ¶ ～를 읽다 read an address in response 〔reply〕 / 졸업식에서 누가 ～를 했지 Who gave the address in reply at the graduation?

**답사**(踏査) 《미지의 땅 등》 (an) exploration; 《측량》 a survey; 《실지의》 a field investigation; reconnaissance. ～하다 explore; make explorations into; survey; make a survey 《of》; investigate. ¶ 그 섬을 현지 ～하다 make an on-the-spot survey of the island; explore the island / 학생들은 고적 ～를 했다 The students made a field investigation of the historic scene. ◉ ～대 an exploring party.

**답서**(答書) an answer. ＝답장(答狀).

**답습**(踏襲) following 《the earlier policy》. ～하다 follow in 《*a person's*》 footsteps; follow suit; follow 《the policy of the former Cabinet》; imitate (모방하다). ¶ 종래의 전통을 ～하다 follow 〔stick to〕 an old tradition / 신임 사장은 전 사장의 방식을 ～할 것이다 The new president will continue the course set by the former president.

**답신**(答申) a report. ～하다 submit a report; report (back) the findings 《of the committee》 to 《the President》. ◉ ～서 a (written) report. ～안(案) the draft of a report.

**답신**(答信) a reply; an answer; 《전신의》 a reply telegram. ～하다 answer 〔reply to〕 a letter.

**답안**(答案) 《용지》 a paper; an answer 〔examination〕 paper; 《해답》 an answer. ¶ 잘 된 ～ a good paper / 백지 ～ a blank paper / 영어 ～ a paper in English / ～을 내다 hand 〔give, turn〕 in *one's* (answer) paper / ～을 채점하다 mark 〔grade〕 examination papers.

**답장**(答狀) a reply (letter); a written reply; an answer 〔a reply〕 to a letter. ～하다 answer 〔reply to〕 a letter; send a reply to 《*a person, a person's* letter》. ¶ ～을 내다 answer 〔reply to〕 a letter; send a reply / ～을 내지 않다 leave a letter unanswered / ～을 기다립니다 Please oblige me with an answer. / 즉시 ～해 주십시오 Please answer my letter by return of post. / 그 편지에 ～이 없다 There has been no answer to the letter.

**답전**(答電) a reply telegram; an answer to a telegram. ～하다 reply by telegraph; send a wire in reply; telegraph in return; wire an answer.

**답지**(遝至) ～하다 rush 〔sweep, pour〕 in; be flooded 〔deluged〕 with; throng to; storm; come pouring 〔snowing〕 in. ¶ 주문이 ～하다 have a rush of orders / 신청이 ～하다 be deluged with applications 〔offers〕 / 축전이 ～했다 Congratulations came snowing in.

**-답지않다** (be) unlike; unbecoming; unworthy of; improper; unusual 《with》; out of keeping 《with》. ¶ 신사답지 않은 ungentlemanly / 학생답지 않은 행동 a conduct unbecoming in 〔to〕 a student / 공무원답지 않은 행실 behavior unworthy of a government official / 그 사람답지 않은 행동이었다 His behavior was out of character. 「impulse〕.

**답치기놓다** act recklessly 〔blindly, on

**답파**(踏破) traveling on foot extensively; tramping all over. ～하다 tramp all over; traverse 〔travel over〕 《a country》; travel on foot. ¶ 전국을 ～하다 tramp 〔walk, hike〕 all over the country / 실크로드를 ～해보는 것이 그의 어릴 때부터의 꿈이었다 Ever since childhood it had been his dream to travel (along) the Silk Road.

**답하다**(答—) answer; reply; give an answer 〔a reply〕; respond 《to》 (반응). ¶ 답할 수 없는 질문 an unanswerable 〔insoluble〕 question / 질문에 ～ answer a question / 환호에 ～ respond to the cheers / 답하지 않다 make no answer 〔reply〕 / 그녀는 긍정적〔부정적〕으로 답했다 She answered in the 「affirmative 〔negative〕. / 이 질문에 답해 주시오 Answer me this question. / 우리 학급의 아무도 그 질문에 답할 수 없었다 No one in the class could answer the question.

> **용법** **answer** 구두·문서·행동 따위로 「답하다」란 뜻이 되는 가장 일반적인 말. **reply** answer보다 격식차린 말. 받은 편지·질문 등에 대한 막연한 답이 아니라, 질문의 내용·요점 등에 대해 하나하나 답하는 경우는 answer가 아니라 reply를 써야 함. **respond** answer, reply보다 더 격식차린 말. 요청·호명·충고·기대 등에 대해 즉각적으로 나타내는 반응을 뜻하는 말.

**닷** five. ¶ 닷 말 five *mal.*

**닷새** ① 《5일》 five days. ② 《초닷새》 the fifth day of the month.

**당**(唐) 《중국 왕조의 이름》 Tang (618-907).

**당**(糖) sugar. ¶ 혈액 속의 당 blood sugar / 소변에 당이 나오다 sugar is found in *one's* urine / 소변의 당을 검사하다 examine the urine for sugar.

**당**(黨) a (political) party (정당); a faction (분파); a clique (파벌); a group (집단); a league (동맹).
¶ 당간부 a party official / 당의 중진 leaders of a party / 당의 내분 a factional strife in a party / 당 출신의 장관 a minister of party extraction / 당 3역(役) the party triumvirate / 당내의 파벌 an intraparty faction / 당에 들어가다〔가입하다〕 join a party / 당을 조직하다〔결성하다〕 form a party / 당의 방침에 따르다 toe the party line / 당에서 탈퇴하다 leave 〔withdraw from〕 a party / 당을 해산하다 dissolve the party / 당에 끌어들이다 win 《*a person*》 over to *one's* party / 그들은 당의 세력을 확장하려 하고 있다 They are trying to extend party prestige.
◉ 당대회 a party convention. 당본부 party headquarters. 당정책조정회의 a policy coordination meeting of the party. 당정치국 《옛 소련 공산당의》 (communist) party's politburo.

**당-**(當) ① 《바로 그·이》 this; that; the present; at issue; the said; 《the one》 in question; the proper; the appropriate; 《age》 at the time. ¶ 당사(社) this firm / 당역(驛) this station / 당자 the person in question; the said person; the person concerned.
② 《현재》 ¶ 당 20세, 20 years old at the time.

**-당**(當) per...; (for) each. ¶ 1인당 per *capita* (L.) 〔head〕; for each person / 인구 1인당 per head of population / 톤당 per ton / 1페이지당 낱말 수 the number of words to a page / 비용은 1인당 2만원이었다 The cost came out as twenty thousand won a head.

**당고**(當故) ～하다 lose *one's* parents; go into mourning for *one's* parents.

**당고모**(堂姑母) *one's* grandfather's niece on his brother's side; an aunt (who is *one's* father's cousin).

**당구**(撞球) billiards; pills 《영》; pool (내기 당구). ¶ ～치다 play (at) billiards; have a game of billiards / ～를 치는 사람 a billiard player; a cueist / ～에서 이기다〔지다〕 win 〔lose〕 a game of billiards.
◉ ～공 a billiard ball. ～대 a billiard table; a pool table. ～장 a billiard hall 〔room〕; pool room 《미》 (도박공의). ～채 a (billiard) cue.

**당국**(當局) the authorities. ¶ 관계 ～ the authorities concerned / 학교 ～ the school authorities / 경찰〔정부〕 ～ the police 〔government〕 authorities / 군〔군수사〕 ～ the military 〔army investigation〕 authorities / ～의 명에 의하여 by order of the authorities / ～의 허가를 얻다 obtain the sanction of the authorities. ◉ ～자 ＝당국.

**당권**(黨權) party hegemony; 《당수직》 the party presidency. ¶ ～에 도전하다 challenge the party presidency / ～ 경합에 나서다 compete with 《*a person*》 for the party presidency.
◉ ～싸움 a strife for party hegemony.

**당규**(黨規) the party rules 〔regulations〕.

**당근** 『식물』 a carrot. ¶ ～과 채찍 《보수와 벌》 (the) carrot and (the) stick / 아무를 설득하기 위해 ～과 채찍을 함께 쓰다 use (a combination of) (the) carrot and (the) stick to persuade *a person.*

**당기**(當期) the (current) term. ◉ ～결산 the settlement of accounts for the present term. ～배당 the dividend for this term. ～손익 the profits and losses for the current term. ～순이익 the net income.

**당기**(黨紀) party discipline. ¶ ～를 바로잡다 tighten party discipline / ～를 어지럽히다 lower 〔breach〕 party discipline. ◉ ～위원회 a disciplinary committee.

**당기다**[1] ① 《끌다》 pull; draw; drag; tug; haul; jerk.

> 용법 **pull** 물건을 「끌다」의 일반적인 말. draw에 비해 순간적이고 힘이 들어 있음. **draw** 물건을 잡아당기는 데 그다지 많은 힘을 들이지 않아도 됨을 나타냄. **drag** 무거운 것을 질질 끌다. **tug** 힘을 들여 당기다. **haul** 무거운 물체 따위를 서서히 끌다. 기계로 끄는 경우에도 쓰임. **jerk** 갑자기 홱 잡아당기다.

¶ 그물을 ～ haul in a net / 밧줄을 ～ draw 〔pull〕 the rope / 소매를 ～ pull 〔tug〕 《*a person*》 by the sleeve / 활을 팽팽히 ～ draw 〔bend〕 a bow to the full / 방아쇠를 ～ pull the trigger 《at, on》 / 밧줄을 홱 ～ give the rope a jerk / 난로 곁으로 의자를 ～ draw a chair up to the stove / 자석은 쇠를 당긴다 A magnet attracts iron. ② 《켕기다》 stretch 《a rope》 tight; strain; tighten 《a rope》. ¶ 밧줄을 팽팽히 ～ tighten 〔strain〕 a rope; stretch a rope tight / 너무 당기면 끊어진다 If you strain it too hard, it will break. ③ 《기일을》 make earlier; advance; move 《a date》 up 〔forward〕. ⇨ 앞당기다. ¶ 기일을 이틀 ～ advance the date by two days / 결혼 날짜를 사흘 ～ shift the wedding date three days ahead. ④ 《불을》 light up; fire up. ¶ 초에 불을 ～ light up a candle. ⑤ 《마음이》 be attracted; be moved 《by》.

**당기다**[2] 《입맛이》 stimulate 〔whet, appeal to〕 《*one's* appetite》; 《*one's* appetite》 be stimulated. ¶ 입맛 당기는 음식 appetizing food / 입맛이 ～ have a good appetite / 환자는 입맛이 당기기 시작했다 The patient has begun to have a good appetite.

**당김음**(—音) 〖음악〗 a syncopation.

**당나귀**(唐—) a donkey; an ass. ¶ 수탕나귀 a jackass / 암탕나귀 a jennet; a genet.

**당나라**(唐—) 〖역사〗 Tang. ¶ ～ 때 the Tang age.

**당내**(堂內) 《일가》 *one's* near relatives; 《불당 안》 within the temple; (intra-) temple.

**당내**(黨內) within the party; (intra-) party. ¶ ～의 사정 the intraparty situation / ～의 알력 intraparty conflict 〔trouble〕.

**당년**(當年) 《금년》 this 〔the current〕 year; 《그 해》 that year. ¶ 그녀는 ～15세이다 She is fifteen years old (this year). ◉ ～치 products of the year; the year's growth. ～치기 goods which last only one year; one year's wear.

**당뇨**(糖尿) 〖의학〗 glycosuria; glucosuria. ◉ ～병 diabetes (mellitus); sugar diabetes: ～병 증세 diabetic symptoms / ～병 환자 a diabetic.

**당닭**(唐—) 〖조류〗 a bantam; 《사람》 a short fat man; a humpty-dumpty.

**당당하다**(堂堂—) ① 《어연번듯하다》 (be) grand; stately; magnificent; majestic; imposing (위압하는); commanding (위풍당당한); splendid (화려한); dignified (위엄 있는).

> 용법 **grand** 규모·위엄·균형미에서 사람에게 강한 인상을 주는 경우에 씀. **stately** 위엄·기품이 있으며 강하고 인상적인 경우에 씀. **magnificent** 웅대하고 화려한 뜻으로 씀. **majestic** 위엄·기품·위대함 등의 인상이 짙은 경우에 쓰임.

¶ 당당한 문장 majestic sentences / 당당한 저택 a grand 〔magnificent〕 mansion / 당당한 체격 a splendid physique / 당당한 태도 a dignified attitude / 풍채가 당당한 신사 a gentleman of a commanding presence.

② 《정정당당하다》 (be) fair; justifiable; square; open; fair and square; open and above board. ¶ 당당한 권리 a lawful 〔legitimate〕 right / 당당한 승부 fair play / 당당한 이론 a fair and square argument / 당당한 이유 a fair 〔good〕 reason.

**당당히**(堂堂—) ① 《훌륭히》 grandly; splendidly; magnificently; majestically; in a dignified manner; with (great) dignity; with an imposing air; with pomp and glory. ¶ ～ 개선하다 return from a victorious campaign in glory / ～ 행진하다 march in grand style / 시험에 ～ 합격하다 pass an examination with flying colors / 정문으로 ～ 들어가다 enter at the main gate in state. ② 《떳떳이》 fairly; justifiably; squarely; openly. ¶ ～ 싸우다 fight openly 〔on the square〕; play fair / 의견을 ～ 주장하다 defend *one's* opinion like a man / 경기에 ～ 이기다 play fair and win a game; win a game fairly.

**당대**(當代) ① 《한평생》 *one's* lifetime. ¶ ～에 모은 재산 a fortune *one* has amassed in *one's* lifetime / ～에 부자가 되다 get rich in *one's* own lifetime. ② 《시대》 the present age 〔generation〕; those days. ¶ ～의 대음악가 a great musician of the day / ～에 드물게 보는 정치가 a statesman of rare caliber 「of the day 〔in the present age〕/ ~ 제일의 미인 the reigning beauty.

**당도**(當到) arrival; coming. ~하다 arrive 《at》; come upon; present itself; occur; get to; gain 《*one's* destination》. ¶목전에 ~한 위험 a pressing danger / 기회가 ~하다 a chance presents itself / 곤란이 ~하다 difficulties fall upon *one.*

**당도**(糖度) saccharinity.

**당돌하다**(唐突―) ① 《안차다》 (be) plucky (담력 있는); bold (대담한); spunky (용감한); fearless (겁 없는). ¶작아도 ~ Though small, he is plucky. ② 《주제넘다》 (be) forward; presumptuous; rude. ¶당돌한 말 a desultory remark / 어른 앞에서 그렇게 말하는 것은 당돌한 짓이다 It is rude of you to talk like that to your elders. / 당돌한 말씀이지만 그 일은 제가 해보겠습니다 It may be presumptuous of me, but I shall try to handle the matter.

**당두하다**(當頭―) draw near; be imminent; be near at hand. ⇨박두.

**당락**(當落) the result of an election; success (or defeat) in an election. ¶~ 가능성이 반반인 후보자 a candidate whose chances are 「even 〔fifty-fifty〕/ ~ 여부는 반반이다 have only a fifty=fifty chance of success in the election / ~은 내일 정오면 확실해진다 The result(s) of the election will be clear by noon tomorrow.

**당랑**(螳螂) 〖곤충〗《사마귀》 a (praying) mantis (*pl.* -tes, ~es). ◉ ~거철(拒轍) It is like the fly trying to bite the tortoise.

**당략**(黨略) party politics; a party policy. ¶~상 as a party policy.

**당량**(當量) 〖화학〗 an equivalent.

**당로**(當路) those in authority; the authorities. ⇨요로(要路).

**당론**(黨論) the view 〔platform〕 of a party; a party platform; a party opinion. ¶~이 …에 기울다 the platform of a party is favorable for….

**당류**(糖類) sugars; 〖화학〗 saccharide.

**당리**(黨利) the party interests. ¶~를 도모하다 promote 〔advance〕 the party interests. ◉ ~당략(黨略) party interests and tactics; party politics: ~ 당략에 치우치다 be too much swayed by the party interests; pursue the party interests.

**당면**(唐麪) Chinese noodles.

**당면**(當面) facing; confrontation. ~하다 face; confront; be confronted 〔faced〕 with. ¶~한 《절박한》 urgent; present; pressing; immediate; impending / ~한 문제 a question of the moment 〔hour〕; the matter 〔question〕 in hand / ~한 급한 일 an urgent 〔a burning, a pressing〕 question; a problem calling for immediate 「solution 〔attention〕/ 우리 나라가 ~한 문제 the problems with which our country is confronted / ~한 온갖 시련과 도전을 극복하다 surmount various ordeals and challenges facing 《the our country》/ ~한 소요에 응하는 데는 그것으로 충분하다 That's enough to meet the immediate 〔pressing〕 need.

**당명**(黨命) an order of a party; a party order 〔policy〕. ¶~을 어기다 act against a party policy.

**당목**(唐木) Chinese cotton goods; cotton (cloth).

**당무**(黨務) party affairs. ¶~를 처리하다 manage 〔conduct〕 party affairs / 그 당은 원내 대책 협의를 위해 ~회의를 소집할 예정이다 The party is to call a meeting of its executive committee to discuss the party's floor strategy. ◉ ~위원 an executive member of a party: ~ 위원회 the executive committee of a party. ~회의 a meeting of the executive members of a party.

**당밀**(糖蜜) syrup (순수한); golden syrup (저순도의); molasses 《미》; (black) treacle 《영》.

**당번**(當番) 《의무·일》 duty; watch; turn (차례); 《사람》 a person on duty 〔watch〕. ~하다 be on 「duty 〔watch, a shift〕. ¶~이 끝나다 be off duty / 오늘 ~은 누구냐 Who is on duty today? / (오늘은) 내가 ~이다 I am on duty (today). / 내일은 네가 ~이다 It is your turn to be on duty tomorrow. / 매주 한 번씩 ~을 한다 I have to be on duty once a week. / 내주는 내가 청소 ~이다 It's my turn to do the cleaning next week. ◉ ~표 a roster. 청소~ *one's* turn 〔duty〕 for sweeping.

**당부**(當付) a request; an entreaty. ~하다 ask 〔request, charge, tell, bid〕 《*a person*》 to *do* 《*something*》. ¶뒷일을 ~하다 ask 《*a person*》 to take care of future affairs / 신신 ~하다 ask earnestly; entreat / 이 말씀을 전하라는 ~를 받고 왔습니다 I was told to see and tell you this.

**당부**(當否) right or wrong (옳고 그름); propriety or impropriety (적부); justice or unjustice (정당·부당).

**당분**(糖分) sugar content; (the amount

of) sugar. ¶ 콩의 ～ the sugar content in the bean / ～이 많은 식품 sugar-rich food(s); food(s) with a higher sugar content / ～이 적은 포도 grapes low in sugar / ～을 함유하다 contain sugar / ～을 섭취하다 take in 〔absorb〕 sugar / 오줌에 가끔 ～이 섞여 나오다 have sugar in the urine off and on / 오줌의 ～을 검사하다 examine 《*a person's*》 urine for sugar / ～은 가급적 먹지 않는 것이 좋겠습니다 You may as well be moderate in eating sugary food. ◉ ～ 측정기 a saccharometer.

**당분간**(當分間) 《지금 현재》 for the present; 《얼마 동안》 for some time (to come); for a while; for the time being. ¶ ～ 바쁘다 I am rather busy for the present. / 이 돈만 있으면 ～ 꾸려나갈 수 있다 I can do with this amount of money for the time being. / ～ 비는 오지 않을 게다 It will not rain for some time. / 그 환자는 ～ 면회 사절이다 The patient is not allowed to see anyone for some time.

**당비**(黨費) party expenditure 〔expenses〕; expenditure 〔expenses〕 of a party; 《당원이 내는》 party fee. ¶ ～를 내다 contribute toward party expenditure.

**당비름**(唐—) 〖식물〗 a Joseph's coat.

**당사**(當社) our company 〔firm〕.

**당사**(黨舍) the headquarters of a party.

**당사국**(當事國) the country concerned.

**당사자**(當事者) the person 〔party〕 concerned; an interested party; a party 《to a suit》. ¶ ～간의 해결 settlement out of court / ～ 간에 협상하다 negotiate with persons concerned / 직접 관계 있는 ～ parties immediately interested / 결론은 ～간 협의에 맡겨졌다 The conclusion was left (up) to a conference between the persons 〔parties〕 concerned. ◉ ～일동 all concerned. 결혼～ the contracting parties in a marriage.

**당선**(當選) ① 《선거에》 being elected; winning an election. ～하다 be elected; win the election; win a seat in the National Assembly; be returned 《to the National Assembly》; be voted into office. ¶ ～ 가망이 있는 후보자 a candidate in the winning; a strong candidate / ～권 내에 들다 be in the running; have a fair chance of success / ～권 밖이다 be out of the running / ～이 확실하다 be sure of being returned / 백표 차로 ～되다 win the election by a majority of 100 votes / 최고 득표로 ～되다 be elected at the head of the poll / 대통령에 ～되다 win the presidency / 의장〔시장〕에 ～되다 be elected chairperson 〔mayor〕 / 그의 ～은 무효가 되었다 His election was invalidated 〔annulled〕.
② 《현상에》 winning a prize. ～하다 win a prize; [사물이 주어] be accepted 〔selected〕. ¶ 그녀는 현상 논문에서 1등으로 ～되었다 She won the first prize in the prize essay contest.
◉ ～무효 annulment of *one's* election; invalidity of election return: ～ 무효 소송 an election petition. ～소설 a prize novel. ～자 a successful candidate; the elected [총칭]; 《현상의》 a prizewinner. ～작 a prizewinner; a prizewinning work: ～작가 a prizewinner. 무투표～ being elected without voting: 그는 무투표로 시장에 ～되었다 He was elected mayor without voting.

**당세**(當世) the present time 〔day, age〕; the day; the time.

**당세**(黨勢) the strength 〔size, prestige〕 of a party; party influence. ¶ ～를 확장하다 expand the party strength; enhance the party prestige / ～가 침체하다 The party is at a low ebb.

**당수**(黨首) the leader 〔head〕 of a political party. ¶ 3～의 회담 a conference 〔talk〕 among the leaders of three political parties.

**당숙**(堂叔) a male cousin of *one's* father; an uncle.

**당시**(唐詩) poems of Tang period; Tang poetry.

**당시**(當時) at that 〔the〕 time; then; in those days 〔times〕. ¶ ～의 then; of those days / ～의 국무총리 the then Prime Minister / ～의 대학생 university students of those days / 내란 ～ in those days of civil war / 그 소설은 ～에 대단한 인기였다 The novel had a great vogue in its day. / ～에는 비행기 같은 것은 없었다 In those days there were no such things as airplanes. / 그 ～ 그녀는 아직 학생이었다 She was still at school 「then 〔at that time〕. / ～의 그에겐 1만원이 큰 돈이었다 In those days 10,000 won was a big amount for him.

**당신**(當身) ① 《2인칭》 you; 《부부·애인 등의 호칭》 (my) dear; (my) darling. ¶ ～의 친구 your friend; a friend of yours. ② 《그 어른》 he; himself. ¶ 할아버지 ～께서 손수 지으신 집이다 This is the house which my grandfather built himself.

**당아욱**(唐—) 『식물』 a (common) mallow.

**당연하다**(當然—) (be) fair and proper; right(ful); reasonable; natural; expected; be a matter of course; be no wonder. ¶ 당연한 일 a matter of course / 당연한 결과 a natural 〔an expected, a logical〕 result 〔outcome〕 / 당연한 권리 an undoubted right / 당연한 의무 an inevitable duty / 당연한 일로 받아들이다 take 《*a thing*》 as a matter of course / 이치상 ~ be in the nature of things; stand to reason / 그가 화를 내는 것은 ~ It is natural that he should be angry. *or* He may well be angry. / 그가 벌〔상〕을 받는 것은 ~ He deserves punishment 〔praise〕. / 빚진 돈을 갚는 것은 ~ One ought to pay what one owes. / 네가 그렇게 말하는 것도 ~ You may well say so. / 네가 그렇게 생각하는 것은 ~ You have good reason to think so. / 네가 그것을 믿는 것은 ~ It is natural for you to believe it. / 그의 죽음은 당연하다고 생각했다 I felt his death served him right. / 그가 그 제안을 거절하는 것은 ~ It stands to reason that he should decline the offer.

**당연히**(當然—) justly; properly; naturally; as a matter of course; deservedly; necessarily; of course. ¶ ~ …이라고 생각하다 take it for granted that… / ~ 받아야 할 것을 받다 get 〔have〕 *one's* due 〔deserts〕 / 그는 ~ 벌을 받아야 한다 He deserves punishment.

**당원**(黨員) a member of a party; a party man 〔member〕; a partisan. ¶ ~이 되다 join a party / 그들은 평~이다 They are the rank and file of that party. ◉ ~명부 a list of the party members.

**당월**(當月) this month; the said 〔present〕 month; that month.

**당위**(當爲) 『철학』 what should be; what *one* should do.

**당의**(糖衣) 『약』 sugar-coating. ¶ ~의 sugar-coated / 알약에 ~를 입히다 sugar-coat a pill. ◉ ~정(錠) a sugar-coated pill 〔tablet〕.

**당의**(黨議) 『회의』 a party council; 《결의》 a party decision; 《강령》 a party policy 〔principle〕. ¶ ~에 의해서 결정되다 be decided at a party council.

**당인**(黨人) ＝당원(黨員). ◉ ~근성 partisan spirit.

**당일**(當日) (on) the 〔that〕 day; (on) the appointed day; (at) the date named. ¶ ~의 날씨 the weather of the day / ~한(限) 식권 a meal ticket valid for the day / ~한(限) 유효표 a day ticket / ~ 판매한 표 a ticket sold on the day 《of the performance》 / ~ 우천시에는 If it should 〔In case of〕 rain on that day… / ~ 세탁 《게시》 One day laundry. / 발행 ~한 유효 《표시》 Available 〔Good〕 for the day of issue only.

**당일치기**(當日—) ¶ ~ 여행 a day's trip / ~로 다녀오다 go and return in one day; return on the same day; make a day's trip 《to》 / 버스로 경주까지 ~로 갔다 올 수 있을까요 Can I get to Kyŏngju and back in a day by bus?

**당자**(當者) the person concerned 〔involved, in question〕; the concerned party.

**당장**(當場) 《즉시》 on the spot; then and there; here and now; immediately; promptly; at once. ¶ ~ 필요한 것 an immediate need / 돈을 ~ 갚으라 하다 demand 《*a person*》 pay the money back immediately / ~ 그 자리에서 처형하다 execute 《*a person*》 on the spot 〔right then and there〕 / ~ 일에 착수해라 Get (down) to work at once. / ~ 나가라 Get out right now. / ~ 시작하라 Start it without delay. / 돈이 ~ 필요하다 I want the money right now. / ~이라도 비가 올 것 같다 It may begin to rain at any moment.

**당쟁**(黨爭) party strife 〔rivalry〕; a party 〔an intraparty〕 conflict. ¶ ~에 초연하다 be above 「party strife 〔partisan wrangling〕 / ~을 일삼다 be given to party squabbles.

**당적**(黨籍) the party register. ¶ ~에 있다 be on the list of party members; belong to a party / ~을 가지다 affiliate *oneself* to 〔with〕 a political party / ~에서 떠나다 leave 〔secede from〕 the party; disaffiliate *oneself* from the party / ~에서 제적하다 strike 《*a person's*》 name off the party register; expel 《*a person*》 from the party / ~을 옮기다 come 〔go〕 over to another party. ◉ ~ 증명서 a certificate of party membership.

**당정협의**(黨政協議) a government-ruling party session; a special cabinet and ruling party consultative session.

**당조짐하다** keep a close watch on 《*a person's* conduct》; put 《*a person*》 under strict discipline; supervise strictly.

**당좌**(當座) 《예금》 a current deposit 〔account〕. ¶ ~를 트다 open a current account with a bank; open a banking 〔bank〕 account 《미》/ ~에 예금하다 deposit *one's* money on current account. ◉ ~계정 a current account (생략 C/A). ~대부금 a call loan; call money. ~대월 an overdraft; an overdrawing account. ~수표 a check 《미》; a cheque 《영》. ~예금 a checking 〔current〕 account 〔deposit〕.

**당지**(唐紙) ricepaper; Chinese paper.

**당지**(當地) this place 〔district, city, town〕; (down) here. ¶ ~에 오시거든 꼭 들러 주십시오 Please drop in when you happen to be in this area 〔town〕.

**당지기**(堂—) the janitor of 「a private school 〔a temple〕.

**당지다** be pressed and hardened; become 〔get〕 hard 〔solid〕 by pressure.

**당직**(當直) being on duty 〔watch〕. ~하다 be on (night) duty; carry on duty; keep watch. ¶ ~을 교대하다 relieve the watch / ~을 인계하다〔받다〕 hand 〔take〕 over a duty / ~이다 be on (night) duty; be on watch.
◉ ~선원 an officer on watch 〔duty〕. ~수당 pay for night duty. ~실 a night duty room. ~원 a person on duty 〔watch〕; a duty man. ~의사 a duty doctor; 《야간의》 a night doctor. ~장교 an orderly officer; an officer of the day 〔guard〕; 《해군의》 a watch officer. ~표 a watch bill 〔list〕.

**당직**(黨職) a party post. ◉ ~개편 a reshuffle 〔reorganization〕 of the party's hierarchy. ~자 a party executive; an executive staff member of a party.

**당질**(堂姪) a son of a male cousin. ◉ ~녀 a daughter of a male cousin with the same surname.

**당집**(堂—) a temple; a shrine.

**당차다** be small but sturdy built.

**당착**(撞着) (a) contradiction; (an) inconsistency; clash; conflict. ⇨ 모순. ~하다 be contradictory 《to》; be inconsistent 《with》; clash; conflict 《with》. ◉ 자가~ self-contradiction.

**당첨**(當籤) prize winning. ~하다 win a prize; draw a winning 〔lucky〕 number. ¶ 일등에 ~하다 win first prize / 복권에 ~되다 win a prize in a (public) lottery. ◉ ~권 a winning 〔prize〕 ticket. ~률 the ratio of winning numbers. ~번호 a winning 〔lucky〕 number. ~자 the winner of the prize; the drawer of the lucky number: 즉석복권 ~자 an instant lottery winner.

**당초**(當初) = 애초.

**당초문**(唐草紋) an arabesque (pattern, design).

**당치않다**(當—) 《불합리하다》 (be) unreasonable; absurd; 《부당하다》 (be) undeserved; unjust; unfair; improper; unjustified; unlawful; unmerited; undue; preposterous (터무니없는). ¶ 당치 않은 값 an unreasonable 〔exorbitant〕 price / 당치 않은 벌 undeserved punishment / 당치 않은 생각〔말〕 an absurd 〔a preposterous〕 idea 〔remark〕 / 당치 않은 요구 an unjustified 〔unlawful〕 demand / 당치 않은 조치 unfair measures / 당치 않은 소리 (Stuff and) nonsense! *or* How absurd! *or* Don't talk such nonsense. / 그런 당치 않은 소리가 어디 있어 What can be more absurd? / 그가 그런 말을 하다니 ~ It is unreasonable of him to say such a thing.

**당칙**(黨則) the party rules 〔regulations〕.

**당파**(黨派) a party; a faction (당내의 파벌); a school (학파); 《도당》 a clique; a league. ¶ 초~ 외교 supraparty diplomacy / ~적 partisan; factional / 비~적인 nonparty; nonpartisan / ~적 감정 party 〔partisan〕 feeling / ~에 관계없이〔~를 묻지 않고〕 regardless of party affiliation / ~로 갈리다 split into factions / ~를 만들다 form a party 〔faction, clique〕 / ~를 지어 싸우다 dispute in factions / ~에 속하다 belong to a party 〔faction〕 / 그 당에는 몇 개의 유력한 ~가 있다 There are several powerful factions in the party. ◉ ~심 party 〔partisan〕 spirit; partisanship; partyism: ~심이 강한 정치가 a party-spirited 〔factional〕 politician. ~싸움 a party dispute.

**당폐**(黨弊) party evils; party abuses.

**당하다**(當—) ① 《사리에 맞다》 (be) reasonable; rational; sensible; natural; right. ¶ 당한 말을 하다 talk sense.
② 《만나다》 meet with; come up against; be confronted with 〔by〕; face; encounter; 《겪다》 go through; experience; suffer 《pain》; be subjected to. ¶ 불행을 ~ experience 〔encounter〕 a disaster / 사고를 ~ meet with an accident / 큰 손해를 ~ suffer 〔sustain, have〕 a heavy loss / 패배를 ~ suffer a defeat; lose a game 〔war〕 / 어려운 일을 ~ face 〔be confronted by〕 a difficulty; run 〔come〕 up against a diffi-

culty / 그것은 당해 보지 않은 사람이면 모른다 It is beyond the imagination of anyone who has not experienced.
③《감당·필적하다》match; be equal to; be a match for; rival 《*a person*》; compete with. ¶ …에는 당할 수 없다 be no match for 《*a person*》/ 난국에 ∼ tackle a difficult situation / 두 명을 당할 만큼 강하다 be strong enough to be a match for two men / 힘으로는 아무도 그를 당할 수 없다 No one can match him in strength. / 그녀를 당할 사람은 아마 없을 것이다 We shall never see her match.
④《남에게》have 《something undesirable》 done; 《속다》 be taken in; be cheated; be outwitted; 《재해 등을》 be hit 《by》. ¶ 끝내 당했다 I am done for at last. / 감쪽같이 당했다 I was fairly caught. *or* I was fooled. *or* I was taken in.

**-당하다**(當—) suffer; undergo; sustain; be afflicted with. ¶ 공격당하다 be attacked / 구타당하다 be struck; get licked; receive a blow / 배척당하다 get boycotted / 섬멸당하다 be annihilated / 거절당하다 be refused; get turned down.

**당해**(當該) concerned; proper; competent; appropriate. ◉ ∼관청 the appropriate 〔competent, proper〕 authorities; the authorities concerned.

**당헌**(黨憲) the party's constitution.

**당혹**(當惑) ∼하다 be perplexed; be embarrassed; be puzzled 〔baffled〕.

**당혼하다**(當婚—) reach a marriageable age.

**당화**(糖化) 〖화학〗 saccharification. ∼하다 make 〔turn〕 into sugar; saccharify.

**당황하다**(唐惶·唐慌—) be confused 〔flustered, bewildered, embarrassed〕; be flurried 〔upset, hurried〕; lose *one's* head 〔self-possession〕; be perplexed 〔puzzled〕; be at a loss. ¶ 당황하여 confusedly; in a hurry 〔flurry〕; in confusion / 당황케 하다 throw 《*a person*》 into confusion; confuse; embarrass; upset / 당황하여 계산이 틀렸다 In my hurry I made an error in calculation. / 그녀는 위기에 처해도 당황하지 않았다 She remained calm even in the crisis. / 뜻하지 않은 그의 방문에 모두 당황했다 They were upset by his surprise visit. / 그의 얼굴엔 당황하는 기색이 보였다 His face expressed perplexity. / 뜻밖의 질문을 받고 당황했다 I got confused at the unexpected question. / 그는 어떤 일이 닥쳐도 당황하는 일이 없다 He is equal to any occasion. / 나는 가방을 지하철에 놓고 내린 것을 깨닫고 매우 당황했다 I lost my head when I found I had left my bag on the subway train.

**닻** an anchor; 《소형의》 a grapnel. ¶ 닻고리 a ring / 닻줄 a cable; an anchor line / 닻을 감다〔올리다〕 weigh 〔heave up, raise, pull up〕 anchor / 닻을 주다〔내리다〕 drop 〔cast, let fall〕 the anchor; let go the anchor / 닻이 걸리다 an anchor bites 〔holds〕/ 배는 닻을 내리고 있었다 The ship was at anchor.

**닿다** ①《접하다》touch; reach. ¶ 손 닿는〔닿지 않는〕 곳에 within 〔beyond, out of〕 *one's* reach / 눈 닿는 데까지 as far as the eye can reach / 손이 천장에 ∼ *one's* hand reaches the ceiling / 늘어진 가지가 물에 ∼ drooping branches touch the water / 손이 땅에 닿을 때까지 몸을 앞으로 굽혀라 Bend over until your hands touch the ground. / 어린이 손이 닿지 않는 곳에 보관할 것《주의》 Keep out of reach of children.
②《도착하다》reach; arrive 《at, in》; get to. ¶ 무사히 ∼ arrive in safety; 《물건이》 arrive in good condition 〔order〕/ 집에 ∼ get home; reach *one's* house / 배가 목적지에 ∼ a ship reaches its destination / 그는 드디어 목적지에 닿았다 He found his way to the place at length. / 새마을호는 정각에 대전에 닿았다 The Saemaŭl reached 〔got to〕 Taejŏn on schedule. / 이 열차로 가시면 내일 아침 목포에 닿습니다 This train will land you in Mokp'o tomorrow morning. / 짐이 네게 닿았느냐 Has the baggage reached you?
③《연줄이》have pull; have connections. ¶ 저 회사에 연줄이 안 닿느냐 Don't you have any connections in that company? / 그 회사에는 연줄이 닿지 않아 취직할 수 없다 I lack the connections to get a job at the company.
④《이치에》hold up; be sound; 《조리에》 be consistent; hang together. ¶ 조리가 닿지 않는 말을 하다 talk incoherently; utter an incoherent remark / 그의 요구는 사리에 닿지 않는다 His claim hardly stands to reason.

**닿소리** 〖언어〗 a consonant.

**대**[1] 〖식물〗 (a) bamboo. ¶ 대껍질 a bamboo sheath / 대꼬챙이 a pointed bamboo stick / 대나무 세공 bamboo work / 대마디 a bamboo joint 〔node〕/ 대막대 a bamboo stick 〔pole〕/ 대바늘

a bamboo (fiber) needle / 대숲 a bamboo 「thicket 〔glove〕 / 대울타리 a bamboo fence / 대잎 a bamboo blade / 대창 a bamboo spear / 대를 쪼개다 split a bamboo.

**대**[2] ① 《줄기》 a stalk; a stem; a halm (벼 따위); a cane (대나무 따위); 《막대》 a pole; a rod; a staff; 《붓·펜의》 a holder; 《담뱃대》 a (tobacco) pipe. ② 《줏대》 a definite opinion of *one's* own; a conviction; a set idea. ¶ 대가 세다 be stubborn / 대가 약하다 be weak-kneed; be timid; be fainthearted / 대가 센 사람 a man of strong convictions. ③ 《담배의》 a cigaret(te); a pipeful of tobacco; a smoke; a fill (양). ¶ 담배 한 대 a cigarette; a pipeful of tobacco / 담배를 한 대 권하다 offer 《*a person*》 a smoke / 담배를 한 대 피우다 smoke a pipe; have 〔take〕 a smoke.
④ 《주먹 따위》 a blow; a stroke; a hit. ¶ 한 대에 at 「a 〔one〕 blow; with one 「stroke 〔blow〕 / 한 대 먹이다 strike 《*a person*》 a blow; deal 〔give〕 《*a person*》 a blow.

**대**(大) 《큼》 greatness; largeness; bigness; 《크기》 large size; 《거대한》 huge; giant; grand; vast; 《손해 따위의》 heavy. ¶ 대사고 a terrible accident / 대사업 a great enterprise / 대음악회 a grand concert / 대서울 Great Seoul / 대승리 a 「signal 〔sweeping〕 victory / 대우주 macrocosm / 대평원 a vast plain / 실물대 as large as life; life-size / 대를 살리고 소를 죽이다 renounce the small in order to secure the great; amputate a limb to save the body.

**대**(代) ① 《시대》 a time; a period; an age; 《세대》 a generation; a lifetime (일대); 《치세》 a reign; a dynasty (왕조); a family line (가계).
¶ 5대 five generations / 4대조 *one's* ancestor four generations back / 아들대 the filial generation / 아버지 대에는 in *one's* father's time / 2000년대(에) (in) the 2000's / 몇 대에 걸쳐서 for several generations / 대를 잇다 carry on a family line / 대가 끊어지다 a family line breaks; a line dies out / 그녀는 30대이다 She is in her thirties. / 그 가족은 여러 대 동안 같은 집에서 살아왔다 The family has lived in the same house for generations. / 링컨은 미국의 몇 대 대통령입니까 Where does Lincoln stand in the order of the American presidents? *or* What is the number of Lincoln's presidency? ② 《값》 charge; fee; rate; cost. ¶ 도서대 book fee / 양복대 the cost of a suit.

**대**(隊) 《일행》 a party; 《군인의》 a company; a corps (*pl.* corps); a body; a squad; 《악대의》 a band; 《대오》 the ranks; a line; formation. ¶ 대를 짓다 form a 「party 〔body〕 / 비행대 a flying corps / 대대 a battalion / 중대 a company (보병); a battery (포병).

**대**(對) ① 《짝》 a pair; a counterpart; a parallel; a couple (쌍). ② 《상대》 versus (생략 v., vs.); against; between; 《비율》 to; anti-. ¶ 민주주의 대 공산주의 democracy versus communism / 자본가 대 노동자의 투쟁 a struggle of labor against capital / 공대공 〔공대지, 지대공〕 유도탄 an air-to-air 〔an air-to-surface, a ground-to-air〕 guided missile / 대미 무역(관계) 《Korea's》 trade (relations) with the United States / 한국의 대미 정책 Korea's policy toward the United States / 3대 1의 스코어 a score of 3 to 1 / 20대 57의 다수 a majority of 57 against 20 / 5대 3으로 K 팀이 이겼다 The score was five to three in favor of the K team.

**대**(臺) ① 《받침》 a stand; a rest; a rack (걸쳐 놓은); a table (탁자); a support (버팀); a pedestal (비석 따위의). ¶ 악보대 a music stand / 화장대 a dressing table; a toilet-stand; a dresser. ② 《단위》 a car; a cart; a plane. ¶ 소 달구지 세 대 three carts / 비행기 세 대 three airplanes / 다섯 대의 자동차에 분승하다 ride in five separate cars. ③ 《액수》 a level; a mark. ¶ 천만원대에 달하다 rise to the level of 10 million won; reach the 10 million won mark / 수입이 1억 달러대를 돌파했다 Imports have passed $100 million mark. / 광산주(株)가 천원대로 떨어졌다 The mine stocks sagged to the 1,000 won level. ④ 《고대(高臺)》 a heights; an eminence; a hill.

**대가**(大家) ① 《권위자》 a great master; an authority 《on》; a great expert 《on》; 《학문의》 a great scholar. ¶ 인류학의 ∼ an authority on anthropology / 경제학의 ∼ an expert in economics / 음악〔그림〕의 a 「great musician 〔master painter〕 / ∼연(然)하다 pretend to be an authority; pose as an authority; put on the airs of a great master / 그 분야의 ∼로서 인정받고 있다 be 「an acknowledged 〔a recognized〕 「authority on the subject 〔expert in the

line].
② 《번창한 집안》 a big family; an illustrious family; a rich family.
③ 《큰 집》 a big house; a mansion.
◉ 대갓집 a wealthy house; a powerful [distinguished] family.

**대가**(代價) price; cost; (a) charge. ⇨ 값. ¶ ∼를 치르다 pay the price; pay for 《an article》 / 목숨이라는 ∼를 치르고 at the cost of *one's* life / 비싼 ∼를 치르게 하다 [비유적] make 《*a person*》 pay dear 《for》 / 국민은 어떤 ∼를 치르더라도 평화를 얻고 싶어한다 The people want peace 「at all costs [at any price].

**대가**(對價) compensation; value; a consideration (계약상의); 《답례》 (a) return. ¶ …의 ∼로서 in 「compensation [return] for…; as a consideration for… / 충분한 ∼를 받다 get good value 《for》 / ∼성 뇌물을 받다 accept a bribe in 「return [consideration] for service promised.

**대가극**(大歌劇) a grand opera.

**대가다** 《시간에》 get there [arrive] on time (정각에); be [arrive] in time 《for》 (늦지 않게). ¶ 수업 시간에 ∼ arrive at school on time / 약속한 시간에 ∼ present *oneself* at the appointed time.

**대가리** the top; the point; the head; the tip; the skull; the pate. ¶ 생선∼ the jowl / 소[돼지]∼ the head of 「an ox [a pig] / 뱀이 사리를 틀고 ∼를 쳐들고 있었다 A snake lay in a coil with its head raised.

**대가족**(大家族) a big [large] family. ¶ ∼을 거느리고 있다 have a large family to support. ◉ ∼ 제도 a large-family system; an extended family system.

**대각**(對角) 〖수학〗 the opposite angle. ◉ ∼선 a diagonal (line): ∼선의 diagonal / ∼선을 이루어 diagonally / ∼선을 긋다 draw a diagonal. 내∼ the 「inner [interior] opposite angle.

**대각거리다** clack; clatter; keep snapping. ¶ 대각대각 clacking continuously / 그릇이 ∼ dishes are clattering.

**대각하다**(大覺—) perceive absolute truth; attain divine enlightenment.

**대간첩**(對間諜) counter-espionage. ◉ ∼ 작전 《conduct, be engaged in》 a counter-espionage operation: ∼ 작전 본부 the Counter-Infiltration Operations Center; the Counter-Espionage Operations Headquarters.

**대갈** a horseshoe nail. ◉ ∼마치 a farrier's hammer; 《사람》 a person hardened through adversities; a person steeled [inured] to hardships. ∼못 a nail with a big head; a rivet. ∼장군 a man with a big head.

**대갈**(大喝) a loud cry; a great yell. ∼하다 shout (in a thunderous voice) 《at》; thunder [roar] 《at》. ¶ ∼ 일성(一聲) 《in》 a thunderous shout.

**대감**(大監) His [Your] Excellency.

**대감독**(大監督) 〖기독교〗 an archbishop; a primate (영국 국교의).

**대강**(大綱) ⇨ 대강령. ① 《기본 원칙》 fundamental [general] principles; 《formulate》 main lines 《of》; 《개요·대요》 an outline; the substance 《of *one's* speech》. ¶ 사건의 ∼ 줄거리 the substance of the case / 경제 정책의 ∼을 정하다 lay down the fundamental principles of economic policy / ∼을 말하다 outline; give an outline 《of *one's* policies》 / ∼을 파악하다 have a general idea 《of》 / 조약의 ∼에 관해 합의에 이르다 reach agreement on the main substance of the treaty.
② 《대충》 roughly; cursorily; summarily; about; 《거의》 nearly; almost; 《대체로》 in general; generally. ¶ ∼대강 roughly; cursorily; in rough outline / ∼ 어림잡다 make a rough estimate / ∼ 훑어보다 glance over 《a letter》; run over 《papers》; skim 「through [over] 《a letter》; take a cursory view of 《a book》.

**대강**(代講) ∼하다 lecture as a substitute; substitute 《as teacher》; substitute-teach; teach for [in place of] 《*a person*》. ¶ ∼하는 사람 a vicarious [substitute] lecturer / 김 선생의 ∼을 하다 supply [fill] Mr. Kim's place.

**대강령**(大綱領) basic [fundamental] principles; general rules [principles].

**대갚음**(對—) (a) repayment; a return; requital in kind; 《보복》 revenge; retaliation; tit for tat; an eye for an eye. ∼하다 repay; return; requite; retaliate; get even with; give measure for measure; pay back in kind. ¶ 은혜를 ∼하다 return a favor; repay 《*a person*》 for *his* kindness / 원한을 ∼하다 revenge; avenge; give measure for measure / 언젠가는 너에게 ∼하겠다 I'll get even with you one day. *or* I'll pay you back for this one day.

**대개**(大槪) ① 《개요》 an outline; a summary; the substance.
② 《일반적으로》 generally; in general;

usually (대체로); 《대부분》 mostly; most 《of》; for the most part; 《거의》 nearly; about; almost. ¶ ~의 경우에 generally; in most cases / ~ 모두 nearly all; practically all / 나는 ~ 7시에 일어난다 I usually get up at seven. / 학생은 ~ 그 사전을 가지고 있다 Most students have that dictionary. / 나는 일요일에는 ~ 집에 있습니다 I am usually at home on Sunday(s). / 나는 일요일에는 ~ 외출합니다 I go out nearly every Sunday.

**대개념**(大概念) 〖논리〗 a major concept.

**대거**(大擧) 《거사》 a great enterprise; an uprising for a cause; an attack in full force; 《서둚》 doing a job in a great hurry. ~하다 launch a great enterprise; do a job in a great hurry; 《한목에 많이》 [부사] in a body; in (great) force; in a (great) mass; in large numbers; on a large scale. ¶ ~ 공격하다 attack with a large army; launch a large-scale offensive; attempt a great drive.

**대검**(帶劍) 《칼을 참》 wearing a sword (칼차기); 《총검》 a bayonet. ~하다 wear a sword 〔saber〕; be armed with a sword. ¶ ~을 빼다 draw *one's* sword 〔bayonet〕 / ~을 허용〔금지〕하다 allow 〔forbid〕 《*a person*》 to wear a sword.

**대검찰청**(大檢察廳) the Supreme Public Prosecutor's Office. ◉ ~ 중앙 수사부 the Central Investigation Division at the Prosecutor-General's Office.

**대견하다, 대견스럽다** 《부족함이 없다》 (be) sufficient; enough; 《흡족하다》 (be) satisfactory; laudable; admirable; praiseworthy. ¶ 대견스럽게 여기다 feel satisfactorily; take 《it》 laudable 〔admirable〕; think much of 《*a person*》.

**대결**(對決) confrontation; a showdown 《미》. ~하다 confront 《with》; have 〔come to〕 a showdown 《with》. ¶ 아랍과 이스라엘의 ~ the Arab-Israeli confrontation / 여야간의 ~ a confrontation between the ruling party and the opposition parties / ~시키다 confront 《the accused with *his* accuser》; bring 《*a person*》 face to face 《with》 / 가능하다면 ~을 피하고 싶다 I want to avoid a showdown if possible. / 두 사람간의 법정 ~은 피할 수 없었다 A court showdown between the two was inevitable. ◉ ~장면 a confrontation scene. ~정책 confrontation policy.

**대경**(大慶) an occasion for great rejoicing; great happiness.

**대경**(大驚) great astonishment. ~하다 be astonished; be greatly surprised; be startled. ◉ ~ 실색(失色) turning pale from astonishment 〔fear〕: ~ 실색하다 turn pale from astonishment; be greatly startled 〔astonished〕; be taken aback.

**대계**(大系) an outline 《of the Korean history》.

**대계**(大計) a long-range plan; a grand design; a far-reaching 〔far-sighted〕 plan. ¶ 국가의 백년 ~를 세우다 formulate a far-sighted national policy; establish a grand national policy on a long-range bases.

**대고** 《자꾸》 persistently; importunately; unceasingly; without letup; keeping at 《*a thing*》; keeping after 《*a person*》. ¶ ~ 조르다 press 〔importune, badger, pester, keep after〕 《*a person* to do *a thing*》 / ~ 공부하다 keep at *one's* studies; keep studying without letup / ~ 권하다 strongly urge 《*a person* to *do*》; press 《drink》 on 《*a person*》 / 형한테 영화 구경을 가자고 ~ 조르다 keep begging 〔keep after〕 *one's* brother to go to the movies.

**대고모**(大姑母) = 왕고모(王姑母).

**대공** 〖건축〗 a king post.

**대공**(大功) a great merit; meritorious services; a signal deed 〔exploit〕. ¶ ~을 세우다 render meritorious service; distinguish *oneself;* achieve great things.

**대공**(對空) anti-air(craft); ack-ack 《구어》. ◉ ~ 감시병 a spotter; a star-gazer. ~레이더 an air search radar. ~무장 antiaircraft armaments. ~미사일 an antiaircraft missile. ~방어 antiaircraft defense. ~사격 antiaircraft 〔ack-ack〕 fire. ~십자 포화 a box barrage. ~포(砲) an antiaircraft gun: ~ 포화 antiaircraft fire; antiaircraft gunfire; flak.

**대공국**(大公國) the grand duchy.

**대과**(大過) a serious error; a grave mistake; a blunder. ¶ ~ 없이 근무하다 serve 《for twenty years》 without committing 〔free from〕 (any) serious mistakes 〔major blunders〕.

**대과거**(大過去) 〖문법〗 the past perfect tense; the pluperfect (tense).

**대관**(大官) a dignitary; a high official; a bigwig 《구어》.

**대관**(大觀) a comprehensive 〔general〕 view; an overall view. ~하다 take an overall 〔a general〕 view of.

**대관**(戴冠) coronation; crowning. ◉ ~

식 a coronation (ceremony): ~식을 거행하다 perform a coronation.

**대관절**(大關節) 《요컨대》 in brief; in a word; in short; 《도대체》《what, how, why》 on earth; (what) in the world; in the name of God; 《구어》 (what) the devil 〔hell〕. ¶ ~ 너는 누구냐 What on earth are you? / ~ 저게 뭐냐 What in the world is that? / ~ 어디 갔다 오는 거요 Where the hell have you been? / ~ 무엇을 하고 있었나 What in the name of hell have you been doing? / ~ 무슨 일이요 Just what is the matter? *or* What in the world has happened? *or* What the hell? / ~ 무얼 가지고 싸우시오 What on earth are you quarreling about?

**대괄호**(大括弧) 『수학』 (square) brackets.

**대교**(大橋) a grand bridge. ¶ 마포〔반포〕 ~ Mapo 〔Banpo〕 Grand Bridge.

**대구**(大口) 『어류』 a codfish. ◉ ~알 the cod roe. ~탕 cod soup.

**대구**(對句) an antithesis (*pl.* -ses); a couplet; a distich. ¶ ~를 이루다 form 〔make〕 an antithesis 《to, of》.

**대구루루** rolling; rumbling; with a rolling 〔rumbling〕 sound. ~하다 roll; rumble; make a rolling 〔rumbling〕 sound. ¶ ~ 구르다 keep rolling / 통이 마루에서 ~ 굴렀다 The barrel rolled over and over on the floor. / 유리잔이 식탁에서 ~ 굴러 떨어졌다 The glass rolled off the table.

**대국**(大局) the general 〔whole〕 situation. ¶ ~적으로는 generally speaking; on the whole / ~적으로 보다 take a wide 〔large〕 view of 《the situation》; see 《*something*》 in perspective / ~적으로 보면 on a broad survey / ~을 살피다 survey 〔study〕 the general situation / ~에 중대한 영향을 미치다 have an important effect on the whole situation / ~을 잘못 판단하다 take a wrong view of things; miss the main point 〔issue〕 of things / 보다 ~적으로 보고 판단해라 Judge the matter from a wider point of view 〔on a broader basis〕.

**대국**(大國) a big nation 〔country〕; a great power.

**대국**(對局) ① 《난국에의》 facing a situation; confronting 《a difficulty》. ~하다 face a situation; confront a difficulty. ② 《바둑·장기의》 playing a game 《with *a person*》. ~하다 play a game 《with》.

**대군**(大君) a (Royal) prince.

**대군**(大軍) a large 〔big〕 army 〔force〕.

**대군**(大群) a large crowd 〔herd (소, 돼지의), flock (양 따위의), shoal (물고기의), school (물고기, 고래의)〕 《of》. ¶ 철새의 ~ a large flock of migratory birds / 메뚜기의 ~ swarms of locusts.

**대굴대굴** ⇨ 떼굴떼굴.

**대권**(大圈) a great circle. ◉ ~항로 the great circle route 〔track〕. ~항법 great 〔globular〕 circle sailing 〔navigation〕.

**대권**(大權) 《최고 권력》 the supreme power; a prerogative; 《주권》 the sovereign authority; 《통치권》 sovereignty; the governing power. ¶ 국왕의 ~ the royal prerogative / 병마(兵馬)의 ~ the supreme authority over the army / ~을 침해하다 encroach upon the supreme power / (국가) ~을 장악하다 hold the supreme power (of the state); reign supreme. ◉ 비상~ emergency power.

**대궐**(大闕) the royal palace.

**대규모**(大規模) a large 〔grand〕 scale. ¶ ~의 large-scale; grand-scale / ~로 on a large 〔a massive〕 scale; in a big 〔large〕 way / ~의 밀수 smuggling on a large scale / …을 ~로 사용하다 make massive use of... / 그들은 ~ 방공훈련을 했다 They staged a full-scale air defense drill. ◉ ~ 작전 large-scale (military) operations.

**대그락거리다** keep clattering 〔rattling〕. ¶ 그릇이 ~ dishes are clattering away / 연필이 대그락거린다 Pencils keep rattling 《in the pencil case》.

**대그락대그락** clattering 〔rattling〕 repeatedly; clatteringly.

**대그르르하다** ⇨ 대글대글하다.

**대그릇** bamboo ware; a bamboo bowl.

**대극**(大戟) 『식물』 a spurge.

**대근하다**(代勤—) take over the duties 《of a sick colleague》.

**대글대글하다** be rather thick 〔big〕 among the thin 〔small〕 things.

**대금**(大金) a large amount 〔sum〕 of money; an enormous sum of money; a lot of money; big money 《구어》; 《고가》 a great cost. ⇨ 큰돈. ¶ ~을 내다 pay a big sum / 그는 ~을 들여 그 빌딩을 샀다 He bought the building at a great cost.

**대금**(大笒) 『악기』 a large transverse bamboo flute.

**대금**(代金) the 〔(a)〕 price (값); the 〔(a)〕 cost (비용); the 〔a〕 charge (요금); the (purchase) money. ¶ ~을 치르다 pay for 《*a thing*》; pay the price 《for》 / ~을 징수하다 collect bills / ~을 재촉하다 press 《*a person*》 for payment / ~을 계산하다 calculate 〔add up〕 the price / 여기 ~이 있습니다 Here is the money for it. / ~은 필요 없습니다 It is free of charge. *or* We charge nothing for it. / 그 가구는 아직 ~을 지불하지 않았다 That piece of furniture is not paid for yet. / 그에게 차 수리 ~으로 5만원을 청구했다 I charged him fifty thousand won for repairing the car. ◉ ~ 교환 우편 cash on delivery 《영》 (생략 C.O.D. Post); collect on delivery mail 《미》 (생략 C.O.D. mail): ~ 교환 우편으로 소포를 보내다 send a parcel C.O.D.

**대금**(貸金) 《돈놀이》 money-lending; usury (고리의); 《돈》 a loan; an advance (선(급)금). ~하다 lend money; make a loan 〔an advance〕 to. ¶ ~을 회수하다 collect 〔call in〕 loan. ◉ ~업 money-lending business: ~업자 a money-lender; a usurer; a loan shark 《미구어》. 단기~ short(-term) loan. 당좌~ call loan 〔money〕; money at 〔on〕 call. 장기~ time 〔long-term〕 loan.

**대금고**(貸金庫) a safe-deposit box. ⇨ 대여금고. ¶ 은행의 ~에 보석을 보관하다 keep jewelry in a safe-deposit box at a bank.

**대기**(大忌) strong aversion; abhorrence. ~하다 abhor; loathe; shun.

**대기**(大氣) the air; the atmosphere. ¶ ~의 atmospheric / ~중의 산소 atmospheric oxygen; oxygen in the atmosphere / ~상태가 불안정하다 atmospheric conditions are unsettled. ◉ ~관측 aeroscopy. ~론 aerology. ~분류(噴流) an atmospheric jet stream. ~압 the pressure of the atmosphere; atmospheric 〔air, barometic〕 pressure. ~차(差) 『천문』 refraction.

**대기**(大器) 《큰 그릇》 a large vessel; 《인재》 a great talent; a genius; a man of great caliber. ¶ 미완성의 ~ [비유적] a diamond in the rough / ~만성 Great talents mature late. *or* Great success does not usually occur early. / ~만성형 《사람》 a late bloomer 〔developer〕.

**대기**(待機) watching and waiting for a chance; standing by. ~하다 watch and wait 《for a chance》; stand 〔wait〕 「ready 〔in readiness〕 《for, to *do*》; stand by. ¶ ~ 명령을 받다 be ordered to be ready 《for》; be alerted 《for》 / ~를 명하다 alert 《the troops》; order 《*a person*》 to stand by / 자택 ~를 명받다 be told 「to stand by 〔to be on standby〕 at home / ~ 태세를 취하다 assume a watch-and-wait attitude / 경관을 ~시키다 put policemen on the alert / 비상 사태에 대비하여 경찰이 ~하고 있다 The police are on the alert 〔on standby〕 for an emergency. / 그 병원에서는 응급 환자를 대비해서 간호사가 24시간 ~하고 있다 At that hospital nurses stand on twenty-four-hour call in case of emergency. ◉ ~기간 a waiting period. ~발령 an order to leave *one's* post and to wait for further action: ~ 발령되다 be ordered to leave *one's* post and wait for further action. ~상태 stand-by status: ~ 상태에 있다 be standing by ready 《to *do*》; be on alert status. ~실 a waiting room. ~자 명부 a wait(-ing) list: 나를 ~자 명부에 올려 주세요 Put me on your wait list, please. ~차관(借款) stand-by credit: ~ 차관 협정을 맺다 conclude a stand-by credit agreement 《with》.

**대기권**(大氣圈) the atmosphere. ¶ ~ 밖(의 우주) 《from, into》 outer space / ~내 핵실험 an atmospheric nuclear test / ~ 밖으로 나가다 venture into outer space / ~밖으로 로켓을 발사하다 launch a rocket into outer space.

**대기업**(大企業) a large enterprise 〔corporation〕; a conglomerate (계열 회사를 거느린); [총칭] big business; major companies 〔firms〕.

**대기오염**(大氣汚染) air 〔atmospheric〕 pollution 〔contamination〕. ¶ 방사능 낙진에 의한 ~ air pollution by radioactive fallout / 배기 가스에 의한 ~ atmospheric contamination by exhaust gases 〔fumes〕 《from》. ◉ ~도 a degree of air pollution. ~ 방지법 the Air Pollution Control Act; the Clean Air Act 《미》.

**대길**(大吉) great good luck 〔fortune〕; excellent 〔best〕 luck. ~하다 have good luck; (be) auspicious 〔very lucky〕.

**대끼다** be (hard) put to it; be tried; see hardships; rough it; be driven from pillar to post. ¶ 세상 풍파에 ~ go through life's vicissitudes; experience many hardships in life.

**대낚시** pole-and-line fishing.

**대난**(大難) a great misfortune 〔calamity〕; great difficulties.

**대남**(對南) against the South 《Korea》. ¶ ~ 간첩 an espionage agent against the South / ~ 공작 operations against the South / ～ 방송 broadcasting toward the South.

**대납**(代納) payment by proxy. ～하다 pay for another; 《물납하다》 pay in kind.

**대낮** broad daylight; the middle of the day; high noon (정오). ¶ ～에 in the daytime; in the broad daylight / ～처럼 밝다 be as light as noonday; be as bright as day.

**대내**(對內) [형용사적] home; domestic; interior. ◉ ～문제 domestic issues 〔problems〕. ～정책 a domestic policy.

**대농**(大農) 《대농업》 large-scale farming; 《사람》 a big 〔wealthy〕 farmer.

**대뇌**(大腦) 『해부』 the cerebrum (*pl.* ～s, -bra); the brain proper. ¶ ～의 cerebral. ◉ ～막 the cerebral membrane. ～반구 a cerebral hemisphere. ～엽(葉) a cerebral lobe; a lobe of the brain. ～피질 cerebral cortex.

**대님** cloth bands used to tie up the lower ends of trousers; pants-leg ties. ¶ ～을 매다 fasten the bottoms of *one's* trousers with ties.

**대다**[1] ① 《연결·대면하다》 bring into contact; connect; link. ¶ 음극과 양극을 ～ bring the negative pole into contact with the positive / 살 사람과 팔 사람을 ～ bring a buyer into contact with a seller; arrange a meeting between buyer and seller / 홍선생을 좀 대 주십시오 《전화에서》 Will you get me Mr. Hong, please? *or* May I talk to Mr. Hong, please? / 회계과 좀 대 주세요 Put me through to the accounts section, please.

② 《손을》 touch; put (*one's* hand to); lay; place. ¶ 이마에 손을 ～ put *one's* hand to *one's* forehead / 진열품에 손대지 마시오 Don't touch the exhibits.

③ 《입에》 eat; drink; taste. ¶ 그는 술을 전혀 입에 대지 않는다 He does not drink wine at all. / 병든 아이는 아무 것도 입에 대지 않았다 The sick child ate nothing.

④ 《갖다 대다》 put; place; apply; lay; hold; press. ¶ 수화기를 귀에 ～ hold the receiver to *one's* ear / 청진기를 가슴에 ～ put a stethoscope to 《*a person's*》 chest / 화약에 성냥불을 ～ apply a match to powder.

⑤ 《착수·관계하다》 take to; put *one's* hand to 《a task》; set to work; start 《an enterprise》; set about 《*a thing*》; attempt (시도). ¶ 정치에 손을 ～ dabble 〔meddle〕 in politics / 여자에게 손을 ～ have an affair with a woman / 일에 손을 ～ start 〔begin〕 *one's* work; set about *one's* business / 투기에 손을 ～ take to 〔dabble in〕 speculation / 그는 자신 없는 일에는 손을 대지 않는다 He does not attempt a task he doesn't feel equal to.

⑥ 《붙이다》 fix; put; attach; line (옷에 안감을). ¶ 구두에 창을 ～ fix soles on *one's* shoes / 받침대를 ～ set up a prop; prop up a stick / 벽에 판자를 ～ fix a board on the wall / 옷에 헝겊을 ～ put a patch on *one's* clothes / 의복에 털가죽으로 안을 ～ line a garment with fur.

⑦ 《비교하다》 compare 《*a thing*》 with. ¶ 길이를 대보다 compare length / 번역문을 원문과 대보다 compare a translation with original / 그 책은 이 책에 댈 수 없다 That book can't be compared with this one.

⑧ 《귀찮게 굴다》 do; make. ¶ 성화를 ～ behave badly / 등쌀(을) ～ annoy / 그녀가 등쌀 대는 통에 못살겠다 She is so hard upon me.

⑨ 《시간에》 arrive 「in time (때를 맞춰) 〔on time (정각에)〕. ¶ 기차 시간에 ～ be in time for the train / 정각에 ～ 《a train》 come in on time.

⑩ 《…을 향해서》 aim; direct. ¶ 누구의 얼굴에 대고 침을 뱉다 spit in 《*a person's*》 face / 그것은 누굴 대고 하는 말이냐 Who is that remark aimed at?

⑪ 《의지하다》 lean 《*one's* body》 against. ¶ 나무에 등을 ～ rest 〔lean〕 *one's* back against a tree.

**대다**[2] ① 《물을》 draw (water) into; irrigate. ¶ 논에 물을 ～ draw water into a rice paddy; irrigate a rice paddy. ② 《공급·주선하다》 supply; provide; furnish. ¶ 대먹는 싸전 *one's* favorite rice store / 공장에 자재를 ～ supply a factory with materials / 변호사를 ～ provide 《the defendant》 with a lawyer / 아무한테 식량을 ～ provide 〔supply〕 *a person* with food; provide food for *a person* / 아들에게 학비를 ～ provide *one's* son with school expenses.

**대다**[3] ① 《일러주다》 tell; indicate; show; inform of; 《사실대로》 tell (the truth); speak up 〔out〕; confess; spit it out 《구어》. ¶ 글 뜻을 ～ give the meaning of a sentence / 길을 ～ show the way / 증거를 ～ give 〔produce〕 evidence / 사실을 대게 하다 make 《*a person*》 confess 〔own〕 the fact / 그가 알고만 있다면 사실을 기어이 대게 하겠다 If he knows,

I will have it out of him. / 숨기지 말고 바른대로 대라 Be frank with me and tell the truth. ②《핑계를》 make; find. ¶ 핑계를 ~ find 〔make〕 excuses / 그녀는 언제나 그럴 듯한 구실을 댄다 She always make plausible excuses.

**대다**[4] 《배·차 따위를》 pull 〔draw〕 up; bring to; berth 〔moor〕 《alongside》; stop. ¶ 자동차를 현관에 ~ pull a car up to the vestibule; bring 〔draw up〕 a car alongside the porch / 배를 선창에 ~ pull a boat up to the quay; bring a boat alongside the pier.

**대다수**(大多數) the greater part 《of》; the majority (★ 「과반수」의 뜻으로도 쓰임); a large 〔a great, an overwhelming〕 majority; the most part. ¶ ~는 mostly; for the most part / ~를 차지하다 hold 〔form〕 a great majority / ~의 지지를 받다 be supported by the majority / 주민의 ~는 농업에 종사하고 있다 The inhabitants are, for the most part, engaged in farming. / ~의 사람들은 그렇게 생각하지 않는다 Most people don't think so.

**대단원**(大團圓) a denouement; the (grand) finale; the end. ¶ ~의 막을 내리다 come to an end.

**대단찮다** ① 《수·양적으로》 be not many; be not much; be not big. ¶ 재간이 ~ have little ability 〔talent〕 / 손해가 ~ There is no great damage. / 대단찮은 돈이다 It's a small amount of money. / 그의 수입은 ~ His income is very small.
② 《대수롭지 않다》 (be) ordinary; mediocre; run-of-the-mill; 《구어》 be not so hot; be no great shakes. ¶ 대단찮은 학자 a third-rate scholar / 대단찮은 일에 매달리다 stick at trifles / 그는 정치가로는 ~ He is not much of a statesman. *or* He is no great shark as a statesman.
③ 《병세·사정이》 be not serious; be not grave; (be) trivial; slight (하찮음). ¶ 대단찮은 병 a slight illness / 그는 감기가 들었지만 대단찮은 모양이다 His cold does not seem so serious. / 그것은 대단찮은 일이다 It is nothing serious.
④ 《정도가》 be not severe; be not intense; (be) mild; moderate. ¶ 대단찮은 추위 a mild cold spell / 추위는 대단치 않았다 It was not very 〔so〕 cold.

**대단하다** ① 《많다》 (be) many; much; a lot of; a great deal of; considerable; enormous; immense; be a great deal. ¶ 대단한 금액 a vast sum / 대단한 사람들의 무리 a big crowd; an immense crowd of people / 대단한 재산 a considerable fortune / 대단한 출혈 excessive bleeding / 자네 대단한 배짱이로군 You have a lot of guts.
② 《위대하다》 (be) great; grand. ¶ 대단한 학자 a great scholar / 대단한 사람 a great man / 대단한 미인 a stunning beauty / 대단한 것 a valuable thing; a treasure / 그는 대단한 학자가 못된다 He is not much of a scholar. / 그의 능력은 대단한 것이 못된다고 생각한다 I have a low opinion of his abilities.
③ 《중요·심각하다》 (be) important; serious; grave. ¶ 대단한 문제 a serious problem / 대단한 사건 an awful 〔a terrible〕 accident / 병이 ~ be seriously ill / 그것은 우리들 생활에 대단한 영향을 미친다 It has an important influence upon our lives. / 이것은 그리 대단한 일이 아니다 This is not so serious 〔important〕. / 어느 대학을 나왔느냐는 대단한 문제가 아니다 It matters very little what college you graduated from.
④ 《심하다》 (be) severe; intense; terrible. ¶ 대단한 고통 great 〔severe〕 pain / 대단한 더위 terrible heat / 대단한 질투 intense jealousy / 대단한 추위 a severe cold spell / 그는 성이 나면 ~ He is terrible in anger.

**대단히** very; much (★ very는 주로 형용사·부사·현재분사를, much는 동사·과거분사를 수식함); very much; greatly; seriously; terribly; awfully; remarkably; extremely. ⇨ 매우. ¶ ~ 많은 돈 very much money (★ much는 형용사·부사의 비교급과 최상급을 수식함: *much* more money 「훨씬 많은 돈」 / be *much* better 「훨씬 좋다」 / be *much* 〔by far〕 the best 「뛰어나게 좋다」) / ~ 아름다운 여인 a very 〔most〕 beautiful woman / ~ 노하다 be very angry; be awfully mad / ~ 재미있다 be very interesting / ~ 피로하다 be terribly tired / ~ 즐거웠습니다 I had a very 〔really〕 good time. *or* I enjoyed myself very much. / 나는 그것에 ~ 흥미를 가지고 있다 I'm very 〔extremely〕 interested in it.

**대담**(大膽) boldness; daring; intrepidity; hardihood. ~하다 (be) bold; daring; intrepid; dauntless; stout-hearted; fearless (겁 없는); courageous. ¶ ~하게 fearlessly; boldly; daringly / ~(무쌍)한 군인 a dauntless 〔fearless〕 soldier / ~한 무늬가 있는 옷 a dress with a bold pattern / ~한 기도 a bold attempt; an adventurous undertaking / ~하게 나오다 show a bold front / ~하게도 …을 시도하다 make a brave try at 《*a matter, doing*》/ ~하게 행동하다 act boldly / ~한 녀석이다 He has iron nerves 〔nerves of steel〕. *or* How daring of him! / ~하게도 그는 혼자 나갔다 He was bold enough to go all alone. / 그는 때때로 ~한 발언을 한다 He sometimes expresses bold opinions.

**대담**(對談) a talk; a conversation; a dialogue; a *tête-a-tête* (F.); an interview. ~하다 talk 〔converse〕《with》; have a talk 〔an interview〕《with *a person*》; have a *tête-a-tête*. ¶ 나는 브라운 씨와 그 계획에 관해 장시간 ~했다 I had a long talk with Mr. Brown about the project.

**대답**(對答) an answer; a reply; 《응답》 a response; a rejoinder. ~하다 answer; reply; give an answer 〔a reply〕; 《반응》 respond 《to》. ¶ 호의적인 ~ a favorable answer / ~할 말이 없다 have no word in reply / 질문에 ~하다 answer a question / ~을 하지 않다 make no answer 〔reply〕; answer 《*a person*》 nothing / 그렇다고〔그렇지 않다고〕 ~하다 give an affirmative 〔a negative〕 answer; answer in the affirmative 〔negative〕 / 명확〔애매〕한 ~을 하다 give a definite 〔half-hearted〕 answer 《to a question》/ 싫건 좋건 확실한 ~을 해주시오 I should like to have a definite reply, yes or no. / 뭐라고 ~해야 좋을지 몰랐다 I didn't know how to answer. *or* I was at a loss for an answer. / 전화를 했으나 아무런 ~이 없었다 There was no response to my call.

**대대**(大隊) 〖군사〗 a battalion. ¶ ~ 훈련을 하다 go through battalion drill. ◉ ~기(旗) a battalion flag. ~부관 a battalion adjutant. ~장 a battalion commander. 공병~ an engineering battalion. 비행~ a squadron.

**대대**(代代) generation after generation; from generation to generation; for generations; from father to son. ¶ ~의 successive; hereditary / ~로 물려오는 보물 a family treasure; an heirloom / ~로 전해 내려오는 전설 a legend handed down from generation to generation / 선조 ~의 묘지 a family tomb / 이 집안은 ~로 서울에 살고 있다 This family has been in Seoul for generations. / 저 집안은 ~로 변호사다 That family has been lawyers for generations.

**대대적**(大大的) grand; great; wholesale; large-scale; sweeping. ¶ ~으로 on a grand 〔large〕 scale; extensively; in a big way 《구어》/ ~인 검거 a roundup; a wholesale arrest / ~으로 사업을 하다 engage in business on a large scale / ~으로 광고하다 advertise 《*one's* new product》「on a large scale 〔extensively〕; 《신문에》 place a large advertisement in a newspaper / (신문이) ~으로 보도하다 give a lot of space 《to》; give prominent coverage 《to》; treat 《*it*》 as top headline news.

**대덕연구단지**(大德硏究團地) the *Taedŏk* Science Town, a high-tech research center in Korea.

**대도**(大道) ① 〖논리〗 the (right) way; great moral principle. ¶ 천지의 ~ the great law of heaven and earth. ② 《바른 길》 the right path 〔track〕. ◉ ~무문(無門) the right path 〔the great way〕 has no「door 〔hindrance〕.

**대도시**(大都市) a big city.

**대독**(代讀) ~하다 read 《a message》 for 〔on behalf of〕 《*a person*》. ¶ 대통령의 축사를 국무총리가 ~하였다 The congratulatory address of the President was read by the Prime Minister.

**대돈변**(一邊) 10% interest per month.

**대동**(帶同) accompaniment. ~하다 be accompanied by 《*a person*》; take 《*a person*》 (along) 《with *one*》. ¶ 그는 비서를 ~하고 일본으로 떠났다 He left for Japan accompanied by his secretary.

**대동단결**(大同團結) unity in the common interests; a grand union. ~하다 be united; unite 〔form a coalition〕 (regardless of minor differences). ¶ 우리는 공동의 적에 맞서 ~했다 We united against a common enemy.

**대동맥**(大動脈) 〖해부〗 the main artery; the aorta. ¶ ~의 aortic; aortal / [비유적] 경부선은 서울과 부산을 잇는 교통의 ~이다 The Kyŏngbu line is the main artery between Seoul and Pusan. ◉ ~류(瘤) an aortic aneurysm.

**대동사**(代動詞) 〖문법〗 pro-verb.

**대동소이**(大同小異) substantial identity with negligible 〔insignificant〕 differences; general similarity. ~하다 be almost identical 〔nearly alike〕; be substantially the same. ¶ ~한 much 〔nearly〕 alike; almost identical; substantially 〔practically〕 the same / 이것들은 모두 ~하다 These are all much the same. / 양자(兩者)는 ~하다 There is little to choose between the two.

**대두**(大斗) a large-size dry measure; a measure of capacity about half a bushel.

**대두**(大豆) a soybean; a soy(a) (bean).

**대두**(擡頭) raising *one's* 〔its〕 head. ~하다 raise *one's* 〔its〕 head; become conspicuous; gain power; rise. ¶ 민족주의의 ~ the rise of nationalism / 신인들의 ~와 더불어 우리 노인들은 뒤로 물러난다 As new figures come to the fore, we old men drop 〔fall〕 behind. / 그 당시 유력한 상인 계급이 새로이 ~하고 있었다 In those days a powerful merchant class was on the rise.

**대들다** turn 〔fall〕 upon 《*a person*》; defy; go at 《*a person*》; fly 〔lash out〕 at 《*a person*》; stand up to. ¶ 버럭버럭 ~ stand up to 《*a person*》 firmly / 윗사람에게 ~ fly in the face of *one's* boss; turn on *one's* superior / 나는 약속을 어긴 그에게 대들었다 I flew at him for breaking his promise. / …라(고)하면서 ~ challenge 《*a person*》 saying that… / 내게 대들 셈인가 Do you mean to defy 〔be down on〕 me? / 감히 그에게 대들 자는 없다 No one dare lift a finger against him.

**대들보**(大—) ① 〖건축〗 a girder; a crossbeam. ② 《사람》 a mainstay; a pillar; a prop. ¶ 집의 ~를 잃다 lose the mainstay 〔principal breadwinner〕 of a family.

**대등**(對等) (an) equality; an equal 〔a level〕 footing; equal 〔even〕 terms. ~하다 (be) equal; even; equivalent; be on a level with; be on an equal footing 〔terms〕 with. ¶ ~하게 equally; on equal terms 〔on an equal footing〕 《with》 / ~한 상대〔동료〕 *one's* equal / ~한 관계에 있다 be on an equal footing 《with》 / ~한 교제를 하다 associate with 《*a person*》 on equal terms / ~한 계약을 맺다 enter into a contract on equal terms 《with another》 / ~한 게임을 하다 play an even game; be a good match for each other / …와 ~하다 be on 「a level 〔an equal footing〕 with… / ~하게 하다 level; even; equalize 《one to 〔with〕 another》; put 《A》 on a par 〔level〕 《with B》 / ~해지다 get even with; acquire parity with / ~하게 취급하다 treat 《things, men》 on equal terms / 그는 너와 ~한 입장이 아니다 He is not on equal terms with you. / 모든 국민은 ~한 법의 적용을 받는다 All of the people are equal under the law. / 이 분야에서 한국은 이제 일본과 ~한 위치에 있다 Korea has now achieved equality with Japan in this field. ◉ ~조약 a treaty on equal terms.

**대뜸** 《즉시》 at once; immediately; promptly; instantly; 《즉석에서》 on the spot; offhand; right away. ¶ ~ 대답하다 answer at once / ~ 승낙하다 give a ready consent; accept 《an invitation》 immediately / 일을 ~ 해버리다 finish *one's* work at once / 그것을 영어로 무어라 하는지 ~ 나오지 않는다 Right offhand I can't find the English for it.

**대란**(大亂) a serious 〔great〕 disturbance; a great commotion 〔rebellion〕. ¶ ~을 진압하다 suppress 〔quell〕 a great rebellion.

**대략**(大略) ① 《개략》 an outline; a summary; an epitome; the gist. ¶ ~을 말하다 give 「an outline 〔a summary〕 《of》; summarize; sum up; outline / ~은 다음과 같다 It can be summarized as follows. ② 《대충》 roughly 〔broadly〕 (speaking); in broad outline; on the whole; generally. ¶ ~ 실정이 이렇다 Roughly 〔Broadly〕 speaking, that is the actual situation.

**대량**(大量) a large 〔great〕 quantity; enormous volume. ¶ ~으로 in large 〔great〕 quantities; on a massive 〔large〕 scale; in (great) volume / ~ 수출하다 export 《*a thing*》 in large quantities / ~ 구입시 특가 제공 《게시》 Special prices on quantity lots. / 한국은 석유를 ~으로 수입하고 있다 Korea imports petroleum on a massive 〔large〕 scale. ◉ ~검거 a mass arrest. ~구입〔매입〕 bulk purchase; heavy 〔bulk〕 buying: 원료를 싼값으로 ~ 매입하다 buy raw materials in bulk at lower prices. ~생산 mass production; production on a large scale: ~ 생산하다 mass-produce; produce in a great quantity. ~ 생산방식 a mass production method. ~ 수송수단 a large-scale transportation means. ~실업 mass 〔large-scale〕 unemployment. ~주문 bulk 〔large〕 order. ~파괴 (무기) (weapons of) mass destruction. ~학살 genocide; mass murder; massacre. ~해고 mass discharge 〔dismissal〕; voluminous dismissal.

**대령**(大領) 〖육군〗 colonel (생략 Col.); 〖해군〗 a captain (생략 Capt.); 〖공군〗 a colonel 《미》; a group captain 《영》.

**대령**(待令) waiting for an order 〔a

command]; presenting *oneself*. ～하다 wait for an order 〔a command〕; stand ready to carry out an order; present *oneself* 《before an official》.

**대례**(大禮) 《국가의》 a state ceremony; 《대관식》 a coronation; 《결혼식》 a wedding ceremony. ¶ ～를 올리다 hold a wedding. ◉ ～모(帽) a cocked 〔court〕 hat. ～복(服) full 〔court〕 dress; 《부인의》 a *robe décolletée* (F.); 《군인의》 a grand gold-laced uniform; a full=dress uniform. ～사절(使節) the Commissioner of the Coronation.

**대로**(大怒) great anger 〔rage, fury, wrath〕; exasperation. ～하다 get angry; be furious; rage; be enraged; be exasperated (격앙하다); be in a fume 〔huff〕; fly into a passion.

**대로**(大路) a broad way; a main road; a highway; a thoroughfare.

**대로** ① 《…처럼 · …에 따라서》 as; like; just as; in accordance with; the same; in the way 〔manner〕 of (…의 방법으로); in pursuance of; true to; after. (***a***) [동사 뒤에서] ¶ 하고 싶은 ～ as *one* pleases; at will; to *one's* heart's content / 먹고 싶은 ～ 먹다 eat *one's* fill; eat as much as *one* likes / 남이 시키는 ～ 하다 act as *a person* bids; be led by the nose / 하고 싶은 ～ 해라 Do as you like. *or* Have your own way. / 나하는 ～ 해라 Do as I do. / 내가 말한 ～다 I told you! *or* Didn't I tell you so? / 책을 놓인 ～ 두었다 I left the book as it was. / 바른 ～ 말해라 Tell the truth! / 보신 ～ 말씀해 주십시오 Please tell me as you saw it. / 만사 예기한 ～ 일이 순조로웠다 Everything worked as expected. (***b***) [명사 뒤에서] ¶ 규칙～ according to the rule / 글자～ to the letter; literally / 내 명령～ according to my orders; as I tell you / 네 말～ as you say / 예상～ as *one* expected / 마음～ as *one* likes 〔wants, wishes, pleases〕 / 마음～ 할 수 있다면 if I could do as I please / 약속～ as promised; true to *one's* promise / 예정～ as scheduled; according to the schedule / 대본～ 쓰다 write after a copybook / 제멋～ 하다 have everything *one's* own way; do everything at will; do as *one* pleases / 모든 일이 계획～ 진행되었다 Everything went as previously arranged. / 그들은 왕의 명령～ 행동했다 They acted according as the king told them to. / 분부～ 하겠습니다 I'll act upon your words. *or* I'll act as you tell me. ② 《…하면 곧》 as soon as; directly; immediately after. ¶ 날씨가 좋아지는 ～ on the first fine day / 날이 밝는 ～ as soon as the dawn breaks / 형편이 닿는 ～ at *one's* first 〔earliest〕 convenience / 뉴욕에 닿는 ～ on your arrival in New York.

**대롱** ① 《관》 a slender bamboo tube. ② 《물레의》 a spinning bobbin.

**대롱거리다** 《매달려》 dangle; dingle-dangle; sway 〔swing〕 to and fro; hang and swing loosely. ¶ 풍경이 바람에 대롱거린다 A wind-bell is dangling back and forth in the wind.

**대롱대롱** dangling; dingle-dangle; swaying 〔swinging〕 to and fro. ¶ 사과가 가지에 ～ 달려 있다 Apples are dangling from the branches.

**대류**(對流) 〚물리〛 convection current. ◉ ～권(圈) the troposphere. ～식 히터 a convector heater.

**대륙**(大陸) a continent. ¶ ～의〔적인〕 continental / 아시아〔유럽〕 ～ the Continent of Asia 〔Europe〕; the Asian 〔European〕 continent / ～간의 intercontinental / ～적인 인간 a man of easygoing disposition / ～화하다, ～풍이 되다 continentalize; be continentalized / 아시아는 모든 ～ 중에서 가장 크다 Asia is the largest of all the continents of the world.
◉ ～간 탄도탄 intercontinental ballistic missile (생략 ICBM). ～분수계 the continental divide. ～붕(棚) a continental shelf. ～성 기후 continental climate. ～이동설 〚지학〛 the continental drift theory. ～정책 continental politics. ～주의, ～(적) 사상 continentalism. ～ 횡단 철도 a transcontinental railway; a coast-to-coast railroad 《미》.

**대리**(代理) 《행위》 representation; 〚법〛 proxy; 《대리인》 a deputy; a substitute; a representative; an agent (거래·판매의); a proxy; 《법정의》 an attorney. ～하다 act 「for 〔in behalf of〕 《a manager》; take 「*a person's* place 〔the place of *a person*〕; represent; act as 《*a person's*》 proxy; substitute for 《*a person*》.
¶ 교장 ～ the acting principal / 과장 ～ the acting section chief / …의 ～로서 in 〔on〕 behalf of; by deputy 〔proxy〕 / ～시키다 substitute 《*a person*》 for another; make 《*a person*》 *one's* proxy; 《법률》 subrogate / ～를 보내다 send a proxy 〔representative〕 / ～를 보다 act

(as substitute) for; act in《*a person's*》 name / 형을 ~하여 서류에 서명했다 I signed the paper for my brother by proxy. / 지배인이 없는 동안 내가 ~를 봅니다 I'll take our manager's place in his absence. *or* I'll substitute for our manager in his absence. *or* I'll act for the manager in his absence. (★ act as manager이면「지배인으로서 일하다」의 뜻. 즉 act의 주어와 manager는 동일인임). / 나의 ~를 부탁합니다 Please「take my place〔act in my place〕. / 그는 지금 이 연구소에서 소장 ~로 근무하고 있다 He is now a deputy chief in this laboratory.

> 용법 **agent**, **representative** 타인을 위해 업무나 회사의 권리를 대신해서 행하는 사람. **deputy** 공식적으로 직무를 대행하는 사람. 우리말로「…대리」,「부…」로 흔히 번역됨. **proxy** 선거 따위에서의 대리인. **substitute** 가장 일반적으로 흔히 쓰이는「대역」을 뜻하는 말.

◉ ~경작 the cultivation by proxy: 유휴지를 ~ 경작시키다 have《*a person*》 cultivate the idle land by proxy. ~공사(公使) a *chargé d'affaires* (F.). ~권 the right〔power〕of representation〔attorney〕; agency. ~대사 a *chargé d'affaires* (of an embassy); an acting ambassador: 임시 ~ 대사 a *chargé d'affaires ad interim* (L.). ~소송 a lawsuit by proxy〔attorney〕. ~시험 proxy exam(ination). ~업 agency; an agent's business; commission agency; factorage: ~업자 an agent; a factor. ~운전사 a proxy driver. ~운전업 the "rent-a-driver" business. ~위임권 power of attorney. ~위임장 a letter of attorney. ~응시자 a proxy testee. ~인 ⇨ 대리. ~전쟁 a proxy war. ~점 an agency; a commercial agent: 독점 ~점 an exclusive agency; a sole agency《for a company》/ 광고 ~점 an advertising agency〔agent〕. ~투표 voting by proxy; proxy vote. ~판매 sale by agent.

법정 ~인 a legal representative. 전권 ~인 a universal agent. 총~인 a general agent. 판매 ~인 a selling agent.

**대리모**(代理母) a surrogate mother.

**대리석**(大理石) marble. ¶ ~ 기둥 a marble pillar / ~상(像) a marble statue; statue of〔in〕marble / 인조 ~ artificial marble.

**대립**(對立) (a) confrontation《between A and B》; (an) opposition; antagonism (반목); a conflict (의견 등의 충돌); friction (마찰). ~하다 confront (each other); be opposed to; be confronted with. ¶ 두 민족의 ~ the antagonism of one race to another / 격렬한 이해〔노사간〕의 ~ a sharp conflict「of interests〔between labor and management〕/ ~된 의견 (an) opposing〔(a) conflicting〕opinion / 사랑은 증오와 ~한다 Love is opposed to hatred. *or* Love conflicts with hatred. / 중요한 점에서 우리들의 의견은 크게 ~되어 있다 We have widely divided opinions on an important point. / 시어머니와 젊은 며느리 사이에는 미묘한 ~이 자주 생긴다 There is often friction between a young wife and her mother-in-law.

◉ ~개념 a coordinate concept. ~관계 antagonistic relationships. ~유전자〔형질〕allele. ~자 an opponent. ~절(節)〖문법〗a coordinate clause. ~후보 a rival candidate.

**대마**(大馬)〖바둑〗a large group of stones. ¶ ~불사(不死) Large groups of stones are seldom captured.

**대마**(大麻)〖식물〗hemp. ◉ ~씨 hempseed. ~초 marijuana; 《smoke》 cigarettes made of (outlawed) hemp leaf: ~초를 상습적으로 피우다 habitually smoke hemp leaf cigarettes.

**대마루** ①《지붕의》the ridge of the roof. ②《대마루판》the decisive moment; the crucial〔critical〕moment.

**대막대기** a bamboo stick〔pole〕.

**대만**(臺灣) Taiwan; Formosa. ¶ ~의 Formosan. ◉ ~사람 a Formosan; a Taiwanese. ~해협 the Formosa〔Taiwan〕Strait.

**대만원**(大滿員) a full house; 《게시》 House full; Full house; Sold out (매진); Car full (전동차 따위). ⇨ 만원. ¶ ~이다 be more than full; be filled to bursting; be full to the doors (극장 따위가).

**대말**《죽마》a child's hobbyhorse; stilts.

**대망**(大望) a great hope〔ambition, desire〕; an aspiration; *one's* supreme ambition. ¶ ~을 가진 ambitious; aspiring / ~을 품다 be full of ambitions; have〔cherish, harbor, nourish〕an ambition; aim high; have a high aim; aspire after greatness; raise *one's* sights / ~을 이루다 realize *one's* supreme ambition; attain the object〔reach the goal〕of *one's* ambition.

**대망**(待望) expectation; awaiting; anticipation. ~하다 expect; anticipate; wait 〔hope〕 for; look forward to. ¶ ~의 long-awaited; eagerly anticipated; long cherished; long-expected; hoped= for / ~의 여름방학이 왔다 The long= awaited summer vacation has come.

**대매출**(大賣出) a special bargain sale. ¶ 반액〔사은〕 ~ a half-price 〔thank= you〕 bargain sale / 연말 ~ a year-end sale 《at a department store》.

**대맥**(大麥) barley. = 보리.

**대머리** a baldhead; a bald-headed person; a baldpate. ¶ ~의 bald-headed / 젊어서 벗어진 ~ a premature baldhead / 일찍 ~가 된 prematurely bald / ~가 되다 become bald-headed.

**대면**(對面) an interview; a meeting. ~하다 meet; see; interview; have an interview 《with》. ¶ 첫~ the first meeting 〔interview〕 / 오래간만에 ~하다 see *one* after a long interval 〔separation〕 / 부자가 20년 만에 ~했다 Father and son met after twenty years' separation. / 나는 어제 그녀와 첫~을 가졌다 I met her for the first time yesterday. ◉ ~교통 facing 〔oncoming〕 traffic. ~통행 《보행자 입장에서》 walking so as to face the oncoming traffic.

**대명**(大命) an Imperial Order; a Royal command 〔mandate〕. ¶ ~을 내리다 issue a Royal mandate.

**대명**(待命) pending appointment; awaiting orders; 《대기 발령》 being placed on the waiting list. ~하다 await 〔wait for〕 orders; be placed on the waiting list.

**대명사**(大名辭) 〖논리〗 the major term.

**대명사**(代名詞) 〖문법〗 a pronoun; [비유적] a synonym 《for honesty》. ¶ ~의 pronominal / ~로서 pronominally / 그의 이름은 외교적 수완의 ~다 His name is a synonym for diplomatic ability. ◉ 관계〔지시, 의문, 인칭〕~ the relative 〔demonstrative, interrogative, personal〕 pronoun.

**대모**(代母) 〖가톨릭〗 a godmother.

**대모**(玳瑁) 〖동물〗 a hawksbill (turtle). ◉ ~갑(甲) a tortoiseshell: ~갑 세공 tortoiseshell work.

**대모집**(大募集) a wholesale employment; an extensive employment. ~하다 invite a large number of 《students》. ¶ 남녀 공원 ~ 《광고》 Wanted—a large force of factory workers.

**대목** ① 《시기》 the most important occasion; the busiest 〔highest, best〕 season; a rush period 《of business》. ¶ 섣달 ~ the very end of the year; the rush period of the year-end / ~을 보려고 물건을 쌓아 두다 stock goods to provide for the rush period / 시험 ~에 가서 앓다 get sick at the very time when the examination begins. ② 《고비》 the most important occasion 〔spot〕; a critical stage; 《부분》 a part; a passage. ¶ 난해한 ~ a difficult passage / 정국은 마침내 어려운 ~에 이르렀다 The political situation has now reached a critical stage. ◉ ~장 a fair preceding a fete day: 연말 ~장 a fair at the very end of the year.

**대목**(大木) ① 《큰 건축의》 a master carpenter. ② = 목수(木手).

**대목**(臺木) 《접본》 a (parent) stock. ¶ ~에 접붙이다 insert a graft into a stock / ~에 접붙여지다 be grafted on a parent stem.

**대못** 《죽정》 a bamboo peg 〔nail〕. ◉ ~박이 a fool; a blockhead; a dunce.

**대못**(大—) 《큰 못》 a large nail 〔peg〕.

**대문**(大門) the great 〔front〕 gate; the main entrance. ¶ ~을 걸다 bolt the front gate. ◉ ~짝 a gate-door; one door of a gate: 신문에 ~짝만하게 나다 go into headlines.

**대문자**(大文字) ① 《웅대한 글》 master(-ful) writing. ② 《로마자의》 a capital letter; a capital. ¶ ~로 쓰다 write 《a word》 with 〔in〕 capital letters; capitalize 《a letter》 / ~ A, a capital A.

**대문장**(大文章) ① 《글》 masterful writing. ② 《사람》 a master writer; a great master of (literary) style.

**대물**(代物) a substitute. ◉ ~변제 payment in substitutes.

**대물**(對物) objects; reality; [형용사적] objective; real. ◉ ~계약 a real contract. ~담보 security against a thing. ~대부 a loan on security. ~렌즈 an object glass 〔lens〕; an objective. ~배상 책임보험 property damage liability insurance. ~세 a real 〔tangible〕 tax. ~소송 real action. ~신용 real credit.

**대물리다**(代—) hand down 〔leave, transmit, bequeath〕 to *one's* posterity. ¶ 손자에게 재산을 ~ bequeath *one's* property to *one's* grandson.

**대미**(對美) [부사적] toward(s) America 〔the U.S., the United States〕; with America. ¶ 한국 사람의 ~감정 the Korean sentiments toward the Americans. ◉ ~관계 relations with America 〔the U.S.〕. ~무역 trade with the U.S.. ~수출 export(ation) to the

U.S. ～ 수출 자율규제 voluntary restriction 〔curtailment〕 of exports to the U.S. ～의존 reliance upon 〔on〕 the U.S. ～ 일변도 being pro-American throughout; total 〔complete〕 dependence upon the United States: ～ 일변도의 정책 an out-and-out pro-American policy. ～정책 a policy toward the U.S.. ～환율 the won-dollar (exchange) rate; the exchange (rate) on the U.S. dollar.

**대민**(對民) ¶ ～ 봉사활동 service for public welfare.

**대바구니** a bamboo basket.

**대바늘** a bamboo (knitting) needle.

**대받다** retort; contradict 《*a person*》. ¶ 그는 내가 잘못이라고 대받았다 He retorted upon 〔against〕 me, saying I was to blame.

**대받다**(代—) ① 《상속하다》 inherit. ¶ 재산을 ～ inherit some property. ② 《계승하다》 succeed to; continue. ¶ 아버지의 일을 ～ succeed to *one's* father's business.

**대발** a woven bamboo blind.

**대발회**(大發會) 〖증권〗 the first session of the new year.

**대밭** a bamboo grove 〔thicket〕.

**대번(에)** 《단숨에》 at a breath; at a stroke 〔stretch〕; without stopping; 《곧》 at once; immediately; in no time; 《쉽사리》 easily; without difficulty 〔effort〕; without hesitation (서슴지 않고). ¶ ～ 때려눕히다 knock 《*a person*》 down at a single blow / ～ 알아맞히다 guess (right) at once / 나무를 ～ 찍어 넘어뜨리다 fell a tree at a single stroke / ～에 맥주 한 컵을 비우다 drink *one's* beer down 〔up〕 in a single draft 〔gulp〕/ 돈을 ～ 다 써버리다 use up 〔spend〕 *one's* money in no time / 일을 ～ 해치우다 finish *one's* work almost immediately.

**대범스럽다**, **대범하다**(大泛—) be not overly fussy (about trifles); be not easily bothered (by trifles); be generous 《with》; be broad-minded. ¶ 대범한 사람 a broad-minded person / 대범스런 태도 an air of magnanimity; lofty manners; free and open manners / 대범스럽게 행동하다 act magnanimously / 마음을 더 대범하게 가져라 Be more「generous 〔broad-minded〕.

**대법관**(大法官) a justice of the Supreme Court. ¶ 윤 대법원장은 김대통령에게 6명의 새 ～ 후보자를 추천하였다 Chief Justice Yun recommended to President Kim six candidates as new Supreme Court justices.

**대법원**(大法院) the Supreme Court; the Court of Cassation (프랑스의). ¶ ～에 상고하다 appeal to the Supreme Court. ◉ ～장 the Chief Justice; the President of the Supreme Court.

**대법회**(大法會) 〖불교〗 ① 《설법회》 a large Buddhist lecture meeting. ② 《재올림》 Buddhist high mass; a great memorial 〔religious〕 service. ¶ ～를 가지다 celebrate 〔hold〕 high mass.

**대변**(大便) excrements; feces; stools; dung (동물의). ¶ ～을 보다 go to stool; have a bowel movement; relieve 〔ease〕 *oneself;* 《배변하다》 defecate; empty *one's* bowels / ～ 보러 가다 go to the toilet 《미》/ ～이 나오다 *one's* bowels move / ～이 마렵다 want to go to the toilet; have a call of nature; be taken short (갑자기).
◉ ～검사 an examination of the feces: ～ 검사를 하다 examine 《*a person's*》 feces 〔stool〕. ～기 a toilet stool. ～불통 constipation; stoppage of bowel movements.

**대변**(代辯) speaking by proxy. ～하다 speak for 《another》; be a mouthpiece for; act as a spokesman 《of》. ¶ 어머니를 위해 아들이 ～했다 The son spoke「for 〔on behalf of〕 his mother.
◉ ～자 〔인〕 a spokesperson; a mouthpiece; a spokesman (남성); a spokeswoman (여성); a voice (주의 주장의): 국방부 ～인 a spokesman for 〔of〕 the Defense Ministry / 신문은 여론의 ～자가 되어야 한다 The newspaper must speak for the public.

**대변**(貸邊) 〖부기〗 the credit(or) (생략 cr.); the credit side. ¶ ～에 기입하다 enter on the credit side.
◉ ～계정 a credit account. ～잔액 a creditor balance.

**대변**(對邊) 〖수학〗 the opposite side 〔edge〕; the subtense.

**대별**(大別) a general 〔broad〕 classification. ～하다 classify 〔divide〕 roughly 〔broadly〕 《into》; make a general classification 《of》. ¶ 두 종류로 ～하다 divide broadly into two categories / 이들은 세 가지 유형으로 ～된다 These can be classified roughly into three types.

**대보다** compare 《A with 〔to〕 B》; make a comparison 《between A and B》; contrast 《A with B》 (대조하다). ¶ 두 장의 사진을 ～ compare the two photos / 키를 ~ compare heights; measure *oneself* against another / 길고 짧은 것은 대봐야 안다 You can't tell which is longer unless you measure them against each other. / 신구(新舊)의 제품을 대보면 질의 차이가 뚜렷하다 When we compare the new product with the former one, the difference in quality is quite clear.

**대보름(날)**(大—) the 15th of January by the lunar calendar. ◉ ~달 the first full moon on the lunar calendar.

**대복**(大福) great happiness; great luck 「fortune」.

**대본**(大本) the great foundation; the primal basis. ¶ 국가〔인륜〕의 ~ the foundations of the state 〔human morality〕 / 농자 천하지~ Agriculture is the foundation of a nation.

**대본**(貸本) 《책》 a book for rent; a book to loan out; 《빌려줌》 lending books. ◉ ~서점 a lending 〔rental〕 library. ~업 book-lending service: ~업자 a keeper of a lending library.

**대본**(臺本) 《극의》 a (play) script; 《영화의》 a scenario; a (film) script; 《가극의》 a libretto (*pl.* ~s, -ti). ¶ ~을 쓰다 write scripts 〔scenarios〕 / ~ 없는 TV 인터뷰는 ~이 있는 것보다 훨씬 재미있다 Unscripted TV interviews are far more interesting than scripted ones. ◉ ~작가 a script writer. 방송 ~ a script.

**대본산**(大本山) 《절의》 the home 〔main〕 「temple of a Buddhist sect.

**대부**(代父) 〘가톨릭〙 a godfather.

**대부**(貸付) loaning; lending. ~하다 loan; make a loan 〔an advance〕; lend. ¶ 부당 ~ a reckless 〔an improper〕 loan / 신용 ~ a loan on personal pledge; a personal 〔credit〕 loan; an open credit / 은행 ~ a bank loan / 장기〔단기〕 ~ (a) long-term 〔short-term〕 loan 〔credit〕 / 당좌 ~ a call loan. ◉ ~계(원) a loan teller 〔clerk〕. ~계정 a loan account. ~금 a loan; an advance. ~기한 the term of a loan. ~신탁 a loan trust. ~원부(元簿) a loan ledger; a loan book. ~은행 a credit bank. ~이자율 the interest rate on a loan. ~잔액 a debit balance.

**대부분**(大部分) the greater 〔best〕 part 《of》; most 《of》; the majority 《of》. ¶ ~은 mostly; for the most part; mainly; chiefly / 인생의 ~을 시골에서 보내다 spend most 〔the greater part〕 of *one's* life in the country / 손님은 ~ 여자들이었다 The customers were mostly women. / 참석자는 ~ 대학생들이었다 Those present were, for the most part, university students. / ~이 그것에 반대였다 The majority was against it. / 청중은 ~ 어린이였다 The audience consisted mainly of children. / ~의 근대음악은 난해하다 「Most modern music 〔A large part of modern music〕 is difficult to understand. / 학생의 ~이 그 운동에 참가했다 The majority 〔Most〕 of the students took part in the movement.

**대부인**(大夫人) your 〔his〕 (esteemed) mother.

**대북**(對北) ◉ ~방송 broadcasting toward North Korea 〔the north〕.

**대분수**(帶分數) 〘수학〙 a mixed number.

**대불**(大佛) a great image 〔statue〕 of Buddha.

**대비**(大妃) a Queen Mother; a Queen 「Dowager.

**대비**(對比) comparison (비교); contrast (대조). ~하다 compare 〔contrast〕 《two things, A with B》; make a comparison 《between two novels》. ¶ 번역문과 원문을 ~해 보아라 Compare the translation with the original. / 붉은 색과 검은 색의 ~가 인상적이다 The contrast 「of 〔between〕 red and black is very impressive.

**대비**(對備) 《준비》 preparations 《for》 (물품 따위의); provision 《against》 (비축); 《방비》 a defense 《against an attack》. ~하다 prepare 《for》; make preparations 《for》; provide; get 〔have〕 《*a thing*》 ready 《for》; make provision 《for, against》. ¶ 화재에 ~하다 take precautions against a fire / 적의 공격에 ~하다 provide 〔guard〕 *oneself* against an enemy attack / 장래〔비상시〕에 ~하다 prepare for 「the future 〔emergency〕 / 예상 못한 경비 지출에 ~하다 provide for unforeseen expenses / 노후를 ~하기 위해 그는 저금을 시작했다 He's started to save money for his old age.

**대빗** a bamboo comb.

**대사**(大事) ① 《큰일》 a great thing; an important 〔weighty〕 matter 〔issue〕; a serious 〔grave〕 affair (우려할 만한); 《큰 사업》 a grand enterprise; a great undertaking. ¶ ~를 이루다 achieve a great thing 〔deed, work〕 / 이것은 국가의 ~다 《위기》 This is a national crisis. ② 《혼인》 a marriage ceremony; the big event. ¶ ~를 치르다 hold 〔celebrate〕 a marriage 〔wedding〕.

**대사**(大使) an ambassador; an ambassadress (여성). ¶ 주한～ an ambassador to Korea / 스미스 ～부처 Ambassador and Mrs. Smith / 주미 한국 ～ the Korean Ambassador to America / 그는 주영～로 임명되었다 He was appointed ambassador to Great Britain.
◉ ～급(級) 회담 an ambassador-level conference: ～급 회담을 열다 hold「a meeting at ambassadorial level〔an ambassador-level meeting〕. ～부인 an ambassadress.
**대사**(大師) 〖불교〗 a saint; a great Buddhist priest. ¶ 원효～ (the Buddhist) Saint Wonhyo.
**대사**(大蛇) a big snake; a huge〔large〕serpent; an anaconda.
**대사**(大赦) an amnesty. = 사면(赦免).
**대사**(大寫) 〖영화〗 a close-up.
**대사**(代謝) ⇨ 신진 대사(新陳代謝). ◉ ～이상(異常) a metabolic disorder. ～ 작용〔기능〕 metabolism: ～기능이 약하다 have a low metabolic rate.
**대사**(臺辭) 《배우의》 (a) speech; words; *one's* line(s); the lines 《of a play》 (전체 대사). ¶ ～를 말하다 deliver *one's* lines; speak *one's* part〔lines〕/ ～를 잊다 forget *one's* lines; dry up / ～를 틀리다 bungle〔fluff〕*one's* lines〔a line〕/ ～ 없는 역을 하다 do〔have〕a nonspeaking〔walk-on〕part.
**대사관**(大使館) an embassy. ¶ 미국～ the American Embassy / 주미 한국～ the Korean Embassy in Washington, D.C. / ～부 육군〔해군〕 무관 a military〔naval〕*attaché* to an embassy / ～을 설치하다 establish an embassy 《in, at》. ◉ ～ 서기관 a secretary of an embassy. ～원 a member of the embassy staff; the staff of an embassy [총칭]. ～ 참사관 a councilor〔counselor〕of an embassy.
**대사립** a bamboo gate.
**대상**(大祥) the second anniversary of *a person's* death.
**대상**(大喪) death of the king; mourning for the king.
**대상**(大賞) a grand prize; *grand prix* (F.). ¶ 가요〔가수〕～ the annual grand prize awarded to the best song〔singer〕/ ～을 받다 receive〔be awarded〕a grand prize.
**대상**(代償) ① 《변상》 compensation; a price. ～하다 compensate〔indemnify〕《*a person* for a loss》; pay compensation 《for》; 《딴 것으로》 compensate in substitutes. ¶ …의 ～으로 in compensation〔return〕for… / 어떤 ～을 치르더라도 at any price; whatever the cost / 값비싼 ～을 치르다 pay「heavily〔a painful price〕《for *a thing*》. ② 《대리 변상》 vicarious compensation. ～하다 compensate on behalf of 《*a person*》. ◉ ～부전(不全) 〖의학〗 《심장의》 decompensation. ～수입 compensatory imports.「caravan.
**대상**(隊商) a caravan. ¶ 낙타 ～ a camel
**대상**(對象) an object 《of study》; a subject 《of our investigation》; a target 《of criticism》. ¶ 공격의 ～ a target of attack / 과세의 ～ property liable for taxation / 신앙의 ～ the object of worship / 조소의 ～ the butt of ridicule / 연구의 ～ the subject of *one's* study / 고교생을 ～으로 하는 사전 a dictionary (intended) for〔aimed at〕high-school students / 비난의 ～이 되다 become the focus of public censure / 선망의 ～이 되다 become the object of envy / 이것들을 과학적 연구의 ～으로 삼다 make these things an object of scientific study / 5백명의 대학생을 ～으로 정치 의식 조사를 하다 conduct a survey of political awareness on five hundred college students / 조사의 ～이 무엇이냐 What is the subject of the survey? (★ subject 대신 object를 쓰면「조사의 목적」이라는 뜻).
**대상**(帶狀) ¶ ～의 belt-shaped; belt-like. ◉ ～지수(指數) a zonal index. ～포진(疱疹) 〖의학〗 shingles; herpes zoster.
**대생**(對生) 〖식물〗 symmetry; opposition. ¶ ～의 opposite / 이것은 잎이 ～하는 식물이다 This is an opposite-leaved plant. ◉ ～엽(葉) opposite leaves.
**대서**(大暑) ① 《절후》 "midsummer"; the 12th of the 24 seasonal divisions of the year. ② 《더위》 an intense heat.
**대서**(代書) writing「for〔on behalf of〕another. ～하다 write 《a letter》 for 《another》. ◉ ～소〔방〕 a scrivener's office. ～업 scrivenery. ～인 a scribe; a scrivener: ～인한테 써 받다 have 《an application》 written by a scrivener. ⇨ 행정사.
**대서다** ① 《뒤에 서다》 stand close behind 《*a person*》. ② 《대항하다》 stand against; turn against〔upon〕; be pitted against; defy. ¶ 윗사람에게 ～ defy *one's* superior.
**대서양**(大西洋) the Atlantic (Ocean). ¶ ～의 Atlantic / ～ 횡단의 transatlantic. ◉ ～조약 the Atlantic Pact〔Treaty〕.

～함대 the Atlantic Fleet. ～항로 an Atlantic line. ～헌장 the Atlantic Charter. ～ 횡단비행 a transatlantic flight. 북～ 조약기구 the North Atlantic Treaty Organization (생략 NATO).

**대서특필**(大書特筆) special writing 〔mention〕; 《신문 따위의》 featuring. ～하다 mention 〔write〕 especially; 《신문 따위가》 give (special) prominence to; make a feature of; make special mention 《of》. ¶ ～할 만한 《a deed》 deserving 〔worthy of〕 special mention; remarkable; extraordinary. 「footstone.

**대석**(臺石) a pedestal (stone); 《묘의》 a

**대선**(貸船) hiring out boats; 《배》 a boat on hire; a chartered boat. ～하다 hire out a boat; charter a boat 〔ship〕. ¶ 1시간당 2달러로 보트를 ～하다 hire out a boat for two dollar an hour. ◉ ～료 a boat hire fee. ～장 a boat-hiring place.

**대선거구**(大選擧區) a major constituency. ◉ ～제 a major constituency system.

**대설**(大雪) ① 《절후》 the 21st of the 24 seasonal divisions of the year (occurring around December 8th). ② 《눈》 a heavy snow; a tremendous snowfall. ¶ 동해안 지방에는 ～이 내렸다 There was a very heavy snowfall in the areas facing the East Sea.

**대설대** a pipestem

**대성**(大成) 《큰 인물이 됨》 attainment of greatness. ～하다 attain 〔come to〕 greatness; become a great man; be crowned with success (성공하다). ¶ ～할 인물 a man full of promise / 그는 실업계에서 ～했다 He attained greatness in the business world. / 그녀는 대중 가수로서 ～했다 She was crowned with success as a popular singer. ② 《이룸》 completion; accomplishment. ～하다 complete; accomplish; achieve.

**대성**(大聖) 《현인》 a great sage; a *mahatma* (Sans.); 《공자》 Confucius, the Great Sage.

**대성**(大聲) a loud voice 〔cry〕. ⇨ 큰소리 ①. ¶ ～ 통곡하다 weep aloud; wail; mourn in a loud voice.

**대성공**(大成功) a great 〔huge〕 success 〔hit〕; splendid results; a box-office success (흥행의). ¶ ～을 거두다 be prosperous 〔thriving〕; 《장사 따위가》 be doing a flourishing business; 《모임 따위가》 be a success; be very well attended / 그 영화는 ～이었다 The movie was 〔made〕 a great hit 〔success〕.

**대성황**(大盛況) prosperity; a (great) success. ¶ 하기 강습회는 ～이었다 The summer workshop was a great success.

**대세**(大勢) the general situation 《of the world》; the general tendency (추세); the trend; the current. ¶ 세계의 ～ the international situation; the trend of international affairs / ～에 순응〔역행〕하다 swim 〔go〕 with 〔against〕 the tide 〔current〕 / ～를 파악하다 have a grasp of the situation / ～를 결정짓다 bring 《*a matter*》 almost to its final issue / ～를 살피다 take a general view of things; study the general situation / ～가 우리에게 유리〔불리〕하다 The general situation is favorable 〔unfavorable〕 to us. / ～는 이미 결정되었다 The overall situation is no longer in doubt.

**대소**(大小) large and small size; size (크기). ¶ ～에 따라 according to size / ～ 여러 가지의 of various sizes / ～에 불구하고 whether large or small; regardless of size / ～의 차가 있다 be vary in size / ～를 비교하다 compare the size 《of two things》 / ～에 상관없이 값은 같다 They are (of) the same price, regardless of size.

**대소**(大笑) a roar of laughter; a loud laughter; a good 〔hearty〕 laugh. ～하다 laugh aloud; have a good laugh at 〔over〕. ¶ 가가(呵呵) ～하다 break 〔burst〕 into a roar of laughter; laugh heartily / 박장～하다 laugh aloud clapping *one's* hands.

**대소**(代訴) litigation by proxy. ～하다 sue 〔bring suit〕 on behalf of 《*a person*》.

**대소**(對訴) 『법』 a countercharge; a counterclaim. ⇨ 맞고소. ◉ 이혼 ～ a counter divorce action.

**대소동**(大騷動) 《떠들썩함》 a (great) uproar; clamor; 《혼잡》 confusion; (a) turmoil; 《소동》 a great disturbance 〔commotion, fuss〕; a tumult; great excitement (흥분에 의한). ¶ ～을 일으키다 make a fuss; make much ado 《about trifles》 / 그 소식 때문에 ～이 벌어졌다 The news caused 「great excitement 〔a great disturbance〕. / 회합에서 ～이 벌어졌다 There was a great stir at the meeting.

**대소변**(大小便) feces and urine; 《용변》 urination and defecation. ¶ ～을 보다 go to the toilet-room; visit the lavatory; relieve *oneself* 〔nature〕 / 혼자서

는 ~도 보지 못하다 be unable to defecate or urinate by *oneself*.

**대소사**(大小事) matters great and small; all sorts of matters. ¶ ~를 맡기다 leave everything to 《*a person's*》 discretion 〔care〕.

**대소수**(帶小數) 〖수학〗 a mixed decimal.

**대소쿠리** a bamboo basket.

**대속**(代贖) redemption 〔expiation, atonement〕 on behalf of another; 《예수의》 the Redemption; the Atonement. ~하다 redeem; atone for 《*a person*》.

**대손**(貸損) a bad debt; a dead loan. ¶ ~이 된 대출금 a debt unpaid; a bill unsettled / ~이 되다 [돈이 주어] become uncollectable 〔irrecoverable〕. ◉ ~손실 a bad debt loss. ~준비금 a bad debt reserve. ~충당금 the allowance for bad debts.

**대수**(大數) ① 《큰 수》 a big 〔great, large, high〕 number. ② 《대운》 great fortune; good luck.

**대수**(代數) 〖수학〗 algebra; literal arithmetic. ¶ ~적 algebraic(al) / ~적 해법(解法) an algebraical solution / ~로 풀다 solve 《a problem》 in algebra; work out 《a problem》 algebraically. ◉ ~식〔기호, 곡선〕 an algebraic(al) expression 〔sign, curve〕. ~학자 an algebraist. ~함수〔방정식〕 an algebraic(al) function 〔equation〕. 논리~ algebra of logic.

**대수**(對數) 〖수학〗 a logarithm. ⇨ 로그.

**대수롭다** (be) important; valuable; useful. ¶ 대수롭게 여기다 make 〔think〕 much of...; have a high regard for ... / 대수롭지 않다 be of little importance; be trivial 〔trifling, insignificant, useless〕 / 대수롭지 않은 일 a matter of no importance; a trivial affair 〔matter〕 / 대수롭지 않은 물건 a little thing; a trifle; poor stuff / 대수롭지 않은 인간 a good-for-nothing 〔worthless〕 fellow; a person of no importance / 대수롭지 않은 문제를 가지고 야단법석을 떨다 make a big fuss over nothing / 자네가 어느 대학을 나왔건 그것은 대수로운 문제가 아니다 It matters very little what college you graduated from.

**대수술**(大手術) 《have, go through》 a major surgical operation.

**대숲** a bamboo thicket 〔grove〕.

**대승**(大乘) 〖불교〗 *Mahayana* (Sans.); the Great Vehicle. ¶ ~적 견지 a broad view; a broader viewpoint / ~적 견지에서 보다 look at 《the situation》 from a broader viewpoint; take an overall view of 《the state of affairs》. ◉ ~경 the Mahayana Sutras. ~불교 Mahayana (Buddhism).

**대승**(大勝) ① 《썩 나음》 great superiority. ~하다 be much better (than); be far superior 《to》. ② 《이김》 a great 〔signal〕 victory. ~하다 win 〔gain〕 a great 〔signal〕 victory 《over》; 《선거에서》 win a landslide (victory) 《over》. ¶ 10대 0의 ~ a great victory 「with 〔by a score of〕 ten to nought.

**대승리**(大勝利) a sweeping 〔complete, signal〕 victory; 《선거에서》 a landslide. ¶ 공화당의 ~ a Republican landslide.

**대시** ① 《부호》 a dash. ¶ b ~ b′; 〖수학〗 b prime 《미》; b dash 《영》 / ~를 붙이다 put a dash 《after a word》. ② 《돌진》 a dash. ~하다 dash 《up 〔down〕 the stairs》.

**대식**(大食) ① 《끼니》 main meals; breakfast and supper. ② 《많이 먹음》 gluttony; heavy feeding 〔eating〕. ~하다 eat gluttonously; gluttonize; eat like a horse. ¶ ~의 gluttonous / ~은 건강에 나쁘다 Eating too much is bad for (the) health. ◉ ~가 a big 〔large〕 eater; a glutton.

**대신**(大臣) a minister (of state); a cabinet member. ⇨ 장관(長官). ¶ ~의 ministerial / ~직 a portfolio (*pl.* ~s); a ministerial chair.

**대신**(代身) ① 《대용·대리》 substitution; vicariousness; 《사람·사물의》 a substitute; 《대리인》 a proxy; a deputy; 《교대자》 a relief; 《후임》 a replacement. ~하다 act as a substitute 《for》; take 《*a person's*》 place; serve the purpose 《for, of》; replace. ¶ ~(에) instead of...; in place of...; in lieu of... / 그 ~ (에) instead / ~으로 as a substitute / ~이 되다 serve as; do duty for / 내 ~ 오늘 저녁 음악회에 가거라 You go to the concert in my place this evening. / 내 ~ 편지 좀 써 다오 Write a letter for me. / 영어 ~ 독어를 배우겠다 I'll learn German instead of English. / 그 ~ 홍차를 다오 Give me tea instead. / 그녀에게 편지 ~ 전화를 걸었다 I phoned her instead of writing to her. / 어떤 기계도 인간을 ~할 수 없다 No machine can (be a) substitute for a human being. / 그는 수표 ~ 현금을 주었다 He gave us cash 「instead 〔in lieu〕 of a check. / 너 ~ 내가 가겠다 I will go instead 〔in place〕 of you. *or* I will go for you 〔in your place〕. / 요새는 전기

가 가스를 ～한다 Electricity is replacing gas nowadays. / 그를 ～할 사람이 없다 There's nobody who can take his place. / 내일 나 ～ 회의에 참석해 주겠느냐 Would you mind attending tomorrow's meeting 「instead 〔in place〕 of me?

② 《대상(代償)》 compensation; return. ¶ (…하는) ～에〔으로〕 in return (for…); in compensation (for…); in exchange (for…); to make up for / ～에 이 책을 너에게 주겠다 I'll give you this book in return. / 그가 나한테 영어를 가르쳐 주는 ～ 나는 그에게 독어를 가르쳐 준다 I'm teaching him German in return for his teaching me English.

③ 《한편》 but; though. ¶ 값이 비싼 ～ 품질이 좋다 The quality is good though it is expensive. *or* It is dear but the quality is good. / 그는 돈이 있는 ～ 자식이 없다 He doesn't have children but he has money, instead. / 그에게는 적도 많지만 ～ 친구도 많다 He has as many friends as enemies.

**대실**(貸室) a room 〔hall〕 on 〔for〕 hire. ◉ ～료 room charge; hotel charge (호텔의).

**대심**(對審) 〖법〗 a trial (공판); confrontation (대결). ～하다 confront the accused with the accuser.

**대아**(大我) 〖철학〗 absolute ego; the higher self; the inner man; *one's* large self; 〖불교〗 *one's* true self; *Atman* (Sans.).

**대안**(代案) an alternative 《idea, plan, proposal》; a substitute 《measure, bill》. ¶ ～을 제시하다 make 〔suggest〕 an alternative idea 〔plan, measure〕.

**대안**(對岸) the other side of the river; the opposite bank 〔shore〕. ¶ ～에 on the other side; on the opposite bank 〔shore〕 / 그 사건을 ～의 불 보듯하면 안 된다 We must not look upon this case with indifference.

**대안**(對案) a counterproposal; a countermeasure.

**대안렌즈**(對眼—) 〖물리〗 an eye lens; an eyeglass; an eyepiece.

**대액**(大厄) a great misfortune 〔disaster, calamity〕.

**대야** a washbasin; a washbowl.

**-대야** 《…다고 해야》 ¶ 일을 한대야 도와주지 I'll help you only if you exert yourself. / 얼음이 물보다 차대야 말이 되지 To make sense you have to say that ice is colder than water.

**대양**(大洋) the ocean. ¶ ～의 oceanic / ～의 한가운데서 in the middle of the ocean; in mid-ocean 〔mid-sea〕 / 저 ～ 너머의 대륙 a transoceanic continent / ～을 가로질러서 across the ocean / ～을 항해하다 sail 〔plow〕 the ocean. ◉ ～도(島) an oceanic island. ～항로 an ocean line: ～ 항로선 an ocean liner. ～횡단 비행 a transoceanic flight.

**대양주**(大洋州) Oceania; the Oceanic Islands. ◉ ～사람 an Oceanian.

**대어**(大魚) a big 〔large〕 fish. ¶ ～를 놓치다 [비유적] miss a good chance of (winning) success. ◉ ～낚시 big-game fishing. ～상 the award for catching the biggest game fish.

**대어**(大漁) a good 〔rich〕 haul; a large 〔big〕 catch (of fish). ¶ ～를 하다 have a large catch of 《sardine》; make a good haul of 《pollack》. / ～를 빈다 Good fish!

**대언**(大言) big words; big talk; a loud boast. ～하다 talk big; boast; brag. ◉ ～장담 boasting; bragging.

**대업**(大業) ① 《큰 사업》 a great enterprise 〔work〕; a great deed 〔achievement〕. ¶ ～을 맡다 be charged with an important task / ～을 이루다 achieve a great work. ② 《건국》 foundation 〔establishment〕 of a country. ¶ 건국의 ～ the great work of founding the state.

**대여**(貸與) lending; a loan. ～하다 lend; lease; loan. ¶ 무료로 ～하다 lend free; loan 《*a thing*》 without charge / 돈을 ～하다 loan 〔lend〕 《*a person*》 some money. ◉ ～금 a loan. ～자 a lender. ～장학금 a loan scholarship.

**대여섯, 대엿** about five or six.

**대역**(大役) 《임무》 an important duty 〔task〕; 《역할》 a heavy role; an important part; 《사명》 an important mission. ¶ ～을 맡다 undertake 〔accept〕 an important part / ～이 맡겨지다 be given 〔be charged with〕 an important task 〔mission〕 / 그는 햄릿 ～을 멋지게 연기했다 He played the important part of Hamlet splendidly.

**대역**(大逆) high treason. ◉ ～무도 heinous treason; 《시역(弑逆)》 regicide. ～사건 a case of high treason. ～죄 (high) treason; lese-majesty; *lèse-majesté*(F.): ～죄로 사형을 선고받다 be sentenced to death on a charge of high treason.

**대역**(代役) a substitute; 《연극의》 an understudy; 《영화의》 a stand-in. ～하다 play the part for 《*a person*》; stand in 〔for〕; understudy 《the leading actor》; act as a substitute《for》. ¶ 위험한 장면에서는 스턴트맨이 그 배우의 ~을 했다 A stunt man stood in for the actor in a dangerous scene.

**대역**(對譯) a translation printed side by side with the original text; a text《of *Hamlet*》with《*its* Korean》translation printed on the opposite page. ¶ 이 책은 영한~으로 되어 있다 In this book the English original has its Korean translation on the opposite page. ◉ ~판(版) a bilingual edition.

**대연습**(大演習)〖군사〗《hold》grand maneuvers.

**대열**(隊列)《종렬》a column; a file;《횡렬》a rank; a line;《대형》(a) formation. ¶ ~ 정연하게 in regular ranks〔perfect order〕/ ~을 정돈하다 dress〔align〕ranks; line up / ~을 짓다 get〔form〕in line / ~을 지어 행진했다 We marched in line〔file, ranks〕.

**대엿새** about five or six days.

**대영**(對英) [부사적] toward〔with〕Great Britain. ◉ ~무역 trade with Britain. ~정책 policy toward Britain.

**대오**(隊伍) =대열(隊列). ¶ ~를 짓다 form ranks / ~를 지어 행진하다 march in「parade〔grand order〕.

**대오다** come〔arrive, get here〕on time. ¶ 약속한 시간에 ~ come at the appointed time / 여섯 시까지 대오시오 Get here by six.

**대오리** a bamboo strip.

**대오하다**(大悟一) attain divine enlightenment; attain spiritual awakening; form *one's* philosophy of life. ¶ 그는 활연대오했다 Spiritual awakening came to him.

**대왕**(大王) ①《선왕》His Majesty the late King. ②《왕의 존칭》Your〔His〕Majesty; ... the Great. ¶ 세종 ~ Sejong the Great / 알렉산더 ~ Alexander the Great / 염라 ~ *Yama,* the King of Hell.

**대외**(對外) [형용사적] outside; foreign; external; overseas (해외의); (toward) abroad. ◉ ~경제 정책 연구원《한국의》the Korea Institute for International Economic Policy(생략 KIEP). ~관계 foreign〔international〕relations. ~교섭 negotiations with a foreign country. ~군사 판매 차관 the foreign military sales credits (생략 FMSC). ~권익 foreign rights and interests. ~무역 foreign〔overseas〕trade. ~문제 international〔external〕issues. ~방송 a broadcast beamed overseas; broadcasting abroad. ~원조 a foreign aid; an aid to a foreign country: ~원조법《미국의》the Foreign Assistant Act. ~정책 a foreign〔an external〕policy. ~투자 overseas〔external〕investment.

**대요**(大要) a summary; an outline; a résumé; the gist; substance (내용); a synopsis; an epitome (문학 작품·강연의); an abstract (성명·문서·연설의). ¶ 국사 ~ an outline of Korean history / 보고서의 ~ the gist of a report / ~를 말하다 give a summary〔an outline〕《of》; sum up; summarize / 그 계획의 ~를 설명하다 explain an outline of the project / 자네 논문의 ~를 말해보게 Give the summary〔outline〕of your paper.

**대욕**(大慾) avarice; greed. ¶ ~은 무욕(無慾)과 같다 Grasp all, lose all.

**대용**(代用) substitution. ~하다 substitute〔use〕《A》for《B》. ¶ …의 ~으로 in place of...; in substitution for... / …의 ~이 되다 serve for〔as〕; can be used as substitute《for》/ 이 빈 깡통을 재떨이 ~으로 쓰다 use this empty can as an ashtray / 이 궤짝은 식탁 ~이 된다 This box will serve for〔as〕a table. / 석탄이 석유 ~이 될까 Can we substitute coal for oil? ◉ ~가능성 substitutability. ~물, ~품 a substitute (article)《for》. ~식 substitute〔ersatz〕food;《밥의》a rice substitute. ~어〖문법〗a substitute.

**대용**(貸用) using on loan; borrowing. ~하다 take〔use〕on loan; borrow.

**대우**〖농업〗grain planted as a catch crop with wheat or barley. ◉ ~깨〔콩, 팥〕sesame〔beans, redbeans〕planted as a catch crop with wheat〔barley〕.

**대우**(待遇)《처우》treatment;《접대》reception; service (호텔 등의);《급료》pay; salary; remuneration (보수). ~하다 treat; receive; entertain; pay. ¶ 최상의 ~ the red carpet treatment / 이사 ~ 부장 a department chief with board-member status / 과장 ~의《an editor》with section-chief-status / ~가 좋은《손님에게》hospitable;《급료의》well-paid / ~가 좋다〔나쁘다〕be treated warmly〔coldly〕; meet with a friendly〔cold〕reception;《급료의》be well〔poorly〕paid / ~를 개선하다 improve「working〔labor〕conditions; increase the pay (승급하다) / 동등하게 ~하다 treat《*a person*》on the same footing《with〔as〕another》/ 지위에 상당한 ~를 하다 do《*a person*》the honor due to *his* position; do 《*a person*》 due honor / 이 회사는 ~가 좋다〔나쁘다〕 This company pays〔does not pay〕 us well. / 그녀는 호텔에서 친절한〔불친절한〕 ~를 받았다 She received kind〔bad〕 treatment at the hotel. / 그는 그런 친절한 ~를 받으리라고는 생각도 못했다 He little thought that he should meet with such a kind reception.

◉ ~개선 a raise of salary; an improvement of treatment〔labor conditions〕: ~ 개선을 위해 파업하다 go on a strike for better working conditions.

**대우**(對偶) ① 《짝지음》 a pair. ② 〖수학·논리〗 contraposition.

**대우주**(大宇宙) 〖철학〗 the great universe; a macrocosm.

**대우파다** 〖농업〗 plant a catch crop with wheat〔barley〕 in early spring.

**대운**(大運) 《운명》 fate; destiny; 《운수》 great fortune; good luck.

**대웅성**(大熊星) 〖천문〗 (stars of) the Great Bear; Ursa Major.

**대웅전**(大雄殿) 〖불교〗 the main building of a temple; the main hall〔shrine〕.

**대웅좌**(大熊座) 〖천문〗 the Great Bear. 「=큰곰자리.

**대원**(大願) an earnest prayer; *one's* cherished desire. ◉ ~성취 the attainment of *one's* desire.

**대원**(隊員) a member 《of an expedition team》. ¶ 소방~ a member of a fire brigade.

**대원수**(大元帥) the generalissimo; the commander-in-chief. 「principle.

**대원칙**(大原則) the broad〔dominant〕

**대월**(貸越) 《미불》 an outstanding account; 《당좌 예금 등의》 an overdraft. ¶ ~이 되다 remain unpaid〔outstanding〕; overdraw *one's* accounts / ~이 되어 있다 be overdrawn. ◉ ~계정 a creditor account.

**대위**(大尉) 〖육군〗 a captain; 〖해군〗 a lieutenant (생략 Lt., Lieut.); 〖공군〗 a captain 《미》; a flight lieutenant 《영》.

**대위법**(對位法) 〖음악〗 counterpoint. ¶ ~의 contrapuntal 《passages》. ◉ 이중~ double counterpoint.

**대유**(大儒) a great Confucianist; a great scholar.

**대음**(大飮) heavy〔deep〕 drinking; a carouse. ~하다 drink heavily; carouse; have a carouse〔spree〕.

**대응**(對應) ① 《상대·대처》 facing each other; confrontation; opposition. ~하다 face〔confront〕 each other; be opposed 《to》; cope 《with》. ¶ 새로운 정세에 ~하다 cope with the new situation. ② 《상응》 correspondence; symmetry (좌우의). ~하다 correspond 《with, to》; answer to; be equivalent 《to》; be symmetrical. ¶ 1대 1의 ~ 〖수학〗 one-to-one correspondence / 그것에 ~하는 말은 이것이다 This word「corresponds〔is equivalent〕 to that.

◉ ~각 〖수학〗 a homologous〔corresponding〕 angle. ~변 〖수학〗 homologous〔corresponding〕 sides. ~부 〖음악〗 a counterpart. ~책 a countermove; a countermeasure. 동형~ 〖수학〗 isomorphism.

**대의**(大意) 《개략》 the general idea〔meaning〕; an outline; a summary; a résumé (F.); 《요지》 the gist〔purport〕 《of a speech》; the substance. ¶ ~를 간추려 쓰다 make a résumé / 문장의 ~를 파악하다 grasp the general idea of a passage / 이 이론의 ~는 이렇다 In substance〔outline〕, the theory is as follows〔like this〕.

**대의**(大義) 《의리·목적》 a great duty〔cause〕; loyalty; 《정의》 justice; righteousness. ¶ ~를 위해 싸우다 fight for the great〔noble〕 cause 《of freedom》.

◉ ~명분 a just and great cause; *one's* highest duty: ~명분이 서지 않다 cannot be justified; be not justifiable / …라는 ~명분으로 in the cause of…; on the pretext of… / 그들은 ~명분을 찾고 있다 They are looking for a flag to die for. / 그것으로 ~명분이 선다 It gives me a good excuse. *or* It justifies my reason.

**대의**(代議) representation.

◉ ~원 a representative; a delegate (파견 의원). ~정치 representative〔parliamentary〕 government. ~제도 a representative〔parliamentary〕 system.

**대인**(大人) ① 《어른》 an adult; a grown-up person. ¶ ~용 for adult; 《남자》 for men; 《여자》 for women / ~이 되다 grow up to be a man〔woman〕. ② 《거인》 a big man; a giant. ③ 《고관》 a high (government) official; a (high) dignitary. ④ 《대인 군자》 a man of virtue; a noble gentleman; a great man. ¶ 그에게는 ~의 품격이 있다 He impresses us a man of great character. ⑤ 《남의 아버지》 your〔his〕 esteemed father.

**대인**(代印) a seal set by proxy; signing per procuration. ~하다 sign〔set a seal〕 by proxy; affix *one's* seal to 《a paper》 as proxy for 《*a person*》. ¶ ~도 무방하다 Signature 〔Signing〕 per procuration would do. *or* You may get somebody to sign it for you.

**대인**(對人) [부사적] toward 〔with〕 personnel 〔the person〕. ¶ ~의 personnel; personal. ◉ ~공포증 anthrophobia; a morbid fear of meeting people. ~과세 personal tax. ~관계〔신용〕 personal relations 〔credit〕. ~담보 personal security. ~보험 《미》 bodily injury liability insurance.

**대인기**(大人氣) great popularity; a great success; a (big) hit; a boom. ¶ ~를 끌다 be very popular; make a great hit / 그 공연은 ~다 The performance ˹has created a sensation 〔has a great run〕. / 이런 음악은 요즘 젊은이들 사이에 ~다 Music of this kind has achieved great popularity among young people in recent years.

**대인물**(大人物) a great man; a great character 〔figure〕; a man of great ˹caliber. ¶ 그는 ~로 추앙되었다 He was looked up to as a great man.

**대일**(對日) [부사적] toward 〔with〕 Japan. ¶ ~ 외교 관계 diplomatic relations with Japan / 미국의 ~ 외교 방침 the U.S. diplomatic policy toward Japan.
◉ ~감정 the feeling 〔sentiments〕 toward Japan: ~ 감정이 극히 나쁘다 The feeling is very bad toward the Japanese. ~강화 조약 the peace treaty with Japan. ~ 무역〔관계〕 trade 〔relations〕 with Japan: ~ 무역 적자〔흑자〕 the trade deficit 〔surplus〕 between Korea and Japan. ~원조 aid to Japan.

**대임**(大任) 《임무》 a great task; an important charge 〔service, duty〕; 《요직》 an important office 〔position〕; 《책임》 heavy responsibility 〔trust〕; 《사명》 an important mission. ¶ ~을 맡다 undertake a great task / ~을 맡기다 entrust 《*a person*》 with an important duty / ~을 띠고 있다 be charged 〔entrusted〕 with an important duty 〔task〕 / ~을 완수하다 carry through 〔perform, acquit *oneself* of 〕 a great task; fulfill a great mission / 그녀는 흔쾌히 그 ~을 떠맡았다 She was willingly to undertake ˹the heavy responsibility 〔the great task〕.

**대입**(代入) 〚수학〛 substitution. ~하다 substitute 《*ax* for *x*》.

**대입수능시험**(大入修能試驗) the national 〔state-run〕 scholastic achievement examination for college entrance; 《미》 the Scholastic Aptitude Test (생략 SAT).

**대입준비학원**(大入準備學院) a college entrance test preparation institute.

**대자** a bamboo measure 〔rule〕.

**대자**(大字) a large character; 《대문자》 a capital letter.

**대자**(帶磁) 〚물리〛 magnetization. ~하다 become magnetic; be magnetized. ◉ ~율 magnetic susceptibility.

**대자대비**(大慈大悲) 〚불교〛 Buddha's great mercy and compassion. ¶ ~하신 관세음보살 Avalokitesvara of Great Love and Great Mercy.

**대자보**(大字報) a big-character poster. ¶ 많은 학생들이 대학 캠퍼스에 부착된 ~를 읽고 있다 Many students are reading a big-character poster at the college campus.

**대자연**(大自然) nature; (Mighty) Nature; the great outdoors; Mother Nature.

**대작**(大作) a great work; a masterpiece (걸작); a work of large size (대형의).

**대작**(代作) ① 《행위》 composing 〔writing〕 for another; ghostwriting; 《작품》 a vicarious work; a ghostwritten article. ~하다 compose 〔write〕 for 《*a person*》. ¶ 그녀가 그의 논문을 ~하고 있다 She has been ghostwritten his article. ② = 대파(代播).
◉ ~자(者) a ghostwriter.

**대작**(對酌) drinking together. ~하다 drink together; hobnob 《with》.

**대잠**(對潛) ¶ ~(용)의 antisubmarine. ◉ ~초계(기) an antisubmarine patrol (plane).

**대장** a blacksmith; a smith (★ 보통 goldsmith, tinsmith처럼 복합어로 쓰임).
◉ ~간 a blacksmith's shop; a smithy. ~일 smithery; blacksmith work. ~장이 a blacksmith: ~장이 집에 식칼이 논다 《속담》 The tailor's wife is worst clad. *or* The shoemaker's wife goes barefoot.

**대장**(大將) 《계급》 〚육군·공군〛 a general; 〚해군〛 an admiral; 《두령》 a head; a chief; a boss. ◉ ~직 generalship; admiralship.

**대장**(大腸) the large intestine; the colon. ◉ ~균 colitis germs; colon bacillus. ~염 colitis. ~카타르 catarrh of the colon.

**대장**(隊長) a captain; a commander; a leader (지도자). ¶ 탐험 ~ the leader 〔chief〕 of an expedition (team) / 소~ a platoon leader / 중〔대〕~ a company

〔battalion〕 commander.

**대장**(臺帳) a ledger (회계원장); a register (기록부); a land register (토지 대장); an inventory (재고품 대장). ¶ ～에 기입하다 make an entry 《of an item》 in the ledger / 그것을 ～에 기입하는 것을 잊었다 I forgot to put 〔enter〕 it in the register 〔ledger〕.

**대장경**(大藏經) 〖불교〗 the complete collection of Buddhist Scriptures 〔Sutras〕; *Tripitaka.*

**대장부**(大丈夫) a manly 〔brave〕 man; a heroic man. ¶ ～답게 굴라 Behave like a man. *or* Play the man. / ～라면 그런 짓은 못한다 You should be man enough not to do a thing like that.

**대저**(大著) a great work 〔book〕.

**대저울** a beam(-type) balance.

**대적**(大敵) 《강적》 a powerful 〔formidable〕 enemy; 《경쟁자》 a great rival; a formidable opponent 〔competitor〕. ¶ 민주주의의 ～ the most deadly foe of democracy / 그는 나의 ～이다 I have a formidable enemy in him.

**대적**(對敵) ① 《적대》 hostility; antagonism. ～하다 be hostile 《to》; turn against; oppose; be antagonistic 《to》. ② 《맞섬·겨룸》 matching; a match; an equal. ～하다 match; equal; rival. ¶ ～할 사람이 없다 have no equal 〔match, parallel〕; be without a match; be peerless.

**대전**(大典) ① 《의식》 an Imperial 〔a state〕 ceremony 〔function〕. ② 《법전》 a canon. 「마마 = 대전(大殿).

**대전**(大殿) His Majesty the King. ◉ ～

**대전**(大戰) a great war 〔battle〕. ¶ ～전〔후〕의 prewar 〔postwar〕. / 세계 ～ the World War / 제1〔2〕차 세계 ～ World War Ⅰ〔Ⅱ〕; the First 〔Second〕 World War. ◉ ～기념비 a cenotaph.

**대전**(帶電) 〖물리〗 electrification. ～하다 take a 〔an electrical〕 charge. ¶ ～하고 있는 electrified; charged (with electricity); live 《wire》 / +〔−〕로 ～하다 become positively 〔negatively〕 charged. ◉ ～미립자 a charged corpuscle. ～방지제 an anti-static spray. ～체 a charged 〔an electrified〕 body.

**대전**(對戰) ① 《전쟁》 waging war; engagement. ～하다 oppose 〔fight, confront, encounter〕 《the enemy》. ② 《경기·시합 따위》 competition; a match; a bout. ～하다 《시합하다》 play 《a match》 against...; have a game with...; compete 《with》; fight 《with》. ¶ ～시키다 match 〔pit〕 《*a person* against another》 / 작년도의 우승자와 ～하다 have 〔play〕 a game with the championship-holder of last year / 이 두 시합의 승자들이 내일 ～한다 The winners of these two games will meet tomorrow. ◉ ～료 fight money. ～성적 the win=loss records 《between A and B》; the result of a game 〔match〕.

**대전어**(大錢魚) 〖어류〗 a gizzard shad.

**대전제**(大前提) 〖논리〗 the major premise 《of a syllogism》; the sumption.

**대전차**(對戰車) ¶ ～(용)의 antitank. ◉ ～ 미사일 an antitank missile(생략 ATM). ～지뢰 an antitank mine. ～포 an antitank gun; a bazooka. ～호(壕) an antitank trench.

**대절**(貸切) 《미》 reserving; booking; engaging; 《게시》 "Reserved". ⇨ 전세.

**대접** 《그릇》 a (soup) bowl. ¶ 국 한 ～ a bowl of soup / ～에 담아내다 serve in a bowl.

**대접**(待接) ① 《환대》 hospitality; welcome; 《대우》 treatment; (a) reception. ～하다 be hospitable 〔offer *one's* hospitality〕 to 《*a person*》; make 《*a person*》 welcome. ¶ 따뜻한 ～을 받다 be warmly 〔cordially〕 received; be given a cordial reception / 손님을 따뜻이 ～하다 receive guests warmly / 따뜻한 ～에 감사드립니다 I am most grateful for your warm hospitality. ② 《음식 접대》 treatment; entertainment. ～하다 treat; serve; entertain. ¶ 다과 ～을 받다 be served 〔entertained〕 refreshments 〔tea and cakes〕 / 오찬 ～을 받다 be entertained at luncheon / 나는 그들에게 저녁을 ～했다 I treated 〔entertained〕 them to dinner.

**대정맥**(大靜脈) 〖해부〗 the vena cava (*pl.* the venae cavae).

**대제**(大帝) a great emperor. ¶ 피터 ～ Peter the Great. 「fete.

**대제**(大祭) a grand festival; a great

**대제사장**(大祭司長) a high 〔chief〕 priest. 「tide; the spring tide.

**대조**(大潮) the major tide; the flood

**대조**(對照) (a) contrast; (an) antithesis; 《비교》 (a) comparison; (a) collation. ～하다 contrast 〔compare, collate〕 《A with B》; make a comparison 《between A and B》; set 《A》 against 《B》. ¶ 명암의 ～ the contrast between light and shade / ...와 ～적으로 in contrast to... / ～를 이루다 form a contrast; be in 《striking》 contrast 《to, with》 / 두 사본을 ～하다 collate the two manuscripts / 그 번역을 원문과 비교 ~해 보아라 Compare the translation with the original. / 그녀의 반응은 톰의 그것과는 완전히 ~적이었다 Her reaction was a complete contrast to Tom's. / 이 건물은 주변과 뚜렷한 ~를 이루고 있다 This building presents a striking contrast to its surroundings. ◉ ~실험 〖생물〗 a control experiment. ~연구 contrastive study 《of English and Korean》. ~표 a calculating table.

**대족**(大族) a mighty clan 〔family〕; a flourishing 〔prosperous〕 family.

**대종**(大宗) ① 《계통》 the main stock; the lineage of the head family. ② 《주요한 것》 the main items. ¶ ~을 이루다 form its majority. ◉ ~가 the general head family. ~손 the heir of the general head family.

**대종상**(大鐘賞) Grand Bell (best film) 「Awards.

**대좌**(對坐) sitting face to face. ~하다 sit opposite 《to *a person*》; sit face to face 〔*vis-à-vis* (F.)〕 《with *a person*》.

**대좌**(臺座) a pedestal.

**대죄**(大罪) 《종교·도덕상의》 a grave 〔deadly〕 sin; 《법률상의》 a grave offense; a great 〔grave, heinous〕 crime. ¶ ~를 범하다 commit a great crime. ◉ ~인 a felon; a great offender; an atrocious criminal.

**대죄하다**(待罪—) await the official decision on *one's* punishment.

**대주**(大酒) heavy 〔deep, hard〕 drinking; carousal. ◉ ~객 a heavy drinker; a toper; a sot; a soaker.

**대주**(代走) ~하다 〖야구〗 run for another runner. ◉ ~자 a pinch runner.

**대주**(貸主) a lender; a creditor (채권자); a lessor (부동산의).

**대주교**(大主教) 《가톨릭》 an archbishop. ¶ 캔터베리 ~ the Archbishop of Canterbury.

**대주다** ① 《공급하다》 supply 〔provide, furnish〕 《*a person* with *a thing*》; pay 〔meet, cover〕 expenses (비용을). ¶ 용돈을 ~ allow 《*a person*》 pocket money / 아무의 집에 식량과 옷을 ~ supply *a person's* home with food and clothes / 아들에게 학비를 ~ provide *one's* son with school expenses / 장사 밑천을 ~ furnish 《*a person*》 with funds. ② 《일러주다》 let 《*a person*》 know; tell 《*a person*》; tip off (몰래). ¶ 집을 ~ refer 《*a person*》 to a house / 장사의 비결을 ~ let 《*a person*》 know the tricks of trade.

**대중** ① 《겉어림》 a rough estimate 〔calculation〕; 《추측》 (a) conjecture; a guess. ¶ ~(을) 잡다 make a rough estimate / 눈~을 잡다 measure with *one's* eye / 비용의 ~을 잡아보다 estimate the expense / ~이 맞다〔틀리다〕 be right 〔wrong〕 in *one's* conjecture; guess right 〔wrong〕 / 건축비의 ~을 잡다 make a rough estimate of the cost of building 《a house》. ② 《표준》 a standard (to rely on); consistency; 《목표》 a guide; a mark; an aim; 《한도》 measure. ¶ ~을 삼다 set up a standard; aim 《at》 / 등대를 ~삼아 앞으로 나아가다 go on with lighthouse as *one's* guide / 무슨 말인지 ~을 못 잡겠다 I can't make head or tail of it.

**대중**(大衆) the (general) public (★ 《미》에서는 단수 취급); the masses(★ 복수 취급); the people(★ 복수 취급); the mass of the people; the multitude; the grass roots.

> 용법 the **public** 합리적인 판단이 가능한 건전한 민주주의를 지지하는 사람들. the **masses** 사회 기구를 잘 이해하지 못하고 매스컴 장단에 호응하는 사람들. 종종 경멸적인 뜻으로 쓰임. the **people** 국가나 자치 단체를 구성하는 일반 사람들, 특히 선거민. the **multitude** 「다수의 사람들 → 군중」이란 뜻에서 연유된 말. 보통, 무식하고 쉽게 상황·매스컴 따위에 영향을 받는 사람들이란 뜻으로, the masses와 비슷한 뜻으로 쓰임. the **grass roots** 권력이나 특수한 기술·지식을 갖지 않은 일반 사람들. 흔히 「민초」란 뜻으로도 번역됨.

¶ ~적인〔취향의〕 popular; for the masses; for popular use; 《구어》 pop / ~의 소리 public opinion / ~을 위한 정당 a party for the masses / ~의 지지를 얻다 have a support of the public; have mass support / ~을 우롱하다 fool the public / ~에게 호소하다 address the mass of people; appeal to the masses / ~의 마음을 꽉 잡고 있다 have a strong hold on the public mind. ◉ ~가수 a popular singer. ~가요 a popular 〔pop〕 song. ~과세 mass taxation. ~노선 popular line. ~문학 popular literature; sensational literature. ~문화 popular culture. ~사회 (a) mass society. ~성 popularity; popular appeal. ~소설 a popular novel 〔story〕. ~식당 a general eating house 〔place〕; a cheap restaurant. ~심리 mass psychology. ~오락 mass entertainment: 영화의 ∼오락으로서의 가치 the mass entertainment value of cinema production. ∼운동 a mass movement: ∼ 운동을 일으키다 start mass movement 〔people's drive〕. ∼음악 popular music. ∼작가 a popular writer; a pulp writer. ∼잡지 a popular magazine. ∼전달 mass communication. ∼정당 a mass party. ∼정책 a policy toward the masses. ∼집회 a mass rally. ∼차 a popular car (대중 취향의); an economy car (경제적인). ∼판(版) a popular edition. ∼화 popularization: 과학의 ∼화 popularization of science / ∼화하다 popularize; become popularized; make 《*a thing*》 popular.

**대중없다** 《종작없다》 (be) inconsistent; pointless; changeable; unreliable; 《일정치 않다》 (be) unsettled; uncertain; unfixed; vague (애매); 《표준이 없다》 lack a standard. ¶ 대중없는 말 inconsistent 〔pointless〕 remarks; unreliable statements / 우편이 어떤 때는 세 시에, 어떤 때는 다섯시에 오고 해서 시간이 ∼ There's no telling about the mail—sometimes it comes at three and sometimes at five. / 그는 하는 짓이 대중없어 믿을 수가 없다 He is so inconsistent in his behavior that you can never depend upon him. / 시작하는 시간은 ∼ There is no fixed rule about the hour of commencement.

**대증**(對症) allopathy. ◉ ∼약 an allopathic remedy; a specific medicine. ∼요법 〖의학〗 allopathy; allopathic treatment; symptomatic 〔expectant〕 treatment: ∼요법가 an allopathist / ∼요법을 하다 treat symptoms; meet symptoms as they call for attention.

**대지**(大地) the earth; the ground; mother earth 《시어》. ¶ ∼를 밟다 tread on the ground.

**대지**(大志) a great ambition; an aspiration(★ ambition은 특정한 목표나 성공·명성 따위에 대한 야심, aspiration은 동경하는 것이 되고 싶은 포부). ¶ ∼를 품다 have 〔harbor〕 an ambition 《to *do*》/ 소년들아 ∼를 품어라 Boys, be ambitious!

**대지**(大指) the thumb; the big finger.

**대지**(垈地) a site; a (building) lot; a plot of land; ground. ¶ ∼의 선정 the selection of a site / 학교의 ∼ a site for a school / ∼를 찾다〔확보하다〕 look for 〔secure〕 a site 《for a building》/ 내 집의 ∼는 100 평방미터이다 My plot of land is 100 square meters. ◉ ∼면적 plottage.

**대지**(帶紙) a (half-)wrapper. ⇨ 띠지.

**대지**(貸地) leased land; lot 〔land〕 for rent 〔to let 《영》〕.

**대지**(臺地) 《고원》 a plateau; a tableland; a height (높은 언덕).

**대지**(臺紙) 《두꺼운 종이》 ground paper; pasteboard; a board; a mount (사진의); a mat (그림의).

**대지**(對地) anti-ground. ¶ 공∼ 공격 an air-to-ground attack / 지∼미사일 a ground-to-ground missile. ◉ ∼공격 a ground attack; an air raid. ∼속도 《비행기의》 groundspeed.

**대지주**(大地主) a great landlord; a big landowner.

**대지팡이** a bamboo cane 〔stick〕.

**대진**(代診) a locum 《for》. ∼하다 examine 〔diagnose〕 《a patient》 in 〔on〕 behalf of 《another doctor》; act as a locum tenens. ◉ ∼의사 an assistant doctor; a doctor's assistant.

**대진**(對陣) 《군사》 the confrontation 《of armies》. ∼하다 confront 〔face〕 each other; encamp facing each other. ¶ 강을 끼고 ∼하다 confront 〔face〕 each other across a river.

**대질**(對質) 〖법〗 confrontation; face-to-face questioning. ¶ 피고와 원고를 ∼시키다 confront the accused with the accuser; bring the accused face to face with the accuser. ◉ ∼심문 (a) cross-examination.

**대질리다** get defied.

**대집행**(代執行) 〖법〗 execution by proxy.

**대짜**(大—) a big one. ¶ ∼ 못 a big nail / ∼ 물고기를 하나 잡다 catch a big fish.

**대짜배기**(大—) a big 〔gigantic〕 one; an awfully big one; a whopper. ¶ ∼ 그릇 a big dish / ∼로 in 〔into, with〕 a big one; on a large scale / ∼로 한잔하다 have a drink in a large mug / 그는 사소한 일로 아내와 ∼로 다투었다 He had a big quarrel with his wife over trifles.

**대쪽** (a piece of) split bamboo. ¶ 성미가 ∼같은 사람 a straightforward person; a single-minded person.

**대차**(大差) a great 〔wide, big, vast, striking〕 difference; a big discrepancy 〔disparity〕. ¶ ∼가 있다 be much 〔very〕 different 《from》; differ much 〔a great deal〕 《from》/ ∼ 없다 make no great difference; be much the same / ∼를 내다 get a big 〔long〕 lead 《on》/ 양자 사이에는 ∼가 있다 There is a wide difference between the two. / 우리 팀은 5점의 ～로 이겼다 Our team won the game by the wide margin of 5 points. / 총선에서 공화당이 ～로 이겼다 The Republican Party won by a substantial majority in the general election.

**대차**(貸借) 《빌려주고 빌림》 borrowing and lending (★ 보통 borrowing을 먼저 씀); (a) loan; debt and credit (장부상의). ¶ ～를 대조하다 balance / ～를 차감하다 balance account / ～를 결산하다 strike a balance; sum up the debtor and creditor account / 이것으로 ～가 없어진다 This will settle the account. *or* This will「put 〔make〕 us even. ◉ ～계약(서) a charter. ～계정 a debtor and creditor account: ～ 계정서 a current account. ～관계 financial relations; accounts: 두 사람은 ～ 관계가 있다 The two have accounts with each other. / 나는 그와 ～ 관계가 없다 I have no accounts to settle with him. ～기한 the term of a loan. ～대조표 《draw up》 a balance sheet (생략 B/S): ～ 대조표 감사 balance sheet audit. ～소송 an action for debt. ～인 lessor and lessee; debtor and creditor. 국제～결제 the balance of international payments.

**대차륜**(大車輪) 《철봉의》 a giant swing.

**대찰**(大刹) a great 〔noted〕 temple; a large temple.

**대책**(對策) a step; a measure (★ step과 measure는 보통 복수형으로 쓰임); 《대항책》 a countermeasure; a counterplan; a countermove. ¶ ～으로서 as a countermeasure / ～을 강구하다 consider 〔take〕 a countermeasure 〔counterplan〕; devise a countermove; take measures 〔steps〕 to meet 〔cope with〕 the situation / ～을 세우다 work out a countermeasure / ～을 소홀히 하다 neglect to take appropriate measures promptly / 신속한 ～ 강구에 쫓기다 be forced to take prompt measures / 이것이 그 문제에 대한 최선의 ～이다 This is the best way 〔steps〕 dealing with the problem. / 정부는 무역 마찰에 대한 새로운 ～을 마련하겠다고 약속했다 The Government has promised to take new measures against trade friction(s). / 계속 늘어나는 쓰레기 처리를 위해 신속한 ～을 세워야 한다 Prompt measures should be taken to deal with the ever-increasing quantities of garbage. ◉ 비상～ an emergency 〔a drastic〕 measure; urgent measures: 비상 ～을 쓰다 take 〔resort〕 to exceptional 〔extreme〕 measures. 종합～ 《work out》 comprehensive countermeasures 《against》.

**대처승**(帶妻僧) a married Buddhist priest; a non-celibate Buddhist monk.

**대처하다**(對處―) cope 〔deal〕 《with》; tackle; meet; manage. ¶ 식량 부족에 ～ cope with the food shortage / 난국에 ～ cope with a difficult situation 〔crisis〕 / 적의 여하한 위협에도 완전히 대처할 능력이 있다 be completely capable of meeting any enemy threat / 그녀는 그 일에 냉정히 대처했다 She met 〔dealt with〕 the problem calmly.

**대척**(對蹠) 《정반대》 diametrical opposition. ¶ ～의 antipodal; diametrically opposite. ◉ ～점 the antipode. ～지 the antipodes.

**대천**(大川) a big 〔large〕 river.

**대첩**(大捷) a great 〔signal, sweeping〕 victory. ～하다 win a sweeping victory.

**대청**(大青) 『식물』 woad.

**대청**(大廳) the main floored room; a hall. ◉ ～마루 ＝대청(大廳).

**대체**(大體) ① 《요점》 the principal parts; the main 〔chief〕 point(s); the gist; 《취지》 the purport; 《개략》 an outline. ¶ ～의 뜻 general meaning / ～적인 원칙 general principles / ～로 《일반적으로》 on the whole; in the main; by and large; generally (speaking); 《대부분》 for the most part; 《대략》 roughly; in the rough; almost / ～로 끝나다 be「all but 〔almost, nearly〕 over / ～로 다음과 같다 It may be summarized as follows. / 이곳 기후는 ～로 따뜻하다 The climate here is generally mild. / ～로 이렇다 It's something like this. / 나의 의견은 ～로 당신과 같소 My opinion is on the whole the same as yours. / 화재로 인한 손해는 ～로 3백만 원 정도다 The damage caused by the fire is roughly estimated at three million won. / ～로 그의 사업은 잘 되고 있다 By and large his business is going well. / 양국은 ～로 의견의 일치를 보았다 The two 〔Each〕 countries reached an agreement in principle. / ～로 그런 사람이 많다 Generally speaking, there are many people like that.
② ⇨도대체(都大體).

**대체**(代替) alternation; change; substitution (대용). ～하다 alternate 《with》;

be substituted; substitute 《for》. ¶~ 법칙〔원리〕 『경제』 the principle of substitution.
◉ ~물 『법』 a substitute; a fungible. ~식량 substitute food 《for rice》. ~안(案) 《suggest》 an alternative idea. ~ 에너지〔연료〕원(源) substitute energy (sources); energy alternative: 각종 ~ 에너지원의 개발 exploitation of various substitute energy sources / ~ 에너지원을 개발하여 국내 자원을 가장 효과적으로 이용하다 explore alternate energy sources and utilize domestic resources most effectively. ~품 a substitute 《for》; a back-up (긴급시 예비품). ~효과 『경제』 substitution effect.

**대체**(對替) 『경제』 transfer; (ex)change. ~하다 transfer 《accounts》; exchange 《a bill》. ¶ 우편~로 송금하다 send money by postal transfer / 수수료를 아무의 계정으로 ~하다 transfer a commission to *a person's* account.
◉ ~계정 a transfer account: ~ 계정거래 a transfer account transaction. ~저금 〔계좌〕 a transfer savings 〔account〕. ~전표 a transfer slip.

**대추**[1] 《과실》 a jujube; a Chinese date. ¶ 그는 ~씨 같다 [비유적] He is small but hardy. ◉ ~나무 a jujube tree: ~나무 방망이다 《*a person*》 is toughly built / ~ 나무에 연 걸리듯 [비유적] be up to *one's* ears 〔be over head and ears〕 in debt; be deeply in debt.

**대추**[2] 《물려 낸 물건》 《his brother's》 hand-me-downs; 《her sister's》 reach=me-downs 《영》; a used 〔second-hand〕 thing. ¶ 나는 언니의 대추를 입어야 되니까 지겹다 I'm fed up with having to wear my sister's hand-me=downs.

**대출**(貸出) lending; 《금전의》 a loan; an advance (선급·가지급 따위); 《도서의》 lending service. ~하다 make a loan 《to》; lend 〔loan〕 out. ¶ 도서를 ~하다 lend 〔loan〕 a book / 금전을 ~하다 make a loan 《to *a person*》; advance money; make advances / 도서관의 ~을 이용하다 use the lending service of a library / 5부 이자로 ~하다 lend 〔loan〕 money at 5 percent interest / 이 책은 ~합니까 Do you lend out this book? / 그 책은 ~중입니다 The book is out on loan.
◉ ~계 a lending clerk; 《부서》 the lending section 《of a library, bank》. ~금 loaned 〔advanced〕 money. ~도서 loaned books; books on loan; books to be lent out. ~동결 a loan freeze. ~자금 money to lend. 부당~ an illegal advance; a reckless loan. 비상~ emergency advances. 신용~ a loan without security given.

**대충**(代充) supplement by substitution. ~하다 supplement 〔replenish〕 with substitutes.

**대충** 《대강》 roughly; loosely; grossly; 《거의》 almost; nearly; about. ¶ ~ 말하면 speaking roughly; in short / ~ 들려주다 give an outline 《of 》/ ~ 훑어보다 glance 〔look〕 《over》; run 《*one's* eyes》 through / ~ 알고 있다 have a general knowledge 《of 》/ 비용을 ~ 어림잡다 make a rough estimate of expenses / 책을 ~ 읽다 skim through a book / 일을 ~ 하다 make a hasty job of it; do a slapdash job; scamp; give it a lick and a promise / 사건의 전말을 그에게 ~ 이야기했다 I gave him the brief outline of the accident. / (그것을 끝내는 데) ~ 열흘이 걸릴 것이다 Roughly speaking, it will take ten days (to finish it). / 나는 아침마다 몇몇 신문을 ~ 훑어 본다 I run my eyes over several newspapers every morning. / 「자네가 생각나는 것은 이것뿐인가」―「~ 그런 정도야」 "Is this all you can recall?"—"That's about it." / 여비가 ~ 백만 원이 된다 Travel expenses amount to about a million won. / 집은 ~ 다 지었다 The house is nearly finished.

**대충자금**(對充資金) 『경제』 the counterpart fund.

**대취**(大醉) dead drunkenness. ~하다 get dead 〔beastly, blind〕 drunk; be boozy 《속어》; get tanked up 《속어》. ¶ ~한 사람 a drunken person; a drunkard; a drunk / ~해 있다 be beastly 〔dead〕 drunk; be as drunk as a lord 〔fish, fly〕; be blind 《속어》.

**대치**(代置) replacement. ~하다 replace 《A with B》.

**대치**(對峙) confrontation; standing face to face; standing opposite each other. ~하다 confront; face 《the enemy》; stand face to face 《with》. ¶ 쌍방이 ~하여 서로 양보하지 않는다 Neither would yield to the other in their rivalry.

**대칭**(對稱) ① 『수학』 symmetry. ¶ 좌우 ~ bilateral symmetry; bisymmetry / 선〔평면〕 ~ line 〔plane〕 symmetry / ~적(으로) symmetrical(ly) / 좌표의 원점에 대해서 ~을 이루는 두 점 two points which are symmetrical with respect

to the origin. ② 《제2인칭》 the second person.
◉ ～ 대명사 a 2nd-person pronoun; a pronoun of address. ～도형〔률〕 a symmetrical figure 〔law〕. ～면 planes of symmetry. ～배광(配光) 〖전기〗 symmetrical light. ～배열(排列) 〖전기〗 symmetrical arrangement. ～식 a symmetric(al) expression. ～점 a symmetrical point. ～접속(接續) 〖전기〗 push-pull connection. ～축(軸) an axis of symmetry. ～함수〔삼각형〕 a symmetrical function 〔triangle〕. ～ 회로망 〖전기〗 symmetrical network.
**대칼** a bamboo knife.
**대타**(代打) ～하다 〖야구〗 pinch-hit 〔bat〕 《for》. ◉ ～자 a pinch hitter.
**대토**(代土) exchange of land; substitute land.
**대통**(一筒) a bamboo tube.
**대통**(一桶) 《담뱃대의》 the bowl of a tobacco pipe.
**대통**(大通) being wide open; success; prosperity. ～하다 be wide open; succeed; prosper; flourish. ¶ 운이 ～하다 have a spell of extremely good luck.
◉ ～운(運) extremely good luck.
**대통**(大統) the Royal 〔Imperial〕 line. ¶ ～을 잇다 continue the Royal line; succeed to the Throne.
**대통령**(大統領) the President 《of the United States》; the Chief 〔Federal〕 Executive 《미》. ¶ ～의 presidential / ～직〔지위〕 presidency; the presidential chair 〔office〕 / ～의 임기 a presidential term / 레이건 ～ President Reagan / ～에 당선되다 be elected President / ～에 취임하다 be sworn in as President / ～ 각하 《호칭》 Mr. President! / 그는 ～ 선거에 출마한다 He will run for presidency. / 그 전쟁은 카터 ～ 재임 중에 끝났다 The war came to an end during the presidency of Jimmy Carter. / 「케네디 ～은 몇 대 ～이지」—「35대 ～이야」 "What number of President is J.F. Kennedy?"—"He is the 35th President."
◉ ～ 경제 수석 비서관 the senior presidential secretary for economic affairs. ～경호실(장) (the Chief of ) the Office of the Presidential Security (Force). ～ 관저 a presidential residence; an executive mansion; the White House 《미》. ～ 교서 a Presidential message; the president's message. ～ 권한대행 the acting President. ～ 당선자 《취임전의》 the President-elect. ～령 a Presidential decree; an Executive ordinance. ～문장(紋章) the seal of the President. ～ 부인 the First Lady 《미》. ～ 비서 a presidential secretary. ～비서실 the Presidential Secretariat: ～ 비서실장 the Chief Presidential Secretary; the Presidential Secretary-General. ～선거(전) a presidential election (campaign). ～ 안보 보좌관 a presidential aide for security affairs. ～ 예비선거 《미국의》 the presidential primary. ～ 5년 단임제 a five-year single presidential term. ～제 a presidential government. ～ 직선제 a direct presidential election system. ～집무실 the president's office; the Oval Office (미국 백악관 내의). ～ 특별보좌관 a special assistant 《for the Foreign Affairs》 to the President. ～ 특사 a special envoy of President; a presidential envoy: 한·러간의 ～ 특사교환 an exchange of Russo-Korean presidential envoys. ～ 후보자 a candidate for the presidency; a presidential nominee 〔candidate〕.
**대퇴**(大腿) 〖해부〗 the thigh.
◉ ～골(骨) a thighbone; a femur (*pl.* ～s, -mora). ～근(筋) the femoral muscle. ～부 the femoral region.
**대파**(大破) ① 《깨짐》 a great destruction; heavy 〔serious〕 damage; wreck; ruin; havoc dilapidation. ～하다 [자동사] be greatly destroyed 〔dilapidated〕; be heavily damaged; be utterly ruined; be wrecked (배 따위가); be smashed (비행기 따위가). ¶ 배는 태풍 때문에 ～했다 The ship was badly 〔heavily〕 damaged by a typhoon. / 그 사고로 내 차는 ～했다 My car was smashed up in the accident. ② 《쳐부숨》 a crushing defeat. ～하다 [타동사] defeat completely; put to rout; rout 《the enemy》 utterly. ¶ 적의 함대를 ～했다 We have defeated the enemy fleet completely.
**대파**(代播) 〖농업〗 sowing a substitute plant in a dried rice-paddy. ～하다 plant a paddy with 《millet》.
**대판**(大一) ① 《큰 판》 a large 〔big, huge〕 scale. ¶ ～ 싸움 a big fight / ～ 씨름 a big *ssireum* match / ～(으로) 싸우다 fight a big fight. ② 《큰 도량》 generosity; magnanimity.
**대판**(大版) large size 《print, printing, edition》. ¶ ～의 large-sized; of large size.
**대패** 〖공구〗 a plane.

◉ 대팻날 a plane blade 〔iron〕. 대팻밥 (wood) shavings; planing refuse; 《포장용》 excelsior 《미》; wood wool 《영》. 대팻손 the handle of a plane. 대팻집 the wooden body of a plane; a plane stock.

**대패**(大敗) ① 《크게 짐》 a crushing 〔heavy, serious, severe, complete, disastrous, terrible〕 defeat; an utter rout; shellacking 《미속어》. ～하다 sustain 〔suffer, meet with〕 a crushing defeat; be put to rout; be routed; lose a battle completely. ¶ ～시키다 defeat utterly; put to rout; utterly rout 《the enemy》 / 우리 당은 총선거에서 ～했다 Our party sustained a crushing defeat in the general election. ② 《실패》 a great failure.

**대패질** planing; smoothing. ～하다 plane; smooth. ¶ 널판때기에 ～하다 plane a board.

**대포** drinking out of 〔from〕 a large cup. ◉ 대폿잔 a pottery bowl for drinking. 대폿집 a grogshop; a groggery.

**대포**(大砲) ① 《포》 a gun; a cannon; artillery [총칭]. ¶ ～소리 the roaring 〔boom〕 of guns / ～알 a shell / 한 줄로 늘어선 ～ a train of ordnance / ～를 쏘다 fire a gun / 그들은 적을 향해 ～를 쏘았다 They fired their artillery at the enemy. ② 《거짓말》 a lie; a fib; a big 〔tall〕 talk; a high 〔tall〕 tale. ¶ ～를 놓다 talk big; brag; draw 〔shoot〕 a long bow / ～도 어지간히 놓아라 That's enough of your boasting!

**대폭**(大幅) ① 《폭》 full width 〔breadth〕. ¶ 모슬린의 ～한 자 one foot of full width muslin / ～으로 한 야드 a yard of broadcloth. ② [부사] 《많이》 sharply; steeply; greatly; in a big jump. ¶ 가격의 ～인상 a sharp rise 〔increase〕 in prices / 가격의 ～하락 a sharp fall 〔reductions〕 in prices / ～(적인) 삭감 a drastic curtailment 〔cut〕 《of expenses》 / 지출을 ～적으로 줄이다 cut an appropriation sharply / 비 때문에 과일 가격이 ～ 올랐다 The price of fruits has risen sharply because of the rain. / 계획은 ～ 변경되었다 There was a drastic change in the plan.

**대표**(代表) 《대표함》 representation; 《사람》 a representative; a delegate; a delegation(대표단). ～하다 represent; be representative of; stand 〔act〕 for. ¶ ～적인 representative; typical (전형적) / ～적인 한국인 a typical 〔representative〕 Korean / …을 ～해 on 〔in〕 behalf of; for / ～를 보내다 send delegates 〔a delegation〕 《to a conference》 / 집안을 ～하여 인사하다 offer thanks on behalf of the family / 그는 한국을 ～하여 회의에 참석했다 He represented Korea at the conference. / 그는 이 협의회의 한국 ～이다 He is the Korean representative on the council. / ～ 없는 곳에 과세 없다 No taxation without representation. ◉ ～권 (the right of) representation. ～단 a delegation. ～대리 an alternate delegate. ～번호 《전화의》 the key 〔main〕 number; (the) general information number. ～부 『외교』 a mission: 무역 ～부 a trade mission. ～사원(社員) a representative partner; an acting 〔senior〕 partner. ～이사 the chief director; the chairman of board of directors. ～자 an executive. ～작 a masterpiece; *one's* most important work. 졸업생 ～ 《고별사하는》 a valedictorian 《미》. 다수〔소수, 비례〕～제도 a majority 〔minority, proportional〕 representation system.

**대푼** a penny; a tiny sum. ◉ ～변 1 percent interest. ～짜리 a thing of little value. ～쭝 a pennyweight.

**대품**(代―) exchange 〔substitute〕 work.

**대풍**(大風) a high 〔big, strong, violent〕 wind; a gale (질풍).

**대풍**(大豊) a bumper crop 〔harvest〕; an abundant 〔a good, a rich〕 harvest 〔crop〕; a heavy 〔record〕 crop. ¶ 벼농사는 어느 모로 보든지 ～이다 There is every prospect of a very large rice crop. / 금년에는 ～일 것이다 We will have a good 〔rich〕 harvest this year.

**대풍수**(大楓樹) 『식물』 the chaulmoogra tree.

**대풍자**(大楓子) 『한의』 chaulmoogra seeds. ◉ ～유(油) chaulmoogra oil.

**대피**(待避) ～하다 『철도』 shunt; 《공습 따위를》 take shelter 《in, under》. ¶ 폭풍우를 피하여 안전한 항구에 ～하다 《a ship》 find shelter in a safe harbor from a storm / 측선에 ～시키다 shun 《a train》 to the siding. ◉ ～로 《자동차 도로의》 a pull-out; a lay-by. ～선(線) a side track 《미》; a siding; a shunt line. ～소 a shelter: ～소—브레이크 고장 차량 《게시》 Brake problems: Pull out here. ～역 a shunting station. ～호(壕) a shelter; a dugout.

**대필**(代筆) ghostwriting; writing for

《another》. ～하다 write 《a letter》 for 《another》; ghostwrite; write 《a letter》 to 《another's》 dictation. ¶ 어머니의 ～을 하다 write for *one's* mother.

**대하**(大河) a large river. ◉ ～소설 a saga (novel); an epic novel; a long novel; a *roman-fleuve* (F.).

**대하**(大蝦) 〖동물〗 a lobster; a crayfish.

**대하다**(對—) ① 《마주 보다》 face; front; confront; be opposed to; be over against. ¶ 적을 ～ confront an enemy; engage 〔deal with〕 an enemy / 마주 대하고 앉다 sit opposite 《each other》; 《two people》 sit face to face / 그녀와 나는 테이블을 사이에 두고 마주 대하고 앉았다 She and I sat facing each other with a table between us. / 은행과 우체국은 서로 마주 대하고 있다 The bank and the post office stand opposite to each other.

② 《대조하다》 ¶ …에 대한 as opposed to…; in contrast to… / 구어체에 대한 문장체 literary style as opposed to colloquial style / 한국어의 「나라」에 대한 영어는 무엇이냐 What is the English (word) for the Korean "nara"?

③ 《향하다, 관하다》 ¶ …에 대한 toward; to…; against… / 종교에 대한 서적 books on religion / 시사 문제에 대한 강연 a lecture on current affairs / 국가에 대한 의무 *one's* duty to 〔toward〕 *one's* country / 선생님에 대한 태도 *one's* attitude toward *one's* teacher / 문학에 대한 흥미 *one's* interest in literature / 질문에 대한 대답 an answer to a question / 결정에 대한 항의 a protest against a decision / 압력에 대한 저항 resistance against pressure / 자식에 대한 어머니의 사랑 a mother's love for her child.

④ 《상대·대접하다》 see; face; receive; treat. ¶ 사람을 대하기 싫어하다 don't like to see people / …을 따뜻이 ～ receive 《*a person*》 with warmth / 아무를 후히 ～ treat *a person* generously / 그는 우리를 친형제처럼 대했다 He treated us as his brothers.

⑤ 《비교하다》 ¶ …에 대한 compared with…; (as) against… / 1시간에 대하여 10,000원 ten thousand won per hour / 그가 백 표를 얻은데 대해 나는 2백 표를 얻었다 I got two hundred votes to 〔against〕 his one hundred.

⑥ 《대항하다》 resist; oppose; match; take a stand against 《*a person*》 《on an issue》. ¶ 힘에 대해서는 힘으로 맞서라 Oppose force with force.

**대하증**(帶下症) 〖의학〗 leukorrhea.

**대학**(大學) 《종합》 a university; 《단과》 a college. ¶ ～ 1〔2,3,4〕년생 a freshman 〔sophomore, junior, senior〕 《미》 / ～의 자치 university autonomy / ～에 들어가다 enter college; enter a 〔the〕 university / ～에 다니다 go to 〔be in〕 college 〔(the) university〕 / ～을 졸업하다 graduate from 〔at〕 a university / 나는 내년에 ～ 입시에 응시한다 I am going to take the entrance examinations of universities next year. / 어느 ～에 다닙니까 What university do you go to? *or* What university are you in? / 나는 Y ～을 나왔습니다 I graduated from Y University. *or* I am a graduate of Y University. (★ 대학 이름은 Yale University, University of Texas 처럼 대학에 따라 University 라는 말의 위치가 다름. 그러나 우리 나라 대학의 경우는 흔히 「Seoul National 〔Korea〕 University와 같은 형식을 취함.)

◉ ～가(街) a university 〔college〕 town. ～ 교수 a university 〔college〕 professor: ～ 교수단 the college staff; the faculty of a university. ～교육 a university 〔college〕 education: ～교육을 받다 get a college education / ～교육을 받은 college-〔university-〕trained 《engineer》. ～교 총장 a university president; the president (of a university); a chancellor. ～구내 a (university) campus. ～모자 a college cap. ～병원 a university hospital. ～생 a college 〔university〕 student; a college man 〔woman〕; an undergraduate; a collegian. ～생활 college 〔university〕 life. ～ 수학능력시험 the college (academic) aptitude test. ～원 a (post)graduate course; a graduate school 《미》: ～원장 a dean / ～원 학생 a graduate 〔postgraduate〕 student; a graduate member of a university / ～원 과정 the (post)graduate course (of a university) / ～원에서 연구하다 do graduate work. ～입시 a college 〔university〕 entrance examination: ～입시 부정 사건 a college admission exam scandal. ～ 입학정책 the college admission policy. ～ 입학 학력고사 a state-run scholastic achievement test for university and college entrance. ～ 졸업식 the college's 〔university's〕 commencement ceremony 《미》. ～축제 a college 〔university〕 campus festival. ～ 출신자 a university 〔college〕 graduate; a collegian 《미》. ～ 학장 a dean

〔president〕. 문리과〔의과, 법과, 공과, 농과, 사범, 미술, 음악, 치과, 약학, 수의과, 가정, 수산, 항공〕 ~ a college of ⌈liberal arts and sciences 〔medicine, law, engineering, agriculture, education, fine arts, music, dentistry, pharmacy, veterinary medicine, home economics, fisheries, aviation〕. 4년제 ~ the four-year-course colleges and universities. 여자~ a women's university. 유명〔명문〕~ a prestige college 〔university〕.

**대학자**(大學者) a great 〔prominent〕 scholar; a man of great erudition.

**대한**(大旱) a great drought; a long spell of dry weather.

**대한**(大寒) ① 《절후》 the last of the 24 seasonal divisions of the year (= around the 21st of January); the colder season. ② 《추위》 intense cold; the depth of winter.

**대한**(大韓) Korea. ◉ ~ 무역 투자 진흥 공사(公社) The Korea Trade-Investment Promotion Agency (생략 KOTRA). ~ 민국 the Republic of Korea (생략 ROK): ~ 민국을 한반도의 유일한 합법적인 정부로 인정하다 recognize the Republic of Korea as the sole legitimate government in Korean peninsula / ~ 민국 만세 《만세 삼창을 할 때》 "Long Live Korea"; "Hip, hip, hurrah for Korea!" / 우리는 ~ 민국 만세 삼창을 불렀다 We gave three cheers for the Republic of Korea. ~ 상공회의소 the Korea Chamber of Commerce and Industry. ~ 적십자사 Korea National Red Cross. ~ 해협 the Straits of Korea.

**대합**(大蛤) 〖조개류〗 a large clam. ◉ ~ 구이 grilled clam meat in shell. ~찜 steamed clam meat in shell.

**대합실**(待合室) a waiting room; 《호텔 등의》 a lounge; a lobby.

**대항**(對抗) 《적대》 opposition; antagonism; rivalry (경쟁); 《저항》 counteraction; resistance; defiance. ~하다 oppose; antagonize; confront; face; meet; set up 〔pit *oneself*〕 《against》; cope 〔vie〕 《with》; counteract; resist; defy. ¶ 한일 ~ 수영대회〔축구시합〕 the Korea-Japan swimming meet 〔soccer game〕/ …에 ~하여 in opposition to…; in rivalry with…; against… / ~케 하다 pit 〔set up〕 《*a person* against another》 / 정정 당당히 ~하다 show a strong front; play square; face the enemy square / 아무에게는 ~할 수 없다 be no match for *a person;* cannot stand against *a person* / 영어에서 그녀에게 ~할 수 있는 사람은 이 학급에서 아무도 없다 No one in this class can rival 〔equal〕 her in English. *or* She has no equal in English in this class.
◉ ~경기 a match; 《학교간의》 an interschool match 〔game〕. ~력 opposing power. ~운동 a counter movement. ~의식 (a sense of) rivalry; competitiveness: 형제간의 ~ 의식 rivalry between brothers. ~자 an antagonist; a rival; an opponent; an emulator. ~책(策)〔조치〕 a counterplot; a countermeasure: ~책을 강구하다 take countermeasures 《against》. ~행위 a counteraction.

**대해**(大害) great damage 〔loss〕; great harm; great injury. ¶ 곡식에 ~를 주다 cause great damage to the grain.

**대해**(大海) an ocean; a great sea; the main(시어). ¶ 망망한 ~ the boundless expanse of water / ~의 일적(一適) a drop in the bucket 〔ocean〕/ 우물 안 개구리는 ~를 모른다 A frog in the well knows nothing of the great ocean.

**대행**(代行) vicarious execution. ~하다 execute as proxy 《for》; act for 《*a person*》; deputize 〔act as deputy〕 《for the president》. ¶ 학장 ~ an acting president / 업무를 ~하다 do business for 《*a person*》/ 형님을 ~하다 act for *one's* brother. ◉ ~기관 an agency; a substitute machinery. ~ 업무 agency business. ~자(者) a proxy; an agent. 수출〔수입〕 ~업자 an export 〔import〕 agent.

**대행성**(大行星) 〖천문〗 the major planets.

**대헌장**(大憲章) 〖역사〗 the Magna C(h)arta; the Great Charter.

**대형**(大兄) Mr. …; You.

**대형**(大形·大型) a large 〔full〕 size. ¶ ~의 large-〔full-, king-〕sized; of a large size; big; large / 초~의 extra-large / 비행기는 ~화되고 있다 Airplanes are getting larger (and larger) in size.
◉ ~버스 a large-sized bus. ~주(株) large-sized capital stocks; large-capital stocks. ~차 a large-size(d) car. ~트럭 a heavy-duty truck.

**대형**(隊形) (military) formation; order. ¶ ~을 정돈하고 in good formation / ~을 정돈하다 put the formation in good order / ~을 이루다 form ranks / ~을 무너뜨리다〔흐트러뜨리다〕 break rank(s). ◉ 밀집～ (a) close formation. 전투～ battle 〔combat〕 formation: 전투 ～으로 in battle order.

**대화**(大火) a big 〔great〕 fire. ＝큰불.

**대화**(大禍) a great disaster; a calamity. ¶ ～를 입다 meet with a calamity.

**대화**(對話) (a) conversation; a dialogue (두 사람의); a talk; a chat (잡담). ～하다 talk 〔converse〕 with; have a talk 〔conversation〕 with. ¶ ～의 정치 dialogue politics; politics through dialogue / 두 철학자의 ～ a dialogue between two philosophers / 세 사람의 ～ a trialogue / 노사간의 우호적인 ～ friendly dialogue between management and labor / ～와 협상의 모든 문호를 닫다 close all channels for dialogue and negotiations《with》/ 북한측이 아무 전제 조건 없이 ～의 광장으로 나올 것을 촉구하다 urge the North Korean side to come to the dialogue table without any preconditions / 나는 그녀와 ～했다 I talked 〔had a talk〕 with her.
◉ ～극 a dialogic play. ～자 an interviewer; a dialogue partner. ～체 dialogue 〔conversational〕 style: ～체의 dialogic(al); written in dialogue. ～편(編) a book of dialogues. 남북～ the South-North talk 〔dialogue〕; the inter-Korean dialogue: 남북 ～의 재개 resumption of the South-North dialogue.

**대환**(大患) affliction; a disaster; a great misfortune 〔trial〕.

**대황**(大黃)〖식물〗a kind of rhubarb.

**대회**(大會) ① 《큰 모임》 a great 〔large, mass, grand〕 meeting; a rally (집회); a general meeting (총회); 《회의》 a conference; a convention. ¶ ～를 열다 hold a mass meeting; meet in (a) conference / ～에서 연설하다 deliver a speech at a large assembly / 당～를 소집하다 call a party convention / 그 ～에는 만 명 이상의 시민이 참가했다 More than ten thousand citizens attended the mass meeting.
② 《경기》 a meet; a tournament; a tourney. ¶ 전국 스키 ～ a national ski tournament / 전국 테니스 ～ an all-Korea tennis tournament.
◉ ～신기록 《set》 a new meet record. 국제 소년단 ～ a world jamboree. 기념 ～ a commemoration meeting (on a grand scale).

**대흉**(大凶) ① 《불길》 worst luck; the worst of ill luck; extremely bad luck; a great misfortune. ～하다 (be) extremely unlucky; ill-omened; unusually ominous 〔portentous〕; extremely bad. ② 《흉년》 an unusually bad harvest 〔crop〕; great failure of crops. ¶ 금년의 쌀 농사는 ～이다 This year's rice crop has been a big failure.
◉ ～년 an extremely bad year; 《흉작의》 an extremely lean year; a year of an unusually bad harvest.

**대희**(大喜) great delight; exultation; ecstasy. ～하다 be overjoyed; be transported with joy; be ecstatic.

**댁**(宅) ① 《남의 집》 your 〔his〕 esteemed house 〔residence, home〕; 《가족》 your 〔his〕 esteemed family. ¶ 댁이 어디시던가요 Where did you say your house is? / 한씨 댁이 여기입니까 Is this where Mr. Han lives? ② 《당신》 you. ¶ 댁의 성명이 무엇이오 What is your name? / 댁의 말씀이 옳소 You are right. ③ 《남의 부인》 the wife of 《*a person*》; Mrs. .... ¶ 한씨 댁 Mrs. Han; the wife of Mr. Han.

**댁내**(宅內) your 〔his〕 esteemed family. ¶ ～ 모두 안녕하십니까 Is everyone in your family well? / ～ 제절의 만복을 빌겠습니다 With my best wishes for you and your family.

**댁네**(宅―) your 〔his〕 wife.

**댄서** a dancer.

**댄스** a dance; dancing. ¶ ～의 상대 *one's* dancing partner / ～를 하다 dance; have a dance 《with》; perform dance / 저의 ～ 상대가 되어 주시지 않겠습니까 May I have the next 〔this〕 dance with you? ◉ ～교사〔교습소〕 a dancing instructor 〔school〕. ～파티 a dance; a dancing party; a ball (대무도회); a prom (대학·고교에서의) 《미》: ～ 파티를 열다 give a dance 〔ball, dancing party〕 / ～ 파티에 가다 go to a dance; go dancing. ～홀 a dance hall 《미》; a dancing saloon 《영》; a ballroom (호텔·궁전의): 비밀 ～ 홀 an underground dance hall.

**댐** a dam. ¶ 다목적 댐 a multipurpose dam / 발전용 댐 a hydroelectric 〔power〕 dam / 댐을 건설하다 build a dam 《across a river》; dam 《a river》/ 댐이 붕괴되었다 The dam gave away 〔collapsed, broke〕.

**댑싸리**〖식물〗belvedere. ◉ ～비 a belvedere broom.

**댓** about five. ¶ 댓 사람 about five persons / 댓 권 about five volumes.

**댓가지** bamboo branches.

**댓개비** a piece of bamboo; a piece of split bamboo.

**댓돌**(臺—) 〖건축〗 terrace stones.
**댓바람** at a stroke 〔blow〕; at once; immediately; in no time; easily; quickly. ¶ 아무를 ～에 때려 눕히다 knock down *a person* with the first blow / 일을 ～에 해치우다 finish *one's* work at a stroke.
**댓새** about five days.
**댓줄기** a bamboo stalk.
**댓진**(—津) tobacco tar accumulated in a pipe.
**댕강-** ⇨ 댕그랑-.
**댕그랑거리다** tinkle; jingle; clang; cling; ring. ¶ 풍경이 댕그랑거리기 시작하였다 A hanging bell 〔wind bell〕 began to tinkle.
**댕그랑댕그랑** cling-cling; clang-clang; tinkle-tinkle; ting-ting; ting-a-ling; jingling.
**댕기** a pigtail ribbon. ¶ ～를 드리다 wear 〔put on〕 a pigtail ribbon.
**댕기다** 《불이》 catch 〔take〕 (fire); spread to; 《불을》 light 〔make, kindle, ignite〕 (fire). ¶ 마른 나무에는 불이 잘 댕긴다. Dry wood catches fire easily. / 그는 담배를 한 개비 꺼내어 불을 댕겼다 He took out a cigarette and lit it.
**댕돌같다** be hard as a rock; (be) solid; firm.
**더** ① 《보다 많이》 (some) more (양); longer (시간); farther (거리); further (정도) (★ 구어에서는 정도·거리에 다같이 further를 쓰기도 함). ¶ 더 많이 《양》 much 〔a lot of〕 more; 《수》 (a good) many more / 더 비싼 more expensive; dearer / 조금만 더 a little 〔few〕 more / 케이크를 좀더 주시오 Give me some more cake, please. / 좀더 앉았다 가시오 Why don't you stay a little longer? / 좀 더 가면 왼쪽에 그 집이 있다 Go on a little farther and you will find the house on your left. / 나는 더 할 말이 없다 I have nothing further to say. / 더 있느냐 Is there any more? / 밥을 좀더 드릴까요 How about a second helping of rice? / 더 말할 것이 뭐 있느냐 What's left to say? ② 《…보다 더》 more (than); still more. ¶ 이것은 저것보다 더 예쁘다 This is more beautiful than that. / 그는 나보다 키가 더 크다 He is taller than I. / 작년보다 더 춥다 It is colder than last year. / 내일 날씨는 더 나빠지겠다 The weather for tomorrow will be even worse. / 그녀는 나이보다 더 늙어 보인다 She looks older than she really is. / 그는 나보다 일을 더 빨리 한다 He is a quicker worker than I (am). *or* He works more quickly than I (do).
**더가다** 《거리》 go 〔walk〕 beyond; get ahead; 《정도》 exceed; go farther; last longer; be more than; 《시계가》 go too fast; gain time. ¶ 시계가 더 간다 The watch gains time 〔goes too fast〕. / 조금 더 가서 쉬자 Let us walk a little farther before we take a rest. / 나는 이 모자에 마음이 더 간다 I like this hat better. / 경치에 정신이 팔려 나도 모르게 한 정거장을 더 갔다 I was so much lost in the fine scenery along the line that I rode past one station.
**더구나** besides; moreover; further; in addition; into the bargain; to boot; what's more; more; still more; all the more; to make matters 〔things〕 worse (설상가상으로). ¶ ～ 눈마저 몹시 내렸다 To make things 〔matters〕 worse, it was snowing hard. / 비가 오는데 ～ 바람까지 분다 It is raining and, what's more, the wind is blowing too. / 학벌도 없으려니와 경험은～없다 He has no scholarship, to say nothing of experience. / 그 집이 마음에 들지 않았다. ～ 값도 너무 비쌌다 I didn't like the house, moreover 〔besides〕, the price was too high.
**더군다나** ⇨ 더구나.
**더그매** an empty space below the roof.
**더그아웃** 〖야구〗 a dugout.
**더껑이** film; skim; scum; cream. ¶ 죽에 ～가 지다 a skim forms on the porridge / ～를 걷어내다 skim 《off》.
**더께** accumulated dirt; layers of dirt; scum.
**더넘스럽다** be a bit too large 〔big〕; be a little too much.
**더느다** braid 《string, thread》 in two plies.
**-더니** ① 《원인》 as now it has been observed that…; … and now 〔then〕; … but now 〔then〕. ¶ 한참 쉬었더니 몸이 거뜬하다 I've had a bit of rest and now I feel wonderfully refreshed. / 바람이 불더니 비가 온다 First the wind and now the rain. / 비가 오더니 날이 따뜻해졌다 It's been raining and now it's turned warm. / 그는 한번 가더니 소식이 없다 We've had no word from him at all since he left. / 알아봤더니 그는 2년 전에 죽었다 I found out that he has been dead for two years. ② 《회상·감상조》 it used to be that… but 〔and〕 now…. ¶ 옛날엔 가을이면 사슴이 내려오더니 In days gone by, the deer used to come down in

autumn (but not any more). / 그 전에는 이곳이 연못이더니 This used to be a pond.

**더더구나, 더더군다나** ⇨ 더구나.

**더덕** 〖식물〗 *Codonopsis lanceolata* (학명). ◉ ~구이 grilled *deodeok*. ~바심 crushing *deodeok* root.

**더덕더덕** ⇨ 다닥다닥.

**더덜거리다** stammer; falter; stutter.

**더덜이** increasing and decreasing; adding and subtracting.

**더뎅이** a scab; a slough. ¶ 부스럼에 ~가 앉다 a scab forms over a boil.

**더듬거리다** ① 《손으로》 be groping 《for》; be feeling 《after, for》; fumble 《for》. ¶ 지팡이로 길을 더듬거리며 가다 go along feeling *one's* way with a cane / 책을 찾느라 어두운 방을 ~ be groping for a book in a dark room. ② 《말을》 stammer; stutter; falter. ¶ 더듬거리며 stammeringly; stutteringly / 더듬거리며 말하다 stammer out 《an apology》 / 그는 몹시 더듬거린다 He stammers badly.

**더듬다** ① 《말을》 stammer (말이 막혀서); stutter (습관적으로); falter (머뭇거리며); have an impediment in *one's* speech. ¶ 말을 ~ stammer. ② 《손으로》 grope 《for》; feel 《after, for》; fumble 《for》. ¶ 더듬으며 가다 grope 〔feel〕 *one's* way 《in the dark》; go feeling 《along the wall》 / 전등의 스위치를 더듬어 찾다 grope 〔fumble, feel〕 for a light switch / 바위 틈을 더듬어 게를 잡다 feel 〔reach〕 between the rock and catch the crab / 잔돈이 있나 주머니를 더듬어 보다 fumble 〔feel, fish〕 in *one's* pocket for a coin. ③ 《근원·기억을》 trace; tread; follow; explore. ¶ 인류의 역사를 ~ trace the history of mankind / 기억을 ~ try to recall / 우리는 강의 수원까지 더듬어 갔다 We traced the river to its source. / 기억을 더듬어 어렸을 때의 일에 대해서 써 보았다 I wrote about my childhood, searching my memory.

**더듬더듬** ① 《말을》 stammering; stuttering; faltering. ¶ ~ 말하다 stammer; stutter / ~ 읽다 falter over 《a passage》. ② 《손으로》 by feel; gropingly.

**더듬이**[1] 《말더듬이》 a stutterer; a stammerer.

**더듬이**[2] 〖동물〗 a tentacle; a feeler; a "hand"; an antenna; a palpus; a barbel (물고기의).

**더듬적거리다** be stammering 〔stuttering, faltering〕 in. ¶ 말을 ~ stammer 〔stutter, falter〕 in *one's* speech.

**더듬적더듬적** stammering; stuttering; faltering.

**더디** late; behind time 〔schedule〕. ¶ 목적지에 ~ 닿다 reach *one's* destination late 〔behind time〕 / 예정보다 1시간 ~ 도착했다 I got there one hour late 〔later than scheduled〕.

**더디다** ① 《걸음 따위가》 be slow 《in, of, at》; be tardy 《at》; be slowed down; (be) retarded. ¶ 걸음이 ~ be slow of foot; be slow-footed; go at a slow pace / 진보가 ~ be slow in progress; make slow progress. ② 《늦다》 (be) late; be behind time 〔schedule〕; take a long time. ¶ 돌아오는 것이 ~ be late 〔slow〕 in coming back; be gone a long time / 이 열차는 꽤 더디군 This is an awfully slow train, isn't it? / 금년에는 봄이 ~ Spring is late in coming this year. *or* Spring comes late this year.

**-더라** 《회상·감상조》 it has been observed that…; it is known that…; as we all know; I hear 〔have been told〕 that…; I noticed that…; 《…인 것 같다》 they say; it is said. ¶ 그이가 아까 저리 가더라 He was (noticed to be) going that way little while ago. / 어제는 퍽 춥더라 It was quite cold yesterday (I found). / 그는 머지 않아 미국에 간다더라 They say he's going to America soon.

**-더라도** 《비록》 even if; even though (it has been observed that…); although; admitting 〔granting, supposing〕 that; whatever may. ¶ 아무리 적더라도 no matter how small it may be / 아무리 곤란하더라도 however hard it may be / 무슨 일이 있더라도 whatever happens; under any circumstances / 비록 자네가 옳다고 하더라도 even if you are in the right / 설사 그가 취해 있었다 치더라도 granting that he was drunk / 비를 흠뻑 맞더라도 가야겠다 I have to go even if I get drenched in the rain. / 일주일 안에 된다고 하더라도 때는 늦다 Even if it is finished in a week, it will not be in time. / 나무는 있다 치더라도 극히 조금밖에 없다 There are very few trees, if any. / 그는 그 돈을 전부는 아니더라도 절반 이상이나 써 버렸다 He has spent more than half the money, if not all.

**-더라면** 《가정·희망》 if only…; if it had been…; I wish. ¶ 그 구두가 좀더 컸더라면 내 발에 맞을 텐데 If the shoes had been a little bigger, they would have fit my feet. / 그 일을 했더라면 좋

았을 것을 I wish he had done it (but he didn't).

**더러**[1] ① 《얼마쯤》 some; somewhat; a little (양); a few (수). ¶ 세상에는 그런 사람이 ~ 있다 There are some people like that. / 그는 외국에 나가서 ~ 배운 것도 있다 He has been abroad and has learned a thing or two. / 모임에는 여자들도 ~ 있었다 There were a few women at the meeting, too. ② 《이따금》 occasionally; from time to time; now and then; once in a while. ¶ 나한테도 ~ 놀러 오너라 Why don't you come and see me once in a while? / 가다가는 그런 일이 ~ 생긴다 Occasionally such a thing happens. / ~ 길에서 그를 만난다 I sometimes see him on the street. / 의견의 차이도 ~ 생긴다 Differences of opinion may arise from time to time.

**더러**[2] 《…에게》 to 《*a person*》; toward. ¶ 아버지께서 나~ 심부름 가라고 하신다 Father tells me to go on an errand. / 선생님께서 나~ 공부 잘하라고 하셨다 My teacher gave the advice to me that I should work hard.

**더러워지다** ① 《불결해지다》 get 〔become〕 dirty 〔filthy〕; be 〔get, become〕 soiled; be stained (얼룩지다); be polluted (오염되다). ¶ 땀으로 더러워진 셔츠 a shirt stained with sweat / 잉크로 더러워진 책상 a desk spotted with ink / 매연으로 더러워진 공기 air polluted with smoke / 더러워진 옷 soiled 〔dirty, unclean〕 clothes / 검댕으로 더러워진 얼굴 a face smudged with soot / 흰 양말은 쉬이 더러워진다 White socks get dirty easily. ② 《지조 따위가》 become mean 〔low, base, sordid, dirty〕; become corrupt (도의심이). ¶ 마음이 ~ become mean-spirited 〔base=minded〕 / 사람이 ~ become a low 〔base, mean, dirty〕 character / 생각이 ~ come to have mean ideas. ③ 《이름·명성이》 be soiled 〔sullied, stained, tarnished, dishonored, disgraced〕. ¶ 이름이 ~ *one's* name 〔reputation〕 is soiled 〔sullied〕 / 가문(家門)이 ~ *one's* family name is stained 〔disgraced〕. ④ 《순결이》 become unchaste; lose *one's* chastity 〔purity〕; be dishonored. ¶ 몸이 ~ lose *one's* chastity; stain *one's* virtue.

**더럭** all at once; at a stroke. ¶ 겁이 ~ 나다 be 「seized with fear 〔struck with awe〕 all of a sudden; get into a funk / ~ 죽다 drop dead.

**더럭더럭** pertinaciously; persistently; tenaciously; importunately. ¶ ~ 재촉하다 make an importunate demand 《for payment》 / ~ 조르다 keep teasing 〔pestering〕 《*a person*》 for 《*a thing*》 / 소년은 어머니에게 로봇 장난감을 사달라고 ~ 졸랐다 The boy insistently begged his mother to buy him a toy robot.

**더럼타다** be easy to dirty 〔soil, stain〕; be easily soiled; be liable to become dirty. ¶ 더럼타는 옷 clothes easy to get soiled / 흰 양말은 쉽게 더럼탄다 White socks soil easily.

**더럽다** ① 《불결》 (be) dirty; filthy; foul; grimy; soiled; squalid; shabby; stained; unclean. ¶ 더러운 옷 dirty clothes / 더러운 방 a messy room / 더러운 변소 a filthy toilet / 더러운 공기 foul air / 더러운 손으로 만지지 마라 Keep your dirty hands off it.
② 《야비》 (be) mean; base; low; sordid; dirty 《미》. ¶ 더러운 놈 a mean 〔low〕 fellow; a dirty guy 〔dog〕 / 더러운 마음 a low mind / 더러운 생각 a mean idea / 더러운 돈 filthy lucre / 더러운 수법을 쓰다 use a mean trick; be sneaky / 돈만 바라고 일하다니 ~ It is sordid of you to work just for money.
③ 《추잡》 (be) obscene; indecent; filthy; nasty. ¶ 더러운 이야기 a filthy talk / 행태가 ~ be coarse 〔gross〕 in *one's* ways.
④ 《인색》 (be) stingy; niggardly; miserly; close-fisted. ¶ 돈에 더러운 사람 a stingy 〔close-fisted〕 fellow; a miser / 돈에 더러운 사람이라 그는 기부를 안 할 것이다 Because he is stingy, he won't contribute any money.

**더럽히다** ① 《불결하다》 soil; stain; taint; befoul; blemish; make dirty. ¶ 옷을 ~ soil *one's* clothes / 방을 ~ get a room dirty / 물을 ~ make water dirty; 담배 연기는 방 안의 공기를 더럽힌다 Cigarette smoke pollutes the air in the room.
② 《이름·명성 따위를》 disgrace; dishonor; bring disgrace 《upon》; sully; tarnish. ¶ 명성을 ~ soil *one's* reputation / 가문을 ~ bring disgrace upon *one's* family / 조상의 이름을 ~ disgrace the good name of *one's* ancestors / 그런 행위는 우리 학교의 전통을 더럽히게 될 것이다 Such a deed would disgrace 〔defile〕 the tradition of our school.
③ 《순결을》 dishonor 《a woman》; outrage; violate. ¶ 여자를 ~ violate a woman / 여자가 (남자에게) 몸을 ~ lose

*one's* chastity 〔purity〕; stain *one's* virtue.

**더미** a heap; a pile; an accumulation; a stack. ¶ 돌～ a pile of rocks / 쓰레기 ～ a rubbish heap / 볏짚 ～ a stack of straws / 산～처럼 쌓다 pile 《*things*》 mountain high; gather 《*things*》 into a heap.

**더미씌우다** shift the burden of responsibility 《onto *a person*》; throw the blame 《on *a person*》; pass the buck. ¶ 그는 책임을 친구에게 더미씌웠다 He passed the buck onto his friend.

**더버기** ¶ 온몸이 흙～가 되다 be covered with mud from top to toe 〔head to foot〕/ 옷이 잉크～가 되다 have got ink all over *one's* clothes.

**더벅머리** 《머리》 disheveled 〔unkempt〕 hair; bushy hair; 《아이》 a child; a lad (who still has his hair loose).

**더부룩이** in tufts; tufty; bushy; fringy; thick(ly). ¶ 머리털이 ～ 자라다 *one's* hair grows thick; *one's* hair get tufty.

**더부룩하다** ① 《풀·나무가 우거짐》 (be) tufty; fringy; bushy; thick. ¶ 더부룩한 머리 tufty 〔thick〕 hair / 마당에 풀이 더 부룩하게 자랐다 The garden is overgrown with grass 〔weeds〕. ② 《배가 부르다》 (be) 〔feel〕 bloated; feel stodgy; feel 〔sit〕 heavy on the stomach; remain undigested. ¶ 속이 ～ feel bloated.

**더부살이** a resident 〔living-in〕 servant. ¶ ～ 환자(還子) 걱정 《속담》 worrying about things which are none of *one's* concern / ～를 살다〔하다〕 be hired as a living-in servant.

**더북더북** in bunch; in grove. ～하다 be in bunch; be in grove; (be) thick; dense. ¶ 풀이 ～한 언덕 a hill thickly covered with grass.

**더불다** ① 《함께 하다》 do together; partake 《of》. ② 《동행하다》 take 《*a person*》 with (데리고 가다); bring 《*a person*》 with (데리고 오다); be accompanied 《by》; be attended 《by》; accompany; go 《with》.

**더불어** ① 《함께》 together; with; side by side. ¶ 그와 ～ 기쁨〔슬픔〕을 함께 하다 share *one's* joy 〔sorrow〕 with him / 친구와 ～ 산보를 가다 go for a walk with a friend. ② 《상대하여》 with; against. ¶ 그와 ～ 바둑을 두었다 I played a game of *paduk* with him. / 그와 ～ 다툴 필요가 없다 You needn't quarrel with him.

**더블** double. ◉ ～베드 a double bed. ～상의(上衣) a double-breasted coat. ～스틸 『야구』 a double steal. ～플레이 『야구』 a double play; a twin killing. ～헤더 『야구』 a double-header.

**더블린** 《아일랜드의 수도》 Dublin.

**더블유비시** 《세계 권투 평의회》 WBC. 〔< *W*orld *B*oxing *C*ouncil〕

**더블유비에이** 《세계 권투 연맹》 WBA. 〔< *W*orld *B*oxing *A*ssociation〕

**더블유에이치오** 《세계 보건 기구》 WHO. 〔<the *W*orld *H*ealth *O*rganization〕

**더블유티오** 《세계 무역 기구》 WTO. 〔<the *W*orld *T*rade *O*rganization〕

**더빙** 《필름·테이프의 재녹음》 dubbing. ～하다 dub 《a tape》; copy 〔duplicate〕 (복제를 만들다). ¶ 비디오 테이프를 ～하다 duplicate a video (tape).

**더뻑** rashly; recklessly; blindly; thoughtlessly; impetuously. ¶ ～ 내닫다 run off recklessly; dash 〔rush〕 off / 일에 ～ 달려들다 tackle a job recklessly.

**더뻑거리다** act 〔behave〕 rashly 〔recklessly〕; act on impulse; be impetuous. ¶ 그는 더뻑거려 실수가 많다 Being rash, he makes mistakes.

**더뻑더뻑** rashly; recklessly. ¶ 아무 일에나 달려들다 try recklessly to do everything / 돈을 ～ 쓰다 spend money recklessly 〔like water〕.

**더새다** put up 《at an inn》; spend 〔pass〕 a night (on *one's* way); stay for the night.

**더스트 슈트** a trash 〔refuse, rubbish〕 〔(disposal) chute.

**더없이** most of all; best (of all); supremely. ¶ ～ 아름다운 꽃 the finest flower imaginable / ～ 기뻐하다 be delighted beyond measure / 지금은 ～ 좋은 기분이다 I've never felt better.

**더욱** 《한층 더》 more; more and more; still 〔much〕 more; all the more; 《부정의 경우》 less and less; still 〔much〕 less (★ still과 much는 형용사 또는 부사의 비교급과 함께 쓰임. still은 비교급의 앞뒤 어디에 두어도 좋음: still more 〔less, fewer, taller〕; more 〔less, fewer, taller〕 still). ¶ ～더 still more / ～ 중요한 것은 what is more important / ～ 공부하다 work harder / ～ 노력하다 make (even) greater efforts / ～ 작아지다 grow less and less / 높이 올라갈수록 공기는 ～ 희박해진다 The higher we go, the thinner the air is. / 그것은 ～ 곤란한 문제다 That is a problem still more difficult. / 네가 같이 가겠다니 ～ 좋다 It is the better since you will go with me. / 2월에는 ～ 추워질 것이다 It will get much 〔still〕 colder in February.

**더욱더욱** 《증가》 more and more; increasingly; 《감소》 less and less. ¶ 그 텔레비전 프로그램은 ~ 재미있어졌다 The TV program has become more and more interesting. / 날이 ~ 짧아지고 있다 The days are getting shorter and shorter.

**더욱이** ① = 더욱. ② 《그 위에》 besides; moreover; in addition (to that); particularly; especially; into the bargain; on top of (that); what's more; more than all. ¶ ~ 좋은 것은 what is better / ~ 곤란한 것은 to make matters worse; what is worse / 그는 잘 알아듣는 데다가 ~ 한번 배운 것은 잊어버리지 않는다 He learns easily, and what is more, he remembers what he has learnt.

**더워하다** be sensitive to the heat; feel hot 〔heat〕; suffer from the heat; swelter. ¶ 어린애가 더워하는 것 같다 The baby seems to feel hot. / 그는 살이 쪄서 유달리 더워한다 Being so fat, he is particularly susceptible to the heat.

**더위** ① 《날씨》 the heat; hot weather. ¶ 찌는 듯한 ~ steaming 〔sweltering〕 heat / 무더운 ~ sultry 〔oppressive〕 heat / 한낮의 ~ 속에 in the heat of the midday / ~가 시작되다 hot weather sets in / ~를 식히다 beat the heat / ~가 물러가다 hot weather comes to an end / ~에 견디다 stand 〔bear, withstand〕 the heat / ~에 못 견디다 succumb to the heat / ~에 약하다 be sensitive to the heat / ~를 피하다 avoid 〔escape〕 the heat / ~를 잊기 위해 맥주 한잔을 하다 have a glass of beer to dispel 〔kill〕 the heat / 오늘 ~는 대단하다 It's terribly hot today. / 이 ~에 외출은 하고 싶지 않다 I don't like to go out in this heat 〔such hot weather〕. ② 《병》 sunstroke; heatstroke; illness from the heat. ¶ ~를 먹다 be affected by the heat; suffer from hot weather; be ill from the heat; be sunstruck (일사병에 걸리다).

**더위잡다** grasp at 《*a thing*》; clutch at 《*a thing*》.

**더치다** ① 《병세가》 become worse; be aggravated. ¶ 병이 ~ *one's* illness worsens; take a bad turn; take a turn for the worse. ② = 덧들이다.

**더펄개** a shaggy dog; 《애완견》 a poodle.

**더펄거리다** ① 《머리 따위가》 bounce 〔fly〕 up and down. ¶ 머리가 ~ *one's* hair is bouncing up and down. ② 《사람이》 act 〔behave〕 helter-skelter; never sit down long enough to get anything done.

**더펄더펄** bouncing up and down.

**더펄머리** bouncing hair.

**더펄이** a helter-skelter person; a person who is flying off in all directions at once; one who never sits down long enough to get anything done.

**더하기** 〖수학〗 addition.

**더하다**[1] 《비교해서》 (be) more. ¶ 더한 값 a higher price / 크기가 ~ be bigger / 독하기는 그것보다 이 술이 ~ This liquor is stronger than that. / 형도 어지간히 잔소리가 많지만 어머니는 ~ Brother is grumbling a lot but mother is worse.

**더하다**[2] ① [자동사] 《심해지다》 become 〔get〕 worse; worsen; grow harder; increase in violence; get serious; gather strength; go from bad to worse; be aggravated; grow in intensity; become intensified. ¶ 추위가 ~ get colder / 곤란이 ~ become more difficult / 두통이 ~ *one's* headache becomes worse / 병세가 ~ *one's* illness takes a turn for the worse. ② [타동사] 《보태다》 add (up); sum up. ¶ 하나에 둘을 ~ add two to one / 3에 4를 더하라 Add 4 to 3. / 15에 25를 더하면 40이다 Twenty-five added to fifteen makes 〔is, equals〕 forty. ③ [타동사] 《늘리다》 increase; augment; add to; enlarge. ¶ 속력을 ~ speed up; accelerate; gain in velocity; gather speed / 세력을 ~ gain power; gain in influence.

**더한층**(─層) still 〔much〕 more; all the more; 《부정》 still 〔much〕 less. ⇨ 가일층. ¶ 사태는 ~ 심각해졌다 Things have got(ten) even worse. / 그에게 ~ 노력할 것을 약속했다 I promised him that I would make greater efforts.

**더할 나위 없다** 《완전하다》 (be) perfect; 《탁월하다》 (be) unsurpassed; 《최상이다》 (be) the finest 〔best, greatest, highest, most〕 《최악이다》 (be) the worst. ¶ 더할 나위 없이 perfectly; supremely; thoroughly; extremely; all the way; immensely; with no room for further improvement 〔deterioration〕 / 더할 나위 없이 사랑스러운 as lovely as can be / 나는 더할 나위 없이 행복했다 I was perfectly happy. / 이것은 우리 연구에 더할 나위 없이 필요한 자료다 This is just the thing we need

for our studies. / 하이킹에 더할 나위 없는 날씨였다 It was an ideal day 〔weather〕 for hiking. / 그녀는 아내로서 ~ She is everything that a wife should be. *or* She is all that can be desired as a wife. 「*etc.*).
**덕** a shelf 〔rack〕 (for drying grain,
**덕**(德) ① 《미덕》 virtue; goodness; moral excellence. ¶ 덕이 있다 be virtuous 〔respectable〕 / 덕 있는 사람 a virtuous man 〔woman〕; a man 〔woman〕 of virtue 〔high moral character〕 / 덕을 닦다 cultivate virtue 〔virtuous habits〕 / 덕을 갖추다 possess virtue / 덕에 감화되다 be influenced by *a person's* virtue. ② = 덕택. ③ = 공덕.
**덕기**(德氣) virtuous mien; virtue; goodness. ¶ ~ 있다 have a virtuous mien; be virtuous.
**덕담**(德談) well wishing remarks.
**덕대** 『광업』 a miner who rents part of a mine to work; a subcontract miner. ◉ ~갱 a rented part of a mine.
**덕량**(德量) a virtuous mind; generosity; broad-mindedness.
**덕망**(德望) (a) moral influence; a reputation for virtue; high moral repute. ¶ ~이 있다 be reputed 〔renowned〕 for *one's* virtues. ◉ ~가 a man of high moral repute.
**덕분**(德分) indebtedness. = 덕택(德澤).
**덕석** a straw mat for covering the back of an ox (to protect against cold); a straw rug for cattle.
**덕석밤** a large wide chestnut.
**덕성**(德性) moral character 〔nature〕; a kindly nature; a good heart; a virtuous character. ¶ ~을 함양하다 cultivate 〔foster〕 moral 〔noble〕 character / ~스럽다 be good-natured 〔kind-hearted, virtuous〕.
**덕수궁**(德壽宮) the *Tŏksu* Palace.
**덕스럽다**(德—) look virtuous; (be) virtuous; respectable; benignant; gracious. ¶ 덕스럽게 생기다 have respectable features.
**덕육**(德育) moral education; moral culture 〔training〕; character building. ¶ ~을 중히 여기다 attach much importance to moral culture / ~과 지육(知育)은 병행시켜야 한다 The cultivation of moral habits should go with that of intellect.
**덕의**(德義) morality; moral integrity; probity. ¶ ~를 존중하다 have a high sense of honor / 그는 ~를 중히 여기는 사람이다 He is a man of strict morality.
**덕적덕적** thickly covered. ¶ 그녀는 늘 분을 ~ 바른다 She always powders her face thickly.
**덕지덕지** layer after layer 《of accumulated dirt》; thick 《with dirt》; encrusted. ¶ 때가 ~ 끼다 be covered thick 〔encrusted〕 with dirt.
**덕택**(德澤) 《신세》 indebtedness; 《은혜》 (a) favor; (a) benefit; 《친절》 kindness; 《도움》 help; aid; assistance; 《후원》 support; backing. ¶ ~으로 thanks to; 《원인》 owing to; due to; 《이유》 because of; 《도움·후원 등으로》 through 《*a person's*》 patronage 〔support, good offices, favor, help〕 / 근면한 ~ the fruit 〔result〕 of *one's* labor / 그녀의 원조〔노력〕 ~으로 성공하다 succeed through her aid 〔efforts〕 / 아버지 ~에 잘 산다 He is indebted to his father for his comfortable life. / 자네 〔그 기계〕 ~에 예정대로 모든 일을 끝낼 수 있었네 Thanks to 「you 〔the machine〕, I finished the whole job on schedule. / 이 일을 잘 해낼 수 있었던 것은 모두 자네 ~일세 We owe our success in this work entirely to you. / 그것은 오로지 하느님의 ~이라고 생각한다 I believe that it was only by the grace of God. / 오늘 이렇게 된 것은 모두 아버지 ~이다 What I am today, I owe to my father.
**덕행**(德行) virtuous 〔moral〕 conduct; virtue. ¶ ~이 높은 사람 a man of virtue; a noble-minded man / ~으로 알려지다 be renowned for *one's* virtue.
**덕화**(德化) moral reform 〔influence〕. ~하다 influence 〔reform〕 by virtuous example.
**덖다**[1] 《찌들다》 become dirty 〔filthy〕; be soiled. ¶ 때가 ~ get dirty. 「oil).
**덖다**[2] 《볶다》 parch; panfry (without
**-던가** 《의문·의심》 ¶ 그걸 어디에 두었던가 Where did I leave it? / 그것이 크던가 작던가 Was it large or small (I wonder)? / 얼마나 크던가 How big was it? / 내가 왜 그리 했던가 후회됩니다 I have come to worry over why I did that.
**-던걸** 《지난 일의 회상》 ¶ 그는 말을 잘 하던걸 He spoke well, after all! / 금강산을 가보니 좋던걸 I have been to see Mt. *Kumkang* and found them very beautiful indeed.
**-던데** ① 《회상》 ¶ 그는 프랑스어도 공부하던데 아마 번역가가 되려는가 보지. He has 〔is known to have〕 been study-

ing French also—maybe he's going to become a translator ! / 아까 그가 오던데 어찌 이 자리에 보이지 않는가 I saw him on his way here a little while ago—how come he isn't here ? / 어제 보니까 아무도 없던데 누가 이런 짓을 해 놓았을까 I didn't see anybody around here yesterday, so who could have done this ?
② [종결어미] ¶ 그것은 어렵던데 I found it difficult. / 손해는 염려했던 것보다 대단치 않던데 The loss was far less than we feared. / 자네 아들이 공부를 잘 하던데 But I have found your son doing quite well in school. (Why do you worry ?)

**-던들** [결과의 반대 가정] ¶ 빨리 의사에게 보였던들 그는 죽지 않았을 텐데 If he had seen the doctor right away, he wouldn't have died. / 당신의 도움이 없었던들 나는 실패했을 것이다 If it had not been for 〔But for, 《문어》 Had it not been for〕 your help, I should have failed.

**던적스럽다** 《비열하다》 (be) mean; low; base; sordid; despicable; 《추잡하다》 (be) indecent; obscene; filthy; dirty. ¶ 던적스러운 사람 a man of low character 〔base mind〕; a mean-spirited person / 던적스러운 생각 a mean thought / 던적스러운 얘기 filthy 〔indecent〕 talk / 보수를 바라다니 ~ It is mean of you to wish for recompense.

**던져두다** ① 《방치하다》 put 〔throw〕 to one side; leave. ¶ 책을 방구석에 ~ leave a book to a corner of the room. ② 《일을》 lay 〔put〕 aside; leave 《*one's* work》 undone; neglect. ¶ 하던 일을 ~ lay aside *one's* work unfinished / 그녀는 집안 일을 던져두고 파티에 갔다 She went to the party neglecting her household work.

**-던지** 《지난 일의 회상·의심》 ¶ 값이 얼마였던지 기억이 안 난다 I don't remember how much it was. / 그녀가 누구였던지 생각이 안 난다 I can't remember who she was. / 우연이었는지 고의였던지 하여튼 그녀는 여기 왔다 She came here anyway, whether by accident or by design.

**던지다** ① 《내던지다》 throw; cast; toss (가볍게 위로); 《세게》 fling; hurl; pitch (겨냥하여). ¶ 돌을 ~ throw a stone 《at a dog》 / 볼을 ~ throw 〔pitch〕 a ball / 던질 채비를 하다 『야구』 set *oneself* for the throw / 주사위를 ~ roll 〔cast〕 dice / 강에 몸을 ~ drown *oneself* in a river / 소년은 개에게 뼈를 던져 주었다 The boy tossed the dog a bone. / 투수는 커브 공을 던졌다 The pitcher delivered a curve ball.
② 《투표하다》 vote for (찬성); vote against (반대); cast (a vote); poll; ballot. ¶ 깨끗한 한 표를 ~ cast an honest 〔a clean〕 vote 《for》.
③ 《투신하다》 throw *oneself* into 《a movement》; devote *oneself* to 《*a matter*》; enter 〔launch〕 into 《business》. ¶ 정계에 몸을 ~ enter 〔go into〕 politics / 사회 운동에 몸을 ~ fling *oneself* into a social movement / 좀더 네 일에 몸을 던져 일해라 I want you to put more of your heart into your work.
④ 《영향을 주다》 affect; have an effect 〔influence〕 《on》. ¶ 장관의 발언은 경제계에 큰 파문을 던졌다 The Minister's statement 「caused a sensation 〔created a stir〕 in the economic world.

**던지럽다** (be) mean; base; foul; filthy.

**덜** less; incompletely; little. ¶ 덜 구워진 underdone; half-done; 《생선·고기가》 half-roasted; 《빵이》 half-baked / 덜 마른 half-dried / 덜 삶은 underdone; half-done; half-cooked / 덜 취한 half-tipsy; half-drunk / 덜 마른 나무 unseasoned wood / 덜 익은 과일 unripe 〔green〕 fruit / 이 고기는 덜 구워졌다 This meet is underdone. / 오늘은 어제보다 덜 춥다 It is less cold today than yesterday. / 잠을 조금 덜 잤더니 정신이 흐릿하다 I feel groggy because I had little sleep. / 이 책은 생각했던 것보다 덜 재미있다 This book is less interesting than I expected.

**덜거덕-** ⇨ ＝달가닥-.

**덜꿩나무** 『식물』 beech viburnum.

**덜다** ① 《빼다》 subtract; deduct; take off 〔away, from〕; remove. ¶ 그릇의 물을 ~ take some water from a bowl / 스물에서 열 다섯을 ~ subtract 15 from 20 / 너무 많으니 좀 덜어라 It is too much, remove some. ② 《경감하다》 lessen; lighten; mitigate; alleviate; dispel; allay; 《절약하다》 save; curtail; spare; cut down (감축). ¶ 고통을 ~ mitigate 〔alleviate, lighten〕 *one's* pain 〔affliction〕 / 불안을 ~ allay misgivings 〔apprehension〕 / 근심을 ~ relax *one's* attention; give relief to the mental strain / 생활의 낭비를 ~ leave out 〔omit, eliminate〕 the squandering 〔waste〕 of life / 시간을 〔수고를〕 ~ save time 〔trouble〕 / 기계는 노력을 던다 Machinery dispenses with labor. / 그

렇게 하면 비용을 덜 수 있다 You will be able to cut down your expenses in that way. / 이것으로 가스 요금의 5할을 덜게 된다 This will save you fifty percent on 〔of〕 your gas bill.

**덜덜**[1] 《떠는 모양》 trembling(ly); shivering(ly); shaking(ly); quivering(ly). ¶ 무릎을 ~ 떨며 with trembling knees / ~ 떨다 tremble; shiver / 추워서 ~ 떨다 shiver with cold / 무서워서 ~ 떨다 tremble with 〔for〕 fear; shudder in horror / 추워서〔무서워서〕 이가 ~ 떨리다 say an ape's paternoster / 손이 ~ 떨려 글을 쓸 수 없었다 I could not write as my hand shook. / 무릎이 ~ 떨린다 My knees shake under me. / 아버지는 화가 나서 손을 ~ 떨었다 My father's hands tremored in anger.

**덜덜**[2] 《구르는 소리》 rattling; clattering. ¶ ~ 소리나다 rattle; clatter / 수레가 ~ 거리며 길을 지나갔다 A cart rattled along the road.

**덜되다** ① 《사람이》 be no good; be not up to the mark; be a failure; be a complete botch; leave much to be desired. ¶ 덜된 사람 a good-for-nothing fellow; a person who is no good; a wretched fellow; a greenhorn / 덜된 수작을 하다 talk nonsense. ② 《미완성이다》 (be) incomplete; be not finished; be not completely done; 《덜 익다》 be not ripe. ¶ 덜된 과일 unripe 〔green〕 fruit / 일이 ~ *one's* work is not finished / 밥이 아직 ~ the rice is not ready 〔cooked〕 yet / 덜된 채로 두다 leave 《*a thing*》 unfinished / 조사가 아직 덜되어 있다 The investigation is not thorough-going enough.

**덜렁거리다** ① ⇨ 달랑거리다①. ② 《까불다》 act frivolously; be restless; be always on the go 〔move〕; conduct 〔behave〕 *oneself* flippantly. ¶ 덜렁거리는 사람 a flighty person / 덜렁거리며 돌아다니다 go around restlessly; flutter 〔flit〕 around; can't sit still a minute.

**덜렁말** a skittish horse.

**덜렁쇠** a frivolous 〔flippant, flighty, heedless〕 person; a restless person; a fidget.

**덜렁하다** ① ⇨ 달랑거리다①. ② 《가슴이》 feel a shock; get a start; be much surprised 〔frightened, alarmed, startled〕; get the wind up; have *one's* heart in *one's* mouth; feel *one's* heart stop. ¶ 가슴이 ~ be extremely startled; jump out of *one's* skin / 그가 나를 부르러 보냈을 때 가슴이 덜렁했다 When he sent 〔called〕 for me, I had my heart in my mouth. / 그 소식을 듣고 가슴이 덜렁했다 I was startled at the news. *or* The news gave me quite a turn.

**덜름하다** 《옷이》 (be) rather short.

**덜리다** ① 《덜어지다》 be subtracted; deducted; taken off 〔away, from〕. ② 《경감되다》 be reduced; become less; lessen; decrease; become lower; be mitigated; be alleviated; be eased. ¶ 걱정이 ~ *one's* anxiety is eased / 고통이 ~ *one's* pain is mitigated 〔eased, alleviated, lightened〕 / 불안이 ~ *one's* misgiving 〔apprehension〕 is allayed.

**덜먹다** ① 《다 먹지 않다》 do not eat all (served). ② 《실컷 먹지 않다》 do not satisfy *one's* hunger; be moderate in eating. ③ 《행동이》 act improperly and waywardly.

**덜미** the back of the neck; the nape; the scruff (of *one's* neck). ⇨ 뒷덜미.

**덜미잡이** grabbing by the back 〔scruff〕 of *a person's* neck. ~하다 grab 〔take, seize〕 by the back 〔scruff〕 of *a person's* neck.

**덜미잡다** ① = 덜미잡이하다. ② 《재촉하다》 press 《*a person*》 hotly.

**덜밉지않다** be not so bad (in looks); (be) rather good-looking; be rather fond of.

**덜어내다** take out of 〔from, away〕. ¶ 가마니에서 쌀을 ~ take some rice out of a rice bag / 그릇에서 밥을 ~ take some rice out of a bowl.

**덜커덕** ① 《부딪쳐 나는 소리》 ~하다 click; thump; plump; bump; thud. ¶ ~ 소리 내며 with a thud 〔thump〕; plump heavily; with a bump 〔flump〕 / 문이 ~하다 a door clicks / ~ 떨어지다 fall plump 〔with a flump〕; fall heavily; flump / 창문이 ~ 닫히다 a window shuts with a click.
② 《가슴이》 ~하다 feel a shock; be startled; get shocked 《at, by》; have *one's* heart in *one's* mouth. ¶ 그의 말에 가슴이 ~ 내려 앉았다 His words shocked me. / 그 소식을 듣고 가슴이 ~ 했다 The news gave me a start. / 전보라면 언제나 가슴이 ~ 내려 앉는다 A telegram always gives me a turn.

**덜커덕거리다** keep clicking; rattle; clatter. ¶ 덜커덕거리는 창문 a rattling window / 짐수레가 덜커덕거리며 가다 a cart clatters along.

**덜커덕덜커덕** clicking; rattling; clattering.

**덜커덩** with a bang; with a crash; rattling; clattering. ～하다 bang; crash; thud; bump. ¶ ～ 수화기를 내려놓다 slam 〔bang〕 down the receiver / 문을 ～ 닫다 shut a door with a bang / 문이 ～하다 a door bangs.

**덜커덩거리다** keep banging 〔crashing, rattling, clattering〕. ¶ 기차는 덜커덩거리며 건널목을 지났다 The train rattled over the crossing. / 유리창이 바람에 덜커덩거린다 A window is rattling in the wind.

**덜컥-, 덜컹-** ⇨덜커덕-, 덜커덩-.

**덜퍽부리다** shout loud and act mean.

**덜퍽스럽다** (be) buxom; portly; ample. ¶ 몸이 ～ be buxom.

**덜퍽지다** (be) plentiful; rich; 《몸집이》 (be) buxom; portly; plump; corpulent; stout.

**덜하다** ① [자동사] lessen; decrease; diminish. ¶ 그 약 덕택에 아픔이 ～ The medicine eased 〔alleviated〕 the pain. / 추위가 덜해졌다 It has got 〔grown, become〕 less cold. ② [타동사] lessen; diminish; decrease. ¶ 지출을 ～ curtail 〔cut down〕 (*one's*) expenses. ③ 《견주어서》 (be) less. ¶ 올해의 수확은 작년보다 상당히 덜하겠다 This year's crop will fall much short of last year's

**덤** an extra; an addition; 《경품》 something thrown-in. ¶ 덤으로 in addition 《to》; on top of 《*a thing*》; into the bargain; besides; moreover / …을 덤으로 주다 throw in 《*a thing*》 for free / 덤으로 몇 개 더 주시오 Throw in a few more, please. / 이것은 덤으로 드립니다 This is a free 〔an uncharged〕 addition. / 그 옷을 사시는 분에게는 스카프를 덤으로 드립니다 If you buy the clothes, 「you'll be given a scarf as an extra 〔I'll throw in this scarf for free〕.

**덤덤탄**(―彈) a dumdum bullet; a soft-nosed bullet.

**덤덤하다** remain 〔keep〕 silent; hold *one's* tongue; keep dumb 〔mum〕. ¶ 덤덤하니 앉아 있다 sit in silence.

**덤받이** a child of *one's* wife by a previous marriage; a child by *one's* former husband.

**덤벙** with a splash 〔plop〕. ～하다 make a splash 〔splatter〕. ¶ 물에 ～ 떨어지다 drop in the water with a plop; fall plop into the water / 그는 머리부터 ～ 뛰어들었다 He dived in head first with a splash.

**덤벙거리다** ① 《까불다》 act frivolously 〔rashly, lightly, carelessly, hastily〕; bustle; make a fuss. ¶ 아무 일에나 ～ stick *one's* nose into everything / 조심해라, ～가는 그릇 깰라 Be careful—you will break the dish if you handle it so carelessly. ② 《물을》 splash; splatter; dabble. ¶ 덤벙거리며 걷다 go splashing 《through the mud》/ 발을 물에 담그고 ～ dabble *one's* feet in the water.

**덤벙덤벙** ① 《경솔히》 frivolously; rashly; lightly; hastily; carelessly. ¶ 아무 일에나 ～ 대들다 poke *one's* nose into everything. ② 《물을》 splashing; splattering.

**덤벼들다** ① 《달려들다》 fly 〔spring, leap, jump〕 to 〔at, on〕; pounce on 〔at〕. ⇨덤비다 ②. ¶ 아무의 제안에 ～ jump at *a person's* offer; seize on *a person's* proposal / 개가 나에게 덤벼들었다 A dog pounced at me. / 그는 그 기회를 놓칠세라 덤벼들었다 He grasped at the opportunity. / 집에 가니 아이들이 반가워 덤벼들었다 When I arrived home, the children flew to me. ② 《일에》 go 〔get, proceed〕 to work; set *oneself* to work; tackle 《a task》; cope with 《a problem》. ¶ 그녀는 즉시 그 일에 덤벼들었다 She flung herself into the work with determination. / 여럿이 덤벼들어 일을 순식간에 해치웠다 Several of them went at the work and made short work of it.

**덤부렁듬쑥** thick; dense; overgrown; luxuriant; in luxurious growth. ～하다 (be) thick; overgrown; luxuriant.

**덤불** a bush; a thicket; a shrub. ¶ 가시～ 길을 걸어가다 tread a thorny bush.

**덤불자작이** 〚식물〛 a birch.

**덤불혼인**(―婚姻) marriage between two people already related by marriage.

**덤비다** ① 《서둘다》 hurry; act helter-skelter; act hurriedly 〔hastily〕; be hasty 〔hurried〕. ¶ 덤비지 말고 calmly; with composure; unflustered / 너무 ～가 다칠라 You might get hurt if you hurry too much. / 급하게 덤빌 일이 아니었다 There was no urgency about the job. / 덤비지 마라 Don't be so hasty 〔in a hurry〕! *or* Take your time! *or* Steady! *or* Take it easy! *or* Keep your shirt on! 《구어》. ② 《대들다》 turn 〔fall〕 on 《*a person*》; fly at; challenge 《*a person*》 to 《a fight》; pick a quarrel with 《*a person*》; retort; attack; go at. ⇨덤벼들다. ¶ 적에게 ～ go at 〔attack〕 an enemy / 비호같이 ～ spring at 《*a person*》 with tiger-like ferocity / 그들은 서로 맹렬히 상대에게 덤볐다

They set about each other fiercely. / 덤비려면 덤벼 봐라 Come at me. *or* Now come on! *or* Come and get me if you can. / 자 몽땅 덤벼라 Go ahead, the whole pack of you!

**덤터기** blame-shifting; passing the buck 《미구어》. ¶ ~ 쓰다 have the blame shifted on to *oneself* / ~ 씌우다 shift the blame on to 《*a person*》; pass the buck 《미구어》.

**덤프차**(一車), **덤프트럭** a dump truck.

**덤핑** 《투매》 dumping. ~하다 dump 《goods》; sell 《goods》 at sacrifice prices 《in overseas markets》. ¶ 한국산 비디오 필름에 대한 반~ 조사 the anti-dumping probe into Korean-made video film / 외국제 강철에 대한 ~ 방지책 anti-dumping measures against foreign steel / 과잉물자를 외국시장에서 ~하다 dump the surplus goods in foreign markets / ~ 공세를 취하다 conduct offensive dumping 《on overseas markets》. ◉ ~방지 관세 anti-dumping duties. ~시장 a dumping market 〔field〕. 반~법 an anti-dumping act 〔law〕.

**덥다** (be) hot; warm (★ hot는 미국에서, warm은 영국에서 흔히 씀); feel hot 〔warm〕. ¶ 더운 물 hot water / 더운 방 a warm 〔hot〕 room / 더운 날 a hot 〔warm〕 day / 더울 때 먹다 eat 《food》 hot; drink 《*sul*》 hot / 몸이 덥다 have a fever 〔temperature〕 / 더워서 땀이 나다 sweat with the heat / 날이 ~ It is hot 〔warm〕. / 더워졌다 It has become hotter 〔warmer〕. *or* It has got 〔grown〕 hot 〔warm〕. / 더워서 죽겠다 I am dying of the heat. *or* The heat is unbearable. *or* I can't stand the heat. / 오늘도 덥겠다 We're going to have another hot day. / 지금이 한창 더울 때다 The summer 〔air〕 is now at it's hottest. / 푹푹 찌는 듯이 ~ It is scorching 〔steaming〕 hot. / 덥기 전에 외출하자 Let's go out before it gets hot. / 더워서 잠을 잘 수 없다 It's so hot (that) I can't sleep.

**덥석** with a quick movement; quickly; suddenly; hastily; greedily; 《단단히》 tightly. ¶ ~ 물다 snap 《at》 / 손을 ~ 쥐다 clasp 〔grasp〕 《*a person's*》 hand suddenly; give 《*a person*》 a grip / 과자를 한 줌 ~ 움켜쥐다 grab handful of cake / 사자가 고기를 ~ 물었다 The lion snapped up a piece of meat.

**덥적거리다** ① 《남의 일에》 interfere 《in *a matter,* with *a person*》; meddle with everything; step in; butt in; poke *one's* nose into everything. ¶ 덥적거리기 좋아하는 사람 a meddlesome person; a busybody / 그는 무슨 일에나 덥적거린다 He meddles with everything. *or* He pokes his nose into everything. / 주제넘게 덥적거리지 마라 You keep out of this. *or* It is none of your business. ② 《붙임성 있게》 do all sorts of nice 〔ingratiating〕 things; make ingratiating gestures; go out of *one's* way to be nice. ¶ 그녀는 누구에게나 덥적거렸다 She was very friendly 〔affable〕 to everybody.

**덥적덥적** ① 《남의 일에》 trying one thing after another; meddling with everything; poking *one's* nose into everything. ¶ 그는 ~ 남의 일에 간섭하는 버릇이 있다 He has a way of meddling in other people's business. ② 《붙임성 있게》 doing all sorts of nice 〔ingratiating〕 things; making ingratiating gestures; going out of *one's* way to be nice.

**덧** 《짧은 시간》 a short space of time 〔while〕; a spell. ⇨ 어느덧. ¶ 덧없는 세월 flying 〔quick-passing〕 time.

**덧가지** a double branch.

**덧거름** fertilizer given to growing plants; additional fertilizer.

**덧거리** ① 《추가물》 an additional thing 〔work〕; extra thing 〔work〕. ~하다 put 〔throw〕 in an additional thing 〔work〕. ② 《말》 an exaggeration. ~하다 exaggerate; overstate. ¶ 그는 ~가 심하다 He is prone to exaggerate. *or* He always exaggerates. ◉ ~질 《덧얹음》 putting 〔throwing〕 in an additional thing; 《말의》 exaggeration; overstatement.

**덧거칠다** 《일이》 be going amiss 〔wrong〕; (be) worsening.

**덧걸다** hang 《*a thing*》 on top 《of something else》. 「top 《of》.

**덧걸리다** be added on; be hung on

**덧걸이** 《씨름》 an armlock trip. ¶ ~를 걸다, ~질하다 trip a wrestler with an armlock.

**덧게비** an extra thing 〔person〕; a burden; a nuisance. ¶ ~치다 make *oneself* a nuisance; give trouble.

**덧깔다** spread 《*a thing*》 on top 《of》.

**덧나다**[1] ① 《병이》 become worse; take a bad turn; take a turn for the worse; be aggravated; 《곪다》 form 〔generate〕 pus; fester. ¶ 병이 ~ an illness is aggravated; *one's* condition takes a turn for the worse / 종기가 ~ a boil gets worse. ② 《성나다》 be offended; get *one's* back up; have *one's* blood up; be provoked (into fury); fly into a temper; fly off the handle; get angry 〔mad〕.

**덧나다**[2] 《이가》 grow on top 《of another》; grow extra; grow from the common root; grow to one side; shoot off; deviate. ¶ 이가 ~ have a double 〔side〕 tooth; grow a snag tooth.

**덧날** an extra blade on top of a plane. ¶ 대패에 ~을 끼우다 attach an extra blade to a plane. ◉ ~막이 a metal band over the extra blade.

**덧내다** 《병을》 cause to take a bad turn; make worse; aggravate; inflame. ¶ 종기를 건드려 ~ make a boil worse by fiddling with it; make a pimple inflamed by fiddling with it.

**덧니** a side tooth (grown from the root of another tooth); a snaggletooth (벋니); a double tooth (겹친 이). ◉ ~박이 a person with a side tooth.

**덧달다** hang on top 《of another》. ¶ 덧달리다 be hung on top. 「a layer》.

**덧대다** add 〔join〕 《on a board, a prop,

**덧들이다** ① 《감정을》 provoke 《*a person*》 to anger; hurt 《*a person's*》 feeling. ¶ 아무의 감정을 ~ offend *a person;* make *a person* angry. ② 《잠을》 keep 《*a person*》 from getting back to sleep.

**덧문**(—門) 《문·창의》 an outer 〔a double〕 door 〔window〕.

**덧버선** outer socks.

**덧붙다** attach 〔stick〕 on in addition.

**덧붙이다** ① 《더 붙이다》 attach; stick; fix; affix; put; join 《on top of another》. ¶ 소포를 짐에 덧붙여 보내다 send a parcel along with 《*a person's*》 baggage / 벽에 널판자를 ~ fix planks of wood on a wall / 종이를 ~ paste a piece of paper on 《another》; paste two sheets of paper together. ② 《보태어 말하다》 add 〔put in, throw in〕 《*a thing*》 extra; add 《one thing to another》; append. ¶ 덧붙여 말하다 add; make an additional remark / 한 말씀 덧붙이겠습니다 Let me add a few more words to make sure. / 「단, 확실치는 않다」고 그는 덧붙였다 "But I am not sure," he added. / 그녀의 설명에 아무 것도 덧붙일 것이 없다 I have nothing 「to add to 〔to say about〕 her explanation. 「clipper.

**덧빗** an iron comb added to a hair-

**덧셈** addition. ~하다 add up 《figures》.

**덧소금** added salt (before setting to pickle). 「《미》.

**덧신** overshoes; galoshes; gumshoes

**덧신다** put on 〔wear〕 《*a thing*》 over *one's* shoes. 「wearing on *one's* head.

**덧쓰다** put 《*a thing*》 over what *one* is

**덧양말**(—洋襪) an extra pair of socks worn over the regular ones.

**덧없다** ① 《속절없이 빠르다》 (be) short=lived; transient; transitory; ephemeral; be quick in passing; be all too soon. ¶ 덧없는 세월 flying 〔quick passing〕 time / 덧없는 사랑 a short-lived love / 덧없이 지나가는 인생 transient 〔ephemeral〕 life / 이 세상의 행복이란 모두가 얼마나 덧없는 것이냐 How transient all happiness is in this world ! ② 《무상하다》 (be) vain; hopeless; uncertain; changeable; mutable; evanescent. ¶ 인생의 덧없음 the frailty of life / 덧없는 세상 the uncertain 〔changeable〕 world / 나는 한때 성공에 대한 덧없는 희망을 가졌었다 I once had a vain hope of success. / 인생은 덧없는 것이다 All is vanity in life. *or* Life is but an empty dream. ③ 《자취·근거 없음》 (be) unfounded; baseless; false; be without leaving any trace.

**덧없이** fleetingly; transiently; evanescently; quickly; transitorily; all too soon; before *one* knows it. ¶ 세월이 ~ 가다 time passes before we know it / 인생이 ~ 가다 life comes to an end all too soon.

**덧입다** put on 〔wear〕 《a coat》 over a garment. 「regular coat.

**덧저고리** an extra coat worn over *one's*

**덧짐** an added 〔extra〕 load.

**덩굴** a vine (포도 따위의); a tendril (덩굴손); a creeper (담쟁이의); a runner (딸기·고구마의); a bine (특히 hop 의). ¶ ~지다 creep; put on vines; grow creepers / ~이 뻗다 a vine creeps 〔climbs, trails, trains〕 / 포도 덩굴이 나무를 감고 있다 Grapevine twines about the tree. ◉ ~손 a tendril; a cirrus.

**덩그렇다** ① 《높다·헌거롭다》 (be) high and big; stately; imposing. ¶ 집을 덩그렇게 높이 짓다 build a house tall / 언덕 위에 덩그렇게 지은 집이 한 채 서 있다 An imposing house towers high over the hill. ② 《텅비다》 (be) big and hollow. ¶ 덩그런 집 a big and empty house / 그 방은 가구가 없어 ~ The room is bare of furniture.

**덩달다** follow《*others*》blindly. ¶ 덩달은 가격 인상 the follow-up price hikes / 큰애가 우니 작은애도 덩달아 운다 The elder child is crying, and the younger one「pulls the same trick〔follows suit〕.

**덩더꿍** tum-tum; tum-tumming; tum-de-dum. ¶ ~이 소출 a happy-go-lucky way of life.

**덩덩** tum-tum; tum-tumming. ¶ ~ 북을 울리다 beat a drum tum-tum / ~ 하니 굿만 여겨《속담》ready to expect「a nice party〔a good thing〕out of every possible situation.

**덩덩그렇다** ①《헌거롭다》(be) ever so high and big; most imposing. ②《텅 비다》(be) huge and empty.

**덩실거리다** dance lively〔sprightly, merrily, cheerfully〕; skip about. ¶ 기뻐서 ~ dance about with joy.

**덩실덩실**《dancing》lively; joyfully; merrily; gaily; light-heartedly; cheerfully. ¶ ~ 춤추다 dance joyfully.

**덩어리** a lump; a mass (★ lump는 비교적 작은 덩어리, mass는 같은 종류의 물건이 많이 모인 덩어리); a block (돌이나 나무의); a chunk (고기·치즈의); a clod (흙의). ¶ 금~ a lump〔nugget〕of gold (주조되지 않은); a gold ingot (주조된) / 점토~ a lump of clay / 빵~ a loaf of bread / 진흙~ a cake of mud / 골칫~ a troublesome fellow / 그는 욕심~다 He is avarice itself. / 큰 바위~가 길을 막았다 A mass of rock blocked the road.

**덩어리지다** lump; mass; form a mass; conglomerate. ¶ 흙이 ~ dirt lumps / 얼음이~ ice forms into a mass / 전분은 너무 급히 끓이면 덩어리진다 Cornstarch will lump if boiled too fast.

**덩이** a lump; a mass; a clod; a nugget; a piece.

**덩치** bulk; size; volume. ¶ ~가 크다 be bulky; be big; be voluminous; be of a large build / ~가 큰 사람 a big〔bulky〕person / ~가 큰 짐 a big〔bulky〕piece of baggage / ~ 크고 꾀 있는 놈 없다 Big head, little wit.

**덫** a trap; a snare; a hook; a gin;《계략》a trick. ¶ 쥐덫 a rattrap; a mousetrap / 덫을 놓다 lay〔set〕a trap / 덫에 걸리다 be caught in a trap; fall into a snare; be ensnared; be entrapped / 덫으로 잡다 entrap; snare; gin; ensnare; catch in a trap / 제가 놓은 덫에 제가 걸리다 be caught in *one's* own snare; be hoist with *one's* own petard / 나는 덫에 걸렸다 I fell into a trap. (★ 비유적인 뜻으로는 trap을 쓰는 것이 보통임.) / 감쪽같이 덫에 걸렸다 I was clean〔quite〕taken in.

**덮개**《침구》bedding; bedclothes; a quilt; (bed) covers; a coverlet; a comfort(er); a cover (보호를 위한); covering (덮어씌우는 것). ¶ ~가 있는 covered / ~가 없는 uncovered; bare / ~를 하다 cover / ~를 벗기다 take the cover off《*something*》; uncover.

**덮다** ①《씌우다》cover《with》; put《*a thing*》on; veil;《휩싸다》cover up; overspread; blanket;《뚜껑을》cover; cap; put《the lid》on; shut down《the lid》(★ shut은 뚜껑이 붙어 있는 경우, put은 뚜껑이 떨어져 있는 경우에 씀). ¶ 산꼭대기를 덮은 구름 clouds hanging over the top of the mountain / 이불을 ~ put on bedclothes; cover *oneself* with bedclothes; draw bedclothes over / 나무 뿌리를 흙으로 ~ cover the root of a tree with earth / 뚜껑을 ~ put a lid on / 사용하지 않을 때는 커버로 덮어놓아라 Put the cover on it when you're not using it. / 짙은 구름이 산봉우리를 덮었다 Thick cloud(s) overspread the mountaintop. / 눈이 들판을 온통 덮었다 Snow clothes the fields. *or* The fields were covered with snow.
②《엄폐하다》hide; conceal; cover up《for》. ¶ 죄를 덮어두다 cover up《*a person's*》crime; keep《*a person's*》crime secret / 아들의 잘못을 덮어 주다 cover up for *one's* son / 그의 실패는 덮어둘 수 없는 사실이다 His failure is a fact that cannot be concealed.
③《펼쳐진 것을》shut; close. ¶ 책을 ~ close a book.

**덮어놓고** without asking〔giving〕any reason〔explanation〕; without any cause〔reason〕; causelessly; thoughtlessly; recklessly; arbitrarily. ¶ ~ 가자고 하다 ask《*a person*》to go without telling why / ~ 치다 hit《*a person*》without giving any explanation; up and hit《*a person*》/ ~ 열넉 냥 금 give a random judgment / 사람을 ~ 비판하지 말아라 Don't criticize people indiscriminately. / 아버지는 ~ 나만 잘못했다 하신다 Father automatically says I am the one to blame whatever happens. / ~ 한꺼번에 이것저것 일을 시작하려 하지 마라 Stop trying to start so many matters off at the same time.

**덮어두다** shut *one's* eyes 《to》; take no notice 《of》; keep 《*a thing*》 from *one;* pass 《*a matter*》 over unnoticed; let 《*a matter*》 go unchallenged; overlook; wink 〔connive〕 at 《*a person's* wrongdoings》. ¶ 아무의 잘못을 ~ shut *one's* eyes to *a person's* fault; overlook *a person's* mistakes / 이것은 그대로 덮어둘 수 없다 We should not let this pass without protest. *or* This should not be passed unmentioned. / 불쌍하니까 이번만은 덮어둔다 For pity's sake I will let the matter pass for this time. / 중대한 실수가 아니니 덮어둘 수 있다고 생각한다 It's not a serious error, we can let it pass, I think.

**덮어쓰다** be wrongly 〔falsely〕 accused 《of stealing》. = 뒤집어쓰다 ②.

**덮어씌우다** ① 《가림》 cover 《*a thing* with...》; put 《*a thing*》 over 〔on〕; plate 《*a thing* with gold》. ② 《죄를》 charge 《*a person* with a blame》; pin 《a fault on *a person*》; accuse *a person* of 《theft》 falsely; make a false charge 《of espionage》 against *a person;* 《구어》 frame. ¶ 누구에게든 부당하게 덮어씌우지 마라 Don't accuse anyone unjustly.

**덮이다** 《얹히다》 be put on; 《가리다》 be covered with; be veiled; be hidden; be concealed; 《싸이다》 be wrapped; be enfolded. ¶ 뚜껑이 ~ a lid is put on; be lidded / 눈으로 ~ be covered with snow / 하늘이 구름으로 덮여 있다 The sky is covered with clouds. / 산꼭대기는 구름으로 덮여 있다 The mountain peak is wrapped in clouds.

**덮치기** 《새그물》 a large fowler's 〔fowling〕 net; a bird net with double handles.

**덮치다** ① 《겹쳐 누르다》 throw 〔cast, pop〕 《*a thing*》 over; hold 〔get〕 《*a person*》 down; pin 《*a person*》 to the floor; overlap one another; 《습격하다》 attack; raid; fall on (불운 따위가); descend on; swoop down 〔on〕; seize. ¶ 그물로 새를 ~ throw a net over birds; catch birds with a net / 솔개가 병아리를 ~ a kite swoops down 〔falls〕 on a chicken / 사내가 여자를 ~ a man attacks a woman / 적의 병영을 ~ make a raid upon the enemy's camp / 노름판을 ~ raid a gambling den / 폭풍우가 갑자기 배를 덮쳤다 A storm overtook the ship.
② 《여러 가지 일이》 《several things》 happen 〔come〕 all at the same time; be pressed for business; suffer from pressure of business. ¶ 여러 가지 일이 ~ have many things to do all at the same time; things come all bunched up at once / 여러 가지 불행이 ~ have several misfortunes together / 엎친 데 덮친다 Misfortunes never come singly. / 혼사에 장사가 덮쳤다 They had a wedding and a funeral one after the other.

**데** ① 《곳》 a place; a point; a spot; 《특징》 a feature; an aspect; 《대목》 a passage (문장 따위의); a part (부분). ¶ 위험한 데 a dangerous spot / 표 파는 데 a ticket-seller's; a ticket window / 남들이 있는 데에서 in the presence of others; in public / 앉을 데가 없다 There is nowhere to sit. / 그녀는 여자다운 데가 없다 There is nothing feminine 〔womanly〕 about her. / 가는 데가 어디냐 Where is the place you are going to? / 여기는 젊은 사람들이 오는 데가 아니다 This is no place for young people. / 이 도시는 해발 2천 피트나 되는 데에 있다 The town is situated 2,000 ft. above sea level.
② 《경우》 a case; a circumstance; 《경우에》 in case of 〔that〕...; when.... ¶ 이것은 머리 아픈 데에 먹는 약이다 This is the medicine you take when you have a headache.

**-데** [종결어미] it has been observed that...; it is known that...; I noticed that.... ¶ 구경꾼이 많이 오데 (We noticed that) lots of people were coming to see the sight. / 경치가 과연 좋데 The scenery sure was grand!

**데꺽** ① 《소리》 cracking; snapping; with a crack; with a snap. ¶ 지팡이가 ~ 부러지다 *one's* stick breaks with a snap. ② 《손쉽게》 without any trouble; with ease; quickly and easily; just like that; in a snap. ¶ 그는 그 문제를 ~ 풀었다 He solved the problem just like a snap. *or* The problem was a snap for him.

**데꺽거리다** crack; clatter; rattle; keep snapping. ¶ 그릇이 ~ dishes are clattering.

**데꺽데꺽** clattering; rattling.

**데니어** 《실 굵기》 a denier (생략 D, d). ¶ 40 ~의 양말, 40-denier stockings.

**데다** ① 《불·열에》 get 〔be〕 burned 〔scalded〕; have a burn; scald 〔burn〕 *oneself.* ¶ 덴 자국 a scar of a burn / 덴 데 쓰이는 연고 an ointment for burns and scalds / 난로에 손을 ~ burn *one's* hand on a stove / 뜨거운 물에 손을 ~ scald *one's* hand with hot water / 욕조의 물은 델 정도로 뜨거웠다 The water in the bathtub was scalding hot. ② 《혼나다》 have had a bitter experience 《with》; suffer 《from》; have had enough 《of》; find 〔know〕 《*a thing*》 to *one's* cost; get *one's* fingers burned 《on》. ¶ 너의 장난에는 아주 데었다 I've had plenty 〔enough〕 of your mischief. / 그 사람한테는 한번 단단히 데었다 I have had some very bitter experiences with him. / 데 봐서 알지만 말벌에 쏘이면 몹시 아프다 Wasps' stings are serious, as I know to my cost.

**데데하다** (be) poor; trashy; good-for-nothing; worthless; unsatisfactory. ¶ 데데한 사람 a good-for-nothing person / 데데한 수작 useless remarks; nonsense / 데데한 물건 poor stuff; trash; rubbish / 데데하게 굴다 act foolishly / 두 사람은 데데한 일로 잘 싸운다 The two often quarrel over a trifle.

**데되다** be unsatisfactory (in quality); lack something; be short of perfection; leave something to be desired; be somewhat defective.

**데드볼** 〚야구〛 a pitch that hits the batter. ¶ ~을 맞다 be hit by a pitched ball / ~로 1루에 나가다 get to first hit by a pitched ball.

**데려가다** take 《*a person*》 along; take 〔lead〕 《*a person*》 away 〔off〕; carry 《*a person*》 off; 《연행》 walk 《*a person*》 off; 《유괴하다》 kidnap 《a child》. ¶ 아이를 아저씨 댁에 ~ take a child to *one's* uncle's / 너를 길잡이로 데려가겠다 I'll take you along as a guide. / 데려가 주시오 Let me go with you. / 매일 아침 그는 양을 목장으로 데려갔다 Every morning he led the sheep to the pasture. / 경찰관이 그녀를 경찰서로 데려갔다 A policeman took her along with him to the police station. *or* A policeman walked her off to the police station.

**데려오다** bring 《*a person*》 along; bring 《*a person*》 with *one*. ¶ 아이를 학교에서 집으로 ~ bring *one's* child home from school / 의사를 ~ bring a doctor 《along with *one*》 / 그는 아들을 함께 데려왔다 He brought his son with him.

**데리다** 《거느리다》 get accompanied by; be attended by; take 《*a person*》 along with *one*. ¶ 아이들을 데리고 있는 부인 a woman with children / 개를 데리고 산책하다 take *one's* dog for a walk / 그를 서둘러 병원으로 데리고 가다 rush him to a hospital / 가족을 데리고 있다 be accompanied by *one's* family / 가족을 데리고 피난하다 flee with *one's* family / 수행원을 데리고 회의에 참석하다 attend a meeting accompanied by *one's* aids / 어머니는 아이를 데리고 공원에 갔다 The mother took her child to the park.

**데릴사위** a son-in-law taken into the family; one adopted as husband for an heiress. ¶ ~가 되다〔로 들어가다〕 marry an heiress; marry into *one's* wife's family.

**데릴사윗감** ① 《귀염 못 받는》 a person who is likely to be disliked. ② 《얌전한》 a young man of exemplary life.

**데마고기** 《선동행위》 demagoguery; demagogy; demagogism; a groundless story; a false 〔an unfounded〕 rumor; grapevine 《미구어》. ¶ ~를 퍼뜨리다 set a false rumor afloat; circulate a false rumor 〔report〕.

**데면데면하다** ① 《조심성 없다》 (be) careless; thoughtless; heedless; inattentive; negligent. ¶ 일을 데면데면히 하지 말고 좀 잘 해라 Don't make a careless job of it—I want it done carefully.
② 《붙임성 없다》 (be) stiff; distant; cold; standoffish. ¶ 데면데면하게 대하다 treat 《*a person*》 stiffly; assume 〔put on〕 a cool air 《toward》 / 두 사람 사이는 좀 데면데면해졌다 They are not getting along as well as they used to. *or* A certain coolness has come over their relationship.

**데모** a demonstration (시위 행진); a rally (집회). ~하다 demonstrate 《against nuclear tests》. ¶ ~ 만능의 풍조 almighty demonstration trend / 반전(反戰) ~ an antiwar demonstration / ~에 가담하다 join a demonstration / ~를 해산시키다〔진압하다〕 disperse 〔put down〕 a demonstration.
◉ ~대 (a group of ) demonstrators. ~행진 《stage》 a demonstration parade.

**데모크라시** democracy. ⇨ 민주주의. ¶ ~의 democratic.

**데밀다** push 《it》 in.

**데뷔** a *début* (F.). ~하다 make *one's* debut 《on the stage》; debut. ¶ 그녀는 이번 가을에 음악계〔연예계〕에 ~할 것이다 She will make her debut in 「the musical world 〔the show business〕

this autumn. / 그녀가 가수로 ～한 것은 5년 전이었다 It was five years ago that she made her debut as a singer.

**데삶다** boil 《an egg》 soft 〔lightly〕; parboil. ¶ 데삶은 underdone; half-done; half-cooked; half-boiled; rare / 데삶은 달걀 a half-〔soft-〕boiled egg; a half-done egg; a half-poached egg.

**데생** 〖미술〗 a *dessin* (F.); a (rough) sketch. ¶ 그는 그 정물 ～을 했다 He made a rough sketch of a still life.

**데생기다** be immature; be raw.

**데설궂다** (be) rude; unrefined; unmannered; rough; loose.

**데스마스크** a death mask. ¶ ～를 뜨다 make a death mask 《of》.

**데스크** 《책상》 a desk; the (registry) desk (호텔의); 〖신문〗 《사람》 a copy editor; a subeditor; 《미》 a deskman. ◉ ～톱 비디오〔컴퓨터〕 a desktop video 〔computer〕.

**데시-** 《10분의 1》 deci-. ¶ 데시그램 a decigram (생략 dg) / 데시미터 a decimeter (생략 dm) / 데시리터 a deciliter (생략 dl) / 데시벨 a decibel (생략 dB, db).

**데시기다** eat reluctantly 〔unwillingly〕. ¶ 그녀는 입맛이 떨어져 음식을 데시기기만 했다 She had no appetite and only picked at her food.

**데알다** have a superficial 〔little〕 knowledge 《about》; know superficially 〔sketchily〕; know a little.

**데우다** warm 〔heat〕 (up); make warm. ¶ 다시 ～ rewarm; reheat; warm 《*something*》 up 〔over 《미》〕 / 물을 ～ heat water / 술을 데워 마시다 drink wine hot / 국을〔우유를〕 ～ warm up soup 〔milk〕 / 밥을 데워 먹다 eat a rice meal warm.

**데이비스컵** 〖테니스〗 the Davis cup. ◉ ～ (쟁탈)전 the Davis cup tournament.

**데이터** data (*sing.* -tum) (★ 미국에서는 흔히 this data처럼 단수로도 쓰임). ¶ ～를 입력〔출력〕하다 input 〔output〕 data / …에 관한 ～를 모으다 gather data on…. ◉ ～뱅크 a data bank. ～베이스 a database. ～전송 a data transmission 〔transfer〕. ～처리 data processing: ～처리 장치 a data processor; a data processing device 〔machine〕. ～통신 data communication: ～통신 장치 data communications equipment.

**데이트** a date. ～하다 date (with) 《a handsome boy》; have 〔make〕 a date 《with》. ¶ 수잔나는 오늘밤 나의 ～ 상대다 Susanna is my date for tonight.

**데익다** (be) half-cooked〔-done〕; rare.

**데치다** ① 《삶아 내다》 boil slightly; parboil; scald. ¶ 푸성귀를 끓는 물에 ～ parboil vegetables in hot water. ② 《혼내다》 chastise; punish severely.

**데카-** 《10배의 뜻》 deca-. ¶ 데카리터 a decaliter / 데카미터 a decameter.

**데카당** a decadent (사람). ◉ ～문학 decadent literature. ～파 the decadents.

**데카당스** decadence.

**데커레이션** (a) decoration. ¶ 크리스마스 ～ Christmas decoration. ◉ ～케이크 (a) decorated 〔party〕 cake; (a) fancy cake.

**데탕트** 《긴장 완화》 *détente* (F.).

**데퉁바리** a clumsy oaf.

**데퉁스럽다, 데퉁맞다** (be) clumsy; awkward.

**덱데구루루** ⇨ 땍때구루루.

**덴가슴** a 「deeply-shocked 〔horrow-stricken〕 state of mind; a regrettable 〔painful, nightmarish〕 memory. ¶ 불에 ～이다 have a nightmarish memory of fire / 나는 빚 보증인이란 것에 ～을 안고 있다 I know to my cost what it is to stand behind another's loan.

**덴겁하다** be confused 〔flustered, flurried〕; lose *one's* presence of mind; get rattled. ¶ 덴겁해서 in a fluster.

**덴마크** Denmark. ¶ ～의 Danish. ◉ ～말 Danish. ～사람 a Dane.

**덴버** 《미국의 도시》 Denver.

**델라웨어** 《미국의 주》 Delaware (생략 Del.).

**델리킷** ¶ ～한 입장 a delicate situation / 그것은 (신중을 요하는) ～한 문제이다 It's a delicate problem.

**델린저 현상**(―現象) 〖물리〗 the Dellinger phenomenon.

**델타** 〖지리〗 a delta. ¶ ～ 지대 a delta region / 나일 강의 ～ the Nile Delta.

**도**(度) ① 《각도의》 a degree. ¶ 75도의 각 an angle of 75 degrees.
② 《경위도》 a degree. ¶ 북위〔남위〕 38도, 38 degrees 〔38°〕 north 〔south〕 latitude; latitude 38° N 〔S〕 / 동경 20도 longitude 20° E / 서울은 동경 127°, 북위 37° 50′에 있다 The longitude of Seoul is a hundred twenty-seven degrees east and its latitude is thirty-seven degrees fifty minutes north.
③ 《온도》 a degree. ¶ 체온이 40도까지 올라갔다 His temperature was 〔rose〕 as high as forty degrees. / 온도계는 그늘진 곳에서 섭씨 10도이다 The mercury 〔thermometer〕 registers 〔stands at〕 10°C in the shade. / 이 지방에서는

영하 20도의 기온이 보통이다 In this region temperatures of 20° below zero are common. / 물은 섭씨 100도에서 끓는다 Water boils at 100°C. (★ 100°C는 a 〔one〕 hundred degrees Centigrade라고 읽음.).
④ 《렌즈의》 a degree; a unit measuring the diopter of a lens. ⇨도수. ¶ 18도의 안경 spectacles of 18 degrees.
⑤ 《알코올의》 percent. ¶ 25도 소주 *soju* containing 25% alcohol.
⑥ 《회수(回數)》 a time. ⇨도수. ¶ 2색도 인쇄 two-color printing / 3도 인쇄하다 print in three colors.
⑦ 《정도》 a degree; (an) extent; a measure; a limit; moderation (절도). ¶ 도를 지키다 be moderate; use moderation; keep within bounds; be temperate / 도를 지나치다 go to excess 〔to extremes〕; go too far 《in》; exceed the limits; be intemperate; go beyond 〔out of〕 the bounds 《of moderation》 / 운동도 도를 지나치면 몸에 해롭다 Too much exercise is bad for your health. / 술을 먹어도 도를 지나쳐서는 안 된다 You should refrain from excessive drinking. / 무슨 일이고 도를 넘으면 해가 된다 If you go beyond the bounds in anything, it will do you harm. / 그녀의 농담은 도가 지나친 것 같다 I'm afraid she has carried her joke too far.

**도**(道) ① 《행정 구역》 a province; a district; a *do.* ¶ 도(립)의 provincial 《hospitals》 / 경기도 Kyŏnggi-do / 도당국 the provincial authorities / 도행정(行政) provincial administration. ② 《도리》 the way; 《도의·가르침》 morality; a moral doctrine 〔principle〕; teachings; doctrines; 《진리》 truth; reason; justice; 《종교상의》 a religious doctrine; a religion; 《지켜야 할》 *one's* duty. ¶ 공자의 도를 펴다 expound the teachings 〔doctrines〕 of Confucius; preach 〔propagate〕 Confucianism / 도를 구하다 seek after truth / 도를 닦다 cultivate *one's* moral 〔religious〕 sense / 도를 깨닫다 perceive a truth; realize a religious truth. ③ 《기예·방술의》 a way; an art. ¶ 궁도 archery; bowmanship.

**도** ① 《역시》 so; also; too; 《부정》 not... either. ¶ 「그는 정직하다」—「나도 그렇다」 "He is honest."—"So am I." (★ So am I.는 I를 올림조로 말함) / 「나는 그가 올거라고 생각한다」—「나도 그렇게 생각한다」 "I think he will come."—"So do I." / 「그녀는 일찍 일어난다」—「그녀의 오빠도 그래」 "She is an early riser."—"So is her brother." / 그녀도 그것을 원한다 She wants it, too. *or* She, too, wants it. *or* She also wants it. *or* She wants it also. (★ too와 also의 위치 및 콤마의 유무에 주의할 것) / 「아유 목말라」—「나도 그래」 "I am very thirsty."—"I 〔Me〕, too." / 나도 가겠다 I will go too. / 내일도 좋다 Tomorrow will be all right too. / 그는 선생님이 아니며 그녀도 선생님이 아니다 He isn't a teacher and she isn't either 〔neither is she〕. / 「나는 낚시질이 싫다」—「나도 그렇다〔싫다〕」 "I don't like fishing."—"Neither 〔Nor〕 do I." (★ and가 긍정문을 연결시킬 때에는 too 또는 so를 쓰고, 부정문을 연결시킬 경우엔 either 또는 neither를 씀. and 뒤에서는 she isn't〔can't〕와 같이 생략형으로 씀) / 당신이 안 가겠다면 나도 안 가겠소 If you don't go, I will not either. / 내가 바보라면 너도 바보다 If I'm a fool, you are another.
② 《…도 …도》 and; as well as; both... and (+긍정); (n)either... (n)or... (+부정). ¶ 나도 동생도 가겠다 Both I and my little brother will go. / 나도 아우도 안 가겠다 Neither I nor my little brother will go. / 그 사람도 나도 부자가 아니다 Neither he nor I am rich. *or* He is not rich, nor am I. / 떡도 엿도 먹었다 They ate both the rice cakes and the taffy. / 떡도 엿도 안 먹었다 They didn't eat either the rice cakes or the taffy. / 그는 영어도 알고 불어도 안다 He understands both French and English. / 그는 불어를 말할 수도 있고 쓸 수도 있다 He speaks French, and writes it as well. / 나는 불어도 독일어도 못한다 I can speak neither French nor German. / 보고싶기도 하고 두렵기도 하다 I'm divided between curiosity and dread in seeing it. / 볼만도 하고 들을 만도 하다 It is both worth seeing and worth hearing. / 바람도 불고 비도 온다 The wind is blowing and it is raining too. / 그녀도 그녀의 어머니도 아프다 She as well as her mother is ill. / 갈 수도 없고 안 갈 수도 없다 I can't go and yet I can't get out of going. / 바람이 불 듯도 하고 비가 올 듯도 하다 It looks as though it might blow or it might rain.
③ 《…조차도·…라 할지라도·아직도》 even; yet; still; even though; even if; at all; indeed. ¶ 아무리 비가 심하게 오

더라도 however 〔no matter how〕 hard it may rain / 아직도 젊다 They are still young. / 아직도 잔다 He's still asleep. / 한번도 잘 한 날이 없었다 There wasn't even one day when he did it well. / 신문도 읽을 줄 모른다 He can't read even a newspaper. / 백화점에서도 못 산다 You can't buy it even in department stores. / 근심이 되어 밤에 잠도 안 온다 I feel so anxious (that) I can't sleep even at night. / 아무 것도 없다 There is nothing. *or* We have nothing. / 아무도 안 왔다 Nobody came at all.

**-도**(度) 《연도》 a year (period); a term. ¶ 금년도 the current year / 내년도 next year / 2000년도 예산 the budget of the fiscal year of 2000 / 1990년도 졸업생 a graduate of the year 1990.

**도가**(都家) 《동업자의 집합소》 a club house of the same traders; a gathering place of business men in the same field; 《도매상》 a wholesale store 〔house〕. ¶ 술~ a brewery; a distillery.

**도가니**[1] a melting pot; a crucible. ¶ 정쟁(政爭)의 ~ the whirlpool of political strife / 쇠를 ~에 넣고 녹이다 melt metal in a crucible / 흥분의 ~가 되다 go wild with excitement; turn into a scene of wild excitement / 미국은 거대한 인종의 ~다 The United States is a great melting pot of races.

**도가니**[2] 《쇠무릎》 the knee bone of an ox; beef from around the knee bone.

**도가머리** a crest 《of a bird》; a bird with a crest; 《사람》 a person with crested hair.

**도가자류**(道家者流) a Taoist; members of the Taoist school.

**도각**(倒閣) overthrowing the Cabinet. ¶ ~ 운동을 일으키다 start a movement to overthrow the Cabinet.

**도감**(圖鑑) a pictorial 〔an illustrated〕 book 《of the Korean flora》; a picture book. ¶ 동물〔식물〕 ~ an illustrated animal 〔plant〕 book / 과학 ~ a picture book of science.

**도강**(渡江) crossing a river. ~하다 cross a river. ¶ ~ 작전을 강행하다 force river= crossing operations. ◉ ~훈련 a river= crossing exercise.

**도개교**(跳開橋) a bascule bridge.

**도거리** the gross; bulk; mass. ¶ ~로 together; in a lump; in one lot; in the gross; in bulk; *en massé* (F.) / ~일 job work; a work done by the job 〔by contract〕 / 일을 ~로 맡아 하다 do work by the job / ~로 사다 buy 《*thing*》 in (the) mass 〔lot, bulk〕.

**도계**(道界) the province limits; the boundary line between provinces.

**도공**(刀工) a swordsmith.

**도공**(陶工) a potter; a ceramist; a porcelain maker; a pottery worker.

**도관**(陶棺) an earthenware coffin. = 옹관(甕棺). 「따위의》 a conduit; a pipe.

**도관**(導管) ①《식물의》 a vessel. ②《물

**도괴**(倒壞) collapse; destruction. ~하다 collapse; be destroyed; fall (down); tear down; demolish; destroy; crumble. ¶ 지진으로 300호의 집들이 ~되었다 Three hundred houses were destroyed by the earthquake.

**도교**(道敎) Taoism. ¶ ~ 신자 a Taoist.

**도구**(道具) ①《공구》 a tool; an instrument; an implement; a utensil (주방용); an outfit; a kit 《구어》; 《무대의》 scenery (대도구); props (소도구).

> (용법) **tool** 통상, 동력 없이 손으로 사용하는 망치·드릴 따위. 특히 목공·미장공 등이 사용하는 도구. **instrument** 의료용 메스·가위·온도계 따위. 정밀한 학술적인 일에 사용되는 동력이 필요 없는 도구. **implement** tool보다 크기가 큰 것. 특히 그 구조가 간단한 괭이·쟁기 따위. **utensil** 요리·청소 따위에 사용되는 가정용 도구를 칭하는 좀 딱딱한 표현의 말. **outfit, kit** 어떤 특정한 일·목적 등에 필요한 도구의 한 벌.

¶ 주방 ~ kitchen utensils / 가재 ~ household goods / 차(茶) ~ tea things / 화장~ *one's* cosmetic paraphernalia / 목공용 ~ a carpenter's tool 〔outfit, kit〕 / 낚시 ~ a fishing outfit / ~상자 a toolbox.

② 《수단·방편》 a means; a tool. ¶ 선전~ an instrument of propaganda / 그는 목적을 이루기 위해 나를 ~로 삼았다 He made a cat's-paw of me to accomplish his desire. / 언어는 사상 전달의 ~다 Language is the vehicle of thought.

**도국**(島國) an island country. ⇨ 섬나라.

**도굴**(盜掘) 《불법 채광》 illegal 〔bootleg〕 mining; 《고분 등의》 tomb 〔grave〕 robbery; illegal excavation. ~하다 mine by stealth 〔illegally〕; dig out by stealth; rob a tomb 〔grave〕. ¶ 국보를 ~하다 illegally excavate national treasures.

◉ ~범 a tomb robber. ~품 illegally

excavated articles.

**도규**(刀圭) ① 《약숟갈》 a medicine spoon. ② 《의술》 medicine; the medical art. ◉ ～가 a medical man. ～계 the medical world 〔profession〕; medical circles. ～술 = 의술.

**도금**(鍍金) 《금속의》 plating; gilding (금도금); coating. ～하다 plate; gild. ¶ 전기 ～ electroplating / 금〔은〕～한 숟가락 a gold-〔silver-〕plated spoon / 금으로 ～한 반지 a gold-plated ring / 금～하다 gild; plate 《a metal》 with gold / 동을 은으로 ～하다 plate copper with silver / 크롬으로 전기 ～하다 electroplate with chromium / ～한 것이 벗겨졌다 The gilt comes 〔is, rubs〕 off.
◉ ～공 a (gold-)plater; a gilder. ～술 the art of plating. ～액(液) a plating solution. ～제품 plated ware.

**도급**(都給) a contract (for work); undertaking. ¶ ～으로 《be built》 by 〔under〕 contract; 《be paid》 by the job / 일을 ～주다 give out a contract for the work; put the work out to contract / …에게 ～을 맡기다〔주다〕 give 《*a person*》 a contract 《for》; let a contract 《to *a person*》; form 《the work》 out 《to *a person*》 / ～을 맡다 contract 〔undertake〕 《to *do,* for the work》; get 〔receive〕 a contract / 주택 건축을 ～ 맡고 있다 have a contract to build a house / ～으로 다리를 놓다 build a bridge by 〔on〕 contract / 그 회사는 우리집 수리를 400만 원으로 ～맡았다 The company made a contract with me to renovate my house at four million won. / 우리는 새 박물관 건설을 그 공동 기업체에 ～주었다 We gave the contract to build the new museum to that joint venture.
◉ ～가격 a contract price. ～계약 《make》 a contract (for work). ～업 the contracting business. ～인 a contractor; 《특히 건축의》 a housebuilder. ～일 contract work; work 〔a job〕 done by contract. ～입찰 a contract tender. ～제도 the contract work system. (공동) ～제 a joint contract system.

**도기**(陶器) earthenware (도기·토기); pottery (도기류); ceramics [총칭]; china; chinaware (도자기, 특히 접시, 그릇 등) (★ 이상 어느 것이나 셀 때는 a piece of..., two pieces of...처럼 쓰는 것이 보통임). ¶ ～(제)의 china; ceramic / ～에 유약을 칠하다 glaze earthenware.
◉ ～공장 a pottery. ～상(商) a crokery dealer; a china dealer 〔shop, store〕.

**도깨그릇** ⇨ 독[1].

**도깨비** 《요괴》 a bog(e)y; a (hob-)goblin; a bugbear (나쁜 아이를 잡아먹는다는); a bugaboo 《미》; 《괴물》 a monster; 《유령》 a ghost; a phantom; a specter; an apparition. ¶ ～가 나오는 집 a haunted house / ～가 나오다 be haunted (by a goblin) / ～ 땅마련하듯 build a castle in the air / ～도 수풀이 있어야 모인다고 한다 It is necessary to have something to fall back on for a person to achieve anything. / ～를 사귀었나 [비유적] Where is all your money coming from? / ～ 장난 같다 There is no knowing what is what. / 저 낡은 집에는 ～가 나온다고 한다 That old house is said to be haunted by goblins 〔a ghost〕.

**도깨비바늘** 『식물』 Spanish grass 〔needles〕.

**도깨비부채** 『식물』 a bronzeleaf.

**도깨비불** ① 《인에 의한 야광》 phosphorescence; phosphorus; a corpse candle 〔light〕; a death fire; 《귀신의 불빛》 a will-o'-the-wisp; a jack-o'-lantern. ② 《원인 불명의》 a fire of unknown origin.

**도꼬마리** 『식물』 a cocklebur.

**도끼** an ax(e); 《손도끼》 a hatchet; 《자르고 빼개고 하는》 a chopper. ¶ 큰 ～ a big hatchet / 얼음 깨는 ～ an ice ax / 믿는 ～에 발등 찍히다 《속담》 Be betrayed by a trusted follower. *or* Stabbed in the back. ◉ ～자루 an ax handle. ～질 wielding an ax: ～질하다 wield an ax.

**도끼눈** glaring eyes; staring with hatred. ¶ ～을 한 사람 an eagle-eyed person / ～을 하고 보다 glare fiercely at; glower at; look angrily at; scowl at 〔on〕.

**도난**(盜難) (a) robbery; (a) theft; (a) burglary (야간의). ¶ ～에 의한 손실 《상점 등의》 pilferage (loss) / ～방지용의 antitheft 《devices》; burglarproof 《doors》 / ～을 당하다 [집이 주어] get 〔be〕 robbed 《of money》; be burglarized; [물건이 주어] be stolen / 경찰에 ～신고를 하다 report a burglary 〔theft〕 to the police / ～ 사건의 건수가 최근에는 감소되었다 Theft 〔Robbery, Burglary〕 cases have recently decreased in number. / 어젯밤에 이 아파트에서 ～사건이 있었다 There was a theft in this apartment house last night. / 우리집은 한 달에 3번이나 ～을 당했다 My house was burglarized three times

in one month.
◉ ～경보기 a burglar alarm. ～방지 자물쇠 a burglarproof 〔an antitheft〕 lock. ～보험 burglary 〔theft〕 insurance. ～사건 a case of robbery. ～신고 a robbery report. ～예방 burglarproof. ～차량 missing vehicles. ～품 a stolen article; stolen property 〔goods〕. ～피해자 a victim of theft.

**도내**(道內) the inside of a province; within a province; provincial.

**도넛** a doughnut; a donut 《미》. ◉ ～판 (레코드) a (standard) 45-rpm record; an EP record. ～화 현상 the 〔a〕 hollowing-out effect (도심부의 공동화); (urban) sprawl (도시 주변부의 확대). 잼 ～ a jam doughnut.

**도닐다** walk around; ramble about.

**도다리** 『어류』 a flounder; a sole.

**도달**(到達) arrival; reaching; attainment (달성). ～하다 arrive 《in, at, on》; reach; get to; come to; attain. ¶ 한밤중에 목적지에 ～하다 reach the destination at midnight / 같은 결론에 ～하다 come to 〔arrive at, reach〕 the same conclusion / 그녀의 그림은 완성 단계에 ～했다 Her painting attained (to) perfection.

**도담도담** 《growing up》 well; nicely.

**도당**(徒黨) 《배타적인》 a clique; a faction (정당 따위의); 《범죄에 관계되는》 a band; a gang; 《같은 부류》 a league. ¶ ～을 짓다〔꾸미다〕 band 〔gang〕 together; form a faction 〔league〕; conspire 《with》. ◉ ～근성 cliquism: ～근성이 강한 cliquey.

**도대체**(都大體) in the world; 《how, what, why》 on earth 〔the hell, the devil, the deuce〕; at all. ¶ ～ 너는 누구냐 Who on earth are you? / ～ 어딜 가니 Where the hell do you think you are going? / ～ 모를 일이다 I can't understand it at all. / ～ 그의 말은 알아들을 수가 없다 I can't understand him at all. / 그 사람은 ～ 영어를 아는가 Does he know any English at all? / ～ 그녀는 재산이 있는가 Has she any property at all? / 너 ～ 여기서 뭣을 하느냐 What on earth are you doing here? / ～ 무슨 일이냐 Whatever is the matter? *or* What the deuce is the matter? / ～ 그 책이 어디 갔지 Where has the book gone to anyway? / ～ 무얼 가지고 싸우느냐 What the dickens are you quarrelling about? / ～ 무슨 영문인지 알지 못하겠다 I don't know what the hell this is all about. / ～ 어떻게 하란 말인가 What on earth do you expect me to do?

**도덕**(道德) morality; morals (★ 보통 복수형으로 단수 취급함). ¶ ～적(인) moral; moralistic; ethical / ～상 morally; from a moral point of view / ～상의 moral; moralistic; ethical / ～상의 죄인 a moral offender; a sinner / ～적 감화〔기준〕 moral influence 〔standards〕 / ～적 위험 『보험』 moral hazard / ～적 제재 moral restraint 〔sanctions〕 / ～적으로 설명하다 moralize.
◉ ～가 a virtuous man; a man of virtue; a moralist: ～가 인 체하다 assume a virtuous air. ～감정 ethical emotion. ～관념 a moral sense: ～관념이 강한 사람 a person of 「strict morals 〔moral principles〕; a highly virtuous person. ～교육 moral education. ～군자 a gentleman renowned for his virtue. ～률 (a) moral law; (an) ethical code. ～문제 a moral question. ～심 a sense of morality. ～원리 moral principles. ～의식 moral consciousness: ～의식의 결여 lack of moral sense; amorality. ～재무장 운동 the Moral Re-Armament (생략 MRA). ～주의 moralism. ～철학 moral philosophy; ethics.

**도도하다** (be) haughty; proud; arrogant; overbearing; insolent; stuck-up 《구어》; uppish 《영구어》. ¶ 도도히 haughtily; proudly; arrogantly / 도도한 태도 a haughty attitude / 도도하게 굴다 behave *oneself* haughtily; take 〔assume〕 an overbearing attitude; hold *one's* head very high.

**도도하다**(陶陶—) 《흥이》 (be) happy; jolly; pleased. ¶ 취흥이 ～ be gay with wine; be gloriously drunk.

**도도하다**(滔滔—) ① 《강물이》 flow with a rush; run in rushing torrents. ¶ 도도히 《water flows》 with a rush; in rushing torrents; in a vast 〔broad〕 expanse / 탁류가 도도히 흐른다 The muddy water rushes on in a vast expanse. ② 《변설이》 (be) eloquent; fluent; effusive; flowing. ¶ 도도히 flowingly; eloquently; fluently; effusively / 도도한 변설 a flood of eloquence 〔words〕; flowing eloquence / 도도히 말하다 speak eloquently 〔fluently〕; pour forth a flood of eloquence / 그는 자기의 의견을 도도하게 말했다 He expressed his opinion eloquently 〔fluently〕.

**도독하다** ⇨ 두둑하다.

**도두** high. ¶ 둑을 ~쌓다 build a dike high / 볏가리를 ~ 쌓다 heap the sheaves of rice high / ~ 뛰다 jump as high as *one* can.

**도두보다, 도두뵈다** ⇨ 돋보다, 돋보이다.

**도둑** 《사람》 a thief; a robber (강도); a burglar (밤도둑); a housebreaker (주택 침입 강도); pilferer (좀도둑); a shoplifter (들치기); 《행위》 ⇨ 도둑질. ¶ 자동차 ~ a car thief / ~맞다 [사람이 주어] have 《*a thing*》 stolen; be robbed of 《*one's* purse》; [사물이 주어] be stolen / ~이 매를 들다 impute *one's* blame to others / ~놈 개 꾸짖듯하다 mumble; whisper (as if afraid of being overheard) / 나는 지갑을 소매치기에게 ~맞았다 I had my wallet stolen by a pickpocket. / ~이야 Stop thief! *or* Help! A thief! / 어젯밤에 집에 ~이 들었다 A thief 〔burglar〕 broke into our house last night. *or* Our house was robbed last night. / 어젯밤 옆집에 ~이 들어 현금과 보석을 훔쳐갔다 Last night a burglar broke into next door and took their money and jewels. / 우리 집에는 ~에 대비하여 개를 기르고 있다 We keep a dog as a precaution against burglars. / ~이 제 발 저리다 《속담》 A thief has a bad conscience and is apt to give himself away. / ~맞고 사립 고친다 《속담》 It is like closing the stable door after the horse has bolted. / ~의 씨가 따로 없다 《속담》 Thieves are made, not born. / ~의 집에도 되가 있다 Even thieves have their standard of good and evil. / ~놈 개에게 물린 셈 One who has done wrong can hardly complain at censure or humiliation. / ~을 맞으려면 개도 안 짖는다 《속담》 When you are unlucky, everything goes wrong for you. ◉ ~고양이 an alley cat; a stray cat. ~놈 a thief; a robber. ~장가 a secret marriage.

**도둑질** theft; robbery; burglary; stealing. ~하다 steal 《*a thing* from *a person*》; thieve; commit theft; pilfer 《*a thing* from shop》; filch; 《강탈》 rob 《*a person* of *a thing*》; 《구어》 pinch; snitch; lift. ⇨ 훔치다. ¶ 가난 때문에 저지른 ~ theft through poverty / ~하러 들어 가다 break into 《*a* house》; burglarize 《*a* house》 / 상점의 물건을 ~하다 lift articles in a store / ~도 손이 맞아야 한다 《속담》 Harmonious cooperation is everything in accomplishing something. / 늦게 배운 ~이 날새는 줄 모른다 《속담》 One is apt to become overly engrossed in work or a hobby begun late in life.

**도둑합례**(一合禮) a secret marriage; a private wedding. ~하다 get married secretly; be privately married.

**도드라지다** ① [형용사적] (be) swollen; protuberant; be heaved up; (be) raised; high; embossed; 《현저하다》 (be) conspicuous; prominent; outstanding; striking; remarkable. ¶ 도드라진 눈 goggle 〔protuberant〕 eyes; bulging eyes / 도드라진 장식 embossments / 도드라진 보기 a remarkable example / 길 가운데가 ~ the middle of the road is high / 이 꽃에는 몇가지 도드라진 특징이 있다 This flower has some striking 〔conspicuous〕 features. ② [자동사적] swell; protrude; heave (up); rise; be embossed. ¶ 뾰루지가 도드라졌다 A boil is swollen up.

**도떼기시장**(一市場) an open-air market; a flea market.

**도라지** ① 『식물』 a broad bellflower; a Chinese balloonflower. ② 《뿌리》 the root of a broad bellflower; platycodon. ¶ ~를 캐다 dig up the roots of bellflowers. ◉ ~나물 seasoned roots of broad bellflowers.

**도락**(道樂) ① 《취미》 a hobby; a pastime; pleasure; *one's* favorite amusement 〔diversion〕. ¶ ~으로 하다 do 《*a thing*》 「as a hobby 〔for pleasure〕 / ~으로 우표를 수집하다 collect stamps 「as a pastime 〔for fun〕 / 장미 가꾸는 것이 그의 ~이다 Growing roses is his hobby. ② 《방탕》 dissipation; debauchery. ¶ ~에 빠지다 be dissipated; debauch *oneself;* lead a 「dissipated 〔fast〕 life; 《구어》 sow *one's* wild oats.

**도란도란** murmuring together; in whispers. ⇨ 두런두런.

**도랑** 《배수로》 a ditch; a dike; 《하수구》 a drain; a gutter (길가의). ¶ ~을 파다 dig a ditch; ditch / ~을 치다 clear out a ditch; ditch / ~을 메우다 fill in a ditch / ~에 빠지다 fall into the ditch / ~을 파서 물이 빠지게 했다 We dug a ditch to drain off the water. ◉ ~물 ditch water. ~창 a gutter; a drain: ~창에 박히다 be thrown 〔crushed〕 into a gutter; be laid in a gutter.

**도랑치마** a short skirt.

**도래**(到來) arrival; advent (중요한 일 등의). ~하다 come; arrive; 《기회가》 present 〔offer〕 itself. ¶ 호기가 ~하기를 기다리다 wait for a good opportunity / 마침내 행동을 취할 때가 ~했다 Now is the time for us to take action.

**도래**(渡來) coming across the sea; 《사람의》 a visit; 《사물의》 introduction; importation; influx. ~하다 come over 〔across〕 the sea; cross over 《to Korea》; visit 《this country》; be introduced 《into a country》. ¶ 외국인의 ~ an influx of foreign visitors / 불교의 ~ the introduction of Buddhism 《into Korea》.

**도래떡** a large-sized round rice cake.

**도래매듭** a double knot.

**도래방석**(一方席) a round cushion.

**도래샘** a swirling fountain 〔spring〕.

**도래솔** pine trees surrounding a grave.

**도래송곳** ① 《큰 구멍 내는》 a two-groove 〔double-edged〕 drill. ② = 나사송곳.

**도량**(度量) magnanimity (배짱이 큼); liberality (활수함); generosity (관대함); broad-mindedness (도량이 큼). ¶ ~이 넓은 magnanimous; generous; liberal; broad-minded / ~이 좁은 narrow-〔small-〕minded; ungenerous; mean-spirited / ~이 있다 be magnanimous 〔large-minded, liberal, generous〕 / 그는 새로운 사상을 받아 들이기에는 너무나 ~이 좁았다 He was too hidebound to accept new ideas.

**도량**(跳梁) rampancy; domination. ~하다 be rampant; be dominant; thrive. ¶ 동네 사람들은 폭력배의 ~을 허용치 않았다 The townspeople did not let gangsters have their own way.

**도량**(道場) 『불교』 a Buddhist seminary.

**도량형**(度量衡) weights and measures. ◉ ~ 검사관 a sealer (of weights and measures). ~ 검사소 the Weights and Measures Examination Institute; the Bureau of Standards. ~기(器) measuring instruments. ~동맹 a standards union. ~법 measurement. ~표 tables of weights and measures. ~학 metrology. 미터 ~법 the metric system of weights and measures.

**도레미파** the musical scale; 《음계명》 do, re, mi, fa, sol, la and si. ¶ ~로 노래하다 (sing) sol-fa / ~를 연습하다 practice scales 《on the piano》. ◉ ~연습 a solfège; a solfeggio (*pl.* -gi, ~s). ~창법 Solmization; sol-fa.

**도려내다** scrape out; cut out 〔off, away〕; hollow out; cleave; excise (종기 따위를); gouge (끌로). ¶ 사과의 썩은 곳을 ~ scrape out spoiled 〔sour〕 parts of apples / 통나무를 도려내어 카누를 만들다 hollow a canoe out of a log.

**도련**(刀鍊) cutting the edge (of paper) even; trimming. ~하다, ~치다 trim; cut the edge 《of paper》 even. ◉ ~칼 a paper-trimming knife.

**도련님** ① 《도령의 존칭》 a young gentleman; an unmarried boy (as addressed by servants); 《호칭》 Young Master. ② 《시동생》 an unmarried younger brother of *one's* husband; a young brother-in-law. ¶ ~은 당나귀가 제격이다 《속담》 a proper thing for a proper status. ◉ ~천량 a tidy sum saved up by avoided extravagances.

**도령** 《총각》 a bachelor; a young man; an unmarried man; a boy. ◉ ~귀신 the ghost of a bachelor.

**도령**(道令) 《행정 명령》 a provincial ordinance; the order of a province.

**도로**(徒勞) a lost 〔waste of〕 labor; vain 〔sterile, fruitless〕 effort; vain 〔empty〕 attempt. ¶ ~에 그치다 prove abortive 〔fruitless〕; end in a waste of labor; come to nothing / 홍수로 그들의 노력은 ~에 그치고 말았다 The flood brought all their efforts to nothing. ◉ ~무익(無益) vain 〔sterile〕 effort; toiling in vain.

**도로**(道路) a road; a street (가로); a highway; an avenue; a thoroughfare (큰 길); the route (노정).

> 용법 **road** 도시와 도시, 마을과 마을을 잇는 도로. **street** 한쪽 또는 양쪽에 상점이나 건물 등이 이어져 있는 도심의 거리. **highway** 주로 《미》에서 사용되는 말로 「간선 도로」, 즉 우리 나라의 「국도」나 「도에서 관리하는 도로」 등을 뜻함. **avenue** 도로 양쪽에 가로수가 있는 도심의 거리. 미국에서는 도심지의 「큰 거리」를 말하며, boulevard라고도 한다. 또 뉴욕에서는 동서로 뻗은 거리를 street, 남북으로 통한 것을 avenue라고 한다. **thoroughfare** 격식차린 말로 「넓게 뚫린 큰 도로」란 뜻. 큰 도시 내의 「주요 도로」란 의미로 흔히 쓰임.

¶ ~상에서 on the road; on 〔in 《영》〕 the street / ~를 따라 《go》 along the road / ~를 개통하다〔막다〕 open 〔block〕 a road / ~를 보수하다 repair 〔mend, improve〕 a road / ~를 횡단하다 cross the road / ~ 수리중 《게시》 Street closed for repairs. / ~가 붐빈다 The roads 〔streets〕 are crowded 〔busy〕. *or* There's a lot of traffic on the street. / 이 근처는 ~ 사정이 나쁘다 The roads are bad around here.

◉ ～건설 road building. ～계획 a road plan. ～공사《수리》 street improvement; road repairing;《건설》 road construction 〔building〕: ～공사중《게시문》 Under Construction. ～교통량 road capacity. ～교통법 the Road Traffic (Control) Law. ～교통통제 a highway traffic control. ～망(網) a network of roads: ～망 확충 expansion 〔supplementation〕 of road networks. ～보수 road repairs. ～이정표 a milepost; a milestone. ～인부(人夫) a roadman. ～정보(情報) traffic information. ～정비계획 a road maintenance and improvement project. ～지도 a road 〔street〕 map《of Pusan》. ～청소 street cleaning. ～청소부 a street cleaner; a scavenger. ～포장 pavement (of a road, street). ～표지(標識) a road sign; a highway route marker. 한국～공사 the Korea Highway Corporation.

**도로** ①《다시》 (over) again; back. ¶ ～가다 retrace *one's* steps; go back; turn back / 오던 길을 ～ 가다 go back over *one's* way 〔where *one* came〕 / 잃었던 돈을 ～ 찾다 get *one's* lost money back / ～ 주다 give《*a thing*》 back; return《*a thing*》 / ～ 데려오다 bring back. ②《전처럼》 as before 〔ever, usual〕; as it was. ¶ 제자리에 ～ 갖다 놓다 put《*a thing*》 back in its place 〔where it was〕 / 그 책을 책장에 ～ 꽂아라 Replace the books on the shelves. / 그들은 싸웠으나 ～ 친해졌다 They quarreled but are now friends again. / 그녀는 ～ 건강해졌다 She is quite all right again. *or* She is now as healthy as before.

**도로아미타불**(一阿彌陀佛) a relapse; a setback. ¶ ～이다 be no better than what *one* used to be; wind up just where *one* started; have lost all *one* gained / ～이 되다 lose all (that) *one* has gained.

**-도록** ①《목적》 so that; in order to 〔that…〕; (so as) to; so 〔in order〕 that *one* may…; that *one* may…. ¶ …하지 않도록 (so as) not to; that… may not; lest… should / 그런 일이 없도록 조심하다 be on *one's* guard so that such a thing will not happen / 그녀에게 말하지 않도록 주의해라 Take care not to tell her. / 급행열차 시간에 늦지 않도록 빨리 일어났다 I got up early「so as to 〔in order to〕 be in time for the express. / 집은 신선한 공기와 햇빛이 많이 들어오도록 지어져야 한다 Houses should be built so as to admit plenty of light as well as of fresh air. / 일곱 시에 아침 밥을 먹도록 해 주시오 Please prepare my breakfast so that I may have it at seven. ②《…때까지》 to the point where; till; until (a result). ¶ 밤 늦도록 till late at night / 죽도록 사랑하다 love《*a person*》 to death / 백 살이 되도록 살다 live to be a hundred / 눈물이 나도록 웃었다 I laughed till the tears ran down

**참고** 도로·교통 관련어들

▶ 중심가《미》 a main street;《영》 a high street / 주요 도로 a thoroughfare / 작은〔좁은〕 도로 a lane; an alley / 뒷골목 a back street / 상점 거리 a shopping street.

▶ 고속 도로 a superhighway《미》; a freeway《미서부》; an expressway《미동부》; a motorway《영》/ 유료 고속 도로 a toll road; a turnpike / (미국의) 대륙 횡단 고속 도로 a transcontinental highway / 주간(州間) 고속 도로 an interstate highway /진입〔출구〕 램프 an entrance 〔exit〕 ramp / 진입로 an entrance lane / 요금 징수소 a tollgate; a tollbooth; a turnpike / 휴게소 a rest area.

▶ 교통 미국은 우측통행 (keep to the right), 영국은 좌측통행 (keep to the left)이다. 미국에서는 대개의 경우, 십자로에서 우회전하려는 경우, 좌측 도로에 직진해 오는 차가 없거나, 시간적 여유가 있을 때는 신호가 빨간등이라도 횡단 보도 (crosswalk)의 안전이 확인되면 우회전할 수 있다. 단, 신호에「적신호 우회전 금지」 No (Right) Turn on Red의 표시가 있으면 기다려야 한다.

▶ 교차점 an intersection; a crossing; a crossroad(s) / 교통 신호 a traffic signal 〔light〕 / (보행자용) 지하도 an underground (passage) / 일방교통 one-way traffic / (보행자용) 육교 an overpass / 차선 a lane / 8차선 도로 an 8-lane highway / 버스 전용 차선 a bus lane / 중앙 분리대 a median strip《미》; a central reserve《영》/ 갓길 shoulder.

▶ 주차장 a parking lot; a car park《영》/ 주차 미터 a parking meter / 주차 금지 구역《레커차 견인 구역》 a towaway zone; no parking area / 주유소 a gas station《미》; a service 〔filling, petrol《영》〕 station.

my face.
③ 《되도록…》 as… as possible; as… as *one* can. ¶ 내일 아침에는 되도록 일찍 일어나겠다 I'll get up as early as possible tomorrow morning. / 되도록 일찍 가거라 Go as soon as you can.

**도롱고리** 〖식물〗 a variety of millet.

**도롱뇽** 〖동물〗 a (giant) salamander; 《영원(蠑螈)》 a newt; a water lizard.

**도롱이** a rain cape made of straw, miscanthus, *etc.*; a straw raincoat.

**도료**(塗料) paint(s); coating(s); colors; pigments. ¶ 야광(夜光)〔발광(發光)〕 ~ luminous paint. ◉ ~분무기 a paint sprayer; a spray gun. ~상(점) a paint store.

**도루**(盜壘) 〖야구〗 base stealing; a stolen base (스코어 기록시). ~하다 steal a base. ¶ ~에 실패하다 be caught stealing / 2루에 ~하다 steal second; steal into the second base.

**도루묵** 〖어류〗 a hard-finned sandfish.

**도륙**(屠戮) massacre; slaughter. ~하다 massacre; slaughter.

**도르다**[1] 《토하다》 throw up; vomit; cast up; spew; spue; disgorge. ¶ 먹은 것을 ~ throw up what *one* has eaten.

**도르다**[2] 《분배하다》 distribute; hand round 〔out〕; deal out; serve round 〔out〕; 《배달하다》 deliver; send round 〔out〕; 《할당하다》 assign; allot; apportion. ¶ 배급품을 ~ distribute rations / 선물을 ~ hand out 〔round〕 presents / 신문을 ~ deliver newspapers / 초대장을 ~ send out invitations / 카드를 ~ deal (out) cards / 길에서 광고를 ~ distribute circulars on the road.

**도르다**[3] 《변통하다》 manage; contrive; tide over; shift and contrive; make shift; scratch along; 《융통하다》 accommodate 《*a person* with money》; advance 《money to *a person*》; lend. ¶ 돈을 ~ manage to get money; get money somehow / 자금을 ~ finance 《an enterprise》.

**도르다**[4] 《속이다》 get round 《*a person*》 with fair words; talk 《*a person*》 out of 〔into〕; deceive; dupe; take in.

**도르래** ① 《장난감》 pinwheel top. ② 《활차》 a pulley.

**도르르** round; with a twirl; coiling. ¶ 종이를 ~ 감다 roll paper round; twirl up paper / 실이 ~ 풀리다 thread is twirled off a reel.

**도리** 〖건축〗 a beam; a crossbeam; a girder 「(교량 따위의).

**도리**(道理) ① 《정당한 이치》 reason (사리); right (바른길); propriety (타당); truth (진리); justice (정의); principle (원리). ¶ ~상 in reason; in 〔by, from〕 the nature of things; as a matter of course / ~에 맞다 be reasonable; stand to reason; be consistent with reason / ~에 벗어나다 be unreasonable; be against reason; be contrary to 〔inconsistent with〕 reason.
② 《의무》 a duty; obligation. ¶ 자식으로서의 ~ filial duty; duty as a son / 어버이된 ~로서 자식을 교육시킬 의무가 있다 It is in nature of things that parents should put children to school. / 그런 짓을 하는 것은 학생의 ~가 아니다 It is not proper for a student to do such a thing.
③ 《방도》 a way; a method; an alternative (대안); 《수단》 a measure; a means. ¶ (할) ~가 없다 have no way (of *do*ing, to *do*) / 별 ~가 없다 There is no other way. *or* There is no alternative. / 기다릴 수밖에 딴 ~가 없다 You have nothing to do but wait. / 잠자코 있을 수밖에 ~가 없었다 There was nothing for it but to hold my tongue.

**도리기** a Dutch treat. ~하다 eat 《a 「feast》 as a Dutch treat.

**도리깨** ① 《농기구》 a flail. ② 《쇠도리깨》 a flail 《a kind of weapon》.
◉ ~질 flailing: ~질 하다 flail; beat with a flail. ~침 mouth watering; saliva produced by a desire to eat. 도리깻장부 the handle of a flail.

**도리다** ① 《베내다》 cut (out) round; gouge; scoop out; hollow out (구멍을); bore. ¶ 판자 가운데를 톱으로 ~ cut out a part of a plank with a circular saw / 상처를 칼로 ~ gouge out a wound with a knife.
② 《삭제하다》 strike 〔cross〕 out; erase; cancel. ¶ 명부에서 이름을 ~ cross 〔strike〕 a name from a list.

**도리도리** 《아기에게》 Shake-shake!

**도리머리** shaking *one's* head as a sign of negation 〔denial〕.

**도리스식**(一式) 〖건축〗 Doris (type, style). ¶ ~의 Doric 《order》.

**도리어** 《반대로》 on the contrary; instead; the other way round; 《오히려》 rather; all the more; all the better 〔worse〕. ¶ ~ 좋다〔나쁘다〕 be so much the better 〔worse〕 / 내가 ~ 미안하오 I should be the one to ask your pardon. / ~ 아우가 형보다도 크다 Contrary to what you might expect, the younger brother is taller than the older one. / 약간의 술은 ~ 약이다 A little drink does you more good than harm. / 그를 칭찬은 커녕 ~ 비난해야만 하겠다 Far from praising him, I must positively blame him. / 그가 알랑거리는 것이 ~ 밉다 I hate him all the more for his flattery. / 그 약을 먹고 나서 ~ 병이 악화됐다 I am all the worse for the medicine I have taken. / ~ 병세를 악화시켰다 It only made the patient worse.

**도리질** ~하다 《a child》 shake *its* head for fun from side to side.

**도림장이**(—匠—) an wood engraver.

**도림질** engraving (wood).

**도립**(倒立) standing on *one's* head (and hands); 《체조》 hand-standing. ~하다 stand on *one's* head (and hands); do a handstand. ⇨ 물구나무서다. ¶ ~해서 걷다 walk on *one's* hands.

**도립**(道立) ¶ ~의 provincial. ◉ ~공원 a provincial park. ~병원 a provincial hospital.

**도마** a chopping board [block]; a kitchen board. ¶ ~에 오른 고기 the game [jig] is up; nothing can be done now; "the fat is in the fire"; no way to pull through / ~ 위의 고기가 칼을 무서워하랴 《속담》 Nothing is dreadful to a person who is in the jaws of death.

**도마름**(都—) a head supervisor of tenant farmers.

**도마뱀** 『동물』 a lizard; a bluetail (미국산). ◉ ~붙이 a gecko (*pl.* ~(e)s); a wall lizard. ~자리 『천문』 the Lizard; Lacerta.

**도막** = 토막.

**도말**(塗抹) ~하다 ① 《발라 지우다》 paint out; blot out; 《칠하다》 paint over; smear (기름으로). ② 《변통하여 꾸리다》 patch up; make shift; temporize.
◉ ~제 a liniment; an embrocation.

**도망**(逃亡) escape; flight; runaway; getaway; desertion (탈영). ~가다, ~치다, ~하다 escape; run away; take to *one's* heel; flee; fly (★ flee의 대용임. 과거·과거분사형은 fled를 씀); abscond 《from》; take flight. ¶ ~중인 범죄자 a criminal 「on the run [at large] / ~을 꾀하다 attempt [make an attempt] to run away; try to escape / 간신히 ~치다 have a narrow escape / 뿔뿔이 ~가다 fly in all direction; disperse / 채 ~가지 못하다 fail to escape [get off]; be left behind / 살짝 ~치다 slip off [away] / 슬그머니 ~치다 sneak [steal] away; slink off / 허둥지둥 ~가다 beat a hasty retreat; rush [skip] away; make a quick escape; show a clean pair of heels; flee hurriedly; scamper off [away] / 감시의 눈을 속여서 ~하다 slip *one's* guard / 국외로 ~가다 fly the country; flee from a country / 밤을 타서 ~치다 flee by night; decamp at night; take to moonlight flitting / 아내를 두고 정부와 ~하다 elope with *one's* mistress deserting *one's* wife / 빚을 지고 ~하다 run away with *one's* debts unpaid; give *one's* creditors the slip / 말이 ~치다 the horse runs away; the horse gets [breaks] loose / 죄수가 교도소에서 ~치다 a prisoner breaks out of jail.
◉ ~꾼[자] a runaway; an absconder; a deserter; a fugitive; an escapee: ~꾼의 봇짐 a large and loose bundle. ~병 a runaway soldier; a deserter; a soldier over the hill.

**도망범죄인**(逃亡犯罪人) 『법』 a fugitive from justice; a criminal who has broken out of jail. ◉ ~인도 extradition.

**도맡다** ① 《혼자서》 take all upon *oneself;* answer for (the whole thing); shoulder 《*something*》 alone; hold *oneself* responsible for (the whole thing). ¶ 모든 책임을 혼자서 ~ take the whole responsibility alone / 빚을 ~ hold *oneself* liable for a debt; shoulder all the debts alone / 그는 동네 싸움을 혼자 도맡아 한다 He takes on all the fights in the village. / 거래상의 손실은 회사에서 도맡는다 The losses on the transactions will be met by the company. / 내가 도맡아 만사 잘 해 나가겠다 I will see (to it) that all goes well.
② 《몰아서》 take over (the whole). ¶ 가게에 있는 물건을 전부 ~ take over all the goods in the store / A사가 B사의 사업 전체를 ~ company A takes over the entire business of company B.

**도매**(都賣) wholesale; (the) wholesale trade [business] (도매업). ~하다 sell 《*a thing*》 wholesale 《at 60% of the retail price》. ¶ ~와 소매 wholesale and retail / ~로 팔다[사다] sell [buy] 《*a thing*》 wholesale / 반값으로 ~하다 sell wholesale at 50 percent of the price / 이 책상은 ~로 3만 원이다 This desk is worth thirty thousand won at [by] wholesale.
◉ ~가격 a trade [wholesale] price: ~ 가격으로 드리겠습니다 We will give it to you at wholesale (price). ~물가(지수) wholesale price (index). ~상

《사람》 a wholesale dealer; 《영업》 a wholesale business 〔trade〕: ～상을 하다 carry on a wholesale trade. ～시장 a wholesale market.

**도면**(圖面) a drawing; a plan 《of a ship》 (설계도); a sketch (간단한); a blueprint (청사진). ¶ ～을 그리다 draw a plan.

**도모**(圖謀) planning; devising; contriving; designing; scheming. ～하다 《계획하다》 plan; scheme; devise (궁리하다); contrive (연구하다); plot (음모 등을); 《애쓰다》 strive 〔labor〕 for. ⇨ 꾀하다. ¶ 자살을 ～하다 contemplate suicide / 자기의 이익을 ～하다 seek *one's* own interests / 공익을 ～하다 strive for the public good / 우리는 그들과 화해를 ～했다 We planned out the reconciliation with them. / 일을 ～함은 인간이요 일의 성사는 하늘에 달렸다 Man proposes, God disposes.

**도목수**(都木手) a master carpenter.

**도무지** [부정적으로] (not) at all; (not) in the least; (not) the slightest; (not) whatever; 《전혀》 utterly; entirely. ¶ ～알 수 없다 I can not understand it at all. / 그녀는 ～ 힘이 없다 She is as weak as a kitten. / 그는 ～ 부끄러운 줄 모른다 He is lost to all sense of shame. / 그녀는 상식이라곤 ～ 없다 She has not a bit of common sense. / 거기에는 ～ 간 일이 없소 I was never there at all. / 그의 말은 ～ 알아들을 수가 없다 I can't catch 〔understand〕 him at all. *or* I have no 〔not the remotest〕 idea of what he means. / 그 일에 대해서는 ～ 모릅니다 I don't have the remotest idea of it. / 그에게서 ～소식이 없었다 I heard nothing from him. / 그를 ～ 만나보질 못했다 I have seen nothing of him. / 거짓말이라 ～ 믿을 수가 없다 It's all a lie—I can't believe it at all. / ～ 그를 믿을 수가 없다 I cannot bring myself to believe him. / 그의 이름이 ～ 생각나지 않았다 I could not, for the life of me, recollect 〔remember〕 his name. / 이 창문이 ～ 열리지 않는다 This window will not open. (★ will not은 주어의 강한 거부를 나타냄).

**도미** 〖어류〗 a sea bream; a gold bream; a red snapper. ◉ ～조림 braised sea bream with soy sauce. ～찜 steamed sea bream. 도밋국 sea-bream soup.

**도미**(渡美) going (over) to America; a visit 〔an emigration〕 to America. ～하다 go (out) to America; visit America; emigrate to America (이주). ¶ ～ 유학생 a Korean student studying in the U.S. ◉ ～실업단 a party of businessmen visiting America 《for inspection》. ～의원단 a parliamentary mission to America; a party of representatives visiting America.

**도미노** dominoes. ◉ ～이론 the domino theory. ～효과 a 〔the〕 domino effect.

**도미니카** Dominica. ¶ ～의 Dominican. ◉ ～공화국 The Dominican Republic. ～사람 a Dominican.

**도민**(島民) the inhabitants of an island; the islanders.

**도민**(道民) an inhabitant 〔resident〕 of a province. ¶ ～회 an association 〔a society〕 of people from 《Hwanghae》 Province.

**도박** 〖식물〗 a kind of red algae (*Grateloupia elliptica*).

**도박**(賭博) ① 《노름》 gambling; gaming. ～하다 gamble; play for money 〔stakes〕. ¶ ～에 빠지다 gamble deeply / ～으로 돈을 잃다 gamble away *one's* money / 사기 ～을 하다 swindle at cards / ～으로 살림을 망치다 lose *one's* fortune at dice / 큰 ～을 하다 play for high stakes; gamble heavily. ② [비유적] a venture; a risky 〔hazardous〕 attempt; a hazard; a risk. ¶ ～을 하다 take the risks 〔chances〕; run a risk; stake 〔venture〕 *one's* life; risk *one's* neck.
◉ ～꾼 a gambler. ～상습자 a confirmed 〔a habitual, an inveterate〕 gambler. ～성 a penchant for gambling; an inclination to gambling: ～성을 띤 오락 게임 a recreational game bordering on gambling. ～장 a gambling house 〔room, den (비밀의)〕; a casino. ～죄 a gambling offense; a betting; a gaming. 사기～ fraudulent 〔crooked〕 gambling: 사기～꾼 a cardsharper; a rook; a swindler; a cheat.

**도발**(挑發) provocation; incitement; excitement; stirring up. ～하다 provoke; excite; incite; stir up; arouse. ¶ ～적인 provocative 《acts》; suggestive 《novels》 / 호기심을 ～하다 excite *one's* curiosity / 전쟁을 ～하다 provoke a war / ～적인 언사를 쓰다 employ provocative language 〔words〕/ ～적인 태도를 취하다 take a provocative attitude / 그것은 우리에 대한 그의 ～적 행위이다 It's his provocative action against us. / 우리는 ～을 당해 그들과 전쟁을 했다 We were provoked to fight a war with them. / 우리는 그들의 어떠한 ~도 무찌를 준비가 되어 있다 We are ready to annihilate any type of provocative acts created by them. / 그의 말은 다소 ~적이었다 His remarks were rather provocative. (★ 성적인 도발의 뜻으로도 쓰임).

**도배**(島配) exile; banishment. ~하다 exile; banish 《a criminal》 to an island. ¶ ~되다 be exiled 〔banished〕 to an island.

**도배**(徒輩) a gang; a party; a group; a set; a lot.

**도배**(塗褙) papering 《walls and ceiling》. ~하다 paper 《walls and ceiling》. ¶ 벽〔천정〕을 ~하다 paper the wall 〔ceiling〕; hang paper on the wall 〔ceiling〕/ 방을 새로 ~하다 repaper a room. ◉ ~장이 a paperhanger. ~지 wallpaper.

**도배장판**(塗褙壯板) papering walls, ceiling, and hypocausted floor. ~하다 paper walls, ceiling, and hypocausted floor.

**도버** 《영국의 항구》 Dover. ◉ ~ 해협 the Strait of Dover.

**도벌**(盜伐) the secret felling of trees; the illegal cutting of trees; stealing 〔hijacking〕 timber. ~하다 fell 〔cut down〕 trees in secret; steal 〔"hijack"〕 timber; cut down trees without (a) license. ¶ 산림 ~ 사건 a forest tree theft scandal.

**도범**(盜犯) 《행위》 robbery; theft; burglary; 《사람》 a thief; a burglar; a robber.

**도법**(圖法) drawing; draftsmanship.

**도벽**(盜癖) thievish habits; a propensity for theft; a proclivity to steal; sticky fingers 《구어》; 〖의학〗 kleptomania. ¶ ~이 있는 사람 a kleptomaniac / 그에겐 ~이 있다 He has thievish habits.

**도벽**(塗壁) covering (a wall) with plaster; plastering. ~하다 plaster a wall.

**도별**(道別) classification 〔classified〕 by province. ◉ ~인구표 a population chart (broken down) by province.

**도보**(徒步) walking; going on foot; pedestrianism. ¶ ~로 on foot; afoot; heel-and-toe / ~로 가다 walk 《to a place》; go on foot; foot it; tramp / ~로 통학하다 walk to school; go to school on foot / ~로 여행하다 travel on foot; make a journey on foot / 거기까지 ~로 20분쯤 걸린다 It takes (you) about twenty minutes to 「walk there 〔go there on foot〕. / ~ 여행은 혼자 하는 것이 좋다 A walking tour should be conducted alone. ◉ ~경주 a foot 〔walking〕 race. ~여행 a journey on foot; a walking tour: ~ 여행가 a traveler on foot; a pedestrian traveler; walking tourist. ~운동 pedestrian exercise. ~자 a pedestrian. ~주의 pedestrianism.

**도복**(道服) the garment of a Taoist.

**도본**(圖本) a drawing. ⇨ 도면(圖面).

**도부**(到付) 《행상》 itinerant hawking; peddling. ~하다, ~치다 peddle; hawk; engage in an itinerant trade. ◉ ~꾼, 도붓장사 peddling; itinerant hawking: 도붓장사하다 engage in peddling; be a peddler. 도붓장수 a peddler; a hawker.

**도불**(渡佛) going to France; a visit to France. ~하다 go to France.

**도비**(徒費) waste; wastefulness. ~하다 cast away; waste.

**도사**(道士) 《도를 깨달은 사람》 a Taoist (도교의); an enlightened Buddhist (불교의); 《도를 닦는 사람》 an ascetic.

**도사**(導師) a spiritual guide 〔teacher〕 in Buddhism.

**도사공**(都沙工) a chief boatman.

**도사리다** ① 《다리를》 cross (*one's* feet); sit 〔squat〕 cross-legged; 《뱀 따위가》 coil *itself* (up). ¶ 도사리고 있는 뱀 a snake in a coil / 도사리고 앉다 sit cross-legged. ② 《마음을》 calm (*one's* mind); calm down. ¶ 마음을 ~ calm *one's* mind; compose *oneself*. ③ 《생각·감정이》 lurk 《in *one's* mind》; be harbored 〔rooted〕. ¶ 그녀에겐 나에 대한 나쁜 감정이 도사리고 있다 She harbors ill feeling against me. / 두 집안 사이에 도사리고 있는 반목의 뿌리를 도저히 끊을 수가 없었다 Nothing could resolve the 「deep-rooted 〔long-standing〕 feud between the two families.

**도산**(倒産)[1] 《파산》 bankruptcy; insolvency; a (company) failure. ~하다 go 〔become〕 bankrupt 〔insolvent〕; go under. ¶ ~ 회사의 수 the number of business failures 〔bankruptcies〕/ 불경기로 많은 회사가 ~했다 Owing to the depression, a lot of companies were bankrupt. / 금년들어 중소 기업의 ~이 증가하였다 There have been more bankruptcies of smaller firms this year.

**도산**(倒産)[2] 〖의학〗 cross birth. ~하다 have a cross birth.

**도산매**(都散賣) wholesale and retail.

**도살**(屠殺) slaughter; butchery; massacre (학살). ~하다 slaughter 《a pig》; butcher. ¶ 양(羊)들이 식육용으로 ~되었다 The sheep were butchered for meat. ◉ ~업 butchery. ~자 a butcher. ～장 a slaughterhouse; a butchery; an *abattoir* (F.).

**도상**(途上) = 도중. ¶ 발전 ～에 있는 나라들 developing countries; countries on their way to development.

**도상**(道床) 『토목』 a roadbed.

**도상**(圖上) ¶ ～ 작전 a war game; tactics on the map(s).

**도색**(桃色) ① 《색깔》 rose (color); pink. ¶ ～의 rose-colored; rosy; pink. ② 《색정》 love; obscenity. ¶ ～적인 《성적인》 erotic; sexy; obscene (외설한).
◉ ～문학 erotic 〔obscene〕 literature; pornography. ～본(本) an obscene book; [집합적] erotica. ～사진 an obscene 〔a steamy〕 photo; a French postcard. ～영화 a sex film; blue movies 《속어》. ～유희 sex play; an amorous affair. ～잡지 a pornographic magazine; a yellow journal.

**도서**(島嶼) islands; isles; islets. ◉ ～민 an islander; an islesman.

**도서**(圖書) books. ¶ 참고 ～ reference books / 추천 ～ recommended books / 교양〔신간〕 ～ cultural 〔new〕 books / 많은 ～를 구입하다〔모으다〕 buy 〔collect〕 a large number of books.
◉ ～대여업 book-lending business: ～대여업자 a keeper of a lending library. ～대여점 a lending 〔rental〕 library. ～대출 데스크 a circulation desk. ～목록 a catalogue of books 〔publications〕. ～상품권 a book coupon 〔token 《영》〕 《for 10,000 won》. ～실 a library (room). ～열람권 a library permit. ～열람료 a library admission fee. ～열람실 a reading room. ～열람 용지 a call slip. ～열람인 a reader; a visitor 《to the library》. ～출판업 the publishing business: ～ 출판업자 a publisher. ～출판회사 a publishing company 〔concern〕. ～카드 a book card. 국제 표준 ～번호 International Standard Book Number (생략 ISBN). 한국～전시회 the Korean books exhibition 〔fair〕.

**도서관**(圖書館) a library. ¶ ～의 책 a library book / 공공〔대출, 무료〕 ～ a public 〔lending, free〕 library / ～에 다니다 frequent a library / ～에서 책을 찾다 search a library / ～에서 책을 빌리다 take 〔borrow〕 a book from a library; get a book out of a library / 그 ～의 이용자는 일년에 약 10만 명이다 The library is consulted annually by about 100,000 persons.
◉ ～교육 library education. ～사서 a librarian; a library clerk. ～장 the director 〔curator〕 of a library; the chief librarian. ～학 library science; librarianship 《영》. ～행정 library administration. 국립 중앙～ the National Central Library. 대학〔학교〕 ～ a university 〔school〕 library.

**도서다** ① 《바람이》 change; shift; veer. ¶ 바람이 남쪽으로 도섰다 The wind shifted to the south. ② 《태아가》 (a fetus) begin to turn (in the womb). ③ 《되돌아서다》 turn 〔come〕 back; return; double (back) on *one's* tracks. ④ 《젖이》 a mother's milk starts flowing after childbirth; (the mammary gland) become ready for breast=feeding.

**도선**(渡船) a ferry; a ferryboat. ◉ ～료 ferriage; a ferry charge. ～장 a ferry (station).

**도선**(導船) pilotage; piloting. ～하다 pilot 《a boat》. ◉ ～사 a pilot.

**도선**(導線) the leading 〔conducting〕 wire.

**도설**(圖說) an illustration; an explanatory diagram 《of insects》; a diagrammatic chart.

**도섭** fickleness; caprice; fancy; whim. ～스럽다 (be) fickle; capricious; changeable; whimsical. ¶ ～을 부리다 show fickleness.

**도섭**(徒涉) wading. ～하다 wade 《across a river》; ford 《a river》.

**도성**(都城) a capital city (수도); a castle town.

**도소주**(屠蘇酒) spiced liquor 〔mulled wine〕 drunk on New Year's Day.

**도수**(度數) ① 《횟수》 (the number of) times; (a) frequency. ② 《온도 등의》 the degree; 《안경의》 a degree; a diopter. ¶ 안경 ～ the power of glasses / ～가 높은 안경 glasses with heavy lenses; powerful 〔strong, thick〕 spectacles / 안경 ～를 높이다 use stronger lenses / 안경 ～를 맞추다 adjust the lenses to *one's* eyes / 안경 ～가 맞지 않다 lenses do not agree with *one's* eyes / 꽤 ～ 높은 안경을 쓰다 wear glasses of a pretty high degree 〔with very heavy lenses〕. ③ 《알코올의》 proof. ¶ ～(가) 높은 위스키 high-proof whisky. ◉ ～분포 『통계』 frequency distribution. ～요금 《전화의》 message rates; the call charge. ～제 《전화의》 the message 〔call〕 rate system.

**도수**(徒手) bare hands. ⇨ 맨손, 맨주먹.

**도수**(導水) water conveyance. ～하다 conduct water 《into》. ◉ ～관 an aqueduct. ～로 a raceway; a water canal.

**도수리구멍** 〖공업〗 a fire-hole on the side of a kiln.

**도술**(道術) Taoist magic; magical arts.

**도스르다** brace *oneself* (up); gird *oneself* 《for *something*, to do *something*》; gird up *one's* loins.

**도승**(道僧) a Buddhist priest who has attained spiritual enlightenment.

**도시**(都市) a city; a town; 《대도시》 a metropolis.

> **용법** **city**는 크고도 중요한 town을 가리키며 **town**은 도시로서 아직 시(市)로 승격되지 않은 것을 이름. 이러한 구별은 영국에서는 비교적 충실히 지켜지고 있으나 미국에서는 흔히 city를 씀. **metropolis** 나라·주·지방 따위의 「대도시·주요 도시」를 일컬음. 그러나 반드시 capital과 일치하는 것은 아님.

¶ ~의 city; urban; municipal / ~의 경관〔경치〕 a cityscape; a townscape / 거대 ~ a megalopolis; a megapolis / 대학 ~ a university 〔college〕 city / ~의 발달 the growth of cities; urban growth / 소~ small towns / 전원~ a garden 〔rural〕 city / 살기 편한 ~ a hospitable city / 인구의 ~ 집중 경향 the cityward tendency of the population / ~ 게릴라 an urban guerrilla / ~화 urbanization / ~화하다 citify; urbanize / 인구 300만의 대~ a large 〔big〕 city with a population of three million / 뉴욕시는 미국 제1의 대~다 New York City is the largest city in the U.S.

◉ ~가계 조사 urban family income and expenditure survey. ~가스 city gas. ~개량 civic improvement. ~개조 urban renewal. ~경제 urban economy. ~공학 urban engineering 〔construction〕: ~공학과 urban engineering 〔construction〕 department. ~교통 urban transport 〔transportation〕. ~국가 a city-state. ~대항 축구시합 the 《national》 intercity 《nonprofessional》 soccer tournament 〔championship series〕. ~문제 an urban problem. ~미 the beauty of a city. ~발달 the growth of cities 〔urban communities〕. ~방송 broadcasting over city; an urban program. ~방위 civilian defense. ~사회학 urban sociology. ~생활 city 〔urban〕 life: ~생활자 a city dweller; an urbanite; [총칭] city people / ~생활을 하다 live in town. ~영세민 low-income urban people. ~위생 urban sanitation. ~인 a city dweller; an urbanite; townspeople; townsfolk. ~인구 urban population: ~인구 분산 city population dispersion; population decentralization. ~재개발 계획 urban redevelopment projects; the 〔a〕 massive urban renewal program. ~재정 municipal finance. ~전입 inflow into urban areas. ~제휴 (a) town affiliation. ~지역 urban areas. ~폐기물 municipal waste. ~행정 municipal administration.

**도시**(圖示) illustration; graphic(al) representation. ~하다 illustrate; show by a diagram; show in a graphic form

**도시계획**(都市計劃) urban planning; city planning 《미》; town planning 《영》. ¶ ~이 잘 되어 있는 도시 a well=planned city / ~을 시행하다 carry out city planning. ◉ ~과 City-Planning Section. ~구역 a town planning area. ~법 the Town Planning and Zoning Act. ~위원회 the City-Planning Committee.

**도시락** 《옛날의》 a small willow basket (for carrying food); a lunch basket 〔package〕; 《현대의》 a lunch box. ¶ ~을 먹다 eat 〔take〕 *one's* lunch / ~을 만들다 make 〔prepare, fix 《구어》〕 a lunch box / ~을 싸다 pack a lunch basket / ~을 가지고 가다 take 〔carry, bring〕 a lunch with *one*. ◉ ~밥 food packed in a lunch box.

**도식**(圖式) a diagram; a graph; 〖철학〗 a schema (*pl.* ~ta); a plan; 〖논리〗 a figure. ¶ ~으로 나타내다 display in graph 〔diagram, diagrammatic, schematic〕 form; put into the form of a diagram 〔graph〕; schematize; diagrammatize. ◉ ~화 diagraming; graphing; schematizaton.

**도식하다**(徒食—) 《무위도식》 eat the bread of idleness; live an idle life; live in idleness; idle away *one's* time.

**도신**(刀身) a sword blade.

**도심**(盜心) an impulse to steal; a thieving 〔larcenous〕 propensity.

**도심**(都心) the heart 〔center〕 of a city (★ 도시의 심장부에 해당하는 중심에는 heart, 기하학적인 중심지에는 center를 씀); downtown areas; the downtown. ¶ ~의 호텔 a midtown hotel / 서울 ~에 살다 live in downtown Seoul / ~ 지역의 교통 체증을 덜다 ease traffic jams in the downtown area / ~은 땅값이 비싸

다 Land prices in central 《Seoul》 are high. / 관청은 대개 서울 ~에 있다 Most government offices are (located) in the heart 〔center〕 of Seoul. ◉ ~지대 the downtown 〔midtown〕 area.

**도안**(圖案) a design; a plan; a pattern. ¶ ~을 만들다 design; draw a design 《for》 / ~을 모집하다 collect 〔invite〕 designs by prize competition / ~을 그리다, ~화하다 draw 〔make〕 a design of 《flowers》 / 그녀는 자수용 ~을 그리고 있다 She designs patterns for embroidery. ◉ ~가 a designer. ~용지 design paper.

**도액**(度厄) exorcism. ~하다 exorcise; rid of 〔neutralize, temper〕 evil influence; drive 〔get rid of〕 *one's* evils.

**도야**(陶冶) cultivation; molding; training; education. ~하다 cultivate; mold; train; build up. ¶ 인격을 ~하다 build up 〔cultivate, form〕 *one's* character.

**도약**(跳躍) a spring; a jump; a leap; a skip; jumping. ~하다 spring; jump; leap; skip; prance (말이). ¶ 호랑이는 ~력이 강하다 The tiger is a powerful jumper. / 야망은 미래에 대한 ~판이나 같다 Ambition is like a springboard for one's future.
◉ ~경기 jumping. ~단계 〚경제〛 the take-off stage: 경제 발전의 초기 ~단계에 들어서 있다 be in the early stage of take-off for economic development. ~대 a springboard. ~운동 a jumping exercise. ~종목 a jumping event. ~판 a springboard.

**도양**(渡洋) [형용사적] transoceanic.
◉ ~작전 transoceanic 〔overseas〕 military operations. ~폭격 overseas 〔ocean-hopping〕 bombing; transoceanic bombing 〔air raids〕.

**도어** a door. ⇨ 문(門). ◉ ~맨 《호텔 따위의》 a doorman.

**도열**(堵列) a line (of men). ~하다 line 〔be drawn〕 up; form a line. ¶ ~시키다 line 《people》 along 《the street》 / 길 양쪽에 ~하다 line either side of the road. 「rice blight.

**도열병**(稻熱病) 〚식물〛 rice blast disease;

**도영**(渡英) going (overseas) to England; a visit 〔trip〕 to England. ~하다 go to England.

**도예**(陶藝) ceramic art; ceramics. ◉ ~가 a potter; a ceramic artist; a ceramì(ci)st. ~품 works of pottery 〔ceramic art〕.

**도와**(陶瓦) an unglazed tile.

**도와주다** ① 《조력하다》 help; aid; assist; 《후원하다》 support; give support 《to》; back (up). ¶ 숙제를 ~ help 《*a person*》 with 〔in〕 *his* homework / 소화를 ~ aid 〔promote〕 (the) digestion / 차에 오르는〔내리는〕 것을 ~ help 《*a person*》 into 〔out of〕 a car; help 《*a person*》 onto 〔off〕 a bus / 그녀가 사다리에서 내려오는 것을 도와 주었다 I helped her (to) climb down the ladder. / 나를 좀 도와 주실 수 없겠습니까 Could you help me out? *or* I wonder if you could help me out? ② 《구제하다》 relieve; save; rescue; give relief to; give 《*a person*》 a helping hand; help 《*a person*》 out of difficulties. ¶ 가난한 사람을 ~ relieve 〔extend a helping hand to〕 the poor; succor the needy / 강물에 뛰어들어 물에 빠진 소년을 ~ jump into the river and save 〔rescue〕 a drowning boy.

**도외시**(度外視) ~하다 disregard; ignore; neglect; overlook; leave 《*a thing*》 out of consideration; take no account of 《*a thing*》. ¶ 여론을 ~하다 disregard public opinion / 그는 비용을 ~하고 이 집을 지었다 He had this house built irrespective 〔regardless〕 of expenses. / 이 가격은 채산〔이익〕을 ~하고 정한 것이다 This price was set with profit left out of consideration. 「bill.

**도요(새)** 〚조류〛 a snipe (bird); a long-

**도용**(盜用) 《금전의》 peculation; embezzlement; misappropriation; 《물건 따위의》 surreptitious use; using by stealth; 《특허의》 theft; illegal use. ~하다 appropriate 《public money to *one's* own use》; embezzle; steal; make (a) fraudulent use 《of *a person's* registered design》; plagiarize 《*a person's* book》. ¶ 전기를 ~하다 make fraudulent use of electricity; steal electric current / 남의 아이디어를 ~하다 plagiarize another's idea / 프로그램 ~이 종종 문제가 된다 The theft of programs is an issue that often arises. / 수년 동안 시장은 많은 액수의 공금을 ~해 왔다 For years the mayor has been 「embezzling 〔misappropriating〕 large sums of public money.

**도움** aid; help; assistance; 《구조》 rescue; 《구제》 relief; 《후원》 support; 《효용》 use; service; good; utility. ¶ 자네 ~으로 with 〔by〕 your kind assistance / 친구의 ~을 얻어서 with the assistance 〔help〕 of a friend / ~이 되다 be of help; be helpful to; be an aid; be useful 〔of use〕 / ~이 되지 않

다 be of no use 〔service, avail〕; be useless; be good for nothing; avail nothing / ～을 요청하다 ask 《*a person*》 for help; ask for 《*a person's*》 help; turn 〔look〕 to 《*a person*》 for help / …의 ～을 얻다 enlist 〔obtain, receive〕 the aid of… / ～을 주다 lend 《*a person*》 assistance; render 〔extend〕 help / 크게〔많은〕 ～이 되다 be of much help; be a great help / 나는 자네 ～이 필요하다 I need your help. / 그녀는 큰 소리로 ～을 구했다 She cried (out) for help. / 그는 누구의 ～도 받지 않았다 He had no help from anyone. / ～이 되어 드릴 수 있다면 다행이겠습니다 I shall be happy to be of (any) service to you.

**도움닫기** 《스포츠》 an approach run. ◉ ～높이뛰기 a (running) high jump. ～멀리뛰기 a (running) long jump.

**도원경**(桃源境) an earthly paradise; Shangri-La, Shangri-la.

**도읍**(都邑) ① 《서울》 the capital. ② 《도시》 a city; a town. ～하다 set up the capital 《at》; 《a dynasty》 holds its court 《at》. ◉ ～지 the seat of government.

**도의**(道義) (public) morality; moral justice; moral principles. ¶ ～적 moral / ～적으로, ～상 morally (speaking); from a moral sense / ～의 퇴폐 demoralization; moral decadence / ～상 …해야 하다 be bound in honor to *do* / ～에 어긋나다 be against public morals / ～를 중히 여기다 have high 〔strong〕 moral sense / ～가 땅에 떨어졌다 Morality has lost its hold on the people. *or* People have lost their sense of morality.
◉ ～심 moral sense: ～심에 호소하다 appeal to 《*a person's*》 moral sense. ～앙양 enhancement of morality. ～정치 《establish》 moral politics.

**도의적 책임**(道義的責任) moral responsibility; a moral obligation. ¶ ～을 지다 take moral responsibility 《for》 / ～을 지고 사표를 제출하다 tender *one's* resignation, taking moral responsibility 《for》; 《사직하다》 resign *one's* post 〔office〕, taking moral responsibility 《for》.

**도의회**(道議會) a provincial assembly 〔council〕. ◉ ～ 의원 a member of a provincial assembly; a provincial councilman.

**도일**(渡日) going to Japan; a visit 〔trip〕 to Japan. ～하다 go to Japan.

**도임하다**(到任—) arrive at 〔arrive to assume〕 *one's* new post.

**도입**(導入) introduction; induction; invitation; importation; import. ～하다 introduce 《foreign capital》; induce; invite; import. ¶ 외국으로부터 새 기술을 ～하다 introduce 〔import〕 new technology from abroad. ◉ ～부 『음악』 the introduction.

**도자기**(陶瓷器) ceramics; chinaware; pottery; china and porcelain. ¶ ～ 장사를 하고 있다 be in the china trade. ◉ ～공 a ceramist; a potter. ～공장 a pottery (factory). ～ 제조업 ceramics.

**도작**(盜作) 《행위》 plagiarism; 《작품》 a plagiarism; a crib. ～하다 plagiarize.

**도작**(稻作) 『농업』 rice culture 〔farming〕.

**도장**(道場) 《체육관》 a drill hall; a gymnasium (*pl.* ～s, -sia); an exercise hall. ◉ 태권도〔유도〕～ a t'aekwondo 〔judo〕 hall.

**도장**(塗裝) coating; painting. ～하다 coat with paint. ◉ ～공 a painter. ～공사 painting; painter's work. ～재(材) coating materials.

**도장**(圖章) a seal; a stamp. ¶ ～을 찍다 seal; affix 〔put, stamp〕 *one's* seal 《to》 / ～을 새기다 make 〔engrave〕 a seal; 《새겨 받다》 have *one's* seal cut 〔engraved〕 / ～을 위조하다 counterfeit a seal / ～이 찍혀 있다 《the documents》 bear the stamp 〔seal〕 《of》 / 이름 밑에 ～을 찍으시오 Please put your seal under your name.
◉ ～ 주머니 a seal-case. ～포〔방〕 a seal-engraver's 〔maker's〕 shop.

**도장방**(—房) 《규방》 a *boudoir* (F.).

**도저하다**(到底—) ① 《썩 좋다》 (be) good; fine; excellent. ¶ 학문이 ～ have an excellent scholarship. ② 《극진하다》 (be) perfect; thorough. ¶ 부모에 대한 효성이 ～ be devoted to *one's* parents.

**도저히**(到底—) 《아무리 …해도》 (not) at all; (cannot) possibly; by no means; hardly; 《전혀》 quite; utterly; absolutely. ¶ ～ 비교가 안되다 cannot for a moment compare with; it is beyond all comparison / ～ 있을 수 없다 it is most unlikely 〔out of the bounds of possibility〕 that… / 그 시는 ～ 이해할 수가 없다 I cannot understand the poem at all. / 나는 그런 일은 ～ 할 수 없다 I cannot possibly do such a thing. / ～ 우리가 이길 가망이 없다 There is 「no 〔hardly any〕 hope of our winning. / 그것은 ～ 불가능하다 It is absolutely impossible. / 해결은 ～ 불가

능하다 No settlement is remotely possible. / 그것은 ～ 승낙할 수 없다 I can't possibly consent to it. / 그에게는 ～ 상대가 될 수 없다 I am no match for him.

**도적**(盜賊) ＝도둑.

**도전**(挑戰) challenge; defiance (반항); provocation (도발). ～하다 challenge; make 〔give〕 a challenge 《to》; defy; bid defiance 《to》; provoke a battle. ¶ ～적 challenging; defiant; aggressive / ～적 태도를 취하다 take 〔assume〕 a defiant 〔provocative〕 attitude 《toward》/ ～에 응하다 accept 〔take〕 a challenge; take up the glove / 세계 기록에 ～하다 challenge the world record / 나는 수영에서 세계 기록에 ～할 생각이다 I'm going to establish a new world record for swimming. / 그는 나에게 한 번 더 승부를 겨루자고 ～해왔다 He challenged me to (have) one more game. / 아무도 그의 ～에 응하지 않았다 No one took up his challenge. / 국방부의 한 고위 관리는 지난 주말 판문점에서 있었던 북한의 도발적인 행동은 한반도에서의 평화와 안정을 위협하는 중대한 ～이 된다고 경고했다 A high-ranking Defense Ministry official warned that North Korea's provocative actions late last week at the Panmunjŏm constitute a grave challenge which threatens the peace and stability on the Korean Peninsula.
◉ ～자 a challenger: ～자의 자격을 얻다 fill the requirements for challenging (a champion). ～장 a (written) challenge; a cartel.

**도전**(盜電) surreptitious use of electricity; stealing power. ～하다 make surreptitious use of electricity; tap the wires; steal power.

**도전**(導電) electric conduction; conduction of electricity. ◉ ～율 conductivity. ～체 an electric conductor.

**도정**(道政) provincial government 〔administration〕.

**도정**(道程) mileage; a distance; a route; a path; 《여정》 a journey; an itinerary. ¶ 60킬로미터의 ～ a distance of sixty kilometers; a sixty kilometers' journey.

**도정**(搗精) polishing 《rice》 by pounding. ～하다 polish 《rice》 by pounding.
◉ ～공장 a rice-polishing mill.

**도제**(徒弟) an apprentice. ¶ ～로 보내다 apprentice 《*one's* son to a carpenter》/ ～가 되다 be apprenticed to; apprentice *oneself* to; be articled to / ～를 두다 take apprentices.
◉ ～기간 *one's* apprenticeship. ～연한 *one's* term of service. ～제도 an apprentice system; apprenticeship.

**도제**(陶製) ¶ ～의 china; made of china; ceramic; earthen. ◉ ～ 파이프 a clay pipe.

**도주**(逃走) ＝도망. ◉ ～범 a fugitive from justice.

**도중**(途中) ¶ ～의 역(驛) stations on 〔along〕 the route; way 〔intermediate〕 stations / ～(에) 《도상》 on the way 《to, from》; on *one's* way 《to》; on the road; *en route* 《to, for》; on route 《to, from》; in transit (수송중); 《중도에》 halfway; midway / 식사 ～에 in the middle 〔course〕 of a meal / 이야기하던 ～에 in the midst 〔middle〕 of *one's* talk; in the middle of a conversation; midway through a conversation / 집에 돌아가는 ～에 on *one's* way 〔midway〕 home; *en route* home / 학교〔일하러〕 가는 ～(에) on *one's* way to school 〔work〕/ ～까지 바래다 주다 go part of the way to see 《*a person*》 off; put 〔set〕 《*a person*》 on *his* way / ～에 그만두다 give up halfway; do not go all the way / ～에 되돌아오다 turn back halfway 〔midway〕/ ～에 들르다 stop off 《at》/ 영화를 상영되는～에 보다 see a movie from halfway 〔partway 《미》〕 through / 나는 ～에 부산에서 일박할 생각이다 I will stop overnight in Pusan. / 하던 말을 ～에 끊다 break the threads of a talk / ～ 어디선가 무슨 일이 있었던 게 틀림없다 Something must have happened somewhere along the way. / 남이 말하고 있는～에 끼어들지 마라 Don't interrupt others while they are talking. / 시간이 너무 늦어서 회의는 ～에 그만뒀다 We cut short the meeting, as it was getting too late. ◉ ～계시(計時) clocking partway times 〔lap times〕 《in a race》.

**도중하차**(途中下車) a stopover; a layover 《미》. ～하다 stop over 《at》; make a stopover; break *one's* journey 《at》; stop off 《at》; lay over 《미》. ¶ 대구에서 ～하다 break *one's* (railroad) journey at Taegu / ～무효 《주의》 No stopover (is allowed) on this ticket.
◉ ～역 a stopover station.

**도지**(賭地) 《논밭·집터》 sharecrop land.

**도지다**[1] ① 《심하다》 (be) severe; hard; extreme; intense. ¶ 욕이 ～ be extreme in abusing 《*a person*》. ② 《단

단하다》(be) hard; strained.

**도지다**[2] [병이 주어] a relapse occurs; get worse; [사람이 주어] suffer a setback; have 〔suffer〕 a relapse; become serious again. ¶ 감기가 ~ a cold gets worse / 그는 무리하여 병이 도졌다 He got a relapse through strain. / 그의 감기는 도져서 폐렴이 되었다 His cold developed into pneumonia.

**도지사**(道知事) the governor of a province; a provincial governor.

**도착**(到着) arrival; reaching. ~하다 arrive《at the station, in Paris, on the scene》; reach; get to; 《편지·물건 따위가》 come to hand; 《항해》 fetch. ¶ ~순으로 in order of arrival / ~하는 대로 on *one's* arrival; as soon as *one* arrives; upon arrival / 현장에 ~하다 《an ambulance》 arrive on 〔get to〕 the scene / 무사히 ~하다 arrive in safety; 《물건 따위가》 arrive in good condition 〔order〕 / 이 열차는 서울에 몇 시에 ~합니까 What time is this train to arrive in Seoul? / 우리는〔열차는〕 오전 11시에 서울역에 ~할 예정입니다 We are 〔The train is (scheduled)〕 to arrive at Seoul Station at 11 a.m. (★ 차장이나 승객이 이야기할 때는 보통 we를 쓴다) / 비행기의 ~이 눈보라로 지연되었다 The arrival of the airplane has been delayed because of snow storm. / 네 편지는 아직 ~하지 않았다 Your letter has not reached me yet.
◉ ~성명 an arrival statement. ~역 an arrival station. ~ 예정 시간 the estimated time of arrival (생략 ETA). ~지점 *one's* destination; a place of arrival; 〖군사〗 the objective point. ~ 플랫폼〔라운지〕 an arrival platform 〔lounge〕. ~항 a port of arrival.

**도착**(倒錯) 《정신병》 perversion; inversion (성(性) 도착). ◉ 성~ sexual perversion 〔inversion〕: 성 ~자 a sexual pervert 〔invert〕.

**도처(에)**(到處(―)) everywhere; in every place; all over; throughout 《the country》; wherever *one* goes; far and wide; in all directions; in every quarter; on every hand; on all sides. ¶ 세계 도처로부터 from all parts 〔every corner〕 of the world / 그는 도처에서 환영을 받았다 He was welcomed wherever he went. / 비슷한 광경을 도처에서 볼 수 있다 A similar sight meets our eyes at every turn. / 그 회사는 전국 도처에 지점이 있다 That company has its branches in almost all parts of the country. / 로마에는 도처에 유적이 있다 Rome abounds with relics.

**도처낭패**(到處狼狽) failure whatever *one* attempts. ~하다 fail in every attempt. ¶ 그는 ~했다 Everything he put his hand turned out to be a failure.

**도청**(盜聽) 《전화의》 (wire) tapping; a wiretap; 《엿들음》 eavesdropping. ~하다 tap 《a telephone wire》; listen in 《on the enemy's communication line》; eavesdrop (on) 《a conversation》; bug 《미구어》. ¶ 경찰은 피의자의 전화를 ~했다 The police put a tap on the suspect's telephone.
◉ ~기〔장치〕 a concealed microphone (대화의); a wiretapping device (전화의); a wall-snooper (벽에 장치한); a bug 《미구어》. ~사건 a wiretap scandal. ~자 a wiretapper.

**도청**(道廳) a provincial office 〔government〕. ◉ ~ 소재지 the seat of a provincial office; a provincial seat.

**도체**(導體) 〖물리〗 a conductor (열·전기의); a medium (매개). ¶ 반~ a semiconductor / 부(不)~ a nonconductor.

**도축**(屠畜) butchery. ⇨ 도살(屠殺).

**도취**(陶醉) ① 《술·승리 따위에 의한》 intoxication. ~하다 be 〔get〕 intoxicated. ¶ 성공〔술〕에 ~하다 be intoxicated with success 〔from wine〕 / 그들은 승리에 ~하여 밤새 마시고 춤추었다 Intoxicated by their victory, they drank and danced all night. ② 《사물에》 rapture; fascination. ~하다 be fascinated 〔charmed〕 《by the beautiful music》; be carried away 《by》; be in rapture 〔ecstacies〕 《over》; be lost in rapture. ¶ 자연의 아름다움에 ~하다 be fascinated by the beauty of nature.
◉ 자기~ self-intoxication; narcissism: 자기~자 a narcissist.

**도치**(倒置) inversion; (placing) upside-down; reverse. ~하다 invert; reverse; put upside-down. ◉ ~문 〖문법〗 an inverted sentence. ~법 (grammatical) inversion.

**도킹** 《우주선의》 docking. ~하다 dock 《with the command module》. ¶ ~시키다 dock 《two spaceships》 / ~ 조작을 하다 perform a 《successful》 docking maneuver / ~을 풀다 undock.

**도탄**(塗炭) dire distress; great misery. ¶ ~에 빠지다 be reduced to the greatest misery; fall into extreme distress / ~에 빠진 백성을 구하다 save the people from distress.

**도태**(淘汰) 〚생물〛 selection; 《가려내기》 weeding 〔combing〕 out; sift 《the good from the bad》; 《인원정리》 dismissal (해고); a shake-up 《구어》. ~하다 select; curtail; weed 〔comb〕 out; get weeded out; be combed out; dismiss. ¶ 남아도는 인원을 ~시키다 weed out useless employees; dismiss superfluous personnel. ◉ ~작용 a sifting=〔weeding-〕out process.

**도토**(陶土) potter's clay; kaoline; porcelain 〔china〕 clay.

**도토리** an acorn. ¶ 개밥에 ~ an outcast; an ostracized 〔a left-out〕 person / 그들은 ~ 키재기다 They are more or less on the same level, and no one is outstanding. *or* They are all alike. ◉ ~ 깍정이〔받침〕 the cup of an acorn. ~묵 acorn jelly.

**도톨도톨** granulated; lumpy; rough; uneven. ¶ ~한 나무껍질 a rugged bark / ~한 피부 rough skin / ~하게 만든 가죽 granulated leather / 얼굴에 여드름이 ~나다 *one's* face is covered with pimples.

**도통**(都統) ① 《도합》 in all; all together; totally; all told. ⇨ 도합. ② 《전혀》 (not) at all; absolutely. ¶ ~ 모르다 know not at all / 요즘 그녀를 ~ 못 만난다 I have seen nothing of her lately.

**도통**(道通) spiritual enlightenment. ~하다 be spiritually enlightened; attain spiritual enlightenment. ¶ 그 일에 ~하다 be well 〔deeply〕 versed in the matter; be conversant with the matter.

**도판**(圖版) a plate; a figure; an illustration.

**도포**(塗布) application. ~하다 spread; apply 《an ointment to》. ◉ ~약 《연고》 an ointment; 《물약》 a liniment.

**도포**(道袍) Korean full-dress attire (in olden days).

**도표**(道標) a signpost; a guidepost; a fingerpost (손가락 모양의); a road sign; a milestone (이정표).

**도표**(圖表) a chart; a graph; a diagram. ¶ ~의 diagrammatic(al); graphic / 역사〔통계〕~ a historical 〔statistical〕 chart / ~로 나타내다 put 《figures》 into the form of a diagram; diagrammatize; chart; represent by a chart.

**도품**(盜品) stolen goods 〔merchandise〕; pilferage [집합적]; swag 《속어》.

**도피**(逃避) (an) escape; (a) flight; (an) evasion (회피). ~하다 escape; fly; flee (★ 최근 flee의 현재형은 미국에서는 쓰이나 영국에서는 일상어로서 fly가 쓰임); take flight; evade. ¶ 자본의 ~ flight of capital; capital flight / 현실로부터 ~하다 escape from reality / 사회로부터 ~하다 seclude *oneself* from society / 대륙으로 ~하다 disappear to 〔seek asylum on〕 the Continent. ◉ ~구 a way of escape; an outlet. ~문학 escapist literature. ~생활 《live》 a life of escape from the world. ~여행 a runaway flight 〔trip〕; an escape journey. ~자 a runaway; a fugitive; a refugee. ~장소 a place of refuge; a bolt hole. ~주의 escapism: ~주의자 an escapist.

**도핑** doping; drug use. ¶ ~테스트 a dope test; a drug check 〔test〕.

**도하**(都下) the capital; the metropolis. ¶ ~의 in the capital 〔metropolis〕; in Seoul / ~의 각 중학교 the middle schools in the capital.

**도하**(渡河) crossing a river. ~하다 cross a river. ◉ ~작전 《force》 a river=crossing operation. ~지점 a crossing point; a point of passage.

**도학**(道學) moral philosophy; ethics. ◉ ~군자 a virtuous gentleman; a man of virtue. ~자 a moralist.

**도한**(盜汗) night sweating; nightly sweats. ¶ ~이 나다 have night sweats; sweat at night.

**도합**(都合) the total; the sum total; [부사적] in all; all told; altogether. ¶ ~ 2백 명 (a total of) 200 persons in all / ~ 12명의 수행원 a suit of retainers twelve in all / 그녀의 지출은 ~ 200 달러에 달했다 Her expenses reached a total of 200 dollars.

**도항**(渡航) a passage; a voyage; a sailing; a crossing. ~하다 make a passage 〔voyage〕 《to》; go over 〔across〕 《to》; go abroad 〔overseas〕 (외국으로). ¶ ~ 절차를 밟다 go through the formalities for *one's* trip 《to America》. ◉ ~자 a passenger.

**도해**(圖解) a diagram (설명용의); an illustration (삽화). ~하다 illustrate 《in graphic form by picture》; show with 〔by〕 a diagram. ¶ ~로 위성의 궤도를 보여주다 show the orbit of a satellite using a picture / ~하면 다음과 같다 It is graphically shown as follows. ◉ ~ 백과사전 an illustrated 〔iconographical〕 encyclopedia. ~법 iconography; illustration. ~사전 a picture dictionary. 곤충~ explanatory diagrams of insects.

**도형**(圖形) a figure; a diagram; a device. ¶ 입체〔기하학적〕 ～ a solid 〔geometrical〕 figure / ～으로 나타내다 show in 〔by〕 a diagram; figure. ◉ ～ 기하학 descriptive geometry.

**도화**(桃花) a peach blossom.

**도화**(圖畫) 《그리기》 drawing (연필·펜으로 그린); painting (물감으로 그린); 《그림》 a drawing; a painting; a picture. ¶ ～를 그리다 draw a picture. ◉ ～지 drawing paper.

**도화선**(導火線) 《화약의》 a (detonating) fuse; a (powder) train; 《사건의 원인》 an incentive; a cause. ¶ ～에 불을 붙이다 light 〔fire〕 the fuse 《of》 / ～이 되다 prove an incentive to; give rise to; cause; occasion; touch off / 대폭동의 ～이 되다 prove an incentive to mass revolt; give rise to 〔lead up to〕 mass riots / 한 경찰관의 발포가 대폭동의 ～이 되었다 A shot fired by a policeman sparked 〔triggered〕 off a great riot.

**도회**(都會) a city; a town. (★ 행정권을 가진 자치체의 도시를 city, 시골에 대비한 뜻으로의 도시를 town이라 함). ⇨ 도시(都市). ¶ ～의 city; town; urban / ～풍의 urban; urbane (세련된) / ～에서 자란 town-〔city-〕bred / ～화하다 citify; urbanize / 서울은 대～다 Seoul is a large 〔big, huge〕 city. / 그녀는 ～에서 자랐다 She was raised in a city. ◉ ～병 a city disease. ～생활 city 〔town, urban〕 life. ～인 a city dweller; a townsman. ～지 urban areas; a city; a town.

**도흔**(刀痕) a sword cut 〔scar〕.

**독**[1] an earthenware pot; a jar; a jug. ¶ 독 안에 든 쥐가 되다 be in a fine fix; be quite in a helpless situation / 밑빠진 독에 물붓기 be like throwing water on thirsty soil; be nothing more than a drop in the bucket / 이제는 도망 못간다. 너희들은 독안에 든 쥐다 You have no chance to get away. We've got you here.

**독**(毒) ① 《성분》 a poison; a poisonous substance; 《독약》 a poisonous drug 〔medicine〕; (a) poison; a toxicant; 《동물의》 (a) venom; 《병독》 a virus. ¶ 강렬한 독 a strong 〔powerful〕 poison / 치명적인 독 a deadly poison / 독을 넣은 음료 a poisoned drink / 독이 있다 be poisonous 〔virulent, toxic, noxious〕 / 독이 없다 be innocuous 〔harmless〕 / 독을 타다 administer poison to; put poison in 《the coffee》; poison 《a well》 / 독을 마시다〔먹다〕 take poison / 독을 마시고 자살하다 commit suicide 〔kill *oneself*〕 by (taking) poison / 독을 제거하다 neutralize 〔counteract〕 poison / 독이 퍼지다 a poison takes effect / 독이 전신에 돌았다 The poison passed into the whole system. / 이 열매에는 독이 있다 This berry is poisonous.
② 《해독》 harm; injury; virus; bad effects. ¶ 독이 되다 prove 〔be〕 poisonous 〔injurious, harmful〕 / 청소년에게 독이 되는 읽을거리를 추방하자 Let's get rid of readings which may corrupt the youth.
③ 《독기》 malice; spite; ferocity. ¶ 독이 서린 비평 malicious criticism.

**독**[2] a dock. ⇨ 선거(船渠). ¶ 독에 들어가다 (go into) dock / 배를 독에 들이다 dock a vessel; put a ship into dock / (배가) 독에서 나오다 come out of dock. ◉ 독 사용료 dockage; dock dues. 건(乾)〔부(浮)〕독 a dry 〔floating〕 dock.

**독가스**(毒—) poison(ous) gas; toxic 〔noxious〕 gas. ¶ ～를 사용하다 use poison gas / ～로 죽다 be gassed. ◉ ～ 공격 a gas attack. ～ 마스크 a gas mask. ～ 사형실 a gas chamber. ～전(戰) (poison-)gas warfare. ～탄(彈) a (poison-)gas bomb (폭탄); a (poison-)gas shell (포탄).

**독감**(毒感) influenza; (the) flu; a bad cold; grippe. ¶ ～에 걸리다 contract influenza; catch 〔get〕 (the) flu / ～을 앓고 있다 have 〔be suffering from〕 influenza; have flu; be sick with the flu / ～ 예방 접종을 받다 get a vaccination against influenza; get a flu shot 《구어》/ 전국적으로 ～이 유행하고 있다 Influenza is raging throughout the country.

**독거**(獨居) solitary life; living alone; solitude. ～하다 lead a solitary life; live alone; live in solitude.

**독경**(讀經) 〖불교〗 reading scriptures; sutra chanting. ～하다 read 〔chant〕 the Buddhist scripture 〔sutra text〕; read a service.

**독계**(毒計) a wicked design; an evil scheme; a trick. ¶ ～를 꾸미다 make a wicked 〔an evil〕 design / ～에 빠지다 fall into *one's* wicked trap.

**독과점**(獨寡占) monopoly and oligopoly. ◉ ～업체 a monopolistic (industrial) firm 〔enterprise〕. ～품목 monopoly-oligopoly (products) items: ~품목으로 지정하다 designate as monopolistic and oligopolistic items.

**독극물**(毒劇物) toxic chemicals. ¶ 식품 회사 ~ 협박범을 엄단하다 deal sternly with extortionists threatening food companies with poison-lacing.

**독기**(毒氣) ① 《독기운》 noxious air; poisonous vapor 〔gas〕; 《독성》 poisonous character; virulence. ¶ ~가 있는 poisonous / ~를 빼다 clear away poisonous vapors. ② 《악의》 malice; spite. ¶ ~를 품다 be malicious; be spiteful / ~ 있는 말 malicious 〔spiteful〕 remarks / 그의 말에는 ~가 있다 His remarks are poisoned with acrimony. *or* His word stings.

**독나방**(毒—) 〖곤충〗 a poisonous moth.

**독납**(督納) tax dunning. ~하다 dun for taxes; press for tax payment.

**독녀**(獨女) the only daughter. ⇨ 외딸.

**독농가**(篤農家) a diligent 〔productive〕 farmer; a most efficient farming producer.

**독단**(獨斷) an arbitrary decision; dogmatism (주장). ~하다 decide arbitrarily; decide on *one's* own judgment 〔discretion〕; act on *one's* own authority 〔responsibility〕. ¶ ~적인 dogmatic; arbitrary; peremptory / 아무와도 상의 않고 ~으로 행동하다 act arbitrarily without consultation / ~적이어서 다른 사람의 의견을 듣지 않다 be too opinionated to listen to what others say / 사물을 ~적인 방식으로 보는 것은 위험하다 It's dangerous to have an arbitrary 〔a dogmatic〕 viewpoint. ◉ ~가 a self-willed person; a dogmatist. ~론 〖철학〗 dogmatism; a dogma.

**독담당**(獨擔當) ~하다 take sole charge of; assume sole responsibility for.

**독도**(獨島) *Tokto* Island. ¶ ~는 우리땅 *Tokto* is our land. / 우리는 우리의 섬, ~의 주권에 대한 어떠한 도전도 단호히 격퇴하여야 한다 We have to firmly and resolutely repel any challenge to the sovereignty of our island, *Tokto*.

**독두**(禿頭) =대머리. ◉ ~병 〖의학〗 alopecia.

**독려**(督勵) encouragement. ~하다 encourage; stimulate; urge. ¶ 부하를 ~하여 일을 서둘다 urge *one's* men to push 〔rush〕 the work / 코치는 그들이 최선을 다하도록 ~했다 The coach encouraged them to do their best.

**독력**(獨力) *one's* own efforts; single-handed efforts. ¶ ~으로 by *one's* own efforts; single-handed; for 〔by〕 *oneself;* unaided; independently / ~으로 하다 do *something* single-handed; do on *one's* own / 누구나 혼자서 그것도 ~으로 살 수는 없다 No one can live all by and for himself.

**독립**(獨立) ① 《자립》 independence; self-help (자조); self-reliance (자립); self-support (자활). ~하다 become independent; stand on *one's* own legs; stand alone; paddle *one's* own canoe. ¶ ~하여 생계를 꾸려가다 support *oneself;* earn *one's* own living; keep house for *oneself* / ~하여 장사를 시작하다 start *oneself* in business; set up business on *one's* own account / ~하여 살 만한 수입이 있다 earn enough to live on *one's* own.

② 《정치적》 independence; freedom. ~하다 become free and independent. ¶ ~을 선언하다 declare independence / ~을 인정하다 recognize the independence 《of》 / ~을 시켜 주다 give independence 《to》 / ~을 획득하다 〔잃다〕 gain 〔lose〕 *one's* independence.

③ 《분리》 separation; isolation (고립). ~하다 be separated from; separate *oneself* from; be isolated. ¶ ~하여 separately; in isolation / 그 건물은 다른 것과 ~돼 있다 The building is separated from the rest.

◉ ~가옥 a detached 〔separate〕 house. ~국(가) an independent country; a sovereign state. ~군 an army for national independence. ~기념관 Independence Hall. ~기념일 《미국의》 the Independence Day (★ 7월 4일). ~문 the Independent Arch 〔Gate〕. ~변수(變數) 〖수학〗 an independent variable. ~부정사 〖문법〗 an absolute infinitive. ~분사구문 〖문법〗 an absolute participial construction. ~생활 an independent life. ~선언 《미국의》 the Declaration of Independence. ~심〔정신〕 an independent spirit. ~운동 an independence movement. ~전쟁 《미국의》 the Revolutionary War; the War of Independence. ~주의 independentism; separatism (분리주의). ~채산제(採算制) the independent profit system; the self-supporting 〔autonomous〕 accounting system: ~채산제로 on a self-paying basis. ~투사 a fighter for national independence: 국립묘지 ~투사의 묘 the tombs of independence fighters at the National Cemetery.

**독립국가연합**(獨立國家聯合) the Commonwealth of Independent States (생략 CIS).

**독립독행**(獨立獨行) independence; self-reliance; self-help. ～하다 rely on *oneself;* be self-reliant; paddle *one's* own canoe; cut *one's* own way; be *one's* own master.

**독립자영**(獨立自營) independent management. ～하다 manage 〔run〕 independently.

**독립자존**(獨立自存) independence and self-existence. ～하다 be self-existent; be self-sufficient.

**독립자활**(獨立自活) independence and self-support. ～하다 support *oneself.*

**독메**(獨—) a small mountain all by itself in the remote countryside.

**독무**(獨舞) a solo dance.

**독무대**(獨舞臺) 《경쟁자가 없음》 *one's* unrivaled sphere of activity; being without a rival; 《독판치다》 *one's* monopoly; being the sole master of the stage 〔field〕; 《혼자 연기함》 playing alone 〔by *oneself*〕. ¶ ～를 이루다 have the stage all to *oneself;* be 〔stand〕 without a rival / 그 경주는 그의 ～였다 He 「had no rivals 〔was without rivals〕 in the race. / 정계는 그의 ～다 He has the political stage all to himself. *or* He reigned supreme in the political world. / 토론회는 그의 ～였다 In the panel discussion he outshone all the participants. / 패션 이야기만 나오면 그녀의 ～다 When it comes to fashion, no one can match her.

**독물**(毒物) ① 《독·독약》 poison; 《유독물질》 poisonous stuff; a toxic 〔poisonous〕 substance. ¶ 위 속에서 아무런 ～도 검출되지 않았다 No poisonous substance was detected in the stomach. ② 《사람》 a vicious 〔ferocious, spiteful〕 person. ◉ ～검출 detection of poisonous matter. ～ 공포증 〖정신의학〗 toxiphobia. ～학 toxicology.

**독미나리**(毒—) 〖식물〗 a water hemlock.

**독방**(獨房) a single room; a room to *oneself;* a solitary 〔an isolated〕 cell (교도소의). ¶ ～살이 living in a single room; solitary confinement / ～에 감금되다 be placed in solitary confinement / ～을 쓰다 occupy a room to *oneself.* ◉ ～감금 solitary confinement 〔imprisonment〕.

**독백**(獨白) a monolog(ue); a soliloquy. ～하다 soliloquize; perform a monolog; say to *oneself;* utter a soliloquy. ◉ ～극 a monodrama.

**독버섯**(毒—) a toadstool; a poisonous mushroom.

**독벌레**(毒—) a poisonous insect.

**독법**(讀法) 《읽는 방법》 a way of reading 《Shakespeare》; a reading; how to read; 《발음》 pronunciation; 《해석》 a reading; an interpretation.

**독보적**(獨步的) (be) unique; peerless; unrivaled; matchless; unchallenged. ¶ ～ 위치에 있다 hold 〔stand in〕 a unique position / 그는 희극 배우로서 ～인 존재였다 As a comedian he stood without a peer.

**독본**(讀本) a reader; a reading book. ¶ 부～ a supplementary 〔side〕 reader / 영어 ～ an English reader.

**독부**(毒婦) a wicked 〔an evil〕 woman.

**독불**(獨佛) France and Germany. ¶ ～의 Franco-German.

**독불장군**(獨不將軍) ① 《제 주장하는》 a man of self-assertion; a self-satisfied person; a self-righteous man; a stubborn fellow (고집통이). ② 《겉도는 사람》 an isolated person; a person who is left out; an outcast.

**독사**(毒蛇) a venomous 〔poisonous〕 snake; a viper.

**독살**(毒殺) poisoning. ～하다 poison 《*a person*》; kill 〔murder〕 《a dog, *a person*》 with 〔by〕 poison. ◉ ～사건 a poisoning case. ～자 a poisoner.

**독살림**(獨—) an independent life. ～하다 live independently; keep house for *oneself.* ¶ 부모를 떠나 ～하다 live independently of *one's* parents; support *oneself* without relying on *one's* parents.

**독살부리다**(毒殺—) give vent to *one's* spite; act spitefully; act wickedly 〔in a vicious manner〕.

**독살스럽다**(毒殺—) (be) venomous; wicked; malicious; spiteful; vicious. ¶ 독살스럽게 spitefully; malignantly; virulently / 독살스러운 여편네 a spiteful woman; a vicious woman / 독살스럽게 말하다 use spiteful 〔virulent〕 language / 독살스럽게 욕하다 abuse wickedly 〔viciously〕.

**독살풀이**(毒殺—) ～하다 go at 《*a person*》 in a wicked manner; give vent to *one's* spite.

**독생자**(獨生子) 〖기독교〗 (Jesus Christ,) the only begotten Son (of God).

**독서**(讀書) reading. ～하다 read a book. ¶ ～용 안경 reading glasses / ～를 좋아하는 사람 a booklover / ～를 좋아하다

be fond of reading; take kindly to books / ～삼매에 빠지다 be buried in books; be absorbed in reading / 널리 ～하다 read widely 〔extensively〕 / 밤늦게까지 ～하다 sit up late reading books / 요즘 젊은이들은 별로 ～를 하지 않는다 Young people nowadays do not do much reading.

◉ ～가 a reader; a great reader (다독가); a man of wide reading (독서 범위가 넓은 사람). ～경향 readers' interest. ～계(界) the reading public 〔world〕. ～광(狂) a bookworm; a literary glutton. ～력 《cultivate》 *one's* reading ability. ～법 a method of reading (a book). ～실 a reading room; a private library. ～욕(慾) a desire for reading. ～주간 Book Week. ～회 a reading club 〔circle〕.

**독선**(獨善) self-righteousness〔-importance〕; self-complacency. ¶ ～적(인) self-righteous 《behavior》; self-opinionated; self-complacent / ～적으로 self-righteously / ～과 특권 의식에 사로잡혀 법의 침해를 정당화하다 justify any violation of law out of self-righteousness and sense of privilege / 그는 종종 ～적으로 행동한다 He often behaves 「self-righteously 〔complacently, in a self-centered manner〕. ◉ ～적 관료(官僚) self-righteous bureaucrats. ～주의 self-righteousness.

**독설**(毒舌) a malicious 〔venomous, poisonous〕 tongue. ¶ ～을 퍼붓다 speak with acrimony; use *one's* malicious tongue; make blistering remarks 《about, on》; wag *one's* slanderous tongue 《at》; give 《*a person*》 a tongue=lashing.

◉ ～가 a malicious person: 그는 ～가다 He has a spiteful 〔sharp〕 tongue.

**독성**(毒性) virulence; toxicity; toxic 〔poisonous〕 character. ¶ ～이 있는 virulent; poisonous; toxic; toxicant / ～이 없는 nonpoisonous; nontoxic; nonvirulent. ◉ ～기준 a toxity level.

**독소**(毒素) a toxin; poisonous substance 〔matter〕. ¶ ～ 조항 a poisonous clause 〔article〕. ◉ 항(抗)～an antitoxin.

**독송**(讀誦) recitation; intonation. ～하다 read aloud; recite; intone.

**독수**(毒手) a dastardly 〔dirty〕 trick; an evil ruse; vicious means 〔clutch〕; a trap. ¶ 악한의 ～에 걸리다〔를 벗어나다〕 fall into 〔escape from〕 the clutches 〔claws〕 of a villain.

**독수공방**(獨守空房) a woman's solitary life in her husband's absence; living in solitude. ～하다 live alone; lead a solitary life; remain true to *one's* husband in his absence. ¶ ～을 지키는 아내 a grass widow; a lonely wife.

**독수리**(禿—) an eagle; a vulture.

**독순술**(讀脣術) lip-reading. ¶ ～로 해독하다 lip-read.

**독습**(獨習) self-study; self-teaching. ⇨ 자습(自習). ¶ 기타를 ～하다 learn to play 〔practice on〕 the guitar by *oneself.*

**독시**(毒矢) a poisoned arrow.

**독시하다**(毒弑—) poison 《*one's* superior》; kill 《*one's* superior》 by poison.

**독식**(獨食) monopoly. ～하다 monopolize; engross; have 〔keep〕 《*a thing*》 to *oneself.*

**독신**(獨身) a single life; bachelorhood (남자); spinsterhood (여자); celibacy (종교적인). ¶ ～의 single; unmarried / ～이다 be 〔remain〕 single; be unmarried / ～으로 살다 live 〔stay〕 single; live 〔lead〕 a bachelor's 〔spinster's〕 life; bach (it) 《미속어》 / ～으로 마음편하게 살다 live in single blessedness / (이혼하여) 다시 ～이 되다 return to single status / 평생을 ～으로 살다 remain unmarried for life; continue single all *one's* life; live and die single / 저분은 ～입니까 아니면 결혼한 사람입니까 Is he a bachelor or a married man?

◉ ～귀족 a well-off unattached young man 〔woman〕. ～생활 a single 〔an unmarried〕 life; celibacy. ～숙부〔숙모〕 *one's* 「bachelor uncle 〔maiden aunt〕. ～자 an unmarried person; a single man 〔woman〕; 《남자》 a bachelor; a lone wolf 《속어》; 《여자》 a spinster; a bachelor girl; an old maid (나이 먹은): ～자 아파트 《live in》 a bachelor apartment. ～주의 celibacy; bachelorism; 《여자의》 old-maidism: ～주의자 a celibate; a celibatarian.

**독신**(篤信) earnest belief; devotion. ～하다 believe earnestly; be devoted to 《a religion》. ◉ ～자 a devotee 《of》; a devout believer 《in》.

**독신**(瀆神) blasphemy. ～하다 blaspheme 《the name of God》.

**독실**(篤實) sincerity; faithfulness. ～하다 (be) sincere; earnest; faithful; true. ¶ ～한 사람 a man of sincerity; a true gentleman; good men and true [총칭]. 「roomette (침대차의).

**독실**(獨室) a single 〔private〕 room; a

**독심**(毒心) malice; spite; venom. ¶ ～을 먹다 be filled with spite.

**독심술**(讀心術) mind 〔thought〕 reading; telepathy. ◉ ～사(師) a mind 〔thought〕 reader; a telepathist.

**독아**(毒牙) a (poison) fang. ¶ …의 ～에 걸리다 fall a victim 〔prey〕 to…; fall 〔get〕 into the claws 〔clutches〕 of…; be made a victim of….

**독액**(毒液) poisonous liquid 〔juice, sap, medicine〕; venom (독사 등의).

**독약**(毒藥) (a) poisonous drug 〔medicine〕; (a) poison. ¶ ～을 타다 put poison into 《food》; mix poison in / ～을 먹다 take poison / ～을 먹이다 poison 《*a person*》. ◉ ～학 toxicology.

**독어**(獨語) German; the German language. ◉ ～독문학과 the department of German language and literature.

**독연**(獨演) a solo performance; a recital; a solo (*pl.* ～s, -li). ⇨ 독주(獨奏).

**독염**(毒焰) a poisonous flame.

**독오르다**(毒—) become spiteful 〔venomous〕.

**독일**(獨逸) Germany. ¶ ～의 German; Germanic. ◉ ～계 미국인 a German=American. ～어 German; the German language. ～ 연방 공화국 the Federal Republic of Germany. ～인 a German; the Germans [총칭]; a Jerry 《영군 속어》.

**독자**(獨子) the 〔*one's*〕 only son.

**독자**(獨自) *one's* self. ¶ ～의 《개인의》 individual; personal; 《유일한》 unique; 《독특한》 (of) *one's* own; original / ～적인 personal; individual; independent 《views, standpoint, position, *etc.*》/ ～적인 입장에서 from an independent standpoint / ～적인 문체 an original 〔a peculiar, a unique〕 style / ～적인 행동을 취하다 go *one's* own way; act independently of others / 이윽고 그들은 ～적인 방법으로 사업을 시작했다 Soon they started business in a fashion unique to themselves. ◉ ～성 individuality; originality. ～조사 an independent investigation 《of》.

**독자**(讀者) [일반적] a reader; the reading public (독서계); 《신문·잡지의》 a reader; a subscriber (구독자); the audience [총칭]. ¶ ～의 소리 the reader's voice / ～가 많다 《신문·잡지의》 have a large circle of subscribers; have 〔enjoy〕 a large circulation; 《책의》 be widely read / ～들이 원하는 것을 찾아내기 위해 계획된 전국적인 ～ 여론 조사 a nationwide readership survey designed to find out what readers want / 개정판에서는 ～의 견해가 반영되어 있다 Readers' comments and opinions are reflected in the revised edition.
◉ ～란 the readers' column; letters to the editor. ～층 a class of readers; a readership: 이 잡지들은 각각 ～층이 다르다 Each of these magazines has its own class of subscribers.

**독작하다**(獨酌—) drink alone; drink without a companion; drink by *oneself.*

**독장수셈** an unreliable account; a fruitless 〔vain〕 effort. ¶ ～을 하다 count chickens before they are hatched; sell the skin before one has killed the bear.

**독장치다**(獨場—) play a one-man show; reign supreme in a field; prove *oneself* to be sole master of a situation; stand without rivals; 《독점》 monopolize. ¶ 문예계에서 ～ reign supreme in the literary world / 토론회에서 ～ take over a discussion / 이야기를 독장쳐서 하다 monopolize the talk.

**독재**(獨裁) dictatorship; despotism; autocracy; absolute rule. ～하다 have 《a country》 under *one's* despotic rule; hold an absolute authority 《over》. ¶ ～적(으로) dictatorial(ly); despotic(ally); autocratic(ally) / 당시 우리 나라는 군부 ～가 행해지고 있었다 Our country was under a military dictatorship in those days.
◉ ～국가 a despotic 〔an autocratic〕 state; a dictatorship. ～군주 a despotic monarch; a despot; an absolute ruler: ～ 군주국 an absolute monarchy. ～자 a dictator; an autocrat; a despot. ～정치 dictatorship; dictatorial government: ～ 정치를 펴다 establish 〔set up〕 a dictatorship; impose one=man rule 《on》. ～주의 dictatorship; despotism.

**독전**(督戰) urging the soldiers to fight vigorously; leading in battle. ～하다 urge the soldiers to fight; lead in battle. ◉ ～대 a supervising unit.

**독점**(獨占) exclusive possession; monopoly; monopolization. ～하다 monopolize 《power》; 《고어》 engross 《the market》; keep 〔have〕 《*a thing*》 to *oneself;* enjoy an exclusive possession 〔use〕 of. ⇨ 독차지. ¶ ～적 monopolistic; exclusive / ～ 규제 및 공정 거래에 관한 법률 the Monopoly Regulations

and Fair Trade Law / 시장을 ～하다 monopolize a market / 이야기를 ～하다 monopolize the conversation / 방을 ～하다 have a room all to *oneself* / 이익을 ～하다 monopolize the gains; get all the benefits without division / …의 사랑을 ～하다 monopolize 〔engross〕 *a person's* love / 인기를 ～하다 have a lock 〔monopoly〕 on popularity / 그 기업은 시장을 ～했다 That enterprise monopolized the market.
◉ ～가격 a monopoly price. ～권 (the right to) a monopoly; an exclusive 〔a sole〕 right. ～금지법 《be against》 the Antimonopoly 〔Antitrust〕 Law 〔Act〕: 저 회사는 ～ 금지법 위반으로 고발되었다 That company was charged with (a) violation of the Antimonopoly Law. ～사업〔기업〕 a monopolistic enterprise 〔undertaking〕. ～시장 a monopolistic market. ～욕 a desire to have entire 〔exclusive〕 possession: 그녀는 ～욕이 강하다 She always wants to keep everything all for herself. ～이윤(利潤) monopoly profit. ～자 a monopolizer; a monopolist; a sole owner. ～자본(주의) monopolistic capital(ism): ～자본이 지배하는 산업 monopoly-controlled industries. ～주의 monopolism. ～화 monopolization. ～회사 a monopoly.

**독점판매**(獨占販賣) an exclusive sale. ～하다 make an exclusive sale 《of》. ¶ ～권을 주다 give the sole selling rights 〔the franchise〕 / ～의 특약을 맺다 enter into a special contract for the sole agency / 그 회사는 석유 ～권을 갖고 있다 The firm has a monopoly on 〔of〕 oil sales. ◉ ～점 a sole agent 〔agency〕.

**독종**(毒種) 《사람》 a malicious 〔venomous〕 person; a brute; a person of fierce character; 《짐승》 a fierce animal.

**독주**(毒酒) ① 《독한 술》 hard liquor; strong spirits. ② 《독약을 탄》 poisoned liquor.

**독주**(獨走) 《혼자 뜀》 running alone; 《앞질러 달림》 running far ahead of 《*a person*》; a walkover 《구어》. ～하다 run alone without a rival; leave others far behind; have a walkover. ¶ B팀이 선두로 ～하고 있다 B team is on top now. / 마지막 한 바퀴는 그녀의 ～였다 She left all the other runners far behind on the last lap. / 이번 선거는 그의 ～가 될 것이다 He will be elected virtually unopposed this time.

**독주**(獨奏) 〖음악〗 a recital; a solo (*pl.* ～s, -li). ～하다 play 〔perform, give〕 a solo; play 《it》 solo 〔unaccompanied〕. ◉ ～곡 a solo. ～자 a soloist. ～회 《give, have》 a solo; a recital: 피아노 ～회 a piano solo 〔recital〕.

**독지가**(篤志家) 《자선가》 a benevolent 〔charitable〕 person; a philanthropist; a volunteer (자원봉사자); a supporter. ¶ 익명의 ～ an anonymous benefactor / ～들의 찬조를 바라다 solicit the support of those who are specially interested in the project.

**독직**(瀆職) (official) corruption; corrupt practices; 《수회》 bribery; malversation; graft 《미》. ～하다 practice corruption; receive a bribe; graft 《미》. ¶ 그는 ～ 혐의를 받고 있었다 He was suspected of having taken the bribe. / 그는 ～을 철저히 조사했다 He investigated the corruption thoroughly. ◉ ～공무원 a corrupt public official; a grafter 《미》. ～사건 a corruption scandal; a bribery case. ～죄 bribery; a charge of misconduct in office. ～행위 corrupt practices.

**독차지**(獨—) exclusive possession; having 〔keeping〕 all to *oneself;* monopolizing. ～하다 have 〔keep〕 all to *oneself;* possess exclusively; monopolize; engross. ⇨ 독점. ¶ 유산을 ～하다 have all the inheritance to *oneself* / 아버지의 사랑을 ～하다 get all of *one's* father's love / 이익을 ～하다 take all the profit / 그는 상을 ～했다 He carried away all the prizes.

**독창**(獨唱) a (vocal) solo; a recital. ～하다 sing a solo; give a vocal solo. ◉ ～곡 a solo piece. ～자 a soloist. ～회 a (solo) vocal recital.

**독창**(獨創) originality. ～하다 create uniquely; originate. ¶ ～적(인) (being) unique; original; creative / ～적인 연구 a trailblazing study / 그녀에겐 ～적인 데가 있다 She has an original mind. / 이것은 실로 ～적인 아이디어다 This is quite an original idea. / 우리는 좀더 ～적인 작품을 기대하고 있다 We are expecting more original works.
◉ ～력 creative power 〔talent〕; originality: ～력을 기르다 develop originality / ～력을 보이다 show originality 《in》 / ～력이 없다 be wanting 〔lacking〕 in originality. ～성 originality: 그는 ～성이 풍부하다 He is rich in originality.

**독채**(獨—) 《live in》「an unshared 〔a separate〕 house.

**독초**(毒草) 《독풀》 a poisonous herb; a noxious plant 〔weed〕; 《담배》 strong tobacco.

**독촉**(督促) pressing; a demand; dunning; a call (세금 등의). ~하다 press 《*a person* for》; urge 《*a person* to *do*》; 《빚을》 dun 《*a person* for the payment of a debt》; remind 《*a person*》 of 《a debt》. ¶ 그에게 빚의 상환을 ~했다 I pressed 〔pushed〕 him for payment of his debt. / 그에게 속히 답장하라고 ~했다 I demanded a prompt answer of him. / 그에게 속히 오도록 ~하겠다 I'll urge him to come quickly. ◉ ~장 a demand note; 《지불의》 a collection letter; a (letter of) reminder; 《빚의》 a dunning letter 〔note〕; a dun.

**독충**(毒蟲) a poisonous 〔noxious〕 insect.

**독침**(毒針) 《곤충 등의》 a poison sting(-er); 《바늘》 a poisoned needle.

**독탕**(獨湯) a private bath. ¶ ~에서 목욕하다 take a bath at a private bathroom.

**독특**(獨特) ~하다 (be) peculiar 《to》 (고유한); unique (달리 없는); original; special; characteristic 《of》 (특징 있는). ¶ 그의 ~한 웅변 his inimitable eloquence / ~한 방법으로 《solve a problem》 in *one's* own way / 오렌지에는 ~한 향기가 있다 The orange has a scent all 〔of〕 its own. *or* The orange has a characteristic smell. / 이 관습은 한국의 ~한 것이다 This custom is 〔This is a custom〕 unique 〔peculiar〕 to Korea.

**독파**(讀破) ~하다 read 《a book》 (all the way) through; go through; finish 《a book》. ¶ 수많은 책을 ~하다 read a world of books.

**독판**(獨—) *one's* unrivaled sphere of activity; monopoly. ⇨독무대. ¶ ~(을) 치다 stand unchallenged 〔unrivaled〕; monopolize.

**독필**(毒筆) a spiteful pen; a pen dipped in gall. ¶ ~을 휘두르다 dip *one's* pen in gall; wield a spiteful pen; write 〔attack〕 with acrimony 〔rancor, bitterness〕.

**독하다**(毒—) ① 《유독하다》 (be) poisonous; harmful; injurious; baneful; noxious. ¶ 독한 가스 poisonous gas. ② 《맛·성질이》 (be) strong; severe; intense; sharp. ¶ 독한 냄새 sharp odor 《of medicine》 / 독한 담배〔술〕 strong tobacco 〔drink〕 / 독한 감기 a bad cold. ③ 《표독하다》 (be) vicious; spiteful; bitter; malicious; venomous; atrocious. ¶ 독한 여자 a spiteful 〔vicious〕 woman / 독한 짓 an atrocious act / 독한 말을 하다 use spiteful 〔malicious〕 language. ④ 《꿋꿋하다》 (be) firm; dogged; tough; unflinching; unyielding. ¶ 독한 마음 firm resolution; stout-heartedness; a dogged spirit / 마음을 독하게 먹고 공부하다 study with firm resolve.

**독학**(篤學) a love of learning; devotion to *one's* studies. ~하다 devote *oneself* to *one's* studies; study hard. ¶ ~의 studious; assiduous; hard-working; given 〔devoted〕 to study. ◉ ~자 a devoted scholar; a man of erudition; a diligent student.

**독학**(獨學) self-study; self-teaching; self-education. ~하다 study by *oneself;* teach *oneself* 《English》; learn untutored; educate *oneself;* study 《English》 without a teacher. ¶ ~의 self-educated; self-taught; unschooled 《experts》 / ~으로 읽고 쓰기를 배우다 teach *oneself* how to read and write / ~으로 독일어를 배우다 learn 〔study〕 German「without a teacher 〔on *one's* own, by *oneself*〕. ◉ ~자 a self-educated 〔self-taught〕 man; a learner without a teacher; an autodidact.

**독해력**(讀解力) ability to read and understand; (reading) comprehension.

**독행**(篤行) 《독실한 행실》 a good deed; upright conduct; 《자선행위》 an act of charity; a benevolent 〔warm-hearted〕 act.

**독혈**(毒血) 〖한의〗 bad 〔toxic〕 blood. ◉ ~증 〖의학〗 toxemia; blood poisoning.

**독회**(讀會) a reading. ¶ 의안은 제 2~ 생략으로 가결되었다 The bill was passed, the discussion stage having been dispensed with. ◉ 제1 ~ the 1st reading; the committee stage: 의안은 제1 ~에 회부되었다 The bill was read for the first time. 제2〔3〕 ~ the 2nd 〔3rd〕 reading; the discussion 〔voting〕 stage.

**독후감**(讀後感) *one's* impressions of a book 〔an article, *etc.*〕.

**돈**[1] 《금전》 money; 《현금》 cash; ready money; 《금화》 gold; 《경화》 (a) coin; 《지폐》 a bill 《미》; a bank note 《영》; 《금액》 a sum; 《재산》 wealth; riches. ¶ 많은〔적은〕 돈 a large 〔small〕 sum of money / 돈 걱정 financial 〔money〕 worries / 돈 문제 a matter of money; money matters / 돈타령 talking about money all the time / 부정한 돈 ill-gotten money / 돈 때문에 일하다 work merely for money / 돈과 인연이 없다 be doomed to poverty.

> (용법) 보통, 「돈」이라고 막연히 말할 때는 불가산명사인 money를 쓴다. 「경화」나 「지폐」를 개별적으로 말할 때는 a 500-won coin (500원 짜리 동전), a thousand-won bill (천원짜리 지폐)처럼 가산명사로 취급된다. 또, moneys 또는 monies로 복수형을 쓰게 되면 특별한 뜻이 된다. different moneys of different countries (여러나라의 갖가지 돈) / tax moneys(세수입) / foreign aid monies(외국 원조 자금)

¶ 인간 만사 돈 세상 Money is everything. *or* Money governs 〔Gold rules〕 the world. / 돈 떨어지니 정 떨어진다 When poverty comes in at the door, love flies out at the window. *or* Out of pocket, out of mind. / 쉽게 번 돈은 쉽게 없어진다 Ill got, ill spent. *or* Lightly come, lightly go. / 돈은 돌고 도는것 Money changes hands. *or* Money moves from pocket to pocket. *or* Money comes and goes. / 돈만 있으면 개도 멍첨지라 《속담》 Money often makes the man. / 돈만 있으면 귀신도 부릴 수 있다 Money makes the world go round. *or* Money (is the key that) opens all doors. *or* Money makes the mare (to) go.

돈의: 돈의 money; monetary; pecuniary / 돈의 힘 the power of money 〔wealth〕 / 돈의 힘으로 by force of money / 이것은 결국 돈의 문제이다 It is after all a matter of money.

돈이: 돈이 많이 드는 자동차 money-eating〔-consuming〕 automobiles / 돈이 되는〔안되는〕 일 profitable 〔unprofitable〕 work; a job that pays 〔doesn't pay〕 / 돈이 있다 have (a lot of) money; be rich; be well off; be in funds 〔cash〕 / 돈이 없다 have no money; be poor; be badly off; be out of funds 〔cash〕 / 돈이 남아돌다 have more money than one can spend; be rolling in money 《구어》 / 돈이 생기다 get the money; grow 〔get〕 rich / 돈이 모이다 come to have some money / 돈이 필요하다 be in want 〔need〕 of money / 당장 돈이 필요하다 need ready money / 돈이 마르다 money is scarce / 돈이 들다 take 〔cost〕 (*one*) a lot of money; be expensive / 돈이 되다 be profitable; be paying; be lucrative.

¶ 돈이 원수다 All is because of money. *or* Lack of money is one's sorrow. / 돈이 돈을 번다 Money begets 〔makes〕 money. / 돈이 장사라 《속담》 Money is power. / 돈이 행세하는 세상이다 Money talks in this world of ours. / 돈이 암만 있어도 행복은 못 산다 No amount of money can buy happiness. / 걱정 말게 돈이면 안되는 게 없다네 Don't worry. Money talks. / 차 수리에 많은 돈이 들었다 It cost me a lot of money to 「repair my car 〔have my car repaired〕. / 돈이 필요하시다면 언제든 말씀만 하십시오 If it's money you need, you only have to ask. / 마침 가진 돈이 없다 I have no cash on me now.

돈에: 돈에 궁하다〔쪼들리다〕 be pinched 〔hard pressed〕 for money; be in want 〔need〕 of money; be in financial difficulties / 돈에 몸을 팔다 sell *oneself* / 돈에 정신이 없다 be eager for money; be mercenary / 돈에 눈이 어두워지다 be blind with money; be lured 〔tempted〕 by gold / 돈에 맛을 들이다 get a taste for money; love money / 사랑에 속고 돈에 울다 be lucky neither at cards nor at love.

돈을: 돈을 벌다 make 〔earn〕 money / 돈을 많이 벌다 make 〔amass〕 a fortune; make a pile (of money) / 돈을 크게 벌 수 있는 일거리 a lucrative 〔profitable〕 work; a fat job; a gainful work / 돈을 모으다 save money; put money by; lay by money; amass money / 돈을 변통하다 get money somehow; manage to raise money / 돈을 꾸다 borrow money / 돈을 갚다 repay; pay back; return money / 돈을 꾸어 주다 lend 〔loan 《미》〕 《*a person*》 money / 돈을 은행에 예금하다 put 〔deposit〕 money in a bank / 돈을 아무에게 맡기다 trust *a person* with money / 돈을 내다 《지불》 pay 《for》; 《기부》 contribute money to; 《투자》 invest in; 《출자》 finance; offer money / 돈을 들이다 put in money; spend money 《on clothes》 / 돈을 마련하다 raise money; get the money ready / 돈을 요령있게 쓰다 spend money well; make the most of *one's* money; turn *one's* money to good account / 돈을 물쓰듯〔낭비〕하다 spend 〔squander〕 money

like water; spend money like it grows on trees / 돈을 활용 않고 놔두다 leave *one's* money idle / 돈을 걸다 bet money 《on》; bet with money / 돈을 먹이다 《뇌물》 bribe; grease the hand 〔palm〕 of 《*a person*》 / 돈을 구하려고 쩔쩔 매다 be at a loss how to raise money / 돈을 구하려고 동분서주하다 busy *oneself* to get a loan / 담보물을 잡히고 돈을 빌리다 borrow money on *one's* property.
¶ 그녀는 아이들 교육에는 돈을 아끼지 않는다 She doesn't begrudge what she has to pay for her children's education. / 당신을 위해서라면 기꺼이 돈을 내겠다 Since it's you who's asking for money, I'll gladly let you have it.
돈으로: 돈으로 매수 안 되는 사람 a soul above money / 돈으로 바꾸다 turn 〔convert〕 《*a thing*》 into money; cash 《a check》 / 돈으로 살 수 없다 cannot be got 〔had〕 for money.
¶ 돈으로 된다면야 얼마든지 내겠다 I will go to any expense if money can settle it. / 「이 세상에 돈으로 안 움직일 사람 있나」라고 그는 빈정거렸다 He said cynically that every man has his price.

**돈²** 《무게》 a *ton* (3.7565 grams).

**돈가스**(豚—) a pork cutlet.

**돈구멍** 《돈줄》 a source of money; a source of income. ¶ ～을 뚫다 find a way of getting 〔raising, borrowing〕 some money.

**돈궤**(—櫃) a cash 〔money〕 box; a 「strongbox.

**돈꿰미** 《옛날, 엽전 따위의》 a string for threading coins.

**돈내기** a bet; 《도박》 gambling. ～하다 bet; stake; gamble.

**돈냥**(—兩) a small sum of money; some money; a pretty 〔fine〕 penny. ¶ ～이나 있는 사람 a well-to-do person.

**돈놀이** moneylending; usury (고리 대금). ～하다 loan; lend money at interest; run a moneylending business; 《고리의》 practice usury. ◉ ～꾼 a moneylender; a usurer.

**돈단무심**(頓斷無心) ～하다 pay no attention to; be indifferent about 〔to〕.

**돈대**(墩臺) an eminence; a high 〔an elevated〕 ground; heights.

**돈더미** a heap of money. ¶ ～에 올라앉다 suddenly get 〔become〕 rich.

**돈독**(—毒) an unhealthy taste for money. ¶ ～이 오른 사람 a person of mercenary spirit; a moneygrubber / ～이 오르다 become mercenary; acquire an unhealthy taste for money.

**돈독**(敦篤) ～하다 (be) sincere; simple and honest; courteous; friendly. ¶ 한미 관계를 ～히 하다 promote friendly relations between Korea and America / 삼촌은 우정이 ～한 사람이다 My uncle is true to his friends.

**돈맛** a taste for money; a love of money. ¶ ～을 알다 come to love money; learn the value 〔charm〕 of money / ～을 들이다 get 〔acquire〕 a taste for money; love money.

**돈머리** ① 《액수》 an amount of money; a sum (of money). ¶ ～수가 크다 be a large amount of money; be a tidy sum. ② 《일정액》 a given 〔definite〕 amount 〔sum〕 of money. ¶ ～가 들어맞다 a sum is correct / ～가 모자라다 be short (a certain sum) / ～를 맞추다 round the sum off.

**돈모**(豚毛) swine bristles.

**돈바르다** (be) narrow-minded; fussy; be hard to please.

**돈방석**(—方席) ¶ ～에 앉다 have a plenty of money; be well-off; be 「very rich 〔independently wealthy〕.

**돈벌이** moneymaking; earning 〔making〕 money. ～하다 make 〔earn〕 money. ¶ ～에 급급하다 be too much bent on moneymaking / ～에 약삭빠르다 be a shrewd man of business / ～를 잘하다 be clever at making money / ～ 잘 하는 사람 a moneymaker; a golden thumb 《속어》 / 그 일은 돈벌잇감이다 There is money in that job. *or* That's a fat job. / 그는 ～라면 무슨 짓이라도 한다 He'll do anything for money. / ～에만 급급하는 대학들이 있다는 것은 유감스런 일이다 It's regrettable that there are some money=hungry colleges.

**돈벼락** sudden 〔mushroom〕 wealth. ¶ ～을 맞다 strike it rich; gain quick riches; suddenly get 〔become〕 rich.

**돈복**(—福) luck with money. ¶ ～이 있다 be blessed with a chance to make money / ～이 터지다 hit a source of wealth.

**돈사**(豚舍) a pigsty; a pigpen.

**돈사**(頓死) a sudden death. ⇨ 급사.

**돈세탁**(—洗濯) money laundering. ¶ 그는 미국에서 마약 거래와 ～으로 무기 징역에 400만 달러의 벌금형을 선고받았다 He has been sentenced to life imprisonment and fined ＄4 million for drug trafficking and money laundering in U.S.

**돈수**(頓首) 《편지 맺음말》 Yours sincerely; Yours very respectfully.

**돈아**(豚兒) my son; my boy.

**돈육**(豚肉) pork.

**돈좌**(頓挫) a setback; a hitch. ~하다 be frustrated; be held up; be checked 〔deadlocked〕; be brought to a standstill.

**돈주머니** a purse; a moneybag; a pocketbook 《미》. ¶ ~가 가볍다 have a light purse / ~가 텅 비다 *one's* purse becomes empty / ~가 바닥이 나다 spend *one's* last penny; spend all the money *one* has / ~를 졸라매다〔풀어놓다〕 tighten 〔loosen〕 the purse strings / ~의 끈을 꽉 쥐고 있다 hold 〔control〕 the purse strings.

**돈줄** a line of credit; a source of money. ¶ ~을 잡다 find a supplier of funds 〔a financial supporter〕 / ~이 떨어지다 lose *one's* financial backing.

**돈지갑**(—紙匣) a purse; a pocketbook; a wallet 《미》.

**돈지랄하다** spend money in a crazy way.

**돈질** handling the money in gambling. ~하다 handle the money in gambling.

**돈치기** 《play》 chuck-farthing; coin=tossing.

**돈키호테** Don Quixote. ¶ ~식의 quixotic.

**돈팔이** ① 《돈벌이》 obsession with making money. ② ⇨돌팔이.

**돈표**(—票) a voucher; a check.

**돈푼** little money; a small sum of money; a small fortune; peanuts 《속어》. ¶ ~깨나 모으다 save a pretty penny; make a small fortune / 그는 ~이나 있는지 모르나 큰돈은 없을 게다 He may have some money but not much, I bet. / 그는 ~이나 있다고 빼긴다 He is proud of the "peanuts" he has.

**돈후안** 《방탕아》 a Don Juan; a libertine.

**돋구다** ① 《높이다》 raise; make higher; 《흙 따위를》 heap 〔pile〕 up. ¶ 안경 도수를 ~ make *one's* eyeglasses stronger / 흙을 ~ heap up earth. ② 《자극하다》 excite; incite; stimulate; stir up. ¶ 수요를 ~ whip up demand / 식욕을 ~ whet 〔stimulate〕 *one's* appetite; give an edge to *one's* appetite / 흥미를 ~ (a)rouse 〔excite, stir up〕 《*a person's*》 interest 《in》.

**돋다** ① 《해·달이》 come up; rise. ¶ 해는 동쪽에서 돋는다 The sun rises in the east. ② 《싹 따위가》 grow; sprout; bud; spring up; come up. ¶ 날개가 ~ grow wings / 싹〔움〕이 ~ put out 〔forth〕 buds 〔shoots〕; come into bud / 이가 ~ a tooth 「develops 〔come through〕; [사람이 주어] cut a tooth; teethe (젖먹이의) / 풀이 ~ grass grows 〔sprouts〕; put forth 〔push out〕 new shoots. ③ 《피부에》 come out; form; erupt. ¶ 두드러기가 ~ *one's* nettle rash has erupted 〔broken out〕 / 그런 것을 먹으면 두드러기가 돋는다 That would bring you out in a rash.

**돋보기** ① 《노안경》 spectacles for the aged; farsighted (eye)glasses. ② 《안경》 (reading) glasses; spectacles. ¶ ~를 끼다 wear 〔put on〕 (reading) glasses / ~안경 필요하신 분 1번 창구에 말씀해 주십시오 《게시》 Reading glasses available at window 1. ③ 《화경》 a magnifying glass; a magnifier. ¶ ~로 보다 see through a magnifying glass.

**돋보다** see with a favorable eye; see in a favorable light.

**돋보이다, 돋뵈다** look better (than actually is); set off; look 〔show〕 to advantage; make a fine show. ¶ 돋보이게 하다 set 《it》 off (to advantage); show 《it》 to advantage; make 《*a thing*》 look better / 가구를 이렇게 놓으니 훨씬 돋보인다 The furniture looks much better in this position. / 회색 옷은 붉은 타이를 돋보이게 한다 A gray suit tends to set off a red tie nicely. / 그녀는 흰 드레스를 입으니 훨씬 돋보인다 She looks to advantage in white dress. / 그 옷은 그녀의 자태를 한층 더 돋뵈게 한다 The clothes set off her figure to advantage. / 그 목걸이는 당신 드레스를 매우 돋보이게 한다 The necklace sets your dress off very well.

**돋우다** ① 《심지를》 raise; turn 《*a thing*》 up. ¶ (등잔의) 심지를 ~ turn up the wick (of a lamp).

② (***a***) 《높이다》 raise; make higher; bank. ¶ 땅을 ~ raise the ground level / 길을 ~ bank the road / 베개를 ~ make *one's* pillow higher; raise *one's* pillow. (***b***) 《목청을》 raise; lift; elevate. ¶ 목청을 ~ raise (lift) *one's* voice / 목청을 돋우어 꾸짖다 rebuke 《*a person*》 with a raised voice / 그런 사소한 일에 목청을 돋울 필요는 없다 You need not shout at such a trifle. *or* You ought to be more quiet about so small a matter.

③ 《기운 등을》 raise; lift; elevate; heighten; encourage; cheer up;

invigorate. ¶ 기운을 ~ raise 〔lift〕 *one's* spirits; cheer up / 사기를 ~ raise 〔improve, lift〕 the morale 《of the men》; 《사물이》 give a stimulus to the fighting spirit 《of the men》 / 용기를 ~ encourage; embolden; give 《*a person*》 courage. ④ 《감정 등을》 incite; stimulate; gall; excite; stir up; provoke; aggravate. ¶ 감정을 ~ stimulate 〔stir up〕 《another's》 feelings 〔sentiment〕 / 화를 ~ make 《*a person*》 madder; aggravate 《*a person's*》 anger; provoke 《*a person*》 to anger; offend 《*a person*》. ⑤ 《부추기다》 incite 〔instigate〕 *a person* 《to *do*》; egg 〔spur〕 *a person* on 《to *do*》. ¶ 싸움을 ~ egg 《*a person*》 on to fight with 《*another*》; make 《*persons*》 quarrel.

**돋을무늬** a raised figure; an embossed figure. ¶ ~를 내다 raise; emboss.

**돋을볕** morning sunshine.

**돋을새김** 〖조각〗 a (carved 〔sculptured〕) relief; (a) relief sculpture 〔carving〕. ⇨부조(浮彫).

**돋치다** 《나오다》 grow; rise 〔sprout〕 up; come out 〔up〕. ¶ 가시 돋친 말 harsh language; stinging 〔cutting, biting, barbed〕 words / 날개가 ~ grow wings / 날개 돋치듯 팔리다 sell like hot cakes 〔wildfire〕.

**돌**[1] ① 《첫돌》 the first birthday 〔anniversary〕. ¶ 돌을 맞다 mark 〔celebrate〕 *one's* first birthday / 돌이 다가오다 the first anniversary is coming around. ② 《주년(周年)》 an anniversary; one full year. ¶ 다섯 돌 the fifth anniversary 《of》 / 창립 한 돌 맞이 기념 행사를 하다 observe the first anniversary of the opening / 집을 지은 지 두 돌이 된다 It is two years since I built the house.

**돌**[2] (a) stone; 《조약돌》 a pebble; a rock 《미》; a grit (쌀 등에 섞인); a flint (라이터 돌); 《보석》 a precious stone; a jewel. ¶ 둥근 돌 a round stone 〔pebble〕 / 모난 돌 a square stone / 돌이 많은 stony; full of stones; pebbly 《beaches》 / 돌로 쌓은 둑 a bank of stone / 돌집 a stone(-built) house / 돌에 새기다 carve 〔cut〕 in stone / 돌을 갈다 dress stone / 돌을 깔다 pave 《the road》 with stone / 돌을 던지다 throw a stone at 《a dog》; pelt 《*a person*》 with stones / 채석장에서 돌을 떠내다 quarry stone from a stone pit / 돌이 되다 turn to stone; petrify (석질화) / 돌을 줍다 pick up a stone 〔rock〕 / 도로에는 돌이 깔려 있다 The road is paved 〔flagged〕 with stone.

**돌가루** crushed rock; stone dust.

**돌감** a wild persimmon. ◉ ~나무 a wild persimmon tree.

**돌개바람** 《회오리 바람》 a whirlwind; a twister; a cyclone; a tornado.

**돌격**(突擊) a charge; a rush; an onrush; a dash; an assault (강습). ~하다 charge 《at, on》; make a dash at; rush 〔dash〕 《at》; make an assault upon; raid. ¶ 적을 향해 ~하다 make a dash at the enemy / 적진에 ~하다 rush 〔charge〕 the enemy's position. ◉ ~나팔 charge. ~대 shock troops; a storming party; commandos; raiders. ~전 a charge; an assault; an onslaught; a raid.

**돌결** the grain of a stone. ¶ ~이 곱다 〔거칠다〕 the stone has a fine 〔coarse〕 grain.

**돌계단**(一階段) (a flight of) stone steps; a stone stairway; a stone step (한 단). ¶ ~을 오르다〔내리다〕 go up 〔down〕 the stone steps / ~을 올라가면 학교 건물이 있다 A flight of stone steps leads (you) to a school building.

**돌계집** a barren 〔sterile〕 woman.

**돌고드름** 〖광물〗 a stalactite.

**돌고래**[1] 〖동물〗 a dolphin; a porpoise; a sea hog 〔pig〕. ◉ ~자리 〖천문〗 the Dolphin; Delphinus.

**돌고래**[2] 《방고래》 all-stone flues (of a Korean hypocaust).

**돌곪기다** 《a tumor》 fester within.

**돌공이** a stone pestle.

**돌관**(突貫) a charge; a rush. ~하다 charge 《on》; rush 《at》. ◉ ~공사 rush work; a rush job: ~공사를 하다 rush the construction work / ~공사로 집을 짓다 throw up a house.

**돌기**(突起) a projection; a protrusion; a protuberance; a swelling; 〖동물·식물〗 a process; a boss; 〖해부〗 a promontory. ~하다 stick out; rise; project; protrude; form a projection. ¶ ~한 projecting; protuberant; salient.

**돌기둥** a stone pillar 〔column〕.

**돌기와** a slate; slabs of stone for roofing. ◉ ~집 a slate-roofed house.

**돌김** 〖식물〗 laver stuck to underwater stone.

**돌나물** 〖식물〗 a sedum; a stonecrop.

**돌날** a baby's first birthday.

**돌능금** a wild apple; a crab apple.

**돌다** ① 《회전하다》 turn (round, around); go round; rotate; revolve; spin. ¶ 뱅뱅 ~ circle round; turn round and round; wheel / 팽이가 ~ a top spins / 시계 바늘과 반대 쪽으로 ~ turn 〔revolve〕 anticlockwise / 독수리가 빙빙 ~ an eagle circles 〔wheels〕 round / 지구는 태양의 주위를 돈다 The earth goes 〔moves, travels, revolves〕 around the sun. / 바퀴는 축을 중심으로 돈다 The wheel revolves on its axis. / 방이 눈 앞에서 빙글빙글 도는 것 같았다 It seemed to me that the room was spinning around. / 선풍기가 윙윙 돌고 있었다 The electric fan was working busily.

② 《순회하다》 make a round; walk *one's* beat; go *one's* rounds; patrol; 《유람하다》 tour 《Europe》; make a tour 《of Europe》; travel about 〔around〕. ¶ 공원을 한 바퀴 ~ take a walk around the park / 단골 거래처를 ~ go the rounds of *one's* customers / 담당 구역을 ~ make 〔go〕 *one's* rounds / 영업 사원이 주문받으러 지방을 ~ a salesman goes round the country for orders / 산책삼아 시내를 한 바퀴 ~ go round the city for a walk / 인사를 하며 ~ make a round of calls 〔visits〕 / 영남 지역을 ~ make a tour of the Yŏngnam district / 순경이 순찰을 돌고 있다 The policeman is 「on 〔patrolling, covering〕 his beat.

③ 《순환·유통하다》 circulate; pass current. ¶ 《물건이》 여러 손을 돌고 돌아 passing through many hands / 피는 체내를 돈다 Blood circulates through the body. / 약간의 위조지폐가 돌고 있다고 한다 It is said that some forged notes are in circulation. / 불경기로 돈이 잘 돌지 않는다 Money is tight owing to the business depression.

④ 《몸의 기능이》 work; function. ¶ 혀가 잘 ~ have a glib tongue; be quite a talker / 혀가 잘 돌지 않다 be tongue=tied; be unable to speak distinctly; *one's* speech is slurred (술취했을 때); have an impediment in *one's* speech (언어장애) / 머리가 잘 ~ *one's* brain works well; be quick-〔sharp-〕witted / 머리가 잘 돌지 않다 *one's* brain doesn't work well; be slow-witted 〔dull〕.

⑤ 《약·술기운 등이》 take effect. ¶ 기운이 돌기 시작하다 begin to feel the effect 《of》 / 술기운이 ~ be under the influence of liquor; be tipsy / 나는 취기가 꽤 돌았다 I was quite drunk. / 독이 온몸에 돌았다 The poison has passed into his system.

⑥ 《현기증이 나다》 be dizzy; get 〔feel〕 giddy. ¶ 눈이 핑핑 ~ be 〔feel〕 dizzy; feel 〔grow〕 vertiginous / 눈이 돌 정도로 바쁘다 I'm in a whirl of business. *or* I'm as busy as a bee.

⑦ 《회람되다》 pass 《from hand to hand》; 《돌아오다》 come 〔go〕 round; 《배부되다》 be distributed. ¶ 회람이 ~ a circular passes / 내 차례가 돌아왔다 My turn has come (around). / 다시 봄이 돌아왔다 Spring has come around again.

⑧ 《돌림병이》 prevail; be prevalent 〔wide-spread, epidemic〕. ¶ 감기가 ~ a cold is making the rounds / 온 동네에 홍역이 돌고 있다 Measles is raging throughout the village.

⑨ 《소문이》 circulate; be abroad; run 〔be〕 current; be put in circulation. ¶ 소문이 ~ a rumor is abroad / …이라는 소문이 돌고 있다 a rumor is abroad 〔current〕 about….

⑩ 《소생하다》 come round; be restored. ¶ 맥이 ~ *one's* pulse regains its beat 〔picks up its beat again〕 / 의식이 ~ regain 〔recover〕 consciousness; recover *one's* senses.

⑪ 《방향을 바꾸다》 turn; turn about; go around. ¶ 왼쪽으로 ~ turn to the left; turn left / 뒤로 ~ turn (a)round / 모퉁이를 ~ turn 〔go round〕 a corner / 반대당으로 ~ go into opposition / 정부 지지로 ~ swing over to the Administration.

⑫ 《우회하다》 go 〔come〕 round; go a long way round; take a roundabout way; make a detour; 《경유하다》 go 〔come〕 《home》 via 〔by way of〕. ¶ 우체국으로 ~ go round by the post office / 뒷문으로 돌아오시오 Come round to the back door. / 적의 배후로 ~ move around to the back of the enemy / 그녀는 알래스카를 돌아 귀국했다 She has returned home 「via 〔by way of〕 Alaska.

⑬ 《정신이》 go 〔run〕 mad; go 〔become〕 crazy 〔insane〕; lose *one's* mind 〔senses〕; 《구어》 go off *one's* head. ¶ 아무를 돌게 하다 drive *a person* mad 〔crazy, nuts〕 / 그녀는 너무나 슬퍼서 정신이 돌았다 She went 「mad 〔out of her mind〕 with grief. / 그런 짓을 하다니 자네 돌았나 You are mad 〔crazy〕 to do such a thing. *or* It is crazy of you to do a thing like that. ⑭ 《기타》 ¶ 눈물이 핑 ～ tears「come to 〔gather in〕 *one's* eyes; *one's* eyes swim 〔dim〕 with tears / 윤기가 ～ be glossy / 얼굴에 화색이 ～ have a good 〔healthy〕 complexion; look well; look rosy 《미》.

**돌다리** a stone bridge. ¶ ～도 두드려보고 건너다 look before *one* leaps; act with the utmost caution; make assurance double sure.

**돌담** a stone wall. ¶ ～을 두르다 surround with a stone wall.

**돌담불** a pile of stones; a rock pile.

**돌대** 《회전축》 the axis of rotation; a pivot.

**돌대가리** ① 《우둔》 a stupid person 〔fellow〕; a blockhead. ② 《완고》 a stubborn 〔an obstinate〕 person.

**돌덩이** a piece of stone; a stone. ¶ ～ 같다 be as hard as a rock 〔granite〕.

**돌도끼** a stone ax.

**돌돌** ① 《마는 모양》 into a roll 〔scroll, ball〕. ¶ 옷자락이 ～ 말리다 the edge of a coat are rolled up / 종이를 ～ 말다 roll up 〔twirl〕 a piece of paper / 잎새가 ～ 말리다 leaves are all curled up. ② 《구르는 모양》 rolling. ¶ ～ 구르다 roll over and over. ③ 《뭉치는 모양》 ¶ ～ 뭉치다 solidify in unity.

**돌돔** 〖어류〗 a parrotfish.

**돌떡** rice cake made for a baby's first birthday.

**돌라가다** pilfer; filch; steal; commit a theft. ¶ 볏단을 ～ steal a sheaf of rice / 우산을 ～ filch an umbrella.

**돌라놓다** ① 《둘러놓다》 put 《*things*》 in a circle. ② 《돌려놓다》 set 《*a thing*》 aside; put 《*a thing*》 aside.

**돌라맞추다** 《다른 것으로》 fix 《*a thing*》 as a substitute; make 《*a thing*》 a substitute; substitute; use 《*a thing* for》; turn 《*a thing* into》. ¶ 책상을 식탁으로 ～ turn a desk into a dinner table.

**돌라매다** ① 《새끼줄을》 tie 《*a thing*》 around. ¶ 허리에 밧줄을 ～ tie a rope around *one's* waist. ② 《이자를》 convert interest into principal.

**돌라방치다** substitute 《*a thing* for another》; make shift 《with》.

**돌라서다** stand in a circle.

**돌라주다** hand round; distribute; share (out); serve out 〔round〕; deal out 〔round〕. ¶ 배급품을 ～ distribute rations / 전단을 ～ distribute handbills / 선물을 ～ share gifts 《among》.

**돌라치다** ⇨ 돌라방치다.

**돌려내다** ① 《꾀어 빼내다》 lure 〔decoy〕 《*a person*》 out; entice 《*a person*》 away 《from》. ¶ 곰을 굴에서 ～ lure a bear out of its den / M회사에서 여배우를 ～ 《돈으로》 hire a screen actress away from M company / 그들은 그녀를 그 회사에서 돌려내려고 하였다 They tried to entice her away from the company. ② 《따돌리다》 leave 《*a person*》 out (in the cold); cast out.

**돌려놓다** change direction; turn (around); put the other way round. ¶ 책상을 ～ put a desk the other way round.

**돌려보내다** return; send back; let 《*a person*》 go back. ¶ 손님을 ～ turn away a guest (at the door) / 사자(使者)를 ～ send a messenger back / 아내를 친정에 ～ send back *one's* wife to her parents / 그 상품이 견본과 달라서 돌려보냈다 The article was sent back as not being up to sample. / 그를 어머니에게 돌려보내라 Send him back to his mother. / 불량품일 경우에는 돌려보낼 수 있다 You can return the goods if they are defective.

**돌려보다** read 《a magazine》 in turn; send 《a circular》 round 《to all the members》; pass 《a book》 around and read it; circulate 《a letter》 among 《the members》. ¶「전쟁과 평화」 비디오 테이프를 ～ watch a video "War and Peace" in turn.

**돌려쓰다** borrow 《money, *things*》.

**돌려주다** ① 《반환하다》 return 《*a thing*》; give 〔pay〕 《*a thing*》 back. ¶ 빌린 책을 ～ return 《*a person*》 a borrowed book / 돈을 ～ return the borrowed money; pay the money back / 빚은 이 달 10일까지 돌려주어야 한다 The debt is due on the 10th of this month. ② 《융통하다》 lend; advance 《money》; finance. ¶ 돈을 ～ lend money 《to *a person*》; accommodate 《*a person*》 with a loan / 자금을 ～ finance a business 〔an enterprise〕.

**돌리다**[1] ① 《회전시키다》 turn; spin; trundle; revolve 《a wheel》; wheel; rotate 《a propeller》; push 〔pull, move〕 *a thing* round. ¶ 굴렁쇠를 ～ trundle a hoop / 다이얼을 ～ turn 〔spin〕 a dial; dial / 시계 바늘을 ～ turn the hands of a watch / 팽이를 ～ spin a top.
② 《방향을 바꾸다》 turn (about); veer (round); shift; wheel; sheer (배가). ¶ 눈길을 ～ turn *one's* eyes (away)

《from, to》/ 발길을 ~ turn back; retrace 〔turn〕 *one's* steps / 뱃머리를 ~ veer a boat / 얼굴을 홱 ~ turn 〔screw〕 *one's* head around / 화제를 ~ change the subject 〔topic〕 (of conversation); shift the conversation / 기수(機首)를 남쪽으로 ~ take a southern course; turn south(ward); head for the south.
③ 《차례로》 send round 《a circular》; pass 《*a thing*》 round 〔about〕; hand round 〔on〕. ¶ 다음으로 ~ pass on to the next / 술잔을 ~ pass a glass of wine round; circulate the wine cup / 케이크를 ~ hand 〔pass〕 round cakes / 회람을 ~ send out a circular / 잡지를 돌려가며 보다 read a magazine in turn.
④ 《회부하다》 transmit; send round 《a bill to》; refer 《*a matter* to》. ¶ 사건을 딴 부처로 ~ refer a matter to another office / 서류를 담당계원에게 ~ send round the papers 〔send the papers over〕 to the man in charge.
⑤ 《전임시키다》 transfer. ¶ 회계과로 ~ transfer 《*a person*》 to the accounting section.
⑥ 《도르다》 distribute; deal out; serve out 〔round〕; deliver; send out. ¶ 신문을 ~ deliver newspapers / 초대장을 ~ send out invitations.
⑦ 《마음·주의를 바꾸다》 change; alter; turn; divert. ¶ 마음을 ~ change *one's* mind; divert *one's* attention 《to》/ 마음을 돌려 새사람이 되다 turn over a new leaf; mend *one's* ways / 마음을 돌리게 하느라고 몹시 애쓰다 have a hard time trying to make 《*a person*》 change *his* mind / 일반의 관심을 복잡한 국내 문제로부터 외부 세계로 ~ divert the public attention from its complicated domestic trouble to the outside world / 그의 제의를 거절할까 했으나 마음을 돌려 받아들이기로 했다 I intended to decline his offer, but on second thought I decided to accept it.
⑧ (***a***) 《원인·책임을 넘기다》 attribute 〔ascribe〕 《*a matter*》 to; put 《*one's* failure》 down to 《*a person*》; impute 《a crime》 to 《*a person*》. ¶ …의 책임으로 ~ lay the responsibility on; throw the blame at the door of 《*a person*》/ 성공을 행운에 ~ attribute 〔credit〕 *one's* success to luck / 실패를 불운의 탓으로 ~ ascribe 〔impute〕 *one's* failure to bad luck / 회사의 파산은 방만한 경영의 탓으로 돌릴 수 있다 The bankruptcy of the company can be attributed to lax management. (***b***) 《영광을 넘기다》 bring; yield; concede. ¶ 승리의 영광을 조국에 ~ yield 〔give〕 the palm (of victory) to *one's* fatherland / 영광을 모교에 ~ bring glory to *one's* alma mater.
⑨ 《가동·운영하다》 operate; work; run. ¶ 기계를 ~ set a machine in motion; work 〔operate〕 a machine / 공장을 ~ operate a plant.
⑩ 《뒤로 미루다》 defer; postpone; put *something* off; let 《*a matter*》 wait; leave *something* over; leave *something* until later; delay 《*do*ing》 till later. ¶ …보다 뒤로 돌려지다 take a back seat to 《another problem》/ 어려운 문제는 뒤로 돌리자 Let's leave the difficult problems till later. / 싫은 일은 뒤로 돌리기가 쉽다 People are apt to postpone the work they dislike. / 그건 나중으로 돌려도 된다 That can wait. *or* You can let it wait.
⑪ 《돌려쓰다》 divert 《*a thing* to some other purpose》; appropriate 〔apply〕 《to》. ¶ 학비로 ~ apply 《money》 toward *one's* school expenses / 소모품비를 인건비로 ~ appropriate wear and tear expenses for personnel use.
⑫ 《기타》 ¶ 농담으로 ~ take 《*something*》 as a joke / 백지로 ~ 《새롭게 시작하다》 start 「afresh 〔anew〕; make a fresh start; 《원상태로》 get back to normal 〔where *one* was at the start〕; return to 《its》 former state.

**돌리다**[2] ① (***a***) 《병이》 improve; turn the corner; ease; pass the crisis; be over the hump. ¶ 병이 ~ take a favorable turn; improve; become 〔get〕 better. (***b***) 《쉬다》 rest; pause for breath. ¶ 잠시 숨을 ~ take 〔have〕 a rest 〔breather〕/ 한숨 ~ breathe 〔give〕 a sigh of relief; get out of a difficult situation / 빚을 다 갚아서 이젠 숨 좀 돌리겠다 I can breathe easy now that I have paid all my debts. ② 《변통하다》 lend; advance 《money to *a person*》; accommodate 《*a person* with a loan》; borrow; get 《a loan》. ¶ 3만원쯤 돌릴 수 없을까요 Can you afford to lend me 30,000 won? / 은행에서 백만원을 돌렸다 I got a loan of one million won from the bank.

**돌림** ① 《차례로 돌아감》 something done by turns 〔in rotation〕; something passed round; rotation 《of》. ¶ ~으로 alternately; by turns; by 〔in〕 rotation / ~으로 한 턱씩 내다 treat《*one's* friends》to《dinners》in rotation / 우리는 ~으로 당번을 한다 We are on duty in turns. ② ⇨돌림병. ◉ ~병 an epidemic; a catching〔a contagious, an infectious〕disease: ~병이 발생하다 an epidemic breaks out. ~자(字) a part of a name which is common to the same generation of a family. ~쟁이 a person left out; a person excluded〔estranged, alienated, shunned〕by his company. ~턱 a treat given by turns; giving a treat in rotation. ~편지 a circular letter; a round robin.

**돌멘**《고인돌》a dolmen; a cromlech.

**돌멩이** a (single) stone; a cobble (-stone). ◉ ~질 stone-throwing〔=slinging〕: ~질하다 sling〔throw〕a stone《at》; stone; pelt《*a person*》with stones; pelt stones《at》.

**돌무더기** a pile〔heap〕of stones.

**돌무덤** a stone grave; a cairn.

**돌묵상어**〚어류〛a bone shark; a basking shark.

**돌미나리**〚식물〛a wild parsley.

**돌미륵**(一彌勒) a stone Buddha.

**돌반지기** gritty rice.

**돌발**(突發) an〔a sudden〕outbreak; (out-)burst. ~하다 break out; burst forth; occur〔happen〕suddenly. ¶~적(으로) sudden(ly); unforeseen(ly); unexpected(ly) / 중동에서 전쟁이 ~했다 A war broke out in the Middle East. ◉ ~사건〔사고〕a sudden happening; an unforeseen〔unexpected〕occurrence〔incident〕; an accident: 구급대는 ~사고에 대비하여 24시간 대기한다 The rescue party are on duty for twenty-four hours a day in preparation for the unexpected.

**돌방**(一房) a room made of stone.

**돌밭** a stony place.

**돌배**〚식물〛a wild pear.

**돌변**(突變) a sudden change〔turn〕. ~하다 change suddenly; take a sudden turn;《병이》take a sudden turn for the worse; take a serious turn. ¶날씨가 ~했다 The weather suddenly changed. / 부저가 ~을 알렸다 The buzzer sounded an emergency. / 그때부터 나에 대한 그의 태도가 ~했다 From that time his attitude toward me underwent a sudden change.

**돌보다** take care of; help; aid; give assistance《to》; look after; attend to〔on〕. ¶돌보아 주는 사람 one who cares for another; a caretaker / 가축을 ~ manage cattle / 일을 ~ take care of *one's* work; attend to *one's* work / 아기를 잘 ~ take good care of a baby; look after a baby well / 환자를 ~ look after〔tend to〕a patient / 가정을 돌보지 않다 neglect〔think little of〕*one's* home / 내가 없는 동안 아기 좀 돌봐 주세요 Please look after〔nurse〕the baby while I am away. *or* Will you please baby-sit while I am out? / 그를 돌보는 이가 아무도 없다 No one takes care of him. *or* He has nobody to look after him. / 몇달전 나는 한 가족을 위해 집과 개를 돌봐 주기로 하였다 A few months ago, I agreed to house-and-dog-sit for a family.

**돌부리** a jagged edge〔point〕of a stone. ¶~를 차면 발부리만 아프다《속담》Don't cut off your nose to spite your face.

**돌부처** ① a stone (image of) Buddha. ¶~같이 말이 없다 be as silent〔taciturn〕as a stone Buddha. ② an insensitive and stubborn person.

**돌비**(一碑) a stone monument〔tablet〕; a tombstone.

**돌비** Dolby. ◉ ~시스템 Dolby system: ~시스템으로 녹음된 카세트 a Dolbyized cassette.

**돌비늘**〚광물〛mica; isinglass.

**돌사닥다리** a stony mountain path.

**돌산**(一山) a rocky mountain;《채석장》a quarry; a stone pit.

**돌삼**〚식물〛a wild hemp.

**돌상**(一床) a table laid in celebration of a baby's first birthday.

**돌샘** a rock spring.

**돌소금**〚광물〛rock salt. = 암염(岩塩).

**돌솜**〚광물〛asbestos. = 석면(石綿). ◉ ~타일 an asbestos tile.

**돌순**(一筍)〚지질〛a stalagmite. = 석순(石筍).

**돌싸움** a mock fight with stone missiles. ~하다 play at war with stone missiles.

**돌쌓기**〚건축〛(stone) masonry; masonwork.

**돌아가다** ①《본래의 장소로》return; go〔get, be〕back; come back (말하는 상대에게); leave (떠나다). ¶집으로 ~ go (back) home / 고향으로 ~ return to *one's* native place / 걸어서〔서둘러〕집으로 ~ walk〔hurry〕home / 집에 자동차로 ~ go home by car; drive home / 돌아갈 채비를 하다 prepare for going home / 이제 돌아가야겠습니다 I must be going now. *or* I must say good-bye now. / 그는 어젯밤 늦게 집으로 돌

아갔다 He went home late last night. ②《본디 상태로》 return to. ¶ 먼저 이야기로〔직업으로〕 ~ return to *one's* 「story 〔old job〕/ (죽어서) 흙으로 ~ fall back to dust / 다시 소년으로 돌아가고 싶다 I wish I were a boy again. ③《끝나다》 end 《in》. ¶ 수포로 ~ end in「smoke 〔nothing〕; end in failure; 「come to 〔go for〕 nothing; prove fruitless / 전쟁은 적의 승리로 ~ the battle ends in the enemy's victory. ④《책임·욕 따위가》 fall 《upon》; attribute 《to》; ascribe 《to》; set 〔put〕 down 《to》. ¶ 실패의 책임이 그에게로 돌아갔다 The failure was ascribed「on 〔upon〕 his fault. / 아들의 잘못으로 욕이 아버지한테 돌아갔다 The misdemeanor of the son brought disgrace to his father. / 그것을 하면 책임은 너한테 돌아간다 If you do that, you will be held responsible for it. ⑤《복구·회복하다》 return 〔be restored〕 《to》; revert 《to》. ¶ 이전 상태로 ~ return to the former state / 본디 몸으로 ~ be restored to health. ⑥《죽다》 die; pass away; depart from this life. ¶ 아버지께서 돌아가신 지 20년이 된다 It is twenty years since my father died. ⑦《우회하다》 go a long way round; take a roundabout way. ⑧《작동·작용하다》 work; operate. ¶ 기계가 잘 돌아가지 않는다 The machine does not work well. / 오늘은 내 머리가 잘 돌아간다 My brain is working well today.

**돌아눕다** 《한 번》 turn over in *one's* sleep; 《여러 번》 toss about in bed.

**돌아다니다** ①《싸다니다》 go 〔walk〕 around 〔about〕; pace around; wander 〔gad, roam〕 about; 《맹수·도둑 따위가》 prowl 《about》. ¶ 어슬렁어슬렁 ~ stroll 〔wander, loiter〕 about; take a stroll / 하는 일 없이 ~ gad about idly / 연설하며 ~ go around making speeches; make a speaking tour / 산으로 ~ wander about in the mountains / 이리저리 ~ wander from place to place; knock about here and there / 어디를 돌아다녔느냐 Where have you been wandering about? ②《소문 따위가》 get「around 〔about〕; spread; circulate; be diffused; 《병·사상 따위가》 pervade; prevail; 《유행하다》 come into fashion; become popular. ¶ 온 읍내에 나쁜 소문이 ~ A bad rumor goes round all over the town.

**돌아들다** ①《되돌아옴》 come back; return; find *one's* way back to. ¶ 저녁이 되면 새들이 제 둥지로 돌아든다 In the evening the birds fly back to their nests. ②《물이》 curve in; make a bend; make a turn this way. ¶ 물이 산 밑으로 돌아든다 The river curves in toward the foot of the mountain.

**돌아보다** ①《뒤를》 look back 《at》; turn 〔look〕 around. ¶ 홱 ~ wheel about; turn face about / 흘끗 ~ take a backward glance 《at》/ 그녀는 뒤도 안 돌아보고 방을 나갔다 She went out of the room without looking back. / 그 소녀는 몇번이고 그 고양이를 돌아보았다 The girl was looking back at the cat over and over again. / 그녀가 지나가면 모두가 돌아본다 When she passed, everybody turned around to look at her. ②《회상하다》 look back 《on》; reflect 《on》; reminisce; 《반성하다》 think back on 《*something*》; examine *oneself;* reflect on *oneself.* ¶ 지난일을 ~ look back upon the past / 고생하던 때를 돌아다보다 look back upon hard times / 과거를 돌아보니 부끄럽게 여겨질 때가 있다 I am sometimes ashamed on looking back upon the past. / 나의 학생 시절을 돌아보면, 내가 얼마나 많은 시간을 낭비했는가를 깨닫게 된다 When I think back on my student days, I realize how much time I wasted. ③ = 돌보다.

**돌아서다** ①《등을 보이다》 turn backward; turn *one's* back to 〔on〕 《*a person*》; 《방향을 바꾸다》 turn round 《toward》; turn about. ¶ 그녀는 나를 보고 돌아섰다 She turned her back upon me. / 그녀는 갑작스레 돌아서서 나를 보았다 She suddenly turned around and looked at me. ②《등지다》 turn *one's* back on; turn against; break up with; fall out with; be「alienated 〔estranged〕 from; dissent. ③《병이》 improve; take a turn for the better.

**돌아앉다** sit down with *one's* back toward 《*a person*》.

**돌아오다** ①《귀환하다》 return; come back; get 〔be〕 back. ¶ 돌아오지 않는 다리 "Bridge of No Return" / 돌아오지 않는 청춘 the irrevocable youth / 회사에서 ~ come home from the「office 〔business〕/ 성공하여 고향에 ~ return to *one's* native place in glory / 다시는 돌아오지 못할 길을 떠나다 go on *one's* last journey; depart from this world; die / 그는 고향을 떠나 두 번 다시 돌아오

지 않았다 He left the country never to return. / 그는 3시경에 돌아올 것으로 생각됩니다 We expect him back at about three o'clock. / 곧 돌아옴《게시》 Will be back soon.
② 《원상태로》 return 《to》; 《제정신이》 come to; come round. ¶ 차례가 ~ *one's* turn comes (round) / 제정신이 ~ come to *oneself;* recover *one's* senses / 잃어버린 시계가 주인에게 돌아왔다 The lost watch was returned to the owner. / 정신이 돌아와 주위를 살펴보니 아무도 없었다 When I came to (myself) and looked around I found I was alone.
③ 《책임 따위가》 fall on; be brought. ¶ 책임이 ~ a responsibility fall on *one's* shoulders / 욕이 ~ disgrace is brought upon *one.*

**돌알** 《수정알》 the crystal lens of glasses; 《삶은 달걀》 a hard-boiled egg.

**돌연**(突然) [부사적으로] abruptly; suddenly; on a sudden; all of a sudden; unexpectedly; all at once; without warning 〔notice〕. ~하다 (be) sudden; abrupt; unexpected; unlooked-for; be a surprise. ¶ ~한 방문 a surprise 〔an unexpected〕 visit / ~한 사고 an unexpected occurrence; a sudden accident / ~한 질문 an abrupt question / ~ 사직하다 resign without (giving) notice / ~ 나타나다 burst upon the scene 〔view〕 / 형이 ~ 미국에서 귀국했다 My brother came back from America unexpectedly. ◉ ~변이 〖생물〗 (a) mutation: ~변이설(說) the thcory of mutation / ~변이체 a mutant / ~변이를 일으키다 mutate; sport. ~사(死) a sudden death: 그녀의 ~사에 가족 모두가 충격을 받았다 Her sudden death shocked all the family.

**돌옷** rock moss.

**돌우물** a stone well.

**돌이키다** ⇨ 돌아보다. ① 《고개를》 turn 〔look〕 round; turn *one's* head 〔face〕; face about. ② 《회상하다》 look back on 〔to〕; reminisce about; review; retrospect; 《반성하다》 reflect upon *oneself;* think back on 《*something*》; examine *oneself.* ¶ 돌이켜 생각하니 on (further) reflection; on second thought(s); to look at 《*the matter*》 from a different angle / 과거를 돌이켜보다 think back to the past days; look back upon the past / 매일 세 차례씩 자신의 행동을 돌이켜보다 (try to) reflect on *one's* actions thrice daily / 돌이켜보아 양심에 찔리는 데가 없다 have an easy 〔a clear〕 conscience / 돌이켜보아 후회될 바가 없다 have no regret for what *one* has done / 청춘시절을 돌이켜보다 reminisce about *one's* youth.
③ 《마음을》 change 《*one's* mind》; make 《*a person*》 change 《*his* mind》; get 《*a person*》 to change 《*his* mind》; 《재고하다》 reconsider; reflect on; think better of.
④ 《원상태로》 get back; regain; recover; retrieve; restore; recuperate; undo. ¶ 돌이킬 수 없는 irrevocable; irreparable; irreclaimable; beyond 〔past〕 retrieve / 돌이킬 수 없는 과거 the irrevocable past / 돌이킬 수 없는 손실 an irreparable 〔irrecoverable〕 loss / 돌이킬 수 없는 잘못을 저지르다 commit 〔make〕 an irreparable mistake / 이미 저지른 일은 돌이킬 수 없다 What is done cannot be undone. *or* What is done, is done.

**돌입**(突入) ~하다 rush 〔dash, run, break〕 in 〔into〕; storm into 《the palace》; 《개시하다》 plunge 《into》. ¶ 적진에 ~하다 charge 〔dash〕 into the enemy's position / 파업에 ~하다 rush into a strike; come 〔go〕 out on strike / 두 나라는 전쟁에 ~했다 Two nations broke into war.

**돌잔치** the banquet given on a baby's first birthday.

**돌잡히다** let the baby celebrate his first birthday by choosing one thing from the table where the food and gifts are.

**돌쟁이** a one-year-old baby.

**돌절구** a stone mortar. ¶ ~도 밑 빠질 때가 있다 《속담》 Nothing lasts forever.

**돌중방**(一中枋) a stone sill at the entrance to an alley.

**돌진**(突進) a rush; a dash; an onrush; a charge. ~하다 rush 《at, for, to》; dash 〔charge〕 《at》; make a dash 〔dart〕 《at》. ¶ 적을 향해 ~하다 charge 〔rush〕 at the enemy; make a dash at the enemy / 비상구 쪽을 향해 ~하다 dash 〔make a dash〕 toward the emergency exit / 멧돼지가 우리를 향해 ~해 왔다 The wild boar was rushing toward us.

**돌집** a stone house 〔building〕.

**돌짬** a crevice 〔crack, chink〕 in rock.

**돌쩌귀** a hinge. ¶ 수톨쩌귀 the pintle of a hinge; a pivot / 암톨쩌귀 the gudgeon of a hinge; a pan / ~에 녹이 슬지 않는다 《속담》 A rolling stone gathers no moss.

**돌출**(突出) ① 《튀어나옴》 projection; protrusion. ～하다 project; jut 〔stick〕 out. ¶ ～한 projecting; protuberant; projected / 그 곶은 호를 그리며 남동쪽으로 ～해 있다 The cape juts 〔runs〕 out south-eastward in an arc. ② 《두드러짐》 prominence. ～하다 stand out; be prominent; 《의표를 찌르다》 take 〔catch〕 《*a person*》 by surprise; do something unexpected. ¶ …을 ～케 하다 bring ... into prominence / 그는 종종 ～된 행동을 한다 He often does things that surprise people. ◉ ～물 a projection. ～부 a projecting part; a salient (part); 〖군사〗 a salience; a perimeter (전선의); 〖지리〗 a spur (산·바위 따위의).

**돌층계**(—層階) a stone step; a flight of stone steps.

**돌칼** 〖고고학〗 a stone blade.

**돌탑**(—塔) a stone tower 〔pagoda〕.

**돌파**(突破) ① 《뚫고 나감》 breaking through. ～하다 break 〔smash〕 through. ¶ 적진〔비상선〕을 ～하다 break through the enemy's line 〔police cordon〕. ② 《넘어섬》 passing; exceed. ～하다 pass; exceed; rise above. ¶ 10만원대를 ～하다 pass 〔break〕 the hundred thousand won mark 〔line〕 / 지원자는 천 명을 ～했다 The number of the applicants exceeded one thousand. ③ 《극복》 surmounting. ～하다 surmount; overcome; get over. ¶ 난관을 ～하다 surmount 〔overcome, get over〕 difficulties / 입시의 난관을 ～하다 pass a difficult entrance examination 《to a college》.
◉ ～작전 〖군사〗 breakthrough operations. 중앙～ a frontal breakthrough.

**돌파구**(突破口) a breakthrough; a breach. ¶ ～를 만들다 break a path 《for *one's* attack》; open the way 《for resuming negotiation》; find a way out 《to》; breach / 경제 파탄으로 인해 점증하는 국민들의 불만을 완화시키기 위한 ～를 찾다 find a breakthrough for easing of an ever-mounting popular discontent caused by its ensuing economic fiasco / 그가 공격의 ～를 열었다 He ⌈broke a path 〔opened the way〕 for our attack.

**돌팔매** a throwing stone. ◉ ～질 stone throwing: ～질하다 throw stones.

**돌팔이** 《떠돌이 장사꾼》 a wandering tradesman; an itinerant trader; 《엉터리 전문가》 an unqualified specialist 〔expert〕. ◉ ～선생 an unqualified teacher. ～의사 a traveling healer; a quack doctor.

**돌팥** 〖식물〗 a wild red-bean.

**돌풍**(突風) a (sudden) gust of wind; a squall; a blast of wind. ¶ ～에 간판이 날려 넘어지다 The signboard was blown over by a gust of wind. / ～ 지역 《게시》 Sudden wind change ahead.

**돌피** 〖식물〗 a wild millet.

**돔** 〖건축〗 a dome. ¶ ～구장(球場) a domed baseball stadium.

**돔바르다** 《인식하다》 (be) stingy; niggardly; close-fisted; 《인정없다》 (be) unfeeling; coldhearted; heartless. ¶ 돔바르게 굴다 skin 〔flay〕 a flint; lead a niggardly life.

**돔발상어** 〖어류〗 a dogfish; a mudfish.

**돕다** ① 《조력하다》 help; aid; assist; give 〔lend〕 a helping hand; 《후원하다》 support; give support 《to》; back (up). ¶ 아무를 ～ help *a person* / 일을 ～ help 《*a person*》 with 〔in〕 *his* work / 길 찾는 것을 ～ help 《*a person*》 to find *his* way / 형은 내 숙제를 도와주었다 My brother helped me with my homework. / 나는 자네를 전폭적으로 도울 생각이다 I will back you up one hundred percent. / 나는 할머니가 계단 오르시는 것을 도왔다 I aided an old lady in climbing the stairs. / 하늘은 용감한 자를 돕는다 Heaven favors the brave. / 하늘은 스스로 돕는 자를 돕는다 Heaven helps those who help themselves. / 식량으로 가난한 나라들을 돕자 Let's aid poor countries with food. / 나는 선생님이 시험지 채점하는 것을 도왔다 I assisted the teacher with 〔in〕 grading the exam papers.
② 《구조하다》 save; rescue; 《구제하다》 relieve. ¶ 물에 빠진 사람을 ～ save 〔rescue〕 a drowning man / 가난한 사람을 ～ relieve the poor.
③ 《조장하다》 promote; contribute 《to》; conduce to. ¶ 소화를 ～ promote 〔aid〕 digestion / 운동은 건강을 돕는다 Exercise is conducive to good health. / 그는 우리 도시의 산업 발전을 크게 도왔다 He contributed greatly to the industrial growth of our town.

**돗바늘** a matting needle; a darning needle.

**돗자리** a (rush) mat; matting [총칭]. ¶ ～를 깔다〔치다〕 spread 〔make〕 a mat / 꽃～ a figured mat; a fancy matting.

**동**[1] ① 《묶음》 a bundle; a bunch; a load. ¶ 먹 한 동 a bunch of 〔10〕 ink sticks / 붓 한 동 a bundle of 〔10〕 writing brushes / 곶감 한 동 a load of

〔10,000〕 dried persimmons / 무명 두 동 two bundles 〔100 *p'il*〕 of cotton cloth. ② 《윷놀이의》 one of the four rounds necessary to complete a game of *yut.*

**동**[2] ① 《조리·이치》 reason; logic; coherence. ¶ 동이 닿다 square with logic; stand to reason; be reasonable; be logical 〔coherent〕 / 동 닿지 않는 말 unreasonable 〔illogical, incoherent〕 remarks / 그가 말하는 바는 동이 닿지 않는다 He is not governed by logic. ② 《동안》 (a space of ) time; a period; a span; an interval. ¶ 동이 뜨다 have a space 《between》; the interval is longer than usual; be far 「between 〔apart〕 / 동을 띄우다 leave a longer interval than usual / 전기 요금 받으러 오는 것이 이번은 좀 동이 뜨다 They are later than usual this time in collecting the electricity bill. ③ 《옷의》 a cuff. ¶ 소맷동, 끝동 the cuff of a sleeve. ④ 《상추의》 a lettuce stalk.

**동**(東) east. ⇨동쪽. ¶ 동향집 a house facing east / 동의 east; eastern / 동으로 가다 go east 〔eastward〕 / 동이 튼다 Day breaks 〔dawns〕. ◉ 동반구 the Eastern Hemisphere. 동아시아 East Asia. 동측 the east 〔eastern〕 side; 《동서 양진영의》 the East; the Eastern bloc. 동풍 an east 〔easterly〕 wind.

**동**(棟) 《집채》 ¶ 두동 two houses 〔buildings〕 / 한동 30호(戶)의 아파트 an apartment house composed of thirty apartments / H아파트 7동701호, H Apt. 7-dong No. 701; 7-701, H Apt.

**동**(洞) 《행정구역》 a *dong;* a street; a block; a village.

**동**(胴) ① 《갑옷의》 the plastron; the body armor. ② 《몸의》 (the trunk of ) the body. ¶ 저고리의 동이 길다 The coat has a long waist.

**동**(銅) copper (기호 Cu). ¶ 동전 a copper (coin) / 동을 함유한 coppery / 동을 입히다 copper; cover 〔coat〕 《*a thing*》 with copper. ◉ 동관 a copper pipe 〔tube〕. 동메달 a bronze medal. 동세공 copperwork. 동세공인 a coppersmith.

**동**(同) the same; the corresponding; 《상기의》 the said; the above. ¶ 동세대 the same generation / 동인물 the said person / 동갑의 사람들 people of the same age / 작년 동일 the corresponding 〔same〕 date of last year / 동사(同社) the said corporation / 동량의 물 an equal amount of water / 동시각에 at the same time / 동일동시에 at the same time on the same day / 동일에 on the same day.

**동가**(同價) the same price.

**동가리톱** a crosscut saw.

**동가식서가숙**(東家食西家宿) 《떠도는 사람》 a vagabond; a wanderer; a man with no fixed abode. ~하다 lead a vagabond 〔wandering〕 life; live as a tramp.

**동갈하다**(恫喝—) threaten; intimidate.

**동감**(同感) 《같은 감정》 the same sentiment; sympathy; the same feeling; 《같은 의견》 agreement; concurrence. ~하다 《공감하다》 sympathize 《with》; feel the same way; share 《*a person's*》 feeling; 《동의하다》 agree 《with》; be of the same opinion 《as》. ¶ 그 점에 대해서는 나도 ~이다 I'm with you on that. / 나도 당신과 전적으로 ~입니다 I quite agree with you. *or* I feel the same way as you do. *or* That's my opinion, too. / 그의 견해에 대해서 많은 동료들이 ~하고 있는 것은 아니다 It is not that many of his colleagues 「share 〔are in agreement with〕 his view.

**동갑**(同甲) the same age; *a person* 〔*persons*〕 of the same age; contemporaries. ¶ 그와 나는 ~이다 He and I are of the same age. / 그들은 모두 ~이다 They are all (of ) an age.

**동갓** 〖식물〗 a kind of mustard.

**동강** a piece; a part. ¶ ~나다 go 〔be broken〕 to pieces 〔parts〕 / ~치다 cut 《*a thing*》 into pieces / 연필이 두 ~나다 a pencil is broken into two pieces / 막대를 세 ~으로 자르다 cut a stick into three pieces. ◉ ~치마 a short 〔knee-length〕 skirt.

**동강동강** into pieces; piece by piece. ¶ 막대를 ~ 자르다 cut a stick into pieces / 엿이 ~ 부러지다 a rice-candy bar is broken into pieces.

**동개** a quiver (for arrows). ◉ ~살 an arrow with a large feather.

**동갱**(銅坑) a copper mine.

**동거**(同居) living together; living in the same house. ~하다 live 〔stay〕 with 《a family》; live together; share the same house 《with》; live under the same roof. ¶ 나는 아저씨와 ~하고 있다 I live with my uncle. *or* I am staying at my uncle's. / 우리는 3대가 ~하고 있다 Three generations of my family are living together. ◉ ~인 an inmate; a lodger; a roomer 《미》.

**동거리**(同距離) the same distance; an equal distance.

**동격**(同格) the same rank; the same status; an equal footing; equality; 〚문법〛 apposition. ¶ 자기와 ~인 사람 *one's* equal; *one's* peer / …와 ~이다 be on「a par 〔an equal footing〕 with…; 〚문법〛 be in apposition to… / 오늘날 여성들은 남성과 ~인 입장에 서고 싶어한다 Woman today want to be on an equal footing with men.
◉ ~명사 a noun in apposition. ~어 an appositive; a word in apposition.

**동결**(凍結) freezing; a freeze 《of, on》. ~하다 freeze (up). ¶ 임금 ~ 정책 a wage-freeze policy / ~을 해체하다 unfreeze; defreeze / 임금과 물가를 60일간 ~하다 impose a 60-day freeze on wages and prices / 예산안이 작년 수준으로 ~되었다 The budget bill was frozen at last year's level. / 그의 해외 재산은 ~되었다 His assets abroad were frozen. / 오늘은 추워서 강이 완전히 ~되었다 It's cold today and the river is frozen over.
◉ ~건조 lyophilization. ~방지제 an antifreeze. ~자산 frozen assets.

**동경**(東經) the east longitude. ¶ ~ 180도 the 180th degree of east longitude; the international date line / ~ 30도 20분 《at》 30 degrees 20 minutes east longitude; Long. 30° 20E (★ longitude thirty degrees twenty minutes east로 읽음).

**동경**(銅鏡) a copper mirror.

**동경**(憧憬) (a) yearning; (a) longing. ~하다 long 〔wish〕 for; yearn 〔hanker〕 after 〔for〕; thirst for 《wealth》; 《숭배하다》 admire; adore. ¶ ~의 대상 an idol 《of teenage girls》 / ~의 땅 a longed-for place / 영화배우를 ~하다 admire a movie star / 도시 생활을 ~하다 hanker after city life / 은근히 ~하다 have a secret admiration / 그는 학생들의 ~의 대상이다 He has the admiration of his 〔the〕 students. / 대부분의 사람들은 아름다움을 ~한다 Most people have a yearning for beauty.

**동계**(冬季) the winter season; winter; wintertime. ¶ ~에는 in winter; during the winter months / ~용으로 《preserve》 for winter use. ◉ ~방학, ~휴가 the winter holidays 〔vacation〕. ~올림픽 the Winter Olympics.

**동계**(同系) ¶ ~의 《혈연적으로》 akin 《to》; of the same (ethnic) stock; 《회사 따위가》 affiliated 《concerns》; 《학문이》 cognate 《sciences》 / 물리학과 천문학 같은 ~의 과학 cognate sciences, such as physics and astronomy. ◉ ~색 a similar color: ~색의 스커트 a similar-colored skirt. ~회사 an affiliated company.

**동계**(動悸) beating 〔thumping, throbbing〕 of the heart; heartbeats; 《병·운동에 의한》 palpitations. ~하다 throb; beat; palpitate; flutter (고르지 않게). ¶ ~가 심하다 *one's* heart beats violently / 긴장하면 ~가 빨라진다 Nervousness「speeds up 〔increases〕 the heartbeat 〔pulse〕.

**동고동락**(同苦同樂) suffering and rejoicing together. ~하다 share *one's* joys and sorrows; share *one's* fortunes 〔lot〕 《with》; share the pleasures and pains of life 《with》. ¶ 우리는 ~해 온 사이다 We've been through a lot together. *or* We have been great friends both in joy and sorrow.

**동고리** a small round willow basket.

**동고비** 〚조류〛 a nuthatch.

**동곳** a topknot pin; a hairpin (worn by men). ¶ ~을 꽂다 wear a hairpin in *one's* topknot.

**동공**(瞳孔) 〚해부〛 the pupil of the eye. ◉ ~막 the pupillary membrane. ~확대〔축소〕 the dila(ta)tion 〔contraction〕 of the pupil.

**동공이체**(同工異體) equal excellence in workmanship though different in style.

**동관**(同官) a colleague; a fellow official.

**동광**(銅鑛) 〚광물〛 a copper mine; 《광석》 copper ore; crude copper.

**동구**(東歐) Eastern Europe. ◉ ~권 the east European bloc.

**동구**(洞口) a village entrance; the approach to a village. ¶ ~밖 the outskirts of a village.

**동국**(同國) 《같은 나라》 the same country; 《그 나라》 that country. ◉ ~인 a fellow countryman; a compatriot.

**동국**(東國) an eastern country; 《한국》 the Nation of the East; Korea.

**동굴**(洞窟) a cave; a cavern; a grotto (*pl.* ~s, ~es); 《동물의》 a den. ¶ ~에 사는 사람 a cave dweller / ~을 탐험하다 explore a cave; spelunk (취미로).
◉ ~벽화 a wall painting in a cave; 〚고고학〛 a graffito. ~예술 cave art. ~탐험가 a caver; a spelunker (취미로 하는). ~학 speleology: ~학자 a speleologist.

**동궁**(東宮) 《세자》 the Crown Prince; 《세자궁》 the Palace of the Crown Prince.

¶ ～ 전하 His 〔Your〕 Highness the Crown Prince.

**동권**(同權) equal rights; the same right; equality of rights; 《법률상의》 isonomy. ◉ 남녀～ equal rights for men and women; the equality of the sexes (in law): 남녀 ～주의 feminism / 남녀 ～주의자 a feminist.

**동그라미** ① 《원》 a circle; a ring; 《고리》 a loop; 《영》 a zero. ¶ ～를 그리다 draw 〔describe〕 a circle / ～로 두르다 encircle; enclose 《a word》 with a circle; put a circle around 《a word》 / 담배 연기로 ～를 만들어 뿜다 blow a curling wreath of smoke; blow smoke-rings / 바른 말에 ～를 쳐라 「Put a circle 〔Encircle〕 the correct word. ② 《돈의 속어》 money; 《속어》 clink; tin; the needful; dough. ◉ ～표 the circle symbol(기호 ○).

**동그라지다** fall 〔tumble〕 down 〔over〕; fall to the ground; fall 〔roll〕 head over heels (거꾸로). ¶ 미끄러져 ～ slip and fall 「down 〔head over heels〕 / 그녀는 나무 그루터기에 걸려 동그라졌다 She tumbled over the stump of a tree.

**동그랗다** (be) round (원형의); circular (환상의); 《공 모양의》 globular; spherical. ¶ 동그란 모양의 것 a round shape; a round-shaped thing / 동그란 지붕 a dome / 동그란 얼굴 a round face / 동그란 눈 round eyes / 눈을 동그랗게 뜨고 말하다 speak with *one's* eyes wide open / 우리 동그랗게 둘러 앉읍시다 Let's sit in a circle.

**동그마니** ① 《홀로》 lonely; solitarily; all alone. ¶ 넓은 방에 홀로 ～ 앉아 있다 sit all alone in a hall. ② 《홀가분히》 easily; lightly.

**동그스름하다** (be) roundish; somewhat round. ¶ 동그스름한 얼굴 a roundish face / 동그스름하게 하다 round; make 《*a thing*》 round; 《깎아서》 round off 《a corner》.

**동글납작하다** (be) round and flat. ¶ 동글납작한 얼굴 a round and flat face / 떡을 동글납작하게 만들다 make a rice cake round and flat.

**동글동글** ① 《도는 모양》 round and round; rolling; turning. ¶ ～ 돌아가다 turn 〔go〕 round and round; twirl; spin. ② 《둥근 모양》 round. ～하다 be all round 〔circular, globular, spherical〕. ¶ ～한 조약돌 round pebbles / ～한 눈깔사탕 round pieces of taffy.

**동글반반하다** (be) round and flat.

**동급**(同級) 《같은 등급》 the same rank 〔level〕; equality; 《학급의》 the same class 〔grade〕. ¶ 나를 그런 녀석들과 ～으로 생각지 마라 Don't rank me among those kind of people. / 지식에 관한 한 저 두 사람은 ～이다 Those two are on a par as far as knowledge is concerned. ◉ ～생 a classmate; a class-fellow: 나는 그와 ～생이다 I am in the same class with him.

**동긋하다** (be) roundish; rather round.

**동기**(冬期) ＝ 동계(冬季).

**동기**(同氣) brothers and sisters; siblings. ¶ ～간 sibling relationship / ～간의 우애 brotherly 〔sisterly〕 affection; fraternal love / ～간이다 be siblings; be brothers 〔sisters〕; be brother(s) and sister(s).

**동기**(同期) the same 〔corresponding〕 period; 《학교의》 the same class. ¶ 작년 ～에 비하면 as compared with the corresponding 〔same〕 period of last year / 작년 ～와 비교할 때 자동차 수요는 어떻습니까 How is the demand for cars compared with the same period (of) last year? / 우리는 학교〔대학〕 ～다 We were in the same class at school 〔college〕. / 그와 나는 입사 ～다 He and I entered the company in the same year.

◉ ～생 a classmate; graduates in the same year; 《be》 *one's* contemporary at college (대학의).

**동기**(動機) a motive; an inducement 《to *do*》; an incentive 《to an action, to *doing*》. (★ motive는 심리적·감정적인 자극. incentive는 외부적인 자극을 의미함). ¶ 행위〔범죄〕의 ～ the motive of a deed 〔crime〕 / 사악한 ～ a sinister motive / 불순한 ～ an ulterior motive / …이 ～가 되어 prompted 〔motivated, actuated〕 by... / 금전상의〔이기적인〕 ～에서 from mercenary 〔selfish〕 motives / …의 ～가 되다 motivate; prompt; actuate / 어떤 ～로 자살했을까 What motivated 〔moved〕 him to commit suicide? / 이런 일을 하게 된 ～는 무엇이냐 What caused 〔motivated〕 you to do this? / 사소한 사건이 전쟁을 야기시키는 ～가 되는 수도 있다 A quite trivial incident can trigger off a war.

◉ ～론 《논리》 motivism. ～부여 motivation 《to do; for doing》: ～부여가 강할 수록 영어 학습은 효과가 난다 The stronger the motivation, the more quickly a student will learn English. ～분석〔조사〕 motivation research.

**동기**(童妓) a young 〔child〕 *gisaeng;* a (young) apprentice *gisaeng.*

**동기**(銅器) a copper 〔bronze〕 utensil; copperware [총칭]. ◉ ～시대 the Bronze Age.

**동끊기다** ① 《동안이》 an interval (of time, period, space) is cut off. ② 《뒤가》 be cut off without supply.

**동나다** run out; run short 《of》; be out; be exhausted; 《상품이》 be sold out; be out of stock. ¶ 석유가 ～ be 〔run〕 out of kerosene; kerosene is out of stock / 휘발유가 동났다 We have run getting out of gas(oline). *or* The gas has run out.

**동나무** firewood sold by the bundle.

**동남**(東南) (the) southeast(생략 SE). ¶ ～의 southeast 《side》; southeastern 《district》; southeasterly 《wind》/ ～으로 southeastwards. ◉ ～동 southeast by east; east-southeast (생략 E.S.E.). ～풍 a southeast 〔southeasterly〕 wind; a southeaster. ～향 facing southeast.

**동남아시아**(東南—) Southeast Asia. ¶ ～사람 Southeast Asians. ◉ ～ 국가연합 the Association of Southeast Asian Nations (생략 ASEAN). ～ 조약기구 the Southeast Asia Treaty Organization (생략 SEATO).

**동내**(洞內) inside a village. ¶ 온 ～가 뒤집히다 the whole village is in an uproar.

**동냥** ① 《구걸》 begging; mendicancy (승려의). ～하다 beg 《rice, money》; beg *one's* bread; go out begging. ¶ ～다니다 go (about) begging; go around as a beggar. ② 《주는 금품》 rice 〔money〕 given to 「a beggar 〔a begging monk〕; alms. ¶ ～을 주다 give rice 〔money〕 to a beggar 〔a begging monk〕 / ～을 받다 receive rice 〔money〕 as a beggar / ～은 아니 주고 쪽박만 깬다 only find faults with 《*a person*》 without complying with *his* request. ◉ ～자루 a beggar's bag. ～중 a mendicant; a begging priest 〔monk〕; a fakir. ～질 begging; mendicancy: ～질하다 beg 《rice, money》; beg *one's* bread; go out begging.

**동냥아치** a beggar; a mendicant. ¶ ～ 쪽박깨진 셈 be at a loss having lost *one's* stock-in-trade.

**동네**(洞—) a 〔*one's*〕 village; the neighborhood. ¶ 큰 ～ a large village / 작은 ～ a hamlet / ～ 어귀에서 on the outskirts of a village / ～ 사람 a villager; villagers; [집합적] village people 〔folk(s)〕 / ～ 어른 elders of *one's* village / ～의 소문 (a) neighborhood gossip / ～ 색시 믿고 장가 못 든다《속담》 Wanting the improbable often leads to frustration. / 온 ～사람들이 그것을 구경하러 나왔다 The whole village turned out to see it.

**동년**(同年) 《같은 해》 《in》 the same year; 《그해》 《in》 that 〔the said〕 year; 《동갑》 the same age. ¶ 그녀는 그의 형과 ～생이다 She was born in the same year as his brother. / ～, 나는 A사에 입사했다 In the same year I joined A company.

**동년배**(同年輩) (about) the same age. ¶ ～의 사람들 people (of) about the same age / ～이다 be (of) the same age as *a person;* be as old as *a person* / 그들은 ～처럼 보인다 They seem to be of the same age.

**동녘**(東—) the east. ¶ ～ 하늘 the eastern sky / ～이 밝아지다 The light of the day is peeping in the east. *or* Morning 〔Day〕 dawns.

**동단**(東端) the eastern end; the eastern extremity 〔tip〕.

**동당거리다** ⇨ 둥덩거리다.

**동닿다** ① 《조리가 맞다》 be coherent 〔consistent〕; be reasonable 〔logical〕; stand to reason; 《일치하다》 coincide with; fit in. ¶ 동닿지 않는 말 illogical 〔incoherent, unreasonable〕 remarks; (self-)contradictory statements / 이야기가 ～ the remark 〔story〕 「stands to reason 〔accords with reason, makes sense〕 / 동닿지 않는 말을 하다 talk incoherently; say incoherent 〔illogical〕 things; talk nonsense. ② 《이어지다》 come 〔follow〕 in succession.

**동대다** ① 《안 끊어지게》 make follow in regular succession. ¶ 학비를 다달이 동대서 보내다 send *a person's* school expenses regularly every month / 이 쌀을 가지고는 다음 추수 때까지 동댈 수가 없다 The rice won't last until next harvest time. ② 《조리가 맞게 하다》 make fit in; make 《*one's* story》 coherent 〔logical, consistent〕; make 《it》 reasonable 〔logical, plausible〕. ¶ 이야기를 ～ make a story consistent 〔plausible〕.

**동대문**(東大門) *Dongdaemun;* the East 「Gate (in Seoul).

**동댕이치다** ① 《내던지다》 throw 〔cast, hurl, fling〕 away. ¶ 홧김에 재떨이를 ～ throw away 〔fling, hurl〕 an ash tray in anger. ② 《그만두다》 throw over

〔up〕; give up; abandon; chuck up 《구어》. ¶ 일을 중도에 ～ give up *one's* work halfway through / 일자리를 ～ throw over *one's* job / 지위를 ～ throw up *one's* office 〔position〕.

**동동** 《발을》 jumping up and down 《from cold, impatience》. ¶ 발을 ～ 구르다 stamp (*one's* feet) on the ground / 추워서 발을 ～ 구르다 jump up and down for cold / 발을 ～ 구르며 분해하다 stamp with vexation 〔chagrin〕. 「구르다.

**동동거리다** ⇨ 동동. ¶ 발을 ～ ⇨ 발을 동동

**동등**(同等) 《평등》 equality; 《지위가》 coordination; the same rank; 《수준이》 a par; 《동일》 oneness; 《등가·등량》 equivalence. ～하다 (be) equal; be of the same rank; (be) equivalent. ¶ ～한 equal; coordinate; equivalent / ～한 권리 equal rights / ～한 물건 an equivalent / ～한 사람 *one's* equal / ～한 입장에서 on an equal footing / ～하게 equally; coordinately / ～하게 대하다 treat 《*them*》 equally; make no discrimination of 《*a person*》 / ～하게 하다 equalize 《all, *a person* with another》; place 《*persons*》 on an equal footing / 대학 졸업 또는 ～한 학력을 가진 자 college graduates or the equivalent / 그는 우리와 ～한 입장에서 이야기한다 He talks with us on equal terms.

**동떨어지다** 《거리가》 be far 〔wide, poles〕 apart; be remote 〔a long way〕 from; be distant 《from》; 《성상(性狀) 등이》 be much removed 《from》; be (widely) different 《from》. ¶ 동떨어지게 (by) far; out of the ordinary; out 〔far〕 and away; a long way / 마을에서 동떨어진 곳 a place far apart from a village / 동떨어진 소리 a statement wide of the mark; an absurd 〔a nonsensical〕 remark / 나는 내 취미와는 동떨어진 일을 하고 있다 I am engaged in a work quite alien to my taste. / 그의 이야기는 사실과 크게 동떨어진다 His story 「is quite different from what actually happened 〔is far from being the whole truth〕.

**동뜨다** ① 《뛰어나다》 (be) superior; extraordinary; exceptional; be far better 〔ahead〕; be far and away. ¶ 동뜨게 (by) far; out of the ordinary; extraordinarily; exceptionally / 영어를 동뜨게 잘하다 be exceptionally good at English / 재간이 ～ have an extraordinary talent. ② 《사이가 뜨다》 have a space between; have a longer interval than usual; be few and far between; be far apart. ¶ 밤이 늦어 버스가 ～ The hour is late and the buses are few and far between. / 두 동네 사이가 ～ The two villages are far apart from each other.

**동락**(同樂) enjoying together; sharing *one's* joy 《with》. ¶ 동고～하다 share *one's* joys and sorrows 《with》.

**동란**(動亂) a disturbance; an upheaval; a riot; 《전쟁》 a war. ¶ ～의 중동 war=〔strife-〕torn Middle East / ～을 일으키다 cause a disturbance 〔riot〕; rise in riot / ～을 진압하다 quell a disturbance 〔riot〕.

**동량지재**(棟梁之材) the pillar 《of a state》; the chief support.

**동력**(動力) 〖기술〗 (motive) power; 〖역학〗 dynamic (force); 〖물리〗 moment. ¶ ～으로 움직이는 power-driven 《machine》 / ～을 공급하다 supply (electric) power 《to a factory》; power 《a factory》 / ～으로 움직이다 move under (motor) power.
◉ ～계(計) a dynamometer. ～ 공급시설 power equipment. ～료 power rate. ～사정 power situation 〔condition〕. ～선 a power line. ～송신선 a power transmission line. ～원(源) a power source: 원자력이라는 새로운 ～원 a new type of power source called atomic energy. ～장치 《특정 기계 등의》 a power plant 〔system〕. ～학 power science; dynamics. ～회선 a power circuit. 한국 ～ 자원연구소 the Korea Institute of Energy and Resources (생략 KIER).

**동렬**(同列) (being of) the same rank 〔class〕. ¶ …와 ～에 두다 put in the same category with; place on the same level with.

**동료**(同僚) a colleague; an associate; a fellow worker 〔official〕; a co-worker; a companion; a comrade (동지). ¶ ～장교 a fellow officer / 회사의 ～ a colleague 「at work 〔in *one's* office〕 / 그녀는 ～들과 잘 어울린다 She gets on 〔along〕 well with her colleagues.

**동류**(同類) ① 《같은 종류》 the same class 〔kind, category〕; the like(s) 《of》. ¶ ～의 of the same class / …와 ～이다 belong to the same class with; be in the same category as; be allied to. ② 《한패》 an accomplice; a confederate; a gang; a pack. ¶ 그도 ～임에 틀림없다 He must be one of the party. ◉ ～의식 consciousness of kind: ～ 의식설 theory of consciousness of kind. ～항 〖수학〗 a similar 〔like〕 term.

**동륜**(動輪) 〖기계〗 a driving 〔traction〕 wheel.

**동률**(同率) the same ratio.

**동리**(洞里) the neighborhood. = 동네.

**동마루**(棟—) 〖건축〗 a tile-roof ridge.

**동막이하다**(垌—) embank; shore up.

**동맥**(動脈) 〖해부〗 an artery; 《주요 교통로》 the main traffic route. ¶ ～의 arterial / ～이 경화되다 the artery hardens / ～은 혈액을 심장에서 체내의 각 부분으로 운반한다 Arteries carry blood from the heart to other parts of the body. / 철도는 우리나라 산업의 ～이라 할 수 있다 The national railroads are regarded as the industrial arteries of our country.
◉ ～경화증 〖의학〗 arteriosclerosis (*pl.* -roses); 《suffer from》 hardening of the arteries: 시(市)행정은 ～경화증에 걸려 있다 [비유적] The city administration has become「too inflexible 〔too set in its ways〕. ～관 an arterial tube. ～류(瘤) an aneurysm. ～염 arteritis. ～혈 arterial blood. ～혈화(血化) arterialization: ～혈화하다 arterialize.

**동맹**(同盟) 《조약》 an alliance; 《연합》 a league; a union; (a political) confederation. ～하다 be allied 〔leagued〕 《with》; league together 《with》; form 〔enter into〕 a union 〔an alliance〕 《with》. ¶ 2국〔3국〕 ～ a dual 〔a triple〕 alliance / 금주 ～ a temperance union / …와 ～하여 in alliance with… / ～을 맺다 ally *oneself* 《with》; be allied 《with》; form a league 〔union〕; conclude 〔enter into〕 an alliance 《with》 / 일본은 제2차 대전에서 독일과 ～을 맺고 있었다 Japan was allied with Germany in World War Ⅱ. ◉ ～국 an ally; an allied country 〔power〕; a confederate. ～군 allied forces; the allies. ～자 an ally. ～조약 a treaty of alliance. ～휴교 a college 〔school〕 strike.

**동맹파업**(同盟罷業) a (labor) strike; a walkout 《미》; a turnout 《영》. ～하다 strike; go on (a) strike; walk out. ¶ ～중이다 be on (a) strike; A strike is on. / ～을 중지하다 call off a strike / 임금 인상을 요구하여 ～에 들어가다 go on strike for higher wages 〔pay〕 / K회사의 ～은 거의 두 달이나 계속되었다 The strike at the K Company has been on for nearly two months. ◉ ～자 a striker; a turnout 《영》. ～파괴자 a strike breaker; a blackleg 《영》; a scab; a rat 《속어》.

**동메달**(銅—) a bronze medal. ¶ ～ 획득자 a bronze medal winner; a bronze medalist.

**동면**(冬眠) 〖동물〗 hibernation; winter sleep. ～하다 hibernate. ¶ ～하고 있다 be in hibernation; lie dormant.
◉ ～동물 hibernating animals; hibernants. ～장소 winter quarters; a hibernaculum (*pl.* -la).

**동명**(同名) the same name.
◉ ～이인(異人) a different person of the same name; *one's* namesake: 그녀는 ～이인임이 밝혀졌다 She turned out to be a different person of the same name.

**동명사**(動名詞) 〖문법〗 a gerund. ¶ ～의 gerundial.

**동무** 《친구》 a friend; a mate; a companion; a comrade; 《구어》 a pal; a chum. ～하다 keep company 《with》; keep 《*a person*》 company; accompany; be a companion to. ¶ 길～ a fellow traveler / 말～ a companion to talk with / 길～하다 keep 《*a person*》 company on *his* journey / ～가 되다 become friends. ◉ ～장사 business in partnership: ～장사하다 do business in partnership. ～장수 traders in partnership.

**동문**(同文) the same script 〔wording〕; 《of》 an identical text. ¶ ～의 편지를 두 통 내다 send a message in duplicate / 이하 ～ The rest 〔following〕 is the same as above. *or* Same as above.
◉ ～전보 a multiple 〔an identical〕 telegram. ～통첩(通牒) an identic 〔a circular〕 note.

**동문**(同門) 《동창》 a fellow student 〔disciple〕; a classmate; 《졸업생》 an alumnus (*pl.* -ni); an alumna (*pl.* -nae) (여자). ◉ ～회 an alumni association.

**동문서답**(東問西答) an incoherent answer; an irrelevant reply. ～하다 answer incoherently; reply irrelevantly. ¶ 자네 말은 아주 ～이군 What you say is irrelevant.

**동문수학**(同門受學) ～하다 study under the same teacher 《with》; be a fellow student 《with》.

**동물**(動物) an animal; a living creature; 《들짐승》 a beast; animal life [총칭]. ¶ ～적인 bestial; brutal(잔인한) / ～적인 본능 (an) animal

instinct / ～ 애호의 날 Be-kind-to-Animals Day / 야생 ～ wild animals / ～을 기르다〔길들이다〕 keep 〔domesticate〕 animals / ～을 사랑하다 be kind to animals / 아무를 ～ 취급하다 treat *a person* like a beast / 인간은 이성이 있는 ～이다 Man is a rational 「animal 〔being〕. / 인간은 사회적 ～이다 Man is a social animal.
◉ ～계 the animal kingdom 〔world〕. ～병원 a veterinary hospital. ～분류학 zootaxy; zoological taxonomy. ～상(相) the fauna 《of Africa》. ～생태학 zoo-ecology. ～숭배 zoolatry; animal worship. ～실험 experiments on 〔with, using〕 animals. ～심리학 animal psychology. ～애호 kindness to animal: ～ 애호가 an animal lover. ～ 애호협회 the Society for the Prevention of Cruelty to Animals (생략 SPCA). ～원(園) a zoo; zoological gardens: 아이들을 ～원에 데리고 가다 take *one's* children to the zoo. ～지리학 zoogeography; animal geography. ～학 zoology: ～학자 a zoologist. ～학대 cruelty to animals. ～해부학 zootomy; animal anatomy. ～행동학 ethology. ～화 an animal painting.

**동물성**(動物性) animal nature; animality. ◉ ～ 단백질 animal protein(s). ～섬유 an animal fiber. ～식품 animal food. ～지방 animal fat(s).

**동미남**(東微南) east by south (생략 EbS).

**동미북**(東微北) east by north (생략 EbN).

**동민**(洞民) the people 〔inhabitants〕 of a *dong;* the village folk; the villagers.

**동바리** 〖건축〗 a short pillar propping up a veranda floor 〔a low bench〕.

**동박새** 〖조류〗 a white-eye (bird).

**동반**(同伴) company. ～하다 accompany; go (in company) with; take 《*a person*》 with; be accompanied by. ¶ 아내를 ～하여 with 〔accompanied by〕 *one's* wife / 그는 가족 ～이다 He is accompanied by his family. / 그는 부부～으로 미국에 갔다 He went to America taking his wife with him. ◉ ～자 *one's* companion; *one's* partner: ～자 없는 미성년자는 입장하지 못한다 Unescorted minors are not admitted. *or* No admittance to unescorted minors.

**동반구**(東半球) the Eastern Hemisphere.

**동반자살**(同伴自殺) 《남녀의》 a joint suicide 《with a woman》; a lovers' suicide; a double suicide; 《한 집안의》 a (whole) family suicide. ¶ 연탄가스로 ～을 기도하다 plan a 《family》 suicide by a briquet gas. ◉ 모자 ～ a mass suicide of a mother and children. ～미수 an attempted double suicide.

**동방**(東方) the east; the eastward; the Orient (동양). ¶ ～예의지국 the country of courteous people in the East; Korea / ～으로 (to the) eastward; toward the east / 빛은 ～으로부터 Light from the East (타고르의 시구). ◉ ～교회 the Eastern (Orthodox) Church.

**동방**(東邦) an eastern country; an Oriental nation; Korea (한국).

**동방**(洞房) ① 《침실》 a bedroom. ② 《신방》 a bridal room. ③ 《화촉동방》 sharing bed on the bridal 〔first〕 night. ◉ ～화촉 ⇨ 동방 ③.

**동방구리** a fat-bellied jar.

**동배** dividing up duties on a hunt.

**동배**(同輩) *one's* equal; a peer; a fellow; a comrade; a colleague. ¶ ～ 중에서 뛰어나다 rise above *one's* fellows.

**동백**(冬柏) 〖식물〗 camellia seeds. ◉ ～기름〔유〕 camellia oil (used to dress hair). ～꽃 a camellia (blossom). ～나무 a camellia (plant).

**동병**(同病) the same disease. ¶ ～상련(相憐) Fellow sufferers sympathize with 〔pity〕 each other. *or* Misery loves company.

**동병**(動兵) military mobilization. ～하다 mobilize.

**동복**(冬服) winter clothes 〔clothing〕; winter wear; 《여성의》 a winter dress.

**동복**(同腹) children born of the same mother. ¶ ～의 uterine (이부 동모(異父同母)의). ◉ ～누이 sisters born of the same mother. ～형제 brothers born of the same mother; uterine brothers.

**동복**(童僕) a page; a boy servant.

**동봉**(同封) ～하다 enclose 〔inclose〕 《a letter》. ¶ ～한 편지 the enclosed 〔accompanying〕 letter / ～해 보내다 be sent under the same cover / 십만 원짜리 수표를 ～합니다 We are enclosing a check for 100,000 won (herewith). *or* 《상용문에서》 Enclosed please find a check for 100,000 won. / 당신의 편지와 ～하신 것을 잘 받았습니다 I have received your letter with its enclosure. / 여기 원서를 ～합니다 I enclose my application herewith.
◉ ～서류 enclosures (생략 encls.).

**동부** ① 〖식물〗 a cowpea. ② 《씨》 ripe cowpeas. ◉ ～고물 ground-up cowpeas (used to coat cakes). ～묵 cowpea paste 〔jelly〕.

**동부**(東部) the eastern part; 《미국의》 the East. ¶ ~의 eastern / ~ 해안 the east coast / ~의 여러 주 《미국의》 the Eastern States / ~로 가다 go (to) east / 그녀는 ~ 출신이다 She is from the East.

**동부**(胴部) the body; the trunk; 《조상(彫像)의》 the torso (*pl.* -(e)s, -si); 《기계의》 the drum; the barrel.

**동부인**(同夫人) going out with *one's* wife. ~하다 go out with *one's* wife; take *one's* wife along; accompany 〔be accompanied by〕 *one's* wife. ¶ ~하여 왕림해 주시기 바랍니다 Please come to see us with your wife. *or* 《의례적》 We request the pleasure of your company and that of Mrs. 《Kim》.

**동북**(東北) northeast (생략 NE). ¶ ~의 northeast(ern); northeasterly / ~으로 northeastward. ◉ ~동 east-northeast (생략 E.N.E.). ~지방 the northeastern provinces 〔districts〕. ~풍 the northeast wind; a north easter. ~향 facing northeast; having a northeast exposure.

**동분모**(同分母) 〚수학〛 the same denominator.

**동분서주**(東奔西走) being terribly busy. ~하다 busy *oneself* 《about *something*, to *do*》; run 〔bustle〕 about; be always 〔constantly〕 on the move. ¶ 그는 사업일로 ~하고 있다 He is flying around on business. / 시장은 산업체 유치를 위해 ~하고 있다 The mayor is busy going here and there visiting people, trying to persuade an industrial company to set up its plant in the city.

**동사**(同社) the same company; the said 〔above(-mentioned)〕 firm.

**동사**(凍死) death from (exposure to) cold. ~하다 die of 〔from〕 cold; freeze 〔be frozen〕 to death. ¶ 그는 산속에서 오도가도 못하게 되어 ~했다 He was stranded in the mountains and froze to death. ◉ ~자 a person frozen to death.

**동사**(動詞) 〚문법〛 a verb. ¶ ~의 verbal / ~의 변화〔활용〕 conjugation / 완전〔불완전〕 ~ a complete 〔an incomplete〕 verb / 이 부류의 ~는 같은 형식으로 변화한다 The verbs of this class are conjugated in the same way.

**동사무소**(洞事務所) a town-block office; a *dong* 〔village〕 office.

**동산** a garden; 《산》 a hill (near a village). ◉ ~바치 a gardener.

**동산**(動産) 〚법〛 movable property; movables; personal property 〔estate〕. ◉ ~반환소송 a 〔an action of〕 detinue. ~보험 property insurance. ~압류 distraint; personal distress.

**동산**(銅山) a copper mine.

**동삼삭**(冬三朔) the three winter months.

**동상**(同上) the same as (the) above; ditto (생략 do.). ¶ ~의 above-mentioned.

**동상**(凍傷) frostbite; chilblains (★ frostbite보다 가벼운). ¶ ~에 걸린 손가락 frostbitten fingers / ~에 걸리다 be 〔get〕 frostbitten; have frostbite / 왼쪽 귀가 ~에 걸리다 get *one's* left ear frostbitten / 그녀는 얼굴에 심한 ~이 걸려 있었다 She was suffering from a severe attack of frostbite on her face. ◉ ~자 a frostbitten person.

**동상**(銅像) a bronze statue; a statue in bronze; a bronze image. ¶ ~을 세우다 erect 〔set up〕 a bronze statue / 고명한 시인의 ~이 세워졌다 The bronze statue of a famous poet was put up 〔built, erected〕.

**동상례**(東床禮) a wedding reception at the bride's house.

**동색**(同色) ① 《빛깔》 the same color. ¶ 상하 ~의 옷 a jacket and pants of the same color. ② 《당파》 fellow members of a party.

**동색**(銅色) copper color. ¶ ~의 copper-colored. ◉ ~인(人) a redskin. ~인종 the copper-colored race.

**동생**(同生) a younger brother 〔sister〕; *one's* little brother 〔sister〕. ¶ 막내~ *one's* youngest brother 〔sister〕 / 나한테 ~이 생겼다 I have got a baby brother 〔sister〕.

**동생공사**(同生共死) ~하다 share the fate with others. ¶ 모두 ~의 운명이다 be all in the same boat.

**동서**(同書) the same 〔said〕 book. ¶ ~에서 《출처》 *ib.*; *ibid.* [< *ibidem* (L.)]

**동서**(同棲) 《남녀의》 cohabitation; 《같이 삶》 living together. ~하다 cohabit 《with》; live together 〔with〕; share bed and board 《with》. ¶ 젊은 남녀의 ~ cohabitation of young men and women / 그는 그녀와 반년간 ~했다 He cohabited with her for half a year. / 요즘은 결혼하지 않고 ~ 생활을 하는 것이 꽤 일반화된 것 같다 It seems that living together without getting married is pretty common these days. ◉ ~자 a cohabiter; a cohabitant.

**동서**(同壻) 《남자》 the husband of *one's* wife's sister; a brother-in-law; 《여자》

the wife of *one's* husband's brother; a sister-in-law.

**동서**(東西) 《동과 서》 east and west; 《동서양》 the East and the West; the Orient and the Occident. ¶ ～간의 관계 East-West relations / 약 ～50 마일 about 50 miles from east to west / ～를 막론하고 throughout the world; for all countries of the world / ～고금을 막론하고 across the ages and countries of the world; for all 「ages and countries 〔time and spaces〕/ ～로 흐르다 run east and west / ～로 펼쳐져 있다 extend east and west / ～도 분간 못하다 don't know *one's* right from left / ～간의 긴장을 완화하다 ease the tensions between the east and the west / 그 섬은 ～로 길게 뻗어 있다 The island stretches east to west. / 한강은 서울을 ～로 흐르고 있다 The Han River runs through Seoul from east to west. / 이 진리는～ 고금에 두루 통한다 The truth is applicable to all times and places. *or* The truth holds true in all ages and countries.
◉ ～남북 the four cardinal points; north, south, east and west (★ 영어에서는 우리말과 달리 이런 순서로 말함); the four points of the compass: 이 광장에서는 4개의 길이 ～남북으로 뻗어 있다 Four streets radiate from the plaza to the four points of the compass.

**동석**(同席) ～하다 sit together; sit with 《*a person*》; sit in company 〔at the same table〕 《with》; share a table with 《*a person*》 (식당 등에서). ¶ 나도 ～했다 I was present, too. *or* I was (one of those) present. / 그 사람과는 ～하고 싶지 않다 I don't like to be in his company. ◉ ～자 those present; the (present) company: ～자는 모두 여성이었다 Those present were all women.

**동석**(凍石) 〖광물〗 soapstone; steatite.

**동선**(同船) the same ship. ～하다 board the same ship 《with *a person*》; be on the same ship 《with》; take the same ship. ◉ ～자 a fellow passenger; a shipmate (선원).

**동선**(銅線) copper wire 〔wiring〕.

**동설**(同說) the same 〔said〕 theory 〔opinion, view〕.

**동성**(同性) 《남녀의》 the same sex. ¶ ～의 of the same sex / 그녀는 ～간에 인기가 있다 She is popular among her own sex. ◉ ～(연)애 homosexual love; homosexuality; 《여성간의》 lesbianism; sapphism: ～(연)애를 하다 fall in unnatural love 《with》; make homosexual love 《with》. ～연애자 a homosexual; a homo 《속어》; 《남》 a gay; 《여》 a lesbian.

**동성**(同姓) the same surname 〔family name〕. ¶ ～의 사람 a namesake.
◉ ～동명 《*a person* with》 the same family and personal name: 그는 나와 ～동명이다 He is my namesake. *or* He has the same family and given names as mine. ～동본 the same surname and the same family origin. ～인 a person of the same surname as *oneself*.

**동소체**(同素體) 〖화학〗 an allotrope.

**동수**(同數) the same number. ¶ ～의 as many 《as...》; of the same number / 찬반 ～의 투표 a 《50-50》 tie vote / 찬반 ～인 경우는 재투표 한다 In case of a tie, there will be another vote. / A반과 B반의 학생수는 ～이다 There are the same number of students in classes A and B.

**동숙**(同宿) lodging together. ～하다 lodge in the same house; 《호텔에》 stay at the same hotel 《with》. ¶ 대학에서 그들은 ～했다 They roomed together at college. / 그와 나는 당분간 ～하게 됐다 He is to stay with me for the present. ◉ ～인 《하숙의》 a fellow lodger 〔boarder〕; 《호텔의》 a fellow guest.

**동승**(同乘) riding together. ～하다 ride together 《with》; ride with 《*a person* in the same carriage》; take the same car 〔train〕; share a car 《with》. ¶ 나는 그와 ～하여 공항에 갔다 I went to the airport in the same car with him. ◉ ～자 a fellow rider 〔passenger〕; a flight companion (비행기의).

**동시**(同時) the same time. ¶ ～의 simultaneous; concurrent.
◉～개설 신용장 a back-to-back 「letter of credit 〔L/C〕. ～녹음 synchronous recording. ～발생 synchronism; simultaneity; concurrence. ～발표 simultaneous announcement 〔release〕: ～발표하다 be released simultaneously. ～방송 〖라디오·TV〗 simultaneous broadcasting; a simulcast. ～상영 a double feature; a two-picture program. ～선거 a double election. ～성 simultaneity. ～통역 《일》 《carry out》 simultaneous interpreting; 《provide》 a simultaneous translation; 《사람》 a

simultaneous interpreter: 5개국어 ~ 통역 설비 five-language simultaneous interpretation facilities.

**동시**(凍屍) a frozen corpse 〔body〕.

**동시**(童詩) children's verse; (a) nursery rime 〔rhyme〕.

**동시대**(同時代) the same age 〔period〕. ¶ ~의 of the same age 〔period〕; contemporary 《with》 / ~에 in the same age 〔period〕 / ~의 사람 a contemporary / ~의 작가들 contemporary writers / 금동(琴童)은 춘원과 ~의 사람이었다 Kŭmdong was contemporary with Ch'unwon. / 그들은 우리와 ~의 사람들이다 They are our contemporaries. / 코페르니쿠스의 학설은 ~ 사람들에게는 이해되지 않았다 The Copernican theory was not understood at all by his contemporaries.

**동시에**(同時一) ① 《같은 때에》 at the same time 《as》; simultaneously; concurrently 《with》. ¶ …과 ~ 발생하다 happen 〔come〕 together; coincide with; synchronize 〔concur〕 with / 지진과 ~ 사방에서 화재가 일어났다 Simultaneously with the earthquake there broke out fire on all sides. / 나와 B군은 ~ 입학했다 I entered the school at the same time 〔in the same year〕 as B. / 두 주자는 거의 ~ 골인했다 The two runners reached the goal line at the same time.
② 《…하기도 …하기도》 both… and; not only… but also; 《한편》 while; on the other hand; as well as. ¶ 재간이 있는 ~ 부지런하다 be both talented and industrious / 이 책은 흥미도 있고 ~ 유익도 하다 This book is instructive as well as interesting. *or* This book is both instructive and interesting. / 등산은 즐거운 운동이지만 ~ 위험도 하다 Mountain climbing is a pleasant sport, but it is dangerous, too. / 그는 학자인 ~ 예술가다 He is a scholar and artist. (★ 동일인이므로 artist의 관사는 불필요).
③ 《한꺼번에》 at a time; at once. ¶ ~ 두 가지 일을 하지 마라 Don't do two things at a time.
④ 《…하자마자》 as soon as. ¶ 나를 봄과 ~ 그는 도망쳤다 The moment he saw me, he ran away.

**동식물**(動植物) animals and plants. ¶ 아프리카의 ~군(群) the fauna and flora of Africa / 많은 ~이 멸종 위기에 놓여있다 A lot of animals and plants are 「in danger of 〔on the verge of〕 extinction.

**동실**(同室) the same room. ◉ ~자 a roommate.

**동심**(同心) 《같은 마음》 the same mind; 《마음이 같음》 like-mindedness; unanimity; accord; agreement; 《중심이 같음》 concentricity. ~하다 share one mind; be of one heart; be of the same mind. ¶ 두 사람은 ~ 일체다 The two are practically of a mind. / 우승을 하려면 우리 팀은 ~일체가 되어야 한다 In order to win the championship, our team must function as one mind and one body.
◉ ~원 『수학』 a concentric circle. ~협력 cooperation in harmony; working with one mind: ~ 협력하다 cooperate in harmony; unite efforts in perfect accord; work with one mind.

**동심**(童心) the child's mind 〔heart〕; the innocence of a child. ¶ ~으로 돌아가다 be 〔become〕 a child again; retrieve *one's* childish innocence / ~을 잃다 lose *one's* childish innocence / ~에 상처를 주다 hurt the feelings of children; offend the child heart; disillusion a child / 그는 ~으로 돌아가 어린이들과 함께 놀았다 Feeling like a child again, he played with children.

**동씨**(同氏) the said person; he. ¶ ~의 말에 의하면 according to him; in his opinion.

**동아** 『식물』 a wax gourd; a white gourd (melon). ¶ ~ 속 썩는 것은 밭 임자도 모른다 《속담》 The anxiety deep in one's mind escapes the notice of even the most intimate friend.

**동아**(冬芽) 『식물』 a winter bud.

**동아**(東亞) East Asia; 《동양》 the East; 《극동》 the Far East. ¶ ~의 (Far) Eastern.

**동아리** ① 《부분》 a part; a portion. ¶ 아랫〔윗〕 ~ the lower 〔upper〕 part. ② 《무리》 a group; a set; gang; 《서클》 a society; a club. ¶ 춤 ~ a dance group / 그녀는 대학교 영화 ~에 들어갔다 She joined the university film society.

**동아시아**(東一) East Asia. ¶ ~ 국가들 〔문제〕 East Asian countries 〔affairs〕.

**동아줄** a rope; a line; a stay (배의). ¶ 용의자의 두 손은 ~로 묶여 있었다 The suspect's hands were tied with rope.

**동안** ① 《사이》 a space (of time); a period; a while; an interval; [부사적] in; for 《a week, three days》; during

《the vacation》; between; within. ¶ 한 주일 ～ for (a period of) a week / 5년 ～ for (the space of) five years / 잠깐 ～ a little while; for a short time; in 〔for〕 a (little) while / 오랫～ for a long time; for long / 얼마～ for some time / 사는 ～ while *one* lives / 여러 해 ～ for (many) years / 전쟁～ 내내 throughout the war; while the war lasted / 지난 5년 ～에 in the past 〔last〕 five years / 그 ～에 meanwhile; in the meantime / 그 ～ 안녕하셨습니까 How have you been since I saw you last? / 그녀는 아주 잠깐 ～에 식사를 준비했다 She prepared the meal in a very short time. / 여름 방학 ～ 삼촌 댁에 가 있었다 I stayed with my uncle during summer vacation. / 최근 10년 ～ 과학에서 눈부신 발전을 했다 Remarkable progress has been made in science in 〔for〕 the last ten years. (★ in three weeks, in the last ten years를 각기 these three weeks, these ten years로 함은 예스러운 말투. for these weeks라고는 보통 안함) / 그녀는 그 ～ 내내 잠자코 있었다 She kept silent 「all the while 〔the whole time〕.
② 《…하는 동안》 while 《*doing*》; as long as; meanwhile; in the meantime; in (the course of). ¶ 우리가 일하는 ～에 아무 방해도 없었다 There was no disturbance at all while we were working. / 내가 대학에서 공부하는 ～ 여러 가지 좋은 경험을 많이 했다 While studying at college, I had all sorts of pleasant experiences. / 집을 비운 ～에 그녀가 찾아왔다 She came to my house 「while I was out 〔in my absence〕. / 내가 살아 있는 ～은 너를 도와주겠다 As long as I live 〔am alive〕, I will help you. / 내가 그 곳에 머무는 ～은 날씨가 좋았다 It was fine while I was staying there.

**동안**(東岸) the east coast; the east bank 《of a river》.

**동안**(童顔) a baby face; a boyish 〔girlish〕 face. ¶ ～의 baby-faced; boyish= 〔girlish-〕looking / 그는 아직도 ～이다 He still has a childish face. *or* He is still boyish-looking.

**동안 뜨다** have an interval 〔a space〕 between; have a longer interval than usual; be few and far between; be far apart. ⇨ 동뜨다.

**동압력**(動壓力) dynamic pressure.

**동액**(同額) the same amount 〔sum〕 《of money》; a like sum. ¶ ～의 of the same amount; 《액면이 같은》 equivalent in amount / 남녀 ～의 급료 the salary paid equally to men and women.

**동양**(東洋) the East; the Orient. ¶ ～의 Eastern; Oriental; of the East 〔Orient〕 / ～풍의 Oriental / ～식〔풍〕으로 하다 Orientalize / 그녀는 ～적인 미인이다 She has Oriental beauty.
◉ ～구(區) 〖생물〗 the Oriental region 〔realm〕. ～무역 Eastern trade. ～문명〔미술〕 Oriental civilization 〔art〕. ～문제 an Oriental 〔Eastern〕 question. ～문화 Oriental culture. ～사 Oriental history. ～사람 an Oriental; the Orientals [총칭]; the gook 《경멸》. ～사상 Eastern ideas; Orientalism. ～식 Orientalism; 《건물》 Oriental style. ～인 ＝동양 사람. ～인종 Oriental races. ～제국(諸國) the Eastern 〔Oriental〕 countries. ～태평양 권투 연맹 the Oriental and Pacific 〔Oriental-Pacific〕 Boxing Federation (생략 OPBF). ～통(通) an Orientalist; an authority on Oriental affairs. ～학 Oriental studies: ～학자 an Orientalist. ～화(化) Orientalization: ～화하다 Orientalize. ～화(畫) an Oriental painting 〔drawing〕.

**동어**(一魚) 《숭어새끼》 a young mullet.

**동업**(同業) the same trade 〔profession〕; the same line of business. ～하다 do business in partnership 《with》; run business together. ¶ ～지 조선일보 the Chosun Ilbo, our contemporary / ～인 김씨 Mr. Kim, who is in the same line of business as ours.

**동업자**(同業者) 《개인의》 a person in the same 「trade as *one* 〔line of business〕; a fellow trader 〔businessman〕; 《공동 영업의》 a partner; an associate; [총칭] the profession (의사·변호사 등의); the trade 〔craft〕 (상인·기능인 등의); a contemporary (신문 등의). ¶ ～가 많은 장사 a crowded trade / ～ 할인 trade discount / 우리는 ～이다 We are in the same line of business 〔trade〕.

**동여매다** ＝동이다.

**동역학**(動力學) 〖물리〗 kinetics; dynamics.

**동옷** ＝동저고리.

**동요**(動搖) ① 《물리적인 흔들림》 tremble; shake; shaking; trembling; quaking; 《배의》 roll; rolling (좌우로); pitching (상하로). ～하다 shake; quake; tremble; 《배가》 pitch and roll; 《차·마

차 따위가》 jolt. ¶ 배의 ~ the rolling of a ship. ② 《마음의》 unrest; restlessness (불안); 《인심·사회적인》 agitation; disturbance; a stir. ~하다 《마음이》 be unsettled; be agitated; become restless; 《결심이》 waver; 《갈팡질팡하다》 vacillate 《between》; 《세상이》 be disturbed. ¶ 정계의 ~ unrest in the political world; political disturbance / 물가의 ~ fluctuation in prices / 마음의 ~ restlessness of mind / 사상의 ~ an agitation of thought / ~를 일으키다 [사물이 주어] cause 〔create〕 unrest; [사람이 주어] get 〔become〕 restless; get shaken / 전국적으로 민심이 ~하고 있다 There is public unrest throughout the country. / 그의 죽음은 정치적인 ~를 일으켰다 His death led to political unrest. / 그 문제에 대해서 그들은 ~하고 있다 They are agitated over the question. / 정계에 ~의 조짐이 있다 There are signs of an upheaval in the political world. / 그 소식을 듣고 그는 마음의 ~를 감출 수 없었다 Hearing the news, he wasn't able to hide his state of agitation.

**동요**(童謠) a nursery rhyme 〔song〕; a children's song. ◉ ~작가 a writer of children's songs. ~집 nursery rhymes.

**동우**(同友) like-minded friends; a comrade; a colleague; a fellow member.

**동원**(動員) mobilization. ~하다 mobilize 《troops》; set in motion; call out 《300 policemen》; 《물건을》 bring 《*something*》 into play; call 〔press〕 《*something*》 into service. ¶ 강제 ~ compulsory mobilization 《of students》/ 노동력의 ~ labor mobilization / ~을 해제하다 demobilize / 경찰 전원을 ~하여 폭동에 대비했다 All the police were sent out on the alert for the riot. / 그 영화는 총 10만명의 관객을 ~했다 The film drew audiences totaling 100,000 people. / 그 연구를 추진하기 위해 고성능 컴퓨터가 ~되었다 They had recourse to high-efficiency computers in order to push forward their research. ◉ ~계획 a mobilization plan. ~령 《issue》 a mobilization order: 국가 ~령 《promulate》 National Mobilization Order. ~해제 demobilization; 〖군사〗 redeployment.

**동월**(同月) the same 〔said〕 month. ¶ ~ 15일에 on the 15th of the same month.

**동위**(同位) the same rank 〔position〕; 〖수학〗 the same digit. ¶ ~의 coordinate 《with *a person*》 in rank. ◉ ~각 〖수학〗 the corresponding angles. ~원소 〖물리〗 an isotope: 방사성 ~ 원소 a radioisotope; a radioactive isotope.

**동유**(桐油) tung oil. ◉ ~지 oilpaper.

**동음**(同音) the same sound; 〖음악〗 homophony. ¶ ~ 이의(異義)의 homonymous. ◉ ~어 a homophone (★ 동음이면서 철자가 다른 것도 포함). ~이의어 a homonym (★ 발음과 철자가 같은 것).

**동의**(同義) the same meaning; synonymy; synonymity. ¶ ~의 synonymous; synonymic(al). ◉ ~어 a synonym: 'happy'는 본래 'lucky'와 ~어였다 'Happy' used to be synonymous with 'lucky'.

**동의**(同意) 《일치》 agreement; 《같은 의견》 the same opinion; 《승낙》 consent; assent; 《찬성》 approval. ~하다 agree 《with, to》 (★ with는 사람, to는 사물일 때 흔히 쓰임. 그러나 agree with a plan 〔what he says〕도 잘 쓰임. 단, agree to *a person*이라고는 하지 않음); consent 〔assent〕 to 《a proposal》; approve of 《what you say》; subscribe to 《an opinion, a plan》. ¶ ~를 얻다 obtain 《*a person's*》 consent 〔approval〕 / ~를 얻어서 with the consent 《of *a person*》 / 제안에 ~하다 agree 〔accede〕 to a proposal / 고개를 끄떡여 ~를 나타내다 nod 《*one's* head》 in assent / 나는 기꺼이 그 안에 ~했다 I willingly consented to the plan. / 그에게 전적으로 ~할 수는 없다 I cannot go all the way with him. / 그 점에 관해서는 너에게 ~한다 I agree with you on that point. / 그는 아들의 결혼에 ~하지 않았다 He did not approve of his son's marriage. / 미성년자가 결혼하자면 부모의 ~를 얻어야 한다 Marriage between minors requires parental consent. ◉ ~서 a written consent. ~자 an assenter; an approver.

**동의**(胴衣) 《동옷》 a man's jacket; 《조끼》 a vest; a waistcoat; 《구어》 a weskit.

**동의**(動議) a motion. ~하다 make 〔bring forward, put〕 a motion; move 《that...》. ¶ 긴급 ~ an urgent 〔emergency〕 motion / B씨의 ~로 on Mr. B's motion / ~가 성립하다〔부결되다〕 a motion is carried 〔rejected〕/ ~를 채택하다 adopt a motion / ~를 철회하다 withdraw a motion / ~에 찬성하다 second a motion / 휴회의 ~를 내다 make a motion to adjourn / 토론 종결의 ~를 내다 move the closure

《영》〔cloture《미》〕/ 나는 그 ～에 찬성〔반대〕 투표를 했다 I voted for 〔against〕 the motion. / 의안을 즉시 표결할 것을 ～합니다 Mr. Chairman, I move that the bill be put to the vote immediately. ◉ ～제출자 a mover.

**동이** a 〔an earthenware〕 jar. ¶ 물～ a water jar.

**동이다** tie 〔do〕 up; bind; fasten; cord; chain (사슬로). ¶ 끈으로 꾸러미를～ tie up a bundle with string / 볏단을 ～ bind rice into a sheaf / 죄인을 포승으로 ～ tie a criminal with a rope.

**동인**(同人) ①《뜻이 같은 사람》people of kindred spirits; a group; a coterie; 《개인》a (fellow) member; fellow members. ¶ 문학～ a literary coterie 〔group〕/ 잡지 "창조"의 ～ a member of a literary group which publishes a magazine "Ch'angjo". ②《그 사람》the same 〔said〕 person; the person in question. ◉ ～잡지 a literary coterie magazine.

**동인**(動因) a motive; motivation; a drive; a cause; an incentive《to an action》. ¶ 이 범죄의 ～ the motive for this crime / 개인적〔금전적〕 ～에서 from personal 〔mercenary〕 motives / 굶주림은 행동을 일으키는 강한 ～이다 Hunger is a strong drive to action.

**동인도**(東印度) the East Indies. ¶ ～회사 〖역사〗 the East India Company.

**동일**(同一) identity; sameness. ～하다 (be) identical《with》; be the same《as》; be one and the same. ¶ ～하게 equally; without discrimination / ～ 노동에 대한 ～ 임금 equal pay for equal work / ～하게 취급하다 treat《men》 without discrimination / ～ 인물임을 확인하다 identify《*a person*》 as… / ～ 수준에 있다 be on the same level 《with》/ 지킬 박사와 하이드씨는 ～인물이다 Dr. Jekyll and Mr. Hyde are one and the same person. / 개와 늑대는 ～ 종류에 속한다 The dog belongs to same family as the wolf.
◉ ～개념 an identical conception. ～성 identity; oneness; sameness. ～원리 the principle of identity. ～인물 the same person.

**동일시**(同一視) ～하다 identify《*a thing*》 with《another》; treat《*matters*》 without discrimination; regard《A》 in the same light as《B》; put on a par 《with》; put《*a thing*》 in the same category 〔class〕. ¶ 시장은 시민의 이익을 자신의 번영과 ～했다 The mayor identified the interests of the citizens with his own prosperity. / 나는 저런 사람들과 ～되고 싶지 않다 I don't like to be classed with them.

**동자**(童子) a (little) boy; a child. ¶ ～라도 그것은 안다 Even a child knows it. ◉ ～기둥 〖건축〗 a post. ～중 a boy monk 〔bonze〕; a priestling.

**동작**(動作) action; movement(s); motion; 《거동》 bearing; behavior; manners; gesture (몸짓). ～하다 move; act. ¶ 느린 ～ slow motion 〔movement〕/ ～이 민첩하다〔느리다〕 be quick 〔slow〕 in action 〔movement〕/ 그녀는 ～이 매우 우아하다 She is very graceful in her movements.

**동장**(洞長) a *dong* 〔village〕 headman.

**동장군**(冬將軍) General Winter; Jack Frost; a severe 〔rigorous〕 winter. ¶ ～이 오기 전에 before General Winter 〔Jack Frost〕 comes.

**동저고리** a men's coat; a jacket. ¶ 동저고릿바람으로 나다니다 go around in informal 〔casual〕 wear; go around in *one's* shirtsleeves.

**동적**(動的) dynamic; kinetic. ¶ ～인 표현 dynamic expressions / ～인 느낌 a dynamic feeling. ◉ ～밀도《인구의》 dynamic density.

**동전**(銅錢) a copper coin; a copper; 《경화》 a coin. ¶ 십원짜리 ～ a ten-won coin 〔piece〕/ ～의 앞면〔뒷면〕 heads 〔tails〕 of a coin / (공중 전화의) ～ 넣는 구멍《drop a coin in》 a slot / ～으로 치르다 pay in coins / ～ 한 푼 없다 haven't a penny 〔cent〕; have no money at all / ～ 한 푼 안 남기고 다 쓰다 spend all the money *one* has; spend *one's* last cent / 자동 판매기에 500원짜리 ～을 넣다 put 〔drop〕 a 500-won coin in the vending machine / ～ 교환기—가동중《게시》 Coin changer—in operation / ～은 현관 판매대에 준비되어 있습니다《게시》 Coin exchange at cashier's counter in entrance. / ～을 바꾸어 드립니다 Change made here. / 그들은 누가 먼저 가느냐를 ～을 던져서 정했다 They tossed a coin to decide who would go first. ◉ ～지갑 a coin 〔change〕 purse. ～통 a coin box.

**동전기**(動電氣) 〖물리〗 current 〔dynamic, voltaic, kinetic〕 electricity.

**동절**(冬節) the winter season; winter; wintertime.

**동점**(同點) the same grade 〔mark, score〕; 《경기의》 a tie; a draw (무승

부). ¶ ~이 되다 tie with…; tie 〔even〕 the score with… / ~으로 만들다 tie the score; score the tying run (야구에서) / ~으로 비기다 draw 《with》 / 시합은 3대 3의 ~으로 끝났다 The game finished in a tie with a score of 3 to 3. *or* The game ended in「a 3-to-3 tie 〔a tie, 3 to 3〕. / 나는 영어 시험에서 그녀와 ~이었다 I got the same score as she did on 〔in〕 the English test. ◉ ~결승전 a play-off. ~타(打) 〖야구〗 a game-tying hit; a score-tying blast. ~홈런 a game-tying「home run 〔homer〕.

**동점**(東漸) eastern penetration; eastward advance 〔movement〕. ~하다 proceed eastward; move 〔expand〕 eastward. ◉ 서세(西勢)~ Eastern penetration of Western powers.

**동정** a collar strip (attached to the top border of a Korean coat). ¶ ~을 달다 attach a collar strip onto a coat.

**동정**(同情) sympathy; compassion; pity (연민). ~하다 sympathize with 《*a person*》; feel 〔have〕 sympathy 《for》; pity 《*a person*》; feel pity 〔compassion〕 for 《*a person*》; have compassion on 《*a person*》. ¶ ~적인 sympathetic; compassionate; warmhearted / ~하여 sympathetically; in sympathy / 깊은〔따뜻한〕 ~ deep 〔warm〕 sympathy / ~을 나타내다 show *one's* sympathy 〔pity〕 《for》 / …에 대해 ~을 표시하다 express sympathy with… / ~을 사다〔받다〕 win 〔gain〕 《*a person's*》 sympathy / ~을 잃다 lose 《*a person's*》 sympathy / ~을 베풀다 extend *one's* sympathy 《to》 / ~할 만하다 deserve 《*a person's*》 pity 〔sympathy〕 / 진심으로 ~하다 sympathize from the bottom of *one's* heart / 아무의 어려운 처지에 ~하다 have compassion for *a person's* hard lot; sympathize with *a person* in *his* predicament / 자네에게 ~하고 있네 My sympathies are with you. / 일반의 ~이 그에게로 쏠렸다 Public sympathies were centered on him. ◉ ~자 a sympathizer; a well-wisher. ~파업 《go on》 a sympathy strike: ~파업을 하다 go on strike in sympathy 《with》. ~표 a sympathy vote: ~표를 모으다 collect sympathy votes.

**동정**(童貞) virginity. ¶ ~을 잃다 lose *one's* virginity / ~을 지키다 keep *one's* virginity. ◉ ~남 a (male) virgin. ~녀 a virgin; 《성모》 the (Blessed) Virgin; the Virgin Mary. ~생식 〖생물〗 virgin generation; parthenogenesis. ~설 the Virgin Birth.

**동정**(動靜) movements 《of the enemy》; a state of things (정세); the goings-on (실정); *one's* doings. ¶ 정계의 ~ the development of political affairs / 적의 ~을 살피다 feel out 〔watch〕 the movements of the enemy / 나는 그녀의 그 후 ~은 모른다 I have no idea about what has become of her since then. / 그녀의 ~을 알려 주십시오 Please let me know how she is getting on.

**동정심**(同情心) sympathy; a sympathetic feeling. ¶ ~ 있는 sympathetic; warm-hearted / ~ 없는 unsympathetic; cold-hearted / ~이 일어나다 be moved to sympathy / ~에 호소하다 appeal to 《*a person's*》 sympathy / 그에 대해서 ~이 일어났다 Sympathy with him swelled up in my heart.

**동제**(銅製) ¶ ~의 copper; made of copper / ~메달 a copper medal. ◉ ~품 copper goods 〔manufactures〕.

**동조**(同調) ① 《보조 맞춤》 alignment. ~하다 align *oneself* 《with》; follow suit; fall in 〔come into〕 line 《with》; side 《with》; sympathize 《with》. ¶ ~자 a sympathizer; a fellow traveler / 프랑스에 ~하다 follow France's line / 남의 의견에 ~하다 sympathize with *a person's* opinion / 나는 이 방침에 ~하지 않는다 I do not sympathize this policy. / 그가 위원을 그만두자, 다른 사람들도 모두 이에 ~하였다 When he resigned from the committee, all the rest followed suit. ② 〖전기〗 tuning; 〖영화〗 synchronism. ~하다 tune in to 《a TV show》. ¶ (음성·화면이) ~하지 않다 do not synchronize; 《구어》 be out of sync 《with》. ◉ ~기(器) a tuner.

**동족**(同族) 《종족》 the same race 〔tribe〕; 《동포》 brethren; 《혈족》 the same blood; consanguinity; 《일족》 the same family. ◉ ~결혼 endogamy. ~목적어 〖문법〗 a cognate object. ~어(語) cognate languages. ~체 〖화학〗 a homologue. ~회사 a family concern 〔firm〕; an affiliated concern.

**동족상잔**(同族相殘) a fratricidal war; an internecine struggle. ~하다 engage in a fratricidal war; make an internecine struggle against one another. ¶ ~의 비극을 겪다 experience the tragedy of a fratricidal war.

**동종**(同種) the same kind 〔sort〕. ¶ ~의 of the same kind 〔sort〕 / ~의 나

무 a tree of the same kind [species] / ~의 범죄가 늘고 있다 Crimes of the same kind have increased.

◉ ~동문(同文) the same race and language; homogeneity in race and characters. ~번식 〖생물〗 close breeding; inbreeding.

**동죄**(同罪) the same crime [offense, sin].

**동주**(同舟) (taking) the same boat. ⇨ 오월동주. ~하다 take the same boat 《with》; share a boat; be a fellow passenger.

**동중국해**(東中國海) the East China Sea.

**동중원소**(同重元素) 〖화학〗 an isobar.

**동지**(冬至) the winter solstice.

◉ ~선(線) 〖천문〗 the Tropic of Capricorn. ~섣달 the 11th and 12th lunar months; the coldest winter months. ~점(點) 〖천문〗 the solstitial point; the point of solstice. ~팥죽 red-bean gruel taken on the winter solstice. 동짓달 the 11th lunar month.

**동지**(同地) 《같은 곳》 the same place [district]; 《그곳》 the said place.

**동지**(同志) 《뜻이 같음》 the same mind; a congenial spirit; 《사람》 a like-minded person; a comrade; a fellow member; a kindred spirit. ¶ ~를 규합하다 muster men under *one's* banner; rally kindred spirits; appeal to like-minded people / 김 씨와 몇몇 ~들은 당내에서 새로운 집단을 결성했다 Mr. Kim and some like-minded colleagues formed a new group within the party.

**동진**(東進) marching [proceeding] east; easting (천체의). ~하다 march [go] eastward; proceed east.

**동질**(同質) the same quality [nature]; homogeneity(동종). ¶ ~의 of the same quality; homogeneous / 민족의 ~성 national homogeneity / ~의 제품 products of the same quality / 문화적으로 ~인 이웃 나라 a culturally homogeneous neighbor country.

◉ ~이상 〖광물〗《현상》 polymorphism; 《개체》 a polymorph. ~이체(異體) 〖화학〗 allotropy.

**동쪽**(東—) the east(ern) side; the eastward; (the) east. ¶ ~의 east; eastern; easterly / ~에 in the east; to the east; on the east (접하여) / ~으로 to the east [eastward]; eastward / ~에서 부는 바람 an east [easterly] wind / ~으로 가다 go east [eastward] / ~에서 바람이 불고 있다 The east wind is blowing. / 그는 인천시의 ~에 살고 있다 He lives in the east of Incheon City. / 배는 ~으로 항진했다 The ship sailed east [eastward]. / ~하늘이 밝아온다 The eastern sky is becoming light. / 해는 ~에서 뜨고 서쪽으로 진다 The sun rises in the east and sets in the west. / 우리 마을은 시내에서 15마일 ~에 있다 Our village is [lies] 15 miles east of the town. / 한국은 ~으로 동해에 면해 있다 Korea faces the East Sea on the east. / 동래는 부산의 ~에 있느냐, 서쪽에 있느냐 Is Dongnae to the east of Busan or to the west of it?

**동차**(同次) ¶ ~ 방정식 a homogeneous equation / ~식 a homogeneous expression.

**동참**(同參) participation. ~하다 participate 《in》; take part 《in》. ¶ 그녀도 그 계획에 ~했다 She participated in the project, too. ◉ ~자 a participant.

**동창**(同窓) a schoolmate. ⇨ 동창생. ¶ 우리는 ~이다 We attended [graduated from] the same school. *or* We were at school together. / 그와 나는 대학 ~이다 He is an alumnus of my college. *or* He and I studied at the same college. *or* He and I are graduates of the same college.

◉ ~생 a fellow student; a schoolmate; 《동기생》 a classmate; 《졸업생》 a graduate; an old boy [girl]; 《미》 an alumnus (*pl.* -ni) (남); an alumna (*pl.* -nae) (여). ~회 《조직》 《미》 an alumni association; 《영》 an old boys' [girls'] association; 《회합》 a class reunion (동기생의); 《미》 an alumni meeting [reunion]: ~회 명부 the membership list of an alumni association / ~회지(誌) an alumni bulletin.

**동창**(東窓) a window facing east; the east window.

**동천**(東天) the eastern sky; the sky in the east.

**동철**(冬鐵) 《나막신의》 crampons; spikes (on shoes); 《말편자의》 horseshoe spikes.

**동체**(同體) 《한 물체》 the same substance; 《한 몸》 one body.

**동체**(胴體) the body; the trunk (조각상의); the torso (*pl.* ~s, -si); 〖항공〗 the body; the fuselage; an airframe.

◉ ~착륙 belly-landing: ~ 착륙하다 make a belly-landing; bellyland 《a plane》.

**동체**(動體) a body in motion; a moving body. ◉ ~사진 a photochronograph.

**동축**(同軸) the same axle. ◉ ～원 coaxal 〔coaxial〕 circles. ～케이블 a coaxial cable.

**동치**(同値) 〖수학〗 the equivalent.

**동치다** bind up; tie up.

**동치미** chopped radishes pickled in salt water; watery radish kimchi.

**동침**(一鍼) 〖한의〗 an acupuncture needle.

**동침**(同寢) ～하다 sleep together; share 「the same bed 《with》.

**동태**(凍太) a frozen pollack.

**동태**(動態) movement 《of the population》. ¶ 여론의 ～ the drift 〔trend〕 of public opinion / 적의 ～를 주시하다 watch the movements of the enemy / 5년마다 인구 ～를 조사하다 investigate the movement of population every five years. ◉ ～경제 dynamic economy. ～통계 dynamic statistics: 인구의 ～통계 vital statistics.

**동통**(疼痛) a (sharp) pain; an ache. ¶ 손에 심한 ～을 느끼다 have a terrible pain in *one's* hand.

**동트기**(東—) daybreak; dawn.

**동트다**(東—) 《the day》 break; dawn. ¶ 동틀 무렵에 출발하다 start at the first gray of dawn; set out at the crack of dawn.

**동티** 〖민속〗 an evil from the subterranean gods by disturbing the earth; trouble brought upon *oneself* gratuitously. ¶ ～ 나다 incur the divine wrath; bring evil 〔a curse〕 upon; inflict an evil on.

**동파**(同派) 《같은 파》 the same school 〔faction, sect, clique〕; 《그 파》 the said clan 〔faction〕.

**동파**(凍破) ～하다 be frozen to burst 「〔rupture〕.

**동판**(銅版) 〖인쇄〗 a copperplate; a copperplate print; a mezzotint. ◉ ～인쇄 (copper)plate printing. ～조각(술) chalcography; copperplate engraving. ～화 a copperplate print.

**동편**(東便) the east 〔eastern〕 side.

**동포**(同胞) 《형제》 brothers; sisters; brethren; 《겨레》 fellow countrymen 〔citizen〕; compatriots. ¶ 해외 ～ countrymen and countrywomen overseas 〔abroad〕 / 재미 ～ Korean residents in the U.S. / 5천만 ～에게 고함 A word for our fifty-million compatriots! ◉ ～애 brotherly 〔fraternal〕 love; fraternity: ～애를 보이다 show 〔display〕 *one's* fraternal 〔brotherly〕 love.

**동풍**(東風) the east wind; an easterly wind.

**동하다**(動—) ① 《움직이다》 move; stir; budge; shift. ② 《마음이》 (***a***) 《감동·욕망 등이》 be moved 〔touched〕; be 〔feel〕 inclined to 《*do*》. ¶ 구미가 동하는 appetizing 《dish》; tempting 《offer》 / 동하기 쉽다 be nervous; be easily moved 〔affected, agitated, excited〕 / 구미가 ～ 《식욕이》 feel an appetite 《for》; 《욕심이》 have an itch 〔desire〕 《for, to *do*》; want 《to *do*》; have a (great) mind 《to *do*》 / 욕정이 ～ feel lust for women / 그 지위에 몹시 구미가 ～ I have a great yearning for the post. / 그녀의 말에 그의 마음은 크게 동했다 Her words moved 〔touched〕 him largely. (***b***) 《흔들리다》 be shaken 〔perturbed〕; be upset. ¶ 동하기 쉽다 be easily agitated 〔excited〕 《by》; be susceptible 《to》 / 마음이 동하지 않다 keep calm; remain unruffled 〔unperturbed〕 / 그녀는 전혀 동하는 기색을 보이지 않았다 Her manner showed no signs of being upset. *or* She didn't look perturbed in the slightest. ③ 《병이 도지다》 come back; recur; [사람이 주어] have 〔suffer〕 a relapse. ¶ 그녀는 무리를 했기 때문에 병이 다시 동했다 She had a relapse through over- ⌊work.

**동하중**(動荷重) live load.

**동학**(同學) a fellow scholar 〔researcher, student〕; a classmate.

**동항**(同行) 《같은 항렬》 the same degree of relationship.

**동항**(凍港) an icebound port. ¶ 부～ an 「ice-free port.

**동해**(東海) the East Sea.

**동해**(凍害) frost damage.

**동해안**(東海岸) the east coast.

**동행**(同行) going together; traveling together. ～하다 go 《to a place》 along 《with *a person*》; accompany *a person* 《to a place》; go in company 《with》; go in *a person's* company; go 〔come〕 with 《*a person*》; travel together 《with *a person*》. ¶ ～하는 세 사람 a party of three (travelers) / 경찰서까지 ～을 요구하다 ask 《*a person*》 to come 〔go〕 to the police station / 그와 ～하여 시내까지 갔다 I accompanied 〔went with〕 him to town. ◉ ～자 a fellow traveler; a (traveling) companion: ～자의 한 사람 one of the party.

**동향**(同鄕) the same native place; the same district 〔town, village, province〕. ¶ 그와 나는 ～이다 He comes from the same province as I. *or* He is from the same province as 「me 〔I am〕. ◉ ～인 a person from the same 「province 〔part of the country〕.

**동향**(東向) an eastern exposure 〔aspect〕; facing east; eastward. ～하다 face east; look toward the east. ◉ ～집 a house facing east. ～판 a ground 〔lot〕 facing east.

**동향**(動向) a tendency; a trend; a movement (움직임). ¶ 경제 ～에 매우 민감하다 be very responsive to economic trends / 여론의 ～에 주의하다 watch the trend of public opinion / 정치가는 시대의 ～에 민감해야 한다 Politicians must be sensitive to the movements of the times. / 이 한 가지 일로 정계의 ～을 알 수 있다 This straw shows in which way the wind is blowing in the political world.

**동혈**(洞穴) a cave; a cavern; a grotto.

**동형**(同型) the same type 〔pattern〕; a similar type. ¶ ～이다 be of the same type / 두 사람은 ～의 컴퓨터를 샀다 The two bought computers of the same style.

**동형**(同形) the same shape; 〖생물·화학〗 isomorphism. ¶ ～의 《be》 of the same shape 〔kind〕; isomorphic / 좌우 ～의 symmetrical.

**동호**(同好) the same taste. ～하다 share the same tastes. ◉ ～인 people sharing the same tastes; people interested in the same subject. ～회 a club; an association: 낚시 ～회 an (amateur) anglers' club / 음악～회 a music lovers' society / 스키 ～회 an amateur ski club.

**동화**(同化) assimilation; 〖생물〗 anabolism (식물의); adaptation. ～하다 assimilate 《with, to》; adapt *oneself* 《to》. ¶ ～할 수 있는 assimilable / ～하기 어렵다 be hard to assimilate / 외국 풍습에 ～하다 adapt *oneself* to foreign customs / 다양한 외국 문화를 ～하다 assimilate a variety of foreign cultures.
◉ ～력 assimilative power. ～성 assimilability. ～작용 〖생물·생리·지질〗 (the process of) assimilation; anabolism. ～조직 an assimilation tissue.

**동화**(動畫) an animation; an animated film 〔cartoon〕. ◉ ～제작자 an animator.

**동화**(童話) a fairy tale; a nursery tale 〔story〕; a juvenile 〔children's〕 story. ◉ ～극 a children's 〔juvenile〕 play. ～작가 a writer of juvenile stories; a fairy-tale writer.

**동화**(銅貨) a copper coin 〔piece〕; a copper; copper coinage [총칭].

**동활차**(動滑車) a movable pulley.

**동회**(洞會) a *dong* 〔village〕 office. ⇨ 동사무소.

**돛** a sail; a canvas. ¶ 삼각돛 a jib / 바람을 가득 받은 돛 a full sail / 돛을 올리다 hoist 〔put up, spread〕 a sail / 돛을 내리다 lower 〔take down〕 a sail / 돛을 펴다〔감다〕 unfurl 〔furl〕 a sail / 순풍에 돛을 달고 달리다 sail before the wind; be under easy sail / 순풍에 돛을 단 듯 모든 것이 잘 되어 간다 Everything goes very well; It's all plain sailing.

**돛단배** a sailer; a sailing ship.

**돛대** a mast; a stick. ¶ ～를 잃은 배 a dismasted vessel.

**돛새치** 〖어류〗 a sailfish.

**돼지** ① 《가축》 a pig (★ 미국에서는 특히 새끼 돼지); a hog (★ 불깐 수컷. 미국에서는 성장한 돼지); a boar (불까지 않은 수퇘지); a sow (새끼를 낳은 암퇘지); a grunter; swine [총칭]; 《식육용의》 a pork pig; a porker (어린 것). ¶ 한 배 ～새끼 a farrow; a litter of pigs / ～를 치다 raise hogs; breed pigs / 그는 돼지처럼 게걸스럽게 먹는다 He makes a pig of himself. *or* He eats like a hog 〔pig〕. / ～에 진주 《속담》 To cast 〔throw〕 pearls before swine. *or* It's like casting pearls before swine. ② [비유적] a greedy 〔grasping〕 person; a hog; a glutton; a great eater. ◉ ～가죽 pigskin. ～고기 pork; pig meat. ～기름 lard (★ 소의 기름은 tallow). ～떡 a mess; a filthy 〔dirty〕 thing. ～우리 a pigsty; a pigpen; a hogpen 《미》: ～우리 같은 집 a shack; a wretched hovel. ～저금통 a piggy bank. ～풀 〖식물〗 a hogweed.

**되** 《곡식 되는》 a measure; a measuring cup 〔basket〕; a dry measure; 《액체 되는》 a liquid measure; 《계량 단위》 a unit of measure; a *toe* (＝1 / 10 *mal*, 10 *hop*). ¶ 쌀 넉 되 four *toe* of rice / 되로 팔다 sell by the measure / 되를 속이다 give short measure / 되를 넉넉하게 주다 give good measure / 되로 주고 말로 받는다 《속담》 be revenged ten times harder; sow the wind and reap the whirlwind (성서에서) / 되글을 가지고 말글로 써 먹는다 《속담》 turn *one's* small learning to best advantage; make the most of *one's* meager knowledge.

**되-** 《다시·도리어·도로》 back; again; backward; reversely; conversely;

instead; on the contrary; in return. ¶ 되묻다 ask in return / 되씹다 chew again (and again); ruminate / 되찾다 regain; get back / 되돌려주다 return; give 〔hand〕 back / 되돌아가다 go back; return / 되생각하다 think over again; reconsider / 되사다 buy back; repurchase; redeem / 되싣다 reship / 되치다 strike back / 되튀다 rebound; spring back.

**-되** ① 《…이지만》 though; although; even though. ¶ 그는 전력을 다했으되 though he did his utmost 〔best〕; in spite of 〔after, with〕 all his efforts / 나이는 먹었으되 though he is old; old as he is / 그는 훌륭한 학자이긴 하되 fine scholar as he is / 집이 남향이되 동으로 좀 치우쳤다 The house faces south but leans slightly to the east. / 돈은 많되 쓸 줄을 모른다 He has lots of money but he doesn't know how to spend it. ② 《…이나 정말》 and that; and indeed; 《조건·금지 등을 나타내어》 if; but. ¶ 비가 오되 억수같이 온다 It is raining and really raining hard. / 바람이 불되 몹시 분다 The wind is blowing and very hard too. / 그는 키가 크되 여간 큰 키가 아니다 He is tall and even unusually tall. / 오기는 오되 혼자 오너라 If you want to come, bring nobody with you. / 보기는 보되 만지지는 마라 You may look at it, but don't touch it!

**되갈다** ① 《논밭을》 replow; replough 《영》. ② 《가루 따위를》 regrind.

**되감다** roll 《it》 back up 〔again〕.

**되강오리** 〖조류〗 = 농병아리.

**되개고마리** 〖조류〗 a red-tailed shrike.

**되걸리다** 《병에》 contract 《a disease》 again; be seized 〔afflicted〕 with again; come down with another case 《of》. ¶ 감기에 ~ catch cold again; recatch a cold; catch more cold.

**되게** 《몹시》 very; exceedingly; extraordinarily; hard; severely; heavily; bitterly; extremely; awfully. ¶ ~ 덥다 be very hot / ~ 걱정되다 be much worried / ~ 무섭다 be quite dreadful.

**되넘기다** 《되팔다》 resell (right after *one* has bought); buy 《*something*》 and sell it again 《to》. ¶ 사과를 과수원에서 사서 소매상에게 ~ buy apples from an orchard and sell them to a retailer.

**되놈** 《중국인의 낮춤말》 a Chinese; [경멸적] a Chinaman; a Chink 《속어》.

**되뇌다** keep repeating 《words》; say over again. ¶ 남의 말을 ~ echo 〔repeat〕 《*a person's*》 words / 같은 소리를 ~ harp on the same string; repeat the same thing.

**되는대로** ① (***a***) 《함부로》 at random; at haphazard; irresponsibly. ¶ ~ 대답하다 make a random answer; answer at 〔by〕 haphazard / ~ 지껄이다 talk irresponsibly 〔at random〕; say anything that comes into *one's* head; talk wild. (***b***) 《정성 없이》 lukewarmly; halfheartedly. ¶ 일을 ~ 하다 scamp 〔fudge, slur over〕 *one's* work. ② 《되어가는 대로》 ¶ ~ 살아가다 ride with the tide; live in a happy-go-lucky way; resign *oneself* to fate.

**되다**[1] ① 《어떤 상태·위치·지위 등에 이르다》 become; get; grow; be; go.

> 용법 **become** 「…이 되다」란 뜻으로, **get**와 함께 가장 흔히 쓰이는 말. get이 더 구어적인 표현. 회화에서 become은 주로 명사 앞에서 쓰임. 형용사 (과거분사 포함) 앞에는 become보다 get를 쓰는 것이 일반적: become angry보다는 get angry가 더 구어적. **grow** 점점 어떤 상태로 「되어가다」라고 과정을 뜻하는 말. **be** 「…이다」란 상태를 뜻하는 경우가 많으나, 「…이 되다」란 become의 뜻으로도 많이 쓰임. be동사 단독으로 become의 뜻이 되는 경우도 있으나, 「동사+to be+명사」 또는 「be+과거분사」의 형태가 더 일반적: 「나는 이제 대학 2년생이 되었다」 I'm a sophomore now. / 「나는 선생님이 되고 싶다」 I want to 「be」 〔become〕 a teacher. / 「앓게 되다」 be taken ill. **go** 주로 바람직하지 않은 상태로의 변화나 급격한 또는 뚜렷한 변화를 뜻하는 경우가 많음: 「대머리가 되다」 go bald.

¶ 버릇이 ~ grow into a habit / 부자가 ~ become a rich man; get rich / 3학년이 ~ become a third-year student / 어른이 ~ come of age; grow up to be a man; attain *one's* majority 〔adulthood〕 / 외교관이 ~ enter the diplomatic service / 장관이 ~ become a cabinet minister / 장님이〔미치광이가〕 ~ go blind 〔mad〕 / 희생이 ~ fall a victim 《to》 / 작가가 되고 싶다 wish to be a writer / 커서 무엇이 되고 싶니 What would you like 〔are you going〕 to be when you grow up? / 그는 정치가가 되기 위해 교직을 포기했다 He gave up his teaching job to become a politician. / 그는 훌륭한 청년이 되었

다 He has grown up to be a fine young man.

② 《…하게 되다》 begin to 《*do*》; come to 《*do*》; get to 《*do*》; 《…할 수 있게 되다》 learn to *do*. ¶ 좋아하게 ～ begin 〔get, come〕 to like 《*a thing*》; take a fancy to 《a man》/ 좋아하지 않게 ～ cease to like 《*a thing*》/ 싫어하게 ～ conceive a dislike for 《*a person*》/ 나는 피아노를 잘 칠 수 있게 되고 싶다 I want to learn to play the piano well. / 곧 너는 헤엄을 칠 수 있게 될 게다 You will soon learn to swim. / 자넨 어떻게 담배를 피우게 되었는가 How did you come to start smoking?

③ 《어느 시기에 이르다》 be; come; set in. ¶ 봄이 되면 when spring comes / 이제 곧 9시가 된다 It'll soon be nine o'clock. / 우리 아들은 이번 생일로 5살이 된다 Our son will be five years old on his next birthday. / 장마철이 되었다 The rainy season has set in.

④ 《변화하여 …이 되다》 turn into 〔out〕; change 《into》; develop; get 《better》. ¶ 물이 수증기가 ～ water turns 〔changes〕 into vapor / 푸른빛이 초록으로 ～ blue changes 〔passes, fades〕 into green / 감기가 폐렴이 ～ a cold develops into 〔leads to〕 pneumonia / 병이 완쾌 ～ get 〔be〕 quite well again / 물이 산소와 수소로 분해～ water resolves into oxygen and hydrogen / 애벌레가 나방이 되었다 The caterpillar changed into a moth.

⑤ 《지나다》 pass; elapse; be (since). ¶ 그가 미국 간 지 3년 된다 It is three years since he went to America. / 우리가 저 나무를 심은 지 5년이 된다 It is five years since we planted that tree. / 얼마나 오래 됩니까 How long has it been?

⑥ 《어떤 수에 이르다》 number; amount to; run up to; make; be; 《무게가》 weigh; 《용적·넓이·크기가》 measure; 《면적이》 cover. ¶ 그 수효는 약 500이나 된다 They number about five hundred. *or* They are about five hundred in number. / 그는 키가 5피트 4인치가 된다 He is five feet four inches tall. *or* He stands five feet four. / 몸무게가 60킬로나 된다 I weigh sixty kilograms. / 강은 폭이 10미터나 된다 The river measures 〔is〕 ten meters across. / 농장은 약 3천 평방미터가 된다 The farm covers about three thousand square meters.

⑦ 《결과가 되다》 turn out (to be); prove (to be); result in. ¶ 만사는 우리가 바라던 대로 되었다 Everything turned out as we had hoped. / 꿈이 현실로 되었다 The dream has come true. / 좋은 날씨가 되었다 The weather turned fine. / 머리의 상처가 그녀에게 치명상이 되었다 The injury to the head proved fatal to her. / 투표 결과는 어떻게 되었느냐 How did the voting turn 〔come〕 out? / 그런 짓을 하면 너는 파멸된다 That would lead to your ruin. / 경기는 무승부가 되었다 The match resulted in a draw.

⑧ 《구성되다》 consist 《of》; be composed 〔formed〕 《of》; be made up 《of》. ¶ 이 소설은 3부로 되어 있다 This novel has three parts. / 미국은 50개의 주로 되어 있다 The United States 「is made up 〔consists〕 of fifty states. / 물은 산소와 수소로 되어 있다 Water consists 〔is composed〕 of oxygen and hydrogen.

⑨ 《성취·완성되다》 be made 〔finished, completed, attained, accomplished〕; succeed; 《준비가》 be ready. ¶ 일이 뜻대로 ～ succeed in *one's* attempt / 식사 준비가 되었습니다 Dinner is ready. / 도로 공사가 다 되었다 The road construction has been completed. / 되고 안 되고는 오직 너의 노력 여하에 달려 있다 Whether you succeed or not depends entirely on your efforts.

⑩ 《생육·홍성하다》 grow; thrive; prosper. ¶ 채소가 잘 ～ vegetables grow well 《in this soil》/ 장사가 잘 ～ do good 〔prosperous〕 business; business is good / 집안이 잘 ～ a family is prosperous; a family thrives / 집안이 잘 안 되어 간다 A family is going downhill.

⑪ 《쓸모있다·알맞다》 serve the purpose; will do; work; be all right. ¶ 그 돈이면 되겠다 That amount of money will do. / 이 지팡이는 무기가 된다 This stick will serve as a weapon. / 「이 짧은 끈으로 되겠습니까」—「예, 됩니다」 "Will this short string do?"—"Yes, it will do." / 「뭐 좀 쓸 것이 필요한데」—「이 연필이면 되겠습니까」 "I want something to write with."—"Does this pencil serve your purpose?" / 그렇게 해서야 되겠니 That won't do. *or* You shouldn't do that. / 이것은 안 되겠네 This one's no good! / 그것은 말이 되지 않는다 That is nonsense 〔absurd〕.

⑫ 《없이 때우다》 can do without; can dispense with. ¶ 한일 사전은 없어도 됩

니다 I can do without a Korean-Japanese dictionary.
⑬《역할·구실을 하다》act as; serve as; play the role of. ¶ 햄릿이 ~ play the role 〔take the part〕 of Hamlet / 알코올은 소독약이 된다 Alcohol acts as a disinfectant.
⑭《…의 관계》¶ 그는 내 조카가 된다 He stands to me in the relation of nephew. *or* He is my nephew.
⑮《관용적 표현》¶ 그것은 내게 좋은 약〔교훈〕이 되었다 It was a lesson to me. *or* It taught me a lesson. / 때가 오면 그리 되겠지 All will be done in good time. / 떠들어봐야 일이 어떻게 되는 것 아니다 Shouting wouldn't mend matters. *or* Shouting will get you nowhere.

**되다**[2] 《되질하다》measure. ¶ 되〔말〕로 ~ measure in *toe* 〔*mal*〕; measure《rice》with a measure / 되어(서) 팔다 sell by measure / 후하게 ~ give a good measure.

**되다**[3] ①《질지 않다》(be) thick; hard. ¶ 된 밥 hard-boiled rice / 된 죽〔풀〕 thick gruel 〔paste〕 / 죽을 되게 쑤다 make the gruel thick.
②《심하다》(be) severe; intense; heavy. ¶ 된 서리 heavy frost / 된 추위 intensely cold weather / 된 형벌 severe punishment / 되게 꾸짖다 scold severely / 되게 혼내주다 give《*a person*》a ˹hard time 〔good licking〕; teach《*a person*》a lesson; defeat *one's* opponent badly / 되게 아프다 be very 〔extremely〕 painful / 되게 춥다 be very 〔intensely〕 cold / 되게 때리다 strike《*a person*》hard / 되게 얻어맞다 be beaten hard / 되게 걱정하다 worry very much / 그날 밤엔 된 서리가 내렸다 There was a hard frost that night. / 되게 추운데 Bitterly cold, isn't it?
③《벅차다》(be) hard; trying; bitter; tough. ¶ 된 일 hard work; a tough job / 된 고비 the worst 〔hardest〕 part; a crisis; a crucial 〔critical〕 stage; the hump / 일의 된 고비를 넘기다 be through with the hardest part of a job / 병의 된 고비를 넘기다 pass the crisis 〔critical stage〕 of an illness.

**-되다** ① [동사적 명사에 붙어] become; get to be; be. ¶ 걱정되다 be worried 〔anxious〕 about / 확인되다 be ascertained / 판명되다 become clear 〔plain〕 / 시작되다 begin; have a beginning / 해결되다 get solved 〔resolved〕 / 자리가 준비되다 a table is ready / 건강은 완전히 회복되셨습니까 Is your health completely recovered? ② [형용사·부사적 어근에 붙어] be. ¶ 망녕되다 be silly; be nonsensical; be unreasonable / 속되다 be vulgar 〔common〕 / 참되다 be true / 헛되다 be false; be in vain; be futile.

**되다랗다** (be) quite thick 〔heavy〕.

**되대패** a round 〔circular〕 plane.

**되도록** ①《될 수 있는 대로》as... as possible; as... as *one* can; 《될 수 있으면》if possible; if it can be so arranged; if circumstances allow; [부정] no more than *one* can help. ¶ ~ 일찍 가거라 Go as soon as you can. / ~ 빨리 달려라 Run as fast as possible 〔you can〕. / ~ 빨리 오너라 Please come as early as you can. / ~ 시간을 유효하게 쓰시오 Make the best (use) of your time. / ~ 늦지 않도록 해라 Don't be longer than you can help. ②《될 수 있게》(so as) to; so that it may.... ¶ 교사가 ~ 돕다 help《*a person*》(to) become a teacher / 일등이 ~ 힘쓰다 try hard to win the first prize《in a race》.

**되돌아가다** ①《길을》go back《to》; return《to》; turn back. ¶ 온 길을 ~ retrace *one's* steps; go back over *one's* way; return 〔turn back〕 the way *one* has come / 도중에서 ~ turn back halfway / 나쁜 날씨 때문에 비행기는 김포로 되돌아갔다 The plane turned back to Kimpo airport due to bad weather. ②《본디 상태로》return《to》; go back《to》; revert《to》. ¶ 본론으로 ~ return to *one's* main point / 이전 직업으로 ~ return to *one's* former business / 옛 버릇으로 ~ return to *one's* old habits / 제자리로 ~ return to 〔go back to〕 *one's* seat / 한 번 파괴된 자연은 쉽게 원상태로 되돌아가지 못한다 Nature, once destroyed, will not easily return to its former state.

**되돌아보다** ①《뒤를》look 〔turn〕 around; turn about; look back《at》. ¶ 잠깐 ~ take a backward glance《at》; cast a hasty glance backward 〔behind〕; look back for a second / 되돌아보지도 않고 방을 나가다 go out of the room without looking back / 그녀는 갑자기 되돌아보며 나에게 말을 걸었다 She suddenly turned around and talked to me. ②《과거를》look back on 〔to〕; reminisce (회상하다); think back on; reflect on (반성하다). ¶ 과거를 ~ look back over the past; think back on the old days; think backward / 자기가 걸어온 길을 ~ look back over *one's* career / 나의 소년 시절을 되돌아보니 그때가 그립다 Looking back upon my boyhood, I long for it.

**되돌아오다** come 〔get〕 back 《to》; turn back 《to》; return 《to》; be sent back (반송되다); be restored 〔recovered〕 (회복되다). ¶ 제정신으로 ~ recover 〔come to〕 *one's* senses; come to (*oneself*) / 본제(本題)로 ~ revert 〔return〕 to the subject / 우리는 떠났던 곳으로 되돌아왔다 We retraced our steps to where we started. / 잃은 물건이 주인에게 되돌아왔다 The lost article was returned to its owner.

**되들고되나다** 《the crowd》 come and go; throng in and out.

**되들다** raise *one's* face defiantly.

**되똑거리다** totter; be unstable; shake; be shaky. ¶ 상다리가 ~ the leg of a table is shaky / 하이힐을 신고 ~ totter (along) on high heels.

**되똑되똑** totteringly; unstably; unsteadily; shakily; with tottering steps. ¶ 어린애가 몇발짝 ~ 걸었다 The baby took a few tottering steps.

**되뜨다** go against reason; be irrational 〔absurd, illogical〕.

**되롱거리다** dangle; sway.

**되롱되롱** ¶ 사과가 가지에 ~ 달려 있다 Apples are dangling from the branches.

**되묻다** 《다시 묻다》 ask again; repeat *one's* question; 《반문하다》 ask a question in return; ask back. ¶ 나는 무의식적으로 그에게 되물었다 I asked him the same question back involuntarily. / 그녀는 나의 질문에는 대답하지 않고, 너라면 어떻게 하겠느냐고 되물었다 She didn't answer my question, but instead asked me (back) what would I do in her place. 「return.

**되밀다** push 〔bear〕 back; push in

**되바라지다** ① 《그릇이》 (be) open; shallow. ¶ 되바라진 그릇 a shallow dish. ② 《편협하다》 (be) shallow; narrow=minded; hard; intolerant; illiberal. ¶ 되바라진 사람 a shallow 〔narrow=minded〕 person. ③ 《깜찍하다》 (be) overly smart 〔bright〕; precocious; pert; saucy; forward. ¶ 되바라진 아이 a precocious child / 되바라진 소리를 하다 say pert things. 「again; reprint.

**되박다** print 〔inlay, drive in, *etc.*〕

**되받다** 《도로 받다》 receive 〔get〕 《*a thing*》 back; 《반항하다》 stand up to a scolding; scold back; retort; answer 《*a person*》 back.

**되받아치다** hit 〔beat〕 《*a person*》 back 《on the head》; strike back; return a blow 《to》; deliver a counterblow 《against》.

**되부르다** call back; recall.

**되사다** buy 《*a thing*》 back; repurchase. ¶ 나는 그녀에게 판 차를 되사려고 한다 I'll buy back the car I sold her.

**되살다** ① 《먹은 것이》 be heavy on *one's* stomach; feel uncomfortable (because of indigestion). ② 《소생하다》 revive; return 〔come back〕 to life; come to *oneself*; 《불이》 be rekindled; flame 〔blaze, burn〕 up. ¶ 인공 호흡으로 되살아나다 be resuscitated 〔revived〕 by artificial respiration / 죽어가던 뱀이 ~ a dying snake comes back to life / 꺼져가던 불이 ~ a dying fire flames up again / 비가 와서 초목이 되살아났다 The rain has reinvigorated the withered plants. ③ 《헤어졌던 부부가》 be reunited 《with her former husband》; return to the former relations 《with a wife》.

**되살리다** 《사람을》 raise 《*a person*》 from the death; recall 〔restore〕 《*a person*》 to life; bring 《*a person*》 (back) to life 〔to 《*his*》 senses〕; bring life to 《*a person*》; revive; resuscitate 《from death》; 《기억 등을》 wake 〔recall, bring back〕 《*one's* memories》; 《식물 따위를》 freshen. 「again.

**되살피다** re-examine; look back over it

**되새** 〖조류〗 a brambling.

**되새기다** 《음식물을》 chew over and over again (because of poor appetite); 《소 등이》 ruminate; chew the cud; [비유적] ruminate 《about, of, on, upon, over》; think 《*a matter*》 over; meditate 《on》. ¶ 소가 먹은 것을 되새기고 있다 The cow is 「ruminating 〔chewing its cud〕. / 그녀는 선생님의 말씀을 여러 차례 되새겼다 She 「chewed over 〔ruminated upon〕 what her teacher had said. / 남녀노소 할 것 없이 잠시 고통스러웠던 한국전쟁의 역사를 되새겼다 Men and women, old and young alike, thought over the painful history of the Korean War for a while.

**되새김질** 《소 따위의》 rumination. ~하다 ruminate; chew the cud.

**되세우다** make 《a fallen thing》 stand again; stand 〔erect, raise〕 《*something*》 again; 《재건하다》 rebuild;

reconstruct.

**되솔새** 〖조류〗 a pale-legged willow warbler.

**되술래잡다** counterattack; put the blame on 《another》. 「terattacked」.

**되술래잡히다** be counterblamed 〔coun-

**되쏘다** 《총을》 shoot back; shoot again; refire; 《반사하다》 reflect; 《말로》 retort 〔retaliate〕 《upon》.

**되쏘아보다** stare back; glare back.

**되씌우다** shuffle *one's* 《responsibility》 off onto 《another's》 shoulder; lay 〔put, shift〕 《the blame》 on 《*a person*》; lay 《a fault》 at another's door. ¶ 너는 네 잘못을 나에게 되씌우려 한다 You are trying to put the blame on me when you are to blame yourself.

**되씹다** ① 《말을》 repeat; reiterate; say over and over again. ¶ 한 말을 ~ repeat *oneself*. ② = 되새기다.

**되알지다** ① 《억짓손이 세다》 (be) aggressive; pushing; pushy. ② 《벅차다》 be more than *one* can do; be beyond *one's* power 〔ability〕.

**되양되양하다** (be) flippant; frivolous.

**되어가다** ① 《일이》 go (on); progress; advance. ¶ 잘 ~ go (on) well; make (good) progress; be well under way; go on smoothly 〔without a hitch〕 / 일이 잘 ~ make good headway with *one's* work; an attempt is going to be successful / 되어가는 대로 하다 follow a hit-or-miss method; have the haphazard way of doing everything / 되어가는 대로 내버려두다 leave 《*a matter*》 to take 〔run〕 its own course / 혼담은 생각대로 잘 되어갔다 Engagement and marriage went ahead 「like clockwork 〔without a hitch〕. / 「일은 잘 되어가고 있습니까」—「예, 순조롭습니다」 "How is your work? Going smoothly?"—"Yes, just fine." ② 《완성을 향해》 be being made; be getting finished 〔completed〕. ¶ 일이 다 되어간다 The work is being finished. ③ 《시일·때가》 be getting; be setting in. ¶ 어른이 ~ be on the threshold of adulthood / 정오가 되어간다 It is getting on for noon. / 그가 미국으로 떠난 지 3년이 되어간다 It is almost three years since he went to America.

**되잖다** (be) poor; worthless; absurd; nonsensical; no good. ⇨ 되지 못하다. ¶ 되잖은 물건 poor 〔wretched〕 stuff / 되잖은 수작 absurd remark; nonsense / 되잖은 녀석 a wretched fellow; a good-for-nothing / 되잖은 핑계 a poor 〔lame〕 excuse.

**되지기**[1] 《밥》 reheated rice.

**되지기**[2] 《논밭》 a paddy field wide enough to plant one *toe* of seed rice.

**되지못하다** ① 《미달》 be short of; be not up to; be less than; be under. ¶ 열 살이 ~ be under ten (years old) / 그는 미국 간 지 반 년이 되지못하여 다시 돌아왔다 He came back home less than half a year after he went to America. / 기부금은 합계 100만원도 되지못했다 The donations came to a little less than a million won.
② 《미완성》 be not made; be not finished 〔completed, attained, accomplished〕; (be) unsuccessful; fall through. ¶ 일이 다 ~ a job is not finished; a plan fails 〔falls through〕.
③ 《격이》 be not able 〔fit〕 to become; be not successful (in being); be not worthy of. ¶ 학자가 ~ be not worthy of being called a scholar / 지식만으로서는 교사가 되지못한다 Knowledge alone does not qualify one for 〔to be〕 a teacher.
④ 《되잖다》 (be) no good; good-for-nothing; be not up to the mark; be not proper; be not decent; 《건방지다》 (be) impudent; presumptuous; pert; saucy. ¶ 되지못한 녀석 a good-for-nothing; a presumptuous fellow / 되지못하게 굴다 behave badly 〔improperly, indecently〕; play the scoundrel.

**되지빠귀** 〖조류〗 a gray-backed thrush.

**되직하다** be somewhat thick; be a bit too hard; stodgy. ¶ 풀이 ~ the paste is a bit thick / 밥을 되직하게 짓다 cook rice a bit hard.

**되질** measuring with a *toe*. ~하다 measure with a *toe*.

**되짚어** back; retracing 〔returning〕 right away. ¶ ~ 가다 go 〔turn〕 back right away; double upon *one's* steps / ~ 오다 come 〔turn〕 right back / ~ 보내다 send right back / ~ 회답해 주시기 바랍니다 Please answer my letter by return (of) mail 〔post 《영》〕.

**되찾다** 《다시 찾다》 take 〔get, win〕 back; regain; have 《it》 back; recover; restore; retrieve. ¶ 영토를 ~ recover territory / (빼앗긴 것을) 아무에게서 ~ take back 《*something*》 from *a person* / 이전의 지위를 ~ retrieve *one's* former position / 질서를 ~ restore 〔reestablish〕 order / 건강〔명성, 마음의 안정〕을 ~ get back 〔recover, regain〕 *one's* health 〔reputation, composure〕/ 그는 예전 생활을 되찾고 싶었다 He wanted the old life back. / 정부는 경제회복 대책에 대한 국민의 신뢰를 되찾는데 성공했다 The government succeeded in「winning back 〔recovering〕 public confidence in its plan for economic recovery.

**되치이다** ① 《반대로 당하다》 be counterattacked 〔retorted, retaliated〕; be given tit for tat; be riposted in kind. ② 《일이》 go for wool and come home shorn else; a thing turns out to be contrary to *one's* hope.

**되통스럽다** ⇨ 뒤퉁스럽다.

**되풀이**[1] 《반복》 doing 〔going〕 over again; (a) repetition; a repeat; reiteration; 《노래의》 a refrain. ～하다 do 〔go〕 over again; repeat; reiterate. ¶ ～하여 repeatedly; over again; over and over (again); again 〔time〕 and again / 말을 ～하다 repeat *oneself;* say over again; harp on the same string / 잘못을 ～하다 repeat 〔duplicate〕 *one's* mistake; make the same mistake again 〔twice〕/ 책을 세 번 ～하여 읽다 read a book three times over / 역사는 ～된다 History repeats itself. *or* History is the record of repetition. / 인생은 ～될 수 없다 You cannot live (your life) twice. / 같은 잘못을 ～하지 마라 Don't make the same error twice.

**되풀이**[2] 《계산》 figuring out the cost 《of *something*》 by the *toe;* 《되로 팖》 selling by the *toe.* ～하다 figure 〔sell〕 by the *toe.*

**된똥** hard stools 〔feces, excrements〕.

**된마파람** 《뱃사람 말》 a southeast wind.

**된매** a severe beating. ¶ ～를 맞다 be severely beaten.

**된바람** ① 《뱃사람 말》 a north 〔northerly〕 wind. ② 《강풍》 a strong 〔severe, violent〕 wind; a rushing wind.

**된밥** hard-boiled rice.

**된새(바람)** 《뱃사람 말》 a northeast(erly) wind.

**된서리** a heavy 〔hard, severe〕 frost. ¶ ～ 맞다 suffer from a heavy frost; 《타격받다》 suffer a bitter blow; receive a setback; be hit hard / 그는 이번 장사에 ～ 맞았다 He suffered quite a setback on the last deal. / 면직물 업계는 그 일로 인해 ～를 맞았다 The cotton industry was hard hit by it.

**된서방**(一書房) a hard 〔severe, harsh〕 husband. ¶ ～ 맞다 get married to a harsh husband; [비유적] suffer an ordeal; have a great trouble; be faced with a great difficulty.

**된소리** 〖음성〗 a fortis (*pl.* fortes).

**된장**(一醬) *toenjang,* the Korean soybean paste. ¶ ～국 beanpaste soup / ～찌개 soybean-paste pot stew / ～에 풋고추 박히듯 sticking to one place / 한국의 ～과 청국장은 항암 작용이 매우 높다는 것을 한 연구에서 재확인했다 A study reaffirmed that the Korean *toenjang* 〔soybean paste〕 and its liquid version, *chŏnggugjang,* are highly effective in fighting cancer.

**된풀** thick paste.

**된하늬** 《뱃사람 말》 a northwest(erly) wind.

**될뻔댁**(一宅) a person who just missed a chance of becoming somebody.

**될성부르다** (be) promising. ¶ 일이 ～ bid fair to succeed / 될성부른 나무는 떡잎부터 알아본다 《속담》 Sandalwood is fragrant even in seed leaf. *or* Genius displays itself even in childhood.

**될수있는대로** 《가급적》 as... as possible 〔practicable〕; as... as *one* can 〔may〕; 《될 수 있으면》 if possible 〔practicable, feasible〕; if it can be so arranged; if circumstances allow; [부정의 경우] as little 〔few〕 as possible. ⇨ 가급적. ¶ ～ 빨리 as quickly 〔promptly〕 as possible; with the least possible delay; as soon as possible; at *one's* earliest (possible) convenience; at the first opportunity / ～ 많이 as much 〔many〕 as possible / ～ 싸게 팔다 sell as cheaply as possible / ～ 빨리 회답을 주십시오 Please reply at your earliest convenience. *or* Please let me have your answer as soon as possible.

**됨됨이** ① 《사람》 the man; *one's* nature 〔disposition〕; *one's* character; *one's* personality. ¶ ～가 정직하다 be honest by nature 〔in character〕/ 그는 사람 ～가 근실하다 He is serious-minded by nature. / 그는 사람 ～가 변변치 못하다 He is not much good. *or* He hasn't much on the ball. / 그의 연설 속에는 그의 사람 ～가 여실히 나타나 있다 His personality comes out clearly in his speech. ② 《물건》 make; makeup; workmanship. ¶ ～가 좋다 It is「a good make 〔a well made〕. / ～가 시원찮다 The make is poor.

**됫밀** odd grain left over when measuring with a *toe.*

**됫박** a gourd bowl used as a measure; 《되》 a *toe.* ¶ 쌀을 ~으로 사다 buy rice 「by the *toe* 〔in small quantities〕. ◉ ~질 measuring with a gourd bowl; buying by the gourd bowl: ~질하다 measure with a gourd bowl; buy rice by the gourd bowl; buy rice in small quantity.

**됫술** about one *toe* of rice wine; rice wine sold by the *toe.*

**두** two; a couple 《of》. ¶ 두 가지 《종류》 two kinds 《of》; 《방법》 two ways / 두 내외 a (married) couple; husband 〔man〕 and wife / 두 배 double; two times / 두 번 twice; again; two times / 두 번째 a second time / 두 번째 아내 a second wife / 우유 두 잔 two glasses of milk / 두 가지 해석이 가능하다 can be interpreted in two ways; admit of two different reading.

**두**(頭) 《마리》 head (단복수 동형). ¶ 소 여섯 두 six head of cattle.

**두각**(頭角) 《뛰어남》 prominence; conspicuousness. ¶ ~을 나타내다 cut 〔make〕 a conspicuous 〔brilliant〕 figure 《in》; distinguish *oneself;* stand head and shoulders (above others); stand out 《above》 / 유능한 지휘관으로 ~을 나타내다 distinguish *oneself* as an able commander 《among *one's* comrades》 / 실업계에서 ~을 나타내다 become distinguished in business circles / 그는 뛰어난 재능으로 ~을 나타내고 있다 He stands out among men for his brilliant ability 〔talent〕. / 그는 지금 신진 화가로서 ~을 나타내고 있다 He is now cutting a brilliant figure as a young painter.

**두개**(頭蓋) 〖해부〗 the cranium (*pl.* ~s, -nia); the brainpan. ¶ ~의 cranial; cephalic. ◉ ~골 the skull; the cranial bone: ~골을 다치다 suffer a skull fracture; have *one's* skull fractured. ~근 cranial muscles. ~절개술 craniotomy.

**두건**(頭巾) a hempen hood for a mourner.

**두겁** a cap; 《붓두껍》 a writing-brush cap.

**두겁조상**(—祖上) *one's* most distinguished ancestor.

**두견**(杜鵑) ① 〖조류〗 a cuckoo. ② 《진달래》 an azalea.

**두고두고** 《오래도록》 (for) long; for a long time; for a good while; 《여러 차례》 many times; from time to time; over and over (again); again 〔time〕 and again. ¶ ~ 생각하다 think continually of 〔about〕 《*something*》 / ~ 쓸 수 있다 can be used for a long time / 과자를 ~ 먹다 dip into *one's* supply of cakes from time to time; eat cakes sparingly / 잘못한 것을 ~ 나무라다 refer time and again to the mistake *one* once made / 그것은 ~ 쓸 수 있다 It can be used for a long time. / 은혜는 평생 동안 ~ 잊지 않겠습니다 I shall be grateful to you as long as I live. / 이 일은 ~ 잊지 않을 것이다 I shall never forget it. *or* It will live in my memory for ever. / 「나 당신과 결혼하기로 했어. 그래 주겠어」—「자기를 좋아하긴 하지만, 당장 대답할 수는 없어」—「물론이지, ~ 생각해봐」 "I've made up my mind to marry you. Will you?"—"I like you, but I can't tell you right now."—"Of course, you can't. Sleep on it".

**두고보다** watch (intently); watch 〔keep watch〕 over. ⇨ 지켜보다. ¶ 그 사건의 추이를 ~ watch the development 〔course〕 of the event / 어디 두고 보자 You shall smart for this. *or* You will have to pay for this.

**두고오다** leave... (behind); put... in 《a place》 and forget where (it is); mislay. ¶ 우산을 ~ mislay *one's* umbrella / 회사 책상 위에 라이터를 두고 왔다 I left my lighter on my office desk.

**두골**(頭骨) the cranial bones; the skull. ⇨ 두개골.

**두그르르** with a single roll.

**두근거리다** palpitate; throb; beat (fast); pound; go pit-a-pat; pit-a-pat; feel nervous; be agitated. ¶ 두근거리는 가슴 a palpitating 〔throbbing, beating〕 heart / 가슴을 두근거리며 with a beating 〔palpitating〕 heart / 가슴이 ~ *one's* heart palpitates 〔goes pit-a-pat〕 / 두근거리는 가슴을 가라앉히다 calm *one's* agitated breast; collect *oneself* / 나는 그 소식을 듣고 가슴이 두근거렸다 My heart beat quickly at the news. *or* The news made my heart thump. / 나는 가슴을 두근거리며 보고 있었다 I watched it 「with my heart beating fast 〔pounding against my chest〕.

**두근두근** pit-a-pat; palpitating; throbbing. ~하다 = 두근거리다.

**두길(마)보기** opportunism; fence-sitting; a wait-and-see policy.

**두길마보다** wait and see (how the wind blows); sit on the fence; wait for the cat to jump.

**두꺼비** 〖동물〗 a toad. ¶ ~ 파리 잡아먹듯 be ready to eat anything / ~ 꽁지만하

다 be tiny. ◉ ～ 씨름 a tie game.

**두꺼비집** 〖전기〗 a fuse box; a (safety) cutout.

**두껍다** (be) thick; heavy; bulky; stout. ¶ 두껍게 thickly / 두꺼운 책 a thick book / 두꺼운 벽 a thick 〔heavy〕 wall / 낯짝이 ～ be brazen(-faced); be impudent 〔shameless, cheeky〕 / 두껍게 썰다 cut 《meat》 into thick slices / 두껍게 입다 put on warm clothes / 두껍게 하다 thicken; make 《*a thing*》 thick(er).

**두껍다리** a small nameless stone bridge on a ditch in an alley.

**두껍닫이** 〖건축〗 a sliding door pocket; a shutter box.

**두께** thickness. ¶ ～가 두껍다〔얇다〕 be thick 〔thin〕 / ～가 세 치다 be three *ch'i* thick; have a thickness of three *ch'i* / ～가 얼마나 되느냐 How thick is it? *or* What is its thickness?

**두남두다** ① 《도와주다》 forgive 《*a person's* mistake》 and help 《*him*》. ② = 편〔역성〕들다.

**두뇌**(頭腦) brains; a head. ¶ 냉정한 ～ cool brains / 치밀〔산만〕한 ～ close 〔loose〕 head / 예민한 ～ an acute intellect / ～ 플레이 a play with brains / ～가 명석하다 be clear-headed; have a clear head / ～가 명석한 사람 a clear-headed person; a person with a clear head; a bright person / ～를 요하다 require brains / ～를 짜다 beat 〔cudgel, rack〕 *one's* brains / 수학적인 ～를 갖고 있다 have a mathematical brain / 그의 ～는 실무에 적합하다 He has a good head for (practical) business. / 이 일을 해내려면 우수한 ～가 필요하다 It takes an excellent brain to accomplish this task. / 너의 ～ 회전은 정말 마음에 든다 I love the way your mind works.

◉ ～노동 brainwork: ～노동자 a brain-worker; a mental laborer. ～유출 brain drain; an outflow of brain. ～집단 a group of brains; a think tank.

**두다**[1] ① 《놓다》 put 《down》; place; set; lay (옆으로). ¶ 책을 책상 위에 ～ put 〔place〕 a book on a desk.

② 《보존하다》 keep; store (up); hold. ¶ 돈을 금고에 ～ keep money in a safe / 귀중품은 어디에 둡니까 Where do you keep your valuables? / 이 생선은 내일까지 둬도 괜찮을까 Will this fish keep overnight?

③ 《뒤에 두다》 leave (behind); forget. ¶ 책을 집에 두고 오다 leave *one's* book (behind) at home / 모자를 차 안에 두고 왔다 I left my hat in the car.

④ 《그대로 두다》 leave; allow; let; keep; have; leave over; set aside (예비로). ¶ 책을 책상 위에 놓아 ～ leave the book on the desk / 일을 하지 않고 ～ leave *one's* work undone / 하고 싶은 말을 하지 않은 채 ～ leave unsaid what *one* would rather say / 그대로 두어라 Leave it as it is. *or* Leave it alone 〔be〕. / 그를 놀려 둘 순 없다 I cannot have him idle. / 남겨 두었다가 내일 먹어라 Save some for tomorrow.

⑤ 《데리고 있다》 keep; employ; engage; have; 《묵게 하다》 lodge. ¶ 사람을 ～ employ a person; keep a servant / 양자를 ～ adopt a son / 하숙생을 ～ take in a boarder / 바깥채에 사람을 ～ rent a room in the outer wing.

⑥ 《설치하다》 set up; establish; place. ¶ 분과 위원회를 ～ organize 〔set up〕 a subcommittee / 사무실을 ～ set up 〔have〕 《its》 office 《in, on》 / 각 대학에 도서관을 ～ set up a library at each university / 각부에 장관을 ～ place 〔assign〕 a Minister over each ministry.

⑦ 《차이·중점을》 place; put; lay. ¶ 중점을 ～ put emphasis 《on》; lay (a) stress 《on》 / 차이를 ～ make a difference 〔discrimination〕.

⑧ 《간격을》 leave a space 《between》. ¶ 벽을 사이에 두고 on the other side of the wall; with a wall between / 일정한 간격을 두고 at regular intervals / 1미터 사이를 두고 심다 plant 《a tree》 at intervals of one meter; one meter apart 《from each other》 / 석 달을 두고 만나지 못하다 have not seen for three months.

⑨ 《마음에》 bear; entertain; cherish; set on; have; hold. ¶ 마음에 ～ have a mind to; fix 〔set〕 *one's* mind on; 《이성 등에서》 let *one's* heart go out to 《a woman》; feel some inclination toward 《a man》 / 염두에 ～ bear 〔have, keep〕 《*something*》 in mind / 학문에 뜻을 ～ set *one's* heart on learning / 마음에 두고 잊지 않다 hold 《*the matter*》 in remembrance; bear in mind.

⑩ 《다짐을》 (give a) pledge.

⑪ 《수결을 쓰다》 sign 《a document》; put *one's* written seal 〔signature〕 to.

⑫ 《바둑·장기를》 play 《chess, ***paduk***》; move 《a chessman》. ¶ 장기를 ～ play (a game of) *changgi* 《with》 / 자네가

둘 차례야 The next move is with you. ⑬ 《넣다》 put in; add; stuff. ¶ 밥에 팥을 ～ put redbeans in the rice / 솜을 ～ pad 〔stuff〕 《a garment》 with cotton.
⑭ 《지칭하다》 name; mean. ¶ 너를 두고 하는 말이다 It means you. / 특히 누구를 두고 한 말은 아니다 I meant no one in particular.

**두다**[2] [조동사] 《동작의 결과를 이어감을 뜻하는 말》 ¶ 나 하는 것을 잘 봐 두게 Now look carefully at the way I am doing it (so I won't have to show you again). / 내 말을 잘 들어 두어라 Pay attention to what I'm going to say. / 그녀 마음대로 하게 내버려 두자 Let her have her own way. / 맛은 없으나 그냥 먹어 두자 It is not tasty but let's eat it up anyway. / 그 방법을 알아두면 써먹을 날이 있을 거다 If you learn how to do it, you would have a chance to make use of it.

**두다리** ¶ ～ 걸치다 have it both ways; sit on the fence; straddle / ～ 걸쳤다가 실패하다 fall between two stools.

**두더지** 〖동물〗 a mole. ¶ ～ 혼인 같다 cherish an impossible 〔empty〕 hope; build a castle in the air. ◉ ～가죽 a moleskin. ～전술 tunneling tactics; an underground campaign.

**두덜거리다** grumble 《at》; complain 《about》. ⇨ 투덜거리다.

**두덜두덜** with grumbling; complaining.

**두덩** 《논·밭의》 a bank; a levee; a mound. ¶ 논～ a levee / 밭～ a bank around a field / ～에 누운 소 [비유적] a person 「in easy circumstances 〔"living in clover"〕. ◉ ～톱 a short fat-bellied saw.

**두동지다** (be) contradictory; inconsistent; incoherent.

**두두룩이** ① 《수북하게》 high; protuberantly; in a heap 〔pile〕. ¶ 흙을 ～ 쌓아 올리다 pile earth up into a small mound. ② 《많이》 much; plenty; satisfactorily. ¶ 돈을 ～ 집어주다 give plenty of money / 팁을 ～ 주다 give a generous tip; tip freely.

**두두룩하다** (be) swollen; raised; elevated; heaved; high. ¶ 두두룩한 돈지갑 a plump purse.

**두둑** 《밭 사이의 경계》 a bank; an embankment; a levee; 《이랑》 a ridge. ¶ 논～ a levee; the ridge of a rice paddy / 밭～ a bank around a field.

**두둑이** ＝ 두두룩이.

**두둑하다** ① 《두껍다》 be somewhat thick; (be) heavy. ¶ 밖이 꽤 추우니 두둑이 입고 가거라 It's pretty cold outside, so you'd better bundle up well. ② 《풍부하다》 (be) ample; plenty; satisfactory. ¶ 두둑한 사례 an ample reward 〔fee〕 / 돈이 ～ have plenty of money; be flush of money; have a plump purse.

**두둔하다** back up 《the weak》; give support; stand by; side 《with》; take sides 《with》. ¶ (싸움에서) 자기 애를 ～ back *one's* own child up (in a quarrel) / 부하를 두둔하여 말하다 talk 「in favor of 〔in defense of〕 *one's* subordinate / 약자를 ～ stand by the weak / 늘 그를 두둔만 하지 마라 Don't always take sides with him.

**두둥둥** tee-dum-dum.

**두둥실** floating gently 〔lightly〕; buoyantly; in an airy manner. ¶ ～ 뜨다 waft 《on the wind》; float 《in the air》 / 기구가 ～ 높이 떠 있다 A balloon is floating high up in the air. / 흰 구름이 ～ 떠 있다 White clouds are floating lightly in the sky. / 낙하산이 펴지자 내 몸이 ～ 공중에 뜨는 것을 느꼈다 The parachute opened and I felt my body floating lightly in the air.

**두드러기** 〖의학〗 hives; nettle rash; urticaria. ¶ ～가 돋다〔나다〕 get nettle rash; have urticaria; form wheals; break out in a rash / 또 ～가 났다 My nettle rash has broken out 〔erupted〕 again. / 그런 것을 먹으면 ～가 난다 That would bring you out in a rash. / 먹은 생선이 맞지 않았는지 온몸에 ～가 돋았다 The fish I ate seems to have had a bad effect on me, for now I have a breaking-out all over my body.

**두드러지다** ① 《뚜렷하다》 (be) notable; conspicuous; marked; salient; striking; remarkable; outstanding; noticeable; considerable; [동사적] stand out; cut a conspicuous figure; come to the fore. ¶ 두드러진 공적 distinguished services / 두드러진 차이 a sharp 〔striking〕 difference / 두드러진 특징 prominent characteristics; salient features / 두드러지게 remarkably; strikingly; conspicuously; markedly; considerably / 성적이 두드러지게 좋다 be far ahead of the others 《in *one's* studies》; stand high 《in *one's* class》 / …와는 두드러지게 다르다 show a sharp contrast to…; be a far cry from… / 이렇다하게 두드러진 데가 없다

cut no striking figure 《in *one's* class》/ 두드러진 진보를 보이다 show marked improvement 《in》. ② 《내밀다》 swell; protrude; heave; rise; be embossed; become elevated. ¶ 뾰루지가 ～ a boil is swollen up.

**두드리다** 《치다》 strike; beat; hit; knock 《on the door》; rap 《on the table》; 《가볍게》 pat 《a dog, *a person* on the arm》; tap 《on the window, *a person* on the shoulder》; 《세게》 bang 《on 〔at〕 the door》; pound 《the table》 (되풀이해서). ¶ (의사가) 가슴을 ～ tap 〔sound〕 《a patient's》 chest / 문을 ～ knock 〔rap〕 at the door / 문을 가볍게 〔세게〕 ～ tap 〔pound, rap〕 at the door / 대문을 (세게) ～ thunder at the gate / 북을 ～ beat a drum / 어깨를 ～ pat 〔tap〕 《*a person*》 (up)on the shoulder / 화가 나서 책상을 ～ pound 〔thump〕 the table in anger / 못을 두드려 박다 drive 〔hammer〕 in a nail / 누군가가 문을 두드리고 있다 Someone is knocking at the door. *or* There is a knock at the door.

**두들기다** strike repeatedly; beat; pound; batter; give 〔deal〕 repeated blows. ¶ 두들겨 부수다 break 〔batter〕 down 《a house》/ 두들겨 쫓아내다 throw 〔kick〕 《*a person*》 out (of the house) / 두들겨 패 죽이다 beat 〔flog〕 *a person* to death; beat the life out of *a person* / 그는 신문에서 호되게 두들겨 맞았다 He was attacked 〔severely criticized〕 in the newspapers.

**두량**(斗量) ① the measurement of quantity 《by a *mal* or *toe* measure》. ② disposition of an affair to a satisfactory conclusion.

**두런거리다** murmur together; whisper in a group 〔to each other〕; speak in undertones; exchange whispers.

**두런두런** murmuring together; in whispers. ¶ ～ 이야기하다 ⇨ 두런거리다.

**두렁** a ridge between (rice) fields; a levee. ¶ 논～ a levee; the ridge of a rice paddy / ～에 든 소 [비유적] have plenty to eat wherever *one* goes.

**두렁이** swaddling clothes.

**두렁허리** 『어류』 a kind of freshwater eel.

**두레** ① 《물푸는》 a water scooper (used in irrigation). ② ＝두레박. ◉ ～우물 a deep 〔draw〕 well.

**두레박** a well bucket. ¶ ～으로 물을 푸다 draw water 《from a well》 with a bucket. ◉ ～줄 a well rope. ～틀 a (well) sweep; a shadoof.

**두레박질** drawing water with a well bucket. ～하다 draw water 《from a well》 with a bucket.

**두레질** ～하다 irrigate with water scoops.

**두려빠지다** come off (from a center); an entire area sinks.

**두려움** 《공포》 fear; (a) dread; terror; (a) fright; horror; 《염려》 anxiety; apprehension; 《외경》 awe; reverence; veneration. ¶ ～으로〔때문에〕 out of fear; from 〔with〕 fear; driven by fear; in horror; in fright / ～에 휩싸이다 be terrified; be seized with fear; be terror-〔panic-〕stricken; 《위엄에》 be struck with awe / ～을 모르다 be fearless 〔dauntless〕; be intrepid / ～으로 떨다 tremble with fear; tremble like a leaf in terror / ～에 질려 실신하다 faint in terror / ～에 말문이 막히다 be struck dumb with fright / ～이 일게 하다 arouse fear into 《*a person's*》 heart; scare; 《위엄에》 rouse awe in 《*a person*》; hold 《*a person*》 in awe 《of 》/ 그는 ～을 모르는 녀석이다 He does not know what fear is.

**두려워하다** ① (***a***) 《무서워하다》 fear; dread; be afraid 〔fearful〕 of; be frightened 〔terrified, scared〕 at; feel a horror 〔dread〕 of. ¶ 뱀을 ～ be afraid of snakes; have a horror of snakes / 몹시 ～ have a holy horror of; be in mortal fear of / 두려워하지 않다 be fearless; know no fear / 죽음을 두려워하지 않다 be not afraid of death; defy death / …을 항상 ～ be 〔live〕 in constant fear of… / 너는 아무것도 두려워할 것 없다 You have nothing to fear. / 잘못한 것이 없으니 조금도 두려워할 것이 없다 My conscience is clear and I have nothing to be afraid of. / 실수가 두려워 말하는 것을 피하면 영어 회화의 숙달은 부지하세월이다 You will never speak English well if you avoid speaking for fear of making mistakes. (***b***) 《염려하다》 fear; be afraid of; apprehend; be apprehensive of. ¶ 병이 날까 ～ be in fear of falling ill / 입시에 떨어질까 ～ be afraid 〔apprehensive〕 failing in an entrance exam. ② 《경외하다》 fear; stand in fear 〔awe〕 《of》. ¶ 크게 두려워하는 선장 the much-feared captain / 어른을 ～ stand in awe of *one's* elders / 두려워하게 하다 inspire 《*a person*》 with awe; keep 《*a person*》 in awe.

**두렵다** ① 《무섭다》 (be) fearful; hor-

rible; frightened; scared; terrified; [서술적] be afraid of. ¶ 두려워서 몸을 떨다〔움츠리다〕 shudder 〔shrink〕 with fear / 두려워 달아나다 run away through fear / 두려워지다 be seized with fear; get frightened 〔scared〕 《at》 / 나는 그 사람이 ~ I am afraid of him. / 나는 죽음이 ~ I am afraid to die. (★ "I am afraid to die.와 I am afraid of dying.의 뜻의 차이"—전자는 「두려워 죽을 수 없다」(=I don't dare to die.)의 뜻이며 후자는 「죽는 것이 아닌가 걱정이다」(=I am afraid lest I should die.)의 뜻임). ② 《경외스럽다》 (be) awesome; be awed 〔feared, awe-stricken〕. ¶ 두려워서 고개를 못 들다 be too much awed to raise *one's* head / 후생이 ~ *one's* juniors are to be feared; young students deserve respect.
③ 《…하지 않을까》 be feared 〔apprehended〕; be afraid of; there is a danger of. ¶ …이 두려워 for fear of 《losing money》; lest 《*one*》 should; from fear 《of punishment》 / 다칠까 ~ There is a danger of being injured. / 사고가 날까 ~ I am afraid an accident might happen.

**두령**(頭領) a boss; a chief; a leader; a head.

**두루** 《골고루》 round; all around; all over; throughout; widely; extensively; 《널리》 far and wide; generally; universally. ¶ ~ 아는 사실 a matter of universal 〔common〕 knowledge; a fact known to the general public / ~ 살피다 look all around carefully / ~ 찾다 search everywhere; make a wide search / ~ 알리다 let all the people know; inform everyone / 시내를 ~ 안내하다 take 《*a person*》 all over the city / 전국을 ~ 돌아다니다 go around all over the country / 여러 방면의 서적을 ~ 섭렵하다 read through books covering all sorts of fields / 그의 명성은 ~ 알려져 있다 His reputation is known far and wide.

**두루마기** a traditional Korean man's outer coat 〔overcoat〕.

**두루마리** a roll of (letter) paper; a scroll. ◉ ~화장지 a toilet roll; a roll of toilet paper.

**두루뭉수리** ① 《사물》 an object of nondescript shape; unshapely thing; a mess. ¶ ~를 만들어 놓다 make a mess out of it. ② 《사람》 a nondescript person; a good-for-nothing fellow.

**두루미** 〖조류〗 a crane. ¶ ~ 꽁지 같다 have a short thick beard. ◉ ~자리 〖천문〗 the Crane.

**두루미냉이** 〖식물〗 a Chinese artichoke.

**두루춘풍**(一春風) always being genial to everybody; 《사람》 a person who is nice to everybody. ¶ ~이다 be always genial to everybody.

**두루치기** using the same thing for a variety of purposes. ¶ ~ 일꾼 a factotum; an all-rounder; a jack-of-all-trades.

**두류**(逗留) a stay; a stop. ⇨ 체류(滯留). ¶ 장기 ~하다 make a long stay. ◉ ~객(客) a guest; a house guest; a sojourner.

**두르다** ① (***a***) 《둘러싸다》 put around; surround 《with, by》; enclose 《with, in》; encircle; hem 〔shut〕 in. ¶ 돌담을 ~ enclose 《a house》 with a stone wall / 성벽을 두른 도시 a walled town / 병풍을 ~ set up a screen all around / 울타리를 ~ fence round 《a garden》. (***b***) 《입다·차다》 wear 〔wrap〕 about *one;* engird(le). ¶ 완장을 ~ wear an armband / 치마를 ~ put on *one's* 〔wear a〕 skirt / 허리에 혁대를 ~ bind a belt about 〔round〕 *one's* waist.
② 《돌리다》 turn 《a wheel》; wheel; revolve; whirl 《a stick》.
③ 《마음대로 다루다》 wield; make a puppet of 《*a person*》; have 《*a person*》 under perfect control; turn 《*a person*》 round *one's* little finger.
④ 《변통하다》 contrive; manage to. ¶ 돈을 ~ (manage to) raise money; borrow money; find funds / 돈을 둘러주다 lend money; accommodate 《*a person*》 with money.
⑤ 《속이다》 deceive; cheat; gloss over. ¶ 둘러대다 employ subterfuges; explain away.

**두르르** ① 《말리는 모양》 round; with a twirl. ¶ 종이를 ~ 말다 roll paper / 양탄자를 ~ 말다 roll up a carpet. ② 《구르는 모양》 rolling. ¶ ~ 구르다 roll (about); tumble about.

**두르풍**(一風) a cape; a shawl.

**두름** 《물고기·채소의》 a string 《of fish, of dried vegetables》; bunches of vegetables. ¶ 청어 두 ~ two strings of herring.

**두름성**(一性) 《주변》 resourcefulness; versatility; adaptability; manipulation. ¶ ~ 있는 사람 a resourceful man; a man of ability / ~이 있는 shifty; resourceful / ~이 없는 shiftless; resourceless / ~ 있게 행동하다 take proper steps to meet the situation / 그는 ~이 있어 돈을 잘 마련한다 He is resourceful and very good at raising money. / 그는 ~ 있는 사람이다 He is a versatile person. *or* He knows how to adapt himself to circumstances.

**두릅** 《두릅나무 순》 fatsia shoots. ◉ ~나무 〖식물〗 a Japanese angelica tree; a fatsia.

**두리기둥** 〖건축〗 a column; a (cylindrical) pillar.

**두리목**(一木) rounded lumber 〔timber〕.

**두리반**(一盤) a large round dining table.

**두리번거리다** stare about; look around nervously 〔restlessly〕. ¶눈을 ~ goggle 〔roll〕 *one's* eyes / 누가 보고 있지나 않나 하고 ~ look 〔stare〕 around to see whether anybody is watching him / 그녀는 신기한 듯 실내를 두리번거렸다 She looked around inside the room restlessly but curiously.

**두리번두리번** (nervously) looking around time and again (with *one's* eyes wide open 〔with a startled look〕). ¶~ 둘러보다 keep looking around nervously; stare around.

**두마음** double heartedness; double-dealing; treachery; duplicity. ¶~이 있는 double-faced〔-dealing〕; treacherous / ~이 없는 single-hearted; sincere (성실한) / ~을 품다 carry two faces (under one hood); play a double game.

**두말** 《이랬다저랬다》 duplicity; equivocation; a double tongue. ~하다 be double-tongued; break 〔go back on〕 *one's* word 〔promise〕; say this and that. ¶~ 말고 without saying anything further / ~ 않고 without complain 〔grumbling, a murmur〕 / 한입으로~하다 keep two tongues in one mouth; tell a lie / ~하지 않다 keep *one's* word; be as good as *one's* word / ~ 못 하다 be dumbfounded 〔nonplussed〕; be struck dumb / ~ 못 하게 하다 strike 《*a person*》 dumb; bring 《*a person*》 to a nonplus.

**두말 없이** without saying anything further; without any complaint 〔trouble〕; with no further ado. ¶~ 승낙하다 give a ready consent; consent readily / 그에게 돈말을 했더니 ~ 빌려주더라 When I asked him to lend me some money, he did so without a moment's hesitation. / 그 뒤부터 그들은 ~ 잘 산다 Since then, they get along without more ado.

**두멍** 《큰 솥》 a large iron pot used to store water; 《동이》 a large water jar.

**두메** an out-of-the-way village 〔district〕; a remote country place; the back country; the backwoods. ¶~에서 살다 live in the back country 〔remote countryside〕. ◉ 두멧구석 an out-of-the-way corner of a mountain district; a remote backwoods. 두멧사람 a person who lives in an out-of-the-way place; a backwoodsman; hill folk.

**두목**(頭目) a leader; a chief; a boss; a headman; 《괴수》 a ringleader; a kingpin. ¶폭도〔도둑〕의 ~ the ringleader of a mob 〔robbers〕 / 소매치기의~ a master pickpocket / ~과 부하 a boss and his henchmen / …를 ~으로 하는 with… at its head.

**두묘**(痘苗) 〖의학〗 vaccine; the vaccine lymph 〔virus〕.

**두문불출**(杜門不出) ~하다 lead a solitary life; confine *oneself* at home; stay indoors.

**두문자**(頭文字) 《머리글자》 an initial (letter).

**두미**(頭尾) the head and the tail; beginning and end. ¶~ 없다 be incoherent 〔rambling, desultory〕 / ~ 없는 이야기를 하다 say incoherent things; tell an incoherent story.

**두발**(頭髮) (*one's*) hair; the hair (on the head).

**두방망이질** pounding 〔throbbing, beating〕 of *one's* heart. ¶가슴이 ~치다 *one's* heart beat quick 〔fast〕 《at, with》.

**두번** 《2회의》 twice; two times; 《다시》 again; 《두번째》 the second time. ¶한 달에 ~ twice a month / ~ 다시 없는 기회 a golden opportunity / 흰 에나멜을 ~ 바르다 give two coats of white enamel / 나는 이 책을 ~ 읽었다 I've read this book twice 〔two times〕. ◉ ~째 the second time: ~째로 for the second time / ~째 아내 *one's* second wife / 뒤에서 ~째 열(列) the second row from the rear / 그가 이곳에 온 것은 이번이 ~째다 This is his second visit here. / 그에게 주의를 준 것은 이번이 ~째다 This is the second time (that) I've warned him. / 왼쪽에서 ~째 사람은 누구입니까 Who is the second (person) from the left?

**두벌갈이** 〖농업〗 a second sowing 〔plowing〕. ~하다 sow twice; till a second time; plow 〔plough 《영》〕 again.

**두벌솎음** thinning vegetables out for

the second time; 《푸성귀》 vegetables 〔greens〕 thinned out for the second time. ～하다 thin vegetables out for the second time.

**두벌주검** an examined 〔a dissected〕 corpse. ～하다 have an autopsy.

**두부**(豆腐) bean 〔soybean〕 curd. ¶ ～ 한 모 a cake of bean curd; a bean-curd cake / ～ 살에 바늘 뼈 《속담》 be very delicate 〔fragile〕. ◉ ～장수 a bean-curd dealer 〔seller, maker〕. ～튀김 fried bean curd.

**두부**(頭部) the head. ¶ ～의 cephalic / 그는 어제 교통 사고로 ～에 부상을 입었다 He was injured in 〔on〕 the head in a traffic accident yesterday.

**두사이** ① 《간격》 an interval between two places; a space between two 《*things*》. ¶ ～에 끼이다 get in between; be caught in the middle; be sandwiched between. ② 《관계》 the relation(ship) 〔terms〕 between two persons. ¶ ～가 좋다 be good friends; be on good terms / ～가 나쁘다 be on bad terms; be in bad with each other / ～를 가르다 keep 《two persons》 apart; 《이간》 alienate; estrange; part 《two lovers》 / ～에 들다 go between; intervene between two parties / ～가 버그러지다 be alienated 〔estranged〕 from each other; have a falling-out; split up.

**두상화**(頭狀花) 『식물』 a capitate(d) flower; a caput (*pl.* capita); a capitulum (*pl.* -la); a flower head.

**두서**(頭書) a superscription. ¶ ～의 superscribed; 《상기의》 above-mentioned.

**두서**(頭緖) ① 《일의》 a clue; the first step; the beginning; the commencement. ¶ 일의 ～를 잡다 get a clue to a matter. ② 《조리》 consistence; coherence; order; coherency. ¶ ～ 없는 rambling; incoherent; desultory; silly; absurd / ～ 없는 이야기 a rambling 〔wild, silly〕 talk / ～ 없이 incoherently; inchoately; in a rambling manner / ～ 없는 말을 하다 talk in a rambling way; wander in *one's* talk; talk to no purpose / 네 말은 ～가 없다 What you say is confused 〔does not make sense〕.

**두서너** two or three-or-four; a few. ¶ ～ 마디 a few word / ～ 번 two or three times / 책 ～ 권 a few books / ～ 사람 a few people / ～집 건너 a few doors away / ～ 마디만 말씀 드리겠습니다 Allow me to speak just a few words.

**두서넛** two or three; a few.

**두손** two hands; both hands. ¶ ～ 들다 [비유적] give up; throw up *one's* hands; give in; admit *one's* defeat / ～으로 쥐다 〔들다〕 hold 《*a thing*》 in both hands / ～ 모아 빌다〔축원하다〕 pray with *one's* hands pressed together; pray with palms put together / ～을 벌리다〔내밀다〕 open 〔extend〕 *one's* hands.

**두손매무리** doing things slapdash. ～하다 scamp *one's* work; do *one's* work in a slipshod 〔slapdash〕 manner.

**두약**(杜若) 『식물』 an alpinia tree.

**두어** about two; a couple of. ¶ ～ 달 about two months / ～ 마디 a few words / ～ 사람 a couple of people.

**두어두다** 《내버려두다》 leave 《*a matter*》 as it is 〔stands〕; let 〔leave〕 《*a person*》 alone. ¶ 그가 울겠다, 가만 두어두어라 Leave him alone or he will cry.

**두억시니** 『민속』 a demon; a devil.

**두엄** 《거름》 compost; barnyard 〔farmyard〕 manure; muck. ¶ ～을 주다 manure 〔compost〕 《a field》. ◉ ～걸채 a muck rack. ～더미 a manure pile. ～발치 a muck bog. ～자리 a compost yard 〔dump〕.

**두운**(頭韻) alliteration. ¶ ～을 맞추다 alliterate. ◉ ～법 alliteration.

**두유**(豆乳) soybean milk.

**두이레** the fourteenth day of a baby's life 〔birth〕.

**두절**(杜絶) stoppage; cessation; interruption; suspension. ～하다 be stopped; be cut off; be interrupted; be blocked; cease; be paralyzed. ¶ 공급이 ～되다 [사람이 주어] be cut off from the supply / 소식이 ～되다 hear nothing from / 눈보라로 교통이 ～됐다 Traffic was held up 〔paralyzed〕 by the snow storms. / 이 거리는 10시가 지나면 사람 왕래가 ～된다 This street is deserted after ten. / 이달 8일부터 교통은 거의 ～되었다 Traffic has been almost entirely interrupted since the 8th of this month.

**두족류**(頭足類) 『동물』 the Cephalopoda. ¶ ～의 동물 a cephalopod.

**두주**(斗酒) kegs of wine. ¶ ～를 불사하다 be ready to drink gallons of wine; drink like a fish.

**두주**(頭註) headnotes.

**두텁다** 《정리·인정 등이》 (be) warm; cordial; affectionate; deep; hearty. ¶ 두터운 우정 a warm 〔deep〕 friendship / 정리가 ～ be true to *one's* friends / 인정이 ～ have a warm 〔feeling〕 heart / 우의를 두텁게 하다 deepen the friendship / 그녀는 신앙심이 ～ She is a religious woman.

**두통**(頭痛) a headache; 〖의학〗 cephalalgia. ¶ 빠개지는 듯한 ～ a splitting 〔racking〕 headache / 가벼운 ～ a slight headache / ～이 나다 have a headache / ～이 심하다 have 〔suffer from〕 a bad headache / ～을 호소하다 complain of a headache.

**두통거리**(頭痛—) a headache; a worry; a thorn in *one's* side 〔flesh〕; a source 〔cause〕 of trouble 〔anxiety〕. ¶ 항상 떠나지 않는 ～ a constant source of brain-racking troubles 《to》 / 애가 말을 듣지 않아 ～다 The child's disobedience 〔stubbornness〕 is a headache to me. / 교통 문제는 아주 ～다 The traffic problem is a real headache. / 그는 집안의 ～다 He is a great distress to the family. / 이 문제는 우리들 최대의 ～다 This problem is our biggest headache.

**두툴두툴** uneven(ly); rough(ly). ⇨ 도톨도톨.

**두툼하다** be rather 〔somewhat〕 thick. ¶ 두툼한 책 a thick 〔bulky, stout〕 book / 두툼한 입술 full lips / 두툼하게 자르다 cut 《meat》 into thick slices.

**두한족열**(頭寒足熱) keeping the head cool and the feet warm (for health).

**두호**(斗護) patronage; protection; favor. ～하다 patronize; protect; favor; look after; side with; shield. ¶ 약자를 ～하다 protect the weak.

**두흔**(痘痕) a pockmark; a pit. ¶ ～이 있다 be pitted 〔pockmarked〕.

**둑** a bank; an embankment; a dike; 《논둑》 a ridge between rice paddies; a levee. ¶ 둑길 a causeway; a bank path; a dike / 갯둑 the bank 〔embankment〕 of an estuary; a dike / 둑을 쌓다 build 〔construct〕 a dike; embank 《a river》 / 둑이 터지다〔무너지다〕 a bank breaks 〔gives way〕 / 논둑을 거닐다 walk on a paddy levee.

**둔각**(鈍角) 〖기하〗 an obtuse angle.
◉ ～삼각형 an obtuse triangle.

**둔감**(鈍感) dullness; insensibility; stolidity. ～하다 (be) dull; stolid; thick-skinned; insensible 《to, of》; dumb 《미속어》. ¶ ～해지다 《사람이》 become insensitive; 《감각이》 become dull / 그는 ～해서 남의 기분을 모른다 He is insensitive to other people's feelings. / 그녀는 자기 소문에 대해 ～했다 She was deaf to the gossip around her.

**둔갑**(遁甲) ～하다 take the form 〔shape〕 《of》; turn 〔change, transform〕 *oneself* into 《*something*》. ¶ 사람으로 ～한 여우 a fox in the shape of man; a fox in human shape / (여우가) 여자로 ～하다 take 〔assume〕 the shape of a woman; change 《*itself*》 into a woman.

**둔갑술**(遁甲術) 〖민속〗 the occult art by which *one* is said to render *himself* invisible to others; the art of changing *oneself* into.

**둔기**(鈍器) a dull 〔blunt〕 weapon. ¶ ～로 살해되다 be killed with a blunt instrument.

**둔덕** a hilly spot. ¶ ～(이) 지다 become hilly.

**둔부**(臀部) the buttocks; the posterior; the hips; the rump 《of a horse》; the backside; the behind. ¶ ～가 크다 be wide-〔full-, broad-〕hipped.

**둔사**(遁辭) evasive remarks; a subterfuge; an excuse; an evasive answer. ¶ ～를 늘어놓다 give an evasive answer; excuse *oneself* / 그것은 단지 ～에 지나지 않는다 It is nothing but a mere excuse for evasion.

**둔세**(遁世) seclusion 〔retirement〕 from the world. ～하다 seclude *oneself* 〔retire〕 from the world; escape from life; renounce the (secular) world. ¶ ～생활을 하다 live secluded 〔in seclusion〕 from the world.

**둔재**(鈍才) dullness; 《사람》 a dull 〔dull-witted〕 person; a dunce. ¶ ～의 dull; slow-〔dull-〕witted; stupid.

**둔전**(屯田) 〖고제도〗 a farm cultivated by troops regularly stationed in the area. ◉ ～병 a farm soldier.

**둔주**(遁走) running away; flight. ～하다 run away; take (to) flight.
◉ ～곡(曲) 〖음악〗 a fugue.

**둔치** the level-upped riverside; the high-water-level land by the river.

**둔탁하다**(鈍濁—) 《사람이》 (be) slow; dull; stupid; 《소리 등이》 (be) dull; thick; dead. ¶ 둔탁한 소리 a dead sound.

**둔통**(鈍痛) a dull pain. ¶ 위(胃)에 ～을 느끼다 feel a dull pain in the stomach.

**둔팍하다**(鈍—) (be) slow-witted; stolid; stupid; dull.

**둔패기** a slow-witted 〔dull〕 person.

**둔하다**(鈍—) ① 《성질·머리가》 (be) dull; thick; slow; thick-〔slow-〕headed. ¶ 둔한 사내 a dull 〔stupid〕 fellow; a dullard / 감각이 ～ be insensitive; be

thick-skinned / 머리가 ~ have a dull head; be dull(-brained) / 그는 둔해서 상황을 깨닫지 못한다 He doesn't realize the situation because he's 「not very bright 〔slow on the uptake〕.
② 《동작·상태 등이》 (be) slow; sluggish; inactive; inert. ¶ 동작이 ~ be slow in movement; be a slow coach.
③ 《소리가》 (be) thick; dull. ¶ 둔한 소리를 내다 make a thick 〔dull〕 sound.

**둔해지다**(鈍—) become 〔grow〕 dull; become blunt; 《동작이》 become sluggish. ¶ 솜씨가 ~ become less capable; get out of practice (연습 부족으로) / 술을 먹으면 머리가 둔해진다 Drinking dulls the senses 〔muddles one's brains〕. / 나이를 먹으니 사리 판단이 둔해졌다 As I grew older, it got harder to catch on things.

**둔화**(鈍化) blunting 《of sensibility》; slowdown 《in the economy》. ~하다 become 〔grow〕 dull; become blunt; 《약화되다》 be weakened; weaken. ¶ 이 도표는 우리나라 경제의 ~를 나타내고 있다 This diagram shows a slowdown in our country's economy.

**둘** two. ¶ 둘로 in two 〔half〕 / 둘씩 two at a time; by 〔in〕 twos; two by 〔and〕 two / 둘 다 both (...and...); [부정] neither (...nor...) / 둘 걸러 in every third place / 둘 중 하나 one of the two; one between the two / 둘도 없는 《유일한》 unique; only; 《비길데 없는》 peerless; matchless; unparalleled; unrivaled / 둘로 접은 two-fold; twice-folded / 둘도 없는 친구 a unique friend; a friend there's no one like in the whole world / 둘로 나누다〔자르다, 쪼개다〕 divide 〔cut, break〕 《*a thing*》 in two 〔into two parts〕 / 둘 중에서 하나를 고르다 choose between the two / 둘도 없는 친구다 be a David and Jonathan 〔Damon and Pythias〕 / 이런 건축물은 둘도 없다 This is the most unique architecture. / 둘만으론 부족하다 Two is not enough. / 이렇게 편리한 것은 둘도 없다 There can be nothing more convenient than this. / 둘은 잘 어울리는 부부다 They are a well-matched couple. / 둘 다 괜찮다 Both are all right. *or* Either will do. / 둘 다 좋지 않다 Neither of them is 〔are〕 good. (★ Both of them are not good.라고 하면 '둘 다 괜찮다는 것은 아니다'라는 의미가 됨. not이 both와 더불어 쓰이면 부분 부정, neither와 함께 쓰이면 전체 부정) / 그들은 둘 다 미인이다 They are both pretty.

**둘**— 《새끼 못 배는》 sterile; barren. ¶ 둘암탉〔암소〕 a sterile hen 〔cow〕.

**둘되다** (be) stupid; dull(-witted); insensible; thick(-headed); blunt; curt.

**둘둘** ⇨ 돌돌. ¶ ~ 감다 wind 《a rope》 round 《*a thing*》.

**둘러대다** ① 《말을》 put 〔cook〕 up 《an excuse》; gloss over 〔cover up〕 《*one's* fault》; make an excuse 《for》; explain away. ¶ 그럴 듯한 이유를 ~ cook up a good reason; manage to gloss over 《*one's* mistake》 / 그녀는 돈을 갚지 못한 이유를 둘러댔다 She put up good reasons why she hasn't been able to return the money.
② 《변통하다》 manage; make shift; shift and contrive; devise. ¶ 돈을 ~ get money somehow; make up a sum / 여기저기서 둘러대어 가까스로 500만 원을 만들었다 I barely managed to raise five million won from various sources.

**둘러막다** fence in; enclose 《with, in》; surround 《with, by》; hem 〔shut〕 in; rope off (밧줄로). ¶ 돌담으로 집을 ~ enclose a house with stone walls / 병풍으로 ~ set up a screen all around / 철조망으로 ~ fence 《the land》 with barbed wire.

**둘러메다** bear 〔carry〕 on *one's* shoulder; fling 《*a thing*》 around *one's* shoulders. ¶ 어깨에 가방을 ~ carry a bag over *one's* shoulder / 그는 등에 보따리를 둘러메고 있었다 He had 〔was carrying〕 a bundle on his back.

**둘러보다** look (a)round 〔about〕; look over; take 〔give〕 a look 〔glance〕 around; make a survey 《of》; survey. ¶ 좌중을 ~ look around the people present; make a survey of the company; look from one to another / 집을 한 번 ~ take a look around a house / 그는 방안을 둘러보았다 He looked (a)round the room.

**둘러서다** stand in a circle; gather about. ¶ 그들은 부장을 중심으로 빙 둘러섰다 They stood in a circle around the boss.

**둘러싸다** ① 《빙》 enclose; surround; encircle; envelop; beset; 《사람들이》 crowd round; close 〔cluster, throng〕 around 《*a person*》; 《포위하다》 besiege; lay siege to. ¶ 난로를 ~ gather about 〔round〕 a stove / 적진을 ~ lay siege to the enemy position / 담으로〔울타리로〕 ~ enclose 〔gird〕 《*a house*》 with a「wall〔fence〕/ 멀리서 ~ surround《the enemy》at a distance / 테이블을 둘러싸고 앉다 sit〔be seated〕around the table / 군중이 그의 차를 둘러쌌다 A crowd surrounded his car. ②《관계·문제를》surround. ¶ …을 둘러싸고 centering〔pivoting〕around…; in connection with; concerning… / 그를 둘러싼 세 사람의 여인 the three women around him / 지급을 둘러싸고 말다툼을 하다 have a dispute over〔concerning〕the payment.

**둘러싸이다** be besieged〔invested, surrounded〕; be enclosed〔girded〕. ¶ 친구에 둘러싸여 with *one's* friends around《*one*》/ 구경꾼에 ~ be surrounded〔crowded round〕by spectators / 삼면이 바다로 둘러싸여 있다 be surrounded by sea on three sides / 숲으로 둘러싸인 호수 a lake encircled with〔by〕woods / 그 집은 수목에 둘러싸여 있다 The house is shut in by trees. / 그는 열띤 청중에 둘러싸여 서 있었다 He stood surrounded by an eager crowd of listeners.

**둘러쌓다** pile《*things*》up in a circle.

**둘러쓰다** ①《머리에》wear《it》around *one's* head;《몸에》get《it》all over *oneself;*《물을》pour〔dash〕《water》over〔(up)on〕*oneself;*《먼지를》be covered with《dust》. ¶ 담요를 ~ wrap *oneself* up in a blanket. ②《변통하다》borrow《money, *things*》.

**둘러앉다** sit (a)round; sit in a ring〔circle〕; gather around in a circle. ¶ 난롯가에 ~ sit around a stove / 방안에 빙 ~ sit around a room in a circle.

**둘러엎다** overturn; upset; overthrow;《하던 일을》do away with. ¶ 밥상을 ~ overturn a dining table / 커피잔을 ~ upset〔tip over〕the coffee cup / 살림을 ~ do away with a home; break up a household / 장사를 ~ give〔wind〕up *one's* business.

**둘러차다**《허리에》attach〔tie〕《*a thing*》around *one's* waist.

**둘러치다**[1] ①《내던지다》throw hard; fling; hurl. ¶ 땅바닥에 ~ hurl〔throw〕《*a person*》to the ground / 둘러치나 메어치나 일반이다 [비유적] It makes no difference whichever you choose. ②《때리다》thrash; swish; bring down; hit. ¶ 몽둥이로 ~ bring a club down on《*a person*》.

**둘러치다**[2]《두르다》put around; enclose; surround; encircle; stretch《wires》around. ¶ 벽에 병풍을 ~ put a screen around the wall / 운동장에 울짱을 ~ palisade a playground; enclose a playground with a picket fence.

**둘레** girth; circumference. ¶ 나무 ~ the girth of a tree / 지구의 ~ the distance round the earth / ~가 5킬로미터 five kilometers round〔in circumference, in girth〕/ 연못 ~를 한 바퀴 돌다 go〔walk〕(a)round a pond /「이 연못의 ~는 얼마나 됩니까」—「약 500 미터입니다」"How big is this pond round?"—"It is about 500 meters round." / 이 호수는 ~가 10마일이다 The lake is ten miles around〔in circumference〕. / 지구는 태양의 ~를 돈다 The earth turns〔goes, moves〕around the sun.

**둘레둘레** ¶ 주위를 ~ 살피다 stare around; look about *one* wanderingly.

**둘리다** ①《둘레에》be surrounded〔encircled, enclosed, encompassed〕. ¶ 집에 널판장이 ~ a house is surrounded by a board fence / 동네가 산으로 사면이 둘려 있다 The village is surrounded by mountains on all sides. ②《몸에》be put round; be wrapped (up) in; be worn. ¶ 머리에 수건이 ~ A towel is worn round *one's* head. ③《휘둘리다》be controlled; be swayed; be wielded; be at *one's* beck and call. ¶ 아무한테 ~ be swayed by *a person;* be wrapped around *a person's* finger.

**둘째** the second; number two (생략 No. 2). ¶ ~로 secondly; in the second place / 둘쨋번 집 the second house / 앞에서 둘쨋번 자리 the second seat from the front / 끝에서 ~ 동생 the youngest brother but one / 그는 ~로 왔다 He came in second. *or* He was the second to arrive. / 용모는 ~ 문제다 Personal appearance is of secondary importance. / 미국에서 ~로 큰 주(州) the second-biggest state in the U.S. / 그는 ~로 시험에 합격했다 He was the second to pass the examination. *or* He passed the examination second on the list. ◉ ~손가락 a forefinger; an index finger.

**둘치** a sterile female animal.

**둘하다** (be) clumsy; awkward; gawky. ¶ 둘한 사람 a clumsy〔gawky〕person / 둘한 솜씨 poor skill.

**둥**[1]〖음악〗the second note of the native Korean musical scale.

**둥**[2]《하는 듯 마는 듯》may or may not

have *done* (with equal likehood); may or may not be; appear 「to have *done* or not to have *done* 〔to be or not to be〕. ¶ 남의 말을 듣는 둥 마는 둥 하다 listen to a person in an absent sort of way / 비가 온 둥 만 둥 하다 We've had no rain to speak of. / 바빠서 조반을 먹는 둥 마는 둥 하고 집을 나왔다 I was in such a hurry that I left home with hardly any breakfast.

**둥개다** 《쩔쩔매다》 be hard up; have a hard time; labor 〔slave〕 over; find difficulty to deal with; be embarrassed 《with》; do not know what to do 《with》; be quite at a loss. ¶ 둥개게 하다 drive 《*a person*》 to *his* wit's end; give 《*a person*》 a lot of trouble / 일을 ~ slave over *one's* work; have a hard time doing *one's* work.

**둥구나무** a large old shade tree.

**둥굴대** a rounded strickle 〔grain-leveler.〕

**둥굴레** 〖식물〗 a Solomon's seal.

**둥굴이** a stripped log. 「a tumble.

**둥그러지다** tumble 《over, down》; have

**둥그스름하다** (be) roundish.

**둥글다** (be) round; globular; spherical; circular. ¶ 둥근 얼굴 a round 〔moon〕 face / 둥근 달 a round (full) moon / 둥글게 앉다 sit in a ring 〔circle〕 / 둥글게 자르다 cut 《*a thing*》 round / 지구는 ~ The earth is spherical 〔round〕.

**둥글둥글** ① 《모양이》 ~하다 be all round 〔circular, globular, spherical〕. ② 《원만》 ~하다 (be) harmonious; well-rounded; ami(c)able; sociable. ¶ (성격이) ~한 사람 a smooth-mannered person; a man of affability / 그의 성격이 ~해졌다 The corners of his character have been rounded off. *or* His character has become mellow.

**둥글리다** round; make 《*a thing*》 round; round off (깎아서). ¶ 책상 모서리를 ~ round off the edge of a table.

**둥글뭉수레하다** (be) round and blunt=tipped.

**둥글번번하다** (be) round and flat.

**둥덩거리다** keep beating (a drum); beat boom-boom; rataplan; tom-tom. ¶ 북을 ~ keep beating 〔booming〕 a drum. 「buoyantly.

**둥덩실** floating high up in the air;

**둥둥**[1] 《북소리》 boom-boom; drumming; rub-a-dub(-dub); thumping; rat-a=tat(-tat). ¶ 북을 ~ 울리다 beat a drum boom-boom.

**둥둥**[2] 《아기 어르는 소리》 "Rock-a=bye-baby!"

**둥실둥실** 《뜨다》 floating light(ly) 〔buoyant(ly)〕. ¶ 배가 ~ 뜨다 a boat is floating buoyantly.

**둥실둥실하다** 《살찌다》 (be) rotund; plump; corpulent. ¶ 둥실둥실한 얼굴 a round 〔plumpy〕 face / 둥실둥실하게 살찌다 be plump 〔portly, corpulent〕.

**둥싯거리다** move slowly 〔sluggishly〕; waddle. ¶ 몸이 비대해서 ~ be fat and move slow.

**둥싯둥싯** slowly; sluggishly; lazily; with waddling step 〔gaits〕. ¶ ~ 걷다 waddle; walk 〔move〕 with an awkward, swaying motion. 「saddle.

**둥어리막대** a stick attached to a pack-

**둥우리** a basket 〔crate〕 made of straw, bamboo or the like. ◉ ~장수 a beef peddler. 대~ a bamboo basket.

**둥지** a nest. ¶ ~를 치다〔틀다〕 build a nest; nest / 새들은 저녁 일찌감치 ~로 돌아온다 Birds fly home to roost early in the evening.

**둥치** 《밑동》 the base (of a tree trunk); (the part near) the root. ¶ 나무 밑~를 자르다 cut down a tree (close) at the base; 《톱으로》 saw off a tree at the root.

**둥치다** ① 《동이다》 wrap up; tie up together. ② 《깎아내다》 cut off the worthless part; trim.

**뒈지다** 《속어》 kick the bucket; kick off; drop dead. ¶ 너 같은 건 어서 뒈져라 Drop dead, you bastard. *or* To hell with you! *or* Go to hell!

**뒝벌** 〖곤충〗 a bumblebee.

**뒤** ① 《뒤쪽》 the back; the rear. ¶ 뒤의 back; hind; rear / 맨 뒤의 hindmost.

뒤에: 뒤에서〔로〕 behind; at the back 〔in the rear〕 《of》; 《미》 in back 《of》; after; backward / 바로 뒤에 close behind; on 〔over〕 the neck of / 행렬 맨 뒤에 at the tail of a queue / 뒤에 남다 stay 〔remain〕 behind / 뒤에 숨다 hide *oneself* behind 《the door》.

뒤로: 뒤로 넘어지다 fall down backward / 뒤로 돌다 get (around) behind 《a tree》 / 뒤로 처지다 drop 〔lag, trail〕 behind 《the others》 / 고향을 뒤로 하다 leave *one's* home behind / 뒤로 물러나서 아무를 지나가게 하다 step back to let *a person* though / 뒤로 살그머니 다가가다 「sneak up 〔creep〕 behind 《*a person*》.

뒤에서: 뒤에서 밀다 push 《a cart》; 《후

원하다》 support 〔back up, bolster up〕《*a person*》/ 뒤에서 붙잡다 grab 《*a person*》 from behind.

뒤를: 뒤를 돌아(다)보다 look back 〔around〕《at》; look behind / 뒤를 따라가다 go behind 〔in the wake of〕; follow 《*a person*》; go after 《*a person*》; follow 〔tag〕 at 《*a person's*》 heel / 뒤를 좇아 달리다 run after 《*a person*》.

¶ 뒤에서 누가 부른다 Someone is calling from behind. / 2보 뒤로 《구령》 Two steps backwards! / 뒤로 돌아 《구령》 Turn to the right about! *or* About turn! / 바위 뒤로부터 한 척의 보트가 희미한 달빛 속에 나타났다 From behind the rock, a boat came out into the weak moonlight.

② 《행적》 a trace 〔track〕; a trail. ¶ 뒤를 밟다 track 〔shadow〕《*a person*》; dog 《*a person's*》 steps; follow in 《*a person's*》 track; trail 《*a person*》/ 뒤를 좇다 follow (up); pursue; run after.

③ 《시간적으로》 (***a***) 《나중·이후》 ¶ 뒤의 later; subsequent / 그 뒤(로) since then; thereafter; after that / 그 뒤 곧 soon after that / 그 뒤 죽〔내내〕 ever since / 훨씬 뒤에 long after / 닷새 뒤 five days later 〔after(wards)〕/ 십 년 뒤 ten years after; after ten years. (***b***) 《앞으로》 future; hence. ¶ 지금부터 2주일 뒤에 two weeks hence 〔from now〕/ 뒤를 위해 대비하다 provide for the future / 50년 뒤의 세계 the world 50 years hence.

뒤에: 뒤에 after; afterwards; later (on); subsequently; by and by; after a time 〔while〕/ 2, 3일 뒤에 after a few days; a few days after 〔later〕 (★ a few days later이면 「…보다 2, 3일 늦어서」의 뜻) / 아침 식사 뒤에 after breakfast / 그로부터 2, 3분 지난 뒤에 a few minutes after that.

¶ 그것은 뒤에 안 일이다 It was discovered afterwards. / 그는 뒤에 온다 He will come later 〔afterwards〕. (★ He will come after.는 틀림) / 뒤에 가겠다 I'll come later. / 그는 뒤에 큰 사람이 되었다 He became a great man later on. / 그 뒤 그로부터 소식이 없다 I have not heard from him since. / 뒤에 볼 나무는 그루를 돋운다 《속담》 One who thinks of the future never fails to prepare himself for it.

④ 《순서적으로》 ¶ 뒤의 the next; the following; the succeeding; the latter (후자의) / 뒤로 next; after / 뒤로 돌리다 〔미루다〕 put off; let 《*a matter*》 wait 〔stand over〕; hold over; sidetrack 《*a matter*》.

⑤ 《뒤의 일》 future affairs. ¶ 뒤를 부탁하다 entrust 《*a person*》 with future affairs; ask 《*a person*》 to look after *one's* affairs while *one* is away.

⑥ 《죽은 후(後)》 after *one's* death. ¶ 뒷일 affairs after *one's* death / 뒤에 남은 가족 the bereaved family / 뒤에 남다 survive 《*one's* parents》/ 처자식을 뒤에 남기고 죽다 die leaving *one's* wife and children behind / 뒷일을 부탁하다 give 《*a person*》 the charge of the affairs after *one's* death.

⑦ 《배후》 the back. ¶ 뒤에서 behind 《*a person's*》 back; 《몰래》 in secret; 《없는 곳에서》 in 《*a person's*》 absence; 《이면에서》 behind the scenes / 뒤에서 공작하다〔조종하다〕 maneuver behind the scenes; pull the strings (from behind) / 뒤에서 욕하다 speak ill of 《*a person*》 「behind *his* back 〔in *his* absence〕.

⑧ 《집착》 tenacity. ¶ 그는 성은 잘 내지만 뒤가 없는 사람이다 He is quick to get angry and quick to get over it.

⑨ 《결과·뒤끝》 the end; consequences; results; aftermath. ¶ 그렇게 하면 뒤가 재미없다 You will have to pay dearly for doing so. / 뒤야 어찌 되든 내가 알 바 아니다 I don't care 「about the consequences 〔for what may come of it〕. / 이 술은 뒤가 좋지 않다 This liquor leaves 〔has〕 nasty aftereffects.

⑩ 《후사》 a successor; 《자손》 a descendant; offspring; descent; posterity. ¶ 그 집은 뒤가 끊겼다 The family line broke.

⑪ 《계승》 what is left behind by a predecessor; the footsteps 《of》. ¶ …의 뒤를 이어 following (in the steps of); in succession to… / 뒤를 이을 사람 an heir; an heiress (여자) / 뒤를 잇다 succeed to 〔take over〕《*a person's* business》; succeed 《*one's* father as the head of the family》; 《후임》 succeed 《*a person*》 at a post 〔in a position〕; step into 《*a person's*》 shoes / 전임자의 뒤를 이어 사업을 운영하다 step into the shoes of *one's* predecessor and run the business.

⑫ 《돌봄·대줌》 what is wanted; needs. ¶ 뒤를 대다 supply 《*a person's*》 needs; keep in supply; supply money / 공부하는 아들의 뒤를 대다 pay school expenses for *one's* son / 장사하는 사람

의 뒤를 대다 supply a merchant with funds / 뒤를 봐 주다 look after; take care 〔charge〕 of; look to the needs 《of》/ 뒤 대기가 힘들다 be very hard to keep 《it》 in supply for 《*a person*》. ⑬ 《대변》 feces; excrement; stool; a bowel movement. ¶ 뒤가 마렵다 feel like having a bowel movement; have an urge to go to the bathroom / 뒤를 보다 go to stool; relieve 〔ease〕 *oneself;* relieve nature / 뒤가 순하다〔굳다〕 have an easy 〔a hard〕 bowel movement. ⑭ 《나머지·여타》 the rest; the remainder; the sequel (계속). ¶ 뒤에 남다 be left over / 뒤는 상상에 맡긴다 The rest may be left for you to imagine. *or* You may guess the rest.

**뒤구르다** ① 《총 따위가》 recoil; kick; rebound. ¶ 총이 몹시 뒤구른다 The gun kicks badly. ② 《일의 뒤끝을》 wind up 〔fix, settle〕 with care. ¶ 일을 ~ wind up a job and make sure that everything is all right.

**뒤까불다** jump 〔shake〕 up and down; act 〔bear *oneself*〕 frivolously 〔silly〕. ¶ 뒤까불지 말고 좀 점잖게 굴어라 Don't be so silly, try to behave like a gentleman.

**뒤꼍** the backyard; the back (side); out in back. ¶ (집) ~에서 놀다 play in the backyard; play out in back.

**뒤꽁무니** the rear end. ¶ ~가 빠지게 달아나다 take to *one's* heels; turn tail and run away / 그는 처녀 ~를 쫓아다닌다 He runs after girls. *or* He is a skirt chaser. ⇨ 꽁무니.

**뒤꽂이** a chignon ornament.

**뒤꿈치** the heel. ¶ 구두 ~ the heel of a shoe / 구두 ~가 닳았다 The shoes are down at heels. *or* The heels of (my) boots are worn out.

**뒤끓다** ① 《물이》 seethe; boil up 〔over〕; come to a boil. ¶ 물이 뒤끓고 있다 The water is seething. / 주전자의 물이 뒤끓는다 The water of kettle is boiling up. ② 《우글거리다》 swarm; be crowded 〔jammed〕 《with people》. ¶ 구더기가 ~ be alive 〔infested〕 with maggots / 도둑이 ~ be infested with robbers / 세밑이면 백화점은 쇼핑객으로 뒤끓는다 The department stores are crowded with shoppers at the end of the year. ③ 《소란하다》 seethe; ferment; be in an uproar 〔a ferment〕. ¶ 흥분으로 ~ seethe 〔be agog〕 with excitement 《over》/ 전쟁이 터질 것이란 소문으로 국내가 뒤끓었다 Rumors of war caused national ferment.

**뒤끝** 《결말》 the end (of an affair); a conclusion; 《해결》 (a) settlement; 《후유증》 aftereffect. ¶ (일의) ~을 맺다 wind up 《an affair》; bring 《*a matter*》 to an end; finish / 그는 일을 벌여만 놓고 ~을 못 맺는다 He always fails to finish the job he has undertaken. / 이 술은 ~이 깨끗치 않다 This liquor has 〔leaves〕 nasty aftereffects.

**뒤내다** become sick 〔weary〕 《of》; shrink (back) 《at, from》; hang 〔hold〕 back; back out of 《an agreement》.

**뒤넘기치다** throw down; throw 〔fling〕 《*a person*》 backward(s); 《뒤엎다》 upset; overturn. ¶ 아무를 ~ throw *a person* down / 밥상을 ~ overturn a dining table.

**뒤넘다** fall 〔be thrown〕 on *one's* back; go over; tumble down; overturn; turn over; upset.

**뒤넘스럽다** be stuck-up; (be) impertinent; presumptuous; overbearing; pert; impudent; cheeky; saucy.

**뒤놀다** ① 《흔들리다》 shake; sway; totter; be shaky 〔rickety〕; 《까불리다》 roll 〔pitch〕 heavily. ¶ 책상다리가 ~ the legs of a table are rickety / 물결에 배가 ~ a boat rolls heavily in the waves. ② 《돌아다니다》 wander; roam; rove.

**뒤늦다** be way late 〔overdue〕; be too late; be belated; be delayed. ¶ 뒤늦게 too late; behind time; at the eleventh hour; belatedly / 뒤늦은 경고 a belated 〔an eleventh-hour〕 warning / 뒤늦은 사과를 하다 offer a belated apology.

**뒤대** the northern part 《of a country》; the north(ern district); the northland.

**뒤대다**[1] 《대주다》 supply 《*a person* with》; provide 《*a person* with》. ¶ 아들 학비를 ~ supply *one's* son with school expenses / 아우 집의 식량을 ~ provide *one's* brother with rice / 종이를 ~ keep paper in constant supply.

**뒤대다**[2] 《비뚜로 말하다》 misinform; tell a lie; make a false statement.

**뒤덮다** cover 《with, over》; hang over; put on; overspread; veil. ¶ 눈이 산을 ~ snow covers 〔blankets〕 the mountains / 이불을 ~ put on bedclothes; cover 《*oneself*》 with bedclothes / 흐린 하늘이 바다를 뒤덮고 있었다 The overcast sky hung low over the sea.

**뒤덮이다** be covered (all over) 《with》;

be overspread; be hung over. ¶ 얼음에 ~ be coated 〔covered〕 with ice / 온통 눈으로 ~ be blanketed 〔covered all over〕 with snow / 구름에 ~ be clouded over; be overcast / 신록으로 ~ be clothed in fresh verdure / 하늘은 구름으로 뒤덮여 있다 The sky is overcast. / 담은 담쟁이 덩굴로 뒤덮여 있다 The wall is overgrown with ivy. / 테이블은 먼지로 뒤덮여 있었다 The table was covered 〔coated〕 with dust.

**뒤돌아보다** look back 〔round〕 《at》; turn about to see; turn *one's* head 〔face〕; look over *one's* shoulder; 《회고》 reflect 〔look back〕 《on, upon》. ¶ 과거를 ~ look back upon *one's* past / 뒤돌아보지 말고 어서 갈 길을 가자 Let us go on our way without looking back. / 뒤돌아보니 그는 아직도 손을 흔들고 있었다 I turned around 〔looked back〕 to find him still waving his hand.

**뒤두다** ① 《후일로 밀다》 leave for the future; set aside for later. ② 《여유를 두다》 keep later dealings 〔consideration〕 in mind. ¶ 뒤를 두고 잘라 말하지 않다 avoid saying anything definite with later dealings in mind.

**뒤둥그러지다** ① 《뒤틀리다》 be twisted 〔contorted〕 all out of shape; be warped 〔distorted〕. ② 《생각·성질이》 be perverse; be twisted 〔perverted〕.

**뒤따르다** follow (up); go 〔run〕 after 《another》; accompany (수행); continue; 《행렬 등을》 bring 〔close〕 up the rear; 《미행하다》 follow; trail; shadow (그림자처럼). ¶ …을 뒤따라 자살하다 commit suicide to follow 《*someone* in death》 / 누군가 나를 뒤따르고 있는 것 같다 Someone seems to be following 〔trailing〕 me. / 한 떼의 기마 경관이 뒤따랐다 A group of mounted policemen brought up the rear. / 많은 소년과 소녀들이 서커스 행렬을 뒤따랐다 Many boys and girls tailed after the circus procession.

**뒤딱지** the back lid 《of a watch》.

**뒤떠들다** make much noise; be noisy; fuss 《over》; stir.

**뒤떨어지다** ① 《처지다》 (***a***) 《능력 등이》 fall 〔drop, get, lag〕 behind 《*a person something*》; be behind; be backward; be behindhand; prove (*oneself*) inferior to 《*a person*》; fall below 〔back〕; yield to 《*a person*》. ¶ 문화가 ~ be backward 〔lag behind〕 in culture / 시대〔유행〕에 ~ be behind the times 〔fashion〕 / 일이 ~ be behind in *one's* work / 경주에서 다른 선수들한테 ~ fall behind 〔be outstripped by〕 the other runners in a race / 다른 학생들보다 공부가 ~ be behind the other students in *one's* studies / 다른 애들보다 지능이 훨씬 ~ be far beneath 〔greatly inferior to〕 the other children in intelligence / 유행에 뒤떨어지지 않도록 하다 keep up with the fashion (of the day); keep pace with the current style / 그 나라는 여러 점에 있어 다른 나라한테 뒤떨어져 있다 The country lags behind other countries in many respects. (***b***) 《낙오되다》 drop 〔fall〕 out; straggle. ¶ 행군에서 ~ fall out while on the march. ② 《뒤에 남다》 remain 〔stay〕 behind.

**뒤뚱거리다** be shaky 〔unsteady〕; totter; stagger; falter.

**뒤뚱뒤뚱** staggeringly; unsteadily. ¶ ~ 걷다 walk with faltering steps.

**뒤뚱발이** a person who totters along.

**뒤뜰** a rear garden; a backyard 《미》.

**뒤로돌아** 《구령》 About face! ¶ 학생들은 일제히 ~를 했다 Students 「turned around 〔about-faced〕 all together.

**뒤룩거리다** ① 《눈알을》 goggle. ¶ 눈을 ~ goggle 〔roll〕 *one's* eyes 《on》 / 눈을 뒤룩거리며 주위를 둘러보다 look around staringly. ② 《몸을》 sway; waddle. ¶ 몸을 ~ sway *one's* body. ③ 《성이 나서》 make angry gestures; jerk with anger.

**뒤룩뒤룩** 《눈알을》 glaring; 《몸을》 swaying; waddling; 《성이 나서》 jerking with anger; in a huff. ¶ ~ 걷다 walk swaying *one's* body.

**뒤미처** right 〔immediately〕 after; soon 〔shortly〕 after; without intermission 〔a break〕; close on the heels 《of》. ¶ ~ 좇아가다 follow 《*a person*》 right after *one* has left / ~ 그도 사직했다 He too, soon after the other, resigned his post.

**뒤바꾸다** take 〔put〕 the wrong one; (make a) mistake; reverse; switch; invert; get 《it》 backwards. ¶ 순서를 ~ reverse the order; make a mistake in the sequence / 신을 뒤바꿔 신다 put *one's* shoes on the wrong way round; have the right shoe on the wrong foot (좌우를); wear another's shoes (남의 신을).

**뒤바뀌다** be taken 〔put〕 in the wrong way; be mistaken; be reversed 〔switched〕; be mixed up. ¶ 순서가 ~

be topsy-turvy; be out of order / 신이 다른 사람 것과 ～ wear another's shoes by mistake / 이야기 순서가 뒤바뀌었습니다만… I should have said this first, but… / 상황이 뒤바뀌었다 The situation reversed itself.

**뒤바르다** 《종이 따위를》 paste (up) all over; 《분 따위를》 paint 〔powder〕 《*one's* face》 thick(ly); put on thick make-up; 《칠 따위를》 daub all over; (be-)smear.

**뒤받다** stand up to a scolding; scold back; talk 〔answer〕 back to 《*a person*》; retort.

**뒤밟다** track; shadow; tail; trail; dog 《*a person's* steps》; follow 《in *a person's* track》; get on 《*a person's*》 tail. ¶ 뒤밟게 하다 put a dog on the trail / 형사에게 뒤밟게 하다 set a detective on 《*a person, a person's* track》 / 비밀 경찰이 밤낮으로 나를 뒤밟고 있다 The secret police are shadowing me night and day.

**뒤버무리다** mix 《up, in》; add. ¶ 나물을 ～ mix up vegetables; toss a salad.

**뒤범벅** a mess; a hotchpotch; a jumble; a medley; a muddle; a pell-mell. ～되다 be mixed up; be jumbled together; be in a mess; be confused. ¶ ～을 만들다 mix up; jumble together; make a mess.

**뒤보다** ① 《용변보다》 evacuate the 〔move *one's*〕 bowels; go to stool; ease *oneself;* do *one's* needs. ¶ 뒤보러 가다 go to the closet 〔toilet, lavatory〕. ② ⇨ 뒤보아주다.

**뒤보아주다** take care of; look 〔see〕 after; help. ¶ 어머니 없는 애를 ～ take care of a motherless child / 장사하는 사람을 ～ help a merchant with funds.

**뒤뿔치다** work under 《*a person*》; do hackwork 《for》.

**뒤서다** ① 《뒤따르다》 follow; follow at 《*a person's*》 heels; accompany; go 〔come〕 with. ② ＝ 뒤지다[2].

**뒤섞다** mix (up); add in; jumble together 〔up〕; make a mess; compound 《this and that》; mingle together; blend. ¶ 흙에 모래를 ～ mix earth with sand / 카드짝을 ～ shuffle a pack of cards / 이것을 다른 책과 뒤섞지 말아 주십시오 Don't mix this book with the others.

**뒤섞이다** be mixed 〔jumbled〕 《up, together》; be added in; be made a mess of; become blended; be intermingled. ¶ 옷이 모두 뒤섞여 있다 Clothes are all in disarray. / 책이 모두 뒤섞여 있다 The books are all mixed up. / 서류가 뒤섞이지 않도록 주의하시오 See (to it) that the papers do not get mixed. / 책상 위에는 책과 서류가 한데 뒤섞여 있었다 Books and papers were all jumbled together 〔in a jumble〕 on the desk.

**뒤숭숭하다** ① 《혼란하다》 (***a***) 《분위기 등이》 (be) busy; bustling; restless; confused. ¶ 뒤숭숭한 느낌 a sense of restlessness / 뒤숭숭한 도시 생활 the flurry of city life / 뒤숭숭한 하루를 보내다 pass a restless day / 아버지의 급환으로 집안이 ～ There is confusion at home owing to the sudden illness of father. (***b***) 《세상이》 (be) noisy; turbulent; troubled; agitated; disturbed. ¶ 뒤숭숭한 시대 troubled 〔turbulent, unsettled〕 times. ② (***a***) 《마음이》 (be) nervous; distracted; disturbed; restless; be ill at ease. ¶ 마음이 뒤숭숭해 아무 것도 못 하겠다 I am restless and don't feel like doing anything. (***b***) 《물건이》 (be) messy; confused; disarrayed; untidy. ¶ 뒤숭숭한 방 a messy room; a room in disorder.

**뒤스럭거리다** ① 《변덕부리다》 act fickle; be capricious 〔whimsical〕. ② 《뒤지다》 rummage; ransack; feel 〔fumble〕 for. ¶ 뒤스럭뒤스럭 fumbling; rummaging.

**뒤스럭스럽다** be always excited 〔hotheaded〕 and noisy.

**뒤스르다** arrange; manage skillfully; make (a) shift; put things in order.

**뒤엉키다** ① 《실·줄 따위가》 get 〔become〕 entangled; get 〔become〕 raveled. ¶ 뒤엉킨 실을 풀다 untie entangled knots; unravel a thread. ② 《이야기 등이》 get confused 〔mixed〕; get tangled; 《사건 등이》 get complicated; become involved. ¶ 뒤엉킨 문제를 해결하다 settle a complicated problem / 그 사건에는 여러가지 복잡한 사정이 뒤엉켜 있다 The case is entangled with various complicated circumstances.

**뒤엎다** ① 《전복시키다》 upset; overturn; turn over; 《결정을》 overrule; reverse. ¶ 정설을 ～ explode 〔overthrow〕 the established theory / 판결을 ～ overrule a decision; reverse 〔repeal〕 a sentence. ② 《타도하다》 overthrow; subvert. ¶ 현정부를 ～ overthrow the present government.

**뒤웅박** a gourd (cut at the top with the meat removed).

**뒤잇다** follow; succeed (one another);

come one after another. ¶ 뒤이어 later on; following that successively; one after another / 인사에 뒤이어 축배를 들었다 Following 〔After〕 the congratulations, we drank a toast.

**뒤적거리다, 뒤적이다** ransack; rummage 《in》; 《더듬어서》 fumble 〔feel, fish〕 《in》; browse (책 따위를). ¶ 서랍을 ~ ransack 〔rummage in〕 a drawer 《for》/ 호주머니를 ~ fumble in *one's* pocket 《for》; go through 《*a person's*》 pocket (훔치기 위해) / 책을 ~ browse through a book.

**뒤져내다** rummage 《out》; hunt out; seek 〔search〕 out. ¶ 서랍에서 돈을 ~ rummage money from a drawer/ 벽장에서 감춰 둔 과자를 ~ seek out cakes put away in a wall cupboard.

**뒤져보다** look 〔search〕 《for》; hunt (up); make a search 《for》; rummage 〔fumble〕 《for》. ¶ 서랍을 ~ rummage in a drawer 《to see if there is any money》/ 창고를 ~ search a warehouse 《to see if there is any rice concealed (there)》/ 있을 만한 곳은 모두 뒤져 보았으나 못찾았다 I hunted in all the likely places, but I failed to find it.

**뒤조지다** double-check; make sure; make double-sure; affirm; confirm.

**뒤주** a wooden rice chest 〔bin〕; a grain box.

**뒤죽박죽** topsy-turvy; higgledy-piggledy; pell-mell; all mixed up; all jumbled up; in a mess; in confusion; in disorder. ¶ ~인 상태 a topsy=turvy confusion; topsy-turvydom / ~이 되다 get mixed up; get confused / ~을 만들다 mix up; make a mess of; turn 《*things*》 topsy-turvy / 서가의 책이 ~이 되었다 Books on the shelf are all mixed up. / 원고가 방에 흩어져 ~이 되었다 The manuscript sheets are scattered pell-mell all over the room. / 번호순으로 돼 있으니 ~이 안 되도록 해라 They are in numerical order, so please don't jumble them.

**뒤쥐** 『동물』 a shrew(mouse).

**뒤지**(—紙) toilet 〔privy〕 paper; a toilet roll (두루마리).

**뒤지다**[1] 《찾다》 search; rummage; fumble. ¶ 아무의 몸을 ~ search *a person* 《for a weapon》/ 서랍을 ~ rummage (in) the drawer 《for》/ 주머니를 ~ fumble in *one's* pocket; search 〔dig into〕 *one's* pocket / 집안을 ~ search a house 《for *something*》/ 샅샅이 ~ search every corner; look in every nook and cranny / 있을 만한 곳은 모조리 뒤졌다 I looked for it in every likely place.

**뒤지다**[2] 《뒤떨어지다》 lag 〔fall, drop〕 behind 《another》; fall back; be behind 《others》; be backward 《in》; be outstripped 《by》; yield 《to》; 《시대에》 be in arrear of (the) times. ¶ 지능이 뒤지는 아이 a backward 〔(mentally) retarded〕 child / 시대〔유행〕에 ~ be behind the times 〔fashion〕; be out of style / 남에게 뒤지지 않다 yield 〔be second〕 to none / 시류에 뒤지지 않다 keep in touch with the world / 시류에 뒤지지 않도록 하다 keep abreast of the times / 뒤지지 않고 따라가다 keep up with 《*a person*》/ 그 나라는 문화가 뒤지고 있다 The country is backward in civilization. / 우리들은 예방 의학에서 뒤져 있다 We lag behind in preventive medicine. / 국내 자동차 제조업자들은 기술면에서 외국 생산업자들에게 크게 뒤져 있다 The local car makers are far behind foreign manufacturers in terms of technology.

**뒤집개질** turning 《*a thing*》 over 〔upside down, topsy-turvy〕. ~하다 turn 《it》 over.

**뒤집고핥다** know 「inside out 〔in detail〕; know 〔understand〕 thoroughly; have a full knowledge 《of》; be quite at home.

**뒤집다** ① 《안팎을》 turn the other way; turn out 〔over〕; turn inside 〔wrongside〕 out; turn outside in; 《위아래를》 turn 《*a thing*》 upside down. ¶ 뒤집어 말하면 to put 《it》 the other way; stated reversely / 팬케이크를 ~ turn 〔flip〕 a pancake / 스웨터를 뒤집어 입다 put on sweaters inside out / 답안용지를 뒤집어 놓다 turn the answer sheet over; put *one's* examination paper face down / 양말을 뒤집어 신다 put on *one's* socks wrongside out / 접시를 뒤집어(서) 놓다 turn a dish over. ② 《뒤엎다》 (***a***) 《사물을》 upset; overturn; turn over. (***b***) 《바꾸다》 change; 《좌절시키다》 frustrate; baffle; 《결정을》 overrule; reverse; upset. ¶ 계획을 ~ upset a plan; balk 《*a person*》 in *one's* plan; change 〔vary〕 *one's* plan (바꾸다) / 판결을 ~ overrule a decision / 학설을 ~ upset 〔overthrow〕 a theory. ③ 《순서를》 reverse; invert; switch. ¶ 순서를 ~ reverse 〔change〕 the order. ④ 《혼란시키다》 throw into confusion;

《형세를》 reverse; turn the tables. ¶ 그 소식은 장내를 발칵 뒤집어 놓았다 The news threw the audience into utter confusion.

**뒤집어쓰다** ① 《몸에》 (***a***) 《푹 덮다·가리다》 cover 《with》; put on; wear; draw 〔pull〕 《*a thing*》 over *one's* head. ¶ 복면을 ～ mask *oneself;* cover 〔muffle (up)〕 *one's* face / 이불을 ～ cover *oneself* with bedclothes; pull *one's* quilt over *one's* head. (***b***) 《물·먼지 등을》 pour 《water》 on 《*oneself* 》; be covered 《with》; 《물결을》 be washed 《by》. ¶ (찬)물을 ～ pour 〔dash〕 water over 〔(up)on〕 *oneself* / 먼지를 ～ be covered with dust / (배가) 파도를 ～ ship water 〔a sea〕; be flooded by waves / 온몸에 흙탕물을 ～ be splashed all over with muddy water. ② 《책임·허물을》 take 《blame》 upon *oneself.* ¶ 남의 죄를 ～ take another's blame upon *oneself* / 억울한 죄를 ～ be falsely accused.

**뒤집어씌우다** 《덮다》 cover 《with》; put 《*a thing*》 on; 《책임·죄를》 charge 《*a person*》 with 《a blame》; put 〔lay, pin〕 《the blame》 on 《*a person*》; fix 〔shuffle off 〕 《*one's* responsibility》 on 《*a person*》.

**뒤집히다** ① (***a***) 《안팎이》 be turned inside out; be turned over; 《거꾸로》 be turned upside down. ¶ (우산 따위가) 바람에 ～ be blown inside out / (옷 등이) 뒤집혀 있다 be wrong side out. (***b***) 《순서가》 be reversed; be changed 〔switched〕. ¶ 순서가 뒤집혔다 The order is reversed 〔changed〕. ② 《전복되다》 (***a***) 《사물이》 be overturned; be turned over; be upset; 《배가》 capsize; overturn; turn turtle; 《쓰러지다》 tumble down; topple over 〔down〕; be upset. ¶ 계획이 ～ a plan is upset / 배가 뒤집혔다 The boat overturned. / 꽃병이 뒤집혔다 The vase has been upset. / 현정부는 곧 뒤집힐지도 모른다 The present government might be tumbled from power before long. (***b***) 《결정·학설 따위가》 be reversed; be overruled 〔exploded〕; 《역전되다》 be reversed. ¶ 뒤집힌 학설 an exploded 〔overthrown〕 theory / 형세가 뒤집혔다 The situation was reversed. ③ 《야단이 나다》 ferment; throw into confusion; be turned topsy-turvy. ¶ 주인이 죽자 집안은 발칵 뒤집혔다 The master's death threw the whole house into utter confusion. / 그 소식에 온 마을이 발칵 뒤집혔다 The news set the whole village in an uproar. ④ 《속이》 feel sick 〔nausea〕; 《정신이》 go 〔run〕 mad. ¶ 눈이 ～ lose *one's* head; be beside *oneself* / 배가 고파 눈이 뒤집힐 것 같다 be almost frantic with hunger.

**뒤쫓다** follow up; chase; pursue; run after 《*a person*》. ¶ 범인을 ～ pursue a criminal / 형사는 사흘 동안이나 용의자를 뒤쫓았다 The (police) detective followed the suspect for three days.

**뒤차**(―車) 《다음 차》 the next 〔later〕 train; the following car; 《끝차》 a car in the rear; a rear car.

**뒤채**[1] 《집채》 a backhouse; the back wing.

**뒤채**[2] 《가마의》 the rear handbars of a sedan chair.

**뒤채다** be in excess; be found 〔met with〕 everywhere; 《발길에 걸리다》 get in *one's* way.

**뒤처리**(―處理) putting 《*things*》 to rights 〔in order〕; after-measures; settlement 《of an affair》. ～하다 wind up 《an affair》; put 《*things*》 in order; dispose of. ¶ 사건의 ～를 하다 settle 〔wind up〕 an affair / 파산한 회사의 ～를 하다 wind 〔clear〕 up the affairs of an insolvent company.

**뒤처지다** be behind 《*a person*》; lag 〔fall〕 behind 《*a person* in *something*》; be tardy 《at, in》; 《시작이》 make a slow start.

**뒤쳐지다** be turned over.

**뒤축** the heel of the foot; 《신·버선의》 the heel of shoes 〔socks〕. ¶ ～이 높은〔낮은〕 신 high-〔low-〕heeled shoes / ～을 대다 put a heel on; heel / 구두 ～이 닳다 shoes are worn down at the heel.

**뒤치다** turn 《over》; 《잠자리에서》 turn over 〔round〕 in sleep; toss 〔roll〕 about in bed. ¶ 엎어진 삽을 ～ turn over an upturned spade / 잠을 못 자고 몸을 ～ toss and turn sleepless in bed.

**뒤치다꺼리** ① 《돌봄》 helping (from behind); taking care of; looking after; providing; supplying. ～하다 help (from behind); provide; supply; take care of. ¶ 애들 ～를 하다 take care of *one's* children / 동생의 살림 ～를 하다 provide *one's* brother's family (with daily necessities). ② 《뒤처리》 clearing 〔winding〕 up.

**뒤탈**(―頉) later trouble; future 〔further〕 difficulty. ¶ ～이 두려워 for fear of later troubles / ～이 없도록 so as to prevent any trouble that might occur in future; so there will be no future troubles / ～이 없도록 하다 leave no seeds of future trouble / 모두 해결되어 ～은 없었다 Everything was settled and there was no further 〔more〕 trouble.

**뒤통수** the back of the head; 〖의학〗 the occiput; occipital region. ¶ ～를 치다 hit the back of *one's* head; 《낙심하다》 get dispirited 〔disappointed〕; lose heart.

**뒤통스럽다** (be) clumsy; bungling; thick; thick-headed; obtuse. ¶ 뒤통스러운 사람 a bungler; a botcher / 뒤통스러운 짓 a blunder / 그는 뒤통스러워 일을 잘 저지른다 He is such a thick-headed fellow that he makes a bungle of everything he does.

**뒤틀다** ① 《비틀다》 twist; wrench; screw; distort. ¶ 팔을 ～ wrench 〔twist〕 《*a person's*》 arm; give a twist to 《*a person's*》 arm / 고통으로 몸을 ～ writhe in great agony (with *one's* hands clenched). ② 《방해하다》 thwart; baffle; foil; frustrate. ¶ 남의 계획을 뒤틀어 놓다 thwart *a person's* plan.

**뒤틀리다** ① 《비틀리다》 be wrenched; be 〔get〕 twisted; be wricked; be warped; be distorted. ¶ 목재가 말라 ～ timber is warped by heat / 성질이 ～ become crooked 〔perverse〕; be 〔get〕 warped. ② 《일이》 be thwarted 〔baffled〕; be frustrated; be foiled. ¶ 계획이 ～ a plan is thwarted.

**뒤틀어지다** ① 《물건이》 《it》 twist; warp; 《일이》 fail; go amiss 〔awry, wrong〕; miss. ¶ 팔다리가 ～ *one's* limbs twist / 계획이 ～ a plan misses 〔goes wrong, fails〕. ② ＝틀어지다 ③.

**뒤틈바리** a blunt rude person; a careless 〔an imprudent〕 fellow; a rough.

**뒤폭**(―幅) ① 《옷의》 the back (piece) of a garment. ② 《가구 따위의》 the back (piece) of a box 〔chest〕.

**뒤표지**(―表紙) the back 〔reverse〕 cover (of a book).

**뒤품** the shoulder width of a garment.

**뒤흔들다** ① 《몹시 흔들다》 shake hard 〔violently〕; sway 〔swing〕 hard. ¶ 열매를 따려고 나무를 ～ shake fruits off a tree; shake down fruits / 지축을 뒤흔드는 굉음 a deep earthshaking rumble / 지진이 건물을 뒤흔들었다 The earthquake shook the building. / 나는 동생의 어깨를 뒤흔들어 깨웠다 I shook my brother by the shoulder to wake him. ② 《어지럽히다》 disturb; stir; agitate. ¶ 마음을 ～ disturb *a person's* 〔*one's*〕 mind / 세상을 ～ cause 〔create〕 a stir; disturb 〔upset〕 the world / 정계를 ～ cause a sensation in the political world.

**뒤흔들리다** ① 《사물이》 be shaken 〔swayed〕 hard. ¶ 지진으로 집이 ～ houses are shaken by the earthquake / 길이 나빠 차가 ～ a car sways because of the rough road. ② 《동요되다》 be disturbed; be stirred; be agitated. ¶ 마음이 ～ *one's* mind is disturbed.

**뒷간**(―間) ＝변소. ¶ ～에 갈 적 맘 다르고 올 적 맘 다르다 《속담》 "Danger past, God forgotten." *or* Once on shore, we pray no more.

**뒷갈망** dealing with the aftermath; setting 《*matters*》 right; settlement; winding-up; straightening things out; after-adjustment; putting in order. ～하다 deal with the aftermath; clean up a mess; settle the matter 〔problem〕; wind up; straighten 《*matters*》 out.

**뒷갈이** plowing the field after harvesting.

**뒷거래**(―去來) 《매매》 black market 〔underground〕 dealings; black-marketing; 《비밀 교섭》 secret dealings; an undercover 〔a secret〕 arrangement. ⇨ 암거래. ～하다 《매매》 sell 〔buy〕 《goods》 on the black market; black-market; 《비밀 교섭》 have 〔make〕 secret dealings with. ¶ 그는 ～로 큰 돈을 벌었다고 한다 He is said to have made a lot of money by black-marketing.

**뒷걱정하다** worry about an aftermath.

**뒷걸음질** stepping 〔walking, moving〕 backward. ～하다 step 〔walk, move〕 backward.

**뒷걸음치다** step 〔walk, move〕 backward; retrograde; back down; 《무서워서》 flinch; shrink back 〔away〕 《from》; draw back 《from danger》. ¶ 말이 뱀을 보고 ～ a horse shies 〔jibs〕 at the sight of a snake / 뒷걸음치지 마라 No hanging back!

**뒷고대** the back of a collar.

**뒷골목** a back alley 〔street〕; a by-street.

**뒷공론**(―公論) ① 《비평·험담》 backbiting; speaking ill of 〔criticizing〕 others behind their backs. ～하다 backbite 《*a person*》; speak ill of 〔criticize〕 《*a person*》 behind *his* back; say unkind 〔spiteful〕 things about 《*a person*》 behind *his* back; stab 《*a* *person*》 in the back. ②《일 끝난 뒤의》 idle discussion after *something* is over; 《속어》 a postmortem; "a rehashing". ～하다 discuss 《*something*》 after it is over; hold a futile debate after the event; rehash events; go over 《*a thing*》 again.

**뒷구멍** 《뒷문》 a back door; a back way; a rear entry; 《부정 수단》 an illegitimate way. ¶ ～ 영업 illegal [back door] business / ～으로 하는 계약 a backdoor contract / ～으로 도망치다 escape by the back door / ～으로 돈을 대다 give 《*a person*》 money out the back door / ～으로 돈을 먹이다 bribe 《a *person*》 secretly / ～으로 입학하다 buy *one's* way into school; obtain [get] a back-door admission to a college.

**뒷굽** ① ⇨ 뒷발굽. ②《신의》 the heel of a shoe.

**뒷그림자** 《그림자》 a shadow behind; 《뒷모습》 the sight [appearance] of *one's* back.

**뒷길** ① 《길》 a back-street; a by-road (샛길). ②《장래》 *one's* future (prospects). ¶～을 보아 용서하다 forgive 《*a person*》 for the sake of *his* future.

**뒷날** the future; a later day; later (on); afterward; the days to come; someday; another day. ⇨ 후일. ¶ ～을 기약하고 헤어지다 part in the hopes of meeting again; 《일을 미루고》 part from 《*a person*》 deferring the matter to some future occasion / ～ 가서 후회하지 마라 Make sure you're not sorry in the future. / ～ 다시 봅시다 See you again someday.

**뒷다리** a hind [rear] leg (★ 앞뒤 짝을 이루는 것은 hinder가 아닌 hind를 씀). ¶～로 서다 stand [rear up] on 《its》 hind legs [feet]; sit up (개가); ramp (말이) / 말이 ～로 섰다 The horse stood on its hind legs.

**뒷다리잡히다** be at 《*a person's*》 mercy; be in 《*a person's*》 clutches. ¶말 실수로 뒷다리를 잡혔다 I was blamed for a slip of the tongue.

**뒷담당**(―擔當) answering [taking responsibility] for the aftermath; taking care [charge] of the rest of 《it》. ～하다 answer [take responsibility] for the aftermath 《of *an affair*》; take care [charge] of the rest. ¶ 싸움의 ～을 하다 take care of any troubles resulting from a fight / 일이 잘못되면 ～은 내가 하겠다 If anything goes wrong, I will take care of it.

**뒷대문**(―大門) the back-entrance [-gate]; a rear gate.

**뒷덜미** the nape; the scruff; the back of *one's* neck. ¶ ～를 잡다 take [seize, grasp] 《*a person*》 by the nape of *his* neck.

**뒷돈** ①《준비금》 reserve funds; extra funds; ready money. ②《밑천》 supply of money; funds; capital; stakes. ¶ 장사 ～을 대다 supply 《*a person*》 with capital for business / 노름 ～을 대다 supply 《*a person*》 with gambling stakes.

**뒷동산** a garden [park] in the back of a house [building]; a hill at the back 《of *one's* home, of the village》.

**뒷마감** winding-up; bringing to a finish; completion; conclusion. ～하다 wind up; bring to a finish; complete; conclude. ¶ 일을 ～하다 wind up a job; finish *one's* work / 회계를 ～하다 close an account.

**뒷마구리** the rear crossbar of a pack-saddle.

**뒷마당** a backyard; a rear garden; a back lot.

**뒷마무리** ⇨ 마무리.

**뒷말** ＝ 뒷공론.

**뒷맛** an aftertaste. ¶ ～이 좋다 [깨끗하다] have [leave] a pleasant [clean] aftertaste / ～이 나쁘다 have [leave] an unpleasant [a nasty, a bad] aftertaste.

**뒷맵시** *one's* appearance [figure] from the back. ¶ ～가 곱다 look fine from behind / ～가 없다 look poor from behind.

**뒷머리** ① 《물건의》 the back part 《of》; the back end. ¶ 책상 ～ the back part of a table. ② 《행렬의》 the rear; the end. ¶ 줄의 ～ the end [rear] of a row / 행렬의 ～ the rear of a procession.

**뒷면**(―面) ① 《이면》 the reverse [other] side; the back (side); 《내면》 the inside. ¶ 엽서의 ～ 《on》 the back of a postcard / ～을 보시오 《게시》 See back page. *or* See the reverse side. *or* Please turn over (생략 P.T.O.). ② 《동전의》 the tail; the reverse 《of a coin》.

**뒷모습**(―貌襲) the appearance [figure] from behind; the sight of 《*a person's*》 back. ¶ ～이 꼭 형과 같다 look just like *one's* brother from behind / 그가 달려가는 ～을 보았다 I caught sight of his back as he ran along.

**뒷모양**(―貌樣) ① ＝ 뒷모습. ② 《체면》 the "face" that will result; embarrassment *one* will get into.

**뒷목** leavings 〔grain left over〕 after threshing.

**뒷문**(—門) a back 〔rear〕 gate; a postern (gate). ¶ ~으로 입학하다 obtain a backdoor admission 《to a college》 / ~으로 도망치다 escape by the back door.

**뒷물** bathing *one's* private parts; a hip bath; a sitz bath. ~하다 bathe *one's* private parts; take a sitz bath.

**뒷밀이** ① 《일》 pushing a cart from behind; boosting 《속어》. ~하다 push 《a cart》 from behind. ② 《사람》 a person who pushes a cart from behind; a pusher; a pushman.

**뒷바닥** 《신발의》 the back of a shoe sole.

**뒷바라지** helping 《*a person*》 from behind by providing him with 《*something*》; looking after; giving aids; taking care of. ~하다 help 《a family》 out; look after; take care of. ¶ 아들의 살림 ~를 하다 provide *one's* son with daily necessaries.

**뒷바퀴** a back 〔rear〕 wheel.

**뒷받침** 《후원》 backing; backup; support; 《증명》 proof; substantiation; 《보증》 guarantee; endorsement. ~하다 back (up); support; endorse; substantiate; prove; give substance to 《words》; add support to 《the rumor》. ¶ ~하는 사람 a backer; a supporter; a protector; a patron / 유력한 ~ strong backing / 증거의 ~이 없는 자백 a naked 〔an incorroborated〕 confession / 사실의 ~이 있는 주장 an argument based on facts / 견해를 ~하다 endorse 《*a person's*》 view / 진술을 ~하다 substantiate a statement / 말을 행동으로 ~하다 back up *one's* words with deeds / 통계로 주장을 ~하다 fortify *one's* case with statistics / 사실을 ~하는 증거를 확보하다 secure evidence supporting the fact / 그것을 ~할 이론이 없다 There is no theory to prove it. / 당신이 말하는 것을 ~할 증거가 있습니까 Do you have any evidence to back up what you are saying? / 그에게는 형의 ~이 있었다 He had a brother at his back.

**뒷발** ① 《발》 a hind foot; heels; 《다리》 a hind leg. ¶ ~로 차다 kick with *one's* heel / ~로 흙을 차다 scratch up the dirt with its hind legs. ② 《발길》 the back of *one's* foot; *one's* heel.

**뒷발굽** 《동물의》 a back 〔hind〕 hoof.

**뒷발질** kicking with *one's* heel. ~하다 kick with *one's* heel. 「in the back.

**뒷방**(—房) a back 〔rear〕 room; a room

**뒷배보다** help 《*a person*》 from behind.

**뒷보증**(—保證) an endorsement for transfer; an endorsement to order; *visé* (F.). ⇨ 배서(背書).

**뒷북치다** fuss about belatedly; pother after the event.

**뒷사람** a person behind; 《뒷세대》 a person of a later generation; generations to come.

**뒷산**(—山) a hill at the back 《of the village, of *one's* house》.

**뒷생각** afterthoughts; hindsight; worries about the future.

**뒷소문**(—所聞) an after-talk; gossip 〔a rumor〕 following the event.

**뒷손** accepting 《it》 「on the sly 〔under the counter, from the back door〕; getting bribed. ¶ ~ 벌리다 be ready to accept on the sly; be open to bribery.

**뒷손가락질** ~하다 point after 《*a person*》; point a finger of scorn at 《*a person*》; talk about 《*a person*》 with scorn. ¶ ~을 받다 have depreciating words uttered behind *one's* back; be an object of social contempt; be talked of (in contempt) / ~당하지 않도록 노력하다 try to keep *one's* character above reproach.

**뒷손없다** be careless 〔slipshod〕 about finishing things up; (be) loose; negligent.

**뒷수습**(—收拾) settlement 《of an affair》. ⇨ 뒤처리, 뒷갈망. ¶ 사건의 ~을 하다 settle an affair.

**뒷심** ① 《뒤에서 도와주는》 help 〔aid, assistance〕 from behind; backing=up; protection; support. ¶ ~이 든든하다 have a good backing / 장사하는 데 삼촌의 지위가 적지 않은 ~이 된다 The social position of his uncle makes no little help to him in doing business. ② 《저력》 latent 〔potential〕 energy 〔power〕. ¶ ~이 있는 strong; energetic; powerful.

**뒷이야기** a sequel 《to the event》.

**뒷일** ① 《뒤의 일》 later happenings; the aftermath of an event; the rest; the sequel. ¶ 소송 ~을 처리하다 dispose of the aftermath of a lawsuit / ~은 네게 맡기겠다 I will leave the rest to you. / ~에 대해서는 책임질 수 없다 I will not take any responsibility for what may happen later on.

② (***a***) 《장래의》 future (affairs). ¶ ～을 부탁하다 《없는 동안의》 ask 《another》 to look after *one's* affairs while *one* is gone; entrust 《another》 with future affairs / 먼 ～을 생각하다 have future in view; 《자손의 일을》 have the welfare 〔interests〕 of posterity at heart / ～이야 누가 알 수 있나 There is no knowing what will happen in the future. / 그는 친구들에게 ～을 부탁하고 먼 길을 떠났다 He went on a long journey asking his friends to take care of anything that might come up. (***b***) 《사후의》 affairs after *one's* death. ¶ ～을 걱정하다 worry about *things* 〔*one's* family〕 after *one's* death / ～을 부탁하다 entrust 《*a person*》 with the affairs after *one's* death; give 《another》 the charge of the affairs after *one's* death.

**뒷자락** the rear skirt; the back hem of *one's* clothes.

**뒷자리** a back 〔rear〕 seat.

**뒷전** ① 《굿의》 the last of the 12 stages of an exorcism. ¶ ～ 놀다 《무당이》 perform the last stage of an exorcism. ② 《뒤·배후》 the back; the rear. ¶ ～에서 behind 《*a person's*》 back; in 《*a person's*》 absence (없는 데서); behind the scenes / ～에서 욕하다 speak ill of 《*a person*》 behind *his* back 〔in *his* absence〕; backbite 《*a person*》 / ～에 앉아 조종하다 pull the wires 〔strings〕 (from behind) / 멀리 ～에 앉다 sit far back. ③ 《미룸》 negligence. ¶ ～으로 미루다 lay aside; neglect; leave 《*a matter*》 to be dealt later on / 공부를 ～으로 돌리다 neglect 〔ignore〕 *one's* studies. ◉ ～ 풀이 performing the last stage of an exorcism: ～ 풀이하다 finish the exorcism.

**뒷정리**(—整理) arrangements for the conclusion 〔end〕. ～하다 arrange to end 〔conclude〕; put 《*things*》 in order; clear away (청소); dispose of (처리); clear the table (식사의).

**뒷조사**(—調査) a detailed 〔secret〕 investigation. ～하다 investigate in secret.

**뒷줄** the row behind; a back 〔rear〕 row.

**뒷지느러미** 『어류』 an anal fin.

**뒷질** pitching; rocking. ～하다 《a ship》 pitch; 《a boat》 rock back and forth.

**뒷짐** folding *one's* hands behind *one's* back. ¶ ～지다 fold *one's* hands behind *one's* back / ～ 지우다 make 《*a person*》 fold *his* hands behind *his* back; 《결박짓다》 tie 《*a person's*》 arms behind *his* back.

**뒷짐결박**(—結縛) ～하다 tie 〔bind〕 《*a person's*》 arms behind *his* back. ¶ ～을 당하다 have *one's* hands tied behind *his* back.

**뒷집** the house 「right 〔in the〕 back of *one's* own; the house adjoining in the back.

**뒹굴다** ① 《누워서》 lie down; throw *oneself* down; roll over. ¶ 자리 속에서 ～ roll in bed / 잔디밭에서 ～ throw *oneself* down on the lawn. / 트럭이 옆으로 뒹굴었다 The truck turned over on its side. ② 《빈둥대다》 idle 〔loaf〕 away (*one's* time); loaf around; live at ease. ¶ 그는 아무 것도 않고 뒹굴고 있다 He leads an idle life. / 그녀는 낮에는 집에서 뒹군다 She idles her time away at home in the daytime.

**듀스** 『테니스』 《go to》 deuce.

**듀엣** 『음악』 《이중창〔주〕》 a duet.

**드나나나** whether *one* is at home or stays out; wherever *one* goes. ¶ ～ 걱정거리뿐이다 I have nothing but troubles, whether at home or out.

**드나들다** ① 《출입하다》 come in and go out; go 〔come〕 in and out; frequent (자주). ¶ 드나드는 배 ships going in and out / 사람들이 자주 ～ people are coming in and out all the time / 술집에 자주 ～「hang out at 〔hang around〕 a bar; frequent a pub / 마음대로 드나들 수 있다 have free access 《to》; have the run of 《the house》 / 우리 집에는 매일 드나드는 사람이 많다 We have 「a lot 〔lots〕 of visitors every day. ② 《갈아들다》 be frequently changed. ¶ 그 집에는 가정부가 자주 드나든다 Housemaids are frequently changed in that family. ③ 《들쭉날쭉하다》 be crooked; be indented; be not straight; go in and out. ¶ 드나듦이 심한 해안선 a much indented coastline / 모를 심은 줄이 드나들어 들쭉날쭉하다 The row of planted rice is irregular.

**드난** 《주로 여자》 living out as a servant 〔laborer, charwoman〕; a daily domestic service. ¶ ～ 살다 live out as a servant 〔laborer, charwoman〕. ◉ ～꾼 a daily 〔live-out〕 servant 〔laborer, charwoman〕. ～살이 living out as a servant 〔laborer, charwoman〕.

**드날리다** ① 《집어서》 hold 〔pick〕 up 《*something*》 and make 《it》 fly. ② 《이름·명성을》 make *oneself* famous. ¶ 명

성을 ~ have *one's* reputation raised; win a 「for and wide 〔world-wide〕 reputation. ⇨ 들날리다 ①.

**드넓다** (be) spacious; large; wide; open; vast; extensive. ¶ 드넓은 홀 a large 〔spacious〕 hall / 드넓은 뜰 an extensive 〔a spacious〕 garden / 드넓은 바다 a vast ocean; a broad expanse of sea.

**드높다** (be) high; tall; lofty; eminent. ¶ 하늘에 드높이 high up in the air; way up in the sky 《미》/ 그의 영업 방침에대해 비난의 목소리가 ~ His business practices are loudly attacked.

**드디어** at last; at length; in the end; finally; ultimately; eventually; in the long run; [부정문에서] after all. ⇨ 마침내. ¶ ~ 승리를 거두다 gain the final victory / 우리는 ~ 산 정상에 도달했다 At length, we reached the top of the mountain.

**드라마** a drama. ¶ 인간~ a human drama / 텔레비전 ~ a teleplay; a television play.

**드라이** dry. ◉ ~ 아이스 dry ice. ~ 클리닝 dry cleaning: ~ 클리닝하다 dry=clean; dry-cleanse / 이것을 ~ 클리닝해 주시겠습니까 Will you have this dry=cleaned please?

**드라이버** 《운전기사》 a driver; 〖골프〗 a driver; 《나사돌리개》 a screwdriver.

**드라이브** a drive. ~하다 drive; take 〔have〕 a drive 《to》. ¶ ~하러 가다 go for a drive / 그들은 자동차로 ~ 나갔다 They went for a drive in a motorcar. ◉ ~웨이 a driveway.

**드라이브인** (a) drive-in. ◉ ~극장 a drive-in theater. ~식당 a drive-in 〔roadside〕 restaurant. ~은행 a drive=in bank.

**드라이어** a (hair) drier; a dryer.

**드래프트** 〖야구〗 a draft. ¶ 그는 롯데(구단)에서 ~ 1위로 지명되었다 He was chosen as the Lottes' number one draft pick 〔choice〕. ◉ ~제 the draft system.

**드러나다** ① 《알려지다》 become known 〔famous, prominent, conspicuous〕. ¶ 드러나게 prominently; preeminently; conspicuously / 이름이 세상에 ~ become famous in the world / 업적이 ~ *one's* achievements become known.
② 《나타나다》 (***a***) 《사물이》 come into view; come out; appear; crop out; emerge 《from》; be exposed; be bared. ¶ 광맥이 ~ a mineral vein 「crops out 〔appears〕/ 어깨가 ~ *one's* shoulders are exposed 〔bared〕. (***b***) 《성질·표정이》 reveal 〔show〕 itself; be revealed; come in evidence; find expression 《in》; be expressed. ¶ 마각〔본성〕이 ~ show 「the cloven hoof 〔*one's* true colors〕/ 그녀의 얼굴에 기쁜 빛이 드러났다 A look of pleasure came to her face. /술을 마시면 본성이 드러난다 Wine 〔Liquor〕 reveals *one's* true self.
③ 《감춘 것이》 come 〔be〕 out; be found (out); be laid bare; be discovered; be detected; be disclosed 〔revealed〕; be exposed; come 〔be brought〕 to light. ¶ 거짓말이 ~ *one's* lie is detected; *one's* falsehood is found out / 비밀이 ~ a secret is revealed 〔exposed, disclosed〕; a secret gets 〔leaks〕 out / 죄상이 하나하나 ~ the facts about *one's* crime are brought to light one by one / 그의 전과가 드러났다 His criminal record came to light. / 비밀 결사 조직이 드러났다 The system of the secret society was discovered. / 음모가 드러났다 The plot has been laid bare.

**드러내다** ① (***a***) 《보이다》 show; indicate; manifest; display; exhibit; 《입증하다》 prove; speak for; bespeak. ¶ 솜씨를 ~ display *one's* skill / 차이를 ~ bring out the differences / 이 점이 그의 정직함을 드러내고 있다 This 「proves 〔speaks for〕 his honesty. (***b***) 《명성·두각을》 distinguish. ¶ 두각을 ~ cut 〔make〕 a conspicuous 〔brilliant〕 figure 《in》; distinguish *oneself* / 이름을 ~ have *one's* name up.
② 《노출하다》 (***a***) 《속엣것을》 expose; bare; lay bare 〔open〕. ¶ 가슴을 드러낸 bare-bosomed 《waitress》; topless / 넓적다리를 ~ bare 〔expose〕 *one's* thigh / 속살을 ~ expose *one's* bare skin / 이를 ~ show 〔bare〕 *one's* teeth; grin / 드러내놓고 반대하다 oppose publicly; offer an open opposition. (***b***) 《성질·본색을》 show; reveal; betray; express; disclose. ¶ 본색〔본성〕을 ~ show *one's* true colors 〔character〕; give *oneself* away / 본심을 ~ disclose *one's* real intention; reveal *one's* real motive / 속셈을 ~ show 〔reveal〕 *one's* hand; put *one's* cards on the table / 정체를 ~ throw off 「the mask 〔*one's* disguise〕; unveil 〔reveal〕 *oneself* / 얼굴에 성난 빛을 ~ betray *one's* anger in his face / 그는 얼굴을 찡그리며 혐오감을 드러냈다 He showed his disgust with a frown. / 그녀는 불만을 드러냈다

She manifested dissatisfaction. ③《폭로하다》 expose; disclose; reveal; lay bare; divulge; bring to light. ¶ 비밀을 ~ reveal 〔divulge, spill〕 a secret / 아무의 잘못을 ~ expose *a person's* mistake 〔wrongdoing〕/ 아무의 흉계를 ~ lay *a person's* evil design bare / 회사 내막을 ~ disclose the inside story of a company.

**드러눕다** lie down; lay *oneself* down; stretch *oneself;* lie on *one's* back; throw *oneself* down. ¶ 드러누운 자세 a recumbent posture / 잔디 위에 ~ stretch *oneself* on a lawn / 드러누워서 책을 보다 read a book lying down《in bed》/ 병으로 ~ be laid up with illness; take to 〔be confined to〕 *one's* bed / 베개를 베고 ~ lie with *one's* head on a pillow.

**드러머**《북치는 사람》a drummer.

**드러쌓이다, 드러쌔다** ①《쌓이다》be heaped up; be piled up; accumulate;《눈·먼지 따위가》lie《on》. ¶ 창고에 쌀이 ~ rice is piled up in a warehouse / 눈이 석 자나 드러쌓였다 The snow lay three feet deep. ②《많다》be plentiful; be full of.

**드럼**[1]《북》a drum.

**드럼**[2]《통》a drum. ¶ 석유 세 ~ three drums of petroleum. ◉ ~통 a drum (can).

**드렁거리다** snore away (through *one's* nose).

**드렁드렁** snoring loudly. ¶ 코를 ~ 골다 snore loudly 〔terribly, horribly〕.

**드레스** a dress. ¶ ~를 입은 여성 a woman in dress. ◉ ~ 메이커 a dressmaker;《남자》a *couturier* (F.);《여자》a *couturière* (F.): ~메이커로 일하다 do dressmaking.

**드레싱** 〖요리〗(a) dressing.

**드레지다** have weight; (be) dignified; stable; imposing; commanding. ¶ 드레진 사람 a person of dignity / 그의 태도에는 어딘지 드레진 데가 있다 There is something dignified in his bearing.

**드롭** 〖야구〗 a drop. ¶ ~을 던지다〔치다〕 hurl 〔hit〕 a drop. ◉ ~킥 〖축구·럭비〗 a dropkick; a drop.

**드롭스**《사탕》drops.

**드르렁거리다** keep snoring through (*one's* nose). ¶ 코를 ~ be snoring away / 드르렁거리기 시작하다 fall to snoring.

**드르렁드르렁** snoring (loudly, heavily). ¶ ~ 코고는 소리 a tremendous rattling snore.

**드르르** ①《미끄럽게》smoothly; slippery; rattling off; rolling along. ¶ ~ 미끄러지다 go slipping; slip / ~ 미끄러져 내려가다 slide down / ~ 열리다 open smoothly. ②《떠는 모양》tremblingly; shiveringly. ¶ ~ 떨다 tremble; vibrate. ③《막힘 없이》smoothly; without a hitch; easily; swimmingly. ¶ 글을 ~ 읽다 read a passage smoothly / 그는 기억력이 좋아 한반 친구 이름을 ~ 왼다 He has a remarkable memory and can rattle off the names of his classmates.

**드리다**[1] ①《주다》give; offer; let《*a person*》have; present《*a thing* to *a person, a person* with *a thing*》. ¶ 선생님께 선물을 ~ give 〔send〕 a present to *one's* teacher / 아버지께 진지를 ~ serve *one's* father with dinner / 맥주 좀 드릴까요 Will you have some beer? / (가게에서) 무엇을 드릴까요 What can I show you, 「sir 〔ma'am〕? *or* May I help you, sir 〔ma'am〕? / 싸게 드리죠 I will let you have it very cheap. ②《정성·의식 등을》offer; hold; observe. ¶ 축하를 ~ offer *one's* congratulations / 불공을 ~ hold a 「Buddhist mass 〔memorial service at a temple〕/ 기도를 ~ offer 〔put up〕 *one's* prayers. ③ 〔조동사〕 do as a favor for a superior. ¶ 보여 ~ submit《*a thing*》for *one's* inspection; let《*a person*》see / 알려 ~ inform《*a person*》of; tell《*a person*》/ 어머니 일을 도와드려라 Help your mother with her work. / 그분께 길을 가리켜 드렸다 I have shown the gentleman the way.

**드리다**[2]《곡식을》winnow (grain from the chaff by blowing air on it).

**드리다**[3]《꼬다》braid; plait (머리 따위를); twist《into a rope, *etc.*》; entwist. ¶ 댕기를 ~ plait *one's* hair into a pigtail / 실을 ~ entwist threads / 세 겹으로 밧줄을 ~ twist three plies into a rope.

**드리다**[4]《방·마루를》set; construct; make; arrange; put in. ¶ 광이 있던 자리에 새로 거실을 하나 드렸다 I have turned (what was) the storeroom into a living room.

**드리다**[5]《가게문을 닫다》shut up; put up the shutters; close (a shop for the day).

**드리블** 〖구기〗 a dribble. ~하다 dribble.

**드리없다** (be) irregular; variable; changeable; be subject to change; be not fixed. ¶ 값이 ~ have no fixed prices; prices are irregular.

**드리없이** irregularly; variably. ¶ ~ 팔다 sell at irregular prices / 수업을 ~ 시작하다 start class at no fixed time.

**드리우다** ① 《늘어뜨리다》 hang (down); let (hang) down; suspend. ¶ 막〔커튼〕을 ~ let a curtain down; hang down a curtain / 그림자를 ~ cast 〔throw〕 a 〔its〕 shadow 《on, over》 / 머리를 ~ let *one's* hair down / 댕기를 ~ wear a ribbon in braided hair. ② 《주다》 give 《to an inferior》; bestow 《on, upon》; grant. ¶ 교훈을 ~ give a (moral) lesson / 은혜를 ~ show 《*a person*》 a favor; bestow a favor 《on》. ③ 《남기다》 leave 《*one's* name, *one's* example》. ¶ 이름을 후세에 ~ leave *one's* name to posterity; immortalize *one's* name; win immortal fame.

**드릴** 《송곳》 a drill.

**드림** a hanging thing (=a streamer, pendant, *etc.*). ¶ ~ 장막 a drop curtain.

**드림셈** payment by installment; a down payment; an installment plan. ¶ ~으로 치르다 pay off by installments.

**드림흥정** transaction by installments. ~하다 buy 〔sell〕 on installments.

**드맑다** (be) very clear.

**드문드문** ① 《시간적》 once in a (long) while; at (rare) intervals; from time to time; occasionally; few and far between. ¶ ~ 찾아오다 come once in a while; show up from time to time / 그런 일이 ~ 있다 Such things happen from time to time. ② 《공간적》 at intervals; sparsely; thinly; scatteringly; sporadically; few and far between. ¶ ~ 있다 be scattered here and there / 나무를 ~ 심다 plant trees at intervals 〔sporadically〕 / 털이 ~ 나다 be thinly haired; be thinly covered with hair / 골짜기에는 집이 ~ 있다 The valley is sparsely dotted with houses. / 관중 가운데에는 낯익은 얼굴들도 ~ 보였다 There was a sprinkling of familiar faces in the audience.

**드물다** 《흔하지 않다》 (be) rare; uncommon; unusual; 《적다》 (be) scarce; few (and far between). ¶ 드물게 rarely; seldom; uncommonly; on rare occasions; at rare intervals / 극히 드물게 very rarely; once in a long while / 드문 물건 a rare thing; a rarity; a curiosity / 드문 일 a rare occurrence; an unusual thing; a rarity / 매우〔극히〕 ~ be phenomenal; be as scarce as hen's teeth / 인가가 ~ be thinly 〔sparsely〕 populated / 그가 집에 있는 일은 ~ We seldom find him at home. / 그가 약속 시간에 늦는 일은 ~ It is unusual for him to be late for the appointed time. / 그녀는 보기 드문 미인이다 She is a (girl of) rare beauty. / 3월달에는 폭풍이 ~ Storms are not frequent in March. / 실로 드문 사건이다 The case is a singular one. / 그는 보기 드문 수재다 He is a once-in-a-century genius. / 그 사람처럼 키가 큰 사람은 ~ He is an exceptionally tall man. / 그녀가 눈물을 보이는 일은 극히 ~ It is very rare 〔unusual〕 for her to shed tears. / 사막에서는 비가 오는 일이 ~ It rarely rains in the desert.

**드새다** pass the night 《at an inn》. ¶ 하룻밤 ~ stay overnight; pass 〔stop (for)〕 the night / 하룻밤 드새기를 청하다 ask 《*a person*》 for a night's lodging.

**드세다** (be) very strong; violent; 《집터가》 have an unlucky aspect; (be) evil; ill-omened. ¶ 성질이 드센 여자 a woman of violent temper.

**드잡이** ① 《격투》 a hand-grip; (coming to) grips; a grapple; grappling; a rough-and-tumble fight; a scrimmage. ~하다 come to grips 《with *a person*》; grapple 《with》. ¶ 서로 ~하다 grapple with each other; come to grips with each other. ② 《빚쟁이의》 seizing *one's* kitchen utensils for a debt; attachment; seizure. ~하다 seize *one's* kitchen utensils for a debt; attach; distrain 《upon》. ③ 《가마채의》 helping a palanquin bearer by shouldering one of the crosspoles. ~하다 help a palanquin bearer out by shouldering one of the crosspoles.

**드티다** 《자리·날짜가》 be extended 〔lengthened, protracted, stretched out〕; 《자리·날짜를》 extend; lengthen; protract; stretch out; make an interval longer. ¶ 돈 갚는 기한을 ~ stretch out the intervals between payments / 출발을 이틀 ~ put off 〔postpone〕 *one's* departure by two days.

**득**(得) ① ⇨ 소득. ② 《이득》 profit; a gain; advantage (유리); benefit (유익). ¶ 득이 되다 turn 〔prove〕 to *one's* profit 〔advantage〕; bring profit 《to》 / 득이 되는 profitable; advantageous; beneficial; economical / 빨리 갚는 것이 득이다 It is to your advantage for you to return the money as soon as possible. / 그런 것을 해도 조금도 득이 되지 않는다 It won't benefit you at all to do that. *or* It will not at all make you better off to do such a thing.

**득** ① 《긋다》《draw a line》 forcefully; with pressure. ¶ 줄을 득 내려긋다 draw a forceful line downward. ② 《긁다》 scraping hard. ¶ 솥 밑을 득 긁다 give the bottom of the oven a hard scrape / 차체(車體)가 철사에 득 긁히다 The car gets a bad body scratch from a wire. ③ 《얼다》 (freeze) hard; solid.

**득남**(得男) the birth of a son. ＝생남(生男). 「녀(生女).

**득녀**(得女) the birth of a daughter. ＝생

**득달같다** 《지체 없다》 (be) prompt; quick; ready; [서술적] be right on time. ¶ 득달같이 대령하다 present *oneself* promptly.

**득도**(得道) ～하다 『불교』 attain Nirvana; achieve spiritual enlightenment 〔awakening〕.

**득돌같다** 《바라는 대로 되다》 (be) quite satisfactory; gratifying; perfect; fine.

**득득** ① 《금·줄을》《drawing a line》 again and again forcefully 〔firmly, fast〕; with repeated pressure. ¶ 줄을 ～ 긋다 draw line after line forcefully. ② 《긁다》 scraping again and again; (scraping, scratching) away hard. ¶ ～ 긁다 scrape and scrape; scratch *oneself* violently. ③ 《얼어붙다》《freeze》 solid all over. ¶ ～ 얼어붙다 freeze up solid all over; be frozen fast.

**득롱망촉**(得隴望蜀) "Give him an inch and he will take an ell."; insatiable ambition; limitless greed.

**득명**(得名) ～하다 gain fame; make *one's* reputation; become famous.

**득문**(得聞) ～하다 hear of; catch wind up; be informed of.

**득세**(得勢) ① 《세력을 얻음》 gaining power 〔strength〕. ～하다 gain 〔acquire, obtain〕 power 〔influence〕; become influential. ¶ 그의 의견이 점점 ～하고 있다 His view is gaining ground. ② 《국면이》 turning to *one's* advantage. ～하다 turn to *one's* advantage; get an opportunity.

**득승**(得勝) a victory; a triumph; a success; a win. ～하다 win a victory; obtain a success; end in *one's* victory. ¶ 경기에서 ～하다 win a game / 투표에서 ～하다 beat 《*a person*》 at the poll.

**득시글득시글** in swarms; swarming. ～하다 be swarming 《with》; be crowded 〔teeming〕 《with》; be alive 《with》; 《벌레 따위》 squirm 〔wriggle about〕 in a swarm. ¶ 구더기 떼가 ～ 끓다 maggots swarm; swarm with maggots / 옷에 이가 ～하다 the clothes are covered with lice all over / 거리에는 사람이 ～ 끓는다 The street is teeming with people.

**득실**(得失) 《얻음과 잃음》 gains and losses; 《이익과 손해》 advantages and disadvantages; 《성패》 success and failure; 《장단점》 merits and demerits. ¶ ～을 떠나서 without considering personal interest / ～을 고려하다 ponder on 〔weigh〕 the merits 〔relative advantages〕 / ～이 거의 반반이다 The gains and losses are about on a par.

**득의**(得意) ① 《뽐냄》 pride; exultation; complacency; triumph; elation. ～하다 take a pride 《in》; be proud 《of》; feel elated; swell up. ¶ ～만면 being all exultant 〔triumphant, elated〕 / ～만면하여 elatedly; triumphantly; in triumph; with self-satisfaction; with a proud air / ～의 웃음을 짓다 smile in triumph. ② 《뜻을 이룸》 prosperity. ¶ ～의 시절에 in *one's* best 〔bright, palmy〕 days / ～의 절정에 있다 be at the summit of *one's* prosperity; be at the zenith of *one's* glory. ◉ ～양양 ＝의기양양. 「the people.

**득인심**(得人心) ～하다 win the hearts of

**득점**(得點) the marks obtained; 《경기의》 the points made; 《야구》 the runs scored; 《총괄적》 a score. ～하다 score (a point); make 〔earn〕 a score. ¶ ～이 없다 score nothing; be scoreless / ～ 없이 끝나다 end scoreless / 대량 ～하다 score many points; make a good score; 『야구』 score a lot of runs / 3대 2의 ～으로 이기다 win with 〔by〕 a score of 3 to 2. / 3대 1의 ～으로 우리가 앞서고 있다 We're leading by a score 3 to 1. / 그의 ～은 95점이었다 He scored 〔earned〕 ninety-five points. ◉ ～ 게시판 a score board. ～자 a scorer. ～표 a scorebook; a scorecard (권투의); a score sheet (야구의). 개인〔팀〕 ～ an individual 〔a team〕 score.

**득책**(得策) the best way 〔policy, plan〕; a wise way; the advisable 〔policy, best〕 thing to *do*. ¶ ～이다 be wise; be advisable 〔politic〕 / 그렇게 하는 편이 ～이다 It is advisable 〔better, wise〕 to do that way. / 그에게 일임하는 것이 ～이라 생각한다 I think it advisable to leave the matter to him.

**득표**(得票) the number of votes obtained 〔polled〕. ～하다 get 〔gain, win] votes. ¶ 남보다 많이〔적게〕 ~하다 run「ahead of 〔behind〕 another's ticket《미》/ 그의 ~수는 다른 후보자보다 훨씬 많았다 His polling score was far larger than that of any other candidate.

◉ ~수 the number of votes; the polling score. ~ 전략 vote-getting tactics. 최고 ~ the highest poll: 최고 ~로 당선되다 be elected《to》 with the highest poll.

**-든가** (either...) or else. ¶ 저녁엔 산책을 나가든가 집에서 소설을 읽든가 했다 Of an evening, I would either go for a walk or read a novel at home.

**든거지 난부자**(—富者) a person who looks rich but is really poor.

**든든하다** ① 《튼튼하다》 (***a***) 《굳세다》 (be) strong; robust; stout. ⇨튼튼하다. (***b***) 《단단하다》 (be) strong; solid; 《안정·안전·공고·견실하다》 (be) stable; secure; steady; solid; sound. ¶ 든든하게 만든 strongly-〔solidly-〕built / 든든한 기초 a solid foundation / 든든한 자리 a safe position / 든든한 회사 a sound business firm / 든든한 담보 a gilt-edged 〔good〕 security / 방비가 ~ be strongly 〔heavily〕 fortified / 방비를 든든하게 하다 strengthen the defenses / 마음을 든든하게 갖다 harden *one's* heart 〔*oneself*〕.

② 《미덥다》 (be) safe; secure; reassuring; reliable; have nothing to worry about. ¶ 든든한 사람 a dependable 〔reliable〕 person / 마음 든든하게 생각하다 [사람이 주어] feel reassured; feel secure 〔confident〕; [사물이 주어] be reassuring 〔encouraging〕 / …을 들으니 ~ it is heartening 〔encouraging〕 to hear that... / 자네가 함께 있어 주면 ~ Your presence inspires me with confidence. *or* I feel safe as long as you stay with me. / 믿을만한 든든한 사람이 있으면 돈을 꿔 주어도 괜찮다 I don't mind loaning money if there is anyone reliable to lend it to.

③ 《배가》 (be) full; compact; substantial; stomachful. ¶ 속이 ~ *one's* stomach is full / 든든하게 먹다 eat *one's* fill 〔to *one's* heart's content〕 / 든든하게 먹어 두다 fortify *oneself* with a meal 《against *something*》.

**든든히** ① (***a***) 《굳세게》 strongly; robustly; stoutly. ¶ ~ 생기다 look strong. (***b***) 《단단히》 strongly; solidly; securely. ¶ ~하다 strengthen; make firm 〔solid〕; solidify / 마음을 ~ 먹다 take courage; keep out *one's* nerve; harden *oneself* / 집을 ~ 짓다 build a house durably.

② 《배부르게》 compactly; substantially. ¶ 밥을 ~ 먹다 eat a substantial meal.

③ 《미덥게》 securely; reassuringly; safely; reliably. ¶ 마음 ~ 생각하다 feel reassured 〔confident, safe, secure〕; be inspired with confidence / 나는 그를 ~ 여겼는데 그렇지도 못하다 I thought he was reliable but I have found he isn't.

**든번**(—番) being on duty. ¶ ~이다 be on duty.

**든벌** home 〔everyday〕 wear; weekday 「clothes.

**든부자 난거지**(—富者—) a person who looks poor but is really rich.

(-)**든지** ① 《…일지라도》 any at all; regardless of which; ... (so)ever. ¶ 무엇을 하든지 whatever (it be found that) *one* does / 언제든지 anytime at all; whatever time it may be / 얼굴이야 어떠하든지 regardless of what 《*a person*》 looks like.

② 《…하더라도》 no matter 《what, who, when, *etc.*》. ¶ 무슨 일이 있든지 오늘밤엔 나가지 마라 Don't go out tonight no matter what happens. / 어디로든지 간에 전지(轉地)를 하시오 Take change of climate, no matter where.

③ 《안가림》 either... or; whether... or.... ¶ 오든지 말든지 whether it comes or not / 이거든지 그거든지 둘 중에 하나를 가지십시오 Take one of the two, either this one or that one. / 가든지 오든지 마음대로 하게 Come or go, whichever you please.

**든직하다** 《사람됨이》 (be) weighty; sedate; composed (침착); dignified (위엄); calm; self-possessed; grave. ¶ 든직한 인물 a man of substance; a sedate man / 그는 든직하여 믿을 만하다 He is a man of dignified character and very reliable.

**든침모**(—針母) a resident seamstress 〔needlewoman〕.

**듣다**[1] 《물방울이》 drop; drip; trickle; flow in drops. ¶ 빗방울이 ~ raindrops fall; it is dripping.

**듣다**[2] ① (***a***) 《소리를》 hear; be heard; listen to; give ear to; lend an ear to; mind. ¶ 강의를 ~ attend a lecture / 라디오를 ~ listen to the radio / 빗소리를 ~ listen to the rain / 연설을 ~ hear a speech; hear 《*a person*》 speak / 음악을 ~ listen to music / 귀를 기울여 ~ listen attentively 〔carefully〕 《to》; listen with pricked ears 《to》; strain *one's* ears / 주의해서 ~ listen to《a speech》attentively; be all ears / 잘못 ~ hear amiss; mishear; hear《it, *him*》wrong; be misinformed《about》/ 듣기 거북하다 be offensive 〔unpleasant, harsh〕 to the ear / 듣기 어렵다 be hard 〔difficult〕 to hear / 듣기 좋다〔싫다〕 be pleasant 〔harsh〕 to the ear / 참고로 들어두다 hear《it》for *one's* information / 듣기 싫은 소리를 하다 say a disagreeable 〔spiteful〕 thing《to》/ 낮말은 새가 듣고 밤말은 쥐가 듣는다《속담》Pitchers 〔Walls〕 have ears. / 듣기 좋은 노래도 한 두 번이지《속담》The best fish smell after three days. / 들으면 병이요 안 들으면 약《속담》Turning a deaf ear to a person's troubles is the best way to get rid of them. (***b***)《소식 등을》hear of; be informed 〔told〕 of 〔about〕; understand; [사물이 주어] come to *one's* ears; reach *one's* knowledge. ¶ 들은 바에 의하면 from what I hear; I hear 〔I am told, we learn〕《that...》/ 별로 들어보지 못한 unfamiliar; strange; new / 많이 들어본 이름 a familiar name / 소문으로 ~ hear of《*a matter*》; know by hearsay / 풍문에 ~ learn 〔have it〕 by hearsay; get wind of / 집 소식을 ~ have word from home / 그런 일은 들어본 적이 없다 I have never heard of such a thing.

② 《남으로부터》(***a***)《좋은 말·나쁜 말을》get; receive. ¶ 꾸중을 ~ be 〔get〕 scolded; get 〔receive〕 a rebuke / 칭찬을 ~ be praised 〔admired, extolled〕《by》; draw praise《from》/ 악평을 ~ be criticized unfavorably. (***b***)《이르는 말 등을》obey; follow; take; listen to;《청·요구 등을》grant; comply with; accede to; hear. ¶ 부모의 말을 ~ obey *one's* parents; mind what *one's* parents say / 청을 들어주다 grant a request 〔favor〕; comply with《*a person's*》request / 들으려 하지 않다 turn a deaf ear to / 남의 말을 듣지 않다 will not listen to what others say; will give no ear to《other's》counsel / 이 아이는 부모의 말을 듣지 않는다 This boy does not obey his parents. / 그는 내 충고를 듣지 않았다 He didn't follow 〔take〕 my advice. *or* He turned a deaf ear to my advice.

③ 《효험이 있다》(***a***)《약효가》take effect; have effect《on》; do《*a person*》good; work. ¶ 약이 ~ a medicine takes effect; a drug works / 약이 듣지 않다 a medicine fails to work; a drug has no effect《on》; a medicine doesn't work / 이건 금세 듣는다 This will have a prompt effect on you. / 이 약은 감기에 잘 듣는다 This medicine is good 〔effective〕 for a cold. *or* This medicine works well for a cold. (***b***)《기계 따위가》be effective; work; act; operate; tell. ¶ 안 ~ have no effect《on》; fail to work / 브레이크가 안 듣는다 The brake refuse to act 〔work〕.

**듣다못해** lacking patience to hear《*a person*》out. ¶ ~ 그에게 화를 냈다 I got tired of listening to him and blew up. / 월급이 적다는 불평을 ~ 나갈테면 나가라고 야단을 쳤다 Sick of 〔Fed up with〕 his grumbling at the low salary, I shouted for him to leave if that is what he wants to do.

**듣보기장사** doing business when the market is good; speculative business.

**듣보다** keep an eye on; set *one's* eyes upon.

**들**[1] ①《벌판》a plain; an uncultivated field;《농장》a farm;《전답》a field. ¶ 넓은 들 a vast field / 들 가운데의 외딴 집 a lone 〔solitary〕 house in the middle of a plain / 들에 나가 일하다 work in field / 들에서 놀다 play in the field. ② [형용사적] 《야생의》field=grow; wild. ¶ 들꽃 a wild flower / 들길 a field path.

**들**[2] 《등등(等等)》and so on 〔forth〕; et cetra (생략 etc., &c.); and 〔or〕 the like; and many other things. ¶ 가령 ...들 such as; for example / 노리개며 책들 toys, books, and what not / 우리는 동물원에 가서 코끼리, 범, 사자, 곰 들을 보았다 We went to the zoo and saw elephants, tigers, lions, bears, and the like.

**들-** 《몹시》hard; violently; heavily; badly; thoroughly. ¶ 들볶다 torment hard.

**-들** [접미사] ¶ 우리들 we; us / 사람들 people; other people / 어린애들 children / 애들아 Hey you people 〔you folks, you all〕! / 이분들은 우리 회사 사람들입니다 These are my colleagues in the company. / 잘들 했다 You all did well. / 놀러들 갑시다 Let's all go out and have some fun. / 다들 갔느냐 Has everybody gone? / 안들 먹느냐 Aren't you folks eating? / 먹기에들 바쁘다 They're all busy eating. / 이리들 오세요 Come this way, you people. / 들어들 오시오 Come in, you people.

**들개** a wild dog; a stray dog (집 없는).

**들것** a stretcher; a litter. ¶ ～으로 나르다 carry 《*a person*》 on a litter 〔stretcher〕.

**들고나다** ① 《참견하다》 poke *one's* nose 《into》; poke 《into》; step into; interfere 《in *a matter,* with *a person*》; meddle 《in, with》. ¶ 남의 일에 들고날 것이 없다 There is no need to stick your nose into other people's business. ② 《물건을》 carry out 《household articles》 for sale to raise money. ¶ 요즈음 자주 가구를 팔려고 들고나는 것을 보니 그가 난봉이 난 모양이다 Since he is frequently carrying out his furniture for sale it looks as though he were leading a wild life these days.

**들고뛰다, 들고튀다** 《달아나다》 (get wind and) run away; take to flight 〔*one's* heels〕; make *one's* escape. ¶ 경관을 보자 도둑은 들고뛰었다 At the sight of the police, the thief took to his heels.

**들고파다** study hard 〔untiringly〕; drudge. ¶ 들고 파는 사람 a grind.

**들국화**(一菊花) a wild chrysanthemum 〔aster〕.

**들기름** perilla oil.

**들길** a path 〔track〕 across a field; a field path.

**들까부르다** ① 《키질》 fan 〔winnow〕 briskly. ② 《흔들다》 move up and down; jolt (차가); pitch and roll; rock (배가).

**들까불다** ⇨ 들까부르다.

**들까불리다** 《키질하다》 be fanned 〔winnowed〕 briskly; 《몹시 흔들다》 jolt; be jolted 〔rocked〕.

**들깨** 〖식물〗 green perilla; 《씨》 perilla seeds.

**들꿩** 〖조류〗 a hazel grouse.

**들끓다** ① 《혼잡하다》 crowd; swarm 《with》; gather 《round》; be jammed 〔crowded〕 《with》. ¶ 시장에는 사람들이 들끓고 있다 The market place are crowded 〔thronged〕 with people. ② 《해로운 것이》 swarm; breed; alive 〔be infested〕 《with》. ¶ 거지가 ～ [장소가 주어] be swarmed 〔crowded〕 with beggers / 구더기가 ～ be infested with maggots / 쥐가 ～ 《a house》 be infested 〔swarming〕 with rats / 도둑이 들끓는 지역 a district infested with thieves. ③ 《소란하다》 seethe 《over》; ferment; be in an uproar. ¶ 그 문제로 온 나라 안이 들끓었다 The whole country seethed over the question.

**들날리다** ① 《이름이》 《*one's* name》 resound; become famous 〔renowned, popular, well-known〕; distinguish *oneself.* ¶ 이름이 온 세상에 ～ be known the world over. ② 《이름을》 make famous 〔well-known〕; distinguish; win a reputation; make a name for *oneself.* ¶ 명성을 ～ come to fame; win fame / 온 세상에 이름을 ～ win a worldwide reputation 〔fame〕.

**들녘** flat country; a plain; the plains; an open field 〔country〕.

**들놀다** swing 〔sway〕 up and down 〔back and forth〕.

**들놀이** a picnic; an outing; a junket 《미》. **～하다** have a picnic; be on a picnic. ¶ ～ 가다 go picnicking.

**들다**[1] ① 《안으로》 (***a***) 《들어가다·오다》 enter; go 〔come〕 in(to); get in(to); walk 〔step〕 in(to); 《물이》 be leaky; make water (배가); 《범위 안에》 come under. ¶ 문틈으로 바람이 드는 방 a drafty room / 물이 ～ [사물이 주어] take 〔let〕 in water / 방안에 ～ enter a room; walk into a room / 범주 안에 ～ fall under 〔come within〕 the category 《of》 / 사정 거리 안에 ～ come within range (of fire) / 잠자리에 ～ go 〔get〕 to bed; retire (to bed); turn in 《속어》 / 안으로 드시지요 Please come in. (***b***) 《집 따위에》 settle 《in》; move in (이사해서); 《투숙하다》 put up 《at》; stop 《at》; lodge in 〔check into〕 《a hotel》. ¶ 새 집에 ～ settle in a new house / 셋방에 ～ rent 〔take〕 a room / (여관에) 손님이 ～ have a lodger / (집 등에) 아직 사람이 들지 않고 있다 still remain unoccupied. (***c***) 《침입하다》 break in; visit. ¶ 간밤에 도둑이 들었다 A burglar broke into my house last night. *or* I had my house broken into last night. (***d***) 《볕이》 shine 〔come〕 《in(to), upon》; strike 《on》. ¶ 저녁 햇살이 드는 방 a room open to sunshine from the west / 볕이 잘 ～ be very sunny; be full of sunshine / 볕이 안 드는 곳에 in a shade 〔sunless〕 place; in the shade. ② (***a***) 《가입하다》 join; associate *oneself* with 《a society》. ¶ 보험에 ～ insure 《*oneself*》; 《영》 assure 《*one's* life》; take out (a policy of) insurance 《on》 / 클럽에 ～ join a club; become a club member; be enrolled in a club / 이 건물은 화재보험에 들어 있다 This building is insured against fire. (***b***) 《시험 등에》 pass 《an examination, a test》; succeed 《in》; be admitted 《to》. ¶ 학교에 ～ be admitted (in)to a school / 그는 K대학 입시에 들었다 He succeeded in 〔passed〕 the entrance examination for K University. ③ 《병이》 fall 〔get〕 ill; be ill 〔afflicted, troubled〕《with》. ¶ 병든 소 sick cattle / 병이 ～ fall ill 〔sick〕; be taken ill; suffer from a disease / 감기가 ～ catch 〔get〕 (a) cold.

④《담기다》 contain; hold; 《포함되다》 be included; be counted 《among》. ¶ 계산에 ～ count; be taken into account / 한 가마에는 쌀 열 말이 든다 A bag holds ten *mal* of rice. / 이 병에 극약이 들어 있다 This bottle contains a powerful drug. / 표에는 내 이름도 들어 있다 The list includes my name. / 이 상자는 많이 든다 This box holds great deal. / 그 중에는 나도 들어 있었다 I was among them. / 이 잡비는 셈에 들어 있다 This miscellaneous expenses are included in the account.

⑤ 《수용하다》 can accommodate 〔house〕; hold 《so many people》. ¶ 이 홀에는 백 명이 들 수 있다 This hall can accommodate a hundred guests. *or* This hall「seats 〔has a seating capacity of〕 one hundred.

⑥《소요되다》 take; need; require; cost. ¶ 공이 든 작품「an elaborate 〔a painstaking〕 piece of work / 시간이 드는 time-consuming / 돈이 얼마 들더라도 at any cost; regardless of expense / 돈 〔밑천〕이 ～ cost 《*one*》 much money; be expensive / 만 원이 ～ cost a ten thousand won / 시간이 ～ take (up) time; require (a lot of ) time / 힘(이) ～ be hard 〔difficult, tough〕; require hard work / 이 집을 짓는 데 6개월이 들었다 It took six months to build this house. / 그건 얼마나 들었나 What 〔How much〕 did it cost (you)? / 여행비용은 제(諸)잡비를 포함해서 50만원 이상이나 들었다 The trip cost more than 500,000 won including incidental expenses. / 이 기관차는 기름이 많이 든다 This engine consumes much oil. / 이것저것 모두 돈 드는 일뿐이다 There are a lot of drains on my purse.

⑦《상태로 되다》 become; get; be visited. ¶ 멍이 ～ get bruised / 버릇이 ～ get 〔fall〕 into a habit 《of》; get in the way 《of *do*ing》; acquire 〔pick up〕 a habit 《of 》/ 잠이 ～ go 〔get〕 to sleep; fall asleep / 재난이 ～ suffer 〔be visited by〕 a calamity / 잡념이 ～ be a victim of idle 〔worldly〕 thoughts / 정신이 ～ come to *oneself* 〔*one's* senses〕; recover 〔regain〕 consciousness / 정이 ～ become 〔get〕 intimate 《with》; become attached to 《a woman》; come to love 《*a person*》/ 철이 ～ become possessed of discretion; get some sense / 풍년〔흉년〕이 ～ have a good 〔lean〕 year; have a bumper 〔poor〕 harvest / 그는 눈 언저리에 멍이 들어 있었다 He had a black eye. / 그는 죽을 것 같은 생각이 들었다 He felt as if he were going to die.

⑧《때·운 따위가》 set in; begin; come round; be visited. ¶ 봄이 들면 when spring comes (round) / 복날이 ～ the dog days「come round 〔begin〕 / 운이 ～ be visited by good luck; fortune turns in *one's* way / 장마가 ～ the wet weather 〔rainy season〕 sets in / 이 달에 들어 몹시 춥다 The weather has been extremely cold since the beginning of this month. / (축구에서) 후반에 들어 곧 동점이 되었다 The score was tied a short way into the second half.

⑨《물들다》 dye; be dyed; take (up) color; be tainted 《with》 (악습에). ¶ 검게 물이 ～ be dyed black / 물이 잘 ～ 〔안 ～〕 dye 〔take dye〕 well 〔badly〕.

⑩《마음에》 be satisfied 〔pleased〕 《with》; [사물이 주어] be satisfactory; be acceptable to 《*a person*》; be to *one's* taste 〔satisfaction〕; suit 〔catch, take, strike〕 *one's* fancy; find favor with 《*a person*》; be in *one's* favor; impress 《*a person*》 favorably; like. ¶ 마음에 들도록 to *one's* satisfaction; (so as) to please 《*a person*》/ 마음에 드는 집 a house to *one's* taste; a house *one* likes / 마음에 드는 여자 a woman after *one's* heart 〔fancy〕; a woman *one* likes 〔takes to〕 / 하녀가 주인의 눈에 ～ a maid finds favor with her master / 마음에 들지 않다 be not to *one's* taste 〔liking〕; be unacceptable; be unsatisfactory / 저 그림이 마음에 든다 That picture appeals to my taste. / 놈의 하는 짓이 (통) 마음에 들지 않는다 I hate the way he behaves. *or* I don't like what he is doing.

⑪《맛이》 set in; get a taste 《to it》; get tasty; become edible; get ripe; ripen; become mellow. ¶ 사과가 맛이 ～ an apple gets some flavor in it; an apple is ripe / 술의 맛이 ～ wine mellows.

⑫《시중·주선·편을》 do. ¶ 아무의 시중을 ～「wait on 〔attend〕 *a person* / 중매를 ～ serve as go-between / 아무의 역성〔편〕을 ～ side with *a person*.

**들다**[2] 《날붙이가》 cut (well); be sharp. ¶ 잘 드는〔잘 안 드는〕 칼 a sharp 〔blunt〕 knife / 잘 안 ～ be dull 〔blunt〕 / 칼이 잘 ～ 〔들지 않다〕 a knife cuts well

〔poorly〕/(날이) 들지 않게 되다 become dull 〔blunt〕.

**들다**[3] 《나이가》 grow older; grow 〔get, become〕 old; take 〔put〕 on years; be well up in years; be advanced in years 〔ages〕. ¶ 나이 든 사람 a (fairly) old man / 훨씬 나이 들어 뵌다 You look much older than your age. / 나이 들면 철이 좀 들까 I wonder if he will become more sensible when he gets older. / 나이가 듦에 따라 백발이 늘었다 As I grew older, much of my hair turned gray.

**들다**[4] ① 《날씨가》 clear away 〔up, off〕. ¶ 날이 ~ it 〔the weather〕 clears up; it stops raining / 날이 들 것 같다 It looks as if it will clear up. ② 《땀이》 subside; cease; stop. ¶ 땀이 ~ stop sweating.

**들다**[5] ① 《손에》 hold; take; have; have 《*a thing*》 in *one's* hand; carry; have 〔take〕 with 〔about〕 *one*. ¶ 칼을 빼들고 with a naked blade in *one's* hand / 펜을 ~ take up *one's* pen / (손에) 들고 다니다 carry (about) 《*a thing*》/ 손에 지팡이를 ~ carry a walking stick / 손에 책을 ~ have a book in *one's* hand / 손에 촛불을 ~ hold a lighted candle in *one's* hand / 그는 언제나 카메라를 들고 다닌다 He always carries a camera with him. / 강도는 식칼을 들고 있었다 The burglar was armed with a kitchen knife.

② 《올리다》 raise; lift (up); put up; hold up. ¶ 무거운 돌을 ~ lift a heavy stone / 머리를 ~ put up 〔raise, lift〕 *one's* head / 얼굴을 ~ look up / 손을 ~ put 〔lift, hold〕 up *one's* hand; raise *one's* hand.

③ 《사실·예를》 cite; state; name; mention; give 《an example》; produce 《evidence》. ¶ 예를 들면 for example (생략 e.g.); for instance / 예를 ~ give an example; cite 「an instance 〔a case in point〕/ 이유를 ~ state the reason 《for》/ 증거를 ~ produce 〔adduce〕 evidence / 아무의 이름을 ~ mention 〔give〕 *a person's* name / 그 이유를 드시오 Give your reasons for it. / 뜰의 꽃 이름을 전부 들어라 Name all the flowers in the garden.

④ 《먹다》 have; take; eat; drink. ¶ 더 드시지요 Will you take another helping? / 맛있게 드십시오 Enjoy your meal, sir. / 저녁 식사로 무엇을 드셨습니까 What did you have for supper? / 많이 드십시오 Help yourself, please.

**들두드리다** beat 〔hit, knock〕 hard; strike blow after blow. ¶ 문을 ~ pound on a door / 아무를 ~ beat *a person* 「black and blue 〔to a jelly〕.

**들들** ⇨ 달달[1].

**들떠들다** 《people》 make noise; raise a 「clamor.

**들뜨다** ① 《붙은 것이》 come undone 〔off〕; get loose; curl up at the end. ¶ 장판이 ~ a layer of laminated paper comes undone from the floor / 자릿귀가 ~ the end of a mat curls. ② 《마음이》 grow restless; be unsteady; (*one's* mind) wanders 〔drifts〕. ¶ 들뜬 마음 a restless heart / 마음이 ~ tread upon air; walk on air / 봄이 되면 마음이 들뜨기 쉽다 One's mind is apt to wander when spring comes. / 마음이 들떠 일을 제대로 할 수 없다 I can't keep my mind on my work the way I should. / 그런 들뜬 정신으로는 성공할 수 없다 You can never be sure of success if you are so unsteady in mind. ③ 《살이》 look yellow and swollen. ¶ 독감 끝에 얼굴이 누렇게 들떴다 My face got all yellow and swollen after my bad cold.

**들락날락** ~하다 come and go incessantly; go in and out frequently; frequent.

**들랑거리다** keep coming and going; frequent.

**들러리** ① 《신랑의》 a best man; a groomsman; 《신부의》 a bridesmaid. ¶ ~ 서다 serve as a best man 〔bridesmaid〕. ② [비유적] a foil; a setoff. ¶ ~를 서다 serve as a foil.

**들러붙다** ① 《부착》 stick 〔cling, adhere, cleave〕 to. ¶ 찰싹 ~ stick fast to / 껌이 마루에 ~ chewing gum sticks to the floor / 찰싹 들러붙어 떨어지지 않다 stick fast and won't 「come off 〔go away〕; stick like a bur / 페인트칠은 아직 들러붙는다 The paint is still sticky. ② 《사람 등에》 stand 〔keep〕 close to; cling fast 《to *a person*》; stick together. ¶ 귀찮게 ~ hang about 〔around〕 《*a person*》; pester 《*a person*》 to death.

**들레다** clamor; make a noise; create an uproar; be boisterous.

**들려주다** 《알리다》 let 《*a person*》 hear 〔know〕 《of》; tell; inform 《*a person* of》; 《읽어서》 read to 《*a person*》; 《연주하여》 play for 《*a person*》; give 《*a person*》 a tune; 《노래를 불러》 sing for 《*a person*》. ¶ 이야기를 ~ tell a story / 시를 ~ read a poem to 《*a person*》/ 노래 한 곡 들려주시오 Sing us a song. / 이것은 아이들에게 들려줄 이야기가 아니

다 This is not a story for children.

**들르다** drop 〔step〕 in 《at *a person's* house, on *a person*》; drop into 〔by〕 《a store》; stop in 〔at〕; call 《at *a person's* house, on *a person*》; look in 《at *a person's* house》; stop by 《미》. ¶ 잠깐 ～ pay 《*a person*》 a casual visit; run in 《to *a person*》 / 주막에 ～ stop in at the inn / 커피 마시러 다방에 ～ drop into a coffee shop for a (cup of) coffee / 대구에 ～ stop off at Taegu / (가는) 도중에 ～ stop in 《at another's home》 on *one's* way / 시간이 있거든 나에게 한번 들르시오 Drop in to「see me 〔look me up〕 when you have time. / 이쪽으로 오시게 되면 들러 주시오 If you happen to come this way, please drop in. / 학교 가는 길에 형의 집에 들러라 Call at your brother's house on your way to school.

**들리다**[1] ① 《귀에》 (***a***) 《소리가》 [사람이 주어] (can) hear 《*a person* speaking》; [소리가 주어] be heard 〔audible〕; meet 〔greet〕 the ear; reach 〔fall on〕 *one's* ear. ¶ 들리는〔안 들리는〕 곳에서 in 〔out of 〕 *one's* hearing; within 〔out of 〕 hearing 〔earshot〕; within 〔out of 〕 the sound of / 부르면 들리는 거리에 있다 be within hearing distance / 들리지 않다 [사람이 주어] cannot hear 《*a person,* what *a person* say》; [소리가 주어] cannot be heard; be inaudible / 들리지 않게 되다 《귀가》 lose *one's* hearing; 《소리가》 die away; be out of hearing / 천둥 소리가 들린다 You can hear thunder. / 안 들리니 좀더 크게 말하여라 Speak louder—I can't hear you. / 전화가 잘 들리지 않는다 The telephone isn't clear. / 그는 오른쪽 귀가 잘 들리지 않는다 He has a hearing trouble in his right ear. (***b***) 《…같이》 sound; seem; ring. ¶ 역설적으로 ～ sound paradoxical / 그것은 빈정대는〔비꼬는〕 투로 들린다 It sounds sarcastic 〔ironical〕. / 그 이야기는 진정으로 들리지 않는다 The story doesn't ring true. / 그 말은 조금 이상하게 들린다 The remark strikes me a bit strange. / 이상하게 들릴지 모르나 그 말은 신용할 만하다 Strange as it may sound, the story is credible.
② 《소문이》 be said; be rumored; come to *one's* ears 〔knowledge〕. ¶ 들리는 바에 의하면 according to a report 〔rumor〕; from what I hear; I'm told 《that…》 / 소문에 ～ be talked 〔gossiped〕 about / 그들이 이혼했다는 소문이 들린다 It is rumored that they have been divorced. / 그가 돈을 많이 벌었다는 말이 들린다 They say he has made a lot of money.

**들리다**[2] ① 《병이》 suffer from; be attacked by; be beseized with; be inflicted with; catch. ¶ 감기(가) ～ suffer from a cold; have an attack of flu. ② 《귀신이》 be possessed with 〔by〕; be obsessed 〔haunted〕 by; be bewitched. ¶ 귀신 들린 devil-possessed / 무엇에 들린 것처럼 like *one* possessed; as if *one* was possessed / 그는 악마에 들려 있다 He is possessed with an evil spirit.

**들리다**[3] 《위로》 be lifted (up); be raised. ¶ 테이블 다리가 ～ a leg of the table is lifted / 몸이 공중에 ～ *a person* gets lifted up in the air.

**들리다**[4] 《들게 하다》 let 《*a person*》 raise 〔lift〕 《*a thing*》; 《운반시키다》 get 《*a person*》 to take 〔carry〕 《*a thing*》; make 〔have〕 《*a person*》 hold 《*a thing*》. ¶ 보따리를 ～ have 《*a person*》 carry a bundle / 하녀에게 선물을 들려 보내다 send a present by the maid.

**들먹거리다** ① 《물체가》 move up and down; shake. ¶ 바위가 ～ a rock moves up and down; a rock shakes.
② 《몸·마음이》 《*one's* shoulders, buttocks》 move up and down; become restless; be eager 《to *do*》; be excited 〔tempted〕 《to *do*》; be inclined 《to *do*》. ¶ 궁둥이가 ～ *one's* buttocks move up and down; become restless / 어깨가 ～ *one's* shoulders twitch; become restless; become buoyant / 한 대 때리고 싶어 팔이 ～ *one's* hands itch to deal 《*a person*》 a blow / 좋은 소식에 마음이 ～ be buoyed up by good news.
③ 《물체를》 move 《a heavy thing》 up and down; shake 《*a thing*》. ¶ 바위를 ～ shake a rock.
④ 《몸·마음을》 move 《*one's* shoulders, buttocks》 up and down; 《충동질》 make 《*a person*》 restless; stir up; egg 《*a person*》 on; incite; instigate. ¶ 어깨를 ～ move 〔twitch〕 *one's* shoulders restlessly / 남의 마음을 ～ make *a person* restless; move *a person* to *do;* make *a person* eager to *do;* fire *a person's* interest; excite *a person* / 근로자를 들먹거려 파업을 일으키게 하다 instigate workers to go on strike.
⑤ 《언급하다》 mention; refer to; speak of; specify by name. ¶ 그의 이름까지 들먹거릴 필요야 없지 않니 You don't

have to mention his name.

**들먹들먹** in a moving up and down; shakingly; 《마음이》 restlessly; buoyantly; excitedly.

**들먹이다** ＝들먹거리다.

**들메** tying straw sandals to *one's* feet. ◉ ～끈 strings used to tie straw sandals to *one's* feet; shoe-string.

**들보** 〖건축〗 a crossbeam; a girder.

**들볶다** annoy; harass; torment hard; be hard on 《*a person*》; treat 《*a person*》 harshly; be cruel to. ¶ 들볶이다 be tormented; be annoyed; be handled roughly; meet with harsh usage / 몹시 ～ torment 《*a person*》 to death / 며느리를 들볶아 내쫓다 torment 〔tease, worry〕 *one's* daughter-in-law out of the house / 빚쟁이에게 들볶이다 be tormented 〔hounded〕 by a (pressing) creditor.

**들부셔내다** clean up; wash up 〔out〕. ¶ 요강을 ～ clean a chamber pot.

**들부수다** break 《*a thing*》 to pieces; knock to pieces; smash up; crush; destroy; 《계획 따위를》 frustrate; ruin. ¶ 그릇을 ～ smash dishes / 닥치는 대로 ～ destroy everything *one* can lay *one's* hands on.

**들비비다** rub hard.

**들뽕나무** 〖식물〗 a wild mulberry tree.

**들살** 〖건축〗 a prop; a stay; a support.

**들새** a field 〔wild〕 bird; wild fowl [총칭].

**들소** a wild ox; a bison.

**들숨** the air *one* breathes in; air that is being inhaled; inhalation. ¶ ～ 날숨 inhalation and exhalation; breathing / ～ 날숨 없다 be in a fix 〔quandary〕.

**들썩거리다, 들썩이다** ＝들먹거리다.

**들썩하다** ① 《약간 들리다》 be turned up 〔lifted, raised〕 slightly; be slightly tilted. ¶ 책귀가 ～ the corner of a book is a bit turned up. ② 《떠들썩하다》 (be) noisy; boisterous. ③ 《그럴듯하다》 (be) plausible; specious.

**들썽거리다** itch 〔die〕 to *do;* be impatient; be eager. ¶ 치고 싶어 마음이 ～ feel impatient to attack; 《팔이》 *one's* hands itch to deal 《*a person*》 a blow.

**들쑤시다** ⇨들이쑤시다.

**들쓰다** ① 《덮어쓰다》 put 《*something*》 on all over *oneself;* pull up all over *oneself.* ¶ 담요를 머리까지 ～ pull a blanket over *one's* head / 그는 담요를 머리까지 들쓰고 자고 있다 He is sleeping with his head (buried) under a blanket. ② 《물 따위를》 be covered with; be poured on; pour 《water》 on *oneself.* ¶ 먼지를 ～ be covered with dust / 물을 ～ pour water upon *oneself,* 《튀는 물을》 water splashes all over *one's* body / (배가) 파도를 ～ ship water; be flooded by waves. ③ 《모자 등을》 wear (on *one's* head) casually. ¶ 모자를 들쓰고 나서다 go out wearing a hat casually. ④ 《비난·허물 등을》 take 《blame, responsibility》 upon *oneself.* ¶ 남의 죄를 ～ take another's guilt upon *oneself.*

**들씌우다** ① 《덮어씌우다》 put on 〔cover〕 《*something*》 all over; pull 《*something*》 all over. ¶ 머리에 이불을 ～ pull bedclothes over 《*a person's*》 head. ② 《물 따위를》 cover 《*a person*》 all over with; put 《water》 all over 《*a person*》. ¶ 물을 ～ pour water on 〔over〕 《*a person*》. ③ 《모자 등을》 put 《it》 on 《*a person's*》 head casually. ¶ 어린애에게 모자를 서둘러 들씌우고 데리고 나가다 take a child out with a hat hastily pulled over his head. ④ 《비난·허물을》 impute (a fault) to 《another》; lay 〔put, fix〕 (the blame) on 《another》; shift 《responsibility》 to 《another》. ¶ 죄를 남에게 ～ lay the guilt on another.

**들어가다**[1] ① 《안으로》 enter; go in(to); get in(to); turn in; walk 〔step〕 in(to); find *one's* way into; let *oneself* in. ¶ 방으로 ～ go into a room / 사지(死地)로 ～ go into the jaws of death / 새 생활로 ～ enter upon a new life / 숲속으로 ～ take to the woods / 정문〔뒷문〕으로 ～ enter at the front 〔back〕 door / 그는 창문으로 가만히〔몰래〕 들어갔다 He stole 〔slipped〕 in through the window. / 잔디밭에 들어가지 말 것 《게시》 Keep off (the grass). / 들어가도 괜찮습니까 May I come in? (★ go in 이라고는 하지 않으며 상대방의 입장이 되어 come in이라고 함). / 집은 길에서 좀 들어가 있다 The house is a little way off the road.

② 《틈·속·사이에》 go through; penetrate; be lodged; be inserted. ¶ 뚫고 ～ penetrate into / 바늘귀에 실이 ～ a thread goes through the eye of a needle; a needle is threaded / 이 낱말이 그 두 낱말 사이에 들어간다 This word goes 〔is to be inserted〕 between those two words.

③ 《특정한 곳에》 (***a***) 《입회·투신하다》 join; go into; associate *oneself* with 《a society》; 《회사에》 join; go to work for 《a firm》; find 〔take〕 service in

〔with〕; be employed 《by》. ¶ 관계(官界)에 ～ go into government service / 실업계에 ～ go into business; enter upon a business career / 클럽에 ～ join a club; become a club member / 회사에 ～ enter a company's service / 김 군은 이번에 외교통상부에 들어갔다 Mr. Kim has found a position in the Ministry of Foreign Affairs and Trade. (***b***) 《입학하다》 enter 〔be admitted to〕 《a school》; get into. ¶ 대학에 ～ enter 〔get into〕 a college; register at a college 《미》 / 이 대학은 들어가기가 꽤 어렵다 This university is rather hard to get into.

④ 《수용하다》 hold; accommodate; house. ¶ 이 자루에는 서 말이 들어간다 This sack holds three *mal.* / 이 방은 오십 명이 들어간다 This room accommodates 〔seats, has a seating capacity of〕 fifty people.

⑤ 《포함·함유하다》 include; contain; hold. ¶ 요금에는 세금도 들어가 있다 The tax is included in the price. / 이 음료에는 알코올이 들어가 있지 않다 This drink contains no alcohol.

⑥ 《돈이》 be put in; be spent; be sunk; cost. ⇨ 들다[1] ⑥.

⑦ 《움푹하다》 become hollow; be sunk(en); sag. ¶ 쑥 들어간 눈 sunken 〔deep-set〕 eyes / 배가 고파 눈이 ～ *one's* eyes grow hollow with hunger.

⑧ 《시작되다》 begin; set in. ¶ 내일부터 겨울 방학에 들어간다 The winter vacation begins tomorrow. / 장마철에 들어갔다 The rainy season has set in.

**들어가다**[2] 《가져가다》 filch; lift; steal; swipe; take 〔carry〕 away; take 〔bear〕 off; make off 《with》. ¶ 남의 우산을 ～ ⌈make off with 〔take〕 another's umbrella / 좀도둑이 세간 몇 개를 들어갔다 A petty thief swiped some of our household goods.

**들어내다** ① 《내놓다》 lift out; take 〔bring, carry〕 out; remove. ¶ 뜰에 의자를 ～ bring a chair into the garden / 화재가 나면 안전을 위해 이 상자를 먼저 들어내야 한다 In case of fire, this case must be removed for safety first of all. ② 《쫓아내다》 drag out; turn 〔throw, thrust〕 out; chuck out.

**들어맞다** ① 《적합하다》 fit (in) perfectly; fit like a glove; fit 〔suit〕 《*me*》 to a T. ¶ 몸에 꼭 들어맞는 well-fitting 《clothes》; tight-fitting 《dress》 / 옷이 몸에 ～ the clothes fit perfectly / 장부가 장붓구멍에 ～ the tenon fits snug in the mortise / 가구가 취미에 ～ a piece of furniture suits *one's* taste to a T / 원어의 뜻에 꼭 들어맞지 않는다 It does not convey the exact meaning of the original word.

② 《일치하다》 fit together; agree 《with》; tally 〔square〕 with; be in accord with. ¶ (의견·말 등이) 딱 ～ be in perfect accord 《with》 / 두 사람의 이야기가 들어맞는다 The accounts of the two people tally with each other. / 그의 모습은 범인의 인상서와 들어맞는다 His features answer to the description of the criminal.

③ 《정확하다》 be right; be correct. ¶ 셈이 딱 들어맞는다 The accounts are perfectly correct.

④ 《적중하다》 hit the mark; make a good hit; hit it right; hit the nail on the head; 《맞히다》 guess right; 《예상이》 come true; turn out true; take; work. ¶ 화살이 과녁에 ～ an arrow hits the mark / 꿈〔예언〕이 ～ a dream 〔prophesy〕 comes true / 예상이 ～ a conjecture turns out true / 계획이 ～ a plan 〔scheme〕 works / 네 말이 들어맞았다 You guessed right. *or* You hit the nail on the head.

⑤ 《적용되다》 apply 《to》; be applicable 《to》; hold true 〔good〕; conform to. ¶ 같은 규칙이 이 경우에도 들어맞는다 The same rule holds good here.

**들어먹다** eat up; eat out; run 〔go〕 through; use up. ¶ 장사를 ～ wind 〔give〕 up *one's* business / 재산을 ～ run through *one's* fortune / 도박으로 〔술로〕 전재산을 ～ gamble 〔drink〕 away *one's* fortune.

**들어박히다** ① 《들어가 박히다》 get 〔be〕 stuck; be caught 〔bogged〕 《in》; be driven in (못 따위가). ¶ 개울에 ～ 《a car》 be stuck 〔mired〕 in a ditch / 진창에 ～ be caught 〔stuck〕 in the mud / 못이 ～ a nail is driven in.

② 《빽빽하다》 be crowded 〔packed〕 《with》; 《사람 등이》 be jam-packed 《with》; 《별이》 be studded 〔strewn〕 《with》. ¶ 집들이 빽빽이 들어박힌 지역 a closely built-up area / 집들이 빽빽이 ～ be crowded with houses.

③ 《나오지 않다》 shut *oneself* up 《in the house》; confine *oneself* to 〔in〕 《a room》; remain 〔keep〕 indoors. ¶ 집에만 들어박혀 있는 사람 a stay-at-home; a homebody / 방에 ～ keep to *one's* room / 서재에 ～ shut *oneself* up in *one's* study.

**들어번쩍** ～하다 command 〔have, meet with〕 a ready sale; sell 〔go〕 (off) like hot cakes. ¶ 그 제품은 ～했다 The products sold like hot cakes.

**들어붓다** ① 《물을》 pour (down); fall heavily. ¶ 들어붓듯 쏟아지는 비 a pouring 〔streaming, torrential〕 rain; a downpour (of rain) / 비가 사뭇 ～ It rains hard 〔in torrents〕. *or* It rains cats and dogs. / 가마에 물을 ～ pour water into an iron pot / 아무에게 물을 ～ pour water on *a person* / 주전자의 물을 ～ pour water out of a kettle. ② 《술을》 drink heavily 〔copiously〕; quaff; guzzle; gulp down. ¶ 술을 ～ drink 《liquor》 heavily / 술을 단숨에 ～ drain *one's* glass 《of liquor》 at a gulp.

**들어서다** ① 《안으로》 enter; step 〔tread〕 in; stand 〔set foot〕 inside; go 〔get〕 into. ¶ 구내에 ～ enter the premises / 집안으로 ～ step 〔walk〕 into a house. ② 《대들다》 defy; put 〔set〕 *oneself* against; stand up to. ③ 《수효에》 come up to (a certain fixed number). ¶ 돈이 제 머릿수에 ～ The money adds up to the expected amount. ④ 《계통·자리에》 succeed to; accede to; take a position (as). ¶ 후임으로 ～ succeed 《*a person*》 「at a post 〔in a position〕; sit in *a person's* place; step into 《*a person's*》 shoes. ⑤ 《접어들다》 begin; set in. ¶ 장마철에 ～ The rainy season sets in. ⑥ 《건물이》 come into being 〔existence〕. ¶ 집이 빽빽이 ～ be crowded 〔packed〕 with houses / 번화가에는 큰 건물들이 쭉 들어섰다 Many great buildings stood in a row on the busy street.

**들어앉다** ① 《안쪽으로》 go 〔come〕 in and sit; sit inside closer. ¶ 방안에 ～ get into a room and sit down / 이리 들어앉으시오 Come in and sit down closer. ② 《자리에》 settle down; become. ¶ 과장으로 ～ become a section chief / 본실로 ～ 《a concubine》 become 《*a person's*》 legal wife / (아무의) 자리에 ～ take 《a *person's*》 place. ③ 《은퇴하다》 retire. ¶ 사업을 그만두고 ～ retire from business. ④ 《깊숙이》 stand back; be secluded; be retired. ¶ 집이 거리에서 좀 들어앉은 곳에 있다 My house stands 「a little way back from 〔a little way off〕 the street.

**들어오다** ① 《안으로》 come in(to); enter; get in; let *oneself* in; 《도둑 등이》 break in(to). ¶ 도둑이 ～ a burglar breaks into 《*a person's*》 house / 모기가 ～ mosquitoes come in / 집으로 ～ come in(to) the house / 들어오게 하다 admit; let 《*a person*》 into 《a room》 / 들어오세요 Come in, please. *or* Step 〔Walk〕 in, please. / 내 우산 속으로 들어오시오 Share 〔Come under〕 my umbrella, please. / 바람이 들어오게 창문 좀 열어라 Open the window to let in air. / 열차가 들어왔다 The train came 〔pulled〕 in. / 들어오지 마시오 《게시》 No trespassing! / 관계자 외에는 들어오지 마시오 《게시》 No admittance except on business. *or* No unauthorized entry allowed.
② 《끼다》 come in 《between》. ¶ 두 사람 사이로 ～ come in between two people.
③ 《입학·입회》 join; enter; participate in. ¶ 대학에 ～ enter college / 우리 클럽에 ～ join our club / 사원 한 사람이 새로 들어왔다 A new member joined our company.
④ 《수입이》 have; get; receive. ¶ 월(月) 100만원의 수입이 ～ have a monthly income of 1,000,000 won / 과외 수입이 들어오면 그것을 사주마 I'll buy it for you, when I get my extra income.
⑤ 《감각에》 (***a***) 《눈에》 come in sight; come into view; meet the 〔*one's*〕 eye. (***b***) 《귀에》 reach 〔come to〕 *one's* ears; come to *one's* knowledge.
⑥ 《시설되다》 be laid on; be installed. ¶ 이 방에는 직접 수도가 들어와 있다 The tap water is laid on direct to this room.

**들어올리다** lift (up); raise; hold up.

**들어주다** grant 《a request, a favor》; comply with 《*a person's* request》; answer 〔hear〕 《*a person's* prayer》. ¶ 청을 들어주지 않다 turn a deaf ear to 《*a person's*》 request.

**들어차다** fill; be filled; be full of; be replete 〔loaded〕 with; be packed; be stuffed; teem 〔swarm〕 with; overflow with. ¶ 꽉 ～ be chock-full; be packed (to the) full / 방에 사람이 ～ a room is 「full of 〔crowded with〕 people / 이 곳은 집들이 들어찼다 This is a built-up area.

**들엉기다** coagulate; congeal; condense; 「solidify.

**들엎드리다** shut *oneself* 《in *one's* room》; confine *oneself* 《to a room》; stay at home; keep 〔stay〕 indoors. ¶ 일요일에는 늘 집에 들엎드려 있다 I usually stay 〔keep〕 indoors on Sunday.

**들여가다** 《안으로》 bring 〔take〕 in; carry in; 《사다》 buy; get. ¶ 땔나무를 집에 ～ carry firewood into *one's* house / 사과

를 좀 들여가시지요 Won't you take 〔buy〕 some of the apples?

**들여놓다** ① 《안으로》 take 〔carry〕 in (and put down); put in; bring in; take 《to》. ¶ 빨래를 ~ take in washings / 차고에 차를 ~ run a car into a garage / 책상을 이 방에 들여놓으시오 Bring the desk in this room. ② 《사들이다》 purchase; buy (in); lay in 《a stock》; stock; take in. ¶ 식량을 ~ lay in provisions / 가게에 모직물을 ~ stock *one's* shop with woolen goods. ③ 《발을》 set foot 《in》; put *one's* foot 《in(to), on》; step into. ¶ 진탕 속에 발을 ~ step into the mire / 정계에 발을 ~ enter upon a political career / 두번 다시 그런곳에 발을 들여놓지 마라 Don't step 〔set your foot〕 in such a place again.

**들여다보다** ① 《안·속을》 look in(to); peep 〔peek〕 into; peep through; get a peep at. ¶ 문에서 ~ peep 〔put *one's* head〕 in at the door / 방안을 ~ peep into a room / 열쇠 구멍으로 ~ look through a keyhole / 우물 속을 ~ look down the well; take a look into the well / 울타리 너머로 ~ look over a fence 《at》 / 창문으로 ~ look 〔peek〕 in at the window / 틈으로 ~ peep through a crevice 《in the wall》. ② 《들르다》 look 〔drop, call, pop〕 in; look 《*a person*》 up. ¶ 가게를 ~ show *one's* nose in a shop; look in at a store / 도중에 그를 잠깐 들여다보았다 I dropped in to see him on my way. ③ 《자세히》 look into; examine carefully; scrutinize; 《빤히》 gaze 《on》. ¶ 얼굴을 ~ look 〔gaze〕 into 《*a person's*》 face; look 《*a person*》 in the face; fix *one's* eyes on 《*a person's*》 face / 책을 ~ look into a book; read a book / 지문을 ~ scrutinize the fingerprints.

**들여다보이다** be transparent; be easily seen through. ¶ 속이 들여다보이는 거짓말 an obvious 〔a transparent, a thinly-veiled〕 lie / 속살이 들여다보이는 블라우스 a see-through blouse / 속이 빤히 들여다뵈는 짓을 하다 resort to a shallow trick.

**들여디디다** set (foot) in; put (*one's* foot) into 〔inside〕; step in. ¶ 개골창에 발을 잘못 ~ step into a ditch by mistake / 위험한 곳에 발을 ~ set foot in a dangerous spot.

**들여보내다** send in; let 〔allow〕 《*a person*》 in; admit. ¶ 뒷문으로 ~ let 〔allow〕 《*a person*》 into the house by the backdoor / 선물을 ~ send in a present / 통행권을 가진 사람만을 ~ admit only those who have a pass / 들여보내지 않다 close 〔shut〕 the door against 〔to〕 《*a person*》 / 그 사람을 들여보내라 Send 〔Show〕 him in. / 이 증명만 있으면 거저 들여보낸다 This certificate will gain you free admission.

**들여앉히다** 《여자를》 have 〔make, let〕 《a woman》 settle down in *one's* home. ¶ 회사에서 일하던 아내를 집에 ~ have *one's* wife stay at home and give up her office job / 기생을 첩으로 ~ get a *kisaeng* to settle down as *one's* concubine.

**들여오다** ① 《안으로》 bring in; carry in; take in. ¶ 책을 서재로 ~ bring 〔carry〕 books into *one's* study / 차내에 위험물을 들여오지 마시오 《게시》 Don't take dangerous articles onto the bus. ② 《사들이다》 buy in; get (in); 《수입하다》 import. ¶ 외국에서 ~ get 〔procure, order〕 from abroad / 미국에서 밀을 ~ import wheat from America / 채소는 모퉁이의 채소가게에서 들여온다 We get vegetables from the greengrocery at the corner.

**들은귀** ① 《경험》 picked-up experience. ② 《지식》 useful knowledge picked up by keeping *one's* ears open. ¶ ~가 밝다 have alert ears.

**들은풍월**(—風月) ideas picked up here and there; knowledge acquired 〔picked up〕 by listening to others.

**들음직하다** be worth hearing; be worth listening to. ¶ 들음직한 설교 a sermon worth listening to.

**-들이** (capable of) holding...; containing. ¶ 서 말들이 자루 a sack holding three *mal;* a 3-*mal* bag / 2리터들이 병 a two-liter bottle; a bottle capable of containing 2 liters.

**들이굽다** be bent in. ¶ 팔이 들이굽지 내굽나 《속담》 Blood is thicker than water.

**들이끼우다** put 《*something*》 into 「an opening 〔a gap〕; put 《*something*》 in between.

**들이끼이다** be put 〔caught〕 in between; be put into 「an opening 〔a gap〕.

**들이다** ① 《안으로》 let 〔allow〕 in; admit. ¶ 집에 ~ let 《*a person*》 into *one's* house / 방에 새 공기를 ~ let fresh air into the room; air the room / 손님을 응접실로 모셔 ~ show 〔usher〕 a guest into the drawing room / 사람을 방에 들이지 않다 admit no one to *one's* room; keep people out of *one's* room / 어느

누구도 방안에 들이지 마라 Don't let anybody come into the room.
②《입회시키다》 let join; let participate; admit; let in. ¶ 새 회원을 ~ admit a new member.
③《일꾼·양자를》 employ《a residential servant》; adopt; take into the family. ¶ 새 가정부를 ~ engage 〔take on, hire〕 a new housekeeper / 조카를 양자로 ~ adopt *one's* nephew as a son.
④《맛을》 get 〔acquire〕 a taste《for》; take to; take a liking《to》. ¶ 돈에 맛을 ~ get a taste for money / 도박에 맛을 ~ take to gambling / 일단 마약에 맛을 들이면 끊기가 힘들다 Once you get into the drug habit, it is very difficult to give it up. / 그는 18세라는 이른 나이에 이미 술에 맛을 들였다 He acquired a taste for liquor at the early age of eighteen.
⑤《잠을》 invite 〔induce〕 (sleep); put《*a person*》 to (sleep); make《*a person*》 sleep. ¶ 어린애를 잠~ put a child to sleep.
⑥《물감을》 dye. ¶ 옷〔머리〕에 검정 물을 ~ dye *one's* clothes 〔hair〕 black.
⑦《길들이다》 impart (training to); tame; domesticate; break in.
⑧《힘·노력·비용을》 put in; spend; lay out; take pains 〔trouble〕; make efforts. ¶ 큰 돈을 들여서 at a great cost / 힘들여서 with great efforts; with difficulty / 돈을 ~ put in money; spend money / 힘을 ~ put in effort; throw *oneself* into / 2억원을 들여 집을 짓다 spend two hundred million won to build a house / 그녀는 옷에 돈을 많이 들인다 She spends a great deal of money on dress. / 이 탁자를 만드는 데 많은 공을 들였다 I have put a lot of work into making this table.
⑨《땀을》 let (sweat) cool off; cool *oneself;* cool off. ¶ 땀 좀 들이고 일을 하자 Let's stop and cool off before going on with the work.

**들이닥치다** ①《바싹》 approach; draw 〔come〕 near; be close 〔near〕 at hand; 《위험 따위가》 be impending 〔imminent〕. ¶ 눈 앞에 들이닥친 위험「an imminent 〔a pressing〕 danger / 곧 폭풍이 들이닥칠 것 같다 A storm is imminent. ②《사람이》 be visited suddenly; make 〔rush〕 for; storm《a place》; rush in. ¶ 뜻하지 않은 손님이 ~ be visited by unexpected guests / 적병이 ~ be suddenly attacked by the enemy.

**들이대다** ①《대들다》 resist openly; defy; protest; rebel 〔oppose〕 against《*a person*》. ¶ 그는 상사에게 정면으로 들이댔다 He defied his boss to his face. / 그는 월급을 올려야 한다고 주인한테 들이댔다 He protested to his master that his salary ought to be raised.
②《코앞에》 thrust《*a thing*》 before《*a person*》; put 〔place〕《*a thing*》 under《*a person's*》 nose; point《a gun》 at 〔to, toward〕. ¶ 권총을 ~ point 〔aim〕 a revolver at《*a person*》/ 단도를 들이대고 협박하다 threaten《*a person*》 with a dagger / 증거를 ~「bring forward 〔thrust〕 evidence《at *a person*》/ 코앞에 주먹을 ~ thrust *one's* fist in《*another's*》 face.
③《공급하다》 supply《*a person*》 continuously《with》; provide《*a person*》 constantly《with》. ¶ 물자를 ~ keep things in constant supply.

**들이덤비다** ①《서둘다》 act very hurriedly 〔hastily〕; bustle; busy *oneself* with; be terribly hurried 〔hasty〕; be terribly flustered. ⇨ 덤비다 ①. ¶ 여럿이 들이덤벼 일을 잠깐 동안에 해치웠다 Several people flung themselves into the job and got it done in no time.
②《덤벼들다》 go at《it》 hard; set upon 〔attack, assault〕 furiously; fall 〔turn〕 upon《*a person*》; defy; challenge. ¶ 아무에게 ~ attack *a person* / 윗사람에게 ~ challenge *one's* superior / 맹렬한 기세로 ~ spring at《*a person*》 with tiger-like ferocity.

**들이마시다** ①《액체를》 drink (in); suck in; slurp up; gulp down. ¶ 물을 ~ drink water / 국을 ~ slurp 〔gulp down〕 soup / 맥주 한 조끼를 단숨에 ~ chug-a-lug a jug of beer / 맥주 한 컵을 단숨에 ~ drink up a glass of beer at one gulp. ②《기체를》 breathe in; inhale; draw in. ¶ 신선한 공기를 ~ breathe in fresh air / 독기를 ~ inhale poisonous fumes / 산소를 들이마시고 이산화탄소를 내뱉다 inhale oxygen and exhale carbon dioxide / 담배 연기를 깊이 ~ inhale cigarette smoke.

**들이맞추다** fix 〔fit〕 it in(to); get 〔put, let〕 it in. ¶ 미닫이에 유리를 ~ fit a windowpane in a sliding door.

**들이몰다** ①《몰아넣다》 drive 〔chase〕《into》; shoo in. ¶ 닭을 닭장에 ~ shoo chickens into the coop / 돼지를 울 안으로 ~ drive a pig in the pigsty / 궁지로 ~ drive《*a person*》 into a corner; corner《*a person*》/ 궁지에 들이몰려 있다 have *one's* back to 〔against〕 the wall; be cornered. ② 《차마를》 drive fast 〔violently〕; make 〔let〕 run. ¶ 말을 ~ gallop a horse; go galloping / 차를 ~ hasten 〔drive fast〕 to 《a place》 in a car.

**들이몰리다** ① 《안쪽으로》 be driven in. ¶ 소가 외양간으로 ~ a cow is driven into the barn. ② 《호되게》 be called to account; be taken to task; be roundly scolded. ¶ 책임을 등한히 했다고 ~ be scolded for neglecting *one's* duty. ③ 《떼지어》 crowd; throng; flock together; swarm. ¶ 공원에 사람이 ~ a park is crowded with people.

**들이밀다** ① 《안으로》 push 〔force, shove, squeeze〕 into. ¶ 승객들을 만원 버스 안으로 ~ squeeze passengers into a crowded bus. ② 《냅다》 push hard; thrust hard; shove hard. ¶ 아무를 ~ give *a person* a shove 〔push〕.

**들이밀리다** ① 《안으로》 be pushed 〔thrust, shoved〕 in(to). ¶ 방 한 구석에 ~ be pushed into the corner of a room. ② 《한 곳으로》 crowd; flock; swarm; come 〔get〕 together; rush. ¶ 사람들이 백화점에 ~ people crowd into 〔rush to〕 the department store / 사람들이 사방에서 ~ people flock from all quarters / 어제 은행에 돈을 찾으러 사람들이 들이밀렸다 Yesterday there was a rush on the bank to withdraw money.

**들이박다** drive 〔knock, strike〕 《*a thing*》 in(to); ram 《a stake》 into 《the ground》; wedge in (쐐기를). ¶ 못을 ~ drive 〔hammer〕 a nail into 《a wall》.

**들이받다** run 〔strike, knock, hit, bump〕 against 〔into〕; collide with; butt; bunt (into); bunt hard. ¶ 전주를 ~ hit an electric pole / 나무를 ~ run into a tree / 머리로 ~ give 《*a person*》 a butt of head / (머리로) 가슴을 ~ butt 《*a person*》 in the chest / 머리를 벽에 ~ knock 〔bump〕 *one's* head against the wall / 소가 뿔로 ~ a bull bunts 《*a person*》 with its horns / 트럭이 소형차를 들이받았다 A truck bumped into a small car.

**들이부수다** destroy; break 《*a thing*》 into pieces; tear down; smash. ¶ 낡은 집을 ~ tear down a shabby house.

**들이불다** ① 《이쪽·안으로》 blow this way; blow 《in(to)》. ② 《세차게》 blow hard. ¶ 바람이 ~ a wind blows hard.

**들이붓다** ① 《쏟아붓다》 pour into. ¶ 솥에 물을 ~ pour water into a kettle. ② 《계속해서》 pour continuously 〔profusely〕.

**들이빨다** suck hard; suck in; inhale; imbibe. ¶ 빨대로 소다수를 ~ suck on soda water with a straw / 젖을 ~ suck the breast hard.

**들이세우다** ① 《안에》 take 〔bring, carry〕 《*a thing*》 in and stand 《it》 up. ¶ 우산을 실내에 ~ bring an umbrella into a room and stand it up. ② 《지위에》 place; appoint; install 《*a person* in a position》. ¶ 아무를 과장으로 ~ install *a person* as section chief.

**들이쉬다** 《숨을》 inhale; inspire; breathe in; draw 《a breath》. ¶ 숨을 ~ draw *one's* breath; breathe in 《air》 / 숨을 깊이 ~ draw a deep breath; breathe (in) deep.

**들이쌓이다** lie in a heap; be piled on top of one another; lie 〔be〕 heaped up; collect. ¶ 창고에 쌀이 ~ rice lies heaped up in a warehouse / 테이블 위에 먼지가 ~ dust collects 〔is thick〕 on the table.

**들이쑤시다** ① 《아프다》 smart; tingle; throb with pain; fester; ache. ¶ 골머리가 ~ have a severe headache / 곪은 손가락이 ~ a festered finger smarts / 온몸이 ~ have a severe pain throughout *one's* body.
② 《구멍 따위를》 poke hard at; pick; peck; prod. ¶ 이를 ~ pick *one's* teeth / 담뱃대를 ~ poke the stem of a pipe.
③ 《선동하다》 instigate; incite; stir up. ¶ 들이쑤셔 싸움을 붙이다 stir up 《the people》 to fight.
④ 《뒤지다》 rummage 〔ransack〕 《in a drawer》; dig out; poke and pry 《into》. ¶ 남의 비밀을 ~ poke and pry into another's secret.

**들이조르다** importune 〔beg, press, pester〕 《*a person* for *a thing, a person* to *do*》 relentlessly.

**들이지르다** ① 《세게 지르다》 (***a***) 《주먹 등으로》 strike 〔beat, hit〕 hard; 《칼 따위로》 push 〔thrust〕 hard. ¶ 칼로 아무의 가슴을 ~ thrust a knife into *a person's* chest; stab *a person* in the chest. (***b***) 《발길로》 kick hard; give a hard kick 《on the shin》. ¶ 옆구리를 ~ give a hard kick on the side.
② 《소리를》 yell; shout; cry (out); raise 〔lift up, strain, pitch〕 *one's* voice.

**들이차다** 《안으로》 kick in; 《세차게》 kick hard.

**들이치다**[1] 《바람 등이》 blow 〔sweep〕 in (-to); 《비 등이》 drive into 〔through〕. ¶ 비가 들이치지 않도록 하다 shut out the rain / 비가 열린 창문으로 들이쳤다 The rain blew in from the open window. / 바람이 세차게 방안으로 들이치고 있다 The wind is blowing furiously into the room.

**들이치다**[2] 《습격》 attack; assault; storm; raid. ¶ 경관이 도박 소굴을 ~ policemen raid 〔make a raid on〕 a gambling den / 성안의 적군을 ~ attack the enemy in the castle.

**들이켜다** 《마시다》 drink down 〔up〕; drain (a cup); gulp down; toss 〔quaff〕 off. ¶ 물을 꿀꺽꿀꺽 ~ gulp down water / 단숨에 ~ empty 《*one's* glass》 in one draft; drink 《a glass of wine》 at a gulp / 한 방울도 안 남기고 ~ drink 《a glass of water》 to the last drop / 단숨에 들이켜라 Drink it up, please! *or* Bottom up!

**들이키다** 《다그다》 pull in; take in; draw in; tug in; put closer 〔nearer〕. ¶ 발을 ~ draw in *one's* legs / 나무를 담 가까이 들이켜 심다 plant trees closer to a wall / 테이블을 한 구석으로 들이켜 놓다 draw a table over into the corner of a room.

**들이퍼붓다** ① 《물을》 pour 《water》 hard; 《눈비가 쏟아지다》 rain 〔snow〕 hard on; pour 〔rain〕 down hard. ¶ 비가 ~ rain in torrents 〔buckets〕; rain cats and dogs. ② 《폭격·질문 등을》 bombard hard; 《욕설을》 heap abuses upon 《*a person*》.

**들일** farm work; work in the fields; field 〔farm〕 labor. ¶ ~ 나가다 go to work in the field / ~을 하다 do farm work; work on the farm.

**들입다** 《몹시》 hard; rashly; recklessly; forcibly; ceaselessly; like mad. ¶ ~ 공부하다 study hard (without letup); dig into *one's* subject / ~ 밀다 give a hard push / ~ 캐묻다 pound 〔prod〕 with questions; ask questions one after another / 아무를 ~ 패다 beat *a person* hard 〔black-and-blue〕.

**들장미**(—薔薇) a wild rose; a brier.

**들쥐** a field mouse.

**들짐승** a wild 〔feral〕 animal.

**들쩍지근하다** be somewhat sweet; (be) sweetish.

**들쭉** 〖식물〗 blueberries. ◉ ~나무 a 「blueberry.

**들쭉날쭉** uneven; jagged; indented; serrated. ~하다 (be) uneven 〔jagged, indented, serrated〕. ¶ ~한 해안선 an indented coastline / 잎새 가장자리가 ~하다 a leaf is serrated at its ends.

**들차다** be sound in mind and body; be strong and firm.

**들창**(—窓) a window which can be 「raised up 〔propped〕 open. ◉ ~눈이 a person who is always lifting his eyelids. ~코 an upturned 〔a turned-up〕 nose; 《사람》 a person with an upturned nose.

**들척지근하다** ⇨ 들쩍지근하다.

**들추다** ① 《폭로하다》 disclose 〔divulge, let out〕 《a secret》; uncover; reveal; expose; dig up 〔into〕; rake up 《*a person's*》 past; ferret out 《*a person's* secret》. ¶ 남의 비밀을 ~ disclose another's secret / 아무의 잘못을 ~ expose *a person's* fault / 정체를 ~ reveal 《*a person's*》 true character / 남의 조상을 들추어 말하다 take a dig at another's ancestors. ② 《뒤지다》 search; ransack; rummage. ¶ 책을 찾느라고 온 방을 ~ turn a room upside-down looking for a book / 연필이 있나 하고 서랍을 ~ rummage in a drawer for a pencil.

**들추어내다** ① 《폭로하다》 expose; disclose; uncover; reveal; dig up 〔into〕; lay bare; bring a secret to light. ¶ 아무의 비밀을 ~ dig into *a person's* secret / 아무의 불미한 과거를 ~ dig up *a person's* disreputable past / 그의 비행을 들추어냈다 I exposed his dark deed. ② 《찾아내다》 find out; seek out; hunt out; rummage out. ¶ 서랍에서 돈을 ~ rummage money out of a drawer / 방안에서 감춰 둔 장물을 ~ 「hunt out 〔find〕 the stolen goods hidden in a room.

**들치기** 《행위》 shoplifting; 《사람》 a shoplifter. ¶ ~하다 lift 〔steal〕 goods in a store; shoplift / ~ 상습범 a habitual shoplifter / ~하다가 잡히다 be caught shoplifting.

**들치다** raise; lift; hold up (the end of). ¶ 이불을 ~ hold up an end of a blanket.

**들큰거리다** 《비위를》 say disagreeable things; make irritating remarks; hurt *a person's* feelings; hurt 〔offend〕 *a person.*

**들큼하다** (be) sweetish; be somewhat 「〔unpleasantly〕 sweet.

**들키다** be found (out); be discovered 〔detected, caught〕 《*doing*, in the act of *doing*》. ¶ 들키지 않고 without being discovered 〔noticed〕; 《sneak in》 unobserved; 《get away》 unnoticed; 《escape》 undetected / 들키지 않도록 하다 keep from being seen / 장난하다 선생님한테 ~ be caught up to some mischief by the teacher / 저울눈을 속

이다가 ~ be detected giving short measure / 우산을 훔치다가 ~ be caught in the act of filching an umbrella / 그는 도둑질 현장을 들켰다 He was caught red-handed stealing. / 들키지 않도록 울 밑에 숨어라 Just keep down under the hedge so (that) nobody can see you. / 그들은 들킬 염려가 없었다 They were safe from detection.

**들타작**(一打作) threshing in the field.

**들통**(一桶) a pail; a bucket.

**들통나다** become known; be found out; come to light; be exposed 〔revealed, discovered, detected〕; leak 〔get〕 out. ¶ 음모가 들통났다 The plot came to light. / 비밀이 곧 들통났다 The secret soon「leaked out 〔came out〕. / 그가 바람을 피우고 있는 것이 아내에게 들통났다 His wife found out that he had been「unfaithful to 〔cheating on〕 her.

**들판** a plain; a field. ¶ ~에 나가 일하다 work in the field.

**듬뿍** much; plenty; lots; full (to the brim); brimfully. ¶ 설탕 큰 술 하나 ~ a rounded tablespoonful of sugar / 컵에 ~ 따르다 fill the cup to the brim / 버터를 ~ 바르다 spread butter thick《on a slice of bread》/ 팁을 ~ 주다 tip《a porter》handsomely / 붓에 먹물을 ~ 칠하다 take up a full 〔generous〕 brushful of ink / 우리는 음식을 ~ 먹었다 We had food and drink in plenty.

**듬성듬성** sparsely; thinly; scatteredly; sporadically; here and there. ¶ 털이 ~ 나다 hair grows thinly / 나무를 ~ 심다 plant trees sparsely.

**듬쑥** full; greedily. ¶ 과자를 손에 ~ 그러쥐다 grasp a greedy handful of cake / 장작을 한 아름 ~ 그러안다 hold an armful of firewood in *one's* arms.

**듬쑥하다** ① = 든직하다. ②《많다》(be) full (of); fill. ¶ 밥을 그릇에 듬쑥히 담다 fill a bowl full of rice.

**듯** ¶…듯 마는〔만, 말〕 듯하다 it hardly seems one way or the other; it hardly feels as if; *one* hardly knows whether / 밥이 적어 먹은 듯 만 듯하다 There was so little rice I hardly feel as if I had eaten any. / 어젯밤은 모기에 물려 자는 듯 마는 듯했다 I was bitten by mosquitoes so much that I got hardly any sleep last night. / 비가 올 듯 말 듯하다 There's no telling whether it will rain or not. *or* It may rain or then again it may not.

**듯싶다**《것 같다》look (like); feel like; seem as if; "it seems (to me) that…". ¶ 그는 학생인 ~ He looks like a student. / 좀 클 ~ Something tells me it will be a bit too big. / 범이라도 잡을 ~ I feel so strong I could even catch a tiger. / 벼슬이라도 한 듯싶은 모양이구나 You act as if you had become a government official or something. / 주인인 듯싶은 사람이 나왔다 A man, apparently the master of the house, came out.

**듯(이)** 〔부사적〕 as if; as though; like; as. ¶ 기쁜 듯이 joyfully; with a glad look / 슬픈 듯이 sadly; with a sad air / 사뭇 만족스러운 듯이 with evident satisfaction / 빚을 줄 듯이 말하다 talk as if *one* would give a loan / 큰일이나 하는 듯이 야단법석이다 fuss about as if *one* is doing an important job / 한 대 칠 듯이 덤벼들다 go at《*a person*》as if about to hit *him* / 그는 죽은 듯이 가만히 있었다 He remained motionless as if he were dead. / 그는 아무 일도 없었던 듯이 행동했다 He behaved as if nothing had happened.

**-듯(이)** 〔어미〕 like; as; as if 〔though〕. ¶ 자기 아들 사랑하듯이 사랑하다 love《a child》like *one's* own / 네 형이 하듯이 해라 Do as your brother does. / 삶이 있듯이 죽음도 있다 As a man lives, so he dies.

**듯하다** ①《…인〔할〕 것 같다》seem; appear; look (like); sound (like);《마치 …인〔할〕 것 같다》seem as if; look as though.

> 용법 **seem**「마음에 …라고 생각되다」라고 말하는 사람의「주관」을 말하려고 할 때 쓰임. **appear**「외관상으로는 …하게 보이지만 실제로는 그렇지 않을지도 모른다」라는 뜻을 내포함. **look**「눈으로 보니 …하게 보이다」란 뜻으로 객관적인 사항에 관해 쓰임. **sound**「…인 것처럼 들리다, 생각되다」란 뜻으로 회화에서 자주 쓰임.

¶ 정직한 사람인 ~ look honest; look like an honest man / 그녀는 병든 ~ She seems to be sick. *or* It seems that she is sick. / 발화 장소는 부엌인 ~ It appears that the fire broke out in the kitchen. / 비가 올 ~ It looks like rain. *or* It is likely to rain. / 잡지 기사는 아무래도 정말인 ~ What the magazine says really appears 〔seems〕 to be true. / 저것은 트럼펫 소리인 ~ That sounds like a trumpet. / 어머니는 그 소식을 듣고 안심하신 듯했다 My

mother seemed to be relieved to hear that news. / 그는 아직 살아 있는 ~ He seems to be still alive. *or* It seems that he is still alive.
② 《당장 …할 것 같다》 be ready 《to *do*》; threaten 《to *do*》; be on the verge of 《*do*ing》. ¶ 이제라도 비를 퍼부을 듯한 구름 threatening clouds / 금방 피어날 듯한 장미 a rose just ready to burst / 슬퍼서 가슴이 미어질 듯했다 My heart almost burst with grief. / 당장이라도 비가 쏟아질 ~ It is threatening to rain.

**-듯하다** be like; be as (if). ¶ 가랑잎에 불붙듯하다 flare up like tinder; get mad at the drop of a hat / 다람쥐 쳇바퀴 돌듯하다 go round and round like a squirrel in on the frame of a sieve / 구렁이 담 넘어가듯하다 succeed in an unnoticed way / 가난한 집에 제사 돌아오듯하다 come around as often as the bill collectors.

**등** ① 《사람·동물의》 the back. ¶ 등을 맞대고 눕다 lie back to back 《with *a person*》/ 등을 돌리다 turn *one's* back 《to, on》; give the back to 《*a person*》; run 〔walk〕 out on 《*a person*》/ 서로 등을 돌리고 앉다 sit back to back 《with》/ 적에게 등을 보이다 turn *one's* back on the enemy; [비유적] turn tail (도망치다); beat a retreat / 등이 가렵다 My back is itching.
② 《뒤쪽》 the back; the back end 〔side〕. ¶ 의자의 등 the back of a chair / 벽을 등지고 with *one's* back to 〔against〕 the wall / 등 뒤에 서다 stand in the back / 저고리 등이 닳다 the back of *one's* coat is worn out / 등이 더우랴 배가 부르랴 《속담》 It won't 「bring you anything profitable 〔do you any good〕.

**등**(等) ① 《등급》 a class; a grade; a degree; a rank. ¶ 1〔2, 3〕등 the first 〔second, third〕 class 〔grade〕/ 1등상 the first prize / 등을 매기다 grade; graduate; classify / 1등으로 졸업하다 graduate first on the list / 등 안에 들다 be up to a grade; be in a class / 등외로 떨어지다 fall under the regular grade / 죄를 한 등 감하다 downgrade the sentence by one degree; reduce the penalty by one degree / 3등 기차로 여행하다 go 〔travel〕 third class on a train / 그 자동차 회사의 무쏘는 파리—다카 랠리에서 8등을 차지했다 Musso of the Motor Co. has captured eighth place in Paris-Darkar Rally.
② 《…따위》 and so 「on 〔forth〕; et cetera (★ etc., &c.로 생략하여 and so forth 〔on〕이라고 읽는 것이 보통임); and what not; and the like; and all that 〔the rest, the like〕; and such like. ¶ 한국, 중국, 일본 등 세 나라에서 in these three countries of Korea, China, and Japan / 그들은 나의 연령, 성명 등을 물었다 They asked my age, my name, and so on. / 그는 나에게 돈을 달라는 등 여러 가지로 귀찮게 군다 He bothers me with requests for money and so on.

**등**(燈) a lamp; a lantern; a light. ¶ 등불 lamplight / 등을 켜다 make a light; light a lamp; light up 《a room》; 《전등을》 turn 〔switch〕 on the (electric) light / 등을 끄다 put out the light 〔lamp〕; 《전등의》 turn off the light / 등이 꺼졌다 The light 「has gone out 〔is out〕.

**등**(藤) 〖식물〗 a rattan; a cane. ¶ 등의자 a rattan chair / 등지팡이 a cane stick.

**등가**(等價) an equal value; 〖화학〗 equivalence; 《무역·금융의》 parity. ¶ ~의 of equal value; 〖화학〗 equivalent.
◉ ~량 〖화학〗 an equivalent.

**등각**(等角) 〖수학〗 equal angles. ◉ ~삼각형 an equiangular triangle. ~선 an isogonic line.

**등갈퀴나물** 〖식물〗 a cow vetch.

**등갓**(燈—) a lamp shade.

**등거리**(等距離) an equal distance; equidistance. ¶ ~의 equally distant 《from, both from A and B》; equidistant / ~에 at equal distances.
◉ ~외교 an equidistance 〔even-handed〕 diplomacy. ~외교 정책 a policy of dealing equally 《with A and B》; equal distance diplomacy.

**등걸** a stump; a stub. ¶ 나뭇~을 캐내다 dig up the stump of a tree.
◉ ~불 a stump fire; 《깜부기불》 embers; a dying 〔low〕 fire. ~숯 charcoal made from stumps.

**등걸잠** sleeping with *one's* clothes on and without any covering. ¶ ~자다 sleep with *one's* clothes on, without any covering.

**등겨** rice chaff.

**등고선**(等高線) a contour (line). ¶ ~을 넣다〔표시하다〕 contour; represent in contour. ◉ ~지도 a contour(-line) map.

**등골** ① 《등줄기》 the hollow along the spine; the hollow of the back. ¶ ~에 땀이 나다 be given a hard time / ~이 오싹하다 [사물이 주어] send a chill

〔shiver〕 down *one's* spine / ～이 오싹해지다 be chilled to the marrow / 나는 ～이 오싹했다 I felt a cold chill pass through me. *or* A shiver ran through my limbs. ② 《척수》 the spinal cord 〔marrow〕. ¶ ～이 빠지다 suffer extremely; have a very hard time of it / 자금을 조달하느라 ～이 빠지게 일하다 take great pains to raise the money 《for the business》 / ～ 뽑다 exact 〔wring, extort, squeeze〕 《money》 from 《*a person*》 / 사내의 ～을 뽑다 squeeze a man dry; bleed a man white / 여자한테 ～을 뽑히다 be squeezed dry 〔bled white〕 by a woman.

**등과**(登科) 《옛 제도》 passing the higher civil service examination. ～하다 pass the higher civil service examination.

**등교**(登校) attending school. ～하다 attend 〔go to〕 school. ¶ ～시에는 차 조심해라 Watch for the passing traffic when you are on your way to school. ◉ ～거부 refusal to attend school.

**등귀**(騰貴) a rise 《in prices》. ⇨ 앙등.

**등극**(登極) enthronement; accession to the throne. ～하다 ascend 〔accede〕 to the throne; come to the throne.

**등글개첩**(—妾) a young mistress of an old man.

**등긁이** a (wooden) back scratcher.

**등급**(等級) a class; a grade; an order; a rank; a degree; 《별의》 magnitude. ¶ ～별의 graduated 《admission fees》 / ～을 매기다 grade; classify / 이 상품에는 품질에 따라 ABC로 ～이 매겨져 있다 These articles are graded A, B and C according to quality.

**등기**(登記) registration; registry. ～하다 register; have 《*a thing*》 registered; effect 〔make〕 registration. ¶ ～가 되어 있다 be registered; be on the record / ～필 《표시》 Registered. / 그는 새로 지은 집을 자기 명의로 ～했다 He has the newly-built house registered in his name. ◉ ～료 a registration fee. ～말소 cancellation of registration. ～번호 the registered number. ～부 a register. ～사항 matters required to be registered. ～소 a registry (office). ～용지 a registration form 〔blank〕. ～절차 the formalities of registration. ～필증 a registration certificate. 국내〔국제〕～ domestic 〔international〕 registration. 선적～ registration of nationality (of a ship).

**등기우편**(登記郵便) registered mail 〔post 《영》〕. ¶ ～ 영수증 a registration receipt / ～으로 부치다 send 《a letter》 registered / ～으로 하다 have 〔get〕 《a letter》 registered. ◉ ～료 a registration 〔registry〕 fee.

**등꽃**(藤—) wisteria blossoms.

**등나무**(藤—) a wisteria; a wistaria. ◉ ～덩굴 a wisteria vine. ～시렁 a wisteria trellis.

**등단**(登壇) ～하다 take 〔ascend, go onto, mount〕 the platform; proceed to the platform. ¶ 총리가 ～했다 The Prime Minister mounted the platform.

**등달다** get all hot and bothered; fret 〔stew〕 《about》; be impatient 〔irritated〕; be upset; be in a stew; be held in suspense. ¶ 등달아 있다 be in a fret 〔chafe〕 / 가만 있거라 돈을 잃어 등이 단다 Let me alone—I am upset over losing (at gambling). / 그는 꿔준 돈을 받지 못해 등달아한다 He is all hot and bothered because he can't collect the money he lent out.

**등닿다** ① 《등대다》 have backing; be supported; lean on; depend upon; shelter *oneself* under 〔rely upon〕 《the man of influence》. ¶ 그는 서울에 등닿는 친척이 있어 몸을 의지하러 갔다 He has a relative to depend upon in Seoul and has gone there to live with him. ② 《마소의 등이》 be grazed; be abraded; be chafed; be rubbed raw.

**등대**(等待) waiting. ～하다 wait for; await; be 〔get〕 ready for 《an order》.

**등대**(燈臺) a lighthouse; a beacon; 《시》 a pharos. ◉ ～선 a lightship; a floating lighthouse. ～지기 a lighthouse keeper. 등댓불 a beacon lamp; lights.

**등대다** lean 〔depend, rely, count, fall back〕 on 《*a person's*》 authority 〔influence, power〕; look 〔turn〕 to 《*a person*》 for help. ¶ 아버지의 세력에 등을 대고 뽐내다 give *oneself* airs under the shelter of *one's* father's influence / 그는 관계(官界)에 등댈 유력한 몇 사람이 있다 He has several men of influence he can count on in the government. / 자네는 언제든 그에게 등댈 수 있다 You can always rely 〔count〕 on him.

**등덜미** the upper part of the back; the nape 〔scruff〕 of the neck. ¶ ～를 잡다 take 〔seize〕 《*a person*》 by the scruff of the neck.

**등등**(等等) et cetera (생략 etc.); and so on; and so forth; and all that sort of thing. ¶ 그녀의 핸드백 속에는 콤팩트, 빗, 휴지, 지갑 ～이 들어 있다 Her handbag contains a compact, a comb, wastepaper, a purse, and so forth. / 그녀는 자동차를 사야 한다 집을 사야 한다는 ~의 요구를 하고 있다 She insists I buy a car, I buy a house, and so on.

**등등거리**(藤―) a rattan undershirt (worn in summer to keep sweat from coat).

**등등하다**(騰騰―) (be) triumphant; exultant; be on *one's* high horse; be riding high. ¶ 기세가 ~ show *one's* nerve; wear a high hat; be in high spirits / 노기 ~ be in wild rage; be furious.

**등딱지** a shell; 《거북·게 따위의》 carapace.

**등락**(騰落) rise and fall; fluctuations. ¶ 주가(株價)의 ~ the fluctuations of stock prices.

**등량**(等量) the same 〔equal〕 quantity; 〖화학〗 equivalence. ¶ ~의 of the same quantity; equivalent.

**등록**(登錄) registration; entry. ~하다 register 《with an office》; enter; make an entry; enroll; put on record; 《해 받다》 have 《*a thing*》 registered; obtain 《a place》 in a register. ¶ 주민~ resident registration / 유권자의 ~ the registration of voters / 대장에 ~하다 enter in the cadaster / 상표를 ~하다 register a trademark 《with the Patent Office》 / 회원으로 ~하다 enroll 〔register〕 as a member / ~필 《표시》 Registered. / 그녀는 아직 그 클럽에 ~되어 있지 않다 She has not registered for the club yet. / 그 디자인은 특허청에 ~되어 있다 The design is registered with the Patent Office.
◉ ~금 a registration fee; 《학교의》 tuition (fees). ~번호 a registered number. ~법 the registration law. ~부 a register. ~상표 a registered trademark. ~세 a registration tax 〔fee〕. ~의장(意匠) a registered design. ~인〔자〕 a registrant. ~제 registration system. ~증 a certificate of registration.

**등롱**(燈籠) 《달아 놓는》 a hanging 〔garden〕 lantern; 《들고 다니는》 a hand lantern; 《신전의》 a dedicatory 〔sacred〕 lantern. ¶ 석~ a stone lantern / ~에 불을 켜다 light a hanging lantern.
◉ ~꾼 a lantern bearer.

**등마루** 《등뼈의》 the ridge of the spine.

**등메** a rush mat fringed with cloth.

**등바대** a neckband sewed in unlined garments.

**등반**(登攀) climbing. ~하다 climb (up); scale; make the 〔an〕 ascent of. ¶ 한라산 ~을 하다 climb 〔make an ascent of〕 Mt. Halla. ◉ ~대 a climbing party. ~자 a climber.

**등받이** ① = 등거리. ② 《의자의》 the back 「of a chair.

**등번호** 《야구》 a player's 〔uniform〕 number; 《경주》 a racing number.

**등변**(等邊) 〖수학〗 equal sides. ¶ ~의 equilateral. ◉ ~삼각형 an equilateral triangle. ~형 an equilateral (figure).

**등본**(謄本) a (certified) copy; a transcript; a duplicate. ¶ 호적~ a (certified) copy of *one's* 「domiciliary 〔family〕 register / ~을 뜨다 obtain 〔get, make〕 a certified copy / ~을 신청하다 apply for a copy.

**등분**(等分) 《같은 부분》 equal parts 〔proportions〕; 《등분하기》 division into equal parts. ~하다 divide equally 〔into equal parts〕; share 《the profits》 equally 《with》; deal out equally 〔into equal portion〕. ¶ ~으로 equally; in(to) equal parts / 4~하다 divide 《*something*》 into quarters / 비용을 ~하다 share the expenses equally with 《*a person*》 / 재산을 자식들에게 ~하다 divide the property equally among *one's* children.

**등불**(燈―) a light; a lamp(light). ¶ ~을 켜다〔끄다〕 light 〔put out〕 a lamp / ~아래서 글을 읽다 read by lamplight.

**등비**(等比) 〖수학〗 equal ratio; geometric ratio. ◉ ~급수 geometric(al) progression: ~ 급수적으로 in a geometric ratio. ~수열 geometric(al) series.

**등뼈** the backbone; the chine; the spine. ◉ ~동물 a vertebrate.

**등사**(謄寫) copy; transcription; reproduction. ~하다 copy; make a copy 《of》; transcribe; reproduce.
◉ ~물 mimeographed material. ~원지 stencil paper; a stencil. ~지 carbon paper (복사용의). ~판, ~기 a mimeograph; a copying machine: ~기로 밀다 mimeograph; run off 《70 copies》 on a mimeograph.

**등산**(登山) (mountain) climbing; mountaineering. ~하다 climb 〔ascend, scale, go up〕 a mountain; make an ascent of a mountain; go mountain=climbing (★ climb에는 애써서 「오르다」라는 뜻이 있어 낮은 산에 오를 때는 go up이 더 알맞음. climb up은 보다 더 노력이 드는 감이 강해 크고 험준한 산에 씀). ¶ 나는 때때로 혼자 ~을 간다 I sometimes go mountain climbing alone. / 경험이 적은 ~객들이 산을 우습게 보는 경향이 있

다 Inexperienced mountain climbers are apt to underestimate the dangers of mountains.
◉ ～가 a mountaineer; an alpinist. ～객 a mountain climber. ～길[로] a mountain trail; a path up a mountain: 이 산에는 ～로가 셋 있다 There are three trails leading to the top of this mountain. ～모 an alpine cap [hat]. ～시즌[철] the mountaineering season. ～열 a passion [craze] for mountaineering. ～장비 mountain-climbing equipment. ～전차[철도] a mountain trolley [railway]. ～지팡이 an alpenstock. ～화 mountain-climbing boots. ｢have a stiff back.

**등살바르다** have stiff back muscles;

**등색**(橙色) orange (color). ¶ ～의 orange-colored.

**등성마루** 〖생물〗 the ridge 《of the spine》; the top of the back; the line of the backbone.

**등성이** the back; a ridge; 《산등성이》 the ridge of a mountain.

**등세**(騰勢) an upward tendency; a rising trend. ¶ 물가가 ～를 보이고 있다 Prices are on the rise [advance].

**등세공**(藤細工) rattanwork; canework.

**등속**(等速) equal speed; 〖물리〗 uniform velocity. ◉ ～운동 uniform motion.

**등속**(等屬) and so forth [on]; and the like; and what not; and such like; et cetera (생략 etc, &c.). ¶ 과자～ cakes and the like.

**등솔기** the seam on the back of a coat.

**등수**(等數) ① 《차례》 a grade; a rank; a class. ¶ ～를 매기다 grade; graduate; get ratings 《for, on》. ② 《같은 수》 an equal number.

**등식**(等式) 〖수학〗 an equality.

**등신**(等身) life-size; full-length. ¶ ～(대)의 life-size(d); as large as life / ～대보다 큰 동상 a larger-than-life bronze statue / 이 초상은 ～대이다 This portrait is life-sized. ◉ ～상(像) a life-size statue.

**등신**(等神) a fool; a stupid person; a dunce; a noodle; a blockhead; a stick 《구어》. ¶ ～ 같은 stupid; foolish / ～같은 짓을 하다 do a stupid thing; make a fool of *oneself*.

**등심**(一心) 《쇠고기의》 a fillet; sirloin (of beef). ¶ ～스테이크 a sirloin steak.

**등심**(燈心) a (lamp) wick.

**등심초**(燈心草) 〖식물〗 a rush.

**등쌀** annoying; pestering; bothering; harassing; molesting; needling. ¶ 모기 ～에 잠을 잘 수가 없다 The mosquitoes are so annoying that I can't sleep. / 이 애 ～에 못 견디겠다 I cannot suffer the pestering nature of this child any more. / 시어머니 ～에 시집을 못살고 쫓겨왔다 She couldn't take her mother-in-law's nagging, so she left her husband and came home.

**등쌀대다** bother; annoy; pester; harass; molest; needle. ¶ 계모가 등쌀대는 통에 못살겠다 My stepmother's persistent harrassment is ｢more than I can bear [too much for me]. ｢isobar (line).

**등압선**(等壓線) an isobaric line; an

**등에** 〖곤충〗 a gadfly; a horsefly.

**등온선**(等溫線) 〖기상〗 an isothermal (line); an isotherm.

**등외**(等外) a failure; 《경기의》 an also-ran. ¶ ～의 《경기에서》 unplaced; 《품질이》 offgrade; substandard / ～로 처지다 be [run] unplaced; fail to win a prize; be eliminated (예선에서); be judged to be below standard (품평회 등에서) / 그녀는 최선을 다했지만 ～가 되었다 She did her best but ｢failed to place [ended up an also-ran].

**등용**(登用·登庸) 《임용》 (an) appointment; (an) assignment; 《승진》 promotion. ～하다 appoint [assign] 《*a person* to a position》; promote 《*a person* to a higher position》. ¶ 인재를 ～하다 engage men of ability / 법관에 ～되다 be appointed (as a) judge; be promoted [raised] to the bench / 인재 ～의 길을 열다 open the offices to talent; make all careers open to talent / 회사의 활성화를 위해 유망한 신인을 ～하기로 결정했다 It was decided that we should make full use of promising new recruits in order to breathe new life into our company.

**등용문**(登龍門) a gateway to success 《in a career》; an opening to honors; a narrow opening to highly-prized membership 《of a profession》. ¶ 젊은 이들의～ the gateway to success in a career for young people / 이 콩쿠르는 많은 음악가들의 ～역할을 해 왔다 Success in this contest has been the first step to a successful career for a number of musicians.

**등원**(登院) ～하다 attend the House.

**등위**(等位) a rank; a class; a grade.
◉ ～접속사[절] a coordinate conjunction [clause]. ｢oil 《영》.

**등유**(燈油) lamp oil; kerosene; paraffin

**등의자**(藤椅子) a rattan chair.

**등자**(—子) 《말 탈 때의》 stirrups. ¶ ～에 발을 걸치다 have 〔rest〕 *one's* feet on the stirrups / ～에 발을 헛 걸치다 miss *one's* stirrups.

**등잔**(燈盞) an oil cup for a lamp; a lampoil container. ¶ ～불 a lamplight / ～ 밑이 어둡다 《속담》 We are apt to overlook important things that lie near hand. *or* It is often difficult to see what's right in front of your eyes.

**등장**(登場) ① 『연극』 entrance on the stage; entry. ～하다 enter the stage; come onstage; appear 《on the television》; make an entrance. ¶ (리어왕) ～ Enter (King Lear). ② 《나타남》 advent; appearance. ～하다 appear on the scene; make an appearance; enter the field. ¶ 신무기의 ～ the advent of new weapons / 노인학은 비교적 새롭게 ～한 학문이다 Gerontology 「is a fairly new arrival 〔is something of a newcomer〕 in the scientific field.
◉ ～순 order of appearance. ～인물 *dramatis personae* (L.); the characters 《in a play 〔novel〕》.

**등재**(登載) registration; record. ～하다 register; record.

**등정**(登頂) ～하다 reach 〔get to〕 the top 〔summit〕 of a mountain. ¶ 마나슬루 산 ～에 성공하다 conquer the summit of Mt. Manaslu.

**등정**(登程) starting 〔setting out〕 on a journey; departure. ～하다 start 〔set out〕 on a journey; depart.

**등줄기** the line of the backbone. ¶ ～가 아프다 have a pain in *one's* back / ～에 식은 땀이 흘렀다 I felt a chill go down my spine.

**등지**(等地) (and) like places. ¶ 마산 ～ Masan and like places.

**등지느러미** a dorsal fin.

**등지다** ① 《틀어지다》 be(come) alienated 〔estranged〕 《from》; break (up) 〔split〕 《with》; fall out 《with》. ¶ …와 등지고 있다 be on bad terms with…; be at odds with…; 《미구어》 be at outs 〔on the outs〕 with… / 형제가 서로 등진 지 오래다 It has been a long time that the two brothers are at odds. / 그들은 서로 등져서 내왕하지 않는다 They are at odds with each other and are no longer on visiting terms.
② 《배반하다》 rise 〔turn〕 against 〔(up)on〕; betray; 《돌아서다》 turn *one's* back on; leave (떠나다). ¶ 고향을 ～ leave *one's* home behind 《*one*》 / 나라를 ～ turn against *one's* country; leave *one's* native country / 세상을 ～ turn *one's* back on the world; forsake 〔hide *oneself* from〕 the world; die (죽다) / 친구를 ～ turn against *one's* friend / 아직 젊은 나이에 그녀는 세상을 등지고 수녀가 되었다 Though still young, she renounced the world and became a nun. / 그는 세상의 부귀를 등지고 은퇴해 산다 He leads a secluded life having put aside worldly fame and wealth.
③ 《등뒤로 하다》 《*one's* back》 lean against. ¶ 벽을 등지고 with *one's* back against the wall / 등진 가재 a person who is relying on another's authority 〔power, influence〕 / 벽을 등지고 서다 stand 「leaning 〔with *one's* back〕 against a wall / 그 도시는 산을 등지고 있다 The town has 〔lies with〕 hills at the back.

**등질**(等質) homogeneity. ¶ ～의 homogeneous.

**등짐** a pack 〔burden〕 carried on *one's* back. ¶ ～을 지고 with a burden on *one's* back / ～을 지다 carry a burden on *one's* back. ◉ ～장수 a pack-peddler.

**등차**(等差) equal difference; gradation (차등). ◉ ～급수〔수열〕 『수학』 arithmetical progression 〔series〕. ～세〔세율〕 discriminating duty 〔rates〕; graded duty 〔tariff〕.

**등창**(—瘡) 『한의』 an abscess 〔a tumor〕 on *one's* back.

**등청**(登廳) ～하다 attend the office; go to the office; go to work.

**등촉**(燈燭) a lamplight and a candlelight; a lighted lamp; a light.

**등축**(等軸) an equal axis (*pl.* axes). ¶ ～의 『물리·생물』 isodiametric.

**등치**(等値) equal value; 『논리』 equipollence. ¶ ～의 equivalent; equipollence.

**등치다** ① 《때리다》 pat 〔slap〕 《*a person*》 on the back. ② 《빼앗다》 extort 《money by threat》; blackmail 《*a person* of *his* money》; squeeze; bully 〔wring, screw〕 《money out of *a person*》; racketeer. ¶ 등쳐먹는 놈 a blackmailer; an extortioner / 아무를 ～ browbeat *a person* out of money; hector *a person* out of *his* money; bully 〔screw〕 money out of *a person* / 등쳐 먹고 살다 live by racketeering / 등치고 간 내먹다 drive 《*a person*》 into an awkward situation and proceed to take advantage of it / 등치고 배 문지르다 do 《*a person*》 harm by both threatening and coaxing.

**등친**(等親) ＝친등(親等).

**등태** a straw-mesh container carrying a burden on the back.

**등판**(登板) ～하다 〖야구〗 take the plate 〔mound〕; go to the mound.

**등피**(燈皮) 《유리 꺼펑이》 a lamp chimney; a globe (둥근). ¶ ～를 씌우다 put a chimney on 《a lamp》.

**등하불명**(燈下不明) One has to go abroad to get news of home. ⇨등잔.

**등한**(等閑) ～하다 (be) negligent; careless. ¶ ～히 negligently; carelessly / ～히 하다 neglect 《*one's* studies》; give no heed 《to》; slight 《a guest》; disregard; make light 〔little〕 《of》; leave to chance / 교육을 ～히 하다 neglect *one's* education / 일을〔직무를〕 ～히 하다 slight 〔neglect〕 *one's* work 〔duties〕 / ～시하다 neglect; be neglectful of; be negligent in; slight.

**등허리** 《등과 허리》 the back and the waist; 《허리의 등쪽》 the back of the waist.

**등화**(燈火) a light; a lamplight. ¶ ～ 가친(可親)하다 sit reading far into the night / ～ 가친의 계절 the best season for reading. ◉ ～관제 control of lights; a blackout; a brownout; a dimout: ～관제하다 black out. ～신호 signaling with a lantern 〔flash light, torch〕.

**-디** ① 《-더냐》 have it been observed that…?; be it known that…?; did you hear that…?; have you been told that…?; did you notice that…?; have you found that…? ¶ 싼 것이 있디 Did you notice if they had any cheap ones? / 얼마나 크디 How big was it? ② 《강조》 really be; be ever so; be very 〔quite〕. ¶ 검디검다 be real black / 크디크다 be ever so big.

**디기탈리스** 〖식물〗 a foxglove; 〖약〗 digitalis.

**디너** (a) dinner. ¶ ～에 초대 받았다 I was invited to dinner. ◉ ～쇼 a dinner with a floor show.

**디데이** 《공격·계획 등의 개시일》 (the) D-day.

**디도서**(—書) 〖성서〗 the Epistle of St. Paul to Titus; Titus (생략 Tit.).

**디디다** ① 《땅을》 step on; tread on. ¶ 땅을 ～ step on the ground; tread the soil / 외국땅에 발을 ～ step 〔set foot〕 on foreign soil; visit a foreign land / 첫발을 내～ make the first step 《toward》 / 한 발짝 내～ take a step forward / 정계에 발을 내～ enter upon a political career / 새로운 인생으로 한 발짝 내～ embark on a new career 〔life〕 / 발을 헛〔잘못〕 ～ miss *one's* foot 〔step〕; lose *one's* footing; take 〔make〕 a false step. ② 《누룩을》 tread malted flour paste into cakes.

**디디디** 《시외 자동 전화》 D.D.D. [<*di*rect *d*istant *d*ialing]

**디디티** D.D.T. [<*d*ichloro-*d*iphenyl-*t*richloro-ethane]

**디딜방아** a treadmill; a mortar (worked by treading).

**디딤돌** a stepstone; 《수단》 a stepping-stone; a step. ¶ ～을 밟고 over stepping-stones / 장차 출세하는 ～이 되다 serve as a stepping-stone for future success / 실패를 성공의 ～로 삼다 make *one's* failure a stepping-stone to success.

**디램** 〖컴퓨터〗 《동적램》 DRAM. [<*d*ynamic *r*andom *a*ccess *m*emory]

**디렉터** a director.

**디멘션** 〖물리〗 a dimension.

**디모데** 〖성서〗 ◉ ～전서〔후서〕 The First 〔Second〕 Epistle of St. Paul to Timothy; Ⅰ〔Ⅱ〕 Timothy (생략 Tim.).

**디밀다** ⇨들이밀다.

**디버그** 〖컴퓨터〗 《프로그램 고치기》 debug; debugging.

**디비** 〖컴퓨터〗 《축적된 기록 정보》 DB [<*d*ata *b*ase]; 《방송》 digital broadcasting.

**디스카운트** (a) discount. ¶ 그녀는 정가에서 20% ～해 줬다 She gave 〔allowed〕 a discount of 20% off the fixed prices. ◉ ～ 세일 a discount sale.

**디스코** 〖음악〗 disco.

**디스코테크** a discotheque.

**디스크**[1] 〖의학〗 hernia of an intervertebral disk; a ruptured disk.

**디스크**[2] a disk; a disc. ◉ ～ 드라이브 〖컴퓨터〗 《디스크를 움직여 읽고 쓰는 장치》 a disk drive. ～자키 〖방송〗 a disk 〔disc〕 jockey; a deejay 《구어》.

**디스템퍼** 〖의학〗 distemper.

**디스토마** 《편충》 a distoma; flukes; 《병》 distomiasis. ¶ 간～ distoma hepaticum.

**디스포저** 《싱크대의 음식 찌꺼기 분쇄 장치》 a disposer.

**디스플레이장치**(—裝置) 〖컴퓨터〗 《정보 표시 장치》 a display unit.

**디아스타아제** 〖생화학〗 diastase.

**디아이와이** DIY. [<*d*o *i*t *y*ourself]

**디엔에이** 《디옥시리보 핵산》 DNA. [<*d*eoxyribo*n*ucleic *a*cid]

**디자이너** a designer; a stylist 《미》. ¶ 공업〔상업〕～ an industrial 〔a commercial〕 designer / 의상 ～ a dress designer / 인테리어 ～ an interior designer.

**디자인** designing; a design. ～하다 design; make 〔draw〕 a plan 《of》. ¶ ～료 a design fee / 이 옷은 김 씨의

~에 따라 만든 것이다 This dress has been made to Mr. Kim's design.

**디저트** a dessert. ¶ ~용 나이프〔접시, 스푼〕 a dessert knife 〔plate, spoon〕 / 아이스크림이 ~로 나왔다 Ice cream was served as dessert.

**디젤** ① 《독일의 기계 기사》 Rudolf Diesel (1858-1913). ② 《기관》 a diesel. ¶~엔진을 동력으로 하는 배 a diesel-powered〔-driven〕 vessel. ◉ ~기관 a diesel 〔Diesel〕 engine. ~동차 a diesel railcar. ~전기 기관차 a diesel-electric locomotive.

**디지털** digital. ◉ ~비디오 디스크 a digital video disc (생략 DVD). ~스케일 a digital scale. ~시계 a digital clock. ~오디오 디스크 a digital audio disc (생략 DAD). ~전화 a digital telephone. ~카메라 a digital camera. ~컴퓨터〔계산기〕 a digital computer. ~텔레비전 a digital television. ~통신 digital communication. ~팩시밀리 a digital facsimile.

**디티피** 《탁상출판》 DTP. [<the *d*esk*t*op *p*ublishing]

**디프테리아** 『의학』 diphtheria. ¶ ~ 예방의 antidiphtheritic / ~의 증상 diphtherial symptoms. ◉ ~혈청 antidiphtheria serum.

**디플레(이션)** 『경제』 deflation. ◉ ~정책 a deflationary policy.

**디피이** 《현상, 인화, 확대》 D.P.E. [<*de*veloping, *p*rinting, and *e*nlarging]

**딜러** a dealer. ¶ 중고차~ a dealer in used cars; a used-car dealer.

**딜럭스** deluxe 《cars》. ¶ ~한 식사 a deluxe meal / ~한 여행을 하다 travel first-class. ◉ ~판(版) an edition deluxe; a deluxe edition. ~호텔 a hotel deluxe.

**딜레마** a dilemma. ¶ ~에 빠지다 fall into 〔be on the horns of〕 a dilemma; be (caught) in a dilemma.

**딜레탕트** a dilettante. (*pl.* -ti, -tes).

**딩딩하다** ① 《힘이》 (be) strong; robust; sturdy; stout. ¶ 노인이 아직 ~ The old man is still hale and hearty. ② 《단단하다》 (be) hard; solid; firm; 《팽팽하다》 be stretched to the full; (be) tense; taut. ¶ 젖이 불어 ~ a breast is swollen with milk / 배가 불러 ~ have a full stomach / 종기가 밑이 들어 ~ The abscess is deep-rooted and hard. ③ 《기반이》 (be) stable; secure; solid. ¶ 딩딩한 부자 a fabulously rich person / 살림이 ~ be well off / 재정적 배경이 ~ have a stable backing of finance.

**딩크족**(―族) 《아이를 갖지 않는 맞벌이 부부》 DINKs. [<*D*ouble *I*ncome *N*o *K*ids]

**따갑다** ① ⇨뜨겁다. ② 《쑤시다》 (be) stinging; tingling; prickly; pricking; have a tingling pain. ¶ 눈이 ~ have a stabbing pain in *one's* eye / 뙤약볕에 살이 ~ *one's* skin smarts under the sun's rays / 벌한테 쏘인 데가 ~ The spot stung by the bee is tingling. / 귀가 따갑도록 욕을 먹었다 He had his head scolded off.

**따귀** ⇨ 뺨따귀. ¶ ~를 때리다 slap 《*a person*》 on the cheek; give 《*a person*》 a box on the ear / ~를 맞다 get a box on the ear.

**따끈따끈** ~하다 (be) warm; hot; hot from the oven (빵 따위); [서술적] glow (with warmth). ¶ ~한 만두 a steaming hot bun / ~한 고구마 a pipping hot sweet potato.

**따끈하다** (be) hot; heated; warm; be nice and warm. ¶ 따끈한 커피 hot coffee / 나는 따끈한 음식이 좋다 I like my food hot.

**따끈히** (so that it is) hot; good and hot. ¶ 물을 ~ 끓이다 boil water good and hot / 술을 ~ 데우다 warm up *sul* 〔wine〕 in 《a kettle》; heat wine / 우유를 ~ 데우다 scald milk warmly.

**따끔거리다** sting; prick; tingle; be stinging; be tingling; smart 《with pain》. ¶ 귀가 ~ have a sharp pain in *one's* ear / 종기가 ~ a boil is excruciating / 목이 ~ have a sore throat.

**따끔따끔** stinging; pricking; tingling; piercingly painful; excruciating. ¶ ~ 아프다 have a sharp 〔stabbing. tingling〕 pain; be stinging / 옆구리가 ~ 쑤신다 I have stitches 〔a stick〕 in my side. / 상처가 ~ 쑤신다 The cut smarts.

**따끔령**(―令) a strict order.

**따끔하다** ① 《쑤시다》 (be) piercingly painful; stinging; pricking; burning; smarting; tingling. ¶ 따끔하게 아프다 have a prick / 바늘로 따끔하게 찌르다 prick with a needle. ② 《호되다》 (be) sharp; harsh; severe; caustic; vitriolic; incisive; cutting; bitter. ¶ 따끔한 비평 (a) harsh 〔caustic, hotly worded〕 criticism / 따끔하게 비꼬는 말을 하다 deliver 《*a person*》 pinprick; make a cutting remark 〔sarcasm〕 《at》 / 따끔하게 꾸지람을 듣다 be severely 〔warmly, roundly〕 scolded / 따끔한 맛을 보다 have a bitter experience 〔a hard time of it〕 / 따끔한 맛을 뵈다 give 〔teach〕

《*a person*》 a lesson; give 《*a person*》 a good thrashing / 따끔하게 혼을 내다 make 《*a person*》 smart 〔sweat〕 《for it》.

**따님** your 〔his〕 daughter.

**따다**[1] ① 《붙은 것·달린 것을》 pick; pluck; nip 〔pinch, trim〕 《off》; gather (따 모으다). ¶ 꽃을 ~ pluck 〔pick〕 a flower / 딸기를 ~ pick strawberries / 사과를 ~ pick 〔gather〕 apples / 싹을 ~ nip buds / 나무 열매를 ~ gather nuts.
② 《터뜨리다》 open; lance. ¶ 곪은 데를 ~ open a boil.
③ 《요약하다》 pick out; sum up; summarize; digest; epitomize. ¶ 요점을 ~ pick out the main points; sum up; put it in a nutshell.
④ 《인용하다》 quote 《from a book》; cite 《an instance》; 《표절하다》 plagiarize; 《구어》 crib. ¶ 남의 글귀를 ~ crib another's words; plagiarize / 춘향전에서 ~ make selections 〔quote a passage〕 from the *Ch'unhyangjŏn*.
⑤ 《얻다·받다》 get; take; obtain; gain; score. ¶ 금메달을 ~ be awarded a gold medal / 만점을 ~ get 〔win〕 full marks 《in》 / 면허를 ~ obtain 〔secure〕 a license / 자격을 ~ obtain a qualification 《for》; qualify 《to, for》 / 좋은 점수를 ~ get 〔obtain〕 good marks / 학위를 ~ get 〔take, receive〕 a degree.
⑥ 《돈을》 gain; get; win 《by gambling》. ¶ 노름에서 돈을 ~ win money in gambling.

**따다**[2] ① 《만나주지 않다》 pretend to be out; feign absence; be "not at home" to 《a caller》; refuse to see 《a caller pretending to be away from home》. ¶ 그는 귀찮은 손님이 오면 언제나 따버린다 He is always out to unwelcome guests. ② 《따돌리다》 leave 《*a person*》 out; reject; exclude; 《미행자 등을》 give 《*a person*》 the slip; shake off 《*a person* following *one*》; throw 〔put〕 《a detective》 off the scent 〔track〕. ¶ 그들은 나를 따버리고 자기들만 소풍갔다 They all went off on a picnic, leaving me out.

**따다**[3] 《다르다》 be not related; (be) irrelevant; different; another. ⇨ 딴[2]. ¶ 딴 문제 an irrelevant question; quite another question.

**따돌리다** leave 《*a person*》 out (in the cold); exclude; shun; boycott; shut 《*a person*》 out; 《사회적으로》 ostracize. ¶ 동네에서 따돌림을 받다 be excluded from the village life / 나를 따돌리고 저희들끼리만 모임을 가졌다 They left me out of their meeting. / 그는 반친구들에게 따돌림을 받고 있다 He is excluded 〔alienated〕 from his classmates. *or* He is shunned by his classmates. / 무슨 이유인지 그는 회사의 동료들로부터 따돌림을 받고 있다 For some reasons or others, he is given the cold shoulder by his colleagues at the office.

**따뜻이** ① 《덥게》 warm(ly); hot. ¶ 방을 ~ 데우다 heat a room warm; warm (up) a room / 몸을 ~하다 keep *oneself* warm; clothe warm. ② 《온정으로》 warmly; kindly; warm-heartedly. ¶ ~ 대하다〔대접하다〕 treat 〔entertain〕 《*a person*》 warmly / ~ 맞이하다 give 《*a person*》 a warm reception; receive 《*a person*》 warmly 〔cordially, with warm hands〕 / 사람들은 피난민을 ~ 맞았다 People received 〔welcomed〕 the refugees warmly.

**따뜻하다** ① 《덥다》 (be) warm; mild. ¶ 따뜻한 겨울 a mild 〔soft〕 winter / 따뜻한 날씨 warm weather / 따뜻한 방 a warm room / 따뜻한 옷 warm clothes / 따뜻해지다 get warm; warm (up); grow warmer / 오늘은 ~ It's nice and warm today. (★ 단지 warm을 쓰면 '덥다'의 뜻에 가깝다) / 나날이 따뜻해지고 있다 It's getting warmer day by day. ② 《음식이》 (be) hot. ¶ 따뜻한 우유 hot milk / 따뜻할 때 먹어라 Eat it while it's hot. ③ 《마음이》 (be) kind; warm; genial; cordial; warm-hearted. ¶ 따뜻한 가정 a cheerful 〔sweet〕 home / 따뜻한 동정 warm sympathy / 따뜻한 마음 a warm 〔kindly〕 heart / 따뜻한 환영을 받다 receive a cordial 〔warm, hearty〕 welcome / 따뜻한 손길을 뻗치다 extend kindly help to 《the poor》 / 그는 마음이 따뜻한 사람이었다 He was a warm-hearted man. / 나는 부모〔형제〕의 따뜻한 정을 모른다 I am a stranger to parental 〔fraternal〕 affection. *or* I don't know what it is to have parental 〔fraternal〕 love. / 우선 따뜻한 대접에 감사드립니다 First, I'd like to thank you for your hearty hospitality. ④ 《색이》 ¶ 따뜻한 색 a warm color.

**따라가다** ① 《사람·길 등을》 follow; follow (close) on the heels of 《*a person*》; 《함께》 go along 《with》; accompany; 《뒤를 밟다》 shadow; tag 〔trail〕 along. ¶ 길을 ~ follow a path 〔road〕 / 사절단을 ~ accompany a delegation; join the retinue of a mission / 아버지를 ~ go along with *one's* father; follow *one's* father / 우리는 그의 바로 뒤를 따라갔다

We followed close behind him. / 개는 주인 뒤를 따라갔다 The dog tagged along after his master.
②《남 하는 대로》 follow; follow suit; obey; act upon. ⇨ 따르다[1] ②.
③《뒤지지 않게》 catch up with 〔to〕; keep up 〔pace〕 with. ¶ 앞서 가는 사람을 ~ catch up with a person ahead / 너무 빨리 걸어서 따라가지 못하겠다 You walk so fast I can't keep up with you. / 강의가 너무 어려워서 따라갈 수 없었다 The lecture was too difficult for me to follow.
④《겨루다》 compete with; be a match for; stand abreast with《*a person*》; equal; rival. ¶ 따라갈 사람이 없다 be peerless; have no equal 〔peer〕; stand unrivaled 〔unequaled, unsurpassed〕《among *one's* contemporaries》/ 영어에 있어서 그를 따라갈 사람이 없다 No one can compete 〔compare〕 with him in English.

**따라다니다** 《함께》 follow 《*a person*》; accompany; 《뒤를》 follow (up); tag along after; track 〔shadow, run after〕《*a person*》; 《성가시게》 follow; prowl 〔hacker〕《after》; dangle《about, after, round》. ¶ 여자 꽁무니를 ~ chase after a girl; hang about a girl / 형사가 ~ be shadowed by a plainclothesman / 그 소년은 언제나 누나 뒤를 따라다닌다 The boy is always tagging along after his big sister. / 그녀의 꽁무니를 따라다닌 남자도 많았다 Many a man chased around after her.

**따라붙다** overtake; catch 〔come〕 up 《with》; 《점차》 gain on 〔upon〕. ¶ 그 분야에서 미국 수준에 ~ catch up with the United States in the field / 순찰차가 우리 차를 따라붙고 있었다 A squad car was gaining on us.

**따라서** ①《그러므로》 accordingly; consequently; therefore; hence; for this 〔that〕 reason; so that. ¶ 그 물건은 품질이 좋고 ~ 값도 비싸다 The article is of fine quality, and therefore its price is high. / 그는 놀고만 있고 ~ 학교 성적도 나쁘다 He is idling all the day with the consequence that his school record is very poor.
②《…에 따라》 in accordance with; in conformity to 〔with〕; according to; in line with. ¶ 희망에 ~ in compliance with *one's* wishes / 당신 지시에 ~ in accordance with your instructions / 지위〔능력〕에 ~ according to *one's* position 〔ability〕/ 필요에 ~ as occasion calls 〔demands〕; as the need arises / 법에 ~ 처벌하다 punish according to 〔in accordance with〕 the law / 관습에 ~ 행동하다 behave according to 〔conform to〕 custom / 그는 자기의 신조에 ~ 행동했다 He acted up to his principle. / 우리는 규칙에 ~ 경기를 해야 한다 We must play the game according to its rules.
③《…함에 따라》 in proportion to 〔as〕; according as; as. ¶ 날이 지남에 ~ as days go by; as time passes; with the passing 〔lapse〕 of time / 수입이 늚에 ~ according 〔in proportion〕 as *one's* income increases / 문명이 발달함에 ~ as civilization progresses; with the progress of civilization / 나이가 많아짐에 ~ 그는 고집이 더욱 세어졌다 The older he grew, the more obstinate he became.
④《끼고》 along; by; alongside《of》; parallel to 〔with〕. ¶ 강둑을 ~ 가다 go along the river bank / (도로가) 해안을 ~ 나 있다《the road》 skirt 〔run along〕 the coast / 돌담을 ~ 10분쯤 걸어가자 곧 바닷가가 나왔다 We walked along the stone wall for about ten minutes, and soon came to the shore.
⑤《모방하여》 after《the example of》; in 〔after〕 the manner of; in imitation of. ¶ 선례에 ~ 하다 follow a precedent / (발음 연습 등에서) 나를 ~ 하세요 Repeat after me.

**따라오다** ①《함께》 come along with; follow; tag along《with *a person*》; accompany; 《좇아오다》 keep up with; follow on the heels of. ¶ 나를 따라오너라 Follow 〔Come with〕 me. / 그는 교육 사절단을 따라왔다 He has come accompanying an educational mission. / 내가 먼저 가고 아이들이 뒤에 따라왔다 I went first and the children tagged along 〔behind〕.
②《남이 하는 대로》 follow (suit); do likewise 〔the same〕; be modeled《on》. ¶ 만일 미국이 찬성하면 영국도 이에 따라올 것이다 If the U.S. agrees, Britain will follow suit.
③《겨루다》 compete; rival; equal; be a match for. ¶ 따라올 사람이 없다 have no equal 〔match〕; stand unrivaled / 영어에서 네가 날 따라오려면 아직 멀었다 It will be a long time before you can take me on in English.

**따라잡다** = 따라붙다.

**따라지** ①《난쟁이》 a dwarf; a pigmy; a shorty; a midget. ②《노름의》 one point; the lowest point (in a card game). ③ 《따분한 존재》 a miserable existence.

◉ ~목숨 a life lived under another's thumbs; slavish life; a life in bond. ~신세 a wretched life; a life of bare substance.

**따로** ① 《별개로》 separately; apart. ¶ …와는 ~ apart 〔aside, separately, independently〕 from… / ~ 살다 live separately / ~ 두다 keep 〔set〕 《*a thing*》 separately 〔apart〕 / 방을 ~ 잡아두다 reserve a room separately 《for》; set apart a room 《for》 / 그녀는 남동생 몫으로 케이크를 ~ 남겨 두었다 She set aside some cakes for her brother.
② 《여분·별도》 extra; additionally; in addition; besides. ¶ 그에게는 ~ 20만 원의 수입이 있다 He has an extra 〔additional〕 income of two hundred thousand won. / 방세는 5만 원이고 식비는 ~ 낸다 Lodging costs 50,000 won and board extra. / 더 좋은 좌석을 원한다면 ~ 돈을 내야 합니다 You must pay extra if you want a better seat.
③ 《특별히》 specially; particularly. ⇨ 별로. ¶ ~ 볼 일〔말할 것〕은 없다 I have nothing particular to do 〔say〕. / ~ 이렇다 할 이유는 없다 I have no particular reason for it. / ~ 이렇다 할 일은 일어나지 않았다 Nothing mentionable has happened.

**따로나다** 《살림을》 establish 〔set up〕 a branch family; make a separate home.

**따로내다** 《살림을》 make 《*a person*》 establish a separate home. ¶ 아우를 ~ have 〔let〕 *one's* younger brother establish a separate home.

**따로따로** separately; severally; respectively; individually; apart. ¶ 길을 ~ 가다 go respective 〔several〕 ways / ~ 싸다 wrap up separately / ~ 두다 keep 《*things*》 separate / ~ 돌아가다 go home separately 〔each *one's* own way〕 / ~ 행동하다 act individually / 죄수를 ~ 가두다 keep prisoners separate from each other / 입장료를 ~ 내다 pay admission one by one; pay each for *one's* own ticket / 함께 오지 말고 ~ 오너라 Come one by one, not in a group. / 그 형제는 ~ 살고 있다 The brothers live apart 〔each by himself〕. / 계산은 ~ 해주세요 Give us separate bills, please. / 이 브로치 두 개는 ~ 싸 주세요 Please wrap up these two brooches separately.

**따르다**[1] ① 《따라가다》 (***a***) 《뒤를》 follow; go after; follow on the heels of 《*a person*》; 《뒤를 밟다》 shadow 《the suspect》; dog 《*a person's*》 steps; track; trace; 《수행하다》 follow; go with; accompany. ¶ 아무의 뒤를 ~ follow *a person;* go after *a person;* follow on the heels of *a person* / 엄마 뒤를 ~ tag along after *one's* mother / (행렬 등의) 뒤를 ~ follow 〔bring〕 up the rear. (***b***) 《시류·유행 등을》 follow; go with; pursue. ¶ 대세를 ~ follow the general trend; swim with the tide / 시류에 ~ go with the stream 〔tide〕 / 유행을 ~ follow 〔run after〕 the fashion.
② 《본뜨다》 follow; follow suit; model *oneself* 《on, after》; tread in 《*a person's*》 steps. ¶ 선례를 ~ follow a precedent / 선인을 ~ follow in the footsteps 〔wake〕 of *one's* forefathers / 표준에 ~ be conformable to a standard.
③ 《복종하다》 obey; be obedient to 《*a person*》; come 〔keep〕 to heel; 《굴하다》 yield 〔submit〕 to; give in to 《*a person's* view》. ¶ 따르지 않다 disobey / 아무의 의견에 ~ defer to *a person's* opinion / 당 방침에 ~ toe 〔follow〕 the party line / 조건〔설득〕에 ~ yield to conditions 〔persuasion〕 / 지시에 ~ obey 〔follow〕 《another's》 directions / 그는 상사의 명령에 따랐다 He obeyed his boss's orders.
④ 《준수하다》 observe; obey; abide by; conform to 《custom》; act upon 《*a person's* advice》. ¶ 다수결에 ~ abide by the decision of the majority / 법을 따르지 않다 defy the law / 국법에 ~ obey 〔be obedient〕 the law.
⑤ 《응하다》 comply with; accede to. ¶ 요구에 ~ comply with 《*a person's*》 request / 규칙에 ~ comply with the rule; play by the rules (경기의) / 제안에 ~ accede to a proposal.
⑥ 《견주다》 compete with; rival; equal; be a match for; stand up to. ¶ 따를 자가 없다 have no equal 〔peer〕; stand unrivaled 〔unequaled〕.
⑦ 《붙좇다》 take to 《*a person*》; get attached to; be fond of; 《인기가 있어》 be made much of; be a favorite with; be tamed (동물이). ¶ 여자들이 ~ be much sought after by girls 〔women〕 / 아이들이 나를 잘 따른다 Children take to me. / 어린애가 아버지를 잘 따른다 The child is fond of his father. / 그는 부하들이 잘 따른다 He is loved by his men. / 이 개는 누구에게나 잘 따른다 This dog is easily tamed to anybody.

⑧《수반하다》 follow; ensue; go with; accompany; attend; be followed [attended] by. ¶ 불면에 따르는 우울 melancholy attendant on sleeplessness / 여러 가지 어려움이 ~ be attended with various difficulties / 성공에는 흔히 고생이 따른다 Success often attends hard work. / 우주 여행에는 큰 위험이 따른다 Traveling in space involves great risks. / 재물을 가지면 여러 가지 근심이 따른다 Wealth brings with it a number of anxieties.
⑨《의거하다》 be based [founded, grounded] on 《*something*》. ¶ 따라야 할 기준 a rule to go by; an authoritative rule / 사실에 따른 이야기 a story based on fact / 관례에 따라「in conformity with [according to] custom / 규칙에 따라 pursuant to regulations / 충동에 따라 움직이다 act on impulse.

**따르다**[2] 《액체를》 pour 《in, out, into》; fill 《a cup with tea》; put 《water》 in 《a bowl》. ¶ 찻종에 차를 ~ pour tea into a cup / 주전자의 물을 ~ pour water out of a kettle / 잔에 술을 ~ fill a glass with wine / 내가 포도주를 따라 드리지요 Let me help you to some wine. / 그녀는 보온병에서 더운 커피를 잔에 따랐다 She poured hot coffee into the cup from [out of] the thermos.

**따름** 《…할》 just; only. ¶ …ㄹ ~이다 it is just [only] that… / 그는 담배만 피울 ~이었다 He was just (sitting there) smoking. / 애만 쓸 ~이다 I'm just trying, that's all. / 나는 그에게 전화를 했을 ~이다 I had merely telephoned him.

**따리** 《아첨》 flattery; toadying, fawning; adulation; 《미구어》 apple-polishing; 《구어》 soft-soap. ¶ ~(를) 붙이다 flatter; curry favor with; fawn on. ◉ ~꾼 a flatterer; a sycophant; a toady.

**따먹다** ①《과일을》 pick 《an apple》 and eat. ②《바둑·장기 등에서》 take [catch, get] a piece.

**따발총**(一發銃) a Russian submachine「gun.

**따분하다** ①《느른하다》 (be, feel) languid; listless; dull; enervated. ¶ 날씨가 더워 ~ The warm weather makes me feel listless. ②《지루하다》 (be) boring; tiresome; wearisome; irksome; dull; tedious; insipid; 《구어》 dreary; monotonous (단조로운). ¶ 따분한 날씨 dull [gloomy] weather / 따분한 문체 a tedious [monotonous] style / 따분한 사람[것] a boring person [thing]; a bore / 따분한 생활 an insipid (daily) life; a bare living (가난한) / 따분한 세상 the dreary world; wearisome life / 따분한 이야기 a boring tale; dull talk; an insipid conversation / 따분한 얼굴을 하다 look bored; wear a bored look / 따분해지다 become weary [tired] 《of》; be bored 《by, with》; find 《*a matter*》 dull [monotonous]. ③《난처하다》 (be) embarrassing; awkward; helpless (처량하다). ¶ 돈이 없어서 ~ be hard up for money / 이거 참 따분하게 됐군 This is an awkward situation [position]. *or* Things have come to a peculiar pass.

**따사롭다** (be) pretty warm; warmish. ¶ 햇살은 ~ It's pretty warm in the sun. / 봄의 따사로운 햇살을 받고 산책했다 I took a walk in the warm spring sunlight.

**따스하다** (be) warm; mild. ¶ 따스한 물 warm water / 따스한 겨울 a soft [mild, green] winter / 따스한 날씨 warm [mild] weather / 따스한 방 a warm room / 따스해지다 grow [get] warmer / 몸을 따스하게 하다 keep *oneself* warm.

**따습다** (be) comfortably warm; nice and warm.

**따오기** 〖조류〗 a crested ibis.

**따옴표**(一標) quotation marks; 《구어》 quotes. ¶ 큰 ~ double quotation marks / 작은 ~ single quotation marks / ~를 찍다 put in quotes [quotation marks].

**따위** ①《등등》 and so on [forth]; et cetera (생략 etc.); and [or] the like; and many other things. ¶ 사과, 배 ~ apples, pears, and what not / 농작물 ~ agricultural products and the like / 나는 그 상점에서 빵, 커피, 설탕 ~를 샀다 I bought bread, coffee, sugar and so「on [forth] at the store.
②《…같은》 … and such like; such 《*a thing*》 like [as]…; the like 《of…》; (of ) the sort. ¶ 그림·조각 ~ 미술품 works of art such as paintings and sculptures / 이[그, 저] ~ 《*a thing, a person*》 of this [that] sort; such a one; this kind 《of》; this sort 《of》 / 이 ~ 물건 an article of this kind [sort] / 너 ~ your like; the likes of you / 우리 ~에게는 for such as we; for the likes of us / 나는 그림이나 음악 ~는 흥미가 없다 I don't take much interest in such things as painting and music. / 너 ~는 그것을 하지 못한다 You never could do it. / 그는 결코 거짓말 ~를 할 사람이 아니었다 He was

never known to tell a lie. / 감기가 들면 두통, 기침, 신열, 콧물 ～의 증세가 나타난다 A cold produces such symptoms as headache, coughs, fever and sniveling.

**따지다** ① 《가리다》 distinguish 〔discriminate〕 《between right and wrong》; bring 《it》 out 《who is right and who is wrong》. ¶ 좋은 책과 그렇지 못한 책을 ～ discriminate good books from poor ones. ② 《따져묻다》 question (closely); query; call 《*a matter*》 in question; demand an explanation of; inquire of 《*a person*》 about 《*a matter*》; press 〔drive〕 a question; press 《*a person*》 for 〔about〕; examine; cross-examine. ¶ 미심쩍은 점을 ～ have a doubtful point explained by 《*a person*》 / 사실 여부를 ～ inquire into the truth of the matter / 그들이 따지고 드는 통에 그는 자기가 했다고 자백했다 Driven into a corner by their questioning, he admitted that he had done it! ③ 《셈하다》 calculate; count; reckon; figure; compute. ¶ 이자를 ～ compute 〔reckon〕 interest / 비용을 ～ calculate expenses / 손익을 ～ figure up accounts; reckon the profits and losses.

**딱** ① 《소리》 with a bang 〔bump, slam, crash, pop, crack, rap, snap〕. ～하다 bang; slam; crack; crash; pop; go bang 〔slam, crack, crash, pop〕. ¶ 딱 부러지다 break with a snap; snap / 막대기로 딱 때리다 whack 〔thwack〕 《*a person*》 with a stick / 머리를 딱 때리다 rap 《*a person*》 on the head / 머리를 문틀에 딱 부딪치다 bump 〔bang〕 *one's* head against the doorframe. ② 《바라짐·벌림》 with an outward thrust; wide-open. ¶ 가슴이 딱 바라지다 have a broad chest; be broad of chest / 눈을 딱 부릅뜨다 open *one's* eyes wide (as in anger) / 입을 딱 벌리고 with *one's* mouth wide open; agape / 놀라서 입을 딱 벌리다 be agape with wonder 〔surprise〕. ③ 《꼭》 (***a***) 《사물·수량·크기 등이》 perfectly; exactly; to a T; to a nicety; to a hair; like a glove; 《미구어》 on the nose. ¶ 딱 맞는 모자 a close-fitting cap / 딱 들어맞는 말 an apt remark; the right word 《for》 / 옷이 딱 맞다 *one's* clothes fit 「perfectly 〔to a T〕 / 과녁을 딱 맞히다 hit the mark on the nose / 당신이 딱 알아맞혔어요 You've guessed right. / 두 사람의 이야기가 딱 들어맞는다 The accounts of the two men square with each other perfectly. (***b***) 《시간적으로》 exactly; punctually; precisely; just; sharp; to the minute; 《미구어》 on the nose. ¶ 딱 3시에 시작하다 begin at three sharp / 시계가 딱 맞다 a watch keeps good 〔exact〕 time / 제시간에 딱 나타나다 arrive right on time; show up on the dot. (***c***) 《단지·다만》 just; only. ¶ 딱 백 원 just one hundred won / 딱 한 마디만 하다 say just a word / 딱 한 잔만 더 마시다 have just one more glass (of wine). ④ 《버티는 꼴》 firmly; doggedly; stubbornly. ¶ 딱 버티고 서다 stand firmly; won't budge an inch. ⑤ 《단호히》 decisively; resolutely; flatly; firmly; definitely; positively; 《전혀》 (not) by any means; 《영원히·아주》 once for all. ¶ 딱 잘라 거절하다 decline positively; refuse 《*a person's* request》 flatly; give a flat refusal / 딱 결심하다 make up *one's* mind definitely 〔once and for all〕; make a firm resolution / 딱 잘라 말하다 speak flatly / 담배를 딱 끊다 give up smoking once (and) for all / 그런 일은 딱 질색이야 I wouldn't do it for anything.

**딱다그르르** rolling; rumbling; thundering; pounding. ¶ ～ 구르다 roll over and over.

**딱따구리** 〖조류〗 a woodpecker.

**딱따깨비** 〖곤충〗 a kind of grasshopper.

**딱딱** ① 《마주치는 소리》 with repeated bangs 〔crashes, cracks, thuds, smashes〕. ¶ 손뼉을 ～ 치다 clap *one's* hands / 그는 손가락마디를 꺾어서 ～ 소리내는 버릇이 있었다 He had a habit of cracking his finger joints. ② 《부러지는 소리》 snapping continuously. ¶ 나뭇가지가 ～ 부러지다 branches snap from the tree one after another.

**딱딱거리다** snarl 〔snap〕 《at》; dress 《*a person*》 down; 《미구어》 call down; nag 《at》. ¶ 그녀는 늘 남편에게 딱딱거린다 She always snaps at her husband. / 나에게 그런 식으로 딱딱거리지 마시오 Don't snarl at me like that.

**딱딱이** 《나무토막》 wooden clappers. ¶ ～를 치다 beat 〔strike〕 clappers; clap wooden clappers.

**딱딱하다** ① 《단단하다》 (***a***) 《물체가》 (be) hard; solid; dry and hard (말라서). ¶ 딱딱한 나무 hard wood / 딱딱한 의자 〔침대〕 a hard chair 〔bed〕 / 딱딱한 껍질 solid 〔hard〕 shell / 딱딱해지다 become hard 〔hardened, solid〕; harden; be dried and hardened. (***b***) 《질기다》

(be) tough; stiff. ¶ 꼬투리가 딱딱한 완두 tough-skinned green peas / 딱딱한 표지의 책 a book with a stiff cover. ② 《태도·규칙·분위기 등이》 (be) stiff; stiff as a ramrod; stiff-mannered; angular; 《엄격하다》 (be) strict; rigid; hard and fast; 《분위기가》 (be) uncomfortable; (be) formal; strained. ¶ 딱딱한 규칙 rigid regulations; hard-and=fast rules / 딱딱한 법률 용어 cramp law terms / 딱딱한 분위기 an uncomfortable atmosphere / 딱딱한 사람 a strait-laced 〔stiff-necked〕 person; a very formal person / 딱딱한 태도 a stiff manner 〔carriage〕 / 딱딱하게 말하다 speak 〔talk〕 formally; speak like a book / (태도가) 딱딱해지다 freeze up / 딱딱하지 않다 be free and easy / 이 학교 학생들은 딱딱한 규칙에 꼼짝없이 얽매여 있다 The students of this school are strictly bound by hard-and-fast rules. ③ 《문장 등이》 (be) stiff; bookish. ¶ 딱딱한 문장 a bookish 〔stiff〕 style / 그의 소설은 문장이 ~ His novel is written in a stiff style.

**딱바라지다** 《몸이》 be short and plump 〔thick〕; be stocky 〔stockily built〕; 《그릇이》 be wide and shallow. ¶ 딱바라진 중년 남자 a stockily-built middle-aged man.

**딱부릅뜨다** glare 《at》; goggle 《at》. ¶ 눈을 딱부릅뜨고 with glaring 〔angry〕 eyes.

**딱부리** 《눈》 bulging eyes; 《사람》 a pop-eyed person. = 눈딱부리.

**딱새** 〖조류〗 a (crested) flycatcher; a pewee; a redstart. ¶ 검은~ a stonechat / 노랑~ a robin-flycatcher / 유리~ a bush-robin; a Siberian blue-tail.

**딱성냥** a lucifer 〔friction〕 match. ¶ ~을 긋다 strike 〔light〕 a friction match.

**딱장받다** 《도둑을》 torture 《a suspect》; put 《a thief》 on the rack; make 《a suspect》 confess *his* crime; make 《*a person*》 admit *himself* guilty.

**딱정벌레** a (ground) beetle.

**딱지**[1] ① 《상처의》 a (dried) scab; a slough. ¶ ~가 앉다 scab; a scab forms over 《a boil》 / ~가 떨어지다 a scab 「peels away 〔comes off〕. ② 《종이의》 a fleck in paper. ¶ 종이에 ~가 붙어 있다 There is a fleck in the paper. ③ 《껍데기》 a shell; a crust; 《거북·게의》 a carapace. ¶ 게~ a crab shell / 거북의 등~ a tortoise 〔turtle〕 shell; a carapace / 소라~ the shell of a turban shell. ④ 《시계의》 a (watch) case. ¶ 금~ 시계 a gold watch; a watch in a gold case / 시계 뒤 ~ the back of a watch case.

**딱지**[2] (a) rejection; (a) refusal. ¶ ~ 놓다 reject; refuse; snub; give 《*a person*》 a rebuff 〔setdown〕; 《구혼자에게》 give 《a suitor》 the mitten; kick 《*a person's* proposal》 / ~ 맞다 be refused 〔spurned, rejected〕; suffer 〔meet with〕 a rebuff; get snubbed; 《구혼자가》 get the mitten; be kicked / 시험에서 ~ 맞다 be rejected 〔get plucked〕 in the examination.

**딱지**(―紙) ① 《우표·증지 따위》 a stamp; a sticker; a label; a tag (꼬리표); a ticket (교통 위반의). ¶ 우표 ~ a postage stamp / ~ 붙은 marked; notorious; on the blacklist / ~ 붙은 사람 an ex-convict; a (well-known) black-guard; a notorious scoundrel / (교통 순경이) ~를 떼다 give 《a driver》 a ticket; ticket a traffic offender / 주차〔속도〕 위반 ~를 받다 get a parking 〔speeding〕 ticket / 운전 부주의로 ~를 떼이다 be ticketed for careless driving. ② 《놀이딱지》 a pasteboard card. ¶ ~치기를 하다 play a game of slapping a pasteboard card down on the ground in order to turn over that of *one's* opponent. ◉ ~장수 《암표상》 a (ticket) scalper.

**딱총**(―銃) a popgun; 《폭죽》 a fire-「cracker.

**딱총나무** (―銃―) an elder (tree).

**딱하다** ① 《가엾다》 (be) pitiful; pitiable; poor; be too bad; be a pity 〔shame〕. ¶ 딱하게도 sorry 〔sad〕 to say / 딱하게 여기어 out of pity 〔sympathy〕; in pity 《of》 / 보기에 ~ be pitiful to see / 딱하게 여기다 feel 「pity 〔sorry, compassion〕 for 《*a person*》; pity; take 〔have〕 pity 〔compassion〕 《on》 / 딱한 사정을 호소하다 appeal for *one's* sympathy; plead for mercy / 딱할 정도로 바싹 마르다 be miserably thin; be pathetically lean / 몸이 편치 못하다니 ~ It is too bad that you are not feeling well. / 그 광경은 보기에도 딱했다 The sight was painful even to look at.
② 《난처하다》 (be) awkward; embarrassing; annoying; be embarrassed; be at a loss; be in a fix. ¶ 딱한 처지〔입장〕 an embarrassing 〔awkward〕 situation / 딱한 처지에 있다 be awkwardly situated; be in a (miserable) plight 〔predicament〕 / 딱하게도 나는 영어를 잘 알지 못한다 The trouble is that I don't know English very well. / 나의 딱한 입장도 좀 생각해 주게 You

might have a little consideration for my painful position. / 일이 딱하게 됐다 Things have come to a pretty pass.

**딴**[1] 《…로서는》 as; as for (*oneself*); on *one's* part; in *one's* own estimation; in *one's* own way. ¶ 내 딴은 as for myself; on my part; in my thought / 그는 제 딴엔 잘 한다고 생각하고 있다 He fancies himself to be doing it well. / 내 딴엔 최선을 다한다고 한 것이 이 모양이 되었소 Poor as the job is, I have done my best. / 네 딴에는 학자라고 생각하고 있을는지는 모르나 학자가 되기에는 아직 멀었다 You may fancy yourself a scholar, but you have a long way to go before you become one.

**딴**[2] 《다른》 another; (the) other; different; separate; irrelevant. ¶ 딴 날 some other day / 딴 돈 money set aside for another purpose / 딴 방법 another method; a different way / 딴 수작 irrelevant remarks / 어디 딴 곳 some other place; somewhere else / 딴 때에 at another time; in some other time / 딴 가게에서는 at other stores / 딴 종이에 쓰다 write on 「another 〔a separate〕 sheet / 언젠가 딴 날 올 수 없습니까 Can't you come any other day? / 딴 이야기를 합시다 Let us change the subject. / 딴 종이에 문제의 해답만을 써라 Write only the answers to the questions on a separate sheet of paper.

**딴것** 《다른 것》 a different thing; something else; another one; other things; the other; (the) others. (★ another는 an+other로서 「나머지 몇 개 중의 하나」, the other는 「둘 중의 나머지 하나」, the others는 「둘 이상의 나머지」의 뜻). ¶ ～은 젖혀 놓고 first of all; above all; before everything / (이것 말고) ～으로 몇 개 주시오 Give me some others. / 이 스웨터는 마음에 안 드는데, ～을 보여 주시오 I don't like this sweater. Please show me another. / ～은 미루어 쉽게 알 수 있다 The rest can be easily imagined.

**딴꽃가루받이** 〖식물〗 cross-pollination. ¶ ～시키다 cross-pollinate.

**딴데** another place; other places; a different place; some other place; somewhere else; elsewhere. ¶ ～에서 at 〔in〕 another 〔some other〕 place / ～를 보다 look 「away 〔aside〕; take *one's* eyes off 《*one's* book》 / 말을 ～로 돌리다 change the subject / 저 가게가 ～보다 싸다 They sell much cheaper than other stores. / 나는 지금 ～ 약속이 있어서 못 가겠다 I have an engagement now somewhere else so I won't be able to go. / 나는 도서관과 그 밖에 ～에서 자료를 수집했다 I collected the data in the library and elsewhere.

**딴따라패**(—牌) 《연예인을 속되게 이르는 말》 people in 「show business 〔the entertainment world〕.

**딴마음** 《딴생각》 any other intention; 《속셈》 an ulterior motive; a secret purpose; 《반심》 duplicity; treachery; 《악의》 malice; ill will. ¶ ～이 있는 double-faced; double-dealing; treacherous / ～을 갖다〔품다〕 have 「an ulterior motive 〔an axe to grind〕; harbor 〔have〕 a 「secret 〔treacherous〕 intention / ～이 없다 have no ulterior motives; be 「sincere 〔single-hearted, devoted〕 / ～이 없음을 분명히 하다 establish *one's* innocence / 그는 ～이 있어서 그런 것을 나에게 주었는지 모른다 He may have some ulterior motive in giving me such a thing.

**딴말** 《딴소리》 an 「irrelevant 〔improper〕 remark; an absurd remark; 《뒤집는 말》 a double tongue. ¶ ～을 하다 be double-tongued; 《약속을 어기다》 「back out of 〔go back on〕 *one's* word / ～하고 있다 You are 「going 〔flying〕 off 「at 〔on〕 a tangent. / ～ 말고 요점만 말해라 Keep to the point! / 굳게 약속했으니 그도 이제 ～은 하지 않겠지 Since he gave his firm promise, he cannot 「break 〔go back on〕 his word.

**딴맛** a different taste; 《색다른》 a 「particular 〔peculiar, changed〕 taste.

**딴머리** 《덧대어 얹는》 a wig; false hair.

**딴사람** ① 《다른 사람》 another person; other people; (the) others. ¶ ～들 the others; the rest 《of the company》 / ～은 모르거니와 나로서는 for my own part; I don't know about others, but… / 그것은 누군가 ～이 해야 한다 Somebody else ought to do that. / ～은 아무도 모릅니다 Nobody else knows it. / ～ 아닌 당신의 부탁이니 최선을 다하겠습니다 Since the request comes from you (and none other), I will try my best. ② 《달라진 사람》 a changed 「being 〔man〕; a 「new 〔different〕 being. ¶ 그는 이제 아주 ～이 되었다 He is quite an another 〔a different〕 man now. / 전과 비교해 보면 아주 ～ 같다 He looks quite different from what he was. / 수염을 깎더니 아주 ～이 되었다 He looked quite a different person after shaving off his beard.

**딴살림** living apart; a separate living.

～하다 live apart《from》; live in a separate house. ¶～을 차리다 establish a separate home; 《첩을 두다》 keep 〔set up〕 house for mistress / 형제가 각기 ～한다 Each brother has own home.

**딴생각** 《다른》 another idea; a different intention; 《엉뚱한》 an ulterior motive; a secret purpose. ¶～을 품다 have 「an ulterior motive 〔an axe to grind〕.

**딴소리** ＝딴말.

**딴은** 《하기야》 really; indeed; to be sure; I see; well (yes); as for that. ¶～… 하지만 그러나 … it is true …, but … / ～ 옳은 말이오 Indeed you are right. *or* Indeed, so it is. / ～ 그렇군 I see, that's the reason. / ～ 네 말도 그럴듯하다 Hearing what you say, it sounds quite reasonable.

**딴전** 《상관없는 딴 짓을 하다》 irrelevant remarks; an irrelevant act; evading the issue; beating around the bush; going off on a tangent; missing the point. ¶～부리다 make irrelevant remarks; go off on a tangent; get off the subject; do 《*something*》 beside the issue; 《시치미 떼다》 pretend not to know; pretend to be ignorant of; play the innocent / ～ 보다 do another work; neglect *one's* main duty.

**딴죽** 《씨름에서》 a "leg-bracket"; a leg-trip. ¶～걸다 trip 《*a person*》 (up); bracket *one's* leg with a foot / 제 ～에 제가 넘어지다 trip *oneself* up; be hoist with *one's* own petard.

**딴죽치다** ① 《발로》 hit 《*a person*》 on the leg with *one's* foot. ② 《어기다》 「back out of 〔disregard〕 an agreement.

**딴쪽** 《다른 쪽》 another 〔a different〕 direction; the other side.

**딴청** ＝딴전.

**딴판** a completely different state of affairs; a quite unrelated situation. ¶아주 ～이다 be quite unlike 〔different〕; be as different as chalk from cheese / (정세 따위가) ～이 되다 change completely 〔entirely, altogether〕; undergo a (complete) change / 내 예상과는 ～이다 It is quite different from what I expected.

**딸** a daughter. ¶첫딸 *one's* first daughter / 귀여운 딸 *one's* pet daughter / 막내딸 *one's* last daughter / 딸 없는 사위 having the form without the substance / 딸을 낳다 give birth to a daughter / 딸을 시집보내다 marry off *one's* daughter.

**딸기** a berry; strawberries. ¶～를 따다 pick berries. ◉ ～밭 a strawberry field 〔patch (작은)〕. ～술 strawberry wine. ～잼 strawberry jam. ～코 a red-spotted〔-speckled〕 swollen nose; a strawberry nose. ～크림 strawberry and cream. 「the hiccups.

**딸꾹거리다** hiccup (and hiccup); have

**딸꾹딸꾹** with repeated hiccups.

**딸꾹질** (repeated) hiccupping; a hiccup. ～하다 hiccup; have the hiccups. ¶～을 시작하다 get the hiccups; have an attack of hiccups / ～을 참다 catch a hiccup / ～을 하면서 말하다 say between hiccups / ～이 좀처럼 멈추지 않았다 The hiccups wouldn't stop. *or* I couldn't stop my hiccups.

**딸랑－** ⇨ 달랑－.

**딸리다** ① 《붙어 있다》 belong to; be attached to. ¶가구 딸린 셋집 a furnished house to let / 이 열차에는 식당차가 딸려 있다 There is a dining car attached to this train. ② 《남 밑에》 be dependent 《on, upon》; depend 《on》; hang 《on》; be attended 《on》. ¶딸린 가족이 많다 have a large family to support; have many dependents / 형에게 딸려 살다 depend upon *one's* brother for support / 간호사가 딸려 있다 be attended by a nurse. ③ 《딸리거나 지니고 가다》 take 〔bring〕 along; send 《*a person*》 accompanied by 《another》. ¶어린애에게 유모를 딸려 보내다 send a child accompanied by his 〔her〕 nurse.

**딸자식** (―子息) 《남에게》 my daughter.

**땀**[1] 《흘리는》 sweat; perspiration (★ 점잖은 대화에서는 sweat 보다 perspiration을 씀). ¶구슬땀 beads of sweat / 식은땀 a cold sweat; night sweat / 진땀 a sticky 〔clammy〕 sweat / 땀의 결정 the fruits of *one's* labor 〔hard work〕.

땀을: 땀을 흘려 번 돈 money earned by the sweat of *one's* brow; honestly earned money / 땀을 많이 흘리는 사람 a great sweater / 땀을 흘리다 sweat; perspire / 땀을 흘리고 있다 be in a sweat; be sweaty / 땀을 뻘뻘 흘리다 be running 〔streaming〕 with sweat / 진땀을 흘리다 have a sticky sweat; 《혼나다·애먹다》 have a hard time of it / 이마의 땀을 씻다 mop *one's* brow; wipe (the) perspiration from *one's* forehead / 목욕탕에 들어가 땀을 빼다 wash off *one's* sweat in the bath / 땀을 잘 흘리다 sweat easily 〔freely〕.

땀에: 땀에 (흠뻑) 젖다 be wet with perspiration; be drenched 〔soaked〕 in 〔with〕 sweat; be covered with sweat /

땀에 흠뻑 젖어 sweated all over; bathed in perspiration; drenched in sweat.
땀이: 땀이 나다 [사람이 주어] sweat; perspire / 땀이 많이 나다 sweat profusely 〔freely〕; perspire violently / 땀이 쏟아지다 [사람이 주어] break out in sweat; burst into a violent sweat / 옷에 땀이 흠뻑 배다 *one's* clothes are soaked with sweat; *one's* clothes are all sweaty / 등골에 땀이 나다 have perspiration on *one's* back; 《무섭거나 망신으로》 be extremely frightened; be terribly ashamed.
¶ 그는 이마에 구슬땀을 흘리고 있었다 Drops of sweat stood on his forehead. *or* I saw the sweat beading on his forehead. / 손에 땀을 쥐고 경기를 구경했다 I watched the game「breathlessly 〔in breathless suspense〕. / 땀을 흠뻑 흘리면 감기는 낫는다 A good sweat will cure your cold. / 사람이란 이마에 땀을 흘리며 일해야 한다 Man must「work 〔earn his bread〕 by 〔in〕 the sweat of his brow.

**땀²** 《바느질의》 a stitch.

**땀기**(―氣) a bit 〔trace〕 of sweat; moisture with sweat. ¶ 손에 ~가 있다 have a bit of sweat in *one's* palm; *one's* palm is a bit moist 〔sweaty〕.

**땀나다** sweat; perspire; get「in a sweat 〔into perspiration〕; the sweat comes out; 《힘들다》 be hard 〔toilsome〕; take pains. ¶ 땀나는 일 a hard 〔an onerous〕 job; a thing hard to bear; a horrible sweat.

**땀내** the smell 〔reek〕 of sweat. ¶ ~ 나다 smell sweaty; stink of sweat / ~ 나는 옷 garments stinking with sweat; 《wear》 sweaty clothes.

**땀내다** sweat 《a patient》; work up a sweat; induce perspiration; throw 《*a person*》 into a sweat. ¶ 이불을 쓰고 ~ work up a sweat covering *oneself* with bedclothes / 땀을 내어 감기를 떼다 sweat out a cold.

**땀들이다** cool *oneself;* dry *one's* sweat.

**땀띠** prickly heat; (a) heat rash 《미》. ¶ ~가 돋다 have heat rash; suffer from prickly heat / ~가 슬다 heat rash「goes away 〔disappears〕. ◉ ~약 talcum 〔prickly heat〕 powder.

**땀받이** an undergarment for soaking sweat up; 《모자 안쪽의》 a sweatband; 《말안장 밑의》 sweat cloth.

**땀방울** beads of sweat. ¶ 이마에 ~이 맺히다 beads of sweat stand on *one's* brow.

**땀빼다** 《수고하다》 sweat 《with heavy work》; 《애먹다》 suffer severely; sweat (it out); have a hard time of it. ¶ 일하느라 ~ have a hard time in doing a job / 일을 잘못해 놓고 땀뺐다 I sweated for mistake I have made. / 아버지한테 꾸중을 듣느라 땀뺐다 I had to sweat through a lecture from my father. / 변명하느라 그는 땀뺐다 He was all of a sweat trying to explain. 「gland.

**땀샘** 〖해부〗 a sweat 〔perspiratory〕

**땀질** plucking (out) unnecessary things with chisel 〔knife〕. ~하다 chisel 〔cut〕 out 〔away〕.

**땅¹** ① 《대지·지면》 the earth; the ground; land (육지). ¶ 땅을 고르다 roll 〔level〕 the ground; grade the ground / 땅을 파다 dig in the ground; 《농사》 do farming / 땅에 묻다 bury 《*a thing*》 in the ground / 땅이 꺼지다 the ground「gives way 〔collapses〕 / 땅에 앉다〔눕다〕 squat 〔lie down〕 on the (bare) ground / 땅이 흔들리는 것을 느꼈다 I felt the earth shake.
② 《영토》 (a) territory; a land. ¶ 땅을 넓히다 extend *one's* territory / 이국 땅에서 죽다 die in a strange land / 외국 땅을 밟다 tread 〔set foot〕 on foreign soil / 미국 땅을 밟아 본 일이 없다 I have never been to America.
③ 《토지》 land; a piece of land 〔real estate〕; a lot; an estate. ¶ 개인땅 privately-owned land / 땅부자 a great land owner / 땅을 가지다〔팔다, 사다, 빌리다〕 own 〔sell, buy, lease〕 a lot / 나는 서울 교외에 200평방 미터의 땅을 샀다 I bought a 200 square-meter lot in the suburbs of Seoul.
④ 《토양》 soil; earth; land. ¶ 기름진〔메마른〕 땅 fertile 〔sterile〕 soil / 땅을 갈다 till the soil 〔ground〕; cultivate land / 땅을 걸우다 enrich 〔fertilize〕 the soil / 땅이 벼농사에 적당치 않다 The soil is not fit for rice culture.
⑤ [비유적으로] ¶ 오늘날 도덕은 땅에 떨어졌다 Morality has disappeared these days. / 그의 명성은 땅에 떨어졌다 He has entirely lost his reputation. / 그의 위신은 땅에 떨어졌다 His prestige has gone. / 두 사람의 사고 방식에는 하늘과 땅만큼의 차이가 있다 There is a world of difference between their ways of thinking.
◉ 땅문서 a land registration certificate. 땅사기꾼 a land swindler; a fake land broker. 땅사기 사건 a land fraud case. 땅투기 land speculation.

**땅**[2] ①《총소리》 bang; with a bang. ¶ 총을 땅 쏘다 bang a gun. ②《쇳소리》 clang; with a clang.

**땅강아지** 〖곤충〗 a mole cricket.

**땅개** 《개》 a dog built short; 《사람》 a man of short stature.

**땅거미**[1] 《황혼》 twilight; dusk; 《시어》 the gloaming. ¶ ～ 질 때에 at dusk [twilight]; in the (evening) twilight / ～가 진다 The dusk gathers.

**땅거미**[2] 〖동물〗 a ground-[an earth-]spider.

**땅광** a cellar.

**땅굴**(一窟) a tunnel; an underground way [passage]. ¶ ～공사 tunneling work / ～을 파다 dig [cut, bore, build] a tunnel 《through a mountain》.

**땅굽성**(一性) 〖식물〗 (positive) geotropism. ＝향지성.

**땅기다** get [grow, become] stiff. ¶ 옆구리가 ～ feel stiff in the side; *one's* side is stiff / 어깨가 ～ have a stiff shoulder; *one's* shoulders are stiff.

**땅꽈리** 〖식물〗 a ground cherry.

**땅꾼** 《뱀 잡는》 a snake-catcher.

**땅내** the smell of soil; smelling of the ground. ¶ ～ 맡다 《동물이》 settle down in a place; 《식물이》 take root.

**땅덩이** land; the earth (지구); a territory (국토). ¶ ～ 위에 살고 있는 모든 인류 all mankind living on the earth.

**땅딸막하다** (be) short and fat [thick]; thick-set; dumpy; stocky; stockily [chunkily] built. ¶ 중년의 땅딸막한 사람 a stockily-built middle-aged man.

**땅딸보** a dumpy [stocky] person; a stockily [chunkily] built fellow.

**땅땅** 《총소리》 bang-bang; 《쇳소리》 clanging; clang-clang. ¶ 총을 ～ 쏘다 keep banging a gun / ～ 쇠를 벼르다 beat iron clang-clang.

**땅땅거리다** ① 《큰소리치다》 talk big [high and mighty, tall, overbearingly, high-handedly, imperiously]. ¶ 땅땅거린다고 무서워할 내가 아니다 I am not the man to flinch at your high-handed talk. / 그는 일 년만 있으면 큰 돈을 모은다고 땅땅거리고 있다 He is bragging that he can make big money within a year. ② ⇨ 떵떵거리다 ②.

**땅뙈기** a patch of land; a small plot [piece] of field [land]; a lot. ¶ 그가 가진 ～란 얼마 안 된다 He has just a few small patches.

**땅마지기** a few acres of field. ¶ 그 사람 자기네 살아갈 ～나 가졌다 He has a few acres of field, just enough to support his family.

**땅바닥** the bare ground. ¶ ～에 앉다 sit [squat] on the bare ground.

**땅버들** 〖식물〗《갯버들》 a sallow; a pussy willow.

**땅벌** 〖곤충〗 a digger wasp; a sphex.

**땅벌레** 〖곤충〗 a grub.

**땅볼** 〖야구〗 a grounder; a ground ball. ¶ 내야 ～ an infield grounder / 느린 ～ a slow grounder / ～을 치다[잡다] knock [take] a grounder / ～의 안타를 치다 hit into the dirt / ～을 치고 아웃되다 ground out 《to third》.

**땅빈대** 〖식물〗 a spurge; a euphorbia.

**땅세**(一貰) land rent.

**땅속** ¶ ～의[에] in [under] the ground; underground / ～의 보물 buried [underground] treasure / ～에서 파내다 dig 《*a thing*》 out of the ground; unearth.

**땅울림** rumbling of the earth. ～하다 hear an underground rumbling.

**땅임자** a landowner; a landholder.

**땅재주**(一才一) tumbling; a somersault. ¶ ～를 넘다 tumble; perform a somersault; somersault.

**땅질성**(一性) 〖식물〗 negative geotropism. ¶ ～의 geotropic.

**땅콩** a peanut; a groundnut. ◉ ～버터 peanut butter. ～오일 peanut oil. ～장수 a peanuts vendor.

**땅파기** ① digging the soil. ② 《바보짓》 a silly attempt to bicker with a block-head.

**땅파먹다** do farm [mine] work for a living; engage in farming [mining]; dig (dirt) for a living.

**땅풍뎅이** 〖곤충〗 a groundbeetle.

**땋다** braid 《*one's* hair》; plait. ¶ 머리를 ～ braid *one's* hair; 《땋아 늘이다》 wear *one's* hair in a braid [a plait, two plaits] (down the back) / 머리를 땋아 늘인 처녀 a girl in pigtails.

**때**[1] ① 《시간》 time; an hour. ¶ 때가 지나면 in (the course of) time / 때가 흐름[지남]에 따라 as time goes on; with the passing [passage] of time / 때가 되면 in due (course of) time / …와 때를 같이하여(서) at the same time [moment]; concurrently [simultaneously] with / 때를 어기지 않고 punctually; on time / 때를 가리지 않고 at all times / 때를 정하여 at a fixed time; at regular intervals / 때마침 just at the right moment / 때 가는 줄 모르다 be「unconscious of [oblivious to] the passage [lapse, flight] of time / 때를 보내다 pass *one's* time; spend time 《in》/ 때를 아끼다 watch [be careful of] the time; be sparing of time / 때를 알리다

《시계가》 strike the hour; 《홰치다》 crow; announce the dawn / 때를 어기다 be behind time; be not punctual; be late / 때를 어기지 않다 be on time; be punctual / 이제 자야 할 때다 It is time to go to bed. *or* It is time (that) you went to bed. (★ subjunctive를 써서 반드시 you went가 됨. 과거형이 아님).
② 《경우》 a case; an occasion; 《시기》 time; a moment; a season. ¶ 꽃필 때 the flower season / 위험한 때 a time of danger / 전쟁 때 in wartime / 젊었을 때 in *one's* youth; when young / 추수 때 the harvest time / 마침 좋은 때에 just at the right moment; in the nick of time / …한 때는 in time 〔case, the event〕 of… / 때에 따라서 as occasion requires 〔demands〕; as the case may be / 급한 일이 있을 때에는 in the day of trouble; should emergency arise / 때와 경우에 따라 according to the time and circumstances; should time and circumstances permit / 그를 만났을 때 그 이야기를 했다 I told him about it when I saw him. / 그런 쓸데없는 말을 하고 있을 때가 아니다 This is no time for such idle talk. / 그 때에는 의사의 진찰을 받는 것이 좋다 In that case, you had better consult your doctor. / 바로 그때 구급차가 왔다 The ambulance arrived at that moment 〔time〕. / 그러한 기분이 들 때도 있다 There are times when I feel that way. / 이제 이 문제에 대해 생각해야 할 때이다 It's high time (that) this question were gone into.
③ 《기회》 an opportunity; a chance; time. ¶ 때를 못 만난 영웅 an unappreciated hero / 때를 얻지 못한 사람 a person who is out of tune with the times / 다른 때 (at) another time; some other time / 때를 보아 at a favorable opportunity / 때를 얻은, 때에 알맞은 timely; well-timed; opportune; seasonable / 때를 기다리다 wait 〔bide〕 *one's* time; wait for a favorable chance / 때를 놓치다 miss an opportunity / 때를 만나다 have a favorable opportunity; the time is in *one's* favor; get a chance; find an opportunity / 때를 엿보다 watch for an opportunity 〔a chance〕; watch and wait / 때를 타다 avail *oneself* of an opportunity / 자 때가 왔다 Now the time 〔the chance〕 has come. *or* Now is the time 〔chance〕. / 때가 이롭지 못하다 It is not a favorable moment. / 때를 놓치지 마라 Make hay while the sun shines. *or* Strike the iron while it is hot.
④ 《그 당시》 ¶ 그때 then; in those days; at the 〔that〕 time / 그때의 대통령 then President / 서울에 있을 때 when 〔while〕 I was in Seoul / 어렸을 때부터 since *one's* childhood / 그때 그는 프랑스에 있었다 He was in France then. / 그때 그는 여섯 살이었다 He was six years old at that time.
⑤ 《치세》 a reign. ¶ 세종 대왕 때에 in the reign of Sejong the Great.
⑥ 《끼니》 a mealtime; a meal. ¶ 때를 거르다 go without a meal / 간신히 때를 잇다 live from hand to mouth; get a bare livelihood; eke out a miserable existence / 때를 걸렀더니 시장하다 Having skipped a meal, I am hungry. / 하루 한 때밖에 못 먹었다 I had only one meal a day.

**때**[2] ① 《더러움》 dirt; filth; grime; 《물 때》 scum; scale. ¶ 때투성이의 dirty; filthy; grimy / 때가 묻다〔끼다〕 have dirt (on it); get dirty 〔filthy〕; become dirty 〔filthy, grimy, soiled〕; be stained with dirt / 때를 비벼 없애다 scrub off the dirt / 때를 씻다 wash off the dirt / 때를 벗다 become clean; get free of dirt / 때가 빠진다 Dirt comes off. ② 《메부수수함》 unrefinedness; rusticity; 《촌티》 provinciality. ¶ 때벗은 polished (in manners); refined; urbane; free from boorishness / 때를 못 벗은 unpolished; unrefined; uncouth; rustic; 《사람이 촌티 나는》 provincial / 때를 벗다 become polished 〔refined, smart〕; be free from vulgarity 〔boorishness〕 / 그 소녀는 시골에서 와서 아직 때를 벗지 못했다 The girl hasn't got the hayseed out of her hair yet. ③ 《인색》 meanness. ¶ 하는 짓이 때가 끼었다 There is something mean in what he does. ④ 《오명》 a false 〔an unjust〕 charge; a slur; a stain; a blot; disgrace; dishonor. ¶ 때를 벗다 clear *oneself* of a false charge 《of theft》; wipe out 〔away〕 a stain 〔blot〕 on *one's* name.
◉ 때밀이 a body-scrubber (in the public bathhouse).

**때가다** 《잡혀가다》 be taken to 《the police station》; be arrested 〔nabbed〕.

**때구루루** rolling; rumbling. ⇨ 대구루루.

**때그락–** ⇨ 대그락–.

**때까치** 〖조류〗 a butcherbird; a shrike.

**때깔** an attractive shape and color of cloth.

**때곱재기** (bits of ) dirt; filth; grime.

**때꾼하다** be sunken 〔hollow〕 (from exhaustion). ¶ 때꾼한 눈 sunken 〔hollow〕 eyes.

**때다**[1] ① 《잡히다》 be caught; be arrested; be rounded up. ¶ 소매치기가 경찰에 때들어갔다 A pickpocket was arrested by the police. ② 《배척당하다》 be rejected 〔ostracized, boycotted〕.

**때다**[2] 《불을》 kindle; burn 《coal, wood》; make 〔build〕 《a fire》; heat with 《a fire》. ¶ 난로를 ～ make a fire in the stove / 석탄〔장작〕을 ～ burn coal 〔wood〕 / 방에 불을 ～ heat a (hypocausted) room / 땔 것이 없다 have nothing to make a fire with.

**때다**[3] ⇨ 때우다.

**때때로** sometimes; at times; occasionally; (every) now and then; once in a while; at intervals; from time to time.

> 용법 **sometimes** 가장 일반적인 말. 문장 안에서의 위치는 대개 일반동사의 앞, be동사의 뒤, 조동사의 뒤, 때로는 문두에 온다. **at times** occasionally와 거의 같은 뜻. **occasionally** 가끔 기회 있을 때마다 일어난다는 뜻. **now and then** 되풀이해서 불규칙적으로 일어난다는 뜻. 앞에 every를 붙이면 강조하는 뜻이 됨. **once in a while** occasionally와 거의 같은 뜻으로 구어적인 표현. **at intervals** 「사이·간격」을 두고의 뜻. **from time to time** 좀 문어적인 말로 「어느 정도의 정해진 간격을 두고」의 뜻.

¶ ～ 들르다 drop in once in a while / ～ 방문하다 call on 《*a person*》 from time to time / ～ 편지가 온다 There is a letter now and then / 틈이 있을 때 나는 ～ 그림을 그린다 I sometimes paint pictures when I am free. / 그녀는 ～ 늦는다 She is sometimes late.

**때때옷** a colorful festive dress for children.

**때때중** a young Buddhist monk.

**때려눕히다** knock 〔strike〕 《*a person*》 down 〔out〕; floor 《*a person*》 with a blow; beat to *a person's* knee; stretch 《*a person*》 on the ground. ¶ 상대를 한 방에 ～ knock *one's* opponent down 〔floor *one's* opponent〕 with a blow.

**때려부수다** knock 《*a thing*》 to pieces; smash (up); shatter; wreck 《a building》; break 〔batter, tear〕 down 《a house》; [비유적] give a crushing defeat. ¶ 인종 차별의 벽을 ～ batter down racial barriers / 그는 울타리를 때려부쉈다 He smashed down the fence.

**때려죽이다** beat 〔flog〕 《*a person*》 to death; beat the life out of 《*a person*》.

**때려치우다** give 〔throw〕 up; quit; abandon; relinquish. ¶ 학교를 ～ give up 〔withdraw from〕 school / 장사를 ～ quit *one's* business / 직장을 ～ throw up *one's* job.

**때로(는)** sometimes; at times; in some cases; on (some) occasion; once in a while; occasionally. ¶ 나는 ～ 일찍 일어날 때도 있다 Sometimes, I get up early. / ～ 울고 싶을 때도 있다 Sometimes I feel like crying.

**때리다** ① 《치다》 hit; beat; thump; punch; strike; knock; give 《*a person*》 a blow; slap (손바닥으로); 《몽둥이로 계속해서》 thrash; 《곤봉으로》 club. ¶ 머리를 ～ hit 《*a person*》 on the head / 빰을 ～ slap 《*a person*》 on the cheek / 얼굴〔등〕을 ～ hit 〔slap〕 《*a person*》 in the face 〔on the back〕 / 실컷 ～ give 《*a person*》 a good beating / 주먹으로 마구 ～ rain 〔shower〕 blows on 《*a person*》 / 철썩 ～ bop; whop; whap 《구어》 / 빗발이 창문을 세차게 때렸다 The rain lashed 〔beat〕 against the window. ② 《비난하다》 attack; censure; criticize. ¶ 정부 정책을 맹렬히 때리는 연설 a powerful speech attacking government policy.

**때마침** at the right moment; in the (very) nick of time; in good time; just in time 〔season〕; timely; seasonably; opportunely; fortunately; luckily; as good luck would have it. ¶ ～ 들어오다 come in at just the right moment / ～ 나타나다 make 「a timely 〔an opportune〕 appearance.

**때맞다** (be) timely; well-timed; seasonable; opportune. ¶ 때맞은 비 a timely rain / 때맞은 말 a seasonable 〔an opportune〕 remark.

**때문** ¶ … ～에 《원인·이유》 because (of); on account of; owing to; by 〔for the〕 reason of; as; since; for; from; through; by; due to; with; 《덕분에》 thanks to / 그〔이〕 ～에 for that 〔this〕 reason / 무엇 ～에 for what reason 〔purpose〕; what ... for; why; 《근거》 on what ground / 부주의〔태만〕 ～에 through carelessness 〔negligence〕 / 지진 ～에 as a result of the earthquake / …이 없기 ～에 《이유》 for want 〔lack〕 of; 《원인》 from want 〔lack〕 of / 굶주림 ～에 죽다 die of 〔from〕 hunger / 악천후 ～에 비행기는 연착했다 Due to bad weather the plane was late. / 그녀의

성공은 열심히 일한 ～이다 Her success is due to hard work. / 무엇 ～에 왔느냐 What have you come here for? / 너 ～에 무척 걱정했다 You have caused me great anxiety. / 병 ～에 못 왔다 Illness kept me from coming. / 그 사고는 운전자의 부주의 ～에 일어났다 The accident 「happened through 〔was caused by〕 the driver's carelessness. / 그가 힘써 주었기 ～에 우리는 기대 이상의 성공을 거두었다 Thanks to his efforts, we achieved greater success than we had expected.

**때묻다** 《몸·물건이》 become dirty 〔filthy〕; be soiled; 《마음이》 be mean 〔stingy, foul-minded, dirty-minded〕. ¶ 때묻은 stained; blemished; marred / 때묻은 정치인 a tainted politician; an unsavory political old-timer / 때묻지 않은 clean; spotless; stainless; pure / 때묻지 않은 정치가 a clean 〔an unpolluted〕 politician.

**때물** unrefinedness; dirt; boorishness; rudeness; rusticity. ¶ ～(을) 벗다 be urbane; be refined; be polished.

**때아닌** untimely; unseasonable; inopportune. ¶ ～ 꽃 《핌》 off-season flowering; 《꽃》 a blossom out of season / ～ 꽃이 피다 bloom out of season; bloom again / ～ 천둥 소리에 놀라다 be surprised at the unseasonable thunder.

**때없이** at any time; regardless of the time; "just any old time"; irregularly; at irregular intervals. ¶ ～ 밥을 달라고 하다 ask for 〔claim〕 food at any time.

**때우다** ① 《땜질》 solder; tinker; braze. ¶ 주전자를 ～ solder 〔repair〕 a kettle. ② 《깁다》 patch; darn. ③ 《임시 변통으로》 make shift 《with》; manage 《with》; substitute. ¶ …없이 ～ dispense with …; do 〔manage〕 without… / 도넛으로 점심을 ～ substitute doughnuts for regular lunch; make a lunch of doughnuts.

**때죽나무** 〖식물〗 a snowbell.

**땍때구루루** rattling; clattering; rolling; rumbling. ¶ ～ 구르다 roll over and over.

**땔감** fuel; firewood (장작).

**땔나무** firewood; wood for fuel. ¶ ～를 하다 gather 〔collect〕 firewood. ◉ ～꾼 a firewood gatherer; 《순박한 사람을 놓으로》 a naive 〔guileless〕 person.

**땜** 《액땜》 riddance; getting rid of (a preordained misfortune by suffering one of lesser severity). ¶ 수〔팔자〕땜하다 use up *one's* bad luck on something relatively innocuous.

**땜가게** a tinker shop; a soldering shop.

**땜납** solder; pewter. ¶ ～으로 붙이다 solder.

**땜인두** a soldering iron.

**땜일** soldering; tinkering. ～하다 solder; tinker.

**땜장이** (—匠—) a tinker.

**땜질** tinkering; soldering; repairing; mending; patching. ～하다 = 때우다①.

**땟국** dirt; filth; grime. ¶ 얼굴에 ～이 끼다 have dirt on *one's* face.

**땟물** ① 《자태》 *one's* looks; a figure; *one's* appearance. ¶ ～이 훤하다 have a good figure; be handsome. ② 《씻어낸》 dirty water; dirt.

**땟솔** a bath brush; a scrub brush.

**땡**[1] ① 《땡땡구리》 two cards of the same kind; a pair. ② 《행운》 a piece 〔stroke〕 of good luck 〔fortune〕; a lucky break falling with a windfall. ⇨ 땡잡다.

**땡**[2] 《소리》 with a clang.

**땡감** 《덜 익은 감》 an unripe 〔astringent〕 persimmon.

**땡땡** clanging 〔clinging〕 repeatedly; ding-dong; clang-clang. ¶ 종이 ～ 치다 a bell is clanging away / 종을 ～ 치다 keep clanging a bell / 시계가 ～ 치다 a clock is chiming.

**땡땡이**[1] 《장난감》 a toy drum. ◉ ～중 a mendicant priest who goes around clanging a gong.

**땡땡이**[2] loafing; idling. ¶ ～부리는 사람 a loafer; an idler / ～부리다 loaf (on the job) / ～부리다 들켜서 목이 짤리다 be fired because *one* is caught loafing on the job.

**땡땡하다** ① 《팽팽하다》 (be) tight. ② 《속이》 (be) hard; compact; solid; hale and hearty; vigorous. ¶ 땡땡한 감 a hard persimmon / 종기가 부어 ～ a tumor is swollen and hard.

**땡잡다** hit the jackpot; run into good luck; get a break; strike a bonanza; 《구어》 make a killing 《in stocks》. ¶ 그는 그 사업에 투자하여 땡(을) 잡았다 He had invested in the business and made a killing.

**땡추절** a temple housing unworthy 〔fallen〕 monks.

**땡추중** a fallen monk.

**떠가다** float away. ¶ (구름이) 하늘에 ～ scud across the sky.

**떠꺼머리총각** an old bachelor with a pigtail.

**떠나다** ① 《있던 데서》 (*a*) 《출발하다》 start; leave; depart 《from》; set out 〔off〕; take leave of; go away 〔off〕; 《열차 등이》 pull out; 《비행기가》 take off; 《배가》 set sail; sail out; clear 《port》. ¶ 고향을 ～ leave *one's* native

place; leave home / 광주로 ~ leave 〔depart〕 for Kwangju / 여행길을 ~ start on journey; leave on a trip / (열차가) 정거장을 ~ leave 〔get clear of〕 the station / 한국을 ~ leave 〔depart from〕 Korea / 아침 일찍 ~ start early in the morning / 도시를 떠나 여름 별장으로 향하다 leave the city for a summer house / 경비병은 밤새도록 초소를 떠나지 않았다 The guard did not leave his post all night long. / 이제 떠날 시간이다 It's time for us to leave. (***b***) 《물러나다》 leave 〔quit〕 《*one's* post》; resign (from) 《*one's* post》. ¶ 공직을 ~ resign 〔retire〕 from public life / 회사를 ~ leave 〔quit〕 the company / 왕위를 ~ abdicate the throne 〔crown〕 / 그가 직장을 떠난 지 거의 1년이 됐다 It's almost a year since he left his job.
② 《떨어지다》 separate; part from 〔with〕. ¶ 멀리 떠나 살다 live far apart / 책상 곁을 떠나지 않다 be chained to *one's* desk / 그 아이는 엄마 곁을 떠나지 않는다 The child is always at his mother's side. / 그는 이해득실을 떠나 그 일에 헌신하고 있다 He is devoted to the work 「unselfishly 〔from a disinterested motive〕.
③ 《머릿속·마음에서》 be estranged from; be away from; 《잊다》 be out of *one's* head; forget. ¶ 마음에서 떠나지 않다 [사물이 주어] haunt; be ever present in *one's* mind; [사람이 주어] be unable to forget / 그녀의 어두운 얼굴이 내 마음에서 떠나지 않는다 Her dark face haunts me. / 민심은 현정부에서 떠나 있다 「Public sentiment is 〔Popular feelings are〕 estranged from the government. / 그의 마음이 아내를 떠난 지 오래다 It is a long time since he felt love for his wife.
④ 《죽다》 ¶ 세상을 ~ depart (from) this life; pass away; die.

**떠내다** ① 《액체를》 scoop (out, up); dip (out, up); ladle (out, up) (국자로); spoon up 〔out〕 (숟갈로). ¶ 물고기를 뜰채로 ~ scoop fish with a landing net. ② 《초목 등을》 scoop up; 《돌을》 quarry (out). ¶ 뗏장을 ~ scoop up a piece of sod 〔turf〕.

**떠내려가다** be carried 〔washed, swept〕 away; drift away 〔down〕; get adrift. ¶ 하류로 ~ be carried down the river / 홍수에 ~ 《a bridge》 be swept away by a flood.

**떠다니다** ① 《공중·물 위를》 fly about; float (about); drift (about); be adrift 《with the current》. ¶ 뭉게구름이 하늘에 떠다닌다 Fleecy clouds are floating in the sky. / 파도에 밀려 이리저리 ~ drift about at the mercy of the waves / 연못 위에 고니가 떠다닌다 A swan is floating about on the pond. ② wander. ⇨ 떠돌다.

**떠다밀다** ① 《밀다》 push (away, aside, by); thrust (away, aside); shove (away, aside); force aside. ¶ 문을 ~ push 〔give a push〕 at the door / 아무를 옆으로 ~ shove *a person* aside / 사람들을 떠다밀며 나아가다 elbow *one's* way through a crowd / 아무를 떠다밀어 물 속에 빠뜨리다 push *a person* into the water / 사람들에게 떠다밀려 지하철을 타다 be jostled aboard a subway. ② 《제 일을 남에게》 push 《a job, a responsibility》 onto 《*another*》; put 《the blame》 on another; shift 《the blame》 on someone else.

**떠돌다** ① 《방랑하다》 wander about; roam; rove; drift. ¶ 떠도는 사람 = 떠돌이 / 떠도는 wandering; roaming / 여기저기 떠돌아다니다 wander 〔roam〕 about from place to place. ② 《소문이》 get about 〔abroad, around〕; be rumored. ¶ 떠도는 이야기 a rumor; gossip; hearsay / 거리에 떠도는 이야기 the street gossip; the talk of the town / 그녀가 이혼했다는 소문이 떠돌고 있다 There is a story going around that she has divorced. / 그가 뇌물을 먹었다는 이야기가 떠돈다 Rumor has it that he has accepted bribes.

**떠돌이** a wanderer; a vagabond; a vagrant; 《미》 hobo. ¶ ~노동자 a wandering laborer; 《미》 a floater / ~생활 a wandering 〔nomadic, vagrant〕 life / ~생활을 하다 lead 〔live〕 a vagrant life.

**떠들다**[1] ① 《시끄럽게》 make a noise; make 〔raise, kick up〕 a racket; be noisy 〔boisterous〕; 《지껄이다》 talk glibly; rattle on; wag *one's* tongue; 《하찮은 일로》 make a fuss 〔fuss up 《미》〕 《about trifles》; make much ado 《about nothing》. ¶ 신문에서 ~ be noised about in the newspaper / 너무 떠든다고 야단 맞았다 We were told off for making so much noise. / 시끄럽다, 떠들지 마라 Quiet down! *or* Don't be noisy! *or* Be quiet!
② 《요구·반대하다》 clamor 《for, against》. ¶ 입장을 시키라고 ~ clamor for admission / 노동 시간을 단축하라고 떠들고 있다 They are clamoring for shorter working hours.

③ 《소란부리다》 kick up a row; make a scene; create a disturbance. ¶ 의원들은 의장이 사직해야 한다고 떠들었다 The assemblymen kicked up a row and demanded that the speaker resign.
④ 《소문나다》 be rumored; be gossiped about. ¶ 세상에서는 내가 뇌물을 먹었다고 떠드나 나는 동전 한푼 받은 일이 없다 It is rumored that I took a bribe, but I have never accepted a red cent.
⑤ 《신나게》 go on a racket; have a spree; make merry; be on the spree. ¶ 그들은 술이 취해 떠들었다 They were drunk and made merry.
⑥ 《흥분하다》 be excited. ¶ 조금도 떠들지 않고 calmly; showing no excitement; with perfect composure / 그 소식을 접하고 그들은 떠들었다 They were excited by the news.

**떠들다**[2] 《쳐들다》 turn up 〔lift, raise〕 an edge of 《an object》. ¶ 이불을 떠들고 어린애를 들여다보다 lift up a corner of the quilt and look into the baby.

**떠들썩거리다** ⇨ 떠들다[1], 떠들썩하다[2]. ¶ 하나도 떠들썩거릴 일이 아니다 It's nothing to make「a great fuss 〔a song and dance〕 about. / 종업원들이 월급 올려 달라고 떠들썩거리고 있다 The employees are making an uproar clamoring for a raise of their salaries. / 학생들이 시험을 치르지 않겠다고 떠들썩거린다 The students are agitating against having an examination.

**떠들썩하다**[1] 《떠들려 있다》 《a corner》 be lifted up; be raised. ¶ 이불귀가 ～ The end of the quilt is raised.

**떠들썩하다**[2] ① 《시끄럽다》 (be) noisy; boisterous; uproarious; clamorous; be in a hubbub. ¶ 떠들썩하게 noisily; boisterously; clamorously / 떠들썩한 교실 a noisy classroom / 떠들썩한 환락가 a boisterous entertainment area / 몹시 떠들썩도 하다 What a racket! / 헌법 논의로 세상이 ～ The world is boisterous over the controversy of the Constitution. ② 《뒤숭숭하다》 (be) troubled; unquiet; turbulent; tumultuous; agitated; disturbed. ¶ 세상을 떠들썩하게 하다 create 〔cause〕 quite a sensation / 참으로 떠들썩한 세상이로고 What troubled times we live in! ③ 《소문이》 be abroad; be noised about; be making the rounds. ¶ 온 동네가 떠들썩한 소문 a rumor making the rounds of the village.

**떠들어대다** ⇨ 떠들다[1], 떠들썩거리다. ¶ 하찮은 일을 가지고 ～ make a fuss about 〔over〕 trifles / 그 사건을 신문에서는 크게 떠들어댔다 The case made a lot of noise in the papers.

**떠들치다** ① 《한 귀를》 turn up 〔lift, raise〕 the corner 〔end〕 of 《an object》. ¶ 이불을 ～ lift up a quilt / 바위를 ～ lift up (one side of) a rock. ② 《비밀을》 disclose; divulge; reveal; expose. ¶ 비밀을 ～ reveal a secret / 회사의 내부 사정을 ～ make a public disclosure of the inside affairs of a company.

**떠듬거리다** ⇨ 더듬거리다.

**떠름하다** ① 《맛이》 (be) somewhat astringent 〔puckery〕; sour; bitter; mouth-puckering. ¶ 떠름한 감 a puckery 〔sour〕 persimmon / 떠름한 차 bitter 〔over-stewed〕 tea / 떠름한 포도주 rough wine. ② 《내키지 않다》 be indisposed 《to (do) the work》; be reluctant 《to *do*》; be in no mood 《to *do*》; 《달갑지 않다》 (be) glum; sour; sullen. ¶ 떠름한 얼굴을 하다 look glum; pull 〔make〕 sour face / 떠름하게 대답하다 make a reluctant answer / 어두운 길을 혼자 가기가 ～ I am scared of going my way alone in the dark. ③ 《꺼림하다》 be 〔feel〕 leery; be 〔feel〕 wary; 《걸리다》 [사람이 주어] be 〔feel〕 anxious 〔uneasy〕 《about》; [사물이 주어] weigh on 〔upon〕 *one's* mind; be on *one's* mind. ¶ 떠름한 음식 food to be leery of; suspicious 〔doubtful〕 food / 떠름한 사람 a person to be leery of; a suspicious 〔doubtful〕 person / 그의 말이 무척 ～ His words weigh heavily on my mind.

**떠맡기다** entrust 〔leave〕 《*a matter*》 to 《*a person*》; put 《*a thing*》 into 《*a person's*》 hands; impose 《*a matter*》 on others; saddle 《*a person*》 with. ¶ 일을 억지로 ～ force work on 《*a person*》 / 가게 일을 딴 사람들에게 ～ leave management of a shop in other people's hands / 말썽거리를 ～ saddle 《*a person*》 with an encumbrance / 그 문제는 전적으로 그의 판단에 떠맡겨졌다 The matter was left entirely to his judgment. / 그는 어린 아들을 친척한테 떠맡기고 미국으로 건너갔다 He went over to America entrusting his little son to his relatives.

**떠맡다** 《일을》 undertake; assume; take on 《a task》; take 《a job》 on *oneself;* accept; 《계승하다》 take over 《*a per-*

*son's* business》; 《책임을》 answer for; take responsibility for; hold *oneself* responsible for; 《담당하다》 take charge of; charge *oneself* with; 《보증하다》 guarantee 《*a person's* character》. ¶ 사장 자리를 ～ accept 〔take on〕 the post of president / 부채를 ～ hold *oneself* liable for a debt / (변호사가) 사건을 ～ undertake 〔be entrusted with〕 a case / 싸움 중재를 ～ take upon *oneself* to settle a quarrel / 책임〔손실〕을 ～ assume the responsibility 〔loss〕 / 모든 책임을 혼자 ～ bear the whole responsibility 《for》 / 그는 그것을 할 책임을 떠맡았다 He charged himself with the responsibility of doing it. / 그것은 제가 떠맡죠 Leave the matter to me. *or* I'll see to it.

**떠메다** lift 《*a thing*》 up on *one's* shoulder. ¶ 그는 힘들여 쌀부대를 떠멨다 He lifted a rice bag up on his shoulder with an effort.

**떠밀다** ⇨ 떼밀다.

**떠받다** 《머리나 뿔로》 butt; 《뿔·엄니로》 gore. ¶ 머리로 ～ butt 《*a person*》 with *one's* head / (뿔로) 떠받아 죽이다 gore 《*a person*》 to death / 쇠뿔에 떠받히다 be gored by a bull.

**떠받들다** ① 《쳐들어 올리다》 lift (up); raise (up); hold up (high). ¶ 어린애를 두 손으로 ～ lift 〔hold up〕 a baby with both hands. ② 《공경하다》 serve dutifully; take good care of; have a great regard 《for》; 《소중히 하다》 make much of; hold 《a person》 dear. ¶ 부모를 ～ be filial to *one's* parents; be a good son 〔daughter〕 to *one's* parents / 남편을 ～ take good care of *one's* husband. ③ 《추대하다》 set up; set 〔put〕 《*a person*》 on pedestal; 《옹립하다》 give support 《to》; back (up). ¶ 아무를 두목으로 떠받들고 with *a person* at the head 〔as a figurehead〕 / 스승으로 ～ look up to 《*a person*》 as *one's* teacher / 회장으로 ～ set up 《*a person*》 as chairman / 마을 사람들은 그를 어른으로 떠받들고 있다 The villagers revere him as an elder.

**떠받치다** support; prop (up); bolster; shore up. ¶ 벽을 기둥으로 ～ support 〔prop up〕 a wall with a post.

**떠버리** 《수다쟁이》 a chatterbox; a nonstop talker; a gossip; 《허풍선이》 a braggart; a boaster; a gasbag 《구어》.

**떠벌리다** ① 《과장하다》 talk big; brag; exaggerate; 《구어》 pile it on. ¶ 이야기를 ～ talk big; exaggerate a story. ② 《크게 차리다》 do 〔set up〕 《*a thing*》 on a large scale. ¶ 잔치를 ～ give a feast on a large scale.

**떠보다** ① 《달아 보다》 measure; weigh 《a piece of baggage》; check the weight. ② 《사람을》 (***a***) 《인품을》 size up 《*a person*》. ¶ 아무의 사람됨을 ～ size up the caliber of *a person;* try *a person's* caliber. (***b***) 《남의 속을》 sound (out); fathom; feel. ¶ 속을 ～ probe 〔try to find out〕 《*a person's*》 intention; sound 《*a person*》 on 〔about〕 《*a matter*》 / 의견을 ～ explore 《*a person's*》 views; sound 《*a person's*》 opinion / 나는 그녀의 얼굴을 쳐다보면서 속마음을 떠보려고 했다 I gazed into her face, trying to sound 〔feel〕 her out. / 그녀와 결혼할 것인지 그에게 의사를 떠보았으나 아직 작정 못하고 있는 것 같더라 I sounded him out as to whether he would marry the girl, but he seems to be still undecided whether to marry or to stay single.

**떠오르다** ① 《물 위에》 surface; break the surface; be afloat (again); rise 〔come〕 to the surface. ¶ (가라앉은) 배를 떠오르게 하다 set a boat afloat; refloat a boat / 잠수함이 해면에 떠올랐다 The submarine 「came up 〔rose〕 to the surface of the sea.
② 《공중에》 rise; come up; rise to 〔in〕 the sky. ¶ 해가 수평선 위로 떠올랐다 The sun rose above the horizon.
③ 《생각 등이》 [사물이 주어] occur to 〔flash upon, strike〕 《*a person*》; come 〔spring〕 to mind; come across *one's* mind; [사람이 주어] hit upon 《an idea》. ¶ 생각이 ～ an idea flashed upon 〔came to, struck〕 me / 옛 기억이 ～ an old memory comes back to *one's* mind / 죽은 친구의 모습이 눈앞에 ～ the image of a dead friend floats before *one's* eyes / 좋은 생각이 문득 떠올랐다 A bright idea 「struck me 〔flashed across my mind〕. *or* I was struck with a bright idea. *or* I hit upon a bright idea. / 이상한 생각이 문득 떠올랐다 A strange idea 「crossed 〔flashed into〕 my mind. / 그녀를 방문해야겠다는 생각이 떠올랐다 It occurred to me to visit her.
④ 《웃음 따위가》 play about. ¶ 입가에 웃음이 ～ begin to smile; a smile plays about *one's* lips.
⑤ 《표면화하다》 come to the front. ¶ 수사선상에 몇 명의 남자가 용의자로 떠올랐다 Several men arose as suspects in the course of investigations.

**떠죽거리다** 《젠체하고》 boast; talk big; 《짐짓 사양하다》 make an outward show of declining.

**떠죽떠죽** boastfully.

**떠지껄하다** chatter noisily; be noisy 〔clamorous〕. ¶ 떠지껄하게 noisily.

**떠지다** 《*one's* eyes》 come open; become awake; [비유적] come to *one's* senses; be awakened 《to》.

**떡** rice cake. ¶ 그림의 떡 《be nothing but》 pie in the sky / 떡 해 먹을 집안 《속담》 a discorded family by the domestic trouble / 떡을 빚다 shape dough for cakes / 떡을 치다 pound steamed rice into cake / 떡 주무르듯 하다 have 《*a person*》 (completely) at *one's* mercy; have 《*a person*》 at *one's* beck and call; lead 《*a person*》 by the nose / 떡 줄 사람은 아무 말도 없는데 김칫국부터 마신다 《속담》 get excited over a treat which may not be forthcoming; It is rash to sell the bird on the bough. / 이게 웬 떡이냐 What a welcome windfall! *or* It's a gift from the gods. / 그것은 누워서 떡 먹기다 It's a piece of cake. *or* That's (as) easy as pie.

**떡가래** a bar 〔stick〕 of rice cake.

**떡가루** rice flour. ¶ ~를 반죽하다 knead dough / ~를 빻다 pound rice into flour / ~를 찌다 steam rice flour.

**떡갈나무** 『식물』 an oak (tree).

**떡값** the price of rice cake; 《보너스》 a bonus; 《뇌물》 a (small amount of) bribe; palm oil; good-will money.

**떡고물** bean flour for coating 〔covering〕 rice cake.

**떡국** rice-cake soup (prepared with slices of rice cake, beef, eggs, *etc.*).

**떡만두국** rice cake and dumpling soup.

**떡메** a mallet used to pound steamed rice for cake.

**떡밥** (a) paste bait; paste.

**떡방아** a rice-flour mill. ¶ ~를 찧다 make rice flour; pound rice into flour.

**떡벌어지다** ① 《퍼지다》 (be) wide; broad. ⇨딱바라지다. ¶ 가슴이 ~ have a broad chest; be broad-chested / 어깨가 ~ be broad-shouldered. ② 《소문이》 spread (abroad); get about 〔abroad, around〕; get 〔take〕 air. ③ 《틈 따위가》 open wide; gape; be wide open; burst 〔split〕 open (터져서). ¶ 놀라서 입이 ~ be agape with wonder 〔surprise〕.

**떡보** a person who loves rice cakes.

**떡볶이** a broiled dish of sliced rice cake, meat and hot seasoning.

**떡산적**(—散炙) a spit-roasted 〔skewered〕 sliced rice cake and meat.

**떡살** various forms used to press patterns 〔designs, markings〕 into rice cake.

**떡소** stuffing (for rice cakes).

**떡심** 《심줄》 tendons 〔gristle〕 and tough parts of beef; 《사람》 a tough 〔brawny, stubborn〕 person.

**떡쌀** rice for making rice cake.

**떡쑥** 『식물』 a cottonweed; a cudweed.

**떡잎** 『식물』 a seed leaf; a cotyledon. ¶ 될성 부른 나무는 ~부터 알아본다 《속담》 Genius will assert itself at an early age. *or* Genius displays itself even in childhood.

**떡판**(—板) ① 《널빤지》 a piece of thick board upon which the lump of pounded rice cake is placed. ② 《엉덩이》 a woman's buttocks 〔broad hips〕.

**떤꾸밈음**(—音) 『음악』 a trill.

**떨거덕** ⇨ 달가닥.

**떨거지** *one's* relatives 〔kinsmen〕.

**떨기** 《꽃 등》 a bunch; a cluster; 《식물》 a plant. ¶ 한 ~ 꽃 a bunch of flowers. ◉ ~나무 a shrub; a bush.

**떨다**[1] 《몸을》 tremble; quiver; shiver; quake; shake; 《전율하다》 shudder; thrill; 《목소리를》 wobble; 《진동하다》 vibrate.

> 용법 **tremble** 걱정·공포 따위로 사람이 떨 때, **quiver** 사람이나 나뭇잎·불꽃 따위가 가볍게 떨 때, **shiver** 사람이 추위·공포로 떨 때, **shake** 땅·집 따위 물건의 흔들림을 말하며, 사람에게 쓰는 경우는 비유적 용법으로서 무의식적으로 떨 때 씀. **shudder** 공포로 몹시 떨 때 씀.

¶ 노여움으로 ~ tremble with rage / 무서워서 ~ tremble with fear / 손을 ~ tremble *one's* hands / 사지를 ~ tremble in every limb / 추워서 ~ shiver 〔shake〕 with cold / 그 광경을 보고 ~ shudder 〔tremble〕 at the sight / 무서워 떨게 하다 make 《*a person*》 shiver; terrify / 와들와들〔사시나무 떨듯〕 ~ shake 〔tremble〕 all over; tremble like an aspen leaf / 그의 목소리는 흥분으로 떨고 있었다 His voice was shaking with excitement. / 그녀의 입술은 추워서 떨고 있었다 Her lips were quivering in the cold. / 그는 유혈 장면을 보고 치를 떨었다 He shuddered at the bloody sight. *or* The bloody sight made him shiver.

**떨다**[2] ① 《붙은 것을》 remove; beat 〔shake, brush〕 off. ¶ 담요〔자리〕를 ~ shake 〔beat〕 a blanket 〔mat〕 / 먼지를

～ dust 《furniture》; shake off the dust; brush off 《a hat》 / 비듬을 ～ remove dandruff / 바지에 묻은 눈을 ～ beat the snow from *one's* trousers / 파이프의 재를 ～ knock the ash off *one's* pipe / 자리를 떨고 일어서다 leave *one's* seat brusquely.
② 《적합치 않은 것을》 weed out; eliminate; sift out; screen out.
③ 《공제하다》 take off 〔away〕; deduct; knock 〔strike〕 off. ¶ 월급에서 세금을 ～ deduct tax from *one's* salary.
④ 《팔다 남은 것을》 clear out 〔off〕; get rid of stock; close out; 《비우다》 empty. ¶ 남은 물건을 ～ clear out remaining stocks / 재고품을 ～ get rid of *one's* stock; have a clearance sale / 주머니를 ～ empty *one's* purse.
⑤ 《우수리를》 take 〔knock, round〕 off; neglect; omit. ¶ 우수리를 ～ omit 〔round off〕 fractions / 우수리를 떨고 3천원만 치르다 pay only 3,000 won knocking off the odd sum.

**떨다**[3] 《애교·엄살 따위》 do; display; show. ¶ 극성 ～ run to extreme / 방정 ～ act frivolously / 애교를 ～ behave attractively; display *one's* charm / 수다를 ～ wag *one's* tongue; rattle on / 엄살을 ～ pretend to be in pain.

**떨떠름하다** ⇨ 떠름하다.

**떨떨하다** ① 《천하다》 (be) mean; shabby; unbecoming; [서술적] be below the mark. ¶ 떨떨한 사내 a good-for-nothing (fellow). ② 《내키지 않다》 be disinclined 《to *do*》; be reluctant 《to *do*》; leery; wary; be in no mood 《to *do*》; don't feel like *do*ing; feel uneasy 《about》. ¶ 그 음식 먹기가 ～ I don't feel like eating the food.

**떨리다**[1] 《몸이》 tremble; quiver; shiver; quake; shake; 《음성이》 wobble; quaver; 《이가》 chatter. ¶ 떨리는 목소리 《with》 a trembling 〔tremulous〕 voice / 떨리는 손 trembling 〔shaky〕 hands / 손이 ～ *one's* hands tremble 〔shake〕 / 사지가 ～ tremble in every limb / 덜덜 ～ be all of 〔in〕 a tremble; be (up)on the tremble / 무서워서 ～ tremble with fear; shiver with fright / 분해서 ～ tremble with indignation / 추워서 ～ shiver with 〔from〕 cold; quiver from cold / 떨리는 목소리로 노래하다 sing in a quavery voice / 그녀는 흥분해서 입술이 떨렸다 Her lips were quivering with emotion. / 그 생각만 해도 치가 떨린다 The very thought of it gives me the shudders. / 그의 목소리는 노여움으로 떨렸다 His voice trembled with anger.

**떨리다**[2] ① 《떨어지다》 be shaken off; be beaten 〔thrown〕 off; fall 〔come〕 off. ¶ 담요의 먼지가 잘 안 떨린다 The dust in the blanket won't come off. ② 《떨려나다》 be plucked 〔excluded, eliminated, removed, left out〕. ¶ 지원자는 시험에서 50명 이상이 떨리었다 More than fifty candidates were plucked in the examination. ③ 《해고되다》 be dismissed; be laid off.

**떨어내다** shake 〔strike〕 off; beat 〔brush〕 off. ¶ 담요에서 먼지를 ～ beat dust out of a blanket / 나뭇가지에서 마른 나뭇잎을 ～ shake dead leaves off the branches of a tree.

**떨어뜨리다** ① 《아래로》 drop; throw down; let fall; dump; 《고개를》 hang 〔drop〕 (*one's* head); droop. ¶ 고개를 떨어뜨리고 with a hanging head; with *one's* head dropped / 보따리를 이층에서 아래로 ～ drop a bundle 〔throw a bundle down〕 from upstairs / 잔을 ～ drop a cup; let a cup slip 〔drop〕 / 폭탄을 ～ drop bombs 《on》 / 구호품을 낙하산으로 ～ drop relief supplies by parachute.
② 《놓치다》 let slip; drop; miss (*one's* hold). ¶ 공을 ～ miss 〔muff, fumble〕 a ball; fail to catch a ball.
③ 《분실하다》 drop; lose. ¶ 돈지갑을 길에 ～ lose *one's* wallet on the road.
④ 《하락시키다》 (***a***) 《가치·신용·인기·지위 등을》 debase; abase; degrade; depreciate; reduce; lower; take from 《the value》. ¶ 가치를 ～ detract 〔impair〕 the value; depreciate / 값을 ～ lower 〔slash, put down〕 the price / 위신을 ～ lose *one's* prestige / 인기를 ～ [사물이 주어] lower 〔injure〕 *one's* popularity / 지위를 ～ degrade; demote; reduce 《an officer》 to lower grade / 품격을 ～ demean *oneself;* lose dignity / 신용을 ～ lose 《*a person's*》 confidence; lose credit 《with *a person*》; fall into discredit 《with》. (***b***) 《정도·질을》 lower; make worse; deteriorate; debase. ¶ 상품의 질을 ～ lower 〔debase, deteriorate〕 the quality of goods / 강의의 수준을〔정도를〕 ～ make *one's* lecture easier to follow.
⑤ 《속도 등을》 lessen; decrease; reduce. ¶ 속력을 ～ slow down *one's* car / 열차는 속력을 떨어뜨렸다 The train slowed down 〔up〕 its speed.
⑥ 《소비하다》 spend; scatter. ¶ 외국 관광객이 떨어뜨리고 가는 돈 the dollar

〔money〕 scattered 〔spent〕 by the foreign tourists.
⑦ 《시험에서》 reject 《a candidate》; flunk; fail. ¶ 지원자의 반수를 ～ fail half the candidates.
⑧ 《함락시키다》 take; capture; reduce; carry. ¶ 요새를 ～ capture 〔reduce〕 a fort / 적의 진지를 ～ carry an enemy position.
⑨ 《앞지르다》 leave behind; outstrip; outrun; get 〔pull〕 ahead of. ¶ 경주에서 다른 선수를 ～ outrun 〔get ahead of〕 the other runners in a race.
⑩ 《해뜨리다》 wear out. ¶ 옷을〔구두를〕 ～ wear out *one's* 「clothes 〔shoes〕.
⑪ 《바닥나다》 exhaust; run out; use up. ¶ 돈을 ～ run out of money / 쌀을 ～ use the rice up; run 「out 〔short〕 of rice.
⑫ 《경매에서》 knock 《*a thing*》 down 《to *a person*》 (경매인이); make a successful bid 《for *a thing*》 (응찰인이).

**떨어먹다** eat up; spend the last cent; run 〔go〕 through. ¶ 가산을 다 ～ squander 〔eat up〕 *one's* fortune; run through *one's* fortune 《in idleness》 / 저금을 다 ～ use up *one's* savings / 가졌던 돈을 ～ go through all *one's* money / 형은 부모가 남겨 놓은 재산을 다 떨어먹었다 My elder brother ran through the fortune left by our parents. *or* My brother spent all the money our parents had left him.

**떨어지다** ① 《밑으로》 fall; drop; have a fall; come 〔go〕 down; 《비행기가》 crash; be down; 《액체가》 drip. ¶ 거꾸로 ～ fall headlong 〔head foremost〕 / 쿵하고 땅에 ～ fall on the ground with a thud / 털썩 ～ fall 「plump 〔flop〕 / 나무에서 ～ fall 〔drop〕 from a tree / 말에서 ～ 「fall from 〔come off〕 a horse / 벼랑에서 ～ fall over a 「precipice 〔cliff〕 / 배에서 바다로 ～ fall overboard / 차가 강에 떨어졌다 The car fell 「into 〔in〕 the river. / 계단에서 떨어져 다리가 부러졌다 I fell down the stairs and broke my leg. / 헬리콥터는 산에 떨어졌다 The helicopter crashed into the mountains. / 처마에서 빗물이 똑똑 떨어지고 있다 Rainwater is dripping from the eaves.
② 《몸에서》 slip; drop. ¶ 손에서 ～ fall 「out of 〔drop from〕 *one's* hand / 쥐었던 책이 ～ a book falls out of *one's* hand / 지갑이 주머니에서 ～ a pocketbook slips out of *one's* pocket.
③ 《해가 지다》 set; sink; go down. ¶ 해가 서산에 ～ the sun goes down behind the (western) mountains / 해가 지평선 아래로 ～ the sun 「sinks 〔dips〕 below the horizon.
④ 《하락하다》 (***a***) 《온도·열이》 fall; drop; go down; descend. ¶ 온도가 ～ the 「temperature 〔mercury〕 falls 〔drops〕; fall 〔drop〕 in temperature / 열이 ～ *one's* fever 「subsides 〔goes down, abates, falls〕. (***b***) 《값이》 become lower; fall; drop; go down; sag; decline. ¶ 물가가 ～ prices 「fall 〔go down〕; [물건이 주어] fall 〔go down〕 in prices / 천원이 ～ fall off by 1,000 won / 물가는 오르기만 하고 떨어지는 일이 없다 「Prices do nothing but rise 〔Prices go up all the time〕, they never come down. (***c***) 《가치·신용·품격 등이》 fall in 「value 〔merit〕, depreciate; be debased; be impaired; be detracted. ¶ 물건의 가치가 ～ the value of things is 「lowered 〔lessened〕 / 사람의 품격이 ～ debase 〔degrade〕 *oneself;* lose *one's* dignity / 신용이 ～ lose public confidence / 위신이 ～ lose *one's* prestige. (***d***) 《감퇴하다》 go down; decrease; diminish; fall 《in *one's* estimation》. ¶ 속력이 ～ lose in speed / 손님이 ～ [가게가 주어] lose (its) customers 〔custom〕; [손님이 주어] fall away / 인기가 ～ lose *one's* popularity; fall in popularity; *one's* popularity wanes / 매상이 떨어졌다 The sales have dropped off. / 그의 명성이 떨어지고 있다 His reputation is on the wane. / 실수입이 5퍼센트로 떨어졌다 The real income has declined by 5 percent. (***e***) 《성적이》 go down. ¶ (석차가) 다섯째로 ～ 「go down to 〔slip into〕 the fifth place / 나는 지난 시험에서 석차가 5등이나 떨어졌다 I 「dropped 〔went down〕 five places in class after the last examination. (***f***) 《지위·계급이》 be demoted 《to》; be degraded 《from》; be reduced to a lower rank.
⑤ 《질 따위가》 become worse; deteriorate; be debased; 《못하다》 be inferior 《to》; fall behind 《another》; do not come up to. ¶ 품질이 ～ the quality is debased; be inferior in quality / 기술이 ～ *one's* skill falls off / 기술로는 그에게 떨어진다 I am not his equal in skill. / 그의 타고난 재주는 아무에게도 떨어지지 않았다 In natural gifts he fell behind none. / 가격은 전과 같으나 질이 떨어졌다 The price is the same, but they have lowered the quality.
⑥ 《거리가》 be distant 《from, away from, off》; 《떨어져 있다》 be 「apart 〔sep-

arated〕《from》; 《간격이》 keep off. ¶ 멀리 떨어진 far; faraway; far-off; remote / 멀리 떨어진 곳에 a long way away 〔off〕; far away 《from》; at a long 〔great〕 distance / 2미터씩 떨어져서 at intervals of two meters / 다른 사람들과 떨어져 앉다 sit apart from the others / 가족과 떨어져 살다 live separated from *one's* family / 역은 이곳에서 3킬로 떨어진 곳에 있다 The station is three kilometers away from here. / 그 집은 딴 집들과 떨어져 있었다 The house stood apart from others. / 그는 우리집에서 좀 떨어진 곳에 산다 He lives (at) some way 〔distance〕 from my house.
⑦ 《붙은 것이》 come off; come 〔fall〕 apart; be off; become disjoined; be removed. ¶ 표지가 떨어진 책 a book with the covers off / 단추가 ～ a button comes off / 책상 다리가 ～ a leg of the table 「comes off 〔is disjoined〕」.
⑧ 《헤어지다》 separate 《from》; part from 〔with〕. ¶ 떨어질래야 떨어질 수 없는 사이다 be hand and glove with each other; be inseparable from each other.
⑨ 《함락하다》 fall; be reduced. ¶ 적의 수중에 ～ fall 〔pass〕 into the enemy's hands. ⇨함락.
⑩ 《손에 넘어가다》 fall into; be carried away; be won. ¶ 남의 수중에 ～ fall 〔pass〕 into another's hands / 입찰은 우리에게 떨어졌다 Our tender was accepted. / 경매의 결과 그 명화는 그의 손에 떨어졌다 The famous picture was set up at auction and was knocked down to him.
⑪ 《술수에》 fall into; be caught; be deceived. ¶ 계략에 ～ be entrapped; fall a prey to 《*a person's*》 plot; fall into (another's) snare / 속임수에 ～ be taken; be tricked / 유혹에 ～ yield to 〔fall into〕 temptation.
⑫ 《남다》 be left over 〔behind〕. ¶ 집에 혼자 떨어져 있다 be left behind alone in the house / 그 빚을 갚고도 떨어지는 돈이 좀 있다 There is a comfortable little sum left over after paying the debt.
⑬ 《뒤떨어지다》 fall 〔drop, get, lag〕 behind; be outstripped; be outrun; be backward 《in》; be behindhand. ¶ 경주에서 다른 선수한테 ～ fall behind another runner in a race; be outrun by another runner in a race / 앓아서 공부가 ～ be behind in *one's* studies because of an illness / 그는 다른 학생보다 영어가 떨어진다 He is behind the other students in English.
⑭ 《실패하다》 fail; be defeated 〔unsuccessful〕; lose. ¶ 시험에 ～ fail 〔flunk〕 in an examination / 선거에 ～ be defeated in an election; lose 〔fail in〕 an election / 선발에 ～ be rejected; be not accepted.
⑮ 《해지다》 wear 〔be worn〕 out; get 〔become〕 threadbare. ¶ 떨어진 옷 threadbare clothes / 옷이 ～ *one's* clothes are worn out / 구두가 ～ *one's* shoes are worn out.
⑯ 《바닥나다》 be exhausted; run out; get 〔run〕 out of; be 〔run〕 short of; be out; be out of stock. ¶ 기름이 ～ run out of oil; the oil is all gone 〔used up〕 / 돈이 ～ run out of money; have no money left / 쌀이 ～ rice is exhausted; run out of rice / 식량이 떨어졌다 We have run out of provisions. *or* Our provisions have run out. / 화제가 떨어졌다 We have nothing more to talk about.
⑰ 《유산하다》 abort; miscarry. ¶ 애가 ～ have an abortion 〔a miscarriage〕.
⑱ 《부합하다·나뉘다》 tally with; 《a number》 divide evenly; be evenly divisible. ¶ 책 수효가 생각했던 수와 맞아 떨어진다 The number of the books tallies with what I had expected. / 12는 3으로 나뉘어 떨어진다. Twelve is evenly divided by 3.
⑲ 《끝나다》 get finished; be completed. ¶ 일이 내일이면 떨어진다 The work will be finished tomorrow.
⑳ 《숨이》 breathe *one's* last (breath); expire; die. ¶ 그는 막 숨이 떨어지려는 참이었다 He lay at the point of death.
㉑ 《병·습관이》 be shaken off; be got rid of. ¶ 버릇이 ～ be cured of a habit; get out of a habit / 병이 ～ get over *one's* illness; be cured of a disease / 감기가 떨어지지 않는다 I can't shake off my cold. / 나쁜 버릇은 좀처럼 떨어지지 않는다 A bad habit is hard to get rid of.
㉒ 《고립하다》 isolate. ¶ 혼자 떨어져 살다 live 〔lead〕 an isolated life.
㉓ 《터지다》 tear; break; split; rend. ¶ 귀청이 떨어질 것 같은 ear-splitting; deafening; ear-piercing.

**떨이** clearance 〔sacrifice, cut-price〕 goods; a bargain; remnant articles sold at marked-down prices.
◉ ～판 a clearance sale; a rummage 〔remnant〕 sale.

**떨치다**[1] ① [자동사] resound; be widely felt 〔known〕; be wielded. ¶ 명망이 전국에 ~ be「popular 〔widely known〕 throughout the country; the whole country rings with 《*a person's*》 name / 태풍이 맹위를 떨쳤다 The typhoon raged in all its fury. ② [타동사] make well known in the world; win; wield (power, influence, *etc.*). ¶ 문명(文名)을 ~ win literary fame; make a name for *oneself* as an author / 용맹을 ~ win fame as a brave man / 명성을 천하에 ~ make a noise in the world; win a worldwide reputation / 나라의 위세가 이웃 나라까지 ~ a country wields its power over its neighbors.

**떨치다**[2] 《먼지 따위를》 shake off 《dust》; whisk 《dust》 off 〔away〕; 《몸을》 shake 〔tear〕 *oneself* away 〔free〕 《from》. ¶ 그의 손을 떨치고 방을 나왔다 I shook off his hand and went out of the room. / 잡념을 떨치고 더 열심히 공부해라 Free your mind from worldly thoughts and work harder.

**떫다** (be) astringent; rough. ¶ 떫은 감 a astringent persimmon / 떫은 맛을 빼다 remove the astringency 〔tannin〕 of 《a persimmon》.

**떳떳이** ① 《옳게》 honorably; in an honorable way; with a clear 〔a clean, an easy〕 conscience; openly; aboveboard. ② 《정당하게》 justly; fairly; equitably. ¶ ~ 행동하다 act fair and square; play fair / ~ 해라 Do fair business 〔play〕.

**떳떳하다** 《올바르다》 (be) honorable; have a clear 〔a clean, an easy〕 conscience; (be) open; aboveboard; 《정당하다》 (be) just; fair; rightful; equitable. ¶ 떳떳한 방법 fair means; the proper way / 떳떳한 경기 fair play / 떳떳한 요구 a fair demand / 떳떳한 처사 a fair deal / 떳떳한 행동 an honorable deed; an aboveboard action / 양심에 비추어 ~ have an easy 〔a clear〕 conscience / 떳떳한 부부가 되다 become man and wife in the sight of Heaven 〔before all the world〕; become a legitimate 〔legally united〕 couple / 떳떳한 몸이 되다 《혐의 등이 풀려서》 have *one's* innocence established; be cleared from the charge / 빚을 갚지 않는 것은 떳떳하지 못한 일이다 It is not honorable not to pay *one's* debts. / 그녀는 우리에게 도움을 청하는 것을 떳떳하게 여기지 않았다 She was too proud to ask for our help.

**떵떵거리다** ① ⇨ 땅땅거리다 ①. ② 《호화롭게》 live in grand 〔extravagant〕 style; live like a prince. ¶ 그는 이제 큰 집을 사서 떵떵거리며 산다 Now he has bought himself a mansion and is living on the fat of the land.

**떼**[1] [일반적] a group; a crowd; a throng; a multitude; a party; 《폭도 따위의》 a mob; a gang; 《동물의》 a herd (특히 소, 말 따위); a flock (양 따위의); a pack (사냥개나 이리 등의); a drove (이동하는 동물); a pod (바다 표범 따위); 《새의》 a flock; a bevy (작은 새 따위); 《벌레의》 a swarm; a cloud (메뚜기 따위); 《물고기의》 a shoal; a school. ¶ 떼를 지어 in crowds 〔groups, flocks, swarms, *etc.*〕 / 떼를 짓다 make 〔form〕 a group; flock 〔throng〕 together; gang up / 떼를 지어 오다 come「in a group 〔in groups, in crowds, in swarms, in packs, in a flock〕 / 떼지어 덤비다 attack all in a bunch.

**떼**[2] 《잔디》 sod; turf. ¶ 떼를 뜨다 cut out sod 〔turf〕 / 떼를 입히다 sod; turf.

**떼**[3] 《뗏목》 a raft. ¶ 떼를 엮다 make a raft 《of》; make... into a raft / 떼로 나르다 raft 《timber》 / 떼를 띄워 보내다 send a raft along the stream.

**떼**[4] 《억지》 an impossible 〔unreasonable, unjustifiable〕 demand 〔claim, assertion〕; an importunate 〔an insistent, a persistent〕 demand 〔claim, assertion〕; keeping after 《*a person*》 for *something;* insisting on. ¶ 떼를 쓰다 ask for the impossible; be fretful; talk peevishly; pester 《*a person* to *do*》; importune 〔tease〕 《*a person* for *a thing*》; be impervious to reason / 그 애는 아버지 보고 사진기를 사달라고 떼를 쓴다 The boy keeps after his father to buy him a camera. / 꿔 간 돈이 3만원인데 2만원이라고 떼를 쓴다 He keeps insisting that he owes me only 20,000 won when he really owes me 30,000. / 그 애는 쩍하면 떼쓴다 The child is always crying over something. / 떼만 쓰면 장사냐 Stubbornness will get you nowhere.

**떼거지** ① 《떼지어 다니는》 beggars going around in a bunch. ② 《재해로 생긴》 a great number of people who have turned beggars owing to a natural calamity; a large group of victims of a disaster. ¶ 전쟁 때문에 갑자기 ~가 생겼다 The war has brought about a great number of beggars all at once.

**떼과부**(—寡婦) a number 〔lot〕 of widows. ¶ 전쟁으로 ~가 생겼다 The war widowed many women.

**떼굴떼굴** rolling 〔rumbling〕 continuously. ¶ ～구르다 roll over and over / ～ 굴러 떨어지다 roll 〔tumble〕 down / 둥근 통이 땅 위를 ～ 굴렀다 The barrel rolled over and over on the ground.

**떼다**[1] ① 《걸린, 끼운, 붙은 것을》 remove; take off 〔away〕; detach 《a stamp from a sheet》; dismantle 《equipment》; tear 〔strip〕 off. ¶ 간판을 ～ remove a signboard / 눈곱을 ～ rub 〔wipe〕 the matter from *one's* eyes / (포좌에서) 대포를 ～ demount a gun / 미닫이를 ～ take out 〔off〕 a sliding door / 우표를 ～ take the stamp off (an envelope) / 달력 한 장을 ～ tear off a leaf from a calendar / 그녀는 포스터를 모두 떼었다 She tore off all the posters (on the wall).
② 《떼어놓다》 (***a***) 《간격을》 leave a space; space 《*a thing*》 out. ¶ 2미터씩 사이를 떼어 at intervals of two meters / 줄과 줄 사이를 ～ leave space between the lines / 두 줄씩 ～ leave out every two lines / 한 줄씩 떼어서 쓰다 write on every other line / 나무를 4미터씩 떼어서 심다 plant trees four meters apart. (***b***) 《갈라놓다》 take 〔keep〕 apart; part; separate; draw 〔pull, set〕 《*persons, things*》 apart. ¶ 개를 각각 떼어놓다 keep the dogs apart / 기관차를 열차에서 ～ detach a locomotive from a train / 맞붙어 싸우는 두 사람을 떼어놓다 separate two fighting persons; pull apart the two grappling persons / 사랑하는 두 사람을 떼어놓다 separate the pair of lovers / 이 사전에서 한시도 손을 뗄 수가 없다 I cannot do without this dictionary.
③ 《공제하다》 take away 〔off〕; deduct; knock 〔strike〕 off. ¶ 세금을 떼고 월 100만원의 수입 a monthly income of one million won after tax deduction / 선이자를 떼고 빌려 주다 loan money with interest deducted in advance / 봉급에서 ～ deduct 《a sum》 from *one's* salary; take 《a sum》 off *one's* pay.
④ 《바람직하지 않은 것을》 (***a***) 《아이를》 have an (artificial) abortion; induce abortion; commit feticide. (***b***) 《병·버릇 따위를》 get rid of; wean; cure. ¶ 못된 버릇을 ～ get over a bad habits; get rid 〔break *oneself*〕 of bad habits / 학질을 ～ cure malaria; [비유적] get 〔be〕 rid of a nuisance; rid *oneself* of a nuisance.
⑤ 《젖을》 wean 《a baby from 「the breast 〔its mother〕》.
⑥ 《떼어두다》 set aside 〔apart〕; put by; lay aside 〔by, away, off〕; 《나중을 위해》 save; spare; reserve 《*something*》 for hereafter. ¶ 차 살만한 돈을 떼어두다 spare money enough to buy a car / 만일의 경우를 위해 돈을 떼어놓다 reserve 〔save〕 money for 「emergencies 〔a rainy day〕 / 노후를 위해 돈을 따로 떼어두다 put aside 〔save〕 some money for old age.
⑦ 《봉한 것을》 open; unseal; break 〔open〕 the seal; cut 《a letter》 open. ¶ 봉한 마개를 ～ pull out a stop 〔bung〕; uncork 《a bottle》 / 편지 봉투를 ～ open 〔unseal〕 a letter.
⑧ 《거절하다》 refuse; reject; decline. ¶ 청하는 것을 잡아～ refuse 〔turn down〕 a request / 그의 청을 뗄 수 없었다 I could not decline his request.
⑨ 《수표·어음 등을》 draw 《a bill on *a person*》; tear off 《a chit》; issue 〔make out〕 《a check in favor of *a person*》. ¶ 100만원 짜리 수표를 ～ write 〔make out, issue〕 a check for one million won / 은행 앞으로 백만원짜리 수표를 ～ draw a check on a bank for 1,000,000 won / 50만원의 어음을 그녀 앞으로 뗐다 I drew a bill on her for 500,000 won.
⑩ 《시치미를》 assume; put on (an air of); pose as; pretend; act. ⇨ 시치미[1].
⑪ 《코를》 have the door slammed in *one's* face; get a rebuff. ⇨ 코떼다.
⑫ 《끝내다》 finish up. ¶ 책을 ～ finish (reading, studying) a book / 일손을 ～ finish *one's* work; knock off work (for the day).
⑬ 《…에서 손을》 sever connection 《with》; extract *oneself* 《from》; wash *one's* hand 《of》; withdraw *oneself* 《from》. ¶ 계약에서 손을 ～ draw back from a contract / 나는 그 사업에서 손을 떼었다 I washed my hands of the business.

**떼다**[2] = 떼이다.

**떼도둑** a gang of robbers; a pack of thieves.

**떼먹다** ⇨ 떼어먹다.

**떼밀다** push; shove; give a push 〔shove〕. ¶ 아무를 ～ push 〔shove〕 *a person* / 떼밀고 들어가다 force *one's* way into / 문을 떼밀어 열다 push the door open / 벼랑〔기차〕에서 떼밀어 떨어뜨리다 push 《*a person*》 「over the cliff 〔off the train〕 / 떼밀지 마시오 Stop shoving.

**떼새** 〖조류〗 a plover; 《새떼》 birds in flock; a flock of birds.

**떼송장** a lot of corpses 〔bodies〕.

**떼쓰다** ask for the impossible ⇨ 떼[4].

**떼어놓다** ① 《갈라놓다》 pull 〔draw〕 《*persons, things*》 apart; separate 〔part〕 《*persons, things*》; 《격리하다》 isolate 《*a thing*》; 《이간하다》 estrange; 《뒤에 남기다》 leave behind. ¶ 떼어놓고 가다 leave 《*a person*》 behind / 싸움하는 사람을 ~ pull combatants 〔fighting persons〕 apart / 사랑하는 두 사람을 ~ separate the pair of lovers. ② 《경주에서》 run 《two meters》 ahead 《of *a person*》; have a lead on 《*a person*》.

**떼어먹다** 《갚지 않다》 do not pay 《*one's* debt 〔bill〕》; welsh on 《*one's* debt》; bilk 《*a person*》 out of 《debt》; evade payment; fail to pay; 《착복하다》 embezzle; divert to *one's* own ends. ¶ 공금을 ~ embezzle 〔pocket〕 public money / 빚을 ~ welsh 〔run out〕 on a debt / 셈을 ~ bilk 〔jump〕 a bill; shirk payment of a bill / 술값을 ~ do not pay *one's* drink; leave *one's* bar bill unpaid / 빚을 떼먹고 달아나다 bolt away without paying *one's* debts.

**떼이다** have a loan 〔bill, debt〕 unpaid; be welshed on; become irrecoverable; be dishonored. ¶ 떼인 외상값 a credit bill left unpaid.

**떼쟁이** an insistent person; a person who always makes impossible 〔unreasonable, unjustifiable〕 demands 〔claims〕; a child who keeps always after 《*a person*》 for 《*a thing*》.

**떼죽음** massive death 《of》. ~하다 die in a mass. ¶ ~을 당하다 suffer a massive death / 낚시터에서 많은 물고기가 ~한 것이 발견되었다 A large number of fish have been found dead in a fishing pool.

**떼짓다** form groups; make up a group; flock; band together. ¶ 떼(를) 지어 in groups 〔crowds, packs, flights, swarms, flocks〕.

**떼치다** ① 《물리치다》 push away 〔aside〕; thrust away 〔aside〕; brush 〔force〕 aside; 《잡힌 몸을》 shake *oneself* free of 《*a person's* grasp》; tear *oneself* away 《from》. ¶ 우는 애를 떼치고 밖으로 나가다 go out pushing aside a crying child. ② 《거절하다》 refuse; brush aside; reject; turn down. ¶ 요구를 ~ refuse 〔brush aside〕 a request.

**뗏목**(—木) a raft. ¶ ~을 엮다 make a raft 《of logs》 / ~으로 나르다 carry 《*a thing*》 on a raft; raft (timber) / 통나무를 ~으로 엮어 띄워보내다 raft logs down the river.

**뗏장** a piece 〔chunk〕 of sod 〔turf〕.

**뗑겅–** ⇨ 댕그랑–.

**또** ① 《그리고·또한》 and; also; too; as well; (not only)… also; (both)… and; again; besides; moreover; what is more; into the bargain. ¶ 그의 가족으로는 아버지 어머니가 있고 또 할아버지 할머니가 계시다 He has his parents and grandparents in his family. / 그는 군인이요 또 학자다 He is (both) a soldier and a scholar. / 그 밖에 또 다른 비용이 있을 것도 생각해야 한다 In addition, you have to take into consideration that there will be some other expenses. / 비 오는데 또 바람까지 분다 It is raining and, what's more, the wind is blowing (too). / 그는 오늘도 또 나타나지 않았다 He didn't show up again today. ② 《다시》 once more; again; repeatedly. ¶ 또 한 번 once again 〔more〕 / 일을 또 시작하다 begin *one's* work again; resume *one's* work / 부산에 또 불이 났다 There was another fire in Pusan. / 또 놀러 오시오 Come and see me again. / 돈을 또 달란다 He is asking money again. / 담배를 또 하나 주시오 May I have another cigarette, please? / 또 무엇을 드릴까요 《장사꾼이 손님에게》 Anything else? / 또 한 번만 일러주시오 Please tell me once more. / 또 뵙겠습니다 I hope to see you again. ③ 《다른 한편》 while; on the other hand; 《생각밖에》 contrary to 《expectations, *etc.*》. ¶ 그녀는 영리하지만, 또 실수도 가끔 저지른다 She is clever, but on the other hand she often makes mistakes. / 제 형은 키가 큰데 저 애는 또 저렇게 작다 He is so small while his brother is very tall. / 난 또 누구라구 Well, it is you! (I thought it was somebody else.) / 다른 사람이라면 또 몰라도, 그 만은 의심할 여지가 없다 However it may be with other people, he is quite above suspicion.

**또그르르** with a single roll.

**또는** or (else); (either…) or; 《딴 말로》 in other words. ¶ 내일 ~ 모레 tomorrow or the day after / 이달 ~ 내달에 either this month or next / 그 사람이나 ~ 내가 가기로 되어 있다 He or I am to go. (★ 동사의 수는 그것에 가장 가까운 주어에 일치시킴).

**또다시** 《또》 again; once more (한 번 더); twice (두 번); afresh (다시); over again. ¶ ~ …하다 repeat; do… over again / (읽은 책을) ~ 읽다 read 《a book) (all over) again / ～ 침묵에 빠지다 relapse into silence / 이런 실책은 ～ 안하겠습니다 I swear that I shall never repeat the same error. / 그가 내 집에 ～는 발을 못 붙이게 하겠다 He shall not set foot again in my house.

**또닥거리다** beat; rap; knock; tap; patter. ¶ 등을 ～ pat 《*a person*》 〔give 《*a person*》 a tap〕 on the back / 연필을 가지고 책상을 ～ be tapping on a table with a pencil.

**또닥또닥** tap-tap; rat-tat-tat; tapping. ～하다 tap. ⇨ 또닥거리다.

**또랑또랑하다** (be) very clear; bright; distinct. ¶ 또랑또랑한 목소리로 in a clear 〔ringing, sonorous〕 voice / 어린 애들의 또랑또랑한 목소리가 들린다 I hear the clear voices of children.

**또래** (of) the age; (of) the size. ¶ 고 ～ 몇이 나를 찾아왔었다 A group of boys of that age had been here to see me. / 고 ～를 몇 개 더 사다 주오 Buy a few more of that size. / 모두 그 ～다 All of them are of the same age (나이) 〔size (크기)〕.

**또렷또렷** ～하다 be all clear 〔distinct, vivid〕. ¶ 글씨를 ～ 쓰다 write a clear hand / ～한 목소리로 말하다 speak in a clear voice / (발음을) ～하게 하다 speak distinctly; articulate.

**또렷이** clearly; distinctly; vividly; plainly; explicitly.

**또렷하다** ⇨ 뚜렷하다.

**또바기** 《한결같이》 without fail; punctually; regularly. ¶ 그에게는 언제나 ～ 존대해 말한다 I never fail to address him in honorifics.

**또박또박** ① 《정확히》 neatly; exactly; correctly; accurately; carefully. ～하다 (be) neat; exact; careful. ¶ ～ 쓴 글씨 neat writing; a neat hand / 글씨를 ～ 쓰다 write neatly / 개수(個數)를 ～ 세서 받다 count the number exactly and then take them. ② 《거르지 않고》 punctually; regularly. ¶ ～ 제시간에 대오다 come on time punctually / 빚을 ～ 갚다 pay *one's* debt regularly.

**또한** besides; moreover; also; too; as well; either; likewise; both… and; [부정구문] neither; nor; not… either. (★ also, too는 문장 안·문장 끝 어디에도 올 수 있는데, 문장 끝에 오는 too는 그 앞에 콤마로 끊을 수 있음. as well은 문장 끝에 오고, neither, nor는 주어·동사의 도치를 일으킴.) ¶ 재미도 있고 ～ 교훈적이다 be 「both 〔at once〕 interesting and instructive / 용기도 있고 ～ 슬기도 있다 be no less brave than intelligent / 그녀는 아름다울 뿐 아니라 ～ 착하다 She is beautiful and good, too. / 나도 ～ 그런 일은 하기 싫다 Neither do I wish to do such a thing. / 그것도 ～ 문제다 That is also a problem. / 이것도 ～ 쉽지 않다 This isn't easy, either. / 이 책은 재미도 없고 ～ 교훈적이지도 않다 This book is neither interesting nor instructive.

**똑**[1] 《두드리는 소리》 with a tap 〔rap, thud〕; 《부러지는 소리》 with a (light) snap. ～하다 tap; rap; snap. ¶ 대통으로 머리를 똑 때리다 rap 《*a person's*》 head with the bowl of a pipe / 똑 부러지다 snap (off); break with a snap / 나뭇가지를 똑 꺾다 snap off a twig / 똑하고 땅 위에 떨어지다 fall to the ground with a light tap.

**똑**[2] 《꼭·아주 다》 just; right; exactly; precisely; completely. ¶ 똑 제시간에 대오다 arrive 〔come〕 right on time / 돈이 똑 떨어지다 run out of money completely; spend *one's* last cent.

**똑같다** (be) just 〔exactly〕 alike; absolutely identical 《with》; exactly the same 《as》; be the exact image 〔likeness〕 《of》. ¶ 똑같은 날에 on the very same day / 똑같은 말을 몇번이고 되풀이하다 say the same thing again and again; harp on the same string / 나도 당신과 똑같은 생각이오 Your thoughts echo mine. / 형제가 ～ The brothers are exactly alike.

**똑같이** equally; evenly (한결같이); impartially (공평하게); indiscriminately (차별 없이); alike; similarly; in the same way; likewise. ¶ ～ 보인다 look alike / 두 자매는 ～ 예쁘다 The two sisters are equally pretty. / 돈을 ～ 나눠 주시오 Please divide the money equally.

**똑딱거리다** tick; ticktock; rap-rap; knock; patter. ¶ 시계가 ～ a clock ticks / 똑딱선이 똑딱거리며 지나간다 A steamboat is chugging along. / 시계가 똑딱거리는 소리 외에는 모두가 조용하였다 All was silent save for the ticking of the clock.

**똑딱단추** a snap fastener. ¶ ～를 채우다 close a snap fastener; fasten a snap.

**똑딱똑딱** ticktock; ticktack; click-clack; ticking; pattering.

**똑딱선**(一船) a steamboat; a motorboat.

**똑똑** ① 《물이》 dropping one by one; pattering; dripping. ¶ ～ 떨어지다 drip; dribble; trickle; fall in drops / 눈물이 ～ 떨어지다 tears drop one by one / 핏방울이 ～ 떨어지다 blood drips drop by drop. ② 《부러짐》 with snaps. ¶ 나

뭇가지가 ～ 부러지다 branches are broken with snaps. ③《두드림》 rapping; knocking. ¶ 문을 ～ 두드리다 rap 〔knock〕 at the door / 책상을 ～ 두드리다 rap on a desk.

**똑똑하다** ①《분명하다》 (be) clear; distinct. ¶ 똑똑한 글씨 clear writing; a clean hand / 똑똑한 발음 distinct pronunciation / 똑똑한 인쇄 clear printing. ②《사람이》 (be) clever; bright; smart; intelligent; shrewd (빈틈없다). ¶ (얼굴이) 똑똑해 보이는 intelligent-looking / 똑똑한 아이 a bright boy 〔girl〕 / 똑똑한 처사 intelligent management; wise handling / 머리가 ～ have a clear head; be clear-headed; be bright / 똑똑한 체하다 try to appear smart; pretend to be wise.

**똑똑히** ①《분명히》 clearly; distinctly; definitely. ¶ ～ 들리다 be clearly heard / ～ 말하다 speak clearly; say definitely / ～ 발음하다 pronounce clearly 〔distinctly〕 / ～ 인쇄하다 print clearly. ②《영리·현명하게》 brightly; smartly; intelligently; well. ¶ 사람이 ～ 생기다 look bright 〔smart〕 / 일을 ～ 처리하다 dispose of a matter intelligently.

**똑바로** ①《곧게》 straight; in a straight line; directly; upright; erect. ¶ ～ 걷다 walk straight / ～ 서다 stand upright 〔erect〕; stand up straight / 자세를 ～ 하다 straighten *oneself* / 글씨를 ～ 쓰다 write in a straight line / ～ 집으로 가다 go straight home. ②《바른대로》 straight; upright; honestly; frankly; without concealment; correctly. ¶ ～ 말하면 to tell the truth; to be frank 〔honest〕 with you / ～ 말하다 tell the truth; speak without concealment; speak out frankly / ～ 발음하다 pronounce correctly / ～ 살아가다 live straight; lead an honest life / 사물을 ～ 보도록 해라 Look at the matter in the right.

**똑바르다** ①《곧다》 (be) (dead) straight; 《직립하다》 (be) upright; erect. ¶ 똑바른 길 a straight road. ②《바르다》 (be) honest; upright; right(eous); frank. ⇨올바르다. ¶ 똑바른 길을 걷다 tread the right path.

**똘기** an unripe 〔a green〕 fruit.

**똘똘이** a bright child; a clever boy 〔girl〕.

**똘똘하다** (be) clever; bright; smart. ¶ 똘똘한 아이 a bright 〔clever〕 boy 〔girl〕.

**똥** ①《대변》 excrements; feces; stools; dung; droppings; shit 《비어》. ¶ 새똥 bird droppings / 마소의 똥 cow and horse dung / 똥 푸는 사람 a night-soil man / 똥을 누다 defecate; empty 〔evacuate〕 *one's* bowels; relieve nature 〔*oneself*〕 / 똥을 치우다 remove 〔collect〕 night soil / 똥을 푸다 dip up night soil / 똥이 마렵다 feel a bowel urge; have a call of nature / 똥 누러 갈 적 마음 다르고 올 적 마음 다르다 《속담》 Once on shore, we pray no more. *or* The danger past and God forgotten. / 똥 묻은 개가 겨 묻은 개 나무란다 《속담》 The pot calls the kettle black. / 똥은 건드릴수록 구린내만 난다 《속담》 You can't expect anything good from the company of a bad man. / 똥이 무서워 피하랴, 더러워서 피하지 《속담》 Shun bad people as you would become filthy. ②《더껑이》 scum. ¶ 이똥 impurities on the teeth; tartar (치석).

**똥값** a dirt-cheap price. ¶ ～으로 for almost nothing; 《obtain》 for a song; at a wretched price; dirt-〔dog=〕cheap / ～으로 팔다 sell dirt-cheap; sell for a mere 〔an old〕 song.

**똥개** a mongrel; a stray dog.

**똥거름** dung-manure; "night soil". ◉ ～장수 a carrier of night soil; a honey-bucket man.

**똥구멍** the anus; the rectum; the anal orifice 〔passage〕. ¶ ～으로 호박씨 깐다 behave slyly 〔craftily〕.

**똥그라미** ①《원》 a circle; a ring. ②《돈》 money; coin.

**똥끝** the tip(s) of excrement. ¶ ～(이) 타다 feel anxious 〔worried〕; worry *oneself* (sick); be fidgeted 《about》.

**똥독**(一毒) poison 〔virulence〕 in excrement; rash caused by excrement. ¶ ～(이) 오르다 get a rash from touching excrement.

**똥똥하다** ＝뚱뚱하다.

**똥바가지** a dung dipper; a dipper for night soil.

**똥배** a big paunch; a potbelly.

**똥배짱** foolhardiness; daredevil(t)ry; reckless courage 〔bravery〕.

**똥싸개** a child who is not able to control his bowel movements; a pants=soiler

**똥싸다** 《혼나다》 have a hard 〔bad〕 time; have a hell of time; be put to it. ¶ 숙제를 끝내느라 똥쌌다 I had a hell of time getting the homework done.

**똥오줌** feces and urins; excretions; body wastes; "night soil". ¶ ～을 함부로 갈기다 relieve *oneself* just anywhere / 환자의 ~을 받아내다 take care of the body wastes of a patient.

**똥줄** drops from the bowels in an urgent evacuation. ¶ ~ 당기다 [비유적] be frightened out of *one's* wits; be scared to death; be scared shitless 《비어》 / ~ 빠지다 《크게 혼나다》 have a hard time (of it); have a terrible 〔dreadful, bitter〕 experience.

**똥집** ① 《큰 창자》 the large intestine. ② 《체중》 *one's* body weight. ③ 《위》 the stomach.

**똥차**(—車) a night soil wagon (cart); a dung cart; a honey cart 《속어》; 《고장 잘 나는 차》 a ramshackle car(t); a shabby car; a jalop(p)y 《구어》.

**똥창맞다** see eye to eye with; be of a mind; be congenial 《to, with》.

**똥칠하다**(—漆—) smear dung; 《망신하다》 disgrace. ¶ 얼굴에 ~ disgrace *one's* name; bring disgrace on 《*a person*》; stain 〔sully〕 《*a person's*》 good name.

**똥통**(—桶) a honey bucket; a dung tub; a manure pail.

**똥파리** a bottle-green fly; a dung fly.

**똬리** a head-pad (made of straw, grass or cloth used by women to carry burdens on their heads). ◉ ~쇠 a (metal) washer.

**뙈기** 《논밭의》 a patch 《of a field 〔paddy〕》; a small piece 《of land》. ¶ 밭〔논〕 한 ~ a patch of field 〔rice paddy〕 / 논 ~나 가지다 have a few patches of rice paddy.

**뙤다** snap off; break off. ¶ 그물코가 ~ the mesh of a net breaks off / 바늘귀가 ~ the eye of a needle snaps 〔breaks〕 off.

**뙤약볕** the scorching sun; the glaring 〔blazing〕 sunshine. ¶ ~을 쬐다 expose *oneself* to strong sunshine / ~을 받으며 걷다 walk under the burning 〔blazing〕 sun.

**뙤창(문)**(—窓(門)) a door with a small window in it.

**뚜껑** ① 《덮개》 a lid; a cover; a cap (병·만년필의); a case (시계의). ¶ 상자 ~ the lid of a box / ~ 달린 lidded; covered / ~ 없는 lidless; open / ~을 닫아두다 keep 《*a thing*》 covered / ~을 열다 open; uncover; lift 〔take off, undo〕 the lid 〔cover〕; [비유적] open (시작되다); make public 〔known〕 (발표하다) / ~을 하다〔닫다〕 cover; cap; close; put on 〔shut down〕 the lid / ~이 덮이다 be covered 〔lidded〕; have a lid 〔cover〕 on / ~이 닫혀 있다 It has a lid on. *or* It is covered. / ~을 열어 볼 때까지는 아무도 뭐라 말할 수 없다 No one can tell 〔predict〕 how it will turn out (until it actually happens). *or* We cannot make a prediction until we see how it turns out. ② 《속어》 《모자》 a cap; a hat.

**뚜뚜** toot-toot; hoot-hoot; 《자동차가》 honk-honk. ¶ 기적을 ~ 울리다 toot a steam whistle / 경적을 ~ 울리다 toot *one's* horn / 나팔을 ~ 불다 toot a bugle 〔trumpet〕 / (차가) 경적을 ~ 울리며 달리다 run hooting 〔honking〕.

**뚜렷이** clearly; distinctly; vividly; 《두드러지게》 remarkably; strikingly; markedly. ¶ ~ 감소하다 decrease markedly; show a marked decrease / ~ 구별하다 distinguish clearly; make a clear distinction 《between》 / ~ 생각나다 come back to *one* vividly / ~ 인쇄하다 print clearly.

**뚜렷하다** (be) clear; vivid; distinct; plain; definite; evident; obvious; 《두드러지다》 (be) remarkable; marked; striking; considerable. ⇨ 두드러지다. ¶ 뚜렷한 구별 a sharp 〔clear〕 distinction / 뚜렷한 기억 a vivid recollection / 뚜렷한 글씨 clear handwriting; a clear hand / 뚜렷한 대조 a striking 〔sharp〕 contrast / 뚜렷한 사실 a plain 〔an obvious〕 fact / 뚜렷한 인상 a vivid impression / 뚜렷한 증거 clear evidence; an evident 〔a positive〕 proof / 뚜렷한 영상 a clear 〔distinct〕 image / 뚜렷한 개성 a distinct personality / 윤곽이 뚜렷한 용모 clear-cut features / 두 낱말 사이에는 뚜렷한 차이가 있다 There is a distinct difference between the two words.

**뚜벅거리다** strut 〔swagger〕 (along). ¶ 뚜벅거리는 걸음 a strutting gait.

**뚜벅뚜벅** strutting(ly); with a strutting gait. ¶ ~ 걷다 strut; swagger / 그 배우는 무대 위를 ~ 걸어다녔다 The actor strutted about the stage.

**뚜쟁이** a pimp; a pander; 《중매인》 a matchmaker. ¶ ~ 노릇하다 act as a pimp; pimp; pander; act as go-between.

**뚝** ① 《떨어지는 모양》 with a thump 〔thud, whack〕. ~하다 thud; thump; whack. ¶ 조롱박이 땅에 뚝 떨어졌다 A gourd dropped with a thud on the ground. / 짐이 선반에서 뚝 떨어졌다 A package fell down with a thud from the shelf.
② 《부러지거나 끊어지는 모양》 snap; with a (heavy) snap. ~하다 snap. ¶

뚝 끊어지다 come snap (off) / 뚝 부러지다 be broken with a snap; break 〔snap〕 short / 실을 뚝 끊다 snap a piece of thread in two / 그는 자기 바이올린의 현 하나가 뚝 끊어지는 소리를 들었다 He heard one of the strings of his violin snap. / 돛대가 뚝 부러졌다 The mast snapped off. / 밧줄의 가장 약한 곳이 뚝 끊어졌다 The rope snapped at the weakest point.
③ 《갑자기》 suddenly; abruptly; unexpectedly. ¶ 뚝 그치다 stop suddenly; come to a dead stop / 인기가 뚝 떨어지다 have a sudden fall in *one's* popularity / 그의 소식이 뚝 끊어졌다 He dropped his correspondence with me. / 시세가 뚝 떨어졌다 Prices came down with a run. / 내 발자국 소리에 벌레 소리가 뚝 그쳤다 At my footsteps the insects suddenly ceased to sing.

**뚝뚝** ⇨ 똑똑. ¶ 그녀는 눈물을 ~ 흘렸다 She shed tears drop by drop. *or* Her tears fell in drops.

**뚝뚝하다** 《성격·태도·말씨 등이》 (be) unaffable; blunt; stiff; rough; tough; obstinate; persistent; strong. ⇨ 무뚝뚝하다. ¶ 뚝뚝하게 대답하다 give a blunt 〔curt〕 answer / 뚝뚝하게 말을 하다 speak with asperity / 그는 뚝뚝해서 다루기에 힘이 든다 He is stiff 〔bullheaded〕 and very hard to deal with. / 그는 뚝뚝해서 남에게 좋은 인상을 주지 못한다 He is so rough that he usually gives people a bad impression.

**뚝배기** an unglazed earthenware bowl. ¶ ~보다 장맛이 좋다 《속담》 Though the appearance is poor, the substance is good. 「testy.

**뚝별나다** (be) quick-tempered; touchy;

**뚝별씨** 《성질》 quick 〔hot〕 temper; touchiness; testiness; 《사람》 a testy person.

**뚝심** great physical strength 〔power〕; latent 〔potential〕 power; 《버틸 힘》 staying power; endurance. ¶ ~ 센 사람 a man of mighty sinews / ~이 있다 be endowed with brute force; be mighty strong / 그는 ~이 있어서 그만한 짐은 십리라도 지고 간다 He is so strong that he can easily carry such a bundle on his back as far as ten *ri*. / 그 경기에서 그는 ~이 있음을 보여주었다 In the game he showed himself to be a resourceful player.

**뚫다** ① 《통하게 하다》 (**a**) 《구멍을》 bore; make 《a hole》; dig; drill (송곳 등으로); 《꿰뚫다》 go 〔pass, thrust〕 through; cut through; pierce; penetrate. ¶ 3루를 뚫는 안타 a single past third / 얼음에 구멍을 ~ pierce a hole in the ice / 벽에 구멍을 ~ make 〔bore〕 a hole in the wall 《with a drill》 / 천정을 ~ go through the ceiling / 산에 터널을 ~ dig 〔cut, build〕 a tunnel through a mountain; tunnel a hill / 탄알이 벽을 뚫었다 The bullet pierced 〔went through〕 the wall. (**b**) 《막힌 것을》 open up; open 《a path through a wood》; pass 〔run〕 through. ¶ 길을 ~ break 〔open up〕 a road / (막힌) 토관을 ~ make water run through earthen pipes.
② 《헤어나다》 (**a**) 《어려움 등을》 weather; find 〔see〕 *one's* way out of 《the difficulty》; cut 〔fight〕 *one's* way through 《the enemy》; get over 《a barrier》; get out of 《trouble》. ¶ 난관을 ~ find *one's* way out of a difficulty; get over a difficulty / 적의 포위망을 ~ cut 〔fight〕 *one's* way through the besieging enemy / 위기를 뚫고 나가다 come 〔struggle〕 through a crisis. (**b**) 《법·감시 등을》 evade; avoid; get around. ¶ 감시망을 ~ evade the vigilance of the guard / 법망을 ~ evade 〔avoid, elude〕 the law; dodge the law / 법망을 뚫고 계속해서 죄를 범하다 commit one crime after another without falling into the clutches of the law.
③ 《곬을》 find (a way). ¶ 금맥을 ~ spot 〔locate〕 gold deposits / 돈 구멍을 ~ find a way to get money / 취직 자리를 ~ find 〔get〕 a job.
④ 《이치를》 attain; get at; master. ¶ 학문의 깊은 이치를 ~ master 〔penetrate〕 the secrets of learning.

**뚫리다** ① 《구멍이》 be pierced 〔bored, perforated, drilled, penetrated〕; get opened up. ¶ 구멍이 ~ a hole is made / 길이 ~ a road is made 〔open〕; a way is found / 터널이 ~ a tunnel is made 〔bored, driven, excavated, built, cut〕 / 그 터널이 뚫리기까지는 아직 1년쯤 더 남았다 It will be one year or so before the tunnel is driven through. / 돈 구멍이 ~ [비유적] a way is found to get money. ② 《이치가》 be attained; be mastered. ¶ 학문의 깊은 이치가 ~ the secrets of learning are mastered 〔penetrated〕.

**뚫어내다** 《구멍을》 pierce out; bore out; manage to pierce 〔bore, perforate, penetrate〕. ¶ 산에 터널을 ~ laboriously cut 〔drive, build〕 a tunnel through a mountain / 송곳으로 두꺼운 판자에 구멍을 ~ bore out a hole with a drill through a thick board. / 돈 구멍을 ~ [비유적] manage to find a way 〔find out a way〕 to raise money.

**뚫어새기다** cut out 《a perforated wooden pattern》.

**뚫어지게 보다** stare 〔gaze〕 《at》; look hard 《at》; fix 〔fasten〕 *one's* eyes 《on》. ¶ 아무를 ~ look at *a person* with a penetrating 〔piercing〕 stare / 아무의 얼굴을 ~ stare *a person* in the face / 그녀는 내 눈을 뚫어지게 보았다 She looked deep into my eyes.

**뚫어지다** ① 《동작》 bore; drill; pierce; perforate; penetrate; be bored 〔drilled, penetrated, pierced, perforated〕. ¶ 벽에 구멍이 ~ a hole is made 〔drilled〕 through a wall / 이 송곳은 도무지 뚫어지지 않는다 This drill won't bore at all. ② 《결과》 a hole is made; be torn 〔broken, worn out〕. ¶ 신발이 ~ *one's* shoes are worn out / 장지에 구멍이 ~ a paper sliding door is torn.

**뚱기다** snap (it) out 〔let 《it》 go〕 with elastic force; let spring back; let resile.

**뚱기치다** give 《it》 a hard snap.

**뚱딴지**[1] ① 《애자》 an insulator. ② 《사람》 a blunt 〔dull〕 person; a log; a blockhead. ③ 《엉뚱함》 a preposterous 〔an unexpected, an irrelevant〕 person 〔thing〕. ¶ ~ 같다 be exorbitant; be absurd 〔irrelevant〕 / ~ 같은 생각 a wild 〔crazy〕 idea; an eccentric notion / ~ 같은 질문 in irrelevant question / ~ 같은 소리를 하다 say something ridiculous 〔eccentric〕 / ~ 같은 소리 마라 Don't be so ridiculous! *or* Nonsense!

**뚱딴지**[2] 〖식물〗 a Jerusalem artichoke.

**뚱땅거리다** keep drumming and twanging. ¶ 뚱땅거리며 놀다 make merry (boisterously); make whoopee; go on 〔have〕 a spree.

**뚱땅뚱땅** drumming and twanging.

**뚱뚱보** a fat 〔a plump, an obese, a corpulent〕 person; 《구어》 a fatty; Fatty (호칭). ¶ ~의 fat; fleshy; plump / 그녀는 ~다 She is a fat piece.

**뚱뚱하다** ① 《사람이》 (be) fat; stout; plump; corpulent; portly (중년이); obese; chubby; overweight. (★ fat는 「지방질의→뚱뚱한」의 뜻으로 혐오감이 함축되어 있어 여성에게는 쓰지 않음. stout는 「건강미 있게 체격이 듬직한」이란 좋은 뜻이 있어 남녀에게 흔히 자주 쓰임. plump는 둥글둥글하니 느낌이 좋게 「살이 찐」의 뜻. 여성에게 쓰이는 가장 무난한 표현은 rather overweight 임). ¶ 뚱뚱한 여인〔신사〕 a stout lady 〔gentleman〕 / 뚱뚱한 환자 an overweight patient / 뚱뚱해지다 fatten; grow corpulent 〔stout〕; become fat; put on weight. ② 《배 따위가》 (be) full; be swollen up. ¶ 배가 ~ be potbellied; have a full stomach; 《임부가》 be big with child.

**뚱보** ① 《뚱한 사람》 a dull 〔taciturn, glum, sulky〕 person. ② ⇨ 뚱뚱보.

**뚱하다** ① 《성질이》 (be) taciturn; reserved; uncommunicative. ¶ 뚱하여 말이 적다 be reserved and taciturn. ② 《심술나서》 (be) moody; glum; sullen; sulky. ¶ 뚱한 얼굴을 하다 look sullen 〔glum〕 / 그는 내가 돈을 주지 않는다고 뚱해서 앉아 있다 He is sitting there all glum because I have refused to give him the money.

**뛰놀다** jump about; skip (about); romp 〔gambol, frolic, caper〕 about; cut capers. ¶ 어린애들이 놀이터에서 뛰놀고 있다 The children are romping about on the playground. / 토끼들이 뛰놀고 있었다 The rabbits were leaping and hopping about.

**뛰다**[1] ① 《달리다》 run; rush; dash; race. ¶ 뛰어서 running; at a run / 뛰어가다 go running; go at a run; run 《to》; rush 《for》 / 뛰어오다 come running 〔on the run〕 / 뛰어서 귀가하다 run 〔race, fly〕 home; come home at a run / 집에서 여기까지 줄곧 뛰어왔다 I have run all the way from home. / 그는 층계를 뛰어 올라갔다〔내려갔다〕 He dashed up 〔down〕 the stairs.
② 《도약하다》 jump; leap; spring; bound; hop (한 발로). ¶ 뛰어서 with a jump; in a leap / (한번) 껑충 ~ make a leap 〔bound〕; give a spring / 가볍게 ~ take a slight jump; leap lightly / 기뻐서 ~ leap 〔jump〕 for joy; dance with joy.
③ 《물가가》 rise suddenly; go 〔run〕 up; jump (abruptly); shoot up; make a jump. ¶ 물가가 하룻밤 사이에 뛰었다 The prices shot up overnight. / 원유가가 1배럴당 20달러로 뛰었다 The price of oil has jumped to $20 a barrel. / 부동산 가격이 갑자기 뛰었다 Real property values went up suddenly.
④ 《뛰어넘다》 jump 〔vault, leap, spring〕 over; fly over. ¶ 담을 뛰어넘다 clear 〔jump over〕 a fence / 도랑을 뛰

어 건너다 jump 〔leap〕 over a ditch. ⑤《순서를》 skip (over); jump (over); omit. ¶ 3페이지를 건너 ~ skip page three / (책의) 어려운 구절을 건너 ~ skip 〔jump〕 (over) difficult passages. ⑥《물고기가》 break the water (물 속에서); be still full of life (잡은 것이).

**뛰다**[2] ①《물 따위가》 splash; spatter. ¶ 옷에 잉크가 ~ *one's* clothes are splashed with ink / 진흙이 내 바지에 튀었다 The mud splashed my trousers. / 프라이팬에서 기름이 튀었다 Oil spattered out of the frying pan. ②《달아나다》 run away 〔off〕; flee; escape; get away; take (to) flight; take to *one's* heels; make off. ¶ 한국에서 미국으로 ~ escape from Korea to America.

**뛰다**[3] ①《그네를》 get on 〔sit in〕 a swing. ¶ 그네를 뛰며 놀다 play on the swing. ②《널을》 seesaw. ¶ 널(을) ~ play seesaw 〔teeter-totter〕; seesaw.

**뛰다**[4] 《가슴이》 beat; throb; palpitate; 《맥박이》 pulsate. ¶ 맥박이 ~ *one's* pulse beats / 가슴이 ~ *one's* heart beats / 내 이름을 부르는 소리에 가슴이 뛰었다 When I heard my name called, my heart went pit-a-pat.

**뛰어가다** run; rush; dash; dart; race. ¶ 학교에 ~ run to school / 단숨에 ~ dash in a breath 〔with one breath〕.

**뛰어나가다** run 〔rush, dash, dart〕 out; 《도약하여》 jump 〔leap〕 out. ¶ 뒤에서 앞으로 ~ run forward from the rear / 밖으로〔뜰로〕 ~ rush out into the street 〔garden〕 / 방에서 ~ rush out of a room / (짐승이) 우리에서 ~ break 〔jump〕 out of a cage / 집을 ~ dart 〔rush〕 out of a house; 《가출하다》 run away from home; fly from *one's* home / 나는 그 행렬을 보려고 뛰어나갔다 I ran out to see the parade.

**뛰어나다** be better than; surpass; excel; exceed; be superior to; outdo; shine; 《우수하다》 be excellent; 《탁월하다》 stand conspicuous 〔out〕; tower above 《others》; distinguish *oneself;* be preeminent 〔outstanding〕.
¶ 뛰어난 outstanding; eminent (탁월한); prominent; distinguished; excellent (우수한); noted (유명한) / 뛰어나게 out 〔far〕 and away; by far; preeminently; out of the ordinary / 뛰어난 사람 an outstanding person / 뛰어난 재간 a distinguished talent / 뛰어난 학자 an eminent scholar / 뛰어난 업적 an outstanding 〔a brilliant〕 achievement / 수학에 ~ be excellent in mathematics / 영어에 ~ excel (all of us) in English / 남보다 역량이 ~ surpass 〔excel〕 others in ability / 한 가지 기예에 ~ be a master of an art / 한 반에서 그중 ~ stand out among 〔tower above〕 *one's* classmates / 그는 시험에서 뛰어난 성적을 올렸다 He distinguished himself in the examination. / 그녀는 외국어에 ~ She shines at 〔in〕 foreign languages.

**뛰어내리다** jump 〔leap, spring〕 down; jump 〔leap〕 off 〔from〕. ¶ 말에서 ~ leap from a horse; swing from a saddle / 창문에서 ~ leap out of a window / 달리는 열차에서 ~ jump off a running 〔moving〕 train / 2층에서 ~ jump 〔leap〕 down from the second floor / 5층에서 뛰어내려 자살하다 commit suicide by leaping 〔leap to *one's* death〕 from the fifth floor / 그는 10미터 높이에서 뛰어내렸다 He jumped 〔leaped〕 from a height of ten meters.

**뛰어넘다** ①《껑충》 jump 〔leap, spring〕 over; vault 《over》. ¶ 도랑을 ~ jump 〔leap〕 over the ditch / 담을 ~ clear 〔jump over〕 a fence / 장애물을 ~ clear 〔take〕 a hurdle / 그는 2미터 20을 뛰어넘어 높이뛰기에서 우승했다 He cleared the bar at 2.20 meters to win the high jump (event). ②《순서를》 skip 《over》; jump over. ¶ 10페이지에서 15페이지로 ~ skip from page 10 to 15 / 그는 나를 뛰어넘어 승진했다 He has been promoted over my head.

**뛰어다니다** ①《깡충깡충》 jump about; gambol; skip; frisk; romp. ¶ 강아지가 눈위를 뛰어다니고 있다 A pup is romping about in the snow. ②《바삐》 rush 〔run〕 about; fly about; hustle 〔bustle〕 about; be on the run; run around; busy *oneself* 《*do*ing》. ¶ 일자리를 찾느라 온종일 뛰어다녔다 I spent all day running around to look for a job. / 우리는 기금을 모으려고 뛰어다녔다 We busied ourselves raising funds. / 여기저기 뛰어다녀서 가까스로 5만 원을 마련했다 By much bustling here and there, I managed to raise fifty thousand won.

**뛰어들다** ①《도약》 jump 〔leap, spring〕 in(to); rush 〔dash, run〕 in; plunge 〔dive〕 into (물 속에). ¶ 다리에서 강으로 ~ jump off the bridge into the river / 물속으로 ~ go 〔plunge〕 into the water; take the water / 별안간 ~ make a sudden rush into 《a room》 / 철길에 ~ throw *oneself* on a track / 창문으로

방에 ～ jump into a room through the window / 그는 아이를 구하려고 불속으로 뛰어들었다 He ran 〔rushed〕 into the fire to save the child. ② 《남의 일에》 thrust *oneself* into; poke *one's* nose into; 《구어》 butt in. ¶ 싸움에 ～ thrust *oneself* into a quarrel.

**뛰어들어오다** dash 〔rush, run〕 in; burst into 《a room》. ¶ 우리가 방에서 이야기하고 있는데 그가 뛰어들어왔다 He dashed into the room where we were talking.

**뛰어오다** run 〔rush, dash, dart〕 along this way; come running. ¶ 한 아이가 우리에게 뛰어왔다 A child came running to us. / 집에서 여기까지 죽 뛰어왔다 I have run here all the way from home.

**뛰어오르다** jump 〔leap, spring〕 up; bounce; bound; 《물가가》 rise suddenly; jump; soar; make a jump; shoot up. ¶ 연단에 ～ spring up on a platform / 뛰어올라 타다 jump into 《a running car》; jump on 《a running horse》 / 여우는 포도를 따려고 여러 번 뛰어올랐다 The fox jumped many times to try to reach the grapes. / 휘발유 가격이 밤새 뛰어올랐다 The price of gasoline shot up overnight.

**뜀** 《달리기》 running; 《도약》 jumping; leaping; springing; skipping; vaulting. ¶ 뜀 뛰다 《달리다》 run; run a race; 《도약하다》 jump; leap; vault; spring.

**뜀뛰기** jumping. ◉ ～선수 a jumper. ～운동 a jumping exercise.

**뜀박질** ① ＝달음박질. ② ＝뜀뛰기.

**뜀틀** a vaulting 〔long〕 horse; a buck. ◉ ～운동 the vaulting 〔long〕 horse.

**뜨개것** knitted goods 〔work〕.

**뜨개바늘** a knitting needle 〔stick〕; 《코바늘》 a (crochet) hook.

**뜨개실** knitting yarn; wool. ¶ ～로 양말을 뜨다 knit wool into socks; knit socks out of wool.

**뜨개질** knitting; knitwork; 《코바늘의》 crochet. ～하다 knit; do *one's* knitting. ¶ ～한 장갑 hand-knitted gloves / 그녀는 아침부터 ～하고 있었다 She has been knitting since morning.

**뜨거워지다** get 〔become〕 hot; grow 〔get〕 warm; heat (up). ¶ 눈시울이 ～ be moved to tears / 엔진이 (정상보다) 뜨거워지기 시작했다 The engine has started to heat up.

**뜨거워하다** feel 《it》 hot; find 《it》 hot.

**뜨겁다** ① 《무엇이》 (be) hot; burning; heated. ¶ 뜨거운 국 hot soup / 몹시 뜨거운 커피 piping hot coffee / 뜨거운 눈물을 흘리다 shed hot tears / 햇볕이 ～ the sun is hot / 목욕물이 좀 지나치게 ～ The bath is a little too hot. / 부끄러워 얼굴이 ～ My face burns with shame / 증세(增稅) 문제는 정당 간에 뜨거운 감자처럼 처리 곤란한 문제이다 The issue of raising taxes is a hot potato among political parties. ② 《연애 관계가》 be madly in love 《with》; be hot 《on》; be sweet 《on》. ¶ 두 사람은 뜨거운 사이다 They are sweet on 〔deeply in love with〕 each other.

**-뜨기** one; guy; thing. ¶ 사팔뜨기 a cross-eyed 〔squint-eyed〕 person / 시골뜨기 a country bumpkin / 칠뜨기 a moron; an idiot / 얼뜨기 a half-wit.

**뜨끈뜨끈하다** (be) piping 〔burning〕 hot. ¶ 뜨끈뜨끈한 군고구마 sweet potatoes fresh from the oven.

**뜨끈하다** (be) fairly hot. ¶ 뜨끈한 국 warm soup / 국을 뜨끈하게 데우다 warm 〔heat〕 (up) soup.

**뜨내기** ① 《사람》 a wanderer; a vagabond; a vagrant; a tramp; a hobo; 《일꾼》 a wandering 〔casual〕 laborer; (구어) a floater. ② 《일》 a job done off and on; an odd job. ¶ ～로 행상하다 go around peddling things off and on / ～로 일해서 살아가다 get along by doing odd jobs. ◉ ～손님 a stray 〔chance, casual〕 visitor 〔customer〕; a transient guest.

**뜨내기장사** a business done off and on; a casual 〔temporary〕 business. ～하다 do a business off and on. ¶ 그는 ～로 돈깨나 모았다 He has amassed quite a sum of money by doing odd business.

**뜨다**[1] ① 《동작이 느리다》 (be) slow; sluggish; tardy; slack; 《경사 따위가》 gentle. ¶ 시계가 ～ a watch is slow 〔loses time〕 / 걸음이 ～ be slow-footed; be slow of foot; be a slow walker / 일이 ～ be slow at *one's* work; be a slow worker / 지붕의 물매가 너무 ～ The roof is pitched too gentle. / 그녀는 계산이 ～ She is slow at accounts.

② 《둔하다》 (be) dull; slow-〔dull-〕witted; be slow 《of understanding 〔learning〕》. ¶ 눈치가 ～ be slow at sensing a situation; have a slow perception / 깨우침이 ～ be slow to learn 〔in understanding〕.

③ 《입이》 (be) taciturn; reticent; be slow (to speak). ¶ 입이 ～ be taciturn; be incommunicative; be slow of

speech / 입이 뜬 사람 a man of few words; a silent man.
④ 《칼날이》 (be) blunt; dull. ¶ 칼날이 ~ the edge of a knife is blunt.
⑤ 《다리미가》 be slow to heat up.

**뜨다**[2] ① 《물·하늘에》 float 《on the water, in the air》. ¶ 물 위에 떠 있는 나뭇잎 leaves floating on the water / 물에 거품이 ~ bubbles float on the water / 하늘에 구름이 ~ clouds float in the sky / (공중에) 두둥실 ~ waft / 뒤집힌 보트를 붙들고 떠 있다 keep afloat by clinging to an overturned boat / 얼음은 물에 뜬다 Ice floats on the water. / 애드벌룬이 공중에 떠 있었다 An advertising balloon was floating in the air.
② 《해·달이》 rise; come up; 《무지개가》 span; hang 《in》. ¶ 해가〔달이〕 ~ the sun 〔moon〕 rises / 별이 하나씩 떴다 The stars came out one by one. / 하늘에 무지개가 떠 있다 A rainbow spans 〔hangs in〕 the sky.
③ 《연이》 (a kite) floats away free (after its string has been cut to disentangle it from another string).
④ 《벌어지다》 (***a***) 《들뜨다》 be detached; get 〔break〕 loose; come off 〔apart〕; be disjoined. ¶ 장판이 ~ a layer of oilpaper comes off the floor / 구들장이 ~ a slab of floor stone gets loose / 이가 (들) ~ [원인이 주어] set *one's* teeth on edge; loosen *one's* teeth. (***b***) 《틈새가》 have a gap 〔an opening〕. ¶ 잇새가 ~ have gaps between the teeth. (***c***) 《두 사람 관계가》 be estranged. ¶ 부부 사이가 ~ The man and wife are estranged from each other. *or* The couple do not get on well with each other.
⑤ 《사이가》 (***a***) 《공간적으로》 be 〔get〕 separated; be distant 〔apart〕 《from》. ¶ 십리나 사이가 ~ be ten *ri* away / 사이를 뜨게 하다 leave a space; space out / 우리 집과 그의 집은 거리가 상당히 떠 있다 My house and his are quite separated from each other. (***b***) 《시간적으로》 have an interval 《of time》; be few and far between. ¶ 사이가 3년 ~ be at an interval of three years / 일요일이라 시내 버스가 ~ Since it is Sunday, the city-bus service is slow.
⑥ 《빌려준 것》 become irrecoverable; be lost for good. ¶ 나는 그에게 빌려준 돈이 떠서 손해를 보았다 I suffered a loss because the money I lent him was dissipated.

**뜨다**[3] ① 《썩다》 become (hot and) stale 〔stuffy〕; be 〔get〕 musty; grow moldy; mold; turn bad 《from heat》. ¶ 날이 더워 창고에 둔 쌀이 떴다 The rice kept in the warehouse has become stale because of warm weather. ② 《얼굴이》 become sallow and bloated 〔swollen〕. ¶ 누렇게 뜬 얼굴 a bloated face / 너무 집에만 들어박혀 있었더니 얼굴이 다 떴다 Since I have shut myself in the house all the time, my face has grown all sallow. ③ 《발효하다》 ferment; undergo fermentation.

**뜨다**[4] 《뜸을》 burn 《moxa》 on 《the skin》; cauterize 《the skin》 with moxa; give 《*a person*》 moxa treatment.

**뜨다**[5] 《있던 곳을》 leave 《a place》; go away 〔off〕; depart 《from》; move 《out of a place》; clear out. ¶ 고향을 ~ leave *one's* hometown / 동네를 ~ leave a village / 서울을 ~ leave Seoul / 세상을 ~ depart (from) this life; pass away; die / 자리를 ~ leave 〔quit〕 *one's* seat / 자리를 뜨지 않고 있다 keep *one's* seat / 이곳은 살기가 힘들어 조만간 떠야겠다 Since it is so hard to get along here, I shall have to clear out sooner or later.

**뜨다**[6] ① 《떼어내다》 cut out. ¶ 강에서 얼음을 ~ cut out ice blocks from a river / 석재를 ~ cut out 〔quarry〕 stone / 떼를 ~ cut sod.
② 《푸다》 scoop (up); dip (up); ladle out (국자로); spoon up 〔out〕 (숟가락으로). ¶ 국자로 국을 ~ ladle soup; dip up soup with a ladle / 물고기를 사내끼로 ~ scoop fish with a landing net / 솥에서 더운 물을 떠내다 dip hot water out of a cauldron / 물을 손으로 떠 마시다 drink water out of *one's* cupped hands.
③ 《종이 따위를》 make 〔manufacture〕 《paper》; make paste 《into cake forms》. ¶ 김을 ~ make laver.
④ 《수란을》 poach 《eggs》.
⑤ 《각뜨다》 cut 《in, into》. ¶ 소를 잡아 각을 ~ cut a butchered ox into several parts.
⑥ 《저미다》 slice 《meat》; cut into slices. ¶ 포를 ~ cut meat into slices 《to be dried》.
⑦ 《옷감을》 buy 《a piece of cloth to make clothes》. ¶ 장에 가거든 옷감 한 감 떠다 주시오 When you go to the marketplace, please get me a piece of cloth to make into a dress.

**뜨다**[7] ① 《눈을》 open (*one's* eyes). ¶ 눈을 크게 뜨고 《look at》 with *one's* eyes wide open / 눈을 ～ open *one's* eyes; 《아침에》 wake (up); awake; 《자각하다》 be awakened 《to》 / 성에 눈을 ～ become aware 〔conscious〕 of sex; be sexually awakened / 엄연한 현실에 눈을 ～ awake to the stern realities of life. ② 《청각을》 open; prick up 《*one's* ears》. ¶ 귀를 ～ hear; catch; learn; begin to understand / 음악에 귀를 ～ begin to appreciate music / 아기가 귀를 ～ a baby begins to hear.

**뜨다**[8] ① 《떠서 만들다》 (***a***) 《그물을》 make 《a net》; net. ¶ 그물을 ～ make a net; net. (***b***) 《짜다》 knit; do *one's* knitting; crochet (코바늘로). ¶ 양말〔장갑〕을 ～ knit stockings 〔gloves〕 《out of wool》. ② 《깁다》 stitch; sew. ¶ 터진 데를 한두 바늘 ～ put one or two stitches in a rip; sew up a rip with one or two stitches. ③ 《문신하다》 tattoo 《the skin, a flower on *one's* arm》. ¶ 아무의 등에 용의 문신을 ～ tattoo a dragon on *a person's* back.

**뜨다**[9] 《받다》 horn; toss; butt. ¶ 황소가 뿔로 ～ a bull tosses 《*a person*》 with his horns.

**뜨다**[10] ① 《본을》 copy; copy out; copy from; imitate. ¶ 버선 본을 ～ copy the pattern of socks 《from the original model》 / 본을 떠서 그리다 paint from a copy / 아무의 나쁜 점을 본 ～ copy *a person's* bad points; imitate 〔follow〕 *a person's* bad example. ② 《도면 따위를》 trace; draw; copy. ¶ 사본을 ～ copy; make a copy 《of》. ③ 《지형(紙型) 따위를》 make; take. ¶ 지형을 ～ make 〔take〕 a papier-mâché mold 《of》.

**뜨덤뜨덤** falteringly; with difficulty; stammering(ly). ⇨ 더듬더듬.

**뜨듯하다, 뜨뜻하다** (be) warm; hot. ¶ 뜨듯한 날씨 warm weather / 뜨듯한 방〔옷〕 a warm room 〔clothes〕 / 뜨듯해지다 get 〔become〕 warm / 뜨듯하게 하다 warm 〔heat〕 up / 방을 뜨듯하게 덥히다 heat a room warm.

**뜨뜻미지근하다** 《온도가》 (be) lukewarm; tepid; 《태도가》 (be) halfhearted; lukewarm; 《너무 온건하다》 (be) too lenient 〔mild〕. ¶ 뜨뜻미지근한 태도를 취하다 adopt a lukewarm attitude 《toward》; turn lukewarm 《toward》.

**뜨락** a garden; a yard. ⇨ 뜰.

**뜨막하다** be long 《since》; have a long interval 《between》; be few and far between. ¶ 오늘은 일요일이라서 버스가 ～ Since it is Sunday, the buses are running few and far between.

**뜨물** water in which rice has been washed.

**뜨악하다** (be) unwilling; reluctant; be disinclined 《to *do*》. ¶ 나는 거기에 가는 것이 어쩐지 ～ I'm not very keen on going there.

**뜨음하다** (be) infrequent; have a rather long interval; have a longer interval than usual. ¶ 발길이 ～ come 〔visit〕 less often 〔frequently〕 (than before) / 집 소식이 ～ have not heard from home for quite a long time / 옆집 사람들의 싸움이 요즘은 좀 ～ The next-door people don't quarrel as often as they used to these days. / 적의 포화가 뜨음해졌다 The enemy's fire slackened a little.

**뜨이다** ① 《눈이》 (come) open; be opened; wake (up); awake; 《귀가》 prick up; take an interest. ¶ 아침 다섯 시에 눈이 ～ awake at five in the morning / 귀가 ～ *one's* ears prick up 《with surprise 〔pleasure〕》 / 눈이 ～ wake (up); awake; [비유적] come 〔be brought〕 to *one's* senses; awake(n) 《to》 / 눈이 번쩍 ～ awake suddenly; be wide awake / 현실에 눈이 ～ awake to the realities of life / 성에 눈이 ～ become aware 〔conscious〕 to sex; be sexually awakened / 음악〔그림〕에 귀가 〔눈이〕 ～ begin to appreciate music 〔painting〕 / 그 소리를 들으니 귀가 번쩍 뜨인다 Hearing that is a pleasant surprise.
② 《눈에》 be seen; attract 〔catch〕 *one's* 〔*a person's*〕 attention 〔eye〕; strike 〔catch〕 the eye 《of》; greet 〔meet, fall〕 under *one's* 〔*a person's*〕 eyes; 《두드러지다》 be prominent 〔conspicuous〕; stand out conspicuously; be striking 〔remarkable〕. ¶ 눈에 뜨이게 conspicuously; strikingly; remarkably; markedly; noticeably / 눈에 뜨이지 않게 in a quiet 〔a modest, an inconspicuous〕 way; so as not to attract attention; quietly / 눈에 뜨이게 아름다운 미인 an attractive beauty; a woman of striking 〔dazzling〕 beauty / 눈에 ～ attract (*one's*) attention; draw notice; catch 〔strike〕 *one's* eyes / 눈에 뜨이는 곳에 게시하다 put up 《a notice》 in a conspicuous place / 눈에 뜨이게 잘 생기다 be remarkably good-looking / 눈에 뜨이게 건강이 쇠약해지다 *one's* health declines noticeably / 그는 눈에 뜨이게 향상했다 He has made remarkable progress. / 그의 이마에 있

는 상처가 흉하게 눈에 뜨인다 The scar on his forehead shows horribly. / 사진기를 들고 나오다가 아버지 눈에 뜨였다 I was taking the camera with me when I was detected by my father.

**뜬구름** 《구름》 a drifting 〔floating〕 cloud; a cloud drift; [비유적] transitoriness (덧없음); transience; evanescence (of life). ¶ ～ 같은 인생 transient 〔ephemeral〕 life; the transience of human life / 인생이란 ～이다 Life is but an empty dream.

**뜬눈** unsleeping 〔wide-awake〕 eyes. ¶ ～으로 밤을 새우다 sit up all night; cannot get a wink of sleep; do not sleep a wink; be wakeful all night; pass 〔have〕 a sleepless night (잠이 안와서) / 어젯밤은 ～으로 새웠다 I couldn't sleep a wink last night.

**뜬벌이** ～하다 earn *one's* living by doing odd jobs.

**뜬세상**(一世上) the (transitory) world; transient 〔fleeting〕 life.

**뜬소문**(一所聞) a groundless rumor; an unfounded report; a *canard* (F.). ¶ …라는 ～이 돌아다니다 a groundless rumor is going around that….

**뜬숯** used charcoal; cinders.

**뜬재물**(一財物) wealth happened upon 〔come by〕 casually; wealth won without effort; a windfall. ¶ ～이 나에게 굴러 들어왔다 I unexpectedly came into a large fortune.

**뜯게질** unsewing 〔ripping the seams out of〕 worn-out clothes.

**뜯기다**[1] ① 《물리다》 be bitten. ¶ 벼룩에게 뜯긴 자리 a fleabite / 나는 밤새도록 모기한테 뜯겼다 I was bitten by mosquitos all through the night. ② 《빼앗기다》 have 《*a thing*》 bitten off; be plucked 〔fleeced〕 《of》; be exacted 〔extorted, squeezed〕 《by》. ¶ 돈을 ～ be fleeced of money 《by a sharper》. ③ 《잃다》 lose. ¶ 노름에서 ～ lose money in gambling; gamble away *one's* money. ④ 《뜯어지다》 be torn. ¶ 옷이 못에 걸려 ～ have *one's* clothes torn on a nail.

**뜯기다**[2] 《마소에게 풀을》 graze 《cattle》; put 〔turn〕 《cattle》 to grass; put 《sheep》 to grazing; pasture. ¶ 소에게 풀을 ～ put a cow on grass; put cattle to graze 〔to pasture, to feed on growing grass〕.

**뜯다** ① 《떼어내다》 (***a***) 《잡아떼다》 tear (out); pick; pluck; pull out; take apart. ¶ 닭의 털을 ～ pluck a chicken / 뜰의 잡초를 ～ weed the garden; pull up weeds in the garden. (***b***) 《뜯어내다》 tear apart; take apart; pull to pieces; break up; disjoint; dismantle; disassemble. ¶ 공장을 ～ dismantle a factory / 기계를 ～ strip a machine (down) / 시계를 ～ take a watch apart 〔to pieces〕. (***c***) 《꿰맨 것을》 unsew; unstitch. ¶ 옷을 ～ unsew clothes / 솔기를 ～ undo a seam; unsew / 뜯어진 솔기를 꿰매다 mend an open seam. ② 《뜯어먹다》 bite; graze; eat. ¶ 불갈비를 ～ eat roast ribs of beef / 소가 풀을 ～ the cattle graze / 빵조각을 크게 물어 ～ bite off a large chunk of bread. ③ 《돈을》 pluck; fleece; extort 《money from *a person*》. ¶ 아무한테 돈을 ～ pluck 〔fleece〕 *a person* of *his* money / 친구에게서 용돈을 ～ pester 〔press〕 *one's* friend for pocket money. ④ 《노름판에서》 gain; get; receive. ¶ 노름판에서 돈을 ～ take a (free) cut of the winnings; receive a tip from each gambler. ⑤ 《현악기 줄을》 play; pluck (the string of); pick. ¶ 가야금을 ～ play a *kayagŭm* (= Korean harp).

**뜯어고치다** ① 《해체하여》 tear 〔take〕 apart and mend 〔repair〕; 《개조하다》 reconstruct; rebuild; remodel. ¶ 옷을 ～ mend *one's* clothes; have *one's* suit remodeled / 헌 집을 ～ rebuild 〔reconstruct〕 an old house / 방을 ～ remodel a room. ② 《시정하다》 look over and change 〔alter〕; revise 《the plan》; reform; remake; remedy; 《조직·정책 따위를》 rearrange; reorganize; reshuffle. ¶ 악폐를 ～ reform abuses; redress evils / 못된 버릇을 ～ 《자기의》 get over a bad habit; 《남의》 break 〔cure〕 《*a person*》 of a bad habit / 법령을 ～ revise an ordinance.

**뜯어내다** ① 《붙은 것을》 take off 〔away〕; pick (off); tear 〔pluck, rip, strip〕 off. ¶ 달력 한 장을 ～ tear off a leaf from a calendar / 옷에서 실밥을 ～ remove the stitches from clothes / 솔기를 ～ undo 〔rip up〕 a seam; cut a seam open / 옷의 안찝을 ～ rip off 〔out〕 the lining / 잡풀을 ～ pluck up weeds. ② 《분해·해체하다》 break 《*a thing*》 up; disjoint; dismantle; disassemble; disintegrate; pull 〔take〕 《*a thing*》 to pieces; strip 《*a thing*》 down; 《건축물을》 demolish; pull 〔take〕 down. ¶ 기계를 ～ take a machine to pieces / 뜯어내어 운반하다 convey 《a machine》 in section / 지붕을 ~ strip the roof of tiles; unroof of a house. ③《금품을》 extort; pluck; fleece. ¶ 남편한테서 돈을 ~ pluck *one's* husband of his money; tease *one's* husband for money.

**뜯어말리다** pull apart《fighters》; stop 《a fight》. ¶ 싸움을 ~ pull combatants 〔quarreling persons〕 apart; stop a rough-and-tumble fight.

**뜯어먹다** ①《먹다》(***a***)《풀을》feed on grass; graze (on). (***b***)《입으로》eat 〔bite〕 off; gnaw; nibble at 〔on〕;《손으로》tear off《*something*》with *one's* hands and eat《it》. ¶ 구운 닭고기를 ~ nibble on a roasted chicken / 뼈에 붙은 고기를 ~ gnaw the meat off a bone. ②《희생으로 하여》live on 〔off〕 《*a person*》; impose a burden of livelihood on《*a person*》; sponge on. ¶ 딸을 뜯어먹고 살다 live on *one's* daughter; make sacrifice of *one's* own daughter.

**뜯어버리다** 《내버리다》 tear 《*a thing*》 off and throw it away; take 《*a thing*》 apart 〔to pieces〕 and throw it away;《제거하다》clear《*a thing*》away; remove.

**뜯어벌이다** ① 《벌여놓다》 take 〔tear, pull〕 to pieces; dismantle; take 《a machine》 apart; open up. ②《얘기를》 tell in an irritating fashion; narrate 〔relate, describe〕 in a disagreeable 〔an impudent〕 manner.

**뜯어보다** ①《봉한 것을》open《*a thing*》 〔tear《*a thing*》open〕 and look at it. ¶ 편지를 ~ tear a letter open; cut open a letter; open a letter and read it. ② 《살펴보다》 look at 《*a thing*》 from every angle; scrutinize carefully; examine 〔inspect〕 in detail; make a close inspection 《of *a thing*》. ¶ 아무의 얼굴을 ~ scrutinize *a person's* face carefully / 집을 이모저모로 ~ look a house over thoroughly. ③《간신히 읽다》 read 〔construe〕 with difficulty; falter (in reading). ¶ 편지를 간신히 ~ read a letter with difficulty.

**뜰** a garden; a yard; a ground. ¶ 뜰 우물 a well in the yard / 앞〔뒤〕뜰 a front 〔back〕 yard / 안뜰 a courtyard.

**뜰아래채** an outer (and less important) wing of a house.

**뜰아랫방**(─房) a room in an outer and less important wing of a house.

**뜸**[1]《짚 따위로 엮은》a rush mat; rush matting. ¶ 뜸으로 지붕을 이은 집 a rush-thatched cottage.

**뜸**[2] 〖한의〗 moxa cautery; moxibustion. ¶ 뜸 자국 a mark made by moxa cautery / 뜸 자리 spots on the body suitable for moxa cautery / 뜸뜨다 cauterize《the skin》with moxa; burn moxa on《the skin》; apply moxa《to》.

**뜸**[3] 《밥 등의》 ¶ (밥에) 뜸이 들다 be steamed (to a proper degree).

**뜸들이다** ① 《음식물을》 cook 〔steam〕 thoroughly. ¶ 밥을 ~ steam boiled rice; give 〔allow〕 boiled rice to settle; let rice steam for a while after being cooked. ② 《일할 때》 give a necessary interval of time; give time (enough); give a pause. ¶ 일을 뜸들여 하다 allow enough time to get a job done.

**뜸베질** 《소의》 horning; a butt. ~하다 「horn; butt.

**뜸부기** 〖조류〗 a mud hen; a water rail 〔cock〕.

**뜸직뜸직** 《언행이》 slowly; gravely; solemnly; in a dignified manner. ¶ ~ 말하다 speak solemn words; measure *one's* words / 걸음을 ~ 걷다 walk slowly; walk with dignified 〔measured〕 steps.

**뜸직하다** (be) slow; measured; grave; solemn; dignified; imposing; commanding.

**뜸직이** slowly; gravely; solemnly.

**뜸질** 《뜸뜨기》 cauterizing with moxa; moxa cautery. ~하다 cauterize 《the skin》 with moxa; give 《*a person*》 moxa treatment.

**뜸집** a rush-thatch(ed) hut 〔cottage〕.

**뜸하다** ⇨ 뜨음하다.

**뜻** ① 《의향》 an intention; an intent; 《마음》 a 〔*one's*〕 mind; an idea; a thought; a wish; a want. ¶ …할 뜻이 있다, …할 뜻을 갖다 have an intention 《of》; be inclined to *do;* have a mind to *do;* intend to *do* / 뜻을 말하다 〔밝히다〕 reveal 〔express, announce, declare, disclose〕 *one's* intention; speak *one's* mind / 사장의 뜻에 따르다 follow the instructions of the president; yield to the president's wishes / 남의 뜻을 떠보다 sound *a person's* views / 뜻이 서로 통하다 come to 〔arrive at〕 an understanding; understand each other / 장사할 뜻은 조금도 없다 I don't have the slightest intention of going into business. / 너는 부모의 뜻을 어겨서는 안된다 You shouldn't do anything against your parent's wishes. / 뜻있는 분들의 참석을 환영합니다 Those interested are welcome to attend.

② 《목적·희망》 an aim; an object; a purpose; (a) hope; a wish; 《의지》 mind; (a) will. ¶ 큰 뜻 an ambition; an aspiration / 뜻을 세우다 set an aim in life; fix a purpose; make up *one's* mind 《to *do*》; be determined to 《*do*》 / 뜻을 높이 가지다 aim high / 뜻을 이루다 attain *one's* aim 〔object〕; reach *one's* goal; accomplish 〔fulfill〕 *one's* purpose; achieve 〔succeed in〕 *one's* object; realize *one's* aspiration / 아무의 뜻을 어기다 act against *a person's* will / 아버지의 뜻을 잇다 take over the will of *one's* father / 모든 일이 뜻대로 되지 않다 everything goes wrong 《for *one*》 / 만사가 내 뜻대로 되었다 Everything went with me. / 그는 뜻을 이루지 못하고 죽었다 He died before he could realize his dream. *or* He did not live long enough to realize his aspiration(s). / 연작(燕雀)이 어찌 홍곡(鴻鵠)의 뜻을 알리요 A man must be a hero to understand a hero. *or* How can the sparrow soar with the eagle.

③ 《의미》 meaning; a sense; significance; 《취지》 import; purport; effect; point; purpose. ¶ 뜻있는 significant; meaningful / 뜻없는 senseless; meaningless / 말 뜻 the meaning of a word; the meaning of what *one* says / 보통 뜻 the ordinary meaning; the usual sense / 숨은 뜻 a hidden 〔latent〕 meaning / 뜻이 통하지 않는 말 senseless talk / 뜻의 미묘한 차이 a delicate shade of meaning / …라는 뜻의 편지 a letter to the effect that… / 좁은〔넓은, 엄밀한, 글자대로의〕 뜻으로 in a narrow 〔broad, strict, literal〕 sense / 어떤 뜻에서는 in a (certain) sense; in a way / 뜻을 곡해하다 pervert 〔twist〕 the meaning / 뜻을 해석하다 interpret the meaning / 뜻을 잘못 해석하다 mistake the meaning; misinterpret; misconstrue / 뜻이 없다 be meaningless; be senseless; be devoid of meaning; be nonsense / 뜻이 깊다 have deep 〔profound〕 meaning; be full of meaning; be significant; be meaningful / 뜻이 분명하다 the meaning is clear; have an obvious meaning / 뜻이 애매하다 have an ambiguous 〔obscure〕 meaning; be vague / 넓은 뜻으로 쓰다 use it in a broad 〔general〕 sense / 좋은 뜻으로 해석하다 take it in a favorable sense; put a good construction on 《what *one* says》; take 《it》 well / 나쁜 뜻으로 해석하다 take 《what *one* says》 in a bad sense; put a bad construction on 《what *one* says》; take 《it》 ill / 뜻있는 (듯한) 시선을 힐끔 주다 shoot a meaning glance at 《*a person*》 / 그녀는 뜻있는 (듯한) 미소를 지었다 She gave a meaningful smile. / 그건 무슨 뜻이냐 What do you mean by that? / 이 문장의 뜻은 전혀 알 수가 없다 I can make nothing of this passage. / 잘 있다는 뜻의 편지를 받았다 I received a letter to the effect that he is getting along well. / 내말을 그런 뜻으로 받아들여서는 곤란하다 You must not take my words that way. / 나쁜 뜻으로 말한 것이 아니니 나쁘게 생각지 마라 Don't get me wrong—I had nothing bad in mind.

**뜻글자**(―字) an ideograph.

**뜻대로** *one's* own way; just as wished 〔hoped〕; just as intended 〔meant〕; as *one* wishes 〔expects〕; as was expected. ¶ ～ 되다 come up to *one's* expectations; turn out satisfactory; turn out just as *one* wished / ～ 안 되다 fall short of *one's* expectations 〔hopes〕 / ～ 하다 do as *one* pleases 〔likes〕; have 《*a thing*》 *one's* own way / ～ 되지 않는 세상 life full of vexations / 만사가 ～ 되었다 Everything worked out just as I had planned. *or* Everything went my (own) way. / 만사가 ～ 되지 않았다 Everything has gone wrong with me. / 일이란 좀처럼 ～ 되는 것이 아니다 Things seldom come up to our expectations.

**뜻맞다** ① 《뜻이 맞다》 agree 〔hit it off 《구어》〕 《with *a person*》; see eye to eye 《with》; be of a mind; be like=minded. ¶ 뜻맞는 친구 a congenial friend; a friend *one* likes / 서로 ～ see eye to eye with each other / 그들은 뜻이 맞는다 They are like-minded. / 김군과 나는 뜻맞는 사이다 We are congenial spirits, Mr. Kim and I.

② 《마음에 들다》 be satisfactory; be acceptable to 《*a person*》; be to *one's* taste 〔liking〕; be after *one's* heart; suit 〔please, catch, take, capture, strike〕 《*a person's*》 fancy. ⇨ 마음 ②.

**뜻밖** being contrary to *one's* expectation; a surprise. ¶ ～의 unexpected; unanticipated; unforeseen; unlooked=for; unsuspected / ～에(도) unexpectedly; accidentally; surprisingly; to *one's* surprise / ～에 빨리 earlier than (was) expected / ～의 결과 an unexpected result / ~의 일 an unexpected happening; an unforeseen occurrence / ~의 사건 an unlooked-for event; an accident / ~의 소식 surprising news / ~의 손님 an unexpected guest / ~이라 생각할지 모르겠으나 contrary to what you might think / ~의 재난을 만나다 suffer an unexpected misfortune / …은전혀 ~이다 be surprised 《at, to hear that …》; be disappointed 《in》 / ~에도 …하게 되다 happen 〔chance〕 to *do* / ~의 사람이 찾아오다 have an unexpected caller / 그의 방문은 전혀 ~이었다 His visit was a great surprise to me. / 이런 데서 만나다니 정말 ~이군요 I never dreamed to see you here, of all places. / ~에 시간이 걸렸다 It took more time than I (had) expected. / 매상이 ~에 적었다 The sale did not come up to our expectations. / 그것은 천만 ~이다 That is a great surprise. *or* That is a bolt from the blue.

**뜻받다** meet 《*a person's*》 request; comply with 《*a person's*》 wish; yield to 〔obey〕 《*a person's*》 wishes. ¶ 부모의 뜻을 받아 하라는 대로 하다 yield to *one's* parents and do what they say; obey *one's* parents.

**뜻있게** meaningfully; sensibly; in a meaningful or sensible way; with meaning or purpose. ¶ 돈을 좀 ~ 써라 Spend your money sensibly 〔usefully, to good purpose〕.

**뜻하다** ① 《마음먹다》 intend to *do;* aim 《at *something,* to *do*》; set *one's* heart 〔mind〕 on 《learning》; aspire to 〔after〕 《fame》; have an ambition 《to *do*》; 《결심하다》 resolve to *do;* make up *one's* mind 《to *do*》. ¶ 외교관을 ~ aspire 〔aim〕 to be a (career) diplomat / 그는 뜻한 바를 이루기 위해 열심히 노력했다 He tried hard to 「attain his aim 〔achieve his purpose〕 ② 《의미하다》 mean; signify; imply. ¶ 그것은 무엇을 뜻하느냐 What does it mean 〔signify〕? / 침묵은 때때로 동의를 뜻한다 Silence often implies consent. / 그러한 실험은 인류의 파멸을 뜻할 수도 있다 Such experiment might spell the end of the human race.

**띄다** ① ⇨뜨이다. ② ⇨띄우다.

**띄어쓰기** spacing words. ~하다 ⇨띄어쓰다.

**띄어쓰다** write leaving space (between the words); separate the words; leave spaces; space 《lines》. ¶ 한자 한자 ~ space out words / 한 줄씩 ~ write on every other 〔second〕 line.

**띄엄띄엄** ① 《드문드문》 sparsely; thinly; scatteredly; 《사이를 두고》 at intervals; intermittently. ¶ ~ 읽다 skip 《in reading》; read skippingly; read 「at random 〔desultorily〕 / 나무를 ~ 심다 plant trees at considerable intervals / 인가가 ~ 있다 be sparsely dotted with houses. ② 《느릿느릿》 slowly 《walk》; sluggishly. ¶ 걸음을 ~ 걷다 walk very slowly / ~ 걸어도 황소 걸음 slow but steady; slow but sure.

**띄우다**[1] ① 《공중에》 fly 《*a thing*》; let 《*a thing*》 fly; send 《*a thing*》 up. ¶ 연을 ~ fly 〔send up〕 a kite / 광고 풍선을 ~ float an advertising balloon. ② 《물위에》 float; set 《a boat》 afloat; sail; waft (나뭇잎 따위를); launch (진수하다). ¶ 뗏목을 ~ float a log raft 《down a river》 / 배를 ~ set a boat afloat; sail a boat; launch a boat. ③ 《얼굴에》 express; let show; look 《sad, angry》. ¶ 얼굴에 근심의 빛을 띄우고 with a gloomy brow; with a worried look / 입가에 미소를 띄우고 with a smile (playing) about *one's* lips / 눈에 기쁜 빛을 띄우고 with *one's* eyes beaming with joy / 만면에 웃음을 ~ smile all over *one's* face; be beaming 〔radiant〕 with smiles. ④ 《편지를》 send; dispatch. ¶ 편지를 ~ send a letter; post 〔mail〕 a letter.

**띄우다**[2] 《훈김으로》 ferment; mold; sweat (담뱃잎 따위를); make 《*a thing*》 〔let 《*a thing*》 get〕 stale from the heat. ¶ 누룩을〔메주를〕 ~ ferment malt 〔steamed soybean lumps〕.

**띄우다**[3] 《사이를》 space; leave 《an interval》; leave space 《between》. ¶ 사이를 띄워서 at intervals; sparsely / 석 자 사이를 띄워서 나무를 심다 plant trees 3 *ja* apart / 줄〔행〕 사이를 ~ leave space between the lines; space the lines / 두 줄씩 ~ leave out every two lines.

**띠** ① 《허리의》 a belt; a sash (여자·어린이용의). ¶ 허리띠 a waistband; a girdle / 가죽띠 a leather belt; a band / 띠를 매다 tie a belt 〔sash〕 / 띠를 조르다 tighten *one's* belt / 띠를 풀다 untie 〔undo〕 a sash. ② 《물건 매는》 a (drawing) string; a binder; twine. ③ 《아기 업는》 a "papoose" 〔baby-carrying〕 band. ④ 《탄생한 해의》 the zodiacal sign *one* was born under. ¶ 그녀는 말띠이다 She was born in the year of Horse. ⑤ 《화투의》 a five-point card in the flower card game.

**띠다** ① 《띠를》 wear 《a belt, a girdle》. ¶ 띠를 ～ wear a belt; girdle *oneself*. ② 《지니다》 carry; be armed with. ¶ 몸에 비수를 ～ be armed with a dagger. ③ 《용무를》 be charged with 《a duty》; be entrusted with; be invested 〔clothed〕 with 《authority》; have. ¶ 공무를 띠고 on official business / 용무를 띠고 여행하다 go on a trip for business purposes / 중대한 사명을 ～ be entrusted with 〔have〕 an important mission. ④ 《빛·기색을》 have; wear; assume; put on; show; present; exhibit. ¶ 노기를 띤 말 sharp 〔angry〕 words / 붉은 빛을 띤 자주 purple tinged with red; purple with a dash of red / 걱정하는 빛을 띠고 with an expression of worry / 붉은 빛을 ～ be tinged with red; be reddish; have a tinge of red / 걱정하는 빛을 ～ look worried; have a worried look / 술기운을 ～ be under the influence of liquor; be tipsy / 활기를 ～ present an animated appearance; liven up.

**띠앗머리** sibling 〔brotherly, sisterly〕 affection; fraternal love; love among brothers and sisters. ¶ ～ 없다 lack in brotherly 〔sisterly〕 affection.

**띠종이, 띠지**(—紙) a strip of paper; a money band (돈다발 묶는).

**띠톱** a band 〔belt〕 saw.

**띵띵하다** ⇨ 딩딩하다.

**띵하다** 《아파서》 have a deep-seated 〔dull〕 pain; 《머리가 흐리다》 (be) dull; muddled; fuzzy; muzzy; numb. ¶ 머리가 ～ have a dull headache; feel heavy in the head; feel *one's* head muddled / 밤샘을 했더니 머리가 ～ My head is fuzzy because I stayed up all night. / 과음하면 머리가 띵해진다 Excessive drinking muddles *one's* brains.

**-ㄹ** ① [일반적 사실을 나타내는 전성어미] ¶ 할 일 things to do / 잘 시간 the time to go to bed / 팔 집〔자동차〕 a house 〔a car〕 for sale / 쓸 돈 the money to spend / 나한테 편지를 쓸 사람들 persons to write letters to me / 내가 편지를 쓸 사람들 persons for me to write letters to / 그것은 어찌할 도리가 없다 There's nothing to be done about it. / 너를 볼 때마다 자네 어머니 생각이 난다 You always remind me of your mother. / 나는 어찌할 바를 몰랐다 I did not know what to do.
② [미래의 일을 나타내는 전성어미] ¶ 올봄 the coming spring / 자동차를 팔 사람 the man who will sell the car / 시집 갈 여자 a bride-to-be / 비가 올 징조 《atmospheric》 signs of rain / 나는 비행기로 갈 생각이다 I intend to go by plane.

**-ㄹ걸** ① 《추측》 I should 〔dare〕 say; perhaps; probably; maybe; I guess. ¶ 아닐걸 I should say not. / 그 집은 꽤 비쌀걸 But that house will be very expensive! / 이것으로 충분할걸 This will probably be enough. / 네가 나보다 더 클걸 I think 〔guess〕 you are taller than I. / 그는 지금 집에서 공부하고 있을걸 I guess he is studying at home now. / 그 모자는 나한테 좀 클걸 I guess the hat is a bit too big for me.
② 《후회》 (I wish I had) but... (I didn't). ¶ 말을 할걸 If only I had spoken! / 그 책을 살걸 I wish I'd bought that book. / 그가 했더라면 좋았을걸 I wish he'd done it, anyway (but he didn't do it).

**-ㄹ 것같다** 《사물에 대한 추측》 it seems that it will be 〔*do*〕; it is like the one 〔thing〕 that will be 〔*do*〕; be likely to; probably; 《막 …할 것 같다》 threaten 《to *do*》; be about to 《*do*》; 《…같이 보이다》 look; appear.
¶ 곧 울음을 터뜨릴 것 같다 be ready to cry; be almost in tears / 그가 올 것 같다 He seems to be coming. / 그는 올 것 같지 않다 He is not likely to come. /비가 올 것 같다 It looks like rain. / 이 책은 재미있을 것 같다 This book seems interesting. / 저 차는 그다지 비쌀 것 같지 않다 That car doesn't seem to be very expensive. / 그는 절망한 나머지 미칠 것 같았다 He was almost beside himself with despair. / 그들은 그것을 승낙할 것 같지 않다 There is little likelihood of their giving consent to it.

**-ㄹ게** I will do right away (I promise). ¶ 잠깐 다녀올게—기다리고 있거라 Please wait here—I'll be right back. / 내가 얼른 보고 줄게—잠깐만 보여 줘 Please show it to me for a moment—I'll give it right back to you. / 내가 이따 문을 닫을게 I'll shut the door a little later.

**-ㄹ까** ① 《의문·의심》 I wonder; I am afraid; I fear (★ I am afraid; I fear는 주로 못마땅한 일에 대해 씀: I fear it is too late. 「너무 늦은 게 아닐까」); whether it is to be 〔*do*〕; will it be?; will it *do?* ¶ 그게 정말일까 I wonder if 〔whether〕 it can be true. *or* Can it be true? / 지금 몇 시나 되었을까 What time is it, I wonder? / 설마 그럴까 Really? *or* You don't say! / 그는 어떤 사람일까 What is he? / 그는 누구일까 Who is he? / 내일도 날이 흐릴까 Will it be cloudy again tomorrow? / 그가 왜 이리 올까 Why is he coming this way? / 그는 올까 I wonder if he is coming. / 그가 이 제의를 거절한다면 어떻게 될까 If he should refuse the proposal, what would happen? / 나는 이 달 월급으로 시계를 하나 살까 망설이고 있다 I'm toying with the idea of buying a watch with this month's pay.
② 《…할까요》 shall we *do?* ¶ 갈까(요) Shall we go? / 자, 공원에나 갈까 Now, let's go to the park, shall we? / 걸어서 갈까 Shall we go on foot? *or* What do you say to going on foot? / 자전거를 타고 갈까요, 걸어갈까요 Shall we ride our bikes or walk? / 위스키 한 잔 하는 게 어떨까 How about having a glass of whisky?

**-ㄹ까 말까** ① 《주저》 ¶ 일요일에 그녀를 방문할까 말까 망설였다 I hesitated about calling on her on Sunday. / 나는 그녀

의 초대에 응할까 말까 망설였다 I had 〔felt〕 some hesitation in accepting her invitation.

② 《미달》 ¶ 만원이 될까말까 한 돈 a sum less than ten thousand won / 그 일은 한 시간이 될까말까 해서 끝났다 The work was finished in a little under an hour.

**-ㄹ까 보냐** ¶ 어찌 그런 일이 있을까 보냐 How can it 〔that〕 be? / 누가 그런 짓을 할까 보냐 Who would do such a thing?

**-ㄹ까 보다** 《불확실한 의사》 ¶ 책이나 읽을까 보다 I would rather read. / 오늘 저녁에는 외식이나 할까보다 I feel like eating out this evening.

**-ㄹ까봐** 《우려》 for fear of; fearful of. ¶ 또 실패할까봐 걱정이다 I'm afraid I shall fail again. / 그는 죽을까봐 두려웠다 He was afraid of dying.

**-ㄹ까 하다** be thinking of *do*ing. ¶ 저녁 식사 후에 테니스를 칠까 한다 I'm thinking of playing tennis after supper. / 점심 시간 전에 선생님을 찾아뵐까 한다 Before lunchtime I think I'll go to see the teacher. / 나는 사직할까 합니다 I have half a mind to resign.

**-ㄹ꼬** ¶ 그는 왜 안 올꼬 I wonder why he doesn't come. / 그것이 무엇일꼬 What could it be? / 그는 어떻게 되었을꼬 I wonder what has become of him. / 그는 어찌 이렇게 늦을꼬 Why is it 〔How is it〕 (that) he is so late?

**-ㄹ는지** 《불확실》 if...; whether it will be 〔*do*〕. ¶ 그것을 팔는지 물어볼까 Shall we ask them if they are going to sell it?

**-ㄹ는지도 모르다**, **-ㄹ는지요** I wonder; whether (it)...; maybe 〔perhaps〕 (it) will *do*. ¶ 비가 올는지(요) I wonder if it's going to rain. / 그가 갈는지(도) 모른다 Maybe he will go.

**-ㄹ 듯이** as if 〔as though〕 to *do* 〔be〕; tending to. ¶ 그는 금방이라도 나를 때릴 듯이 노려보았다 He glared at me as if he were going to strike me at any moment / 그는 죽을 듯이 신음했다 He groaned as if he were going to die.

**-ㄹ라** ¶ 빨리 가거라 기차를 놓칠라 Hurry up, or you will not be in time for the train. / 공부 좀 부지런히 하거라 낙제할라 Work hard, or you will fail in the examination. / 조심해라 넘어질라 Be careful lest you (should) fall down. / 병날라 그만 먹어라 Stop eating before you get sick. / 비가 올라 우산을 가지고 가거라 Take your umbrella, in case it should rain.

**-ㄹ라치면** whenever; if. ¶ 봄이 될라치면 이 산에는 꽃이 많이 핀다 When spring comes, many flowers bloom on this mountain. / 일요일 같은 때 동물원에 가볼라치면 사람이 굉장히 많다 If you visit the zoo on a Sunday, you will find a lot of people there.

**-ㄹ락 말락** ¶ 월급이 70만 원 될락 말락 한다 I have a salary a bit short of 700,000 won. / 잠이 들락 말락 한다 I keep falling asleep. *or* I'm half asleep. / 소리가 들릴락 말락 멀리 사라진다 Hardly to be heard, the sound fades away in the distance. / 그의 이름이 생각 날락 말락 입에서 뱅뱅 돌기만 한다 His name is on the tip of my tongue, but I just can't think of it. / 그는 말을 할락 말락 한다 He is hesitating whether to say anything.

**-ㄹ 만큼** 《정도》 enough to *do*; as much as necessary for *do*ing. ¶ 나는 집을 지을 만큼 돈이 없다 I haven't got money enough to build a house. / 나는 아직 한국말로 연설을 할 만큼 능통하지 못하다 I don't know Korean well enough yet to make a speech in it. / 배가 안 고플 만큼 먹었다 I have eaten enough not to feel hungry. / 그는 일어설 수 없을 만큼 취해 있었다 He was so drunk that he could not stand up.

**-ㄹ 만한** worth; enough. ¶ 볼 만한 그림 a picture worth seeing / 그 책은 읽을 만한 가치가 있다 That book is worth reading. / 우리는 점심을 먹을 만한 시간도 없다 We don't have time enough to have lunch. / 그 일은 공을 들일 만한 가치가 없다 The work is not worth the trouble.

**-ㄹ망정** ¶ 그가 비록 가난할망정 poor as he is / 그가 비록 늙었을망정 though he is old; old as he is / 그는 몸은 약할망정 의지는 강하다 He may be weak in body but he has a strong will. / 굶어 죽을망정 도둑질은 안 한다 I'd rather starve than steal. / 빌어 먹을망정 그에게 신세는 안 지겠다 Even if I were brought to begging, I would never ask a favor of him.

**-ㄹ 모양**(—模樣) ¶ … 할 모양이다 appear about to *do*; seem 〔look〕 as if it will *do*; show signs of becoming 〔going to be〕; look like / 그는 돌아오지 않을 모양이다 There is no sign of his return. / 쌀값이 내릴 모양이다 There are indica-

ㄹ

tions that the price of rice will fall. / 비가 올 모양이다 It looks like rain.

**-ㄹ 바에** if 〔since〕 *one* is to *do;* if it is arranged that; if *one* is obliged to *do;* if it's a matter of *do*ing.
¶ 이왕 떠날 바엔 주저할 것이 무엇 있나 Since we are leaving, why shilly=shally? / 이왕 할 바엔 힘껏 해라 If you do it at all, do it with all your might. / 싸울 바엔 최후까지 싸워라 If you do fight, fight it out. / 돈을 줄 바에는 되도록 빨리 주시오 If you are going to let me have the money, please give it to me as soon as possible.

**-ㄹ 바에야** if (only) *one* is to *do.*
¶ 어차피 꾸중을 들을 바에야 솔직하게 말씀이나 여쭐 것을 As long as I was going to get scolded anyway, I might as well have told him just what I thought.

**-ㄹ 밖에** ¶ 할 일이 없으니 책이나 읽을 밖에 I have nothing to do but read. / 돈이 없으니 빚을 낼 밖에 도리가 없다 Since I am broken, I've got to get a loan. / 그가 하도 어이없는 수작을 하니 웃을 밖에 His remark is so absurd that 「I can't do anything but laugh 〔I can't help laughing〕.

**-ㄹ뿐더러** not only... but (also); as well as.
¶ 그는 시인일뿐더러 화가이기도 하다 He is both at once a poet and a painter. *or* He is a poet as well as a painter. / 그는 영어를 말할뿐더러 불어도 한다 He speaks not only English but also French. / 그것은 경제적일뿐더러 몸에도 좋다 It is not only economical but also good for your health.

**-ㄹ세** you know; I (can) tell you.
¶ 오늘이 오월 초하루일세 It is the first of May, I (can) tell you.

**-ㄹ세라** lest (should); for fear (that).
¶ 그는 비를 만날세라 우산을 가지고 갔다 He took his umbrella for fear of being caught in the rain.

**-ㄹ세 말이지** there's no danger of; there's hardly any chance 〔likelihood〕 that; I tell you there's no likelihood.
¶ 비가 올세 말이지 It will be all right if it rains, but it won't. / 그놈이 사람일세 말이지 He isn't even a human being.

**-ㄹ수록** increasingly with (being, *do*ing); the more 〔the better, the bigger, *etc.*〕... the more... (★ 「…하면 할수록 점점 …해지다」는 (the+비교급, the+비교급)의 형태로 나타냄).
¶ 빠르면 빠를수록 좋다 The sooner, the better. / 많으면 많을수록 좋다 The more, the better. / 갈수록 태산이라 One calamity followed close on the heels of another. *or* Out of the frying pan into the fire. / 클수록 좋다 The bigger, the better. / 이 책은 읽을수록 재미있다 The more I read this book, the more interesting it is. / 생각하면 생각할수록 점점 더 모르겠다 The more I think, the less I understand. / 사람은 가지면 가질수록 욕심이 더 난다 The more one gets, the more one wants.

**-ㄹ 수 없다** cannot; be unable to *do;* 《사물이》 be too much for; cannot afford to *do* (여유가 없다).
¶ 폭풍우로 출발할 수 없다 The storm prevents us from starting. / 나는 그런 사치는 할 수 없다 I cannot afford such luxury. / 그건 도저히 참을 수 없다 It is more than I can bear. / 그 회답은 지체할 수 없다 The answer admits no delay. / 그것은 너무 어려워서 할 수 없다 It is too difficult for me to do. *or* It is too much for me. / 우리는 그들의 조건을 받아들일 수 없다 We cannot accept their terms. *or* It is impossible for us to accept their terms. *or* Their terms are impossible for us to accept.

**-ㄹ 수 있다** 《사람의 능력》 can *do;* be able to *do;* be capable of *do*ing; be equal to the task; [물건이 주어] be in *one's* power; be possible; be practicable.
¶ 할〔될〕 수 있으면 if possible; if circumstances allow / 될 수 있는 한 to the best of *one's* ability; as far as possible 〔*one* can〕 / 될 수 있는 대로 as... as possible; as... as *one* can / 될 수 있는 대로 빨리 as soon 〔quickly〕 as possible / 내가 할 수 있는 일이면 무엇이든지 하겠다 I will do anything in my power. / 그는 자신의 수입으로 남 부럽지 않게 생활할 수 있다 His income enables him to live a decent life. / 누구나 이 문제에 대해 의견을 말할 수 있다 Everyone is entitled to give 〔state, express〕 his opinion on this subject. / 내일은 올 수 있을 겁니다 I shall be able to come tomorrow. / 될 수 있으면 내일까지 마쳐 주시오 Please finish it by tomorrow, if you can.

**-ㄹ 양으로** with the expectation of *do*ing; with a view to *do*ing; in order to *do;* with the intention of *do*ing. ¶

그는 친구를 찾아볼 양으로 서울에 왔다 He came to Seoul with the idea of seeing his friend. / 사전을 한 권 만들 양으로 자료를 모으고 있다 I am gathering data with a view to compiling a dictionary.

**-ㄹ 양이면** if it is the intention 〔idea〕; of *do*ing; if *one* is going to *do.* ¶ 북극에 갈 양이면 한 달은 걸리겠다 It will take one month to get to the North Pole. / 구경을 다 할 양이면 몇 날이 걸릴지 모르겠구나 There's no telling how many days it will take if we do all the sightseeing.

**-ㄹ 줄** ① 《능력》 ¶ …할 줄 안다 can *do;* be able 〔competent〕 to *do;* be capable of *do*ing; be good 《at》 / 피아노를 칠 줄 안다 can 〔know how to〕 play the piano / 그녀는 그것을 나보다 더 잘 할 줄 안다 She is better able to do it than I am. / 그는 거짓말을 할 줄 모르는 사람이다 He is not a man to tell lies. ② 《예상 밖》 ¶ 여기서 당신을 만날 줄은 몰랐다 This is the last place to expect to meet you. *or* Fancy meeting you here. / 그런 못된 놈일 줄은 몰랐다 Who should have imagined him to be such a rascal?

**-ㄹ 지** whether … (or); if. ¶ 그가 올지 안 올지 모르겠다 There's no knowing 〔telling〕 whether he will show up or not. *or* I'm not sure if he will come. / 장차 무슨 일이 생길지 짐작을 못 하겠다 There is no guessing what will happen in the future. / 그렇게 시간이 많을지 모르겠다 I wonder if I'll have that much time to spare. / 나는 나의 운명을 웃어야 할지 울어야 할지 모르겠다 I don't know whether to laugh or cry at my lot. / 출세할지 못할지는 우리의 노력 여하에 달렸다 Whether or not 〔no〕 we succeed in life depends on our own efforts. (★ 명사절이 글머리에 나올 때는 if가 아니라 whether를 씀) / 내일 비나 오지 않을지 I am afraid it will rain tomorrow. / 가야 할지 어쩔지 나는 모르겠다 I don't know whether to go (or not).

**-ㄹ 지나** it is proper 〔right〕 to *do*…, but…. ¶ 죄를 보아서는 엄벌에 처할지나 In view of the crime, it is proper to inflict a severe punishment, but….

**-ㄹ 지니라** it is proper 〔right〕 to *do.* ¶ 학생은 공부에 힘쓸지니라 It is proper for students to devote themselves to their studies.

**-ㄹ 지도 모르다** may; 《어쩌면》 might (★ might도 may와 같은 뜻으로 쓰이는 경우가 있으나 추측의 확실성은 may보다는 희박함 : It may be true. 「정말일지도 모른다」; It might be true. 「어쩌면 정말인지도 모른다」); it is possible (that)…; maybe 〔perhaps〕 it will be 〔*do*〕. ¶ 그는 갈지도 모른다 Perhaps he will go. / 그 문제는 네게 좀 어려울지도 모른다 The question may be a little difficult for you. / 오후에는 비나 눈이 올지도 모른다 Perhaps it may rain or snow this afternoon. / 내가 틀렸을지도 모른다 I'm afraid I am wrong. / 어쩌면 사실일지도 모른다 It may be true, though I am not sure. / 내가 그렇게 말했을지도 모른다 I may have told that way. / 그녀는 50이 넘었을지도 모른다 She is over fifty, I should think 〔say〕. / 그가 도와주지 않았더라면 목숨을 잃었을지도 모른다 I might possibly have lost my life if he had not helped me.

**-ㄹ 지라** ought to *do;* must; shall; should. ¶ 부모를 공경할지라 You should obey your parents. / 간음하지 말지라 Thou shalt not commit adultery.

**-ㄹ 지라도** even though 〔if〕; although; (even) admitting that…. ¶ 눈이 올지라도 even if it snows 〔should snow〕 / 사실일지라도 granting it to be true; granted it is true / 아무리 고단할지라도 however 〔no matter how〕 tired *one* may be / 어떤 일이 생길지라도 whatever 〔no matter what〕 may happen / 결과가 어찌 될지라도 whatever the consequence may be / 아무리 돈이 많이 있을지라도 however 〔no matter how〕 rich he may be 〔is〕 / 아무리 가난할지라도 도둑질해서는 안 된다 Granting that one is very poor, that cannot be an excuse for his theft. / 삼수 갑산을 갈지라도 할 말은 해야겠다 I have to speak my mind now, no matter how far I may be sent in exile for doing so. / 몸은 약할지라도 마음은 단단해야 한다 You should be firm in mind even though you are weak in body.

**-ㄹ 지어다** should; ought to *do;* must. ¶ 도둑질하지 말지어다 Thou shalt not steal. / 국민된 자는 병역 의무를 다할지어다 It shall be the duty of every body to undergo military service

**-ㄹ 지언정** even if 〔though〕; rather 〔sooner〕 than. ¶ 굶어 죽을지언정 그에게 신세는 안지겠다 Even if I starve to death, I won't ask a favor of him. / 죽을지언정 구속은 안 받겠다 I'd rather die than be confined. / 낙제를 할지언정 커닝은 안 한다 I would rather fail than cheat.

**-ㄹ진대** if; in case《of》;《조건》provided that;《-ㄹ 것 같으면》judging from. ¶ 입신양명 못 할진대 돈이나 벌리라 If I couldn't rise to eminence, I would rather amass a fortune. / 내가 볼진대 그는 승산이 없다 In my opinion 〔From what I know of him〕 the chances are against him.

**-ㄹ 테다** will; intend to; expect to; mean to; be going to; be supposed to; be expected to.
¶ 나는 오늘 떠날 테다 I would start today. / 세 시까지는 그가 올 테지 He is expected to be here by three o'clock. / 그것은 지금쯤 준비되어 있을 텐데 It ought to be ready by now. / 너는 그것을 벌써 오래 전에 했어야 할 텐데 You ought to have done it long ago. / 나는 오전중에 돌아올 테다 I will be back before noon.

**라** 〖음악〗 ①《계이름》la. ②《라음》re; D. ◉ 라단조〔장조〕 D minor 〔major〕.

**라고** ①《내용》(saying) that it is; calling it (by name); "quote".
¶ 존이～ 하는 사람 a man named 〔called〕 John / 누가 뭐～ 하든 whatever others 〔people〕 may say《about, of》/ 이 꽃은 영어로 무어～ 하느냐 What do they call this flower in English? / 이것이 진달래～ 하는 꽃이다 This is a flower called the azalea. / 자네가 가는 곳이 어디～ 그랬나 Where did you say it was that you are going? / 그 당시 한국을 고려～ 불렀다 They called Korea "Goryeo" at that time.
②《비꼬는 투》¶ 이것을 잡지～ 샀더니 읽을 것이 하나도 없다 I bought this "magazine" and can't find a thing in it to read.

**-라고** ¶ 너보고 어서 오라고 야단이 났다 They are raising the roof for you to come at once. / 그에게 이것을 보라고 하시오 Tell him to take a look at this.

**라고는** ¶ 한국에는 호수～ 별로 없다 Korea has no lakes to speak of. / 내 소유～ 거의 없다 I have few things I can call my own.

**-라고도** also; in a sense; so to speak. ¶ … 라고도 하다 be equally said … / … 라고도 할 수 있는 as it may be called / 한국은 「고요한 아침의 나라」라고도 한다 Korea is also known as "the land of morning calm". / 출생은 죽음의 시작이라고도 할 수 있다 Birth is, so to speak 〔in a sense〕, the beginning of death.

**-라고 해서** ¶ 부자라고해서 반드시 행복한 것은 아니다 The rich are not always happy. / 반짝이는 것이라고해서 모두 금은 아니다 All that glitters is not gold.

**-라기 보다** rather《than》; more of…. ¶그는 직업 외교관이라기보다(는) 학자이다 He is 「a scholar rather than 〔more of a scholar than〕 a career diplomat.

**라놀린** 〖화학〗 lanolin(e).

**라는** ¶ 철수～ 소년 a boy called 〔named〕 Cheolsu / T～ 좋은 친구가 있다 have a good friend in Mr. T.

**-라는** ¶ 하지 말라는 충고 an advice not to do / 하라는 대로 하라 Do as you are told. / … 하라는 명령을 받고 있다 be under orders to do.

**-라니** ¶ 벽화라니 무슨 벽화 말인가 By murals, what kind of murals do you mean?

**-라니까** ①《강조하여》I tell you; I assure you. ¶ 정말이라니까 I mean it. *or* I'm telling you. *or* I'm not kidding. / 빨리 가라니까 Go quick, I tell you.
②《…라고 하니까》¶ 그에게 들어오라니까 싫다고 하더라 I asked him in, but he refused.

**라니냐** 〖기상〗《남미 페루의 적도 부근 중부 태평양 해역의 해면 수온이 평년보다 1～2도 낮아지는 현상》La Niña.

**-라도** 《…까지도》even; the very;《설사 …일지라도》though; even if; however;《어떤 …이라도》any.
¶ 비가 오더라도 even if it rains / 결과가 어찌 되더라도 whatever the consequence may be / 내가 아니더라도 besides me / 아무리 돈이 많더라도 however 〔no matter how〕 rich he may be / 어린애라도 그것을 안다 Even a child can know it. / 그는 모든 것을 다 알기라도 하듯이 말한다 He speaks as if he knew everything. / 꿈에라도 보고 지고 I wish I could see you even in a dream. / 그 둘 중 어느 쪽이라도 좋다 Either of them will do. / 어떤 아이라도 그런 것은 한다 Any child can do it.

**라돈** 〖화학〗 radon (기호 Rn).
◉ ～가스 radon gas. ～계(計) a radonoscope.

**라듐** 〖화학〗 radium (기호 Ra).
◉ ～광천(요법) a radium spring (treatment). ～방사선 radium rays.

**라드** 《요리용 돼지기름》lard. ◉ ～유(油)

lard oil.

**라든지** 《나열》 and; or; and so on; and the like; 《선택》 either... or. ¶ 사과～배～ 하는 여러 가지 것들 apples, pears and various other things.

**-라든지** or; whether 〔either〕 ... or. ¶ 우리는 그에게 그 일을 하라든지 말라든지 결정을 내려줘야 한다 We must decide whether to make him do the work or not.

**라디안** 〖수학〗 radian.

**라디에이터** 《방열기》 a radiator.

**라디오** radio 《미》; wireless 《영》; 《수신장치》 a radio; a 「radio 〔wireless〕 set. ¶ ～ 겸용 전축 a 「radio gramophone / ～를 듣다 listen to the radio; hear 「on 〔over〕 the radio / ～를 틀다〔끄다〕 turn the radio 「on 〔off〕 / ～의 주파수를 맞추다 tune in a frequency / ～ 소리를 높게〔낮게〕 하다 turn the radio 「up 〔down〕 / ～에 출연하다 go on the 「radio 〔air〕 / 이 ～로 외국 방송을 들을 수 있나 Can we get foreign stations on this set? / 나는 매일 ～강좌를 듣는다 I listen to a radio 《English》 course 〔programs〕 everyday.
◉ ～강연 a radio 「talk 〔address〕. ～강좌 a radio 《English》 course. ～녹음 radio transcription. ～뉴스 the news on the radio; radio news. ～드라마 a radio 「drama 〔play〕. ～로케이터 a radio locator. ～방송 radio broadcasting; a radio broadcast (1회): ～ 방송국 a radio (broadcasting) station / ～ 방송을 하다 broadcast; speak on the 「radio 〔air〕; talk over the radio. ～송신기 a (radio) transmitter; 《자동차용》 an autoradio 《미》. ～수신기 a (radio) receiver; radio (set). ～아나운서 a radio announcer. ～전파 radio waves. ～존데 〖기상〗 a radiosonde. ～ 좌담회 a radio forum. ～중계 hookup 《미》; relay: ～ 중계 방송 a 《nationwide》 hookup; a relay broadcast. ～ 청취자 a radio 「listener 〔audience〕. ～체조 radio 「cal(l)isthenics 〔gymnastic exercises〕. ～코미디 a radio comedy. ～프로 a radio program. ～해설자 a radio commentator.

**라르고** 〖음악〗 largo.

**라마** 《라마승》 a lama. ◉ ～교 Lamaism: ～교도 a Lamaist; a Lamaite. ～사원 a lamasery.

**라마단** 《이슬람교의 금식 기도의 달》 Ramadan.

**라면**[1] 《국수》 *ramyon;* instant noodles; Chinese noodles in soup. ¶ ～ 수프 soup bases of *ramyon* / 수재민을 돕기 위해 상당량의 ～과 기타 구호품이 보내졌다 Considerable amount of *ramyon* and other relief goods had been sent out to extend a helping hand to the flood victims.

**라면**[2] 《가정·조건》 if it be; supposing; provided. ¶ 내가 새～ 너에게 날아가련만 If I were a bird, I'd fly to you.

**-라면** ¶ 가라면 가 Go 「as you are told 〔as I tell you〕.

**라벤더** 〖식물〗 a lavender. ◉ ～향수〔유(油)〕 lavender water.

**라벨** a label. a sticker 《미》. ¶ ～을 붙이다 label 《a bottle》; attach 〔affix〕 a label to 《a bottle》; put a label on 《a box》 / 그는 전과자라는 ～이 붙었다 He was 「branded 〔labeled〕 as an ex-convict.

**라서** ¶ 뉘～ 나를 이기리요 Who indeed can best me? *or* Who would dare to best me? / 막내～ 그가 더 귀엽다 I love him all the better because of the youngest.

**라스베이거스** 《미국의 도시》 Las Vegas.

**라스트** the last.
◉ ～스퍼트 the last spurt. ～신 the last scene. ～이닝 〖야구〗 the last inning.

**라야, 라야만** [조사] ¶ 너라야 능히 그 일을 할 수 있다 It is you that can do the job. *or* No one but you can do it. / 건강을 잃고 난 뒤(에)～ 그 고마움을 안다 You only realize the value of health when you have lost it.

**-라야** [연결어미] only; not ... until. ¶ 달은 밤이라야 빛을 낸다 The moon shines only at night.

**라오스** Laos. ¶ ～의 Laotian. ◉ ～사람 a Laotian.

**라우드스피커** a loud speaker. ＝확성기.

**라운드** 〖권투〗 a round. ¶ 제 5～ 1분 17초만에 《be knocked out》 at 1:17 of the fifth round.

**라운지** 《호텔 등의》 a lounge.

**라이거** a liger. [＜*li*on＋ti*ger*]

**라이너** 〖야구〗 a liner; a line drive; 《안옷감》 (a) liner.
¶ ～를 치다 hit 〔drive〕 a liner / 3루 쪽으로 ～를 쳐서 병살당하다 line to third for a double play / 헬멧 ～ a helmet liner.

**라이노타이프** 〖인쇄〗 a linotype.

**라이닝** 〖기계〗 lining; 《옷의 안감》 lining.

**라이덴병**(―甁) 〖물리〗 a Leyden jar.

**라이따이한** a person of half-Korean and half-Vietnamese.

**라이벌** a rival. ◉ ～의식 a competitive

spirit; a spirit of competition 〔rivalry, emulation〕.

**라이베리아** 《아프리카의 공화국》 Liberia. ¶~의 Liberian.
◉ ~사람 a Liberian.

**라이브** live.
¶~ 녹음 a live recording / ~콘서트 a live concert.

**라이브러리** a library.

**라이선스** a license 《미》; a licence 《영》.
◉~료 a license fee. ~생산 licensed production.

**라이스** rice.
◉ ~페이퍼 rice paper. 카레~ curry and rice; curried rice.

**라이온** a lion; a lioness (암컷).

**라이온스클럽** Lions Club (*l*iberty, *i*ntelligence, *o*ur *n*ation's *s*afety의 생략).

**라이카** 《상표명》 a Leica (camera).

**라이터** 《불 켜는》 a (cigarette) lighter; 《문필가》 a writer.
¶~돌 a lighter flint / 가스〔기름〕~ a gas 〔an oil〕 lighter / ~를 켜다 light a lighter / 이 ~는 불이 안 켜진다 This (cigarette) lighter fails to work.
◉ ~기름 lighter oil 〔fluid〕.

**라이트**[1] ① 〖야구〗 the right field; 《우익수》 a right fielder. ¶~ 플라이를 치다 fly to right.
② 〖권투〗 a right 《to the jaw》. ¶ 턱에 강한 ~를 먹이다 deal 〔land〕 a hard right to the jaw.
◉~윙 〖축구〗 the right wing.

**라이트**[2] ① 《빛》 light; 《등불》 a (car) light. ¶~를 끄〔켜〕시오 Turn off 〔on〕 lights.
② 《체급》 the lightweight class. ¶~급 선수 a lightweight 《boxer》.

**라이트**[3] 《비행기 발명가 형제》 Wilbur Wright (1867-1912); Orville Wright (1871-1948).

**라이트밴** 《창이 있는》 a station wagon; 《영》 an estate car; 《창이 없는》 a light van 〔truck〕.

**라이프** 《생명·인생》 (a) life.
◉ ~보트 a lifeboat (구명정). ~워크 《필생사업》 *one's* lifework 〔life's work〕. ~재킷 a life jacket.

**라이프사이언스** 《생명과학》 life sciences.

**라이프사이클** a life cycle.
¶ 평균 수명이 길어져 정년 퇴직 후의 생활이 ~의 중요 부분을 더 많이 차지하게 되었다 Thanks to the increased average life expectancy, life after retirement has become an increasingly significant part of the total life cycle.

**라이프스타일** a life-style.

**라이플**(총)(—(銃)) a rifle.

**라인** 《줄》 a line; 《컨베이어 시스템의》 an assembly line.
◉ ~댄서 《a troop of》 precision dancers. ~댄스 precision dancing. ~드라이브 a line drive 〔liner〕. ~즈맨 a linesman (선심). ~프린터 〖컴퓨터〗 a line printer.

**라인강**(—江) the Rhine (River).

**라인업** 《야구·축구에서》 the 《starting》 line-up 《of a team》.
¶ ~을 소개〔발표〕하다 announce the lineup 《of the Yankees》.

**라일락** 〖식물〗 a lilac.

**라조**(—調) 〖음악〗 D.

**라커룸** 《체육 시설의》 a locker room; 《옷 보관함》 a locker.
¶ 배구 연습이 끝나면 그녀는 항상 ~에 누워 있었다 After volleyball practice she always laid herself down in the locker room.

**라켓** a racket; a bat 〔paddle〕 (탁구의).

**라텍스** 《고무 나무의 유즙》 latex.

**라트비아** 《동유럽의 공화국》 Latvia. ¶~의 Latvian.
◉ ~사람 a Latvian.

**라틴** Latin. ¶~의 Latin.
◉ ~문학 Latin literature. ~민족 the Latin races. ~아메리카 Latin America: ~ 아메리카의 Latin-American / ~ 아메리카계의 사람 Hispanics. ~어 the Latin language: ~어학자 a Latinist; a Latin scholar. ~음악 Latin music.

**-락**(말락) ⇨ -으락.

**락타아제** 〖화학〗 lactase.

**락토오스** 〖화학〗 lactose; milksugar.

**란** ¶ 동기란 간단하다 As for motive, that is simple. / 진리란 무엇인가 What is truth?

**란**(—欄) = 난(欄). ¶ 가정란 the domestic affairs section 〔columns〕/ 광고〔문예〕란 the advertisement 〔literary〕 column.

**-란** ⇨ -라는.
¶ 날보고 어떻게 하란 말인가 What do you want me to do?

**란도셀** [< *ransel* (D.)] a knapsack; a satchel.
¶ ~을 메다 carry a knapsack on *one's* back.

**-람** ¶ 내가 가야 할 이유가 뭐람 Why should I go of all things?

**람바다** 〖음악·춤〗 lambada.

**람보** 《영화의 주인공》 Rambo; 《비유적으로 불사신·독불장군》 a rambo.

**랍비** 《유대교 율법사》 a rabbi.

**랑** and; or; and so on 〔forth〕; etc.; 《함

께》 (together) with. ¶ 너랑 나랑 you and me / 친구랑 이야기하다 talk with a friend.

**랑데부** a rendezvous; a date 《미》. ¶ ~를 하다 meet 《*a person*》 as arranged; have a date 《with》 / 궤도상에서 ~하다 rendezvous in orbit 《with》; have an orbital rendezvous 《with》 / 두 우주선의 ~는 성공적이었다고 보도되었다 The successful rendezvous of the two spaceships was reported.

**-래** they say; I hear. ¶ 그녀의 오빠는 변호사래 I hear that her brother is a lawyer. / 그이가 뭐래 What did he say?

**래글런** a raglan. ¶ ~ 소매 raglan sleeves.

**-래서** ¶ 그가 저녁을 먹으러 오래서 갔다 I went to his house, being invited to dinner. / 그를 오래서 같이 놀자 Let's ask him to come to play with us.

**-래서야** ¶ 이래서야 됩니까 You shouldn't do this. / 두 달도 못 되어 그만두래서야 되겠소 It is unreasonable that you should ask me to quit within two months. / 이것이 1,000원어치래서야 말이 됩니까 Are you kidding to say that this is worth 1,000 won?

**-래야** must; have to; should; ought to.
¶ 사람을 보내서 그를 오래야 되겠다 I must send a person for him. / 그래야 마땅하지 You should do so. *or* It should be so.

**래커** lacquer.
¶ ~를 칠하다 lacquer; coat 《*a thing*》 with lacquer.

**랙깍지벌레** 〖곤충〗 a lac insect.

**랜덤샘플링** 《무작위 표본추출(법)》 random sampling.

**랜싯** 《외과》 a lancet.

**랜턴** 《서양식 제등》 a lantern.

**랠리** 《장거리 자동차 경주》 a rally. ¶ 제18회 파리-다카르 ~ the 18th Paris-Dakar Rally.

**램** 〖컴퓨터〗 《임의 접근 기억장치》 RAM. [< *r*andom *a*ccess *m*emory]

**램프**[1] a lamp.
◉ 석유~ an oil lamp. 알코올~ an alcohol 〔a spirit〕 lamp.

**램프**[2] 《입체교차로 따위의 진입로》 a ramp.

**랩**[1] 〖음악〗 《리듬에 맞춰 말하듯이 부르는 흑인 음악》 rap (music).
◉ 랩가수 a rapper. 랩그룹 a rap group.

**랩**[2] 《연구실·실습실》 a laboratory; a lab 《구어》. ¶ 랭귀지~ a language lab.

**랩소디** 〖음악〗 a rhapsody.

**랩타임** 〖경기〗 《트랙의 일주·경영 코스의 왕복에 요하는 시간》 the lap time. ¶ 300 미터의~ the 300 meter lap time.

**랩톱** 〖컴퓨터〗 ¶ ~형의 lap-top / ~형 컴퓨터 a lap-top computer.

**랭크** 《계급·지위》 (a) rank. ¶ 제1위에 ~되다 be ranked No. 1; be given the first rank.

**랭크앤드파일** 《장교에 대한 병사들·지도자에 대한 일반 대중》 the rank and file.

**랭킹** 《순위》 ranking.
¶ 국제〔국내〕~ international 〔national〕 ranking / ~ 1위를 차지하다 take the first ranking / 그는 매년 상위 ~에 든다 He is in the top ranking group every year.

**-랴** ① 《반어》 ¶ 내가 설마 그러랴 I would never do so. / 그가 감히 그런 말을 했으랴 How could he dare to say so? / 그것이 어찌 저절로 움직이랴 It can't move by 〔of〕 itself. *or* How can it move of 〔by〕 itself?
② 《문의》 ¶ 걸어가랴 Shall I go on foot? / 돈을 주랴 Do you want some money? *or* Shall I give you some money?

**-량**(量) volume; quantity; (an) amount.
¶ 교통량 traffic volume / 생산량 an output 《of a factory》.

**-러** ⇨ -으러. ¶ 낚시하러 가다 go fishing / 너를 보러 왔다 I have come to see you.

**러너** 〖야구〗 a runner.
¶~를 내보내다 send a runner / ~를 일소하다 clear the bases 《with a three-base hit》.

**러닝** running (race).
◉ ~메이트 a running mate. ~셔츠 an (athletic) undershirt; 《영》 running vest; a sleeveless undershirt. ~슈즈 《a pair of》 running shoes; spiked shoes. ~홈런 an inside-the-park home run.

**러버** 《고무》 rubber.

**러브** love.
◉ ~게임 《테니스에서》 a love game. ~레터 a love letter. ~신 a love scene. ~호텔 a love hotel; a hotel catering to couples wishing to make love in a limited time.

**러셀** 《영국의 철학자》 Bertrand Russell (1872-1970).

**러셀(차)** (—(車)) 《제설차》 a Russel 〔wedge-type〕 snowplow.

**러시아** Russia.
◉ ~사람 a Russian. ~어 Russian

(language).

**러시아워** the rush hour(s). ¶ 아침〔저녁〕의 ~ 동안에 during the「morning 〔evening〕 rush hours.

**러키** lucky.
◉ ~ 세븐 『야구』 the lucky seventh: ~ 세븐에서 전세를 만회하다 get back (on the opposing team) in the "lucky" seventh. ~존 the lucky zone.

**럭비** 《스포츠》 Rugby (football); rugger 《영구어》.
◉ ~공 a Rugby ball.

**럭스** 『물리』 《밝기의 단위》 a lux.

**런던** 《영국의 수도》 London.
◉ ~ 국제 금융선물거래소 『금융』 the London International Financial Futures Exchange. ~사람 a Londoner; a cockney. ~사투리 cockney accent. ~영어 cockney (English). ~탑 the Tower of London.

**런치** lunch. ◉ ~타임 《at》 lunchtime.

**럼** 《술》 rum. ◉ 럼주(酒) = 럼.

**레가타** 《요트레이스》 a regatta.

**레귤러** regular; 《정식 선수》 a regular player.
◉ ~멤버 a regular member. ~ 포지션 regular position.

**레그혼** 《닭의 품종》 a leghorn.

**레늄** 『화학』 rhenium (기호 Re).

**레닌** 《러시아의 혁명가》 Nikolai Lenin (1870-1924).
◉ ~주의 Leninism: ~주의자 a Leninite.

**레더** leather; 《모조가죽》 imitation leather.
◉ ~코트 a leather coat. ~클로스 leathercloth.

**레드카드** 『축구』 《주심이 퇴장을 명하는 카드》 a red card.

**레디메이드** 《기성복의》 ready-made. ¶ ~의 ready-to-wear; ready-made / ~의 옷 ready-made clothes; store-bought clothes.

**레디믹스** 『건축』 ready-mix.

**레모네이드** 《레몬즙 음료》 lemonade.

**레몬** 『식물』 a lemon. ◉ ~산(酸) citric acid. ~스쿼시 lemon squash. ~유 lemon oil. ~즙〔주스〕 lemon juice. ~차(茶)〔티〕 lemon tea.

**레바논** 《중동의 공화국》 (the Republic of ) Lebanon. ¶ ~의 Lebanese. ◉ ~사람 a Lebanese.

**레벨** a level. ¶ ~이 높다〔낮다〕 be on a high 〔low〕 level / 높은 ~에 이르다 attain a high level / ~을 높이다〔낮추다〕 level up 〔down〕.

**레스토랑** a restaurant. ¶ ~경영자 a restaurateur. ◉ ~시어터 a restaurant theater.

**레슨** a lesson. ¶ 피아노 ~ a piano lesson; a lesson in piano / 바이올린 ~을 받다 take 〔have〕 a violin lesson.

**레슬러** a wrestler.

**레슬링** 《스포츠》 wrestling. ◉ ~선수 a wrestler; a matman 《미구어》.

**레위기**(—記) 『구약』 (The Book of) Leviticus (생략 Lev.).

**레이** 《하와이의 화환》 a lei. ¶ ~를 목에 걸다 put on a lei round *one's* neck.

**레이더** (a) radar. 〔< *ra*dio *d*etecting *a*nd *r*anging〕 ¶ ~에 잡히다 show up on the radar screen.
◉ ~기지 a radar base 〔site, station〕. ~돔 a radar dome; a radome. ~망 a radar fence 〔screen, network〕. ~시설 a radar installation. ~유도미사일 a radar-guided missile. ~장치 a radar device 〔set, system〕.

**레이디** a lady. ◉ 퍼스트~ the First Lady.

**레이디퍼스트** Ladies first; deference toward women.

**레이서** a racer; a racing driver.

**레이스**[1] 《경주》 a race.
◉ ~코스 a race course.

**레이스**[2] 《수예품》 lace; lacework. ¶ ~를 달다 trim with lace. ◉ ~실 cotton thread. ~장식 enlacement; lacing.

**레이싱카** a (miniature) racing car; a (miniature) racer.

**레이아웃** 《인쇄·도안의》 (a) layout. ¶ 우리는 이 책에서 사진 ~에 특별히 신경을 썼다 We took special care of the layout of pictures in this book.

**레이오프** 《일시적 해고》 a layoff. ¶ 불황으로 근로자의 2할을 ~시켰다 On account of business recession, they laid off twenty percent of their workers.

**레이온** 《인조견사》 rayon; artificial silk.
◉ ~직물 rayon fabric.

**레이저** 『물리』 《빛의 증폭 장치》 (a) laser. 〔< *l*ight *a*mplification by *s*timulated *e*mission of *r*adiation〕 ◉ ~광선 a laser beam; laser light. ~디스크 『컴퓨터』 a laser disk. ~메스 a laser knife. ~병기 a laser weapon. ~수술 laser surgery. ~용접기 a laser-operated welder. ~통신 (a) laser communication. ~프린터 a laser printer. ~핵융합 laser fusion.

**레이트** 《율》 a rate. ¶ 환(換)~ the exchange rate; the rate of exchange.

**레인슈즈** a rain shoes.

**레인지** a (cooking) range, a cookstove

《미》; an oven. ¶ 가스～ a gas range 〔stove〕/ 전자～ a microwave (oven).

**레인코트** a raincoat; 《벨트 달린》 a trench coat; a waterproof; 《고무 입힌》 a mac(k)intosh; 《갠 날에도 입는》 a weatherall.

**레일** a rail; a (railway) line; a (railroad) track 《미》. ¶ ～을 깔다〔떼다〕 lay 〔rip up〕 rails. 「누수 현상).

**레임덕** a lame duck (집권 말기의 권력

**레저** leisure; leisure time amusement. ◉ ～붐 a leisure boom. ～산업 the leisure industry. ～시설 leisure facilities. ～용 차량 a recreational vehicle (RV). ～용품 equipment for leisure time amusement.

**레즈비언** 《여성 동성애자》 a lesbian; a female homosexual; a les 《구어》.

**레지스탕스** resistance (activity).

**레지스터** 《등록(부)·등기》 a register. ¶ 여자 ～ a cash-register girl / ～ 오피스 《호적 등기소》 a register office.

**레커차**(一車) a wrecker; a wrecking car; a tow truck 《미》. ¶ ～에 끌려가다 be towed by a wrecker.

**레코드** ① 《기록》 a record; a mark. ⇨ 기록(記錄). ② 《축음기의》 a (phonograph, gramophone) record; a disk; a disc. ¶ ～를 틀다 put a record on the player; play a record / ～에 취입하다 disc 《*one's* singing》; record 《a speech》 on a disk / 그 ～판 한 장만 주시오 I want a copy of that record. ◉ ～수집가 a discophile. ～음악 record(ed) 〔disk〕 music; a canned music 《구어》: ～음악 시간 《라디오의》 a disk hour. ～콘서트 a record concert; a disk recital. ～플레이어 a record player; a phonoplayer.

**레크리에이션** (a) recreation. ◉ ～센터 a recreation center. ～시설 facilities for recreation; recreational facilities. ～차 a recreational vehicle (생략 RV).

**레터** a letter. ¶ 팬～ a fan letter.

**레터링** 《글자 도안의》 lettering.

**레테르** 《상표》 a label; a sticker 《미》. ⇨ 라벨.

> 참고 「레테르」의 유래와 **label**: 우리말의 「레테르」는 네덜란드어에서 들어온 말. 영어로는 label 이라고 해야 한다. 따라서 「상자에 레테르를 붙이다」는 put a label on the box 라고 한다. 「…라는 낙인을 찍다」라는 비유적인 뜻으로 쓸 경우는 He was labeled 〔branded〕 as a boaster. (그는 허풍쟁이라는 레테르가 붙여졌다).

¶ ～를 붙이다 label 《a bottle》; attach 〔affix〕 a label to 《a bottle》; put a label on 《a box》/ 전과자라는 ～가 붙다 《평가》 be branded 〔labeled〕 as an ex-convict.

**레토르트** 〖화학〗 《실험용 기구》 a retort.

**레퍼리** 《심판》 a referee. ¶ ～를 보다 referee 《a match》; act as referee.

**레퍼토리** 《연주 곡목》 a repertory; a repertoire. ¶ 폭넓은 ～를 가지고 있다 have a large repertory / ～에 들어 있지 않다 be not in *one's* repertory.

**레프트** 〖야구〗 《좌익》 left field; 《좌익수》 a left fielder; 〖권투〗 a left 《to the jaw》. ¶ ～에 플라이를 치다 hit a fly to left field. ◉ ～윙 the left wing. ～잽 a left jab.

**렌즈** a lens (*pl.* ～es). ¶ ～의 중심 the optical center / ～를 맞추다 train the lens 《on》/ ～를 …에 돌리다 direct the lens to… / (카메라의) ～를 조르다 stop down 《a lens》. ◉ 줌～ a zoom lens. 표준～ a standard 〔normal〕 lens. 합성～ a compound lens.

**렌치** a wrench.

**렌터카** a rental car; a Rent-a-car (상표 이름). ◉ ～업자 a car-rental agent.

**-려고** ¶ 집을 사려고 은행에서 빚을 냈다 I took out a loan from the bank in order to buy a house.

**-려기에** as; because; since. ¶ 비가 오려기에 우산을 갖고 왔다 I took an umbrella with me, because it was going to rain. / 그가 부모님이 보고 싶어 집에 가려기에 허락했다 I gave him permission to go home as he was anxious to see his parents.

**-려나** ¶ 언제 돈을 주려나 When shall I have the money? / 자네 오늘 저녁 산책하러 오려나 Will you come for a walk this evening? / 대관절 내게 무엇을 시키려나 What on earth do you expect me to do?

**-려네** I will; I intend 〔mean〕 to *do;* I am going to *do.* ¶ 나는 그것을 하려네 I am going to do it. / 이 선물을 자네에게 주려네 This gift is intended for you. / 나는 어떤 희생을 치르더라도 목적을 달성하려네 I will accomplish my purpose at any cost.

**-려느냐** ¶ 너는 무엇이 되려느냐 What are you going to be? / 그것으로 무엇을 하려느냐 What are you going to do with it? / 어느 것을 가지려느냐 Which will you take? / 언제 가려느냐 When will you go?

**-려는** ¶ 나는 자네 일에 간섭하려는 의사는

없네 I have no mind to meddle with your affair. / 너를 속이려는 생각은 털끝만큼도 없다 I don't have 「the slightest intention 〔the least idea〕 to cheat you. / 이것은 이제 우리가 만나려는 소녀의 사진이다 This is the picture of a girl whom we are going to see.

**-려는가** ¶ 자네는 무엇을 하려는가 What are you going to do? / 언제 떠나려는가 When are you going to leave? *or* When do you intend to leave? / 얼마 동안 이곳에 머무르려는가 How long do you plan to remain here?

**-려는데** ¶ 막 외출을 하려는데 그녀가 들어왔다 She came in just as I was going out. / 퇴근하려는데 외국인이 나에게 영어로 말을 걸었다 Just as I was leaving the office I was spoken to by a foreigner in English.

**-려는지** ¶ 나는 그가 가려는지 안 가려는지 모른다 I don't know whether he wants to go or not. / 그가 직접 오려는지 모르겠다 I am uncertain whether he will come himself or not.

**-려니** ¶ 우리는 그가 시험에 합격하려니 생각했다 We expected that he would pass the examination. / 그들이 진심으로 환영해 주려니 생각했다 I imagined that they would give me a hearty welcome. / 그는 곧 나으려니 생각했다 He thought that he should soon recover.

**-려니와** ① 《또한》 not only ... but; as well as; moreover. ¶ 그는 정치가도 아니려니와 학자도 아니다 He is neither a politician nor a scholar. / 취직도 하려니와 곧 결혼도 하겠다 Besides getting a job, I'll get married soon. ② 《한편》 on the other hand; while. ¶ 바이올린은 오래 된 것일수록 좋으려니와 달걀은 새것일수록 좋다 The older a violin the better, on the other hand, eggs cannot be too new.

**-려다가** ¶ 소풍을 가려다가 날씨가 흐려서 그만두었다 As it was cloudy, I gave up the idea of going on a picnic. / 교사가 되려다가 마음을 바꿨다 Teaching was my original intention, but I have changed my mind.

**-려도** ¶ 가려도 사정이 있어서 못 간다 Circumstances do not permit of my going. / 아무리 하려도 할 수 없다 However much I may try, I cannot do it.

**-려면** ¶ 옳게 구경하려면 하루종일 걸릴 게다 To see it properly would take a whole day.

**-려면야** ¶ 하려면야 할 수 있다 I could, if I would. / 이기려면야 이길 수 있다 I could win, if I would.

**-려무나** do please; come now; may; had better. ¶ 내 사전을 쓰고 싶으면 쓰려무나 You may use my dictionary if you like. / 좀더 누워 있으려무나 You had better take a little more rest.

**-려야** ¶ 나는 웃지 않으려야 웃지 않을 수 없었다 I could not help laughing. *or* I could not but laugh. / 잊으려야 잊을 수 없다 I shall never forget.

**-려오** I will 〔would〕. ¶ 당신이 가면 나도 따라가려오 If you go, I will accompany you. / 나라를 위해서는 힘을 다 바치려오 I would do anything for my country. / 다시는 그런 짓을 안 하려오 I will never do such a thing again.

**-련** ¶ 매 맛을 보련 Are you looking for a taste of the whip?

**-련다** ¶ 나는 내일 가련다 I'm going to go tomorrow.

**-렴** ⇨-려무나.

**-렵니까** ¶ 댁에 계시렵니까 Shall you be at home? / 언제 이곳을 떠나시렵니까 When are you leaving here? / 함께 영화 구경 가시지 않으렵니까 Won't you go to the movies with me? / 신문을 잠깐 빌려 주시렵니까 Will you please lend me the newspaper for a moment?

**-렷다** 《틀림 없음·추측·다짐》 be sure 〔bound〕 to happen; will surely happen; will likely 〔probably〕 happen; probably be. ¶ 비가 와도 그는 오렷다 He's bound to come even if it rains. / 그가 오는 것만은 사실이렷다 I'm sure he is coming—there's no question about that.

**-령**(領) a territory; a possession; a dominion; a protectorate; a fief.

**-령**(嶺) a ridge; a (mountain) pass. ¶ 한계령 the Hangyeryŏng pass.

**로** ① 《수단》 by; by means of; with; in; on. ¶ 잉크로 쓰다 write in ink / 연필로 쓰다 write with a pencil (★ 도구에는 with, 재료를 나타내는 물질명사에는 in 이 붙음) / 열차로 by train / 영어로 쓰다 write 《a novel》 in English / 도보로 on foot.

② 《원료·재료》 from; of; out of. ¶ 포도주는 포도로 만든다 Wine is made from grapes. / 이 집은 벽돌로 되어 있다 This house is made 〔built〕 of bricks. / 석유로 여러 가지 물건을 만든다 We make lots of things out of petroleum.

③ 《원인·이유》 for; as; from; through; because of; due to. ¶ 부주의로 through 〔due to〕 *one's* careless-

ness / 과로로 죽다 die from overwork / 암으로 죽다 die of cancer / 병으로 학교를 쉬다 absent from school because of illness.
④《지위·신분·자격》 as; for. ⇨으로서. ¶ 맏이로 태어나다 be born eldest / 비서로 고용하다 engage 《*a person*》 as a secretary.
⑤《변화·결과》 into; to; for. ¶ 산이 바다로 변하더라도 though mountains turn to sea.
⑥《방향》 to; toward; for. ⇨으로. ¶ 목포로 가는 차 the train for Mokp'o / 모든 길은 로마로 통한다 All roads lead to Rome.
⑦《근거·기준》 by; from. ¶ 무게로 by weight / 다스로 by the dozen / 주급제로 일하다 work by the week / 내 시계로 10시다 It's ten by my watch.
⑧《구성·성립》 of. ¶ …로 되다 be composed of; consist of; be made of / 이 드라마는 10부로 되어 있다 This drama consists of ten parts.

**로가리듬** 〖수학〗 a logarithm. ⇨로그.

**-로고** ¶ 알 수 없는 일이로고 What a mystery it is! / 참 고얀 놈이로고 How wicked he is! / 참으로 뻔뻔스런 놈이로고 How impudent he is! / 참으로 해괴한 일이로고 What a strange thing it is!

**로고스** 〖철학〗《우주 법칙》 logos.

**-로구먼** ¶ 벌써 두시로구먼 It is already two o'clock! / 참 아름다운 경치로구먼 What a (beautiful) sight (it is)!

**-로군** ¶ 정말 예쁜 여자로군 Truly, she is a fair woman. / 그것 참 좋은 생각이로군 It's a really good idea. / 그는 신용할 수 있는 인물이 아니로군 He is not a man to be relied upon.

**로그** 〖수학〗 a logarithm; a log. ¶ 30의 ~ log. 30; the logarithm of 30 / 자연〔상용〕~ a natural 〔common〕 logarithm. ◉ ~표 a logarithmic table; a log table. ~ 함수 a logarithmic function.

**로는** ①《로서는》 ¶ 나의 견해로는 in my opinion; to my thinking / 영어로는 그것을 무엇이라고 합니까 What is the English for it? *or* What do you call it in English? ②《…점에서는》 ¶ 그는 영어 연설로는 누구에게도 지지 않는다 When it comes to making speeches in English, he doesn't lose to anyone. / 경치가 아름답기로는 그곳이 국내 제일이다 For scenic beauty, it is the best place in the country. ③《…에 의하면》 ¶ 내가 아는 바로는 so far as I know; to my knowledge / 내 시계로는 대체로 여섯시다 It is about six by my watch.

**-로다** ¶ 그것은 경사로다 It is a matter of congratulation. / 그이야말로 신사로다 What a gentleman he is!

**로도** ¶ 거기는 기차~갈 수 있고 자동차~갈 수 있다 You can get there either by train or by car.

**-로되** ⇨ -이로되.

**로듐** 〖화학〗 rhodium (기호 Rh).

**로드게임** 《원정 경기》 a road game.

**로드레이스** 《자전거의》 a road race; (bicycle) road-racing.

**로드맵** 《운전자용 지도》 a road map.

**로드쇼** 〖영화〗 a road show; a (special) first-run showing 《of a film》.

**로드아일랜드** 《미국의 주》 Rhode Island (생략 R.I.).

**로드워크** 《노상 트레이닝》 roadwork; 《도로 공사》 roadworks.

**로란** 《배·항공기의 자기 위치 측정장치》 loran. [< *lo*ng *ra*nge *n*avigation]

**로마** 《이탈리아의 수도》 Roma; Rome. ¶ ~의 Roman / ~는 하루 아침에 이루어진 것이 아니다 Rome was not built in a day. ◉ ~가톨릭(교) Roman Catholicism: ~ 가톨릭교도 a Roman Catholic / ~ 가톨릭교회 the Roman Catholic Church. ~교황 the Pope; the Holy Father. ~법 the Roman Law. ~사람 a Roman. ~서(書) 〖신약〗 the (Pauline) Epistle to the Romans. ~숫자 Roman numerals. ~자(字) Roman letters; the Roman 〔Latin〕 alphabet: 한글을 ~자로 표기하다 Romanize Korean / ~자 표기 the Romanization; writing Korean in roman characters. (신성) ~제국 the (Holy) Roman Empire.

**로마네스크** 〖건축〗 Romanesque 《architecture》. ◉ ~건축〔양식〕 romanesque architecture 〔style〕.

**로맨스** a romance; a love affair; affairs of the heart (연애 사건); a love story. ¶ ~그레이의 신사 a gentleman with silver-gray hair; an elderly gentleman in his second youth. ◉ ~시트 a seat for two; a love seat. ~카 a deluxe coach.

**로맨스어** (―語) a Romance language.

**로맨티시스트** a romanticist.

**로맨티시즘** romanticism.

**로맨틱** romantic. ~하다 (be) romantic. ¶ ~한 일생 a romantic career.

**로봇** a robot; 《허수아비 같은 사람》 a figurehead. ¶ ~ 같은 존재 a robotal existence; a figurehead / ~화하다 robotize / ~ 조종의 비행기 a robot-controlled airplane. ◉ ~공학 robotics. ~산업 robotics industry. ~학 robotology. 산업용~ an industrial robot.

**로비** a lobby; a lounge.
◉ ~스트 a lobbyist. ~활동 a lobbying activity: 미국 의회의 지지를 얻기 위해 ~활동을 강화하다 intensify lobbying activities to win the U.S. Congress support / ~ 활동을 벌여 상원에서 법안을 통과시키다 lobby a bill through the Senate.

**로빈후드** 《영국의 의적(義賊)》 Robin Hood.

**로빙** 《테니스》 lobbing. ~하다 lob 《a ball》.

**로서** ① 《기능·자격》 as; for; in the capacity of 〔as〕. ¶ 대표~ as a representative 《of our company》. ② 《인정된, 알려진, 생각된 상태·신분》 to be; as; that; knowing it as; in view of. ¶ 교사~의 책임 *one's* duty as a teacher / 나~는 as for me; on my (own) part; for my part / 더 이상 너를 내 친구~ 생각하지 않겠다 I will not think of you as my friend any more. / 네가 내게 복종을 강요하려 한다면 나~도 가만히 있을 수가 없다 If you try to coerce me into obedience, I just can't stay quiet. / 그는 정치가보다는 소설가~ 더 잘 알려져 있다 He is better known as a novelist than as a statesman.

**로션** (a) lotion. ¶ 헤어~ hair lotion / 스킨~ skin lotion / 애프터 셰이브 ~ after-shave lotion / 핸드~ hand lotion.

**로스** 《손실》 loss. ¶ 시간의 ~를 벌충하다 make up for lost time / 우리는 유통 과정의 ~를 가능한 한 줄이려고 노력했다 We made an effort to hold the loss to a minimum during the distribution process.

**로스앤젤레스** 《미국의 도시》 Los Angeles (생략 LA).

**로스타임** injury time; loss time.

**로스트** roast (meat). ◉ ~비프〔치킨〕 roast beef 〔chicken〕.

**로스트 제너레이션** the Lost Generation.

**로써** 《도구》 with; 《수단》 by; by means of; through; 《재료》 with; of. ¶ 나무〔돌〕~ 짓다 build 《it》 of wood 〔stone〕 / 감사의 뜻을 말~ 표현하다 express *one's* thanks in words; put *one's* grateful feelings into words / 문서~ 통지하다 inform 〔notify〕 《*a person*》 in writing 〔by letter〕 / 문필~ 생활하다 write for living / 이~ 폐회사를 대신하고자 합니다 With this I would like to conclude my closing address.

**로열박스** a royal box.

**로열젤리** royal jelly.

**로열티** a royalty. ¶ 그 작가는 그의 책 한 권마다 10%의 ~를 받는다 The writer gets a 10% royalty on each copy of his book.

**로이드** 《남자 이름》 Lloyd. ◉ ~감정서 a Lloyd's survey report. ~감정인 a Lloyd's surveyor. ~선급(船級) 증명서 a Lloyd's list. ~선급 협회 Lloyd's Register of British and Foreign Shipping.

**로이드안경**(—眼鏡) round glasses with thick plastic rims.

**로이터** Reuter. ◉ ~ 통신사 Reuters; the Reuter's News Agency; Reuter's Ltd. ~특파원 a Reuters' correspondent 《in Seoul》.

**로자리오** 〖가톨릭〗 a rosary.

**로제타석**(—石) the Rosetta stone.

**로진백** 〖야구〗 《송진가루 주머니》 a rosin bag.

**로카** ROKA. [<*R*epublic *o*f *K*orea *A*rmy]

**로커** a locker. ◉ ~룸 a locker room. 코인~ a coin-operated locker.

**로커빌리** 〖음악〗 《록과 컨트리 뮤직을 섞은 음악》 rockabilly. ◉ ~가수 a rockabilly singer.

**로컬** local. ¶ ~타임 local time (현지 시간).

> 용법 영어의 local은 「현지의, 본고장의, 어느 지방의」란 뜻이며, 우리말의 「시골」이란 뜻은 전혀 없음. 「시골의」 뜻은 rural.

◉ ~뉴스 local news. ~방송 a local broadcast. ~선 《철도 따위의》 a local line. ~옵션 local option. ~컬러 local color. ~판 a localnews section 〔page〕. ~프로 a local program.

**로케(이션)** 〖영화〗 a location; a location scene. ¶ ~가다 go on 〔out for〕 location / ~중이다 be on location / 우리는 다음주 제주도로 ~을 떠난다 We'll go over to Cheju on location next week. ◉ ~팀 a location unit. ~헌팅 location hunting.

**로켓** a rocket. ¶ 역추진〔감속〕~ a retro-rocket; a decelaration 〔retarding, braking〕 rocket / 부스터〔증속〕~ a booster rocket / 달〔우주〕~ a moon 〔space〕 rocket / ~을 쏴 올리다 launch a rocket / ~으로 인공 위성을 궤도에 올리다 rocket a satellite into orbit / ~이 발사되었다 The rocket was launched. / ~을 타고 달로 날아갔으면 좋겠다 I wish I could take a rocket to the moon.
◉ ~공학 rocketry. ~기사 a rocke-

teer. ∼발사장〔대〕 a launching「site 〔pad〕. ∼발사 장치 a rocket launcher. ∼비행기 a rocket plane. ∼실험장 a rocket field. ∼엔진 a rocket engine. ∼연료 rocket fuel. ∼추진 rocket propulsion: ∼ 추진의 rocket-propelled. ∼탄 a rocket bomb. ∼포 a rocket gun; a rocket launcher (보병용).

> 참고 1, 2 … 다단계 로켓의 영어 표기: 로켓에는 1단식〔계〕 로켓부터 시작해서 2단식, 3단식, … 다단식 로켓 등이 있는데, 각 단의 명칭은 the first-stage 〔the second-stage, a three-stage, a multistage〕 rocket, 마지막 단의 로켓은 the final-stage rocket임.

**로코코** 〖건축·미술〗 rococo《architecture》.
**로큰롤** 《춤·곡》 rock-'n'-roll; rock-and=roll. ¶ ∼을 열광적으로 추고 있는 젊은이들 youngsters rock-'n'-rolling frantically.
**로키산맥**(一山脈) 《북아메리카의》 the Rocky Mountains; the Rockies.
**로터리** a rotary; a traffic circle《미》; a roundabout《영》. ◉ ∼엔진 a rotary engine. ∼클럽 a Rotary Club: 국제 ∼ 클럽 the Rotary International / ∼ 클럽 회원 a Rotarian.
**로테이션** rotation. ¶ ∼으로 《*do something*》 by 〔in〕 rotation / ∼에 들어 있다 be in the rotation / ∼에서 제외되다 be put out of the rotation.
**로프** (a) rope; (a) cord. ¶ …을 ∼로 동이다 rope《a trunk, a man to a tree》.
**-로 하여금** ¶ …로 하여금 …을 시키다《강제로》 make《*a person do*》; cause《*a person* to *do*》; force 〔compel〕《*a person* to *do*》;《의뢰하여》 let《*a person do*》;《허락》 allow《*a person* to *do*》/ 그∼ 편지를 부치게 하다 get him to post a letter / 나는 그∼ 일을 하게 했다 I had him do the work. *or* I got him to do the work. *or* I「had 〔got〕 the work done by him.
**로힐** low-heeled 〔flat〕 shoes.
**록** 〖음악〗《로큰롤》 rock. ¶ 록 콘서트 a rock concert / 록 스타 a rock star.
**록아웃** 《경영자가 행하는 공장 폐쇄》 (a) lockout. ∼하다 lockout; carry out a lockout.
**록클라이밍** 《암벽 등반》 rock climbing.
**록펠러** 《미국의 석유왕》 John Davison Rockefeller (1839-1937). ◉ ∼ 재단 the Rockefeller Foundation.
**론** 〖상업〗《대부금》 loan.
**-론**(論) 《논설》 an essay; a treatise; a comment; a leading article;《논의》 argument; discussion; discourse; debate; controversy. ¶ 예술론 an essay on art / 한자 폐지론 a controversy over the abolition of Chinese characters.「form.
**론도** 〖음악〗 a rondo. ◉ ∼ 형식 a rondo
**론코트** 《잔디 구장》 a lawn court.
**론테니스** lawn tennis.
**롤러** a roller; a roll; 〖사진〗 a squeegee. ¶ ∼로 고르다 smooth《the ground》 with a roller. ◉ ∼블레이드 (a pair of) roller blades. ∼스케이트 《기구》 (a pair of) roller skates;《놀이》 roller skating: ∼ 스케이트장 a roller-skating rink / ∼ 스케이트를 타다 roller-skate; skate on wheels. ∼코스터 《유원지의》 a roller coaster.
**롤링** 《배의》 rolling; a roll. ∼하다 roll.
**롤백** ¶ ∼ 작전 a rollback operation / ∼ 정책 a rollback policy.
**롤빵** a roll (of bread).
**롬** 〖컴퓨터〗《판독 전용 메모리》 ROM. [<*r*ead *o*nly *m*emory]
**롬퍼스** 《아이들의 놀이옷》 rompers.
**-롭다** be; be characterized by. ¶ 향기롭다 be fragrant / 호화롭다 be「brilliant 〔gaudy〕/ 해롭다 be injurious; be harmful; be noxious / 새롭다 be new.
**롱런** 〖영화·연극〗 a long run. ¶ 그 연극은 15개월이나 ∼하였다 The play had a long run of fifteen months.
**롱비치** 《미국의 도시》 Long Beach.
**롱스커트** a long skirt.
**롱펠로** 《미국의 시인》 Henry Wadsworth Longfellow (1807-82).
**롱플레잉(레코드)** a long-playing (record) (생략 LP).
**롱홀** 〖골프〗 a par-5 hole.
**뢴트겐** 《독일의 물리학자》 Wilhelm Konrad「Roentgen 〔Röntgen〕 (1845-1923);《뢴트겐선》 Roentgen rays; X=rays. ⇨ 엑스선.
**-료**(一料) ①《요금》 a charge; a rate; a fee. ¶ 입장료 an admission fee. ②《재료》 a material. ¶ 조미료 a seasoning.
**루마니아** Romania; Roumania. ¶ ∼의 Romanian; Roumanian. ◉ ∼ 사람 a Romanian; a Roumanian.
**루미네선스** 〖물리〗 luminescence.
**루브르** 《파리의 박물관》 the Louvre (Museum).
**루블** 《러시아 화폐》 a r(o)uble.
**루비** ① 〖광물〗 a ruby. ② 〖인쇄〗 a small size of print; 5½ pt. size. ◉ ∼반지 a ring set with a ruby; a

ruby ring.

**루스** loose. ～하다 (be) loose; slovenly. ¶그는 ～한 사람이다 He is an untidy man. / 그녀는 돈 씀씀이가 ～하다 She is a spendthrift. *or* She is careless with money.

**루스리프** 《공책》 a loose-leaf notebook; 《종이》 loose-leaf paper.

**루스벨트** ① 《미국 제26대 대통령》 Theodore Roosevelt (1858-1919). ② 《미국 제32대 대통령, ①의 조카》 Franklin Delano Roosevelt (1882-1945).

**루이사이트** 〖화학〗 lewisite.

**루이지애나** 《미국의 주》 Louisiana (생략 La.).

**루주** *rouge* (F.); (a) lipstick. ¶새빨갛게 ～를 칠한 입술 thickly rouged lips / ～를 바르다 put on rouge.

**루지** 《경기용 소형 썰매》 a luge; a (Swiss) toboggan.

**루키** 《신인》 a rookie.

**-루타**(壘打) 〖야구〗 a base hit. ¶2루타를 치다 make a two-base hit.

**루터** 《독일의 종교 개혁가》 Martin Luther (1483-1546). ◉ ～파 교회 a Lutheran church. ～파 신자 a Lutheran.

**루트** ① 《경로》 a route; a channel. ¶정식〔비밀, 부정한〕～ legitimate 〔secret, illegal〕 channels 《of supply》 / 외교～를 통해서 through diplomatic channels. ② 〖수학〗 root. ¶～4, the root of 4 (표기 √4).

**루프** (a) loop. ◉ ～안테나 a loop antenna.

**루피** 《인도의 화폐 단위》 a rupee (생략 R, Re).

**룰** 《규칙》 a rule. ¶룰에 따라서 according to the rules / 룰을 어기다 be against the rules / 룰대로 하다 do what the rules prescribe.

**룰렛** 《도박》 roulette; a roulette (기구); 《양재용》 roulette.

**룸** a room. ¶베드룸 a bedroom. ◉ 룸메이트 a roommate. 룸서비스 room service.

**룸바** 〖음악〗 rhumba.

**룸펜** a tramp; a hobo 《미》; a bum; 《실업자》 a jobless 〔an unemployed〕 person. [<Lumpen 《독》] ◉ ～생활 a hobo's life.

**룻기**(一記) 《구약》 (the Book of ) Ruth.

**-류**(流) ① 《형》 a style; a type; a mode; a manner; a way. ¶자기류 *one's* own fashion / 한국인류의 생각 Korean modes of thought / 피카소류의 그림 a picture 「after 〔in the style of〕 Picasso. ② 《유파》 a school. ¶프로이트류의 심리학 the Freudian school of psychology. ③ 《등급》 a class; a rate; order. ¶2류 출판사 a second-rate publishing company / 일류 시인 a poet of the first order.

**-류**(類) ① 〖생물〗 《강(綱)》 a class (of insects, ferns); 〖생물〗 《목(目)》 an order (of carnivores, hymenoptera). ② 《종류》 a kind; a sort; a variety; a class; 〖논리〗 a genus. ¶귤류 oranges; citrus fruits.

**류머티즘** 〖의학〗 rheumatism; rheumatic trouble. ¶～에 걸리다〔의 기가 있다〕 have an attack 〔a touch〕 of rheumatism. ◉ 급성〔만성〕～ acute 〔chronic〕 rheumatism.

**륙색** a rucksack; a knapsack. ¶～을 걸머지다 carry a rucksack on *one's* back.

**르네상스** the Renaissance. ¶～ 양식의 Renaissance / ～는 근대 문명의 여명이다 Renaissance is the dawn of modern civilization. ◉ ～건축 Renaissance architecture. ～양식 Renaissance style.

**르완다** 《아프리카의 공화국》 《the Republic of》 Rwanda.

**르포(르타주)** 《do, write》 *reportage* (F.); a report 《on》.

**를** [조사] ⇨을. ¶기회를 타다 seize 〔take advantage of〕 an opportunity / 때를 기다리다 bide *one's* time; wait for 〔await〕 the time / 어디를 가나 wherever *one* goes 〔*one* may go〕 / 송씨를 상대로 with Mr. Song for a counterpart 〔an opposite number〕 / 거리를 걷다 walk (down) the street / 그가 나를 오랄 까닭이 있나 I see no reason why he should ask me to come. / 그는 그녀를 그의 며느리로 삼았다 He made her his daughter-in-law.

**리** 《…할 리》 (good) reason; possibility. ¶그가 못올 리가 없다 There is no reason why he can't come. / 그럴 리가 있나, 믿지 못하겠는 걸 How can that be? I can't believe it. / 그 말이 거짓말일 리가 없다 That couldn't be a lie. / 그게 정말일 리가 없다 That cannot be true. / 그가 그런 어리석은 말을 했을 리가 없다 He cannot have said such a foolish thing.

**-리**(裡) amid(st); in. ¶암암리에 secretly; covertly / 갈채리에 단(壇)을 내리다 leave a platform amidst 〔in〕 the applause of the audience.

**리골레토** 〖음악〗 *rigoletto* (It.).

**리그** a 《baseball》 league. ◉ ～전 a league game 〔match〕; the league series 〔tournament〕: 고교 농구 ～전 the High School Basketball League. 메이저〔마이너〕～ the Major 〔Minor〕

League.

**-리까** ⇨-으리까. ¶ 지금 곧 가리까 Shall I go right now? / 어떻게 하리까 What shall I do?

**리넨** linen. ¶ ~제의 linen《cloth》.

**리놀륨**《마루용 합성재》linoleum.

**-리다** ①《즐거이 하겠소》(I) will gladly *do*. ¶ 내가 하리다〔읽으리다〕 I'll be glad to do〔read〕it. / 그 일은 내가 맡아 보리다 I'll take care of that matter. ②《…할 것이다》will probably be〔*do*〕. ¶ 손해를 보신다면 내가 책임지리다 I'll answer for your possible losses. / 빨리 가시오, 기차를 놓치리다 Hurry up, or you will miss the train.

**리더** ①《지도자》a leader. ¶ 그는 그 그룹의 ~이다 He is the leader of the group. ②《책의》a reader. ◉ ~십 leadership.

**리드** ①《앞섬》a lead. ~하다 lead《*a person* in a race》; take the lead; have a lead. ¶ 근소한 차이로 ~하다 lead by a narrow margin / 5대 0으로 ~하다 lead by 5 to 0; have a five to zero lead / 우리 팀이 2점 ~하고 있다 Our team is now leading by two points. / 그는 2위의 주자를 100미터 ~하고 있었다 He had a lead of 100 meters over the second runner. ②《이끎다》¶ 댄스에서 상대를 ~하다 lead *one's* partner in a dance. ③《악기의》a reed. ¶ ~오르간 a reed organ / ~악기 a reed instrument.

**리듬** rhythm. ¶ ~ 있는 rhythmic; rhythmical / ~을 타다 get into the rhythm / 빠른 ~으로 노래하다 sing in quick rhythm / 그녀는 ~감이 좋다 She has good rhythm. ◉ ~감 rhythmic sense; a sense of rhythm. ~앤드 블루스〚음악〛rhythm and blues (생략 R and B). ~체조 rhythm callisthenics.

**리딩히터**〚야구〛a leading hitter.

**리라**《이탈리아의 화폐 단위》a lira (*pl.* lire) (생략 L).

**-리라**《추측》may〔might〕《be, *do*》; must; I suppose〔think〕; possibly;《의지》will; shall. ¶ 그는 꼭 성공하리라 He is sure to succeed. / 그렇지 않았다면 그는 아마도 목숨을 잃었으리라 Otherwise he might possibly have lost his life. / 그 놈을 이번만은 놓치지 않으리라 He shall not escape me this time.

**-리라고(는)** (think, suppose, expect) that…. ¶ 나는 그가 꼭 성공하리라고 믿는다 I am sure (that) he will succeed. / 네가 오리라고는 생각지 못했다 I had no idea (that) you were coming.

**리리시즘** lyricism.

**리릭**《서정시》a lyric.

**리모컨** ⇨리모트컨트롤.

**리모트컨트롤**〚기계·전기〛remote control. ~하다 remote-control《a rocket》. ¶ ~로 조작하다 operate《a machine》by remote control. ◉ ~장치 a remote-controlled device.

**리무진**《고급 대형 승용차》a limousine.

**리바운드**《농구에서》a rebound. ¶ 평균 7, 8개의 ~를 잡아내다 pull down an average of 7-8 rebounds.

**리바이벌**《재생》(a) revival. ¶ 19세기에 바로크 음악의 ~이 잠시 있었다 There was a short revival of baroque music in the 19th century.

**리베이트** a rebate; rate-off《구어》;《수수료》a commission; a kickback; a drawback. ¶ ~를 받다 receive a rebate; get a kickback《미구어》/ 판매원은 총 매상액의 7%의 ~를 받았다 The salesman got a 7 percent commission on all sales.

**리벳** a rivet. ¶ ~으로 고정시키다 fasten《*a thing*》with rivets.

**리보 금리**(一金利)《런던 은행간 거래 금리》LIBOR. [<*L*ondon *I*nternational *B*ank *O*ffered *R*ate]

**리보플라빈**〚생화학〛riboflavin; vitamin $B_2$.

**리보핵산**(一核酸) ribonucleic acid (생략 RNA).

**리본** a ribbon. ¶ 머리에 ~을 달다 wear a ribbon in *one's* hair / 머리를 ~으로 매다 tie *one's* hair with a ribbon.

**리볼버**《회전식 연발 권총》a revolver.

**리뷰** a review. ◉ 북 ~ a book review.

**리비도**〚심리〛《성(性)본능》libido.

**리비아**《아프리카의 공화국》Libya;《공식 명칭》Socialist People's Libyan Arab Jamahiriya. ¶ ~의 Libyan. ◉ ~사람 a Libyan.

**리빙키친**《취사 겸용 거실》a living-room=cum-kitchen.

**리사이클링**《재활용》recycling. ~하다 recycle; reuse. ¶ 알루미늄 깡통을 ~하다 recycle aluminum cans.

**리사이틀**〚음악〛a recital. ¶ ~을 열다 give a《piano》recital.

**리서치** research. ~하다 do research《on》.

**리셉션** a reception. ¶ ~을 베풀다 give〔hold〕a reception.

**리스산업**(一産業) leasing industry.

**리스크** (a) risk. ¶ 영업상의 ~ a business risk / ~를 무릅쓰다 run a risk. ◉ ~캐피털 risk capital.

**리스트** a list. ¶ ~를 만들다 make a list

《of》; list / ～에 올리다 put 《*a person*》 on the list / 그의 이름이 ～에 올라 있었다 His name was on the list.

**리스트럭처링** 〖경제〗 《사업 구조 개조》 restructuring.

**리시버** 〖무선〗 a receiver.

**리시브** 《스포츠》 receiving. ～하다 receive 《the served ball》.

**리아스식**(—式) 〖지리〗 ria (type). ¶ ～해안 a rias coast.

**리어카** a rear-car; a handcart; a push-cart; a bicycle「cart [trailer].

**리얼** real. ◉ 리얼리스트 realist. 리얼리스틱 realistic. 리얼리즘 realism.

**리엔지니어링** 《기계 따위의 개량·재설계》 reengineering.

**-리요** ¶ 어찌 말로 다할 수 있으리요 No language can express it. *or* It is beyond description. / 그 소식을 들으면 그가 얼마나 기뻐하리요 How glad he will be to hear it!

**리저브** 《예약》 a reservation. ～하다 reserve 《a room》; book 《a hotel》.

**리조트** 《행락지》 a resort. ¶ 여름[겨울]의 ～ a「summer [winter] resort. ◉ ～호텔 a resort hotel.

**리치** 〖권투〗 reach. ¶ ～가 길다 have a long reach.

**리케차** 〖생물〗 《균》 a rickettisia (*pl.* -ae).

**리코더** 《녹음기》 a recorder. ¶ 타임 ～ a time recorder.

**리코딩** recording.

**리콜** 《소환·해임·결함 상품의 회수》 (a) recall. ～하다 recall. ¶ ～제 the recall system / 우리 나라 대사의 ～ the recall of our ambassador / 결함 제품의 ～작전 the recall operation of faulty products / 500대의 차가 안전성에 결함이 있어 ～되었다 Five hundred cars were recalled for safety reasons. ◉ ～제 the recall system.

**리퀘스트** a request. ¶ ～곡 a request「tune [song]. ◉ ～프로(그램) 〖방송〗 a request program.

**리큐어** 《술》 liqueur. ¶ ～잔 a liqueur glass.

**리크** 《새는 것·구멍·양》 a leak; leakage. ¶ 가스[뉴스] ～ a「gas [news] leak.

**리클라이닝 시트** 《등을 젖힐 수 있는 좌석》 a reclining seat.

**리타이어** retire 《from》; drop out 《of》 (경기에서).

**리터** 《용량 단위》 a liter (생략 l., lit.).

**리턴매치** 〖권투〗 a return match.

**리투아니아** 《동유럽의 공화국》 (the Republic of) Lithuania. ¶ ～의 Lithuanian.

**리튬** 〖화학〗 lithium.

**리트머스** 〖화학〗 litmus. ◉ ～시험지 《test with》 litmus paper. ～액 litmus solution.

**리포터** 《보조기자·통신원》 a reporter. ¶ 연예 ～ a 《TV》 reporter on show business.

**리포트** 《학생의 제출물》 a paper; a term paper; 《보고》 a report. ¶ 내주 월요일까지 ～를 제출하시오 Your papers must be handed in by next Monday. / 나는 프랑스 혁명에 관한 ～를 써야 한다 I have to write a paper on the French Revolution.

> 용법 영어의 **report**는 공적인 보고·보도의 뜻. 대학생들이 교수에게 내는 학과에 관련된 숙제나 논문 따위의 제출물은 **paper**, **term paper** 라고 함. 학술 논문은 **treatise**, 소논문은 **essay**, 졸업 논문은 **graduation thesis** 라고 함.

**리프트** a lift; 《스키장의》 a「ski [chair] lift.

**리플레이션** 〖경제〗 《통화 재팽창》 reflation.

**리플릿** 《광고용의 1매짜리 인쇄물》 a leaflet.

**리허설** rehearsal; a dry run 《속어》. ¶ ～을 하다 rehearse a play; put a play into rehearsal; practice / 배우들은 첫공연에 대비하여 ～을 거듭 했다 The actors have rehearsed the play many times for the opening day.

**리히터지진계**(—地震計) the Richter scale.

**리히텐슈타인** 《오스트리아와 스위스 국경에 있는 공국》 (the Principality of) Liechtenstein.

**린스** a (hair) rinse. ～하다 rinse 《*one's* hair》; give 《*one's* hair》 a rinse.

**린치** lynch; lynching; torture. ¶ ～를 가하다 lynch [torture] 《*a person*》; (gang up on *a person* and) beat *him* up / 그들은 배신자에게 ～를 가했다 They lynched the traitor.

> 용법 **lynch**, **lynching**은「사적 처형」이란 뜻으로 살인 행위를 뜻함. 단순히「사적 제재」 또는「집단 폭행」을 뜻하는 우리말의「린치」와는 상당한 뜻의 차이가 있음.

**릴** 《낚시·테이프 따위의》 a 《fishing》 reel; 《필름의》 a reel; a spool. ◉ 릴낚싯대 a (fishing) rod and reel.

**릴레이** a relay (race). ¶ 400미터 ～ a 400-meter relay. ◉ ～경주＝릴레이.

**릴리프** relief. ～하다 relieve. ¶ ～로 활약하다 work in relief. ◉ ～피처 《구원 투수》 a relief pitcher; a reliever.

**림프** 〖해부〗 lymph.
◉ ～관 a lymphatic vessel〔duct〕. ～샘〔선(腺)〕 a lymphatic gland; a lymph node: ～선염 inflam-mation of the lymphatic gland / ～선이 붓다 develop swollen lymphatic glands. ～액 lymph.

**립스틱** a lipstick. ⇨루주.

**링** 〖권투〗 the ring; 《체조의》 flying rings; 《피임용》 an intrauterine (contraceptive) device (생략 IU(C)D); 《반지》 a ring. ◉ 링사이드 《sit at》 the ringside: 링사이드에 앉다 sit at the ringside.

**링거** ◉ ～액 〖의학〗 Ringer's solution〔fluid〕. ～주사 《give》 an injection of Ringer's solution.

**링컨** 《미국 16대 대통령》 Abraham Lincoln (1805-65).

**링크** ① 〖경제〗 a link; 〖컴퓨터〗《연결》 a link. ② 《스케이트장》 a rink. ◉ ～가공제 a link process system. ～제(制) 〖경제〗《수출입 등에서의》 a link system: …을 ～제로 하다 place … on link system.

**링크스** (golf) links.

**-ㅁ세** 《하겠네》 I will gladly 《do it for you》; let me *do.* ¶ 내 나중에 감세 I'll be along later. / 곧 갚음세 I'll pay you back right away. / 나중에 전화를 함세 I'll 「call you up 〔telephone you〕 later. / 우리들의 결정을 자네에게 꼭 알려 줌세 We shall let you know our decision.

**마**[1] 《남쪽》 the south (뱃사람들의 말). ¶ 마파람 the south wind; a souther.

**마**[2] 〖식물〗 a yam.

**마**[3] 〖음악〗 mi. ¶ 마음 E / 내림마 E flat (기호 E♭) / 올림마 E sharp (기호 E#).

**마**(麻) 〖식물〗 a hemp; flax(아마); jute (황마). ◉ 마직 hemp; linen(린넨); jute(황저포).

**마**(馬) a horse. ⇨ 말.

**마**(魔) a demon; an evil spirit 〔influence〕. ¶ 마의 건널목 a fatal 〔an accident-prone〕 (railroad) crossing / 마의 호수 an enchanted 〔treacherous〕 lake / 마의 금요일 an unlucky Friday / 마가 끼어 tempted by an evil spirit; unluckily; as ill luck would have it / 마가 들다〔끼다〕 be possessed by a demon; be tempted by an evil spirit; come under the influence of an evil spirit; be bewitched 〔jinxed〕 / 일에 마가 들다〔끼다〕 *one's* plan is jinxed / 무슨 마가 끼었는지 그는 은행에서 5백만원을 횡령했다 I wonder what could have possessed him to have embezzled five million won from the bank.

**마**(碼) a yard (=91.44cm). ¶ 마에 얼마로 팔다 sell 《a fabric》 by the yard.

**-마**(魔) a devil of a man; a (human) fiend. ¶ 살인마 a devilish homicide; a cutthroat.

**마가린** margarine; oleo 《미》; marge 《영구어》.

**마가목** 〖식물〗 a mountain ash; a rowan.

**마가복음**(一福音) 〖성서〗 (the gospel of ) Mark.

**마각**(馬脚) *one's* true character. ¶ ∼을 드러내다 betray *oneself;* show the cloven hoof; reveal *one's* true character 〔colors, nature〕; give *oneself* away / 그는 그만 ∼을 드러내고 말았다 He revealed his 「true nature 〔real self 〕 unconsciously.

**마갈궁**(磨羯宮) 〖천문〗 the Goat; Capricorn.

**마감** a close; closing; a deadline. ∼하다 close; bring to a close; finish. ¶ 편집의 ∼ editorial deadline; the time for going to press; the final editing / ∼ 후에 도착한 원고 late 〔belated〕 manuscripts / 일을 ∼하다 finish a job / 원고를 ∼하다 accept no more manuscripts; go to press with the manuscripts on hand / 신청은 ∼되었다 The time for application has closed. / 예약 ∼은 이달 30일입니다 The subscription list closes on the 30th inst. / 응모 ∼은 오후 4시입니다 The deadline 〔closing time〕 for applications is 4 p.m. / T대학은 어제 원서를 ∼하였다 T University stopped accepting applications yesterday. / ∼은 언제죠 When is the deadline?
◉ ∼날〔기일〕 the closing 〔last〕 day; the final date; the deadline. ∼시간 the closing hour; 《신문 기사의》 the copy deadline: ∼시간〔날짜〕에 대다 meet 〔make〕 the deadline / ∼시간〔날짜〕까지 대지 못하다 miss the deadline. 모집∼ the close of the subscription. 원고∼ the deadline for the manuscript. 일∼ finishing a job. 장부∼ the closing of books.

**마개** a stopper; a stopple; a cork; a plug. ¶ ∼를 막다 cork; plug / ∼를 따다〔뽑다〕 uncork 《a bottle》; open a cap; remove a stopper.
◉ ∼뽑이 a corkscrew; a cap 〔bottle〕 opener. 귀∼ an earplug; an ear stopper; an ear stopple.

**마고자** an outer coat worn by men over their upper garment.

**마구**(馬具) horse equipment; horse 〔riding〕 gear. ¶ ∼를 달다〔벗기다〕 harness 〔unharness〕 《a horse》 / ∼를 단 harnessed 《horse》.
◉ ∼상 《사람》 a harness maker; a saddler; 《장사》 a harnessry; a saddler's shop; a saddlery.

**마구** ① 《함부로》 carelessly; recklessly; rashly (무모하게); at random (되는대로); haphazardly; without discretion

(신중하지 않게); indiscriminately (무차별하게); slapdash; hit-or-miss; blindly (무턱대고). ¶ 글씨를 ~ 쓰다 write carelessly 〔sloppily〕 / 돈을 ~ 쓰다 spend money recklessly 〔like water〕; lavish *one's* money 《on》 / 말을 ~하다 talk at random; be rough-spoken / 사람을 ~ 다루다 handle 《*a person*》 roughly; manhandle / 일을 ~하다 do a half-baked 〔slapdash〕 job of it / 아무것이나 ~ 먹다 eat anything without discrimination; be omnivorous / 약속을 ~하다 make a profusion of promises / 총을 ~ 쏘다 fire blindly 〔at random〕 / 상품을 ~ 다뤄서는 안 된다 Don't handle the goods roughly.
② 《몹시》 hard; much. ¶ 사람을 ~ 때리다 beat 《*a person*》 up 〔wildly〕; belabor 《*a person*》 (with a stick) / 욕을 ~ 해대다 heap abuses on 《*a person*》.

**마구(간)** (馬廐(間)) a stable; a barn. ¶ ~에 넣다 stable 《a horse》; put 〔lodge〕 《a horse》 in a stable.

**마구리** end pieces; caps on both ends. ◉ ~판 a device for squaring wooden end pieces.

**마구잡이** 《행동》 random 〔haphazard, careless〕 behavior; 《선택》 random choice. ¶ 일을 ~로 하다 do *one's* work carelessly; do a slapdash job of it / 학생을 ~로 입학시키다 admit any number of students indiscriminately / 책을 ~로 읽다 read books at random.

**마굴** (魔窟) 《악마의》 a lair of devils; 《악한의》 a den (of rascals); an underworld hangout; 《창녀의》 a brothel; a house of ill repute; the brothel districts; 《아편굴》 an opium den.

**마권** (馬券) a betting ticket 〔slip〕 《on a horse》. ¶ 적중〔미적중〕 ~ a winning 〔losing〕 ticket / ~을 사다 buy a betting 〔pari-mutuel〕 ticket.
◉ ~매표구 a betting booth 〔window〕; a ticket window 〔office〕. ~세 horse-race tax. ~업자 a bookmaker.

**마귀** (魔鬼) ① 《악마》 an evil spirit; a devil; a demon. ¶ ~같은 demoniac; fiendish; diabolic / ~를 쫓아내다 drive out evil spirits. ② 〖기독교〗 the Devil; a Satan. ◉ ~할멈 a witch; a hag; a harridan.

**마그나카르타** 〖역사〗 Magna C(h)arta.

**마그네슘** 〖화학〗 magnesium (기호 Mg); 《사진의》 flash powder. ◉ ~광 magnesium light. 산화~ magnesium oxide; magnesia. 염화~ magnesium chloride.

**마그네시아** 〖화학〗 magnesia (산화마그네슘).

**마그네틱** magnetic. ◉ ~테이프 a magnetic tape.

**마그넷** a magnet.

**마그마** 〖지질〗 magma (*pl.* ~s, ~ta).

**마나님** an elderly lady; an old woman; 《호칭》 madam; your (good) lady.

**마냥** ① 《실컷·만판》 till full; to satiety; to *one's* heart's content. ¶ ~ 즐기다 enjoy to *one's* heart's content / ~ 먹었다 I have eaten all I wanted. ② 《그저》 solely; only; but; intently; 《끝없이》 endlessly; ceaselessly. ¶ ~ 그리워하다 solely long for 《*one's* lover》 / ~ 어리석기만 하다 be in a bottomless ignorance / ~ 돈벌 궁리만 하다 be solely bent on moneymaking / ~ 울고만 있다 do nothing but cry / 그는 ~ 게으름을 피고 있다 He is always idle. ③ 《내내》 to the full(est) extent; all the way; 《느긋하게》 slowly; draggingly. ¶ ~ 끌다 drag on / 집까지 ~ 걸었다 I walked all the way to my house.

**마네킹** a mannequin; a manikin.
◉ ~걸 a manikin girl. ~인형 a window dummy 《미》.

**마녀** (魔女) a witch; a sorceress; 《여자 악마》 a she-devil〔-demon〕. ◉ ~사냥 a witch-hunt; witch hunting.

**마노** (瑪瑙) 〖광물〗 agate. ¶ ~브로치 an agate brooch.

**마누라** ① 《자기 아내》 *one's* wife; 《호칭》 my dear; honey; darling. ¶ ~를 얻다 take 《a woman》 to wife; make 《a woman》 *one's* wife / 그는 ~에게 꼭 쥐어지낸다 He is a henpecked husband. ② 《노파》 an old woman; the old hag.

**마는** but; only; (al)though. ¶ 가고 싶지 ~ 바빠서 못 가겠다 I should like to go, only (that) I'm too busy. / 돈은 있습니다~ 지금 당장 빌려드리진 못하겠습니다 I have the money but I can't lend it to you right now.

**마늘** 〖식물〗 a garlic; 《조미용》 garlic. ¶ ~ 냄새가 나는 garlicky; smelling of garlic / ~을 듬뿍 넣고 맛을 낸 요리 a dish thickly flavored with garlic.
◉ ~모 a trigonal shape. ~장아찌 pickled garlics. ~종 the stalk 〔stem〕 of a garlic. ~쪽 a clove of a garlic.

**마니교** (摩尼教) Manich(a)eism.

**마니아** 《상태》 a mania; a craze 《for》; 《사람》 a 《dance》 maniac; an 《audio》 enthusiast; a 〔an enthusiastic〕 fan; 《구어》 a buff. (★ 「마니아」는 영어의 mania에서 유래된 것이나, 이 낱말은 「이상할

정도로 극단의 열광자」란 강한 뜻이 있기 때문에, 단순히 「…에 열중하는 사람」의 뜻으로는 거의 쓰이지 않음). ¶ 그는 영화 ~다 He is a film buff.

**마닐라** 《필리핀의 수도》 Manil(l)a.
◉ ~로프 Manila rope. ~삼 Manila hemp. ~지 Manila paper.

**마님** madam; My Lady.

**–마님** Your 〔His〕 Excellency; My Lord. ¶ 대감〔영감〕마님 My Lord.

**마다**[1] 《짓찧다》 hit; smash; crush.

**마다**[2] [조사] each; every; all. ¶ 날~ every day / 이틀~ every other day / 집집~ each and every house / 페이지 ~ page after page; every page / 3년 ~ every three years; every third year / 곳곳 ~ everywhere / 갈 적~ every time *one* goes / 식구 한 명이 늘 때~ for each additional number of the family / 십년~ 증가하다 increase with every decade / 사람~ 그를 칭찬한다 Everybody praises him. / 버스는 5분~ 떠납니다 The buses start every five minutes. / 그녀는 만나는 사람~ 그 이야기를 한다 She tells the story to everybody she meets.

**마다가스카르** 《아프리카 남동의 섬나라》 Madagascar (Island) (공화국).

**마다하다** mind 《*do*ing》; hate; dislike; decline 《an offer》. ¶ …하기를 마다하지 않다 do not mind 《*do*ing》; be ready 〔willing〕 to 《*do*》 / 마다 할 수가 없다 have no word to decline; do not know how to decline / 그는 부엌일도 마다하지 않았다 He didn't mind doing kitchen work. / 그 젊은이는 자유를 위해서라면 죽음도 마다하지 않았다 The young man was ready to die for liberty.

**마담** a madam; 《요정 등의》 a proprietress (주인); the manageress 《of a saloon》 (고용된). ◉ 얼굴~ the manageress 《of a tea room》 who has a large circle of acquaintances.

**마당** ① 《뜰》 a yard; a court. ¶ 뒷~ the backyard / 신부집 ~에서 결혼식을 올리다 hold a wedding ceremony in the bride's house. ② 《곳》 a place; a ground. ¶ 토론의 ~ a place for debating 〔discussion〕. ③ 《타작 마당》 a threshing ground; the yard (as used for threshing). ④ 《경우》 an occasion; a case; a juncture (시기); a situation; 《때》 the moment. ¶ 이 ~에 on this occasion; at this time 〔juncture〕 / 떠나는 ~에 at the time of *one's* departure / 이 위급한 ~에 그게 무슨 짓이냐 What a hell are you doing at this emergency? / 이 ~에 그런 핑계가 통할 줄 아느냐 When things have got to this state, do you still think you can talk your way out of it? ⑤ 《판소리 등의》 an episode. ¶ 봉산 탈춤 일곱 ~ 중의 하나 one of the seven episodes of the *Pongsan* Mask Dance.
◉ ~맥질 smoothing the threshing ground before harvest time: ~맥질하다 smooth the threshing ground. ~발 a wide-sized (human) foot. ~비 a yard broom. ~질 threshing in the yard: ~질하다 thresh in the yard / 볏~질 threshing rice.

**마대**(麻袋) a gunny 〔hemp〕 sack; a sandbag (모래주머니).

**마도로스** [< *matroos* (D.)] a sailor; a seaman. ◉ ~파이프 a (tobacco) pipe.

**마도요** 〖조류〗 the Indian curlew.

**마도위**(馬—) a horse broker.

**마돈나** 《성모》 the Madonna; 《애인》 the lady *one* adores. ¶ ~상 a Madonna.

**마되질** measuring. ~하다 measure (with *mal* and *toe*).

**마드무아젤** a *mademoiselle* (*pl. mesdemoiselles*) (F.)(생략 Mlle, *pl.* Mlles); Miss; a young lady.

**마들가리** ① 《나무의》 twigs; sticks; dead branches; tinder. ② 《해진 옷의》 seams of a worn-out garment. ③ 《홑맺힘》 kinks in straw-rope 〔thread〕.

**마들다**(魔—) get possessed by a demon.

**마디** ① 《식물의》 a joint; a node; a knot; a knob. ¶ 나무 ~ a gnarl; a knar / 대나무~ a joint of bamboo; a bamboo joint (from node to node) / ~ 없는 나무 clean 〔clear〕 timber; timber without a knot / ~가 많다 be full of knots; be knotty 〔knobby, gnarled〕. ② 《관절》 a joint; a knuckle (손가락·무릎의). ¶ 다릿~ the leg joint / 손가락 ~ a knuckle / 팔~가 부러지다 *one's* arm is broken at the joint. ③ 《말·노래의》 a word; a phrase; a song; a tune. ¶ 한~ 부르다 sing a tune / 한 ~ 하겠다 I'll say a word. / 노래 한 ~만 하시오 Please favor us with a song.

**마디다** (be) durable; long-lasting; long=wearing. ¶ 값싼 비단은 마디지 못하다 Cheap silk has not much endurance. / 이 옷들은 마디어 오래 입을 수 있다 These clothes will wear well.

**마디마디** ① 《식물의》 all the joints 〔nodes〕; every joint 〔node〕. ② 《관절

의》 all the joints; every joint (of the body). ¶ ～가 아프다 every joint aches; feel pain in every joint. ③《말·노래의》 all the words 〔phrases〕; every word 〔phrase, tune〕.

**마디지다** have nodes 〔joints〕; be gnarled 〔knotty〕; be full of knots. ¶ 마디진 손 knobby fingers / 마디진 솔 a gnarled pine.

**마디충**(一蟲) 〖곤충〗 a rice (stem) borer.

**마디풀** 〖식물〗 a knotgrass; a knotweed.

**마따나** as; just; just as 《*a person*》 say. ¶ 자네 말～ 옛날에는 여기에 연못이 있었네 As you say, there was a pond here in old(en) times. / 옛말 ～ 암탉이 울면 집안이 망하는 법이다 As the old saying goes, "when the woman wears the trousers the family goes to ruin".

**마땅하다** ①《적합하다》 (be) becoming; befitting; right; appropriate; apposite; suitable; 《상당하다》 (be) fair; reasonable. ¶ 마땅한 값에 사다 buy at a reasonable price / 마땅한 사람과 결혼하다 marry a suitable person / 마땅한 예를 들다 give a good 〔an appropriate〕 example / 마땅한 조건으로 계약하다 make a contract on fair terms / 그 자리에 마땅한 사람이다 be the very man 〔just the one〕 for the place; be the right man for the position.
② 《당연하다》 (be) right; proper; reasonable; 《의당》 ought to; should. ¶ 부모의 말을 순종해야 ～ You ought to obey your parents. / 그의 죄는 죽어 ～ His crime deserves certain death. / 너는 그 책임을 지고 사직을 해야 ～ Of course you should resign, holding yourself responsible for it. / 너는 내게 감사해야 ～ You ought to thank me for it.
③ 《만족스럽다》 (be) satisfactory; pleasing; gratifying. ¶ 못마땅해 하다 be dissatisfied with / 며느리를 못 마땅해 하다 be dissatisfied with *one's* daughter-in-law / 마땅찮은 얼굴을 하다 look displeased; turn glum / 나는 그 결과가 마땅찮다 I am not satisfied with the result.

**마땅히** ① 《적당히》 suitably; adequately; appropriately; properly; reasonably. ¶ 값을 ～ 부르다 bid a reasonable price. ② 《의당히》 justly; properly; naturally; necessarily; of necessity; deservedly; of course; as a matter of course. ¶ ～ …해야 하다 ought to 《*do*》; it is proper that 《*one*》 should 《*do*》 / 너는 ～ 벌을 받아야겠다 You deserve punishment. / 상관의 명령에 ～ 복종해야 한다 You must naturally obey the orders of your superiors.

**마뜩찮다** (be) disagreeable; offensive. ¶ 마뜩찮은 소리를 하다 say something disagreeable 〔offensive〕.

**마뜩하다** (be) satisfactory; agreeable; acceptable. ¶ 마뜩한 디자인이 없다 None of these patterns suits my fancy.

**마라톤** a marathon (race). ¶ ～을 하다 run a marathon. ◉ ～경주 a marathon race: ～경주에 나가다 run in a marathon race. ～선수 a marathon runner; a marathoner.

**마래미** 〖어류〗 a young yellowtail.

**마량**(馬糧) fodder; feed; forage; hay.

**마력**(馬力) 《단위》 horsepower (생략 h.p., hp). ¶ 50～의 발동기 a motor of 50 hp / ～을 올리다 push the power up / 이 모터는 100 ～입니다 This motor develops 〔has a capacity of〕 100 hp. / 이 기계에는 55～의 모터가 달려 있다 This machine is equipped with a motor of 55 hp.

**마력**(魔力) 《매력》 (a) mysterious charm; enchanting power; 《이상한 힘》 magic 〔magical〕 powers; magic. ¶ 숫자의～ the magic of numbers / ～을 지닌 charming; fascinating; bewitching / ～에 걸리다〔홀리다〕 fall under 〔be bound by〕 a magic spell; find *oneself* under the charm 《of》.

**마련** ① 《준비》 preparation; provision; arrangement; 《장만》 purchase. ～하다 prepare; provide; furnish; have 《*a thing*》 ready; arrange; make arrangement 《for》; 《사다》 buy 〔get〕 《what is necessary》; 《계획을》 plan; work out. ¶ K씨를 위해 특별히 ～된 행사 an event specially arranged to honor Mr. K / 계획을 ～하다 work out a scheme / 새옷을 ～하다 get 〔buy〕 a new suit(사다); have a new suit made(만들게 하다) / 술자리를 ～하다 give 〔prepare〕 a drinking party / 집을 ～하다 get 〔purchase〕 a house / …을 ～해 주다 provide 《*a person*》 with; furnish 《*a person*》 for.
② 《변통》 management; contrivance; makeshift. ～하다 manage to *do;* contrive; arrange; make shift; see to. ¶ 구실을 ～하다 invent an excuse 《of》 / 돈을 ～하다 get money somehow; make up a sum; raise money 〔funds〕 / 돈을 ～하기 위해 뛰어다니다 get about to

raise money / 어떻게 ～해 볼게 I will try and manage to get it. / 정오까진 꼭 좀 ～해 주게 Be sure to get it ready by noon. / 30만원만 ～해줄 수 없겠나 Can't you come up with just some 300,000 won? *or* Can you afford to lend me some 300,000 won?

③ 《당연》 ¶ …하게 ～이다 be certain 〔sure, bound〕 《to *do*》; 《숙명적으로》 inevitably to 〔be〕; be doomed 〔destined〕 《to》; be a matter of course / 생명 있는 것은 죽게 ～이다 Life is subject to decay. / 약은 쓰기 ～이다 Why a medicine tastes bad is a matter of course.

**마렵다** feel an urge to urinate 〔defecate〕; have a call of nature; want to relieve *oneself*. ¶ 똥이 ～ have to defecate; feel the call of nature; feel like going to stool; want to relieve *oneself* / 오줌이 ～ have a 〔feel the〕 need to urinate / 엄마 오줌 마려워 Mommy, I want to do my needs.

**마로니에** 『식물』 a *marronnier* (F.); a horse chestnut (tree).

**마루** ① 『건축』 a wooden floor. ¶ ～를 놓다 floor; put in flooring; board the floor / ～를 뜯다 tear 〔rip〕 up the floor. ② 《지붕·산의》 a ridge. ¶ 산～ the ridge of a mountain.
◉ ～방 a floored room; a room with a wooden floor. ～운동 『체조』 floor exercise. ～청 a flooring; a floorboard. 마룻대 『건축』 a ridge pole. 마룻바닥 《sit on》 the floor.

**마루터기, 마루턱** the top; the summit; the peak. ¶ 산～ the peak of a mountain / 지붕～ the top of a roof. ◉ 고갯～ the summit of a pass.

**마르다**[1] ① 《건조하다》 (***a***) 《젖은것·물기가》 dry (up); be parched up (바싹); run 〔get, become, go〕 dry (우물·흐르는 물이); 《목재가》 be seasoned. ¶ 말라붙은 우물 a dry well / 잘 마른 재목 well-seasoned timber / 바싹 ～ dry up; be dried up; parch / 쉽게 ～ dry easily 〔fast〕 / 샘〔우물〕이 ～ spring 〔well〕 dries up 〔runs dry〕 / 세탁이 쉽고 금새 ～ be easy to wash and quick to dry / 논이 말라서 갈라지다 the rice paddy is all parched and cracked / 옷이 말랐다 The clothes have dried. (***b***) 《목·입이》 be 〔feel〕 thirsty; be parched (up); parch. ¶ 바싹 마른 입술 parched lips / 목이 ～ be thirsty; have a dry throat. (***c***) 《시들어 죽다》 wither; die; be dead. ¶ 마른 가지 a dead 〔withered〕 branch 〔twig〕 / 마른 잎을 따다 rip off dead leaves.
② 《야위다》 grow gaunt 〔slim〕; become thin 〔lean〕; be wasted 〔emaciated〕; lose flesh (병으로); pine away (슬픔·사랑으로). ¶ 마른 사람 a thin 〔lean, skinny, scrawny, scraggy〕 person / 걱정으로 ～ worry *oneself* to a frazzle / 잘 먹지 못해 ～ be wasted with hunger / 전보다 훨씬 마르셨군요 You have got much thinner than you were. / 그는 병으로 옛모습을 찾아볼 수 없게 말랐다 He has worn away to a shadow because of sickness.
③ 《고갈되다》 run out; be exhausted; be used up. ¶ 돈이 ～ have no money left; money is tight 〔scarce, in short supply〕 / 호주머니가 ～ have a cold 〔light〕 purse; feel the draught 《구어》; be low in (*one's*) pocket.

**마르다**[2] 《옷감·재목을》 cut out. ¶ 옷을 ～ cut out clothes / 상의(上衣)를 치수에 맞추어 ～ cut out a coat to measure / 재목을 치수에 맞추어 ～ cut lumber to measure.

**마르크** a mark; a Deutche mark (생략 DM).

**마르크스** 《독일의 경제학자》 Karl Heinrich Marx (1818-83). ◉ ～레닌주의 Marxism-Leninism. ～주의 Marxism: ～주의자 a Marxist.

**마른갈이** 『농업』 plowing 〔ploughing 《영》〕 a rice field while it is dry. ～하다 plow a rice field while it is dry.

**마른걸레** a dust cloth; a dry mop. ¶ ～질하다 wipe with a dry mop 〔cloth〕.

**마른기침** a dry cough; a hack(ing). ～하다 make a dry 〔hacking〕 cough.

**마른날** a clear 〔fine〕 day.

**마른반찬**(—飯饌) dried meat 〔fish〕 eaten with rice (as side dishes).

**마른밥** 《뭉친 밥》 a rice-ball; 《국 없는》 rice eaten without soup.

**마른버짐** 『의학』 psoriasis.

**마른번개** lightning in a clear blue sky.

**마른빨래** ～하다 rub the dirt off the clothes.

**마른신** 《기름에 결지 않은》 unoiled leather shoes; 《마른 땅에 신는》 dry-weather shoes.

**마른안주**(—按酒) a (simple) relish of dried meat and fish taken with wine 〔beer〕; a snack.

**마른옴** 『의학』 the itch; scabies.

**마른일** the part of housework in which you don't get your fingers wet. ～하다 do the dry part of the housework.

**마른입** ①《국물 안 먹은》a mouth that has had no soup. ② = 잔입.

**마른천둥** thunder in a clear blue sky.

**마른침** ¶ ~을 삼키다 hold 〔catch〕 *one's* breath; strain *one's* attention / ~을 삼키며 발표를 기다리다 wait for the announcement breathlessly.

**마른하늘** the clear blue sky. ¶ ~에 생벼락 a bolt from the blue; a bombshell; a thunderbolt.

**마른행주** a dish towel.

**마름**[1]《이엉 단》a bundle of woven straw for thatching.

**마름**[2]〖식물〗a water chestnut 〔caltrop〕.

**마름**[3]《사람》the supervisor 〔manager〕 of the tenant farms.

**마름모** a lozenge; a diamond (shape); 〖수학〗a rhombus (*pl.* ~es, -bi). ¶ ~의 lozenge 〔diamond〕-shaped; lozenged; rhombic. ◉ ~꼴 무늬 a diaper pattern.

**마름쇠** a caltrop; a caltrap.

**마름자** a tailor's yardstick.

**마름질** cutting (out). ~하다 cut out 《lumber, clothes》. ¶ ~이 바느질보다 어렵다고 한다 Cutting is said to require more skill than tailoring.

**마리** the number 《of animals》; a head 〔단복수 동형〕. ¶ 새 한 ~ a bird / 소 두 ~ two (head of) cows / 물고기 세 ~ three fish / 마릿수를 세다 count the number 《of animals》; count noses 《of sheep》.

**마리아** Mary; Maria. ◉ 성모 ~ the (Blessed) Virgin Mary; the Holy Mother.

**마리아나제도**(一諸島)《서태평양의 제도》the Mariana Islands.

**마리화나**《환각제》marihuana; marijuana; grass 《미속어》. ¶ ~를 피우다 smoke marijuana.

**마림바**《악기》a marimba.

**마마**[1](媽媽) ①《천연두》smallpox. ¶ ~에 걸리다 have smallpox; be attacked by 〔suffer from〕 smallpox. ②《역신 마마》plague. ◉ 마맛자국 a pockmark; a pit: 얼굴에 마맛자국이 있다 *one's* face is pitted with smallpox 〔marked by smallpox〕.

**마마**[2](媽媽) ①《경칭》Your 〔His〕 Majesty; Your 〔His〕 Highness. ②《귀인의 첩》Madame. ◉ 동궁~ the (Crown) Prince; His Highness. 상감~ the King; His Majesty.

**마멋**〖동물〗a marmot(te).

**마멸**(磨滅) defacement; wear (and tear); abrasion. ~하다 deface; wear down 〔away, out〕; be worn down 〔away, out〕. ¶ ~된 타이어 a worn-out tire / (돌계단 등이) 사람 발길에 ~되다 wear down under the tread 《of》 / 돌에 새긴 문자가 완전히 ~돼 있다 The inscription on the stone has been worn out 〔defaced completely〕. ◉ ~제 abrasive.

**마모**(磨耗) wear (and tear); frictional wear; abrasion. ~하다 be worn away 〔out, down〕. ¶ ~되기 마련이다 be subject to wear / 베어링이 ~되어 있다 The bearings are worn down 〔away〕.

**마무르다** ①《끝손질하다》give 〔put, add〕 the final 〔finishing〕 touch; touch up; do up; finish off. ¶ 멍석을 ~「give the final touches to 〔finish up〕 a straw mat / 바느질을 ~ make 〔sew〕 the final stitches. ②《뒤끝을》settle; bring 《*a matter*》 to a finish; finish (off, up); complete; conclude; get through with. ¶ 문장을 솜씨 있게 ~ round off a sentence / 일을 ~ finish 〔get through with〕 *one's* work / (일) 끝을 ~ finish up; come to the end; be through.

**마무리** finish; the finishing touches 〔strokes〕; completion; conclusion. ~하다 give the finishing 〔last〕 touches; touch up. ¶ ~가 잘 되다 the finish is good / 이 보석함은 ~가 좋다 This jewel case has a good finish. / 만사는 ~가 중요하다 All's well that ends well. / 그것을 4시까지 ~ 해 주시오 Please get it finished by four. ◉ ~공 a finisher. ~ 기계 a finishing machine. ~대패 a finishing plane. ~줄 a smooth file. ~칠 last coating.

**마물**(魔物) a demon; a devil; an evil spirit; a thing of evil. ¶ 여자는 ~이야 Woman is a bewitching creature.

**마바리**(馬—) ①《짐말》a horse carrying a burden; a packhorse. ②《짐》a horse load 〔burden〕. ③《수확》harvesting two *seom* of grain on a one=*majigi* plot of land. ◉ ~꾼 a packhorse driver; a pack-horse man 〔peddler〕.

**마방**(馬房) a horse stable; a livery stable; 《주막집》a wineshop with stable facilities. ◉ ~집 a liveryman's; a stableman's.

**마법**(魔法) magic; the black art. ⇨ 마술(魔術).

**마부**(馬夫) a footman; a groom; a stableman; a horse driver; a carter.

**마분**(馬糞) horse dung; horse droppings. ◉ ～지 strawboard; millboard.

**마블** 《대리석》 marble.

**마비**(痲痺) paralysis; numbness; palsy. ～되다 be paralyzed; go numb; be benumbed 〔palsied, numbed〕 《with cold》.

> **용법** **paralyze** 신체의 마비, 비유적으로는 활동 불능의 뜻. **numb**, **benumb** 특히 추위 따위로 감각이 없어진다는 뜻: 그녀의 발은 추위로 마비되었다 Her feet were benumbed by the cold. / 눈보라로 도시의 기능이 마비되어 있다 The city is paralyzed by the snowstorm. **palsy** paralysis와 같은 뜻의 고어적인 표현.

¶ ～성의 paralytic 《polio》; paralyzing 《poison》 / ～시키다 paralyze / 국회의 기능을 ～시키다 hamstring the House / 양심을 ～시키다 atrophy 《*a person's*》 conscience / 그는 뇌혈전증으로 왼발이 ～되어 있다 His left leg has been paralyzed since he was afflicted with cerebral thrombosis. / 추위로 손가락이 ～되었다 My fingers got numb with cold. / 그의 양심이 ～돼 있다 His conscience is atrophied. *or* He has no scruples. / 그는 정의감이 완전히 ～되어 있다 He has no sense of justice at all. / 전국의 수송망은 ～ 상태에 빠졌다 The nationwide transportation system is now paralyzed. / 파업으로 산업이 ～되었다 The strike paralyzed the industry.
◉ ～약 an anesthetic. 뇌성～ cerebral palsy. 소아～ infantile paralysis; polio 《구어》. 심장～ heart failure. 안면～ facial paralysis. 전신〔국부〕～ general 〔local〕 paralysis.

**마비풍**(馬脾風) 〖한의〗 diphtheria.

**마사지** massage. ¶ ～를 하다 massage 《*a person* on the arm》; give 《*a person*》 a massage / 매일 밤 얼굴을 ～하다 massage *one's* face every night.
◉ ～사 《남자》 a masseur [mæsə́ːr]; 《여자》 a masseuse [mæsə́ːz]; 《남녀공통》 a massagist; a massager. ～요법 massotherapy.

**마사회**(馬事會) ◉ 한국～ the Korea Racing Authority.

**마상**(馬上) horseback. ¶ ～에서 on horseback / ～에서 소리치다 call out to 《*a person*》 from on *one's* horse.
◉ ～객 a rider; an equestrian.

**마상이** 《작은 배》 a (small) boat; a skiff; 《통나무배》 a dugout; a canoe.

**마성**(魔性) devilishness. ¶ ～의 fiendish; devilish / ～을 지닌 여자 a temptress; an enchantress.

**마셜제도**(一諸島) 《서태평양의 섬》 the Marshall Islands.

**마소** horses and cattle. ¶ ～처럼 부리다 drive 〔work〕 《*a person*》 hard.

**마손**(磨損) wear and tear; friction loss; abrasion. ～하다 wear (away).

**마수** 《그날 운수》 the luck of the day judged from the first sale. ¶ ～가 좋다〔나쁘다〕 the first sale bodes good 〔bad〕 luck for the day's business.

**마수**(魔手) an evil hand. ¶ ～에 걸리다 fall a victim to 《*a person*》; be made a victim of 《*a person*》 / ～를 뻗치다 exert *one's* evil influence; attempt to victimize 《*a person*》; make a victim of 《*a person*》.

**마수걸이** the first sale of the day; the first transaction at the beginning of a business. ～하다 make the first sale of the day; make the first transaction at the beginning of a business. ¶ ～로 수박 한 개를 팔다 sell a watermelon as the first sale / ～니 싸게 팔겠소 You are the first buyer, so I'll sell it cheap for luck.

**마술**(馬術) horsemanship; (the art of) riding; 《곡마술》 equestrianism. ¶ ～의 대가 a master horseman / ～의 연습 riding practice 〔lessons〕; equestrian exercises / ～에 능하다 be at home in the saddle; be a good horseman / ～을 배우다〔가르치다〕 take 〔give〕 lessons in horsemanship. ◉ ～경기 a riding 〔an equestrian〕 event. 고등～ high school; *haute école* (F.). 종합～ 《올림픽의》 the three-day events.

**마술**(魔術) magic (arts); the black art; sorcery; witchcraft. ¶ ～을 부리다 use 〔practice〕 magic; conjure; juggle / ～로 …하게 하다 conjure 《*a person*》 into 《*doing something*》. ◉ ～사〔쟁이〕 a magician; a conjurer; a wizard; a sorcerer; 《여자》 a witch; a sorceress.

**마스카라** 《apply》 mascara 《to *one's* eyelashes》. ¶ ～를 짙게 칠한 눈 eyes heavy with mascara.

**마스코트** a mascot. ¶ 그 팀의 ～는 호랑이다 The team's mascot is a tiger.

**마스크** ① 《탈》 a mask; 《병균·먼지를 막기 위한》 a gauze mask over the mouth and nose; a flu mask (감기용). ¶ ～를 쓰다 wear a mask. ② features; looks. = 용모. ¶ 그 가수는 ～가 좋다 The singer has good 〔attractive] features.

**마스터** 《주인》 a master; 《경영자》 the proprietor. ∼하다 《숙달하다》 master 《English》; get the thorough knowledge 《of》. ◉ ∼키 a master key. ∼플랜 a master plan.

**마스트** 《돛대》 a mast. ¶ ∼가 셋인 배 a three-masted ship.

**마시다** ① 《음료를》 drink; take; have; 《삼키다》 swallow; take down. ¶ 물을 ∼ drink water / 술을 한 잔 ∼ drink a glass of wine / 차를 ∼ take tea / 벌컥벌컥 ∼ gulp down; guzzle / 단숨에 ∼ drink down; drink in one draft / 한입에 ∼ swallow at a gulp; drink off / 한 잔 ∼ have a drink; wet *one's* whistle / 홀짝홀짝 ∼ drink in little sips / 차를 마시며 이야기하다 talk over a cup of tea / 실컷 ∼ drink to *one's* heart's content / 마시지 못함 《게시》 Unfit for drinking. / 무엇을 마시겠습니까 What will you have 〔drink, have to drink〕? *or* What do you want to drink ? / 커피를 한 잔 마시니 졸음이 달아났다 A cup of coffee made me wide awake. / 술을 마시고 차를 운전하는 것은 교통 규칙 위반이다 Driving under the influence of alcohol is a violation of the traffic rules. / 이틀간이나 먹지도 마시지도 못하고 해상을 표류했다 We drifted over the sea for two days with nothing to eat or drink.
② 《공기를》 breathe in; inhale. ¶ 담배 연기를 들이 ∼ inhale tobacco smoke / 신선한 공기를 마음껏 (들이) ∼ breathe fresh air to the full.

**마신**(魔神) a devil; an evil spirit; Satan; the Devil.

**마애불**(磨崖佛) a rock cliff Buddha; a Buddha image carved on a cliff.

**마약**(痲藥) a drug; a narcotic; dope 《구어》; junk 《구어》.

> 용법 **drug** 본래 약·약제의 뜻이지만, 「마약」을 가리키는 경우가 더 많음. **narcotic** 마취제·최면제를 말하며, 「아편」 따위의 마약을 뜻함. **dope** 구어로서 「마약」의 뜻. **junk** 특히 마약의 일종인 「헤로인(heroin)」을 가리킴.

¶ ∼ 관련 범죄 narcotic-related crimes / ∼에 중독되다 become addicted to narcotics; be 〔go〕 hooked 《미속어》/ ∼을 밀매하다 peddle 〔traffic〕 drug / ∼을 맞다 take 〔inject〕 a drug 〔narcotic〕 / ∼을 흡입하다 inhale a narcotic / 그는 ∼에 중독돼 있다 He is on dope.
◉ ∼거래 traffic in drugs. ∼근절 캠페인 a Campaign to Uproot Drug Abuse. ∼남용 drug abuse: ∼ 남용자 a drug abuser. ∼단속 a dope check; narcotic control: ∼ 단속법 『법』 the Narcotics Control Law / ∼ 단속관 a narcotics agent. ∼밀매 drug traffic; dope peddling 《속어》; traffic in drugs: ∼ 밀매자 a drug peddler; a narcotic 〔drug〕 trafficker; a dope pusher 《구어》. ∼범죄 narcotics crimes. ∼중독 narcotics 〔drug〕 addiction: ∼중독자 a drug 〔narcotic〕 addict; a narcotic; a junkie 《속어》/ 그는 ∼ 중독자가 되었다 He became a drug addict. *or* He became addicted (to drugs). 한국 ∼퇴치 운동 본부 the Korean Antidrug Campaign Center.

**마왕**(魔王) ① the Devil; Satan; the Prince of Darkness. ② 『불교』 an evil spirit.

**마요네즈** mayonnaise. ¶ ∼를 치다 dress 《asparagus》 with mayonnaise.

**마우스피스** a mouthpiece.

**마운드** 『야구』 the mound; the pitcher's plate. ¶ ∼에 서다 be on the mound; take the mound / ∼에서 내려오다 leave the mound.

**마을** a village; a hamlet; a rural community. ¶ 이웃∼ a neighboring village / 외딴 ∼ an isolated village; a remote village. ◉ ∼금고 a village fund. ∼문고 a village library. ∼버스 a shuttle bus. ∼사람 village people: 온 ∼ 사람들이 그것을 구경하러 나왔다 The whole village turned out to see it.

**마을가다** visit *one's* neighboring village; visit *one's* neighborhood 《for an evening chat》. 「neighborhood》.

**마을꾼** a habitual frequenter 《to *one's*

**마음** ① 《정신》 (the) mind; (the) spirit; mentality; 《생각》 an idea; (a) thought.

> 용법 **mind** 이지적으로 생각하는 지적 활동을 뜻하는 「마음」. 머리·두뇌로 바꿔 말할 수 있는 말. **spirit** 육체와 대비되는, 즉 flesh (육체)로부터의 독립을 강조, 「정신」을 뜻하는 「마음」. **heart** 사랑·슬픔 따위의 감정이 깃들어 있는 「마음」.

¶ ∼과 육체 the mind and the body / 어린 ∼ a child's 〔childish〕 mind / ∼의 양식 mental food 〔nourishment〕 / ∼의 탓 a trick 「of senses 〔of the imagination〕/ ～의 평화 peace of mind / 어린 ～에도 무척 슬펐다 Though I was a child, I felt very sad. / ～은 급하지만 몸이 말을 안 듣는다 The spirit is willing but the flesh is weak. / 그것은 자네 ～ 탓이야 That's the mere fancy of yours. *or* It's all in your mind. / 그녀는 입이 거칠지만 ～은 착하다 She has a foul tongue, but is, at heart, a good girl.

마음이: ～이 좋은 사람 a gentle-minded person / ～이 넓은〔좁은〕 사람 a broad-minded 〔narrow-minded〕 person; a generous 〔petty〕 person / ～이 기쁘다 be glad (at heart) / ～이 놓이다 be 〔feel〕 relieved; feel at ease; be assured / ～이 들뜨다 feel excited 〔elated〕 / ～이 변하다 change *one's* mind; undergo a change of heart; be unfaithful; 《남녀간에》 grow out of love 《with》 / ～이 쓰이다 be worried 〔concerned, anxious〕 《about》 / ～이 커지다 become emboldened; lose 《*one's*》 timidity / ～이 끌리다 be attracted 《by》; take (an) interest 《in》 / 어머니가 얼마나 고생하셨는가를 생각하면 ～이 아프다 It pains me to think of how much my mother suffered.

마음에: ～에 걸리다 [사물이 주어] weigh (up)on 〔trouble〕 *one's* mind; worry 《*one*》; [사람이 주어] be anxious 〔nervous〕 《about》; feel uneasy 《about》 / ～에 그리다 imagine; draw a mental picture 《of》; picture 《the new house》 in *one's* mind / ～에 든든하다 feel safe 〔secure, reassured〕 / ～에 떠오르다 hit upon; think of; [사물이 주어] occur to 《*one*》; come across 〔to〕 *one's* mind / ～에 새기다 engrave 《an image》 〔print 《*a thing*》〕 on *one's* memory / ～에 거리끼다 have scruples about 《*doing*》 / (…하려고) ～에 정하고 있다 have *one's* heart 〔mind〕 set on 《*doing*》 / 내일의 시험이 ～에 걸려서 그는 잠을 잘 수 없었다 He couldn't sleep because tomorrow's test was on his mind. / 그는 행복한 결혼 생활을 ～에 그리고 있었다 He has 「pictured to himself 〔imagined〕 a happy married life. / 그 광경은 그녀의 ～에 깊이 새겨졌다 The scene was deeply etched in her mind.

마음을: ～을 (하나로) 합하여 with one accord / ～을 가라앉히다 calm 〔compose〕 *oneself;* collect *one's* scattered mind / ～을 고쳐먹다 turn over a new leaf; reform (*oneself*) / ～을 괴롭히다 trouble *one's* mind / ～을 긴장시키다 strain *one's* nerves / ～을 놓다 feel at rest 〔ease〕; feel 〔be〕 relieved / ～을 다잡다 brace *oneself* up / ～을 떠보다 sound 《*a person*》 on 〔about〕 《*a matter*》; probe 〔try to find out〕 《*a person's*》 intention / ～을 쏟다 put 〔pour〕 *one's* heart (and soul) into; concentrate on; give *one's* whole mind 《to》 / ～을 알아채다 read another's mind / ～을 잡다 take hold of *oneself;* control 〔check〕 *oneself;* pull *oneself* together; keep the presence of mind; recover *one's* composure / ～을 정하다 make up *one's* mind; resolve 《to》 / ～을 졸이다 worry (*oneself*) 《about》; be held in suspense; be in a fidget / ～을 편히 하다 set *one's* mind at ease; set *one's* heart at rest / ～(을) 잡아 개 장사다 be a backslider; be still addicted to *one's* old vices / ～을 끌다 attract; allure; appeal to (*one's* curiosity); attract *one's* attention.

② 《기분·느낌》 a mood; a feeling; 《심정》 (the) heart. ¶ ～을 모질게 먹다 harden 〔steel〕 *one's* heart 〔*oneself*〕 《against pity》 / ～을 빼앗다 fascinate; bewitch; captivate / ～을 빼앗기다 be fascinated 〔captivated〕 《by》; lose *one's* heart 《to》 / ～ 아파하다 grieve 《about, at, for》; be grieved 《at》 / (아무의) ～을 움직이다 move 《*a person*》; touch 《*a person's* heart》 / ～을 주다 share *one's* confidence 《with》; trust *oneself* 《to》 / ～을 털어놓다 open 〔bare〕 *one's* heart 《to》; unbosom *oneself* 《to》 / …할 ～이 없다 be in no mood to *do* / ～을 상하게 하다 hurt 《*a person's*》 feelings / 그녀는 바로 그에게 ～을 빼앗겼다 She instantly fell in love with the man. *or* The man fascinated her at once. / 가까스로 ～을 가라앉히고 그의 말에 귀를 기울였다 With some difficulty I got my feelings under control and listened to him.

③ 《사려》 thought; 《인정》 consideration; sympathy; tenderness; heart; kindness. ¶ ～을 쓰다 be sympathetic; be considerate / (남의) ～을 헤아리다 feel for; sympathize with; enter into another's feeling / 제 아들에게 늘 ～을 써 주셔서 감사합니다 Thank you for constant consideration to my son.

④ 《진심·마음속》 heart; wholeheart-

edness; sincerity. ¶ 따뜻한 ~ a warm heart / ~으로부터의, ~을 담은 hearty; heartfelt; wholehearted; sincere; warm / ~속 깊이 deep down in *one's* heart / ~속으로는 at 〔in〕 the back of *one's* mind / ~속으로 inwardly; secretly; in *one's* heart / ~에 품다 cherish; harbor; entertain / ~속으로 웃다 laugh in *one's* sleeve / ~을 담다 give *one's* whole mind (to) / ~은 좋은 사내다 be a good fellow at bottom 〔heart〕 / 여자에게 ~을 허락하다 give *oneself* up to a woman / ~을 담아 인사를 하다 express *one's* deepest gratitude; thank 《*a person*》 with *one's* whole heart.
⑤ 《의향·의도》 will; intention; inclination; plan; design; mind; heart. ¶ 갈 ~이 있다 have a mind to go / ~은 굴뚝 같다 have a great mind to; be eager to / …할 ~이 없다 have no mind to *do;* have no inclination for; don't feel like *do*ing / ~에도 없는 소리를 하다 say what *one* does not mean / 오늘은 도무지 일할 ~이 없다 I don't feel like working today. / 그의 기분을 해칠 ~은 없었다 I never meant to hurt him.
⑥ 《취미·기호》 fancy; taste; liking; mind; heart. ¶ ~에 들다 be to *one's* liking; be after *one's* fancy; be satisfactory; be acceptable; suit 〔catch, take, strike〕 *one's* fancy 〔taste〕; please; be in *one's* favor; find favor with 《*a person*》; impress favorably / ~에 들지 않다 be disagreeable to 《*a person*》; be not to 《*a person's*》 liking; go against the grain 〔stomach〕; be unsatisfactory; be displeased 〔dissatisfied〕 with 《*something*》 / ~에 맞는 일 congenial work / ~에 드는 옷 clothes to *one's* taste / ~에 드는 여자 a woman after *one's* heart.

**마음가짐** ① 《마음 태도》 *one's* mental attitude; 《마음 준비》 preparation. ¶ 만일의 경우에 대비한 ~이 돼 있다 I am prepared for the worst. ② 《결심》 determination; resolution; resolve.

**마음결** a cast 〔turn〕 of mind; grain; temper; nature; disposition. ¶ ~이 곱다 be tender-hearted; be sweet-tempered; be of gentle disposition / ~이 사납다 be bad-tempered.

**마음껏** 《실컷》 to *one's* heart's content; to *one's* satisfaction; as much as *one* likes; as *one* wishes 〔pleases〕; to the full. ¶ ~ 먹다 eat *one's* fill; eat all *one* can / ~ 울다 cry *one's* heart out; weep *oneself* out / 그들은 휴일을 ~ 즐겼다 They enjoyed the holiday to their hearts' content.

**마음내키다** feel inclined 《to *do*》; be willing 《to *do*》; feel like 《*do*ing》; be in the mood 《for *do*ing, to *do*》. ¶ 마음이 내키지 않다 be reluctant 《to *do*》; be in no mood 〔humor〕 《to *do,* for *do*ing》; be shy of 《*do*ing》; have no inclination 《to *do*》 / 마음내키지 않는 대답을 하다 give a halfhearted answer / 그녀와 만나는 것이 마음내키지 않는다 I don't feel like meeting her. / 그곳에 가는 것이 그다지 마음내키지 않는다 I'm not very keen on going there.

**마음놓다** ① 《안심하다》 set *one's* heart 〔mind〕 at ease; relax; take it easy. ¶ 마음 놓고 without anxiety 〔worry〕; free from care; with mind at ease; with security; freely / 마음놓고 살다 have 〔lead〕 a carefree life; live with security / 잘 있으니 마음놓으십시오 Please set your heart at ease because I am getting along well. / 대단한 일이 아니니 마음놓으십시오 Relax—it isn't anything serious. / 그 점에 대해서는 마음놓으십시오 Set your mind at ease about that. / 그 사람이면 마음놓고 일을 맡길 수 있다 You may trust him to do the work for you.
② 《방심하다》 relax *one's* attention; slacken 〔let up in〕 *one's* effort; be off *one's* guard; be inattentive; be negligent. ¶ 마음놓지 않다 be on (*one's*) guard; have (all) *one's* wits about *one;* be on the lookout; keep a sharp watch; be wide awake.

**마음대로** as *one* wishes 〔pleases, likes〕; of *one's* own accord (독단으로); freely (자유로이); at *one's* own discretion (재량껏). ~하다 have *one's* (own) way 《in everything》; *do* what *one* pleases; *do* as *one* pleases. ¶ ~이다 be at *one's* option; be within *one's* discretion / …의 ~ 되다 be at the mercy of *one;* be at *one's* beck and call; be in *one's* power / ~ 되지 않다 be beyond *one's* control; be unable to have *one's* own way 《in》 / ~ 쓰다 make free use of 《*a person's* pen》 / 아무를 ~ 조종하다 lead *a person* by the nose / ~ 드세요 Please help yourself. / 그건 자네 ~일세 You can suit yourself. *or* It's up to you. / 그렇다면 ~ 해라 Then do as you please! *or* Consult your own convenience. / 그것은 내 ~ 결정할 수 없습니다 I can't settle it on my own authority. / 나는 그들이 제 ~ 하게 내버려 둔다 I let them have their way. / 그렇게 네 ~는 안 될걸 You are counting without your host. / 너는 ~ 이 방을 써도 좋다 You are at liberty to use this room. / 구워먹든 쪄먹든 네 ~ 해라 You may do what you like with your own. / 나는 그를 ~ 할 수 있다 I can twist 〔turn〕 him round my little finger.

**마음든든하다** be secure; feel secure 〔safe, reassured〕; [사물이 주어] be reassuring 〔encouraging〕. ¶ …을 들으니 ~ it is heartening 〔encouraging〕 to hear that… / 자네가 곁에 있으면 ~ Your presence is reassuring to me. *or* I feel encouraged by your presence. / 그런 말씀을 들으니 마음 든든합니다 Your words give me great relief 〔are very encouraging to me〕. *or* That is a very reassuring remark. / 네가 함께 가 준다면 훨씬 ~ If you come along with me, I'll feel much more secure.

**마음먹다** ① 《의도하다》 intend to; have a mind to; plan to; want to; be going to. ¶ 아들을 대학에 보내려고 마음먹고 있다 I am going to send my son to college. / 만사가 마음 먹은 대로 되었다 Everything turned out as I wished 〔wanted, planned〕. / 그 글을 쓰려고 마음 먹기는 했으나 아직 못하고 있다 I have been intending to write the article, but I just haven't gotten around to it yet.
② 《결심하다》 make up *one's* mind; be determined 〔resolved〕 《to *do*》; make a resolution. ¶ 굳게 ~ be firmly determined / 마음 먹은 대로 실행하다 act up to *one's* resolution / 큰 마음 먹고 …하다 treat *oneself* to … / 큰 마음 먹고 백만 원을 기부하다 generously donate a million won / 한 번 마음먹었으면 그대로 하는 것이 좋다 If you have once made up your mind, you had better follow it. / 그는 위대한 학자가 되려고 단단히 마음 먹고 있다 He is firmly determined to become a great scholar. / 하려고 마음 먹으면 못 할 일이 없다 Where there is a will, there is a way.

**마음보** will; intention; motive; nature; temper; 《흔히 나쁜 뜻》 disposition. ¶ ~ 사나운 사람 a crab; a bear; a dog in the manger / ~ 사나운 여자 a cat; a shrew; a witch; a she-devil / ~가 고약한 mean; ill-natured; bad / ~가 사납다 be evil-minded; be ill-willed; be ill-disposed / ~ 사납게 굴다 behave with evil intention; behave maliciously 〔crossly, ill-naturedly〕.

**마음속** (deep within) *one's* heart; the bottom of *one's* heart; *one's* innermost thoughts; *one's* bosom. ¶ ~에서 우러나오는 말 words flowing out of *one's* heart / ~으로는 in *one's* heart; inwardly / ~ 깊이 deep down in the heart of; in the secret corner of *one's* heart; in *one's* heart of hearts / ~ 깊이 사무치다 sink deep into *one's* heart / ~에 품다 cherish; harbor / ~에 묻어두다 keep 《the story》 to *oneself* / ~을 꿰뚫어보다 read 《*a person's*》 inmost thoughts; see through 《*a person's*》 intention 〔heart〕; see 《*a person*》 inside and out / ~을 들여다보다 read 《*a person's*》 mind / ~을 떠보다 sound (out) 《*a person* on a subject》 / ~을 털어 놓다 speak 〔tell〕 *one's* (inmost) mind; unbosom *oneself* 《to》.

**마음쓰다** ① 《생각·연구하다》 use *one's* mind 〔head〕; work *one's* brain. ② 《배려해주다》 be thoughtful of 〔for〕; think of. ③ 《유의·걱정하다》 pay attention 《to》; give heed 《to》; mind; care 〔worry〕 《about》. ¶ 환자로 하여금 …에 마음(을) 쓰지 않게 하다 turn the patient's thought away from….

**마음씨** (a) nature; (a) temper; (a) disposition. ¶ ~가 좋다 be a nice sort of person; be good-natured; have a good disposition; be good at heart / ~가 나쁘다 be ill-natured 〔cross, malicious, crabbed〕; be ill=〔bad-〕tempered; be an unpleasant sort of person / ~가 더럽다 be mean; be dirty / ~를 곱게 쓰다 act with good intentions; behave good-naturedly / 그녀는 ~가 곱다 She has a sweet 〔good〕 disposition. / 그녀는 ~는 고우나 센스가 부족하다 She has a good heart, but not much sense. *or* She is naturally sweet-tempered, but hasn't much sense.

**마음졸이다** trouble *oneself*; worry (*oneself*) 《about》; feel uneasy 《about》; be nervous 《about》; be worried 〔anxious〕 《about, for》. ¶ 마음 졸이게 하다 worry; fidget; fret 《*a person's*》 heart; keep 〔hold〕 《*a person*》 into a flutter / 실패할까봐 ~ be nervous at the possibility that *one* might fail / 그 아이 때문에 늘 마음졸이고 있다 I'm always worrying about that child. / 네가 늦어서 매우 마음졸였다 I was irritated at your delay.

**마음죄이다** be worried; be anxious 〔concerned, nervous〕《about》; fret; stew; be upset; fear. ¶ 마음죄이는 판국 a tense 〔jittery〕 situation / 그가 무사히 돌아올지 마음죄인다 I am worried whether he will get back safely. / 결과가 어떻게 될지 몹시 마음죄인다 I am nervous about the results.

**마이너스** 〖수학〗 minus; 《음극》 the negative pole; the cathode; 《결손》 a deficit; a deficiency; 《결점》 a defect; 《불리한 점》 a disadvantage; a drawback 《to the project》; a handicap (★ 영어에서는 「결점」, 「불리」의 뜻으로 minus를 쓰는 경우는 거의 없음). ¶ ～가 되다 《결손》 suffer a loss; 《불리》 be disadvantageous 〔prove a disadvantage〕 《to》; handicap 《*a person*》 / 10 ～ 3은 7, Ten minus three leaves 〔is, equals〕 seven. / 그것은 그에겐 ～가 될 것이다 That will work against him. / ～곱하기 ～는 플러스가 된다 Minus times minus is plus. / 오늘 아침은 기온이 ～ 8도까지 내려갔다 The temperature went down to eight degrees below zero this morning. / 이 달은 가계가 ～다 We can't make both ends meet this month. / 지난 해의 우리 영업은 ～였다 Our business was in red last year. ◉ ～부호 a minus (sign). ～성장 negative (economic) growth: ～성장률 a negative growth rate. ～이온 minus ion.

**마이동풍**(馬耳東風) being like preaching to the wind; turning a deaf ear to what *one* says. ¶ ～이다 turn a deaf ear to...; pay no attention to 《*a person's* advice》 / 아무리 그에게 충고했으나 ～이었다 He turned a deaf ear to my repeated advice. *or* Everything I said was lost on him.

**마이신** 《약》 streptomycin.

**마이애미** 《미국의 도시》 Miami.

**마이카** *one's* own car; a private car.

**마이크로미터** a micrometer; micrometer callipers.

**마이크로버스** a microbus; a minibus.

**마이크로웨이브** ＝마이크로파.

**마이크로일렉트로닉스** microelectronics.

**마이크로자료실**(一資料室) the micro-material room.

**마이크로칩** a microchip.

**마이크로카메라** a microcamera.

**마이크로컴퓨터** a microcomputer.

**마이크로톰** 《현미경 관찰용 박편 절단기》 a microtome.

**마이크로파**(一波) 〖물리〗 a microwave. ◉ ～분광학 microwave spectroscopy.

**마이크(로폰)** a microphone; a mike. ¶ ～ 앞에 서다 speak at the microphone / ～를 통해 인사하다 speak over the microphone / ～ 앞에서 얼다 suffer mike fright / ～ 시험 중 입니다 Testing. One, two, three, four. ◉ ～공포증 mike fright. ～이동 장치 〖영화〗 a sound boom (촬영중 음향 조절용). 무선～ a wireless microphone.

**마이크로프로그램** 〖컴퓨터〗 a microprogram.

**마이크로프로세서** a microprocessor.

**마이크로필름** a microfilm. ◉ ～리더 a microfilm reader. ～ 영사기〔현상기〕 a microfilm projector 〔processor〕. ～카메라 a microfilm camera.

**마일** a mile (＝1.6 km). ¶ 한 시간에 4 ～을 가다 cover 〔do, make〕 four miles in an hour / 시속 60～로 달리다 run at (the rate 〔speed〕 of ) sixty miles per hour; run 60mph 〔m.p.h.〕 / 이 차는 최고 시속 100～ 까지 낼 수 있다 This car can make a hundred miles an hour at maximum speed. ◉ ～수 mileage.

**마작**(麻雀), **마장** ma(h)-jong(g). ～하다 play mah-jongg. ¶ ～의 패 a mah=jongg tile. ◉ ～꾼 a mah-jongg player. ～놀이방 a mah-jongg parlor.

**마저** ① 《남김없이 모두》 without leaving any; with all the rest; all; with everything else. ¶ 일을 ～ 해치우다 finish all the rest of work / 재고품을 ～ 팔아 치우다 sell off all the stock left over / ～ 듣다 hear the last of it / 이것까지 ～ 드십시오 Please eat this last one up too. ② 《…까지도》 even; to; as 〔so〕 far as; up to; to the limit; to the extent of. ¶ 제 이름 ～ 못 쓰다 cannot so much as sign *one's* own name / 그는 집～ 팔았다 He went so far as to sell his house. / 이제 늙어 걸음～ 제대로 걸을 수 없다 I'm now too old even to walk properly. / 하인들～ 그를 업신여긴다 Even his servants despise him.

**마적**(馬賊) mounted thieves 〔bandits〕.

**마전**[1] 《표백》 bleaching. ～하다 bleach. ◉ ～장이 a bleacher; a laundryman. ～터 a bleaching establishment; a laundry.

**마전**[2] 《곡식을 되는》 a grain-measuring place.

**마조**(一調) 〖음악〗 the tone E. ◉ 마장〔단〕조 E major 〔minor〕.

**마조히즘** 〖의학〗 masochism.
**마주** (right, directly) opposite; face to face; facing each other; just across (from each other). ¶ ~ 바라보다 look each other in the face; confront each other / ~ 놓다 set 《*things*》 opposite (to) each other.
**마주르카** 《폴란드의 춤》 mazurka.
**마주보다** be opposite 《to》; face each other; confront. ¶ 은행과 우체국은 서로 마주보고 있다 The bank and the post office stand opposite to each other.
**마주서다** stand face to face; stand right opposite; stand facing right ahead; confront. ⇨ 맞서다.
**마주앉다** sit face to face 〔tête-à-tête〕 《with *a person*》; sit across the table from 《*a person*》; sit opposite to 《*a person*》. ¶ 마주앉아(서) 식사를 하다 have a tête-à-tête dinner; dine tête-à-tête / 마주앉아 이야기하다 talk face to face 《with *a person*》 / 우리는 서로 마주 앉았다 We sat facing each other. *or* We sat face to face (with each other).
**마주잡다** ⇨ 맞잡다.
**마주치다** ① 《충돌하다》 collide 《with》; crash together 〔against, into〕; run against 〔into〕; knock 〔bump, dash〕 against. ⇨ 부딪치다. ② 《조우하다》 come on 〔across〕; hit 〔chance〕 upon; run 〔bump〕 into; meet with; face; confront. ¶ 딱 ~ come plump; come face to face / 노상에서 친구와 ~ meet (up with) a friend on *one's* way / 막다른 골목에서 원수와 ~ confront an enemy in a blind alley / 우리의 눈길이 마주쳤다 Our eyes met.
**마주하다** be opposite 《to》. ¶ 책상을 마주하고 앉다 sit opposite the table.
**마중** going 〔coming〕 out to meet 《*a person*》. ¶ ~나가다 go out to meet 〔greet〕 《*a person*》 / ~을 받다 be met 〔greeted〕 《at the airport》 / 많은 친구들이 정거장에 ~나왔다 Many friends came down to see me at the station. / 공항에 ~나가겠습니다 I'll come to meet you at the airport. / 주인이 몸소 현관까지 ~나왔다 The master of the house came out in person to greet me at the door. / 사람을 역에 ~ 보내겠다 I will send someone to meet you at the station.
**마중물** priming water. ¶ 펌프에 ~을 붓다 fetch 〔prime〕 the pump.
**마지기** a patch of field requiring one *mal* of seed; a *majigi.* ¶ 논 한 ~ a patch of rice paddy.
**마지막** 《최후》 the last; the end; the conclusion. ¶ ~의 last; final; concluding / ~날 the last 〔final〕 day; the closing 〔concluding〕 day / ~말 *one's* dying words / ~ 사람 the last man / ~ 수단 the last resort / ~ 싸움 the final struggle; the last battle / ~에 lastly; finally; at last; in the end / ~으로 lastly; (for) the last time / ~을 고하다 end; come to an end 〔a close〕; mark 《its》 end 〔conclusion〕; wind up / 맨 ~에〔으로〕 오다 come last 〔at the end〕; bring up the rear 〔the tail end〕 / ~까지 to the end; to the last / 영화를 ~까지 보다 sit out 〔through〕 a movie / ~까지 저항하다 resist to the end / ~까지 싸우다 fight it out / ~으로 이것만은 말해두고 싶다 In conclusion, I'd like to say this. / 무슨 일이 있어도 ~까지 버틸 작정이다 Whatever happens, I will hold out to the end. / 자, 이것이 ~이다〔남아 있는 전부다〕 Well, this is all I have 〔this is all that is left〕.
**마지못하다** be forced 〔obliged, compelled〕 to *do;* be under the necessity 〔compulsion〕 of; be driven by dire 〔sheer〕 necessity to. ¶ 마지못할 사정 compelling 〔unavoidable〕 circumstances; dire 〔sheer〕 necessity / 마지못하여 unavoidably; inevitably; out of 〔from〕 necessity; under compulsion (강제되어); against *one's* will; reluctantly / 마지못해 …하다 be compelled 〔forced, obliged〕 to 《*do*》; be hard put to it to 《*do*》 / 마지못해 승낙하다 give an unwilling consent / 마지못해 최후의 수단을 취하다 be driven 〔impelled〕 to extreme measures / 마지못해서 그에게 돈을 꾸어 주었다 I couldn't help lending him the money.
**마지않다** can never 《thank》 enough. ¶ 기다려 마지 않던 the long-waited for / 감사해 ~ can never thank 《*a person*》 enough; offer *one's* heartfelt thanks / 축하해 ~ offer *one's* sincerest congratulation / 행운을 빌어 마지 않습니다 I really 〔sincerely〕 wish you 「good luck 〔every happiness〕.
**마진**(痲疹) 〖한의〗 《홍역》 measles.
**마진** a margin 《of profit》. ¶ 큰폭의 ~ 《with》 a large 〔wide〕 margin / 약간의 ~ a slim 〔narrow, small, thin〕 margin / ~폭이 크다〔작다〕 leave a large 〔slim〕 margin of profit / 그 값으로는 ~이 박하다 The price leaves no mar-

gin of profit. / 약 장사는 ~이 크다 The profit margin is wide in the drug business. ◉ ~제(制) the margin system.

**마차**(馬車) a carriage; a coach; 《짐마차》 a cart (2륜의); a wagon (4륜의); 《역마차》 a stagecoach; 《포장마차》 a covered wagon; 《경주용 마차》 a chariot. ¶ 쌍두〔4두〕~ a carriage and pair 〔four〕/ ~를 타다 ride in 〔on〕 a carriage / ~로 가다 go by carriage / 말 한 필이 끄는 ~ a one-horse carriage. ◉ ~길 a carriage-way. ~말 a carriage horse; 《짐마차의》 a cart horse. ~삯 carriage fare; cartage.

**마찬가지** 《동일》 the (very) same; selfsame; one and the same. ¶ ~의 the same; like; identical; similar; equal; equivalent / ~로 in the same manner 〔way〕; alike; likewise; equally; similarly; as well / ~ 조건으로 on equal terms / ~다 be the same; be identical; be equal; be equivalent; be uniform; be similar 〔like, alike〕/ 거의 ~다 be much 〔almost〕 the same 《as》; there is not much to choose between 《them》/ 죽은거나 ~다 be as good as dead / 도둑이나 ~다 be no better than a thief / 그녀가 무엇을 하든 내게는 ~다 It's all the same to me what she does. / 그녀가 오건 안 오건 ~다 It makes no difference whether she comes or not. / 당신들 남자들이란 모두 ~야 You men are all alike. / 그것은 새 것이나 ~다 That is as good as new. / 이 증서는 휴지 조각이나 ~다 This bond is little 〔no〕 better than waste paper. / 어느 쪽을 택하든 ~다 There is no difference between the two (ways). / 내 삶은 항상 ~다 My life is always the same. / B씨의 경우도 ~다 The same may be said of Mr. B. / 일은 끝난 것이나 ~ The work is as good as finished. / 거부하지 않는 것은 용인하는 것이나 ~ Giving no refusal is equivalent to acceptance.

**마찰**(摩擦) friction; rubbing; 《알력》 friction; trouble; discord; feud. ~하다 rub 《against, with》; chafe 《the skin》. ¶ ~을 막다 prevent friction / ~을 피하다〔없애다〕 avoid 〔remove〕 friction / 건포〔냉수〕 ~을 하다 have a rubdown with a dry 〔cold wet〕 towel / ~이 생기다 cause friction 《between》/ ~을 줄이다 diminish 〔reduce〕 friction / 나뭇조각을 ~시켜 불을 피우다 make fire by rubbing two pieces of wood together / 복잡한 인간관계는 당연히 ~을 낳는다 Obviously, complex human relationships cause friction. / ~로 로프가 끊어졌다 Friction caused the rope to break. ◉ ~계수 the coefficient of friction. ~력 frictional force; friction. ~손실 〖물리·공학〗 friction loss. ~열 frictional heat. ~음 a frictional sound; 〖음성〗 a fricative (sound). ~저항 frictional resistance. ~적 실업 frictional unemployment. ~전기 frictional electricity. 무역~ trade friction 〔dispute〕.

**마천루**(摩天樓) a skyscraper.

**마초**(馬草) fodder; forage. ¶ ~를 주다 feed a horse; give a horse fodder.

**마취**(痲醉) anesthesia; narcotism. ~하다 put 《*a person*》 under anesthesia; anesthetize 《*a person*》; give (an) anesthetic 《to》; put 《*a person*》 to sleep (with an anesthetic). ¶ 전신〔국부〕~ general 〔local〕 anesthesia / ~된 상태에서 while anesthetized; in the anesthetized condition / ~에서 깨어나다 come out 〔wake up〕 from the anesthetic / ~가 듣지 않았다 The anesthetic did not work. / 한 시간 후면 ~가 풀립니다 The effect of the anesthetic will wear off in an hour. ◉ ~과(科) the anesthesia department. ~법 a method of anesthesia. ~상태 narcosis: 반~ 상태 twilight sleep. ~약〔제〕 an anesthetic; a narcotic. ~요법 narcotherapy. ~작용 narcotism; narcotic influence. ~전문의 an anesthetist; an anesthesiologist. ~총 a tranquilizing gun. ~학 anesthesiology.

**마치**[1] 《장도리》 a small 〔claw〕 hammer; 《망치》 a hammer. ⇨망치.

**마치**[2] a march. ¶ 웨딩~ a wedding march / 더블~ a double march (구보).

**마치**[3] 《처럼》 as; just like; as if. ¶ ~여우같이 간교하다 be crafty as a fox / ~미치광이 같다 《사람이》 look as if *one* were mad / ~ 죽은 것 같다 look as if dead; be more dead than alive / ~한 대 얻어맞은 것처럼 머리가 띵하다 I feel as if I had been hit on the head. / 그는 ~ 경찰관처럼 보였다 He looked just like a police officer. / 그는 ~ 술취한 사람처럼 걷고 있었다 He was walking as if he were drunk.

**마치다**[1] ① 《닿다》 be struck; hit; be obstructed; be stuck. ¶ 말뚝이 바위에 마치어 들어가지 않는다 The stake has hit a rock and won't drive in any deeper. ② 《걸리다》 pinch; feel an acute pain. ¶ 구두가 ~ *one's* shoes pinch / 구두에 발이 ~ *one's* feet are pinched by *one's* shoes / 마룻바닥이 등에 ~ 《lying on》 the floor hurts *one's* back.

**마치다**[2] 《끝내다》 end; finish; complete; bring to a close 〔an end〕; make an end of; get 〔be〕 through 《with》; get 《it》 over with; 《수행하다》 accomplish; 《졸업하다》 graduate 《from》. ¶ 일을 ~ finish 〔be through with〕 *one's* work / 볼일을 ~ make an end of *one's* business / 연설을 ~ conclude 〔end off〕 a speech / 대학 과정을 ~ complete 〔finish, pass through〕 a 〔*one's*〕 university course; complete college / 양로원에서 생애를 ~ end *one's* days in an old people's home / 식사를 마치면 나갑시다 Let's leave when we finish eating. / 회의를 마친 것은 밤 12시가 지나서였다 It was after midnight by the time the meeting 「ended 〔was over〕.

**마침** just in time; at the right moment; in the nick of time; opportunely; fortunately; luckily; as good luck would have it; just. ¶ ~ 그때에 just at the time; just then / ~ 갖고 있다 happen to have on hand; have on hand / ~ 잘 왔다 You have come at just the right moment. / ~ 가진 돈이 없다 Unfortunately I have no money with me. / ~ 그때에 그가 거기 있었다 He happened to be there then. / 가물었던 차에 ~ 비가 왔다 We had a timely 〔needed〕 rain after a long dry spell. / ~ 사람이 지나다가 나를 물에서 건져 주었다 As good luck would have it, a man came along and helped me out of the water. / ~ 자네를 만나러 가던 길이었다 I was just coming to see you.

**마침가락** the very thing 〔person〕 wanted; the right thing 〔person〕; just the thing 〔person〕. ¶ 그에게 ~인 일 the work he is best fitted to undertake / 그는 이 일에 ~인 사람이다 He is just the person for this job. / 그녀는 네 아내로 아주 ~이다 She is the right girl for you to marry. / 그 상자는 쌀궤로 ~이다 The box will make a nice rice chest.

**마침내** at last; at length; at long last; finally; in the end; ultimately; eventually; after all. ¶ 나의 꿈은 ~ 실현되었다 My dream has finally 〔at last〕 come true. / 그는 ~ 이해하게 되었다 At length he came to understand. / ~ 일이 끝났다 The work has come to an end at last. / ~ 전쟁이 터지고 말았다 A war broke out at last.

**마침표**(一標) a period; a full stop. ¶ ~를 찍다 put a period 《to》.

**마카로니** macaroni. ◉ ~ 웨스턴 an Italian 〔a spaghetti〕 western.

**마케팅** 〖경제〗 marketing. ◉ ~리서치 marketing research. ~채널 a marketing channel. ~코스트 《유통비》 marketing cost.

**마켓** a market. ¶ ~을 개척하다 develop 〔create〕 a market. ◉ ~셰어 《시장점유율》 market share. ~텀스 《시장조건》 market terms. 슈퍼~ a super market; a superette (작은).

**마크** ① a mark; 《상표》 a trademark; 《레테르》 a label; 《표지》 a badge. ¶ ~를 달다 mark; put a mark 《on》. ② 《감시》 ~하다 watch; keep *one's* eye 《on *a thing*》. ¶ 그녀는 교사로부터 문제 학생으로 ~당하고 있었다 She was marked down by the teacher as a problem student. ③ 《구기에서》 ~하다 mark 〔guard, check 《미》〕 《a certain player》. ¶ 4번 선수를 ~해라 Guard the No. 4 player. ④ 《기록하다》 ¶ 세계 신기록을 ~하다 set a new world record.

**마키아벨리즘** 《정치 목적을 위한 권모술수 「주의》 Machiavellism.

**마태복음**(一福音) 〖성서〗 (the Gospel of) Matthew (생략 Matt.).

**마티네** 《연극·영화의 낮 흥행》 a matinee; a matinée. ◉ ~흥행 a matinee performance.

**마티니** 《칵테일의 일종》 martini.

**마파람** the south 〔southerly〕 wind. ¶ ~에 게눈 감추듯 eat something up in no time at all.

**마편초**(馬鞭草) 〖식물〗 verbena.

**마포**(麻布) hemp cloth. ⇨ 삼베.

**마피아** 《범죄조직》 the Mafia. ◉ ~단원 a Mafioso (*pl.* -si, ~s).

**마필**(馬匹) horses. ¶ ~을 보충하다 supply remounts. ◉ ~개량 horse improvement.

**마하** 〖물리〗 Mach (number) (생략 M). ¶ ~ 2로 날다 travel at Mach 2.

**마호가니** 〖식물〗 mahogany.

**마호메트** 《이슬람교의 개조》 Muhammad, Muhammed (570-632). ◉ ~교(敎) Islamism. = 이슬람교.

**마흔** forty. ⇨ 사십.

**막**(膜) a film; 《점막》 a membrane. ¶ 막상(膜狀)의 membranous / 기름의 엷은

막 a film of oil.

**막**(幕) ①《가건물》a booth; a shack; a temporary erection; a hut; a shed. ¶ 막을 짓다 put up a shed 〔booth〕.
②《장막·휘장》a tent; a curtain; a hanging screen; hangings. ¶ 막을 치다 set up 〔stretch〕 a tent / 막을 거두다 fold up a tent / 막을 올리다 raise 〔draw up〕 a curtain / 막을 내리다 lower 〔drop, pull down, let down〕 a curtain / 막을 옆으로 당기다 pull 〔draw〕 aside a curtain / 새로운 시대의 막이 올랐다 A new age 〔era〕 has started.
③《연극의》an act. ¶ 첫막 the first 〔opening〕 act; Act I / 끝막 the last act / 3막 6장의 극 a play in three acts and six scenes / 막이 열리다 the curtain goes up 〔is raised〕; the first act begins.
④《끝장》an end; a close; a conclusion. ¶ 전쟁은 막을 내렸다 The war has come to an end. / 이것으로 3개월간에 걸친 노동 쟁의도 막을 내렸다 This ended a labor dispute extending over three months.

**막**[1] 《방금》just; just 〔right〕 at the moment. ¶ 막 …하려던 참이다 be about to 《*do*》; be on the point of 《*do*ing》/ 영화는 지금 막 시작했다 The movie has just started 〔started just now〕. (★ just는 과거형·현재완료형 어느 쪽도 다 수식하지만, just now는 과거에만 씀) / 막 손님이 왔다 A guest has just come. / 막 나가려는 참에 비가 쏟아졌다 I was just going out when it started pouring down. / 지금 막 도착했다 I have just arrived. / 그는 막 외출하려던 참이었다 He was just going out.

**막**[2] ⇨ 마구. ¶ 막 살다 lead a rough 〔wild〕 sort of life / 막 때리다 strike 《*a person*》 blindly / (총을) 막 쏘아대다 fire 〔shoot〕 at random.

**막가다** 《행동이》 behave rambunctiously 〔recklessly〕. ¶ 막가는 놈 an outlaw; a desperado.

**막간**(幕間) an interval (between acts or scenes); an intermission 《미》. ¶ 연극의 ~에 during the intermission between the acts of a play. ◉ ~극 an interlude; a skit between acts.

**막강하다**(莫强—) (be) mighty; enormously powerful. ¶ 막강한 군사력 great military strength / 막강한 전함 a mighty battleship / 막강한 나라 the most powerful nation / 적의 병력은 막강했다 The enemy were in great strength.

**막걸리** unstrained 〔raw, crude〕 rice wine; *makkŏlli.*

**막과자**(—菓子) coarse confectionery; cheap candy 〔sweets 《영》〕.

**막깎다** cut 《*one's* hair》 short; give a crew cut. ¶ 머리를 ~ have *one's* hair cut short; get a crew cut.

**막나이** 《막치무명》 rough muslin.

**막내** the lastborn; the youngest child. ◉ ~둥이 *one's* darling baby child: ~둥이 응석받듯 humor 《*a person*》 indulgently. ~딸 the last 〔youngest〕 daughter. ~며느리 the wife of *one's* last 〔youngest〕 son. ~아들 the last 〔youngest〕 son. ~아우〔동생〕 the last 〔youngest〕 brother 〔sister〕. 막냇누이 the last 〔youngest〕 sister. 막냇사위 the youngest son-in-law. 막냇자식 the youngest child.

**막노동**(—勞動) rough work; physical labor. = 막일.

**막다** ①《틀어막다》stop up (구멍 등을); fill (up) (틈을); close up 《an opening》. ¶ 구멍을 ~ stop 〔fill〕 up a hole; stop a gap / 귀를 ~ cover 〔fill, stop〕 *one's* ears / 병마개를 ~ cork 〔put the stopper on; cap〕 a bottle / 틈을 종이로 ~ close up an opening with paper / 솜으로 귀를 ~ fill 〔stop, wad〕 *one's* ears with cotton / 담벽의 갈라진 틈을 시멘트로 막았다 I filled (up) the crack in the wall with cement.
② 《…못하게》 (***a***) 《방지하다》 keep away 〔off, out, back〕; prevent; 《금지하다》forbid 《*a person* to *do*》; prohibit 《*a person* from *do*ing》; 《비밀이 안 새게》 silence 《*a person*》; buy 《*a person's*》 silence. ¶ 도난을 ~ prevent theft / 발언을 ~ prohibit 《*a person*》 from speaking / 입을 ~ forbid 《*a person*》 to mention 《it》; stop 《*a person's*》 mouth; muzzle 〔gag〕 《*a person*》/ 전염을 ~ prevent infection / 강물의 범람을 ~ keep the river from overflowing / 추위를 ~ keep out 〔off〕 the cold / 어린애가 난로불에 가까이 못 가게 ~ keep a child away from the fire. (***b***) 《방어·저지하다》 hold 〔keep〕 《the enemy》 in check 〔at bay〕; hold back 〔off〕; ward off; defend; check; arrest; curb. ¶ 위험을 ~ stave off a danger / 적의 퇴로를 ~ cut 〔hold〕 off the enemy's retreat / 그의 신속한 행동은 큰 사고를 막았다 His prompt action prevented a serious accident. (***c***) 《차단하다》 block 〔obstruct〕 《the entrance》; intercept 〔screen〕 《light》;

dam up (흐름을). ¶ 강물을 ~ dam up a river / 길을 ~ block 〔bar〕 the way; bar the passage; obstruct 〔stand in〕 《*a person's*》 way / 바람을 ~ shut out the wind; screen 《a house》 from the wind / 남의 말을 (가로) ~ cut 《*a person*》 short; intercept 《*a person*》 / 앞길을 ~ cross 《*a person's*》 path; head 《*a person*》 off / 통행을 ~ close (up) a road; block a street.
③ 《칸을》 screen off; partition; compart. ¶ 칸을 ~ partition a room / 휘장으로 칸을 ~ screen off part of a room.
④ 《둘러막다》 enclose; fence (round); rail off (가로대로); rope off (줄로). ¶ 뜰을 울타리로 ~ enclose a garden with a fence.

**막다르다** be closed at one end; (be) blind. ¶ 막다른 집 a house at the end of a blind alley 〔dead-end street〕/ 막다른 곳에 이르다 come to the end 《of》; reach a dead end / 곧바로 가면 길의 막다른 곳에 그것이 있다 Keep straight on, and you will find it at the end of the road.

**막다른골**(목) a blind 〔dead〕 alley; a dead-end (road). ¶ ~에 다다르다 run into a blind alley; come to a dead-end; be driven to the last extremity; come to a deadlock / ~에 다다른 국면을 타개하다 bring a deadlock to an end; break the deadlock.

**막대그래프** a bar graph.

**막대기** a piece of wood; a stick; a staff; a cane. ¶ ~로 때리다 beat 〔strike〕 《*a person*》 with a stick.

**막대패** a jack plane; a fore plane. ◉ ~질 jack-planing: ~질하다 use a fore plane 《after a saw》.

**막대하다**(莫大―) (be) huge; enormous; immense; colossal; tremendous; stupendous. ¶ 막대한 금액〔돈〕 a colossal 〔huge〕 sum; a great 〔vast〕 sum of money / 막대한 부(富) immense wealth / 막대한 비용 an enormous 〔immense〕 expense / 막대한 빚 a vast 〔mammoth〕 debt / 막대한 손실 a tremendous 〔an enormous〕 loss / 오랜 불경기로 실업계는 막대한 타격을 받고 있다 Business suffers greatly from a long-continued depression. / 그는 아버지로부터 막대한 유산을 상속받았다 He inherited a huge 〔a vast〕 fortune from his father. / 막대한 액수의 돈이 그 프로젝트에 투입되었다 A huge 〔great〕 amount of money was put into the project.

**막도장**(―圖章) an unofficial (small-sized) seal.

**막되다** (be) ill-bred; ill-mannered; boorish; lawless; wild. ¶ 막된 놈 an ill-bred 〔ill-mannered〕 fellow; a wild guy / 막된 말 rude language; a rude way of speaking / 막되게 굴다 behave badly 〔rudely, wildly〕.

**막둥이** ① 《막내》 the last 〔youngest〕 son. ② 《잔심부름꾼》 a boy servant; a page.

**막론하다**(莫論―) go without question; be a matter of course; be needless to say; there is no need to speak of. ¶ …을 막론하고 not to speak of...; to say nothing of... / 남녀 노소를 막론하고 regardless 〔irrespective〕 of sex and age / 지위의 고하를 막론하고 irrespective of rank / 결과의 여하를 막론하고 no matter what the consequences may be.

**막료**(幕僚) the staff [총칭]; a staff officer.

**막막하다**(寞寞―) 《쓸쓸하다》 (be) desolate; dreary; deserted; 《외롭다》 (be) lonely; lonesome; 《막연하다》 helpless. ¶ 살 길이 ~ do not know how to maintain life / 어찌해야 좋을 지 ~ be at a loss what to do.

**막막하다**(漠漠―) (be) vast; boundless. ¶ 막막한 사막 a vast expanse of desert.

**막말** a blunt remark 〔speech〕; rude 〔rough〕 talk; rough stuff. ~하다 speak roughly; put it bluntly. ¶ ~로 개수작이지 무어냐 To put it bluntly, that is utter nonsense, isn't it?

**막무가내**(莫無可奈) ¶ ~로 obstinately; stubbornly; resolutely; firmly / ~로 듣지 않다 refuse flatly 〔point-blank〕; will not listen 《to》; turn a deaf ear 《to》 / 그는 ~로 자기 의견을 굽히지 않았다 He stuck to his own opinion. / 아무리 사정을 하여도 ~였다 I tried very hard to persuade him, but he won't listen.

**막바지** the very end; the (dead) end; the extremity; the last moment (위기). ¶ 길의 ~ the dead end of a road / 언덕의 ~ the top of a hill / ~에 몰리다 be driven 〔brought〕 to bay; be driven to the last moment 〔extremity〕/ ~에 몰아넣다 drive 《*a person*》 to bay / 우리는 ~에서 역전승을 했다 We turned the tables and won at the last moment.

**막벌다** earn wages as a day laborer.

**막벌이** ~하다 earn wages as a day 〔physical, manual〕 laborer. ◉ ~꾼 a day laborer; an odd-jobber.

**막부득이**(莫不得已) unavoidably; inevitably; irresistibly; necessarily. ¶ ~한 경우에는 in an unavoidable case; if necessary.

**막사**(幕舍) a barracks; a camp.

**막살다** lead a rough 〔careless, haphazard, wild, reckless〕 sort of life; lead a grubby life.

**막상** 《급기야》 ultimately; in the last analysis; 《실제로》 really; in reality 〔actuality〕; when you get (right) down to it. ¶ ~ 때가 닥치면 if the time comes; at the last moment; at a push; 《절박하면》 when *one* is put to the push / ~ 팔려고 하니 값이 안 오른다 When I comes to sell them, they bring in but a little amount. / ~ 찾으려고 하니 좀처럼 눈에 안 띈다 When *one* comes to look for it, *one* finds it very hard to come at. / ~ 때가 되니 그녀는 겁이 나고 말았다 She lost her nerve at the last moment. / ~ 실행에 들어 간다면 돈이 엄청나게 들테지 When the time comes 〔When it comes time〕 to carry it out, it will require a great deal of money

**막상막하**(莫上莫下) nothing better and nothing worse. ~하다 (both) are the same; (be) alike. ¶ ~의 열전 a well-matched contest; a neck and neck race / 그 둘은 ~다 There is little difference 〔little to choose〕 between the two. / 두 사람의 기술은 ~이다 The two are on a par with each other in skill.

**막새** ① 《수키와》 convex tiles at the edge of eaves. ② 《암·수키와》 (both concave and convex) tiles at the edge of eaves.

**막심하다**(莫甚—) be at the furthest extreme; (be) immense; tremendous; extreme. ¶ 막심한 손해 a tremendous 〔heavy〕 loss / 곤란이 ~ have tremendous difficulties / 막심한 타격을 입다 suffer a hard blow / 후회가 ~ I regret it very much.

**막아내다** keep away 〔out, off, back〕; ward off; check; hold in check; hold 「off 〔at bay〕; forestall; prevent; defend *oneself* against; protect 《from, against》; shield 《from》. ¶ 불길을 ~ check the fire; hold the fire in check / 적을 ~ defend 《*oneself*, the country》 against an enemy; bear the brunt of the enemy / 화살을 ~ ward off an arrow.

**막역**(莫逆) intimacy; familiarity; closeness. ~하다 (be) intimate; familiar; close. ¶ ~한 친구 an intimate 〔a close〕 friend; a bosom friend / ~한 사이 close 〔intimate〕 relations / ~한 사이다 be a David and Jonathan 〔Damon and Pythias〕.

**막연하다**(漠然—) (be) vague; obscure; ambiguous; dim; hazy. ¶ 막연히 vaguely; obscurely; dimly; hazily; ambiguously / 막연한 대답을 하다 give a vague answer / 막연한 말을 하다 speak in general terms / 막연한 불안에 사로잡히다 be overcome with a nameless fear / …에 대한 막연한 동경 a vague longing for ... / 나는 막연하게 그 일을 기억하고 있을 뿐이다 I have but a faint remembrance of it. *or* It dimly lives in my memory. / 그는 취직할 수 있으려니 하는 막연한 생각으로 상경했다 He came up to Seoul in vague hopes of finding some job.

**막이** damming up; banking up; protection against. ¶ 방패~ warding off; defending / 보~ banking up a paddy / 서리~ a shelter against 〔a protection from〕 frost / 액~ preventing 〔forestalling〕 misfortune; warding off evil.

**막일** physical labor; rough work; chore; toil. ~하다 labor; toil; slave; do rough work. ◉ ~꾼 a (physical) laborer; an odd-jobber; a handyman.

**막자** a medicine pestle. ◉ ~사발 a mortar.

**막장** 《탄광의》 ① 《채벽》 a blind end 〔front〕 in a mine gallery; a coal 〔pit, working〕 face. ② 《작업》 mining; exploitation work. ~하다 engage in mine exploitation; mine. ◉ ~일 mining (work): ~일하다 mine; do mining.

**막중하다**(莫重—) (be) grave; very 〔extremely〕 important. ¶ 막중한 책임 a weighty 〔heavy〕 responsibility / 막중한 사명을 띠다 be charged with very important mission.

**막지르다** ① 《앞길을》 block; bar. ¶ 길을 ~ block 《*a person's*》 way; bar 《*a person's*》 passage / 앞길을 ~ cross 《*a person's*》 path; head 《*a person*》 off; stand in 《*a person's*》 way. ② 《냅다지르다》 thrust 〔jab, stab, push, kick〕 at random 〔with force〕; shout loudly (소리를). ¶ 소리를 ~ yell out; shout and yell.

**막질리다** ① 《길을》 be barred; be blocked. ¶ 길을 ~ have *one's* way blocked. ② 《넵다》 get thrust 〔jabbed, stabbed, pushed, kicked〕 at random 〔with force〕.

**막차**(一車) the last car 〔bus, train〕. ¶ ~를 놓치다 miss the last train 〔bus〕.

**막초**(一草) coarse 〔poor-quality, cheap〕 tobacco.

**막치** a coarse 〔crude, low-grade〕 article; poor stuff; junk 《미구어》.

**막판** ① 《마지막 판》 the last round; the final scene; 《선거전 등의》 last-ditch; last-phase; 《중대한 때》 the last 〔critical〕 moment. ¶ ~에 와서 at the last moment 〔eleventh hour〕 / ~에 접어들다 be on the last stage of 《*do*ing》 / 그는 정작 ~에 가서 주저앉아 버렸다 He lost heart at the last moment. / 마침내 그는 ~에 몰렸다 He was driven to bay at last. ② 《뒤범벅 판》 a haphazard scene; a mess.

**막후**(幕後) behind the curtain. ¶ ~의 인물 a man behind the scene / ~의 역할 a behind-the-scenes role / ~에서 협상하다 confer 〔negotiate〕 behind closed doors / ~에서 조종하다 maneuver behind the scenes; pull (the) wires 〔strings〕 (from behind).
◉ ~공작 behind-the-scene maneuvering: ~공작을 하다 maneuver behind the scene. ~교섭〔흥정〕 behind-the-scenes negotiations 〔dealings〕.

**막히다** ① 《구멍 따위가》 get stopped up; be clogged; be choked 〔filled〕 up; be 〔get〕 blocked; be closed. ¶ 굴뚝이 ~ a chimney is choked up 《with soot》 / 파이프가 ~ a pipe is clogged / 수챗구멍이 ~ a gutter is choked 《with debris》 / 숨이 ~ be choked 〔suffocated, stifled〕 / 하수도가 ~ a drain is stopped up / 코가 ~ *one's* nose is stuffy; have a stuffed-up nose / 요도(尿道)가 ~ have trouble urinating 《by urinary calculuses》.
② 《길·말·생각이》 be stopped 〔blocked, barred〕; be cut off; be interrupted; be held up; be stuck. ¶ 막힌 사람 a blockhead; a thickhead / 교통이 ~ traffic is held up 〔jammed, blocked, interrupted〕 / 길이 ~ a road is blocked; have no way / 말이 ~ be stuck for a word; be at a loss for words; get tongue-tied / 앞길이 ~ be at the end of a road; have no way out; be stalled; be deadlocked; have no opportunity / 막혔음, 통과 못함 《게시》 Dead end.
③ 《칸이》 be partitioned; be compartmented; 《가로놓임》 lie across. ¶ 벽으로 ~ be partitioned with a wall / 앞이 강으로 ~ a river lies across the path ahead; have a river ahead / 뒤가 산으로 ~ be walled in from behind by a mountain; have a mountain behind.

**만**(卍) 〖불교〗 ① 《표지》 a Buddhist emblem; the Buddhist cross. ② 《글자》 a swastika; a fylfot; a gammadion.

**만**(萬) ten thousand; a myriad; very many; all. ¶ 만에 하나 one in ten thousand; very rarely / 만에 하나라도 by any chance / 만사람 a myriad of people; all the people / 수십만 hundreds of thousands / 은혜의 만분의 일이라도 갚겠습니다 I would dearly wish to pay back even an infinitesimal part of your kindness to me.

**만**(滿) just; full; fully; to a day. ¶ 만 5년 full five years / 만 15세 fifteen years old / 만 3일간 (for) a full 〔whole〕 three days; (for) three whole 〔full〕 days / 나이를 만으로 세다 count 《*a person's*》 age in full 〔in completed years〕 / 만 20세에 2,3개월이 모자라다 want some months of twenty / 그가 한국을 떠난 지 만 3년이 된다 It is a full three years since he left Korea. / 그는 이달 15일로 만 20세가 된다 He completes his twentieth year on the 15th of this month. / 벌써 만 5년이 된다 It is now five years to a day.

**만**(灣) a bay; a gulf. ¶ 만을 이루다 form a bay. ◉ 경기만 Kyŏnggi Bay; the Bay of Kyŏnggi.

**만**[1] 《때의 경과》 after the lapse of…; interval. ¶ 3년 만에 귀향하다 come home after three year's absence / 닷새 만에 목욕하다 take a bath after five days / 반년 만에 술을 마시다 drink wine after half-a-year's abstinence / 오래간 만입니다 It is a long time since I saw you last. / 그녀를 만난 것은 5년 만이다 It's been five years since I saw her last.

**만**[2] ① 《다만·뿐》 only; just. ¶ 한국어만을 하는 사회 a society that talks only Korean / 만 원만 있으면 if only we had ten thousand won / 밥만 먹다 eat only rice / 정군만 왔다 Only Mr. Chŏng came. / 혼자만 알고 계세요 Keep it to yourself. / 하나만 주시오 Give me just one. / 나만이 잘못했습니까 Am I the only one to blame? / 그것만은 못 하

겠다 I'll do anything but that. / 그는 재간이 있을 뿐만 아니라 부지런도 하다 He is not only talented, but hard-working as well. / 나혼자만의 문제라면 간단하지 It would be simple if it concerned only me. / 그 사람만이 안다 He's the only one that knows. / 너는 공부만 하면 된다 You have only to work hard. / 보기만 해도 기분이 나빠진다 The mere sight of it makes me sick. / 그는 불평만 하고 있다 He is always complaining. *or* He does nothing but complain. / 오직 그만이 그것을 할 수 있다 He alone 〔Only he〕 can do it.

② 《만큼》 just; to the extent of; as much as. ¶ 석 자만 주시오 Just give me 3 *ja.* / 이만 하면 라디오를 살 수 있다 The amount will be enough to buy a radio. / 그만 일로 화낼 것은 없네 Don't be offended at such a trifle. / 그만 빚으로 무슨 걱정을 하나 Don't worry about that nominal debt. / 그만 돈이 없나 You mean you don't have that amount of money?

**만가**(輓歌) 《장례의》 a funeral song; 《애가》 an elegy; a dirge.

**만감**(萬感) all sorts of thoughts; a thousand emotions. ¶ ~이 교차하다 a thousand emotions 「crowd in upon 〔are crowding into〕 *one's* mind / 그는 ~이 복받쳐 말도 안 나왔다 He was speechless as a thousand emotions crowded in upon him.

**만강**(萬康) peace; tranquility; security; welfare; health. ¶ 댁내의 ~을 빕니다 I offer prayers for peace and prosperity to your family.

**만강**(滿腔) a full heart; fullheartedness; wholeheartedness. ¶ ~의 wholehearted; heartfelt / ~의 사의를 표하다 tender *one's* heartfelt thanks; express *one's* deep gratitude.

**만개**(滿開) full bloom. = 만발.

**만경**(萬頃) vast(ness); enormous (-ness); extensive(ness); boundless (-ness); immense(ness). ◉ ~창파 the boundless expanse of water.

**만고**(萬古) 《옛날》 all antiquity; 《영원》 perpetuity; eternity. ¶ ~의 영웅 a hero for all ages 〔time〕 / ~에 유례 없는 unique for all generations.

◉ ~불멸 being imperishable; lasting forever. ~불변 being unchangeable; staying the same forever. ~불역(不易) being immutable; invariable. ~불후(不朽) being immortal; remaining intact 〔undecayed〕 forever: ~ 불후의 명작 an immortal work. ~절색(絶色) a peerless beauty. ~절창(絶唱) an unparalleled 〔a peerless〕 singer. ~풍상(風霜) all kinds of hardships and privations: ~ 풍상을 다 겪다 undergo all sorts of hardships.

**만곡**(彎曲) 《곡선》 a curve; a bow; 《구부러짐》 a bend; a crook; curvature. ~하다 (be) curved; bent; bowed; crooked. ¶ 척추의 ~ the curvature of the spine / 안쪽〔바깥쪽〕으로 ~하다 in-〔out〕curved. ◉ ~부 the bend 《of an arm, of a river》. ~성 시야(視野) 〖의학〗 curvature myopia.

**만구**(灣口) the mouth of a bay; the bay entrance.

**만국**(萬國) all nations; all (the) countries on earth; the whole world. ¶ ~의 international; universal.

◉ ~기 the flags of all nations; [총칭] bunting (장식용의): ~기를 장식한 운동장 the playground decked with bunting. ~박람회 an international exposition; a world('s) fair. ~신호 the international code signals. ~우편 연합 the Universal Postal Union (생략 UPU). ~음성 기호 the international phonetic alphabet (생략 IPA).

**만금**(萬金) an immense sum of money. ¶ ~으로도 바꿀 수 없다 be invaluable; be priceless.

**만기**(萬機) ① 《정무》 all the affairs of state. ¶ ~ 총람하다 conduct all State affairs / ~ 친람하다 attend to the affairs of the State. ② 《기틀》 all the politically important key points. ③ 《기밀》 all (sorts of) secrets; all confidential matters.

**만기**(滿期) the expiration 《of term》; (the) maturity 《of a bill》. ¶ ~가 되다 《임기가》 expire; run out; 《복무가》 complete *one's* term of service; serve out *one's* time; 《어음 따위가》 mature; be 〔become, fall〕 due / 임기가〔계약이〕 ~가 되었다 My term of office 〔The contract〕 has expired. / 이 어음은 3개월이면 ~가 된다 The bill is 〔falls〕 due in three months. / 이 계약은 이달 말에 ~가 된다 The contract runs out at the end of this month.

◉ ~배당 〖생명보험〗 a maturity dividend. ~병(兵) a time-expired soldier. ~상환 redemption at 〔on〕 maturity. ~석방 release 《of a prisoner》 on the expiration of prison term. ~어음 a matured bill. ~일 the day of maturity; the due date; expiration date: 서면으로 통보하면 ~일 3개월 전까지는 계약을 해지할 수 있습니다《계약 해지 예고 조항》 With written notification, we can dissolve the contract three months prior to its expiration date. ~제대 discharge on expiration of term of service.

**만끽**(滿喫) ~하다 eat to *one's* fill; have enough《of》; enjoy《*a thing*》 fully [to the full]; do ample justice《to》. ¶ 지난 일요일에는 전원의 봄을 ~했다 Last Sunday we enjoyed spring in the countryside to the full. / 저 식당에서는 진짜 이탈리아 요리를 ~할 수 있다 We can have our fill of genuine Italian food at that restaurant.

**만나다** ①《조우하다》 meet; meet with (★ meet with는「우연히 만나다(= encounter)」의 뜻이며, meet는「우연히 만나다」「약속하고 만나다」그 어느 쪽이든 씀); encounter; come upon [across]; be faced with; be confronted by; suffer; experience. ¶ 노상에서 친구를 ~ meet a friend on *one's* way / 우연히 ~ come [run] across《*a person*》; meet《*a person*》 by chance; fall in with《*a person*》/ 적을 ~ encounter an enemy / 폭풍우를 ~ be overtaken by a storm / 귀가 도중 소나기를 만났다 I was caught in a shower on my way home. / 옛 제자들을 극장에서 우연히 만났다 I happened to meet my former students at a theater.
②《사람을 보다》 see; meet; interview; have an interview with. ¶ 만나러 가다 go「to [and] see《*a person*》; go to meet《*a person*》/ 친구를 만나러 가는 길이다 be on *one's* way to see a friend / 애인을 ~ have a rendezvous with *one's* lover [sweetheart] / 두 사람을 만나게 해주다 arrange a meeting between the two / 만나 본 일이 없는 사람이다 He is quite a stranger (to me). / 직접 만나 뵙고 의논드릴 일이 있습니다 I have something about which I want to confer personally with you. / 그 사람은 만나지 않도록 해라 Keep yourself out of his sight. / 얼마나 너를 만나고 싶었는지 모른다 I have missed you very badly. / 누구를 만나려는 겁니까 Who would you like to see? / 그녀는 지배인을 만나고 싶다고 했다 She wanted to see the manager. *or* She asked for the manager.
③《걸리다》 find《lodgings》. ¶ 호텔을 잘 ~ find a good hotel.
④《알게 되다》 become acquainted《with》; strike up an acquaintance《with》; get to know; come in contact《with》. ¶ 그들은 3년 전에 만나 결혼하였다 They got to know each other three years ago and then got married. / 그와 만나게 된 것이 내 악운의 시초였다 Getting acquainted with him was the beginning of my bad luck.
⑤《선·도로 따위가》 join; cross; intersect. ¶ 두 선이 만나는 점 the point of intersection; the junction of two lines / 두 길은 거기서 만난다 The two roads join there.

**만난**(萬難) innumerable difficulties; all obstacles; thousand and one difficulties. ¶ ~을 무릅쓰다 surmount [overcome] all difficulties / ~을 무릅쓰고 at all costs [hazards, risks]; through thick and thin; at any cost / 우리는 ~을 무릅쓰고 평화를 실현해야 한다 We have to establish peace no matter how much it may cost.

**만날** always; every day; all the time; incessantly; continuously; continually. ¶ ~ 빈둥거리고 있다 always idle *one's* time away / ~ 서로 싸우기만 하다 quarrel with each other all the time / ~ 비가 온다 It rains continuously. / 그는 ~ 부모에게 걱정만 끼친다 He is a constant source of anxiety to his parents.

**만년**(晩年) *one's* later [declining, last] years. ¶ ~에 late in life; in *one's* latter [later, closing] years / ~을 불우하게 보내다 live the rest of *one's* life in obscurity / 그녀는 ~에 행복했다 She was happy in her last years. / 이 교향곡은 그의 ~ 작품이다 He wrote this symphony in his latter years.

**만년**(萬年) ten thousand years; perpetuity; eternity. ¶ ~지계(之計) a plan for the ages / ~지택(之宅) a substantial building; a strongly-built house / ~ 평사원이다 be a permanent [eternal] clerk. ◉ ~조수 an assistant never promoted. ~후보 an ever-unsuccessful candidate.

**만년설**(萬年雪) perpetual [permanent] snow (field);《고산의》 an icecap. ¶ 극지의 ~ polar icecaps.

**만년필**(萬年筆) a fountain pen. ¶ ~에 잉크를 넣다 (re)fill a fountain pen / ~에 잉크가 떨어지다 a fountain pen「has run out of ink [is dry].

**만능**(萬能) omnipotence; being almighty; having an all-round capability. ¶ ～의 almighty; omnipotent; 《다용도의》 all-purpose; 《다방면의》 all-round / ～하신 신 Almighty God / 기계 ～의 시대 the age of machinery / 그는 ～이다 He can manage everything. / 부(富)가 ～은 아니다 Wealth is not everything. / 지금은 황금 ～의 세상이다 Money is everything nowadays. / 과학 기술은 이미 ～이 아니라고 나는 생각한다 I no longer think that technology is a panacea.

◉ ～공(工) an all-round mechanic. ～공구 an all-purpose tool. ～선수 an all-(a)round athlete 〔player〕; an all-rounder: ～보결 선수 a utility player.

**만다라**(曼陀羅) 〖불교〗 *mandala* (Sans.); Buddha's picture.

**만단**(萬端) all sorts of affairs; 《온갖 방법》 every (possible) means. ¶ ～의 준비를 갖추다 make every preparation; get everything ready.

**만담**(漫談) a comic chat 〔dialogue〕. ～하다 have a comic chat. ◉ ～가 a comic storyteller; a comedian; a gagman.

**만당**(滿堂) 《장소》 the whole house 〔hall〕; 《사람》 all the audience. ¶ ～의 갈채를 받다 carry 〔bring down〕 the house / ～의 신사 숙녀 여러분 To all of you, ladies and gentlemen! / ～은 물을 끼얹은 듯 조용해졌다 A hush fell over the crowded hall.

**만대**(萬代) all generations; all ages; eternity. ¶ ～에 for all ages; forever; everlastingly; eternally / ～에 전하다 be remembered for ages to come; live forever in the lips of people.

**만돌린** 〖악기〗 a mandolin. ¶ ～을 타다 play (on) the mandolin. ◉ ～연주자 a mandolinist.

**만두**(饅頭) a bun stuffed with seasoned meat and vegetables; dumplings. ¶ ～를 빚다 make a stuffed bun. ◉ ～국 dumpling soup. ～소 bun stuffing. 찐～ steamed meat dumplings. 팥～ a steamed bun stuffed with sweet bean paste; a bean-jam bun.

**만득하다**(晩得—) beget a child in *one's* later years.

**만들다** ① 《…을 재료로》 (***a***) 《제조·생산하다》 make; manufacture; produce. ¶ 나무로 책상을 ～ make a desk of wood / 자동차를 ～ manufacture 〔produce〕 cars 〔automobiles〕 / 철강은 철로 만들어진다 Steel is made from iron. (★ 원칙적으로 원료가 변질되는 경우는 make... from, 변질되지 않는 경우는 make (out) of처럼 사용됨) / 이 테이블은 참나무로 만들어져 있다 This table is made (out) of oak. (★ 수동일 때에는 흔히 out가 생략됨). (***b***) 《양조》 brew 《wine》; distill 《whisky》. ¶ 쌀로 술을 ～ make wine from rice. (***c***) 《음식을》 prepare; fix; cook. ¶ 음식을 ～ fix 〔prepare〕 some food; make 〔cook〕 a dish / 혼자 요리를 만들어 먹었다 I cooked and ate (the food) by myself. / 무엇 좀 맛있는 것을 만들어 줘야지 I will prepare something nice for you. (***d***) 《주조하다》 coin; cast; strike. ¶ 화폐를 ～ coin money; mint 〔strike〕 coins / 청동으로 상(像)을 ～ cast a statue in bronze.

② 《되게 하다》 make; make 《a musician》 of 《*a person*》; 《…로 몰다》 turn 《*a person*》 into; 《…로 바꾸다》 change 〔turn, convert〕 《one thing into another》. ¶ 아들을 의사로 ～ make a physician of *one's* son / 아무를 도둑으로 ～ make 《*a person*》 into a thief / 바보로 ～ 《놀리다》 make a fool of 《*a person*》 / 밥을 죽으로 ～ turn rice into gruel / 수술을 잘못해서 불구로 ～ cripple 《*a person*》 with a poorly performed operation.

③ 《작성하다》 make out; draw up; make; frame; write 〔compose〕 《a story, a poem》 (시문·가사 등을). ¶ 서류〔계약서〕를 ～ draw up a document 〔contract〕 / 초고를 ～ make 〔prepare〕 a draft / 책을 ～ make 〔write〕 a book / 이 프로는 어린이를 대상으로 만들어졌다 This program was prepared for children.

④ 《건설하다》 make; build; erect; construct. ¶ 길을 ～ build a road / 공원을 ～ make 〔lay out〕 a park / 새 고속도로가 만들어지고 있다 A new expressway is now under construction.

⑤ 《조직·창립·형성하다》 set up; organize; form; establish. ¶ 규칙을 ～ make a rule / 학교를 ～ establish 〔found〕 a school / 사업체를 ～ set up a business company / 우리 네 사람은 새 회사를 만들었다 The four of us established a new company. / 우리는 학교에 사진부를 만들었다 We organized 〔formed〕 a camera club in the school.

⑥ 《도야·육성하다》 cultivate; foster; build up; train. ¶ 사람을 ～ bring 《*a person*》 up into a fine man; make a man (of him) / 선량한 시민으로 ～ build up 〔train〕 good citizens.

⑦ 《조작하다》 make up; invent; fab-

ricate. ¶ 만든 이야기 a made-up 〔an invented〕 story / 만들어서 하는 말 a fabrication / 학교에 지각한 구실을 얼렁뚱땅 만들어 내다 hastily invent an excuse for being late for school.
⑧ 《창조하다》 make; create; invent (창제). ¶ 음악을〔노래를〕 ～ compose music 〔a song〕/ 하느님께서 이 땅 위에 만물을 만드시다 God creates all creatures here below.
⑨ 《…하게 하다》 make 〔have, let〕 《*a person do*》; get 〔induce, cause, force〕 《*a person* to *do*》. ¶ 가게 ～ make 《*a person*》 go; induce 《*a person*》 to go / 믿게 ～ make 《*a person*》 believe 《in》/ 기계가 돌아가게 ～ set a machine to work (in operation) / 자진해서 기부를 하게 ～ induce 《*a person*》 to donate of *his* own accord.

**만듦새** make; workmanship; craftsmanship. ¶ 옷 ～가 좋다 The make of the coat is fine. / 이 옷은 ～가 별로 좋지 않다 This dress is of poor workmanship.

**만료**(滿了) the expiration 〔expiry〕 《of a term》; termination 《of office》. ～하다 expire; fall 〔become〕 due; come to an end; complete. ¶ 임기 ～일 the day *one's* term of office expires 〔runs out〕/ 그는 형기 ～로 출소했다 He left prison at the expiration of his term. ◉ ～일 the expiration date.

**만루**(滿壘) 〖야구〗 a full 〔loaded〕 base. ¶ ～가 되다 the bases are full / 노아웃〔투아웃〕에 ～가 되었다 The bases are loaded 〔filled〕 with none 〔two〕 out. ◉ ～홈런 a bases-loaded homer; a home run with the bases loaded; a grand slam 《미》: 역전 ～홈런을 치다 hit a grand slam to win the losing game.

**만류**(挽留) holding back; detaining. ～하다 hold back; prevent; detain; dissuade 《*a person* from *do*ing》. ¶ 싸우지 말라고 ～하다 hold 《*a person*》 from wrangling; dissuade 《*a person*》 from fighting / 사임을 ～하다 persuade 《*a person*》 to remain in office / 소매를 잡고 ～하다 detain 《*a person*》 by the sleeve / 타일러 ～하다 dissuade 《*a person*》 from 《*do*ing》; talk 《*a person*》 out of 《*do*ing》.

**만류**(灣流) 〖지리〗 the Gulf Stream.

**만리**(萬里) a long distance. ¶ ～ 창파를 건너서 오다 come from afar over the sea. ◉ ～장성(長城) the Great Wall of China. ～장천(長天) the high heavens. 만릿길 a long way 〔journey〕.

**만만하다** ① 《무르다》 (be) soft; tender supple. ② 《다루기가》 be easy (to deal with); easy-going; be ready to yield; be not firm. ¶ 만만한 사람 a person easy to deal with; an easy-going person; an easy mark; a pushover / 만만한 일 an easy job / 만만하게 보다 hold 《*a person*》 cheap; think 《*a person*》 an easy man to deal with; make slight of 《*a person*》; take 《*things*》 easy / 만만치 않은 상대를 만나다 catch a Tartar / 그는 만만치 않다 He is a hard 〔tough〕 fellow. ③ 《대수롭지 않다》 (be) negligible; slight; insignificant; be of no account 〔importance〕. ¶ 만만찮은 적〔상대〕 a strong enemy 〔antagonist〕/ …을 만만하게 여기다 treat 《*a matter*》 as of little account.

**만만하다**(滿滿―) (be) filling; abounding; be full of; be brimful with; be filled with. ¶ 패기 ～ be full of ambition; be brimming with enterprise / 자신이 ～ be full of self-confidence.

**만만히** ① 《무르게》 softly; tenderly; (so it is) soft 〔tender〕. ② 《쉽게》 easily; readily. ¶ 그 여자는 ～ 네게서 떨어지지 않을 게다 The girl won't readily let you go. ③ 《우습게》 negligently; slightingly. ¶ ～ 보다〔여기다〕 make light of; undervalue; hold 《*a person*》 cheap; don't make very much of 《*a person*》/ 그거 ～ 여길 일이 아니다 That is not a matter to be 「slighted 〔taken lightly〕. / 상대를 ～ 보지 마라 Don't underestimate 〔underrate〕 your opponent. / 내가 그렇게 ～ 보이느냐 Do you see any green in my eye?

**만면**(滿面) the whole face. ¶ ～에 미소를 띄우고 smiling all over *one's* face; with *one's* face beaming with a smile / 희색이 ～하다 *one's* face beams with joy; glee is written all over *one's* face. ◉ ～수색(愁色) a face full of anxiety: ～ 수색을 띄다 be full of anxiety 〔worry〕. ～수참(羞慚) a face filled with shame: ～ 수참하다 be filled with shame. ～희색(喜色) a face beaming with joy.

**만무하다**(萬無―) cannot be; be not likely at all that...; be out of the question; there is no reason why. ¶ 네가 그것을 모를 리 ～ I cannot believe that you know nothing about it. / 그럴 리가 ～ That is impossible. *or* That cannot be so. / 사실일 리가 ～

It cannot be true.

**만물** the final weeding of a rice paddy.

**만물**(萬物) all things; all creation. ¶ ~의 영장 the lord of all creation.
◉ ~ 박사 a well-informed person; a walking dictionary; a Jack-of-all=trades. ~상(商) a general store. 우주 ~ all things in the universe; the whole of creation.

**만민**(萬民) all the people; the whole nation. ◉ ~법 *jus gentium* (L.).

**만반**(萬般) all kinds; every sort. ¶ ~의 준비〔태세〕를 갖추다 make every 〔full, thorough〕 preparation 《for》.

**만발**(滿發) full bloom. ~하다 come into full bloom; be in full bloom 〔blossom〕; be at 《their》 best. ¶ 꽃이 ~해 있다 The flowers are 「in full bloom 〔at their best〕.

**만방**(萬方) all directions; every way; all possible means. ¶ ~으로 손을 쓰다 try all 〔every〕 means available; exhaust all possible means; leave no stone unturned.

**만방**(萬邦) all nations of the world.

**만병**(萬病) all kinds of diseases. ¶ 감기는 ~의 근원이다 A cold may lead to all kinds of illness. ◉ ~통치(약) a remedy for every ill; a panacea; a cure-all: 이 세상에는 ~통치약이란 없다 There is no cure-all in the world.

**만병초**(萬病草) 〖식물〗 a rhododendron.

**만복**(滿腹) a full stomach; satiety. ¶ ~이 되도록 먹다 eat 「*one's* full 〔to *one's* heart's content〕. ◉ ~감 a feeling of fullness 〔plenitude〕 《after a meal》: ~감을 주는 식사 a filling meal.

**만복**(萬福) great fortune; supreme happiness; all kinds of good luck. ¶ 소문(笑門) ~래 Fortune comes to a merry home. *or* Laugh and grow fat. / 댁내의 ~을 빕니다 I pray for all blessings on your family.

**만부당**(萬不當) = 천만부당.

**만부득이**(萬不得已) ⇨ 부득이(不得已).

**만분지일**(萬分之一) one in ten thousand; a ten-thousandth. ¶ 은혜의 ~이라도 보답할까 합니다 I will do my bit, however little, to repay your kindness.

**만사**(萬事) everything; all things; all affairs; all. ¶ ~에 in all things / ~를 좌지우지하다 manage 〔take control of〕 everything / ~ 오케이 Everything's O.K. 《미》 *or* All's well. 《영》 / ~가 돈이면 다다 Money is all in all 〔everything〕. *or* Money makes the mare (to) go. / ~가 끝장 났다 It's all finished for me. / 인간 ~ 새옹지마 Inscrutable are the ways of Heaven. / ~가 잘 되어간다 All goes well. / ~에 주의해라 You must be careful in every respect. / ~ 제쳐놓고 동창회에 참석해 주시기 바랍니다 Please do everything you can to 「come to 〔attend〕 the alumni meeting.

**만사여의**(萬事如意) ~하다 everything turns out as *one* wishes; all goes well.

**만사태평**(萬事太平) 《잘 됨》 all going well; 《걱정 없음》 nonchalance; indifference; being carefree. ~하다 all goes well; be nonchalant.

**만사형통**(萬事亨通) being prosperous in everything; all going well. ~하다 all goes well; be prosperous in everything.

**만삭**(滿朔) completion of time for childbirth; (the month of) parturiency. ~하다 《*one's* delivery time》 come due; come to *one's* time of parturition. ¶ ~이 되다 come to her time (of parturition) / 그녀는 지금 ~이다 Her time is near now. *or* She is near her time.

**만산**(滿山) the whole mountain. ~하다 cover the whole mountain.

**만상**(萬象) all kinds of phenomena; all things in the universe.

**만석꾼**(萬石—) a person who has a 10,000-bushel crop; a millionaire.

**만성**(晩成) maturing late; being slow in maturing. ~하다 mature late; be slow in maturing. ¶ 대기 ~형의 사람 a late developer 〔bloomer〕.

**만성**(慢性) 〖의학〗 chronicity; (being) chronic. ¶ ~의, ~적 chronic; deep=seated / ~적 실업 chronic unemployment / ~적 인플레이션〔불황〕 chronic inflation 〔depression〕 / ~이 되다 become chronic 《with *a person*》; pass into a chronic state / 나의 천식은 ~입니다 Asthma is chronic with me. / 그녀는 ~ 위궤양이다 She has a chronic stomach ulcer.
◉ ~병 《suffer from》 a chronic disease. ~신부전 chronic renal failure. ~위장병 chronic dyspepsia. ~환자 a chronic 〔an established〕 invalid. ~후두염 clergyman's sore throat.

**만세**(萬世) all ages 〔generations〕; 《영겁》 eternity. ¶ ~에 이르도록 through all ages to come / ~에 전하다 be transmitted to all ages.

**만세**(萬歲) ① 《만년》 ten thousand

years; a long time. ②《외침》hurrah; cheers; long live...; *vivat* (L.). ¶ ~ 삼창하다 give three cheers for《*a person*》(★ Hip, hip, hurrah! 를 세 번 반복함) / 대통령 ~ Long live the President! / 국왕 ~ Hurrah for the King! / 휴가 ~ Hurrah for the holidays!

◉ ~력(曆) a perpetual almanac 〔calendar〕.

**만수**(滿水) ¶ ~가 되다 be filled (to the brim) with water / 댐이 ~가 되었다 The dam is now full of water.

**만수**(萬壽) longevity. ◉ ~무강 a long life; longevity: ~무강하다 live long; enjoy longevity.

**만수받이** ①《무당의》a shamanic episode at which one shaman echoing the sounds of another shaman. ②《좋게 받아 줌》putting up with 〔overlooking〕 misbehavior.

**만시지탄**(晩時之歎) repenting of *one's* missing a chance.

**만신** a female shaman.

**만신**(滿身) the whole 〔entire〕 body. ¶ ~에 all over *one's* body; from head to foot / ~창이(瘡痍)가 되다 be covered all over with wounds / ~의 힘을 다해 당기다 heave with all *one's* might and main.

**만심**(慢心) self-conceit; pride. ¶ ~을 갖다 be bloated 〔inflated〕 with pride; be 〔get〕 conceited; be puffed up / 조그만 성공으로 ~을 갖다 conceit *oneself* over minor successes / 그는 잔뜩 ~하고 있다 He is eaten up with pride.

**만안**(萬安) peace; tranquility; security; welfare; health. ~하다 (be) peaceful; tranquil; secure. ¶ 댁내 ~하시기를 기원합니다 I offer prayers for peace and prosperity to your family.

**만약**(萬若) = 만일.

**만연**(蔓延) spread; spreading; prevalence. ~하다 spread; prevail; be prevalent 〔widespread〕. ¶ 전염병의 ~ the spread of an epidemic / 질병이 ~되고 있는 난민수용소 a disease-ridden refugee camp / 병의 ~을 막다 check 〔prevent〕 the spread of a disease / 지금 악성 감기가 ~되고 있다 A bad cold is (going) about now. / 이 그릇된 생각이 ~돼 있다 This misconception is widespread.

**만연히**(漫然―) ①《목적 없이》aimlessly; desultorily; in a rambling 〔desultory〕 way. ¶ ~ 독서하다 read at random / ~ 대학에 들어가다 go to college aimlessly / 세월을 ~ 보내서는 안 된다 Don't idle away your time. ②《맺힌데 없이》loosely. ③《질펀히》lengthily; longwindedly; endlessly.

**만용**(蠻勇) foolhardiness; recklessness; venturous 〔animal, brute〕 courage. ¶ ~을 부리다 display a reckless courage.

**만우절**(萬愚節) April Fools' Day.

**만원**(滿員) no vacancy;《극장의》a full 〔packed〕 house;《게시문》House Full; Full House; Sold out (표의 매진). ¶ ~ 관객 a capacity crowd 〔audience〕 / ~을 이루다 be full; be packed; draw a full house / ~패를 달다 put up a "Full Up" notice / 버스마다 ~이었다 Every bus was loaded to its full capacity. / 극장은 ~을 이루는 성황이다 The theater is drawing a full house. / 나는 매일 ~ 버스를 타고 통학한다 Everyday I go to school in 〔on〕 the crowded bus. / 모든 호텔이 초~이었다 All the hotels were packed 「full 〔to the roof〕. / 좌석 ~《게시》Standing room only. (생략 S.R.O.) *or* House full.

◉ ~버스 a jam-packed bus. ~열차 a packed 〔jam-packed, full〕 train.

**만월**(滿月) a full moon. ¶ ~이다 the moon is (at the) full / 그날 밤은 ~이었다 The moon was full that night.

**만유**(萬有) all things in the universe; the whole of creation. ◉ ~의지론(意志論)『철학』pantheism. ~인력 universal gravitation: ~ 인력의 법칙 the law of universal gravitation.

**만유**(漫遊) a tour; a pleasure trip. ~하다 tour; make a tour. ¶ 세계를 ~하다 tour the world; make a tour of the world.

**만이**(蠻夷) barbarians; savages.

**만인**(萬人) every man; all people; everyone. ¶ 이것은 ~이 다 인정하는 바이다 This fact is universally recognized 〔accepted〕.

**만인**(蠻人) a savage; a barbarian.

**만일**(萬一) ①《만의 하나·극히 드문 일》ten thousand to one; (an) emergency; a rare possibility. ¶ ~에 대비하다 provide 〔make provision〕 against 「a rainy day 〔an emergency〕; prepare for the worst / ~에 대비하여 저축하다 save money against 〔for〕 a rainy day; provide 〔put *something* aside〕 against an emergency.

만일의: ~의 경우 a most unexpected situation; an emergency / ~의 경우에는 if anything 〔the worst〕 should 〔does〕 happen; if the worst comes to the worst; in case of 〔in an〕 emergency / ～의 경우의 대책 an emergency measure; a contingency plan / ～의 사태를 각오하고 있다 be prepared for the worst / 그에게 ～의 경우가 생기면, 즉시 나에게 전화해 주시오 In case anything happens to him, call me immediately. / ～의 경우에는 이 빨간 단추를 누르시오 Push this button in an emergency.

만일을: ～을 위해서 for caution's sake; by way of precaution / ～을 위해서 우비를 갖고 가시오 You had better take a raincoat (just) in case. / ～을 위해서 그 일을 경찰에 신고했다 I reported the matter to the police for caution's sake.

② [부사적] 《만약》 if; provided 〔supposing, suppose〕 (that); in case (of, that) (…의 경우에는); by any chance; by any possibility.

(***a***) [현재·장래에 관해서의 바람·가정] 《직설법 현재 또는 가정법 현재를 써서》 ¶ ～ 괜찮으시다면 if you 「like 〔don't mind〕 / ～ 내일 비가 오면 나는 안 갑니다 If it rains 〔rain〕 tomorrow, I will not go there. (★ 조건절 속에서는 미래형 대신 현재형이 쓰이므로 If it rains... 로 하는 것이 보통임) / ～ 그 소문이 사실이라면 신문이 보도할 테지 If the rumor is true, the papers will report it. (★ 구어에서는 직설법 현재로 나타내는 것이 보통임).

★ *a*) *if*-clause 안에서는 단순미래를 보이는 will, shall은 생략되지만, 의지미래의 will은 남김: If you *will* cook the dinner, I'll wash the dishes. 「당신이 음식을 만들면 나는 접시를 닦겠다」. *b*) 습관적인 일을 말할 때에는 주절 속에도 현재 시제가 쓰임: If he has plenty of time, he usually *does* very well in his exams. 「시간이 충분하면 대개 그는 시험을 잘 친다」.

(***b***) [현재의 사실에 반대의 가정·상상] 《가정법 과거를 써서》 ¶ ～ 내가 자네라면 이 집을 살지도 모르는데 If I were 〔was〕 you, I might buy this house. / ～ 자네가 내 입장에 처한다면 어떻게 하겠나 If you were in my shoes, what would you do? / ～ 그렇다면 나는 얼마나 행복할까 If it was 〔were 《문어》〕 so, how happy I should be! / ～ 그 못된 버릇만 없다면 그를 추천할 텐데 If he had not that bad habit, I would recommend him. / ～ 태양이 없다면 아무 것도 생존 못할 게다 If it were not for 〔But for, Were it not for 《문어》〕 the sun, nothing could live. (★ 가정법 과거에 있어서는 *if*-clause의 동사는 인칭·수에 관계없이 were를 씀. 다만, 구어에서는 if I were you, ...; if it were not for... 따위 몇몇 관용화된 표현 이외는 직설법 과거를 쓰며, 단수(특히 부정형)에는 was를 쓰는 경향이 강함).

(***c***) [실현성이 적은 현재·미래의 일] 《가정법 과거를 써서》 ¶ ～ 누가 백만 원을 준다면 어떻게 하겠느냐 If someone were to 〔should〕 give you a million won, what would you do? (★ 이 경우의 were to는 순전한 가정을 표시하며, was to로 할 수 없음).

(***d***) [현재·미래에 관해서의 강한 의심] 《가정법 미래를 써서》 ¶ ～ 비가 온다고 하더라도 나는 가겠습니다 I will 〔shall 《영》〕 go even if it should rain. / ～ 그렇게 해 주신다면 대단히 고맙겠습니다만 If you would kindly do so, I should be much obliged. (★ 가정법 현재와의 의미의 차이에 주의. 더욱 강한 의심을 나타냄).

(***e***) [과거의 사실에 반하는 가정·바람] 《가정법 과거완료를 써서》 ¶ ～ 또 한 번 해 보았더라면 그는 성공했을는지도 모른다 If he had tried 〔Had he tried〕 once more, he might have succeeded. / ～ 당신의 도움이 없었다면 나는 실패했을 테죠 If it had not been for 〔But for, Had it not been for〕 your help, I should have failed. / ～ 마음대로 고를 수 있었다면 자넨 무슨 직업을 택했을까 If you could have had your choice, which job would you have taken?

**만입**(彎入) embayment; 《해안선의》 an indentation. ～하다 curve in. ¶ 바다는 육지에 깊이 ～해 있다 An arm of the sea penetrates far into the land.

**만자**(卍字) a swastika; a fylfot (pattern); a gammadion. ◉ ～창(窓) a window with a swastika-shaped frame.

**만장**(萬丈) ten thousand fathoms deep 〔high〕; unfathomable height 〔depth〕. ¶ 파란 ～한 full of ups and downs; with many vicissitudes / 파란 ～한 생애 a checkered career; an eventful life / ～의 기염을 토하다 give full vent to *one's* feelings; talk big 〔tall〕; give an eloquent speech / 그는 쉬지 않고 30분간 ～의 기염을 토했다 He went on talking for half an hour without a pause. ◉ ～봉(峰) a lofty peak; an alp.

**만장**(輓章·挽丈) a funeral ode; an elegy; a paper 〔silk〕 streamer on which a funeral ode is written.

**만장**(滿場) the whole house 〔hall〕; the

whole assembly 〔audience〕. ¶ ~의 갈채를 받다 bring down the (whole) house / 그의 연설은 ~의 청중에게 깊은 감명을 주었다 His speech impressed the whole audience deeply.

**만장일치**(滿場一致) unanimity (of the whole assembly). ¶ ~로 《전원 찬성으로》 unanimously; with one consent 〔accord〕; by a unanimous consent; with unanimous approval; 《반대 없이》 without a single dissenting voice / 그 법안은 ~로 가결되었다 The bill was passed「unanimously 〔by unanimous consent〕.

**만재**(滿載) a full load 〔cargo〕. ~하다 carry a full cargo; be loaded to capacity 《with》; be fully loaded 《with》; carry 〔have〕 a full load 〔cargo〕 《of 》; 《기사를》 be full of 《fresh news》. ¶ 석탄을 ~하고 carrying 〔with〕 a full cargo of coal on board / 이 잡지는 항공기에 관한 기사를 ~하고 있다 This magazine is packed with information on aircraft. / 그 배는 전자 기기를 ~하고 있었다 The ship was carrying a full cargo of electronic equipment. / 신선한 야채를 ~한 트럭이 잇달아 밖으로 나갔다 One truck after another went out, loaded to capacity with fresh vegetables. ◉ ~흘수 gauge; full 〔load〕 draft: ~ 흘수선 a load line 〔waterline〕; the Plimsoll line / ~흘수선표 the Plimsoll mark; a load-line mark.

**만적거리다** finger; handle; fumble with; play 〔toy〕 with. ⇨ 만지작거리다.

**만적만적** fingering; handling; fumbling; toying; tampering.

**만전**(萬全) absolute security; perfection. ¶ ~의 safe; perfect; 《튼튼한》 secure; 《틀림없는》 infallible / ~지계(之計)〔지책(之策)〕 a perfect plan; the best possible measure / ~을 기하다 make assurance doubly secure / ~지책을 강구하다 take all possible measures to ensure 《the success of a project》; adopt the safest policy 〔most prudent course〕; use a sure card / 태풍에 대비하여 ~의 방책을 강구했다 All possible measures were taken against the typhoon.

**만점**(滿點) ① 《득점》 full marks; a perfect score. ¶ ~을 받다 get full marks / ~을 주다 give full marks; mark 《*a person*》 perfect / 백점 ~으로 채점하다 mark examination papers out of 100 / 백점 ~에서 85점을 따다 get 〔score〕 85 percent; get 〔obtain〕 85 out of 100.
② 《그만임》 perfection. ¶ ~의 perfect; entirely satisfactory / 영양 ~의 먹거리 very nourishing 〔nutritious〕 food / 서비스 ~이다 The service is quite satisfactory. / 이만하면 ~이다 This is all that could be desired. / 이 호텔은 서비스 ~이다 They give excellent service at this hotel. / 국회에서의 그의 연설은 ~이었다 His speech in the National Assembly was as fine as it could be.

**만조**(滿朝) the entire (royal) court. ◉ ~백관 all the (civil and military) officials of the court.

**만조**(滿潮) high water; (a) high tide; (a) full 〔flood〕 tide. ¶ ~시에 at high 〔full〕 tide; at high water / ~는 오후 2시다 The tide is full at 2 p.m. *or* High tide is at two o'clock in the afternoon.

**만족**(滿足) ① satisfaction; contentment; gratification; content. ~하다, ~스럽다 be satisfied 〔pleased, happy, contented〕 《with》; be gratified 《by, with》; content *oneself* 《with》.

> (용법) **satisfaction** 욕망·필요·식욕 따위가 충족되는 일로 느끼는 기쁨·즐거움의 뜻. **contentment** 바람·욕망 따위가 모두 충족된 것은 아니지만, 그런대로 족하다고 느끼는 편안한 마음의 상태. **content** 한정된 관용구에서 쓰이며, 시적·문학적 표현의 용어. **gratification** 격식을 갖춘 말.

¶ ~한 satisfactory / ~하게 satisfactorily / ~케 하다〔시키다〕 satisfy; gratify 《*one's* desires》; give 《*a person*》 satisfaction / 야심을 ~시키다 gratify *one's* ambition / ~의 뜻을 표명하다 express *one's* satisfaction 《at, with》/ 나는 그 결과에 ~하고 있다 I'm happy 〔pleased〕 with the result. *or* I content myself with the result. / 이것이라면 틀림없이 ~하실테죠 I am sure you will find it satisfactory. / 제안은 대다수의 사람들이 ~해 하는 것이어야 한다 The proposal should be acceptable to most people. / 나는 현상태에 ~하고 있다 I'm happy with the way it is. / 그것은 모두가 만족하도록 해결되었다 It was settled to the satisfaction of all. / 행복이란 ~하는 데 있다 Happiness consists in satisfaction 〔contentment〕. / 그 협상은 ~스러운 것이었

다 The negotiations were satisfactory. / 그녀는 자신의 호기심을 ～시키기 위해 그것을 했다 She did it to gratify her curiosity.
② 《충분》 ¶ ～한 enough; sufficient / 네가 그것으로 ～하다면 나도 ～스럽다 If it's good enough for you, it's got to be good enough for me. / 이것으로 ～스러운 설명이 되었다고 생각한다 I believe this is a sufficient explanation.
◉ ～감 a feeling of satisfaction.

**만족**(蠻族) a savage tribe.

**만종**(晩鐘) the evening bell; a vesper bell; a curfew.

**만좌**(滿座) the entire assembled party; the whole company. ¶ ～한 사람들 앞에(서) in public; in front of everyone; publicly / ～한 사람들 앞에서 창피를 당하다 be insulted publicly; be put to shame in front of the whole company.

**만주**(滿洲) Manchuria. ¶ ～의 Manchurian. ◉ ～말 Manchu; the Manchu language. ～문자 the Manchu script.

**만지**(蠻地) a savage land; a barbaric region.

**만지다** 《손·손가락으로》 finger; touch; pass *one's* hand over; 《만져서 알아냄》 feel; 《손대어 고침》 handle. ¶ 책을 ～ touch a book / 수염을 ～ stroke *one's* beard / 배를 ～ rub *one's* belly / 만지지 마시오 《게시》 Hands off.

**만지작거리다** keep fingering 〔handling, touching〕; fumble with; 《갖고 놀다》 monkey 〔fool〕 around with; toy 〔play〕 with; tamper with. ¶ 골동품을 ～ dabble in curios / 자물쇠를 ～ fumble with 〔at〕 a lock / 콧수염을 ～ twiddle *one's* moustache / 아기는 장난감 차를 만지작거리고 있었다 The baby was fingering a toy car.

**만지작만지작** fingering; handling; touching; fumbling; toying; tampering; monkeying 〔fooling〕 around.

**만찬**(晩餐) dinner; supper; the evening meal. (★ dinner는 하루 중의 중요한 식사를 가리키며 지금은 보통 만찬의 뜻으로 쓰이지만 반드시 저녁 식사와 일치하는 것은 아님). ¶ 최후의 ～ the Last Supper / ～에 초대하다 ask 〔invite〕 《*a person*》 to dinner / ～을 들다 dine; sup; have 〔take〕 dinner 〔supper〕.
◉ ～회 《give, hold》 a dinner party.

**만천하**(滿天下) the whole world. ¶ ～에 in the whole world 〔country〕; throughout the realm; 《announce》 publicly / ～에 사죄하다 apologize before the whole nation 《for what *one* has done》 / ～에 알려지다 be known (all) the world over; be universally known / 이리하여 그의 용감한 행동은 ～에 널리 알려졌다 In this way, his bravery was known to the whole world.

**만초**(蔓草) a vine; a creeper; a climber; a trailing 〔climbing〕 plant.

**만추**(晩秋) late autumn 〔fall〕. ¶ ～에 in late fall; late in autumn.

**만춘**(晩春) late spring.

**만취**(滿醉·漫醉) dead drunkenness; carousal. ～하다 be 〔get〕 dead-drunk; 《미구어》 be boozed (up); be zonked (out); get soused. ¶ ～자 a drunken person; a drunk / 그는 파티에서 종종 ～가 된다 He often gets dead drunk at a party.

**만큼** ① 《비교》 as... as; equal to; 〔부정〕 not so... as; less than (…만큼 …하지 않다). (★ 부정문에서는 not so... as 대신 not as... as가 흔히 쓰임. 그러나 형식을 존중하는 문장에서는 not so... as가 주로 쓰임). ¶ 오늘은 어제～ 춥지 않다 Today is not so cold as yesterday. / 너도 그～ 할 수 있다 You can do as well as he. / 누구는 너～ 못하는 줄 아느냐 Do you think anyone can't do as well as you? / 나도 하기만 하면 그 사람～ 한답니다 If I devoted myself to it, I could do as much 〔as well〕 as he. / 이것도 그것～ 좋다 This one is as good as that. / 예상했던 것～ 나쁘지는 않다 It is not so bad as I expected. / 그는 겉보기～ 나이를 먹지 않았다 He is less old than he looks. / 이～ 재미있는 책은 없다 No book is more interesting than this one. *or* This is the most interesting book. / 쇠～ 유용한 금속은 없다 No metal is so useful as iron. / 저들～ 닮은 형제도 드물다 No two brothers can resemble each other more than they do. / 노력한 ～의 보답은 있었다 Our efforts were rewarded.
② 《정도》 an extent; a degree; 《…할 정도》 so much that; enough to. ¶ 그〔이〕～ to that 〔this〕 extent; as much as that 〔this〕; that 〔this〕 much / 얼마～ how much; to what extent 〔degree〕 / 큰 집을 지을 ～ 돈이 없다 I don't have money enough to build a big house. / 범이라도 잡을 ～ 날래다 He is swift enough to catch a tiger. / 싫증이 날 ～ 먹었다 I have eaten it 「so often 〔so much〕 that I am sick of it. / 그는 일어서지 못할 ～ 술이 취했다

He was so drunk that he could not stand up. / 나는 송선생에게 충고할 ~ 친하지 않다 I'm not a good enough friend of Mr. Song's to offer him advice. / 나는 그에게 변통할 수 있는 ~의 돈을 꾸어 주었다 I lent him what money I could raise.

③ 《원인·이유·근거》 ¶ 직업이 직업이니 ~ 복장을 화려하게 입어야만 한다 I must be gaily dressed, because of my profession. / 그녀는 힘들게 세상을 살아 온 사람인 ~ 동정심이 있다 She is sympathetic, as she has seen much of life.

**만큼만** (just) as much as.

**만판** ① 《마음껏》 to *one's* heart's content; as much as *one* wishes 〔wants〕; to the full; heartily. ¶ ~ 마시다〔먹다〕 drink 〔eat〕 *one's* fill / 인생을 ~ 즐기다 enjoy life to the full / 나는 휴일을 ~ 즐겼다 I enjoyed the holiday to my heart's content. ② 《오직·마냥》 entirely; solely; wholly; simply. ¶ ~ 놀기만 하다 spends all *one's* time loafing; do nothing but idle *one's* time away.

**만평**(漫評) 《생각나는 대로 하는 비평》 a desultory 〔rambling〕 criticism; literary gossip; 《만화 따위로의》 a satire (comic); a caricature. ~하다 review randomly; criticize desultorily; gossip 《on literary works》. ◉ 시사~ rambling comments on current events; current notes.

**만필**(漫筆) stray 〔random, rambling〕 notes; random jottings; 《신문·잡지의》 *causeries*(F.).

**만하**(晩夏) late summer.

**만하다** ① 《족하다》 be sufficient 《to *do*》; be... enough 《to》. ¶ 쉴 만한 공원 a park that is a good place to relax in / 먹을 ~ be good to eat; be eatable / 아들을 대학에 보낼 만한 재산이 있다 He is rich enough to send his son to college.

② 《가치가 있다》 be (well) worth 《*doing*》; be worthy of 《mention》; be worth while to; deserve 《praise》. (★ worth는 다음 세 가지 쓰임이 보통임. It is worth doing. It is worth while to do. To do this is worth while. worthy는 「of+명사 또는 부정사」의 형식으로 쓰임). ¶ 가볼 만한 곳 a place worth visiting / 만날 만한 사람 a man worth meeting / 가질 ~ be worth having 〔owning〕 / 살 ~ be (well) worth buying / 입을 ~ be (well) worth wearing; be (quite) wearable / 읽을 ~ be readable; be worth reading (★ The book is worth while reading.은 잘못) / 주목할 ~ be worthy of note / 칭찬할 ~ deserve praise / 볼 만도 하고 들을 만도 하다 be both worth seeing and worth hearing / 그의 용감한 행위는 크게 칭찬할 ~ His brave conduct deserves 〔entitles him to〕 high praise. / 그 전람회는 볼 ~ The exhibition is worth seeing. *or* It is worth while seeing the exhibition. (★ 이 때의 it는 seeing 이하를 받는 관용구적 표현).

③ 《때가》 be at the point of (*doing*); have reached the stage (when *one* can *do*). ¶ 그는 한창 일할 만한 나이에 죽었다 He died just at the age when he can lead an active life.

**-만하다** 《같은 정도의 비교》 be to the extent of; be as big 〔little〕 as; be as much 〔little〕 as; be the size of; 《더하지 않다》 be not more (than). ¶ 새알만하다 be the size of a bird's-egg; be as small as a bird's-egg / 호랑이만하다 be as big as a tiger / 그 크기가 이만하다 Its size is this big. / 그 쥐는 강아지만하다 The rat is the size of a puppy dog. / 그만한 것쯤 알고 있다 I know as much. / 환자의 병세는 그저 그만하다 The patient's condition is neither better nor worse.

**만학**(晩學) learning late in life. ~하다 learn late in life. ¶ 그는 ~했다 He 「took up 〔began〕 learning late in life. / ~이지만 그의 어학 실력은 대단하다 He has a marvelous linguistic knowledge which he acquired in his later years. ◉ ~자 a late learner.

**만행**(蠻行) barbarity; savagery; brutality; an atrocity; a savage deed. ¶ ~을 저지르다 commit an act of brutality / 그들의 ~을 규탄하다 impeach them for their brutalities.

**만혼**(晩婚) marrying late; (a) late marriage. ~하다 get married late.

**만화**(漫畫) a caricature (인물 풍자만화); a cartoon (시사 풍자만화); 《보통, 연속된 4컷의》 a comic strip; a strip cartoon 《영》; [일반적] a funny picture; 《미구어》 comics; funnies.

¶ ~화하다 make a caricature of; caricature; cartoon; adapt 《a fairy story》 into a comic strip; make a comic-strip version of 《Animal Farm》 / ~식으로 in cartoon fashion / TV에서 ~를 보다 see a 〔an animated〕 cartoon on television.

> 용법 **caricature** 풍자적인 한 장면의 만화. 주로 인물을 다루며, 하나의 미술품으로 제작됨. **cartoon** 주로 시사 풍자 만화. 대개 한 장면의 그림으로 끝나며, 통상 caption이 붙는다. **comic strip** 통상 4개의 장면이 연속되어 이루어지는 하나의 만화. 신문·잡지 따위에 실리는 연재 만화. 때로는 이것을 cartoon이라고 하는 경우도 있으나 일반적이 아님.

◉ ~가 a cartoonist; a comic artist; a caricaturist. ~란 a comic section 《of a newspaper》; 《미구어》 funnies. ~영화 an animated 〔a movie〕 cartoon; a cartoon film. ~잡지 a comic magazine; a comic 《구어》. ~책 a comic book. 불량~ substandard comic books 〔comics〕.

**만화경**(萬華鏡) a kaleidoscope. ¶ ~ 같은 kaleidoscopic.

**만화방창**(萬化方暢) luxuriant growth of all things in spring. ~하다 《in spring》 all things grow luxuriantly.

**만회**(挽回) retrieval; recovery; restoration. ~하다 recover 《*one's* losses》; retrieve 《*one's* fortunes》; restore 《*one's* reputation》; 《따라잡다》 catch up 《with》. ¶ ~하기 어려운 irretrievable; irrecoverable / 퇴세를 ~하다 recover from the discouraging 〔difficult〕 situation / 우리는 세력을 ~해야 한다 We should recover 〔regain〕 our power. / 이 승부〔형세〕는 ~할 수 없다 It is impossible to「turn the tables 〔reverse the situation〕. / 그는 곧 그의 명예를 ~했다 He recovered his reputation soon. / 그는 인기를 ~하기 위해 필사적이었다 He made a desperate attempt to regain his popularity. / 명예는 한번 잃으면 ~하기가 매우 어렵다 Honor, once lost, is virtually impossible to retrieve. ◉ ~책(策) measures for retrieving 《*one's* lost credit》.

**많다** ① 《수가》 (be) many; numerous; 《양이》 much; abundant (풍부); full. ¶ 많은 《수가》 many; many a; numerous; a good 〔great〕 many; 《양이》 much; a good 〔great〕 deal of; plentiful; 《수·양》 lots 〔a lot〕 of; heaps 〔a heap〕 of; plenty of / 많은 사람 many 〔lots of〕 people / 많은 물 much 〔lots of〕 water / 수가〔양이〕 많아지다 increase in number 〔quantity〕 / 이 곳은 비가 ~ We have much rain here. / 많으면 많을수록 좋다 The more, the better. / 그렇게 생각하는 사람이 ~ Many people think so. / 못에 물고기가 ~ There are lots of fish in the pond. *or* This pond「abounds with 〔is full of〕 fish. / 미국엔 석유가 ~ The United States is rich in oil. / 한국에는 경치 좋은 곳이 ~ Korea has many scenic spots. / 이 경험으로 우리는 많은 것을 배웠다 We learned much from this experience.
② 《잦다》 (be) frequent; often; prevalent; current; common; be rife with. ¶ 일본에는 지진이 ~ Japan has frequent earthquakes. / 요새 동네에 도난 사건이 ~ The village has been rife with theft lately. / 이 병은 어린이에게 ~ This disease often attacks children. *or* Children are subject to this disease.

**많이** ① 《다수·다량》 much; a lot; in plenty; plentifully; in large numbers 〔quantities〕; in profusion; in abundance. ¶ 많이는 largely; mostly; for the most part; chiefly / 돈을 ~ 쓰다 spend much 〔a lot of〕 money / 사람을 ~ 쓰다 employ a large number of people / 금이 ~ 나다 gold is produced in large quantities / 비가 ~ 오다 get a lot of rain; have frequent rain / 할 일이 ~ 있다 There are so 〔too〕 many things to do. / 우리는 돈을 ~ 갖고 있다 We have money in abundance.
② 《흔히》 often; frequently. ¶ 어린이가 이 병에 ~ 걸린다 Children often get 〔come down with〕 this disease.

**맏-** 《첫째》 firstborn; first; eldest. ¶ 맏누이 the eldest sister / 맏딸 the first daughter; the eldest daughter / 맏며느리 the wife of *one's* eldest son.

**맏물** the first (product) of the season; the first cut; the first supply 《of tomatoes》. ¶ ~ 꽁치 early mackerel pikes / ~ 사과 the first apples of the season; the early apples / ~ 상추 lettuce from the first cut; the first lettuce of the season / ~ 딸기를 먹다 eat early strawberries; eat strawberries for the first time in the season.

**맏배** the firstborn (of animals); the first hatch 〔litter〕. ◉ ~돼지 the first litter of pigs. ~병아리 chickens of the first hatch. 「〔eldest〕 daughter.

**맏사위** the husband of *one's* firstborn

**맏상제**(―喪制) the chief mourner; the eldest son of the deceased.

**맏아들** the firstborn 〔eldest〕 son.

**맏이** the firstborn 《son》; the eldest 《child》. ¶ ~로 태어나다 be born first;

be the eldest.

**맏형**(一兄) the eldest brother.

**말**[1] ①《곡식을 되는》 a *mal;* a measure containing about 18 liters. ¶ 말로 되다 measure《rice》 with a *mal.* ②《단위》 a *mal;* a unit of measure(= about 18 liters). ¶ 되로 주고 말로 받다《득보다》 throw a sprat to catch a whale; give an egg to gain an ox;《봉변당하다》 sow the wind and reap the whirlwind.

**말**[2] 〖동물〗 a horse; a pony (몸집이 작은 조랑말 따위). ¶ 경주말 a race horse; a racer / 연자말 a horse working in a flour mill / 말을 기르다 keep a horse / 말을 타다 ride a horse; mount 〔get on〕 a horse / 말타고 가다 「go on 〔ride〕 horseback / 말에서 내리다 dismount (from) horse; 「alight from 〔get off〕 a horse / 말을 달리다 gallop a horse; spur a horse on / 말을 길들이다 break in a horse / 말을 조련하다 train a horse / 말에서 떨어지다 「fall off 〔be thrown from〕 *one's* horse / 말을 멈추다 「pull up 〔hold in〕 a horse; draw rein / 말에 안장을 얹다 saddle a horse / 말에 편자를 박다 shoe a horse / 말 갈 데 소 갈 데 다 다녔다 have been going around everywhere; have trod every cowpath / 말 살에 쇠 살 talk incongruously; talk nonsense / 말 갈 데 소 간다《속담》 One goes where one shouldn't. / 말타면 경마 잡히고 싶다《속담》 Give him an inch and he'll take a mile. *or* The more one has, the more one wants.

**말**[3] 〖식물〗 a duckweed.

**말**[4] 《장기·윷 따위의》 a marker in chess; checkers; a piece; a man.

**말**[5] ①《언어》 language; speech; a word (낱말); a term (용어); a language (국어); a dialect (방언). ¶ 외국말 a foreign language / 자기 나라 말 *one's* native language; the vernacular / 우리〔한국〕말 Korean; the Korean language / 상말 vulgar speech / 서울말 Seoul speech / 시골말 a local dialect; dialect speech; country 〔rustic, rural〕 speech / 표준말 the standard language.

②《담화》 a talk; a speech; a conversation; a chat;《언사》 what *one* says 〔said〕; a remark; a statement. ¶ 말의 장벽 a language barrier / 가시돋친 말 harsh language; a caustic remark; stinging words / 동정의 말 a word of sympathy / 말 없이 in silence; without a word;《무단으로》 without (previous) notice / 말과 속이 다르다 do not mean what one says.

말로: 말로 나타내다 express《*one's* thanks》 in words; put《*one's* feelings》 into words / 생각을 말로 나타내다 express 〔verbalize〕 *one's* thoughts; put *one's* thoughts into words / 말로는 나타낼 수 없다 be too《beautiful》 for words / 말로 표현할 수 없을 정도로 beyond words; more than tongue can tell / 말로 다할 수 없는 inexpressible; indescribable; untold; beyond 〔past〕 all description / 보통〔의학상의〕 말로 말하면 in common 〔medical〕 parlance / 조용한 말로 in a calm tone.

말에: 말에 궁하다 be at a loss for words / 말에 가시가 있다 have a harsh tongue; 《words》 carry a sting / 남의 말에 넘어가다 be cajoled 〔wheedled〕; be taken in by《*a person's*》 glib talk.

말을: 말을 하다 ⇨ 말하다 / 말을 걸다〔건네다〕 speak 〔call〕 to; address; accost; hail《*a person*》/ 말을 꺼내다 begin to talk; start a talk; broach a subject; break the ice / 말을 꾸미다 use fine language; use fair words; adorn *one's* words; euphemize; talk in fine language / 말을 돌리다 switch the conversation; change the subject / 말을 머뭇거리다 hesitate to say 〔speak〕; be reluctant to say; falter / 말을 도맡아 하다 do all the talking; monopolize 〔take over〕 the conversation / 말을 삼가다〔조심하다〕 be careful 「in *one's* speech 〔of *one's* language〕; weigh 〔spare〕 *one's* words; govern 〔restrain〕 *one's* tongue; be prudent in utterance / 말을 어기다 break *one's* word 〔promise, appointment〕; eat *one's* words; go back on *one's* words / 말을 잇다 go on; continue to talk / 말을 잘 하다 have a glib tongue; be a glib talker / 말을 잘못 하다 make a mistake in the use 〔choice〕 of words; make a slip 〔lapse〕 of the tongue; speak wrongly 〔amiss, incorrectly〕 / 말을 주고 받다 have a word《with》; pass a few (friendly) words《with》; exchange words《with》/ 말을 못하게 되다 be deprived of *one's* power of speech; lose *one's* speech 〔tongue〕 / 남의 말을 그대로 믿다 take《*a person*》 at *his* word; accept another's word as it means / 감사〔환영〕의 말을 하다 say a few words of gratitude 〔welcome〕 《to》/ 말을 바꿔 하면 in other words;

that is (to say); to put it in another way.

말이: 말이 거칠다 be rough of 〔in〕 speech; be rough-spoken / 말이 격해지다 argue with increasing vehemence; come to high words / 말이 많다 be wordy 〔loquacious, garrulous〕; be very talkative; speak too much / 말이 많은 사람 a talkative 〔wordy, verbose, loquacious〕 person; a man of many words; a chatterbox (여자) / 말이 적다 be taciturn; be (a man) of few words / 말이 서투르다 be a poor speaker; be poor at talking / 말이 상스럽다 be vulgar in speech / 말이 통하다 a language is spoken; make *oneself* understood / 말이 통하지 않다 cannot make *oneself* understood / 말이 다르다 a remark does not tally; talk a different story / 대답할 말이 없다 have no word in reply; words fail 《*one*》 to reply / 적절한 말이 생각나지 않다 cannot find 「a proper 〔an apt〕 expression; cannot express 《*a thing*》 properly / 이을 말이 막히다 be stuck for something to say; run out of topics of conversation.

¶ 그의 말은 이렇다 This is what he said. / 말과 행동이 다르다 What he says is one thing and what he does is another. / 이 아이는 아직 말을 못한다 This child cannot talk yet. / 가는 말이 고와야 오는 말이 곱다 《속담》 Nice words for nice words. / 호랑이도 제 말하면 온다 《속담》 Talk of the devil, and he is sure to appear. / 말 한마디에 천냥 빚도 갚는다 《속담》 One should be wary of *one's* words. *or* Your tongue can make or break you. / 낮말은 새가 듣고 밤 말은 쥐가 듣는다 《속담》 Walls have ears. *or* Refrain from speaking ill of other people. / 쉬운 말로 설명 좀 해주게 Explain it in plain 〔simple〕 words 〔terms〕. / 죽은 사람은 말이 없다 Dead men tell no tales.

③ 《잔소리》 a scolding; a reprimand; a lecture (훈계조의); bickering (말다툼의); a complaint (불만); a criticism. ¶ 너 그렇게 하면 아버지한테 말듣는다 You will 「hear from 〔be scolded by〕 your father if you do that. / 거기 길을 막으면 동네 사람들이 말을 할 것이다 If you block the road, the villagers will complain. / 말 많은 집은 장맛도 쓰다 《속담》 Everything goes wrong in a bickering family. / 그는 언제나 투덜투덜 말이 많다 He is always grumbling.

④ 《소문》 a rumor; gossip; hearsay; town talk. ¶ …하다는 말이 있다 it is said 〔rumored, gossiped〕 that…; they say; I hear / 말이 돌다 word is getting around / 말이 나다 a rumor is started; the word is out (that…) / 말이 퍼지다 word spreads / 말을 내다 start a rumor.

⑤ 《이야기》 a story; a tale; a saying. ¶ 옛말 an old tale; an old saying / 옛말 그른 데 없다 Old sayings 「never fail 〔are always true〕.

⑥ 《전갈》 a message. ¶ 말을 전하다 deliver 〔give〕 a message / 전할 말을 남기다 leave a message 《with *a person*》 / 전할 말이라도 있습니까 Would you like to leave a message?

⑦ 《의미·경우》 meaning; import; the case. ¶ 그거 어떻게 된 말이요 What do you mean by that? *or* What are you talking about? / 이렇게 됐단 말일세 It boils down to this. *or* It is a case of this.

⑧ 《주장》 *one's* say; what *one* has to say; a claim; a complaint (불평). ¶ 양쪽 말을 듣다 hear both sides.

**-말**(末) the end; the close. ¶ 5회말 《야구에서》 the second half 〔bottom〕 of the fifth inning / 4월말에 at the end of April / 5월말경에 toward 〔about〕 the end of May; in late May / 세기말에 at the close of the century.

**말갈기** a (horse's) mane.

**말갛다** (be) clear; transparent; lucid. ¶ 푸르고 말간 물 the clear-blue water / 말간 눈 clear eyes / 말간 국 clear soup; *consommé* (F.).

**말개지다** become clear; clear up; get 「clean.

**말거리** ① a cause of troubles. ⇨말썽거리. ② 《화제》 a topic 〔subject〕 of conversation. ⇨화제.

**말거머리** 〖동물〗 a horseleech.

**말경**(末境) 《끝판》 the end; the close; 《말년》 the declining years of *one's* life.

**말고** [보조사] 《아니고》 not… but…; instead of; except; but. ¶ 이것~도 또 다른 것이 있지 않습니까 You have another besides this, surely? / 이것~ 좀더 가는 줄은 없느냐 Don't you have any thinner strings than this?

**-말고** ¶ 그렇고말고 Certainly. *or* Of course. *or* It's just as you say. *or* Oh yes, to be sure! *or* Yes, indeed. *or* Sure.

**말고기자반**(—佐飯) a drunken man

with a red face.

**말고삐** reins; a bridle. ¶ ～를 잡다 hold 〔lead〕 《a horse》 by the bridle; hold 〔take over〕 the reins 《of》 / ～를 당기다 tighten 〔pull up, draw in〕 the reins; rein in 《a horse》 / ～를 당겨 말을 세우다 rein in 〔back〕 *one's* horse / ～를 늦추다 loosen 〔slacken, let out〕 the reins; give the reins to 《a horse》 / ～를 늦추지 않다 [비유적] keep a tight rein on.

**말곰** 〚동물〛 a Manchurian bear.

**말공대**(一恭待) addressing in honorifics. ～하다 pay respect by addressing in honorifics; address in honorifics.

**말괄량이** a romping 〔bouncing〕 girl; a tomboy; a hoyden; a minx. ¶ ～ 같은 tomboyish; hoydenish.

**말구유** a manger; a horse trough.

**말구종**(一驅從) a groom; a footman.

**말굳다** stammer; stutter; falter.

**말굴레** a bridle; a headgear; a halter. ¶ ～를 씌우다 bridle a horse.

**말굽** ① 《발톱》 a horse's hoof. ¶ ～모양의 horseshoe-shaped / 갈라진 ～ a cloven hoof / ～소리 the beat 〔sound, clatter〕 of horse hoofs; hoof-beats. ② 《편자》 a horseshoe. ¶ ～을 박다 put on a horseshoe; shoe (a horse). ◉ ～옹두리 the horseshoe-shaped kneecap of an ox. ～자석 a horseshoe magnet. ～추녀 a horseshoe-shaped piece of wood attached to the ends of eaves.

**말귀** 《말뜻》 the meaning of what *one* says; 《알아듣는 능력》 hearing; 《이해력》 understanding; comprehension; the uptake; an ear (for words). ¶ ～가 빠르다〔어둡다〕 be quick-〔dull-〕witted; be quick 〔slow〕「on the uptake 〔to understand, of understanding〕; be quick 〔slow〕 in understanding what 《*a person*》 says / ～를 못 알아듣다 can't make out what *one* says / 자네, 참 ～가 어둡군 그래 I say, you are slow on the uptake.

**말기**(末期) the end; the close; the last 〔closing〕 years 〔period, days〕; the last 〔terminal〕 stage 《of communism》. ¶ ～적인 decadent / ～ 증상의 환자 a terminal patient; a patient in the terminal stage / 19세기 ～에 at the close of the 19th century / 전화는 19세기 ～에 발명되었다 The telephone was invented at the end 〔close〕 of the 19th century. / 현대의 물질 문명은 이미 ～적 증상을 나타내고 있다 Modern material civilization has already shown signs of a downfall. / 그것은 조선 ～에 일어난 일이다 It happened in the late Joseon dynasty era. ◉ ～암 terminal cancer: ～암 환자 a terminal cancer patient. ～증상 terminal symptoms.

**말꼬리** ¶ 남의 ～를 붙잡고 늘어지다 trip 《*a person*》 up with 〔catch 《*a person*》 in〕 *his* own words / 그녀는 언제나 상대의 ～를 잡고 늘어지는데 능란하다 She is always quick to jump on any slip of the tongue by her opponent.

**말꼬투리** ¶ ～를 잡다 pounce on every slip of the tougue; catch 《*a person*》 in his own words / 남의 ～를 잡지마라 Quit 〔Stop〕 your habit of picking on people.

**말꼴** fodder; provender; forage. ¶～을 주다 fodder 〔give fodder to〕 a horse.

**말끄러미** ⇨ 물끄러미.

**말끔** 《남김없이 모두》 all; completely; thoroughly; entirely; quite; utterly. ¶ 세간을 ～ 치우다 carry off all the furniture / 빚을 ～ 청산하다 clear off *one's* debts.

**말끔하다** 《옷차림 따위가》 (be) clean; tidy; neat; trim; 《용모 따위가》 (be) comely; lovely. ¶ 말끔한 용모의 소녀 a lovely 〔comely〕 little girl / 말끔한 옷차림을 하고 있다 be neatly dressed.

**말끔히** clean(ly); clearly; neatly. ¶ 마당을 ～ 쓸다 sweep a garden clean / 방을 ～ 치우다 put a room in order; tidy 〔do up, straighten up〕 a room neatly / 얼굴을 ～ 씻다 wash *one's* face clean / 얼굴이 ～ 생기다 have a nice face / 아 이런, 그것을 ～ 잊고 있었다 Oh, shucks ! I forgot all about it.

**말끝** the end of *one's* words 〔speech〕. ¶ ～을 흐리다 speak ambiguously 〔evasively〕; leave *one's* statement vague; prevaricate; slur the end of *one's* words / 그는 ～마다 그 소리다 He never opens his mouth without saying it.

**말나다** ① 《화제에 오르다》 be brought into conversation; become 〔be〕 a topic 〔subject〕 of conversation; be talked about. ¶ 새 학교를 세우자고 말이 난 것은 육성회 석상에서였다 It was at the P.T.A. meeting that the proposal to found a new school was made. ② 《소문이》 be rumored 《that》; be talked 〔gossiped〕 about; become the talk 《of the town》; 《비밀이》 come

〔be, slip, leak〕 out; transpire; be disclosed. ¶ 말날까 두려우니 아무한테도 이야기 말게 Don't tell anybody about it—I'm afraid of its leaking out.

**말내다** ① 《의견·제안을》 broach 《a subject》; propose; 《얘기삼아》 bring into the conversation; begin to talk about; 《소문을》 start a rumor. ¶ 내일 산책 가자고 김군이 말을 냈다 Kim suggested going out for a walk tomorrow. / 그 말을 낸 사람이 누군지 좀 알았으면 좋겠다 I'd give a pretty penny to know who started the rumor. / 누가 말냈는지 모르지만 아무 근거없는 이야기다 I don't know who started the story, but it is entirely groundless. ② 《비밀을》 let out 《a secret》; disclose; divulge; reveal; expose. ¶ 말내지 않다 keep 《a secret》; keep 《*a matter*》 to *oneself;* never let 《*the matter*》 pass *one's* lips / 절대 말을 내선 안돼 Say nothing to any one. *or* Keep it strictly to yourself.

**말년**(末年) ① 《생애의》 *one's* later 〔latter, declining〕 years; the last part of *one's* life. ¶ ～에 late in life; in *one's* last 〔closing〕 years / 그녀의 ～은 행복하였다 She was happy in her last years. / 그는 ～을 쓸쓸히 지냈다 He lived unknown toward the end of his life. ② ＝말기(末期).

**말눈치** ① 《말의 뜻》 an implication; a suggestion; a nuance; a hint; a tip. ¶ ～를 모르다 can't take the hint / 사직할 듯한 ～다 hint at *one's* resignation. ② 《이해》 catching 〔understanding〕 what *one* says; taking a hint 〔tip〕. ¶ ～가 빠르다 catch on quick; be quick to take a hint.

**말다**[1] 《둘둘》 wind (up); roll (up); furl (기·텐트 따위를); reel (실을). ¶ 두루마리를 ～ roll a roll of paper / 담배를 ～ roll a cigarette / 융단을 ～ roll up a carpet / 돛을 ～ furl a sail.

**말다**[2] 《국·물에》 put 《rice》 into soup 〔water〕; mix 《food》 with soup. ¶ 국수를 ～ put noodles into soup; prepare noodles.

**말다**[3] 《그만두다》 stop; cease; drop; quit; leave 〔lay〕 off; give up (단념하다). ¶ 일을 하다가 ～ leave 〔knock〕 off work; lay aside *one's* work; leave 《*a thing*》 half-done 〔unfinished〕 / 말았더라면 좋았을걸 I wish I had not done with it. / 비가 오다 말았다 It started to rain and then stopped. / 내버려 두어라 — 싸우다 말겠지 Leave them alone — they won't fight long.

**말다**[4] [조동사] ① 《금지》 don't; keep 〔refrain〕 from 《doing》; avoid. ¶ 가지 마라 Don't go. / 가지 말자 Let's not go. / 마음을 놓지 말게 Don't fall asleep at the switch, now. / 서슴지 말고 전화해 주십시오 Don't hesitate to telephone me. / 놀지 말고 일합시다 Let's cut out the loafing and get to work. ② 《…로 끝나다》 end up 《*do*ing》; finally *do.* ¶ 술로 그는 죽고 말았다 Drink ended him. / 필경 싸움이 벌어지고 말겠구나 I am afraid there will be a fight after all. / 이 일은 꼭 해 놓고야 말겠다 I will get this job done if it kills me!

**말다툼** a dispute; an argument; a wrangle; a quarrel; a squabble (사소한). ～하다 quarrel 《with》; have 「an argument 〔a quarrel, a dispute〕 《with》; argue 《with》. ¶ ～이 격해졌다 Words ran high. / ～은 종종 드잡이로 변한다 Quarrels are often followed by fights. / 그는 그녀와 하찮은 일로 ～하였다 He argued with 〔against〕 her about a trifle.

**말단**(末端) the end; the tip. ¶ 행정기구의 ～ the smallest unit of the administrative organization; a government office in direct contract with the public / 사장의 뜻이 ～까지 전해지지 않았다 The president's intention did not reach the rank and file.
◉ ～공무원 a petty 〔minor〕 official; the lowest echelon of public officials; rank and file officials. ～관절 『해부』 terminal joints. ～기관 terminal offices 〔organs〕. ～기구 the smallest unit of an organization. ～사원 a minor clerk. ～장치 a (data communication) terminal.

**말대꾸** ① 《응수》 a reply; a response; a back answer; a retort (반박). ～하다 retort; talk back. ¶ 그는 「나와는 상관없는 일이야」라고 ～했다 "It's no concern of mine," he retorted. ② ⇨말대답.

**말대답**(一對答) a back talk; a retort; a crack 《미속어》. ～하다 talk back to 《*a person*》; answer 《*a person*》 back; retort; give 《*a person*》 back talk. ¶ 더이상 ～하지 마라 No more of your back talk. / 어른한테 ～해서는 못 쓴다 You shouldn't talk back to your elders. / 나의 ～으로 아버님께서 노하셨다 My father got angry with me for talking 〔answering him〕 back. / 그녀는 아이들의 ～을 용서치 않았다 She never let her children answer (her) back.

**말더듬다** stammer; stutter; mumble (우물우물); falter 《out, forth》. ¶ 말을 더듬으며 변명하다 mumble (out) an excuse / 그는 몹시 말을 더듬는다 He has a terrible stutter. / 그는 말을 더듬으며 사과했다 He stammered (out) an apology.

**말더듬이** a stammerer; a stutterer.
◉ ～교정기 an articulator.

**말동무** someone to talk to; a companion.

**말되다** ① 《사리에 맞다》 make sense; stand to reason. ¶ 말도 되지 않는 소리 nonsense; rubbish. ② 《합의되다》 come to an understanding; reach an agreement; come to terms. ¶ 그 집을 사기로 말이 되었다 We came to terms on (buying) the house. ③ 《말썽이 되다》 become the object of criticism 〔complaint〕; cause trouble.

**말똥가리** 〖조류〗 a buzzard.

**말똥거리다** roll (*one's* eyes) vacantly. ¶ 누운 채 눈을 말똥거리며 천장만 바라보다 lie with a vacant stare at the ceiling.

**말똥말똥** with (vacant) fixed eyes; unblinkingly; blankly; in a daze. ¶ ～ 쳐다보다 look 《*a person*》 full in the face; stare (hard) 《at》 / (잠은 안오고) 눈이 ～하다 be wakeful; be wide=awake.

**말뚝** a stake; a post; a picket (울타리용); 《토목용의》 a pile (대형); [집합적] piling. ¶ ～을 박다 drive in a stake 〔pile, picket〕; hammer a pile in(to) 《the ground》 / ～을 세우다 put 〔set〕 up a post / ～을 뽑다 pull up a stake / 말은 ～에 묶여 있다 The horse is tethered to a stake. ◉ ～잠 《잠》 sleeping while sitting upright. ～잠(簪) 《비녀》 a kind of metal hairpin.

**말뜨다** be slow of 〔in *one's*〕 speech.

**말뜻** the meaning of a word.

**말라깽이** a lean 〔skinny〕 person; a scarecrow; a bag of bones 《구어》.

**말라리아** 〖의학〗 malaria. ¶ ～에 걸린 malarial; malarian; malarious / ～에 걸리다 catch 〔contract〕 malaria; develop malaria.
◉ ～모기 a malarial 〔malaria-bearing〕 mosquito. ～열 malarial fever. ～예방약 an anti-malarial tablet; a malaria=prevention pill. ～요법 a malarial fever treatment. ～원충 a malarial parasite; a plasmodium (*pl.* -dia). ～환자 a malaria patient.

**말라빠지다** become thin 〔lean, emaciated〕; grow gaunt; get skinny; lose weight 〔flesh〕. ¶ 몹시 말라빠진 as lean as a rake / 병으로 말라빠진 sick and emaciated / 말라빠진 팔 a thin and weak arm.

**말라위** 《아프리카의 공화국》 Malawi.

**말라죽다** 《초목이》 wither; dry up; be blighted. ¶ 말라죽은 나무 a blighted 〔withered〕 tree.

**말라카해협**(一海峽) 《말레이 반도 남부의》 the Strait of Malacca.

**말랑거리다** be(come) soft; get tender. ¶ 말랑거리는 감 a soft ripe persimmon.

**말랑말랑하다** be all soft; be (nice) and tender. ¶ 말랑말랑하게 softly; tenderly / 말랑말랑한 고기 tender meat / 말랑말랑하게 삶은 콩 beans cooked (until they are) tender / 촉감이 ～ feel soft; be soft 〔tender〕 to the touch / 그 고기를 말랑말랑하도록 삶아라 Boil the meat till it becomes soft.

**말레이** Malay(a). ¶ ～의 Malay(an).
◉ ～군도 the Malay Archipelago. ～반도 the Malay Peninsula. ～사람 a Malay(an). ～어 the Malay(an) language.

**말레이시아** 《동남아의 나라》 Malaysia.
◉ ～사람 a Malaysian. ～연방 the Federation of Malaysia.

**말려들다** be dragged 《into》; be 〔get〕 involved 〔entangled, implicated〕 《in》; involve 〔embroil〕 *oneself* 《in》; get mixed up 《in》. ¶ 기계에 ～ be caught in a machine / 분쟁에 ～ be(come) embroiled in a dispute; be involved in trouble / 싸움에 ～ 「become embroiled 〔get mixed up〕 in a quarrel / 음모〔범죄〕에 ～ be implicated in 「a conspiracy 〔the crime〕 / 전쟁에 ～ be drawn 〔dragged〕 into a war; be involved in a war / 그런 일에는 말려들고 싶지 않다 I don't like to be mixed up in such a business.

**말로**(末路) the last days 《of a hero》; the end 《of *one's* life》; 《운명》 *one's* fate. ¶ 인생의 ～ the end of *one's* career / 그의 ～는 비참하였다 His last days were miserable. *or* He died a miserable death. / 그의 ～를 가엾게 생각하다 I feel pity for his last days.

**말리**(茉莉) 〖식물〗 a jasmin(e); a jessamine.

**말리** 《아프리카의 공화국》 (the Republic of) Mali.

**말리다**[1] ① 《만류하다》 put a stop to 《*a person's doing*》; persuade *a person* 《not to *do*》; dissuade 《*a person*》 from *do*ing. ¶ 말리는 것도 듣지 않고 in defiance 〔spite〕 of 《*a person's*》 warnings / 싸움을 ~ stop a quarrel / 사표 내려는 것을 ~ dissuade 《*a person*》 from tendering *his* resignation. ② 《금지하다》 prohibit 《*a person*》 from 《*do*ing》; forbid 《*a person* to *do*》; prevent. ¶ 나무를 베지 못하게 ~ prohibit 《people》 from cutting the forest trees.

**말리다**[2] ① 《건조시키다》 dry (up); air 《clothes, mats》 (바람에); make 〔let〕 dry; desiccate 《milk, soup》; 《초목을》 blight (시들게 하다); 《재목을》 season (건조시키다). ¶ 말린 물고기 dried fish / 젖은 옷을 널어 ~ hang wet clothes (out) to dry / 빨래를 햇볕에 ~ dry the washing in the sun / 양말을 스토브에 ~ dry socks over a stove / 재목은 공기에 노출시켜 말린다 Timber is seasoned by exposure to the air. ② 《물을 빼다》 drain off 〔away〕; draw off water. ¶ 연못의 물을 ~ drain a pond dry; pump a pond dry.

**말리다**[3] 《둘둘》 be rolled 〔curled〕 (up). ¶ 치맛자락이 ~ the end of a skirt is rolled.

**말마디** a phrase; a clause; a bit 〔piece〕 of speech 〔talk〕; 《꾸지람》 a rebuke; a scolding. ¶ ~나 듣다 get a good scolding / 그 사람 ~깨나 할 줄 안다 He is quite a good speaker. / 그처럼 늦게 귀가하면 어머니한테 ~깨나 듣겠군 You will catch it from your mother if you come home so late at night.

**말막음** ~하다 hush up; shut 《*a person*》 up; get avoid 〔forestall〕 《*a person's*》 words; muzzle 《*a person*》. ¶ ~으로 10만원을 지불하다 pay 〔give〕 《*a person*》 a hundred thousand won for hush money / 꾸중을 듣지 않게 ~이나 해야겠다 I have to figure out some way to get around a scolding.

**말머리** the beginning of *one's* speech 〔talk〕; *one's* first few words; the subject of *one's* speech. ¶ ~를 돌리다 change the subject of *one's* speech; shift the topic of conversation.

**말먹이** fodder; hay; forage. ⇨ 말꼴.

**말몰이꾼** a pack-horse driver.

**말문**(一門) ¶ ~을 열다 break the silence; open the conversation / ~이 막히다 be struck dumb; be dumfounded; be at a loss for words / 존은 낸시에게 데이트를 신청하고 싶었지만 ~이 막혀 아무 말도 못했다 John wanted to ask Nancy for a date, but he was tongue-tied.

**말미** time (to spare); leave (of absence); furlough. ¶ ~를 주다 give 〔grant〕 leave (of absence) / ~를 얻다 get 〔be granted〕 a leave of absence / ~를 얻어 고향에 돌아가다 go home on furlough / 하루 ~를 주셨으면 좋겠습니다 I should like to get a day's leave.

**말미**(末尾) the close; the end. ¶ 보고서의 ~에 at the end of the report / 편지 ~에 인삿말을 덧붙이다 add a word of thanks at the end of the letter.

**말미암다** 《유래》 come 〔arise〕 from; be derived 《from》; 《원인》 be due to; be caused by. ¶ 말미암아 owing to; because of; on account of; due to / 부주의로 말미암은 사고 an accident due to carelessness / 비로 말미암아 오지 못하였다 I couldn't come because of the rain.

**말미잘** 〖동물〗 a sea anemone; a sea-flower.

**말발굽** a horse's hoof. ⇨ 말굽.

**말방울** a horse bell.

**말버릇** 《말하는 방식》 *one's* manner of speaking; *one's* way 〔habit〕 of talking; 《늘 하는 말》 *one's* favorite phrase; *one's* pet saying. ¶ ~이 고약하다 be rude in speech; be violent-tongued / ~이 거칠다 be rough in speech / 「바로 그거야」라는 것이 그의 ~이다 "Quite so" is a pet phrase of his.

**말버짐** 〖한의〗 ringworm; fungus.

**말벌** 〖곤충〗 a wasp; a (yellow) hornet.

**말벗** a companion to chat with; someone to talk to 〔with〕. ¶ ~이 되다 keep 《*a person*》 company / ~이 없어 따분하다 be bored with nobody to talk to / ~이 있었으면 좋겠다 I want to have someone to talk with.

**말보** talkativeness from a usually taciturn person. ¶ ~가 터지다 begin to talk freely; break the ice.

**말복**(末伏) the third of the three periods of summer doldrums; the last of the dog days.

**말본** grammar. ⇨ 문법(文法).

**말사**(末寺) 〖불교〗 a branch temple.

**말산**(一酸) 〖화학〗 malic acid.

**말살**(抹殺) 《삭제·말소》 erasure; obliteration; cancel; 《숙청·살해》 purge; liquidation. ~하다 《삭제하다》 rub 〔blot〕 out; cross out; strike off; erase; efface; obliterate; 《숙청·살해하다》 purge; liquidate; get rid of; kill. ¶ 기록에서 이름을 ~하다 cross 〔strike〕 a name off the 《criminal》 list; erase a name from the 《criminal》 list / 정적을

~하려는 그들의 기도는 실패했다 Their plot to liquidate their political rivals failed.

**말상**(一相) 《얼굴》 a long face; 《사람》 a person with a long face. ¶~이다 be long-〔horse-〕faced.

**말상대**(一相對) a companion; someone to talk to; a conversational partner. ¶ 그녀는 나의 할머님의 좋은 ~다 She makes a good companion for my grandmother.

**말석**(末席) 《끝자리》 the lowest seat 〔place〕; the seat furthest from the seat of honor; 《낮은 지위》 the lowest 〔bottom〕 rank. ¶~에 앉다 sit at the foot of the table / 클럽에서 나는 항상 ~이다 I'm always at the bottom of the club. / ~을 더럽히다 《겸양의 말》 be humbly present 《at》; have the honor of being a member 《of》.

**말세**(末世) a 〔this〕 degenerate 〔corrupt〕 age; the end of the world. ¶이 쯤되면 세상도 ~다 The world is going to the dogs. *or* This reminds us of the age of decadence we live in. / 법관이 죄를 범한다면 ~지 If a judge commits a crime, it's the end of the world.

**말소**(抹消) erasure; effacement. ~하다 erase; efface; strike 〔cross〕 out. ¶ 등기의 ~ cancelation of registration / 형(刑)의 기록을 ~하다 erase the penalty from the records / 우리는 명부에서 그의 이름을 ~했다 We struck 〔crossed〕 out his name from the list.

**말소리** a voice. ¶~를 낮추어 in whispers; under *one's* breath / ~가 높다 have a loud voice; talk in a loud voice / 이웃집에서 ~가 들려 온다 The voices of people next door can be heard. / 창밖에서 그의 ~가 들렸다 I heard him talking outside the window.

**말속** the meaning 〔implication〕 of *one's* words; what is behind *one's* words.

**말속**(末俗) customs of a degenerate age; degenerate customs.

**말솜씨** *one's* ability to speak 〔talk〕; eloquence. ¶~가 좋다 be good at speaking 〔talking〕; be eloquent; have a fluent tongue / ~가 없다 be poor at speaking 〔talking〕; be a poor speaker.

**말수**(一數) ¶~가 적은 사람 a man of few words; a silent man / ~가 적다 be silent; be taciturn 〔reticent〕 / ~가 많다 be talkative 〔loquacious〕; talk 〔be given to talking〕 too much / 그는 ~가 많다 He is a chatterbox 〔talkative man〕.

**말승냥이** 《늑대》 a wolf; 《키가 큰 사람》 a tall person.

**말실수**(一失手) a slip of the tongue; a verbal lapse; an impropriety in speech. ¶~를 하다 make a slip of the tongue; *one's* tongue slips; commit an impropriety in speech; use improper language 〔words〕 / ~를 사과하다 apologize for an inadvertent remark / 아무래도 내가 ~를 한 것 같다 I seem to have made a slip of the tongue about it.

**말썽** trouble(s); difficulties; 《논쟁》 a quarrel; a dispute. ¶~을 부리다 accuse 《*a person*》 deliberately 〔falsely〕; make a deliberate 〔false〕 charge 《against》/ ~을 일으키다 cause trouble; lead to a dispute / 저 집은 ~이 끊이지 않는다 They have constant domestic trouble. / 이 일로 ~이 생길지도 모른다 Difficulties may arise out of this affair.

◉ ~거리 a cause 〔source〕 of trouble; a matter for complaint: ~거리가 되다 become 「a source of trouble 〔a matter for complaint〕 / 우리 집의 ~거리는 저 작은 놈이다 The younger boy is the one who is always causing us trouble. ~꾸러기〔꾼〕 a troublemaker; a grumbler.

**말쑥이** neatly; tidily; nicely; smartly. ¶옷을 ~ 차려입다 dress *oneself* up smartly / 방을 ~ 치우다 tidy *one's* room up neatly.

**말쑥하다** (be) clean; neat; smart; nice. ¶ 말쑥한 방 a clean room / 말쑥한 얼굴 nice features / 말쑥한 집 a nice house / 그녀는 언제나 옷차림이 ~ She is always neatly dressed.

**말씀** words; speech; talk; saying. ~하다 speak; talk; say; tell. ¶ 선생님의 ~ what *one's* teacher says / ~하시는 중 실례입니다만 Excuse my 〔me for〕 interrupting you, but... / ~을 통 이해할 수 없습니다 I find no sense in what you say. / 잠시 드릴 ~이 있는데요 May I have a word with you? / 빨리 ~하세요 Tell me quick. / 먼저 ~하십시오 You speak first, please. / 다시 한번 ~해 주십시오 Please say that again. *or* Will you repeat? *or* I beg your pardon. (★ 이 경우는 끝을 올림조로 함. 내림조로 하면 「용서하십시오」, 「실례했습

니다」가 됨.) / 외람된 ～이지만, 저는 찬성할 수 없습니다 I'm afraid you will think me impertinent to say so, but I can't agree with you.

**말씨** *one's* choice of words; *one's* way of speaking; wording; speech; language; an accent (억양). ¶ 점잖은 ～ refined speech 〔diction〕 / 난폭한 ～ rude language / 순 함경도 ～ a broad Hamgyeong-do accent / ～가 공손한〔거친〕 사람 a civil-〔rough-〕spoken person / ～를 조심하다 be careful in *one's* 「speech 〔choice of words〕; watch *one's* language / ～가 얌전하다 be polite 〔refined〕 in speech / ～가 상스럽다 be rough of speech / ～가 투박하다 be crude in speech / 사람의 성격은 그 ～로 알 수 있다 You will be judged by your speech.

**말아니다** ①《당찮다》 don't make sense; (be) nonsense; absurd; unreasonable. ¶ 그건 말도 아니다 That's nonsense. / 이제 와서 돈을 갚지 못하겠다는 것은 말이 아니다 After all this time, it is unreasonable of you to say you can't return the money. ②《형편없다》 (be) miserable; wretched; [서술적] be in very bad shape 〔condition〕. ¶ 말 아닌 생활 a miserable life / 생활이 ～ lead a miserable 〔wretched〕 life / 형편이 ～ be in a piteous plight / 체면이 ～ utterly lose *one's* face 〔prestige〕 / 그 사람 요즘 건강이 ～ He is in 「pretty bad shape 〔very poor health〕 these days.

**말안되다** (be) absurd; unreasonable; nonsense. ¶ 말(도) 안 되는 소리 마라 Don't be absurd. / 제 자식을 버리다니 말(도) 안 되는 소리다 It is outrageous to desert *one's* own child.

**말야** I mean; you-know; you-see; uh; that is. ¶ 돈을 십만 원이나 잃었단 ～ You see I lost one hundred thousand won or so. / 그렇게 해선 안 된단 ～ You shouldn't do as you are doing. / 그 사람은 ～ 그다지 믿지 못할 사람이야 He is—uh—none too reliable a person. 「majority.

**말없다** silent. ¶ 말없는 대중 the silent

**말없이** 《묵묵히》 without saying anything; in silence; silently; without a word; without notice (통고 없이). ¶ ～ 앉아 있다 be sitting in silence / 아무 ～ 결근하다 absent *oneself* 《from office》 without notice / 그에게 돈을 빌려 달라니까 ～ 빌려 주었다 He lent me the money without a word when I asked him. / 그는 다른 사람들의 입방아를 개의치 않고 ～ 연구에 몰두했다 He devoted himself to his research regardless of other people's tittle-tattle.

**말엽**(末葉) the close (of an age); the end. ¶ 20세기 ～에 toward the close of the 20th century. 「elderberry.

**말오줌나무** 〖식물〗 an elder (tree); an

**말일**(末日) the last day; the end 《of May》. ¶ ～에 on the last day / 신청 마감은 이달 ～까지입니다 The deadline for the application is the end of this month.

**말장난** a play upon words; a word-play; a pun. ～하다 play upon words.

**말재간**(一才幹) ＝말재주.

**말재주** (a) talent for speaking; the gift of the gab; eloquence (능변). ¶ ～가 있다 have the gift of the gab; be good 〔clever〕 at speaking; be gifted with eloquence; have a talent for speaking / ～가 없다 be awkward in speaking; be poor at speaking.

**말전주** 《이간질》 talebearing; mischief-making; setting people at variance. ～하다 tell tales; make mischief. ◉ ～꾼 a mischief-maker.

**말조심**(一操心) care in speaking. ～하다 be careful of *one's* speech; watch *one's* tongue.

**말주변** talking ability; the gift of the gab. ¶ ～이 있는 glib-tongued / ～이 좋다 have a ready tongue; have the gift of the gab / ～이 없다 be awkward in expressing *oneself;* be clumsy in the use of language; be a poor talker.

**말죽**(一粥) boiled horse-feed. ◉ ～통(桶) a horse-feed 〔forage〕 tub.

**말즘** 〖식물〗 a curly pondweed; a water-caltrop.

**말직**(末職) a petty office; a small post; the lowest position.

**말질** ①《남의 말》 taletelling; gossiping; criticism. ～하다 tell tales (about others); gossip. ¶ ～ 잘하는 사람 a telltale; a gossip(monger); a busybody. ②《말다툼》 a quarrel; a dispute. ～하다 quarrel 《with *a person*》; dispute.

**말짜**(末一) 《물건》 things of the lowest quality; the worst stuff; 《사람》 an ill-mannered fellow; a low fellow.

**말짱하다** ①《온전하다》 (be) whole; complete; intact; 《흠 없다》 flawless; spotless; perfect; be free from damage 〔blemish〕; 《깨끗하다》 tidy; clean.

¶ 말짱한 옷 spotless 〔clean〕 clothes / 말짱한 그릇 a dish in perfect condition / 사지가 말짱한 동안은 so long as *one* can yet work; as long as *one* can move about. ② 《정신이》 (be) sane; sound; [서술적] be in *one's* senses; 《취하지 않고》 (be) dead sober; [서술적] be not drunk. ¶ 정신이 ~ have a clear mind; be sound in mind; have *one's* senses; be in *one's* right mind.

**말짱히** safely; without a flaw 〔blemish〕; in perfect shape.

**말째**(末—) the last; the bottom; the tail end. ⇨ 꼴찌.

**말참견**(—參見) interference; meddling. ~하다 put in a word; cut 〔break, butt〕 in; 「interfere in 〔meddle with〕 《another's affair》; 《구어》 put 〔shove〕 *one's* oar in; 《구어》 poke 〔thrust〕 *one's* nose. ¶ 쓸데없는 ~ 말게 None of your lips! *or* Mind your own business! / ~ 말고 너 할 일이나 해라 We can do without your remarks —mind your own business. / 남이 이야기하고 있는데 ~ 하는 것은 예의 없는 짓이다 It is rude to cut in while others are talking.

**말채찍** a horsewhip. ◉ ~질 whipping a horse: ~질하다 whip a horse.

**말초**(末梢) 《가지끝》 the tip of a twig; 《말단》 a tip; 〚해부〛 the periphery. ¶ ~적 trifling; trivial; insignificant; 〚해부〛 distal; peripheral / ~적인 일에 구애받다 stick at trifles; be meticulous. ◉ ~신경(계) a peripheral nerve (system).

**말총** horsehair.

**말치레** nice-talk; using fair 〔honeyed〕 words; making a specious remark; lip service 〔homage〕. ~하다 nice-talk; use fair 〔honeyed〕 words; make a specious remark. ¶ ~만의 찬사 an insincere compliment / ~만 번드르르한 smooth-tongued; oily; fair-spoken.

**말코** 《베틀의》 the loom roller on which finished material is rolled up; 《사람의》 a muzzle-shaped nose.

**말코지** a branched hanger 〔hook〕.

**말투**(—套) the way *one* talks; *one's* way of talking; *one's* manner of speech. ¶ 야비한 ~ a mean 〔low〕 expression / ~가 거칠다 use harsh 〔violent〕 language; be rough in *one's* speech / ~가 사납다 have a nasty way of talking / 사람의 성격은 그의 ~로 안다 You will be judged by your speech. / 그는 무엇이나 다 알고 있는 듯한 ~였다 He talked as if he knew everything. / 그는 머지 않아 사직할 듯한 ~였다 He hinted at his resignation in the near future.

**말파리** 〚곤충〛 a botfly; a horsefly.

**말판** a game board; 《윷·주사위》 a *yut* 〔dice〕 board.

**말편자** a horseshoe. ¶ ~를 박다 shoe a horse.

**말하다** ① 《이야기를》 talk; speak; converse; have a talk 〔chat〕 with. ¶ 말하기 어려운 듯이 hesitatingly; falteringly / 어린애가 말하기 시작하다 a child starts to talk / 서로 말이나 하는 사이다 be on speaking terms with each other / 더듬더듬 ~ speak in a faltering voice / 너와 말할 시간이 없다 I have no time to talk with you. / 말하기는 쉬우나 행하기는 어렵다 It is easier to preach than to practice.
② 《언급하다》 tell; say; speak of; state; mention; relate; narrate; describe; express. ¶ 말할 수 없는 unspeakable; unutterable; inexpressible / 위에 말한 바와 같이 as said 〔stated, described, shown〕 above / (무어라) 말할 수 없다 be indescribable; be unspeakable 〔inexpressible〕; be beyond expression / 아무를 좋게〔나쁘게〕 ~ speak well 〔ill〕 of *a person* / 고쳐 ~ improve *one's* expressions 〔wording〕; correct *one's* misstatement / 잠시 자네에게 말할 게 있다 I'd like to have a word with you for a minute. / 그가 겪은 어려움은 몇마디로 다 말할 수 없다 The troubles he took cannot be told in a few words. / 이 사람이 앞서 말한 그 친구다 This is the friend I was telling you about. / 남자답게 졌다고 말해라 Acknowledge your defeat with good grace! / 너에게만 말한다 This is for your ear alone. *or* This is between the two of us. / 그건 이렇게도 말할 수 있다 That could be put this way, too. / 얼굴은 그 사람의 성격을 말한다 A man's face expresses his character. / 이 사실은 그의 부지런함을 말해 주고 있다 This fact speaks for his diligence. / 염려말게, 아무에게도 말하지 않을게 Don't worry. My lips are sealed. / 어떻게 말해야 좋을지 몰랐다 I didn't know how to put it. *or* I had no words for it. / 내일 일은 뭐라고 말할 수 없다 There is no saying 〔telling〕 what may happen tomorrow.
③ 《부탁하다》 ask; beg; wish; hope. ¶ 말하기 거북한 hard to ask / 그에게 말하면 무엇이나 들어준다 He is a very

obliging 〔accommodating〕 man. / 돈 꾸어 달라고 말하기 거북했다 I found it rather awkward to ask for money.
④《불평·꾸지람 따위를》 bring 《*a matter*》 to 《*a person's*》 attention; advise; complain; protest; scold. ¶ 불평을 ～ complain; voice *one's* discontent / 말하고 싶은 것을 참다 bite *one's* tongue / 그 애가 말을 듣지 않으니 한번 단단히 나무라시오 I want you to give the boy a sound scolding, he is so disobedient. / 암만 말해도 그는 들으려 하지 않는다 Give him all the advice in the world, he won't listen.
⑤《상의하다》 consult 《*a person*》; discuss 《*a thing*》 《with》. ¶ 선생님께 말씀 드려봤느냐 Did you talk to 〔consult〕 your teacher about it? *or* Did you discuss it with your teacher?
⑥《어떤 언어를》 speak. ¶ 어설픈 불어로 ～ speak in broken French / 영어를 유창히 ～ speak English fluently; be a fluent speaker of English.

**말하자면** ①《따져 말하면》 if we are to speak about it at all; when you get right down to it; if we must say; if you ask me; to put it in plain 〔blunt〕 terms. ¶ ～ 네가 잘못이다 If you ask me, it's you who are to blame. / 그것은 ～ 사기지 무엇이냐 To put it in plain terms, that is pure swindling and nothing else. ②《이를테면》 so to speak; as it were; in other words; we might say; as much as to say; or rather; in a sense. ¶ 이순신 장군은 ～ 한국의 넬슨이다 Admiral Yi Sunshin is, so to speak, the Nelson of Korea.

**말할 것도 없다** ¶ …은 ～ it is needless to say that…; it need scarcely 〔hardly〕 be said that…; it goes without saying that 《money cannot buy happiness》/ …은 말할 것도 없고 not to mention 〔speak of〕; to say nothing of; let alone / 말할 것도 없이 그는 약속을 지켰다 「Needless to say 〔Of course〕, he kept his promise. / 그녀는 영어는 말할 것도 없고 일어와 중국어도 말한다 She can speak Japanese and Chinese, to say nothing of English.

**말향**(抹香) incense (powder).

**맑다** ①《흐리지 않다》 (***a***)《물·공기·소리·사물 등이》 (be) clear; clean; limpid; pure; fresh (신선한). ¶ 맑고 푸른 하늘 the clear blue sky / 맑은 국물 clear soup / 맑은 눈 clear eyes / 맑은 목소리〔음색〕 a clear voice 〔note〕 / 바위 틈을 흐르는 맑은 시냇물 a small clean stream among the rocks / 맑은 수정 pure crystal / 맑은 공기를 마시다 breathe 〔have〕 fresh air / 맑아지다 (become) clear 〔clean〕 / 맑게 하다 clear 《the water》; make clear / 종소리가 맑게 울린다 The bell rings loud and clear. / 물이 맑으면 고기가 아니 산다《속담》 Clear water does not breed fish. *or* Strict integrity leaves *one* isolated. (***b***)《날씨가》 (be) fine; clear; fair. ¶ 맑은 날씨 fine 〔fair〕 weather / 맑은 하늘 a clear sky / 맑은 아침 a fine 〔beautiful〕 morning / 《날씨가》 맑아지다 clear (up); become clear.
②《처세·생활·환경 등이》 (be) clean; honest; innocent; clear; pure; 《청빈하다》 (be) poor (but honest). ¶ 맑은 사람 a man of integrity / 맑은 생애 a career with a clean record / 맑은 생활 a pure 〔an honest〕 life / 양심이 ～ have a clear conscience / 직장이 ～ there is no extra benefits out of *one's* position.
③《정신·기분 등이》 (be) clear; pure; fresh; refreshing. ¶ 맑은 마음 a lucid mind; a pure heart / 맑은 정신 a clear 〔fresh〕 mind; a good memory / 기분이 맑아지다 feel refreshed; feel purified / 기분이 맑지 않다 feel depressed 〔down〕.

**맑디맑다** (be) very clear; be as clear as can be 〔as crystal〕.

**맑스그레하다** (be) somewhat 〔rather〕 clear.

**맑은소리** a voiceless sound.

**맑은술** refined rice wine.

**맑은장국**(—醬—) clear meat soup; bouillon.

**맘마** 《소아어》 food; rice.

**맘보** 『음악』 a mambo. ¶ ～를 추다 mambo. ◉ ～바지 drainpipe trousers.

**맙소사** Oh, no!; Good God!; Good gracious 〔heavens〕!

**맛**[1] ①《음식의》 (a) taste; (a) flavor; (a) savor (풍미). ⇨ 맛보다. ¶ 매운 맛 a hot 〔biting, spicy〕 taste / 신맛 a sour taste / 맛이 있다〔좋다〕 be tasty 〔savory〕; taste good 〔nice〕; have a good flavor; be delicious / 맛이 없다〔나쁘다〕 be untasty; taste bad 〔flat〕; be unsavory; be unpalatable; be flavorless 〔insipid, jejune〕 / 맛을 내다 season 《food with salt and pepper》 (양념 등으로); flavor 《food with onions》 (풍미를) / 맛을 알다 (be able to) appreciate 《delicacies》 / …맛이 나다 taste 〔savor〕 of 《orange》 / 맛이 변하다 become stale; 《시어지다》 turn

sour / 맛이 어떻습니까 How does it taste? *or* What does it taste like? / 무엇이고 먹어 봐야 그 맛을 알 수 있다 The proof of the pudding is in the eating.
② 《사물에서 느끼는》 relish; taste; interest; pleasure; delight(s). ¶ 돈 맛 a taste for money / 여자 맛 an interest in women / 시의 맛 the pleasures 〔delights〕 of poetry / (…에) 맛을 들이다 get 〔acquire〕 a taste for; take a liking for 〔to〕 / 글 맛을 알다 「have a relish for 〔appreciate〕 literature.
③ 《경험》 experience; the taste 《of》. ¶ 맛보다 experience; go through / 인생의 쓴맛을 보다 taste the bitterness of life; go through the hardship of life / 쓴맛 단맛 다 알다 know 〔have tasted〕 the bitters and sweets of life; have been through the mill / 성공의 맛을 알다 taste the benefits of success; know what it is like to succeed / 그는 가난의 맛을 아직 모른다 He doesn't know the taste of poverty yet.
④ 《혼쭐내다》 ¶ 맛을 보여주다 teach 《*a person*》 a lesson; make 《*a person*》 smart 〔sweat〕 《for it》.
⑤ 《기타》 ¶ 하필 오늘 가야 맛이냐 Why do you have to choose to go today necessarily?

**맛**[2] 〖조개류〗 a razor clam.

**맛김** seasoned laver.

**맛깔스럽다** ① 《맛이》 (be) tasty; palatable; agreeable. ¶ 맛깔스러운 음식 an agreeable food. ② 《마음에》 be to *one's* taste; be after *one's* fancy; (be) satisfactory; acceptable.

**맛나다** 《맛있다》 (be) tasty; delicious; savory; 《맛이 돌다》 taste good 〔nice〕; have a good flavor. ¶ 맛난 음식 tasty 〔delicious〕 food.

**맛난이** ① 《조미료》 sauce; flavoring; seasoning; something to bring out the flavor. ② 《음식》 delicious food.

**맛들다** pick up flavor; become good to eat 〔drink〕; become tasty; grow ripe; ripen. ¶ 술이 맛들었다 The wine is properly aged.

**맛들이다** ① 《음식을》 season 〔flavor〕 with; give a flavor to; make 《*something*》 ripe 〔mature〕 enough to eat 〔drink〕. ¶ 김치를 ~ get the kimchi well pickled / 술을 ~ make wine mature; age wine. ② 《재미를》 get 〔acquire, develop〕 a taste 《for》; take a liking 《for, to》. ¶ …에 맛을 들여 encouraged 〔emboldened〕 by 《*one's* first success》 / 돈에 ~ get a taste for money / 도박에 ~ take to gambling / 주색에 한번 맛들이면 좀처럼 헤어나지 못한다 Once you pick up a taste for wine and women, you will find it very hard to give up. / 여우가 한번 닭에 맛들이면 꼭 다시 찾아온다 If foxes once taste a chicken, they will never fail to come back again.

**맛맛으로** according to *one's* pleasure 〔taste, desire〕. ¶ ~ 골라 먹어라 Help yourself according to your taste.

**맛보다** ① 《시식하다》 taste; try 〔have〕 a taste of; sample. ¶ 음식을 ~ taste the food / 술을 ~ sample 〔try the flavor of〕 the wine / 간을 ~ taste 《*something*》 to see if it needs any

> **참고** 음식물의 맛을 나타내는 영어 표현
>
> 1. 달다 (be) sweet; sugary; have a sweet taste: 단맛이 나는 간장 (sweet=and-)mild soy sauce / 단맛이 나는 와인 sweet wine / 달콤새콤하다 be 〔taste〕 sweet and sour / 달콤매콤하다 be 〔taste〕 sweetly 「tangy 〔pepperish, hot〕 / 달콤한 냄새가 나다 smell sweet; be fragrant.
> 2. 쓰다 (be) bitter; have a bitter taste: 쓴 약 a bitter medicine / 맥주의 씁쓸한 맛 the slight bitterness of beer / 약간 쓴 맛이 나다 be 〔taste〕 slightly bitter / 달콤씁쓸하다 be bittersweet / 블랙 커피는 내게 너무 쓰다 Black coffee is too bitter for me.
> 3. 시다 (be) sour; acid; tart; have a sour 〔acid〕 taste: 신 포도 a sour grape / 신 사과 a tart apple / 신 레몬 an acid lemon / 시큼하다 be 〔taste〕 rather acid.
> 4. 맵다 (be) hot; pungent; spicy; have a hot 〔tangy, pepperish, pungent〕 taste: 매운 김치 hot kimchi / 톡 쏘는 매콤한 소스 a rich and pungent sauce / 이 카레는 내겐 너무 맵다 This curry is too hot for me.
> 5. 짜다 (be) salty; salted; have a salty taste: 짠 음식 salty food.
> 6. 떫다 (be) astringent: 떫은 감 an astrigent persimmon / 떫은 와인 rough 〔harsh〕 wine.
> 7. 기타: 부드럽다 (be) smooth; mild; mellow / 담백하다 (be) plain; simple / 느끼하다 (be) heavy / 느끼한 요리는 위에 부담을 준다 Heavy food is not easily digested.

salt. ② 《겪다》 experience; learn; taste. ¶ 가난을 ~ taste 〔experience〕 poverty; learn when it is to be poor / 인생의 쓰라림을 ~ go through life's hardships.

**맛부리다** 《싱겁게 굴다》 behave insipidly.

**맛살** 《조개의》 the meat inside a razor clam.

**맛없다** ① 《음식이》 (be) untasty; unpalatable; tasteless; flavorless; insipid; [동사적] taste bad 〔flat〕. ¶ 맛없는 음식 tasteless food; a flat food / 맛없는 과일 fruit flat to taste. ② 《재미·흥미가》 (be) uninteresting; dull; dry; flat; insipid. ¶ 맛없이 살아가다 lead a dull life.

**맛있다** ① 《음식이》 (be) tasty; delicious; good 《to eat》; palatable. ¶ 맛있는 음식 tasty food / 맛있게 먹다 eat with gusto 〔relish〕. ② 《재미가》 (be) interesting; delightful; fun.

**맛장수** an insipid 〔a prosaic〕 person.

**맛젓** pickled razor clams.

**망**(望) ① 《동정을 살핌》 watch; lookout; guard; observation; vigilance. ¶ 망보는 사람 a watchman; a guard; a lookout; a keeper / 망을 보다〔서다〕 watch; keep a watch 〔lookout〕; stand guard; look out for; be on the lookout / 망을 세우다 set a watch; place a guard; keep guard. ② 《만월》 a full moon. ③ 《보름》 the 15th day of the lunar month.

**망**(網) ① 《그물》 a net; [총칭] netting. ¶ 머리망 a hairnet / 철조망 barbed-wire entanglements / 망을 뜨다 make 〔weave〕 a net; net / 망에 걸리다 be caught in a net / 망을 치다 stretch 〔lay, set〕 a net. ② 《조직》 a network. ¶ 수사망을 펴다 spread 〔put〕 a dragnet. ◉ 방송망 a radio network. 철도〔통신〕망 a railway 〔communication〕 network.

**망가뜨리다** ① 《파괴하다》 break; destroy; demolish; smash; damage; ruin; wreck. ② 《건강·기계 따위를》 ruin 《*one's* health》; put 《a machine》 out of order. ¶ 그는 과로로 몸을 망가뜨렸다 His health failed owing to overwork. ③ 《계획 따위를》 spoil; upset; frustrate; mar. ¶ 그의 조심성 없는 말이 혼담을 망가뜨렸다 His careless remark spoiled the plans for marriage.

**망각**(忘却) lapse of memory; forgetfulness; oblivion. ~하다 forget; be forgetful 〔oblivious〕 of. ¶ ~의 늪으로 빠지다 sink 〔fall, pass〕 into oblivion / 의무를 ~하다 neglect *one's* duties; be unmindful of *one's* duties / 격분한 나머지 자기 자신을 ~하다 forget *oneself* in a fit of passion.

**망간** 〖화학〗 manganese (기호 Mn). ¶ ~의 manganic. ◉ ~강(鋼) manganese steel. ~산 manganic acid. ~철 ferromanganese.

**망거**(妄擧) a reckless 〔foolhardy, rash〕 act; an ill-advised attempt.

**망건**(網巾) a *mang-gŏn;* a horsehair-woven headband. ◉ ~골 a *mang-gŏn* mold 〔block〕. ~당 the top of a *mang-gŏn:* ~당줄 *mang-gŏn* strings. ~장이 a *mang-gŏn* maker 〔weaver〕.

**망계**(妄計) a foolhardy 〔rash〕 plan; a reckless scheme; an ill-advised project.

**망고** 〖식물〗 a mango (*pl.* ~es, ~s).

**망국**(亡國) the ruin of *one's* country; national ruin 〔decay〕. ¶ ~적인 《politics》 ruinous to *one's* country / ~지본(之本) the cause of national ruin / ~지탄(之歎) lamentation 〔grief〕 over the national ruin. ◉ ~민족 a ruined people; a homeless race.

**망그러뜨리다** put out of shape; ruin; spoil; break; destroy. ¶ 모자를 밟아 ~ ruin a hat by stepping on it / 장난감을 ~ break a toy / 책상을 ~ destroy a table. ⇨망가뜨리다.

**망그러지다** be put out of shape; be ruined; be spoilt; be destroyed; be broken. ¶ 망그러진 차 a disabled car / 모자가 ~ a hat is ruined 〔is crushed out of shape〕 / 장난감이 ~ a toy gets broken / 책상이 ~ a table is destroyed / 망그러지지 않도록 다루다 handle 《an article》 with care.

**망극**(罔極) ① 《은혜가》 being immeasurable 〔extreme, infinite〕. ¶ ~한 은혜 a great favor 〔love〕 《of *one's* parents》 / 성은이 ~하옵니다 Inscrutable are the king's favors. ② 《슬픔이》 the greatest grief beyond expression 《at the death of the king or *one's* parents》. ¶ 얼마나 ~하십니까 Please let me offer my condolence to you on this sad event. ◉ ~지통(之痛) great grief 〔lamentation〕.

**망나니** ① 《참수인》 an executioner; a head cutter. ② 《못된 사람》 a wretch; a rogue; a rake; a villain; a scoundrel; a rowdy; a public nuisance. ¶ 에이 ~ 자식 You damn rascal!

**망녀**(亡女) ① 《딸》 *one's* late 〔deceased〕

daughter. ② 《망골 계집》 an illmannered woman; a bad woman.

**망년회**(忘年會) a year-end (dinner) party. ¶ ~를 열다 hold a year-end party; give a party to see the year out.

**망념**(妄念) ⇨ 망상(妄想).

**망녕그물** a net for catching rabbits or pheasants; a fowling net.

**망대**(望臺) a watchtower. =망루(望樓).

**망동**(妄動) a rash act; imprudent action. ~하다 act imprudently 〔rashly〕. ⇨ 경거(망동).

**망둥이** 〖어류〗 a goby. ¶ ~ 제 동무 잡아먹는다 work harm to *one's* own fellows.

**망라**(網羅) ~하다 《포함하다》 include 〔comprehend, contain〕 everything; cover all 《the facts》; 《모으다》 collect all 《the items》; bring together. ¶ 모든 문제점을 ~하다 covers all the questions / 이 사전은 한국어의 구어적 표현들을 ~하고 있다 This dictionary contains all Korean colloquialisms. / 그 모임엔 사회 각층의 인사가 ~되어 있다 Every class of society is represented at the meeting.

**망령**(亡靈) a departed spirit 〔soul〕.

**망령**(妄靈) dotage; senility; *one's* second childhood; 《병적인》 senile dementia 〔psychosis〕. ~되다〔스럽다〕 (be) absurd; unreasonable. ~들다 be in *one's* dotage 〔in *one's* second childhood〕; grow 〔become〕 senile; grow mentally weak. ~부리다 《노인이》 behave like a child; behave unreasonably 〔foolishly〕. ¶ ~된 말 an absurd remark / ~든 노인 an old man in his dotage; a dotard.

**망론**(妄論) a foolish opinion; an absurd view; ridiculous talk; balderdash.

**망루**(望樓) a lookout; a watchtower; an observation tower.

**망막**(網膜) 〖해부〗 the retina (*pl.* ~s, -nae). ◉ ~검시경 a retinoscope; a skiascope. ~검시법 retinoscopy; skiascopy. ~박리(剝離) 《have 〔suffer from〕》 detachment of the retina. ~염(炎) 〖의학〗 retinitis. ~화상(火傷) a retinal burn.

**망망**(茫茫) ~하다 (be) vast; boundless; extensive. ¶ 망망한 바다 a boundless 〔an immense〕 expanse of water.

**망명**(亡命) 《국외 추방》 exile; 《적국으로의 도망》 defection. ~하다 flee from 〔defect from〕 *one's* own country for political reasons (★ defect나 defector (망명자)는 seek refuge, refugee 등과는 달리, 국가 기밀을 쥐고 있는 사람이 망명하여, 그 기밀을 적국에 팔아 넘긴다는 뉘앙스가 있음); seek refuge in a foreign country; exile *oneself*. ¶ 미국으로 ~하다 seek 〔take〕 refuge in the United States / ~ 생활을 하다 live in exile / 정치적 ~을 하다 take 〔seek〕 political asylum 《in France》 / 정치적 ~을 요청하다 ask for political asylum 《in a third country》. ◉ ~객 a political exile. ~자 a fugitive; an exile; a refugee; a defector. ~정권 an exiled regime. ~정부 a government in exile. ~죄인 a fugitive from the law.

**망발**(妄發) a reckless remark; thoughtless words; an unreasonable 〔absurd〕 speech. ~하다 make an absurd remark; make a blunder. ◉ ~풀이 a treat given to make up for *one's* reckless remarks.

**망부**(亡父) *one's* late 〔deceased〕 father.

**망부**(亡夫) *one's* late 〔deceased〕 husband.

**망부석**(望夫石) the legendary stone on which a faithful wife stood waiting for her husband until she perished.

**망사**(網紗) gauze.

**망상**(妄想) a wild 〔vagrant〕 fancy; a fantasy; a fantastic idea; wanton thoughts; a delusion. ¶ ~에 빠지다 be lost in wild fancies; spin a daydream; give *oneself* over to wild fancies / ~을 품다 nurse delusions; hold delusions in the mind / ~에 사로잡히다 be obsessed by delusions / ~에 시달리다 suffer from delusions. ◉ ~증〔광〕 〖의학〗 paranoia.

**망상**(網狀) net shape; reticulation. ¶ ~의 reticulate; reticulated; net-shaped / ~을 이루다 reticulate. ◉ ~막 the reticulum (*pl.* -la). ~맥(脈) 〖식물〗 netted 〔reticulate〕 venation. ~섬유 〖식물〗 a reticulum. ~조직 〖해부〗 a retiform tissue; a reticulum.

**망상스럽다** ① 《경솔하다》 (be) frivolous; flippant. ② 《요망스럽다》 (be) wicked; tricky; sly.

**망새** 〖건축〗 a decorative ridge-end tile.

**망석중이** ① 《꼭두각시》 a puppet; a marionette. ② 《사람》 a puppet (for another).

**망설망설** hesitatingly; waveringly. ~하다 shilly-shally; dilly-dally. ¶ ~ 결정을 짓지 못하다 hover in indecision; hang back from making a decision.

**망설이다** hesitate; waver; vacillate;

hover; scruple; be shilly-shally; be irresolute; flinch 〔shrink〕《from》. ¶ 망설이지 않고 without hesitation 〔wavering〕; resolutely / 갈까 말까 ~ can't make up *one's* mind whether to go or not / 확실한 답변을 ~ hesitate to give a definite answer.

**망성어**(望星魚) 『어류』 a surffish.

**망쇄**(忙殺) busyness. ~하다 (be) terribly busy; busily occupied.

**망신**(亡身) loss of reputation; losing face; dishonor; disgrace; humiliation. ~하다 lose face 〔*one's* reputation〕; disgrace *oneself;* humiliate *oneslf;* be mortified. ~스럽다 (be) humiliating; disgraceful. ¶ ~을 당하다 disgrace *oneself* in public; be put to shame / 집안 ~을 외부에 드러내다 wash *one's* dirty linen in public / ~시키다 disgrace; humiliate; mortify; bring into dishonor; put 《*a person*》 out of countenance / 집안 ~ 시키다 bring shame 〔digrace〕 on *one's* family. ◉ ~살(煞) ill luck to bring disgrace.

**망신**(妄信) blind belief; credulity. ~하다 believe blindly; be credulous.

**망실**(亡失) loss. ~하다 loss; miss.

**망아지** a pony; a foal; a colt (수컷); a filly (암컷).

**망양지탄**(望洋之歎) lamenting *one's* inablility (to cope with a situation); a feeling of 「hopelessness 〔total incapacity〕. ¶ ~이 있다 feel *one's* object to be unattainable; lament *one's* incapacity.

**망언**(妄言) an absurd remark; foolish talk; a blunder. ~하다 make an absurd remark; talk foolishly; make a blunder. ¶ ~다사(多謝) 《편지 등에서》 Please forgive me for expressing my opinion so boldly.

**망연자실**(茫然自失) abstraction; stupefaction; entrancement. ~하다 [서술적] be distract; be stupefied 〔stunned〕 《at, by》; be at a loss; be at *one's* wits' end. ¶ 그녀는 그 소식을 듣자, ~하여 그 자리에 서 있었다 On hearing the news, she stood there 「in dumb surprise 〔vacantly〕.

**망연하다**(茫然—) ① ＝아득하다. ② 《멍하다》 (be) vacant; blank; abstracted; [서술적] be in a daze. ¶ 망연히 vacantly; blankly; abstractedly; absentmindedly; in a daze / 망연한 나머지 어찌할 바를 모르다 be quite at a loss what to do.

**망외**(望外) beyond *one's* expectation 〔hope〕. ¶ ~의 unexpected; unforeseen / ~의 성공 an unlooked-for success.

**망운**(亡運) evil luck which will bring ruin. ¶ ~이 들다 *one's* star is on the wane.

**망울** ① 《덩어리》 a lump; a ball; a bulb; a kernel; a stone. ¶ 젖~ lumps around teats 〔nipples〕 / ~지다 get lumpy; have lumps; form a ball 〔lump〕. ② 《꽃의》 a bud; a flower bud. ③ 《림프선의》 an inflammation 〔a swelling〕 of a lymphatic gland; lymphadenitis. ¶ ~ 서다 have lymphadenitis; have a swollen lymphatic gland.

**망원가늠자**(望遠—) a telescopic sight. ¶ ~가 달린 소총 a telescopic rifle.

**망원경**(望遠鏡) a telescope; 《쌍안경》 a binocular; field glasses. ¶ ~으로 보다 look at 《a star》 through a telescope / ~을 눈에 맞추다 adjust a telescope to *one's* eye / ~을 들여다보다 look in a telescope. ◉ 광학〔굴절〕~ an optical 〔a refracting〕 telescope. 반사~ a reflecting telescope. 적외선~ a infrared telescope. 전파~ a radio telescope. 천체 ~ an astronomical telescope. 태양 관측용~ a helioscope.

**망원렌즈**(望遠—) a telephoto lens.

**망원분광기**(望遠分光器) 《천체 스펙트럼의》 a telespectroscope.

**망원사진**(望遠寫眞) a telephotograph. ◉ ~기 a telecamera.

**망인**(亡人) the dead. ⇨ 망자.

**망일**(望日) a full-moon day; 《보름날》 the fifteenth day of the lunar month.

**망자**(亡者) a dead person; the departed; the deceased. ¶ ~의 영혼을 달래다〔위로하다〕 console the spirit of the deceased.

**망조**(亡兆) an omen of ruin. ¶ ~가 들다 show signs of ruin; be doomed to ruin.

**망종**(芒種) ① 《곡식》 grain with an awn. ② 《절후》 *Mangjong;* one of the 24 seasonal divisions (around 5 June).

**망주석**(望柱石) a pair of stone posts in 「front of a tomb.

**망중한**(忙中閑) leisure in the intervals of *one's* work; some odd moments of leisure (to be found) in *one's* busy life. ¶ ~을 즐기다 enjoy an interval of leisure snatched from busy life.

**망지소조하다**(罔知所措—) be at a loss; do not know what to do.

**망처**(亡妻) *one's* late 〔deceased〕 wife.

**망측**(罔測) ~하다 《해괴하다》 (be) absurd; inordinate; 《상스럽다》 (be) indecent; low; vulgar; 《추잡하다》 (be) nasty; vicious; obscene; offensive; disgusting; 《꼴이》 (be) ugly; unsightly. ¶ ~한 생각 an inordinate idea / ~한 소리 an absurd 〔a spicy〕 story; an indecent 〔a low〕 talk / 여자에게 ~한 소리를 하다 say ugly things 〔make an obscene remark〕 to a girl / 그런 ~한 소리 하지 마라 Don't say such nasty things.

**망치** a hammer (금속제의); a mallet (나무의); a sledge (hammer) (두손으로 사용하는); a gavel (의장이 쓰는). ¶ 큰 ~ a maul; a sledge hammer / ~로 두드리다 hammer; strike 〔beat〕 with a hammer. ◉ ~자루 the handle of a hammer. ~질 hammering: ~질하다 hammer.

**망치다** ruin; mar; spoil; destroy; wreck; make a mess 〔muddle〕 of; play havoc with; play the devil 〔deuce〕 with; 《구어》 mess 〔foul 《미》〕 *something* up. ¶ 계획을 ~ spoil 〔ruin〕 a plan / 농작물을 ~ 《폭풍우 따위가》 make havoc of the crops / 비에 모자를 ~ ruin *one's* hat in the rain / 개가 화단을 ~ a dog plays havoc with 〔makes a mess of〕 a flower bed / 일생을 ~ be ruined for life; blast *one's* career; make a failure 〔mess〕 of *one's* life / 그는 술로 몸을 망쳤다 Wine was his ruin.

**망칠**(望七) 61 years old.

**망태기**(網—) a net 〔mesh〕 bag.

**망토** a mantle; a cloak; a cape; a shawl.

**망판**(網版) 〖인쇄·사진〗 a halftone; a halftone plate 〔block〕.

**망하다**(亡—) ① 《멸망하다》 perish; cease to exist; die out. ¶ 함께 ~ fall 〔be ruined〕 together; share the same fate / 망할 위험에 처해 있다 be in danger of perishing / 핵전쟁이 일어나면 인류는 망한다 If there is a nuclear war, the human race will perish. ② 《영락하다》 go to ruin; come 〔go〕 down in the world; fall low; be in reduced circumstance; 《회사 따위가》 fail. ¶ 망한 집안 a family now fallen on evil days / 망한 사람 《구어》 a down-and-out; a man down on his luck / 집안이 ~ a family goes down / 회사가 ~ a company fails / 술로 ~ go to the dogs with drink / 그 은행은 작년에 망했다 The bank failed last year. / 그의 낭비로 집안이 망했다 The family was ruined by his extravagant habits. ③ 《고약하다》 be wretched; be hard to deal with. ¶ 그 책은 읽기 ~ The book is hard to read. / 망할 놈의 말이 길을 가줘야지 What can I do with the wretched nag—it is so slow!

**망향**(望鄕) homesickness; nostalgia. ¶ ~의 homesick / ~병에 걸리다 become 〔get, feel〕 homesick 《for》; have a feeling of homesickness; long for the sight of *one's* home / 그녀는 그 노래를 듣자 ~의 염(念)에 사로 잡혔다 She got homesick on hearing the song.

**망혼**(亡魂) the spirit 〔soul〕 of the dead. ¶ ~을 위로하다 solace 〔pacify〕 the departed soul.

**맞-** facing; directly opposite; direct; straight; together; jointly; each other; mutually. ¶ 맞구멍 a hole on the opposite side / 맞바람 a head wind.

**맞갖다** be to *one's* taste 〔liking〕; (be) likable; agreeable; satisfactory. ¶ 맞갖은 집 a house to *one's* taste / 맞갖은 음식 tasty food / 맞갖은 여자 a girl after *one's* heart.

**맞갖잖다** (be) distasteful; offensive; disagreeable; unsatisfactory; undesirable; go against the grain. ¶ 맞갖잖은 사람 a disagreeable person / 맞갖잖은 수작 an offensive remark; a remark hard to stomach / 맞갖잖은 음식 distasteful 〔unpleasant〕 food.

**맞걸다** ① 《마주 걸다》 interlock; lock 〔link〕 together. ② 《노름판에서》 stake the same amount (of money) as the other party; stake 〔bet〕 against.

**맞걸리다** ① 《두 물건이》 be linked together; be coupled. ¶ 차량 연결기가 ~ the couplers of cars are engaged 〔joined〕. ② 《두 사람이》 be pitted against each other; be matched 〔faced〕 with each other; be out for fight 〔competition〕. ¶ 둘이 결승전에서 ~ the two are pitted against each other in the final match.

**맞고소**(—告訴) a cross 〔counter〕 action; a counterclaim 《for damages》; a countercharge. ~하다 bring a counter action 《for, against》; counterclaim; countercharge.

**맞교대**(—交代) two shifts. ◉ ~작업 operating with two shifts.

**맞꼭지각**(—角) 〖수학〗 vertical angles.

**맞다**[1] ① 《옳다·정확하다》 be right; be correct; 《시계가》 keep good time; 《계산·장부끝이》 balance. ¶ 맞는 답 a

correct 〔right〕 answer / 맞지 않다 be wrong 〔incorrect〕 / 내 시계는 항상 ~ My watch keeps good time. / 계산이 아무리 해도 안 맞는다 These figures don't add up. / 내 계산은 잘 맞는다 I find the accounts all right. / 네 대답은 ~ Your answer is right 〔correct〕. / 맞았어 That's right.
② 《의견·내용 등이 일치하다》 agree 《with》; coincide 〔tally〕 《with》; be in accord 《with》; be in keeping 《with》; conform 《with》. ¶ 가풍에 ~ conform with a family custom 〔tradition〕 / 규격에 ~ be up to standard / 조건에 ~ meet the conditions / 서로 이야기가〔마음이〕 ~ agree with each other / 너의 주장은 논리에 안 맞는다 Your argument is illogical. / 그 기획에 관해 그들의 의견이 맞지 않았다 They didn't agree on the project. / 그녀의 이야기는 네 말과 딱 맞는다 Her account (of it) corresponds 〔tallies〕 perfectly with yours. / 모습이 인상서와 맞는다 The features answer the description.
③ 《적합하다》 《모양·치수가》 fit; 《기호·체질 따위가》 suit; be suited to; become; 《기후·음식 따위가》 agree with. ¶ (사이즈가) 몸에 맞는〔안 맞는〕 옷 well= 〔ill-〕fitting clothes / 기호에 ~ suit 〔be to *one's*〕 taste / 목적에 ~ serve 〔suit〕 *one's* purpose / 입에 맞는〔맞지 않는〕 음식 an agreeable 〔a disagreeable〕 food / 이상에 ~ meet *one's* ideal; measure up to the ideal / 취미에 맞는 직업 an occupation to *one's* liking / 비위에 맞지 않다 be hard to stomach; go against the grain / 이 구두는 나에게 꼭 맞는다 These shoes fit me very well. / 이곳 기후는 내 체질에 맞지 않는다 The climate here doesn't agree with my constitution. / 맞는지 한번 입어 보세요 Just try it on for size. / 「한국 요리가 입에 맞습니까」—「아주 잘 맞습니다」 "Does Korean food suit your taste ?"—"Nothing suits me better".
④ 《조화하다》 go well 《with》; match well 《with》; harmonize 《with》; be in harmony 《with》; be in tune 《with》 (곡조가); 《어울리다》 become; befit; be suitable 〔becoming〕. ¶ 발이〔보조가〕 ~ fall into step / 발이 맞지 않다 get 〔walk〕 out of step; break step / 장단이〔곡조가〕 맞지 않다 get out of tune; be out of tune 《with》 / 그 넥타이는 양복에 잘 맞는다 The tie goes well with your coat. / 이 카펫은 벽지와 잘 맞지 않는다 This carpet doesn't match 〔go well with〕 the wallpaper. / 빨간 옷은 그녀에게 잘 맞는다 A red dress becomes 〔looks good on〕 her. / 이 요리는 그 술에 잘 맞는다 This dish goes very well with the liquor.
⑤ 《구멍 등에》 fit. ¶ 쐐기가 구멍에 ~ a wedge fits in a hole / 열쇠가 자물쇠에 맞는다 The key fits the lock.
⑥ 《마음에》 be congenial 《to, with》; be like-minded; get along well 《with》. ¶ 마음이 ~ be of one mind; agree with each other; be in harmony / 마음이 맞는 친구 a congenial friend; a friend (quite) after *one's* own heart / …이 맞지 않다 disagree 《with》; be in discord 《with》; do not get along well 《with》 / (남녀가) 눈이 ~ fall in love 《with each other》 / 손이 ~ go nicely with each other / 도둑질도 손이 맞아야 한다 Even theft requires a good partner.
⑦ 《수지가》 pay (off); be profitable. ¶ 수지가 ~ both ends meet; pay (off) / 수지맞는 장사 a paying 〔profitable〕 business; a business that pays (off) / 그것을 천 달러 이하로 팔아서는 수지가 맞지 않는다 It wouldn't pay to sell it for less than 1,000 dollars.
⑧ 《들어맞다》 (***a***) 《명중·적중하다》 strike 《on》; hit (the mark); make a good hit; 《예상 등이》 prove (to be) right; come true. ¶ 꿈이 ~ a dream comes true / 예언이 ~ a prophecy comes true 〔comes to pass〕 / 짐작이 ~ *one's* guess is right; make a good guess; guess right / 《탄환·화살이》 과녁의 한가운데에 ~ hit the target in the center; hit the bull's eye / 《주먹 등이》 어깨〔눈, 머리〕에 ~ hit 《*a person*》 on the shoulder 〔in the eye, on the head〕 / 《탄알 따위가》 맞지 않다 miss 《*a person*, the target》; go wide (of the mark) / 오늘 일기 예보는 맞았다 Today's weather forecast proved right. (***b***) 《당첨되다》 draw; win 《in a lottery》. ¶ 복권이 ~ win (a prize) in a lottery; get 〔draw〕 a lottery prize.

**맞다²** ① 《손님·사람을》 meet; go (out) to meet; receive 《a visitor》; greet; make 《*a person*》 welcome; 《때를》 greet; see. ¶ …를 정거장에 나가 ~ meet 《*a person*》 at the station; go to the station to meet 《*a person*》 / …를 반가이 ~ welcome 《*a person*》; receive 《*a person*》 with delight / …를 따뜻이 ~

give 《*a person*》 a warm reception 〔welcome〕; greet 《*a person*》 with smile / 설을 ~ greet the New Year / 묵은 해를 보내고 새해를 ~ see the old year out and the new year in / 40세의 생일을 맞다 see *one's* 40th birthday come round / 청중은 박수로 그를 맞았다 The audience greeted 〔welcomed〕 him with applause.
② 《맞아들이다》 take; invite; call in; 《초빙하다》 engage; hire. ¶ 사위를 ~ take a son-in-law into *one's* family; find a husband for *one's* daughter / 아내를 ~ take a wife; get married / 양자를 ~ adopt a son / 새 교장을 ~ have a new principal 〔headmaster〕 come / 의사를 ~ call in a doctor / 전문가를 ~ engage an expert / 그들은 그녀를 따뜻이 집안으로 맞아들였다 They warmly invited her into their house.
③ 《비바람 등을》 be exposed to; expose *oneself* to. ¶ 밤이슬을 ~ be exposed 〔expose *oneself*〕 to the night dew / 비를 ~ be exposed to rain / 비바람을 ~ be exposed to the weather / 비맞지 않도록 하다 keep 《the clothing》 from the rain.
④ 《당하다》 meet with; come across; encounter; suffer 《from》. ¶ 도둑(을) ~ [사람이 주어] have 《*something*》 stolen; be robbed of 《*one's* purse》; [물건이 주어] be stolen / 벼락을 ~ be struck by lightning / 야단(을) ~ get 〔have〕 a scolding; catch it / 위기를 ~ face 〔be confronted by〕 a crisis / 퇴짜(를) ~ get rejected.
⑤ 《얻어맞다》 be hit by 〔on〕; be struck; be beaten; be knocked; get a blow 〔punch〕; be shot (총을). ¶ 매를 ~ be struck 〔beaten〕; be flogged 〔lashed, whipped〕 (회초리·채찍 등으로) / 뺨을 ~ be boxed on the ears / 볼기를 ~ be spanked 〔flogged〕 (on the buttocks) / 머리를 ~ be struck on the head / 콧등을 ~ be hit in the nose.
⑥ 《주사를》 get 〔have, receive〕 《an injection》; take 《a needle》; 《침을》 get acupunctured; 《도장·검인을》 receive 《a stamp of approval》. ¶ 팔에 모르핀 주사를 ~ get 〔have〕 a morphine shot in 〔on〕 the arm / 장티푸스 예방 주사를 ~ be inoculated 〔injected〕 against typhus.
⑦ 《점수를》 get 《points, a mark》. ¶ 시험에서 만점을 ~ win 〔get〕 a full mark in an exam.
⑧ 《상대하다》 meet 〔confront〕 《the enemy》. ¶ 앞뒤로 적을 ~ be hemmed in by the enemy / 적을 맞아서 싸우다 fight to repulse the attack of the enemy.

**맞닥뜨리다** be faced with; be confronted with; encounter. ¶ 난관에 ~ face 〔run up against〕 a difficulty; be confronted by a difficulty / 막다른 골목에 ~ run 〔come〕 right into a dead end / 원수와 외나무 다리에서 ~ encounter an enemy on a log bridge.

**맞닥치다** come face to face with; encounter; meet with. ¶ 원수와 노상에서 ~ encounter an enemy on *one's* way / 장애에 ~ be confronted with a difficult problem; hit 〔run into〕 a snag.

**맞담배** ¶ ~ 피우다, ~질하다 smoke to *a person's* face; sit smoking together.

**맞당기다** draw 〔pull〕 each other; pull 〔drag, tug, haul〕 《a rope》 from both sides. ¶ 줄이 맞당겨 끊어지다 a rope is pulled apart from both sides.

**맞닿다** come in contact 〔touch〕 《with》; touch (with) each other. ¶ 땅과 하늘이 맞닿은 지평선 the horizon where the earth and (the) sky seem to meet / 하늘과 바다가 서로 ~ sky and water merge into each other / 두 사람의 손이 맞닿았다 Their hands touched 〔met〕.

**맞대다** ① 《마주 대다》 bring into contact (with each other); 《마주 대하다》 come 〔sit〕 face to face 《with》. ¶ 무릎을 맞대고 앉다 sit knee to knee with 《*a person*》; sit opposite each other / 이마를 ~ bring 〔put〕 brows together; sit together face to face / …와 얼굴을 ~ come 〔be〕 face to face with… / 음극을 양극에 ~ put the cathode in contact with the anode / 맞대고 욕하다 abuse 《*a person*》 to his face 〔into *his* teeth〕 / 그와 서로 얼굴을 맞대고 의논해 보렴 Why don't you talk face to face with him? / 그와 매일 얼굴을 맞대고 일한다 I work face to face with him everyday.
② 《대면시키다》 bring 《two persons》 into contact with each other; confront 《*a person*》 with 《another》; bring 〔join〕 together. ¶ 살 사람과 팔 사람을 ~ bring buyer and seller together / 원고와 피고를 ~ confront the accused with his accuser; bring the accused face to face with his accuser.
③ 《양쪽에》 fix 〔put〕 on both sides.

**맞대면**(—對面) a face-to-face interview 〔meeting〕. ∼하다 interview 〔meet〕 face to face. ¶ 재판장은 피고와 증인을 ∼시키기로 했다 The chief justice decided to confront the accused with the witness.

**맞대하다**(—對—) face 〔confront〕 each other. ¶ 맞대하고 앉다 take a seat opposite (to) 《*a person*》/ 맞대하고 이야기하다 have a face-to-face chat 《with》.

**맞돈** cash payment; payment in cash; cash (down). ¶ ∼을 내다 pay in cash / ∼ 주고 사다 buy 《*a thing*》 for cash / ∼으로 사고 팔다 deal in cash.

**맞들다** ① 《마주 들다》 lift (up) together; hold up 《*a thing*》 together. ¶ 테이블을 ∼ lift a table together. ② 《협력하다》 cooperate 《with》; work together; join hands 〔forces〕 《with》. ¶ 일을 서로 맞들어 하다 cooperate 〔help one another〕 in doing a job / 백지장도 맞들면 낫다 《속담》 Many hands make light work.

**맞뚫다** bore 〔drill, penetrate〕 《a hole》 from both sides.

**맞먹다** 《필적하다》 be a match for; match; be equal to; 《상당하다》 be worthy to; be equivalent to. ¶ 맞먹을 자가 없다 have no equal 〔match〕; be unrivaled / 3 개월 급여와 맞먹는 보너스 a bonus equivalent to three month's pay / 1 달러는 천 이백원과 맞먹는다 A dollar is equivalent to 1,200 won. / 두 사람의 실력은 맞먹는다 The two are equally matched in ability.

**맞물다** ① 《서로 물다》 bite each other; 〖치과〗 occlude; 《아래 윗니가》 meet well. ¶ 잘 맞물리지 않다 don't quite bite evenly; 《my teeth》 don't meet properly. ② 《톱니바퀴 따위가》 gear 《into, with》; engage 《with》; mesh 《with》; (inter)lock. ¶ 기어가 서로 맞물려 있다〔있지 않다〕 be「in 〔out of〕 gear 〔mesh〕 / 맞물리게 하다 engage 《cogwheels》 / X 톱니바퀴가 Y 톱니바퀴와 맞물렸다 The wheel X engages with the wheel Y.

**맞바꾸다** exchange (one thing for another); barter 〔trade〕 《A for B》; 《구어》 swap 《stamps》. ¶ 시계와 카메라를 ∼ exchange a watch for a camera / 쌀과 기계를 ∼ barter 〔trade〕 rice for machines.

**맞바둑** an unhandicapped *paduk* game. ¶ ∼을 두다 play *paduk* on an even basis; play on an equal footing.

**맞바람** a contrary 〔head〕 wind; an adverse 〔unfavorable〕 wind. ¶ 배가 ∼을 받아 잘 가지 못한다 The ship is held back by a head wind. / ∼이 분다 The wind is against us.

**맞받다** ① 《정면으로》 receive 〔face〕 directly. ¶ 햇빛을 ∼ receive the direct sunlight. ② 《응수하다》 give 《*a person*》 tit for tat; (make a) retort. ¶ 상대방의 악담에 굴하지 않고 그도 날카롭게 맞받았다 Undaunted by his opponent's abuse, he retorted as sharply. ③ 《들이받다》 run 〔clash〕 against 〔into〕; collide head-on 《with》. ¶ 둘이 이마를 ∼ two people bump their heads together.

**맞받이** the opposite spot 〔side〕. ¶∼ 언덕 a hill opposite / 길 건너 ∼집 a house right across the street.

**맞배지기** 〖씨름〗 counter-lifting.

**맞벌이** working together (for a living); working in double harness. ∼하다 work together for a living; earn a livelihood together; work 〔run〕 in double harness. ¶ ∼ 가정 a double-income 〔two-income〕 family; a two-bread-winner house 〔family〕 / ∼생활 two-income living / 그들은 ∼를 하고 있다 They both (go out to) work. / 우리는 ∼해서 월수입이 200만원이다 Between us, we earn two million won a month. / 남편만의 수입으로 가족을 부양하기 힘들어서 요즘은 ∼ 가정이 흔해졌다 The two-income family is commonplace today, as few husbands can support their family on a single paycheck.

◉ ∼부부 a working couple; a two paycheck couple: 자식이 없는 ∼ 부부 double income no kids (생략 DINKs).

**맞벽**(—壁) 〖건축〗 the outer layer of a 2-layer wall.

**맞보다** look at each other; look each other in the face. ¶ 맞보고 웃다 smile at each other / 그들은 맞보기만 하고 아무 말도 않는다 They are just watching each other without saying a word.

**맞부딪치다** hit 〔strike〕 against; run 〔bump, smash, crash〕 into; collide 〔have a collision〕 《with》. ¶ 버스와 트럭이 ∼ a bus collides with a truck; a bus and a truck run into each other / 두 대의 차가 정면으로 맞부딪쳤다 Two cars collied head-on.

**맞붙다** ① 《한데》 stick 〔cling, glue〕 together. ¶ 두 집이 맞붙어 있다 The two houses stand close to each other. / 둘은 밤낮 맞붙어 (돌아) 다닌다 They always stick together. / 종이가 맞붙어 떨어지지 않는다 The two pieces of paper are stuck 〔glued〕 so hard that they won't come apart. ② 《싸우다·씨름하다》 grapple 〔wrestle, tackle〕 with; come to grips with; be matched 《with》 (경기에서). ¶ 맞붙어 씨름하다 wrestle with each other / 맞붙어 싸우다 come to grips with each other / 어려운 문제와 ~ tackle 〔grapple with〕 a difficult problem.

**맞붙들다** catch 〔hold〕 together 〔each other〕; 〖권투〗 clinch. ¶ 어깨를 양쪽에서 ~ hold 《*a person*》 by both shoulders.

**맞붙이다** ① 《사람을》 bring 《them》 into contact; 《경기 등에서》 match 〔pit〕 《A》 against 《B》. ② 《붙이다》 stick 〔plaster, fix〕 together. ¶ 종이 두 장을 풀로 ~ put two sheets of paper together with glue.

**맞붙잡다** seize 〔grasp〕 each other.

**맞비겨떨어지다** balance; come out even; both ends meet. ¶ 셈이 ~ the accounts balance.

**맞상**(—床) a table for two. ⇨ 겸상.

**맞상대**(—相對) direct confrontation.

**맞서다** ① 《마주서다》 stand face to face 《with》; face; confront. ¶ 테이블을 사이에 두고 ~ face 《*a person*》 across the table / 과감히 위험에 ~ boldly confront the danger / 어려운 일에 (피하지 않고) ~ face anything difficult.
② 《대항하다》 stand 〔rise〕 against; oppose; stand up to; 《싸우다》 fight (against); put *oneself* against. ¶ 힘에는 힘으로 ~ meet 〔counter〕 force with force / 용감히 적과 맞서 싸우다 fight bravely against the enemy / …에 감연히〔정면으로〕 ~ face up squarely to 《a problem》; bear 〔take〕 the full brunt 《of an attack》 / 그에게 맞서 대항하지 않으면, 그는 너를 계속 괴롭힐 것이다 If you don't stand up to him, he's just going to keep on bullying you.
③ 《견주다》 cope with; match. ¶ 테니스로는 그와 맞설 사람이 없다 There is no one who can match him in tennis.

**맞선** an interview 〔a meeting〕 with a view to marriage; a marriage meeting. ¶ ~ 보다 have an interview with *one's* prospective bride 〔bridegroom〕; [한쪽이 주어] be formally introduced to *one's* prospective marriage partner; [두 사람이 주어] 「be formally introduced 〔meet each other〕 with a view to marriage.

**맞소송**(—訴訟) a counter-suit 〔-action, 「-complaint〕.

**맞수**(—手) a (good) match 〔rival〕; a worthy opponent. ¶ 서양 장기의 ~ *one's* equal in chess.

**맞아들이다** show 〔usher〕 《*a person*》 in(to). ⇨ 맞다[2]①, ②.

**맞아떨어지다** tally; be correct. ¶ 계산이 ~ a calculation is correct; the figures tally.

**맞은쪽, 맞은편**(—便) 《위치》 the opposite 〔other〕 side; 《상대편》 the opposite 〔other〕 party. ¶ 강 ~ the other side of the river; across the river / 길 ~집 a house opposite 〔across the road〕 / 병원 바로 ~에 살다 live just opposite (to) the hospital / 바람이 ~에서 불어오다 have a headwind.

**맞이** meeting; reception; welcoming. ~하다 ⇨ 맞다[2]. ¶ 손님 ~ reception of guests / 달 ~ enjoying the moon / 신년 ~ greeting the New Year / 아내를 ~하다 get married; take a wife / 정거장에 나가 손님을 ~하다 go to the station to meet a guest / 집에 손님을 ~하다 show a guest into *one's* house / 환호로 ~하다 receive 《*a per-son*》 with cheers.

**맞잡다** ① 《서로 잡다》 take 〔hold〕 together. ¶ 손에 손을 맞잡고 hand in hand 《with》 / 테이블을 맞잡아 들다 lift a table together. ② 《드잡이하다》 grapple with each other. ¶ 서로 맞잡고 싸우다 come to grips with each other / 머리끄덩이를 ~ grab each other by the hair. ③ 《협력하다》 cooperate 《with》; work together; collaborate 《with》. ¶ 서로 손을 맞잡고 사업을 하다 do a business in cooperation with each other.

**맞잡이** a (good) match; an equal; 《서로 같음》 the same; self-same. ¶ 레슬링의 ~ a match in wrestling.

**맞장구치다** chime in 《with *a person*》; echo 《another's words》; listen with repeated expressions of assent. ¶ 그는 그녀의 이야기를 들으면서 자주 맞장구쳤다 He was expressing his agreements at frequent intervals as he listened to her.

**맞장기**(—將棋) even-match *janggi;* an unhandicapped *janggi*-game. ¶ ~를 두다 play *janggi* on even terms.

**맞절** mutual bowing. ~하다 bow to each other; greet each other.

**맞접다** fold on itself; fold in half.

**맞추다** ①《짜맞추다》fit into; assemble; put together; fix up; put (pieces) together. ¶ 뜯어놓은 시계를 ~ reassemble a watch / 테이블에 다리를 ~ put legs on a table / 모형 비행기를 짜~ build 〔put together〕 a model plane. ②《맞게 하다》set 〔fit, suit, adapt, conform〕《*a thing* to another》; adjust 《a radio dial》 tune 《to》. ¶ 보조를 ~ keep 〔fall into〕 step 《with》/ 수지를 ~ balance *one's* income and outlay; make 〔gain〕 a profit / 피아노 반주에 맞추어 노래하다 sing to piano accompaniment / 바이올린의 선율을 피아노에 ~ tune the violin to the piano / 라디오를 KBS FM에 ~ tune the radio in to KBS FM / 자명종을 6시 반에 ~ set the alarm for six thirty / 쌍안경을 눈에 ~ adjust the binoculars (correctly) to suit *one's* eyes / 안경 도수를 ~ adjust *one's* lens prescription / 음악에 맞추어 손뼉을 치다 clap *one's* hands (in time) to the music. ③《적합하게 하다》fit 〔adjust〕《A to B》; bring 《A》 into line 《with B》; 《조화시키다》 match 《colors》; 《동조하다》 act in line 〔go along〕《with the party's policy》. ¶ 비위를 ~ curry favor with 《*a person*》; flatter 〔please〕《*a person*》/ 세인의 기호에 ~ suit 〔hit〕 the taste of the public / 몸에 맞추어 드레스를 만들다 have a dress made to measure / 넥타이를 옷에 ~ make a match of tie with *one's* suit / 그는 당론에 맞추어 이 문제에 관한 정견을 발표했다 He set forth his political views on the matter in line with the decisions of the Party. ④《주문하다》order; give an order 《to》; place an order 《with》. ¶ 새로 맞춘 양복 a suit newly made to order; a tailor〔custom〕-made suit / 구두를 ~ have a pair of shoes on order / 양복점에서 양복을 ~ place an order with a tailor shop; have a tailor make *one's* suit / 그는 옷을 모두 맞추어서 입는다 He has all his suits made to order. ⑤《대조하다》compare 〔check〕《A》 with 《B》; check *something* 《with, against》. ¶ 원문과 ~ compare 《a translation》 with the original / 원부(原簿)와 맞춰 보게 Check it up with the ledger. / 답을 내것과 맞춰 봐라 Check your answers with mine. ⑥《접합시키다》set 《a broken leg》; join; connect; put together. ¶ 뼈를 ~ set a fracture 〔a broken bone〕/ 삔 데를 ~ set a dislocation. ⑦《마주 대다》touch. ¶ 입을 ~ kiss 《a girl on the mouth》/ 볼에 입을 ~ kiss 《*a person*》 on the cheek.

**맞춤** 《양복의》 an article ordered; a thing made to order; a custom-made article. ¶ ~의 tailor-made; ordered; custom-made. ◉ ~옷 a suit made to measure 〔order〕; a custom suit.

**맞춤법**(一法) the rules of spelling; orthography. ¶ 한글~ the spelling system of *Hangul;* the rules of Korean spelling 〔orthography〕/ ~을 익히다 learn a correct spelling / ~에 맞추어 쓰다 spell correctly according to the rules of orthography. ◉ ~통일안 a draft for unified 〔standardized〕 spelling system. 「equal terms.

**맞혼인**(—婚姻) a marriage arranged on

**맞흥정** a first-hand 〔direct〕 transaction 〔dealings, bargain〕. ~하다 make a direct 〔buyer-to-seller〕 deal.

**맞히다** ①《알아맞히다》guess right; make a good guess; give a right answer; hit the truth. ¶ 잘못 ~ guess wrong / 답을 ~ hit the answer / 바로 알아 맞혔다 You have hit the nail right on the head. ②《명중시키다》hit 《the mark》. ¶ 바로 ~ hit the nail on the head; make a good hit / 화살을 과녁에 ~ hit the mark with an arrow / 빗〔못〕~ miss the mark / 탄환은 표적의 한가운데를 맞혔다 The bullet hit the target right in the center. ③《비·바람 따위를》 expose to; leave out in 《the weather》. ¶ 눈을〔비를〕~ expose to 〔leave out in〕 the snow 〔rain〕/ 비를 맞히지 않도록 하다 protect 〔keep〕《*a thing*》 from the rain.

**맡기다** ①《보관시키다》leave 《*a thing*》 in 《*a person's*》 care 〔charge〕; deposit 《*a thing*》 with 《*a person*》; entrust 《*a person*》 with 《*a thing*》; entrust 《*a thing*》 to 《*a person*》; put 〔place〕《*a thing*》 under 《*a person's*》 care 〔charge〕. ¶ 귀중품을 ~ place valuables in 《*a person's*》 custody; entrust valuables to 〔with〕《*a person*》/ 돈을 은행에 ~ put 〔deposit〕 money in a bank / 아무에게 돈을 ~ entrust *a person* with *one's* money / 짐을 ~ check *one's* baggage; leave *one's* luggage 《in a left-luggage office》/ 어린아이를 ~ leave a child in *a person's* care; farm out a child 《on》/ 집을 이웃 사람에게 ~ leave *one's* house in charge of a

neighbor / 우산은 휴대품 보관소에 맡겨 주십시오 Check your umbrella at the cloakroom, please.
② 《위임·위탁하다》 entrust 〔leave〕 《*a matter*》 (up) to 《*a person*》; entrust 《*a person*》 with 《a task》; trust 《*a person*》 with 《*a thing*》; leave 《*a thing*》 to 《*a person's*》 care. ¶ 경영을 ~ leave its management in 《*a person's*》 hands / 일을 ~ entrust 《*a person*》 with a task; give 〔assign〕 the job to 《*a person*》 / 전권을 ~ entrust 《*a person*》 with a power of attorney / 책임을 ~ place responsibility on 《*a person*》 / 우리는 이 문제의 조사를 경찰에 맡겼다 We put this investigations of the matter into the hands of the police. / 그는 상점의 운영을 아들에게 맡길 것이다 He will leave the management of the store in the hands of his son. / 그 일은 제게 맡기세요 You can count on me for that.
③ 《방임하다》 leave 《*a person* to do *something*》; let 《*a person* do *something*》. ¶ 몸을 (내)~ submit 〔resign〕 *oneself* to 《*another's*》 will; give *oneself* to 《*a person*》 / 상상에 ~ leave 《*a thing*》 to the imagination / 운을 하늘에 ~ resign 〔abandon〕 *oneself* to *one's* fate; leave 《*a matter*》 to chance; trust to luck 〔chance〕 / 그 문제는 전적으로 그의 판단에 맡겨졌다 The matter was left entirely to his judgment.

**맡다**[1] ① 《보관하다》 keep; receive 《*a thing*》 in trust 〔custody〕; be entrusted with 《*a thing*》; take charge of 《*a thing*》; take 《*a thing*》 in 〔under *one's*〕 charge. ¶ 맡은 돈 money left in *one's* keeping / 이 돈 좀 맡아 주시오 Keep this money for me. / 찾으러 올 때까지 맡고 있겠다 I'll keep 〔take care of〕 it till you call for it.
② 《책임·담당·감독 등을》 undertake; take 〔assume, have〕 charge 《of》; be in charge 《of》; take 〔have〕 《*something*》 under 〔in〕 *one's* charge; take 《a task》 upon *oneself*. ¶ 맡고 있는 아이 a child who is in 〔under〕 *one's* care / 그 사무를 맡은 사람 a man in charge of the business / 어린애를 ~ take care of a child / 중책을 ~ assume a heavy responsibility / 창고를 ~ take charge of a warehouse / 《변호사가》 사건 맡기를 거절하다 refuse to undertake a case / 《학교에서》 영어를 ~ hold classes in English / 6학년을 맡고 있다 I am in charge of the sixth grade.
③ 《허가를》 get; receive; secure. ¶ 자동차 운전 면허를 ~ get a driver's license / 담당 의사의 허가를 ~ get permission from the physician in charge / 허가를 맡고 영업하다 do business under license.

**맡다**[2] ① 《냄새를》 smell; scent; sniff. ¶ 냄새를 ~ smell 《a flower》; take a smell 《at》; have a smell of; catch a whiff 《of》 / 향수 냄새를 ~ smell (at) 〔have a smell of〕 the perfume / 이 장미꽃 향기 좀 맡아 보세요 Have a smell of 〔at〕 this rose. / 감기가 들어서 냄새를 못 맡는다 I can not smell, because I have a cold. ② 《낌새를》 sense; suspect; get wind 〔scent〕 of 《a plot》; smell out 《the secret》. ¶ 계획을 냄새 ~ get wind of a plan / 그는 돈 있는 것을 냄새 맡고 나를 찾아 왔다 He sensed that I had money and came to see me.

**매**[1] ① 《때리는》 a whip; a rod; a cane (막대기); a lash (채찍). ¶ 매를 때리다 whip; flog; lash / 매를 맞다 be whipped 〔licked, flogged〕; be lashed; be thrashed 〔struck, beaten, slapped〕 / 죄인에게 50대의 매를 때리다 give a criminal fifty lashes. ② 《매질》 whipping; lashing; flogging. ¶ 혹독한 매 a hard whipping; a good lick / 사정 없는 매 merciless flogging / 매도 먼저 맞는 놈이 낫다 《속담》 You had better face your difficulties as early as possible.

**매**[2] ① 《맷돌》 a millstone. ② 《매통》 a wooden mill for hulling rice.

**매**[3] 〖조류〗 a hawk; a falcon (수렵용의). ◉ 매부리 《사람》 a falconer. 매사냥 falconry: 매사냥을 하다 hunt with a falcon. 매파 《강경파》 the hawks; the hard-liners; 《개인》 a hawk; a hard-liner.

**매**[4] 《울음소리》 bleating; baa. ¶ 양이 매 울다 a sheep bleats 〔goes baa〕.

**매-** quite; much (the same). ¶ 매한가지다 be much about the same.

**매-**(每) each; every. ¶ 매달 every 〔each〕 month / 매초〔분〕 per second 〔minute〕 / 매페이지에 page after page; every page.

**-매** shape; form; cast. ¶ 몸매 *one's* figure 〔shape〕; *one's* carriage / 눈매 the expression 〔cast〕 of *one's* eyes; *one's* eyes.

**-매**(枚) sheets 《of paper》.

**매가**(買價) the purchase price; 〖증권〗 a bid price.

**매가**(賣家) a house for 〔on〕 sale.

**매가**(賣價) a selling price. ¶ 이것을 ~의 반액으로 드리죠 I offer this at half the sale price.

**매가오리** 〚어류〛 an eagle ray.

**매각**(賣却) sale; disposal (by sale). ~하다 sell (off); dispose of. ¶ 그는 집을 ~했다 He sold his house. *or* He disposed of his house by sale. / 나는 집을 ~하는 데 4개월 이상 걸렸다 The sale of my house took more than four months. ◉ ~계정 sales account. ~공고 a public notice of sale. ~대금 proceeds from sale. ~물 something to sell; an article 「to dispose of 〔for sale〕. ~인 a seller. ~조건 terms of sale. ~처분 disposal 〔disposition〕 by sale. ~통지 a notice of sale. ~필 《게시》 Sold.

**매개**(每個) each one; apiece.

**매개**(媒介) intermediation; mediation; agency; good offices (주선). ~하다 mediate 《between two parties》; act as (a) go-between; 《전염병을》 transmit 《disease》; carry 《germs》. ¶ …의 ~로 through the medium 〔good offices〕 of... / 말라리아는 모기의 ~로 전염된다 Malaria is carried by mosquito(e)s. *or* Mosquito(e)s transmit malaria. / 그들의 우정은 음악을 ~로 하여 맺어졌다 They became close friends through music. ◉ ~물 a medium (*pl.* -dia); 《병균의》 a carrier; a vector (곤충). ~변수(變數) 〚수학〛 a parameter. ~자 a mediator; an agent; 《거래의》 a middleman.

**매개념**(媒概念) 〚논리〛 the middle con「cept 〔term〕.

**매거**(枚擧) enumeration. ~하다 enumerate; list; mention one by one. ¶ 일일이 ~할 수 없다 be too many to mention 〔enumerate〕; be too numerous to mention / 이런 종류의 범죄는 너무 흔해서 ~할 수가 없다 Crimes of this kind are too frequent 〔common〕 to enumerate.

**매거진** 《잡지》 a magazine.

**매관매직**(賣官賣職) trafficking of official posts. ~하다 traffic in government posts.

**매국**(賣國) betrayal of 〔treachery to, selling〕 *one's* country. ~하다 betray 〔sell〕 *one's* country. ¶ ~적인 traitorous / ~적인 행위 an act of treachery (against *one's* country); a traitorous act. ◉ ~노(奴) a traitor (to *one's* country); a betrayer (of *one's* country).

**매기**(買氣) 〚증권〛 a bullish 〔buying〕 sentiment 〔feeling〕. ¶ 부동산 ~ a real estate boom / ~가 있다 be in the buying mood / ~가 적다 be a lack of buying sentiment / ~가 왕성한 시장 a bull market.

**매기**(每期) every term; each period; 《회기》 each 〔every〕 session.

**매기다** 《값을》 put 〔mark〕 a price 《on *a thing*》; 《경매 따위에서》 offer 〔bid〕; 《등급을》 grade; classify; give 《marks》 (점수를); 《번호를》 number. ¶ 높은 값을 ~ set the price high; put a high price on 《*a thing*》 / 수입품에 높은 관세를 ~ charge 〔impose, levy〕 high duties on imports.

**매끄럽다** ① 《반드럽다》 (be) smooth; sleek; slick. ¶ 매끄러운 털 a glassy fur / 매끄러운 표면 smooth surface. ② ⇨ 미끄럽다.

**매나니** ① 《맨손》 an empty 〔a bare〕 hand. ¶ ~로 with empty hands. ② 《맨밥》 a meal without side dishes.

**매너** manners. ¶ ~가 좋은 well-mannered / ~가 좋다 have good manners; be well-mannered / ~가 나쁘다 have no manners; be bad-〔ill-〕mannered / 무대 ~가 좋다 have good stage manners; deport *oneself* properly on the stage.

**매너리즘** a mannerism. ¶ ~에 빠지다 fall into mannerism; become stereotyped; 《구어》 get into 〔be stuck in〕 a groove.

**매년**(每年) every year; annually; per year (1년마다). ¶ ~ 한 번 once a year / ~의 yearly; annual / 이 고장은 ~ 홍수가 진다 Flood is practically an annual occurrence in this district. / ~ 이맘때가 되면 눈이 내리기 시작한다 It always begins to snow at this time of year.

**매니저** a manager. ¶ 그는 ~가 되었다 He was installed as manager.

**매니지먼트** 《경영》 management. ¶ 그 사업은 ~가 부실해서 실패했다 The business failed owing to poor management. ◉ ~ 컨설턴트 a management consultant.

**매니큐어** 《미조술》 (a) manicure; 《미조액》 nail polish 〔varnish 《영》〕. ~하다 《스스로》 manicure; do manicuring; 《남이 해주다》 have 〔get〕 a manicure 《on *one's* nails》. ¶ 손톱에 ~를 바르다 polish *one's* nails / ~를 지우다 remove the polish from *one's* nails.

**매다**[1] ① 《묶다·동이다》 bind; tie 〔do〕 up; fasten; lash 《two things together》. ¶ 구두끈을 ~ tie up *one's* shoelaces; tie 〔do up〕 *one's* shoes / 넥타이를 ~

tie a necktie / 상처를 동여 ~ bind up a wound / 상자를 끈으로 ~ cord (up) a box / 소포를 ~ string a parcel / 허리띠를 ~ fasten *one's* belt.
② 《잡아매다》 tie; fasten; chain (사슬로); 《배를》 moor; tie up; 《개 따위를》 keep on a leash. ¶ A를 B에 ~ make fast A to B; leash 〔chain〕 A to B / 개를 ~ keep a dog on a leash / 돛을 돛대에 ~ fasten sails to the mast / 배를 부두에 ~ moor a ship 〔make a ship fast〕 to the quay / 소를 나무에 ~ tie 〔fasten〕 a cow to a tree.
③ 《달아매다》 (***a***) 《목을》 hang (to death). ¶ 목을 ~ hang *oneself* 《on a tree; commit suicide by hanging *oneself* / 목을 매어 죽이다 strangle 《*a person*》 to death. (***b***) 《가설》 make; fix. ¶ 선반을 ~ make a shelf; fix a shelf 《to a wall》. (***c***) 《줄을》 stretch; extend. ¶ 그네를 ~ put up a swing / 줄을 팽팽하게 ~ stretch a rope tight.
④ 《구속하다》 bind; tie down; fetter; restrict; confine.
⑤ 《만들다》 put together; create; make. ¶ 붓을 ~ make a brush / 책을 ~ bind 〔make〕 a book.

**매다**[2] 《김을》 weed. ¶ 김을 ~ weed; pull weed; do the weeding / 논을 ~ weed a rice paddy.

**매달** (每—) every month. ¶ ~의 monthly / ~두 번씩 twice a month / 그는 ~ 월급의 20%를 저축한다 He saves 20 percent of his pay every month.

**매달다** ① 《달아매다》 hang (up); suspend. ¶ 등을 처마 끝에 ~ hang a lamp at the eaves / 아무를 나뭇 가지에 ~ hang *a person* on the branch of a tree. ② 《일·직장에》 tie *oneself* down 《to》; bind 〔chain, yoke〕 *oneself* to; restrict 〔confine〕 *oneself* to. ¶ 회사에 목숨을 ~ be tied hand and soul to the company; be dependent upon *one's* company for *one's* livelihood.

**매달리다** ① 《늘어지다》 hang down 《from》; be suspended 《from》; dangle; swing. ¶ 철봉에 ~ hang down from the horizontal bar / 허공에 ~ hang in the air / 어깨에 ~ hang on 《another's》 shoulders / 나무에 사과가 주렁주렁 매달려 있다 Apples are dangling all over the apple tree. / 매달린 개가 누워 있는 개를 웃는다 《속담》 The pot calls the kettle black.
② 《붙잡고 늘어지다》 cling to; hang on; hold on to. ¶ 소매에 ~ cling to 《*a person's*》 sleeve / (버스 등의) 손잡이에 ~ hang on to a strap / 밧줄에 ~ hold on to a rope / 어린애가 엄마한테 매달렸다 The child clung to his mother.
③ 《달라붙다》 hold on to; stick to; cling to. ¶ 일에 ~ stick at 〔to, with〕 a job / 지위에 ~ cling to *one's* position.
④ 《딸리다》 depend 〔rely〕 on. ¶ 매달린 식구 family dependents / 매달린 식구가 많다 have a big family to support; have many mouths to feed / 그녀는 매달린 애가 셋이 있다 She has three dependent children.
⑤ 《애원하다》 entreat 〔implore〕 《*a person* to *do,* for *something*》; appeal to; make a pathotic appeal 《to》. ¶ 도와달라고 ~ look to 《*a person*》 for help / 놓아달라고 경찰에게 ~ implore a policeman for *one's* release / 자비심에 ~ appeal to 《*a person*》 for mercy.

**매대기** smearing 〔daubing〕 all over 《with》. ~치다 smear 〔daub〕 all over; besmear. ¶ 벽에 진흙을 ~치다 smear a wall all over with mud / 얼굴에 분을 ~치다 daub *one's* face all over with powder; powder *one's* face thick.

**매도** (罵倒) abuse; invective. ~하다 abuse; revile; rail 《against》; hurl abuse 〔invective〕 《at》; call 《*a person*》 names; condemn. ¶ 그는 그녀를 ~했다 He hurled abuse at her. / 그들은 모두 그녀의 나쁜 짓을 ~했다 They all condemned her for her misdeed.

**매도** (賣渡) sale and delivery. ~하다 sell 《*a thing*》 (over) to 《*a person*》; deliver; 《어음 따위를》 negotiate 《a bill》. ◉ ~가격 a sale 〔selling〕 price. ~계약 a contract for selling. ~인 a seller; 〖법〗 a vendor. ~증서 a bill of sale.

**매독** (梅毒) 〖의학〗 syphilis. ¶ ~성의 syphilitic / 선천성 ~ congenital 〔hereditary〕 syphilis / ~에 걸리다 contract 〔catch, get〕 syphilis; become (a) syphilitic. ◉ ~검사 an examination of syphilis. ~환자 a syphilitic (person).

**매듭** a knot; a tie; 《세공》 knotwork. ¶ ~을 맺다 knot; tie 〔make〕 a knot / ~을 풀다 unknot; untie 〔undo〕 a knot / ~이 풀리다 A knot comes undone 〔gets loose〕.

**매듭짓다** ① 《끈 따위를》 knot; make 〔tie〕 a knot. ② 《결말을》 settle; conclude; put an end 《to》; bring 《*a matter*》 to an end; put a stop 《to》.

¶ 일을 ~ conclude 〔finish〕 *one's* work / 원만히 ~ come to an amicable settlement / 살인 사건의 수사가 마침내 매듭지어졌다 The murder investigation has at long last come to an end. / 학원 분쟁은 아직 매듭지어지지 않았다 The campus dispute has not been settled yet.

**매력**(魅力) (an) attraction; (a) charm; (a) fascination; (an) appeal; allure; glamor. ¶ ~적인 charming; fascinating; attractive / ~적인 여성 a charming 〔attractive〕 woman / ~이 없는 unattractive; have no appeal 《to》; unglamorous / 여성적인 ~ feminity; feminine attraction / 성적 ~ 《emanate》 a sex appeal / ~이 없는 여자 a plain 〔homely〕 woman / ~이 있다 appeal 《to》; have an appeal 〔a fascination〕 《to》; have something attractive 《about *one*》; hold a fascination 《for》/ …에 ~을 느끼다 be fascinated 〔charmed〕 by... / 이런 일은 나에게 별로 ~이 없다 This kind of work does not appeal to me. / 그에게는 인간적인 ~이 있다 He has personal magnetism 〔charm〕. / 아름다운 눈이 그녀의 큰 ~ 중의 하나다 Her beautiful eyes are among her greatest charms.

**매료**(魅了) ~하다 charm; fascinate; captivate; enchant; cast a spell 《on》; hold 《the audience》 spellbound. ¶ 그의 연설은 청중을 ~시켰다 His speech held the audience spellbound. / 그녀의 우아함은 파티석상의 모든 사람을 ~했다 Her graciousness charmed everyone at the party.

**매립**(埋立) (land) reclamation; filling-up. ~하다 fill up 《a pond with earth》; fill in 《a moat》; reclaim 《land from the sea》. ¶ 간석지의 ~ reclamation of the foreshore / 신공항 건설을 위해 바다를 ~하다 reclaim land from the sea to build a new airport / 그 공업 단지는 바다를 ~하여 만든 것이다 The industrial park was formed by reclaiming from the sea. ◉ ~공사 land reclamation work. ~지 reclaimed land 〔ground〕; a landfill (쓰레기의); a land reclamation site (매립 중인).

**매만지다** adjust 《*one's* dress》; trim; smooth (down); primp (up). ¶ 머리를 ~ smooth down *one's* hair / 옷을 ~ adjust 〔straighten〕 *one's* clothes; tidy 〔fix 《미》〕 *oneself.*

**매맛** a taste of the whip; whipping; flogging. ¶ 너 ~ 좀 봐야겠다 I shall have to give you a taste of the whip.

**매맞다** be whipped 〔lashed〕; suffer a whipping; get flogged. ¶ 그런 짓을 하면 매맞는다 If you do such a thing, you will get whipped. / 또 매맞고 싶니 Do you want another thrashing?

**매매**(賣買) buying and selling; purchase and sale; 《거래》 trade; dealings; a transaction; a bargain. ~하다 buy and sell; deal 〔trade〕 《in》; traffic 《in drugs》. ¶ 가까스로 ~를 약정하다 manage to strike 〔close〕 a bargain 《with a certain company》/ 그는 부동산 ~를 하고 있다 He deals in real estate. / 그것은 그램 당 얼마로 ~된다 It is sold at so much a gram. / 그는 마약 ~로 체포되었다 He was arrested for trafficking drugs. / 증권거래소에서는 약 200만주의 주식 ~가 있었다 About two million shares changed hands on the security exchange. ◉ ~가격 sale 〔selling〕 price. ~계약 a sales contract; a bargain; a contract for 〔of〕 sale. ~액 a turnover; sales amount. ~조건 terms of sale. ~증서 a bill of sale. 부정~ an illegal bargain 〔transaction〕. 위장~ a wash sale (주식의).

**매머드** a mammoth. ◉ ~건물 a massive 〔colossal〕 building. ~기업 a mammoth enterprise. ~도시 a megalopolis; a huge city. ~탱커 a gigantic tanker; a supertanker.

**매명**(賣名) self-advertisement; self-publicity. ~하다 publicize 〔advertise〕 *oneself;* seek publicity. ¶ ~을 위해 for publicity's sake; in order to have *one's* name up / ~을 일삼다 seek 〔court, strive for〕 publicity. ◉ ~행위 an act of self-advertisement.

**매몰**(埋沒) burying. ~하다 bury 《in, under》. ¶ 눈 속에 ~되다 be buried under snow.

**매몰스럽다** (be) unkind; cold; hard; callous; heartless. ¶ 매몰스럽게 cold-heartedly; curtly; icily; coldly / 매몰스러운 태도 a cold 〔an unfriendly〕 attitude; a distant air / 매몰스럽게 굴다 be short with 《*a person*》; give 《*a person*》 the cold shoulder.

**매몰차다** (be) very unkind; very cold; hard; harsh; callous; heartless.

**매무새** the appearance of *one's* dress. ¶ ~를 고치다 adjust *one's* dress; tidy (up) *oneself* / ~가 단정하다 keep *oneself* neat and trim; look neat and tidy.

**매무시** adjusting 〔primping〕 of the attire. ～하다 adjust 〔primp, tidy〕 *oneself;* make *one's* toilet. ¶ 단정하게 ～하다 make *oneself* look neat and tidy.

**매문**(賣文) literary hackwork. ～하다 sell *one's* writing; make a living with *one's* pen. ¶ ～을 업으로 하다 be engaged in literary hackwork.
◉ ～업자 a penny-a-liner; a hack-writer; a literary journeyman.

**매물**(賣物) an article for 〔on〕 sale; 《게시》 For sale. ¶ ～로 내놓다 put 《*a thing*》 on the market; offer 〔put up〕 《*a thing*》 for sale; place 《*a thing*》 on sale / 이 제품은 ～이 아니다 This product is not salable 〔marketable〕.

**매미** 〖곤충〗 a cicada (*pl.* ～s, -dae); a balm cricket; a locust 《미》. ¶ ～의 허물 the cast-off shell of a cicada / ～가 울다 a cicada chirrs / ～의 우는 소리 the chirring of a cicada / ～의 합창 소리 the chirring of cicadas in chorus.

**매방**(買方) a buyer; a purchaser; 〖증권〗 a bull; bull operators.

**매방**(賣方) a seller; the selling side; 〖증권〗 a bear.

**매번**(每番) 《매회》 every 〔each〕 time; 《자주》 very often; frequently; 《늘》 always. ¶ ～ 폐를 끼쳐 죄송합니다 I am sorry to trouble you so often 〔frequently〕. / 여러 차례 해 보았으나 ～ 실패했다 I made several attempts only to fail as many times.

**매복**(埋伏) 《숨어 있음》 lying in ambush; 《복병》 an ambush. ～하다 lie in ambush; ambush; waylay; lay an ambush. ¶ ～했다가 공격하다 attack 《enemy》 from ambush.

**매복**(賣卜) ～하다 sell 〔tell〕 fortunes; practice divination.

**매부**(妹夫) *one's* sister's husband; *one's* brother-in-law.

**매부리**[1] 《매 부리는 사람》 a falconer; a hawker.

**매부리**[2] 《매의 부리》 a hawk's beak 〔bill〕. ¶ ～ 같은 hawkbilled. ◉ ～코 a hooknose; a hooked 〔an aquiline〕 nose.

**매사**(每事) every 〔each〕 business 〔affair, matter〕; every circumstance; each undertaking; each plan. ¶ ～에 《만사에》 in everything; 《어김없이》 always; 《변함없이》 invariably / 그는 ～에 성공했다 He succeeded in everything he attempted. / ～는 불여(不如) 튼튼 All business should be carefully attended to so that it never fails. ◉ ～불성 failing in every undertaking.

**매사냥** hawking; falconry. ～하다 hunt with a hawk; go hawking; hawk.
◉ ～꾼 a falconer; a hawker.

**매사추세츠** 《미국의 주》 Massachusetts (생략 Mass.).

**매삭**(每朔) every month; monthly.

**매상**(買上) buying; purchase; 《정부의》 procurement. ～하다 buy; purchase. ¶ 정부의 ～ 가격 the Government's buying 〔purchasing〕 price 《for rice》.

**매상**(賣上) sales; selling; 《수익·매상고》 the proceeds; takings. ¶ 그날의 ～ the day's takings / 어제는 50만 원의 ～을 올렸다 The sales of yesterday totaled 500,000 won. / 오늘 ～은 어제보다 많았다 Today's sale was larger than yesterday's. ◉ ～계정 (a) sales account. ～금 the amount sold; the sales; the proceeds (of sales): 학교 축제의 ～금 the proceeds from the school festival. ～세 sales tax. ～장부 sales book. ～전표 a sales slip.

**매상고**(賣上高) sales; sales volume; the takings 〔proceeds〕. ¶ 매달 영업의 ～는 얼마나 오릅니까 How much does your business bring in every month?
◉ 순～ the net sales. 총～ the gross sales.

**매석**(賣惜) ～하다 hold back 《goods》 from the market; hold off selling 《goods》; be unwilling 〔indisposed〕 to sell *something* (in expectation of better prices). ¶ 생산자는 가격 상승을 예상하고 ～행위를 하고 있다 Producers are holding off selling in anticipation of a rise in price.

**매설**(埋設) laying. ～하다 lay 《a cable》 underground 〔under the ground〕.
◉ ～선 underground wiring.

**매섭다** (be) severe; strict; fierce; violent. ¶ 매서운 공격 a severe attack; a bitter criticism (비난) / 매서운 눈초리 hard eyes / 매섭게 생기다 look sharp; look fierce.

**매세**(買勢) bullish sentiment. ¶ 주식 시장은 ～가 강하다 The stock market is very inclined to be bullish. *or* The mood in the stock market is very bullish.

**매세**(賣勢) 《팔림세》 bearish sentiment; selling support.

**매수**(枚數) the number of sheets 〔leaves〕.

**매수**(買收) ① 《매입》 purchase; buying up. ～하다 purchase; buy up. ¶ 토지

를 ~하다 buy 〔purchase〕 land / 그 회사는 작은 회사를 ~하여 성장해 왔다 That company has been growing by buying up small businesses / 그 출판사는 미국의 대부호에게 ~되었다 That publishing company was bought up by an American billionaire.
② 《뇌물로》 bribery; buying. ~하다 bribe 《*a person*》; win 《*a person*》 over by bribery; buy 《*a person*》 (off). ¶ ~할 수 있는 bribable / 국회 의원을 ~하다 buy off some members of the National Assembly / 유권자를 ~하다 buy voters 〔votes〕 / 경영자측에 ~당하다 be bought over to the management / 돈에 ~당할 내가 아니다 Money can't buy me.
◉ ~가격 a purchase price. ~계획 a purchasing plan. ~운동 an agitation 〔effort〕 for buying 《*a person*》 off. ~합병 《기업의》 mergers and acquisitions (M & A).

**매수**(買受) buying (over); acquiring by purchase. ~하다 acquire 《*a thing*》 by purchase; purchase; buy over; take over. ◉ ~대금 the price (paid). ~인 a purchaser; 『법』 a vendee.

**매스게임** massed calisthenics 〔gymnastics〕 (★ mass game은 우리식 영어).

**매스미디어** the (mass) media.

**매스컴** the mass media; mass communications; the press; journalism. ¶ ~에서 떠들어대다 receive 〔get〕 a lot of publicity in the media 〔press〕 / ~을 타고 싶어하다〔경원하다〕 seek 〔avoid〕 press publicity / 사건을 ~에서 떠들어댈 것이 두려워 행방을 감추다 disappear somewhere for fear that the media would get a lot of attention from the media.

**매시**(每時) every hour; per hour. ¶ ~50 마일의 속도로 at a speed of 50 miles per hour; at 50 mph 〔m.p.h.〕.

**매시근하다** (be) weary; languid; worn out; exhausted.

**매식**(買食) 《행위》 eating at a restaurant; 《음식》 a paid meal. ~하다 eat 〔have a meal〕 at a restaurant. ⌈cot.

**매실**(梅實) a *maesil;* a Japanese apri-

**매실매실하다** (be) sly; crafty; foxy.

**매씨**(妹氏) ① 《남의 누이》 your esteemed sister. ② 《손윗누이》 *one's* elder sister.

**매암돌다** 《돌다》 spin *oneself* round; whirl (till dizzy); 《발전이 없다》 remain in obscurity. ¶ 평사원으로 ~ remain 〔live the humdrum life of〕 a mere clerk.

**매암돌리다** 《제자리에서》 spin 《*a person*》 round; whirl 《*a person*》 round; 《이리저리》 keep 《*a person*》 hopping on one errand after another; send 《*a person*》 on a wild goose chase.

**매암쇠** the rynd 〔rind〕 of a millstone.

**매약**(賣約) a sales contract. ~하다 make a sales contract; contract to sell. ¶ ~필 《게시》 Sold.

**매약**(賣藥) a patent medicine; a drug. ~하다 sell a patent medicine. ◉ ~상 《사람》 a druggist; 《상점》 a drugstore. ~ 행상인 a medicine peddler.

**매양**(每—) always; every 〔all the〕 time. ¶ ~ 놀고만 있다 be always playing 〔idle〕; do nothing but play.

**매연**(煤煙) 《그을음·연기》 (sooty) smoke; soot and smoke; soot; smut; 《자동차의》 exhaust gas; automobile exhaust fumes. ¶ ~이 많은〔적은〕 도시 a smoky 〔smokeless〕 city / ~으로 더러워진 벽 a smutty 〔smoke-stained〕 wall / ~을 뿜어내다 fume out exhaust gas / 자동차의 ~이 스모그 현상의 주요 원인의 하나로 꼽히고 있다 Automobile exhaust fumes are blamed as one of the major causes of smog. ◉ ~공해 smoke pollution. ~농도계 a smoke indicator. ~업소 an industrial establishment causing smoke pollution. ~차량 harmful-gas emitting vehicles: ~차량을 엄중 단속하다 exercise strict control over vehicles with faulty exhausts that produce harmful fume.

**매염**(媒染) mordanting; fixing colors by means of mordant. ~하다 mordant 《*a thing*》; treat 《*a thing*》 with a mordant. ◉ ~료〔제〕 a mordant; a fixative: ~제를 사용하다 mordant 《*a thing*》; treat 《*a thing*》 with a mordant. ~성 (quality of) mordancy: ~성의 mordant. ~염료 mordant dyes.

**매우** very; exceedingly; remarkably; extraordinarily; so; really; terribly; awfully; badly; much.
¶ ~ 많은 돈 very much money / ~아름다운 여인 a very 〔most〕 beautiful woman / ~ 빨리 much too fast / ~ 놀랍게도 to *one's* great surprise / ~ 크다 be extremely large / ~ 아름답다 be quite beautiful / ~ 피곤하다 be very tired / ~ 감사하고 있다 be much obliged 《to you》 / 오늘은 ~ 덥다 It is awfully 〔so, very, terribly〕 hot today. / 그녀를 만나 ~ 기뻤다 I was really glad to see her. / 네가 없어 ~ 섭섭하다 I miss you badly. / 그는 ~ 놀

란 표정이었다 He wore a very surprised expression. / 그는 ~ 영리해 보였다 He looked extremely smart to me.

**매운바람** a sharp 〔biting, cutting〕 wind.

**매운탕**(―湯) a pepper-pot soup.

**매월**(每月) every 〔each〕 month. ¶ ~의 monthly / ~ 두 번 twice a month.

**매음**(賣淫) prostitution; harlotry. ~하다 practice prostitution; prostitute *oneself;* become 〔be〕 a prostitute; go 〔be〕 on the street.

◉ ~굴 a brothel; a whorehouse; a hot house 《속어》. ~녀 a harlot; a prostitute; a whore; a hooker 《미속어》; a call girl. ~방지법 the Anti-Prostitution Law. ~행위 prostitution.

**매이다** ① 《끈으로》 be tied; be fastened. ¶ 구두끈이 ~ shoelaces are fastened; *one's* shoes are tied / 소가 나무에 매여 있다 A cow is tied to a tree. ② 《목이》 be strangled; be hanged 《to death》. ③ 《얽매이다》 be restricted 〔bound, tied〕. ¶ 규칙에 ~ be bound by a rule / 일에 ~ be chained 〔tied down〕 to *one's* work 〔business〕 / 시간에 ~ be restricted by time; have very little time to call *one's* own / 나는 무엇에나 매인다는 것은 질색이다 I can't stand being tied down. *or* I am impatient of any restriction.

**매인**(每人) every 〔each〕 person. ¶ ~당 for each person; per capita 〔head〕 / ~당 두개씩 주어라 Give them two apiece.

**매인목숨** not being *one's* own boss; being an underling 〔a slave〕; an underling; a slave. ¶ ~이다 be not *one's* own master / ~이라 시간이 자유롭지 않다 Since I am not my own boss, I have no time to myself at all. / 회사에 ~이 되어 일요일밖에는 틈을 낼 수가 없다 Since I am an employee of the company, I have only Sundays to myself.

**매일**(每日) every 〔each〕 day. ¶ ~의 daily; everyday / ~ 정해진 일 a daily routine / ~ 하는 일 daily work / ~ 《되풀이 해서》 day after day; day in day out; 《날이 갈수록》 day by day; from day to day; with each passing day / ~ 오전 중에 every morning / 이런 일이란 ~ 일어나는 것이 아니다 This sort of thing doesn't happen every day. / ~이 그저 그 타령이었다 One day was just like another.

**매일반**(―一般) all the same. ⇨매한가지.

**매입**(買入) buying; (a) purchase. ~하다 purchase; buy in 〔up〕. ¶ 대량으로 ~하다 make a large purchase of 《rice》 / 돈을 다른 토지를 ~하는 데 돌리다 apply the money to purchase the other lands / 고본 고가 ~ 《게시》 Secondhand books bought at good prices. ◉ ~가격 〔원가〕 the purchase price. ~계획 a purchasing plan. ~상환 redemption 〔repayment〕 by purchase. ~소각 〖증권〗 optional redemption; retirement of shares. ~주문〖증권〗 buy 〔purchase〕 orders. ~환율 a buying rate of exchange; a buying exchange quotation.

**매자나무** 〖식물〗 a Korean barbery.

**매자목**(賣子木) 〖식물〗 a snowbell (plant); a storax.

**매작지근하다** ＝미지근하다.

**매장**(埋葬) ① 《시체의》 burial; interment. ~하다 bury; inter; lay 《*a person*》 to rest.

② 《사회적인》 social ostracism. ~하다 ostracize; expel 〔oust〕 《*a person*》 from society; treat 《*a person*》 as a social outcast. ¶ ~되다 be ousted 〔excluded〕 from society; become a social outcast / 그런 자는 사회에서 ~되어야 한다 He ought to be ostracized from society.

◉ ~비 cost of burial. ~식 《perform》 the burial service. ~신고 the report of a burial. ~지 a burial ground; 《묘지》 a cemetery; a graveyard. ~허가증 a burial permit.

**매장**(埋藏) 《묻어 감춤》 burying underground. ~하다 bury 〔hide〕 《*a thing*》 underground. ¶ ~되어 있다 lie under the ground / 이 산에는 꽤 많은 광물이 ~되어 있다 There are rich mineral deposit in these hills.

◉ ~량 reserves: 석탄〔석유〕의 ~량 coal 〔oil〕 deposits; the estimated amount of coal 〔oil〕 deposits. ~물 something buried 《in the ground》; 《광물 따위의》 a 《coal》 deposit. ~지대 a 《coal》 field.

**매장**(賣場) 《파는 장소》 a selling area; 《백화점 따위의》 the 《jewelry》 counter; the 《food》 floor; the 《menswear》 department. ¶ 그녀는 화장품 ~에서 일한다 She clerks behind the cosmetic counter. ◉ ~감독 a floor 〔section〕 manager; a floorwalker 《미》; a shopwalker 《영》. ~판매원 a sales clerk.

**매절**(賣切) being sold out. ⇨매진(賣盡). ~하다 sell out. ¶ ~되다 be sold out; go out of stock.

**매점**(買占) buying up; a corner(ing). ~하다 buy up 《all the coffee in the market》; corner the market 《in wheat》; corner 〔make a corner in〕 《silver, the shares of Company B》. ◉ 시장~ market cornering.

**매점**(賣店) a stand; a booth; a stall; a store 《미》. ¶ 신문~ a newsstand 《미》/ 역의 ~ a station stall / 학교 ~ 《미》 school store / ~을 내다 install a booth; set up a stand.

**매정하다, 매정스럽다** (be) unkind; hard-〔cold-〕hearted; cold; heartless. ¶ 매정한 말 cruel 〔unkind〕 words; harsh things / 매정하게 거절하다 give a flat 〔point-blank〕 refusal; spurn 《a demand》 point-blank 〔bluntly〕 / 매정한 소리를 하다 speak heartlessly; say a harsh thing / 매정하게 굴다 treat 《*a person*》 coldly 〔in a cold way〕 / 나는 그런 매정한 짓은 못한다 It is not in my heart to be so cruel.

**매제**(妹弟) *one's* younger sister's husband; a brother-in-law.

**매조지** (putting on) the finishing touches; the finish.

**매주**(每週) every 〔each〕 week; weekly; per week (1주마다). ¶ ~의 weekly / ~한 차례 once a week / ~ 토요일 every Saturday.

**매주**(買主) 《사람》 a buyer; a purchaser; 〖법〗 a vendee; 〖증권〗 a bull; bull operators. ¶ 그 신제품에는 곧 ~가 나타날 것이다 You'll find ready buyers for the new products. ◉ ~시장 a buyers' market.

**매주**(賣主) a seller; a vendor; 〖증권〗 a bear; 〖법〗 a bargainer. ◉ ~시장 a sellers' market.

**매직** magic. ◉ ~아이 《라디오 등의》《상표명》 a Magic Eye. ~유리 one-way glass. ~ 잉크 (a kind of) marking ink; 《상표명》 Magic Ink. ~핸드 〖전자공학〗 a magic hand; a manipulator.

**매진**(賣盡) selling out. ~하다 sell 〔clear〕 out; run out of 《merchandise》. ¶ ~되다 be sold out; be cleared (off, out); be 〔go〕 out of stock / 금일 ~ 《게시》 Sold out today. / 승차권 ~《게시》 Tickets sold out. / 좌석이 ~되었다 Every seat was booked. / 광고낸 품목이 ~되었다 The advertised items are sold out.

**매진**(邁進) pushing on. ~하다 push on 〔forward〕; struggle on; 《노력》 strive 《for》. ¶ 우리는 다음 승리를 향해 ~할 것을 약속했다 We promised to push on toward the next victory.

**매질** whipping; lashing; flogging; beating. ~하다 whip; lash; flog; beat.

**매질**(媒質) 〖물리〗 a medium.

**매체**(媒體) 〖물리〗 a medium (*pl.* ~s, -dia); a vehicle 《of sound》. ¶ 광고~ a medium of advertisement / 대중~ the mass media / 공기는 소리의 ~이다 Air is the vehicle of sound. / 텔레비전은 매스컴의 가장 중요한 ~ 중 하나이다 Television is one of the most important media of mass communication.

**매초**(每秒) every 〔per〕 second. ¶ ~10미터의 속도로 at a velocity 〔speed〕 of 10 meters per second.

**매초롬하다** possess a healthy beauty.

**매축**(埋築) (land) reclamation. ⇨ 매립.

**매춘**(賣春) prostitution. ⇨ 매음(賣淫).

**매출**(賣出) (a) sale; selling. ⇨ 매상(賣上). ~하다 sell off 〔out〕; offer 《*a thing*》 for sale; place 《*a thing*》 on the market; put 《*a thing*》 on sale. ¶ 연말 대~ the year-end (bargain) sale / 특가〔염가〕~ a 「special 〔bargain, discount〕 sale / 이 신제품은 내일부터 ~된다 This new product will go on sale tomorrow. / 신형차의 ~은 연말까지 연기되었다 The launch of the new car (onto the market) has been postponed until the end of the year. ◉ ~가격 an offering price. ~광고 an advertisement of the opening sale.

**매캐하다** ① 《연기내가》 (be) smoky. ¶ 방이 ~ a room is smoky. ② 《곰팡내가》 (be) musty; moldy; fusty. ¶ 매캐한 곰팡내가 나다 smell musty 〔fusty〕.

**매콤하다** (be) somewhat hot; peppery; pungent; sharp. ¶ 매콤한 냄새 a peppery smell / 「이 카레는 맛이 어떻지」—「너무 매콤해」 "How do you like this curry?"—"It's too hot for me."

**매크로** 《매우 큰》 macro-. ¶ ~ 세계의 macrocosmic 《laws of the universe》. ◉ ~경제학 macroeconomics: ~경제학적인 macroeconomic. ~바이오틱스 《장수 식사법》 macrobiotics. ~코즘 《대우주》 the macrocosm.

**매트** a 《floor》 mat. ¶ 도어~ a doormat.

**매트리스** a mattress.

**매파**(—派) 《강경파》 the hawks; a hard-liner. ¶ 의회 내의 ~와 비둘기파 the hawks and the doves in the Congress.

**매파**(媒婆) an old woman go-between 〔matchmaker〕.

**매판자본**(買辦資本) comprador capital. ¶ 이 나라의 경제적 근대화를 위해선 ~이 민족 자본으로 대체되어야 한다 National capital must replace the comprador capital if this country is to attain its economic modernization.

**매팔자**(一八字) easy circumstances.

**매표**(賣票) selling of tickets. ～하다 sell tickets. ¶ ～ 시간 09:00—17:00 《게시》 Ticket sales hours 9:00 AM—5:00 PM. ◉ ～구 a ticket window. ～소 a ticket office 〔box〕; 《영》 a booking office; a box office (극장의). ～원 a ticket agent 〔girl〕.

**매품**(賣品) an article for sale; 《게시》 「For sale.

**매한가지** sameness. ¶ ～의 the same; all the same; much the same / 오늘 가나 내일 가나 ～다 It makes no difference whether you go today or tomorrow. / 엎어지나 젖혀지나 ～다 It is six of one and half a dozen of the other.

**매형**(妹兄) *one's* elder sister's husband; 「*one's* brother-in-law.

**매호**(每戶) every 〔each〕 house(hold).

**매호**(每號) every 〔each〕 number 〔issue〕.

**매혹**(魅惑) (a) fascination; (a) charm. ～하다 fascinate; captivate; bewitch; charm. ¶ ～적인 charming; bewitching; captivating; fascinating / ～적인 여자 a glamorous 〔an enchanting〕 woman / ～적인 미소 a bewitching smile / 사람을 ～하는 일종의 마력이 있다 possess a magical power of charming people / 여자의 매력에 ～당하다 fall under the spell of a girl's charms; fall a victim to a woman's charms.

**매화**(梅花) 〖식물〗 a Japanese apricot tree (나무); an *maehwa* blossom (꽃). ◉ ～주 (a) *maehwa* wine.

**매회**(每回) each 〔every〕 time; each 〔every〕 round (권투 따위) 〔inning (야구 따위)〕. ¶ 우리팀은 ～ 득점했다 Our team scored one or more runs every inning.

**매흙** a fine gray loam (for plastering). ¶ ～질하다 plaster a wall with gray loam.

**맥**(脈) ① 《맥박》 the pulse; pulsation. ¶ 맥이 뛰는 곳 the places (on a human body) where the pulse can be felt / 맥이 고르다〔고르지 못하다〕 the pulse is regular 〔irregular〕 / 맥이 끊어지다 the pulse 「stops 〔ceases to beat〕 / 맥이 뛰다 the pulse beats; pulsate / 맥이 빠르다 have a quick 〔rapid〕 pulse; the pulse beats 〔goes〕 fast / 맥이 느리다 have a slow pulse / 맥이 약하다 the pulse is weak 〔feeble〕 / 맥을 보다 《진맥》 feel 〔take〕 《*a person's*》 pulse; 《살핌》 sound out 《*a person*》; feel out 《a situation》 / 맥도 모르고 침통 흔든다 try to do 〔cope with〕 something without knowing anything about it.
② 《광맥》 a (mineral) vein. ¶ 맥을 뚫다 《광맥을》 open up a vein of ore / 맥을 찾아내다 strike a vein of ore.
③ 《풍수지리의》 a favorable location where the spirits of the dragons are supposed to converge.
④ 《생기·힘》 spirit; vigor. ¶ 여자 앞에서 맥을 못추다 get weak-kneed in the presence of a woman / 맥이 풀리다 lose *one's* energy 〔vigor〕; fall into low spirits; be dispirited.

**맥각**(麥角) 〖식물〗 ergot. ◉ ～소 ergotine. ～중독 ergotism.

**맥고**(麥藁) (a) barley 〔wheat〕 straw. ◉ ～ 모자 a straw hat.

**맥농**(麥農) cultivation of barley 〔wheat〕; barley 〔wheat〕 farming.

**맥도**(脈度) (a) pulse (frequency); a pulse rate.

**맥동**(脈動) 〖물리〗 pulsation.

**맥락**(脈絡) ① 〖해부·생물〗 the veins; the system of veins. ② 《사물의》 a thread 〔line〕 of connection; a chain of reasoning; logical connection; coherence; the context (문맥). ¶ ～이 없는 incoherent; disconnected; disjointed / 그의 이야기는 ～이 닿지 않아 이해하기 어려웠다 His speech was difficult to understand because it was so disjointed. ◉ ～막 〖해부〗 the choroid.

**맥량**(麥涼) the cool weather at the barley ripening 〔harvest〕 season.

**맥량**(麥糧) barley of summer provisions.

**맥류**(麥類) a sorts of barley (barley, wheat, oats, *etc.*).

**맥리**(脈理) ① 《문맥의》 logical connection; coherence; the context. ② 《진맥의》 the diagnostic theory of the pulse.

**맥맥이**(脈脈—) continuously; uninterruptedly; unbrokenly. ¶ ～ 이어오는 우리의 전통 our unbroken tradition / 평화 운동의 정신은 ～ 이어질 것이다 The spirit of the peace movement will live on.

**맥맥하다** ① 《코가》 (be) stuffy; be stuffed-〔bunged-〕up. ¶ 코가 ～ *one's* nose is stuffy; have a stuffed-up nose. ② 《생각이》 be stuck 《for an idea》; be at a loss 《for ideas》; be at *one's* wit's end. ¶ 생각이 ～ be stuck for an idea.

**맥박**(脈搏) 〖생리〗 the pulse; pulsation; the beat of the pulse; 《the regularity of》 a blood beat. ⇨맥(脈)①. ¶ ~이 정상이다 The pulse is normal. / ~이 120으로 뛰어 올랐다 The pulse mounted to 120. ◉ ~계 a pulsimeter; a sphygmometer. ~수 《1분간의》 the pulse (rate); a pulse count. 결체성(結滯性) ~ intermittent pulse.

**맥보다**(脈—) ① 《진맥하다》 feel 〔have *one's* fingers on〕 《*a person's*》 pulse. ② 《살피다》 sound out 《*a person's* view》; feel 〔sound〕 《*a person* on a subject》.

**맥분**(麥粉) (wheat) flour.

**맥빠지다**(脈—) ① 《기운없다》 feel weak 〔feeble〕; be tired 〔exhausted〕; be worn out. ¶ 맥빠진 얼굴을 하다 look languid / 한 삼십 리 걸었더니 맥이 빠진다 Having walked 30 *ri* or so, I feel pretty tired. ② 《낙심하다》 be dispirited 〔disappointed, depressed, discouraged〕; be damped; be disheartened. ¶ 그 소식을 듣고 맥(이)빠져 버렸다 The news damped my spirits. / 시험 결과를 보고 나는 맥(이) 빠졌다 I felt greatly disappointed at the result of the examination.

**맥시** a maxi; a maxi-skirt〔-coat〕. ¶ ~ 오더 《대량 주문》 a maxiorder.

**맥시류**(脈翅類) 〖곤충〗 Neuroptera.

**맥아**(麥芽) malt. ◉ ~당 maltose; malt sugar.

**맥암**(脈岩) 〖지질〗 a dyke rock.

**맥없다**(脈—) 《기운없다》 (be) weak; feeble; feel tired 〔exhausted, enervated, worn out, done in〕; 《풀죽다》 (be) dispirited; dejected; be in low spirits; be in the dumps; feel blue.

**맥없이**(脈—) ① 《기운없이》 weakly; feebly; spiritlessly; in low spirits; helplessly; disappointedly; 《쉽게》 easily; without difficulty. ¶ ~ 쓰러지다 fall down helplessly / ~ 앉다 sit exhausted; sit dejected / 맥없이 지다 be easily beaten 《in the match》. ② 《공연히》 without any reason; for no reason. ¶ ~ 울다 start crying at the least little thing.

**맥작**(麥作) 《재배》 cultivation of 「barley 〔wheat, *etc.*〕; barley culture; 《수확》 a barley crop.

**맥주**(麥酒) beer; ale. ¶ 생~ draft beer 《미》; draught beer 《영》 / 흑~ dark 〔black〕 beer; porter; stout / ~ 한 조끼 a jug 〔mug〕 of beer / ~의 거품 froth 〔bubbles〕 on beer / ~를 한잔 하다 have a (glass of) beer / 김빠진 ~ stale 〔flat〕 beer / 김빠진 ~ 같다 be as insipid as stale beer / ~ 두 잔 주시오 Two beers, please. / 그는 ~ 한 잔에 취해버렸다 He got drunk on a single glass of beer. ◉ ~병 a beer bottle. ~양조 beer brewing: ~양조장 a beer brewery. ~조끼 a beer jug. ~집〔홀〕 an ale-house; a beer hall. ~통 a beer barrel. 깡통〔캔〕~ canned beer. 병~ bottled beer.

**맥줄**(脈—) an artery.

**맥쩍다** ① 《따분하다》 (be) bored; tedious; dull. ¶ 할 일이 없어 ~ With nothing to do, I am bored to death. ② 《낯이 없다》 be ashamed of *oneself;* be put out of countenance. ¶ 돈을 더 꾸어 달라기가 ~ I feel constrained to ask for more money.

**맥추**(麥秋) the harvest time for barley; June.

**맥파**(脈波) 〖의학〗 a pulse wave. ◉ ~계 a sphygmograph.

**맥풀리다**(脈—) = 맥빠지다.

**맨**[1] 《오로지》 exclusively; nothing but 〔else〕; just; full of. ¶ 구경거리는 없고 맨 사람뿐이다 There is nothing to see but lots of people. / 연못에 맨 물고기다 The pond is full of fish 〔swarms with fish〕.

**맨**[2] 《제일》 (ut)most; the very; extreme. ¶ 맨 처음〔먼저〕 at the very first; first of all; before every thing else; before all others; right at the start / 맨 꼴지 the very last 〔bottom〕; the tail (end) / 맨 꼭대기에 on the top 《of》; the highest / 맨 나중에 at the very end 〔last〕; last of all; behind all others / 맨 아래에 at the very bottom; the lowest / 맨 왼편 집 a house at the very left; the house way at the left / 그것은 복도 맨 끝에 있습니다 It's way down at the end of the hall.

**맨-** [접두사] bare; naked. ¶ 맨발 bare feet / 맨손 an empty 〔a bare〕 hand / ~바닥 the bare floor.

**맨꽁무니** 《빈털터리》 without resources; empty-handed. ¶ ~로 장사를 시작하다 start a business without a cent to back *one* up.

**맨끝** the (very) end 〔last〕. ¶ ~의 final; concluding; closing / 편지의 ~에 at the close of a letter; in closing *one's* letter / 책의 ~ 페이지 the last page of a book.

**맨나중** the very last 〔end〕. ¶ ~의 final; terminal / ~에 in conclusion; finally /

그는 ~에 왔다 He arrived last.

**맨둥맨둥하다** (be) treeless; bare; bald.

**맨뒤** the very last 〔end〕; the tail (end). ¶ 줄 ~에 서 있다 be at the tail of a queue.

**맨드라미** 〖식물〗 a cockscomb.

**맨땅** 《sit on》 the bare ground.

**맨머리** 《아무것도 안 쓴》 a bare head; a hatless head; 《쪽진 머리》 a hairdo done without any false hair. ¶ ~로 나가다 go out bareheaded; go out without putting on a hat.

**맨먼저** at the very first 〔beginning〕; first of all. ¶ ~의 foremost; first / 그가 ~왔다 He was the first to come. / 그의 이름이 ~ 나와 있다 His name leads the list. / 아침에 일어나면 ~ 냉수욕을 한다 I take a cold bath first of all in the morning.

**맨몸** ① 《알몸》 a naked body; nudity; nakedness; a nude. ¶ ~으로 naked (-ly); in *one's* birthday suit; in the raw; stark-naked / ~이 되다 become naked; strip; strip *oneself* naked; strip to the skin / ~으로 자다 sleep naked; sleep in the raw. ② 《무일푼》 being penniless. ¶ ~이 되다 become penniless; go broke.

**맨몸뚱이** a naked body. ⇨ 맨몸.

**맨밑** the very bottom. ¶ ~의 the lowest; the bottommost.

**맨바닥** the bare floor 〔ground〕.

**맨발** bare feet. ¶ ~의 barefoot(ed) / ~이 되다 become barefooted / ~로 다니다 go 〔walk around〕 barefoot 〔in *one's* bare feet〕.

**맨밥** rice without any side dishes. ¶ ~을 먹다 eat rice alone; eat rice without any side dishes at all.

**맨션** a mansion (★ 영어의 맨션은 보통 부호의 대저택을 말함). ◉ ~아파트 a luxury apartment; an apartment house of a better class; a condominium.

**맨손** an empty 〔a bare〕 hand. ⇨ 맨주먹. ¶ ~으로 돌아오다 return empty-handed / ~으로 고기를 잡다 catch a fish with *one's* bare hands. ◉ ~ 체조 free gymnastics 〔exercise〕.

**맨숭맨숭하다** ① 《털이 없다》 (be) hairless; bare; bald. ¶ 턱이 ~ be beardless; have no beard; have a bald chin. ② 《나무가 없다》 (be) treeless; bare; bald. ③ 《안 취하다》 (be) unintoxicated; sober. ¶ 자네가 술을 얼마나 마셨는지 모르겠지만 아직 맨숭맨숭하군 그래 I don't know how much you have drunk, but you seem none the worse for it.

**맨아래** the very bottom. ¶ ~의 the lowest; the nethermost; the undermost; the bottommost.

**맨앞** the van; the head; the foremost; the (very) front. ¶ ~의 foremost / ~에 at the head 《of》 / ~에서 걷다 walk at the head 《of》 / 행렬의 ~에 서 있다 be in the van 〔front〕 of parade 〔procession〕.

**맨위** the (very) top; the summit; the peak. ¶ ~의 topmost; uppermost; highest / ~ 선반 the top shelf.

**맨입** an empty mouth 〔stomach〕. ¶ ~에 술을 하다 drink on an empty stomach / ~으로 집을 나왔다 I left home without eating.

**맨주먹** a naked fist; an empty fist; a bare 〔an empty〕 hand. ¶ ~으로 with empty hands; bare-handed; with *one's* naked fists; unarmed (무기없이) / ~으로 싸우다 fight with *one's* own naked fists / ~으로 장사를 시작하다 start a business with practically nothing / ~으로 범을 잡다 kill a tiger with *one's* naked fists / ~으로 큰 돈을 모으다 make a fortune starting with nothing.

**맨처음** the (very) first; the outset; the beginning; the earliest; the original. ¶ ~에 at first; at 〔in〕 the beginning / ~에 오다 come first; be the first to come / ~에 김씨의 연설이 있었다 The meeting opened with Mr. Kim's address.

**맨투맨** one-to-one. ¶ ~ 방어작전을 쓰다 use 〔adopt〕 a man-to-man defence.

**맨틀피스** 《벽난로의 선반》 a mantelpiece.

**맨해튼** ① 《뉴욕의》 Manhattan. ② 《칵테일》 manhattan (cocktail).

**맨홀** a manhole. ◉ ~ 뚜껑 a manhole cover.

**맬더스** 《영국의 경제학자》 Thomas Robert Malthus (1766-1834). ◉ ~학설 Malthusianism.

**맴돌다** whirl; spin round. ⇨ 매암돌다.

**맴맴** chirping (of a cicada). ¶ 매미가 ~ 울다 a cicada is chirping.

**맵다** ① 《맛이》 (be) hot; pungent; sharp; spicy. ¶ 매운 소스 a pungent sauce / 국이 ~ the soup is hot. ② 《혹독하다》 (be) severe; strict. ¶ 매운 추위 severe cold (weather) / 사람이 ~ be a hard man.

**맵시** stylishness; shapeliness; form; appearance. ¶ ~ 있는 몸매 a handsome 〔graceful〕 figure / ~ 없는 구두

ugly 〔shapeless〕 shoes / 옷을 ~ 있게 입다 wear *one's* clothes stylishly; dress *oneself* in good shape / 그녀는 언제나 옷 ~에 신경을 쓴다 She always keeps herself 「neat 〔tidy〕. *or* She is always careful about her appearance. ◉ 몸~ *one's* 「figure 〔carriage〕.

**맵싸하다** (be) pungent; acrid; peppery. ¶ 목이 ~ My throat feels terribly irritated.

**맷돌** a (hand) mill; a millstone; a quern. ◉ ~중쇠 the pivot and gudgeon of a millstone. ~질 grinding grain in a stone 「mill 〔mortar〕: ~질하다 grind grain in a stone mill.

**맷방석**(一方席) a round straw mat.

**맹격**(猛擊) a 「fierce 〔furious, heavy〕 attack 〔assault〕; a hard blow. ¶ ~을 가하다 make 〔launch〕 a 「violent 〔fierce〕 attack 《on 〔against〕 the enemy》; deal 《*a person*》 a hard blow.

**맹견**(猛犬) a 「fierce 〔ferocious〕 dog. ¶ ~ 주의《게시》 "Beware of the Dog!"

**맹공(격)**(猛攻(擊)) a 「violent 〔heavy〕 attack. ~하다 attack violently; make a vigorous attack 《on》. ¶ ~을 받다 come under heavy attack.

**맹그로브** 『식물』 a mangrove.

**맹근하다** be somewhat warm.

**맹금**(猛禽) a bird of prey; a predatory 〔raptorial〕 bird. ◉ ~류 Raptors.

**맹꽁맹꽁** croaking (of a frog).

**맹꽁이** ① 『동물』 a kind of small round frog. ¶ ~ 결박한 것 같다 be a humpty-dumpty. ② 《맹추》 a bird-brain; a simpleton; a blockhead. ◉ ~ 자물쇠 a padlock.

**맹도견**(盲導犬) a guide dog; a Seeing-Eye dog.

**맹독**(猛毒) (a) deadly poison. ¶ ~성의 fatally poisonous / ~을 가진 뱀 a highly poisonous snake / ~이 있다 be virulently poisonous.

**맹랑**(孟浪) ~하다 ① 《허망하다》 (be) false; untrue; 《믿을 수 없다》 (be) incredible; unbelievable; 《근거없다》 (be) unfounded; groundless; unreliable; 《터무니없다》 (be) absurd; fabulous; nonsensical; unreasonable. ¶ ~한 이야기 an incredible story / ~한 소문을 퍼뜨리다 set wild rumors afloat / 일이 ~하게 되다 a plan is unexpectedly frustrated; a plan gets 「spoiled 〔hits a snag〕 / 나라고, 천만에, 누가 그런 ~한 소리를 하더냐 I? Not half! Whoever told you such a silly story as that? ② 《만만치 않다》 be tougher than *one* had expected; be harder to tackle than *one* had expected; be not negligible; be no 「mean 〔small〕. ¶ ~한 아이 a shrewd child / 일이 ~하다 This is a little too hard to solve. *or* This is rather tough.

**맹렬**(猛烈) ~하다 (be) violent; furious; fierce; feverish; intense; vehement; 《경쟁 따위가》 keen; 《비바람 따위가》 heavy. ¶ ~히 violently; fiercely; intensely; furiously; vehemently; madly / ~한 반대 strong opposition / ~한 연습 heavy 〔intensive, rigorous〕 training 〔practice〕; hard training / ~한 경쟁 (a) keen competition / ~한 일격 a smashing blow / ~한 속도로 at a 「terrific 〔breakneck〕 speed / 불법에 대하여 ~한 항의를 하다 make a vehement protest against injustice / ~히 공격하다 make a fierce attack 《on》; attack 《*a person*》 ferociously / ~히 싸우다 fight 「desperately 〔hotly〕 / ~히 일하다 work like a beaver / 그는 시험에 대비하여 ~히 공부하였다 He studied like mad for the examination. ◉ ~ 사원 「a dedicated 〔an enthusiastic〕 worker; an eager beaver employee.

**맹목**(盲目) blindness. ¶ ~적(으로) blind(ly); reckless(ly); ignorant(ly) / ~적인 사랑〔숭배〕 a blind 「love 〔devotion〕 / 교리를 ~적으로 믿다 have blind faith in the doctrine / 그녀는 아들에게 ~적인 애정을 쏟고 있다 She loves her son blindly. / 사랑은 ~적인 것, 사랑에 빠진 자는 때때로 이성적으로 생각하거나 행동할 수 없게 된다 Love is blind, those who fall in love are unable at times to think or act rationally. ◉ ~비행 a blind flight; blind 〔instrument〕 flying. ~착륙 blind 〔instrument〕 landing.

**맹문모르다** do not understand the matter at all; have no grasp of the situation; have no sense. ¶ 맹문도 모르고 덤벼들다 rush 〔plunge〕 into 《*something*》 without slightest information of it.

**맹문이** a person who doesn't understand the situation at all; a person who has no sense. ¶ 그런 ~는 처음 보았다 I have never seen a man so utterly devoid of sense as he.

**맹물** plain 〔tasteless〕 water; insipid 〔flat〕 stuff; dishwater; 《사람》 a dull person; a jellyfish. ¶ 이것은 맥주가 아니고 ~이다 This isn't beer—it's dishwater! / 그 사람은 ～이다 He is a dull drink of water.

**맹반격**(猛反擊) ～하다 make a violent 「counterattack 《on》.

**맹방**(盟邦) an ally; an allied power; a confederate (state); a league (of allies).

**맹사**(盲射) random firing 〔shooting〕; a shot in the dark. ～하다 fire 〔shoot〕 at random; fire blindly.

**맹사**(猛射) a heavy fire; severe 〔hot〕 firing. ～하다 rain a heavy fire on 《the enemy》.

**맹성**(猛省) serious reflection 〔reconsideration〕; penitence 《for *one's* wrongdoing》. ～하다 reflect on 〔reconsider〕 《*a thing*》 seriously. ¶ ～을 촉구하다 urge 《*a person*》 to reflect seriously on *his* conduct.

**맹세** an oath; a pledge; a vow. ～하다 swear; take an oath; give 〔pledge〕 *one's* word; make a vow; promise 《to *do*》. ¶ ～코 upon 〔on〕 my word 〔honor〕; by God / 신 앞에 ～하다 swear by God / ～를 지키다〔어기다〕 keep 〔break〕 *one's* vow 〔pledge, oath〕 / 굳게 ～하다 make solemn vow / 마음 속으로 ～하다 swear within *oneself;* promise *oneself* / 비밀을 지킬 것을 ～하다 pledge 〔bind〕 *oneself* to secrecy; promise to keep a secret / (남에게) 반드시 ～를 지킬 것을 약속케 하다 pledge 《*a person*》 to keep *his* oath / 순결을 지킬 것을 ～하다 take a vow of chastity / 금주를〔금연을〕 ～하다 swear off drinking 〔smoking〕 / 충성을 ～하다 pledge 「allegiance 〔*one's* loyalty〕 《to》 / ～코 약속을 지키겠다 I swear I'll keep my promise. / 그는 앞으로 행실을 고칠 것을 ～했다 He took a pledge to mend his ways in the future. / 나는 가지 않겠다. ～코 안 간다 I won't go. Not on my life!

**맹세지거리** swearing in vulgar language. ～하다 swear profanely; utter curses.

**맹수**(猛獸) a fierce animal; a savage 〔wild〕 beast. ◉ ～사냥 big-game hunting: ～사냥을 하다 shoot big game; go big-game hunting; go on (a) safari. ～조련사 a tamer 〔trainer〕 of wild animals.

**맹습**(猛襲) a vigorous 〔fierce, heavy, hot〕 attack; a violent assault. ～하다 make a fierce attack 《on》.

**맹신**(盲信) blind 〔unquestioning〕 acceptance 《of a theory》; an unquestioning belief; (blind) faith. ～하다 give hasty credit 《to a rumor》; believe blindly 《in astrology》; be credulous. ¶ 마을 사람들은 그 오래된 미신을 ～하고 있다 The villagers are credulous about the old superstition.

**맹아**(盲啞) the blind and dumb. ◉ ～교육 education for the blind and dumb. ～학교 a blind and dumb school.

**맹아**(萌芽) 《싹》 a sprout; 《발아》 a germination; 《징조》 a sign.

**맹약**(盟約) 《서약》 a pledge; a covenant; 《협정》 a pact; 《동맹》 an alliance; a league. ～하다 make 〔form, conclude〕 a pact 《with》; form an alliance. ◉ ～국(國) a pact member; a confederate state.

**맹연습**(猛練習) hard 〔intensive〕 training. ～하다 do hard training; train hard; carry out vigorous practice 〔exercises〕. ¶ 시합을 앞두고 2개월간 ～을 하다 train hard for two months for the fight.

**맹위**(猛威) fierceness; ferocity; fury. ¶ ～를 떨치다 《사람이》 go on a 〔be on the〕 rampage; exercise an overwhelming influence 《over》; 《사물이》 rage; be rampant; play 〔work〕 havoc 《with》 / 폭풍우가 하루 종일 ～를 떨쳤다 The violent storm raged all day long. / 독감이 지금 ～를 떨치고 있다 Influenza is now raging.

**맹인**(盲人) a blind (person); [총칭] the blind. ◉ ～교육 blind education; education of the blind.

**맹자**(孟子) 《사람》 Mencius; 《책》 the Works 〔the Discourses〕 of Mencius.

**맹장**(盲腸) 〖해부〗 the cecum; the blind gut; 《충양돌기》 the (vermi-form) appendix (*pl.* ～es, -dices); ¶ ～을 떼어내다 have *one's* appendix removed 〔out〕 / ～이 터지다 His appendix perforated 〔burst〕. ◉ ～염 〖의학〗 appendicitis; cecitis: ～염 수술 (an) appendectomy / ～염 수술을 받다 have an operation for appendicitis.

**맹장**(猛將) a brave general; a dauntless leader; a veteran fighter.

**맹점**(盲點) 《망막상의》 a blind spot; 〖의학〗 a scotoma (*pl.* ～s, ～ta); [비유적] a blind spot 〔point〕; 《피하는 길》 a loophole. ¶ 법의 ～ a loophole 〔blind spot〕 in the law; a legal loophole / ～을 찌르다 pinpoint 〔put *one's* finger on〕 a 《*person's*》 weak point 〔blind spot〕 / 그들은 내 이론의 ～을 공격했다 They attacked the weak point in my theory. / 그는 법의 ～을 이용하여 큰 돈을 벌었다 He made a huge sum of money by「taking advantage of a blind point of law 〔imposing on a loophole in the law〕.

**맹종**(盲從) blind 〔unquestioning〕 obedience 〔submission, deference〕. ～하다 obey 〔follow, submit〕 blindly. ¶ 상급자라고 해서 그들에게 ～할 필요는 없다 You need not follow them blindly because they are your superiors.

**맹주**(盟主) the leader of a confederation 〔confederacy, league〕; the leading power. ¶ ～가 되다 become the leader《of》; hold sway over.

**맹진**(猛進) a dash; a drive. ～하다 dash 〔make a bold dash〕 forward; run headlong; make a drive《on》; push forward vigorously.

**맹추** a stupid 〔thickheaded〕 person; a blockhead; a dullard.

**맹타**(猛打) a heavy 〔hammer〕 blow; 〖야구〗 a heavy hit; slugging. ～하다 hit hard; give a heavy hit. ¶ ～를 퍼붓다 〖야구〗 hit hard; pump out hits; hammer《a pitcher》; 〖권투〗 make a punching bag out of《*one's* opponent》. ◉ ～자 a heavy batter 〔hitter〕; a slugger.

**맹탕** 《국물》 insipid 〔watery〕 soup; 《사람》 a dull 〔flat〕 person. ¶ 이 국은 ～이다 This soup is mere wash.

**맹폭**(盲爆) blind 〔indiscriminate〕 bombing. ～하다 bomb 〔bombard〕 blindly.

**맹폭**(猛爆) heavy bombing 〔bombardment〕; an intensive 〔a heavy〕 air raid. ～하다 bomb 〔bombard〕 heavily.

**맹호**(猛虎) a fierce 〔ferocious〕 tiger.

**맹화**(猛火) raging 〔roaring〕 flames; 《큰불》 a devastating fire. ¶ ～속에 뛰어들다 rush into raging flames.

**맹활동**(猛活動) vigorous activity. ～하다 act vigorously; be in full activity.

**맹훈련**(猛訓鍊) intense 〔hard〕 training. ～하다 carry out intense training; train hard.

**맹휴**(盟休) a strike; a school strike (학교의). ～하다 go on strike; down *one's* books (학교에서).

**맺다** ① 《끈·매듭을》 tie (up); knot; fasten (together); bind. ⇨매다. ¶ 매듭을 ～ make 〔tie〕 a knot

② 《열매를》 bear; produce. ¶ 열매를 ～ bear fruit; [비유적] go to seed; produce a result; come 〔be brought〕 to fruition / 우리들의 노력은 열매를 맺었다 Our efforts bore fruit.

③ 《끝을》 conclude; finish; close; wind up. ¶ 토론을 끝 ～ close a debate / 그는 감사하다는 말로 연설을 끝맺었다 He concluded 〔wound up〕 his speech with a few words of thanks.

④ 《원한을》 bear; cherish; nurse; harbor. ¶ 원한을 ～ bear《*a person*》a grudge; harbor an enmity《toward》.

⑤ 《관계 등을》 form《a connection with》; enter 〔come〕 into《a relationship with》; 《계약을》 make《a contract》; close《a bargain》; 《조약을》 conclude《a treaty》; 《제휴하다》 ally 〔league〕《with》; unite 〔link (up)〕《with》. ¶ 계약을 ～ make 〔conclude, enter into, place〕 a contract《with》; sign a contract / 동맹을 ～ form 〔enter into〕 an alliance《with》/ 인연을 ～ form a connection / 부부의 인연을 ～ tie the nuptial 〔marriage〕 knot / 우정을 ～ cultivate 〔contract, form〕 friendship with《*a person*》/ 의형제를 ～ become sworn brothers / 조약을 ～ conclude 〔make up〕 a treaty《with》/ 남녀가 결혼으로 맺어지다 be united in marriage.

**맺음말** closing 〔concluding〕 remarks; 「conclusion.

**맺히다** ① 《매듭이》 be tied; be knotted; be fastened. ¶ 매듭이 ～ a knot is tied 〔made〕; be knotted; have a knot in it.

② 《열매가》 bear《fruit》; come into bearing; fruit; seed; 《익다》 ripen; grow 〔become〕 ripe; be in fruit. ¶ 이 나무는 가을에 열매가 맺힌다 This tree bears fruit in the fall / 우리의 노력은 이제야 열매가 맺혔다 Our effort bore fruit at last.

③ 《원한 따위가》 be pent up; be rooted; smolder. ¶ 맺힌 원한 a deep grudge; pent-up rancor / 원한이 ～ have a long smoldering grudge / 맺힌 울분을 터뜨리다 let out 〔relieve, vent〕 *one's* pent-up rancor 〔feelings〕.

④ 《이슬·눈물·피가》 form. ¶ 이슬이 ～ dew forms; be dewy; be covered with dew / 눈물이 ～ tear forms; have tears (in *one's* eyes) / 피가 ～ blood gathers; 《피부에》 be bruised / 풀잎에 이슬이 ～ dewdrops form on the blades.

**맺힌데** 《피의》 a bruised 〔contused〕 spot; 《감정의》 ill 〔bad〕 feeling; a deep-set rancor. ¶ 마음에 ～가 있다 have something 〔ill feeling〕《against *a person*》.

**머** aw; mmh, huh; well; gee; gee whiz; darn-it; shucks; so there. ¶ 시

계 하나 꼭 사줘야 돼 며 Gee—you gotta buy me a watch!

**머금다** ① 《입에》 keep 〔hold〕 《*a thing*》 in *one's* mouth. ¶ 물을 머금고 with *one's* mouth full of water. ② 《마음에》 bear 〔keep〕 《*something*》 in mind; entertain; harbor; have. ¶ 원한을 ~ bear 《*a person*》 a grudge. ③ 《눈물·이슬을》 form; have. ¶ 눈물을 ~ have tears in *one's* eyes; tears stand in *one's* eyes / 이슬을 ~ have dew on it; be wet with dew; be dewy / 그녀는 두 눈에 그득히 눈물을 머금고 있었다 Her eyes were filled with tears. ④ 《웃음을》 express; have; show; display. ¶ 웃음을 ~ have a smile on *one's* lips; *one's* face beams 〔shines〕 with joy.

**머나멀다** 《거리가》 (be) very far away 〔off〕; in the distance. ¶ 머나먼 곳 a faraway place; a place faraway / 머나먼 길 a long long road 〔distance〕 / 머나먼 길 오시느라 수고가 많으셨소이다 Thank you for taking the trouble to come all this distance.

**머다랗다** (be) rather far 〔distant〕; rather long.

**머드** 《진흙》 mud. ◉ ~배스 《진흙 목욕》 mud bath. ~패드 mud pad.

**머드러기** a big one; a large piece of fruit; a large fish.

**머루** 〖식물〗 wild grapes; wild grape-vines.

**머름** 〖건축〗 a wainscot; a baseboard.

**머리** ① 《두부》 the head. ¶ ~에서 발끝까지 from head 〔crown〕 to toe; from top to bottom / ~ 뒤로 두 손을 대고 with *one's* hands behind *one's* head.

머리가: ~가 무겁다 feel heavy in the head; feel depressed / ~가 아프다 have a headache / ~가 어찔어찔하다 feel dizzy 〔giddy〕; have a giddy head; *one's* head swims 〔spins〕 / ~가 욱신거리다 be racked with a headache; have a splitting headache.

머리를: ~를 가로젓다 shake *one's* head (in denial) / ~를 긁다 scratch *one's* head / ~를 끄떡이다 nod *one's* head (in assent) / ~를 (쳐)들다 raise 〔lift up, hold up〕 *one's* head / ~를 들지 못하다 be unable to lift up *one's* head; be cowed 〔ashamed〕 / ~를 때리다 hit 《*a person*》 on the head / ~를 부딪치다 butt heads with 《another》 / ~를 숙이고 있다 keep *one's* head down / ~를 공손히 숙이고 with a respectful 〔low〕 bow / ~를 축 늘어뜨리다 hang (down) *one's* head / ~를 쓰다듬다 pat 《*a person*》 on the head; stroke 《*a person's*》 head / ~를 두 손에 파묻다〔으로 감싸다〕 bury 〔hold〕 *one's* head in *one's* hands / ~를 맞대고 의논하다 put 《their》 heads together.

¶ 그녀는 나보다 ~ 하나가 더 크다 She is taller than I by a head. / ~가 천근처럼 무겁다 I feel like my head weighs a ton.

② 《두뇌》 a head; brains; mind (정신). ¶ 명석한 ~ a clear head / ~ 회전이 빠른 사람 a quick-thinking person / ~ 회전이 느리다〔빠르다〕 be slow=〔quick-〕witted; have a slow 〔an agile〕 mind.

머리가: ~가 낡다 have old-fashioned ideas / ~가 이상하다 be crazy; be out of *one's* mind; be off *one's* head / ~가 이상해지다 *one's* mind goes funny; *one's* brain stops working properly / ~가 예민하다〔둔하다〕 be sharp=〔slow-〕witted / ~가 좋다 be clever; be bright; have brains; have a good brain; 《구어》 be brainy / ~가 나쁘다 be stupid; be dull; have no brains; 《구어》 be dumb; 《구어》 be thick / ~가 필요하다 require 〔need〕 brains / 수학의 ~가 있다 have a head for mathematics.

머리에: ~에 그리다〔떠올리다〕 picture 《*something*》; imagine; envisage 《*something*》 / (생각이) ~에 떠오르다 come 〔spring〕 to mind; come into 〔enter〕 *one's* head; occur to *one* / ~에 넣다 《고려하다》 take 《*something*》 into consideration 〔account〕; 《잊지 않다》 bear 〔keep〕 《*something*》 in mind / ~(속)에 남아 있다 stay in *one's* mind / (생각이) ~(속)에 스치다 flash across *one* 〔*one's* mind〕; flash into *one's* mind.

머리를: ~를 쓰다〔굴리다〕 use *one's* head 〔brain(s)〕; use 〔work〕 *one's* wit(s); exercise *one's* brains 〔intellect〕; set *one's* wits to work / ~를 쓰는 일 brainwork; mental work / ~를 썩이다 《생각으로》 rack 〔cudgel〕 *one's* brains 《to *do*, over a question》; 《근심으로》 be worried 《about, over》 / ~를 혹사하다 overwork 〔overtax, strain〕 *one's* brain.

¶ 자네 오늘 ~가 좀 이상한게 아냐 You're not thinking straight, are you? / 그의 참을성에는 ~가 수그러진다 I take off my hat to him 〔I really respect him〕 for his perseverance. / 아무리 ~를 짜봤지만, 끝내 그는 그 수수께끼를 풀 수 없었다 Hard as he cudgeled his

brains, he couldn't find the solution to that puzzle. / 그런 하잘것없는 문제를 가지고 ～를 혹사할 필요는 없다 You don't have 「to overtax your brain 〔to use your brains too much〕 with such a useless matter.
③ 《끝·꼭대기》 the top; the head; the point; the tip; the end (part). ¶ 책상～ the top of a table / 끝～ the end (part); the end piece / 기둥～ the top of a pillar.
④ 《첫머리》 the beginning. ¶ 첫 ～부터 다시 세다 count over 〔again〕 from the beginning.
⑤ 《머리털》 the hair (of *one's* head). ¶ ～를 가르다 part *one's* hair / ～를 깎다 cut *one's* hair; 《이발사 등에게》 have *one's* hair cut; get a haircut / ～를 손질하다 trim *one's* hair; 《시킬 때》 be having *one's* hair trimmed / ～를 땋다 braid *one's* hair / ～를 빗다 comb *one's* hair; tidy up *one's* hair / ～를 지지다 frizz 〔frizzle, curl〕 *one's* hair / ～를 쪽찌다 do *one's* hair in a chignon / ～를 풀다 let *one's* hair down; undo the hair; 《거상》 go into mourning / ～ 손질을 좀 더 정성껏 하게 You should take a bit more care of your hair.
⑥ 《위에 서는 사람》 the head 《of a department》.
◉ ～말 a preface; a foreword; an introduction; a preamble: ～말을 쓰다 write a preface 《to》. ～뼈 the skull. ～쓰개 a headpiece; headgear; a hood. ～채 a long tress of hair. ～형 a hair style. 머릿기름 《물기름》 hair oil; 《포마드》 pomade. 머릿수건 a (head) kerchief; a babushka. 머릿장(欌) a chest 〔wardrobe〕 set at the bedside.

**머리감다** wash *one's* hair; have a shampoo.

**머리끄덩이** the lock 〔clump〕 of *one's* hair. ¶ ～를 잡다 grab 《*a person*》 by the hair.

**머리끝** 《머리털의 끝》 the ends of *one's* hair; 《정수리》 the crown (of the head). ¶ ～에서 발끝까지 from head to foot; from top to toe / ～까지 화가 치밀어 있다 fly 〔get〕 into a rage 〔passion〕; be in towering rage.

**머리띠** a headband; 《여자용》 a hairlace. ¶ ～를 매다 wear 〔tie〕 a band around *one's* head.

**머리맡** *one's* bedside 〔pillow-side〕. ¶ ～에(서) at 〔by〕 *one's* 〔*a person's*〕 bedside; at the head of *one's* bed / ～에 부르다 call 《*a person*》 to *one's* bedside.

**머리얹다** ① 《머리를》 put up *one's* hair; do *one's* hair in a chignon; 《혼인》 attain womanhood; get married. ② 《기생이》 lose *one's* virginity; be deflowered. ¶ 머리 얹히다 initiate a *kisaeng* to sex; deflower a *kisaeng*.

**머리염색**(一染色) a hair dye. ◉ ～약 hairdye.

**머리치장**(一治粧) hairdo; hairdressing. ～하다 「do up 〔dress〕 *one's* hair.

**머리카락, 머리칼, 머리털** a hair (of *one's* head). ¶ 흰 ～ a white hair / 굵은 ～ a coarse 〔thick〕 hair / ～이 세다 *one's* hair turns gray / ～을 염색하다 dye *one's* hair (black); have *one's* hair dyed. / ～ 뒤에서 숨바꼭질한다 《속담》 Try to pull the wool over a 《*a person's*》 eyes. / 그 무시무시한 광경에 ～이 곤두섰다 My hair stood on end at the frightful sight.

**머리통** the bulk of *one's* head. ¶ ～이 크다 have a big head.

**머리핀** a hairpin; a barrette; a bobby pin.

**머릿골** 〖해부〗 the brain; brains; gray matter.

**머릿니** head lice; vermin in the hair. ¶ ～가 끓다 be swarming with head lice.

**머릿살** nerves of the head. ¶ ～(이) 아프다 be a headache; be troublesome; have a headache / ～(을) 앓다 be troubled; be annoyed 《with》.

**머릿수**(一數) the number of persons; a head 〔nose〕 count. ¶ ～를 세다 count the number of persons present; count heads 〔noses〕 / ～가 많다〔적다〕 there are 〔is〕 a large 〔small〕 number 《of 》; be large 〔small〕 in number / ～를 채우다〔늘리다, 줄이다〕 make up 〔increase, reduce〕 the number.

**머무르다** stop; stay; put up 《at》; 《직책 따위에》 remain; stay. ¶ 여관에 ～ stop 〔put up〕 at an inn / 친구 집에 ～ stay at a friend's home / 현직에 ～ remain in (*one's* present) office.

**머무적거리다** hesitate 《about, to do》; waver 《between》; think twice 《about》; flinch 〔shrink〕 《from》. ¶ 얼른 대답을 못 하고 ～ be tardy in answer / 결단을 못 내리고 ～ be hesitant 〔puzzled over〕 to make a decision.

**머무적머무적** hesitating(ly); hesitant(ly); wavering(ly); irresolutely.

**머슴** a farmhand; a farm servant

〔worker, laborer〕; a ranch hand 《미》. ¶ ～(을) 살다 become 〔serve as〕 a farm servant / ～을 두다 keep a farmhand. ◉ ～방 a farmhand's room. ～살이 working 〔serving〕 as a farmhand: ～살이하다 work 〔hire on〕 as a farmhand. ～애 《어린 머슴》 a boy farm servant; a boy farmhand; 《사내아이》 a boy; a lad.

**머시** whats-it; whose-it(s); what-do=you-call it. ¶ 그 사람 이름이 ～더라, 어제 찾아왔던 사람 말야 What was the name of that man—the man who was here yesterday, I mean? / ～냐 그 글자 찍는 기계 좀 보여 주게 Let me see that ...uh... gadget that writes letters. / 그 머신가 하는 사람 죽었다네 That guy, whats-his-name, I hear he died.

**머쓱하다** ① 《키가》 (be) lanky; spindly; gangling; rangy. ¶ 키가 머쓱하니 크다 be tall and lanky. ② 《기가 죽다》 be discouraged 〔dejected〕; look embarrassed; droop; feel small.

**머위** 『식물』 a butterbur.

**머저리** a fool; an ass; a simpleton.

**머줍다** (be) dull; slow; sluggish.

**머지않아** 《오래잖아》 soon; before long; in the near future.

**머천다이징** 《상품화 계획》 merchandising.

**머츰하다** stop 〔cease〕 for a while. ¶ 비가 ～ It stops raining for a while. *or* The rain lets up for a moment.

**머큐로크롬** 《빨간약》 mercurochrome.

**머플러** 《소음 장치·목도리》 a muffler.

**먹** 《먹물》 India(n) 〔Chinese〕 ink; 《고체의》 an ink stick; an ink-cake. ¶ 먹 한 자루 a cake 〔stick〕 of Chinese ink / 먹을 듬뿍 묻힌 붓 an ink-filled 〔ink-laden〕 brush / 먹을 갈다 grind an ink-cake / 먹을 묻히다 《붓에》 dip in ink; 《얼굴 등에》 smear 〔stain〕 with ink.

**먹거리** food; foodstuffs. ⇨ 먹을거리.

**먹구름** dark 〔black〕 clouds. ¶ ～이 하늘을 덮었다 The sky is overspread with dark clouds.

**먹그림** 《묵화》 an Indian-ink drawing; a black-and-white painting.

**먹놓다** chalk out; mark (measure lines on lumber) with ink. ¶ 치수를 ～ mark out the measurements.

**먹다**[1] ① 《음식을》 eat; take; have; 《속어》 feed *one's* face. ¶ 밥을 ～ eat rice; take 〔have〕 *one's* meal / 게걸스럽게 ～ eat greedily 〔avidly〕; devour; gorge 《on》 / 놀고 ～ eat idle bread; live 〔lead〕 an idle life / 맛있게 ～ eat with relish 〔gusto〕 / 배불리 ～ eat 〔have〕 *one's* fill; eat to *one's* heart's content / 하루 세끼 ～ eat three times a day; take three meals a day / 한입에 ～ eat at a mouthful; wolf it (down) / 먹고 달아나다 run away without paying for *one's* food / 이 버섯은 먹을 수 있다 This mushroom is 「edible 〔good to eat〕. *or* This mushroom can be eaten. / 소는 풀을 먹는다 Cows feed on grass. / 식탁에는 다 먹을 수 없을 만큼의 요리가 있었다 On the table there were more good dishes than I could eat. / 며칠 전에는 프랑스 요리를 먹어보았다 The other day I tried some French dishes. / 그는 사흘 동안 아무 것도 먹지 않았다 He has taken no food for three days. / 아침을 일찍 먹었다 We took an early breakfast. / 참 잘 먹었습니다 I've had enough, thank you. / 먹기는 파발이 먹고 뛰기는 역마가 뛴다 《속담》 One who has stood idle takes the lion's share while the other who has worked hard goes unrewarded. / 먹는 개도 아니 때린다 《속담》 Refrain from beating or scolding a person while he is at his meal. / 먹지 않는 종, 투기 없는 아내 《속담》 Don't expect too much (the impossible) of human nature.
② 《먹고살다》 live 《on, by》; subsist 《on》; make 〔earn〕 *one's* living. ¶ 먹고 살기가 어렵다 find it hard to make *one's* living / 먹기 위해 일하다 work for *one's* bread / 월 50만 원으로는 먹고 살 수 없다 I cannot live on 500,000 won a month. / 그는 빌어먹고 있다 He subsist entirely by begging. / 나는 가족을 먹여 살릴 만큼의 수입이 있다 My income is good enough to support my family.
③ 《물·약 따위를》 drink; take; have. ¶ 약을 ～ take medicine(s) / 술을 ～ drink wine / (아이가) 젖을 ～ suck (its mother's) breast / 물을 한 모금 ～ have 〔take〕 a drink 〔gulf〕 of water 《from》 / 술은 먹되, 먹히지는 마라 You may drink, but don't let the drink take over.
④ 《벌레 따위가》 eat into; be worm=eaten; be moth-eaten; be decayed. ¶ 좀〔벌레〕 먹은 moth-〔worm-〕eaten / 좀 먹은 책 moth-eaten book / 벌레 먹은 이 a decayed tooth / 옷에 좀이 먹었다 The moths have eaten holes in my clothes.

⑤ 《남의 것·재물을》 take; seize; appropriate; devour; swallow up; make 《it》 *one's* own unjustly 〔illegally〕. ¶ 남의 재물을 ~ take another's property; make another's property *one's* own illegally / 공금을 ~ embezzle; misuse public funds / 그는 내 돈 만원을 먹었다 He cheated me out of ten thousand won.
⑥ 《이문·구문을》 get; take; receive; have. ¶ 구문을 ~ get a commission 《on the sale of…》 / 이익의 3할을 ~ get a 30% of the profit.
⑦ 《욕·겁을》 get; undergo; suffer; catch. ¶ 욕을 ~ get a scolding; catch it 《속어》; be abused 〔reviled, insulted〕 / 겁을 ~ get scared; be intimidated / 겁을 먹고 소리지르다 shriek in fear; cry in terror.
⑧ 《나이를》 grow old(er); get (years of age); acquire (age). ¶ 나이를 먹어 감에 따라 as we advance in age / 어지간히 나이 먹은 사나이 a rather old man / …보다 두 살 더 ~ be two years older than….
⑨ 《더위를》 be affected by the (summer) heat; suffer from hot weather; be ill from the heat.
⑩ 《판돈 따위를》 win 〔take〕 《the wager》. ¶ 5달러의 판돈을 ~ win 〔take〕 the wager five dollars.
⑪ 《주먹 따위를》 ¶ 한 대 ~ be given a blow 《on the head》.
⑫ 《녹(祿) 따위를》 receive; be given. ¶ 녹을 ~ receive a stipend; get a salary 《from》.
⑬ 《마음을》 fix; set; make; intend 〔determine, decide〕 《to *do*》. ¶ 마음(을) ~ make up *one's* mind 《to *do*》; put *one's* heart 《into》; set 〔keep〕 *one's* mind 〔heart〕 《on》; take special care / 화가가 되려고 마음 ~ determine on becoming a painter / 나는 끝까지 싸우기로 마음먹고 있다 I am determined to fight to the last.
⑭ 《기타》 ¶ 먹느냐 먹히느냐의 투쟁 a life-and-death struggle; a struggle with no quarter given or taken / 이것은 바로 먹느냐 먹히느냐의 판국이다 This is a kill-or-be-killed situation.

**먹다**[2] ① 《칼날 따위가》 bite 〔cut〕 well. ¶ 톱이 잘 ~ a saw bites 〔cuts〕 well; a saw is sharp / 대패가 잘 먹지 않다 a plane doesn't bite 〔cut〕 well; a plane is blunt. ② 《맷돌이》 grind (well). ¶ 맷돌이 잘 ~ a millstone grinds well. ③ 《색깔·풀 따위가》 dye (well); soak in (well). ¶ 천에 물이 잘 ~ the cloth dyes well. ④ 《씨아가》 gin (well). ¶ 씨아가 잘 ~ a cotton gin gins well / 먹지 않는 씨아에서 소리만 난다 《속담》 Make a great fuss but get nothing done. *or* All talk, no work. ⑤ 《들다》 cost; be spent; be consumed. ¶ 돈이 많이 먹히다 be costly; be expensive / 기름이 많이 ~ oil is consumed in large quantities.

**먹다**[3] 《귀가》 lose *one's* hearing; become 〔go〕 deaf; be deafened. ¶ 한쪽 귀가 ~ become deaf 「of an 〔in one〕 ear / 그는 아주 귀가 먹었다 He is stone-deaf. *or* He is as deaf as door.

**먹먹하다** 《귀가》 (be) deaf; deafened; silent; stunned. ¶ 귀가 ~ be deaf; be deafened / 시끄러운 소리에 귀가 ~ be deafened 〔stunned〕 by noise.

**먹물** ① 《먹의》 India(n) 〔Chinese〕 ink. ¶ ~이 묻다 be stained with Chinese ink. ② 《검은 물》 inky 〔black〕 water; 《오징어·낙지의》 ink 〔sepia〕 《of a cuttlefish》.

**먹빛** an ink(y) black.

**먹새** ⇨먹음새 ②.

**먹성**(一性) capacity for eating; appetite. ¶ ~이 좋다 have a good 〔large〕 appetite; be omnivorous.

**먹실** 《실》 a string stained with ink; a string dyed black. ¶ ~넣다 《남에게》 tattoo 《a dragon on *a person's* back》; 《자기에게》 have 《a dragon》 tattooed 《on *one's* back》.

**먹은금** the cost price; price; cost. ¶ ~에 팔다 sell at cost / ~보다 싸게 팔다 sell below cost.

**먹을거리** food; something to eat; foodstuffs; provisions (양식). ⇨식량.

**먹음새** ① 《조리법》 cooking; cookery; cuisine. ¶ 그 집 ~가 아주 훌륭하다 Their cooking is simply wonderful. ② 《먹는 태도》 way of eating; appetite (식욕). ¶ ~가 좋다 be a hearty eater; eat well.

**먹음직스럽다** (be) delicious-looking; appetizing; tempting. ¶ 먹음직스러워 보이다 look delicious; be tempting; make *one's* mouth water / 그 파이는 ~ That pie tempts me (the appetite).

**먹이** 《사료》 food; feed; 《맹수의》 a prey; 《물고기·새의》 bait (미끼). ¶ (동물에게) ~를 주는 시간 feeding time / 병아리 ~ chicken food / ~를 주다 feed 《an animal》 / 말에게 ~로 밀과 귀리를 주었다 feed wheats and oats to the horse. / (맹수 따위가) ~를 찾아 헤매다 seek for prey; roam about in quest

of food / 가엾은 염소는 늑대의 ~가 되었다 The poor goat fell prey to a wolf. / 동물에게 ~를 주지 마시오 《게시》 Don't feed the animals.
◉ ~사슬 〖생물〗 food chain. ~통(桶) a feed bucket; a feeding trough.

**먹이다**[1] ① 《음식을》 let 《*someone*》 eat 〔drink〕; feed 《an animal on》; serve 《*a person* with》; treat 《*a person* to》; entertain 《*a person*》 with. ¶ 배불리 ~ let 《*a person*》 have *his* fill; feed up / 너무 ~ overfeed 《*one's* pets》 / 억지로 ~ force food upon 《*a person*》; force 《*a person*》 to eat / 소에게 풀을 ~ feed a cow (on) grass / 어린애에게 젖을 ~ give breast to a baby; suckle a baby / 일꾼에게 밥을 ~ give 〔offer〕 meal to a worker; serve a worker with meal / 억지로 약을 ~ force 《*a person*》 to take medicine / 내가 가난한 학생이었을 때, 그녀는 자주 식당에서 저녁 식사를 먹여주었다 When I was a poor student, she often treated me to dinner at a restaurant.
② 《부양·사육》 support; provide for; keep; maintain; feed; raise; rear. ¶ 거저 ~ feed 《*a person*》 for nothing; give free meals / 소를 ~ raise a cow / 개를 ~ keep a dog / 당신은 정말로 이 박봉으로 7인 가족을 먹일 수 있다고 생각하는가 Do you really think that I can feed a family of 7 on this miserable salary?
③ 《뇌물을》 bribe with; grease 〔oil〕 *a person's* palm 《with》. ¶ 아무에게 돈을 ~ bribe *a person;* slip money into *a person's* hands / 먹여서 입을 막다 bribe 《*a person*》 into secrecy; buy 《*a person's*》 tongue.
④ 《때리다》 give; administer. ¶ 한 대 ~ give a blow; deal 《*a person*》 a blow / 귀싸대기를 한 대 ~ box 《*a person's*》 ear(s); let 《*a person*》 have it on the cheek / 주먹을 ~ strike with *one's* fist; land 〔deal〕 《*a person*》 a punch 《on》.
⑤ 《피해·겁·욕을》 make 《*a person*》 suffer with; inflict 《on *a person*》. ¶ 겁을 ~ scare 〔intimidate〕 《*a person*》 / 아무를 욕 ~ let *a person* get a scolding; cause *a person* to be abused.

**먹이다**[2] ① 《색을》 dye 《*a thing*》 with. ¶ 검정물을 ~ dye 《*a thing*》 black. ② 《풀을》 apply (starch); starch 《linen》. ¶ 셔츠에 풀을 ~ starch *one's* shirt / 이것에 풀 좀 먹여 주시오 I want this to be starched. ③ 《기름을》 oil 《*a thing*》 with. ¶ 기름 먹인 천 oil cloth / 장판에 기름을 ~ oil floor paper. ④ 《밀·초를》 wax 《*a thing*》 with. ⑤ 《기계에》 put 《*a thing*》 in; feed 《*a thing*》 at; feed 《*a thing*》 with. ¶ 씨아에 솜을 ~ feed a gin with cotton; feed cotton to a gin / 작두에 풀을 ~ feed a haycutter with hay. ⑥ 《돈을 들이다》 put 《money》 in; spend 《money on furniture》.

**먹자** a carpenter's square (for drawing ink lines).

**먹자판** 《먹고 떠드는 자리》 a spree; boisterous merrimaking; a scene of riotous eating; a big feast; 《구어》 high jinks; 《향락적인 생각》 the pleasure-first〔-seeking〕 way of life. ¶ ~을 벌이다 go on a spree; be 〔go〕 on the razzle.

**먹장** a piece 〔stick〕 of Chinese ink. ¶ ~ 갈아 부은 듯하다 be black as ink 〔pitch〕. ◉ ~ 구름 = 먹구름.

**먹줄** ① 《실》 an 〔a carpenter's〕 inking line 〔string〕. ② 《금》 a carpenter's inkline. ¶ ~ 띄우다 stretch out an inking line / ~ 친 듯하다 be straight and even. ◉ ~꼭지 the point at the tip of an ink-line.

**먹지**(―紙) carbon paper; copying paper.

**먹칠**(―漆) smearing with Chinese ink. ~하다 smear with Chinese ink; 《명예 따위에》 disgrace; bring disgrace on *one;* sully *one's* reputation; mar; 《계획 따위에》 spoil; throw a wet ruin; make a mess of. ¶ 인격에 ~을 하다 impair *one's* dignity / 명성에 ~을 하다 tarnish *one's* reputation; cast a slur on *one's* fame.

**먹칼** an inking spatula (of a carpenter).

**먹통**(―桶) an ink-pad; an inkwell; an inkpot; 《바보》 a fool.

**먹투성이** a thing smeared all over with Chinese ink. ¶ 옷이 ~가 되다 *one's* clothes are all smeared with Chinese ink.

**먹황새** 〖조류〗 a black-headed stork.

**먹히다** ① 《먹음을 당하다》 get eaten; be eaten up 《by》; be swallowed up; be devoured; be consumed. ¶ 먹느냐 먹히느냐의 싸움 a life-and-death struggle; a struggle with no quarter given or taken / 쥐가 고양이한테 ~ a rat is eaten by a cat. ② 《음식이》 can be eaten 〔drunk〕; get consumed. ¶ 밥이 많이 ~ have a good appetite for rice / 오늘은 술이 먹히지 않는다 I can't drink much today. *or* I don't feel like having a drink today. ③《돈이》 be put in; be spent; require; cost. ¶ 비싸게 ~ come 〔prove to be〕 expensive / 싸게 ~ cost little; come cheap / 비용이 3만원 ~ it costs 30,000 won in expense. ④《빼앗기다》 be cheated of; be taken for; lose. ¶ 돈을 ~ be cheated of money by 《*a person*》; lost *one's* money to 《*a person*》 / 그 사람한테 돈을 빌려 주었다가는 먹히기가 쉽다 You will probably never see the money again if you lend it him.

**먼가래** a temporary burial of one who has died away from home.

**먼가래질** throwing dirt far away when spading.

**먼길** a long way 〔journey〕; all this 〔that〕 distance. ¶ ~을 떠나다 go a long way; make a long journey / 일부러 ~을 오시느라 수고하셨습니다 It is very kind of you to come all this distance.

**먼나라** a remote 〔distant, faraway〕 「country 〔land〕.

**먼눈**[1] 《소경의》 a blind eye.

**먼눈**[2] 《먼 곳을 보는》 a far-off 〔faraway〕 look in *one's* eyes. ¶ ~을 팔다 have a faraway look in *one's* eyes.

**먼데** 《먼 곳》 a far-off place; 《변소》 a toilet; a privy. ¶ ~서 in the distance; at a distance; far off; a long way off / ~서 오다 come 「a long way 〔from afar〕 / ~로 가다 go far away.

**먼동** the eastern sky of an early morning; the dawning sky. ¶ ~이 트다 day breaks 〔cracks〕; it 〔day, morning〕 dawns in the east / ~이 틀 때에 at dawn 〔daybreak〕; at break of a day; at (the) crack of a day / ~이 트기 전에 before dawn 〔daybreak〕.

**먼로주의**(一主義) the Monroe Doctrine; Monroeism.

**먼바다** the high seas; the open sea.

**먼발치(기)** a spot far off. ¶ ~에서는 (when viewed) from a distance / ~로 보다 have a distant view 《of》 / ~에서 보면 모든 것이 아름답게 보인다 Distance lends enchantment to all views.

**먼빛으로** from a distance; from afar. ¶ ~ 보다 view from a distance / ~보면 when viewed from a distance; to gaze at a distance.

**먼산**(一山) a distant mountain. ◉ ~바라기 a person with a far-away look in the eyes.

**먼일** distant events; future 〔coming〕 events. ¶ ~을 예상하다 anticipate what is to come / ~을 생각하다 think of the future; look forward into the future.

**먼저** ①《앞서》 first; ahead. ¶ ~ 가다 go first; go before others; go ahead / ~ 먹다 take 〔eat〕 first; eat before others / ~ 실례합니다 Please excuse my going first. *or* I'm afraid I must 「be leaving 〔be off〕 now. / ~ 가십시오 Please go first. *or* After you. / 내가 제일 ~ 수학 문제를 풀었다 I solved all my mathematical problems far in advance of others. / 그가 제일 ~ 왔다 He was the first man 「to arrive 〔who arrived〕.
②《우선》 first of all; above all; before everything else. ¶ ~ 빚을 갚아야겠다 I have to pay my debts before everything else. / ~ 하숙집부터 정해 놓아야 했다 The first thing to be done was to secure lodgings.
③《미리》 earlier; before; in advance; beforehand. ¶ ~ 떠나다 leave earlier / 돈을 ~ 준비하다 get the money ready beforehand / 돈을 ~ 지불하다 pay in advance.
④《전에》 (sometime) ago; previously; before; formerly. ¶ ~ 빌려 간 돈 the money you borrowed from me / ~ 말한 바와 같이 as previously stated; as noted 〔said〕 above / ~ 그렇게 말한 일이 있지 않는가 Didn't you say that sometime ago?

**먼저께** the other day; sometime ago.

**먼지** dust; a mote (티끌). ¶ ~투성이의 full of dust; covered with dust; dusty 《road》 / ~ 속에서 in the dust / ~가 끼다 dust gathers 〔collects〕; be 〔become〕 dusty / ~가 많다 be dusty 〔dust-covered〕 / ~가 일다 dust rises; it is dusty / ~를 쓸다 sweep 〔brush〕 the dust 《off the shelves》 / ~를 일으키다 raise 〔stir up〕 dust / ~를 털다 dust; 「brush away 〔beat off〕 dust / 책상은 ~가 덮여 있다 The desk is covered with dust. / 자동차가 지나면서 ~를 일으켰다 The car raised dust as it passed. / 방 구석에는 ~가 쌓이기 쉽다 Dust is apt to collect in the corners of a room. / 비로 ~가 가라앉았다 The rain has settled the dust. ◉ ~떨이 a duster.

**멀거니** absent-minded(ly); blank(ly); vacant(ly); with a blank 〔far-off〕 look; with an abstracted air. ¶ ~ 바라보다 「look vacantly 〔gaze blankly〕 《at *a person*》 / ~ 앉아 있다 be sitting absent-mindedly.

**멀건이** an absent-minded person.

**멀겋다** ① 《흐릿하게 맑다》 (be) dull; lusterless; be a bit clear; be not quite clear; be (unpleasantly) pale. ¶ 멀건 하늘 a dull 〔pale〕 sky. ② 《묽다》 (be) dishwater-colored; look watery. ¶ 멀건 우유 washy milk / 국이 ~ soup looks thin 〔watery〕.

**멀게지다** clear a bit; go from dark to dull; become paler 〔clearer〕; 《묽어지다》 become watery 〔thin〕.

**멀구슬나무** 〖식물〗 a bead tree.

**멀다**[1] ① 《거리가》 (be) far; distant; remote; far-off; faraway. ¶ 먼 거리 a long distance / 먼 길 a long way 〔distance, journey〕 / 먼 곳에 far away 〔off〕; a long way off; afar; in the distance / 멀지 않은 곳에 not far away 〔off〕 《from》 / 갈 길이 ~ have a long way to go / 학교는 집에서 꽤 ~ The school is 「quite a distance 〔long way〕 off from my house. / 여기서 집까지는 ~ My house is far from here. ② 《관계가》 (be) distant. ¶ 먼 친척 a distant 〔remote〕 relative / 멀고도 가까운 것이 남녀의 사이다 Distant yet so close is the relationship between man and woman. / 자주 안 보면 마음조차 멀어진다 Out of sight, out of mind. / 먼 친척보다는 이웃 사촌이 낫다 A good neighbor is better than a brother far off.
③ 《시간적으로》 (be) remote. ¶ 먼 옛적 the old far-off days; remote antiquity / 먼 장래 the remote 〔far-off, distant〕 future / 머지않아 before long; one of these days; 《조만간》 in the near future / 인간은 먼 옛날부터 불을 쓸 줄 알았다 From the remote antiquity man has known how to use fire. / 그날도 머지않았다 The day will not be far distant.
④ 《정도가》 be no match 《for》; be far inferior 《to》; 《미숙련》 (be) poor; unskilled. ¶ 일이 완성되려면 아직 멀었다 Their work is still far from being finished. / 내 영어 실력은 형을 따라가려면 멀었다 In point of the ability in English, I'm far behind my brother.

**멀다**[2] 《눈이》 become 〔go〕 blind; lose *one's* eyesight; 《귀가》 go deaf; lose *one's* hearing. ¶ 먼 눈 a blind eye / 돈에 눈이 멀어서 blinded by the lure of money / 한쪽 귀가〔눈이〕 ~ be 「deaf 〔blind〕 in one ear 〔eye〕.

**멀떠구니** 《새의 모이주머니》 a craw; a crop.

**멀뚱멀뚱** ① 《눈이》 vacantly; blankly; absent-mindedly; dazedly. ~하다 (be) vacant; blank; absent-minded. ¶ ~한 눈 vacant eyes / ~ 바라보다 gaze at 《*a thing*》 vacantly; stare in silent wander 《at》.
② 《국물이》 ~하다 (be) thin; watery; sloppy. ¶ ~한 국 thin 〔watery〕 soup.

**멀리** far; far off 〔away〕; afar; 「in the 〔at a〕 distance; a long way off. ¶ ~ 떨어져 있는 마을 a distant 〔a far-off〕 village; a village 「a long way off 〔far away〕 / ~ (떨어져) 산다 live 「far away 〔at a distance〕 / ~ 여행하다 travel far; make a long journey / ~ 바라보다 look at something from afar; get a distant view / ~서 오다 come a long 「way 〔distance〕; come from afar 〔a great distance〕 / 그 탑은 ~서도 보인다 The tower can be seen from afar. / ~ 불빛이 보였다 A light was seen in the distance. / ~서 대포 소리가 들려 왔다 「We heard guns 〔Guns were heard〕 afar 〔in the distance〕. / ~ 에베레스트산이 보였다 Mount Everest could be seen in the distance. / 저 ~ 산이 보이기 시작했다 A mountain became visible far in the distance. / 그 애는 혼자서 어딘가 ~ 간 것 같았다 The child seemed to have gone far away alone. / 그 소문은 ~까지 퍼졌다 The rumor spread far and wide. / 그의 농장은 시내에서 멀리 떨어져 있다 His farm is a long way from the town.

**멀리뛰기** the running broad 〔long 「《영》〕 jump.

**멀리하다** 《경원하다》 keep away 《from》; keep 《*a person*》 「at a distance 〔at an arm's length〕; keep clear of 《*a person*》; shun; avoid 《sweets》; 《절제하다》 abstain 《from drinking》. ¶ 못된 친구를 ~ avoid 〔keep away from〕 bad company / 주색을 ~ 「keep away from 〔swear off〕 wine and women; give up liquor and sex / 사람을 멀리하고 밀담하다 have a talk behind closed door / 그는 요즘 그녀를 멀리한다 He keeps her at arm's length these days.

**멀미** ① 《배·차 따위의》 (motion) sickness; nausea; queasiness. ~하다 feel 〔be〕 sick; suffer from motion sickness. ¶ 뱃~ seasickness / 비행기 ~ airsickness / 차~ carsickness / 사람 ~를 하다 feel sick from being in a crowd / 차〔비행기〕 ~를 하다 get 〔feel〕 carsick 〔airsick〕 / 나는 뱃~를 잘 한다

I get seasick easily.
② 《진저리》 being fed up 《with》; being sick 《of》. ~나다 be 〔feel〕 disgusted 《with, at》; be sick (and tired) 《of》; 《구어》 be fed up 《with》. ¶ 그 일에는 이제 ~가 난다 I am beginning to get fed up with the work.
◉ ~ 봉투 a barf bag: 「나 ~ 봉투가 하나 필요한데요」—「좌석주머니에 하나 들어 있습니다」 "I need a barf bag."—"There's one in your seat pocket."

**멀쑥하다** 《키가》 (be) lean and tall; 《묽다》 (be) watery; thin. ¶ 키가 ~ be lanky 〔spindling, skinny〕 / 멀쑥한 국 watery soup.

**멀어지다** ① 《거리가》 go away 《from》; withdraw 《from》; recede in the distance; 《소리가》 die away; grow faint. ¶ 비행기는 이륙하자 점점 시야에서 멀어져 갔다 The plane took off and soon disappeared from view. / 그들의 목소리는 점점 멀어져 갔다 Their voices gradually died 〔faded〕 away in the distance. ② 《관계가》 be 〔become〕 estranged 〔alienated〕 《from》; drift apart 《from each other》. ¶ 도시 생활에서 ~ estrange *oneself* from city life / 두 사람 사이는 점차 멀어졌다 The two have gradually become estranged / 결혼 후 그들의 사이는 점점 멀어졌다 After their marriage, they gradually drifted apart.

**멀쩡하다** ① ⇨ 말짱하다. ② 《뻔뻔스럽다》 (be) shameless; impudent; brazen; 《구어》 cheeky; 《미구어》 nervy. ¶ 멀쩡한 놈 a cheeky 〔an impudent〕 fellow; a brazen-faced fellow / 멀쩡한 거짓말을 하다 lie in 〔through〕 *one's* teeth 〔throat〕; tell a barefaced lie / 멀쩡하게도 …하다 have the cheek 〔nerve, impudence〕 to *do;* be shameless 〔impudent〕 enough to *do.*

**멀찍멀찍** far apart; with a long interval 《between》; at a good distance; some distance apart. ¶ ~ 떨어져 앉다 take seats some distance apart / 나무를 ~ 심다 plant trees at a good distance from each other.

**멀찍이** pretty far; rather distant; far apart; far enough. ¶ ~ 사이를 두다 leave a pretty long interval 《between》 / 나무를 집에서 ~ 심다 plant a tree rather far from the house / ~ 떨어져서 동네가 있다 There is a village quite a way off.

**멀찍하다** (be) pretty far; rather distant; be some distance away 〔apart〕.

**멀티-** 《다수의, 많은》 multi-. ◉ ~내셔날 《다국적의》 multinational. ~미디어 《혼합미디어》 multimedia (TV·슬라이드·테이프 등의 병용). ~채널 《다채널》 multichannel 《stereo》.

**멈추다** ① 《…이》 stop; cease; come to an end; 《정지》 stop; halt; come to a stop 〔stand, halt〕; 《엔진이》 go dead. ¶ 멈춰 있다 be at a standstill; be standing 《at a bus stop》 / 비가 ~ cease 〔stop〕 raining / 갑자기 ~ stop short 〔dead〕; come to a sudden stop 〔halt〕 / (기계 장치가) 자동적으로 ~ shut *itself* off / 서서히 ~ come to a smooth stop / 버스가 갑자기 멈춰 섰다 The bus made a sudden stop. / 출혈이 여간해서 멈추질 않는다 The blood will not stop flowing. / 딸꾹질이 멈추지 않았다 The hiccups would not stop. / 빨간 신호에 버스가 멈춰 섰다 The bus stopped at a red light. / 통증이 멈췄느냐 Is the pain gone ? *or* Has the pain left you ?
② 《…을》 stop; cease; put a stop 〔an end〕 to; bring to a stop 〔halt, standstill〕; hold up 〔on〕. ¶ 말을 ~ 「pull up 〔rein in〕 a horse; bring *one's* horse to a stop / …에 눈길을 ~ take notice 《of》; let *one's* eyes rest 《on》 / 발걸음을 ~ stop; halt; make a stop; stand still / 이야기를 ~ stop 〔cease〕 talking / 일손을 ~ stop work; rest from *one's* work 〔labor〕 / 차를 ~ stop a car; bring a car to a halt.

**멈칫거리다** hesitate 《at, to》; waver; draw 〔fall, shrink〕 back; flinch 《from》. ¶ 방에 들어서지 않고 ~ hesitate to enter a room; linger at the door / 갑자기 개가 짖어대서 그는 멈칫거렸다 He shrank back as the dog suddenly started barking. / 권총을 보자 대담한 그도 멈칫거렸다 Brave as he was, he flinched at the sight of the pistol.

**멈칫멈칫** hesitating(ly); hesitant(ly); slow(ly); dilly-dally; lingering(ly). ¶ ~ 대답을 않다 hesitate to answer / ~ 자리에서 일어서지 않다 be slow to leave *one's* seat.

**멈칫하다** 《갑자기 멈추다》 ⇨ 멈칫거리다. ¶ 발을 ~ come 〔bring *one's* feet〕 to a sudden halt / 하던 말을 ~ suddenly stop talking for a moment / 주먹을 맞고 ~ wince under the blow.

**멋** ① 《운치·아취》 taste; elegance; grace; (a) charm; 《사물의 진미》 flavor; relish; savor; 《세련·풍류》 refinement; elegance; 《짜릿한 맛》 gusto; zest; delight; pleasure; 《독특한 기품》 aroma. ¶ 노래의 멋 the flavor of a song / 시의 멋 the delights 〔pleasure〕 of poetry / 인생의 멋 the zest of living / 멋있는 tasteful; elegant; charming; graceful; refined / 멋없는 tasteless; inelegant; vulgar; prosaic; dry / 멋없는 연주 an insipid performance / 멋있는 말 a topping remark; a witty saying; a witticism / 멋없는 말 a vapid 〔an uninteresting〕 remark / 멋있는 노래 a song full of gusto 〔life〕 / 멋있는 춤 a dance full of zest 〔grace〕 / 멋을 모르는 사람 a prosaic person / 멋있는 사람 a person of refined taste / (…의) 멋을 알다 have a taste 《for》; relish; appreciate 《the fun, beauty, interest of》 / (…의) 멋을 모르다 have no taste 〔relish〕 《for》; have no appreciation 《of》; do not delight 《in》 / 현대 음악은 멋이 없다 Modern music has no attractive features. / 저 산이 풍경에 멋을 더해주고 있다 That mountain adds charm to the landscape. / 이 집의 정원은 꽤나 멋이 있다 The garden of this house is quite elegant. / 노송 하나가 정원에 멋을 더하고 있다 An old pine tree graced the garden.

② 《맵시》 dandyism; foppishness; 《허영》 show. ¶ 멋이 있는 stylish; smart (-looking); fashionable; *chic* (F.) / 멋있는 사람 dandy / 안경을 멋으로 쓰다 wear spectacles 〔glasses〕 for show / 모자를 멋으로 비스듬이 쓰고 있다 be wearing *one's* hat stylishly at a rakish angle.

**멋거리** dandification; foppishness; foppery.

**멋내다** spruce up. ⇨멋부리다.

**멋대로** 《마음 내키는 대로》 as *one* pleases 〔likes, wishes, chooses〕; selfishly; willfully; by choice 〔preference〕; 《자기 편한 대로》 《behave》 in a self-serving manner; 《자유 의사로》 freely; of *one's* (own) free will; of *one's* own accord; 《독단으로》 at *one's* (own) discretion; arbitrarily; 《무단히》 without leave 〔permission〕. ¶ ~ 굴다〔하다〕 go 〔have〕 *one's* own way 《in》; do what *one* likes 〔pleases〕; do as *one* pleases / ~하게 내버려 두다 let 《*a person*》 have his own way / 남의 물건을 ~ 쓰다 make free use of 《*a person's*》 things; appropriate 《*a person's*》 things for *one's* own use / 그녀는 그 일을 내 ~하게 했다 She gave me a free hand to do the job. / 그런 일을 내가 ~ 결정할 수는 없다 I cannot settle it on my own authority. / 네 ~ 해라 Suit yourself.

**멋들다** get interesting; take on flavor 〔charm〕; be beautiful 〔charming, fascinating〕; be captivating 〔sexy〕.

**멋들어지다** be full of fun 〔beauty, grace, interest〕; be full of gusto; (be) thrilling; exciting; delightful; captivating; fascinating; dashing; dramatic. ¶ 멋들어진 노래 a song full of gusto; a fascinating song / 멋들어지게 with gusto 〔zest〕; interestingly; fascinatingly / 멋들어진 연주 a tiptop 〔topping, swell〕 performance / 영어를 멋들어지게 하다 have a wonderful command of English / 멋들어지게 해내다 come off with flying colors; make a great success of / 멋들어지게 춤추다 dance with gusto; dance beautifully / 수양버들이 멋들어지게 늘어지다 a weeping willow droops gracefully.

**멋모르다** be ignorant 《of》; have no conception 〔idea〕 《of》; be quite unconscious 《of》. ¶ 멋모르는 사이에 without *one's* knowledge (of it); before *one* is aware (of it) / 멋모르고 달려들다 try to go at *somebody* 〔*something*〕 without knowing anything about *him* 〔*it*〕.

**멋부리다** spruce up; smarten 〔prettify, fancy, liven〕 up. ¶ 옷에 ~ dress stylishly 〔smartly〕; spruce 〔smarten〕 *oneself* up / 오늘은 굉장히 멋부리셨군요 You are all dressed up today, aren't you?

**멋없다** lack flavor; (be) insipid; uninteresting; dry; dull; flat; vapid; jejune; unsavory; wishy-washy; poor. ¶ 멋없는 사람 a dull 〔an uninteresting〕 person / 멋없는 문체 a dull 〔dry, jejune〕 style / 멋없이 굴다 act awkwardly; be ungainly; be unseemly / 애가 멋없이 키만 크다 The boy has height but that's about all.

**멋있다** 《맵시가 있다》 (be) stylish; fashionable; smart; polished; foppish; 《풍치 있다》 (be) tasty; tasteful; elegant; fine; chic. ¶ 멋있는 모자 a fanciful hat / 그녀는 멋있는 데가 있다 There is something chic about her.

**멋쟁이** a dandy; a fop; a swell; a dude; a classy 〔sharp〕 dresser; a fancy pants 《미구어》.

**멋지다** 《근사하다》 be fairly good; be very smart 〔cute 《미구어》〕; 《훌륭하다》 (be) fine; splendid; nice; neat; 《맵시·

태도 등이》 (be) stylish; smart; polished; foppish; dandyish; 《미구어》 (be) swell; high-toned; posh 《영구어》. ⇨멋들어지다. ¶ 멋진 물건 a stunner; a rare find / 멋진 미인 a smashing beauty / 멋진 생각 a smart 〔capital〕 idea / 멋진 솜씨 great 〔wonderful〕 skill / 멋진 아파트 a cute apartment / 멋진 플레이 a fine play / 멋져 보이다 look chic / 멋지게 성공을 하다 achieve brilliant success / 멋지게 차려 입다 be dressed in exquisite taste / 그 옷을 입으면 멋져 보인다 You look quite smart in that dress. / 그보다 더 멋진 일이 어디 있겠소 What could be nicer?

**멋질리다** become sluttish 〔slatternly, loose〕; get foppish 〔vain〕 《of appearances》. ¶ 멋질린 계집 a loose woman; a slattern; a vain 〔modish〕 woman.

**멋쩍다** ① ＝멋없다. ② 《거북하다》 (be) awkward; clumsy; stiff; constrained; feel uncomfortable; feel ill at ease; (be) embarrassed. ¶ 멋쩍은 듯이, 멋쩍게 awkwardly; stiffly; embarrassedly; bashfully / 멋쩍은 듯이 웃다 smile sheepishly / 혼자 가기가 좀 ～ It is sort of awkward to go there all alone. / 또 부탁하기가 ～ I am embarrassed to ask a further favor. / 오늘 아침 열차에서 치한으로 오인받았다. 어찌나 멋쩍었는지 말이 안 나왔다 Someone took me for a sex maniac in the train this morning. It's so embarrassing that I couldn't defend myself.

**멍** ① 《타박상》 a bruise; a contusion. ¶ 멍이 들다 have 〔get〕 a bruise / 눈에 멍이 들다 have a black eye / 멍이 들도록 때리다 beat 《*a person*》 black and blue. ② 《일의 탈》 a real snag; deep-rooted trouble; a serious hitch 〔setback〕; an insuperable obstacle. ⇨멍들다②.

**멍게** 〖동물〗 a sea squirt; an ascidian.

**멍군, 멍** a defensive move against a check-mate; "out of check". ～하다 make a defensive move against a checkmate; get out of check. ¶ 멍군 장군, 장이야 멍이야 It is hard to tell which of the two is wrong.

**멍들다** ① 《피맺힘》 have 〔suffer〕 a bruise; be bruised; have 〔suffer〕 an internal injury. ¶ 눈에 ～ have 〔get〕 a black eye / 전신이 ～ be black and blue all over / 맞아서 ～ be bruised by a blow / 그녀의 모진 말이 그의 마음을 크게 멍들게 했다 Her severe remarks hurt him badly. *or* Her harsh words bruised his feelings. ② 《일이》 suffer a serious hitch 〔setback〕; run into a real snag 〔an insuperable obstacle〕.

**멍멍** bowwow. ～거리다 bowwow; bark. ¶ 개가 ～ 짖다 a dog goes 〔barks〕 bowwow.

**멍멍개** 《소아어》 a bowwow; a doggie.

**멍멍하다** keep being deafened 《by the din》; stay stunned 〔dazed〕. ¶ 멍멍히 silently; as if stunned. ⇨멍하니.

**멍석** a straw mat; [총칭] straw matting. ¶ ～을 깔다 spread a straw mat 《on the ground》.

**멍석딸기** 〖식물〗 a white flowering raspberry.

**멍에** a yoke (bar). ¶ ～를 메우다 yoke 《an ox》; put a yoke on; put 《an ox》 to the yoke / ～를 짊어지다 come 〔be〕 under a yoke / ～를 벗다 throw 〔shake, cast〕 off the yoke 《of》; [비유적] free *oneself* from restraint.

**멍청이** a stupid 〔thick-headed〕 person; a dullard; a dunce; a fool; a blockhead.

**멍청하다** (be) stupid; foolish; silly; dull-witted; boneheaded. ¶ 멍청히 blankly; vacantly / 멍청한 얼굴 a stupid face 〔look〕; a foolish face; vacant look / 멍청한 짓을 하다 do a stupid thing; make an ass of *oneself* / 멍청한 얼굴을 하다 look stupefied 〔blank〕 / …을 멍청히 쳐다보다 gaze foolishly at 《*something*》 / 놀라서 멍청해지다 be stupefied with terror / 일을 않고 멍청히 앉아 있다 sit on *one's* hands.

**멍텅구리** ① ＝멍청이. ② 《병》 an ugly bottle (holding a bit more than a *toe*).

**멍하니** ① 《넋잃고》 absent-mindedly; vacantly; blankly; with a far-away look; in a daze; in a stunned look. ¶ ～ 앉아 있다 be sitting absent-mindedly / ～ 바라보다 gaze blankly 〔with vacant eyes〕 / ～ 경치를 바라보다 look absently at the landscape / 그녀는 ～ 그를 바라보았다 She turned bemused eyes toward him. / 그는 ～ 밖을 내다보고 서 있었다 He stood gazing vacantly out the window. ② 《하는 일 없이》 idly; aimlessly. ¶ ～ 시간만 보내다 idle *one's* time away; let time slip by.

**멍하다** (be) absent-minded; vacant; blank; stunned; dazed; deafened. ¶ 멍한 얼굴 a vacant face / 귀가 ～ be deafened 《by a noise》/ 정신이 ～ be in a daze; be stunned / 멍한 얼굴로 쳐다보다 gaze at 《*a thing*》 vacantly / 멍해지다 be absent-minded 〔abstracted, dazed, stupefied〕/ 그 소식은 너무나 충격적이어서 그는 잠시 멍해 있었다 The news was such a shock to him that for a while he remained stupefied.

**메**[1] 《망치》 a mallet (목제); a hammer; 《큰 것》 a sledge hammer; a maul. ¶ 메로 치다 hammer; strike with a hammer.

**메**[2] 《제삿밥》 rice offered to the gods or to departed spirits.

**메가바이트** 〚컴퓨터〛《정보의 기억 단위》 a megabyte (생략 MB).

**메가버시티** 《거대 대학교》 a megaversity.

**메가사이클** 〚물리〛 = 메가헤르츠.

**메가톤** 《100만 톤》 a megaton (생략 MT). ¶ ～급의 수소 폭탄 a hydrogen bomb in the megaton range.

**메가폰** 《확성기》 a megaphone. ¶ ～을 잡다 〚영화〛 direct the production of a movie.

**메가헤르츠** 〚물리〛《주파수 단위》 a megahertz (생략 MHz).

**메갈로폴리스** 《거대 도시》 a megalopolis.

**메공이** a hammer-shaped pounder.

**메귀리** 〚식물〛 oats.

**메기** 〚어류〛 a catfish; a bullhead; a horn(ed) pout. ◉ ～수염 a slender drooping moustache. ～입 a big (long) mouth; 《사람》 a bigmouthed person.

**메기다**[1] ① 《소리를》 lead (a song). ¶ 소리를 ～ lead a song 〔chant〕. ② 《톱질에서》 take the lead (on a two-man saw). ¶ 톱을 ～ take the lead on a two-man saw.

**메기다**[2] ① 《화살을》 fix; put. ¶ 화살을 ～ fix an arrow in *one's* bow; put an arrow 「on the string 〔to the bow〕; notch 〔nock〕 an arrow. ② 《윷놀이》 move 《a *yut* marker》. ¶ 말을 ～ move a *yut* piece.

**메기장** nonglutionous Indian millet.

**메꽃** ① 〚식물〛 a convolvulus; a bindweed. ② 《꽃》 the flower of a convolvulus.

**메꾼** a hammerer; a blacksmith.

**메꿎다** (be) willful 〔stubborn〕 and ill-tempered.

**메뉴** 《차림표》 a menu; a (menu) card; a bill of fare. ¶ ～에 있다 be on the menu / ～를 좀 보여〔갖다〕주세요 「May I see 〔Bring me〕 the menu, please?

**메다**[1] ① 《막히다》 be 〔get〕 choked 〔filled, plugged, stopped〕 (up); be 〔get〕 blocked; get clogged; be stuffed (up). ¶ 목이 ～ *one's* throat is choked; feel choked / 하수구가 ～ a sewage pipe 「stops up 〔gets stopped up〕/ 코가 ～ *one's* nose is stuffy / 목이 메게 울다 be choked with tears; sob / 파이프가 메었다 The pipe is clogged. / 길은 사람들로 꽉 메어졌다 The street is crowded with people. / 굴뚝이 그을음으로 메었다 The chimney is choked up with soot. ② [타동사] ⇨ 메우다[1].

**메다**[2] ① 《어깨에》 shoulder 《a gun》; carry 〔take, bear〕 《a load》 on *one's* shoulder. ¶ 총을 메고 with a gun (up)on 〔across〕 *one's* shoulder; gun on shoulder. ② ⇨ 메우다[2].

**메달** a medal. ¶ ～권에 들다〔권에서 탈락하다〕 enter 〔drop out of〕 the range of winning a medal / ～을 획득하다 win a medal.

◉ ～순위 medal standings. ～획득자 a medalist; a medal winner. 금〔은, 동〕 ～ a gold 〔silver, bronze〕 medal: 한국은 마라톤 경주에서 금～을 땄다 Korea won the gold medal in a marathon race.

**메달리스트** a medalist.

**메들리** 〚음악·경기〛《그러모은 것·혼성곡 따위》 a medley. ¶ 400미터 개인 ～ the individual 400-meter medley (race) / 그녀는 크리스마스 노래를 ～로 불렀다 She sang a medley of Christmas songs. ◉ ～릴레이 a medley relay 〔race〕.

**메떡** cakes made from nonglutinous grain.

**메떨어지다** (be) boorish; unrefined.

**메뚜기** 〚곤충〛 [총칭] a grasshopper; 《벼메뚜기》 a locust.

**메뜨다** (be) sluggish; slow-moving.

**메리고라운드** 《회전 목마》 a merry-go-round; 《미》 a carousel; 《영》 a roundabout.

**메리노** 《양모》 merino; 《직물》 a merino (*pl.* ～s). ◉ ～양 a merino (sheep).

**메리야스** [< *medias* (Sp.)] knitted 〔knit〕 (cotton) goods; knitwear; knitwork. ¶ ～ 셔츠 a knit(ted) undershirt.

◉ ～공장 a knitting mill. ～의류 knitwear; 《영》 hosiery. ～직조 jersey; stockinet(te): ～ 직조의 스웨터 a jersey sweater. ～천 knitted fabrics.

**메리트** 《장점·가치·이익》 a merit; an advantage. ¶ 그런 일을 해 봤자 대단한 ～는 없다 There isn't much merit in doing so.

**메린스** 《면직물의 하나》 *merinos* (Sp.). 「muslin.

**메릴랜드** 《미국의 주》 Maryland (생략 Md.).

**메마르다** (be) dried up; shriveled; withered; arid; 《불모》 (be) barren; sterile; infertile; 《마음이》 (be) severe; harsh. ¶ 메마른 땅 dry 〔sterile〕 soil; arid 〔sterile, infertile〕 land / 내 감정은 메마른 것 같다 I feel drained of emotion.

**메모** a memo (*pl.* ~s); a memorandum (*pl.* ~s, -da). ~하다 make a note 《of》; take notes 《of a lecture》; note down; write a memo notes 《about》. ¶ ~를 보면서 답변하다 give an answer from *one's* notes / 그는 ~ 없이 이야기했다 He spoke without notes. / 그의 주소를 ~해 두었다 I took a note of his address. ◉ ~용지 scratch 〔memo〕 paper. ~장 a memo 〔note〕 pad.

**메모리** a memory. ¶ 세계 최초의 기가바이트 컴퓨터 ~ 칩 the world's first gigabyte computer memory chip / 요즘의 개인용 컴퓨터는 3.2기가바이트 이상의 ~를 갖고 있다 Recently most personal computers have at least 3.2 gigabyte of memory.

**메밀** 〖식물〗 buckwheat. ◉ ~가루 buckwheat flour. ~국수 buckwheat noodles. ~묵 buckwheat paste 〔jelly〕.

**메부수수하다** (be) countrified; hayseedy; rustic; boorish. ¶ 메부수수한 계집아이 a boorish girl.

**메서디스트** 〖기독교〗 《감리교 신자》 Methodist(s).

**메소포타미아** 〖지리〗 Mesopotamia. ¶ ~의 Mesopotamian.

**메숲지다** (be) thick; dense; luxuriant; bushy.

**메스** [<*mes* (Port.)] a scalpel; a surgical 〔surgeon's〕 knife. ¶ …에 ~를 대다 《외과 의사가》 perform an operation on 《a patient for appendicitis》; [비유적] make a searching inquiry into 《a graft case》 / 지금이 바로 불평등 세제(稅制)에 대하여 ~를 가할 때다 It's high time that we took drastic measures to reform the unfair tax system.

**메스껍다** ① 《역겹다》 be sick 《at the stomach》; feel sick 〔nausea〕; be nauseated 〔sickened〕; feel queasy; feel like vomiting. ¶ 메스꺼운 냄새 a sickening smell / 이제 떡은 보기만해도 ~ Even the sight of a rice-cake makes me sick. ② 《눈에 거슬리다》 (be) sickening; stomach-turning; nauseating; revolting; disgusting; abominable. ¶ 메스꺼운 수작 a disgusting remark / 메스꺼운 아첨 nauseating 〔sickening〕 flattery / 메스껍게 굴다 act 〔behave〕 disgustingly.

**메슥거리다** feel sick; feel like throwing up. ¶ 속이 ~ feel sick to *one's* stomach.

**메슥메슥하다** be sick 《at the stomach》; have nausea. ¶ 속이 ~ feel sick.

**메시아** 《구세주》 the Messiah.

**메시지** a message. ¶ 축하 ~를 보내다 send a congratulatory message / 그녀에게 ~를 남기다 leave a message for her.

**메신저** a messenger. ◉ ~보이 a messenger boy.

**메아리** an echo (in the mountains). ¶ ~치다 echo; resound; reverberate; be echoed / 여자의 비명 소리가 긴 복도에서 ~쳤다 A woman's scream echoed through the long passage. / 그의 총소리가 온 산에 ~쳤다 The report of his gun 「echoed over 〔reverberated through〕 the hills.

**메어치다** throw 《*a person*》 over *one's* shoulder; throw 《*a person*》 to the ground; get 〔knock〕 《*a person*》 down.

**메역취** 〖식물〗 (the European) goldenrod.

**메우다**[1] ① 《구멍·틈 등을》 fill up; plug (up); stop up; fill 〔cover〕 in; 《안 통하게》 choke up (모래 등이); jam (군중 등이). ¶ 구멍을 ~ block 〔stop〕 up a hole; stop a gap / 바다를 ~ reclaim a foreshore; recover land from sea / 갈라진 틈새를 ~ fill up a crack with 《*a thing*》 / 여백을 ~ fill in a space 〔blank〕. ② 《모자라는 것을》 supply; make up for; 《결함을》 stop 〔fill up〕 《a gap》; offset 《a fault》. ¶ 결원을 ~ fill a vacant place; fill up a vacancy. ③ 《벌충하다》 compensate for; make up 〔amend〕 《for》; make good; atone for 《*one's* sin》; supplement 《*one's* income by doing…》. ¶ 결손을 ~ make good the loss / 부족액을 ~ replenish a shortage; 「make up 〔supply〕 the deficit / 손실을 ~ make up 〔compensate〕 for the loss.

**메우다**[2] ① 《테를》 ¶ (통에) 테를 ~ hoop 《a tub》; bind (a tub) with hoops. ② 《북을》 ¶ 북을 ~ put the skin 〔head〕 on a drum; make a drum. ③ 《쳇불을》 ¶ 체를 ~ fix a sieve net on its frame; make a sieve. ④ 《멍에를》 yoke; put a yoke 《on an ox》; put 《an ox》 to the yoke. ⑤ 《짐을》 make 《*a person*》 carry 《a bundle》 on *his* shoulder 〔back〕.

**메이다** ① 《테를》 make 《*a person*》 put a hoop on a tub. ② 《북을》 make 《*a person*》 put the skin 〔head〕 on a drum; have《*a person*》make a drum. ③《체를》have《*a person*》fix a sieve net on its frame.

**메이데이**《노동절》《celebrate》May Day; 《구조 신호》《call out, pick up》a mayday; a Mayday. ¶ ~ 집회〔행진〕에 참가하다 participate in〔join〕the May Day rally〔march〕.

**메이저**〚전자 공학〛《전자파 증폭기》a maser. [< *m*icrowave *a*mplification by *s*timulated *e*mission of *r*adiation]

**메이저리그**〚야구〛《미》the major leagues; the majors. ¶ ~의 선수 a major league player; a major-leaguer.

**메이커**《제조업자》a maker (★ 우리나라에서 「메이커」는 회사를 가리키지만, 영어의 maker는 개인을 가리켜 watchmaker나 dressmaker처럼 합성어로 쓰이는 일도 많음); a manufacturer. ¶ 자동차 ~ an automobile manufacturer / L사는 한국 유수의 식품 ~이다 Company L is one of the top food-products companies in Korea. ◉ ~제품 articles manufactured by well-known makers; brand-name merchandise: ~제품이 아닌 of a little-known brand / 당점에서는 ~제품만을 취급합니다 We handle only the best brands of articles.

**메이크업** ①《화장》(a) makeup. ~하다 make (*oneself*) up; put on *one's* makeup. ¶ ~을 한 남우 an actor in his makeup / ~을 지우다 clean off 〔remove〕*one's* makeup / ~을 고치다 fix *one's* makeup; 《구어》powder *one's* nose / ~을 잘 하다〔못 하다〕be good 〔poor〕at makeup / 그녀는 ~하는데 시간이 많이 걸린다 It takes her a lot of times to put on her makeup. ②《신문·잡지의》make-up; lay-out.

**메인** ①《미국의 주》Maine (생략 Me.). ②《주요한, 주된》main. ¶ 이 요리가 오늘밤의 ~이다 This is the main dish of this evening. ◉ ~라인《간선 철도·도로》a main line. ~마스트 the mainmast. ~스타디움 the main stadium. ~ 스탠드 the grandstand; the main stand. ~스트리트 the main street. ~오피스《본점·본사》the main office. ~이벤트 the main event. ~ 테이블 the main〔head〕table. ~프레임〚컴퓨터〛《중앙처리장치》a main frame.

**메조**〚식물〛nonglutinous〔regular〕millet.

**메조소프라노**〚음악〛mezzo-soprano. ◉ ~ 가수 a mezzo-soprano.

**메주** soybean malt (for making soybean paste and sauce). ¶ ~를 쑤다 steam soybeans for making soybean malt / 콩으로 ~를 쑨대도 곧이듣지 않다 do not accept a story at the face value; do not believe a story to be true. ◉ ~콩 malt soybeans. 메줏덩이 a ball〔block〕of soybean malt.

**메지다** (be) nonglutinous; be not sticky.

**메질** hammering; pounding. ~하다 hammer《on》; pound《on》

**메추라기**〚조류〛a quail. ¶ ~떼 a flock of quails. ◉ ~도요〚조류〛a snipe.

**메치다** ⇨ 메어치다.

**메카**《이슬람교의 성지》Mecca; 《동경의 땅·발상지》a mecca《for artists》. ¶ 한국은 태권도의 ~이다 Korea is the mecca of *t'aekwondo*.

**메커니즘**《기계장치·기구》a mechanism. ¶ 인체의 ~ the mechanism of the human body / 현대 사회의 ~은 복잡하다 The structure of present society is complicated.

**메탄**〚화학〛methane. ◉ ~가스 methane (gas); marsh gas.

**메탄올**〚화학〛methanol; methyl alcohol.

**메트로놈**〚음악〛a metronome.

**메틸**〚화학〛methyl. ◉ ~ 알코올 methyl alcohol; wood alcohol.

**멕시코** Mexico. ¶ ~의 Mexican. ◉ ~만 the Gulf of Mexico: ~만류 the Gulf Stream. ~사람 a Mexican. ~시티《멕시코의 수도》Mexico City.

**멘델**《식물학자》Gregor Johann Mendel (1822-84). ◉ ~법칙〚생물〛Mendel's laws; Mendelism.

**멘스**〚생리〛the menses; menstruation.

**멘탈테스트** a mental test〔examination〕. ¶ ~를 하다 conduct〔give, hold〕a mental〔an intelligence〕test.

**멘톨**〚화학〛menthol.

**멘히르**〚고고학〛《선돌》a menhir.

**멜대** a carrying pole. ¶ ~로 메다 carry 《it》on a pole.

**멜라닌**〚생화학〛melanin. ◉ ~색소 melanic pigment.

**멜로드라마**〚연극〛a melodrama; a soap opera《구어》. ¶ ~ 같은 melodramatic. ◉ ~ 작가 a melodramatist.

**멜로디**〚음악〛a melody; a tune. ¶ 아름다운〔귀에 익은〕~ a sweet〔familiar〕melody / 옛 ~를 흥얼거리다 hum an old tune / 그는 그 노래말에 ~를 붙였다 He wrote the melody〔tune〕of the song lyrics.

**멜론**〚식물〛a melon.

**멜빵** a rope〔strap〕for carrying something on *one's* shoulder; a shoulder strap; 《총의》a sling; 《바지의》braces 《영》; (a pair of) suspenders《미》. ◉ ~붕대 a sling; a suspensory: 팔에 ~붕대를 메고 있다 have *one's* arm in a sling.

**멤버** a member. ¶ 위원회의 ~이다 be a member of the committee; be on the committee. ◉ ~십 membership. 베스트 ~ the best members 〔players〕《of a team》. 스타팅~ a starting 〔an opening〕 lineup. 정규~ a regular member.
**멥쌀** nonglutinous 〔regular〕 rice.
**멧갓** ① 《산림》 a forested mountain. ② 《말림갓》 a forest preserve.
**멧닭** 〖조류〗 a Ussurian black-cock.
**멧대추** a jujube. ◉ ~나무 a jujube tree.
**멧도요** 〖조류〗 a woodcock.
**멧돼지** 〖동물〗 a wild boar.
**멧부리** a peak; the top 〔ridge〕 of a mountain.
**멧부엉이** a hick; a country bumpkin; a boor.
**멧새** ① 《산새》 a mountain bird. ② 〖조류〗 a meadow bunting.
**멧종다리** 〖조류〗 a mountain hedge=sparrow.
**며** [접속조사] ¶ 사과며 포도며 기타 과일들 apples, grapes and many other fruits.
**-며** 《연결》 and; or; 《동시》 while; as; between; over; with. ¶ 비가 오며 말며 하다 rain off and on / 울며 말하다 tell between sobs / 그의 누이는 얼굴도 고우며 품행도 얌전하다 His sister is both good-looking and well-behaved.
**며느리** a daughter-in-law. ¶ ~를 맞다 〔보다〕 get a wife for *one's* son / ~를 시집살이시키다 ill-treat 〔be hard〕 on *one's* daughter-in-law / ~가 미우면 손자까지 밉다 《속담》 He who hates Peter harms his dog. *or* Love me, love my dog. / ~ 사랑은 시아버지, 사위 사랑은 장모 《속담》 A daughter-in-law is loved most by her father-in-law, and a son-in-law by his mother-in=law.
**며느리발톱** 〖동물〗 a cockspur; a spur; a calcar.
**며느리밥풀** 〖식물〗 a cowwheat.
**며칟날** what day (of the month); the date. ¶ 오늘이 ~이냐 What day (of the month) is it today?
**며칠** ① ⇨ 며칟날. ② 《일수》 how many days; how long; several 〔a few〕 days (수일). ¶ ~ 동안 for days / ~ 전 some time ago; the other day / ~ 전부터 for the last few days; lately; recently / 그녀는 ~ 전부터 병으로 누워 있다 She has been ill in bed these several days. / 그 일을 하는데 ~ 걸리겠소 How many days will it take to get the work done? / 비가 ~을 두고 왔다 We have had a long spell of rainy weather. / 여기에 ~이나 머물꺼야 How long will you stay here? / 올해도 이제 ~ 안 남았다 There are but a few days left (in) this year.
**멱**[1] 《목》 a throat; a gullet. ¶ 돼지 멱따는 소리 a squealing sound; a squeal; a squeak / 멱을 따다 cut 《a fowl's》 gullet; cut 《*a person's*》 throat.
**멱**[2] 〖장기〗 a *janggi* 〔Korean chess〕 piece located in a position which blocks another piece from making a move. ¶ 멱장기 a *janggi* 〔Korean chess〕 move against the rule.
**멱**(冪) 〖수학〗 power. ¶ 멱수 an exponent.
**멱살** the throat; 《옷깃》 a collar. ¶ ~을 잡다〔움켜쥐다〕 seize 《*a person*》 by the collar 〔by the lapels〕; grab 《*a person's*》 throat.
**멱씨름** grappling at each other's throats. ~하다 grapple at each other's throats.
**면**[1](面) ① 《얼굴》 a face. ¶ ~을 맞대고 face to face / 면전에서 in the presence 《of *a person*》; before 《*a person*》. ② 《가면》 a mask; 《검도 등의》 a face guard. ¶ 면을 쓰다〔벗다〕 put on 〔take off〕 a mask.
③ 《국면》 an aspect; a side; a phase; 《관점》 a respect. ¶ 재정면에서의 원조 financial support / 모든 면에서 in every respect / 그 문제를 다른 면에서 생각해 보자 Let's think about the problem from a different aspect 〔angle〕. / 인생의 밝은 면을 보는 것이 중요하다 It's important to see the bright side of life.
④ 《표면》 a surface; 《평면》 a plane; 《곡면》 a curved surface; a face (다면체의). ¶ 평평한〔거친, 매끈한〕 면 a flat 〔rough, smooth〕 surface; (레코드의) B면 the B-side; the flip side (★ 특히 겉면이 히트곡일 때) / 입방체에는 몇개의 ~이 있느냐 How many surfaces does a cube have?
⑤ 《신문·책의》 a page. ¶ 제1면 the front page / 광고면 a page of advertisements / 너는 신문의 무슨 면을 먼저 보느냐 What page 〔columns〕 of the newspaper do you look at first of all? / 나는 신문의 사회면에만 흥미가 있다 I find interest only in the social page in a newspaper.
**면**[2](面) 《행정구역》 a *myeon* (as a subdivision of a *gun*); a township; a subcounty. ◉ ~소재지 the seat of a *myeon* 〔township〕 office.
**면**(綿) cotton. ⇨ 무명.
**-면** ⇨ -으면. ¶ 비가 오면 if it rains / 깨끗이 본다면 이 책을 빌려주지 You may borrow this book as long as you

keep it clean. / 내일 오면 그것에 관해 나한테 말해라 Speak to me about it when you come tomorrow. / 사귀면 사귈수록 너는 그를 좋아하게 될 것이다 The more you get to know him, the more you like him.

**면경**(面鏡) a hand mirror; a small looking glass.

**면구스럽다, 면구하다**(面灸—) (be) shamefaced; abashed; [서술적] feel awkward 〔embarrassed, nervous, ashamed〕. ¶ 그런 일로 표창을 받게 되어 ～ I feel embarrassed to be officially commended for such a thing.

**면나다**(面—) 《체면이 서다》 win 〔gain〕 honor; get credit; be honored. ¶ 면나는 face-saving 《concession》.

**면내다**(面—) bring honor 〔credit〕 《to》; do 《*a person*》 proud; save 《*a person's*》 face. ¶ 면내는데 급급하다 be too concerned about *one's* own personal honor.

**면담**(面談) an interview; a talk. ～하다 meet and talk 《with》; have an interview 〔a talk〕 《with》; talk personally 《with》. ¶ …와 개인 ～하다 have a personal interview with… / 상세한 것은 ～ 후 결정 《광고》 Particulars 〔Details〕 to be arranged personally. / 나는 내일 사장과 ～하기로 되어 있다 I'll have 「an interview 〔a talk〕 with the president tomorrow.

**면대**(面對) a face-to-face confrontation. ～하다 meet 〔come〕 face to face 《with》; face 〔confront〕 each other. ¶ ～하여 face to face; to 《*a person's*》 face / ～해 앉다 sit face to face 《with》; sit opposite 《each other》 / ～하여 욕설을 퍼붓다 abuse 《*a person*》 to his face; cast a reproach into *one's* teeth / 그와 ～해서 그런 말을 할 사람은 우리 중에 아무도 없다 None of us dare to say such a thing to his face.

**면도**(面刀) 《칼》 a razor; 《면도질》 shaving. ～하다 shave *oneself;* 《이발관에서》 get 〔have〕 a shave; get *oneself* shaved 《by》. ¶ 갓 ～한 얼굴 a freshly-shaved face / 깨끗이 ～한 얼굴 a clean-shaven face / ～하지 않은 얼굴 an unshaven face / ～만 해주시오 I want only a shave. ◉ ～날 a razor blade: ～날같이 날카로운 as keen as razors / ～날을 세우다 sharpen 〔hone, strap〕 a razor blade / 그는 ～날처럼 날카롭다 He is (as) sharp as a razor(blade). ～솔〔거울〕 a shaving brush 〔mirror〕.

**면려**(勉勵) exertion; endeavor; industry; assiduity. ～하다 exert *oneself;* work hard; be industrious.

**면류**(麵類) noodles.

**면류관**(冕旒冠) a (royal) crown; a diadem. ◉ 가시～《그리스도의》 the crown of thorns. 「fern.

**면마**(綿馬) 『식물』 an aspidium; a male

**면면**(綿綿) continuity; endlessness. ～하다 (be) continuous; unbroken; endless. ¶ ～히 without a break; continuously; ceaselessly / 이 가문은 11세기부터 ～히 이어져 왔다 The line of this family has been unbroken since the eleventh century.

**면면**(面面) 《여러 사람》 every one; each one; all. ¶ 위원회의 ～ each member of the committee; every one of the committee / 참석한 ～ 모두가 명사들이었다 All those present were distinguished men.

**면모**(面貌) 《얼굴의 모양》 looks; a countenance; features; facial linements; 《사물의 겉모습》 (an) appearance; an aspect; a phase. ¶ ～를 일신하다 change the appearance 《of》; change 《*a thing*》 out of all recognition; undergo a complete change / 새로운 ～를 띠다 assume a new aspect 〔phase〕 / 고속도로의 개통으로 그 도시의 ～가 일신됐다 The expressway has completely changed the appearance of the city.

**면목**(面目) ① 《모습》 an appearance; an aspect. ⇨ 면모. ② 《체면》 face; honor; (a) reputation; prestige; 《위엄》 dignity. ¶ ～을 세우다 save *one's* face 〔honor, dignity〕 / ～을 잃다 disgrace *oneself;* lose face; be in disgrace; be put out of countenance / ～을 지키다 preserve 〔maintain〕 *one's* honor 〔dignity〕 / ～을 되찾다 recover *one's* face / 정말 ～ 없습니다 I feel heartily ashamed. *or* I am really ashamed of myself. / 그를 볼 ～이 없다 I am ashamed to meet him. / 그 계획이 실패하면 ～을 잃게 될 것이다 You will lose face if you fail with the project.

**면밀**(綿密) ～하다 《세밀하다》 (be) detailed; minute; 《세심하다》 (be) scrupulous; meticulous; 《치밀하다》 (be) close; elaborate; 《철저하다》 (be) thorough. ¶ ～히 minutely; closely; thoroughly; scrupulously; carefully; elaborately / ～한 관찰 minute observation / ～한 계획 a detailed plan / ～한 검사 a close 〔thorough〕 examination / ～한 사람 a scrupulous person / ～한 계산 accurate calculation / ～한 묘사 a close description / ～한 보고서 a detailed report / ～히 조사하다 make a close investigation 《of》/ 우리들은 ～한 계획을 세우고나서 행동했다 We took action after making a careful plan.

**면바르다**(面—) 《반듯하다》 (be) even; level; well-formed; nice and neat; 《차림새가》 (be) well-featured.

**면박**(面駁) confutation to 《*a person's*》 face. ～하다 confute 〔reproach〕 to 《*a person's*》 face; cast 〔throw〕 a reproach in 《*a person's*》 teeth. ¶ 남편은 아내를 ～했다 The husband abused his wife to her face.

**면방**(**적**)(綿紡(績)) cotton spinning.

**면벽**(面壁) 『불교』 practicing Zen facing the wall. ¶ ～을 하다 sit in (religious) contemplation 〔mediation〕 in front of the wall.

**면봉**(綿棒) 《치료용의》 a swab; an absorbent cotton swab (fixed to a stick).

**면부득**(免不得) ～하다 be unavoidable 〔inevitable, inescapable〕. ⇨ 불가피.

**면분**(面分) a casual acquaintance; knowing by sight. ¶ ～이 있다 know by sight.

**면사**(免死) escape from death. ～하다 escape death.

**면사**(綿絲) cotton yarn (직조용); cotton thread (바느질용).

**면사무소**(面事務所) a *myeon* 〔township〕 office.

**면사포**(面紗布) a wedding 〔bridal〕 veil.

**면상**(面上) *one's* face. ¶ ～을 치다 strike 《*a person*》 on the face / ～에 흉이 지다 have a scar on the face.

**면상**(面相) physiognomy; a countenance; features; looks.

**-면서** ① 《동작의 진행》 …ing; 《동시에》 as; while; over; during; with. ¶ 지난 날을 얘기하면서 talking about bygone days / 한잔 마시면서 얘기하다 talk over a bottle of wine; drink wine while talking / 울면서 말하다 tell between sobs. ② 《불구하고》 (al)though; and yet; still; in spite of; for all that. ¶ 나쁜 일인 줄 알면서 though I knew it was wrong / 큰 부자이면서도 그의 욕심은 한이 없다 「Although he is rich 〔With all his riches〕, he is still avaricious.

**면서기**(面書記) a *myeon* official; an official of township office.

**면세**(免稅) exemption from taxation; tax exemption. ～하다 exempt 《*a thing*》 from taxation. ¶ ～가 되다 be exempted from taxation / ～로 되어 있다 be free of tax / ～로 사다 buy 《*a thing*》 duty-free / 외교관은 ～의 혜택을 누린다 Foreign diplomats are given immunity from taxation. / ～로 위스키를 살 수 있습니까 Can I get the whisky tax-free? ◉ ～소득 tax-free income. ～수입품 (duty-)free imports. ～점(店) a duty-free shop. ～점(點) the tax exemption limit 〔point〕: ～점을 인상〔인하〕하다 raise 〔lower〕 the tax exemption limit. ～품(品) duty-〔tax=〕free goods; duty-free articles (수입품): ～품의 위스키 duty-free whiskey.

**면소**(免訴) dismissal 《of a case》; acquittal 〔discharge, release〕 《of a prisoner》. ～하다 dismiss 《a case》; acquit 〔release〕 《a prisoner》. ¶ ～되다 be acquitted; be discharged; be released.

**면수**(面數) the number of pages.

**면식**(面識) acquaintance. ¶ ～이 있다 be personally acquainted 《with》; know (personally) / 일～도 없는 사람 a total 〔perfect〕 stranger / 나는 그와는 ～이 있다 I am acquainted with him. / 그와는 전혀 ～이 없다 He is quite a stranger to me.

**면실**(棉實) cottonseed. ◉ ～유 cottonseed oil.

**면양**(綿羊·緬羊) a sheep (*pl.* ～).

**면업**(綿業) the cotton industry.

**면역**(免役) 《노역의》 exemption from public labor; 《병역의》 exemption from military service; immunity from conscription. ～하다 be exempted from public labor 〔military service〕.

**면역**(免疫) 『의학』 immunity (from a disease). ¶ 자연～ natural immunity / 인공～ artificial immunity / ～이 되다 「gain (an) immunity 〔become immune〕 《to, against, from》; [비유적] be callous to 《scolding》; be not affected by 《criticism》 / ～이 되어 있다 be immune 《to, against, from》/ ～시키다 immunize 〔confer immunity on〕 *a person* 《against a disease》/ 나는 홍역에 ～되었다 I am immune to 〔from〕 measles. / 그는 감기엔 ～된 것 같다 He seems immune from influenza. / 백신 주사를 맞으면 소아마비에 ～이 된다 Vaccination immunizes people against polio. / 저 아이들은 어머니의 잔소리에 ～되어 있다 [비유적] Those children are immune to their mother's nagging.
◉ ～기간 a period of immunity. ～반응 (an) immune reaction. ～성 immu-

nity: ～성이 없는 nonimmune / ～성을 주다 confer immunity《on the patient》; immunize《*a person*》against a disease / ～성을 얻다 gain 〔secure〕 immunity. ～유전학 immunogenetics. ～자 an immune person. ～저항체 an immunity resistant. ～주사 (a protective) inoculation. ～체 an immune body: 자가 ～체 an autoimmune body. ～학 immunology. ～혈청 an immune serum.

**면욕**(免辱) ～하다 escape a humiliation 〔shame〕.

**면작**(棉作)《재배》cotton culture; cultivation of cotton;《수확》the cotton harvest 〔crop〕.

**면장**(免狀)《면허장》a license; a certificate; a permit; a charter;《졸업·개업의》a diploma;《사면장》a letter of pardon. ¶ ～을 받다 get 〔obtain〕 *one's* diploma 〔license〕.

**면장**(面長) the chief of *myeon* 〔township〕.

**면적**(面積) (an) area; square measure; size《of land》. ¶ 총～ the gross area / 넓은〔좁은〕～ a large 〔small, limited〕 area / 삼각형의 ～ the area of a triangle / ～을 구하다 square / ～이 7평방 마일이다 cover 〔have〕 an area of seven square miles / 이 회의장의 ～은 600평방 피트이다 The area of this floor is 600 square feet. *or* This floor has an area of 600 square feet. ◉ ～계(計) a planimeter; a planometer.

**면전**(面前) ¶ ～에서 in the presence《of》; before《*a person*》/ 사람들 ～에서 in public; in the presence of others / 그는 사람들 ～에서 책망당했다 He was scolded in the presence of people. / 아이들 ～에서 그런 이야기하지 마라 Don't say such things in front of the children. / 나의 ～에서 그녀의 이야기를 하지 마시오 Please don't speak of her in my presence.

**면접**(面接) an interview; interviewing. ～하다 interview; have an interview with《*a person*》. ¶ 개인～ an individual interview / 취직 ～을 받다 have an interview 〔be interviewed〕 for a job / ～을 위해, 10월 10일에 회사로 나와 주십시오 Please come to the office for an interview on October 10. ◉ ～시간 the hours for interviews. ～시험 an interview; an oral test 〔examination〕;《대학에서의》a viva voce examination;《구어》a viva: ～시험을 치르다 undergo an oral examination; have an interview / ～ 시험을 실시하다 hold an oral examination. ～자《하는 사람》an interviewer;《받는 사람》an interviewee.

**면제**(免除) (an) exemption; release; remission. ～하다 exempt《*a person* a duty》; discharge《*a person* from taxation》. ¶ 일부〔전액〕～ partial 〔total〕 exemption / 입학〔입회〕금～ exemption of the entrance fee / 벌금을 반액～하다 remit a fine to half of the amount / 병역을 ～받다 be exempted from military service / 그는 수업료를 ～받고 있다 He is exempted from school tuition. / 이들 물품은 관세가 ～되어 있다 These goods are exempt from customs 〔import duties〕. / 40세 이상 되는 사람은 병역이 ～되었다 Those who were forty years old and over were excused 〔exempted〕 from military service.

**면제품**(綿製品) cotton goods 〔stuff〕.

**면종**(面從) eyeservice; obedience to《*a person*》only in *his* presence. ～하다 pay eyeservice《to》; obey《*a person*》only in *his* presence; acquiesce in word only. ◉ ～복배(腹背) false obedience; (a) Judas kiss.

**면죄**(免罪) acquittal; remission of sin; 『가톨릭』a papal indulgence. ～하다 acquit. ¶ ～되다 be acquited《of the charge》. ◉ ～부(符)《서양사》an indulgence; a pardon.

**면지**(面紙)《책의》the inside 〔reverse〕 of the《front, back》cover of a book.

**면직**(免職) dismissal 〔removal〕 from office; deprivation of office; discharge. ～하다 dismiss 〔remove〕《*a person*》(from office); discharge《*a person*》(from *his* duties); relieve《*a person*》of *his* office 〔post〕. ¶ ～되다 be dismissed 〔removed〕 from office; be discharged; be relieved of *one's* post; lose *one's* position / 직무 태만으로 ～되다 be dismissed for negligence in *one's* duties; be fired from *one's* job through neglect of duty / 그는 뇌물을 받아서 ～되었다 He was dismissed 〔discharged〕 from office for accepting bribes.

**면직물**(綿織物) cotton fabrics 〔textiles, cloth〕. ◉ ～업자 cotton weavers.

**면질**(面質) confrontation. ⇨ 대질(對質).

**면책**(免責) exemption 〔immunity〕 from responsibility 〔obligation〕. ～하다 exempt 〔discharge〕《*a person*》from responsibility. ¶ ～되다 receive immunity from responsibility; become immune from obligation. ◉ ～조항

an escape 〔exemption〕 clause. ～특권《외교관의》 diplomatic immunity; 《국회 의원의》 the privilege of exemption from liability 《for *one's* speech in the House》: ～ 특권이 있다 have the privilege of exemption from liability 《for *one's* speech in the House》.

**면책**(面責) (a) personal reproof 〔reprimand〕. ～하다 reprove 《*a person*》 to *his* face; reprimand 《*a person*》 personally.

**면치레**(面―) saving 〔keeping up〕 appearances; saving *one's* face. ～하다 keep up appearance; put up a good front; assume the appearance 《of》.

**면포**(綿布) cotton cloth 〔stuff〕.
◉ ～류 cotton piece goods. ～상(商) a dealer in cotton goods.

**면하다**(免―) ① 《모면하다》 (***a***) 《피하다》 escape 《danger》; be saved 〔rescued〕 from 《drowning》. ¶ 부상을 ～ escape 〔get off〕 injury / 위기를 ～ get through a crisis / 위험을 ～ escape 〔get out of〕 danger / 죽음을 ～ escape death; be saved from death / 처벌을 ～ escape punishment; go 〔get off〕 scot-free / 그의 집은 소실을 면했다 His house was saved from the fire. / 다행히 내 차는 사고를 면했다 Fortunately my car missed being involved in the accident. (***b***) 《회피하다》 avoid 《an accident》; escape 《responsibility》; evade 《*one's* duty》; elude 《taxation》; excuse *oneself* from. ¶ 면할 수 없는 unavoidable; inevitable; inescapable / 책임을 면하려 하다 shirk 〔shift off〕 *one's* responsibility; try to evade *one's* duty. / 그들의 행위는 비판을 면하지 못했다 Their conduct is not safe from criticism.
② 《면제되다〔하다〕》 be exempted from 《taxation》; be immune from 《punishment》; be released from; be relieved of. ¶ 병역〔징집〕을 ～ be exempted from military service 〔draft〕 / 빚을 ～ acquit *oneself* of a debt / 책임을 ～ be relieved of a responsibility 〔*one's* post〕 / 벌금을 반액으로 ～ remit a fine to half the amount.
③ 《고통·욕·시달림 등을》 get rid of; rid *oneself* of; overcome. ¶ 성가심을 ～ get 〔be〕 rid of a nuisance; rid *oneself* of a nuisance / 욕을 ～ save *one's* face; avoid dishonor / 고통을 면하려고 하다 seek relief from suffering.
④ 《겨우 …하다》 manage to escape with difficulty; barely avoid; have a narrow escape; escape narrowly. ¶ 주림을 ～ barely avoid hunger; just manage to keep body and soul together.

**면하다**(面―) 《향하다》 face (on); front (on); look out on (to); open on (to) (출입문이); 《직면하다》 confront; face. ¶ 바다에 면해 있는 건물 a building facing the sea / 창이 길에 ～ a window looks out on the street / 우리집은 바다에 면해 있다 My house looks 〔faces〕 toward the sea. / 그 집은 거리에 면해 있다 The house faces 〔front on〕 the street. / 파리는 센 강에 면한 도시이다 Paris is a city (standing) on the River Seine.

**면학**(勉學) study; pursuit of knowledge; academic pursuit. ～하다 study; pursue *one's* studies. ◉ ～ 분위기 the studious atmosphere on campus; the campus atmosphere fit for study: ～분위기를 조성하다 create an academic atmosphere. ～풍토 《promote》 a hard-studying campus climate.

**면허**(免許) a permission; a license. ～하다 permit; license; authorize. ¶ ～가 있는〔없는〕 licensed 〔unlicensed〕 / 자동차 운전 ～시험 an auto-license examination 〔test〕 / 개업의의 ～ a license to practice medicine / ～를 얻다〔따다〕 obtain 〔take, get〕 a license. ◉ ～기간 a term of license. ～날짜 the date of license. ～료 a license fee. ～세 taxation on a licensed business. ～영업 a licensed business. ～장 a license. ⇨ 면허증. ～제 a license system. ～행정처분 administrative actions on permits. 제조～ manufacturing license.

**면허증**(免許證) a license; a certificate (증명서); a permit (허가증); a charter (특허장); 《자동차의》 a driver's license; a driving licence 《영》. ¶ 가(假)〔임시〕 ～ a temporary license; 《자동차의》 a learner's license; a provisional licence 《영》 / ～ 소지자 a licenseholder; a licensee / ～을 내주다 grant 〔issue〕 a license 〔certificate〕 / ～을 따다 obtain 〔take out〕 a license / ～을 갖고 있다 hold a license / ～을 취소〔정지〕당하다 get 〔be〕 disqualified; have *one's* license canceled 〔suspended〕 / 운전 ～을 갱신하다 renew *one's* driver's license / 「운전 ～을 보여주십시오」―「예, 여기 있습니다」 "Let me see your driver's license."—"Here it is."

**면화**(棉花) 〖식물〗 a cotton. ◉ ～씨 a

cottonseed: ~씨 기름 cottonseed oil.

**면화약**(綿火藥) guncotton; nitrocotton.

**면회**(面會) an interview; a meeting. ~하다 see; meet; receive 《a guest》; have an interview 《with》. ¶ ~를 요청하다 ask for an interview 《with》; ask 《*a person*》 to see 《*one*》; request an interview 《with》 / ~를 사절하다 decline 〔refuse〕 to see 《a caller》 / ~ 사절 《게시》 No visitors (allowed). *or* Visitors 〔Interviews〕 declined. *or* Do not disturb (수업·연구 중에) / 작업중 ~사절 《게시》 Interviews declined during working hours. / 환자는 중태이므로 ~를 사절합니다 The patient is in such a critical condition that no one is allowed to see *her*. / K씨를 ~하고 싶습니다 I would like to see Mr. K.
◉ ~시간 the visiting hours. ~실 a visiting room. ~인 a visitor; a caller. ~일 an at-home 〔a visiting〕 day; a receiving 〔reception〕 day.

**멸공**(滅共) crushing communism; rooting up communists. ◉ ~정신 the spirit to crush communism; the "Defeat Communism" spirit: ~ 정신을 강화하다 strengthen 《the nation's》 anti-Communist stand.

**멸구** 〖곤충〗 a rice insect; a leafhopper.

**멸균**(滅菌) pasteurization; sterilization. ⇨ 살균. ~하다 pasteurize; sterilize. ¶ ~된 거즈 sterilized gauze. ◉ ~력 sterilizing 〔germicidal〕 power. ~작용 sterilizing action 〔power〕.

**멸도**(滅度) 〖불교〗 Nirvana; the final emancipation.

**멸망**(滅亡) a downfall; a fall; ruin; collapse; destruction. ~하다 fall; go to ruin; be destroyed 〔ruined〕; perish; cease to exist; go out of existence. ¶ ~해 가는 민족 a dying race / 로마 제국의 ~ the fall of the Roman Empire / ~시키다 ruin; destroy; overthrow; wipe out of existence / ~의 길을 걷다 be on the way to collapse 〔ruin〕 / ~에 직면하다 be on the brink 〔verge〕 of ruin / 핵전쟁이 일어나면 인류는 지상에서 ~할지도 모른다 The human race may perish from the earth if a nuclear war breaks out.

**멸문**(滅門) extermination of a whole family; destruction of all *one's* kinsfolk. ¶ ~지화 a disaster that wipes out a whole family.

**멸사봉공**(滅私奉公) selfless devotion (to *one's* country).

**멸시**(蔑視) contempt; disdain; disregard. ~하다 despise; slight; disregard; disdain; look down upon 〔at〕; hold 《*a person*》 in contempt; make light 〔little〕 of. ¶ ~당하다 be held in contempt 〔irreverence〕 / 그는 너를 ~하고 있다 He looks down upon you. / 그가 가난하다고 ~해서는 안 된다 You should not 「despise 〔look down upon〕 him because he is poor.

**멸족**(滅族) extermination of a tribe 〔family〕. ~하다 exterminate 《*a person's*》 whole family 〔kinsfolk〕; wipe 〔put〕 a tribe out of existence; 《멸망하다》 《a tribe, a family》 become extinct.

**멸종**(滅種) extermination of a stock 〔race〕. ~하다 exterminate a stock; 《멸망하다》 《a stock, a race》 be exterminated; become extinct. ¶ 공룡은 ~된 동물이다 The dinosaur is an extinct animal.

**멸치** 〖어류〗 an anchovy. ◉ ~젓 salted 〔pickled〕 anchovies.

**멸하다**(滅―) ruin; destroy; exterminate; annihilate. ¶ 적을 ~ destroy 〔ruin〕 an enemy / 해충을 ~ exterminate noxious insects.

**명**(名) ① 《사람수》 persons. ¶ 전부 30명 thirty persons all told 〔in all〕. ② [접두어] famous; noted; excellent; great; celebrated. ¶ 명판결 a judicious decision / 명판사 an able 〔a wise〕 judge / 명연주 an excellent performance / 명투수 a star pitcher.

**명**(命) ① 《목숨》 *one's* life. ¶ 명이 길다 live long; have a long life; last long / 제 명에 죽다 die a natural death / 이래서는 제 명대로 못 살겠다 This will bring me to an early grave. / 그는 명(命)이 얼마 안 남은 것 같다 He does look like he's got one foot in the grave. ② ⇨ 운명. ③ 《명령》 an order; a command; 《지시》 an instruction. ¶ 당국의 명에 의하여 by order of the authorities / 명을 받다 receive orders 《from *a person*》; be ordered 《by *a person*》 / 명에 따르다〔거역하다〕 obey 〔disobey〕 《*a person's*》 orders.

**명**(銘) ① 《예술품 등의 작자명》 a signature. ¶ 명을 새긴 칼 a sword with the name of the maker inscribed on it / 작품에 명을 넣다 inscribe 〔engrave〕 *one's* name on *one's* work; sign. ② 《묘비명》 an epitaph; an inscription. ¶ 돌에 명을 새기다 engrave an inscription on a stone. ③ 《경계의 말》 a

motto (*pl.* ～(e)s); a maxim. ¶ 좌우명 *one's* (favorite) motto. 「dynasty.
**명**(明) 《중국의 왕조》 Ming; the Ming
**명가**(名家) ① 《명문》 a distinguished 〔prestigious〕 family. ¶ ～의 자녀 children born of a good family / 그는 ～의 출신이다 He comes of a distinguished family. ② 《명사》 an eminent personage; a great master (대가).
**명가**(名歌) 《뛰어난 시가》 an excellent poem; 《유명한 시가》 a celebrated 〔famous〕 poem.
**명가수**(名歌手) a renowned 〔famous〕 singer; a great singer.
**명견**(名犬) a fine 〔good〕 dog.
**명견만리**(明見萬里) 《have》 deep insight; far-sighted capacity.
**명경지수**(明鏡止水) 《마음에 거리낌이 없는 것》 a mind as serene 「as a polished mirror 〔as still water〕; a mind undisturbed by evil thoughts. ¶ ～와 같다 The mind is as bright and clean as a stainless mirror.
**명곡**(名曲) an excellent 〔exquisite〕 piece of music; a famous work of 《classical》 music. ¶ ～을 감상하다 appreciate an excellent piece of music.
**명공**(名工) a skillful workman 〔craftsman〕; a master hand; an expert workman.
**명과**(銘果) 《이름이 널리 알려진》 a cake of a well-known brand; 《고급과자》 an exellent cake.
**명관**(名官) a celebrated governor; a wise 〔an intelligent〕 magistrate.
**명관**(明官) a good 〔wise〕 governor 〔magistrate, government official〕. ¶ 구관이 ～이다 《속담》 The first governor is always better. *or* [비유적] There is nothing like the first love.
**명구**(名句) a well-chosen 〔nice, memorable〕 phrase 〔line〕; a wise saying (명언). ◉ ～집 a collection of famous sayings.
**명군**(明君) a bright king; a wise ruler.
**명궁**(名弓) 《사람》 a famous archer; an expert bowman; 《활》 a noted bow.
**명금**(鳴禽) 〖조류〗 a singing bird; a songbird. ◉ ～류 the songbirds.
**명기**(名妓) a celebrated *kisaeng*. 「cle.
**명기**(名器) a famous 〔an excellent〕 arti-
**명기**(明記) ～하다 write 〔state, define〕 clearly 〔expressly〕; spell out; specify (조문 등으로). ¶ 규칙에 ～된 바와 같이 as defined 〔specified〕 in the regulations / 신앙의 자유는 헌법에 ～되어 있다 Freedom of religion is spelled out in the Constitution. 「⇨ 내년.
**명년**(明年) next year; the coming year.
**명단**(名單) a roll 〔list, register〕 of names. ¶ 초대자의 ～ a list of guests invited / ～을 만들다 make a list 《of members》 / ～에 올라 있다 be on the list; be listed / ～에 올리다 put 《names》 on the list.
**명단**(明斷) a clear judgment. ¶ ～을 내리다 pass 〔make〕 a clear judgment 《of, on》.
**명담**(名談) a felicitous 〔well-phrased, witty〕 remark; a wise 〔golden〕 saying. ¶ 그것은 ～인데 That's well said.
**명답**(名答) a splendid 〔brilliant, clever〕 answer; an excellent answer. ～하다 answer 〔reply〕 brilliantly. ¶ ～입니다 You said it. *or* You've hit it.
**명당**(明堂) ① 《왕의 정전》 the king's audience hall. ② 《무덤앞의 평지》 the flat space in front of a grave. ③ 《좋은 묏자리》 a propitious site for a grave; 《좋은 자리》 an ideal 〔excellent〕 spot 《for》.
**명도**(明渡) delivery; surrender; evacuation. ⇨ 인도(引渡). ～하다 vacate 《a house》; evacuate 《a town》; surrender 《a castle》. ¶ ～를 요구하다 ask 《*a person*》 to vacate 《the house》 / ～를 통지하다 give 《the tenant》 notice to quit / 집의 소유권을 ～하다 transfer the ownership of the house to 《*a person*》. ◉ ～소송 an eviction suit; dispossession proceedings. ～신청 a petition for eviction.
**명도**(冥途) Hades; the world of the dead; the underworld; the other world; the realm of shades. ¶ ～에 들다 leave this world; go down to the nether world.
**명동**(鳴動) rumbling. ¶ 태산 ～에 서일필(鼠一匹) 《속담》 Much cry and little wool. *or* Much ado about nothing.
**명란**(明卵) spawn 〔roe〕 of a pollack. ◉ ～젓 salted pollack roe.
**명랑**(明朗) brightness; clearness; cheerfulness. ～하다 (be) bright; clear; cheerful; sunny. ¶ ～하게 merrily; cheerfully; jovially; light-heartedly; in a gay spirit / ～한 목소리로 in a clear voice / ～한 가정 a merry home / ～한 사람 a sunny 〔an open-hearted〕 person; a gay and jovial person / ～한 아가씨 a cheerful girl / ～해지다 become merry 〔gay, light-hearted, cheerful〕 / ～하게 하다 make bright; brighten up / ～하게 지내다

live gaily; lead a merry life / ～하게 노래하다 sing merrily / ～한 사람이다 be a man of sunny disposition.

**명령**(命令) 《분부》 an order; a command; bidding; 《법령》 an ordinance; a decree; a (public) injunction; 《지시》 a direction; 《훈령》 an instruction. ～하다 order; command; direct; instruct; tell; charge.

> 용법 **order, command** 권력을 가진 인물이 「명령하다」의 뜻이지만, order는 일시적·독단적으로 명령한다는 뜻이고, command는 공식적으로 직무상의 명령을 내리는 것. **direct, instruct** 일·상업·외교 관계 등에서 「명령·지시·지휘하다」 등의 뜻이지만 direct는 강제의 뜻이 강하고, instruct는 격식차린 느낌의 말. **tell** order, command, direct 등의 일상어로서, Don't tell me to do or not to do (나한테 이래라 저래라 하지 마시오).처럼 「…하시오」 정도의 명령의 뜻을 갖고 있음. **charge** 「의무로서 …하라고 명령하다」의 뜻.

¶ ～적으로 imperatively; peremptorily / ～대로 as ordered; according to an order / ～에 의하여 by order 《of》 / ～을 내리다 issue an order; give order / ～대로 하다 do as *one* is told; act on 《*a person's*》 order / ～조로 말하다 speak in a commanding 〔an authoritative〕 tone / ～을 무시하다 ignore an order 〔a decree〕 / ～을 실행하다 carry out an order / ～을 어기다 disobey an order; act contrary to *another's* order; violate a command / ～을 철회하다 withdraw a command 〔an order〕 / ～을 받다 take 〔receive, get〕 orders 《from》 / ～에 따르다 obey *a person's* order / 양심의 ～에 따르다 obey the dictates of (*one's*) conscience / 진군 ～을 내리다 give a marching order / ～에 따르지 않는 자는 처벌받는다 The ones who do not obey the order will be punished. / ～이 내리는 대로 출발할 준비가 되어 있습니다 I am ready to leave anytime the order comes. / 심판은 그 선수에게 퇴장 ～을 내렸다 The referee ordered the player off the field. / 경찰은 그들에게 물러가라고 ～했다 The policemen ordered them back. / 차는 경찰관의 정지 ～을 무시하고 내달렸다 The car sped on, ignoring the policeman's order to stop.
◉ ～계통 a line 〔chain〕 of command; a command system. ～문 〖문법〗 an imperative sentence. ～법 〖문법〗 the imperative mood. ～서 an order; 〖법〗 a precept. ～위반 violation of an order. ～자 a commander; a dictator.

**명론**(名論) a convincing 〔sound, telling〕 argument; a well-founded theory; an excellent opinion. ◉ ～탁설(卓說) an original opinion worth listening to.

**명료**(明瞭) clearness; plainness; lucidity; distinctness. ～하다 (be) clear; plain; obvious; evident; distinct; 《문체 등이》 (be) lucid; 《글자체 등이》 (be) legible. ¶ ～하게 clearly; plainly; obviously; evidently; distinctly; lucidly; legibly / ～하게 답변하다 give a definite answer / ～하게 쓰다 write legibly / ～하게 하다 make 《*a thing*》 clear; clarify / ～하게 발음하다 pronounce distinctly. ◉ ～도 〖통신〗 clarity; articulation: ～도 지수 an articulation index.

**명리**(名利) fame and wealth 〔fortune〕; riches and honor. ¶ ～에 뜻이 없다 be indifferent to fame and wealth / ～에 급급하다 be running after fame and wealth; be constantly striving 〔hankering〕 after fame and wealth.
◉ ～심 worldly interests.

**명마**(名馬) a fine horse; an excellent 〔good〕 steed.

**명망**(名望) reputation; repute; renown; popularity (인망). ¶ ～이 있는 reputed; renowned; popular / ～을 얻다 gain 〔win〕 fame; win 〔build up〕 a reputation / ～을 잃다 fall in public estimation; lose *one's* reputation 〔popularity〕 / ～이 있다 have a reputation; be well-reputed; be popular.
◉ ～가 a man of high repute; a man standing high in public esteem.

**명맥**(命脈) life; the thread of life; existence. ¶ ～이 다하다 die (out); come to an end; go out; expire / ～을 이어가다〔유지하다〕 《사람이》 remain alive; maintain life; 《풍습 따위가》 stay 〔remain〕 in existence / 간신히 ～을 이어가다 have only a spark of life left in *one* / 그 회사는 간신히 ～을 유지하고 있다 The company is barely keeping its head above water.

**명멸**(明滅) flickering; blinking; glimmering. ～하다 flicker; blink; glimmer; come on and off. ¶～하는 등불 a flickering light. ◉ ～신호 a blinking signal.

**명명**(命名) naming; christening. ～하다 give a name 《to》; name; 《의식과 함께 사람·배 등을》 christen. ¶ 복동이라고 ～하다 name 《a boy》 Poktong / 그 배는 퀸이라고 ～되었다 The ship was named Queen. *or* We named the ship Queen. ◉ ～법 《학술상의》 nomenclature. ～식 a naming 〔christening〕 ceremony. ～자 the christener.

**명명백백**(明明白白) ⇨ 명백. ¶ ～한 as clear as day 〔daylight, the sun at noonday〕; quite obvious.

**명모**(明眸) bright eyes. ◉ ～호치 starry eyes and pearly teeth: ～호치의 여성 a beautiful woman; a beauty.

**명목**(名目) 《명칭》 a name; 《구실》 a pretext. ¶ ～상의, ～뿐인 nominal; in name only / ～상의 사장 a nominal 〔figurehead〕 president; a president in name only / ～상의 이유 the ostensible reason / …라는 ～으로 under the name 〔pretext〕 of... / ～에 지나지 않다 be just nominal; be in name only / 무슨 ～이든 만들어서 (up)on some pretext or other / 그는 정치 헌금이라는 ～으로 정치가에게 뇌물을 제공했다 He offered a bribe to a politician under the pretext 〔excuse〕 of giving a political donation. ◉ ～국민소득 nominal national income. ～론 〖철학〗 nominalism. ～성장률 nominal growth rate. ～임금 nominal wages. ～ 자본 nominal capital.

**명문**(名文) an excellent composition; a fine piece of prose; a noted composition (유명한 글); (a piece of) prose in an exquisite style; a beautiful passage (미문). ¶ ～이다 be well written; be high in literary merit / ～을 쓰다 write 〔have〕 a fine style; be a good writer. ◉ ～가 a fine prose writer; a master of literary style; a stylist. ～구(句) a witty 〔a happy, an apt〕 remark; a well-worded saying; an epigram; an aphorism. ～집 a choice collection of prose; an anthology of literary gems.

**명문**(名門) a distinguished 〔a reputable, an illustrious〕 family; a noble family; a family with a long lineage. ¶ ～ 출신이다 come from 〔of〕 a distinguished family; be born into 〔of〕 a noble family; be a man of high birth / ～ 출신의 사람 a man of a good family; a man of noble birth. ◉ ～거족(巨族) mighty clans. ～교 a school with a high (academic) reputation; a prestige school; a top-prestige school: 야구의 ～(고)교 a (high) school famous for its excellent baseball team / 하버드는 ～교이다 Harvard is a prestigious 〔distinguished〕 university.

**명문**(明文) 《조문》 an express provision 〔statement〕; a specific proviso. 《증서》 a written contract; a deed. ¶ ～화하다 put 《*something*》 in the statutory form / ～으로 규정되어 있다 be expressly stipulated in the text / 제외한다는 ～이 없으면 if it is not expressly excluded / 이 문제에 관해서는 법률에 ～화 되어 있지 않다 This subject is not provided for in the law. *or* There is no provision in the law on this subject. ◉ ～규정 (a) substantive enactment.

**명물**(名物) ① 《명산물》 a well-known 〔famous〕 product; 《특산물》 a special product; a (local) speciality. ¶ 대구 ～의 사과 the apple which Taegu is noted for / 안성의 ～은 유기이다 Ansŏng is famous for its brass. / 이 지방의 ～은 무엇입니까 What is this locality famous for? ② 《이름난 사람·것》 an institution; a feature; an attraction. ¶ 읍내에서 ～인 사나이 a popular figure in town / 이 식당의 ～요리 the speciality of this restaurant / 안개는 런던의 ～이다 The fog is a thing which London is famous for. / 그 축제는 런던의 ～ 중의 하나이다 The festival is one of the attractions of London.

**명미하다**(明媚—) (be) beautiful; picturesque. ¶ 풍광(風光) 명미한 땅 a place of scenic beauty; a picturesque site.

**명민**(明敏) sagacity; intelligence; perspicacity. ～하다 (be) sagacious; shrewd; intelligent; perspicacious. ¶ 그의 동생은 두뇌가 ～하다 His brother 「is clear-headed 〔has a clear head〕.

**명반**(明礬) alum. ◉ ～석 alum stone; alunite.

**명백**(明白) clearness; plainness; obviousness; distinctness. ～하다 (be) plain; clear; obvious; manifest; distinct; unmistakable. ¶ ～히 clearly; plainly; obviously; evidently / ～히 말하자면 in plain terms / ～한 사실 an obvious fact; a plain truth / ～한 증거 an evident proof / ～해지다 become clear / ～하게 하다 make 《*something*》 clear; define; clarify / ～히 진술하다 state clearly 〔plainly〕 / 그것은 극히 ～

한 일이다 That is as clear as daylight.

**명복**(冥福) happiness in the other world; heavenly bliss. ¶ ～을 빌다 pray for the happiness 〔bliss〕 of the dead; pray for the repose of 《*a person's*》 soul / 그의 ～을 빕니다 May his soul rest in peace!

**명부**(名簿) a register 〔list, roll〕 of names; a nominal list 〔register, roll〕; a roster. ⇨ 명단. ¶ 신입생〔선거인〕 ～ a register of「freshmen 〔electors〕 / 학급 ～ a class list / ～를 작성하다 make 〔prepare〕 a list 《of members》 / ～에 기입하다〔올리다〕 put 〔enter〕 《*a person's* name》 on the roll; register 《*a person's* name》; enroll 《*a person*》 (on the list) / 방문자 ～에 이름을 쓰다 write *one's* name in the visitors' book / ～에서 지우다〔삭제하다〕 cross 《*a person's* name》 off 〔out〕 from the list; remove 〔erase, cancel〕 《*a person's* name》 from the list.

◉ 기부자～ a subscription list.

**명부**(冥府) ＝ 명도(冥途).

**명분**(名分) *one's* moral obligations 〔duty〕; 《정당성》 (moral) justification; 《이유》 a just cause. ¶ ～이 안 서는 행동 an unjustifiable act / ～을 밝히다 clearly define *one's* moral obligations; fulfill *one's* specified duty / ～을 세우다 justify *oneself* 〔*one's* conduct〕 / ～이 서지 않다 cannot be justified; be hardly justifiable.

**명사**(名士) a prominent person 〔figure〕; a personage; a celebrity; 《구어》 a big name. ¶ 사회 ～ the elite of society / 각계의 ～ notables of all spheres of social activity / 경제계의 ～ a prominent figure in business circles / 당대의 ～들 prominent men of the time / 문단의 ～ a big name in literary circles; a famous 〔noted〕 writer / 정계의 ～ a prominent figure in politics; a noted politician / 학계의 ～ a distinguished scholar; a prominent figure in the academic world.

**명사**(名詞) 〖문법〗 a noun. ¶ ～의 nominal / 보통〔고유, 물질, 추상, 집합〕～ a common 〔a proper, a material, an abstract, a collective〕 noun. ◉ ～구(句)〔절〕 a noun phrase 〔clause〕. ～화 nominalization: ～화하다 nominalize.

**명사**(名辭) 〖논리〗 a term; a name.

◉ 대〔소〕～ the major 〔minor〕 term.

**명산**(名山) a well-known 〔noted, celebrated〕 mountain. ◉ ～대천 splendid mountains and rivers.

**명산**(名産) a well-known 〔noted, special〕 (local) product; a speciality (of the district). ¶ 대구의 ～은 사과다 Taegu is famous for its apple. *or* The apple is a speciality of Taegu.

**명상**(瞑想) meditation; contemplation. ～하다 meditate 〔muse〕 《on》; contemplate. ¶ ～적인 meditative; contemplative / ～생활 a contemplative life / ～에 잠기다 be lost 〔sunk〕 in meditation / 철학적인 문제에 관하여 ～하다 meditate on 〔contemplate〕 a philosophical problem. ◉ ～록 meditations.

**명색**(名色) ＝ 명목(名目). ¶ ～만의 nominal / ～뿐인 자유 the shadow of freedom / ～이 대학 교수인데 그런 일은 할 수 없다 It would impair the prestige of a college professor to do such a thing.

**명석**(明晳) lucidity; clearness; clarity. ～하다 (be) lucid; clear; distinct. ¶ ～치 못한 indistinct; vague / 두뇌가 ～하다 be clear-headed; be bright; have a clear head.

**명성**(名聲) fame; renown; (a) reputation; honor and distinction; popularity (인망). ¶ ～있는 renowned; noted; celebrated / ～이 자자한 사람 a man「with a great reputation 〔of great renown〕 / ～이 높다 be famous; be highly reputed; be celebrated / ～을 얻다 win 〔gain, acquire〕 a reputation; attain 〔win〕 fame / ～을 높이다〔잃다〕 enhance 〔lose〕 *one's* reputation / ～을 손상시키다 [원인이 주어] hurt 〔damage〕 *one's* reputation / ～을 쌓다 build up a solid reputation / ～이 올라가다 rise in fame / ～을 구하다 seek fame / 세계적인 ～을 얻다 achieve 〔enjoy〕 a world-wide reputation / 그녀는 힘겹게 ～을 유지했다 She managed to maintain her reputation. / 그의 ～은 국내외에 쟁쟁하다 His name is known both at home and abroad.

**명성**(明星) ＝ 샛별.

**명세**(明細) particulars 《on, about》; details 《about》; specifics. ～하다 (be) particular; minute; detailed; full. ¶ ～한 보고서를 만들다 make a detailed report 《on》 / 지출의 ～를 보고하다 render an account of payments 〔all money spent〕 / 합계 30만원, 그 ～는 다음과 같다 It totals 300,000 won, made up as follows.

◉ ～서 《계산 등의》 a detailed 〔full〕

statement; 《시방서》 specifications: 내용 ～서 a detailed statement of contents / 설계 ～서 building specifications / 지출 ～서 a bill of expenditures / 선적 ～서 shipping specifications. ～표 an itemized account.

**명소**(名所) a famous 〔noted〕 place; sights (to see); a place of interest; a beauty 〔scenic〕 spot (명승지). ¶ 관광 ～ a tourist attraction / ～를 구경하다 do 〔see〕 the sights 《of Seoul》 / ～를 안내하다 show 《*a person*》 the sights 《of Kyŏngju》; take 《*a person*》 to places of interest 《in an old city》 / 내일 런던의 ～를 구경하고 싶습니다 I'd like to make a tour of famous sites in London tomorrow. ◉ ～안내서 a guide to the sights.

**명수**(名手) 《사람》 an expert; an adept; a master 〔capital〕 hand; 《바둑·장기 등의 수》 an excellent 〔a clever〕 move. ¶ 사격의 ～ a good 〔an expert〕 marksman; a sharpshooter / 피아노의 ～ an accomplished pianist / 거짓말의 ～ a big liar / 그가 피리의 ～라며 He is a skillful performer on the flute, isn't he?

**명수**(命數) 《운명》 *one's* fate; destiny; 《수명》 *one's* (natural) span of life; one's length of days. ¶ ～가 다하다 *one's* time has come; *one's* time 〔life〕 has ended / 자기 ～를 알다 know *one's* doom; know that *one* is dying 〔is near death〕.

**명승**(名勝) scenic beauty; noted scenery. ¶ ～을 보존하다 preserve scenic beauty. ◉ ～고적 places of natural beauty and historic interest: ～고적이 많다 be rich in scenic and historic interest. ～지 a scenic spot; a place of scenic beauty; a famous sight: ～지를 답사하다 explore the natural beauty of the place.

**명승**(名僧) a celebrated 〔distinguished〕 Buddhist monk.

**명시**(明示) clear statement; elucidation. ～하다 express 〔state, describe〕 clearly; demonstrate plainly; point out specifically; specify. ¶ ～하지 않은 《as yet》 unspecified / 그 기획에 필요한 금액을 ～하다 specify the amount of money needed for the project.

**명시**(明視) clear 〔right〕 perception; clear vision. ～하다 see 《*a thing*》 clearly; see in a clear light; be clear-visioned. ◉ ～거리 the visibility distance. ～도 〖물리〗 luminance.

**명실**(名實) name and reality 〔deed〕. ¶ ～공히 both in name and reality; both nominally and virtually / ～상부하다 be true to *its* name; live up to *its* reputation / ～상부하지 않다 The reality does not agree with 〔falls short of〕 the name. / 그는 ～공히 그 운동의 지도자다 He is the leader of the movement in reality as well as in name.

**명심**(銘心) ～하다 inscribe 《*something*》 in *one's* memory; keep 〔bear〕 《*a matter*》 in mind; have 《*a matter*》 branded on *one's* mind. ¶ ～할만한 말 words which are worth remembering / 그 일을 항상 ～해야 한다 It must always be borne in mind. / 지각하면 안된다는 점을 ～해라 Keep 〔Bear〕 it in mind that you must not be late for work.

**명아주** 〖식물〗 wild spinach; a goosefoot.

**명안**(名案) a good 〔wonderful, great〕 idea 〔plan〕; a splended suggestion. ¶ ～이 떠오르다 hit on 〔have〕 a good idea / 무슨 ～이 없겠느냐 Can you think of anything better? *or* Have you got a better idea? / 그것 참 ～이다 That's an idea. *or* Good idea!

**명암**(明暗) light and darkness 〔shade〕. ¶ 인생의 ～ the bright and dark sides 〔phases〕 of life / ～을 분명히 나타내다 show a clear contrast between light and shade / 그녀 운명의 ～은 그 선택으로 결정됐다 [비유적] The choice decided her fate. ◉ ～도 brightness; light intensity. ～등 an occulting light. ～법 〖미술〗 shading; chiaroscuro.

**명약관화**(明若觀火) being as clear as daylight. ～하다 be as clear as day 〔daylight〕; quite obvious; be plain enough.

**명언**(名言) a wise 〔golden〕 saying; a witty 〔an apt〕 remark. ¶ 불후의 ～ an immortal saying / 예로부터 전해져 오는 ～ an old saying / ～을 말하다 make wise 〔witty, apt〕 remarks / 그거 과연 ～이군 That's well 〔aptly, wisely〕 said. ◉ ～집 analects.

**명언**(明言) a definite statement; (a) declaration. ～하다 declare; say definitely; state positively; assert.

**명역**(名譯) an excellent 〔admirable〕 translation.

**명연기**(名演技) good acting; an excellent 〔a fine〕 performance.

**명예**(名譽) 《영예》 honor; glory; credit distinction; 《명성》 fame; reputation; a good name. ¶ ～로운 지위 an hon-

orable position / ～에 관련된 사항 a point of honor / ～를 중히 여기는 사람 a man of honor / ～가 되다 be a credit 〔an honor〕 to 《the school》; do 〔bring〕 honor 〔credit〕 to 《*a person*》; be to *one's* honor / ～를 얻다 gain 〔win, attain〕 honor / ～를 주다 award honor to 《*a person*》; bestow 〔confer〕 honor on 《*a person*》 / ～를 잃다 lose *one's* honor / ～를 손상하다 bring disgrace on 《*a person*》; stain 《*a person's*》 honor; injure 〔impair〕 《*a person's*》 reputation / ～를 존중하다 value 〔prize〕 honor 《above everything else》 / ～를 회복하다 retrieve 〔redeem〕 *one's* (lost) honor; regain 〔recover〕 *one's* reputation / ～에 영향을 주다 affect *one's* honor 〔reputation〕 《of》 / ～를 위하여 싸우다 fight for the honor 《of》 / …에 ～를 걸다 wage *one's* reputation on... / …하는 것을 ～로 여기다 feel it an honor to *do* / ～를 걸고 약속을 지키겠다 On my honor, I will keep my promise. / 그는 ～롭게 죽었다 He died a glorious death.
◉ ～교수 an honorary 〔emeritus〕 professor; a professor emeritus 〔emerita (여)〕. ～박사(학위) an honorary doctoral degree. ～시민 an honorary citizen. ～심〔욕〕 a desire for fame; aspirations after fame. ～(의) 전당 《야구의》 the (Baseball) Hall of Fame. ～제도 《사관 학교의》 the honor system. ～직 an honorary post 〔office〕. ～총장 an honorary president; a president-emeritus 《of Korea University》. ～퇴직 voluntary resignation 〔retirement〕; quitting *one's* job voluntarily. ～학위 an honorary degree. ～혁명 〖역사〗 the Glorious 〔Bloodless〕 Revolution. ～회복 regaining *one's* impaired reputation. ～회장〔회원〕 an honorary chairperson 〔member〕. ～훼손 defamation of character; 《문서에 의한》 (a) libel; 《구두의》 (a) slander: ～훼손으로 고소하다 sue 《*a person*》 for libel.

**명왕성**(冥王星) 〖천문〗 Pluto.

**명우**(名優) a famous 〔celebrated〕 actor 〔actress〕; a great star. ¶ ～가 되다 rise to stardom.

**명월**(明月) a bright moon. ¶ 중추 ～ the harvest moon.

**명유**(名儒) a well-known Confucianist; a prominent scholar; a scholar of note.

**명의**(名義) 《이름》 a name; 《명분》 moral obligations. ¶ ～상(은) nominally; in name / ～만의 사장 a president in name only / 딸 ～의 예금 money deposited in the name of *one's* daughter / 타인 ～로 under disguised ownership / ～를 바꾸다 change the holder 《of》; transfer the title to 《*one's* wife》 / 내 집은 장남 ～로 되어 있다 My house is in my first son's name.
◉ ～도용(盜用) an illegal use of other's name. ～변경 title transfer; transfer of the name 《of an estate》; entry of a change of holders. ～인 the holder 《of a title deed》.

**명의**(名醫) a skilled physician; a great doctor; 《유명한 의사》 a well-known 〔celebrated〕 doctor.

**명인**(名人) a noted person; a (past) master 《in, of》; a master-hand; an expert 《at, in》. ¶ 바둑의 ～ 《국수》 the champion *paduk* player; 《명수》 an expert *paduk* player / 피리의 ～ a master-flutist / 변장의 ～ an expert in disguise / ～의 경지에 이르다 master 《an art》; attain 〔achieve〕 mastery 《in》; become a master-hand 《at》 / ～의 기량을 보이면서 with a mastery skill. ◉ ～기질 the spirit of a master artist: ～기질을 지니고 있다 have a character typical of a master artist. ～전 《바둑의》 the professional *paduk* 〔*go*〕 players' championship series.

**명일**(名日) a festive day; a national holiday.

**명일**(明日) tomorrow. ⇨ 내일.

**명일**(命日) the anniversary of 《*a person's*》 death.

**명작**(名作) a masterpiece; a fine piece 《of literature》; a fine work 《of art》. ¶ 근래 최고의 ～ the greatest masterpiece in recent years / 세계적으로 알려진 ～ works known the world over.

**명장**(名匠) a master-hand; a master craftsman 〔artisan〕; a skillful workman.

**명장**(名將) a distinguished 〔famous〕 general; an illustrious admiral; a great commander.

**명재상**(名宰相) an able premier.

**명저**(名著) 《훌륭한 책》 a great 〔fine〕 book; 《걸작》 a masterpiece. ¶ 고금의 ～ ancient and modern classics.

**명절**(名節) ① 《날》 a festive day; a national holiday; red-letter days. ¶ 실상 정월 ～ 기분은 그믐날 밤부터 시작된다 In reality, the festive mood begins on the eve of the New Year's

Day. ② 《명분과 절의》 moral obligation and justice.
**명정**(酩酊) drunkenness; intoxication. ~하다 be intoxicated; be in a drunken condition; get drunk.
**명정**(銘旌) a flag 〔banner〕 with an inscription of the name and the rank of the dead.
**명제**(命題) 〖논리〗 a proposition; a thesis (*pl.* -ses); a statement; 《제목》 a given subject for a composition. ¶ 긍정〔부정〕~ an affirmative 〔a negative〕 proposition / 정언(定言)〔가언(假言)〕~ a categorical 〔a hypothetical〕 proposition. ◉ ~함수 a propositional 〔sentential〕 function.
**명조**(明朝) ① 《내일 아침》 tomorrow morning. ② 〖역사〗 《중국 왕조》 the Ming dynasty. ③ 《활자체》 Ming-style printing type.
**명주**(明紬) silk. ◉ ~붙이 silks. ~실 silk thread. ~옷 silk clothes.
**명주**(銘酒) liquor of famous 〔noted〕 brand; high-quality liquor.
**명주조개**(明紬—) 〖조개류〗 a round clam.
**명줄**(命—) the span of life. ⇨수명.
**명중**(命中) a hit. ~하다 hit 《the mark》; strike home; tell. ¶ 목표에 ~하다 hit the bull's-eye; hit the target / ~하지 않다 miss 《the mark》; go wide (of the mark) / 총알은 과녁의 한 복판에 ~하였다 The bullet hit the target right in the center. / 돌멩이가 그의 머리에 ~했다 The stone hit him on the head. ◉ ~률 an accuracy rate. ~탄 a (direct) hit; a telling shot.
**명징**(明澄) clearness; lucidity. ~하다 (be) clear; lucid.
**명찰**(名札) 《이름표》 a nameplate; 《가슴에 다는》 a name card; 《좌석의》 a place card; 《문패》 a doorplate; 《짐·옷의》 an identification tag 〔label〕. ¶ ~을 달다 attach 〔affix〕 a name tag 《to》.
**명찰**(名刹) a famous 〔noted〕 temple.
**명찰**(明察) keen insight; clear judgment; discernment; keen perception. ~하다 have a keen insight 《into *a matter*》; discern; see through. ¶ ~을 바랍니다 I leave it to your good 〔clear〕 judgment.
**명창**(名唱) 《노래》 a famous song; 《사람》 a master singer; a noted 〔great, celebrated〕 singer.
**명철**(明哲) sagacity; intelligence. ~하다 (be) sagacious; intelligent.
**명추**(明秋) next fall 〔autumn〕.
**명춘**(明春) next spring.
**명충**(螟蟲) = 마디충. 「solar plexus.
**명치** the pit of stomach; 《구어》 the
**명칭**(名稱) a name; a title; a term. ¶ 법률상의 ~ a legal name / ~을 붙이다 (give a) name; term; designate / ~을 바꾸다 change the name; rename.
**명콤비**(名—) 《make》 an excellent pair; 《form》 an ideal combination. ¶ ~를 이루다 form 〔make〕 a good pair.
**명쾌**(明快) lucidity; explicitness. ~하다 (be) lucid; explicit; clear-cut. ¶ ~하게 clearly; lucidly; explicitly / ~한 답변〔해석〕 a lucid answer 〔interpretation〕 / 하고자 하는 말을 ~하게 말하다 make *oneself* clear / ~한 지시를 내리다 give explicit directions / 질문에 대한 그의 답변은 ~했다 His answer to the question was quite to the point.
**명태**(明太) 〖어류〗 an Alaska pollack.
**명토**(名—) pointing out; indication. ¶ ~(를) 박다 point out; indicate.
**명패**(名牌) a nameplate. ⇨명찰.
**명품**(名品) a fine article; a perfect gem; 《명작》 a masterpiece.
**명필**(名筆) 《글씨》 an excellent handwriting; superb calligraphy; 《사람》 a noted calligrapher; a good hand 《at writing characters》. ¶ 그는 상당한 ~이다 He writes a very good hand.
**명하다**(命—) ① 《명령하다》 order; command; give orders; issue a command; direct; tell 《*a person*》 to *do;* bid 《*a person*》 *do.* ¶ 퇴장을 ~ order 《*a person*》 out / 양심이 명하는 바에 따르다 obey the dictates of conscience / 명하는 대로 하다 follow orders; do as *one* is told 《to *do*》 / 즉시 귀가할 것을 명한다 I order you to go home immediately. ② 《임명하다》 appoint; name 《*a person*》 to 《a post》. ⇨임명.
**명함**(名銜) a visiting card; 《미》 a calling card; 《업무용》 a business card. ¶ ~을 내놓다 give 〔present〕 *one's* card 《to》; 《방문처 현관에서》 send in 〔up〕 *one's* card / ~을 주고 받다 exchange cards / 사장에게 주라고 ~을 접수원에게 주고 오다 leave *one's* card for the president with the receptionist / ~을 주시면 전해 드리겠습니다 If you give me your card, I'll take it in. ◉ ~판 《사진》 *a carte de visite*; photograph size 《8.3 cm×5.4 cm》.
**명현**(名賢) a noted wise man 〔sage〕.
**명화**(名花) ① 《아름다운 꽃》 a beautiful flower. ② 《미인》 a celebrated beauty. ¶ 사교계의 ~ a society belle.
**명화**(名畫) ① 《훌륭한 그림》 a master-

piece of painting; 《널리 알려진 그림》 a famous 〔celebrated, great〕 picture. ¶ 거장이 그린 역사적 ～ old master paintings. ②《훌륭한 영화》 an excellent film. ¶ 왕년의 ～ a film classic.

**명확**(明確) definiteness; clearness; precision. ～하다 (be) definite; clear; precise; distinct. ¶ ～히 definitely; distinctly; precisely; clearly / ～한 설명 a definite 〔clear-cut〕 explanation / 이 점을 ～히 하다 clear up 〔clarify〕 this point / 권한과 책임의 한계를 ～히 하다 establish clear-cut lines of authority and responsibility / 나는 이 점을 ～히 하고 싶다 I want you to make this point clear. / 그는 그 문제에 관한 자신의 입장을 ～히 하였다 He clarified his stand on the issue. / 그의 답변은 ～하지가 않았다 His answer 「was ambiguous 〔lacked clarity〕.

**명후년**(明後年) the year after next.

**명후일**(明後日) the day after tomorrow.

**몇** 《얼마나》 how many 《days》 (수); how much (양·금액); how far (거리); how long (시일); at what time (시간); how old (연령); 《다소》 some; several; a little 〔few〕. ¶ 몇 사람 how many people; several people (★ 같은 말이라도 용법이 다름에 주의할 것: 실패한 사람도 몇 사람된다 Some 〔Several persons〕 have failed. 성공한 사람은 몇 사람 안 된다 Few (men) succeeded. 몇 사람이라도 채용하겠다 I will employ any number of persons.) / 일년 몇 개월 one year and some months / 30 몇 마일 thirty and some odd miles / 50 몇 달러 fifty-odd dollars / 몇 십〔백, 천, 만, 십만〕이나 되는 사람들 dozens 〔hundreds, thousands, tens of thousands, hundreds of thousands〕 of people / 몇 주일씩이나 for weeks; week after week / 오후 다섯 시 몇 분인가의 열차 the five=something p.m. train / 그 사람이 70 몇 살 때의 in his seventy-somethingth year / 몇 자 적다 write a few words / 그는 몇 시냐고 물었다 He asked the time. / 몇 시 차를 탈까요 What 〔Which〕 train shall we take? / 그는 몇 살인가 How old is he? *or* What is his age? / 몇 십 마리나 되는 양이 죽었다 The sheep died by scores.

**몇가지** how many kinds 〔ways〕; several kinds 〔ways〕. ¶ ～로 in various ways / ～로 해석할 수 있는 말 a word of variable construction / 그건 ～나 있습니까 How many kinds of it are there? / 그건 ～로도 해석할 수 있다 It may be construed in several ways.

**몇몇** some; several. ¶ ～ 사람 some 〔several〕 persons / 우리들의 ～은 이성을 잃었다 Some of us lost our heads. / 우리들 중의 ～은 걸어서 돌아가기로 했다 Several of us decided to walk home.

**몇번**(一番) ① 《번호》 what number? ¶ 당신은 ～입니까 What is your number? / 댁의 전화 번호는 ～입니까 What is your telephone number? / 당신 아버지는 왼쪽에서 ～째입니까 Where is your father from the left? ② 《횟수》 how often; several times. ¶ ～이고 any number of times; (very) often; frequently; many times; over and over again; repeatedly / ～이고 해보아도 however often *one* may try / 이 그림은 ～봐도 물리지 않는다 I never get weary of looking at this picture. / 나는 그곳에 ～ 가본 적이 있다 I have been there a number of times. / 그는 ～이고 실패한 끝에 성공했다 He finally succeeded after a series of failures.

**몇시**(一時) when?; what time? ¶ ～에 (at) what time? / ～까지 by what time? / ～까지라도 till all hours / 지금 ～냐 What time is it (now)? *or* Do you have the time? *or* What is the time?

**몇시간**(一時間) how many hours?; how long?; some 〔several〕 hours. ¶ ～ 동안이나 for hours / ～이나 계속해서 for hours together 〔on end〕 / 여기서 부산까지 ～ 걸립니까 How long does it take from here to Pusan?

**몇월**(一月) ¶ ～에 in what month (of the year)? / 당신은 ～생입니까 In what month of the year were you born?

**몇해** 《몇년간》 how many years?; how long? ¶ ～ 동안이나 for years / 그는 미국에 ～ 있지 않았다 He didn't stay long 〔many years〕 in America.

**모**[1] 《벼의》 a young rice plant; rice=sprouts; 《모종》 a seedling; 《묘목》 a sapling; a young plant 〔tree〕. ¶ 모를 심다 transplant rice seedlings; set 〔bed〕 out rice plants / 모낼 때 rice=planting season. ◉ 모판 a seedbed; a seed plot.

**모**[2] ① (각) an angle. ¶ 모가 난 angular; angled / 세모(꼴) a triangle / 네모(꼴) a square; a quadrangle; a quadrilateral / 모가 나다 ⇨ 모나다 ①. ② 《모서리》 an edge; an angle; a corner. ¶ 모를 세우다 make angular; sharpen the edge / 모를 죽이다 round off an angle;

take the edge off. ③《인품이 모남》 the rough edges 《of *one's* character》; abrasiveness. ¶모가 난 abrasive 《personality》; difficult 《people》 / 모가 나지 않은 affable; sociable / 모난 데가 없어지다 [사물이 주어] smooth 《down》 the rough edges of *one's* character; [사람이 주어] become mature 〔mellow〕; mature; mellow / 사람들과 어울려 지내게 되면 그의 모난 데도 없어지게 될 것이다 Associating with other people will 「smooth down his rough edges 〔make him better company〕.

**모**[3] 《윷》 the 5 points made by throwing the four *yut* sticks so that all four faces are down.

**모**[4] 《두부 셀 때》 a cake; a block; a square. ¶두부 한 모 a bean-curd cake.

**모**(毛) ① 《털》 hair; wool; fur. ¶모양말 woolen socks. ② 《단위》 a *mo* (= one-tenth of a *ri*).

**모**(母) 《*one's*》 mother. ¶모비행기 《유도탄을 발사하는》 a parent plane / 모회사 a parent company.

**모**(某) 《모씨》 a certain person; Mr. So-and-so; someone; 《어떤》 a; one; certain. ¶모처 a certain place / 모 은행 a certain bank / 김모 a certain Kim; a 〔one〕 Mr. Kim; a man called Kim / 모 박사 Doctor So-and-so; Doctor What's-his-name 《구어》 / 작년 5월 모일에 on a certain day in May last year.

**모가비** 《인부 등의 우두머리》 a foreman; 「a head; a boss.

**모가지** the neck. ⇨ 목[1]. ¶~가 달아나다 *one's* head is cut off; get decapitated; 《해고당하다》 be 「fired 〔sacked 《구어》, dismissed〕; 《영구어》 get 〔be given〕 the sack / ~를 자르다 《해고하다》 fire; 《구어》 sack; dismiss; 《영구어》 give 《a worker》 the sack.

**모가치** a share; a portion; 《구어》 a 「cut. ⇨ 몫.

**모감주나무** 〖식물〗 a goldenrain (tree); a Chinese bladdernut.

**모개** ¶~로 all together; in the lump 〔gross〕 / ~로 사다 buy 《*things*》 in (the) mass. ◉ ~흥정 wholesale dealing; a package deal: ~ 흥정하다 make a package deal.

**모걸음질** sidling. ~하다 walk sideways; 「sidle.

**모겟돈** a (good) round sum; a sizable sum 〔amount〕 (of money).

**모경**(暮景) an evening scene.

**모계**(母系) the maternal line; the mother's side. ¶~의 maternal; on the mother's side. ◉ ~가족 a maternal family. ~사회 a matrilineal society. ~친척 the relatives on the maternal side.

**모계**(謀計) an artifice; a trick; a plot; a scheme; a stratagem. ¶~를 꾸미다 plot; conspire / 적의 ~에 빠지다 fall a prey to the enemy's stratagem; play into the enemy's hands.

**모골**(毛骨) hair and bone. ¶~이 송연하다 a shudder runs through *one;* [사람이 주어] shudder 《at》; [사물이 주어] make *one* shudder; make *one's* hair stand on end.

**모공**(毛孔) the (skin) pores.

**모과** 〖식물〗 the fruit of a Chinese quince. ◉ ~나무 a Chinese quince.

**모관**(毛管) a capillary (tube). ◉ ~현상 ⇨ 모세관 현상.

**모교**(母校) the school 〔university〕 *one* graduated from; *one's* old school; *one's alma mater* (L.) (주로 대학). ¶선생님의 ~는 하버드 대학이다 Harvard is our teacher's alma mater. *or* Our teacher graduated from Harvard University. ◉ ~애 almamaterism.

**모국**(母國) *one's* mother country; *one's* homeland. ¶~을 방문하다 visit *one's* mother country / 그녀는 마침내 ~ 한국의 땅을 밟았다 She has finally come home to Korea.
◉ ~관광단 a tourist party on a visit to their homeland. ~어 *one's* mother tongue; *one's* native language: 영어를 ~어처럼 구사하다 speak English like *one's* mother tongue. 재일동포 ~ 방문단 a home-visiting group of Korean residents in Japan.

**모군**(募軍) ① 《공사판의》 a construction worker; a navvy; a coolie. ¶~ 서다 become a construction worker; work as a coolie. ② = 모병.

**모권**(母權) maternal rights 〔authority〕; matriarchy. ¶~을 신장하다 raise 〔promote〕 the status of motherhood.
◉ ~사회 the matriarchal society. ~시대 the matriarchal stage. ~제 matriarchy.

**모근**(毛根) the root 〔bulb〕 of a hair; a hair root. ¶~을 이식하다 implant a hair.

**모금** 《마실 것의》 a gulp; a sip (차 따위의); 《한 모금》 《미》 a draft 〔draught 《영》〕; 《담배의》 a puff 《at》. ¶한 ~ 마시다 take a sip 《of tea, wine》 / 한 ~을 꿀꺽 마시다 drink 《beer》 at a single draft 〔in one gulp, in one swallow〕 / 담배를 한 ~ 빨다 puff at *one's* cigar 〔cigarette〕.

**모금**(募金) fund raising; collection of contributions 《for》; invitation 〔collection〕 of subscriptions. ～하다 raise 〔invite〕 subscriptions 《for》; collect contributions. ¶ 가두～ a street collection of subscriptions / 그들은 회관 재건을 위해 ～하고 있다 They are raising money for the rebuilding of the hall / 그들은 태풍 이재민을 위해 ～했다 They collected some money for the sufferers from the typhoon.
◉ ～목표액 the amount「of money to be raised 〔of contributions to be collected〕. ～운동 《start》 a fund-raising campaign; a drive to obtain funds 《for》. ～함 a donation box.

**모기** 〖곤충〗 a mosquito. ¶ ～ 떼 a swarm of mosquitoes / ～한테 물리다 be bitten 〔stung〕 by mosquitoes / ～에게 물린 자국 a mosquito bite / ～가 많다 [장소가 주어] swarm with mosquitoes / ～가 앵앵거리다 mosquitoes buzz / ～를 쫓다 drive away mosquitoes / ～를 잡다 swat 〔slap〕 mosquitoes / ～보고 칼 빼기 《속담》 much ado about nothing; making a mountain out of a molehill. ◉ ～향 a mosquito (repellent) stick 〔coil〕. 모깃소리 《in》 a very thin 〔faint〕 voice.

**모기둥** 〖건축〗 a square pillar.

**모기장**(一帳) a mosquito net. ¶ ～을 치다〔걷다〕 put up 〔take down〕 a mosquito net / ～ 안에서 자다 sleep under a mosquito net.

**모깃불** a smudge (fire); a mosquito fumigator 〔smoker〕. ¶ ～을 피우다 make a smudge (to keep mosquitoes off); smoke mosquitoes away 〔out〕; keep off mosquitoes with smoke.

**모나다** ① 《모양이》 be 〔get to be〕 angular; be angulated 〔angled, edged, pointed〕. ¶ 모난 기둥 a square pillar / 모난 얼굴 a squarish face / 모나게 깎다 sharpen the edges; cut squarely / 모난 돌이 정 맞는다 《속담》 A tall tree catches much wind. ② 《말·행동·성품 따위가》 be angular 〔stiff, harsh, severe〕; be unsociable 〔unaffable, uncompromising〕. ¶ (성격이) 모난 사람 a harsh person; an unsociable person / 모난 말 a sharp 〔biting〕 remark / 모나지 않은 affable; sociable / 말이 모가 나다 speak in harsh language / 모나게 굴다 behave 〔act〕 harshly 〔unsociably〕. ③ 《두드러지다》 be 〔become〕 conspicuous 〔striking〕. ¶ 모난 점 conspicuous points / 모난 행동 odd behavior. ④ 《유효하다》 be useful 〔effective〕. ¶ 돈을 모나게 쓰다 put money to a good use; spend money「well 〔to good cause〕.

**모나리자** 《다빈치가 그린 여인초상화》 the Mona Lisa; La Gioconda.

**모내기** rice-planting; rice transplantation. ～하다 ＝모내다[1]. ¶ ～에 바쁘다 be busy planting the rice. ◉ ～철 the rice-planting season.

**모내다**[1] 〖농업〗 transplant rice seedlings; set 〔bed〕 out rice plants.

**모내다**[2] 《각을 내다》 make angular; make square; give squares 〔edges〕 to; put corners on. ¶ 기둥을 ～ make a pillar square.

**모녀**(母女) mother and daughter. ¶ ～간 between 〔the relation of〕 mother and daughter.

**모년**(某年) a certain year.

**모노드라마** 〖연극〗 a monodrama.

**모노레일** 《궤도》 a monorail; 《차량》 a monorail train 〔car〕. ¶ ～로 가다 go by monorail. ◉ 현수식〔승마식〕 ～ a suspended 〔mounted〕 type monorailroad.

**모놀로그** a monologue; a soliloquy.

**모눈종이** plotting paper; graph paper 《미》; section paper 《영》. ¶ 3 밀리～ paper ruled into 3-millimeter squares.

**모니터** a monitor. ◉ ～스크린 《감시장치》 monitor screen. ～제 〖방송〗 a monitor system.

**모닝** morning. ◉ ～드레스 a morning dress. ～서비스 cut-price service during the morning hours. ～코트 a morning coat. ～콜 a wake-up call; a morning call (★ 의사의 오전 중 왕진이란 뜻도 있음): ～콜하다 give 〔make〕 a wake-up call.

**모다기-** all at once; from all sides. ¶ 모다기령(令) orders coming from everywhere all at once / 모다깃매 blows from all sides.

**모닥불** a fire in the open air; an open-air fire; a bonfire. ¶ ～을 놓다 build up a fire; make a bonfire.

**모당**(母堂) ＝대부인.

**모더니스트** a modernist. 「modernism.

**모더니즘** modernism. ¶ 포스트 ～ post-

**모던** modern. ◉ ～걸〔보이〕 a modern girl 〔boy〕. ～댄스〔발레〕 modern dance 〔ballet〕. ～아트 the modern art. ～재즈 modern jazz.

**모데라토** 〖음악〗 *moderato* (It.).

**모델** a model. ¶ 화가의 ～ an artist's

model / 패션 ~ a fashion model / 사진 ~ a photo 〔photographer's〕 model / …을 ~로 하여 《work, paint》 from a model / …을 ~로 해서 그린 초상화 a portrait painted from sittings given by… / ~이 되다 act as a model; pose for an artist; sit for a painter / 이 소설의 주인공은 A씨가 ~이다 The hero of this novel is modelled after Mr. A. / 그 소녀는 직업이 ~이다 The girl is a professional model. / 그 차는 여러 번 ~을 바꿨다 The car went through a number of model changes. / 전후의 한국 민주주의는 미국을 ~로 삼아 왔다 Post-war democracy in Korea has been modeled on that of the United States. ◉ ~소설 a *roman à clef* (F.). ~스쿨 a model school. ~체인지 a model change; (a) restyling; 《구어》 face lifting; 《구어》 a face-lift: ~체인지를 하다 bring out a new model. ~케이스 a model case. ~하우스 a model 〔show〕 house.

**모뎀** 『컴퓨터』 《변복조 장치》 a modem. [< *mo*dulator-*dem*odulator]

**모도리** a shrewd 〔calculating〕 fellow.

**모독**(冒瀆) blasphemy; (a) sacrilege; (a) profanation; desecration. ~하다 blaspheme; desecrate; profane; defile. ¶ 신을 ~하다 blaspheme against God / 국가의 명예를 ~하다 profane the honor of *one's* country / 인간성을 ~하다 defame humanity.

**모두** [명사적] all; everything; everybody; everyone; [부사적] in all; all told; all together; one and all; in a body; without the exception; *en masse* (F.); by 〔in〕 the gross. (★ all은 복수동사로 받으며 every-는 단수동사로 받음). ¶ 아이들은 ~ all the children / ~ 7명〔개〕 seven in all / 우리 셋이 ~ everyone of us three / 빚을 ~ 갚다 pay 〔repay〕 all *one's* debts / 준비를 ~ 갖추다 make every preparation 《for》; be all set 〔ready〕 《for》 / ~ 같은 소리를 했다 All said the same thing. / ~ 놀랐다 All were surprised. / ~ 반대다 All are against it. / ~ 몇 명이요 How many are there in all? / ~ 그 노래를 부릅시다 Let's sing the song together. / 그 상품은 ~해서 7백만 원으로 평가되었다 The goods were valued in the gross at 7,000,000 won. / ~ 3만 원이오 It is 30,000 won, all told. / ~ 가져가거라 Take the whole lot. / 저분들은 ~ 독신이다 They are bachelors without exception. / 우리 일행은 ~ 다섯이었다 There were five of us, all told. / ~ 이런 식으로 하는 거다 Do everything in this way. / 그 일은 ~ 알고 있다 I have heard all about it. / 용돈을 ~ 써 버렸다 He has spent the last penny of his pocket money. / 회원은 ~ 출석했다 The members are all present. / ~ 사겠다 I'll buy them all 〔by the gross〕. / ~ 내 잘못이다 It's all my fault. / 그 문제는 이제 ~ 완전히 해결되었다 The problem is now completely solved. / 우리 형제는 ~ 키가 크지 않다 None of my brothers are tall. (★"이것을 All my brothers are not tall. 로 하면 안 되는가?" —all, every, both 따위에 not가 오면 부분부정이 되어「모두 키가 큰 것은 아니다」의 뜻이 되므로 그렇게 할 수 없음.) / 그의 두 친구가 ~ 친절하다고는 할 수 없다 Both of his friends are not kind. (★「둘이 다 친절하지 않다」는 Neither of his friends are kind.임.) / 그것이 인생의 ~가 아니다 That is not everything in life. ◉ ~먹기 《도박 등에서》 winner-take-all.

**모두**(冒頭) the head paragraph; the beginning; the opening. ¶ 연설의 ~에 at the opening of *one's* speech / ~의 한 구절 one of the opening paragraphs / ~에 싣다 give 《an article》 at the beginning.

**모두뜀** leaping with both feet.

**모두머리** doing *one's* hair up in a chignon with a strand of braided hair.

**모둠냄비** a stew 〔chowder 《미》〕 cooked at the table.

**모듈** a module.

**모드레짚다** swim with a kind of crawl stroke.

**모든** all; whole; every; each and every; every possible. ¶ ~ 사람 all the people; everybody / ~ 종류의 물건 all sorts of things / ~ 방향으로 in every direction; in all directions / ~ 경우에 in all cases; on every (and any) occasion; on all occasions / ~점으로 보아 in all respects 〔points〕; in every way 〔point〕 / ~ 경우를 생각하다 consider all the situations imaginable / 자기의 ~것을 바치다 devote 〔offer, give〕 *oneself* entirely 《to》 / ~ 수단을 다하다 try every possible mean / 문제를 ~ 각도에서 검토하다 study a problem from all angles / ~점에서 이쪽이 낫다 This is better from every point of view.

**모들뜨기** a cross-eyed person. ◉ ~눈 cross-eye; 『의학』 internal 〔convergent〕 strabismus.

**모들뜨다** look with both eyes turning toward the nose; have cross-eyes. ¶ 눈을 ~ look cross eyed.

**모뜨다** imitate; copy; ape; mimic. ¶ 아무의 행동을 ~ imitate *a person's* conduct.

**모라토리엄** 〖금융〗《지불유예》 moratorium. ◉ ~증후군 《채무 기피 증세》 moratorium syndrome.

**모락모락** ⇨ 무럭무럭.

**모란**(牡丹) 〖식물〗 a (tree) peony. ◉ ~꽃 a peony blossom.

**모란채**(牡丹菜) 〖식물〗 a cauliflower.

**모랄** 《도덕》 morals; moral sense; ethics.

**모랄리스트** 《도덕가》 a moralist.

**모래** sand; grit (굵은); a grain of sand (한 알). ¶ ~가 많은 sandy / 쌀에 ~가 있다 rice has grits in it / ~가 눈에 들다 get 「some 〔a few grains of〕 sand in *one's* eye / ~를 뿌리다 sand 《a road》; sprinkle 《a road》 with sand / ~ 위를 걷다 walk on the sand / ~로 닦다 sand 《a metal bar》 / ~알을 씹는 것 같다 be as tasteless as sawdust / 바닥에 ~를 깔다 sand the floor / 바닷가의 ~알처럼 많다 be numberless as the sands on the seashore / ~ 장난을 하다 play with sand. ◉ ~땅 a sandy place; 《토양》 sandy soil. ~먼지 《raise》 a cloud of (sand) dust. ~무더기 piles of sand; sand dunes. ~바람 《모래가 섞인》 a sand=laden wind; 《폭풍》 a sandstorm; 《모래 먼지》 a sand cloud; a dust cloud. ~밭 a sandy-soil field. ~벌판 a sandy plain; the sands. ~사장 a sandy beach; the sands. ~시계 sandglass; an hourglass. ~언덕 a sand dune; a sand hill. ~욕(浴) 《동물의》 a dust bath 〔bathing〕; ~주머니 a sandbag; 《조류의》 a gizzard. ~찜 a sand bath: ~찜질하다 take a sand bath. ~ 채취장 a sandpit. ~톱 a sandbank (in a river); a sandy beach. ~틀 a sand mold. ~판 《놀이터》 a sandbox. ~펄 a marsh 〔swamp〕 covered with sand. ~포대 a sandbag. 모랫길 a path on the sand; a sandy road.

**모래강변**(—江邊) 《물가》 a sandy shore 《along a river》; a sandy beach.

**모래무지** 〖어류〗 a false 〔goby〕 minnow.

**모래집** 〖해부〗 the amnion. ◉ ~물 amniotic fluid.

**모략**(謀略) 《계략》 a stratagem; a trick; 《음모》 a plot; an intrigue; a scheme; machinations. ¶ ~을 꾸미다 work out 〔form〕 a plot 《to *do,* against》; plan a stratagem; devise a trick / ~에 걸리다 fall into a snare; be caught in a trap. ◉ ~가(家) a schemer. ~ 선전 tricky propaganda.

**모레** the day after tomorrow. ◉ ~ 아침〔저녁〕 the morning 〔evening〕 after next.

**모로** ① 《비껴서》 obliquelly; slantwise; diagonally; aslant. ¶ ~ 그은 줄 a line drawn at 〔on〕 a slant / ~ 자르다 cut diagonally / ~보다 give 《*a person*》 a sidelong glance. ② 《옆으로》 sideways. ¶ ~ 걷다 walk sideways / ~ 드러눕다 lie on *one's* side / ~ 가도 서울만 가면 된다 《속담》 The end justifies the means.

**모로코** Morocco. ¶ ~의 Moroccan. ◉ ~가죽 Morocco leather. ~사람 Moroccan.

**모롱이**[1] 《산의》 a spur of a hill.

**모롱이**[2] 〖어류〗 ① 《웅어》 a young *Coilia ectenes* fish. ② 《숭어》 a young gray mullet.

**모루** an anvil (block). ◉ ~채 《쇠메》 a 「hammer; a sledge.

**모르다** ① 《알지 못함》 do not know; cannot tell (미리); be ignorant of; be unaware of; be not informed about; be not familiar with; be not acquainted with. ¶ 모르는 곳 an unfamiliar place / 모르는 사람 a stranger / 모르는 말 a word 〔language〕 *one* doesn't know / 모르고 without knowing 《it》; unwittingly / 모르는 사이에 before *one* knows 〔is aware of〕 it; without *one's* knowledge; 《잠행성 병 따위가 진행되는 것을》 insidiously / 글을 ~ be ignorant; be illiterate / 어쩔 줄(을) ~ do not know what to do; be at a loss; be at *one's* wit's end / 전혀 ~ know nothing 《about》; have no idea 《of how》 / 끝까지 모른다고 버티다 stoutly maintain *one's* ignorance / 하나만 알고 둘은 ~ know only one side 《of the *matter*》 / 나는 그것을 전혀 모릅니다 I haven't got the slightest 〔faintest〕 idea about it. / 그가 그런 범죄를 저질렀다는 것을 나는 전혀 몰랐다 I had no idea he had committed such a crime. / 무슨 일이 일어날지 모르겠다 There is no telling 〔knowing〕 what may happen. *or* What may happen is anyone's guess. / 모른다고 시치미떼도 소용 없어 It's no use feigning ignorance. / 모르는 것이 약 《속담》 Where ignorance is bliss, 'tis folly to be wise. (★ 'tis는 it is의 단축형.) / 그들도

이 문제에 관해서는 우리처럼 모르고 있다 They are as much in the dark about this affair as we are.
② 《이해 못함》 do not understand; have no idea of; do not know. ¶ 글뜻을 ~ do not understand the meaning of a sentence / 조금도 ~ do not understand at all; do not have the slightest idea 〔inkling〕 of / 도무지 모르겠다 It is above 〔beyond, past〕 my comprehension 〔head〕. / 무어가 무언지 모르겠다 I can't tell which is which. / 그의 평론은 어려워서 나는 모르겠다 His essays are too difficult for me to understand.
③ 《인식 못함》 do not appreciate; do not recognize; ignore; disregard 《of》; slight. ¶ 돈을 ~ do not appreciate the value of money; be indifferent to money / 어른을 ~ do not recognize the prestige of *one's* elders; slight 〔do not pay due respect to〕 *one's* elders / 중요성을 ~ do not recognize the importance 《of》.
④ 《깨닫지 못함》 fail to realize 〔see, perceive, notice〕; ignore; be unaware 〔unconscious〕 《of》; be not conscious of; be blind to. ¶ 저도 모르게 in spite of *oneself;* involuntarily / 자기 잘못을 ~ be blind to *one's* own faults 〔mistakes〕; do not realize *one's* own mistake / 위험한 줄을 ~ do not realize the danger / 음모가 있을 줄은 몰랐다 I little suspected a plot.
⑤ 《느끼지 못함》 do not feel; be unconscious of; be insensible of 〔to〕; be impervious to. ¶ 은혜를 ~ be ungrateful / 부끄러움을 ~ be impervious to shame; be dead 〔lost〕 to shame; be shameless / 고마운 줄을 ~ be insensible to kindness; be ungrateful / 그곳은 더위를 모르는 데다 The place is free from the summer heat. / 건강의 고마움을 ~ do not know what a good thing it is to keep *oneself* fit; do not appreciate the blessing of health.
⑥ 《무경험》 have no experience; be ignorant of. ¶ 가난을 ~ be ignorant of 〔free from〕 poverty / 여자를 ~ have had no experience with women; be indifferent to women / 세상을 ~ be unversed in the ways of the world; be ignorant of the world.
⑦ 《기억하지 못함》 do not remember. ¶ 「너 저사람 알 것 같니」—「아니, 모르겠는데」 "Do you remember him?"— "No, I don't".
⑧ 《무관계·냉담》 have nothing to do with; be not concerned with; turn *one's* back on; (deliberately) ignore. ¶ 난 모르겠다—너 좋을 대로 해라 Do as you like.—I'll have nothing to do with it. / 나는 모르는 일이다 I have nothing to do with it. *or* It's no concern of mine. / 네가 한 일은 난 모른다 I can't help what you have done. / 그 녀석이 어찌 되건 난 모르겠다 I don't 「give 〔care〕 a damn what becomes of him.

**모르면모르되** if I guess right; most probably 〔likely〕; I may be wrong but I think. ¶ ~ 50은 넘었을 게다 If my guess is right, he must be over fifty.

**모르모트** 〖동물〗 a guinea pig.

**모르몬교**(—敎) Mormonism. ◉ ~도 a Mormon.

**모르쇠** 《불가지론》 know-nothingism; 《벙어리 노릇》 playing dumb. ¶ ~ 잡다 play dumb; pretend not to know; feign ignorance.

**모르타르** mortar. ¶ ~를 바른 mortared.

**모르핀** morphine. ◉ ~주사 a morphine injection. ~중독 《상용》 morphine addiction; morphinism; 《급성》 morphine poisoning.

**모른체하다** 《시치미떼다》 feign 〔affect〕 ignorance; pretend not to know; play innocent; 《무관심》 look on 《*a thing*》 with indifference; take no notice 《of *a person*》; assume an unconcerned air; be indifferent 《to》; 《길에서》 cut 《*a person*》 (dead); look the other way. ¶ 모른 체하고 with an unconcerned air; as if nothing had happened (아무 일도 없었던 듯이); as if *one* knew nothing about it (시치미떼고) / 남이 곤경에 처한 것을 ~ look coolly on a person in distress; look on a distressed person with folded hands / 거리에서 만나도 ~ pretend not to recognize 《*a person*》 in the street; cut 《*a person*》 (dead) in the street.

**모름지기** it is proper that *one* should 《do》; should 《*do*》; ought to 《*do*》. ¶ ~ 네 가족을 돌봐야 한다 It is only proper that you should take care of your own family. / ~ 믿는 바를 행해야 한다 It is imperative 〔proper〕 that you should carry your conviction into effect.

**모름하다** 《생선이》 (be) stale; bad.

**모리**(謀利) 《부당한 이익》 an excessive 〔unfair〕 profit; 《행위》 profiteering. ~하다 profiteer 《from》; make excessive

〔undue〕 profits. ¶ ~를 단속하다 control profiteering. ◉ ~간상배 a profiteering scoundrel. ~배 a profiteer: 전쟁 ~배 a war profiteer.

**모리셔스** 《아프리카의 자치국》 Mauritius.

**모리타니** 《아프리카의 공화국》 Mauritania.

**모멘트** 〚물리〛 moment. ¶ ~의 momental / 힘의 ~ the moment of a force; torque. ◉ 관성~ moment of inertia.

**모면**(謀免) shirking; evasion; eluding; escape. ~하다 escape; avoid; evade; shirk; elude; be saved 〔rescued〕 from 《drowning》. ¶ ~할 수 없는 unavoidable 《disasters》; inevitable 《fact》 / 간신히 ~하다 have a narrow escape / 죽음을 ~하다 escape death; be saved from death / 책임을 ~하다 evade *one's* responsibility / 처벌을 ~하다 escape punishment; go scot-free / 화재를 ~하다 be saved from the fire / 나는 간신히 정면 충돌을 ~했다 I barely escaped a head-on collision. / 그는 가까스로 파산을 ~하여 체면을 지켰다 He staved off bankruptcy, keeping his dignity.

**모멸**(侮蔑) scorn; disdain; contempt. ~하다 scorn; disdain; despise; contemn. ¶ ~적인 눈빛 a contemptuous look / ~적으로 생각하다 hold 《*a person*》 in contempt.

**모모**(某某) =아무아무. ◉ ~인(人) a certain number of persons; Messrs. So-and-so.

**모모한**(某某―) worthy of mentioning; celebrated; well-known. ¶ ~ 인사 a celebrity; a man of mark 〔distinction〕.

**모물**(毛物) 《털가죽》 fur; 《제품》 a fur; fur goods. ◉ ~전 a fur store.

**모반**(母斑) a birthmark; 〚의학〛 a n(a)evus.

**모반**(謀叛) an insurrection; a rebellion; a revolt; treason (역모). ~하다 revolt 〔rebel, plot, conspire, rise〕 《against》; rise in rebellion 〔revolt〕 《against》. ¶ ~을 꾀하다 plot a rebellion 《against》. ◉ ~자 a rebel; an insurgent; a traitor. ~죄 treason.

**모발**(毛髮) hair. ¶ ~이 빠지다 hair falls out 〔off〕; [사람이 주어] lose *one's* hair. ◉ ~습도계 a hair hygrometer. ~영양제 a hair tonic.

**모방**(模倣) imitation; copying. ~하다 imitate; copy 《from, after》; model after 〔on〕; pattern 《after》; follow an example 《of 》. ¶ ~적인 imitative; mimic / 원숭이의 ~하는 버릇 the mimicking habits of a monkey / …을 ~하여 after the model 〔manner〕 of...; in imitation of... / ~하여 만들다 make 《*a thing*》 on the model of 《another》; model 《*a thing*》 after 《another》 / 이것은 그것을 ~한 것이다 This is modelled on that. / 우리는 ~에 의해서 많은 것을 배운다 We learn many things by imitations. / 그의 독특한 필치는 ~할 수가 없다 His unique style defies imitation. / 그는 교묘하게 그 유명한 작가의 문체를 ~하였다 He wrote well in imitation of the famous writer's style. ◉ ~문명 imitated civilization. ~범죄 a copycat crime. ~본능 the instinct of imitation. ~설 the imitation theory. ~성 imitative nature: ~성이 많다 be full of imitative nature. ~예술 imitative arts. ~자 an imitator; a copier; a copycat.

**모범**(模範) a model; an example; an exemplar; a paragon; a pattern; a mirror. ¶ ~적인 model; exemplary / ~적인 행위 an exemplary deed / ~적인 남편〔아내〕 a model husband 〔wife〕 / …을 ~으로 하여 after the example of...; on the model of... / ~을 보이다 show 〔give〕 a fine example 《of》; set 〔offer〕 an example 《to *a person*》; set the pattern 《for》 / ~이 되다 be a good example 《to others》; become an example 《of》 / …을 ~으로 삼다 model 〔pattern〕 after 《*a person*》; follow the example of 《*a person*》; pattern *oneself* on 〔after〕 《*a person*》 / 저 분을 ~으로 삼아라 Make him your model. *or* Make a model of him. / 그의 용감한 행위는 타의 ~이 되었다 His brave deed served as a pattern for others. / 부모는 자식들의 좋은 ~이 되어야 한다 Parents should set a good example for their children. ◉ ~경기 an exhibition game. ~공무원〔시민, 용사, 운전기사〕 the exemplary official 〔citizen, soldier, driver〕. ~답안〔회답〕 a model paper 〔answer〕. ~림 a model forest. ~마을 a model village. ~생〔청년〕 a model 〔an exemplary〕 student 〔young man〕. ~수(囚) a model 〔well-behaved〕 prisoner.

**모법**(母法) (a) mother 〔parent〕 law.

**모병**(募兵) recruiting; enlistment of soldiers; 《징병》 conscription; drafting. ~하다 recruit 〔draft, conscript〕 soldiers. ¶ 그는 지원병으로 ~에 응했다 He enlisted as a volunteer in the army 〔navy〕. ◉ ～관 a recruiting officer.

모본단(模本緞) damask (silk); satin 「damask.

모붓다 sow rice seed 《on a seedbed》.

모빌 『미술』 a mobile.

모빌유(―油) lubrication oil; (a) lubri- 「cant.

모사(毛絲) woolen yarn; worsted (yarn); wool. ¶ ～로 양말을 짜다 knit wool into socks; knit socks out of wool.

모사(模寫) 《베낌》 copying; 《베낀 것》 a copy; a reproduction; a facsimile; a replica (조각·주화 등의). ～하다 copy (out) 《a picture》; trace; facsimile; reproduce. ¶ 라파엘의 ～ a copy from Raphael / 이것은 유럽 명화의 ～물이다 These are the copies 〔reproductions〕 of famous European paintings.

모사(謀士) a schemer; a strategist; a tactician; a resourceful man. ¶ 정계의 ～ a wily politician.

모사(謀事) scheming; planning; plotting. ～하다 plan; make a plan; design; scheme; plot (음모를). ¶ ～는 재인(在人)이요 성사는 재천(在天) 《속담》 Man proposes; God disposes.

◉ ～꾼 a schemer. 「설탕.

모사탕(―砂糖) cube 〔lump〕 sugar. ＝각

모살(謀殺) premeditated 〔willful〕 murder. ～하다 murder; kill 《*a person*》 with malice aforethought. ◉ ～범 a murderer. ～사건 a murder case.

모살미수(謀殺未遂) an attempted murder. ～하다 fail in an attempt to murder. ◉ ～범 an attempted murderer.

모새 fine sand. 「gloom〕.

모색(暮色) evening twilight 〔dusk,

모색(摸索) groping. ～하다 grope 《for》; fumble 《for》. ¶ 암중～하다 grope (about) in the dark / 살인 사건의 단서를 ～하다 grope for some clue to the murder / 평화적 통일을 ～하다 explore ways toward peaceful unification / 많은 과학자가 그 문제의 해결책을 ～하고 있다 Many scientists are searching for a solution to that problem.

모생약(毛生藥) a hair restorer 〔grower〕.

모서리 a corner; an edge; an angle. ¶ 책상 ～ the corner 〔edge〕 of a desk / ～를 후리다 round off a corner 〔an edge.〕

모선(母船) a mother ship 〔vessel〕; a depot ship; 《우주선의》 a command module (사령실). ¶ 포경(捕鯨)～ a whaling mother ship; a mother whaler.

모성(母性) motherhood; maternity. ¶ ～적인 여성 a motherly woman. ◉ ～보호 protection of motherhood. ～본능 maternal instinct(s): 그녀는 자신의 ～ 본능에 눈을 떴다 She became aware of her motherly instincts. ～애 maternal affection; mother('s) 〔motherly〕 love. ～예찬 adoration of motherhood. ～유전 maternal inheritance. ～형 a motherly type of woman.

모세 Moses. ¶ ～의 율법 the Law of Moses; the Mosaic Law / ～의 십계명 the Ten Commandments.

모세관(毛細管) 《관》 a capillary (tube); 《혈관》 a capillary (vessel). ◉ ～벽 a capillary wall. ～인력(引力) capillary attraction. ～척력(斥力) capillary repulsion. ～현상 capillary action 〔phenomenon〕; capillarity.

모세포(母細胞) a mother cell.

모세혈관(毛細血管) 『해부』 a capillary (vessel).

모션 a motion. ¶ 슬로～ slow motion / ～이 큰 투수 a pitcher with a big motion / …하려는 ～을 쓰다 make a motion 《to》.

모손(耗損) wear and tear; friction loss; abrasion. ～하다 wear away 〔off〕; undergo friction loss; suffer abrasion.

모순(矛盾) 《일관성 없음》 (an) inconsistency; 《불일치》 (a) discrepancy; 《상반됨》 (a) contradiction; 《대립》 (a) conflict 《of evidence》. ¶ 말의 ～ contradiction in terms / ～되다 contradict; be contradictory 《to》; be inconsistent 〔incompatible〕 《with》; conflict 《with》; be at variance 《with》 / ～되는 contradictory 《to each other》; conflicting; inconsistent; incompatible 《with》 / ～되지 않는 consistent / ～된 증언 conflicting testimonies / ～된 말을 하다 contradict *oneself;* make a contradictory statement / ～ 투성이다 be full of inconsistencies / 이 세상은～ 덩어리다 This is a world of contradictions. / 현실과 이상은 종종 ～된다 The reality often contradicts the ideal. / 그의 행동은 그의 말과 ～된다 His actions are contradictory to his words. / 그것은 헌법 정신에 ～된다 That would be inconsistent with the spirit of the Constitution.

◉ ～개념 a contradictory concept. ～명사(名辭) contradictory terms. ～율 the law 〔principle〕 of contradiction.

모숨 a handful 《of grass, straw, *etc.*》; a lock; a tuft.

모스부호(―符號) the Morse code 〔alphabet〕. ¶ ～로 송신하다 send Morse code; communicate 〔signal〕 in Morse code.

**모스크** 《이슬람교 사원》 a mosque.

**모스크바** 《러시아의 수도》 Moscow. ¶ ～시민 Muscovite.

**모슬린** 〖직물〗 (muslin) delaine. ⇨ 메린스.

**모습** ① 《몸매·생김새》 a figure; a form; 《형태·모양》 a shape; 《영상》 an image. ¶ 걷는 ～ the walking figure 《of *a person*》 / 사람의 얼굴 ～을 한 바위 a rock in the shape of a human face / 한라산의 아름다운 ～ the beautiful shape of Mt. Halla / 지구는 오렌지와 같은 ～을 하고 있다 The earth is like an orange in shape. / 그 여인은 우아한 ～을 하고 있다 The lady has a graceful figure. / 그의 ～이 아직도 눈에 선하다 His image is still vivid in my mind. / 그는 인간의 ～을 한 악마이다 He is a devil in human form. / 그녀는 자기 ～을 거울에 비추어 보았다 She looked at her own image in the mirror. / 그의 ～이 어둠 속으로 사라졌다 His figure vanished into darkness.
② 《모양·양상》 a state; a condition; an aspect; a picture (관념적인 모습). ¶ 너의 있는 그대로의 ～을 그녀에게 보여라 You should show her what you really are. / 이 책은 농민의 참～을 그리고 있다 This book gives a true picture of farmers' lives. / 그는 한국의 참～을 해외에 소개하기 위해 애쓰고 있다 He is trying to introduce Korea to other countries as it really is. / 오랜만에 그녀를 만났는데 옛모습은 전혀 없었다 I met her after a long absence and found her quite another person.
③ 《외모·존재》 (personal) appearance; guise; 《자세》 a pose; a posture. ¶ 앉아〔서〕 있는 ～으로 in a sitting 〔standing〕 posture / ～이 안 보이는 invisible / ～을 나타내다 appear; show *oneself;* make *one's* appearance; show 〔turn〕 up; come 「in sight 〔into view〕 / 완전히 ～을 나타내다 come into full view / ～이 사라지다 disappear; go 〔fade〕 away; vanish from the 「sight 〔sense〕 / ～을 바꾸다 disguise *oneself* 《as a woman》 / ～을 감추다 hide *oneself* 《behind the door》 / ～을 감추고 있다 be in hiding / 초라한 ～을 하고 있다 look shabby; be shabbily dressed / 이 ～으로는 사람들 앞에 나갈 수 없다 I can't go out looking like this. *or* I am not fit to be seen. / 그녀는 어느 날 갑자기 ～을 감췄다 One day she suddenly disappeared. / 겉～만으로 사람을 판단해서는 안 된다 You can't judge a person from 〔by〕 the way he looks. / 그녀의 뒷～은 어머니와 똑같다 She looks exactly like her mother from the back. / 두 시간이나 기다렸지만 그녀는 ～을 나타내지 않았다 We waited for two hours, but she didn't show 〔turn〕 up.

**모시** ① 《옷감》 ramie cloth 〔fabric〕. ② 《모시풀》 a ramie; a Chinese silk plant. ◉ ～실 ramie yarn. ～옷 ramie clothes.

**모시**(某時) a certain 〔an undisclosed〕 time.

**모시다** ① 《섬기다》 attend 〔wait〕 on 《*a person*》; serve. ¶ 부모를 ～ have *one's* parents with *one;* wait upon *one's* parents; be filial to *one's* parents.
② 《청해 오다》 have 《*a person*》 come; call in; invite. ¶ 선생님을 모시어 오다 invite a teacher 《to a village》 / 선생님을 모임에 ～ have *one's* teacher at a meeting; invite *one's* teacher to a meeting / 의사를 모시러 보내다 send for a doctor / 우리는 각 분야의 전문가를 여럿 모시고 그들의 의견을 기탄없이 발표하게 했다 We called in several experts in different fields and had them express their opinions freely.
③ 《정해진 곳으로》 take 《*a person*》 over 〔to〕; show 《*a person*》 in 〔over〕; 《함께 가다》 go 《with》; accompany. ¶ 손님을 방으로 ～ show a guest into a room / 어른을 모시고 가다 accompany *one's* elder / 그 부인을 이층으로 모셔라 Show the lady upstairs. / 도중까지 모셔다 드리죠 I'll go part of the way with you.
④ 《신으로》 deify; worship; 《사당을》 enshrine; dedicate 《a shrine》 to; set up. ¶ 조상을 ～ worship *one's* ancestors / 할아버지의 위패를 사당에 ～ set up grandfather's mortuary tablet in the family shrine.
⑤ 《받들다》 set 《*a person*》 up 《as》; put 《*a person*》 on a pedestal; have 《*a person*》 over. ¶ 사장으로 ～ set 《*a person*》 up as president / 총재로 ～ install 《*a person*》 as the president; 《모시고 있다》 be under the presidency of 《*a person*》 / 우리 협회는 김박사를 회장으로 모시고 있다 Our society has Dr. Kim as its president.

**모시조개** 〖조개류〗 a short-necked clam.

**모시항라**(一亢羅) coase 〔loosely-woven〕 ramie cloth.

**모씨**(某氏) Mr. So-and-so; Mr. X; a

certain gentleman.

**모암**(母岩) 〖광산〗 ground; a matrix (*pl.* ~es, -trices); 〖토목〗 a parent 〔mother〕 rock.

**모야**(暮夜) a dark night; late at night.

**모양**(模樣·貌樣) ① 《형태》 a shape; a form. ¶ 코 ~ the shape of *one's* nose / 희한한 ~의 돌 stones of unusual forms / ~을 이루다 take shape; get 〔put〕 into shape / ~이 변하다 change shape 〔form〕 / ~이 망그러지다 〔망그러지지 않다〕 get out of 〔hold its〕 shape / 하늘에 동물 ~의 구름이 몇 개 떠 있다 There are some clouds in the shape of animals in the sky.
② 《생김새·맵시》 appearance; a look; an air. ¶ ~이 좋다 look nice 〔well〕; be shapely; be well-shaped〔-formed〕 / ~이 나쁘다 look bad 〔poor〕; be shapeless; be misshaped; be ill=formed / ~(이) 사납다 look unseemly 〔awkward, indecent, improper〕; be offensive (to the eye); look bad; be unsightly; be unbecoming / ~을 내다 adorn *oneself;* decorate; dress up / ~이 나다 look nice 〔pretty〕; look jolly / ~이 안 나다 look out of shape / ~을 바꾸다〔일신하다〕 《개조하다》 remodel; renew; 《변경하다》 alter; change.
③ 《체면》 face; dignity; appearance; decency; honor; reputation. ¶ ~이 말이 아니다 be disgraced; be put out of countenance / 그걸 그에게 말하면 내 ~은 무엇이 되겠나 What about my dignity if you tell him about that?
④ 《형편·상태》 the state 〔situation, aspect, phase, position〕 of affairs; circumstances; progress; things; matters; doings. ¶ 이 ~으로 나가면 if things go at this rate / ~을 살피다 see how the wind blows; see how things stand; watch 〔see〕 the run of events / 일 돼가는 ~을 보다 see how things go; observe the progress 〔trend〕 of an affair / 하는 ~을 보다 see how 《*a person*》 acts 〔reacts〕; observe 《*a person's*》 attitude toward 《*a matter*》.
⑤ 《전망·징후》 a sign; a symptom; an indication; 《외관》 (an) appearance; a look; an air. ¶ …할 ~이다 look like …; be likely to *do;* seem about to be; it seems 〔appears〕 that … / 피곤한 ~이다 look tired / 그녀는 외출한 ~이다 She seems to be out. / 그가 이 소년의 형인 ~이다 He seems to be this boy's older brother. / 비가 올 ~이다 It looks like rain. *or* It is threatening to rain. / 그는 혼자 가는 ~이다 He seems to be going alone. / 이의가 있는 ~이다 There seems to be an objection. / 쌀값이 내릴 ~이다 There are indications that the price of rice will fall. / 그는 아픈 ~이다 It seems 〔appears〕 that he is sick. / 회의는 난항을 겪고 있는 ~이다 It seems that troubles is brewing in the meeting.
⑥ 《방식》 a way; a manner. ¶ 그 ~으로 like that; that way; in that manner / 이 ~으로 해라 Do it this way.

**모양근**(毛樣筋) 〖해부〗 a ciliary muscle.

**모양새**(模樣—) ① 《됨됨이》 (a) shape; (a) figure; a form; an appearance. ¶ ~가 예쁘다 be nice-looking; look nice 〔pretty〕; be shapely; be well=shaped; be well-formed / ~가 나쁘다 be bad-looking; be ugly; be misshapen / ~를 내다 try to look good / ~ 좋게 만들다 make 《*a thing*》 so that *it* looks nice 〔attractive〕. ② 《체면》 (an) appearance; face; dignity; honor. ⇨ 모양.

**모양체**(毛樣體) 〖해부〗 a ciliary body. ◉ ~염 〖의학〗 cyclitis.

**모어**(母語) *one's* mother tongue. ⇨ 모국어.

**모여들다** gather 〔flock〕 (together); come 〔get〕 together; crowd 〔swarm, flock〕 in; cluster. ¶ 주위에 ~ gather 〔crowd, flock, swarm, cluster〕 about 〔around〕 / 사방에서 ~ flock from all quarters / 구경꾼이 운동장에 ~ spectators crowd into a playground / 설탕 그릇에 개미떼가 모여든다 Ants swarm over a sugar bowl. / 아이들이 요술쟁이를 구경하려고 모여들었다 Children gathered to watch the magician.

**모옥**(茅屋) a thatched cottage 〔hut〕.

**모욕**(侮辱) (an) insult; contempt; affront; indignity. ~하다 insult; affront; treat 《*a person*》 with contempt; wound 《*a person's*》 pride. ¶ ~적인 말 《make》 insulting remarks / ~을 당하다 suffer an insult 〔affront〕; be insulted; be put to shame / ~을 참다 brook 〔bear, pocket〕 an insult / 갖은 ~을 주다 heap insults upon 《*a person*》; level insults at 《*a person*》 / 이 이상의 ~은 참을 수 없다 This is the last insult I can bear. / 그것은 내게 대한 ~이다 It is an affront 〔a slap in the face〕 to me. / 「그런 ~에는 참을 수 없다」—「흥분하지 말게」 "I can't put up with such

an insult."—"Don't get so excited."
◉ ~죄 contempt: 법정 ~죄로 기소되다 be charged with contempt of court.

참고 「모욕하다」와 상관되는 낱말들
**insult** 「모욕하다」란 뜻의 가장 일반적인 말. 거만한 태도로 모욕을 가해서 상대의 마음을 상하게 하거나 부끄러움을 느끼게 한다는 뜻. **despise** 정도가 낮다든가, 가치가 없다, 좋지 않다, 보잘것없다 따위로 상대를 「멸시하다」란 뜻. 약간 문어적인 낱말이다. **look down upon** 〔**on**〕 despise의 구어적 표현으로 가장 일상적인 말. **contempt** 명사로서 despise보다 뜻의 강도가 높은 말. 꼭 말로 하지 않더라도, 「저급하고 치사하고 창피스럽다」는 격렬한 모욕·멸시의 뜻을 나타낸다. **disdain** 「멸시·경멸하다」란 뜻인데, 그것을 태도로 나타낸다는 뜻이 포함되어 있다.

**모우**(暮雨) rain at nightfall.

**모월**(某月) a certain month. ¶ ~ 모일에 on a certain day of a certain month.

**모유**(母乳) mother's milk; breast milk. ¶ ~로 자란 아이 a breast-fed child / ~로 기르다 breast-feed《a baby》; feed《a baby》on mother's milk; rear《a baby》at the breast / ~로 키우기 계몽운동을 강화하다 strengthen enlightenment campaigns stressing breast feeding / 그녀는 아이들을 모두 ~로 키웠다 She breast-fed all of her children. ◉ ~포육(哺育) breast feeding; maternal 〔natural〕 feeding.

**모으다** ①《집합시키다》gather; bring 〔get〕《people》together;《불러서》call《people》together;《회합에》assemble;《모집하다》recruit 〔draft〕《soldiers》. ¶ 일꾼을 ~ recruit workmen / 더 많은 사람들을 모아라 Get more people together. / 이 기획의 성패는 새 회원을 얼마만큼 모으냐에 달려 있다 The success of our scheme depends on how many new members we can recruit to the club.
②《수집하다》gather; collect; make a collection of;《모금하다》raise. ¶ 우표를 ~ collect 〔make a collection of〕 stamps / 재료를 ~ gather materials《for *one's* book》/ 기부금을 ~ collect contributions / 네가 할 일은 이에 관한 정보를 모으는 일이다 What you have to do is to gather information about this. / 온갖 수를 다 써서 그 자금을 모아야 한다 We must raise the funds in every way we can.
③《집중하다》concentrate; focus《on》. ¶ 정신〔힘〕을 ~ concentrate *one's* attention 〔strength〕 on / 광선을 초점에다 ~ concentrate rays of light into a focus.
④《끌다》draw; attract. ¶ 사람들의 눈길을 ~ attract public gaze / 그녀의 공연은 언제나 많은 관중을 모은다 Her performances always draw 〔attract〕 a large crowd.
⑤《그러모으다》bring 〔put〕 together; heap up; pile up. ¶ 재를 ~ heap up ashes.
⑥《저축하다》accumulate; amass; make; save; lay up; store. ¶ 어렵게 모은 돈 *one's* hard-saved money / 돈을 ~ save 〔accumulate〕 money / 큰 돈을 ~ amass a fortune / 돈을 모아 두다 put 〔set, lay〕 money aside; store 〔lay〕 up money.
⑦《조각을》assemble; join 〔group, unite〕 together; piece 〔fit〕 together. ¶ 부품을 모아서 자동차를 조립하다 assemble (parts into) a car / 헝겊 조각을 모아 이불을 만들다 piece together bits of cloth to make a patchwork quilt.

**모음**(母音) 〖음성〗 a vowel (sound). ¶ 단(單)~ a monophthong / 이중~ a diphthong / 반~ a semivowel / ~화하다 vocalize.
◉ ~변화 vowel gradation; (vowel) mutation. ~조직 a vowel system. ~조화 vowel harmony.

**모음곡**(一曲) 〖음악〗 a suite. ¶ 발레~ a ballet suite.

**모의**(模擬) imitation. ¶ ~의 imitation; mock; mimic; sham; simulated / 월면(月面) 착륙 ~실험 a simulated moon landing. ◉ ~국회 a mock assembly. ~법정 a moot court; a practice courtroom. ~ 비행 훈련 장치 a simulator. ~시험〔고사〕 a mock 〔trial〕 examination. ~ 재판 a moot. ~전 a mock 〔sham〕 battle. ~전투 연습 exercises under simulated combat conditions. ~투표 a straw vote 〔poll〕.

**모의**(謀議) conference;《음모》a plot; a conspiracy. ~하다 consult together《about》; confer;《음모를》plot 〔conspire〕 together. ¶ 반란을 ~하다 conspire to rise in revolt / 그 비밀 조직은 대통령 암살을 ~했다 The secret organization plotted the assassination of the President. ◉ 공동~ a joint conspiracy.

**모이** feed; food. ¶ 닭~ chicken feed / 새~ bird feed; birdseed / ~주는 시간

feeding time / ～를 주다 feed; give food 《to》 / ～를 먹다 feed (*itself*) / 참새～로 빵부스러기를 주다 feed crumbs to sparrows / 겨울동안 들새를 위해서 ～를 바깥에 놓아두었다 We put out food for the birds during the winter. / 이 새의 ～는 무엇입니까 What does this bird feed on? ◉ ～통 a feeder.

**모이다** ① 《집합하다》 gather 〔flock〕 (together); come 〔get〕 together; 《떼지어》 crowd; swarm. ¶ …의 둘레에 ～ gather 〔crowd, flock, swarm, cluster〕 about 〔around〕 / 어린이들이 운동장에 ～ children flock to the playground / 장터에 사람들이 ～ people crowd into a market / 모여 《구령》 Line up! *or* Fall in! / 거리에 사람이 많이 모였다 The street was crowded with people. *or* There was a large crowd on 〔in〕 the street. / 다들 모였나 Has everybody come? *or* Is everybody here?

② 《회합하다》 meet; assemble; congregate. ¶ 모인 사람들 those present 《at a party》 / 회의를 위해 ～ meet 〔assemble〕 for a meeting / 어디로 모일까 Where shall we meet? / 우리는 한 달에 두 번 모인다 We meet twice a month.

③ 《물건·돈이》 collect; accumulate; be collected; be accumulated; be amassed; be saved (up). ¶ 모인 돈 the money collected; the contributions 《for》 / 눈이 모여 수북이 쌓이다 snow piles up into a heap / 돈이～ money is saved (up) / 돈을 모으려 해도 모이지를 않는다 Although I try to save money, it just won't accumulate.

④ 《집중하다》 center 《in, at, on》; concentrate 《on》; 《한 점에》 converge 《on》; be focused 《on》. ¶ 모두의 시선이 그에게 모였다 All eyes were turned 〔centered〕 on him. / 세간의 동정이 그 소년에게로 모였다 Public sympathy focused on the boy. *or* The boy attracted a great deal of public sympathy.

**모인**(某人) a certain person; Mr. So-and-so.

**모일**(某日) a certain day.

**모임** a (social) gathering; a meeting; a party; an assembly; a get-together 《구어》. ¶ 동네 ～ a gathering of neighbors / ～에 나가다 attend 〔be present at〕 a meeting / ～에 불참하다 fail to attend 〔be absent from〕 a meeting / ～을 갖다 have 〔hold〕 a meeting / ～이 있다 A meeting will be held. / 다음 ～에는 참석하는 것이 좋을게다 You had better be present at the next meeting.

**모자**(母子) mother and child. ¶ ～의 정 maternal and filial affection / ～가 다 건재하다 Both mother and child are 「doing fine 〔in good condition〕.
◉ ～가정 a mother-and-child family; a fatherless family. ～보건법 the Mother and Child Health Law. ～ 보건 센터 a mother-child health center.

**모자**(帽子) a hat (테 있는); a cap (테 없는); [총칭] headgear. ¶ ～챙 the visor 〔shade〕 of a cap / ～테 the brim of a hat / ～리본 a hatband / 테 넓은 ～ a broad-brimmed hat / ～를 손에 들고 hat in hand / ～를 쓴 채로 with *one's* hat on / ～를 쓰지 않고 without a hat on / ～를 쓰다〔벗다〕 put on 〔take off〕 a hat / ～를 쓰지 않고 있다 be bareheaded; be without a hat / ～를 써보다 try on a hat / ～를 씌우다 hat 〔cap〕 《*a person*》 / ～를 벗기다 unhat 〔uncap〕 《*a person*》 / ～를 비스듬히 쓰다 cock *one's* hat; wear *one's* hat at an angle / ～를 젖혀 쓰다 wear *one's* hat on the back of *one's* head / ～를 푹 눌러 쓰다 wear *one's* hat deep; pull *one's* hat over *one's* eyes / ～를 벗고 인사하다 take off 〔raise, lift〕 *one's* hat 《to *a person*》 / ～를 벗지 않다 keep *one's* hat on / ～를 벗으시오 《게시》 Off with your hat. *or* Please remove hats. *or* Take hats off. *or* Hats off.
◉ ～걸이 a hatrack; a hatrail; a hatstand. ～상 《사람》 a hatter; a milliner (여성용의); 《가게》 a hat shop. ～상자 a hatbox; a hat case. ～제조업자 a hatmaker.

**모자라다** ① 《부족하다》 be 〔come, fall, run〕 short of; be not enough; be insufficient 〔deficient〕; lack; be lacking; want. ¶ 다섯 명이 ～ want 〔need〕 five men; be five men short / 돈이 ～ be short of money / (만 원에서) 100원 ～ be 100 won short (of 10,000 won) / 생각이 ～ lack judgment / 식량이 ～ be short of provisions / 역량이 ～ be wanting in ability / 기술이 ～ lack 〔be deficient in〕 skill / 영양이 ～ be undernourished; lack adequate food / 영어 실력이 ～ be 「weak in 〔poor at, no good at〕 English / 일손이 ～ be short of hands; be shorthanded; be undermanned / 키가 ～ be not tall enough / (돈이) 얼

마나 모자라는가 How much is wanting? / 6피트에 3인치 모자란다 It wants three inches of six feet. / 아직 모자라는 것이 있다 Something is wanting. / 투표 결과는 과반수에 5표 모자란다 The vote lacks five of being a majority. / 정족수에 5명이 모자란다 Five more members are needed for a quorum. ② 《우둔하다》 《*one's* intelligence》 be below the average; be half-witted; be dull; be stupid; 《구어》 be soft 〔weak〕 in the head. ¶ 그는 좀 모자란다 He is a little stupid 〔weak in the head〕.

**모자반** 〖식물〗 a gulfweed; a sargasso (weed).

**모자이크** a mosaic. ¶ ～식 포장도로 a mosaic pavement. ◉ ～결정 a mosaic crystal. ～무늬 mosaic: ～무늬 바닥 a tessellated floor. ～병(病) mosaic (disease). ～세공 mosaic work.

**모작패** 〖광산〗 a share-mining system.

**모잠비크** 《아프리카의 공화국》 Mozambique.

**모쟁이** 〖어류〗 a young gray mullet.

**모정**(母情) maternal affection 〔love〕; mother('s) love.

**모정**(慕情) longing 《for》; love 《for》; affection 《for, toward》. ¶ 어머니와 자식에 대한 ～ longing for mother and child / ～을 품다 have a longing 《for home》.

**모제르총**(—銃) 《상표명》 a Mauser. ¶ ～식 총 a Mauser-action gun.

**모조**(模造) imitation. ～하다 imitate; make an imitation 《of》; 《위조》 counterfeit. ¶ ～의 imitation; fake(d); 《인조의》 artificial / 그릇에 가득 담긴 식탁 위의 ～과일 a bowl of artificial fruit on the table / 그들은 수정으로 ～다이아몬드를 만들었다 They made an imitation diamond out of crystal. ◉ ～가죽 imitation leather. ～금(金) imitation gold. ～식품 《진열장용》 the wax and plastic replicas of menu offerings (displayed in restaurant windows). ～지(紙) imitation vellum; vellum paper. ～진주〔보석〕 an imitation pearl 〔gem〕. ～품 an imitation; a replica; 《가짜》 a sham; a counterfeit; a fake: 그의 미술 소장품에는 ～품도 있었다 His art collection included counterfeits.

**모조리** all; without (a single) exception; thoroughly; completely; entirely; wholly; from the beginning to the end; all the way. ¶ ～ 가져가다 take away everything (*one* can lay hands on) / ～ 검거하다 make a wholesale arrest 《of the gangsters》 / 그들을 ～ 사형에 처하다 put every last one of them to death / ～ 털어놓다 make a clean breast of 《*a matter*》 / 세간이 ～ 타다 lose every stick of furniture in a fire / 책을 처음부터 끝까지 ～ 외다 memorize a book from cover to cover / 전답을 ～ 팔아 버리다 sell all *one's* (real) estate; make a clean sweep of *one's* real estate / 가진 물건을 ～ 도둑맞았다 My personal effects were stolen (right down) to the last article. / 위원들은 ～ 반대였다 No one of the committee was favorable to it.

**모종** 〖농업〗 a seedling; 《나무의》 a sapling; a young plant; a nursery tree; a set. ～하다, ～내다 plant 〔transplant〕 a seedling; bed out; plant out. ¶ 토마토 ～ a young tomato plant / 딸기 ～ a set of strawberry. ◉ ～비 a timely rain for transplanting seedlings. ～삽 a (garden) trowel.

**모종**(某種) a certain kind. ¶ ～의 a certain; unnamed; some / ～의 이유로 for a certain reason / ～의 혐의를 받다 be 〔lie〕 under some suspicion.

**모주** a hard 〔heavy〕 drinker; a tippler; a drunkard; a boozer 《속어》; a thirsty soul. ◉ ～꾼〔망태〕 ⇨ 모주.

**모주**(母酒) 《밑술》 crude 〔raw〕 liquor; 《재강》 lees; dregs.

**모지**(某地) 《at》 a certain place; 《at》 an unnamed place. ¶ 강원도 ～에서 somewhere in Kangwon-do.

**모지다** 《성품이》 (be) angular. ⇨ 모나다.

**모지라지다** wear down to a stump; wear out; be worn out; get stumpy 〔blunt〕. ¶ 모지라진 worn-out; stumped; stubby 《pencils》.

**모지락스럽다** (be) cruel; harsh; heartless; hard; rough; cold-hearted. ¶ 모지락스러운 짓을 하다 do a cruel 〔nasty〕 thing.

**모지랑붓** a worn-out writing brush.

**모지랑비** a worn-out 〔stumpy〕 broom.

**모지랑이** a worn-out one 〔brush, broom, *etc.*〕; a stump.

**모직**(毛織) woolen fabric 〔cloth〕; worsted fabric. ¶ ～의 woolen. ◉ ～물 woolen fabrics 〔cloth, textiles〕; woolen goods: ～물상(商) a woolen merchant 〔draper 《영》〕 / ～물 제조업자 a woolen manufacturer / ～물 공업 the woolen textile industry / ～공장 a woolen mill.

**모진 목숨** *one's* damned 〔contemptible〕

life; *one's* wretched 〔miserable〕 life; *one's* woeful 〔sad〕 lot. ¶ ~을 어쩌지 못하다 have to bear *one's* wretched life; cannot escape *one's* contemptible existence / ~이 아직도 붙어 있소 I am still prolonging this damned life of mine.

**모질다** ① 《잔인함》 (be) harsh; cruel; brutal; merciless; heartless; ruthless; atrocious. ¶ 모진 말 harsh remarks / 모진 사람 a brutal person; a heartless person; a brute / 모질게 굴다 act ruthlessly / 모질게 대하다 treat 《*a person*》 harshly; deal harshly with 《*a person*》; be cruel 〔hard〕 to 《*a person*》 / 그는 그 아이를 모질게 대했다 He treated the child badly 〔cruelly〕. / 그런 모진 소리를 하지마라 Don't say such a merciless thing.
② 《베겨 냄》 (be) hard; tough; die-hard. ¶ 모진 사람 a die-hard; a tough guy / 재난에 모질게 견디다 bear a calamity with fortitude / 마음을 모질게 먹다 steel 〔harden〕 *one's* heart 〔*oneself*〕 《against pity》 / 그는 모질어 겁이 없다 He is too tough to be afraid of anything.
③ 《바람·날씨 따위》 (be) wretched; hard; severe; bitter. ¶ 모진 바람 a wretched 〔hard〕 wind / 모진 추위〔더위, 날씨〕 a severe cold 〔heat, weather〕.

**모질음** harshness; hardness; toughness. ¶ ~을 쓰다 fight hard; struggle 《against pain 〔agony〕》.

**모집**(募集) 《사람의》 enlistment; recruitment; enrollment; 《기금 따위의》 raising; collection; 《채권 따위》 floatation. ~하다 enlist; recruit; enroll; 《기금 등을》 raise; collect; invite; 《공채를》 float. ¶ 공채를 ~하다 float 〔raise〕 a (public) loan / 기금을 ~하다 raise funds; invite a subscription 《for a fund, to *do*》 / 사무원을 ~하다 invite applications for the position of clerk / 지원자를 ~하다 receive applications 《for a post, for admission to a school》 / 현상 소설을 ~하다 hold a prize contest for novels; open a prize-list for novels / 새 회원을 ~하다 recruit new members / ~에 응하다 respond to an invitation; apply for the position offered / 자선 사업을 위한 기부금을 ~하다 collect contributions 〔money〕 for charities / 새 병원의 건축 자금을 ~하다 raise a fund for a new hospital / 점원 ~ 《게시》 Clerks wanted. / 학생 ~ 《게시》 New students invited. / 사무원 1명 ~에 100명이 지원했다 One hundred people applied for the position of a clerk. / 다음 달부터 입주자 ~을 시작한다 We will put in an advertisement of tenants next month. / 저 대학에서는 지금 학생을 ~ 중이다 That college is now advertising for students.
◉ ~광고 an advertisement for subscription; a want ad: ~ 광고를 내다 advertise 《for》. ~방법 a method of recruitment. ~액 the amount to be raised. ~요강 an application handbook; 《지침》 guidelines for applicants; 《입학의》 a list of entrance requirements; a prospectus 《of a school for candidates》. ~인원 《단체·클럽 등》 the number of new members to be enrolled in a society; 《학교의》 the number 《of students》 to be admitted to a school. 기금 ~ 운동 a drive to raise funds.

**모집다** ① 《허물 따위를》 point out specifically; put *one's* finger on; indicate. ¶ 남의 허물을 ~ point out 〔indicate〕 *a person's* mistake 〔error〕.
② 《모조리 집다》 grasp 〔hold〕 all.

**모집단**(母集團) 『통계』 population; a universe.

**모차르트** 《오스트리아의 작곡가》 Wolfgang Amadeus Mozart (1756-91).

**모착하다** (be) short and fat 〔chubby, plump〕.

**모창하다**(模唱—) mimic 《*a person's*》 song 〔way of singing〕.

**모채**(募債) loan floatation; the raising of a loan. ~하다 float 〔raise, issue〕 a loan. ◉ ~액 the amount of a loan. ~인수 underwriting. ~조건 the terms of loan floatation.

**모처**(某處) a certain place; unnamed quarters; an undisclosed spot; somewhere. ¶ 시내 ~에서 somewhere in the city.

**모처럼** ① 《오랜만에》 after a long time 〔interval, silence, absence, separation〕; 《고대했던》 long-awaited; much awaited. ¶ ~ 좋은 날씨 fine weather after a long spell 《of rain》; the first fine weather in many days / 그들은 ~ 서로 만나 대단히 기뻐했다 They were very pleased to see each other after a long separation. / 나는 ~ 부산에 갔다 I went to Pusan after a long interval. / ~의 휴가를 비 때문에 망쳤다 The rain spoiled the much-awaited holidays.
② 《애써서》 with (much) trouble 〔effort〕; at great pains. ¶ ~ 모은 돈을

어리석게도 다 써버렸다 I was foolish enough to spend the money I had saved at no small pains. / ～의 노력이 수포로 돌아갔다 All my effort came to nothing.
③《친절하게도》(so) kindly; with special kindness; 《특별히》 specially; on purpose (일부러). ¶ ～ 말씀〔권〕하시기에 as 〔since〕 you so kindly offer 〔recommend〕 it / ～ 주시는 것이니 받겠습니다 Thank you for your kind gift. / ～의 말씀이지만 응할 수가 없습니다 I am sorry but I have to decline your kind offer. / ～의 충고도 그에게는 쇠귀에 경읽기였다 All my kind advice fell flat on him. / ～ 찾아오셨는데 뵙지 못해서 미안합니다 I am terribly sorry I was not here to see when you were so kind to come all the way to visit. / ～ 초대해 주셨는데 공교롭게도 선약 때문에 응하지 못해 유감입니다 Many thanks for your kind invitation, but a previous engagement unfortunately compels me to decline.

**모체**(母體) 《어머니 몸》 the mother's body; the mother; 《주체》 the parent (body); a base; 《균류의》 a matrix (*pl.* -trices, ～es). ¶ ～ 보호를 위해 for the health of the mother / …을 ～로 하다 stem 〔branch〕 from / 태아를 꺼내지 않으면 ～가 위험하다 Unless the fetus is extracted, the mother's life is in danger. / 프랑스 말은 라틴어를 ～로 하여 발달되었다 French has developed from Latin.
◉ ～발아 『식물』 viviparity. ～전염 hereditary transmission.

**모춤** 『농업』 a bundle of rice seedlings.

**모춤하다** be a little too much 〔long〕.

**모친**(母親) *one's* mother. ◉ ～상 mourning for *one's* mother; *one's* mother's death: ～상을 당하다 have *one's* mother 〔die.

**모카** 《커피》 mocha.

**모탕** ①《장작 팰 때의》 a wooden block on which firewood is cut. ②《굄목》 wooden blocks on which things are piled up. ◉ ～세(貰) storage charges.

**모태**(母胎) ① 『해부』 the mother's womb; the uterus (자궁). ¶ ～ 내의 생명 antenatal life / ～를 떠나다 leave the mother's womb. ②《발생·발전의 토대》 the matrix. ¶ 로마는 서양 문명의 ～이었다 Rome was the matrix of Western civilization.

**모택동**(毛澤東) Mao Tse-tung 〔Zedong〕 (1893-1976). ◉ ～사상 Maoism; Mao's thought(s).

**모터** a motor; an engine. ◉ ～바이크 a motorbike. ～보트 a motorboat. ～사이클 a motorcycle. ～쇼 a motor show. ～케이드 《자동차 행렬》 a motorcade. ～풀 a motor pool. ～홈 《이동 주택차》 a motor home.

**모텔** 《자동차 여행자용 호텔》 a motel. 〔<*mo*tor+ho*tel*〕

**모토** a motto. ¶ …을 ～로 하다 make it *one's* motto 《to *do*》 / 「정직은 최선의 방책」이라는 것이 나의 ～이다 "Honesty is the best policy" is my motto.

**모투저기다** save up little by little.

**모퉁이** a corner; a turn; a turning place. ¶ ～의 가게 a store on 〔at〕 the corner; a corner store / ～를 돌아서 셋째 집 the third house round the corner / ～를 돌다 turn 〔take, go round〕 a corner; round the corner / ～에 있다 stand 〔be〕 on 〔at〕 the corner 《of a street》 / 첫번째 길 ～를 왼쪽으로 돌아가시오 Take the first turn 〔turning〕 to the left.
◉ ～집 a house at the corner. 모퉁잇돌 『건축』 a cornerstone (주춧돌).

**모티브** 《동기》 a motive; 《예술 작품의 주제》 a motif (F.)

**모판**(一板) 『농업』 a nursery; (an individual) seedbed; a rice seedbed.

**모포**(毛布) a blanket; a rug. ⇨ 담요.

**모표**(帽標) a badge on a cap; a cap badge.

**모피**(毛皮) a fur (보드라운); a fell; a skin (거친); a pelt (생피). ¶ ～ 외투를 입은 부인 a lady in furs; a fur coated lady. ◉ ～류 furriery. ～목도리 a fur comforter 〔wrap〕. ～상 《직업》 furriery; 《사람》 a furrier; a fur dealer. ～제품 furs; fur goods. ～코트 a fur coat.

**모필**(毛筆) a writing 〔painting〕 brush; a hairbrush; a hair pencil.
◉ ～화 a hair-pencil picture.

**모함**(母艦) a mother 〔depot〕 ship. ¶ 잠수～ a submarine tender 〔depot ship〕 / 항공～ an aircraft carrier.

**모함**(謀陷) a plot to do injury; slander; calumny. ～하다 intrigue against; plot to injure; snare; entrap. ¶ ～에 빠지다 fall into a snare 〔trap〕; be caught in a trap; be entrapped / 남을 ～하려다 도리어 자기가 구렁에 빠지다 be caught in *one's* own trap; be hoist with *one's* own petard.

**모항**(母港) a home port.

**모해**(謀害) a plot 〔scheme〕 to do harm. ～하다 plot to harm.

**모험**(冒險) an adventure; a risky attempt; a hazard; a venture; a risk. ～하다 venture《on》; risk; take a chance; run a risk 〔the hazard〕; make a venture. ¶ ～적인 adventurous; hazardous; risky / ～적인 사업 a risky enterprise 〔undertaking〕; venture business / ～을 즐기는 사람 an adventurous person; a lover of adventure / ～한 번 해보다 run a risk; take a chance / 목숨을 걸고 ～하다 venture *one's* life; risk *one's* neck / 공연한 ～을 하다 take risks unnecessarily / 무모한 ～을 하다 take a leap in the dark / 이런 시점에서 공연한 ～을 할 필요는 없겠다 At this point, there is no sense in taking chances. / 그것은 좀 지나친 ～이 아닐까 I fear it is too hazardous a step to take. / 때로는 다소의 ～도 필요하다 Sometimes it is necessary to take 〔run〕 some risks. / 지금 주식에 투자하는 것은 ～이라고 생각한다 I am afraid that investing money in stocks now is risky.
◉ ～가 an adventurer. ～담 a tale 〔an account〕 of *one's* adventure; an adventure story. ～대 a body of adventurers. ～성 adventurousness; riskiness. ～소설 an adventure novel 〔story〕. ～심 an adventurous spirit; the spirit of adventure. ～자본《위험부담의》a venture 〔risk〕 capital. ～주의 adventurism. ～주의자 an adventurist.

**모형**(模型) a model; a dummy; a pattern; a mold (주물 등의). ¶ 군함의 ～ a model 〔miniature〕 warship / 작은 ～ a miniature / 축척 ～ a scale model / 실물 크기의 ～ a life-size model《of》; a full-scale mockup《of an airplane》/ ～을 뜨다〔만들다〕 model; make a model《of》/ 그의 취미는 범선 ～을 만드는 것이다 His hobby is to make models of sailing ships.
◉ ～도 a model picture. ～비행기〔자동차〕 a model 〔miniature〕 plane 〔car〕. ～실험 an experiment with a model; a model test; model-testing. ～제작자 a patternmaker. ～주택 a model house. ～지도《입체의》a relief map; a model map.

**모형**(母型) 〚인쇄〛 a matrix.

**모호하다**(模糊—)《애매하다》(be) vague; dim; hazy; faint; obscure; indistinct; blurred; ambiguous; equivocal. ¶ ～하게 dimly; faintly; obscurely; indistinctly; in a haze / 모호하게 대답하다 give a vague 〔dubious〕 answer / 모호한 말을 하다 speak ambiguously; equivocate / 모호한 변명을 하다 give a vague 〔an equivocal〕 explanation / 모호한 태도를 취하다 maintain an uncertain 〔a dubious〕 attitude《toward》; do not commit *oneself*.

**모회사**(母會社) a parent company; a holding company 〔corporation〕.

**목**[1] ①《모가지》a neck; a head (머리). ¶ 기다란 목 a long 〔slender〕 neck / 짧은 목 a short neck / 가느다란 목 a scraggy neck / 굵은 목 a heavy 〔thick〕 neck; a bull neck / 목을 매다 hang *oneself*《on a tree》; strangle *oneself*《with a cord》/ …밖으로 목을 내밀다 stick 〔poke〕 *one's* head out of《the window》/ 목을 길게 빼다 crane *one's* head; rubberneck《미구어》/ ～에 매달리다 throw both arms round《*a person's*》neck / 목이 잘리다《해고》be discharged; be fired《구어》; get the sack《영구어》/ 목을 베다〔치다〕 cut off《*a person's*》head; behead; decapitate; [비유적] fire (해고하다) / 목졸라 죽이다 strangle《*a person*》to death / 목을 비틀다 wring the neck《of a chicken》; wring《*a person's*》neck / 목을 움츠리다 duck *one's* head.
②《목구멍》a throat; a gullet; a windpipe. ¶ 목에 걸리다 stick 〔lodge〕 in *one's* throat / 가시가 목에 걸리다 have 〔get〕 a fish bone stuck in *one's* throat / 목이 마르다 be 〔feel〕 thirsty; have a dry throat; be dry / 목이 메다 be choked 〔stifled〕《by, with》/ 목이 아프다 have a sore throat / 목이 쉬다 have a hoarse throat; have a frog in *one's* throat / 목메어 울다 be choked with tears; sob / 목놓아 울다 weep with abandon / 목을 축이다 quench 〔relieve〕 *one's* thirst; wet *one's* whistle / 목이 말라 죽겠다 I am as dry as a herring. *or* I am parched with thirst.
③《좁은 부분·요충》a neck; a narrow part 〔point〕; a narrowing; an important part 〔point〕. ¶ 길목 a narrowing 〔squeeze, bottleneck〕 in a road; a key position (on the road); a strategic point / 버선목 the ankle of a sock / 병목 the neck of a bottle; the bottleneck / 여울목 the narrow throat of a stream.
④《곡식의》the neck of a stalk of grain.

**목**[2] 〚광산〛 gold ore found (on refining) to contain an admixture of silver or lead; slag; dross.

**목**(目) ①《항목》 an item; a sub-item; a division; a class. ②《동식물의 분류》 an order. ¶ 같은 목에 속하는 동물〔식물〕 co-ordinal animal 〔plant〕 (★ 식물학에서는 -ales, 동물학에서는 -acea를 붙여 목을 표시함). ③《바둑의》 a piece (돌); a cross (집).

**목가**(牧歌) a pastoral song 〔poem〕. ¶ ~적인 pastoral; bucolic / ~적인 풍경 a pastoral 〔an idyllic〕 scene. ◉ ~시 an idyl(l); a pastoral poem.

**목각**(木刻) 《조각》 wood engraving 〔carving〕; 《목각화》 a woodcut; a wood=block print; 《활자》 a block letter. ~하다 engrave on wood. ◉ ~술 woodcraft. ~인형 a wooden doll.

**목간**(沐間) 《목욕》 (taking) a bath; bathing; 《목욕간》 a bathroom. ~하다 take 〔have〕 a bath; have a tub 《영》. ¶ ~하러 가다 go to a public bath (house) / ~시키다 give a bath 《to a baby》; bath 《a baby》 / ~물이 준비되었다 The bath is ready. ◉ ~통 a bath; a tub; a bathtub 《미》.

**목걸이** neckwear; a neckpiece; a necklet; a necklace; 《개의》 a collar; 《장식품》 a rivière. ¶ 진주 ~ a pearl necklace / ~를 하다 wear a necklace / ~를 달다 put a collar on 《a dog》 / 개의 ~를 잡아끌다 drag a dog by the collar.

**목검**(木劍) a wooden sword.

**목격**(目擊) witnessing. ~하다 witness; see with *one's* own eyes; observe. ¶ ~되다 come under *one's* 〔*a person's*〕 eyes 〔notice, observation〕 / 끔찍한 광경을 ~하다 witness a horrible scene / 나는 그 교통 사고를 ~했다 I saw the traffic accident with my own eyes. ◉ ~담 an eyewitness account; a first-hand report. ~자 a witness; an eyewitness: 그 사고의 ~자는 없었다 There were no witnesses 〔eyewitnesses〕 to the accident.

**목곧다** 《완고하다》 (be) stiff-necked.

**목곧이** a stiff-necked person.

**목공**(木工) 《사람》 a carpenter; a woodworker; a craftman in wood; a joiner (소목); 《일》 woodwork(ing). ◉ ~기계〔공구〕 a woodworking machine 〔tool〕. ~선반 woodprocessing lathe. ~소 a carpentry shop; a woodworking shop 〔plant〕; 《제재소》 a sawmill. ~술 carpentry; woodcraft. ~품 woodwork.

**목관**(木棺) a wooden coffin.

**목관**(木管) a wooden pipe. ◉ ~악기 a woodwind instrument; the woodwind.

**목구멍** a throat; a gullet; a windpipe. ¶ ~이 아프다 have a sore throat / ~이 막히다 be choked 《with》 / ~까지 치밀어 왔지만 차마 나는 그 말을 그에게 할 수 없었다 I almost blurted it out, but I couldn't bring myself to tell him. / ~이 포도청 《속담》 Hunger makes any man a criminal.

**목귀질하다** plane off the corners 〔edges〕.

**목금**(木琴) 《악기》 a xylophone. ¶ ~주자 a xylophonist.

**목기**(木器) a wooden vessel; [총칭] woodenware. ◉ ~전 a woodenware store.

**목다리**(木—) 《a pair of》 crutches. ⇨ 목발.

**목다심** soothing *one's* throat.

**목달이** ①《버선》 the neck of Korean socks formed with the inner cloth. ②《다 해진》 worn-out socks. ◉ ~양말 knee-length stockings.

**목대잡다** direct; supervise; command; boss 《around, about》 《구어》.

**목대잡이** a director; a supervisor; a commander; an overseer.

**목덜미** the nape; the back 〔scruff〕 (of the neck). ¶ ~를 잡다 take 〔seize, grab, grasp〕 《*a person*》 「by the scruff of his neck 〔by the collar〕; collar 《*a person*》.

**목도** 《일》 carrying 《a weight》 with a pole jointly shouldered by two 〔four〕 persons; 《막대기》 a carrying pole. ~하다 carry 《a weight》 with a pole shouldered by two 〔four〕 persons. ◉ ~꾼 the pole-bearers.

**목도**(木刀) a wooden knife 〔sword, stick〕.

**목도**(目睹) = 목격(目擊).

**목도리** a neckpiece; a neckcloth; muffler; a comforter; a scarf. ¶ 밖이 추우니 ~를 하고 가는 것이 좋을게다 It is cold outside, so you had better 「wear muffler 〔put a scarf on〕.

**목돈** ①《모갯돈》 a sizable sum 〔amount〕 of money; a good round sum. ¶ ~으로 백만원 a round sum of one million won / ~을 좀 만들다 scrape together some money / ~을 만들 수가 없다 I can't make up a good round sum. / 그는 ~을 은행에서 꺼냈다 He drew a large 〔sizable〕 sum of money from the bank. / 나에게 ~이 있다 I have a sizable sum (of money). ②《무당에 주는》 advance payment to a shaman for an exorcism.

**목돌림** a catching 〔an infectious〕 sore throat.

**목동**(牧童) a herdboy; 《미》 a ranch

hand; 《양의》 a shepherd boy; 《소의》 a cowboy; a cowpuncher 《미구어》.

**목련**(木蓮) 〖식물〗 a (lily) magnolia. ◉ ~화 a magnolia blossom.

**목례**(目禮) a nod (of greeting); nodding. ~하다 nod 《to》; give a glance in salute; greet with *one's* eyes; greet with a nod. ¶ ~를 주고 받다 exchange nods 《with》 / 복도에서 만났을 때 그녀는 ~를 했다 She greeted me with her eyes when we met in the corridor.

**목로**(木壚) a long and narrow table to set *one's* drink on (in a bar). ◉ ~술집, 목롯집 a stand-up bar; a saloon; 《영》 a public house; 《영구어》 a pub.

**목록**(目錄) ① 《상품·장서의》 a list 《of articles》; a catalog(ue); 《재산·재고품의》 an inventory. ¶ ~을 만들다 make 〔draw up〕 a list 〔inventory〕 《of 》; list; catalog / 장서의 ~을 만들다 catalog a library / ~에 올리다 catalog 《articles》; put 〔place〕 《goods》 on the catalog / ~에 있다 be on 〔in〕 the catalog / 그 상점에서 상품 ~을 보내왔다 The store sent us a catalog of their merchandise. ② 《목차》 contents.

**목리**(木理) 《나뭇결》 the grain (of wood); 《나이테》 the annual rings of a tree.

**목마**(木馬) a wooden horse; 《흔들 목마》 a rocking horse; a rocker; a hobbyhorse. ¶ 트로이의 ~ the Trojan horse / 회전~ a merry-go-round; 《영》 a roundabout.

**목마르다** ① 《갈증나다》 (be) thirsty; get 〔feel〕 thirsty; feel 〔be〕 dry. ¶ (술마신 뒤에) 목이 말라 물을 마시다 cool *one's* coppers / (목이) 탈듯이 ~ be parched with thirst / 목마른 것을 덜다 quench 〔relieve〕 *one's* thirst. ② 《갈망하다》 have a thirst for 《money, knowledge》; be thirsty after 〔for, of〕; thirst 〔hunger, crave, yearn〕 for 《money》; hanker after. ¶ 목마르게 기다리다 be on the tiptoe of expectation; look eagerly for / 목마르게 기다린 비 long-awaited rain; the long-looked-for rain.

**목말** riding 《*a person's*》 shoulders. ~타다 ride on 《*a person's*》 shoulders; ride pickaback 〔piggyback〕 《on *a person*》. ~태우다 give 《a child》 a ride on *one's* shoulders; ride 〔have, hold〕 《*a person*》 on *one's* shoulders; ride 〔carry〕 《a child》 pickaback. ¶ ~을 태우고 걷다 carry 《a child》 on *one's* shoulders.

**목매다** ① 《남을》 strangle; hang 《*a person*》 by the neck. ¶ 나뭇가지에 ~ hang 《*a person*》 on the branch of a tree / 수건으로 목매어 죽이다 strangle 《*a person*》 to death with a towel. ② 《스스로》 strangle *oneself;* hang *oneself.* ¶ 나무에 ~ hang *oneself* on a tree / 들보에 ~ hang *oneself* from a beam of *one's* house.

**목메다** be choked 〔stifled, suffocated〕 《with, by》; be stuck 《with》. ¶ 목메인 소리로 in a choked 〔choking〕 voice / 설움에 ~ be choked with sorrow / 목메어 물을 마셔야겠다 I am choking—I'll have to drink some water.

**목면**(木綿) ① cotton. ⇨무명. ② 〖식물〗 a cotton plant. ⇨목화.

**목물** washing *one's* neck and back; a bust bath. ~하다 have *one's* neck and back washed; take a bust bath.

**목민**(牧民) governing the people. ◉ ~관 a governor.

**목발**(木―) 《a pair of 》 crutches. ¶ ~을 짚고 걷다 go 〔walk〕 on crutches.

**목본**(木本) a woody plant; 〖식물〗 an arbor.

**목부**(牧夫) a pasture employee; a herdsman.

**목부용**(木芙蓉) 〖식물〗 a cotton rosemallow.

**목불인견**(目不忍見) ¶ ~이다 cannot bear 〔endure〕 to see; be unable to stand the sight of; be extremely pitiful / 그 참상은 ~이었다 The tragic sight was simply appalling. / 그 무서운 광경은 참으로 ~이었다 I could hardly bear 〔endure〕 to look at the dreadful scene.

**목비** a spell of heavy rain at rice-planting season.

**목사**(牧師) a minister; a clergyman; a pastor; a vicar 《미》; a rector; a parson; 《교목·군목 등》 a chaplain; [총칭] the clergy.

> 용법 **minister** 미국에서는 「프로테스탄트(Protestant)의 목사」. 영국에서는 「비국교파·장로 교회의 목사」란 뜻. **clergyman** 영국에서는 「국교회의 목사」를 가리키나, 미국에서는 「성직자 전반」을 뜻함. **parson** 「영국 국교회의 교구 목사」란 뜻이나 구어에서는 일반적으로 Protestant의 목사를 말한다. **pastor** 「교구·교회의 목사」로 특히 로마 가톨릭·영국 및 스코틀랜드 국교 이외의 성직자를 가리킨다. **rector** 「영국 국교회의 교구 목사」. **vicar** 「미국 성공회의 회당 목사, 영국 국교회의 rector 대리를 담당하는 목사」를 뜻한다.

¶ ～가 되다 become a clergyman; enter the ministry; take (holy) orders; go into the church / 그는 ～다 He is in holy orders. / 김 ～님 Reverend Kim; Rev. Kim. ◉ ～관(館) a rectory; a parsonage. ～직 order(s); ministry.

**목상**(木像) 《망석중이》 a dummy; a wooden figure; 《조각품》 a wooden statue 〔image〕.

**목새**[1] 《모래》 fine soft sand pile carried in by the currents.

**목새**[2] 〖농업〗 rice-plant fever.

**목석**(木石) 《나무와 돌》 trees 〔sticks〕 and stones; 《생명 없는 것》 inanimate objects; 《무감정》 insensibility; unsusceptibility; hardheartedness; callousness. ¶ ～ 같은 unimpressionable; insensible; unsusceptible; impassive / ～ 같은 사람 an insensible person / ～이 아니다 be sentient; be a sentient being / 나라고 해서 ～은 아니야 I am not a stock nor a stone. *or* I am made of flesh and blood.

**목선**(木船) a wooden boat 〔ship〕.

**목성**(木星) 〖천문〗 Jupiter.

**목세루**(木—) cotton serge.

**목소리**[1] a voice; a tone. ¶ 가는 ～ a thin 〔faint〕 voice / 고운 ～ a sweet 〔beautiful, melodious〕 voice / 굵은 ～ a deep 〔full〕 voice / 낭랑한 ～ a sonorous voice / 높은〔낮은〕 ～ a loud 〔low〕 voice / 맑은 ～ a clear 〔silvery, ringing〕 voice / 새된 ～ a shrill voice / 성난 ～ an angry voice / 쉰 ～ a husky 〔hoarse〕 voice / 큰 ～ a loud voice / 작은 ～ whispers; a low 〔small〕 voice / 쩌렁쩌렁한 ～ a resonant voice / 귀에 거슬리는 ～ a harsh 〔grating〕 voice / 듣기 싫은 ～ an ugly 〔discordant〕 voice.

목소리가: ～가 들리는〔안 들리는〕 곳에 within 〔beyond, out of〕 hearing 〔call, earshot〕 / ～가 좋다 have a sweet 〔fine〕 voice / ～가 나쁘다 have a poor voice / ～가 높다〔낮다〕 speak in a loud 〔low〕 voice / ～가 나오지 않다 *one's* voice fails; lose *one's* voice; be out of voice / ～가 쉬다 *one's* voice becomes husky 〔hoarse〕 / ～가 쉬도록 말을 하다 talk *oneself* hoarse.

목소리로: 거친 ～로 in an angry voice / 낮은 ～로 in a low voice; in a quiet tone; in an undertone; in whispers / 높은〔큰〕 ～로 in a loud voice; loudly / 슬픈 ～로 in a sad voice / 한〔같은〕 ～로 with one voice; in chorus 〔unison〕.

목소리를: ～를 낮추어 in whispers; under *one's* breath / ～를 거칠게 하여 in an angry tone / ～를 떨며 in a quivering 〔quaking〕 voice / ～를 낮추다〔죽이다〕 lower 〔drop, sink〕 *one's* voice / ～를 높이다 raise 〔lift〕 *one's* voice; raise *one's* pitch / ～를 좋게 하다 improve 〔cultivate〕 *one's* voice / 남의 ～를 알아듣다 recognize another's voice / ～를 자랑하다 be proud of *one's* voice.

¶ 그들은 ～를 높여 교육 제도 개혁의 필요성을 강조했다 They emphasized the necessity of reforming the educational system.

**목소리**[2] 〖음성〗 《후두음》 a guttural.

**목수**(木手) a carpenter. ¶ 도～ a master carpenter. ◉ ～연장 carpenter's tools; a carpenter's outfit 〔kit〕. ～일 carpentry: ～일을 하다 do carpentering; carpenter.

**목수**(木髓) 《고갱이》 pith.

**목숨** 《생명》 life; the breath of life; 《수명》 *one's* life span.

¶ 귀한 ～ *one's* precious 〔dear〕 life / 천한 ～ *one's* abject life / 모진 ～ *one's* wretched 〔damned〕 life / 초로같은 ～ a frail life; a life as tenuous as the dew on the grass / 둘도 없는 ～ *one's* most precious life; *one's* dear life.

목숨이: ～이 붙어 있는 한 as 〔so〕 long as *one* 「lives 〔is alive〕 / ～이 끊어지다 breathe *one's* last; be dead / ～이 붙어 있다 be alive (and breathing); *one's* life is spared; still live / ～이 다할 때까지 싸우다 fight to the last drop of *one's* blood / ～이 아깝다 *one's* life is dear (to *one*); hold *one's* life dear / ～이 위태롭다 be in peril of *one's* life.

목숨에: ～에 관계되다 endanger 〔imperil〕 *one's* life; be dangerous to life; be 〔prove〕 fatal 《to》; be the death 《of》 / ～에 관계되는 부상〔병〕 a mortal 〔fatal〕 injury 〔disease〕 / ～에 관계되는 중대한 일 an important affair which might endanger *one's* life.

목숨을: ～을 건지다 escape death; be saved (from death); survive (살아남다); pull through (환자가) / ～을 간신히 건지다 have a narrow escape (from death) / ～을 걸다 risk 〔hazard〕 *one's* life; risk *one's* neck / ～을 걸고 at the risk of *one's* life / ～을 걸고 맹세하다 swear on *one's* life / ～을 끊다 《남의》 take 《*a person's*》 life; kill; 《스스로》 take *one's* own life; kill *oneself* / ～을 노리다 seek 《*a person's*》 life; plot《*a person's*》death; make an attempt on《*a person's*》life / ~을 (내)던지다 throw away *one's* life; lay down〔give up〕*one's* life; die《for》/ ~을 돌보지 않다 disregard *one's* life / ~을 바치다「give *one's* life〔sacrifice *oneself*〕for / ~을 부지하다 maintain〔sustain〕*one's* life / ~을 빌다 ask〔plead, appeal〕for *one's* life; beg *one's* life; 《포로 등이》ask for〔cry〕quarter / ~을 빼앗다 take《*a person's*》life; kill / ~을 빼앗기다 be〔get〕killed / ~을 살리다 spare〔save〕《*a person's*》life; save《*a person*》from death / ~을 소중히 여기다 value *one's* life; hold *one's* life dear / ~을 가벼이 여기다 slight *one's* life / ~을 아끼다 grudge *one's* life; be afraid of death / ~을 위태롭게 하다 endanger〔imperil〕《*a person's, one's*》life / ~을 이어가다 support *oneself;* keep on living; (manage to) keep body and soul together / ~을 잃다 lose *one's* life.

¶ 그녀는 부상을 입었지만 ~을 잃을 정도는 아니었다 Her injury was not fatal. *or* Though she was injured, she was not in danger of losing her life. / ~만은 살려주십시오 For mercy's sake, spare me! / 사람의 ~은 초로와 같다 Man's life is as transient as dew. / 수술 덕분에 ~을 건졌다 The success of the operation gave me a new lease of life. / 그는 호기심 때문에 하마터면 ~을 잃을 뻔했다 His curiosity nearly cost him his life. / 이 세상에서 사람의 ~만큼 중요한 것은 없다 Nothing in the world is more precious than human life. / 그는 술 때문에 ~을 잃었다 Drinking was the cause of his death. *or* He lost his life because of drinking.

**목쉬다** become hoarse〔husky〕; [사람이 주어] talk *oneself* hoarse. ¶ 목쉰 소리 a hoarse〔husky〕voice / 목쉰 소리로 huskily; hoarsely / 목이 쉬어 말이 안 나오다 be too hoarse to speak.

**목양**(牧羊) sheep breeding〔raising, farming〕. ◉ ~견 a sheep〔shepherd〕dog. ~신 a goat god; Pan. ~자 a sheep raiser; a shepherd; 《미》a sheepman; 《영》a sheep farmer. ~장 a sheeprun; a sheep range《미》.

**목양말**(木洋襪) cotton socks〔stockings〕.

**목요일**(木曜日) Thursday (생략 Thur(s).).

**목욕**(沐浴) bathing; a bath. ~하다 bathe; take〔have〕a bath; wash *oneself.* ¶ ~하기 좋아하다 be fond of bath / ~하러 가다 go to the (public) bath〔bathhouse〕/ ~시키다 give《a baby》a bath; bathe《a baby》/ 하루 두 번 ~하다 take two baths a day. ◉ ~간〔실〕a bathroom. ~값〔비, 료〕a bathhouse charge. ~물 (hot) water for a bath; bath water: ~물을 데우다 heat the bath / ~물이 준비됐다 The bath is ready. ~재계 ablutions: ~ 재계하다 perform〔make〕*one's* ablutions; purify *oneself.* ~탕 a bathhouse; a public bath. ~통 a bathtub: ~통에 들어가다 soak in a bathtub; sink into a bath.

**목우**(木偶) a wooden figure〔doll〕; a wooden image〔statue, idol〕.

**목운동**(―運動) a neck exercise.

**목자**(牧者) ① 《양치는》a shepherd. ② 《목사》a pastor; a minister; a clergyman.

**목잠**(木簪) an ornamental wooden hairpin.

**목잠기다** hoarsen; lose *one's* voice; grow〔go, become〕hoarse.

**목장**(牧場) a ranch《미》; a stock farm; a pasture; a meadow.

> (용법) **stock farm, ranch**「소·말·양 따위를 사육하는 농장」이란 뜻이지만, ranch는 미국에 있는「대규모의 농장」을 말하며, 또「특정 가축의 사육장」이란 뜻도 있다. **pasture**「가축을 방목(放牧)하는 목장」, **meadow**「건초용 목초 재배지」란 뜻.

¶ ~ 일꾼 a ranch hand; a cowhand / ~을 경영하다 conduct〔run〕a ranch / ~에 놓아 기르다 put〔send, turn (out)〕《cattle》to pasture / ~에서 일하다 work on a ranch〔stock farm〕; ranch / ~ 여기저기에서 소들이 한가로이 풀을 뜯고 있다 Cows are grazing peacefully here and there in the pasture. ◉ ~주인 the owner of a stock farm; 《미》a cattleman; a rancher; a ranchman.

**목재**(木材) wood; 《제재한》lumber《미》; timber《영》; 《통나무》a log; 《각목》square lumber. ◉ ~공업 the lumber industry. ~벌채업 lumbering. ~벌채인부 a timberman; 《미》a lumberman; a lumberjack. ~상 a lumber〔timber〕merchant. ~소 a sawmill; a timber mill. ~운반선(船) a lumber carrier. ~저장소 a lumberyard; a woodyard.

**목적**(目的) a purpose; an aim; an

object; an objective; 《목표》 a goal; an end; 《의도》 an intention.

> 용법 **purpose** 명확한 의도와 강한 결의를 수반하는 목적을 나타내는 가장 일반적인 말. **object** 특정한 행위나 노력의 대상이 되는 구체적인 사항, 목표를 강조하는 말. **goal** 「결승점」이란 뜻에서 전화(轉化)된 낱말로, 노력과 인내에 의해 도달하는 목표. **end** 「최종 목표」, 동기에 중점을 둔 낱말로서, 잘 짜여진 계획과 수단으로 도달하게 되는 목적을 말한다. means(수단)와 상대되는 말. **aim** 어떤 계획, 행동에 의해 실현하려는 구체적인 명확한 목표를 나타내는 말.

¶ ～과 수단 ends and means / ～이 없는 aimless; purposeless / 확고한 ～ a fixed 〔set〕 purpose / 공동의 ～ a common cause.

목적에: ～에 맞다 answer 〔be fit for〕 the purpose; serve *one's* purpose; suit *one's* end / ～에 맞지 않다 be unfit for the purpose.

목적으로: …할 ～으로 with the object 〔intention〕 of 《*do*ing》; with a view 〔an eye〕 to 《*do*ing》; with the view of 《*do*ing》; for the purpose of 《*do*ing》; in a bid 《to》 / 군사상의 ～으로 for military purposes / 이러한 ～으로 for this purpose; to this end; with this (end) in view / 무슨 ～으로 what for?; for what purpose / …을 ～으로 하다 aim 《at》; have 《*something*》 for *one's* object / 생명 보험금을 탈 ～으로 남편을 독살하다 poison *one's* husband in a bid to collect *his* life insurance money.

목적을: ～을 갖다 have an object; have an end in view / ～을 달하다〔이루다〕 achieve 〔carry out〕 *one's* aim 〔purpose〕; accomplish *one's* purpose; attain *one's* object; succeed in *do*ing 〔*something*〕; gain *one's* end / ～을 바꾸다〔바꾸지 않다〕 change 〔stick to〕 *one's* purpose / ～을 벗어나다 wander from *one's* purpose / ～을 정하다 set up a purpose / …을 ～으로 하다 aim at ...; have 《*a thing*》 for *one's* object / ～에 들어맞다 answer the purpose; serve *one's* purpose(s) 〔end(s)〕.

¶ 본협회의 ～은 …에 있다 The object of the association shall be...; The association has for its object.... / 그것은 ～한 것과 다르다 It is unfit for the purpose. / 발표할 ～으로 쓴 것은 아니다 This was written with no eye for publication. / 그는 확고한 ～이 있어 한 것은 아니다 He did not do it on set purpose. / ～은 수단을 정당화한다 The end justifies the means. / 인생의 참다운 ～은 무엇인가 What is the real aim of life? / 그는 무슨 ～으로 여기에 왔는가 What has he come here for? / 그녀는 언어학을 연구할 ～으로 이 대학에 왔다 She came to this college for the purpose of studying linguistics. / 아무런 ～없이 대학에 입학하는 학생들이 많다 Many students enter college without any purpose 〔aim〕. / 대체 무슨 ～으로 그런 짓을 하느냐 What on earth do you do such a thing?

◉ ～격 〚문법〛 the objective case. ～론 〚철학〛 teleology. ～물 the object (matter). ～세 an object tax; a special purpose tax. ～어 an object (to a verb): 간접〔직접〕 ～어 〚문법〛 an indirect 〔a direct〕 object. ～의식 a sense of purpose: 그는 분명한 ～ 의식을 가지고 그 캠프에 참가하였다 He took part in the camp with a clear sense of purpose. ～지 *one's* destination; *one's* journey's end; the 〔*one's*〕 goal: ～지에 도달하다 arrive at *one's* destination; reach the end of *one's* journey.

**목전**(目前) ¶ ～의 before 〔under〕 *one's* eyes; immediate; imminent / ～의 위험 an imminent danger / ～에 under 〔before〕 *one's* nose 〔eyes〕; in *one's* presence / 시험을〔선거를〕 ～에 두고 with the examination 〔election〕 just before *one* 〔near at hand〕 / …의 ～에서 in the presence of...; before 〔under〕 *one's* very eyes / ～에 닥치다 be near 〔close〕 at hand; be imminent; be just ahead / ～의 이익을 꾀하다〔좇다〕 seek immediate gain; be after 「immediate profit 〔quick profit〕; adopt a short-sighted policy / ～의 일밖에 생각 못하다 take only a shortsighted view of things / 시험을 ～에 두고 맹렬히 공부하다 study hard with the examination close at hand.

**목정**(木精) methanol ⇨ 메탄올.

**목젖** the uvula (*pl.* ～s, -lae).

**목제**(木製) ¶ ～의 made of wood; wooden / 이 책상은 ～이다 This is a wooden desk. *or* This desk is made of wood.

◉ ～인형 a wooden doll. ～품 wooden ware 〔articles〕; wood products; woodwork.

**목조**(木造) ¶ ～의 built 〔made〕 of wood; wooden / 그의 집은 ～다 His house is built of wood. ◉ ～가옥〔건물〕 a wooden house; 《미》 a frame house 〔building〕. ～건축 a wooden building.

**목조르기** 〖레슬링〗 a nelson; strangle-hold (반칙).

**목줄** (낚시의) a snell; a leader 《미》.

**목줄기** ⇨ 목덜미.

**목질**(木質) ¶ ～의 woody; ligneous. ◉ ～부 the wood; the woody parts 《of a plant》; 〖식물〗 the xylem. ～섬유 woody fiber. ～조직 woody tissue. ～화(化) lignification.

**목찌르다** stab 《*a person*》 in the throat; pierce *a person's* neck. 「레 ③.

**목차**(目次) (a table of ) contents. ⇨ 차

**목책**(木柵) 《set up》 a wooden fence 〔barricade〕 《around》.

**목청** ① 《성대》 the vocal cords. ¶ ～을 울리다 vibrate the vocal cords. ② 《목소리》 *one's* voice. ¶ ～껏 《call》 at the top of *one's* voice / ～이 좋다 have a lovely 〔sweet〕 voice / ～이 나쁘다 have a poor voice / ～을 돋우다 raise 〔lift (up)〕 *one's* voice; raise *one's* pitch / 그녀는 도와달라고 ～껏 외쳤다 She 「cried out 〔shouted, screamed〕 for help at the top of her voice.

**목초**(牧草) grass; pasture; pasturage. ¶ 그들은 ～를 찾아 가축과 함께 이동한다 They move with their livestock following the grazing. ◉ ～지 a pasture; pasture land; grassland; a meadow: 소가 ～지에서 풀을 뜯어 먹고 있다 The cattle are grazing in the pasture.

**목축**(牧畜) stock raising 〔farming〕; livestock farming; cattle breeding. ～하다 raise 〔rear〕 livestock; raise cattle; engage in stock-farming. ◉ ～시대 the pastoral age. ～업 stock=farming; cattle-breeding: ～업자 a stock farmer; a cattle breeder; a grazier; 《미》 a rancher; a ranchman. ～지대 cattle land.

**목측**(目測) eye 〔visual〕 measurement. ～하다 measure with the eye. ¶ ～을 잘못하다 measure 《the length》 wrongly by eye; fail to measure the exact distance with *one's* eye / 아무의 신장을 ～하다 measure *a person's* height with the eye / 그 나무의 높이는 ～으로 약 8미터는 된다 The tree is about eight meters tall by eye measurement. ◉ ～거리 distance measured with the eye.

**목침**(木枕) a wooden pillow.

**목탁**(木鐸) ① 〖불교〗 a 「woodblock 〔wooden〕 gong 《in a Buddhist temple》. ¶ ～을 두드리다 sound 〔beat〕 a wooden gong. ② 《사회의》 a leader; a teacher; a guide of the public. ¶ 사회의 ～이 되다 become a leader of society 〔the public〕 / 사회의 ～이 되어야 할 신문 the press that should lead the public.

**목탄**(木炭) ① 《숯》 charcoal. ② 〖미술〗 《a pencil of 》 charcoal fusain. ◉ ～가스 charcoal gas. ～지 charcoal paper. ～화 《draw》 a charcoal (drawing); a fusain.

**목판**(木板) 《음식을 나르는》 a wooden tray 〔platter〕; 《널판》 a board. ◉ ～차 《무개 화차》 an open wagon.

**목판**(木版) a wood (printing) block; an engraving woodblock. ¶ ～으로 인쇄하다 make a print from a woodblock. ◉ ～본 《책》 a book printed from woodblocks. ～인쇄 (wood-)block printing: ～인쇄의 block-printed 《cards》. ～조각 wood engraving; woodcutting; xylography. ～화 a woodcut; a (wood-)block print; a woodprint: 채색 ～화 a colored wood print.

**목포수**(一砲手) a hunter lying in wait for animals.

**목표**(目標) 《표지》 a mark; a sign; 《표적》 a target; 《목적》 an aim; a goal; an object; an objective. ～하다 aim 《at, to》; have 《*something*》 in *one's* mind. ¶ 장기～ a long-range objective; a long-term aim / 이달의 판매 ～ our sales target for this month / …을 ～로 《study》 for …; 《study hard》 with an eye 〔a view〕 《to becoming a lawyer》 / …을 ～로 하다 take aim at…; have… as *one's* object / ～에 맞춰 놓다 put 《the spacecraft》 on target / 좋은 ～가 되다 present a fine target 《for》 / ～에 달하다 reach 〔attain〕 the goal / ～에 미달하다 be wide 〔short〕 of the goal / ～를 정하다 set a goal / 10% 증산을 ～로 하다 set a goal of ten percent increase in production / ～를 높은 데 두다 aim high; set *one's* sights high / 그들은 예정보다 빨리 ～를 달성했다 They attained their goal ahead of time. / 생산고는 당초 ～에 미달하였다 The output failed to reach the target we had set first. / 소방서를 ～로 이 길을 곧바로 가세요 Please go straight on this street with the fire station for your guide. / 「너의 장래 ～는 무엇이냐」―「어머니와

같은 훌륭한 교사가 되는 것이다」 "What is your goal in the future?"—"To be an outstanding teacher like my mother."
◉ ～기일《계획 등의》《set》 a target date. ～숫자 a target figure. ～시간《계획 등의》 target time. ～액 the target; the goal: 월생산 ～액 the target for monthly output / ～액을 돌파하다 pass the target; exceed the goal. ～연도 the goal year. ～일《공사 따위》 the target day. ～지점 『군사』 the target spot; the objective 〔an aiming〕 point: ～ 지점에 정확하게 착륙하다 land (right) on target; make an accurate 〔on-target〕 landing. ～탑《비행장의》 a pylon.

**목하**(目下) now; at present; at the (present) moment. ¶ ～의 급무(急務) an urgent necessity of the day; a pressing need of the hour.

**목형**(木型) a wooden model 〔form, pattern〕. ◉ ～공 a patternmaker.

**목화**(木花) cotton; cotton wool 《미》; raw cotton; a cotton plant. ¶ ～를 따다 pick cotton 《from a cotton plant》 / ～를 틀다, ～씨를 빼다 gin cotton. ◉ ～꽃 a cotton flower. ～송이 a cotton ball. ～씨 a cottonseed. ～재배 cotton growing.

**몫** ① [일반적] a share; a portion; a cut 《구어》; a quota (책임분); an allotment (할당분); a split 《구어》. ¶ 내 몫 my share / 세 몫으로 나누다 divide 〔split〕 into three portions / 한몫 차지하다 take a share; get a rake=off / 한몫 끼다 have a share 《in》; share 《in the profits》 / 한몫 주다 give a share 《to》 / 자기 몫을 요구하다 claim *one's* share 《in the profits》 / 부당하게 몫을 차지하다 take an excessive share 〔a lion's share〕 / 동생 몫으로 남겨두다 leave a portion aside for *one's* brother / 내 몫을 줘 Give me my share. / 이것이 자네 몫의 전부다 This much has fallen to your lot. / 각자 자기몫을 받았다 A share was allotted to each.
② 『수학』 the quotient (생략 q.). ¶ 6 나누기 3의 몫은 얼마냐 What is the quotient of 6 divided by 3?

**몫몫이** each 〔every〕 share 〔portion〕; into shares 〔portions〕; share by share. ¶ ～ 공평히 나누다 divide into equal shares / ～ 차지하다 take each *one's* own share.

**몬순** 『기상』 a monsoon.

**몬태나** 《미국의 주》 Montana (생략 Mont.).

**몬트리올** 《캐나다의 도시》 Montreal. ¶ ～의정서 the Montreal Protocol.

**몰** 『화학』 a mol(e); a gram molecule.

**몰각하다**(沒却—) disregard; ignore; forget. ¶ 처음의 목적을 ～ forget 〔lose sight of〕 *one's* original object / 법의 정신이 몰각되어 있다 The spirit of the law is ignored.

**몰강스럽다** (be) cruel; brutal; harsh; pitiless.

**몰골** unshapeliness; shapelessness. ¶ ～사납다 be ill-shaped〔-formed〕; be unshapely 〔ungainly, shapeless, unseemly, indecent〕; be offensive to the eye / ～ 사나운 짓 unseemly 〔improper〕 behavior / ～ 사나운 복장을 하다 be shabbily dressed 《in》 / 이게 무슨 ～이냐 What a wretched state you are in! *or* How miserable you look!

**몰교섭**(沒交涉) ① 《교섭이 없음》 lack of relation. ¶ ～이다 have no connection with; have nothing to do with; be independent of; stand aloof from / 그는 사회와는 ～이다 He keeps aloof from society. ② 《무간섭》 noninterference; nonintervention.

**몰다** ① 《마소·차 따위를》 drive 《a car》; urge 《a horse》 on 《with a whip》. ¶ 소를 ～ drive a cow / 말을 마구간에 몰아넣다 drive a horse into a stable / 자동차〔마차〕를 ～ drive a car 〔horse-cart〕 / 자동차를 몰고 현장에 급히 달려가다 rush 〔hasten〕 to the scene in a car / 그는 자기 차를 몰고 출근한다 He drives his car to work.
② 《뒤쫓다》 pursue; chase 《after》; give a chase 《to》; run 〔go〕 after; hunt up; 《사냥개로》 course. ¶ 토끼를 ～ chase a hare / 물고기를 그물 안으로 ～ chase fish into a net.
③ 《궁지에》 corner; drive 《into》. ¶ 궁지〔막다른 골목〕에 ～ drive 《*a person*》 into a corner; drive 《*a person*》 to the wall; corner 《*a person*》.
④ 《죄인으로》 reproach; take to task; call to account; put 《*a person*》 hard to it; charge with; accuse of. ¶ 살인죄로 ～ charge 《*a person*》 with 〔accuse 《*a person*》 of〕 murder / 역적으로 ～ denounce 《*a person*》 as a traitor.

**몰두**(沒頭) absorption 《in》. ～하다 be devoted to; devote *oneself* to; give *oneself* up to; be absorbed 〔engrossed, immersed, lost, buried〕 in; immerse *oneself* 《in》. ¶ 그는 연구에 ～하고 있었다 He was absorbed 〔lost〕 in his research. *or* He gave himself up 〔devoted himself〕 to his research. /

그녀는 한평생 전쟁 고아를 돌보는 데 ~ 했다 She gave her whole life to taking care of war orphans.

**몰디브** 《인도양의 독립국》 Maldives.

**몰라보다** cannot 〔fail to〕 recognize; show no appreciation of. ¶ 몰라볼만큼 변하다 change beyond 〔out of〕 recognition; look as if 《he, it》 were another person 〔thing〕; be altered 〔transformed〕 beyond recognition / 몰라뵈서 죄송합니다 Pardon me, but I could not recognize you for the moment. *or* Sorry for not recognizing you sooner. / 오랫동안 만나지 않은 탓에 그를 몰라보았다 Since I hadn't seen him for a long time, I failed to recognize him. / 너무 달라져서 몰라보겠다 You have changed so much that I can hardly recognize you.

**몰락**(沒落) 《파멸》 a fall; ruin; (a) downfall; 《파산》 bankruptcy. ~하다 fall; go to ruin; go under; be ruined; 《파산하다》 go bankrupt. ¶ 집안의 ~ the ruin of *one's* family / 로마 제국의 ~ the fall of the Roman Empire / ~한 사람 a ruined person / ~시키다 ruin; bring 〔reduce〕 to ruin; put the skids under / 이것 때문에 그는 아주 ~해버리고 말았다 This has completed his ruin. / 그는 지금은 ~했지만 한때는 날렸다 He is now down-and-out, but he has seen better days.

**몰래** secretly; in secret; privately; stealthily; by stealth; quietly; furtively; on the quiet 〔sly〕 《구어》. ¶ 집안 사람 ~ without the knowledge of *one's* people 〔folks〕 / ~ 눈짓하다 give a furtive wink / ~ 도망치다 steal away; slip off 〔away〕 / ~ 뒤를 밟다 shadow 《*a person*》 stealthily / ~ 만나다 meet secretly; have a clandestine meeting / ~알려 주다 tell *a person* secretly 《about *a thing*》 / ~ 방을 나오다 slip out of the room / ~보다 steal a glance 〔look〕 《at》; cast a stealthy glance 《on》; look 〔glance〕 furtively 《at》 / ~ 빠져 나가다 get away by stealth; slip out; sneak out / ~ 읽다 read 《a letter》 by stealth / ~ 재미를 보다 take *one's* pleasure on the sly / 기차를 ~ 타다 steal a ride on a train / 그는 발소리를 죽이고 ~ 들어왔다 He came in with stealthy 〔noiseless〕 steps. ◉ ~카메라 a hidden camera.

**몰려가다** ① 《쫓겨감》 be driven 〔pushed, pressed〕. ¶ 소가 외양간으로 ~ A cow is driven toward a cowshed. ② 《떼지어감》 throng (to) 《a place》; flock 〔crowd, swarm, cluster〕 toward; go in flocks 〔crowds〕; storm 《a store》. ¶ 장터로 ~ flock toward the marketplace / 그 설교를 들으려고 사람들이 교회로 몰려갔다 People thronged the church to hear the sermon.

**몰려나다** ① 《쫓겨나다》 be expelled; be put 〔gotten, turned, sent, driven〕 out; 《지위에서》 be ousted; 《셋집에서》 be evicted 《from a rented house》. ¶ 회사에서 ~ be kicked out of a company / 동네에서 ~ be driven out of *one's* village; be ostracized by the village community. ② 《떼지어 나가다》 come (out) in crowds 〔flocks, swarms〕; turn out en masse.

**몰려다니다** ① 《쫓기어》 be driven 〔chased〕 about 〔around〕. ② 《떼지어》 move about 〔around〕 in crowds 〔flocks, swarms, packs, shoals〕. ¶ 애들이 ~ Children are loafing around in groups 〔bunches〕. / 물고기 떼가 ~ Fish move around in shoals.

**몰려들다** ① 《쫓겨오다》 be driven 〔chased, pressed, pushed〕 into. ② 《여럿이》 besiege 《a house》; crowd 《a house, into a house》; come in crowds 〔flocks〕; swarm; gather; throng to 《the door》. ¶ 방 안으로 ~ crowd into a room / 새떼가 나무에 ~ Birds flock to a tree / 손님들이 특매품을 구하려고 몰려들었다 Customers crowded in to look for bargains. / 군중이 좁은 길에 잔뜩 몰려 들었다 A crowd of people stuffed the narrow lane.

**몰려오다** ① 《쫓겨》 come driven 〔pushed, pressed, chased〕; be pushed 〔chased, driven, pressed〕 this way. ② 《떼지어》 come in flocks 〔crowds, swarms, packs, en masse〕; flock 〔crowd, swarm〕 this way. ¶ 우르르 ~ come swarming about / 사방에서 ~ flock from all 〔various〕 quarters / 여름이 되면 그곳에 많은 사람이 몰려 온다 In summer the place attracts many visitors. / 피난민들이 몰려온다 Refugees come pouring in.

**몰리다** ① 《밀리다》 be driven 〔pushed, pressed〕. ¶ 방 한 구석으로 ~ be driven into the corner of a room / 시간에 ~ be pressed for time / 일에 ~ be swamped 〔pressed, busy〕 with work / 집안일에 ~ be kept at domestic cares / (바둑 등에서) 초읽기에 ~ be pressed by countdown.
② 《쫓기다》 be pursued; be chased;

《사냥에서》 be hunted up; be coursed. ¶ 토끼가 개한테 ～ a rabbit is chased 〔hunted up, coursed〕 by a dog / 도둑이 막다른 골목으로 ～ a thief is driven into a blind alley.
③ 《어려운 처지에》 be pressed 〔pinched〕 for; be hard up for; be at a loss. ¶ 대답에 ～ be at a loss for an answer / 돈에 ～ be pressed for money / 자금에 ～ be hard up for funds.
④ 《죄로》 be accused of; be charged with; be blamed for. ¶ 살인죄로 몰리어 《be tried》 on a charge of murder / 역적으로 ～ be accused of 〔charged with〕 treason.
⑤ 《한 곳에》 come 〔get, draw〕 together; gather together; group 〔flock, crowd, swarm〕 together; cluster; throng; storm; surge. ¶ 사람이 한쪽으로 ～ people crowd to one side / 돈이 한 곳으로 ～ money flows into one place; money is poorly distributed / 사인을 받으려고 ～ crowd around 〔press around〕 《a famous singer》 for 《*his*》 autograph / 많은 군중이 경기장으로 몰렸다 A big crowd surged in the stadium.

**몰리브덴** 〖화학〗 molybdenum (기호 Mo). ◉ ～강(鋼) molybdenum steel. ～광(鑛) molybdenite.

**몰박다** put 〔fix〕 all in one place; group (together).

**몰사**(沒死) extinction; dying out. ～하다 become extinct; die out; cease to exist; be annihilated. ¶ ～ 직전에 있다 be (now) in danger of extinction / 산사태로 가족이 ～했다 The whole family was buried to death by a landslide.

**몰살**(沒殺) massacre; slaughter; annihilation; extermination. ～하다 massacre; kill to a man; annihilate; exterminate. ¶ 적을 ～하다 annihilate the enemy / 온 가족을 ～하다 murder the whole family.

**몰상식**(沒常識) lack of common sense; absurdity; thoughtlessness; senselessness. ～하다 have no common sense; (be) senseless; thoughtless; absurd. ¶ ～도 이만저만 아니다 be utterly absurd; be ridiculous / 그는 ～하다 He has no 〔is short of, is lacking in, lacks〕 common sense.

**몰수**(沒收) confiscation; forfeiture (과실·범죄등의 처벌로서); seizure (압수). ～하다 confiscate (국고에); forfeit; seize. ¶ ～되다 forfeit; be confiscated / 재산을 ～하다 confisate *a person's* property / ～를 면제받다 be exempt from confiscation / 부정행위로 취득한 토지를 ～당하다 forfeit the land *one* acquired by illegal means / 경찰은 밀수품을 즉각 ～ 했다 The police seized the smuggled goods immediately. / 그의 재산의 일부는 국가에 ～당했다 Part of his property was confiscated by the state. ◉ ～경기〔게임〕〖야구〗 a forfeited game. ～자 a confiscator; a seizor. ～품 a confiscated article 〔property〕; a forfeit(ure).

**몰식자**(沒食子) 〖한의〗 a gallnut. ◉ ～산(酸) 〖생화학〗 gallic acid.

**몰아**(沒我) self-effacement; selflessness; self-renunciation. ¶ ～적 self-effacing; selfless / ～의 경지에 이르다 rise above self; attain a state transcending self.

**몰아** (all) in all; all together; in a body; en masse (F.); in the aggregate; in a lump; as a whole 〔group〕; by the gross 〔lot〕; in bulk; collectively. ¶ 한데 ～서 《전부》 altogether; in the gross 〔lump〕; on the whole; 《포함》 including; inclusive of / 일주일치 식료품을 ～사다 buy food in bulk for the whole week.

**몰아가다** ① 《몰고 감》 drive (away). ¶ 소를 들로 ～ drive a cow out to pasture / 바람이 구름을 ～ a wind drives clouds away 〔along〕 / 말을 급히 ～ urge a horse forward 〔on〕 / 자살로 ～ drive 《*a person*》 to 〔to commit〕 suicide. ② 《휩쓸어 감》 take away in bulk 〔en masse, by the lot〕; buy 《*things*》 as a lot. ¶ 가게의 연필을 ～ take away 〔buy up〕 all the pencils a store has.

**몰아내다** ① 《내쫓다》 drive 〔press, push, shove〕 out; turn 〔send, put〕 out; rout; 《구어》 kick 〔throw〕 《*a person*》 out; bounce 《미》; 《지위에서》 oust 〔expel〕 《*a person* from a position》; 《셋집 등에서》 evict 〔eject〕 《a tenant》 from 《the house》; ostracize (추방). ¶ 교장 자리에서 ～ oust 《*a person*》 from the position of principal / 방에서 ～ put 《*a person*》 out of the room; show 《*a person*》 the door; turn 《*a person*》 out-of-doors / 관사에서 ～ evict 《*a person*》 from an official residence / 왕을 왕위에서 ～ dethrone a king / 반대파를 몰아내려고 하다 try to oust the objectors 《from》. ② 《사냥에서》 chase 〔hunt〕 out; run 《a hare》 (down). ¶ 사냥개가 사슴을 숲에서 ～ a hound chases a deer out of the bush.

**몰아넣다** ①《안으로》 drive in(to); press 〔push, chase〕 in(to). ¶ 방안으로 ~ push 《*a person*》 into a room / 닭을 닭장 안으로 ~ drive the chickens into the henhouse. ②《궁지에》 corner; get 〔drive〕 into a (tight) corner; put into a fix. ¶ 궁지에 ~ corner 《*a person*》; drive 《*a person*》 into a corner; drive 《*a person*》 to the wall / 우리는 드디어 용의자를 막다른 골목에 몰아넣었다 We finally tracked 〔ran〕 down the suspect in a blind ally. ③《한데》 put 〔push, press, cram, jam〕 all into. ¶ 학생을 한 교실에 ~ put 〔cram〕 all the students into one classroom. ④《전쟁 따위에》 draw 〔drag〕 《a nation》 into 《a war》.

**몰아대다** ①《막 해냄》 squelch; talk 〔put, get〕 《*a person*》 down; give 《*a person*》 a setdown; refute; blame; call to account 〔task〕. ¶ 약속 불이행을 ~ reproach 《*a person*》 for breaking *his* promise. ②《재촉》 drive 〔press〕 hard; urge 〔spur〕 on; hasten 《*a person*》. ¶ 돈 내라고 ~ press 《*a person*》 for payment of money / 일을 빨리 하라고 ~ press 《*a person*》 「to make a quick job of it 〔to speed up the work〕.

**몰아들이다** ① drive in(to); chase in(to). ⇨ 몰아넣다. ②《휩쓸어》 take all in bulk; buy up the (whole) lot. ¶ 장터의 쌀을 몽땅 ~ buy up all the rice in the marketplace.

**몰아받다** ①《한꺼번에》 receive 〔get〕 《it》 all at one time 〔in a lump〕. ¶ 빚을 ~ collect the debt in a lump sum. ②《도맡아》 receive all 《as a representative of other people》; engross; monopolize. ¶ 수석 학생이 동급생의 졸업장을 몰아받는다 The top student receives the diplomas on behalf of his classmates.

**몰아붙이다** ①《한쪽으로》 put 〔push, press〕 《it》 all to one side. ¶ 서류를 책상 한 편에 ~ shove papers off to one side of the desk. ②《한 곳에》 put 〔fix, stick, paste, post〕 《it》 all in one place. ¶ 게시를 벽 한 구석에 ~ put up 〔post〕 all the notices in one corner of a wall.

**몰아사다** buy in a lump 〔in the aggregate〕; buy in bulk 〔quantity〕.

**몰아세우다** 《훌닦다》 berate; blame heavily; take 《*a person*》 to task; call to account; put hard to it; give 《*a person*》 a hard time (of it). ¶ 잘못했다고 ~ give 《*a person*》 a hard time (of it) over *his* mistake / 빚을 빨리 갚지 않는다고 ~ berate 《*a person*》 for the delay in paying *his* debt / 자식을 명문 대학에 들어가라고 몰아세우는 것은 부모의 이기심이다 It's egoistic of parents to press their children to go to a famous university.

**몰아오다** ① [자동사적] 《한꺼번에》 come all at one time. ¶ 오랜 가뭄 끝에 큰비가 몰아왔다 There was a heavy rain all at one time after a long spell of dry weather. ② [타동사적] 《몰고 옴》 drive; chase; rush 《along》; 《휩쓸어 옴》 take 〔buy up〕 the whole lot. ¶ 바람이 소낙비를 ~ a wind brings a shower along.

**몰아주다** 《한꺼번에》 give 《it》 〔pay 《it》 up〕 all at once; give 〔pay up〕 the whole amount. ¶ 1년 생활비를 ~ give 《*a person*》 the living expenses for one year in a lump sum.

**몰아치다** ①《바람 등이》 blow against 〔on〕; blow hard; rage; storm. ¶ 바람이 몰아치는 언덕 a wind-swept height / 밤새도록 폭풍이 몰아쳤다 A storm raged all night. ②《한꺼번에》 do 《work》 all at once; do in one sweep 〔swoop〕. ¶ 밀린 일을 ~ get caught up on *one's* work in one big push / 시험 공부를 ~ cram for an examination. ③《몰아붙이다》 put all to one side 〔in one place〕.

**몰약**(沒藥) myrrh.

**몰염치**(沒廉恥) = 파렴치.

**몰이** chasing; beating 《out》; running. ~하다 chase; beat; hunt out 〔up〕; run 《a fox》 (down). ◉ ~꾼 a chaser; a beater. ~포수 a chaser (in hunting).

**몰이해**(沒理解) lack of understanding 〔sympathy〕. ¶ ~한 unfeeling; heartless; unsympathizing.

**몰인정**(沒人情) want of sympathy; heartlessness. ~하다 (be) cruel; pitiless; ruthless; inhuman; cold-hearted; heartless. ¶ ~한 사람 a heartless 〔an unfeeling〕 person; a brute / ~한 짓을 하다 act 〔behave〕 callously; treat 《*a person*》 cruelly / 나는 저렇게 ~한 짓은 못 하겠다 It is not in my nature 〔I was not born〕 to do such a cruel thing.

**몰입**(沒入) ①《몰두》 absorption 《in》. ~하다 be absorbed 〔immersed〕 in 《*one's* work》; devote *oneself* 《to》. ¶ 일

에 ～하다 be absorbed [immersed] in *one's* work / 그 청년은 사색에 ～하고 있었다 The young man was absorbed in thought. ② 《몰수》 confiscation; seizure; forfeiture. ～하다 confiscate; seize; forfeit.

**몰지각**(沒知覺) indiscretion; thoughtlessness. ～하다 (be) indiscreet; thoughtless; senseless.

**몰취미**(沒趣味) lack of taste; tastelessness. ～하다 be lacking in taste; (be) tasteless; insipid; dull. ¶ ～한 사람 a man of no taste; a prosaic man / ～하게 장식된 방 a room furnished in very poor taste.

**몰타** 《지중해의 섬나라》 Malta.

**몰풍치**(沒風致) tastelessness; lack of artistic effect. ～하다 (be) tasteless; unpleasing; unstimulating; be lacking in artistic effect.

**몰하다**(歿—) die; pass away. ⇨ 죽다.

**몰후**(歿後) after *a person's* death.

**몸** ① 《몸뚱이》 the body; 《골격》 frame; 《체격》 physique; build; 《체질》 constitution; 《자기》 oneself; 《육체·살》 flesh. ¶ 몸의 bodily; physical / 몸의 구조[발육] the bodily structure [development] / 몸 둘 바를 모르다 do not know what to do with oneself.

몸이: 몸이 큰 big; large; big-bodied; largesized; of large build / 몸이 큰 남자 a man of large build / 몸이 작은 small(-sized); short / 몸이 비대한 fat; stout; corpulent / 몸이 가냘픈 thin; slender; slim(-figured) / 몸이 나다 grow fat; put on weight / 몸이 단단[튼튼]하다 have a strong constitution [frame, physique]; have a solid build; be sturdy; be strong / 몸이 약하다 have a weak constitution [frame, physique]; be delicately built; be physically weak [delicate, puny] / 몸이 좋다 be well-built / 몸이 건장하다 have a sturdy constitution; be of sturdy build; be husky / 몸이 나른하다 feel tired and languid / 몸이 감당 못 하다 be not physically strong enough 《to *do*》 / 몸이 가루가 되도록 일하다 work like a bee; work assiduously [laboriously].

몸에: 온 몸에 on all over (the body); from head to foot / 몸에 걸치다 put on; wrap *oneself* in / 몸에 지니다 have [keep] 《*a thing*》 on *one's* person; carry 《*a thing*》 about [on] *one*; wear 《a gun》 / 몸에 맞다 《옷이》 fit *one;* 《기후 등이》 suit *one;* agree with *one* / 몸에 손대다 touch *a person's* body.

몸을: 몸을 씻다[닦다] wash [dry] *oneself* / 몸을 굽히다 bend *one's* body forward / 침대에 몸을 펴고 눕다 lie (at) full length on the bed / 몸을 단련하다 strengthen [harden] *one's* body; build up *one's* body / 몸을 더럽히다 《여자가》 lose her chastity [purity]; stain her virtue / 몸을 던지다 throw *oneself* into / 몸을 떨다 shiver 《with cold》; tremble 《for fear》; quiver 《with emotion》; shudder 《with terror》 / 몸을 망치다[그르치다] ruin *oneself;* go astray / 몸을 맡기다 give *oneself* up 《to》; place *oneself* at 《*a person's*》 disposal; put *oneself* into 《*a person's*》 hands / 몸을 바치다 devote *oneself* [*one's* life] to; sacrifice *oneself* [*one's* life]; 《여자가》 give herself to 《a man》 / 몸을 붙일 곳이 없다 have nobody to turn to (for help); have no place to go / 몸을 숨기다 conceal [hide] *oneself* / 몸을 쉬다 have [take] a rest; rest (*oneself*) / 몸을 쓰다듬다 stroke [pat, caress] 《*a person's*》 body / 몸을 아끼다 spare *oneself* [*one's* efforts] / 몸을 의지하다 lean [rely] on; find shelter with 《*a person*》; stay with 《*a person*》 / 몸을 팔다 sell *oneself* 《into slavery》; sell *herself;* prostitute *oneself* / 몸을 편안히 하다 make *oneself* comfortable; ease *oneself* / 몸을 허락하다 surrender her chastity to 《a man》; give [submit] *herself* to 《a man》.

¶ 몸이 두 개라도 모자란다 I am too busy even if I had two bodies. / 그녀는 홀몸이 아니다 《임신중》 She is with child [in the family way]. / 운동을 하고 났더니 온몸이 쑤시고 아팠다 I had aches and pains all over after physical exercise. / 이 옷은 몸에 맞는다 This coat fits me. *or* This coat is a good fit for me. 《미》 / 기름진 음식은 내 몸에 맞지 않는다 Greasy food doesn't agree with me. / 그녀의 몸의 곡선은 아름답다 She is built with beautiful curves.

② 《몸통》 the body; the trunk (of the body). ¶ 여자 머리에 사자 몸을 가진 괴물 a monster having a woman's head and a lion's body; 〚그神〛 《스핑크스》 the Sphinx.

③ 《건강》 health; 《체질》 constitution.

몸이: 몸이 건강하다 be in good health; be quite well; be [feel] fit / 몸이 나빠지다 break down in health; injure *one's* health / 몸이 아프다 be sick [ill];

《구어》 be out of sorts; be in a bad way / 몸이 약해지다 become weak; be run down; *one's* health fails / 몸이 좋아지다 get well 〔better〕; improve in health / 몸이 좋지 않다 feel unwell / 몸이 회복되다 be well again; be restored to health; regain *one's* health.
몸을: 몸을 상하다 injure 〔lose〕 *one's* health; make *oneself* ill (무리하여) / 몸을 조심하다 be careful about *one's* health; take good care of *oneself;* pay attention to *one's* health / 몸을 회복하다 regain 〔recover〕 *one's* health; be restored to health; get well again.
몸에: 몸에 좋다〔나쁘다〕 be good 〔bad〕 for the health; be wholesome 〔unwholesome〕; be beneficial 〔injurious〕 to *one's* health.
¶ 이렇게 바빠서는 몸이 지탱 못한다 I cannot stand such a strain of business. / 그는 몸이 완전히 회복되지 않았다 He has not recovered completely. / 담배는 몸에 해롭다 Smoking is bad for your health. / 그는 과음으로 몸을 망쳤다 He ruined his health by drinking too much.
④《습관》¶ 몸에 익다 be accustomed to; be familiar with / 일이 몸에 배다 be accustomed to a job; be used to work / 재산이 몸에 붙지 않다 be a stranger to money; be doomed to poverty.
⑤《신분》 *one's* status;《사람》 a person; a personage. ¶ 귀한 몸 a high personage; a person of high rank 〔of noble birth〕; an important figure / 천한 몸 a person of low 〔humble〕 birth / 종의 몸 *one's* status as a slave; a slave / 첩의 몸에서 난 아들 a son begotten by a concubine.
⑥《월경》 menstruation; the menses. ¶ 몸을 하다 menstruate. ⇨몸하다.
⑦《도자기의》 pottery which remains to be glazed; a raw-clay pot.

**몸가짐** 《품행》 behavior; morals; conduct; 《행동》 action. ¶ ～을 조심하다 be prudent in *one's* conduct / ～이 얌전하다〔좋다〕 behave well; behave *oneself* / ～이 점잖다 have gentlemanly behavior; behave like a gentleman / ～이 나쁘다 be ill-conducted; misconduct *oneself;* lead a loose life; be loose in *one's* behavior / ～이 좋지 않은 사내 a man of loose morals / ～을 바르게 해라 Behave yourself!

**몸가축** taking care of *one's* personal appearance; keeping *oneself* neat. ～하다 pay attention to personal appearance; take care of *one's* personal appearance; keep *oneself* neat.

**몸값** money paid for a person sold as a slave-servant 〔prostitute〕 (인신 매매의); (a) ransom. ¶ ～을 요구하다 demand a ransom 《for a hostage》 / ～을 지급하다 pay the ransom 《for》 / ～을 치르고 빼내다 redeem 《*a person*》 by paying the ransom / 그들은 승객을 인질로 ～을 요구했다 They held the passengers to 〔for〕 ransom.

**몸꼴** *one's* figure 〔build〕; 《체격》 physique; frame; make; construction. ¶ ～이 건장한 strongly-built; 《men》 of robust build / ～이 가냘프다 be slight of build.

**몸나다** grow fat 〔corpulent, portly, stout〕; put on weight 〔flesh〕; fatten.

**몸닦달** training *oneself;* hardening *one's* body; inuring *oneself;* self-discipline. ～하다 train 〔inure〕 *oneself* 《to》.

**몸단장**(一丹粧) decorating 〔embellishing〕 *oneself*. ～하다 dress 〔equip〕 *oneself;* outfit *oneself*. ¶ 그녀는 서둘러 ～을 하였다 She dressed herself in a hurry. / 나는 리셉션을 위해 ～을 했다 I got myself ready for the reception.

**몸달다** be impatient 《at, for》; be irritated 《at, by, with》; fret 〔fidget〕 《about》; be in a fret 〔fidget〕 《about, over》; be eager 《for victory, to make up the loss》. ¶ 몸달게 하다 give 《*a person*》 the fidgets / 실패는 그를 몹시 몸달게 했다 His failure really irritated him. / 젊은이들은 빨리 출발하고 싶어 몸달아 했다 Young men were impatient to start at once.

**몸담다** participate in; be concerned in; concern *oneself* in 〔with〕; take part in; have a hand in; 《종사하다》 engage *oneself* in. ¶ 그는 부동산업에 몸담고 있다 He is concerned with the real estate business. / 그녀는 교직에 몸담고 있다 She engages herself in teaching.

**몸두다** stay 〔live〕 in; take shelter with. ¶ 몸둘 곳이 없다 have no place to live 〔stay〕 in; do not know where to put *oneself* / (부끄러워) 몸둘 바를 모르겠습니다 I am deeply ashamed of myself. *or* I really don't know where to look.

**몸때** 《월경 때》 the time of menstruation; the menstrual period.

**몸뚱이** the body; frame. ⇨몸.

**몸매** *one's* figure 〔shape, form, carriage〕. ¶ 균형 잡힌 ～ a well-proportioned figure 〔form〕/ 날씬한 ～ a slender figure / ～가 예쁘다 have a nice 〔good〕 figure.

**몸받다** take upon *oneself* 《the task of a superior》.

**몸보신**(—補身) invigorating 〔nurturing〕 *one's* body; restoring health of the body. ～하다 invigorate *one's* body. ¶ ～약 a tonic medicine.

**몸부림** writhing; kicking and screaming; struggle; wriggle. ～하다〔치다〕 struggle; writhe (in agony); wriggle; flounder; be convulsed 《with pain》. ¶ 괴로워서 ～치다 writhe in a desperate agony / 아무리 ～쳐도 소용없다 It's no use struggling and writhing. / 나는 결박을 벗어나려고 ～ 쳤다 I struggled to free myself from my bonds.

**몸살** illness from fatigue 〔exhaustion〕; general fatigue (from overwork). ¶ ～이 나다 suffer from fatigue; fall in from overwork / ～로 눕다 take to *one's* bed from fatigue. ◉ ～풀이 rest.

**몸서리** 《무섭거나 혼이나서》 a shudder; a shiver; shuddering; 《싫증으로》 being sick of. ～나다〔치다〕 shudder 《at, with》; shiver 《with cold》; tremble 《with fear》; be sick (and tired) 《of hearing her complaints》. ¶ (공포 따위로) ～나는〔쳐지는〕 frightful; terrible; horrible; shocking / 듣기만 해도 ～나다 shudder at the mere mention 〔thought〕 of 《*a person's* voice》/ 이제 그 일엔 ～가 난다 I am sick and tired of that business. / 생각만 해도 ～ 난다 The mere thought of it makes me shudder. / 그것은 ～쳐지는 광경이었다 It was a frightful 〔shocking〕 scene.

**몸소** personally; in person; (by) *oneself*. ¶ ～ 방문하다 make a personal call 《on, at》/ ～ 지휘하다 take 〔assume〕 personal command 《of》; be in personal command 《of》/ ～ 지도하다 take personal direction / ～가다 go (by) *oneself* / ～해라 Do it for yourself. / 그는 부하들에게 ～ 시범을 보였다 He personally set an example to his inferiors.

**몸수색**(—搜索) a body-searching; a frisk(ing). ～하다 search; frisk. ¶ 감춘 무기가 없는지 ～을 하다 search 《*a person*》 for a hidden weapon.

**몸쓰다** perform a feat.

**몸엣것** 《월경》 menstrual blood 〔discharge, flow〕.

**몸있다** menstruate; have *one's* period.

**몸져눕다** be confined to bed with a serious illness; be bedridden; take to *one's* bed; be ill 〔sick〕 in bed.

**몸조리**(—調理) care of health; recuperation (병후의). ～하다 take good care 〔be careful〕 of *one's* health; recuperate 〔recruit〕 *oneself* (병후에). ¶ 산후의 ～ postpartum care / ～하기 위하여 for (the good of) *one's* health; for recuperation / ～를 안하다 be careless of 〔neglect〕 *one's* health.

**몸조심**(—操心) 《건강을 위해》 taking care of *oneself;* being cautious about *one's* health; 《언행을》 behaving *oneself;* being cautious about *one's* behavior. ～하다 《건강을 위해》 take care of *oneself;* 《언행을》 behave *oneself.*

**몸종** a lady's personal maidservant.

**몸주체** body control; handling *oneself;* taking care of *oneself.* ¶ 늙어서 자기 ～를 못하다 be too old and feeble to take care of *oneself.*

**몸집** the body; the frame; the bulk; *one's* build. ¶ ～이 크다 be big of frame; be large-limbed / 작은〔큰〕 ～ small 〔large〕 stature 〔build〕/ ～이 큰 녀석 such a bulky fellow / ～이 호리호리한 소녀 a girl of slender frame / ～이 통통하다 be pudgy / ～이 뚱뚱하다 be fat 〔stout, portly〕/ ～이 가냘프다 be slim; be of slender build / 그는 ～이 건장하다 He has a strong build.

**몸짓** a gesture; (a) gesticulation; (a) motion. ～하다 make gestures; gesticulate; move *one's* body; motion. ¶ 과장된 ～으로 with exaggerated 〔dramatic, expansive〕 gestures / ～으로 나타내다 express 《*oneself*》 by gesture 〔in pantomime〕; gesture 《the size of a box》/ ～으로 흉내내다 imitate by gesture; mimic with gestures / ～을 섞어 설명하다 accompany *one's* explanation with actions; use (a lot of) gestures when 《he》 explains / ～으로 가라고〔앉으라고〕 하다 motion 《*a person*》 away 〔to a seat〕/ 그 댄서의 ～은 우아하다 The dancer has graceful motions. / 그는 과장된 ～으로 이야기했다 He spoke with large 〔exaggerated〕 gestures. / 그는 ～으로 찬성을〔반대를〕 표시했다 He signaled assent 〔dissent〕. / 그는 일어설 듯한 ～을 했다 He made as if to stand up. /「서로 어떻게 의사소통을 하셨는지요」—「손짓과 ～으로 했습니다」"How did you understand each other?"—"We communicated with signs and gestures."

**몸차림** dress; equipment; outfit; a

getup. ～하다 dress *oneself;* equip *oneself* 《for》; dress up; get properly dressed.

**몸채** 《집의》 the main house 〔building〕.

**몸치장**(一治粧) decking *oneself* out; getting 〔trimming〕 *oneself* up; embellishing *oneself.* ～하다 dress 〔attire, adorn〕 *oneself;* deck 〔fit〕 *oneself* out; trim *oneself* up. ¶ 보석으로 ～하다 deck *oneself* out with jewels; bejewel *oneself.*

**몸통** the trunk; the bulk of *one's* body; the body. ¶ ～이 절구통 같다 be fat as mortar barrel.

**몸풀다** 《해산》 be delivered of 《a baby》; give birth 《to a baby》; 《피로를》 take 〔have〕 a rest; relax; relieve *one's* fatigue.

**몸하다** menstruate; have *one's* (menstrual) period.

**몹시** ① 《대단히》 awfully; terribly; very; greatly; highly; immensely; exceedingly; excessively. ¶ ～ 가난하다 be awfully poor / ～ 감동하다 be deeply touched / ～ 기뻐하다 be highly 〔much〕 pleased; be hugely delighted / ～ 덥다 be exceedingly 〔unusually, extremely〕 hot / ～ 바쁘다 be very busy 《with work》; be pressed 《with *one's* business》 / ～ 서두르다 be in a great hurry / ～ 아름답다 be terribly beautiful / ～ 어둡다 be awfully dark / ～ 춥다 be awfully cold / ～ 피로하다 be very tired (★ tired는 동사적 성격을 잃을 형용사로 보기 때문에 much보다는 very가 바른 용법임. 또 pleased, delighted, surprised, worried 따위에도 much 대신 very를 흔히 씀) / ～화내다 blow *one's* top; be mad with anger / 그대가 없어 ～ 쓸쓸하다 I miss you very much. / ～ 운이 좋았다 I had capital luck. / ～ 더워서 상의를 벗었다 It was so hot that I took my coat off.
② 《심하게》 hard; severely; badly; bitterly; harshly; cruelly. ¶ ～ 심하게 굴다 behave cruelly; act harshly; be hard 《on》 / ～ 꾸짖다 scold severely / 날씨가 ～ 나빠지다 it grows violent 〔stormy〕 / ～ 머리가 아프다 have a severe headache / ～ 울다 cry bitterly / ～ 취하다 be heavily 〔dead〕 drunk; be quite boozy 《미구어》 / 사람을 ～ 부리다 drive a person hard / 피를 ～ 흘리다 bleed badly / ～ 피곤하다 be dead tired; be utterly exhausted / …이 없어서 ～ 곤란을 겪고 있다 be badly in want of...; be hard up for 《money》 / ～ 춥군요 Bitterly cold, isn't it? / 비가 ～ 온다 It rains hard 〔fiercely〕.

**몹쓸** ① 《도덕적으로》 bad; evil; immoral; sinful; wicked; ill-natured. ¶ ～ 놈 a wicked guy; a crook; a rascal / ～ 짓 a wrong; an evil deed; a misdeed; a vice / ～ 녀석과 어울리다 keep bad company; associate with a bad fellow / ～ 짓을 하다 do 〔work〕 evil; do wrong 《to 〔by〕 *a person*》; do 《*a person*》 harm; do 《*something*》 wrong; commit a crime 〔sin〕 / 그렇게 순진한 여자를 속이다니 너도 참 ～ 놈이다 How wicked you are to deceive such an innocent girl! ② 《악성의》 bad; malignant; virulent; nasty; severe. ¶ ～ 감기 a bad cold; a severe cold / ～병 a virulent disease.

**못**[1] 《박는》 a nail. ¶ 못 대가리 a nailhead / 나무못 a (wooden) peg / 납작못 a tack / 침목못 a spike / 못뽑이 pincers; a nail puller / 못에 찔린 상처 a nail wound 〔puncture〕 / 못에 걸다 put 〔hang〕 《a hat》 on a hook; hang 《a coat》 on a peg / 못에 발바닥을 찔리다 run a nail into the sole of *one's* foot / 못을 박다〔치다〕 drive a nail 《in》; hammer a nail 《into》; nail down / 가슴에 못을 박다 ⇨ 못박다 / 못을 뽑다 extract 〔pull out, draw out〕 a nail; unnail / 못에 옷이 걸렸다 The nail caught his dress.

**못**[2] 《손발의》 a callosity; a callus; a corn (주로 발의). ¶ 못이 생기다〔박이다〕 become callous; be callused; get 〔have〕 a corn 《on》 / 손가락에 못이 박이다 a callosity has formed on my finger / 귀에 못이 박이도록 듣다 be sick 〔tired〕 of hearing 《*something*》; hear more than enough of 《*something*》 / 귀가 못이 박이도록 말해주다 drum a lesson into *one's* head.

**못**[3] 《연못》 a pond; a pool; 《저수지》 a reservoir. ¶ 못을 파다 dig a pond / 못을 메우다 fill in a pond.

**못**[4] 《불가·불능》 not (possibly); definitely not; never; under no circumstances; cannot; won't; unable 《to *do*》. ¶ 못 가겠다 I can't go. *or* I won't go. / 어두워서 책을 못 읽겠다 It is too dark to read a book. / 나는 더 이상 못 참겠다 I can no longer endure 〔bear〕 this quietly. / 그 책은 가져가지 못한다 You are not allowed to take the book. / 나를 버리고는 가지 못해요 I will not let you go leaving me behind.

**못걸이** a bar of wood with nails on it

for hanging things; a hook; a peg.

**못나다** ①《어리석다》(be) dull(-witted); stupid; be no good. ¶ 못난 짓을 하다 do a stupid 〔foolish〕; act foolishly; commit a folly. ②《생김새가》(be) ugly; bad-looking; plain; homely. ¶ 얼굴이 못났다〔못나가도 했다〕 have an ugly 〔a real ugly〕 face.

**못난이** a stupid person; a good-for-nothing (fellow); a no-account; a no-good; a coward (겁쟁이).

**못내** forever; unforgettably; always; constantly; eternally. ¶ ～ 서러워하다 be in constant sorrow / ～ 잊지 못하다 never forget; hold *a person's* memory ever dear.

**못되다**[1] ①《덜되다》 be not done 〔through, over, ready〕; (be) unfinished. ¶ 일이 아직 ～ a job is not yet done. ②《미달하다》 be short 〔inside〕 of; be not up to; do not reach 〔make〕. ¶ 2년이 못되어 in less than two years / 1 마일도 ～ be inside 〔a little short〕 of a mile; be less than a mile; be a short mile / 20세가 ～ be under twenty years of age / 월급이 100만원이 ～ *one's* salary is under one million won / 60이 못되어 죽다 die before sixty. ③《여위다》 look poor; be in bad shape. ¶ 건강이 ～ *one's* health is in very bad shape; suffer from ill health / 앓고 나서 얼굴이 ～ look poor after *one's* illness. ④《기울다》 get worse; decline. ¶ 나라 형편이 ～ a country is in an awful condition 〔in a mess〕 / 집안이 ～ a family goes downhill / 못되어 가다 be on the decline 〔wane〕; be on the down-grade.

**못되다**[2] 《나쁘다》(be) bad; bad-natured; evil; wicked; wrong. ¶ 못된 놈 a bad egg; a rascal / 못된 짓 an evil deed; a misdeed; a wrong act; misbehavior; a vice / 못되게 굴다 do wrong; do a dishonest act; misbehave *oneself* / 못된 짓을 꾸미다 plot evil / 못된 동무와 사귀다 keep bad company; associate with a bad fellow / 못된 일에 가담하다 「be a party to 〔take part in〕 evil-doing / 못된 송아지 엉덩이에 뿔난다《속담》 A no-good person is 「acting up 〔putting on airs〕. *or* The lean weed lifts its head high.

**못마땅하다** (be) unsatisfactory; be not to *one's* liking; (be) distasteful; disagreeable to《*a person*》; offensive; go against the grain; be displeased 〔dissatisfied〕 with; do not like. ¶ 못마땅한 말 distasteful 〔disagreeable〕 remarks / 못마땅한 사람 an unacceptable 〔undesirable〕 person / 못마땅한 듯이 with a displeased look; in ill humor / 그 음식이 ～ That food is unsatisfactory 〔disagreeable〕 to me / 못마땅한 얼굴을 하다 make a sour 〔wry〕 face; frown 〔scowl〕 at《*a person*》; show *one's* displeasure《at》/ 못마땅해하다 be displeased 〔dissatisfied, disgruntled〕 with / 못마땅한 소리를 하다 say something offensive 〔disagreeable, unpleasant〕/ 그의 말이 못마땅하다 His words 「cut me to the quick 〔get on my nerves〕. / 무엇이 그렇게 못마땅한가 What makes you so displeased?

**못박다** 《못을 박다》 drive a nail in;《상처주다》 wound《*a person's*》 feelings; hurt《*a person*》;《강조·다짐하다》 call《*a person's*》 attention《to》; tell《*a person*》 emphatically《of, about》; remind《*a person*》 of《*something*》;《고정하다》 fix《the date》; set; peg. ¶ 십자가에 ～ crucify《*a person*》/ 가격을 3천원으로 ～ peg the price at three thousand won / 회합 장소를 ～ fix the place for the meeting / 그녀의 말은 그의 가슴에 못을 박았다 She deeply hurt his feelings with the remark.

**못박이다** ①《손발에》 get 〔have〕 a corn 〔callus, bunion〕. ¶ 손바닥에 ～ have a callus on the palm of *one's* hand / 발바닥에 못이 박이다 have a corn on the sole of *one's* foot. ②《시선·발 따위가》 stand riveted to the spot. ¶ 그 자리에 ～ stand transfixed on 〔riveted to〕 the spot.

**못박히다** 《가슴 속에》 go 〔cut〕 deep (in *one's* heart); be stung to the quick; feel a deep rancor 〔grudge〕. ¶ 가슴에 ～ be hurt deep in *one's* heart; be deeply wounded / 원한이 깊이 ～ harbor a deep grudge 〔rancor〕 against《*a person*》.

**못보다** overlook; make an oversight; pass by 〔over〕; fail to notice.

**못 본 체하다** pretend not to see;《눈감아주다》 connive 〔wink, blink〕 at; overlook; close *one's* eyes《to》;《돌보지 않다》 neglect; slight; do not care for; show indifference to. ¶ 잘못을 보고도 ～ overlook 〔slur (over)〕《*a person's*》 fault / 곤경에 처한 친구를 ～ leave *one's* friend in the lurch; fail a friend in *his* need / 길에서 보고도 ～ cut《*a per-*

*son*》 (dead) in the street / 매수된 경찰관은 그 도둑을 보고도 못 본 체하였다 The bribed policeman applied a blind eye to the theft. /「저런! 토니잖아」—「맞아, 우리 그를 못 본 체하자」 "Oh! There's Tony."—"I know, let's make as if we don't see him."

**못비** a timely 〔sufficient〕 rain for transplanting young rice plants.

**못뽑이** a nail puller 〔extractor〕; a claw hammer; (a carpenter's) pincers.

**못살게굴다** tease; treat badly; torment; ill-treat; be hard upon 《*a person*》. ¶ 그녀는 며느리에게 못살게 군다 She is hard on her daughter-in-law.

**못살다** be badly off; live in poverty. ¶ 못사는 사람 a poor person; [집합적] the poor (and needy).

**못생기다** ① 《얼굴이》 (be) ugly; bad-looking; plain; homely. ¶ 못생긴 사람 an ugly person / 얼굴이 ～ have an ugly face; have homely features / 저 여자는 못생겼다 She looks homely 〔plain〕. ② 《어리석다》 (be) stupid; foolish; good-for-nothing.

**못쓰다** ① 《행위 따위가》 (be) bad; wrong; improper; no-good; worthless; 《해서는 안되다》 must 〔shall〕 not 《*do*》; ought not to 《*do*》; should not 《*do*》. ¶ 사람이 못쓰게 되다 a person gets bad 〔worse〕; 《병으로》 a person becomes poor in health; a person is in bad shape / 너 그러면 못쓴다 You shouldn't do that. *or* It is wrong 〔improper〕 for you to do that. ② 《사물이》 (be) bad; inferior; poor; coarse; unusable; unsuitable; inadequate; be out of order. ¶ 못쓸 물건 a bad 〔poor〕 goods; an unusable 〔unsuitable〕 article / 못쓰게 하다 spoil; ruin; destroy; rot 《구어》 / 못쓰게 되다 be spoilt; be ruined.

**못자리** ① 《모판》 a rice seedbed 〔seed-plot〕. ¶ ～를 내다 prepare a rice seed-plot. ② 《씨뿌림》 sowing rice seeds. ～하다 sow rice seeds (in seed-plot).

**못줄** 『농업』 a guide line for setting out rows of rice seedlings.

**못지않다** be not inferior 《to》; be just as good (as); be no less (than). ¶ A는 B에 ～ A is as good as B. / 그는 나에 못지 않게 힘이 세다 He is just as strong as I am. / 오늘도 어제 못지 않게 춥다 Today is just as cold as yesterday was. / 그의 어학 재능은 학급 내의 누구 ～ He is inferior 〔second〕 to none in linguistic talent in his class. / 오락은 일에 못지 않게 필요하다 Recreation is no less necessary than work. / 국산품은 외국 제품 ～ Our product is not inferior to those produced abroad.

**못질** nailing. ～하다 drive (in) a nail.

**못하다**[1] 《비해서》 be lower 《in degree, quality, quantity》; be inferior 《to》; (be) worse; be not so good 〔strong, beautiful, much〕 as. ¶ 보기에 …만 ～ compare unfavorably with / 남보다 훨씬 ～ be far beneath the other / 이 꽃은 저 꽃만 ～ This flower is not up to that one 《in beauty》. / 자식은 나쁜 아내만 ～ Having a son is not quite the same as having even a bad wife.

**못하다**[2] 《할 수 없다》 cannot; be unable 《to *do*》; cannot possibly *do;* will not (★ will not, won't는 명령·권유를 나타냄); refuse to *do;* do not; never do; 《하지 못하다》 fail 《to》; miss 《*do*ing》; 《잘못하다》 be poor 〔bad, weak〕. ¶ 가지 ～ cannot 〔will not〕 go; fail to go / 먹지 ～ can 〔will〕 not eat / 읽기와 쓰기를 ～ be not able 〔unable〕 to read and write / 승진하지 ～ fail to promote / 알아맞히지 ～ guess wrong 〔amiss〕 / 일을 ～ can't 〔won't〕 work / 너무 어려워서 못하겠다 It is too difficult for me to do. *or* It is utterly beyond my power. / 나는 수학을 못한다 I am weak 〔poor〕 in mathematics. *or* Mathematics is my weak point. / 그는 화가 나서 말을 못했다 He was speechless with anger 〔rage〕. / 그는 그 여자가 어리석다는 것을 알아채지 못했다 He didn't see her to be foolish.

**못하다**[3] 《…하지 않다》 be (definitely) not. ¶ 물이 맑지 ～ The water is not clear. / 그는 유능하지 ～ He is lacking in ability. / 그는 사람이 착하지는 못하지만 괜찮다 He isn't a very good person, but that does not matter.

**몽골** Mongolia. ¶ ～의 Mongol; Mongolian; Mongolic. ◉ ～말[1] Mongolian (language); Mongol. ～말[2] the Mongolian horse. ～문자 Mongolian script 〔literature〕. ～반(斑) 《어린아이의》 a Mongol(ian) spot. ～사람 a Mongol(ian). ～인종 the Mongolian race. 내〔외〕～ Inner 〔Outer〕 Mongolia.

**몽구리** ① 《까까머리》 a close-cropped head; a clean-shaven head. ② 《중》 a Buddhist monk.

**몽구스** 『동물』 a mongoose (*pl.* -ses).

**몽근벼** awnless 〔beardless〕 rice grains.

**몽근짐** a heavy 〔weighty〕 load for its bulk.

**몽글다** 《낟알이》 (be) awnless; beardless; be clean of foreign elements; (be) stripped.

**몽글리다** ① 《꺼끄러기를》 take 〔clear〕 away awns 〔foreign elements〕 from grains. ¶ 벼를 ~ strip an ear of rice; strip rice of awns. ② 《단련》 inure; harden. ¶ 몸을 ~ inure *oneself* to; harden the body. ③ 《옷맵시》 trim 〔spruce〕 *oneself* up; preen *oneself*.

**몽글몽글하다** (be) clotty; lumpy. ¶ 풀이 ~ paste is lumpy 〔is full of lumps〕 / 림프선이 부어 ~ lymphatic glands are swollen and lumpy.

**몽깃돌** a killick.

**몽니** greed; avarice; rapacity. ¶ ~ 궂다, ~ 사납다 be greedy 〔avaricious, rapacious, covetous〕 / ~ 부리다 act greedy; show *one's* greedy. ◉ ~쟁이 a greedy 〔grasping〕 person; a hog 《구어》.

**몽달귀**(一鬼) the ghost of a bachelor.

**몽당붓** a worn-out writing brush.

**몽당비** a worn-out broom; a stump of a broom.

**몽당이** 《모지랑이》 a worn-down〔-out〕 stump; 《실뭉치》 a ball of thread.

**몽당치마** a short skirt.

**몽둥이** a heavy stick; a club; a cudgel. ¶ ~로 치다 beat 《*a person*》 with a heavy stick; club 〔cudgel〕 《*a person*》 / ~로 얻어맞다 get beaten with a heavy stick; be clubbed; be cudgeled / ~로 때려 죽이다 club 《*a person*》 to death.

**몽둥이세례**(一洗禮) beating severely with a heavy stick; clubbing; cudgeling. ¶ ~를 주다 beat 《*a person*》 with a heavy stick; club; cudgel / ~를 받다 get beaten with a heavy stick; be clubbed.

**몽따다** pretend not to know; assume ignorance; play the innocent.

**몽땅** in 〔by〕 the lump; in chunks; in a lot; all; entirely; completely. ¶ ~ 털리다 be robbed of all *one* has / ~ 가져가다 take everything away / 돈을 ~ 써버리다 spend all the money *one* has / 투기로 돈을 ~ 날리다 lose the whole of *one's* money in speculation. / 도둑이 들어와 현금을 ~ 털어갔다 A burglar broke in and took all the cash I had in the house.

**몽똑몽똑** stumpily; stubbily; bluntly. ~하다 be all stumpy 〔stubby, blunt〕.

**몽롱하다**(朦朧一) (be) dim; faint; unclear; indistinct; obscure; hazy; dizzy; vague. ¶ 몽롱하게 dimly; indistinctly; vaguely; fuzzily / 몽롱하게 보이다 loom; appear indistinctly / 의식이 ~ have a dim consciousness / 높은 열로 의식이 몽롱해지다 grow faint from fever / 하도 오래 전 일이라 기억이 ~ It was such a long time ago and 〔that〕 I only have a vague memory of it.

**몽매**(蒙昧) ignorance. ~하다 (be) ignorant; unenlightened; benighted; uncivilized. ¶ 무지 ~한 사람들 benighted 〔unenlightened〕 people.

**몽매**(夢寐) sleeping and dreaming. ¶ ~간에도 even while asleep; awake or asleep / ~간에도 잊지 못하다 do not forget 《*something*》 even in sleep 〔even for a moment〕.

**몽상**(蒙喪) mourning. ~하다 observe 〔go into, take to〕 mourning 《for *one's* father》.

**몽상**(夢想) a daydream; a dream; a vision; a wild fancy; a fantasy. ~하다 dream 《of, that…》; daydream; indulge in reveries. ¶ ~도 못할 undreamt-of / ~에 잠기다 be lost in wild fancies; be lost in reveries; spin a daydream. ◉ ~가 a dreamer; a visionary.

**몽설**(夢泄) a nocturnal emission; 《구어》 a wet dream. ~하다 have a nocturnal emission; have a wet dream.

**몽실몽실** 《통통함》 ~하다 (be) plump; round; fleshy; chubby; lumpy. ¶ ~한 몸 a fleshy body / ~한 젖가슴 the smooth and corpulent breast / ~ 살찌다 be fat and plump / ~ 살찐 어린애 a chubby child.

**몽유병**(夢遊病) 〖의학〗 somnambulism; sleepwalking. ◉ ~자 a sleepwalker; a somnambulist.

**몽정**(夢精) a wet dream. ⇨ 몽설(夢泄).

**몽진**(蒙塵) = 파천(播遷).

**몽짜스럽다, 몽짜치다** be more subtle than *one* might think; be deeper 〔smarter〕 than *one* looks.

**몽총하다** ① 《푸접없다》 (be) blunt; cold; indifferent; unaffable; crusty. ¶ 몽총한 사람 a blunt 〔cold, crusty〕 person / 몽총한 짓 a blunt thing to do. ② 《몽톡하다》 (be) (short and) stubby; blunt.

**몽치** a short thick club; a cudgel. ¶ ~로 때리다 beat 《*a person*》 with a club; cudgel 〔club〕 《*a person*》 / ~로 얻어맞다 get beaten with a club; be clubbed; be cudgeled.

**몽타주** (a) montage. ¶ ~를 만들다 montage 《photo prints》. ◉ ~사진 《make》 a composite picture; 《compose》 a montage picture 〔photograph〕; a photomontage; an identikit picture: 경찰은 도망간 간첩의 ~ 사진을 배포했다 The police distributed identikit pictures of the fleeing agent.

**몽혼**(朦昏) anesthesia. ⇨ 마취(痲醉).

**몽환**(夢幻) dreams and phantasms; (a) fantasy; visions. ◉ ~곡 a fantasia. ~극 a dream play.

**뫼** ① 《무덤》 a grave; a tomb; a sepulcher. ¶ 선산에 뫼를 쓰다 bury in the family ground / 뫼를 파내다 dig open a grave. ② 《산》 a hill; a mountain.

**묏자리** a grave site. ¶ ~를 구하다〔잡다〕 look for 〔choose〕 a grave site / ~를 정하다 designate 〔fix〕 a grave site.

**묘**(卯) 〖민속〗 ① 《십이지의》 the Sign of the Hare 〔Rabbit〕; the 4th of the 12 Earth's Branches. ② ⇨ 묘방(卯方). ③ ⇨ 묘시(卯時).

**묘**(妙) a mystery; a miracle; a wonder; 《교묘》 adroitness. ¶ 조화(造化)의 묘 the mystery of nature 〔creation〕.

**묘**(墓) a grave. ⇨ 무덤.

**묘**(廟) 《사당》 a shrine; 《능》 a mausoleum.

**묘계**(妙計) = 묘책(妙策).

**묘구도적**(墓丘盜賊) 《무덤을 파는》 a grave robber; a plunderer of a grave; 《송장을 파내는》 a body snatcher.

**묘기**(妙技) 《솜씨》 exquisite skill; 《연기 따위》 a wonderful performance; 《서커스 따위》 a splendid feat; a stunt; 《스포츠의》 a fine play. ¶ 공중의 ~ an aerial stunt / ~를 보이다 exhibit 〔display〕 *one's* feats; perform a wonderful feat / 관중들은 그녀의 ~에 큰 박수를 보냈다 The audience gave her a big hand for her wonderful performance.

**묘령**(妙齡) blooming age; young 〔early〕 womanhood; the flower 〔prime〕 of youth. ¶ ~의 여성 a blooming girl; a young lady; a woman of eligible age / ~에 달하다 attain budding womanhood; arrive at a marriageable age.

**묘리**(妙理) an abstruse principle; a profound law; a knack. ¶ ~를 터득하다 get at the fundamental principle; get the knack 《of》.

**묘막**(墓幕) a hut built near a grave.

**묘망**(渺茫) ~하다 (be) vast and far-reaching; boundless; unlimited.

**묘목**(苗木) a sapling; a seedling; a young plant; a nursery tree; a set. ¶ ~ 상자 a flat / ~을 심다 plant a seedling / 서리로 인해 ~이 죽었다 The frost has killed the seedlings.

**묘미**(妙味) 《맛·매력》 exquisiteness; (exquisite) beauty; (a) charm; a subtle 〔nice〕 point; (one of the) niceties. ¶ ~를 맛보다 appreciate the beauty 《of》; relish the real pleasure 《of scuba diving》 / 그의 문체(文體)에는 말할 수 없는 ~가 있다 There is an indescribable 〔a haunting〕 charm in his style. / 이것이 낚시의 ~다 This is the real charm 〔thrill〕 of fishing.

**묘방**(卯方) 〖민속〗 the Direction of the Hare; east.

**묘방**(妙方) ① 《약방문》 an excellent 〔a secret〕 prescription. ② = 묘법 ①.

**묘법**(妙法) ① 《방법》 an excellent means 〔method〕. ② 《불법》 the marvelous 〔wonderful〕 law of Buddha.

**묘비**(墓碑) a tombstone; a gravestone; a funerary slab. ¶ ~명(銘) an epitaph; an inscription on a tombstone / ~를 세우다 set up a tombstone 《over a grave overlooking the village》.

**묘사**(描寫) delineation; depiction; description; 《그림으로》 representation; portrayal. ~하다 delineate; depict; describe; represent; portray; picture. ¶ 감각적〔사실적, 심리적〕 ~ a sensational 〔realistic, psychological〕 description / 전원 생활을 ~한 소설 a novel depicting rural life / 성격을 ~하다 portray character / 여실히 ~하다 give a living 〔graphic〕 description 《of》 / 완전히 ~하다 give a complete 〔full〕 description 《of》 / 장면을 ~하다 describe 〔depict〕 a scene / 그는 수필에서 그 장면을 생생히〔세밀하게〕 ~하였다 He vividly 〔minutely〕 described 〔depicted〕 the scene in his essay. *or* In his essay he gave a vivid 〔minute〕 description 〔depiction〕 of the scene. / 영화에서 그 인물은 실제 이상으로 용감하게 ~되어 있었다 In the movie the man was portrayed as more courageous than he really was. ◉ ~력 the power of description.

**묘상**(苗床) ① 《모종판》 a seedbed; a nursery; a seed-plot. ② = 못자리 ①.

**묘소**(墓所) 《산소》 a graveyard; a burial ground.

**묘수**(妙手) ① 《사람》 an expert; a master 《of》; an adept. ② 《바둑 따위의》 an excellent 〔clever〕 move.

**묘시**(卯時)〖민속〗the Watch of the Hare. ① the 4th of the 12 double-hours (=the period between 5 and 7 a.m.). ② the 7th of the 24 hours (=5:30-6:30 a.m.).

**묘안**(妙案) an excellent plan〔scheme〕; an ingenious design〔device〕; a wonderful〔bright〕idea. ¶ ～을 생각해 내다 hit on〔be struck with〕a capital idea; a bright idea strikes *one* / ～이 좀처럼 떠오르지 않는다 Bright ideas never occur to me.

**묘안석**(猫眼石)〖광물〗(a) cat's-eye.

**묘약**(妙藥) a specific; a wonder〔miracle〕drug; a golden〔sovereign〕remedy《for》. ¶ 두통의 ～ an excellent remedy for headaches.

**묘역**(墓域) the boundaries of a grave.

**묘연하다**(杳然—) ①《거리가》be far away. ②《기억이》(be) dim; vague; indistinct;《소식이》(be) unknown; missing. ¶ 소식이 ～ hear nothing from《*a person*》.

**묘제**(墓祭) a memorial service held before the grave.

**묘지**(墓地) a graveyard; a burial ground;《공동묘지》a cemetery;《성당·교회 부속의》a churchyard. ¶ 공원～ a cemetery park / 국립～ the National Cemetery / ～에 매장하다 bury in the cemetery / 정부는 공동 ～에 있는 묘의 크기와 존속 기간에 더 엄격한 제한들을 가할 수 있는 장례와 ～에 관한 법률을 개정하려 하고 있다 The government is seeking to revise the law governing funerals and graveyards which would place stricter restrictions on the size of tombs and the duration period of tombs in public cemeteries. ◉ 무연(無緣)～ a potter's field. 외국인～ a foreigners' cemetery. 유엔～ the U.N. Memorial Cemetery.

**묘지**(墓誌) an epitaph; an inscription on a tomb. ◉ ～명(銘) an inscription on a tomb; an epitaph.

**묘지기**(墓—) a grave keeper.

**묘책**(妙策) an excellent plan; an ingenious〔a clever〕scheme. ⇨ 묘안(妙案).

**묘판**(苗板) = 못자리 ①.

**묘포**(苗圃)〖농업〗a seedbed; a nursery〔(garden).

**묘하다**(妙—) ①《썩 잘되다》(be) exquisite; marvelous. ¶ 묘하게 되다 be exquisitely made. ②《이상하다》(be) strange; queer; odd. ¶ 묘한 것 a curious thing; an oddity / 묘한 말 a strange remark; a rare〔wonderful〕remark; an appropriate remark / 묘한 버릇 a queer〔peculiar〕habit / 묘한 행동 strange〔eccentric, odd, peculiar〕behavior / 묘한 사람 a strange person; an eccentric / 묘하게도 curious〔strange〕to say〔relate〕; curiously〔strangely〕enough / 일이 묘하게 되려니까 by a curious coincidence / 묘하게 보이다〔들리다〕seem〔sound〕strange / 묘한 기분이 들다 feel strange / 묘한 소리를 하다 say strange things / 묘한 얼굴을 하다 make a queer face; give a queer look / 어제 묘한 일이 생겼다 A curious thing happened to me yesterday. / 묘하게도 그녀는 그 계획을 알고 있다 Strange to say, she knows (about) the plan. / 그 여자가 묘하게 마음에 걸렸다 I felt anxious about her, though I knew not why. / 우리가 여기서 만나다니 묘하군 It is strange that we should meet here. (★ 뜻밖이란 기분을 나타내는 It is... that—에서 that-clause 속에는 보통 should를 씀) / 시골에 가면 아직도 묘한 풍습들이 많이 남아있다 When you go into the countryside, you will find that there are many strange customs that still survive.

**묘혈**(墓穴) a grave. ¶ 스스로 ～을 파다 dig *one's* own grave; bring about *one's* own ruin; dig a pit for *oneself*.

**무**[1]〖한의〗an acute periostitis.

**무**[2]〖식물〗a radish; an icicle radish. ¶ ～밑동 같다 be all alone in this world / ～쪽 같다 be ugly〔ill-favored〕; look plain〔homely〕. ◉ ～김치《prepare》radish roots kimchi. ～말랭이 dried radish slices. ～장아찌 dried radish slices seasoned with soysauce and spices. ～진디〖곤충〗a cabbage aphis〔aphid〕. ～짠지 radish pickle; pickled radish. ～채 radish shreds〔strips〕; shredded radish. ～청 the green part of a radish; radish leaves.

**무**(戊)〖民俗〗the 5th of the 10 Heaven's Stems.

**무**(武)《무예》military〔martial〕arts;《군사》military affairs; warfare. ¶ 무를 닦다 train *oneself* in military〔martial〕arts; cultivate the arts of war / 무를 숭상하다 pursue the policy of militarism; glorify the military.

**무**(無) ①《없음》nothing; naught; nil; nihility; zero. ¶ 무가 되다 come to naught〔nothing〕; go for nothing / 무에서 유(有)는 생기지 않는다 Nothing comes of nothing. *or* You cannot create anything out of nothing. / 희망은 무로 돌아갔다 My hope was reduced to zero. ② [접두어로] not having; lacking; un-; -less. ¶ 무관계 being unconnected 〔unrelated, irrelevant〕.

**무가내**(無可奈), **무가내하**(無可奈何) having no alternative. ⇨ 막무가내. ¶ ～다 be at *one's* wits' 〔wit's〕 end; there is no alternative; be all up with *one;* be helpless.

**무가당**(無加糖) ¶ ～의 sugar-free; unsweetened; sugarless 《orange juice》.

**무가치**(無價値) worthlessness; valuelessness. ～하다 (be) worthless; valueless; be of no value. ¶ ～한 설명으로 시간을 낭비하다 waste time making nugatory 〔worthless〕 comments.

**무간섭**(無干涉) nonintervention; *laissez-faire* (F.). ◉ ～주의 a hands-off policy; a *laissez-faire* 〔let-alone〕 policy; a policy of noninterference.

**무간하다**(無間—) (be) intimate; familiar; friendly; close 《to *one's* bosom》. ¶ 무간한 친구 a bosom friend / 무간하게 지내다 be on an intimate footing with 《*a person*》; be thick with 《*a person*》; be on good 〔friendly〕 terms with... / 우리들은 무간한 사이다 We are on intimate terms.

**무감각**(無感覺) insensibility; 《무감동》 callousness; apathy; callosity. ～하다 (be) insensible; senseless; callous; apathetic. ¶ ～하게 되다 go 〔get, become〕 numbed 〔senseless〕; be benumbed / 통증에 ～하다 be insensible to pain / 남의 고생에 ～하다 be callous 〔apathetic〕 to the sufferings of others / 추위로 손가락이 ～하게 되었다 My fingers are numbed with cold. ◉ ～증 『의학』 anesthesia.

**무감사**(無鑑査) ¶ ～의 《a painting》 not submitted to the jury 〔selecting committee〕.

**무개**(無蓋) ¶ ～의 unlidded; uncovered; open. ◉ ～대차(臺車) a push car; a flatcar. ～자동차 an open car; 《속어》 a breezer. ～화차(貨車) 《미》 a flatcar; a gondola; an open freight car.

**무거리** coarse flour (left over in the sieve); shorts of flour; screenings. ¶ ～ 고추장 thick red-pepper paste made of coarse soypaste flour.

**무겁** the mound behind a target.

**무겁다** ① 《무게가》 (be) heavy; weighty; ponderous. ¶ 무거운 돌〔가방〕 a heavy stone 〔bag〕 / 무거운 짐〔부담〕 a heavy 〔weighty〕 burden / 무겁게 하다 make 《*a thing*》 heavier; add to *its* weight / 무거워지다 get 〔become, grow〕 heavy 〔heavier〕; increase in weight / 무거워 보이는 heavy-looking 《package》.
② 《언행이》 (be) grave; serious; quiet; prudent; discreet. ¶ 입이 무거운 사람 a closemouthed 〔tight-lipped〕 person / 입이 ～ be taciturn; be slow of speech; be a man of few words / 그는 보기보다 언행이 무거운 사람이다 He is more prudent person than he appears to be.
③ 《기분이》 (be, feel) heavy; depressed; dull; languid. ¶ 무거운 마음으로 with a heavy heart / 마음이 ～ have a heavy heart; be depressed in spirits / 머리가 ～ feel heavy in the head; *one's* head feels heavy; have a thick head on *one* 《구어》 / 발걸음이 ～ walk with leaden foot; tread heavily; drag *oneself* / 어깨가 ～ have a heavy feeling in the shoulders; feel a heavy load in *one's* mind.
④ 《병이》 (be) serious; critical; 《죄가》 (be) grave; grievous; serious 《crimes》; 《벌이》 (be) severe. ¶ 무거운 벌 a heavy 〔severe〕 punishment / 무거운 병 a serious 〔severe〕 illness 〔disease〕; a disease of a serious nature / 무거운 죄 a grave charge; a capital offense / 병이 ～ be seriously ill.
⑤ 《중대하다》 (be) important; weighty; momentous; grave. ¶ 무거운 사명 an important mission / 무거운 책임 a grave 〔heavy, great〕 responsibility / 무거운 책임을 맡기다 trust 〔place〕 《*a person*》 with a heavy responsibility.

**무게** ① 《중량》 weight; heft 《미구어》. ¶ 엄청난 ～ a heavy 〔lumping〕 weight / ～가 늘다 gain 〔pick up〕 (in) weight; put on weight / ～가 서 근 나가다 weight three *kŭn;* have the weight of three *kŭn* / ～가 있다 be heavy; be weighty / ～가 60킬로이다 be sixty kilograms in weight; weigh sixty kilograms / ～로 깨지다 break under the weight / ～로 내려앉다 collapse 〔give way〕 beneath 〔under the weight of〕 《the people》 / ～로 팔다 sell by weight / ～를 달다 weigh 《*a thing*》 / 손으로 ～를 가늠해 보다 heft 《*a thing*》; weigh in *one's* hand / ～를 지탱하다 bear the weight.
② 《언행의》 weight; importance; dignity; authority; prestige. ¶ ～가 없는 unimposing; undignified / ～가 있다

carry weight; have dignity 〔prestige〕; be important; be dignified / ~ 있는 말 a remark carrying weight 〔authority, conviction〕/ ~ 있는 사람 a dignified person; a person of dignity / 그 사람 말은 ~가 있다 What he says carries weight 〔authority, conviction〕. ◉ ~ 중심 a center of balance; 〖물리〗 the center of gravity. ⇨ 중심(重心).

**무결근**(無缺勤) = 무결석(無缺席).

**무결석**(無缺席) perfect attendance; whole 〔regular〕 attendance. ¶ 3년간 내내 ~이다 attend 《school》 for three years without missing a single day / 그는 10년간 무지각· ~으로 근무했다 He worked at the office without missing a single day or being late for ten years. ◉ ~자 a non-absentee; a regular attendant.

**무경쟁**(無競爭) ¶ ~으로 without competition; without a rival; 《반대없이》 unopposed.

**무경험**(無經驗) inexperience; want 〔lack〕 of experience. ¶ ~의 inexperienced; unpracticed; untrained; green 《구어》/ ~이다 have no experience 《in teaching》/ 그녀는 ~때문에 새로운 사업에 실패했다 She was hampered in the new job by her lack of experience. ◉ ~자 an inexperienced person; a green 〔an untrained〕 hand: ~자 환영 《광고에서》 Help wanted. Experience not necessary.

**무계획**(無計劃) being planless. ~하다 (be) unplanned; planless; haphazard; reckless; unmethodical. ¶ ~한 지출 reckless expenditure / ~한 생산 unplanned production / 그런 ~한 행동으로는 아무 것도 실현하지 못한다 You would not realize anything by such a rash act. / ~적인 개발이 격심한 교통 체증의 주요 원인 중 하나이다 The lack of a development plan is one of the main causes of the severe traffic congestion. / ~적인 벌채가 홍수의 원인이었다 Uncontrolled 〔Unplanned〕 logging 「was the cause of the flood.

**무고**(無故) 《무사》 being without mishap; freedom from trouble 〔a disease〕. ~하다 have no trouble; (be) safe; well; [서술적] be all right. ¶ ~하게 지내다 get along well; live in peace.

**무고**(無辜) innocence; blamelessness. ~하다 (be) innocent; guiltless. ¶ ~한 백성 innocent people / 그 마을의 반수 이상의 ~한 주민들이 게릴라들에 의해 학살당했다 More than half (of) the innocent residents of the village were massacred by the guerrillas.

**무고**(誣告) 〖법〗 a false charge 〔accusation〕; 《문서상의》 a libel; 《구두상의》 a slander; a calumny. ~하다 make a false charge 〔accusation〕; accuse 《*a person*》 falsely; slander. ¶ 절도를 했다는 ~ a false accusation of theft against 《*a person*》. ◉ ~자 a false accuser; a calumniator. ~죄 a calumny: ~죄로 고소당하다 be sued on charges of making a false accusation.

**무곡**(舞曲) 《무용곡》 《a piece of》 dance music; 《음악과 춤》 music and dance.

**무골충**(無骨蟲) 《벌레》 boneless worms; 《사람》 a spineless 〔wishy-washy〕 person. 「natured person.

**무골호인**(無骨好人) an excessively good=

**무공**(武功) military exploits 〔merits, feats〕; feats of arms; a distinguished military service. ¶ ~을 세우다 render distinguished military services; distinguish *oneself* in war. ◉ ~훈장 the Order of Military Merit: 화랑〔태극〕 ~ 훈장을 받다 be awarded the Order of Military Merit *Hwarang* 〔*Taegŭk*〕. 「examination.

**무과**(武科) 〖역사〗 the military service

**무과실**(無過失) ◉ ~(손해)배상책임 no=fault liability for compensation. ~책임 liability without fault; strict 〔absolute〕 liability. ~책임주의 principle 〔doctrine〕 of strict 〔absolute〕 liability.

**무관**(武官) 《육군·해군》 a military 〔naval〕 officer. ¶ 대사관 근무 ~ a military 〔naval〕 attaché to an embassy.

**무관(계)**(無關(係)) no connection; no relation. ~하다 (be) unrelated; irrelevant 《to》; unconnected; [서술적] have no connection 〔relation〕 《with》; have nothing to do 《with》. ¶ 그 문제와 ~한 사항 a matter foreign to the question / 나는 그것과 ~하다 I have nothing to do with it. *or* I have no relation 〔connection〕 with it. / 이 사건에 대해서 나는 전연 ~합니다 I have neither part nor lot in the affair. / 그가 무엇을 하든 나와는 ~하다 It matters little to me whatever he may do. / 나는 그 회사와는 ~하다 I am not connected with the company. / 당신이 말하는 것은 토의 중인 문제와 ~합니다 What you are saying is irrelevant to the problem under discussion.

**무관심**(無關心) apathy; indifference;

unconcern; nonchalance; callousness; lacking interest 《in》. ～하다 (be) indifferent 《to》; unconcerned 〔careless〕 《about》; unmindful 《of》; apathetic; callous; have no interest 《in》. ¶ 정치적 ～ political apathy / 교육에 대한 일반의 ～ the indifference of the general public toward education / 옷차림에 ～하다 be careless about *one's* personal appearance / 사소한 일에 ～하다 do not trouble *oneself* about trifling matters / ～한 체하다 pretend to be indifferent 《to》; assume the air of indifference; affect 〔feign〕 indifference / 그는 정치에는 전혀 ～하다 He doesn't have the least interest in politics. / 그녀는 옷차림에 전혀 ～하다 She is quite indifferent to what she wears. *or* She doesn't 「care 〔pay any attention to〕 what she wears. / 당신은 자식들의 교육에 대해 어쩌면 그렇게도 ～할 수가 있습니까 How can you 「be so uninterested 〔take so little interest〕 in the education of your own children?

**무교육**(無教育) ¶ ～의 uneducated; illiterate; ignorant. ◉ ～자 uneducated person.

**무교회**(無教會) ◉ ～운동〔주의〕 the non-church movement.

**무구**(無垢) purity; innocence. ～하다 《섞인 것이 없는》 (be) pure; 《더럽힌 것이 없는》 spotless 〔immaculate〕; 《순진한》 innocent. ¶ ～한 처녀 an innocent 〔immaculate〕 virgin / ～한 동심으로 돌아가다 retrieve *one's* childish innocence.

**무국적**(無國籍) statelessness. ¶ ～의 stateless / ～자 a stateless person; 《국적을 잃은 사람》 a person who has lost his nationality.

**무궁**(無窮) eternity; infinity. ～하다 (be) limitless; unlimited; eternal; infinite; endless; boundless. ¶ ～히 infinitely; eternally; forever.

**무궁무진**(無窮無盡) infinitude; endlessness. ～하다 (be) infinite; endless; boundless.

**무궁화**(無窮花) 〖식물〗 a rose of Sharon; an althea. ¶ 한국 소설 「～꽃이 피었습니다」의 일어 번역판이 일본에서 곧 출간될 것이라고 한다 It is said that a Japanese translation 〔version〕 of the Korean novel, "Roses of Sharon have Blossomed" will soon be published in Japan. ◉ ～대훈장(大勳章) the Grand Order of *Mugunghwa*. ～동산 the beautiful land of Korea. ～위성 the *Mugunghwa* Satellite.

**무궤도**(無軌道) 《궤도가 없는》 lacking tracks; 《상도를 벗어난》 aberration; recklessness; rashness. ～하다 《궤도가 없다》 (be) railless; unrailed; trackless; 《상도를 벗어나다》 (be) wild; extravagant; aberrant; unbridled (억제할 수 없는). ¶ ～한 생활 a loose 〔dissolute, dissipated, fast〕 life / 우리는 그의 ～한 행실을 간과해서는 안 된다 We should not overlook his reckless 〔dissipated, unprincipled〕 behavior. ◉ ～전차 a trackless tram 〔trolley car〕.

**무균**(無菌) 〖의학〗 asepsis. ¶ ～의 without bacilli; germless; 《살균한》 sterilized; pasteurized; aseptic. ¶ 이 방은 ～상태로 유지되어 있다 This room is kept in a germless condition. ◉ ～상태 an aseptic 〔a germfree〕 condition; an asepsis. ～수술 aseptic surgery. ～실 a germfree 〔sterilized〕 room; an aseptic room. ～우유 pasteurized 〔sterilized〕 milk.

**무극**(無極) 《무한》 being limitless; boundless; 〖물리〗 without poles; lacking poles; nonpolar. ◉ ～결합 nonpolar union. ～(성) 분자 〖화학〗 a nonpolar molecule.

**무근**(無根) groundlessness; baselessness. ～하다 (be) groundless; unfounded; baseless; false. ¶ ～지설 a groundless 〔wild〕 rumor / 김 선생이 사직한다는 소문은 사실 ～이었다 The rumor that Mr. Kim would quit our company proved (to be) unfounded.

**무급**(無給) ¶ ～의 unpaid; unsalaried; without salary; 《명예직의》 honorary / ～이다 be allowed no pay / ～으로 일하다 work 〔serve〕 without pay / 견습기간중은 ～이다 You will receive no pay 〔No salary will be paid〕 while you are on probation.

**무기**(武技) martial 〔warlike〕 arts.

**무기**(武器) arms; a weapon (★ arms는 창이나 칼 따위 전투용의 것. weapon은 arms를 포함한 넓은 뜻으로 쓰임); 〖집합적〗 ordnance. ¶ ～거래 사기 사건 an arms deal fraud case / ～를 들다 take up arms; arm *oneself* / ～를 가지고 있다 be armed; carry 〔bear〕 arms / ～를 빼앗다 disarm 《*a person*》 of his weapons / ～를 버리다 lay down 〔give up〕 *one's* arms / 벌에는 침이란 ～가 있다 The bee is armed with a sting. / 눈물은 여자의 ～다 Tears are women's weapon.

◉ ～경쟁 the arms race: 갈수록 치열해지는 ～ 경쟁 the ever-mounting arms race. ～고(庫) an armory; ordnance stores. ～구입 arms purchase. ～대여 lend-lease; lease-lend: ～ 대여법 《미국의》 the Lend-Lease Act. ～불법 소지 《be arrested on charges of》 illegal possession of weapon. ～원조 arms 〔military〕 aid. ～제조 weaponry; arms production. ～판매 arms sale; sales of arms.

**무기**(無期) no time limit. ¶ ～의 unlimited; indefinite / ～ 휴회가 되다 be adjourned *sine die* 〔for an indefinite period〕 / 그 학생은 ～ 정학을 받았다 The student has been suspended from school for an indefinite period. ◉ ～공채(公債) a perpetual public loan. ～연기 (an) indefinite postponement: ～ 연기가 되다 be postponed 〔put off〕 indefinitely 〔for an indefinite period〕. ～징역 penal servitude for life; life imprisonment; a life sentence: ～징역수 a lifetimer / ～ 징역을 선고받다 be sentenced to penal servitude for life. ～형(刑) penal servitude for life 〔for an indefinite term〕.

**무기**(無機) ¶ ～의 inorganic; mineral / ～ 성분 the mineral content 《of》. ◉ ～계 the inorganic world. ～물〔체〕 an inorganic substance. ～산 a mineral 〔an inorganic〕 acid. ～안료(顔料) a mineral pigment. ～영양 mineral nutrition. ～질 《무기물》 inorganic matter; 《광물질》 mineral matter: ～질 질소〔칼륨, 인산〕 비료 inorganic nitrogeneous 〔potassic, phosphoric〕 fertilizer. ～화학 inorganic chemistry. ～화합물 an inorganic compound.

**무기력**(無氣力) languor. ～하다 《활기 없는》 (be) spiritless; nerveless; 《활발치 못한》 inactive; 《무감동의》 (be) apathetic 《about, to》; 《해이해진》 (be) languid; 《둔하고 활기 없는》 (be) sluggish; dull; 《대가 약한》 (be) weak-kneed; 《구어》 gutless. ¶ 나이를 먹어 ～하다 be infirm 〔feeble〕 with age / ～하게 하다 enervate; emasculate / 그는 언제나 ～하다 He is always inactive. *or* He never feel like doing anything. / 그는 온건하고 좋은 사람이지만 어딘가 ～한 데가 있다 He is gentle and good, but a rather spiritless person.

**무기명**(無記名) ¶ ～의 unsigned; unregistered; uninscribed; blank; unidentified; anonymous (익명의) / 이 앙케트는 ～으로 제출하십시오 Please submit this questionnaire unsigned. ◉ ～공채〔사채, 증권〕 a bearer bond 〔security, debenture〕. ～식: ～식의 blank 《endorsement》; 《소지인 지급의》 《a check》 payable to bearer; bearer 《checks》. ～어음 a blank bill. ～예금 an uninscribed deposit. ～주식 bearer shares; uninscribed shares 〔stocks〕. ～투표 a secret 〔an unsigned〕 vote; secret voting; a secret ballot: ～ 투표로 의장을 뽑다 select the chairperson by secret ballot 〔voting〕.

**무기음**(無氣音) 〖언어〗 unaspirated sounds.

**무기한**(無期限) ¶ ～의 limitless; indefinite; without term / ～으로 indefinitely; for an indefinite period / 그 모임은 ～ 연기되었다 The meeting was postponed 「indefinitely 〔for an indefinite period〕. / 이 조약은 ～ 유효하다 This treaty will be effective indefinitely. ◉ ～대부금 an advance 〔a loan〕 without a fixed date for settlement. ～파업 a no-time-limit strike; a strike for an indefinite period: 조합은 ～ 파업에 들어갔다 The union went out on strike for an indefinite period.

**무꾸리(질)** 〖민속〗 a shaman's rites; a kind of shamanistic divination. ～하다 have a shaman perform a *mukkuri;* have *one's* fortune told by a shaman.

**무난**(無難) ① 《어렵지 않음》 being easy. ¶ ～히 quite easily; with ease; without (any) difficulty 〔trouble〕 / ～히 이기다 win an easy victory 《over》; walk over; win hands down 《미구어》. ② 《그런대로 좋은》 faultlessness. ¶ 이 정도면 ～하다 This may pass. *or* This is passable. / 그것은 그 나름대로 ～하다 It's well enough in its way. / 쓰레기를 줄여야 할 필요성에 대한 그의 논점은 ～히 받아들여졌다. His point about the need to reduce wastes was well taken.

**무남독녀**(無男獨女) an only daughter. ¶ ～에게 장가들다 marry 〔get married to〕 《*a person's*》 only daughter.

**무너뜨리다** pull down 《a house》; tear down; break down; destroy; demolish. ¶ 담을 ～ demolish 〔pull down〕 a wall / 산을 무너뜨려 길을 내다 cut a road through a hill / 적의 방어선을 ～ succeed in breaking through the enemy's defense line.

**무너지다** collapse; crumble; fall 〔break〕 down; give way; fall 〔drop〕 to pieces; be destroyed. ¶ 무너져 내리다 tumble down / 담이 ~ a wall falls down / 비로 둑이 ~ a dike is destroyed 〔washed out〕 by the rain / 벽이 무너지기 시작했다 The wall has begun to crumble. / 그 둑은 언제 무너질지 모른다 The embankment may go any moment. / 태풍으로 많은 집들이 무너졌다 Many houses were destroyed by the typhoon.

**무녀**(巫女) a female shaman. ⇨ 무당.

**무녀리** 《첫새끼》 the first-born of a litter; 《사람》 a stupid fellow; a soft fool.

**무념무상**(無念無想) 〖불교〗 freedom from all (worldly) thoughts. ¶ ~의 경지에 이르다 rid *oneself* of all worldly thoughts; attain (a) perfect serenity of mind.

**무농약야채**(無農藥野菜) chemical-free vegetables; 《유기 재배의》 organic vegetables.

**무뇌증**(無腦症) 〖의학〗 anencephaly; ⌈anencephalia.

**무뇨증**(無尿症) 〖의학〗 anuria.

**무능**(無能) 《무재능》 lack of talent; 《무능력》 lack of ability; incompetency. ~하다 (be) incompetent; incapable; good-for-nothing. ¶ (생활력이 없는) ~한 남편 a do-nothing 〔incompetent〕 husband / ~한 사람 a good-for-nothing (fellow); a man of no ability; an incompetent person / ~한 정권 a do-nothing 〔an inefficient〕 government / ~하여 파면되다 be dismissed for incompetency / ~을 드러내다 betray *one's* incompetency 〔incapacity〕 《for》 / 이 사건으로 공무원들이 얼마나 ~한 지가 드러났다 This incident brought to light how incompetent government officials are. / 야당은 물가 정책을 다루는 정부의 ~함을 공격했다 The Opposition party attacked the government for its inefficiency over price policies.

**무능력**(無能力) lack of ability; incompetence; inefficiency; incapacity. ~하다 be lacking in ability; (be) inefficient; incompetent; incapable.
◉ ~자 an incompetent (person); 《법률상의》 a person without (legal) capacity.

**무늬** 《도안》 a pattern; a design; a figure; 《깃털의》 markings 《of a bird's plumage》. ¶ 꽃~ a flower 〔floral〕 pattern / ~ 있는 《a blouse》 with a 《rose》 pattern 〔figure〕 / ~를 넣다 put on 〔decorate with〕 a pattern; draw 〔paint, describe〕 a pattern 《on》; pattern; figure / ~를 넣어 짜다 weave in figures 〔patterns〕 / 줄 ~가 있는 셔츠 a shirt with a stripped pattern / 모자이크 ~ a design in mosaic / 이 깔개에는 장미 ~가 있다 This rug has a rose pattern.

**무단**(武斷) militarism. ◉ ~정치 military government; government by the bayonet; an iron rule: ~정치를 하다 govern by the bayonet. ~주의 militarism.

**무단**(無斷) ¶ ~히, ~으로 without (due) notice (예고 없이); without leave 〔permission〕 (허가 없이); without asking (양해를 얻지 않고); without knowledge (of ...) (알리지 않고) / 남의 물건을 ~으로 사용하다 make free use of another's possessions / ~히 차용하다 borrow without asking 〔the owner's permission〕 / ~ 출입 금지 Don't enter 《the building》 without permission. *or* 《게시》 No trespassing. / ~ 전재 금지 《게시》 All rights reserved.
◉ ~결근〔결석〕 absence without due notice 〔without leave〕: ~ 결석하다 play truant; stay away 《from school》 without leave; play hookey 《미》; cut a lecture / ~ 결근하다 absent *oneself* 〔stay away〕 《from *one's* office》 without leave. ~복사본 a pirate edition. ~사용 illegal use. ~이탈〔외출〕 《미군속》 AWOL. 〔< *a*bsent 〔*a*bsence〕 *w*ith*o*ut *l*eave〕

**무담보**(無擔保) ¶ ~의 unsecured; naked; without collateral 〔security〕 / ~로 대출하다 grant 《*a person*》 a loan without collateral. ◉ ~대부금 an unsecured loan. ~사채 a naked 〔an unsecured〕 debenture.

**무당** an exorcist; a (female) shaman; a witch; a spiritualistic medium. ¶ ~이 제굿 못하고 소경이 저 죽을 날 모른다 《속담》 The fortune-teller cannot tell his own fortune.

**무당개구리** 〖동물〗 a red-bellied frog.

**무당벌레** 〖곤충〗 a ladybird; a ladybug; a lady beetle.

**무당새** 〖조류〗 a yellow bunting.

**무당서방** ① 《무당의 남편》 the husband of a shaman. ② 《공것 바라는》 a man who likes to have things for nothing 〔free of charge〕.

**무당선두리** 〖곤충〗 a whirligig (beetle).

**무당파**(無黨派) political independents.

**무대** 《해류》 a (water) current; an ocean current.

**무대**(舞臺) 《연극의》 stage; 《활동의》 *one's* field of action; *one's* sphere 《of activity》; a stage; 《분야》 a field; 《소설의》 a scene 《of a story》. ¶ 세계 외교의 ~ the stage of the world's diplomacy / ~에 서다 appear on the stage 〔before the footlights〕; 《배우가 되다》 go on the stage; tread the boards / ~에 올리다 stage 《a play》; present 〔bring, put〕 《a play》 on the stage / ~에서 물러나다 go 〔come〕 offstage; 《은퇴》 retire from 〔quit〕 the stage / ~에서 얼다 have stage fright / ~가 바뀌다 the scene shifts 〔changes〕 / 국제 ~에서 활약하다 take an active part in the international arena / 첫 ~를 밟다 make *one's* debut; make *one's* first appearance on the stage / 그는 세계를 ~로 활약한다 The wide world is his stage. / ~는 바뀌어 1934년의 파리이다 The scene has changed and it is now Paris in 1934. / 자네가 ~생활을 했었으리라고는 믿어지지 않는다 I can't believe you used to appear on the stage. / 이 각본을 ~에 올리면 어떨까 I wonder how this play will go on the stage. / 그의 활동 ~는 매우 넓다 His sphere of activity is very large. / 그는 세계 외교 ~에서 활약하고 있다 He is active on the world diplomatic scene. / 그 소설의 ~는 미국의 남부다 「The setting for that novel 〔The scene of the story〕 is laid in the South. (★ the South는 미국의 남부를 지칭.)

◉ ~감독 a stage director 〔manager〕: ~ 감독을 하다 stage-manage. ~극 a stage drama 〔play〕. ~기교 stagecraft. ~뒤 a backstage; behind the scenes. ~배우 a stage actor 〔actress (여)〕. ~생활 a stage 〔theatrical〕 career. ~연습 《have》 a (full) dress rehearsal. ~예술 theatrical art. ~의상 a stage 〔theatrical〕 costume. ~장치 (stage) setting; the set(s) 〔properties (소품)〕: ~ 장치가 a scenic designer / ~장치를 하다 set the stage. ~조명 stage lighting 〔illumination〕. ~중계 a stage relay; a direct broadcast 〔telecast〕 from the theater. ~효과 stage effect; scenic effects.

**무더기** a pile; a heap; a lot; a deposit. ¶ 사과 한 ~ a pile of apples / 한 ~에 천원 1,000 won a lot / 한 ~에 3,000원 하는 딸기 strawberries sold at three thousand won a pile / ~로 쌓아올리다 pile 〔heap〕 up / ~로 쌓이다 be piled 〔heaped〕 up / ~로 팔다〔사다〕 sell 〔buy〕 by the lot / 그들은 생필품을 ~로 사갰다 They bought up a large quantity of daily 〔living〕 necessities.

◉ ~돈 a pile 〔a lump sum〕 of money: ~돈을 벌다〔잡다〕 make *one's* pile (of money); heap up riches.

**무더기무더기** in piles; in heaps; heap by heap. ¶ 돌이 ~ 쌓이다 stones are deposited in heaps.

**무더위** sultriness; (high) humidity; sultry 〔sweltering, humid〕 weather. ¶ 대단한 ~다 be awfully sultry; be steaming.

**무덕**(無德) lack of virtue. ~하다 be lacking in virtue.

**무던하다** 《사람·정도가》 (be) quite satisfactory; quite good 〔nice〕; generous; liberal; serviceable; passable. ¶ 무던한 물건 quite a good article / 무던한 사람 quite a nice man / 그만하면 ~ That will serve the purpose. / 야, 그 값이 무던하구나 Oh, that's quite a high price!

**무던히** ① 《좋게》 quite nicely; quite satisfactorily. ¶ 그는 우리 애들한테 ~ 굴었다 He was quite nice to our children. ② 《어지간히》 quite; fairly; extremely; exceedingly. ¶ ~ 많다 be quite a lot / ~ 크다 be quite big / ~ 애를 쓰다 make considerable efforts.

**무덤** a grave; a tomb; a sepulcher. ¶ ~ 파는 사람 a gravedigger / ~을 파다 dig a grave / ~에 묻다 bury in a grave / ~을 파헤치다 dig open a grave; 《고분 등》 excavate a tomb / 그가 한 짓은 스스로 ~을 파는 것과 같다 What he did was like digging his own grave. *or* What he did was suicidal.

**무덥다** (be) sultry; sweltering; steaming; humid; muggy; hot and damp; sticky; (rather) hot; stifling. ¶ 무더운 날씨 sultry 〔muggy〕 weather / 이 방은 ~ This room is hot and damp. / 어제는 무더웠으나 오늘은 한결 선선하다 It was stifling yesterday, but it is cooler today.

**무도**(武道) ① 《도》 chivalry; knighthood. ② 《무예》 martial 〔military〕 arts; military science.

**무도**(無道) ~하다 (be) wicked; evil; inhuman; miscreant; immoral; unreasonable; outrageous. ¶ ~한 짓 a cruel deed; an inhuman act.

**무도**(舞蹈) a dance; dancing. ～하다 dance; perform a dance. ◉ ～곡 dance music. ～병(病) 〖의학〗 St. Vitus's dance; chorea. ～장 a dance 〔dancing〕 hall; a ballroom. ～화(靴) dancing shoes; pumps. ～회 a ball; a dance; a dancing party: 가면 ～회 a masked ball; a masquerade / ～회를 열다 give a dance 〔ball〕.

**무독**(無毒) ① 《무해》 being nonpoisonous 〔nontoxic〕; innocuousness; innoxiousness; harmlessness. ～하다 (be) nonpoisonous; nontoxic; harmless; innoxious; innocent (of harm). ② 《성질》 gentleness; mildness. ～하다 (be) gentle; mild.

**무두장이** a tanner.

**무두질** ① 《모피의》 tanning; tawing; dressing skin. ～하다 tan; dress; taw. ¶ ～하지 않은 untanned 〔raw〕 《hide》. ② 《쓰림》 a grinding 〔pricking, gnawing, piercing, stabbing, burning〕 pain 《in stomach》. ～하다 grind; gnaw; prick; pierce; stab; burn. ¶ 뱃속에서 ～하다 have a gnawing pain in *one's* stomach; 《시장해서》 be awfully hungry.

**무드** a mood; an atmosphere. ¶ ～있는 식당 a restaurant with atmosphere / ～를 조성하다 create 〔set〕 a mood / 이 커피숍의 ～는 매우 좋다 This coffee shop 「is quite pleasant 〔has a good atmosphere〕. ◉ ～음악 mood(y) music.

**무득무실**(無得無失) "no gain no loss".

**무득점**(無得點) being without a score. ¶ ～의 scoreless; 《야구》 runless / ～으로 끝나다 end scoreless 〔runless〕 / ～으로 완봉하다 shut out 《the opposing team》; 《구어》 whitewash 《*one's* opponents》 / 《야구에서》 상대팀을 8회까지 ～으로 봉쇄했다 We held them runless for eight innings.

**무디다** ① 《날붙이가》 (be) blunt; dull; 《소리 따위가》 dim. ¶ 무딘 면도날 a dull razor blade / 무딘 소리 a dim 〔dull〕 sound / 칼날을 무디게 하다 turn 〔blunt〕 the edge of a sword / 무언가가 쿵하는 무딘 소리와 함께 땅에 떨어졌다 Something fell to the ground with a dull thud.
② 《머리·감각·움직임이》 (be) dull; slow (움직임이). ¶ 머리가 무딘 사람 a dull 〔dense, slow-witted〕 person; a dullard; a slow coach / 감각이〔센스가〕 ～ have dull senses; be slow to notice; have a slow perception / 결심을 무디게 하다 weaken 《*a person's*》 determination; shake 〔stagger, dampen〕 《*a person's*》 resolve 〔resolution〕; discourage 《*a person*》 from *do*ing / 그는 머리가 무뎌서 상황을 깨닫지 못한다 He doesn't realize the situation because he's slow on the uptake. / 나는 등에 무딘 통증을 느꼈다 I felt a dull pain in my back.
③ 《말이》 (be) blunt; brusque. ¶ 무딘 말 a brusque remark / 말을 무디게 하다 talk bluntly.

**무디어지다** ① 《날붙이가》 grow 〔become〕 dull; get 〔become〕 blunt 〔dull〕; dull. ② 《기세·움직임·감각·기술 따위가》 become dull. ¶ 감각이〔센스가〕 ～ become less perceptive; become insensitive 《to》 / 결심이 ～ *one's* determination weakens 〔falters, wavers, is weakened〕; have *one's* resolve 〔revolution〕 shaken; waver 〔be shaken〕 in *one's* resolve / 솜씨가 ～ become less shrewd 〔capable〕; get out of practice / 그는 연습 부족으로 투구(投球)가 무디어졌다 His pitching has rusted through lack of training.

**무뚝뚝하다** (be) blunt; brusque; abrupt; curt. ¶ 무뚝뚝한 사람 a blunt 〔brusque〕 person; a bad mixer 《미》; an oyster / 무뚝뚝하게 굴다 act brusquely / 무뚝뚝하게 말하다 talk bluntly; speak stiffly / 무뚝뚝한 대답을 하다 give *a person* a curt 〔blunt〕 reply.

**무량**(無量) ～하다 (be) immeasurable; infinite; inestimable. ¶ 감개가 ～하다 *one* 〔*one's* heart〕 is filled with deep emotion. ◉ ～대복 infinite happiness. ～수(壽) constant 〔eternal〕 life.

**무량수전**(無量壽殿) 〖불교〗 the Hall of Eternal Life; the *Muryangsujŏn.*

**무럭무럭** ① 《자람》 rapidly; perceptibly; well. ¶ ～ 자라다 grow fast; grow up quickly 〔rapidly, healthily〕 / 나무가 ～ 자라다 a tree grows well. ② 《김·연기 따위가》 thickly; densely. ¶ 김이 ～ 나다 puff steam / 김이 ～ 나는 음식〔만두〕 a steaming dish 〔bun〕 / 그 요리에서는 김이 ～ 오르고 있었다 Steam was rising from the (hot) dishes.

**무려**(無慮) to the prodigious 〔vast〕 number of; as many 〔much〕 as; no less than. ¶ ～ 3천 명 as many as three thousand people / ～ 2천 명이나 되는 사람들이 홍수로 집을 잃었다 As many as 2,000 people lost their houses by the flood. / ～ 3만의 관중이

야구장에 모였다 No less than 30,000 spectators were present at the baseball field.

**무력**(武力) force of arms; military power; (armed) force; the sword. ¶ ～으로 by (force of) arms; at the point of the bayonet / ～을 쓰지 않고 without an appeal to arms / ～에 호소하다 appeal 〔resort〕 to arms; use force / ～으로 굴복시키다 keep《people》in submission by the saber 〔sword〕 / ～으로 해결하다 settle《an affair》by force / ～을 과시하다 make a show of force; demonstrate muscles / 그 문제는 ～에 의하지 않고 평화리에 해결되었다 The trouble has been peacefully settled without the use of force.

◉ ～간섭 armed interference 〔intervention〕. ～개입 armed intervention: 그들은 그 국제 분쟁에 ～ 개입했다 They meddled in that international conflict by using military force. *or* They intervened militarily in that international conflict. ～공격〔항쟁〕 an armed attack 〔strife〕. ～도발 a military 〔an armed〕 provocation: 적의 ～ 도발을 분쇄하다 smash the enemy's armed provocations. ～외교 power diplomacy; diplomacy backed by force. ～전 armed hostilities. ～정치 power politics; rule of force. ～충돌 an armed clash 〔conflict〕: ～충돌을 피하다 avoid an armed clash. ～행사 the use of armed force. ～혁명 an armed revolution.

**무력**(無力)《힘이 없음》powerlessness; helplessness;《무능》incompetence. ～하다 (be) powerless; impotent; incompetent; helpless; [서술적] have no power 〔influence〕.

> 용법 **powerless** 외부 또는 다른 힘이 너무 강해서 자신이 무력한 경우. **impotent** 자기 자신의 힘이 없어서 무력한 경우. **helpless** 자기 스스로는 어쩔 수 없어서, 손을 드는 무력한 경우.

¶ ～한 군대 ineffective troops / 적의 공격에 ～하다 be helpless against the enemy's attack / ～하게 하다 incapacitate; debilitate; neutralize《enemy defense》/ 나는 아주 ～해서 당신에게 힘이 되어 드릴 수 없을 것 같군요 I am completely powerless so I'm afraid I can't be of any help to you.

◉ ～감 a feeling of helplessness 〔ineffectualness〕.

**무렵**《때》time;《쯤》about; around; toward(s);《…할 무렵》about the time when.... ¶ ～에 at the time; on the occasion; when; as / 꽃 필 ～ the flower season / 그 ～ in those days; then; at that time / 해질 ～ toward evening; at sunset 〔sundown《미》〕/ 1986년 ～부터 since around 1986 / 그 ～ 저는 고교생이었습니다 I was a high school student in those days 〔at that time, then〕.

**무례**(無禮) rudeness; impoliteness; discourtesy; a breach of etiquette; insolence (불손); an insult (모욕). ～하다 (be) impolite; discourteous; rude; insolent; impertinent.

¶ ～한 말을 하다 say *something* rude to *a person;* make an insulting remark / ～한 짓을 하다 be rude《to》; act insultingly《to》/ ～하게도 …하다 have the impertinence to《*do*》; be rude enough to《*do*》/ 왜 이렇게 ～하지 How can you be so rude? / 여성에 대해 ～한 짓을 하지 마라 Don't be rude to a lady. / ～하게도 그는 나를 무시했다 He was rude enough to ignore me. / 이야기를 하는 도중에 퇴장하는 것은 상대에게 ～한 짓이다 Walking out during a speech is an affront to the speaker. / 그의 ～함을 이 이상 참을 수 없다 I can't「put up 〔stand〕 with his insolence any longer. / 저의 ～함을 부디 용서해 주십시오 I sincerely apologize to you for my lack of courtesy.

**무뢰한**(無賴漢) a ruffian; a rowdy; a bum; a roughneck; a rough《영》.

**무료**(無料) no charge. ¶ ～의 free (of charge); gratuitous / ～로 free (of charge); for nothing; gratis; without a fee / ～로 보내다 send《*a thing*》free / ～로 제공되다 be offered free 〔without cost, for nothing〕/ 이 팸플릿은 ～입니다 There is no charge for this pamphlet. / 그것은 ～로 드립니다 You can get it free. *or* It is free (of charge). / 사신 물건은 ～로 배달해 드립니다 Articles bought here will be delivered free of charge. / 견본은 청구하시는 대로 ～ 우송합니다 Patterns are sent post free on request. / ～ 서비스합니다 Service is all free. / 입장〔운임〕 ～《게시》Admission 〔Carriage〕 Free. / 6세 미만 ～《게시》Admission free for children under six. / ～ 증정《게시》Free gift.

◉ ～배달 free delivery (생략 FD). ～봉사 free service; 《자발적인》 volunteer work. ～숙박소 a free public hostelry. ～승차권 a (free) pass. ～입장권〔관람권〕 a free pass 〔ticket〕; a complimentary ticket. ～입장자〔관람자〕 a free visitor; a deadhead 《미》. ～증정 offering 〔giving〕 without payment 〔free of charge〕: ～증정하다 offer 《*a thing*》 free of charge; give for nothing. ～진료소 a free clinic.

**무료**(無聊) ennui; tedium; wearisomeness. ～하다 (be) bored; tedious; wearisome; [서술적] suffer from ennui. ¶ ～함을 달래다 beguile tedious hours; beguile the tedium; relieve *oneself* from ennui 《by》; while away 〔kill〕 the time.

**무루**(無漏) without exception; with no omission; to everybody; one and all.

**무르녹다** ① 《무르익다》 (***a***) 《과일이》 get 〔become〕 fully ripe; be overmature 〔overripe〕. ¶ 무르녹은 감 a fully ripened persimmon. (***b***) 《기회가》 be ripe for 《action》; mature; 《음모 등이》 come to a head. ¶ 기회가 무르녹기를 기다리다 wait for a ripe opportunity. ② 《녹음 등이》 be deep; 《수목이》 be at its best. ¶ 신록이 ～ the fresh green (of spring) is at its best; spring is at its greenest.

**무르다**[1] ① 《물건이》 (be) soft; tender; flabby; flaccid. ¶ 무른 복숭아 a soft peach / 무른 살 flabby 〔flaccid〕 muscles. ② 《사람이》 (be) weak; feeble; infirm; pliable; yielding; unresisting; 《엄하지 않다》 (be) indulgent; soft; generous; be not strict. ¶ 아내에게 무른 남편 an uxorious 〔a doting〕 husband / 자식에게 무른 부친 an indulgent father / 여자에게 ～ be spoony on a woman; have a weakness 〔soft spot〕 for girls / 정에 ～ be easily moved (to tears); be tenderhearted / 그는 사람이 물러 좀처럼 "아니"란 말을 못 한다 He is a weak sort of person unable to say "no" on most occasions.

**무르다**[2] ① 《과일 따위가》 get soft; become tender. ¶ 복숭아가 ～ A peach gets soft. ② 《삶은 것이》 get soft; become tender; be well-cooked. ¶ 무른 감자 a well-cooked potato / 잘 ～ be boiled quite soft / 알맞게 ～ be done to a turn / 잘 물렀습니까 Is it cooked well? *or* Is it well-done?

**무르다**[3] ① 《산 것을》 take back 〔redeem〕 money; cancelling a purchase; get a refund; 《판 것을》 give back 〔return〕 money; cancelling a sale; give a refund. ¶ 집을 샀다가 ～ cancel the purchase of a house; return the house *one* (has) bought and get the money back / 팔았던 시계를 물러 주다 accept the return of a watch (and refund the sales price). ② 《삭치다》 cancel 〔offset〕 each other's accounts. ¶ 주고 받을 것을 ～ cancel the debts each owes the other. ③ 《장기·바둑에서》 retract a move.

**무르익다** ① 《과일·술이》 get ripe; (be) fully ripened; mellow. ¶ 무르익은 감 a fully ripened persimmon / 무르익은 술 mellow wine. ② 《기회가》 become 〔be〕 ripe 《for》; (be) ripe; matured. ¶ 기회가 무르익기를 기다리다 wait till the time is ripe 《for》 / 때는 무르익었다 The opportunity has ripened 〔matured〕. *or* The time is ripe (for it).

**무릅쓰다** risk; brave 〔defy, face〕 《a danger》; venture; run a risk 〔hazard〕; dare. ¶ …을 무릅쓰고 in spite of; despite; in defiance of; at the risk of; in the face 〔teeth〕 of / 비바람을 ～ brave 〔dare, defy〕 the wind and rain; weather a storm / 위험을 ～ brave 〔dare, defy〕 a danger; run a risk / 비를 무릅쓰고 학교에 가다 go to school in spite of the rain / 죽음을 무릅쓰고 저항하다 face death to resist / 나는 생명의 위험을 무릅쓰고 그녀를 구하려 했다 I tried to save her at the risk of my life. / 그는 부모의 반대를 무릅쓰고 결혼했다 He got married in spite of his parents' opposition.

**무릇**[1] 〖식물〗 a squill.

**무릇**[2] generally speaking; as a general rule; in general. ¶ ～ 사람이란 것 a man in general / ～ 사람이란 해야 할 본분이 있는 법이다 All men have their duties.

**무릉도원**(武陵桃源) an Arcadia; a Utopia; the Happy Valley.

**무릎** a knee; a lap; 《옷 따위의》 the knee. (★ lap는 앉았을 때의 허리에서 무릎까지의 부분을 말하며, 어린아이 따위를 올려 놓는 곳). ¶ ～깊이 knee-deep / ～을 베개삼아〔베고〕 with *one's* head on another's lap / ～을 구부리고 on *one's* bended knees / ～으로 기다 go on *one's* knees / ～으로 서다 rise on the knees / 물이 ～까지 차다 stand 〔sink〕 knee-deep in the water / ～을 꿇다 kneel down; fall on *one's* knees;

bend *one's* knees; 《예배볼 때》 genuflect; 《굴복》 bend 〔bow〕 the knee to 〔before〕 《*a person*》; yield 《to》; surrender / ∼을 꿇고 애원하다 implore on *one's* (bended) knees / ∼을 맞대(고 앉)다 sit 〔get〕 knee to knee 《with》 / ∼을 치다 slap 〔hit, pat〕 *one's* lap 《with glee or admiration》; be full of glee 〔admiration〕 / ∼을 치며 기뻐하다 be in high spirits; express *one's* great joy / ∼을 맞대고 이야기하다 have a familiar 〔heart-to=heart〕 talk 《with》; talk face to face / ∼을 베다 lay 〔rest, pillow〕 *one's* head on 〔in〕 《*a person's*》 lap / ∼ 위에 앉다 sit on 《*a person's*》 lap / 아이를 ∼에 안다 hold a child in 〔on〕 *one's* lap / ∼까지 내려오는 스커트 a knee-length skirt / 눈이 ∼까지 쌓였다 The snow lay knee-deep. / 그는 도랑에 빠져 ∼을 다쳤다 Falling into a ditch, he was wounded in the knee. / 바지의 ∼이 닳았다 My trousers are (worn) out at the knees. / 무서워서 ∼이 덜덜 떨렸다 My knees shook under me with fear.
◉ ∼덮개 a lap robe 《미》; a travelling rug 《영》. ∼마디〔관절〕 a knee joint. ∼뼈 the kneepan; the kneecap.

**무릎맞춤** a confrontation (for purposes of cross-examination). ⇨ 대질(對質).

**무릎반사**(一反射) 〖의학〗 a knee jerk; a 「patellar reflex.

**무리**[1] ① 《사람의》 a group; a crowd; a throng; 《폭도·악당의》 a mob; a gang; 《짐승의》 a herd (소·말·사슴 따위); a flock (양·토끼); a pack (사냥개·이리 따위); 《새 떼》 a flock; a covey (메추라기); 《곤충 따위》 a swarm; a cloud (메뚜기·파리 따위); 《고기 떼》 a shoal; a school. ¶ 사람의 ∼ a crowd of people / 양의 ∼ a flock of sheep / 고등어의 ∼ a school of mackerel / 열 사람 스무 사람씩 ∼를 지어 in groups of ten to twenty / ∼를 짓다 group; form 「a group 〔groups〕 / ∼를 지어 다니다 move around in crowds 〔pack, flock, swarm, mass〕 / ∼를 지어 날아가다 fly in a flock. ② 《도당》 a company; a group; a gang. ¶ ∼를 짓다 gang together; form a gang / ∼를 지어 in a gang / 김씨와 그의 ∼가 도당을 짓다 Mr. Kim and his crowd gang up together. ①, ② ⇨떼[1]. ③ 《생산물의 시기》 the season 《of prevalence for fish, *etc.*》. ¶ 청어 ∼ the herring season.

**무리**[2] 《앙금》 water-soaked rice ground into settlings 〔sediments〕. ◉ ∼떡 rice cakes made of *muri*. 무릿가루 flour of dried *muri*.

**무리**[3] 《해·달의》 a halo; a ring; a circle. ¶ 달∼ the halo of the moon.

**무리**(無理) ① 《이치에 맞지 않음》 unreasonableness; unnaturalness. ∼하다 (be) unreasonable; unjust (부당하다); (be) unnatural (부자연스럽다). ¶ ∼하게 unreasonably; unjustly / ∼ 없는 《타당한》 reasonable; justifiable; 《자연스러운》 natural / ∼를 하다 go against nature / ∼한 요구를 하다 ask too much of 《*a person*》; make an unreasonable demand of 《*a person*》 / 그건 ∼한 주문이다 That's expecting 〔asking〕 too much. / 이 이상 바라는 것은 ∼다 You can't reasonably wish for more. / 네가 그녀를 싫어하는 것도 ∼는 아니다 It is natural 〔no wonder〕 that you should dislike her. *or* You have good reason to dislike her. / 당신이 그렇게 말하는 것도 ∼는 아니요 You may well say so. / ∼한 소리 하지 마라 Stop being unreasonable. / 그녀가 그렇게 멋지니, 그가 좋아하는 것도 ∼가 아니다 She's so nice, I can't blame him for liking her.
② 《불가능》 impossibility. ∼하다 (be) impossible; beyond *one's* power. ¶ ∼한 일을 시도하다 attempt the impossible; try to do something beyond *one's* power / 그 일은 한 사람으로는 ∼다 The job is too much for one person.
③ 《억지·강제》 compulsion. ∼하다 (be) compulsory; forcible; forced. ¶ ∼하게 by force; forcibly; compulsorily; 《좋든 싫든》 willy-nilly; against *one's* will / ∼하게 당기다 pull by force / ∼하게 물을 먹이다 force water down 《*a person's*》 throat / ∼하게 …시키다 compel 〔force〕 《*a person*》 to 《*do*》; force 〔drive〕 《*a person*》 into 《*do*ing》 / 저 때문에 너무 ∼를 하셨습니다 You have made too many sacrifices for me.
④ 《과도》 excessiveness; immoderation; 《과로》 overstrain; overwork. ∼하다 (be) excessive; immoderate; too 《difficult》. ¶ ∼를 하다 strain 〔overdo〕 *oneself;* overstrain 〔overwork〕 *oneself;* overtax *oneself* / ∼를 하게 하다 put a strain on 《*a person*》 / ∼를 해서 사다 go to all length 〔any length〕 to buy 《*something*》; scrape together a sufficient amount of money to purchase 《*something*》 / ∼하지 말게 Take it easy. / ∼를 하면 못쓴다 It won't do to

try to overreach yourself. / ~를 해서 몸이 안 좋다 The overstrain affected my health. / 그 일은 나에겐 ~다 I am not equal to the task.
◉ ~방정식 〖수학〗 an irrational equation. ~수 an irrational 〔a surd〕 number. ~식 〖수학〗 an irrational expression.

**무마**(撫摩) ① 《어루만짐》 stroking; patting. ~하다 pat; stroke; smooth down. ② 《달램》 soothing; coaxing; pacifying; appeasing. ~하다 soothe; coax; pacify; appease; calm (down); quiet. ¶ 노여움을 ~시키다 soothe 〔pacify〕 《*a person's*》 rage / 아무를 잘 ~하여 체념시키다 coax *a person* 「to give it up 〔into giving it up〕.

**무말랭이** dried strips of radish.

**무면허**(無免許) ¶ ~로 without license 〔licence 《영》, permit, certificate〕 / ~의 unlicensed; without a license.
◉ ~운전 unlicensed driving; driving without a license: ~운전사 an unlicensed driver / 그는 ~ 운전을 했다 He drove a car without a license. / 그는 ~ 운전으로 경찰에 잡혔다 He was caught by the police for driving without a license. ~ 의사 an unlicensed practitioner.

**무명** cotton cloth 〔fabric〕; cotton.
◉ ~베 cotton cloth; muslin. ~실 cotton thread 〔yarn〕. ~옷 cotton clothes.

**무명**(無名) ¶ ~의 nameless; unnamed; anonymous (익명의); 《알려지지 않은》 unknown; obscure / 그는 그때까지 ~이었다 He was still an unknown. / 당시 ~의 한 청년이던 한씨는 그 소설을 쓰고 일약 유명인이 되었다 Mr. Han, then a youth without reputation, leaped into fame by writing that novel.
◉ ~골(骨) the innominate bone; the hipbone. ~씨 an anonym(ous person); an unidentified person: ~씨로부터 편지를 받다 receive an anonymous letter. ~용사 an unknown soldier: ~ 용사의 무덤 the Tomb of the Unknown (Soldier). ~인(사)〔작가〕 an obscure individual 〔writer〕; a nameless person 〔writer〕. ~지(指) the fourth finger; the ring finger.

**무모**(無毛) ¶ ~의 hairless. ◉ ~증 〖의학〗 atrichosis (*pl.* -choses); atrichia.

**무모**(無謀) ~하다 《무작정의》 (be) resourceless; reckless; 《경솔한》 rash; 《무분별한》 imprudent; thoughtless. ¶ ~하게도 recklessly; rashly; thoughtlessly / ~한 사나이 a reckless fellow; a daredevil / ~한 시도 a reckless attempt; a wild 〔mad〕 scheme / ~한 짓을 하다 do reckless thing; do something rash; take a leap into the dark / 참 ~한 짓도 했군 What a rash thing you have done! / ~한 짓일랑 하지 마라 Look before you leap. / ~한 운전은 하지 마세요 Don't drive recklessly. / 그 조그마한 무명 회사에 투자하는 것은 아주 ~한 짓이었다 It was just a shot in the dark to invest in that small unknown company.

**무문근**(無紋筋) 〖해부〗 an unstriated muscle.

**무미**(無味) ~하다 (be) tasteless; insipid; flat; vapid. ¶ ~ 무취 무색(無臭無色)의 tasteless, odorless and colorless.

**무미건조**(無味乾燥) dryness; dullness; tastelessness. ~하다 (be) dry; dry-as-dust; dull; flat; tasteless; insipid. ¶ ~한 강의 a dull 〔dry-as-dust〕 lecture / ~한 문체 a bald style / ~한 생활 prosaic 〔cut-and-dried〕 life / 그의 이야기는 아주 ~하다 His speech is 「dry as dust 〔uninteresting〕.

**무미류**(無尾類) 〖동물〗 an anuran.

**무미익기**(無尾翼機) a tailless airplane.

**무반**(武班) the military nobility.

**무반동**(無反動) ¶ ~총〔포〕 〖군사〗 a recoilless rifle 〔gun〕.

**무반주**(無伴奏) ¶ ~의 〖음악〗 unaccompanied 《cello sonata》.

**무방비**(無防備) ¶ ~의 defenseless; unfortified; naked / ~상태 《leave a town in》 a defenseless state. ◉ ~도시 an open city; an unfortified city.

**무방침**(無方針) lack of fixed policy.

**무방하다**(無妨—) 《해가 없다》 do 《*a person*》 no harm; 《상관없다》 be no hindrance; do not matter; make no difference; 《해도 좋다》 may; can; be all right; be allowed to 《*do*》. ¶ …함은 무방하다 be not precluded from 《*do*ing》; may... / 술담배는 약간 해도 무방할 겁니다 A little alcohol or tobacco will do you no harm.

**무배당**(無配當) ¶ ~의 non-dividend; without dividend / ~이다 No dividend is paid 《on the stocks》. / 그 회사는 부득불 ~이 될 수밖에 없는 처지가 되었다 The company was forced 「to pass its dividend 〔to suspend dividends〕.
◉ ~주(株) a non-dividend stock.

**무법**(無法) lawlessness; unlawfulness; injustice. ~하다 (be) unlawful; lawless; outrageous (난폭한); 《부당한》

unreasonable; exorbitant. ¶ ~의 《불법》 unlawful; lawless; 《난폭》 outrageous; 《부당》 unreasonable; exorbitant / ~한 조치 an unlawful measure / ~한 짓을 하다 act unlawfully; do 《*a person*》 wrong. ◉ ~상태 《be in》 a lawless state 〔condition〕; 《be under》 a reign of violence. ~자 an outrageous fellow; an outlaw. ~지대 a disturbed 〔lawless〕 area. ~천지 a lawless world. ~행위 the act of hooliganism.

**무변**(無邊) ① 《무한》 infinity; limitlessness; boundlessness. ~하다 (be) limitless; boundless; infinite. ¶ 광대 ~한 vast and boundless. ② 《무이자》 being free of 〔bearing no〕 interest.
◉ ~대해(大海) a boundless ocean. ~전(錢) a passive 〔flat〕 debt; interest-free money; a loan without interest.

**무변화**(無變化) changelessness; 《단조로움》 monotony. ¶ ~의 unchanging; unchanged; monotonous.

**무병**(無病) ~하다 be free from diseases; be healthy (and sound); be 「well 〔in good health〕.

**무보수**(無報酬) nonpayment. ¶ ~의 free; gratuitous / ~로 without pay 〔recompense, reward〕; 《무료로》 free of charge; for nothing / ~로 일하다 work without pay; give *one's* service free / ~로 가르치다 teach 「free 〔without a fee〕 / 그녀는 ~로 도서관에서 일하고 있다 She is working at the library 「for no pay 〔without pay, on a voluntary basis〕.

**무복**(巫卜) shamans and fortune-tellers; sorceresses and soothsayers.

**무복친**(無服親) distant relatives (for whom *one* wears no mourning).

**무분별**(無分別) indiscretion; imprudence; recklessness; thoughtlessness. ~하다 (be) indiscreet; thoughtless; reckless. ¶ ~하게도 thoughtlessly; indiscreetly; imprudently; recklessly / ~한 짓을 하다 do something rash; commit a rash act; act rashly / ~하게도 …하다 have the imprudence 〔indiscretion〕 to 《*do*》; be thoughtless enough to 《*do*》 / ~하게도 그는 소지금을 다 써버렸다 He was foolish enough to spend all his money. / 그는 그런 어리석은 짓을 할 만큼 ~하지는 않다 He has more sense than to do such a foolish thing.

**무불간섭**(無不干涉) indiscreet meddling in everything; indiscreet interference. ~하다 always nose into; meddle constantly.

**무비**(武備) armaments; military preparations.

**무비**(無比) incomparableness; peerlessness. ~하다 (be) incomparable; matchless; peerless; unrivaled. ¶ 당대 ~의 unparalleled by *one's* contemporaries.

**무비판**(無批判) ¶ ~적(으로) uncritical(-ly); unquestioning(ly); indiscriminate(ly) / 정치가가 하는 말을 ~적으로 믿어서는 안된다 We should not believe uncritically what politicians say.

**무사**(武士) a warrior; a soldier; a knight. ◉ ~도 chivalry; knighthood (기사도).

**무사**(無死) 〖야구〗 no down 〔out〕; none out. ◉ ~ 만루 full bases with no outs: ~ 만루의 찬스를 놓치다 let slip a big chance of victory in no down, full bases.

**무사**(無私) impartiality. ~하다 (be) unselfish; impartial; disinterested; selfless. ¶ 공평 ~한 fair and disinterested.

**무사**(無事) 《안전》 being without mishap 〔accident〕; safety; security; 《평온》 peace; 《건강》 good health. ~하다 《안전하다》 (be) safe; secure; 《평온》 (be) peaceful; quiet; be (*do*ing) well. ¶ ~히 safely; in safety; without mishap 〔accident〕; all right / ~히 끝나다 pass off without mischance; be carried out all right / ~히 도착하다 《물건이》 arrive in good condition / ~히 돌아오다 come back safe / ~히 있다 be in good health; live in peace / ~히 지내다 get along well; be enjoying good health / ~히 빠져나오다〔피하다〕 make good *one's* escape; escape without harm / ~히 해결나다 come to a satisfactory conclusion / ~히 임무를 마치다 carry out *one's* duty 〔mission〕; acquit *oneself* of a task / 그날 밤은 ~히 지나갔다 The night passed unevently. / 그래 가지고는 ~히 끝나지 않을걸 That won't fix up the matter at all, I fear. / 배는 ~히 항구로 피난했다 The ship found safe shelter in a harbor. / 그는 ~히 집에 돌아갔다 He returned home safe 〔in safety〕. (★ arrive, return 따위의 동사에는 부사 safely 대신 형용사 safe가 쓰임. 뜻은 같지만 return safe가 구어적임) / 그렇게 하는 것이 ~하겠는걸 It would be safer to do so. / 불이 났지만 금고는 ~했다 The safe remained intact in the fire. / 그 문제는 ~히 해결되었다 The problem was settled peacefully. / 졸업식은 ～히 끝났다 The commencement went off without a hitch. ◉ ～안일주의 a peace-at-any-price principle 〔policy〕; an easygoing attitude: 그는 만사가 ～ 안일주의이다 He always avoids trouble at any cost.

**무사고**(無事故) ¶ ～의 accident-free / ～로 without an accident / 그는 20년간 ～인 모범운전사로 표창되었다 He was officially commended as an excellent driver because he had no accident for twenty years. ◉ ～비행〔운전〕 accident-free flying 〔driving〕; flying 〔driving〕 without an accident.

**무사마귀** 〚의학〛 a wart; a verruca (*pl.* -cae). ¶ ～투성이의 warty / ～가 나다 have a wart; a wart forms 〔grows〕.

**무사분열**(無絲分裂) 〚생물〛 amitosis.

**무사분주**(無事奔走) ～하다 be very busy about nothing; be busy with nothing in particular.

**무사태평**(無事泰平) 《평안》 tranquility; peace; 《태평》 being easy(going) 〔carefree〕. ～하다 (be) peaceful; tranquil; easy(going); free from care. ¶ 시험 날짜가 박두했는데 어찌 그리 ～할 수 있는가 How can you take it easy when the examination is so near.

**무산**(無産) ¶ ～의 propertyless; unpropertied. ◉ ～계급 the proletariat; proletarians; the propertyless 〔unpropertied〕 (class). ～대중 the proletariat (class). ～자 a proletarian; 《집합적》 the have-nots 《구어》. ～정당 a proletarian party.

**무산**(霧散) dissipating 〔vanishing〕 like the mists. ～하다 dissipate; vanish; be dispelled; disperse.

**무삶이** 〚농업〛 ① 《고르기》 softening a rice field with water. ② 《갈기》 plowing a rice field wet.

**무상**(無上) ¶ ～의 supreme; the highest; the greatest; the best / 그것은 저에게 ～의 영광입니다 I deem it the highest honor I could aspire to.

**무상**(無常) mutability; transience; uncertainty. ～하다 (be) uncertain; mutable; transient; vain. ¶ ～의 uncertain; mutable; transient / 인생의 ～ the frailty of life / 인생은 ～하다 All is vanity in life. *or* Man's life is transitory. *or* Nothing is certain in this world. / 인생의 ～함이여, 아침에 홍안인데 저녁에는 백골 Life is too uncertain. Here today, gone tomorrow.

**무상**(無償) ¶ ～의〔으로〕 gratis; free (of charge); for nothing; without compensation 〔pay〕; 〚법〛 gratuitous(-ly) / 수재민들에게 모포가 ～으로 배급되었다 Blankets were distributed free of charge to flood victims. ◉ ～계약 a gratuitous contract; a nude pact 〔contract〕. ～교부 《주식》 delivery without compensation. ～배급 free distribution. ～양도 a gratuitous conveyance. ～원조 a grant; grant-type aid. ～주(株) a stock dividend; bonus stock. ～증자 free issue of new shares.

**무상출입**(無常出入) ～하다 go in and out constantly; frequent; visit freely; have free access to 《*a person's* house》.

**무색**(一色) dyed color. ◉ ～옷 clothes made of colored cloth.

**무색**(無色) ① 《빛깔없음》 lack of color; colorlessness. ¶ ～의 colorless; achromatic / ～ 투명한 액체 a colorless transparent liquid / ～으로 하다 make 《*a thing*》 colorless; achromatize. ② 《무안》 shame; disgrace. ～하다 (be) ashamed; feel shame. ¶ ～케 하다 put 《*a person*》「in the shade 〔to shame〕; outshine 《*a person*》 / 네 솜씨는 전문가를 ～케 할 정도다 Your skill would put a professional「to shame 〔in the shade〕.

**무생물**(無生物) an inanimate object 〔being〕; a lifeless 〔nonliving〕 thing. ◉ ～계 inanimate nature 〔world〕. ～시대 〚지질〛 the azoic age 〔era〕. ～학 abiology.

**무서리** the first 〔early〕 frost. ¶ ～가 내리다 have the first frost of the year.

**무서움** (a) fear; fright; terror; dread; horror. ¶ ～을 모르는 fearless; dauntless; intrepid / ～을 타다 be easily frightened / ～을 참다 bear *one's* fear / ～이 없다 have 〔feel〕 no fear.

**무서워하다** fear; dread; be afraid 〔fearful〕 《of》; be frightened 〔scared, terrified〕 《at》; be nervous about. ¶ 무서워하지 않다 be not afraid 《of》; have no fear 《of》; defy 《death》 / 지진을 몹시 ～ dread 〔be very timid of〕 earthquake / 무서워할 것 없다 You have nothing「to fear 〔to be afraid of〕. / 그는 개가 무서워 접근하지 않았다 He was afraid to come near the dog.

**무석인**(武石人) a stone statue of a warrior (standing) in front of a royal tomb.

**무선**(無線) radio; wireless. ¶ ～으로 송신하다 send a message by radio

〔wireless〕/ ～으로 연락을 취하고 있다 be in radio contact《with》/ ～으로 긴급 연락이 들어왔다 An urgent message was received on the radio.
◉ ～검파기 a radiodetector. ～공학 radio engineering. ～관리법 Wireless Control Law. ～국 a radio 〔wireless〕 station. ～기술 radio techniques. ～방송 radio broadcasting; radiocasting《미》. ～방위계(方位計) a radiogoniometer. ～방향탐지 radio-direction-finding (생략 R.D.F.): ～방향 탐지기 a radio compass; a radio direction finder. ～사진전송 radiophotography. ～송신 wireless transmission: ～송신기 a wireless transmitter. ～실 a radio=room; a wireless room. ～위치 표지 〖항공〗 a marker (radio) beacon. ～장치 a wireless installation. ～전보 a wireless (telegram, message); a radio-telegram; a radiogram《미》: ～전보를 치다 send a radio 〔wireless〕; radio 〔wireless〕 a message. ～전송사진 a radiophoto; a photoradiogram. ～제어 radio control. ～조종 wireless 〔radio, remote〕 control: ～ 조종하다 radiocontrol; control by wireless 〔radio〕/ ～ 조종기 a radio-controlled plane; 《무선 유도 비행기》 a ground=to-air pilotless aircraft (생략 GAPA). ～주파수 radio frequency. ～중계 radio relay: ～ 중계국 a radio relay station. ～통신 radio 〔wireless〕 communication: ～ 통신국 a radio communication station / ～통신 방해 jamming (of wireless) / ～통신사 a radio operator; a radioman / ～통신 인구 《이용자수》 wireless-communication population. ～표지 a raido beacon. ～호출기 a pager 〔beeper〕; a radio pager.

**무선전신**(無線電信) wireless telegraphy; radiotelegraphy. ¶ ～으로 by radio 〔wireless〕/ ～을 치다 telegraph by wireless; radio / (선박이) ～ 설비를 갖추다 carry radio 〔wireless〕/ 구조를 요청하는 ～을 받다 pick up wireless calls for help 《from a wrecked ship》/ A와 B 사이에 직통 ～이 개통되었다 Direct wireless communication has been established between A and B. ◉ ～국 a radio 〔wireless〕 station. ～기 a radio 〔wireless〕 apparatus; a wireless telegraph 〔set〕. ～기사 a radiotelegraphist; a radio 〔wireless〕 operator; a radioman.

**무선전화**(無線電話) a wireless telephone 〔set〕; radiotelephony; 《전화기》 a radiotelephone; a cordless phone; a cellular phone. ¶ ～로 말하다 talk over the radiophone 〔by wireless〕; have a wireless talk 《with》/ ～를 걸다 telephone 〔talk〕 by wireless; radiotelephone 《to》. ◉ ～국 a radio station. ～시설 a radiotelephone service 〔system〕. ～통신 a radiotelephone message. 다중 채널 ～기 a multichannel radiophone. 휴대용 ～기 a walkie=talkie; a cellular phone.

**무섬타다** be easily frightened; scare 「easily.

**무섭다** ① 《끔찍하다》 (be) terrible; fearful; frightful; dreadful; horrible; 《섬뜩하다》 (be) grim; uncanny; 《사납다·흉악하다》 (be) fierce; ferocious; savage. ¶ 무서운 광경 a horrible scene; a dreadful sight / 무서운 동물 a fierce animal / 무서운 독 a dreadful poison / 무서운 무기 a formidable weapon / 무서운 병 a 「deadly 〔horrible〕 disease / 무서운 영화 a horror movie / 무섭게 terribly; horribly; awfully / 무서워서 도망치다 run away through fear / 무서워서 떨다 tremble 〔recoil〕 with fear / 무서워서 소리치다 shriek in fear 〔terror〕; cry out for fear / 무서워서 말도 못하다 cannot speak for fear / 무서워서 움츠리다 shrink for fear / 무섭게 노려보다 glare at 《*a person*》 fiercely; browbeat 《*a person*》/ 무서운 눈으로 보다 look menacingly 《at *a person*》/ 무섭게 하다 frighten; terrify; scare / 무서워지다 be seized with fear.
② 《대단·지독하다》 (be) awful; terrible; frightful; 《엄청나다》 tremendous; formidable; stupendous; terrific 《구어》; enormous. ¶ 무서운 구두쇠 an awful miser / 무서운 인파 a tremendous crowd; an enormous turnout (of people) / 무서운 정력 prodigious energy / 무서운 힘 stupendous force / 무서운 속도로 at a furious 〔terrific〕 speed / 무섭게 춥다 be terribly 〔awfully〕 cold / 무섭게 서둘다 be in an awful rush / 습관은 ～ A habit is something not to be lightly treated.
③ 《두렵다》 be afraid 《of, that》; be apprehensive (lest); be scared 〔frightened〕. ¶ 무서움을 모르다 fear nothing; be fearless 〔dauntless, intrepid〕/ 감기 들까 ～ I am afraid of catching a cold. / 무서워 죽을 뻔했다 I was scared to death. / 무서울 것 없다 There's nothing to be afraid of (for me).

**무성**(無性) ¶ ～의 〖생물〗 agamous; agamic; sexless; asexual; neutral 《flowers》. ◉ ～번식 agamogenesis. ～생식 asexual reproduction. ～세대 an asexual generation. ～식물 a neuter (plant). ～아(芽) a gemma (*pl.* -mae). ～화(花) 〖식물〗 a neuter flower.

**무성**(無聲) ¶ ～의 silent; voiceless. ◉ ～방전(放電) silent discharge. ～음 〖음성〗 a voiceless sound. ～자음 〖음성〗 a voiceless consonant.

**무성영화**(無聲映畫) a silent film 〔motion picture〕. ◉ ～ 시대 the silent picture days.

**무성의**(無誠意) insincerity. ～하다 (be) insincere; untrustworthy; fickle; 《people》 lacking in good faith; 《구어》 shifty. ¶ ～한 짓을 하다 act in bad faith / 그건 너무 ～한 행동이 아닌가 Your conduct betrays a lack of good faith.

**무성하다**(茂盛一) (be) exuberant; luxuriant; thick; close-grown. ¶ 나무가 무성한 산 a thickly-〔well-〕wooded hill / 잎이 무성한 나무 a leafy tree; a tree thick 〔thickly covered〕 with leaves / 풀이 ～ be thick 〔densely covered〕 with grass / 무성하게 자라다 [초목이 주어] grow thick(ly) 〔luxuriantly〕; [장소가 주어] be thickly covered with 《trees》; be overgrown with 《weeds》.

**무세**(無稅) ¶ ～의 (tax-)free; duty-free; untaxed; taxless / ～로 free of duties; duty-free / ～ 수입을 허가하다 allow the free entry 《of goods》; admit 《goods》 free of duty / 저 상점에서는 ～로 전기 제품들을 살 수 있다 You can buy electric appliances tax-free at that store. ◉ ～ 수입 free entry: ～수입품 duty-free imports; articles on the free list. ～품 duty-free goods; a tax-free article; goods free of duty.

**무소** 〖동물〗 a rhinoceros; a rhino 《구어》. ◉ 일각(一角)〔인도〕～ an 〔a great〕 Indian rhinoceros; a great one-horned rhinoceros.

**무소**(誣訴) 〖법〗 false accusation; a trumped-up charge. ～하다 accuse 《*a person*》 falsely; make a false accusation 《against *a person*》.

**무소득**(無所得) no gain 〔income〕; no benefit. ～하다 gain little 《from, by》; get little benefit 《from》; be little benefited 《by》.

**무소부지**(無所不知) omniscience. ～하다 be omniscient; know everything.

**무소불능**(無所不能) omnipotence; almightiness. ～하다 (be) omnipotent; almighty.

**무소불위**(無所不爲) omnipotence. ⇨ 무소불능.

**무소속**(無所屬) ¶ ～의 affiliated with no party; independent; unattached; 《중립의》 neutral / ～이다 be independent; be not a party man 《미구어》/ 그는 ～으로 입후보했다 He ran as an independent candidate. *or* He ran as a candidate, independent of any party. ◉ ～ 의원 an independent (member); a nonpartisan representative. ～자 a free lance(r). ～후보 an independent candidate.

**무소식**(無消息) no news 《from *a person*》. ¶ ～이다 hear nothing from 《*a person*》; have no news from / ～이 희소식 《속담》 No news is good news.

**무솔다** 《푸성귀가》 decay from the dampness.

**무쇠** cast iron; iron.

**무수**(無水) 〖화학〗 [형용사적] anhydrous. ◉ ～규산 silicic (acid) anhydride; silica. ～물(物) an anhydride.

**무수**(無數) being innumerable 〔numberless, countless〕. ～하다 (be) innumerable; countless; numberless. ¶ ～히 countlessly; innumerably; without 〔out of〕 number; in countless numbers / 밤하늘에는 ～한 별들이 반짝이고 있었다 The myriads of stars were twinkling in the night sky.

**무수기** the difference in water level between ebb and flood tides.

**무수리**[1] 《궁중의》 a court lady's maid.

**무수리**[2] 〖조류〗 an adjutant bird 〔stork〕.

**무수입**(無收入) ¶ ～으로 without (any) income.

**무수정**(無修正) ¶ ～으로 without revision 〔amendment〕 / 법안을 ～으로 통과시키다 pass the bill with no revision.

**무숙자**(無宿者) a homeless vagabond 〔wanderer〕; a tramp; a vagrant; 《미구어》 a hobo.

**무순**(無順) ¶ ～의 disorderly; out of order / ～으로 without order; in random 〔unalphabetical〕 order.

**무술**(戊戌) 〖민속〗 the 35th binary term of the sexagenary cycle.

**무술**(巫術) 《practice》 shamanism.

**무술**(武術) military 〔martial〕 arts. ¶ ～사범 a master of military arts / ～에 조예가 좀 있다 have some military accomplishments.

**무쉬** the 9th and 24th days of the lunar month, when the flood tide begins after the ebb tide.

**무슨** what; what kind of; some; some kind of. ¶ ～일 《의문》 what; 《어떤 일》 something; 《만사》 everything / ～ 일에

도 in all things / ~ 일에나 in anything and everything / ~ 까닭에 why; for what reason / ~ 일이 있건〔일어나든〕 no matter what happens〔may happen〕; whatever happens / ~ 일이 있으면 if anything〔the unexpected〕 should happen《to *a person*》; in case of emergency〔need〕/ ~ 일이냐 What is the matter with you? *or* What's up? *or* What's the matter? / ~ 일이 생겼습니까 What happened? *or* Did something happen? *or* What's the trouble? / ~ 일로 오셨습니까 What can I do for you? *or* Is there anything I can do for you? / ~일이고 열심히 해야 한다 Whatever (kind of) job it is, you should do it wholeheartedly. / ~ 명안이 없는가 Can you think of some good plan? / 그것을 공부해서 ~ 소용이 있는가 What is the use〔good〕of studying it? / ~ 음식을 이렇게 많이 차리셨습니까 My, what a lot of nice food you have fixed for us! / ~ 일을 그렇게 더디게 하시오 Why are you so slow with the work! / 언제 ~일이 있을지 모른다 Anything can happen any time. *or* You can never tell what will happen. / ~ 사람이 그렇게 게으르담 What a lazy man he is〔you are〕! / 남이 ~ 말을 하든 상관 안 해 I don't mind what people say of me. / ~ 수를 써서라도 그를 데리고 오게 You must force him to come here by all means. / ~일이 있으면 곧 전화를 하게 Call me immediately if anything happens. / 김선생님께 ~ 전할 말씀이라도 있습니까 Is there any message for Mr. Kim?

**무슨 일이 있어도**《긍정》by all〔any, all possible〕means; at any cost; at all costs〔risks〕; whatever happens; by some means or other; must needs《*do*》; needs must《*do*》(★ needs는 부사. must needs나 needs must나 거의 같게 쓰이지만 후자는 약간 고체. must needs는 종종「아무리 해도 …라고 하여 말을 듣지 않다」의 뜻을 가짐);《부정》by no means; on no account. ¶ 그는 ~ 거기 머물러야 한다고 강하게 주장했다 He strongly insisted that he should stay there. / ~ 끝까지 해내는 거다 Go through with it by all means〔at any cost〕! / ~그것을 내놓을 수는 없다 I won't part with it for anything in the world.

**무승부**(無勝負) a tie; a draw; a drawn game; an undecided match. ¶ ~가 되다, ~로 끝나다 end in a draw〔tie〕.

**무시**(無視) disregard《for rules》; neglect《of consequences》. ~하다 disregard; ignore; pay no attention〔heed〕《to》; take no account〔notice〕《of》; set《the rules》at naught. ¶ …을 ~하고 in disregard of…; in defiance of… / 교통신호를 ~ 하고 against the traffic signal / 남의 기분을 ~하다 pay no attention to other people's feelings / 규칙을 ~하다 flout〔defy〕 the rules / 문법을 ~하다 do violence to grammar / 민의(民意)를 ~하다 override the wishes of the people / 이 문제는 ~할 수 없다 This problem cannot be bypassed. / 그는 ~할 수 없는 존재다 He is a man to be reckoned with. / 나의 경고는 ~되었다 My warning was disregarded〔went unheeded〕. / 그는 나의 충고를 ~ 했다 He took no notice of my advice. / 그는 윗사람에게 ~당했다 He was ignored by his superior.

**무시근하다** (be) lazy and slipshod; loose; slovenly; sloppy.

**무시로**(無時—) at any time; at all times; in an unpredictable way.

**무시류**(無翅類)〖곤충〗Aptera.

**무시무시하다** (be) horrible; terrible; frightful; dreadful; ghastly. ¶ 무시무시한 광경 a terrible〔ghastly〕scene / 전투 뒤의 고요는 무시무시했다 The silence after the battle was ghastly.

**무시험**(無試驗) ¶ ~의 free of examination / 운동 선수로서의 재능이 있어서 그는 대학에 ~으로 입학했다 His talent as an athlete enabled him to enter the university without taking an examination. ◉ ~검정 getting a certificate without examination. ~입학제도 a test-free admission system. ~진학〔입학〕admission to a school without examination.

**무식**(無識) ignorance; illiteracy. ~하다 (be) ignorant; illiterate. ¶ ~한 사람 an ignorant person; an ignoramus / ~한 탓으로 due to ignorance / ~을 드러내다 betray〔expose〕*one's* ignorance. ◉ ~쟁이 an ignorant man.

**무신**(戊申)〖민속〗the 45th binary term of the sexagenary cycle.

**무신경**(無神經) insensibility; insensitivity;《냉담》apathy. ~하다 (be) insensible (남의 감정에 대해); inconsiderate; apathetic; stolid; callous《to》; thick-skinned (비난·모욕 등에). ¶ 수모당해도 ~이다 be insensible〔lost〕 to shame / 그는 여자의 미묘한

감정 따위에 대해서는 ~하다 He is apathetic to delicate woman's feelings. / 그는 남이 무어라 하건 ~이다 He is too thick-skinned to mind what others say. / 식사 중에 그런 이야기를 꺼내다니, ~ 하기 짝이 없다 It's too inconsiderate of you to bring up such a subject during the meal.

**무신고**(無申告) ¶ ~로 without (previous) notice; without leave. ◉ ~ 데모 an unsanctioned demonstration. ~ 집회 a meeting held without previous notice. 「an atheist; an unbeliever.

**무신론**(無神論) 〖철학〗 atheism. ◉ ~자

**무실점**(無失點) ¶ ~으로 without losing a point / ~을 기록하다 record no losing point 〔score〕.

**무심**(無心) ① 《생각 없음》 inadvertence; heedlessness; absentmindedness. ~하다 (be) unwitting; inadvertent; unintentional; absentminded; unconscious. ¶ ~히, ~코, ~결에 unintentionally; undesignedly; 《문득》 casually; in a casual way; incidentally; accidentally; 《부주의하게》 carelessly; unguardedly; 《자기도 모르게》 unconsciously; in spite of *oneself;* 《뜻하지 않게》 unexpectedly; (all) unawares; 《순진하게》 innocently / ~코 한 말 a casual remark; an inadvertent remark / ~히 말하다 speak lightly / ~히 바라보다 look ahead casually / ~코 시계를 들여다보다 glance casually at *one's* watch / ~코 비밀을 누설하다 reveal a secret 「carelessly 〔in an unguarded moment〕 / ~코 서랍을 열어보니… When I happened to open the drawer, … / 나는 ~코 그녀를 보았다 I took a casual glance at her. / ~코 한 말이 가장 가까운 친구를 소원하게 하는 수가 있다 A few light words sometimes estrange the closest friends. ② 〖불교〗 absence of the worldly desires.

**무쌍**(無雙) peerlessness; matchlessness. ~하다 (be) peerless; matchless; unrival(l)ed; unparalleled; incomparable; unique. ¶ 용감 ~한 사람 a man of great prowess.

**무아**(無我) self-effacement; annihilation of self; absence of ego. ¶ ~의 unselfish; 《이타적인》 altruistic; 《망아의》 ecstatic / ~의 경지 absolute altruism / ~의 경지에 이르다 attain the state of perfect selflessness; rise above (the) self; be in ecstasies. ◉ ~경(境) ecstasy; transport. ~애 selfless love; absolute altruism. ~의식 〖정신분석〗 the id.

**무악**(舞樂) 〖음악〗 court dance music.

**무안**(無顔) shame; disgrace. ~하다 be ashamed 《of *oneself*》; feel shame; lose face. ¶ ~을 주다 put 《*a person*》 to shame 〔the blush〕 / ~을 당하다 be put to shame; disgrace *oneself;* be humiliated / 그리 말하시면 제가 ~합니다 You make me blush. / 그는 몹시 ~해 했다 He was filled with shame.

**무안타**(無安打) 〖야구〗 no hit. ¶ ~ 무득점의 경기 a no-hit, no-run game / 그 투수는 상대 팀을 ~로 봉쇄했다 The pitcher kept 〔held〕 the opposing team hitless.

**무양무양하다** (be) inflexible 《in personality》; hidebound.

**무어** ① 《무엇》 what; which; something. ¶ 이건 대체 ~야 Whatever is this object? / 저 친구가 하긴 무얼 해 What can he do? *or* I am blessed if he can do anything. / 너 ~ 좀 먹어야지 Surely you have to eat something, don't you?
② 《감탄·놀람》 what! 〔?〕 … ? 〔!〕; why !; how …! ¶ ~그 사람이 죽었어 What! Is he dead? / ~ 얼마요 What! How much did you say it is? / ~ 내가 잘 못했다고 What? I am wrong! / ~ 그가 교통사고를 당했다고 What! You say he had a traffic accident?
③ 《여러 말 할것 없다는 뜻으로 덧붙여서》 ¶ ~ 괜찮아 Never mind! *or* I don't care. / ~ 힘들 것 없어 Why, nothing is easier. / 세상이란 ~그런 거지 Such is the way of the world. / 누워서 떡 먹기지 ~ Why, nothing is easier. / 돈이 ~ 여간 들어야지 It is so expensive, you see.
④ 《무어니 무어니 해도…》 say what you will; indeed; let me tell you. ¶ ~니 ~니 해도 뱀만큼 싫은 것은 없어 If there is one thing I hate 〔dislike〕 more than another, it is a snake.

**무어라** ¶ ~ 하든 whatever others may say 《about, of》; after all / ~ (말)할 수 없다 《단언 못함》 One cannot tell. *or* God 〔Heaven only〕 knows!; 《형용키가 어려움》 be unspeakable; be inexpressible 〔indescribable〕 / ~ 대답을 할까요 What answer shall I make? / ~ 사과드릴 말이 없습니다 I don't know how to apologize to you. / ~ 감사의 말씀을 드려야 할지 모르겠습니다 I can never thank you enough. / 내일 회의에 참석할 수 있을지

어떨지 ～ 말할 수 없다 I can't say for sure whether or not I can attend the meeting tomorrow. (★ whether 절이 길 때는 or not은 흔히 whether 뒤에 옴).

**무언**(無言) silence; muteness; taciturnity. ¶～의 silent; speechless; tacit; mute; dumb / ～으로 silently; in silence; mutely; without speaking / ～의 용사 silent [dead] war heroes / ～의 반항[항거] passive resistance. ◉ ～극(劇) a pantomime; a dumb show.

**무엄**(無嚴) ～하다 (be) rude; outrageous; impertinent; insolent; 《버릇 없다》 (be) presumptuous; forward. ¶～한 놈 an outrageous [insolent] fellow / ～하게도 …하다 have the impertinence to 《*do*》; be rude enough to 《*do*》.

**무엇** what; which; something; anything. ¶～이든 anything; whatever; everything / ～이라 말할 수 없는 indescribable; unspeakable; beyond expression / ～ 하러 what for / ～을 하든 간에 in all things / ～을 먹겠소 What do you want to eat? *or* Do you want something to eat? / 내가 네게 ～을 감추겠니 Would I hide anything from you? *or* I am telling you the whole truth. / 그는 ～ 하는 사람이냐 What is he? / 너 ～ 하러 왔느냐 What have you come for? / ～이고 하겠습니다 I will do anything. / 그녀는 ～인지 사가지고 왔다 She's bought something or other.

**무엇보다** above all (things); before everything (else); first of all; more than anything else; of all things. ¶낚시를 ～도 좋아하다 like fishing better than anything else / 등산은 다른 ～도 재미있다 Nothing is more interesting than (mountain) climbing. / ～도 그것은 빌 클린턴에 대한 국민들의 신임 투표였다 First and foremost, it was a referendum on Bill Clinton.

**무엇이든** 《어느것이든》 any; anything; 《모두》 everything; all; whatever. ¶～ 좋아하는 것을 고르다 choose anything [whatever] *one* likes / 붉은 꽃이면 ～ 좋다[괜찮다] Any red flower will do. / ～좋아하는 것이 있으면 잡수세요 Help yourself to whatever you please. / 시킬 일이 있으면 ～ 말하세요 If there is anything I can do for you, please don't hesitate to ask me.

**무엇하다** 《거북하다》 be awkward; be hard to say [describe, put into words]; be embarrassing; be unsatisfactory. ¶그 일은 내가 하기는 좀 ～ It is awkward for me to do that myself.

**무엇하면** 《원한다면은》 if you like [wish, please, prefer]; 《할 수 있다면》 if I can; if possible; 《필요하면》 if necessary; 《편리하면》 if (it is) convenient (for you); if it suits you. ¶～ 그만둬도 괜찮네 You can give it up, if you don't like it.

**무엇하지만** ¶이렇게 말하기는 ～ excuse me for my frankness, but…; to be frank with you; it may be rude to say so, but… / 나 자신이 그렇게 말하는 것도 ～ if I may be permitted to say so; though I say it who shouldn't. / 무엇하지만 돈 만 원만 빌려 주시오 (I shouldn't but) May I ask you to lend me ten thousand won?

**무역**(貿易) (foreign) trade; export and import business; commerce (★ 국내의 「상업」의 뜻으로도 쓰임). ～하다 trade 《with》; have trade relation 《with》. ¶～의 균형 the balance of trade / 점증하는 ～의 불균형 the growing trade imbalance / ～에 종사하다 engage in foreign trade / ～을 하다 conduct [carry on] trade / ～을 시작하다 open (up) trade 《with》 / ～을 육성하다 foster trade / ～을 자유화하다 liberalize (external) trade / ～을 재개하다 reopen trade / ～을 증진[확대]하다 increase [expand] foreign trade / 한국의 대미(對美)～ Korea's trade with the United States / 한중～ trade between Korea and China; Korea=China trade / 우리 회사는 외국 ～을 하고 있다 Our company is engaged in foreign trade. / 한국의 대(對)중국 ～은 해마다 그 규모가 커지고 있다 Korea's trade with China is growing larger year after year. / 한국의 대중국 ～의 흑자는 10억 달러에 달했다 Korea's trade surplus with China amounted to $ 1 billion. / 그 나라의 ～ 전망은 결코 밝지 않다 The outlook for the country's trade is far from bright. / 한국은 ～을 자유화하도록 요구받고 있다 Korea is being asked to liberalize trade.

◉ ～결손[적자] a trade deficit: ～결손[적자]의 개선 the improvement of the trade deficit. ～경쟁국 a trade rival. ～관리 (foreign) trade control. ～량 the volume of trade. ～마찰 a trade friction [conflict]: 한일간의 ～ 마찰을 방지할 대책을 마련하다 work out measures to prevent trade frictions between Korea and Japan. ~박람회 a trade fair: 제7회 서울 국제 ~ 박람회 the 7th Seoul International Trade Fair ('94). ~보복 trade reprisals 《against》. ~불균형 a trade imbalance. ~사절단 a trade mission. ~상 《사람》 a trader; a trading merchant; 《회사》 a trading firm; an exporter (수출상); an importer (수입상): ~상을 하고 있다 be in the export-import business. ~상대국 a trading partner. ~상사 a trading firm 〔concern, company〕: 종합 ~ 상사 a general trading company (생략 GTC.) ~수지 the balance of trade; the trade balance: ~ 수지의 적자 trade loss. ~액 the amount of trade. ~어음 a trade bill 〔paper〕. ~업 trade 〔trading〕 business: ~업계 trading circles. ~역조 adverse balance of trade; trade imbalance 《in Japan's favor》: ~ 역조의 시정 the rectification of the trade imbalance 《now in Japan's favor》. ~연보 a trade yearbook; annual trade returns. ~외 수입 earnings on 〔income from〕 invisibles. ~외 수지 the invisible trade balance: ~외 수지 적자 the invisible trade deficit. ~자금 〔기금〕 a foreign trade fund; a commercial fund. ~자유화 trade liberalization. ~장벽 a trade barrier: 미국의 오랜 대북한 ~ 장벽 the long-standing barriers to U.S. trade with North Korea / 가능한 한 ~장벽 제거에 노력하다 make efforts to remove as many trade barriers as possible. ~정보 trade information. ~정책 a trade policy: 보호〔자유〕 ~ 정책 protective 〔free〕 trade policies. ~ 조건 terms of trade. ~통계 foreign trade statistics. ~품 trade goods; imports (수입품); exports (수출품). ~학과 《대학의》 the Department of Trade. ~항 a trading port. ~ 허가장 a permit for trading. ~ 협력 기구 the Organization for Trade Cooperation (생략 O.T.C). ~협정 a trade agreement: 한미 ~ 협정 a trade agreement between Korea and the United States. ~회사= ~상사. ~흑자 a trade surplus.

대한 ~ 투자 진흥 공사 the Korea Trade-Investment Promotion Agency (생략 KOTRA). 미국 ~ 대표부 the U.S. Trade Representative. 세계 ~ 기구 the World Trade Organization (생략 WTO). 한국 ~협회 the Korea International Trade Association (생략 KITA). 한중~ trade between Korea and China; Sino-Korean trade.

**무역풍**(貿易風) the trade wind; monsoon. ◉ 겨울〔여름〕 ~ dry 〔wet〕 monsoon. 반대 ~ an antitrade wind.

**무연**(無煙) [형용사적] smokeless. ◉ ~탄 anthracite (coal); hard coal 《미》. ~화약 smokeless powder.

**무연고**(無緣故) ¶ ~의 without relative; unrelated; having no surviving relatives. ◉ ~분묘 a neglected 〔forlorn, deserted〕 grave.

**무염**(無塩) ¶ ~의 saltless; salt-free; unsalted. ◉ ~식 a salt-free diet.

**무영등**(無影燈) 《외과용》 an astral lamp.

**무예**(武藝) military 〔martial, warlike〕 arts; feats of arms. ¶ ~에 능한 사람 a master of martial arts / ~를 닦다 practice military arts.

**무오**(戊午) 〖민속〗 the 55th binary term of the sexagenary cycle.

**무욕**(無慾) freedom from avarice. ~하다 (be) unselfish; unavaricious; disinterested; free from avarice.

**무용**(武勇) bravery; valor; prowess. ¶ ~으로 명성이 높은 무사 a warrior famed for his valor. ◉ ~담 a tale 〔an account〕 of *one's* heroic exploits.

**무용**(無用) uselessness; needlessness. ~하다 《쓸모없다》 (be) useless; no good; of no use 〔avail〕; 《필요없다》 (be) needless; unnecessary. ¶ ~지물(之物) a useless thing; a good-for-nothing; a fifth wheel / ~자 출입 금지 《게시》 No admittance except on business. *or* No unauthorized entry allowed. *or* Off limits to unauthorized personnel.

**무용**(舞踊) dancing; a dance. ~하다 dance; perform a dance. ¶ ~을 배우다 take lessons in dancing. ◉ ~가 a dancer; a dancing master 〔mistress〕. ~극 a dance drama. ~단 a *corps de ballet* (F.); a ballet 〔dance〕 troupe: 국립 (고전) ~단 the National (Classical) Dance Company. ~연구소 a dancing school.

**무운**(武運) the fortune(s) of war. ¶ ~이 없다 be unfortunate in war / ~을 빌다 pray for 《*a person's*》 good fortune in battle.

**무운**(無韻) ¶ ~의 unrhymed; blank. ◉ ~시(詩) a blank 〔an unrhymed〕 verse.

**무위**(無爲) idleness; doing nothing; inactivity. ¶ ~하게 idly; in idleness /

～한 생활《live》 a life of ease; an idle life / ～무책(無策)의 정부 a do-nothing government / ～로 끝나다 come to nothing. ◉ ～도식 an idle life: ～도식하다 eat the bread of idleness; live an idle life; idle 〔loaf〕 *one's* time away.

**무유증**(無乳症) 〖의학〗 agalactia.

**무의무신**(無依無信) lack of integrity and trust. ～하다 be unfaithful and untrustworthy.

**무의무탁**(無依無托) having no place to turn to; having no one to depend on. ～하다 have no place to turn to; have no one to depend 〔rely〕 on; (be) homeless; lonely. ¶ ～한 떠돌이 a homeless 〔helpless〕 wanderer.

**무의미**(無意味) ～하다 《의미없다》 (be) meaningless; insignificant; pointless; 《무익하다》 (be) purposeless; 《당치않다》 (be) absurd; senseless; nonsensical. ¶ ～한 생활 a meaningless life / ～한 말을 하다 talk nonsense / ～한 생활을 하다 live to no purpose / 이런 ～한 논쟁은 그만두자 Let's put an end to this meaningless 〔senseless〕 argument. / 연하장 같은 것은 ～하다는 사람도 있다 Some say that the New Year's complimentary note is mere formalism.

**무의식**(無意識) unconsciousness; involuntariness; 〖정신분석〗 the unconscious. ¶ ～적인 unconscious; involuntary; 《기계적인》 mechanical; automatic / ～적인 동작 an involuntary action / ～적으로 unconsciously; mechanically; automatically; 《나쁜 줄 모르고》 without knowing what *one* is doing / ～중에 while *one* is unconscious 《of it》; before *one* knows 《it》/ ～중에 그것을 했다 I did it involuntarily. / 나이를 먹으면 ～적으로 행동하는 일이 많아진다 When we are old, we tend to act more and more out of mere habit. ◉ ～상태 an unconscious state 〔condition〕: ～상태에 빠지다 fall into unconsciousness.

**무의촌**(無醫村) a doctorless village.

**무의탁**(無依托) having no one to depend 〔rely〕 on. ⇨ 무의무탁. ◉ ～노인 a senior citizen who does not have dependents; an old man without dependents.

**무이자**(無利子) no interest. ¶ ～의 free of interest; bearing no interest / ～로 without interest; interest-free / ～로 돈을 빌려주다 lend money without taking interest. ◉ ～공채(公債) flat 〔passive〕 bonds.

**무익**(無益) uselessness; unprofitableness; futility. ～하다 (be) useless; unprofitable; no good; fruitless; futile. ¶ ～한 토론 a futile argument / 백해～하다 do more harm than good / ～한 살생 (the) wanton destruction of life / ～한 살생을 하다 kill 《animals》 wantonly.

**무인**(戊寅) 〖민속〗 the 15th binary term of the sexagenary cycle.

**무인**(武人) a soldier; a warrior.

**무인**(拇印) a thumbmark; a thumbprint. ¶ 서류에 ～을 찍다 put a thumb 〔make a thumb imprint〕 on the papers; seal a paper with *one's* thumb.

**무인**(無人) ¶ ～의 manless; unmanned; uninhabited; deserted. ◉ ～건널목 an unattended (railroad) crossing. ～도(島) an uninhabited 〔a desert〕 island. ～비행기 a pilotless 〔radio-controlled〕 (air) plane. ～위성 an unmanned satellite. ～지대 no-man's land. ～판매기 a self-service stand; a vending machine.

**무인지경**(無人之境) no-man's land; an uninhabited region. ¶ ～을 가듯 진격하다 carry 〔sweep〕 everything before *one;* advance with irresistible force.

**무일푼**(無一一) being penniless. ¶ ～이 되다 become 〔find *oneself*〕 penniless; loss everything; 《미구어》 go (clean) broke; lose *one's* shirt / 거의 ～으로 장사를 시작하다 start business with practically nothing.

**무임**(無賃) ¶ ～으로 free (of charge); charge-free; carriage-free (짐이). ◉ ～승객 a free passenger; a deadhead 《미》.

**무임소**(無任所) ¶ ～의 without portfolio; unassigned. ◉ ～장관 a minister without portfolio.

**무임승차**(無賃乘車) a free ride; deadheading 《미》. ～하다 ride free (of charge); have a free ride; travel deadhead 《미》; 《몰래》 steal a ride 《on a train》. ◉ ～권 a free pass.

**무자**(戊子) 〖민속〗 the 25th binary term of the sexagenary cycle.

**무자각**(無自覺) ¶ ～한 insensible 《of》; blind 《to》; unconscious 《of *one's* responsibility》/ 우리는 자신들의 결점에는 ～할 때가 종종 있다 We are often blind to our own faults.

**무자격**(無資格) disqualification; 〖법〗

incapacity; incompetence. ~하다 (be) disqualified; unqualified; 《무면허》 (be) unlicensed. ¶ 그는 교사로서 ~이다 He is unqualified as a teacher.
◉ ~교사 an unlicensed 〔unqualified〕 teacher. ~자 a man without qualification; 〖법〗 an incompetent.

**무자력**(無資力) want 〔lack〕 of funds; lack of means; insolvency. ◉ ~자 a person without funds 〔means〕; an insolvent.

**무자맥질** diving; ducking. ~하다 dive 《into, in, under》 water; duck 《down》; go 〔swim〕 underwater.

**무자본**(無資本) ¶ ~으로 without capital 〔funds〕; with nothing to start with.

**무자비**(無慈悲) mercilessness; cruelty. ~하다 (be) merciless; cruel; ruthless; pitiless; heartless; hard-hearted. ¶ ~한 짓을 하다 do a cruel thing / 그들의 탄원은 ~하게 거절당했다 Their plea was heartlessly rejected.

**무자식**(無子息) ~하다 (be) childless; heirless; [서술적] have no children 〔issue〕. ¶ ~ 상팔자 《속담》 Love of children is an eternal encumbrance.

**무자위** a water pump.

**무작위**(無作爲) 〖통계〗 ¶ ~로 unintentionally; at random / ~화하다 randomize / ~로 표본을 추출했다 We chose samples at random. ◉ ~표본 〖통계〗 a random sample. ~(표본)추출 (법) random sampling.

**무작정**(無酌定) lack of any definite plan; lack of definite view in mind; recklessness; rashness; [부사적] with no particular plan 〔view〕 in mind; recklessly; blindly. ~하다 (be) aimless; planless; rash; reckless; [서술적] lack any definite plan; have no particular view in mind; be without any goal in mind. ¶ ~ 돈을 쓰다 spend money recklessly / 그는 ~ 상경했다 He went up to Seoul with no definite object.

**무작하다** be ignorant and boorish.

**무장**(武將) a general; a warlord.

**무장**(武裝) 《국가의》 armaments; 《병사의》 equipments. ~하다 arm 《*oneself* with》; equip 《an army》; bear 〔take up〕 arms; militarize 《a country》. ¶ 비~지대 a demilitarized zone / ~하고 있다 be armed 《with》; be under arms / ~ 봉기하다 take up arms 《against》; rise in arms / 총으로 ~하다 arm *oneself* with rifle.
◉ ~간첩 an armed (espionage) agent; an armed infiltrator: ~ 간첩선 an armed espionage ship. ~경관 an armed policeman; [집합적] armed police. ~공비 an armed communist guerrilla 〔commando〕; an armed Red bandit: ~ 공비의 침투 infiltration of armed commandos 《into》. ~평화 〔중립〕 armed peace 〔neutrality〕. ~폭동 armed revolt. ~해제 demilitarization; disarmament: ~을 해제하다 disarm; dismantle 《a fortress》; demilitarize 《a nation》. 완전~ 《in》 full kit.

**무장지졸**(無將之卒) a leaderless army.

**무재**(無才) lacking ability; incompetence. ~하다 be lacking in ability; (be) untalented; incompetent.
◉ ~인 an untalented person.

**무저항**(無抵抗) nonresistance; passive obedience. ¶ ~의 unresistant; nonresistant / ~으로 without resistance; without making 〔offering〕 any resistance. ◉ ~주의 the principle of nonresistance: ~ 주의자 a nonresistant.

**무적**(無敵) ¶ ~의 matchless; unrivaled; unequaled; invincible / ~의 용사 a man of matchless valor / 그 팀은 ~이다 The team is unrivaled 〔invincible〕. / 체스에서 그는 ~이다 No one can match him at chess. ◉ ~함대 〖역사〗 the Invincible Armada.

**무적**(無籍) absence of a registered domicile; lack of a record. ◉ ~자 a person without a registered domicile.

**무적**(霧笛) 《고동》 a fog siren; a foghorn.

**무전**(無電) wireless 《영》; radio. ¶ ~으로 by wireless 〔radio〕 / ~을 치다 radio a message 《미》; send a message by radio 〔wireless〕 / ~으로 유도(誘導)하다 talk down 《a plane》 / 그 배는 ~으로 구조를 청해왔다 The ship radioed for help. ◉ ~국 a wireless 〔radio〕 station. ~기사 a wireless 〔radio〕 operator. ~실 a wireless room; a radioroom. ~탑 a radio tower.

**무전**(無錢) being moneyless 〔penniless〕. ◉ ~여행 a penniless trip; a vagabond journey; hitchhiking 《미》: ~ 여행가 a hitchhiker / ~ 여행하다 travel without spending any money; work *one's* way 《through a country》; hitchhike. ~취식 jumping a restaurant bill: ~ 취식하다 bilk on a restaurant bill; bilk a restaurant 〔bar〕 out of its money; jump a restaurant bill.

**무절제**(無節制) intemperance; excesses; immoderation; incontinency. ～하다 (be) immoderate; intemperate; incontinent. ¶ ～한 생활을 하다 lead an intemperate life.

**무절조**(無節操) inconstancy; unchastity. ～하다 (be) inconstant; unchaste.

**무정**(無情) heartlessness; pitilessness; hardness; cruelty; apathy. ～하다《박정하다》(be) heartless; pitiless;《냉혹하다》(be) cold-hearted; callous; harsh; cruel. ¶ ～하게도 heartlessly; cruelly / 그는 ～하게도 곤경에 처해 있는 친구를 모른 체했다 He was cold-hearted enough to let down a friend in need. / 너는 ～한 사람이다 You are heartless 〔merciless〕. ◉ ～세월 fleeting 〔transient〕 time.

**무정견**(無定見) (a) lack of fixed 〔steadfast〕 principles. ～하다 be lacking a fixed principle; have no fixed views of *one's* own; have no settled opinion. ¶ 정부는 ～한 농업 정책을 수정해야 한다 The government should rectify the lack of a fixed policy for agriculture.

**무정란**(無精卵) 『생물』 an unfertilized egg; a wind egg.

**무정부**(無政府) anarchy. ¶ ～의 anarchic. ◉ ～ 상태 《be in》 a state of anarchy. ～주의 anarchism: ～주의자 an anarchist.

**무정위**(無定位) ¶ ～의 『물리』 astatic. ◉ ～검류계 an astatic galvanometer. ～조속기(調速機) an astatic governor. ～침(針) an astatic needle.

**무정형**(無定形) shapelessness. ～하다 (be) formless; shapeless; amorphous. ◉ ～물질〔금속〕 an amorphous substance 〔metal〕. ～상태 amorphous state. ～탄소 amorphous carbon.

**무제**(無題) 《예술 작품 따위의》 no title. ¶ ～의 titleless; without a title.

**무제한**(無制限) unlimitedness; unrestrictedness. ～하다 (be) unlimited; unrestricted; free. ¶ ～으로 without any restriction; freely; without reserve / 수입을 ～으로 확대하다 expand import without restriction / 수화물의 중량에 대해서는 ～이다 There is no weight limit for baggage. ◉ ～급 《유도 등의》 the open-weight division. ～법화(法貨) unlimited legal tender. ～입국 unrestricted admission 《of immigrants》.

**무조건**(無條件) ¶ ～의 unconditional; unqualified; absolute / ～으로 unconditionally; unqualifiedly; without reservation / ～ 받아들이다 accept 《another's statement》 without reserve / ～ 승낙하다 give an unqualified consent / 그들은 우리의 제안을 ～ 받아들였다 They accepted our proposal without any condition. ◉ ～반사 『심리』 (an) unconditioned reflex. ～항복 unconditional surrender.

**무족목**(無足目) 『동물』 Apoda.

**무좀** 『의학』 athlete's foot: tinea (pedis). ¶ ～에 걸리다 have athlete's foot.

**무종교**(無宗教) no religion. ¶ ～의 irreligious; with no religious faith; atheistic / 나는 ～(자)입니다 I am a member of no religion. ◉ ～자 a person with no religion 〔religious faith〕; an atheist; an unbeliever.

**무종아리** the lower part of the calf.

**무죄**(無罪) being not guilty; innocence; guiltlessness. ～하다 (be) innocent; guiltless; be not guilty. ¶ ～가 되다 be found 「not guilty 〔innocent〕; be acquitted 《of the crime》 / ～로 하다〔를 선고하다〕 find 〔declare〕 《*a person*》 not guilty; acquit 《*a person*》 / ～를 주장하다 assert 〔claim, maintain〕 *one's* innocence; plead not guilty 《to a crime》 / ～ 선고를 받다 be given a verdict of "not guilty" / 간신히 ～가 되다 narrowly escape conviction / 그는 수뢰혐의로 기소되었으나 ～가 되었다 He was charged with bribery but found innocent (of it). *or* He was charged with bribery but acquitted of the charge. ◉ ～석방 acquittal (and discharge): ～석방하다 acquit 《*a person*》 of the charge / ～ 석방이 되다 be found innocent and acquitted 〔released〕. ～판결 a decision of "not guilty": ～ 판결을 하다 find 〔declare〕 《*a person*》 not guilty.

**무주**(無主) being ownerless. ◉ ～고혼(孤魂) a forlorn wandering spirit (who lacks posterity). ～공처(空處) an unowned land; a deserted lot.

**무주정**(無酒精) ¶ ～의 nonalcoholic. ◉ ～음료 a nonalcoholic beverage; a soft drink.

**무주택**(無住宅) being homeless. ◉ ～서민층 the homeless masses. ～자 a houseless 〔homeless〕 person; houseless people. ～증명서 a certificate verifying 《*a person's*》 homeless status.

**무중력**(無重力) weightlessness; zero gravity. ¶ ～의 weightless; zero-gravity. ◉ ～비행 a weightless flight. ～

상태 a state of weightlessness 〔non-gravitation〕; a weightless 〔gravity=free〕 state: ～ 상태로 in a weightless stage; under weightless condition; at 〔in〕 zero G / ～ 상태로 되다 go 〔become〕 weightless / 그들은 ～ 상태에서 몇가지 실험을 했다 They made some experiments 「in the condition of weightlessness 〔at zero gravity〕.

**무지** not quite enough grain to fill a bushel sack.

**무지**(拇指) 《엄지》 a thumb.

**무지**(無地) solid color. ¶ ～의 plain; unfigured; solid 《black》; self-colored / 그의 넥타이는 검정색 ～였다 His tie was solid black. ◉ ～천 plain 〔solid=color〕 cloth; cloth without a pattern.

**무지**(無知) ignorance; illiteracy (문맹). ～하다 (be) ignorant; stupid; uninformed. ¶ ～ 몽매한 백성 unenlightened people / 자신의 ～를 드러내다 betray *one's* ignorance / 나는 컴퓨터에 관해서는 정말 ～하다 I'm quite ignorant about the computer. / 그는 ～로 인해 죄를 저질렀다 His crime was committed through ignorance.

**무지각**(無知覺) insensibility; indiscretion; thoughtlessness. ～하다 (be) insensible. ¶ ～한 짓을 하다 do something rash; commit an imprudence; act indiscreetly.

**무지개** a rainbow. ¶ ～가 뜨다 a rainbow forms 〔appears〕; have a rainbow. ◉ 쌍～ a double 〔coupled〕 rainbow.

**무지근하다** feel heavy 〔dull〕. ¶ 뒤가 ～ *one's* bowels are stuffy; be constipated / 머리가 ～ feel heavy in the head.

**무지기** an underwear skirt; a slip.

**무지러지다** wear down to a stump; wear out; be worn out; get stumpy 〔blunt〕. ¶ 붓이 ～ a writing brush wears out.

**무지렁이** a stupid person; a dunce; a moron; a rustic; a dull tool.

**무지르다** cut off 〔away〕. ¶ 나뭇가지를 ～ cut branches off a tree; cut away branches from a tree.

**무지막지**(無知莫知) ～하다 (be) ignorant and uncouth. ¶ ～하게 굴다 act 〔behave〕 rudely; be wild.

**무지몰각**(無知沒覺) ignorance and lack of understanding. ～하다 (be) utterly ignorant; know nothing.

**무지몽매**(無知蒙昧) lack of enlightenment. ～하다 (be) unenlightened; benighted.

**무직**(無職) ¶ ～의 unemployed; without occupation; out of work / ～이다 be unemployed 〔jobless〕; be out of work; lack a regular occupation / 그는 지금 ～이다 He is jobless 〔out of work〕 now. *or* He has no job now. ◉ ～자 a jobless man; the unemployed.

**무직하다** ⇨ 무지근하다.

**무진**(戊辰) the 5th binary term of the sexagenary cycle.

**무진**(無盡) 《다함이 없음》 (with) no end; no limit. ～하다 (be) unending; unlimited.

**무진동** 〖광물〗 copper containing over 50% iron sulfide.

**무진장**(無盡藏) ～하다 《다함이 없다》 (be) inexhaustible; 《한도가 없다》 (be) unlimited; boundless; have no end; 《풍부하다》 (be) abundant. ¶ ～한 천연자원 inexhaustible natural resources / 이 곳의 석탄은 ～이다 The coal mine here has inexhaustible deposits. / 태양에너지는 ～이다 Solar energy is inexhaustible.

**무질리다** be cut off 〔out, away〕. ¶ 나뭇가지가 ～ branches are cut off from a tree.

**무질서**(無秩序) 《혼란》 disorder; lawlessness; confusion; 《혼돈》 chaos. ～하다 (be) disordered; lawless; confused; chaotic. ¶ 폭동으로 도시는 ～상태에 빠졌다 The city was thrown into complete chaos by the rioting.

**무집게** a pair of pincers; nippers.

**무찌르다** ① 《마구 죽이다》 wipe out; kill off; mow 〔cut〕 down. ¶ 적 수백을 ～ mow down hundreds of the enemy. ② 《공격·격파하다》 launch 〔make〕 an attack on; beat; defeat; crush; smash; conquer (정복하다). ¶ 상대를 ～ clobber *one's* opponent / 적을 ～ defeat 〔crush〕 the enemy / 우리는 상대팀을 3대 0으로 무찔렀다 We defeated out opponents three (to) nothing.

**무찔리다** ① 《살육당하다》 get killed off; be 〔get〕 mowed down. ② 《공격당하다》 be attacked; be defeated; be devastated (짓밟히다). ¶ 성이 적에게 ～ A castle is assaulted 〔devastated〕 by the enemy.

**무차별**(無差別) indiscrimination; nondiscrimination; no distinction. ～하다 (be) indiscriminate; equal. ¶ ～하게 indiscriminately; equally; without distinction / ～하게 다루다 be impartial 《to》; treat equally / 남녀 ～로 without distinction of sex / 통행인에게 ～ 사격을 가하다 fire indiscriminately at passersby. ◉ ～폭격〔검거〕 indiscriminate bombing 〔arrest〕.

**무착륙**(無着陸) ¶ ～의 nonstop; without alighting. ◉ ～비행 a nonstop flight: ～비행을 하다 make a nonstop flight; fly nonstop 《to》.

**무참**(無慚) shame; disgrace. ～하다 be 〔feel〕 ashamed; feel mortified.

**무참**(無慘) ～하다 《무자비하다》 (be) cold-blooded; merciless; pitiless; ruthless; 《잔인하다》 (be) cruel; atrocious; 《비참하다》 (be) tragic; miserable. ¶ ～하게 mercilessly; cruelly; atrociously; pitilessly; without pity 〔mercy〕; in cold blood / ～히도 사람을 죽이다 commit murder in cold blood / ～한 최후를 마치다 die a tragic 〔cruel〕 death / 그것은 보기에도 ～한 광경이었다 It was a horrible 〔an appalling〕 scene to look at.

**무책**(無策) lack of policy. ⇨ 속수무책.

**무책임**(無責任) 《책임이 없음》 irresponsibility; 《책임감이 없음》 lack of a sense of responsibility. ～하다 (be) irresponsible. ¶ ～하게 irresponsibly; without a sense of responsibility / ～한 사람〔행위〕 an irresponsible person 〔conduct〕 / ～한 말을 하다 make an irresponsible statement 〔remark〕 / ～하기 짝없다 be utterly irresponsible 《for》 / 저 사람은 ～하다 He lacks a 〔has no〕 sense of responsibility. / 그런 ～한 행동을 못 본 체 할 수는 없다 I can't shut my eyes to such irresponsible conduct. / 우리 회사는 ～한 회사가 아닙니다. 한국에서 이미 20년 간이나 사업을 해 왔으니까요 Our company is no fly-by-night. We've been operating in Korea for 20 years. (★ fly-by-night는 「야반 도주」를 뜻한다. 「빚지고 밤에 도주하는」 무책임한 회사가 아니라는 재미있는 표현이다.)

**무척** very (much); exceedingly; greatly; awfully; highly; extremely. ¶ ～ 덥다 be awfully 〔terribly, very〕 hot / ～손해보다 suffer a great loss / ～ 즐거웠다 I've had such a good time. / ～행복하다 I'm so happy. / 그 소식을 듣고 그녀는 ～ 기뻐했다 She was very glad to hear the news. / 그녀를 ～ 만나보고 싶다 I'm impatient to see her. *or* I'm dying to see her. / 나는 ～ 화가 났다 I got excessively 〔extremely〕 angry.

**무척추동물**(無脊椎動物) 〖동물〗 an invertebrate (animal).

**무체**(無體) ¶ ～의 incorporeal; intangible. ◉ ～동산 a chose in action. ～물 an immaterial being. ～재산(권) intangible property; intellectual property (right). ⇨ 지적재산(권).

**무춤하다** halt; stop short; hold back *one's* steps; start (back); shrink (back) 《from》. ¶ 뱀을 보고 ～ stop short at the sight of a snake.

**무취**(無臭) (being) odor-free 〔odorless, scentless〕. ～하다 (be) ordorless; scentless. ¶ 무색 ～의 colorless and ordorless.

**무취미**(無趣味) lack of taste. ⇨ 몰취미. ¶ ～한 dry; dull; prosaic.

**무치다** season 〔dress〕 《vegetables》 with 《some condiments》. ¶ 나물을 ～ season vegetable.

**무크** a mook. [< *m*agazine+b*ook*]

**무턱대고** 《이유 없이》 without reason; for no good reason; 《준비 없이》 with no prearrangement; with no preparation; 《수단·능력도 없이》 with no resources 〔capability〕; 《무모하게》 thoughtlessly (생각 없이); rashly; recklessly; 《마구잡이로》 blindly; at random (닥치는대로). ¶ ～ 귀여워하다 dote on 《a child》 blindly / ～돈을 쓰다 spend money recklessly 〔like water〕 / ～ (남을) 믿다 believe 《what people say》 too readily; be credulous / ～(총을) 쏘다 shoot without aim; fire blindly; shoot indiscriminately (무차별하게) / ～ 반대하다 be violently opposed 《to》 / ～ 돌진하다 push on furiously; make a reckless dash 《at, into》 / ～ 사업을 시작하다 go into a business with nothing to back *one* up / ～ 시험을 치러 보다 try taking an examination cold 〔without any preparation〕 / ～ 책망하다 scold 《*a person*》 for no good reason.

**무테**(無—) ¶ ～의 rimless. ◉ ～안경 (a pair of) rimless glasses.

**무통**(無痛) painlessness; 〖의학〗 indolence. ◉ ～ 분만 painless delivery 〔childbirth〕.

**무투표**(無投票) ¶ ～로 without voting 〔a vote〕 / 그는 ～로 의장에 뽑혔다 He was chosen as chairperson without a vote. ◉ ～당선 being elected 《chairperson》 without voting. ～당선 지구 a district uncontested in election.

**무트로** 《한목에 많이》 in a lump at one time; a large amount 《of *something*》 at one time.

**무판화**(無瓣花) 〖식물〗 an apetalous flower.

**무패**(無敗) no defeat; a clean record 〔score〕. ¶ ～의 전적이다 have a record of all wins and no defeats; have a clean slate with no mark of defeat.

**무표정**(無表情) absence 〔lack〕 of expression. ～하다 (be) expressionless; blank; unrevealing. ¶ ～한 얼굴 an expressionless 〔wooden〕 face; a poker face 《구어》; a wooden look; a dead pan 《구어》/ 그는 어떤 질문에도 ～하게 답했다 He answered any question expressionlessly.

**무풍**(無風) 《바람이 없음》 ¶ ～의 windless; calm / ～ 상태 a (dead) calm; (a state of) windlessness / 현재 노사간 관계는 ～상태이다 [비유적] There is no dispute between labor and management at the moment. ◉ ～대(帶) the calm latitudes; 《아열대의》 the horse latitudes; 《적도의》 the doldrums: 정치적 ～대 political doldrums. ～수역 the (region of) calms.

**무학**(無學) illiteracy; ignorance; lack of schooling. ～하다 (be) illiterate (문맹); ignorant (무식); 《배우지 못하다》 (be) uneducated; unlettered; unschooled. ¶ 그는 ～ 이지만 위대한 예술가였다 Although illiterate, he was a great artist.

**무한**(無限) infinity; the infinite; 《영원》 eternity; infinitude. ～하다 (be) infinite; boundless; limitless; unlimited; endless; immeasurable; inexhaustible. ¶ ～히 infinitely; boundlessly; endlessly; without limitation; eternally / ～한 감사 unbounded gratitude / ～한 공간 the infinite space / ～한 우주 boundless 〔endless〕 universe / ～한 욕망 unbounded desires / ～한 보고(寶庫) an inexhaustible mine of wealth 〔treasure〕 / ～한 즐거움을 주다 give no end of pleasure / ～한 가능성을 지니다 have boundless potentialities 《for》/ 수요는 ～히 증가할 것이다 The demand will probably increase to an unlimited extent. / 우주는 ～히 넓다 The universe is immeasurably vast. / 그의 힘은 ～하다 His strength is boundless. / 그녀의 욕망은 ～하다 Her greed knows no bounds. ◉ ～경쟁시대 the age of limitless competition. ～공간 infinite space. ～궤도 an endless track; a caterpillar 《tractor》. ～급수(級數) 〖수학〗 an infinite series. ～대(大) infinity: ～대의 infinite. ～량 infinite quantity. ～소 the infinitesimal: ～소의 infinitesimal. ～소수 an infinite decimal. ～집합 〖수학〗 an infinite set. ～책임 unlimited liability: ～ 책임 회사 an unlimited (liability) company / ～ 책임 사원 a general partner; a partner with unlimited liability.

**무한정**(無限定) infinity; unlimitedness; [부사적] unlimitedly; endlessly. ¶ ～이다 there is no end to 〔of〕; know no limits 〔end, bounds〕/ ～ 학생으로 남고 싶다 I wish I could remain a student forever.

**무함**(誣陷) falsely implicating a person in a charge 〔crime〕. ～하다 falsely implicate.

**무항산**(無恒産) ¶ ～이면 무항심(無恒心)이다 A real property, a real purpose. *or* Competency is for constancy of mind.

**무해**(無害) harmlessness; 《약의》 innocuousness; 《식품의》 innoxiousness. ～하다 (be) harmless; innocuous; innoxious. ¶ 이 제초제(除草劑)는 인간에게는 ～하다 This weed killer does not harm human beings. / 소량의 술은 ～하다 A little alcohol will do you no harm. ◉ 인축(人畜) ～ No harm 〔Harmless〕 to men and beasts.

**무해무득**(無害無得) no gain no loss. ～하다 be neither gain nor loss; be neither advantageous nor disadvantageous; be neither harmful nor useful.

**무허가**(無許可) no permit. ¶ ～로 without a permit 〔license〕/ ～로 영업을 하다 engage in business without a license 〔permit〕. ◉ ～건물 an unauthorized 〔unlicensed〕 house 〔building〕. ～판매〔제조〕 nonlicensed sale 〔production〕. ～판잣집 an illegal shack.

**무혈**(無血) ¶ ～의 bloodless; without bloodshed / ～의 승리 a bloodless victory. ◉ ～점령 a bloodless 〔an uncontested〕 occupation. ～혁명〔쿠데타〕 a bloodless revolution 〔coup d'état〕.

**무협**(武俠) chivalry; heroism. ¶ ～적인 chivalrous; chivalric; heroic.

**무형**(無形) formlessness; shapelessness. ¶ ～의 《추상적인》 abstract; 《비물질적인》 immaterial; incorporeal; 《정신적인》 moral; spiritual; 《형체 없는》 intangible; 《눈에 안 보이는》 invisible / ～의 원조〔이익〕 moral support 〔gains〕/ 유형～의 손실 tangible and intangible losses / 지식은 ～의 재산이다 Knowledge is a moral 〔an intangible〕 asset. / 그 분으로부터는 유형～의 은고(恩顧)를 입고 있다 I am indebted to him morally as well as materially. ◉ ～문화재 intangible cultural assets 〔property〕. ～물 an immaterial being; a shapeless thing. ～자산〔재산〕 intangible 〔immaterial〕 property 〔assets〕; intangibles: ～ 고정(固定) 자산 intangible fixed assets / ～ 자산은 평가가 어렵다 Intangibles are hard to value.

**무호동중이작호**(無虎洞中狸作虎) In the land of the blind a one-eyed man is king. *or* When the cat's away, the mice will play.

**무화과**(無花果) a fig (열매); a fig tree (나무).

**무환수입**〔**수출**〕(無換輸入〔輸出〕) no-draft import 〔export〕; import 〔export〕 without foreign exchange 〔draft〕; free import 〔export〕.

**무환자**(無患子) 〖식물〗 a soapberry (tree).

**무효**(無效) invalidity; nullity.

¶ ～의 invalid; (null and) void; 《통용 안 되는》 unavailable; 《효과 없는》 ineffectual; futile / ～가 되다 become 「(null and) void 〔ineffective〕; become invalid; be of no use 〔avail〕; be no longer good / ～로 하다 annul; invalidate; nullify; make (null and) void / 강요된 약속은 ～다 A promise made under compulsion is not binding./ 도중하차하면 이 차표는 ～가 된다 If you break your journey, this ticket will cease to be valid. / 그 투표지는 ～로 한다 That (voting) paper shall not be counted. / K씨의 당선은 ～가 되었다 Mr. K's election was declared invalid. / 유언은 법정에서 ～라고 선언되었다 The will was declared void by the court. / 당신의 여권은 기한이 지났기 때문에 ～이다 Your passport is out of date and invalid. / 그는 집세를 내지 않아서 임대 계약이 ～가 되었다 His lease lapsed when he didn't pay the rent.

◉ ～계약 a void 〔an invalid〕 contract. ～소송 nullity suit: 결혼 ～ 소송 a nullity suit. ～수표 an invalid check. ～전력 reactive power; wattless power. ～조항 〖법〗 an irritant clause; an irritancy. ～투표 an invalid 〔a spoilt, a null and void〕 vote. ～화 invalidation; 〖법〗 defeasance.

**무후하다**(無後—) be childless 〔heirless〕.

**무훈**(武勳) military merits. ＝무공.

**무휴**(無休) (having) no holiday. ¶ 연중 ～(이다) be open throughout the year; 《게시》 Open throughout the year. *or* Open 365 days.

**무흠**(無欠) 《흠이 없음》 flawlessness. ～하다 (be) flawless; free from blemish; impeccable.

**무희**(舞姬) a dancing girl; a dancer.

**묵** jelly. ◉ 녹두묵 green-pea jelly. 메밀묵 buckwheat jelly.

**묵계**(默契) a tacit 〔secret〕 understanding; an implicit 〔undisclosed〕 agreement. ～하다 agree tacitly; make a tacit agreement 《with》. ¶ ～하에 《do *something*》 on a tacit understanding / …사이에 ～가 되어 있다 A tacit understanding exists between ….

**묵고**(默考) ＝묵상(默想).

**묵과**(默過) connivance. ～하다 overlook; look over; pass over 《*a matter*》 in silence; let 《it》 pass 〔go〕; connive 《at》. ¶ 잘못을 ～하다 overlook 〔slur (over)〕 《*a person's*》 fault / 밀렵자를 ～하다 shut *one's* eyes to a poacher / 이대로 ～할 수는 없다 I cannot pass it over in silence. / 총리의 연설 중 다음의 말은 ～해서는 안 된다 The following remarks made by the Prime Minister in his address should not go unheeded.

**묵낙**(默諾) tacit consent 〔admission, permission〕; acquiescence. ～하다 consent tacitly 《to》; give tacit consent; acquiesce 《in》. ⇨ 묵인.

**묵념**(默念) ① ＝묵상(默想). ② ＝묵도(默禱). ¶ …에 대하여 일분간 ～하다 pay one minute's silent tribute 《to》; observe 〔offer〕 a one-minute silent prayer for 《the war dead》.

**묵다**[1] ① 《오래되다》 get old; be antiquated; be out of date; be old-fashioned; be outdated; be outmoded; outworn; 《음식이》 be stale. ¶ 묵은 관습 an old custom; a wormeaten custom / 묵은 빚 an old debt; a debt of long standing / 묵은 사상 a moss=grown idea; an old-fashioned idea / 묵은 쌀 old 〔long-stored〕 rice / 묵은 학설 an outdated 〔obsolete〕 theory / 케케 묵은 생각 a completely outmoded idea / 케케 묵은 수작 an old story; a hackneyed remark / 케케 ～ be hackneyed; be threadbare.

② 《낙제하여》 be off; lead a life away from; 《유급하다》 stay back (in the class); remain (in the original class). ¶ 입학 시험에 떨어져 일년 묵었다 I 「was off 〔led a life away from〕 school for one year because of a failure at entrance exams.

③ 《자본 등이》 lie idle; 《상품이》 remain unsold 《on the shelf》. ¶ 묵고 있는 밭 a field lying idle; an idle field.

**묵다**[2] 《숙박》 stay 《at, in, with》; lodge 《in, with》; put up 《at》; stop 《at, in》 《미구어》 (★ at, in에는 장소, with에는 사람이 계속됨). ¶ 하룻밤 ~ stay overnight; pass the night; stop for the night / 여관에 ~ stay 〔put up, stop, lodge〕 at an inn; stop (at a hotel); register 〔check in〕 at a hotel / 하룻밤 묵어 가기를 청하다 ask for a night's lodging / 나는 A호텔에 묵을 예정입니다 I'm going to stay at the A Hotel. / 그는 조선 호텔에 묵고 있다 He is registered 〔checked in〕 at the Chosun Hotel. / 나는 호반의 호텔에 묵었다 I put up 〔checked in〕 at a hotel by the lake. / 우연히 우리는 같은 호텔에 묵었다 We happened to put up at the same hotel.

**묵도**(默禱) a silent prayer. ~하다 pray silently 〔in silence〕; offer a silent prayer.

**묵독**(默讀) silent reading; reading to *oneself*. ~하다 read silently 〔to *oneself*〕.

**묵례**(默禮) a silent bow 〔obeisance〕; a nod; nodding. ~하다 make a (silent) bow 《to》; (greet with a) nod; bow in silence. ¶ 서로 ~하다 exchange nods 〔bows〕 / 그들은 살짝 모자를 치켜 들며 서로 ~하였다 They saluted each other by raising hats. / 그 뒤로 그들은 서로 정중하게 ~만 할 뿐 말을 주고받는 일은 전혀 없었다 From then on, they merely bowed civilly each other without exchanging so much as a word.

**묵묵**(默默) ~하다 (be) silent; mute; tacit. ¶ ~히 silently; in (stony) silence; mutely; tacitly / ~ 부답(不答)하다 be silent and make no response.

**묵비권**(默秘權) the right of silence; 《미》 the Fifth Amendment (★ 미국 헌법 수정 제5조에 자기에게 불리한 증언을 거부할 수 있는 권리가 보장되어 있음). ¶ ~을 행사하다 stand mute; exercise 〔use〕 *one's* right to keep silence; 《미》 take the Fifth (Amendment) / 그 피의자는 ~을 행사하여 범행의 자백을 거부했다 The suspected person refused to confess to the offence by exploiting his right to remain silent.

**묵살**(默殺) ~하다 take no notice of; ignore 《*a person's* remarks by keeping silence》; pass (over) 《*a matter*》 in 〔with〕 silence. ¶ 의안을 ~하다 pigeonhole 〔shelve〕 a bill / 제안을 ~하다 smother up 〔burke〕 a proposal / 반대 의견을 ~하다 ignore objections / 항의를 ~하다 turn a deaf ear to protests / ~되다 be ignored; meet with disregard.

**묵상**(默想) meditation; contemplation. ~하다 meditate 《on》; muse 《on》; contemplate. ¶ ~에 잠기다 be lost in deep contemplation; be buried in deep meditation.

**묵새기다** make a long stay without doing much.

**묵수**(默守) adherence. ~하다 adhere to; stick 〔cling, keep〕 to 《old customs》.

**묵시**(默示) revelation. ~하다 reveal. ◉ ~록(錄) ⇨ 계시록(啓示錄).

**묵시**(默視) a silent watching. ~하다 overlook; pass over; watch 〔look at〕 silently; remain a passive spectator; tolerate; let go unchallenged. ¶ 그 사실은 ~할 수가 없다 I can't shut my eyes to the fact.

**묵은세배**(―歲拜) bowing *one's* greeting to elders on New Year's Eve.

**묵은해** the old year; the past year(s); the year that has been rung out. ¶ ~를 보내고 새해를 맞이하다 speed 〔ring out〕 the old year and greet 〔ring in〕 the new year.

**묵음**(默音) ¶ ~의 silent; 『음성』 mute.

**묵이** an old thing; old stuff.

**묵인**(默認) tacit 〔silent〕 approval 〔consent〕; tacit permission; 『법』 connivance; toleration. ~하다 approve 〔permit〕 tacitly; give (a) tacit consent 〔permission〕; connive 〔wink〕 at; pass over; tolerate. ¶ …의 ~ 아래 with 《*a person's*》 connivance / 이런 부패가 ~되다니 참 한탄할 노릇이다 It is a matter for sincere regret that such corruption should be overlooked. / 그들의 행위는 너무나도 악질이어서 ~할 수는 없다 Their conduct 〔behavior〕 is so unethical 〔outrageous〕 that we can't overlook it.

**묵정밭** a fallow field that has gone to waste.

**묵정이** old stuff; stuff that has been laid aside for a long time.

**묵종**(默從) acquiescence; passive 〔silent〕 obedience. ~하다 obey passively; acquiesce 《in》; submit tamely 〔unprotestingly〕 《to》.

**묵주**(默珠) 『가톨릭』 a rosary.

**묵주머니** ① 《묵의》 a jelly bag. ② 《일의》 a mess; a wreck. ¶ 일을 ~로 만들다 make a mess of 《it》.

**묵즙**(墨汁) liquid Chinese ink; India ink.

**묵지**(墨紙) copying paper; carbon paper. ¶ ~를 대고 쓰다 take a carbon copy.

**묵직이** heavily. ¶ 짐을 ~ 싣다 load a heavy cargo; pack a weighty load.

**묵직하다** ① 《무게가》 (be) rather heavy 〔massive, weighty〕. ¶ 묵직한 지갑 a substantially heavy purse; a filled up purse. ② 《몸가짐이》 (be) rather grave 〔serious〕. ¶ 묵직한 느낌을 주는 사람 a man of great presence.

**묵허**(默許) tacit permission 〔consent〕; connivance. =묵인(默認). ¶ ~를 얻다 get 《*a person's*》 tacit consent.

**묵화**(墨畫) an India(n)-ink drawing; a black-and-white painting; a monochrome painting.

**묵히다** 《쓰지 않고》 leave unused; leave wasted; 《상품·자본 등을》 let 《goods》 lie idle; keep 《money》 idle. ¶ 쌀을 ~ leave rice unused / 땅을 ~ lay land 〔soil〕 fallow; keep a land idle / 돈〔물건〕을 ~ let funds 〔goods〕 lie idle / 돈을 은행에 묵혀두는 일은 없어야 한다 You should not let your money lie idle in the bank. / 묵혀 없애느니 써서 없애는 게 낫다 Better wear out than rust out.

**묶다** ① 《동여서》 bind; tie; fasten; cord (끈으로); chain (사슬로); 《묶음으로》 tie 〔do〕 up; bundle; bunch; sheave. ¶ 꾸러미〔다발〕로 ~ tie up in a bundle; tie into a bundle / 머리를 ~ bind *one's* hair up / 범인을 ~ tie a criminal with cords / 볏단을 ~ sheave straw; bind 〔tie up〕 straw into a sheaf / 소포를 ~ string a parcel / 지폐를 ~ wad bank notes together / 짚단을 ~ bundle straws. ② 《속박·제약하다》 bind; fetter; tie; restrict; restrain; chain. ⇨ 묶이다①. ¶ 규칙으로 ~ restrict 《*a person*》 by rules.

**묶음** a bundle; a bunch; 《볏단》 a sheaf; 《장작》 a fagot; 《건초·짚》 a truss; 《새끼 따위》 a coil. ¶ 장작 한 ~ a bundle of firewood / 짚 한 ~ a bundle 〔sheaf〕 of straw / 꽃〔열쇠〕 한 ~ a bunch of flowers 〔keys〕 / 서류 한 ~ a bunch 〔sheaf〕 of papers / 돈 한 ~ a bundle 〔roll〕 of paper money 〔bank notes〕 / 한 ~에 만원 ten thousand won a bundle / ~으로 하다 (make a) bundle; bunch; tie 〔do〕 up in bundles; bunch 〔pack〕 into a bundle / ~으로 팔다 sell by the bundle 〔bunch〕.

**묶이다** ① 《물건이》 be fastened together; be bound 〔tied, trussed, bundled, bunched, sheaved〕. ¶ 짐이 단단히 ~ a bundle is tied up tight. ② 《사람이》 be bound 〔tied up, fettered, chained〕. ¶ 손발이 ~ *one's* hands and feet are tied up / 두 손을 뒤로 묶이어 with *one's* hands tied behind / 우리는 팔다리가 튼튼한 밧줄로 묶이었다 Our legs and arms were bound with stout cord. ③ 《속박되다》 be tied 〔fettered〕 by; be bound 〔restricted, restrained〕 by; be chained 《to》. ¶ 규칙에 ~ be screwed down to a rule; be bound by a rule / 시간에 ~ be restricted by time; have very little time to call *one's* own / 의리에 ~ be fettered by the bonds of obligation / 일에 ~ be chained 〔fettered, tied down〕 to *one's* business 〔work〕; be tied up in *one's* business; be chained to the desk / 나에 대한 그녀의 애정에 묶이어 나는 그녀 곁을 떠날 수가 없었다 Chained to her by her love for me, I could not bring myself to leave her.

**문**(文) ① 《문장》 writings; a composition; a sentence (문법상의); style (문체). ¶ 서술문 a declarative sentence / 명문이다 be well written; be high in literary merit. ② 《문학·학문》 literature; letters; the pen. ¶ 문은 무(武)보다 강하다 The pen is mightier than the sword. ③ 《신발의》 footgear size (=2.64cm). ¶ 10문짜리 고무신 size 10 rubber shoes.

**문**(門) ① 《출입문》 a gateway; a gate (대문); a door (방문); a sliding door (미닫이·장지문); a window (창문). ¶ 들어가는 문 the gate 〔door〕 in (to) 《a house》; the entrance / 나가는 문 the gate 〔door〕 out; the exit / 문을 두드리다 knock 〔tap, rap〕 at the door / 문을 열다〔닫다〕 open 〔close, shut〕 the door / 열쇠로 문을 열다 unlock a door (with a key) / 문을 열어주다 open a gate 《for *a person*》 / 문을 꼭 닫으시오 Close the door after you. *or* Not to be left open. *or* Please keep the door closed. / 문에 함부로 손대지 마시오 《게시》 No tampering with the door. ② 《생물 분류의》 『동물』 a phylum (*pl.* -la); 『식물』 a division. ③ 《해부의》 a hilum (*pl.* -la). ④ 《대포 셀 때》 a cannon. ¶ 대포 수문 several pieces of ordnance.

● 좁은 문 《기독교에서》 the strait gate 《to heaven》.

**문**(紋) = 무늬.

**문**(問) a problem; a question (in a test). ¶ 제1문 the first question.

**문간**(門間) the gate section; the space just within a gate. ¶ ~에 들어서다 step just inside the gate. ◉ ~방 a room in the gate section. 〔drawers〕.

**문갑**(文匣) a stationery chest (of

**문경지교**(刎頸之交) sworn 〔devoted, bosom〕 friendship. ¶ ~를 맺다 pledge to eternal 〔close〕 friendship.

**문고**(文庫) a library; 《기록 보존의》 archives. ◉ ~본(本) a pocket edition; a paperback: ~본으로 읽다 read 《a novel》 in paperback. ~판 a book size slightly smaller than pocket-book size. 마을~ a village library.

**문고리**(門—) an iron-ring handle (attached to a door); a door fastener; a (door)pull; 《미닫이의》 a catch. ¶ ~를 걸다 fasten 〔lock, latch〕 a door.

**문과**[1](文科) 《인문과》 the department of liberal arts; the literary course. ¶ ~대학 a college of liberal arts.

**문과**[2](文科) 《과거》 the civil service examination under the dynasty. ¶ ~에 급제하다 pass the civil service examination.

**문관**(文官) a civil official; a civil servant; a civilian; [총칭] the civil service. ◉ ~우위(優位) the superiority 〔priority〕 of civil service to military service.

**문교**(文敎) education; educational affairs. ◉ ~정책 an educational policy.

**문구**(文句) ＝글귀. ¶ 명~ a clever 〔happy〕 expression; a famous quotation / 선전~ a catchphrase.

**문구**(文具) stationery; writing materials.

**문구멍**(門—) a rip in a door 〔window〕.

**문기둥**(門—) a doorpost; a gatepost.

**문단**(文段) a paragraph.

**문단**(文壇) the literary world; literary circles; the world of letters. ¶ ~경향 literary trends / ~의 거성 a literary magnate; the most prominent figure in the literary world / ~의 총아 a popular writer / ~에 나가다 start 〔enter upon〕 a literary career; make *one's* debut in letters / ~에 이름을 떨치다 win literary fame; make a name in literature / ~에서 지반을 굳히다 establish *oneself* in the literary world.

**문단속**(門團束) locking a door 〔gate〕; securing a door. ~하다 lock a door properly; secure a door. ¶ ~을 잘하다 fasten the doors securely / 도둑이 들지 않도록 ~을 철저히 하시오 Bolt your door fast against possible burglary.

**문답**(問答) questions and answers; a dialogue (대화); a catechism (문답식 교수). ~하다 exchange questions and answers; hold a dialogue 〔conversation〕; catechize. ¶ ~식으로 catechetically; in the form of questions and answers / 이 역사책은 ~식으로 쓰여져 있다 This history book is written in question and answer form. ◉ ~식 교수법 the interrogatory method of teaching.

**문대다** ＝문지르다.

**문덕(문덕)** falling apart 〔crumbling〕 (from decomposition); in lumps; into pieces.

**문도**(門徒) a disciple; a follower.

**문둥병**(—病) leprosy. ⇨ 나병(癩病).

**문둥이** a leper.

**문드러지다** 《썩어서》 rot 《away, off》; decay; be disintegrated 〔decomposed〕; 《피부·상처 따위가》 be sore; be inflamed; 《곪다》 fester; ulcerate; 《너무 익어서》 be overripe; 《해지다》 be worn out. ¶ 문드러진 빨간 피부 ulcerated tender red skin / 너무 익어 문드러진 감 an overripe persimmon / 살이 썩어 ~ flesh rots off / 상처가 ~ a wound festers 〔is inflamed〕 / 시체는 무섭게 썩어 문드러져 있었다 The corpse was in a fearful state of decomposition.

**문뜩** 《갑자기》 suddenly; 《우연히》 by (any) chance; casually (무심코); unexpectedly (생각지 않게); 《아무 생각 없이》 unintentionally. ¶ ~ 생각나다 〔머리에 떠오르다〕 occur to 《*one*》; flash across *one's* mind; hit upon 《an idea》 / ~ 깨닫다 it occurs to *one* 《that》 / ~ 밖을 내다보다 look out casually / ~ 옛일이 생각났다 An old memory suddenly returned to me. / ~ 좋은 생각이 떠올랐다 A good idea suddenly struck 〔occured to〕 me. / 나는 ~ 뒤를 돌아다 보았다 I cast a casual look over my shoulder. / ~ 우산을 두고 온 것이 생각났다 It struck me that I had left my umbrella. / 돌아가신 어머님 생각이 ~문뜩 난다 The memory of my late mother revives unexpectedly from time to time.

**문란**(紊亂) disorder; confusion; disorganization. ~하다 (be) disordered; confused; loose; disorderly; [서술적] be in disorder. ¶ ~한 가정 a disorderly household / 풍기를 ~케 하다 corrupt public morals / 풍기가 ~하다 Discipline is lax 〔loose〕. / 국가 재정이 극도

로 ~해져있다 The national finances are in extreme confusion.

**문례**(文例) a model (sentence); an example 《for writing》. ¶ ~를 들다 give an example / ~가 풍부하다 be full of illustrative examples.

**문루**(門樓) the upper story of a castle 〔city〕 gate.

**문리**(文理) ① 《문장의 조리》 the construction 〔style〕 of classical Chinese; the context. ② 《깨달아 아는 길》 the line of thought. ③ 《문과와 이과》 liberal arts and sciences. ◉ ~과 대학 the College of Liberal Arts and Sciences.

**문맥**(文脈) the context 《of a passage》; the line of thought. ¶ ~상의 contextual / ~으로 뜻을 파악하다 grasp the meaning 《of a word》 from the context / ~에 따라서는 다른 해석도 가능하다 It could read differently in another 〔a different〕 context. / 그 낱말이 어떤 뜻인지 ~으로 추측하여라 Guess what the word means from the context.

**문맹**(文盲) illiteracy; 《사람》 an unlettered person; an illiterate. ¶ ~의 ignorant; unlettered; illiterate / 무학 ~인 사람 a person who is uneducated 〔ignorant〕 and illiterate. ◉ ~률 《lower》 the illiteracy rate. ~퇴치 the eradication of illiteracy; a crusade against illiteracy: ~ 퇴치 운동 the illiteracy eradication campaign.

**문면**(文面) the contents 〔purport〕 of a letter. ¶ ~에 의하면 according to (the text of) the letter 〔what the letter says〕 / 그 서류의 ~상으로는 on the face of the document / 편지의 ~은 다음과 같다 The letter reads as follows.

**문명**(文名) literary fame. ¶ ~을 떨치다 win literary fame; make a name for *oneself* as an author.

**문명**(文明) (a) civilization; (a) culture (문화). ~하다 (be) civilized; enlightened.

> **용법** **civilization** 원시적인 상태를 벗어나 정신적·물질적으로 고도로 발달한 개화의 상태. **culture** 「문화」의 뜻으로, 각각의 민족이 독자적으로 만들어 낸 종교·기술·습관 등의 생활 양식을 가리킴. 특히 정신면에서의 활동에 중점이 두어짐. 우리말의 「문명」에 잘 상응하는 영어는 civilization임.

¶ 고도의 ~ a high civilization / ~의 이기(利器) modern conveniences / 기계〔물질〕~ machine 〔material〕 civilization / 서양 ~ Western civilization / ~이 발달하다〔뒤떨어지다〕 be advanced 〔backward〕 in civilization; be high 〔low〕 in the scale of civilization / ~이 발달함에 따라 with the advance of civilization / 외국의 ~을 받아들이다 adopt 〔introduce〕 the foreign civilization / 이러한 ~ 시대에도 even in these enlightened times / 컴퓨터는 가장 큰 ~의 이기이다 The computer is the greatest of all modern conveniences.

◉ ~개화 civilization and enlightenment. ~국 a civilized country. ~병 diseases of 〔resulting from〕 civilization. ~ 비평 criticism on civilization. ~사 the history of civilization (★ 저서는 부정관사 a). ~사회 a civilized society. 근대 ~(의 산물) (a product of) modern civilization.

**문묘**(文廟) a Confucian shrine.

**문무**(文武) civil 〔literary〕 and military arts; the pen and (the) sword. ¶ ~겸전하다 have both literary and military accomplishments; be both a good warrior and a good scholar / ~겸비한 사람으로 알려져 있다 be known as a man of literary and military accomplishments. ◉ ~(백)관 civil and military officials.

**문문하다** ① 《무르다》 (be) soft; tender; supple. ¶ 문문한 가죽 soft leather / 문문한 고기 tender meat. ② 《만만하다》 (be) easy (to deal with); be ready to yield; (be) soft; be not firm; (be) easygoing. ¶ 문문한 사람 a person easy to deal with; an easy mark; a pushover / 문문히 보다 look on 《*a person*》 as a softy; think little of 《*a person*》; make light of 《*a person*》.

**문물**(文物) civilization (문명); culture (문화); institutions (제도); things (사물). ¶ 서양의 ~ Occidental 〔Western〕 civilization 〔culture〕; things Western.

**문미**(門楣) 〚건축〛 the lintel of a door.

**문민**(文民) a civilian. ◉ ~정부 a civilian government.

**문밖**(門—) ① 《문의 바깥》 the outside of a house 〔door, gate〕. ¶ ~에서 놀다 play outside near the door. ② 《성문 밖·교외》 outside the city gate; the suburbs 〔outskirts〕 of a city. ¶ 서울 ~에 살다 live in the suburbs of Seoul.

**문발**(門—) a door screen 〔blind〕.

**문방구**(文房具) (an article of) stationery; writing materials. ◉ ～상《사람》 a stationer. ～점 a stationery shop 〔store〕; a stationer's (shop, store).

**문벌**(門閥) 《가문》 birth; lineage; pedigree; 《명문》 high 〔noble〕 lineage; a good 〔distinguished〕 family. ¶ ～좋은 집안에 태어나다 come of a good family; be of noble 〔high〕 birth.

**문법**(文法) grammar; rules of composition. ¶ ～적(으로)grammatical(ly) / ～상의 잘못 a grammatical mistake / ～에 맞다 be grammatical / ～에 안맞다 be ungrammatical; violate grammar / ～상 맞다 be grammatically correct / ～에 맞추다 grammatize / ～에 맞는〔안 맞는〕 어법을 쓰다 use good 〔bad〕 grammar / ～에 구애받다〔받지 않다〕 adhere to 〔be free of〕 grammar. ◉ ～책 a grammar (book). ～학자 a grammarian. 국～ Korean grammar. 비교〔일반〕～ comparative 〔general〕 grammar.

**문병**(問病) an inquiry after a sick person; a visit to a sick person. ～하다 inquire 〔(go to) ask〕 after a sick person; visit 〔call on〕 《*a person*》 in *his* sickbed. ¶ 입원 중인 친구를 ～하다 visit 〔call on〕 a friend in hospital; visit a friend in hospital to ask after his health. ◉ ～객 a visitor (asking after *a person's* health).

**문복**(問卜) ～하다 have *one's* fortune told; consult a fortuneteller.

**문빗장**(門—) a door latch; a gate bar; a bolt. ¶ ～을 지르다 bar 〔bolt〕 (a gate) / ～을 벗기다 unbar 〔unbolt〕 (a gate).

**문사**(文士) ＝문인(文人).

**문살**(門—) the frame of a paper sliding door.

**문상**(問喪) a call of condolence; a condolatory call. ～하다 condole with 《*a person* on *his* bereavement》; offer 〔express〕 *one's* condolence to 《*a person* on a sad event》. ¶ ～(을) 가다 make a call to express *one's* condolence 〔sympathy〕; call at 〔go to〕 《*a person's*》 home to offer *one's* condolence 《on a sad event》 / ～을 받다 receive callers for condolence. ◉ ～객 a person calling to express his sympathy; a condoler.

**문서**(文書) 《서류》 a document; 《통신》 letters; notes; 《기록》 archives; a record; a missive (공문서). ¶ ～(형식으)로 in 〔by〕 writing; in written form / ～화하다 commit to 〔put in〕 writing / ～로 정식 보고했다 We made the report formally in writing. / 회답은 ～로 하여 주시기바랍니다 You are requested to answer in written form. / 노사간의 결정은 ～화하지 않으면 무효가 된다 The agreement between labor and management will be invalid unless it is specified in written terms. ◉ ～과(課) 《관청》 the archives and documents section; 《회사》 the correspondence section. ～보관함 a file cabinet. ～손괴(損壞) 〖법〗 spoliation. ～위조(죄) forgery of documents; falsification. ～철(綴) a file: ～철 표지 a folder. 공～ official documents. 극비～ a topsecret document.

**문선**(文選) ① 《시문집》 a selection of literary works; an anthology. ② 〖인쇄〗 type-picking. ～하다 pick types. ◉ ～공 a type picker.

**문설주**(門—) 〖건축〗 the side posts of a door 〔window, gate〕; a gatepost.

**문세**(文勢) force of (literary) style.

**문소리**(門—) a sound 〔noise〕 made by opening or shutting a door. ¶ ～가 난다 I hear the door.

**문수**(文殊) 〖佛教〗 *Mañjuśri;* the *bodhisattva* of wisdom and intellect. ◉ ～보살 ＝ 문수(文殊).

**문수**(文數) the size of shoes; shoe size.

**문신**(文臣) a civil minister 〔vassal〕.

**문신**(文身) tattooing; a tattoo. ～하다 tattoo 《a dragon on *a person's* back》 (남에게); have 《an anchor》 tattooed 《on *one's* arm》 (자기에게). ¶ 등에 ～하다 have *one's* back tattooed.

**문안**(門—) ① 《문의 안》 within the gate; inside the gate 〔door〕. ② 《성내》 inside the city gate; the city proper. ¶ ～ 사람 a person who lives in the city / ～에 살다 live in the city.

**문안**(文案) 《의안 따위》 a draft 《미》; a draught 《영》; a sketch; an outline. ¶ ～을 작성하다 draft; make 〔draw up, prepare〕 a draft 《for》. ◉ ～작성자 a drafter; a draftsman.

**문안**(問安) an asking 〔inquiry〕 after the health of another; sending kind regards. ～하다 send kind regards; pay *one's* respects to 《*a person*》; inquire 〔ask〕 after 《*a person's*》 health. ¶ ～하러 가다 call on 《*a person*》 to inquire after *his* health. ◉ ～편지 a letter conveying the compliments of the season.

**문약**(文弱) literary indulgence to the neglect of martial arts; effeminacy. ¶ ~에 빠지다 sink into effeminacy; become effeminate.

**문어**(文魚) 〖동물〗 an octopus. ¶ ~발식으로 기업을 확장하다 expand *one's* business lines as an octopus spreads its arms. ◉ ~통발 an octopus trap.

**문어**(文語) literary 〔written〕 language; 《낱말·표현》 a literary 「word 〔expression〕. ◉ ~체 literary 〔book〕 style.

**문얼굴**(門—) 〖건축〗 a framework of a door; a doorframe.

**문예**(文藝) literature; literary art; art and literature. ¶ ~에 조예가 깊다 be well versed in art and literature. ◉ ~기자 a literary writer. ~독본 literary selections; a literary reader. ~란 a literary 「column 〔page, section〕. ~부흥 the revival of learning; the Renaissance. ~사조 the trend of literary thoughts. ~영화 literary 「pictures 〔films〕. ~인 a literary man; a man of letters. ~작품 literary 「works 〔productions〕. ~잡지 a literary magazine. ~평론 (an essay in) literary criticism: ~평론가 a literary critic; a book reviewer. ~학 the science of literature. ~활동 literary activity. 한국 ~진흥원 the Korean Culture and Arts Foundation.

**문외한**(門外漢) 《국외자》 an outsider; 《영역 밖의》 a layman; a nonspecialist. ¶ ~의 생각 a layman's idea / 그는 전혀 ~이다 He is a rank outsider. / 프랑스 문학에 관해서는 아주 ~입니다 French literature is not at all in my line 〔is entirely outside my field〕.

**문우**(文友) a literary 「friend 〔associate〕; a fellow writer.

**문의**(文義·文意) the meaning of a 「passage 〔sentence〕; the purport of a 「phrase 〔passage〕. ¶ ~를 파악하다 grasp the meaning of a passage.

**문의**(問議) (an) inquiry; (a) reference (특히 신원·신용 등의). ~하다 make inquiries 《at an office about *a matter*》; inquire 《of *a person* about *a matter*》; refer 《to *a person* for *something*》; ask 《*a person*》 for information. ¶ ~해 보니 on inquiry / ~를 받다 receive an inquiry 《about》 / 전화로 ~하다 make an inquiry by telephone / ~편지를 보내다 send a letter of inquiry / ~했으나 회답이 없다 hear nothing in reply to *one's* inquiry / 그녀의 인품에 관해 그녀의 전 고용주에게 ~를 했다 I have referred to her former employer concerning her character. / 사무실에 ~하십시오 Please inquire at the office. / 자세한 내용은 우체국 창구에 ~하시기 바랍니다 For further details, please contact the post office. / 전화 ~에 대해서는 대답할 수 없습니다 We are unable to handle any inquiries over the phone. / 자세한 것은 김 교수님께 ~하라는 말을 들었습니다 I was referred to Prof. Kim for the detailed information. ◉ ~서(書) a letter of inquiry. ~처(處) 《인물·신용 따위의》 a reference.

**문인**(文人) a literary man; a man of letters; cultured person (교양인). ◉ ~극 a theatrical performance by men of letters. ~사회 literary circles; the *literati* (L.). ~협회 the Literary Men's Association. ~화(畫) a painting by a literary artist after the Southern School of Chinese painting.

**문인**(門人) a pupil; a disciple; a follower; [집합적] 《have》 a 《large》 following.

**문자**[1](文字) ① 《글귀》 a phrase. ② 《숙어》 an idiomatic phrase, especially from the Chinese classics. ¶ ~를 잘 쓰다 be much given to 「quoting 〔using〕 phrases from classical Chinese.

**문자**[2](文字) 《글자》 a letter; a character (한자); figures. ¶ 대〔소〕~ a 「capital 〔small〕 letter / 표의 ~ an ideograph; an ideogram / 표음 ~ a phonogram / ~에 구애되다 adhere to the letter 《of the law》 / ~그대로 해석하다 interpret 《a passage》 literally 〔to the letter〕; take a word in its literal sense / ~그대로 무일푼이다 I am literally penniless. ◉ ~다중방송 teletext. ~언어 a written language. ~판 a dial (plate); 《시계의》 the face 《of a watch》; the clockface.

**문장**(文章) 《글》 a sentence; 《작문》 a composition; a piece of writing; an essay (수필); a prose (산문); 《논설》 an article; 《문체》 writings; (a) style. ¶ ~이 능하다〔서툴다〕 have 〔write in〕 a 「good 〔bad〕 style; be a good 〔poor〕 writer / ~을 다듬다 polish (up) *one's* style / ~을 짓다 write 〔make〕 a composition. ◉ ~가 a 「fine 〔good〕 writer; a stylist. ~구조 the sentence structure. ~론〔구성법〕 syntax. ~분석 a sentence analysis. ~체 written 〔uncolloquial〕 style.

**문장**(紋章) a crest; a heraldic emblem 〔device〕; a coat of arms; armorial bearings.
**문장부**(門—) 〖건축〗 a door pivot.
**문재**(文才) literary talent 〔ability〕. ¶ ~가 있다 have a talent for writing.
**문전**(文典) a grammar; a grammar book.
**문전**(門前) 《in》 front of a gate. ¶ ~ 걸식하다 beg 《*one's*》 bread from door to door; go out begging / ~ 성시(成市)를 이루다 be crowded 〔thronged〕 with callers; have a constant stream of visitors / ~ 축객(逐客)하다 turn a visitor away at the door; refuse to see 《*a person*》; be not at home to 《a caller》.
**문제**(問題) a question; a problem; a subject (주제); a topic (화제); an affair; a matter (사건); trouble (분규); an issue (논의 대상).
¶ 귀찮은 ~ a vexed question / 주어진 ~ a given question 〔problem〕 / 당면한 ~ the question 〔point〕 at issue / 연구 ~ a subject of 〔for〕 inquiry 〔study〕 / 당황케 하는 ~ a puzzling question / 지엽적인 ~ side issues / 미해결 ~ an open 〔undecided, unsettled〕 question / 해결해야 할 여러~ many problems awaiting solution / 손도 못대고 있는 ~ an untouched subject / 금전상의 ~ a matter of money / 생사의 ~ a matter of life and death / 시간의 ~ a question 〔matter〕 of time / 중대한 ~ a matter of 〔for〕 grave concern / 중심 ~ the central issue 〔problem〕 / ~ 가 되지 않는다 be beside the question; be out of the question.
문제가: ~가 되다 become an issue; be at issue; come into question; cause 〔give rise to〕 public discussion; 《표면화하다》 come to 「a head 〔the fore〕 / ~가〔도〕 안 되다 《대수롭지 않다》 matter little; count for nothing / …에는 많은 ~가 있다 there are a lot of problems about 《our system》.
문제의: ~의 인물 the man in question; a controversial figure (문제가 많은 사람) / ~의 발단은… the question was posed when….
문제에: ~에 답하다 answer a question / ~에 깊이 들어가다 go deep into a subject / ~에 부딪치다 meet 〔encounter〕 a problem / 이 ~에 관한 저서 works on this subject / 여러 가지 ~에 걸치다 cover a wide range of subjects.
문제를: ~를 일으키다 cause trouble 〔problems〕; raise a question; give rise to public discussion (세상에) / ~를 내다 set 〔give〕 a question; present a problem / ~를 다루다 handle 〔treat〕 a subject 〔problem〕 / ~를 풀다〔해결하다〕 solve 〔work out〕 a problem; settle a question.
¶ 그것으로 ~는 해결이다 That settles the case 〔matter〕. / 그것은 돈과 시간의 ~다 It's a question of money and time. / 계획이 잘될지 어떨지 ~다 It is an open question whether the scheme will come off or not. / 환경 보호는 오늘날 가장 중요한 ~중 하나다 Environmental protection is one of the most crucial topics today. / ~는 그가 그만한 돈을 낼 수 있느냐에 있다 The question 〔point〕 is whether he can afford to pay that much money. / 성공하느냐 못하느냐가 ~다 It is questionable whether he will succeed or not. / 공식 석상에서의 그의 발언이 ~가 되었다 His statement in public brought on much criticism. / 시험에는 응용 ~가 많이 나왔다 A lot of applied problems 〔questions〕 were given in the exam. / 그것은 중대한 국제 ~가 되었다 It turned into a grave international issue. / 그는 끊임없이 ~를 일으켰다 He was in continual trouble. / 급료 ~는 결정을 보지 못할 것이다 The matter of salary will be left open 〔remain undecided〕.
◉ ~소설〔극〕 a problem novel 〔play〕. ~아(兒) a problem child. ~영역 a problem area. ~은행 an item pool. ~의식 《have》 a critical mind; an awareness of the issues 〔problems involved〕. ~점 the point at issue; a controversial 〔moot〕 point: 이 방법에 관해서는 몇가지 ~점이 지적되고 있다 Several problems have been pointed out concerning this method. ~집 a collection of problems. ~해결능력 *one's* problem-solving powers.
**문제화**(問題化) ~하다 become an issue; come into question; 《표면화》 come to a head 〔the fore〕; 《말썽》 cause 〔give rise to〕 trouble.
**문조**(文鳥) 〖조류〗 a paddy(bird).
**문죄**(問罪) (an) accusation; indictment. ~하다 accuse 《*a person*》 of a crime.
**문주란**(文珠蘭) 〖식물〗 a crinum.
**문중**(門中) *one's* (whole) family; a clan;

*one's* close relatives; kinsmen.

**문지기**(門—) a gatekeeper; a gateman; a doorman.

**문지도리**(門—) the hinges of a door [gate]; a pivot of a door.

**문지르다** rub; scour; scrub. ¶ 문질러 없애다 rub off; scrape off [away, out] / 헝겊으로 문질러 광을 내다 polish with a dry cloth / 마루를 걸레로 ~ scrub a floor with a floorcloth.

**문지방**(門地枋) 〖건축〗 a doorsill (방의); the threshold (대문의). ¶ ~을 넘다 cross the threshold / ~이 닳도록 찾아다니다 call upon 《*a person*》 repeatedly; pay frequent visits to 《her house》; visit 《*a person*》 a number of times.

**문직**(紋織) figured texture.

**문진**(文鎭) a paperweight.

**문질리다** 《남을 시켜》 make 《*a person*》 rub [scrub]; 《피동》 be rubbed; be scrubbed.

**문집**(文集) a collection of works; an anthology; a prose collection. ◉ 송강(松江)~ a collection of Song-gang's works.

**문짝**(門—) (a leaf [flap] of) a door. ¶ ~을 열어 젖뜨리다 push [pull] the door open.

**문책**(文責) ¶ ~은 기자에게 있음 The reporter is responsible for the wording and content of this [the] article.

**문책**(問責) (a) censure; (a) reproof; reprimand. ~하다 take [call] 《*a person*》 to task 《for *do*ing, about *something*》; call [bring] 《*a person*》 to account; reprove; reprehend; rebuke; censure. ¶ 대통령은 총리의 실언을 ~했다 President censured the Prime Minister for his slip of the tongue.

**문체**(文體) (a) (literary) style. ¶ 쉬운 ~(로) (in) an easy [a plain] style / 세련된[조잡한] ~ a polished [rough] style / 간결[화려, 우아]한 ~ a concise [a florid, an elegant] style / …의 ~를 본떠서 in the style of 《*a person*》 / ~를 다듬다 polish *one's* style / 쉬운 ~로 써있다 be written in an easy [a plain] style / 그의 소설은 간결한 ~로 쓰여져 있다 His novels are written in a clear style. ◉ ~론(論) stylistics.

**문초**(問招) questioning [interrogating] 《a criminal》; an inquiry. ~하다 question 《a criminal》; investigate; inquire [make an inquiry] into; examine. ¶ ~ 중이다 be under examination [investigation] / 죄인을 ~하다 examine a criminal / 엄중한 ~를 하다 conduct a strict examination / 경찰의 ~를 받다 be examined [questioned] by the police. ◉ ~실 《경찰의》 an interrogation room.

**문치**(文治) civil administration; administration by civilians. ¶ ~ 정책 a policy of civilian government. ◉ ~주의 the principles of civilian government.

**문치**(門齒) 〖해부〗 foretooth; an incisor.

**문치적거리다** act shilly-shally; mess around without getting anything done.

**문치적문치적** shily-shally; dilly-dally.

**문턱**(門—) a threshold; a doorsill. ¶ ~에 걸터앉다 sit on a doorsill.

**문투**(文套) a literary style [form].

**문틀**(門—) the framework of a door; a doorframe.

**문틈**(門—) a chink [crevice] in the door [window, gate]; door crevice. ¶ ~으로 들여다보다 peep [look] in through a chink [crevice] in the door.

**문패**(門牌) a doorplate; a nameplate; a plate. ¶ ~를 달다 put up a nameplate on [at] the door.

**문풍지**(門風紙) weather strips.

**문필**(文筆) literary art; writing. ¶ ~로 먹고 살다 live by *one's* pen; make a profession of literature / ~에 종사하다 be engaged in literary work; follow the profession of letters / ~에 재능이 있다 have a talent for writing. ◉ ~가 a writer; a man of letters.

**문하**(門下) [형용사적] under 《*a person's*》 instruction [guidance, tuition]; studying under 《*a person*》. ◉ ~생[인] a pupil; a disciple; a follower.

**문학**(文學) literature; letters. ¶ 영[불, 국]~ English [French, Korean] literature / ~ 운동 a literary movement / ~에 뜻을 두다 aspire to literary honors / ~에 소양이 있다 have literary culture / ~에 취미가 있다 have a taste for literature / ~ 이야기를 하다 talk [discuss] literature / 그는 대학에서 국~을 전공했다 He majored in Korean literature at the University. ◉ ~가 a literary man; a man of letters. ~개론 an introduction to literature. ~계 the literary world; literary circles; the world of letters. ~론 《이론》 the theory of literature; 《논문》 a literary essay; a treatise on litereture. ~박사 Doctor of Literature

(생략 D. Litt., Litt. D.); 《사람》 a doctor of literature. ～부 the department 〔faculty〕 of literature: ～부장 the dean of the literary department / ～부 학생 a lit student 〔boy, girl〕 《미구어》. ～사(士) Bachelor of Arts (생략 B.A., A.B.); 《사람》 a bachelor of arts. ～사(史) the history of 《English》 literature. ～상(賞) a literary award. ～석사 Master of Arts (생략 M.A., A.M.); 《사람》 a master of arts. ～소녀 a young lady of literary interests. ～예술 literary art(s). ～자 a scholar of literature; a writer; a man of letters: 불(佛)～자 a scholar of French literature. ～작품〔잡지〕 a literary work 〔magazine〕. ～ 청년 a young lover of literature; a young literary enthusiast 〔aspirant〕. 국민～ national literature.

**문헌**(文獻) literature 《on》; (documentary) records; documents; 《전거(典據)》 an authority. ¶ 의학에 관한 ～ the medical literature / 이 문제에 관한 ～ the literature on this subject / 여러 ～을 조사하다 refer to sundry records / 나는 그 문제에 관한 ～을 전부 조사했다 I researched all the literature on the subject.
◉ ～학 (the science of) bibliography; philology. ～ 학자 a philologist.

**문형**(文型) a sentence pattern. ¶ 기본 ～ a basic sentence pattern.

**문호**(文豪) a great 〔an eminent〕 writer; a great man of letters; a literary giant. ¶ 지금까지 몇몇 ～들이 이와 동일한 주제로 작품을 남기고 있다 Some of the great names in literature have written on this same subject.

**문호**(門戶) the door. ¶ ～를 개방하다 open 〔throw open〕 the 〔*one's*〕 door 《to, for》 / ～를 폐쇄하다 shut 〔close〕 the door 《to, on》 / 그 클럽은 여성에게 ～를 개방했다 The club opened its doors to women. ◉ ～ 개방주의〔정책〕 the open-door policy 〔principle〕.

**문화**(文化) culture; civilization (문명). ¶ 고도의 ～ a high level of culture; a high cultural level 〔standard〕 / ～의 발달 advance of culture / ～의 전파 culture diffusion / 한국 ～의 전통 Korean cultural tradition / 이(異)～의 수용 the adoption of foreign culture / ～가 발달하다 become civilized; advance in civilization / ～가 뒤(떨어)지다 be backward in civilization; be at a low level of culture / 외국의 ～를 섭취하다 absorb 〔take in〕 foreign culture / ～ 분야의 공로자 a person who has performed distinguished services in the field of culture / 이(異)～ 간의 커뮤니케이션 cross-cultured communication.
◉ ～공로자 a person who has contributed to culture. ～교류 cultural exchange 〔relations〕: 국가간의 ～ 교류를 도모하다 promote cultural exchange 〔interchange〕 between 〔among〕 nations. ～국가 a cultured 〔civilized〕 nation. ～국민 civilized citizens. ～권 a culture 〔cultural〕 area. ～단체 a cultural organization. ～부 《신문사의》 the culture desk. ～사(史) (a) cultural history. ～사업 a cultural enterprise; cultural work. ～사절 a cultural delegate 〔envoy, mission〕. ～생활 《live》 a civilized 〔decent〕 life; a reasonable standard of living. ～수준 a cultural level 〔standard〕: 국가의 ～ 수준이 높다〔낮다〕 be high 〔low〕 in national standards of culture. ～시설 cultural institutions 〔facilities〕. ～양식 〖사회〗 a culture pattern. ～영화 an educational 〔a cultural〕 film. ～유산 (a) cultural heritage. ～인 a man of culture; a cultured 〔cultivated〕 man. ～인류학 cultural anthropology. ～자산 cultural assets 〔wealth〕. ～제 a cultural festival. ～주택 a modern 〔an up-to-date〕 house. ～체육관광부 the Ministry of Culture, Sports and Tourism: ～체육관광부 장관 the Minister of Culture, Sports and Tourism. ～혁명 《중국의》 the (Great) Cultural Revolution. ～협정 a cultural agreement. ～활동 cultural activities. ～회관 a cultural center; a lyceum 《미》. ～훈장 the Order for Cultural Merit.

**문화재**(文化財) cultural assets 〔properties〕; 《한국의》 Korean relics. ¶ ～(의) 보호〔관리〕 protection 〔preservation〕 of cultural properties / 도(道) 지정 ～ province-designated cultural properties / 주요 ～로 지정되다 be designated as an important cultural property 〔asset〕 / 지난날 일본으로 가져간 많은 우리 나라 ～들이 한 일본인 수집가의 노력으로 한국에 되돌아 왔다 Many Korean relics taken to Japan in the past have returned to Korea thanks to the effort of a private Japanese collector. ◉ ～관리국 the Cultural Property Preservation Bureau. ～보호법 the Cultural Properties Protection Law. ～청 the Cultural Properties Administration. 무형〔유형〕~ intangible 〔tangible〕 cultural assets. 인간~ human Cultural assets.

**문후**(問候) inquiring (by letter) after another's well-being; paying *one's* respect to《*a person*》(by letter). ~하다 write a letter《to》.

**묻다**[1] 《붙다》 stick《to》; be stuck; adhere《to》; be covered; be stained 〔smeared〕《with》. ¶ 피 묻은 옷 bloodstained clothes / 잉크가 묻어 있다 be stained 〔smeared〕 with ink / 바지에 진흙이 묻어 있다 Your trousers are muddy. / 용의자가 피 묻은 셔츠를 빨고 있는 것을 이웃 사람이 목격했다 A neighbor saw the suspect washing a bloodstained shirt.

**묻다**[2] ①《파묻다》bury《in, under》; inter; inhume. ¶ 김칫독을 ~ bury a kimchi jar in the ground; put a kimchi jar into the ground / 시신을 ~ bury a corpse 〔body〕/ 손수건에 얼굴을 묻고 울다 weep 〔cry〕 into *one's* handkerchief / 공사 인부는 토관을 묻었다 The workmen sank earthen pipes. ②《숨기다》conceal; hide; keep《*something*》to *oneself* (가슴 속에); keep《*a matter*》under wraps. ¶ 살인 사건을 비밀로 묻어 두다 keep a murder case secret / 나는 그 비밀을 죽을 때까지 가슴 속에 묻어둘 작정이다 I'll keep the secret to myself all my life.

**묻다**[3] ①《질문》¶ 다시 ~ inquire again / 문장의 뜻을 ~ ask the meaning of a sentence / 자세한 내용을 ~ ask about the details / 전문가한테 ~ consult an expert / 귀찮게 자꾸 ~ annoy《*a person*》with repeated questions; pester《*a person*》with questions. ②《책임을》charge《*a person*》with《responsibility》; call《*a person*》to account. ¶ 죄를 ~ accuse《*a person*》of a crime. ③《문제삼다》care. ¶일의 성패를 묻지 않다 do not care about success or failure; do not care whether *one* succeeds or fails / 능률만 오른다면 비용은 묻지 않겠다 We don't care about the expense 〔cost〕, if it increases efficiency. ④《안부를》inquire 〔ask〕 after《*a person's* health》; inquire about. ¶소식을 ~ ask how《*a person*》is getting along; ask for news about《*a person*》.

**묻히다**[1] 《묻게 하다》smear; stain; cover. ¶ 구두에 흙을 ~ get 〔have〕 mud on *one's* shoes / 떡에 콩가루를 ~ cover a rice cake with bean flour / 붓에 먹을 ~ dip a writing brush in Chinese ink / 손에 잉크를 ~ stain *one's* hands with ink; get 〔have〕 *one's* hands stained with ink / 굽기에 앞서 고기에 빵가루를 묻혔다 I coated the meat with bread crumbs.

**묻히다**[2] 《파묻히다》get 〔be〕 buried《in, under》;《숨겨지다》be concealed《from》; be kept secret《from》; be smothered 〔hushed〕 up (사건 등이). ¶ 산채로 ~ be buried 〔entombed〕 alive / 망각 속에 ~ be buried in oblivion / 그 사건은 완전히 묻혀버렸다 The matter has been covered 〔hushed〕 up. / 그는 공원 묘지에 묻혔다 He was buried 〔laid to rest〕 in the park cemetery.

**물**[1] ① [일반적] water. ¶ 찬〔더운〕물 cold 〔hot〕 water / 짠〔단〕물 salty 〔fresh〕 water / 오염된〔정수한〕 물 polluted 〔purified〕 water / 끓인〔마시는〕 물 boiled 〔drinking〕 water / 물탱크 a water tank / 물로 희석하다 water down; dilute; put water in《*one's* wine》.

물이: 물이 풍부한 a well-watered《mountain》/ 물이 새지 않다 be waterproof; be watertight / 물이 새지 않도록 하다 make《it》watertight / 물이 부족하다 be short of water / 수돗물이 안 나오다 no water comes from the tap.

물에: 물에 담그다 dip 〔soak〕 in the water / 물에 헹구다 cleanse 〔rinse〕 with water.

물을: 물을 긷다 draw water《from a well》/ 물을 끼얹다 sprinkle 〔dash〕 water《over *a person's* face》; pour water《on a fire》/ (논에) 물을 대다 irrigate 〔draw water into〕 (a paddy) / 물을 뒤집어 쓰다 pour water on *oneself* / 물을 뜨다〔푸다〕 draw water《from》; dip 〔scoop〕 up water / 물을 붓다 pour water into / 물을 빼다 drain off《a pool》/ 물을 뿌리다 sprinkle water《on a dusty path》; water《the garden》/ 물을 엎지르다 spill water / 물을 주다 water《a horse, a flower》/ 물을 짜내다 squeeze 〔wring〕《a towel》dry / 물을 채우다 fill《a tub》with water / 물을 타다 add water《to》;《술 따위에》dilute《whisky》with water; water down; put water in《*one's* wine》; take 〔mix〕 water with《*one's* whisky》/ 물을 탄 우유 watered 〔diluted〕 milk / (수도의) 물을 틀다〔잠그다〕 turn on 〔off〕 the water.

¶ 엎지른 물이다《속담》It is no use crying over spilt milk. / 강〔우물〕에 물이 말라 버렸다 The river 〔well〕 has

run dry. / 내 구두는 물이 스민다 My shoes leak 〔let in water〕. / 물은 낮은 데로 흐른다 It is the nature of water to run downhill. / 물이 맑으면 고기가 없다 A man with no faults is not easy to get along with.
② 《액체 모양의 것》 (a) liquid; (a) fluid (유동체); juice(즙). ¶ 물약 liquid medicine / 과일 물 fruit juice / 무릎에 물이 괴다 have water on the knee; fluid collects under *one's* kneecap.
③ 《홍수·범람》 a flood; (an) inundation. ¶ (큰) 물이 나다 have a flood; there is a flood; be flooded / 물에 잠기다 be submerged; be flooded 〔swamped〕 / 물이 빠졌다 The water 〔flood〕 has receded. *or* The (level of the) river has fallen.
④ 《나무의》 sap; juice. ¶ 나무에 물이 오르다 the sap rises 〔runs〕 in a tree. ◉ 물오염 water pollution.

**물**[2] 《색깔》 dyed color. ¶ 검정물을 들이다 dye black / 물을 빼다 bleach; take the color out / 물이 날다 the color fades / 물이 들다 dye. ⇨ 물들다.

**물**[3] ① 《빨래의》 a period between one wash and another; a wash; the number of times clothes have been washed. ¶ 새물 옷, 첫물 옷 new clothes that have yet to be laundered / 한물 빤 옷 clothes that have been washed once. ② 《과일·해산물의》 the season; a crop; a catch; a flush. ¶ 첫물 상치 the first flush of lettuce / 만물 사과 the first crop of apples / 끝물 고등어 the last catch of mackerel / 배가 한물지다 pears are「in full flush 〔at their best〕. ③ 《누에의》 a hatch 〔batch〕 of silkworms. ¶ 첫물 누에 the first hatch of silkworms.

**물가** the edge of the water; the water's edge; the waterside; the shore; the beach. ¶ ～에서 at the water's edge; close to 〔at the edge of 〕 the water.

**물가**(物價) price(s). ¶ ～의 등귀〔상승〕 a rise 〔an advance〕 in prices / ～의 하락 a fall in prices / ～가 오르다 prices rise 〔go up〕 / ～가 내리다 prices fall 〔come down〕 / ～가 계속 뛰어오르고 있다 prices keep on soaring / ～를 올리다 raise 〔advance〕 prices / ～를 내리다 lower 〔reduce, bring down〕 prices / ～를 안정시키다 stabilize prices / ～를 현실화하다 rationalize the price structure / ～의 변동이 크다 prices fluctuate widely / ～가 비싸다〔싸다〕 Prices are high 〔low〕. (★ Price are dear 〔cheap〕.라고는 하지 않음) / ～가 한없이 오르고 있다 The prices are skyrocketing. / ～가 바닥 시세를 보였다 Prices have hit rock-bottom. / 「도쿄는 ～가 매우 높다면서요」—「그렇습니다. 생활비가 많이 들지요」 "I hear prices are terribly high in Tokyo."—"That's right. It's very expensive to live there." ◉ ～고(高) high prices of commodities. ～급등 a rapid 〔galloping〕 rise in prices. ～대책〔정책〕 a (commodity) price policy. ～동결(凍結) pegging 〔freezing〕 of prices: ～를 동결시키다 peg prices. ～등귀 a rise in price. ～변동 price fluctuation. ～수당 a commodity price allowance; an allowance for price increase. ～수준 the price level. ～악순환 the price spiral. ～안정 price stabilization: ～ 안정선 a price stabilization zone / 튼튼한 ～ 안정에 바탕을 둔 지속적인 경제 성장을 추구하다 pursue sustained economic growth based on the firm foundation of price stabilization / ～ 안정에 우선권을 두다 place top priority on stabilizing prices / ～ 안정을 이룩하다 attain price stability. ～인상 a price hike. ～인하 a price reduction: ～ 인하 운동 a cut=price drive; a cut-the-price campaign. ～정책 a price policy: 저 ～정책 a low-price policy. ～지수 a price index: 도매〔소비자〕 ～ 지수 a wholesale 〔consumer〕 price index. ～체계 a price structure 〔system〕. ～통제 price control(s). ～파동 violent price fluctuations. ～표 a price list. ～하락 a fall in prices. 주요～ prices of staple commodities.

**물갈래** a branch 〔fork〕 of a river; the place where a stream divides. ¶ ～가 둘로 갈라지다 fork into two rivers 〔streams〕.

**물갈이** ① 〖농업〗 plowing a paddy with water in it. ～하다 plow a paddy with water in it. ② 《인원의 교체》 a change; relief. ～하다 change; replace 《an old thing with a new one》. ¶ 총회에서 이사진의 ～가 단행되었다 The members of the board were changed 〔replaced〕 at the general meeting.

**물갈퀴** a web; a webfoot (물갈퀴 발).

**물감** dyestuffs; dyes; colors. ¶ 천연〔합성〕 ～ natural 〔synthetic〕 colors / 그림 ～ oil colors (유화의) / ～을 들이다 dye / ～이 잘 먹다 (take) dye well; dye fast.

**물개** 〖동물〗 a fur seal (해구); an otter (수달).

**물거름** 《액체 거름》 liquid fertilizer 〔manure〕. ◉ ~통 a night soil bucket; a honey bucket 《미속어》.

**물거리**(—距離) distance by water; navigable distance at high tide.

**물거미** 〚동물〛 a water spider. ◉ ~ 뒷다리 [비유적] a tall skinny person.

**물거품** a bubble; foam; froth. ¶ ~ 같은 명성 a bubble reputation / ~이 되다 come to naught 〔nothing〕; end (up) 〔result〕 in failure; end 〔go up〕 in smoke / ~이 지다 bubble; foam; froth / ~처럼 사라지다 burst like a bubble; end 〔go up〕 in smoke / 그의 노력은 모두 ~으로 돌아갔다 All his efforts came to nothing 〔naught〕.

**물건**(物件) ① 《일반 유형물》 a thing; an object; 《물품》 an article; goods; 《재료》 stuff; (a) material; stock (재고품); 《소유물》 a possession. ¶ 온갖 종류의 ~ all sorts of goods / 저 상점에서는 여러 가지 ~을 판다 They sell a wide variety of things in that store. / 이것은 내 ~이오 This is mine. / ~에 욕심을 내지 마라 Don't lust for things. / 화재 중에 갖고 나온 ~은 단지 책 한 권뿐이었다 The only object rescued from the fire was a book. ② 《품질》 quality. ¶ ~이 좋다 be of 「good 〔fine〕 quality / ~이 나쁘다 be of 「bad 〔poor, coarse〕 quality / 이 자전거는 좋지 않군요. 더 나은 ~을 사주세요 This bicycle is not good. Buy me a better one. ◉ 증거~ material evidence.

**물걸레** a damp house 〔floor〕 cloth; a wet mop. ¶ ~질하다 wipe with a damp cloth 〔wet duster〕.

**물것** biting insects.

**물결** ① 《파도》 a wave; a sea (of waves). ¶ ~ 소리 the sound 〔roar〕 of the waves / 큰 ~ a surge; a billow / 잔~ a ripple / 밀려오는 ~ a surf; a comber / 거친 ~ wild 〔raging〕 waves; a rough 〔heavy〕 sea / 잔잔한 ~ gentle waves / ~이 일다 the sea gets up; waves rise / ~이 자다 the sea goes down; waves subside / ~이 치다 waves undulate / ~에 떠다니다 drift on the waves / ~에 휩쓸리다 be washed 〔carried〕 away by the waves / ~을 뒤집어쓰다 be washed by the waves; ship a wave / ~을 타다 ride on the waves / ~을 거슬러 나아가다 stem the waves / ~을 헤치고 나아가다 plow 〔cleave〕 through the waves / ~이 해변에 밀어닥치고 있다 waves are lapping the beach / ~이 높다 The waves are high. *or* The seas are running high / 큰 ~이 바위에 부딪혀 부서졌다 The big waves 〔billows〕 broke 「against 〔on〕 the rocks. ② 《물결 같은 것》 a stream; (a) flow. ¶ (누런) 황금의 ~ the golden waves of 《barley》 / 사람의 ~ a torrent of people / 차(車)의 ~ a stream of cars / 그의 사업은 시대의 ~을 탔다 His business went with 〔rode on〕 the tide of the times.

**물결치다** move in waves; rise and fall (like waves); wave; roll; undulate; dash 《against》. ¶ 물결치는 대로 at the mercy of the waves / 물결치는 바다 a rolling sea / 바람에 ~ waves rise in the wind / 절벽을 향해 파도가 ~ waves dash against 〔break on〕 the foot of a cliff / 밀이 바람에 ~ wheat undulates in the wind.

**물경**(勿驚) surprisingly (enough); it will surprise you but...; you would be surprised but...; startling; shocking. ¶ 쌓인 빚이 ~ 천만 원이었다 The debt went on increasing, reaching at last a surprising amount of ten million won.

**물계**(物—) ① 《시세》 the current price; the selling price. ② 《물정》 the way things are 〔stand〕; what's what. ¶ ~를 알다〔모르다〕 understand 〔fail to understand〕 things.

**물고**(物故) 《유명 인사의 죽음》 death (of an eminent or notorious person); 《죄인의 죽음》 putting 〔being put〕 to death. ¶ ~나다 die; be dead / ~내다 kill 《*a person*》; put 《*a person*》 to death.

**물고기** a fish; [집합적] fish. (★ fish는 보통 단수형으로 또 집합적으로도 쓰이는데, 복수형 fishes는 특히 물고기의 종류를 말할 때 씀: one fish, many fish (동일 종류); all kind of fishes(모든 종류)). ¶ ~를 잡다 fish; catch fish / ~를 낚다 fish; angle (for fish) / 이 강에는 ~가 많다 This river abounds 〔teems〕 with fish. ◉ ~떼 a shoal of fishes. ~뼈 a fish bone.

**물고기자리** 〚천문〛 the Pisces; the 「Fishes.

**물고늘어지다** ① 《이빨로》 bite at something and hang on to it. ¶ 팔을 ~ sink *one's* teeth in the arm and hangs on. ② 《집요하게》 stick to; hang 〔hold〕 on to; get a firm grip on 《*one's* rival》; latch on to 《구어》. ¶ 끝까지 ~

stick to *one's* last / 말꼬리를 ~ catch 《*a person*》 in *his* own words; cavil at 《*a person's*》 words / 계속 질문해서 (상대를) ~ harass 《*a person*》 with repeated interpellations 〔questions〕/ 그는 잇단 질문으로 집요하게 국무총리를 물고 늘어졌다 He hounded the Prime Minister persistently, asking him one question after another.

**물고동** 《수도꼭지》 a tap; 《미》 a faucet. ¶ ~을 틀다〔잠그다〕 turn on 〔off〕 a faucet 〔tap〕.

**물곬** a channel; a water course; a drain. ¶ 도랑에 ~을 내다 make a drain in a ditch / ~이 메다 a drain is stopped up.

**물구나무서다** stand on *one's* hands; do a handstand. ¶ 물구나무서기 《체조》 handstanding; a handstand / 물구나무서서 걷다 walk on *one's* hands.

**물구덩이** a 《stagnant》 pool; a puddle. ¶ ~가 생기다 a pool forms / ~를 피해서 길을 걷다 walk along the road avoiding the puddles / 큰 비가 오면 사방에 ~가 생긴다 There come out small muddy pools here and there after a heavy rain.

**물굽성**(一性) 〖식물〗 hydrotropism. ◉ 양성〔음성〕~ positive 〔negative〕 hydrotropism.

**물굽이** a bend 〔curve〕 in a river 〔stream〕. ¶ ~ 지다 (a river) has a bend; bend; wind; curve.

**물권**(物權) 〖법〗 a real right; *jus in rem* (L). ¶ ~ 표시 조항 a habendum (*pl.* -da) / ~의 설정〔이전〕 the creation 〔transfer〕 of a real right. ◉ ~법 the Law of Realty. ~행위 reality right action.

**물귀신**(一鬼神) a water demon. ¶ ~이 되다 drown; be drowned (to death).

**물긋하다** 《묽다》 (be) somewhat thin 〔watery, washy〕.

**물기**(一氣) 《습기》 moisture; dampness; wetness; 《과일 등의》 juiciness; succulences. ¶ ~가 많은 배 a pear full of juice; a juicy pear / ~가 있는 moist; damp; wet; watery; 《과일 등》 succulent; juicy / ~ 없는 dry; husky; parched; drained 《channel》/ ~를 짜내다 squeeze 〔wring〕 《a towel》 dry / ~를 제거하다 dehydrate; 《탈수하여 건조시키다》 desiccate; dry (up). 「리 ②.

**물기근**(一飢饉) a water famine. ⇨ 물난

**물기둥** a column of water; a water column 〔spout〕. ¶ 거대한 ~이 치솟았다 There went up a huge column of water.

**물기름** 《두발용의》 hair oil.

**물길** a waterway; a watercourse; a 「water 〔sea〕 route. ¶ ~로 삼백 리 three hundred *ri* by water / ~을 따라 항해하다 sail along a waterway.

**물까치** 〖조류〗 a blue magpie.

**물꼬** a sluice (gate); an irrigation gate. ¶ ~를 트다 sluice water out of paddy.

**물끄러미** staring (with fixed eyes). ¶ 얼굴을 ~ 쳐다보다 stare 《*a person*》 in the face; look hard 〔steadily〕 at 《*a person's*》 face; gaze intently at 《*a person's*》 face.

**물난리**(一亂離) ① 《홍수》 a flood disaster. ¶ ~가 나다 have a flood disaster; suffer from a flood / 이번 ~에 많은 사람이 죽었다 Many people lost their lives in the recent flood. ② 《물부족》 a water famine; the shortage of water supply.

**물납**(物納) payment in kind. ~하다 pay 〔tax〕 with goods 〔in kind〕. ¶ 상속세를 부동산으로 ~하다 pay (an) inheritance tax in real estate. ◉ ~세(稅) tax payment in kind.

**물내리다** 《체질하다》 resift rice flour on a loose sieve while pouring water over it.

**물놀이** ① 《잔물결이 읾》 rippling 〔wrinkling〕 of water. ~하다 ripple; wrinkle. ② =물장난. ③ 《행락》 a waterside excursion; a boating excursion (뱃놀이). ¶ ~ 가다 go on a waterside 〔boat〕 excursion; go swimming.

**물다**[1] ① 《동물이》 bite 《at》; snap 《at》. ¶ 개가 ~ a dog bites 《*a person*》/ 다리를~ bite 《*a person*》 in the leg / 물어뜯다 bite 〔gnaw〕 off; cut off with the teeth / 물어 죽이다 bite to death. ② 《물고기가》 bite 〔nibble〕 《at》; take a bait. ¶ 미끼를 ~ take 〔rise to〕 the bait 〔fly〕; snap at the bait / 오늘은 고기가 잘 문다 The fish are biting well today. ③ 《물것이》 bite; sting. ¶ 모기가 문다 Mosquitoes bite. / 벼룩이 문 데가 가렵다 The flea-bite itches. ④ 《언어 차지하다》 get; catch; find. ¶ 계집이 사내를 ~ a woman 「gets 〔latches onto〕 a man. ⑤ 《입에》 take 〔hold〕 《*a thing*》 in *one's* mouth; hold 〔have〕 《*a thing*》 between *one's* teeth. ¶ 담배〔파이프〕를 입에 물고 with a cigarette 〔pipe〕 in *one's* mouth / 실을 입에 ~ hold a

thread between the teeth / 고양이가 생선을 물고 달아났다 A cat ran away with some fish.
⑥《톱니바퀴가》 gear《with, into》; be in gear《with》.

**물다**[2] ①《돈을》 pay; repay. ¶ 벌금을 ~ pay a fine; pay *one's* penalty 〔forfeit〕/ 빚을 ~ pay 〔repay〕 *one's* debt / 세금을 ~ pay a tax 〔duty〕《on》/ 책값을 ~ pay for a book / 자기 돈으로 ~ pay for《*a thing*》 out of *one's* own pocket. ②《보상·배상》 compensate; 〔make reparation〕 for《damage》; pay for《damage》; indemnify《*a person*》 for《*his* losses》. ¶ 그 꽃병을 깨었으니 값을 물어 주어야 한다 You broke the vase and you'll have to pay for it.

**물다**[3] 《상하다》 rot; go bad; stale. ¶ 살이 ~ *one's* skin rots.

**물덤벙술덤벙** blindly; aimlessly; at random; without knowing anything about《it》; naively. ~하다 act blindly 〔naively〕.

**물독** a water jar 〔pot〕.

**물동**(物動) mobilization of materials. ◉ ~계획 a materials mobilization plan; a program for the mobilization of material resources. ~량 the quantity of goods transported.

**물동이** a water pitcher 〔jar〕.

**물두부**(—豆腐) boiled bean curds.

**물들다** ①《색깔이》 dye; get 〔be〕 dyed; take (up) color; be tinged《with red》(엷게);《얼룩지다》 get stained 〔smeared〕. ¶ 꺼멓게 ~ be dyed black / 물이 잘 들다 dye 〔take dye〕 well 〔fast〕/ (옷에) 잉크가 ~ be stained with ink / 서쪽 하늘이 지는 해로 붉게 물들었다 The western sky is dyed red by the setting sun. / 이 천은 잘 물들지 않는다 This cloth will not dye well. / 그의 셔츠는 피로 물들어 있었다 His shirt was stained with blood.
②《감염·감화되다》 be imbued 〔infected〕《with》; be tainted 〔stained, contaminated〕《with》; be influenced《by》. ¶ 악에 ~ be 「tainted with 〔steeped in〕 vice; sink in vice; 「fall into 〔be given to〕 evil ways / 도시풍에 ~ be imbued with urban 〔city〕 manners / 사회주의에 ~ be tinged 〔infected〕 with socialism / …에 물들기 쉽다 have an aptitude to《vice》/ 젊은 이들은 외국 문화에 지나치게 물들기 쉽다 Young people are apt to be over-influenced by foreign culture. / 아이들이 사회악에 물들지 않도록 막아야 한다 We must prevent children from being infected with 〔by〕 the social evils.

**물들이다** ①《물들게 하다》 dye. ¶ 머리를 검게 ~ dye *one's* hair (in) black / 손톱을 빨갛게 ~ paint *one's* nails red / 그녀는 머리를 갈색으로 물들였다《남의 손으로》 She has her hair dyed brown. / 지는 해가 하늘을 장미빛으로 물들이고 있다 The setting sun tinges the sky with rosy flush. ②《채색하다》 color; paint《*one's* face》; tinge (엷게). ¶ 피로 ~ stain《*one's* hands》 with blood / 얼굴을 붉게 ~ 〔붉히다〕 blush; turn red 〔crimson〕/ 부상당한 사람의 피가 땅을 빨갛게 물들였다 The blood of the injured man dyed the ground red.

**물딱총**(—銃) a water pistol 〔gun〕; a squirt gun. ¶ ~을 쏘다 shoot《*a person*》 with a water pistol; squirt a water pistol《at》.

**물때**[1] 《조수 시간》 tide time; 《밀물》 the high tide. ¶ ~를 기다리다 wait for 「the high tide 〔the favorable tide〕《to set sail》/ ~를 놓치다 miss the high tide.

**물때**[2] 《물의》 fur; (boiler) scale; (an) incrustation; slime; scum. ¶ ~를 벗기다 clean fur《from》; scrape off the fur / ~가 끼다 fur (forms)《on》; scale; be covered with fur 〔scale〕.

**물때까치** 〖조류〗 a Chinese great grey shrike.

**물떼새** 〖조류〗 a plover.

**물똥튀기다** splash water.

**물량**(物量) the amount 〔quantity〕 of materials 〔resources〕. ¶ ~의 우세 material superiority 〔advantage〕/ ~의 힘을 과시하다 let *one's* material superiority tell on《the enemy》/ ~으로 압도하다 overwhelm《the enemy》 with material superiority / 그들은 압도적인 ~의 우세를 바탕으로 우리에게 총공세를 가해 왔다 They launched an all-out attack on us relying on their overwhelming material advantage. ◉ 총괄 ~ 방식 〖경제〗 the market basket formula.

**물러가다** ①《뒤로》 move back(ward); draw 〔step〕 back; 《후퇴하다》 pull 〔fall〕 back; retreat; withdraw《from》; recede《from》. ¶ 한발짝 뒤로 ~ take a step backward / 적이 ~ the enemy retreats / 군대는 도시에서 물러갔다 The troops withdrew from the town.
②《자리에서》 retire; withdraw《from》; leave; 《어른·상사·높은 사람 앞에서》 bow *oneself* off. ¶ 물러가라고 명하다 order《*a person*》 away / 잠자코〔말없이〕 ~

take French leave; leave without saying a word 〔anything〕/ 아버지 앞에서 ～ withdraw from the presence of *one's* father / 국왕 앞에서 ～ bow *oneself* away from the king's presence / 당장 물러가거라 Get out of here right away. / 구경꾼들은 하나, 둘 물러갔다 The spectators dropped off one by one. / 그만 물러가야겠습니다 I think I must be off.
③ 《그만두다·은퇴하다·사임하다》 withdraw 〔retire〕 《from》; resign 《*one's* post》. ¶ 공직에서 ～ resign 〔withdraw〕 from public office.
④ 《끝나다·소멸하다》 pass; be gone; be over; leave. ¶ 위기가 ～ the crisis passes / 추위가 물러갔다 The cold weather is over 〔gone〕. / 태풍은 물러갔다 The typhoon is over.
⑤ 《연기되다》 be put off; be postponed; be held over; be set back.

**물러나다** ① 《벌어지다》 come loose; come out; come undone. ¶ 탁자 다리가 ～ a leg of the table comes loose. ② 《철수·퇴출》 withdraw 《from》; retreat; retire; leave; 《물러서다》 step 〔stand〕 back; back. ¶ 식탁에서 ～ withdraw 〔retire〕 from the table / 사람 앞에서 ～ withdraw from 《*a person's*》 presence / 적이 성에서 삼십리 ～ the enemy retreats thirty *ri* away from the castle / 이렇게 되면 물러날래야 물러날 수 없다 I am in for it now. *or* I have gone too far to retreat. *or* I cannot withdraw 〔turn back〕 now. ③ 《은퇴·사직》 retire; resign; quit. ¶ 공직을 ～ retire 〔resign〕 from public life / 정계에서 ～ retire from political life; withdraw from the political arena / 직(職)을 ～ resign *one's* office 〔position〕; quit *one's* job / 그는 정계에서 물러날 것이라고 한다 I hear that he is going to retire from 〔leave〕 the political world.

**물러서다** ① 《뒤로》 back; move off; step 〔stand〕 back 〔aside〕; get out of the way; 《후퇴하다》 withdraw; retreat; recede. ¶ 한 걸음 ～ stand back a step / 뒤로 ～ move off to the rear / 사람이 지나가게 ～ make way for *a person* / (이젠) 물러설 수가 없다 go too far to retreat; be in for it; cannot back out. ② 《은퇴·사직하다》 resign; retire; leave. ⇨ 물러나다 ③. ③ 《양보하다》 concede 《to》; yield. ¶ 한 치도 물러서지 않다 do not yield an inch.

**물러앉다** ① 《자리를》 draw 〔move〕 *one's* seat back; sit back. ¶ 이 애가 앉을 수 있게 좀 물러앉아 주겠니 Would you mind sitting back a bit so that this child may have a seat? ② 《관직 따위에서》 retire; resign; leave. ⇨ 물러나다 ③.

**물러오다** retrace *one's* steps; come 〔turn〕 back; retreat; recede; retrogress. ¶ 가던 길을 ～ retrace *one's* step 〔way〕.

**물러지다** ① 《물건이》 get soft; grow tender; soften. ¶ 감이 ～ a persimmon softens up. ② ＝누그러지다.

**물렁팥죽**(—粥) ① 《사람》 a softy; a sissy; a milksop; a pushover. ② 《물건》 soft stuff.

**물렁하다** ① ⇨ 말랑말랑하다. ② 《성질이》 (be) yielding; flaccid; weak.

**물레** a spinning wheel; 《도자기용의》 a potter's wheel. ◉ ～바퀴 the wheel of a 「spinning wheel 〔water mill〕. ～방아 a water mill. ～질 spinning: ～질하다 spin yarn 〔thread〕. 물렛줄 a spinning-wheel belt.

**물려받다** inherit 《*a thing* from *a person*》; take over 《another's duties, a task》; succeed to; be (the) heir to 《an estate》. ¶ 아버지 사업을 ～ take over 〔succeed to〕 *one's* father's business / 재산을 ～ inherit 〔come into, step into〕 a fortune / 선임자로부터 사무를 ～ take over *one's* duties from *one's* predecessor / 그는 가업을 물려 받았다 He has taken over his family business 〔trade〕. / 그의 재능은 어머니로부터 물려받은 것이다 His genius comes from his mother.

**물려주다** hand 〔turn, make〕 over; transfer; leave (남기다); abdicate (왕위를); bequeath (동산을); devise (부동산을). ¶ 권리를 ～ devolve rights on 《*a person*》/ 아들에게 사업을 ～ turn the business over to *one's* son / 재산을 아들한테 ～ hand over *one's* property to *one's* son / 소유권을 형에게 ～ yield *one's* right of possession to *one's* brother / 왕자에게 왕위를 ～ abdicate the throne in favor of his son.

**물려지내다** be in 《*a person's*》 clutches; be at 《*a person's*》 mercy; be under *a person's* thumb.

**물력**(物力) 《물건의 힘》 material power; 《재료와 노력》 materials and efforts.

**물론**(勿論) (as a matter) of course; to be sure; undoubtedly; naturally; needless to say. ¶ 그는 학식은 ～ 경험도 많다 He has experience as well as knowledge. / …함〔임〕은 ～이다 There is no doubt that…. *or* It goes without saying that…. / ～이지 Of course! / ～ 아니다〔틀린다〕 Of course not. / 가느냐고, ～이지 Will I go, you say? Sure, I will.

**물류**(物流) 〖경제〗 (physical) distribution. ⇨ 유통. ¶ ～시스템이 복잡해서 물가가 내리지 않는다 The reason prices don't go down is because of the intricate distribution system 〔network〕. ◉ ～관리 (the) 「administrative control 〔administration〕 of physical distribution. ～비(용) (physical) distribution costs: 높은 ～비용을 깎아내리기 위해 기반 시설을 확장하다 expand infrastructure to pare down high distribution 〔logistics〕 costs. ～산업 the distribution industry.

**물리**(物理) 《사물의 이치》 the laws of nature; physical laws; 《물리학》 physics. ¶ ～적 ⇨ 물리적 / 이론〔응용〕～ theoretical 〔applied〕 physics. ◉ ～광학 physical optics. ～실험 《make》 an experiment in physics. ～치료〔요법〕 physiotherapy; physical therapy 〔treatment〕. ～화학 physical chemistry; 《물리와 화학》 physics and chemistry.

**물리다**[1] 《싫증나다》 have had enough; be fed up 《with》; get sick 《of》; be 〔get, grow〕 tired 《of》; lose interest 《in》; want nothing more to do 《with》. ¶ 물리도록 to satiety; to *one's* fill / 물리도록 먹다 eat to satiety; eat *one's* fill / 물릴 줄을 모르다 be insatiable / 국수 요리에 ～ be fed up with noodle dishes / 소설 읽기에 ～ get sick of reading novels / 물리게 하다 satiate; surfeit; bore; weary / 단 것도 자주 먹으면 물린다 Sweets served too often cloy the palate. / 이 그림은 아무리 봐도 물리지 않는다 I never get weary of looking at this picture.

**물리다**[2] 《푹 익히다》 cook soft 〔tender〕.

**물리다**[3] ① 《연기하다》 put off; postpone; defer. ¶ 기한을 ～ extend the term 《from… to…》 / 회합 날짜를 ～ postpone (the date of) a meeting / 하루하루 ～ put off from day to day. ② 《옮기다》 change direction; shift; move 〔put〕 back. ¶ 의자를 뒤로 ～ push *one's* chair back / 차를 뒤로 ～ pull a car back. ③ ＝물려주다.

**물리다**[4] 《치우다》 clear; take 〔put〕 away; remove. ¶ 밥상을 ～ clear 〔take away〕 the table.

**물리다**[5] 《잡귀를》 exorcise; expel; dispel. ¶ 악귀를 ～ exorcise evil spirits / 굿을 하여 집안의 악귀를 ～ drive evil spirits out of a household with shaman rites.

**물리다**[6] 《동물·벌레에》 get bitten. ¶ 모기에 물린 자리 a mosquito bite / 독사에 물려서 죽다 die from a viper bite / 미친 개한테 ～ be bitten by a mad dog / 모기에 ～ be bitten 〔stung〕 by a mosquito.

**물리다**[7] 《배상시키다》 make 《*a person*》 compensate 〔reimburse〕. ¶ 깨뜨린 그릇 값을 ～ make 《*a person*》 pay a broken dish / 농작물에 끼친 손해를 ～ make 《*a person*》 pay compensation for the damage done to *one's* crops.

**물리적**(物理的) physical. ¶ ～ 법칙〔변화, 현상〕 a physical law 〔change, phenomenon〕 / ～ 성질 physical properties / ～인 physical / ～으로 physically / 이 현상에 관하여는 아직 ～인 설명이 되어 있지 않다 There is not a physical explanation for this phenomenon yet. / 그것을 이틀 안으로 끝내는 것은 ～으로 불가능하다 It's physically impossible for us to finish it in two days.

**물리치다** ① 《거절하다》 refuse; reject; turn down. ¶ 요구를 ～ refuse 〔turn down〕 a request; reject a demand / 제의를 ～ turn down 〔spurn, wave away〕 an offer / 탄원을 ～ reject a plea / 뇌물 주겠다는 제의를 ～ turn down the offer of a bribe. ② 《격퇴하다》 drive back 〔away〕; beat off 〔back〕; repel; repulse. ¶ 적을 ～ repulse 〔drive away〕 the enemy. ③ 《승부에서》 defeat; beat. ¶ 최고 경쟁자를 ～ beat the No.1 contender / 선거에서 다른 후보를 ～ defeat another candidate in an election. ④ 《멀리하다》 keep away; make 《*a person*》 leave *one;* order 〔tell〕 《*a person*》 to withdraw from *one's* presence. ¶ 사람을 물리치고 밀담하다 get 《*a person*》 off for a private talk; meet 〔talk〕 behind closed doors.

**물리학**(物理學) physics; physical science. ¶ 이론〔응용〕～ theoretical 〔applied〕 physics / ～적인 physical. ◉ ～기구 physical instruments. ～자 a physicist.

**물림** ① 〖건축〗 an extra space of half a *kan* added to a regular room as a kind of porch. ② 《물려 받거나 주는 일》 transfer; conveyance; assignment. ¶ ～재산 property bequeathed by *one's* forefathers; the family fortune; the inheritance / ～옷 clothes handed down; a hand-me-down.

**물림쇠** a staple; a metal band; a clamp.

**물마** flood on the ground (caused by rain).

**물마루** the crest (of waves); a wave 「crest.

**물만두**(一饅頭) a stuffed dumpling cooked in hot water; boiled ravioli.

**물말이** ① 《밥》 cooked rice served in water. ② 《젖은 것》 a thing drenched with water.

**물맛** the taste of water. ¶ ～이 짜다 The water tastes salty.

**물망**(物望) popular prospects 〔favor〕. ¶ ～에 오르다 win public support; rise in 〔to〕 popularity / 후보 ～에 오른 사람 a 《Democratic》 prospect; a prospective candidate.

**물망초**(勿忘草) 〖식물〗 a forget-me-not.

**물맞이** taking 〔drinking, bathing in〕 mineral water.

**물매**[1] 《매질》 hard flogging 〔whipping〕. ¶ ～ 맞다 be flogged hard / ～ 치다 punish 《*a person*》 with a good sound flogging.

**물매**[2] 《경사》 a slope; a slant; a pitch. ¶ 지붕의 ～가 싸다 A roof has a steep enough slant to it. / 지붕의 ～가 뜨다 The roof is not steep enough.

**물매질** flogging 〔whipping〕 hard. ～하다 flog 〔lash, whip〕 《*a person*》 hard.

**물멀미** dizziness 〔vertigo〕 caused by looking at a vast expanse of water; seasickness. ～하다 feel dizzy 〔seasick〕.

**물목** ① 《물어귀》 a point at which the water flows out; a point at which a side stream branches off; the fork of a river 〔stream〕; a narrows. ¶ ～을 지키다 stand watch at the fork of a river. ② 〖광물〗 the spot where gold dust pans thickest.

**물목**(物目) a catalog(ue) of goods.

**물문**(一門) 《수문》 a sluice; a water gate; a floodgate; a gate (운하의).

**물물교환**(物物交換) barter; bartering. ～하다 barter 《A for B》; trade 《old newspapers》 for 《toilet paper》. ¶ ～으로 by barter; on the barter system / 그들은 식량과 총을 ～했다 They bartered food for guns.

**물밀다** 《조수가》 rise; flow; come in. ¶ 물밀 때 the flow of the tide; tide time / 물밀듯이 몰려오는 군중 a surging crowd of people / 물밀듯이 밀어닥치다 surge forward in crowds.

**물밑** the bottom of water 〔sea, river〕. ¶ ～ 교섭〔협상〕 a 「secret 〔behind-the-scenes〕 negotiation.

**물바가지** a gourd for dipping water.

**물받이** a gutter at the eaves; an eave(s) trough.

**물방개** 〖곤충〗 a diving beetle.

**물방아** ① 《방아》 a water mill 〔wheel〕. ¶ ～를 돌리다 operate a water 「mill 〔wheel〕. ② 《방아두레박》 water wheel buckets. ◉ 물방앗간 a water mill.

**물방울** a drop of water; a waterdrop. ◉ ～무늬 polka dots 《on cloth》: ～무늬의 a polka-dot(ted) 《neckties》.

**물뱀** 〖동물〗 a water snake; a sea snake (바다뱀). ◉ ～자리 〖천문〗 the Water Snake; Hydrus.

**물베개** a (rubber) water pillow.

**물벼락** pouring 〔splashing〕 water on 《*a person*》 suddenly; dousing 《*a person*》 with water. ¶ ～(을) 맞다 get doused; get a dousing; be suddenly poured over with water.

**물벼룩** 〖동물〗 a water flea.

**물병**(一甁) a water bottle 〔flask〕. ◉ ～자리 〖천문〗 the Water Bearer; Aquarius. 유리～ a carafe.

**물보라** spray (of water). ¶ 폭포의 ～ the spray of a waterfall / ～를 일으키다 raise spray; send up clouds of spray.

**물볼기** flogging 〔whipping〕 women with their underwear drenched. ¶ ～(를) 치다 give a woman a wet flogging.

**물부리** 《담뱃대의》 the mouthpiece; 《궐련의》 a cigarette holder.

**물분**(一粉) a liquid makeup 〔face-paint〕; a facepowder fluid; a liquid cosmetic.

**물불** fire and water. ¶ ～을 안 가리다 go through fire and water; stick to it through thick and thin / 그를 위해서라면 ～을 안 가리겠다 I will go through fire and water for his sake. / 우리는 ～을 안 가릴 각오다 We are ready to face any hardship.

**물빛** ① 《물감의》 dye color; dyed color. ② 《남색》 aquamarine; light blue; water green.

**물살** the current 〔flow〕 of water. ¶ ～이 세다 a current is strong 〔swift〕 / ～이 센〔빠른〕 강 a fast-flowing river.

**물상**(物象) 《사물》 an object; 《현상》 material phenomena; 《학과》 the science of inanimate nature.

**물새** ① 《수금》 a waterfowl; a water bird; an aquatic bird. ② ⇨ 물총새.

**물색**(物色) ① 《물건의 빛깔》 the color of a thing; 《물들인 빛》 dyed color. ② 《고름》 selecting; 《찾음》 looking for. ～하다 《고르다》 choose; select; pick out; single out; take *one's* pick; 《찾다》 look for; search for; hunt up. ¶ 아냇감을 ～하다 look for a wife / 일자리를 ～하다 hunt for a job / 후임자를 ～하다 look for a successor to 《*a person*》/ 우리는 곧 결혼하게 되어 있어서 알맞은 집을 ～중이다 Since we're getting married soon, we've been looking for a suitable house.

**물색없다** (be) unreasonable; absurd.

**물샐틈없다** ① 《꼭 막히다》 (be) watertight. ② 《완벽하다》 (be) strict; rigorous; watertight. ¶ 물샐틈없는 방위 태세 a watertight defense position / 물샐틈없는 변론 a watertight argument / 물샐틈없는 수비 《야구에서》 airtight fielding 《미》/ 물샐틈없는 경계망을 펴다 throw a tight cordon 〔net〕 around; [장소가 주어] be closely guarded / 경찰은 물샐틈없는 수사망을 폈다 The police put up a dragnet.

**물성**(物性) 〖물리〗 properties of matter.

**물세**(物稅) 〖법〗 a property tax; a real tax.

**물세례**(―洗禮) ① 〖기독교〗 baptism. ② ＝물벼락.

**물소** 〖동물〗 a (water) buffalo.

**물소리** the sound of flowing water; murmurs of stream.

**물속** ¶ ～의 underwater / ～에 in the water; under water; at the bottom 〔below the surface〕 of the water / ～ 깊이 가라앉다 sink deep down to the bottom of the water / ～으로 뛰어들다 jump 〔plunge〕 into the water / (실수로) ～에 풍덩 빠지다 get 〔have〕 a ducking / 아무를 ～에 처박다 give *a person* a ducking.

**물수건**(―手巾) a wet towel; a steamed towel; a small damp towel.

**물수란**(―水卵) a poached egg.

**물수리** 〖조류〗 an osprey; a fish hawk.

**물수제비** duck(s) and drake(s). ¶ ～(를) 뜨다 skip stones; play duck(s) and drake(s).

**물시계**(―時計) a water clock.

**물신**(物神) a fetish. ◉ ～ 숭배 fetishism; fetishistic religion.

**물실호기**(勿失好機) ～하다 do not miss 〔lose, let slip〕 a chance. ¶ ～하라 Strike while the iron is hot. *or* Make hay while the sun shines.

**물심양면**(物心兩面) ¶ ～으로 both materially and morally; physically and spiritually / ～의 도움을 받다 receive support, both moral and material, from 《*a person*》/ 나는 자네를 ～으로 돕고 싶네 I'd like to help you both materially and morally.

**물싸움** 《논물의》 an irrigation 〔a water=rights〕 dispute. ～하다 dispute about 〔over〕 the water-rights.

**물써다** ebb; go out; be on the ebb. ¶ 물썰 때 at the ebb.

**물썽하다** (be) gullible; be easy to be fooled; be not formidable; (be) unstubborn; feeble.

**물쑥** 〖식물〗 a kind of wormwood 「〔artemisia〕.

**물쓰듯하다** spend 《money》「unsparingly 〔like water〕; be a free spender. ¶ 돈을 물쓰듯하는 사람 an extravagant person; a spendthrift; a big 〔lavish〕 spender / 여자에게 미쳐서 돈을 ～ spend money unsparingly on a woman.

**물씬거리다** ① 《물체가》 be 〔become〕 soft 〔tender〕. ② 《냄새가》 smell nice 〔strong〕; be strongly scented with; reek with. ¶ 향수 냄새가 ～ be strongly scented 〔reek〕 with perfume.

**물씬물씬하다** 《물렁물렁하다》 (be) soft; tender; squashy; 《냄새가》 smell strongly 〔prodigally〕; give off a strong smell; 《악취가》 reek 《of》; stink 《of fish》.

**물씬하다** ① 《부드럽다》 (be) soft; tender. ¶ 물씬한 고기 meat cooked tender. ② 《냄새가》 be nicely 〔strongly〕 scented.

**물아**(物我) 〖철학〗 objects and self; the ego and the non-ego.

**물아래** a down-river area; the lower part of a river.

**물안개** wet 〔rainy〕 fog; water fog.

**물안경**(―眼鏡) 《a pair of》 (diver's) goggles.

**물알** soft unripe grain. ¶ ～ 들다 develop into soft unripe grain.

**물앵두** a fruit of the honeysuckle. ◉ ～나무 〖식물〗 a honeysuckle.

**물약**(―藥) a liquid medicine.

**물어내다** ① ＝물어주다. ② 《퍼뜨리다》 air 〔let out〕 family secrets; rattle the skeleton in the family closet; wash *one's* dirty linen in public.

**물어넣다** reimburse; refund; repay; compensate for. ¶ 유용한 회사 돈을 ～ repay misappropriated company funds.

**물어떼다** bite off; gnaw off 〔away〕; tear 〔cut〕 off with *one's* teeth. ¶ 떡을

한입 ～ bite off a mouthful of rice cake.

**물어뜯다** bite (hard); bite 〔tear〕 off. ¶ 코를 ～ bite 《*a person's*》 nose.

**물어보다** ask 《*a person* about *something*》; inquire 《of *a person* about *a matter*》; question; find out; ascertain (by inquiry). ¶ 길을 ～ ask the way 《to》; inquire for the way / 귀찮게 ～ plague 《*a person*》 with questions / 안부를 ～ ask 〔inquire〕 after 《*a person*》 / 이유를 ～ inquire 〔ask (for), demand〕 the reason / 좀 물어 볼 말이 있습니다 May I ask you some questions? *or* I have some questions to ask you.

**물어주다** pay 《for》; make good; compensate. ¶ 잃어버린 책을 ～ pay 〔compensate〕 for the book *one* has lost / 아들 빚을 ～ pay 〔settle〕 *one's* son's debt.

**물억새** 〖식물〗 a common reed.

**물역**(物役) 《건축 재료》 construction materials. ◉ ～장사 a dealer in construction materials.

**물엿** glutinous starch syrup.

**물오르다** ① 《나무에》 《sap》 rise. ¶ 봄이 되어 나무에 물이 오르기 시작한다 Spring has come and the sap of trees begin to rise. ② 《사람이》 get rich; make money; get ahead (in life); rise.

**물오리** 〖조류〗 a wild duck; a mallard.

**물오리나무** 〖식물〗 a Siberian alder.

**물외** a (water) cucumber.

**물욕**(物慾) 《속된 욕심》 worldly desires; love of gain. ¶ ～에 사로잡힌 worldly=〔earthly-〕minded; blinded by love of gain / 그는 ～이 강한 사람이다 He is greedy for worldly riches.

**물위** ① ＝수면(水面). ¶ ～에 떠오르다 「come up 〔rise〕 to the surface; break (the) surface. ② 《상류》 an up-river area; an upper stream.

**물유리**(—琉璃) 〖화학〗 water 〔liquid, soluble〕 glass.

**물음** a question; an inquiry. ¶ 다음 ～에 답하시오 Answer the following questions. ◉ ～꼴 the question 〔interrogative〕 form 《of a verb》. ～표 a question 〔an interrogation〕 mark.

**물의**(物議) 《뭇사람의 평판》 public criticism; public discussion; 《논의·분쟁》 controversy. ¶ ～를 빚다〔일으키다〕 arouse 〔evoke〕 criticism; give rise to public censure; bring on public criticism; stir up trouble / 그의 발언은 ～를 일으켰다 His remarks caused 〔gave rise to〕 a discussion. / 장관의 수회 행위는 국민들의 거센 ～를 빚어냈다 The minister's corruption aroused a storm of public criticism.

**물이꾸럭** paying off some other's loss 〔debt〕. ～하다 pay off 《for another》.

**물이끼** 〖식물〗 (a) sphagnum (*pl.* -na); bog moss.

**물자**(物資) 《물품·재화》 goods; 《상품》 commodities; 《필수품》 necessities; 《원료》 raw materials; 《자원》 resources; 《공급물》 supplies. ¶ ～의 수급 supply and demand of goods / ～의 부족 a shortage of goods 〔materials, commodities〕 / ～를 공급받다 get a supply of goods / ～를 확보하다 secure 〔ensure〕 the supply of goods / ～를 보급하다 give 〔furnish〕 supplies 《to》; supply goods 《to》 / ～를 아낍시다 《게시》 Save Supplies. / 그 나라는 ～가 부족하다 The country is poor in resources. / 구호 ～가 그 나라에 보내졌다 Relief supplies were sent to the country.
◉ ～동원 mobilization of materials. ～활용 utilization of materials. 생활～ the necessities of life; basic necessities 〔essentials〕; vital 〔essential〕 goods: 생활 ～가 부족하다 We're running short of the necessities of life.

**물자동차**(—自動車) 《살수차》 a street sprinkler; a sprinkler truck; 《급수차》 a water-supply wagon.

**물자체**(物自體) 〖철학〗 a thing-in-itself; a *Ding-an-sich* (G.).

**물잡다** draw water into (a paddy); supply (a paddy) with water; irrigate (a paddy).

**물장구** ① 《장단》 drumming on gourd vessels turned over on the water. ② 《헤엄칠 때》 the beating; the flutter kick; the thrash. ¶ ～치다 make flutters 〔flutter kicks〕; swim with the thrash.

**물장난** playing 〔dabbling〕 in water. ～하다 play 〔dabble〕 in water.

**물장사** 《술집 영업》 a gay trade. ¶ ～를 하는 여자 a woman of the gay world.

**물장수** a water-carrier; a water-seller.

**물적**(物的) physical; material. ◉ ～원조 a material help 〔aid, support〕. ～자원 material 〔physical〕 resources. ～증거 physical 〔material, real〕 evidence: ～증거로 확보하다 seize 《*something*》 as material evidence.

**물정**(物情) 《사물의》 the state of things; the conditions of affairs; 《세태의》

public feeling; the world. ¶ 세상 ~을 모르다〔에 어둡다〕 be ignorant 〔know little〕 of the world / 세상 ~에 밝다 know much of the world; be wise in the ways of the world; be a man of the world.

**물주**(物主) ① 《자본주·전주》 a financier; a financial supporter. ② 《노름판의》 the banker.

**물주다** give water 《to》; water. ¶ 나무에 ~ water a plant.

**물줄기** ① 《흐름》 a watercourse; a stream; a current; a flow. ¶ ~가 두 갈래로 갈리다 a water branches off into two streams. ② 《내뿜는》 a spout 〔jet, gush〕 of water. ¶ ~가 세게 뻗치다 water spouts 〔gushes〕 out.

**물증**(物證) real 〔material〕 evidence.

**물지게** a water-toting device (strapped to the back).

**물질**(物質) matter; substance; material.

> 용법 **matter** 「정신」을 뜻하는 mind, spirit에 대응하는 낱말로 「공간을 점유하는 모든 것」에 두루 쓰인다. **substance** matter의 본질적 구성물, 즉 화학적 특성을 가진 특정의 matter를 말한다. **material** 사용을 목적으로 하는 특정의 matter, 즉 「원료」를 나타낸다.

¶ ~ 불멸의 법칙 〖물리〗 the law of conservation of matter. ⇨질량. / ~은 고체, 액체, 기체로 변화한다 Matter can change into a solid, liquid and gas. / 눈과 얼음은 동일한 ~이다 Snow and ice are the same substance.

◉ ~계 the physical 〔material〕 world. ~대사 〖생물〗 metabolism. ~명사 〖문법〗 a material noun. ~문명 material civilization. ~주의 materialism: ~주의자 a materialist. 반(反)~ 〖물리〗 antimatter.

**물질적**(物質的) material; physical; objective. ¶ ~인 material; physical / ~ 번영 material prosperity / ~인 원조 material aid 〔help〕 / ~인 존재 materiality / ~인 생각 a materialistic view / ~으로 유복하다 be comfortably 〔well〕 off / ~으로 곤란받다 be badly off; be in needy circumstances / 과학은 ~인 문제를 다루고, 종교는 정신적인 문제를 다룬다 In science we deal with physical matters, and in church with the spiritual. *or* Science deals with the physical, while religion deals with the spirit. / 그는 ~으로 축복받고 있다 He is blessed with material comforts.

**물집** 《피부의》 a (water) blister. ¶ ~이 생기다 get 〔have〕 a blister 《on *one's* foot》 / ~이 터졌다 The blister has broken 〔burst〕.

**물짝지근하다** 《일하는 태도가》 (be) stalemated; stagnant; dull; tedious.

**물쨍하다** 《사람이》 (be) very soft; be quite a sissy; be a milksop.

**물찌똥** 《똥》 watery 〔loose〕 feces. ¶ ~을 싸다 have loose bowels.

**물차**(―車) 《살수차》 a street sprinkler; a sprinkler cart; 《급수차》 a water wagon.

**물참** 《만조》 the high tide.

**물참나무** 〖식물〗 a kind of oak.

**물체**(物體) a body; a physical solid; an object; substance; 〖법〗 a material object. ¶ 미확인 비행 ~ an unidentified flying object (생략 UFO).

**물초** getting wet all over; dripping wet. ¶ ~가 되다 get wet 「all over 〔to the skin〕.

**물총새**(―銃―) 〖조류〗 a kingfisher.

**물치** 〖어류〗 a frigate mackerel.

**물컥**(물컥) with a strong stench; stinking(ly). ¶ 물고기 썩은 냄새가 ~ 나다 stink of rotten 〔decayed〕 fish.

**물컹거리다** be very soft 〔squashy〕; be(come) too soft; lose texture. ¶ 고기가 상해서 물컹거린다 The meat has gone bad and lost its texture.

**물컹**(물컹) softly; squashily. ~하다 (be) soft; squashy. ¶ 무엇인가 ~한 것을 밟았다 I felt something squash under my feet.

**물컹이** ① 《물건》 soft stuff; overripe stuff. ② 《사람》 a softy; a weakling; a sissy; a milksop.

**물쿠다** be(come) sultry 〔sweltering, steaming hot〕.

**물크러지다** 《너무 익어》 be reduced to jelly 〔pulp〕; 《썩어》 decompose.

**물큰**(물큰) with a strong smell 〔stench〕; pungent; 《악취가》 stinking; reeking. ¶ 향수내가 ~ 나다 the pungent smell of perfume hits *one's* nose.

**물타작**(―打作) ~하다 threst the rice before it dries.

**물통**(―桶) a water pail 〔bucket〕; a water tank.

**물퉁이** ① 《물건》 a thing which is water-soaked and swollen. ② 《사람》 a fatty but frail person.

**물퍼붓듯** as if pouring water; in torrents. ¶ 비가 ~ 하다 it rains in torrents.

**물표**(物標) a (baggage) check; a tally.

**물푸레**(나무) 〖식물〗 an ash tree.

**물품**(物品) articles; things; commodities; goods. ¶ 온갖 ~ all sorts of goods; goods of every description. ◉ ~목록 a list of goods; a catalog(ue); an inventory (재고 조사의): ~ 목록을 작성하다 itemize. ~세 a commodity tax: 《판매세》 a sales tax: ~세법 the Commodity Tax Law.

**물행주** a (wet) dishrag 〔dishcloth〕.

**물홈** the groove of a paper sliding door.

**물화**(物貨) goods; commodities; merchandise.

**물활론**(物活論) 〖철학〗 hylozoism; animism. ◉ ~자 an animist; a hylozoist.

**묽다** 《농도》 (be) watery; washy 《milk》; thin 《coffee, porridge, paste》; sloppy 《food》. ¶ 묽게 하다 make 《*something*》 thin(ner); water 《soup》 down / 페인트를 묽게 하다 thin down paint / 국물을 묽게 하다 dilute the broth 〔soup〕.

**묽디묽다** be very 〔ever so〕 watery; be as thin as can be.

**뭇**[1] 《큰 작살》 a large fish spear.

**뭇**[2] 《묶음》 a bundle 《of ten fish》; a bunch; a sheaf. ¶ 청어 두 뭇 two bundles of herrings / 장작 한 뭇 a bundle of firewood / 볏짚 한 뭇 a sheaf of rice straw.

**뭇**[3] 《여러》 many; all; all sorts of. ¶ 뭇 사내의 노리개가 되다 be made a plaything of all men.

**뭇매** (several) beating all at one time; beating up; drubbing. ¶ ~질하다 gang up on 《*a person*》 and beat *him* up; join in giving 《*a person*》 a thrashing / ~를 맞다 get a pelting rain of kicks and blows.

**뭇발길** ① 《발길질》 kicking 《*a person*》 from all sides. ¶ ~에 채다 get 〔be under〕 a pelting rain of kicks 《by gangs》. ② 《공박》 attacks from all quarters.

**뭇사람** the people; the public; many people. ¶ ~ 앞에서 before 〔in the presence of〕 others; in public 〔company〕 / ~이 보는 가운데 in public; in the presence of the whole company / ~ 앞에서 꾸짖다 scold 《*a person*》 before others 〔in public〕.

**뭇소리** many voices; many 〔all, all sorts of〕 opinions.

**뭇시선**(一視線) everyone's eyes 〔gaze〕; public gaze. ¶ ~을 끌다〔모으다〕 attract public gaze.

**뭇입** criticism from all 〔many, several〕 people. ⇨ 중구(衆口).

**뭉개다** ① 《으스러뜨리다》 crush; mash; squash; 《밟아》 trample 《*a thing*》 to pieces; 《밟아 끄다》 stub out (담배를). ¶ 밟아 ~ crush 《*a thing*》 by treading on 〔under *one's* feet〕 / 모자를 깔고 ~ sit on a hat (and mash it in) / 불을 밟아 뭉개어 끄다 trample out a fire. ② 《계획·의안 따위를》 shelve; table. ¶ 그들은 법안을 깔아 뭉갰다 They shelved the bill. ③ 《꾸물〔빈둥〕거리다》 dawdle. ¶ 한 자리에서 ~ dawdle at one place. ④ 《쩔쩔매다》 do not know 「what to do with 〔how to deal with〕; be embarrassed; be at a loss; make a mess of. ¶ 일을 ~ do not know how to deal with a matter; find a matter 「beyond *one's* control 〔too much for *one*〕; make a mess of a matter.

**뭉게구름** 〖기상〗 a cumulus (*pl.* -li).

**뭉게뭉게** in clouds; thickly. ¶ ~ 솟아오르는 연기 volumes 〔billows〕 of smoke / ~ 연기를 내뿜다 emit smoke in great profusion / 구름이 ~ 피어오르다 clouds rise up one after another; thick clouds are gathering.

**뭉구리** ① 《까까머리》 a close-cropped head; a shaven head. ② 《중》 a Buddhist monk.

**뭉그대다** linger; dawdle 《over》; 《일을 가지고》 dally away.

**뭉그러뜨리다** crumble; throw 〔knock〕 down. ¶ 담을 ~ crumble a wall / 쌓아 놓은 과일을 ~ throw 〔knock〕 down piled-up fruits.

**뭉그러지다** crumble; collapse; fall down. ¶ 오래된 돌담이 ~ an aged stone wall falls down.

**뭉그적거리다** dawdle 《over》; linger; move listlessly or aimlessly. ¶ 몸을 ~ dawdle; move *one's* body aimlessly / 한 자리에서 ~ dawdle in one place.

**뭉그적뭉그적** dawdling; listlessly; aimlessly. ⇨ 뭉그적거리다.

**뭉근하다** 《a fire》 be low but steady. ¶ 뭉근히 (burn) low 〔slow〕 but steady / 뭉근한 불에 익히다 cook over a slow fire; simmer / 불을 뭉근히 때다 keep a low fire going steadily.

**뭉긋이** 《비스듬히》 (sloped or warped) gently; slightly. ¶ 고개가 ~ 경사지다 a hill is gently sloped.

**뭉긋하다** ① 《기울어지다》 (be) sloping; inclined; gently sloped. ¶ 고개가 ~ a hill slopes gently. ② 《휘어지다》 (be) warped; gently 〔slightly〕 bent. ¶ 막대가 뭉긋하게 휘다 a stick is slightly bent.

**뭉기다** throw 《*a thing, a matter*》 down; destroy; demolish; let 《*a thing*》 fall.

**뭉때리다** ① 《시치미 떼다》 assume ignorance; pretend innocence 〔not to know〕. ② 《안 하다》 deliberately shirk 《a job》.

**뭉떵뭉떵** lump after lump; chunk after chunk; in 〔by〕 the lump; in chunks; in big lumps. ¶ 돈을 ~ 잘리다 lose great chunks of money repeatedly / 떡을 ~ 자르다 cut a rice cake into big chunks.

**뭉뚝하다** (be) stumpy; stubby; blunt. ¶ 뭉뚝한 연필 a stubby pencil / 뭉뚝한 끝 a blunt point 〔edge〕.

**뭉뚱그리다** bundle up crudely; wrap up in a slipshod way; get 〔put, bring〕 together hastily. ¶ 짐을 ~ bundle up a package crudely.

**뭉실뭉실** ⇨ 몽실몽실.

**뭉치** ① 《덩이》 a bundle; a roll; a lump; a clod. ¶ 편지 한 ~ a bundle of letters / 지폐 한 ~ a bundle 〔roll, wad〕 of bank notes; a roll of (paper) money. ② 《뭉치사태》 beef round.

**뭉치다** ① 《단결하다》 unite; hold 〔hang, get, come, stand, group, band〕 together. ¶ 뭉쳐서 in a body 〔force, group〕; in union; in one united body / 네댓명씩 뭉쳐서 in groups 〔knots〕 of four or five / 굳게 ~ be closely banded together; be strongly united / 뭉쳐서 대항하다 stand together against; be united against / 투철한 애국심과 확고한 역사 의식으로 굳게 ~ be firmly united with patriotic spirit and perspectives regarding history / 국가 위기에 모든 정당이 한데 뭉쳤다 All the political parties stood together 〔closed ranks〕 in a national crisis. / 뭉치면 살고 흩어지면 죽는다 United we stand, divided we fall.
② 《합치다》 unite; put 〔gather, group, bind〕 together. ¶ 짚을 뭉쳐 단을 짓다 bind straw together into a bundle / 힘을 ~ cooperate; unite 〔join〕 efforts.
③ 《덩이 짓다》 make a lump; lump together; mass; conglomerate. ¶ 눈을 ~ make snowball; press 〔mass〕 snow into a lump 〔ball〕 / 종이를 (꾸깃꾸깃) ~ crumple (up) a piece of paper into a ball / 흙을 ~ harden earth into a mass.

**뭉크러-** ⇨ 뭉그러-.

**뭉클하다** ① 《먹은 것이》 (be) heavy; stodgy. ¶ 속이 ~ rest 〔sit〕 heavy on *one's* stomach; remain undigested in the stomach. ② 《가슴이》 be filled 《with emotion》; be choked 《with grief》; feel a lump in *one's* throat. ¶ 가슴이 뭉클한 이야기 a touching 〔moving〕 story / 가슴이 뭉클해서 아무 말도 안 나왔다 My heart was too full for words. / 가슴이 뭉클해(져)서 그만 울음이 터질 것 같았다 I was so touched that I almost cried.

**뭉키다** ① 《몰리다》 gather 〔draw, get〕 together; swarm; crowd; cluster. ② 《덩어리짐》 lump; mass; conglomerate. ¶ 풀이 뭉키어 덩이가 되다 paste masses into a lump.

**뭉텅이** a lump; a bundle; a package. ¶ 지폐 ~ a bundle 〔roll, wad〕 of bank notes; a bundle of (paper) money.

**뭍** (the) land; dry land; (the) shore (배에서 본); the mainland (섬 사람이 본). ¶ 뭍바람 a land wind 〔breeze〕 / 뭍벼 dry land rice / 뭍짐승 a land animal / 뭍에 오르다 go ashore 〔on shore〕. ◉ 뭍살이 = 육서(陸棲).

**뭐** ⇨ 무어.

**뭐니 뭐니 해도** all things taken together; when all is said and done; no matter what *one* says; after all. ¶ ~ 생활 조건은 향상되었지 When all is said and done, the living conditions have improved. / ~ 정계에서는 그 사람이 인물이다 After all he is the greatest star in the political world.

**뭣** ⇨ 무엇.

**뮤온** 〚물리〛 a muon.

**뮤지컬** a musical. ◉ ~드라마 a musical drama. ~코미디 a musical comedy; a comic opera.

**뮤직** music. ◉ ~홀 a music hall.

**뮤추얼펀드** 〚경제〛 《투자 신탁 회사》 a mutual fund 《미》.

**-므로** 《까닭으로》 as; so; on account of; since; because; because of 《illness》; owing to; due to. ¶ 그는 몸이 허약하므로 힘든 일은 못 시키겠다 As his health is weak, he cannot be put to heavy work. / 자네가 여기를 떠나므로 나도 떠나겠다 Since you are leaving here, I'll leave here too.

**미**(未) 〚민속〛 ① 《십이지의》 the sign of the sheep; the 8th of the 12 Earth's Branches. ② ⇨ 미방(未方), 미시(未時).

**미**[1](美) beauty; the beautiful. ¶ 남〔여〕성미 masculine 〔feminine〕 beauty / 자연〔육체〕미 natural 〔physical〕 beauty / 미적 감각 a sense of beauty 〔the beautiful].

**미**²(美) 《미국》 (the United States of America.

**미**〖음악〗 mi.

**미-**(未) not yet; un-; in-. ¶ 미완성의 incomplete; unfinished / 미완성 교향곡 the Unfinished Symphony.

**미가**(米價) the price of rice; rice price. ¶ 농민들이 ～ 인상을 요구하였으나 가격은 동결되었다 The farmers demanded the higher price of rice, but it was left as it was. ◉ ～정책 the rice price policy. ～조절 control 〔regulation〕 of the rice price 〔market〕.

**미가공**(未加工) ¶ ～의 raw; crude; unprocessed / ～ 다이아몬드 diamonds in the rough.

**미가서**(一書) 〖성서〗 (The Book of) Micah (생략 Mic.).

**미각**(味覺) the (sense of) taste; the palate. ¶ ～의 계절, 가을 autumn, the season of the pleasures of the table / ～을 만족시키다 please *one's* palate / ～을 돋우다〔자아내다〕 tempt 〔invite〕 the taste; tickle *one's* palate; tempt the appetite / ～이 발달해 있다 have a keen sense of taste; have a delicate palate / ～을 돋우는 음식 tempting 〔appetizing, delicious-looking〕 food. ◉ ～기관 a taste organ. ～세포 a taste 〔gustatory〕 cell. ～신경 a gustatory nerve.

**미간**(未刊) ¶ ～의 unpublished; not yet published.

**미간**(眉間) ⇨ 양미간.

**미감**(美感) a sense of beauty; an esthetic sense.

**미감아**(未感兒) 《나병 따위의》 a child uninfected 《with leprosy》; children of negative lepers (나병의).

**미개**(未開) ① 《문명의》 being uncivilized 〔unenlightened〕. ～하다 (be) uncivilized; barbarous; savage; 《원시적인》 primitive. ② 《꽃의》 ～하다 be not open; be unbloomed; be not in blossom. ◉ ～사회 (a) primitive society. ～인 a savage; a barbarian; a primitive man. ～지 a savage 〔barbaric〕 land; a backward 〔an uncivilized〕 region; 《미개척지》 undeveloped land; untapped territory; virgin soil.

**미개간**(未開墾) ¶ ～의 uncultivated; wild. ◉ ～지 uncultivated land; virgin 〔maiden〕 soil.

**미개발**(未開發) ¶ ～의 undeveloped; unreclaimed; 《저개발》 underdeveloped. ◉ ～국 a backward country; an underdeveloped country. ～지역 an undeveloped area.

**미개척**(未開拓) ¶ ～의 uncultivated; undeveloped; unexploited; untapped; wild; 《학문 따위의》 unexplored / 이것은 ～ 연구 분야다 This is an unexplored field of research. ◉ ～분야 a field still unexplored: ～분야를 연구하다 do research in an unexplored field. ～시장 a (vast) potential market. ～지 undeveloped 〔unreclaimed, waste〕 land; untapped territory; virgin soil.

**미거**(美擧) a praiseworthy undertaking; a commendable 〔laudable〕 act; a good 〔benevolent〕 deed.

**미거하다**(未擧—) (be) indiscreet; foolish; stupid; imbecile; dumb 《미》. ¶ 미거한 자식 a thoughtless son.

**미결**(未決) pendency. ¶ ～의 undecided; pending; open; unsettled; unconvicted (죄수의) / 아직 ～로 남아 있다 be left unsettled; be held in abeyance / 그는 ～인 채로 반년이나 구치소에 갇혀 있다 He has been kept in prison 〔detention〕 half a year pending trial. / 그 문제는 아직 ～이다 The question is still open 〔unsettled〕. ◉ ～감(監) a house of detention. ～구류 detention pending trial: ～구류 일수 the number of days of unconvicted detention. ～문제 a pending 〔an open〕 question; a moot point. ～사항 arrearage; matters yet to be settled. ～서류 pending documents. ～서류함 an in-tray〔-box〕. ～수(囚) a prisoner on remand 〔pending trial〕; an unconvicted prisoner; a prisoner awaiting trial. ～안(案) an unsettled bill; an undecided matter; a pending case.

**미결산**(未決算) ¶ ～의 unsettled 《debt》; unbalanced; open; outstanding. ◉ ～계정(計定) an open 〔unbalanced, outstanding〕 account.

**미결정**(未決定) ¶ ～의 undecided; undetermined / ～이다 be not yet decided (on); be undecided 〔pending〕; be in the air / ～인 채로 남겨두다 leave 《*a matter*》 unsettled 〔at large〕 / 그 건(件)은 ～인 채로 남아 있다 The matter has been left unsettled.

**미결제**(未決濟) ¶ ～의 outstanding; unsettled; unpaid (미불의). ◉ ～ 거래 an incomplete transaction. ～어음 an unsettled bill.

**미경과**(未經過) ¶ ～의 prepaid; prereceived. ◉ ～보험료 a prepaid premium; an unearned premium. ～비용 prepaid expenses.

**미경험**(未經驗) inexperience. ¶～의 inexperienced; unexperienced; green; new. ◉ ～자 a green hand; an inexperienced person; a person new to the job: ～자 환영《광고》 Help wanted. Experience not required. *or* Welcome the inexperienced.

**미곡**(米穀)《쌀》 rice;《곡물》 cereals; grain. ◉ ～도매상 a wholesale grain merchant. ～보유량 rice in stock; rice stocks. ～상 a rice dealer: ～상을 하다 deal in cereals. ～시장 the rice market. ～연도 the rice〔crop〕year. ～창고 a (rice-)granary.

**미골**(尾骨)〖해부〗 the coccyx; the tailbone.

**미공인**(未公認) ¶～의 not yet officially recognized; unofficial; unauthorized. ◉ ～기록 an unofficial record.

**미관**(美觀) a fine〔beautiful〕sight〔spectacle〕; the beauties of nature (자연의). ¶～을 나타내다 present a fine sight / ～을 더하다 add to the beauty《of》/ ～을 해치다 spoil〔mar〕the beauty〔appearance〕《of》/ 그 건물이 도시의 ～을 해친다 The building spoils〔mars〕the beauty〔beautiful sight〕of the town.

**미관**(微官) an obscure〔a low〕position in government. ◉ ～말직 the lowest position in Government.

**미구**(未久) ¶～에 before long; shortly.

**미구불원**(未久不遠) ～하다 be soon; be not far (when...); be close by; near.

**미국**(美國) America; the United States (of America) (생략 U.S.A.); the States; the U.S.(A.); the USA. ¶～의 American; U.S.; Yankee / ～제(製) 자동차 an American-made car; a car made in U.S.A.

◉ ～국기 the American flag; the Stars and Stripes; the Star-Spangled Banner. ～군인 an American soldier; a GI. ～대륙 the American continent; the Americas. ～대외 군사 판매차관 U.S. foreign military sales credits. ～령(領) American territory; an American possession. ～말 American (English); the American language;《일반 미국어》 General American. ～문학 American literature. ～문화원 the U.S.〔American〕Cultural Center. ～본토 stateside; the continental U.S. ～본토의 stateside. ～사람〔인〕 an American;《전형적인》 Uncle Sam;《북부나 New England 지방의》 a Yankee《구어》; the Americans [총칭]. ～산 구매 계획 Buy American Program. ～식품 의약국 the U.S. Food and Drug Administration (생략 U.S. FDA). ～약전 the United States Pharmacopeia (생략 U.S.P.). ～어법 an Americanism. ～영어 American English. ～의 소리 the Voice of America (생략 V.O.A.). ～정부 the U.S. Government; the White House《구어》; the《Clinton》 Administration. ～통상대표부 the United States Trade Representative (생략 USTR). ～화(化) Americanization: ～화하다 Americanize.

**미군**(美軍) the U.S. Armed Forces; American forces; the U.S. Army〔Navy, Air Force〕;《병사》 an American soldier〔sailor, airman〕; a GI. ◉ ～점령 지역 the American-occupied area. ～정 the U.S. Military government. 주한～ the U.S. Forces (stationed) in Korea: 주한 ～의 감축〔철수〕 the reduction〔withdrawal, pullout〕of the U.S. Forces stationed in Korea / 주한 ～의 대폭적인 증강 the large-scale reinforcement of the U.S. (military) forces in Korea.

**미궁**(迷宮) a labyrinth; a maze. ¶～에 빠지다《사건이》 become shrouded〔be wrapped〕in mystery; get complicated / ～에 빠진 살인 사건 an unsolved murder case / 그 사건은 여전히 ～에 빠져 있다 The case is as much in the dark as ever. *or* The case is still unsolved.

**미그**《러시아 제트 전투기》 a MIG jet fighter; a MIG.

**미급하다**(未及―)《미치지 못함》 be not yet reached〔attained〕; do not amount《to》; fall short《of》; be not up to par;《필적하지 못함》 be inferior《to》; fall behind. ¶훨씬～ be far behind《another》; be not nearly so good as《another》/ 미급하지만 돕겠습니다 I will do what little I can to help you. / 우리 나라 공업 생산성은 구미 제국에 비해 훨씬 ～ The productivity of our country falls far short of that of Western countries.

**미기**(美技) a brilliant〔beautiful, neat〕performance;《스포츠》 a fine play.

**미기입**(未記入) ¶～의 unentered《item》. ◉ ～장부 a blank book.

**미꾸라지, 미꾸리**〖어류〗 a loach; a mudfish.

**미끄러뜨리다** let《*a thing*》 slip〔slide, skid〕. ¶발을 ～ miss *one's* footing; have a slip.

**미끄러지다** 《얼음·눈에》 slide; glide; slip; skid; 《시험 따위에》 fail 《in an examination》; get plucked. ¶ 미끄러지지 않도록 한 nonskid 〔skid-proof〕 《shoes》 / 미끄러지듯이 glidingly / 미끄러져 내리다 slide down 《a tree, a slope》 / 미끄러져 넘어지다 slip and fall / 바나나 껍질에 ~ slip on a banana peel / 빙판에서 미끄러져 넘어지다 slip on the ice / 미끄러져 떨어지다 slip off 〔down〕 / 벼랑에서 미끄러져 떨어지다 slip down the cliff / 배가 호수 위를 미끄러져 나간다 A boat glides along the lake. / 어머니는 욕실에서 미끄러져 다치셨다 My mother ⌈slipped 〔had a slip〕 in the bathroom and got hurt.

**미끄럼** sliding; slipping; a slide; a slip; a skid; slippage. ¶ ~ 타다〔지치다〕 《얼음 위에서》 slide 〔skate〕 on the ice; have a slide 〔make slides〕 on the ice; 《눈 위에서》 slide over the snow (in a sleigh) / 《차바퀴의》 ~을 방지하다 prevent 《a wheel》 from slipping / ~ 주의 《게시》 Slippery. ◉ ~방지 장치 a device to prevent slipping 〔skidding〕; 《신발의》 creepers; cleats. ~방지 타이어 a nonskid 〔skidproof〕 tire. ~틀〔대〕 《아이들의》 a slide; a sliding bed: ~틀을 타며 놀다 slide 〔play〕 on a slide.

**미끄럽다** 《반드럽다》 (be) smooth; sleek; slick; 《빙판 따위가》 (be) slippery; oily. ¶ 미끄러운 길 a slippery road / 몹시 ~ be as slippery as an eel / 비가 와서 길이 ~ The path is slippery with the rain. / 길이 미끄러워서 걷기가 어렵다 The street is slippery, and that makes walking difficult. / 빙판길은 미끄러워서 걷기에 위험하다 The frozen street is slippery and dangerous to walk on. / 주의: 바닥이 미끄러움 《게시》 Caution: *Slippery* surface.

**미끈거리다** ① 《반들거리다》 feel smooth 〔slick, sleek〕; be smooth 〔slick, sleek〕. ¶ 종이가 ~ paper is sleek 〔slick〕. ② 《미끄럽다》 feel slippery 〔oily〕; be slippery 〔greasy〕; be slimy. ¶ 미꾸라지는 미끈거린다 Loaches are slippery. / 뱀장어가 미끈거려 손에 잡히지 않는다 Eels are so slippery that we can't hold them.

**미끈미끈** sleekly; slippery; oily; greasily. ~하다 (be) sleek; slippery; slimy; oily; greasy. ⇨ 미끈거리다.

**미끈하다** ① 《사물이》 (be) smooth; sleek; slick. ¶ 미끈한 자동차 a sleek car. ② 《사람이》 (be) good-looking; nice-featured; smart; sleek; 《옷맵시가》 (be) flashy; well-dressed. ¶ 미끈한 얼굴 a sleek 〔fair〕 face; a good-looking 〔handsome〕 face / 다리가 미끈한 여자 a woman with shapely legs / 미끈하게 생기다 be good-looking 〔handsome〕; have nice features / 미끈하게 차리다 be flashily dressed.

**미끼** ① 《낚시의》 a (fish) bait. ¶ 산 ~ a live bait / 새 ~로 갈다 put on a fresh bait / ~를 물다 take a bait / 낚시에 ~를 꿰다 bait 〔put a bait on〕 an angling hook; bait a hook; bait up. ② 《유혹》 a bait; a decoy; a lure. ¶ 여자를 ~로 쓰다 use 〔employ〕 a girl as a decoy 〔bait〕 / ~에 걸려들다 be lured; get decoyed; bite / 닭을 ~로 여우를 잡다 catch a fox with a hen for a decoy / 경품을 ~로 손님을 끌다 attract 〔allure〕 customers by offering a free gift / 승진을 ~로 자기 진영에 끌어들이다 use promotion as a lure to entice 《*a person*》 into *one's* camp. ◉ ~수사 a sting 《미구어》. 낚시 ~ a fish bait; a bait for fish. 떡밥~ (a) paste bait; paste.

**미나리** 〖식물〗 a dropwort. ◉ ~꽝 a dropwort field. ~아재비 a buttercup.

**미나마타병**(一病) 〖의학〗 Minamata disease; a disease caused by industrial mercury poisoning.

**미남**(美男) a handsome man. ⇨ 미남자.

**미남자**(美男子) a handsome man; a good-looking fellow; an Adonis.

**미납**(未納) default in payment; nonpayment. ~하다 leave 《*something*》 unpaid; be in arrears. ◉ ~금〔액〕 the amount in arrears. ~세 back 〔unpaid, delinquent〕 taxes. ~자 a person in arrears; a 《tax》 defaulter.

**미네랄** minerals; 《광천수》 mineral water.

**미네소타** 《미국의 한 주》 Minnesota (생략 Minn.).

**미녀**(美女) a beauty; a belle; a beautiful woman. ¶ 절세의 ~ a woman of unsurpassed beauty.

**미농지**(美濃紙) (a kind of) rice paper.

**미뉴에트** 〖음악〗 a minuet.

**미늘** 《낚시의》 the barb (of a fishhook); 《갑옷의》 metal scales (on a coat of armor). ◉ ~창 a halberd; a forked spear.

**미니** a mini. ◉ ~스커트 a miniskirt. ~카 a minicar. ~카메라 a miniature camera; a minicamera. ~컴퓨터 a minicomputer.

**미니멈** 《최소의 수량·정도》 a 〔the〕 minimum. ◉ ～웨이지 《최저 임금》 minimum wage.

**미니어처** a miniature. ◉ ～세트 〖영화〗 a 「miniature set.

**미다**[1] 《머리털이 빠지다》 get 〔go〕 bald; bald. ¶ 뒷머리가 ～ *one's* head balds in the back.

**미다**[2] 《구멍나다》 tear 〔make〕 a hole in 《paper, leather》; get torn. ¶ 잘못하여 종이를 ～ tear a hole in the paper by mistake.

**미닫이** a sliding door 〔window〕. ◉ ～창 a sliding window.

**미달**(未達) shortage; lack; deficiency; insufficiency. ～하다 be short 《of》; be deficient 《in》; be less than; be under; lack; want. ¶ 연령 ～의 underage / 정족수 ～로 for want 〔in the absence〕 of quorum / 정족수에 ～ 하다 lack 〔want〕 a quorum / 지원자는 아직 정원 ～이다 The number of applicants has not reached the limit yet.

**미담**(美談) a praiseworthy 〔laudable〕 anecdote 〔episode〕; a moving 〔a capital, an inspiring〕 story. ¶ 그 이야기는 오늘날까지 ～으로 전해지고 있다 The story is told down to this day with undiminished admiration.

**미답**(未踏) ¶ ～의 untrodden; unexplored / 전인～의 영역 a region where no man has ever 「explored 〔ventured into〕.

**미덕**(美德) a virtue; a noble attribute; grace (of character). ¶ 겸양의 ～ the virtue of modesty / ～을 쌓다 keep on doing good deeds; accumulate virtues.

**미덥다** (be) reliable; trustworthy; sure-footed; 《희망 있는》 (be) promising. ¶ 앞날이 미더운 사람 a promising person; a person with a great 〔rosy〕 future / 미덥지 않다 be unreliable; be untrustworthy; be not to be depended upon.

**미동**(美童) ① 《예쁜 아이》 a handsome 〔good-looking〕 boy. ② 《남색 상대》 a catamite.

**미동**(微動) a slight movement; a stir; a tremor. ¶ ～도 않다 do not stir 〔move, budge〕 an inch; stand as firm as a rock. ◉ ～계(計) a tromometer. ～기압계 a statoscope. ～측정기 a microdetector.

**미두**(米豆) bucket-shop operation in rice; speculation in rice. ◉ ～장 the rice exchange.

**미들급**(—級) the middleweight class. ¶ ～의 middleweight. ◉ ～선수 a middleweight: ～ 선수권 middleweight championship. ～챔피언 a middleweight champion.

**미등**(尾燈) 《자동차 따위의》 a taillight; a tail lamp 《영》; a rear light.

**미등**(微騰) 〖경제〗 a fractional advance.

**미디** a midi; a midi-skirt.

**미디어** 《언론매체》 media (★ medium의 복수). ¶ 매스～ mass media.

**미라** a mummy. ¶ ～로 만들다 mummy; mummify.

**미락**(微落) 〖경제〗 a fractional decline.

**미란**(靡爛) 《염증》 inflammation; 《부란》 decomposition; 《궤양》 ulceration; fester; erosion. ～하다 be inflamed; ulcerate; fester; be decomposed; decompose. ◉ ～성 가스 irritating poisonous gas; lewisite.

**미란다 룰** 《묵비권·변호사의 도움을 요구할 권리가 있음을 통고하는 규정》 Miranda rule 《미》.

**미래**(未來) ① 《장래》 (the) future; time 〔days〕 to come. ¶ ～의 future; coming; 《years》 to come; prospective / ～에 in (the) future; in days to come; in the womb of time; 《아주 먼》 in the far distant future / ～가 있는 promising; full of promise; hopeful / ～가 있는 교사 a prospective teacher / ～의 남편〔아내〕 *one's* future 〔prospective〕 husband 〔wife〕; the husband-〔wife-〕to-be / ～를 예상하다 anticipate what is to come / ～에 살다 live in the future / ～의 계획을 세우다 form a plan for *one's* future / ～에 무슨 일이 일어날 지 알 수가 없다 No one knows what will happen in the future. / 우리는 ～에 대한 희망을 가져야 한다 We should keep hope for the future. / 대통령은 정부가 ～ 지향적인 자세로 국정을 운영해 나갈 것이라고 말했다 President said that the government will carry out state affairs in a future-oriented manner.

② 《내세》 the future life 〔existence〕; the next 〔other〕 world; the world 〔life〕 to come. ¶ ～를 믿다 believe in a life to come 〔the life after death〕.

③ 〖문법〗 the future tense. ¶ 가까운 ～ 〖문법〗 the immediate future.

◉ ～사(事) future 〔coming〕 events 〔affairs〕. ～상(像) an image of the future. ～완료 〖문법〗 the future perfect (tense). ～인 man of the future world. ～파 《미》 futurism; 《사람》 a futurist. ～학 futurology.

**미량**(微量) a very small amount; a minute quantity; micro. ◉ ～분석

microanalysis. ~영양소 micronutrient. ~천칭 a microbalance. ~측정기 a microdetector. ~화학 microchemistry.

**미레자** 《T자》 a T square. 「smoothing.

**미레질** reverse 〔back-hand〕 planing;

**미려**(美麗) beauty; elegance; gracefulness. ~하다 (be) beautiful; elegant; graceful.

**미력**(微力) feeble power; poor ability (능력); slender means (자금력); little influence (세력). ¶ ~이나마 in spite of *one's* poor ability / ~을 다하다 do *one's* bit 〔best〕; do what (little) *one* can; exert *oneself* to the full.

**미련** 《우둔함》 stupidity; foolishness; asininity. ~하다〔스럽다〕 《우둔하다》 (be) stupid; foolish. ◉ ~쟁이〔퉁이〕 a stupid fool; a senseless fellow; an ass; a blockhead; a ninny.

**미련**(未練) ① 《애착》 lingering attachment 〔affection〕; reluctance 〔being unable〕 to give up; 《후회》 regret. ¶ 아직 ~이 있다 be still attached 《to》; feel 《some》 regret 《for》; have a lingering affection 〔love〕 《for》; be unable to put 《*something, somebody*》 out of *one's* mind / ~이 없다 do not regret 〔have no regrets for〕 giving up 《*a matter*》 / 도시 생활에 ~은 없다 I do not regret giving up city life. / 이제 죽어도 ~은 없다 Now I can die without regret(s). / 그는 그 여자에게 아직도 ~이 남아 있다 Still he cannot give her up. *or* He still has a lingering attachment to her. / 사정이 이렇고 보니 이 세상에 아무 ~도 없다 With things as they are, I have no regrets at giving up this life. / 그는 아무 ~ 없이 회사를 떠나겠다고 말했다 He said he had no regrets about leaving the company.
② 《미숙함》 clumsiness; awkwardness. ~하다 (be) clumsy; awkward.

**미령**(靡寧) indisposition. ~하다 (be) indisposed; unwell; ill.

**미로**(迷路) a maze; a labyrinth. ¶ ~ 같은 labyrinthine; labyrinthian / ~에 빠지다 be lost in a maze; be at a loss / ~를 빠져나오다 thread a maze; go 〔find *one's* way out〕 through a labyrinth. ◉ ~학습 〖심리〗 maze learning.

**미료**(未了) 〔형용사적〕 unfinished; unsettled; pending; incomplete.

**미루나무** 〖식물〗 a poplar.

**미루다** ① 《연기하다》 put 《*something*》 off; postpone; delay; hold off; defer (의도적으로). ¶ 뒤로 ~ let 《*a matter*》 wait 〔stand over〕; 《미》 sidetrack 《*a matter*》; leave 《*something*》 until later; delay 《*doing*》 till later / 결정을 ~ stay 〔suspend〕 judgment 《till》 / 회합 날짜를 ~ put off the date of a meeting / 하루하루 ~ put off from day to day / 일을 뒷날로 ~ put work off; defer *one's* work till a later date / 빚을 갚지 않고 ~ delay paying a debt / 출발을 더는 미룰 수 없다 I can't delay 〔defer〕 the departure any longer. / 그 문제는 다음 회의로 미루어졌다 The issue has been carried over to the next meeting. / 자네, 다음 기회로 미루지 그래 Why don't you wait for the next chance?
② 《남에게》 shift 〔shuffle off, lay〕 《the blame, responsibility for *something* onto *a person*》. ¶ 일을 다른 사람한테 ~ shift 〔shunt〕 a job on to someone else / 죄를〔책임을〕 남에게 ~ put 〔lay, fix〕 the blame on 《*a person*》; lay the blame at 《*a person's*》 door; 《구어》 pass the buck to 《*a person*》 / 책임을 서로 ~ shift the responsibility back and forth; keep passing the buck 《구어》 / 자기 잘못을 남에게 ~ lay *one's* mistakes at another's doorstep.
③ 《헤아리다》 infer 〔deduce, gather〕 《from》; guess; conjecture; judge 《by, from》. ¶ 이것으로 미루어 보아 judging from this / 미루어 헤아리다 infer; conjecture; judge 《from》; draw an inference 《from》; 《남의 마음을》 enter into 《*a person's*》 feelings / 그의 거동으로 미루어 점잖은 사람인 것을 알겠다 I see from his behavior that he is a gentleman. / 나머지는 미루어 알 수 있다 The rest may be inferred. *or* From this one may judge the rest.

**미루적거리다** postpone; delay; defer; procrastinate; put off. ¶ 일을 ~ delay *one's* work / ~가 기회를 놓치다 dally away *one's* opportunity.

**미륵**(彌勒) 〖불교〗 *Maitreya* (Sans.) (= the Merciful Buddha); 《돌부처》 a stone statue of Buddha.

**미리** beforehand; in advance; previously; in anticipation 《of》. ¶ ~ 계획을 세우다 plan ahead / 돈을 ~ 받다 take money in advance / ~ 주의를 주다 give 《*a person*》 a warning / ~ 준비해 두다 make preliminary arrangements 《for》; have 《*something*》 ready beforehand; make preparations in advance / ～ 통지하다 give《*a person*》previous notice《of》/ ～ 허가를 얻다 obtain a permit in advance / 출발을 ～ 알려 주십시오 Let me know the time of your departure beforehand. / 짐은 ～ 부쳐 두십시오 Send your baggage in advance〔beforehand〕. / ～ 전화로 그가 집에 있을지 여부를 알아두었더라면 좋았을 텐데 I wish I had asked by telephone beforehand whether he would be at home or not.

**미립**(微粒) a fine grain; a particle. ◉ ～운(雲)〖기상〗a virga. ～체(體)〖생물〗a microsome (세포내의).

**미립자**(微粒子) a (minute) particle;〖물리〗a corpuscle. ¶ ～의 corpuscular. ◉ ～설(說) the corpuscular theory of light. ～전류 a corpuscular current. ～필름 a fine-grained film. ～현상 a corpuscular phenomenon.

**미만**(未滿) ¶ ～의 under; below; less than / 만원 ～ less than〔not exceeding〕10,000 won / 6세 ～의 유아 children under six (years of age); children under the age of six / 12세 ～ 어린이 700원《게시》700 won for a child under 12. *or* Children under 12 ₩ 700 / 18세 ～ 입장불가《게시》No one under eighteen (is) admitted.

**미망**(迷妄) an illusion; a delusion; a fallacy. ¶ ～에서 깨어나다 be disillusioned; awake from a delusion〔an illusion〕/ ～을 깨뜨리다 dispel an illusion; explode a fallacy.

**미망인**(未亡人) a widow; a dowager. ¶ 전쟁 ～ a war widow; a war-bereaved wife / 김씨의 ～ the wife of the late Mr. Kim / ～이 되다 be widowed; lose *one's* husband / 그녀는 남편의 사(死)후, 내내 ～으로 지냈다 She remained a widow after her husband's death.

**미명**(未明) the gray of the morning; early dawn. ¶ ～에 before dawn〔daylight, daybreak〕《on the morning of...》; in the early dawn.

**미명**(美名)《구실》a good〔fair〕name. ¶ …의 ～ 아래 in the name of; under the cloak〔pretext, guise, veil〕of《charity》/ 자선이라는 ～하에 그는 부정한 돈을 거두었다 Under the guise of being a charity he collected dirty money.

**미모**(美貌) good〔attractive〕looks; pretty features; beauty. ¶ ～의 good-looking; beautiful / 드물게 보는 ～의 여인 a woman of rare personal beauty / ～에 사로잡히다 be captivated〔fascinated〕by《*a person's*》charms / 그녀는 (스스로) 자신의 ～를 뽐낸다 She「prides herself on〔is proud of〕her good looks. / 나는 그 여성의 ～에 마음을 빼앗겼다 I was fascinated by the woman's beauty.

**미목**(眉目) features; looks; a face. ¶ ～이 수려하다 be handsome; be good-looking.

**미몽**(迷夢) a delusion; an illusion. ¶ ～에서 깨어나게 하다 disillusion《*a person*》/ ～에서 깨어나다 be disillusioned; come〔be brought〕to *one's* senses.

**미묘**(微妙) delicacy; subtlety; nicety. ～하다 (be) delicate; subtle; nice; fine. ¶ ～한 문제 a delicate matter; a tender subject / ～한 상황 a delicate〔ticklish〕situation / ～한 뜻의 차이 delicate〔nice〕shades of meaning / 동의어의 ～한 뜻의 차이 a subtle difference in meaning between synonymous words / 정국의 ～한 움직임 subtle shifting of the political situation / 그 문제는 좀 ～하다 The matter in question is somewhat delicate. / 나는 지금 ～한 입장에 있다 I am now in a delicate position. / 그들 간에는 ～한 의견의 차이가 생겼다 A subtle〔nice〕difference of opinion has arisen between them.

**미문**(美文) elegant prose; *belles-lettres* (F.). ◉ ～체 a flowery〔an ornate〕style.

**미물**(微物) a creature of no account; a very small creature; a trifle;《미생물》a microbe.

**미미**(美味) relish; a good flavor; deliciousness. ¶ ～의 tasty; delicious.

**미미**(微微) ～하다 (be) slight; tiny; minute; petty;《보잘 것 없다》(be) insignificant; trifling. ¶ ～한 문제 a matter of small importance / ～한 증가〔감소〕an immaterial increase〔decrease〕/ 모금 액수는 ～한 것이었다 The amount of money raised was insignificant / 그 회사는 처음에는 ～한 존재였다 At first the company was a petty affair. *or* The company had but small beginnings.

**미발견**(未發見) ¶ ～의 (as yet) undiscovered.

**미발달**(未發達) ¶ ～의 not yet developed; undeveloped; underdeveloped; of〔at〕an early stage of development.

**미발표**(未發表) ¶ ～의 unpublished; not yet made public / 작품은 ～의 것일 것

Works already published 〔printed〕 elsewhere are not accepted.

**미발행**(未發行) ¶ ~의 not yet issued; unpublished; unissued 《stocks》.

**미방**(未方) 〖민속〗 the Direction of the Sheep(=southwest-by-south).

**미복**(微服) disguise in dress. ¶ ~ 잠행을 하다 travel incognito; go in disguise.

**미봉**(彌縫) patching up; temporizing; tinkering. ~하다 patch up; temporize; gloss over. ¶ ~적으로 해결하다 patch the matter up. ◉ ~책(策) a makeshift; a temporary remedy; a stopgap policy 〔measure〕; a temporizing measure: ~책을 쓰다 adopt a stopgap policy 〔measure〕; resort to a temporary makeshift.

**미부**(尾部) the tail (part).

**미분**(微分) 〖수학〗 differential; differentiation. ~하다 differentiate. ◉ ~계수 a differential coefficient. ~방정식 a differential equation. ~자 a particle; an atom; a corpuscle; a molecule. ~적분학 differential and integral calculus. ~학 differential calculus.

**미분명**(未分明) uncertainty; indefiniteness; lack of clearness. ~하다 (be) uncertain; indefinite; unclear; indistinct.

**미불**(未拂) unpayment; arrearage. ¶ ~의 unpaid; unsettled; outstanding; in arrears / ~로 남아 있다 remain unpaid 〔unsettled, outstanding〕 / ~이 쌓이다 fall into 〔be in〕 arrears 《with *one's* rent》; run up bills 《at the bookseller's》
◉ ~계정(計定) an outstanding 〔unpaid〕 account; an account overdue; 《지급할》 an account payable; 《받을》 an account receivable. ~금 an account not yet paid; arrearages. ~배당금 dividends unclaimed; accumulated dividends. ~봉급 back pay 〔salary〕; pay 〔salary〕 in arrears. ~액(額) an unpaid 〔outstanding〕 amount; (the amount in) arrears. ~이자 interest accrued 〔in arrears〕; outstanding 〔accrued〕 interest (payable). ~잔고 an outstanding balance.

**미불**(美弗) = 미화(美貨) ①.

**미불입**(未拂入) ¶ ~의 unpaid; unsettled; outstanding. ◉ ~주〔자본금〕 unpaid stocks 〔capital〕.

**미비**(未備) 《준비가 안됨》 unpreparedness; 《불완전》 imperfection; defectiveness (결함); 《부족》 lack; deficiency; 《미비점》 a defect; a loophole (법률 등의). ~하다 (be) unprepared; defective; deficient; incomplete. ¶ 제도상의 ~ institutional inertia / 위생 설비의 ~ lack of proper sanitation; poor sanitary facilities / ~한 점을 시정하다 correct 〔remedy〕 a defect; bring 《*a matter*》 to perfection / ~한 점이 많다 There is much to be desired. / 서류가 ~하다 The documents are not properly made out. *or* The documents are invalid 〔incorrect〕. / 법의 ~점을 이용하는 악질적인 사건이 그치지 않고 있다 There is no end of reprehensible 〔shocking〕 cases where people take advantage of loopholes in the law.

**미쁘다** (be) reliable. ⇨ 미덥다.

**미사**(美辭) flowery words; flowers of rhetoric; rhetorical flourishes.
◉ ~여구(麗句) fine phrases; florid language: ~여구를 늘어놓다 use all sorts of flowery words.

**미사**(彌撒) 〖가톨릭〗 a (Christian) mass. ¶ ~를 올리다 say 〔read〕 mass / ~에 나가다 go to mass. ◉ 장엄~ Solemn Mass; *Missa Solemnis* (L.). 진혼~ a requiem mass. 추도~ a memorial mass.

**미사일** 〖군사〗 a missile. ¶ ~을 장비한 missile-carrying 《submarines》 / ~을 발사하다 fire 〔launch〕 a missile / 공대지(空對地) ~ an air-to-surface missile (생략 ASM) / 공대공(空對空) ~ an air-to-air missile (생략 AAM) / 전술〔전략〕용 ~ a tactical 〔strategic〕 missile / 공중 발사 순항 ~ an air-launched cruise missile (생략 ALCM).
◉ ~경쟁 a missile race. ~공학 missilery. ~기지 a missile base 〔station〕; a missile launching site. ~발사대 a missile launching ramp 〔pad〕. ~방어용~ ⇨ 탄도탄 요격 미사일. ~병기 a missile weapon. ~실험 the test-firing of a missile. ~탐지 위성 early-warning satellites. 다핵탄두~ a multiple independently-targeted reentry vehicle (생략 MIRV). 대공~ a surface-to-air 〔an antiaircraft〕 missile. 대륙간~ an intercontinental missile. 수중~ an underwater missile. 열(熱)추적 ~ a heat-seeking missile. 유도~ a guided missile (생략 GM). 전략용~ a strategic missile (생략 SM). 중거리~ an intermediate-range missile. 탄도탄 요격~ an antiballistic missile (생략 ABM). 핵~ a nuclear missile.

대(對)～방위 antimissile defense. 전술 ～ 부대 a tactical missile forces.

**미삼**(尾蔘) tiny-sized ginseng.

**미상**(未詳) being unknown 〔unidentified〕. ～하다 (be) unknown; unidentified; be not ascertained; be not exactly known. ¶ 작자 ～의 anonymous; unidentified / 신원 ～의 unidentified / 피해 정도는 아직 ～이다 The extent of the damage is not yet known 〔has not yet been ascertained〕.

**미상불**(未嘗不) in reality; as a matter of fact; indeed; undoubtedly; certainly. 「outstanding; unredeemed.

**미상환**(未償還) nonredemption. ¶ ～의

**미색**(米色) pale 〔straw〕 yellow.

**미색**(美色) beauty (of a woman); loveliness; charms; 《미인》 a beauty.

**미생물**(微生物) 〖생물〗 a microorganism; a microbe; a germ. ¶ ～의 microbial; microbic. ◉ ～연구소 the Institute of Microbiological Diseases. ～연구실 the Microbiology Laboratory. ～학 microbiology: ～학(상)의 microbiological / ～학자 microbiologist.

**미성**(美聲) a sweet 〔beautiful〕 voice.

**미성년**(未成年) minority; nonage; (legal) infancy. ¶ ～의 minor; infant; juvenile; under age / ～이다 be under age; be in *one's* minority 〔nonage〕 (★ nonage는 법률 용어); be not yet of age. ◉ ～노동 child labor. ～범죄 juvenile delinquency. ～자 a minor; 〖법〗 an infant; a person under age; boys in their minority: ～자 보호법 《violate》 the Minor Protection Law / ～자의 흡연을 〔음주를〕 금하다 prohibit minors from smoking 〔drinking liquor〕.

**미성숙**(未成熟) immaturity; unripeness. ～하다 (be) immature; unripe; unfledged. 「〔product〕.

**미성품**(未成品) an unfinished article

**미세스** 《기혼 여성의 호칭》 Mrs. (*pl.* Mmes). ¶ ～ 브라운 Mrs. Brown.

**미세하다**(微細—) 《매우 작다》 (be) minute; fine; microscopic; 《세밀하다》 (be) minute; detailed; full. ¶ 미세하게 in detail; minutely; fully / 금가루의 미세한 입자 minute particles of gold dust / 미세한 점까지 조사하다 investigate 《*a matter*》 down to the minutest details. 「school.

**미션스쿨** a mission 〔missionary〕

**미소**(微小) ～하다 (be) tiny; infinitesimal (극소한); minute; microscopic. ¶ ～한 생물 a microorganism; a microscopic organism. ◉ ～식물 a microphyte. ～체 a granule; a corpuscle; 〖생물〗 a microcyte.

**미소**(微少) ¶ ～한 very little; a very small amount 《of》.

**미소**(微笑) a (faint) smile. ～하다 smile give a 《friendly》 smile. ¶ 입가에 ～를 띄우고 with a smile on *one's* lips / 만면에 ～를 띄우고 with a broad smile on *one's* face; beaming with a smile / ～짓다 wear a smile 《on *one's* face》; beam with smile / 그녀는 ～로써 찬성〔승낙〕을 표시했다 She smiled her approval 〔agreement〕. / 그녀는 ～를 띄우며 사의를 표했다 She smiled and said "Thank you."

**미소년**(美少年) a handsome youth; a good-looking boy; a fair-faced lad.

**미송**(美松) 〖식물〗 an Oregon 〔a Douglas〕 pine 〔fir〕.

**미수**(未收) ～하다 have not yet collected. ¶ ～의 uncollected; receivable; unearned; deferred. ◉ ～금 an uncollected 〔outstanding〕 amount; an amount receivable; an outstanding fee (요금): ～금 계정 accounts receivable. ～배당금〔이자〕 accrued dividends 〔interest〕 receivable.

**미수**(未遂) ¶ ～의 attempted; unconsummated; unaccomplished / ～로 끝나다 fail 〔end〕 in *one's* attempt 《at murder》 / 방화 ～로 구속되다 be arrested on a charge of attempted incendiarism. ◉ ～범 a would-be criminal. ～죄 an attempted crime.

**미수**(米壽) 88 years of age.

**미수** honeyed 〔sugared〕 water with powder of roast grain in it. ◉ 미숫가루 powder of roast grain.

**미수교국**(未修交國) a nation with which it has no diplomatic ties. ¶ ～과의 관계 개선을 꾸준히 모색하다 endeavor further to improve relations with the nations which 《Seoul》 has no diplomatic ties with.

**미숙**(未熟) ～하다 《과일이》 (be) unripe; immature; green; 《경험이》 (be) inexperienced; unskilled; half-fledged; poor. ¶ 미숙한 사상 an immature thought / 미숙한 솜씨 poor ability / 내 영어는 아직 ～하다 My English is still far from perfect. / 그는 아직 일 솜씨가 ～하다 He is still green at his job. / 그는 운전이 ～하다 He is an unskillful driver. / 이 사과는 아직 ～하다 This apple is still unripe 〔green〕. / 나는 기자로서 아직 ～하다 I'm still inexperienced as a reporter. ◉ ～아 an immature [a premature] baby: ~아 출산 a premature birth. ~자 an inexperienced worker; a greenhorn.

**미숙련**(未熟練) unskillfulness. ◉ ~공(工) an unskilled workman [laborer]; a green hand; [총칭] unskilled labor. ~ 운전기사 an 「amateur [unskilled, inexperienced] driver.

**미술**(美術) art; (the) fine arts. (★ fine arts는 건축·그림·조각·공예를 가리키는데 넓은 뜻으로는 시·음악·무용·극 따위도 포함함.) ¶ 현대 ~ modern art / 조형[장식] ~ plastic [decorative] art / 공업 ~ industrial art / ~적인 artistic(al) / ~적으로 artistically / ~적인 견지에서(보면) from an artistic point of view / ~을 감상하다 appreciate art / 그녀는 ~에 취미가 있다 She has artistic taste. ◉ ~가 an artist. ~감독 〖영화〗 an art director. ~감식안 《have》 an eye for the beautiful; 《have》 an artistic [(a)esthetic] eye. ~감정가 a virtuoso (*pl.* ~s, -si); a connoisseur (of art). ~계 the world of art; art circles. ~공예 artistic handicrafts; arts and crafts; fine and applied arts: ~ 공예품 industrial artworks. ~관 an art museum; an art gallery: 국립 현대 ~관 the National Museum of Modern Art. ~교육 art education. ~대학 a college of fine arts. ~부 《학교의》 an art club. ~사 art history: ~사가(史家) an art historian. ~상 a fine art dealer. ~서[책] an art book. ~애호가 a lover of art. ~전람회 an art exhibition [show]. ~평론가 an art critic. ~품 a work [an object] of art; an art object: ~품 애호가 a curioso (*pl.* ~s, -si) / 수집 ~품 an art collection. ~학교 an art school [academy].

**미스** 《독신 여성》 Miss (*pl.* ~es); a miss; an unmarried woman. ¶ ~ 브라운 Miss 《Mary》 Brown (★ 자매인 경우, Miss Brown이라면 장녀를 지칭하고 차녀 이하는 Miss Mary Brown처럼 이름을 붙여 불러 구분함) / 올드~ an old maid; a spinster (★ 올드미스는 정식 영어가 아님) / 그녀는 아직 ~다 She is 「still single [not married yet]. ◉ ~영 인터내셔널 the Miss Young International Beauty Pageant. ~유니버스 Miss Universe: ~ 유니버스로 뽑히다 be elected Miss Universe; win the Miss Universe title. ~코리아 Miss Korea: ~ 코리아 선발 대회 the Miss Korea Beauty Pageant.

**미스터** 《남자의 경칭》 Mister (생략 Mr.); a mister; a gentleman. ¶ ~김 Mr. [Mr] Kim.

**미스터리** ① 《불가사의·신비》 a mystery. ¶ 그것이 나에겐 아주 ~야 It's a complete mystery to me. ② 《추리소설》 a mystery. ¶ 내 책의 대부분이 ~와 만화책이다 The majority of my books are mysteries and comics.

**미스(테이크)** 《틀린 데》 a miss; a mistake; a slip(-up). ¶ ~를 범하다 mistake; make [commit] a mistake 《in》.

**미스프린트** a misprint.

**미시**(未時) 〖민속〗 the 8th of the 12 double-hours (=the period between 1 and 3 p.m.); the 15th of the 24 hours (=1:30-2:30 p.m.).

**미시**(微視) ¶ ~적(인) microscopic(al) / ~적으로 microscopically. ◉ ~경제학 microeconomics. ~적 분석 (a) microscopic analysis.

**미시간** 《미국 주》 Michigan (생략 Mich.).

**미시시피** 《미국의 주》 Mississippi (생략 Miss.). ◉ ~강 the Mississippi River.

**미식**(美式) 《in》 the American way [manner, fashion]; Americanism. ¶ ~의 American-style. ◉ ~영어 American English. ~축구 American football.

**미식**(美食) dainty [delicious] food; a luxurious [lavish, rich] diet. ~하다 live on dainty [rich, good] food; keep a good table; be an epicure. ◉ ~가 an epicure; a gourmet. ~주의 gourmandism; epicurism.

**미식**(米食) rice diet. ~하다 「live on [eat] rice. ◉ ~인종 a rice-eating people.

**미신**(迷信) (a) superstition; a superstitious belief. ¶ ~적인 superstitious / ~을 믿다 entertain a superstitious belief 《in》 / ~을 타파하다 break down [do away with] a superstition; get rid of all superstitions / ~에 혹하다 be enthralled by a superstition / ~에서 벗어나게 하다 free 《*a person*》 from superstition / 한국에서 4는 불길한 숫자라는 ~이 있다 There is a superstition in Korea that four is an unlucky number. / 당신은 그런 ~을 믿습니까 Do you believe in such a superstition? ◉ ~가 a superstitious person.

**미심**(未審) ~스럽다, ~쩍다, ~하다 (be) doubtful; suspicious; dubious; questionable. ¶ ~쩍은 인물 a suspicious [dubious] character [person] / ~쩍은 점 doubtful points / ~히 여기다 doubt 《*something*》; regard as doubtful / ~쩍은 점을 묻다 make inquiries into doubtful points / ～쩍은 데가 있으면 설명해 드리지요 Let me explain doubtful points if there are any.

**미싱** a sewing machine. ⇨ 재봉틀.

**미아**(迷兒) a missing 〔lost〕 child; a stray child. ¶ ～가 되다 be 〔get〕 lost 《in the crowd》; be missing; 《길에서》 lose the 〔*one's*〕 way / ～를 찾다 search for a missing child. ◉ ～보호소 a home for missing children.

**미안**(美顔) a beautiful face; handsome features. ◉ ～수 a beauty wash 〔lotion〕. ～술 facial 〔beauty〕 treatment; a facial; beauty culture.

**미안하다**(未安—) 《안됐음·유감》 (be) regrettable; regretted; sorry. ¶ 미안하게 생각하다 be 〔feel〕 sorry 《for》; regret; have no excuse 《for》; be conscience-stricken; be penitent 《for》/ 미안하지만 …해 주시겠습니까 I am sorry to trouble you, but…. / 미안합니다 I am sorry for it 〔you〕. *or* 《잘못하거나 실례되는 언동 뒤에》 《미》 Excuse me for…; 《영》 I beg your pardon. / 대단히 미안합니다 I am very sorry. *or* Please excuse me. / 그는 미안하다고 하며 내 청을 거절했다 He declined my request expressing his regrets. / 미안하지만 말씀에 응할 수가 없습니다 I am sorry I can't oblige you. *or* I'm sorry, but I can't comply with your wish. / 미안하지만 같이 갈 수가 없습니다 I regret to say that I can't go with you. / 미안하지만 돈 좀 빌려 주시겠습니까 Could you lend me some money, please? / 기다리시게 해서 미안합니다 I'm sorry to have kept you waiting. / 여러 번씩 오시게 해서 미안합니다 I am sorry to have troubled you to come over so often.

**미안해하다**(未安—) regret; be 〔feel〕 sorry 《for, about, that》; apologize for. ¶ 미안해 할 것 없다 Don't worry about it.

**미약**(媚藥) an aphrodisiac; a philter; a love 〔an amatory〕 potion.

**미약하다**(微弱—) (be) feeble; weak; 「faint.

**미얀마** (the Union of ) Myanmar. ◉ ～사람 a Myanmarese. ～어 Myanmarese.

**미양**(微恙) a slight illness.

**미어**(美語) American English; American; an Americanism (미국식 어법).

**미어지다** be 〔get〕 torn; rip (open); have a hole in it. ¶ 가슴이 미어질 듯한 heart-rending 《grief》; heart=breaking 《sorrow》/ 그녀의 가슴은 슬픔으로 미어졌다 Her heart was torn with sorrow.

**미역**[1] 《목욕》 (outdoor) bathing; a bathe; a swim. ¶ ～ 감다 bathe 《in a river》; have a dip 《in a river》/ 내에 ～ 감으러 가다 go to a stream for a bathe; go bathing in a stream.

**미역**[2] 〖식물〗 brown seaweed. ¶ ～을 따다 gather brown seaweed.

**미역국** seaweed soup. ¶ ～ 먹다 [비유적] get dismissed 〔fired, sacked〕 (해고당하다); fail an exam (낙방하다) / ～ 먹이다 dismiss; fire; sack.

**미연**(未然) ¶ ～에 before 《it》 happens; beforehand; previously / ～에 방지하다 prevent 《a war》; nip 《a difficulty, an evil》 in the bud; kill 〔check〕 《it》 in the egg / ～에 손을 쓴〔조치를 취해 둔〕 것이 운이 좋았다 We were lucky that we had taken steps before anything happened.

**미열**(微熱) a slight fever. ¶ ～이 있다 have a slight fever; be a bit feverish / 저녁이 되면 ～이 나다 get 〔run〕 a slight fever in the evenings.

**미온**(微溫) tepidity; lukewarmness. ¶ ～적인 lukewarm (철저하지 않은); tepid (열의가 식은); 《뜨뜻미지근한》 lax; indifferent / ～적 수단〔정책, 태도〕 a lukewarm measure 〔policy, attitude〕/ 이제까지의 경제 자극책은 너무나 ～적이었다 The measures we have taken so far to stimulate the economy have been too half-hearted.

**미완**(未完) ～하다 have not finished 〔completed〕. ¶ ～의 incomplete; unfinished / ～의 그림 a picture in the rough 〔in the making〕/ ～의 작품 an unfinished work 《of art》; 《미술·문학의》 a torso / ～의 대기(大器) a great talent in the making / ～인 채로 있다 be left unfinished / 연재소설은 마침내 ～으로 끝났다 The serial novel finally stopped without reaching its conclusion.

**미완성**(未完成) incompletion. ⇨ 미완. ◉ ～교향곡 the Unfinished Symphony.

**미용**(美容) beauty art 〔culture〕; cosmetic 〔beauty〕 treatment. ～하다 receive beauty 〔cosmetic〕 treatment. ¶ ～을 위해 다이어트를 하다 diet for beauty; go on a beauty diet / ～을 유지하다 stay in shape.

◉ ～사 a beauty artist; a beautician; a cosmetician; 《머리만지는》 a (woman) hairdresser. ～성형 cosmetic surgery; face-lifting. ～술 beauty art 〔culture〕; cosmetology. ～식 food for beauty. ～실〔원〕 a beauty parlor 〔salon, shop〕; 《영》 a hairdresser's. ～체조 shape-up exercises; calisthenics. ～학교 a beauty school.

**미욱하다** (be) stupid; silly; dull; thick-headed; foolhardy. ¶ 미욱한 사람 a stupid person / 미욱한 짓을 하다 do a stupid thing; act the fool / 그런 거짓말을 하다니 미욱한 짓이었다 It was stupid of me to tell such a lie.

**미움** hate; hatred; enmity; loathing. ¶ ～을 받다 be hated 〔detested, disliked〕 《by》; make *oneself* hated 《by》 / ～ 받는 사람 a person disliked by everyone; a hated person / ～을 사다 incur 《*a person's*》 enmity; become an object of loathing / 그는 어디를 가나 ～을 받는다 He is an unwelcome guest everywhere. / 그런 짓을 하는 것은 남의 ～을 살 뿐이다 To do so 「would simply make people hate you 〔would be to court hatred〕.

**미워하다** hate 《*a person*》; have a hatred for; have a spite against; loathe; detest. ¶ …을 미워하는 나머지 to spite 《*a person*》; out of hatred 《for》; in hatred of 《*a person*》 / 서로 ～ hate each other; be hateful to one another / 그 녀석은 무슨 짓을 하든 미워할 수가 없다 No matter what he does, it is hard to hate him. / 죄는 미워하되 사람은 미워하지 마라 You must hate the criminal act but not the criminal himself as a person. *or* Condemn the offense 〔sin〕, but not the offender 〔sinner〕.

**미음**(米飮) thin gruel of rice 〔millet〕. ¶ ～을 쑤다 prepare thin rice gruel.

**미의식**(美意識) an (a)esthetic sense.

**미익**(尾翼) 《비행기의》 the tail unit.

**미인**(美人) ① 《미녀》 a beauty; a belle; a beautiful woman 〔lady〕; a pretty girl. ¶ 서울 ～ a Seoul belle / 당대 제일의 ～ the reigning beauty / 요염한 ～ a glamour girl 《미》 / 절세의 ～ a woman of unsurpassed beauty / ～박명이다 Beautiful women are often short-lived 〔ill-fated〕. ② 《미국인》 an American. ◉ ～계(計) a badger game: ～계를 쓰다 pull a badger game. ～선발대회 a beauty contest.

**미작**(米作) ① 《벼농사》 rice culture 〔growing〕. ② 《수확》 the rice crop 〔harvest〕. ◉ ～예상 a rice-crop estimate: ～예상 수확량 the estimated rice crop. ～지대 a rice-producing district; a rice country.

**미장**(美粧) cosmetology; beauty culture; beauty treatment. ◉ ～원 a beauty parlor 〔shop, salon〕.

**미장이**(—匠—) a plasterer. ◉ ～일 plastering; plaster work.

**미적**(美的) (a)esthetic. ¶ ～으로 (a)esthetically. ◉ ～가치 esthetic values. ～감각 an esthetic sense: ～ 감각이 전혀 없다 have no eye for the beautiful 〔beauty〕. ～생활 an esthetic life. ～쾌감 esthetic pleasure.

**미적거리다** ① 《내밀다》 keep budging forward; push 〔shove〕 forward bit by bit. ② ⇨ 미루적거리다.

**미적분**(微積分) 〖수학〗 differential and integral calculus; infinitesimal calculus.

**미적지근하다** ⇨ 미지근하다.

**미전**(美展) an art exhibition 〔show〕.

**미점**(美點) a point of beauty; a merit; a virtue; a good quality 〔point〕.

**미정**(未定) ¶ ～의 undecided; unsettled; in abeyance; pending / ～이다 remain unsettled 〔undecided〕; be in abeyance / 갈지 안 갈지 아직 ～이다 It is still undecided whether we go or not. / 연제(演題)～ 《게시》 Subject undecided.

**미제**(未濟) ¶ ～의 pending; unsettled; unfinished; to be settled.

**미제**(美製) ¶ ～의 American-made; made in U.S.A.

**미조**(美爪) manicure. ◉ ～사 a manicurist. ～술 manicure (손톱의); pedicure (발톱의).

**미조직**(未組織) ¶ ～의 unorganized.

**미주**(美洲) the Americas. ◉ ～기구(機構) the Organization of American States (생략 O.A.S.). ～대륙 the American continent(s). ～회의 the Inter-American Conference.

**미주리** 《미국의 주》 Missouri (생략 Mo.).

**미주신경**(迷走神經) 〖해부〗 a vagus 〔pneumogastric〕 nerve; a vagus (*pl.* -gi); a pneumogastric.

**미주알** sphincter muscles of the anus; sphincters; the anus.

**미주알고주알** inquisitively; minutely; to the last details. ¶ ～ 캐묻다 ask inquisitively; question 《*a person*》 down to the most minute details / 그는 나의 계획에 관해서 ～ 캐물었다 He catechized me (to the last detail) about my plan.

**미즈** 《기혼·미혼을 가리지 않고 부르는 여자의 경칭》 Ms.; Ms (*pl.* Mses, Ms's [míziz]). ¶ ～송 Ms. Song.

**미증유**(未曾有) ¶ ～의 unprecedented; unparalleled in history; phenomenal; record-breaking; unheard-of / ～의 대전(大戰) the greatest war on record / ～의 대풍작 a record crop / ～의 대지진 the most disastrous earthquake on record / ～의 사회 변동 an unprecedented social transformation / 그해 세계무역은 ～의 성장을 기록했다 World trade registered an unprecedented growth that year.

**미지**(一紙) 《납지》 wax paper.

**미지**(未知) ¶ ～의 unknown; strange / ～의 세계 the unknown world / ～의 사람들과 만나는 것은 여행의 즐거움 가운데 하나다 Meeting strangers is one of the pleasures of a trip.

**미지근하다** ① 《온도가》 (be) lukewarm; tepid; be not warm enough. ¶ 미지근한 물 tepid 〔lukewarm〕 water / 미지근한 방 a room not warm enough / 물을 미지근히 데우다 get the water lukewarm / 미지근해지다 get 〔become〕 tepid 〔lukewarm〕; get less hot 〔cold〕 / 나는 미지근한 목욕물이 좋다 I like a lukewarm bath. ② 《태도 따위가》 (be) lukewarm; halfhearted; too mild 〔lenient〕; be not strict 〔severe〕 enough. ¶ 미지근한 수단 a halfway measure / 미지근한 태도를 취하다 adopt 〔assume〕 a lukewarm attitude 《toward》; be soft 《on, upon》; show little enthusiasm / 학생들을 너무 미지근하게 다루다 be too easy with *one's* students.

**미지수**(未知數) 〖수학〗 an unknown quantity; the unknown. ¶ 승패는 전혀 ～다 The match is a very open one. / 문단에서 그는 아직 ～다 He is still unknown quantity in the literary world. / 그의 능력은 아직 ～이다 His ability is yet to be known.

**미진**(微塵) fine dust; a particle; a bit; an insignificant thing; a trifle.

**미진**(微震) a slight shock (of an earthquake); a faint earth tremor.
◉ ～계(計) a tromometer; a microseismograph.

**미진하다**(未盡一) (be) unexhausted; incomplete; unfinished. ¶ (마음에) 미진한 데가 있다 have an unsatisfied feeling; miss something.

**미착**(未着) ¶ ～의 not yet arrived; not yet delivered. ◉ ～품 goods to arrive; goods not yet delivered.

**미착수**(未着手) ¶ ～의 not yet started.
◉ ～공사 constructions not yet started 〔under way〕.

**미채**(迷彩) camouflage; dazzle paint. ¶ ～를 하다 camouflage 《a ship》.

**미처** (not) up to that; as far as; to that extent; far enough; early enough; in time; in advance. ¶ ～ 상상도 못 할 beyond the stretch of imagination / 그것까지는 ～ 생각지 못했다 I was not far-sighted enough to think of that. / 그는 ～ 피하지 못해 타 죽었다 He failed to escape and was burnt to death. / 바빠서 ～ 파티 준비를 못했다 I was too busy to arrange things for the party in advance.

**미처리**(未處理) ¶ ～의 《business》 yet 〔left〕 unattended 《to》; 《papers》 yet 〔still〕 to be dealt with; 《matters》 not yet attended to; outstanding; unsettled.

**미처분**(未處分) ¶ ～의 unfinished; unsettled; undisposed-of 《articles》; undivided 《profits》.

**미처치**(未處置) 《치료가》 ¶ ～의 《the wounded》 left untreated / ～된 충치 a bad tooth left untreated.

**미천하다**(微賤一) (be) lowly; humble; obscure; be of low 〔humble〕 origin. ¶ 미천한 신분 a man of obscure birth; a person in humble station.

**미추룸하다** (be) healthy and handsome; healthy and fair; [서술적] shine 〔be sleek〕 with health; have the glow of health.

**미취학**(未就學) ¶ ～의 not (yet) attending school. ◉ ～ 아동 a preschool child; children not attending school.

**미치광이** ① 《광인》 a madman; a lunatic; an insane 〔a crazy〕 person; a bedlamite. ¶ ～처럼 like mad; madly; frantically / ～처럼 떠들다 rave like a madman / ～가 되다 go mad 〔crazy〕; go out of *one's* mind; lose *one's* reason 〔wit, senses〕 《미》. ② 《열광자》 a maniac; an enthusiast; a fanatic; a fan. ◉ ～짓 an act of a madman; sheer insanity 〔madness〕: ～짓을 하다 behave like a madman; act crazy 〔frantic〕. 술～ an inveterate drunkard; an alcoholic; a toper. 춤～ a dance maniac.

**미치다**[1] ① 《정신 이상》 become insane; go mad 〔crazy〕; lose 〔go out of〕 *one's* mind. ¶ 미치게 하다 make 〔drive〕 《*a person*》 mad 〔crazy〕 / 미친 짓을 하다 do crazy 〔foolish, wild, absurd〕 things; make a foolish mistake; misbehave / 미친 듯이 성내다 rave

with anger; get mad and lose *one's* head / 미쳐 날뛰다 run amuck 〔amok〕; rave; rage; rant / 미치지 않고서야 그런 짓을 하겠는가 No one but a madman would do such a thing. / 이런 날씨에 가다니 미친 짓이다 It's crazy 〔It's sheer madness〕 to go out in this kind of weather.
② 《열광》 be crazy 〔mad〕 《about》; be fanatical; be beside *oneself* 《over》; lose *one's* head 《over》; be frantic; be given up 《to》. ¶ 사랑에 ~ be blind with love; be gone in love 《with》; be off *one's* head 《about a girl》 / 여자한테〔영화에〕 ~ be crazy about a girl 〔movies〕 / 정치에 ~ be all wrapped up in politics / 미칠 듯이 기뻐하다 be mad 〔frantic, wild〕 with joy; be overcome with delight; go into raptures; be ecstatic / 미칠 듯이 사랑하다 love 《a girl》 to madness / 그녀는 신흥종교에 미쳐 있다 She is fanatic believer in a new religious sect.

**미치다**[2] 〔자동사〕 ① 《이르다》 reach; attain to; come to; come up to; amount to; mount up to; 《걸치다》 extend 《to, over》; stretch; range over; 《언급하다》 refer to.
¶ 눈이 미치지 않는 곳에 beyond 〔out of〕 *one's* ken / 눈이 미치는 한 as far as the eye can see / 힘이 미치는 한 as much as lies in *one's* power; to the best of *one's* ability / 손이 미치는 곳에 within *one's* reach; in reach / (설명 등이) 상세한 데까지 ~ go 〔enter〕 into details 〔particulars〕 / 생각이 ~ be clever 〔alert, far-sighted〕 enough to think of / 생각이 미치지 못하다 miss; overlook; be not clever 〔alert, far-sighted〕 enough to think of / (세세한 데까지) 손이 ~ attend to everything; leave nothing undone / 손이 미치지 않다 be out of *one's* reach / 손이 미치지 않는 곳에 있다 be beyond *one's* reach; be out of *one's* grasp / 표준에 ~ come up to the standard 〔mark〕 / 표준에 미치지 못하다 come 〔fall〕 short of the standard / 기대에 미치지 못하다 do not come up to *one's* expectations / 힘이 미치지 못하다 be beyond *one's* power 〔reach〕; be above *one's* ability / 거기까지는 생각이 미치지 못했다 I was not far-sighted enough to think of it. / 아무도 거기까지는 미처 생각이 못 미쳤다 Nobody thought so far as that.
② 《재난 등이》 befall; happen 《to *a person*》; be visited. ¶ 위험이 몸에 ~ be in danger; get exposed to 〔be faced with〕 danger / 재난이 몸에 ~ a misfortune befalls 《*a person*》 / 부모에게 누(累)가 ~ *one's* parents are involved in trouble.
③ 《견주다》 match; equal; come up with. ¶ 미치지 못하다 be inferior 《to》; be no match 〔equal〕 《for》; be behind / 미치려면 까마득하다 be far behind another; be not a patch upon another; fall (by) far short of another / 수학에 있어서 그에 미칠 사람이 없다 No one can match him in mathematics. / 내 역량은 도저히 그에게 미치지 못한다 He is far more capable than I am.
④ 〔타동사〕 《영향을》 exert 〔exercise〕 《influence upon》; cause 《harm》; make 《itself》 felt. ¶ 크게 해(害)를 ~ do 〔cause〕 much harm 《to》 / …에 대하여 영향을 ~ affect; have affect on….

**미칭**(美稱) a euphemism.

**미크로네시아** 《태평양의 작은 섬들의 총칭》 Micronesia. ¶ ~의 Micronesian. ◉ ~사람 Micronesian.

**미크론** 《백만분의 1미터》 a micron (*pl.* ~s, -cra).

**미키마우스** 《Walt Disney 만화 주인공》 Mickey Mouse.

**미터** ① 《길이》 a meter. ¶ 길이 5 ~ five meters long 〔in length〕 / 그 수영장은 깊이가 2 ~ 이다 The swimming pool is two meters deep. / 50 ~ 달리기 the fifty-meter dash. ② 《계기》 a meter; a gauge. ¶ ~에 나온 숫자 the meter reading / ~를 검사하다 《고장 유무를》 examine a meter; (사용량을) read 〔inspect〕 a meter / ~를 달다 install a meter / ~를 속이다 tamper with a meter / ~에 나온 요금을 내다 pay the meter.
◉ ~검사원 a meter reader. ~법 the metric system: 우리는 ~법을 채용했다 We went metric. ~사용료 meterage. ~자 a metric rule. ~제(制) a pay-by-the-meter system. ~톤 a metric ton.

**미투리** hemp-cord sandals 〔shoes〕.

**미트** 〖야구〗 a mitt. ¶ 캐처~ catcher's mitt.

**미팅** 《회합》 a meeting; 《남녀의》 a date.

**미풍**(美風) a laudable 〔beautiful, fine〕 custom. ◉ ~양속 good morals and manners: ~양속을 저해하는 행위 an offense against 〔an act injurious to〕 public morals; a disorderly conduct.

**미풍**(微風) a breeze; a gentle 〔light, soft〕 wind; a breath of air. ¶ 오늘은

～이 불고 있다 It is breezy today.

**미필**(未畢) ～하다 have not finished; have not fulfilled. ¶ ～의 unfinished; incomplete; unfulfilled; unexecuted.

**미필적 고의**(未必的故意) 〚법〛 willful 〔conscious〕 negligence; *one's* conscious neglect; *dolus eventualis.*

**미학**(美學) 〚철학〛 (a)esthetics. ¶ ～상의 (a)esthetic / ～적 가치를 지닌 작품 a work of (a)esthetic value. ◉ ～자 an (a)esthetician; an esthete.

**미해결**(未解決) ¶ ～의 unsolved; pending; outstanding; unresolved / ～의 문제 《remain》 an unsolved problem 〔issue〕; an outstanding 〔a pending, an open〕 question; a moot point / ～인 채로 남아 있다 remain unsolved 〔unsettled〕 / ～인 채로 두다 leave 《*a matter*》 unsettled 〔outstanding, open〕; leave 《*a matter*》 at loose ends / 어떻게 그렇게 됐는지 아직도 ～의 문제로 남아있다 How it came about remains an unsolved question.

**미행**(尾行) following; shadowing. ～하다 follow (up); 《구어》 shadow; 《구어》 tail 《after》; dog 《*a person*》. ¶ ～을 당하다 be shadowed 《by a detective》 / ～을 시키다 put a shadow 《on *a person*》 / ～을 따돌리다 《구어》 give *one's* tail the slip; ditch 〔shake off〕 a shadow / 그녀는 누군가가 자기를 ～하고 있음을 알아채고 있었다 She was aware that somebody was following 〔tailing〕 her. ◉ ～자 a shadow(er); a tail.

**미행**(美行) laudable 〔good〕 conduct; a good deed.

**미행**(微行) incognito travelling 〔visiting〕. ～하다 travel 〔visit〕 《a place》 incognito; pay an incognito visit 《to》.

**미혹**(迷惑) confusion; bewilderment; delusion; infatuation. ～하다 be bewildered; be confused; be seduced; be in infatuated 《with》; be captivated 《by》. ¶ 여색(女色)에 ～되다 fall a victim to the charms of a woman; be infatuated with a woman.

**미혼**(未婚) ¶ ～의 unmarried; single / 그는 평생 ～이었다 He remained 〔stayed〕 single all his life. ◉ ～모(母) an unwed 〔unmarried〕 mother; a bachelor mother. ～자 an unmarried person; 《남자》 a bachelor; 《여자》 an unmarried woman; a maiden girl; a bachelor girl.

**미화**(美化) beautification. ～하다 beautify; pretty up; make 《*something*》 beautiful; 《이상화하다》 idealize. ¶ 전쟁을 ～하다 glorify 〔romanticize〕 war. ◉ ～운동: 교내 ～ 운동 a campaign to beautify the school; a campus clean-up campaign. (환경)～원 《도로청소원》 a street cleaner.

**미화**(美貨) ① 《달러》 American money 〔currency〕; the American dollar. ¶ ～로 in American currency 〔money〕 / ～ 1달러에 1,200원, 1,200 won per a U.S. dollar. ② 《상품》 American goods.

**미확인**(未確認) ¶ ～의 yet to be 〔not yet〕 confirmed; unconfirmed; unidentified (정체불명의). ◉ ～보도 news from an unconfirmed source. ～ 비행 물체 an unidentified flying object (생략 UFO). ～정보 unconfirmed information.

**미흡하다**(未洽—) (be) insufficient; unsatisfactory; [서술적] be not quite satisfactory; be somewhat insufficient to satisfy 《*one*》. ¶ 미흡한 감이 들다 feel not quite satisfied; feel that *something* is missing 〔wanting, lacking〕; miss something / 미흡한 점이 있다〔없다〕 leave something 〔nothing〕 to be desired / 그는 아직 기술이 ～ His technique still leaves much to be desired.

**미희**(美姬) a beautiful woman 〔girl〕.

**믹서** a 〔an electric〕 mixer; 《주스 따위를 만드는》 《미》 a blender; 《영》 a liquidizer; 《음향의》 a (sound) mixer.

**-민**(民) 《인민》 the people; 《국민》 a nation; a people; 《민족》 a race. ¶ 유목민 a nomadic race / 이재민 the sufferers 《from a disaster》; the victims 《of a calamity》.

**민가**(民家) 《개인집》 a private house; 《일반집》 a commoner's house.

**민간**(民間) ¶ ～의 《공(公)이 아닌》 private; nonofficial; nongovernment(al); 《군대가 아닌》 civilian; civil; nonmilitary / ～측 the unofficial side / ～에(서) among the people / ～에게 맡기다 leave 《*a matter*》 to private hands / 이것은 ～에 뿌리를 내리고 있는 신앙이다 This is a belief rooted in the people. ◉ ～ 공로자 a social benefactor. ～기업 a private enterprise: ～ 기업 부설 연구소 a research institute run by a private enterprise. ～단체 a private 〔non-governmental〕 organization. ～대표 nongovernment delegates. ～무역 private foreign trade 〔commerce〕. ～방송 a commercial broadcasting: ～ 방송국 a commercial radio station;

《TV의》 a commercial television station. ～사업 a private enterprise 〔business〕. ～설화 popular legends; a folktale; a folk story. ～신앙 a popular 〔folk〕 belief. ～약 a folk medicine. ～어업 협정 an unofficial fishing agreement. ～외교 non-governmental 〔people-to-people〕 diplomacy. ～요법 a folk 〔popular〕 remedy; an old wives' remedy. ～인 a private citizen; a civilian (군인에 대하여): ～인 통제선 ⇨ 민통선. ～자본 private capital 《investment》. ～전승(傳承) a legend; folklore. ～항공 civil aviation: ～항공기 a civil passenger airliner / 비무장 ～ 항공기 an unarmed passenger plane / 국제 ～ 항공 기구 the International Civil Aviation Organization (생략 ICAO).

**민감**(敏感) 《느낌의 예민함》 sensitivity; 《감수성》 sensibility; susceptibility. ～하다 (be) sensitive 《to》; susceptible 《to》. ¶ 열에 ～한 sensitive to heat / ～한 사람 a sensitive person / ～한 기질 a susceptible nature / ～한 기질이다 be touchy; have a thin skin / 더위에 매우 ～하다 be very sensitive 〔susceptible〕 to heat / 딸은 지금 ～한 나이다 My daughter is now at a vulnerable age. ◉ ～도(度) 《계기의》 responsiveness. ～성(性) susceptibility; sensitiveness: 이상 ～성 〖병리〗 allergy.

**민국**(民國) a republic.

**민권**(民權) the people's rights; popular 〔civil〕 rights. ¶ ～을 주장하다 assert the people's rights / ～을 신장〔옹호〕하다 extend 〔defend〕 the people's rights / ～을 유린하다 trample on civil rights. ◉ ～수호 운동 a movement 〔drive〕 for the defense of the people's rights. ～운동 the democratic movement: ～운동가 《미구어》 a civil righter. ～주의 the principle of democracy.

**민꽃식물** 〖식물〗 a cryptogam; a flowerless plant; [총칭] the Cryptogamia.

**민낯** 《화장을 않은 맨 얼굴》 a woman's unpainted face; a face with no make-up on it; a naked face.

**민단**(民團) a foreign settlement group. ◉ 재일본 대한민국～ the Korean Residents Union in Japan.

**민도**(民度) 《문화·수준》 the cultural standard; 《생활 수준》 the standard of living. ¶ 그 국민의 ～는 매우 높다〔낮다〕 The people's standard of living is very high 〔low〕.

**민둥민둥하다** (be) treeless; bare; bald.

**민둥산**(一山) a bare 〔bald〕 mountain.

**민들레** 〖식물〗 a dandelion.

**민란**(民亂) a popular uprising; an insurrection of the people.

**민력**(民力) 《foster, build up》 national power 〔strength〕; the financial resources of the people 〔nation〕 (재력).

**민망하다**(憫惘—) (be) embarrassed; flustered; sorry; sad; feel awkward. ¶ 민망한 생각이 들다 feel sorry 《for》; take 〔have〕 compassion 《on》 / 그의 초라한 모습이란 보기에 민망할 정도였다 He seemed so miserable that I found no words to soothe him.

**민머리** ① 《백두》 a person without office. ② 《대머리》 a bare 〔bald〕 head. ③ 《쪽 안 찐》 undone hair.

**민며느리** a girl brought into *one's* home as a future wife for *one's* son.

**민물** fresh water. ◉ ～고기 a freshwater fish. ～호수 a freshwater lake.

**민박**(民泊) a private residence temporarily taking lodgers; a private house providing bed and meals; 《영》 a guesthouse. ～하다 take lodgings at a private house.

**민방위**(民防衛) civil defense. ◉ ～대 Civil Defense Corps: ～대원 a Civil Defense Corps member. ～본부 《(director of) the Civil Defense Headquarters. ～체제 the civil defense system. ～훈련 a civil defense exercise 〔drill〕.

**민법**(民法) civil law [총칭]; the Civil Law Act (협의의); the Civil Code (법전). ◉ ～학(學) (the study of) civil law: ～학자 a scholar of 〔an authority on〕 the civil law.

**민병**(民兵) 《부대》 a militia; 《개인》 a militiaman(남자); a militiawoman(여자). ◉ ～단(團) a militia corps.

**민복**(民福) national welfare; well-being 〔welfare〕 of the people.

**민본주의**(民本主義) democracy.

**민사**(民事) civil affairs; a civil case. ◉ ～범 a civil offender. ～법원 a civil court. ～사건 a civil case. ～원고〔피고〕 a plaintiff 〔defendant〕. ～재판 a civil trial. ～책임 civil liability.

**민사소송**(民事訴訟) a civil suit 〔action〕. ¶ ～을 제기하다 bring a civil action 《against》. ◉ ～법 the Civil Proceedings Act; the Code of Civil Procedure.

**민생**(民生) the public welfare; the livelihood of the people. ¶ ～의 안정 the stabilization of the people's liveli-

hood / ~안정을 위한 대책이 시급하다 Measures to stabilize the people's livelihood are urgently needed.
◉ ~고(苦) the people's economic plight 〔difficulties〕; [집단적] mass poverty. ~문제 public welfare problems: ~ 문제의 해결을 착실히 추구해 나가다 steadily seek to solve problems concerning the public livelihood.

**민선**(民選) popular election. ¶ ~의 chosen 〔elected〕 by the people; popularly elected. ◉ ~의원 a representative elected 「by the people 〔by popular vote〕. 「the people.

**민성**(民聲) public opinion; the voice of

**민속**(民俗) folk 〔ethnic〕 customs; folkways; manners and customs of the people. ¶ ~의 날 Folklore Day.
◉ ~공예 folkcraft; folk handicraft; folk 〔native〕 art: ~ 공예품 a folkcraft article 〔object〕. ~극 a folk drama 〔play〕. ~무용 a folk dance: 국립 ~ 무용단 the National Folk Ballet Troupe. ~문학 folk literature. ~박물관 《be on display at》 a folklore museum: 국립 ~ 박물관 the National Folklore Museum. ~예능〔예술〕 folk art: ~ 예능 경연 대회 a folk art festival; the Folk Arts Contest / ~ 예술 공연단 folk arts troupes / 전국 ~ 예술 제전 the National Folk Arts Festival. ~음악 folk music. ~자료 《collection of》 folk material; folklore data. ~촌 a (national) folk village: 한국 ~촌 the Korean Folk Village. ~학 folklore: ~ 학자 a folklorist. 한국 ~ 협회 the Korean Folklore Society.

**민속**(敏速) quickness; agility; promptness. ⇨ 신속. ~하다 (be) quick; agile; prompt.

**민수**(民需) public 〔civilian, consumer〕 needs; private 〔civilian〕 demands 〔requirements〕. ◉ ~산업 non-military 〔civilian, consumer〕 industry. ~품 civilian 〔consumer's〕 goods; goods for civil 〔nongovernmental〕 use 〔consumption〕.

**민수기**(民數記) 『성서』 (The Book of) Numbers (생략 Num., Numb.).

**민숭민숭하다** ⇨ 맨숭맨숭하다.

**민심**(民心) popular feelings; public 〔popular〕 sentiment; the mind of the people. ¶ ~의 동요 popular unrest / ~을 거두다〔얻다〕 win popularity; win the confidence of the people / ~을 잃다 lose the support of the people; lose popularity / ~을 동요시키다 create disturbance in the mind of people / ~의 소재를 정확히 파악하다 grasp accurately the whereabouts of the public mind / ~이 동요하고 있다 Restlessness prevails among the people. / 그 정당은 점차로 ~을 잃었다 The political party gradually lost the support of the people.

**민약**(民約) social contract 〔compact〕.
◉ ~설 the theory of social contract.

**민어**(民魚) 『어류』 a croaker; a sciaenoid fish.

**민영**(民營) private management 〔operation〕. ¶ ~의 privately-operated 〔-managed〕 / ~이다 be run by private concerns; be under private management / ~으로 하다 place 〔put〕 《*something*》 under private management; leave 《a railway》 to private enterprise; commit 《an enterprise》 to private hands / ~으로 되다 fall into private hands; come under private management / 그 공사(公社)는 머지 않아 ~으로 바뀌게 되어 있다 That public corporation is supposed to be transferred to the private sector in the near future. ◉ ~사업 a private enterprise 〔business, undertaking〕.

**민영화**(民營化) privatization. ~하다 privatize. ¶ 국유 철도는 2000년대에 분할 ~될 것이다 The national railway corporation will be broken up and privatized in 2000's.

**민완**(敏腕) ability; capability; capacity; shrewdness. ¶ ~한 able; capable; competent; shrewd / ~한 솜씨를 발휘하다 show 〔give full play to〕 *one's* ability; display *one's* uncommon shrewdness. ◉ ~가 a man of ability. ~형사 a competent 〔shrewd〕 police detective.

**민요**(民謠) a folk song; a (folk) ballad; folk singing. ◉ ~가수 a folk singer. ~대회 a hootenanny 《미》.

**민요**(民擾) a popular uprising; an insurrection; a revolt.

**민원**(民怨) popular enmity; popular complaint(s); public discontent. ¶ ~을 사다 incur the enmity of the people / ~의 대상이 되다 become a target of public grievance.

**민원**(民願) a civil appeal 〔petition〕. ¶ 각종 ~ 사항을 처리하다 deal with various civil petitions. ◉ ~봉사실 a civil petition section. ~사무〔업무〕 civil affairs administration. ~상담소 a civil affairs office; the Civil Service Consultation Center. ~서류 civil affair documents: ~ 서류의 간소화 simplification of civil affair documents. ~실 the Public Service Center. ~안내(실) the Civil Service Information (Room). ~창구 a window for civil petitions.

**민유**(民有) private ownership; [형용사적] privately 〔publicly〕 owned.
◉ ~림 private forest. ~재산 a private property. ~지(地) privated 〔nongovernment〕 land. ~화 privatization: ~화하다 privatize.

**민의**(民意) the will of the people; public 〔popular〕 opinion 〔sentiment〕; a public consensus. ¶ ~를 묻다 seek the judgment of the people; consult the will of the people / ~를 존중〔반영〕하다 respect 〔reflect〕 the will of the people / ~를 수렴하다 collect the public opinions / 수상은 ~를 묻기 위해 국회를 해산했다 The Prime Minister dissolved the Diet to seek the judgment of the people.

**민의원**(民議院) 《하원》 the Lower House; 《미국·일본》 the House of Representatives; 《영국》 the House of Commons; 《프랑스》 the Chamber of Deputies.

**민적**(民籍) 《등록》 census registration; 《등본》 a family register. ⇨ 호적.

**민정**(民政) civil government 〔administration〕 (as opposed to military). ¶ ~을 실시하다 establish a civil government / 그 나라에는 ~이 시행되고 있다 A civil government is established in the country. ◉ ~이양 transfer of power to civil 〔an elected〕 government. ~장관 a civil administrator.

**민정**(民情) the state of the people; the realities of the people's life; popular sentiment 〔feelings〕. ¶ ~을 시찰하다 observe 〔see〕 how the people live.
◉ ~시찰 여행 an inspection 〔observation〕 tour of the people's conditions.

**민족**(民族) a race; a people; a nation; 〚사회〛 an ethnic group. ¶ ~의 national; racial / ~의 이동 (a) racial migration; (a) folk movement / ~의 화합 national reconciliation / ~적 우월감 racism; ethnocentrism / ~적(인) 편견 racial prejudice / ~의 동질성 national homogeneity / 한국 ~ the Korean people.
◉ ~감정 a national sentiment 《toward》. ~국가 a nation-state. ~문제 a racial problem. ~문화 national culture. ~성 racial traits; national characteristics. ~심리학 folk 〔ethnic〕 psychology. ~언어학 ethnolinguistics. ~운동 a racial movement; a national movement 《for independence》. ~음악 ethnic music. ~의상 native 〔ethnic〕 costume. ~의식 national 〔ethnic, racial〕 consciousness: 발전 도상국에서는 ~ 의식이 강하다 Racial consciousness is high among the developing countries. ~자본 national 〔domestic〕 capital. ~적 긍지 a national pride. ~적 비극 national tragedy. ~적 일체감 the sense of national homogeneity. ~정신 the racial 〔national〕 spirit. ~주의 nationalism; racialism: ~ 주의자 a nationalist; a racialist. ~주체성 national identity. ~진영 the nationalist camp 〔bloc〕. ~통일연구원 the Research Institute for National Unification (생략 RINU). ~학 ethnology: ~학 학자 an ethnologist. ~해방 national liberation: ~해방 전선 the National Liberation Front (생략 NLF).
다~ 국가 a multinational 〔multiracial〕 country. 단일 ~ 국가 a racially homogeneous nation.

**민족두리** an unjeweled 〔a plain〕 *tchokturi* (=woman's black headpiece).

**민족자결**(民族自決) (the) self-determination of peoples. ¶ ~ 원칙에 입각한 남북한간의 직접 회담 the direct talks between south and north Korea based on the principle of the national self-determination. ◉ ~주의 the principle of self-determination of peoples.

**민주**(民主) popular rule; democracy. ⇨ 민주적. ¶ 반 ~세력 the antidemocratic forces 《in a country》.
◉ ~공화국 a democratic republic. ~국 a democratic country. ~당 《미국의》 the Democratic Party; the Democrats: ~ 당원 a Democrat. ~사상 democratic ideas. ~전선 a democratic front. ~정당 a democratic party. ~정체(政體) democracy. ~정치 a democratic form of government. ~제도 a democratic system. ~ 평화 통일 자문 회의 the Advisory Council on Democratic and Peaceful Unification (생략 ACDPU). ~혁명 a democratic revolution.

**민주적**(民主的) democratic. ¶ ~인 democratic / 반~인 antidemocratic / 비~인 undemocratic / ~으로 democratically / 그 문제에 관해서 ∼으로 투표가 행해졌다 A vote was democratically taken on the question.

**민주주의**(民主主義) democracy; democratism; democratic principles. ¶ ∼가 이 땅에 뿌리를 내리도록 온갖 노력을 쏟다 exert all efforts to have democracy take deep roots in this soil. ◉ ∼자 a democrat; a democratist. ∼ 혁명 = 민주혁명. 의회〔사회, 민족적, 교도〕∼ parliamentary 〔social, national, guided〕 democracy. 직접〔간접〕∼ direct 〔indirect〕 democracy.

**민주화**(民主化) democratization. ∼하다 democratize. ¶ 교육의 ∼ democratization of education / ∼된 나라 a democratized country / 1980년의 광주 ∼ 운동 a pro-democracy movement in Kwangju in 1980. ◉ ∼추진협의회 the Council for the Promotion of Democracy (생략 CPD).

**민중**(民衆) the people; the general public; the masses; the populace. ¶ ∼적 popular; democratic / 그는 ∼의 적이다 He is a public enemy. / 그의 정책은 ∼의 지지를 얻었다 His policies were supported by the people. *or* His policies earned popular support. / 그의 생각은 일반 ∼에게는 받아들여지지 않았다 His ideas were not accepted by the people at large.
◉ ∼대회 a mass meeting; a people's rally. ∼심리 popular psychology. ∼ 예술 popular arts; mass arts. ∼오락 mass entertainment 〔recreation〕; popular amusements. ∼운동 a popular movement. ∼투쟁 a mass struggle. ∼화 popularization: ∼ 화하다 popularize.

**민짜** a plain things; an artless article.

**민첩**(敏捷) quickness; promptitude; agility; alacrity; nimbleness. ∼하다 《동작이》 (be) quick; prompt; agile; nimble; 《성질이》 (be) sharp; acute; alive. ¶ ∼하게 quickly; with agility; smartly / 행동이 ∼하다 be quick 〔prompt〕 in action.

**민통선**(民統線) the civilian passage restriction line; the farming restriction line (in Korea); the Civilian Control Line (생략 CCL). ¶ 군당국은 철원 지역의 ∼을 재조정할 예정이다 The military authorities will readjust the Civilian Control Line 〔CCL〕 in the Ch'ŏrwon area.

**민틋하다** (be) even and smooth.

**민폐**(民弊) public harm 〔damage〕; an abuse suffered by the public; a public nuisance. ¶ ∼를 끼치다 cause a nuisance to the people.

**민하다** (be) senseless; thoughtless; stupid; silly; foolish.

**민항**(民航) ⇨민간 항공. ◉ ∼기(機) an aircraft of civil aviation.

**민화**(民話) a folktale; a folk story.

**민화**(民畫) 《a piece of》 folk painting.

**민활**(敏活) quickness. = 민속(敏速).

**믿다** ① 《사실로》 believe; accept 《a remark》 as true 〔truth〕; give credit 〔credence〕 to; put 〔place〕 credit in; 《확신하다》 be confident 〔sure〕 《of, that》; be convinced of 《a fact》; be persuaded 《of, that》. ¶ 믿을 수 있는 credible; believable / 믿을 수 없는 incredible; unbelievable; doubtful / 나의 믿는 바로는 to the best of my belief; in my opinion / 성공을 ∼ be confident of success / 굳게 믿어 의심치 않다 firmly believe 《that...》; have a firm belief 《that..., in》 / 정말로 ∼ take 《*a thing*》 for truth; believe 《a statement》 (to be true) / 남의 말을 (그대로) ∼ believe what a person says; take a person at his word; take a person's word for it / (남의 말을) 잘 ∼ be credulous; be ready to believe anything *one* hears / (남의 말을) 잘 믿지 않다 be incredulous 《of, about》; be skeptical 《about》 / 나는 도무지 믿어지지 않는다 I'm rather inclined to doubt it. / 그것을 도저히 믿을 수가 없다 I cannot bring myself to believe it. / 그의 말을 믿을 수가 없다 I cannot believe him. *or* I cannot take his word. / 네 말은 아무도 믿을 사람이 없다 Who would believe it? *or* Tell that to the Jews. / 그는 신의 존재를 믿고 있다 He is positive as to the existence of God. / 지식은 힘이라고 나는 믿는다 It is my firm belief that knowledge is power.
② 《신용하다》 trust; believe 〔put *one's* trust〕 in 《*a person*》; put 〔place〕 confidence in; 《신뢰하다》 rely 〔depend〕 on 《*a person*》; have faith in; 《기대다》 count (up)on; look 〔turn〕 to 《*a person*》 for help; lean 〔reckon, calculate〕 on; 《기대하다》 expect. ¶ ...을 믿고 on the strength of...; relying on ... / 믿을 만한 사람 a reliable 〔trustworthy〕 person / 믿을 만한 보도〔소식통〕 a reliable report 〔source〕 / 믿을 곳 *one's* resort; a person *one* can turn to for help / 믿을 수 없는 이야기

an unbelievable 〔incredible〕 story / 믿을 만하다 be reliable; be trustworthy; be authentic; be authoritative / 권력을 ～ turn to 〔lean on〕 *one's* power / 아무를 ～《신뢰》 trust in *a person;* 《의지하다》 look to *a person* for help; rely 〔depend〕 upon *a person* / 요행을 ～ rely on chance / 자기 힘을 ～ have confidence in 〔rely on〕 *one's* strength / 아버지 재산을 ～ lay *one's* account with *one's* father's property / 아들을 집안의 기둥으로 ～ rely on *one's* son as the prop and stay of the family / 믿지 못할 것을 ～ lean on 〔turn to〕 a broken reed; hope against hope / 믿을 사람이 없다 have no one to turn to / 고모를 믿고 상경하다 come up to Seoul, counting on *one's* aunt's help / 나는 자네를 믿네 I believe in you. (★ in이 없으면 「자네 말을 믿는다」는 뜻이 됨) / 자네를 믿고 부탁하네 I make this request with full confidence in you. / 믿을 사람이라고는 너 하나밖에 없다 You are the only person I can trust. *or* I have no one but you to turn to for help. / 그는 믿을 수 없다 We cannot trust him. *or* He is not reliable. *or* He cannot be depended upon. / 우리는 자네 원조를 믿고 있네 We rely on your support. / 나를 너무 믿지 말게 Don't expect too much of me. / 자기의 역량을 너무 믿어서는 안되네 You shouldn't place too much confidence in your ability. / 그는 어려울 때 믿을 수 있는 사람이다 He will not fail you in time of need.
③《신앙하다》 believe 《in》; have belief 《in》; have faith 《in》; embrace; confess faith 《in》. ¶ 믿는 사람 a believer; an adherent / 기독교를 ～ believe in Christianity / 하느님을 ～ believe in God / 그들은 신을 믿고 있다 They have faith in God. *or* They are pious people. / 나는 귀신 따위를 믿지 않는다 I don't believe in ghosts.

**믿음** ①《믿는 마음》 trust; confidence; credit; credence. ¶ ～을 두다 trust 《in *a person*》; put confidence 〔trust〕 《in》; put faith 《in》 / ～을 잃다 lose credit 《with》; lose the confidence. ②《신앙》 belief; faith. ¶ ～이 없는 사람 an impious person; an infidel / ～이 두텁다 be pious; be devout; have a strong 〔deep〕 faith / ～이 약하다 be weak in faith.

**믿음성**(―性) reliability; dependability; trustworthiness. ¶ ～ 있다 be reliable; be dependable; be trustworthy / ～ 없다 be unreliable 〔undependable, untrustworthy〕 / 이 소식은 ～이 있다 This news is reliable.

**믿음직하다**《신뢰할 수 있다》 (be) reliable; dependable; 《마음든든하다》 trustworthy; authentic; 《장래가》 (be) hopeful; promising. ¶ 믿음직한 사람 a promising man; a person of promise / 믿음직한 친구 a steadfast friend / …을 매우 믿음직하게 생각하다 repose 〔place〕 great trust in 《*a person*》; hope 〔expect〕 much from 《*a person*》.

**밀**[1] 〖식물〗 wheat; corn 《영》. ◉ 밀밭 a wheat field.

**밀**[2] ①《밀랍》 beeswax; (yellow) wax. ②〖광물〗 minerals refined out of ore rock.

**밀가루** (wheat) flour. ¶ 된 ～ 반죽 stiff dough.

**밀감**(蜜柑) 〖식물〗 a mandarin orange; a tangerine. ◉ ～화채 tangerine punch.

**밀계**(密啓) a secret report to the throne. ～하다 secretly report to the throne.

**밀계**(密計) a secret plan 〔plot, design, scheme〕. ¶ ～를 꾸미다 plot secretly; frame 〔weave〕 a secret plot.

**밀고**(密告) (secret) information 《against》; an anonymous report 〔notice〕; (a) betrayal. ～하다 inform 《on, against》; tell 《on *a person*》; tip 《*a person*》 off 《about *something*》; betray; 《속어》 squeal 《on *a person*》; 《영속어》 blow the gaff 《to the police》. ¶ ～를 받다 receive secret information 《from》 / 그는 친구를 경찰에 ～ 했다 He informed on 〔against〕 his friend to the police. / 공범자가 경찰에 ～했다 The accomplice squealed to the cops. ◉ ～자 an informer; a betrayer.

**밀고나(아)가다** 《앞으로》 push 〔press〕 on(ward); shove along 〔on〕; force *one's* way 《through, to》; 《추진하다》 push on 〔ahead〕 《with a plan》; go 〔move〕 ahead with 《a project》; 《끝까지》 push through; carry 《it》 through. ¶ 대담하게 ～ brave 〔breast〕 it out / 자기 생각을 ～ persist in *one's* opinion; hold on to *one's* belief.

**밀교**(密教) 〖불교〗 esoteric Buddhism.

**밀국수** wheat vermicelli; noodles.

**밀기름** a pomade made of beeswax and sesame oil.

**밀기울** (wheat) bran.

**밀깜부기** a smut ear of wheat.

**밀낫** a reaping hook.

**밀다** ①《떠밀다》 push; thrust; shove; elbow (팔꿈치로). ¶ 문을 ~ (give a) push at the door / 배를 삿대로 ~ shove a boat with a pole / 수레를 ~ push 〔wheel〕 a cart / 등뒤에서 ~ push 《*a person*》 from behind / 밀고 들어가다 force *oneself* 〔*one's* way〕 into / (밑에서) 밀어주다 give 《*a person*》 a hoist 〔boost〕 / 탁자를 앞으로 ~ thrust a table forward / 밀어 넘어뜨리다〔떨어뜨리다, 올리다〕 push down 〔off, up〕 / 서로 ~ jostle one another / 밀고 밀리는 대혼잡이다 be packed to overflowing; be crowded 〔jammed〕 with people.
②《면도로》 shave; 《이발사 등이》 get 〔have〕 a shave; 《대패로》 plane 《a board》. ¶ 대패로 판자를 반반하게 ~ plane a board smooth / 수염을 ~ shave *oneself;* 《남이 밀어주다》 get *oneself* shaved 《by》.
③ 《때를》 rub; scrub; wash. ¶ 등을 ~ wash 《*a person's*》 back / 때를 ~ wash 〔rub〕 off the dirt.
④ 《추천하다》 recommend; propose; 《후원하다》 support; boost 《미》. ¶ 뒤에서 ~ back 〔bolster〕 up 《*a person*》 / 다른 후보를 ~ recommend another candidate / 회장으로 ~ propose 《*a person*》 for 〔as〕 *one's* president / 그녀를 가정교사로 ~ put in a good word for her as a (private) tutor.
⑤ ⇨ 미루다.

**밀담**(密談) a secret 〔subdued, clandestine〕 conversation; a confidential talk; a tête-à-tête. ~하다 talk secretly 〔behind closed doors〕 《with》; have a confidential talk 《with》.

**밀대** ①《막대》 a push stick. ②《총의》 the recoil mechanism 《on a carbine》.

**밀도**(密度) density; consistency. ¶ 인구 ~ population density / ~ 있는 강의 a substantial lecture / ~가 높은 dense 《metal》; of high density / 이 지역의 인구 ~는 높다〔낮다〕 This district is densely 〔sparsely〕 populated. ◉ ~계 a densimeter. ~측정 densimetry.

**밀도살**(密屠殺) illegal butchery. ~하다 slaughter 《cattle》 clandestinely 〔in secret〕. ¶ ~ 행위를 적발하다 pick up illegal butchery practices.

**밀떡** a wheat ointment 〔plaster〕 (to be applied to a wound).

**밀뜨리다** push 〔shove〕 off; thrust. ¶ 아무를 ~ push *a person* off.

**밀랍**(蜜蠟) beeswax; (yellow) wax.

**밀레니엄** 《1천년의 기간》 a millennium. ◉ ~버그 〖컴퓨터〗 a millennium bug.

**밀려나다** 《밖으로》 be pushed 〔forced〕 out; 《지위 등에서》 be ousted 〔expelled, dislodged〕 《from》; be squeezed 〔shoved〕 out of; 《하위로》 be relegated 《to》. ¶ 사장자리에서 ~ be squeezed out of the president's seat / 회사에서 ~ get shoved 〔pushed〕 out of *one's* job with the company / 시대의 흐름에서 ~ be swept irresistibly by the current of the times.

**밀려들다** advance 〔press〕 on 《a castle》; make 〔rush〕 for 《the door》; rush 〔surge, crowd〕 into; 《쇄도》 rush 〔throng〕 to 《a place》; make a rush for 《a place》; 《파도가》 beat 〔surge, rush〕 upon 《the shore》. ¶ 밀려드는 파도 advancing 〔surging〕 waves / 주문이 ~ have a rush 〔flood〕 of orders / 신청이 ~ [사람·단체가 주어] be flooded 〔deluged〕 with applications 〔offers〕 / 조수가 밀려든다 The tide is flowing. / 예금자들이 은행으로 밀려들었다 The depositors besieged the bank. *or* The bank had a rush of depositors.

**밀렵**(密獵) (game-)poaching. ~하다 poach (for) 《pheasants, salmons》; steal game. ¶ 보호 동물을 ~하다 poach protected animals. ◉ ~선(船) a poaching boat. ~자, ~꾼 a poacher.

**밀리** milli-. ◉ ~그램 a milligram(me) (생략 mg, mgm). ~리터 a milliliter (생략 ml). ~미크론 a millimicron (생략 m$\mu$). ~미터 a millimeter (생략 mm). ~바 a millibar (생략 mb).

**밀리다** ①《떠밀림》 be pushed; be shoved; be thrust. ¶ 밀고 밀리는 경쟁〔싸움〕 a dingdong race 〔fight〕; a seesaw struggle 〔battle〕 / 인파에 ~ be swept along in the crowd / 물결에 이리저리 ~ be tossed about by the seas; be at the mercy of the waves / 북적이는 방에서 밀려나오다 be crowded out of the room.
②《깎임》 get shaved; shave (수염이); be planed; plane (대패로). ¶ 송판이 잘 ~ a board planes well.
③《일이》 be left undone; be behind 《with, in》; be in arrears 《with》; 《교통의 흐름이》 be congested. ¶ 밀린 일 piled-up work; a (great) backlog of work / 일이 ~ work accumulate; be behind in 〔be in arrears with〕 *one's* work / 일이 산더미처럼 밀려 있다 There

is a good deal of work left undone. *or* I've got a lot of work piled up now. / 밀린 일을 처리해야 한다 I have some unfinished work to dispose of. *or* I have backlog of work to get through.
④《내야할 돈이》 fall into arrears; be in arrears《with》; be left unpaid; be overdue; be outstanding. ¶ 밀린 돈 arrears / 밀린 이자 an interest on arrears / 지급이 ~ run up a bill; be in arrears with payment / 집세가 ~ be behind 〔in arrears〕 with *one's* rent; get behinded with *one's* rent; fail to pay *one's* rent / 그는 집세가 반년이나 밀려 있다 He is six months behind 〔in arrears〕 with his rent.

**밀림**(密林) a thick 〔dense〕 forest; a jungle. ¶ 안데스산(山)의 동쪽 경사지는 ~으로 뒤덮여 있다 The eastern slopes of the Andes are heavily forested.
◉ ~지대 a jungle area.

**밀막다** refuse under a pretense; decline on the pretext of something.

**밀매**(密賣) an illicit sale《of》; illicit traffic《in》; smuggling; 《술의》 bootlegging《미》. ~하다 sell《*something*》 secretly; smuggle; bootleg. ¶ 경찰은 마약~ 적발에 나섰다 The police set about exposing the illicit drug trade.
◉ ~자 a smuggler; a secret 〔an illicit〕 dealer; 《술의》 a bootlegger. ~장소《술의》 a bootleggery; a blind pig 〔tiger〕《미》. ~품 smuggled goods.

**밀매매**(密賣買) illicit traffic《in》. ~하다 engage in illicit traffic《in》; deal secretly《in》.

**밀매음**(密賣淫) unlicensed prostitution. ~하다 engage in unlicensed prostitution. ◉ ~녀 an unlicensed prostitute.

**밀모**(密謀) a plot; an underhand design 〔intrigue〕; a conspiracy (공모). ~하다 plot; conspire.

**밀무역**(密貿易) smuggling. ~하다 smuggle (in, out). ◉ ~업자 a smuggler.

**밀물**《물이 들어옴》 the inflow 〔rising〕 of the tide; 《조수》 the flowing 〔rising, swelling〕 tide. ¶ ~ 때에 at high tide / ~이 되다〔들어오다〕 the tide rises; the tide is at its flow.

**밀방망이** a rolling pin (to flatten dough).

**밀범벅** wheat-and-pumpkin pudding.

**밀보리** wheat and barley. = 쌀보리.

**밀봉**(密封) ~하다 seal up; seal tightly 〔hermetically〕; make 〔keep〕《a box》 airtight (공기가 들어가지 않게). ◉ ~교육 secret 〔clandestine〕 training.

**밀사**(密使) a secret envoy 〔messenger〕; a secret (service) agent. ¶ ~로 보내다 send《*a person*》 on a secret mission.

**밀생**(密生) thick growth《of trees》. ~하다 grow thick 〔in clusters〕; be thickly wooded.

**밀서**(密書) a secret message; a secret note 〔letter〕. ¶ ~를 지니다 bear 〔carry〕 a secret message.

**밀선**(密船) a smuggler (vessel).

**밀송**(密送) ~하다 send 〔dispatch〕 secretly 〔in secret〕.

**밀수**(密輸) smuggling; contraband trade. ~하다《밀수입》 smuggle《goods》 in(to)《the country》; import through illegal channels; 《밀수출》 smuggle《goods》 abroad; export unlawfully; run《guns》《미》. ¶ 금제품을 ~하다 run contraband goods / 마약을 국내〔국외〕로 ~하다 smuggle drugs in 〔abroad〕 / 정부는 마약의 ~ 방지에 노력했다 The government tried to prevent the smuggling of drugs.
◉ ~감시선 a revenue cutter; a contraband-control vessel. ~단 a gang of smugglers; a smuggling ring: 4인조 ~단 a four-man《gold》 smuggling ring. ~선 a smuggling vessel; a smuggler. ~업자 a smuggler. ~품 contraband 〔smuggled〕 goods; contraband: ~품은 압수된다 contraband is subject to confiscation.

**밀수제비** pieces of flour dough boiled with meat soup.

**밀실**(密室) a secret room 〔chamber〕; a closet. ¶ ~에서 behind 〔with〕 closed doors / ~에 감금하다 keep《*a person*》 in solitary 〔close〕 confinement / ~에서 밀담하다 closet *oneself* with《another》; be closeted together.
◉ ~공포증 claustrophobia. ~살인 a murder in a shut-up room: ~살인 사건 a locked-room murder case. ~정치 closed-door politics. ~회의 a closed-door session.

**밀약**(密約) a secret promise 〔understanding〕; a secret agreement 〔treaty〕. ¶ ~을 맺다 conclude 〔enter into〕 a secret treaty《with》; contract a secret pact / 두 나라 사이에 ~이 있다 A secret understanding exists between the two countries. / 그들은 우리와 ~을 맺었다 They have made a secret understanding. / 기자회견에서

대통령은 적과의 ～을 부정했다 At the press conference the President denied having made a secret treaty with the enemy.

**밀어**(密語) a confidential talk. ⇨ 밀담.

**밀어**(密漁) poaching. ～하다 poach (for) 《fish》. ¶ 연어를 ～하다 poach salmon. ◉ ～선 a poaching vessel. ～자 a poacher.

**밀어내기** pushing 〔pressing〕 out; 《야구의》 a forced-in run; a run scored with the batter getting a walk. ¶ ～로 1점을 내주다 force in a run (with a base-loaded walk); force in the third-base runner.

**밀어내다** push 〔thrust, force, press〕 out. ¶ 링 밖으로 ～ thrust 〔push〕 《*one's* opponent》 out of the ring / 동료를 밀어내고 출세하다 win promotion at the expense of *one's* colleagues.

**밀어붙이다** ① 《물건을》 push to one side; move 《*a thing*》 aside 〔out of the way〕; 《사람을》 push 〔drive〕 《*a person*》 to; push 〔thrust〕 against; pin against; press hard. ¶ 벽쪽으로 ～ drive 《*a person*》 to the wall. ② 《계획·일을》 push 〔force, carry〕 《*one's* plan》 through.

**밀어젖히다** push 〔thrust〕 away 〔aside〕; force 〔push〕 aside 〔out of the way〕; elbow 《*a person*》 out 〔aside, to one side〕 (팔꿈치로). ¶ 사람을 ～ push people aside.

**밀어치기** 『당구』 a follow shot.

**밀월**(蜜月) a honeymoon. ¶ 두 나라간의 ～ 시대 a honeymoon period between the two countries. ◉ ～여행 a honeymoon trip: ～여행자 honeymooners.

**밀의**(密議) a secret 〔closed-door〕 conference; a private consultation; a conclave. ～하다 confer in private 《with》; hold a secret conference 〔chamber council〕. ¶ ～중이다 be in conclave / ～를 거듭하다 get 〔put 《their》 heads〕 together in secret consultation(s).

**밀입국**(密入國) illegal entry into a country; smuggling *oneself* into 《a country》. ～하다 smuggle *oneself* into 《a country》; enter 《Korea》 illegally; 《밀항으로》 stow away. ¶ 멕시코 국경을 넘어 미국으로 ～시키다 smuggle 《*a person*》 into the United States over the Mexican border. ◉ ～자 an illegal entrant; a stowaway (밀항자).

**밀장지**(—障—) a sliding door; a sliding partition.

**밀전병**(—煎餠) a grilled wheat cake.

**밀접**(密接) ～하다 (be) close 《to》; intimate 《with》. ¶ ～한 관계 a close connection 《between》; close ties / …와 ～한 관계가 있다 be closely connected with 〔related to〕…; be in close connection with… / ～한 관계를 맺다 come 〔be brought〕 into close relation 《with》; be brought closer together / 이것은 우리들의 생활과 ～한 관계가 있다 This has a close relation to our life.

**밀정**(密偵) a spy; a secret agent. ¶ 적을 위하여 ～ 노릇을 하다 spy for the enemy.

**밀조**(密造) illicit manufacture; 《술의》 unlawful brewing. ～하다 manufacture 〔distill〕 illicitly; brew unlawfully. ¶ 위스키를 ～하다 brew whisky secretly 〔illicitly〕.

**밀주**(密酒) home-brewed wine; 《미구어》 moonshine; bootleg. ◉ ～제조자 an illicit distiller; 《미구어》 a moonshiner; a bootlegger.

**밀집**(密集) ～하다 mass; crowd; swarm; close up; be in close 〔tight〕 formation. ¶ 가옥의 ～지대 a (densely) built-up area / ～하여 나아가다 advance in mass formation 〔shoulder to shoulder〕 / 인가가 ～되어 있다 The houses stand roof by roof 〔close together〕 / 한국의 인구는 서울과 그 주변에 ～되어 있다 The population of Korea is concentrated in Seoul and its suburbs. ◉ ～대형 a close order; (a) close formation. ～부대 massed troops. ～훈련 close-order drill. 인구～지역 an overpopulated 〔overcrowded, overpeopled〕 area.

**밀짚** (a) wheat 〔barley〕 straw. ◉ ～모자 a straw hat. ～세공 strawwork.

**밀착**(密着) close adhesion. ～하다 stick (fast) 《to》; adhere (closely) 《to》. ¶ ～시키다 stick 《A》 fast to 《B》; weld 《together》 / 사건을 ～ 취재하다 Keep up *one's* close coverage of a case. ◉ ～법 『사진』 contact printing. ～인화 a contact print 〔copy〕. ～(인화)지 contact paper.

**밀초**(蜜—) a wax candle.

**밀치다** push; shove; thrust. ¶ 아무를 ～ push a person; give a person a shove / 옆으로 ～ push 〔thrust〕 aside / 밀치고 나아가다 push on; shove along; thrust 〔force, elbow〕 *one's* way.

**밀치락달치락** ～하다 push and shove; hustle and jostle. ¶ ～하는 군중 a milling crowd 〔throng〕; a jostling crowd / 사람들은 서로 ～하며 열차에 올라탔다 The people got into the train with a lot of pushing and shoving.

**밀칙**(密勅) a secret order from the king.

**밀크** (cow's) milk. ◉ ～커피 white coffee; *café au lait* (F.).

**밀타승**(密陀僧) 〖화학〗《일산화납》 litharge.

**밀탐**(密探) ～하다 spy 《on *a person*, into a secret》; make secret inquiries; be engaged in espionage.

**밀통**(密通) ① 《간통》 an illicit intercourse; adultery. ～하다 commit adultery 《with》. ② ＝내통(內通). ◉ ～자 an adulterer (남자); an adulteress (여자); 《내통자》 a betrayer.

**밀폐**(密閉) ～하다 shut tight(ly); cover 〔close〕 up tight; make 〔keep〕 air=tight; seal up. ¶ ～된 상자 an airtight box / 뚜껑을 덮어 ～하다 cover tightly with the lid / 잼은 ～한 용기에 넣어서 보존하십시오 Please store jam in an airtight container.

**밀항**(密航) a secret passage; stowing away; smuggling *oneself*. ～하다 stow away 《on a steamer》; steal a passage 《to》; sail in secret; smuggle *oneself* 《into, out of》 (★ 입국은 into…, 출국은 out of…를 쓰며, 배나 비행기 속에 숨어서 밀항하는 것을 말한다. stow away는 자동사임). ¶ 일본으로 ～을 꾀하다 attempt to smuggle *oneself* into Japan / 그는 ～해서 국외로 도망치려고 했다 He plotted to stow away to escape from the country. ◉ ～단속법 the Stowaway Control Law: ～ 단속법을 어긴 죄로 검찰에 의해 기소되다 be indicted by prosecution on charge of violating the Stowaway Control Law. ～선 a smuggler. ～자 a stowaway.

**밀행**(密行) going secretly; a prowl. ～하다 prowl 《about》; go secretly 《to》.

**밀회**(密會) a clandestine 〔secret〕 meeting; a tryst; a rendezvous. ～하다 meet 《*a person*》 secretly 〔in secret〕; have a secret meeting 《with》; rendezvous. ◉ ～장소 a secret meeting-place.

**밉광스럽다** (be) very hateful 〔abominable〕.

**밉다** (be) hateful; detestable; abominable; disgusting; loathsome; repulsive; spiteful. ¶ 미운 사람 an odious person; a detestable 〔hateful〕 fellow / 미운 짓 spiteful conduct / 밉게 굴다 behave 〔act〕 detestably 〔abominably〕 / 그 녀석 주는 것 없이 미운 놈이다 I just don't like him. *or* I don't know why, but that man rubs me (up) the wrong way. / 그 애는 지금이 한창 미울 때다 He is in his naughty boyhood. / 죄가 밉지 사람이 미운 것은 아니다 Condemn the offense, but pity the offender.

**밉살맞다** ＝밉살스럽다.

**밉살스럽다** (be) hateful; detestable; disgustings; spiteful; repulsive; insolent. ¶ 밉살스럽게 hatefully; in a hateful manner; with (obvious) hatred / 밉살스러운 말투 an insolent tone / 밉살스러운 얼굴 a repulsive countenance; a hateful look / 밉살스럽게 말하다 use malicious language / 밉살스러운 말을 하다 say spiteful things 《to》; talk spitefully 〔provokingly〕 / 밉살스럽도록 침착하다 remain provokingly calm / 참 밉살스러운 놈이군 What a repulsive 〔an odious〕 wretch he is!

**밉상**(—相) a disgusting 〔repulsive〕 face 〔countenance〕.

**밋밋하다** (be) long and slender; straight and smooth; smooth and flat. ¶ 밋밋이 long and slender; straight and smooth / 밋밋한 얼굴 a flat, expressionless face / 밋밋한 턱 a beardless chin / 밋밋하게 자란 나무 a slender and upright tree.

**밍근하다** (be) lukewarm; tepid.

**밍밍하다** (be) tasteless; flat; weak; thin; watery. ¶ 밍밍한 국 thin soup / 밍밍한 맥주 flat beer / 맥주가 김이 빠져 밍밍해졌다 The beer has become 〔gone〕 flat.

**밍크** 〖동물〗 a mink. ◉ ～모피 mink. ～목도리 a mink stole. ～코트 《wear》 a mink (coat).

**및** and (also); both… and; as well as. ¶ A및 B, (both) A and B; B as well as A / A, B 및 C도 후보자로 받아들여졌다 A, B and C as well have been accepted as candidates.

**밑** ① 《아랫쪽》 the lower part; the bottom; the foot; the base. ¶ 밑에서 다섯째 줄에 in the fifth line from the bottom / 밑에서 받치다 support 《*a thing*》 from below.

밑의: 밑의 under; lower / 바로 밑의 directly 〔just, right〕 under / 책상 오른쪽 밑의 서랍 the lower right drawer of a desk.

밑에: 밑에 under; below; beneath; underneath (바로 밑); down / 눈 밑에 below *one's* eyes (★ under를 쓰면 「눈 앞」의 뜻) / 다리 밑에 under 〔beneath〕 a bridge (★ below를 쓰면 「다리의 하류」라는 뜻) / 나무 밑에 under a tree / 비탈

밑에 at the foot of a slope / 산 밑에 at the foot 〔base〕 of a hill / 계단 밑에 at the bottom of the stairs / 밑에 놓다 put 〔lay, set〕 *a thing* down / 밑의 층에 살고 있다 live downstairs / 스웨터 밑에 받쳐 입다 wear 《a shirt》 under(-neath) *one's* sweater / 나무 밑에 피하다 take shelter under a tree.

밑으로: 밑으로 down(ward) / 밑으로 내려가다 go 〔come〕 down; go 〔come〕 downstairs (아랫층으로) / 밑으로 내려보내다 let 《*a thing*》 down / 밑으로 떨어지다 fall down; fall to the ground (지상에) / 지평선 밑으로 지다 sink 〔go down〕 below the horizon.

밑을: 다리밑을 지나다 pass under a bridge / 밑을 보다 look down; lower *one's* eyes.

¶ 그것은 이 돌 밑에 묻혀 있다 It is buried beneath this stone. / 그가 테이블 밑에서 나왔다 He came out from under the table. / 개는 식탁 밑에 몸을 숨겼다 The dog hid itself under the table. /그들은 낙엽 더미 밑에 묻힌 그녀의 시신을 발견했다 They found her body buried under 〔beneath〕 a pile of dead leaves. / 그는 밑에서 당신을 기다리고 있습니다 He is downstairs waiting for you.

② 《속·바닥》 the bottom 《of a bottle》; the bed 《of a river》. ¶ 바다 밑 the bottom of the sea; the sea bottom / 밑을 떼어내다 knock the bottom 《of a box》 out / 바다 밑에 가라앉다 sink 〔go down〕 to the bottom of the sea / 밑에 닿다 hit the bottom; touch the bottom (발이) / 밑빠진 독에 물붓기 vain 〔wasted〕 efforts; It would be like throwing water on thirsty soil. / 통의 밑이 쑥 빠졌다 The bottom came 〔fell clean〕 out of the cask. *or* The bottom of the cask has come out. / 물이 하도 맑아서 밑바닥까지 보였다 The water was so clear that I could see the bottom.

③ 《계급·지위·나이의》 ¶ 밑의 lower; subordinate; 《이하의》 below; under / 밑에서 두번째 아이 the second youngest of *one's* children / (남의) 밑에 있다 be subordinate to 《*a person*》 / (아무의) 밑에서 일하다 work under 《*a person*》; play second fiddle to 《*a person*》 / 대위는 소령보다 한 계급 밑이다 A captain is one rank below a major. / 그는 나보다 두 살 밑이다 He is two years my junior. *or* He is two years younger than me 〔I am〕. / 그는 밑의 사람에게는 항상 다정했다 He was always friendly 〔kind〕 to his subordinates.

④ 《…을 받고》 (***a***) 《지휘·지시·감독·보호》 under; at. ¶ …밑에 under the command 〔direction, supervision〕 of …; under… / 부모 밑에(서) 《grow up》 under *one's* parental roof / 부모 밑을 떠나다 leave *one's* parental roof; live away from *one's* parents / 나는 수년간 김 교수님 밑에서 공부했다 I studied under Professor Kim for several years. / 그는 B대학에서 양 교수의 지도 밑에 연구를 계속했다 He pursued his studies under Professor Yang at B university. / 용장(勇將) 밑에 약졸은 없다 The follower is only as good as his leader. (***b***) 《행사 등의 후원·협찬》 under. ¶ …의 주최 밑에 under the auspices 〔sponsoring〕 《of》 / 시민 문화제가 시(市)의 후원 밑에 열렸다 The citizens' cultural festival was held under the sponsorship of the city. (***c***) 《영향·조건》 ¶ 그들은 악조건 밑에서 일하고 있었다 They were working under bad conditions. / 1만원 밑으로는 팔 수 없습니다 I can't sell it under 〔for less than〕 10,000 won.

⑤ 《근거·근본》 the root; the basis; the foundation; the origin. ¶ 밑도 끝도 없는 소문 a groundless rumor; an unfounded gossip.

⑥ 《밑둥지·뿌리》 the root; the base. ¶ 나무 밑 the base of a tree / 귀밑까지 빨개지다 blush to the roots of *one's* hair.

⑦ 《음부》 the private parts; the secrets; 《궁둥이》 the buttocks; the hips. ¶ 밑이 질기다 stay too long; outstay 〔overstay〕 *one's* welcome. ¶ 제 밑 들어 남보이기 wash *one's* dirty linen in public.

⑧ 〖수학〗 a base; a radix.

**밑각** (一角) 〖수학〗 a base angle.

**밑감** 《원료》 raw materials.

**밑거름** 〖농업〗 manure given at sowing 〔planting〕 time; initial 〔base〕 manure. ¶ ∼이 되다 [비유적] make a sacrifice of *oneself* 《for》; sacrifice *oneself* 《for》.

**밑구멍** 《밑의 구멍》 a hole at the bottom; 《항문》 the anus; the asshole; 《음부》 the vulva.

**밑그림** a rough sketch; a draft; a design. ¶ 자수의 ∼ a design for embroidery / ∼에 따라 조각하다 carve on a design / ∼을 그리다 make a rough sketch 《of》; make a design 《of》; design; draft.

**밑넓이** 〖수학〗 the bottom dimensions.

**밑돌다** be less 〔lower〕 than; be 〔fall〕 below 《the average》. ¶ (결과가) 예상을 ～ fall short of *one's* expectation(s) / 올해 쌀 수확은 평년작을 밑돌았다 The rice crop of this year is below the average one. / 매상이 예상을 대폭 밑돌았다 The sales are much lower 〔less〕 than expected.

**밑동** the lower part; the root; the base. ¶ 나무 ～ the root 〔lower part〕 of a tree / 기둥 ～ the lower part 〔base〕 of a column / 나무를 ～에서 자르다 cut down a tree (close) at the base; 《톱으로》 saw off a tree at the root.

**밑면**(一面) 〖수학〗 the base.

**밑바닥** ① 《물건의》 the bottom; the base; the bed 《of a river》. ¶ 구두의 ～ the sole of a shoe / 독의 ～ the bottom of a jar / 솥 ～에 검댕이 앉다 soot gathers on the bottom of a pot. ② 《생활·환경 등의》 the (rock) bottom; the nadir 《of *one's* fortune》; 《사회의》 the lowest stratum of society. ¶ 사회 ～의 사람들 people at the bottom of the social scale; the submerged tenth / ～으로부터 출세하다 rise out of the depths. ◉ ～생활 life in the gutter 〔slums〕; a life of bare subsistence: ～ 생활을 하는 사람들 the submerged tenth; the scum of society.

**밑바탕** 《기초》 groundwork; a foundation; a grounding; 《성격·본성》 *one's* real 〔original〕 nature; *one's* true character 〔colors〕. ¶ 학설의 ～을 이루는 이론 a doctrine underlying a theory / ～이 좋지 못하다 be bad 〔wicked〕 by nature / ～이 되어 있다 have a good grounding 《in》; be well grounded 《in》 / ～이 드러나다 reveal *one's* true character; show 〔come out〕 *one's* true colors.

**밑받침** ① 《밑에 까는》 an underlay; a desk pad (책상 위의); a celluloid board (노트의); a clipboard. ② 《버팀》 an under support; a stay 〔support〕 at the base. ¶ 기둥의 ～ a stay at the base of a pillar / 담의 ～ a support at the base of a wall.

**밑밥** 《낚시의》 a ground bait.

**밑변**(一邊) 〖수학〗 the base.

**밑불** starter fire; live charcoal to make a fire.

**밑술** crude liquor; raw spirits.

**밑씨** 〖식물〗 an ovule.

**밑씻개** toilet paper 〔tissue〕.

**밑알** a nest egg.

**밑조사**(一調査) 《예비 조사》 a preliminary investigation; spadework.

**밑줄** an underline. ¶ …에 ～을 치다〔긋다〕 underline 〔underscore〕 (a word) / ～을 친 부분 an underlined 〔underscored〕 part.

**밑줄기** the lower part of a stem 〔stalk〕.

**밑지다** lose (money) 《over》; suffer 〔incur〕 a loss. ¶ 밑지는 장사 a losing 〔an unprofitable〕 business / 장사해서 ～ lose by *one's* business / 밑지고 팔다 sell 《*a thing*》 below cost 〔at a loss〕; sell 《articles》 at the sacrifice of *one's* own interest / 밑져야 본전이다 be none the worse for the loss / 그렇게 하면 크게 밑진다 It involves a big loss. / 그는 절대로 밑지는 일은 하지 않는 사내다 He never acts against his own interests. / 「그 거래에서는 이익을 좀 보셨습니까」—「천만에요, 10만 원이나 밑졌는 걸요」 "Did you make a profit out of that transaction ?"—"No way. I lost 〔suffered a loss of 〕 100,000 won over it."

**밑질기다** stay (too) long; overstay *one's* time. ¶ 밑질긴 사람 a sticker / 밑(이) 질겨 환영을 못 받다 outstay 〔wear out〕 *one's* welcome.

**밑창** the bottom piece; the outsole 《of a shoe》.

**밑천** ① 《자본》 capital; fund; 《원금》 the principal. ¶ ～을 들이다 lay out money 《on》; put 〔sink〕 money 《in》; invest capital 《on》 / ～을 뽑다 earn as much at the capital invested; recover *one's* investment; get *one's* money's worth / ～을 잘리다 be unable to cover the cost / ～이 빠지지 않다 fail to return the original investment / 장사 ～을 대다 provide 《*a person*》 with capital / 장사 ～을 들어먹다 eat up all the funds *one* has / 장사를 하려 해도 ～이 없다 I have nothing to start business with. / ～이 없으면 장사도 못한다 One can make nothing out of nothing. ② [비유적] *one's* original investment in words. ¶ 그에게 한 마디 했다가 ～도 못찾았다 He cut me (down) with a sharp rejoinder. ③ 《성기》 *one's* penis; *one's* equipment.

**밑층**(一層) the bottom layer; 《건물의》 the down floor(s); the downstairs; the ground floor (일층).

**밑판**(一板) the bottom board plate.

**밑화장**(一化粧) a makeup base; a foundation.

# ㅂ

**-ㅂ니까** Is 《he, she, it》 ...?; Are 《you, they》 ...?; Do 《you》 ...?; What is [are] ...? ¶ 비쌉니까 Is it expensive? / 그가 갑니까 Is he going? / 그들은 놉니까 Are they playing? / '무궁화'를 영어로 뭐라고 합니까 What is the English for '*mugunghwa*'?

**-ㅂ니다** be; do. ¶ 저는 교사입니다 I am a teacher. / 바람이 불고 있습니다 The wind is blowing. / 나는 내 핸디캡을 극복하기 위해 최선을 다합니다 I do my best to overcome my handicap.

**-ㅂ디까** have it been observed that ...?; be it known that...?; did you hear [have you been told] that...?; did you notice that...?; have you found that...? ¶ 그 시계가 잘 간다고 합디까 Did they say that the watch runs OK? / 그가 당신에게 무엇이라 합디까 What did he say to you?

**-ㅂ디다** they say (that)...; it is known [said] that...; as I [we all] know...; I hear [am told] that...; I noticed [understand] that...; I've found out that.... ¶ 그렇다고 합디다 So I understand. *or* It is said to be so. / 당신 시계는 수리하는 데 한 이틀 걸린다고 합디다 They said your watch would take about two days to repair.

**-ㅂ시다** let's. ¶ 갑시다 Let's go. / 놉시다 Let's play. / 그 문제는 한 잔 하면서 이야기합시다 Let's discuss the matter over a drink.

**바**[1] 〚음악〛 fa; F. ¶ 올림 바조 F sharp (기호 F#) / 내림 바조 F flat (기호 F♭) / 바 장조 F major / 바 단조 F minor.

**바**[2] 《밧줄》 a rope; a hawser (배 매는); a tether (마소용의); 《끈》 a cord; a string; a line. ¶ 바를 치다 stretch a rope.

**바**[3] ① 《방법》 a way; means; 《범위》 an extent; 《일》 a thing; that...; what. ¶ 할 바를 모르다 don't know [be at a loss] what to do / 위에 말한 바와 같이 as stated [mentioned] above / 내가 아는 바로는 as [so] far as I know; to the best of my knowledge / 그것은 네가 알 바 아니다 It is no concern of yours. *or* It's none of your business. / 그것은 바로 네가 바라던 바 아니냐 Isn't that just what you have wished for? / 그것은 내가 예상했던 바다 It is what I expected. ② 《…하였는데》 ¶ 우리 몇 사람이 그 회를 주최하였던 바 의외의 대성황을 이뤘다 A few of us sponsored the society and it has prospered beyond our expectations.

**바**[4] 《술집》 a bar(room); a bar parlor; 《미》 a saloon; 《영구어》 a pub; 《영》 a public house. ◉ ~걸 a bar hostess; 《미》 a bar girl. ~텐더 《미》 a bartender; 《영》 a barman; 《미》 a barkeep(er) (★ 바의 주인이라는 뜻도 있음).

**바**[5] ① 《가로대·쇠막대기》 a bar. ② 〚기상〛 a bar. ⇨ 밀리바.

**바가지** ① 《그릇》 a gourd (dipper); a calabash. ¶ ~로 물을 푸다 dip water with a gourd dipper. ② 《요금의》 overcharging; an exorbitant [unreasonable] price; a rip-off 《구어》. ⇨ 바가지쓰다, 바가지씌우다. ¶ 「주스 캔 한 개에 3달러라고요」—「~로군요」 "Three dollars for a can of juice?"—"What a rip-off!" ③ 《아옹거림》 nagging; snarling. ¶ ~를 긁다 nag [yap] 《at husband》; keep after 《husband》 / ~ 긁는 아내[여자] a nagging wife [woman]. ◉ ~요금 overcharging prices.

**바가지쓰다** be overcharged 《for》; be charged high; be made to pay through the nose; pay exorbitantly. ¶ 엄청나게 바가지 썼다 They rushed me shockingly. / 택시 운전사에게 바가지 쓰지 않도록 조심하게 Be careful not to be ripped off by the taxi driver.

**바가지씌우다** overcharge 《a foreigner》; make undue [indecent] profits; ask [charge] exorbitant [unreasonable] prices. ¶ 바가지 씌우는 업소 a clip joint / 좀 바가지 씌우는 것 같군요 I'm afraid you've charged me a bit too much.

**바각** with a scrape. ~거리다 《…이》 scrape and scrape; scratch and scratch; make a scraping noise; 《…을》 scrape 《against》; scratch 《at》.

**바겐** 《특매품》 a bargain; 《특매》 a sale.

◉ ～세일 a bargain sale.

**바곳**[1] 《송곳》 a drill 〔an awl, a gimlet〕 with a metal side-handle.

**바곳**[2] 〖식물〗 a monkshood (plant); a wolfsbane; an aconite.

**바구니** a wicker 〔bamboo〕 basket. ¶ 장～ a shopping basket.

**바구미** 〖곤충〗 a rice 〔black〕 weevil.

**바그너** 《독일의 작곡가》 Wilhelm Richard Wagner (1813-83). ¶～풍〔작〕의 Wagnerian.

**바그다드** 《이라크의 수도》 Bag(h)dad.

**바그르르** ① 《물이》 simmeringly; at a rolling boil. ～하다 simmer. ¶ 물이 ～ 끓다 water simmers. ② 《거품이》 bubbling; foaming; frothing. ～하다 bubble up; foam; froth. ¶ 비누 거품이 ～ 일어나다 suds bubble up.

**바글거리다** ① 《끓다》 seethe; boil (over, up); 《거품이》 bubble up; rise in bubbles. ② 《북적거리다》 bustle; be crowded 〔thronged〕 《with people》; 《벌레가》 squirm 〔wriggle about〕 in swarm. ¶ 설탕 주위에 개미가 바글거린다 A swarm of ants surrounded the sugar. ③ 《마음이》 become irritated 〔nervous〕; fret (and fume).

**바깥** ① 《바깥쪽·외부》 the outside; the exterior. ¶～의 outer; outside; outward; exterior; external / ～으로 outwards / ～으로부터의 영향 exterior influences / ～에서 문을 잠그다 lock the door from the outside / 자기의 의견을 말할 때에는 감정을 ～에 나타내지 않도록 해야 한다 You should try not to show your emotions when you express your opinion. ② 《옥외》 the outdoors; out-of-door; the open (air). ¶～의 out-door / 창～을 보다 《창에서》 look out of 〔《미》 look out〕 the window; 《창 너머로》 look out through the window / ～에서 놀다 play outside 〔outdoors, in the open〕 / ～에 나가다 go out (of doors) / ～에 나가지 않다 keep 〔stay〕 indoors; stay in / ～에서 식사하다 eat 〔dine〕 out / ～은 매우 춥다 It is very cold outside. / 그는 좀처럼 ～ 출입을 하지 않는다 He seldom goes out. *or* He is a real stay-at-home. / 집에만 있기 때문에 ～ 일은 모른다 I always stay at home, so I don't know what happens in the streets. ③ 《남성》 male; *one's* husband.

◉ ～공기 the (outside) air: ～ 공기를 쐬다 get out in the air. ～뜰 the outer garden 〔yard〕. ～문 《앞면에》 the front door; 《대문》 the outer 〔outside〕 gate. ～방 a room in the outer wing of a house. ～부모 *one's* male parent; *one's* father. ～사돈 the father of *one's* son-in-law 〔daughter-in-law〕. ～소문 rumors circulating in society; gossip; what is being voiced abroad; the talk of the town. ～소식 news (in general circulation); information; the news of the day: ～ 소식에 어둡다 be unfamiliar with what is going on in the outside world; be in the dark when it comes to world events. ～식구 male members of a family. ～심부름 an errand: ～ 심부름하다 run 〔go out on〕 an errand / ～ 심부름 보내다 send out on an errand. ～양반〔어른〕 the master (of the house); the husband. ～일 outdoor work. ～쪽 the outside; the outer side; the exterior. ～채 an outhouse; an out-building; an annex; a side building.

**바꾸다** ① 《변경하다》 change; alter (★ 보통 change는 「전면적으로 바꾸다」, alter는 「부분적으로 손질하다」라는 뜻); shift; convert; vary; reverse 《positions》; 〖음악〗 《높이·음성을》 modulate. ¶ 역사의 흐름을 바꾼 사건 events that changed the course of history / 생각〔직업, 복장, 화제〕을 ～ change *one's* mind 〔job, clothes, subject〕 / 계획을 ～ vary *one's* plans / 방향을 ～ turn 《in another direction》; change *one's* course / 방침을 ～ alter *one's* policy / 테이블의 위치를 ～ move a table; alter 〔change〕 the position of the table / 습관을 좀처럼 바꾸지 않다 be conservative in *one's* habits / 또 일자리를 바꿨느냐 Did you change jobs again? / 너의 스케줄을 좀 바꿀 수 없겠느냐 Can't you change your schedule somehow?
② 《고치다》 reform 《a system》; revise 《a law》; remold 《a rule》; amend 《a regulation》; restyle 《a policy》.
③ 《교환하다》 exchange; barter 《one thing for another》; 《전환하다》 change; turn; convert 《one thing into another》; 《변형·변질하다》 change 《the shape of》; transform 《a barn into a garage》; transmute. ¶ 돈을 ～ change money / 달러를 원화로 ～ change dollars into won / 현금으로 ～ convert 《*one's* clothes》 into cash / 수표를 현금으로 ～ cash a check / 시계를 돈으로 ～ swap a watch for money / 만원 지폐를 천원짜리로 ～ change 〔break〕 a 10,000-won note into 1,000-won notes / 물건과 물건을

~ trade 〔barter, swap〕 one thing for another / 자리를 ~ change seats 《with another》/ 생명은 돈과 바꿀 수 없다 Life cannot be bartered for gold. / 건강은 무엇과도 바꿀 수 없다 Nothing can take the place of health. *or* Nothing is more precious than health.
④《갱신하다》 renew; 《대체하다》 replace 《A with B》; put 《A》 in place of 《B》; substitute 《A》 for 《B》. ¶ 헌 매트 커버를 새것으로 ~ replace the covers of old mats with new ones / 물탱크 속의 물을 ~ renew water in a tank / 헌 타이어를 새것으로 ~ replace the old worn tire with a new one / 무엇인가 딴 물건으로 바꿀 수 없습니까 Could I have 〔take〕 something else instead?
⑤《피륙을 사다》 buy 〈cloth〉. ¶ 비단 다섯 자를 ~ purchase five *cha* of silk.
⑥《전화에서》 ¶ …씨 좀 바꿔 주십시오 May I speak to…? *or* I'd like to speak 〔talk〕 to…. *or* Get me… please.

**바꿈질** ①《물물·의견 따위》 act of exchanging; exchange; barter; swap(-ping); ~하다 〈make an〉 exchange; swap 《watches》 with 《*a person*》; swap 《A》 for 《B》. ②《갊》 act of changing; change; switch; replacement. ~하다 switch; replace.

**바꿔** ¶ ~ 말하다 say in other words; put 《it》 〈in〉 another way / ~ 말하면 in other words; that is to say; namely / 옷을 ~ 입다 change clothes / 입장을 ~ 생각하다 put *oneself* in 《*a person's*》 place 〔shoes〕 / 〈손에 든 것을〉 ~ 들다 pass 《*a thing*》 from one hand to another.

**바꿔치다** substitute 《one thing for another》 〈fraudulently〉; change 《one thing for another》 〈secretly〉. ¶ 지폐를 위조 지폐와 ~ substitute forged notes for genuine ones.

**바뀌다** change; be 〔get〕 changed; undergo a change; alter; be altered; shift; turn; vary 〈여러 가지로〉; 《수정되다》 be amended 〔revised〕; 《…로 변형되다》 change 〔turn〕 《into》; be turned 〔transformed〕 《into》.
¶ 바뀌지 않다 be 〔remain〕 unchanged; be the same 〈as before〉 / 바뀐 아이 a changeling; an elf child / 이야기가 ~ pass 〈on〉 to another subject / 주소가 ~ have *one's* address changed / 해가 ~ the 〈old〉 year goes out; the 〈new〉 year comes in; the year changes / 그녀는 쉬이 마음이 바뀐다 She easily changes her mind. *or* she is fickle. / 눈물이 흐느낌으로 바뀌었다 The tears turned into sobs. / 내 서류 가방이 바뀌었다 I had my briefcase changed. /그 땅은 소유주가 여러 번 바뀌었다 The land has changed owners many times. / 점심 메뉴는 매일 바뀐다 The lunch menu varies from day to day. / 그녀의 기분은 절망에서 희망으로 바뀌었다 Her mood passed from despair to hope. / 미움이 애정으로 바뀌었다 Hatred gave way to love.

**바나나** a banana. ¶ ~ 껍질을 벗기다 peel 〈off the skin of〉 a banana. ◉ ~송이 a bunch of bananas.

**바나듐** 〖화학〗 vanadium 〈기호 V〉.

**바느질** needlework; sewing. ~하다 do needlework; sew. ¶ ~을 잘 하다〔~이 서툴다〕 be good 〔poor〕 at needlework; be clever 〔awkward〕 with the needle / ~로 생계를 꾸리다 earn *one's* living by needlework / ~솜씨가 곱다 〔거칠다〕 *one's* needlework is fine 〔coarse〕. ◉ ~거리 sewing; a dress to be made. ~삯 sewing charges. ~상자 a sewing kit; a needlework box. ~손 needlework. ~자 a measure for sewing. ~품 needlework 〈as labor〉.

**바늘** ①《바느질용》 a needle; 《핀》 a pin; 《한 바늘》 a stitch. ¶ ~로 찌르는 듯한 아픔 a stinging pain / ~로 찌르다 prick with a needle / ~에 실을 꿰다 thread a needle / ~에 손가락을 찔리다 prick 《*one's* finger》 with a needle / ~을 꽂다 stick 〔drive〕 a pin / 상처를 여섯 ~ 꿰매다 put six stitches in the wound 〔on *one's* gash〕 / ~ 가는 데 실 간다 《속담》 be indispensable adjuncts 《of》; always go with / ~ 도둑이 소도둑 된다 《속담》 He who steals a pin will steal an ox. / 그는 ~만한 일을 홍두깨만큼 늘여서 말한다 He makes a mountain out of a molehill.
②《시계의》 a hand; 《계기의》 a pointer; 《낚시의》 a hook; 《레코드용의》 a needle; a stylus; 《주사기의》 a needle. ¶ 이 시계에는 ~이 세 개 있다 This clock has three hands.
◉ ~겨레 a needle pad; a pincushion. ~구멍 a hole made by a needle. ~귀 the eye of a needle; a needle eye. ~밥 thread remnants. ~방석 (1) = 바늘겨레. (2) [비유적] a bed of nails: ~방석에 앉은 것 같다 I feel as if I had sat 〔stood〕 on tacks 〔thorns〕. ~쌈 a packet of needles.

**바다** ① the sea; an ocean 〈대양〉. ¶ ~

건너 beyond 〔across〕 the sea / 거울 같은 ~ a sea smooth as a mirror / 고요한 ~ a calm 〔placid〕 sea / 끝없는 ~ a boundless (expanse of the) sea / 푸른 ~ blue expanse of water; blue water / ~ 생활 life on the sea; seafaring life; marine life / ~가 없는 나라 a landlocked country / ~를 건너다 cross the sea / ~에 나가다 《배가》 go 〔sail〕 out to sea; put 〔set〕 out to sea / ~에 던지다 throw 《*a thing*》 into the sea; throw 《goods》 overboard (배에서); jettison (해난 때) / ~에〔로〕 떨어지다 fall into the sea; 《배에서》 fall overboard / ~에 뛰어들다 jump 〔plunge〕 into the sea; fall overboard (배에서) / ~에 면하다 face 〔front〕 the sea / ~에 몸을 던지다 drown *oneself* in the sea; throw *oneself* overboard (배에서) / (배가) ~를 항행하다 sail on the sea / ~ 위를 날다 fly over the sea / ~가 거칠어질 것 같다 There is going to be a heavy 〔rough〕 sea. / 한국은 삼면이 ~로 둘러싸인 나라다 Korea is a country surrounded by the sea 「on three sides 〔on all sides but one〕. ② [비유적] a wide expanse. ¶ 불~ a sea of flames / 피~ a pool of blood / 주변 일대는 불~가 되었다 The fire blazed on all sides. *or* The whole area was in flames.

◉ ~낚시 sea fishing. ~내음〔냄새〕 the tang of sea air. ~밑 the bottom 〔floor, bed〕 of the sea; the seabed. 바닷가 the seashore; the beach: 바닷가를 거닐다 ramble 〔stroll〕 about the beach. 바닷길 a sea route. 바닷말 seaweeds. 바닷물 seawater; the salt sea. 바닷바람 a sea wind; a sea breeze: 바닷바람을 쐬다 enjoy the 《cool》 breeze that comes from the sea. 바닷새 a seabird; marine birds.

**바다거북** 〖동물〗 a large (sea) turtle.

**바다뱀** 〖동물〗 a sea snake 〔serpent〕.
◉ ~자리 〖천문〗 the Water Snake; Hydra.

**바다비오리** 〖조류〗 a red-breasted merganser.

**바다사자**(―獅子) 〖동물〗 a Steller's sea lion.

**바다오리** 〖조류〗 a (common) murre; a guillemot.

**바다제비** 〖조류〗 a (stormy) petrel.

**바다짐승** a marine 〔sea〕 animal.

**바다표범** 〖동물〗 a seal; an earless seal.

**바닥** ① 《평면》 the floor; the ground; the flat. ¶ 방 ~ floor (of a room) / 손 ~ palm (of a hand) / 평평한 ~ the flat (of the ground) / 마룻~에 on the floor / 땅~에 눕다 lie on the ground 〔earth〕. ② 《밑부분》 the bottom; the bed 《of a river·lake》; the sole 《of a shoe》. ¶ 이중 ~의 double-bottomed / (물속) ~에 닿다 touch bottom (발이); find bottom (닻이) / ~에 이르다 reach the bottom / (저수지 등이) ~을 드러내기 시작하다 begin to bare its bottom / 이 찻잔은 ~에 금이 갔다 There is a crack in the bottom of this teacup. ③ 《고갈》 the end of *one's* resources; exhaustion; drain. ⇨ 바닥나다. ④ 《시세》 ⇨ 바닥(시)세. ⑤ 《짜임새》 weave; texture. ¶ ~이 고운〔거친〕 fine 〔coarse〕 in texture. ⑥ 《번잡한 곳》 a congested 〔built-up〕 area. ¶ 서울 ~ the Seoul area / 장~ the market area; a marketplace.

◉ ~(시)세 the (rock-)bottom price; the bedrock price: ~시세에 이르다 reach 〔strike〕 (the) bottom. ~짐 ballast: ~짐을 싣다 ballast a ship; take on ballast.

**바닥나다** be drained 〔exhausted, used up, consumed〕; run 〔be, give〕 out of stock; be all gone; be sold out. ¶ 그 물건은 바닥났다 The stock is exhausted. / 식량이 바닥나고 있다 We are running out of food supplies 〔provisions〕. / 그들의 선거 자금은 마침내 바닥났다 They finally ran out of electoral funds.

**바닥내다** allow 《*a thing*》 to run out; run out of. ¶ 식량을 ~ let provisions out of stock.

**바닥보다** 《밑천이》 run out of capital 〔fund〕; 《실패하다》 fail.

**바닷가재** 〖동물〗 a lobster.

**바닷개** 〖동물〗 a fur seal. ⇨ 물개.

**바닷게** 〖동물〗 a sea crab.

**바닷물고기** a sea fish; a saltwater fish.

**바닷새** a seabird; a seafowl.

**바대** a reinforcement strip sewed inside a jacket 〔an undershirt〕.

**바동-** ⇨ 버둥-.

**바둑** *paduk; go.* ¶ ~(을) 두다 play 〔have a game of〕 *paduk*.

◉ ~돌 a *paduk* 〔*go*〕 stone. ~무늬 a figure 〔design〕 with black and white spots; a speckled design. ~판 a *paduk* 〔*go*〕 board: ~판 무늬 check; checkers.

**바둑말** 〖동물〗 a dappled horse; a piebald.

**바둑이** a black and white dog; a dog spotted with black and white; 《개이름》 "Spot(ty)".

**바드득** creakily; gratingly; raspingly. ～거리다〔대다〕 creak; grate; rasp; squeak. ¶ 이를 ～갈다 grate *one's* teeth.

**바득바득** ⇨부득부득.

**바들바들** ⇨부들부들.

**바디** a reed; a yarn guide.

**바디탑 컴퓨터** 《음성 인식 컴퓨터》 a bodytop computer.

**바라**(哱囉) ① 《자바라》 small cymbals. ② 《소라》 a small gong.

**바라다** ① 《소원하다》 desire; wish; hope; 《원하다》 want; crave 〔wish〕 for; aspire to 〔after〕; 《관심을 가지다》 care for (★ 주로 의문·부정형에 쓰임).

> 용법 **desire**는 격식차린 말투로 주어의 의지·의도를, **wish**는 desire보다 소원하는 강도가 좀 약하고, hope에 비해 실현성이 좀 약한 소원을 뜻함. **hope**는 실현 가능한 것을 기대한다는 뜻일 때 흔히 쓰임. **want** 필요·결핍 등으로 「원한다」는 뜻. **aspire after** 〔**to**〕 강하게 「열망하다」는 뜻.

¶ 행복과 건강을 ～ desire 〔wish for〕 happiness and health / 세계 평화를 ～ wish for world peace / 유명해지기를 ～ aspire after 〔to〕 fame; crave 〔hanker〕 for fame / 성공을 ～ wish for 〔hope for, desire〕 *one's* success / 바라건대 It is to be desired 〔hoped〕 that...; I hope that.... / 부귀도 명예도 바라지 않는다 I don't care for wealth or fame. / 그것은 바라던 바다 That is just what I wished for. / 내일까지 마쳐 주기 바라네 I want 〔wish〕 you to finish it by tomorrow. / 그녀는 다시 한 번 고향의 산과 개울을 보기를 바라고 있다 She wishes to see the mountains and streams of her birthplace again. ② 《기대·예기하다》 expect; hope 《that..., for *something*》; look for; look forward to; anticipate; count on; reckon on. ¶ …을 바라고 《희망하여》 hoping 《that...》; in the hope 《of *do*ing, that...》; 《기대하며》 in anticipation of ... / 요행을 ～ hope against hope; rely on chance / 용서를 ～ hope for *one's* pardon / 당신의 조력을 바랄 수 있을까요 Can we reckon on your help? / 모든 일이 잘 되기를 바란다 I hope everything will come out all right. / 그에게 크게 바랄 것은 없다 You cannot expect much 〔great things〕 of him. / 우리는 보다 나은 생활을 바라고 있다 We all hope for a better life. / 나는 너의 도움을 바라고 있었다 I have expected you to help me. *or* I have been looking forward to your assistance. ③ 《간원·부탁하다》 beg; request; entreat; hope; implore; desire. ¶ 은혜를 베풀어 주기를 ～ ask a favor 《of *a person*》 / 내 작문을 보아주기 바란다 I wish you would look over my composition. / 진열품에 손대지 마시기를 바랍니다 Visitors are requested not to touch the exhibits. / 그들은 정부의 보조를 바랐다 They asked for government aid. / 재고하여 주시기를 바랍니다 I would appreciate it if you would think about it again. ④ 《선택하다》 prefer; choose; 《좋아하다》 like. ¶ 부귀보다 행복을 바란다 I prefer happiness to wealth. / 노예가 되느니 차라리 죽음을 바란다 I'd choose death rather than slavery. / 무엇이든 바라는 것은 주겠다 You shall have anything you like. / 그녀는 스스로가 바라서 그와 결혼했다 She married him of her own choice.

**바라문**(婆羅門) a Brahman; Brahmanism. ◉ ～교 Brahmanism.

**바라밀다**(婆羅蜜多) 〖불교〗 Paramita; entrance into Nirvana.

**바라보다** ① 《건너다보다》 see; look at; watch; 《응시하다》 gaze at 〔on, into〕; stare at; 《관망하다》 view; take a view 《of》; 《방관하다》 look on. ¶ (우두커니) 구름을 ～ gaze vacantly at the clouds / (우두커니) 창 밖을 ～ look out the window (absent-mindedly) / 뚫어지게 ～ look hard 《at》; gaze intently 《at》; goggle 《at》 / 달을 ～ gaze 〔look〕 at the moon / 남의 얼굴을 ～ look into another's face; gaze on another's face / 망원경으로 지평선을 ～ sweep 〔scan, rake〕 the horizon with a telescope / 나는 군중이 지나가는 것을 바라보고 있었다 I was watching the crowd pass. ② 《나이가》 be close 〔hard〕 upon; be getting on for 〔to〕. ¶ 나이 50을 ～ be getting on for fifty. ③ 《기대하다》 expect; hope 〔look〕 for; count on 〔upon〕. ¶ 미래를 ～ look forward to the future / 그는 성공을 바라보고 최선을 다했다 He did his best to succeed.

**바라보이다** be looked over; command; overlook; 《눈에 들어오다》 come in sight; come into view. ¶ 멀리 삼각산이 ～ command a distant view of Mt. *Samkag* / 집은 바다가 바라보이는 언덕 위에 있다 The house stands on a hill overlooking the sea. / 호텔에서 호수가 잘 바라보인다 The hotel has a good command 〔view〕 of the lake.

**바라지** attentive care; looking after; provision; supply; assistance. ～하다 take care 〔charge〕 of; attend to; care for; provide 〔supply, furnish〕《*a person* with》; look to the needs 《of》. ¶ 자식 ～ provision for *one's* son; care for *one's* child / 옷 ～하다 provide 《*a person*》 with clothes.

**바라지다**[1] ①《몸이》 (be) short and fat; thickset; stumpy; have a stocky build. ¶ 바라진 사람 a stocky man. ② 《그릇이》 (be) shallow. ¶ 바라진 접시 a shallow dish. ③ ＝되바라지다.

**바라지다**[2] 《벌어지다》 widen; open (out); be wide open; 《갈라지다》 split off; be separated.

**바라크** 〔<barracks 《영》〕 a temporary shelter; a hut; a shack. ¶ ～를 짓다 build 〔put up〕 a shack.

**바락** ⇨버럭.

**바락바락** desperately; frantically. ¶ ～ 기를 쓰다 make desperate efforts; struggle 〔strive〕 frantically / 그는 무엇에 화가 났는지 갑자기 나에게 ～ 대들었다 Suddenly he lost all his mind, and flashed out at me for no reason.

**바람**[1] ①《공기의 흐름》 a wind; a current of air; a breeze (미풍); a gale (질풍); storm (폭풍); a current (선풍기 등의). ¶ ～이 부는 windy / ～이 없는 windless / 일진의 ～ a gust 〔blast〕 of wind / 맞 ～ a contrary 〔head, adverse〕 wind / 변덕스러운 ～ a choppy 〔fickle〕 wind / 살을 에는 듯한 ～ a biting 〔cutting, nipping〕 wind / 세게 부는 ～ a rattling wind / 휙 부는 ～ a puff of wind; a piping 〔whistling〕 wind / 회오리 ～ a whirlwind / ～의 방향이 바뀌다 shift; veer /세찬 ～ 속을 걷다 walk in a high wind.

바람이: ～이 불다 the wind blows; it is windy / ～이 그치다 the wind stops blowing; blow itself out / ～이 일다 the wind is getting up / ～이 자다 the wind goes down 〔falls〕 / ～이 들어오지 않도록 하다 prevent the admission of wind; keep out 《cold》 air.

바람에: ～에 물결치는 풀 the grass waving in the wind / 머리를 ～에 나부끼며 with hair flying behind *one* / ～에 나부끼다〔펄럭이다〕 flutter 〔flap, flow, flicker〕 in the wind.

바람을: (돛이) ～을 잔뜩 받고 (under 〔in〕) full sail / ～을 들이다 let 〔admit〕 fresh air 《into》; ventilate; air 《a room》 / ～을 등지고 가다 go before 〔with〕 the wind; go with the wind to *one's* back / ～을 안고 가다 walk in 〔against〕 the wind / ～을 아랑곳하지 않고 《sail》 in the teeth of the wind / ～을 쐬다 expose 《*a thing*》 to the air; air 《clothes》; 《사람이》 expose *oneself* to the wind; ventilate *oneself* in the breeze / 선풍기 ～을 쐬다 sit in the current of an electric fan / 저녁 ～을 쐬다 enjoy the cool of the evening / ～을 타고〔에 날려〕오다 come (floating) on the wind; be blown in.

¶ ～이 윙윙거린다 The wind howls 〔soughs〕. / ～의 방향이 남으로 바뀌었다 The wind has「shifted 〔veered, changed〕 to the south. / 오늘은 ～이 한 점도 없다 There is not a「breath 〔stir〕 of air today. / ～에 모자가 날렸다 I had my hat blown off. / 나뭇가지가 ～에 흔들리고 있다 The branches are swaying about in the wind. / ～이 불어 등불이 꺼졌다 The wind blew out the light.

②《외풍》 a draft; a draught 《영》; air (외기). ¶ ～을 막다 cut off the drafts / ～이 들어온다 I feel a draft. *or* It's airy here. / ～이 문 새로 들어온다 Drafts come in through the chinks in the door.

③《공기》 air. ¶ ～이 빠진 타이어 a flat 〔deflated〕 tire / ～을 넣다 fill with air; pump up 《a tire》.

④《들뜬 마음》 fickleness; unfaithfulness; inconstancy; caprice; capriciousness. ⇨바람나다. ¶ ～난 fickle; unfaithful; inconstant; wanton / ～난 여자 a wanton 〔an easy〕 woman; a woman of loose morals / ～ 피우다 play with love; lead a fast 〔dissolute〕 life; play the wanton; have an affair with 《*a person*》 / 그는 결코 ～을 피우지 않는다 He is entirely faithful to his wife. / 그녀는 남편이 ～ 피우는 것을 알고 있었다 She was aware of her husband's unfaithfulness.

⑤《중풍》 palsy; paralysis (*pl.* -ses). ⇨바람맞다 ①.

⑥《허풍》 bragging; a big 〔tall〕 talk; a whopping lie. ¶ ～이 센 친구 a braggart; a boaster.

⑦ [비유적] ¶ 무슨 ～이 불었는지 somehow or other; for some reason or other; I don't know why but... / 정계에 새 ～을 불어넣다 breath 〔blow〕「a fresh breeze 〔new life〕 into the political situation / 무슨 ～이 불어 여길 찾아왔나 How does it happen that you're here? / 무슨 ～이 불었는지 그는 나에게 편지를 보내왔다 I wonder what put the idea of writing to me into his head.

◉ ～구멍 an air hole; a vent; a wind hole; an air shaft. ～기 the force 〔feel〕 of the wind; 《들뜬 마음》 inconstancy; fickleness; wantonness. ～둥이 (1) 《허풍선이》 a windbag; a gasbag; a braggart; someone full of hot air. (2) 《바람 피우는》 a flirt; 《남자》 a playboy; a philanderer; 《여자》 a fickle woman; a coquette.. ～막이 a windscreen; a windbreak; a shelter from the wind. ～세 wind force 〔velocity〕. ～잡이 = 바람둥이(1).

**바람**[2] 《길이》 the length of an arm-span (=about two yards). ¶ 새끼 한 ～ two yards of rope.

**바람**[3] ① 《계제·사품》 (in) conjunction 《with》; (in the) process 《of》; (as a) consequence 《of》; (as a) result 《of》; an impetus; a momentum; influence; a motive. ¶ 일어나는 ～에 in (the act of) rising / 떠드는 ～에 as a result 〔consequence〕 of confusion / 자동차를 피하려는 ～에 발목을 삐었다 I sprained my ankle (in the process of) trying to dodge a car. / 취한 ～에 그는 상관과 다투었다 Under the influence of alcohol, he argued with his boss. ② 《차림》 the state of not being properly dressed; with(out) *one's* ... on. ¶ 셔츠 ～으로 in shirt sleeves; without *one's* coat on.

**바람**[4] 《소망》 *one's* dearest wish; *one's* hearts' desire. ¶ 오랜 세월의 ～ *something* that *one* has wanted 〔wished〕 to do for a long time; *one's* long=cherished desire / 내집 마련은 우리의 오랜 ～이었다 Owning a home of our own was a dream for years.

**바람개비** ① 《풍향계》 a (weather) vane; a weathercock. ¶ ～가 바람에 돈다 The vane is turning with the wind. ② 《팔랑개비》 a pinwheel. ③ 〖조류〗 = 쏙독새.

**바람결** ① 《바람에 불려》 ¶ ～에 carried on 〔come on, riding, back of〕 the wind / ～에 새 소리가 들린다 The wind brings the chirping of birds. ② 《풍편》 (getting) wind of an affair; rumor; hearsay. ¶ ～에 들으니 I heard say that ...; A little bird told me that...; Rumor has it that...; It has come to my ears that...; The wind brought the news that... / ～에 들으니 두 사람은 머지 않아 결혼한다고 한다 Rumor has it that they're getting married soon. / 그 소식은 ～에 들었다 A little bird told me about it.

**바람꽃** ① 《뽀얀 기운》 a hazy atmosphere around the top of a distant mountain presaging a high wind. ② 〖식물〗 an anemone.

**바람기**(一氣) ① 《바람의 기운》 the force 〔feel〕 of wind. ② 《들뜬 마음》 ⇨ 바람[1] ④. ¶ ～가 있는 사람 a person of 「loose morals 〔easy virtue〕; a wanton woman (여자).

**바람나다** ① 《들뜨다》 lead a loose life; be unfaithful; take to amours; have a secret love affairs. ② 《능률나다》 warm up; get warmed up; get under way; really get started.

**바람들다** ① 《푸성귀가》 get pulpy; get soft inside; get soggy. ¶ 바람든 무 a pulpy radish. ② 《바람나다》 become indiscreet; take up a gay life; take to amours; play with love. ¶ 바람든 여자 a *demimondaine* (F.); a fast woman; high stepper / 바람든 남자 a gay blade 〔dog〕; a man-about=town. ③ 《일·계획이》 be upset; fail; be spoiled; be hindered; go wrong.

**바람맞다** ① 《중풍》 be stricken with paralysis; have a stroke. ⇨ 바람[1] ⑤. ¶ 그는 바람을 맞아 오른쪽 반신을 못 쓴다 He is paralyzed 〔benumbed〕 on his right side with palsy. ② 《속다·허황됨을 당하다》 be deceived 〔cheated〕; be swindled; be rejected 《by a beloved》; get the cold shoulder 《from》. ¶ 여자한테 ～ be spurned 〔scorned〕 by a woman. ③ 《기대에 어그러지다》 be disappointed 《by》; 《헛기다리다》 wait 〔be kept waiting〕 for 《*a person*》 in vain. ④ 《바람들다》 become indiscreet; take up a gay life; lead a loose life.

**바람맞히다** reject 《a suitor》; give the cold shoulder 《to》; give the gate 《to》; 《기다리는 사람을》 keep 《*a person*》 waiting in vain; 《미구어》 stand 《*a person*》 up. ¶ 그는 나를 바람맞혔다 He stood me up. / 나는그를 두 시간이나 기다렸는데 오지 않았다. 결국 바람맞았지 I waited for him for two hours, but he didn't come. In short, I was stood up.

**바람받이** a place exposed to the wind; a wind-swept place. ¶ ～의 wind=swept; bleak; exposed to the wind /

~에 있는 집 a house exposed to the winds.

**바람자다** ① 《바람이》 the wind dies down; the breeze stops blowing. ② 《들뜬 마음이》 calm down; quiet down.

**바람잡다** ① 《들뜨다》 take up a wild 〔fast〕 life; be fickle; commit absurdity; take to amours; 《구어》 burn *one's* candle at both ends. ② 《허황하다》 conceive a wild hope 〔scheme〕; throw straw against the wind; take a shot in the dark.

**바람직하다** (be) desirable; advisable. ¶ 바람직한 일 a desirable thing; a matter to be desired / 바람직하지 않은 인물 an undesirable person / 자네 혼자 거기 가는 것은 바람직하지 않다 It is not advisable for you to go there alone. / 암에 대한 정기 검진을 받는 것은 ~ It is desirable that you should have a periodic checkup for cancer.

**바랑** ① 《배낭》 a knapsack; a rucksack; a packsack 《미》. ② 《중의》 a 《bonze's》 sac. ¶ ~을 지다 carry a sac on *one's* back.

**바래다** ① 《빛깔이》 fade; discolor; get washed out; grow faint. ¶ 색이 바랜 faded; discolored / 바래지 않는 fadeproof; color-fast; standing 《color》 / 색이 바랜 청바지 a pair of faded jeans / 잘 바래는 색 fugitive colors / 바래지 않는 색 fast 〔unfading〕 colors / 커튼이 햇빛에 바랬다 The sun faded the curtains. *or* The curtains were discolored by the sun. ② 《희게하다》 bleach; blanch; wash out (dye). ¶ 무명을 ~ bleach cotton / 빨래를 햇볕에 ~ bleach laundry in the sun.

**바래(다)주다** see 〔take〕 《*a person* to a place》; escort; see 《*a person*》 off; send off. ¶ 집까지 ~ see 《*a person*》 home; 《차로》 take 《*a person*》 home 《in *one's* car》 / 역까지 ~ see 《*a person*》 to 〔as far as〕 the station / 공항까지 바래다주러 가다 go to the airport to see 《*a person*》 off.

**바레인제도**(一諸島) 《페르시아 만의 섬》 Bahrein 〔Bahrain〕 Islands.

**바로**[1] ① 《바르게》 (***a***) 《정당하게》 justly; rightly; properly (합당하게); 《틀림없이》 correctly; 《진실되게》 honestly; truly; truthfully. ¶ ~ 말하면 properly 〔strictly, frankly〕 speaking; to tell the truth / ~ 대답하다 give a correct answer; answer right / ~ 맞히다 hit the nail (right) on the head; 《알아맞히다》 guess right; make a good guess / ~ 발음하다 pronounce correctly. (***b***) 《똑바로》 straight; upright. ¶ ~ 앉다 sit straight 〔upright〕 / ~ 서다 stand straight 〔upright〕 / 책상 위에 ~ 놓다 put 《*a thing*》 right on the desk / 모자를 ~ 써라 Put your hat on straight / 자세를 ~ 하시오 Hold yourself straight.

② 《곧·곧장》 right away; straight away; immediately; directly; at once; with no delay; in a jiffy 《구어》. ¶ 지금 ~ right now; this very moment / ~ 용건으로 들어가다 plunge at once into business / ~ 집으로 돌아가다 go straight home / 그이가 왔다가 ~ 갔다 He was here but left immediately. / 서울에 도착하는 대로 ~ 전화 주시오 Please call me as soon as you arrive in Seoul. / 그는 아침 식사 후 ~ 집을 떠났다 He left the house right after breakfast.

③ 《꼭·정확히》 just; right; exactly; precisely; 《정말로》 really; truly; duly; 《확실히》 surely; certainly; quite; 《불과》 only; but. ¶ ~ 가까이에 close 〔near〕 by; close at hand; quite near 《the house》 / ~ 그때에 just then; just at that moment / ~ 눈앞에서 right in front of *one;* right under *one's* nose / ~ 위에 just 〔right〕 above 〔overhead〕 / ~ 밑에 right 〔just〕 under / ~ 다섯 시에 just 〔exactly〕 at five (o'clock) / ~ 어젯밤에 just 〔only〕 last night / ~ 한복판에 right in the center; in the very center / ~ 한 시 (정각) exactly one o'clock (sharp) / ~ 맞은편 건물 a building just opposite 〔in front〕 / 그는 ~ 이웃에 살고 있다 He lives quite near 〔close〕 by. / ~ 이 근처에서 그를 보았다 I saw him just about here. / 학교 ~ 앞에서 사고가 났다 There was an accident right in front of the school.

④ 《다름아닌》 no doubt; undoubtedly; 《바로 그》 the very.... ¶ 그것을 부순 사람은 ~ 그 학생이다 There is no doubt that he is the student who broke it. / 이것은 내가 잃어버린 ~ 그 반지다 This is the very ring (that) I lost. / 그것은 다름아닌 ~ 부사장이었다 It was no less a person than the vice president.

⑤ 《마치》 as (if); just as (though). ¶ ~ 뭐나 아는 듯이 말한다 You talk as if you knew something. / 너는 ~ 성난 것 같구나 You look as if you were angry!

⑥《구령》 Eyes front!; As you were! ¶「우로 나란히」—「～」 Eyes right!—Eyes front!

**바로**[2] 《곳》 right about this 〔that〕 place. ¶ 이〔그〕 ～에 about 〔around〕 here 〔there〕.

**바로미터** 《청우계》 a barometer; 《추측의 표준》 a barometer; an indicator. ¶ 건축 활동은 상황(商況)의 ～이다 Building activity is a barometer of business conditions.

**바로잡다** ① 《굽은 것을》 straighten; make straight 〔right〕. ¶ 자세를 ～ straighten *oneself* / 굽은 등뼈를 ～ straighten *one's* bent backbone. ② 《잘못된 것을》 correct; redress; reform; rectify; amend; set right; set 〔put, bring〕 to rights. ¶ 바로잡을 수 없는 incorrigible 《habits》; irremediable 《defects》 / 마음을 ～ reform *oneself*; straighten *oneself* out / 행실을 ～ mend *one's* ways; amend *one's* conduct; correct *one's* behavior / 그릇된 생각을 ～ put 《*a person*》 right in *his* ideas; undeceive 《*a person*》 (of *his* misconception); 《구어》 put 〔set〕 《*a person*》 straight / 악폐를 ～ reform abuses; redress evils / 못된 버릇을 ～ get rid of 〔get over〕 a bad habit; break 〔cure〕 *oneself* of a bad habit; 《남의》 break 〔cure〕 《*a person*》 of a bad habit / 난시를 안경으로 ～ correct *one's* astigmatism by glasses.

**바로크** 〖건축〗 baroque. ¶ ～식 건물 a baroque house. ◉ ～건축 baroque architecture. ～양식 the Baroque; the baroque style. ～음악 baroque music.

**바륨** 〖화학〗 barium (기호 Ba). ¶ 위의 X선 검사를 위해 ～을 먹이다 give 《*a person*》 a barium meal before a stomach X-ray.

**바르다**[1] ① 《곧다》 (be) straight; straightforward; 《곧추》 upright; erect. ¶ 바른 자세로 in a correct 〔good〕 posture; in an erect 〔upright〕 posture / 자세를 바르게 하다 straighten *oneself* / 그림이 바르냐 Is the picture straight? / 의자에 바른 자세로 앉으시오 Sit up (straight) in the chair. ② 《옳다》 (***a***) 《정당하다》 (be) right; rightful. ¶ 마음이 바른 right-minded; upright / 바른 행동 right conduct / 바른 결론 a right conclusion / 바른 일을 하다 do the right thing; do (what is) right / 방식이 ～〔바르지 않다〕 go about 《*a thing*》 in the right 〔wrong〕 way / 우리 아버지의 판단은 언제나 ～ My father's judgment is never wrong. (***b***) 《정의롭다》 (be) righteous; just. ¶ 바른 길을 걷다 follow 〔tread〕 the path of virtue; pursue an honest career / 그들의 요구는 결코 바르다고 할 수 없다 Their demands are far from just. (***c***) 《참되다》 (be) honest; upright; truthful. ¶ 바른 사람 an honest 〔a just〕 man / 바른 말을 하다 tell 〔speak〕 the truth; tell what is right. (***d***) 《알맞다》 (be) proper. ¶ 바른 방식 the proper way; the correct method / 바르게 행동하다 behave properly 〔correctly〕 / 식사할 때의 바른 자세를 보여 주겠다 I'll show you how to sit properly at (the) table. (***e***) 《틀림없다》 (be) correct; 《정확하다》 (be) accurate; exact. ¶ 바른 답 a correct answer / 바른 계측〔통계〕 accurate measurements 〔statistics〕. ③ 《햇볕이》 (be) sunny. ¶ 양지 바른 곳 a sunny place.

**바르다**[2] ① 《붙이다》 stick; paste; plaster; 《장지문 등을》 paper; 《고약·연고 등을》 apply 《to》. ¶ 고약을〔연고를〕 ～ apply 「a plaster 〔ointment〕 《to a wound》; put 「a plaster 〔ointment〕 《on a cut》 / 종이를 ～ paper 《a box》; paste paper 《on》 / 벽에 포스터를 ～ plaster a poster on the wall / 방에 하늘색 벽지를 ～ paper a room in blue; cover the walls of a room with blue wallpaper. ② 《칠하다》 paint; plaster (회반죽을); varnish (니스를); lacquer (옻을); coat (페인트 등을); rub in (문질러). ¶ 기름을 ～ grease 《a machine》; oil 《a sword》 / 벽을 ～ plaster a wall / 분을 더덕더덕 ～ powder 〔paint〕 *one's* face thick; wear a heavy 〔put on thick〕 makeup / 빵에 버터를 ～ spread bread with butter; spread butter on bread / 종이에 풀을 ～ put paste on a sheet of paper / 피부에 문질러 바르시오 Rub it into the skin.

**바르다**[3] ＝발라내다.

**바르르** ① 《끓는 소리》 bubbling; in bubbles; seething; boiling; fizzing. ¶ ～ 끓다 be hissing hot / ～ 끓기 시작하다 come to a bubbling boil. ② 《성냄》 in a huff; in a sudden fit of anger. ¶ ～ 성이 나다 flare up in anger; boil up. ③ 《타오름》 in a sudden burst of flame. ¶ ～ 타오르다 burst into flames. ④ 《떪》 shivering; trembling; quivering. ¶ 추워서 ～ 떨다 shiver with cold / 무서워서 ～ 떨다 tremble with fear.

**바르샤바** 《폴란드의 수도》 Warsaw. ◉ ～조약 the Warsaw Pact.

**바른길** ① 《곧은 길》 a straight way. ② 《옳은 길》 the path of right 〔virtue, duty〕; the right path 〔track〕; (the path of) righteousness. ¶ ～로 인도하다 guide 《*a person*》 into the right path / ～로 가게 하다 set 《*a person*》 on the right track / ～로 돌아오다 get back on the right track / ～을 밟다 tread (on) the path of righteousness; pursue an honest career; keep to the right path / ～을 벗어나다 stray 〔deviate〕 from the right path / 한 번 ～을 벗어나면 되돌아오기가 어렵다 Once you stray from the right path, you will find it difficult to get back on to it.

**바른말** 《옳은 말》 a reasonable 〔right, proper〕 word; 《직언》 plain speaking; a straight talk. ～하다 speak reasonably; speak plainly; speak without reserve. ¶ ～하는 사람 an outspoken 〔a plain-spoken〕 person / 그는 항상 ～을 한다 He always speak reasonably. / ～은 귀에 거슬린다 《속담》 Outspoken advice is 〔sounds〕 harsh to the ear. *or* A good medicine 「tastes bitter 〔is bitter to the taste〕.

**바리**[1] ① 《밥그릇》 a brass rice bowl. ② ＝바리때. ◉ ～때 a wooden rice bowl used by temple priests. ～전(廛) a brassware shop.

**바리**[2] 《짐을 세는 단위》 a load 〔pack〕 《of *things*》. ¶ 장작 두 ～ two loads of firewood / 그는 달구지에 나무 한 ～를 실었다 He put a load of wood in the cart. *or* He loaded the cart with wood. ◉ ～나무 firewood loaded on a horse 〔an ox〕. ～무 radishes 〔turnips〕 loaded on a horse 〔an ox〕 (to take around and sell).

**바리새** ◉ ～인 a Pharisee: ～인의 Pharisaic; Pharisaical. ～주의〔파〕 Pharisaism.

**바리캉** 〔＜*barriquant* 《프》〕 hair 〔barber's〕 clippers.

**바리케이드** a barricade. ¶ ～를 치다〔쌓다〕 set up a barricade 《across the street》; barricade 《a place》 / ～로 봉쇄하다 block with a barricade / ～를 돌파하다 break through a barricade.

**바리콘** 〖전기〗 a variable condenser.

**바리톤** 〖음악〗 baritone (남성 중음부); a baritone (가수). ¶ 목소리가 ～이다 have a baritone voice.

**바림** 〖미술〗 shadings 〔gradations〕 (of a color); shading off. ～하다 shade off; gradate. ¶ 배경을 ～한 초상화 a vignette / 바다 색을 ～하다 gradate the color of the sea.

**바바리(코트)** a trench coat; a Burberry 「(상표명).

**바베큐** ⇨ 바비큐.

**바벨** 〖성서〗 Babel. ◉ ～탑 the Tower 「of Babel.

**바보** a fool; a stupid person; a simpleton; 《멍텅구리》 a blockhead; 《저능자》 a moron; 《백치》 an idiot; a donkey; an ass; 《멍청이》 a dunce; a dullard; a dolt; a ninny; a booby; 《구어》 a goose; a chump. ¶ 지독한 ～ a big 〔damned〕 fool; an idiot / ～같은 생각 a foolish idea / ～ 같은 foolish; silly; stupid; idiotic (★ '바보같은'의 뜻으로, silly는 듣는이가 느끼는 감이 부드러운 편인데 반하여 stupid는 상대자의 우둔함을 지적하기 때문에 감정을 상하게 할 우려가 있음. foolish는 '도리어 상식에 어긋난'의 뜻이며 주로 말이나 행동에 대해서 씀) / ～ 같은 소리를 하다 talk nonsense 〔rubbish〕; sound like an idiot / ～ 같은 짓을 하다 do a foolish 〔silly〕 thing; play 〔act〕 the fool; commit a folly / ～라고 부르다 call 《*a person*》 a fool / ～ 같다 be foolish; be like a fool / ～ 같이 굴다 play 〔act〕 the fool; play the ass; make a fool of *oneself* / ～같이 보이다 look stupid 〔foolish〕; have a stupid look / ～ 취급을 하다 make a fool of 《*a person*》 / ～같은 소리하고 있네 You are talking rubbish. *or* Nonsense! / ～짓 좀 작작해라 Don't be quite so stupid. *or* Cut out the foolishness. / 이 ～야 You idiot 〔fool, old donkey〕! / 그런 일을 할 만큼 ～는 아니다 I know better than to do such a thing. / 나는 너에게 ～ 취급을 당하지는 않겠다 I'm not going to be made a fool of by you. / 이 ～ 얼간아 Silly idiot! / 너야 말로 최고의 ～로구나 You're an out-and-out fool.

**바비큐** 《통구이》 a barbecue. ¶ ～로 하다 barbecue 《meat》.

**바빌로니아** 《고대 제국》 Babylonia. ¶ ～의 Babylonian. ◉ ～사람 a Babylonian.

**바빌론** 《바빌로니아의 수도》 Bybylon. ◉ ～유수(幽囚) Babylonian captivity 〔exile〕.

**바쁘다** ① 《틈이 없다》 (be) busy; occupied; engaged; be (all) tied up. ¶ 바쁘게 busily; in a hurried manner; like a busy bee / 바쁜 일정 a crowded 〔heavy〕 schedule / 바쁜 하루 a busy day / 바쁘게 움직이다〔일하다〕 busy *oneself* 《with, about, *doing*》 / 늘 ～ be always kept busy / 바쁜 생활을 하다 lead a busy life / 일하기에 ~ be busy working / 사무〔짐꾸리기〕에 ~ be busy with *one's* office work 〔packing〕/ 시험 준비로 ~ be busy preparing for the examination (★ be busy to prepare for...라고는 안 씀) / 이 일 저 일로~ be busy with one thing or another / 눈이 핑핑 돌 정도로 ~ be in a whirl of business / 눈코 뜰 새 없이 ~ be (as) busy as a bee; move about busily with pressure of work / 하는 일 없이 ~ be busy about nothing; busy *oneself* with nothing; be busy with nothing to mention in particular / 잠잘 틈도 없이 ~ be too busy to get enough sleep / 나는 지금 ~ I'm tied up right now. / 오늘은 종일 바빴다 I've had a busy day today. / 그는 잠시도 앉아 있을 새 없이 ~ He is too busy to let the grass grow under his feet. / 연말이 다가오면 공연히 ~ When the year is drawing to an end, we are busy without anything particular to do. / 늘 바쁘시군요 I see you are busy 〔keeping busy〕 as usual. / 너무 바빠 숨 돌릴 틈도 없다 I am so busy I can't catch my breath. / 바빠 아무와도 면회를 할 수 없다고 일러라 Tell the man I am too busy to see anybody. ② 《급하다》 (be) pressing; urgent; immediate. ¶ 바쁜 일 a pressing work; urgent business / 바쁜 주문 an urgent order / 바쁜 걸음으로 with hurried steps; at a quick pace / 바쁘시면 5일 내로 해 올리겠습니다 If you are in a hurry, I'll do it in five days.

**바삐** ① 《쉴 새 없이》 busily; industriously. ¶ ~ 일하다 work busily; be busy at 〔with〕 work / ~ 지내다 live a busy life. ② 《급히》 hurriedly; hastily (허둥지둥); in haste; in a rush; in a hurry; 《지체없이》 without delay. ¶ 한시 ~ in great haste; without a moment's delay / ~ 가다〔내려가다, 돌아오다, 들어오다〕 hurry along 〔down, back, in〕 / ~ 가버리다 hurry off 〔away〕 / ~ 걷다 walk with hurried steps / ~ 굴다 behave hurriedly; hurry; hasten; rush; 《재촉하다》 press; urge (on) / ~ 먹다 take a hasty 〔hurried〕 meal / ~ 쓰다 write in haste / ~ …하다 hasten to *do;* lose no time in *do*ing / ~ 서둘러라 Hurry up! *or* Make haste! *or* Be quick! / 왜 그리 ~ 서두르냐 Why are you in such a hurry? *or* What's the rush? / ~ 서두를 필요 없다 There is no hurry.

**바삭** 《밟힐 때 소리》 with a rustle 〔crinkle〕; rustlingly; 《깨물 때 소리》 with a crunch. ~하다 give a rustle 〔crinkle〕; crunch.

**바삭거리다** rustle (and rustle); crinkle; crunch (again and again). ¶ 가랑잎이 바람에 바삭거린다 The fallen leaves rustle in the breeze. / 어떤 남자가 바삭거리며 덤불 속에서 나왔다 A man came rustling out of the thicket.

**바삭바삭** rustlingly; with a rustle; crinkling; crunching; 《단단한 것이 부서지는 소리》 crips; crunch. ¶ ~하게 기름에 튀긴 생선 a fish fried crisp / ~하다 《비스킷 따위가》 be crisp / ~하게 되다 get 〔become〕 crisp; crisp (up) / ~ 소리를 내다 rustle 《in the wind》; crump (밟힌 눈이) / 서리를 ~ 밟다 crunch the frost / ~하게 타다 be burnt to a crisp / (빵 등이) ~하다 be dry and crumbling / 토스트를 ~하게 굽다 crisp toast.

**바셀린** 《상표명》 Vaseline; petroleum jelly; petrolatum.

**바소** 〖한의〗 a lancet.

**바소쿠리** a wicker basket used as a dirt-carrier.

**바수다** ⇨ 부수다.

**바순** 〖음악〗 a bassoon. ◉ ~ 연주자 a bassoonist.

**바스** a bath. ◉ ~룸 a bathroom. ~타월 a bath towel.

**바스대다** move about restlessly; be never still; be restless 〔fidgety〕. ¶ 바스대는 아이 a restless child / 바스대지 마라 Don't fidget.

**바스락** with a rustle; with a low 〔soft〕 sound. ~하다 make a rustle sound.

**바스락거리다** make rustling sound; rustle. ¶ 나뭇잎이 바람에 바스락거린다 The leaves are rustling in the wind.

**바스락바스락** rustlingly; with a rustle. ~하다 rustle.

**바스러뜨리다** smash; crush; break (into pieces).

**바스러지다** 《부서지다》 crumble; fall to pieces; be broken to pieces; break 〔crush〕 to pieces; be smashed to powder. ¶ 빵이 ~ bread crumbles.

**바스스** 《crumple, crumble, rise, ruffle》 gently 〔softly, lightly〕. ¶ ~ 잠자리에서 일어나다 get lightly out of bed.

**바스켓** a basket. ◉ ~볼 《농구》 《play》 basketball; a basketball (공).

**바슬바슬** crumbling(ly). ~하다 (be) crumbly. ¶ 과자가 너무 말라서 만지는 대로 ~ 부스러진다 The cake is so dry, it crumbles when you touch it.

**바심** ① 《풋바심》 threshing and milling unripe grain. ~하다 thresh grain before it is ripe. ② 《바심질》 trimming lumber; smoothing the surface of lumber. ∼하다 trim 〔dress, smooth〕 lumber.

**바싹** ① 《물기가 없게》 《dried up》 completely; in a parched manner; scorched; burnt up 〔off〕; burnt dry. ¶ ∼ 마른 입술 parched lips / ∼ 마른 우물 a dried-up well / ∼ 마르다 dry up; be dried up (completely); be parched; run dry (우물 따위가) / 목이 ∼ 마르다 be parched with thirst / ∼ 볶다 parch 〔roast〕 《beans》 crisp 〔well enough〕 / 가뭄으로 땅이 ∼ 말랐다 The earth is dried up because of the drought.
② 《몸이 마른》 haggardly; thinly. ¶ ∼ 마른 haggard; gaunt; skinny; rawboned; emaciated / ∼ 마른 얼굴 haggard 〔emaciated〕 face / ∼ 마른 사람 a scrag / 몸이 ∼ 마르다 be reduced to a skeleton 〔shadow〕; be nothing but skin and bones / 그는 앓고 나서 ∼ 말랐다 He lost much weight because of illness.
③ 《죄는 모양》 《approach》 closely; close to; fast; tightly; firmly. ¶ ∼ 껴안다 hug 《a child》 to *one's* breast / ∼ 다가앉다 sit closer to 《*a person*》 / ∼ 동이다〔묶다〕 bind 〔tie〕 《*a thing*》 fast 《with a rope》 / ∼ 달려들다 edge in; move in on / ∼ 땅에 엎드리다 lie on *one's* face close to the ground; hug the ground / 띠를 ∼ 죄다 tighten a belt fast / 몸을 벽에 ∼ 붙이고 있다 keep up against the wall / 그들은 벤치에 ∼ 붙어 앉았다 They sat close together on the bench.
④ 《당기는 모양》 《cut》 short; to the quick; 《줄이는 모양》 to the bone; to the minimum. ¶ 손톱을 ∼ 깎다 cut a nail short 〔to the quick〕 / 생활비를 ∼ 줄이다 curtail 〔cut down〕 *one's* living expenses to the bone / 회사는 인건비를 ∼ 줄였다 The company cut its labor costs to the minimum.

**바야흐로** ① 《한창》 in full operation; at the height 《of》; 《바로》 just; now; really. ¶ ∼ 가을이다 Autumn is really here. *or* Autumn has come. / 휴전 회담이 ∼ 진행중이다 The truce talks are in full swing. / ∼ 독서의 계절이다 Right now is the time to read books. ② 《이제 막》 《be》 about to 《*do*》; on the point 〔brink, verge〕 《of *do*ing》; almost; nearly; 《be, come》 near 《*do*ing》. ¶ ∼ 하려 하다 be about 〔be just going〕 to *do;* be on the point 〔brink, verge〕 of *do*ing / 해가 ∼ 지려고 한다 The sun is just about to set. *or* The sun is near setting.

**-바에야** 《이왕 …이면》 at all; 《차라리》 rather; sooner… than; as soon. ¶ 이왕 그만둘 바에야 if you give it up at all / 항복할 바에야 죽겠다 I would rather die than surrender. / 어차피 할 바에야 철저히 해라 If you do it at all, do it thoroughly.

**-바와 같이** as; like. ¶ 생각한 바와 같이 as one expected 〔feared〕 / 아시는〔말씀하시는〕 바와 같이 as you know 〔say〕 / 그가 하는 일로 알 수 있는 바와 같이 조심성 있는 사람이다 He is careful as his work shows.

**바운드** bounce; bound. ∼하다 bounce; bound. ¶ 공을 원 ∼로 잡다 catch a ball on the first bounce 〔bound〕 / 공은 ∼하여 삼루수 머리 위를 넘어갔다 The ball bounded 〔bounced〕 over the third baseman.

**바울** 《예수의 사도》 St. Paul(?–67? A.D.).

**바위** a rock; a crag (울퉁불퉁한). ¶ 흔들∼ a rocking stone; a logan stone / ∼투성이의〔가 많은〕 rocky; cragged; craggy / 물에 침식된 ∼ water-worn rocks / 나무뿌리와 ∼를 잡고 오르다 clamber up by roots and rocks / 기선은 ∼에 충돌했다 The steamer was dashed against a rock. / 파도가 ∼에 부서지고 있다 The waves are breaking on the rocks. ◉ ∼굴 a (rock) cave; a cavern. ∼너설 sharp 〔jagged〕 edges of a rock. ∼산 a rocky mountain; a crag. ∼옹두라지 a spur 〔sharp jut, sharp projection〕 of a rock; a jag of a rock. ∼타기 rock-climbing.

**바위솔** 〖식물〗 a houseleek.

**바위옷** 〖식물〗 rock moss; lichen. ¶ ∼이 끼다 《rock》 gather moss.

**바위제비** 〖조류〗 a martin; a martlet.

**바위종다리** 〖조류〗 a hedge sparrow.

**바위채송화**(―菜松花) 〖식물〗 a sedum; a stone-crop.

**바위취** 〖식물〗 a saxifrage.

**바윗돌** a block of rock; a rock block.

**바음자리표**(―音―標) 〖음악〗 the F 〔bass〕 clef.

**바이러스** a virus. ¶ 감기 ∼ the common cold virus / B형 ∼성 간염 viral hepatitis type B. ◉ ∼병 a virus 〔viral〕 disease. ∼학 virology: ∼학자 a virologist. ∼혈증 〖의학〗 viremia.

**바이마르** 《독일의 도시》 Weimar. ◉ ∼ 헌법 the Weimar Constitution.

**바이블** the Bible. ¶ ～에 손을 얹고 맹세하다 swear on the Bible.
**바이스** 〖기계〗 a「vise〔vice《영》〕.
**바이애슬론** 《스키 경기》 biathlon. ¶ ～선수 a biathlete.
**바이어** a buyer; a buying agent from abroad. ¶ ～와 상담(商談)을 하다 have a business talk with a buyer.
**바이없다** ①《방법 등이》(be) not at all; not by any means; not in the least. ¶ 방법이 ～ be quite at a loss (as to) what to do; be at *one's* wit's end / 이제 할 방법이 ～ There is nothing that can be done. *or* It's「all up with〔all over for〕me. ②《비길 데 없다》(be) incomparable; limitless; 《대단하다》(be) extreme. ¶ 영광스럽기 ～ feel〔be〕most〔greatly〕honored / 기쁘기 ～ be delighted beyond measure / 위험하기 ～ be extremely dangerous / 아버지의 기쁨은 바이없었다 Father's joy knew no bounds.
**바이오리듬** (a) biorhythm.
**바이오세라믹스** bioceramics.
**바이오테크놀로지** biotechnology.
**바이올리니스트** a violinist; a fiddler.
**바이올린** a violin; a fiddle. ¶ ～의 대가 a master violinist / ～의 활 a (fiddle) bow / ～을 켜다 play the violin. ◉ ～독주 a violin solo; a solo on the violin. ～연주자 a violinist; a fiddler. ～협주곡 a violin concerto.
**바이칼호**(―湖) Lake Baikal.
**바이킹** ①〖역사〗a Viking. ②〖요리〗smorgasbord.
**바이트** 〖컴퓨터〗a byte.
**바인더** 《문방구·농기계》 a binder.
**바일병**(―病) 〖의학〗 Weil's disease.
**바자**[1] 《울타리용》 rough-woven「sticks〔reeds, bamboos〕to make a fence. ◉ ～울 a rough-woven《bamboo》fence. 바잣문 a twig gate in a bamboo fence.
**바자**[2] 《자선시》 a bazaar. ¶ 자선 ～ a charity bazaar / ～를 열다 open〔hold〕a bazaar / 교회는 고아들을 위해 ～를 열었다 The church hold a bazaar for (the) orphans.
**바작바작** ①《소리》 with a sizzling; cracking; crackling. ¶ ～ 소리 내다 crack / ～ 타다 burn crackling / 밥이 솥에서 ～ 탄다 The rice is sizzling in the pot. / 벽난로에서 불이 ～ 소리를 내며 탔다 A fire crackled in the hearth. ②《초조》 in a state of「apprehension〔anxiety〕; fretting; 《구어》 in a stew. ¶ 속이 ～ 타다 be devoured by anxiety / 마음을 ～ 죄다 be held in suspense.
**바장이다** stroll aimlessly. ⇨ 버정이다.
**바제도병**(―病) 〖의학〗 Basedow's disease.
**바조**(―調) 〖음악〗 the note F. ¶ 바장〔단〕조 F「major〔minor〕.
**바주카포**(―砲) a bazooka (gun).
**바지** (a pair of) trousers; pants《미》; slacks (평상복); breeches (주로 짧은 것); knicker(bocker)s. ¶ 승마용 ～ riding breeches / 접어 올린 ～단 the「cuffs《미》〔turnups《영》〕on trousers / ～단을 접다 turn up the trousers at the bottom / ～를 입다 put on *one's* trousers / ～를 벗다 take off *one's* trousers / ～ 단추를 채우다 button up *one's* trousers / ～를 다리다 press *one's* trousers / ～의 지퍼를 채우다〔풀다〕「zip up〔unzip〕*one's* trousers / ～에 주름을 세우다 crease *one's* trousers / ～ 단추가 안 채워져 있다 trousers are unbuttoned. ◉ ～걸이 a trouser hanger. ～멜빵 suspenders《미》; braces《영》. ～저고리 trouser and coat; [비유적] a man of no guts; a good-for-nothing; 《명목만의 인물》 a figurehead: ～ 저고리만 다닌다 He has no backbone. *or* He is a straw man. ～주머니 a trouser pocket. 바짓가랑이 a「trouser〔pant〕leg: ～를 걷어 올리다 roll up *one's* trouser legs.
**바지락(조개)** 〖조개류〗 a thin-shelled surf clam.
**바지랑대** a wash-line pole; a clothes pole.
**바지런-** ⇨ 부지런-.
**바지지, 바지직** with a「hiss〔rip〕. ～하다 give〔let out〕a「hiss〔rip〕; hiss; rip. ～거리다 hiss (and hiss); keep ripping; fizz.
**바짝** ⇨ 바싹.
**-바치** a maker; an artisan; a worker; a mechanic. ¶ 갖바치 a maker of leather shoes / 성냥바치 a blacksmith.
**바치다**[1] ①《드리다》 give《to a superior》; offer; present; make a present《of》; dedicate (건물·서적 따위를); devote (노력·시간·돈 따위를); consecrate (신에게); give up (심신을). ¶ 뇌물을 ～ bribe《*a person*》; offer a bribe / 일생을 ～ devote〔dedicate, consecrate, give〕*one's* life《to art》/ 일신을 ～ devote〔commit〕*oneself* to《a work》; give *oneself* up; give *one's* whole-hearted devotion《to》/ 나라를 위해 목숨을 ～ sacrifice *oneself* for *one's* country; give〔lay down〕*one's* life for (the sake of) *one's* country / 신께 제물을 ～ offer a sacrifice to

God / 애인에게 모든 것을 ~ give *one's* all to *one's* lover / 이 책을 한 선생님께 바칩니다 This book I dedicate to Mr. Han. / 그녀는 그에게 헌신적인 사랑을 바쳤다 She loved him「devotedly〔with her heart and soul〕. / 그는 여가를 오로지 저술에 바쳤다 He dedicated all his spare time to writing.
② 《납부하다》 pay. ¶ 세금을 ~ pay *one's*「taxes〔a tax〕/ 공과금을 ~ pay public imposts.
③ [조동사] do 《*a thing*》 for someone superior. ¶ 선생님께 숙제를 해 ~ hand in *one's* homework to *one's* teacher.

**바치다**[2] 《지나치게 즐기다》 be addicted to; be「overly fond of〔preoccupied with〕; have an excessive liking for; be「crazy〔mad, wild〕about. ¶ 계집을 ~ be wild about women; be girl-crazy / 색을 ~ have an excessive liking for sexual pleasure.

**바캉스** [< *vacances* (F.)] 《미》 (a) vacation; 《영》 holidays. ¶ ~철 a「vacation〔holiday〕season.

**바커스** 〖그神〗 Bacchus.

**바퀴**[1] ① 《수레의》 a wheel; 《가구에 달린》 a caster. ¶ 자전거 ~ wheels of a bicycle / 앞〔뒷〕 ~ the「front〔rear〕wheels / (비행기의) 앞~ a nosewheel / ~달린 가구 furniture mounted on casters / ~를 달다 fix a wheel / 그 짐마차는 너무 빨리 달리는 바람에 ~가 빠져 버렸다 The wagon ran so fast (that) the wheel came off. ② 《도는 횟수》 a turn; a round; 《회전》 a turn; a rotation. ¶ 한 ~ 돌다 take a「round〔cycle〕; make〔take〕a turn; go round; 《담당 구역을》 go〔make, do〕*one's* rounds / 세계를 한 ~ 돌다 travel round the world / 공원을 한 ~ 돌다 take a walk around the park / 그 비행기는 착륙 전에 비행장을 두 ~ 돌았다 The plane circled the airport twice before landing. ◉ ~살 a spoke 《of a wheel》. ~의자 a wheelchair. ~자국 a rut; a wheel track; a furrow (깊은): ~자국을 남기다 (make a) rut. ~통 the hub (of a wheel).

**바퀴**[2] 〖곤충〗 a cockroach; a roach. ¶ ~가 우글거리는 부엌 a cockroach-ridden kitchen.

**바탕**[1] ① 《성질》 nature; character; (a) disposition; (a) temperament; 《소지》 the making; 《체질》 (physical) constitution. ¶ ~이 좋은 사람 a man of good disposition / ~이 약질이다 be of a delicate constitution.
② 《밑바탕》 (***a***) 《기본 바탕》 (the) ground; field; 《직물의》 texture; weave. ¶ 노란 ~에 푸른 무늬 a blue design on a yellow ground / 옷감의 ~이 곱다 be of fine「texture〔weave〕. (***b***) 《기반·기초》 foundation; basis; 《학문 등의》 a grounding 《in》. ¶ ~을 두다 base; be based on / ~이 되어 있다 have a grounding 《in Latin》/ 물가 안정의 ~위에 지속적인 경제 성장을 추구하다 pursue continued economic growth on the foundation of price stabilization / 이 이야기는 작가의 개인적 체험에 ~을 두고 있다 This story is based on the writer's personal experience.

**바탕**[2] 《동안》 a spell of action; a bout; a turn; a round; a set; [부사적] for a「time〔while, spell〕; for some time. ¶ 씨름 한 ~ a bout of wrestling / 한 ~ 놀았다 We played a round. / 비가 한 ~ 왔다 There was a shower for some time. / 우리는 한 ~ 이야기 꽃을 피웠다 We enjoyed chatting for a while.

**바터** barter. ◉ ~무역 barter trade. ~제(制) the barter system.

**바텐더** 《미》 a bartender; 《영》 a barman; 《미》 a barkeep(er) (매니저 겸).

**바통** a baton. ¶ ~을 넘기다 pass〔hand over〕the baton 《to》; 《작업 등의》 hand over 《*one's* duties to》/ ~을 물려받다 receive〔accept〕the baton 《from》; 《작업 등의》 take over the baton 《from》.

**바투** close; closely; near. ¶ ~ 앉다 sit close / ~ 쓰다 write closely / 머리를 ~ 깎다 cut the hair「close〔short〕/ 시간이 ~ 다가온다 The time draws near.

**바특이** ① 《바싹》 a little bit close(ly); close to; right by. ¶ 손톱을 ~ 깎다 cut *one's* nails close. ② 《국물을》 thick. ¶ 국물을 ~ 끓이다 boil down the soup; make the soup a bit thick(er).

**바특하다** be not watery; be a bit thick. ¶ 밀가루로 국을 바특하게 할 수 있다 You can thicken the soup with flour.

**바티칸** 《교황청》 the Vatican. ◉ ~시국(市國) the Vatican City.

**박**[1] 〖식물〗 a gourd; a calabash (호리병박). ¶ 박꽃 a gourd flower / 박속 the flesh of a gourd / 박을 타다 cut〔split〕a gourd in two.

**박**[2] ① 《긁거나 가는 소리》 with a「rasp〔grate, scrape, grind〕. ② 《찢는 소리》 with a rip.

**박**(泊) stay. ¶ 1박 2식(食)에 30,000원 thirty thousand won a night including two meals / 1박하다 pass〔spend〕

a night 《at, in》; stay overnight 《at, in》; 「put up 〔lodge〕 《at a hotel》 for the night.

**박**(箔) leaf; foil. ¶ 금박 gold leaf / 박을 입히다 put 《silver》 leaf 《over》.

**박격포**(迫擊砲) 〖군사〗 a trench mortar. ¶ ~탄 a mortar shell.

**박공**(膊栱) 〖건축〗 a gable.
◉ ~널 a bargeboard. ~벽 a gable end 〔wall〕. ~지붕〔창〕 a gable roof 〔window〕.

**박구기** a gourd dipper 〔ladle〕.

**박다** ① 《못 따위를》 drive 〔strike, knock〕 《in, into》; ram down 《a stake》; wedge in (쐐기 등을). ¶ 못을 ~ drive 〔hammer〕 a nail into 《a wall》; drive a nail home (대가리까지) / 땅에 말뚝을 ~ drive a stake into the ground / 나무에 쐐기를 ~ hammer a wedge into a log.
② 《소를》 fill 《rice cake》 with 《bean jam》; stuff 《a bun》 with 《meat and vegetables》. ¶ 떡에 소를 ~ stuff a rice cake; fill a rice cake with stuffing; put stuffing in a rice cake.
③ 《사진을》 take 《a photograph》; 《인쇄하다》 print; put 《a book》 into print 〔press〕; impress; get 《*a thing*》 printed. ¶ 명함을 ~ have *one's* cards printed / 사진을 ~ take a picture / 백부를 ~ print 〔strike off〕 100 copies.
④ 《찍어내다》 make 〔cut out〕 《cookies, cakes》 in a shape; shape.
⑤ 《바느질》 sew (by backstitch); sew 《*a thing*》 by hand 〔with a machine〕; hand-〔machine-〕stitch 《*a thing*》. ¶ 이불을 ~ stitch a quilt.
⑥ 《끼워넣다》 (***a***) 《보석 따위를》 fix; mount 《a gem, *etc.*》; inlay; set; enchase. ¶ 거미발에 보석알을 ~ mount a jewel in a setting / 반지에 진주를 ~ set a pearl in a ring; set a ring with a pearl / 상아에 금을 ~ inlay gold on ivory. (***b***) 《장부촉을》 tail; house.

**박달(나무)** 〖식물〗 a birch.

**박대**(薄待) cold treatment; poor entertainment; inhospitality; a cool reception. ⇨ 푸대접. ~하다 treat 《*a person*》 coldly; give 〔show〕 《*a person*》 the cold shoulder; 《손님을》 give 《*a person*》 a cold reception. ¶ ~받다 be treated unkindly 〔coldly〕; get a freezing reception.

**박덕**(薄德) want 〔lack〕 of virtue. ~하다 have little virtue. ⇨ 부덕(不德).

**박동**(搏動) 《맥박》 (a) pulsation; 《심장의》 (a) palpitation; (a) pulsebeat; (an) ictus (*pl.* -tuses, -tus). ◉ ~계 a sphygmograph.

**박두**(迫頭) ~하다 draw near; approach; be near 〔close〕 at hand; impend; be imminent. ¶ 위기가 ~하다 be faced with a crisis / 시험이 ~했다 The examination is near at hand.

**박람회**(博覽會) an exhibition; an exposition 《미》; a fair 《미》. ◉ ~장 the exhibition grounds; fairgrounds 《미》. ~출품자 an exhibitor.

**박래품**(舶來品) imports; imported goods; foreign-made articles.

**박력**(迫力) force; power; punch 《구어》. ¶ ~이 있다 be powerful 〔impressive〕; be moving; strongly appeal 《to》 / ~이 없다 lack power 〔punch〕 / 그의 연설은 ~이 없다 His speeches lack punch. / 그의 말에는 ~이 넘쳐흘렀다 There was plenty of punch in his remarks.

**박리**(剝離) peeling off; exfoliation; excoriation. ~하다 come off; peel off; scale off; exfoliate; excoriate. ◉ 망막 ~ 〖의학〗 separation of the retina; *amotio retinae*.

**박리**(薄利) small profits; a narrow margin (of profit). ¶ ~로 팔다 sell at small profits. ◉ ~다매(多賣) small profits 「with quick returns 〔with a good turnover〕; quick sales at small profits; a nimble penny: ~ 다매주의 a quick-returns policy.

**박막**(薄膜) a thin film; 〖해부〗 a thin membrane; a pellicle. ◉ ~집적회로 a thin-film integrated circuit. ~트랜지스터 액정 표시 장치 a thin film transistor liquid crystal display (생략 TFT LCD).

**박멸**(撲滅) eradication; extermination. ~하다 stamp out; eradicate; 《구제(驅除)》 exterminate. ¶ 콜레라의 ~ the eradication of cholera / 전염병을 ~하다 stamp out infectious diseases / 해충을 ~하다 exterminate vermin.
◉ ~책 an exterminatory measure. 결핵 ~운동 a crusade against tuberculosis; an anti-T.B. drive.

**박명**(薄命) ① 《불행》 ill luck; a sad 〔hapless〕 fate. ~하다 (be) unfortunate; unlucky; ill-fated〔-starred〕. ¶ 자신의 ~함을 한탄하다 grieve over 〔lament〕 *one's* ill luck. ② 《단명》 a short life. ¶ 가인〔미인〕 ~ Beauty and long life seldom go hand in hand.

**박물**(博物) ① 《넓은 견문》 having wide knowledge. ② ⇨ 박물학. ◉ ~관 a

museum: 국립 민속 ~관 the National Folklore Museum / 국립 중앙 ~관 the National Museum of Korea. ~군자 a man of erudition. ~표본 a specimen of natural history. ~학 natural history; the study of nature: ~학자 a naturalist.

**박박**[1] ①《갉음》 crunch; 《긁음》 grate; rasp; 《가려워서 긁음》 scratch; 《문지름》 scrub; 《이를 갊》 grind; gnash. ¶ ~ 갉다 crunch (on) 《a bone》 / ~ 소리를 내다 grate 《on the stone》; make a rasping noise 〔sound〕 / ~ 긁다 scratch 《a mosquito bite》 / 이를 ~ 갈다 grind 〔gnash〕 *one's* teeth 《while *one* is asleep, with vexation》 / 바가지를 ~ 긁다 (a wife) nag 《at》. ②《찢음》 with a sound as of tearing cloth to pieces. ¶ 그는 그 편지를 ~ 찢었다 He tore the letter to pieces.

**박박**[2] ①《얽음》 (pockmarked) all over; solid (with pockmarks). ¶ 그의 얼굴은 ~ 얽었다 His face is all covered with pockmarks. ②《짧게》 (having *one's* hair cut) close. ¶ 머리를 ~ 깎다 have *one's* hair cut 〔cropped〕 short.

**박복**(薄福) being unlucky; being unfortunate; misfortune; ill-luck; sad fate. ~하다 (be) unlucky; unfortunate; ill-fated〔-starred〕. ¶ ~한 여인 an ill-starred woman / ~하게 태어나다 be born under an unlucky star / 자신의 ~함을 슬퍼하다〔한탄하다〕 grieve over *one's* ill 〔tough〕 luck.

**박봉**(薄俸) a small 〔meager, scanty, low〕 salary; a poor pay; a pittance. ¶ ~ 근로자 an underpaid 〔a poorly paid〕 workman / ~을 받다 draw a small pay / ~으로 생활하다 live on a small salary / ~으로 일하다 work at a small pay / 그는 ~을 받고 있다 He is ill 〔poorly〕 paid.

**박빙**(薄氷) thin 〔filmy〕 ice; a thin coat of ice.

**박사**(博士) a doctor; a Ph. D.; Dr. ...; [비유적] an expert; a learned man. ¶ 홍 ~ Dr. Hong. ◉ ~과정 the doctor's course 《in economics》. ~논문 a doctoral dissertation 〔thesis〕; a thesis for a doctorate. ~학위 a doctor's degree; a doctorate: ~ 학위를 수여하다 confer a doctorate on 《*a person*》 / ~ 학위를 따다 obtain 〔take〕 「a degree of doctor 〔a doctorate〕 《in economics at Korea University》.

**박살** 《조각조각 부서짐》 ¶ ~내다 break 〔crush, smash〕 《*a thing*》 to pieces 〔to atoms, to smithereens〕 / ~나다 come 〔be broken〕 to pieces.

**박살**(撲殺) clubbing 〔beating〕 《*a person*》 to death. ~하다 club 〔beat, strike, knock〕 《*a person*》 dead; club to death; kill with blow.

**박새** 〖조류〗 a great-tit. ¶ 쇠~ a marsh-tit / 진~ a coal-tit.

**박색**(薄色) an ugly look 〔face〕; an ugly-looking woman; a plain woman. ¶ 둘도 없는 ~이다 be ugly enough to stop a clock.

**박속** the insides 〔edible part〕 of a gourd. ¶ ~ 같은 이 even teeth.

**박수** a male shaman 〔diviner, sorcerer〕.

**박수**(拍手) a handclap; (a) clapping of hands. ~하다 clap *one's* hands (in applause); 《구어》 give 《*a person*》 a 《big》 hand. ¶ ~ 치는 사람 a clapper; a claquer; a person clapping / 우레 같은 ~ 속에 amidst 「a thunderous clapping of hands 〔a storm of applause〕 / ~를 보내다 give 《*a person*》 a clap / 일어서서 ~를 보내다 give 《*a person*》 a standing ovation / ~로써 맞이하다 clap 《*a person*》 in; welcome 〔greet〕 《*a person*》 with a clapping of hands / 열렬한 ~를 받다 receive warm 〔loud〕 applause 《from》; 《구어》 get a big hand / 한 씨에게 열렬한 ~를 부탁합니다 May I ask you to give a big hand to Mr. Han. / ~가 멎다〔뜸해졌다〕 The clapping 「died down 〔thinned out〕. / 그 결의는 만장의 ~로써 채택되었다 The resolution was adopted with a general clapping of hands. ◉ ~부대 a claquer; claque [총칭].

**박수갈채**(拍手喝采) cheers; applause; plaudits. ~하다 clap *one's* hands in applause; applaud 《*a person*, an act》 with hands; give 《*a person*》 a clap and cheers.

**박식**(博識) erudition; extensive 〔wide, encyclopedic〕 knowledge. ~하다 be erudite 〔well-informed, learned〕.

**박신거리다** swarm; crowd; throng. ¶ 사람들로 ~ be crowded 〔thronged〕 with people.

**박신박신** in swarms; in crowds. ¶ (벌레 등이) ~ 들끓다 squirm 〔wriggle about〕 in swarm; [장소가 주어] crawl with 《worms》.

**박애**(博愛) philanthropy; benevolence; humanity; charity. ~하다 love (mankind); engage in philanthropy. ¶ ~의 philanthropic; benevolent; humane; charitable. ◉ ~사업 philanthropic 〔charitable〕 work. ~주의 philanthropism: ～주의자 a philanthropist.

**박약**(薄弱) ～하다 《의지·성격이》 (be) fainthearted; pusillanimous; 《근거 따위가》 (be) flimsy; weak; unsubstantial. ¶ 의지가 ～하다 have a weak will; be weak-willed / 그 주장은 근거가 ～하다 The claim is based on flimsy 〔tenuous〕 grounds.

**박음질** a backstitch; sewing; sewing machine stitches. ～하다 backstitch.

**-박이** 《박혀 있는 사람·물건》 an inlaid 〔imprinted〕 one; one with something stuck 〔pressed〕 in or attached 〔fixed on〕. ¶ 쌍열박이 a double-barreled gun / 덧니박이 a person who has a double 〔redundant〕 tooth / 점박이 a person with a mole 〔birthmark〕.

**박이다**[1] ① 《속에》 get stuck in 〔embedded〕; run 《a thorn》 into (가시 등이); 《마음에》 sink deeply into *one's* mind; remain deep in *one's* mind. ¶ 못이 박인 손가락 a finger with a callosity / 엄지손에 가시가 박였다 I've got a splinter in my thumb. / 그 날의 애처로운 광경이 뇌리에 깊이 박여 잊을 수가 없다 The pitiable scenes of the day are indelibly engraved on my mind. ② 《몸에 배다》 get 〔fall〕 into a habit 《of》; form 〔pick up〕 a habit 《of》. ¶ 계속하면 인이 박이는 약 a habit-forming drug / 담배에 인이 ～ contract the habit of smoking. ③ 《죽치다》 stay at home. ⇨ 틀어박히다.

**박이다**[2] 《인쇄하다》 let 〔put into〕 print; 《사진을》 have 〔get〕 *one's* photograph taken. ¶ 책을 ～ print a book.

**박이부정**(博而不精) ¶ ～이라 Jack of all trades and master of none.

**박자**(拍子) 〚음악〛 beat; time; measure; number. ¶ 2〔3, 4〕 ～ duple 〔triple, quadruple〕 time / 4분의 2〔8 분의 6〕 ～ two-quarters 〔six-eighths〕 time / ～를 맞추어 in measured time; keeping time with / ～를 맞추다 keep (good) time with 〔to〕 《the music》 / 발로 ～를 맞추다 beat 〔keep〕 time with *one's* foot.

**박장대소**(拍掌大笑) applause mingled with laughter. ～하다 engage in applause mingled with laughter; laugh aloud clapping *one's* hands.

**박절기**(拍節器) 〚음악〛 a metronome.

**박절하다**(迫切—) 《야박함》 (be) exacting; cold-hearted; unfeeling; heartless; inhuman; strict; severe; inconsiderate; relentless; unsparing. ¶ 박절한 사람 a hard-hearted 〔a unsympathetical〕 person / 박절한 말을 하다 speak cruelly 〔heartlessly〕; say a harsh thing / 박절한 처사를 하다 behave callously; treat 《*a person*》 cruelly / 박절하게 거절하다 give a flat 〔point-blank〕 refusal / 나로서는 그런 박절한 짓은 할 수 없다 It is not in my nature to do such a cruel thing.

**박정**(薄情) cold-heartedness; coolness of heart; hard-heartedness; cruelty; heartlessness. ～하다〔스럽다〕 (be) heartless; cold-hearted. ⇨ 박절하다.

**박제**(剝製) stuffing; mounting; 《물건》 a stuffed 〔mounted〕 specimen. ¶ ～한 stuffed / ～한 새 a stuffed bird / ～로 하다 stuff 〔mount〕 《a bird》.
◉ ～사 a taxidermist. ～술 taxidermy.

**박주**(薄酒) poor 〔untasty〕 liquor; unpalatable *sul;* rotgut 《속어》.

**박주가리** 〚식물〛 a milkweed

**박쥐** 〚동물〛 a bat; a flittermouse.
◉ ～오입쟁이 a secret whoremonger; a night lifer. ～우산 an umbrella.

**박진**(迫眞) truthfulness to life; verisimilitude. ～하다 be true to life 〔nature〕; be lifelike. ¶ ～한 realistic 《performances》 / ～하게 with 《great》 verisimilitude. ◉ ～감〔성〕 ⇨ 박진(迫眞).

**박차**(拍車) a spur; a rowel spur; 《촉진》 acceleration; speeding up. ¶ ～ 달린 장화 spurred boots / 장화에 ～를 달다 spur *one's* boots / 말에 ～를 가하다 set 〔put〕 spurs to *one's* horse; spur (on) *one's* horse / ～를 가하다 [비유적] spur 〔urge〕 《*a person*》 《to *do;* into action》; accelerate; give impetus to.

**박차다** kick out hard; give a vigorous kick; kick away 〔off〕; 《거절》 reject 《a proposal》; give a rebuff; turn down 《a proposal》. ¶ 굴러오는 복을～ toss aside a piece of good luck / 자리를 박차고 떠나다 leave 〔fling out of〕 the room indignantly / 모든 장애(障碍)를 박차고 나아가다 go ahead sweeping aside all obstacles.

**박치기** butting. ～하다 butt 《at, against》; bump 〔knock〕 *one's* head against 《*a person*》; give a butt (of a head) 《to *a person*》; 《서로》 knock 〔bump〕 heads together.

**박타다** ① 《박을》 split a gourd in two. ② 《바라던 일이》 fall 〔come〕 short of *one's* expectation; run counter to *one's* expectation; disappoint *one;* be spoiled; come to nothing.

**박탈**(剝脫) coming off; peeling off; exfoliation (금박 따위의); 《피부의》 excoriation; desquamation (표피의). ～하다 fall 〔come〕 off; peel 〔scale〕 off; exfoliate; excoriate; desquamate. ⇨ 벗기어지다 ②.

**박탈**(剝奪) 《재산·권리 따위》 deprivation; divestiture; dispossession; deplumation; 《죄·과실에 의한》 forfeit; forfeiture. ～하다 deprive 〔strip〕 《*a person*》 of 《*his* office》; divest 《*a person*》 of 《*his* rank》. ¶ 시민권을 ～하다 deprive 《*a person*》 of *his* civil rights / 계급을 ～하다 divest 《*a person*》 of *his* rank; strip 《*a person*》 of *his* honors; degrade / (벌로서) ～당하다 forfeit 《*one's* civil rights》; lose as a forfeit; be deprived of 《*one's* rank》/ 특권을 ～당하다 be shorn of *one's* privileges / 부정행위로 그는 관직을 ～당했다 Because of his dishonest conduct, he was divested of his office. / 그들은 그의 일체의 권리를 ～했다 They deprived him of all his rights.

**박태기나무** 〖식물〗 a redbud; a Judas tree.

**박테리아** a bacterium (*pl.* -ria). ＝세균.

**박토**(薄土) barren 〔poor〕 soil; infertile 〔sterile〕 land.

**박판**(薄板) a thin plate 〔board〕; a sheet.

**박편**(薄片) a thin leaf 〔layer〕; a scale.

**박피**(薄皮) a thin skin; a pellicle; 《피막》 membrane 《액체의》 a film.

**박하**(薄荷) 〖식물〗 peppermint; mint. ◉ ～껌 peppermint 〔spearmint〕 gum. ～뇌(腦) menthol. ～담배 a mentholated cigarette. ～사탕 peppermint (candy). ～수 peppermint solution. ～유 peppermint oil. ～정 menthol crystals; mint camphor.

**박하다**(薄—) ① 《인색하다》 (be) illiberal; stingy; niggardly; tight; hard; 《평가가》 be severe 〔strict〕 in marking. ¶ 점수가 ～ be strict 〔severe〕 in marking; be chary of marks / 박하게 굴지 마라 Don't be so stingy. ② 《인정이》 (be) heartless; unfeeling; inhuman; cold-blooded; hard. ¶ 인심이 ～ be inhospitable; be unkind. ③ 《두께가 얇다》 thin. ⇨ 얇다. ④ 《적다》 (be) scanty; meager. ¶ 급여가 ～ be ill 〔poorly〕 paid; [직장이 주어] do not pay good wages / 이익이 ～ the profit 〔margin〕 is small.

**박학**(博學) erudition; extensive learning; wide knowledge. ～하다 (be) erudite; well-read; learned. ¶ ～한 사람 an erudite; a man of erudition / ～다재하다 be very learned and talented; have profound learning and great ability. ◉ ～다문(多聞)〔다식(多識)〕 being erudite and well-informed: ～다식한 사람 a well-informed man with broad vision.

**박해**(迫害) oppression; persecution; torment. ～하다 oppress; persecute; torment. ¶ 종교상의 ～ religious persecution / ～를 받다 suffer 〔be subjected to〕 oppression 〔persecution〕; be persecuted; be oppressed / 그만이 ～에 대항했다 He alone 「resisted 〔struggled against〕 the oppression. ◉ ～자 an oppressor; a persecutor.

**박히다** ① 《들어가 꽂힘》 get stuck 〔imbedded, driven in〕. ¶ 손에 가시가 ～ a thorn gets stuck into *one's* finger / 벽에 못이 박혀 있다 There is a nail stuck in the wall. / 탄알이 기둥에 박혔다 The bullet lodged in the pillar. ② 《찍히다》 be taken (사진이); be printed (인쇄물이). ¶ 사진이 잘 박혔다 The photo came out good.

**밖** ① 《바깥쪽》 the outside; 《외부》 the exterior; 《집 밖》 the outdoors; the open (air). ¶ 밖의 outer; outside; external; exterior; outward; outdoor / 밖에 out; outside; without; out of doors / 집 밖 (the) outside of a house / 집 밖에서 outside the house; out of doors; outdoors / 밖의 일 outdoor work / 밖에 나가다 go out (of doors); go out into the open air / 밖에서 놀다 play outdoors; be out playing / 밖에서 보다 look at 《*a thing*》 from without 〔the outside〕/ 밖에서 식사하다 dine 〔eat〕 out / 창 밖을 내다보다 《창에서》 look out (of) the window; 《창 너머로》 look out through the window / 밖에서 문을 잠그다 lock the door from the outside / 밖에서 열다 open 《the door》 from the outside / 밖은 꽤 춥다 It is rather cold out of doors. / 머리를 창 밖으로 내밀지 마라 Don't put your head out of the window. / 우리 비밀이 밖으로 새고 있다 Our secrets are leaking out. / 그는 감정을 밖으로 드러내지 않는다 He keeps his feelings to himself.
② 《이외》 outside of (a limit); (with the) exception 《of》; 《다른》 else; 《다만 …뿐》 only; but; no more than; merely; barely. ¶ 그 밖에 besides; in addition 《to》/ …밖에(는) 《제외》 except; excepting; but; save; with the excepton of / 한 번밖에 only 〔but〕 once / 그 밖의 것 rest; other; another / 그 밖의 사람들 the rest; the

others / 하나밖에 없는 몸 the only body we have / …밖에 없다 there is nothing but…; nothing except; only; just / …할 수밖에 없다 have no choice but to *do;* cannot help *do*ing / 이것밖에 없다 This is all I have. / 나는 돈이 2백 원밖에 없다 I have only two hundred won with me. *or* I have no more than 200 won. (★ no more than = only로서 「단, 겨우…」, 「…에 지나지 않다」, 「밖에 없다」라는 뜻이고, not more than = at most로서 「많아야, 기껏해야」라는 뜻임) / 놀랄 수밖에 없다 I cannot help being astonished. / 그것밖엔 모른다 Other than that I know nothing. *or* I know no more than that. / 그 밖의 할 일이 없다 I have nothing else to do. / 그렇게밖엔 해석이 안 된다 I cannot interpret it in any other way. / 그는 그 밖에 돈도 받았다 Besides that he received a sum of money. / 하늘하고 바다밖에 보이지 않았다 There was nothing in sight save sky and sea. / 그것을 할 줄 아는 사람은 너밖에 없다 You alone can do it. / 그는 미치광이로밖엔 생각되지 않는다 I can't 「but think 〔help thinking〕 that he is mad. / 그 밖의 것은 미루어 알 수 있다 The rest may be inferred. / 너밖에 그렇게 말하는 사람이 없다 You are the only one who says so. / 자네밖엔 기댈 사람이 없다 I have no one but you to turn to for help. / 그렇게 할 수밖에 없었다 I could not have acted otherwise.

**반** a flattened sheet 〔layer〕. ¶ 솜반 a flattened layer of cotton.

**반**(反) ① 〖철학〗 antithesis. ② [접두사] anti-. ¶ 반사회적행동 an antisocial act / 반일 운동 an anti-Japanese movement / 반제국주의 anti-imperialism / 반체제(파)의 anti-Establishment.

**반**(半) (a) half; semi-; demi-; hemi-; halfway; partial; incomplete. ¶ 물이 반쯤 있는 half full of water / 반걸음 half a step / 반나절 a quarter of a day / 반 병 half a bottle / 반시간 half an hour / 반 파운드 half a pound; a half pound / 한 다스반 a dozen and a half / 한 배 반 one and a half times; half as much again as / 일의 반 half of *one's* work / 2마일 반 two and a half miles; two miles and a half / 한 시간 반 an hour and a half; one and a half hours / 한 시 반 1:30 o'clock; half past one / 반 농담으로 partly for fun; half in jest / 반 장난으로 half in play; half-heartedly / 반은 병 때문에 반은 운이 나빠서 partly through illness and partly through misfortune / 반으로 가르다 〔반분하다〕 halve; cut in half / 반씩 나누다 go halves 〔shares〕; share 《*something*》 half and half / 경비를 반으로 줄이다 cut (down) the expenditure by half / 그의 일은 아직 반도 끝나지 않았다 His work is not half done 〔finished〕 yet. / 그의 성공은 반은 운이다 His success is 「partly 〔in part〕 due to luck. / 적어도 반은 왔다 We have covered at least a half of the way. / 달걀의 반은 곯았다 Half of the eggs are rotten. (★ half는 다음에 오는 명사·대명사의 수에 따라 뒤에 오는 동사의 단수·복수가 결정됨) / 그는 시간의 반은 낭비하였다 He wasted half his time. / 시작이 반이다 《속담》 "Well begun is half done."

**반**(班) a company; a set; a team; a group; a party; 《학급》 a class; 《동네의》 a neighborhood association; 〖군사〗 a section; a squad. ¶ 영어반 the English class / 상급〔하급〕반 the senior 〔junior〕 class / 수사반 a criminal investigation squad / 연구반 a research team / 학생을 세 반으로 나누다 divide the students into three classes.

**반가공품**(半加工品) semi-finished〔-processed, -manufactured〕 goods.

**반가부좌**(半跏趺坐) sitting cross-legged with one leg put under the other.

**반가움** delight; joy; gladness.

**반가워하다** be glad 〔pleased, delighted〕 about 《*do*ing》; 《기뻐하다》 rejoice in; take pleasure in 《*do*ing》. ¶ 소식을 듣고 ~ be overjoyed at hearing a news / 편지를 받고 ~ be glad to get a letter 《from home》 / 그는 나를 보고 반가워했다 He rejoiced to see me.

**반가이** gladly; joyfully; delightedly; with joy 〔pleasure〕. ¶ ~ 맞이하다 welcome 《*a person*》 gladly.

**반감**(反感) 《혐오감》 (an) antipathy; 《나쁜 감정》 ill 〔bad, hard〕 feeling; an antagonistic feeling; a feeling of revolt; (a) revulsion of feeling; 《적의》 hostility.
¶ 두 사람 사이의 ~ a mutual antipathy between two persons / ~을 사다 rouse 〔provoke〕 《*a person's*》 antipathy; incur 《another's》 ill feeling; invite 《*a person's*》 hostility / ~을 자아내다 provoke antipathy / ~을 품다 harbor 〔come to have〕 ill feeling 《toward》; feel antipathy 《against》;

have an antipathy 《to》; entertain antipathy 《against》 / 몹시 ~을 갖다 be strongly opposed 《to》; have a strong antipathy 《to》 / 그는 나에게 ~을 가지고 있는 듯하다 He seems to have 「ill feeling 〔an antipathy〕 toward me.

**반감**(半減) a reduction by half; a cut by 〔in〕 half. ~하다 reduce 〔cut〕 by half 〔50 per cent〕; halve; 《값을》 take off half the price; 《반으로 줄다》 be halved; be cut in half; be reduced by half; decrease to half. ¶ 경비를 ~하다 cut down the expenditure by half / 그 가치가 ~했다 It's only worth half what it was. / 인플레이션으로 실수입이 ~했다 My real income was cut in half by the inflation. / 그 계획에 대한 흥미가 ~했다 I lost half my interest in the project.
◉ ~기 〖물리〗 a half-life (of a radioactive element); a half(-life) period: 생물학적 ~기 a biologic(al) half-life.

**반갑다** (be) glad; joyful; happy; pleased; welcome; be delighted 《to meet》; be pleasant 《to know》. ¶ 반가운 소식 happy 〔glad, joyful〕 news; good tidings / 반가운 손님 a welcome guest / 반갑잖은 손님 an unwelcome guest / 반가워서 for joy / 반갑게 웃다 smile gleefully; laugh with joy / 반갑게 맞이하다 give 《*a person*》 a joyous welcome / 반갑기도 하고 슬프기도 하다 have mixed feelings of joy and sorry / 편지는 반갑게 읽었습니다 I have read your letter with pleasure. / 그의 성공한 소식을 듣고 반가웠다 I was glad to hear of his success. / 반갑게도 길에서 옛 친구를 만났다 To my joy, I met one of my old chums on the street. / 만나뵈어 반갑습니다 (1) I'm glad to see you. (2) 《처음 대면할 때》 I'm glad to meet you. (★ 이 말은 「처음 뵙겠습니다」 How do you do?를 말한 다음 흔히 계속됨. Glad to meet you.로도 생략할 수 있음. 이에 대한 답은 마찬가지로 I'm glad to meet you.이지만 you에 보통 강세를 줌).

**반값**(半—) half the price; a half price. ¶ ~으로 at half-price; at half the price; at 50% off the regular price / ~으로 깎아주다 take off half the price / ~으로 하다 cut 〔reduce〕 the price by half / ~에 사다 buy 《*a thing*》 at its half value 〔for half the price〕 / ~에 팔다 sell 《*a thing*》 at half-price / 12세 미만의 어린이는 ~이다 Children under twelve are half fare.

**반개**(半個) (a) half; half a piece. ¶ 사과 ~ half (of) an apple.

**반개**(半開) ① 《문이》 being half 〔partly〕 open; being ajar. ~하다 be half 〔partly〕 open; be ajar; half-open. ¶ ~된 창문 a half-open window. ② 《꽃이》 being half in bloom; being half open 〔out〕. ~하다 be half in bloom; be half open 〔out〕.

**반거(들)충이**(半—) a half-baked 〔half=learnt〕 person; a smatterer; a sciolist; a man of half 〔superficial〕 knowledge. ¶ ~의 superficial; half-learnt; shallow.

**반격**(反擊) a counterattack; a counterblow; a counteroffensive; 《경기의》 a rally. ~하다 counterattack; make a counterattack 《on the enemy》; fight back 《against》; strike back 《at》; rally. ¶ ~으로 나가다 launch a counterattack 《on, against》; mount a counteroffensive 《against》 / (경기에서) 멋진 ~을 펼치다 stage a magnificent rally / 우리는 ~의 준비가 되어 있다 We are ready to fight 〔strike〕 back now. / 우리 군은 격렬하게 ~을 가했다 Our forces launched a heavy 〔strong〕 counterattack. ◉ ~기지 a retaliation base. ~작전 counterattack operations.

**반경**(半徑) a radius (*pl.* -dii); a semidiameter. ¶ 행동~ a radius of action 〔operation〕 / ~ 3마일 이내〔밖〕에 within 〔outside〕 the radius of three miles 《of, from》 / ~ 5 cm의 원을 그리다 draw a circle of 5-centimeter radius; describe a circle with the radius of 5 centimeters / 태풍의 중심으로부터 ~ 100 km 이내에서는 순간 풍속 30미터의 돌풍이 불고 있다 Gusts of up to 30 meters per second are blowing within a 100 kilometer radius of the typhoon's center.

**반고리관**(半—管) 〖해부〗 the semicircular 「canals.

**반고체**(半固體) a semisolid.

**반골**(反骨) an 「uncompromising 〔unyielding〕 attitude of mind. ◉ ~정신 an unyielding spirit.

**반공**(反共) anti-Communism. ¶ ~ 선전 anti-Communist propaganda / ~의 보루를 구축하다 build a bulwark against communism.
◉ ~교육 anti-Communist education. ~법 the Anti-Communist Law. ~사상 anti-Communism: ~ 사상을 고취하다 infuse strong anti-Communist idea 〔thought〕 《into the mind of the public》. ~운동〔정책, 태세〕 an anti=

Communist movement 〔policy, stand〕. ～전선 the anti-Communist front. ～정신 anti-Communist spirit. ～주의자 an anti-Communist. ～포로 the anti-Communist prisoners of war. 아시아 ～연맹 the Asian People's Anti-Communist League (생략 APACL). 한국～연맹 the Korea Anti-Communist League (생략 KACL).

**반공**(反攻) a counterattack. ⇨ 반격.

**반공일**(半空日) a half-holiday; Saturday.

**반과거**(半過去) 〖문법〗 the imperfect tense.

**반관반민**(半官半民) semi-government(al) management. ¶ ～의 semiofficial; semi-governmental / ～으로 semiofficially / ～의 기구 a semi-governmental organization. ◉ ～회사 a semi-governmental corporation.

**반괴**(半壞) partial destruction. ～하다 be partially 〔partly〕 destroyed.

**반구**(半球) a hemisphere. ¶ 동〔서, 남, 북〕～ the Eastern 〔Western, Southern, Northern〕 Hemisphere.

**반국가적**(反國家的) antinational; antistate 《activities》.

**반군**(叛軍) rebel 〔mutinous〕 troops; a rebel 〔an insurgent〕 army.

**반군국주의**(反軍國主義) antimilitarism.

**반권위주의**(反權威主義) antiauthoritarianism ¶ ～의 antiauthoritarian.

**반금속**(半金屬) 〖화학〗 semimetals. ¶ ～의 semimetalic.

**반기** refreshments on a tray to be passed around at the end of a party or ceremony. ～하다 pass the refreshments around at the end of a party 〔ceremony〕.

**반기**(反旗·叛旗) a standard 〔banner〕 of revolt 〔rebellion〕. ¶ ～를 들다 raise 〔unfurl〕 the standard of revolt; rise in revolt 《against》; take up arms 《against》; rise 〔revolt〕 《against》 / 환경 단체들은 그 제안에 ～를 들고 일어섰다 Environmental groups rose up against the proposal.

**반기**(半期) a half term 〔year〕. ¶ 상〔하〕～ the first 〔latter〕 half of the year / ～의 half-yearly; semiannual / ～마다 semiannually; half-yearly. ◉ ～결산 the half-yearly settlement 〔accounts〕. ～배당 a semiannual dividend.

**반기**(半旗) a flag at half-mast. ¶ ～를 걸다 hang 〔hoist, fly〕 a flag at half-mast〔-staff〕; half-mast a flag / 조의를 표하기 위해 관청 건물에 ～를 게양하고 있다 In order to express their condolence they are flying flags at half-mast on official buildings.

**반기다** rejoice to see 〔hear〕; be delighted at 〔with〕; be pleased 《at》; be glad 《of》. ¶ 반기는 얼굴로 with a look of joy on *one's* face / 손님을 ～ be delighted to see a guest; joyfully welcome the visitor.

**반기생**(半寄生) 〖생물〗 semiparasitism. ¶ ～의 hemiparasitic; semiparasitic. ◉ ～생물 a hemiparasite.

**반나마**(半—) more than 〔over〕 half.

**반나절**(半—) several hours (of the day); a quarter (of a day); half the morning. ¶ 어제는 ～을 독서로 보냈다 Yesterday I spent a quarter of the day reading.

**반나체**(半裸體) ¶ ～의 half-naked; seminude; seminaked. ◉ ～화 a seminude (picture).

**반날**(半—) half a day; a half day 《미》.

**반납**(返納) return; restoration. ～하다 return; give back; restore. ¶ 이 책은 내주까지 ～하게 되어 있다 This book is due 〔to be returned〕 next week.

**반년**(半年) half a year; a half year; six months. ¶ ～마다 half-yearly; semiannually; every half year / 이 보고서를 쓰는 데 ～ 걸렸다 It took me a half year to write this report.

**반닫이**(半—) a clothes chest which has upper half of the front board hinged.

**반달**(半—) ① 《달》 a half moon; 〖천문〗 a dichotomy. ¶ ～ 모양의 semicircular; semilunar. ② 《연의》 a crescent-shaped kite tail. ③ 《속 손톱》 a lunule; a lunula (*pl.* -lae). ④ 《보름 동안》 a half month; two weeks; a fortnight. ¶ ～치〔분〕의 semimonthly 《pay》 / 잡지를 ～에 한 번씩 내다 publish a magazine semimonthly. ◉ ～꼴 a semicircle.

**반달리즘** 《문화·공공시설의 파괴 행위》 Vandalism.

**반당**(反黨) 《행위》 antiparty activities. ¶ ～ 행위를 하다 engage in antiparty activities; oppose the party. ◉ ～분자 antiparty elements.

**반대**(反對) ① 《역(逆)》 the reverse; the opposite; the contrary. ¶ ～의 opposite 《direction》; reverse 《side》; contrary 《opinion》; adverse 《wind》 / ～로 《역으로》 the other 〔wrong〕 way; 《방향》 in the opposite direction; 《이에 반해》 on the contrary / ～되는 소문 a rumor to the contrary / ~ 방향에서 오다 come from the opposite direction / 나의 생각은 정~였다 I thought quite the opposite. / 사실은 그와 정~다 The reverse is the case. /어둠의 ~는 무엇입니까 What is the opposite 〔contrary〕 of dark? / 그와 ~로 동생은 근면하다 He is idle while his brother is diligent. / 오스트레일리아의 계절은 우리 나라와 정~다 The seasons in Australia are just opposite to ours. / 흑은 백의 ~이다 Black is the opposite of white. / 그녀는 내 명령에 ~되는 일을 했다 She did the reverse of what I ordered.

② 《반항》 opposition; resistance; antagonism; objection; kick 《구어》. ~하다 oppose; be opposed 《to》; offer opposition 《to》; object to 〔against〕; take exception 《to》; raise 〔make〕 an objection 《to》; take a stand 《against》; stand 〔be〕 《against》; antagonize; set *oneself* 《against》; kick 《구어》. ¶ ~의 opposite; contrary; hostile / …에 ~하여 in opposition 《to》; in defiance 《of》; against… / 한 사람도 ~하지 않고 unanimously; by common consent / 개혁에 ~하는 사람 a man hostile to reform / ~를 받다〔에 부딪치다〕 meet with 〔run into〕 opposition; be opposed 《by》 / ~를 외치다 cry against 《a policy》; raise an objection 《to, against》 / ~ 의사를 표명하다 declare *oneself* (to be) against 《a policy》; come out against 《a proposal》 / ~를 위한 반대를 하다 oppose「for opposition's sake 〔for the sake of opposition〕 / 끝까지 ~하다 stubbornly oppose 《a scheme》; hold out 《against *a person's* order》 / 그들은 내가 하는 일에는 무엇이든 ~한다 They are all against me whatever I do. / 자네가 어느 편을 택하든지 나는 ~하지 않겠네 Whichever you may take, I will not object to it. / ~ 의견을 가진 분은 안 계십니까 Do you have anything to say against it? / 그의 양친은 그 혼담에 ~하고 있다 His parents are opposed to the match. / 아내는 부업을 갖겠다지만 나는 ~한다 My wife is going to get part time job, but I will put my foot down. / 그 제안은 노조의 강경한 ~에 부딪쳤다 The proposal ran into strong opposition from the labor union.

◉ ~개념 a contrary concept. ~급부 〖법〗 a return service; a consideration. ~당(黨) the opposition (party); a party in opposition. ~론 an opposite opinion 〔view〕; a counterargument; an argument against 《a proposal》. ~명사 〖논리〗 contrary terms; opposites; contraries. ~명제 a contrary (proposition); an opposite. ~방향 the opposite direction. ~색 an antagonistic 〔opposing〕 color. ~설 an opposite view 〔opinion〕; a counterview. ~세력 counterforce. ~신문 〖법〗 (a) cross-examination: ~ 신문하다 cross-examine; cross-question. ~어 an antonym. ~운동 a counter action 〔movement〕; a movement 〔campaign〕 against 《a measure》. ~의견 《이의》 objection; 〖법〗 a dissenting opinion. ~자 an opponent; a dissenter; an objector; a kicker 《구어》. ~제안 《make》 a counterproposal. ~투표 negative voting; blackballing: ~ 투표하다 vote against 《a measure》; blackball 《an applicant》. ~파 an opposition faction; a dissident group. ~편 the opposite side; 《딴 쪽》 the other side: 우리는 달의 ~편을 볼 수 없다 We cannot see the other side of the moon. ~표 a negative 〔dissenting〕 vote.

**반대기** a flattened「dumpling 〔cooked vegetable ball〕. ◉ ~떡 a flattened rice dumpling.

**반덤핑**(反—) 〖경제〗 antidumping. ◉ ~관세 antidumping tariffs. ~법 antidumping act. ~조치 antidumping measures.

**반도**(半島) a peninsula. ¶ ~의 peninsular / 한~ the Korean Peninsula / 바다로 돌출한 ~ a peninsula jutting out into the sea / 한국은 호랑이 모양의 ~이다 Korea is a peninsula shaped like a tiger.

**반도**(叛徒) rebels; insurgents. ¶ 그는 거기서 ~들의 습격을 받았다 He was attacked there by the rebels 〔revolters〕.

**반도덕적**(反道德的) anti-moral. ¶ ~ 행위 anti-moral conduct.

**반도미**(半搗米) half-polished〔-cleaned〕 rice.

**반도체**(半導體) 〖물리〗 a semiconductor. ¶ 64메가 디램 ~ a 64 mega DRAM semiconductor / 금속 산화막 ~ a metal-oxide semiconductor / ~ 생산 기술 semiconductor production technology. ◉ ~소자 〖컴퓨터〗 a semiconductor device. ~재료 연구실 the Semiconductor Materials Laboratory.

**반독립**(半獨立) partial independence; semi-independence. ◉ ～국 a semi-independent state [country].

**반동**(反動) (a) reaction; counteraction; 《총 따위의》 kick; recoil. ～하다 react; rebound; kick; recoil. ¶ ～적(인) reactionary / ～으로 as a reaction / ～적인 정치가[인] a reactionary politician / ～을 일으키다 cause [occasion] a reaction / 이 총은 ～이 적다 This gun kicks only slightly. / 호경기의 ～으로 공황이 오는 경우가 많다 As a reaction from business boom, you often see a panic. ◉ ～내각 a reactionary Cabinet. ～력 reaction. ～분자 reactionary elements. ～사상 a reactionary thought [idea]. ～정부 a reactionary government. ～주의 reactionism: ～주의자 a reactionary. 무～총 a recoilless rifle.

**반두** 《그물》 a scoop net.

**반드럽다** ① 《물건이》 (be) smooth (and shining); glossy; sleek; glazed. ¶ 반드러운 종이 sleek paper / 대리석같이 ～ be as smooth as marble / 반드럽게 하다 (make) smooth. ② 《사람됨이》 (be) slick; shrewd; smart. ¶ 반드러운 사람 a smart guy; a slick operator.

**반드르르** glossily; smoothly; sleekly. ～하다 (be) smooth; glossy; sleek. ¶ ～ 윤기 흐르는 머리 glossy [sleek] hair / 마루를 얼음장같이 ～(하게) 닦다 polish a floor as smooth as a sheet of ice.

**반드시** ① 《꼭》 certainly; surely; without fail. ¶ ～ …하다 be sure to *do;* never fail to *do; do* without fail / 그들은 ～ 우리를 구하러 온다 They will surely [certainly] come to rescue us. *or* They are sure to come to rescue us. / 우리 팀은 ～ 이긴다 Our team is bound [certain, sure] to win. / 식사 전에는 ～ 손을 씻어라 Be sure to wash your hands before a meal. / 그는 ～ 성공한다 He is sure to succeed. / 아침 식사 전에 ～ 한 시간 산책을 한다 I make it a rule to take an hour's walk before breakfast.
② 《늘》 always; invariably; habitually. ¶ 크리스마스에는 ～ 매출이 오른다 Inevitably, sales go up at Christmas. / 나는 출발하기 전에 ～ 기름을 점검한다 I always check my oil before starting. / 그들은 만나기만 하면 ～ 싸운다 They never meet without quarreling. / 부자라고 해서 ～ 행복한 것은 아니다 The rich are not always happy.
③ 《기필코》 by all means; at any price; at all costs; 《필연코》 inevitably; necessarily. ¶ 그를 ～ 시험을 치게 하시오 Let him take the examination by all means. / 우리는 ～ 그를 구해 낼 것이다 We will save [rescue] him at any price. / 전쟁은 ～ 불행을 가져온다 War necessarily brings disaster. / 번쩍이는 것이 ～ 다 금은 아니다 《속담》 All is not gold that glitters.

**반들거리다** ① 《건방지게 굴다》 be smartish; conceited; 《교활하다》 be cunning [crafty]; 《게으름 피우다》 idle; loaf; 《미》 goldbrick [goof off] 《on the job》. ② 《윤나다》 glisten; shine; have a gloss. ¶ 잘 닦아 반들거리는 복도 a well-polished corridor.

**반들반들** smoothly. ¶ 무릎이 닳아 ～한 바지 trousers worn shiny in the knees.

**반듯반듯하다** be all squared away.

**반듯이** so as to be sqare and level; in an even form [position]; straight; in a straight line; square; orderly; 《직립》 upright; erect; 《수직》 perpendicularly; vertically. ¶ ～ 하다 straighten; make 《*a thing*》 erect (세우다) / ～ 눕다 lie on *one's* back / ～ 서다 stand straight [upright] / ～ 앉다 sit straight [squarely, erect] / 연필을 ～ 잡다 hold a pencil right / 몸을 ～ 가누다, 자세를 ～ 하다 hold *oneself* straight; straighten *oneself* / ～ 놓아라 Place it on end.

**반듯하다** ① 《바르다》 (be) straight; square and level; even; 《정돈돼 있다》 (be) right; orderly; be in good order; be straightened up; 《복장 등이》 (be) neat. ¶ 네모 반듯한 상자 a perfectly square box / 상체를 반듯하게 펴다 straighten *one's* upper body / 책상을 반듯하게 놓다 set a desk right; put [set] a desk in order. ② 《반반하다》 (***a***) 《흠 없다》 (be) flawless; 《당당하다》 (be) respectable; decent. ¶ 반듯한 집안 a respectable family. (***b***) 《생김새가》 (be) of fine make; nice-[good-]looking; comely. ¶ 용모가 ～ have regular [comely] features / 반듯한 얼굴 a fine-featured face.

**반등**(反騰) 〖증권〗 a reactionary rise; a rebound; a rally. ～하다 rise in reaction; rally; rebound. ¶ 주가의 급～ a sharp rebound in stock prices.

**반딧불** the glow [glimmer] of a firefly. ¶ ～이 어둠 속에서 반짝인다 Fireflies glow in the dark.

**반딧불이** 《개똥벌레》 a firefly; a glowfly; a lightning bug 《미》.

**반락**(反落) 〚증권〛 a reactionary fall 《in stock prices》; a fall in reaction. ~하다 fall 〔drop〕 in reaction; fall 〔slip〕 back.

**반란**(反亂·叛亂) a rebellion; a revolt; an insurrection; 《봉기》 a rising; an uprising. ¶ ~을 일으키다 rise 〔break out〕 in revolt 〔rebellion〕; rebel 〔revolt, rise〕 《against》 / ~을 진압하다 get under 〔put down, suppress, pacify, quell〕 a revolt 〔rebellion〕 / ~이 일어났다 A revolt 〔rebellion〕 broke out. ◉ ~군 a rebel army; the rebel forces; insurgent 〔mutinous〕 troops. ~부대 insurgent troops. ~자 an insurgent; a rebel.

**반려**(伴侶) a companion; a partner; an associate; a mate. ¶ 일생의 ~ 《get》 a life partner; *one's* companion through life; *one's* spouse (배우자).

**반려**(返戾) return; giving back. ~하다 return; give back; restore. ¶ 사표를 ~하다 refuse 〔return〕 《*a person's*》 resignation.

**반론**(反論) a counterargument; an objection; a refutation. ~하다 refute; make an objection 《to》; utter an objection 《against》. ¶ ~을 펴다 bring 〔put, set〕 forward 〔forth〕 a counterargument / 그의 학설에 대해 갖가지 ~이 있다 There are all kinds of opposing argument against his theory. / 그의 의견에 ~을 제기하는 사람은 없었다 Nobody objected to 〔argued against〕 what he said.

**반만**(半萬) half a myriad; five thousand. ◉ ~년 five millennia; 5,000 years: ~년 역사 a 5,000-year-old history.

**반말**(半—) 《거친 말》 crude language; rough talk; words lacking in respect; impolite speech; slipshod 〔slovenly, insolent〕 speech; 《얕잡은 말》 a neutral style of speech (ignoring social differences). ~하다 talk roughly 〔slovenly〕; speak impolitely; use the low forms of speech 《to》.

**반면**(反面) the other side; the other hand; the reverse; the contrary; the opposite. ¶ ~에 on the other hand; on the other side; while on the other / 싼 ~에 좋지 않다 It's cheep, but on the other hand it isn't good.

**반면**(半面) ① 《얼굴의》 half the face; a half face; a profile (옆 얼굴). ¶ ~상(像) a profile; a silhouette (그림자 그림). ② 《사물의》 one side; a half; 《다른 면》 the other side. ¶ ~의 진리 a half truth / 생활의 ~ one side of *one's* living / 문제의 ~만을 보다 look at 〔on〕 only one side of the question / 어두운 〔약한〕 ~을 갖다 have *one's* dark 〔weak〕 side / 그의 성품에는 사람들이 잘 모르는 ~이 있다 The other side of his personality is hardly known to the world.

**반면**(盤面) 《바둑·장기의》 the face of a board; 《음반의》 the surface of a record. ¶ ~이 유리〔불리〕하다 The game is favorable 〔unfavorable〕.

**반모음**(半母音) 〚음성〛 a semivowel.

**반목**(反目) hostility; antagonism; variance; enmity; feud (장기간의). ~하다 be in antagonism 《with》; be at odds 〔variance〕 《with》; feud 《with》; be at feud 〔enmity〕 《with》; be at daggers drawn 《with》; do not see eye-to-eye 《with》. ¶ 양자간의 ~ antagonism between the two / 서로 ~하다 be hostile to each other / 양자간의 ~이 공공연히 계속되었다 The two have been at open defiance with each other. / 두 집안은 오랫 동안 서로 ~해 왔다 The two families have been at odds with each other for a long time.

**반몫**(半—) a half-share; half a (man's) portion 〔share〕.

**반문**(反問) a counter-question; a cross-question. ~하다 ask a question in return; ask back; 《반대신문하다》 cross-question; cross-examine. ¶ "그것은 무슨 뜻이죠" 라고 나는 ~했다 "What do you mean by that ?" I asked in return.

**반문**(斑紋) a spot; a speck; a speckle (많은); 《새·짐승의 깃털·가죽의》 marking(s). ¶ ~이 있다 be spotted 〔specked, speckled〕; be mottled / 표범은 황갈색 털가죽에 검은 ~이 있다 The leopard has a tawny skin covered with dark spots.

**반물** a dark 〔deep〕 blue; navy blue. ◉ ~집 a dyehouse (where they dye cloth navy blue). ~치마 a navy-blue skirt.

**반물질**(反物質) 〚물리〛 antimatter.

**반미**(反美) ¶ ~의 anti-American / ~ 선동을 하다 stir anti-American feeling. ◉ ~감정 an anti-American sentiment 〔feeling〕. ~시위 anti-U.S. demonstrations. ~주의 anti-Yankeeism; anti-Americanism: ~주의자 an anti-American.

**반미**(飯米) cooking rice; rice for meal.

◉ ～콩 cooking beans.

**반미개**(半未開) semi-barbarism. ◉ ～국 a semi-civilized country. ～인 semi-barbarous people; a semi-barbarian.

**반미치광이**(半—) a half-crazed person; a slightly mad person.

**반민주적**(反民主的) anti-democratic. ¶ ～ 입법 anti-democratic legislation.

**반바닥** the base of the thumb.

**반바지**(半—) short pants 〔trousers〕; knee trousers 〔pants〕; knee breeches (무릎 밑에서 홀친). ¶ ～ 차림의 소년들 boys with knee-length pants.

**반박**(反駁) (a) refutation; (a) confutation; (a) retort; (a) contradiction; 〖법〗 rebuttal. ～하다 refute; confute; retort; contradict; rebut. ¶ ～의 여지가 없는 irrefutable / 내가 이야기를 끝내자 그들은 일제히 나를 ～하기 시작했다 As soon as I concluded my speech, they started refuting me. ◉ ～(성명)서 a written refutation 〔retort〕.

**반반**(半半) ① 《절반》 half-and-half; a tossup (가능성의). ¶ ～으로〔씩〕 half-and-half; in half 〔halves〕; fifty-fifty / ～으로 나누다 halve; go halves 〔shares〕 《with *a person* in the profits》; split fifty-fifty; divide 《*a thing*》 into equal parts / ～으로 섞다 mix 《milk and coffee》 half-and-half / 소금과 설탕을 ～씩 넣다 put in sugar and salt half-and-half; add equal amounts of sugar and salt / ～으로 하자 Let's go fifty-fifty. *or* I will go halves with you. / 승산은 ～이다 The chances stand even. *or* It is a tossup. / 정부 제안에 대한 국민의 반응은 찬반이 ～이다 The people's reaction 〔response〕 to the Government's proposal is half in favor and half against. ② 《반의 반》 half of half; a quarter; a fourth.

**반반하다** ① 《반듯하다》 (be) smooth; even; regular; level; flat. ¶ 반반한 표면 a smooth surface / 반반하게 하다 level (down 〔up, off〕); flatten; even; make even 〔smooth〕; roll (금속 등을). ② 《인물이》 (be) nice-looking; comely; attractive; handsome. ¶ 반반한 여자 a nice-looking woman / 얼굴이 ～ have regular 〔clear-cut〕 features; be good-looking. ③ 《문벌이》 (be) respectable; good; decent. ¶ 집안이 ～ come from a good family.

**반발**(反撥) ① 《되퉁김》 rebounding; a backlash; 〖물리〗 repulsion. ～하다 repel; repulse; bound 〔spring〕 back; rebound / 자석의 같은 극은 서로 ～한다 The same poles of magnets repel each other. ② 《반항》 opposition; resistance; insubordination. ～하다 oppose; resist; be offended 《by》; rebel 《against》. ¶ 크게 ～을 느끼고 있다 be in great reaction 《against》 / 나는 그의 말에 ～을 느꼈다 I felt repulsion toward his remarks. ◉ ～력 force of repulsion. ～작용 repulsion.

**반백**(半白) ¶ ～의 half-white; grayish; 《머리가》 grizzled; pepper-and-salt; streaked 〔shot〕 with gray / ～의 사나이 a man with grizzled hair.
◉ ～노인 a grizzled old man.

**반백**(半百) half a hundred; half a century; 50 years 「old 〔of age〕.

**반벙어리**(半—) a half-mute; one who lisps; a mumbler; a stammerer.

**반병신**(半病身) ① 《반불구자》 a half-cripple; a semi-paralytic; a partially handicapped person. ② 《반편》 a half-wit.

**반보**(半步) half a step; a half step.

**반복**(反復) repetition; (re)iteration; repeat. ～하다 repeat; reiterate; iterate; do 《*something*》 over again. ¶ ～하여 repeatedly; over again; again and again / ～하여 말하다 say over again; repeat *oneself* / 역사는 ～한다 History is the record of repetition. *or* History repeats itself. ◉ ～기호 〖음악〗 a sign of repetition; a repeat. ～발생 〖생물〗 palingenesis. ～설 〖철학〗 the recapitulation theory. ～시험 a repeat test. ～연습 repeated practice: ～ 연습은 학생에게 가장 긴요하다 Repeated practice is of the first importance to the students.

**반복**(反覆) 《언행의》 fickleness; inconstancy; 《생각의》 repeated switching 《of *one's* opinion, decision, *etc.*》. ～하다 switch 〔shift〕 again and again. ◉ ～무상(無常) inconstancy; instability.

**반봉건**(半封建) semi-feudalism. ◉ ～사상〔사회〕 a semi-feudalistic idea 〔society〕.

**반분**(半分) 《나눔》 halving. ～하다 《나누다》 halve; divide into halves; go halves 〔shares, fifty-fifty〕 《with *a person* in *a thing*》; 《자르다》 cut in (-to) halves. ¶ 이익을 ～하다 share the profit equally; go fifty-fifty on 〔in〕 the profit / 서로 ～하자 Let's share it equally.

**반비례**(反比例) 〖수학〗 inverse proportion 〔ratio〕 《to》; reciprocal proportion 〔ratio〕. ～하다 be in inverse proportion 〔ratio〕《to》; be inversely proportional 《to》. ¶ …에 ～하여 in inverse proportion 〔ratio〕 to…; inversely proportional to… / 기온은 높이에 ～한다 Temperature is in inverse 「proportion 〔ratio〕 to altitude.

**반빗**(飯—) a woman 〔female〕 cooking servant in charge of making side dishes. ◉ ～간(間) a kitchen. ～아치 an official side-dish cook (in the palace).

**반사**(反射) reflection; reflexion《영》; reverberation; 《생리적》 a reflex. ～하다 reflect; throw back; reverberate. ¶ ～적인 reflective; reflexive / ～적으로 reflectively; by reflex / 거울은 빛을 ～한다 A mirror reflects light. / 달은 태양의 빛을 ～하여 빛난다 The moon shines by the reflected light of the sun. / 나는 ～적으로 일어났다 I stood up as if by (a) reflex action. ◉ ～각〔선〕 the angle 〔line〕 of reflection. ～경 a reflector; a reflecting mirror. ～광 reflected light. ～광선 reflected rays. ～광학(光學) catoptrics. ～기(器) a reflector. ～능〔력〕 reflective power. ～등 a reverberator. ～로(爐) a reverberator; a reverberatory furnace 〔kiln〕. ～망원경 a reflecting telescope; a reflector. ～면 a specular surface. ～상(像) a reflected image. ～성 reflexibility ～신경 a reflexes. ～열 reflected heat. ～운동 a reflex movement 〔motion〕; a reflex. ～율 reflexibility. ～작용 a reflex (action). ～체 a reflector. ～카메라 a reflex camera. ～파 a reflected wave. ～현미경 a reflecting microscope.

**반사회적**(反社會的) antisocial. ¶ 무정부주의자의 ～ 학설 the anarchist's antisocial teachings.

**반삭**(半朔) half a month; a half month.

**반상**(班常) the nobles and the commoners; the high and the low(ly).

**반상(기)**(飯床(器)) a set of dishes for a table; a table service; a dinner set.

**반상회**(班常會) a neighborhood meeting; a monthly neighbors' meeting.

**반색하다** show great joy; rejoice 《in, at》; be delighted 《in》; light up with joy; be 〔become〕 all smiles; be glad of; delight in. ¶ 반색하며 옛친구를 맞다 receive *one's* old friend with 「great joy 〔open arms〕.

**반생**(半生) half *one's* life; half a lifetime. ¶ 전〔후〕～ the former 〔latter〕 half of *one's* life / ～을 보내다 spend half a lifetime / 그는 그 연구에 ～을 바쳤다 He devoted half his life to the research.

**반생반사**(半生半死) ¶ ～의 half-alive and half-dead; half-dead; all but dead; more dead than alive.

**반석**(盤石) a huge rock; 《견고》 firmness. ¶ ～같이 as firm 〔steadfast〕 as a rock / ～ 같은 adamantine (견고한) / 국기(國基)를 ～ 위에 올려 놓다 place 〔set up〕 *one's* country on a stable foundation.

**반설음**(半舌音) ＝ 반혓소리.

**반성**(反省) ① 《내성》 self-examination; reflection; introspection; reconsideration (재고). ～하다 think 《*something*》 over; search *one's* conscience; reflect on *one's* past conduct; reconsider; 《후회하다》 regret; be sorry 《for》. ¶ ～적 심리 reflective psychology / ～하고 〔해 보니〕 on second thought(s); on reflection / ～을 촉구하다 ask 〔urge〕 《*a person*》 to reconsider 《*a matter*》; call on 《*a person*》 to reflect on *his* past conduct / 정부의 ～을 촉구하다 demand the government's reconsideration / 나는 내가 한 일을 ～했다 I reflected on what I had done. / 그는 ～의 빛이라고는 없다 He shows no sign of regret 〔remorse〕 (for what he did). ② 《자기 관찰》 self-observation. ～하다 observe *one's* self.

**반세기**(半世紀) half a century.

**반소**(反訴) 〖법〗 a cross action; a counteraction; a countersuit; a counterclaim; a countercharge. ～하다 counterclaim; bring a cross action; file a countersuit. ¶ 손해 배상의 ～ a counterclaim for damages / ～를 제기하다 ＝ ～하다. ◉ ～인 a counterclaimant. ～장 a cross bill.

**반소**(半燒) partial destruction (by fire). ～하다 be partially destroyed (by fire); be partially 〔half〕 burnt. ¶ 옆집에서 난 불로 우리 집도 ～했다 The fire, which broke out in the neighboring house, burnt down half of my house.

**반소경**(半—) (being) half-blind; 《사람》 a person of dimsighted 〔purblind eyes〕; 《문맹자》 an unlettered 〔illiterate〕 person.

**반소매**(半—) a half-〔short-〕sleeve; a half-length sleeve. ¶ ～의 half-〔short-〕sleeved / ～ 셔츠〔블라우스〕 a shirt 〔blouse〕 with short(-length) sleeves; a half-〔short-〕sleeved shirt 〔blouse〕.

**반송**(返送) sending back; return. ～하다 send back; return. ¶ 선편으로 ～하다 ship back / 발송자에게 ～하다 return to the sender / 주소 불명 우편물은 ～된다 The mail, if its address is unknown, will be sent back 〔returned〕. ◉ ～료 《우편의》 return postage. ～화물〔운임〕 return cargo 〔freight〕.
**반송**(搬送) conveyance. ～하다 convey; carry. ◉ ～파(波) a carrier wave.
**반송장**(半—) a person half dead (from age and infirmity); a person who has one foot in the grave; a good-for-nothing old man 〔woman〕.
**반송하다**(伴送—) send 《*a thing*》 along with.
**반수**(半數) half the number; half 《of the members》. ¶ 위원 ～의 재선출 the reelection of half the committee / ～를 넘다 be more than half the number; show 〔hold〕 a majority / 학생의 ～는 기숙사 생활을 하고 있다 Half (of) the students live in the dormitory.
**반숙**(半熟) [형용사적] half-〔soft-〕boiled; half-cooked; half-done. ～하다 boil 《an egg》 soft 〔lightly〕; be half-boiled 〔half-done〕. ¶ ～ 달걀 a half-〔soft-〕boiled egg; a half-done egg.
**반시**(半時) 《반시간》 half an hour.
**반시간**(半時間) half an hour; a half hour 《미》; thirty minutes.
**반시류**(半翅類) 〖곤충〗 Hemiptera.
**반식민지**(半植民地) ¶ ～ 국가 a semicolonial state / ～ 상태 semicolonialism.
**반신**(半身) 《상하의》 half (of) the body; half-length; 《좌우의》 one side of the body. ¶ 상〔하〕～ the upper 〔lower〕 half of the body / 좌〔우〕～ the left 〔right〕 side of the body / 왼쪽 ～이 마비되다 be paralyzed on the left side of the body.
◉ ～불수 paralysis of one lateral half of the body; hemiplegia: ～불수가 되다 be paralyzed on one side. ～사진 a half-length photograph; a vignette. ～상 a half-length statue 〔portrait〕; a half figure; a bust.
**반신**(半神) ◉ ～반수 a half-god and half-beast. ～반인 a demigod.
**반신**(返信) 《질문 등에 대한 정식 답변》 a reply; an answer; a reply telegram (전신의). ～하다 answer 〔reply to〕 a letter; send a reply. ◉ ～료 postage for a reply; return postage. ～용 봉투 a stamped addressed envelope. ～용 엽서 a reply (postal) card.
**반신**(叛臣) a rebel retainer 〔courtier〕; a traitorous 〔rebellious〕 minister.
**반신반의**(半信半疑) ～하다 be half in doubt; be suspicious 〔doubtful〕 of; halfway doubt. ¶ ～의 incredulous; dubious; half in doubt / ～로 half in doubt; doubtfully; dubiously / 그녀는 ～하는 눈치였다 She looked incredulous. / 나는 ～하며 그의 이야기를 듣고 있었다 I was half in doubt listening to his talk. *or* I couldn't quite believe his words.
**반실하다**(半失—) lose 〔waste〕 half; half-lose; half-waste. ¶ 반실되다 be half-lost 〔half-wasted〕.
**반심**(叛心) a rebel's 〔rebellious〕 heart; treacherous mind; the intention to revolt. ¶ ～을 품다 harbor rebellious intentions; be treacherous 《against, to》.
**반암**(斑岩) 〖지질〗 porphyry.
**반액**(半額) 《정가의 절반》 half (the) price; 《운임 등》 half (the) fare; 《입장료 등》 a half-rate; half the amount 〔sum〕. ¶ ～으로 at half the price 〔fare〕; at half-price / ～으로 하다 reduce the price 〔fare〕 by half; cut the price by half; make a fifty percent discount / 12 세 미만의 어린이는 ～입니다 Children under twelve are allowed half rates.
**반야심경**(般若心經) 〖불교〗 the *Prajñā-para-mitā-sutra* (Sans.).
**반양성자**(反陽性子) 〖물리〗 an antiproton.
**반어**(反語) 《비꼬기》 an irony; an ironical expression; 《수사적 의문》 a rhetorical question; 《반의어》 a word in reverse; an antonym. ¶ ～적(인) ironic; ironical / ～를 쓰다 speak ironically / "fine"이라는 말은 곧잘 ～로 쓰인다 The word "fine" is often used ironically.
**반역**(反逆·叛逆) (high) treason; breach of faith 〔allegiance〕; treachery; (an) insurrection; (a) rebellion; (a) revolt; insurgency; mutiny. ～하다 turn traitor; revolt 〔rebel〕 《against》; rise in revolt 〔mutiny〕. ¶ ～적 treasonous; rebellious; treacherous / ～을 꾀하다 plot treason 《against》; conspire 《against》 / 그들은 국왕에게 ～했다 They rebelled 〔revolted〕 against the King.
◉ ～자 a traitor; an insurgent; a rebel; a plotter; a mutineer. ～죄 (high) treason: ～죄를 범한 guilty of high treason / ～죄로 처형되다 be executed for treason.
**반열**(班列) (a) rank; order. ¶ …의 ～에 들다 rank 〔be ranked〕 among…;

take *one's* place among… / 귀족의 ~에 오르다 be raised to 〔on〕 the peerage / 강국의 ~에 들다 rank among the Great Powers.

**반영**(反英) ¶ ~의 anti-British. ◉ ~운동 an anti-British movement. ~주의 《take》 an anti-British stand; anti=Britishism.

**반영**(反映) reflection. ~하다 《…을》 reflect; 《…이》 be reflected 《in》. ¶ 여론의 ~ a reflex of public opinion / 이 책은 시대를 ~하고 있다 This book is a mirror of the times. / 법률은 일국의 도의를 ~한다 Laws reflect the morals of a country. / 국민의 여론은 여간해서 국회에 ~되지 않는다 It takes time for public opinion to be reflected in the National Assembly. / 신문은 세태의 흐름을 ~한다 The press is the mirror of society. / 높은 범죄 발생률은 불안정한 사회를 ~한다 A high crime rate is a reflection of an unstable society. / 이 드라마의 대화는 오늘날 젊은이들이 쓰는 말투를 여실히 ~해 주고 있다 The dialog in this drama vividly reflects the conversational style of young people today.

**반영구적**(半永久的) (being) semi-permanent. ¶ ~인 건물 a semi-permanent building.

**반올림**(半—) ~하다 round 《a figure》 off 《to the nearest whole number》; 《소수점 이하를》 count fractions of .5 and over as a unit and cut away the rest. ¶ 0.5 이상의 끝수를 ~하다 raise fractions not lower than 0.5 to a unit.

**반원**(半圓) a half circle; a semicircle. ¶ ~을 그리다 make 〔draw〕 a half-circle; describe a semicircle. ◉ ~주(周) a semicircumference. ~형 a semicircle; a hemicycle: ~형의 semicircular; half-round.

**반월**(半月) a half moon. ⇨ 반달. ◉ ~기(旗) the crescent. ~형 a semicircle; a half-moon: ~형의 semicircular; semilunar; crescent(-shaped).

**반유대**(反—) ¶ ~의 anti-Semitic. ◉ ~주의 anti-Semitism: ~주의자 an anti-Semite; a Jew biter.

**반유동체**(半流動體) 〖화학〗 a semiliquid; a semifluid.

**반음**(半音) 〖음악〗 a (chromatic) semitone; a half tone; a half step. ¶ ~올리다〔내리다〕 sharp 〔flat〕 《a tone》 / …보다 ~ 높다〔낮다〕 be a half tone higher 〔lower〕 than…; be higher 〔lower〕 in pitch by a half tone than…. ◉ ~계 a chromatic scale. ~정 a chromatic interval; a semitone. ~표 a half note; 《영》 a minim.

**반응**(反應) 〖화학〗 (a) reaction; 《반작용》 counteraction; 《반향》 a response; 《효과》 an effect. ~하다 react 《to, on》; act 《on, upon》; respond 《to》. ¶ 핵〔연쇄〕 ~ a nuclear 〔chain〕 reaction / 자극에 대한 ~ response to a stimulus / ~이 없다 show no reactions; have no effect 《on》; make 〔give〕 no response; be impassive / ~이 없는 irresponsive; ineffectual; unresisting / ~을 일으키다 act 《on》; produce a response / 알칼리성의 ~을 보이다 show an alkaline reaction / 꾸짖어도 그는 전혀 ~이 없다 Scolding has no effect on him at all. / 신경은 자극에 ~한다 Nerves respond to a stimulus. / 그 소식을 듣고 그는 어떻게 ~했습니까 How did he react to the news? / 주사를 놓았지만 환자는 아무런 ~도 없었다 The injection had no (responsive) effect upon the patient. / 우리들의 호소에 대해 그들은 아무런 ~도 없었다 We got no response to our appeal from them. *or* They didn't respond to our appeal at all. ◉ ~기(器) 〖생물〗 an effector. ~물질 〖화학〗 a reactant. ~속도 reaction velocity. ~시간 a latent period; reaction time. ~실험 a reaction experiment. ~열 heat of reaction. ~체질 a reactor.

**반의반**(半—半) one fourth; a quarter.

**반의식**(半意識) 〖심리〗 subconsciousness. ¶ ~적 subconscious; half-conscious.

**반의어**(反意語) 〖언어〗 an antonym.

**반일**(半—) a half-day's work; a half=time job; half the work.

**반일**(反日) ¶ ~의 anti-Japanese. ◉ ~감정 an anti-Japanese sentiment 〔feeling〕.

**반일**(半日) half a day; a half day.

**반입**(搬入) carrying 〔taking, bringing〕 in. ~하다 carry 〔take, bring, send〕 《*a thing*》 in. ¶ 출품된 작품이 속속 전시회장에 ~되었다 The works for exhibition were brought into the hall one after another. ◉ ~일 《전람회 등의》 the days 〔period〕 (designated) for the sending in of exhibits.

**반입자**(反粒子) an antiparticle.

**반자** 〖건축〗 ceiling. ¶ ~를 드리다 ceil; board a ceiling; put up 〔hang〕 a ceiling. ◉ ~널 a ceiling board

〔panel〕. ~지 the ceiling paper. ~틀 a ceiling joist.

**반자성**(反磁性) 〖물리〗 diamagnetism. ¶ ~의 diamagnetic.
◉ ~체 a diamagnetic (substance).

**반작용**(反作用) 〖물리〗 (a) reaction; (a) counteraction. ¶ ~의〔적〕 reactive; counteractive / 작용과 ~ action and reaction / ~을 보이다 react 《upon》/ ~을 일으키다 cause a reaction / 그것의 ~으로 이것이 일어났다 This came to happen as a reaction of that. / 작용이 있으면 반드시 ~이 뒤따른다 Action is always followed by reaction.

**반장**(班長) a squad 〔section, group〕 leader; 《학급의》 a monitor; a class president; 《작업의》 a foreman; 《동네의》 the head of a neighborhood association.

**반장화**(半長靴) half boots; short boots.

**반전**(反戰) (being) antiwar; renunciation of war. ¶ ~의 antiwar / ~을 외치다 cry against war.
◉ ~데모 an antiwar demonstration. ~론 pacifism; opposition to war: ~론자 a pacifist; a peace advocate; a dove. ~사상 an antiwar sentiment 〔ideas〕. ~운동 an antiwar campaign 〔movement, protests〕. ~주의 pacifism: ~주의자 a pacifist. ~파 an antiwar faction 〔elements〕; the dove.

**반전**(反轉) ① 《돎》 turning in the reverse direction. ~하다 turn 〔revolve〕 in the reverse direction; turn reversely 〔the other way around〕. ② 《방향이 뒤바뀜》 reversal. ~하다 reverse (itself); be reversed; reverse *one's* 〔*its*〕 course. ¶ 형세는 ~되었다 The situation has reversed (itself). / 테이프는 마지막에 이르면 자동적으로 ~한다 When the tape cames to the end, it automatically reverses.
◉ ~필름 reversal film. ~현상 〖사진〗 reversal; solarization. 급~ 〖항공〗 a split turn. 급상승~ 〖항공〗 wing over.

**반절**(半—) a half bow.

**반절**(半折) ① 《접음》 halving; folding in the middle; cutting into two. ~하다 halve; cut in(to) two; fold in the middle. ② 《반쪽》 a half sheet of paper; half size.

**반점**(斑點) a spot; a speck; a speckle (많은 경우); 《짐승 가죽·새 깃털 등의》 marking(s); a fleck. ¶ ~이 있는 spotted; specked; speckled / ~이 있다 be covered with spots; be speckled.

**반정**(反正) ① 《왕에게》 reforming the government by deposing the king 〔present ruler〕; taking over the throne after dethroning a wicked king. ~하다 depose 〔replace〕 the ruler; take over the throne. ② 《회복·쇄신》 restoration; renovation. ~하다 bring back to a proper 〔normal〕 condition; restore order.

**반정립**(反定立) 〖철학〗 antithesis.

**반정부**(反政府) ¶ ~의 antigovernment antiministerial / ~ 활동 혐의로 구속되다 be arrested on 〔under〕 suspicion of antigovernment activities.
◉ ~당 an opposition party. ~신문 an antigovernment newspaper.

**반정신**(半艇身) half a (boat's) length. ¶ ~의 차로 이기다 win a race by half a length.

**반제**(反帝) anti-imperial(ism).
◉ ~(국주의)운동 the anti-imperialist movement. ~사상 anti-imperialist ideas 〔thought〕. ~주의 anti-imperialism. ~투쟁 the struggle against imperialism.

**반제**(返濟) (a) payment; (a) repayment; refundment; return.

**반제품**(半製品) half-〔semi-〕finished goods.

**반주**(半周) a semicircle; a hemicycle. ~하다 go half round 《a place》.

**반주**(伴奏) an accompaniment. ~하다 play 《*a person's*》 accompaniment 《on the piano》; accompany 《*a person* on the piano》. ¶ 관현악의 ~ an orchestral accompaniment / A의 ~로 노래하다 sing with A's accompaniment / 무~로 노래하다 sing without instrumental accompaniment / 피아노 ~에 맞추어 노래하다 sing to a piano accompaniment / 피아노로 바이올린의 ~를 하다 accompany the violin on the piano
◉ ~부 the accompaniment. ~자 an accompanist.

**반주**(飯酒) liquor with *one's* food 〔meals〕; liquor taken at meal time.

**반주권국**(半主權國) a semi-dependent country.

**반주그레하다** (be) rather nice-looking. ¶ 반주그레하게 생긴 여자 a comely woman.

**반죽** kneading; dough; paste. ~하다 knead 《flour》; work 《clay》. ¶ 밀가루를 (되게) ~하다 knead flour into (stiff) dough. ◉ ~그릇 a kneading trough.

**반죽음**(半—) being half-dead〔-killed〕; 《모진 고비》 extremely hard 〔trying〕

circumstances. ～하다 be nearly 〔all but〕 killed; suffer terribly. ¶ ～을 만들다 half-kill; beat 〔flog〕 《*a person*》 nearly to death / ～이 되다 be more dead than alive / 대파된 차에서 구출되었을 때 그는 ～이 되어 있었다 When he was rescued from wrecked car, he was more dead than alive.

**반죽좋다** (be) audacious; brazen; impudent; shameless; unabashed; saucy. ¶ 반죽좋게 …하다 have the cheek 〔face, nerve, impudence〕 to *do.*

**반증**(反證) (a) proof to the contrary; disproof; counterevidence. ¶ ～을 들다 〔제시하다〕 produce counterevidence; prove the contrary 〔negative〕; disprove / 진술의 ～으로서 증거를 제시하다 offer evidence against 〔in disproof of〕 a statement / 검찰측 증거에 대한 ～을 제시하다 disprove the evidence submitted by the prosecution / 그에 대한 ～이 없다 There is no evidence to disprove it.

**반지**(斑指) a (finger) ring. ¶ 금〔다이아몬드〕～ a gold 〔diamond〕 ring / ～낀 손가락 a ringed finger / ～를 끼다 put 〔slip〕 a ring on *one's* finger; pass a ring over a finger / ～를 끼고 있다 have 〔wear〕 a ring on *one's* finger / ～를 빼다 take 〔slip〕 a ring off *one's* finger. ◉ ～자국 a ring mark 《on the finger》.

**반지기**(半—) [형용사적] adulterated with. ¶ 모래〔돌, 겨, 뉘〕 ～ 쌀 hulled rice with sand 〔stones, husks, bran〕 in it.

**반지랍다** (be) smooth and glossy; sleek. ¶ 반지랍게 하다 (make) smooth; 《기름 따위로》 lubricate.

**반지르르** glossily; sleekly; lustrously. ¶ 머리에 기름을 ～ 바르다 oil *one's* hair till it shines.

**반지름**(半—) 〖수학〗 a radius; a semidiameter. ⇨ 반경(半徑).

**반지빠르다** ① 《교만하다》 (be) snobbish; affected; stuck-up; offensive; pert; presumptuous; impudent; impertinent; saucy. ¶ 반지빠른 자식 an impertinent 〔a saucy〕 fellow; a conceited pup; a snob. ② 《어중간하다》 (be) good neither for one thing nor the other; inadequate; inappropriate; troublesome; inconvenient; awkward (다루기가). ¶ 옷감이 치마 만들기에는 짧고, 저고리 만들기에는 길어 ～ The cloth is an awkward size—too short to make a skirt and too long to make a coat.

**반직업적**(半職業的) semi-professional. ¶ ～인 운동 선수 a semi-professional athlete 〔player〕.

**반짇고리** a workbox; a sewing box; a housewife (★발음은 [hʌ́zif]).

**반질거리다** ① 《매끈하다》 be slippery 〔sleek, smooth, oily, glossy〕. ¶ 새로 왁스를 먹여서 마루가 반질거린다 The floor, newly waxed, is slippery. ② 《교활하다》 be sly 〔slick, wily, crafty, cunning〕.

**반질반질** ① 《매끈함》 sleekly; smoothly; in an oily 〔slippery〕 fashion. ～하다 (be) slippery; smooth; sleek. ¶ ～한 대머리 a head as bald as an egg. ② 《교활함》 slyly; craftly; artfully; cunningly. ～하다 (be) sly; crafty; cunning.

**반짝** 《빛 따위가》 with a flash; 《감각·의식 따위가》 suddenly; with a start; 《들어올리는 모양》 easily; with no effort. ⇨ 번쩍.

**반짝반짝** brilliantly; glitteringly; dazzlingly. ～하다 glitter; gleam; glisten; sparkle; twinkle; flash; shine. ¶ ～하는 별 twinkling stars / ～ 빛나는 보석 glittering jewels / 구둣솔로 ～ 윤이나게 구두를 닦다 polish *one's* shoes to a bright shine with a brush / 그녀는 부엌살림을 ～ 윤이나게 닦아 놓았다 She put a good shine on all her kitchen utensils.

**반짝이다** shine; glitter; be bright 〔brilliant〕; twinkle (별 따위가); glimmer (멀리서). ¶ 반짝이는 눈 twinkling eyes / 반짝이는 보석 sparkling gems / 금처럼 ～ glitter like gold / 햇빛에 거울을 ～ flash a mirror in the sun(light) / 먼데서 불빛이 반짝인다 A light is glimmering from afar. / 풀잎에 이슬이 맺혀(서) 반짝였다 The dewdrops sparkled 〔glistened〕 on the leaves. / 그녀의 보석이 남포 불빛에 반짝였다 Her jewels shone in the lamplight.

**반쪽**(半—) (a) half.

**반쯤**(半—) (about) half; halfway. ¶ 눈을 ～ 뜨고 with *one's* eyes slightly open / ～ 되는 곳에 《be》 somewhere in between / 나는 그 책을 아직 ～밖에 읽지 못했다 I have read only half the book.

**반찬**(飯饌) dishes to go with the rice; a side dish; subsidiary food. (★ 영미의 식사에는 우리처럼 주식인 「밥」과 「반찬」이란 개념이 따로 없다. 우리의 주식인 「밥」은 영미에서는 「빵」이 아니라, 「고기·생선」 따위를 가리킨다). ¶ 고기 ～ a meat dish / 맛있는 ～ a delicious dish / 생선 ～으로 밥을 먹다 eat rice with fish / 시장이 ～이다 《속담》 Hunger is the best sauce. ◉ ～가게 a grocery (store); a grocer's (shop). ～거리 groceries; materials for making side dishes.

**반창고**(絆瘡膏) 《미》 an adhesive bandage; 《영》 a sticking plaster; a Band-Aid (상표명). ¶ ～를 붙이다 apply a sticking plaster 《to the wound》.

**반체제**(反體制) anti-Establishment. ◉ ～운동 an anti-Establishment movement. ～인사 a dissident. ～작가 a dissident 〔an anti-Establishment〕 writer. ～주의자 an anti-Establishmentarian. ～파 people who are against the Establishment; anti-Establishment groups.

**반추**(反芻) rumination. ～하다 ruminate; chew the cud. ¶ 그는 선생님 말씀을 ～했다 He chewed over 〔ruminated upon〕 what his teacher had said. ◉ ～동물 a ruminant. ～위(胃) the ruminant stomach.

**반출**(搬出) carrying 〔taking〕 out. ～하다 carry 〔take〕 out. ¶ 한국 문화재는 국외 ～이 금지되어 있다 Korean laws prohibit taking cultural assets out of Korean territory.

**반취**(半醉) half-drunkenness; slight intoxication. ～하다 be half-drunk; be half-tipsy; slightly intoxicated.

**반칙**(反則) (an) infringement 〔violation〕 of rules; breaking the rules; 《경기에서의》 (a) foul play; a foul. ～하다 break 〔violate, infringe, act against〕 the rules; foul; play foul; commit a foul. ¶ ～의 foul; against the rules; contrary to the regulations / ～으로 퇴장당하다 foul out of the game / (상대의) ～을 주장하다 lodge a foul against 《a rival》; claim a foul / ～패하다 lose a game on foul / 그것은 ～이다 It is against the rule(s). ◉ ～금 a fine. ～자 an offender.

**반침**(半寢) a small room attached to a large room; a closet.

**반코트**(半—) a topcoat; a topper.

**반타작**(半打作) 〖농업〗 sharing 《the crops》 half-and-half 《with the landowner》. ～하다 share equally 〔half-and-half〕 with the landowner; share the crop equally.

**반토**(礬土) 〖화학〗 alumina; alum.

**반투명**(半透明) translucency; semi-transparency. ～하다 (be) semi-transparent; translucent. ◉ ～체 a translucent; a semitransparent body.

**반파**(半破) partial destruction. ¶ ～되다 be partially 〔partly〕 destroyed.

**반편**(半偏) a half-wit; a fool; a blockhead; a simpleton. ～스럽다 (be) slow-〔half-〕witted; foolish; stupid; silly. ¶ ～노릇〔짓〕 a foolish action; foolishness; foolery / ～이 ＝반편 / ～같은 수작 foolish talk; an absurd story / ～ 노릇〔짓〕하다 do 《*a thing*》 foolish 〔stupid, silly〕; play the fool; make a fool of *oneself*.

**반포**(頒布) distribution; circulation; 《공포》 promulgation. ～하다 distribute; spread; circulate; promulgate.

**반푼**(半—) a farthing. ¶ ～어치 값어치도 없다 be not worth a farthing 〔penny〕.

**반품**(半—) half a day's work.

**반품**(返品) returned goods 〔merchandise〕; articles sent back; 《결함 따위로 회수된 물품》 recalled goods. ～하다 return 《goods》. ¶ 그 잡지는 ～이 많다 Quite a number of copies of the magazine return unsold from the market. / 불량품은 ～이 가능합니다 You can return the goods if they are defective. / ～ 사절 《게시》 All Sales Final.

**반하다**[1] ① 《이성에게》 fall in love 《with》; be enamored 《of》; lose *one's* heart 《to》; be attached 《to》; fall for; be taken 《with her, by her beauty》; take a fancy 《to》. ¶ 반한 여자 a woman of *one's* heart / 서로 ～ be in love with each other / 홀딱 ～ be deeply 〔madly〕 in love with; be head and ears 〔fall head over heels〕 in love 《with》; 《속어》 be dead gone on 《a girl》 / 여자에게 ～ fall for a girl / 한 눈에 ～ fall in love with 《*a person*》 at first sight / 그 여자가 반한 것은 그의 사람됨이 아니라 그의 돈이다 It is not him she is in love with; it's his money. / 반한 눈에는 곰보도 일색 Love blinds a man to all imperfection(s). ② 《감탄하여 끌리다》 be charmed 〔attracted〕; admire; 《넋을 잃다》 be entranced 〔enraptured〕. ¶ 인품에 ～ be charmed 〔taken〕 by 《*a person's*》 personality / 여자의 아름다움에 ～ be charmed by a girl's beauty / 그녀의 손재주에는 반하겠다 I just adore the way she uses her hands!

**반하다**[2] ⇨ 빤하다.

**반하다**(反—) ① 《어긋나다》 go 〔be〕 against; 《반대하다》 be opposed to; be contrary to; run counter to. ¶ …에

반하여〔반해서〕 against; contrary to…; in opposition 〔contradiction〕 to… / 이에 반하여 on the contrary; on the other hand; while / 기대에 ～ be against 〔contrary to〕 *one's* expectation(s) 〔wishes〕 / 그 조치는 우리들의 이익에 반한다 The measure is adverse to our interests. / 그는 자기 의사〔희망〕에 반하여 그 학교로 갔다 He was forced to enter that school against his will 〔wishes〕.

② 《위반하다》 violate; infringe. ¶ 규칙에 ～ be against the rules; violate 〔infringe〕 a rule / 규칙에 반하는 행위는 중벌에 처해진다 Conduct which is against the regulation shall be heavily punished. / 총리는 테러 행위는 국제 사회의 법과 질서에 반하는 것이라고 말했다 Prime Minister said the terrorist act runs counter to law and order in the international community.

**반하다**(叛—) rebel 〔revolt〕 against 《the ruler》; rise in revolt against 《the government》; turn traitor to 《*one's* country》.

**반합**(飯盒) 《군인용》 a (soldier's) canteen; a messtin; a mess kit.

**반항**(反抗) 《저항》 resistance; revolt; 《반대》 opposition; 《도전》 defiance; 《불복종》 disobedience; mutiny (상관에 대한 저항); 《반란》 rebellion; 《적대》 hostility; antagonism. ～하다 《저항하다》 oppose; resist; offer resistance to; 《따르지 않다》 disobey; 《도전하다》 defy; bid defiance 《to》; 《적대하다》 antagonize; be antagonistic 《to》; rebel 《against》. ¶ ～적인 아이 a disobedient 〔rebellious〕 child / ～적 정신 a rebel spirit / ～적(인) rebellious; defiant; antagonistic; hostile / ～적으로 defiantly; hostilely; rebelliously / …에 ～하여 in opposition to; in defiance of / 권위에 ～하다 revolt against authority / ～적 태도를 취하다 take 〔assume〕 a defiant 〔hostile〕 attitude 《toward》; set *one's* face 《against》 / 주인에게 ～하다 lift a hand against *one's* master / 요즘 그녀는 자주 부모에게 ～한다 These days she often disobeys her parents. / 요즘 부모에게 ～하여 가출하는 아이들이 늘고 있다 Recently more and more children have been leaving home in defiance of their parents.

◉ ～기 a rebellious age; the period of rebelliousness; the negative phase: 대부분의 아이들은 사춘기에 제2 ～기에 들어간다 Most children reach the second rebellious age in their lives at puberty. ～심 the spirit of insubordination; a rebellious spirit 〔mind〕.

**반향**(反響) 《음향》 an echo; reverberation(s); 《영향》 repercussions; influence; 《반응》 reflection; an echo; a response; (a) reaction. ～하다 echo; reecho; resound; reverberate; be reflected; affect. ¶ ～이 있다 find 〔have〕 an echo 〔a response〕 《in》; be echoed 《abroad》; be reflected 《on》 / ～이 없다 have no response 〔echo〕 《to》 / ～이 없는 unechoic / ～을 불러일으키다 evoke 〔call forth〕 an echo 〔a response〕 《in》; be responded to 《by》; create a sensation (대단한) / 그의 변설은 청중에게 아무런 ～을 일으키지 못했다 His oratorical efforts evoked no response in his audience. / 그 뉴스는 대단한 ～을 일으켰다 The news created 〔caused〕 a great sensation.

**반혁명**(反革命) a counterrevolution. ¶ ～의 counterrevolutionary.

◉ ～운동 an anti-revolutionary movement. ～파 an anti-revolutionaries.

**반혓소리**(半—) 〖언어〗 a semi-lingual 〔lateral〕 sound.

**반환**(返還) return; restoration; retrocession (영토의); restitution (원소유자에게); repayment(부채의). ～하다 give 〔hand〕 back; return; restore; retrocede; repay; replace. ¶ 빌려 본 책을 ～하다 return 《*a person*》 a borrowed book / …의 ～을 요구하다 demand 〔reclaim〕 the return of… / 도난당한 서류는 얼마 안 가서 소유주에게 ～되었다 The stolen document was soon restored to its owner. ◉ ～점 《마라톤의》 《at》 the turn; the turning point.

**반흘림**(半—) 《서체의》 semi-cursive writing.

**받다**[1] ① 《주는 것·오는 것을》 receive; get; accept; take; have; be given; be presented 《with》; obtain 《support from abroad》; 《수여되다》 be awarded; [사물이 주어] come 〔be〕 to hand. ¶ 연금을 받는 사람 a recipient of a pension / …을 받는 대로(곧) on receipt of 《goods》 / 교육을 ～ receive 〔get〕 an education; be educated 〔trained〕 《by》 / 냉대〔우대〕를 ～ be given a cold 〔warm〕 reception / 사과를 ～ accept an apology / 뇌물을 ～ take 〔receive, accept〕 a bribe; be bribed / 만점을 ～ get 〔score〕 full marks / 면허를 ～ obtain 〔take out〕 a license / 방문을 ～

have a visit 《from》 / 선물을 ~ receive 〔accept〕 a present 《from》; be presented with a gift / 신청을 ~ receive 〔accept〕 applications 〔subscriptions〕 / 전화를 ~ answer 〔get〕 a telephone call; have a (telephone) call from 《*a person*》 / 주문을 ~ receive an order / 허가를 ~ get 〔obtain〕 permission / 좋은 교육을 ~ receive a good education / 피아노 레슨을 ~ take lessons in 〔on the〕 piano / 이 학교는 매년 백 명의 신입생을 받는다 This school admits 100 new students each year. / 이달 14일부의 귀하의 서한을 받았습니다 I have received your letter of the 14th inst. *or* Thank you very much for your letter of the 14th inst. / 물품을 받는 대로 대금을 지불하겠습니다 I will pay the money on 〔upon〕 receipt of the goods. / 받으시는 대로 연락을 주십시오 Please acknowledge (your) receipt.

> 용법 **receive** 제공되거나 배달되는 물건을 수동적으로 「받다, 입수하다」란 뜻. **get** receive와 같은 뜻이며, 구어로서 아주 흔히 사용되는 말. 그러나 품위와 격식을 갖춘 느낌을 주려면 receive가 더 알맞음. **accept** 제공되는 물건·신청·초대 따위를 동의해서 받아들이는 일에 쓰이며 take보다 격식을 차린 느낌이 있는 말. **take** accept와 거의 같은 뜻의 말로서, 원칙적으로는 찬성하지만 그렇다고 기꺼이 받아들이는 것은 아니라는 뉘앙스가 있음.

② 《요금·값을》 charge; ask; 《급료 등을》 be paid 〔given〕; take; receive; 《세금을》 collect 《taxes》. ¶ 한끼 식사에 5천 원 ~ charge 5,000 won for one meal / 비싸게 ~ overcharge; charge too much 〔high〕 / 봉급을 ~ receive a salary; get paid; draw a salary 《of 800,000 won》.

③ 《당하다》 receive 《an insult》; suffer 《an jury》; sustain 《damage》; be subject to; incur 《a loss》. ¶ 공습을 ~ have an air raid; be raided / 모욕을 ~ suffer an insult 〔affront〕; be insulted / 벌을 ~ suffer 〔incur〕 punishment; be punished / 타격을 ~ be (hard) hit; suffer 〔receive〕 a (severe) blow / 혐의를 ~ fall 〔come〕 under suspicion; be suspected 《of》 / 그 소설은 많은 비판을 받았다 The novel was subjected to severe criticism.

④ 《치료·수술 등을》 undergo; go through. ¶ 치료를 ~ receive 〔undergo〕 medical treatment; be treated; receive medical attention / 맹장염 수술을 ~ undergo 〔have〕 an operation for appendicitis.

⑤ 《받아〔막아〕내다》 catch 《a ball》; take 〔accept〕 《a pass》; stop. ¶ 공을 맨손으로 ~ catch 〔stop〕 a ball with *one's* bare hands / 공을 못 ~ miss 〔fail to catch〕 a ball.

⑥ 《그릇에 담다》 put 〔take〕 in. ¶ 물을 한 통 ~ pour water into a bucket; get water in a bucket / 빗물을 물통에 ~ catch the rainwater in the bucket.

⑦ 《우산 따위를》 hold 《an umbrella》 over *one's* head; hold up; put up. ¶ 우산을 ~ carry an umbrella 《in the rain》; put up an umbrella / 양산을 ~ hold a parasol over *one's* head.

⑧ 《뿔·머리로》 butt; gore; hit head against; bang (with head); toss; knock down. ¶ 염소가 가슴을 ~ a goat butts 《*a person*》 in the chest / 머리로 문을 ~ bump *one's* head against the door.

⑨ 《뒤를 잇다》 inherit; succeed; follow; take over. ¶ 숙모의 유산을 1만달러 ~ inherit ten thousand dollars from *one's* aunt / 나는 그의 일을 넘겨 받아 사장이 되었다 I took over his work and became president.

⑩ 《사다》 (***a***) 《그릇에》 buy 《*anything* you can put in a container》. ¶ 술 한 병을 ~ get a bottle of rice wine. (***b***) 《소매상이》 buy 《*things*》 in a mass 〔by the gross〕 《and sell》. ¶ 받아서 팔다 retail.

⑪ 《아기를》 deliver 《a woman of a child》; assist 《a woman》 in 〔at〕 childbirth. ¶ 간호사가 아기를 받았다 A nurse delivered a child.

⑫ 《햇빛 따위를》 bask 《in the sun》; be bathed 《in the moonlight》; shine on 〔into〕; 《바람을》 catch. ¶ 달빛을 받은 호수 a lake in the moonlight / 햇빛을 받는 곳 a place in the sun; a sunny place / 햇빛을 받지 않는 곳에 두다 put 《*a thing*》 in the shade; keep 《*a thing*》 out of the sun / 이 방은 햇빛을 안 받는다 This room gets no sunshine.

⑬ 《기타》 ¶ 질문을 ~ be questioned; answer a question (응하다) / 하숙생을 ~ take in lodgers / 나는 프랑스어 강습을 받고 있다 I am taking a course in French. / 그들은 복지 원조〔생활 보호〕를 받고 있다 They are on welfare.

**받다**[2] 《구미에 맞다》 agree with 《*a person*》; suit *one's* palate 〔taste〕; set (well). ¶ 음식이 잘 ~ eat well; have a good appetite / 음식이 안 ~ lose *one's* appetite; have a poor appetite; *one's* stomach revolts against food / 좋은 음식이지만 입에 받지 않는다 The food is very nice but it does not agree with me.

**받들다** ① 《받쳐들다》 lift (up); hold up; uphold. ¶ 무거운 돌을 두 손으로 ~ hold up a heavy rock with both hands. ② 《지지하다》 uphold; support; 《보좌하다》 assist; aid; help; 《추대하다》 have 《*a person*》 over; 《승복하다》 obey 《with respect》; 《명을》 receive 《a command》. ¶ 아무의 명령을 받들고 in obedience to 〔in pursuance of〕 *a person's* order / 총재로 ~ have 《*a person*》 as 〔for〕 president / 정부를 ~ support the government / 어린 왕을 받들어 나라를 다스리다 help the young king rule 〔run〕 the country. ③ 《공경하다》 treat 《*a person*》 with deference; hold 《*a person*》 in reverence; look up to; venerate; esteem. ¶ 윗사람을 ~ honor 〔wait on, attend on〕 *one's* superiors / 늙은 부모를 ~ attend on *one's* old parents / 선배로 ~ look up to 《*a person*》 as *one's* elder / 스승을 지극히 ~ hold *one's* master in great esteem.

**받들어총**(一銃) presenting arms; 《구령》 Present arms! ~하다 present arms. ¶ ~을 하고 《stand》 at the present arms.

**받아넘기다** parry; elude; fend off; turn aside; dodge. ¶ 아무의 질문을 교묘히 ~ 「parry cleverly 〔evade, dodge〕 a *person's* question / 그는 짓궂은 질문을 잘 받아 넘겼다 He skillfully turned aside the embarrassing questions.

**받아들이다** 《받다》 accept 《a proposal》; receive 《*a person*》; 《동의하다》 assent to; comply with; 《들어 주다》 listen to; grant 〔go along with〕 《*a person's* request》; 《…뜻으로》 accept; take; 《믿다》 believe; 《이해하다》 understand; 《도입하다》 introduce. ¶ 받아들일 태세 preparedness 〔readiness〕 to receive 《new personnel》 / 받아들일 태세를 갖추다 get ready 〔make preparation〕 to receive / 새 학설을 ~ accept a new theory / 사실로 ~ take 《*a thing*》 for truth; accept 《a remark》 as true / 충고를 ~ follow 《*a person's*》 advice / 있는 그대로 ~ take 《*things*》 as *they* are / 미국의 생활 양식을 ~ adopt the American way of life / 할리우드 유행을 ~ introduce a Hollywood fashion / 일반적으로 받아들여지다 be generally accepted; find 〔win, gain, meet with〕 general acceptance / 받아들이기 쉽다〔어렵다〕 [사물이 주어] be acceptable 〔unacceptable〕 to *one* / 난민을 ~ accept refugees / 그렇게밖에는 받아들일 수 없다 It cannot be viewed in another light. / 이 설은 아직 다수의 학자에게는 받아들여지지 않고 있다 This theory has not yet found acceptance with most scholars.

**받아쓰기** (a) dictation; writing to dictation. ~하다 have dictation. ¶ ~를 시키다 give dictation 《to》.

**받아쓰다** write 〔take, put, note〕 down; take down from dictation. ¶ 강의를 ~ take notes of a lecture; write from a lecture / 연설을 속기로 ~ take down a speech in shorthand / 받아쓰게 하다 dictate 《a passage》 to 《*a person*》; have 《*a person*》 take 《*a matter*》 down / 이 편지는 그가 말하는 대로 받아 쓴 것이다 I wrote the letter at his dictation.

**받아치다** strike 〔hit〕 back; 〖권투〗 counter; give a counterblow.

**받을어음** bills receivable (생략 B/R, b.r.).

**받치다** ① 《괴다》 prop 《up》; bolster; put something for support 《under》; underpin; hold up 《with》. ¶ 기둥으로 ~ support 《a wall》 with a post / 바지랑대로 빨랫줄을 ~ prop the clothesline with a long stick / 지붕을 ~ give support to a roof / 글 쓰는 데 받칠 것 좀 주십시오 Give me something to lay under writing paper. ② 〖언어〗 attach 〔place〕 a consonant 〔consonants〕 under a vowel. ③ 《배기다》 be hard; pinch. ¶ 의자가 등에 ~ a seat is hard on *one's* back. ④ 《감정이 치밀다》 well up within *one;* surge (up); be filled 《with》; [사물이 주어] fill *one's* heart with 《anger》. ¶ 그녀 가슴에 분이 받쳤다 A feeling of anger surged up in her. ⑤ 《우산 따위를》 = 받다[1] ⑦.

**받침** ① 《괴는 물건》 something for support; a support; a fulcrum (*pl.* -s, -cra); a (hot) pad; a mat; a prop; underpinning; 《책받침》 a cardboard (used under writing paper); a celluloid board. ¶ ~을 괴다 put a support 《under》; underpin / 책상 다리 밑에 ~을 괴다 put a support under a table leg / 지렛대 밑에 ~을 괴다 put a

fulcrum under the lever.
② 〖언어〗 a "final" (consonant or consonant cluster) on the end of a Korean orthographic syllable.
◉ ~대 a prop; a support; a strut; a crosspiece; a beam; underpinning. ~접시 a saucer.

**받히다** be butted; be gored; be struck; be hit; be knocked 《by》. ¶ 소에게 ~ be gored by a bull / 택시에 ~ be ｢run over 〔hit, knocked down〕 by a taxicab.

**발**[1] ① 《사람의》 a foot (*pl.* feet) (발목 아래 부분); a leg (발목 윗부분); a paw (개·고양이 따위의); tentacles; arms (문어·오징어의). ¶ 머리에서 발끝까지 from head to toe 〔foot〕/ 발로 짓밟다 trample under foot / 발을 걸다 trip 《*a person* with *one's* foot》/ 발을 다치다 get hurt in the foot; injure *one's* foot / 발을 동동 구르다 stamp (*one's* feet) on the ground / 발을 들여 놓다 set foot 《in》; put *one's* foot 《into, inside》/ 발을 밟다 step 〔tread〕 on 《*another's*》 foot 〔toes〕/ 발을 삐다 sprain *one's* foot / 발을 앞으로 내밀다 put *one's* foot 〔feet〕 forward / 발을 잘못 디디다 miss *one's* footing; slip / 발을 질질 끌다 drag *one's* (weary) feet / 발이 아프다 have a sore foot; be footsore / 발이 저리다 *one's* foot has gone to sleep; *one's* foot is asleep / 그를 다시는 내 집에 발들여놓지 못하게 하겠다 He shall never darken my doors. *or* He shall not set foot again in my house.
② 《걸음》 walking; walk; step (보조); pace (보속). ¶ 발이 빠른 동물 a swift-footed 〔light-footed〕 animal / 발이 재다〔빠르다〕 be swift of foot; have fast legs; be quick-footed; be a fast 〔quick〕 walker / 발이 느리다 be slow of foot; be a slow walker / …와 발을 맞추다 keep step with…; match pace with… / 발을 멈추다 stop (walking); halt (★ stop to 《*do*》는 ｢…하기 위해 멈추다｣의 뜻이므로 stop to walk라고는 할 수 없음).
③ 《발걸음》 a step; a stride. ¶ 한 발 앞으로 나서다〔뒤로 물러나다〕 take a step forward 〔backward〕.
④ [비유적] ¶ 발(길)을 끊다 cease to visit / 발을 빼다 break 《with》; cut *one's* ties 《with》; sever *one's* connection 《with》; wash *one's* hands of; turn *one's* back on / 발이 길다 be just in time for a treat; be lucky enough to come by a treat / 발이 짧다 be so unlucky as to miss a treat; just miss a treat; come too late for a treat / 발이 넓다 enjoy a wide acquaintance; have a large number of social connections; get around (a lot); know half the people in town; can call everybody by his first name / (교통 두절로) 발이 묶이다 be deprived of means of transit; be stranded; be tied up / 제발로 서다 stand on *one's* own legs; be independent / 제발로 서게 하다 set 《*a person*》 on *his* feet; make 《*a person*》 independent.
⑤ 《물건의》 the lower end 《of a table》; the foot; the leg. ¶ 세 발 달린 원탁 a three-legged round table.

**발**[2] 《가리는》 a bamboo 〔rattan〕 blind; a reed screen. ¶ 발을 치다 hang a bamboo blind 〔curtain〕/ 발을 내리다 〔걷어 올리다〕 let down 〔roll up〕 the blinds.

**발**[3] 《천의》 texture; weave. ¶ 발이 굵다 〔가늘다〕 be loose-woven 〔close-woven〕/ 발이 곱다〔거칠다〕 be fine 〔coarse〕 in texture.

**발**[4] 《길이》 the span of out-stretched arms; a fathom. ¶ 발로 뽑다 span 《it》 off / 발이 크다 have a large arm span / 밧줄 두 ~ two fathoms of rope.

**발**(發) ① 《탄환 따위의》 a round; a shot (소총의); a shell (대포의). ¶ 탄약 30발, 30 rounds of ｢ammunition 〔ball cartridge〕/ 6연발의 권총 a six-chambered revolver; a six-shooter / 10발 쏘다 fire 10 shots 〔rounds〕/ 세 ~의 총성을 들었다 I heard three shots. ② 《엔진의 수》 ¶ 4발 제트기 a four-engined jet / 쌍발기 a twin-engined plane.

**-발**(發) ① 《출발》 leaving…; from…. ¶ 부산발 leaving (from) Busan / 9시 30분발 열차 the 9:30 〔nine-thirty〕 train / 광주발 급행 an express (train) from Gwangju / 1월 1일 부산발 기선 the steamer leaving Busan on 1st Jan. / 서울발 뉴욕행 202편 flight number 202 from Seoul to New York. ② 《발신》 ¶ 5월 1일발 전신 the cable dated May 1st / 뉴욕발 보도 a news report under a New York dateline; a news report datelined New York / 런던발 9월 9일자 편지 a letter dated September 9th, from London.

**발가락** a toe. ¶ 새끼 ~ a little toe / 엄지 ~ a big toe / (신발의) ~끝이 보이는

peep-toe(d).

**발가벗기다** 《옷을》 strip 《*a person*》「naked 〔of *his* clothes〕; undress 《a baby》; denude; 《모두 빼앗다》 make 《*a person*》 penniless 〔broke〕; rob 〔fleece〕 《*a person*》 of all *his* money. ¶ 발가벗겨지다 [사람이 주어] be stripped naked; 《털리다》 be robbed of all *one's* money.

**발가벗다** undress; strip *one's* clothes off; strip *oneself* bare 〔naked〕. ¶ 발가벗고 with nothing on; in the nude; in *one's* bare skin / 발가벗고 헤엄치다 swim stark-naked / 목욕하려고 ~ strip for a bath.

**발각**(發覺) detection; revelation; discovery; disclosure; exposure. ~되다 be found out; be detected; be discovered; be exposed; be disclosed; be revealed; come to 〔be brought to〕 light. ¶ ~을 두려워하여 for fear that it might come to light; lest it should be found out; for fear of detection / 그는 사기를 치려다 ~되었다 He was detected in a fraud. / 3년 전에 그가 저지른 나쁜 짓이 ~되었다 The evil he did three years ago has「become known 〔been disclosed〕.

**발간**(發刊) publication; issue; issuance 《미》. ~하다 publish; bring out; issue; 《창간하다》 start 《a magazine》; launch 《a newspaper》. ¶ ~되다 be published; come out / 그 책은 언제 ~되느냐 When will the book come out? / 그 사전은 지난 가을에 ~되었다 The dictionary was published 〔came out〕 last autumn.

**발감개** foot-wrappings (in place of socks); foot-cloth.

**발강이** 〖어류〗 a young carp.

**발갛다** (be) bright 〔light〕 red; scarlet; reddish. ¶ 빰이 ~ have red cheeks.

**발개지다** turn bright-red; redden; color; blush (얼굴이). ¶ 얼굴이 ~ blush; flush / (부끄러워서) 귀밑까지 ~ blush to the roots of *one's* hair.

**발걸음** a pace; a step; a gait (★ step은 주로 한 걸음의 보폭을, pace는 걷는 속도, gait는 걷는 모양·보조를 말함). ¶ 가벼운〔무거운〕 ~으로 with a light 〔heavy〕 step / 불안한 ~으로 with an unsteady step 〔gait〕 / 급한 ~으로 at a quick pace; at a trot / ~을 빨리하다〔늦추다〕 quicken 〔slacken〕 *one's* pace / ~을 맞추다 get 〔fall〕 into step 《with》; keep step 《with》; act in concert with; keep 〔hold〕 pace with / ~을 멈추다 stop; halt / ~이 가볍다〔무겁다〕 have light 〔leaden〕 feet / 그들은 ~을 맞추어 걷고 있었다 They were walking in step.

**발걸이** 《의자 따위의》 a rung; 《자전거의》 a pedal; 《발 놓는 데》 a footrest; a foothold; a foot rail.

**발견**(發見) (a) discovery; 《뜻밖의 사실》 revelation; 《발각》 (a) detection. ~하다 discover; make a discovery; find (out); detect; spot; light upon 《a fact》; strike upon 《a theory》; 《우연하게》 chance on; come across. ¶ 과학에서의 대 ~ brilliant discoveries in science / 획기적 ~ an epoch-making discovery / 잘못을 ~하다 detect an error 〔a mistake〕 / …을 ~했다고 주장하다 claim the discovery of... / 시체를 ~하다 recover the body / 시체로 ~되다 be found dead 《in an empty house》 / 진리를 ~하다 get at the truth / 우연히 ~하다 happen to find 〔discover〕; find 〔discover〕 by chance / 그것은 나에게 큰 ~이었다 That was quite a revelation to me. / 골동품상에서 우연히 진귀한 항아리를 ~했다 I lighted on 〔upon〕 a rare vase in a curio shop. / 행방불명이 되었던 등산객들은 무사히 ~되었다 The missing climbers were found alive and well.
◉ ~물 a discovery; a find. ~자 a discoverer; a finder; a detector.

**발광**(發光) emission of light; luminescence; radiation of light. ~하다 emit 〔give forth〕 light; radiate; send out light. ¶ ~하는 luminous; radiant.
◉ ~균 luminous bacteria. ~다이오드 a light-emitting diode (생략 LED). ~도료 luminous 〔luminescent〕 paint. ~동물〔식물〕 a luminous 〔photogenic〕 animal 〔plant〕. ~신호 a flash signal. ~지 luminous paper. ~체 a luminous body; a luminary; a radiant. ~탄 a luminous projectile; a light ball.

**발광**(發狂) ① 《미침》 madness; craziness; insanity; mental derangement. ~하다 go 〔run〕 mad; become insane 〔lunatic, crazy〕; become mentally deranged; lose *one's* head 〔mind, reason, wits, sense〕; go out of *one's* mind. ¶ ~케 하다 drive 《*a person*》 mad 〔crazy〕; craze 《*a person*》 / 그는 극도의 공포로 ~했다 He went mad 〔became insane〕 because of 〔out of〕 extreme fear. *or* Extreme fear drove him mad. ② 《지랄》 a crazy act; wild behavior 〔doings〕.

**발구르다** stamp *one's* feet. ¶ 발을 (동동) 구르며 분해하다 stamp with vexation 〔mortification, chagrin〕.

**발군**(拔群) ¶ ～의 distinguished; preeminent; outstanding; conspicuous; exceptional; unique; of distinction / ～의 성적으로 with honors; with an exceptional record / ～의 공을 세우다 render distinguished services; make a unique 〔signal〕 contribution; distinguish *oneself.*

**발굴**(發掘) ① 《유적의》 (an) excavation; unearthing; a dig; 《시체의》 exhumation. ～하다 dig (out, up); excavate; unearth; 《시체를》 exhume; disentomb; untomb; disinter. ¶ 시체를 ～하다 exhume 〔dig up〕 a corpse / 고분을 ～하다 excavate an ancient tomb / 그들은 지난 여름 그 유적을 ～했다 They unearthed the ruins this past summer. ② 《인재의》 ～하다 scout for 〔pick out〕 《talent》. ¶ 묻혀 있는 인재를 ～하다 dig up hidden talent.
◉ ～자 an excavator; a digger. ～지 the digs; a findspot. ～팀 an excavation team. ～품 an excavation; a find. ～현장 the excavation scene 〔site〕. 석유 ～권 an oil concession.

**발굽** ⇨굽. ¶ 말～ 소리 the sound of a horse's hoofs; the clatter of hoofs.

**발권**(發券) the issue of banknotes. ～하다 issue banknotes. ◉ ～액 the amount of notes issued. ～은행 the bank of issue.

**발그레하다** be tinged with red; (be) reddish; flushed; ruddy; somewhat red. ¶ 얼굴이 ～ *one's* face「is in a glow 〔is flushed〕 《with》 / 기뻐서 그녀의 얼굴이 발그레했다 Her face was aglow with delight.

**발그림자** a trace; a track; a footmark; a trail; a shadow. ¶ ～도 안 비치다 not a shadow 《of *a person*》 is to be seen / ～도 얼씬 안 하다 cease to visit; never come; do not appear.

**발그스름하다** (be) reddish; somewhat red.

**발급**(發給) ～하다 issue. ¶ 여권을 ～하다 issue a passport.

**발긋발긋** splashed with red; red all over; red here and there.

**발긋발긋하다** be dotted with red spots.

**발기**(發起) 《솔선》 initiation; 《사업의》 promotion; 《계획》 projection; 《제의》 a proposal; a suggestion; 《주최》 auspices. ～하다 initiate; promote; project; propose; suggest. ¶ …의 ～로 at the proposition 〔proposal, suggestion〕 of…; 《주최》 under the auspices 〔sponsorship〕 of… / 회사 설립을 ～하다 promote an organization of a company. ◉ ～이득 benefit of initiators. ～인 《회의 따위의》 a promoter; an originator; 《계획의》 a proposer; a sponsor; a projector: ～인주 founder's 〔promoter's〕 shares; management shares / ～인회 a meeting of promoters.

**발기**(勃起) 《음경의》 (an) erection. ～하다 get erect 〔hard, stiff, rigid〕; get 〔have〕 an erection; stand erect; become rigid 〔stiff〕. ¶ ～성의 erectile / ～력 감퇴 impotency. ◉ ～근(筋) an erector (muscle).

**발기다** open up 《a clam》; crack open; shell; tear to pieces. ¶ 콩을 ～ shell peas / 밤을 ～ split the outer covering of the chestnut / …의 불(알)을 ～ castrate.

**발기발기** to pieces; to shreds. ¶ ～ 찢다 tear to pieces.

**발길** ① 《차는 힘》 (the force of) a kick. ¶ 말 ～에 채다 get kicked by a horse. ② 《걸음》 a step. ¶ ～을 끊다 cease to visit / ～을 돌리다 turn *one's* steps 〔heel〕; turn back; retrace *one's* steps / ～을 재촉하다 quicken *one's* pace 〔steps〕 / ～ 닿는 대로 가다 go wherever *one's* steps lead *one;* walk at random; follow *one's* nose / ～이 멀어지다 come 〔visit〕 less frequently (than before) / ～이 잦다 frequent 《a place》; make frequent calls 《on *a person,* at a place》.
◉ ～질 a kick 《at *something*》: ～질하다 kick; give 《*a person*》 a kick.

**발깍** ① 《갑자기 성내는 모양》 suddenly; all of a sudden; all at once; out of the blue. ¶ ～ 성내다 suddenly take offense; lose *one's* temper; fly into a passion 〔(sudden) rage〕; 《속어》 blow *one's* top 〔stack 《미》〕. ② 《뒤집히다》 topsy-turvy; in a state of confusion; in a turmoil 〔hubbub〕; all every-which-way; in a mass. ¶ 집안이 ～ 뒤집히다 a house is (all) topsy-turvy 〔(all) messed up, (all) torn up〕 / 서울이 ～ 뒤집혔다 All Seoul was in an uproar.

**발깍거리다** ① 《술 따위가》 bubble up (in fermentation, boiling). ¶ 탁주가 ～ the rice liquor is bubbling up (as it ferments); be bubbling a brew; be brewing a bubble. ② 《진흙 따위를》 make mud squash 〔squish〕 underfoot. ¶ 진흙을 ～ squash mud under *one's* feet.

**발끈** 《get angry》 all of a sudden; with a burst 《of anger》; in a fit of passion; in a rage. ～하다 flare up; fly into a rage. ¶ ～하는 temper-trigger 《구어》 / ～해서 소리를 지르다 yell out in anger / 모욕을 당하자 그는 ～했다 He flew into a rage at the insulting remark. / 그 말을 듣고 나는 앞뒤 생각없이 ～ 화를 냈다 At that word I flew into a blind rage.

**발끈거리다** burst into a rage readily; get mad easily; be quick to flare 〔flame〕 up; flare 〔flame〕 up 《at the drop of a hat》. ¶ 그는 발끈거리기를 잘 한다 He is quick-tempered 〔hot-tempered〕. *or* He is touchy 〔testy〕.

**발끝** the tip of a toe; a tiptoe; 《구두·양말 등의》 a toe. ¶ 머리 끝에서 ～까지 from top 〔head〕 to toe 〔foot〕 / ～으로 걷다 (walk on) tiptoe / ～으로 서다 stand on tiptoe.

**발단**(發端) ① 《말머리》 opening *one's* mouth. ～하다 open *one's* mouth. ② 《실마리》 the opening; the start; the beginning; the commencement; the outset; the origin. ～하다 originate from 〔in〕; begin; start from; be originated. ¶ 사건의 ～ the origin of an affair / 사건의 ～을 조사하다 trace a matter to its origin / 그 싸움의 ～부터 이야기해 봐라 Tell me about the quarrel from the very beginning. / 사태의 ～은 무엇이었습니까 what started it? *or* How did it start?

**발달**(發達) ① 《성장·발육》 development; growth. ～하다 grow; develop. ¶ 잘 ～된 well-developed; highly-developed / 심신의 ～ mental and physical development / ～시키다 develop; advance / …의 ～을 돕다〔저해하다〕 promote 〔arrest, retard〕 the development 〔growth〕 of... / 수영은 신체 각부의 근육을 ～시킨다 Swimming develops many different muscles. / 언어의 ～은 진화의 자연적인 한 과정이다 The development of language is a natural part of the evolutionary process. / 열대성 저기압이 태풍으로 ～했다 The tropical low (pressure area) developed into a typhoon. ② 《진보》 progress; advance(ment). ～하다 (make) progress; advance; evolve. ¶ 학술의 ～ advancement of learning / 인지(人知)〔근대 과학〕의 ～ the advancement of human knowledge 〔modern science〕 / 공업의 ～ the development of industry / 문화의 ～ cultural progress / 도시의 급속한 ～ the rapid growth of cities / 현저히〔급속히〕 ～하다 make remarkable 〔rapid〕 progress 〔growth〕 / 서울은 교통이 ～된 대도시이다 Seoul is a big city with a developed transport system. / 과학이 급속히 ～했다 Science has made rapid strides. / 한국의 중공업은 근년 눈부신 ～을 이룩했다 Korea's heavy industries have made remarkable progress in recent years. ◉ ～단계 a developmental stage. ～심리학 genetic 〔developmental〕 psychology.

**발돋움** standing on tiptoe; 《발판》 something to stand on. ～하다 stand on tiptoe; stretch *oneself*. ¶ 한 남자가 ～하고 집안을 엿보는 것을 보았다 I saw a man standing on tiptoe looking into the house.

**발동**(發動) 《기계의》 motion; 《권력·무력 등의》 exercise; operation. ～하다 《기계를》 move; put in motion; 《행사하다》 exercise; invoke; put in action; put 《a law》 into operation (실시). ¶ 사법권을 ～하다 put in action the judicial power / 강권을 ～하다 take strong measures 《against》; institute vigorous action 《against》; invoke legal power 《against》 / 규약 제9조를 ～하다 invoke Article 9 of the covenant / 국권을 ～하다 exercise the right of the state 〔state's right〕. ◉ ～력 motive power 〔force〕.

**발동기**(發動機) a motor; an engine. ¶ 백 마력의 ～ a motor with 100 horsepower. ◉ ～선 a motorboat; 《디젤 엔진의》 a motor ship.

**발뒤꿈치** the heel. ¶ ～도 따를 수 없다 be far inferior 《to》; be no match 《for》; cannot hold a candle 《to》 / 나는 모든 점에서 네 ～도 따라갈 수 없다 I am no match for you in every respect.

**발등** the instep. ¶ ～을 밟다 tread on 《*a person's*》 foot / 우선 ～의 불을 꺼야만 했다 It got so I had to do something about it quickly.

**발딱-** ⇨ 벌떡-.

**발라내다** shell; clean; tear 〔peel, strip, take〕 off; pare; hull 《peas》; crack 《a chestnut》. ¶ 생선 가시를 ～ clean 〔bone〕 a fish / 살구씨를 ～ remove the stone 〔pit〕 from an apricot; pit an apricot / 닭고기를 ～ take chicken meat off the bones.

**발라맞추다** cajole; wheedle; coax; flatter; adulate; curry favor with《*one's* superior》; court《*a person's*》favor; hang upon《*a person's*》sleeves; oil *one's* tongue.

**발라먹다**《알맹이·뼈를》shell and eat《nuts》; bone and eat《a fish》: [비유적] wheedle; (sweet-)talk《*a person*》out of《*a thing*》; coax《*a thing*》out of《*a person*》; get《*a thing*》by being nice to《*a person*》.

**발랄라이카**〖악기〗a balalaika.

**발랄하다**(潑剌—)《활발》(be) lively; sprightly; animated; fresh; full of life; vivid (with life); vigorous. ¶ 재기(才氣) 발랄한 사람 a man of keen intellect / 생기 ～ be full of vigor〔go, vim, vitality, animation〕; be full of pep; be peppy〔lively〕.

**발랑-** ⇨ 벌렁-.

**발레** ballet. ¶ ～를 배우다〔가르치다〕take〔give〕ballet lessons. ◉ ～단 a ballet (company); a *corps de ballet* (F.): ～단 단장 a ballet master〔mistress〕/ 국립 ～단 the National Ballet Company. ～댄서 a《male, female》ballet dancer. ～학교 a ballet school.

**발레리나** a ballerina (*pl.* ～s, -rine).

**발렌타인 데이** Valentine Day; (Saint) Valentine's Day.

**발령**(發令)《명령》giving an (official) order;〖법〗《사령》an (official) announcement of appointment;《반포》(an) official announcement; proclamation; gazetting《영》. ～하다 give an official order; proclaim a law〔decree〕; announce officially《*one's* appointment》; issue《orders》. ¶ 그의 과장 임명은 5월 1일부로 ～되었다 His appointment to the post of section chief was announced on May 1. / 우리 회사는 3월 1일부로 인사 이동을 ～했다 Our company announced personnel changes on March 1. / 공습 경보가 ～ 중이다 A warning of an air-raid has been issued. ◉ ～장 a letter〔warrant, writ〕of appointment.

**발로**(發露) (an) expression; (a) manifestation; exhibition. ～하다 manifest〔express, reveal, show〕itself; become manifest. ¶ 애국심의 ～ an expression〔a manifestation〕of patriotism / 따뜻한 우정의 ～ an expression of the warm friendship《between》.

**발론**(發論) a motion; a proposal. ～하다 move; make a motion; propose; introduce a proposal. ¶ ～할 것이 있다 have a proposal to make. ◉ ～자 a proposer; a mover; an introducer; a broacher.

**발름하다** (be) slightly open. ¶ 입이 ～ have *one's* mouth slightly open.

**발리**《테니스·축구》a volley. ¶ 공을 ～로 치다〔차다〕hit〔kick〕a ball on the volley.

**발리볼**《배구》volleyball;《공》a volley-ball.

**발맞다** keep in step《with》; be in step; fall into step. ¶ 발맞지 않다 be out of step.

**발맞추다**《속도를》keep pace《with》;《좌우의 발을》fall〔get〕into step《with》;《행동상》act〔work〕in concert《with》. ¶ 발맞추어 걷다 march〔walk〕in step〔line〕《with》; walk with measured tread.

**발매** lumber〔timber《영》〕cutting; felling《trees》; deforestation; lumbering《미》. ⇨ 벌채(伐採). ～하다 fell《trees》; hew (down); cut lumber; cut down; lumber. ¶ ～를 넣다 start lumber cutting; start felling《trees》/ ～를 놓다 cut down a whole stand of trees at one stretch. ◉ ～치 firewood gathered after cutting a large tree.

**발매**(發賣) sale; putting on sale. ～하다 sell; put《*things*》on the market〔on sale〕; make available; release《a new record》. ¶ ～중이다 be on sale〔on the market〕/ 책의 ～를 금하다 suppress〔ban〕a book; place a book under the ban; (put a) ban on the book / 그 잡지는 오늘 ～된다 The magazine is out today. / 그 책은 5,000원에 ～되고 있다 The book is on sale for 5,000 won. / 그 상품은 이젠 ～되고 있지 않다 The article is not sold anymore. ◉ ～금지 prohibition of sale; suppression《of a book》: ～ 금지가 되다 be suppressed; be placed under a ban. ～부수 circulation. ～일〔시기〕the date of issue. ～처 a sales〔selling〕agency.

**발명**(發明) ① invention;《새 고안》contrivance. ～하다 invent; make an invention; devise; contrive. ¶ ～의 날 the Invention Day / 신～의 newly-invented / ～의 천재 inventive genius / ～의 재간이 있다 have an inventive genius / ～을 실용화하다 put the invention to practical use / ～을 상용화하다 commercialize *one's* invention / 필요는 ～의 어머니다 Necessity is the mother of invention. / 에디슨은 전등을 ～했다 Edison invented the electric lamp. / 새로 ～된 엔진은 곧 실용화 될 것이다

The newly invented engine will soon be put to practical use. / 증기 기관은 누가 발명했지 Who invented the steam engine?
② 《변명》 defense; exculpation; vindication; explanation. ⇨ 변명. ～하다 explain 《*oneself* for》; exculpate *oneself;* offer *one's* apology for; clear *oneself* 《of the charge》; justify *oneself.* ¶ 나의 행동에 대해서는 아무런 ～도 하지 않겠다 I will say nothing in explanation 〔justification〕 of my conduct.
◉ ～가〔자〕 an inventor. ～품 an invention; a contrivance; a device.

**발목** an ankle. ¶ ～을 삐다 sprain *one's* ankle / ～을 잡히다 《일에》 be busy 《with work》; be pressed 《with business》; be chained 〔fettered, tied〕 to *one's* business; 《약점이 있어》 be carped at a fault; give a handle to the enemy; be taken advantage of.

**발묘**(拔錨) weighing anchor. ～하다 raise 〔weigh, pull up〕 anchor; (set) sail 《from》; get under way.

**발문**(跋文) an epilog(ue); a postscript 《to a book》.

**발밑** ¶ ～에 under *one's* feet; at *one's* feet / 어두워서 ～도 보이지 않다 be so dark that *one* can't see where *his* feet are going.

**발바닥** the sole of a foot.

**발바리** a pug-dog; a spaniel (dog); a 「Pekinese.

**발바심** 〖농업〗 threshing by treading; foot threshing. ～하다 thresh grain with *one's* feet; tread the crops under foot.

**발발**[1] ⇨ 벌벌.

**발발**[2] 《삭아서》 《tear, break》 easily; asunder. ～하다 tear easily. ¶ 테이블보가 낡아서 ～ 나간다 The tablecloth is so old that it tears easily.

**발발**(勃發) an outbreak; an outburst; a sudden occurrence. ～하다 break 〔burst〕 out; occur 〔arise〕 suddenly. ¶ 소요와 폭동이 여러 곳에서 ～했다 Riots and disturbances broke out in many places. / 내란이 ～했다 A civil war broke out. / 세계 제2차 대전은 1939년에 ～했다 World War II broke out in 1939.

**발밭다** (be) quick 《to take advantage of an opportunity》; "never miss a trick"; (be) wide-awake to 《*one's* own interests》.

**발버둥이치다** 《아기가》 flutter *one's* feet; kick and struggle; be restless; can't sit still; 《몸부림치다》 squirm; wriggle; flounder; struggle; 《헛애를 쓰다》 make vain efforts; make a useless struggle. ¶ 아무리 발버둥이쳐 봤자 소용없다 It is no use struggling and wriggling / 그녀는 발버둥이치면 칠수록 깊은 곳으로 빠져들어갔다 She struggled only to fall into a depth.

**발버둥질** squirming; struggling; floundering; wriggling. ～ 치다 flutter *one's* feet; kick and struggle; make a useless struggle 《against》. ⇨ 발버둥이치다.

**발벗다** ① 《맨발이다》 be barefoot(ed); have bare feet. ② 〔비유적〕 ¶ 발벗고 나서다 throw *oneself* into 《*a matter*》 with enthusiasm; become involved in 《*a matter*》 actively 〔enthusiastically〕; take a positive attitude 《toward》 / 정부는 불황에 대처하기 위해 발벗고 나섰다 The government took positive measures to deal with the recession.

**발병**(—病) a foot disease 〔trouble〕; sore feet; a pain in the foot. ¶ ～이 나다 *one's* feet get sore; be footsore.

**발병**(發病) the outbreak of 《*a person's*》 illness; an attack (of a disease); 《중풍 따위의》 a stroke. ～하다 be attacked with a disease; be taken ill; fall ill 〔sick〕; get sick. ¶ ～초기에 in the incipient 〔first〕 stage 《of a disease》 / 3월 5일 ～ Fell ill on March 5.

**발복**(發福) a change in fortune (for the better). ～하다 *one's* luck changes for the better; things 「look 〔are looking〕 up for 《*a person*》; be in luck's way; fortune turns in 《*a person's*》 favor.

**발본**(拔本) ① 《원인의》 eradication. ～하다 eradicate; root out. ¶ ～적 개혁을 하다 make a radical 〔drastic〕 reform / ～적 조치를 취하다 adopt drastic measures / 사태를 개선하기 위해서는 ～적인 대책을 강구할 필요가 있다 We have to take drastic measures to improve the situation. ② 《밑천 뽑음》 getting back *one's* capital 《from an investment》. ～하다 get back *one's* capital 《from an investment》; earn as much as the capital invested.

**발본색원**(拔本塞源) eradication of sources of evil. ～하다 eradicate the root of evil; lay the ax to the root of evil.

**발부리** the tip of a toe; tiptoe; 《구두의》 a toe. ¶ ～로 걷다 walk on tiptoe(s) / 돌에 ～를 채다 trip on 〔over〕 a stone.

**발빼다** wash *one's* hands of; sever connections with; break (off) with; break away from; withdraw *oneself* 《from》; cease to do with 《it》. ¶ 그는 하루빨리 그 부정한 사업에서 발을 빼기로 결심했다 He decided to wash his hands of the shady business as soon as possible.

**발뺌** an evasive answer; an evasion; a subterfuge; 《구실》 an excuse. ～하다 make 〔give〕 an evasive answer; talk *oneself* out of 《the difficulty》; explain away 《the incriminating signature》; find 〔cook up〕 an excuse. ¶ ～을 잘 하다 be good at finding excuses 〔subterfuges〕 / 너의 이런 해명은 ～에 불과하다 This explanation of yours is nothing but an excuse. / 그는 자신의 과실을 비서탓으로 돌리고 ～했다 He made an excuse for his fault by blaming his secretary.

**발사**(發射) 《발포》 discharge; firing; shooting; 《로켓의》 launching; blast-off; lift-off. ～하다 discharge 〔fire, let off〕 《a gun》; shoot 《a rifle, a bullet from a rifle》; launch 〔blastoff, send up〕 《a guided missile》. ¶ 총을 ～하다 fire a gun / 일제히 ～하다 fire a volley; fire by volleys / 인공 위성을 ～하다 launch 〔blast-off〕 an artificial satellite 《into space》 / 경찰관은 범인을 향해 권총을 ～했다 The policeman fired his pistol at the criminal. / 잠수함에서 미사일이 ～되었다 A missile was launched from the submarine.
◉ ～각 the angle of fire. ～관 《어뢰의》 a torpedo 〔launching〕 tube. ～ 단계 the launch phase. ～대〔장〕 《로켓 따위의》 a launch(ing) pad 〔site〕. ～물〔체〕 a projectile. ～속도 rapidity of fire. ～시간 《로켓의》 the lift-off time. ～시험 proof firing. ～용 로켓 《우주선 따위의》 a booster (rocket); a launch(-ing) vehicle. ～음 a crack 《of a pistol》; a crackle 《of a carbine》. ～장치 《미사일의》 a launcher. ～탑 a launch tower.

**발산**(發散) ① 《수증기·악취 따위의》 emission; exhalation; 《빛·열 따위의》 radiation; emanation. ～하다 emit; emanate; send forth; give out; radiate; exhale. ¶ 불이 ～하는 열과 연기 heat and smoke emitted by fire / 악취를 ～하다 emit 〔send out〕 a foul odor / 향기를 ～하다 give out 〔diffuse〕 a sweet fragrance. ② 《정력 따위의》 explosion. ～하다 give vent 《to》; let off; release. ¶ 젊음을 ～하다 radiate youthfulness / 평소의 울분을 ～하다 release *one's* pent-up emotions. ③ 『수학·물리』 divergence. ～하다 diverge.
◉ ～광속(光束) a divergent pencil of rays. ～급수(級數) a divergent series. ～렌즈 a diverging lens. ～물 an emanation.

**발상**(發喪) ～하다 announce a death (by starting wailing).

**발상**(發想) ① 《생각》 a way of thinking. ¶ 한국적인 ～ the Korean way of thinking. ② 《착상》 an idea; 《구상》 a conception. ¶ …으로부터 ～을 얻다 get an 〔the〕 idea 《for *one's* work》 from…; be inspired by… / 그것은 매우 참신한 ～이다 That's a very novel idea. ③ 《음악의 표현》 expression. ¶ ～기호 expression mark.

**발상지**(發祥地) the birthplace 《of jazz music》; where *something* started; the place of origin; the cradle 《of civilization》. ¶ 고대 문명의 ～는 황하나 나일강과 같은 큰 강의 유역이다 Ancient civilizations were born along the banks of great waterways such as the Nile and the Yellow River.

**발샅** the space between the toes. ¶ ～의 때꼽재기 a thing unworthy of attention; a thing too insignificant 〔low〕 to mention.

**발색제**(發色劑) a color former; a coupler.

**발생**(發生) 《일어남·생김》 occurrence; (an) outbreak; 《비롯됨》 origination; genesis; birth; 《출현》 appearance; 《생물·열·전기 등의》 generation; production; 《자람》 growth; 『생물』 development. ～하다 《일어나다·생기다》 occur; happen; spring 〔crop〕 up; break out; come into existence 〔being〕; be generated; be produced; originate 〔come〕 《from》; 《자라다》 grow; 《번식하다》 breed. ¶ 문명의 ～ the dawn of civilization / 사건〔지진〕의 ～ the occurrence of an event 〔earthquake〕 / 파리의 ～을 막다 prevent the breeding of flies / 해충이 ～했다 Harmful insects developed. / 역 앞에서 차 충돌 사고가 ～했다 A car collision happened in front of the station. / 그 시에 콜레라가 ～했다 Cholera broke out in the city.
◉ ～기(器) a generator. ～로(爐) 《가스의》 a gas generator 〔producer〕: ～로가스 air gas; producer gas. ～론 the evolution 〔development〕 theory. ～률 the incidence. ～생리학〔심리학〕 genetic biology 〔psychology〕. ～장치 《가스 등의》 a producer. ～주의 『회계』 the

accrual basis. ～지(地) the place of origin; the birthplace; the cradle 《of civilization》. ～학 genetics; embryology: ～학적 genetic. 개체～ ontogeny. 신～ c(a)enogenesis.

**발설**(發說) divulging; revealing; disclosing; announcement; publication. ～하다 divulge; reveal; disclose; announce; make public; make known; give out. ¶ 비밀을 ～하다 let out 〔divulge〕 a secret / 이것을 ～하지 마라 Keep this secret.

**발성**(發聲) utterance; speaking; vocalization; exclamation; ejaculation. ～하다 utter 〔produce〕 a (speech) sound; make voice; speak; vocalize; exclaim; ejaculate. ¶ 그는 ～이 좋지 않다 He has poor vocalization.
◉ ～기 a speaker; a talking apparatus. ～기관 a vocal organ. ～법 vocalization. ～연습 vocal exercises. ～영화 a talking picture 〔film〕; a talkie. ～장치 a mechanism of voice production.

**발소리** the sound of footsteps; a footstep; a footfall; a step; a tread. ¶ ～를 내며 with noisy (foot)steps / ～를 내지 않고 with silent steps; 《walk》 without making a sound / ～를 죽이고 《walk》 soft-footed; 《살금살금》 with stealthy steps; stealthily / ～를 내다 let *one's* foot-steps resound 〔echo〕; make sound as *one* walks / ～가 들리다 hear (the sound of ) 《*a person's*》 footsteps / 그는 ～를 죽이고 방으로 들어왔다 He stole into the room with stealthy steps. / ～가 사라졌다 The footsteps died away.

**발송**(發送) sending; forwarding; dispatch; shipping 《미》. ～하다 《물품을》 send out 〔forth〕; forward; dispatch; ship; 《우편물을》 mail out 《미》; post 《영》. ¶ 소화물을 ～하다 send out 〔off〕 a parcel / 물품을 선편으로 ～하다 send goods by surface mail / 당회사는 화물을 이미 런던으로 ～했습니다 Our company has already shipped the cargo for London. / 항공편으로 그 책을 ～하겠습니다 I will send the book (off) by airmail.
◉ ～계(원) a forwarding 〔shipping 《미》〕 clerk; a mail clerk (우편물의). ～문서 dispatched documents. ～부 the dispatch division 〔department〕. ～역 a forwarding station. ～은행 the forwarding 〔sending, remitting〕 bank. ～인 a sender; 《출하주》 a consignor. ～항(港) a port of dispatch.

**발쇠** informing on others. ～서다 inform on. ◉ ～꾼 an informer; a spy.

**발신**(發信) 《소식의》 dispatch of a message 〔letter〕; 《전신의》 sending 〔dispatch of 〕 a telegram. ～하다 dispatch 《a message》; send 《a letter, a telegram》; communicate; telegraph; wire. ¶ 이 편지는 서울 ～이다 This letter was mailed 〔posted〕 in Seoul. / 조난당한 배는 SOS를 ～했다 The wrecked ship sent an SOS.
◉ ～국 the sending office 〔station〕. ～기 a transmitter. ～신호〔회선〕 a transmitting signal 〔circuit〕. ～음 《전화의》 a dial tone; 《무전 따위의》 a signal. ～인 《편지의》 an addresser; 《전신 등의》 the sender 《of a telegram》. ～지 the place of dispatch.

**발심**(發心) ① 〖불교〗 religious 〔spiritual〕 awakening; conversion; good resolution. ～하다 be converted 《to Buddhism》; become religious; experience religion; have spiritual awakening. ② 《마음먹음》 resolution. ～하다 intend to 《*do*》; make up *one's* mind to 《*do*》; resolve 《to *do*, on an act》.

**발싸개** socks; feet wraps. ¶ 거지～ 같은 놈아 You filthy scum!

**발싸심** fidgeting; twisting *oneself* in various ways to relieve *one's* ennui. ～하다 fidget.

**발씨** familiarity to *one's* feet; skill with *one's* feet; *one's* manner of walking; a step. ¶ 경쾌한 ～로 with springy steps.

**발씨름** ankle 〔shin〕 wrestling.

**발씨익다** (be) well known; practiced; familiar. ¶ 발씨익은 길 a well-known course; a well-acquainted road; a familiar path.

**발아**(發芽) sprouting; budding; germination; shooting. ～하다 germinate; be germinant; sprout (out); bud (out); put out 〔forth〕 buds. ¶ 봄비로 씨앗이 ～했다 The spring rain germinated the seeds. ◉ ～기(期) a germinating period. ～력 germinative power.

**발악**(發惡) 《모진 말》 revilement; abusive language; 《모진 짓》 brutal 〔merciless〕 behavior; 《버둥댐》 a desperate struggle. ～하다 《모진 말하다》 use abusive language; revile; rail against 〔at〕; rave; inveigh 《against》; 《모진 짓하다》 behave violently; act frantically; 《버둥대다》 get 〔become〕 desperate; make frantic efforts. ¶ 최후의 ～ the last-ditch fight 〔struggle〕/ 그는 경찰의 포위망을 뚫으려고 ~했다 He struggled desperately to cut his way through the besieging police.

**발안**(發案) ①《생각해 냄》 (initiating) an idea; (originating) a plan; a proposition; a proposal (발의); a suggestion. ~하다 initiate 《an idea》; originate; suggest; make a suggestion; propose; form 〔strike out〕 a plan; devise (고안하다); invent (발명하다). ¶ 아무의 ~으로 at *a person's* suggestion 〔initiative〕; at the suggestion of 《Mr. Kim》/ 그것은 그녀의 ~이었다 It was her idea. /「그것은 누구의 ~이지」—「나의 ~이다」 "Whose idea 〔plan〕 is it?" —"It's mine." ②《동의》 a motion. ~하다 move.
◉ ~권 the right to submit a bill to the National Assembly. ~자 a proposer; an originator; the inventor.

**발암**(發癌) 〖의학〗 carcinogenesis; the production of cancer. ¶ ~성의 carcinogenic; cancerogenic; cancer-causing〔-forming, -producing〕. ◉ ~물질 a carcinogenic 〔cancerogenic〕 substance; a carcinogen; a cancer=causing 〔-producing, -inducing〕 agent: 고사리는 ~ 물질을 갖고 있음이 판명되었다 The bracken has been determined to contain a carcinogen.

**발언**(發言) (an) utterance; speaking. (a) speech; a remark; a statement; 《제언》 a proposal. ~하다 speak; utter; open *one's* mouth; take the floor (의원이); propose. ¶ ~을 요청하다 ask permission to speak; ask for comments; invite a comment 〔an opinion〕/ ~의 기회를 잃다 lose the opportunity of speaking / ~을 금지하다 prohibit 《*a person*》 from speaking / ~을 취소하다 retract *one's* words / ~을 허용하다 allow 《*a person*》 to speak / ~ 시간을 제한하다 limit on questioning time; limit time on questioning 《in the House》; set a time limit on questioning / 회의 중 한 마디도 ~하지 않다 remain quite silent throughout the conference / 그가 ~할 차례다 He has the floor. / 그는 대담한 ~을 했다 He made a daring remark.
◉ ~자 a speaker; 《동의의》 a mover.

**발언권**(發言權) the right to speak; (the right to) a voice; a say; 《의원의》 the floor 《미》. ¶ ~이 있다〔없다〕 have a voice 〔no voice〕 《in *the matter*》/ (의원이) ~을 얻다 get the floor; catch the Speaker's eye / ~을 얻지 못하다 be denied a voice / (아무와) 대등한 ~을 요구하다 claim 〔demand〕 an equal voice with *a person* / 그는 그 건에 대해서는 ~이 없다 He has no voice 〔say〕 in the matter. / 의장은 그에게 ~을 주었다 The chairman gave him the floor. / 그에게도 ~을 주어라 Let him have his say.

**발연**(發煙) emitting smoke; fuming. ~하다 smoke; emit smoke; fume.
◉ ~병기 smoke arms. ~제 a fumigant; a smoke generating agent. ~탄 a smoke shell 〔bomb〕. ~통(筒) 《신호용》 a smoke candle.

**발열**(發熱) ①《기계의》 generation of heat. ~하다 generate heat. ②《신체의》 pyrexia; (an attack of) fever; calorification (동물체의). ~하다 develop a fever; become feverish; be attacked with fever; run a temperature. ¶ 갑자기 ~하다 have a sudden attack of fever; suddenly become feverish / 그는 감기로 ~이 있었다 He ran a fever with a cold. ◉ ~량 caloric 〔heating〕 value. ~력 caloric power. ~물질 a pyrogen. ~반응 exothermic reaction. ~요법 fever therapy. ~체 a heating element 〔unit〕; a pyrogen.

**발원**(發源) 《물의》 the source; the (fountain)head; 《사물의》 the origin; the beginning; the root. ~하다 rise 〔flow, come〕 《from》; spring 《up, from》; originate 《in》; have its origin 《in》. ¶ (강이) 호수에서 ~하다 rise 〔flow, come〕 from a lake; take 《its》 rise 〔source〕 from a lake / 한강은 태백산맥에서 ~한다 The Han River 「has its source in 〔flows from〕 the Taebaek Mountains.
◉ ~지 the source; the head of a river; a headspring: 강의 ~를 찾다 trace a river to 〔as far as〕 its source.

**발원**(發願) a prayer 《to a deity》. ~하다 offer a prayer 《to a deity》; make a petition 〔vow〕 《to a god》.

**발육**(發育) growth; development. ~하다 grow; develop. ¶ 한창 ~하는 아이 a growing child / 충분히 ~한 fully-grown; fully-developed / ~이 좋다 be well grown / ~이 나쁘다 be undergrown; be underdeveloped / ~이 빠르다〔늦다〕 grow rapidly 〔slowly〕/ ~을 돕다〔방해하다〕 promote 〔retard〕 the growth 《of》/ 지적〔신체적〕 ~이 늦은 아이 a mentally 〔physically〕 retarded child / 물·햇빛·공기는 식물의 ~을 돕는다 Water, sunlight and air help to develop plants. / 금년은 일기가 불순해서 벼의 ~이 늦다 Due to the unseasonable weather, the rice this year is not growing well〔properly〕.

◉ ~기 the period of growth〔development〕. ~기관 a developmental organ. ~부전(不全) incomplete development; abortion; 〖병리〗 hypoplasia: ~부전의 underdeveloped; undergrown.

**발음**(發音) (a) pronunciation; enunciation; articulation. ~하다 pronounce; enunciate; articulate. ¶ ~대로 phonetically / 또렷한〔정확한〕 ~ clear〔correct〕 pronunciation / 틀린 ~ mispronunciation / ~이 또렷한 사람 an articulator / ~대로의 철자법 phonetic spelling / 올바르게 ~하다 pronounce correctly / 잘못 ~하다 mispronounce 《a word》/ ~이 좋다〔나쁘다〕 have a good〔bad〕 pronunciation; *one's* pronunciation is good〔bad〕/ ~하지 않는 문자 a silent letter / 나는 ~을 교정받았다 I had my pronunciation corrected. / listen의 t는 발음하지 않는다 The “t” in “listen” is not pronounced. *or* We don't sound the “t” in “listen”. / 그것은 두번째 음절에 악센트를 주어 ~한다 It is pronounced with an accent on the second syllable.

◉ ~기관 a speech〔vocal〕 organ. ~기호 a phonetic symbol〔sign, alphabet〕. ~사전 a pronouncing dictionary. ~연습 practice〔drill〕 in pronunciation. ~학 phonetics (음성학); phonology (음운학): ~학자 a phonetician.

**발의**(發意) 《의견·계획의》 an initiative; a suggestion; 《창의》 an original idea; a design; a device. ~하다 make a suggestion; originate 《an idea》. ¶ …의 ~로 on the initiative of.

**발의**(發議) a proposal; a suggestion; a proposition; 《동의》 a motion. ~하다 propose; suggest; move; make a proposal. ¶ …의 ~로 at the instance〔suggestion〕 of...; on the motion of; at 《*a person's*》 suggestion〔proposal〕/ 이 계획을 ~한 것은 김씨였다 It was Mr. Kim who initiated this plan.

◉ ~권 the initiative 《of amendments of the constitution》: 직접 ~권 the direct initiative. ~자 the (original) proposer; the originator; the mover.

**발인**(發靷) the departure of the hearse (from home for the burial). ~하다 carry out the bier for burial; the hearse leaves home 《for a cemetery》; carry the coffin out of the house. ¶ 오전 9시 ~ The hearse is to〔scheduled to〕 leave home at 9 a.m.

**발자국** a footprint; a footmark; a spoor (짐승의); a track 《미》; a trace (종적). ¶ 눈 위에 또렷이 남은 ~ footmarks printed off distinctly in the snow / ~을 남기다 leave *one's* footprints / ~을 따라가다 follow 《*a person's*》 footsteps〔tracks〕; track 《*a person*, an animal》; trace 《a criminal's》 tracks〔footmarks〕/ 경관은 범인의 ~을 뒤쫓고 있다 The police are tracing the footmarks of the culprit〔offender〕.

**발자취** ① 《공헌》 a contribution; 《업적》 an achievement; 《발자국》 a footprint; a footmark; a track; *one's* marks. ¶ 역사에 ~를 남기다 leave *one's* marks on history / 그는 과학 분야에서 위대한 ~를 남겼다 He left a legacy of great contributions to science. ② 《걸어온 길》 a course. ¶ 지난 20년간의 ~를 회고하다 think of〔recollect〕 the course *one* has followed for twenty years.

**발작**(發作) a fit; a spasm; an attack; a paroxysm (주기적); an ictus; 《경련》 convulsions. ~하다 have a fit〔spasm〕. ¶ ~적인 spasmodic; fitful / ~적으로 by fits (and starts); fitfully; spasmodically; on a sudden impulse / 격렬한〔가벼운〕 ~ a violent〔mild〕 fit〔stroke〕 《of apoplexy》/ ~적(인) 정신이상 a temporary derangement of the mind / ~을 일으키다 have a fit〔spasm〕《of》/ ~적으로 울다〔웃다〕 have fits of weeping〔laughter〕; cry〔laugh〕 hysterically; burst into a spasm〔fit〕 of weeping〔laughter〕/ 그는 심장 ~을 일으켰다 He had a heart attack. / 절망에 빠진 그녀는 ~적으로 자살을 기도했다 She tried to kill herself in a fit of despair.

**발장구** 《수영에서》 the beating; the flutter (kick); the thrash. ~치다 thrash〔beat〕 *one's* legs in water; flutter *one's* feet.

**발장단**(—長短) beating time with the foot. ¶ ~을 치다 beat〔mark〕 time 《to the music》 with *one's* foot.

**발적**(發赤) 〖의학〗 flare; rubefaction.

◉ ~제 a rubefacient.

**발전**(發展) ① 《발달》 development; growth (성장); 《뻗어남》 expansion; extension; evolution (단계적). ~하다 develop; grow; expand; extend; evolve. ¶ 공업의 ~ industrial growth / 산업의 ~을 꾀하다 foster (the growth of) industry / ～을 저해하다 hamper 〔arrest〕 the growth 《of trade》/ 해외로 ～하다 expand overseas; extend 《*its*》 activities overseas / (도시가) 교외로 ～하다 expand over the surrounding country / 사업을 ～시키다 develop 〔expand〕 *one's* business / 사태의 ～을 지켜보다 watch the development of the situation / 이야기가 의외의 방향으로 ～했다 The conversation took an unexpected turn. / 그는 회사 ～에 크게 공헌했다 He contributed much to the growth of the company. / 사태는 유리하게 ～했다 The situation has developed in our favor. / 이 사업은 크게 ～할 가능성이 있다 This enterprise has great possibilities.

② 《번영함》 prosperity. ～하다 prosper; flourish; be prosperous. ¶ 사업의 ～ the prosperity of business / 귀사의 ～을 기원합니다 We wish for the prosperity of your firm. / 최근 이 도시는 크게 ～했다 This town has become much larger and more brisk.

◉ ～ 도상국 a developing country 〔nation〕. ～성 possibilities; possibility of future growth: ～성 있는 promising; 《a company》 with (bright) futures / ～성(이) 있는 사업〔기업〕 promising business 〔an enterprise〕 with futures.

**발전**(發電) 《전기의》 the generation of electricity; power generation. ～하다 generate electricity; produce electric power. ¶ 원자력 ～ atomic 〔nuclear〕 power generation. ◉ ～기관 《생물의》 an electric organ. ～실 a generator 〔power〕 room. ～자 an armature. ～차 a power source car. ～체 a charged body; an electrified body.

**발전기**(發電機) a 〔an electric〕 dynamo; a (power) generator; an electric generator. ¶ 교류〔직류〕 ～ an alternating 〔a direct〕 current dynamo; an A.C. 〔a D.C.〕 generator / 수력〔화력〕 ～ a hydro 〔thermal〕 generator / 열핵 ～ a thermonuclear generator.

**발전소**(發電所) a power plant 〔station〕; a powerhouse; a generating plant 〔station〕. ¶ 수력〔화력〕 ～ a hydroelectric 〔thermoelectric〕 power plant 〔station〕/ 열병합 ～ a combined heat and power plant / 원자력 ～ a nuclear 〔an atomic〕 power plant 〔station〕/ 자가 ～an isolated 〔a home〕 power plant.

**발전적**(發展的) expansive; developmental; growing. ¶ ～ 해산〔해체〕 the dissolution of several sections into a new organization / ～ 해체를 하다 be dissolved 〔absorbed〕 into a new organization.

**발정**(發情) sexual excitement; 《동물의》 estrus; heat (암컷의); rut (수컷의). ～하다 get sexually excited; 《암컷이》 come 〔go〕 into heat; get on heat; 《수컷이》 rut; go 〔come〕 into rut. ¶ ～하지 않은 anestrous / ～한 암소 a cow in 〔on〕 heat / ～해 있다 be in 〔on, at〕 heat 〔rut〕. ◉ ～기 (the age of) puberty; 《동물의》 the mating 〔rutting〕 season; estrus.

**발족**(發足) a start; starting; 《사업 따위의》 inauguration. ～하다 (make a) start; be inaugurated. ¶ 새로 ～하다 make a new start 《in》; start afresh / 회사가 ～하다 a company is inaugurated / 그 단체는 ～한지 얼마 안 되었다 That association started operations recently. / 정부는 곧 신5개년 계획을 ～시킨다 The Government will start 〔launch, embark on〕 a new five-year plan soon.

**발주**(發注) (placing) an order; ordering. ～하다 place an order 《with *a person* for an article》; order 《an article from England》; give 《*a person*》 an order 《for an article》. ¶ 우리는 새로운 스테레오를 생산자에게 ～했다 We ordered new stereos from the manufacturer. / 그 책들은 이미 ～해 놓았습니다 Those books are already on order. / 영국의 제작자에게 ～한 기계가 3개월 후에 도착했다 The machines I ordered from a British manufacturer arrived three months later.

**발주저리** wearing messy 〔dirty〕 socks.

**발진**(發疹) 〖의학〗 (an) eruption; (an) efflorescence; 《부스럼》 a rash; an exanthem. ～하다 break out (in a rash); come out (in spots); erupt; effloresce. ¶ ～성의 eruptive 《fever》/ 가슴에 ～이 생겼다 A rash appeared 〔came out〕 on the chest. ◉ ～티푸스 typhus (fever).

**발진**(發進) departure; takeoff (항공기의); the launching (로켓의); liftoff (헬리콥터 등의). ～하다 leave; depart 《from》; take 〔lift〕 off; scramble (요격을 위해 긴급히). ¶ 육상 기지에서 ～하는 landbased 《fighters》/ 그 우주 왕복선은 순조롭게 ～했다 The space shuttle lifted off without a hitch.

**발진기**(發振器) 〖물리〗 an oscillator.

**발짝** a step; a pace. ¶ 한～ 한～ step

by step / 한~ 앞으로 나오다〔뒤로 물러나다〕 take a step forward 〔backward〕 / 너무 지쳐서 더는 한 ~도 나아갈 수 없었다 I was so tired that I couldn't take another step.

**발짧다** be late for 《dinner, *etc.*》; just miss 《*something*》; (be) unlucky; unfortunate.

**발쭉거리다** keep on slightly opening and shutting. ¶ 입을 발쭉거리며 웃다〔울다〕 pucker up and smile 〔cry〕.

**발쭉이** (with mouth) half open; with lips slightly parted; with a smile.

**발쭉하다** 《mouth》 be half open; be slightly parted. ¶ 입을 발쭉하게 벌리다 half open *one's* mouth.

**발차**(發車) departure; the starting 《of a train》; 《차장의 소리》 All aboard! ~하다 start 《from》; depart 《from Seoul》; leave 《the station》; pull out 《of the station》. ¶ ~를 알리다 call a train / 막 ~하려는 때에 역에 닿다 get to the station just as the train is going to leave / 열차는 3번 선에서 ~했다 The train left from Track No. 3. / 버스는 몇 분마다 ~합니까 How often does the bus leave here?
◉ ~계(원) a starter. ~시간 the time for departure. ~신호 a starting signal; a signal for departure. ~ 플랫홈 a departure platform.

**발착**(發着) departure and arrival. ~하다 come and go; arrive and depart. ¶ 열차의 ~ 시간 arrival and departure times of trains. ◉ ~ 시간표 a timetable; a 《railroad》 schedule 《미》.

**발췌**(拔萃) 《뽑아냄》 extraction; excerption; 《골라냄》 selection; 《뽑아낸 것》 an extract; an excerpt; 《적요》 an abstract; a summary; 《선집》 a selection. ~하다 extract 《from》; make an extract 《from》; excerpt 《from》; select 《from》; make an abstract 《of》.
¶ 신문의 ~ a press cutting; a newspaper clipping / 잡지의 ~(물) an extract from a magazine / 편지의 한 구절을 ~하다 transcribe 〔quote〕 a passage from a letter / 이 1절은 성서에서 ~한 것이다 This passage is an extract 〔excerpt〕 from the Bible.
◉ ~ 개헌안 the selected amendment bill to the Constitution. ~검사 a random inspection. ~곡(曲) a musical selection.

**발치** 《방의》 the side of a room where *one's* feet ordinarily lie when *he* sleeps; 《발쪽의》 the area where the feet lie.
◉ 발칫잠 sleeping at the feet of others; sleeping in a corner of the room.

**발칙하다** 《무례하다》 (be) rude; impertinent; insolent; 《괘씸하다》 (be) unpardonable; inexcusable; outrageous. ¶ 발칙한 녀석 a rude 〔an insolent〕 fellow / 발칙하게 굴다 behave impertinently 〔improperly, outrageously〕; 《남에게》 take liberties 《with》 / 발칙하게 여기다 hold 《*a person*》 culpable / 이런 편지를 보내다니 발칙한 녀석 같으니 What an insolent fellow he is to write me such a letter!

**발칸** ¶ ~의 Balkan. ◉ ~반도 the Balkan Peninsula. ~제국 the Balkan States; the Balkans.

**발코니** a balcony. ¶ ~로 나가다 go out on the balcony / ~로 나가 시원한 바람을 쐬다 enjoy the cool air out on the balcony.

**발타다** 《a young animal》 try its legs for the first time.

**발탁**(拔擢) selection 《of *a person*》; choice 《of personnel》; an exceptional promotion (승진). ~하다 select; pick 〔single, sift〕 out; choose 《out of》; promote. ¶ 50명 중에서 두 사람을 ~하다 choose two out of 50 / 그는 과장으로 ~되었다 He was selected 〔promoted〕 to a section chief. / 아마추어 아가씨가 영화의 여주인공으로 ~되었다 A young amateur girl was singled out to be the heroine of the movie.
◉ ~승진 promotion by selection: ~승진되다 be picked out for promotion.

**발톱** 《사람의》 a toenail; 《금수의》 a claw; 《맹금의》 a talon. ¶ ~이 있는 clawed; taloned; nailed / ~으로 할퀴다 scratch with the claws; claw (at) / (고양이 등이) ~을 갈다 sharpen 〔whet〕 *its* claws / ~을 감추다 draw in *its* claws.

**발트** ¶ ~의 Baltic. ◉ ~삼국 the Baltic States. ~해 the Baltic Sea.

**발틀** a treadle 〔foot-operated〕 sewing machine.

**발파**(發破) blasting. ~하다 blast; blow 《*it*》 up with dynamite. ¶ ~ 장치를 하다 set dynamite 《to》 / 광산에서 바위를 ~하다 blast rocks in a mine. ◉ ~공(工) a blaster. ~약 a blasting powder 〔charge〕; a shot. ~점화 장치 a portfire.

**발판**(一板) ① 《건축 공사용》 a scaffold; scaffolding; 《발 놓는 자리》 (a) footing; a foothold. ¶ ~용 통나무 a scaffolding pole / ~용 판자 a footing board / ~을 만들다〔구축하다〕 establish a foothold 〔footing〕 / ~을 얻다 get 〔gain, secure〕 a foothold / ~을 굳히다 gain 〔secure〕

a firm foothold 《in the industry》/ 한 발마다 ~을 확인하면서 암벽을 기어오르다 climb a rocky cliff testing the footing for each step / 건물 둘레에 공사용 ~을 설치하다 set up scaffolding around the building / 그는 금융계에 ~을 확보했다〔잃었다〕 He secured 〔lost〕 his footing in financial circles.

② 《발돋움 받침》 a step; a stool; a footstool; a footboard; a stepladder. ¶ ~ 위에 오르다 mount 〔get on〕 a stool / 아이는 ~에 올라서서 선반 위의 과자에 손을 뻗쳤다 The child stood on a footstool to reach for the cakes on the shelf.

③ 《수단》 a stepping-stone; a springboard. ¶ 아무를 ~으로 이용하다 make a stepping-stone of *a person*; use *a person* as a stepping-stone 《to *one's* own success》/ A를 B에 이르는 ~으로 보다 look on A as a stepping-stone to B.

**발포**(發布) promulgation; proclamation; issue. ~하다 promulgate; proclaim; issue; publish; announce. ¶ 헌법의 ~ the promulgation of the constitution / 대한민국 헌법은 1948년 7월 17일에 ~되었다 The Constitution of Korea was promulgated on July 17, 1948.

**발포**(發泡) foaming; foamy effluence; effervescence. ⇨ 거품. ~하다 foam; froth; bubble (up); effervesce. ¶ ~시키다 foam; froth; bubble (up).

◉ ~스티렌 수지 styrene foam; expanded polystyrene; Styrofoam (상표명). ~정(錠) a foam tablet. ~제 a blowing 〔foaming〕 agent.

**발포**(發砲) firing; the discharge of a gun. ~하다 fire 《on》; open fire 《on》; discharge 〔fire off〕 a gun. ¶ 그는 부하에게 ~를 명령했다 He ordered his men to open fire.

◉ ~사건 a shooting incident 〔case〕.

**발표**(發表) (an) announcement; publication; 《성명》 a statement; a communiqué. ~하다 announce; make public; publish; lay 《*a matter*》 before the public; issue 《a statement》; express; release. ¶ 신문 ~ a press 〔news〕 release / 중간 ~ an interim announcement / 미~된 작품 an unpublished work / 정식 ~ a formal announcement / 성명서를 ~하다 announce a statement / 연구를 ~하다 《출판물로》 publish the results of *one's* research; 《학회 등에서》 read a paper 《at an academic meeting》/ 의견을 ~하다 express *one's* view / 약혼을 ~하다 announce *one's* engagement / 새로운 학설을 ~하다 put forward a new theory / 정견을 ~하다 state 〔set forth〕 *one's* political views / 당의 방침을 ~하다 publish 〔set forth〕 a party line / ~를 보류하다 withhold an announcement / 투표 결과를 ~하다 declare the results of the poll / 학생이 조사한 것을 학급에서 ~하다 present the results of *one's* research to the class; read *one's* report to the class / 시험 성적이 ~되었다 The results of the examination have been announced. / 정부는 경제 정책을 ~했다 The government released its economic plan. / 그녀는 학회에서 연구를 ~했다 She presented her research at the academic meeting.

**발하다**(發—) ① 《발산하다》 issue forth 〔out〕; emit; give out 〔off〕 (냄새 등을); emanate (빛을); radiate (빛·열 따위를). ¶ 향기를 ~ give out 〔emit〕 a fragrant 〔sweet〕 smell / 태양은 빛과 열을 발한다 The sun sends out light and heat. / 그는 문학계에서 이채를 발한다 He cuts an eminent 〔a brilliant〕 figure in the literary world. ② 《명령을》 issue; give; send in; 《법령 등을》 issue; publish; send 〔give〕 out; 《소리를》 utter; give utterance to. ¶ 명령을 ~ give an order / 경보를 ~ sound the alarm / 계엄령을 ~ declare martial law / 격문을 ~ send a circular. ③ 《보내다》 dispatch; send (out, forth) 《a troop》.

**발한**(發汗) sweating; perspiration; hidrosis (약·병으로 인한); 『의학』 diaphoresis. ~하다 perspire; sweat. ¶ ~시키다 induce perspiration; sweat 《a patient》; throw 《*a person*》 into a sweat.

◉ ~작용 perspiration; sweating. ~제 a sweating medicine; a diaphoretic; a sudorific.

**발항**(發航) =출항(出航). ◉ ~지 a home port; a port of departure.

**발행**(發行) ① 《발간》 publication; issue. ~하다 publish 《a magazine》; issue; bring out; put into circulation. ¶ 매월〔월2회, 매주〕 ~의 잡지 a monthly 〔a semi-monthly, a weekly〕 (magazine) / ~을 금지〔정지〕하다 prohibit 〔suspend〕 publication / 그 책은 ~이 금지되었다 The publication of the book was banned. / 그 책은 언제 ~됩니까 When will the book come out?

② 《어음 따위의》 drawing; issue. ~하다 draw; issue. ¶ 어음을 ~하다 draw a bill 〔draft〕 《upon *a person* for

500,000 won》/ 은행 앞으로 10만원의 수표를 ～하다 draw a check on a bank for 100,000 won.
③《지폐·주권 등의》 issue; flo(a)tation (채권의). ～하다 issue 《banknotes》; float 《a bond》. ¶ 우표를〔주권을〕 ～하다 issue new stamps 〔shares〕/ 증명서를 ～하다 issue a certificate / 새 화폐를 ～하다 put new currency in circulation.
◉ ～가격 an issue price; 《증권 따위의》 an issue par. ～고 (amount of) circulation; 《공채·지폐 따위의》 the amount of issue. ～권 the right of publication. ～금지 prohibition of publication. ～소〔처〕 a publishing office; the publishers. ～인〔자〕 a publisher; a drawer 《of a bill》; a remitter 《of a money order》; an issuer 《of a check》. ～일 the issued date; the date of issue 〔publication〕. ～정지 suspension of publication: 신문의 ～정지를 해제하다 cancel the suspension of a newspaper. ～지 《어음 등의》 a place of drawing 〔issue〕.

**발행부수**(發行部數) 《신문 따위의》 a circulation; 《단행본의》 copies printed. ¶ ～ 50만 《have》 a circulation of 500,000 / 세계 최고의 ～를 가진 신문 the paper with the heftiest circulation in the world / ～가 많다〔적다〕 have a large 〔limited, small〕 circulation.

**발허리** the arch of the foot.

**발현**(發現) revelation; a manifestation. ～하다 《…이》 be revealed; be manifested; manifest itself; 《…을》 reveal; manifest. ¶ 애국심의 ～ a manifestation of *one's* love for (*one's*) country.

**발호**(跋扈) rampancy; prevalence; domination; predominance; presumption. ～하다 run 〔be〕 rampant 《among people, *etc.*》; prevail; dominate; domineer over; reign supreme; lord it over; ride triumphantly over. ¶ 군벌의 ～ the rampancy of the military clique / 최근 폭력단의 ～가 눈에 띄게 두드러졌다 The gangsters' rampancy has come to the fore recently.

**발화**(發火) ①《점화》 the production of fire; ignition (인화); combustion (연소). ～하다 《…이》 ignite; catch 〔take〕 fire. ¶ 자연 ～ spontaneous combustion / ～시키다 ignite; enkindle; set fire to 《the fuel》/ ～하기 쉽다 be (in)flammable 〔combustible〕; ignitable / 셀룰로이드는 매우 ～하기 쉽다 Celluloid is very combustible. / 황은 비교적 낮은 온도에서 ～한다 Sulfur ignites 〔burns〕 at a relatively low temperature.
②《화재》 an outbreak of fire. ～하다 《…이》 a fire breaks out. ¶ ～의 원인 the origin 〔cause〕 of a fire / …에서 ～하다 the fire starts from... / 맨앞의 객차에서 ～했다 The fire originated in the first car of the train.
③《발사》 discharge; firing 《of a volley》; detonation 《of a charge》. ～하다 《…이》 go off; be discharged; be detonated.
◉ ～기(器) an exploder. ～약 a detonator. ～온도 the ignition temperature. ～장치 an ignition device. ～전(栓) a spark plug. ～점 the ignition 〔combustion〕 point; 《기름의》 the firing 〔burning〕 point; 《분쟁의》 the flash point.

**발효**(發效) coming into effect; effectuation. ～하다 become effective; come 〔go〕 into effect 〔force, operation〕. ¶ 평화 조약의 ～에 따라 with the effectuation of the peace treaty / 조약은 내년 1월부터 ～한다 The treaty will go into effect next January.

**발효**(醱酵) fermentation; ferment. ～하다 ferment; undergo fermentation. ¶ ～하고 있다 be in ferment; be fermenting / ～시키다 ferment; leaven / 포도를 ～시키다 ferment grapes / 이스트로 밀가루 반죽을 ～시키다 leaven dough with yeast / 된장은 콩을 ～시켜 만든다 *Toenjang* is made from fermented soybeans. ◉ ～균 a ferment fungus. ～력〔성〕 fermentability. ～방지제 an antiferment. ～법 zymotechnics. ～소(素) yeast; ferment; leaven. ～작용 fermentation. ～학 zymology.

**발휘**(發揮) display; exhibition; manifestation; demonstration. ～하다 display; show; exhibit (공중 앞에서); demonstrate (증명해 보이다). ¶ 실력을 ～하다 show 〔display〕 *one's* real ability / 재질〔능력〕을 충분히 ～하다 give full play 〔swing, scope〕 to *one's* ability; bring *one's* genius 〔ability〕 into full play / 정치가로서의 수완을 ～하다 prove *oneself* an able politician / 마침내 그녀는 실력을 ～할 수 있는 기회를 얻었다 Finally she's got a chance to show 〔demonstrate〕 her real abilities 〔what she can do〕. / 그 일은 자네의 능력을 충분히 ～할 수 있는 기회를 줄 것이다 The job will give you a chance to display your ability to the full.

**발흥**(勃興) a sudden 〔meteoric〕 rise; a

sudden increase in the power 《of》. ～하다 rise suddenly; rise into power. ¶ 고구려의 ～ the rise of *Koguryŏ* / 신세력의 ～ the rise of a new power.

**밝기** (the degree of) brightness. ⇨ 광도(光度).

**밝다**[1] ①《빛이》 (be) light; bright. ¶ 밝게 bright(ly); brilliantly; with brightness / 밝은 곳에서 in the light / 밝은 동안에 while it is (still) light; during the light hours; before dark / 밝은 방 a light 〔bright〕 room; 《조명으로》 a well-lighted room / 밝은 햇빛 bright sunlight / 달 밝은 밤 a bright moonlit night / 대낮처럼 ～ be as bright as day / 밝게 하다 brighten; lighten; light up; make brighter / 밝아지다 lighten; grow 〔get〕 light; light up / 등불을 밝게 하다 make the lamp brighter / 6시 반인데도 밖은 아직 ～ It is now six-thirty, but it is still light outside. / 이 전등은 ～ 〔밝지 않다〕 This lamp gives a good 〔bad〕 light. / 하늘이 밝아온다 The sky is brightening.
②《빛깔이》 bright. ¶ 밝은 색 bright colors / 밝은 빨강 bright red.
③《눈·귀가》 (be) sharp; keen; acute; quick. ¶ 밝은 눈〔귀〕 acute vision 〔hearing〕; good 〔sharp〕 eyes 〔ears〕 / 귀가 ～ have a good hearing; have a sharp ear; be quick of hearing / 눈이 ～ have keen 〔good〕 eyesight; be sharp-eyed 〔quick-sighted〕 / 개는 아주 귀가 ～ The dog has sharp ears.
④《잘 알다》 be familiar 《with》; be well acquainted 《with》; be (well) versed 《in》; be conversant 《with》; be well posted up 《in》; know well 《about》. ¶ (그 방면에) 밝은 사람 an expert 《in, at》; a connoisseur 《of curios》 / 계수에 ～ be good at figures / 문학에 ～ 「be well read in 〔know a lot about〕 literature / 법률에 ～ be learned in the law / 사무에 ～ be well versed in business methods / 사정에 ～ be well-informed 《of》 / 세상 물정에 ～ know much of the world; be a man of the world / 주변 지리에 ～ know *one's* way around here; know every inch of the neighborhood / 그는 중국 사정에 ～ He is well up in 〔well informed about〕 Chinese affairs.
⑤《기분·성격 등이》 (be) cheerful; sunny; bright; happy; 《전망 따위가》 (be) bright; promising; rosy. ¶ 밝은 기분 《with》 a happy 〔light〕 heart; 《in》 a cheerful mood / 밝은 성격 a sunny 〔cheerful〕 disposition / 밝은 미래〔전망〕 a bright 〔rosy〕 future; a bright outlook for the future / 밝은 표정 a cheerful 〔bright〕 look / 밝아지다 brighten (up) / 기분이 밝아지다 feel light at heart; feel happy / 앞날이 ～ have a bright 〔rosy〕 future ahead 〔before *one*〕 / 전망이 ～ The prospects are bright. / 무역의 전망이 ～ There is a good outlook for foreign trade. / 사물의 밝은 면을 보도록 해야 한다 You should try to look on the sunny side of things.
⑥《공정하다》 (be) clean. ¶ 밝은 사회 a community in peace and prosperity / 밝은 정치 clean politics / 사회를 밝게 하다 make *one's* society orderly and decent.

**밝다**[2] 《날이 새다》 dawn; (day) break. ¶ 밝아오는 하늘 the dawning sky / 날이 밝기 전에 일어나다 rise before (it is) light / 날이 ～ day dawn 〔break, crack〕 / 날이 밝아온다 Morning dawns. *or* Day breaks. / 새해가 밝아온다 The New Year begins. / 날이 밝자 비는 그쳤다 By dawn, the rain had stopped.

**밝을녘** peep of dawn 〔day〕; daybreak; dawn; the early hours of the morning. ¶ ～에 at (the peep of) dawn; at break of day; toward daybreak / ～까지 공부하다 study till the morning light.

**밝히다**[1] ①《분명히 하다》 make 《*a matter*》 clear 〔plain〕; clear (up) 《the cause》; clarify 〔define〕 《*one's* attitude》; throw 〔shed〕 light on 《*a matter*》; explain; 《공개하다》 bring 《*a matter*》 to light; bring out; make 《*a matter*》 public; 《파헤쳐서》 dig up; bare 〔uncover, discover〕 《the truth, the mystery》; disclose 〔reveal, divulge〕 《a secret》; 《확인하다》 ascertain 《*a matter*》; verify. ¶ 계획을 ～ lay the scheme bare 〔open〕 / 사리를 ～ reason with 《*a person*》 / 신분을 ～ prove 〔disclose〕 *one's* identity / 심중을 ～ open 〔bare〕 *one's* heart 《to》; unbosom *oneself* 《to》 / 이름을 ～ disclose *one's* name / …의 뜻을 ～ explain the meaning 《of》 / 태도를 ～ clarify *one's* attitude; make *one's* attitude clear / 자기 입장을 ～ define 〔clarify〕 *one's* position / 밝혀지다 become clear 〔plain〕; 《알려지다》 be (made) known; come 〔be brought〕 to light; 《판명되다》 prove 〔turn out〕 《to be…》; be identified 《as…》 / 그의 죄상이 밝혀졌다 His crime has been brought to light. / 그의 사인(死因)은

아직 밝혀지지 않고 있다 The cause of his death is yet unknown. / 피해자의 신원이 밝혀지지 않았다 The victim is not yet identified. / 돈의 용도는 한푼이라도 다 밝혀주기 바란다 I want you to account for every penny you spend.
② 《환하게 하다》 brighten; lighten; light (up); make brighter. ¶ 가로등을 ～ light on 〔up〕 street lights / 그 거리는 전등이 훤히 밝혀져 있다 The street is brightly lit up. / 그는 손전등으로 내가 가는 길을 밝혀 주었다 He lighted the way for me with a flashlight.

**밝히다**[2] 《밤을 지내다》 pass 〔spend〕 《a night》. ¶ 밤을 ～ stay 〔sit〕 up all night; keep 〔remain〕 awake all night; keep vigil; see the dawn in; pass 〔spend〕 a night / 한 밤을 이야기로 ～ talk the night away / 술로 하룻밤을 ～ drink all night; drink the night away / 하룻밤을 눈물로 ～ pass a whole night in tears; weep all night / 다음날의 시험 준비로 꼬박 밤을 밝혔다 I sat 〔stayed〕 up all night for the test on the next day.

**밞다** ① 《팔로》 measure off 《the length of a piece of cloth or the like》 in double-arm spans. ② 《걸음으로》 measure 《a distance》 in paces; pace off 《a distance》.

**밟다** ① 《디디다》 (***a***) 《발로》 step on; tread (up)on (with the feet); trample (up)on; stamp. ¶ 보리를 ～ step 〔tread〕 on the seedling of barley / 남의 발을 ～ tread 〔step〕 on another's foot / 헛 ～ miss *one's* step; slip / 살얼음을 ～ tread on thin ice / 외국 땅을 ～ step 〔set foot〕 on foreign soil / 전철을 ～ make 〔repeat〕 the same error 〔mistake〕 (as another person did) / 브레이크를 ～ step on the brake / 액셀러레이터를 천천히 ～ press the accelerator pedal slowly / 페달을 ～ work a pedal 〔treadle〕; pedal 《*one's* bicycle》 / 마구 짓～ trample under foot; trample down; tread on / (땅을) 밟아 다지다〔고르다〕 tread down 《the earth》; level 《the earth》 by treading down / 잔디를 밟지 마시오 《게시》 Keep off the grass. / 이봐요, 발을 밟지 말아요 Hi! Get off my feet. / 미안합니다. 제가 선생의 발을 밟았나요 Sorry! Did I step on your feet? (***b***) 《경험하다》 ¶ 무대를 ～ tread the boards 〔stage〕 / 첫무대를 ～ make *one's* first appearance on the stage; make *one's* debut.
② 《남의 뒤를》 follow; track; shadow; tail; get on 《*a person's*》 tail; dog 《*one's* steps》. ¶ 형사로 하여금 뒤를 밟게 하다 set a detective on 《*a person*('s track)》.
③ 《순서·절차 따위를》 go through 《formalities, red tape》; undergo; 《끝내다》 complete 〔finish〕 《a procedure, a course》. ¶ 절차를 ～ go through 〔comply with〕 formalities / 대학 과정을 ～ complete a course at the university; receive a university education / 정규 과정을 ～ complete a regular course.

**밟히다** be stepped on; get 〔be〕 trampled on; be trod upon. ¶ 나는 열차 안에서 발을 밟혔다 I had my foot stepped 〔trodden〕 on in the train.

**밤**[1] ① 《야간》 night; nighttime; 《저녁》 evening. ¶ 밤의 night; nocturnal (야행성의) / 오늘밤 tonight; this evening / 어젯밤 last night / 전날 밤 the previous night / 내일 밤 tomorrow night / 밤의 고요 the stillness of the night / 밤의 서울 Seoul by night / 밤에 at night; in the evening; 《밤중에》 in the night; 《밤에는》 by night / 밤을 타서 under cover 〔the cloak〕 of night / 토요일 밤에 on Saturday night 〔evening〕 / 4월 5일 밤에 on the evening 〔night〕 of April 5 / 밤 여덟 시에 at eight o'clock in the evening; at eight of the evening / 밤이 깊도록 《work》 till late at night; far into the night / 밤이 되기 전에 before dark 〔nightfall, dusk〕 / 밤이 되면 when (the) night 「falls 〔comes on, closes in〕 / 밤이고 낮이고 night and day / 밤을 새우다 pass a night without sleep; sit 〔stay〕 up all night / 이야기로 밤을 새우다 talk the night away / 밤이 되었다 Night falls. *or* Evening sets 〔closes〕 in. / 밤이 아주 깊었다 The night is far advanced.
② 《행사》 an evening. ¶ 모차르트의 밤 Mozart evening 〔*Abend* (G.)〕 / 음악의 밤 《have》 a musical evening.

**밤**[2] 《열매》 a chestnut; a nut. ¶ 밤 따러 가다 go gathering nuts; go chestnut gathering / 밤을 까다 crack a chestnut.

**밤**[3] 《놋그릇 틀》 a mold 〔cast〕 for brasswares.

**밤거리** night streets; the town at night. ¶ ～의 여인 a streetwalker; a street girl.

**밤길** a walk at night; a night trip; a journey by night. ¶ ～을 가다 go 〔travel〕 by 〔at〕 night; make a night trip / ～을 여자 혼자 나다니는 것은 위험하다 It is unsafe for a woman to go out alone at night.

**밤나무** a chestnut tree.

**밤낚시** night fishing 〔angling〕. ～하다 go fishing by night; drop a line at night. ◉ ～꾼 a night angler.

**밤낮** ①《밤과 낮》 night and day; day and night. ②《밤낮을 가리지 않고》 night and day; always; all the time; day in, day out. ¶ 그는 ～(으로) 공부한다 He works (at his studies) night and day.

**밤놀이** night life 〔pleasure, amusement〕; entertainment 〔amusement〕 at night. ～하다 have fun at night; indulge in some night life. ¶ ～ 나가다 go out in the evening《for pleasure》.

**밤눈**[1] 《보는 힘》 night vision. ¶ ～이 밝다 have the eyes of a cat / ～이 어둡다 suffer from night blindness; be blind (as a bat) at night.

**밤눈**[2] 《내리는 눈》 snow in the night.

**밤느정이, 밤늦** a chestnut blossom.

**밤늦다** (be) late at night. ¶ 밤늦게 late at night / 밤늦게까지 far into the night; till late at night / 밤늦도록 공부하다 work at《*one's* studies》 far into the night; burn the midnight oil.

**밤대거리** night shift; night crew; night relief. ¶ ～로 나가다〔일하다〕 work on the night shift.

**밤도와** all night through; all through 〔throughout〕 the night; all hours of the night. ¶ ～ 일하다 work on into the night; work all night; work without having a wink of sleep.

**밤들다** it gets dark; darkness draws around; night closes in 〔sets in〕; the night deepens 〔advances, grows darker〕. ¶ 밤이 들어서야 공부한다 I don't study till the night is well along.

**밤똥** having a bowel movement at night; going to the lavatory 〔bathroom〕 at night.

**밤마다** every night; night after night; nightly. ¶ 두 사람은 ～ 데이트를 했다 The two dated every night.

**밤바람** 《상쾌한》 a night breeze; 《좀 거센》 a night wind. ¶ ～을 쐬다 be exposed to a night wind / ～이 살을 에었다 The night wind cut me to the bone.

**밤볼** 《토실한 뺨》 chubby 〔plump〕 cheeks.

**밤비** rain in the night. ¶ ～에 자란 사람 a person who is "soft in the head"; a (soft) fool.

**밤사이, 밤새** the nighttime. ¶ ～에 during the night; overnight / ～의 폭우로 owing to the heavy rain that has been falling since last night / 집에 ～ 도둑이 들었다 My house was broken into during the night.

**밤새도록, 밤새껏** all night long 〔through〕; all (the) night through; throughout 〔all through〕 the night; the whole night; overnight. ¶ ～ 일하다 work all night / ～ 마시다 make a night of it / ～ 한잠 자지 않다 sit up all night; do not sleep a wink the whole night / 나는 ～ 잠을 이루지 못했다 I remained awake all the night through. / ～ 이가 몹시 아팠다 All night long my tooth ached terribly. / 어머니는 병든 아이 걱정으로 ～ 눈을 붙이지 못했다 The mother's concern over her sick child kept her awake all night.

**밤새(우)다** stay 〔sit, be〕 up all night; see the dawn in; keep vigil; hold awake. ¶ 뜬 눈으로 ～ cannot get a wink of sleep; pass a sleepless night / 밤새워 끝내다 finish《*a thing*》 by working at night (through) / 밤새워 바느질하다 sew all night long / 밤새워 병구완하다 nurse《an invalid》 with sleepless devotion; sit up with《an invalid》 all the night through / 밤새워 일하다 sit up all night working; work all night / 그들은 카드 놀이로 밤새웠다 They sat up all night playing cards.

**밤새움, 밤샘** staying 〔sitting〕 up all night; keeping 〔remaining〕 awake all night; an all-night vigil 〔sitting〕. ～하다 stay 〔sit〕 up all night; keep vigil. ¶ ～은 건강에 나쁘다 Staying up all night is bad for your health.

**밤색**(―色) ¶ ～의 chestnut(-colored); maroon; sorrel 〔bay〕《horse》.

**밤소경** night blindness; 《사람》 a night-blind person.

**밤소일**(―消日) a night out; a night on the town; night amusement 〔pleasure〕. ～하다 have a night on the town; go out for an evening's fun; amuse *oneself* by night.

**밤손님** a night prowler; a (night) thief; a burglar; a night bird. ¶ 어젯밤 집에 ～이 들었다 A burglar broke into my house last night. *or* My house was 〔I had my house〕 broken into last night.

**밤송이** a chestnut bur(r).

**밤안개** a night fog 〔mist〕.

**밤알** a (single) chestnut.

**밤얽이** a kind of knot (like a double bowknot). ¶ ～를 치다 tie a double bowknot.

**밤이슬** (the) evening 〔night〕 dew; the dampness of the night. ¶ ～ 맞는 놈

a prowler; a burglar / ~ 맞다 be wet with night dew; be exposed to the night dampness.

**밤일** night work; night shift. ~하다 work at night; do night work.

**밤자갈** pebbles (for paving).

**밤잔물** a bowl of water kept overnight at the bedside. ⇨ 자리끼.

**밤잠** sleeping at night; night sleep.

**밤재우다** keep overnight.

**밤주악** a stuffed griddle-cake made of chestnut flour and honey.

**밤중**(—中) the dead of night; midnight. ¶ ~에 at (mid)night; in the middle of the night; at 〔in the〕 dead of night; at night time; in the deep of night / ~까지 till the middle of the night; far into the night; until the small hours (of the morning) / 이 ~에 어디 가려느냐 Where do you think (you're) going at this time of night?

**밤차**(—車) a night train; an owl train 《미》; a night bus.

**밤참** a late 〔(mid)night〕 snack. ¶ ~을 먹다 have a night snack.

**밤톨** a (single) chestnut; a thing the size of a chestnut. ¶ ~만하다 be as big as a chestnut; be a chestnut size.

**밤하늘** a night 〔nocturnal〕 sky. ¶ ~을 쳐다보다 look up at the night sky / 그는 ~에 반짝이는 별을 쳐다보며 크게 한 숨을 쉬었다 He gave a deep sigh, looking up at the stars shining in the night sky.

**밥**[1] ① 《지은 밥》 (***a***) 《쌀밥》 boiled 〔cooked〕 rice. ¶ 밥 한 그릇 a bowl of rice / 밥을 담다〔푸다〕 serve rice / 밥을 짓다 boil 〔cook〕 rice / 밥이 뜸들다 rice is steamed (to a proper degree). (***b***) 《잡곡밥》 boiled rice and cereals. ¶ 조밥 boiled millet.

② 《식사》 a meal; food. ¶ 밥 때 mealtime; dinner time / 밥을 먹다 take 〔have, eat〕 a meal; sit 〔be〕 at table / 밥을 함께 먹다 eat 〔dine〕 together / 밖에서 밥을 먹다 eat 〔dine〕 out / 정해진 시간에 밥 먹다 have regular mealtime.

③ 《생계》 living; livelihood; bread. ¶ 밥을 먹다 make 〔earn〕 *one's* 〔a〕 living; eat *one's* bread / 밥도 먹을 수 없다 be unable to earn *one's* bread; cannot make a living / 밥을 먹게 해주다 put 《*a person*》 in the way of making a living.

④ 《먹이》 feed; food; bait; prey. ¶ 돼지밥 hog feed / 고기밥이 되다 be sent to the bottom; be drowned 《at sea》; become food for fishes / 쥐는 고양이의 밥이다 Mice are the prey of cats.

⑤ 《희생물》 a victim; a prey; 《만만한 상대》 a pigeon; a gull; an easy mark. ¶ …의 밥이 되다 fall a prey 〔victim〕 to / 밥으로 삼다 exploit 《*a person*》; prey upon; make a victim of 《a girl》.

**밥**[2] 《부스러기》 waste material produced in cutting, *etc.* ¶ 톱밥 sawdust / 대팻밥 shavings (from a plane) / 끌밥 chisel dust / 가윗밥 waste pieces (of cut cloth); cuttings; scraps / 실밥 waste thread.

**밥값** the price for a meal; food expenses; board (하숙의). ¶ 그는 ~도 못 한다 He is a good-for-nothing.

**밥그릇** a rice bowl. ¶ 밥을 ~에 담다 serve 〔put〕 rice in a bowl; fill a bowl with rice.

**밥내다** torture a confession out of 《a criminal》.

**밥맛** ① 《밥의 맛》 the flavor of rice. ② 《식욕》 appetite. ¶ ~이 있다 have a good appetite / ~이 없다 have no 〔a poor〕 appetite / ~ 나게 하다 arouse 〔whet, stimulate, sharpen〕 *one's* appetite.

**밥물** ① 《밥 짓는》 water for boiling rice. ② 《넘치는》 rice-water. ¶ ~이 넘다 the rice-water is boiling over.

**밥밑** beans 〔barley, *etc.*〕 boiled with rice. ◉ ~콩 choice beans (suitable for cooking with rice).

**밥벌레** a good-for-nothing (fellow); a do-nothing; a drone; an idler; a useless mouth. ¶ 너는 ~다 You are not worth your salt.

**밥벌이** means of a scanty livelihood; a job; breadwinning; earning *one's* bread. ~하다 gain *one's* livelihood; earn *one's* bread; make a living. ¶ ~가 되다 earn *one* enough to eat / ~가 안되다 cannot 〔can hardly〕 manage (to live) on *one's* income; be in needy 〔straitened〕 circumstances / ~가 떨어지다 lose *one's* means of livelihood / ~를 시켜주다 put 《*a person*》 in the way of making a living / 그는 겨우 ~나 하고 있다 He makes a bare living. / 당장 ~가 없다 I'm out of job right now. / 이 장사는 ~가 안된다 This business doesn't pay.

**밥빼기** a baby that is suddenly weaned (because of a new pregnancy) and overstuffs itself on rice.

**밥상**(—床) a dining 〔an eating〕 table; a (dinner) table. ¶ ~을 차리다 set the table / ～을 받다〔에 앉다〕 sit down to *one's* dinner; sit at 〔sit down to〕 table / ～을 올리다 set a meal before 《*a person*》/ ～을 치우다 clear the table / ～에는 온갖 종류의 산해진미가 차려져 있었다 All sorts of delicacies were served on the table.

**밥솥** a rice pot 〔cooker〕; a pot 〔cooker〕 for boiling rice.

**밥술** a spoonful of (boiled) rice; meager food. ¶ ～이나 먹으려고 일을 하다 do the job just to keep 「the wolf from the door 〔body and soul together〕/ 그는 아르바이트로 겨우 ～이나 먹고 산다 He 「gets a bare livelihood 〔ekes out a miserable existence〕 on the income from his part-time job.

**밥쌀** rice for boiling; eating rice.

**밥알** a grain of boiled rice.

**밥장사** restaurant business; selling meals. ～하다 run a restaurant; sell meals; run an eating house.

**밥장수** one who runs a restaurant 〔an eating house〕; one who sells meals.

**밥주걱** a wooden paddle 〔scoop〕 for serving rice.

**밥주머니** a good-for-nothing. ⇨ 밥통 ③.

**밥줄** a means of livelihood; a source of income; *one's* occupation. ¶ ～이 끊어지다 lose *one's* means of livelihood 〔job〕.

**밥집** an eating house; a cheap restaurant.

**밥짓다** ① boil rice; cook food; prepare a meal. ② 《a crab》 foam at the mouth.

**밥통**(―桶) ① 《밥 담는》 a boiled-rice container 〔tub〕. ② 《위》 the stomach. ③ 《밥벌레》 a good-for-nothing; 《바보》 a fool; an ass.

**밥투정** grumbling over 〔at〕 meals. ～하다 grumble over 〔at〕 meals; complain about the inadequacy of *one's* food. ¶ 밥 한 그릇을 다 먹고도 ～을 하는구나 You had a whole bowlful and yet you are grumbling over it.

**밥풀** grains of boiled rice (used as paste 〔starch〕); rice paste. ◉ ～강정 a rice-coated fried cake. ～과자 a honey cake coated with popped rice.

**밥풀질** pasting 〔starching〕 with boiled rice grains. ～하다 paste 〔starch〕 with boiled rice grains.

**밧줄** a rope; a line. ¶ 세 가닥으로 꼰 ～ three-ply rope / ～로 당기다 pull with a rope / ～을 당기다 draw 〔pull〕 the rope; haul at 〔upon〕 a rope; 《두 손으로 번갈아》 haul in 〔up〕 a rope / ～을 치다 stretch a rope; rope / ～을 타고 내려오다 climb down a rope.

**방**(房) ① 《거처하는》 a room; a chamber. ¶ 방세 a room rent; rent / 셋방 a room 「for rent 〔to let 《영》〕/ 볕이 잘 드는 방 a sunny room / 빈 방 an unoccupied room / 방이 셋 있는 집 a three-room(ed) house / 2〔3〕인용 방 《호텔 따위의》 a twin〔triple〕(-bedded) room / 방에 세들다 hire a room; rent a room 《from》/ 방을 세주다 rent 〔let 《영》〕 a room 《to》/ 방으로 모시다 show 《*a person*》 into a room / 방을 예약하다 reserve a room 《at a hotel》/ 방을 비우다 vacate a room; leave a room / 한 방을 같이 쓰다 share a room 《with》/ 이 방은 나의 서재이다 This room serves for my study. / 빈 방이 있습니까 Do you have a vacant room? ② [명사 뒤에서] shop; shopkeeper's; store. ¶ 은방 a silversmith's.

**방**(榜) ① 《방목》 the list of successful candidates (in the higher civil service examination). ② 《방문》 a placard; a public 〔an official〕 notice.

**방**(放) 《탄알 수》 a round; 《소총의》 a shot; 《대포의》 a shell; 《펀치의》 a punch. ¶ 열 방 쏘다 fire ten rounds 〔shots〕/ 한 방의 포성 a roar of cannon / 주먹으로 머리를 여러 방 얻어맞다 be punched on the head several times.

**-방**(方) ① 《방위》 direction. ¶ 동방 east. ② [명사 뒤에서] 《in》 care of (생략 c/o). ¶ 한일환 씨방, 김홍식 씨 Mr. Kim Hong-shik c/o Mr. Han Il-hwan.

**방가**(放歌) singing loudly. ～하다 sing loudly 〔boisterously〕.

**방갈로** 『건축』 a bungalow.

**방값**(房―) 《방세》 room rent; rent; 《숙박료》 room charge.

**방갓**(方―) a wide-brimmed mourning hat made of bamboo splits; a bamboo hat worn by mourners. ◉ ～쟁이 a person wearing a wide-brimmed mourning hat.

**방게** 『동물』 a kind of small crab.

**방계**(傍系) a collateral family 〔line〕. ¶ ～의 《직계에 대한》 collateral; 《부차적인·모회사에 대한》 subsidiary. ◉ ～비속〔존속〕 a collateral descendant 〔ascendant〕. ～인족(姻族) collateral relatives-in-law. ～친족 collateral relatives 〔relations〕. ～혈족 collateral relatives 〔relations〕 by blood. ～회사 a subsidiary 〔an affiliated〕 company.

**방고래**(房―) a flue of an *ondol* 〔a hypocaust〕. ¶ ～를 놓다 lay a system of flues in the floor of a room / ～가 메다

the flue of a hypocaust is clogged up.

**방공**(防共) defense against communism; anti-Comintern. ～하다 fight 〔defend against〕 communism. ◉ ～국가 an anticommunist nation. ～전선 a defense line against the spread of communism.

**방공**(防空) air 〔aerial〕 defense; antiaircraft defense; interception. ◉ ～감시원 an air 〔air-raid〕 warden. ～시설 air defenses; anti-air-raid establishments; air defense facilities. ～연습〔훈련〕《민간의》 an anti-air-raid 〔air defense〕 drill; 《군부의》 air defense maneuvers 〔exercises〕: 민〔군민 합동〕～ 훈련 a civil 〔a military-civil joint〕 air defense drill. ～체제 an air defense setup 〔system〕. ～호 an air-raid shelter 〔trench〕; a dugout: ～호에 들어가다 shelter *oneself* in a dugout. 한국 ～식별 구역 Korean Air Defense Identification Zone (생략 KADIZ).

**방과**(放課) dismissal of a class. ～하다 《school》 be over; let out; be dismissed. ¶ ～ 후 after-school hours; after school (is over) / ～ 후 나는 곧잘 도서관에서 독서로 시간을 보냈다 I would often spend my time reading in the library after school was over.

**방관**(傍觀) looking on as a spectator (to a scene); onlooking. ～하다 look on (unconcernedly); sit as a spectator; remain indifferent 〔impassive〕 《to》; remain a (mere) spectator 〔an idle onlooker〕; stand by and watch; stand by idly. ¶ 수수～하다 remain an unconcerned spectator; look on with folded arms / ～적(인) 태도를 취하다 assume the attitude of an onlooker; assume an indifferent attitude 《to, toward》 / 그들이 굶어 죽어가고 있는데 어떻게 ～할 수 있는가 How can we stand 〔sit〕 by and look on 〔watch〕 them dying of hunger?
◉ ～인〔자〕 a looker-on (*pl.* lookers-); an onlooker; a bystander; an idle spectator.

**방광**(膀胱) 〖해부〗 the (urinary) bladder; the vesica. ◉ ～결석 a bladder-stone; a cystolith. ～경 a cystoscope. ～염 cystitis; inflammation of the (urinary) bladder. ～카타르 catarrh of the bladder. ～파열 rupture of the bladder.

**방구들**(房—) a hypocaust; underfloor heating system.

**방구리** a water jug. ¶ 옹～ a small water jug.

**방구매기** 〖건축〗 making the eaves swell out in the middle by cutting the middle rafter(s) longer.

**방구멍** the center hole of a kite.

**방구석**(房—) 《방의 구석》 a corner of a room; 《방안》 the interior of a room; a room. ¶ ～에 in a room; indoors / 언제나 ～에 틀어박혀 있다 I stay cooped up in my room at all times.

**방귀** wind (in the bowels); gas; a fart 《속어》. ¶ ～를 뀌다 break 〔pass〕 wind; (let a) fart / ～ 뀐 놈이 성낸다 get angry at others for *one's* own mistakes; evil-doers' audacity / ～가 잦으면 똥싸기 쉽다 《속담》 Repeated small irregularities lead to serious consequences 〔troubles〕. *or* Talk of the devil and he is sure to appear.

**방그레** with a gentle 〔bland〕 smile; with a smile; smilingly; beamingly. ¶ ～ 웃다 smile sweetly; smile a sweet smile; beam 《upon *a person*》 / ～ 웃으며 맞이하다 smile 《*a person*》 a welcome / 그녀는 ～ 웃으며 인사를 했다 She greeted me with a smile.

**방글거리다** smile gently; beam. ⇨ 벙글거리다. ¶ 방글거리는 얼굴 a beaming face.

**방글라데시** 《인도 동쪽의 공화국》 Bangladesh.

**방글방글** with a gentle 〔bland〕 smile; smilingly; beamingly. ⇨ 벙글벙글.

**방금**(方今) right 〔just〕 now; just this minute; this very minute; just 〔but〕 a moment ago. ¶ ～ 말씀 드린 것처럼 as I have just said; as I told you a moment ago / 어머니는 ～ 나가셨습니다 My mother went out just now. / ～ 그를 만났다 I saw him just now. (★ just now는 주로 과거형과 함께, just는 현재완료형과 함께 쓰임). / ～ 이곳을 지나간 그분은 누굽니까 Who is the man that has just passed here?

**방긋** with a (sudden) smile. ¶ ～ 웃다 smile a beautiful smile; beam 《upon *a person*》; smile 《at *a person*》; smile radiantly 《at》 / 그녀는 자기도 모르게 ～ 웃었다 An unconscious smile came to her lips.

**방긋거리다** smile 《at》; beam 《upon》; look happy. ¶ 그녀는 방긋거리며 우리를 보고 있었다 She watched us with a sweet smile on her face.

**방긋방긋** smiling; beaming.

**방긋이** ① 《웃다》 with a (sudden) smile; smilingly; beamingly. ¶ ～ 웃다 smile 《at *a person*》; beam 《upon *a person*》. ⇨ 방그레. ② 《열다》 《set a door》 gently ajar; 《a flower》 half-opened; half=

blown; in blossom. ¶ 미닫이를 ~ 열다 open a sliding door a little / 그녀는 문을 ~ 열고 들여다 보았다 She opened the door gently and peeped in. / 장미꽃이 ~ 피었다 The rose is half-blown 〔half in bloom〕.

**방긋하다** (be) half-opening; slightly open; be blossoming forth. ¶ 문이 ~ The door is ajar. 「ruin.

**방나다** go bankrupt; face (financial)

**방나다**(榜─) ① 《일이》 become known; be decided. ② 《명단 등이》 be made public.

**방년**(芳年) the sweet age 《of a young girl》. ¶ ~ 20세의 처녀 a girl of sweet twenty.

**방놓다**(房─) add 〔renovate〕 a room; 《온돌을》 fix a hypocaust 〔*ondol*〕 floor in the room.

**방뇨**(放尿) urination; micturition; pissing 《속어》. ~하다 urinate; pass urine; make water; piss 《속어》.

**방담**(放談) 《혼자서 하는》 a random talk; 《둘 이상이 하는》 (a) random 〔free〕 conversation; 《격식을 차리지 않는》 an informal talk. ¶ 시사 ~ an at-random commentary on current issues 〔topics〕. ◉ ~회 a gabfest 《미구어》; a bull session 《구어》.

**방대**(厖大) ~하다 (be) bulky; massive; enormous; gigantic; huge; stupendous; colossal; extensive; mammoth. ¶ ~한 계획 a huge-scale 〔stupendous〕 program / ~한 예산 a huge 〔stupendous〕 budget / ~한 자료 massive material; a mass 〔mountain〕 of matrial 〔data〕 / ~한 지출 massive expenditures / ~한 책 a bulky volume; a voluminous book / ~한 정보량 an enormous amount of information.

**방도**(方道·方途) a means; a way; ways and means; a measure; a method. ¶ 돈 버는 ~ how to make money; the art of making money / ~를 생각해 내다 develop 〔devise〕 a method 《to *do*》; figure out a way 《to *do*》 / ~를 세우다 formulate 〔draw up〕 a plan / 어찌할 ~를 모르다 be (quite) at a loss what to do; be at *one's* wit's end / (달리) ~가 없다 There is no other choice. *or* There is no alternative.

**방독**(防毒) keeping away poisonous substances; protecting *oneself* from poison. ~하다 keep away poisonous substances; protect *oneself* from poison. ¶ ~의 antigas; gasproof. ◉ ~마스크〔면〕 an anti-gas mask; a gas mask 〔helmet〕; a nose cap; a respirator 《영》. ~실 an anti-gas room 〔shelter〕; a gas-proof shelter; a gas-tight shelter. 「quadruped).

**방둥이** the rump; the buttock (of a

**방랑**(放浪) wandering; roaming; roving; a Bohemian life. ~하다 wander 〔roam〕 about; rove; tramp; drift; lead a Bohemian life. ¶ ~길에 오르다 set out on a wandering 〔aimless〕 journey / 세상을 ~하다 go gypsying about the world; knock about the world 《구어》 / 그는 몇달 동안이나 유럽을 ~하고 있었다 He has been wandering all over Europe for many months. ◉ ~객〔자〕 a wanderer; a vagabond; a vagrant; a hobo; a Bohemian. ~벽 vagrant habits; the habit of wandering about; 《suffer from》 wanderlust; vagabondism: ~벽이 있다 have (a) wanderlust. ~생활 the life of a vagabond; a wandering 〔vagrant〕 life; a Bohemian 〔Gypsy〕 life: ~생활을 하다 lead a wandering 〔vagabond〕 life. ~시(詩) Bohemian poetry.

**방략**(方略) a policy; a stratagem; a maneuver 〔manoeuvre 《영》〕; move; 《수단》 a means; 《계획》 a plan; a scheme; a design; a program. ¶ ~을 정하다〔꾸미다〕 map up a scheme; frame a plan.

**방론**(放論) a harangue; a rant. ~하다 harangue; rant; speak irresponsibly.

**방류**(放流) discharge. ~하다 《물을》 discharge; 《고기를》 stock 〔plant〕 《a river》 with 《fish》; release fish into 《a river》. ¶ 우리는 강에 잉어를 ~했다 We stocked the river with carp. / 그들은 수문을 열고 물을 ~했다 They opened the flood-gate and discharged 〔let out〕 water.

**방리**(方里) a square *ri*.

**방만**(放漫) ~하다 《야무지지 못하다》 (be) loose; 《칠칠치 못하다》 (be) lax; 《무책임하다》 (be) irresponsible; 《터무니없다》 (be) reckless. ¶ ~한 생활 《lead》 a loose life / ~한 대출 a reckless loan / ~한 경영 lax management / ~한 재정 정책 a free-spending economic policy; an irresponsible financial policy.

**방망이** a club; 《경찰관의》 a billy (club); a truncheon; 《무기로 쓰는》 a cudgel. ¶ 다듬잇~ (a pair of) wooden fulling sticks / 빨랫~ a wooden laundry paddle / 요술 ~ the magic mallet 〔wand〕. ◉ ~질 beating with a paddle 〔club〕 《in washing, smoothing cloth》: ~질하다 beat with a paddle

〔club〕; 《가슴이》《*one's* heart》 beat fast; go pit-a-pat; palpitate.

**방매**(放賣) = 매출. ◉ ~가(家) a house for 〔on〕 sale.

**방면**(方面) ① 《지역》 a quarter; a district; 《방향》 a direction; a way; a side. ¶ 제주 ~ the Cheju districts / 각 ~ all quarters; all sides / 부산 ~에〔으로〕 in the direction of Pusan / 각(各) ~에서 from all 〔every〕 quarters; in all directions / 범인은 부산 ~으로 도주했다 The criminal ran away 「in the direction of Pusan 〔towards Pusan〕. ② 《분야》 a field; a line; a sphere; 《국면》 an aspect; a phase; 《각도》 an angle; a source (원천). ¶ 문학 ~ the literary field / 각 ~에서 《견지·각도》 from every point of view; from all angles; 《뉴스 따위》 from various sources / 의학〔운동〕 ~에서는 in the field of medicine 〔sports〕 / 장사 ~에서 in the way of business / 모든 ~에서 고찰하다 consider 《a question》 from all aspects 〔bearings〕 / 그의 관심은 운동 ~에 있는 것 같다 His interest appears to lie in the direction of sports. / 어떤 ~의 일을 하고 계십니까 What field 〔kind of business〕 are you in? / 그는 여러 ~에 아는 사람이 많다 He is acquainted with people of 「all classes 〔various walks of life〕. / 그는 그 ~에서는 꽤 유명하다 He is quite well-known in the field 〔line〕.

**방면**(放免) 《석방》 release; discharge; liberation; 《무죄 방면》 acquittal. ~하다 release; discharge; liberate; set 《*a person*》 free; acquit 《*a person* of the charge》. ¶ 죄수를 ~하다 set a prisoner free; let go a prisoner / 재판관은 훈계를 주고〔벌금만으로〕 그를 ~했다 The judge let him off 「with a warning 〔merely with a fine〕.
◉ 무죄~ acquittal (and discharge): 그는 무죄~이 되었다 He was set free from the charge. *or* He was finally found not guilty and released.

**방명**(芳名) 《경칭》 《your, his》 esteemed 〔honored〕 name; 《명성》 a good 〔fair〕 name 〔reputation, fame〕. ¶ ~을 천추에 남기다 win immortal fame.
◉ ~록 a guest book; a visitors' register 〔list〕; a list of acquaintances.

**방모**(紡毛) 《빗질한 양털》 carded wool; 《털실을 뽑음》 carding 〔spinning〕 wool.
◉ ~사 woolen yarn.

**방목**(放牧) pasturage; grazing. ~하다 graze 《cattle》; pasture; put 《cattle》 (out) to pasture; put 〔turn out〕 《cattle》 to grass. ◉ ~권 herbage. ~지 pastureland; grazing land.

**방문**(房門) a chamber-〔room-〕door.

**방문**(訪問) a call; a visit; 《기자의》 an interview. ~하다 visit; make a call; call on 《*a person*》; call at 《a house》; pay 〔make〕 a visit 《to》; go to see 《*a person*》; interview (기자가).
¶ 관저로 장관을 ~하다 call on a Minister at his official residence / ~차(次) 나가다 go out for a visit; go on a visit to 《*a person*》 / 호별(戶別) ~을 하다 make house-to-house calls / 인사차 ~하다 pay a courtesy call / (교사가) 가정 ~을 하다 call at *one's* students' home / 후에 그를 ~하겠다 I shall call on him later. / 오늘은 ~할 곳이 많다 I have many 〔a number of〕 calls to make today. / 우리의 수도인 서울은 금년 '한국 방문의 해'를 맞이하여 새로운 면모를 보이려고 애쓰고 있다 Our capital, Seoul, is trying to wear a new look on the occasion of the "Visit Korea Year" this year.
◉ ~객 a caller; a visitor: ~객을 만나다〔사절하다〕 see 〔refuse to see〕 a visitor. ~기사(記事) an interview. ~기자 an interviewer; a reporter. ~외교 diplomacy through personal visitation. ~판매 door-to-door sales.

**방문**(榜文) a placard; a public 〔an official〕 notice; a government notification. ¶ ~을 내붙이다 put up 〔post〕 a notice.

**방문단**(訪問團) a group 〔team〕 of visitors. ¶ 재일 동포 모국 ~ a group of Korean residents in Japan who are visiting their fatherland.

**방물** women's merchandise items; fancy goods. ◉ ~장사 selling women's items from door to door. ~장수 a peddler of women's items.

**방미**(訪美) a visit to the United States. ¶ ~길에〔중에〕 on *one's* way 〔while on a visit〕 to America / ~길에 오르다 leave for America 〔the United States〕.

**방바닥**(房—) the floor of a room. ¶ 맨 ~ a bare floor / ~이 차다 The floor is cold.

**방방곡곡**(坊坊曲曲) all over the country; every nook and corner 〔cranny〕 of the land; everywhere throughout the country. ¶ ~에 throughout the length and breadth of the land; in all parts of the country / ~에서 from every quaters; from every nook and corner (of the land) / ～에 알려지다 be 〔become〕 known far and wide 〔all over the country〕.

**방백**(傍白) an 〔a stage〕 aside. ¶ ～으로 말하다 say in an aside.

**방범**(防犯) prevention of crimes; crime prevention. ～하다 prevent crimes; take preventive measures against crimes. ¶ ～은 범인 체포보다 더 중요하다 Prevention of crime is more important than arresting criminals.
◉ ～대원 a night 〔security〕 guard; the public night 〔security〕 guards. ～대책 anti-crime measures: 전면적인 ～대책을 세우다 work out 〔set up〕 overall anti-crime measures. ～벨 a burglar alarm 〔bell〕. ～비 nightwatch dues. ～주간 Crime Prevention Week. ～카메라 a security camera. ～훈련 a crime prevention drill.

**방법**(方法) a way; a method; a manner; 《방책》 a plan; a system; 《방안》 a device; a scheme; 《수단》 a means; 《과정》 a process; 《절차》 a procedure; 《방침》 a plan; a program; 《조치》 a step; a measure; 《처방》 a recipe; a formula (*pl.* ～s, -lae).

> 용법 **way** 어떤 목적을 달성하기 위한 방법을 나타내는 가장 일반적인 낱말, 아래 열거한 여러 낱말들의 대용으로도 쓰임. **method** 논리적·조직적·과학적으로 조리 정연한 방법을 뜻하는 낱말. **manner** 개인적 또는 특수한 형태의 독특한 방법을 뜻하는 말. **system** 시종 일관되게 하나의 체계를 이루고, 규칙에 따라 계통이 세워진 method를 뜻하는 말. **means** 무언가를 하기 위한 구체적인 수단을 뜻하는 말. **procedure** 어떤 일을 행함에 있어서, 그 진행의 순서를 「방법」이라고 부를 때, 쓰이는 말. **measure**, **step** 무언가 대상이 되는 일이나 사건이 있고, 이것에 대한 조치·수단 등을 나타내는 말.

¶ 새 ～ a new method / 가장 좋은 ～ the best method 〔way〕 / …하는 ～ how to 《make, swim》; a method of *do*ing; a way (in which) to *do*.
방법으로: 여러 가지 ～으로 by various methods 〔means〕; by this means or that / 이러한〔올바른〕 ～으로 in this 〔the right〕 way / 일정한 ～으로 in a certain way; on a fixed plan / 올바른〔틀린〕 ～으로 하다 do 《*a thing*》 in the proper 〔wrong〕 way / 어떤 ～으로 이것을 할 수 있는지 모르다 do not know by what means this can be done.
방법을: ～을 그르치다 take a mistaken step 《in》 / ～을 생각해 내다 develop 〔devise〕 a method 《to *do*》; figure out a way 《to *do*》 / ～을 정하다 fix upon a plan / ～을 찾아내다 find a way 《to *do*》 / ～을 취하다 take measures 〔steps〕 to 《*do*》 / 여러 ～을 연구하다 discuss ways and means 《of》.
¶ 그 밖에 다른 ～이 없다 There is no alternative. *or* There is no other way for it. / 어떤 ～으로 하면 좋을까요 How shall I do it?
◉ ～론 methodology. ～연구 a study of methods; method studies.

**방벽**(防壁) a barrier; a barricade; a protective 〔defensive〕 wall; a bulwark.

**방부**(防腐) preservation from 〔against〕 decay; prevention of 〔against〕 putrefaction; antisepsis; preservation; 《시체의》 embalmment. ～하다 preserve (from decay); prevent putrefaction; embalm. ¶ ～(성)의 antiseptic / 목재의 ～보존 preservation of timber against decay. ◉ ～제 an antiseptic; a preservative: 식품 ～제 a food preservative. ～처리 preservative treatment: ～처리를 하다 give 《*something*》 a preservative treatment; 《시체에》 embalm; preserve.

**방불**(彷彿·髣髴) a close resemblance; looking alike. ～하다 (be) alike; resemble closely; 〔서술적〕 bear a close resemblance 《to》. ¶ ～하게 하다 remind 《*a person*》 of 《*something*》; be suggestive of / 그 기동훈련은 실전을 ～케 했다 The maneuvers were suggestive of the spectators of actual warfare.

**방비**(房―) an indoor broom.

**방비**(防備) defense 〔defence 《영》〕; defensive works; defensive preparations. ～하다 make defensive preparations; fortify 《a town》; defend 《against, from》; guard. ¶ ～가 된〔안 된〕 fortified 〔unfortified, defenseless〕 / ～가 없다 be defenseless; be unguarded / ～에 만전을 기하다 make full defensive preparations / ～를 강화하다 reinforce 〔strengthen〕 the defenses 《of a country》.

**방빙**(防氷) ～하다 deice.

**방사**(房事) sexual intercourse. ～하다 have sexual intercourse. ¶ ～를 삼가다 abstain from sexual intercourse; practice continence. ◉ ～과도 sexual excess 〔intemperance〕.

**방사**(放射) ① 《빛·열의》 emission; radiation (복사); emanation (라듐 등의). ～하다 radiate; emit; emanate. ¶ 열을 사방으로 ～하다 radiate heat on all sides. ② = 발사(發射). ◉ ～각 an angle of radiation. ～계 a radiometer. ～기(器) an ejector. ～물 an emission. ～에너지 radiant energy. ～열 radiant heat. ～화학 radiochemistry.

**방사**(放飼) pasturage; grazing. ～하다 《방목하다》 pasture 〔graze〕 《cattle》; put 《cattle》 to grass; 《개 따위를》 leave 《a dog》 at large; give 《a dog》 free run of 《*one's* house》; keep 《a pig》 loose.

**방사능**(放射能) radioactivity. ¶ ～이 있는 radioactive / ～이 없는 inactive / ～의 영향 radiation effects 《from nuclear tests》 / ～에 오염된 야채 vegetables contaminated by radioactivity / ～을 쐰 사람 an irradiated person / 공기 중의 ～ atmospheric radioactivity / ～의 강도 intensity of radioactivity; radioactive level / 인공〔잔존〕 ～ artificial 〔residual〕 radioactivity / 내(耐) ～ 복(服) a radiationproof suit.
◉ ～검사 radioactivity check. ～경보기 an exposure badge. ～낙진〔재〕 radioactive fallout 〔dust, ashes〕. ～농도 기준 a radioactivity concentration guide. ～방어 시설 a fallout shelter. ～비〔구름〕 radioactive rain 〔cloud〕. ～사고 a radiation accident. ～시험 radioscopy. ～오염 radioactive contamination 〔pollution〕. ～이론 the theory of radioactivity. ～장애 〖의학〗 radiation sickness; a radiation disease. ～차폐벽 a radiation shield. ～측정 radiological monitoring: ～측정기 a radiation detector. ～허용 한도 the maximum permissible exposure to radiation.

**방사림**(防沙林) trees planted to arrest sand-shifting.

**방사상**(放射狀) ¶ ～의 radiate(d); radial / ～으로 radiately; radially; in a radial pattern; like the spokes of a wheel / ～으로 뻗다 radiate in all directions. ◉ ～ 도로 radial roads; roads radiating in all directions.

**방사선**(放射線) radiation; radial 〔radiant〕 rays; radioactive rays (방사능 광선). ¶ ～의 강도 radiation intensity / ～에 민감한 radiosensitive / ～에 노출되다 be exposed to radiation; be irradiated / ～을 쬐다 irradiate; apply radiation to 《the affected part》 / ～치료를 받다 undergo radiological 〔receive radiation〕 treatment.
◉ ～계수관 a radiation counter. ～과(科) the department of radiology. ～기사 a radiologist. ～누출 a radiation leak. ～량 (a) radiological dosage. ～병 radiation disease 〔sickness〕. ～사진 a radiograph: ～사진술 radiography. ～열상(熱傷) a radiation burn. ～요법(療法) radiotherapy; radiation therapy. ～(의)학 radiology. ～장애 a radiation hazard. ～차폐 a radiation shield. ～치료 의사 a radiotherapist. ～화학 radiation chemistry.

**방사성**(放射性) radioactivity. ¶ ～의 radioactive / ～ 탄소에 의한 연대 측정 radiocarbon dating. ◉ ～낙진 radioactive fallout. ～ 동위 원소 a radioactive isotope; a radioisotope. ～물질 a radioactive substance. ～원소 a radioactive element; a radioelement. ～폐기물 radioactive waste; nuclear waste; 《구어》 hot soup.

**방생**(放生) 〖불교〗 the release 〔setting free〕 of captive birds or animals.

**방석**(方席) a (floor) cushion. ¶ ～을 깔다〔에 앉다〕 sit 〔seat *oneself*, be seated〕 on a cushion. ◉ 수(繡)～ an embroidered cushion.

**방설**(防雪) protection from 〔against〕 snow. ◉ ～공사 snow protection work. ～림 (a stand of trees that serves as) a snowbreak; a snow(break) forest. ～벽 a snowwall; a snowbreak wall. ～책(柵) a snow fence.

**방성대곡**(放聲大哭) = 방성통곡.

**방성통곡**(放聲痛哭) weeping loudly and bitterly. ～하다 weep loudly and bitterly; lament; wail; grieve 《over, for》.

**방세**(房貰) a room rent. ¶ ～를 올리다 raise the (room) rent / ～ 3만원을 내다 pay 30,000 won for *one's* room 〔lodging〕 / ～는 얼마입니까 How much do you charge for the room? *or* What is the rent (for the room)? / 이 ～는 비싸다〔싸다〕 The rent of this room is high 〔low〕.

**방세간**(房―) room furniture; furnishings.

**방송**(放送) 《radio, television》 broadcasting; a 《radio, TV》 broadcast (한 회의). ～하다 《방송국이》 broadcast 《by radio, television》; send 〔put〕 《the news》 on the air; aircast 《미》; 《사람이》 speak through the air; speak over 〔through〕 the radio; go 〔come〕 on the air; go on radio 〔television〕. ¶ ～을 끝내다 sign off / (라디오) ～을 듣다 listen to the radio broadcast; listen in 《on the radio》 / ～을 재개하

다 get back on the air / ～중이다〔중이 아니다〕 be on 〔off〕 the air / 강연을 ～하다 broadcast a lecture / 5시에 국무총리가 ～에 나온다 The premier will be on the air at five. / ～중이오니 출입을 삼가주시기 바랍니다 《게시》 No entrance: on air. / 그 프로는 오늘밤 9시에 TV〔라디오〕로 ～된다 The program will be broadcast on television 〔the radio〕 from nine this evening. / 그 아마추어 노래자랑 대회는 전국에 중계 ～된다 The amateur singing contest is to be broadcasted over a nationwide hookup. / 나는 그 사고에 관해 12시 뉴스 ～에서 들었다 I heard about the accident on the twelve o'clock news (cast).

◉ ～극 a radio 〔TV〕 drama; a broadcast play. ～금지 용어 a banned word; a word which is not allowed to be used on the air 〔on the TV or radio〕. ～기사(技師) a radio 〔television〕 engineer. ～기자 a network reporter 〔journalist〕; a (network) reporter on camera; a radio 〔TV〕 reporter 〔newsman〕. ～망 a 《radio, TV》 network; a (TV) circuit. ～방해 jamming. ～법 the Broadcast Act. ～사업 the broadcasting industry. ～순서〔프로〕 a radio 〔TV〕 program: 주요 ～ 순서 radio 〔TV〕 highlights. ～시간 《어떤 프로의》 the (broadcasting) time 《for》; the length 《of a program》; 《방송국의》 broadcasting hours; air time. ～시청자 a (TV) viewer; a televiewer. ～실 a 《radio, TV》 studio; a broadcasting room; 《항공사의》 a public address booth; an announcement room (안내 방송의). ～연설 a radio 〔TV〕 speech 〔address〕. ～위성 a broadcasting satellite. ～윤리위원회 the Broadcasting Ethics Commission. ～음악회 an air 〔a radio, a TV〕 concert. ～자 a broadcaster; a radiocaster; 《TV의》 a telecaster. ～저널리즘 network journalism. ～종료 sign-off. ～주파수 radio frequency. ～중단 《속어》 dead air; a dead spot. ～청취자 a (radio) listener; a radio subscriber. ～토론회 a radio forum; a TV debate. ～통신 대학 the Air and Correspondence College. ～프로 a broadcast program. ～해설 위원 a news commentator. ～협회 the Broadcasting Corporation.

생～ a live broadcast 〔program〕. 시험～ an experimental broadcast. 재～ a rebroadcast. 제1〔2〕～ (a broadcast on) the First 〔Second〕 Program. 한국 ～공사(公社) the Korea Broadcasting System (생략 KBS).

**방송국**(放送局) a broadcasting station; a radio 〔TV〕 station. ◉ 중앙〔지방〕～ a key 〔local〕 station.

**방수**(防水) ① 《큰 물의》 prevention of flood; flood control. ～하다 control 〔prevent〕 flood. ¶ ～설비 flood protection works. ② 《스며드는 물의》 waterproof(ing); watertight. ～하다 make 《cloth》 water-tight; waterproof 《cloth》. ¶ ～의 waterproof; watertight; water-resistant / ～ 시트 a waterproof sheet / 내 코트는 ～가 된다 My coat is waterproof.

◉ ～대책 a flood prevention measure; an anti-flood measure. ～모 a waterproof hat; 《뱃사람의》 a tarp(aulin). ～문 a watertight door. ～시계 a waterproof watch. ～실 a watertight compartment. ～외투 a waterproof coat; a raincoat 《미》; a mackintosh. ～장치 a waterproof device; waterproofing. ～제 waterproof agent. ～처리〔가공〕 waterproofing: ～ 처리가 된 문 a watertight door / 종이봉지를 ～ 처리하다 make a paper bag watertight. ～포(布) waterproof cloth; tarpaulin; oilskin. ～화 (a pair of) watertight shoes; rainshoes.

**방수**(放水) discharge; water-drainage. ～하다 《배수》 discharge 《water》; drain water off; 《살수》 spray water; hose 《a burning building》. ◉ ～관 a drainpipe; offlet. ～로 《배수로》 a drain; a (drainage) canal; a flood control channel (홍수 조절용의); a sluiceway (저수지 등의). ～문 a drainage gate. ～차 a water truck; a water cannon car. ～펌프 a drain pump.

**방술**(方術) ① 《방법과 기술》 method(s) and technique(s); art(s). ② 《마법》 Taoist magic (arts); necromancy.

**방습**(防濕) dampproofing; moisture-proofing. ¶ ～의 dampproof; moistureproof / 이 상자는 ～되어 있다 This box is dampproof. ◉ ～공사 a dampproofing work. ～제 a desiccant; a desiccating agent.

**방시레** ＝방그레.

**방식**(方式) 《형식》 a formula (*pl.* ～s, -lae); a form; 《양식》 a mode; 《방법》 a method; a system (계통적); 《절차》 formalities; a procedure; 《관례》 usage. ¶ 일정한 ～으로 in an established 〔a regular〕 form / ～대로 in proper 〔due〕

form / ~에 따르다〔어긋나다〕 follow 〔run counter to〕 the established form 〔usage〕 / ~을 세우다 introduce a method 《into》; methodize; systematize / 새로운 분류 ~ a new system of classification / 옳은 ~을 취하다 adopt a correct form / 일정한 ~에 따라 그 행사는 거행되었다 The ceremony was held according to a regular form.

**방식**(防蝕) protection against corrosion. ¶ ~의 corrosion-proof; corrosion-resistant / ~처리를 하다 treat with an anticorrosive; do corrosion protection work. ◉ ~제 anticorrosive. ~케이블 a corrosion-proof cable. ~피막 corrosion protective covering.

**방실거리다** smile (sweetly 〔radiantly〕); beam with a smile. ¶ 아기는 어머니에게 방실거렸다 The infant smiled (radiantly) at his 〔her〕 mother.

**방실방실** smilingly; beamingly; with a smile. ¶ ~ 웃는 얼굴 a smiling 〔beaming〕 face.

**방심**(放心) ① 《얼빠짐》 absence of mind; an abstracted state of mind; abstraction; absent-mindedness. ~하다 be absent-minded; let *one's* mind wander. ¶ ~하여 absent-mindedly; abstractedly; with an air of abstraction / ~상태에 있다 be in an abstracted state of mind / 그는 ~한 얼굴로 멍하니 거기 앉아 있었다 He just sat there with a blank look on his face.
② 《부주의》 carelessness; inattention; incautiousness; 《불의》 unpreparedness. ~하다 be careless; be unwatchful; relax *one's* attention; be off *one's* guard. ¶ ~않는 cautious; watchful; alert / ~하지 않다 be on *one's* guard; be alert 〔attentive〕; be on the lookout; be wide-awake; keep sharp watch / ~하게 하다 throw 〔put〕 《*a person*》 off *his* guard / ~을 틈타다 take 《*a person*》 off *his* guard; take advantage of 《*a person's*》 unguarded moment / ~한 틈을 찔리다 be taken off *one's* guard; be caught asleep 〔napping〕; be taken at a disadvantage / ~은 금물 Danger comes when you least expect it. *or* Carelessness is our greatest enemy. *or* Overconfidence can be very dangerous.
③ 《안심》 relief 〔freedom〕 from care or anxiety. ⇨ 안심(安心).

**방심**(傍心) 〖수학〗 an excenter.

**방아** a (grinding) mill; a mortar. ¶ ~를 찧다 beat 〔pound〕 《rice》 in a mortar; mill grain. ◉ ~굴대 the wheel shaft of a mill. ~꾼 a miller. ~두레박 a sweep-well bucket. ~벌레 〖곤충〗 a click beetle; a skipjack; a snapping beetle. ~확 the mortar of a mill. 방앗간 a mill. 방앗공이 a pestle; a pounder: 방앗공이로 찧다 pound 《rice》 with a pestle.

**방아깨비** 〖곤충〗 an Oriental longheaded locust.

**방아쇠** the trigger 《of a gun》. ¶ ~를 당기다 pull 〔press〕 the trigger; trigger 《a rifle》.

**방아타령**(一打令) a miller's song.

**방안**(方案) a plan; a device; a scheme; a program. ¶ ~을 세우다 draw up 〔formulate〕 a plan; lay out 〔frame〕 a scheme.

**방약무인**(傍若無人) overbearance; arrogance; audacity; effrontery; outrage; insolence; defiance. ~하다 (be) overbearing; arrogant; domineering; audacious; outrageous; insolent. ¶ ~하게 굴다 behave outrageously; conduct *oneself* recklessly; have *one's* own way (in defiance of others); act as if *one* owns the place / ~하게도 …하다 have the cheek 〔impudence〕 to 《*do*》.

**방어**(防禦) defense 〔defence 《영》〕; safeguard; protection. ~하다 defend; protect; bulwark; shield; safeguard. ¶ ~의 defensive; protective / ~가 안 된 defenseless; undefended / ~가 잘 된 well-fortified / 공격에 대비한 ~ a defense against an attack / 최종 ~선 the last defense line / ~에 나서다 stand on the defensive / 타이틀을 ~하다 defend the title / ~ 태세를 취하다 be ready to keep off any attack; assume a posture of defense / 목숨을 바쳐 ~하다 defend 〔protect〕 at the sacrifice of *one's* life / 공격은 최상의 ~ A good offense is the best defense. *or* The best way to defend is to attack.
◉ ~갑판 an ironclad 〔a protective〕 deck. ~공사 《군사》 defense 〔defensive〕 works; defenses; fortifications. ~구역 a sector of defense. ~동맹 a defense alliance. ~력 defensive power 〔strength〕. ~망 a torpedo net. ~물 a shield; a protector; a bulwark (방파제 등의). ~병기〔무기〕 defensive equipment; a defensive weapon. ~선〔지역〕 a line 〔section〕 of defense: ~선을 사수하다 hold the line of defense to the last. ~수단 defensive measures. ~율(率) 〖야구〗 《pitcher's》 earned run

average (생략 ERA). ～자세〖검도·권투〗guard; a posture of defense: ～자세를 취하다 guard; be on guard. ～전 a defensive fight; a defensive war. ～진지 a defensive position. ～포화 defensive fire. 공세〔수세〕～ an offensive〔a passive〕defense. 대인～〖스포츠〗man-to-man defense. 밀집～〖스포츠〗tight defense. 지역～〖스포츠〗zone defense.

**방어**(魴魚)〖어류〗a yellowtail.

**방언**(方言)《표준어에 대하여》a (regional) dialect; a dialect word; 《그 지방 특유의 언어》a provincialism. ¶ ～의 dialectical; provincial / 지역〔사회, 계급〕～ a regional〔social, class〕dialect / 호남 ～ the Honam dialect.
◉ ～경계선 the dialect boundary. ～연구 dialect study. ～지도 a dialect atlas〔map〕. ～지리학 dialect geography. ～학 dialectology. ～학자 a dialectologist.

**방역**(防疫) prevention of epidemics〔infectious diseases〕; disinfection; quarantine. ～하다 take preventive measures against (epidemics); prevent an epidemic of. ¶ ～에 힘쓰다 strive hard for the prevention of epidemics / ～ 조치를 취하다 take preventive measures against epidemics / 콜레라가 발생했기 때문에 관계 당국은 즉각 ～ 조치를 취했다 As cholera broke out, the authorities concerned immediately took preventive measures against it.
◉ ～과 《정부 기구》the Communicable〔Infectious〕Disease Control Division. ～관 an epidemic control commissioner; a health official. ～대책 anti-epidemic measure: ～ 대책 위원회 the Infectious Disease Prevention〔Control〕Commission. ～선(線) a (sanitary) cordon.

**방연광**(方鉛鑛)〖광물〗galena.

**방열**(防熱) protection against heat. ¶ ～의 heat-resisting〔-resistant〕.
◉ ～복 heat-proof clothes.

**방열**(放熱)《열》radiant heat; 《작용》radiation (of heat). ～하다 radiate heat. ◉ ～기 a radiator.

**방영**(放映) televising《a movie》. ～하다 televise; telecast. ¶ 그 뉴스 프로는 지금 ～중이다 The news program「is now being telecast〔is on the air〕.
◉ ～권 the televising right.

**방울** ①《종》a (small) bell. ¶ ～ 소리 the tinkle of a bell / ～을 달다 tie〔attach〕a bell; bell《a cat》/ ～을 울리다 jingle〔tinkle, ring〕a bell / ～이 울린다 A bell tinkles〔jingles〕. ②《물방울》a drop. ¶ 눈물 ～ a teardrop / 빗방울 raindrops / 이슬 ～ a dewdrop / 잉크 한 ～ a drop〔blob〕of ink / ～이 떨어지다 drip; trickle; fall in drops / 그 때 그녀는 눈물 한 ～도 흘리지 않았다 She did not shed a single teardrop at that time. ◉ ～눈 big, round eyes; bulbous eyes.

**방울방울** drop by drop; in drops; dribbly. ¶ ～ 떨어지다 drip〔drop〕《from》; fall in drops.

**방울뱀**〖동물〗a rattlesnake.

**방울새**〖조류〗a greenfinch.

**방울지다** form a drop. ¶ 방울져 떨어지다 drip; drop; trickle; dribble; fall in drops.

**방울집게** (a pair of) pincers; a nail-puller.

**방위**(方位)《나침반의》a point of the compass; a compass direction〔bearing〕; a direction; 《진행 방향의》a course; 〖천문·해양〗azimuth. ¶ 나침반으로〔태양을 보고〕～를 정하다 find〔get〕*one's* position〔bearings〕「with a compass〔from the sun〕.
◉ ～각〖천문·측량〗an azimuth angle; 《편각》a declination. ～계기 orientation instruments. ～권(圈) an azimuth circle. ～기선(基線) the lubber's line. ～기점 the lubber's mark〔point〕. ～나침반 an azimuth compass〔stabilizer〕. ～의(儀)〖항해〗a pelorus. ～차(差) an azimuthal error. ～측정기《비행기의》an azimuth finder. ～판 a plotting board; a director; an offset angle solver. ～표 a traverse table. 기본～ the cardinal points. 진(眞)～〖항공〗the true heading〔bearing〕.

**방위**(防衛) defense〔defence《영》〕; safeguard; protection. ～하다 defend《against》; protect; safeguard; shield. ¶ 자기 ～를 위해 in self-defense / ～의 제일선 the first line of defense《against》/ ～를 강화하다 build up〔strengthen〕defenses / ～를 분담하다 share the defense load《with the U.S.》/ ～선을 펴다 stretch a defensive cordon《against》/ ～ 자세를 취하다 take a posture of defense / 이 나라를 적의 침략으로부터 ～하는 데 가장 좋은 방법은 무엇일까 What is the best way to defend this country against enemy invasion?
◉ ～계획 a defense plan〔program〕. ～공약《its》defense commitment: ～공약에 따르다 live up to its defense

commitment 《to》. ～군 a defense corps; defence forces. ～기구 a defense mechanism. ～대 a defense corps 〔force〕. ～동맹 a defensive alliance. ～력 defense capacity 〔capabilities〕; defensive strength: 국경의 ～력을 증강하다 strengthen *one's* defenses on the border. ～비 (national) defense expenses 〔costs〕. ～산업 the defense 〔munitions, war〕 industry: ～산업을 육성하다 develop the defense industry. ～성금 a defense fund donated 《by》; a donated defense fund. ～세 the defense tax. ～소집 the defense call-up; the defensive mobilization. ～수단 measures to defend 《*oneself*》: ～수단을 강구하다 adopt some measures to defend *oneself* against 《pollution》. ～시설 defense facilities. ～예산 defense budget. ～조약 a defense treaty. ～지출 defense spending. ～진지 a defensive position. ～체제 a defense setup 〔system〕. ～포장(褒章) a Defense Medal. ～해역 the defense waters. ～협정 a (mutual) defense pact; a defense agreement. 민간～ civilian defense. 지상～ ground defense.

**방음**(防音) soundproofing; sound absorption 〔insulation〕. ～하다 (make it) soundproof; insulate 〔absorb〕 sound. ¶ 나는 ～된 방에서 매일 피아노를 연습한다 I practice the piano in a soundproof room every day. ◉ ～구조 soundproof construction. ～벽 soundproofing walls; sound absorbing walls. ～시설 soundproof facilities. ～실 a soundproof chamber 〔room〕. ～유리 soundproof glass. ～장치 soundproof equipment 〔device〕; a sound insulator; 《소음 장치》 a silencer (총의): ～장치를 하다 make 《a room》 soundproof. ～재(材) sound=proofing 〔deadening, absorbing〕 material. ～타일 acoustic tiles.

**방임**(放任) noninterference; nonintervention; *laissez-faire;* do-as-you-please. ～하다 《일을》 leave 《*a matter*》 to take *its* own course; 《사람을》 leave 《*a person*》 to *himself;* give 《*a person*》 a free hand; give a free rein to; 《간섭하지 않다》 do not interfere 《with》. ¶ 아이들을 ～하는 부모들이 너무 많다 Too many parents「neglect their children 〔let their children do as they like〕. / 우리는 사태를 ～할 수 없다 We cannot leave the matter to take its own course. *or* We cannot leave the matter to itself.

**방임주의**(放任主義) a let-alone 〔noninterference, permissive, *laissez-faire*〕 policy; a hands-off policy; a liberal 〔tolerant〕 attitude. ¶ 자식들을 ～로 키우다 rear children on the "let-alone" principle.

**방자** invoking evil 〔curses〕 upon 《*a person*》; imprecation; cursing; damning. ～하다 curse; execrate; wish ill of 《*a person*》.

**방자**(房子) a servant; a footman; a「valet.

**방자**(放恣) impudence; uppishness; self-indulgence; license; willfulness. ～스럽다〔하다〕 (be) impudent (건방진); uppish (뽐내는); self-indulgent (제멋대로 구는); licentious (방종한). ¶ ～하게 굴다 behave as *one* pleases.

**방잠망**(防潛網) an antisubmarine net.

**방장**(方丈) 『불교』 ① 《주지》 a head priest. ② 《처소》 the residential quarters of a high priest.

**방재**(防材) a (wooden) boom. ¶ 항구에 ～를 부설하다 bar the harbor entrance.

**방재**(防災) disaster prevention; prevention 〔protection〕 against disasters. ～하다 prevent 〔fend off〕 disasters 〔calamities〕. ¶ ～를 위하여 온갖 노력을 다하다 make every effort to prevent disasters. ◉ ～계획 a plan for preventing disaster. ～대책 disaster prevention measures (★ 복수형으로). ～용품 emergency supplies. ～훈련 a disaster 〔an emergency〕 drill.

**방적**(紡績) (cotton-)spinning. ◉ ～견사 spun silk. ～공 a spinner; a cotton-mill hand. ～공장 a cotton 〔spinning〕 mill; a spinnery. ～기(계) a spinning machine 〔jenny〕; [총칭] spinning machinery. ～사(絲) cotton yarn. ～업 the spinning industry: ～업자 a cotton spinner. ～인견 rayon yarn; spun rayon. ～회사 a spinning company.

**방전**(放電) 『물리』 (a) discharge of electricity; (an) electric discharge. ～하다 discharge electricity. ¶ 공중〔불꽃, 진공〕～ atmospheric 〔spark, vacuum〕 discharge / ～시키다 discharge 《a Leyden jar》. ◉ ～거리 striking distance. ～관〔구(球), 등〕 a discharge tube 〔ball, lamp〕. ～율〔수〕 discharge rate 〔number〕. ～자(子) a discharger. ～전류〔전압〕 discharge current 〔voltage〕.

**방점**(傍點) a (side) dot 〔mark〕. ¶ ～을

찍다 mark with a side dot / 강조하는 글자에 ～을 찍다 put dots over 〔alongside〕 the letters to be emphasized.

**방접원**(傍接圓) 〖수학〗 an escribed circle; an excircle.

**방정** flightiness; light-headness; levity; frivolity; giddiness; a rash act. ¶ ～떨다 act frivolously 〔rashly〕; behave in a giddy way; go on in a giddy rein / ～떨지 마라 Be serious. / 네가 방정을 떨어 일을 망쳤다 Your flippant attitude spoiled our work.
◉ ～꾼〔꾸러기〕 a light-headed person; a flighty person; a giddy one.

**방정**(方正) 《언행의》 uprightness; irreproachableness. ～하다 (be) irreproachable; upright; good; excellent; correct. ¶ 품행 ～한 사람 a man of excellent character; a man of good 〔irreproachable〕 conduct / ～히 《behave, conduct *oneself*》 uprightly; irreproachably; squarely.

**방정맞다** ① 《경망스럽다》 (be) flighty; rash; light-headed; frivolous; giddy; unreliable. ¶ 방정맞은 여자 a flighty woman; a giddy girl; a silly woman. ② 《불길하다》 (be) ominous; inauspicious; invite the wrath of God. ¶ 집을 나서면서 방정맞은 생각이 들었다 As I left home, I had an ominous feeling 〔a feeling that something bad was going to happen〕.

**방정식**(方程式) 〖수학〗 an equation. ¶ 1 〔2, 3〕차 ～ a simple 〔quadratic, cubic〕 equation; an equation of the first 〔second, third〕 degree / 고차～ an equation of higher degree / 대수 〔화학〕～ an algebraic(al) 〔a chemical〕 equation / 미분～ a differential equation / 연립～ simultaneous equations / 2항～ a binomial equation / ～을 만들다 set up an equation; equate one term with 〔to〕 another / ～을 풀다 solve 〔work out〕 an equation.

**방제**(防除) 《해충 등의》 prevention of the breeding and extermination 《of flies》; control 《of insect pests》. ～하다 prevent; control.

**방조**(幇助) aid; help; backing; assistance; 《범죄의》 aiding and abetting. ～하다 aid; assist; help; back up; pander; 《범죄를》 abet 《*a person*》 in a crime; aid and abet. ◉ ～자 a supporter; 《범죄의》 an abettor. ～죄 〖법〗 aiding and abetting: 자살 ～죄 aiding and abetting suicide.

**방조문**(防潮門) a tide gate.

**방조제**(防潮堤) a tide embankment; a seawall; a sea dike.

**방종**(放縱) self-indulgence; license; dissoluteness; dissolution; looseness; debauchery. ～하다 (be) licentious; unbridled; dissolute; unrestrained; loose; [서술적] be 〔act〕 self-indulgent. ¶ ～에 흐르다 be given (up) to self-indulgence 〔dissolution〕 / ～한 생활을 하다 lead 〔live〕 a dissolute 〔loose〕 life; 《예술가의》 lead a Bohemian life / 자유를 ～으로 착각하다 take freedom for license.

**방주**(方舟) an ark. ¶ 노아의 ～ Noah's ark.

**방주**(旁註) marginal 〔side〕 notes; marginalia. ¶ ～를 달다 make marginal notes 《to the text》; margin.

**방죽**(防—) a bank; an embankment; a dike 〔dyke〕; a levee; a causeway (둑길). ¶ ～을 쌓다 construct 〔build (up), throw up〕 a bank 《for》; embank 《a river》; dike 《a pond》 / ～이 터지다 a bank gives way 〔breaks〕 / 강물이 넘쳐 ～이 무너졌다 The river overflowed and its bank was washed away.

**방증**(傍證) 《보강 증거》 supporting evidence; corroboration; circumstantial evidence (상황 증거). ¶ ～으로서 as supporting evidence 《of》; in corroboration 《of》 / ～을 수집하다 collect supporting 〔circumstantial〕 evidence / 변호사는 이 사진을 우리에게 유리한 ～으로 사용했다 The attorney used this picture as supporting evidence for us. / 경찰은 살인 사건의 용의자를 체포하고 ～수집에 나섰다 Arresting a suspect in the murder case, police began collecting circumstantial evidence.

**방지**(防止) prevention; check; preclusion. ～하다 prevent; check; hold 〔keep〕 《*a matter*》 in check; preserve 《*a thing* from decay》; nip in the bud (미연에). ¶ 범죄 ～ crime prevention / 소음 ～ prevention of street noises / 화재 ～ fire prevention / 청소년 범죄 ～에 노력하다 make an effort to prevent juvenile crime / 사고를 ～하다 prevent an accident / 병의 만연을 ～하다 check 〔arrest〕 the spread of a disease / 효과적으로 ～하다 prevent 〔check〕 effectively / 전쟁 ～에 노력하다 try to prevent the war. ◉ ～책(策) a preventive measure: 인플레 ～책 an anti-inflation policy / 어떤 ～책을 강구하다 take some preventive measures.

**방직**(紡織) spinning and weaving. ~하다 spin and weave.
◉ ~(공)업 textile industry [manufacturing]: ~업자 a textile manufacturer. ~기 spinning and weaving machinery; spindles and looms.

**방진**(方陣) 《군대의》 a square formation; a phalanx (고대 그리스의); 《수학의》 a magic square. ¶ ~을 펴다 form a phalanx / ~을 풀다 break a square.

**방진**(防塵) protection against dust. ¶ ~의 dustproof; dust-tight. ◉ ~막(膜) a dust layer. ~안경 (a pair of) dust goggles [dustproof glasses]. ~장치 a dustproof device [system].

**방책**(方策) a plan (방안); a scheme (책략); 《방침》 a policy; 《수단》 a means; a measure. ¶ 최선의 ~ the best policy / ~이 다하다 be at the end of *one's* tether; be at *one's* wit's [wits'] end / ~을 세우다 form [lay down] a scheme / ~을 짜내다 think [work] out a plan / 범죄 방지를 위한 ~을 긴급히 강구하다 take urgent measures to prevent crime.

**방책**(防柵) a palisade; a barricade; a barrier; a stockade. ¶ ~을 두르다 barricade; palisade; set [put] up a palisade.

**방첩**(防諜) anti-espionage; counterespionage; counterintelligence 《미》; prevention of 《political, military》 espionage. ◉ ~대 Counter-Intelligence Corps (생략 C.I.C.).

**방청**(防錆) rust preventing. ¶ ~의 rustproof; anticorrosive. ◉ ~도료 anticorrosive [rust-resisting] paint. ~유 rust preventing oil. ~제 an anticorrosive; a rust preventive.

**방청**(傍聽) hearing; listening 《to》; attendance. ~하다 hear; listen to; 《참석하여》 attend 《a trial》; audit; sit in on. ¶ ~이 금지된 회의 a meeting closed to the public / 개회 중인 국회를 ~하다 visit the National Assembly in session / ~을 금하다 exclude the public from a meeting; 《법원에서》 clear the court; try a case with closed doors / ~을 허가하다 try a case with open doors / 그 사건의 공판은 일반의 ~이 허용되었다 The public were admitted to the court when the case was tried.
◉ ~권 an admission ticket; 《의회의》 an order. ~료 the admission fee. ~석 seats for visitors [the public]; public galleries; 《의회·법정 따위의》 an observers' [a visitors'] gallery. ~인 a hearer; an auditor; [총칭] an audience: 《재판장이》 ~인 전원의 퇴정을 명하다 order the public to be excluded from the court; order the court to be cleared.

**방초**(芳草) green grass; fragrant flowers.

**방추**(方錐) ① 《송곳》 a square drill. ② ⇨ 방추형.

**방추**(紡錘) a spindle. ¶ ~형(의) spindle-shape(d); spindly.

**방추형**(方錐形) a square pyramid. ¶ ~의 pyramidal.

**방축**(放逐) expulsion; banishment; ostracism. ⇨ 축출, 추방.

**방축**(防築) ⇨ 방죽.

**방축**(防縮) ¶ ~의 shrink-proof. ◉ ~가공 non-shrink treatment; shrink-resistant finish: ~ 가공한 preshrunk 《fabrics》; 《상표명》 Sanforized.

**방출**(放出) ① 《물자의》 release 《of goods》. ~하다 release. ¶ 정부 보유 미의 ~ the release of government-stocked rice / 수입 양곡의 ~ 허가 the permission for releases of imported food-stuff. ② 《배출》 discharge; effluence (폐수의); 《열·빛 등의》 emission; radiation. ~하다 discharge 《water》; give off 《heat》; radiate 《energy》; emit 《gas》. ◉ ~물자 release goods [commodities].

**방충**(防蟲) ¶ ~의 moth-proof.
◉ ~망 an insect net; a mosquito net (모기장). ~제 an insecticide (살충제); an insect repellent (곤충 등을 막는); a mothball (좀약).

**방취**(防臭) deodorization. ~하다 deodorize. ◉ ~제 a deodorizer; a deodorant. ~판(瓣) a stink [stench] trap; a gas trap; 《하수구의》 a drain trap.

**방치**(放置) leaving [letting] alone; 《등한시》 negligence. ~하다 let 《*a thing, a person*》 alone; leave 《*a matter*》 as it is [stands]; leave 《*a matter*》 to chance; leave 《*a thing*》 to take *its* own course; neglect. ¶ ~한 차 a car left by its owner; a illegally parked car / 병을 ~해 두다 leave the disease untreated / 일을 ~해 두다 leave *one's* work undone / 채마밭을 ~하다 leave the vegetable garden uncared for / 이 문제는 ~할 수 없다 This question cannot be left alone [unattended, as it is]. / 상황은 ~할 수 없을 정도로 심각하다 The situation is too serious to be ignored.

**방침**(方針) 《방향》 *one's* course 《of action》; a line; 《계획》 a plan; 《정책》

a (line of ) policy; 《주의》 a principle; 《목적》 an aim; an object (in view). ¶ 일정한 ～《follow》 a definite「policy 〔object in view〕/ 국가〔교육, 시정〕～ a national 〔an educational, an administrative〕 policy / …을 ～으로 하다〔삼다〕 make a point of 《*doing*》; make it a principle 〔rule〕 《to *do*》/ 무시험이 이 학교의 ～이다 It is the policy of this school not to give the students any examination.

방침에: 당의 ～에 따르다 toe 〔follow, hew to〕 the party line / 선임자의 ～에 따르다 act on the same lines as *one's* predecessor; tread in the steps of *one's* predecessor / 일정한 ～에 따라 나아가다 pursue 〔follow〕 a definite policy.

방침을: ～을 그르치다 take a wrong course 〔policy〕/ ～을 바꾸다 change 〔shift〕 *one's* course 〔policy〕/ ～을 세우다 frame a plan; map out *one's* course; formulate *one's* policy; decide on *one's* policy / 사업의 기본 ～을 정하다 lay the first line of the work / 장래 ～을 세우다 shape *one's* course for the future / 정부는 외교 ～을 변경할 모양이다 The government is likely to revise its foreign policy.

**방콕** 《타이의 수도》 Bangkok.

**방탄**(防彈) bulletproofing; bomb-proofing; protection against bullets. ～하다 shield from bullets. ¶ ～의 bulletproof; bombproof; shotproof.
◉ ～내각(內閣) a bulletproof cabinet. ～복〔조끼〕 a bulletproof jacket 〔vest〕. ～실〔헬멧〕 a bombproof room 〔helmet〕. ～유리 bulletproof glass. ～창(窓) a bullet-resistant window.

**방탕**(放蕩) dissipation; prodigality; debauchery; vicious courses. ～하다 (be) dissipated; dissolute; prodigal; 《젊었을 때》 sow *one's* wild oats. ¶ ～하게 dissipatedly; dissolutely; prodigally / ～한 자식 a prodigal son 〔cat〕/ ～에 빠지다 abandon *oneself* to dissipation; give *oneself* up to dissipation 〔dissolute habits, wild ways〕; indulge *oneself* in debauchery / ～하여 몸을 망치다 be ruined by dissipation / ～한 생활을 하다 live a fast life; lead a dissipated life / ～한 생활을 그만두다 give up *one's* fast living. ◉ ～생활 a fast 〔dissipated〕 life; fast living. ～아〔자〕 a fast liver; a libertine; a prodigal; a debauchee; a rake.

**방파제**(防波堤) a breakwater; a seawall; a bulwark. ¶ ～를 쌓다 build a breakwater / 그토록 어려운 상황에서 아버지는 그에게 ～가 되어 주었다 His father was a bulwark to him in such difficult situations.

**방패**(防牌) a (warrior's) shield; a buckler (작고 둥근). ¶ ～ 모양의 shield=shaped / 법을 ～로 삼아 sheltering behind the law / …을 ～삼다 use 《a tree》 as a shield 《against bullets》; hide 〔screen〕 *oneself* behind 《*a thing*》/ ～막이하다 defend 〔shield〕 from; ward off. ◉ 인간～ human shields 《against air strikes》.

**방편**(方便) ① 《편법》 an expedient; a shift; a means (수단); an instrument (도구). ¶ 목적을 위한 ～ a means to an end / 일시적 ～ a temporary expedient; a makeshift; a stopgap (measure) / ～을 쓰다, ～으로 하다 use 《*a thing, a person*》 as an instrument; make a cat's-paw of / 거짓말도 한 ～일 수 있다 Circumstances may justify a lie.
② 〖불교〗 expediencies for promulgating Buddhism.

**방풍**(防風) protection against wind.
◉ ～림 《plant》 a windbreak (forest); a shelterbelt. ～유리 a windshield (자동차 따위의).

**방학**(放學) school holidays; a vacation (from classes). ～하다 go 〔be〕 on vacation; close 〔break up〕 the school 《for a vacation》; have holidays. ¶ 여름〔겨울〕 ～ the summer 〔winter〕 vacation / 언제부터 ～이냐 When are you to break up 《for the spring》? / 우리 학교는 내일부터 여름 ～에 들어간다 Our school begins its summer vacation tomorrow.

**방한**(防寒) protection against the cold. ～하다 keep the cold away; ward off 〔protect against〕 the cold. ¶ ～ 준비를 하다「make provisions for 〔take precautions against〕 the cold / ～용으로는 확실히 모피가 제일이다 For keeping out the cold, fur is certainly the best.
◉ ～구 an outfit for cold weather. ～모 a winter cap. ～복 winter clothes; clothes for cold weather. ～설비 facilities 〔provisions〕 against the cold. ～외투 an overcoat for cold weather. ～화 arctic boots 〔shoes〕; arctics 《미》.

**방한**(訪韓) a visit to Korea. ～하다 visit 〔come to, go to〕 Korea. ¶ ～중인 Y씨 Mr. Y who is on a visit to 〔in〕 Korea.

**방해**(妨害) (a) disturbance; (an)

obstruction (장애); (an) interruptions (가로막음); interference (간섭); check (저지); jamming (전파의). ～하다 disturb 《*a person's* sleep》; interrupt; interfere with; obstruct 〔hinder〕 《*a person* from *doing*, *a person* in *his* work》; hamper; prevent; clog; jam. ¶ 공부를 ～하다 disturb 《*a person*》 in *his* study / 교통을 ～하다 obstruct traffic; bar the way / 안면〔치안〕을 ～하다 disturb *one's* sleep 〔public peace〕 / 영업을 ～하다 interrupt the conduct of business / 의사(議事) 진행을 ～하다 obstruct proceedings; filibuster 《미》 / 방송전파를 ～하다 jam broadcasts (다른 전파로); interfere with radio 〔TV〕 reception (엔진 등이) / ～가 되다 get 〔stand, be〕 in the way; be a hindrance to; be a drag on / 성공〔출세〕에 ～가 되다 be an obstacle to *one's* success 〔advancement〕; stand in *one's* way to success 〔advancement〕 / 공무 집행을 ～하다 interfere with 《a public official》 in carrying out 〔the performance, the exercise〕 of *his* duty / 나의 일을 ～하지 마라 Get out of my way. / 그는 우리들의 계획을 ～했다 He obstructed 〔blocked〕 our plan. ◉ ～공작 sabotage. ～방송 (radio) jamming. ～행위 (an) interference; (an) obstruction.

**방해물**(妨害物) an obstacle; a hindrance; an impediment; a check; a drag. ¶ ～을 제거하다 remove 〔get rid of〕 an obstacle; do away with a nuisance / ～이 되다 become a drag 《on *a person*》.

**방해석**(方解石) 『광물』 calcite; calcspar.

**방향**(方向) ① 《방위》 a direction; bearings; 《침로》 a course; a line. ¶ 조류의 ～ the drift of a current / …의 ～으로〔에〕 in the direction of…; toward… / 같은 ～으로 in the same direction / 반대 ～에〔으로〕 in a contrary 〔an opposite〕 direction / ～을 취하다〔유지하다〕 take 〔hold〕 *one's* course / ～을 바꾸다 change direction; turn to a different direction; put 〔bring〕 《a ship》 about; change 〔shift〕 *one's* course; turn / ～이 바뀌다 turn; shift; veer (round) / ～을 잃다 lose 〔be out of〕 *one's* bearings; cannot find *one's* way / ～을 잘못 잡다 go in the wrong direction; 《배가》 take the wrong course / 바람이 어느 ～으로 불고 있습니까 Which way 〔In which direction〕 is the wind blowing? / 우리들은 동네와는 반대 ～으로 나아갔다 We made our way in the opposite direction to the village.

② 《방침·진로》 *one's* course 〔aim, object〕. ¶ 인생의 ～ the course of *one's* life / ～을 잘못 잡다 choose the wrong career; make an error in choosing *one's* career / ～을 바꾸다 change *one's* object 〔course〕 / 장래 ～을 정하다 decide on 〔map out〕 *one's* future course / 그녀의 말이 내 인생의 방향을 결정했다고 말할 수 있다 I can say that her words determined the course of my life.

◉ ～감각 a sense of direction: ～ 감각의 상실 loss of orientation / ～ 감각이 예민하다〔둔하다〕 have a good 〔poor〕 sense of direction. ～전환 a change 〔shift〕 of direction (방위의); 《방침·진로의》 a change of principle 〔policy, object〕; a turnabout; a switch 《in a policy》: ～ 전환하다 change 〔shift〕 *one's* course. ～지시기 《자동차의》 a traffic indicator; a turn signal; blinkers 《미》; winkers 《영》. ～타 《비행기의》 a (vertical) rudder. ～탐지기 (a) radar (set); a direction finder: 자동 ～ 탐지기 an automatic direction finder (생략 A.D.F.).

**방향**(芳香) (an) aroma; (a) fragrance (꽃 등의); (a) perfume (향수의); a sweet smell. ¶ ～이 있는 aromatic; fragrant; sweet-smelling / ～을 발산하다 give out fragrance; smell sweet; spread 〔send forth〕 fragrance; diffuse an aroma.

◉ ～유 a fragrant 〔an essential〕 oil (향수의 원료). ～제 an aromatic. ～족 화합물 a compound of the aromatic class; an aromatic compound.

**방혈**(放血) bloodletting. ～하다 bleed.

**방형**(方形) a square. ¶ ～의 square (= shaped).

**방호**(防護) protection; guard; custody. ～하다 protect; guard; have custody of. ◉ ～벽 a protective wall. ～자 a protector; a custodian.

**방화**(防火) fire prevention; prevention against fires; fireproofing. ～하다 prevent fire; take anti-fire measures. ¶ ～의 fireproof / ～재로 보호된 fire-retarded / ～에 힘쓰다 try to prevent the spread of a fire / ～ 대책을 강구하다 take fire prevention measures.

◉ ～건축물 a fireproof building 〔construction〕. ～구조 《건물의》 fireproof construction: 시청은 ～구조로 되어 있

다 The city hall is fireproof. ~기구 fire-fighting equipments. ~대(帶) a fire belt; a firebreak 《미》. ~도료(塗料) a fireproof [resistant] paint. ~림 a belt of trees planted as a firebreak. ~문 a fire door: ~문, 열지 마시오 《게시》 Fire door—Keep door closed. ~벽 (a) fire wall. ~사(砂) sand reserved for fire fighting. ~선 a firebreak; a fire-arresting line. ~설비 fire prevention equipment. ~셔터 a fireproof shutter. ~시설 fire prevention facilities; anti-fire facilities: ~시설을 갖추지 않은 건물 a building equipped with no anti-fire facilities. ~용수 water supply for fire-fighting use; water for extinguishing fires. ~장치 fire-prevention device: ~ 장치를 하다 make anti-fire provisions. ~전(栓) a fireplug; a hydrant. ~훈련[연습] a fire drill.

**방화**(邦貨) 《화폐》 Korean money [currency]; 《화물》 Korean goods. ¶ ~로 환산하다 convert 《dollar》 into Korean currency.

**방화**(邦畫) a Korean film [movie].

**방화**(放火) 《죄》 incendiarism; arson; 《화재》 an incendiary fire; a fire of incendiary origin. ~하다 set fire to 《a house》; set 《a house》 on fire; raise a fire; commit arson [incendiarism]. ¶ 그는 그 건물에 ~했다 He set fire to the building. / 그 화재는 ~에 의한 것이었다 The fire was incendiary. / 그는 ~ 혐의로 조사를 받았다 He was examined on suspicion of arson. ◉ ~광 incendiary mania; pyromania; 《사람》 an incendiary maniac; a pyromaniac. ~범(犯) 《죄》 arson; incendiarism; 《범인》 an incendiary; an arsonist; a firebug 《구어》. ~용의자 an arson-suspect. ~죄 arson; incendiarism.

**방황**(彷徨) wandering; roaming. ~하다 wander about; roam (about); rove; knock about. ⇨ 헤매다. ¶ ~하는 wandering; roaming; straying / ~하는 사람 a wanderer; a vagabond / 이곳 저곳을 ~하다 wander from place to place / 들녘을 ~하다 wander over the field.

**밭** a (dry) field; a farm; a patch (소규모의); a (kitchen) garden (남새밭); an orchard (과수원); a plantation (대규모의). ¶ 감자밭 a potato plot [field] / 딸기밭 a strawberry field [patch] / 배추밭 a cabbage patch / 옥수수밭 a corn field / 꽃밭 a flower garden / 사과밭 an apple orchard / 대밭 a bamboo grove [thicket] / 커피밭 a coffee plantation / 솔밭 a pine grove / 포도밭 a vineyard / 풀밭 a grass field; a lawn / 채소밭 《가정용》 a vegetable [kitchen] garden; 《시판용》 a truck farm 《미》; a market garden 《영》 / 밭을 갈다 cultivate [plow, till] the soil / 밭에 나가다 go (out) into the fields / 밭에 나가 일하다 work out in the fields / 밭에 오이씨를 뿌리다 sow cucumber seeds in the field / 밭농사를 짓다 crop a field 《with wheat》.

**밭갈이** plowing [cultivation] (of a field); tillage. ~하다 plow; till; cultivate; work 《the soil》.

**밭걷이** harvest. ~하다 harvest. ¶ ~에 바쁘다 be busy with the harvest.

**밭고랑, 밭골** a furrow. ¶ ~을 짓다 make furrows; furrow.

**밭곡식**(―穀食) the crops of a field; dry field crop; a harvest. ¶ ~이 잘[안] 되다 have a good [poor] dry-field crop.

**밭귀** a corner of a field.

**밭날갈이** a field so large it takes several days to get it plowed.

**밭농사**(―農事) 《일》 dry-field farming; upland agriculture; 《작물》 dry field crop. ~하다 do dry-field farming.

**밭다**[1] ① 《시간·공간적으로》 (be) very [too] close [near]; [서술적] be pressed for time. ¶ 시간이 ~ time is pressing; be pushed for time / 책장과 책상 사이가 밭으니 좀 사이를 떼어라 The bookcase and the desk are too close together, leave a space between them. ② 《인색하다》 (be) too thrifty; illiberal; stingy; niggardly; close(fisted). ¶ 사람이 ~ be a stingy fellow; be tight; be a tightward.
③ 《기침이》 (be) dry; hacking; habitual; consumptive. ¶ 밭은 기침을 하다 have a dry [hacking] cough.

**밭다**[2] 《졸아붙다》 boil away to nothing.

**밭다**[3] 《체에》 filter; strain; drain. ¶ 술을 ~ strain rice wine / 커피 찌끼를 밭아내다 strain coffee to remove the grounds.

**밭도랑, 밭돌** a ditch in a dry field. ¶ ~을 내다 make ditches in a dry field.

**밭두둑** a ridge (marking the boundaries between fields). 「of a field.

**밭둑** an embankment around the end

**밭떼기** the speculative vegetables

bought in lump sums at fields.

**밭매기** weeding a dry field. ～하다 weed (in) a dry field.

**밭머리** the both ends of a field at right angles to the ridges and ditches.

**밭벼** dry-field rice; upland 〔hill〕 rice.

**밭보리** barley (grown in a dry field).

**밭이다** be 〔get〕 filtered 〔strained〕 《through》.

**밭이랑** a ridge; plowed rows in a field.

**밭일** farming; field 〔farm〕 work. ～하다 do farm work; work in the fields.

**밭장다리** ¶ ～로 걷다 toe out; walk with *one's* toes turned out.

**밭치다** ⇨밭다[3].

**배**[1] ① 《복부》 the belly; the stomach (위); the bowels (장); 《소아어》 *one's* tummy; 〚해부〛 the abdomen. ¶ 배의 abdominal; ventral; 〚의학〛 alvine / 배에 힘을 주다 bear down; apply a strain to the stomach; 《온 힘을》 put *one's* whole strength in the abdomen / (배가 고파) 뱃속에서 꾸루룩 소리가 나다 make *one's* empty stomach churn.

배가: 배가 나온 potbellied; bigbellied / 배가 고프다 be 〔feel〕 hungry / 배가 거북하다 feel heavy in the stomach; have gas on the stomach (가스가 차서) / 배가 나오다 develop a potbelly; get a fat tummy / 배가 나와 있다 have a big paunch; be paunchy; be pot-bellied; be thick in the middle (중년이 되어) / 배가 부르다 (1) 《많이 먹어서》 be full of stomach; (2) ＝배가 나오다, 배가 나와 있다 / 배가 탈나다 have 〔get〕 stomach trouble / 배가 아프다 have a stomachache; have a pain in the stomach; have the gripes (갑자기).

배를: 배를 곯리다 work up an appetite / 배를 불리다〔채우다〕 satisfy *one's* appetite; appease *one's* hunger; stuff out the belly; [비유적] enrich *oneself;* feather *one's* nest (제 배만) / 배를 앓다 have stomach trouble / 배를 주리다 be 〔go, feel〕 hungry; be famished.

¶ 배를 움켜잡고 웃었다 I held my sides 〔I shook〕 with laughter. / 배가 고파서는 일을 할 수 없다 One cannot work on an empty stomach. / 우리들은 배(가)부르게 식사했다 We had a hearty meal. / 「나 요즘 배가 나왔어」—「운동을 좀 해야겠군」 "I've gotten fat around the waist recently."—"You need some exercise."

② 《시샘》 jealousy; envy. ¶ 배가 아프다, 배를 앓다 be green with envy / 배아파하다 be jealous 〔envious〕 《of another's success》; feel intense jealousy 《toward》 / 왜, 배가 아프냐 Why, are you jealous?

③ 《태내》 *one's* source of birth; *one's* mother's womb. ¶ 배가 다르다 be born of a different mother; be half-blooded / 배가 부르다 《임신해서》 be pregnant 〔expecting〕; be large with a child / 그 형제〔자매〕는 배가 다르다 They are half brothers 〔sisters〕.

④ 《마음》 (a) heart; (a) mind; (an) intention (의도); courage (담력). ⇨ 뱃속. ¶ 배가 맞다 ⇨ 배맞다.

⑤ 《중배》 the belly; the bilge 〔bulge〕. ¶ 통의 불룩한 배 the belly of a cask.

⑥ 《새끼 낳는 회수》 a litter. ¶ 한 배에 at one birth / 한 배에 낳은 열 마리의 새끼 돼지 ten little pigs at a litter.

**배**[2] 《타는》 a ship; a boat; a vessel (대형의); 《기선》 a steamer; a steamship (생략 S.S.); a liner (정기선); a barge (거룻배); [총칭] shipping; (water) craft. ¶ 배로 《go》 by ship 〔boat〕; 《travel》 by sea / 배안에(서) in a ship; on board (a ship); aboard / 배 안을 샅샅이 from stem to stern / 미국 가는 배 a ship bound for America / 오징어잡이 배 a ship to angle for cuttle-fish / 둘이 젓는 배 a two-oared boat / 배가 떠나다 a ship sets sail; sail; leave (a) port / 배가 항구에 닿다 a ship arrives in (a) port / 배로 미국에 가다 take ship to America; go to America 「by ship 〔on a ship〕 / 배를 젓다 row (a boat) / 배를 타다, 배에 오르다 get 〔go〕 on board a ship 〔boat〕; board 〔take〕 a ship; take ship / 배에서 내리다 leave 〔get off〕 a ship; land 《at》; disembark / 많은 관광객이 배에서 내렸다 A lot of sightseers disembarked. / 물품은 배로 한국에 보내겠다 The goods will be shipped to Korea. / 배는 언제 (항구에) 도착합니까 When will the ship arrive in port? / 사공이 많으면 배가 산으로 올라간다 《속담》 Too many cooks spoil the broth.

**배**[3] 《과일》 a pear; a pear tree (나무). ¶ 배 먹고 이 닦기 "killing two birds with one stone". 「＝씨눈.

**배**(胚) 〚동물·식물〛 an embryo; a germ.

**배**(倍) ① 《갑절》 two times; twice; double; twofold. ¶ 배의 double; twice; two times 《미》; twofold / 그 배 되는 수〔양〕 twice as many 〔much〕 as that; twice the number 〔quantity〕 / 1배 반 one and half times / 배가 되다 double / 값을 배나 받다 charge double prices / 값의 배를 치르다 pay double 〔twice〕 the price; repay double the original amount / 크기〔길이〕가 배다 be twice as large 〔long〕 as; be twice the size 〔length〕 of / 이건 이전 값의 배다 This costs double what it did before. / 집세는 3년 전의 배가 올랐다 The house rent is twice as high as three years ago. / 아기는 1년만에 체중이 배로 늘었다 The baby doubled its weight in a year. / 그의 재산은 나의 배나 된다 His fortune doubles mine.

② 《곱》 times (as much); multiples of; ...times; -fold (★ 모든 기수(基數)에 ...times, -fold를 붙일 수 있음. 77배 seventy-seven times; seventy-sevenfold). ¶ 2배 twice; two times (as much); double / 3배 three times (as much); treble; thrice; threefold / 4〔5〕배 four 〔five〕 times; fourfold 〔fivefold〕; quadruple 〔quintuple〕 / 6배 sextuple / 7배 septuple / 8배 octuple / 9배 nonuple / 10배 decuple / 백 배 centuple / (배율이) 1,500배의 현미경 a microscope of 1,500 magnifications / 3배로 하다〔가 되다〕 treble; 〔be trebled〕 / 수를 〔양을〕 10배하다 increase the number 〔quantity〕 by ten times / 3의 5배는 15이다 Five times three is fifteen. / 1,000은 100의 몇 배냐 How many times a hundred is a thousand? *or* How many times does a hundred go into a thousand? / 3을 몇 배하면 24가 되느냐 What times 3 is 24? / 그것은 길이가 폭의 1.5배이다 It is one-and-a-half times as long as it is wide. / 나는 받은 친절을 몇 배로 갚을 것이다 I will repay many times over the kindness I have received.

**배가**(倍加) doubling (두 배로); redoubling (증대). ~하다 double (itself); increase double 〔twofold〕; be doubled; make double. ¶ 노력을 ~하다 redouble *one's* exertions / 수입을 ~하다 double the income / 전력을 ~하다 make 《*one's* team》 far more 〔doubly〕 competitive.

**배갈** 《고량주》 Chinese kaoliang spirit 〔liquor〕.

**배겨나다** bear up; put up 《with》; stand (up to); suffer patiently 《through》. ¶ 높은 열에 ~ stand 〔bear up against〕 high temperature / 온갖 고생 속에서 ~ put up with all sorts of hardship / 심한 육체 노동에 배겨날 수 없다 be not strong enough to stand hard labor.

**배겨내다** endure; bear up; hold (up); keep. ⇨ 배기다[2].

**배격**(排擊) rejection; denouncement; denunciation. ~하다 reject; denounce; drive out; show strong disapproval of; exclude. ¶ 테러리즘을 ~하다 reject 〔denounce〕 terrorism / 외국 제품은 우리의 정책에 의해 ~당할 것이다 Foreign products will be driven out according to our new policy.

**배경**(背景) ① 《배후》 a background; a backdrop. ¶ 고대 한국을 ~으로 한 영화 a movie with ancient Korea as its setting / 산을 ~으로 해서 사진을 찍다 photograph 《*a thing, a person*》 with a hill for a background / 저녁 하늘을 ~으로 탑이 뚜렷이 보인다 The tower is seen sharply against the evening sky.

② 《무대의》 scenery; a setting; a scene. ¶ ~을 바꾸다 shift the scenes / ~을 그리다 paint scenes (무대의).

③ 《후원》 backing; support; pull 《미구어》; the context. ¶ 정치적 ~ political backing 〔affiliations, connections, support, pull〕 / 사회적 ~ social background / 유력한 ~ strong backing; a strong backer (사람) / ~이 없다 have no "pull" behind (*one*) / 경제적 ~이 없다 have no economic backing 〔support〕 / ~이 되다 back up; support; give support to; be at 《*a person's*》 back.

◉ ~막 a backdrop. ~음악 background (music). ~화 scene painting; a set scene: ~ 화가 a scene painter.

**배고프다** (be) hungry; sharp-set; feel 〔get〕 hungry. ¶ 배가 고파서 pressed by hunger / 배고파하다 complain of hunger / 배고파서는 일할 수 없다 cannot work on an empty stomach / 배고파 죽을 지경이다 be dying with hunger; I'm simply starving. / 배고픈 놈더러 요기시키란다 《속담》 beg (favor) from those worse off than *oneself* / 어린이들을 배고프게 해서는 안 된다 Children must not go hungry.

**배곯다** have an empty stomach. ¶ 그는 배곯고 지낸다 He always goes hungry.

**배공**(胚孔) 〖동·식물〗 a foramen; the alimentary cavity of an embryo.

**배관**(配管) pipe laying; [총칭] piping; 《배관공사》 piping work; plumbing. ~하다 lay 〔arrange〕 pipes. ◉ ~공 a plumber. ~공사 plumbing; piping work. ~도(圖) a piping diagram.

**배광**(背光) = 후광. ◉ ~성 〖생물〗 negative phototropism.

**배교**(背敎) the abandonment of *one's* (religious) faith; apostasy; renegation. ~하다 renegade; become an apostate. ◉ ~자 a renegade; an apostate; a backslider.

**배구**(排球) volleyball. ~하다 play volleyball. ◉ ~경기[코트] a volleyball game [court]. ~공 a volleyball. ~선수 a volleyball player. 대한 ~ 협회 the Korea Amateur Volleyball Association.

**배금**(拜金) the worship of money; mammon(ism). ◉ ~주의 mammonism; money worship: ~주의자 a mammonist; a money worshipper; a mammonite.

**배급**(配給) distribution (분배); supply (공급); rationing (통제품의). ~하다 distribute《*things* among》; supply《*a person*》 with《*things*》; deal out;《통제품을》 ration. ¶ (식량) ~을 타다 draw *one's* rations / ~ 대상에서 제외되다 come off the ration list / 전쟁 중에 설탕이 ~되었다 During the war, sugar was rationed. / 생산물은 도매업자에 의해 소매상에게 ~된다 Products are distributed to retailers by wholesalers. / 식량 ~이 줄었다 [지연되었다] Food ration has been 「cut [delayed]. ◉ ~기관 a distribution organ; a distributing agency [mechanism]. ~량 a ration. ~루트 a distribution channel [route]. ~미[쌀] rationed rice. ~소 a distribution center; a distributing station [point]. ~자 a distributor. ~제도[조직] a distribution [rationing] system [structure]. ~통장 a ration book. ~통제 distribution control. ~표 a ration ticket [coupon]. ~품 rationed goods. ~회사《영화 따위》 a distributing agency.

**배기**(排氣) exhaust; exhaustion; evacuation;《배출 기체》 used steam; exhaust (steam, gas);《통풍》 ventilation. ~하다 exhaust; draw (air) out; ventilate. ◉ ~가스 exhaust gas [fumes]; (engine) exhaust: 자동차의 ~ 가스 car fumes / ~가스의 규제 control of exhaust gas / ~ 가스로 대기를 오염시키다 pollute the air with exhaust fumes. ~갱(坑) an upcast. ~관《엔진의》 an exhaust pipe. ~구 a vent;《환기창》 a ventilator; an exhaust port [outlet]. ~량 (engine) displacement: ~량 1,500cc의 차 a car of 1,500cc displacement. ~장치 a device for exhausting gases; an exhauster. ~판(瓣)[밸브] a cutout;《엔진의》 an exhaust valve. ~펌프 an air pump.

**배기다**[1]《마치다》 be hard on; pinch; squeeze. ¶ 등이 ~《a seat》 be hard on *one's* back.

**배기다**[2]《견디다》 endure; suffer; bear [put up] with; tolerate; hold (up). ¶ 배길 수 있는 bearable; endurable; tolerable / 배길 수 없는 unbearable; intolerable; insufferable; unendurable; beyond *one's* perseverance; past bearing / …하지 않고는 못 ~ cannot help [keep from]《*doing*》; cannot but《*do*》/ 나로서는 배겨낼 수 없다 It is more than I can bear. *or* I can't stand it any more. / 그는 어떤 일을 시켜봐도 오래 배기지 못한다 He cannot stick to any job for long. / 올 여름의 더위는 정말 배길 수 없다 I simply can't bear the heat of this summer. / 그런 식사로는 몸이 배겨내지 못할 걸 You cannot keep yourself in good health on such a diet.

**배꼽** ①《몸의》 the navel;《구어》 the belly button. ¶ 내민[불거진] ~ a protruding navel / 오목한 ~ a deep [sunken] navel / ~이 빠지도록 웃다 laugh like anything; laugh *oneself* into convulsions / 배보다 ~이 크다《속담》 Subsidiary [Incidental] expenses surpass the original outlay. ②《열매의》 the calyx (*pl.* ~es, calyces) of a fruit. ◉ ~노리 parts around the navel. ~쟁이 a person who has a protruding navel. ~참외 a melon with a protruding calyx.

**배끗거리다** ①《어긋나다》 fail to fit smoothly; do not join properly; will not go in as it should. ②《일이》 go amiss [astray, awry, wrong, haywire《구어》]; get out of line. ¶ 우리의 계획은 배끗거렸다 Our plans have gone awry.

**배끗배끗** ①《어긋나다》 not fitting properly; not going in as it should; not joining smoothly. ②《일이》 (going) amiss; astray; awry; wrong; (getting) out of line. ¶ 일이 ~ 잘 안된다 The thing just doesn't turn out right.

**배나무** a pear tree.

**배낭**(胚囊) 『식물』 an embryo sac.

**배낭**(背囊) a knapsack (군용·여행용); a backpack; a packsack (여행용); a rucksack (등산용). ¶ ~을 메다[지다] strap on a knapsack / ~을 벗다 take off a knapsack / ~에 넣다 pack a knapsack with《*things*》; pack《*things*》in a knapsack.

**배내-** ①《타고난》(in)born; from 〔by〕 birth; congenital. ¶ 배냇병신 a congenital deformity 〔idiot (바보)〕. ②《갓난아이의》of a newborn baby; a baby's. ¶ ～옷 baby 〔swaddling〕 clothes / 배냇냄새 the smell of a new=born infant / 배냇니 a milk tooth; the first set of teeth / 배냇머리 downy hair of a baby; uncut baby hair / 배냇짓 the twitching of a newborn baby's face while asleep. ③《배 안의》inside *one's* stomach 〔bowels〕.

**배내똥** ①《갓난아이의》first excrement of a newborn baby. ②《죽을 때의》last excrement of a dying person.

**배내밀다** reject《*a person's* offer》; refuse *one's* help with haughty disdain; turn up *one's* nose at; sneer 《at》.

**배뇨**(排尿)〖의학〗urination. ～하다 urinate; pass 〔discharge〕 *one's* urine; pass 〔make〕 water. ◉ ～과다증 polyuria. ～통(痛) dysuria.

**배니싱크림** vanishing cream.

**배다**[1] ①《촘촘하다》(be) close; compact; 《조밀하다》(be) dense; thick. ¶ 올이 밴 옷감 a fabric of (a) close texture / 나무를 배게 심다 plant trees close together / 씨를 배게 뿌리다 sow seeds thickly / 나무 사이가 너무～ The space between the trees is too close. ②《속이 차다》(be) closely packed; be pack (to the) full; (be) chock-full; be filled up.

**배다**[2] ①《젖다》soak《through, into》; sink《into》; permeate. ¶ 땀이 밴 옷을 입고 with sweating clothes on / 물이 테이블보에 ～ water soaks into the tablecloth / 땀이 셔츠에 ～ *one's* shirt is「soaked through with perspiration 〔wet with sweat〕/ 담배 냄새가 몸에 ～ be「reeking with 〔reek of〕 tobacco / …이 배어 있다 be saturated 〔stained〕 with… / 붕대에 피가 배었다 The bandage was saturated with blood. ②《버릇·일 등이》get used《to》; grow 〔get, become〕 accustomed《to》; be familiar《with》; become habituated 《to》. ¶ 몸에 밴 일 a familiar job; a job *one* has had some experience with / 못된 버릇이 몸에 ～ take to bad habits / 그는 그런 일이 몸에 밴 사람이다 He is an old hand at such work.

**배다**[3]《아이를》conceive; get 〔become〕 pregnant. ¶ 아이를 ～ conceive a child; be pregnant; be (big) with child; be in the family way / 새끼를 ～ be with young; be knocked up《미속어》/ 배지 아니한 아이를 낳으라 한다《속담》make an unreasonable 〔impossible〕 request.

**배다**[4] ⇨ 배우다.

**배다르다** be born of a different mother. ¶ 배다른 형제 half-brothers〔-sisters〕; a brother 〔sister〕 by a different mother (★ 아비 다른 형제도 half=brother〔-sister〕라고 함).

**배다리** a pontoon 〔floating〕 bridge. ¶ (강에) ～를 놓다 build a pontoon bridge (across a river). ◉ 배다릿집 a house with a suspension bridge in front of the gate.

**배달**(配達) delivery; distribution (배포). ～하다 deliver; distribute; carry. ¶ 우유를〔신문을〕 ～하다 deliver 〔carry〕 milk 〔newspaper〕 to《houses》/ 음식을 ～하다 deliver 〔supply〕 dishes to order / 구입한 물건을 ～받다 have *one's* purchase delivered / 그 편지는 잘못～되었다 The letter was delivered to the wrong address. / ～신속《음식점의 게시》Dishes delivered quickly to order. / 언제 ～해 주시겠습니까 When may I expect delivery? / ～ 불능시에 발송인에게 반환하십시오 In case of nondelivery, please return to the sender. / ～ 즉시 대금 지급함 Cash will be paid on delivery. / 시내는 무료 ～이다 Goods are delivered free within the city limits. / 우편은 하루에 두 번 ～된다 The mail 〔post《영》〕 is delivered twice a day.
◉ ～구역 a《postal》delivery zone. ～료 a delivery 〔an express〕 charge. ～불능편지 a dead letter; a blind letter (주소 불명으로). ～원 a deliveryman; a distributor; a carrier; 《우편의》a mailman; 《영》a postman; 《신문의》a newsman; a newsboy; 《우유의》a milkman. ～증명서 a delivery certificate 〔receipt〕. ～증명우편 certified mail. ～차 a delivery wagon 〔van〕. ～착오 misdelivery; miscarriage. ～처《장소》the destination; 《사람》a receiver. ～확인 confirmation of delivery. 시내～ local delivery.

**배달**(倍達) the name of Korea in ancient times. ◉ ～겨레〔민족〕 the Korean race 〔people〕.

**배당**(配當)《배분·할당》(an) apportionment; an allotment; a share (몫); a dividend (주식의); a bonus (이익의); a disbursement《to a policyholder》(보

험의); 《인원 등의》 a quota; distribution. ～하다 apportion 《to》; allot 《to》; divide; share; pay a dividend. ¶ 무～ non dividend (생략 non div.) / 우선～ a preferred dividend / 주식～ a stock dividend / 1할을 ～하다 pay a dividend of 10 percent / 이익 ～에 참여하다 share 〔participate〕 in the profits / 그 주식의 ～은 5퍼센트이다 The stocks pay five percent. *or* A dividend of five percent is paid on the stocks. / 금년은 주식의 ～이 적다 The stocks do not pay much this year.
◉ ～ 공제 a tax credit for dividends received. ～금〔액〕 a dividend; a share: 특별 ～금 a plum; a bonus 《on stocks》; an extra dividend 《on stocks》 / ～액을 발표하다 declare a dividend. ～락 ex dividend (생략 ex div.); dividend off 《미》. ～률 a dividend rate. ～부(附) cum dividend (생략 cum div.); dividend on 《미》. ～소득 income from dividends. ～소득세 dividend income tax. ～안 a proposed dividend arrangement; a plan 〔scheme〕 of distribution. ～주 a dividend yielding stock.

**배당체**(配糖體) 〖화학〗 glycoside; glucoside; saponin.

**배덕**(背德) immorality; a lapse from virtue. ¶ ～의 immoral; corrupt.
◉ ～자 an immoral 〔a depraved〕 person. ～행위 immoral conduct; an immoral act.

**배돌다** keep to *oneself;* avoid mixing with people; keep aloof from others.

**배동바지** the time when the rice plant starts having grains.

**배두렁이** =두렁이.

**배둥근대패** a "round-bellied" plane.

**배드민턴** 《스포츠》 badminton. ¶ ～공 a shuttlecock; a bird. ◉ 대한 ～ 협회 the Korea Badminton Association.

**배때기** the abdomen; the belly. ⇨ 배[1].

**배때벗다** become 〔be〕 insolent; be uppity 《구어》.

**배란**(排卵) 〖생물〗 ovulation. ～하다 ovulate. ¶ ～기 an ovulatory phase.
◉ ～일 the ovulation day. ～촉진제 a fertility 〔an ovulatory〕 drug.

**배래** the offing; the open sea.

**배래(기)** ① 《물고기의》 the belly of fish. ② 《옷소매의》 the saggy under-part of a coat-arm running from the armpit to the sleeve; the strip of cloth along the sleeve-seam.

**배럴** 《용량 단위》 a barrel.

**배려**(配慮) care (보살핌); concern (관심); regard (마음씀); consideration (헤아림); trouble (진력); good offices (알선). ～하다 take the trouble; consider; take ... into consideration; see (to it) 《that ...》 ¶ 세심한 ～ careful concern; thoughtful consideration; scrupulous care / …의 ～로 through the good offices of... / ～해 주셔서 감사합니다 I am obliged to you for your 「trouble 〔good offices〕. *or* Thank you very much for your kind consideration. / 그는 남의 감정에 대한 ～가 거의 없다 He has very little regard for the feelings of others. / 그의 ～로 그 물품을 입수할 수 있었다 I managed to obtain the article through his good offices.

**배례**(拜禮) respectful salutation; worship. ～하다 bow down; worship.

**배리**(背理) unreasonableness; irrationality; absurdity. ¶ ～의 unreasonable; irrational; absurd; contrary to reason; unnatural.

**배릿-** ⇨ 비릿-.

**배막**(胚膜) 〖동물〗 a germinal 〔an embryonic〕 membrane.

**배맞다** ① 《남녀가》 make an illicit love 《to》; commit adultery 《with》. ¶ 그들은 배가 맞아 달아났다 They fell in love and ran away. ② 《못된 짓에》 conspire 《with》; get in collusion 《with》; be in cahoots 《with》.

**배메기** 〖농업〗 ⇨ 반타작.

**배면**(背面) the back; the rear. ◉ ～공격 an attack from the rear; a rear attack: 우리는 ～ 공격을 당했다 We were attacked in the rear. ～뛰기 《높이뛰기의》 a backward jump 〔dive〕; the Fosbury flop. ～비행 an inverted flight.

**배명**(拜命) ～하다 《명령을》 (humbly) receive an order; get the word 《미》; 《임명(任命)을》 (humbly) accept 〔receive〕 an appointment; be appointed (to the post of ...).

**배문자**(背文字) the titling 《on the spine of a book》.

**배미** ⇨ 논배미. ¶ 논 두 ～ two strips of paddy; two paddies.

**배밀이** 《아기의》 crawl; creeping. ～하다 crawl 〔creep, move〕 on 《its》 stomach.

**배반**(背反) ① 《저버림》 (a) treachery; (a) betrayal. ～하다 betray; go back on 《*a person*》; double-cross; play 《*a person*》 false 〔foul〕; sell 《*a person*》

down the river《구어》;《변절하다》change sides; go〔act〕against《*one's* principles》; desert *one's*「cause〔principles〕; turn *one's* coat. ¶ 신뢰를 ~하다 betray《another's》trust / 친구를 ~하다 turn against *one's* friend / (여자가) 남자를 ~하다 jilt a man / 아내에게 ~당하다 be betrayed by *one's* wife. ②《반역》disobedience; revolt; rebellion. ~하다 disobey; rebel〔revolt〕against; turn traitor to; turn〔rise〕against〔on, upon〕. ¶ 나라를 ~하다 turn traitor to *one's* country.
◉ ~자 a betrayer; a traitor; a squealer《속어》; a turncoat (변절자); an informer (밀고자); a strike breaker (파업파괴자).

**배반**(胚盤)〖생물〗the germinal disk;「the blastodisc.

**배배** ⇨ 비비.

**배번**(背番) a「player's〔uniform〕number. ⇨ 등번호.

**배변**(排便) evacuation; defecation; passage; a movement. ~하다 open〔empty, move, evacuate〕the bowels; evacuate. ¶ 매일 ~을 합니까 Do you have a (bowel) movement every day? *or* Do your bowels move every day?
◉ ~ 곤란증 dyschezia; dyschesia.

**배복**(拜伏) prostrating *oneself.* ~하다 humbly prostrate *oneself.*

**배본**(配本) distribution of (subscribed) books. ~하다 distribute (subscribed) books. ¶ 그 전집의 제1권이 ~되었다 The first volume of the series was distributed.

**배부**(配付) distribution. ~하다 distribute《among, to》; give「out〔about〕; deal〔pass〕out. ¶ 학생들에게 시험지를 ~하다 hand〔give〕out the examination papers to the students / 학생들은 가두에서 통행인에게 전단을 ~했다 The students distributed handbills to passersby on the street. / 각 위원에게 서류가 ~되었다 Documents〔Papers〕were distributed to each member of the committee.

**배부르다** ①《양이 차다》(be) full; satiated; [서술적] have a full stomach; have the stomach full; have enough of;「be cloyed〔be fed up〕with. ¶ 배부르게 먹다 eat *one's*「fill〔bellyful〕; eat heartily; have a hearty meal. ②《넉넉하다》(be) affluent; well-off; "well-fixed". ¶ 배부른 소리를 하다 talk high and mighty. ③《아이를 배다》conceive; get〔become〕pregnant.

**배부른 흥정** a take-it-or-leave-it「sale〔deal, proposition〕; an indifference to the outcome《of a transaction》. ¶ ~을 하다 make a take-it-or-leave-it deal《with》; do not care whether *one* makes a deal or not; be indifferent to the outcome of a transaction; [비유적] adopt an attitude of indifference to《*a thing*》.

**배분**(配分)《분배》distribution; division;《할당》allotment; allocation; a share (배당). ~하다 distribute《to, among》; divide《among》; share; apportion〔allot〕《to》; weigh out (일정량을). ¶ 그 돈은 그들에게 똑같이 ~되었다 The money was evenly distributed among them. / 이익을 셋〔둘〕이서 ~하다 divide the profit「among the three〔between the two〕.

**배불뚝이** a potbellied person; "an old potbelly"; a person with a potbelly.

**배불리** heartily; to *one's* heart's content. ¶ ~ 먹다 eat〔have, take〕*one's* fill; eat heartily.

**배불리다** fill *one's* stomach;《사복을 채우다》enrich *oneself.* ¶ 남의 것으로 (자기를) ~ stuff〔fill〕*one's* (own) pocket〔purse〕; feather *one's* (own) nest.

**배붙이기** cloth woven from silk and cotton with silk on the outside.

**배비**(配備) ⇨ 배치(配置).

**배사**(背斜)〖지질〗an anticline. ¶ ~의 anticlinal. ◉ ~구조 anticline structures. ~습곡〔축〕an anticlinal fold〔axis〕.

**배상**(拜上)《편지에서》"Yours truly";「"From".

**배상**(賠償) compensation; reparation; (an) indemnity; recompense. ~하다 indemnify; recompense〔compensate〕《for》; make reparation《for》; give compensation《for》; make satisfaction《for》; pay for《damage》.
¶ …의 ~으로 in compensation for…; in reparation of… / ~을 받아 내다 take〔obtain, exact〕reparations〔indemnities〕/ ~을 요구하다 demand「reparation〔compensation〕《for》; claim indemnity《for》; claim《against a company》for compensation; seek redress / 손해를 ~하다 pay for damage (done); indemnify《*a person*》for「damages〔losses〕/ 손해 ~을 받기 위해 소송하다 sue《*a person*》for indemnity / 그를 상대로 손해 ~ 청구 소송을 제기할 작정이다 We will bring an action against him for the damage we have suffered.
◉ ~금 a compensation; an indemnity;《특히, 전쟁의》reparations(★ 보통

복수꾈); 《손해의》 damages(★ 보통 복수꼴): ~금을 요구〔지급〕하다 claim 〔pay〕 reparations. ~문제 《discuss》 reparations problems. ~요구 a claim for compensation. ~의무〔책임〕 a liability for reparation. ~자 an indemnifier; a compensator; an indemnitor. ~주의 (the theory of punishment as) social reparation. ~책임보험 liability insurance. ~청구권 the right to demand compensation. ~협정 a reparations treaty. 금전~ reparations in cash.

**배상꾼** a person who is insolent and sly.

**배상부리다** act conceited and cunning; be insolent and sly.

**배색**(配色) a color scheme; the arrangement of colors; coloring. ~하다 do the colors 〔coloring, color scheme〕; arrange 〔match〕 colors. ¶ ~이 좋다 The colors go together well. / 넥타이와 양복 저고리의 ~이 좋다 The color of your tie matches your coat well. *or* Your tie and coat match well. / 그녀는 뛰어난 ~ 감각으로 디자인한다 She designs with sensible coloring.

**배서**(背書) (an) endorsement. ~하다 endorse 《a check》; back 《a bill》. ¶ ~가 있는〔없는〕 endorsed 〔unendorsed〕 / 어음〔수표〕에 ~하다 endorse (*one's* name on) a bill 〔check〕 / 여기에 ~해 주시면 좋겠습니다 Would you please endorse it on the back?
◉ ~양도 a transfer 《of a bill》 by endorsement. ~인 an endorser: 피~인 an endorsee.

**배석**(陪席) ~하다 have the honor of sitting 〔attending〕 with 《*one's* superior》. ¶ 그는 백악관의 성탄절 만찬회에 ~했다 He had the honor of attending the Christmas dinner at the White House. ◉ ~자 an attendant. ~판사 an associate judge; a puisne judge; an assessor.

**배선**(配線) (electrical) wiring; distributing wires. ~하다 wire 《a house》. ¶ 전기의 ~ electric wiring / 이 기계는 ~이 복잡하다 There's a lot of wiring in this machine. / 이 집은 아직 전기〔전화〕 ~이 되어 있지 않다 We haven't wired this house for electricity 〔telephones〕. ◉ ~공사 wiring work. ~도 a wiring diagram. ~반(盤) a distribution board; 《전자 계산기》 a plugboard. ~손료 a charge for wear and tear on the service wire.

**배설**(排泄) 《내보냄》 excretion; evacuation; discharge. ~하다 excrete; evacuate; discharge; purge. ¶ ~ 촉진의 evacuant / 신장은 신진대사로 인한 노폐물을 ~한다 Kidneys excrete the waste products of metabolism.
◉ ~강(腔) a cloaca (*pl.* -cae); an atrium (*pl.* -ria). ~관 an emunctory; a nephridium (*pl.* -dia). ~기관 an excretive 〔excretory〕 organ. ~로 an excretory passage. ~물 excrements (대변); excretion(s) (대소변·땀 등의); output (대변 이외의). ~선(腺) an excretory gland. ~작용 evacuation; discharging function; the excretory process.

**배설**(排設) arrangement. ~하다 arrange 《vessels of offering on the altar》.

**배소**(焙燒) calcination; torrefaction. ~하다 calcinate; calcine; roast; torrefy. ◉ ~로(爐) a calcinating furnace; a calciner.

**배속**(配屬) assignment; attachment. ~하다 assign 《*a person*》 for a post; attach 《an officer to a regiment》. ~되다 be attached 《to》; get posted. ¶ 보병 연대에 ~된 포병 장교 a gunnery officer attached to an infantry regiment / 그는 영업부에 ~되었다 He was assigned to the sales department.

**배수**(倍數) ① 〖수학〗 a multiple. ¶ 9는 3의 ~이다 Nine is a multiple of three. / 4와 6은 2의 ~이다, 4 and 6 are multiples of 2. ② 《갑절》 a double number. ◉ ~비례 multiple proportion. ~성 〖생물〗 polyploidy. ~염색체 a diploid.

**배수**(排水) ① 《물을 빼냄》 draining; drainage; pumping out (펌프로); bailing (파래박으로); sewerage (하수설비에 의한). ~하다 drain (off); dike (도랑으로); pump out; bail 《out a boat》. ¶ ~가 잘 (안) 되다 (do not) flow 〔drain〕 well; be (not) drained well / 이 도랑은 ~가 잘 된다〔안 된다〕 This ditch drains 〔does not drain〕 well. / 우리는 ~할 도랑을 팠다 We dug ditches to drain the water off. / 이 택지는 ~ 설비가 불완전하다 The sewage arrangements at this housing site are incomplete. ② 《선박의》 displacement. ~하다 displace 《300 tons of water》.
◉ ~공사 drainage work(s). ~관 a drainpipe; a watershoot; a waste pipe; a drain: 부엌의 ~관 a kitchen drain / 목욕탕의 ~관이 막혀 있다 The drainpipe in the bathroom is stopped

up. ～구(口) a drain-outlet. ～기 a drainer. ～량 (amount of) displacement: 그 배는 ～량이 2만 톤이다 The ship「has a displacement of 20,000 tons〔displaces 20,000 tons〕. ～로〔구(溝)〕 an overflow; a drain〔drainage〕 ditch; a drain; a sewer. ～설비 drainage. ～작업 draining (work); pumping out. ～톤수 displacement (tonnage). ～펌프 a drain〔drainage〕 pump.

**배수**(配水) supply〔distribution〕 of water; water supply〔service〕. ～하다 distribute〔supply〕 water《to》. ¶ 이 지역은 시로부터의 ～가 안 된다 This area has no distribution of tap water from the city. / 물 탱크차가 각 가정에 ～했다 The tank truck〔lorry〕 supplied water to each family. ◉ ～관 a water〔conduit〕 pipe; a conduit: ～본관 a water〔service〕 main.

**배수진**(背水陣) ①《싸움》 ¶ ～을 치다〔펴다〕 have *one's* retreat cut off; fight with *one's* back to the wall〔sea〕; burn *one's* boats; burn the bridges behind *one* / ～을 치고 싸우는 길 밖에 없다 We have no alternative but to fight with our backs to the wall. ②《진법》 a position taken up with a river behind the troops.

**배승**(陪乘) riding in the same vehicle with a superior. ～하다 ride in the same vehicle (with a superior).

**배시**(陪侍) ～하다 keep company with (a superior); attend〔wait〕 upon. ¶ 주군 곁에 ～하다 wait upon *one's* lord; serve at court.

**배식**(陪食) ～하다 have the honor of dining with《*one's* superior》.

**배신**(背信) betrayal; infidelity. ～하다 betray《*a person's*》 confidence; break faith with. ¶ ～적인 unfaithful; treacherous / 그에게 ～당한 기분이다 I feel that I have been betrayed by him. / 믿었던 친구의 ～ 때문에 그는 사람들을 아주 불신하게 되었다 His trusted friend's betrayal made him deeply mistrustful of people. ◉ ～자 a betrayer; a turncoat (변절자); a traitor. ～행위 a breach of faith; an abuse of confidence: 그가 어떤 구실을 대더라도, 그것은 명백한 ～ 행위이다 No matter what excuses he makes, it is clearly an act of treachery.

**배심**(背心) a rebellious heart; a traitorous mind; a rebellious〔treacherous〕 intention.

**배심**(陪審)《배석함》 (sitting as) jury. ～하다 hold jury; participate in a trial as a juryman; serve〔sit〕 on a jury. ¶ ～ 구성의 절차 the proceedings of composing a jury / ～의 평결이 나왔다 The jury has reached a verdict. ◉ ～재판 a trial by jury. ～제도 the jury system.

**배심원**(陪審員)《개인》 a juryman; a juror; [총칭] a jury (★ 집합적으로 쓰일 때는 단수취급, 구성원을 가리킬 때는 복수취급을 함). ¶ ～의 판결 a verdict / ～을 선임하다 impanel〔empanel〕 a jury / ～이 되다 sit〔serve〕 on a jury; do jury duty / ～은 피고의 유죄를 인정했다 The jury found the accused guilty. / 그 살인 사건에 관하여 ～의 의견이 갈라졌다 The jury were divided in opinion on the murder case. ◉ ～석 the jury box. 대～ a grand juror. 보결～ a talesman. 소～ a petty juror.

**배씸** the sides of a ship and their rims.

**배아**(胚芽)〖식물〗 an embryo bud; a germ. ◉ ～미 rice with embryo buds; rice with germs.

**배알** ①《창자》 the intestines; the bowels; the guts (물고기의). ¶ 생선의 ～을 뽑다 remove the guts from a fish. ②《부아》 exasperation; anger. ¶ ～이 꼴리다 feel vexed〔annoyed〕《with *a person,* at *a thing*》; feel irritated〔injured〕; be sore《at, about》.

**배알**(拜謁) an audience《with the king》; seeing a superior. ～하다 have an audience with《the king》; see《a queen》; be received in audience《by the king》. ¶ 그는 국왕을 ～할 수 있었다 He was received in audience by the King. *or* The King granted him an audience.

**배앓이** stomach trouble(s); colic (급성의); the gripes《구어》. ¶ ～를 하다 have (a) stomachache〔stomach trouble〕.

**배액**(倍額) double the amount〔charge, fee, price〕《of》; a double sum; twice the cost. ¶ 요금의 ～을 물다 pay double (the fare) / 1등은 2등 운임의 ～이다 The first-class fare is double〔twice〕 the second-class (one). ◉ ～지급조항 〖보험〗 the double indemnity clause.

**배양**(培養) ①《기름》 cultivation; nurture; culture (세균 등의). ～하다 cultivate; culture; nurture; rear; raise; grow. ¶ 세균을 ～하다 culture〔incubate, cultivate] bacteria. ② 《양성》 cultivation. ∼하다 cultivate; foster; develop; educate. ¶ 인재를 ∼하다 foster men to be competent / 심성을 ∼하다 cultivate [develop] *one's* mind. ◉ ∼가 a grower; a cultivator; a culturist. ∼균 cultured bacteria; (bacterial) cultures. ∼기(基) a culture medium; a medium. ∼법 a method of cultivation; a method of culture (세균의). ∼소(所) a nursery; a culture ground; a farm. ∼시험[검사] a culture test. ∼액 a culture fluid [solution]. ∼접시 〖미생물〗 a culture dish [plate]. ∼토 culture soil; compost.

**배역**(背逆) betrayal; turning against [upon]; rebels. ∼하다 betray; turn against [upon]; rebel against.

**배역**(配役) the cast 《of a play》; casting (행위). ¶ ∼ 중의 아역 스타들 juvenile stars in the cast / ∼을 정하다 cast 《the actors》 for a part; cast [assign] the parts 《of a play to the actors》 / ∼을 바꾸다 alter the cast / 이 영화의 ∼은 좋다[나쁘다] 「This picture is [The parts in this picture are] well cast [miscast]. (★ 이 cast는 「역을 맡기다」라는 동사의 과거분사임).

**배열**(排列·配列) arrangement; disposition; disposal; grouping. ∼하다 arrange; dispose; array (군대 등을); put [place, set] in order. ¶ 편리한 ∼로 in handy arrangement / ABC순으로 ∼하다 arrange 《words》 in alphabetical order [alphabetically, in ABC order] / 그것들은 연대순으로 ∼되어 있다 They are arranged in chronological order.

**배엽**(胚葉) 〖동물〗 germ [germinal, embryonic] layers. ¶ 내∼ an endoderm / 외∼ an ectoderm; an exoderm / 중∼ a mesoderm.

**배영**(背泳) the backstroke. ∼하다 swim on *one's* back; do the backstroke; (swim) backstroke. ◉ ∼선수 a backstroke swimmer.

**배영**(排英) ¶ ∼ 감정 anti-British sentiment.

**배외**(排外) ¶ ∼적인 anti-foreign; anti=alien; chauvinistic. ◉ ∼사상 anti=foreign ideas [feeling, sentiment]; chauvinism (맹목적 애국주의); xenophobia (외국 혐오); exclusionism (배타주의). ∼운동 an anti-foreign movement [agitation].

**배우**(俳優) 《연기자》 a player; an actor (남자); an actress (여자). ¶ 인기 ∼ a star; a star actor [actress] / 영화 ∼ a movie [cinema, film, screen] actor [actress] / 영화 ∼ 지망자 an aspirant to a screen career / ∼가 되다 become an actor [actress]; 「go on [take to] the stage; appear before the footlights / ∼를 그만두다 「retire from [come off] the stage / 그녀는 18세에 ∼가 되었다 She became an actress at the age of 18. ◉ ∼학교 a school of acting. 무대[연극]∼ a stage actor [actress]. 주연 ∼ a leading actor [actress]

**배우다** learn; study (★ learn은 「경험·학습에 의해 익힌다」는 뜻이고 study는 「계통적으로 본질·이론 따위를 연구·학습한다」는 뜻); be taught; take lessons 《in, on》; take a course in; be trained in; practice [practise 《영》] (연습); draw a lesson [instruction] 《from》 (교훈을). ¶ 그림을 ∼ study painting / 바이올린을 ∼ take violin lessons / 선생에게 ∼ study under [with] a teacher / 수영[자동차 운전]을 ∼ learn how to 「swim [drive a car] / 요리법[미용술, 양재법]을 ∼ take lessons in 「culinary art [cosmetics, dressmaking] / 음악을 ∼ take music lessons 《from *a person*》; take [have] lessons in music / 장사를 ∼ be trained in business / 피아노를 ∼ take lessons on the piano / 영어를 미국인에게서 ∼ learn English from [study English under] an American / 완전히 ∼ learn to perfection; master / 책으로 ∼ learn from books / 남을 보고 ∼ learn 《*something*》 from another / 배우게 하다 get 《*one's* daughter》 to take lessons in 《English》; get 《*a person*》 trained [drilled] in / 배우기 쉽다[어렵다] be easy [difficult, hard] to learn / 배운 도둑질 같다 be like second nature 《to *a person*, for *a person* to do *something*》 / 그는 한국어를 빨리 배운다 He is quick to pick up Korean. / 그들에게서는 배울 것이 아무 것도 없다 There is nothing to be learned [We have nothing to learn] from them. / 누구에게서 한국어를 배우셨습니까 Who(m) did you study Korean with? *or* Who(m) did you learn Korean from? / 그의 저서를 읽고 배운 점이 많다 I have learned a great deal from his writings.

**배우자**(配偶子) 〖생물〗 a gamete.

**배우자**(配偶者) a mate (아내 또는 남편); *one's* husband (남편); *one's* wife (아내); a life partner; a life's companion; 〖법률〗 a spouse; a consort (국왕·

여왕의). ¶ 적당한 ～를 고르다 choose a suitable match 《for *one*》/ 그는 좋은 ～를 얻었다 He has got a good wife. / 그녀는 그의 성실한 ～였다 She has been a faithful mate to him.

**배움** learning; study. ¶ ～의 길 (the pursuit of) learning. ◉ ～터 a school; *one's* learning site 〔shelter〕; the cradle of *one's* study.

**배움배움** scholarly attainments; scholarship; learning; "book learning". ¶ ～이 없다 be illiterate / ～이 많다 be learned; be erudite.

**배웅** seeing 《*a person*》 off; a send-off. ～하다 see 《*a person*》 off; give 《*a person*》 a (good) send-off; see 《*a person*》 partway on *his* way. ¶ ～ 나가다 go 《to the station》 to see 《*a person*》 off / 손님을 현관까지 ～하다 see 〔show, follow, accompany〕 a visitor to the porch / 그는 아내의 ～을 받으며 김포 공항을 떠났다 He flew off from Kimp'o Airport with his wife seeing him off. / 이 손님을 ～해 드려라 Go a little way with our departing guest.

**배유**(胚乳) ＝배젖(胚—).

**배율**(倍率) 〖광학〗 magnification; magnifying power. ¶ 6 ～의 쌍안경 field glasses of six magnifications; a 6-power binoculars / 높은〔낮은〕 ～의 《a telescope》 of high 〔low〕 (magnifying) power.

**배은망덕**(背恩忘德) ingratitude; ungratefulness. ～하다 forget a favor 〔kindness〕; be ungrateful; lose *one's* gratitude 《to》. ¶ ～한 사람 an ungrateful man; an ingrate / ～한 짓을 하다 act ungratefully.

**배음**(倍音) 〖물리〗 harmonics; 〖음악〗 an overtone; a harmonic (overtone).

**배일**(排日) anti-Japanese; the exclusion of the Japanese. ～하다 exclude 〔oppose〕 the Japanese; be anti-Japanese. ¶ 그 나라에서는 ～ 감정이 강하다 An anti-Japanese feeling runs high in that country. ◉ ～론자 an anti-Japanist. ～사상 An anti-Japanese thought. ～운동〔감정〕 an anti-Japanese movement 〔feeling, sentiment〕.

**배일성**(背日性) ＝해질성(—性).

**배임**(背任) breach of trust 〔faith〕; malpractice (의사 등의); malfeasance (공무원의); misappropriation (횡령). ◉ ～죄 breach of trust 〔faith〕; misfeasance in office; misappropriation: ～죄로 기소되다 be charged with breach of trust 〔malfeasance〕/ 그는 회사에 거액의 손해를 끼친 ～죄로 기소되었다 He was indicted on a charge of breach of trust causing huge losses to his company. ～행위 an act in violation of *one's* duty.

**배자**(褙子) a women's waistcoat.

**배전**(倍前) ¶ ～의 more than ever; all the more; increased; redoubled / ～의 노력을 하다 redouble *one's* exertions; make redoubled efforts / ～의 애고(愛顧)를 바랍니다 We (would like to) solicit your increased 〔further〕 patronage 〔favor〕.

**배전**(配電) supply of electric power; electric 〔power〕 supply; power distribution; distribution of electricity. ～하다 supply electricity; distribute power. ¶ 그들은 낮에 3시간 동안 ～을 중단했다 They 「cut off the electric supply 〔stopped supplying electricity〕 for three hours in the daytime. ◉ ～기 a (power) distributor. ～반(盤) a switchboard; a distributing board; a panelboard. ～선 a 〔an electricity〕 main; a main(s) cable; a service wire. ～소 a power distribution station. ～회사 a power distribution company.

**배점**(配點) distribution of marks; the allotment 〔allocation〕 of marks. ～하다 allot 《15 points》 to 《a question》. ¶ 각 문제에 대한 ～은 몇 점입니까 How many points are allotted to each question?

**배정**(配定) (an) assignment; (an) allotment; (an) allocation; (a) apportionment; a quota. ～하다 assign; allot; allocate; apportion; parcel 〔map〕 out. ¶ 방을 ～하다 assign rooms 《to *persons*》/ 시간을 ～하다 divide 〔map out〕 *one's* time / 일을 ～하다 assign 《*a person*》 for a task / 그는 자기에게 ～된 일을 마치기 위해 최선을 다했다 He did his best to finish the work assigned to him.

**배젖**(胚—) 〖식물〗 an albumen; an endosperm. ¶ ～이 있는 albuminous.

**배제**(排除) exclusion; removal; eliminating; 〖법〗 abatement. ～하다 exclude; remove; eliminate; make 〔do〕 away with; oust. ¶ …을 ～하고 to the exclusion of... / 정실을 ～하다 set aside personal considerations; eliminate favoritism / 회담에서 정치 문제를 ～하다 eliminate politics from the conference / 우리 마을에서 폭력을 ～하자 Let's exclude 〔remove〕 violence from our town. / 우리는 어떤 일이 있든 장애를 ～해야 한다 We must remove 〔get rid of〕 the obstacles no matter what may come.

**배제**(配劑) dispensation; prescription.

**배종**(胚種) 〖동물·식물〗 a germ; a germinal vesicle. ◉ ～세포 a germ(inal) cell.

**배주**(胚珠) an ovule. ＝밑씨.

**배중률**(排中律) 〖논리〗 the law of the excluded middle.

**배증**(倍增) (a) doubling; growing 〔increasing〕 double; a twofold increase. ～하다 double; be doubled; grow 〔increase〕 double; become twice as much 〔many, large〕 as…. ¶ ～시키다 double 《*one's* income》 / 수입이 3년 사이에 ～하였다 My income doubled in three years.

**배지** a badge. ¶ 학교 ～ a school badge / ～를 달다 wear 〔put on, bear〕 a badge.

**배지기** 《씨름》 a belly grab; a belly throw.

**배지느러미** 〖어류〗 the ventral fin.

**배지성**(背地性) ＝ 땅질성(一性).

**배진**(配陣) battle array 〔formation, disposition〕; a lineup (운동 개시 전의). ～하다 dispose 〔deploy〕 troops in battle array.

**배질** ① 《노질》 rowing; boating. ～하다 row; boat. ② 《졸기》 a nod. ～하다 nod.

**배짱** ① 《속마음》 a hidden thought; an ulterior motive; *one's* real intention; an *arrière-pensée* (F.). ¶ 말은 그러나 ～은 다르다 That's what he says (but I know better). / 무슨 ～인지 도무지 모르겠다 I cannot quite see his motive 〔idea〕. ② 《뱃심》 boldness; daring; audacity; pluck; nerve; cheek; grit 《미》; "brass"; (self-)confidence; assurance; being sure of *oneself; sang-froid* (F.); guts 《구어》. ¶ ～이 있다 be bold 〔confident〕; have iron nerves; have a lot of guts / ～이 없다 lack nerve 〔confidence, assurance〕; have no guts / ～이 세다〔두둑하다〕 have much 〔a lot of〕 nerve; have iron nerves; be cheeky 〔brazen-faced〕 / ～을 부리다 brave 《it》 out; have *one's* own way.

**배차**(配車) the allocation of buses 〔freight cars〕. ～하다 allocate 〔send out, dispatch〕 buses 〔freight cars〕; operate 〔run〕 cars. ¶ 새 택시가 각 영업소에 ～되었다 A brand-new taxicab was allocated in each taxi station. ◉ ～계(원) a dispatcher.

**배참** venting *one's* anger (for being scolded) on 《someone else》. ～하다 vent *one's* anger 〔take *one's* pique out〕 on 《another》.

**배척**(排斥) rejection; expulsion; exclusion; boycott. ～하다 keep 〔drive〕 out; reject; exclude; expel; proscribe; boycott; pip 《구어》. ¶ 모두에게 ～당하다 be scorned 〔shunned, left〕 by all / 그러한 잘못된 생각은 ～되어야 한다 Such a mistaken idea must be rejected. / 일본 제품이 ～당했다 Japanese goods were boycotted.
◉ ～운동 a boycott (campaign); an expulsion agitation: 사치품 ～ 운동 an anti-luxury movement / 일본 상품에 대한 ～ 운동 the boycott of 〔against〕 Japanese goods.

**배추** a Chinese 〔white〕 cabbage.
◉ ～김치 cabbage kimchi; pickled cabbage. ～꼬랑이 cabbage root. ～속대 cabbage heart. ～찜 Chinese cabbage boiled with pork, bean sprouts, and seasoning.

**배추흰나비** 〖곤충〗 a small 〔cabbage〕 white; a cabbage butterfly.

**배출**(排出) discharge (안에 있는 것을 밖으로); exhaust (가스·증기를); excretion (배설). ～하다 draw off; discharge; transpire; exhaust; issue; eliminate (생리적으로). ¶ 공기의 ～ deflation of air / 가스〔연기·액체〕를 ～하다 discharge gas 〔smoke, liquid〕 / 노폐물을 체외로 ～하다 eliminate 〔excrete〕 waste matter from the body / 그 오수는 하수도로 ～된다 The filthy water is discharged into the sewers.
◉ ～관 a discharge 〔an exhaust〕 pipe; a drain pipe. ～구 an issue; an outlet: ～구를 찾다 《감정 따위》 find (a) vent 《for *one's* anger》. ～기준 《수질의》 an effluent standard; 《대기의》 an emission standard. ～물 waste matter; industrial waste (공장의). ～밸브 an exhaust valve.

**배출**(輩出) ～하다 come forward in succession; appear one after another; produce a large 〔great〕 number of 《scholars》. ¶ 속속 ～하다 come forth 〔turn out〕 in great numbers / 그 대학에서는 다수의 우수한 학자를 ～했다 That university has produced many great scholars.

**배치** 《도자기·과자 등의 한 가마분》 a batch 《of cookies》; 《한 다발·묶음》 a batch 《of letters》; 〖컴퓨터〗 《일괄 처리할 수 있는 job》 a batch. ◉ ～파일 〖컴

퓨터』 a batch pile. ～프로그램 『컴퓨터』 a batch program. ～프로세싱 『컴퓨터』《일괄처리》 batch processing. ～플랜트 《콘크리트 일괄 조합 공장》 a batch plant.

**배치**(背馳) contrariety; inconsistency (불일치); contradiction (모순). ～하다 be contrary 《to》; run counter 《to》; contradict 《each other》; go 〔be〕 against. ¶ 완전히 사실과 ～되다 be totally opposed to facts / 새 시책은 종래의 방침에 ～되는 것이 아니다 The new measure is not out of line with our customary policy. / 갓 수입된 이런 풍습은 우리의 전통적인 것에 ～된다 These customs and manners just introduced run counter to our traditional ones.

**배치**(配置) arrangement; disposition; stationing; posting; placement. ～하다 arrange; 《부서에》 post; station; put 《missiles》 in position. ¶ 공격〔방어〕～offensive 〔defensive〕 disposition / 인원 ～ disposition of men / 구역간 ～ inter-area placement / ～가 좋다〔나쁘다〕 be well 〔badly〕 arranged / 군대를 ～하다 place 〔station〕 troops 《in the provinces》 / 정원석의 ～가 멋이 있다 The stones in this garden are tastefully placed. / 경찰이 길을 따라 ～되었다 The police were stationed along the route. / 이 방의 가구 ～는 좋다〔나쁘다〕 The arrangement of the furniture is good 〔bad〕 in this room. ◉ ～계획 《도시 계획 등의》 block planning; 『건축』 plot planning. ～도 『기계』 an arrangement plan; 『건축』 a plot 〔block〕 plan.

**배타**(排他) exclusion 《of others》. ¶ ～적(인) exclusive; 《당파적인》 clannish; cliquish / ～적인 태도를 취하다 take an unfriendly attitude 《toward》 / 저 마을 사람들은 ～적이다 The villagers are not friendly to strangers. / 거류하는 많은 외국인이 한국은 너무 ～적인 사회라고 불평한다 Many foreign residents complain that Korea is a very exclusive society. ◉ ～론자 an exclusionist. ～적 경제 수역 ⇨ 수역. ～주의 exclusivism; exclusionism; cliquism: ～주의자 an exclusivist; an exclusionist.

**배탈**(一頉) a stomach disorder; a stomach upset 〔trouble〕. ¶ ～ 나다 have stomach trouble; suffer from indigestion / ～을 일으키다 put the stomach out of order; disorder 〔upset, spoil〕 the stomach.

**배태**(胚胎) ～하다 《임신》 conceive; become pregnant; 《기인·기원》 originate 《in》; have 《its》 origin 《in》; arise 〔spring〕 《from》; result 《from》. ¶ 민주주의 원리의 ～ the germination of democratic principle / 훗날의 재앙들은 이미 거기에 ～해 있었다 It was there that many later ills originated.

**배터** 『야구』 a batter; a batsman; a hitter. ＝타자. ◉ ～박스 a batter's box: ～박스에 서다 be at bat; come up to bat.

**배터리** ① 《전지》 a battery. ¶ 자동차의 ～ a car battery. ② 『야구』 the battery. ¶ ～간의 사인 a battery sign.

**배턴** a baton. ¶ ～을 넘기다 hand over 〔pass〕 the baton 《to the next runner》; 《일 등을》 hand over 《*one's* duties to *a person*》; have 《*a person*》 take over 《a job》 / ～을 이어받다 accept 〔receive〕 the baton 《from》; 《일 등을》 take over 《*a person's* duties》.
◉ ～터치 a baton pass; a handover.

**배퉁기다** turn up *one's* nose 《at》.

**배트** 『야구』 a (baseball) bat. ¶ ～를 휘두르다 swing *one's* bat.

**배팅** 『야구』 batting. ◉ ～오더 the batting order.

**배편**(一便) (a) shipping service; 《우편물》 surface 〔sea〕 mail. ¶ ～으로 by ship 〔steamer, water, sea〕 / ～으로 보내다 send 《*a thing*》 by boat; 《우편》 send 《a letter》 by surface 〔sea〕 mail / ～이 나는 대로 보내다 send 《*things*》 by the first available ship 〔vessel〕 / 다음 ～을 기다리다 wait for the next boat / 그 섬으로 가는 ～이 있습니까 Is there (a) steamer service to the island? / 마침 홍도로 가는 ～이 있어서 그 배에 탔다 I took passage in a steamer which happened to be bound for Hongdo.

**배포**(排布·排鋪) 《배짱》 scale 〔breadth〕 of thinking; 《계획》 a plan 〔scheme〕 (in *one's* mind). ¶ ～가 크다 think on a large scale; have a big idea / ～가 유하다 be hard to ruffle 〔discompose〕; be unconcerned with trifles; be nonchalant 〔impassive〕 / 가슴에 딴 ～가 들어 있다 have some plot in *one's* mind; have an axe to grind.

**배포**(配布) distribution. ～하다 distribute (widely) 《among, to》; deal out. ¶ 통지서가 집집마다 ～되었다 A notice was distributed to each household. / 그들은 길거리에서 통행인에게 전단을 ～했다 They distributed bills to passers=

by on 〔in〕 the street. ◉ ～망(網) a network of distribution.

**배필**(配匹) a spouse; a mate; *one's* husband 〔wife〕. ¶ 천생 ～이다 be a well-matched couple 〔pair〕.

**배합**(配合) ① 《조합》 combination; arrangement; 《조화》 match; harmony. ～하다 combine; arrange; match; harmonize; tone (색을). ¶ 색의 ～ the combination 〔arrangement〕 of colors; a color scheme 〔harmony〕 / ～이 잘 된 well-matched; harmonious / ～이 잘 안 된 ill-matched; inharmonious / ～되다 be matched 〔harmonized〕 / 이 색깔은 ～이 좋다〔나쁘다〕 These colors match well 〔do not match〕. ② 《혼합》 mixture; blending; compounding (약품 등의). ～하다 mix; compound; blend. ¶ ～이 되다 get mixed 〔compounded〕 / 약의 ～을 잘못 하다 make a mistake in compounding the medicine / 이 비료는 무엇을 ～했습니까 What does this fertilizer contain? ◉ ～비료 (a) compound fertilizer. ～사료 assorted 〔mixed〕 feed.

**배행**(陪行) ～하다 accompany 〔follow〕 *one's* superior.

**배혁**(背革) 〖제책〗 quarter binding; a leatherback. ◉ ～본 a quarter-bound 〔leatherbacked〕 book.

**배화교**(拜火敎) 〖종교〗 fire worship; Zoroastrianism; Parsiism. ◉ ～도 a fire worshipper; a Zoroastrian; a Parsi.

**배회**(徘徊) ～하다 《싸다니다》 wander 〔roam, ramble, knock〕 about; 《헤매다》 loiter (about, along); hang around 〔about〕 《구어》; saunter; hover (about); prowl (about) (동정을 살피며). ¶ 여기저기를 ～하다 wander from place to place / 그는 종종 길거리를 ～한다 He often wanders 〔roams, hangs〕 about the streets. / ～ 금지 《게시》 No loitering.

**배후**(背後) the back; the rear. ¶ ～에 behind; at the rear 〔back〕 《of》; back of... / ～에서 조종하는 사람 a wirepuller. ⇨～인물〔조종자〕 / ～에서 조종하다 pull the wires 〔strings〕 (from behind); maneuver behind the scenes / 적의 ～를 찌르다 attack the enemy in the rear 〔from behind〕 / ～에 정계의 유력자가 있다 have a powerful political figure behind *one* / 사건의 ～관계를 조사하다 inquire into the background of the case; inquire into the hidden circumstances that led up to the case; 《흑막을》 investigate who is pulling the wires / 그 정치가의 ～에는 유권자의 강력한 지지가 있다 There is the strong support of the electorate behind 〔backing〕 that stateman. ◉ ～인물〔조종자〕 a wirepuller; a man behind the scenes.

**백**(白) ① 《백색》 white. ¶ 백을 흑이라고 하다 call white black. ② 《흰 바둑돌》 a white (*baduk*) stone. ¶ ～을 쥐다 occupy the superior side of board.

**백**(百) a 〔one〕 hundred (★ hundred나 thousand는 앞에 2 이상의 수사가 오더라도 단수형임. 다만, 부정수를 나타낼 때는 many hundreds 「수백」과 같이 복수형이 됨. 그러나 million은 a hundred millions처럼 복수형이 보통). ¶ 몇 백씩이나 by hundreds / 백 번 a hundred times / 백 번째(의) the hundredth / 100살 먹은 사람 a centenarian / 몇 백 명이나 되는 사람들 hundreds of men / 100단위로 세다 count by the hundred.

**백**[1] ① 《뒤》 back. ② 《후원》 backing; support; 《후원자》 a supporter; a patron; a backer. ¶ 그에게는 유력한 ～이 있다 He has an influential supporter. ③ 《스포츠》 a back player (후위).

**백**[2] a bag.

**백가서**(百家書) the books of various philosophers and scholars.

**백각**(百―) 〖광물〗 《흰 석영》 white quartz.

**백건**(白鍵) a white key; a natural.

**백계**(百計) all 〔every〕 means; all resources. ¶ ～가 다하다 exhaust all resources 〔means〕; be on *one's* 〔the〕 beam-ends; be at *one's* last shift; be at *one's* wit's 〔wits'〕 end; come to the end of *one's* rope / ～를 다 쓰다 try every 〔all〕 means conceivable 〔available〕; try every possible means; leave no stone unturned.
◉ ～무책 helplessness.

**백계러시아인**(白系―人) a (White) Russian *émigré*. 「《영》).

**백곡**(百穀) all kind(s) of grain 〔corn

**백골**(白骨) ① 《뼈》 a white 〔bleached〕 bone; a skeleton. ¶～난망이다 be very grateful / 은혜는 ～난망입니다 Your kindness will never be forgotten. ② 《목기류》 wooden vessels (not yet lacquered).

**백곰**(白―) a white 〔polar〕 bear.

**백과**(百科) all branches of knowledge. ◉ ～사전 an encyclop(a)edia; an encyclop(a)edic dictionary: ～ 사전적 지식 encyclopedic knowledge / ～사전

에서 찾아 보았다 I consulted an encyclopedia. ～전서 a complete encyclopedia; an encyclopedia (set).

**백관**(百官) all the government officials. ¶ 문무～ civil and military officials; all the officials of both services.

**백구**(白鷗) 〖조류〗 a sea gull. ⇨ 갈매기.

**백군**(白軍) ① 〖역사〗 the White Russian Army (at the time of the Russian Revolution). ② 《경기에서》 the white team; the white(s).

**백귀야행**(百鬼夜行) ～하다 evil people are rampant; be a veritable pandemonium; present a most scandalous scene 〔sight〕.

**백그라운드** 〖연극〗 the background.

**백금**(白金) white gold; 〖화학〗 platinum (기호 Pt); platina.

**백기**(白旗) 《흰 기》 a white flag; 《휴전의》 a truce flag; a flag of truce; 《항복의》 a flag of surrender. ¶ ～를 들다 display 〔raise〕 a flag of truce; hang out a white flag; give a signal for surrender.

**백날**(百一) ① ＝백일(百日). ② 《허구한 날》 all the time. ¶ ～ 걱정만 끼치다 be a constant source of anxiety 《to *one's* parents》 / 바다 경치는 ～ 보아도 좋다 I never get tired of looking out over the sea.

**백납**(白一) 〖한의〗 leucoderma; vitiligo. ¶ ～ 먹다 have leucoderma.

**백내장**(白內障) 〖의학〗 cataract. ¶ 노인성 ～ senile cataract / ～에 걸린 눈 an eye affected with cataract.

**백넘버** 《운동복의》 a player's 〔uniform〕 number; a jersey number. (★ back number는 「묵은 호의 잡지, 시대에 뒤진 물건〔사람〕의 뜻). ¶「내가 좋아하는 야구 선수는 스티브 맨스필드야」—「그의 ～는 몇 번이지」 "My favorite baseball player is Steve Mansfield." — "What's his player's 〔jersey〕 number?"

**백네트** 〖야구〗 backstop.

**백년**(百年) 《한 세기》 a 〔one〕 hundred years; a century; 《한평생》 *one's* whole life; 《긴 세월》 quite a number of years. ¶ 국가 ～의 대계 《draw up》 a far-sighted national policy 〔program〕; a long-range plan for the nation / ～하청(河淸)(격이다) It's like waiting for pigs to fly.
◉ ～가약 a marriage bond; a conjugal tie: ～가약을 맺다 tie the nuptial knot; become man and wife for weal and woe; cast in *one's* lot with a partner for life. ～제 a centennial (anniversary) 《미》; a centenary 《영》. ～해로 living together to an old age; growing gray together: ～해로하다 live (happily) together to an old age.

**백단향**(白檀香) 〖식물〗 (Indian) sandalwood.

**백당**(白糖) white 〔refined〕 sugar.

**백대**(百代) one hundred generations; a very long time. 「whites 《속어》.

**백대하**(白帶下) 〖의학〗 leucorrh(o)ea;

**백도**(白桃) a white peach.

**백랍**(白蠟) 〖약〗 insect wax; white 〔refined〕 wax. ◉ ～벌레 a wax(-depositing) insect. ～초 a candle made of white 〔refined〕 wax.

**백랍**(白鑞) 《땜납》 pewter; solder.

**백련**(白蓮) ① 《연꽃》 a white lotus. ② ⇨ 백목련.

**백로**(白露) ① 《이슬》 white dew. ② 《절기》 the 15th of the 24 seasonal divisions (＝around 8 September).

**백로**(白鷺) 〖조류〗 a white heron.

**백리**(白痢) 〖한의〗 dysentery with diarrhea that becomes white with mucus.

**백마**(白馬) a white horse.

**백막**(白膜) 《눈의》 the albuginea. ＝공막(鞏膜). ◉ ～염 albuginitis.

**백만**(百萬) a 〔one〕 million. ¶ ～ 인〔원〕 one million persons 〔won〕 / ～분의 1, one 〔a〕 millionth; one part per million; 1 ppm / 수～의 개미들 millions of ants / ～분의 1 지도 a map on a scale of one to a million /「～인의 천문학」《책이름》 *Astronomy for the Million* / (숫자·액수 등이) ～대에 이르다 reach the seven-figure mark.
◉ ～장자 a millionaire; a multimillionaire. 「horn; a novice.

**백면서생**(白面書生) a stripling; a green-

**백모**(伯母) the wife of *one's* father's elder brother; an aunt.

**백목련**(白木蓮) 〖식물〗 a yulan.

**백묵**(白墨) chalk. ⇨ 분필.

**백문불여일견**(百聞不如一見) 《속담》 Seeing is believing. *or* There is nothing like seeing for oneself. *or* A picture is worth a thousand words.

**백미**(白米) polished 〔cleaned〕 rice. ¶ ～에 뉘 섞이듯 하다 《속담》 be very rare.

**백미**(白眉) the finest (example) 《of》; the best 《of》. ¶ 이것은 한국 소설 중의 ～라고 생각한다 I believe this is one of the best Korean novels.

**백미러** a rearview 〔rear-vision〕 mirror (★ back mirror는 한국식 영어). ¶ ～로 보다 watch through the rearview mirror.

**백반**(白斑) ① 《반점》 a white spot. ② 《태양의》 a facula (*pl.* -lae).
**백반**(白飯) cooked 〔boiled〕 rice.
**백반**(白礬) 〚화학〛 alum.
**백발**(白髮) gray 〔grey 《영》〕 hair (반백의); snowy 〔white, silvery〕 hair (전백의). ¶ ～의 white-〔gray-〕haired / ～이 희끗희끗한 streaked with gray / ～이 많이 섞인 grizzled / ～이 되다 [머리가 주어] turn gray; [사람이 주어] grow gray / 내 머리카락이 조금씩 ～이 되기 시작한다 My hair is beginning to go gray 〔to show white streaks〕. / 그는 완전히 ～이 되었다 His hair is completely white. ◉ ～노인 a white-haired〔-headed〕 old person.
**백발백중**(百發百中) hitting 〔making〕 the bull's-eye one 〔a〕 hundred percent; all hits; infallibility. ～하다 never miss the target 〔mark〕; never fail; (be) infallible. ¶ 총알이 ～하였다 Every shot told. / 그는 ～의 명사수다 He is a dead 〔crack〕 shot. *or* He never misses the mark. / 그 의사의 진단은 ～이다 That doctor never makes a wrong diagnosis.
**백방**(百方) 《방향》 every direction; all sides; 《방법》 various ways. ¶ ～으로 《갖가지 방법으로》 in every way; by all means; 《여러 방향으로》 in all directions 〔quarters〕 / ～으로 힘쓰다 bend 〔make〕 every effort; do everything in *one's* power / ～으로 손을 쓰다 try all 〔every〕 means available; exhaust all possible means; leave no stone unturned / ～으로 위로하다 console 《*a person*》 in every way / ～으로 사람을 찾다 look all around 〔all over〕 for a person.
**백배**(百拜) ～하다 bow a hundred times; bow many times. ¶ ～ 사례를 하다 bow *one's* thanks a hundred times; thank heartily; offer a thousand thanks / ～ 사죄하다 bow a hundred apologies; make a humble apology; humbly beg 《*a person's*》 pardon.
**백배**(百倍) a 〔one〕 hundred times; a 〔one〕 hundredfold. ～하다 increase 《a number》 a hundredfold 〔a hundred times〕; multiply 《a number》 by one hundred; centuple. ¶ ～의 centuple; one 〔a〕 hundredfold / 그 소식을 듣고 용기 ～했다 The news inspired us with fresh courage. *or* We perked up at the news.
**백병전**(白兵戰) hand-to-hand fighting; a hand-to-hand fight; close 〔hand-to-hand〕 combat; fighting with swords and bayonets. ¶ ～을 벌이다 fight hand to hand 《with》.
**백부**(伯父) an uncle; *one's* father's elder brother. 「on.
**백부장**(百夫長) 《고대 로마의》 a centuri-
**백분**(百分) one-hundredth part; per cent. ～하다 divide 《it》 into a hundred parts. ¶ ～의 centesimal; percent / ～의 1, a 〔one〕 hundredth; one percent / 100분의 10, ten hundredths; ten percent. ◉ ～도표 a centesimal scale. ～율〔비〕 a percent(age).
**백분**(白粉) 《화장분》 face powder; 《가루》 white powder; flour.
**백사**(白沙) white sand. ◉ ～기(器) white earthenware 〔porcelain〕. ～장 a white sandy beach; the white sands. ～지 white sandy soil.
**백사**(百事) all kinds of matters 〔things〕. ⇨ 만사. ¶ ～불성하다 fail at everything / ～가 잘 되어 간다 All goes well.
**백삼**(白蔘) white ginseng.
**백색**(白色) ① 《흰색》 white color. ¶ ～의 white(-colored). ② 《보수주의자》 the white 〔right〕 wing. ◉ ～광 white light. ～스모그 〚기상〛 white smog. ～인종 the white race(s); white people; Caucasians. ～테러 〚역사〛 the White Terror.
**백서**(白書) a white paper 《on》; a white book 《on》. ¶ 경제〔외교, 농업〕～ 《publish, issue》 an economic 〔a diplomatic, an agriculture〕 white paper.
**백선**(白癬) 〚의학〛 favus; ringworm; the tinea.
**백설**(白雪) (white) snow. ¶ ～ 같은 snowy; snow-white; white as snow / ～에 덮인 산 a snow-capped mountain. ◉ ～공주 《동화》 the Snow White. ～총이 a snow-white horse with black lips.
**백설기**(白一) steamed rice-cake.
**백설탕**(白雪糖) white 〔refined〕 sugar.
**백성**(百姓) 《국민》 the people; the populace; the nation. ¶ 만〔온〕～ all 〔an entire〕 people; the people of all nations / ～의 소리 the voice of the nation.
**백세**(百世) one hundred generations; all generations; forever.
**백세**(百歲) 《백년》 one hundred years; 《백 살》 a hundred years of age. ¶ ～의 노인 a centenarian.
**백수**(百獸) all kinds of animals. ¶ 사자는 ～의 왕이다 The lion is the king of

beasts.

**백수건달**(白手乾達) an out-and-out libertine; a good-for-nothing; a debauchee.

**백숙**(白熟) fish 〔meat, fowl〕 boiled in plain water. ¶ 영계～ chicken boiled with rice.

**백스윙**《야구·골프 등의》(a) backswing.

**백스트레치**《육상경기·경마의》《미》 the backstretch; 《영》 the back straight.

**백스트로크**《배영》《swim with》 a backstroke.

**백스핀**《당구·골프 등의》 backspin. ¶ 공에 ～을 넣다 put backspin on the ball.

**백신**〖의학〗 vaccine. ¶ 유행성 감기 예방 ～을 접종하다 vaccinate 〔inoculate〕 《a child》 against influenza / 소아마비용 생～ a live polio vaccine. ◉ ～주사 vaccine injection; vaccination.

**백씨**(伯氏) your 〔his〕 esteemed elder brother.

**백악**(白堊) chalk; chalkstone; 《흰 벽》 a white wall. ◉ ～관 《미국의》 the White House. ～기(紀) 〖지질〗 the Cretaceous (period). ～질 《치아의》 cement: ～질의 chalky; cretaceous. ～층(層) a chalk bed 〔layer〕. ～토 malm.

**백안시**(白眼視) ～하다 look coldly on 《*a person*》; look askance at; look with indifference; have 〔take〕 a prejudiced view 《of》; frown 《upon》 (흘겨보다). ¶ 세상을 ～하다 take refuge in cynicism; turn *one's* back on the world; affect a detached irony.

**백야**(白夜) nights under the midnight sun; the midnight sun; 〖기상〗 the white night.

**백약**(百藥) all kinds 〔sorts〕 of medicines; sundry 〔multifarious〕 medicines 〔remedies〕. ¶ ～지장(之長) the best of all medicines / ～이 무효하다 All remedies fail. *or* All medicines prove useless.

**백양**(白羊) a white sheep 〔goat〕. ◉ ～궁(宮) 〖천문〗 Aries; the Ram.

**백양**(白楊) 〖식물〗 a (white) poplar; a white asp 〔aspen〕.

**백업** support; backing. ～하다 back 《*a person*》 up; support. ¶ 젊은이들이 그 캠페인을 ～했다 Young people supported 〔backed〕 the campaign. / 투수는 1루수를 ～했다 The pitcher backed up the first baseman. ◉ ～파일 〖컴퓨터〗 a backup file.

**백연**(白鉛) white lead; ceruse. ◉ ～광 〖광물〗 cerusite.

**백열**(白熱) ① 《높은 온도》 white heat; incandescence; white glow. ¶ ～(화)하다〔되다〕 become white-hot; be incandescent; glow white. ② 《열을 띰》 enthusiasm; the climax (경기 따위의). ¶ ～화하다〔되다〕 grow 〔get〕 excited; become heated (토론 등이). ◉ ～광 incandescent light. ～등 an incandescent electric lamp 〔light〕; a glow lamp. ～전 hot fighting; a close game 〔contest〕: ～전을 벌이다 put on a thrilling 〔blistering〕 game 〔race〕 / 그 시합은 ～전이었다 The game was hotly contested. ～점 《reach》 a white=heat point 〔the climax〕.

**백엽상**(百葉箱) 〖기상〗 an instrument screen 〔shelter〕; a ventilated case for meteorological instruments.

**백옥**(白玉) a white gem.

**백운모**(白雲母) 〖광물〗 white mica; muscovite.

**백운석**(白雲石) 〖광물〗 dolomite.

**백의**(白衣) ① 《옷》 white clothes; a white robe 〔dress〕; a white overall 〔coat, apron〕 (의사 등이 입는). ¶ ～의 in white / ～를 입은 여인 a woman in white. ② 《벼슬 없는 선비》 a scholar without a government position; a commoner. ¶ ～ 종군하다 serve in a war as a commoner. ③ 〖불교〗 《속인》 a layman. ◉ ～민족 the white-clad folk; the Korean people. ～용사 a hero in white; a white-clad wounded veteran 〔soldier〕. ～천사 an angel in white; a nurse.

**백인**(白人) ① 《백인종》 a white man 〔woman〕; a Caucasian; a white. ¶ ～에 의한 지배 white rule 〔domination〕 《in Africa》/ ～으로 통하다 《혼혈 흑인 등이》 pass off as 〔for〕 white. ② 《피부 색소 결핍증》 an albino. ◉ ～여자 a European woman 〔lady〕. ～종 the white race; the whites. ～지상주의자 a white supremacist.

**백인백색**(百人百色) So many men, so many minds.

**백일**(白日) a bright day; broad daylight; the daytime; the light of day. ¶ ～하에 드러나다 be brought to light; be exposed 「to the light of day 〔to the public eye〕 / 청천 ～의 몸이 되다 be cleared of the charge / 사건의 모든 진상이 ～하에 드러났다 All the truth of the affairs have been brought to light. ◉ ～몽 a daydream; daydreaming; a reverie: 그는 ～몽을 꾸고 있다 He indulges in daydreaming. ～장 a literary writing contest; an essay contest: 주부 ～장 an essay contest for housewives.

**백일**(百日) 《아기의》 the hundredth day of a newborn baby; 《백일간》 one hundred days. ◉ ～기도 prayer for a hundred days. ～잔치 the feast 〔celebration〕 of a hundred-day-old baby. ～재(齋) 〖불교〗 a Buddhist memorial service on the one hundredth day after 《*a person's*》 death. ～천하 a hundred-day reign; a very brief reign. ～해(咳) whooping cough; 〖의학〗 pertussis.

**백일초**(百日草) 〖식물〗 a garden zinnia.

**백일홍**(百日紅) 〖식물〗 a crape myrtle; an Indian lilac.

**백자**(白瓷) a white porcelain.

**백작**(伯爵) a count; an earl 《영》. ◉ ～부인 a countess.

**백장** ① 《최하층민》 a member of the lowest class (which once engaged chiefly in execution, grave digging, and wickerwork). ¶ ～이 버들잎을 물고 죽는다 《속담》 A low occupation 〔social status〕 stays with one through life. *or* The leopard can not change its spots. ② 《도살자》 a butcher. ¶ 개～ a dogcatcher; a dog killer.

**백전**(百戰) 《with》 a hundred battles. ¶ 그는 ～의 용사다 He is a hero who won every battle. ◉ ～노장 a veteran (of many battles); an old-timer: 그는 ～노장이다 He is an old veteran.

**백전백승**(百戰百勝) an ever-victorious record; invincibility. ～하다 win every battle (that is fought); be ever-victorious. ¶ ～의 ever-victorious; unbeaten / ～의 군대 an invincible army.

**백절불굴**(百折不屈) ¶ ～의 unbending; unflinching; indomitable; indefatigable / ～의 정신 an indomitable spirit.

**백점**(百點) one 〔a〕 hundred points; 《만점》 a perfect paper; full marks. ¶ 영어에서 ～을 받다 get full marks for English; get a perfect score in English / ～만점에서 90점을 받다 obtain 90 points out of a possible 100 / 100점 만점으로 학생들의 성적을 평가하다 grade the students out of 〔on a scale of〕 a hundred / 너라면 그녀에게 100점 만점에 몇 점을 주겠니 How many points would you give her out of a hundred?

**백정**(白丁) ⇨ 백장.

**백조**(白鳥) 《고니》 a swan; a cob (swan) (수컷); a pen (암컷); a cygnet (새끼). ¶ ～의 노래 a swan song / ～의 호수 《발레》 *Swan Lake*. ◉ ～자리 〖천문〗 the Swan; Cygnus.

**백주**(白晝) broad 〔full〕 daylight; the daytime. ¶ ～에 in broad 〔open〕 daylight / 강도들은 대담하게도 ～에 은행에서 5천만 원을 털었다 The gangsters audaciously robbed the bank of fifty million won in broad daylight.

**백중**(百中) the Buddhist All Souls' Day 《mid July by the lunar calendar》. ◉ ～맞이 the Buddhist mass for the repose of the dead on the 15th of July by the lunar calendar. ～물 rainfall around the time of *paekchung*.

**백중**(伯仲) ① 《만형과 그 다음》 *one's* eldest and second eldest brothers. ② 《우열이 없음》 being equal; being even 《with》; being on a par 《with》. ～하다 (be) equal; even 《with》; be on a par 《with》; be evenly-matched; [동사적] match 《each other》. ¶ ～한 기량이다 be evenly matched in skill / 양당의 세력은 ～하다 The two parties are equally balanced in power. / 양팀의 실력은 ～했다 The two teams were perfectly matched.
◉ ～숙계(叔季) the first, second, third, and fourth of brothers.

**백지**(白紙) ① 《흰 종이》 white paper; 《한지》 Korean paper made from mulberry fiber. ¶ 얼굴이 ～장 같다 look as white as a sheet / ～장도 맞들면 낫다 《속담》 Cooperation makes work easier. *or* Two heads are better than one. ② 《기입하지 않은》 a blank paper; a (blank) sheet of paper. ¶ ～답안을 내다 give 〔hand〕 in a blank (answer) paper. ③ 《백지 상태》 a clean slate. ¶ ～(상태)에서 시작하다 start with a clean slate; start afresh / 지난 일은 모두 잊고 ～상태에서 시작하는 것이 좋다 You had better forget all the past and start with a clean slate.
◉ ～동맹 giving in blank examination papers as a student protest strike. ～위임 《give》 carte blanche 《in *a matter*》. ～위임장 a blank power of attorney; a carte blanche (F.). ～투표 《cast》 a blank vote 〔ballot〕.

**백지도**(白地圖) a blank 〔an outline〕 map.

**백지수표**(白地手票) a blank check.

**백지어음**(白地—) a blank bill.

**백차**(白車) a (police) patrol car; a squad 〔cruise, prowl〕 car; a cruiser.

**백척간두**(百尺竿頭) the last extremity; an eleventh hour. ¶ ~에 서다 be in a dire extremity; be driven 〔reduced〕 to the last extremity; be brought 〔driven〕 to bay.

**백철광**(白鐵鑛) 〖광물〗 white iron pyrites; 「marcasite.

**백청**(白淸) refined honey.

**백출**(百出) ~하다 arise 〔pop up, appear〕 in great numbers. ¶ 의론이 ~하다 all kinds 〔hundreds〕 of arguments pop up / 그 문제로 의론이 ~했다 The matter 「became the subject of heated 〔provoked hot〕 discussion.

**백치**(白痴·白癡) 《상태》 idiocy; 《사람》 an idiot. ¶ 그는 ~인 체했다 He feigned idiocy.

**백탄**(白炭) fine 〔hard〕 charcoal.

**백태**(白苔) 〖한의〗 《혀의》 the fur 〔coat〕 《on the tongue》; 《눈의》 a morbid clouding of the lens of the eye. ¶ ~가 끼다 《*one's* tongue》 be furred 〔coated〕.

**백태**(百態) various phases. ¶ 미인 ~ various poses of glamor girls / 인생 ~ various phases of life / 백인 ~ So many men, so many minds.

**백토**(白土) white clay; *terra alba* (L.).

**백통**(白―) nickel; white brass.
◉ ~돈〔전〕 a nickel (coin).

**백판**(白板) ① 《무일푼》 having nothing; "clean"; "utter". ② 《흰 널판》 a white board. ◉ ~건달 a penniless wretch.

**백팔**(百八) 〖불교〗 one hundred eight.
◉ ~ 번뇌 the hundred-and-eight torments of mankind; the 108 passions (a) man is subject to. ~염주 a Buddhist rosary of 108 beads.

**백팔십도**(百八十度) one hundred and eighty degrees (각도); a full half circle (방향). ¶ ~ 전환하다 perform a hundred-and-eight degree turn; do 〔make〕 a complete turnabout 〔about=face〕; reverse *one's* course 〔opinion〕; make a radical 〔complete〕 change 《in *one's* policy》 / 새 정부는 정책을 ~ 전환했다 The new government did an about-face in its policy.

**백퍼센트**(百―) one hundred percent; 100 percent; 100%. ¶ 효과 ~다 be 100 percent efficacious / 나는 ~ 이길 자신이 있다 I am one hundred percent confident of winning. / 너의 의견에 ~ 찬성이다 I agree with your opinion 100 percent. *or* I'm with you all the way.

**백포도주**(白葡萄酒) white wine; 《라인산의》 Rhine wine; hock; 《스페인산의》 sherry.

**백학**(白鶴) 〖조류〗 a crane.

**백합**(百合) 〖식물〗 《나리》 a lily. ◉ ~꽃 a lily blossom. ~뿌리 a lily bulb.

**백해무익**(百害無益) a hundred harms without a single gain. ~하다 be very harmful; be utterly destructive; do more harm than good; it produces all evil and no good. ¶ 그것은 내게는 ~이다 It is more injurious than beneficial for me. / 담배는 ~하다 Smoking will have innumerable harmful effects without doing any good at all.

**백핸드** 《테니스·탁구의》 a backhand stroke 〔drive〕. ¶ ~로 치다 hit 《the ball》 backhand.

**백혈구**(白血球) a white blood cell; a white corpuscle; a leukocyte. ¶ ~의 leukocytic. ◉ ~감소증 leukopenia. ~수 the number of leukocytes; a 〔*one's*〕 white cell count. ~증가증 leukocytosis. ~형성 leukopoiesis.

**백혈병**(白血病) 〖병리〗 leuk(a)emia, leukosis.

**백형**(伯兄) *one's* eldest 〔oldest 《미》〕 「brother.

**백호**(白濠) White Australia. ◉ ~주의 the "White Australia" principle 〔policy〕.

**백화**(白話) "pai hua"; colloquial 〔spoken, vernacular〕 Chinese.
◉ ~문 written colloquial Chinese. ~문학 literature in colloquial Chinese.

**백화**(百花) all kinds 〔sorts〕 of flowers. ¶ ~난만하다 all kinds of flowers are in full bloom; 《the field》 be ablaze with all sorts of flowers. ◉ ~제방(齊放)운동 the "Hundred Flowers" Campaign.

**백화점**(百貨店) a department store 《미》; the stores 《영》. ¶ 뉴욕 시의 대형 ~들 major department stores in New York City / ~으로 물건 사러 가다 go shopping at a department store (★ to a department store라고는 하지 않음).

**백화현상**(白化現象) 〖식물〗 chlorosis; 〖동물〗 albinism.

**밴** ① 〖컴퓨터〗 《부가가치 통신망》 VAN. [<*v*alue *a*dded *n*etwork] ② 《트럭》 a van; a delivery van (상업용).

**밴댕이** 〖어류〗 a large-eyed herring.

**밴드** ① 《띠·끈》 a band; a strap; 《혁대》 a belt. ② 《악단·악대》 a band; a brass band (취주악의). ◉ ~마스터 a bandmaster. ~맨 a band(s)man. 「effect.

**밴드왜건 효과**(―效果) 〖경제〗 bandwagon

**밴앨런대**(―帶) 〖물리〗 《지구를 둘러 싼 도

넌형 방사능대》 the Van Allen (radiation) belt. 「자 a banjoist.

**밴조** 〖악기〗 a banjo (*pl.* -(e)s). ◉ ～주

**밴텀급**(―級) 《권투에서의》 the bantamweight class. ¶ ～ 선수 a bantamweight. 「el.

**밸러스트** 《바닥짐》 ballast; 《자갈》 grav-

**밸런스** balance. ⇨ 균형. ¶ ～가 잡힌 well-balanced / ～를 유지하다〔잃다〕 keep 〔lose〕 balance. ◉ ～시트 a balance sheet (생략 b.s.).

**밸류** value. ¶ 네임 ～가 있는 작가 a writer with a great reputation 〔of great renown〕.

**밸브** a valve. ¶ 사용 후 ～를 누르시오 Press the valve after use. ◉ ～장치 valve gear. ～콕 a valve cock.

**뱀** a snake; a serpent (구렁이); a viper (독사). ¶ 뱀 같은 snaky; serpentine / 뱀껍질 (a) snakeskin / 뱀의 허물 the slough 〔cast skin〕 of a snake / 뱀 부리는 사람 a snake charmer / 뱀에 물려 죽다 die from a snake bite; die of the bite of a snake / 뱀에 놀란 사람 은 새끼줄만 봐도 놀란다 A burnt child dreads the fire. ◉ 뱀자리 〖천문〗 the Serpent; the Snake.

**뱀딸기** 〖식물〗 an Indian strawberry.

**뱀뱀이** upbringing; training; discipline. ¶ 그 소녀는 ～가 있다〔없다〕 That girl is well-〔ill-〕bred.

**뱀잠자리** 〖곤충〗 a dobsonfly.

**뱀장어**(―長魚) 〖어류〗 an eel. ¶ 민물 ～ a fresh-water eel.

**뱀혀** 〖식물〗 a kind of cinquefoil.

**뱁새** 〖조류〗 a Korean crow-tit. ¶ ～가 황새를 따라가면 다리가 찢어진다 《속담》 Tailor your ambitions to the measure of your abilities. *or* People ruin themselves by trying to ape their betters. / ～가 황새 따라가려고 하지 마라 Stop trying to keep up with the Joneses. (★ the Joneses는 「잘 사는 이웃」을 가리킴.) ◉ ～눈이 a person with tiny downward-slanted eyes.

**뱁티스트** a Baptist. ⇨ 침례.

**뱃가죽** abdominal 「muscles 〔flesh, skin〕. ⇨ 뱃살.

**뱃고동** a boat whistle; a gong. ¶ 출항의 ～소리가 울려 퍼졌다 The departure gong sounded.

**뱃길** a (ship's) course; a waterway; a channel (해협); 《항로》 a sea route; a seaway. ¶ 3일이 걸리는 ～ a three days' passage 〔crossing〕 / ～로 가다 go by water 〔ship〕; take ship 《to》.

**뱃노래** a boat(man's) 〔sailor's〕 song; a sea song; a chant(e)y; a barcarole (곤돌라의). ¶ ～를 부르다 sing a boating song.

**뱃놀이** a boating (excursion); a boat ride 《미》; yachting; a row (보트젓기). ～하다 enjoy boating 〔a boat ride〕. ¶ ～ 가다 go for a boat ride; go for a sail 〔row〕; go rowing 〔boating〕.

**뱃대끈** ① 《여자의》 a drawstring (for a woman's drawers). ② 《마소의》 a (saddle-)girth; a bellyband; a cinch 《주로 미》. ¶ ～을 조르다 tighten the girth.

**뱃머리** the bow(s) (★ 복수형으로 쓰이는 경우가 많음); the prow; the head. ¶ ～ 방향으로 on the bow / ～에서 고물까지 from stem to stern / ～부터 가라앉다 sink by the head / ～를 향하다 head 《for》 / ～를 돌리다 wind 〔veer〕 a ship.

**뱃멀미** (qualms of ) seasickness; nausea. ～하다 get 〔become〕 seasick. ¶ ～를 하지 않는〔하는〕 사람 a good 〔bad, poor〕 sailor.

**뱃밥** oakum; pledget; caulking. ¶ ～을 메우다 caulk 《a boat》; stop up 《seams》 with oakum.

**뱃병**(―病) stomach trouble; intestinal upsets. ¶ ～이 나다 have stomach trouble; have a stomach upset.

**뱃사공**(―沙工) a boatman. ⇨ 사공.

**뱃사람** a sailor; a seaman; a mariner. ¶ 노련한 ～ an old sailor 〔salt〕 / ～말 sailor's language / ～의 생활 a sailor's life; a seafaring life / ～이 되다 become a sailor; go to sea / 그는 ～이 되고 싶어한다 He wants to be a sailor 〔to go to sea〕.

**뱃삯** 《승객의》 passage money; a fare; 《나룻배의》 ferriage; ferryboat charge; 《용선료》 charterage; 《화물의》 freight; freightage. ¶ 부산까지 ～이 얼마입니까 How much is the fare to Pusan?

**뱃살** flesh 〔skin〕 of belly 〔stomach〕. ¶ ～을 잡다 shake with laughter; be convulsed with laughter; split *one's* side / 연사의 재담으로 청중은 ～을 잡았다 The audience split their sides by speaker's funny stories.

**뱃소리** a boatman's song. ⇨ 뱃노래.

**뱃속** ① 《배의 속》 the inside of the stomach; the stomach. ¶ ～이 비다 have an empty stomach / ～이 좋지 않다 *one's* bowels are out of order; have a stomach trouble. ② 《속마음》 (a) mind; (a) heart; (an) intention. ¶ ～이 검은 evil-hearted; wicked; crafty; scheming / ～을 떠보다 sound 《*a person*》 (out) 《on *a thing*》 / ～을 들여다 보다 read 〔fathom〕 《*a person's*》 thoughts.

**뱃심** push; nerve; pluck; brazen effrontery; impudence. ¶ ～좋은 사람 a man of nerve / ～(이) 좋다 have a lot of nerve; be brazenfaced 〔cheeky〕 / ～좋게도 …하다 have the nerve 〔cheek〕 to 《*do*》 / 대단한 ～이다 What a nerve he's got! *or* What (a) cheek! / 커피 한 잔을 시켜 놓고 3시간을 버티는 ～이 내게는 없다 I haven't got the nerve to make a cup of coffee stretch over three hours.

**뱃일** work aboard ship. ～하다 work on board.

**뱃전** the side of a boat 〔ship〕; a ship's side; the gunwale. ¶ ～이 기울어지다 a boat tips 〔lists〕 to one side.

**뱃줄** a hawser; a mooring cable.

**뱃짐** a (ship's) cargo; a lading; load; a freight; freightage. ¶ ～을 부리다 discharge 〔unload〕 a ship 〔cargo from a ship〕 / ～을 싣다 stow the cargo; load a ship; take in cargo.

**뱅그르르** ⇨ 빙그르르.

**뱅글뱅글** ⇨ 빙글빙글.

**뱅어**(一魚) 〖어류〗 a whitebait. ◉ ～젓 salted whitebait. ～포 dried slices of seasoned whitebait.

**-뱅이** a person; a fellow; one. ¶ 가난뱅이 a poor man / 비렁뱅이 a beggar / 주정뱅이 a drunken man / 게으름뱅이 an idle 〔a lazy〕 fellow.

**뱅충맞다** 《똘똘치 못하다》 (be) clumsy; timid; fainthearted; 《어리석다》 (be) stupid; dull; thickheaded. ¶ 뱅충맞게 clumsily; timidly; stupidly.

**뱅충이** a clumsy person; "a big ox"; a stupid person; a dolt; a weak-kneed fellow.

**뱅크** a bank. ◉ ～론 a bank loan.

**뱉다** ① 《입 밖으로》 spew; spit out. ¶ (내)뱉듯이 말하다 snap 〔rap〕 out / 침을 ～ spit 《on》; expectorate / 그 놈에게 침이라도 뱉어 주고 싶었다 I would have spat on 〔at〕 him. / 길에 침을 뱉지 마라 Don't spit on the street. ② 《기침하여》 cough up 〔out〕 (phlegm). ¶ 가래를 ～ cough out 〔bring up〕 phlegm. ③ [비유적] give up 《stolen goods》; surrender; disgorge. ¶ 착복한 돈을 뱉어 내다 surrender the embezzled money / 그는 불법으로 취득한 것을 뱉어 냈다 He has disgorged what he got illegally.

**버겁다** be too big 〔thick, bulky〕 to handle; be beyond *one's* capacity 〔control〕. ¶ 버거운 상대 a strong opponent; a tough customer 《미구어》 / 이것은 그에게 버거운 일이다 This job is beyond his capacity 〔power〕. *or* He is not equal to this job.

**버그** 〖컴퓨터〗 《결점·고장》 a bug.

**버그러뜨리다** loosen; crack; split. ¶ 의자를 ～ break a chair.

**버그러지다** split apart; fissure; come loose; separate. ¶ 책상 다리가 ～ the table leg comes loose / 틈이 ～ a split 〔crack〕 gets wider.

**버글거리다** ① 《끓다》 boil; seethe; simmer. ② 《거품이》 bubble up. ¶ 비누거품이 ～ suds bubble up. ③ 《많이 모여》 swarm 〔be crowded〕 《with》; teem 《with》; wriggle 《about》. ¶ 축구장에 사람들이 버글거린다 People are crowded in the soccer field. / 그 늪에는 모기가 버글거린다 The marsh is swarming with mosquitoes.

**버글버글** 《끓다》 boiling; 《거품이》 bubbling up; 《많이 모여》 in swarms 〔crowds〕. ¶ 냄비의 물이 ～ 끓었다 The water bubbled in the pot. / 저 오두막에는 벌레들이 ～하다 That hut is crawling with insects.

**버금** the second (in order); the next. ¶ ～가다 be in the second place; rank 〔be〕 next 〔second〕 to; come next 《to》 / 부산은 서울에 ～가는 대도시이다 Pusan is the greatest 〔largest〕 city next 〔second only〕 to Seoul.

**버너** a burner. ◉ 가스〔석유〕～ a gas 〔an oil〕 burner.

**버둥거리다** (kick and) struggle; wriggle; writhe; flounder 《in the mud》; 《말 따위가》 paw the ground 〔air〕. ¶ 결박에서 벗어나려고 ～ struggle to free *oneself* from *one's* bonds / 어머니가 버둥거리는 아기를 달랬다 The mother soothed her fretful baby. / 버둥거려도 소용이 없다 It is no use, struggle as we may. / 도둑은 경찰관에게 붙잡혀 버둥거렸다 The thief struggled in the policeman's arms.

**버둥버둥** wriggling; struggling.

**버드나무** 〖식물〗 a willow. ¶ ～의 늘어진 가지 long drooping branches of a willow tree.

**버드름하다** (be) protruding 〔sticking out〕 slightly. ¶ 이가 ～ have protruding teeth; have buckteeth.

**버들** 〖식물〗 a willow. ¶ ～ 같은 허리 a slender waist 〔figure〕.
◉ ～개지 a pussy; a catkin; a cat-

tail. ~고리 a hamper; a wicker trunk. ~눈 a willow bud. ~피리 a willow pipe.

**버디** 〖골프〗 a birdie. ¶ 연속 3개의 ~를 잡다 have three consecutive birdies.

**버라이어티** variety. ◉ ~쇼 a variety show; a vaudeville 《미》.

**버럭** 《돌연》 suddenly; all of a sudden; abruptly (불의에). ¶ ~ 소리를 지르다 shout 〔cry〕 suddenly / ~ 화를 내다 fly into a rage 〔passion, temper〕; go 〔fly, get〕 into a tantrum; burst into a fit of anger.

**버력**[1] 《천벌》 the wrath of God; divine retribution. ¶ ~을 입다 be punished by Heaven; incur the wrath of God.

**버력**[2] 〖광산〗 muck; debris. ¶ 감돌과 ~ ore rock and muck. ◉ ~탕 a dump.

**버르르** ⇨ 바르르.

**버르장머리, 버르장이** = 버릇.

**버르적거리다** (kick and) struggle; writhe 《in pain》; wriggle; flounder. ¶ 아파서 몸을 ~ writhe in agony.

**버르적버르적** writhing; squirming; struggling.

**버르집다** ① 《펴서 열다》 push a dent out; cut open; cut and enlarge. ② 《떠벌리다》 expand; enlarge; 《일을》 make serious; aggravate. ¶ 일을 버르집어 놓다 make too much of the matter; carry the matter to a foolish extent; precipitate trouble (악화). ③ 《들추어내다》 disclose 〔divulge, let out〕 《a secret》; expose; lay bare.

**버름버름하다** (be) all loosely fitted; have many cracks 〔crevices〕.

**버름하다** 《틈이》 (be) slightly open; be loosely fitted; have a crack 〔crevice〕 between; 《마음이》 (be) discordant.

**버릇** ① 《습관》 a (personal) habit (무의식적인); a (peculiar) way (행동의 방식); a peculiarity (독특한); a quirk; a vice (못된 버릇). ¶ 나쁜 ~ a bad habit; a vice / 말~ *one's* peculiar way of speaking / 게으른 ~ a habit of idleness / 고칠 수 없는 ~ an incorrigible 〔incurable〕 habit; a confirmed vice / 좀처럼 뗄 수 없는 ~ an inveterate 〔a deeply ingrained〕 habit.

버릇이: ~이 되다 become a habit 《of》; 《선례가 되다》 create a precedent / ~이 붙다 get 〔fall〕 into a habit 《of》; get in the way 《of》; contract 〔acquire, pick up〕 a habit 《of》 / …하는 ~이 있다 have 〔be in〕 the habit of 《biting *one's* nails》; have a way of 《*do*ing》 / 말을 되풀이하는 ~이 있다 have a trick of repeating *oneself* / 우쭐하는 ~이 있다 have the weakness of priding *oneself* 《on》 / ~이 고쳐지다 〔없어지다〕 be cured 〔get out〕 of a habit / 말~이 나쁘다〔없다〕, 입~이 사납다〔나쁘다〕 be foul-tongued; talk vulgarly / 손~이 나쁘다 have a way of taking 〔swiping〕 things; have sticky fingers; be light-fingered; be a kleptomaniac / 술~이 고약하다 be a mean drunk.

버릇을: ~을 고치다 《남의》 cure 《*a person*》 of a habit; get 《*a person*》 out of a habit; 《자기의》 get rid 〔break *oneself*〕 of a habit; get over a habit.

¶ 나는 아침 일찍 일어나는 ~을 들였다 I have cultivated a habit of early rising. / 나쁜 ~은 붙기 쉽고 고치기 힘들다 A bad habit is easy to get into and hard to get rid of. / 그것이 그의 ~이다 It's a habit of his to do that. *or* That's a way he has. / 아이들에게 일찍 일어나는 ~을 들이시오 Make your children form 〔develop, get into〕 the habit of getting up early. / 세 살적 ~이 여든까지 간다 《속담》 "A habit acquired at three will persist to eighty." *or* "What is learned in the cradle is carried to the grave." / 제 ~ 개 못 준다 《속담》 Bad habits are hard to break.

② 《예의》 manners; etiquette; breeding (품행); 《행실》 behavior. ¶ ~없이 rudely / ~ 들이기 training; discipline; breeding / ~을 가르치다 teach 《*a person*》 manners; give 《*a person*》 a lesson / ~이 나쁘다 = 버릇없다.

**버릇없다** (be) ill-bred〔-mannered〕; unmannerly; rude; impertinent; [서술적] be badly brought up. ¶ 버릇없는 아이 an ill-bred boy; a spoilt child / 버릇없는 말을 하다 say rude things / 버릇없이 굴다 behave rudely; be 〔show *oneself*〕 rude 《to》.

**버릇하다** be 〔get〕 accustomed 〔used〕 to 《a job, *do*ing》. ¶ 먹어 ~ get used to eating / 먹어 버릇하지 않은 음식 unaccustomed food; unusual diet.

**버릊다** scatter; kick 〔scratch〕 about; dig open.

**버리다**[1] ① 《내던지다》 throw 〔fling, 《구어》 chuck〕 *a thing* away; cast away 〔off〕 (무용물을); dump (대량의 쓰레기 등을); litter (휴지 등을); junk 《an old TV set》 《미구어》. ¶ 쓰레기를 ~ dump refuse / 음식〔폐물〕을 ~ throw away food 〔waste〕 / 불필요한 책들을 ~ drop

〔throw〕 useless books into the discard / 헌신짝처럼 ~ throw 《*a thing*》 away like an old shoe / 쓰레기를 버리지 마시오 《게시》 No litter(ing), Please. *or* No Dumping Here.
② 《돌보지 않다》 abandon; forsake; desert 〔leave〕 《*one's* family》; discard; turn *one's* back (up)on; lay 〔set〕 aside. ¶ 남편을〔아내를〕 ~ abandon *one's* husband 〔wife〕 / 속세를〔세상을〕 ~ renounce 〔forsake〕 the world; enter the priesthood / 고향을 ~ leave *one's* home town / 곤경에 처한 친구를 ~ turn *one's* back upon a friend in need; fail a friend in *his* need / 아내를 버리고 딴 여자한테로 가다 leave *one's* wife for another woman / 남편에게 버림받다 be deserted 〔left, discarded〕 by *one's* husband.
③ 《포기하다》 give up 《a plan》; abandon 《a game》. ¶ 낡은 생각을 ~ dismiss 〔scrape〕 old idea / 목숨을 ~ lay down *one's* life 《for》 / 왕위를 ~ abdicate the crown / …할 생각을 ~ give up the idea of *do*ing / 지위를 미련 없이 ~ throw up *one's* office 〔position, post〕 without any regrets / 그는 자신의 목숨을 버리며 아이를 구출했다 He sacrificed his life to save the child. / 그는 그 계획을 버리지 않을 수 없었다 He was compelled to abandon his attempt.
④ 《망치다》 mar; spoil; soil; ruin; 《해치다》 harm; impair. ¶ 아이를 ~ spoil a child / 옷을 ~ soil clothes / 과로로〔과음으로〕 건강을 ~ injure 〔impair, ruin〕 *one's* health by overwork 〔excessive drinking〕 / 맛을 ~ spoil the taste 《of》.

**버리다**[2] 〔조동사〕 finish; get through; do completely; get 《it》 done; dispose of 《a job》. ¶ 다 써 ~ use up 《money》; go 〔run〕 through 《*one's* fortune》; run 〔give〕 out of / 음식을 먹어 ~ eat up the food / 잊어 ~ (completely) forget / 장갑을 잃어 ~ lose *one's* gloves / 타 ~ be burnt 〔reduced〕 to ashes / 다 읽어 ~ read through 《a book》; finish reading.

**버림치** stuff to be thrown away 〔discarded〕; junk; waste material; a discard; a reject. ¶ ~도 쓸 때가 있다 There is a time when even junk can be used.

**버마** Burma (★ 1989년 6월 18일에 Myanmar로 개칭). ¶ ~의 Burmese; Burman. ◉ ~말 Burmese. ~ 사람 a Burmese.

**버마재비** 〖곤충〗 a (praying) mantis; a rearhorse.

**버몬트** 《미국의 주》 Vermont (생략 Vt.).

**버무리** food mixed 《with》.

**버무리다** mix together 〔up〕; dress 《vegetables》 with 《other condiment》. ¶ 나물을 ~ dress 〔mix〕 a salad.

**버물다** be mixed up 〔in, with〕 《black-market dealings》; be involved 〔implicated, entangled〕 《in》. ¶ 범죄〔음모〕에 ~ be involved in a crime 〔plot〕.

**버물리다** ① 《버무려지다》 get mixed, mix. ② 《버물게 하다》 get 《*a person*》 to mix. ¶ 나물을 ~ have 〔let〕 《a housemaid》 dress 〔mix〕 a salad.

**버뮤다** 《대서양의 섬》 Bermuda; 《바지의 일종》 Bermuda shorts; Bermudas. ¶ ~의 Bermudian / ~섬 사람 a Bermudian.

**버밍엄** 《영국의 도시》 Birmingham.

**버밍햄** 《미국의 도시》 Birmingham.

**버새** 〖동물〗 a hinny.

**버석-** ⇨ 바삭-.

**버선** traditional Korean socks. ¶ 겹〔솜〕 ~ lined 〔padded〕 socks / ~을 벗다〔신다〕 take off 〔put on〕 *one's* socks. ◉ ~목 the ankle of a sock. ~발 (*one's*) feet in socks; stocking feet: ~발로 뛰쳐 나오다 dash out of the room in *one's* socks 《to greet a visitor》. ~본 a paper pattern for making socks. ~볼 《넓이》 the width of socks; 《헝겊 조각》 a piece of cloth sewed on to mend socks; a sock patch.

**버섯** 〖식물〗 a mushroom; a toadstool (독버섯); a fungus (*pl.* ~es, -gi) (균(菌)). ¶ ~을 따다 gather 〔pick up〕 mushrooms / ~ 따러 가다 go mushroom-gathering 〔mushrooming〕. ◉ ~구름 《핵폭발의》 a mushroom cloud. ~재배(업)자 a mushroom grower.

**버성기다** ① 《틈이》 (be) loosened; loose; be out of order. ¶ 버성긴 그물 a net with large meshes / 사개가 버성기었다 The tenon (of a tenon-and-mortise joint) got loose. ② 《사이가》 (be) estranged; alienated. ¶ 두 사람 사이가 버성기었다 The two are estranged from each other.

**버스** a bus. ¶ 장거리 ~ a long-distance bus 〔coach〕 / 통근~ a commuter bus / 공항~ an airport limousine / ~로 가다 go by bus; take a bus 《to》; 《속어》 bus 《to》 / ~를 타다 「get on 〔board〕 a bus (올라타다); take a ride in a bus; take a bus 《to Chongno》 /

～에서 내리다 get off a bus / ～를 놓치다 miss a bus / 마지막 ～는 언제 떠납니까 When does the last bus leave? / 다음 마을까지 ～편이 있다 The bus goes to 〔as far as〕 the next village. *or* A bus service is available as far as the next village. / ～ 고장으로 학교에 늦었다 I was late for school on account of the bus breakdown. / ～가 붐벼 종점까지 내내 서서 갔다 The bus being crowded, I had to stand all the way to the terminal. / 그는～로 통근한다 He takes the bus to his office. *or* He commutes by bus / 역에서 대학까지 15분마다 ～가 다닌다 Buses run from the station to the college every fifteen minutes.
◉ ～노선 a bus line. ～안내원〔가이드〕 a bus conductor 〔guide〕. ～여행 a bus 〔coach《영》〕 tour. ～요금 a bus fare. ～운전기사 a bus driver. ～ 전용차선 (제도) the 'bus-only' lanes (system); a bus lane. ～정류장 a bus stop. ～카드 a bus card. ～터미널 a bus terminal; a terminal bus station; a depot [díːpou] 《미》. ～토큰 a bus token. ～회사 a bus company.

**버스러지다** ① ⇨ 바스러지다. ② 《벗겨져 떨어지다》 come 〔fall〕 off; peel 〔scale〕 off; be worn off. ¶ 페인트칠이 군데군데 버스러져있다 The paint has peeled 〔fallen〕 away. ③ 《범위 밖으로》 exceed; go beyond; 《벗어나다》 depart 《from》; deviate 〔swerve〕 《from》. ¶ 정도(正道)에서 ～ stray from the right path / 값이 생각했던 것에서 버스러진다 The price is more than I expected.

**버스럭-** ⇨ 바스락-.

**버스트** a bust. ¶ 그녀는 ～가 크다〔작다〕 She has a large 〔small〕 bust. / 그녀는 ～ 82센티, 웨이스트 56센티, 히프 86센티이다 Her dimensions 〔vital statistics 《구어》〕 are 82-56-86 in centimeters.

**버슷하다** 《관계가》 be a bit estranged 〔alienated〕 《from》; do not get on together. ¶ 둘 사이가 ～ The two of them don't get along very well.

**버저** a buzzer. ¶ ～를 울리다 buzz / ～를 누르다 press a buzzer.

**버젓하다** (be) respectable; decent; good; [서술적] be free from shame. ¶ 버젓이 with a good 〔clear〕 conscience / 버젓한 직업 a regular occupation; a respectable work 〔job〕 / 버젓한 집안 a respectable family.

**버정이다** walk idly back and forth; stroll aimlessly 〔idly〕.

**버지니아** 《미국의 주》 Virginia (생략 Va., Virg.).

**버지다** ① 《날붙이에》 get a shallow cut (from a sharp edge). ② 《닳아 찢어지다》 fray; ravel. ¶ 소매가 버졌다 The cuff was frayed.

**버짐** ringworm; pityriasis; psoriasis (마른 버짐).

**버쩍** ＝바싹.

**버찌** 〖식물〗 a cherry; a cherry bob (꼭지가 달린). ◉ ～씨 a cherry stone.

**버캐** (a) crust; fur; (boiler) scale; an incrustation. ¶ 소금〔오줌〕 ～ salt 〔urine〕 incrustations / ～가 끼다 fur; be covered with fur 〔scale〕.

**버클** a (belt) buckle.

**버킷** a bucket. ¶ 한 ～의 물 a bucketful of water (★ a bucket full of water 면 「물이 가득한 버킷」의 뜻).

**버터** butter. ¶ ～바른 빵 bread and butter / 빵에 ～를 바르다 butter *one's* bread; spread bread with butter.
◉ ～나이프 a butter knife 〔spreader〕.

**버터플라이** 《수영》 the butterfly stroke.

**버튼** a button. ⇨ 단추.

**버티다** ① 《겨루다》 resist; oppose; do not give in; stand up to; hold *one's* ground; hold 〔stand〕 out 〔firm〕; 《주장을》 insist 《on, upon》; persist 《in》. ¶ 끝까지 ～ persist to the last; hold out to the end; stand it out; stick to *one's* own opinion (의견을); carry *one's* point (주장을) / 굴하지 않고 ～ hold *one's* ground undauntedly / 떡 버티어 서다 stand in *one's* way; confront / 그는 끝까지 모른다고 버티었다 He obstinately maintained that he had no idea of the matter at all. *or* He insisted on his ignorance. / 쌍방이 다 자기 설을 주장하여 버티었다 The two contending parties remained adamant in asserting their own opinions. / 입구에는 경관이 버티고 있다 A policeman is guarding 〔blocking〕 the entrance. ② 《견뎌내다》 endure; bear up 《under》; stand; hold 《out, on, up》; withstand; keep; stick to it. ¶ 버티어 나가다 endure through; persevere / 모든 어려운 일을 버티어 내다 stand all hardships / 더 버티지를 못하다 cannot hold out any longer / 버틸 힘이 없다 lack tenacity / 좀더 끈기 있게 버티어 보라 Just try to stick to it a little longer. / 그가 어떻게 그렇게 오래 버티었을까 I wonder how he has held out so long. / 이 빌딩은 아무리 큰 지진에도 버틸 수 있다 This building is able to withstand even the biggest earthquake. ③《괴다》 prop 〔bolster, shore〕 up; support 《*a thing*》 with a prop; sustain; hold. ¶ 바지랑대로 빨랫줄을 ~ prop the clothesline with a pole / 막대기로 나무를 ~ prop up a plant with a stick / 기둥으로 벽을 ~ support a wall with a post.

**버팀목**(一木) a wooden support; a prop; a stay. ¶ ~으로 받치다〔버티다〕 prop (up) 《a pillar》; support 《a wall》.

**벅적-** ⇨ 북적-.

**벅차다** ①《힘에 겹다》 be beyond *one's* power; be above *one's* ability; be too much for 《*one*》. ¶ 벅찬 일 work beyond *one's* power; a stiff 〔formidable〕 task / 이 일은 나한테 ~ This work is beyond my endurance. *or* I am not equal to this task. / 그 선수권자는 내게 벅찬 상대였다 The champion was too much for me. ②《가슴이》 be too full for. ¶ 나는 가슴이 벅차서 말을 못 했다 My heart was too full for words. / 그녀는 고마운 생각에 가슴이 벅찼다 She was overwhelmed with gratitude.

**번**(番) ①《당번》 duty; watch; guard; lookout; vigil. ¶ 든〔난〕번 on 〔off〕 duty / 번을 들다 go on watch 〔guard〕 / 번을 서다 keep watch; be on a night watch / 당〔비〕번이다 be on 〔off〕 duty. ②《갈마들기》 (an) alternation; (a) turn; (a) change; (a) shift. ⇨ 번갈아. ③《회수》 a time. ¶ 한번 a time; once; one time / 또 한번 once more; again / 두〔세〕 번 twice 〔thrice〕; two 〔three〕 times / 이〔금〕번 this time; now / 지난번 last time; the other day / 한〔두〕 번째 the first 〔second〕 time / 두 번째 아내 *one's* second wife / 여러 번 many times; many a time / 몇 번이고 again and again. ④《차례》 number (of numerical order). ¶ 1번 number one / 나는 출석부의 15 번이다 I am No. 15 〔the 15th student〕 in the roll book.

**번가루** extra flour in kneading dough properly.

**번각**(飜刻) reprinting; reproduction. ~하다 reprint; reproduce. ◉ ~물(物), ~서(書) a reprint. ~판(版) a reprinted edition; a reproduction.

**번갈아** alternately; by turns; in turn; turn (and turn) about; in rotation 《with》; one after another 〔the other〕. ¶ ~ 하다 take by spell; take spell and spell / ~ 들다 alternate; work in shifts; take turns / ~ 들이다 alternate; shift (them) / ~ 근무하다 do duty by turns / 맥주와 위스키를 ~ 가며 마시다 take beer and whiskey alternately / 아내와 나는 ~ 요리를 한다 My wife and I alternate in cooking. / 그들은 여덟시간마다 ~ (들어서) 일한다 They work (in 〔on〕) eight-hour shifts.

**번개** (a flash of) lightning. ¶ ~ 같다 be like a streak of greased lightning; be quick as a flash 〔as lightning〕 / ~같이 like (a flash of) lightning; like a shot; in a flash / ~ 같은 솜씨 a lightning trick / ~가 번쩍했다 Lightning flashed. *or* There was a flash of lightning. / ~가 잦으면 천둥을 한다 《속담》 When lightning is frequent, thunder will follow. / 그 생각이 ~같이 스쳤다 The idea flashed through my mind.

**번갯불** a bolt of lightning. ¶ ~에 솜 구워 먹겠다 be telling a barefaced lie 〔a whopper〕 / ~에 콩 볶아 먹겠다 be quick 〔nimble〕 in action.

**번거롭다** ①《복잡하다》 (be) complicated; involved; intricate; 《귀찮다》 (be) troublesome; onerous; annoying; cumbersome; vexatious (괴롭다). ¶ 번거로운 문장 an involved style / 번거로운 생활 a vexatious life / 번거로운 절차 red-tape formalities / 법률상의 번거로운 절차 the cumbersome processes of the law / 번거로움을 덜다 save the trouble 《of *do*ing》; save 《*a person*》 trouble / 번거로워하다 find 〔consider〕 《*a thing*》 troublesome / 번거로움을 끼치다 trouble 《*a person*》; give 《*a person*》 trouble / 일을 번거롭게 만들다 complicate matters. ②《어수선하다》 (be) noisy; confused; public. ¶ 이곳은 이목이 너무 ~ This place is too public.

**번거롭히다** 《귀찮게 함》 trouble; bother; keep 《*a person*》 busy; cause 《*a person*》 trouble; put 《*a person*》 into trouble. ¶ 그 일로 그분을 번거롭혔다 I troubled him with the matter.

**번나다**(番一) be through with *one's* duty; be relieved of *one's* watch.

**번뇌**(煩惱) troubles; anxiety; pains; agony; anguish; 〖불교〗 evil passions; worldly 〔carnal〕 desires. ~하다 be in agony; suffer agony; agonize 《over》. ¶ ~를 끊다 renounce worldly desires / ~를 씻다 rarefy *one's* earthly desires / ~에 시달리다 be harassed by passions / ～의 늪에서 헤어나지 못하다 be tossed about on the waves of evil passions.

**번다**(煩多) troublesomeness; onerousness. ～하다, ～스럽다 (be) troublesome; onerous; vexatious.

**번답**(反畓) 〖농업〗 ～하다 convert a dry field into a rice paddy.

**번데기** 〖곤충〗 a pupa (*pl.* ～s, -pae); a chrysalis (*pl.* ～es, -lides). ¶ ～상태 《pass through》 a pupal state / ～로 되다 become a pupa; pupate.

**번드르르** ⇨ 반드르르.

**번드치다** ① 《뒤집다》 turn over; upset; overturn. ② 《마음을》 change 《*one's* mind》; reverse 《a decision》. ¶ 초지를 ～ change *one's* original intention.

**번득이다** 《불빛 등이》 flash; fulgurate; 《빛이》 glitter; gleam; 《생각이》 flash upon 〔across〕 《*one's* mind》; scintillate 《with wit》. ¶ 재치의 번득임 a flash of wit / 가끔 번갯불이 번득였다 There were occasional flashes of lightning. / 그녀의 눈에는 반항의 빛이 번득였다 Her eyes flashed defiance.

**번들다**(番―) be on duty ⇨ 번 ①.

**번듯-** ⇨ 반듯-.

**번롱**(飜弄) ～하다 trifle 〔play, sport, toy〕 《with》; make fun 〔a fool〕 of; make sport of; play fast and loose 《with》; 《파도가》 toss about 《a ship》. ¶ ～당하다 be made a fool of; be trifled with / 풍파에 ～당하다 be tossed about by 〔be at the mercy of〕 the wind and waves / 처녀의 애정을 ～하다니 넌 나쁘다 It's wrong of you to trifle with the girl's affections.

**번망**(煩忙·繁忙) ～하다 be busy; be pressed 〔harassed〕 with busyness.

**번문욕례**(繁文縟禮) red-tape; red-tapism; officialism; bureaucratism.

**번민**(煩悶) agony; worry; anguish. ～하다 agonize; worry; fret; be troubled in mind; be in agony; be worried; languish. ¶ ～ 끝에 병이 나다 worry *oneself* into illness 〔sick〕 / ～ 끝에 죽다 worry *oneself* to death / 사랑으로 ～하다 be lovesick; languish for 〔with〕 love / ～을 잊으려고 술을 마시다 drown *one's* agony in drink / 그는 남몰래 ～하고 있다. He is eating his heart out. / 그녀는 자식의 교육문제〔비행〕때문에 ～하고 있다 She is worried 〔troubled〕 about her son's education 〔bad behavior〕.

**번방**(番房) a room where a guard keeps watch; a guard room.

**번번이**(番番―) each 〔every〕 time; whenever; each occasion; all the time; always. ¶ 올 때마다 ～ each 〔every〕 time *one* comes; whenever 〔as often as〕 *one* calls / 그들은 만날 때마다 ～ 싸운다 They never meet without quarreling. *or* They quarrel every time 〔whenever〕 they meet. / ～ 폐를 끼쳐 죄송합니다 I am sorry to trouble you so often. / 그는 ～ 약속을 어기는데 또 그랬다 He is always breaking his promise and he did it again.

**번복**(飜覆) reversing; changing; upsetting; turning over. ～하다 reverse; change; upset; turn over. ¶ 결심을 ～하다 change *one's* mind / 판결을 ～하다 overrule a decision; reverse 〔repeal〕 a sentence / 전의 의견을 ～하다 reverse an earlier opinion 〔view〕 / 피고는 앞서의 진술을 ～했다 The accused took back his former words.

**번본**(飜本) a reprinted book; a reprint.

**번분수**(繁分數) 〖수학〗 a compound fraction.

**번서다**(番―) go 〔be〕 on duty 〔watch〕; stand guard.

**번성**(蕃盛) 《자손의》 flourishing of posterity; 《수목 등의》 luxuriance of growth; exuberancy. ～하다 flourish; prosper; 《초목이》 grow thick; grow wild 〔rank〕; exuberate. ¶ 집안이 ～하다 have a thriving 〔prosperous〕 family.

**번성**(繁盛) prosperity; flourish; success. ⇨ 번창. ～하다 prosper; flourish; thrive; be prosperous.

**번식**(繁殖) breeding (자손의); reproduction; propagation (동식물의); multiplication; increase; culture (배양). ～하다 propagate 〔reproduce〕 itself; breed; multiply; increase. ¶ 인공 ～ artificial fecundation 〔spawning〕 / 세균의 ～ the propagation of germs / ～시키다 breed / 쥐는 ～이 빠르다 Rats are very fertile animals. *or* Rats propagate themselves very rapidly / 더운 곳에서는 박테리아가 ～하기 쉽다 Bacteria increase 〔multiply〕 rapidly in a hot climate.
◉ ～기 a breeding season. ～기관 a propagative organ. ～력 procreative 〔propagating〕 power; fertility: ～력이 왕성한 prolific 《animal》 / ～력이 있는 fertile; prolific (다산의). ～률 a reproductive rate; a rate of breeding. ～지 breeding grounds.

**번안**(飜案) ① 《안건의》 change; switch; reversal 《of a plan》. ～하다 change 〔reverse〕 《a former plan》; switch.

② 《소설·희곡의》 an adaptation. ~하다 adapt 《a film from a novel》. ¶ 이것은 「리어왕」의 ~이다 This is an adaptation of *King Lear*. ◉ ~소설 an adapted story; an adaptation.

**번역**(飜譯) (a) translation; rendering; a version. ~하다 translate 〔render, turn, put〕 《Korean into English》. ¶ ~하기 어려운 문장 a passage difficult to translate / 명쾌한 ~ a lucid translation / 서투른 ~ a bad 〔poor〕 translation / 틀린 ~ a mistranslation / 원문에 가까운 ~ a translation near the original / ~을 하다 《직업적으로》 do translations / 프랑스어로 ~하다 translate 《Korean》 into French / ~을 잘하다 be good at translating; be a good translator / 잘못 ~하다 mistranslate / 본서의 ~ 복제(複製)를 불허함 "All rights of translation of this book are reserved." / 시의 ~은 어렵다 Poetry does not translate easily. / 그것은 ~할 수 없는 말이다 The word does not bear translation. / 그의 소설은 여러 나라에서〔언어로〕 ~ 되었다 His novels were translated in several countries 〔into several languages〕. ◉ ~가〔자〕 a translator. ~권 the right to translate: ~권을 얻다 secure 〔be given〕 translation rights. ~료 a charge 〔fee〕 for translation. ~문학 literature in translation. ~서〔물, 판〕 a translation; a 《Korean》 version 《of》: 톨스토이의 소설들을 ~판으로 읽다 read Tolstoy's novels in translation.

**번연히**(飜然―, 幡然―) suddenly; all of a sudden. ¶ ~ 깨닫다 realize suddenly; [사물이 주어] suddenly become clear to *one* / 그 말을 듣자 ~ 나의 잘못을 깨달았다 Hearing those words, I suddenly realized that I was wrong.

**번영**(繁榮) prosperity. ~하다 prosper; thrive; flourish; go (on) well. ¶ ~하는 prosperous; flourishing; thriving / 국가의 ~ the prosperity of a country; national prosperity / ~에 이바지하다 benefit prosperity / 더욱 ~하시기를 빕니다 《편지의 맺음말》 With best wishes for your prosperity. / 악인은 망(亡)하고 선인은 ~한다 The wicked fall and the good prosper. ◉ 공동~ common prosperity.

**번의**(飜意) changing *one's* mind; reversing 〔going back on〕 *one's* decision; reconsideration. ~하다 change *one's* mind; reverse *one's* decision; go back on *one's* resolution. ¶ ~를 촉구하다 urge 〔persuade〕 《*a person*》 to reconsider 〔rethink〕.

**번인**(蕃人) 《토인》 an aborigine; 《야만인》 a barbarian; a savage.

**번잡**(煩雜) 《번거로움》 troublesomeness; 《복잡함》 complicatedness; involvedness; 《어수선함》 crowdedness; confusion. ~하다 (be) troublesome; vexatious; annoying; complicated; involved; intricate; crowded; confused. ¶ ~한 형식 complicated formalities / ~한 거리 a crowded street / 그들의 일상생활은 ~한 규칙에 얽매여 있다 Their daily life is bound by complicated rules.

**번전**(反田) 〖농업〗 ~하다 convert a paddy field into a dry field.

**번족**[1](蕃族·繁族) a prosperous family. ~하다 be prosperous.

**번족**[2](蕃族) 《고산족》 the aboriginal tribes of Taiwan.

**번주그레하다** be rather nice looking.

**번죽거리다** behave in an irritating way; annoy; vex; provoke; sorely try; get on 《*a person's*》 nerves.

**번지** 〖농업〗 a soil rake; a kind of farm tool used in soil-leveling.

**번지**(番地) a house 〔lot, street〕 number; the number (of an address). ¶ 정동 1 ~, 1 Chŏng-dong (★ 편지 따위에 주소를 쓸 때 영미 다 함께 번지 앞에 No.는 붙이지 않음) / 같은 ~에 살다 live at the same number / 댁은 몇 ~입니까 What is the number of your house? / 이 편지는 ~수가 틀렸다 This letter is wrongly addressed.

**번지기** 《씨름》 a defensive stance with the wrestler's left or right foot forward.

**번지다** ① 《액체 따위가》 spread; run; blot. ¶ 잉크가 종이에 ~ ink spreads on 〔runs over〕 the paper / 이 종이는 잉크가 번지지 않는다 Ink does not run on this paper / 독이 온 몸에 ~ the poison spreads 〔runs〕 all through the body. ② 《병 따위가》 spread; overspread (온통); 《소문 따위가》 get abroad 〔about〕; go the rounds. ¶ 불이 점점 번졌다 The flames have steadily spread. / 홍역이 이웃 마을로 번졌다 Measles spread to a neighboring village. / 그 소문은 삽시간에 온 마을에 번졌다 The rumor quickly spread through the village. ③ 《일이》 grow; become serious; aggravate. ¶ 나는 그 일이 그렇게 번질 줄은 몰랐다 I didn't expect that it would become such a serious matter. / 폭동은 크게 번지기 전에 진압되었다 The riot was nipped in the bud. / 작은 소동이 점점 심각한 사태로 번졌다 The small disturbance gradually escalated into a major crisis.

**번지럽다** ⇨ 반지랍다.

**번지르르하다** (be) greasy and smooth; glossy; slippery; 《겉만》 (be) deceptive; showy; flashy; oily (말이). ¶ 번지르르한 치사 mere 〔left-handed〕 compliments; 《pay》 lip service / 겉으로만 번지르르한 번영 a specious appearance of prosperity / 겉보기만 ～ be not so good as it looks; be deceptive.

**번지질** 〖농업〗 using a *pŏnji* (=a soil rake). ～하다 do the soil raking.

**번지점프** bungee jumping. ～하다 bungee-jump. ¶ ～란 양다리를 신축성 있는 긴 로프로 묶고 대단히 높은 교량이나 이와 비슷한 구조물에서 뛰어내리는 운동이다 Bungee jumping is the sport of jumping off a very high bridge or similar structure with a long elastic rope tied to *one's* legs.

**번질-** ⇨ 반질-.

**번쩍** ① 《빛 등이》 with a flash. ～하다 give out a flash; flash. ¶ ～ 빛나다 = ～하다 / 눈에서 불이 ～하다 see stars / 햇빛을 받아 거울이 ～ 빛났다 A mirror flashed in the sunlight. ② 《감각기관이》 suddenly; with a start. ¶ 귀가 ～ 뜨이다 strike 〔catch〕 *one's* ears / 눈에 ～ 뜨이다 catch 〔strike〕 *one's* eye; be attractive 〔conspicuous〕 / 정신이 ～ 들다 come to *oneself* with a start. ③ 《들어올림》 lightly; easily; with no effort; 《높이》 high; aloft. ¶ 두 손을 ～ 들고 with *one's* hands high up / 큰 돌을 ～ 들어올리다 lift up a huge stone lightly / 상대를 ～ 들어올리다 hold *one's* opponent high.

**번쩍이다** shine; glitter; be bright 〔brilliant〕; glimmer. ⇨ 반짝이다.

**번차례**(番次例) a turn; an order. ¶ ～를 기다리다 wait for 〔await〕 *one's* turn.

**번창**(繁昌) prosperity; flourish. ～하다 (be) prosperous; flourishing; thriving; successful; do well; do a good business; 《의사·변호사 등이》 have a large practice. ¶ ～하는 가게 a prosperous shop / 사업이〔장사가〕 ～하다 do good business; drive a prosperous trade / ～하게 하다 make prosperous 〔flourishing〕 / 회사의 ～을 기원하다 pray for the prosperity of *one's* firm / 저 가게는 장사가 크게 ～한다 That shop is driving a good 〔splendid〕 business.

**번철**(燔鐵) a frying pan; a frypan.

**번초**(蕃椒) = 고추.

**번트** 〖야구〗 a bunt. ～하다 bunt (the ball). ¶ 드래그 ～ a drag bunt / 희생 ～ a sacrifice bunt / 3루 쪽에 ～하다 bunt down the third-base line / 주자를 ～로 보내다 advance the runner(s) on a bunt / ～ 자세를 취하다 take the bunting position.

**번호**(番號) a number; 《구령》 Number 〔Count〕 off! ¶ ～가 낮은〔높은〕 low= 〔high-〕numbered / ～가 없는 unnumbered; numberless / ～를 매기다〔찍다〕 number; assign 〔give〕 a number 《to》 / ～를 부르다 call out 《*a person's*》 number / (전화) ～를 돌리다 dial a number. ◉ ～순 《in》 numerical order: ～순으로 서다 line up 〔get in line〕 in numerical order. ～(인자)기 a numbering machine. ⇨ 넘버링. ～판 a license 〔number〕 plate; a registration number plate. ～패〔표〕 a number ticket 〔check〕.

**번화**(繁華) prosperity; flourish; 《붐빔》 bustle; liveliness (활기). ～하다 (be) flourishing; thriving; bustling 《street》; busy 〔lively〕 《quarters》. ¶ ～한 거리 a busy street / ～한 도시 a flourishing 〔thriving〕 town / ～해지다 grow prosperous; prosper; flourish; thrive. ◉ ～가 《상점가》 shopping 〔business〕 quarters; a commercial center; a downtown area 《미》; 《환락가》 an amusement quarter; 《사람의 통행이 많은》 a bustling 〔busy〕 street.

**벋가다** go astray; stray 〔deviate, swerve〕 《from》; behave in a contrary 〔perverse〕 way. ¶ 저만한 나이의 소년은 흔히 벋가기 쉽다 A boy at such age is apt to go astray.

**벋나다** stick out; protrude.

**벋놓다** give a free rein 《to》; turn loose.

**벋니** = 뻐드렁니.

**벋다**[1] 《이가》 (be) protruding; protrudent.

**벋다**[2] ⇨ 뻗다[1].

**벋디디다** ① 《발을》 step firmly. ¶ 발을 벋디디고 서다 stand firm(ly) on the ground. ② 《금 밖으로》 step out of bounds.

**벋버스름하다** 《두 사이가》 be at odds with each other; have a gulf between each other.

**벋새** 〖건축〗 a flat tile.

**벋정다리** ⇨ 뻗정다리.

**벌**[1] 《들》 a plain; an open field; a prairie (초원). ¶ 넓은 벌 a large expanse of plains / 황량한 벌 a wilderness; a moor.

**벌**[2] 〖곤충〗 a bee; a honey bee (꿀벌); a wasp (장수말벌); a hornet (말벌); a drone (수펄). ¶ 벌(의) 떼 a swarm of bees / 벌(의) 침 a bee('s) sting / 벌집 a beehive; a honeycomb; a nest of hornets / 벌에 쏘이다 be stung 《on the head》 by a bee / 벌통 주위에 벌떼가 윙윙거리고 있다 Bees are buzzing 〔humming〕 (a)round the hive.

**벌**[3] 《짝》 a suit (of clothes); a set (of dishes); a copy (of a set of documents). ¶ 양복 두 벌 two suits of clothes / 바지 한 벌 a pair of trousers / 찻 잔 한 벌 a tea set; a tea service / 식기 한 벌 a table service / 마구 한 벌 a suit of harness.

**벌**(罰) (a) punishment; (a) penalty (법률상의); retribution (인과응보의). ¶ 벌을 받지 않고 with impunity; scot=free / 벌을 주다〔과하다〕 punish; inflict punishment 〔a penalty〕 《on》; impose a penalty 《upon》; deal 〔mete〕 out punishment 《to》. ⇨ 벌하다 / 벌을 받다 be punished; suffer 〔incur〕 punishment 〔a penalty〕; take the penalty / 벌을 달게 받다 submit to punishment / 벌을 면하다〔받지 않다〕 escape punishment; go unpunished; go scot-free; get away with it / 그가 벌받는 것은 당연하다 The punishment serves him right. / 그런 짓하면 벌받는다 Heaven will punish you for it. / 재범부터는 벌이 무거워진다 Penalties 「go up 〔become heavier〕 after the first offense. / 너는 벌을 면할 수 없다 You cannot go unpunished. / 위반자는 법에 의해 벌을 받았다 The violator was punished according to law.

**벌**(閥) a clique; a faction; a coterie; a clan; a combine; (special, vested) interests; exclusivism; 《종교·학문의》 sectarianism. ¶ 군벌 a military clique / 학벌 an academic clique / 재벌 a *chaebŏl;* a great industrial family; a financial 「combine 〔group〕.

**벌거벗다** ⇨ 발가벗다.

**벌거숭이** a naked body; an unclothed person; a nude (미술품 등의); 《상태》 baldness; being uncovered. ¶ ～의 naked; undressed; unclad; 《알몸의》 starknaked; nude / ～가 되다 become naked; strip *oneself* of *one's* clothes; strip *oneself* naked / ～로 만들다 unclothe; divest; denude; strip 《*a person*》 of *his* clothes / ～로 달아나다 run away naked. ◉ ～산 a bare 〔naked, deforested, treeless〕 mountain.

**벌겋다** ⇨ 발갛다.

**벌게지다** ⇨ 발개지다.

**벌그데데하다** be a dirty red; be a coarse and unpleasant red.

**벌그레하다** ⇨ 발그레하다.

**벌그무레하다** (be) reddish.

**벌그숙숙하다** (be) reddish; ruddy.

**벌그스름하다** (be) reddish.

**벌금**(罰金) a fine (과태료); a (monetary) penalty (범칙금); a forfeit (위약금). ¶ ～을 과해야 할 finable; punishable with 〔by〕 a fine / ～을 부과하다 fine 《*a person* 50,000 won》; punish 《*a person*》 with 〔by〕 a fine; impose a fine on 《*a person*》; assess a fine against 《*a person* for》 / ～으로 때우다 get off 〔be let off〕 with a fine / ～을 물다 pay a fine 〔penalty〕 《of 50,000 won》; pay *one's* penalty / ～을 면제하다 remit a fine / ～을 물게 되다 be fined 《30,000 won for speeding》; incur a fine / ～ 정도로 그친 것이 다행이다 [사람이 주어] be very fortunate to get off with only a fine / 주차 위반으로 5만원의 ～을 물었다 I paid a penalty of 50,000 won for the violation of the parking regulations. / 본규칙의 위반자는 5만원 이하의 ～에 처함 Offenders of this law will be subject to a fine not exceeding fifty thousand won. ◉ ～형 a monetary penalty; amercement.

**벌꿀** honey; mel (약용).

**벌노랑이** 〖식물〗 a bird's-foot trefoil.

**벌다**[1] ① 《틈 따위가》 get wider; spread. ⇨ 벌어지다. ¶ 사이가 ～ the crack spreads 〔gets worse〕. ② 《몸피가》 be too big 《for *something* to hold》.

**벌다**[2] ① 《생계를 위해》 work for *one's* living; earn *one's* bread 〔living〕; 《돈·이득을》 make 〔earn, gain〕 《money》; make 〔get〕 a profit 《from》. ¶ 힘들여 번 돈 hard-earned money / 돈을 ～ earn money / 생활비를 ～ gain 〔make, get〕 a living; work for living / 용돈을 ～ make 〔earn〕 *one's* pocket money / 하루 오만 원 ～ make fifty thousand won a day / 그는 아내가 버는 돈으로 생활한다 He lives on his wife's earnings. / 한 달에 얼마나 버느냐 How much do you earn a month? ② 《시간 등을》 gain 〔earn〕 《time》; make. ¶ 시간을 ～ gain time; play 〔stall〕 for time / 우리는 어떻게든지 시간을 벌어야 한다

We have to gain 〔stall for〕 time. / 몇 점을 벌었느냐 How many points did you gain 〔make〕? ③《자초하다》 ask for; bring 〔draw〕 upon 《*oneself*》; invite; merit. ¶ 매를 ~ incur whipping.

**벌떡** 《일어서는 모양》 suddenly; with a jerk 〔start〕; quickly; rashly; 《자빠지는 모양》 on *one's* back; with the face upward; flat. ¶ ~ 일어서다 start 〔spring, jump〕 to *one's* feet; rise with a spring / 의자에서 ~ 일어서다 jump up from *one's* chair / ~ 나자빠지다 fall on *one's* back; fall face up.

**벌떡거리다** ①《물을》 gulp down; quaff; swig; swill; drink heavily 〔in large draughts〕. ¶ 물을 벌떡거리며 마시다 gulp down a glass of water. ②《가슴·맥박이》 go pit-a-pat; palpitate; throb; beat; pulsate. ¶ 벌떡거리는 가슴 a beating 〔palpitating〕 heart / 여기까지 달려 왔더니 아직도 심장이 벌떡거린다 I ran all the way here, and my heart is still pounding 〔throbbing violently〕.

**벌떡벌떡** ¶ 맥이 ~ 뛰다 *one's* pulse beats / 가슴이 ~ 뛰다 *one's* heart flutters / ~ 마시다 gulp down; drink 《water》 in big gulps; take a long pull 《at the bottle》 a gulp.

**벌렁** on *one's* back. ¶ ~ 드러눕다 lie on *one's* back; lie supine 〔face up〕 / ~ 자빠지다 fall on *one's* back.

**벌렁거리다** 《민첩》 act nimbly; move agilely; behave lightly; 《들떠서》 gad about.

**벌렁코** a flat nose with flared nostrils; a flaring 〔snub〕 nose.

**벌레** 《곤충》 an insect; a bug; 《구더기 따위》 a worm; 《나방 따위》 a moth; 《해충》 vermin [총칭]; 《쐐기》 a caterpillar; 《유충》 a larva (*pl.* -vae). ¶ ~ 먹은 worm-〔moth-〕eaten 《timber》/ ~ 먹은 사과 a wormy apple / ~ 소리 the chirping 〔singing〕 of insects / 구멍을 뚫는 ~ 《나무좀》 a borer / ~가 나다 worms breed / ~가 먹다 be eaten by worms / ~가 꾀다 be invested with vermin; become verminous / ~에 물리다 be bitten by vermin / ~에 쐬다 get stung by an insect / 가을이 되면 ~들이 울기 시작한다 When autumn comes, the insects begin to chirp. ◉ ~그물 = 포충망. ~꾐등불 = 유아등. ~집 a cocoon.

**벌레잡이식물**(―植物) an insectivorous plant.

**벌룩거리다** inflate and deflate 〔swell and subside〕 alternately; quiver; palpitate. ¶ 코를 ~ quiver *one's* nostrils.

**벌룽거리다** ⇨ 벌룩거리다.

**벌름거리다** ⇨ 벌룩거리다.

**벌리다** ①《열다》 open (up); unfold. ¶ 입을 벌리고 with *one's* mouth open / 입을 ~ open *one's* mouth. ②《넓히다》 leave space; widen; 《펴다》 stretch; outstretch; spread. ¶ 날개를 ~ spread 〔expand〕 its wing / 다리를 ~ set *one's* legs apart; spread 〔straddle〕 *one's* legs / 두 다리를 벌리고 with *one's* legs spread out 〔wide apart〕 / 팔을 ~ open *one's* arms / 두 물건의 사이를 ~ widen the space between two things.

**벌린춤** ⇨ 벌인춤.

**벌림새** the mode of display 〔arrangement〕 《of goods, *etc.*》.

**벌매듭** a kind of bowknot; a bee-shaped knot.

**벌모** 〖농업〗 young rice plants growing outside the nursery.

**벌목**(伐木) felling; cutting; logging. ~하다 fell 〔hew, cut down〕 trees; do the felling; lumber. ◉ ~기(期) a felling season. ~꾼〔공〕 a woodcutter; 《미》 a lumber jack. ~작업 felling 〔logging〕 operations.

**벌물** 《논·그릇의》 slopped water; spilt water; overflowing water.

**벌물**(罰―) ①《고문하는》 water torture (pouring water down *a person's* throat). ②《들이켜는》 water gulped down. ¶ ~ 켜듯 하다 take draughts 《of》; "swill" / 그는 맥주를 ~ 켜듯 했다 He swilled the beer down.

**벌바람** wind on an open field.

**벌벌** tremblingly; shiveringly; shakingly; nervously. ¶ ~ 떨다 tremble all over 〔like an aspen leaf〕; 《겁을 먹고》 be afraid 〔nervous〕; be in fear 〔terror〕 / 해고당할까봐 ~ 떨다 be afraid of being sacked / 놀라서〔추워서〕 ~ 떨다 tremble with fright 〔cold〕 / 그는 온몸을 ~ 떨고 있었다 He was trembling 〔shaking〕 all over. / 손이 ~ 떨려 글을 쓸 수 없었다 My hand shook so much 〔badly〕 that I could not write.

**벌부**(筏夫) a raftsman; a rafter.

**벌서다**(罰―) stand in the corner. ¶ 벌세우다 stand 〔put〕 《a child》 in the corner.

**벌써** 《진작》 long ago 〔since〕; 《이미》 already; yet (의문문에서); so soon (어느새). ¶ ~ 열 두 시다 It is twelve o'clock already. / 기차는 ~ 떠났나요 Has the train left yet? / ~ 떠났습니다 It left some time ago. / ~ 찾아뵈었어야 할 것

을 I should have called on you long ago. / 준비는 ~ 다 되어 있다 Preparations were completed long ago. / 내가 도착했을 때 그는 ~ 떠나고 없었다 He had already gone when I arrived.

**벌쐬다** get stung by a bee 〔wasp〕. ¶ 벌쐰 사람 같다 depart abruptly; hurry away 〔off〕.

**벌쓰다**(罰—) suffer 〔incur〕 punishment; 「get punished.

**벌씌우다**(罰—) inflict punishment 〔a penalty〕《on》; punish.

**벌어먹다** earn *one's* bread 〔livelihood〕; work for *one's* living; support *oneself.* ¶ 겨우 벌어먹고 지내다 eke out *one's* livelihood / 붓으로 ~ live by *one's* pen / 정직하게 ~ eat *one's* honest bread / 식구를 벌어먹이다 support 〔maintain〕 *one's* family / 그는 행상을 해서 벌어먹는다 He earns his daily bread by peddling.

**벌어지다** ①《틈이 생기다》 be (wide) open; crack (open); 《밤송이 등이》 burst 〔crack〕 open; 《넓어지다》 widen. ¶ 틈이 ~ a gap widens / (두 사람) 사이가 ~ be alienated 〔estranged〕 from each other / 옷자락이 ~ the lower skirt of *one's* robe rise 《in the wind》 / 밤이 벌어졌다 The chestnuts burst open.
②《일이 터지다》 arise; happen; develop. ¶ (일이) 크게 ~ (an affair) gets serious; assumes a serious proportions / 무슨 일이 벌어질 것 같다 Something is likely to happen. / 싸움이 왜 벌어졌느냐 What is the cause of the quarrel?
③《차이가 나다》 have a 《wide》 margin; differ 《from》; 《경기 등에서》 build up a lead 《on *one's* opponent》. ¶ (차가) 크게 ~ differ greatly 《from》; 《경기에서》 have a long lead 《on》 / 날로 벌어지는 남북 국력의 격차 an ever-yawning north-south gap in national strength / 1등과 마지막 주자 사이의 거리가 꽤 벌어졌다 There is quite a gap between the first and last runners.
④《몸이》 grow stout 〔firm〕. ¶ 어깨가 떡 ~ be square-〔broad-〕shouldered; have broad shoulders.

**벌이** making a living; earning; income; 《일》 work; a job (일자리). ~하다 work for *one's* living; earn *one's* bread. ¶ 밥~하는 사람 《한 집안의》 the breadwinner; the supporter / (장사하여) ~가 되다〔안 되다〕 pay 〔do not pay〕; be profitable 〔unprofitable〕 / ~가 좋다〔시원치 않다〕 have 〔earn〕 a good 〔poor〕 income / ~ 나가다 go to 〔for〕 work / ~를 잘하다 make a good living. ◉ ~터 the place *one* earns *one's* living at. 벌잇줄 a means of (earning a) living; a livelihood; *one's* job: 벌잇줄이 끊어지다 lose *one's* means of livelihood.

**벌이다** ①《시작하다》 open; begin; (make a) start. ¶ 가게를 ~ open 〔run, keep〕 a store / 새로운 사업을 ~ embark upon a new business 〔undertaking〕 / 수사를 ~ enter into investigation.
②《행사·행동·잔치 등을》 hold; give; throw; stage. ¶ 데모를 ~ demonstrate 《against》 / (술)잔치를 ~ hold a banquet; give a feast / 파티를 ~ throw a party / 퍼레이드를 ~ parade 《a street》; march in parade.
③《늘어놓다》 arrange 《goods》; 《진열하다》 display; (put on a) show; spread. ¶ 상품을 진열장에 벌여놓다 arrange goods in a show window.

**벌이줄** a tie string; a tie; a cord.

**벌인춤** a thing or situation that cannot be halted or rejected. ¶ ~이다 You can't give up now. *or* There's no turning back. *or* We have gone 〔come〕 too far to retreat.

**벌점**(罰點) demerit 〔black〕 marks. ¶ ~을 주다 give black marks.

**벌족**(閥族) a distinguished family 〔clan〕. ⇨ 족벌. ◉ ~정치 clan government.

**벌주**(罰酒) some liquor 〔wine〕 forced on 《*a person*》 to drink as a penalty.

**벌주다**(罰—) punish; inflict penalty on 《a culprit》.

**벌집** a (bee)hive; a (honey)comb; a nest of hornets. ¶ ~을 건드리다 stir up 〔arouse〕 a hornet's nest / ~을 쑤신 것 같다 be in utter confusion / 장내는 그 소식 때문에 ~을 쑤신 듯 발칵 뒤집혔다 The news threw the audience into utter confusion.

**벌쩍거리다** ①《움직거리다》 squirm; wriggle. ¶ 아이가 일어나려고 벌쩍거리다 The baby squirms to get up. ②《비벼 빨다》 rub lazily 〔unenergetically〕; scrub softly.

**벌창하다** overflow; flood. ¶ 강물이 ~ a river overflows / 상품이 시장에 ~ the market is flooded with merchandise.

**벌채**(伐採) timber cutting; lumbering 《미》; (tree) felling; deforestation. ~하다 fell; hew 〔chop〕 down; cut (timber); lumber. ¶ 산림을 ~하다 exploit 〔work, cut down〕 a forest / 삼림 ~가 오늘날 심각한 환경문제의 하나가 되어 있다 Deforestation constitutes one of the most serious environmental problems of the day. ◉ ～량 a fall. ～면적 a cutover area.

**벌책**(罰責) rebuke; reprimand. ～하다 rebuke; reprimand. ¶ ～을 당하다 be reprimanded 《for》; be subjected to reprimand.

**벌초**(伐草) ～하다 cut the weeds 〔mow the grass〕 around a grave; tidy up (a grave).

**벌충** making up 《for》; a supplement; compensation; reparation; amends. ～하다 make up 〔amends〕 for; cover 〔make good, balance up〕 《the loss》; supplement; compensate. ¶ 손해를 ～하다 cover 〔make good (for)〕 the loss; make up for the loss; compensate for loss / 허비한 시간을 ～하다 recover 〔make up for〕 lost time / 내가 그 ～을 해주지 I will make it up for the loss.

**벌칙**(罰則) penal regulations 〔clauses〕; punitive provisions. ¶ ～을 적용하다 apply 〔enforce〕 the penal regulations / ～에 저촉되다 infringe the penal regulations / ～에 따라 처벌하다 punish 《*a person*》 according to the penal regulations / 이 법률에는 엄격한 ～이 있다 The law carries severe penalties. ◉ ～규정 penal provisions.

**벌컥** ⇨ 발칵.

**벌타령**(一打令) doing at random 〔without any thought〕; doing as *one* pleases.

**벌통**(一桶) a (wooden) beehive; a hive.

**벌판** a field; 《평원》 a plain; the plains; 《황야》 a wilderness. ⇨ 벌[1].

**벌하다**(罰一) punish; penalize; discipline; give a punishment 《for a crime》; subject 《*a person*》 to punishment 〔a penalty〕; mete out punishment 《to》; bring 《*a person*》 to justice. ¶ 벌받아야 할 행위 punishable conduct; conduct deserving punishment / 엄하게〔무르게〕 ～ punish severely 〔mildly〕 / 가볍게〔무겁게〕 ～ punish lightly 〔heavily〕 / 벌하지 않고 두다 let go unpunished / 아무의 죄를 ～ punish *a person* for *his* crime / 범죄는 법에 의해 벌할 수 있다 Crimes are punishable by the law.

**범** a tiger; a tigress (암컷). ¶ 새끼 범 a tiger kitten; a cub tiger / 자는 범 코침 주기 《속담》 "twisting the lion's tail." *or* "Let sleeping dogs lie." / 범도 제 말 하면 온다 《속담》 Talk of the devil, and he is sure to appear. / 범 없는 골에는 토끼가 스승이라 《속담》 In the valley of the blind the one-eyed is king. / 범(의) 굴에 들어가야 범을 잡는다 《속담》 "Nothing ventured, nothing gained." *or* "You can't go swimming without getting your feet wet." / 범에 날개 《속담》 It makes one invulnerable 〔doublely powerful〕.

**범-**(汎) pan-. ¶ 범독일(주의) Pan-German(ism) / 범민족 대회 a pan-national rally.

**-범**(犯) an offense; a violation; 《사람》 an offender. ¶ 강력범 a violent offense 〔criminal〕 / 살인범 a (convicted) murderer / 방화범 an arsonist / 파렴치범 an infamous criminal / 전과 5범 a man with five previous convictions / 전과 2범이다 be previously convicted two times.

**범고래** 〚동물〛 a grampus; a killer whale; an orc.

**범골**(凡骨) ＝범인(凡人).

**범과**(犯過) a fault; a wrong; wrongdoing. ～하다 do a wrong; commit a fault.

**범국민**(汎國民) ¶ ～적인 pan-national; nationwide. ◉ ～운동 a nationwide campaign 〔movement, drive〕 《for the protection of the environment》.

**범금**(犯禁) violation of restrictions; infringement; transgression; contravention. ～하다 violate restrictions; break a prohibition; transgress; contravene; infringe.

**범나비** 〚곤충〛 a swallowtail (butterfly). 「＝호랑나비.

**범독**(泛讀) reading at random; desultory reading; skimming; scanning (reading material). ～하다 read at random; read desultorily; skip through; skim.

**범띠** 〚민속〛 the attributes of (*one* born in the year of) the Tiger.

**범람**(氾濫) ① 《넘쳐흐름》 inundation; flooding; a deluge; a flood (홍수). ～하다 overflow; flow 〔run〕 over 《the banks》; flood; inundate. ¶ ～하기 쉬운 강 a river prone to rampage / ～해 있다 be in flood 〔spate 《영》〕 / 큰비로 강이 ～했다 The river was flooded by heavy rainstorms. / 강이 ～하여 온 마을이 물에 잠겼다 The whole village was inundated by the flooding of the river. ② 《나돎》 a flood 《of foreign words》; oversupply (공급과잉). ～하다 flood. ¶ 거리에는 자동차가 ～해 있다 There is a flood of cars on the street. / 서점에는 만화책이 ～하고 있다 The bookstores are flooded with comic books.

**범례**(凡例) introductory remarks; explanatory notes; a legend (지도 등의).

**범론**(汎論·泛論) ① 《개괄적》 general

remarks; a summary; an outline; an introduction. ② = 범론(泛論).

**범론**(泛論) a vague remark; a pointless logic.

**범미**(汎美) ¶ ~의 Pan-American. ◉ ~주의 Pan-Americanism. ~회의 Pan-American Congress.

**범방**(犯房) marital intercourse; having sexual intercourse. ~하다 have marital 〔sexual〕 intercourse. ⇨ 방사(房事).

**범백**(凡百) ① 《사물》 all things 〔matters〕. ② 《언행》 *one's* daily behavior; *one's* manners 〔etiquette〕. ¶ ~을 가르치다 tell 《*a person*》 the etiquette / ~을 배우다 learn good 〔take lessons in〕 manners.

**범벅** ① 《음식》 a thick mixed-grain porridge. ② 《뒤죽박죽》 a hotchpotch; a mess; a muddle; a jumble; a complicated affair; a pell-mell; a medley. ¶ ~(이) 되다 be mixed up; be jumbled together; get messed up / 일이 모두 ~이 되었다 Everything got mixed up.

**범범하다**(泛泛—) (be) careless; inattentive.

**범법**(犯法) breaking the law; violation of the law; a transgression; an offense 《against》. ~하다 break the law; violate 〔transgress〕 the law; commit an offence; run counter to rules. ¶ 그들이 하고 있는 것은 ~이 아니다 What they are doing is not against the law. ◉ ~자 a lawbreaker; an offender (against the law). ~행위 an illegal act; a malfeasance (공무원의).

**범부**(凡夫) ① 《속인》 an ordinary person; a common mortal; the common run of men [총칭]. ⇨ 범인(凡人). ② 〖불교〗 an unenlightened person; a common mortal in bondage to his earthly passions.

**범사**(凡事) 《모든 일》 all matters; everything; 《평범한 일》 a commonplace event 〔affair〕; an ordinary matter.

**범살장지** 〖건축〗 a sliding door of crude latticework.

**범상**(凡常) ~하다 (be) ordinary; common; normal; average; commonplace; mediocre. ¶ ~치 않은 extraordinary; out of the common; uncommon / ~한 사람 an average 〔ordinary〕 man / ~치 않은 재능 talents above the average / ~치 않다 be out of the common; rise above mediocrity 〔the common herd〕.

**범서**(凡書) an ordinary 〔a mediocre〕 book.

**범서**(梵書) ① 《범어의》 a book written in Sanskrit 〔Pali〕. ② 〖불교〗 Buddhist scriptures.

**범선**(帆船) a sailing vessel 〔ship, boat〕; a sailer.

**범속**(凡俗) commonness; commonplaceness; banality; platitude; mediocrity; vulgarity. ~하다 (be) common; ordinary; commonplace; mediocre; vulgar. ¶ ~한 생각 a commonplace thought / ~한 사람들 the common crowd 〔people〕; the masses / ~을 초탈하다 rise above 「the common herd 〔the rest of mankind〕.

**범신론**(汎神論) 〖철학〗 pantheism. ¶ ~적 panthesistic. ◉ ~자 a pantheist.

**범심론**(汎心論) 〖철학〗 panpsychism.

**범아귀** the base between the thumb and the index finger 〔forefinger〕.

**범아랍**(汎—) ¶ ~의 Pan-Arab. ◉ ~운동 the Pan-Arab Movement. ~주의 Pan-Arabism.

**범아시아**(汎—) ¶ ~의 Pan-Asiatic. ◉ ~주의 Pan-Asianism.

**범애**(汎愛) = 박애(博愛).

**범어**(梵語) Sanskrit; Pali. ¶ ~의 Sanskrit(ic). ◉ ~학자 a Sanskrit scholar; a Sanskritist.

**범연하다**(泛然—) (be) inattentive; careless; sloppy; heedless; indifferent. ¶ 범연히 indifferently; carelessly.

**범용**(汎用) a wide use. ¶ ~의 all-purpose; general-purpose. ◉ ~컴퓨터 a general-purpose computer.

**범용**(凡庸) mediocrity. ~하다 (be) mediocre; common(place); average; run-of-the-mill; middling. ¶ ~한 사람 an ordinary person / ~한 재주를 가진 사람 a man of mediocre talent.

**범용**(犯用) peculation; misappropriation. ~하다 misappropriate; peculate; divert 《funds》 to private use; use illegally. ¶ 그녀는 협회의 기금을 ~했다 She misappropriated the society's fund.

**범월**(犯越) illegal crossing (of a border); violation of the border. ~하다 illegally cross; violate (a border); invade.

**범위**(範圍) an extent (정도·한도); 《지식·활동 등의》 a range; a scope; a sphere; the province 《of》 (학문·지식 분야); 《한정된 범위》 (the) limits 〔bounds, confines〕 《of》; a boundary (경계선). ¶ 문학의 ~ the realm 〔province〕 of literature / …의 ~ 내에(서) within the limits 〔scope, range, sphere〕 of… / 예산 ~ 내에서 within the budget / ~ 밖에 beyond the limits 〔scope, range〕 《of》; beyond 〔outside〕 the compass of / 내

가 아는 ～에서는 as far as I know / ～가 넓다 be wide ranged; cover a wide range / 모든 ～에 걸치다 run the (whole) gamut 《of》/ ～를 제한〔한정〕하다 set limits 〔bounds〕《to》; fix the limits 《of》; limit; circumscribe / 인지(人知)의 ～를 넘어서다 be beyond the boundary of human knowledge / 지식의 ～를 넓히다 enlarge the range of the knowledge / 교제 ～가 좁다 have a small circle of acquaintance(s) / 좁은 ～에 한정되다 be confined within narrow limits / 그는 독서 ～가 넓다 His reading is of a very wide range. / 그의 세력 ～는 얼마나 되는가 How wide is the sphere 〔range〕 of his influence? / 시험 ～는 10쪽에서 50쪽까지이다 The examination covers pages ten to 〔through〕 fifty.

**범유럽**(汎—) ¶ ～의 Pan-European. ◉ ～주의 Pan-Europeanism.

**범의**(犯意) a criminal 〔guilty〕 intent; malice. ¶ ～가 있는 malicious / ～를 인정하다 recognize 《*a person's*》 criminal intent / ～를 인정할 수 없다 show no criminal intent.

**범의귀** 〖식물〗 a (creeping) saxifrage; a strawberry geranium.

**범인**(凡人) an ordinary person; a common man; an ordinary mortal; a mediocrity; the ordinary 〔general, common〕 run of men [총칭]. ¶ 그것은 ～의 힘으로는 할 수 없다 It is beyond the power of a common mortal.

**범인**(犯人) a criminal; a culprit; an offender; a convict. (★ criminal은 범죄를 범한 사람, offender는 넓은 의미로 위반자도 포함하는 말. convict는 유죄판결을 받은 사람, culprit는 미결수를 말함) ¶ ～을 은닉하다 harbor a criminal / ～을 쫓다 track down a criminal / ～은 아직 잡히지 않고 있다 The criminal is still at large. / ～이 자수했다 The criminal turned himself in. / ～은 현행범으로 체포되었다 The offender 〔criminal〕 was caught 〔arrested〕 in the (very) act. ◉ ～수사 man hunt. ～ 인도 협정 ⇨ 범죄자 상호 인도 협정.

**범자**(梵字) Sanskrit (characters).

**범재**(凡才) 《재주》 common 〔ordinary〕 ability; a mediocrity; 《사람》 a man of no more than ordinary talent; a mediocre person. ⌈rum.

**범절**(凡節) etiquette; proprieties; decorum.

**범종**(梵鐘) the bell of a Buddhist temple; a temple bell.

**범죄**(犯罪) a crime (무거운); an offense (가벼운). ¶ ～(상)의 criminal / ～의 현장 the scene of a crime / ～의 예방 the prevention of crimes; crime prevention / ～의 소추(訴追) criminal prosecution / ～와의 전쟁 a war against crime and violence / ～를 수사하다 investigate a crime / ～를 근절하다〔방지하다〕 eradicate 〔prevent〕 crime / ～를 저지르다 commit a crime / ～에 관련되다 be concerned in the crime / 뉴욕은 ～가 많은 도시이다 New York is a crime-infested city. / 음주 운전은 ～가 된다 Drunk(en) driving constitutes a crime 〔an offense〕. / 그는 저도 모르게 중대 ～를 저질렀다 He had committed a serious crime without knowing what he was doing.
◉ ～감식 criminal identification: ～ 감식자료 materials 〔data〕 for criminal identification / ～ 감식을 하다 identify a criminal. ～건수 the number of crimes committed. ～과학 criminalistics. ～기록 criminal records: 강제적〔의무적〕인 ～ 기록 공개 the mandatory disclosure of criminal records. ～발생률 a crime rate. ～사실 facts constituting an offense. ～사회학 criminal sociology. ～소설 crime stories. ～수사 (a) criminal investigation: ～수사대 a criminal investigation detachment. ～심리학 criminal psychology. ～예방 crime prevention. ～용의자 a suspect; a suspected criminal. ～유형 a crime type. ～인〔자〕 an offender; a criminal; a convict; a con 《속어》; a transgressor: ～자형 a criminal type / 전쟁 ～자 a war criminal. ～자상호인도협정 a bilateral agreement on extradition of criminals. ～조직 a criminal syndicate. ～통계(統計) criminal statistics. ～학 criminology: ～학자 a criminologist. ～행위 a criminal act.

**범주**(帆走) sailing. ～하다 sail; go by sail.

**범주**(範疇) a category; a class. ¶ ～에 넣다 place 《*something*》 under the category 《of》/ 그것들은 모두 Z의 ～에 든다 All of them come within 〔fall under, belong to〕 the category of Z.

**범천**(梵天) 〖불교〗 Brahma-Deva. ◉ ～왕 Brahma (the Creator).

**범칙**(犯則) 《규칙 위반》 a violation of rules; a foul (특히 경기의). ～하다 violate the rules; be against the rules; play foul; foul. ¶ ～ 때문에 지다 lose a game all because of a foul / ～을 하여 퇴장당했다 He was sent off the field for a foul. *or* 《미》 He fouled out of the game. ◉ ～물자 illegal goods; 《밀수품》 a smuggled article. ～자 an offender; a transgressor; a defaulter.

**범칭**(泛稱·汎稱) a general term 〔title〕; a popular name.

**범타**(凡打) 〖야구〗 poor batting. ～하다 hit an easy fly 〔grounder〕 《to》. ¶ ～에 그치다 prove poor at bat.

**범태평양**(汎太平洋) ¶ ～의 Pan-Pacific. ◉ ～ 회의 the Pan-Pacific Conference.

**범퇴**(凡退) ～하다 〖야구〗 be easily put out. ¶ ～시키다 retire 《a batter》 / 3자 ～하다 All the three go out in one-two-three 〔quick〕 order.

**범퍼** 《완충 장치》 a bumper.

**범포**(帆布) canvas; sailcloth.

**범하다**(犯—) ① 《죄악·잘못 등을》 commit; perpetrate; sin against; 《규칙·법률 등을》 violate; infringe; break; trespass 〔offend〕 against. ¶ 과오를 ～ commit 〔make〕 a fault 〔an error〕 / 교칙을 ～ break the school regulations / 저 남자는 살인(죄)를 범했다 That man 「committed 〔is guilty of〕 murder. / 흔히들 벌이 무서워서 죄를 범하지 않는다 The fear of punishment deters many people from crime. ② 《여자를》 rape; violate; 《남의 권리 따위를》 defy; make little of; disregard. ¶ (사람됨이) 범하기 어려운 데가 있다 have something that commands respect.

**범행**(犯行) a crime; an offense; a criminal act. ～하다 commit a crime. ¶ 대담한〔잔인한〕 ～ a bold 〔an atrocious〕 crime / (현장 검증 때의) ～의 재연 a reenactment of the crime / ～을 시인하다〔시인하지 않다〕 plead 「guilty 〔not guilty〕 (법정에서) / ～을 자백하다 confess *one's* crime / ～을 부인하다 deny *one's* having committed the crime / ～은 오전 6시경에 일어난 것으로 추정되었다 It was presumed that the crime took place at about six in the morning. ◉ ～시간 the time of the crime 〔offence〕. ～현장 the scene of the crime 〔offence〕: 형사들은 ～ 현장으로 급히 달려갔다 Detectives sped 〔rushed〕 to the scene of the crime.

**법**(法) ① 《법률》 the law; a rule (법규); 《법전》 a code (of laws).

¶ 법의 날 the Law Day / 법의 정신 the spirit of the law / 법의 효력 the force of the law / 법과 질서 law and order / 법의 지배 the rule of law / 법의 집행 기관 a law enforcement 〔executive〕 agency 〔organ〕 / 법의 적용을 받다 be under the application of the law / 법의 허점을 찌르다 outwit 〔circumvent〕 the law.

법에: 법에 맞다〔어긋나지 않다〕 conform to the law / 법에 맞는 lawful; legal / 법에 어긋나다 be against 〔contrary to〕 the law / 법에 어긋나는 unlawful; illegal / 법에 따라 처리하다 deal with 《*a person*》 according to the law; bring 《*a person*》 to justice (재판으로) / 법(절차)에 따라 처리되다 be dealt with in accordance with the pertinent law / 법에 따라 행동하다 act (up)on the regulation / 법에 호소하다 appeal to the law; invoke (the power of ) the law: take legal action / 법에 저촉되지 않도록 하다 stay on the right side of the law.

법을: 법을 고치다 revise 〔alter〕 the law / 법을 마련하다 legislate; enact a law / 법을 시행하다 enforce a law; bring a law into force / 법을 어기다 break 〔violate〕 the law; go against the law; run counter to the law / 자신에게 유리하게 법을 멋대로 곡해(曲解)하다 twist 〔bend, strain〕 the law to suit *oneself* / 법을 확대 해석하다 stretch the law / 법을 지키다 observe 〔keep, obey〕 the law; abide by the law / 법을 집행하다 administer 〔deal out〕 a law. ¶ 법 앞에서는 만인이 평등하다 All men are equal before the law.

② 《예법》 etiquette; manners; 《도리》 good reason; justification; propriety. ¶ 그런 법은 없다 That's unreasonable. / 그런 법이 어디 있느냐 Where do you find justification for that? *or* What makes you think so? *or* How do you get that way? / 제 일은 제가 하는 법이다 You ought to look after yourself. / 어른한테 그렇게 말하는 법이 아니다 You shouldn't speak like that to your elders. / 그에게 그런 일을 당하고 가만히 있으라는 법은 없다 We should not let him get away with it. / 아버지가 의사라고 너도 의사가 되라는 법은 없다 There is no reason why you should become a doctor (just) because your father is a doctor.

③ 《방법》 a method; a manner; a way how to 《*do*》; 《과정》 a process; 《기술》 an art; technique. ¶ 교수법 a teaching method / 공부하는 법 a method of study / 헤엄치는 법 how to swim / 요리법을 가르치다 teach 《*a person*》 how to cook / 공부하는 법이 틀렸다 You are studying in the wrong way.

④ 〖수학〗 a divisor.

⑤ 〖문법〗 mood. ¶ 직설법 the indica-

tive mood / 가정법 the subjunctive mood.
⑥ 『불교』 ⇨ 불법(佛法).

**법계**(法系) a legal system; a code of law; law. ◉ 로마~ Roman law. 중국~ the Chinese legal system; Chinese law.

**법계**(法界) ① 『불교』 the realm of Buddhism; the universe; 《불교도 사회》 the world 〔circles, society〕 of Buddhists. ② 《법조계》 legal circles; the judicial world; 《영》 the Bench and Bar.

**법과**(法科) 《학부》 the law department; a law course (과정). ¶ ~를 나오다 complete *one's* law course; graduate 《from a university》 in law.
◉ ~대학 a law college; a school of law 《미》: ~대학생 a law student. ~출신 a graduate of a law school.

**법관**(法官) a judicial officer; a judge; [총칭] the judiciary; the bench.

**법권**(法權) a legal right.

**법규**(法規) laws and regulations; enactments. ¶ 현행 ~ the laws in force / ~상 legally; according to the regulation / ~에 비추어 according to (the) law / ~의 불비로 owing to a defect 〔fault〕 in legislation / 상거래에 관한 ~ regulations regarding business transactions / ~상의 절차를 밟다 go through legal formalities / ~에 따라 처벌하다 punish 《*a person*》 according to the law / 교통 ~는 꼭 지켜야 한다 You must obey traffic regulations.

**법당**(法堂) a building that contains a statue of Buddha; a main 〔sermon〕 hall.

**법도**(法度) ① 《법》 a law; a rule; regulations. ¶ ~를 어기다 violate 〔infringe〕 the law. ② 《예법》 courtesy; etiquette; manners. ¶ 그렇게 하면 ~에 어긋난다 It is against etiquette to do so.

**법등**(法燈) 『불교』 ① 《불법》 the light of Buddhism. ② 《등불》 a light offered to the Buddhist altar. ③ 《전통》 Buddhistic tradition 〔heritage〕.

**법랑**(琺瑯) 《유약》 (porcelain) enamel. ¶ ~을 입힌〔먹인〕 냄비 an enameled pot / ~을 입히다 enamel; cover with enamel. ◉ ~질 enamel 《of teeth》. ~철기 an enameled ironware.

**법령**(法令) a law; 《시행령·조례》 an ordinance; [총칭] laws and ordinances; a statute. ¶ ~으로 by law / ~에 의하여 규정되어 있다 be provided for 〔be specified〕 in the law.
◉ ~양식 legal forms. ~ 위반 ordinance violations. ~집 a statute book; a book of statutes; statutes at large; a complete collection of laws and regulations 〔ordinances〕.

**법례**(法例) the law governing the application of laws; rules concerning the application of a law.

**법률**(法律) a law (개별의); [총칭] (the) law. ⇨ 법(法). ¶ ~(상)의 legal; juridical / ~이 인정하는 lawful (합법적인); legal / ~에 어긋나는 unlawful; illegal / …을 금하는 ~ a law against 《gambling》 / ~ 지식이 있는 사람 a person who has legal knowledge / ~을 제정하다 make 〔enact〕 a law / ~을 배우다 《판·검사가 되려고》 read law; 《학문으로서》 study law / ~로 금하다 prohibit by law / ~에 규정되어 있다 be 「provided for 〔specified〕 in the law / 한국에는 문화재 보호를 규정하는 ~이 있다 In Korea, there is a law that provides for the protection of cultural property. / 우리 나라에서는 도박이 ~로 금지되어 있다 Gambling is prohibited by law in our country. / ~의 무지는 받아들여지지 않는다 You cannot be excused if you plead ignorance of the law. *or* Ignorance of the law is no excuse. / ~은 만민에게 공평히 시행되어야 한다 The laws should be carried out with justice to everybody.
◉ ~가 a lawyer (변호사); a judge (판사); a jurist (법률학자). ~고문〔문제〕 a legal adviser 〔question〕. ~사무 the practice of law; legal work 〔business〕; a lawyer's business: ~ 사무소 a law office; a lawyer's office 〔firm〕. ~상담 legal advice: ~ 상담에 응하다 give legal advice / ~ 상담소 a legal information center; 《영》 a law center. ~서 a lawbook. ~안 a (legislative) bill; a draft of a proposed law. ~용어 a legal term. ~위반 a breach 〔violation〕 of the law: ~ 위반이다 be illegal 〔against the law〕. ~이념 the idea of law. ~통 a legal expert; a jurist. ~학 jurisprudence; the science of law. ~행위 a juristic act; a legal action.

**법률상**(法律上) legally; from the legal point of view; in the eye 〔state〕 of the law. ¶ ~ 인정된 lawful; legal; legitimate / ~으로 말하면 legally speaking / ~의 권리 legal rights / ~의 불리한 입장에 있다 be in a legally unfavorable position.

**법리**(法理) a principle of law; legal principles. ¶ ~적(인) juridical; legalistic.
◉ ~학 jurisprudence; the science of

law: ～학의 jurisprudential / ～학자 a jurist; a jurisprudent.

**법망**(法網) the net 〔grip, clutches, hands, toils, meshes〕 of the law. ¶ ～에 걸려들다 fall 〔get〕 into the clutches of the law; be caught in the meshes of the law; be picked up by the law; be brought to justice / ～을 피하다〔뚫다〕 evade 〔avoid, dodge〕 the law; slip from the grip of the law / ～에 걸리지 않고 범죄를 거듭하다 commit one crime after another without falling into the clutches of the law.

**법명**(法名) 〖불교〗 *one's* Buddhist name.

**법무**(法務) ① 〖법〗 judicial affairs. ② 〖불교〗 a clerical duty. ◉ ～관 a law officer; a judiciary; 〖군사〗 a judge advocate. ～부 the Ministry of Justice; the Justice Department 《미》: ～부 장관 the Minister of Justice; the Attorney General 《미》. ～사 a judicial scrivener. ～실 the Legal Affairs Office.

**법문**(法文) ① 《법률》 the law; 《법조문 글귀》 the text 〔letter, wording〕 of the law; written laws; 《법률과 문학》 law and literature. ¶ ～에 명시되어 있다 be specified in the law. ② 〖불교〗 Buddhist writings.

◉ ～화 legalization: ～화하다 put 《*a matter*》 into statutory form; codify; enact 《*a matter*》 into law.

**법문**(法門) 〖불교〗 Buddhism; the Buddhist priesthood; holy orders. ¶ ～에 들어가다 enter the Buddhist priesthood; become Buddhist priest 〔monk〕.

**법복**(法服) ① a robe; a gown; 《법관·변호사의》 a judge's 〔lawyer's〕 gown. ② ＝법의(法衣).

**법사**(法師) a Buddhist priest 〔monk〕; a bonze; 《스승》 the teacher of a Buddhist priest.

**법사위원회**(法司委員會) 《국회의》 the Legislation-Judiciary Committee.

**법석** (a) noise; a clamor; (a) racket; (a) hubbub; (a) fuss; ado. ～하다 be noisy; raise a clamor; make a fuss; fuss 《about》; make much ado. ¶ ～떨다 make a lot of noise 〔a racket〕 / 시시한 일로 ～(을) 떨다 make a fuss about trifles / 술을 마시며 야단～을 부리다 go on a spree. ◉ ～판 a noisy 〔clamorous〕 scene; a clamor.

**법선**(法線) 〖수학〗 a normal. ◉ ～방정식 an equation of normal.

**법수**(法數) 〖수학〗 a divisor.

**법식**(法式) ① 《법도와 양식》 rules and forms; formalities. ¶ 일정한 ～ a regular 〔proper〕 form / ～에 따르다〔어긋나다〕 follow 〔run counter to〕 the established form. ② 《방식》 a formula. ③ 〖불교〗 formalities of a Buddhist ceremony; Buddhist ritual.

**법안**(法案) a (legislative) bill; a measure. ¶ ～을 제출하다 introduce 〔bring in, submit〕 a bill 《to the National Assembly》 / ～을 가결〔부결〕하다 pass 〔reject, throw out〕 a bill / 오랜 토의 끝에 그 ～은 가결〔부결〕되었다 They passed 〔rejected〕 the bill after a long debate. ◉ ～제출권 a right to introduce a bill to the House.

**법어**(法語) 〖불교〗 《설교》 a Buddhist sermon; Buddhist literature; 《불어》 Buddhistic terms; a Buddhist term.

**법열**(法悅) ① 〖불교〗 religious ecstasy 〔exaltation〕. ② 《황홀감》 rapture; an ecstasy; transport. ¶ ～에 잠기다 be in rapture 〔ecstasies〕 《over》; be in ecstasies of delight; be filled with exaltation.

**법왕**(法王) 〖불교〗 *Tathāgata* (Sans.); 「Buddha.

**법요**(法要) 〖불교〗 a Buddhist memorial service. ¶ ～를 올리다 hold a memorial service 《on the second anniversary of *one's* father's death》.

**법원**(法院) a court of justice 〔law〕; a law court; 《건물》 a courthouse. ¶ ～에 출두하다 come into court; appear in court / ～은 그들을 가볍게 처벌하지 말고 엄벌에 처해야 한다 The court should throw the book at them instead of letting them go with a slap on the wrist. (★ 「엄벌에 처하다」를 우리는 일차적으로 punish *them* severely; inflict a severe punishment on *them* 등으로 표현하게 되는데, 미국인들은 「법정 최고형을 선고한다」는 뜻으로 throw the book at… 을 즐겨 쓴다.) ◉ ～서기 a court clerk. ～장 the president 〔presiding officer〕 of a court. ～행정처 the Office of Court Administration.

**법의**(法衣) a Buddhist priest's robe; a sacerdotal 〔clerical〕 robe; canonical dress; canonicals; a vestment.

**법의학**(法醫學) medical jurisprudence; legal 〔forensic〕 medicine. ¶ ～의 medicolegal. ◉ ～교실 a legal medicine lecture room. ～자 a doctor of forensic medicine.

**법익**(法益) the benefit and protection of the law. ¶ ～을 박탈하다 deprive 《*a person*》 of the benefit and protection of the law; outlaw 《*a person*》.

**법인**(法人) a juridical 〔juristic, legal〕

person; a corporation; a corporate body. ¶ ~의 corporative.
◉ ~과세 taxation on juridical persons. ~권 corporate rights. ~단체 a body corporate. ~명의 a corporate name. ~설정 the creating of a juridical person; incorporation. ~세 a corporation tax. ~소득 corporate income: ~소득세 the corporation profit tax. ~신탁 corporation trust. ~자산〔재산〕 corporate assets 〔property〕. ~조직 a corporate organization: 회사를 ~ 조직으로 하다 incorporate a firm. ~주주 an institutional stockholder. 공개~ an open corporation: 공개 ~ 체제 an open corporate structure. 공공~ a public corporation. 단독~ a corporation sole. 사단~ a corporate juridical person; a corporation aggregate. 재단~ a (juridical) foundation; 《미》 a non-profit corporation. 종교~ a religious corporation. 특수~ a corporation having a special status. 학교~ an educational foundation.

**법적**(法的) legal(istic). ¶ ~ 근거 a legal basis / ~으로는 legally (speaking); in the eye of the law / ~ 조처를 취하다 take legal steps 〔action〕; institute legal proceedings / 그에게는 ~ 책임이 없다 He is not legally responsible. / 그것은 ~으로 인정되어 있다 It is legally recognized. / 이 나라에서 뇌사는 아직 ~으로 사람의 죽음으로 인정되지 않고 있다 In this country brain death is not recognized to be human death.
◉ ~근거 a legal basis: 너의 요구는 ~근거가 없다 Your demand has no legal basis. ~조치 legal action. ~하자 a legal flaw. ~효력 《have》 legal force.

**법전**(法典) a code of laws; a law code; a body of law(s). ¶ 현행 ~ the (code of) laws in force / ~을 편찬하다 codify laws. ◉ ~편찬 codification.

**법정**(法廷) a (law) court; a court of justice 〔law〕; a courtroom; a tribunal; the bar; a judgment hall. ¶ ~에서 in court / ~밖에서 out of court / ~에 서다 stand at the bar / ~에서 다투다 take 《*a person*》 to court; argue 《the case》 in court; bring a suit 〔an action〕 《against the Government》 / ~을 열다 hold a court / (사건을) ~으로 끌고 가다 bring 《*a matter*》 before the court; take 〔bring〕 (a case) into court / 죄인을 ~으로 끌어내다 drag a criminal into court / ~ 밖에서 해결하다 settle 《*a matter*》 out of court / 그 증인은 ~에 출두하지 않았다 The witness did not appear in court. / ~은 내주 월요일에 열린다 The court session will be held next Monday. / 그 건은 ~에서 다투게 될 것이다 The matter will be brought to court (for trial).
◉ ~모욕(죄) contempt of court: ~ 모욕죄로 기소되다 be charged with contempt of court. ~투쟁 a court battle. 대〔소〕~ the grand 〔a petty〕 courtroom 〔bench〕.

**법정**(法定) ~하다 provide 〔fix〕 by law; ordain 〔stipulate〕 by law. ¶ ~의 legal; statutory.
◉ ~가격 a legal price. ~과실 legal fruits. ~관리 《be under》 legal management; court receivership. ~구속 기간 the legal deadline for 《*a person's*》 detention. ~권한 legal authority. ~금리 the legal interest rate. ~기간 a legal term 〔period〕. ~기일 legal deadline. ~대리 legal representation: ~ 대리권 the right of legal representation / ~ 대리인 a legal representative. ~득표수 the minimum number of votes required by law for 《*a person*》 to be elected. ~ 상속인 an heir-at-law (*pl.* heirs-); a legal heir 《to》. ~세율 the statutory tariffs. ~수 《회의 정족수》 a quorum. ~운임 a legal fare. ~유예기간 legal delay; days of grace. ~의무 a legal duty. ~이율 the legal rate of interest. ~이자 legal interest. ~재산제 the legal property system. ~적립금〔준비금〕 legal reserves. ~전염병 an infectious disease designated by law; a notifiable disease. ~최고형 the maximum penalty allowable by law 《for》. ~호주상속인 the legal heir to a house; the heir-at-law. ~화폐 legal tender. ~후견인 《*a person's*》 legal guardian. ~휴일 《미》 a legal holiday; 《영》 a bank holiday.

**법제**(法制) legislation; legislative system. ◉ ~사(史) (a) legal history; (a) history of law 〔the legal system〕. ~사법위원회 the Legislation and Judiciary Committee. ~처 the Government Legislation Agency: ~처장 the Director of the Government Legislation Agency.

**법조**(法曹) the legal profession; 《사법관》 judicial officers; 《변호사》 a lawyer; an attorney 《미》.
◉ ~계 law 〔legal〕 circles; the judicial world; 《영》 the Bench and Bar.

**법주**(法主) 〖불교〗 《고승》 a Buddhist

high priest; 《법사》 the teacher of a Buddhist priest; 《종파의》 the head of a Buddhist Sect.

**법치**(法治) constitutional government. ◉ ∼국가 a law-governed country; a constitutional state. ∼사회 a community of law; a law-abiding society. ∼주의 constitutionalism; legalism: ∼주의자 a constitutionalist; a legalist.

**법칙**(法則) a law; a rule (★ 자연과학상의 법칙은 rule이 아니라 모두 law를 씀). ¶ 자연〔운동〕의 ∼ the law of nature 〔motion〕/ 물가는 수요와 공급의 ∼에 따른다 Prices follow the law of supply and demand. / 과학이란 자연의 ∼을 발견하는 것이다 Science is 〔means〕 (the) discovery of a law of nature.

**법통**(法統) 〖불교〗 a religious tradition. ¶ ∼을 잇다 receive the mantle 《of the preceding head of a sect》; succeed to the authority 《in a temple》.

**법하다** ① 《당연》 have good reason 〔justification〕 to be 〔*do*〕. ¶ 그가 성날 법도 하다 He has 「good reason 〔every right〕 to be angry. *or* He should be angry. ② 《상정》 there is reason to expect; it seems reasonable that; it can be expected that; it ought 〔is supposed〕 to be that; 《추측》 it seems likely that. ¶ 그가 올 법한데 He might come. / 그 키 큰 이가 대장일 ∼ That tall one must be the leader. / 비가 올 법도 하다 It looks like rain. / 그 일이 될 ∼ That seems likely to succeed. / 그럴 법한 일이다 That may well be. *or* That is very likely.

**법학**(法學) law; jurisprudence (법률학). ¶ ∼을 배우다 study 〔read〕 law; be educated in law. ◉ ∼도 a law student. ∼박사 《사람》 a doctor of laws; 《학위》 Doctor of Laws (생략 LL.D.). ∼부(部) 《대학의》 the law department; 《미》 a law school (★ 《미》에서는 주로 대학원). ∼사 《사람》 a bachelor of laws; 《학위》 Bachelor of Laws (생략 LL.B.). ∼석사 《사람》 a master of laws; 《학위》 Master of Laws (생략 LL.M.). ∼자 a jurist; a lawyer. ∼통론〔개론〕 a compendium of law; an outline of law. ∼협회 the Jurisprudence Society.

**법호**(法號) 〖불교〗 *one's* (posthumous) Buddhist name.

**법화**(法貨) legal tender; lawful money.

**법화**(法話) 〖불교〗 a Buddhist sermon 〔homily〕. ¶ ∼를 하다 preach a sermon.

**법화경**(法華經) 〖불교〗 the Sutra of the Lotus.

**법회**(法會) 〖불교〗 ① 《설법》 a Buddhist lecture meeting. ② 《재》 a Buddhist mass. ¶ ∼를 열다 hold a Buddhist mass; hold a memorial 〔religious〕 service 《for the dead》.

**벗** 《친구》 a friend; 《반려》 a companion; 《동료》 company. ⇨ 친구. ¶ 오랜〔진실한〕 벗 an old 〔a true〕 friend / 일생의 벗 a lifelong friend / 다년간의 벗 a friend of many years standing / …을 벗삼다 ⇨ 벗하다 / 김 군이라는 좋은 벗을 얻었다 I found a good friend in Kim. / 벗 따라 강남 간다 do anything for *one's* friend's sake; "go through hell and high water with *one's* friend".

**벗개다** 《날이 개다》 clear up.

**벗겨지다** ⇨ 벗기어지다.

**벗기다** ① 《몸에 걸친 것을》 strip 〔divest〕 《*a person*》 of 《*his* clothes》; take 〔strip〕 《*a person's* clothes》 off; unclothe 〔undress〕 《*a person*》; 《거들어서》 help 《*a person*》 off with 〔out of〕 《his overcoat》. ¶ 세관원은 사나이의 옷을 벗기고 몸을 수색했다 The customs officers stripped the man of his clothes and searched him 〔his body〕. / 소녀는 노마님의 외투를 벗겨드렸다 The girl helped the old woman off with her coat.
② 《껍질 등을》 peel (손으로); pare (칼로); shuck 《corn》; hull 《peas》; husk; skin (off); flay; tear 〔peel〕 off (떼어내다). ¶ 나무껍질을 ∼ bark 〔strip the bark from〕 a tree; strip a tree of its bark / 귤 껍질을 ∼ peel an orange / 사과 껍질을 ∼ pare an apple / 바나나 껍질을 ∼ strip the skin from a banana; peel off the skin of a banana / 콩깍지를 ∼ shell 〔pod〕 peas.
③ 《붙어 있거나 덮인 것을》 remove; take off; undo. ¶ 녹을 ∼ get the rust off / 담요를 ∼ take off the blanket / 때를 ∼ rub 〔scrape〕 off the dirt / 가면을 ∼ unmask 〔take off the mask of〕 《a villain》; debunk (정체를) / 뚜껑을 ∼ take off 〔undo〕 the lid; open / 지붕에서 기와를 ∼ remove tiles from the roof / 통의 테를 ∼ unhoop a barrel; take off hoops.
④ 《빗장을》 unbar 〔unbolt〕 《the gate》.

**벗기어지다** ① 《몸에 걸친 것이》 come off. ¶ 단추가 벗겨져 있다 be unbuttoned / 내 장갑이 벗겨지지 않는다 My gloves won't come off. ② 《껍질·가죽이》 get stripped off; peel off; fall 〔come〕 off (칠·비늘 따위가). ¶ 페인트칠이 ∼ the paint peels off. ③ 《덮은 것이》 get removed; be taken off. ④ 《빗장 등이》 be unbarred

〔unbolted〕.

**벗나가다** go beyond the limit; go wrong; deviate 〔swerve〕《from》; go astray; [비유적] behave improperly. ¶ 벗나간 짓 an outrageous act.

**벗다** ① 《몸에 걸친 것을》 take 〔pull〕 《*one's* coat》 off; strip 〔divest〕 *oneself* of 《*one's* shirt》; remove 《*one's* hat》; slip off 《*one's* clothes》 (후딱); pull off 《*one's* gloves》 (잡아 빼듯이); fling 〔throw〕 off 《*one's* boots》 (팽개치듯이). ¶ 급히 ~ rush out of 《*one's* nightgown》/ 모자를〔안경을〕 ~ take off 〔remove〕 *one's* hat 〔the glasses〕/ 가면을 ~ throw off *one's* mask / 옷을 벗다 get undressed; undress 〔unclothe〕 *one-self;* get out of *one's* clothes / 신발을 핵 벗어 던지다 kick off *one's* shoes / 웃통을 벗고 일하다 work bare to the waist / 신은 벗지 않아도 좋다 You may keep your shoes on.
② 《허물을》 slip out of 《its skin》; cast (off) 〔shed〕 《the skin》; slough (off); leave the cocoon (곤충이).
③ 《누명·혐의 등을》 clear 〔divest〕 *one-self* of 《a false charge》. ¶ 누명을 ~ clear *oneself* of a bad name / 오해를 ~ remove a misunderstanding / 혐의를 ~ [사람이 주어] clear *oneself* of the charge 《of theft》; have *one's* innocence established.
④ 《짐을》 unburden *oneself* of; 《책임을》 be freed 〔released〕 from 《*one's* duty》; rid *oneself* of 《responsibility》. ¶ 짐을 ~ take off *one's* load; put *one's* load down.
⑤ 《티·때를》 get rid of "dirt"; get polished 〔refined〕. ¶ 촌티를 벗은 free from boorishness 〔vulgarity〕/ 촌티를 ~ get citified 〔sophisticated, polished〕; "get the hayseed out of his hair" / 어린 티를 ~ grow out of childhood.

**벗어나다** ① 《헤어나다》 get out of 《difficulties》; free *oneself* from 〔of〕 《a bondage》; escape from 《danger》; get rid 〔clear〕 of; rid *oneself* of 《a bad habit》; weather (폭풍우 등을). ¶ 벗어날 수 없는 unavoidable 《disasters》; inevitable 《fate》/ 가난에서 ~ overcome poverty / 구속〔빚, 속박〕에서 ~ free *oneself* from bondage 〔debt, fetters〕/ 궁지를 ~ get out of difficulty 〔trouble〕/ 법망을 ~ slip from the clutches of the law; evade the law / 슬럼프에서 ~ pull *oneself* out of the slump / 악습에서 ~ break *oneself* 〔get rid〕 of a bad habit / 오랜 습관에서 ~ slough off old habits / 위기에서 ~ get 〔pass〕 through a crisis; circumvent a crisis / 재정 위기를 ~ weather a financial crisis / 죽음에서 ~ escape death; be saved from death / 질곡에서 ~ shake off fetters; cast off the yoke 《of》/ 그 민족은 아직 야만적인 상태를 벗어나지 못했다 The people are little removed from barbarism. / 그는 타자를 삼진으로 잡아 핀치를 벗어났다 He worked himself out of a jam by striking out the batter.
② 《눈 밖에 나다》 be out of 《*a person's*》 favor; incur 〔fall under〕 《*a person's*》 displeasure. ¶ 하는 짓이 남의 눈에 ~ *one's* ways fail to find favor in the eyes of another / 그는 하는 일마다 주인의 눈에 벗어났다 Everything he did displeased his employer.
③ 《크게 어그러지다》 depart from; deviate 〔swerve〕 《from》; be contrary to; be against. ¶ 규칙에 ~ be against the rules 〔law〕/ 도리에 ~ be contrary to reason / 예의에 ~ get against etiquette / 인정에 벗어난 짓을 하다 deviate 〔swerve〕 from the path of humanity.
④ 《빗나가다》 miss the mark; go wide 〔astray〕; stray 〔swerve〕 《from》. ¶ 과녁을 ~ miss the target; go wide of the mark / (배가) 침로를 ~ swerve from the course; sheer 《off》/ 이야기가 주제에서 ~ go astray 〔diverge〕 from the main subject / 위성이 지구 궤도를 벗어났다 The satellite 「strayed out of 〔strayed away from〕 its orbit around the earth.

**벗어버리다** ① 《옷 따위를》 take 〔cast, fling, throw〕 《*one's* coat》 off; shed 《*one's* clothes》; kick 《*one's* slippers》 off. ¶ 함부로 ~ throw 《clothes》 in a heap / 아무데(에)나 ~ throw 《clothes》 anywhere. ② 《누명·혐의 등을》 clear 〔divest〕 *oneself* completely 《of》; 《책임 등을》 be freed 〔released〕 from 《*one's* duty》; unburden *oneself* of. ⇨ 벗다[1] ②, ③.

**벗어부치다** slip out of a dress; take 〔cast, throw〕 off. ¶ 웃통을 벗어부치고 일하다 work bare to the waist.

**벗어지다** ① 《몸에 걸친 것이》 come 〔slip〕 off; slip down. ¶ 장갑〔신〕이 벗어지지 않는다 My gloves 〔shoes〕 won't come off. / 치마가 자꾸 벗어진다 My skirt keeps slipping off. ② 《칠·껍질·비늘 등이》 come 〔fall〕 off 《in layers, in scales》; peel 〔scale〕 off; exfoliate; be worn off. ¶ (생선의) 비늘이 ~ scale off / 페인트칠이 ~ the paint comes 〔peels〕 off / 나무껍질이 벗어지고 있다 The bark is peeling off the tree. ③ 《대머리가 되다》 become 〔go, grow〕 bald; lose *one's* hair. ¶ 이마가 벗어진 bald in the front / 그는 젊은 나이에 머리가 벗어졌다 He has become bald-headed prematurely 〔before *one's* time〕. ④ 《피부가》 peel off; be grazed 〔abraded〕. ¶ 무릎이 ~ skin 〔bark〕 *one's* knee; have *one's* knee skinned / 햇볕에 타서 어깨의 살가죽이 벗어졌다 The skin of my shoulders peeled off from too much exposure to the sun.

**벗하다** ① 《벗삼다》 associate 〔keep company〕 with…; make friends 《with》; 「strike up 〔contract〕 a friendship 《with》. ¶ 나는 장애자를 벗하기로 마음먹었다 I resolved to make friends with physically handicapped. ② [비유적] make a companion 《of》; have 《*something*》 for a companion; live with. ¶ 자연을 벗하고 살다 live in communion with nature; live in the bosom of nature / 책을 ~ have books for companions; live with books / 풍월을 벗하고 지내다 live with nature.

**벙거지** 《옛 하인들의》 a felt hat; 《옛 군인의》 a soldier's hat 〔helmet〕; 《모자》 headgear; a hat. ¶ ~ 시울 만지는 소리 vague 〔indistinct, imprecise, fuzzy〕 words.

**벙그레** ⇨ 방그레.

**벙글거리다, 벙긋거리다** (radiantly) smile 《at》; beam 《upon *a person*》; be all smiles; look happy. ¶ 그는 언제 봐도 벙글거리고 있다 No matter when I see him, he's always smiling.

**벙글벙글, 벙긋벙긋** with a broad smile; smilingly; cheerfully. ¶ ~ 웃는 얼굴 a smiling 〔beaming〕 face; a radiant look.

**벙벙하다** be stunned 《by》; be struck dumb with astonishment; be dum(b)-founded 《by》. ¶ 놀라서 어안이 ~ be struck dumb with surprise; be 〔stand〕 aghast / 어처구니가 없어서 ~ feel 〔be〕 utterly shocked 《at》 / 벙벙히 서 있지 (만) 말고 무엇 좀 해라 Don't stand there like a bump on a log—do something! / 그의 어리석음에 어안이 벙벙하여 말이 안 나온다 His stupidity really staggers me.

**벙실거리다** smile sweetly. ⇨ 방글거리다.

**벙어리**[1] 《말 못하는》 a mute; a dumb person; a speech-handicapped person. ¶ ~의 dumb; mute / ~ 냉가슴 앓듯 (하다) suffer in silence / ~가 되다 become dumb; lose *one's* speech / ~ 시늉을 하다 play dumb; play the dummy. ◉ ~장갑 (a pair of) mittens.

**벙어리**[2] 《저금통》 a saving box; 《영》 a moneybox; 《질그릇 저금통》 a piggy bank.

**벙커** 《골프》 a bunker; a sand trap; 〖군사〗 a bunker.

**벙커시유**(―C油) bunker C oil.

**벚꽃** cherry blossoms 〔flowers〕. ◉ ~놀이 a cherry-blossom viewing; 《행락》 a picnic 〔party〕 under the cherry blossoms.

**벚나무** 〖식물〗 a cherry tree.

**베** 《삼베》 hemp cloth; 《무명베》 cotton cloth. ¶ 베를 짜다 weave / 베 짜는 사람 a weaver. ◉ 베실 hemp thread.

**베개** a pillow; a headrest. ¶ (침대용의) 긴 ~ a bolster / ~를 베다 pillow; lay 〔rest〕 *one's* head on a pillow / ~를 베고 with *one's* head on a pillow / ~를 높이 하고 자다 [비유적] sleep with a clear conscience; sleep in peace; sleep free from care 〔fear〕 / 팔~를 베다 pillow 〔rest〕 *one's* head on *one's* arm. ◉ 베갯모 embroidered pads attached to both sides 〔ends〕 of a pillow for decoration. 베갯속 the stuffing of a pillow. 베갯잇 a pillow-case; a pillow-slip; a pillow-cover.

**베갯머리** the end of a pillow; *one's* bedside. ¶ ~에(서) by 〔at〕 《*a person's*》 bedside / ~에 앉다 sit up by 《*a person's*》 bedside.

**베갯밑공사**(―公事) a wife's requests to her husband in private; a curtain lecture. ¶ ~에 안 넘어가다 turn a deaf ear to *one's* wife's private requests.

**베고니아** 〖식물〗 a begonia.

**베끼다** 《옮겨쓰다》 copy; take 〔make〕 a copy 《of》; transcribe (필사); 《모사하다》 trace; copy 《a figure》; reproduce. ¶ (공)책을 ~ copy a (note)book / 책에서 문제를 ~ copy (out) a problem from a book / 이것은 그 편지를 베낀 것이다 This is a copy of the letter.

**베네룩스** Benelux. [<*Be*lgium, *Ne*therlands and *Lux*emburg]

**베네수엘라** 《남미의 공화국》 (the Republic of) Venezuela. ¶ ~의 Venezuelan. ◉ ~사람 a Venezuelan.

**베니스** Venice. ¶ ~의 사람 a Venetian / ~의 상인 《책이름》 *The Merchant of Venice.*

**베니어** veneer (★ 영어의 veneer는 plywood나 가구 등의 겉에 붙이는 상질의 판을 말함). ◉ ~톱 a veneer saw.

**베니어판**(―板) a sheet of plywood; a plywood board; [총칭] plywood. ¶ 벽

에다 ～을 대다 cover the walls with plywood.

**베다¹** 《베개를》 lay 〔rest〕 *one's* head on 《a pillow》; pillow on; use as a pillow. ¶ …을 베고 자다 sleep with *one's* head (pillowed) on 《*a thing*》.

**베다²** 《자르다》 cut (with a sharp-edged instrument); saw (톱으로); clip; shear (가위로); 《풀을》 mow; cut down; 《베어 넘기다》 fell; hew; cut down; 《벼·보리 등을》 reap; gather in; harvest. ¶ 얇게 ～ slice / 잘게 ～ chop up 〔fine〕; cut into pieces; hack to pieces; hackle; hash; mangle (난도질하다) / 나무를 ～ cut down 〔fell〕 a tree / 목을 ～ cut off 《*a person's*》 head; behead 《*a person*》; 《해고하다》 fire; dismiss; 《구어》 sack; 《구어》 give 《a worker》 the sack / 손가락을 ～ cut *one's* finger 《on a knife》/ 고기 한 점을 ～ cut a slice of meat / 면도를 하다가 턱을 베었다 I cut my chin while shaving.

**베다³** 〖불교〗 Veda(s). ◉ ～문학 Vedic literature.

**베도라치** 〖어류〗 a gunnel.

**베드** a bed. ¶ 싱글〔더블〕～ a single 〔double〕 bed. ◉ ～룸 a bedroom. ～메이킹 bedmaking. ～신 a bedroom scene. ～커버 a bedcover; a bedspread. ～타운 a commuter town; a dormitory suburb; 《미》 a bedroom community.

**베드로** 〖성서〗 Saint 〔Simon〕 Peter (? - A.D. 67?). ◉ ～전〔후〕서 The First 〔Second〕 Epistle of St. Peter (생략 I〔II〕 Pet.).

**베란다** a veranda(h); a porch 《미》.

**베레, 베레모**(―帽) a beret. ¶ ～를 비스듬히 눌러쓰다 have a beret pulled on sidewise above *one's* face.

**베르무트** 《백포도주》 verm(o)uth.

**베르사유** 《프랑스의 도시》 Versailles. ◉ ～조약〔궁전〕 the Versailles Treaty 〔Palace〕.

**베른조약**(―條約) the Bern(e) Convention (저작권에 관한).

**베를린** 《독일의 수도》 Berlin. ◉ ～시민 a Berliner. ～장벽 the Berlin Wall.

**베릴륨** 〖화학〗 beryllium(기호 Be).

**베링** 《덴마크의 항해가》 Vitus Bering (1680-1741). ◉ ～해 (the) Bering Sea. ～해협 the Bering Strait.

**베물다** cut 《*a thing*》 off with *one's* teeth; bite 〔gnaw〕 off. ¶ 혀를 ～ bite through 〔off〕 *one's* tongue.

**베스트** the 〔*one's*〕 best. ¶ ～를 다하다 do *one's* best; do all *one* can. ◉ ～드레서 the best dresser; the best-dressed man 〔woman〕. ～멤버 the best members 《of the team》: ～멤버를 갖추다 choose the best members. ～셀러 a best seller; a best-selling book: ～셀러 작가 a best-selling author 〔writer〕. ～텐 the best ten; the ten best 《hitters for the season》.

**베슥거리다** shirk *one's* duties 〔job〕; be backward 《in *doing*》; be reluctant 〔unwilling〕 《to *do*》; take little interest 《in》; have no inclination 《to *do*》.

**베어내다** cut off 〔out, away〕; excise; 《풀을》 mow 《the grass》; cut down. ¶ 고기 한 점을 ～ cut off a slice of meat.

**베어넘기다** 《나무를》 fell 《a tree》; cut 《a tree》 down.

**베어링** 〖기계〗 a bearing. ¶ 롤러 ～ a roller bearing / 볼～ a ball bearing. ◉ ～공업 the (ball and roller) bearing industry.

**베어먹다** cut off and eat. ¶ 케이크를 ～ slice a cake to eat / 사과를 우적우적 ～ munch at an apple.

**베어버리다** cut; cut down. ¶ 단칼에 ～ cut down with one stroke.

**베옷** hempen clothes.

**베이다** get 《it》 cut; get a cut 《on》. ¶ 칼에 손가락을 ～ get a cut on the finger with a knife.

**베이스¹** ① 《기준·토대》 a base; a basis (*pl.* bases); 《화장》 a base. ¶ 임금 ～ a wage base. ② 《기지》 a base. ③ 〖야구〗 a base. ¶ 1〔2, 3〕루 ～ (the) first 〔second, third〕 base. ◉ ～라인 a base line. ～러닝 base running. ～업 a raise of the wage base: ～업을 요구하다 demand a raise (in the wage level).

**베이스²** 〖음악〗 bass (남성의 최저 음역); a bass (악기). ◉ ～가수 a bass (singer). ～기타 a bass guitar.

**베이스볼** 《play》 baseball. ⇨ 야구.

**베이스온볼** 〖야구〗 a base on balls; a walk; a pass. ¶ ～을 내다 give 《a batter》 a base on balls; walk 《a batter》 / ～로 일루에 나가다 get a base 〔walk to first〕 on balls; get a walk.

**베이스캠프** 〖등산〗 a base camp.

**베이식** 〖컴퓨터〗 BASIC; Basic (규격화된 일상어를 사용하는 초급의 프로그래밍 언어). 〔<*B*eginner's *A*ll-purpose *S*ymbolic *I*nstruction *C*ode〕

**베이지** 《담갈색》 beige.

**베이징** 《중국의 수도》 Beijing.

**베이커리** 《빵집》 a bakery.

**베이컨** 《식품》 《a slice of》 bacon. ◉ ～에그 bacon and eggs.

**베이클라이트** 《상표명》 Bakelite.
**베이킹파우더** baking powder.
**베일** a veil. ¶ ～을 쓰고 under the veil of / ～을 쓰다 veil *one's* face; muffle *one's* face in a veil / ～을 쓰고 있다 wear 〔be in〕 a veil / ～을 벗다 unveil; reveal *oneself* / 신비의 ～에 싸여 있다 be veiled 〔wrapped〕 in mystery.
**베짱이** 〖곤충〗 a grasshopper; a katydid. ¶ ～가 운다 Grasshoppers chirp.
**베타** beta; $\beta$. ◉ ～나프톨 betanaphthol. ～선 beta rays. ～입자 beta particles.
**베테랑** a veteran; an expert (숙달자); an old hand (노련한 사람); an old-timer (고참). ¶ 그 방면의 ～ an old-timer in *one's* line / 그는 ～ 외교관이다 He is a veteran 〔seasoned〕 diplomat.
**베트남** 《인도차이나의 공화국》 (the Socialist Republic of ) Vietnam; Viet-Nam. ¶ ～의 Vietnamese. ◉ ～말 Vietnamese. ～사람 a Vietnamese.
**베틀** a loom. ¶ ～로 짜다 weave 《fabric》 on a loom.
**베풀다** ① 《잔치 등을》 hold; give; throw 《a party》 《구어》. ¶ 잔치를 ～ hold a feast 〔banquet〕; give a banquet / 베풀어지다 be held 〔given〕; take place; come off / 떠나기 앞서 그녀는 큰 연회를 베풀었다 Previous to her departure she gave a big party. ② 《은혜 따위를》 grant 《*a person* a favor》; give 《money, things》 in charity; bestow 《a favor on *a person*》; confer on; render. ¶ 은혜를 ～ bestow a favor 《on *a person*》; show 《*a person*》 a favor / 자비를 ～ have mercy 《on》; show 《*a person*》 mercy / 자선을 ～ give alms; render aid 《to *a person*》 / 선정을 ～ govern well; rule wisely / 그는 가난한 사람들에게 자선을 베풀었다 He gave alms to the poor.
**벡터** 〖물리·수학〗 a vector. ◉ ～공간 the vector space. ～함수 a vector function. ～해석 vector analysis.
**벤젠** 〖화학〗 benzene; benzol. ◉ ～핵〔환〕 benzene nucleus 〔ring〕.
**벤진** 〖화학〗 benzine; benzoline.
**벤처기업**〔**비즈니스**〕 a venture business.
**벤처캐피털** 〖경제〗 (a) venture 〔risk 《영》〕 capital.
**벤처컬처** 《적극적·모험적 풍토》 venture culture.
**벤처펀드** venture fund.
**벤치** a bench; 〖야구〗 a (player's) bench (선수석); a dugout; 《감독》 a manager (on the bench). ¶ 선수를 ～로 불러들이다 bench a player.
◉ ～워머 a bench warmer.
**벤틸레이터** a ventilator.
**벨** a bell; a doorbell (현관의). ¶ 벨이 울리는 소리 the sound of the bell; the ringing of the bell / 벨을 누르다 press 〔push, touch〕 the bell 〔button〕 / 벨을 울리다 ring 〔touch〕 the bell / 벨을 울려 하녀〔간호사〕를 부르다 ring for a maid 〔nurse〕 / 벨이 울린다 《손님이다》 There is the bell. / 따르릉 벨이 울렸다 R-r-ring! went the bell. *or* The bell went r-r-ring. / 현관의 벨이 울리고 있다 There is a ring at the door. ◉ ～보이 a bellboy; a bell-hop 《미》.
**벨기에** 《유럽의 왕국》 (the Kingdom of ) Belgium. ¶ ～의 Belgian; Belgic. ◉ ～사람 a Belgian.
**벨로드롬** 《경륜장》 a velodrome.
**벨로루시** (Republic of ) Belarus.
**벨벳** 《옷감》 (a) velvet. ¶ ～과 같은 velvety / ～같은 잔디밭 a velvet lawn / ～처럼 매끄러운 as smooth as velvet.
**벨트** ① 《밴드·기계의》 a belt. ¶ 좌석 ～a seat belt / ～를 매다 fasten 〔buckle (on)〕 *one's* belt / 곧 착륙합니다 ～를 매주십시오 We'll be landing soon. Please fasten your seat belt. ② 《지대》 ¶ 그린 ～ a green belt / 콘～ the Corn Belt. ◉ ～컨베이어 a belt conveyer.
**벵골** 《본래 인도의 주》 Bengal. ¶ ～의 Bengalese; Bengali; Bengalee. ◉ ～만 the Bay of Bengal. ～사람 a Bengalese; a Bengali; a Bengalee.
**벼** 〖식물〗 rice; a rice plant; paddy; 《낟알》 a kernel of (unhusked) rice. ¶ 벼의 그루터기 a rice stubble / 벼베기 rice reaping; harvesting of the rice / 논에 벼를 심다 plant rice in the paddy field / 벼를 베다 mow 〔cut down〕 rice (plants); harvest 〔reap〕 rice / 벼를 타작하다 thresh rice (plants) / 벼가 잘 자라고 있다 The rice is doing well. / 벼는 논에 심는다 Rice is planted in a rice paddy.
**벼농사**(―農事) rice farming. ～하다 do 〔engage in〕 rice farming. ¶ ～의 대풍작 a huge bumper rice crop.
**벼락** thunder (천둥); lightning (번개); a thunderbolt (천둥번개). ⇨ 벼락 맞다. ¶ ～같은 thunderous / ～ 소리 a clap 〔crack〕 of thunder / ～같은 소리를 지르다 thunder out; cry in a thunderous voice / ～이 떨어지다 [장소가 주어] be hit by a stroke of lightning; be struck by lightning; [비유적] get a 《good》 scolding; catch it (hot) 《구

어》/ ~이나 맞아 죽어라 May lightning hit you!

**벼락감투** ①《돈으로 판》official positions sold to individuals to raise government funds. ¶ ~를 쓰다 become a government official overnight. ②《정실의》a government position given to an unqualified person as a political favor; a patronage appointment; a political plum. ¶ ~를 쓰다 go from nobody to government official overnight / ~를 씌우다 make an absurd appointment; give an office as a political plum《to *a person*》.

**벼락공부**(―工夫) cramming; cram. ~하다 cram (up). ¶ 시험 때문에 ~하다 cram 〔get crammed〕 for an examination / 영어를 ~하다 cram (up) English.

**벼락대신**(―大臣) a tough nut (to crack); a tough guy. ¶ 그는 ~이다 He is a tough nut (to crack).

**벼락맞다** be struck 〔hit〕 by lightning. ¶ 벼락 맞은 thunderstruck; thunder-stricken / 벼락 맞아 죽다 be struck dead by lightning / 벼락 맞을 놈 Drop dead! / 벼락 맞을 것 Hell! / 너, 그런 짓 하면 벼락 맞는다 If you do (that), there will be hell to pay!

**벼락부자**(―富者) an overnight 〔a mushroom〕 millionaire; a new rich; a *nouveau riche* (F.); an upstart; the new(ly) rich [총칭]. ¶ 전쟁 경기를 탄 ~ a war-made millionaire; a war profiteer / ~가 되다 gain sudden wealth; become 〔get〕 rich suddenly; strike it rich / 토지로 그는 ~가 되었다 Land made him 「a rich man 〔an upstart〕.

**벼락치기** hasty preparation. ¶ ~의 hastily prepared / ~로 지은 집 a hurriedly constructed building; a jerry-built house / 이제 와서 ~로 공부해 봤자 별수 없을 게다 It's too late now 「to study 〔to cram〕 for the examination.

**벼락치다** lightning strikes 〔hits〕; a thunderbolt falls. ¶ 근처에 벼락(이) 쳤다 The thunderbolt fell close by. / 벼락치는 하늘도 속인다 You can fool anybody if you want to.

**벼랑** a cliff (특히 해안의); a precipice (깎아지른); a bluff (해안이나 계곡의). ¶ ~ 끝 《stand on》 the edge of a precipice; the brink / ~ 끝 정책〔외교〕《구어》brinkmanship / ~을 기어오르다 climb 〔scale〕 a cliff; go over a precipice / ~에서 떨어지다 fall over a precipice 〔a cliff〕; tumble down a precipice / 자동차가 ~에서 바다로 떨어졌다 A car went over the cliff 〔precipice〕 and fell in(to) the sea.

**벼루** 《먹을 가는》an inkstone; an ink slab. ¶ ~에 먹을 갈다 rub an ink stick on the inkstone.

◉ 벼룻돌 (stone used as) an inkstone. 벼룻물 ink(stone) water; water for an inkstone; ink. 벼룻집 《연상(硯箱)》a stationery cabinet; a writing case; 《연갑》an inkstone case.

**벼룩** a flea. ¶ ~에 물리다 be bitten by a flea / ~에 물린 자국 a fleabite / ~에 시달리다 be tormented by fleas / ~을 잡다 catch fleas; hunt fleas / ~의 간을 내어 먹다 skin a flea for its hide.

◉ ~시장 a flea market. ~약 flea powder.

**벼르다** 《마음먹다》intend《to *do*》; plan 《on *do*ing, to *do*》; contemplate 《*do*ing》; be intent 〔bent〕 on 《*do*ing, *something*》; be eager 〔determined〕 《to *do*》. ¶ 죽이려고 ~ contemplate 〔be plotting〕 murder; have (evil) designs on 《*a person's*》 life / 우리는 세계 일주 여행을 벼르고 있다 We are planning to make an around-the=world trip. / 그 소녀는 오랫동안 벼르던 모자를 샀다 The girl bought the hat she had been wanting 〔thinking about〕 for a long time. / "어디 보자" 하고, 그는 벼르며 나갔다 He left, saying "We shall see."

**벼리** ① 《그물의》the guide ropes (at the edge of a fishing net). ② 《책의》contents (목차).

**벼리다** put an edge on 《a knife by forging》; forge a blade on. ¶ 부엌칼을 ~ forge the edge on a kitchen knife.

**벼멸구** 〚곤충〛 a rice insect; a leafhopper.

**벼슬** a government post; official rank. ~하다 take office; enter the government service; obtain a post in the government. ¶ ~이 높다〔낮다〕 be of high 〔low〕 government position; be high 〔low〕 in official rank / ~을 그만두다 resign from government service / ~을 얻다〔잃다〕 secure 〔lose〕 a government position / ~을 올리다 raise 〔promote〕 《*a person*》 in official rank / ~ 자리에 앉아 있다 be in government service; be at service as an official.

**벼슬길** the way (to get) into the government service; government employ 〔service〕. ¶ ～에 오르다 enter government service; start *one's* official career.

**벼슬살이** life as an official; *one's* official life; government service. ～하다 be in government service; serve as a government official. ¶ 그는 30년 동안 ～를 하고 있다 He has been in government service for thirty years.

**벼슬아치** a government 〔public〕 official. ¶ ～가 되다 enter (into) the government service; get employment in a government office / ～ 노릇을 그만두다 leave 〔retire from〕 office.
◉ ～근성 officialism. ～생활 an official life 〔career〕.

**벼훑이** a threshing machine; a rice=thresher.

**벽**(壁) ① a (plastered) wall; 《칸막이》 a partition (wall). ¶ 벽이 있는 walled / 벽을 바르다 plaster a wall / 벽을 사이에 두고 《live》 with a wall between 《us》 / 벽을 칠하다 paint a wall 《white》 / 벽에 그림을 걸다 hang a picture on the wall / 벽에 기대다 lean against the wall / 벽을 치다〔쌓다〕 build a wall. ② 《장벽》 a (blank) wall; a barrier. ¶ (45초대의) 벽을 깨다 break the (45-second) barrier 《for 400 meters》 / (곤란한) 벽에 부딪치다 「run into 〔come up against〕 a stone 〔brick〕 wall; 「come to 〔reach〕 a deadlock / 우리의 목적을 달성하려면 기술상의 벽을 뚫어야 한다 We need a technological breakthrough if we are to achieve our purpose.

**벽**(癖) ① 《버릇》 a habit; a trick; a way; a characteristic. ¶ 도벽 thievish habits; 《구어》 sticky fingers / 방랑벽 the habit of wandering about / 주벽 drinking habits. ② 《기습(奇習)》 a peculiarity; an eccentric habit; an eccentricity; an idiosyncrasy.

**벽개**(劈開) 〖광물〗 cleavage. ～하다 cleave. ◉ ～면 a plane of cleavage.

**벽걸이**(壁—) a wall tapestry; a wall=hanging.

**벽난로**(壁煖爐) a fireplace; a hearth.

**벽돌**(壁—) a (piece of) brick. ¶ 붉은 ～ (a) red brick / ～로 지은 집 a brick house / ～색의 bricky; brick-red / ～로 짓다 build 《a house》 of brick 〔with bricks〕 / ～을 굽다 bake 〔burn, fire, make〕 bricks / ～을 쌓다 lay bricks / 그 길은 ～이 깔려 있다 The road is paved with bricks.
◉ ～공 a bricklayer; a brickmason; 《제조공》 a brickmaker. ～공장 a brickyard; brick works. ～담 a brick wall. ～조각 a brickbat. ～집 a brick (-built) house. 나무～ (a) wood brick. 화장〔오지〕～ (a) dressed 〔glazed〕 brick.

**벽두**(劈頭) ① 《글의》 the opening 《of a book, composition》. ② 《일의》 the first; the outset. ¶ ～에 at the very beginning; in the first place; first of all; to begin 〔start〕 with; at the outset / ～부터 from the start 〔outset〕 / 예산 위원회는 ～부터 격론이 벌어졌다 The budget committee opened with a sharp exchange of words.

**벽력**(霹靂) a peal 〔clap〕 of thunder; a (thunder)bolt. ¶ 청천 ～ a bolt from the blue / ～ 같은 소리를 지르다 roar 〔thunder〕 《at》 / 한밤중에 그녀가 귀가했을 때 그는 그녀에게 ～같이 소리를 질렀다 He thundered 〔barked〕 at her when she got home after midnight.

**벽면**(壁面) the face 〔surface〕 of a wall.

**벽보**(壁報) a wall newspaper; a bill; a poster; a placard. ¶ 괴～ a strange 〔mysterious〕 poster; an illegal bill / ～를 붙이다 put up a bill 〔poster〕; stick a bill 《on a wall》 / ～ 금지 《게시》 Stick 〔Post〕 no bills here.

**벽서**(壁書) writing(s) on a wall.

**벽성**(僻姓) an unusual 〔an odd, a rare〕 surname.

**벽시계**(壁時計) a wall clock.

**벽신문**(壁新聞) a wall newspaper.

**벽안**(碧眼) blue eyes. ¶ ～의 금발 여인 a blue-eyed blonde. ◉ ～자염(紫髯) blue eyes and red beard.

**벽오동**(碧梧桐) 〖식물〗 a Chinese parasol (tree); a Phoenix tree.

**벽옥**(碧玉) 〖광물〗 jasper; green jade.

**벽자**(僻字) an odd and rare character; 「an unusual 〔a queer〕 letter.

**벽장**(壁欌) 〖건축〗 a wall closet 〔cupboard〕; a built-in closet.

**벽장코** a snub 〔pug, flat〕 nose.

**벽지**(僻地) a secluded place; an isolated area; a remote corner of the country; an out-of-the-way place; the backcountry 《미》. ¶ ～에 살다 live in a remote country place / 오늘날 이 나라에서는 어떤 ～에서도 텔레비전을 즐길 수 있다 Today you can enjoy 〔watch〕 television programs in any out-of-the-way place in this country.
◉ ～(학교)교육 (school) education in remote rural areas.

**벽지**(壁紙) wallpaper. ¶ ～를 바르다

wallpaper; paper a wall.

**벽창호**(碧昌—) an obstinate 〔incorrigible〕 person; a pigheaded 〔stubborn〕 person.

**벽촌**(僻村) a remote village; an out-of-the-way hamlet.

**벽토**(壁土) wall mud; plaster; stucco.

**벽해**(碧海) the blue sea; the azure ocean.

**벽화**(壁畫) a mural; a wall 〔mural〕 painting; 《프레스코화》 a fresco (*pl.* ~es, ~s). ¶ 고분의 ~ mural paintings in a tumulus; the ancient tomb mural. ◉ ~가 a muralist; a mural painter.

**변** secret language. ⇨ 변말.

**변**(便) 《대소변》 excreta; excrement; 《대변》 feces; stool; motions. ¶ 묽은〔굳은〕 변 loose 〔hard〕 feces / 변을 보다 evacuate the bowels; ease 〔relieve〕 nature; 《소변을》 urinate; make 〔pass〕 water. ◉ 변검사 an examination of the feces: 변검사를 하다 examine *a person's* feces 〔stool(s)〕.

**변**[1](邊) ① 〖수학〗 a side (다각형의); a member (등식·부등식의). ¶ 삼각형의 세 변 the three sides of a triangle / 정사각형의 네 변의 길이는 같다 The four sides of a square are equal in length. ② 《바둑의》 the side areas (of a *paduk* board). ③ 《과녁의》 the fringe 〔periphery〕 of the bull's-eye of a target. ④ 《가장자리》 a side; an edge; a verge. ¶ 강변 the riverside. ⑤ 《한자의》 the left-side 〔left-hand〕 radical of a Chinese character.

**변**[2](邊) 《변리》 interest (on money). ¶ 비싼〔싼〕 변으로 at a high 〔low〕 rate of interest / 5푼 변이 붙다 bear interest at 5 percent.

**변**(變) 《돌발사》 an incident; a dire happening; 《사고》 an accident; 《재난》 a disaster; a calamity; a misfortune; 《난리》 a disturbance; a change (for the worse). ¶ 변이 나다 an accident 〔incident〕 occurs; something happens / 변을 당하다 have a mishap; meet with an accident / 무슨 변이 났나 왜 안 오지 What can have happened?—Why doesn't he come? / 이런 변을 봤나 Why, I've never known such a thing to happen.

**변격**(變格) irregularity; anomaly; 〖문법〗 irregular conjugation (불규칙 변화).

**변경**(邊境) a frontier (district) (★《미》에서 개척지와 미개척지의 경계 지방); a borderland (국경 지방); 《벽지》 a remote region; outlying districts. ¶ ~에서 《live》 on 〔at〕 the frontier / ~을 침범하다 violate a frontier.

**변경**(變更) (an) alteration; (a) change; 《수정》 (a) modification (일부의); (an) amendment. ~하다 alter; change; modify (일부를); amend. ¶ ~할 수 있는 alterable; changeable / ~할 수 없는 unalterable; unchangeable / 외교 정책의 ~ reorientation of a foreign policy / 항로의 ~ deviation / ~을 가하다 make a change 《in》; make alterations 《in》; make an amendment 《to》 / 날짜를 ~하다 change the date 《of》 / 예정의 일부를 ~하다 change a part of the schedule / 아들 명의로 ~하다 transfer 《property》 to *one's* son / 임대차 계약 조건의 일부를 ~하다 modify the terms of a lease / 예정에 ~ 없음 The schedule remains unchanged. / 마감일은 3월 10일이다. 이것은 절대 ~할 수 없다 The deadline is the 10th of March. That's final. / 기재된 가격은 ~될 수도 있습니다 The prices quoted are subjected to change 〔alteration〕.

**변고**(變故) an incident (사건); an accident (사고); 《재난》 a disaster; a mishap; a calamity; an emergency (돌발적인); (a) trouble. ¶ ~ 없이 지내다 get along with no trouble(s) / ~를 당하다 have a mishap 〔an accident〕 / ~에 대비하다 prepare against a disaster / 그에게 무슨 ~라도 생긴게 아닌지 I am afraid something unforeseen has happened to him.

**변광성**(變光星) 〖천문〗 a variable star.

**변괴**(變怪) ① 《이상한 재변》 an extraordinary calamity 〔disaster〕. ② 《악행》 an extraordinary misdeed.

**변기**(便器) 《변소의》 a toilet stool 〔bowl〕; a urinal (소변용); 《실내의》 a chamber pot; a night chair; a nightstool; a commode; a bedpan (환자용).

**변놀이**(邊—) usury; moneylending. ⇨ 돈놀이.

**변덕**(變德) fickleness; caprice; (a) whim. ~스럽다, ~맞다 (be) capricious; fickle; inconstant; volatile; whimsical; 《날씨》 changeable. ¶ ~스럽게〔맞게〕 capriciously; whimsically; by fits and starts / 일시적 ~ the caprice 〔whim〕 of the moment / ~스러운 날씨 changeable weather / ~을 부리다 behave capriciously / ~이 많다 be capricious; be whimsical / 그녀는 ~이 심하다 She is so capricious. ◉ ~꾸러기〔쟁이〕 a capricious person;

a man of moods; a person who blows hot and cold. 「est.

**변돈**(邊—) a loan; money lent at inter-

**변동**(變動) (a) change; (an) alteration; 《시세 따위의》 fluctuation(s). ～하다 change; undergo a change; fluctuate. ¶ 격심한 ～ a sharp 〔heavy〕 fluctuation; jumps and slumps / 물가의 ～ fluctuations in prices / 정계(政界)의 ～ political change / ～(이) 없는 unchanged; stationary; firm (물가 등의) / ～을 가져오다 bring about a change; take a turn / ～을 겪다〔보이다〕 undergo 〔show〕 a change / 시세 ～이 심하다 The market is subject to sharp 〔wide〕 fluctuations. / 한국 경제는 국제 정세 ～의 영향을 받기 쉽다 The Korean economy is easily affected by changes in the international political situation. / 채소는 다른 식품에 비해서 가격 ～이 심하다 Compared with other categories of food, vegetables suffer sharp fluctuations in price.
◉ ～소득 fluctuating income. ～폭 the range of fluctuation 《in prices》. ～환율 the floating exchange rate 《for the won》: ～환율제 a floating exchange rate system. 대～ a violent 〔radical〕 change; 《사회·정치상의》 a cataclysm.

**변두리**(邊—) ① 《교외》 the outskirts 《of a district, *etc.*》; a suburb. ¶ ～의 suburban; on 〔in, at〕 the outskirts 《of a town》 / 서울 ～(에) (on) the outskirts of Seoul / ～에 살다 live in a suburb. ② 《가장자리》 the outer edge; the border; the margin.

**변란**(變亂) a (social) disturbance; an upheaval; 《반란》 an uprising; a rebellion; 《내란》 (a) civil war; internal disturbances; 《전란》 a war. ¶ 사회의 대～ a social upheaval 〔cataclysm〕.

**변론**(辯論) ① 《논의》 discussion; argument; 《논쟁》 controversy; disputation; 《토론》 debate. ～하다 argue; discuss; debate. ② 《법정의》 pleading; oral proceedings; debate. ～하다 proceed orally; plead (at the bar, before the court). ¶ ～에 들어가다 enter upon debates; open the oral proceedings / ～을 재개하다 reopen the oral proceedings / 피고를 위해 ～하다 argue on behalf of the accused (형사); argue the case for defendant (민사) / ～을 종결하다 conclude *one's* argument.
◉ ～가 a debator; a controversialist; an orator. ～기일 the date for pleading. ～자 a pleader.

**변류기**(變流器) 〖전기〗 a converter; a current transformer.

**변리**(辨理) management; conduct. ～하다 manage 《*a matter*》; dispose of 《*a matter*》; conduct 《a business》.
◉ ～사 a patent attorney. 「(邊).

**변리**(邊利) interest 《on a loan》. ⇨ 변[2]

**변말** secret language; slang; jargon 《of the trade》; 《thieves'》 cant; 《criminals'》 argot. ¶ 그들은 그들만의 ～로 이야기하고 있었다 They were talking in 「a secret language 〔the jargon of their trade〕.

**변명**(辨明) explanation; an excuse; a plea; defense (변호); justification (정당화); vindication (옹호); exculpation (무죄 증명). ～하다 explain 〔excuse〕 *oneself* 《for》; defend *oneself;* make an excuse 《for》; justify *oneself;* exculpate *oneself* 《from a charge》. ¶ ～으로(서) by way of excuse / 괴로운 ～ a pitiful 〔sorry〕 excuse / 그럴 듯한 〔궁색한〕 ～ a plausible 〔lame, clumsy〕 excuse / ～을 듣지 않다 take no excuse 《for》 / 열심히 ～하다 spare no pains to defend *oneself* 〔to apologize〕 / ～이 서지 않다 be inexcusable / 몰랐다고 ～하다 plead ignorance 「as an excuse 〔in excuse〕 / 그는 그녀를 위해 ～했다 He spoke for her. / 그런 ～은 통하지 않는다 You cannot get by with that excuse. *or* No circumstances can justify such an excuse as that. /이제와서 ～해 보았자 소용없다 It is (of) no use trying to excuse yourself now. / 그는 나의 ～을 들으려 하지 않았다 He wouldn't listen to my excuses. / 나는 내가 한 일에 대해 ～할 생각이 없다 I don't intend to explain 「myself 〔what I did〕. ◉ ～서 a written explanation; a letter of explanation.

**변명**(變名) a false 〔an assumed, a fictitious〕 name; an alias; 《이름을 고침》 changing *one's* name. ～하다 assume 〔take on〕 another name; change *one's* name. ¶ (…라는) ～으로 under an assumed 〔a false〕 name 《of》/ ～를 쓰다 use a false 〔different〕 name.

**변모**(變貌) (a) transfiguration; a change in (*one's*) appearance; (a) metamorphosis. ～하다 (come to) look different 《from what *it* used to be》; be transfigured; change 〔adapt〕 *one's* appearance; be metamorphosed 《into》. ¶ 완전히 ～하다 undergo a complete transfiguration 〔metamorphosis, change〕/ 전후 한국 사회는 눈부신 ~를 이루었다 Since the war, the society of Korea has undergone a remarkable change.

**변모없다** 《무례하다》 (be) blunt; rude; 《세련되지 못하다》 (be) unpolished; uncultured; boorish; 《변통성 없다》 (be) inflexible; unadaptable.

**변박**(辨駁) refutation; confutation. ~하다 refute; argue against. ⇨ 논박(論駁). ¶ ~의 여지가 없다 be irrefutable.

**변발**(辮髮) a pigtail; the (Chinese) queue 〔cue〕. ~하다 queue; braid 〔plait 《영》〕 *one's* hair into a pigtail. ¶ ~을 한 pigtailed / ~을 하고 있다 wear a pigtail.

**변방**(邊方) ① 《가장자리 쪽》 edges; sides; side areas. ② =변경(邊境).

**변변치않다** ① 《생김새가》 (be) unattractive; plain; homely. ② 《하찮다》 (be) trifling; insignificant; worthless; useless (쓸모없다). ¶ 변변치 않은 사람 a worthless 〔shiftless, useless〕 fellow; a good-for-nothing / 변변치 않은 책 a book of no value; a worthless 〔boring〕 book. ③ 《초라하다》 (be) poor; miserable; shabby; small; little; coarse. ¶ 변변치 않은 물건 an article of poor quality / 변변치 않은 선물 a small 〔little〕 present 〔gift〕/ 변변치 않은 음식 coarse 〔plain〕 food / 변변치 않습니다만 such as it is / 옷차림이 ~ be shabbily 〔poorly〕 dressed / 변변치 못한 선물입니다만 받아 주십시오 I hope you will accept this little present.

**변변하다** ① 《생김새가》 (be) fairly good-looking; comely; handsome. ¶ 변변하게 생기다 look pretty; be nicely turned-out. ② 《사람·사물이》 (be) fairly good; decent; passable; tolerable; so-so. ¶ 사람이 ~ have a fairly good character / 물건이 ~ the thing is tolerably good / 여기는 변변한 호텔이 없다 There are no decent hotels here. / 그녀는 변변한 치료도 못받고 세상을 떠났다 She died without receiving satisfactory treatment. / 좀더 변변한 것은 없습니까 Don't you have something a little better?

**변변히** well (잘·제대로); properly (알맞게); enough (충분히). ¶ 그는 영어로 편지도 ~ 못 쓴다 He can't write a letter in English properly. *or* He can't write a decent letter in English. / 그는 어찌나 소심한지 사람들 앞에서 ~ 말도 못한다 He is so timid that he scarcely opens his mouth in public. / 며칠 동안 ~ 먹지도 못했다 I have scarcely had anything to eat for the past few days. / 간밤에 ~ 잠도 못잤다 I slept very badly last night.

**변별**(辨別) distinction; discrimination. ~하다 tell 《A from B》; discriminate 〔distinguish〕 《A from B, between A and B》. ¶ 선악을 ~하다 tell 〔know〕 good from bad / 두 색깔의 차이를 ~하다 distinguish between the two colors. ◉ ~력 discriminating power.

**변복**(變服) (a) disguise; disguising *oneself*. ⇨ 변장(變裝). ~하다 disguise *oneself* 《as》; be disguised 《as》.

**변비**(便秘) constipation. ¶ 만성 ~ chronic constipation / ~로 고생하는 사람 a constipated person / ~를 고치다 relieve constipation / ~에 걸리다 be constipated; suffer from constipation / ~가 되었다 My bowels have stopped.

**변사**(辯士) 《연사》 a speaker; 《웅변가》 an eloquent speaker; an orator; 《무성 영화의》 a film interpreter; a movie talker.

**변사**(變死) an unnatural 〔accidental〕 death; a violent death. ~하다 die a violent death; meet with an unnatural death; die by violence; be killed in 〔by〕 an accident; be accidentally killed; die with *one's* boots on. ◉ ~자 a person who has met 〔died〕 an unnatural death; a person killed in an accident; a person accidentally killed.

**변사**(變事) = 이변(異變).

**변상**(辨償) 《배상》 compensation; reparation; 《변제》 (re)payment; reimbursement. ~하다 compensate 《for losses》; reimburse 《for the losses》; repair 《the damage》. ¶ ~을 요구하다 claim 〔demand〕 compensation 《for》/ 당신이 입은 손실에 대해서는 반드시 ~하겠습니다 I will never fail to compensate you for your losses.

**변색**(變色) ① 《빛깔의》 change of color; discoloration; fading (바램). ~하다 change color; become 〔get〕 discolored; discolor; fade; lose 《its》 luster. ¶ ~하지 않는 unfading; fast / 그 색은 ~하지 않는다 The color is fast. ② 《안색의》 change of countenance. ~하다 change countenance; change color.

**변설**(辯舌) speech (연설); eloquence (웅변). ¶ ~이 유창한 eloquent; fluent / ～이 유창하다 have a fluent tongue / 그 후보자는 ～이 실로 유창했다 The candidate spoke very fluently. ◉ ～가 「an eloquent 〔a fluent〕 speaker; an orator.

**변성**(變成) (a) regeneration; (a) metamorphosis. ～하다 regenerate; metamorphose. ◉ ～암(岩) 『지질』 a metamorphic rock: 반상(斑狀) ～암 porphyroid.

**변성**(變姓) ～하다 change *one's* surname.

**변성**(變性) 『의학』 degeneration; 『화학』 denaturation. ～하다 degenerate; get denatured. ◉ ～알코올〔주정〕 methylated 〔denatured〕 spirits 〔alcohol〕. ～제 a denaturant.

**변성**(變聲) the 「change 〔breaking, cracking〕 of voice. ～하다 *one's* voice 「changes 〔breaks, cracks, lowers〕. ¶ 소년은 사춘기가 되면 ～하여 목소리가 굵어진다 A boy's voice breaks and becomes deeper at puberty. ◉ ～기(期) the age at which *one's* voice changes; puberty.

**변성명**(變姓名) ① 《이름을 갊》 changing *one's* (surname and given) name. ～하다 change *one's* (full) name. ② 《가짜 이름》 「an assumed 〔a fictitious〕 name. ～하다 assume another 〔a false〕 name.

**변소**(便所) a lavatory; a water closet (생략 W.C.); 《미》 a toilet (room); a bathroom; a washroom; 《공공장소의》 a restroom; a convenience 《영》; a 「ladies' 〔men's〕 room; 《군대·학교 등의》 a latrine; 《게시》 Gentlemen (남자용); Ladies (여자용). ¶ 공중～ a public lavatory; a street latrine / 수세식 ～ a water closet; a flush toilet / 옥외～ an outhouse; a backhouse; a privy / ～에 가다 go to the 「toilet 〔bath, closet〕; go to stool; 《완곡히》 go to wash *one's* hands / ～에 있다 be at stool / ～에 사람이 있다〔없다〕 The bathroom is 「busy 〔vacant〕. / ～는 어디입니까 Where can I wash my hands? *or* Where is the washroom?

**변속**(變速) a change of speed. ◉ ～기〔장치〕 a gearbox; a transmission. ～기어 a 《five-speed》 derailleur (자동차의 변속 장치); 《자전거의》 a bicycle gearshift. ～레버 a gearshift 《미》; a gear lever 《영》.

**변수**(變數) 『수학』 a variable; a fluent.

**변스럽다**(變—) (be) odd; queer; funny; peculiar. ¶ 변스럽게 굴다 behave 「oddly 〔queerly〕.

**변신**(變身) ① ＝변장. ② 《변태》 (a) metamorphosis; (a) transformation. ～하다 change 〔turn〕 《into》; be 「transformed 〔metamorphosed〕 《into》. ¶ 화려한 ～ transforming *oneself* in a conspicuous way / 동화에서는 동물이 흔히 인간으로 ～한다 In fairy tales animals very often transform themselves into human beings.

**변심**(變心) a change of 「mind 〔heart〕; fickleness; inconstancy; treachery (배신). ～하다 change *one's* mind; prove unfaithful; play 《*a person*》 false; betray 《*a person, a person's* confidence》; turn traitor 《to》. ¶ 그녀는 ～하여 다른 남자에게 갔다 She deserted him and went to live with another man.

**변압**(變壓) 『전기』 transformation. ～하다 transform 《a current》 (in potential); step 《current》 up 〔down〕. ◉ ～기 a 《current》 transformer; a potential transformer. ～탑(塔) a transformer box.

**변온동물**(變溫動物) 『동물』 a 「cold-blooded 〔poikilothermal〕 animal.

**변위**(變位) 『물리』 displacement. ◉ ～전류 a displacement current.

**변음**(變音) 『음악』 a flat.

**변이**(變移) (a) change; (an) alteration; (a) mutation; 『화학』 a conversion. ～하다 change; mutate.

**변이**(變異) 『생물』 (a) variation; (a) modification (비유전성으로서 일시적인). ¶ 돌연～ (a) mutation. ◉ ～설(說) the variation theory. ～종(種) a variable species.

**변장**(變裝) (a) disguise. ～하다 put on a makeup; make up 《as》; disguise *oneself* 《as》; 《가장하다》 masquerade 《as》. ¶ …으로 ～하고 in 〔under〕 the 「disguise 〔guise〕 of 《a merchant》 / 여자로 ～하다〔해 있다〕 「disguise *oneself* 〔be disguised〕 as a woman / 그는 안경과 가짜 콧수염으로 ～했다 He put on 「spectacles 〔glasses〕 and a false mustache for disguise. / 아이들은 여러 동물로 ～했다 The children disguised themselves as various kinds of animals. ◉ ～술 the art of 「disguise 〔camouflage〕.

**변재**(辯才) oratorical 「talent 〔skill〕; eloquence; the gift of gab. ¶ ～가 있는 having the gift of gab; eloquent; fluent / ～가 있다 be gifted with eloquence; have an oratorical talent; have a 「fluent 〔ready〕 tongue / ～가

없다 be awkward in speaking; be a poor speaker.

**변전**(變轉) (a) change; mutation; vicissitudes. ~하다 change; mutate. ¶~ 무쌍한 ever-changing; kaleidoscopic.

**변전소**(變電所) a (transformer) substation.

**변절**(變節) defection; apostasy (종교·주의 등의); tergiversation; 《배반》 (a) betrayal; falling-away; (a) treachery. ~하다 apostatize; tergiversate; turn 〔change〕 *one's* coat; turn round; change sides; desert *one's* cause 〔principles〕. ¶~하지 않다 remain faithful / 쉽게 ~하는 사람은 싫다 I don't like a man who easily changes sides. ◉ ~자 an apostate; a renegade; a turncoat.

**변제**(辨濟) repayment; payment; 《결제》 settlement; 《청산》 liquidation. ~하다 pay (back, off); repay; return; settle; liquidate. ¶빚을 ~하다 pay back what *one* owes; repay *one's* debt. ◉ ~금 repayment; money repaid. ~기간 the term of repayment 〔redemption〕.

**변조**(變調) 〖음악〗 a change of tone; (a) variation; 〖통신〗 (a) modulation (of sound); 《언행의》 irregularity; abnormality; anomaly. ~하다 modulate; change keys. ¶주파수~ frequency modulation (생략 FM) / 진폭~ amplitude modulation (생략 AM) / ~를 가져오다 cease to function properly; 《몸의》 go out of order 〔shape〕. ◉ ~관(管) a modulation tube. ~기 a modulator.

**변조**(變造) 《개조》 alteration; 《위조》 forgery; falsification. ~하다 alter; forge; falsify; raise 〔doctor〕 《a check》. ¶100달러 짜리 지폐를 ~하다 falsify 〔forge〕 100 dollar bills / 공문서를 ~하다 alter official documents / 액면 8만원의 수표를 5백 80만원의 수표로 ~하다 doctor a check with a face value of 80,000 won into a 5.8 million won check. ◉ ~수표 an altered 〔a falsified, a forged, a raised 《미》〕 check 〔cheque 《영》〕. ~자(者) a forger; a falsifier; a 《check》 raiser. ~화폐〔지폐〕 a counterfeit coin 〔bill〕.

**변종**(變種) a variety; a sport; a mutation (돌연변이에 의한); a freak 《of nature》; 《괴물 같은》 a monster. ¶인공~ an artificial variety / 풍토적 ~ a climatic variety.

**변주**(變奏) ~하다 〖음악〗 play a variation 《on a tune 〔theme〕》. ◉ ~곡(變奏曲) 〖음악〗 a (musical) variation.

**변죽**(邊一) a rim; a brim; an edge. ¶~ 울리다 hint 《at》; give 《*a person*》 a hint; allude to 《a fact》; beat about 〔around 《미》〕 the bush.

**변증**(辨證) demonstration (of proof). ~하다 demonstrate. ¶~적 dialectic; dialectical. ◉ ~법 dialectic: ~법적으로 dialectically / ~법적 유물론 dialectic(al) materialism / 유물 ~법 materialistic dialectic.

**변지**(邊地) the edge of land 〔of the world〕; a remote place; 《변경》 a frontier district; the borderland.

**변질**(變質) a change in quality; degeneration; deterioration (품질 등의 악화). ~하다 change in quality; deteriorate; 《음식이》 go bad. ¶더운 날씨에는 식품이 ~되기 쉽다 Food 「spoils 〔goes bad〕 quickly in hot weather. / ~된 화장품을 쓰는 것은 위험하다 It is dangerous to use cosmetics which have deteriorated.

**변질자**(變質者) 《도착자》 a pervert; a deviant; a maniac.

**변천**(變遷) changes (변화); 《추이》 (a) transition; 《성쇠》 vicissitudes; ups and downs 《of life》. ~하다 change; undergo 〔go through〕 changes; shift. ¶시대의 ~ the changes of times / 사회의 ~ social changes / 수많은 ~을 거쳐(서) after many changes / 관습은 시대와 함께 ~한다 Our customs will change with the times.

**변칙**(變則) (an) irregularity; (an) anomaly (예외); 《바뀐 규칙》 a changed regulation. ¶~적인 irregular; anomalous / ~적인 교육 an irregular 〔a picked-up〕 education / ~적인 방법 an irregular method 〔way〕; an unorthodox approach. ◉ ~동사 an irregular verb(불규칙 동사).

**변침**(變針) 〖항해〗 veering. ~하다 veer; turn 〔change, shift〕 *one's* course 《toward》.

**변칭**(變稱) 《바꿈》 changing a name 〔designation〕; 《이름》 a changed name. ~하다 rename; redesignate; change the name of; give another name to.

**변태**(變態) 〖생물〗 a metamorphosis (*pl.* -ses); (a) transformation; 《이상》 (an) abnormality. ¶~적(인) abnormal; perverted / 구더기에서 파리로의 ~ the metamorphosis of a maggot into a fly / 완전〔불완전〕 ~ 〖생물〗 a complete 〔an incomplete〕 metamorpho-

sis / 그의 성격은 ～적인 것 같다 He seems a man of abnormal character.
◉ ～성욕 abnormal sexuality 〔sexual desire〕; sexual perversion: ～성욕자 a (sexual) pervert. ～심리 abnormal mentality: ～심리학 abnormal psychology. ～영업(행위) an abnormal and illegal business activity.

**변통**(變通) 《융통성》 versatility; adaptability; flexibility; 《임기 응변》 contrivance; management; makeshift; arrangement; 《가변성》 changeableness; fickleness. ～하다 (shift and) contrive; manage 《with》; make shift; arrange. ¶ 돈을 ～하다 get money somehow; make up a sum; raise 〔scratch up〕 money / 어떻게든 ～해 보겠다 Somehow I'll manage it.
◉ ～수 a resource; a contrivance; a makeshift; an expedient. 임시～ a temporary 〔rough〕 makeshift.

**변통성**(變通性) versatility; adaptability; flexibility; resourcefulness. ¶ ～ 있는 versatile; adaptable; flexible; resourceful / ～이 없다 be unadaptable 〔hidebound〕; lack (in) versatility.

**변하다**(變—) ① 《…이》 change; undergo a change; be altered; become different; vary (여러가지로); 《…으로 변형하다》 turn 〔change〕 《into》; 《바람이》 come round 〔about〕; shift 《to the east》. ¶ 변하기 쉬운 changeable; unsettled; 《마음이》 capricious; fickle / 마음이 ～ change *one's* mind; undergo a change of heart / 마음이 잘 변하는 여자 a woman of moods; a girl with a fickle mind / 맛이 ～ turn sour 〔stale〕; get high (고기가); food spoils / 모양이 ～ 〔변하지 않다〕 get out of 〔hold〕 its shape / 목소리가 ～ *one's* voice changes 〔breaks〕 / 얼굴빛이 ～ change 「color 〔*one's* countenance〕; turn pale; 《노해서》 go black in the face / 딴판으로 ～ be completely changed / 변하지 않다 be 〔remain〕 unchanged; be 〔remain〕 the same (as before); be constant / 변하지 〔변치〕 않는 unchangeable; constant; steady / 영원히 변치 않는 eternal; everlasting / 그는 지금 전혀 딴 사람으로 변했다 He is quite another man now. / 연민의 정이 노여움으로 변했다 Pity gave place to anger. ② 《…을》 change; make different. ¶ 태도를 ～ change 〔modify〕 *one's* attitude; alter *one's* stand / 얼굴빛을 ～ change color.

**변함없다**(變—) (be) unchanged; constant; steady; show no change; remain unchanged. ¶ 변함없이 without a change; unchangingly; 《여전히》 constantly; as usual 〔before〕; 《무사히》 uneventfully; in peace / 변함없는 사랑 a constant 〔an unfailing〕 love / 변함없는 우정 constant 〔steady〕 friendship / 시간표에 아무런 변함이 없다 There is no change in the timetable.

**변혁**(變革) a change; a reform; a renovation; a revolution; an upheaval. ～하다 change; reform; revolutionize. ¶ 기술상의 ～ a technical renovation / 급속한 산업화에 따르는 광범위한 사회 ～ the wide spectrum of social changes resulting from rapid industrialization / 큰 ～을 가져오다 bring about a revolution 〔a large reform〕 《in the way of life》 / 원자력의 이용은 우리들의 생활 양식에 ～을 가져올 것이다 The use of atomic energy will revolutionize our way of life. / 컴퓨터의 출현은 우리 사회에 급격한 ～을 가져왔다 The advent of computers drastically changed our society.

**변형**(變形) 《형태를 바꿈》 transformation; metamorphosis; modification; variation; deformation; 《바뀐 형태》 a modification; a variety; a variant; a deformity (기형). ～하다 《바꾸다》 change (the shape of ) 《*a thing*》; transform; metamorphose; 《바뀌다》 change 〔turn〕 《into》; be transformed 〔metamorphosed〕 《into》. ¶ 원형이 남지 않을 정도로 ～하다 be disfigured out of 〔beyond〕 all recognition.
◉ ～문법 transformational grammar. ～체 〖동물〗 a plasmodium (*pl.* -dia).

**변호**(辯護) ① 《변명》 defense; vindication; justification (정당화); advocacy (옹호); explanation (해명). ～하다 defend; vindicate; justify; speak in defense of 《another》; speak for 〔in favor of 〕 《*a person*》; put in a (good) word for 《*a person*》. ¶ 자기 ～ self=justification / …을 ～하여 in explanation 〔justification〕 of…; in defense of… / 나는 그런 비난에 대하여 아무 ～도 하지 않았다 I made no defense against those 「accusations 〔charges〕.
② 《법정에서》 defense (피고의); pleading (원·피고의). ～하다 defend 《the litigant》; plead for 〔in favor of 〕 《the accused, a party to a lawsuit》; argue 〔plead〕 the case 《for the defendant》. ¶ ～의 여지가 없는 사건 an indefensi-

ble case / ~를 의뢰하다 ask a lawyer to plead *one's* case; employ a lawyer; take *one's* case to an advocate《영》/ …의 ~를 맡다 take a brief for《*a person*》; undertake to plead for《the defendant》/ 피고의 ~에 나서다 defend the accused; plead [hold a brief] for the defendant / 사건의 ~를 변호사에게 의뢰하는 것이 낫다 You had better get a lawyer to plead your case.
◉ ~권 the right of defense. ~료 a lawyer's fee. ~의뢰인 a client. ~인 a counsel; a pleader; a defender; an advocator: ~인단 the defense counsel / ~인측 증인 a defense witness.

**변호사**(辯護士) a lawyer;《법정의 변호사》a counsel; an counselor《미》; a barrister《영》;《사무 변호사》an attorney (at law)《미》; a solicitor《영》; the bar [총칭]; a public defender (국선의).

> **용법** **lawyer** 변호사의 일반적인 명칭.《미》**counsel**, **counselor**,《영》**barrister** 상급 법원에서 변호를 담당할 수 있는 법정(法廷) 변호사.《미》**attorney**,《영》**solicitor** 하급 법원의 변호사로, 법정 변호사와 소송 의뢰인 사이에서 사무 및 서류 관계를 돕는 사무 변호사. 미국에서는 attorney가 흔히 lawyer의 뜻으로도 쓰이나, 좁은 의미로는 상거래 처리를 위한 의뢰인의 법정 대리인을 가리킨다.

¶ 상대방의 ~ the opposing counsel / ~가 되다 enter the「law [legal profession];《자격을 취득하다》be admitted [called《영》] to the bar / ~를 개업하다「set up [establish *oneself*] as a lawyer; establish a law practice / ~를 대다 engage [employ] (a) counsel [a lawyer] / ~를 업으로 하다 practice law / ~에게 사건을 의뢰하다 give a brief to counsel; take *one's* case to an advocate / 그는 ~가 되려고 공부했다 He studied for the bar. *or* He studied to take up the law. / 피고는 유능한 ~를 채용했다 The defendant has a very able counsel.
◉ ~사무소 a law office. ~수임료 a lawyer's fee. ~시험 the bar examinations. ~회 a bar association. 고문~ a legal adviser; a counselor. 악덕~ a shyster (lawyer). 대한 ~ 협회 Korean Bar Association.

**변화**(變化) ①《바뀜·바꿈》(a) change; (a) variation; (an) alteration (변경); (a) mutation (변전); a transition (변천). ~하다 change; undergo a change; turn《into, to》; shift《into》; alter; vary. ¶ ~하기 쉬운 changeable; variable; liable to variation / ~ 있는 changeful; inconstant / ~ 없는 changeless / ~ 무쌍한 ever-changing; kaleidoscopic; protean / ~ 무쌍한 인생 the kaleidoscope of life / 정세[환경]의 ~ a change「in situation [of circumstances] / 온도의 ~ variation of temperature / 풍향의 ~ a shift of the wind / 날씨의 ~ a change in weather / 점차[서서히] ~하다 change gradually《into》; pass by slight changes《into》;《색채 등이》shade《into》/ ~가 없다 remain unchanged; undergo [suffer] no change / ~를 가져오다 bring on a change / ~를 일으키다 work a change / 정세에 ~가 없다 There is no change in the situation. / 정세는 급격히 ~했다 The situation has changed rapidly. / 이 도시는 지난 10년 동안에 많이 ~했다 This town has changed a great deal in the last ten years.
②《변태·변형》(a) transformation; (a) transfiguration; a metamorphosis (*pl.* -phoses). ~하다 transform (itself)《into》; be「transformed [transfigured]; metamorphose《into》.
③《다양》variety; diversity. ¶ ~ 있는 varied; diversified / ~ 없는 without variety; monotonous (단조로운) / ~를 위해 for the sake of variety / ~ 많은 full of variety; varied / ~ 많은 경치 varied scenery / ~를 곁들이다 add [lend] variety《to》/ ~를 일으키다 start changes / ~를 주다 give variety《to》/ ~를 찾다 seek variety / 나는 ~ 없는 시골 생활에 싫증이 났다 I am tired of the monotonous life in the country. / 그녀는 ~가 많은 생활을 한다 She leads a varied life.
④〖문법〗inflection [inflexion] (어형 변화); declension (격변화); conjugation (동사 활용). ~하다 inflect; decline; conjugate. ¶ 불~의《어미 변화가 없는》indeclinable / 불~ 복수 an unchanged plural / 어형 ~표 a paradigm.
◉ ~계수 the coefficient of variation. ~구(球)〖야구〗a ball thrown for a change of pace;《커브》a curve (ball).

**변환**(變換) change; conversion;〖수학〗transformation. ~하다 change; convert; divert. ¶ ~할 수 있다[없다] be「convertible [inconvertible].

◉ ～기(器) 〖전기〗 a converter; an inverter; a transducer: 전기 음향 ～기 an electroacoustic transducer.

**별** ① 《하늘의》 a star; [총칭] the stars. ¶ 별 같은 starlike; starry; astral / 별빛 starlight / 별 밝은 밤 a starlit 〔starlight〕 night / 별이 총총한 하늘 the starry sky; a sky interspersed 〔strewn〕 with stars / 하늘에 반짝이는 별 twinkling stars in the sky / 눈에서 별이 번쩍하다 see stars / 그것은 하늘에 별 따기다 It is beyond my reach 〔ability〕. *or* It is not easier than picking a star out of the sky. ② 《장성의》 a star; a pip. ¶ 별 둘인 장군 a two-star general; a major general / 별을 달다 become a general.

**별-**(別) 《다른》 different; another; 《별난》 unusual; uncommon; strange. ¶ 별문제 another question; a different case / 별천지 a different world.

**-별**(別) classified by. ¶ 군(郡)별 인구 populations by counties / 직업별 전화부 a classified phone directory / 국적별〔연령별〕로 서시오 Please line up according to your nationality 〔age〕.

**별갑**(鱉甲) tortoiseshell. ¶ ～테 안경 tortoise(shell)-rimmed glasses.
◉ ～세공 tortoiseshell work.

**별개**(別個) a different 〔distinct〕 one; a separate one; another one. ¶ ～의 《개개의》 several; separate; discrete; 《다른》 different; another / ～로 separately / ～의 문제 another question / ～의 죄 separate offenses / 이것과 그것과는 (전연) ～의 것이다 This is one thing, and that is (quite) another. / 이것은 그것과는 ～로 논해야 된다 This must be discussed separately from that. / 자네가 말하는 것은 ～의 문제야 What you are saying is another matter.

**별거**(別居) ① 《부부의》 separation; limited divorce; legal separation. ～하다 live in a separate house; live separately. ¶ ～중인 아내 a separated wife; a grass widow / 남편과 ～하다 live separately from *one's* husband / 스미스 부부는 지금 ～중이다 Mr. and Mrs. Smith are living separately now. ② 《따로 삶》 living apart. ～하다 live away 〔apart〕 《from *one's* family》. ¶ 그녀는 가족과 ～하여 지금 서울에 있다 She is now in Seoul, living apart from her family. ◉ ～수당 a separate allowance; alimony.

**별건**(別件) 《별스러운 일》 an unusual thing 〔event〕; something unusual (심상치 않은); 《별개의 건》 another 〔different, separate〕 matter 〔event〕. ¶ ～으로 구속하다 arrest 《*a person*》 on a separate charge.

**별것**(別—) ① 《진기한 것》 a rarity; an oddity. ¶ 그것은 ～ 아니다 It is no rare thing. *or* It is nothing peculiar. / 그의 능력은 ～ 아니다 I have a low opinion of his ability. / 금강석은 ～ 아니라 석탄의 한 가지다 Diamond is nothing but a kind of coal. ② 《괴상한 것》 an eccentric (person); an unexpected 〔a peculiar〕 incident. ¶ ～ 다봤다 Now I've seen everything! *or* I've never seen such a strange thing. ③ 《별의별 것》 things of various sorts.

**별견**(瞥見) a glance; a glimpse; a cursory view. ～하다 glance 《at》; have 〔take〕 a glance 《at》; catch 〔get〕 a glimpse of; cast a glance over 〔upon〕; glance through (책 등을).

**별고**(別故) ① 《사고》 an untoward event; an accident; something wrong; a trouble. ¶ ～ 없다 《건강에》 be well; 《일에》 be all right; nothing is the matter 《with》 / ～ 없이 in good health; 《get along》 well; 《무사히》 safely; in safety; free from accident 〔sickness〕; without accident 〔mishap〕 / ～ 없으십니까 How are you (getting along)? / 나는 ～ 없이 지내고 있다 I'm (as) well as usual 〔ever〕.
② 《까닭》 a specific reason.

**별과**(別科) a special course 〔department〕. ¶ ～에 들어가다 take a special course.

**별관**(別館) an annex 《to a building》; an extension; an outhouse; an outbuilding. ¶ 호텔의 ～ an annex to a hotel.

**별궁**(別宮) 〖고제도〗 the palace 「of the queen 〔of the wife of the heir-apparent〕; a detached 〔an annexed〕 palace (이궁).

**별기**(別記) a separate paragraph; a separate note. ～하다 write in a separate paragraph; make a separate note 《of》. ¶ ～와 같이 as stated in a separate paragraph; as stated elsewhere.

**별꼴**(別—) an obnoxious thing; an eyesore 《미》. ¶ ～이다, ～ 다 보겠다 What a spectacle 〔sight〕! *or* What a mess! *or* What an eyesore!

**별꽃** 〖식물〗 a chickweed.

**별나다**(別—) (be) peculiar; eccentric;

queer; odd; uncommon; unusual. ¶ 별난 사람 an eccentric; a queer bird; an odd duck / 별난 취미 a taste for odd things; a bizarre taste / 별난 기분이 들다 feel queer / 별나게 굴다 behave eccentrically / 그는 좀 ~ He is a bit queer. / 그녀에게는 별난 버릇이 있다 She has peculiar ways.

**별나라** the land of the stars; the stellar world.

**별납**(別納) separate payment 〔delivery〕. ~하다 pay 〔deliver〕 separately. ¶ 요금~ charges separately paid / 요금~우편으로 보내다 send 《*a thing*》 postpaid 〔post-free《영》〕.

**별다르다**(別—) be of a particular kind; (be) extraordinary. ¶ 별다른 일 something in particular / 별다른 일이 없으면 if you are not otherwise engaged / 별다른 일 없이 학교를 빠지다 absent *oneself* from school without any particular reason / 별다른 일 없이 잘 지냅니다 I am getting along as usual with nothing in particular happening. / 별다른 일 없으면 놀러 오십시오 Visit us if you don't have anything in particular to do. / 그가 지각한 데는 별다른 이유가 없었다 There was no particular reason for his coming late. / 그에겐 아무 별다른 점이 없었다 There was nothing peculiar about him.

**별달리**(別—) differently; otherwise; 《특별히》 particularly; in particular. ¶~ 굴다 behave differently / 내 말을 ~ 생각지 마시오 Don't take my words ill.

**별당**(別堂) ① 《딴 집》 a separate 〔detached〕 house. ② 《절의》 the residence of the superior of a Buddhist temple.

**별도**(別途) 《다른 방면》 a separate way; another way; 《다른 용도》 separate use. ¶ ~의 special; for a special purpose; of a separate item / ~로 separately; apart; 《과외로》 extra; in addition; besides; else / 돈을 ~로 남겨 두다 reserve 〔put aside〕 money for special use / 방을 ~로 잡아두다 reserve a room 《for》; set apart a room 《for》 / 5만원의 ~수입이 있다 have an additional 〔extra〕 income of 50,000 won / …에 관해서는 ~로 정한다 the specifications as to... will be specified elsewhere / ~ 명령이 있을 때까지 기다려라 Wait till you receive another order. / 더 좋은 좌석을 원한다면 ~로 돈을 내야 합니다 You must pay extra if you want a better seat. ◉ ~계정 a special 〔separate〕 account. ~공사 separate work; a separate project. ~수입 a special 〔casual〕 income. ~예금 a special deposit. ~적립금 a special reserve fund. ~지출 a special outlay.

**별도리**(別道理) a better way 〔means〕; a better remedy; an alternative; a choice. ¶ ~ 없이 helplessly; inevitably; reluctantly / …할 수 밖에 ~ 없다 have no choice but to *do;* there is no alternative but to *do* / ~가 없었다 There was no alternative. *or* It couldn't be helped.

**별동**(別棟) another building (separate 〔detached〕 from the main building).

**별동대**(別動隊) a flying column 〔party〕; a detached force 〔corps〕.

**별똥** 《운석》 a meteorite; a meteoric 〔falling〕 stone. ¶ ~이 떨어지다 a meteor falls. ◉ ~별 《유성》 a shooting 〔falling〕 star; a meteor: ~별이다 There goes a shooting star!

**별로**(別—) 《not》 in particular; 《not》 particularly; 《not》 especially; 《그다지》 《not》 very; 《not》 much. ¶ ~ 좋지 않다 be not particularly good / ~ 위험하지는 않다 be not very 〔so〕 dangerous / ~ 춥지 않다 be not especially 〔very〕 cold / ~ 할 말〔일〕도 없다 have nothing particular to say 〔do〕 / ~ 이렇다 할 이유는 없다 I have no particular reason for it. / 그녀는 ~ 외출하지 않는다 She seldom 〔rarely〕 goes out. / 나는 멜론을 ~ 좋아하지 않는다 I don't very much like 〔care for〕 melons.

**별리**(別離) separation; parting. = 이별(離別).

**별말**(別—) an extraordinary 〔unexpected〕 remark; a preposterous 〔an unreasonable, an absurd〕 remark. ~하다 make an extraordinary remark; make a preposterous 〔an absurd, an unreasonable〕 remark. ¶ ~ 다한다 You talk nonsense. *or* Be reasonable. / ~씀 다 하십니다 Don't mention it. *or* Oh no, not at all. / 그가 천재라니 ~ 다 듣겠다 What do you mean "he's a genius"?!

**별명**(別名) another name; a byname; a nickname; an alias (일명); a pseudonym (필명). ¶ ~을 …이라고 하는 also called...; otherwise known as... / ~을 붙이다 nickname 《*a person*》; give 《*a person*》 a nickname; fasten a nickname upon 《*a person*》 / ~으로 부르다 call 《*a person*》 by *his* nickname / 말코란 ～으로 통하다 go by the alias of *malk'o* / 우리는 그녀에게 땅콩이라는 ～을 붙였다 We nicknamed her "Peanut".

**별명**(別命) another 〔a different〕 order. ¶ ～이 있을 때까지 기다려라 Wait for another order.

**별무늬** a star(red) 〔starry〕 design 〔pattern〕.

**별문제**(別問題) another 〔a different〕 question; another thing 〔matter〕; a different story 〔case〕. ¶ …은 ～로 하고 apart 〔aside〕 from… / 그것은 ～이다 That's a different story. *or* That is beside the question. / 예산은 ～로 하고 몇 명의 외국인 강사가 필요한가 Apart from 〔Letting alone〕 the budget, how many foreign instructors do we need?

**별미**(別味) 《맛》 peculiar taste; an exquisite flavor; 《음식》 a delicacy; a dainty; a tidbit.

**별미쩍다**(別味—) (be) queer; odd; peculiar; unusual; abnormal; weird.

**별박이** ① 《말》 a horse with a white spot on its head. ② 《연》 a high-flying paper kite.

**별배**(別杯) a parting cup; a grace cup; a farewell toast; a send-off toast.

**별별**(別別) [형용사적] of various and unusual sorts. ¶ ～ 경험 a varied experience / ～ 사람 all sorts of people in all conditions of life / ～ 일 unusual things of all sorts / ～ 음식 all sorts of rare dishes / ～ 수단을 다 쓰다 try every means available / ～ 일을 다 봤다 I never saw such queer going-on!

**별봉**(別封) (a letter under) separate cover; the accompanying letter 〔document〕. ¶ ～으로 보내다 send 《pictures》 under separate cover.

**별빛** starlight; the stars. ¶ ～을 받으며 in the starlight / ～이 밝다 The stars are shining brightly.

**별사람**(別—) an eccentric; a queer person 〔bird〕; an odd duck; a mess. ¶ ～ 다 보겠다 I have never seen such a mess of man. / 그도 ～은 아니다 He is of the number. *or* He too is not excepted.

**별세**(別世) leaving the world; dying; decease. ～하다 die; decease; pass away; depart this world.

**별세계**(別世界) another world 〔sphere〕; a different world; a fairyland. ¶ ～의 of another world; ultramundane / 마치 ～이다 It is a world in itself. *or* The place makes a world of its own. / 그는 마치 ～ 사람 같다 He looks like a creature from another world. / ～에 온 기분이다 We feel as if we were on another planet.

**별소리** ＝별말.

**별송**(別送) ～하다 send 《*a thing*》 by separate post 〔under separate cover〕. ◉ ～물 《화물의》 unaccompanied goods.

**별수**(別數) ① 《행운》 extraordinary good fortune; special luck. ¶ ～가 나다 run into an unexpected bit of good luck / 거기 가지 마라, ～없을 게다 Don't go there, you won't have any better luck there. / ～없다—가자 We aren't getting anywhere—let's go.
② 《방도》 a special means; a secret key; the secret (to it); the magic word 〔formula〕; the magic touch; an effective way 《to *do a thing*》; the proper technique; the required solution. ¶ 그를 해고하는 수밖에 ～없다 We have no choice but to fire him. / 너도 ～없구나 You don't have any magic formula, either. / 나는 자네에겐 ～가 있는가 했지 Here I thought you would have a special means up your sleeve. / 이젠 ～없다 Now there is no help for it. / 그도 뭐 ～없을 걸 I don't think he has any particular idea about it.

**별스럽다**(別—) ＝별나다.

**별식**(別食) a rare 〔special〕 dish.

**별실**(別室) ① 《딴 방》 another 〔a different〕 room; a special room; a separate room. ¶ ～로 물러가다 withdraw into another room. ② 《첩》 a concubine.

**별안간**(瞥眼間) suddenly; abruptly; all of a sudden; all at once; 《뜻하지 않게》 unexpectedly. ¶ ～ 나타나다 burst on the scene / ～ 죽다 die suddenly / ～ 환해지다 become bright suddenly / ～ 날씨가 변했다 The weather changed all of a sudden. / 버스가 ～ 멈췄다 The bus stopped suddenly. / 그러자 ～ 강풍이 불었다 Then all at once there came a strong wind.

**별일**(別—) an odd thing; a strange thing; a particular thing. ¶ ～ 없이 safely; in safety; without any accident / ～ 없으면 if you don't have anything particular to do / ～ 없이 지내시겠지요 You are getting along all right, I hope. / ～ 없이 잘 지냅니다 I am getting along all right 〔OK〕. / ～ 없으면 좋겠다 There is nothing wrong, I hope. / ～ 다 보겠다 Ridiculous!

**별자리** 〚천문〛 a constellation; an asterism. ¶ 오리온 ～ the constellation of Orion.

**별장**(別莊) a (resort) villa; a country house; a cottage (소규모의) 《미》. ¶ 여름의 ～ a summer house (cottage) 《미》/ 해변가의 ～ a seaside villa.
◉ ～지기 the caretaker of a villa; a villakeeper.

**별정직**(別定職) privileged government position. ◉ ～ 공무원 officials in special government service.

**별종**(別種) a distinct species; a different kind; a special variety. ¶ ～의 of different kind; belonging to a different category.

**별주**(別酒) 《이별주》 a parting drink; one for the road; 《특제 술》 a liquor brewed using a special method.

**별증**(別症) an intercurrent disease; a (medical) complication; a secondary ailment.

**별지**(別紙) an annexed paper; an accompanying 〔a separate, an attached〕 sheet; an annex; an enclosure. ¶ ～의 《동봉한》 enclosed herewith; annexed hereto / ～와 같이 as you will see from the enclosed 〔attached〕 paper; as per enclosure / ～에 기재한 바와 같이 as stated in the attached 〔accompanying〕 paper / ～에 쓰다 write on another 〔a separate〕 sheet / ～와 같이 통지드립니다 We'll inform you as stated in the accompanying paper 〔document〕.

**별책**(別冊) a separate volume; an independent volume 《of a written work》; a separately bound volume; 《잡지 따위의》 an extra number 〔issue〕. ¶ ～으로 되어 있다 be separately bound / ～으로 출판하다 publish as an independent volume / 서류는 항목마다 ～으로 되어 있다 The papers are separately bound for each item. ◉ ～부록 a separate-volume supplement; a (separate) supplement 《to a magazine》.

**별천지**(別天地) another world. ⇨ 별세계.

**별칭**(別稱) another name; a byname.

**별표**(—票) a star; an asterisk (*); a pentagram (☆). ¶ ～가 붙은 asterisked 《words》/ ～를 붙이다 (mark with an) asterisk; star.

**별표**(別表) an attached list 〔sheet, table〕; an appended 〔annexed〕 chart. ◉ ～양식 an attached form.

**별항**(別項) a separate paragraph (다른 단락); another clause 〔provision, section〕 (다른 조문); 《under》 special heading. ¶ ～에 기재된 바와 같이 이것은 법률 위반이다 This is against the law as stated in another clause.

**별행**(別行) another line. ¶ ～을 잡다 write on 〔begin〕 a new line.

**별호**(別號) 《호》 a pen name; pseudonym; 《별명》 a nickname; a byname.

**볍씨** rice seed; seed rice.

**볏**[1] 《새의》 a cockscomb; a comb; a crest 《of a fowl》.

**볏**[2] 《보습의》 a moldboard.

**볏가리** a stack of rice straw.

**볏과식물**(—科植物) (true) grasses.

**볏단** a sheaf of rice.

**볏모** a rice seedling; a young rice plant.

**볏섬** a sack of rice; a straw rice-bag.

**볏짚** rice straw. ¶ ～을 단으로 묶다 tie up 〔bundle〕 rice straw in sheaves / ～을 깔다 spread rice straw / ～으로 지붕을 이다 thatch a roof with rice straw.

**병**(丙) ① 《십간의》 the 3rd of the 10 Heaven's Stems. ② 《성적》 the third grade; C.

**병**(甁) ① 《담는》 a bottle; a vase (화병); a decanter (목이 가는 양주병); a jar (주둥이가 넓은 병); a flask (실험실용); a flagon (식탁용 포도주병); a vial 〔phial〕 (작은 약병). ¶ 병목 the neck of a bottle / 병을 비우다 empty a bottle / 병에 채우다 bottle 《wine》; fill a bottle 《with》/ 이 병은 얼마나 들어가나 How much does this bottle hold? ② 《셀 때》 a bottle 《of》. ¶ 맥주 한 병 a bottle of beer / 병으로 팔다 sell 《*a thing*》 by the bottle / 이 주스는 한 병에 8백원이다 This fruit juice is 800 won a bottle.

**병**(病) ① [일반적] a sickness 《미》; an illness 《영》; a disease; 《가벼운》 an ailment; an indisposition; 《만성의》 a malady; 《국부적인》 a trouble; a complaint; a disorder.
¶ 병난 sick 《미》; ill 《영》; unwell; ailing; diseased; indisposed / 병 때문에 for reason of health; for health reasons; because of 〔owing to, due to〕 *one's* illness / 가벼운 병 a slight 〔minor〕 illness / 중병 a serious 〔severe〕 disease 〔illness〕 / 불치의 병 an incurable illness / 오래 끄는 병 a protracted 〔lingering〕 disease / 잘 낫지 않는 병 an obstinate disease / 소화기 계통의 병 a disorder 〔disease〕 of the digestive system / 마음의 ～ illness of the mind; a mental dis-

ease / 치명적인 ～ a fatal 〔deadly〕 disease / 병문안을 하다 ask 〔inquire〕 after 《*a person's*》 health.

병에: 병에 걸리다 fall 〔get, be taken〕 ill 〔sick〕; be attacked by a disease / 병에 감염되다 catch 〔contract〕 a disease 《from》 / 병에 견디다 bear *one's* illness / 병에 듣다 be of medicinal value / 병에 잘 걸리다 be sickly; be liable to illness 〔a disease〕 / 병에 지다 give way to *one's* disease / 병에 약하다 easily yield to disease.

병이: 병이 나다＝병에 걸리다, 병들다 / 병이 낫다 get well; recover from *one's* illness; be cured of a disease / 병이 옮다 ＝병에 감염되다 / 병이 위독하다 *one's* illness is serious; [사람이 주어] be very 〔critically, seriously〕 ill / 과로로 병이 나다 work *oneself* ill / 과식해서 병이 나다 overeat *oneself* ill.

병으로: 병으로 결근하다 be absent from *one's* duty 〔office〕 owing to illness / 병으로 고생하다 be afflicted 〔troubled〕 with a disease / 병으로 누워있다 be ill 〔sick〕 in bed; be laid up (with illness) / 병으로 죽다 succumb to a disease; die of sickness 〔illness〕; die of 〔from〕 a disease / 병으로 쉰다고 전화하다 call in sick.

병을: 병을 앓다 suffer from a disease; be ill 〔troubled〕 《with》 / 병을 고치다 cure an ailment 〔a disease〕; cure 《*a person*》 of a disease 〔an illness〕 / 병을 구실로 하다 plead illness 〔a disease〕 (as an excuse) / 병을 내버려 두다 neglect a disease; let a disease take its own course / 병을 악화시키다 complicate a disease / 병을 뿌리뽑다 exterminate the germs of a disease / 병을 예방하다 prevent 〔stave off〕 a disease / 병을 옮기다 transmit 〔communicate〕 *one's* illness 〔disease〕 to 《*another*》; infect 《*another*》 / 병을 이기다 survive 〔get over〕 an illness / 병을 진단하다 diagnose a disease / 병을 치료하다 treat a disease / 병을 치료받다 undergo 〔receive〕 medical treatment.

¶ 그녀는 무슨 병이지 What is she suffering from? *or* What is wrong with her? / 나는 병으로 그 모임에 참석지 못했다 I couldn't attend the meeting because of illness. / 그녀의 병은 오래 끌고 있다 Her illness is lingering. / 어머니의 병은 어떻습니까 How is your (sick) mother? / 그녀는 죽을 때까지 병이라는 것을 몰랐다 She never had a day of illness till the one that killed her. *or* Her first illness was her last. / 병에 걸려 봐야 비로소 건강의 고마움을 안다 We do not appreciate the blessing of health till we lose it.

> 용법 **sickness** 《미》에서는 일반적인 「병」을 가리키는 말이지만, 《영》에서는 「병」이외로 「구역질」을 뜻하기도 함. **illness** 《영》에서는 「병」을 뜻하는 가장 일반적인 말. 《미》에서는 약간 격식차린 말로 쓰이며, 비교적 「무거운 병」을 가리킴. **disease** 신체의 기능을 해치는, 병명이 붙는 특정의 「병」을 말함. 따라서 「그는 병에 걸렸다」는 《미》에서는 He is sick. 《영》에서는 He is ill.이 보통. 그러나 《미·영》이 다 함께 명사 앞에서는 a sick man이라 하며 an ill man이라고는 하지 않음. 단, a seriously ill man (중병자)처럼 앞에 부사가 올 때는 sick가 아니고 ill을 씀.

② 《약점》 a weakness (of character); a fault; an infirmity. ¶ 여자를 너무 좋아하는 것이 그의 병이다 His weakness is being too fond of women. / 게으른 것이 그의 병이다 Idleness is his fault. ③ 《사물에 생기는 탈》 trouble. ⇨ 탈(頉).

**병가**(兵家) 《병법가》 a tactician; a strategist; 《군인》 a man of arms; a soldier.

**병가**(病暇) sick leave. ¶ ～를 얻어 쉬고 있다 be on sick leave.

**병갑**(兵甲) arms; armor.

**병객**(病客) a sick 〔sickly〕 person; [총칭] the sick.

**병결**(病缺) absence on account of 〔due to〕 illness.

**병고**(病故) an illness; a sickness; a disease.

**병고**(病苦) the pain 〔torment〕 of sickness; suffering (from illness); illness. ¶ ～에 시달리다 labor under *one's* disease; suffer from *one's* illness / ～를 덜다 relieve *one's* suffering (from illness) / ～를 견디지 못하여 그는 자살했다 Unable to bear the pain of sickness, he killed himself.

**병골**(病骨) a sickly person; a weak 〔delicate〕 person.

**병과**(兵科) a branch of the army; an arm. ◉ ～장교 a combatant officer. 보병～ the infantry (branch). 포병～ the artillery (branch).

**병구**(病軀) a sick body; ill 〔poor〕 health; a sickly constitution. ¶ ～를 무릅쓰고 외출하다 go out in spite of *one's* failing 〔poor〕 health.

**병구완**(病—) nursing; tending 《a sick

person》; care (for the sick). ～하다 nurse; tend; care for; attend on. ¶ 극진한 ～ careful nursing / 자지 않고 ～하다 nurse 《a patient》 all through the night; sit up all night with 《a patient》 / 그녀는 나의 극진한 ～에도 보람없이 어제 저녁에 죽었다 In spite of the devoted nursing I gave, she died last night. / 약도 약이지만 ～이 중요하다 Nursing first, medicine next. *or* Nursing before medicine.

**병권**(兵權) military power 〔authority〕. ¶ ～을 잡다 seize 〔grasp, assume, hold〕 military power.

**병균**(病菌) a (disease) germ; a virus; pathogenic bacteria. ¶ …의 ～을 발견하다 isolate the virus of.... ◉ ～보유자 a disease 〔germ〕 carrier.

**병근**(病根) ① 《병의 근원》 the cause 〔origin〕 of a disease; a morbific agent. ¶ ～을 없애다 exterminate the germs of a disease. ② 《악습》 the root of an evil. ¶ ～을 없애다 strike at the root of an evil.

**병기**(兵器) arms; a weapon (of war); [총칭] ordnance; weaponry. ¶ 공격〔방어〕～ an offensive 〔a defensive〕 weapon / 재래식〔비핵〕～ conventional weapons / 핵～ nuclear weapon. ◉ ～고 an armory. ～장교 an ordnance officer. ～제조 manufacture of arms (and ammunition). ～창 an arsenal; an ordnance depot 《미》. ～학 ordnance science.

**병나다**(病—) ① ＝병들다. ② ⇨ 탈나다.

**병내다**(病—) ① 《병을》 cause 〔bring about〕 illness; make 《*a person*》 sick. ② 《탈을》 put 〔get〕 《*a thing*》 out of order; mess 《*a thing*》 up.

**병단**(兵團) an army corps; a corps.

**병독**(病毒) a virus; a (disease) germ; taint. ¶ ～에 감염되다 get infected; be tainted / ～을 퍼뜨리다 disseminate 〔spread〕 infection / ～이 퍼지는 것을 막다 arrest the spread of a virus. ◉ ～매개 생물 a vector. ～보유자 a germ carrier; a reservoir.

**병동**(病棟) a (sick) ward; 《미》 a pavilion. ¶ 격리～ an isolation ward / 외래〔입원〕～ outpatients'〔inpatients'〕 ward / 일반～ a general ward.

**병들다**(病—) get sick 《미》; fall 〔be taken〕 ill 《영》; be ill 〔troubled〕 《with》. ¶ 병든 sick; ill; in poor health; unwell; diseased / 병든 마음 an aching heart / 병들기 쉽다 be liable to 「illness 〔a disease〕 / 그는 병이 들었다 He is affected by a disease.

**병란**(兵亂) a war; a military disturbance.

**병력**(兵力) 《군대의 힘》 military force 〔power, strength〕; force of arms; 《군인수》 the (numerical) strength of an army; troop strength. ¶ 적의 대 ～ a large enemy force / 100 만의 ～ a force 1,000,000 strong / 200 만의 전시 ～ a war effective of two million / 1개 대대〔중대〕～으로 in battalion 〔company〕 strength / ～을 감축〔증강〕하다 reduce 〔raise, build up〕 its troop strength / 소수의 ～을 거느리고 with a small force / 대 ～으로 쳐들어오다 come in great force / 그들은 계속해 ～을 증가시키고 있다 They keep increasing their military strength.

**병력**(病歷) a case 〔medical, clinical〕 history; the history of a case. ¶ 환자의 ～ the (past) history of a patient / ～을 조사하다 check *a person's* medical 〔clinical〕 history.

**병렬**(竝列) arranging in a row 〔line〕. ～하다 《…이》 stand in a line; be in a row; 《…을》 draw up in a line; arrange 〔place〕 in a row. ◉ ～회로 〖전기〗 a parallel (circuit).

**병리**(病理) pathology. ◉ ～해부학 morbid 〔pathological〕 anatomy.

**병리학**(病理學) pathology. ¶ ～(상)의 pathological. ◉ ～교실 a pathology (class)room. ～자 a pathologist. ～총론〔각론〕 general 〔special〕 pathology.

**병립**(竝立) standing side by side; compatibility; coexistence. ～하다 stand side by side; stand together; coexist 《with》; be consistent 〔compatible〕 《with》. ◉ ～개념 〖논리〗 a coordinate concept.

**병마**(兵馬) ① 《병기와 군마》 arms and war horses; 《군사와 말》 soldiers and horses. ② 《군대·병무》 troops; military affairs. ¶ ～의 대권을 잡다 assume supreme military power.

**병마**(病魔) the demon of ill health; the curse of a disease; a disease. ¶ ～가 덮치다 be taken ill; be seized with a sickness / ～에 시달리다 labor under *one's* disease / ～에 쓰러지다 succumb to a disease; fall a victim to a disease.

**병마개**(甁—) a bottle cap 〔top〕; a cork; a stopper. ¶ ～를 뽑다〔따다〕 uncork; open a bottle; pull out a stopper / ～를 하다 stopper a bottle; put a stopper in a bottle; cork a bottle; put a cap on a bottle / ～를 단단히〔느슨히〕 막다 cork a bottle tightly 〔loosely〕.

**병막**(病幕) a quarantine (station); an isolation hut.

**병명**(病名) the name of a disease. ¶ ～ 미상의 병 an unidentified disease 〔case〕/ ～을 알아내다 diagnose 〔identify〕 a disease / 의사가 ～을 밝히지 못하다 a doctor fails 〔is unable〕 to diagnose a case.

**병목**(甁—) the neck of a bottle; the bottleneck.

**병몰**(病沒) ＝병사(病死).

**병무**(兵務) military 〔conscription〕 affairs. ◉ ～청 the Military Manpower Administration. ～행정 conscription administration.

**병발**(竝發) ①《사건의》 concurrence 《of events》. ～하다 concur; synchronize; take place together; happen 〔break out〕 at the same time. ②《병의》 a complication. ～하다 [새 병이 주어] accompany 《the flu》; [원래의 병이 주어] be complicated by 《another disease》. ¶ 독감이 폐렴을 ～하였다 His influenza grew 〔developed〕 into pneumonia. ◉ ～증 《develop》 a complication; an intercurrent disease; a deuteropathy.

**병법**(兵法) tactics (전술); strategy (전략). ◉ ～가 a military strategist.

**병사**(兵士) a soldier; a private; a serviceman.

**병사**(兵舍) a barracks.

**병사**(兵事) military affairs. ◉ ～계(원) a secretary in charge of military affairs. ～과 a military affairs section.

**병사**(病死) death of 〔from〕 (a) sickness 〔a disease〕. ～하다 die of illness 〔sickness〕; die from a disease. ¶ ～자가 열 명 이상이나 되었다 More than 10 persons died of illness. *or* There were over 10 deaths due to sickness.

**병살**(倂殺) 〖야구〗 a double play. ～하다 make a double play. ¶ ～당하다 be doubled up; have a double play.

**병상**(病床) a sickbed. ¶ ～을 떠나지 못하는 bedrid(den); bedfast 《미》/ ～의 소녀 a bedridden girl / 그녀는 ～에 누워 있다 She is sick 〔ill〕 in bed.
◉ ～일지 《병자의》 a sick person's diary; 《병원의》 the nurse's report; a clinical report 〔diary〕; a sickbed record; a chart.

**병상**(病狀) the condition (of a disease 〔patient〕). ⇨병세.

**병상병**(病傷兵) the sick and wounded (soldiers); the invalid soldiers.

**병색**(病色) sickly appearance.

**병서**(兵書) a book on strategy 〔tactics〕; a book on military science.

**병석**(病席) a sickbed. ¶ ～에 눕다 be ill in bed; be laid up (with illness); lie in *one's* sickbed; be confined to bed / ～에서 일어나다 be out of bed; leave *one's* bed; leave 〔rise from〕 a sickbed.

**병선**(兵船) a warship; a military vessel.

**병설**(竝設) establishment as an annex. ～하다 establish 《a kindergarten》 as an annex 《to the college》.

**병세**(病勢) the condition 〔state〕 of a disease 〔patient〕. ¶ ～가 악화〔호전〕되다 grow worse 〔better〕; take a turn for the worse 〔better〕/ ～가 어지간히 진행되어 있다 *one's* illness is in its advanced stage; [사람이 주어] be far gone in *one's* sickness / 아드님 ～가 좀 어떻습니까 How is your sick son's condition ? / ～에 변화가 없다 There is no change in his condition.

**병소**(病巢) 〖의학〗 a focus (*pl.* ～es, -ci); a lesion. ¶ ～를 적출하다 extract a focus.

**병술**(甁—) bottled liquor; liquor sold by the bottle.

**병술**(丙戌) 〖민속〗 the 23rd binary term of the sexagenary cycle.

**병시**(丙時) 〖민속〗 the 12th of the 24 hour periods (＝10:30-11:30 a.m.).

**병신**(丙申) 〖민속〗 the 33rd binary term of the sexagenary cycle.

**병신**(病身) ① 《불구자》 a deformed 〔maimed〕 person; a deformity; a cripple; a (physically) handicapped person; a disabled person. ¶ ～이 되다 get deformed; get disabled / ～을 만들다 deform; disfigure; maim; cripple / ～으로 태어나다 be born deformed / 전쟁으로 평생 ～이 되다 be crippled 〔maimed, disabled〕 for life in the war.
② 《병든 몸》 a sick body; a chronic invalid (만성 병자).
③ 《바보》 a stupid person; a fool; a good-for-nothing. ¶ ～ 같은 소리 silly talk; nonsense / ～ 같은 짓을 하다 make a fool of *oneself;* act silly / 이 ～아 You blockhead! *or* You big fool ! / ～처럼 굴지 마라 Don't be a fool.
④ [비유적] a defective 〔misshapen〕 thing. ¶ ～으로 만들다 damage 〔spoil, mutilate〕 《*a thing*》; make 《*a thing*》 defective.

**병신구실**(病身—) a behavior to be expected of a defective; a foolish act.

～하다 act 〔play〕 the fool; make an ass of *oneself;* prove to be a fool.

**병실**(病室) a sickroom; a hospital room (병원의); a (sick) ward (병동); an infirmary (학교·공장 따위의); a sick bay 〔berth〕 (함선 내의). ¶ 개인 ～ a private ward / (병원의) 외과 병동 제3 ～ 환자 the patient in Room No. 3 of the surgical ward / ～을 한바퀴 돌다 make a round of the ward.

**병아리** a chick; a chicken; 《한배로 깐》 a brood. ¶ ～를 까다 hatch out chickens. ◉ ～감별기 a chick tester. ～감별사 a chicken sexer.

**병약**(病弱) delicate constitution; (constitutional) weakness; infirmity. ～하다 (be) sickly; constitutionally weak 〔infirm〕; [서술적] have a weak 〔delicate〕 constitution; be an invalid; be in poor health.

**병어** 〖어류〗 a harvest fish. ◉ ～주둥이 a small-mouthed person.

**병역**(兵役) military service; service in the army. ¶ ～을 필한 자 a person who fulfilled *his* (military) service / ～에 복무하다 do 〔undergo〕 military service; serve (*one's* time) in the army 〔navy〕; bear 〔carry〕 arms / ～이 면제되다 be exempted from military service / ～을 기피하다 evade 〔dodge〕 *one's* military service.
◉ ～기피자 a shirker of military service; a slacker 《구어》. ～면제 exemption from (military) service. ～미필자 a person who has not yet completed *his* military duty. ～법 the military service law. ～연한 the term of military service. ～의무 obligatory 〔compulsory〕 military service.

**병영**(兵營) barracks. ◉ ～생활 a barrack 〔an army〕 life.

**병오**(丙午) 〖민속〗 the 43rd binary term of the sexagenary cycle.

**병용**(竝用·倂用) ～하다 use jointly 〔together, in combination〕 《with》; use 《two things》 at the same time. ¶ 가루약과 물약을 ～하다 take a powder medicine with a liquid one together 〔at the same time〕 / 전력회사는 석유와 석탄을 ～하고 있다 The electric power company uses oil with coal.
◉ ～치료 a combined treatment.

**병원**(兵員) strength (of an army, of troops); military personnel. ¶ ～을 증가〔감축〕하다 increase 〔reduce〕 the personnel of army.
◉ ～명부 〖육군〗 a muster roll; an army list; 〖해군〗 a navy list.

**병원**(病院) a hospital; a clinic (진료소); 《미》 a doctor's office (의원); an infirmary (공장 등에 부속된). ¶ 소아과 ～ a children's hospital / 정신～ a mental home 〔hospital, institution〕 / 종합～ a general hospital / 개인～ a private hospital / ～에 다니다 《외래환자로서》 attend (a) hospital; go to (a) hospital / ～에 수용하다 receive 《a patient》 into (a) hospital; admit 《*a person*》 to (a) hospital / ～에 입원하다 enter 〔go into〕 (a) hospital; be hospitalized 《미》 / ～에 입원시키다 send 《*a person*》 to (a) hospital; hospitalize 《*a person*》 / ～에 입원해 있다 be in (the) hospital / ～으로 병문안 가다 visit 〔inquire after, go to see〕 《*a person*》 in hospital (★ hospital은 go to school, go to church 따위에서의 church, school처럼 관사 없이 쓰는 용법이 확립되어 있지 않음. 따라서 go to hospital 또는 go to a hospital 양쪽이 다 사용됨) / ～에서 실습하다 《의대생이》 intern at the 《city》 hospital; be an intern / 그녀는 구급차로 ～에 실려갔다 She was carried to the hospital by ambulance.
◉ ～선 a hospital ship. ～열차 an ambulance train. ～장 the director 〔superintendent, head〕 of a hospital. ～차 an ambulance.

**병원**(病原) 〖의학〗 the cause of a disease; an etiological cause; pathogenesis. ¶ ～의 pathogenic / ～을 알 수 없는 병 a disease of unknown etiology. ◉ ～균 pathogenic bacteria 〔fungi〕; a disease germ; a bacillus (*pl.* -li): ～균을 죽이다〔박멸하다〕 destroy germs / ～균을 발견하다 isolate the bacterium 《of》. ～체 pathogen; a pathogenic organ(ism) 〔microbe〕. ～학 etiology.

**병유하다**(竝有―) combine (one thing with another); possess both 〔together〕; enjoy concomitantly.

**병인**(丙寅) 〖민속〗 the 3rd binary term of the sexagenary cycle.

**병인**(病因) the cause of a disease; an etiological factor. ◉ ～론, ～학 (a)etiology.

**병자**(丙子) 〖민속〗 the 13th binary term of the sexagenary cycle.

**병자**(病者) a sick person; an invalid; 《환자》 a patient; a case; the sick [총칭]. ¶ ～처럼 보이다 look sickly / 금년에는 ～가 많다 The sick rate is heavy this year. / 어젯밤에는 밤새 ～를 간호했

다 Last night I stayed up all night nursing a sick person.

**병작**(竝作) sharecropping on a fifty-fifty basis. ～하다 sharecrop on 50-50 basis. ⇨ 반타작. ◉ ～농 50-50 sharecropping.

**병장**(兵長) a sergeant.

**병적**(病的) unsound; morbid; diseased; pathological; abnormal (변태적). ¶ ～으로 morbidly; pathologically; abnormally / ～인 생각 a morbid thought / ～인 성격 abnormal character / ～소질 diathesis; pathological predisposition / ～으로 좋아하다 have a morbid liking for; have a weakness [passion] for / ～으로 무서워하다 have an abnormal fear《of》/ 마음과 몸이 모두 ～이다 be diseased both in body and mind / 그는 ～으로 시간을 엄수한다 He is morbidly punctual.

**병적**(兵籍) ① 《군적》 a military register; an army roll. ¶ ～에 올리다 enlist [enroll *oneself*] in the army; enter [join] the army [colors]. ② 《군인의 신분》 *one's* military status.
◉ ～부 a muster roll.

**병점**(病占) prognosticating the course of an illness (by divination). ¶ ～을 치다 《a fortuneteller》 prognosticate the course of an illness / ～을 보다 consult 《a fortuneteller》 about *one's* illness.

**병정**(兵丁) a serviceman; a soldier. ¶ ～으로 뽑혀가다 be drafted / ～놀이를 하다 play (at) soldiers.

**병조림**(甁―) bottling. ～하다 bottle 《*a thing*》; seal 《*a thing*》 in a bottle. ¶ ～한 bottled / ～하여 팔다 sell 《vinegar》 in bottles.

**병존**(竝存) coexistence. ～하다 coexist 《with》; be coexistent 《with》; exist together.

**병졸**(兵卒) a private; a (common) soldier; an enlisted man 《미》; [총칭] the ranks; the rank and file. ¶ 일개 ～에서 장군이 되다 rise from the ranks to be a general.

**병종**(丙種) the third class [grade]; grade [class] C.

**병종**(兵種) a branch of the army.

**병주머니**(病―) a bag of woes; a man with miscellaneous ailments.

**병중**(病中) ¶ ～에 during *one's* illness; while *one* is ill [sick] / ～임에도 불구하고 in spite of *one's* sick health; despite *one's* illness / ～이다 be ill in bed.

**병증**(病症) the nature [symptoms] of a disease; a case. ¶ ～을 설명하다 explain *one's* case / 계속되는 기침은 폐결핵의 ～일 수도 있다 A persistent cough may be a symptom of tuberculosis.

**병진**(丙辰) 〖민속〗 the 53rd binary term of the sexagenary cycle.

**병진**(兵塵) the dust of the battlefield; the tumult of war.

**병진**(竝進) ～하다 advance together; keep abreast of 《*a person*》; keep pace with 《*a person*》; advance side by side. ◉ ～운동 〖물리〗 translation.

**병참**(兵站) 〖군사〗 impedimenta; supply trains; logistics.
◉ ～감 the commander of the line of communications; the quartermaster general (생략 Q.M.G.). ～기지 a supply [commissary] base; a base for supplies. ～보급장 a quartermaster depot. ～부[소] the commissariat; a supply department; a quartermaster depot 《미》. ～부대 the Quartermaster Corps; the Material Command 《미》. ～사령부 the Logistic Support Command. ～선 a line of communications; a supply line. ～장교 a commissary; a quartermaster 《미》. ～학[술] logistics.

**병추기**(病―) an invalid; a sickly person.

**병충해**(病蟲害) damages by blight and harmful insects.

**병치**(竝置) juxtaposition. ～하다 put [place] side by side 《with》; juxtapose; place in juxtaposition 《with》. ¶ 두 대의 자동판매기가 ～되었다 Two vending machines were put [placed] side by side.

**병칭**(竝稱) ranking together; classing one with another. ～하다 rank [class] 《*a person*》 with 《another》. ¶ ～되다 be ranked [classed] 《with》.

**병탄**(倂呑) annexation; absorption 《of a small country》; (a) merger. ～하다 annex 《A to B》; absorb; merge; swallow up.

**병통**(病―) trouble 《with a *thing*》; malfunction; something wrong 《with》; a hitch; a snag; a breakdown. ¶ 기계[일]에 ～이 생기다 have trouble with a machine [*one's* work].

**병폐**(病弊) an evil practice; a vice; an evil. ⇨ 폐해. ¶ 사회적[도시의] ～ social [urban] evils [ills].

**병풍**(屛風) a folding screen. ¶ 여섯폭 ～ a folding screen with six panel; a six-fold screen / ～을 치다[두르다] set up a folding screen (all around) / ～

으로 (칸을) 막다 screen off.

**병학**(兵學) military science.

**병합**(倂合) = 합병.

**병해**(病害) 《농작물의》 damage 《to the crop》 caused by blight or other plant disease; crop damage due to disease.

**병행**(竝行) ～하다 《나란히 감》 go side by side 《with》; go abreast 《of》; run parallel 《with》; keep pace 《with》; 《동시에 함》 (two things) 「at the same time 〔side by side〕. ¶ 두 가지 조사를 ～하다 conduct two investigations 「simultaneously 〔side by side〕 / 이 도로는 차 두 대가 ～할 수 없다 Two cars can't go side by side on this road. / 두 가지 일이 ～해서 진행되고 있다 The two jobs 〔projects〕 are going on at the same time.

**병화**(兵火) a fire caused by war; a 「warfare.

**병환**(病患) sickness; illness. ¶ 춘부장의 ～은 어떠시오 How is your (sick) father?

**병후**(病後) convalescence. ¶ ～의 사람 a convalescent person / ～에 after an illness / ～의 쇠약 weakness from *one's* illness / ～에 몸조리를 하다 recuperate *oneself* (after illness) / 그녀는 ～라 체력이 약하다 She is weak after her sickness. / 그녀는 온천에서 ～의 요양을 하고 있다 She is recuperating at a hot spring.

**볕** sunshine; the sun (as heat); the rays of the sun. ¶ 볕이 잘 드는〔안 드는〕 sunny 〔sunless, shady〕 / 볕이 들다 shine 《in(to), upon》; the sun comes 〔shines〕 into 《the room》 / 볕에 말리다 dry 《*a thing*》 in the sun / 볕에 쬐다 expose 《*a thing*》 to the sun / 볕에 타다 be 〔get〕 sunburnt; be (sun)tanned / 볕을 쬐다 take the sun; bask 〔bathe〕 in the sun / 방에 볕이 잘 든다 The sunlight streams 〔pours〕 into the room. / 볕이 따갑다 The sun is burning-hot. / 이 방은 볕이 잘 든다 This room gets a lot of sunlight 〔sunshine〕.

**보** a beam (of wood); a girder (강철의); a crossbeam (횡보).

**보**(步) ① 《걸음》 a pace; a step. ¶ 제1보 the first 〔initial〕 step / 일보 전진〔후퇴〕하다 make a step forward(s) 〔backward(s)〕. ② 《단위》 a measure of length (=6 *cha*).

**보**(保) 《보증》 guaranty; security; a guarantee; a pledge; 《보증인》 a guarantor; a bond; a surety (연대의); a reference (신원의). ¶ 보(를) 두다 co-sign (as a surety) / 보(를) 서다 stand guaranty 〔security〕 《for》; go bond 《for *a person*》 / 보를 세우다 find security 〔surety〕 《for》.

**보**(洑) ① 《저수지》 a dammed pool for irrigation; a reservoir. ② = 봇물.

**보**(褓) ① 《덮거나 싸는》 a cloth for wrapping 〔covering〕. ¶ 상〔테이블〕보 a tablecloth / 책보 a cloth used for wrapping books. ② 《가위바위보의》 "paper".

**-보**(補) assistant; probationary. ¶ 서기보 an assistant secretary; a probationary clerk / 외교관보 a probationary 〔student〕 diplomat / 차관보 an assistant vice-minister 〔undersecretary〕.

**보각**(補角) 〖수학〗 a supplementary angle; a supplement.

**보감**(寶鑑) ① 《책》 a handbook; a thesaurus (*pl.* ～es, -ri); a manual. ② 《모범》 an exemplar; a mirror; a paragon.

**보강**(補强) reinforcement. ～하다 reinforce; strengthen; shore up 《a wall》; build up 《*one's* defenses》; beef up. ¶ 해군을 ～하다 reinforce 〔beef up〕 the navy / 멤버를 늘려서 팀을 ～하다 strengthen the team by increasing its members / 이 교량은 약간의 ～이 필요하다 The bridge needs some reinforcement. ◉ ～공사 reinforcement work. ～증거 〖법〗 (a) corroboration; supporting evidence. ～철재 〖건축〗 armature.

**보강**(補講) a supplementary lecture. ～하다 make up for a missing lecture.

**보건**(保健) 「preservation of 〔keeping〕 good health; health (건강); 《위생》 sanitation; 《학과목》 health education. ¶ ～상의 sanitary; hygienic. ◉ ～대학원 a graduate school of public health. ～물리학 health physics. ～복지부 the Ministry of Health and Welfare. ～사업 public health service. ～소 a public health center. ～시설 health facilities. ～식품 sanitary food. ～위생 hygiene; sanitation. ～음료 a hygienic drink. ～의(醫) a public health doctor. ～제도 the public health system. ～지도 a health guidance. ～체육 a health and physical education. ～행정 public health administration. 국립～연구원 the National Health Institute. 세계～기구 the World Health Organization (생략

WHO).

**보검**(寶劍) 《칼》 a valuable 〔precious〕 sword; 《의장용》 a formal-dress sword; a sword of honor 〔state〕.

**보결**(補缺) filling a vacancy; 《사람》 a substitute; a spare; an alternate 《미》; 《결점의》 supply of deficiency. ~하다 fill (a vacancy); supply 〔make up〕 a deficiency. ¶ ~의 supplementary / ~로 입학하다 be admitted to a school to fill (up) vacancies. ◉ ~모집 invitation for filling vacancies: ~ 모집하다 invite 《students》 to fill vacancies. ~생 a standby student; an alternant candidate (for admission to a school). ~선수 a substitute player; a reserve; a bench warmer (야구의). ~시험 a special entrance examination for standby students.

**보고**(報告) a report; 《간단한》 an account; (a) briefing 《미》; 《통계의》 returns; 《연구·조사 등의》 a memoir. ~하다 report; make 〔submit〕 a report 《of, on》; inform 《*a person*》 of 《an event》; give an account of; 《학회에서》 read a paper. ¶ 문서〔구두〕에 의한 ~ a written 〔an oral〕 report / ~를 받다 be briefed 《on》; get a briefing 《from *a person* on *a matter*》 / 회의 ~를 하다 give a report of the conference / 자초지종을 ~하다 make a full and detailed report / 요약해서 ~하다 make a summary report 《of》 / 나는 지출 ~를 했다 I made a return of money spent. / ~는 다음과 같다 The report runs as follows. / 나는 그 일에 관해 아무런 ~도 받지 못했다 I have received no report on that matter. / 그는 해외 출장에 관한 ~를 요청 받았다 He was asked to give a report of his business trip abroad. ◉ ~문학 *reportage* (F.). ~자 a reporter; a presenter (학회에서의); an informer. ~회 a briefing session. 연차~ an annual report. 중간~ an interim report. 최종~ the final report.

**보고**(寶庫) a treasure house; a treasury; 《땅》 a region rich in natural resources. ¶ 지식의 ~ a treasure house of knowledge 〔information〕 / 바다는 천연 자원의 ~다 The sea is a rich repository of natural resources.

**보고서**(報告書) a (written) report; 《학회의》 a paper; a memoir; 《계수의》 returns; 《협회의》 transactions. ¶ ~를 쓰다〔작성하다〕 make a report 《on》 / ~를 제출하다 send in 〔file〕 a report.

**보관**(保管) custody; charge; keeping; safekeeping; (a) deposit. ~하다 keep; take custody 〔charge〕 《of》; take 《*a thing*》 into *one's* custody; have 《*a thing*》 in *one's* custody 〔keeping〕; hold 《money》 on deposit. ¶ ~되어 있다 be in *one's* safekeeping / ~을 부탁하다, ~시키다 ask 《*a person*》 to keep 《*a thing*》 for 《*one*》; give 《*a thing*》 in the custody of 《*a person*》; give 〔leave〕 《property》 in trust to 《*a person*》 / 영수증을 ~하다 keep 〔preserve〕 a receipt / 물건을 ~하고 있다 have the goods in *one's* custody / 그가 가지러 올 때까지 짐은 내가 ~하지요 I'll take care of the baggage till he calls for it. / 귀중품은 접수계에서 보관합니다 The receptionist will take custody of your valuables. ◉ ~료 a custody fee; charges for custody; 《창고의》 a storage fee; storage. ~물 an article in custody; property in trust. ~소 a depository: 휴대품 ~소 a checkroom; a cloakroom. ~인 a keeper; a custodian; a depositary; 《재산 관리인》 a trustee (관재인). ~증 a deposit receipt; a certificate of custody.

**보교**(步轎) a kind of sedan(-chair); a palanquin. ¶ ~로 가다 go by palanquin / ~를 타다 (have a) ride in a sedan-chair. ◉ ~꾼 a chair-bearer.

**보국**(報國) patriotism; service(s) to *one's* country. ~하다 place *oneself* in the service of *one's* country; render service (to *one's* country); lay down *one's* life (for *one's* country).

**보국안민**(輔國安民) building up the nation and providing for the welfare of the people. ~하다 promote the interests of the nation and provide for the people.

**보국훈장**(保國勳章) the Order of National Security Merit.

**보궐선거**(補闕選擧) an election to fill a vacancy; a by-election 《영》; a special election 《미》.

**보균**(保菌) being infected; carrying germs. ~하다 carry germs; be infected. ◉ ~자 a (disease, germ) carrier; an infected person: 콜레라 ~자 a cholera carrier.

**보그르르** ⇨ 바그르르.

**보글-** ⇨ 버글-.

**보금자리** a nest; a roost; a home. ¶ 사랑의 ~ 《build》 a love nest / ~에 들다

settle in the nest; nest / ～(를) 치다 build a nest; nest 《in a tree》; roost / ～로 돌아가다 go home to roost / ～를 떠나다 leave the roost.

**보급**(普及) diffusion; spread; 《대중화》 popularization. ～하다 spread; diffuse; propagate; popularize. ¶ 텔레비전이 ～됨에 따라(서) with the spread of television / ～되다 become widespread; come into wide use; become popular (일반화되다) / …의 ～을 꾀하다 promote the spread of 《education》 / 새 방법을 ～시키다 generalize the new method / 텔레비전이 거의 각 가정에 ～되었다 TV sets have now found their way into almost all homes. / VTR은 널리 ～되어 있다 Videotape recorders have come into wide use. / 불교는 한자 ～에 도움이 되었다 Buddhism helped the spread of Chinese characters. ◉ ～소 a distributing agency 〔agent〕; a distributor. ～판 a popular 〔cheap〕 edition.

**보급**(補給) supply; replenishment. ～하다 supply; replenish. ¶ 충분한 식량의 ～ a good supply of food / 연료를 ～하다 refuel; replenish fuel / ～이 끊어지다 go 〔run〕 out of supplies; become short of supplies.
◉ ～관 〖군사〗 a supply officer; a quartermaster. ～기지 a supply base 〔depot〕. ～로 a supply route 〔trail〕; a lifeline (유일한). ～선(線) a supply line. ～선(船) a supply ship 〔boat〕.

**보급률**(普及率) the diffusion (rate). ¶ 그 나라는 TV의 ～이 세계 1위다 The country lead the world in the number of television sets in use. / 우리 나라에서 전화의 ～은 부산이 서울에 이어 제2위이다 Pusan is second in our country after Seoul in the percentage of households 〔persons〕 owning a telephone. / 전국의 TV ～은 90%에 달한다 Ninety percent of households in the country now have television sets.

**보기**[1] 《예》 an example; an instance; a case; 《그림으로 된》 an illustration; an illustrative example. ¶ ～를 들다 draw 〔quote〕 an instance 《from》 / …을 ～로 들다 take 《*a thing*》 as an example / 아래의 ～와 같다 It is as in the following examples. / 이것은 좋은 ～다 This is a case in point.

**보기**[2] 《보는 각도》 a way of looking at 《*things*》. ¶ ～에 따라서는 in a way 〔sense〕; viewed from another angle.

**보기**[3] 〖골프〗 bogey. ◉ 더블～ double bogey.

**보기**(寶器) a thing treasured; a treasure.

**보깨다** suffer indigestion; sit heavy on the stomach.

**보꾹** 〖건축〗 the inner part of a roof; the ceiling.

**보나마나** to be sure; undoubtedly; in all probability. ¶ 그녀석 ～ 불합격일 게다 He is sure to fail. *or* I bet he'll flunk.

**보내다** ① 《…에게》 (***a***) 《물품·돈 등을》 send; forward; transmit; consign (상품을); ship (배·차로); dispatch (발송); remit (송금); 《편지를》 post; reply 〔answer〕 (답장을). ¶ 돈을 ～ send money 《to *a person*》; remit 《*a person*》 money / 소포를 ～ send a parcel / 선물을 들려 ～ send 《*a person*》 home with presents / 짐을 ～ send 〔consign〕 goods 《to *a person*》 / 학비를 ～ supply 《*a person*》 with his school expenses / 차를 ～ send a car (round) to 《*a person's* house》 / (편지의) 답장을 ～ answer 〔reply to〕 a letter / (신문 기자가) 기사를 ～ file a story / 찬사를 ～ pay *one's* tribute of praise 《to》 / 이 물건을 집까지 보내주셨으면 싶습니다 I want to have these goods delivered to my home. (***b***) 《사람을》 send; dispatch. ¶ 군대를 ～ dispatch an army 《to》 / 사람을 ～ send a messenger 《to *a person's* house, for *something*》 / 사절을 ～ send 〔dispatch〕 an envoy 《to》 / 심부름 ～ send 《*a person*》 on an errand / 의사를 부르러 ～ send for a doctor / 학교에 ～ send 〔put〕 《a boy》 to school.
② 《배웅하다》 send off; see off. ¶ 손님을 ～ see a guest off / 남편을 보내러 공항까지 가다 go to the airport to see *one's* husband off.
③ 《시간·세월을》 pass 《time, *one's* life》; spend 《*one's* time》; live 〔lead〕 《a life》; kill 〔waste〕 time; while 〔dawdle〕 away. ¶ 시간을 보내기 위하여 to kill time / 말년을 즐겁게 ～ live the rest of *one's* life happily / 비참한 나날을 ～ live 〔lead〕 a wretched life / 빈둥거리며 시간을 ～ dawdle 〔idle〕 away *one's* time / 묵은 해를 보내고 새해를 맞이하다 see the old year out and the new year in / 그는 깨끗한 생애를 보냈다 He led a clean life. / 그는 독서로 하루를 보냈다 He spent the whole day reading.
④ 《그냥》 let 《it》 go; 〖야구〗 let a pitch go by. ¶ (타자가) 공을 그대로 ～ let a

ball go by 〔unstruck〕/ 버스 한 대를 그냥 ~ let a bus go by 《as it was so croweded》; wait for the next bus.

**보너스** a bonus. ⇨상여금. ¶ 월급 2개월분의 ~ a bonus equivalent to two months' pay / 연말 ~ a year-end bonus / ~를 주다 give 《*a person*》 a bonus.

**보는눈** power of observation; a discerning eye. ¶ ~이 있다 have an eye 《for pictures》.

**보늬** astringent skin; the astringent coat (as of chestnuts).

**보닛** 《모자》 a bonnet; 《자동차의》 a hood 《미》; a bonnet 《영》.

**보다**[1] ① [일반적] see; look 《at》; take 〔have〕 a look 《at》; get (a) sight 《of》; 《구어》 set 〔lay〕 eyes 《on》; 《목격하다》 witness. ¶ 보시는 바와 같이 as you see / 언뜻〔얼핏〕 보기에 at the first glance; at first sight / …을 보고 at (the) sight of… / 거울을 ~ look (at *oneself*) in a mirror / 아무의 얼굴을 ~ look *a person* in the face / 뚫어지게 ~ stare (fixedly) at; gaze at 〔on〕; look hard at / 슬쩍 (훔쳐) ~ steal a glance 《at》; cast a furtive glance at 《*a person*》; look at 《*a person*》 furtively / 무심코 ~ happen to see / 무심코 시계를 ~ glance casually at *one's* watch / 언뜻〔얼핏〕 ~ glance at 《*a thing*》 / 언뜻 보이다 get 〔catch〕 a glimpse of / 의심스러운 눈으로 ~ eye 《*a person*》 suspiciously / 자세히〔잘〕 ~ have a good look 《at》 / 주의해서 ~ watch / 차마 (눈뜨고) 볼 수 없다 cannot bear to see; be unable to bear 〔stand〕 the sight of / 보기에도 끔찍하다 be horrible to look at / 보고도 못 본 체하다 《눈감다》 blink 《a fact》; turn a 〔*one's*〕 blind eye to; 《몽따다》 cut 《*a person*》 (dead); pretend not to recognize 《*a person*》 / 보기좋다 be nice to look at; be attractive; be good-looking / 어디 보자 Let me see 〔think〕.... *or* Let me take 〔have〕 a look. / 그것 봐라 (내가 뭐라고 했지) I told you (so)! *or* There you are! / 이것을 보십시오 Please take a look at this. / 어디 두고 보자 You shall smart 〔pay dear〕 for this. / 이것 보십시오 Look here! / 누군지 가 보아라 Go and see who it is. / 자넨 그가 집에 들어가는 것을 보지 못했나 Didn't you see him go into the house? / 술취한 여자는 정말 눈뜨고 볼 수가 없다 What could be more unsightly than a woman in wine! / 그 여자는 꼴도 보기 싫다 I hate the very sight of her. / 그를 어디서 본 듯하다 I fancy I have seen him somewhere before. *or* I remember seeing him once. / 그것은 보면 볼수록 아름답다 The more I look at it, the more beaufitul it looks. / 보는 것 듣는 것이 모두 새로웠다 Everything I saw and heard was new to me.

② 《관찰하다》 observe; look 《at》; view; see; 《시찰하다》 inspect; visit. ¶ 외국인이 본 한국 Korea 「as foreigners see it 〔as seen by foreigners〕 / 내가 보는 바로는〔보기에는〕 from my point of view; as I take 〔see〕 it; the way I see 〔look at〕 it; in my eyes 〔opinion, view〕 / 어디로〔어느 모로〕 보나 in every respect; on all accounts; to all appearances 《미》; to all appearance 《영》 / 볼 줄 아는 사람이 보면 to the initiated 〔trained〕 eye / 대체로 보아(서) on the whole; considered as a whole / …하는 것을 보니 seeing that … / 보는 바가 다르다 look at 〔view〕 《*a matter*》 differently / 호의적으로 ~ take a favorable view 《of》 / 학교를 보러 가다 visit a school; pay a visit of inspection to a school / 나는 그렇게 보지 않는다 I don't view 〔see〕 the matter in that light.

③ 《구경하다》 see 《the sights》; do 《a town》; visit. ¶ 영화를〔연극을〕 ~ see a movie 〔play〕 / 야구〔영화〕를 보러 가다 go to 「see a baseball game 〔the movies〕 / 볼 만하다 be worth seeing 〔visiting〕; be visitable / 볼 것을 다 ~ have done all the sights 《in the town》 / 금강산은 볼만한 곳이 많다 There are lots of 「sights to see 〔places worth seeing〕 in Mt. Kumkang.

④ 《보살피다》 (***a***) 《일을》 attend to 《business》; manage; take; conduct. ¶ 사무를 ~ do 〔attend to〕 business / 일을 ~ conduct affairs; do *one's* job; work / 직무를 ~ perform the duties of an office; attend to *one's* official duties / 내 아내가 집안 일을 본다 My wife manages the household. (***b***) 《돌보다》 take 「charge 〔care〕 of; look 〔see〕 after; watch; 《밥상 등을》 set. ¶ 상을 ~ set the table / 아이를 ~ tend 〔nurse, look after〕 a child; baby-sit 《미》 / 집을 ~ look after a house 《while *a person* is away》 / 내가 없는 사이에 가게 잘 보아라 Keep an eye on the store while I am away.

⑤ 《읽다》 read; see; 《훑어보다》 look

through 〔over〕. ¶ 신문을 ～ read 〔see〕 the papers / 대충 ～ runs *one's* eyes through; glance over / 광고를 보고 사다 buy 《*a thing*》 from advertisement / 이 작문 좀 보아 주십시오 Will you kindly look through this composition? *or* Could you look at this composition?

⑥ 《조사·검사하다》 look over 〔into〕; examine; 《참고하다》 refer to 《a dictionary》. ¶ 보지도 않고 물건을 사다 buy a pig in a poke / 답안지를 ～ look 〔go〕 over the examination papers / 서류를 ～ examine 〔go through〕 the papers / (의사가) 환자를 ～ examine 〔have a look at〕 a patient / 라디오가 고장난 것 같은데, 좀 보아 주겠나 There seems (to be) something wrong with the radio. Will you see to it?

⑦ 《…로 생각하다》 regard 《as》; consider; think of 《as》; take 《for》; look (up)on 《as》; deem; reckon; count 《as, for》. ¶ …(이)라고 ～, …하다고 ～ regard as 《being, *do*ing》 / 그 사태가 중대하다고 ～ regard the situation as serious / 해결된 것으로 ～ look upon 《*a matter*》 as settled / 결석자는 불합격으로 본다 Those who absent themselves will be considered to have failed in the examination. / 그의 실패는 게으름 때문으로 본다 I impute 〔attribute〕 his failure to his laziness. / 그렇게 보는 사람이 대부분이다 Most people take it that way. / 나를 몇 살로 보는가 How old do you take me for? / 우리는 계약이 파기된 것으로 보았다 We considered the contract canceled. / 많은 사람들은 이 소설이 그녀의 대표작이라고 본다 A lot of people regard 〔look upon〕 this novel as her most important work.

⑧ 《당하다》 encounter personally; experience; undergo; go through; suffer; enjoy. ¶ 경사〔불상사〕를 ～ have a happy 〔an unhappy〕 occasion / 손해를 ～ suffer 〔sustain〕 a loss; suffer damage / 욕을 ～ be disgraced; be insulted; have a hard 〔rough〕 time of it / 이익을 ～ make a profit / 재미를 ～ enjoy *oneself;* have a good time; enjoy prosperity / 재미 보십시오 《장사하는 이에게》 I hope you will have lots of business.

⑨ 《치르다》 take 〔sit for〕 《an examination》. ¶ 시험을 ～ take 〔undergo〕 an examination; sit (for) an examination / 시험을 보지 않고 입학하다 be admitted into a school without examination.

⑩ 《누다》 relieve *oneself* 〔nature〕. ¶ 대변을 ～ have a bowel movement / 소변을 ～ urinate; make 〔pass〕 water / 「네 개는 대소변을 가리느냐」—「아직 아냐. 그놈 아무데서나 대소변을 봐」 "Is your dog house-broken 〔house-trained 《영》〕?"—"No, not yet. He has a pee and pooh everywhere."

⑪ 《장을》 buy 〔sell〕 《in the market》. ¶ 장을 ～ deal in the market; do *one's* 〔the〕 marketing / 장보러 가다 go to market; go shopping 〔marketing〕.

⑫ 《값을》 offer 《a price》; name 〔bid〕 a price 《for》. ¶ 값을 5만원으로 ～ make an offer of 50,000 won for.

⑬ 《새 식구를》 get; have. ¶ 며느리〔사위, 손주〕를 ～ get a daughter-in-law 〔son-in-law, grandchild〕 / 자식을 ～ have 〔get〕 a child; beget (아버지가).

⑭ 《사귀다》 have a secret (love) affair with. ¶ 첩을 ～ keep a mistress / 샛서방을 ～ cuckold 〔deceive〕 *one's* husband; have a secret lover.

⑮ 《판단하다》 (***a***) 《…한 사실로써》 judge. ¶ …로써 보면 on the evidence of…; judging from… / 내가 본 바에 틀림은 없다 I am infallible in my judgment. / 내가 보기에 그 회사는 믿을 만하다 In my judgment the company is reliable. (***b***) 《점을》 tell; read; have *one's* fortune told. ¶ 관상을 ～ tell fortunes by physiognomy; read faces; 《보는 사람한테》 have *one's* face read 《by a phrenologist》 / 손금을 ～ read (in) *one's* palm; tell 《*a person's*》 hand; 《보는 사람한테》 have *one's* palm read 《by》 / 나는 사주를 보았다 I had my fortune told by an astrologist.

⑯ 《맡아 보다》 take charge of (담당); deal with (종사); undertake; act as. ¶ 사회를 ～ preside at 〔over〕 《a meeting》; take the chair; 《방송 등의》 act as master of ceremonies 《for》 / 통역을 ～ act as interpreter.

**보다**[2] 《추측》 it seems; I guess. ¶ 비가 올까 ～ It looks like rain. / 비가 오는가 ～ It seems to be raining. / 그는 벌써 왔는가 ～ I guess he is here 〔has come〕 already.

**보다**[3] 《해보다》 try; have a try 《at》. ¶ 구두를 신어 ～ try shoes on / 모자를 써 ～ try on a (new) hat / 한국 음식을 먹어 ～ try out Korean(-style) food / 맞혀 보아라 Try on guess. / 해볼 테면 해보라 Do it, if you dare. / 이 책은 읽어

보니 무척 재미있었다 I found this book very interesting. / 어디 생각 좀 해봅시다 Well, I'll think it over. / 생각해 보십시오 Try and think. *or* Think about it.

**보다**[4] 《비교》 than; rather than; to. ¶ 그렇게 하기～는 rather than do that / ～도 even than; than also 〔either〕 / ～더 more than / ～야 (only if it be) than; if (it's a case of being more, *etc.*) than / ～ 정확히 말하면 to be more exact; to speak more precisely / (…)～ 못하다〔낫다〕 be inferior 〔superior〕 to; be worse 〔better〕 than / 부(富)～ 건강을 중히 여기다 value health above wealth; put health before wealth / 이 기차가 저 기차～ 빠르다 This train is faster than that one. / 그는 내가 생각했던 것～ 키가 컸다 He was taller than I thought he would be. / 힘이 약하다 한들 너～야 약하겠느냐 I may be weak but I'm sure I'm no weaker than you. / 한국의 기후는 독일～ 온화하다 The climate of Korea is milder than that of Germany. / 난 그～ 세 살 어리다 I'm three years younger than him.

**보다못하다** be unable of let 《it》 pass unnoticed; cannot remain indifferent 《to》; cannot stand 《*a thing*》 any longer. ¶ 보다못해 being more than *one* can bear to see; (being) unable to stand (idly) by (any longer) / 시끄럽게 떠드는 아이들을 보다못해 주의를 줬다 I couldn't stand to see the children making a lot of noise, so I told them to stop it.

**보답**(報答) (a) requital; (a) recompense; a reward; a return. ～하다 requite; recompense; return; repay. ¶ …의 ～으로 in return 〔compensation〕 for; for… / 우정에 ～하다 return 《*a person's*》 friendship / 친절에 ～하다 repay 《*a person*》 for *his* kindness / 공로에 ～하다 reward 《*a person*》 for *his* services / 노력에 ～하다 recompense 〔remunerate〕 《*a person*》 for *his* labor / 악을 선으로 ～하다 repay 〔requite〕 evil with good / ～을 못 받다 go unrewarded / 그것은 그에게 당연한 ～이다 That serves him right.

**보도**(步道) a sidewalk 《미》; a pavement 《영》. ¶ 횡단～ a (pedestrian) crossing / ～를 걷다 walk along a sidewalk.

**보도**(報道) news; a report; information; tidings; coverage. ～하다 report; inform 《*a person*》 of; notify 《*a person*》 on. ¶ ～의 자유 freedom of the press / 신문 ～에 의하면 according to the paper 〔the newspaper reports〕; The newspaper says that… / 이미 ～된 바와 같이 as previously 〔already〕 announced 〔reported〕 / …의 ～에 접하다 receive 〔get〕 the news of / 크게 ～되다 go into headlines; hit 〔make〕 (the) headlines / 잘못된 ～를 하다 make an incorrect report 《of》 / 단편적으로 ～하다 make a fragmentary report 《of》 / ～는 정확, 신속해야 한다 News report must be accurate and prompt. / 오늘 신문 ～에 의하면 일본에 대지진이 있었다고 한다 Today's newspaper says 〔reports〕 that a big quake 〔earthquake〕 hit Japan. / 승무원은 전원 사망하였다고 ～되었다 It was reported that all the crew were dead. / 이 신문은 편파적인 ～를 한다 This paper carries biased reports.
◉ ～가치 news value. ～관제 a news blackout; news censorship; a press ban: ～관제를 하다 prohibit 〔ban〕 the publication 《of the news》. ～기관 a news medium; the press; a medium of information. ～기사 a news story. ～기자 a (newspaper) reporter; a newsman. ～반 a press corps. ～본부 a reporting center. ～부 the press section; the public information office. ～사진 a news photo: ～사진 연감 a News Photography Annual; a Press Photos Annual. ～원 a reporter 《for *The Times*》; a newsman. ～전 a reportorial warfare. ～진 reporters; the press; a news front; a reportorial camp. 신문～ a press report.

**보도**(輔導) guidance; direction; protection and guidance. ～하다 guide; direct; lead. ◉ ～과 the guidance section. 직업〔학생〕～ vocational 〔student〕 guidance.

**보도**(寶刀) a treasured 〔sacred〕 sword. ¶ 전가(傳家)의 ～ an heirloom sword.

**보동보동하다** (be) plump; chubby; fleshy; well-fleshed 《cheeks》. ¶ 보동보동하게 살찐 얼굴 a chubby 〔full〕 face.

**보드득** ⇨ 바드득.

**보드랍다** ⇨ 부드럽다.

**보드카** 《러시아산 증류주》 vodka.

**보들보들하다** be very soft 〔tender, smooth, velvety〕. ¶ 보들보들한 살결 a very tender skin.

**보디** 《몸체》 the body. ◉ ～가드 a bodyguard. ～랭귀지 body language. ～블로

〖권투〗 a body blow: ～블로를 치다 deliver a body blow; deal《*a person*》 a blow in the body. ～빌딩 body-building. ～체크 a security check; a frisk (★「보디체크」는 한국식 영어. 영어의 body check는 ice hockey의 용어로 「상대 선수를 몸으로 막는 행위」를 뜻함).

**보따리**(褓—) a bundle. ¶ ～를 싸다 bundle《clothes》; do up in a bundle 〔package〕/ ～를 풀다 undo a bundle. ◉ ～장수 a peddler who carries his wares on his back.

**보라** ⇨ 보랏빛.

**보라매** a hawk that is trained for hawking before it is a year old.

**보람** ①《효력》(an) effect; fruit; (a) result;《가치》worth; usefulness. ¶ ～있는 worth(while); fruitful; effective / ～없는 useless; vain; fruitless; ineffective / ～ 있는 생활 a life worth while to live / ～없는 생활 an empty 〔a useless〕 life / ～없이 to no effect 〔good, avail〕; in vain / 노력한 ～도 없이 in spite of 〔for all〕 *one's* efforts / ～이 있다〔없다〕 be 〔be not〕 worth-while; be 〔be not〕 worth doing; give 〔do not give〕 *one* a sense of satisfaction / 사는 ～을 느끼다 find *oneself* worth living; find *one's* life worth living / 일한 ～이 없었다 I have labored to no purpose 〔in vain〕. / ～이 있는 〔없는〕 생활을 하다 live a meaningful 〔meaningless〕 life / 공부한 ～이 있었다 My study has borne fruit. / 그 약은 먹은 ～이 있었다 The drug has taken effect. / 그런 일을 해 무슨 ～이 있느냐 What is the good of doing it? / 애쓴 ～이 있었다 My pains have been rewarded. / 온 ～은 있었다 It paid me to come. / 좀더 ～ 있는 일을 시켜 주십시오 Please give me a more worth-while 〔challenging〕 job to do.
②《표적》a sign; an indication; a mark; symptom. ¶ ～(이) 뵈다 show 〔give〕 signs《of》.
③《표》a mark 〔note〕 (for future reference).

**보랏빛** violet. ¶ 연～ lilac / 진～ fluorite violet; dark lilac.

**보령**(寶齡) the king's age.

**보로통하다** ⇨ 부루퉁하다.

**보료** a fancy mattress used as cushion.

**보루**(堡壘) a fort; a fortification; a fortress; a stronghold. ¶ ～를 구축하다 fortify; construct 〔raise〕 a fort; construct defense works.

**보류**(保留) reservation; suspension (일시적인). ～하다 reserve; withhold; defer (연기하다). ¶ 계획을 ～하다 hold a plan in abeyance / 발표를 ～하다 withhold an announcement / 당분간 ～하다 wait《*a matter*》out; put《*a matter*》off for the present / 의견을 ～하다 reserve 〔hold back〕 *one's* opinion / 다음 회의까지 ～하다《결정을》defer to the next meeting / 태도를 ～하다 do not commit *oneself;* do not clarify *one's* attitude / 이 문제는 재고하기 위하여 ～되어야 한다 This question is to be reserved for further consideration. ◉ ～조건 a reserve; a reservation: ～조건으로 with reservation / ～조건 없이 제안을 수락하다 accept proposals without reservations. ～조항 a reddendum (*pl.* -da).

**보르네오** 《자바 섬 북방의 섬》 Borneo. ¶ ～의 Bornean.

**보르도** 《포도주》 Bordeaux. ◉ ～액 〖원예〗 Bordeaux mixture 〔liquid〕 (살균용).

**보름** ①《15일 동안》(the space of) fifteen days; a half month. ¶ ～ 안에 in two weeks' time; within a fortnight. ②《보름날》the fifteenth day of the month. ¶ 정월 ～ the 15th of January / ～께 around 〔towards〕 the middle of the month / 개 ～ 쇠듯 missing the good food appropriate to a feast day / ～ 달맞이 놀이 the full-moonrise-watching play. ◉ ～달 a full moon. ～밤 a full-moon night. ～사리《조수》the flood tide occurring on the 15th of the lunar month;《조기》a croaker caught at the time of the flood tide. ～차례(茶禮) the mid-month ancestor memorial service.

**보리** 〖식물〗 barley. ◉ ～고추장 hot-pepper paste made with barley. ～깜부기 smutted barley; barley blight. ～논 a paddy in which barley is grown as a second crop. ～농사 the barley raising 〔farming〕. ～누름 the barley ripening (time). ～밭 a barley field. ～수단(水團) barley flour dumplings mixed with honey. ～수매 가격 the government purchase price of the year's barley crops. ～쌀 a grain of barley; polished barley. ～죽 barley porridge 〔gruel〕. ～차 barley tea 〔water〕. ～타작 barley threshing: ～타작하다 thresh barley. ～풀《cut》grass for barley-field manure. 보릿가루 barley flour. 보릿가을 the barley harvest (time). 보릿겨 barley bran. 보릿고개 the "barley hump"; the spring famine; famine just before the barley harvest in the early summer: 보릿고개를 넘기다 get over the barley hump. 보릿짚 barley straw.

**보리**(菩提) ① 《지혜》 *Bodhi* (Sans.); the Supreme Enlightenment 〔Wisdom〕. ② 《불과(佛果) 달성의 길》 (attainment of) Buddhahood. ◉ ~심(心) a devout disposition; aspiration for Buddhahood.

**보리밥** boiled (rice and) barley. ¶ ~에는 고추장이 제격이다 《속담》 Put humble things with humble things. *or* Like agrees with like. 「shrimp.

**보리새우** 〖동물〗 a mysid; an oppossum

**보리수**(菩提樹) 〖식물〗 《인도의》 a bo tree; a pipal (tree); 《유럽의》 a linden; a lime (tree). 「bors.

**보린**(保隣) mutual help among neigh-

**보링** 《구멍 뚫기》 boring.

**보막이**(洑—) building a dammed pool (of water). ~하다 make a dammed pool.

**보매** apparently; seemingly; judging from the appearances. ¶ ~ 장사치 같다 look like a merchant / ~ 그는 40쯤 되겠다 He looks about forty. / 그녀는 ~ 얌전하다 She looks like a quiet girl. / 그는 ~ 정직한 것 같지만 안 그렇다 He is not as honest as he looks.

**보모**(保姆) a nurse; a nursery governess. ¶ 유치원 ~ a kindergarten teacher.

**보무**(步武) marching steps. ¶ ~당당하게 in fine array / ~당당하다 march on proudly; march in fine array; go on proudly.

**보무라지, 보물** tiny scraps 《of paper, cloth》; tiny bits of thread; lint. ¶ 실~ waste pieces of thread.

**보물**(寶物) a treasure; a highly prized article; valuables. ◉ ~선〔섬〕 a treasure ship 〔island〕. ~찾기 treasure hunting; a treasure hunt.

**보배** a jewel; a treasure; valuables; valuable 〔precious〕 things. ~롭다, ~스럽다 (be) precious; valuable. ¶ 숨은 ~ hidden 〔buried〕 treasure / 집안〔나라〕의 ~ a family 〔national〕 treasure / 어린이는 나라의 ~다 Children are the treasure of the country. / 그는 우리 나라의 ~다 He is a great asset to our country / 구슬이 서말이라도 꿰어야 ~ 《속담》 A book that remains shut is but a block.

**보병**(步兵) 〖군사〗 infantry [총칭]; 《병사》 an infantryman; a foot soldier; a dogface 《미속어》. ◉ ~과 the infantry arm. ~부대 an infantry outfit 〔corps〕. ~사단〔연대, 대대, 중대〕 an infantry division 〔regiment, battalion, company〕. ~전 an infantry action. ~학교 an infantry school.

**보복**(報復) retaliation; (a) reprisal; (a) revenge. ~하다 make 〔carry out〕 a reprisal 《on》; take a reprisal 《against》; retaliate 《an insult upon *a person*》. ¶ ~적인 retaliatory / …의 ~으로(서) in retaliation 〔revenge〕 for…; in 〔by way of〕 reprisal for… / 강력한 ~ 행동을 취하다 take strong retaliatory actions / 똑같은 수법으로 ~하다 retaliate in kind; repay 《*a person*》 in the same coin; serve 《*a person*》 with the same sauce / 이 ~은 꼭 하고야 말 테다 I will pay you out for this. *or* I'll fix you for that. / 노조는 파업으로 회사에 ~했다 The union retaliated against the company by staging a strike. / 그는 ~의 기회를 노렸다 He sought revenge. ◉ ~관세 a retaliative tariff. ~무기 a retaliatory weapon. ~수단 a measure of retaliation; a retaliatory measure. ~정책 a revanchist policy. ~정치 the politics of retaliation. ~조치 《take》 retaliatory measures. ~행위 an act of retaliation. 대량~ the massive retaliation.

**보부상**(褓負商) a peddler 《미》; a pedlar 《영》; a packman. ¶ ~을 하다 peddle.

**보비위**(補脾胃) 《위 보양》 strengthening of stomach and spleen. ~하다 strengthen 〔tone up〕 *one's* stomach; aid digestion; 《비위 맞춤》 propitiate; act obsequiously; curry favor 《with》; flatter.

**보살**(菩薩) ① 《보리살타》 a *Bodhisattva* (Sans.); a Buddhist saint. ¶ 외면은 ~ 내심은 야차 An angel without, a devil within. ② 《나이 먹은 여신도》 a venerable old female believer in Buddhism. ◉ ~할미 a Buddhist nun with unshaved head.

**보살피다** take care of 《*a person*》; look after; watch over. ¶ 집안 일을 ~ manage household affairs / 환자를 ~ attend to 〔on〕 the sick / 그는 나를 친형제처럼 보살펴 준다 He takes quite a brotherly interest in me. *or* He is a real brother to me. / 내 아들을 잘 보살펴 주십시오 Please take good care of my son.

**보상**(報償) (a) compensation; consideration; remuneration. ~하다 recompense; compensate. ◉ ~금 remuneration.

**보상**(補償) (a) compensation; (an) indemnity; indemnification; reparation. ∼하다 compensate 《for》; make good 《the loss》; make compensation 〔reparation〕 for 《the loss》; indemnify 《*a person*》 for 《the damage》. ¶ 상해에 대한 ∼으로 in compensation for *one's* injury / …의 ∼으로서 in compensation for... / ∼을 요구하다 make 〔demand〕 reparation 《for》/ 홍수 피해자들에게 ∼을 하다 compensate those who were hit by the flood / 그는 나의 손해를 ∼하기로 약속했다 He promised to compensate me for 〔against〕 my loss.
◉ ∼안 a compensation bill. ∼작용 〖심리〗 compensation. ∼조치 a compensatory measure; compensation. 수출∼ export compensation. 전면∼ 《demand》 full 〔complete〕 compensation.

**보상금**(補償金) an indemnity; (a) compensation (money). ¶ ∼을 받다 receive compensation (money) 《from》/ ∼을 지급하다 pay compensation to 《*a person* for》/ 1만 달러의 ∼을 내다 pay 〔offer〕 $ 10,000 compensation 《for》; give 10,000 dollars in compensation 《for》.

**보색**(補色) a complementary color.

**보서다**(保―) go 〔give, stand〕 security 《for》. ⇨ 보증.

**보석**(保釋) bail; bailment. ∼하다 let 《a prisoner》 out on bail; bail 《*a person*》 out (of jail) (보석보증금을 내고). ∼되다 be released on bail. ¶∼중에 있다 be under bail; be out on bail / ∼을 허가하다 accept 〔allow〕 bail; admit 《a prisoner》 to bail / 판사는 500만 원을 납입케 하고 ∼을 허가하였다 The judge allowed bail on the payment of 5 million won. ◉ ∼보증금 bail (money): ∼보증금을 내다 give bail 《for》. ∼보증인 a bailsman: ∼보증인이 되다 go bail for 《*a person*》. ∼원(願) an application for bail. ∼증서 a bail bond. 병∼ 《be released on a》 sick bail.

**보석**(寶石) a jewel; a gem; a precious stone.
¶ ∼을 박은 왕관 a jeweled crown; a crown studded with jewels / ∼으로 몸을 장식하다 wear jewelry / ∼을 박다 set a gem in 《a ring》; jewel 《a ring》 with a stone. ◉ ∼공 a lapidary. ∼류 jewelry. ∼반지 a ring set with jewels; a jeweled ring. ∼상 《사람》 a jeweler; 《가게》 a jeweler's (store). ∼상자 a jewel case 〔box〕.

> 용법 **jewel**, **gem** 가공된 보석. jewel에는 귀금속에 gem 또는 precious stone을 박은 고가의 장신구를 의미하는 뜻도 있음. **precious stone** 학술 용어로 가공되지 않은 원석 그대로의 보석을 뜻함. 엄밀하게는 다이아몬드, 에메랄드, 사파이어, 루비 등만을 가리킴.

**보선**(保線) 〖철도〗 line 〔track〕 maintenance; maintenance of rail tracks. ∼하다 keep 〔maintain〕 the tracks in good condition. ◉ ∼공(工) a line(s)-man; a trackman; a platelayer 《영》. ∼공사 track 〔maintenance〕 work. ∼구 a (railroad) section.

**보세**(保稅) ¶ ∼의 in bond; bonded.
◉ ∼가공 bonded processing: ∼가공수출〔무역〕 bonded processing exports 〔trade〕. ∼공장 a bonded factory. ∼지역〔구역〕 a bonded area. ∼창고 a bonded warehouse: ∼창고에 맡기다 bond; store 《goods》 in bond / ∼창고 예치증권 a bonded warehouse warrant / ∼창고 인도 ex bond. ∼화물 bonded goods; goods in bond.

**보송보송하다** (be) dry; dried up 〔out〕. ¶ 보송보송해지다 lose all moisture; dry up / 말라서 ∼ be dried up; be parched.

**보수**(保守) conservativeness; conservatism. ¶ ∼적인 conservative / ∼적인 생각 a conservative idea 〔view〕.
◉ ∼당 the conservative party; the Conservatives; the Right: ∼당원 a Conservative; 《영국의》 a Tory. ∼세력〔파〕 the conservatives; the old liners. ∼정권 a conservative government. ∼주의 conservatism; Toryism: ∼주의자 a conservative; a Tory. ∼진영 a conservative camp.

**보수**(補修) mending; repair. ∼하다 mend; repair; fix. ¶ 공장의 일부를 ∼했다 A part of the factory was repaired. / 부엌은 ∼가 필요하다 The kitchen needs repair. ◉ ∼공사 repair work(s): ∼공사용 재료 repairing 〔mending〕 materials / 하안(河岸) ∼공사 maintenance work on a river bank.

**보수**(報酬) a reward; remuneration; a recompense; a fee (의사·변호사 등의); 《급료》 pay. ¶ …의 ∼로서 in reward 〔recompense, return〕 for... / 무∼로 without pay 〔fee, remuneration〕; for nothing / ∼를 주다 remunerate

〔reward, pay〕《*a person* for *his* labor》/ ~를 받다 be paid《for》/ 그들은 노력에 대한 좋은 ~를 받는다 They receive a good return for their efforts.

**보수계**(步數計) a pedometer.

**보스** a boss; a bossman《미》. ◉ ~정치 boss-ridden 〔machine〕 politics.

**보스턴**《미국의 도시》 Boston. ◉ ~백 a Boston bag; an overnight bag《미》. ~시민 a Bostonian.

**보슬보슬**[1]《눈·비가》《fall》 gently; drizzly. ¶ 눈이 ~ 내리다〔오다〕 it snows gently / 비가 ~ 내리다 it drizzles.

**보슬보슬**[2] ⇨ 바슬바슬.

**보슬비** a drizzle; a misty rain. ¶ ~가 내린다 It is drizzling.

**보습** a plow(share).

**보습**(補習) supplementary lessons; refresher training《미》. ~하다 supplement (education). ◉ ~과 a supplementary course. ~교육 continuation 〔supplementary〕 education. ~학교 a continuation school.

**보시**(布施)《행위》 almsgiving;《금품》 alms; an offering《to a temple 〔Buddhist priest〕》. ~하다 give as a temple offering; make an 〔a monetary〕 offering《to a temple》. ¶ 절에 ~를 바치다 make an 〔a monetary〕 offering to a temple. ◉ 보싯돈 money collected from offerings at a Buddhist temple.

**보시기** a small bowl of porcelain 「〔brass〕.

**보신**(保身) self-protection; keeping *oneself* from harm; self-defense. ~하다 protect *one's* life; protect *oneself*. ¶ 그는 ~에 급급하다 He thinks only of 「self-preservation 〔defending his own interests〕. ◉ ~술 art of self=protection. ~책 the ways 〔techniques〕 of self-protection.

**보신**(補身) ~하다 build *oneself* up by taking tonics. ◉ ~탕 soup of dog's meat.

**보신**(補腎) ~하다 recruit vitality 〔invigorate *oneself*〕 by taking tonics. ◉ ~제 a tonic; an invigorant.

**보쌈김치**(褓—) kimchi wrapped in a large cabbage leaf like a bundle.

**보아** for《*a person's*》 sake; out of consideration for. ¶ 그의 어머니 낯을 ~ out of consideration for his mother / 나를 ~서라도 그를 용서해 주게 Forgive him for my sake.

**보아란듯이** ostentatiously; for show; proudly; to show off. ¶ ~ 행동하다 act demonstratively; cut around《미구어》/ ~ 최신 유행의 옷을 입다 wear a new-look suit just to show off / (이것) ~ 그는 두둑한 지갑을 꺼냈다 He took out his fat purse as if to show it off.

**보아주다** ①《돌보아 주다》 take care 〔charge〕 of; look 〔see〕 after; help. ¶ 아무의 일을 ~ look after *a person* / 집을 ~ take care of the house《during *a person's* absence》/ 나 없는 새에 애들 좀 보아 주십시오 Would you take care of my children while I am away? / 우리 아이의 영어 좀 보아 주시오 Please help my child with his English. ② = 눈감아 주다.

**보아하니** so far as my observation goes; so far as the appearances go; to all appearance; apparently. ¶ ~ 점잖은 분이 왜 이러시오 You look like a gentleman — you should behave yourself better.

**보안**(保安) the maintenance 〔preservation〕 of public security 〔peace〕. ¶ ~상의 위험 security risks. ◉ ~검열 security inspection. ~경찰 public=security police. ~과 the public safety division. ~관 a sheriff《미》: 부~관 a deputy sheriff. ~등 a security light. ~림 a reserved forest; a forest reserve 〔preserve〕. ~사범 national security violators; a public security offender: ~ 관련사범 those who were found guilty of endangering national security. ~설비 safety devices. ~요원《탄광 등의》 the maintenance personnel; a security guard; [일반적인] peace maintenance personnel;《요인 경호의》 security forces [집합적]. ~일반 수칙 security instructions. 국가~법 the National Security Law.

**보암직하다** (be) attractive; eye-catching; appealing; charming; fine.

**-보았자** (even) though 〔if〕...; supposing 〔granting〕 that.... ¶ 좋다고 해보았자 at the best / 불평해보았자 소용없다 It is no use complaining.

**보약**(補藥) a restorative; a tonic; an invigorant.

**보양**(保養) health seeking; preservation of health;《병후의》 recuperation; convalescence. ~하다 take a rest for *one's* health; recuperate (*one's* health); convalesce. ¶ (몸)~을 위해 for (the good of) *one's* health; for recuperation / ~하러 가다 go《to *a place*》 to 「recuperate 〔convalesce〕; go to《a spa》 for *one's* health. ◉ ~소 a sanatorium; a resort house. ～지 a health resort.

**보양**(補陽) ～하다 aid 〔strengthen〕 virility; invigorate 〔vitalize, stimulate〕 *oneself;* take a tonic; pep *oneself* up 《with a tonic》.

◉ ～제(劑) medicine to aid 〔strengthen〕 virility; aphrodisiacs.

**보얗다** ① 《빛깔이》 (be) milky white; pearly; frosty; opaque; cream-colored; be an "off" white. ¶ 살결이 ～ have a pearly skin. ② 《연기·안개가》 (be) hazy; misty; heavy (in the air). ¶ 안개가 ～ the fog is heavy / 방 안이 담배 연기로 ～ The room is heavy with tobacco smoke. / 하늘이 먼지로 ～ The sky is hazy with dust. ③ 《희미하다》 (be) dim; indistinct; blurred; blurry.

**보어**(補語) 〖문법〗 a complement.

◉ 주격〔목적격〕～ a subjective 〔an objective〕 complement.

**보여주다** show; let 《*a person*》 see 〔look at〕 《*a thing*》; display. ¶ 신분증을 보여 주십시오 Please show me your identification card. / 그것 좀 보여 주십시오 Let me have a look at it. / 그는 아무에게도 그것을 보여 주지 않는다 He lets nobody see it. / 그것을 다시 한번 보여 주십시오 Would you please let me 〔Could I〕 have another look at it?

**보옥**(寶玉) a gem. ⇨ 보석(寶石).

**보온**(保溫) keeping 〔retaining〕 warmth; heat 〔thermal〕 insulation. ～하다 retain heat; keep warm. ¶ ～을 위해서 for keeping warmth; to keep 《*a thing*》 warm / ～이 잘 되는 내의 warm underwear; heat-retaining underwear / ～성 시험 a heat-retention test.

◉ ～병(甁) a thermos (bottle, flask); a vacuum bottle: 이 ～병은 보온이 잘 된다 This thermos keeps liquids hot for a long time. ～장치 《자동 조절식의》 a thermostat. ～재(材) lagging (materials); lags.

**보완**(補完) repletion; supplementation; (a) complement. ～하다 complement; supplement; supply 《a want》; make good; make up for. ¶ 상호 ～적인 협력 complementary cooperation / 두 경제의 상호 ～적인 성질 the complementary nature of the two economies / 현행 입시 제도의 약점을 ～하다 make up for the weak points in the current entrance examination system / 일손의 부족을 기계로 ～했다 We used machinery to compensate for the labor shortage. / 부족한 수입을 ～하기 위해 그는 밤에 부업을 했다 He had a side job in the evening in order to supplement his income. ◉ ～설명 《give》 a supplementary explanation. ～재 〖경제〗 complementary goods. ～조치 《take》 complementary measures.

**보우**(保佑) protection; assistance; help; aid. ～하다 protect; assist; help; aid. ¶ 하느님의 ～ providential help; Divine aid.

**보위**(寶位) the throne; the crown. ⇨ 왕위. ¶ ～에 오르다 take 〔accede to〕 the throne.

**보유**(保有) possession; retention. ～하다 possess; hold; keep; retain; maintain. ¶ 핵～국 a nuclear power / 핵무기를 ～하다 hold 〔possess〕 nuclear weapons / 세계 기록〔선수권〕을 ～하다 hold a world record 〔championship〕.

◉ ～량(量) holding amount 〔volume〕: 금 ～량 gold holdings. ～물 tenement; holdings. ～미 rice held in stock: 정부 ～미 the government-stocked 〔=owned〕 rice; the government's rice holdings. ～액〔고〕 holdings: 적정 외환 ～액 an adequate amount of foreign exchange holdings. ～자 a possessor; a holder: 기록 ～자 a record holder. ～주권(株券) holding of shares 〔stocks〕. ～증권 security holdings.

**보유**(補遺) a supplement 《to an encyclopedia》; an appendix (*pl.* ～es, -dices); an addendum (*pl.* -da). ～하다 add a supplement to. ¶ ～의 supplementary.

**보유스름하다** (be) somewhat pearly 〔frosty, misty〕.

**보육**(保育) nurture; upbringing; day care (탁아소 등에서의). ～하다 nurse; nurture; bring up; rear; foster; take care of 《children》.

◉ ～기(器) 《미숙아용의》 an incubator. ～원 a nursery school; a day-care center; a day nursery 《미》. 아동～ childcare; children's education.

**보은**(報恩) requital 〔repayment〕 of kindness; gratitude. ～하다 repay 〔requite〕 《another's》 kindness. ¶ 은사에게 ～하기 위해 in order to repay *one's* teacher's kindness.

**보음**(補陰) 〖한의〗 ～하다 strengthen the negative principle in *one's* nature; counterbalance *one's* virile powers.

◉ ～제 a medicine for counterbalancing *one's* virile powers.

**보이** 《소년》 a boy; 《음식점의》 a waiter;

a potboy (바의); 《호텔의》 a porter; a callboy; a page; a bellboy 《미》; 《기선·여객기의》 a steward; a cabin boy; 《열차의》 a porter 《미》. ◉ ～장(長) a headwaiter; a head porter; a bell captain (호텔의). ～프렌드 a boyfriend.

**보이다**[1] ① 《눈이》 be able to see. ¶ 보이지 않는 눈 a sightless eye / 눈이 보이도록 해주다 restore sight to 《the blind》; restore 《*a person*》 to *his* sight / 고양이는 어둠 속에서도 눈이 보인다 Cats can see in the dark.

② 《눈에》 (***a***) 《눈에 들어오다》 see; catch sight of; [사물이 주어] be seen; be visible; come in sight; be in sight 〔view〕; meet 〔greet〕 the eye; be open to the view; 《나타나다》 appear; turn up; show up; 《오다》 come. ¶ 보이는 곳에서 in (*one's*) sight; within (*one's*) view; within eyeshot of 《*a person*》 / 맨눈에 ～ be visible to the naked eye / 보이지 않다 be not seen; be invisible; be out of sight; be closed to 〔concealed from〕 the view; 《사라지다》 disappear / 육지가 보이지 않는 아득한 바다 위에서 far out on the ocean beyond sight of land / 안 보이게 감추다 hide 《*a thing*》 from *one's* eyes / 무엇이 보이나 What do you see? / 안개 때문에 남산이 보이지 않는다 Namsan is scarcely visible through the fog. / 「김 선생님이 오셨니」—「아직 보이지 않습니다」 "Has Mr. Kim come yet?"—"He hasn't come yet." / 나는 교회가 보이는 곳에서 산다 I live in sight of the church. / 나무 사이로 바다가 보였다 The sea showed 〔was sighted〕 through the trees. / 거리에는 사람하나 보이지 않았다 Not a soul was to be seen on 〔in〕 the street. (***b***) 《발견되다》 [대상이 주어] be found; [사람이 주어] see; can 〔be able to〕 find. ¶ 보이지 않다 《사라지다》 be gone 〔missing〕; be nowhere to be seen / 시계가 보이지 않는다 I can't find my watch. *or* My watch is missing. / 그것이 문헌에 보인다 We find mention of it in literature. / 기부자 명단에는 많은 명사의 이름이 보인다 Among the list of contributors we notice many well-known names.

③ 《…인 듯하다, …로 생각되다》 seem (to be); appear (to be); look 《expensive, as if it is expensive》; look 〔seem〕 like. ¶ 주인으로 보이는 사람 a man who is apparently the master of the house / 정직해 ～ look honest / 장사치처럼 ～ look like a merchant; have the appearance of a merchant / 비가 올 것 같이 보인다 It looks like rain. / 그녀는 아픈 것처럼 보인다 She seems to be ill. / 그 보석은 진짜처럼 보인다 The jewel looks like a genuine one. / 갈 필요가 없을 것 같이 보인다 There seems (to be) no need to go. / 남편보다 부인이 퍽 젊어 보인다 The wife looks much younger than the husband.

**보이다**[2] ① 《…에게》 let 《*a person*》 see 〔look at〕 《*a thing*》; show; 《감춰진 것을》 disclose (to view); reveal 《beautiful white teeth》. ¶ 증명서를 ～ show a certificate / 실례를 ～ give an example; cite an instance / 실력을 ～ show 〔display〕 *one's* ability / 의사에게 ～ consult 〔see〕 a doctor; be examined by a doctor / 좋은 본을 ～ set a good example / 이것을 아무한테도 보이지 마십시오 Don't show this to anyone. / 더 싼 것을 보여 주십시오 Please show me a cheaper one. ② 《전시하다》 exhibit; display; put 〔place〕 《*a thing*》 on display 〔exhibition, show〕; 《공개하다》 throw 《a garden》 open to the public. ¶ 춤을 추어 ～ dance before 《the company》.

**보이스오버** 『영화·TV』 voice-over.

**보이 스카우트** 《단체》 the Boy Scouts; 《단원》 a boy scout. ◉ ～대장 a Scout Leader; the Chief Scout. ～대회 a boy scout rally; a jamboree (국제적인).

**보이콧** boycotting; a boycott. ～하다 stage a boycott; boycott 《Japanese products》. ¶ 우리는 그 회사 제품을 2개월간 ～하기로 했다 We have decided to boycott the firm's products for two months.

**보일락말락** ～하다 catch occasional glimpses of; be hardly seen. ¶ 구름 사이로 달이 ～ 했다 The moon was hardly visible through the clouds.

**보일러** 『기계』 a boiler. ¶ 가스〔기름, 석탄〕～ a gas-〔an oil-, a coal-〕fired boiler. ◉ ～맨 a boiler; a stoker. ～실 a boiler room.

**보자기** a wrapping cloth; a cloth wrapper. ¶ ～에〔로〕 싸다 wrap in a cloth.

**보잘것없다** (be) beneath notice; worthless; insignificant; trifling; trivial; useless. ¶ 보잘것없는 사람 an unworthy person; a worthless fellow / 보잘것없는 물건 a thing of no value; a small thing; a trifle / 보잘것없는 작품 a work of low merit / 보잘것없는 급료와 작업 환경 squalid wages and working conditions / 그 책은 ~ The book is worthless. / 보잘것없는 것이나마 받아 주십시오 Kindly accept this little trifle.

**보장**(保障) guarantee; security. ~하다 guarantee; secure; ensure. ¶ 사회〔집단〕~ social 〔collective〕 security / 평화의 ~ a guarantee of peace / 생활〔안전〕을 ~하다 guarantee 《*a person's*》 living 〔safety〕/ 언론의 자유를 ~하다 secure freedom of speech / 손해가 없도록 ~하다 indemnify 《*a person*》 against 〔from〕 loss / 그의 장래는 ~되어 있다 His future is assured. / 헌법은 언론의 자유를 ~하고 있다 The constitution guarantees freedom of speech. / 그가 성공한다는 ~은 없다 There is no guarantee that he will succeed. ◉ ~제도 a security system. ~조약 a security pact 〔treaty〕: 한미 안전 ~ 조약 the U.S.-Korea Security Treaty. 안전~ 이사회 《U.N.의》 the Security Council (생략 U.N.S.C.).

**보쟁기** 《쟁기》 a plow with a metal blade; 《겨리》 a plow drawn by two oxen.

**보전**(保全) preservation; conservation; maintenance; integrity. ~하다 preserve 〔safeguard〕 the integrity 《of》; preserve 〔keep〕 《*one's* country》 intact; maintain. ¶ 영토〔국토〕의 ~ territorial integrity / 환경을 ~하다 preserve 〔conserve〕 the environment. ◉ ~처분 『법』 a preservative measure.

**보전**(寶典) 《법전》 an important 〔a highly prized〕 code; 《귀중한 책》 a thesaurus; a "treasury" 《of writings》.

**보정**(補正) revision; correction; 『물리』 compensation. ~하다 revise; correct; 『물리』 compensate 《for》.

**보제**(補劑) a restorative. ⇨ 보약(補藥).

**보조**(步調) (a) pace; (a) step. ¶ ~를 맞추어 in step with 《*a person*》/ ~를 맞추다 keep step 《with》; get into step 《with》; match *one's* stride 《to that of ...》; 《일 등의 속도를》 keep pace 《with》; 《협력하다》 act 〔work〕 in concert 《with》/ ~를 흩뜨리다 walk out of step; break step / ~를 빨리하다〔늦추다〕 quicken 〔slacken〕 *one's* pace.

**보조**(補助) assistance; support; help; aid; a supplement (보족). ~하다 assist; help; aid; supplement; subsidize. ¶ ~적인 수단 auxiliary 〔subsidiary, supplementary〕 measures / ~로서 as assistant; in aid 《of》/ ~를 받다 be helped 〔assisted, backed〕 《by》; 《돈을》 be subsidized 《by》/ 국고의 ~를 받다 be subsidized from the national coffers / 생활비를 ~하다 furnish 《*a person*》 with money for *his* support; help 《*a person*》 with *his* living expenses / 학비를 ~하다 help 《*a person*》 with *his* school expenses / 남의 ~로 생활하다 live on the bounty of others / 그들은 정부의 ~로 그 실험을 행하고 있다 They receive financial aid from the government to conduct the experiment. / 그는 시 ~로 생활을 하고 있다 He lives on city welfare. ◉ ~기관 《엔진》 an auxiliary engine; 《기구》 a subsidiary organ. ~기능 an auxiliary function. ~부(簿) a supplementary account book. ~선 《draw》 an addition line. ~어간 a "stem supplement"; a non-final suffix added to an inflectional stem. ~원 a supplementary member; an assistant. ~의자 a spare 〔an extra〕 chair. ~익(翼) 《비행기의》 an aileron. ~자 a supporter; an assistant. ~탱크 《비행기의》 a belly tank. ~함 auxiliary naval vessels. ~화(폐) subsidiary coins.

**보조개** a dimple. ¶ ~ 있는 얼굴 a dimpled face / ~가 지다 dimple; turn on the dimples / 그녀는 웃을 때마다 ~가 진다 Her face dimples when she smiles.

**보조금**(補助金) a subsidy; a grant-in-aid; a bounty. ¶ ~을 주다 give a subsidy 《to》; subsidize; make grants for / ~을 받다 be subsidized 《from》/ 그 산업은 정부로부터 ~을 받고 있다 The industry is subsidized by the government. ◉ 생활~ a supplementary living allowance.

**보족**(補足) supplementation; (a) complement. ~하다 supplement; complement; make good 《a deficiency》. ¶ ~적(인) complementary; supplementary; additional / 상대의 약점을 ~하다 make up for the other's weakness; complement each other's deficiencies.

**보존**(保存) preservation; conservation; storage. ~하다 preserve; conserve; keep 《*a thing*》 from destruction 〔deterioration〕. ¶ 사적의 ~ preservation of historical spots / ~할 수 있다 can be preserved 《long》; will keep / 잘 ~되어 있다 be well preserved; be in fair preservation / ~이 잘 안 되어 있다 be in poor preservation / 천연 자원을 ~하다

conserve natural resources / 훌륭한 전통은 ～되어야 한다 Good traditions should be preserved. / 이 식품은 장기간 ～할 수 있다〔없다〕 This food can 〔cannot〕 be preserved long. / 우리는 전통예능 ～을 위해 노력하고 있다 We try to preserve traditional arts.

> (용법) **keep** 「보존·유지하다」의 가장 일반적인 말. **preserve** keep의 격식차린 말. 물건을 특별한 상태에 두거나 보호책을 강구해서 위해·파괴·부패 따위로부터 지킨다는 뜻. **conserve** 물건을 사용하면서 현상태로 유지한다는 뜻.

◉ ～료 a preservative. ～림 a forest reserve 〔preserve〕. ～비 the expense of preservation. ～식 preserved food; nonperishables. ～혈액 stored blood.

**보좌**(補佐) aid; assistance. ～하다 aid; help; assist; counsel; give advice 《to a superior》. ¶ 회장을 ～하다 assist 〔give counsel to〕 the president / 그는 과장을 ～하는 자리로 승진했다 He was promoted to assistant section chief 〔head〕. ◉ ～관 an aide: 대통령 ～관 a presidential aide. ～인 an assistant; a counselor; an advisor.

**보좌**(寶座) 《왕위》 the throne. ¶ ～에 앉다 sit on the throne; take the royal seat.

**보주**(補註) a supplementary note.

**보증**(保證) 《품질·빚 따위의》 a guarantee; 《상품의》 a warranty; an assurance (확약); 《담보》 (a) security. ～하다 guarantee; answer for; vouch for; warrant; assure. ¶ 지불～수표 a certified check / 정부～채 a government guaranteed bond / ～된 guaranteed; warranted; secured; certified (as genuine) / ～을 서다 stand surety 〔guarantee〕 《for》 / ～을 세우다 find 〔give〕 security 〔surety〕 《for》 / ～할 수 없다 [사람이 주어] be not sure of; cannot vouch for; [사물이 주어] be unwarrantable / 신원〔인물〕을 ～하다 vouch for 《*a person's*》 character; go 〔stand〕 security for 《*a person*》 / 이익을 ～하다 guarantee profit / 품질을 ～하다 guarantee 〔warrant〕 the quality 《of an article》 / 그의 정직함은 제가 ～하죠 I assure you of his honesty. *or* I 「will answer for 〔can vouch for〕 his honesty. / 그건 내가 ～한다 I give you my word for it. / 이 시계는 일년간 ～할 수 있습니다 This watch is guaranteed 〔warranted〕 for one year. / 차용금의 변제는 담보를 제공해서 ～하겠다 I will secure a loan with a pledge. / 내가 산 냉장고는 2년간 ～이 된다 I bought a refrigerator and it came with a two-year guarantee.

◉ ～계약 a contract of suretyship. ～서 a surety certificate; a letter of guarantee; a warranty 《on》: 신용～서 a fidelity guarantee / 재정 ～서 an affidavit of support. ～(적립) 준비금 a guarantee fund. ～채무 suretyship obligations. ～책임 the responsibility of surety.

**보증금**(保證金) security (money); guaranty 〔deposit〕 money; a deposit; 《영》 key money (세들 때의). ¶ ～ 없이 without a deposit / ～을 걸다 make 〔leave〕 a deposit 《of ₩500,000 on *a thing*》; place money on deposit / ～을 떼이다 forfeit the deposit.

◉ 훼손～ 《건물·시설 따위의》 a security deposit.

**보증기간**(保證期間) the term of guarantee; the warranty period. ¶ ～이 얼마나 되지 How long is the guarantee?

**보증인**(保證人) 〖법〗 a guarantor; a surety; a co-signer (연대보증인); 《신원 등의》 a certifier; a reference (신원조회처). ¶ ～이 되다 stand guarantee 〔surety, security〕 《for》; go security 《for》 / ～을 세우다 give 〔find〕 surety 〔security〕 《for》 / ～이 되어 달라고 부탁하다 ask 《*a person*》 to be *one's* guarantor.

**보지** 〖해부〗 the vulva (*pl.* ～s, ～e).

**보지**(保持) maintenance; preservation; retention. ～하다 maintain; keep; preserve; hold. ¶ 비밀을 ～하다 keep a secret / 타이틀을 ～하다 hold the title.

◉ ～자 a holder: 세계 기록 ～자 a world-record holder / 선수권 ～자 a titleholder.

**보직**(補職) assignment to a position; appointment. ～하다 assign 〔appoint〕 《*a person* to the post》. ¶ ～되다 be assigned 〔appointed〕 《to the post of》.

**보채다** cry for 《*something*》; beg 〔whine, tease〕 for 《*things*》; importune; fret; be peevish 〔fussy〕. ¶ 보채는 아기 a fretful baby / 보채는 아이를 달래다 soothe a hurt 〔fretful〕 child / (어린애가) 과자를 달라고 ～ importune 〔badger〕 《*a person*》 for cookies.

**보철**(補綴) 〖치과〗 prosthetic dentistry; dental prosthesis. ¶ 부분～ a partial denture.

**보청기**(補聽器) a hearing aid. ¶ ～를 끼

다 wear a hearing aid.

**보초**(步哨) a sentry; a sentinel; a guard. ¶ ~서다 be on sentry (duty); stand 〔keep〕 sentinel / ~를 세우다 post 《soldiers》 on sentry / ~를 교대시키다 relieve a sentry / 두 병사가 ~를 서고 있다 Two soldiers are standing 〔keeping〕 watch. / 지휘관은 3명의 ~를 세웠다 The commander posted three soldiers on sentry. ◉ ~근무 sentry 〔guard〕 duty. ~병 a guard; a sentry. ~선 a sentry line.

**보충**(補充) supplementation; (a) supplement (추가); replenishment; replacement. ~하다 supplement; fill up; replenish; replace. ¶ 결원을 ~하다 fill (up) a vacancy / 결함을 ~하다 supply 〔cover, make up (for)〕 a deficiency / 식량을 ~하다 get a fresh supply of food / 난로의 연료를 ~했다 I replenished the stove with fuel.
◉ ~대 drafts; reserves. ~문제 a supplementary exercise 〔question〕. ~병 a reservist; a recruit; reserve conscripts: 제1 ~병 a first class reservist. ~수업 supplementary lessons. ~역 reservist duty. ~자 명단 a waiting list. ~증거 〖법〗 adminicle. ~질문 〖법〗 a supplementary question. ~판결 a supplementary judgment.

**보츠와나** 《아프리카의 공화국》 Botswana.

**보측**(步測) pacing. ~하다 pace (off) 《the distance》; measure 《the distance》 by pace.

**보칙**(補則) 〖법〗 supplementary rules.

**보크** 〖야구·당구〗 a ba(u)lk.

**보크사이트** 〖광물〗 bauxite.

**보태다** ① 《보충하다》 supply 《a lack》; make up 《for》; make good; supplement. ¶ 모자라는 것을 ~ make 〔fill〕 up the deficiency / 부족한 월급에 보탬이 되게 하다 help 〔eke〕 out *one's* small income 《by doing a side job》 / 그는 밤일을 해서 모자라는 수입에 보탰다 He supplemented his scanty income by working in the evening. ② 《더하다》 add 《one number to another》. ¶ 하나에 둘을 보태면 셋이 된다 One and two make 〔are〕 three. *or* Two plus one makes three. / 5에 6을 보태라 Add six to five. / 그는 늘 말을 보태서 얘기한다 He always exaggerates.

**보통**(普通) ① 《보통의》 (being) ordinary; common; usual; normal; 《일반의》 general; universal; 《평균》 average; 《보통의 것》 the usual 〔ordinary, normal〕 thing. ¶ ~ 사람 the ordinary 〔common〕 man; the average person / ~이 아닌 uncommon; unusual; extraordinary / ~ 이상의 out of the common 〔ordinary〕 (run); above the average / ~(의) 경우에(는) in ordinary circumstances; usually / ~이다 be the usual thing; be usual / ~ 이상이다 be above the average 〔mediocrity〕 / ~ 이하이다 fall below the average 〔mediocrity〕 / ~ 사람과 다르다 be different from other men; be abnormal / 금년 추위는 ~이 아니다 It is unusually 〔exceptionally, abnormally〕 cold this year.
② [부사적] ordinarily; usually; normally; generally; on the average; as a general 〔usual〕 thing. ¶ ~ 있을 수 있는 일로 생각하다 take 《*a thing*》 as a matter of course / ~ 다섯 시에 일어난다 I usually get up at five. / 우리는 ~ 하루 8시간 일한다 We generally work eight hours a day.
◉ ~개념 an ordinary concept. ~교육 a common 〔general〕 education. ~급행(열차) an ordinary express. ~명사(名詞) 〖문법〗 a common noun. ~명사(名辭) 〖논리〗 a common term. ~법 common law. ~선거 universal 〔popular〕 suffrage; a popular vote 〔election〕. ~열차 an ordinary 〔a local, an accommodation 《미》〕 train. ~예금 an ordinary deposit. ~우편 ordinary mail 〔post〕. ~주(株) a common stock 《미》; an ordinary (share) 《영》.

**보통내기**(普通―) an ordinary person; a mediocrity; the common run of men. ¶ ~가 아니다 be no ordinary person; be (a man of) no ordinary type; be no pushover / ~가 아닌 것 같다 look no 「ordinary 〔common〕 man.

**보퉁이**(褓―) a bundle. ¶ 옷 한 ~ a bundle of clothes / ~를 싸다 make a bundle 〔package〕; bundle 《clothes》 / ~를 풀다 undo a bundle; unpack.

**보트** a (rowing) boat; a rowboat; a shell (레이스용). ¶ ~를 젓다 row a boat / ~에 타다 take 〔get on〕 a boat / ~를 타러 가다 go boating; go for a row / ~를 내리다 launch a boat; 《배에서》 lower a boat.
◉ ~레이스 a boat race; a regatta. ~선수 an oarsman; 《전원》 the (picked) crew; the eight (에이트의). ~피플 《선상 난민》 boat people.

**보편**(普遍) universality; pervasiveness. ¶ ~적(으로) universal(ly); gener-

al(ly) / ~적 진리 universal truth.
◉ ~개념 universal 〔general〕 concept. ~성 universality; catholicity. ~주의 universalism. ~타당성 《be of》 universal validity 〔application〕.

**보폭**(步幅) a step; a stride; a pace.

**보표**(譜表) 〖음악〗 a staff (*pl.* staves); a stave; a score. ◉ ~기법 staff notation.

**보푸라기** nap. ⇨ 보풀.

**보풀** nap; shag; fuzz 《of paper》. ¶ ~이 인 shaggy; nappy / ~을 일으키다 nap; fluff; raise nap 《on cloth》. ◉ ~명주 nubby 〔rough〕 silk.

**보풀다** have a slight nap (on the surface of cloth); have fuzz (on the surface of paper).

**보풀리다** nap; raise a nap 《on cloth》.

**보풀보풀** with a nap; with fuzz. ~하다 (be) nappy; fluffy; downy; fuzzy.

**보필**(輔弼) assistance to the throne. ~하다 assist; counsel; give advice 《to》.

**보하다**(補―) ① 《원기를》 strengthen 《*one's* system》; tone up; build up 《*one's* health》. ② 《관직을》 appoint; assign. ¶ 도지사에 ~ appoint 《*a person*》 (to the post of ) governor.

**보학**(譜學) (the study of ) genealogy. ◉ ~자 a genealogist.

**보합**(步合) 《비율》 rate; ratio; percentage.

**보합**(保合) 〖경제〗 《시세의》 steadiness; no change. ~하다 (keep) balance; remain the same 〔stationary, steady〕. ¶ ~세를 보이다 《the stock prices》 show a steady tone; be firm in tone / 시세는 ~ 상태다 Prices are steady 〔unchanged〕. *or* The market hold 〔remain〕 steady.

**보행**(步行) 《걸어감》 (a) walk; walking. ~하다 walk; go on foot. ¶ ~의 자유를 잃다 be crippled / ~이 어렵다 find it hard to walk; have difficulty in walking / ~ 규칙 위반자를 적발하다 crack down on jaywalkers.
◉ ~객주〔집〕 an inn for foot travelers. ~기(器) 《아기의》 a baby-walker. ~동물 a gressorial (animal); ambulatory animals. ~로 a footpath; a pedestrian passage. ~연습 walking exercises. ~위반 traffic violation by a pedestrian. ~인〔자〕 a walker; a pedestrian; a foot passenger: ~인〔자〕 천국 a pedestrian's paradise; an area of street temporarily closed to vehicle traffic; a (car-free) mall. ~자 전용 교통신호 pedestrian signals 〔lights〕.

**보험**(保險) ① 《보증》 guarantee; security; warranty. ② 《생명·화재 따위의》 insurance; 《영》 assurance. ¶ 임의〔강제〕~ voluntary 〔obligatory〕 insurance / ~에 든 insured; assured 《영》/ ~에 들다 insure 《*oneself*》; insure 《goods, a house》; take out (an) insurance policy / ~에 들어 있다 be insured 《against》; carry 《ten million won》 insurance 《on *one's* life》/ ~을 계약하다 buy 〔take〕 an insurance policy / ~을 해약하다 cancel 〔surrender〕 *one's* insurance policy / ~을 권유하다 canvass for insurance / ~을 신청하다 apply for an insurance policy; open an insurance / 나는 생명 ~에 들었다 I have had my life insured. / 그 집은 2억원의 화재 ~에 들어 있다 The house is insured against fire for 200,000,000 won. / 그녀는 3천만원의 생명 ~에 들어 있다 She has thirty million won in life insurance. / 성형수술은 건강 ~의 대상이 되지 않는다 The health insurance does not cover the plastic surgery.
◉ ~가격 insurance value. ~계약 an insurance contract: ~계약자 a policyholder. ~권유원 《생활 설계사》 an insurance canvasser 〔man〕; an insurance salesman 〔saleswoman〕. ~금액 an insured 〔insurance〕 amount. ~기간 the term insured. ~대리점 an insurance agency. ~료 a premium; an insurance bill 〔due〕: ~료를 지불하다 pay the insurance 《on *one's* life》/ 순~료 a net premium. ~률 premium 〔insurance〕 rates. ~물 property 〔a thing〕 insured; insured goods. ~사기 (an) insurance fraud. ~약관 insurance clauses 〔terms〕. ~업 insurance business; underwriting: ~업자 an insurer; an underwriter. ~의료기관 medical institutions authorized to treat patients with health insurance coverage. ~증서 an insurance policy. ~해약 insurance policy surrender: ~ 해약자 an insurance policy surrenderer. ~회사 an insurance company. 상해〔재해, 양로, 종신〕~ accident(al) 〔casualty, endowment, whole life〕 insurance. 생명〔건강, 화재, 실업, 해상, 자동차, 단체〕~ life 〔health, fire, unemployment, marine, car, group〕 insurance. 피~자 an insured; an assured.

**보험금**(保險金) insurance (money). ¶ 많은 ~을 타다 receive a large insur-

ance 《for》/ ～을 노리고 방화하다 set fire to 《*one's* house》 in order to collect the insurance / 남편의 사망으로 그녀는 3억 원의 ～을 받았다 When her husband died, she received 300 million won insurance.
◉ ～수취인 a beneficiary.

**보헤미아** 《체코의 지방》 Bohemia.

**보헤미안** 《보헤미아 사람》 a Bohemian. ¶ ～의, ～적인 Bohemian / ～기질 Bohemianism.

**보혈**(補血) ～하다 build up 〔nourish〕 the blood. ◉ ～제 a hematic.

**보혈**(寶血) 〚기독교〛 the precious blood (of Jesus).

**보호**(保護) protection; shelter; safeguard; protective custody; 《돌봄》 care; 《보존》 preservation; conservation (유지). ～하다 protect; safeguard; shelter; shield; 《돌보다》 take care of; look after; patronize; 《보존하다》 reserve; preserve; conserve.
¶ 삼림의 ～ conservation of forests / 문화재의 ～ (the) preservation of cultural assets / 야생 동식물의 ～ preservation of wild life / …의 ～아래 under the protection 〔care, guardianship〕 of… / 생명과 재산을 ～하기 위하여 for the protection of lives and property / 자연 ～의 관점에서 from the standpoint of nature conservation / ～를 받다 be protected 《by》; be 〔put *oneself*〕 under 《*a person's*》 protection / 국내 산업을 ～하다 protect home 〔domestic〕 industries / 맡아서 ～하다 take 《*a person*》 under *one's* protection / 경찰에 ～를 요청하다 apply to the policy for protection / 정치적 망명자로서 ～를 요청하다 request (political) asylum 《in the U.S.》/ ～해 주다 provide protection for 《*a person*》; provide shelter / 그는 경찰의 ～를 받고 있다 He is under the police protection. / 비(非)～ 좌회전 《게시》 Left turn at your own risk.
◉ ～관세 a protective duty 〔tariff〕. ～국 a protected state; a protectorate (보호령). ～림 a preserved forest. ～무역 protective 〔protected〕 trade: ～ 무역주의 protectionism / ～무역주의의 벽을 높이다 raise the walls of protectionism 《against》. ～색 protective coloration; a protective color: ～색이 되어 있다 be protectively colored. ～수역 protected waters. ～자 a protector; a protectress (여자); a guardian. ～조(鳥) a protected bird. ～지(역) a reservation; a sanctuary: 야생 동물 ～ 지역 a reservation 〔sanctuary〕 for wild animals.

**보호관찰**(保護觀察) 〚법〛 probation. ¶ ～에 부치다 place 〔put〕 《an offender》 on 〔under〕 probation / 그는 1년간의 ～을 받고 있다 He is under a year's probation. ◉ ～관 a probation officer. ～제도 the probation system.

**보화**(寶貨) (a) treasure. ＝보물(寶物).

**보훈**(報勳) ◉ ～병원 Korea Veterans Hospital; the Patriots and Veterans Hospital. 국가 ～처 the Ministry of Patriots and Veterans Affairs. 한국 ～복지 공단 the Korea Veterans Welfare Corp (생략 KVWC).

**복** 〚어류〛 a puffer; a swellfish; a blowfish; a globefish. ¶ 복의 독(毒) swellfish poison; tetrodotoxin / 복 중독 swellfish poisoning / 복 치듯 in a slovenly way; roughly / 복에 중독되다 be poisoned by swellfish / 복의 이 갈듯하다 gnash *one's* teeth with resentment 〔ill will〕. ◉ 복국 swellfish 〔blowfish〕 soup; potboiled blowfish seasoned with various ingredients.

**복**(伏) ⇨ 복날(伏—).

**복**(福) (good) fortune; (good) luck; blessing; bliss; happiness. ¶ 복된 happy; blessed; felicitous / 복이 많다 〔있다〕 be fortunate; be in luck / 복이 없다 be out of luck; be unfortunate / 복을 주다 bring 《*a person*》 good luck; bless 《*a person*》/ 복을 받다 be blessed 《with riches》/ 복을 빌다 invoke a blessing 《upon *a person*》/ 마음이 가난한 자는 복이 있나니 〚성서〛 Blessed are the poor in spirit. / 어머니는 아들을 위해서 복을 빌었다 The mother invoked a blessing upon her son. / 새해에 복많이 받으십시오 Happy New Year!

**복-**(複) double; complex; compound; composite.

**복각**(伏角) 〚물리〛 a dip 《of the compass》; an inclination. ◉ ～계 an inclinometer. ～ 측원기 a depression range finder. 무～선 《지자기의》 the aclinic line.

**복간**(復刊) reissue; revived publication. ～하다 reissue; revive the publication 《of》. ¶ ～ 잡지 제1호 the first number of a revived magazine.

**복강**(腹腔) 〚해부〛 the abdominal 〔peritoneal〕 cavity.

**복걸**(伏乞) ～하다 prostrate *oneself* and beg; beg from the ground.

**복고**(復古) 《예전대로》 restoration; revival

(of the ancient regime). ～하다 restore; recover. ¶ 왕정～ the restoration of the Royal regime; the Restoration 《영》. ◉ ～론자 a reactionary; an advocate of reaction. ～조(調) a tendency to revert to the old ways; a reactionary tendency. ～주의 reactionism.

**복교**(復校) reinstatement (at school); return to school. ～하다 be reinstated (at school); return to school; be back in school. ¶ ～를 허락하다 allow 《a student》 to return to school; readmit 《a student》 into school / ～되다 get readmitted (into school). ◉ ～조치 《제적생들의》 measures for reinstating the expelled students.

**복구**(復舊) rehabilitation; recovery; restoration; restitution. ～하다 return (to the former condition); be restored (to the original state); be rehabilitated. ¶ ～시키다 restore (to the original state); bring 《*a thing*》 back to its former condition / 평상 상태로 ～하다 return to normalcy / 철도는 곧 ～된다 The railway will be shortly reopened to traffic. *or* The train will resume normal services. / ～될 가능성이 전혀 없다 There is no hope for its restoration. ◉ ～공사 restoration 〔repair〕 work: ～공사중이다 be under repair / ～공사에 착수하다 get 〔set〕 to repair work.

**복굴절**(複屈折) 〖물리〗 double refraction; birefringence.

**복권**(復權) reinstatement; restoration of (civil) rights; rehabilitation. ～하다 get reinstated; be restored to *one's* rights; be rehabilitated. ¶ ～시키다 rehabilitate; reinstate.

**복권**(福券) a lottery ticket. ¶ ～부 채권 a lottery bond / ～ 추첨 a lottery / ～의 당첨 번호 a lucky number / ～이 당첨되다 win (a prize) in a lottery 〔raffle〕; get 〔draw〕 a lottery prize / ～을 사다 buy a lottery ticket; 《사 보다》 take a chance on a raffle / 올림픽 ～ 팜 《게시》 Olympic lottery tickets on sale.

**복귀**(復歸) a return; a comeback; reversion. ～하다 return 《to》; make a comeback; revert; take *one's* old position again; reinstate. ¶ 전전(戰前) 상태로의 ～ a return to prewar condition / 이전 지위로 ～하다 be reinstated 〔reinstalled〕 in *one's* former position 〔post〕 / 원대에 ～하다 rejoin *one's* regiment / 정상으로 ～하다 return to normal(cy) / 직장에 ～하다 return to work / 영화계에 ～하다 make a comeback to the screen.

**복근**(腹筋) abdominal muscles. ¶ ～운동 exercise to strengthen the abdominal muscles.

**복날**(伏―) any one of the three "dog days". ¶～ 개패듯 하다 whip 〔flog〕 《*a person*》 like a dog.

**복닥－** ＝ 북적－.

**복달임**(伏―) ① 《철》 a period of hot weather during July and August. ② 〖민속〗 the custom of eating hot soup in order to repel the summer heat. ～하다 eat hot soup to allay the summer heat.

**복당**(復黨) rejoining the party. ～하다 rejoin the party; be reinstated in the party.

**복대**(腹帶) a health 〔stomach〕 band; 《임부의》 a binder.

**복대기** 〖광물〗 residue left after gold is panned; slag. ¶ ～ 삭히다 extract gold from slag.

**복대기다** ① 《떠들다》 be noisy 〔boisterous, in a bustle〕. ¶ 사람들이 정거장에서 복대긴다 The crowd bustles along in the station. ② 《정신 못 차리다》 be tossed about; be jostled around. ¶ 나는 두 시간 동안이나 사람들 속에서 복대기었다 I was jostled in the crowd for two hours.

**복더위**(伏―) a heat wave during the dog days; a midsummer hot spell.

**복덕**(福德) good luck and virtue; good fortune; happiness and prosperity; 〖불교〗 the reward of virtue. ¶ ～을 갖추다 be perfectly happy and prosperous / ～을 갖춘 사람 a perfect 〔an affable〕 man.

**복덕방**(福德房) a real estate agent; a realtor 《미》; a house-finding agency.

**복도**(複道) a corridor; a passage; a gallery; a hallway 《미》; a lobby (극장의).

**복되다**(福―) ＝ 복스럽다(福―).

**복리**(福利) ＝ 복지(福祉).

**복리**(複利) compound interest. ¶ ～로 계산하다 calculate 〔reckon〕 at compound interest. ◉ ～법 the compound interest method. ～표 a table of compound interest.

**복마**(卜馬) a pack 〔draft, cart〕 horse.

**복마전**(伏魔殿) an abode of demons; a pandemonium; a hotbed (of corruption).

**복막**(腹膜) 〖해부〗 the peritoneum (*pl.*

-nea). ◉ ～염 peritonitis.

**복망**(伏望) ～하다 earnestly desire; humbly beg 〔entreat〕; sincerely hope 《for》. ¶ 선처하시옵기 ～하나이다 I sincerely hope that you will take good care of it.

**복면**(覆面) a mask; a veil. ～하다 mask 〔veil〕 *oneself;* muffle (up) 〔cover〕 *one's* face; have *one's* face masked. ¶ ～강도 a masked burglar 〔robber〕/ ～을 벗다 take *one's* mask off; unmask 〔unveil〕 *oneself.*

**복명**(復命) a report (of *one's* mission). ～하다 report to 《*a person* on *one's* work》; report *one's* mission 《to》. ◉ ～서 a report 《of mission》; a finding.

**복명어음**(複名―) 〚상업〛 a double-name paper; a two-name paper.

**복모음**(複母音) 〚음성〛 a diphthong.

**복무**(服務) (public) service. ～하다 serve; 《복무중》 be in (public) service. ¶ 군(軍)에 ～중이다 be 〔serve〕 in the army 〔navy〕. ◉ ～규정 the office 〔(public) service〕 regulations; 〚군사〛 standing orders. ～기간 the period of (active) service. ～연한 the term of (public) service; the tenure of office.

**복문**(複文) 〚문법〛 a complex sentence.

**복받치다** 《솟아나오다》 well up; gush forth; 《감정이》 be filled 〔seized〕 《with》; [사물이 주어] fill *one's* heart. ¶ 가슴 속에 복받치는 슬픔 the sorrow welling up within *one* / 분이 ～ indignation wells up in *one; one* cannot contain *one's* anger / 갑자기 슬픔이 복받쳐 올랐다 I was suddenly filled with sorrow. 「by.」

**복백**(伏白) 《편지의》 "Humbly presented

**복벗다**(服―) 《탈상하다》 go out of 〔leave off〕 mourning; *one's* mourning period expires.

**복벽**(腹壁) 〚해부〛 the abdominal wall. ◉ ～절개(수술) laparotomy.

**복병**(伏兵) an ambush; an ambuscade; troops in ambush. ¶ ～을 두다 lay 〔make〕 an ambush 《for》/ ～을 만나다 fall into an ambush / 적의 ～이 있다 The enemy are lying in ambush.

**복본위제**(複本位制) 〚경제〛 the double-standard system; bimetallism.

**복부**(腹部) the abdominal region; the abdomen; the belly. ¶ ～의 abdominal / ～가 아프다 have stitches in *one's* side. ◉ ～수술 an abdominal operation; abdominal surgery. ～임신 abdominal pregnancy.

**복부인**(福夫人) a wealthy housewife (chasing after the speculative benefit); women speculators swarming to a place of bidding. 「fraction.」

**복분수**(複分數) a compound 〔complex〕

**복비**(複比) 〚수학〛 compound ratio.

**복비례**(複比例) compound proportion; the double rule of three.

**복사**(伏射) = 엎드려쏴. ◉ ～경기 a prone shooting 〔firing〕 event.

**복사**(複寫) ① reproduction; duplication; reprint(ing). ～하다 reproduce; duplicate; copy; make a duplicate 〔copy〕 of. ¶ 사진을 ～하다 reproduce a photograph / 원고를 ～하다 copy a manuscript / 제록스로 ～하다 make a Xerox copy of 《a letter》 (★ Xerox는 상표명) / 그 송장(送狀)을 ～하시오 Make a copy 〔duplicate〕 of the invoice. / 이 사진을 세 장만 더 ～해 주시오 Please make three more copies of this picture. ② 《복사물》 a reproduction; a duplicate; a copy; a reprint; a facsimile; a transfer. ¶ 고흐의 ～ a copy from Gogh. ◉ ～기 a duplicator; a copying press; a duplicating apparatus; a copier. ～사진 a photostat; a photocopy. ～용 잉크 copying ink. ～지 copying paper; carbon paper. 사진～ photocopy. 사진～기 a photocopier.

**복사**(輻射) 〚물리〛 radiation. ～하다 radiate. ◉ ～가열기 a radiation superheater. ～난방 panel 〔radiant〕 heating. ～선 radiant light; 《광선》 rays of radiant light. ～에너지 radiant energy. ～열 radiant heat; radiation. ～체 a radiator.

**복사뼈** 〚해부〛 the malleolus (*pl.* -li); the anklebone; the talus (*pl.* ～s, -li).

**복상**(服喪) mourning. ～하다 go into 〔take to〕 mourning 《for *a person*》.

**복상**(福相) a happy look; "a face with luck written on it".

**복상**(複像) 〚전자〛 a multiple image; 〚TV〛 a ghost (image).

**복색**(服色) 《옷빛깔·꾸밈새》 the color and style of a uniform 〔an official dress〕; 《의상》 clothes; attire.

**복서** a boxer; a pugilist. ⇨ 권투 선수.

**복선**(伏線) an advance hint; a convert reference; foreshadowing; a foreshadow. ¶ ～을 치다 drop an advance hint; foreshadow 《a coming event》; 《자기 언동에》 allude 《to *something*》 as a preliminary; 《나중일에》 take (precautionary) measures beforehand; forestall (선수치다).

**복선**(複線) 《겹줄》 double lines; 《궤도》 a double track; a two-track line. ¶ ～의 double-track(ed) / ～으로 하다 double-track.
◉ ～공사 double-tracking. 복～ a four-track line; a quadruple track.

**복성**(複姓) double-surname; a 2-syllable family name.

**복성**(複星) 〖천문〗 multiple stars.

**복성스럽다** (be) happy-looking; fat and well-looking; full-faced. ¶ 복성스러운 얼굴 a full face / 얼굴이 ～ have a cherubic face.

**복소수**(複素數) 〖수학〗 a complex number.

**복속**(服屬) ～하다 submit 《to》; obey.

**복수**(復水) condensation; condensed water. ◉ ～기 a condenser. ～판〔펌프〕 a condensing valve 〔pump〕.

**복수**(復讐) revenge; vengeance; vendetta; 《보복》 retaliation; reprisal. ～하다 revenge 〔avenge〕 *oneself* 《on another》; be revenged 〔avenged〕 《on *a person*》; take 〔get, have〕 *one's* revenge 《on *a person*, for the murder》; 《보복하다》 retaliate on 《*one's* foe》; repay 〔requit〕 《a wrong》; pay 〔wipe〕 off old scores. ¶ ～적인 revengeful; vindictive / …에 대한 ～로서 in revenge for 〔of〕… / ～할 기회를 노리다 seek *one's* revenge 〔vengeance〕 on 《*a person*》 for 《a matter》 / ～를 맹세하다 swear revenge 《on, against》 / 아버지의 죽음에 대해서 ～하다 take revenge 〔vengeance〕 for *one's* father's death / 꼭 ～하고 말테다 I will get my revenge. ◉ ～수단 a retaliatory measure. ～심 《burn with》 revengeful thoughts. ～자 a revenger; an avenger. ～전 a battle 〔war〕 of revenge; 《경기의》 a return match 〔game〕.

**복수**(腹水) 〖의학〗 abdominal dropsy; ascites.

**복수**(複數) plural (number). ¶ ～의 plural / ～로 하다 pluralize / "sheep"의 ～는 무엇이냐 What is the plural (form) of "sheep"? / ～의 사람이 동의해야 한다 It is necessary to have more than one person's consent. ◉ ～명사 a plural noun. ～전공 a double major. ～형 〖문법〗 the plural (form).

**복수초**(福壽草) 〖식물〗 an adonis (plant); a pheasant's-eye.

**복술**(卜術) the art of divination; fortune-telling.

**복숭아** a peach. ◉ ～꽃 a peach blossom. ～나무 a peach (tree). ～털 the fuzz on a peach.

**복스** 《무두질한 송아지 가죽》 box calf. ⇨ 박스. ◉ ～구두 shoes 〔boots〕 made of box calf.

**복스럽다**(福—) (be) happy-looking; fat and well-looking; prosperous-looking.

**복슬복슬** (be) fat and shaggy. ⇨ 북슬북슬.

**복습**(復習) (a) review 《of studies》. ～하다 review 《*one's* lesson》; go over 〔through〕 《*one's* lesson》. ¶ 영어를 ～하다 review *one's* English lessons; brush up *one's* English / 그것을 하나하나씩 ～해보는 것이 어떻겠어요 Why don't we go over it point-by-point? ◉ ～시간 review hours. ～용 연습 문제 review exercises.

**복시**(複視) 〖의학〗 diplopia; double vision. ¶ ～의 diploptic.

**복식**(服飾) dress and its ornaments. ◉ ～잡지 a fashion magazine. ～품 accessories (to a dress). 여성용～ ladies' trimmings.

**복식**(複式) 《방식》 multiple forms 〔formulae〕; 〖수학〗 a compound expression 〔formula〕; 〖부기〗 double-entry bookkeeping. ◉ ～경기 a double match. ～기관 a compound engine. ～부기 bookkeeping by double entry; the double entry system. ～테니스 tennis doubles. ～투표 a plural vote.

**복식호흡**(腹式呼吸) abdominal breathing 〔respiration〕; the abdominal type of respiration.

**복신**(福神) the God of Wealth; Billiken; a luck-bringer.

**복싱** boxing. ¶ 프로 ～ professional boxing. ◉ ～경기 a boxing match. ～링 a boxing ring. 섀도～ shadowboxing. 대한 아마추어 ～ 연맹 the Korean Amateur Boxing Federation.

**복쌈**(福—) 〖민속〗 laver-wrapped rice eaten on the 15th of January of the lunar calendar.

**복안**(腹案) a plan 〔scheme〕 (in *one's* mind); an idea. ¶ ～을 세우다 map out 〔draw up, formulate〕 a plan / ～이 서 있다 I have a plan ready.

**복안**(複眼) =겹눈.

**복약**(服藥) taking medicine. ～하다 take medicine. ¶ ～시키다 administer 〔give〕 medicine.

**복어**(—魚) a swellfish. ⇨ 복.

**복역**(服役) ① 《병역》 military service; 《부역》 public service. ～하다 serve *one's* time 〔term〕 in the army 〔in public office〕; be in the service.

② 《징역》 penal servitude. ~하다 serve *one's* sentence 〔term〕; serve *one's* time; serve *one's* prison term. ¶ 만기 ~하다 serve *one's* full time / ~중이다 be serving 〔doing〕 *one's* sentence; be in prison. ◉ ~기간 the term of penal servitude 〔imprisonment〕.

**복염**(伏炎) the midsummer heat (of the "dog days").

**복엽**(複葉) a compound leaf. ◉ ~기(機) a biplane.

**복용**(服用) 《먹는 약의》 taking medicine; internal use 〔application〕. ~하다 take 《medicine》; use 〔apply〕 internally. ¶ 일정량 이상을 ~하다 exceed the prescribed dose / ~시키다 administer 《medicine》 / 1일 3회 식후 ~ To be taken 《a tablet》 three times a day after each meal. / ~하지 마시오 《주의》 Product should not be taken internally. *or* Not to be taken internally. *or* Do not take internally. ◉ ~량 dosage; dose: 최대 ~량 the maximum dose. ~자 a taker.

**복원**(復元) restoration (to the original state); restitution. ~하다 restore 〔be restored〕 to the original state; reconstruct. ◉ ~도 a diagram of a restored building; a reconstruction. ~력 a strength of stability; (a) righting moment (배 따위의). ~작업 restoration (work).

**복원**(復員) demobilization. ~하다 demobilize; be demobilized; be discharged from military service. ◉ ~군인 an ex-serviceman; a demobilized soldier. ~령 demobilization orders.

**복위**(復位) restoration; rehabilitation; reinstatement. ~하다 be restored to the throne. ¶ ~시키다 restore 《a dethroned king》.

**복음**(複音) 〚음성〛 a compound sound.

**복음**(福音) 《기쁜 소식》 glad tidings; good 〔welcome〕 news; a godsend; 〚기독교〛 the (Christian) Gospel. ¶ ~을 전하다 preach the Gospel / 이것은 시민들에게 큰 ~이 될 것이다 This will prove a great boon to the citizens. ◉ ~교회 the Evangelical Church. ~서 the (four) Gospels. ~전도자 an evangelist. ~주의 Evangelism.

**복이나인**(僕伊一) a servant to a lady-in-waiting at court.

**복인수**(複因數) 〚수학〛 compound factors.

**복입다**(服一) wear mourning.

**복자**(福者) a person who is blessed; 〚가톨릭〛 the Blessed.

**복자**(覆字) 〚인쇄〛 a turn (in set type).

**복작-** ⇨ 북적-.

**복잡**(複雜) complexity; complication; intricacy. ~하다 (be) complicated; complex; intricate. ¶ ~ 기괴한 사건 a bizarre and complex case / ~한 기계 an intricate piece of machinery / ~한 기구(機構) intricate 〔complex〕 mechanism 〔structure〕 / ~한 절차 a complicated 〔troublesome〕 procedure / ~한 문장 an involved style / ~한 문제 a knotty 〔an intricate〕 problem; a perplexed question / ~한 일 complicated work / ~한 표현 an expression of mixed feelings / ~해지다 be 〔become〕 complicated / 문제〔사태〕를 ~하게 하다 complicate the issue 〔situation〕 / 그 문제의 이면에는 어떤 ~한 사정이 있음에 틀림없다 There must be some complicated circumstances behind the matter. / 정부의 개입으로 문제는 한층 더 ~해졌다 The intervention of the Government made the issue all the more complicated.

**복장** the center of the thorax 〔chest〕.

**복장**(服裝) (the style of) dress; costume; attire; habiliments; a uniform. ¶ 한국식 ~ Korean-style clothes; the Korean way of dressing / ~이 훌륭하다〔나쁘다〕 be well 〔poorly〕 dressed / 노동자의 ~을 하고 있다 be dressed as a working man / ~을 단정히 하다 《몸차림하다》 dress up (*oneself*); tidy up *one's* dress; make presentable what *one* has on / ~에 개의치 않다 do not care about *one's* dress; be indifferent to *one's* dress / 검소한 ~을 하고 있다 be simply attired / ~ 단정 《게시》 Tidy up your dress. / ~은 자유 《주의사항》 Dress optional. *or* Informal dress. ◉ ~검사 a dress inspection; 《군인의》 a kit inspection. 정식~ formal dress.

**복재기**(服一) a person wearing mourning.

**복쟁이** 〚어류〛 a globefish; a swellfish; a puffer.

**복적**(復籍) ~하다 return to *one's* original domicile 〔family register〕. ¶ ~ 절차를 밟다 go through the formalities of *one's* return to the original domicile 〔family register〕.

**복제**(服制) ① 《거상입는》 the traditional system of mourning attire. ② 《복식》 dress regulation 〔system〕; costume. ¶ ~를 정하다 adopt a definite uniform.

**복제**(複製) a copy; reproduction; duplication; reprinting (책의); 《복제물》 a

reproduction; a facsimile; a duplicate; a replica; a reprint. ～하다 reproduce; make a copy 〔reproduction, replica, facsimile〕 of 《*a thing*》. ¶ 그림을 ～하다 copy a picture / 원본과 똑같이 ～하다 reproduce with complete fidelity / ～ 불허 Reprinting prohibited. *or* All rights reserved.
◉ ～사진 a photocopy. ～인간 a human clone. ～화 a reproduced picture.

**복종**(服從) obedience; submission; subordination. ～하다 obey; be obedient 《to》; submit (*oneself*) 《to》. ¶ ～적(인) obedient; submissive / 맹목적 ～ blind obedience / 명령에 ～하다 obey 《*a person's*》 orders / 부모에게 ～하다 obey *one's* parents / 상사에게 ～하다 be obedient 〔deferential〕 to *one's* superiors / ～시키다 subordinate; subdue; subjugate; get hold of; have 〔hold〕 under *one's* girdle; hold 《*a person*》 in subjection / 명령에 ～시키다 submit 《*a person*》 to *one's* orders / 위협하여 ～시키다 scare 《*a person*》 into submission / 국법에는 반드시 ～해야 한다 We must necessarily be obedient to the laws of the land. / 나는 이런 사람에게는 ～하지 않는다 I am not going to bow down to people of this sort.
◉ ～심 obedience; a submissive spirit. ～훈련 《개의》 obedience training.

**복죄**(服罪) ～하다 submit to a sentence; serve *one's* sentence. ¶ ～치 않다 deny *one's* guilt; plead not guilty.

**복주감투** a kind of winter cap worn by monks or old people.

**복중**(伏中) (the period of) the "dog days"; midsummer.

**복중**(服中) 《during》 the mourning period.

**복지**(伏地) ¶ ～부동(不動)의 자세 《공무원의》 the lying-down-on-the-job attitude of public servants; the easy-goingness in officialdom.

**복지**(服地) cloth; dress material; suiting.

**복지**(福祉) (public) welfare; well-being; prosperity. ¶ 사회〔공공〕 ～ social 〔public〕 welfare / 노인 ～ welfare for the aged / 국민～연금(제도) the national welfare pension (system) / 국민의 ～를 증진하다 promote 「national prosperity 〔the public good〕 / 정부는 국민의 ～ 증진에 노력했다 The government tried to promote the welfare of the people. ◉ ～국가 a welfare state. ～사업 welfare work: ～ 사업가 a welfare worker. ～사회 a welfare society. ～시설 welfare facilities. ～정책 (a) welfare policy; social welfare measures; welfarism. ～제도 welfare system.

**복직**(復職) reinstatement; reappointment. ～하다 be reinstated in 〔come back to〕 *one's* former position; be reappointed 〔reinstalled〕; resume *one's* office. ¶ 해고자 ～ reinstatement of the dismissed / 2개월의 정직이 풀려 그는 지난달 ～했다 After two months' suspension he was reinstated in his former office last month.

**복찜** well-seasoned steamed swellfish.

**복창**(復唱) repetition. ～하다 repeat 《an order》.

**복채**(卜債) a fortune-teller's fee.

**복통**(腹痛) a stomachache; a bellyache; an abdominal pain; a cramp; colic; gripe. ¶ ～을 호소하다 complain of a stomachache / ～이 가라앉다 be cured of stomachache.

**복판** ① 《가운데》 the (very) middle; the center; the heart. ¶ ～에 right 〔just〕 in the middle 〔center〕 《of》; in the midst 《of》 / 상업 지구 ～에 in the heart of the business district / 길 ～을 걷다 walk in 〔keep to〕 the middle of the road / 머리를 ～에서 가르다 part *one's* hair in the middle / 과녁의 ～에 맞다 hit the target right in the center / 서울 시청은 시내 ～에 있다 Seoul city hall is located in the very middle of the city. ② 《고기》 beef attached to the ribs 〔groin, knee bone〕.

**복합**(複合) composition; compositeness; complex. ～하다 compound; mix; be mixed; unite; be united. ¶ ～의 mixed; compound; complex.
◉ ～개념 a complex concept. ～국가 a union of states; a federation; united states. ～기업 a conglomerate. ～명사 a compound noun. ～비료 composite 〔compound, complex〕 fertilizer. ～빌딩 a multiplepurpose building; a building housing a number of 「different business 〔independent business concerns〕. ～사회 a mixed society. ～어 a compound (word). ～영농(營農) combined agriculture. ～오염 multiple contamination 〔pollution〕. ～체 a complex (body).

**복화술**(腹話術) ventriloquy; ventriloquism. ¶ ～을 사용하다 ventriloquize.
◉ ～사 a ventriloquist.

**복활차**(複滑車) a tackle; a compound pulley.

**볶다** ① 《불에》 parch 《beans》; roast 《coffee beans》; panbroil; boil down 《in oil》. ¶ 고기를 ~ roast (minced) meat / 콩을 ~ parch 〔roast〕 beans / 기름에 ~ fry in oil / 볶은 콩이 꽃이 피랴 《속담》 "Don't cry over spilled milk." ② 《못살게》 tease; pester; plague; harass; annoy; treat 《*a person*》 harshly; torment; bully (약한 자를). ¶ 아이가 어머니를 ~ a child pesters his mother / 제발 좀 그렇게 볶지 마세요 Don't be so mean to me.

**볶아대다** keep bothering 〔annoying, pestering〕. ¶ 그 아이는 제 어미를 볶아대고 있다 The child keeps pestering his mother.

**볶아치다** dash off; rush about; hurry (up); hasten. ¶ 일을 제 시간에 끝내려고 ~ rush around frantically trying to finish *one's* work on time.

**볶음** ① 《하기》 panbroiling; roasting; parching. ② 《음식》 any panbroiled 〔roasted〕 food; a roast; a broil.
◉ ~밥 frizzled 〔fried〕 rice: 새우~밥 fried rice with shrimp. 닭~ chopped roast chicken.

**본**(本) ① 《본관》 family origin. ¶ 본이 어디십니까 Where did your family originate in? ② 《본보기》 an example; a model; a pattern (옷 따위의). ¶ 종이로 본을 뜨다 make a pattern out of paper / 드레스의 본을 뜨다 cut out a pattern for a dress. ③ = 본전.

**본-**(本) ① 《본디의》 the original; the basic. ¶ 본값 the (original) cost. ② 《본인》 I; me; myself; *one's* own; my own. ¶ 본국 *one's* 〔my〕 own country. ③ 《이》 this; 《이번》 the present; the current. ¶ 본협약 the present agreement / 본교 this 〔our〕 school / 본회 the present meeting(s). ④ 《주된》 main; chief; principal; head. ¶ 본선 a main line / 본점 a head office. ⑤ 《그·그런》 the above said; the aforementioned; (the) said; such; the; that; those. ¶ 본회 the aforementioned society; said group. ⑥ 《실제의》 real; 《정식의》 regular. ¶ 본명 a real name / 본회의 a plenary session 〔meeting〕; a regular debate.

**본가**(本家) 《본집》 the head 〔main〕 family; 《원조》 the originator; the original maker; 《친정》 《a woman's》 native home.

**본값**(本—) the (original) cost. ¶ ~에 팔다 sell at cost / ~을 건지다 recover the cost.

**본거**(本據) *one's* stronghold; the base; the headquarters. ¶ 생활의 ~ the base and center of *one's* life / 종파의 ~ the headquarters of a religious sect / 적의 ~를 공격했다 We attacked the stronghold of the enemy.

**본거지**(本據地) a stronghold; headquarters; the base of operation. ¶ …을 ~로 하여 with… as the base of operations / 그들은 생활의 ~를 그 마을로 정했다 They settled down in the village.

**본건**(本件) this affair 〔matter, case〕; the case in question; the (pending) case. ¶ ~에 관하여 as to this matter; concerning this matter / ~은 지금 심의 중이다 This case is now under consideration.

**본격**(本格) fundamental rules; propriety. ¶ ~화하다 become serious; get into 《its》 stride; be regularized.
◉ ~소설 a serious novel. ~파 the orthodox school.

**본격적**(本格的) ¶ ~인 full-scale (전면적인); full-dress (정식의); regular; orthodox (정통의); 《진짜의》 genuine; real; 《진심의》 earnest; serious; standard (표준의) / ~인 토의 a full-dress debate / ~인 전쟁 a full-scale war / ~으로 하다 set about 《business》 in earnest; get down to 《*one's* job》 / ~인 장마철로 접어들다 the real rainy season sets in / 영어 회화를 ~으로 배울 작정이다 I intend to study English conversation in good earnest. / ~인 겨울이 다가왔다 The real winter has come. *or* Winter is really here. / ~인 수사가 막 시작되었다 The full-scale investigation has just begun.

**본견**(本絹) pure silk.

**본계약**(本契約) a formal contract 〔agreement〕.

**본고장**(本—) ① 《고향》 *one's* native place; *one's* home town. ¶ 서울은 내가 난 ~이다 Seoul is my birthplace. ② 《본바닥》 a home; a habitat; the (best) place 《for》; 《중심지》 the (productive) center. ¶ 사과〔커피〕의 ~ the home of the apple 〔coffee〕 / 외국어를 ~에서 익히다 learn a foreign language in the country where it is spoken / 파리는 유행의 ~이다 Paris is the birthplace 〔home〕 of fashions.

**본고향**(本故鄕) *one's* native area 〔place〕; *one's* home (ground).

**본과**(本科) a regular course. ¶ ~를 수료하다 finish a regular course.
◉ ~생 a regular 〔full-time〕 student.

**본관**(本官) ① 《자칭》 the present offi-

cial; me; I; we; this office. ②《겸직에 대한》 the principal post 〔official job〕.
**본관**(本貫) *one's* ancestral home.
**본관**(本管) a main (pipe); a (supply) main. ◉ 수도〔가스〕~ a water 〔gas〕 main; a trunk water 〔gas〕 pipe.
**본관**(本館) the main building.
**본교**(本校) 《이 학교》 this 〔our〕 school; 《분교에 대한》 the principal school.
**본국**(本局) ① the head 〔main〕 office; 《전화국의》 the central (office) 《미》; the telephone exchange; 《방송국》 a key station. ¶ ~ 5046, Central 5046 / ~을 부르다 call up (the) Central. ② 《바둑의》 this game 《of *paduk* 〔*go*〕》.
**본국**(本國) *one's* own land; *one's* home 〔native, mother〕 country. ¶ ~으로 돌아가다 go 〔return〕 home / ~으로 송환하다 send 《a foreigner》 back to *his* home country; repatriate 《*a person*》/ 범죄를 저지른 청년은 즉시 ~으로 강제 송환되었다 The young man who had committed a crime was deported to his own country immediately. ◉ ~법 『법』 the law of the domicile. ~송환 repatriation. ~정부 the home government.
**본금**(本金) principal (sum). ⇨ 본전.
**본기억**(―記憶) recognition; remembrance. ¶ ~이 있는 familiar 《face》; well-remembered 《handwriting》/ ~이 없는 unfamiliar; strange / ~이 있다 recognize; know 《*a person*》 by sight; remember (seeing... before) / 그 사람 어디서 ~이 있는 것 같다 I fancy I have seen him somewhere before. *or* I remember seeing him once.
**본남편**(本男便) 《전남편》 *one's* ex-husband; 《남편》 *one's* (real) husband; *one's* legal husband (정당한).
**본년**(本年) this year; the current 〔present〕 year.
**본능**(本能) (an) instinct. ¶ ~적(인) instinctive / ~에 따르다 follow *one's* primitive instincts / ~에 따라서 행동하다 act on instinct / ~을 만족시키다 satisfy *one's* instinct / ~적으로 위험을 감지하다 sense danger 「by instinct 〔instinctively〕 / ~적으로 …을 좋아〔싫어〕하다 have an instinctive 「taste for 〔horror of〕 《*a thing*》/ …하는 ~이 있다 have an instinct for... / 자기 보존의 ~을 갖다 have 〔possess〕 the instinct of self-preservation. ◉ 귀소~ the homing instinct. 원초적 ~ the primordial instinct.
**본당**(本堂) 『불교』 the main building (of a temple); 『가톨릭』 a parish church.
**본대**(本隊) ① 《본부의》 the main body 《of troops》; the main force. ② 《자기 소속의》 the detachment to which *one* belongs; *one's* regular outfit.
**본댁**(本宅) ① 《본집》 your 〔his〕 esteemed home 〔house〕. ② 《정실》 = 본댁네. ◉ ~네 *one's* legal wife.
**본데** experience; discipline; good manners. ¶ ~없다 be ill-bred〔-mannered〕; be rude; have no manners.
**본도**(本道) a main road; a highway.
**본도**(本島) the main island.
**본드** bond; adhesives. ¶~ 흡입 glue 〔bond〕-sniffing.
**본디** originally; from the first; by nature. ¶ ~의 original; primary / ~대로 as before 〔usual〕; as it was before / ~ 상태로 in 《its》 integrity 〔original condition〕/ ~ 착한 사람이다 be a good man by 〔in〕 nature / 깨진 꽃병을 ~ 모습으로 되돌려 놓다 put back the broken vase into its original shape.
**본때** ① 《본보기》 things that can be modeled 〔patterned〕 after. ⇨ 본때 있다. ¶ 그 친구의 옷은 ~가 좋다 The cut of his suit is stylish. / 그녀는 ~가 없다 She's got no figure. ② 《교훈》 a lesson; an object lesson; a warning; an example. ¶ ~를 보이다 make an example 〔a lesson〕 《of》; teach 《*a person*》 a lesson; punish.
**본때있다** (be) exemplary; typical; 《멋있다》 (be) stylish; splendid; excellent. ¶ 본때 있게 잘 하다 do a splendid job of it / 본때 있게 해치우다 come off with flying colors.
**본뜨다**(本―) ① follow; model 《after, on》; copy 《after, from》; pattern 《after》; make 《*a person*》 *one's* model; 《형을》 make a model 《of》; model 《a tooth in wax》. ¶ …을 본떠 after; after the model 〔example〕 of... / 본떠서 만들다 make 《*a thing*》 after the pattern 〔on the model〕 of 《another》; model 《*a thing*》 after 《another》/ 아무를 ~ follow *a person's* example / 미국식을 ~ follow the American style / 이 제도는 지금 독일에서 행해지고 있는 것을 본뜬 것이다 This system is modeled on the one now in use in Germany. ② = 본받다.
**본뜻**(本―) ① 《본래의 의도》 *one's* original purpose; *one's* (real) intention 〔will, motive〕. ¶ ~을 이루다 accom-

plish *one's* purpose; work *one's* will / 그렇게 하는 것은 나의 ～이 아니다 It goes against my heart to do so. *or* It is far from me to do so. ②《의미》 the original meaning 《of a text》; the original import; the literal 〔the basic〕 meaning. ¶ 헌정의 ～ the basic principle of constitutional government / 그 말의 ～을 모르겠다 I can't make out the original meaning of the word.

**본래**(本來) 《원래》 originally; primarily; from the first 〔beginning〕; 《본질적으로》 essentially; fundamentally; in itself; intrinsically; 《자연적으로》 naturally; by nature; 《당연히》 normally; rightfully. ¶ ～의 original; essential; natural / 인간 ～의 성질 human nature / ～ 좋은 것이라도 쓰기에 따라서는 해롭게 된다 A thing good in itself may become harmful by its use. / 이 문제는 ～가 복잡한 문제였다 This was a complicated matter from the beginning. / 그는 ～ 말이 없는 사람이었다 He was by nature a silent man. / 이것은 ～ 그들의 문제이지, 우리들의 문제가 아니다 Properly speaking, this is their concern, not ours.

**본령**(本領) ①《특색》 a characteristic; a feature; 《본분》 the proper province 〔function〕; *one's* duty; 《전문영역》 *one's* line. ②《본성》 the original nature; the real 〔essential〕 character.

**본론**(本論) the main discourse 〔issue, subject〕. ¶ ～으로 들어가기 전에 before taking up the main subject / ～으로 돌아가다 return to the main subject / ～으로 들어가다 proceed 〔go on〕 to the main issue / ～에서 벗어나다 digress from the main point; get off the main track / 그러면 ～으로 들어갑시다 Well, let's get down to the main topic.

**본루**(本壘) 〖야구〗 the home base 〔plate〕. ¶ ～를 밟다 get home / ～로 들어올 기회를 노리다 look for a chance to get home. ◉ ～타 《hit》 a home run; a homer. ⇨ 홈런.

**본류**(本流) the main course 《of a river》; the mainstream; a main current. ¶ 한국 문학의 ～ the main current of Korean literature.

**본말**(本末) root and branch; the means and the end. ¶ 문제의 ～ the relative importance of a question / ～을 전도하다 mistake the means for the end; get *one's* priorities wrong; confuse the order of things; put the cart before the horse.

**본맛** the original taste 〔flavor〕.

**본망**(本望) *one's* heart's dream 〔real desire〕; *one's* long-cherished dream. ⇨ 숙망.

**본명**(本名) *one's* real name; 《필명에 대하여》 *one's* autonym; 《가톨릭》 *one's* Christian 〔baptismal〕 name. ¶ ～으로 under *one's* real name / ～으로 쓴 책 an autonym / ～을 대다 give *one's* real name.

**본무**(本務) ①《본분》 *one's* duty; the proper function. ②《업무》 *one's* (regular) business; *one's* main work. ¶ 먼저 ～에 힘써라 Attend to your business first. *or* Sweep before your own door. ③〖논리〗 moral duty 〔obligation〕. ◉ ～론 deontology.

**본무대**(本舞臺) the regular 〔main〕 stage; the public place.

**본문**(本文) 《본체》 the text 《of a book, of a treaty》; the body 《of a letter》; 《이 글》 this sentence 〔article, passage〕. ¶ ～의 필자 the writer of this article.

**본문제**(本問題) 《본래의》 the original problem 〔question〕; 《기본의》 the fundamental 〔main〕 problem; 《이 문제》 this problem.

**본밑(천)**(本—) capital; funds. ⇨ 밑천.

**본바닥**(本—) 《본디부터 사는 곳》 a native place; a home; a habitat; 《본래의 산지》 the place of origin; the birthplace; the home 《of》; the best place 《for》; the center of production. ¶ ～ 영어 English as it is spoken by its native speaker / ～의 스카치위스키 a genuine Scotch whisky / 커피의 ～ the home of coffee / 차의 ～ a tea-growing center / 외국어를 ～에서 배우다 learn a foreign language in the country where it is spoken / 영국은 대의 정치의 ～이다 England is the birthplace of representative government. ◉ ～ 사람 a native; an indigene: 서울～ 사람이다 be a native of Seoul; be an indigenous Seoulite.

**본바탕**(本—) essence; (real) substance; intrinsic nature; essential quality; *one's* disposition; *one's* true color. ¶ ～이 정직한 naturally honest; honest by nature / ～은 나쁜 사람이 아니다 He is not a rogue at heart.

**본받다**(本—) follow the example 〔model〕 of 《*a person*》; model *oneself* 《on, after》; imitate. ¶ 본받을 만한 행

위 an exemplary conduct / 아무의 덕을 ～ imitate the virtues of *a person* / 그 사람을 본받는 것이 좋겠다 You may as well follow his example.

**본보기**(本—) an example; a model; a pattern. ¶ ～로(서) as an example / 애국심의 좋은 ～ a fine example of patriotism / ～가 될 만한 행실 exemplary conduct / 아무를 ～로 삼다 make an example of *a person.*

**본봉**(本俸) the regular salary 〔pay〕; the basic salary.

**본부**(本部) the head 〔main, home〕 office; the headquarters (★ 단수 취급). ¶ ～를 설치하다 set up the 《investigation》 headquarters 《in》 / ～는 서울에 있다 be headquartered in Seoul / 대학 ～는 구내 중앙에 있다 The administrative building of the university stands in the center of the campus. ◉ ～장(長) the general manager; the director. ～중대 〖군사〗 a headquarters company.

**본분**(本分) *one's* duty 〔part, role〕. ¶ 사람으로서의 ～ *one's* duty as man / ～을 다하다 do 〔perform, discharge, fulfill〕 *one's* duty; do 〔play〕 *one's* part / ～을 게을리하다 neglect 〔fail to *do*〕 *one's* duty / 공무원으로서의 ～을 잊다 neglect *one's* duty as a public servant / 학생으로서의 ～을 잊지말고 행동하라 Conduct yourself bearing in mind your duty as a student.

**본사**(本社) 《주된》 the head 〔main〕 office 《of a firm》; 《당사》 our firm 〔company〕; this company. ¶ ～가 서울에 있는 M 주식회사, M, Inc., headquartered 〔whose head office is〕 in Seoul / ～ 근무가 되다 be transferred 〔assigned〕 to the head office.

**본사**(本寺) 《불교에서》 the temple where *one* first became a Buddhist priest; 《자기가 있는》 this 〔our〕 temple; 《본산》 the main 〔head〕 temple.

**본사내**(本—) ＝본남편(本男便).

**본산**(本山) the head temple of a Buddhist sect; 《교회의》 the cathedral.

**본새**(本—) ① 《생김새》 the original looks; features. ¶ ～가 곱다 be nice-looking; have good features. ② 《바탕》 the nature; basic quality 〔attributes〕. ¶ ～가 사납다 have an ugly nature.

**본색**(本色) ① 《빛깔》 the true 〔natural〕 colors; the original colors. ② 《정체》 *one's* real character; *one's* real intention; the true quality. ¶ ～을 드러내다 reveal *one's* true character; show *one's* true colors; unmask *oneself;* confess *one's* real intention / ～을 숨기다 wear 〔put on〕 a mask; disguise *oneself* / ～이 드러나다 betray *oneself;* betray *one's* true color 〔origin〕.

**본서**(本書) 《이 책》 this book 〔volume〕; the present work 〔book〕; the book 〔volume, work〕 in question; (the) said book.

**본서**(本署) ① 《주된》 a chief station; a principal office; the chief police station (경찰서). ② 《이》 this office 〔station〕.

**본서방** ＝본남편(本男便).

**본선**(本船) 《이 배》 this 〔our〕 ship; 《모선》 a mother 〔depot〕 ship 〔vessel〕. ◉ ～인도 《수출항에서》 free on board (생략 F.O.B., f.o.b.); 《수입항에서》 ex ship: ～인도 가격 the price ex ship.

**본선**(本線) 〖철도〗 the main line; 《간선》 the trunk (line); the main track (측선에 대해서); 《이 선》 this line; 《고속도로 따위에서의 게시》 Through traffic.

**본선**(本選) the final selection.

**본성**(本性) the original nature; *one's* true character 〔real nature〕. ¶ ～을 드러내다 show 〔reveal〕 *one's* character; betray *oneself;* throw off the mask; reveal *one's* true colors; unmask *oneself* / 인간의 ～은 선이다 Man is good by nature. / 아이를 지키는 것은 어머니의 ～이다 It is in the nature of mothers to defend their children.

**본숭만숭하다** 《무관하게 보다》 look on 《*something*》 with an unconcerned air; 《길에서》 cut 《*a person*》 (dead); look the other way; 《얼핏보다》 glance 《over》; take a cursory view 《of》; skim 《over》.

**본시**(本是) originally. ⇨본디.

**본실**(本室) *one's* legal wife; *one's* first wife.

**본심**(本心) 《본마음》 (***a***) 《제마음》 *one's* right mind; *one's* senses. ¶ ～으로 돌아오다 return to *one's* right mind; come to *one's* senses. (***b***) 《진심》 *one's* real 〔true〕 intention; *one's* true self; *one's* conscience (양심); *one's* better nature (바탕). ¶ ～은 at heart 〔bottom〕; in *one's* real being / ～에서 얘기하다 speak from *one's* heart / ～을 드러내다〔밝히다〕 reveal *one's* real intention; betray *oneself;* lay bare *one's* heart; unbosom *oneself* / 그것으로 그의 ～이 드러났다 He betrayed himself by that. / 그게 과연 그의 ～에서 나온 말일까 I wonder if he really meant what he said. / 그는 ～은 좋은

사람이다 He is a good fellow at heart. / 그녀의 ～을 알 수가 없다 I don't know 「her true intention 〔what she is really thinking〕.

**본안**(本案) ① 《원안》 the original bill 〔motion, draft〕; the original plan. ② 《이 안》 this plan 〔bill〕.

**본얼굴**(本—) *one's* original 〔unchanged, unpainted〕 face.

**본업**(本業) *one's* principal 〔main〕 occupation; *one's* regular business 〔work, trade〕. ¶ ～ 외의 일 a side business 〔job〕; a sideline / ～에 힘쓰다 attend to *one's* business / 의사가 ～이다 be a physician by profession / 그의 ～은 축산이다 Livestock breeding is his main occupation.

**본연**(本然) ⇨ 본래. ¶ ～의 자세 the way that one 〔it〕 should be.

**본원**(本源) a source; an origin; the root 《of》; a principle; a cause. ¶ 만물의 ～ the origin 〔first principle〕 of all things / ～을 밝히다 study the origin 《of *a thing*》; trace 《*a thing*》 to *its* source.

**본위**(本位) ① 《통화의》 a (monetary) standard. ② 《기준·중심》 a standard; a principle; 《기초》 a basis (*pl.* bases). ¶ 품질～ quality first / 정치 경제학 ～의 잡지 a magazine devoted to political economy / 영리 ～의 학교 a school run for profit / 자기 ～의 사람〔사고방식〕 a self-centered 「person 〔way of thinking〕 / 남자 ～의 법질서 man first legal order / …을 ～로 하다 make it *one's* principle 〔rule〕 《to *do*》; place 〔put, lay〕 great emphasis 《on》 / 어학 ～로 영어를 배우다 study English on a linguistic basis / 현금 ～로 장사를 하다 do a business on a cash basis / 우리는 품질 ～입니다 Quality first is our motto. / 저 상점은 고객 ～로 장사를 한다 That store puts service to its customers before everything else. *or* They make it their principle to serve customers' interests in that store. / 그 회사는 인물 ～로 채용을 한다 When employing a worker, the company considers his character before 〔over〕 anything else.

◉ ～기호 〖음악〗 《제자리표》 a natural. ～화폐 a standard money 〔coin, currency〕; legal tender. 금〔은〕～ the gold 〔silver〕 standard.

**본의**(本意) ① 《본래 의도》 *one's* original purpose; 《진의》 *one's* real intention 〔will, motive〕. ¶ ～ 아니게 reluctantly; with reluctance; unwillingly; against *one's* will 〔wish〕 / 사직한다는 게 네 ～는 아니겠지 You don't really mean to resign, do you? / ～를 오해하다 misjudge 《*a person's*》 purpose 〔motive〕. ② 《진심》 *one's* heart 〔mind, conscience, better nature〕.

**본이름**(本—) *one's* real 〔original〕 name.

**본인**(本人) ① 《그 사람 자신》 the person himself 〔herself〕; the subject; 《문제의》 the said person; the person in question; 《나·자기》 I; me; myself. ¶ ～ 자신(이) in person; personally / ～의 사진 *one's* own photograph / ～을 만났다 I saw the man himself. / ～이 그렇게 말하고 있다 He says so himself. / 정작 ～은 아무 것도 모른다 He himself knows nothing about it. / 직접 ～에게서 들은 것이므로 사실임에 틀림없다 I heard it directly from the person himself, so it must be true. ② 《대리인에 대하여》 the principal; the constituent. ¶ ～이 출두하다 present *oneself* 《at a court》.

**본임자**(本—) the original owner 〔master〕.

**본적**(本籍) 《원적》 *one's* permanent domicile 〔address〕; *one's* domicile of origin; 《본적지》 *one's* place of register; *one's* home address. ¶ ～을 옮기다 transfer *one's* domicile 《to》 / ～이 서울이다 be legally domiciled in Seoul.

**본전**(本錢) 《원금》 the principal (sum); 《자본·밑천》 capital; fund; 《들어간 돈》 the (original) cost; the cost price. ¶ ～을 건지다〔뽑다〕 recover *one's* investment 〔the cost〕 / ～을〔도〕 못 건지다 fail to return the original investment; suffer a total loss / 밑져야 ～이다 be none the worse for the loss.

**본점**(本店) 《지점에 대하여》 the head 〔main〕 office 〔shop, store〕; 《이 점포》 this store; our shop.

**본제**(本題) the original topic 〔subject〕; the main question 〔issue〕. ¶ ～로 돌아가서 to return (to our subject) / ～로 들어가다 enter into the main question.

**본존**(本尊) 〖불교〗 《주불》 the principal image (of Buddha); 《석가모니불》 Buddha (as the principal image).

**본죄**(本罪) 〖가톨릭〗 an actual 〔a personal〕 sin.

**본주인**(本主人) the original proprietor 〔owner〕.

**본줄기**(本—) the main line 〔plot〕; 《이야기의》 the main thread 《of a story》. ¶ ～에 들어가다 get onto 〔go into〕 the main subject 〔topic, issue〕 / ～에서

벗어나다 stray 〔digress〕 from the main topic.

**본지**(本旨) 《본래의 취지》 the main 〔principal〕 object 〔purport〕; 《참목적》 the true aim; the object in view. ¶ …의 ∼에 맞다 serve 〔answer〕 the purpose of… / 교육의 ∼에 어긋나다 go against 〔be contrary to〕 the true aim of education.

**본지**(本紙) this 〔our〕 newspaper; 《논설 따위에서》 us; we. ¶ ∼의 애독자〔기자〕 our readers 〔correspondent, reporter〕 / ∼에서 이미 보도된 바와 같이 as already reported 「in these columns 〔in our paper〕.

**본지**(本誌) this journal; our magazine.

**본직**(本職) ① 《본업》 *one's* (regular) occupation; *one's* principal business; *one's* regular work 〔job〕. ¶ ∼은 by profession 〔trade〕 / ∼으로 삼다 make 《a carpentry》 *one's* profession / ∼을 소홀히 하다 neglect *one's* regular work / 그의 ∼은 양복장이다 He is a tailor by trade. ② 《관리 등의 자칭》 I; me; myself.

**본질**(本質) real nature; essence; substance (실질); intrinsic 〔essential〕 qualities. ¶ 문제의 ∼ the true nature of the problem / 민주주의의 ∼ the essence of democracy / ∼적(인) essential; substantial / ∼적 속성 an intrinsic attribute / ∼적인 차이 an essential difference / ∼적으로(는) essentially; in essence; in itself; in substance / 외형과 ∼ 모두 in essence as well as in outward form.

**본집**(本—) *one's* (own) home; *one's* parents' home.

**본처**(本妻) *one's* legal 〔lawful〕 wife; *one's* wedded wife.

**본체**(本體) ① 《참모습》 a true form; 《본바탕》 true 〔intrinsic〕 nature; essence. ¶ …을 ∼로 하다 attach primary importance to…; make 《it》 a primary object to 《*do*》 / ∼를 모르다 have no idea of 《its》 true character. ② 《기계 따위의》 the body 〔core〕 《of a machine》. ③ 〖철학〗 the substance (실체); the entity; the thing in itself. ④ 〖불교〗 reality; the principal image of Buddha. ◉ ∼기판 〖컴퓨터〗 a motherboard. ∼론 ontology; substantialism: ∼론의 ontological. 「본체하다.

**본체만체하다** pretend not to see. ⇨ 못

**본초**(本草) 〖한의〗 medic(in)al herbs; 《본초학》 Chinese pharmaceutics; herbal medicine. ¶ ∼ 채집을 하다 herborize; collect herbs. ◉ ∼가 a herb doctor; a herbalist. ∼강목 a botanical list; a flora. ∼학 botany.

**본초자오선**(本初子午線) the first 〔prime〕 meridian.

**본치** figure; appearance.

**본토**(本土) *one's* native country; the mainland; the country proper. ¶ ∼산(産)의 produced on the 《Chinese》 mainland; native 〔indigenous〕 to 《Japan》 proper. ◉ ∼박이 natives; aborigines. ∼방위 home 〔national〕 defense. ∼인 natives; mainlanders; aborigines; autochthons. 중국∼ China proper; Mainland China.

**본형**(本刑) 〖법〗 a regular penalty.

**본형**(本形) the original form 〔shape〕.

**본회담**(本會談) a full-dress talk; the main conference.

**본회의**(本會議) a general meeting; a plenary 〔full〕 session 《of the House》; a full-dress meeting 〔debate〕. ¶ 의안을 ∼에 상정하다 submit a bill to a plenary session; send a bill to the session of the National Assembly.

**볼**[1] ① 《뺨》 a cheek. ¶ 볼이 붉은 red-〔rosy-〕cheeked / 볼을 붉히다 blush; redden / 볼을 비비다 press 〔nestle, rub〕 *one's* cheek against *another's* / 볼을 싸다 cover 〔wrap〕 *one's* cheeks 《with a towel》 / 볼이 홀쭉하다 have a hollow 〔sunken〕 cheeks / 볼이 미어지게 먹다 stuff 〔fill〕 *one's* mouth 《with food》; cram 《food》 into *one's* mouth. ⇨ 뺨. ② 《넓이》 the width (of a long and narrow object). ¶ 볼이 넓은 발 a flat and wide foot / 볼이 좁다〔넓다〕 be narrow 〔wide〕 / 이 구두는 나한테 볼이 너무 좁다 These shoes are too tight for me. ③ 《버선의》 a patch (for cloth socks). ¶ 버선의 볼을 대다〔받다〕 put patches on cloth socks.

**볼**[2] ① 《공》 a ball. ¶ 볼을 던지다 throw 〔deliver, pitch〕 a ball / 볼을 치다〔헛치다〕 hit 〔swing and miss〕 a ball. ② 〖야구〗 a ball (strike zone을 벗어난 공). ¶ (심판이) 볼을 선언하다 call a ball / (투구가) 볼이 되다 get too high 〔low〕; be declared a ball. ◉ 볼보이 a ball boy. 볼카운트 a count.

**볼가심** a bite; a snack; something to chew on. ∼하다 have a snack (to appease *one's* hunger. ¶ ∼할 것 a morsel of food; a bite to eat / 생쥐 ∼할 것도 없다 《속담》 don't have enough for a mouse to chew on; don't have a crumb; be utterly destitute; be as poor as a church mouse.

**볼가지다** ⇨ 불거지다.
**볼강거리다** take a lot of chewing; be chewy 〔leathery, lumpy〕.
**볼강볼강** hard to chew; chewy; leathery; lumpy.
**볼거리** 〖한의〗 mumps (★ 단수 취급). ¶ ~가 나다 get mumps.
**볼그대대하다, 볼그댕댕하다** (be) reddish.
**볼그레하다** (be) reddish; [서술적] be tinged with red.
**볼그무레하다, 볼그속속하다** (be) reddish.
**볼기** the buttocks; the ass 《속어》. ¶ ~를 때리다〔치다〕 spank 《a child》; paddle 《a child's》 bottom; flog 《a culprit's》 buttocks (as a punishment) / ~를 맞다 get spanked. ◉ ~긴살 rump. ~짝 = 볼기.
**볼꼴** outward appearance; show; look. ¶ ~ 사납다 be unsightly; be ugly 〔mean〕 / ~ 사나운 옷차림 unsightly appearance; a shabby dress / ~ 사납게 in an awkward 〔a clumsy〕 manner; unseemly; improperly; badly / ~ 사납게 굴다 behave disgracefully 〔indecently〕; make a sight of *oneself* / 참 ~ 사납다 What a sight!
**볼낯없다** be ashamed to see 《a *person*》; be unable to face 《*one's* sweetheart》; lose (*one's*) face.
**볼레로** 《여성용 웃옷》 a bolero; 〖음악〗 bolero.
**볼록** ◉ ~거울 a convex mirror. ~렌즈 〖물리〗 a convex lens; a convex. ~면(面) a convex surface; a convexity. ~판(版) 〖인쇄〗 letterpress.
**볼록거리다** swell and subside; palpitate.
**볼록하다** ⇨ 불룩하다.
**볼륨** volume. ¶ ~을 높이다〔낮추다〕 turn up 〔down〕 the volume 《on the stereo》.
**볼리비아** 《남미의 공화국》 Bolivia. ¶ ~의 Bolivian. ◉ ~공화국 the Republic of Bolivia. ~사람 a Bolivian.
**볼링** bowling. ¶ ~하러 가다 go bowling. ◉ ~장 a bowling alley.
**볼만하다** 《보암직하다》 be (well) worth seeing; be impressive. ¶ 볼 만한 것 a sight; a spectacle; a feature; a highlight 《미》 / 가 ~ be worth 〔worthy of〕 a visit / 비원은 가 ~ The Secret Garden is well worth seeing. / 그녀의 춤은 볼만했다 Her dance was worth watching. / 그 토론회는 정말 볼만했다 The debate was quite a spectacle.
**볼맞다** ① 《손이 맞다》 work hand in glove together; get along together nicely. ② 《걸맞다》 be well matched; make a good pair.
**볼멘소리** sullen 〔grouchy, sulky〕 words. ¶ ~로 in angry tone / ~로 대답하다 give a sullen answer; answer sulkily.
**볼모** ① 《담보》 a pawn. ⇨ 담보. ② 《인질》 a hostage. ¶ ~로 잡다 take 〔hold〕 《*a person*》 (as a) hostage / ~로 잡히다 be taken 〔held〕 (as a) hostage.
**볼셰비즘** Bolshevism.
**볼셰비키** a Bolshevik (*pl.* ~s, ~i); a Bolshevist.
**볼썽사납다** (be) indecent; unseemly; ungainly.
**볼일** things to be done; things to do; business; 《심부름》 an errand. ¶ ~로 on business; 《심부름》 on an errand / 급한 ~ an urgent 〔a pressing〕 business / ~이 있다 be engaged 《in》; have something to do / ~이 없다 be free; have nothing to do / ~을 보다 do *one's* business; perform 〔carry through, get through〕 *one's* business / ~을 끝내다〔마치다〕 finish 〔settle〕 *one's* business; get through (with) *one's* business / 너에게 ~이 있다 I want to have a word with you. / 내게 무슨 ~이 있느냐 What do you want me for ? / 나는 오늘 저녁 ~이 있다 I have something to do this evening. / 대체 이리 늦은 시간에 무슨 ~이냐 What on earth do you want me for such a late hour ? / ~이 있으시면 언제든지 불러주십시오 Please call me anytime you want me. / 「무슨 ~로 서울에 오셨습니까」—「사업일로 왔습니다」 "What brought you to Seoul ?"—"I've come here on business".
**볼장 다 보다** have done with 《*a thing*》; be ruined. ¶ 이 장사도 이젠 볼장 다 보았다 It is all up with this business.
**볼타전지**(—電池) 〖물리〗 a voltaic battery 〔cell〕; a Volta's cell.
**볼트** ① 〖물리〗 a volt; voltage (볼트수). ¶ 100 ~의 전류 a 100-volt current. ② 《나사못》 a bolt; a screw bolt. ¶ ~로 죄다 bolt up; fasten with a bolt.
**볼티모어** 《미국의 항구》 Baltimore.
**볼펜** a ball-point 〔ballpoint〕 pen.
**볼품** appearance; show; looks; (a) shape. ¶ ~이 좋다 have a good appearance; be graceful / ~이 있다 look nice 〔fine, well〕; make a fine show; be attractive; be pleasing in appearance / ~이 없다〔사납다〕 look poor; have a bad appearance; make a poor show; be unattractive 〔vulgar〕 / 방을 ~있게 꾸미다 make a room look nice / 저 차는 ~이 있다

The car 「has a good shape 〔is very stylish〕.

**볼호령**(一號令) a howl; an angry roar. ~하다 howl; roar《at》.

**봄** spring; springtime. ¶ 봄의 spring; vernal / 봄 같은 springlike / 봄의 따뜻한 햇살 a soft, warm spring sun(-shine) / 인생의 봄 the spring(time) of life / 봄이 되면 in (the) spring; as spring comes round / 이른〔늦은〕 봄에 early 〔late〕 in spring; in early 〔late〕 spring / 봄이 왔다 Spring has come. / 봄이 갔다 Spring is over. / 봄꿩이 제 울음에 죽는다《속담》 The pheasant would not be caught but for its cries. *or* You are digging your own grave. ◉ 봄기운 a feel 〔an air〕 of spring: 봄기운을 느끼다 feel a breath of spring. 봄농사 a spring crop. 봄누에 a spring breed of silkworms. 봄옷 (a suit for) spring wear.

**봄가물**, **봄가뭄** spring drought 〔dry spell〕.

**봄갈이** spring plowing 〔ploughing《영》〕. ~하다 do the spring plowing 〔ploughing〕.

**봄나물** young greens 〔herbs〕. ¶ ~을 캐다 pick young herbs.

**봄날** a spring day; spring weather. ¶ 화창한 ~ the mild days of spring.

**봄내** all through 〔throughout〕 the spring. ¶ ~ 비 한 방울 오지 않았다 We have been without rain the whole spring long.

**봄눈** spring snow. ¶ ~ 슬〔녹〕듯 하다 disappear 〔vanish〕 into thin air; 《음식이》 melt in *one's* mouth; go down 〔digest〕 smoothly.

**봄바람** a spring wind 〔breeze〕.

**봄베** 〔<*Bombe* (G.)〕 a bomb; a cylinder. ◉ 가스~ a gas cylinder.

**봄볕** spring sun(shine).

**봄보리** barley sown in the early spring.

**봄비** spring rain 〔drizzle〕.

**봄빛** spring scene(ry); a spring view.

**봄소식**(一消息) tidings of flowers; news of the cherry trees coming in bloom; a sign 〔herald〕 of spring.

**봄철** the spring season; springtime.

**봄추위** cold weather in early spring; a late frost; the lingering cold in spring.

**봄타다** suffer from spring fever; lose appetite 〔get weaker〕 in spring.

**봅슬레이**《썰매》 a bobsleigh; a bobsled; 《경기》 bobsledding.

**봇논**(洑一) a paddy field watered by a reservoir.

**봇도랑**, **봇돌**(洑一) an irrigation ditch 〔conduit〕.

**봇돌** ①《아궁이의》 a support stone on either side of the fireplace. ②《지붕의》 stone weights over a roof.

**봇둑**(洑一) a dam; levees surrounding a reservoir.

**봇물**(洑一) dam water; water in dammed pool.

**봇줄** draw-cords on a farm animal; a trace.

**봇짐**(褓一) a bundle; a backpack. ¶ ~을 짊어지다 carry a bundle on *one's* back; shoulder a bundle. ◉ ~장수 a peddler who carries his wares on his back.

**봉**[1]《메우는》 a solder patch; plugging (충치의). ¶ 봉(을) 박다 fill up 〔in〕; stop (up); solder on a patch; solder up a hole / 치아에 봉을 해 박다 stop 〔plug〕 a tooth; fill a tooth《with》.

**봉**[2] ⇨ 봉돌.

**봉**(封) ① a paper package; 《약의》 a dose. ¶ 약 한 봉 a packet of medicine / 봉을 짓다 make a parcel 《of *things*》 / 약 한 봉을 먹다 take a dose of medicine. ② = 봉투.

**봉**(鳳) ① ⇨ 봉황. ②《만만한》 a dupe; an easy 〔a soft〕 mark; a gull; a pigeon; a prey; a victim. ¶ 봉으로 삼다 make a sucker out of 《*a person*》 / 봉이 되다 fall an easy victim to 《*a person's* trick》.

**봉건**(封建) ①《봉함》 setting up 《*a person*》 as a feudal lord; enfeoffing. ②《제도》 feudalism. ¶ ~적(인) feudal; feudalistic; 《보수적》 conservative; 《시대에 뒤진》 old-fashioned 《ideas》; 《전제적》 despotic / ~적인 교사 an undemocratic teacher / 그는 ~적이다 He is 「an old fogy 〔too old-fashioned〕. ◉ ~국가 a feudal state. ~군주 a feudal lord; a feudatory. ~사상 a feudalistic idea 〔thought〕. ~시대 the feudal age 〔times〕; the era 〔days〕 of feudalism: 그의 생각은 ~시대의 유물이다 His idea is a relic of the feudal days. ~제도 feudalism; the feudal system 〔regime〕. ~주의 feudalism.

**봉급**(俸給) (a) salary; pay; wages; 《전원의》 the payroll. ¶ 높은〔많은〕 ~ high pay; a high salary / 낮은〔적은〕 ~ small pay; a low 〔small〕 salary / ~을 지급하다 pay 〔give〕 a salary; pay for 《*a person's*》 regular work 〔services〕 / ~을 타다 receive a salary; get paid / ~을 올리다〔내리다〕 raise 〔lower〕 《*a person's*》 salary / ~이 오르

다〔내리다〕 get a raise 〔cut〕 in *one's* salary; have *one's* salary raised 〔reduced〕 / ~이 좋다〔나쁘다〕 be well 〔ill, poorly〕 paid / ~으로 생활하다 live on *one's* salary / 월 백만 원의 ~을 받고 있다 draw a monthly pay of ₩1,000,000 《from a firm》; get ₩1,000,000 a month / ~ 생활을 그만두고 자립하다 become self-employed / ~은 얼마입니까 What is the pay? / 그는 상당한 ~을 받는다 He draws 〔gets〕 a good salary. ◉ ~규정 the salary schedule regulation. ~봉투 a pay envelope. ~생활자 a salaried person; a salary earner. ~일 a payday.

**봉기**(蜂起) a revolt; an uprising; (an) insurrection. ~하다 rise in revolt 〔rebellion, arms〕 《against》; rise 〔revolt〕 《against》. ¶ 농민의 ~ an uprising of the farmers.

**봉납**(奉納) dedication; offering; presentation 《to a deity》; oblation. ~하다 dedicate; offer; present. ◉ ~물 an offering; a votive offering. ~자 an offerer; a dedicator.

**봉놋방**(一房) the lodging room in an inn 〔a tavern〕 where a guest sleep with his fellow lodgers; the inn dormitory.

**봉당**(封堂) an unfloored 〔dirt-floored〕 area between two rooms. ¶ ~을 빌려주니 안방까지 달란다 《속담》 Give him an inch, and he will take an ell. ◉ ~마루 a dirt floor.

**봉독**(奉讀) ~하다 read reverentially.

**봉돌** a weight of stone 〔lead〕 on a fishline; a sinker. ¶ ~을 달다 weight a line.

**봉두난발**(蓬頭亂髮) shaggy 〔unkempt〕 hair.

**봉랍**(封蠟) sealing wax. ¶ ~으로 봉하다 seal 《a letter》 with wax.

**봉밀**(蜂蜜) honey. ⇨ 벌꿀. ◉ ~주(酒) mead.

**봉박다**(封一) add something extra to a package.

**봉변**(逢變) 《변을》 meeting with a mishap; a mishap; a misfortune; 《욕을》 receiving insult; (having) bitter experiences; an insult; humiliation. ~하다 meet with a mishap; be insulted 〔humiliated〕; have bitter experiences; have a hard time of it; have a hell of a time. ¶ 사람들 앞에서 ~을 당하다 be 「humiliated 〔put to shame〕 in public.

**봉봉** 《과자》 *a bonbon* (F.). ◉ 위스키~ a whiskey *bonbon*.

**봉분**(封墳) ~하다 mound 《a grave》; build a mound over a grave.

**봉사**(奉仕) (a) service. ~하다 serve; render services 《to》; give *one's* services (free). ¶ 지역 사회에 ~하다 serve *one's* community. ◉ ~가격 a sacrifice 〔bargain〕 price: ~가격으로 《sell》 at a sacrifice; 《offer》 at a reduced 〔bargain〕 price / ~ 가격으로 제공 《광고》 To be sold at a sacrifice. *or* Slashed prices! ~사업 public welfare work. ~자 one who serves 《the public at large》; a servant 《of the people》. ~활동 voluntary service: ~활동을 하다 do volunteer work 《at an orphanage》. 사회~ public service; service to society: 사회 ~로서 as a service to the public.

**봉사**(奉祀) offering sacrifice to *one's* ancestors. ~하다 offer sacrifice to *one's* ancestors. ◉ ~손(孫) a descendant offering sacrifice to his ancestors.

**봉사**(奉事) 《소경》 a blind person.

**봉서**(封書) a sealed letter. ¶ ~로 under cover; in sealed covers.

**봉선화**(鳳仙花) 〖식물〗 a (garden) balsam; a touch-me-not.

**봉소위**(蜂巢胃) 《반추류의》 a reticulum (*pl.* -la); a honeycomb.

**봉쇄**(封鎖) a blockade; blocking; bottling up; 《동결》 freezing. ~하다 block; blockade 《a port》; block up 《a street》; 〖군사〗 seal 《an area》 off; freeze 《assets》. ¶ 경제~ 《impose》 an economic blockade / 해상 ~ a naval 〔sea〕 blockade / ~를 뚫다 break 〔run, enforce〕 a blockade / ~를 풀다 lift 〔raise〕 a blockade; unfreeze (동결을) / 입구를 ~하다 block the entrance 《to》 / 모든 도로는 ~되었다 All the roads were blocked up. ◉ ~구역〔선〕 a blockade zone 〔line〕. ~예금 restricted 〔frozen〕 accounts 〔deposits〕. ~정책 a blockade policy. ~통화 〖경제〗 blocked currency. ~함대 a blockading squadron 〔fleet〕.

**봉수**(烽燧) a beacon; a signal fire.

**봉안**(奉安) enshrinement. ~하다 enshrine.

**봉양**(奉養) supporting *one's* parents. ~하다 support *one's* parents; serve *one's* parents faithfully. ¶ 노모를 ~할 사람은 그 뿐이다 He is the sole support of his aged mother.

**봉오리** a bud; a button. ¶ ~마다 all the buds; all in bud(s) / ~가 지다 put forth 〔shoot out〕 buds; (be in) bud; have 〔bear〕 buds / ~가 피다

(begin to) open its buds / ~가 맺혀 있다 be in bud. ◉ 꽃~ a flower in bud: 피어나는 꽃~ bursting buds / 꽃~를 꺾다 pluck a flower in the bud; [비유적] pluck the bud of maidenhood.

**봉우리** a peak; a top; a summit. ¶ 산~ a mountain top 〔peak〕.

**봉인**(封印) sealing; a (stamped) seal. ~하다 seal; put the seal (up)on. ¶ ~을 뜯다 break 〔tamper with〕 a seal / ~한 편지 a sealed letter.

**봉작**(封爵) investiture 〔investment〕 with the titles of nobility. ~하다 invest with the titles of nobility; ennoble.

**봉정**(奉呈) dedication; presentation (to a superior). ~하다 dedicate; present; offer.

**봉제**(縫製) needlework; sewing; dressmaking. ~하다 sew; do needlework. ◉ ~공 a needleworker; a dressmaker; a worker in a sewing factory. ~공장 a sewing factory. ~완구 stuffed toys.

**봉죽** assistance; help; aid. ~하다, ~들다 assist; help. ◉ ~꾼 an assistant; a helper; an aide.

**봉지**(封紙) ① 《종이 주머니》 a paper bag. ¶ ~ 바르기 paper-bag making / 그걸 ~에 넣어주십시오 Put it in a paper bag for me. ② 《셀 때》 a pack(-age) 《of》. ¶ 약 한 ~ a packet of medicinal herbs; a (packaged) dose of medicine.

**봉직**(奉職) government 〔public〕 service. ~하다 serve 《at, in》; hold an office 《at, in》; be in the service 《of》; be on the staff 《of a school》.

**봉착**(逢着) ~하다 encounter; face; meet 《with》; be faced 〔confronted〕 《with》; come upon 〔across〕. ¶ 난관에 ~하다 meet with difficulties; find *oneself* in a difficult situation.

**봉창**(封窓) 《봉한 창》 a sealed window; sealing (up) a window (봉하기); 《뚫은 창》 a papered 〔sealed〕 opening in the wall.

**봉창질하다** hoard things; keep 《*something*》 in secret; 《벌충하다》 make up (for a loss); make good; cover.

**봉축**(奉祝) celebration 《of an occasion》. ~하다 celebrate 《an occasion》. ¶ …을 ~하여 in celebration of….

**봉치**(封—) 〖민속〗 wedding gifts sent by the bridegroom's family (to the bride's family). ◉ 봉칫시루 rice cake to celebrate sending 〔receiving〕 a wedding gift.

**봉토**(封土) a fief; feudal land 〔territory〕.

**봉투**(封套) an envelope. ¶ ~의 뚜껑 the flap of an envelope / 투명지가 붙어 있는 ~ a windowed envelope / 주소 성명이 기재된 우표가 붙은 반신용 ~ a self-addressed and stamped return envelope / ~를 뜯다 open 〔break open〕 an envelope cut 《a letter》 open / ~를 봉하다 seal; wafer 《a letter》 / ~에 넣다 put 《a letter》 in an envelope / ~에 주소를 쓰다 address an envelope. ◉ 각〔양〕~ a side-opening envelope. 반신용 ~ a return envelope.

**봉피**(封皮) an envelope; a paper wrapper. ¶ ~를 뜯다 open 〔tear open, unseal〕 the wrapper.

**봉하다**(封—) ① 《문·봉투를》 seal 《a letter》; seal up 《a window》; glue up; fasten. ¶ 봉한〔봉하지 않은〕 편지 a sealed 〔an unsealed〕 letter / 봉하여 보내다 send 《a letter》 under seal / 봉하지 않은 채 부치다 send 《a letter》 unsealed / 봉투를 ~ seal an envelope. ② 《입을》 shut; seal. ¶ 입을 ~ hold *one's* tongue; shut *one's* mouth; seal *one's* lips / 입을 봉하고 말이 없다 keep *one's* lips tight; keep *one's* mouth shut; keep silent / 평론가의 입을 봉하라 Stop critics' mouths!
③ 《구멍을》 close 〔stop〕 up 《a hole》. ¶ 창구멍을 ~ cover a hole in a paper window.
④ 《봉토를》 invest 《*a person*》 with a fief; enfeoff; 《작위를》 confer a peerage.

**봉함**(封緘) a seal; sealing. ~하다 seal (a letter). ¶ ~을 뜯다 break 〔open〕 the seal 〔envelope〕. ◉ ~엽서 a lettercard.

**봉합**(縫合) 〖의학〗 (a) suture; (a) seam. ~하다 suture; seam; stitch (up) 《a wound》. ◉ ~사(絲) 〖외과〗 a suture; a stitching fiber. ~선 a suture; a seam.

**봉행**(奉行) ~하다 do in obedience to 《a superior's order》; obey 《*a person's*》 orders; carry out 《an order》.

**봉헌**(奉獻) dedication; presentation; consecration. ~하다 dedicate 〔consecrate, offer〕 《*a thing*》 to 《a superior, a shrine》. ◉ ~물 votive offerings. ~자 a dedicator.

**봉화**(烽火) a signal fire 〔flare〕; a rocket; a beacon. ¶ ~ 들다 raise a beacon fire / ～를 올리다 light a signal fire; fire 〔send up〕 a rocket as a signal. ◉ ～대〔둑〕 a beacon mound 〔lighthouse〕.

**봉황**(鳳凰) a Chinese phoenix.

**뵈다** ① ⇨보이다. ② = 뵙다.

**뵙다** humbly see 〔meet〕; be presented to; have an audience 〔interview〕 with. ¶ 어제 나는 대통령을 뵈었습니다 I was received by the President yesterday. / 처음 뵙겠습니다 How do you do? / 어디서 한 번 뵌 것 같습니다 I remember seeing 〔having seen〕 you once somewhere. / 이렇게 뵙게 되니 참 반갑습니다 It's good to see you here. *or* I am very glad to have the opportunity of meeting you. / 또 뵙겠습니다 Goodbye—I hope we will meet again. *or* I'll be seeing you again. / 그럼 내일 뵙겠습니다 Well then, I (shall) come tomorrow.

**부**(父) a father.

**부**(否) no; nay(s); negation. ¶ 가부(可否) aye and no; pro and con / 부(否)편이 많았다 The noes had it.

**부**(部) ①《부서》 a department; a bureau; a division; a section. ¶ 경리부 the accountants' department / 국방부 the Ministry 〔Department〕 of National Defense / 도서부《백화점 등의》 the book department 〔section〕. ②《부류》 a class; a category; a bracket. ③《책 셀 때》 a volume; a copy《of a book, magazine, *etc.*》. ¶ 1부 천 원 one thousand won a 〔per〕 copy / 초판 5천 부 a first impression of five thousand copies / 이 책 20부만 보내 주십시오 Please send me twenty copies of this book. ④《부분》 a part; a portion; a section. ¶ 회원의 일부 (a) part of member / 제2부 section Ⅱ / 3부로 된 소설 a novel in three parts.

**부**(富) riches; wealth; a fortune; opulence (부유). ¶ 일국의 부 a nation's wealth / 부의 분배 the distribution of wealth / 부를 쌓다 amass 〔build up〕 a fortune; gather wealth.

**부**(賦) poetical prose; an ode; a prose poem.

**부-**(副) assistant; under-; vice-; sub-; deputy; secondary; subsidiary; accessory; alternate《미》. ¶ 부시장 a deputy mayor / 부의장 a vice-chairman / 부지배인 an assistant manager / 부작용 a side 〔secondary〕 effect.

**-부**(附) ①《날짜》 dated; under the date of. ¶ 이 달 3일〔8월 15일〕부의 편지 a letter dated 3rd inst. 〔Aug. 15th〕. ②《소속》 attached《to》; in attendance《upon》; bearing; belonging《to》. ¶ 대사관부 공군무관 an air *attaché* to the embassy.

**부가**(附加) addition; annexation; supplement. ～하다 add《to》; make additions to;《보충》 supplement;《첨부》 annex; append;《추가》 subjoin. ¶ ～적인 additional; annexed; supplementary; extra.

◉ ～물 an addition; an annex; an appendage; an affix. ～세 an additional tax; a surtax. ～의문〖문법〗 a tag question. ～형(刑) an accessory 〔additional〕 penalty.

**부가가치**(附加價値) added value; value added. ¶ ～가 높은 제품의 생산 the production of high value-added products. ◉ ～세 a tax on value added; a value-added tax (생략 VAT): (상기 요금의) 10%의 봉사료와 10%의 ～세가 가산됩니다 10% service charge and 10% value-added tax will be added. ～통신망 a value-added network.

**부각**〖요리〗 fried kelp.

**부각**(俯角)〖수학〗 a dip; an angle of depression 〔declination〕.

**부각**(浮刻) relief. ～하다 emboss; raise;《새기다》 carve in relief. ¶ ～되다 be embossed; stand out in bold relief; [비유적] be highlighted; be brought to the fore / ～시키다 bring《*a thing*》 into relief / 새 무늬가 ～되어 있다 be embossed with a design of birds.

**부감**(俯瞰) overlooking; looking down. ～하다 overlook; look down upon; command 〔take〕 a bird's-eye view《of》. ◉ ～도 a bird's-eye view《of》; an air 〔aerial〕 view《of》. ～촬영 a crane shot (by a movie camera).

**부갑상선**(副甲狀腺)〖해부〗 the parathyroid (glands). ◉ ～호르몬 parathormone.

**부강**(富强) wealth 〔prosperity〕 and power. ～하다 (be) rich and powerful. ¶ 국가의 ～《promote》 the wealth and power of a nation / 국가의 ～을 꾀하다 strive for national wealth and power.

**부개비잡히다** be badgered into doing something against *one's* will.

**부걱** with a bubble 〔pop〕. ～거리다 bubble; pop (in fermenting).

**부검**(剖檢) a postmortem examination; autopsy. ⇨검시(檢屍).

**부검지** bits 〔shreds〕 of straw.

**부결**(否決) rejection; voting down; negation. ～하다 reject; vote 〔decide〕 against 《a bill》; vote 《a motion》 down; veto (거부하다). ¶ ～되다 be rejected 〔voted down〕; get vetoed 〔killed〕 / 의안을 ～ 하다 reject 〔vote down〕 a bill / 제안은 45대 38표로 ～되었다 The proposal was rejected 〔voted down〕 by a vote of 45 to 38. ◉ ～권 the right of veto; a veto.

**부계**(父系) the paternal side 〔line〕; the male line. ¶ ～의 consanguinean. ◉ ～가족 a paternal 〔patriarchal〕 family. ～사회 a patrilineal society. ～친족 an agnate; a relative on the father's side.

**부고**(訃告) an obituary (notice); an obit; an announcement of 《*a person's*》 death. ¶ ～를 받다 receive a notice of 《*a person's*》 death.

**부고환**(副睾丸) 〖해부〗 the epididymis (*pl.* -mides). 「wealth.

**부골**(富骨) physiognomy denoting

**부과**(賦課) levy; imposition. ～하다 levy 〔impose〕 《a tax on land》; lay 《a tax on an article》. ¶ 소득세를 ～하다 levy 〔impose〕 an income tax 《on》. ◉ ～금 (세관 등의) dues; a levy. ～액 the amount imposed; assessment (사정액). 자동～(세)제 taxation-by=schedule system.

**부관**(副官) an adjutant; an aide(-de=camp). ◉ ～참모 an adjutant general.

**부광**(富鑛) 〖광산〗 a rich mine. ◉ ～대(帶) a bonanza.

**부교**(浮橋) a floating 〔pontoon〕 bridge.

**부교감신경**(副交感神經) 〖해부〗 a parasympathetic (nerve).

**부교수**(副教授) an associate professor.

**부교재**(副教材) an auxiliary textbook.

**부국**(富國) a rich 〔wealthy〕 country. ◉ ～강병 wealth and military power 〔strength〕 of a nation: ～ 강병책 a measure to enrich and strengthen a country.

**부군**(夫君) a 〔*one's*〕 husband.

**부권**(父權) paternal rights. ◉ ～사회 a patriarchal society. ～제도 patriarchy.

**부귀**(富貴) riches and honors; wealth and rank. ～하다 (be) rich and noble. ¶ ～한 집안에 태어나다 be born into a noble and wealthy family; be born with a silver spoon in *one's* mouth / ～ 영화를 누리다 live in splendor. ◉ ～공명(功名) wealth, rank, and fame. ～빈천(貧賤) high and low; men of all ranks.

**부근**(附近) the neighborhood; the vicinity; the environs (근교). ¶ ～의 nearby; neighboring; adjacent / ～에 nearby; in the neighborhood 〔vicinity〕 《of》 / 이 ～에 near 〔around〕 here; in this neighborhood 〔vicinity〕 / ～의 책방에서 at a nearby bookstore / 서울 ～ the vicinity of Seoul; Seoul and (its, the) vicinity / 김형은 이 ～어딘가에 살고 있다 Mr. Kim lives somewhere around here. / 경찰은 범인을 잡기 위해서 그 ～ 일대를 수색하고 있다 The police are running a dragnet around there for the criminal.

**부글거리다** ① 《끓어서》 boil (over); simmer; seethe. ¶ 주전자의 물이 부글거린다 The kettle is singing. ② 《거품이》 bubble. ¶ 거품이 ～ bubble up; rise in bubbles.

**부글부글** ① 《끓어서》 on the simmer; with a sizzling sound. ¶ ～ 끓고 있다 be boiling briskly; be at a simmer. ② 《거품이》 bubbling; foamingly.

**부금**(賦金) a (monthly) installment; a premium (보험의). ¶ 이달치의 ～ this month's installment / 10회로 나눠 ～을 내다 pay in 〔by〕 ten installments. ◉ 상호～ mutual savings account.

**부기** a dolt; a ninny; a stupid fool.

**부기**(附記) an addition; an additional remark 〔note〕; a postscript (생략 P.S., p.s.). ～하다 add 《that...》; append (a note) 《to》; write in addition 《to》.

**부기**(浮氣) (a) swelling (of the skin). ¶ ～를 빠지게 하다 bring 〔take〕 the swelling down 〔away〕 / ～가 가라앉다 〔빠지다〕 The swelling subsides 〔goes down〕.

**부기**(簿記) bookkeeping. ¶ ～를 하다 keep books 〔accounts〕. ◉ ～계원 a bookkeeper; a ledger clerk. ～법 rules of bookkeeping. ～장(帳) an account book. ～학 (the art of ) bookkeeping. 가계〔공장〕～ domestic 〔factory〕 bookkeeping. 단식〔복식〕～ bookkeeping by single 〔double〕 entry. 상업〔공업, 은행〕～ commercial 〔industrial, bank〕 bookkeeping. 「gie.

**부기(우기)** 〖음악〗 boogie; boogie-woo-

**부꾸미** 《전병》 a kind of fried cake made by various flours.

**부끄러워하다** ① 《수줍어하다》 feel 〔be〕 shy; be coy; be bashful; be abashed. ¶ 부끄러워하여 bashfully; shyly / 대답하기를 ～ be too bashful to answer / 그녀는 남자를 부끄러워한다 She is shy around men. / 그녀는 의사에게 진찰받는 것을 몹시 부끄러워했다 She was very shy of consulting a doctor. ② 《창피해하다》 feel shame 《at》; be ashamed 《of》; consider something shameful 〔a shame〕. ¶ 부끄러워하는 표정 an ashamed look / 그녀는 돈이 없는 것을 부끄러워한다 She is ashamed to be without money. / 가난은 부끄러워할 게 못 된다 Poverty is no disgrace.

**부끄럼** ① 《창피》 shame; disgrace; dishonor; ignominy; humiliation (굴욕). ¶ ~을 알다 have a sense of shame; be sensible to shame / ~을 당하다 disgrace *oneself;* humiliate *oneself;* be put to shame / ~을 모르다 have no sense of shame; be dead 〔lost〕 to (all sense of) shame; be shameless / ~을 무릅쓰고 …하다 bear shame to 《*do*》 / 나는 이제 ~이고 뭐고 없다 I am now beyond 〔past〕 all sense of shame 〔decency〕. / 그는 질문하는 것을 ~으로 안다 He thinks it a shame to ask questions. / 그는 ~도 없이 거짓말을 한다 He lies shamelessly. / 나는 ~을 무릅쓰고 그에게 부탁했다 I stooped to ask a favor of him. / 너는 집안에 ~을 끼쳤다 You have brought disgrace upon your family. ② 《수줍음》 shyness; bashfulness; coyness. ¶ ~(을) 타다 feel shy; be bashful; be coy / 그 소녀는 ~을 타서 말도 잘 못한다 The young girl feels too bashful to talk.

**부끄럽다** ① 《수줍다》 (be) shy; bashful; coy; self-conscious; [서술적] be awkward 〔embarrassed〕. ¶ 부끄러운듯이 shyly; bashfully; coyly; awkwardly; embarrassedly; sheepishly / 부끄러운 얼굴을 하다 look shy 〔abashed〕 / 부끄러워 얼굴을 두 손으로 가리다 cover *one's* face with *one's* hands from bashfulness / 남들이 보면 ~ I am 〔feel〕 shy when people are watching me. / 그녀는 부끄러워 그런 말을 할 수 없었다 She was too shy to talk about such things.
② 《창피하다》 (***a***) 《양심·언동이》 (be) shameful; be ashamed 《of》; feel shame 《at》. ¶ 신사로서 부끄러운 일 an act unworthy of a gentleman / 신사로서 부끄럽지 않은 《be》 every inch a gentleman / 신사로서 부끄럽잖은 행동을 하다 act as a gentleman; do a thing worthy of a gentleman / 부끄러워 얼굴을 붉히다 blush 〔flush〕 with shame / 부끄러워 고개를 숙이다 hang *one's* head for shame / 그것은 전문가의 것이라고 해도 부끄럽지 않다 It would do credit to a professional. / 부끄러울 것이 없다 There is nothing to be ashamed of. / 그런 짓을 해서 ~ I am ashamed of doing such a thing. / 부끄러워 그런 일은 못한다 I am ashamed to do so. / 칭찬해 주시니 도리어 부끄럽습니다 Your praises put me to shame. / 말하기 부끄러운 일입니다만… I am ashamed to say that…. *or* To my shame, I must confess that…. (***b***) 《불명예》 (be) disgraceful; dishonorable. ¶ 부끄럽지 않게 살다 live decently; make a decent living / 부끄럽지 않은 옷차림을 하다 be decently dressed / 청빈은 부끄러운 일이 아니다 Honest poverty is no disgrace. / 나는 남에게 신세지는 것을 부끄럽게 여긴다 I consider it beneath my dignity to receive a favor. / 부끄러운 짓 하지 마라 Try not to bring disgrace upon your own head.

**부나비** 〖곤충〗 a tiger moth.

**부낭**(浮囊) 《구명용》 a float; a life preserver 〔saver〕; a life buoy 〔ring〕; 《수영용》 a float; a tire; a swimming ring; 《물고기의》 an air bladder.

**부내**(部內) circles; the department. ¶ ~ 사람 an insider.

**부녀**(父女) father and daughter.

**부녀(자)**(婦女(子)) a woman; [총칭] womenfolk(s). ¶ 부녀자와 같은 womanish; feminine; effeminate / 부녀자를 괴롭히다 bully the fair sex.

**부농**(富農) a rich 〔prosperous〕 farmer.

**부닐다** act amiably 〔friendly, affably〕. ¶ 착착 ~ stick close 《to *a person*》 eager to be helpful.

**부다듯하다** (be) feverish.

**부다페스트** 《헝가리의 수도》 Budapest.

**부닥치다** 《마주치다》 come (up)on 〔across〕; hit on 〔upon〕 《*something*》; 《직면하다》 face; be confronted by; encounter; meet with; come face to face with; run up against. ¶ 난관에 ~ face 〔be confronted by, run up against〕 a difficulty / 반대에 ~ meet with hostility 《from》 / 벽에 ~ run 〔come up〕 against a wall; [비유적] reach a deadlock / 위험에 ~ get into danger / 부닥쳐 보다 have a try; face up 《to》 (맞서보다) / 나는 많은 난관에 부닥쳐 있다 I am confronted with many difficulties. / 한일 관계를 말하게 되면, 반드시 이 문제에 부닥친다 Whenever we discuss Korea-Japan relations, we come up against this problem.

**부단**(不斷) constancy; ceaselessness; continuity. ~하다 (be) constant; continuous; incessant; ceaseless; persistent; perpetual. ¶ ~히 constantly; continually; ceaselessly / ~한 주의 constant attention / ~히 감시하다 keep a constant watch 《over》/ ~히 노력하다 make a ceaseless 〔unremitting〕 efforts; work tirelessly / 무슨 일에나 ~한 노력이 중요하다 It is important to be constantly vigilant in all things.

**부담**(負擔) a burden; a load; a charge (지불의); a responsibility (책임). ~하다 bear 《the expenses》; shoulder 《a burden》; foot 《the bill》; be charged with (비용 따위를). ¶하루 6시간의 수업~ a teaching load of six hours a day / 과중한 ~ a heavy burden / (비용을) 자기 ~으로 at *one's* own expense 〔charge〕; out of *one's* own pocket / 비용을 ~하다 bear 〔shoulder, stand〕 the expense; meet the cost / 비용의 일부를 ~하다 share the cost 〔expenses〕 《with *a person*》/ 손해를 ~하다 account for the loss incurred / …의 ~을 덜어주다 lighten 〔lessen〕 a burden imposed on 《*a person*》/ ~시키다 〔~을 주다〕 burden 〔charge〕 《*a person*》 with 《a task》; impose a burden on 《*a person*》; put a 《severe》 strain on 《*a person's* finances》/ 세금 ~을 줄이다 ease the tax burden; reduce taxes / 일의 ~을 가볍게 하다 relieve 〔lighten〕 the work load / ~에 견디지 못하다 be unable to bear a burden; cannot stand *one's* burden / ~이 되다 be a burden 〔strain, charge〕 《on》; weigh 《on》/ 양친께 이 이상 ~을 주고 싶지 않다 I don't want to be any more burden to my parents. / 그러면 자네 ~이 너무 클텐데 그래 That would make the burden too heavy for you. ◉ ~액 an amount to be borne; *one's* share 《in the expenses》; an allotment; a share. 각자 ~ an equal split; paying each for *his* own account; 《회식 등의》 a Dutch treat: 각자 ~으로 하다 split the account; go Dutch 《구어》/ 비용은 각자 ~이다 Each has to pay his own expenses.

**부당**(不當) injustice; unreasonableness. ~하다 (be) unjust; unfair; improper; unreasonable; unwarrantable; 《과당한》 (be) undeserved; exorbitant; undue. ¶ ~한 값 an unreasonable 〔exorbitant〕 price / ~한 벌 an undeserved punishment / ~한 요구 an exorbitant 〔excessive, unjustified〕 demand / ~한 조처 an unfair dealing / ~한 표시 《상품·내용 등의》 a false 〔misleading〕 description 《of goods 〔contents〕》/ ~한 처벌 an undeserved punishment / ~한 이익을 취하다 make unfair profits / ~한 말을 하다 say unreasonable things; talk unreasonably / ~한 짓을 하다 act unreasonably / 나는 ~한 차별을 받았다 I was a victim of unjust discrimination. / 나는 ~한 결정에 항의했다 I protested against the unfair decision. ◉ ~가정(假定) an unreasonable hypothesis. ~거래 an unfair bargain 〔deal〕. ~과세 unreasonable taxation. ~노동 행위 an unfair labor practice. ~대출(금) an illegal advance (loan). ~이득 an undue 〔excessive〕 profit; excess profits; unjust enrichment; profiteering (행위). ~지출 a misappropriation of (public) funds; an unjust disbursement. ~해고 unfair 〔wrongful〕 dismissal. ~행위 an wrongful act.

**부대**(負袋) a burlap 〔cloth〕 bag; a sack; a gunnysack. ⇨포대. ¶ 밀가루 한 ~ a sack of flour / ~에 담다 put into a bag / ~에서 꺼내다 take 《*a thing*》 out of a bag.

**부대**(附帶) ~하다 accompany; be incidental 〔accessory, appendant〕 to; be attached 〔annexed〕 to. ¶ …에 ~하는 accompanying…; incidental to…. ◉ ~결의 a supplementary 〔an additional〕 resolution. ~계약 an accessory contract. ~공사 appurtenant work. ~권리 《토지 따위에 대한》 an appendant (right). ~비용 incidental expenses. ~사건 a side issue. ~사업 business incidental 《to》; a subsidiary enterprise. ~사항 a supplementary item. ~상소 an incidental appeal (for revision). ~상황 collateral 〔attendant〕 circumstances. ~설비 incidental facilities 〔equipment〕. ~시설 subsidiary facilities. ~요구 a collateral claim. ~조건 a collateral 〔an incidental〕 condition. ~증서 a collateral bond. ~청구 an attendant 〔accessory〕 claim.

**부대**(部隊) a (military) unit; a corps; a force; an outfit; a party; a detachment. ¶보병의 소~ a small force of infantry. ◉ ~기 a guidon; a squad flag. ～명 unit designation. ～장 a commander; the commanding officer (생략 C.O.). ～행진 marching in columns; a column march.

**부대끼다** 《시달리다》 be pestered [tormented] 《by》; be harassed 《by, with》; see [experience] hardships; 《고통받다》 suffer 《from》; be troubled 《with》. ¶ 가난에 ～ be tormented by poverty; feel the pinch of poverty / 깡패에게 ～ be pestered by hoodlums / 더위에 몹시 ～ suffer greatly from the heat / 빚쟁이에게 ～ be tormented by creditors / 세파에 ～ be buffeted about in the world; be tossed about in the storms of life; suffer hardships of life / 느끼한 음식을 먹어서 속이 ～ feel uncomfortable with *one's* stomach loaded with heavy food.

**부덕**(不德) want [lack] of virtue. ～하다 (be) unvirtuous; be short of virtue. ¶ 그것은 모두 내 ～의 탓입니다 I am solely to blame for it. *or* It is all due to my lack of discretion.

**부덕**(婦德) womanly [female] virtues. ¶ ～의 귀감 《be》 a symbol [model, mirror, paragon] of female virtues [womanhood] / ～을 쌓다 cultivate womanly [female] virtues.

**부도**(不渡) failure to honor 《a check》; dishonor; nonpayment. ¶ ～가 나다 be dishonored; bounce 《구어》/ ～를 내다 dishonor [fail to pay] a bill [check] / ～를 내지 않다 manage to honor a bill [check] / (은행이) ～처리하다 dishonor 《a bill》; 《구어》 bounce 《a check》. ◉ ～수표 a dishonored [bad] check; a rubber check 《미속어》. ～어음 a dishonored [bad] bill; a bill of dishonor: ～ 어음을 발행하다 draw a dishonored bill; pass a bad draft. ～통지 a notice of dishonor.

**부도**(附圖) an attached [appended] map [graph, figure].

**부도**(婦道) womanhood; the duty of a woman.

**부도덕**(不道德) (an) immorality (행위); lack of morality; bad morals. ～하다 (be) immoral; unvirtuous; wicked (사악); depraved (타락); profligate. ¶ ～한 행동 immoral conduct / ～한 사내 a man of loose morals / ～한 짓을 하다 act immorally; be guilty of immorality; commit an immoral act.

**부도심**(副都心) a subcenter [secondary center] of a city; a newly emerging city center.

**부도체**(不導體) 『물리』 a nonconductor; a nonconducting substance. ¶ 열[전기]의 ～ a noncondutor of heat [electricity].

**부독본**(副讀本) a supplementary reader.

**부동**(不同) lack of uniformity; inequality; dissimilarity; diversity; disparity; irregularity. ～하다 (be) unequal; uneven; irregular; dissimilar; disparate; divers(e). ¶ 표리가 ～한 double-dealing; double-faced; treacherous / 표리가 ～하다 carry two faces under one hood; play a double game / 순서가 ～하다 be not in order. ◉ 순서～《게시》 No special order is observed.

**부동**(不凍) nonfreezing. ◉ ～액 an antifreezing solution. ～제 an antifreeze (agent). ～항 an ice-free port; a nonfreezing port.

**부동**(不動) immobility; immovability; firmness; stability. ¶ ～의 immovable; immobile; motionless; firm; fixed / ～의 신념 firm belief; unshakable faith / ～의 지위 《hold》 an indisputable [established] position / 우리 방침은 ～이다 Our policy remains unshakable. ◉ ～심 an imperturbable mind. ～자세 an immobile posture; 『군사』 the position at attention: ～자세를 취하다 stand at [come to] attention. ～태 『화학』 the passive state.

**부동**(浮動) floating; fluctuation; wafting. ～하다 float 《in the air》; be a float; 《향기 등이》 waft; be wafted; 《변동하다》 fluctuate 《in price》. ¶ ～하는 floating; unsettled; unsteady. ◉ ～구매력 floating purchasing power. ～성 instability; fluctuation; unsteadiness. ～인구 a floating population. ～자금 floating money [funds]. ～주 floating stocks [shares]. ～투표자 a floating [an undecided] voter; a swing voter: 현재 ～투표자의 수는 유권자의 30%에 달한다 The number of floating voters now stands at 30% of the electorate. ～표 a floating [shifting] vote.

**부동**(符同) grouping together; going (in) cahoots. ～하다 group [gang] together; go (in) cahoots; collude.

**부동명왕**(不動明王) *Acala* (Sans.); the God of Fire.

**부동산**(不動産) real [fixed, immovable] property; immovables; real estate; realty. ¶ ～을 매매하다 deal in real estate / 1억원의 ～을 갖고 있다 have real property worth one hundred

million won / 그는 부모에게서 천만원에 달하는 ~을 물려 받았다 He inherited from his parents real property amounting to ten million won.
◉ ~감정사 a real estate appraiser 〔valuer 《영》〕. ~거래 a real estate transaction: 불법 ~거래를 엄중 감시하다 keep close tabs on illegal real estate transactions. ~권리증 a title deed; a land certificate. ~등기 real=estate registration: ~등기법 the Real Property Registration Act. ~보험 property insurance. ~소득 an income from immovables. ~시가〔과세〕 표준액 the standard value of real estate ⌈based on the current prices 〔computed for tax imposition〕. ~실명제 the real-name property ownership system; the real-name system for real estate trading; the property real=name system. ~양도세 real estate sale 〔transfer〕 tax. ~업 real estate business. ~(중개)업자 a realty dealer; a real estate agent; 《미》 a realtor (공인의); a real estate broker 〔dealer〕. ~취득세 property transaction 〔acquisition〕 tax. ~투기 land 〔real-estate〕 speculation; speculative investment in real estate: ~ 투기 억제 대책 the anti-speculative measures in real estate. ~투자 investment in real estate.

**부두**(埠頭) a wharf (*pl.* wharves, ~s); a quay (안벽); a pier (돌출된 제방). ¶ (배가) ~를 떠나다 move away from the quayside / ~에 배를 대다 bring a boat 〔steamer〕 alongside the quay.
◉ ~노동 조합 a stevedores union; a longshoreman union. ~사용료 wharfage; quayage; pierage. ~세 wharf dues; jettage; quayage. ~인부 a stevedore; a longshoreman; a wharf man. ~창고 a waterfront warehouse. 부둣가 the wharfside; a quay; a pier.

**부둑부둑** pretty well dry; damp-dry; still a bit damp but stiff. ~하다 (be) damp-dry; be dry enough for ironing.

**부둥키다** hold 〔clasp〕 《*a person*》 in *one's* arm(s); embrace 〔hug〕 《*a person*》 closely 〔tightly〕; clasp 《*a person*》 in a tight embrace; 《움켜쥐다》 grasp; clutch. ¶ 아기를 부둥켜 안다 give a baby a hug; hold a baby in *one's* arms / 둘은 부둥켜 안고 울었다 The two threw themselves into each other's arms and wept.

**부드드하다** (be) grasping; stingy; niggardly.

**부드득-** ⇨ 바드득-.

**부드럽다** ① 《촉감이》 (be) soft (to the touch); tender; 《빛 따위가》 (be) mellow; subdued; gentle. ¶ 부드러운 빛 a soft 〔subdued〕 light / 비단처럼 부드러운 살결 skin soft as silk / 녹(綠)과 청(靑)의 부드러운 색조 soft shades of green and blue / 감촉이 ~ be soft 〔smooth〕 to the touch; feel soft. ② 《태도·말씨 등이》 (be) soft; mild; gentle; calm; quiet; amiable. ¶ 부드러운 분위기 friendly 〔congenial〕 atmosphere / 태도가 ~ be of gentle manners / 부드럽게 말하다 talk 〔tell〕 in gentle words; use mild 〔gentle〕 language.

**부드레하다** (be) rather soft; subdued; mild.

**부득부득** stubbornly; obstinately; persistently; importunately. ¶ ~ 조르다 importune 《*a person* for *something*》; ask 《*a person*》 importunately / ~ 우기다 stick stubbornly to *one's* idea; stick doggedly to *one's* own opinion.

**부득불**(不得不) cannot but…; unavoidably; inevitably; necessarily; reluctantly. ¶ ~…하다 be compelled 〔forced〕 to *do;* be under the necessity of *do*ing; be driven by dire necessity to *do* / ~ 최후 수단을 쓰다 be driven 〔impelled〕 to extreme measures / 그는 ~ 그렇게 하지 않으면 안 되었다 Necessity obliged him to that action.

**부득요령** ¶ ~이다 be vague 〔ambiguous, pointless, not to the point〕.

**부득이**(不得已) against *one's* will; unavoidably; inevitably; of 〔out of, from〕 necessity. ~하다 (be) unavoidable; inevitable; obligatory; compelling; cannot be helped. ¶ ~한 사정으로 owing to 〔through〕 unavoidable circumstances / ~한 경우에는 in an unavoidable case; if necessary / ~…하다 be obliged 〔compelled, forced〕 to *do* / ~한 일이다 It can't be helped. / ~해서 그는 이잣돈을 빌렸다 His necessities compelled him to borrow money at interest.

**부들** 『식물』 a cattail; a reed mace.
◉ ~김치 pickled cattail sprouts. ~자리 a bulrush 〔cattail〕 mat.

**부들부들** quiveringly; tremblingly. ¶ ~ 떨다 quiver; shiver; tremble / 추워서 ~ 떨다 shiver with 〔from〕 (the) cold; quiver from (the) cold / 성이 나서 ~ 떨다 tremble with rage / 손이 ~ 떨려

글씨를 쓸 수가 없다 can not write as *one's* hand shakes.
**부들부들하다** = 부드럽다.
**부듯하다** (be) full; tight. ⇨ 뿌듯하다.
**부등**(不等) disparity; inequality. ~하다 (be) unequal; incongruent. ◉ ~속운동 〖물리〗 ununiform 〔accelerated〕 motion. ~식 an inequality: ~식 기호 a sign of inequality (기호 <, >).
**부등가리** an improvised fire shovel.
**부등깃** the soft feathers 〔down〕 of a young bird 〔animal〕.
**부등변**(不等邊) 〖수학〗 ¶ ~의 unequal-sided; inequilateral; scalene. ◉ ~사각형 an irregular quadrilateral; 《영》 a trapezium; a trapezoid. ~삼각형 an inequilateral triangle; a scalene (triangle).
**부디** 《기어이·꼭》 by all means; without fail; in any case; 《바라건대》 please; pray (★ please는 if you please의, pray는 I pray you의 생략으로 모두 동사임.); I beg; (will you) kindly; (please) be kind as to 《*do*》. ¶ ~ 오십시오 Come, by all means. / ~ 안부 전해 주십시오 Please give him my best regard. / ~ 몸조심하십시오 Take good care of yourself. / ~ 그렇게 해주십시오 Will you kindly do so? *or* Do so, if you please.
**부딪다** ① 《맞다》 strike; hit; 《충돌하다》 run against 〔into〕; collide with; run foul of (배가); crash into 〔against, together〕; knock 〔bump, dash〕 against. ¶ 남과 ~ bump into *a person* / (돌 등이) 머리에 ~ strike 〔hit〕 《*a person*》 on the head / 나무에 ~ run into a tree / 벽에 ~ bump 〔hit, bash〕 against the wall / (배가) 암초에 ~ strike 〔run on〕 a sunken rock / 머리를 일부러 벽에 ~ dash *one's* head against the wall / 차를 담에 ~ run 〔crash〕 a car into a wall / 물결이 바위에 부딪쳐 부서진다 The waves break on the rocks. ② 《부닥치다》 (***a***) 《당면하다》 face; face up to; be confronted by. (***b***) 《해보다》 try; risk; take a chance. ¶ 어디, 되든 안되든 부딪쳐 보자 Well, I will try, sink or swim.
**부딪뜨리다** crash 〔smash, bump〕 《into, against, together》. ¶ 자동차를 나무에 ~ crash a car into a tree / 머리를 기둥에 ~ bump 〔knock, hit〕 *one's* head against 〔on〕 the post.
**부딪치다** ⇨ 부딪다.
**부딪히다** be bumped 〔run, dashed〕 against; be bumped 〔crashed, run〕 into. ¶ 배가 바위에 부딪혔다 A boat was dashed against a rock.
**부뚜** winnowing mats. ◉ ~질 winnowing (with mats): ~질하다 winnow.
**부뚜막** a kitchen 〔fireplace〕 range. ¶ ~의 소금도 집어 넣어야 짜다 《속담》 Everything demands some work.
**부라리다** stare (*one's* eyes out); glare 《at, upon》; look with glaring eyes. ¶ 눈을 부라리고 with glaring 〔angry〕 eyes / 눈알을 부라려 침묵시키다 stare 《*a person*》 dumb / 그는 말하면서 무섭게 눈을 부라렸다 He glared fiercely as he spoke.
**부라질** moving a baby's legs back and forth. ~하다 move a baby's legs back and forth; rock a baby.
**부라퀴** ① 《암팡스러운》 a harsh tough person; a shrewd 〔nervy〕 fellow. ② 《이익에 악착같은》 an eager beaver.
**부락**(部落) a (village) community; a village; a settlement. ¶ ~ 단위로 with a village as a unit. ◉ ~민 people of the community; village folk. ~회의 a village meeting. 산간~ a village among the mountains.
**부란**(孵卵) incubation. ~하다 《알이》 be hatched; hatch; 《알을》 hatch (out) 《an egg》; incubate. ◉ ~기(器) an incubator. ~기간 incubation time. 인공~ artificial incubation.
**부란**(腐爛) ulceration; decay; 《시체의》 decomposition. ~하다 ulcerate; decay; rot; decompose.
**부랑**(浮浪) wandering; vagrancy; vagabondage. ~하다 wander 〔stray〕 about; tramp; lead a vagabond 〔hobo〕 life. ¶ ~하는 신세가 되다 be turned adrift in the world. ◉ ~배 roughnecks; hoodlums; the scum of the street. ~아 a juvenile vagrant. ~자 a vagabond; a loafer; a tramp; a hobo; a bum.
**부랴부랴** hurriedly; hastily. ¶ ~ …하다 hasten 〔make haste〕 to 《*do*》; lose no time in 《*do*ing》 / ~ 상경하다 hurry up to Seoul without a moment's delay / 그 소식을 듣자마자 그는 ~ 현장으로 달려갔다 Directly he heard the news he hastened to the spot. / ~ 달려갔으나 이미 늦었다 I rushed to the scene but it was too late.
**부러** deliberately; on purpose; knowingly; intentionally. ⇨ 일부러. ¶ ~ 거짓말을 하다 lie deliberately / 그는 ~ 못 알아 듣는 체했다 He would not understand me. / ~ 한 것은 아니니 용서하시

구려 Pardon me, please, for it was quite accidental.

**부러뜨리다** break (off); snap (딱소리 내며); fracture (뼈를). ¶ 나뭇가지를 ~ break a branch from a tree / 팔을 ~ 《남의》 break 《*a person's*》 arm; 《자기의》 have *one's* 《left》 arm broken / 대지팡이를 무릎에 대고 ~ break a bamboo stick over *one's* knee.

**부러워하다** envy 《*a person, a person's* luck, *a person his* luck》; be envious 〔jealous〕 of; feel envy of. ¶ 부러워하는 눈초리 an envious look / 남이 부러워하게 하다 make others envy 〔envious〕; excite *a person's* envy / 그의 행운을 부러워하지 않는 사람은 없다 Everybody envies him his good fortune. / 사람들은 그를 부러워한다 He is an object of envy.

**부러지다** break; get broken; snap (뚝하고); fracture (뼈가); give way. ¶ 한가운데가 뚝 ~ break in half / 뼈가 ~ have a bone broken; break a bone / 부러진 칼자루에 옻칠하기 doing something useless / 책상 다리 하나가 부러졌다 One of the legs of the table is broken. / 내 몸무게로 나뭇가지가 부러졌다 The branch gave away under me.

**부럼** 〖민속〗 nuts eaten on the 15th day of the first lunar month (to guard *oneself* against boils for a year).

**부럽다** (be, feel) enviable. ¶ 부러운 듯이 enviously; with envy; with envious eyes / 부럽지 않다 be not to be envied; be unenviable / 부럽게 여기지 않다 feel no envy 《at》 / 부러운 듯이 보다 regard 《*a person, a thing*》 with envy; eye 《*something*》 enviously / 자네의 행운〔행복〕이 참 부럽네 How I envy you your luck 〔happiness〕! / 참 ~ How I envy you!

**부레** ① 《물고기의》 an air bladder; a (gas) bladder; a float. ② 《부레풀》 glue made from air bladders; fish glue; isinglass. ◉ ~뜸 treating a kite-string with isinglass. ~질 pasting something with isinglass: ~질하다 paste with isinglass. ~풀 =부레 ②.

**부레끓다** boil 《with rage》; get mad.

**부력**(浮力) 〖물리〗 buoyancy; flo(a)tage; 《비행선 등의》 lifting power; lift. ¶ ~이 있는 buoyant / ~의 중심 the center of buoyancy. ◉ ~계 a buoyancy gauge.

**부력**(富力) wealth; resources.

**부령**(部令) an order 〔a decree〕 from a government ministry. ¶ 교육~ 제2호 Ordinance No. 2 of the Education Ministry.

**부록**(附錄) a supplement; an appendix (*pl.* -dixes, -dices) (권말의); extra; an addendum (*pl.* -da). ¶ 잡지의 ~ a supplement to a magazine; a magazine supplement / ~을 붙이다 add an appendix to 《a book》. ◉ 별책~ a detachable pull-out supplement.

**부루나가다** last longer than expected.

**부루퉁이** a thing which protrudes.

**부루퉁하다** ① 《부어서》 (be) swollen; bloated; bulging. ¶ 부루퉁한 손 a swollen hand / 부루퉁하게 부어오르다 swell up / 얼굴이 ~ have a swollen 〔bloated〕 face. ② 《불만스러워》 (be) sullen; cross; sulky; pouty; sour; morose; peevish. ¶ 부루퉁하여 sullenly; in an angry mood; with a sullen look / 부루퉁한 얼굴 a sullen face 〔look〕 / 부루퉁해 있다 be in the sulks 〔pouts〕; look sulky 〔cross〕 / 부루퉁한 얼굴을 하다 put on a sullen look; wear 〔pull〕 a sulky face / 그는 부루퉁해서 아무런 말이 없었다 He kept a sullen silence.

**부룩** 〖농업〗 ~박다 grow 《beans》 as a catch crop; intercrop. ◉ ~곡식 a catch crop.

**부룩소** a young bull.

**부룬디** 《아프리카의 공화국》 (the Republic of) Burundi.

**부룻** the bulk of a heap; the amount in a heap.

**부류**(浮流) ~하다 float about; drift. ¶ ~ 기뢰를 띄우다〔에 닿다〕 lay 〔strike〕 a floating mine.

**부류**(部類) 《종류》 a class; a kind; 《범주》 a category; 《종족》 a species. ¶ …~에 들다 come 〔fall〕 under the category 〔head〕 of… / 다른 ~에 속하다 belong in different category 〔classification〕 / … ~에 넣다 classify 〔group, catalogue〕 《*a thing*》 with 〔as〕… / 갑과 을을 같은 ~에 넣다 class A with B; put 〔place〕 A in the same category with 〔as〕 B / 그것들은 세 ~로 나뉜다 They can be classified into three kinds.

**부르걷다** roll up 〔back〕 《*one's* sleeves》; tuck 〔lift〕 up. ¶ 팔을 부르걷고 with bare arms; with *one's* sleeves tucked up.

**부르다**[1] ① 《배가》 (be) full. ¶ 배가 부르게 먹다 eat heartily; eat *one's* fill; eat to *one's* heart's contents / 이제 배부르게 먹었습니다 I have had plenty 〔enough〕. ② 《애를 배서》 (be) pregnant; big with 《child》. ¶ 그녀는 배가 ~ She is big with child. ③ 《중배가》 (be) bulgy. ¶ 그 통은 배가 ~ The barrel bulges in the middle.

**부르다**[2] ① 《소리내어》 call; call out 《to》; hail; call after (뒤에서); invoke (신 등을). ¶ 부르면 닿을 거리에 within call 〔earshot〕 / 불러도 들리지 않는 거리에 out of call 〔hail〕; out of hailing 〔calling〕 distance / 이름을 ~ call 《*a person*》 by name / 택시를 ~ call a cab; hail a taxi / 사장님이 부르십니다 The president wants 〔needs〕 you. *or* You are wanted at the president's office. / 아내는 남편을 큰소리로 불렀다 The wife called out for her husband. ② 《오게 하다》 (***a***) 《불러오다》 call 《*a person*》 to *one;* summon (소환하다); 《사람을 보내어》 send for 《a doctor》; call in (불러들이다); 《연예인 등을》 engage; hire. ¶ 가수를 ~ engage a singer 《for the party》 / 벨을 울려 하인을 ~ ring for the servant / 전화로 ~ telephone for 《*a person*》; call 《*a person*》 up on the phone / 부르러 가다 go for; go to fetch / 의사를 부르러 가다 go for the doctor / 의사를 부르러 보내다 send for a doctor / 의사를 불러오다 go and fetch a doctor / 아무를 불러내다〔들이다〕 call *a person* out 〔in〕 / 전화로 K를 부르게 Get K on the phone. *or* Call K to the phone. / 택시를 불러 주시오 Call me a taxi. *or* Call a taxi for me. (***b***) 《청하다》 invite 〔ask〕 《*a person*》 to. ¶ 손님을 잔치에 ~ invite guests to a feast. ③ 《일컫다》 call; name; term (학술상의); style; designate. ¶ …로〔라고〕 ~ call 《it》…; give 《it》 the name of / 애국심이라고 부르는 것 what we call 〔is called〕 patriotism; what goes by the name of patriotism / 이것을 동대문이라고 부른다 This is called *Tongdaemun* 〔East Gate〕. ④ 《값을》 bid 《a price》; offer; set. ¶ 부르는 값 the price asked 〔named〕 / 부르는 값에 사다 buy 《an article》 at the price asked; give the price asked for 《an article》 / 값을 싸게 ~ 《a seller》 set the price low; 《a buyer》 offer a low price / 비싼 값을 ~ charge a high price 《for *a thing*》; ask too much. ⑤ 《노래를》 sing; chant. ¶ 노래를 ~ sing a song / 피아노에 맞추어 노래를 ~ sing to the piano / 노래를 부르기 시작하다 break into song / 노래를 부릅시다 Let us have a song. ⑥ 《외치다》 cry; shout. ¶ 만세를 ~ cry "Hurrah!" 「vociferate.

**부르대다** bawl out; rant and rave;

**부르르** ⇨ 바르르. ¶ ~ 떨다 quiver; tremble; shiver 《with cold》; be all of a tremble.

**부르릉** with a burr 《from a combustion engine》. ~거리다 burr; roar.

**부르심** a summons (*pl.* -es). ¶ 신의 ~ God's calling / ~을 받다 be summoned.

**부르주아** 《개인》 a bourgeois; a man of means; 《계급》 the bourgeoisie; the moneyed class(es) (유산 계급). ◉ ~생활〔문학〕 bourgeois life 〔literature〕. ~취미: ~ 취미의 incongruously high-class 〔elegant, expensive〕; 《구어》 posh.

**부르쥐다** clench. ¶ 주먹을 ~ clench *one's* fist / 주먹을 부르쥐고 치다 strike 《*a person*》 with a clenched fist.

**부르짖다** ① 《소리치다》 shout; exclaim; cry (out); utter 〔give〕 a cry; yell; shriek; scream (비명을). ¶ 성이 나서 ~ shout 〔roar〕 with rage / 목이 쉬도록 ~ shout *oneself* hoarse / 이구동성으로 ~ shout as with one voice. ② 《주장·하소연하다》 cry 《for》; clamor 《for》; advocate. ¶ 개혁을 ~ cry (loudly) for reform / 노동 조건의 개선을 ~ cry for an improvement in working conditions / 산아 제한을 ~ advocate birth control / 임금 인상을 ~ cry for a raise in pay; clamor for higher wages.

**부르짖음** 《외침》 a shout; a cry; an outcry; an exclamation; a yell; a clamor; 《비명》 a shriek; a scream; 《노호》 a roar; a howl. ¶ 개혁의 ~ a cry 〔clamor〕 for reform / 민족의 ~ the voice of the race.

**부르트다** 《물집이 생기다》 rise in blisters; blister; 《부어오르다》 swell up. ¶ 발바닥이 ~ get 〔have〕 a blister on the sole / 손끝이 데어서 부르텄다 My finger tip has blistered from a burn. / 장작을 팼더니 손이 온통 부르텄다 My hands are all blistered from chopping wood.

**부릅뜨다** open (*one's* eyes) with a fierce glare; make (*one's* eyes) glare; stare (*one's* eyes out); glare fiercely. ¶ 눈을 부릅뜨고 with angry 〔glaring〕 eyes / 눈을 부릅뜨고 보다 glare at 〔upon〕 《*a person*》 / 그는 눈을 부릅뜨고 나를 노려보았다 He glared at me with angry eyes.

**부리**[1] 《주둥이》 a bill; a beak; 《끝》 the

tip. ¶ 발～ the tips of the toes / 총～ the muzzle 《of a gun》 / 끝이 구부러진 ～ a hooked beak / ～로 쪼아 구멍을 내다 《birds》 peck a hole 《in the sack》.

**부리**[2] 『민속』 a tutelary spirit. ¶ ～(가) 세다 《한 집안이》 be under strong influence from the guardian spirit.

**부리나케** in a hurry; in haste; hastily; hurriedly; speedily. ¶ ～ 걷다 walk hurriedly / ～ 돌아오다 come back with flying feet; fly back like a shot / ～ 일하다 hurry with *one's* work; make the sparks fly / ～ 계단을 올라〔내려〕가다 rush up 〔down〕 the stairs.

**부리다**[1] ① 《일을 시키다》 make 《*a person,* a horse, *etc.*》 work; work 《*a person*》; set 《*a person*》 to work; manage; use; 《고용하다》 employ. ¶ 하인을 ～ keep a servant; work a servant / 사람을 몹시〔심하게〕 ～ work 〔drive〕 《*a person*》 hard; make 《*a person*》 drudge / 말을 부릴 줄 알다 know how to manage a horse / 소나 말처럼 부려먹다 work 〔drive〕 《*a person*》 hard like a beast of burden; make 《*a person*》 drudge.
② 《조종하다》 work 《a machine》; operate; handle; control. ¶ 기계를 ～ operate a machine / 사람을 부리는 것이 능란하다 be clever in handling *one's* men.
③ 《행사하다》 wield; exercise. ¶ 권력을 ～ exercise *one's* power / 허세를 ～ make a false show of power 〔courage〕; bluff.
④ 《꾀·재주·말썽을》 play 《a trick, a ruse》; do; start 《trouble, *etc.*》. ¶ 수단을 ～ play a trick 〔ruse〕/재주를 ～ exercise *one's* talent; perform a trick.

**부리다**[2] 《짐을》 unload 〔discharge〕 《a ship, a cart》; unpack 《a horse》; clear 《a ship》. ¶짐을 ～ unload cargo 〔goods〕 / 말〔트럭〕에서 짐을 ～ unload a horse 〔a truck〕.

**부리망**(―網) a muzzle. ¶ ～을 씌우다 muzzle 《a cow》; put a muzzle on.

**부리부리하다** (be) big and bright. ¶ 부리부리한 눈 big, bright eyes.

**부마(도위)**(駙馬(都尉)) a royal son-in-law.

**부메랑** a boomerang. ◉ ～효과 『경제』 a boomerang effect: ～효과를 낳다 backfire 《on》; boomerang 《on》 / ～ 효과를 두려워해서 기술 이전을 꺼리다 hesitate on transferring technologies to 《a country》 out of the fear of a boomerang effect.

**부모**(父母) parents (★ 단수형의 parent는 아버지 또는 어머니 한 쪽만의 뜻. 또 「모체」라는 비유적인 뜻: Latin is the parent of the modern Romance language). ¶ ～의 사랑 parental love 〔affection〕 / ～의 마음 the heart of a parent; a parent heart / ～ 슬하에 있다 live under *one's* parental roof 〔care〕 /～를 섬기다〔공경하다〕 serve 〔be respectful toward〕 *one's* parents / 어려서 ～를 여의다 「lose *one's* parents 〔be left an orphan〕 early in life. ◉ ～처자 *one's* parents, wife and children; *one's* family. ～형제 *one's* parents, brothers and sisters.

**부목**(副木) 『의학』 a splint. ¶ ～을 대다 apply a splint 《to》; splint 《an arm》.

**부문**(部門) 《부류》 a class; a group; a head; a department; a section; a category; 《방면》 a branch; a line; a field. ¶ 생활의 모든 ～ every phase of life / ～으로 나누다 classify (into orders); divide into sections / …의 ～에 넣다 classify 《*things*》 under / …의 ～에 들다 fall 〔come〕 under the head of; belong in the classification 〔category〕 of / 철강 ～에서는 P사가 첫째 간다 In the field of steel, P company is top-ranking.

**부박**(浮薄) frivolity; flippancy. ～하다 (be) frivolous; unserious; flippant.

**부보**(訃報) ＝부고(訃告).

**부복**(俯伏) ～하다 prostrate *oneself* 《before》; lie prostrate 《before》.

**부본**(副本) a duplicate; a counterpart; a copy; 《수표장 등의》 a counterfoil; a stub 《미》. ¶ ～을 만들다 make a copy 〔duplicate〕 《of》.

**부부**(夫婦) man 〔husband〕 and wife (★ 이 경우처럼 뜻이 서로 관련되어 있는 2개의 명사가 and로 결합되면 관사가 생략됨: knife and fork / pen and ink); a (married) couple; a pair. ¶ ～의 conjugal; matrimonial / ～ 동반하여 with *one's* wife 〔husband〕 / ～의 애정 married love; conjugal affection / 젊은 ～ a young couple; the young-married [총칭] / 김씨 ～ Mr. and Mrs. Kim / ～의 정리〔인연〕 a marital 〔matrimonial〕 bond; a conjugal tie / 어울리는〔어울리지 않는〕 ～ a well-〔an ill-〕matched couple / ～가 되다 become man and wife / ～의 인연을 맺다 tie the nuptial knot; plight *one's* troth / ～ 행세를 하다 behave as man and wife; pose as if they were a married couple / ～는

한 몸이다 Man and wife are of one flesh. / 그 ～는 금실이 좋다〔좋지 않다〕 The couple 「are happy together 〔live in discord〕. / 저 두 사람은 ～ 사이인가 Are they a married couple? / 저 ～는 지난달 이혼했다 That couple got divorced last month. / 그들은 ～처럼 결혼 피로연에 참석했다 They attended the wedding reception just like man and wife.
◉ ～생활 《live》 a married life. 맞벌이 ～ a couple working together for a living. 신혼～ a newly married couple; the newly wed 《미구어》.

**부부싸움**(夫婦—) a quarrel 〔squabble〕 between husband and wife; a marital dispute. ～하다 quarrel with *one's* husband 〔wife〕; have a marital dispute. ¶ ～은 개도 안 말린다 《속담》 It doesn't pay to act as a mediator for a couple who are having a quarrel.

**부분**(部分) a part; a section; a portion.

> **용법** **part** 전체 중에서 「일부분」을 뜻하는 가장 일반적인 말로, 아래의 두 낱말과 교환 사용해도 뜻의 변화가 없음. **section** 전체를 형성하는 분리된 「한 부분」을 뜻함. 다른 것과의 밀접한 관계를 전제로 함. **portion** 「어떤 한 부분」, 또는 사람이나 어떤 목적을 위해 할당된 부분을 뜻함. (보기) my *portion* of work. (나에게 할당된 일).

¶ ～적(인) partial; 《국지적》 local; 《한정된》 limited / ～적으로 partially; partly; locally / 그의 이야기는 단지 ～적으로만 진실이다 His story is only partially true. / 이 책은 3 ～으로 되어 있다 This book is made up of three parts. / 네 생각은 ～적으로 옳다 You are partly right. / 이 필름에는 삭제된 ～이 있다 Some part of this film have been cut out. ◉ ～부정 〖문법〗 partial negation. ～ 사회 a subgroup of society. ～색맹 partial color blindness. ～식(蝕) a partial eclipse 《of the sun 〔moon〕》. ～품 ⇨ 부품.

**부빙**(浮氷) floating 〔drift〕 ice.

**부사**(副使) a vice-envoy; a deputy delegate.

**부사**(副詞) 〖문법〗 an adverb. ¶ ～적으로 adverbially. ◉ ～구〔절〕 an adverb(ial) phrase 〔clause〕.

**부사령관**(副司令官) a deputy commander(-in-chief).

**부사리** a goring bull.

**부사장**(副社長) a vice-president.

**부산떨다** bustle (up); move about busily.

**부산물**(副産物) a by-product 《of》; a spin-off 《from》 (대규모 연구·사업의); 〖화학〗 the residuum (잔류물). ¶ 연구의 ～ a by-product of research.

**부산하다** ① 《바쁘다》 (be) busy; bustling; restless. ¶ 부산히 busily / 일로 ～ be busy with *one's* work / 사람들이 부산히 드나든다 People bustle in and out. / 세밑은 ～ We feel restless at the year-end. ② 《시끄럽다》 (be) noisy; boisterous; bustling. ¶ 부산히 noisily; boisterously / 부산하게 굴다 make a noise.

**부삽**(—鍤) a fire shovel.

**부상**(父喪) the death of *one's* father; mourning for *one's* father.

**부상**(負傷) an injury; a wound (★ 주로 흉기에 의한). ⇨ 상처. ～하다 be 〔get〕 injured 〔wounded〕; get hurt; sustain 〔suffer〕 an injury. ¶ 가벼운〔심한〕～ a slight 〔serious〕 injury / 팔에 ～을 입다 be injured in the arm; have *one's* arm wounded / ～을 면하다 escape with a whole skin / ～을 입히다 wound 〔injure〕 《*a person*》 / 그는 교통 사고로 ～당했다 He was hurt 〔injured〕 in a traffic accident. ◉ ～병 a wounded soldier. ～자 a wounded 〔an injured〕 person; [총칭] the wounded 〔injured〕; casualties: 그 사고로 ～자 10명이 생겼다 Ten people were injured in the accident. / ～자는 즉시 근처 병원에 수용되었다 The injured person was immediately taken to a neighboring hospital.

**부상**(浮上) ～하다 rise 〔come up〕 to the surface; surface; [비유적] emerge from obscurity; come to the fore. ¶ 잠수함은 천천히 ～했다 The submarine surfaced gradually. *or* The submarine gradually rose 〔came up〕 to the surface. / 그의 인기는 다시 ～했다 He regained his popularity.

**부상**(副賞) a supplementary prize.

**부생**(浮生) 《덧없는 인생》 this fleeting 〔ephemeral, transient〕 life.

**부서**(部署) *one's* post; *one's* place of duty; *one's* quarters (군함 등에서). ¶ 새로운 ～에서 일하다 work at a new post / 새로운 ～로 전속되다 be shifted into a new 「job 〔place of duty〕 / ～를 지키다 keep 〔hold, stick to〕 *one's* post / ～를 떠나다 desert 〔quit〕 *one's* post / 최선을 다해서 자기의 ～를 지켜라 Do your best to keep your post. / 전원 자기 ～에 《구령》 All hands to quarters! *or* To quarters!

**부서**(副署) countersignature. ～하다 countersign; 《배서하다》 endorse; back. ¶ 외교통상부장관이 ～한 영사 임명장 The letter of appointment for the consul countersigned by the Foreign Affairs and Trade Minister.

**부서뜨리다** ⇨ 부스러뜨리다.

**부서지다** break; be broken; crack; be cracked; smash; get smashed; go 〔fall〕 to pieces; collapse. ¶ 부서진 broken; destroyed; damaged / 부서지기 쉬운 easily breaking; easy to break; brittle; fragile; frail; delicate / 부서진 의자 a broken chair / 산산이 ～ be crushed to pieces; be smashed into atoms 〔fragments〕; go all to pieces / 그의 희망은 산산이 부서졌다 His hope was utterly shattered.

**부석**(浮石) pumice (stone); floatstone.

**부석부석** slightly swollen. ～하다 (be) slightly swollen. ¶ 그의 얼굴이 ～하다 His face got slightly swollen.

**부선거**(浮船渠) a floating dock. ◉ ～사용료 the charge for transportation via floating dock. 계안(繫岸)～ an offshore dock.

**부설**(附設) attachment. ～하다 attach 《*something*》 to. ¶ 대학에 연구소를 ～하다 establish a research center attached to a university.
◉ ～기관 an auxiliary organ; an attached 〔affiliated〕 organization. ～도서관 a library attached 《to》.

**부설**(敷設) laying; construction. ～하다 lay (down); construct; build. ¶ 기뢰를 ～하다 lay 〔place〕 a mine / 철도를 ～하다 build 〔construct〕 a railroad.
◉ ～권 a right of construction: 철도 ～권 a railroad concession. ～기뢰 a submarine mine. ～함 a mine layer (기뢰의); a cable repairing ship (케이블의).

**부성**(父性) paternity; fatherhood; the father 《in a person》. ◉ ～애 a paternal love.

**부성분**(副成分) an accessory ingredient.

**부세**(賦稅) taxation; a tax; a duty; a levy. ～하다 tax; levy a tax on.

**부셸** 《단위》 a bushel 《of wheat》 (= 30*l*).

**부속**(附屬) attachment; affiliation. ～하다 be attached to; be affiliated 《with》; belong to; go with. ¶ 이 병원은 H대학에 ～되어 있다 This hospital is attached 〔affiliated〕 to H University.
◉ ～건축물 an annex; an accessory 〔attached〕 building. ～기관 a subsidiary agency; an auxiliary organ; an affiliated organization. ～병원 a hospital in affiliation: 대학 ～ 병원 a hospital attached to a university / 서울 대학교 ～ 병원 the Seoul National University Hospital. ～시설 attached 〔affiliated〕 facilities; accessory structures. ～중〔고등〕학교 a junior 〔senior〕 high school attached to 《the Teachers College》. ～초등학교 an elementary school attached to…. ～품 accessories; fittings: 재봉틀 ～품 attachments for a sawing machine / 자동차 ～품 automobile accessories / 그 기계의 ～품 리스트를 보여 주시오 Show me the list of accessories for that machine. / 이 컴퓨터에는 여러가지 ～품이 있다 There are a variety of accessories that go with this computer. ～합의서 the subsidiary agreements.

**부속물**(附屬物) belongings; a thing attached 《to》; an appendage; a tailpiece; an appurtenance. ¶ 집 및 일체의 ～ a house and all its appurtenances.

**부수**(負數) ＝음수(陰數).

**부수**(部數) 《권수》 the number of copies; 《발행 부수》 circulation; edition. ¶ ～가 많이〔적게〕 나가다 have a large 〔small〕 circulation / ～에 제한이 있다 The number of copies is limited. / 초판의 발행 ～는 3,000부였다 The first edition consisted of 3,000 copies. / 그 신문의 발행 ～는 얼마나 됩니까 How large is the circulation of the newspaper?

**부수**(附隨) ～하다 be annexed 《to》; 《따르다》 accompany; follow; go with; attend 〔be attendant〕 《on》; be collateral 《with》; be incidental 《to》. ¶ ～적인 accompanying; attendant 《on》; incidental 《to》; concomitant / ～적 비용 incidental expenses / 전쟁에 ～되는 재해 the evils accompanying war; the evils that a war drag in its train / 다소의 위험이 ～되다 be attended with some danger / 이에 ～되는 일체의 권리를 포기하다 waive all rights attached thereon / 이런 종류의 위험은 장사에 ～되는 것이다 Such risks are contingent to the trade. / 정치가의 언동에는 사회적, 도의적 책임이 ～된다 A politician's words and deeds are accompanied with social and moral responsibilities. ◉ ～물 a concomitant; an incident (권리·의무 등). ～사건 a dependent event. ～ 사실 a collateral fact. ～서류 appended papers.

～정황 attendant circumstances. ～현상 a concomitant phenomenon.

**부수다** break (down, into pieces); smash; crush; destroy; demolish; 《갈아서》 grind up; 《빻아서》 pound. ¶ 산산이 ～ break to bits 〔pieces〕; shatter 《a window》; smash up / 얼음을 ～ break 〔crack〕 ice / 접시를 ～ break 〔smash〕 a dish / 집을 ～ tear down 〔demolish〕 a house / 자물쇠를 부수고 열다 force open a lock / 창문을 부수고 들어가다 break in through the window.

**부수상**(副首相) a deputy prime minister; a vice-premier.

**부수수하다** (be) loose; disheveled; disorderly; untidy. 「weeds.

**부수식물**(浮水植物) duckweeds; floating

**부수입**(副收入) a side 〔an additional〕 income; income from a side 〔part-time, fill-in〕 job; 《직무상의, 합법적인》 a perquisite; 《구어》 perks. ¶ 그 자리는 여러 가지 ～이 많은 곳이다 The office carries various perquisites.

**부숭부숭하다** ⇨ 보송보송하다.

**부스대다** ⇨ 바스대다.

**부스러기** small fragments; scraps; crumbs; odds and ends; shreds; bits. ◉ 고기～ scraps of meat. 나무～ chips of wood. 빵～ bread crumbs.

**부스러뜨리다** break; smash; crush; shatter. ⇨ 부수다.

**부스러지다** ⇨ 바스러지다.

**부스럭–** ⇨ 바스락–.

**부스럼** a swell; a boil; a tumor; an abscess; a gathering. ¶ ～이 나다 have a boil 《on *one's* foot》; a swelling comes out / 긁어 ～을 만들다 stir up a hornet's nest.

**부스스** ① 《조용히》 quietly; gently; slowly. ¶ 잠자리에서 ～ 일어나다 quietly rise from *one's* bed. ② 《머리·털 등이》 ～하다 (be) disheveled; unkempt; untidy. ¶ ～한 얼굴 a hairly 〔an unshaven〕 face / ～한 머리 disheveled hair.

**부슬부슬**[1] ⇨ 보슬보슬[1], 바슬바슬.

**부슬비** ⇨ 보슬비.

**부시** (a) steel (for striking sparks from flint). ¶ ～(를) 치다 strike fire 〔sparks〕 with 〔out of〕 flint (and steel); get a light from a flint. ◉ ～통 a tinderbox. 부싯깃 tinder (★ 관사 없음). 부싯돌 (a) flint.

**부시다**[1] 《씻다》 wash 《dishes》; rinse; cleanse; clean out. ¶ 병을 ～ wash 〔rinse〕 out a bottle.

**부시다**[2] 《눈이》 (be) dazzling; glaring; blinding; radiant. ¶ 눈이 부시도록 아름다운 여자 a lady of dazzling beauty; a radiant beauty / 눈이 부시게 빛나다 dazzle; glare / 눈이 ～ *one's* eyes are dazzled / 햇빛에 눈이 ～ I am dazzled by the sun. / 조명이 ～ The lights dazzle me. / 자동차의 헤드라이트에 눈이 ～ My eyes are blinded by the headlights.

**부시장**(副市長) a deputy mayor. ¶ 제 1〔2〕 ～ a senior 〔junior〕 deputy mayor.

**부식**(扶植) implantation. ～하다 plant; implant; foster; establish. ¶ 자기 세력을 ～하다 establish 〔extend〕 *one's* influence.

**부식**(腐蝕) corrosion; erosion; 《썩음》 rot; decay; 《녹》 rust. ～하다 corrode; erode; rot; rust (녹슬다); 《녹슬어 들어가다》 eat 《into》. ¶ ～되지 않는 incorrodible; rustless / 녹으로 ～되어 있다 be eaten away with rust / 산은 금속을 ～시킨다 Acid eats into metals. / 이 금속은 ～이 잘 된다 This metal is apt to corrode quickly. ◉ ～방지제 corrosion inhibitor. ～작용 corrosive 〔erosive〕 action; corrosion. ～제 a corrosive (agent); a corroder; a caustic.

**부식(물)**(副食(物)) a side dish; dishes to go with the rice.

**부식토**(腐植土) humus (soil); mold.

**부신**(副腎) 〖해부〗 a (supra)renal gland 〔capsule〕; an adrenal (body, gland).

**부신피질**(副腎皮質) 〖해부〗 the adrenal cortex. ◉ ～호르몬 adrenocortical hormones.

**부실**(不實) ～하다 ① 《몸이》 (be) feeble; weak; delicate; flimsy; be not strong. ¶ 몸이 ～하다 be in delicate health; be weak. ② 《수량이》 (be) short; lacking; poor. ¶ 볏섬이 ～하다 The sack of rice is a little short. ③ 《믿음성이》 (be) unreliable; untrustworthy. ④ 《행위가》 be not sincere 《in *doing*》; be not earnest; (be) unconscientious; be not faithful 《to *one's* duty》. ¶ 그는 일하는 것이 ～하다 He is not a conscientious worker. / 그는 ～하게 일한다 He does not work earnestly. ◉ ～공사 《행위》 illegal 〔faithless〕 construction practices: ～ 공사를 근절하다 uproot illegal construction practices. ～기업 an insolvent enterprise; an improperly-run enterprise; a faltering enterprise: ～ 기업을 정리하다

liquidate 〔reorganize〕 faltering enterprises. ～기재 《장부의》 false 〔fake〕 entries. ～운영〔경영〕 insolvent operation 〔management〕.

**부심**(副審) a sub-referee; a sub-umpire.

**부심**(腐心) ～하다 take great pains 《to *do*》; be at pains 《to *do*》; rack *one's* brains; be bent 〔intent〕 on. ¶ 그녀는 사료 수집에 ～하였다 She has been at great pains to collect historical materials. / 그 운동의 자금 모으기에 크게 ～했다 We took great pains to raise money for the campaign.

**부아** ① 《허파》 the lungs. ② 《분함》 exasperation; anger; rage. ¶ 부앗김에 in a fit of temper 〔anger〕 / ～가 나다, ～를 내다 lose *one's* temper 《with》; fall into a rage; be exasperated; feel offended / ～통이 터지다 get mad; blow *one's* top 〔stack〕; burst into a fit of rage; fly into a fury / 나는 그의 말에 ～가 났다 I was exasperated at his words.

**부양**(扶養) support; maintenance. ～하다 keep up; support; maintain; provide for. ¶ 가족을 ～할 책임이 있다 be under obligation to support *one's* family / 그는 대가족을 ～하고 있다 He has a large family to support. / 인간은 자식을 ～할 의무가 있다 A man is bound to provide for his children.
◉ ～가족 a dependent family: ～가족 공제 tax exemption 〔a tax credit〕 for dependents. ～비 a sustenance allowance; alimony. ～수당 a family allowance. ～의무 the duty of supporting. ～자 a supporter; a sustainer. ～책임자 a person responsible for supporting 《the family》; a breadwinner.

**부양**(浮揚) floating; floatage. ～하다 float 《in the air》; 《경기를》 animate; invigorate; pick up. ¶ 경기를 ～시키다 stimulate the economy / 침몰선을 ～시키다 refloat a sunken vessel.
◉ ～력 buoyancy. ～성 floatability. (경기) ～(정)책 a pump-priming policy 〔measure〕: 경기 침체에 대처하기 위해 부분적 ～책을 쓰다 take partial pump-priming measures to cope with the business slowdown.

**부언**(附言) a postscript; an additional remark. ～하다 add 《that…》; say in addition; remark parenthetically.

**부업**(副業) a side 〔second〕 job; a sideline; (a) side business; a subsidiary business 〔occupation〕. ¶ ～으로(서) as a sideline / 수입이 좋은 ～ a profitable 〔remunerative〕 sideline / ～으로 하다 do 《*a thing*》 on the side / ～을 갖다 hold an off-duty job; have a side business / ～을 장려하다 encourage a subsidiary industry / 요즘 ～으로 양계를 하는 농가가 많다 Nowadays many farmers raise chickens as a sideline.

**부엉부엉** (with a) hoot-hoot! ¶ ～ 울다 「hoot; whoop.

**부엉이** 〖조류〗 a horned 〔an eared〕 owl. ¶ ～가 운다 The owl hoots. / ～ 소리도 제가 듣기에는 좋다고 한다 It is hard to see one's own faults. ◉ ～셈 a foolish calculation.

**부엌** a kitchen; a kitchenette (아파트의 작은). ¶ ～에서 일하다 work in the kitchen; 《가정부로서》 work as a kitchenmaid / ～에 가면 더 먹을까 방에 가면 더 먹을까 torn between a conflict of interests.
◉ ～데기 a kitchenmaid. ～바닥 the kitchen floor. ～세간〔살림〕 kitchen utensils. ～일 《do》 kitchen 〔scullery〕 work. ～칼 a kitchen knife.

**부여**(附與) grant; bestowal; allowance. ～하다 give; grant; allow; bestow 〔confer〕 《a title of nobility》 on 《*a person*》; vest. ¶ 권한을 ～하다 give 《*a person*》 an authority 《to *do*》; authorize *a person* 《to *do*》 / 전권을 ～하다 (in)vest 《*a person*》 with full powers.

**부여**(賦與) endowment. ～하다 endow 〔bless〕 《*a person*》 with. ¶ 재능이 ～되다 be endowed 〔gifted, blessed〕 with talent / 미모와 지력이 ～되어 있다 「have both 〔be endowed with〕 beauty and brains / 우리들에게는 양심이 ～되어 있다 We are all endowed 〔gifted〕 with a conscience.

**부여잡다** grab hard 《at》; seize 《on, upon》; take fast 〔firm〕 hold 《of》.

**부역**(附逆) ～하다 join the rebel army; take sides with the rebels 〔enemy〕.

**부역**(賦役) compulsory 〔statute〕 labor; compulsory service; slave labor; corvée. ¶ ～을 과하다 put 《*a person*》 to slave labor; exact 「statute labor 〔corvée〕 from 《people》.

**부연**(附椽) 〖건축〗 a lean-to; extended 「eaves.

**부연**(敷衍) expatiation; amplification; enlargement; dilatation. ～하다 expatiate 〔dilate, enlarge, extend〕 on 《a subject》; amplify 《the statement》. ¶ 그는 그 문제를 ～하여 설명했다 He dilated upon that subject.

**부엽토**(腐葉土) leaf mold.

**부영사**(副領事) a vice-consul.

**부옇다** ⇨ 보얗다.

**부예지다** get misty 〔hazy〕; become dim 〔obscure〕; get blurred 〔fuzzy〕; shade off; fade (색이). ¶ 부예진 색 a faded 〔dull〕 color / 눈물로 부예진 눈 eyes dim with tear / 안개로 산의 윤곽이 부예졌다 The fog blurred the outline of the hills.

**부용**(芙蓉) 〖식물〗《연꽃》 a lotus; 《목부용》 a cotton rose; a Confederate rose.

**부원**(部員) 《전체》 the staff; 《개인》 a person on the staff; a staff member; a member 《of the staff》; a staff man. ◉ 편집～ (a person on) the editorial staff.

**부원**(富源) sources of wealth.

**부위**(部位) a region; a part.

**부유**(浮游) floating; drifting; 〖물리〗 suspension (고체 입자의). ～하다 float; drift; waft. ◉ ～기뢰 a floating mine. ～물 floating 〔suspended〕 matter 〔particles〕. ～생물 plankton. ～선광 〖광산〗 flotation. ～식물 floating plants.

**부유**(富裕) wealth; richness; affluence. ～하다 (be) wealthy; rich; well-off; well-to-do; [서술적] be well provided for. ¶ ～한 사람 a person of wealth; a well-to-do person / ～한 집안에 태어나다 be born rich; be born of a rich family / ～하게 살다 live in affluence; be well-off. ◉ ～층 the wealthy classes; the rich; the high-income bracket.

**부유스름하다** (be) somewhat pearly; frosty; misty.

**부음**(訃音) an obituary notice; an announcement of death; a report of 《*a person's*》 death. ¶ ～에 접하다 hear 〔be informed〕 of 《*a person's*》 death.

**부응**(副應) ～하다 meet; suit; answer; satisfy; act 〔live〕 up to. ¶ 목적에 ～하다 answer the purpose / …의 희망에 ～하다 meet 〔satisfy, gratify, carry out〕 《*a person's*》 wishes / 기대에 ～토록 노력하겠습니다 I will do my best to act up to your expectation.

**부의**(附議) ～하다 bring 〔take〕 up 《a *matter*》 for discussion; bring 《*a matter*》 before 《a conference》; submit 《a measure》 to 《a council》; refer 《a bill》 to 《a committee》.

**부의**(賻儀) goods 〔gifts〕 to aid in a funeral; a condolence gift 〔money〕. ～하다 offer condolence money 〔goods〕.

**부의장**(副議長) a vice-president〔-chairperson〕; a deputy speaker.

**부이** 《부표》 a buoy; 《구명용》 a life buoy.

**부익부빈익빈**(富益富貧益貧) the rich=get-richer and the poor-get-poorer.

**부인**(夫人) 《아내》 a wife; 《기혼자》 a married lady; a matron; 《경칭》 Mrs. (*pl.* Mmes); Madam.

> 용법 Mrs.는 mistress의 생략이지만 현재에는 Mrs.대신에 mistress를 사용하는 일은 거의 없음. Mrs.는 보통, 남편의 성 앞에 붙임: Mrs. Jones 「존스 씨 부인」 / Mrs. Kim 「김씨 부인」. 다소 격식을 차린 경우라든가 명함·상업 통신문의 수신인에게는 남편의 성명 앞에 붙임: Mrs. Thomas Jones 「토마스 존스 씨 부인」 / Mrs. Kich'un Han 「한 기춘씨 부인」. 미망인 및 법률 문서에 기록할 경우에는 본인의 성명 앞에 붙임: Mrs. Mary Jones 「존스씨 부인 메어리」 / Mrs. Kim Sukcha Han 「한씨 부인 김 숙자」.

¶ ～께서 안녕하십니까 How is your wife? / ～ 더 하실 말씀이 있으십니까 Do you have anything further to say, madam? / ～께 안부 전해 주십시오 Give my best regards to Mrs. ….

**부인**(否認) denial; negation; nonrecognition; repudiation. ～하다 say no 《to》; deny; disavow; disapprove; 《관계·관심 따위를》 disown; disclaim; 《권리·의무 따위를》 repudiate. ¶ 사실을 ～하다 deny a fact / 자기 아이임을 ～하다 disown *one's* own child / 자기 행위를 ～하다 disavow *one's* own action / 진술을 ～하다 contradict a statement / ～할 수 없다 be undeniable / 용의자는 범행을 ～했다 The suspect denied the crime. / 그는 기소 사실을 전면적으로 ～했다 He denied all the indicted facts.

**부인**(婦人) a (married) woman; 《신분·교양이 있는》 a lady (★ 현재는 woman과 함께 여성 일반에게 널리 쓰임). ¶ ～용 for ladies / 신분 있는 ～ a gentlewoman / 중년(의) ～ a middle-aged 〔an elderly〕 woman. ◉ ～과 gynecology: ～과 의사 a gynecologist; a ladies' doctor. ～병 women's disease; women's complaints 〔ailments〕; a female disorder. ～석 seats for ladies. ～회 a women's society 〔association〕.

**부임**(赴任) proceeding to *one's* new post; accession to office. ～하다 start 〔leave, go〕 for *one's* new post; proceed to *one's* post. ¶ 새로 ～해 오신 선

생님 a new 〔newly appointed〕 teacher / ～길에 오르다 start for post; be on the way to *one's* post.
◉ ～지 *one's* place of appointment; *one's* (new) post.

**부자**(父子) father and son.

**부자**(富者) a rich 〔wealthy〕 man; a person of wealth 〔means, property〕; a millionaire (큰부자); [총칭] the rich. ¶ ～가 되다 become 〔get, grow〕 rich; make a fortune 〔pile《구어》〕 / 대단한 ～다 be fabulously rich; have a colossal amount of money; 《구어》 have pots 〔a mint〕 of money.

**부자연**(不自然) unnaturalness; 《인위적》 artificiality. ～하다, ～스럽다 (be) unnatural; artificial (인위적인); forced (무리한); affected (…체 하는). ¶ ～스러운 웃음 a forced smile / ～스러운 표현 an unnatural phrasing / ～스러운 태도 affected manners / ～스런 정중함《with》 studied politeness / 나는 잠시 동안 ～스러운 자세로 서 있어야 했다 I had to stand in an unnatural posture for a while.

**부자유**(不自由) lack of freedom; restriction; inconvenience. ～하다, ～스럽다 (be) restricted; limited; inconvenient; uncomfortable; be not free. ¶ ～한 생활《경제적으로》 a life of want / 몸이 ～스런 사람 a disabled man / 손이 ～스럽다 have trouble in the hand; have lost the use of *one's* hand.

**부자재**(副資材) subsidiary materials.

**부자지** testicles and penis.

**부작용**(副作用) a 《usually adverse》 side effect 《on》; reaction. ¶ 약의 ～ an adverse reaction of a medicine / ～을 일으키다 have 〔produce, cause〕 「(harmful) side effects 〔ill effects〕 / ～이 없다 be free from harmful 「aftereffects 〔side effects〕; produce no ill effects / 이 약은 위에 ～이 없다 This medicine produces no reaction 〔ill effects〕 on the stomach.

**부작위**(不作爲) 〖법〗 forbearance; omission. ◉ ～범(犯) a crime of omission; nonfeasance. ～추출법〖통계〗 random sampling.

**부잔교**(浮棧橋) a floating pier 〔stage〕.

**부잣집**(富者—) a rich 〔wealthy〕 family; 《집》 a rich man's house. ¶ ～ 딸 a bourgeois girl / ～에 장가들다 marry a fortune 〔rich heiress〕 / ～에 태어나다 be born rich; be born with a silver spoon in *one's* mouth.

**부장**(部長) the head 〔chief, director〕 of a department 〔section, division〕 (★ 우리 나라 회사 등에서는 「부」를 department, 「과」를 division, 「계」를 section 등으로 구분짓는 경우가 흔하지만, 영미에서는 이러한 구분이 우리처럼 일정치 않음); a department 〔general〕 manager.
◉ ～검사 a superintendent public prosecutor. 경리〔인사〕～ the chief of the accountants' 〔personal (affairs)〕 department.

**부장품**(副葬品) grave goods; burial accessories.

**부재**(不在) absence. ～하다 be absent; be out (외출 중); be away from 〔be not at〕 home. ¶ ～중에 in 〔during〕 *one's* absence; while *one* is 〔has been〕 away (여행 중에) / 인간성 ～의 교육 dehumanized education / 국민 ～의 정치 government indifferent to the opinions and wishes of the voters 〔electorate〕 / ～중《게시》 Out. / 그는 서울에 가서 ～중이다 He is away in Seoul. / 삼촌댁을 방문했으나 ～중이셨다 I called on my uncle and found him out 〔absent〕. / 교장 선생님이 ～중에는 박 선생님이 그 대리를 보신다 In 〔During〕 the absence of the principal, Mr. Park is in charge of the school.
◉ ～자 an absentee: ～자 투표 voting by mail; 《cast an》 absentee ballot 〔voting〕. ～증명 an alibi. ～지주 an absentee landlord 〔landowner〕.

**부적**(符籍) an amulet; a talisman; a charm. ¶ 액막이 ～ an amulet to avert evils; a charm against evils.

**부적격**(不適格) unfitness; disqualification. ¶ ～의 disqualified 〔unqualified〕 《for》; unfit 《for》 / ～이 되다 be disqualified / 그녀는 불어 교사로는 ～이다 She is not qualified to teach French.
◉ ～자 a person disqualified for 〔unacceptable to〕 《a position》.

**부적당**(不適當) unsuitableness; unfitness; inappropriateness; inadequateness; inadequacy; impropriety. ～하다 (be) unsuitable; unfit 《for》; inappropriate 《to》; inadequate; improper. ¶ ～한 예 an improper 〔inappropriate〕 instance / 그 제안은 ～하다 The proposal is out of place. / 이 표현은 이 경우에 ～하다 This is not a suitable expression 「here 〔for this use〕.

**부적임**(不適任) unfitness. ¶ ～의 unfit 《for》; unqualified 《for》; incompetent 《for》 / 그녀는 그 지위에는 ～이다 She is 「unfit 〔not the right person〕 for the position. ◉ ～자 an unqualified

〔incompetent〕 person.

**부적절**(不適切) inappropriateness; unsuitableness; inadequacy. ～하다 (be) inappropriate; unsuitable; inadequate; be out of place. ¶ 청바지 차림이 이런 장소에는 ～하다 Blue jeans are out of place for this occasion.

**부적합**(不適合) incongruence. ～하다 (be) incongruent; unfit 《for》; inadequate. ¶ 그 땅은 경작하기에는 ～하다 The land is unfit for farming.

**부전**(不全) ¶ ～의 《불완전한》 incomplete; underdeveloped; partial (부분적인) / 발육～ incomplete development. ◉ ～마비 partial paralysis; paresis.

**부전**(不戰) renunciation of war. ◉ ～조약 《conclude》 an antiwar pact; a no-war 〔peace〕 treaty: 그 나라는 러시아와 ～ 조약을 맺었다 The country concluded an antiwar pact with Russia.

**부전**(附箋) a tag; a slip; a label. ¶ ～을 붙이다 tag; label / 편지에 ～이 붙어 돌아오다 a letter comes back with a tag explaining its nondelivery.

**부전나비** 〖곤충〗 a hairstreak; a gossammerwing.

**부전승**(不戰勝) an unearned win. ～하다 win a game by default; draw a bye (상대편 기권 등). ¶ 1회전에서 ～이 되었다 We won without playing in the first game.

**부전자전**(父傳子傳) transmission from father to son. ～하다 transmit from father to son. ¶ ～의 handed down from father to son / ～이다 Like father, like son.

**부전패**(不戰敗) default. ¶ ～가 되다 lose 《a game》 by default; default a game 〔race〕.

**부절따말** a red horse with a black 「mane.

**부절제**(不節制) intemperance; excesses; immoderation. ～하다 be intemperate; commit excesses. ¶ ～한 생활을 하다 lead an intemperate life.

**부점**(附點) 〖음악〗 a dot; a prick; [형용사적] dotted. ◉ ～음표 a dotted note: ～ 2분〔4분〕 음표 a dotted half 〔quarter〕 note.

**부접 못하다** ① 《접근 못 하다》 cannot approach 〔come near to〕 《*a person*》; be kept from approaching; be denied access 《to》. ¶ 부접 못하게 하다 keep *a person* inaccessible 〔unapproachable〕; keep 《*a person*》 away from 《*one, a thing*》. ② 《배겨내지 못 하다》 cannot 〔be unable to〕 stay long; be too warm 〔hot〕 《for *a person*》; cannot stand 〔endure〕. ¶ 그 집에는 가정부가 부접 못 한다 The kitchenmaids won't 〔do not〕 stay long in that family.

**부젓가락** (a pair of ) fire tongs.

**부정**(不正) 《불공정》 injustice; unfairness; iniquity; 《위법》 illegality; unlawfulness; 《비행》 wrong; 《관공리의》 corruption; 《부정직》 dishonesty; 《부당》 impropriety. ～하다 (be) unjust; unfair; foul; wrong; 《위법의》 illegal; unlawful; dishonest (부정직한); false (가짜의). ¶ ～한 돈 ill-gotten money; filthy lucre; graft 《미》 / ～을 바로잡다 remedy 〔redress〕 injustice / ～을 폭로하다 expose injustice 〔dishonest practice〕 / ～한 짓을 하다 do wrong; do a dishonest thing 〔act〕; commit an injustice; 《경기에서》 play foul; 《시험에서》 cheat 《in an examination》 / ～한 방법으로 이기다 win unfairly / ～입학하다 enter 《a university》 through the back door 〔by dishonest means〕 / 그는 ～한 수단으로 돈을 모았다 He made money by unlawful 〔dishonest〕 means.
◉ ～거래 an illegal transaction 〔dealing〕. ～공무원 a corrupt(ed) 〔venal〕 official. ～대부〔대출〕 an illegal 〔a fraudulent〕 loan. ～명색 ill-gotten wealth; wealth achieved by unjust methods. ～부패 irregularities and corruption; abuse of power and graft. ～사건〔수뢰〕 a bribery 〔graft〕 case; a scandal: ～사건이 드러나다 a 《political》 scandal is brought to light. ～선거 a rigged 〔fraudulent〕 election: ～선거 운동 illegal electioneering. ～소득 illegal profits; ill-gotten gains. ～식품 insanitary 〔harmful〕 food. ～업자 an illegal trader; a dishonest businessman. ～저울 a false balance; a tampered weighing machine. ～품 a fraudulent article; an adulterated article; a fraud. ～행위 a dishonest act; an unfair practice; 《시험장에서》 cheating: 시험에서 ～행위를 하다 cheat in the examination.

**부정**(不定) indefiniteness; mutability. ～하다 (be) unsettled; indefinite; unfixed; undecided; 《불규칙의》 (be) irregular; 《변하기 쉬운》 (be) inconstant; changeable. ¶ 그는 주소 ～이다 He has no fixed address. / 나의 수입은 ～하다 I have no regular income.
◉ ～관사〔대명사〕 〖문법〗 an indefinite

article 〔pronoun〕. ～기간 an indefinite period of time. ～방정식 〖수학〗 an indeterminate equation. ～법 〖문법〗 the infinitive mood. ～사 〖문법〗 an infinitive: 분리 ～사 a split infinitive. ～수 an indefinite number. ～수입 an irregular 〔incidental〕 income. ～형 an indeterminate form.

**부정**(不貞) unchastity; unfaithfulness; (conjugal) infidelity. ～하다 (be) unchaste; unfaithful; faithless; false 《to *one's* husband》. ¶ ～한 아내다 be a faithless wife to her husband.

**부정**(不淨) ① 《더러움》 uncleanliness; dirtiness; filthiness; impurity. ～하다 (be) unclean; dirty; filthy; impure; defiled. ② 《기휘(忌諱)할 때의》 an unclean event 《*i.e.* birth or death》 that takes place in the family during the time of purification. ¶ ～나다 〔보다〕 have 〔witness〕 an unclean event (such as a birth or a death) that takes place in the family during the time of purification / ～타다 be subject to 〔suffer from〕 the evil coming from breaking the taboo of uncleanness (during the time of purification). ③ 〖민속〗 the first stage of a shaman rite. ¶ ～치다 perform the first stage of a shaman rite; perform shamanistic exorcism. ◉ ～풀이 a shamanistic exorcism.

**부정**(否定) (a) denial; negation; 《부인》 (a) disavowal. ～하다 deny; say "no" 《to》; contradict. ¶ 이중～ 〖문법〗 double negatives / ～적인 negative; contradictory / ～할 수 없는 undeniable / …을 ～할 수 없다 It cannot be denied that…; There is no denying that… / 그것은 ～할 수 없는 사실이다 That is an undeniable fact. / 당국은 그의 외교 정책을 공공연히 ～했다 The authorities made a public denial of his foreign policy. ◉ ～명제 a negative (proposition). ～문 a negative sentence. ～어 a negative. ～판단 〖논리〗 a negation; a negative assertion 〔proposition〕.

**부정기**(不定期) ¶ ～의 irregular; unfixed; nonscheduled; indeterminate. ◉ ～간(刊) penal servitude for an indeterminate term. ～선 a tramp (steamer); a nonregular liner: ～선을 운항하다 sail a tramp (ship). ～열차 an unscheduled train. ～예금 an irregular deposit. ～편 nonregular service. ～항공 an unscheduled flight: ～항공로 a nonscheduled airline.

**부정당**(不正當) ～하다 (be) improper; wrong; unrighteous; unlawful.

**부정맥**(不整脈) 〖의학〗 arrhythmia; an irregular pulse.

**부정수단**(不正手段) a dishonest 〔an improper, an unfair, a fraudulent, an illicit〕 means; a fraud. ¶ ～으로 by a dishonest means / 그는 목적을 이루기 위해 온갖 ～을 다 썼다 He resorted to any foul means to gain his end.

**부정직**(不正直) dishonesty. ～하다 (be) dishonest. ¶ ～한 행위〔사람〕 a dishonest act 〔person〕.

**부정축재**(不正蓄財) accumulation of wealth by illicit means; amassing of wealth through immoral means. ～하다 accumulate 〔amass〕 wealth by unlawful 〔illicit〕 means; make a fortune by illegal means. ¶ 정부는 부패 공무원의 ～ 재산을 몰수하기 위해 국가 권한을 강화하는 관련 법규의 개정을 고려하고 있다 The government is considering revising relevant laws to empower the state to confiscate illegally gained assets of corrupt civil servants.

**부정확**(不正確) inaccuracy; imprecision. ～하다 (be) inaccurate; incorrect; inexact; imprecise. ¶ ～한 번역 an inaccurate translation / 그는 늘 계산이 ～하다 His calculations are always incorrect. / ～한 정보로 인해 계획이 실패했다 The plan failed because it was based on incorrect information.

**부제**(副題) a subtitle; a subhead(ing).

**부조**(父祖) father and grandfather; 《선조》 ancestors; forefathers. ¶ ～전래의 ancestral; patrimonial.

**부조**(不調) 《건강·컨디션 등의》 a bad condition; a slump; a disorder; 《날씨 등의》 unfavorableness; irregularity. ～하다 (be) unfavorable; irregular; [서술적] be in disorder; 《운동 선수가》 be in a 「bad condition 〔slump 《미》〕; be off 〔out of〕 form. ◉ ～증 ＝월경불순(月經不順).

**부조**(扶助) ① 《잔칫집·상가에의》 providing 《*a person*》 with money 〔things〕 to help pay for a marriage 〔funeral〕 ceremony; a contribution. ～하다 contribute 《toward, to》; give relief to; give congratulatory 〔condolence〕 money 〔goods〕 to aid in a marriage 〔funeral〕. ¶ 상가～ a donation to help out a bereaved family / ～도 말고 젯상 다리나 치지 마라 《속담》 Just keep your hands off my business. ② 《도움》 aid; help; helping out. ～하다 aid; help; assist; support; render 《*a person*》 assistance. ¶ 부모의 ～를 받다 depend on *one's* parents for support. ◉ ～금 congratulatory 〔condolence〕 money; an allowance in aid. 부좃술 a contribution of liquor.

**부조**(浮彫) 〖미술〗 a (carved 〔sculptured〕) relief; (a) relief 〔embossed〕 sculpture 〔carving〕. ～하다 emboss; carve in relief. ¶ 높은〔낮은〕 ～의 상 a sculpture in high 〔low〕 relief. ◉ ～세공 relief 〔raised〕 work.

**부조리**(不條理) irrationality; absurdity; unreasonableness; irregularity. ¶ ～한 irrational; unreasonable / 금융 ～ bank-related irregularities; malpractices at banks / 사회 ～ social irregularities / 온갖 ～를 제거하다 do away with all kinds of irregularities / 공무원들의 각종 ～를 뿌리 뽑다 uproot various irregularities committed by public servants.

**부조화**(不調和) lack of harmony 〔concord, congruity〕; disharmony; incongruity; discord(ance); inharmony. ～하다 (be) inharmonious; disharmonious; discordant; incongruous.

**부족**(不足) 《불충분》 insufficiency; 《모자람》 shortage; deficiency; 《결핍》 want; lack; scantiness; scarcity; dearth. ～하다 (be) insufficient; deficient; wanting; lacking; short; [서술적] [사물이 주어] be not enough; be in short supply; be insufficient; [사람이 주어] be 〔come, drop, fall〕 short 《of》; be in want 〔need〕 《of》; do not have enough 《of》. ¶ 칼슘의 ～ calcium poverty / 물～ lack of water / 화차의 ～ a freight car famine / 수면 ～으로 for want 〔lack〕 of sleep / 자금 ～으로 for 〔by, from, through〕 lack 〔want〕 of funds / 식량이 ～하다〔해지다〕 be 〔run〕 short of provisions / 역량이 ～하다 be wanting in ability / 영양이 ～하다 be undernourished / 일손이 ～하다 be short of hands; be shorthanded / 장비가 ～하다 be ill equipped / 천 원 ～하다 be one thousand won short; come short by one thousand won / (비행기 등이) 연료가 ～하게 되다 run low of fuel / ～한 점이 없다 leave nothing to be desired / ～을 메우다 make good the shortage; make up for a deficiency; cover 〔meet, fill up〕 the shortage 〔deficiency〕 / …로 수입의 ～을 메우다 eke 〔help〕 out *one's* income with 《odd jobs》 / 그는 ～함이 없는 생활을 하고 있다 He lives in plenty. / 자원의 ～은 심각한 문제이다 The shortage of natural resources is a serious problem. / 북부 지방의 최근 홍수는 116명의 인명을 앗아갔고, 심대한 경제적 손실을 주었으며 극심한 식량 ～을 더욱 악화시켰다 The recent floods in the northern part of Korea have claimed 116 lives, inflicted heavy economic damage and worsened a severe shortage of food.
◉ ～액 (amount of ) shortage; amount short; a deficit; the balance due. ～증 〖한의〗 consumption.

**부족**(部族) a tribe. ¶ ～의 tribal / ～사회 a tribal society / ～민 tribesmen; tribal people.

**부존**(賦存) ～하다 be blessed 〔favored〕 《with》. ◉ ～자원 natural resources: ～자원의 부족(을 메우다) (make up for) the shortage of natural resources / ～자원이 많다 be blessed with natural resources.

**부종**(浮腫) ＝부증(浮症).

**부주의**(不注意) carelessness; heedlessness; inattention; lack of care; 《태만》 negligence. ～하다 be careless 〔heedless, incautious〕; be inattentive 〔negligent〕. ¶ 운전～ careless driving / ～하게 carelessly; inattentively; heedlessly; imprudently / ～로 through (*one's*) carelessness / 운전사의 ～로 인한 사고 an accident due to 〔caused by〕 a careless driver / ～로 인한 실수 a careless mistake / ～로〔에서〕 일어나다 arise from carelessness / 내가 정말 ～하였다 It was very careless of me. / 그 교통 사고는 그의 ～로 일어났다 The traffic accident was caused by his carelessness.

**부주제**(副主題) 〖음악〗 the subsidiary (theme).

**부증**(浮症) 〖한의〗 a dropsical swelling; dropsy; (o)edema; anasarca.

**부지**(不知) not knowing; ignorance. ～하다 do not know; be ignorant of.
◉ ～거처(去處) whereabouts unknown; missing. ～기수(其數) being numberless 〔innumerable, countless〕. ～불각(不覺) unconsciously; unwittingly; unaware; without *one's* knowledge; 《본능적으로》 instinctively: ～불각에 나쁜 짓을 하게 되다 drift 〔slip〕 into an evil course. ～불식간(不識間) ＝ 부지중. ～하세월(何歲月) not knowing when 《*a thing*》 is going

to be completed: ～ 하세월이다 Nobody can tell when it will be completed.

**부지**(扶支·扶持) ～하다 hold (out); keep (up); maintain; last; 《견디다》 bear; stand; endure. ¶ 건강을 ～해가는 비결 the secret of maintaining *one's* health / (꺼져가는) 목숨을 가까스로 ～하고 있다 keep 〔linger out〕 a feeble existence / ～ 못하다 cannot stand; be unable to remain / 가까스로 생계를 ～해 나가다 make 〔earn〕 a bare living; 《구어》 scrape a living / 그런 식사론 몸이 ～ 못할 걸세 You cannot keep yourself in good health on such a diet. / 그 녀석 여기서 ～ 못하게 해 놓겠다 I will make it too hot for him.

**부지**(敷地) a (building) site 〔lot〕; (a plot of) ground; a plot. ¶ ～의 선정 the selection of a site 《for》 / ～를 물색〔선정〕하다 look for 〔select, choose〕 a site 《for》 / ～를 확보하다 secure the location 《for》 / 우리집의 ～는 160평방미터이다 My plot of land is 160 square meters. ◉ ～면적 plottage.

**부지깽이** a (fire) poker.

**부지런** industry; diligence; assiduity. ～하다 (be) diligent; industrious; assiduous; hard-working; earnest. ¶ ～한 사람 a hard 〔diligent〕 worker; an earlybird / ～을 피우다, ～(을) 떨다 display diligence; work hard 〔diligently〕 / 그는 ～한 사람이다 He is a hard worker.

**부지런히** diligently; industriously; assiduously; earnestly; 《빈번히》 frequently; often; 《잰걸음으로》 fast; at a quick 〔brisk〕 pace. ¶ ～ 다니다 frequent 《a house》; pay frequent visits 《to》 / ～ 일하다 work hard.

**부지배인**(副支配人) an assistant manager.

**부지중**(不知中) ¶ ～에 unconsciously; unknowingly; (all) unawares; in spite of *oneself;* without knowing it; unintentionally; instinctively / ～에 그리 말했다 The words just escaped my lips.

**부지지, 부지직** ⇨ 바지지.

**부직**(副職) an additional post.

**부진**(不振) dullness; depression; inactivity; stagnation; a slump. ～하다 be dull 〔inactive, depressed, stagnant〕; be at a low ebb; be in a bad way 〔condition〕. ¶ 수출의 ～ inactivity 〔a poor showing〕 of the export trade; a slump in exports / 성적이 ～하다 do poorly 《at school》; show poor 《business》 results / 식욕이 ～하다 have no 〔little, a poor〕 appetite / 장사가 ～하다 (*one's*) business is in a bad way; trade is 「depressed 〔at a low ebb〕 / ～에 빠지다 get into a slump; 《운동선수가》 hit 〔be in〕 a slump / ～에서 헤어나다 come out of a slump / 사업 ～의 타개책을 찾다 find some way out of the 「business depression 〔slump, slack in business〕.

**부진**(不進) poor progress. ～하다 make poor 〔little, scant〕 progress. ¶ 지지 ～하다 make very slow progress; go ahead at a snail's pace.

**부진**(不盡) inexhaustibleness; endlessness. ～하다 (be) inexhaustible; endless. ◉ ～근(수) 〖수학〗 a surd root. ～수 a surd; an irrational number.

**부질간**(一間) a brassworker's furnace.

**부질없다** (be) vain; useless; futile; idle; trivial. ¶ 부질없는 생각 an idle thought / 부질없는 걱정을 하다 worry (*oneself*) unnecessarily / 부질없는 소리를 하다 talk nonsense; utter an absurdity; make an uncalled-for remark / 부질없는 짓을 하다 do a foolish thing; do unwanted things.

**부질없이** idly; to no purpose; in vain. ¶ ～ 기다리다 wait in vain / ～ 돈을 쓰다 waste money / ～ 날을 보내다 live in idleness / ～ 시간을 보내다 idle away *one's* time.

**부집게** fire 〔charcoal〕 nippers; (flame) snuffers; a candle snuffer.

**부쩍** ① ⇨ 바싹. ② 《갑자기》 rapidly; quickly; remarkably; markedly. ¶ ～ 늘다 increase markedly / 수학 실력이 ～ 늘다 make a remarkable improvement in mathematics.

**부차적**(副次的) (being) secondary.

**부착**(附着) sticking; adhesion; cohesion; agglutination. ～하다 adhere 〔stick, attach, cling〕 to. ¶ 해초와 조개가 배 바닥에 ～하다 seaweed and shells cling to the bottom of a ship. ◉ ～력 adhesive power; adhesion. ～어 〖언어〗 an agglutinative language.

**부창부수**(夫唱婦隨) a way of life in which the wife follows the lead set by her husband.

**부채** a fan; a folding fan (쥘부채). ¶ ～를 부치다 fan *oneself;* use a fan. ◉ ～꼭지 the pivot of a fan. ～꼴 fan shape; sector form: ～꼴의 fan=shaped / ～꼴로 fanwise. ～잡이 a blindman's left; the left. ～춤 a dance with a fan 〔fans〕; a fan dance. 부챗살 the ribs of a fan.

**부채**(負債) a debt; liabilities. ¶ 장부상의

～ a book debt / ～가 많이 있다 be heavily in debt; have large 〔immense〕 debts / ～가 없다 be clear 〔free〕 from debts; be out of debts / ～를 남기다 leave debts / ～를 갚다 repay 〔clear off, pay off〕 a debt / ～를 지다 run 〔get, fall〕 in(to) debt; put *oneself* in debt / 10만 원의 ～가 있다 be indebted to 《*a person*》 for 100,000 won / 자넨 ～가 얼마나 되는가 How much do you owe? *or* What is the extent of your liabilities? / 자네 ～ 지불 능력이 있기나 하는 거야 Can you meet your liabilities at all? / 그는 나에게 ～를 탕감해 주었다 He forgave me the debt. *or* He canceled me from the debt. ◉ ～상환 debt redemption. ～액 the amount of debts; indebtedness; liabilities. ～자 a debtor.

**부채질** fanning. ～하다 fan; fan *oneself;* 《선동》 instigate; incite; stir up; 《악화시키다》 make worse; make more serious. ¶ 불난 데 ～하다 add oil to the fire; pour oil on the flame / 허영심을 ～하다 inflate the vanity 《of a woman》 / 교통 체증을 더욱 ～하다 fan the traffic jams even further.

**부처** 《석가모니》 Sakyamuni; Buddha; 《성인》 a Buddhist saint; 《불상》 an image of Buddha; the Buddha; 《사람》 a saint of a man; a saintly person. ¶ ～님 오신 날 the Day of Buddha's Coming / ～님 가운데 토막 같은 사람 a man too saintly to be true; a saint / ～ 밑을 기울이면 삼거웃이 드러난다 《속담》 Everyone has a skeleton in his closet. / ～님한테 설법 《속담》 Teach your grandmother to suck eggs.

**부처**(夫妻) husband and wife; a couple; Mr. and Mrs. ¶ 윌슨 씨 ～ Mr. and Mrs. Wilson; the Wilsons.

**부처꽃** 〖식물〗 a purple loosestrife.

**부척**(副尺) a vernier (scale).

**부쳐지내다** depend 《on *a person*》 for *one's* living; be dependent.

**부촌**(富村) a rich 〔wealthy〕 village.

**부총리**(副總理) a deputy Prime Minister; a vice-premier.

**부총재**(副總裁) a vice-president.

**부추** 〖식물〗 a leek; a scallion. ◉ ～장아찌 leeks soaked in soysauce.

**부추기다** 《선동하다》 stir up; instigate; incite; urge; set 〔spur, egg〕 《*a person*》 on; needle; 《개 따위를》 set 〔turn〕 《a dog》 on 〔at〕 《*a person*》; 《유혹하다》 tempt; entice. ¶ 아무를 부추겨 …하게 하다 set 〔needle〕 *a person* to 《*do*》; incite 〔instigate〕 *a person* to 《an action, *do*》 / 싸움을 ～ egg 《*a person*》 on to fight with 《another》 / 부추겨서 죄를 짓게 하다 abet 《*a person*》 in a crime / 처녀를 부추겨 가출하게 하다 entice a girl away from home.

**부축** helping by holding 《*a person's*》 arms. ～하다 help 《*a person*》; give *one's* arm to. ¶ ～하여 일으키다 help 《*a person*》 up 〔to *his* feet〕 / 부인을 차에서 ～해 내리다 help a lady off 〔out of〕 the car.

**부츠** boots. ¶ ～를 신은 booted.

**부치다**[1] 《힘에》 be beyond *one's* strength 〔power, ability, capacity〕; be too much for 《*one*》. ¶ 힘에 부치는 일 work beyond *one's* power 〔capacity, ability〕 / 그 일은 내 힘에 부친다 I find myself unequal to the task.

**부치다**[2] 《부채를》 fan. ¶ 부채를 ～ use a fan; fan *oneself* / 불을 ～ fan a fire / 숯불을 ～ fan the charcoal fire; fan charcoals into a blaze.

**부치다**[3] ① 《보내다》 send; forward; transmit; consign (상품을); ship (배·차로); dispatch (발송); remit (송금); mail 〔post 《영》〕 《a letter》. ¶ 소포로 ～ send 《*a thing*》 by parcel post / 편지를 ～ send a letter 《to》; mail a letter / 인편에 ～ send 《*a thing*》 through 〔by〕 a person / 기차로 물건을 ～ ship goods by rail / 우편환으로 돈을 ～ remit money by money order. ② 《돌리다》 refer; put; commit; hand over to. ¶ 공판에 ～ commit 《a case》 for trial / 불문에 ～ overlook; pass over / 인쇄에 ～ commit 《it》 to print / 토의에 ～ put 《a question》 to debate; bring 《a question》 up for debate / 회의에 ～ put 〔refer〕 《*a matter*》 to a meeting / 그 사건은 중재에 부쳐질 것이다 The matter will be referred to arbitration.

**부치다**[4] 《논밭을》 cultivate; farm; grow. ¶ 밭을 ～ cultivate a field.

**부치다**[5] 《번철에》 griddle; cook on a griddle; fry. ¶ 달걀을 ～ fry eggs.

**부칙**(附則) additional rules; an additional clause; a supplementary provision.

**부친**(父親) *one's* father.

**부침**(浮沈) 《흥망·성쇠》 rise and fall; ebb and flow; vicissitudes 《of life, fortune》; ups and downs 《of life》; prosperity and adversity. ～하다 rise and fall; ebb and flow; fluctuate; have ups and downs. ¶ ～을 같이하다 cast 〔throw〕 in *one's* lot with 《*a* *person*》; share the smiles and frowns of fortune with 《*a person*》/ 인생에는 ~이 있는 법이다 Life has its ups and downs〔rise and fall〕.

**부침개** a flat cake; panfried food.

**부침하다** sow〔seed〕the field; prepare fields for farming; make a farm.

**부탁**(付託) ① 《맡김》 entrusting; charging; committal; commitment. ~하다 entrust 《*a thing* to *a person*, *a person* with *a thing*》; charge 《*a person* to *do*》; place 《*a thing*, a child》 under 《*a person's*》 charge; commit 《a child》 to 《*a person's*》 care. ¶ 아무에게 일을 ~하다 entrust〔charge〕*a person* with a task / 뒷일을 ~하다 entrust 《*a person*》 with future affairs; give 《*a person*》 the charge of the affairs after *one's* death / 선생님에게 아이 교육을 ~하다 place *one's* child under the care of a teacher.

② 《청함》 asking; a request; a favor; solicitation. ~하다 ask; beg; wish; request; make a request; entreat; implore. ¶ ~을 받고 at another's request / …의 ~으로 at the request of 《*a person*》; at 《*a person's*》 request; by a request from 《*a person*》/ 아무에게 ~해서 through (the courtesy of) *a person* / 친구의 모처럼의 ~이므로 at the pressing request of a friend / ~을 들어주다 comply with〔accede to〕《*a person's*》 request; grant a request; do 《*a person*》 a favor; oblige 《*a person*》/ ~을 거절하다 turn down〔refuse, decline〕《*another's*》 request / 조력을 ~하다 ask 《*a person*》 for help〔assistance〕; look〔turn〕to 《*a person*》 for help / ~이 있다 have a favor to ask of 《*a person*》; wish to make 《*a person*》 a request; wish to ask a favor of 《*a person*》/ ~합니다 Please (do so). / A군을 잘 ~드립니다 I hope you will kindly look after Mr. A. / 이 일을 잘 ~하네 I leave the matter to your discretion. / 이런 일을 ~드려 괜찮을는지요 I hope you will not take it amiss, if I ask you such a thing. / 제 ~ 하나 들어 주시겠습니까 Would you do me a favor? / ~이란 무슨 일인가 What is it that you would have me do? / 제발 가지 말아 주세요. ~입니다 Don't go away, I implore you.

**부탄**[1] 《히말라야 산록의 왕국》 (the Kingdom of) Bhutan. ◉ ~사람 a Bhutanese; a Bhutani (*pl.* ~(s)).

**부탄**[2] 〖화학〗 butane.

**부터** ① 《시간》 from; at; on; in; since (이래); after (이후). (★ from은 현재·과거·미래 어느 것에도 쓰이며 since는 과거에만 사용됨. 따라서 since는 현재〔과거〕 완료와 함께 쓰임).

¶ 아침~ 저녁까지 from morning till evening / 처음~ 끝까지 from beginning to end / 언제~ since when; for how long / 두 시~ 세 시까지 from two to three / 3시 ~는 일이 없다 be free after three o'clock / 다음 ~는 더 조심해라 Be more careful from now on. / 집무 시간: 오전 9시~ 오후 4시까지 Business hours: 9 a.m. — 4 p.m. / 이 법률은 2001년 1월 1일~ 시행한다 This law shall come into force on〔as from〕January 1, 2001. / 역사에 기록되기는 한 3천 년 전~(이)다 It got recorded in history from about 3,000 years ago. / 어릴 때~ 그는 부지런했다 He has been hardworking from his boyhood. (★ 현재완료 문장에는 보통 from을 안 쓰나 from olden times, from *one's* childhood는 예외임).

② 《순서》 beginning with; first; starting from. ¶ … ~ 시작하다 begin with〔at, by, on〕… / 역사~ 공부하다 study beginning with history; study history first / 김씨 댁~ 방문하자 Let's make a round of visits, starting at Mr. Kim's. / 우선 방~ 치우세 Let's start by getting the room cleaned up. / 무엇~ 할까요 What shall I do first? / 너~ 해라 You do first.

③ 《장소》 from; out of; off; through; by; with; at. ¶ 서울~ 부산까지 from Seoul to Pusan / 15페이지 다섯째 줄~ 읽어라 Start reading from line 5, page 15. / 몇 장에서 ~ 시작할까요 What chapter shall we begin with? / 그녀는 방으로 ~ 나왔다 She came out of the room.

④ 《…에게서》 from; of; through. ¶ 친구로~ 온 편지 a letter from a friend 《far away》/ …으로 ~ 독립하다 become independent of…; become self-supporting from… / 자네 얘기는 송군으로 ~ 들었네 I heard of you through Mr. Song.

⑤ 《범위》 (ranging) from 《to…》. ¶ 대체로 2만 원~ 3만 원 사이 all the way from 20,000 won to 30,000 won / 열 살~ 열 다섯 살까지의 아이 children (ranging) from ten to fifteen years old / 초임은 50만원~ 70만원까지다 The commencing salary ranges from 500,000 won to 700,000 won.

**부통령**(副統領) a vice-president (생략 V.P.).

**부티크**《패션 용품점》a boutique.

**부패**(腐敗) ①《썩음》decomposition; rotting; decay; putrefaction. ～하다 rot; go rotten 〔bad〕; putrefy; be decomposed 〔vitiated〕; decay; be spoilt. ¶ ～한 decomposed; putrid; rotten; bad; addled《egg》; tainted《meat》; turned《milk》/ ～하기 쉬운 corruptible; perishable / ～성 화물 perishable cargo / ～하기 쉬운 음식 perishables / ～를 막다 preserve 〔keep〕《*a thing*》from decay / ～하기 쉬움—열을 멀리할 것《게시》Perishable—keep from heat. / 여름에는 식품이 ～하기 쉽다 Foods are apt to「rot 〔go bad〕quickly in summer.
②《타락》corruption; degeneration; degradation; depravity. ～하다 corrupt; rot; degenerate; become corrupt 〔degenerated〕. ¶ 관리의 ～ corruption of government officials / 도덕의 ～ moral taint 〔corruption〕/ ～한 정치가들 corrupt politicians / ～없는 사회 a corruption-free society / 시정(市政)은 수회 행위로 ～되어 있다 The city government has been corrupted through bribery. / 나라의 정치는 ～가 없고 법의 규정이 지켜지는 예측할 수 있는 것이 되어야 한다 The nation's politics must be free of corruption and made to become predictable and ensure the rule of law. / 정부는 중·하위급 공무원에 대한 ～ 척결 운동에 관심을 집중할 것이라고 한다 It is said that the administration will focus its anti-corruption drive on mid-and= lower-level public officials. ◉ ～공무원 a tainted 〔corrupt〕official; a corrupt civil servant. ～균 putrefactive 〔saprogenic〕bacteria. ～물 rotten things; decomposing matter; septic (matter). ～방지제《방부제》an antiseptic; a preservatives. ～산 putrid acid. ～성(性) septicity. ～정치 ward heeling politics. ～추방 운동 an anti= corruption drive.

**부평초**(浮萍草)〖식물〗a duckweed;《떠 있는 풀》a floating weed. ¶ ～ 같은 생활을 하다 lead a precarious life.

**부표**(否票) a "nay" vote; a vote "no"; a negative vote 〔ballot〕. ¶ …에 ～를 던지다 vote against 〔in opposition to〕….

**부표**(浮標)《표지》a (marker) buoy. ◉ ～등 a buoy light. ～설치 buoyage.

**부풀다** ① ⇨ 보풀다. ②《부풀어 오르다》(***a***)《부피가》swell (out, up); get bulky; get big; puff out; fill out (풍선 등이);《팽창하다》become inflated; expand; rise (빵이). ¶ 꽃봉오리가 ～ a bud swells / 살이 ～ flesh swells (up) / 빵이 잘 부풀지 않는다 The bread will not rise. (***b***)《마음이》*one's* bosom heaves; be buoyant《with》. ¶ 그녀는 기대로 가슴이 부풀었다 Expectations heaved her breast. *or* She was buoyant with happy expectations.

**부풀리다** ① ⇨ 보풀리다. ②《부피를》swell (out, up); bulge; fill out; expand;《가스·바람으로》inflate《with gas》; puff; blow up (불어서); raise (이스트로). ¶ 가슴을 ～ heave *one's* breast / (새가) 깃털을 ～ fluff out its plumage / 빵을 ～ raise bread / 풍선을 ～ inflate a toy balloon.

**부품**(部品) parts《of a machine》; spare parts; components. ¶ 자동차 ～ parts of an automobile / 예비 ～ spare parts / 라디오와 ～ a radio set and parts / ～판매업자 a parts supplier / ～을 조립하다 assemble parts into a complete whole.

**부프다** ①《부피가》(be) bulky; voluminous. ¶ 부픈 짐 a bulky package. ②《성질이》(be) impatient; hasty; rash. ¶ 부픈 사람이다 be a rash person.

**부픗하다** ①《부피가》(be) somewhat bulky 〔voluminous〕. ②《말이》(be) exaggerated; magnified.

**부피** bulk; size; volume. ¶ ～가 큰〔있는〕bulky; copious; voluminous; unwieldy; of great bulk 〔size〕/ ～ 큰 물건 articles of a bulky nature.

**부하**(負荷)《짐》a burden; a load;〖전기〗load. ～하다 carry a load 〔burden〕; be loaded. ◉ ～손(損) load loss. ～시험 a load test. ～율 a load factor. ～전동기 a loaded motor.

**부하**(部下) a subordinate; a follower; *one's* men 〔staff〕; men under *one's* charge. ¶ 장교와 ～ an officer and his men / ～ 사병 soldiers 〔men〕under *one's* command / ～가 되다 place *oneself* under《*a person's*》orders / ～를 삼다 place《*a person*》under *one's* orders / …의 ～로서 일하다 serve under《*a person*》/ 당신의 ～가 되고 싶다 I'd like to work under you. / 그는 많은 유능한 ～를 거느리고 있다 He has many able men under him.

**부하다**(富—) ①《부유하다》(be) rich;

wealthy. ② 《몸이》 (be) fat; plump; corpulent.

**부함장**(副艦長) a commander (큰 함선의).

**부합**(符合) coincidence; agreement; correspondence; conformity. ～하다 coincide 〔agree, accord, correspond, conform, tally〕 《with》; be coincident with. ¶ 꼭 ～하다 exactly correspond to / 의견이 ～하다 be in accord with 《*a person's*》 views; concur in opinion 《with *a person*》 / ～하지 않다 do not agree 〔coincide〕 《with》; be inconsistent / 아무의 말과 ～하다 fit in with *a person's* story / (얼굴이) 인상서와 ～하다 《the features》 answer (to) the description / 그의 증언은 사실과 ～한다 His statement tallies 〔fits in〕 with the facts.

**부항**(附缸) cupping a boil. ◉ ～단지 a cupping glass.

**부형**(父兄) *one's* father and (elder) brothers.

**부호**(符號) a mark; a sign; a symbol; a (telegraphic) code. ¶ ～로 쓰다 write 〔jot down〕 in cipher / ～를 붙이다 mark; affix a mark / 그게 무슨 ～이지 What does that symbol stand for? ◉ ～ 분할 다중 접속 〖컴퓨터〗 code division multiple access. ～표 a table of signs; a list of symbols. ～화(化) encoding; encodement: ～화 하다 put 〔convert〕 《information》 into code; encode; code.

**부호**(富豪) a rich 〔wealthy〕 man; a man of wealth; a plutocrat; 《백만 장자》 a millionaire; a billionaire.

**부화**(孵化) hatching; incubation. ～하다 hatch; incubate; sit on 《eggs》. ¶ 병아리를 ～하다 hatch out chickens / 병아리가 ～되다 chickens are (hatched) out. ◉ ～기 an (artificial) incubator. ～장 a hatchery. 인공 ～(법) artificial incubation.

**부화뇌동**(附和雷同) blind following. ～하다 follow blindly; chime in with; follow suit without reflection. ¶ 그는 쉽게 ～할 사람이다 He is apt to follow others blindly. *or* He is easily influenced 〔led〕.

**부활**(復活) 《재생》 revival; rebirth; resurrection; 《재흥》 restoration. ～하다 revive; come to life again; resurrect; be restored 《to the original state》. ¶ 군국주의의 ～ resurgence of militarism / 그리스도의 ～ the Resurrection (of Christ) / ～시키다 revive; resuscitate; restore (to life) / 이전 관계를 ～하다 reestablish former relations / 없어진 풍습을 ～시키다 resurrect an obsolete custom. ◉ ～절 Easter: ～절 전야 Easter eve / ～절 달걀 an Easter egg / ～절 예배 Easter service.

**부회장**(副會長) a vice-president〔-chairman〕.

**부흥**(復興) 《재건》 reconstruction; rehabilitation (복구); 《재흥》 (a) revival; resurgence; restoration; renaissance (문예·예술 등의). ～하다 reconstruct; be reconstructed; rehabilitate; revive; be revived; restore 《to》. ¶ 서울은 잿더미 위에서 ～됐다 Seoul rose from its ashes. / 전후 한국의 눈부신 ～은 세계의 이목을 끌었다 The remarkable recovery 〔rehabilitation〕 of postwar Korea has caught the attention 〔eye〕 of the whole world. ◉ ～목사 a revivalist (preacher). ～사업 reconstruction 〔rehabilitation〕 work. ～회 a revival (service). 경제～ economic revival; an economic comeback.

**북**[1] 《베틀의》 a spindle; a shuttle.

**북**[2] 〖악기〗 a drum; a bass drum (큰); a side 〔high〕 drum (작은). ¶ 북치는 사람 a drummer / 북소리 the sound of a drum / 북을 치다 (beat a) drum / 북은 칠수록 소리가 난다 《속담》 Don't waste argument on such a person.

**북**[3] 《흙》 soil that covers roots; a hill (over roots). ¶ 북을 주다 heap soil around 《a plant》; earth up.

**북**[4] 《소리가》 with a scratch 〔rasp, grate〕; with a rip. ¶ 북 긁다 scratch / 헝겊을 북 찢다 rip a piece of cloth.

**북**(北) north (생략 N). ⇨ 북쪽. ¶ 북의 north; northern; northerly / 북으로 (to the) north; northward(s) / 북으로 가다 go north.

**북경**(北京) Běijing; Peking. ◉ ～원인 〖인류학〗 a Sinanthropus; the Pekin(g) man.

**북괴**(北傀) the North Korean puppet regime. ¶ ～의 끊임없는 군사 위협 the unremitting North Korean military threats.

**북구**(北歐) Northern Europe. ⇨ 북유럽.

**북국**(北國) a northern country. ◉ ～사람 the northerner.

**북극**(北極) 〖지리〗 the North Pole. ¶ ～의 Arctic; polar; pole. ◉ ～고래 〖동물〗 a Greenland whale; a bowhead; a polar whale. ～곰 a polar bear. ～광 ＝극광. ～권 the Arctic Circle 〔Zone〕. ～성 〖천문〗 the Polestar; Polaris; the North Star. ～

양〔해〕 the Arctic Ocean. ~지방 the 「Arctic 〔north polar〕 regions. ~탐험(대) an Arctic expedition (team).

**북녘**(北—) the north(ward); the northern part.

**북단**(北端) the northern 「end 〔extremity〕.

**북대서양**(北大西洋) the North Atlantic (Ocean). ◉ ~ 조약 the North Atlantic 「Treaty 〔Pact〕: ~ 조약 기구 the North Atlantic Treaty Organization (생략 NATO).

**북데기** straw 〔grass〕 refuse; waste 「straw.

**북도**(北道) 《경기도 이북의》 the northern provinces; the provinces north of Gyeonggi; 《남·북도의》 the North (part of a split) province. ◉ 경상~ N. Gyeongsang Province.

**북돋우다** ① 《북주다》 earth up 《plants》; hill (up) 《potatoes》. ② 《원기·힘을》 encourage; urge; stimulate; rouse 《*one's* nerve》; strengthen; invigorate; cheer. ¶ 기운을 ~ fortify *oneself;* strengthen *oneself* / 사기를 ~ heighten 〔stir up, stiffen〕 the morale 《of troops》 / 용기를 ~ encourage; give 《*a person*》 courage; hearten 〔cheer〕 up / 이것이 사기를 북돋우는 최선의 방법이다 This is the best way to raise the morale of the men.

**북동**(北東) northeast (생략 NE). ¶ ~의 northeast(ern) / ~으로 northeastward. ◉ ~풍 a northeasterly wind.

**북두(칠성)**(北斗(七星)) 〖천문〗 the Great Bear; the 「Big 〔Great〕 Dipper; the Plow 《미》; the Ursa Major.

**북류**(北流) ~하다 flow north.

**북면**(北面) ① 《북향》 facing north; 《면》 the north 「side 〔face〕. ~하다 face north. ② 《임금을 섬김》 serving the king as a subject; allegiance. ~하다 serve as a 「subject 〔retainer〕.

**북미**(北美) North America. ⇨ 북아메리카. ◉ 남~ N. and S. America; the two Americas.

**북미동**(北微東) north by east (생략 NbE).

**북미서**(北微西) north by west (생략 「NbW).

**북미주**(北美州) North America.

**북바늘** a guard pin inside a shuttle.

**북반구**(北半球) the Northern hemisphere.

**북방**(北方) 《북쪽》 the north(ward); the northern direction; 《지방》 a northern district. ¶ ~의 northern; northerly / ~에 in (the direction of) the north / ~으로 northwards; toward the north / 그 호수는 서울 ~ 15킬로 지점에 있다 The lake lies 15 kilometers (to the) north of Seoul. ◉ ~민족 a northern race. ~불교 the northern sects of Buddhism. ~정책 a northward policy; a Nordpolitik. ~한계선 the Northern Limit 〔Boundary〕 Line (생략 NLL, NBL).

**북벌**(北伐) an expedition to conquer the north. ~하다 send an expedition to conquer the north.

**북부**(北部) 《in》 the north; the northern part 《of》. ¶ ~산악 지대 the northern mountain area / 뉴욕 주~ upper New York State / 옛날 사당은 시 ~에 있다 The ancient shrine stands 「in 〔to〕 the north of the city. (★ in은 시내에, to는 시외에 있음을 뜻함).

**북북동**(北北東) north-northeast (생략 「NNE).

**북북서**(北北西) north-northwest (생략 NNW).

**북빙양**(北氷洋) the Arctic Ocean.

**북상**(北上) going north; northing. ~하다 go 〔come〕 up north; move northward. ¶ 태풍〔한랭전선〕이 ~중이다 The 「typhoon 〔cold front〕 is moving northward.

**북새** hustle; bustle; commotion; hubbub. ¶ ~놓다 hustle and bustle; make 〔kick up〕 a row; disturb / ~통에 아이를 잃다 lose *one's* child in the 「hustle and bustle 〔confusion of the crowd〕 / ~통에 잠입하다 sneak in during the confusion. ◉ ~판 a confusion; the 「scene 〔site〕 of a commotion.

**북서**(北西) northwest (생략 NW). ⇨ 서북.

**북송**(北送) repatriation to the north. ~하다 repatriate to the north. ◉ ~선(船) a repatriation ship (to the north). 재일 ~교포 a Korean repatriate (to the north) from Japan.

**북슬개** a big shaggy dog.

**북슬북슬하다** (be) plump and hairy; 「shaggy.

**북아메리카**(北—) North America. ◉ ~원주민 an American Indian. ~자유 무역 협정 the North American Free Trade Agreement (생략 NAFTA).

**북안**(北岸) the north(ern) shore 〔coast〕.

**북양**(北洋) the north 「ocean 〔sea〕; the northern waters. ◉ ~어업 north-sea fisheries.

**북어**(北魚) a dried pollack. ◉ ~찜 seasoned and steamed pollack.

**북위**(北緯) the north latitude (생략 N.L.). ¶ ~ 32도 35분에 at 〔in〕 「32 degrees 35 minutes 〔32°35′〕 north latitude (★ latitude thirty-two degrees thirty-five minutes north로 읽음) / 그 당

시 그 배는 ~ 15도 서경 31도 해상에 있었다 The ship was in latitude 15° North and in longitude 31° West at that time.
◉ ~선 north parallel; north latitude.

**북유럽**(北一) Northern Europe. ¶ ~의 Scandinavian; North European. ◉ ~사람 a Scandinavian; a Northern European. ~신화 Norse mythology.

**북잡이** the drummer in a band of mendicant priests.

**북적거리다** bustle; jostle; congest; jam 〔crowd, throng〕 together; be in a bustle 〔commotion〕; be congested 《with》. ¶ 북적거리는 군중 a jostling crowd; a seething mass of people / 북적거리는 거리 a crowded 〔bustling〕 street / 거리는 사람들로 북적거린다 The streets are crowded 〔thronged〕 with people.

**북적북적** in a bustle; full of stir; tumultuously; bustling; jostling; in clamor; in uproar.

**북진**(北進) ~하다 go 〔march〕 north; sail northward.

**북쪽**(北一) the north(ward); the north side. ¶ ~의 north; northern; northerly / ~에 to 〔on〕 the north 《of》; in (the direction of ) the north / ~으로 northward(s); north; toward the north; to the north (★ in the north of는 어떤 지역의 일부분으로 그 「북부에 위치하고 있는」 경우: Russia is in the north of Europe. on the north of는 「…의 북에 접해 있는」 경우: Canada lies on the north of the United States. to the north of는 「…의 북쪽에」의 뜻: Boston is to the north of New York. toward the north는 「북쪽으로」 즉 북쪽으로 접근하는 것이며 반드시 도착의 뜻을 포함하는 것은 아님). / 시의 ~ 20마일 되는 곳에 20 miles (to the) north of the city / ~으로 향해 가다 go north; go towards the north / 어디가 ~이냐 Which way is north?

**북창**(北窓) a north window 〔light〕.

**북채** a drumstick.

**북천**(北天) the northern sky.

**북춤** 《perform》 a drum dance.

**북태평양**(北太平洋) the North Pacific (Ocean).

**북통**(一筒) a drum frame; the (wooden) body of a drum; a drum.

**북편**(北便) the northern part 〔side〕; the north. ¶ ~에 on the north side 《of》.

**북풍**(北風) a north wind; a northerly wind. ¶ 차디찬 ~ a freezing 〔biting, piercing〕 north wind / ~이 살을 에는 듯이 차다 The north wind cuts like a blade. / ~으로 변했다 The wind has gone round 〔turned〕 to the north.

**북한**(北韓) North Korea. ¶ ~ 문제 전문가 an expert on North Korean affairs / 친~의 pro-Pyongyang.

**북해**(北海) 《영국 북쪽의》 the North Sea; 《북쪽의》 a northern sea.

**북행**(北行) going north; northing. ~하다 go (up) north.

**북향**(北向) a northern aspect 〔exposure〕; facing north. ~하다 face (the) north. ◉ ~집 a house facing north.

**북회귀선**(北回歸線) the tropic of Cancer.

**분** as esteemed person. ¶ 손님 두 분 two customers; two guests / 이〔저〕분 this 〔that〕 gentleman 〔lady〕; this 〔that〕 (honored) person / 한두 분 a couple of people / K라는 분 a gentleman named K; a (certain) Mr. K / 그런 이름을 가진 분 a gentleman of that name / 오늘 몇 분이나 오십니까 How many people are you expecting today?

**분**(分) ① 《1 / 10》 one-tenth; a tenth. ⇨푼. ¶ 칠팔분의 가망이 있다 have seven or eight chances out of ten.
② 《시간·각도 등의》 a minute 《of an hour, of a degree》. ¶ 10분 ten minutes / 한 시간 30분 one hour and thirty minutes / 두시 15분 a quarter after 〔past〕 two / 15분 a quarter 《of an hour》; fifteen minutes / 30분 half an hour; 《미》 a half hour; thirty minutes / 3시 25분발(發) 열차 the 3:25 train; the train leaving at 3:25 (★ three twenty-five라고 읽음.) / 북위 30도 10분, 30 degrees 10 minutes north latitude: 30° 10′ N. Lat. / 1시 10분 전입니다 It's a ten minutes to 〔of 《미》, before〕 one. / 7시 20분입니다 It is twenty minuets past seven. *or* It's seven twenty. (★ 「시」와 「분」은 그때 그때의 발음상의 편리에 따라서 둘 다 생략해서 숫자만을 말할 때가 있음. 30분(half)을 경계로 해서 그때까지를 past, 그것을 지나면 to를 쓰는 것이 보통임. 「조금 전」 또는 「조금 지났음」이라고 말할 경우에는 before, 또는 after를 사용함: a little before 〔after〕 three).
③ 《분수·신분》 *one's* lot 〔status, place〕; *one's* social standing; means (자력). ⇨분수. ¶ 분에 만족하다 be contented with *one's* lot / 분에 맞게 살다 live within *one's* means; live up to *one's* income / 선생의 말씀 분에 넘칩니다

Your words are more than I deserve. ④《푼》 10 tael (중국 등지의 중량·화폐 단위); penny (중량). ⑤《본분》 *one's* duty; *one's* part.

**분**(忿) 《분개》 indignation; vexation; chagrin; mortification; 《분격》 ire; wrath; anger; rage. ¶ 분김에 in *one's* vexation 〔mortification〕; out of chagrin; for 〔out of, from〕 spite / (남의) 분을 돋우다 fan 《*a person's*》 anger; add insult to injury / 분을 풀다 wreak *one's* anger 〔vent *one's* spite〕 《on》 / 분을 참지 못하다 lose *one's* temper; get angry; get out of patience.

**분**(盆) 《화분》 a flowerpot. ¶ 분받침 a flower stand / 분에 꽃을 가꾸다 grow a flower in a pot / 분에 심어 놓으면 못된 풀도 화초라 한다 《속담》 Position alone breeds respect.

**분**(粉) toilet 〔face〕 powder; powder. ¶ 분을 바르다 powder 〔paint〕 *one's* face; put powder on *one's* face / 분을 처덕처덕 바르다 make a heavy toilet; paint 《*one's* face》 thick; powder 《*one's* face》 thickly.

**분**(糞) excrement; feces. ⇨ 똥.

**-분**(分) ① 《부분》 a part. ¶ 2분의 1, one-half; a half / 3 분의 1, a third (part); one-third / 3 분의 2, two-thirds / 4 분의 1, one-fourth; a quarter / 4 분의 3, three-fourths; three quarters / 10 분의 7, seven-tenths (★ 2 7/8은 two and seven-eights; 172 / 256는 a hundred and seventy-two over two hundred and fifty-six로 읽음) / 5 만분의 1 지도 a map on the scale of 1:50,000 / 나는 8과 4분의 1의 모자를 쓴다 I wear a size eight-and-a quarter hat. ② 《몫》 a share; a part; a portion; 《일정량》 amount; quantity; enough for; 《함유량》 content; the percentage; supply (비축). ¶ 알코올분 alcoholic content; the percentage of alcohol / 세 사람분의 점심 enough lunch for three persons / 열 사람분의 일 the amount of work sufficient for ten persons / 2 일분의 양식 food for two days / 식사 5인분 dinner for five / 한 겨울분의 땔감 a winter's supply of fuel / 3 일분의 약입니다 Here is medicine for three days.

**분가**(分家) a branch 〔cadet〕 family. ～하다 establish 〔set up〕 a branch family; create a new family.

**분간**(分揀) (a) distinction; discrimination. ～하다 distinguish 〔discriminate〕 《A from B, between A and B》; know 〔can tell〕 《A from B》; 《식별하다》 discern. ¶ ～하기 어려운 indistinguishable / ～을 못 하다 cannot discriminate 〔distinguish〕 《between *things,* A from B》; cannot tell 《A from B》; have no sense of discrimination / ～ 못 할 정도로 beyond 〔out of〕 recognition; indistinguishably / 선악을 ～ 못 하다 cannot distinguish good from evil / 어둠 속에서 사람들 얼굴을 ～하다 distinguish people's faces in the darkness / 그는 전후 사정도 ～ 못할 만큼 술을 마셨다 He drank till his reason was gone. / 뭐가 뭔지 ～을 못 하겠다 I cannot tell which is which.

**분갑**(粉匣) a (powder) compact; a puff case.

**분개**(分介) 『부기』 journalizing. ～하다 journalize. ◉ ～장(帳) 《enter in》 a journal.

**분개**(憤慨) indignation; resentment. ～하다 resent; be enraged 《at 〔against〕 *a thing*, with *a person*》; take offense 《at》; be indignant 《at, over》; burn with indignation; chafe 《at》; get very angry 〔get mad 《구어》〕 《with *a person*, at 〔about〕 *a thing*》; be scandalized 《at, by》. ¶ ～하여 in a rage; in resentment; indignantly / ～시키다 exasperate; enrage; incense; infuriate; provoke; stir 《*a person's*》 blood; rouse 〔stir〕 the gorge 《of *a person*》 / 나는 그의 말을 듣고 ～하였다 I was angry at what he said. / 사장의 불공평한 처사에 ～하여 그는 사직했다 He left the company indignant at the partiality of the president.

**분격**(憤激) exasperation; resentment. ～하다 be exasperated 〔infuriated〕; flare up; get enraged; blow *one's* top; be inflamed by anger.

**분견**(分遣) detachment; detail. ～하다 detach; detail; draft; tell off. ◉ ～대 a detachment; a detached force; a contingent. ～소 an outstation. ～함대 a detached fleet.

**분결같다**(粉—) be smooth and white; be velvety. ¶ 얼굴이 ～ have a fair-skinned face.

**분계**(分界) 《한계》 delimitation; demarcation; 《지계》 the boundary; the border. ～하다 demarcate; delimit; mark the bounds 《of》. ◉ ～선 a boundary line; a demarcation line: ～선을 긋다 draw a demarcation line 《between》.

**분골쇄신**(粉骨碎身) ～하다 ① 《힘쓰다》 do *one's* best; do everything in *one's*

power; exert *oneself* to the utmost; make strenuous efforts. ②《비참하게 죽다》 die tragically; meet (with) a tragic death 〔end〕. 「mill, *etc.*〕.
**분공장**(分工場) a branch factory 〔plant,
**분과**(分科) a department; a section; a branch; a course 《of study》. ¶ 물리학은 과학의 한 ～이다 Physics is a branch of science. ◉ ～위원회 a subcommittee (meeting).
**분과**(分課) a subdivision 《of a section》; a section of a bureau; a section; a branch. ～하다 divide 《an office》; divide 《a bureau》 into sections.
**분관**(分館) an annex; a detached building; 《도서관의》 a branch library.
**분광**(分光) 〖물리〗 a spectrum. ◉ ～계 a spectrometer. ～기 a spectroscope: 질량 ～기 a mass spectrograph. ～분석 spectroscopic 〔spectrum〕 analysis. ～사진 a spectrogram: ～사진기 a spectrograph. ～학 spectroscopy.
**분교**(分校) a branch school. ¶ 이 학교의～ a branch of this school.
**분국**(分局) a branch office 〔bureau〕.
**분권**(分權) decentralization of power 〔authority〕. ～하다 decentralize power. ◉ ～주의 decentralism. 지방～ decentralization.
**분규**(紛糾) a complication; (an) entanglement; an imbroglio; tangle; confusion; distraction; disorder; a trouble (싸움). ¶ 당내의 ～ an intraparty row / ～를 일으키다 cause 〔raise, make〕 trouble; have a 〔get into〕 trouble 《with》/ ～를 거듭하다 pile confusion upon confusion; grow more and more confused / 학원 ～는 아직 결말이 나지 않았다 The campus dispute has not been settled yet.
**분극**(分極) 〖물리〗 polarization. ¶ ～화하다 polarize. ◉ ～작용 polarizing action; polarization. 「apportion.
**분급**(分給) ～하다 distribute; allocate;
**분기**(分岐) divergence; ramification; forking. ～하다 diverge 《from a center, from a main course》; branch off; fork; ramify. ¶ 이 선로는 여기에서 ～하여 광주에 이른다 This line branches off here and leads to Kwangju. ◉ ～선 a branch (line); a spur track; a turnout track. ～점 a diverging 〔turning〕 point; a fork (길의); a crossroad; a junction (철도의).
**분기**(噴氣) ejection; spouting 《of gas》. ～하다 eject; spout; emit. ◉ ～공(孔) 〖지질〗 a fumarole (화산의); 〖기계〗 a steam valve; a gas escape; 《고래의》 a blowhole; a spout.
**분기**(奮起) stirring up; bestirring *oneself*. ～하다 rouse 〔brace〕 *oneself* (up) (to action); be stirred up; bestir *oneself;* come forward; brace *one's* nerve. ¶ ～시키다 stir 〔shake〕 up; rouse 《*a person*》 (in)to activity; brace up 《*a person*》; put 《*a person*》 on his mettle / 톰의 말에 나는 ～했다 I was encouraged by what Tom said.
**분기**(分期) three months (of a year); a quarter year; a quarter of a year. ¶ 3～ 중에 during 〔in〕 the third quarter of the year.
**분김**(忿―) ¶ ～에 in a fit of anger; in (*one's*) mortification; out of vexation 〔chagrin〕; from 〔out of〕 spite / 단지 ～에 집에 방화하다 set fire to a house solely from spite.
**분꽃**(粉―) 〖식물〗 a four-o'clock; a marvel-of-Peru.
**분납**(分納) payment in installments; installment paying 〔delivery〕. ～하다 deliver 《goods》 in installments; pay 《*one's* school fees》 by 〔in〕 installments.
**분내**(粉―) the smell of face powder.
**분네**《분들》 esteemed persons; 《분》 an esteemed person. ¶ 방금 나가신 ～가 누구냐 Who is the man who just left?
**분노**(忿怒·憤怒) anger; wrath; rage; resentment; indignation; exasperation. ～하다 get 〔become〕 angry; fly into a rage; be exasperated 〔indignant〕; flare up; be up in arms 《against》. ¶ ～한 나머지 in a fit of passion 〔fury〕/ ～에 찬 목소리 an angry voice / 끓어오르는 ～와 비탄 a raging indignation and bitterness / ～케 하다 enrage; exasperate; rouse 〔stir〕 the gorge 《of》/ ～에 못 이기다 give way to anger / ～를 가라앉히다 quell 〔appease〕 *one's* anger / ～가 가라앉다 *one's* anger cools; [사람이 주어] relent / ～를 누르다 suppress 〔repress〕 *one's* anger 〔wrath〕/ ～를 사다 incur 〔arouse, provoke〕 《*a person's*》 wrath 〔displeasure〕/ ～를 터뜨리다 betray 〔vent〕 *one's* anger; give vent to *one's* indignation.
**분뇨**(糞尿) excrementitious matter; feces and urine; human waste; excretions; excreta; night soil. ◉ ～관(管) a soil pipe. ～ 소각 장치 a night-soil incinerator. ～수거인 a night-soil man. ～차 a dung cart; a honey wagon. ～

처리 sewage disposal.

**분단**(分團) a (local) branch; a chapter 《of an organization》; a section 《of a class》. ◉ ～학습 group learning.

**분단**(分斷) dividing into sections; division; partition. ～하다 divide (into sections); partition. ¶ 한반도의 비극적인 ～ the tragic division of the Korean peninsula / 한반도의 ～을 영구화하려는 음모 a plot to perpetuate the division of the Korean peninsula.
◉ ～국 a divided country 〔nation〕.

**분담**(分擔) 《일의》 division of labor 〔jobs, a job〕; allotment; 《책임의》 partial responsibility 〔charge〕; taking a share 《in》. ～하다 divide; split up 《a job》; undertake partial responsibility for; take charge of; take a share in; bear a part of 《the expenses, the loss》. ¶ ～된 일 an allotted task / 손해 ～ apportionment of a loss / 비용을 ～하다 bear expenses in common; share expenses 《with one another》/ 비용을 똑같이 ～하다 bear an equal share of the expense / 일을 ～하다 take over a portion of the work; divide work 《among》/ 일을 각자에게 ～시키다 allot a portion of the work to each. ◉ ～금 a share of expenses; allotted charges; a contribution (공동해손의). ～액 an allotment; an allotted amount. ～자 a sharer; a partaker.

**분당**(分黨) secession 《from a political party》; 《당》 a party split; a splinter party. ～하다 secede 《from a political organization》. ◉ ～파 the seceders; the separatists.

**분대** ⇨ 분대질. ◉ ～꾼 a troublemaker; a meddler; an intruder.

**분대**(分隊) 〖군사〗 a squad (육군); a division (해군); a detachment (지대); a party (분견대). ◉ ～장 a squad leader (육군); a division officer (해군).

**분대질** 《참견》 meddling; interference; 《교란·방해》 disturbance; 《말썽》 (making) trouble; 《소란》 fuss; 《귀찮음》 bother; 《폐끼침》 nuisance. ～치다, ～하다 make a nuisance of *oneself;* bother 〔upset, disturb〕 people; meddle; interrupt; interfere.

**분도기**(分度器) a protractor.

**분동**(分銅) a (balance) weight; a counterbalance; a counterweight.
◉ ～저울 a balance.

**분란**(紛亂) 《혼란》 disorder; confusion; 《분쟁》 a trouble. ～하다 [서술적] be in disorder 〔confusion〕; be in a tangle. ¶ ～을 틈타서 in the confusion of the moment; taking advantage of the confusion / ～을 일으키다 cause 〔stir up〕 trouble; make trouble.

**분량**(分量) a quantity; a measure; an amount; a dose (약의). ¶ 많은〔적은〕 ～ a large 〔small〕 quantity 〔dose〕/ ～을 늘리다〔줄이다〕 increase 〔decrease〕 the quantity 《of》/ ～이 늘다〔줄다〕 gain 〔diminish〕 in quantity / ～을 재다 calculate 〔measure〕 the quantity 《of》/ 약의 ～을 잘못 주다 give a wrong dose of medicine; misdose / ～을 정해서 마시다 drink in fixed quantities.

**분력**(分力) 〖물리〗 a component (force).

**분류**(分流) a tributary; a branch. ～하다 branch from 《a large river》.

**분류**(分溜) 〖화학〗 fractional distillation; fractionation. ～하다 fractionate; crack. ◉ ～관 a fractionating column; a distilling tube. ～장치 a fractionator.

**분류**(分類) classification; grouping; assortment; 〖생물〗 diagnosis. ～하다 classify; divide into classes; group; sort; assort. ¶ 물품의 ～ classification of goods / ～하기 곤란한 종(種) a critical species / 두 종류로 ～하다 group 《*things*》 into two classes / 장르별로 ～하다 group by genre / 세세히 ～하다 classify into small groups / 크게 셋으로 ～하다 classify into three large groups / 식물을 각 부문별로 ～하다 classify plants into orders / 알파벳 순으로 ～하다 classify 〔arrange〕 in alphabetical order / 우편물을 ～하다 (as)sort mail. ◉ ～기준 a classificatory criterion. ～목록 a classified catalog(ue). ～번호 a class number (도서 따위의). ～법 a classification system; a system of categorization. ～표 a classified list 〔table〕. ～학 taxonomy; taxology; the science of classification: ～학자 a taxonomist.

**분류**(奔流) a rapid 〔rushing〕 stream; tumbling waters; a torrent; rapids; a flush. ～하다 rush; flush; run with rapidity; dash along. ¶ ～에 휩쓸려 내려가다 be swept away by the torrent.

**분리**(分離) separation; secession; disunion; severance; disjunction; division; split; 《이탈》 detachment; breakaway; 《절연》 isolation; 《흑·백인의》 segregation. ～하다 《떼어놓다》 separate; secede; disjoin; disconnect; split; detach; isolate; segregate; 《떨어지다》 be separated 《from》; be divided 《from》; be isolated 《from》; secede

〔sever〕 *oneself* 《from》. ¶ 중앙 ~대 《도로 상의》 a median strip 《미》; a central reserve 《영》 / ~할 수 없는 inseparable; indivisible / 우유에서 크림을 ~하다 separate cream from milk / 정치와 종교를 ~하다 separate politics from religion.

◉ ~계수법 『수학』 a method of detached coefficients. ~과세 separate taxation. ~기(器) a separator: 원심 ~기 a centrifugal separator. ~론〔주의〕 separatism; secessionism. ~법 a method of chemical separation (화학의). ~불안 『심리』 separation anxiety. ~심리(審理) separate trial. ~주의자 a separatist; a secessionist; 《흑·백인의》 a segregationist. ~파 seceders; separatists. 재산 ~ separation of property.

**분리수거**(分離收去) segregated collection. ¶ 쓰레기 ~ segregated garbage collection; collection of garbage similar in kind.

**분립**(分立) separation; segregation; independence. ~하다 set up independently; become independent 《of》; separate 〔segregate, secede〕 《from》. ¶ A, B, C, D가 ~하고 있다 A, B, C and D are independent of one another. / 그는 자회사를 ~했다 He set up an independent subsidiary company.

**분만**(分娩) parturition; childbirth; delivery. ~하다 give birth to; be delivered of; be brought to bed 《of a child》. ¶ 사내 아이를 ~하다 give birth to 〔be delivered of〕 a boy. ◉ ~실 a delivery 〔labor〕 room; a maternity ward. ~휴가 maternity leave.

**분말**(粉末) powder; dust. ¶ ~의 powdered / ~로 만들다 powder; reduce to 〔grind into〕 powder; pulverize.

**분망**(奔忙) being busy. ~하다 (be) busy; [서술적] be occupied 〔heavily engaged, rushed〕; be pressed 《for time》. ¶ …준비에 ~하다 be very busy preparing for… / …하는 데 몹시 ~하다 be fully occupied 〔be busily engaged〕 in *do*ing.

**분매**(分賣) selling separately 〔singly〕. ~하다 sell 《*things*》 separately 〔singly〕.

**분명**(分明) clearness; obviousness. ~하다 (be) clear; plain; obvious; distinct; patent; explicit; evident; vivid (기억이); 《확실하다》 (be) sure; positive. ¶ ~한 기억 a vivid recollection / ~한 대답 a definite answer / ~한 사실 a plain truth; an obvious fact / ~한 음성 a clear voice / ~한 증거 clear 〔positive〕 evidence; an evident proof / ~해지다 become clear 〔plain〕; come clear 《to *one*》; 《확인되다》 be ascertained 〔confirmed〕; 《알게 되다》 be (made) known; come 〔be brought〕 to light; be revealed 〔bared〕 / ~하지 않다 be indistinct 〔vague, unclear〕; be ill-defined 〔inarticulate〕 / 네가 틀린 것은 ~하다 It is clear that you are all wrong.

**분명히**(分明—) clearly; plainly; distinctly; definitely; evidently; obviously; explicitly; 《확실히》 undoubtedly; positively. ¶ ~ 하다 clarify; make 《*a matter*》 clear 〔plain〕; clear (up) 《the cause》; throw 〔cast, shed〕 light on 《the meaning》 / ~ 말하다 tell frankly 〔pointedly〕 / ~ 기억하고 있다 have a clear recollection of; remember clearly 〔distinctly〕 / 태도를 ~ 하다 define 〔clarify〕 *one's* attitude; make *one's* attitude clear / 태도를 ~ 하지 않다 do not commit *oneself;* be noncommittal 《on an issue》 / ~ 말하면 to put it flatly; to be candid.

**분모**(分母) 『수학』 a denominator. ¶ ~를 없애다 cancel a denominator.

**분묘**(墳墓) a grave; a tomb.

**분무**(噴霧) 『화학』 atomizing. ◉ ~기 a spray(er); a vaporizer; a pulverizer; an atomizer (향수용); a nebulizer (의료용). ~도장(塗裝) spraying; spray painting.

**분문**(噴門) 『해부』 the esophageal 〔cardiac〕 orifice (of the stomach); the cardia.

**분바르다**(粉—) powder 〔paint〕 《*one's* face》. ⇨ 분(粉).

**분받침**(盆—) a pottery flowerpot holder.

**분발**(奮發) strenuous efforts; a spurt; exertion. ~하다 exert *oneself;* make strenuous efforts; put forth *one's* efforts; redouble *one's* efforts; spurt; bestir 〔stir up〕 *oneself.* ¶ 다시 한번 ~하다 make another exertion / 아무를 ~시키다 inspire *a person* with courage; rouse *a person* 《into activity》.

◉ ~심 the spirit of exertion; a strenuous spirit; enthusiasm.

**분방하다**(奔放—) (be) wild; extravagant; free(-spirited); unrestrained. ¶ 분방히〔하게〕 wildly; without restraint / 자유분방하게 살다 lead a free, unrestrained 〔uninhibited〕 life.

**분배**(分配) division; sharing; 《배급》 distribution; 《할당》 allotment; apportionment. ~하다 divide; split; share (out); distribute; portion (out); allocate; allot; give out.

> (용법) **divide** distribute와 share의 두 가지 뜻이 있으나, 목적이나 계획에 따라, 반대나 거절의 표시가 없는 한, 균등하게 「나누다」란 뜻. **share** 물건을 「나누어 주거나 사용하도록 하다」란 뜻. 경험·고통·기쁨 따위 추상적인 것도 서로 나누다란 뜻이 포함됨. 분배자는 분배의 몫을 차지한다는 뜻이 있음. **distribute** 한정되어 있는 수량의 물건을 비슷하게 나누어 준다는 뜻. 배분하는 사람은 몫을 취하지 않는다는 뜻을 함축함. **give out** distribute의 구어적 표현.

¶ 부의 ~ distribution of wealth / ~에 참여하다〔를 받다〕 have 〔get〕 a share of 《*something*》; participate 〔share〕 in 《the profits》/ 식량〔양식〕을 ~하다 serve 〔give〕 out rations; measure out food to 《the poor》/ 재산을 세 자녀에게 균등하게 ~하다 divide *one's* property equally among three children / 이익을 ~해 주다 distribute the profits 《among *one's* employees》/ 강도들은 훔친 물건을 ~했다 The robbers split the loot.
◉ ~금 a dividend. ~론 a theory of distribution. ~액 a share. ~자 a portioner; a distributor.

**분별**(分別) ① 《구분》 division; 《분리》 separation; 《차이의》 distinction; discrimination; 《분류》 classification; assortment. ⇨ 분간(分揀). ~하다 《구분하다》 divide; 《구별하다》 separate; distinguish; discriminate; 《분류하다》 classify; fractionate. ¶ 방향을 ~ 못하다 cannot tell the direction.
② 《사려분별》 discretion; prudence; 《양식》 wisdom; good sense; 《판단》 judgment. ~하다 judge; discern; use 〔exercise〕 discretion. ¶ ~이 있다 be sensible; have discretion 〔good sense〕; know where *one* stands / ~이 있는 discreet; prudent; thoughtful; sensible; wise / ~이 없는 indiscreet; imprudent; thoughtless; ill-advised; rash / ~이 생기다 attain *one's* years of discretion; cut *one's* wisdom teeth / ~을 잃다 lose *one's* wits 〔mind〕; lose control of *oneself* / ~ 없는 짓을 하다 commit a rash act; do something rash /그는 ~ 있는 남자다 He is a man of sense. / 그 정도의 ~은 있어야 하지 않겠느냐 You should know better than that.

**분봉**(分封) 〖역사〗 enfeoffment. ~하다 enfeoff; invest 《*a person*》 with a fief.

**분봉**(分蜂) hiving off; splitting the hive. ~하다 hive off; split the hive.

**분부**(分付·吩咐) the bidding of a superior; an order; a command; 《지시》 directions. ~하다 bid; order; command. ¶ ~대로 하다 do as *one* is bidden 〔told〕; act in obedience to orders / ~를 어김없이 거행하다 carry out orders to the letter / …하라는〔하지 말라는〕 ~를 받다 have orders to 〔not to〕 《*do*》/ 시키실 일이 있으면 언제건 ~만 내리십시오 Whenever you want me, I am at your service.

**분분하다**(紛紛―) 《뒤숭숭하다》 (be) confused; complicated; scattered; pell=mell; tumultuous; noisy; turbulent; 《의견 등이》 (be) diverse; various; divided. ¶ 분분한 세상 a turbulent 〔troubled〕 world; an unsettled world / 의견이 ~ vary 〔be divergent〕 in opinion 《as to》/ 제설(諸說)이 ~ There are diversities of opinions. / 우리는 이 문제에 관해 의견이 ~ We find a wide range of opinion(s) on this point.

**분비**(分泌) 〖생물〗 secretion. ~하다 secrete. ¶ ~를 돕는〔촉진하는〕 secernent; secretive. ◉ ~관 a secretory vessel. ~기관 a secernent; a secretory organ. ~물 a secretion; an exudate. ~선(腺) a secreting gland; a secretor. ~세포 a secreting cell. ~액 secreting fluid; juice. ~작용 secretion.

**분사**(分詞) 〖문법〗 a participle. ◉ ~구〔절〕 a participial phrase 〔clause〕. ~구문 a participial construction. ~형 a participal form. 과거〔현재〕~ a past 〔present〕 participle.

**분사**(憤死) ~하다 die of indignation 〔resentment〕; die in a fit of anger.

**분사**(噴射) jet; spray; injection. ~하다 jet; spout; eject. ¶ 엔진이 화염을 ~한다 The engine jets (out) flames.
◉ ~관〔노즐〕 an injection pipe 〔nozzle〕. ~식 a jet-type: ~식 추진기 a jet propeller. ~추진 jet 〔rocket〕 propulsion: ~추진식 비행기 a jet-propelled 〔jet-engined〕 airplane / ~ 추진 기관 a jet engine.

**분산**(分散) ① 《흩어짐》 breakup; dispersion; decentralization; divergence. ~하다 break up; scatter; disperse; decentralize. ¶ 위험 ~ 〖경제〗 diversification of risks / 산업을 지방으로 ~시키는 것이 필요하다 It is necessary to decentralize industries into the coun-

tryside. ②〖물리〗 dispersion; 〖천문〗 disintegration. ～하다 disperse 《rays into colors》; be dispersed. ¶ 빛의 ～ dispersion of light / 프리즘은 빛을 ～한다 A prism 「breaks up 〔disperses〕 light. ③《파산》 bankruptcy.
◉ ～데이터처리시스템 a distributed data processing system (생략 DDP(S)). ～도 degree of dispersion. ～성 dispersibility. ～율 the index of dispersion. ～투자 diversified investment.

**분상**(粉狀) ¶ ～의 powdered; pulverized; powdery; powder-like.

**분서**(焚書) book burning. ～하다 burn books. ◉ ～갱유 〖역사〗 burning books on the Chinese classics and burying Confucian scholars alive.

**분석**(分析) analysis; 《금속의》 assay; assaying. ～하다 analyze; make an analysis of; reduce 〔break down〕 《*a thing*》 to its elements; resolve; assay 《a drug, an alloy》. ¶ 시료를 ～하다 analyze the sample / 실패의 원인을 ～하다 analyze the cause of failure / 위의 내용물을 ～하다 analyze the stomach contents 《for poison》 / ～한 결과 이것은 비타민 B를 함유하고 있음이 판명되었다 Analysis showed that it contained vitamin B. ◉ ～자 an analyst; an assayer. ～적 사고 analytic thinking. ～표 an analysis table. ～학 analytics: ～학자 an analyst. ～화학 analytical chemistry.

**분설**(分設) establishment of a branch. ～하다 establish 〔set up, install〕 a branch 《of》.

**분성**(分性) 〖물리〗 divisibility.

**분손**(分損) 〖보험〗 partial loss.

**분쇄**(粉碎) pulverization; 〖토목〗 grinding. ～하다 《가루로 하다》 pulverize; reduce to powder; 《부수다》 shatter 〔smash, dash〕 to pieces; break into fragments; crush. ¶ 적의 기도를 ～하다 frustrate an opponent's plan / 적군을 ～하다 crush 〔annihilate〕 the enemy / (상대의) 주장을 ～하다 demolish 《*a person's*》 argument.
◉ ～기 a pulverizer; a grinder; a crusher; a muller; a mill (수동식).

**분쇠**(粉—) lead used in making (skin) powder.

**분수**(分水) the diversion 〔shedding〕 of water. ◉ ～선〔계〕 a watershed.

**분수**[1](分數) ① 《사려 분별》 discretion; propriety; good sense; judgment; discrimination; 《한도》 a limit; bounds. ¶ ～ 없는 indiscreet; imprudent; thoughtless / ～ 있는 sensible; thoughtful; discreet / ～ 없는 짓 a rash act / ～ 없다 have no sense of propriety; be impertinent; be impudent / 그는 ～ 없이 말을 한다 He doesn't know when to shut up. / 농담을 해도 ～가 있지 You carry your joke too far. ② 《분한(分限)》 *one's* lot 〔status〕; *one's* place; *one's* social standing 〔station〕; *one's* means. ¶ ～를 알다 know *one's* place 〔station in life〕 / ～를 모르다 fail to know *oneself* 〔*one's* place〕; be self-conceited / ～를 잊다 forget *oneself;* get above *oneself* / ～를 지키다 keep to *one's* sphere 〔station〕 in life; keep within (due) bounds / ～에 맞게 〔맞지 않게〕 살다 live within 〔above〕 *one's* means / ～에 맞게 기부하다 give *one's* bit.

**분수**[2](分數) 〖수학〗 a fraction; a fractional number. ¶ ～의 fractional / ～로 나누다 fractionize; divide into fractions. ◉ ～방정식 a fractional equation. ～식 a fractional expression. 부분～ partial fractions. 진〔가〕～ a proper 〔an improper〕 fraction.

**분수**(噴水) a jet of water; a fountain. ¶ ～가 솟고 있다 The fountain is playing 〔spouting, spraying〕. / 이 공원의 ～는 평일에는 물이 나오지 않는다 The fountain in this park doesn't run on weekdays. ◉ ～공(孔) a jet; a spout. ～기(器) a waterspout.

**분수령**(分水嶺) 《경계가 되는》 a watershed; a divide; a dividing ridge; 《전환점·고비》 a turning point; a crisis; a hump; a time or event that marks a very important change. ¶ 이 산맥은 이 나라의 ～을 이루고 있다 This range of mountains forms the watershed of the country. / 나폴레옹의 모스크바 후퇴는 그의 생애의 중요한 ～이 되었다 Napoleon's retreat from Moscow was a major watershed in his career.

**분승**(分乘) ～하다 ride separately. ¶ 그들은 네 대의 자동차에 ～해서 출발했다 They split up and set off in four separate cars.

**분식**(粉食) food made from flour. ～하다 eat flour. ¶ ～을 장려하다 encourage the use of flour for food.

**분식**(粉飾) ①《화장》 toilet; makeup; furbelows; showy ornaments. ～하다 paint; make up 《*one's* face》; make *one's* toilet. ②《꾸밈》 embellishment; gilding. ～하다 embellish; adorn; decorate. ¶ ～된 이야기 an embellished account. ◉ ～결산 〖부기〗 fraudulent 〔rigged〕 accounts; a window-dressing settlement (of accounts); window dressing.

**분신**(分身) ① 〖불교〗 an incarnation of the Buddha. ② 《제 2 의 나》 *one's* other self; the *alter ego* (L.).

**분신**(焚身) burning *oneself* to death; self-burning. ～하다 burn *oneself* to death; set *oneself* ablaze to death. ¶ ～을 기도하다 make an attempt to burn *oneself* to death / 경찰의 잔인성에 항의하며 ～한 대학생은 어제 사망하였다 A college student, who burned himself in protest against police brutality, died yesterday.
◉ ～자살(自殺) ＝ 분신(焚身).

**분실**(分室) 《관청의》 a detached office; an annex; 《병원의》 an isolated room 〔ward〕.

**분실**(紛失) loss. ～하다 lose; miss. ¶ ～된 lost; missing / 돈이 ～되다 the money is missing / 반지가 ～되었다 A ring has disappeared 《from the dresser》. / 금고의 돈이 ～된 것을 알았다 I found the money missing from the safe. ◉ ～물 a lost 〔missing〕 article; lost property: ～물 습득자 the finder of a lost article / ～물 안내소 the lost and found office. ～신고 a report of the loss 《of an article》: ～ 신고를 하다 report the loss of an article 《to》. ～자 a loser; the owner of a lost article.

**분야**(分野) a field; a sphere; a division; a branch; *one's* speciality. ¶ 연구 ～ a field 〔an area〕 of study / 학문의 한 ～ a branch of learning / 산업의 각 ～ the various fields of industry / ～가 다르다 be off 〔out of〕 *one's* line 〔beat〕 / 다른 ～로 진출하다 move in another sphere / 새로운 ～를 개척하다 open up a new field / 그것은 내 전문 ～가 아니다 That is out of 〔not in〕 my line. / 대수는 수학의 한～이다 Algebra is a branch of mathematics. / 너의 전문 ～는 무엇이냐 What do you specialize in? *or* What is your 「special field 〔specialty〕?

**분양**(分讓) sale 《of land》 in lots 〔parcels〕; lotting-out; parceling-out. ～하다 sell 《land》 in lots 〔parcels〕; lot 〔parcel〕 out. ¶ 그 땅은 지금 ～중이다 The land is being sold in lots.
◉ ～주택 a house built for sale; a tract house 《미》. ～지 lots for sale; land for sale in lots 〔parcels〕. 변칙 ～ an anomalous distribution 《of》.

**분업**(分業) division of labor 〔work〕; 〖경제〗 specialization. ～하다 divide work 《among》; specialize 《in》. ¶ ～의 시대 the age of specialization / 일을 ～으로 하다 divide 〔parcel out〕 the work / 그들은 그 일을 ～으로 했다 They divided the work among themselves.
◉ 국제～ international division of labor. 의약～ separation of dispensary from medical practice; specialization of dispensary and medical practice.

**분연**(忿然·憤然) ¶ ～(히) in anger; angrily; indignantly; in a rage / ～히 자리를 뜨다 fling away 〔off〕 in a rage; leave in a huff.

**분연(히)**(奮然(―)) resolutely; vigorously; courageously; pluckily. ¶ 분연히 난국과 직면하다 tackle resolutely the difficulty; be determined to face the difficulty.

**분열**(分列) filing off (columns). ～하다 file off. ¶ ～ 행진하다 march in file; troop 《영》.
◉ ～식 a march-past; a defile: ～식을 하다 march in review; march past 《the reviewing stand》; hold a parade; fly past (비행기의).

**분열**(分裂) dissolution; disunion; a split; (a) division; breakup; 《세포의》 disorganization; segmentation; 《원자핵의》 fission; 《종파의》 schism. ～하다 be disunited; be dismembered; be divided; break up; split. ¶ 정당의 ～ the split in a political party / 의식의 ～ dissociation of consciousness / 각파로 ～하다 split 〔break up〕 into several factions / ～시키다 split; break up / 둘로 ～되다 be split in half / 하나의 세포가 ～하여 새로운 세포가 생겨난다 A cell devides into new cells.
◉ ～생식 reproduction by fission; schizogenesis. ～식물 a schizophyte. ～조직 meristem. ～질 schizothymia. ～편(片) a segment.

**분외**(分外) ¶ ～의 beyond *one's* lot 〔status〕; undeserved; unmerited; undue; inordinate / ～의 영광 an underserved honor / ～의 야망 an inordinate ambition.

**분요**(紛擾) confusion. ＝분란.

**분원**(分院) a branch hospital 〔institute〕.

**분위기**(雰圍氣) an atmosphere; an ambience. ¶ 가정적인 ～ a family 〔homey, homely〕 atmosphere / 문학적 ～ a literary atmosphere / 회사의 ～ the atmosphere of the office / 어색한 ～ an uncomfortable atmosphere / 자

유로운 ～에서 in a free atmosphere / ～를 깨뜨리다 destroy 〔mar〕 the atmosphere / 즐거운 ～를 조성하다 create 〔produce〕 a pleasant atmosphere / ～가 마음에 안 든다 The atmosphere is not of my liking. / 나는 그 식당의 조용한 ～를 좋아한다 I like the quiet atmosphere in that restaurant.

**분유**(粉乳) powdered milk; milk powder; dry milk. ¶ ～로 키운 아이 a bottle-fed child / 아기를 ～로 키우다 bottle-feed a baby; feed 〔raise, bring up〕 a baby on the bottle.

**-분의**(分—) a part; a fraction. ¶ 3분의 1, a third (part); one third / 3분의 2, two thirds / 4분의 1, a quarter / 4분의 3, three quarters / 100분의 9, nine hundredths.

**분자**(分子) ① 〚수학〛 a numerator. ② 〚물리·화학〛 a molecule. ¶ ～의 molecular / ～ 구조 molecular structure. ③ 《구성원》 an element; a faction; a set. ¶ 불평〔반동〕～ malcontent 〔reactionary〕 elements / 당내의 부패 ～를 일소하다 purge 〔clear〕 the party of its corrupt elements; purge its corrupt elements from the party / 좋지 못한 ～를 배제하다 eliminate an undesirable element. ◉ ～량 molecular weight. ～력 molecular force. ～생물학 molecular biology. ～선〔살〕 a molecular beam; molecular rays. ～설 the molecular theory. ～시계 〚생물〛 a molecular clock. ～식 a molecular formula (*pl.* -las, -lae). ～인력 molecular attraction.

**분잡**(紛雜) crowdedness; confusion. ～하다 (be) crowded; congested; confused. ¶ ～을 틈타서 in the confusion.

**분장**(分掌) division of duties. ～하다 divide 〔allot〕 《office duties》; take partial charge 《of business》.

**분장**(扮裝) (a) make-up; a getup(별난); impersonation (연기의); disguise (변장). ～하다 make *oneself* up; apply 〔put on〕 a make-up; dress *oneself* up 《as》; disguise (*oneself*) 《as》. ¶ …으로 ～하여 in the guise of… / 여주인공으로 ～하다 「put on a make-up 〔make *oneself* up〕 for a heroine / 여자로 ～하다 be dressed 〔disguised〕 as a woman / 왕은 늙은 농부로 ～하여 적진을 탈출했다 The King disguised himself as an old farmer and escaped through the enemy's lines. ◉ ～사 a make-up artist. ～실 a dressing 〔make-up〕 room.

**분재**(分財) apportioning an inheritance. ～하다 apportion 〔divide up〕 an inheritance. ◉ 분잿깃 *one's* share.

**분재**(盆栽) a dwarfed potted plant; a dwarf(ed) tree in a pot. ～하다 plant 〔grow〕 《a dwarf tree》 in a pot. ¶ ～ 소나무 a dwarf pine tree. ◉ ～가꾸기 raising dwarf trees; dwarf-tree culture.

**분쟁**(分爭) party strife; factional rivalry. ～하다 have party strife; be pitted against one another. ¶ ～으로 분열되다 be torn by factional strife / ～에 끼지 않다 keep clear of 〔stand aloof from〕 party strife.

**분쟁**(紛爭) (a) dispute; trouble; strife. ～하다 have a dispute 《with》; have trouble 《with》. ¶ 국경 ～ a border dispute / 민족 ～ ethnic strife / 학원 ～ a school 〔campus〕 disturbance; student 〔campus〕 unrest / ～의 씨 the seed 〔apple〕 of discord / ～의 초점 the focus of (a) trouble / ～지역 (the) troubled parts 〔areas〕 《of the world》 / ～의 평화적(인) 해결 peaceful settlement of the dispute / ～ 중이다 be in conflict 〔dispute〕 《with》; be at strife 《with》 / ～을 일으키다 cause strife; give rise to complications; raise a trouble 〔dust 《구어》〕 / ～을 조정〔중재〕하다 mediate a dispute / ～을 평화적으로 해결하다 settle a dispute by peaceful means / ～의 씨를 뿌리다 sow the seeds of discord 《among, between》 / 국제간의 ～을 빚어내다 lead to an international trouble / ～의 뿌리는 깊다 The cause of the trouble is deep-rooted 〔deep-seated〕. / 노사간의 ～은 해결되었다 The dispute between labor and management came to a settlement. / 우리는 강대국간의 ～에 휘말려들고 싶지 않다 We do not want to get involved in a strife among big powers. ◉ ～조정자 a trouble shooter. ～처리기관 grievance machinery.

**분전**(奮戰) a plucky 〔brave, desperate〕 fight; hard 〔hot〕 fighting. ～하다 fight desperately 〔bravely, hard〕. ¶ 끝까지 ～하다 fight to the finish; fight it out / 끝까지 ～하다 죽다 die in the last ditch; die game.

**분점**(分店) a branch shop 〔store〕; a branch firm 〔office〕. ¶ 일산 ～ the Ilsan branch / 용산에 ～을 내다 open a branch shop at Yongsan.

**분점**(分點) 〚천문〛 equinoctial points; equinoxes. ¶ 평균 ～ the mean equinox. ◉ ～월 a tropical month.

**분젠** Bunsen. ◉ ～광도계 a Bunsen photometer. ～등〔버너〕 a Bunsen burner.

**분종**(盆種) ～하다 grow plants in pots; pot (up) plants.

**분주**(奔走) ～하다 (be) busy; be busily engaged. ¶ ～하게〔히〕 busily; in a hurried manner; like a busy bee / ～한 생활 《lead》 a bustling life / ～한 하루를 보내다 pass a busy day / 언제나 ～하다 be always kept busy / ～ 다사하다 be busy and rushed with work / ～하게 돌아다니다 run 〔bustle〕 about; be on the run / 그는 늘 ～하다 He always keeps himself busy.

**분지**(盆地) 〖지학〗 a basin; a (round) valley(유역의); a hollow. ¶ ～를 이루다 form a basin / ～는 여름에 덥고 겨울에 춥다 In a basin it is hot in summer and cold in winter.

**분책**(分冊) a fascicle 《of a book》; a separate volume. ～하다 issue 〔print, bind〕 in fascicles. ¶ ～으로 팔다 sell 《the volumes》 「in installments 〔singly〕 / ～으로 간행하다 issue 〔publish〕 《a book》 in parts.

**분첩**(粉貼) 《분 바르는》 a (powder) puff; 《글쓰는》 a kind of cardboard slate for children's writing practice.

**분청사기**(粉青沙器) a grayish-blue-powdered celadon; a celadon covered with grayish-blue powder.

**분초**(分秒) a minute and a second; an instant(순간). ¶ ～를 다투는 문제이다 It admits of no delay. *or* It is a matter of great urgency.

**분출**(噴出) a gush; spouting; a spurt; a violent outflow; 《화산의》 eruption; belch; 《용암의》 extrusion; extravasation. ～하다 《액체를》 gush; spout; blow out; spurt; 《용솟음치다》 well (out, forth); 《뿜어내다》 emit a jet 《of》; eject; belch up (화산·굴뚝이). ¶ 연기를〔화염을〕 ～하다 belch out smoke 〔fire〕 / 물이 관에서 ～하다 water spouts 〔spurts〕 from the pipe / 석유가 유전에서 ～하다 the well spurts oil / 화산은 용암을 ～하고 있다 The volcano is 「spewing out 〔vomiting〕 lava. ◉ ～구 a jet; an exhaust nozzle. ～물 jet (구멍·파이프에서의); ejecta; eruptions (화산의). ～암 an eruptive 〔effusive〕 rock.

**분침**(分針) the minute 〔long〕 hand.

**분칭**(分秤) a small balance (beam).

**분탄**(粉炭) dust 〔slack〕 coal; powdered 〔pulverized〕 coal (석탄가루).

**분탕질**(焚蕩—) dissipation; squandering. ～하다 squander; dissipate.

**분통**(憤痛) resentment; fury; indignation; vexation. ¶ ～(이) 터지다 be greatly vexed 《at》; burst into a fit of rage; get furious; blow *one's* top 《구어》 / 그는 그녀의 말에 ～이 터졌다 He got furious at her remarks.

**분투**(奮鬪) a (hard) struggle; hard fighting; strenuous effort(s). ～하다 fight hard; struggle; strive 《for》; exert *oneself;* make strenuous efforts; make a push. ¶ ～하여 성공하다 fight *one's* way to success / 끝까지 ～하다 fight to the last; fight it out / 선전 ～하다 put up a good fight / 그 계획의 성공을 위해 그녀는 ～했다 She made strenuous efforts to make the plan succeed. ◉ ～노력 violent 〔strenuous〕 efforts. ～정신 a fighting spirit; pluck.

**분파**(分派) a branch; a subbranch; an offshoot; a sect (종파); 《당내의》 a faction. ～하다 divide; branch; form a new sect. ◉ ～주의 factionalism. ～행동〔활동〕 factional action 〔activities〕.

**분패**(憤敗) a defeat by narrow margin.

**분포**(分布) (a) distribution. ～하다 be distributed; range 《from one place to another》. ¶ 수직〔수평〕～ vertical 〔horizontal〕 distribution / 인구 ～ the spread of population / 동식물의 지리적 ～ the geographical distribution of plants and animals / ～가 넓다 be widely distributed / 이들 동물은 전세계에 ～하고 있다 These animals 「range all over the world 〔have a worldwide distribution〕. ◉ ～곡선〔계수〕 〖통계〗 a distribution curve 〔factor〕. ～도 a distribution chart 〔map〕.

**분풀이**(忿—·憤—) giving vent to *one's* indignation; revenge; retaliation. ～하다 vent *one's* anger 〔spite〕 《on》; retaliate; visit 〔work off〕 *one's* anger. ¶ ～로 by way of revenge; to vent *one's* anger 〔spleen〕; in 〔out of, from〕 spite / 돈 차용을 거절당하자 ～로 그는 친구 집 현관문을 찼다 After being refused a loan, he vented his anger by kicking the door of his friend's house.

**분필**(分筆) division of a lot 〔parcel of land〕.

**분필**(粉筆) chalk. ¶ 색～ colored chalk / ～ 한 자루 a piece 〔stick〕 of chalk / ～로 쓰다 write with 〔in〕 chalk; chalk 《*something* on the blackboard》. ◉ ～가루 chalk dust.

**분하다**(憤―·忿―) ①《원통하다》(be) vexing; mortifying. ¶ 분하게도 to *one's* chagrin / 분한 나머지 in *one's* vexation; out of vexation 〔chagrin〕; for spite / 분한 김에 ⇨ 분김에 / 분하게 여기다 be 〔feel〕 mortified 〔chagrined〕《at》 ⇨ 분해하다 / 분해서 눈물을 흘리다 shed tears in *one's* mortification / 아아 ～ How vexing 〔disappointing〕! / 그는 분해서 미칠 지경이었다 He nearly went mad with vexation. / 그의 말을 들으니 분했다 What he said made me mad. / 그의 불공평한 처사가 분해서 나는 사직했다 I quit the job indignant at his favoritism. ②《섭섭하다》(be) regrettable; regretful; regretted; sorry; distressed. ¶ 그를 보지 못해 ～ I am sorry I missed the opportunity of seeing him. / 그는 낙제한 것이 분했다 He was distressed at failing the examination.

**분한**(分限) ①《실용성》 utility; 《경제성》 economical 〔wise, good〕 use. ¶ ～이 있다 be economical / ～이 없다 be uneconomical 〔wasteful〕 / ～ 있게 돈을 써라 Put your money to good use. / 요새는 전보다 돈이 ～ 없다 Nowadays money is worthless than what is used to be. ② ＝ 분수[1](分數) ②.

**분할**(分割) division; partition. ～하다 divide (up); cut 〔carve〕 up; partition; lot out; split; separate. ¶ 토지의 ～ the partition of land / 토지를 ～하다 parcel (out) the land《in lots》/ 토지를 ～하여 팔다 sell *one's* land in lots / ～할 수 없다 be indivisible 〔inseparable〕; be impartible (토지 등을) / 인도는 1947년에 ～되었다 India was partitioned in 1947.
◉ ～매입 installment buying; buying on the installment 〔easy-payment〕 plan《미》. ～법 〖논리〗 partition. ～상속(제) divided succession. ～상환 redemption by installment. ～소유권 divided 〔mixed〕 ownership. ～인도 installment delivery. ～주문 split order. ～통치〔지배〕 divide and rule.

**분할**(分轄) separate control 〔administration, jurisdiction〕. ～하다 control 〔administer〕 separately.

**분할지급**(分割支給) payment in 〔by〕 installments; an installment plan 〔system〕; an easy-payment plan《미》. ¶ ～으로 사다〔팔다〕 buy 〔sell〕 on the installment 〔easy-payment〕 plan / ～으로 자동차를 구입하였다 I bought an automobile 「on the installment plan 〔on time〕.

**분합**(分閤) 〖건축〗 windows 〔sliding doors〕 used to shut the plank-floor room off from the court.

**분해**(分解) ①《해체》 disjointing; dismantling; disassembly; disintegration. ～하다 disjoint; dismantle; disassemble; disintegrate; break down; take 〔pull〕《*a thing*》 to pieces. ¶ 기계를 ～하다 disassemble 〔break up〕 a machine / 시계를 ～하다 take a watch 〔clock〕 apart.
②〖화학〗《환원》 decomposition; resolution; dissolution; degradation. ～하다《환원하다》 resolve (itself)《into》; dissolve《into》; decompose; be decomposed; break down; be reduced to《its components 〔elements〕》. ¶ ～할 수 있는 resoluble; decomposable / ～할 수 없는 irresoluble / 물을 산소와 수소로 ～하다 decompose water into oxygen and hydrogen / 화합물을 원소로 ～하다 reduce 〔resolve〕 a compound into its elements / 이 물질은 대기 중에서 쉽게 ～한다 This substance will readily decompose itself in the air.
③〖물리〗 analysis. ～하다 analyze.
◉ ～도 〖건축〗 a deal drawing. ～사진 〖TV〗 a photographic playback. ～성 resolvability. ～성 플라스틱 degradable plastic: 광～성 플라스틱 light degradable plastic / 생(生)～성 플라스틱 biodegradable plastic. ～수리 an 〔a complete〕 overhaul: ～ 수리를 하다 overhaul《a clock》. ～열 heat of decomposition. ～작용 disintegration; 〖생리〗 catabolism. ～점 〖화학〗 decomposition point. ～효소 〖생화학〗 (a) breakdown enzyme.

**분해하다**(憤―) be 〔feel〕 mortified 〔chagrined, vexed〕《at》; feel chagrin《at》; regret《over, at》; be sorry. ¶ 발을 (동동) 구르며 ～ stamp on the ground with chagrin / 그는 상을 못 탄 것을 분해했다 He was put out that he didn't win a prize.

**분향**(焚香) incense burning. ～하다 burn incense. ¶ 영전에 ～하다 burn 〔offer〕 incense for the dead 〔the repose of the departed soul〕. ◉ 합동 ～소 a joint (memorial) altar.

**분홍**(粉紅) pink (color). ¶ ～색 옷을 입고 있다 be dressed in pink. ◉ ～치마 a pink skirt.

**분화**(分化) differentiation; specialization (특수화). ～하다 differentiate; specialize; be specialized 〔differentiated〕;

branch into. ¶ ~되지 않은, 미~의 unspecialized; undifferentiated; 〖생물〗 undifferent (세포 따위가).

**분화**(噴火) (an) eruption; volcanic activity. ~하다 erupt; burst into eruption; 《화산이》 become active. ¶ ~중이다 be erupting; be active / 맹렬히 ~하다 go into violent eruption. ◉ ~구 a crater. ~산 an erupting [active] volcano.

**분회**(分會) a branch 《of》; a (local) 「chapter.

**붇다** ① 《물에》 swell up; become [grow] sodden; get [grow] soaked. ¶ 불은 swollen; sodden / 더운 물에 불은 손 a hand sodden [swollen] with hot water / 물에 불려두다 keep 《*a thing*》 steeped [soaked] in water / 불리다 steep; soak; sodden; macerate / 콩이 물에 불었다 The soybeans have swollen in the water. ② 《늘다》 (***a***) 《수량이》 increase; multiply; accrue; gain; grow; augment (증대하다); mount [pile] up (부피가); run up (비용·빚 따위가). ¶ 무게가 불어나다 gain in weight / 빚이 불어나다 *one's* debt gets heavy / 수가 불어나다 grow in numbers / 양이 불어나다 increase [grow] in volume; gain in quantity / 식구가 불어나다 the family grows larger / (계속) 불어나고 있다 go on increasing; be on the increase / 이 도시의 인구는 최근 수년 동안에 급속히 불었다 The population of this city has increased rapidly in recent years. (***b***) 《물이》 rise; go up. ¶ 물이 불어난 강 a swollen river; a river in flood / 큰비로 한강 수위가 3미터나 불었다 Owing to the heavy rainfall, the Han River has risen (by) three meters.

**불**[1] ① [일반적] fire; 《화염》 (a) flame; 《밝고 센》 a blaze (★ fire가 「타는 현상」을 나타내는 경우는 관사가 붙지 않을 뿐 아니라 복수형도 없음: Fire burns.). ¶ 불같은 fiery; blazing; burning / 불붙기 쉬운 (in)flammable / 불속 in (the midst of) the flames / 불이 붙다 fire burns; 《집 등에》 catch (on) [take] fire; the fire catches / 불에 태우다 put 《*a thing*》 into a fire; burn.

불을: 불을 끄다 put out 《a fire》; snuff 《a candle》; blow out (불어서) / 불을 때다 make a fire; burn wood [coal]; 《지피다》 put 《fuel》 on fire; feed 《a fire》 with 《coal》 / 불을 붙이다 burn; set 《a piece of paper》 alight; 《발화시키다》 ignite; strike a light (성냥으로); strike fire [a spark] (부싯돌로) / 불을 뿜다 emit fire; 《총이》 fire; 〖야구〗 《타선이》 strike fire / 불을 쓰다 use fire; make use of fire / 불을 피우다 make [kindle, build (up), light, start] a fire / 불을 불어서 일으키다 blow on [at] the fire; fan the fire with *one's* breath / 집에 불을 지르다 set fire to a house; set a house a fire [on fire].

¶ 종이는 불에 잘 탄다 Paper catches fire easily. / 우리는 낙엽을 모아 불을 피웠다 We gathered fallen leaves and made a fire. / 휘발유는 불이 붙기 쉽다 Gasoline is highly inflammable. / 불에 놀란 놈 부지깽이만 보아도 놀란다 《속담》 Once bitten, twice shy. *or* A burnt child dreads the fire.

② 《등불》 a light. ¶ 전깃불 electric light / 불을 켜다 light 《a lamp》; 《전깃불을》 turn [switch, put] on the light / 등잔에 불을 붙이다 light a lamp / 불을 끄다 put out the light [lamp]; 《전등을》 turn [switch] off the light / 불을 켜 놓은 채 잠들다 go to sleep with the light on / 불을 어둡게 하다 dim down an electric light / 불이 켜져 있다 The light is on. / 불이 너무 어둡다 The light is too dim. / 불이 나갔다 The electric light went out. *or* 《퓨즈가 끊어져서》 The light blew. / 등잔불이 꺼졌다 The lamp went out.

③ 《담배·라이터의》 a light. ¶ 불을 붙이다 《성냥으로》 strike a light / 담배에 불을 붙이다 light (up) a cigarette 《from a match》 / 담뱃불을 끄다 put out the cigarette / 불 좀 빌려 주십시오 May I have a light?

④ 《화재》 a fire. ¶ 원인 불명의 불 a fire of unknown origin / 불바다가 되다 become a sheet of fire / 불이 나다 a fire breaks out / 불을 내다 cause [start] a fire / 불을 끄다 put out [extinguish] a fire; bring [get] a fire under control / 불이야 Fire! / 불조심해라 Look out for fire! *or* Take care not to start a fire! / 불은 급속히 번져 나갔다 The fire spread rapidly (from house to house). / 불은 부엌에서 났다 The fire started in the kitchen.

⑤ 《스토브·화로 등의》 a fire; 《화열》 heat. ¶ 불에 올려 놓다 put 《*a thing*》 over a fire.

불을: 불을 끄다 put out the fire / 불을 일으키다 make [build (up), fix] a fire; get a fire going; mend the fire (꺼져가는 불을) / 불을 쑤시다 stir the fire / (꺼지지 않게 재 속에) 불을 묻어두다 bank up the fire; cover char-

coal with ash / 불을 쬐다 「warm *oneself* 〔have a heat〕 at the fire / 불기운을 낮추다 turn the fire low; 《가스의》 lower the flame / 방에 불을 때다 heat (up) the room.
⑥ [비유적] burning passion; flame; fire. ¶ 정열의 불 fire of passion / 복수심에 불타다 thirst for revenge / 눈에서 불이 번쩍 나다 see stars; see a flash of red / 불 보듯 뻔하다 be as clear as 「day 〔crystal〕 / 그는 불같이 노했다 He was red with anger. *or* He flared up.

**불**[2] ① 《음낭》 the scrotal sac; the scrotum. ② 《불알》 the testicles. ¶ 돼지의 불을 까다 castrate a pig. ⇨ 불까다.

**불**[3] 〖농업〗 the side flaps of a loading rack.

**불**(弗) a dollar. ¶ 3불 three dollars.

**불**(佛) ① 《불타》 the Buddha; 《불교의》 Buddhist. ¶ 불구(佛具) Buddhist altar fittings. ② 《프랑스》 France. ¶ 한불 Korea and France; Franco-Korean.

**불-**(不) not; un-; in-; non-; dis-. ¶ 불이익 disadvantage.

**불가**(不可) being not right; being of bad quality. ～하다 be not right; (be) wrong; bad. ¶ 가 20명 ～ 10명 The ayes were 20 and noes 10. / 가도 아니고 ～도 아니다 It is neither good nor bad. / 그것은 ～하다고 생각한다 I don't think that's right.
◉ 가～ right or wrong; good or bad.

**불가**(佛家) ① 《신자·불문》 a Buddhist (family). ② 《절》 a Buddhist temple.

**불가결**(不可缺) indispensability; essential. ～하다 (be) indispensable 《to, for》; essential 〔vital〕 《to》. ¶ 절대 ～한 것이 아니라면 unless enforced by absolute necessity / 공기는 생명에 ～한 것이다 Air is indispensable to life. / 수면과 영양은 건강에 ～하다 Sleep and good food are 「indispensable 〔essential〕 to good health. / 이 계획을 성공시키기 위해서는 너의 도움이 ～하다 Your assistance is vital to the success of this project.

**불가능**(不可能) impossibility. ～하다 (be) impossible; unattainable (달성할 수 없는); impracticable (실행할 수 없는). ¶ ～한 일 an impossibility; an impossible 「thing 〔task〕 / ～한 야망 an unattainable ambition / ～한 일을 꾀하다 attempt 〔try to do〕 the impossible / ～한 일을 요구하다 ask for an impossibility; ask 〔cry, wish〕 for the 「moon 〔stars〕 / ～한 일을 가능케 하다 turn an impossibility into a possibility; make possible what seems to be impossible / 여권 없이는 출국이 ～하다 Without a passport, leaving the country is out of the question. / 그 문제는 해결이 ～하다 It is impossible to settle the matter.

**불가래** a small wooden fire shovel.

**불가리아** Bulgaria. ¶ ～의 Bulgarian.
◉ ～말 Bulgarian. ～사람 a Bulgarian; a Bulgar.

**불가물** a severe drought.

**불가분**(不可分) indivisibility; inseparability. ¶ ～의 indivisible; undetachable; inseparable / ～의 관계 an inseparable relation; an undetachable connection / 흡연과 폐암의 ～의 관련 the inseparable link between smoking and lung cancer / ～의 관계에 있다 be inseparably related 《to each other》.

**불가불**(不可不) inevitably; really ought to; simply must; should at all costs; in any event. ¶ ～ 해야 하다 ought to do; must do / 나는 ～ 내일 떠나야 한다 I really must leave tomorrow. / ～ 가야 한다 I have no choice but to go.

**불가사리** ① 《괴물》 a mythical creature said to eat metal, to expel nightmares, *etc.* ② 〖동물〗 a starfish; an asteroid.

**불가사의**(不可思議) (a) mystery; (a) wonder; 《불가사의한 일》 a marvel; a miracle; a riddle. ～하다 (be) wonderful; marvelous; miraculous; mysterious (신비한); magical (마법 같은).
¶ ～중의 불가사의 the mystery of mysteries; the wonder of wonders / 세계의 7대 ～ the Seven Wonders of the World / ～하게 wonderfully; mysteriously / 우주에는 ～한 일이 많다 The universe is full of wonders. / 생명의 기원은 여전히 ～하다 The origin of life remains a mystery.

**불가시**(不可視) invisibility. ◉ ～광선 〖물리〗 a invisible ray.

**불가역**(不可逆) ¶ ～의〔적〕 irreversible 《changes》. ◉ ～성 irreversibility. ～현상 an irreversible phenomenon.

**불가지**(不可知) unknowableness; inconceivability; inscrutability. ～하다 (be) unknowable; inscrutable; inconceivable; mysterious. ¶ ～적 agnostic(al); nescient. ◉ ～론 〖철학〗 agnosticism: ～론자 an agnostic. ～물(物) an unknowable; the Unknowable.

**불가침**(不可侵) inviolability; nonaggression. ¶ ～의 inviolable / 신성 ～의 sacred and inviolable; sacrosanct 《rights》. ◉ ～권(權) an inviolable right: 영토 ～권 the inviolability of territory. ～선언 a nonaggression declaration. ～조약 《conclude》 a nonaggression pact 〔treaty〕.

**불가피**(不可避) inevitability; unavoidability. ～하다 (be) unescapable; inevitable; unavoidable; ineluctable. ¶ ～한 사정으로 owing to circumstances beyond control; due to some unavoidable circumstances; under unavoidable circumstances / ～하게 …하다 be obliged 〔compelled〕 to *do* / 죽음은 ～하다 Death is inevitable. / 두 나라 사이의 전쟁은 ～하다고 생각된다 War between the two countries seems inevitable.

**불가항력**(不可抗力) an irresistable force; *force majeure* (F.); inevitability; an act of God. ¶ ～의 uncontrollable; beyond (human) control; inevitable; irresistable / ～의 사고 an accident beyond (human) control; an inevitable accident; an act of God / ～으로 발생하다 arise from a cause beyond *one's* control / 당국은 이번의 참사를 ～이라고 말하고 있다 The authorities declare that the accident was inevitable. / 천재(天災)는 ～이다 Natural disasters are beyond human control.

**불가해**(不可解) mysteriousness; (a) mystery; incomprehensibility; inscrutability. ～하다 (be) mysterious; incomprehensible; inexplicable; inscrutable; be beyond comprehension. ¶ ～한 인물 a mystery man; an enigma; a sphinx (*pl.* ～es, sphinges) / ～한 행동 enigmatic behavior / 생명은 ～하다 Life is a mystery.

**불각**(佛閣) ＝불당(佛堂).

**불간섭**(不干涉) nonintervention; noninterference. ◉ ～정책 a nonintervention 〔hands-off〕 policy. ～주의 a nonintervention policy.

**불감증**(不感症) 〖의학〗 frigidity; 《무감각》 insensibility. ¶ ～의 여자 a frigid woman / ～이 되다 grow insensible 《to noise》 / 남의 고통에 대하여 ～이 되다 become callous toward the sufferings of other people / 그는 그러한 비판에는 ～이 되어 있다 He is immune to such criticism. / 주민들 중에는 공해에 대하여 ～에 걸린 사람도 있다 Some of the inhabitants are indifferent to pollution.

**불강아지** a scrawny dog.

**불개** a mythical dog thought to cause eclipses of the sun and the moon.

**불개미** 〖곤충〗 a red ant.

**불개입**(不介入) noninvolvement; nonintervention. ◉ ～정책〔주의〕 a nonintervention 〔noninvolvement〕 policy: 전쟁 ～ 정책을 취하다 take a policy of noninvolvement in the war.

**불거웃** pubic hair.

**불거지다** ① 《속엣것이》 protrude; project; jut 〔stick〕 out; swell 〔bulge〕 out. ¶ 불거진 눈 protruding 〔goggle, pop〕 eyes (퉁방울눈). ② 《숨겼던 것이》 come 〔be〕 out; be laid bare.

**불걱거리다** ① 《씹다》 chew away 《on *something* rubbery》. ② 《빨래를》 scrub.

**불걱불걱** ① 《씹다》 chewing away 《on *something* rubbery》. ② 《빨다》 scrubbing away 《at laundry》.

**불건성유**(不乾性油) non-drying oil.

**불건전**(不健全) unwholesomeness; unsoundness. ～하다 (be) unwholesome; unsound; unhealthy; morbid (병적). ¶ ～한 생각〔사상〕 unwholesome 〔dangerous〕 ideas / ～한 정신 morbid 〔unsound〕 mind / 요즘 많은 아이들이 ～한 오락에 빠져 있다 A lot of boys indulge in unhealthy pastimes these days.

**불경거리다** ⇨ 볼강거리다.

**불경불경** hard to chew; chewy; leathery; lumpy.

**불경이** red cut tobacco.

**불결**(不潔) uncleanliness; filthiness; dirtiness. ～하다 (be) dirty; unclean (-ly); foul; filthy. ¶ ～한 것 dirt; filth / ～한 거리 a dirty 〔squalid〕 street / ～한 물 foul water / ～한 관계 immoral relationship (부도덕한) / ～한 셔츠 an unclean shirt / 부엌이 매우 ～하다 The kitchen is very unsanitary. / 화장실이 참 ～하다 The washroom is really filthy. / ～은 갖가지 병의 근원이다 Various diseases breed in filth. *or* Uncleanliness is the cause of various diseases.

**불경**(不敬) disrespect; irreverence; want of respect; 《모독》 impiety; blasphemy; profanity. ～하다 (be) disrespectful; irreverent; impious; blasphemous. ¶ ～한 말을 하다 make a disrespectful remark; blaspheme 《against》; swear. ◉ ～사건 a lese majesty affair. ～죄 〖법〗 lese majesty. ～행위 lese majesty.

**불경**(佛經) Buddhist scriptures; a sutra. ¶ ～을 외다〔읽다〕 chant 〔recite, read, intone〕 a sutra.

**불경기**(不景氣) 《일반의》 bad 〔hard〕 times; 《장사의》 a business depression; bad business; dull market 〔trade〕; (a) recession (일시적인); 《침체》 dullness; a slump; a slack. ¶ ~인 dull; slack; depressed / 심각한 ~ a serious depression / ~가 되다 grow dull; slacken; [점포 등이 주어] fall on hard times / ~를 모르다 be always prosperous / 실업계는 심각한 ~에 빠져 있다 The business world is in serious depression. / ~일 때는 실업자가 증가한다 When business is depressed, there is usually an increase in unemployment. / 자동차 산업은 지금 ~이다 Times are bad now for the car industry. *or* The car industry is in a depression. / 우리 나라는 심각한 ~를 겪고 있다 We are suffering (from) a serious depression.

**불경제**(不經濟) poor 〔bad〕 economy; want of economy; (a) waste. ¶ ~적인 uneconomical; unthrifty; wasteful / ~적인 사람 an uneconomical 〔a wasteful〕 person / 시간과 노력의 ~ a waste of time and labor.

**불계승**(不計勝) 〖바둑〗 a victory by a wide margin. ~하다 win (a game) by a wide margin.

**불고**(不顧) negligence; indifference. ~하다 disregard; ignore; neglect; be indifferent 《about》; pay no attention; be shameless 〔impudent, brazen-faced〕. ¶ ~ 체면〔체면 ~〕하다 have no regard to *one's* face 〔honor〕 / 염치 ~하고 그에게 일을 부탁했다 I stooped to ask him for it.

**불고기** *pulgogi;* broiled 〔grilled〕 beef (sliced and seasoned).

**불공**(不恭) disrespect; irreverence. ~하다 (be) disrespectful; irreverent; rude.

**불공**(佛供) a Buddhist service 〔prayer〕. ¶ ~ 드리다 offer 〔hold〕 a Buddhist service 〔prayer〕.

**불공대천**(不共戴天) ¶ ~의 원수 an irreconcilable enemy; a sworn 〔mortal, deadly, the dearest〕 foe / 둘은 ~의 원수 사이다 There is a deadly feud between them.

**불공정**(不公正) unfairness; inequity; injustice. ~하다 (be) unfair; inequitable; unjust. ¶ ~하게 unfairly; unjustly; partially / ~한 경쟁〔거래〕 unfair rivalry 〔trade〕 / ~한 재판관 a partial judge / 그의 수법은 ~하고 불공평하다 His method is unjust and unfair.

**불공평**(不公平) unfairness; injustice; inequity; partiality. ~하다 (be) unfair; unjust; inequitable; partial; biased. ¶ ~한 취급 unfair treatment 〔dealing〕 / ~한 세제(稅制) the unfair tax system / ~하게 partially; unfairly; unjustly / ~하게 다루다 treat 《*a person*》 unfairly; discriminate against 《*a person*》 / ~한 조처를 취하다 take partial measures / ~한 짓을 하다 give a bias to *one's* actions; do injustice 《to》 / ~함이 없도록 하다 see that no one will suffer an injustice 〔a disadvantage〕 / 저 심판은 ~하다 That umpire is unfair. *or* That umpire is partial to one of the teams. / 나보고 다 하라니 ~하다 It's unfair to expect me to do all the work. / 너는 나에 대해서 ~하다 You are unfair to me. *or* You treat me unfairly. / 그들은 ~한 판정에 항의했다 They protested against the unfair 〔unjust〕 judgment.

**불과**(不過) just; nothing but; only; merely; but; no more than. ~하다 be no(t) more than; be nothing but. ¶ ~ 10명 no more than 10 people / ~ 이삼십 원에 for a few modest won / ~ 일주일 전에 but 〔only〕 a week ago / 흔히 있는 물건에 ~하다 be nothing but a common article / 구실에 ~하다 That is only an excuse. / 그는 그저 지인에 ~하다 He is nothing but an acquaintance of mine. / 그것은 그저 추측〔소문〕에 ~하다 It is no more than a guess 〔rumor〕. / 나는 해야만 할 일을 한데 ~하다 I only did what I ought to.

**불과**(佛果) 《achieve》 Buddhahood; Nirvana.

**불관**(不關) ~하다 do not care about; be indifferent to; have no concern with; do not meddle 〔interfere〕 in.

**불교**(佛敎) Buddhism. ¶ ~를 믿다 believe in Buddhism. ◉ ~도 a Buddhist. ~ 문학 Buddhist literature. ~문화 Buddhist civilization 〔culture〕. ~미술〔음악〕 Buddhist art 〔music〕. ~조각 Buddhist sculpture. ~청년회 the Young Men's Buddhist Association. ~청년 연합회 the Federation of Young Buddhists Association.

**불구**(不具) ① 《신체상의》 deformity; disability. ¶ ~의 deformed (기형의); crippled (손발을 못 쓰는) (★ 이 두 낱말은 사람에 대한 차별어로 여겨지고 있어 사용하는 것을 삼가는 것이 좋다); disabled (몸이 불편한) / ~가 되다 be disabled. ② 《편지 끝에》 "Yours truly". ◉ ~자 a cripple; a (physically) handicapped person; a disabled person.

**불구대천**(不俱戴天) =불공대천(不共戴天).

**불구속**(不拘束) nonrestraint. ¶ ~으로 in *one's* own custody; without physical restraint / ~ 입건하다〔되다〕 indict 〔be booked〕 without (physical) detention.

**불구하고**(不拘—) ① 《…인데도》 though; although; in spite of; despite; notwithstanding; no matter 《how, what, who, *etc.*》; for 〔with〕 all. ¶ 그럼에도 ~ nevertheless; none the less; for all that / 반대에도 ~ despite (the) opposition / 병중임에도 ~ in spite of *one's* illness / 비가 오는데도 ~ in spite of 〔notwithstanding〕 the rain / 그만큼 이나 학식이 있음에도 ~ for all his learning. ② 《…에 관계없이》 regardless 〔irrespective〕 of; without reference 〔regard〕 to; independent of; whether... or.... ¶ 남녀를〔성별에〕 ~ irrespective of 〔regardless of, without regard to〕 sex; (no matter) whether it is man or woman / 신분의 고하를 ~ irrespective of rank / 국적을 ~ 누구든지 이 대회에 참가할 수 있다 Anyone can take part in this meet, irrespective of his nationality.

**불굴**(不屈) unyieldingness; indomitability; fortitude. ¶ ~의 dauntless; inexhaustible; indomitable; invincible; unyielding; inflexible; indefatigable; unsubdued; sturdy / ~의 용기 stubborn 〔sturdy〕 courage / ~의 의지 a will of iron; an unyielding 〔indomitable〕 will / ~의 정신 an indomitable 〔a dauntless〕 spirit / 역경에도 꺾이지 않고 ~의 정신으로 그는 자기 목적을 관철했다 In the face of adversity he stuck to his purpose with 「great fortitude 〔an indomitable spirit〕.

**불귀객**(不歸客) a dead 〔deceased〕 person. ¶ ~이 되다 pass away; depart (from) this life; go on *one's* last journey.

**불규칙**(不規則) irregularity; unsteadiness. ~하다 (be) irregular; anomalous; unmethodical; unsystematic; unsteady. ¶ ~하게 irregularly; unsystematically; fitfully / ~한 생활을 하다 lead 〔live〕 an irregular life; be irregular in *one's* life. ◉ ~동사 〖문법〗 an irregular verb. ~변화 〖문법〗 irregular conjugation.

**불균형**(不均衡) lack of balance; imbalance; unbalance; disequilibrium; 《어울리지 않은》 disproportion; 《불평등》 inequality; disparity. ~하다 be out of balance; (be) ill-balanced; unbalanced; disproportionate; unequal. ¶ 생활 수준의 ~(an) inequality of living standards / ~한 임금 unequal 〔disproportionate〕 wages / 무역의 ~을 완화하다 reduce the imbalance in trade 《between》 / 경제상의 ~을 시정하다 redress 〔correct〕 economic imbalance.

**불그데데하다** (be) reddish.

**불그레하다** (be) reddish; be tinged with red.

**불그스름하다** (be) reddish.

**불급하다**(不急—) be not urgent; be in no hurry; (be) unpressing; unhurried.

**불긋불긋** with red spots. ⇨ 발긋발긋.

**불기**(—氣) heat of fire. ¶ ~ 없는 unheated; fireless / ~ 없는 방 《in》 an unheated room / 화로에는 ~가 없다 There is no sign of fire in the brazier.

**불기**(不羈) freedom 《from restraint》; liberty; independence. ¶ ~의 free (and independent); unrestrained; unshackled.

**불기**(佛紀) Buddhist Era (생략 B.E.). ¶ ~ 2천 5백년, 2500 B.E. (=1835 A.D.).

**불기둥** a pillar of fire; a column of flames. ¶ ~이 솟다 a pillar of fire shoots up.

**불기소**(不起訴) non-prosecution. ¶ ~로 하다 drop 《a case》; do not prosecute 《*a person*》 / 그는 ~ 되었다 He was not indicted 〔prosecuted〕. *or* The case against him was dropped. ◉ ~처분 a disposition not to institute a public action.

**불기운** (heat of a) fire; 《화력》 force of (a) fire. ¶ ~을 낮추다 turn the fire low; 《가스의》 lower the flame / ~이 더해가다〔떨어지다〕 the fire 「gains force 〔goes down〕.

**불길** flames; a blaze. ¶ 요원의 ~ wildfire; a prairie 〔grass〕 fire / ~이 사납다 the flames are intense; burn fiercely / ~이 오르다 burst into flame; blaze 〔flame〕 up; flare up / 사나운 ~ 속으로 뛰어들다 rush 〔plunge〕 into the raging flames. / ~이 치솟았다 Flames shot up. / ~이 점점 번졌다 The flames steadily spread. / ~은 사방으로 번졌다 The fire spread in all directions. / ~의 번지는 속도가 무섭게 빨랐다 The spread of the flames was alarmingly fast. / 그 집은 순식간에 ~에 휩싸였다 In a moment the house was enveloped in flames. / ~은 다 타서 저절로 꺼졌다 The fire has burnt itself out.

**불길**(不吉) an ill omen; inauspiciousness. ~하다 (be) ill-omened; ominous; unlucky; inauspicious; unpropitious; ill-boding. ¶ ~한 날〔숫자〕 an unlucky day 〔number〕 / ~한 예감〔꿈〕 an ominous presentiment 〔dream〕 / ~한 징조〔조짐〕 an unlucky omen; an ill 〔evil〕 omen / ~한 소리를 하다 croak; say something inauspicious / 집을 나섰을 때 ~한 예감이 들었는데, 그것이 맞아떨어졌다 As I left home I had 「an ominous feeling 〔a feeling that something bad was going to happen, an ominous presentiment〕, which turned out to have been right.

**불김** 《in》 the warmth of a fire. ¶ ~에 젖은 옷이 말랐다 The wet clothes dried out by the fire.

**불깃** burning a swath of trees ahead of a forest fire to prevent its spread; ringing a forest fire with scorched earth.

**불까다** castrate; geld (특히 말을); emasculate; alter 《미》. ¶ 불깐 돼지 a castrated pig / 불깐 말 a gelding; a castrated horse / 불깐 소 a bullock; a castrated bull / 말을 ~ geld a horse.

**불깍쟁이** a real stinker.

**불꽃** ① 《화염》 a flame; a blaze. ¶ ~이 타 오르다 flame 〔blaze〕 up; burst into flame(s) / ~에 (휩)싸이다 be wrapped 〔enveloped〕 in flames. ② 《불똥》 a spark. ¶ ~ 튀다 spark; sparkle; sparks come off (in all directions) / ~ 튀게 하다 spark; give out sparks; throw off sparks; [비유적] have a big argument 《about》 / ~ 튀는 논쟁 a heated discussion; a hot controversy. ③ 《놀이의》 fireworks; firecracker. ¶ ~을 쏘아 올리다 display 〔set off〕 fireworks. ◉ ~놀이 a fireworks display 〔exhibition〕: ~놀이를 하다 let 〔set〕 off fireworks. ~심 the innermost part of a flame.

**불끈** 《get angry》 all of a sudden; with a burst 《of anger》. ~하다 flare up (in anger); be roused to anger; fly 〔get〕 into a passion 〔temper〕 《with》; lose *one's* temper. ¶ ~하여 in a fit of passion; in a (fit of ) rage / 성을 ~ 내다 flare up; fly into a rage / 주먹을 ~ 쥐다 clench *one's* fist / 그는 ~거리는 성미다 He is quick-〔hot-〕tempered.

**불끈불끈** ~하다 burst into a rage readily; get mad easily; flare up at the drop of a hot.

**불나다** a fire breaks out. ¶ 불난 집 a house on fire / 어젯밤에 그 호텔에 불이 났었다 A fire broke out at the hotel last night. / 불난 곳이 어딘가 Where is the fire?

**불난리**(一亂離) the confusion 〔disorder, chaos〕 of a fire. ¶ ~에 다치다 be injured in the confusion of a fire.

**불내다** 《실수로》 cause 〔start〕 a fire; 《고의로》 ⇨불놓다①.

**불놀이** ① ⇨불꽃놀이. ② 《불장난》 playing with fire.

**불놓다** ① 《방화하다》 set fire to 《a house》; set 《a house》 on fire; commit arson. ② 〖광산〗 light a fuse.

**불놓이** shooting (game); game hunting. ~하다 shoot (game); hunt.

**불능**(不能) impossibility; incapability; incapacity; impracticability; lack of ability. ~하다 (be) incapable; impracticable; impossible; be unable 《to》. ¶ 해결 ~인 문제 an insoluble problem / 회답 ~이다 it is impossible to give an answer 《to》 / 이 텔레비전은 수리 ~이다 This television is beyond repair. / 이런 문장은 이해 ~이다 It is impossible to understand this type of sentence. / 대부분의 채권이 회수 ~이 되었다 A lot of loans have become unrecoverable.

**불다**[1] 《바람이》 blow. ¶ 맹렬히〔모질게〕 ~ blow hard; blow a gale; rage / 바람은 북쪽에서 불어온다 The wind 「sits in 〔blows from〕 the north. / 바람이 어느 쪽에서 불어오느냐 Where does the wind sit?

**불다**[2] ① 《입으로》 blow (up); breathe out (입김을); blow out 《a whistle》. ¶ 촛불을 불어 끄다 blow out the candle / 풍선을 ~ blow up 〔inflate〕 a toy balloon / 휘파람을 ~ whistle / (물 따위를) 불어서 식히다 blow into 《*one's* cup of tea》; blow on 《hot water》 (to cool it).
② 《악기를》 blow 〔sound〕 《a trumpet, a bugle》; play (on) 《a flute》. ¶ 피리를 ~ play (on) a flute / 호각을 ~ blow a whistle / 기상 나팔은 여섯 시에 분다 Reveille blows at six.
③ 《자백》 confess 《*one's* crime, that …》; make a confession 《of *one's* crime》; own up 《to an offense》. ¶ 사실대로 ~ confess the truth / 죄를 ~ confess (to) *one's* crime 〔sin〕; con-

fess that *one* has committed a crime; confess *oneself* guilty / 불게 하다 force 〔compel〕 《*a person*》 into confession; make 《*a person*》 admit *himself* guilty / 빨리 불어 Spit it out!

**불단**(佛壇) a Buddhist altar.

**불당**(佛堂) a Buddhist temple 〔shrine, sanctum〕.

**불당그래** a fire rake.

**불덩어리, 불덩이** a ball of fire; a fire-ball; a mass 〔ball〕 of flames. ¶ ～가 되다 《고열로》 have 〔get〕 high fever.

**불도**(佛徒) a Buddhist.

**불도**(佛道) the teaching of Buddha; Buddhist doctrines; Buddhism.
◉ ～수행 (the practice of) Buddhist asceticism.

**불도저** a bulldozer. ¶ ～로 땅을 밀다 bulldoze out.

**불독** a bulldog.

**불돋우개** a wick-raiser.

**불돌** a piece of flat stone used to cover a (charcoal) fire in order to keep it alive for a long time in a brazier.

**불되다** (be) extremely oppressive; intolerably harsh.

**불두덩** 〖해부〗 the pubic region.

**불등걸** a brand; embers; pieces of glowing charcoal.

**불땀** the (potential) heat in a log. ¶ ～이 세다 《장작 등이》 be loaded with heat.

**불땀머리** the well-aired〔-sunned〕 end of a tree 〔log〕.

**불때다** make 〔build〕 a fire; burn wood 〔coal〕. ¶ 방에 ～ heat a room / 아궁이에 ～ make a fire in the fireplace.

**불땔꾼** a perverse fellow; a trouble-maker.

**불똥** ① 《심지의》 the snuff 《of a candlewick》. ② 《불덩이》 sparks. ¶ ～을 뒤집어 쓰다 be covered with sparks / ～을 튀기다 spark; give off sparks / ～이 튀다 spark; sparkle; sparks fly 〔shoot up〕; [비유적] come to involve 《another》.

**불뚝** with a rude burst of anger; flaring up; in a fit of anger 〔temper, passion〕. ¶ 그는 ～ 화를 잘 낸다 He is very quick-tempered. *or* He loses his temper easily.

**불뚝불뚝** with repeated rude bursts of anger; flaring up again and again.

**불뚱거리다** swell up with anger; quiver with rage.

**불뚱이** 《성질》 a hot 〔quick〕 temper; a spasm of temper; a fit of anger; irascibility; 《사람》 a choleric 〔testy, touchy〕 person; a hotspur. ¶ ～(를) 내다 lose *one's* temper 《with *a person*》; get mad 《with, at》 / ～를 누르다 control *one's* temper; keep down *one's* passion.

**불량**(不良) ① 《질의》 badness; inferiority. ～하다 (be) bad; poor; inferior; faulty; deleterious (유해하다); unwholesome (건강에). ¶ 발육이 ～한 어린이 an underdeveloped child / 학교 성적이 ～하다 do badly at school; have a bad 〔poor〕 school record / 품질이 ～하다 The quality is poor.
② 《품성이》 delinquency; wickedness. ～하다 (be) wicked (사악하다); delinquent; depraved (타락하다). ¶ ～해지다 go to the bad; become delinquent; fall low; be degraded; join bad company / (소년 소녀가) ～성을 띠다 be criminally inclined.
◉ ～배 a knave; a hoodlum; a hooligan; a ruffian; 《일당》 a gang of hoodlums; the depraved [총칭]. ～ 상품 고발 센터 Poor Quality Goods Complaint Center. ～소년〔소녀〕 a bad 〔delinquent〕 boy 〔girl〕; a juvenile delinquent. ～식품 subquality 〔substandard〕 foods. ～채권 a bad debt. ～청년 a hooligan; a hoodlum. ～품 inferior 〔defective, shoddy〕 goods; 《불합격품》 a rejected article. ～학생 a disorderly 〔delinquent〕 student. ～화 down fall; degradation: ～화하다 become delinquent; be degraded / 청소년의 ～화를 방지하다 prevent juvenile delinquency.

**불러내다** call 《*a person*》 (out); call 《*a person*》 to 《the office》; 《전화통에》 call 〔ring〕 《*a person*》 up (on the phone); call 《*a person*》 to the telephone; 《법정에》 summon; subpoena; 《호텔·극장 등에서》 page; 《꾀어내다》 decoy; lure; 《마술로》 invoke 〔conjure up〕 《evil spirits》. ¶ 전화로 ～ call 〔ring〕 《*a person*》 up by phone / 그녀는 남편을 호텔 로비로 불러냈다 She had her husband paged in hotel lobby. / 나는 아내를 불러내어 저녁 식사를 함께 했다 I called my wife out and we had dinner together.

**불러들이다** call 〔hail〕 《*a person*》 in(to); have 《*a person*》 in; [비유적] 《초래하다》 bring 《trouble》 on *oneself;* incur 《criticism》. ¶ 위험을 ～ incur danger / 그 학생을 불러들이겠느냐 Will you call the student in?

**불러모으다** call 〔muster〕 together; assemble; convene; rally; summon (together). ¶ 아버지는 가족 모두를 불러모았다 Father called together all the members of the family. / 선생은 학교 운동장에서 놀고 있는 아이들을 불러모았다 The teacher assembled the children playing in the schoolyard.

**불러세우다** call to 《*a person*》 to stop; (call and) stop 《*a person*》; 《손을 들어 택시를》 flag (down); 《보초·경비원 등이》 challenge. ¶ 나는 학생을 불러세웠다 I called to the student to stop. / 경비원은 입구에서 우리를 불러세웠다 We were challenged 〔called to halt〕 at the entrance by a guard. / 그녀는 택시를 불러세웠다 She flagged (down) a taxi.

**불러오다** call 《*a person*》 to *one* 〔*one's* room, *one's* desk, *etc.*〕; 《소환하다》 summon 《*a person*》 to 〔before〕 *one;* 《사람을 시켜》 send for. ¶ 사람을 보내 ~ send 《a man》 for 《*a person*》.

**불러일으키다** call forth; (a)rouse; excite; remind 《*a person* of *something*》. ¶ 기억을 ~ call 《*something*》 to mind 〔memory〕; call back 〔recall〕 《*something*》 to *one's* mind / 여론을 ~ rouse 〔stir up, excite〕 public opinion.

**불려가다** be called (to); be summoned to. ¶ 경찰에 ~ be summoned to the police; get into trouble with the police / 주인 앞에 ~ be called before *one's* master.

**불력**(佛力) the power 〔influence〕 of 「Buddha.

**불로**(不老) perennial 〔eternal〕 youth. ~하다 (be) ever-young 〔ageless〕; unfading; enjoy eternal youth. ¶ ~장수약 the elixir of life.
◉ ~불사 eternal youth and immortality. ~천 a fountain of youth.

**불로소득**(不勞所得) unearned 〔investment〕 income; windfall income; easy money. ◉ ~생활자 a person living on unearned income.

**불로장생**(不老長生) perennial youth and long life 〔longevity〕. ~하다 live ever-young; enjoy eternal youth; be ageless. ¶ ~의 비결 the secret of perennial 〔eternal〕 youth and longevity.

**불로초**(不老草) an elixir of life; a herb bringing eternal youth.

**불룩하다** (be) bulging; baggy; bulgy; inflated; swollen; fat. ¶ 불룩한 지갑 a fat 〔well-stuffed〕 purse / 여성의 불룩한 가슴 the rich 〔well-fleshed〕 breast of a woman / 배가 ~ have a bulging belly; be potbellied / 임신하여 배가 ~ be big with child.

**불륜**(不倫) [일반적] immorality; 《남녀 사이의》 adultery; an adulterous 〔illicit〕 relationship. ¶ ~의 immoral; adulterous; illicit 《love》 / (남녀의) ~ 관계 liaison; immoral intimacy / ~의 사랑 an illicit love affair / ~한 짓을 하다 misconduct *oneself* / 그녀의 남편은 ~을 저지르고 있다 Her husband is 「seeing another woman 〔having an affairs〕. / 그녀는 그 사람과의 ~ 관계를 부인했다 She denied that there had been anything improper in their relationship.

**불리**(不利) disadvantage; a handicap. ~하다 (be) disadvantageous; unfavorable; adverse. ¶ ~한 점 a disadvantage; a handicap; a drawback / …에게 ~하다 be unfavorable to…; tell against… / ~한 조건하에서 under a handicap; in adverse conditions / ~한 처지에 있다 be placed at a disadvantageous position / (형세가) …에게 ~해지다 turn the scale against… / 피고에게 ~한 증언을 하다 testify against the accused / 형세는 그녀에게 ~하다 Things are unfavorable for her. *or* The chances 〔odds〕 are against her.

**불리다**[1] 《배를》 fill. ¶ 배를 ~ fill *one's* stomach; 《사복을 채우다》 line 〔fill, stuff〕 *one's* (own) pocket(s) 〔purse〕; feather *one's* (own) nest; enrich oneself / 공직을 이용하여 자기 배를 ~ line *one's* own pockets taking advantage of *one's* public office.

**불리다**[2] ① 《쇠를》 temper; harden. ¶ 쇠를 ~ temper iron. ② 《곡식을》 winnow; fan. ¶ 곡식을 ~ winnow grain.

**불리다**[3] ① 《부름을 받다》 be called; be summoned 《to》; be invited 《to》. ¶ 선생님에게 불리어 가다 be called before a teacher. ② 《…이라고》 be called; be named.

**불리다**[4] 《바람에》 be blown; blow. ¶ 먼지가 바람에 ~ dust flies in the wind.

**불리다**[5] ① 《액체에》 soak; steep; sodden. ¶ 쌀을 물에 ~ soak rice in water / 물에 불려 두다 keep 《*a thing*》 steeped 〔soaked〕 in water. ② 《증가》 increase 《*one's* fortune》; add to; multiply. ③ 《과장하다》 exaggerate; stretch; magnify.

**불림**[1] 《쇠의》 tempering metal.

**불림**[2] 《공범자의》 informing on *one's* accomplices; ratting.

**불만**(不滿) dissatisfaction; discontent; displeasure; disaffection. ~스럽다 (be) unsatisfactory; displeasing; dissatisfied 〔unsatisfied〕; discontented;

displeased; disaffected; disgruntled. ¶ ~의[스러운] dissatisfied; discontented; displeased; unsatisfactory / 성적(性的) ~ sexual dissatisfaction / ~스러운 결과 an unsatisfactory result / ~이 있는 사람 a man in discontent; a discontented person / …을 ~으로 여기다 be not happy [unhappy] about; be not satisfied 《with》; be displeased 《with》 / ~을 토로하다 complain 《about, of》; grumble 《at, over, about》 / ~을 늘어놓다 air *one's* grievances / ~의 빛을 나타내다 wear a discontented look; betray *one's* dissatisfaction / ~스럽게 여기다, ~을 품다 be displeased [dissatisfied] 《with, at》; feel aggrieved 《at》 / ~을 표명하다 express [signify] *one's* dissatisfaction 《at》; voice *one's* discontent; complain 《of》 / ~이 있다 [사람이 주어] be dissatisfied 《with》; [사물이 주어] leave something to be desired / ~이 없다 [사람이 주어] be content [satisfied] 《with》; have nothing to complain of / 나는 전혀 ~이 없다 I have nothing to complain of. / 지위에 ~을 가지고 있다 I am discontented with my position. / 그 사람이 내게 무슨 ~이 있는지 모르겠어 I wonder if he bears a grudge against me.

**불만족**(不滿足) ⇨ 불만(不滿).

**불매동맹**(不買同盟) a buyer's [shoppers', consumers'] boycott. ¶ ~을 하다 boycott 《a shop, goods》.

**불매운동**(不買運動) a buyers' [consumers'] strike; a civic campaign to boycott some products.

**불면불휴**(不眠不休) ~하다 do without sleep or rest; work day and night; work hard.

**불면증**(不眠症) 〖의학〗 insomnia; sleeplessness. ¶ 과로성 ~ insomnia from exhaustion / ~에 걸리다 suffer from [be troubled with] insomnia. ◉ ~환자 an insomniac.

**불멸**(不滅) immortality; indestructibility; imperishability; athanasia. ~하다 be immortal [indestructible, undying, imperishable, eternal]. ¶ ~의 명성 immortal fame / ~의 명작 a monumental work / ~의 업적 immortal achievements / ~의 시인 the Immortal Bard 《Shakespeare의 이칭》 / 영혼의 ~ immortality of the soul.

**불멸**(佛滅) 〖불교〗 Buddha's death.

**불명**(不明) ① 《사리에》 lack of brightness; dullness; ignorance; lack of perception [wisdom, sagacity, insight]; stupidity. ~하다 (be) unwise; unperceptive; stupid. ¶ ~의 ignorant / 자신의 ~을 부끄럽게 여기다 be shamed of *one's* ignorance. ② 《불분명》 indistinctness; obscurity; ambiguity (모호). ~하다 (be) indistinct; obscure; vague; ambiguous. ¶ 국적 ~의 비행기 a plane of unknown nationality / 신원 ~의 시체 an unidentified body / 원인 ~의 화재 a fire of unknown origin / 원인 ~이다 be unknown; remain unexplained; be a mystery.

**불명**(佛名) ① = 불호 ①. ② 《신자의》 *one's* Buddhist name.

**불명료**(不明瞭) = 불분명.

**불명예**(不名譽) dishonor; disgrace; discredit; ignominy; infamy; shame. ~스럽다 (be) dishonorable; disgraceful; ignoble; ignominious; inglorious; shameful. ¶ ~가 되다[~이다] be a disgrace [dishonor, shame] 《to》; bring disgrace on...; be derogatory to *one's* character / 그것은 우리 가문에 ~스러운 일이다 It brings disgrace upon our family. / ~스럽게도 그의 스캔들이 뉴스거리가 되었다 To his disgrace his scandal was reported in the press. ◉ ~제대 a dishonorable discharge.

**불모**(不毛) 《메마름》 sterility; barrenness. ¶ ~의 barren; sterile; waste / ~의 땅을 개척하다 open [develop] wasteland. ◉ ~지 barren [arid] land; 《황무지》 wasteland; a desert.

**불목** the floor just above the fireplace. ¶ ~에 앉다 sit on the warmest part of the heated room.

**불목**(不睦) 《family》 discord; trouble; dissension; disharmony; 《적대》 hostility; 《숙원》 feud. ~하다 be at enmity [feud, strife, variance, odds] 《with》; be in discord 《with》; be on bad terms 《with》.

**불목하니** 〖불교〗 a cook in a temple; a sexton.

**불무하다**(不無一) be not without...; definitely exist.

**불문**(不問) ~하다 do not ask [question]; ignore; disregard; overlook. ¶ 값의 고하를 ~하고 whatever the cost may be; at any cost / 그 누구임을 ~하고 without distinction [irrespective] of persons / 남녀노소를 ~하고 regardless [irrespective] of sex or age / 다소를 ~하고 however small it may be; large or small; regardless of quantity / ~ 곡직하고 without inquiring into the right or wrong; without any preambles or explanations / ～에 부치다 ignore; disregard; let go; lay aside 《a question》; connive at; pass 《*a matter*》 over; overlook 《*a person's* faults》; leave 《*a matter*》 unnoticed; shut *one's* eyes to / 이 문제는 ～에 부칠 것이 아니다 This should not be passed unnoticed. ◉ ～가지(可知) being understandable without asking.

**불문**(佛文) 《글》 a French sentence; 《문학》 French literature. ◉ ～과 the department of French literature. ～학 French literature.

**불문**(佛門) Buddhism; priesthood. ¶ ～에 들다 enter the Buddhist priesthood; become a Buddhist monk.

**불문율**(不文律) an unwritten law 〔rule〕; common law.

**불문헌법**(不文憲法) an unwritten constitution.

**불미**(不美) ～하다, ～스럽다 (be) ugly; bad; unfavorable; unsavory; unworthy; nasty; scandalous. ¶ ～스러운 사건 a scandalous 〔an ugly〕 case; a scandal / ～스러운 소문 an unsavory rumor; a scandal / 신사로서 ～한 행동 an act unworthy of a gentleman.

**불민**(不敏) incompetency; dullness; slowness; stupidity. ～하다 (be) incompetent; unclever; dull; stupid; be not smart.

**불바다** a sheet 〔sea〕 of flames; a deluge of fire. ¶ ～가 되다 become a sheet of fire / 전쟁이 일어나면 시 전체는 ～가 될 것이다 When a war breaks out the whole city will be engulfed by a deluge of fire.

**불받다** suffer insult and 〔or〕 injury.

**불발**(不發) 《탄환의》 misfire. ～하다 miss fire; misfire; snap (권총이). ¶ ～이 되다 fail to explode 〔go off〕; misfire / ～로 끝나다 《계획 등이》 fall through; miscarry / 포탄은 ～이었다 The shell did not go off. / 계획은 ～로 끝났다 The plan fell through. ◉ ～탄 an unexploded bomb 〔shell〕; 《구어》 a dud (shell): ～탄 처리반 a bomb disposal squad 〔unit〕.

**불밤송이** a chestnut which has dried up and fallen prematurely.

**불범**(不犯) ① 《침범 안 함》 not trespassing 〔encroaching, intruding〕. ～하다 do not trespass 〔encroach, intrude〕 upon. ② 『불교』 abstinence from sexual intercourse. ～하다 abstain from sexual intercourse.

**불법**(不法) 《위법》 unlawfulness; illegality; 《무법·무리함》 lawlessness; outrage; 《부정》 wrong(fulness); injustice; iniquity. ～하다 (be) unlawful; illegal; unjust; iniquitous; wrong; unwarrantable; unwarranted; unjustifiable; unjustified. ¶ ～으로 illegally; unlawfully; wrongfully / ～한 짓을 하다 act unlawfully 〔outrageously〕; do 《*a person*》 wrong; take an illegal act / 그는 ～한 수단으로 그 정보를 입수했다 He got the information by using illegal means.
◉ ～감금 illegal confinement; wrongful detention. ～건축(물) an illegal building. ～몰수 ouster. ～ 선거 운동 an illicit election campaign. ～소지 illegal possession: 무기 ～ 소지 illegal possession of weapon. ～입국 illegal entry; unlawful immigration: ～ 입국자 an illegal entrant 〔immigrant〕 / ～ 입국 외국인 근로자 an illegal-entrant foreign worker. ～점거 unlawful 〔illegal〕 occupation; squatting: ～ 점거자 an unlawful 〔illegal〕 occupant; a squatter. ～점유 unlawful occupation 〔occupancy, use〕. ～집회 an illegal assembly. ～체포 an illegal arrest. ～침입 intrusion; a forcible entry: ～ 침입자 a trespasser / ～ 침입하다 intrude 《into》; trespass 《on, upon》. ～투기(投棄) unlawful dumping 《of garbage》. ～행위 an unlawful 〔illegal〕 act; a delict; a misfeasance: ～ 행위자 a wrongdoer; an offender; a malfeasant.

**불법**(佛法) 《불교》 Buddhism; 《교법》 the law of Buddha; a Buddhist canon.

**불벼락** ① 《번갯불》 a bolt of lightning; a thunderbolt. ② [비유적] a tyrannical decree 〔order〕; a dressing down; a talking-to 《구어》; what for. ¶ ～을 내리다 bark 〔bellow, thunder〕 at 《*a person*》; issue a tyrannical decree; give 《*a person*》 hell 〔what for〕; bawl out / ～을 맞다 get a talking-to; catch 〔get〕 hell 《from》.

**불변**(不變) unchangeability; invariability; immutability; constancy; permanence. ～하다 do not change; be unchangeable 〔invariable, inalterable, immutable, constant, permanent〕. ¶ ～의 법칙 an immutable law / ～의 진리 eternal truth. ◉ ～가속도 uniform acceleration. ～량 『수학』 an invariable; a constant. ～색 a permanent 〔fast, fixed〕 color. ～성 invariability; inalterability. ～자본 constant capital.

**불병풍**(一屛風) a small folding screen to protect a brazier fire from the wind.

**불볕** 《under》 the burning 〔scorching〕 sun. ¶ ～(이) 나다 the sun comes out blazing / ～이다 The sun is burning hot. ◉ ～더위 the sweltering 〔scorching〕 heat of the sun.

**불복**(不服) ① 《판결에 대한》 denial of *one's* guilt; pleading not guilty; 《불만》 dissatisfaction; discontent; 《이의》 an objection; a protest; 《불찬성》 disagreement; 《불평》 a complaint. ～하다 deny *one's* guilt; plead not guilty; be dissatisfied; 《이의를 제기하다》 object to; (enter a) protest against. ¶ 그는 제 일심의 판결에 대하여 ～ 항소했다 He appealed from the finding of the court of the first instance. ② 《불복종》 insubordination; disobedience. ～하다 be insubordinate; be disobedient. ¶ 상관의 지시에 ～하다 do not respond to the instructions given by *one's* senior. ◉ ～상고 an appeal 〔an institution〕 of dissatisfaction (to the Supreme Court). ～항소 an appeal of dissatisfaction (to a higher court).

**불복종**(不服從) disobedience. ⇨ 불복 ②.

**불분명**(不分明) indistinctness; obscurity; ambiguity. ～하다 (be) indistinct; obscure; ambiguous; dim; blurred; inexplicit; unclear. ¶ ～한 발음 inarticulate pronunciation / ～한 태도 an uncertain 〔a noncommittal〕 attitude.

**불붙다** catch (on) 〔take〕 fire; light up; kindle; ignite. ¶ 불붙는 데 키질〔부채질〕하다 make matters worse; cast 〔pour〕 oil on the fire 〔flames〕 / 불붙기 쉽다 be easy 〔quick〕 to catch fire; be combustible; be inflammable.

**불붙이다** set 《*something*》 alight; kindle; ignite; light (up); set on fire; strike (성냥으로); [비유적] touch off 《a quarrel》. ¶ 장작에 ～ kindle wood; light the firewood / 담배에 ～ light (up) a cigarette.

**불비**(不備) deficiency; imperfection; defectiveness; inadequacy; lack (부족). ～하다 (be) defective; faulty; deficient; imperfect; incomplete. ¶ ～한 점 a defect; an omission; a fault; something unsatisfactory; an imperfection / 위생 시설의 ～ lack of proper sanitation / 제도상의 ～ institutional inertia / 서류가 ～하다 The documents are not in order.

**불빛** ① 《빛깔》 the color of a flame; flame color. ② 《빛》 light from fires; firelight; light; rays of light. ¶ ～이 어둡다〔밝다〕 the light is dim 〔bright〕 / (전등의) ～이 약하다 (the bulb) give a poor light / 어둠 속에 ～이 보였다 A light was seen in the dark.

**불사**(不死) immortality; eternal life. ～하다 never die; be immortal. ¶ ～의 immortal; deathless; imperishable / ～불멸 《enjoy》 immortality 〔indestructibility, imperishability, athanasia〕. ◉ ～약 an elixir of life. ～조 the secular bird; the phoenix.

**불사**(佛寺) a Buddhist temple.

**불사**(佛事) Buddhist rituals and services; a Buddhist memorial service. ¶ ～를 행하다 hold a Buddhist service.

**불사르다** burn; commit 《*a thing*》 to the flames; put 《*a thing*》 into fire. ¶ 헌 신문을 ～ burn old newspapers / 쓰레기를 ～ make a bonfire of rubbish; burn garbage / 정열을 ～ burn with passion 〔enthusiasm〕.

**불사신**(不死身) 《아픔을 느끼지 않는》 insensitivity; 《상처를 입지 않는》 an invulnerable body 〔life〕; invulnerability; 《죽지 않는》 immortality. ¶ ～의 invulnerable; immortal; of eternal life / ～이다 have 〔bear〕 a charmed life; be invulnerable 〔immortal〕 / 그녀가 ～이라고 생각하는 것은 어리석다 It is foolish of you to think that she has a charmed life 〔nine lives〕. / 그는 여러 번 사선을 넘어온 ～이다 He is 「an incredibly tough 〔a virtually indestructible〕 man who has survived a life or death crisis more than once.

**불사하다**(不辭一) fail to 〔do not〕 decline; act in an unreserved way. ¶ …하기를 ～ be (quite) willing to *do;* be ready 〔prepared〕 to *do* / 경우에 따라서는 죽음도 불사하겠다 I am ready to die in case of need.

**불상**(不祥) ～하다 (be) ill-omened; ominous; sinister; disgraceful; scandalous. ◉ ～사 an ill 〔unhappy〕 event; an inauspicious 〔a deplorable〕 event; a mishap; a scandal.

**불상**(不詳) being not known 〔clear〕.

**불상**(佛像) an image of Buddha; a Buddhist image 〔statue〕.

**불상놈**(一常一) a very vulgar 〔base, mean, low-down〕 fellow.

**불상정**(不上程) deferment of the introduction of a bill (to the House). ◉ ～안 a motion to defer the (House) deliberation on a bill; a plan to defer the discussion of the issue.

**불서**(佛書) the Buddhist scriptures; Buddhist literature.

**불선명**(不鮮明) obscurity; unclearness; indistinctness; 〖사진〗 blur(ring). ～하다 (be) obscure; indistinct; blurred; be not clear. ¶ 텔레비전의 화면이 ～하다 The TV's picture isn't sharp. *or* The TV is blurry 〔fuzzy〕.

**불설**(佛說) Buddhist doctrine(s); Buddha's teaching(s) 〔sermon(s)〕.

**불성**(佛性) the nature of Buddha; the Buddha-nature.

**불성공**(不成功) lack of success; failure; miscarriage. ～하다 fail at; end in failure; meet with failure; fall through; fall short; prove abortive; fizzle out.

**불성립**(不成立) failure; miscarriage. ～하다 fail; fall through.

**불성실**(不誠實) insincerity; bad faith; unfaithfulness; untruthfulness. ～하다 (be) insincere; unfaithful; untruthful; untrustworthy. ◉ ～신고 《세금의》 《file》 insincere tax returns 《with》.

**불세지재**(不世之才) a man of rare talent; a prodigy; an extraordinary talent 〔gift〕.

**불세출**(不世出) rarity. ¶ ～의 extraordinary; uncommon; unparalleled; matchless / ～의 위인 a great man with few parallels in history.

**불소**(弗素) 〖화학〗 fluorine. ⇨ 플루오르.

**불소하다**(不少―) be not a little 〔few〕; be no small amount 〔quantities〕; (be) quite much; quite many; considerable. ¶ 그에게 힘입은 바가 ～ I owe 「much 〔not a little〕 to his assistance.

**불손**(不遜) haughtiness; arrogance; insolence. ～하다 (be) haughty; arrogant; insolent; presumptuous; assuming; overweening. ¶ ～한 태도 a haughty attitude; an insolent bearing 〔air〕 / ～하게 insolently; with arrogance / ～하게 굴다 behave haughtily.

**불수의**(不隨意) ¶ ～의 involuntary. ◉ ～근(筋) 〖해부〗 an involuntary muscle. ～운동 an involuntary motion 〔movement〕. ～작용 an involuntary action.

**불순**(不純) impurity; adulteration. ～하다 (be) impure; foul; mixed. ¶ ～한 마음 an impure heart / ～한 사상 an undesirable idea / ～한 동기(에서) (from) a dishonest 〔a mixed, a selfish, an interested〕 motive / 자넨 나의 동기가 ～하다는 건가 Do you impeach my motives? ◉ ～분자 an impure element; the subversive elements (파괴분자들): 당내의 ～ 분자 rebellious elements of a party.

**불순**(不順) ～하다 ① 《불순종》 (be) disobedient; rebellious; rude. ② 《날씨가》 (be) unseasonable; changeable; unfavorable. ¶ ～한 날씨 unseasonable 〔unsettled, changeable〕 weather / 일기가 ～해서 on account of the unseasonable weather / 일기 ～한 이때에 in this unseasonable weather / 일기 ～으로 우리들의 출발은 연기되었다 On account of the unseasonable weather our departure was 「postponed 〔put off〕.

**불순물**(不純物) impurities; 〖의학〗 foreign matter. ¶ ～을 없애다 remove 〔get rid of〕 impurities.

**불승인**(不承認) disapproval; veto; 《정권의》 nonrecognition. ¶ ～ 정책의 포기 abandonment of nonrecognition policy.

**불시**(不時) 《때 아님》 being out of season; 《뜻밖》 unexpectedness; suddenness. ¶ ～의 untimely; unexpected; unforeseen; emergent / ～에 unexpectedly; untimely; abruptly; by surprise / ～의 공격 a surprise attack / ～의 죽음 an untimely 〔a sudden〕 death / ～의 경우에 in time of need / ～의 변에 대비하다 provide against emergencies 〔accidents〕 / ～의 경우에 대비해서 돈을 모아두다 put aside money against a rainy day / ～에 덮치다 take 《*a person*》 unawares 〔by surprise〕; 《경찰이 도박장 등을》 raid 〔make a raid upon, move in on〕 《a gambling den》 / ～에 찾아와서 죄송합니다 Please forgive me for coming unannounced.

**불시착**(不時着) a forced 〔an emergency〕 landing. ～하다 make 「a forced 〔an emergency〕 landing 《at》; be ditched (해상에). ¶ 그들은 남해안에 ～하지 않을 수 없었다 They were forced to make a forced landing on the south coast. ◉ ～ 비행장 an emergency landing field.

**불식**(佛式) the Buddhist ritual; Buddhist rites. ¶ ～에 따라 according to 〔with〕 Buddhist rites / ～에 의한 in Buddhist rites.

**불식**(拂拭) ～하다 wipe out; sweep off; clean. ¶ 불명예를 ～하다 wipe out a disgrace / 대화를 통해 있을지도 모를 오

uncalled-for; unjustifiable; unwarrantable; 《지나침》 (be) immoderate; excessive. ¶ ～한 처사 an unfair action 〔dealing〕.

**불완전**(不完全) imperfection; incompleteness; faultiness; defectiveness (결함). ～하다 (be) imperfect; incomplete; faulty; defective. ¶ ～하게 imperfectly; incompletely; defectively / ～한 점 a defect; a fault; an imperfection / ～한 지식 a little 〔smattering〕 knowledge; incomplete 〔imperfect, inadequate〕 knowledge / 다소 ～한 데가 있다 lack 〔want〕 something of perfection; be somewhat defective / 그의 설명은 아주 ～하다 His explanation is far from (being) perfect. / 인간이란 누구나 ～하다 Every man has his faults. *or* No man is perfect.
◉ ～고용 〖경제〗 underemployment. ～독립〔주권〕 incomplete independence 〔sovereignity〕. ～동사 〖문법〗 an incomplete verb: ～ 자동사〔타동사〕 an incomplete intransitive 〔transitive〕 verb. ～명사 a quasi-free noun; a restricted noun. ～변태 〖곤충〗 homomorphism. ～연소 imperfect combustion. ～화 〖식물〗 an incomplete 〔imperfect〕 flower.

**불요불굴**(不撓不屈) tenacity; inflexibility; invincibility; indomitableness. ¶ ～의 tenacious; inflexible; unyielding; invincible; indomitable; dauntless / ～의 노력 untired 〔persistent〕 industry / ～의 정신 an inflexible spirit.

**불요불급**(不要不急) ～하다 be not urgent 〔pressing〕. ¶ ～의 non-urgent / ～의 사업 nonessential enterprises / ～의 계획을 연기하다 postpone non-urgent projects. ◉ ～품 nonessential goods; non-urgently necessary commodities.

**불용**(不用) ～하다 do not use; disuse; discard; junk. ◉ ～품 useless things; a discard; an article in disuse.

**불용성**(不溶性) insolubility. ¶ ～의 insoluble; infusible.

**불우**(不遇) misfortune; ill luck 〔fortune〕; adversity (역경); obscurity (미천함). ～하다 (be) ill-fated; ill-starred; unfortunate; hapless; obscure; unappreciated. ¶ ～한 사람들 people out of luck / ～한 시절 《in》 *one's* dark 〔unfavored〕 days / ～한 처지에 있다 be in adverse circumstances; be in obscurity / ～하게 자라다 grow up in adverse 〔untoward〕 circumstances / 일생을 ～하게 보내다 live in obscurity all *one's* life / ～ 이웃 돕기 (모금) 운동 a "Let's help needy neighbors." (fund-raising) campaign.

**불운**(不運) (a) misfortune; adverse fortune 〔circumstances〕; ill luck; a hapless fate; 《구어》 a bad break. ～하다 (be) unfortunate; unlucky; ill-fated. ¶ ～하게(도) unfortunately; unluckily; as ill luck would have it / ～을 당하다 fall on evil days; meet with a reverse; have bad luck / ～을 한탄하다 feel sorrow at *one's* hard fate 〔lot〕; bemoan *one's* ill luck / ～의 탓이라고 체념하다 accept *one's* fate; resign *oneself* to fate.

**불원**(不遠) 〔부사적〕 ① 《거리》 not far (off). ～하다 be not far 〔far off, distant〕. ¶ ～천리하고 despite the long way. ② 《시간》 before long; soon; shortly. ～하다 be not far in the future. ¶ ～한 장래에 at no (very) distant day 〔date〕; before long; in the near future.

**불유쾌**(不愉快) unpleasantness. ⇨ 불쾌「(不快).

**불은**(佛恩) the grace 〔mercy, kindness〕 of Buddha; Buddha's blessings.

**불응**(不應) nonacceptance; noncompliance; declination; 《거절》 refusal. ～하다 do not 「answer 〔accept, comply with, consent to〕; decline; reject.

**불의**(不意) suddenness; unexpectedness. ¶ ～의 《갑작스러운》 sudden; abrupt; 《우연의》 incidental; casual; 《뜻하지 않은》 unexpected; unlooked-for; unanticipated / ～에 unexpectedly; suddenly; abruptly; all of a sudden; by chance; by surprise / ～의 방문〔내방〕 a surprise visit; an unlooked-for 〔a surprise〕 call / ～의 사건 an unexpected event / ～의 습격 a surprise attack / ～의 습격을 당하다 be taken by surprise; be caught napping 〔unawares〕 / 그의 ～의 질문에 당황했다 I was embarrassed at his abrupt question.

**불의**(不義) ① 《부도덕》 immorality; impropriety; 《부정(不正)》 injustice; unrighteousness; infidelity; 《배신》 perfidy. ¶ ～의 immoral; improper; unjust. ② 《부정(不貞)》 illicit intercourse; unfaithfulness; marital infidelity. ¶ ～의 illicit / ～의 사랑 illicit love / ～의 씨 a child born in sin; a love child / ～의 관계를 맺다 form an illicit connection; misconduct *oneself* 《with》.

**불이익**(不利益) disadvantage; a handicap; a drawback; 《득책이 아님》 inadvisability; inexpediency. ⇨ 불리. ~하다 (be) disadvantageous; unprofitable; unremunerative; inadvisable; inexpedient; unfavorable; be against *one's* interests; 《유해》 (be) detrimental; injurious; prejudicial. ¶ 자기에게 ~이 되는 짓을 하다 act against *one's* own interests.

**불이행**(不履行) nonfulfillment; nonobservance; breach; failure. ~하다 fail to fulfill 〔perform, carry out〕; break 《*one's* promise》. ¶ 계약의 ~ nonfulfillment of a contract / 약속의 ~ failure to 「live up to 〔keep〕 *one's* promise; breach of (*one's*) promise / 의무의 ~ failure in duty; nonperformance of an obligation / 채무의 ~ failure to pay *one's* financial debt; 〖법〗 default / 조약 ~ a treaty violation. ◉ ~자 a defaulter.

**불인가**(不認可) disapprobation; disallowance; disapproval; 《각하》 refusal. ~하다 reject; turn down. ¶ ~되다 be refused; be rejected; be turned down; be disapproved.

**불일**(不一) ~하다 be in disharmony 《with》; (be) irregular; uneven; lack uniformity.

**불일간**(不日間) =불일내(不日內).

**불일내**(不日內) [부사적] shortly; soon; before long; in a short time; in a few days; one of these days. ¶ ~에 찾아 뵙겠습니다 I will come and see you one of these days.

**불일듯이** actively; lively; successfully. ¶ 장사가 ~ 잘되다 *one's* business is thriving.

**불일듯하다** (be) prosperous; thriving; flourishing. ¶ 사업이 ~ *one's* business is spreading 〔growing〕 like wildfire; [사람이 주어] drive a prosperous 〔booming, thriving〕 trade.

**불일치**(不一致) discord(ance); disagreement; dissonance; dissonancy. ~하다 (be) discordant; inharmonious; dissonant; incongruous 《with, to》; be in discord 《with》. ¶ 의견이 ~하다 opinion varies; differ 〔vary〕 in opinion / 그의 행동은 말과 ~한다 His deeds do not 「agree with 〔match〕 his words. *or* He says one thing and does another. ◉ 언행~ the inconsistency of *one's* words with *one's* actions; inconsistency of *one's* speech and action.

**불임**(不姙) ¶ ~의 sterile; barren. ◉ ~수술 sterilization.

**불임증**(不姙症) 〖의학〗 sterility; infertility. ¶ ~의 sterile; barren / ~에 걸리다 become sterile; lose *one's* reproductive power / ~을 고치다 cure 《her》 sterility / ~이다 be sterile; be a barren woman / 나의 아내는 ~인 것 같다 My wife seems to be sterile. ◉ ~치료약 a fertility drug.

**불입**(拂入) (a) payment. ~하다 pay in; pay up 《stocks》. ⇨ 납입.

**불잉걸** burning charcoal.

**불자동차**(一自動車) a fire engine 〔truck〕. ⇨ 소방(자동)차.

**불잡다** 《진화》 subdue flames; check the fire; quench 〔put out〕 a fire.

**불장**(佛葬) a Buddhist funeral. ¶ ~으로 하다 burry 《*a person*》 according to Buddhist rites.

**불장난** ① 《장난》 playing with fire. ~하다 play with fire. ② 《남녀간의》 playing with love; an idle love affair. ~하다 play with love. ¶ 사랑의 ~ an amorous adventure.

**불전**(佛典) the Buddhist classics; 《경전》 the Buddhist scriptures; the sutra. =불경.

**불전**(佛前) before the Buddhist altar.

**불전**(佛殿) a Buddhist sanctum.

**불제**(祓除) exorcism; purification. ~하다 expel 〔drive out〕 《evil spirits》; exorcise 《a place of evil spirits》; purify.

**불제자**(佛弟子) a Buddhist.

**불조심**(一操心) caution 〔guarding〕 against fires; 《게시》 Be careful with fire (주의). ~하다 take care not to start a fire; take precautions against fire; look out for fire.

**불종**(一鐘) a fire bell 〔alarm〕. ¶ ~을 치다 sound an alarm bell.

**불종**(佛鐘) a Buddhist temple bell.

**불좌**(佛座) the seat of a Buddhist idol.

**불지르다** set fire to 《a house》; set 《a house》 on fire.

**불지피다** make 〔build〕 a fire. ¶ 난로〔아궁이〕에 ~ make a fire in the stove 〔fireplace〕.

**불질** ① 《불을 땜》 making a fire. ~하다 make a fire. ② 《총질》 firing 《a gun》. ~하다 fire; shoot.

**불집** a (fire) hazard. ¶ ~을 건드리다 "stir up a hornets' nest"; court danger 〔disaster, defeat〕; do a thing that might lead to something unpleasant.

**불집게** 《심지 자르는》 (fire) snuffers; a

candle snuffer; 《불 집는》 (a pair of) fire nippers〔pincers〕.

**불쩍거리다** rub briskly (the wash(ing)); scrub away (at laundry).

**불쬐다** 《사람이》 warm *oneself* 〔have a heat〕 at the fire; 《사물을》 subject 《*a thing*》 to heat; put 《*a thing*》 over a fire. ¶ 손을 ~ warm *one's* hands over a fire / 불쬐십시오 Please warm yourself at the fire.

**불착**(不着) nonarrival; nondelivery. ¶ ~ 우편물 a miscarried 〔lost〕 letter.

**불찬성**(不贊成) disapproval; disapprobation; disfavor; disagreement; dissension. ~하다 dissent 《from》; disapprove 《of a plan》; express *one's* disapproval 《of》; disagree 〔do not agree〕 《with *a person*, to a proposal》. ¶ 나는 그것에 ~이다 I am against it. / 나는 그 혼담에는 절대 ~이다 I am dead set against that match. / 찬성인지, ~인지를 말하라 Say whether you are for it or against it.
◉ ~자 a disapprover; a dissenter.

**불찰**(不察) negligence; carelessness; lack of attention; thoughtlessness; 《잘못》 a fault; a mistake. ¶ 그런 여자를 아내로 삼은 것이 당신의 ~이오 You made a mistake 〔blunder〕 in marrying such a woman.

**불찰**(佛刹) a Buddhist temple.

**불참**(不參) absence; nonattendance; a failure in attendance; default; nonappearance. ~하다 be absent 《from》; absent *oneself* 《from》; fail to attend; do not appear. ¶ 부득이한 일로 모임에 ~했다 I was prevented by unavoidable business from attending the meeting. / 그는 마라톤에 불참했다 He did not participate in the marathon.
◉ ~자 an absentee. ~통고 a notice of absence.

**불철저**(不徹底) ~하다 (be) inconclusive; be not thorough(going); 《논지 등이》 (be) inconsistent; weak (말·문체·표현 등이); unconvincing (납득이 안 되다); indefinite; halfway; lukewarm. ¶ ~한 논지 the inconsistent point of argument / ~한 수단 halfway measures / 나는 무슨 일이고 ~한 것이 싫다 I hate leaving things half-done. / 그 사고는 사전조사가 ~했기 때문에 일어났다 The accident happened because the preparatory research was not thorough enough.

**불철주야**(不撤晝夜) day and night; around 〔round〕 the clock. ¶ ~ 일하다 work night and day; work double tides 〔shifts〕; put life into *one's* work night and day.

**불청객**(不請客) an uninvited 〔a self-invited, an unbidden〕 guest; a gate-crasher 《미》.

**불청하다**(不聽—) ① 《듣지 않다》 do not listen 〔pay attention〕 to. ② 《불승낙하다》 do not consent to; do not acquiesce in.

**불체포특권**(不逮捕特權) 『법률』 immunity from arrest.

**불초**(不肖) 《아비만 못함》 being unworthy of *one's* father; an unworthy son; 《자칭》 I; me; myself; [형용사적] unworthy 《of》; incapable. ~하다 be unworthy of *one's* father; be not up to 〔comparable with〕 *one's* father. ¶ ~ 소인 I, the unworthy 〔incapable〕 man / ~ 자식 an unworthy son.

**불출**(不出) ① 《못난이》 a stupid person; a good-for-nothing. ② 《안 나감》 confining *oneself* at home. ¶ 두문~하다 keep 〔stay〕 indoors; confine *oneself* at home.

**불충**(不忠) disloyalty; infidelity; failure in *one's* duty 《to the king》; perfidy; treachery; treason. ~하다 (be) disloyal; unfaithful; undutiful; treacherous; perfidious; false; fail in *one's* duty 《to the State》. ◉ ~불효 disloyalty and filial impiety.

**불충분**(不充分) 《부족》 insufficiency; 《불완전》 imperfection; 《부적당》 inadequacy. ~하다 (be) insufficient; not enough; inadequate (부적당하다); unsatisfactory (불만족하다); 《불완전하다》 imperfect; defective; not up to the mark (표준에). ¶ 자금이 ~하다 be short of capital / 보수가 ~하다고 생각하다 be dissatisfied with a remuneration / ~한 점이 있다〔없다〕 leave something 〔nothing〕 to be desired / 공급이 ~하다 The supply is restricted. *or* They are ill provided. / 장비가 ~하다 They are ill equipped. / 조사가 ~하다 An investigation is not thoroughgoing enough. / 아직 그 연구는 ~하다 There is something yet to research. / 증거 ~으로 무죄가 되었다 He was acquitted for lack of evidence. / 나의 영어 지식은 ~합니다 My knowledge of English is quite imperfect.

**불충실**(不忠實) disloyalty; faithlessness; infidelity; dishonesty. ~하다 (be) disloyal; faithless; unfaithful; dishonest; 《몸이》 (be) unhealthy;

unwell.

**불취동성**(不娶同姓) not marrying with one of the same surname; (extended) clan exogamy. ～하다 do not marry with one of the same surname.

**불측지변**(不測之變) an unforeseen accident; an unexpected 〔a sudden〕 calamity.

**불측하다**(不測―) 《헤아릴 수 없다》 (be) inscrutable; unfathomable; 《음흉하다》 (be) bad; wicked. ¶ 불측한 놈 a wicked fellow.

**불치** a hunted animal 〔fowl〕; game; a bag; a catch; a take.

**불치**(不治) 《병》 incurability; malignity. ¶ ～의 incurable; fatal; hopeless; irrecoverable. ◉ ～병 an incurable 〔a fatal〕 disease: ～병과 싸우다 combat with the fatal disease. ～환자 a hopeless case; an invalid for life.

**불친소** a bullock; a steer.

**불친절**(不親切) unkindness; unfriendliness. ～하다 (be) not kind; unfriendly; disobliging; inhospitable. ¶ ～하게 unkindly; in an unkind manner / ～한 상인 a disobliging merchant / 손님에게 ～하다 be inattentive 〔not kind〕 to customers (★ be unkind to *a person*은 「심술궂게 굴다, 매정하게 하다」의 뜻. '불친절하다'는 be not kind to *a person*이 적절함) / 그는 그 외국인에게 ～했다 He was 「not kind 〔unfriendly〕 to the foreigner. / 그 상점은 ～하다 That store gives poor service. *or* They give poor service in that store.

**불침번**(不寢番) night watch; (a) (sleepless, all night) vigil; 《사람》 a night watchman. ¶ ～을 서다 keep a 〔go on the〕 night watch; keep vigil; keep watch by night.

**불컥거리다** squash something wet 「in *one's* hand 〔under *one's* foot〕.

**불컥불컥** squashing something wet 「in *one's* hand 〔under *one's* foot〕.

**불켜다** light (up) 《a lamp》; set 《a lamp》 alight; 《전등을》 turn 〔put 《영》, switch〕 on the light. ¶ 초에 ～ light 〔burn〕 a candle / 불켜져 있다 the lights are on / 밤새도록 불켜두다 keep 「a light burning 〔an electric light turned on〕 all night / 몇시인지 보려고 불켰다 I turned 〔switched〕 on the light to see what time it was.

**불콰하다** (be) ruddy. ¶ 얼굴이 불콰한 사람 a person with a ruddy complexion / 한 잔 술에 얼굴이 ～ *one's* face is slightly flushed with a glass of wine.

**불쾌**(不快) 《마음의》 unpleasantness; displeasure; discomfort; 《몸의》 (an) indisposition; an ailment. ～하다 (be) unpleasant; disagreeable; uncomfortable; 《기분이》 (be) displeased; ill=humored; 《몸이》 (be) not well; indisposed; be out of sorts 〔shape〕. ¶ ～하게 unpleasantly; disagreeably / ～한 날씨 nasty weather / ～한 냄새 an unpleasant smell / ～한 소리 a jarring sound / ～한 말 an ill=favored 〔offensive〕 word / ～한 표정 a displeased look / ～감을 주다 give 《others》 an unpleasant feeling / ～하게 만들다 hurt 《*a person's*》 feelings; give offense 〔umbrage〕 to 《others》 / ～한 얼굴을 하다 look offended 〔hurt〕; look displeased 〔uncomfortable〕 / 그의 말은 나를 아주 ～하게 했다 His words hurt my feelings. *or* His words set my teeth on edge. ◉ ～지수 a temperature-humidity index (생략 THI) (★ 전에는 a discomfort index).

**불타**(佛陀) (the) Buddha. ¶ ～의 가르침 the teachings of Buddha.

**불타다** ① 《불이》 burn; blaze; be in flames (화염에 싸이다). ¶ 불타는 집 a burning 〔blazing〕 house; a house 「on fire 〔in flames〕 / 불타는 석탄 live 〔burning〕 coals / 불타기 쉽다 be easy to burn; catch fire easily; be combustible 〔(in)flammable〕 / 불타지 않다 do not burn (easily); be nonflammable 〔noninflammable, noncombustible〕 / 불타고 있다 be burning; be on fire; be in flames; be ablaze; be aflame / 활활 ～ burn brisky 〔vigorously〕 / 화염을 올리며 ～ burn in flames / 목조 건물은 불타기 쉽다 Wooden houses easily catch fire.
② 《정열 등이》 burn; be aflame. ¶ 불타는 사랑 an ardent 〔a burning〕 love / 복수심에 ～ thirst for revenge / 야심에 ～ be burning with ambition / 증오심에 ～ burn with hatred / 열의에 ～ be afire 〔aflame〕 with enthusiasm / 그들은 향학열에 불타고 있다 They are burning with the desire to learn.

**불탄일**(佛誕日) Buddha's birthday; the Day of Buddha's Coming. ＝부처님 오신 날.

**불탑**(佛塔) a pagoda.

**불통**(不通) ① 《교통·통신의》 impassability; suspension; (a) interruption; a stoppage; a tie-up. ～하다 be suspended; be stopped; be blocked 〔tied-up〕; be interrupted; be cut off.

¶열차 ~ interruption 〔paralysis〕 of the train service / 전화가 ~이다 《특정한 전화》 This phone is out of order. *or* The telephone lines are down. / 눈으로 철도가 ~이 되었다 The railroad was suspended because of the snow. / 산사태로 교통이〔철도가〕 여러 시간 ~이 되었다 The landslide tied up traffic 〔railroad service〕 for several hours. / 시 전체의 전화가 ~되었다 All the telephones in the city were 「cut off 〔disrupted〕.

② 《이해·사정의》 no understanding; unfamiliarity; ignorance. ~하다 have no understanding; be not familiar 〔well acquainted〕 《with》; be ill informed 《of》; be ignorant 《of》. ¶의사가 서로 ~하다 do not understand each other / 세상일에 ~이다 be ignorant of the world; know nothing about the world / 그에겐 사리를 말해도 ~이다 He is dead to reason.

③ 《교제·연락의》 no association; no communication; lack of contact. ~하다 have no association 《with》; be not communicated; lack contact. ¶소식 ~이다 hear nothing from 《*a person*》 / 그들과 연락이 ~된 지 벌써 3일이 된다 It is already three days since they lost contact with us.

**불통일**(不統一) lack of unity 〔coordination〕; disunity; inconstancy; disunion; 《부조화》 disharmony. ~하다 be lacking in unity; be disunited 〔divided〕.

**불퇴전**(不退轉) 〖불교〗 firm belief in Buddha; 《부동의 결의》 unswering determination; a firm resolve. ¶~의 결의 an indomitable resolve / ~의 의지로 resolved to win 〔do〕 or die; with an indomitable resolve.

**불투명**(不透明) opacity. ~하다 (be) opaque; milky; turbid; cloudy; thick; 《전망이》 It is hard to see yet how…. ¶~한 액체 opaque liquid 〔solution〕 / ~한 태도 a questioning 〔an ambiguous, a vague〕 attitude / 앞으로 어떻게 될지 ~하다 It is difficult to say how things will turn out.

◉ ~도(度) 《사진의》 opacity. ~색 an opaque color. ~유리 opaque glass. ~체 an opaque body 〔substance〕.

**불퉁그러지다** bulge; protrude. ¶불퉁그러진 가지 a knotty branch of a tree.

**불퉁불퉁** ① 《내민 꼴》 with lots of knots 〔bumps〕. ~하다 (be) knotty; bumpy. ¶~한 나무 knotty timber.

② 《말》 《speak》 bluntly.

**불퉁스럽다** 《언동이》 (be) rough; blunt; brusque. ¶불퉁스럽고 때때로 적대적인 태도 *one's* abrupt and often antagonizing manner / 말버릇이 ~ talk bluntly; be blunt of speech.

**불퉁하다** (be) bulgy; protuberant.

**불특정**(不特定) ¶~의 unspecific; unspecified; general. ◉ ~기간 《for, over》 an unspecified term. ~다수 many and unspecified persons; the (general) public: 장사란 ~ 다수를 상대로 하는 것이다 Every trade is for unspecified recipients. / 이것은 ~ 다수를 대상으로 하고 있다 This is intended for unspecified individuals.

**불티** sparks (of fire). ¶~가 튀다 spark; sparkle; sparks fly 〔come off〕 / ~가 나다, ~나게 팔리다 command 〔have, meet with〕 a ready sale; sell 〔go〕 (off) like hot cakes.

**불펜** 〖야구〗 a bull pen.

**불편**(不便) ① 《몸 등의》 (an) indisposition; discomfort; malaise. ~하다 (be) uncomfortable; [서술적] be 〔feel〕 unwell 〔ill〕. ¶몸이 ~하다 be not feeling *oneself* 〔very well〕; be out of sorts; be slightly indisposed / 속이 ~하다 have something wrong with *one's* insides / 어디 ~하십니까 Aren't you feeling well?

② 《편리하지 못함》 inconvenience. ~하다 (be) inconvenient; unhandy (다루기가). ★ (in)convenient; (un)handy는 사물이 주어가 되며 사람이 주어가 되지 않음: Are *you* (in)convenient?가 아니고 Is *it* (in)convenient (for 〔to〕 you)?

¶교통이 ~하다 have poor transportation (service); lack traffic facilities; be hard to get to / 휴대하기 ~하다 be unhandy 〔bulky〕 to carry about / ~을 느끼다 feel 〔be put to〕 inconvenience; be inconvenienced / ~을 끼치다〔주다〕 cause 〔give〕 《*a person*》 inconvenience; inconvenience 《*a person*》 / ~을 덜다 mitigate inconvenience / ~을 참다 put up with inconvenience / 쇼핑하기에 ~한 장소 a place inconvenient for shopping / 그는 ~한 곳에 살고 있다 He lives in an inconvenient 〔out-of-the-way〕 place. / 교량이 유실되어서 마을 사람들은 매우 ~하게 되었다 The bridge was washed away to the great inconvenience of the villagers.

**불편부당**(不偏不黨) impartiality; nonpartisanship. ~하다 be impartial

〔nonpartisan〕; be free from party affiliation 〔bias〕. ¶ ～의 《공평한》 fair; impartial; 《편견이 없는》 unbiased; unslanted; independent 《of prejudice》; nonpartisan / ～의 신문 a nonpartisan 〔an impartial〕 newspaper; a newspaper free from party affiliation.

**불평**(不平) discontent; dissatisfaction; displeasure; disaffection (정치상의); a grievance; complaint (★ 구체적인 것을 들어 말하는 경우는 a complaint가 됨); 《속어》 a beef; a bitch; 《구어》 a kick. ～하다 complain of; make a complaint; 《중얼중얼》 grumble at 〔about, over〕 《*one's* food》; murmur at 〔against〕; whimper; grunt; 《구어》 yammer; grouse 《about》; 《구어》 gripe; 《미구어》 kick; 《속어》 beef.

> 용법 **discontent** 보다 일반적인 뿌리 깊은 불평·불만. **dissatisfaction** 흔히 분명한 원인이 있는 일시적인 불평·불만. **grievance** 좀 격식차린 말로, 불평이 되는 고통·비탄의 원인이나 이유 따위. **complaint** 구어적 표현의 말. 불평·불만을 말하는 일 또는 불평의 원인.

¶ ～거리 a complaint / ～스러운 얼굴로 with a discontented look / ～ 한마디 없이 without a murmur 〔complaint〕 / ～스럽게 이야기하다 speak of 《it》 in an injured tone / ～이다 be discontented 〔dissatisfied〕 《with》; be querulous (늘).

불평의: ～의 소리 a murmur; a voice of discontent / ～의 씨 a cause 〔source〕 of dissatisfaction.

불평을: ～을 참다 repress *one's* dissatisfaction / ～을 그치다 leave complaining / ～을 늘어놓다 grumble 《at, over, about》; complain 《about, of》; air *one's* grievances / ～을 터뜨리다 give vent to *one's* dissatisfaction.

불평이: ～이 가득하다 be extremely dissatisfied; be full of complaints / ～이 있다 have complaint to make / 회사에 대해 ～이 있다 have a grievance against the company.

¶ 나는 아무 ～도 없다 I have nothing to complain of. / 그는 늘 ～만 한다 He is a constant 〔confirmed〕 grumbler. *or* He is always complaining. / 무슨 ～이라도 있는가 Do you have something to complain about? / 쌓인 ～이 마침내 폭발했다 The pent-up discontent at last found its vent. / 그녀는 자기 남편이 술을 과음한다고 ～을 했다 She complained that her husband drank too much.

◉ ～가〔객, 꾼〕 a (chronic) grumbler 〔complainer〕; a malcontent; a kicker 《미속어》. ～분자 malcontents; the dissatisfied 〔discontented〕 elements; 《정부 견해에 대한》 a dissident.

**불평등**(不平等) inequality; 《차별》 discrimination. ～하다 (be) unequal; unfair; discriminatory. ¶ ～한 대우 discriminatory 〔unfair〕 treatment / 임금의 ～ wage discrimination / 인종적～ discrimination by race; racial discrimination / 문명국에서도 아직 남녀의 ～한 처우가 남아 있다 Even in civilized countries we still find many cases of 「sexual discrimination 〔unfair treatment of women〕. ◉ ～조약 an unequal 〔a one-sided〕 treaty.

**불포화**(不飽和) unsaturation. ◉ ～기(基) an unsaturated radical. ～용액 an unsaturated solution. ～화합물 an unsaturate; an unsaturated compound.

**불풍나게** busily; repeatedly. ¶ ～ 돌아다니다 bustle around busily.

**불피우다** make 〔build〕 a fire. ¶ 난로에 ～ make a fire in a stove.

**불필요**(不必要) unnecessariness; needlessness. ～하다 (be) unnecessary; needless; unessential; uncalled-for; superfluous. ¶ ～하게 unnecessarily; needlessly / ～한 말 superfluous words / 이런 것은 ～하다 This can be done very well without. *or* We can dispense with this. *or* We can go 〔do〕 without this 《for the present》. / ～한 지출은 절감해야 한다 We must 「cut down on 〔reduce〕 unnecessary expenses. / 변명은 ～하다 There's no need 「for explanation 〔to explain〕.

**불하**(拂下) disposal; (a) sale 《of government property》; (a) transfer 《of state property to private ownership》. ～하다 sell; dispose of; transfer. ¶ 국유지의 ～ sale 〔disposal〕 of national land / 정부는 그 국유림을 ～했다 The government 「disposed of 〔sold〕 the national forest.

◉ ～품 an article (to be) disposed of by the government; articles sold off by the government.

**불학**(佛學) Buddhist learning; Buddhology.

**불학무식**(不學無識) utter ignorance; illiteracy. ～하다 (be) utterly ignorant; illiterate; unlettered; uneducated. ¶ ～한 사람 an utterly ignorant person; an ignoramus.

**불한당**(不汗黨) 《강도》 robbers; brigands; 《악당》 a gang; thugs; rogues; scoundrels.

**불합**(不合) disagreement; discord; disharmony. ～하다 be in disagreement 《with》; be in discord 《with》.

**불합격**(不合格) disqualification; failure; rejection; elimination. ～하다 be disqualified 〔rejected, eliminated〕; come 〔fall〕 short of the mark 〔standard〕; be found ineligible 〔unfit〕 《for》; 《시험에》 fail (in) 〔fail to pass〕 《an examination》; flunk 《미》. ¶ ～되다 = ～하다 / 검사에 ～되다 fail to stand a test; do not pass muster / 신체 검사에 ～되다 fail the physical (examination) / 그는 눈이 나빠서 ～이 되었다 He was rejected 〔disqualified〕 because of his poor eyesight. / 시험관은 지원자의 반수를 ～시켰다 The examiners rejected half the applicants 〔candidates〕. ◉ ～자 a failure; a reject; a disqualified 〔rejected〕 person; an unsuccessful applicant 〔candidate〕. ～품 a rejected article; a reject; off-grade goods; a throw-out.

**불합리**(不合理) irrationality; illogicality; unreasonableness; absurdity. ～하다 (be) irrational; illogical; unreasonable; absurd; preposterous.
¶ ～한 가격 an unreasonable price / ～한 결론〔제도〕 an illogical conclusion 〔system〕 / ～하기 짝없는 out of all reason / 네 말은 ～하다 What you say is absurd. / 너의 의견은 다소 ～하다 Your opinion sounds rather irrational 〔illogical〕. / 그의 학설에는 ～한 점이 몇 가지 있다 There are some illogical points in his theory.

**불행**(不幸) ① 《마음의》 unhappiness; infelicity; misery (큰 불행). ～하다 (be) unhappy; infelicitous; miserable. ¶ ～한 결혼 an unhappy 〔infelicitous〕 marriage / ～한 사람 an unhappy 〔a miserable〕 person; a wretched mortal / ～하게 지내다 lead 〔live〕 a miserable 〔an unhappy〕 life / 아무의 ～을 바라다 wish 《*a person*》 ill 〔harm〕 / 그녀는 ～한 고아들을 돌보았다 She looked after unhappy orphans. ② 《불운》 misfortune; ill fortune 〔luck〕; adversity (역경); 《비참》 (a) misery; 《재앙》 (a) disaster; (a) calamity. ～하다 (be) ill; unfortunate; unlucky; luckless; ill-starred; ill-fated. ¶ ～하게도 unfortunately; unluckily; by misfortune; as ill luck would have it / ～한 소식 ill news / 행 ～ weal or woe / ～의 연속 a series of misfortunes / ～을 당하다 have 〔suffer〕 a misfortune; be hit by misfortune / ～을 면하다 escape misfortune / 자신의 ～을 한탄하다 repine at *one's* misfortune; bewail *one's* misfortune / ～은 겹쳐 오는 법이다 Misfortunes never come singly. / ～하게도 그는 자식을 잃었다 He had the misfortune of losing his son. *or* He unfortunately lost his son. / ～히도 그는 교통사고로 다쳤다 Unfortunately, he was injured in a traffic accident. / ～한 일을 겪게 되신 것 무어라 위로의 말씀을 드려야 할지 모르겠습니다 Please accept my sincere condolence on this sad occasion.

**불행중 다행**(不幸中多幸) a stroke of good luck in the midst of misfortune; one consolation in sadness. ¶ 그 사고로 사망자가 없었다는 것은 ～이다 It is consoling 〔comforting〕 that nobody was killed in the accident.

**불허**(不許) nonpermission; disapprobation; disallowance; disapproval. ～하다 do not permit 〔allow, admit〕; disapprove; disallow; reject; turn down; 《경제 사정이》 cannot afford.
¶ 변명을 ～하다 allow of no excuse / 외출을 ～하다 do not allow 《*a person*》 to go out / 형세는 낙관을 ～한다 The situation does not warrant optimism. / 사태는 일각의 지체도 ～한다 The situation does not admit of a moment's delay. / 그의 작품은 타의 추종을 ～한다 His productions elude all attempts at imitation. / 그런 비싼 사치스런 여행은 우리 경제가 ～한다 We cannot afford such an expensive extravagant journey.
◉ ～복제(複製) All rights reserved. *or* Reprint prohibited. *or* No copy 〔reproduction〕 is allowed without previous permission.

**불허가**(不許可) disapproval. ⇨ 불허.

**불현듯(이)** suddenly. ¶ ～ …하고 싶은 마음이 일어나다 suddenly feel like *doing*; be seized with a sudden desire to *do* / ～ 집 생각이 나다 be overcome with sudden homesickness.

**불협화**(不協和) discord; dissonance; disharmony. ¶ ～의 dissonant; discordant. ◉ ～음 a discord; a dissonance: 경제 마찰 때문에 양국 관계에 ～음이 일어났다 Economic friction has brought a note of discord into the relationship between the two countries.

**불호**(佛號) ① 《부처 이름》 the name of Buddha. ② 《중의》 the name of a Buddhist monk; *one's* name as a Buddhist monk.

**불호령**(一號令) 《명령》 an impetuous order; growling (소리지름); 《꾸짖음》 a roaring scolding. ~하다 growl in a haughty manner; issue an impetuous order; thunder 〔bark, bellow, storm〕 at 《*a person*》. ¶ 자정이 넘어 귀가했더니 아버지의 ~이 떨어졌다 Father barked at me when I got home after midnight.

**불호박**(一琥珀) red amber.

**불혹**(不惑) the age of forty; "the age free from vacillation". ¶ ~을 지나다 be over forty years old.

**불화**(不和) disagreement; discord; dissension; differences; trouble; disunion. ~하다 [서술적] be in discord 《with》; be at odds 〔strife, variance〕 《with》; be on bad terms 《with》. ¶ ~의 discordant; dissentious / 부부간의 ~ a marital 〔matrimonial〕 discord 〔quarrel〕 / 가정 ~ family 〔domestic〕 trouble; discord within the family / ~의 씨 the apple 〔seeds〕 of discord / ~의 씨를 뿌리다 sow (the seeds of) trouble 〔discord〕 / ~해지다 have a quarrel 《with *a person*》; fall out 《with》; become estranged 《from *a person*》 / 둘 사이에는 당분간 ~의 관계가 계속될 것이다 Both of them will remain on bad terms with each other for a while / 청소년 비행은 흔히 가정 ~에 기인한다 A discordant family often causes juvenile delinquency.

**불화**(弗化) 〖화학〗 ⇨ 플루오르화(化).

**불화**(弗貨) dollars; the U.S. dollar.

**불화**(佛畫) a Buddhist painting 〔picture〕.

**불확대**(不擴大) nonexpansion; localization. ◉ ~방침 a nonexpansion policy; a policy of localization: ~ 방침을 취하다 adopt a policy localizing the dispute.

**불확실**(不確實) uncertainty; unreliability. ~하다 (be) uncertain; unreliable; insecure. ¶ ~한 대답 an indefinite 〔uncertain〕 answer / ~한 보도 an unreliable 〔unauthentic〕 report / ~한 사업 a shaky business / ~한 정보원(源) an unreliable source of information / 나는 그런 ~한 사업에 투자하지 않는다 I have no mind to invest in such a precarious business. ◉ ~성 uncertainty: 인생의 ~성 the uncertainty of life.

**불확정**(不確定) indeterminacy; indeterminateness. ~하다 do not decide 〔settle, confirm〕; be indefinite 〔indeterminate, uncertain, undecided, unsettled〕. ¶ 방침은 아직 ~이다 The course to be taken is not yet decided upon. / 그 문제는 아직 ~적이다 That point of the question still remains undecided. / 회의 날짜는 아직 ~이다 The date of the meeting is still uncertain. / ~ 요소가 너무 많다 There are too many indefinite 〔uncertain〕 factors. ◉ ~기간 〖법〗 a time uncertain. ~성 원리 〖물리〗 the uncertainty principle. ~신용장 an unconfirmed letter of credit. ~자산 risky assets.

**불환지폐**(不換紙幣) an inconvertible note; flat money 《미》.

**불활발**(不活潑) inactivity; dullness. ~하다 (be) inactive; stagnant; dull; sluggish; slack. ¶ 이 시기의 시황은 ~하다 Business is dull 〔stagnant〕 this season.

**불활성**(不活性) 〖물리·화학〗 inactivity; inertness. ◉ ~기체〔가스〕 an inert gas.

**불황**(不況) (a) recession; a business 〔trade〕 depression; dull 〔slack〕 business. ¶ ~의 dull; depressed; sluggish; slack; stagnant / 경제의 ~ economic depression / 세계적인 ~ worldwide depression (in business) / ~이다 be depressed 〔dull〕 / ~을 극복하다 overcome 〔get over, get out of〕 the recession / 예견되는 ~에 능동적으로 대처하기 위해 만반의 준비를 갖추다 be fully prepared to cope actively with the expected economic depression / 장사가 ~이다 The market is dull 〔in the doldrums 《구어》〕. *or* Business conditions are depressed. / ~이 점차 회복되어 가고 있다 Business is gradually looking 〔picking〕 up. / 우리 회사는 ~때문에 파산할 지경이다 Our company is almost bankrupt owing to the depression. / ~의 정도가 점점 심각해지고 있다 The depression is becoming more and more serious. / 정부는 대규모적인 ~ 대책을 실시하고 있다 The government is carrying out full-scale counter-recession measures.
◉ ~기(期) a dull 〔a dead, an off〕 season (in trade); a slack time

〔season〕. ～기업 a recession-hit enterprise. ～산업 unpromising industries; a depressed industry. ～시대 depression days; lean years; hard times.

**불효**(不孝) undutifulness 〔impiety〕 《to *one's* parents》; want 〔lack〕 of filial piety; disobedience 《to *one's* parents》. ～하다 be undutiful 〔unfilial, disobedient〕; be ungrateful to 〔neglectful of〕 *one's* parents.

◉ ～자 an undutiful 〔unfilial, ungrateful〕 son 〔daughter〕: 나는 ～자였다 I was not good 〔kind〕 to my parents.

**불효**(拂曉) dawn; daybreak; cockcrow; early morning; 《at》 peep of day.

**불후**(不朽) immortality; imperishability. ～하다 do not die 〔perish, decay〕; last ever; be immortal 〔imperishable, eternal, everlasting〕.

¶ ～의 명작 an immortal work; a masterpiece of lasting merit / ～의 명성을 얻다〔남기다〕 win eternal 〔immortal〕 fame; perpetuate 〔immortalize〕 *one's* name / 이것은 ～의 진리이다 This is an eternal truth. / 그는 이 발견으로 ～의 명성을 얻었다 He won immortal fame with this discovery. *or* This discovery made him immortal.

**불휘발**(不揮發) ¶ ～성의 fixed 《oil》; nonvolatile.

**붉나무** 〖식물〗 a sumac(h).

**붉다** ① 《빛깔이》 (be) red; ruddy; crimson (다홍); scarlet (진홍). ¶ 붉은 뺨 red 〔rosy〕 cheeks / 손톱을 붉게 칠한 여자 a woman with her fingernails painted red / 붉게 물들다 be dyed red / 붉게 물들이다 dye red / 붉어지다 turn red 〔scarlet, crimson〕; redden; color (얼굴이) / 부끄러워 붉어지다 blush with 〔for〕 shame / 성이 나서 붉어지다 be red 〔redden, flush, flushed〕 with anger / 흥분으로 붉어지다 flush up with excitement / 그녀는 붉은 옷을 입고 있었다 She was dressed in red. / 토마토는 익으면 붉어진다 Tomatoes turn red when they are ripe. / 나뭇잎이 붉게 물들었다 The leaves of the trees have turned red. / 서쪽 하늘이 저녁놀로 붉게 물들었다 The western sky is aglow with the setting sun.

② 《사상이》 (be) communistic; red; Red. ¶ 붉은 사상 red ideas; communism / 붉은 물이 들다 turn 〔go〕 Red; turn communistic; 《구어》 get pink.

**붉덩물** a muddy stream. ¶ ～지다 a stream turns muddy.

**붉돔** 〖어류〗 a crimson sea bream.

**붉디붉다** be ever so red; be deep red.

**붉으락푸르락** ～하다 turn alternately pale and red. ¶ 그는 그것을 보고 안색이 ～해졌다 His color came and went at the spectacle.

**붉은거북** 〖동물〗 a loggerhead (turtle).

**붉은광장**(一廣場) the Red Square.

**붉은발** a swollen vein at the site of an infection; a varicose vein. ¶ ～(이) 서다 a swollen vein appears.

**붉은배지빠귀** 〖조류〗 a Korean brown thrush.

**붉은토끼풀** 〖식물〗 a red clover; *Trifolium.*

**붉히다** 《얼굴을》 blush; color (up); redden (*one's* face). ¶ 얼굴을 붉히며 with a blush; blushingly / 귀밑까지 ～ color (up) to the temples / 그녀는 얼굴을 붉혔다 A pink glow mounted to her cheeks. / 그녀는 부끄러워서 얼굴을 붉혔다 She blushed with 〔for〕 shame.

**붐** a boom; (all) the rage. ¶ 조선업계의 붐 a boom in shipbuilding / 최근의 여행 붐 the recent travel boom / 투자 붐 the investment boom / 베이비 붐 a baby boom / 붐이 일다 boom / 붐을 일으키다 touch off a boom / 붐을 타다 ride the crest of the 《building》 boom / 지금은 건축〔관광〕 붐이 일고 있다 A house-building 〔sightseeing〕 boom is on. *or* House-building 〔Tourism〕 is booming now. / 젊은이들 간에는 해외 여행이 붐이다 Traveling abroad is all the rage among young people.

**붐비다** be congested 〔crowded, jammed, packed, thronged〕 《with》; be bustling 〔in a bustle〕. ¶ 붐비는 시간 《출퇴근시》 the rush hour(s) / 붐비는 열차 a crowded train / 손님으로 ～ [가게가 주어] be alive 〔crowded〕 with customers / 이 노선은 항상 붐빈다 There is much traffic on this line. / 입구는 항상 붐빈다 There is always a jam at the door. / 차안은 몹시 붐볐다 The car was jampacked inside. / 거리는 크리스마스 쇼핑객으로 붐비고 있었다 The street was bustling with Christmas shoppers.

**붐하다** ＝희붐하다.

**붓** 《털붓》 a writing brush (모필); a (paint) brush (화필); 《펜》 a pen. ¶ 붓 놀림새 *one's* way of handling a brush; 《필치》 touches; brushwork (화가의) / 붓을 놓다 lay 〔put〕 down *one's* pen; cease to write / 붓을 들다 hold a pen; put pen to paper; write / 붓으로 생활하다 live by *one's* pen; write for *one's* living; make a living by writing / 붓 가는 대로 쓰다 let *one's* pen wander; put down (on paper) whatever comes into *one's* head / 명필은 붓을 탓하지 않는다 A bad workman quarrels with his tools.

**붓꽃** 〖식물〗 an iris; a blue flag.

**붓끝** ① 《필단》 the tip of a (writing) brush; the point of a pen. ¶ ~이 닳았다 The tip of this brush has worn out. ② 《필봉》 the wielding of a pen; *one's* pen. ¶ 그의 ~에 생사가 달렸다 Life and death hang upon his pen.

**붓날다** behave 〔talk〕 in a shallow 〔superficial〕 way.

**붓날리다** make *one's* words 〔deeds〕 superficial; do in a shallow way. ¶ 언행을 ~ be flighty 〔giddy〕.

**붓다**[1] ① 《살이》 swell (up); become bloated 〔swollen〕; tumefy. ¶ 부은 swollen; tumid / 림프선이 ~ develop swollen lymphatic glands / 손가락이 〔얼굴이〕 ~ have a swollen finger 〔face〕 / 울어서 눈이 ~ have *one's* eyes swollen with tears / 각기로 다리가 부었다 My legs are swollen from beriberi. / 다친 팔목이 몹시 부었다 The injured wrist swelled up badly. ② 《성나다》 get angry 《at》; become sullen; get sulky 〔cross, peevish〕. ¶ 부은 얼굴 a sulky face 〔look〕 / 무엇 때문에 부었지 What makes you (so) sulky?

**붓다**[2] ① 《쏟다》 pour 《in(to), on, over》. ¶ 물을 솥에 ~ pour water into a pot; fill a kettle with water. ② 《뿌리다》 sow. ¶ 모판에 씨앗을 ~ sow seeds in a seedbed. ③ 《돈을》 pay in 〔by〕 installments; 《계 등에》 pay *one's* share by installments. ¶ 매달 만 원씩 ~ pay a monthly installment of 10,000 won.

**붓대** a brush handle; the stem 〔body〕 of a writing brush. 「a brush tip.

**붓두껍** a brush cap; a (metal) cap for

**붓방아(질)** fingering *one's* pen while searching ideas. ¶ 붓방아 찧다 finger *one's* pen.

**붓순** 〖식물〗 a Chinese (star) anise.

**붓장난** quill driving; hack writing. ~하다 drive the quill; be a hack writer.

**붓질** making a brush stroke; drawing; painting. ~하다 make strokes with a brush; stroke; paint.

**붓집** a brush case.

**붓통**(一筒) a brush-stand.

**붕** ① 《방귀 소리》 ¶ 방귀를 붕 뀌다 break wind; let a fart; fart; poop. ② 《벌·비행기 등의 소리》 with a hum 〔buzz〕. ③ 《허망하게》 ¶ (계획 등이) 붕 뜨다 end 〔go up〕 in smoke / 도박으로 재산이 붕 뜨다 gamble away *one's* fortune.

**붕괴**(崩壞) (a) collapse; (a) breaking; a breakdown; (a) crumbling; a fall; 《함몰》 a cave-in; 〖물리〗 disintegration. ~하다 collapse; fall (down); give way; break down; crumble; cave 〔fall〕 in (함몰하다); 〖물리〗 disintegrate. ¶ 제방의 ~ the breaking of an embankment / 광산의 갱도가 ~되었다 The mine roof caved in. / 그들은 북한이 당면한 식량 부족과 장기간에 걸친 경제적 어려움에 시달리고 있어서 지금 ~의 초기 단계에 직면했을지도 모른다고 믿고 있다 They believe that North Korea, beset by an immediate food shortage and longer-term economic woes, may now be in the initial stages of a collapse.

**붕긋붕긋** ① 《솟다》《rising》 in little hills 〔bumps〕. ~하다 rise in little hills 〔bumps〕. ② 《배접한 것이》 loosely; bumpily; unevenly. ~하다 (be) loose 〔bumpy, uneven〕 here and there.

**붕긋하다** ① 《솟다》 form a little hill 〔bump〕. ② 《들뜨다》 be a bit loose 〔bumpy, uneven〕.

**붕당**(朋黨) a faction; a clique; a coterie. ¶ ~을 맺다〔이루다〕 form a coterie; clique together.

◉ ~질〔심〕 party spirit; cliquism.

**붕대**(繃帶) a bandage; dressing. ¶~를 하다〔감다〕 bandage 《a hand》; apply a bandage 《to》; bind up 《a wound, a limb》; dress 《a wound》 / 눈에 ~를 한 사람 a person with a bandage over his eyes / ~를 풀다〔떼다〕 unbandage; undress 《a wound》; take a bandage off 《a wound》; remove a bandage / ~를 갈아 대다 change a bandage; renew dressing / 베인 손가락을 ~로 감다 bandage a cut finger / 그는 발에 ~를 했다 He has his foot in bandage.

**붕붕**[1] with a poop-poop-poop!

**붕붕**[2] 《나는 소리》 with buzz 〔hum〕; 《경적 소리》 with honks. ~하다, ~거리다 buzz; honk. ¶ 벌이 ~ 날아다닌다 Bees are buzzing about.

**붕사**(硼砂) 〖화학〗 borax. ◉ ~구(球) 시험 a borax bead test. ~땜 plastering up with borax. 천연~ native borax; tincal.

**붕산**(硼酸) 〖화학〗 boric acid.

◉ ~수 a boric acid solution. ~연고 boric ointment. ~염 a borate.

**붕소**(硼素) 〖화학〗 boron (기호 B).

**붕어** 〖어류〗 a crucian 〔Prussian〕 carp. ◉ ～찜 steamed stuffed carp. ～톱 a saw which has a carp-shaped back.

**붕어**(崩御) the king's death; demise; passing away. ～하다 《the king》 die.

**붕어마름** 〖식물〗 a hornwort.

**붕우**(朋友) a friend; a companion. ◉ ～유신(有信) confidence among friends; confidence should reign over the relation between friends.

**붕장어**(—長魚) 〖어류〗 a conger; a sea eel.

**붕정**(鵬程) a long way; a long distance. ◉ ～만리 a long journey; 《항해》 a long voyage; 《비행》 a long flight; [비유적] a bright future (in front of *one*).

**붙다** ① 《부착하다》 (***a***) 《달라붙다》 stick 《to》; adhere 《to》; attach itself to; be put 〔affixed, posted〕. ¶ 단단히 ～ stick fast 《to》 / 굴은 보통 바위에 붙는다 Oysters usually attach themselves to rocks. / 풀이 잘 ～ The paste sticks well. / 이 편지에는 우표가 붙어 있지 않다 There is no stamp on this letter. / 붙으면 좀처럼 떨어지지 않는다 It sticks like a bur 〔limpet〕. (***b***) 《몸이》 keep 〔stand〕 close 《to》. ¶ 꼭 붙어 서다〔앉다〕 stand 〔sit〕 closely together 〔side by side〕 / 꼭 붙어 걷다 walk abreast 〔side by side〕; walk arm in arm (팔을 끼고) / 벽에 꼭 붙어 서다 stand close to the wall; hug the wall 《미속어》. (***c***) 《이름·낙인 등이》 be dubbed; be labeled. ¶ 무능하다는 딱지가 ～ be branded as a good-for-nothing / 노란 셔츠라는 별명이 ～ be dubbed "Yellow Shirt"; earn *oneself* the nickname of "Yellow Shirt".
② 《인접하다》 adjoin; be adjacent 《to》; border 《on》; abut 《against》. ¶ 서로 붙은 두 방 two adjacent 〔adjoining〕 rooms / 두 집이 서로 붙어 있다 Two houses stand close to each other.
③ 《…밑에》 (***a***) 《종속·추종하다》 attach *oneself* to; belong to; join; 《가담하다》 take sides 〔a side〕 with; side with. ¶ 반대당에 ～ side with the opposite party / 부자에게 ～ attach *oneself* to the rich / 그에게 붙어 있으면 손해는 없다 Under him you will have nothing to lose. / 넌 어느 편에도 붙으면 안된다 You should take neither side. (***b***) 《얹혀 살다》 live with 《*a person* at *his* expense》; be a parasite 《to》; be a dependent 《on》. ¶ 친척집에 붙어 살다 live 〔sponge〕 on *one's* relatives.
④ 《수발들다》 attend 〔wait〕 on; 《동반하다》 accompany; go along with; follow. ¶ 간호사가 붙어 있다 be attended by a nurse / 그에겐 두 명의 비서가 붙어 있다 He has two secretaries.
⑤ 《딸리다》 be joined 〔connected〕 《with》 (연결된); be attached to; join. ¶ 9호실엔 욕실이 붙어 있다 There is a bathroom that goes with Room 9. / 이 열차에는 침대차가 붙어 있다 There is a sleeping car attached to this train.
⑥ 《한 곳에 머물다》 settle (down); come to stay. ¶ 집안에 붙어 있다 stick at home / 자리에 붙어 있다 keep *one's* seat / 그는 좀처럼 집에 붙어 있지 않는다 He seldom stays at home.
⑦ 《생기다》 ¶ 버릇이 ～ get 〔fall〕 into a habit 《of》; pick up 〔form〕 a habit 《of》 / 살이〔몸무게가〕 ～ put on 〔gain in〕 flesh 〔weight〕 / 이자가 ～ bear 〔yield〕 interest / 영어 실력이 ～ become proficient in English.
⑧ 《불이》 catch 〔take〕 《fire》; be ignited. ¶ 이웃집에 불이 붙었다 The neighboring house caught fire. *or* The fire spread to the neighboring house.
⑨ 《시험에》 pass 《an examination》. ¶ 입학 시험에 ～ pass an entrance examination / 학교에 ～ be admitted into a school.
⑩ 《교미하다》 pair; mate; couple; copulate; cover (숫놈이 암놈에게).
⑪ 《귀신이》 be possessed 《by, with》; be obsessed 〔haunted〕 《by》. ¶ 악마가 ～ be possessed by a devil.
⑫ 《세금이》 be dutiable 〔taxable〕; be subject to duty 〔taxation〕; be taxed. ¶ 세금이 붙지 않다 be free of duty; be duty-〔tax-〕free.
⑬ 《기타》 ¶ 일이 손에 안 ～ cannot go about 〔bring *oneself* to〕 work; be in no mood for work / 싸움이 ～ start a quarrel; come to blows.

**붙당기다** grab and pull; yank 《on》; jerk 《along》.

**붙동이다** grab and tie.

**붙들다** catch; seize. ⇨ 붙잡다.

**붙들리다** ① 《체포되다》 be caught 〔arrested, seized, captured〕. ¶ 들치기로 붙들리다 be caught (in the act of) shoplifting 《a book》. ② 《만류당하다》 be stopped; be kept. ⇨ 붙잡히다.

**붙매이다** be detained 〔subordinated〕; be tied 《to》; be bound up 《with》.

**붙박아놓다** fasten 《*a thing*》 immovably; fix firmly; put aside 《in a corner》.

**붙박이** a fixture; a fixed 〔built-in〕

furniture. ¶ ～로 as a fixture; permanently; immovably / 이것은 ～로 되어 있어서 떼어 낼 수가 없다 It is fixed 〔built〕 in, and cannot be taken down. ◉ ～가구 fittings. ～장〔책장〕 a built-in wardrobe 〔bookcase〕. ～창 a blind window; a built-in 〔an immovable〕 window.

**붙박이다** be fastened immovably 〔firmly〕; be put aside in a corner. ¶ 그는 늘 집안에 붙박여 있다 He always sticks at home.

**붙안다** embrace 〔hug〕 《*a person*》 close(ly) 〔hard〕; hold 〔fold, look〕 《a baby》 in *one's* arms.

**붙어다니다** 《뒤를》 follow 《*a person*》 about 〔around〕; dangle about 〔after, round〕 《*a person*》; shadow; hang 〔fasten〕 on 《*a person*》.

**-붙이** ① 《겨레》 the same family; the same blood. ¶ 살붙이 kith and kin / 가까운 일가붙이 a near relative. ② 《동종·동계》 things of 《a class, a group》; things 「made of 〔belonging to〕…」. ¶ 쇠붙이 articles of iron; ironware.

**붙이다** ① 《부착시키다》 (***a***) 《달다》 attach 〔affix, append, fix, tag〕 《one thing to another》; set 〔put, join〕 《one thing to another》; fasten; stitch 〔sew〕 on (꿰매어). ¶ 소포에 꼬리표를 ～ attach 〔fasten〕 a tag to a parcel. (***b***) 《풀 따위로》 stick; paste (up); affix; put; post; glue (아교로); 《고약 등을》 apply 《to》; stick. ¶ 반창고를 ～ apply a sticking plaster 《to the wound》 / 우표를 ～ put a stamp on 《the envelope》; affix 〔stick〕 a stamp 《to a letter》 / 풀로 ～ stick 《*a thing*》 with paste / 벽에 포스터를 ～ stick 〔paste up〕 a poster on the wall / 이곳에 광고를 붙이지 말 것 《게시》 Post 〔Stick 《영》〕 no bills here. (***c***) 《입히거나 깔아서》 cover; line. ¶ 바닥에 타일을 ～ tile a floor; floor 《a room》 with tiles. (***d***) 《바짝》 put 〔place〕 《*a thing*》 close to. ¶ 책상을 붙여 놓다 place 〔put〕 desks side by side. (***e***) 《배·차 등을》 bring to 〔alongside〕; put ashore; 《현관 등에》 draw 〔pull〕 up. ¶ 배를 부두에 ～ bring a ship alongside the quay.

② 《첨부하다》 add; append; attach; annex. ¶ 조건을 ～ attach 〔annex〕 a condition 《to *one's* proposal》; saddle 《*a person*》 with conditions / 경품을 붙여서 팔다 sell articles with a premium / "sir"를 붙이는 것을 잊지 마라 Don't forget to put in the "sir."

③ 《가입시키다》 admit 《*a person* to membership》; let in; take in. ¶ 붙여 주지 않다 keep 《*a person*》 out of a group / 그를 붙이지 말자 Let's not let him in.

④ 《의지하다》 leave (*one's* livelihood) up 《to》; rely on 《*a person*》 for (*one's* care); put *oneself* under 《*a person's*》 care. ¶ 몸 붙일 곳이 없다 have nobody to turn to (for help); have no place to go / 아저씨 집에 몸을 붙이고 있다 I live with my uncle's family.

⑤ 《불을》 light; kindle; ignite; apply 《fire, a flame》 to. ¶ 담배에 불을 ～ light a cigarette.

⑥ 《노름·흥정·싸움을》 bring two parties together for 《an enterprise, a negotiation, *etc.*》; arrange. ¶ 노름을 ～ arrange gambling / 싸움을 ～ make 《*persons*》 quarrel; set 《dogs, *etc.*》 to fighting / 흥정을 ～ arrange a bargain; get two parties to strike a bargain.

⑦ 《내기에서 돈을》 bet 〔stake〕 《money on *a person*》 wager; put.

⑧ 《의견을》 give *one's* opinion; make an additional comment. ¶ 토의에 의견을 ～ give *one's* opinion in a debate.

⑨ 《사람을》 let 《*a person*》 be attended 〔waited upon〕; place. ¶ 감시를 ～ keep 〔place〕 《*a person*》 under guard; place a guard at 《a place》 / 호위를〔경호원을〕 ～ place a bodyguard / 환자에게 간호사를 ～ have a nurse in attendance on a patient.

⑩ 《때리다》 slap. ¶ 따귀를 ～ box 《*a person's*》 ear(s); give 《*a person*》 a box on the ear(s).

⑪ 《교접시키다》 couple; mate; pair 《animals》. ¶ 개를 ～ mate a dog / 암말을 ～ serve a mare.

⑫ 《말을》 speak 〔talk〕 to 《*a person*》; start a conversation with 《*a person*》; address 〔accost〕 《*a person*》.

⑬ 《마음·취미 등을》 acquire; have; take. ¶ 재미를 ～ take (an) interest 《in》; find pleasure 《in》 / 취미를 ～ acquire 〔attain, develop〕 a taste 《for》 〔an interest 《in》〕.

⑭ 《이름을》 name; call; christen (세례명을); style. ¶ 그는 강아지에게 존이라는 이름을 붙였다 He called the puppy John.

**붙임성**(一性) sociability; amiability; affability; kindness; warmth; friendliness; receptiveness. ¶ ～ 있는 affable; sociable / ～ 있는〔없는〕 사람 a person easy 〔hard〕 to get acquainted with / ～ 있는 태도〔친구〕 an affable manner 〔fellow〕 / ～이 있다 be sociable; be easy to approach; be the sort of person you can go to; be receptive.

**붙임줄** 〖음악〗 a tie.

**붙임질** attaching; gluing on 〔together〕. ～하다 attach; glue on 〔together〕.

**붙임틀** a frame used in joining pieces of wood.

**붙임판**(—板) a metal vice for holding pieces of wood which are being joined.

**붙임풀** a kind of paste used in sewing.

**붙임혀** 〖건축〗 an eave prop.

**붙잡다** ① 《손으로》 seize; catch; grasp; grip; clasp; take 〔get, catch〕 hold of. ¶ 꽉 ～ grasp tightly; clutch (hold of) / 손을 ～ grasp 《*a person's*》 hand / 자동차의 손잡이를 ～ hang 〔hold〕 on to a strap / 붙잡고 늘어지다 cling to 《*a person's* sleeve》; hold on to 《a rope》; hang on to / 엄마 치맛자락을 꼭 ～ cling to *one's* mother's skirts / 꼭 붙잡고 있어라 Don't release 〔let go〕 your hold 〔grasp〕 on it.

② 《범인을》 arrest; capture; collar; nab 《속어》. ¶ 도둑을 ～ arrest 〔catch, capture〕 a thief.

③ 《만류하다》 make 《*a person*》 stay; detain; buttonhole 《*a person*》; stop; check. ¶ 손님을 오래 붙잡아 두다 detain 〔keep〕 a guest long / 너를 오래 붙잡지는 않겠다 I won't keep you long. / 그녀는 폭풍에도 불구하고 외출하려는 아들을 붙잡았다 She stopped her son from going out in the storm.

④《일자리를》 get 《a job》; find; obtain.

⑤ 《돕다》 help; aid. ¶ 붙잡아 주다 help; aid; assist; give assistance to.

**붙잡히다** be seized 〔caught, arrested, detained〕. ¶ (범인이) 아직 붙잡히지 않고 있다 remain at liberty 〔large〕.

**붙장**(—欌) a built-in cupboard; a kitchen closet.

**붙좇다** follow (as a disciple or retainer); look up to; respect; revere; follow implicitly. ¶ 스승을 ～ hold *one's* teacher in high esteem.

**뷹달다** be hasty and rough; be reckless; be rough-and-ready.

**뷹대다** behave in a quick and rough 〔a rough-and-ready, an offhanded〕 manner.

**뷔페** a buffet; a refreshment 〔snack〕 「bar.

**뷰티콘테스트** a beauty contest.

**브라보** bravo. ¶ ～를 외치다 bravo.

**브라스밴드** a brass band.

**브라운관**(—管) a cathode-ray tube; a TV (picture) tube; a Braun tube.

**브라질** 《남아메리카의 공화국》 (Federative Republic of ) Brazil. ¶ ～의 Brazilian. ◉ ～사람 a Brazilian.

**브래지어** *a brassiere* (F.); a bra. ¶ ～를 하고 있다 wear a brassiere.

**브랜드** 《상표》 a brand. ¶ 유명 ～ a famous brand / 「샤넬」 같은 이름있는 ～ a name brand like 'Channel'.

**브랜디** 《술》 brandy. ¶ 소다수를〔물을〕 탄 ～ brandy and soda 〔water〕. ◉ ～글래스 a brandy 「glass 〔snifter〕.

**브러시** a brush.

**브레이크**[1] a brake; a brake device (장치). ⇨ 제동(制動). ¶ ～를 걸고〔걸지 않고〕 with the brakes on 〔off〕 / ～를 걸다 apply 〔put on〕 the brakes / ～를 늦추다 take off the brakes / ～를 걸어 멈추다 brake 《a car》 to a stop / ～가 듣지 않았다 The brake did not work. / 나는 ～ 페달을 밟았다 I stepped on the brake (pedal). / ～를 걸어 시속 20km로 낮추다 brake down to 20 (kilometers per hour) / 그 트럭은 급～가 걸리며 멈췄다 The truck braked hard to a stop.

◉ ～등〔라이트〕 a brake light; a stop light. 에어～ an air 〔pneumatic〕 brake. 자동～ an automatic brake. 잠김방지 ～ 장치 (the) Anti-lock Brake System (생략 ABS).

**브레이크**[2] 〖권투〗 a break.

**브레인스토밍** 《아이디어를 서로 내는 학습·회의 방법》 brainstorming.

**브레인 트러스트** a brain trust 《미》.

**브로드웨이** 《뉴욕의》 Broadway.

**브로마이드** 《감광지》 bromide paper; 《사진》 a bromide photograph.

**브로치** a brooch; a breastpin 《미》.

**브로커** a broker. ¶ ～의 구전 brokerage / ～ 노릇을 하다 act as a broker. ◉ 금융～ a money broker. 부동산～ a real estate agent 〔broker〕.

**브롬** 〖화학〗 bromine. ¶ ～을 함유한 bromic / ～으로 처리하다, ～과 화합시키다 brominate; bromize. ◉ ～산 bromic acid. ～수 bromine water. ～적정 bromometry. ～중독 bromism; bromine poisoning. ～지(紙) bromide paper.

**브롬화**(—化) 〖화학〗 bromination. ～하다 brominate. ◉ ～물 a bromide. ～수소 hydrogen bromide (기호 HBr). ～암모늄 ammonium bromide. ～은(銀) silver bromide; bromide of silver (기호 AgBr). ~칼륨 potassium bromide.

**브루나이** 《나라 이름》 Brunei (공식 명칭은 Negara Brunei Darussalam).

**브리지** ① 〚치과〛 a (dental) bridge. ¶ ~를 하다 fix a bridge. ② 〚카드놀이〛¶ ~를 하다 play bridge. ③ 〚레슬링〛 bridge.

**브리핑** (a) briefing. ¶ ~을 하다 give 《*a person*》 a briefing 《on》; brief. ◉ ~차트 a briefing chart.

**브이시아르** 《비디오 카세트 녹화 재생 장치》 a VCR. [< *V*ideo *c*assette *r*ecorder]

**브이아이피** 《중요 인물》 a VIP. [< *v*ery *i*mportant *p*erson]

**브이에이치에프** 〚물리〛 《초단파》 VHF. [< *v*ery *h*igh *f*requency]

**브이톨기**(―機) 〚항공〛 a VTOL aircraft. [< *v*ertical *t*ake-*o*ff and *l*anding aircraft]

**브이티아르** 《비디오 테이프 녹화 장치》 a VTR. [< *v*ideo *t*ape *r*ecorder]

**블라디보스토크** 《러시아의 항구》 Vladivostok.

**블라인드** 《차양》 a blind; a window shade.

**블라우스** 《여성용 상의》 a blouse; a shirtwaist 《미》.

**블랙리스트** 《요주의 인물 일람표》 a blacklist. ¶ ~에 오르다 be (put) on the blacklist; be blacklisted / ~에 올리다 put 《*a person*》 on the blacklist; blacklist 《*a person*》.

**블랙박스** 〚항공〛 《기록 장치 내장 용기》 a black box; an in-flight recorder; a cockpit voice recorder.

**블랙커피** black coffee; 《한 잔》 a black coffee.

**블랙코미디** 《우울하고 불행한 내용의 코미디》 (a) black comedy.

**블랙홀** ① 〚천문〛 《초중력에 의해 빛을 빨아들이는 구멍을 닮은 존재》 a black hole. ② 〚경제〛 《빠져나올 수 없는 상황》 a black hole.

**블랭크** 《공백》 a blank; a gap. ¶ ~를 메우다 fill in the blanks 《of a notebook》; fill the blank 《caused by...》.

**블레이저코트** 《색깔 있는 프란넬 상의》 a blazer.

**블로킹** 〚농구·배구·권투〛 blocking.

**블록** 《시가의 구획》 a block; 《권(圈)》 a *bloc* (F.); 〚건축〛 a concrete 〔cement〕 block. ◉ ~건축 a block building. ~경제 *bloc* economy. 달러~ the dollar *bloc*.

**블론드** blond(e). ¶ ~인 여자 a blonde / ~인 남자 a blond.

**블루** 《푸른색》 blue (color). ◉ ~라운드 〚경제〛 the blue round (생략 BR.). ~벨트 〚환경〛 the blue belt; the environmental protection area in the sea. ~북 a blue book. ~칩 〚증권〛 a blue chip. ~칼라 〚경제〛 a blue color (worker); a physical laborer.

**블루머** 《여성용의 짧은 바지》 bloomers.

**블루스** 〚음악〛 blues. ¶ ~풍의 blue / ~를 부르다 sing blues.

**블루진** (blue) jeans. ¶ ~을 입은 in blue jeans; jeaned 《teen-agers》.

**비**[1] 《내리는》 rain; 《한 번의 강우》 a rain (-fall); a shower (지나는).
¶ 부슬비 a sprinkling rain / 계속 내리는 비 a constant 〔continuous〕 rain / 억수같이 퍼붓는 비 a downpour; a driving 〔pouring〕 rain / 오락가락하는 비 an intermitted rain / 큰 비 a heavy rain / 비가 멈춘 사이에 between rains; during a lull 〔break〕 in the rain / 비가 오든 안 오든 rain or shine / 비를 만나다 be caught in the rain / 비를 막다 keep out 〔exclude〕 the rain / 비를 맞다 be exposed to rain / 비를 맞히다 expose 《*a thing*》 to rain / 비를 맞으며 걷다 walk in the rain / 비를 피하다 take shelter 〔refuge, cover〕 from the rain; shelter (*oneself*) from (the) rain / 비에 젖다 get wet (with rain) / 비가 오다 it rains; rain falls / 비가 새다 the roof leaks / 그녀는 눈물이 비오듯했다 Her eyes rained tears. / 가랑비가 온다 It drizzles. / 비가 올 것 같다 It looks like rain. *or* It threatens to rain. / 비가 오락가락한다 It is raining on and off. / 3시부터 비가 오고 있다 It has been raining since three o'clock. / 올 여름은 비가 많았다〔적었다〕 We have had much 〔little〕 rain this summer. / 비가 계속 왔다 It went on raining. / 비가 몹시 온다 It is raining hard 〔heavily, cats and dogs〕. / 비가 멈췄다〔그쳤다〕 It stopped raining. (★ stop to...는 「...하기 위해서 멈춰서다」의 뜻이므로 It stopped to rain.으로는 뜻을 이루지 못함) / 비가 오기 시작했다 It began 「to rain 〔raining〕. *or* It started raining. / 비 맞지 않게 빨래를 거둬 들여라 Gather up the laundry before it gets rained on. / 비 온 뒤에 땅이 굳어진다 《속담》 After a storm comes a calm. *or* A storm will clear the air.

**비**[2] 《쓰는》 a broom; a besom (마당비). ¶ 빗자루 a broom stick / 비로 쓸다 sweep with a broom.

**비**(比) 《비율》 (a) ratio; proportion; 《비교》 (a) comparison; 《대조》 contrast; 《필적》 an equal; a match. ⇨ 비하다. ¶ A와 B의 비 the ratio of A to B; the ratio A : B.

**비**(妃) ①《왕비》 a queen (consort). ②《태자비》 a crown princess.

**비**(妣) *one's* deceased [late] mother.

**비**(碑)《묘비》 a tombstone; a gravestone;《기념비》 a monument. ¶ 비를 세우다 raise [put up] a tombstone [monument] 《to the memory of...》.

**비-**(非) non-; un-; not-; anti-. ¶ 비공산국 a non-communist country / 비공산화 decommunization / 비금속 a nonmetal / 비논리적 illogical / 비애국적 unpatriotic / 비위생적 unsanitary.

**-비**(費)《비용》 expenses. ¶ 건축[생활]비 the cost of construction [living] / 학비 school expenses [fee].

**비가**(比價)〖경제〗 parity. ¶ 금은의 ~ parity of gold and silver.

**비가**(悲歌) an elegy; a song of sorrow; a dirge; a threnody.

**비각** incompatibles; opposite(s); being (mutually) exclusive; not going together. ¶ 물과 불은 ~이다 Fire and water do not mix.

**비각**(碑閣) a tablet house; a pavilion for a monument.

**비감**(悲感) a sad feeling; sorrow; grief.

**비강**(鼻腔)〖해부〗 the nasal [rhinal] cavity. ◉ ~점막 the nasal mucous membrane.

**비거스렁이** the cool after a rain. ~하다 cool off after a rain.

**비겁**(卑怯) cowardice; poltroonery. ~하다 (be) cowardly; craven; sneaking; dastardly;《남자답지 못하다》(be) unmanly;《비열하다》(be) mean;《부정하다》(be) unfair. ¶ ~한 짓 foul play / ~하게도 …하다 be timid [cowardly] enough to *do* / ~한 짓을 하다 act cowardly [the coward]; act like a coward; behave in a cowardly way; hit below the belt; play a mean trick;《경기 따위에서》 play 《*a person*》 foul / 이제 와서 그런 소릴 하다니 ~하다 It's cowardly of you to say so now. *or* It's mean of you to say such a thing now. ◉ ~자 a coward; a sneaker; a sneak; a poltroon.

**비게질** body scratching (of an animal). ~하다 scratch [rub] its body 《against》.

**비견**(比肩) ~하다 take rank 《with》; bear [stand] comparison 《with》; rank 《with》; be comparable 《with, to》; be equal 《to》. ⇨ 견주다. ¶ 조각가로서 그와 ~할 자는 없다 No one can equal him as a sculptor.

**비견**(鄙見) my humble opinion. ¶ ~으로는 in my humble opinion [view].

**비결**(秘訣) a secret; a key 《to》; the mysteries 《of》. ¶ 건강[행복]의 ~ the secret of health [happiness] / 장사의 ~ the tricks [mystery] of trade / 포장 ~ the mysteries of packing / 얼룩 빼는 ~ a tip for extracting stains / 성공의 ~은 근면과 정직이다 「The secret of [A key to] success is hard work and honesty. / 장수의 ~은 절제다 The secret of longevity is to be moderate in everything.

**비경**(秘境) unexplored [untraveled] regions; a mysterious land. ¶ ~에 발을 들여 놓다 set foot in [on] the unexplored [untrodden] region / 그들은 아마존 ~을 탐험하기 위해 탐험대를 조직했다 They organized an expedition party to explore the mysterious regions around the Amazon.

**비경**(悲境) a sad [miserable] condition; distressing circumstances; adversities; a sad plight [pass]. ¶ ~에 빠지다 be reduced to distress [poor circumstances] / ~에 빠져 있다 be in distress / ~에 빠뜨리다 put *a person* in a bad fix / 내가 ~에 빠져 있을 때 그는 나를 도와주었다 He helped me when I was reduced to adverse circumstances.

**비경**(鼻鏡) a nasal speculum. ◉ ~검사(법) rhinoscopy.

**비경이** a warp beam.

**비계**[1]《돼지의》(hog) fat; lard.

**비계**[2]《건축》 scaffolding; a scaffold. ¶ ~를 설치하다 set up [erect] a scaffolding; scaffold 《a house》; establish a foothold [footing].

**비계**(秘計) a secret plan; a deep plot; secret [underhand] schemes; *one's* best [trump] card. ¶ ~를 쓰다 play *one's* best card.

**비고**(備考) a note; a remark; a reference. ◉ ~란 a reference [remarks] column.

**비곡**(秘曲) an esoteric piece of music; a treasured [precious] musical work.

**비곡**(悲曲) a sad song; a plaintive tune [melody].

**비골**(腓骨)〖해부〗 a fibula (*pl.* ~s, -lae).

**비골**(鼻骨)〖해부〗 the nasal bone.

**비공**(鼻孔)〖해부〗 the nostril; the naris.

**비공개**(非公開) (being) not open to the public. ¶ ~의 private; secret; closed; closed-door / ~ 회의 a closed-door meeting / 그 회의는 ~로 열리게 된다

The meeting will be held behind closed doors. ◉ ～입찰 a closed tender. ～재판 a closed 〔secret〕 trial; a trial held in camera.

**비공식**(非公式) informality; being unofficial. ¶ ～의〔적인〕 unofficial; informal; shirt-sleeve / ～(적)으로 unofficially; informally; off the record (비공개로) / ～ 세계 타이 기록을 수립하다 set the unofficial world tie record 《in》 / 대통령은 그것을 ～으로 말했다 The President said it off the record. ◉ ～견해 an unofficial comment; a personal 〔private〕 opinion. ～경기 an exhibition game 〔match〕. ～방문 an unofficial visit. ～회담 〖외교〗 a conversation.

**비과세**(非課稅) tax exemption. ¶ 이 예금의 이자는 ～이다 The interest on this deposit is tax-free 〔tax-exempt〕. ◉ ～소득 non-taxable income. ～채권 a tax-free bond. ～품 a tax-free 〔duty-free〕 article.

**비과학적**(非科學的) (being) unscientific. ¶ ～으로 unscientifically.

**비관**(悲觀) pessimism. ～하다 be pessimistic 《about, of》; take a pessimistic 〔dim, gloomy〕 view of 《*things*》; look on the dark side of 《life》; 《낙담하다》 be disappointed; lose heart. ¶ 인생을 ～하다 take a gloomy view of life; be weary 〔sick〕 of life; lose interest in *one's* life / 앞날을 ～하다 be 「discouraged about 〔despondent over〕 the 〔*one's*〕 future / 극도로 ～하다 be in the depths of despair / 그는 불치의 병을 ～하고 자살했다 He killed himself, losing all hopes of his recovery. / ～할 것 없다 There's nothing to be pessimistic about. ◉ ～론〔설〕 a pessimistic 〔gloomy〕 view; pessimism: ～론자 a pessimist.

**비관세**(非關稅) ¶ ～장벽 (a) non-tariff barrier (생략 NTB).

**비관적**(悲觀的) pessimistic; dark. ¶ ～으로 pessimistically; darkly / ～으로 보다 take a pessimistic 〔dark〕 view 《of》; paint a dismal picture 《of》; look on the gloomy side 《of》.

**비교**(比較) (a) comparison; a parallel. ～하다 compare 《the two, A with B》 (★ with대신 to도 쓰임); 《대조하다》 set 《one thing》 against 《another》; contrast 《A with B》. ¶ ～도 안 될 만큼 beyond 〔past〕 (all) comparison / …와 ～하면 (as) compared with 〔to〕…; in comparison with…; in contrast to…; against… / ～도 안 되다 there is no comparison between 《the two, A and B》; 《낫다》 be more than a match 《for》; 《못하다》 cannot be compared 《with》; be no match 《for》; cannot stand 〔bear〕 comparison 《with》 / ～될 수 있는 것이 없다 be without 〔beyond, past〕 compare; be unparalleled; stand unrivaled; be unique / A와 B는 ～가 안 된다 A and B are not comparable. *or* A cannot be compared to B. / A와 ～하면 B가 낫다 compared with A, B is better / 나는 번역문을 원문과 ～해 보았다 I compared the translation with the original. *or* I checked the translation against the original. ◉ ～급 〖문법〗 the comparative degree. ～다수 《미》 a plurality; 《영》 a relative majority. ～대조표 a comparative table: ～대차 대조표 a comparative balance sheet. ～문법 comparative grammar. ～문학 comparative literature. ～문화 comparative culture. ～발생학〔생물학, 해부학〕 comparative embryology 〔biology, anatomy〕. ～분석 comparative analysis. ～생산비설 comparative cost theory. ～심리학 comparative psychology. ～언어학 comparative linguistics. ～연구 a comparative study: ～연구법 the comparative method / ～ 연구하다 make a comparative study 《of》. ～연구자 《문학·언어의》 a comparativist; a comparatist. ～우위 comparative advantages.

**비교적**(比較的) comparative(ly); relative(ly). ¶ ～으로 말하면 relatively (speaking); comparatively speaking / 새로 개점한 저 상점은 값이 ～ 싸다 In that newly-opened store things are comparatively cheap.

**비구**(飛球) 〖야구〗 a fly (ball).

**비구니**(比丘尼) a Buddhist nun 〔priestess〕.

**비구름** a rain(-laden) cloud; 〖기상〗 a nimbus (*pl.* ～es, -bi).

**비구승**(比丘僧) a Buddhist monk 〔priest〕.

**비국민**(非國民) an unpatriotic person; a traitor (반역자).

**비군사적**(非軍事的) (being) nonmilitary. ¶ ～인 조약 a nonmilitary treaty.

**비군사화**(非軍事化) demilitarization. ～하다 demilitarize.

**비굴**(卑屈) meanness; servility; lack of moral courage. ～하다 (be) mean (-spirited); 《아첨하는》 obsequious; 《노

예 같은》 servile; subservient; sneaking. ¶ ~한 사람 an unmanly fellow; a sneak(er) / ~한 근성 a servile spirit / ~한 웃음 an obsequious smile / ~한 태도를 취하다 take a servile 〔subservient〕 attitude.

**비극**(悲劇) (a) tragedy; a tragic drama. ¶ ~적(인) tragic; tragical / ~적인 사건 a tragic affair; a tragedy / ~적 장면 a tragic scene / 전쟁이 남긴 ~적인 상처 a tragic legacy left behind by the war / 결손 가정의 ~ a tragedy of a broken home / ~적으로 끝나다 end in a tragedy; end tragically / ~을 공연하다 enact a tragedy / ~이 일어나다 a tragedy takes place / 그가 요절한 것은 이 나라에 있어 크나큰 ~이다 It is a great tragedy 〔extremely regrettable〕 for this country that he died young. / 그것은 정말 ~이었다 That certainly was a tragedy. / 그 사건은 ~적인 결말을 맞이했다 The affair came to a tragic end. *or* The affair ended tragically. ◉ ~배우 a tragedian; a tragic actor 〔actress (여자)〕. ~작가 a tragic dramatist.

**비근하다**(卑近―) (be) common; familiar; simple; plain. ¶ 비근한 예(를 들다) (give) a familiar 〔an everyday〕 example.

**비금비금하다** be much the same.

**비금속**(非金屬) a nonmetal; a metalloid. ¶ ~의 nonmetallic. ◉ ~광물 a nonmetallic mineral. ~광택 nonmetallic luster. ~원소 a nonmetallic element.

**비금속**(卑金屬) a base metal.

**비기다**[1] ①《승부에서》 tie 〔draw〕《with》; come out even; end in a tie 〔draw〕. ¶ 비긴 경기 a tied 〔drawn〕 game / (야구 경기는) 연장전까지 했으나 비겼다 The match went into extra innings and ended in a draw. ②《셈을》 offset 〔cancel〕 each other, come out even 〔balanced〕.

**비기다**[2] 《비유하다》 compare《to》; liken《to》. ¶ 비길 만하다 be comparable to / 시간을 화살에 ~ liken time to an arrow / 인생을 흔히 항해에 비긴다 Life is often compared 〔likened〕 to a voyage.

**비기다**[3] 《때우다》 put《a patch》on.

**비길 데 없다** there is nothing like 〔comparable to〕; be beyond 〔past〕 compare; be《fine》beyond comparison 〔description〕; (be) matchless; peerless; unexampled; unparalleled; unequalled; unrivaled; unique. ¶ 비길 데 없는 장엄함 incomparable magnificence / 경치가 비길 데 없이 아름답다 The scenery is beautiful beyond all description.

**비김수**(―手) 《장기 따위의》 a tying move 〔run, point〕; a draw; a dead heat.

**비꼬다** ①《끈을》 twist (up); entwist; twine. ¶ 실을 비꼬아 노끈을 만들다 twist thread into a string. ②《말을》 give a sarcastic 〔cynical〕 twist to *one's* words. ¶ 비꼬아 말하다 say 〔talk〕 ironically 〔cynically〕; make cynical 〔sarcastic〕 remarks / 늘 그의 말에는 어딘지 비꼬는 데가 있다 What he says has always a touch of irony. / 그 말은 나를 비꼬아 하는 말이다 That remark is a dig 〔an indirect cut〕 at me.

**비꼬이다** ①《끈이》 get twisted. ②《마음이》 be perverse 〔contrary, obstinate〕. ¶ 비꼬인 성질 a crooked disposition / 마음이 비꼬여 있다 be cross-minded; have a perverse mind.

**비꾸러지다** ① 《비뚤어지다》 be quite crooked; be heavily tilted. ②《빗나가다》 go amiss; go awry; miss *one's* way 〔*one's* road, time, goal, *etc.*〕; 《계획 등이》 be upset; go wrong. ¶ 만사가 비꾸러졌다 Everything went athwart 〔awry, crisscross〕. *or* Nothing came up to my expectations.

**비끄러매다** tie《a horse》to《a post》; bind《*a person*》to《a stake》; fasten《a rope》to《a tree》.

**비끗비끗** ⇨ 배끗배끗.

**비끼다** 《비스듬하다》 be bent; lie at an angle; slant; 《빛이》 shine at an angle; slant.

**비나리치다** 《아첨하다》 flatter 〔fawn upon〕《*a person*》; 《비위를 맞추다》 curry favor with《*a person*》.

**비난**(非難) (an adverse) criticism; blame; (a) reproach; (a) censure; reprobation; denunciation; (an) attack (공격). ~하다 criticize unfavorably; censure; blame; reproach; denounce; condemn; attack; charge 〔accuse〕《*a person*》; crack down《on》; rap《속어》.

¶ ~할 만한 blamable; deserving of criticism; reproachable / ~의 대상이 되다 make *oneself* open to criticism; become the focus 〔target〕 of criticism / ~을 초래하다 incur a censure; lay *oneself* open to censure / ~을 면치 못하다 be open to censure 〔criticism] / ~의 여지가 없다 be above [beyond] reproach; have no fault to find with; be impeccable; be irreproachable / ~조로 말하다 speak in reproachful tone [vein] / 그의 행동은 일반의 ~을 초래했다 His conduct laid him open [subjected him] to public censure. / 그들은 지연의 책임이 그에게 있다고 ~했다 They blamed him for the delay. / 친구들 모두가 ~의 눈초리로 나를 보았다 All (of) my friends gave me a reproachful look.

◉ ~자 a critic; a censor; an accuser.

**비너스** 〖로神〗《사랑과 미의 여신》 Venus. ¶ 밀로의 ~ Venus of Milo.

**비녀** an ornamental hairpin. ¶ ~를 꽂다 wear [put on] an ornamental hairpin.

**비녀**(婢女) a woman slave.

**비녀장** a linchpin.

**비논리**(非論理) ¶ ~적(인) irrational; illogical; fallacious; nonsensical; absurd.

**비뇨기**(泌尿器) 〖해부〗 the urinary organs. ◉ ~과 urology; urinology: ~과 의사 a urologist. ~병 urinary diseases.

**비누** soap. ¶ ~ 한 장 a cake of soap / 가루~ soap powder / 세숫~ (a cake of) toilet soap / 세탁~ (a bar of) laundry [washing] soap / 약용~ medicated soap / 역성~ invert soap / 연성~ soft soap / 화장~ beauty soap / 손에 ~질하다 soap *one's* hands / ~로 씻다 wash with soap and water / 얼굴에 ~질을 하다 lather *one's* face.

◉ ~거품 soap bubbles [froth]; suds; lather. ~공장 a soap works. ~방울 soap bubbles. ~제조 soap-making; soap boiling. ~질 soaping: ~질하다 soap. 비눗갑 a soap case [dish]. 비눗물 soapy water; (soap)suds.

**비늘** a scale; a shard. ¶ ~ 모양의 scalelike; imbricate / ~ 있는 scaly; scaled / ~ 없는 scaleless; nude / ~로 덮여 있다 be covered with scales / 생선의 ~을 벗기다 remove the scales from a fish; scale a fish / ~이 떨어지다 scale off.

**비늘구름** 〖기상〗 a cirrocumulus (*pl.* -li). ¶ ~으로 덮인 하늘 a mackerel sky.

**비능률**(非能率) inefficiency. ¶ ~적(인) inefficient / ~적인 생산 방식 an inefficient method of production / 일을 ~적으로 하다 work inefficiently.

**비닐** 〖화학〗 vinyl; polyvinyl resin.

◉ ~보자기 a vinyl wrapper. ~선[튜브] a polyvinyl chloride wire [tube]. ~수지(樹脂) vinyl resin. ~중합체 vinyl polymer. ~하우스 a vinyl plastic hothouse.

**비닐론** vinylon.

**비다**[1] 《속이》 (be) empty; vacant; vacated; unoccupied; hollow; 《시간·스케줄 따위가》 (be) free 《of engagements》.

¶ 빈방[집] 《가구 없는》 an empty room [house]; 《쓰지 않는》 a vacant [an unoccupied] room [house]; 《세놓을》 a room [house] for rent [to let 《영》] / 빈 깡통 an empty can 《미》 [tin 《영》] / 빈 병 an empty bottle / 빈자리 a vacant [an unoccupied] seat; 《결원》 a vacant post; a vacancy / 빈차 an empty car; 《택시의 게시》 For hire. *or* Vacant / 빈 터 vacant land; a vacant ground; a vacant lot; unoccupied ground; an open space / 빈 손으로 with empty hands; empty-handed; without catch (낚시 등에서); without funds (자금 없이) / 머리가 텅 빈 사람 an empty-headed man / 나뭇속이 ~ the tree trunk is hollow / 뱃속이 ~ have an empty stomach; feel empty / 속이 텅 비어 있다 have no substance (실질이 없다) / 손이 ~ have *one's* hands free; be free [unoccupied, disengaged] / 주머니가 비어 있다 have a light [an empty] purse / 빈 곳을 채우다 fill (in) a blank / 이 자리는 비었습니까? Has this seat been taken? / 이 자리는 비어 있습니다 The seat is unoccupied. / 이 열차는 비어 있다 The train is not crowded. / 그를 빈 손으로 돌려 보냈다 I sent him away empty-handed. / 이번 토요일 오후는 스케줄이 비어 있다 I'll be free (from schedule) next Saturday afternoon.

**비다**[2] ⇨ 비우다.

**비단**(非但) merely; simply; only. ¶ ~ …일 뿐 아니라 not only [merely]… but (also); as well as / 그는 ~ 한국에서 뿐 아니라 전 세계에서 유명하다 He is famous not only in Korea but all over the world. / 그의 이론을 뒷받침해 주는 것은 ~ 이 사실뿐만이 아니다 It is not this fact alone that supports his theory.

**비단**(緋緞) silk fabrics; silk(s); satin (공단). ¶ ~의 silk 《stockings》; made of silk; 《비단 같은》 silken 《hair》; silky 《texture》. ◉ ~뱀 〖동물〗 an Indian python; a rock snake. ~실

《바느질용의》 silk thread; 《직물용의》 silk yarn. ～옷 silk dress: ～옷감 silk cloth 〔stuff, fabrics〕. ～이불 silk bedding. ～잉어 〖어류〗 a colored carp. ～장수 a silk merchant 〔trader〕. ～직물 silk goods; silk(s).

**비단결**(緋緞―) the texture of silk; a velvety texture. ¶ ～ 같다 be as soft as velvet / 그녀의 피부는 ～ 같다 Her skin is a velvety texture. / 그녀의 마음은 ～ 같다 She is tender-hearted.

**비당파적**(非黨派的) (being) nonpartisan; nonparty.

**비대**(肥大) 《비만》 fleshiness; corpulence; 〖의학〗 hypertrophy; dilatation. ～하다 (be) fat; fleshy; plump; corpulent; hypertrophous; swollen; enlarged. ¶ ～성의 hypertrophic / 편도선이 ～해 있다 have enlarged tonsils. ◉ 심장～ hypertrophy 〔enlargement〕 of the heart; cardiac hypertrophy.

**비대칭**(非對稱) 〖수학〗 asymmetry; dissymmetry. ¶ ～의 asymmetric(al); dissymmetric(al).

**비도덕적**(非道德的) (being) unmoral; 「immoral.

**비동맹**(非同盟) nonalignment. ◉ ～국(國) a nonaligned nation: ～국 회담 the nonaligned conference / ～국 정상회담 a nonaligned summit conference. ～운동 the nonaligned movement. ～정책 a policy of nonalignment. ～주의 nonalignment.

**비둔**(肥鈍) ～하다 《몸이》 (be) fat; corpulent; fleshy; 《동작이》 (be) slow-moving; clumsy; 《껴입다》 (be) heavily clothed.

**비둘기** 《사육용의》 a pigeon; a dove (특히 야생의). ¶ 통신용～ a carrier-pigeon / ～편으로 by a carrier-pigeon / ～가 울다 coo / ～를 날리다 toss 〔fly, let loose〕 pigeons (into the air) / ～는 평화의 상징이다 The dove is the symbol of peace. ◉ ～장 a pigeon cage 〔house〕; a dovecot(e).

**비둘기파**(―派) the doves; a soft-liner. ¶ ～의 정치가 a dove politician / 의회의 ～와 매파 the doves and the hawks of the Congress.

**비듬** dandruff; scurf. ¶ ～투성이의 scurfy; dandruffy / ～을 떨다 remove dandruff / ～이 생기다 become scurfy / 머리에 ～이 있다 have dandruff. ◉ ～약 a dandruff remover.

**비등**(比等) (being) equal; equal footing. ～하다 be (all) on a par; be about the same; be almost equal. ¶ 그 시대의 10원은 지금의 만 원과 ～하다 The ten won of those days is worth ten thousand won now. / 이것과 그것은 크기가 ～하다 That is almost equal to this in size.

**비등**(沸騰) ① 〖물리〗 boiling; seething; ebullition; effervescence; bubbling. ～하다 《끓다》 boil (up); seethe; 《거품이 일다》 effervesce; bubble. ¶ ～성의 ebullient; effervescent; fizzy / 물은 섭씨 100°에서 ～한다 Water boils 〔comes to the boil〕 at 100° centigrade. ② 《소란·격동》 fermentation; commotion; excitement; agitation; tumult. ～하다 be roused; be 〔become〕 heated 〔excited〕; get agitated; be in a ferment. ¶ 여론이 ～하다 public opinion is aroused 〔agitated〕 / 그 문제를 둘러싸고 논쟁이 ～했다 The matter gave rise to a lot of heated discussion. ◉ ～성 음료 an effervescent drink; a fizz 《미》. ～점 〖물리〗 the boiling point. ＝끓는점.

**비디오** video; 《테이프》 a videotape; 《기기》 a videotape recorder. ¶ 텔레비전 프로를 ～에 녹화하다 videotape a TV program; record a TV program on videotape / ～녹화를 8시에 맞추다 set the video to go on at eight. ◉ ～가게 a videoshop. ～게임 a video game. ～단말표시장치 〖컴퓨터〗 video display terminal (생략 VDT). ～디스크 a videodisc. ～ 소프트웨어 video software. ～아트 video art. ～자키 video jockey (생략 VJ). ～카메라 a video camera; a camcorder. ～카세트 a video cassette 〔cartridge〕: ～카세트 리코더 a video cassette recorder (생략 VCR). ～테이프 (a) videotape: ～테이프 녹화 video tape recording / ～테이프 리코더 a video tape recorder (생략 VTR). ～텍스 a videotex. ～텔 the Videotel (호텔 투숙객용 정보시스템). ～폰 a videophone; a videotelephone. 가정용～ a home video unit.

**비딱거리다** wobble; be shaky 〔rickety〕.

**비딱비딱** wobbly; shaky; rickety.

**비딱하다** (be) inclined; leaning; sloping; slanting; oblique; skew.

**비뚜로** wrong; askew; tilted; obliquely; aslant; slantwise; at an angle; at the wrong angle. ¶ 모자를 ～ 쓰다 cock *one's* hat; wear *one's* hat on one side.

**비뚜름하다** be somewhat crooked 〔wrong, askew〕; be at a bad angle. ¶ 자네, 넥타이가 비뚜름하네 Your tie is 「crooked 〔not straight〕.

**비뚜름히** at a rather bad angle; somewhat crooked 〔wrong, askew〕. ¶ 그림이 ~ 걸렸다 The picture hung askew.

**비뚝거리다** ① 《흔들거리다》 wobble. ¶ 비뚝거리는 의자 a rickety chair / 책상이 ~ the table wobbles. ② 《걸음이》 walk with a shambling motion. ¶ 비뚝거리며 걷다 stagger 〔shamble〕 along; be unsteady on *one's* feet.

**비뚤다** (be) crooked; wrong; tilted; askew; slanting; off-center; [서술적] be at the wrong angle. ¶ 그림〔길〕이 ~ the picture 〔road〕 is crooked / 코가 ~ have a crooked nose.

**비뚤비뚤** crookedly; staggeringly. ¶ ~ 한 길 a winding road.

**비뚤어지다** ① 《기울다》 get 〔become〕 crooked; slant; be tilted; be at a bad angle. ¶ 비뚤어진 코 a crooked nose. ② 《마음 따위가》 be perverse 〔crooked, cross-grained, twisted, warped〕; become distorted. ¶ 비뚤어진 정의감 a perverted sense of justice / 비뚤어진 행동 a crooked deed / 마음이 ~ have a crooked 〔twisted, distorted, warped〕 mind / 그 녀석은 성격이 비뚤어졌다 He has a crook in his character.

**비뚤이** 《사람》 (***a***) 《몸이 비뚤어진》 a person with a twisted body 〔limb〕. (***b***) 《마음이 비뚤어진》 a perverse person; a crank; a crooked stick.

**비래**(飛來) ~하다 fly in; come flying; 《비행기로》 come by air 〔plane〕.

**비럭질** begging. ~하다 go (about) begging; beg.

**비렁뱅이** a beggar; a mendicant. ◉ ~근성 a mean 〔mercenary〕 spirit.

**비련**(悲戀) tragic 〔disappointed〕 love. ¶ ~에 울다 weep over *one's* tragic love.

**비례**(比例) (a) comparison 《with a precedent》; 『수학』 (a) proportion; (a) ratio (비율). ~하다 be proportioned 《to》; be proportionate 〔proportional〕 《to》; be in proportion 《to *one's* ability》. ¶ 급료는 너의 근로 시간에 ~하여 지급하겠다 I'll pay you in proportion to the number of hours you work. ◉ ~대표(제) proportional representation (system). ~배분 proportional allotment 〔allocation〕. ~세 regressive taxation. ~식 a proportional expression; a proportion. ~중항(中項) a mean proportional; a geometric mean. ~할당 제(도) the percentage quota system. 단〔복〕~ simple 〔compound〕 proportion. 정〔반, 역〕~ direct 〔inverse, reciprocal〕 proportion.

**비례**(非禮) impoliteness; impropriety; discourtesy; breach of etiquette; rudeness.

**비로소** 《*do*》 for the first time (after something has happened); not … until 〔till〕…. ¶ 사람은 건강을 잃고서야 ~ 그것이 얼마나 고마운지를 알게 된다 People do not know the blessing of health till they lose it. / 그의 말을 듣고서야 ~ 나는 깨달았다 I realized it for the first time only after he told me. / 화재가 얼마나 무서운지 그 때 ~ 알았다 Then I realized for the first time how horrible a fire was. / 며칠 지나서 ~ 그 사실을 알았다 It was not until a few days later that I learned the truth.

**비록**(秘錄) a secret memoir; a confidential document 〔record〕; (secret) private papers.

**비록** if; even if; (even) though; although; admitting 〔granting, supposing〕 that…. ¶ ~ 농담으로라도 even in fun; even as a joke / ~ 그렇다 할지라도 even if it were so; even so / ~ 아무리 부자일지라도 however 〔no matter how〕 rich *one* may be / ~ 그는 젊지만 though he is young / ~ 나는 가난하지만 poor as I am; though I am poor / ~ 그것이 사실일지라도 역시 잘못은 네 쪽에 있다 Granting it to be true 〔Granted that it is true〕, you are still in the wrong. / ~ 굶어 죽을지언정 그에게 청은 않겠다 Even though I were starving, I would not ask a favor of him.

**비롯하다** 《시작되다》 begin; start; originate 《in》; date 〔arise〕 《from》. ¶ (…을) 비롯해서, 비롯하여 beginning with; including; headed by; from… on down / 시장을 비롯해서 20명이 참석했다 There were twenty present including the mayor. / 이 풍습은 고구려 시대에서 비롯되었다고 한다 This custom is said to date from the Koguryŏ era. / 담임 선생을 비롯하여 많은 여학생이 식에 참석했다 A group of schoolgirls headed by the teacher in charge attended the ceremony.

**비료**(肥料) 《자연의》 manure; 《인조의》 (a) fertilizer; 《퇴비》 compost. ¶ 화학 ~ chemical fertilizer / ~를 주다 manure 《the soil》; put manure 《on, in》; fertilize; spread fertilizer (in the field). ◉ ~공업 the fertilizer industry. ~공장 a fertilizer plant. 「mange.

**비루** 『수의』 mange. ¶ ~ 먹다 get the

**비루**(鄙陋) ～하다 (be) mean; base; low; abject; contemptible. ¶ ～한 근성 a base 〔mean〕 spirit.

**비루스** 〖의학〗 a virus. ⇨ 바이러스.

**비류**(比類) a parallel; a peer; an equal; a match.

**비름** 〖식물〗 an amaranthus.

**비리**(非理) irrationality; unreasonableness; absurdities and irregularities. ¶ ～공무원〔국회의원〕 a government official 〔Representative〕 who is suspected of corruption / ～를 추방하다 drive out absurdities and evil customs.

**비리다** ① 《냄새·맛이》 (be) fishy; [서술적] smell 〔taste〕 fishy. ¶ 비린내 a fish-like 〔fishy〕 smell / 비린내가 나다 smell fishy; stink of fish. ② 《피가》 (be) bloody; smell of blood. ③ [비유적] (be) stingy; niggardly. ¶ 비린 사람 a skinflint; a cheapskate.

**비리비리** thin 〔skinny〕 and dry. ～하다 (be) thin 〔skinny〕 and dry. ¶ ～ 여위다 be nothing but skin and bones.

**비리척지근하다, 비리치근하다** ＝비릿하다.

**비릿비릿** sickening(ly); disgusting(ly). ～하다 (be) sickening; disgusting.

**비릿하다** (be) somewhat fishy; smell a little bloody.

**비마자**(萆麻子) ＝ 피마자.

**비막**(飛膜) 〖생물〗 a flying membrane; a parachute; a patagium (*pl.* -gia).

**비만**(肥滿) corpulence; fatness; obesity. ～하다 (be) corpulent; obese; plump; fat; fleshy 《미》. ¶ ～해지다 become fat; grow corpulent 〔stout〕 / 과식이 그가 ～해진 원인이었다 Overeating made him corpulent. ◉ ～아 an obese 〔a fat, an overweight〕 child. ～증 〖의학〗 obesity. ～형 〖심리〗: ～형의 pyknic / ～형의 사람 a pyknic.

**비말**(飛沫) a splash; a spray 《of water》.

**비망록**(備忘錄) a memorandum (*pl.* -da, ～s); a memo (*pl.* ～s); a memorandum book. ¶ ～에 기입하다 note on a memorandum; enter in a memo / 생각나는 것을 ～에 적어 두었다 I wrote a memo(randum) of the thing that occurred to me.

**비매품**(非賣品) articles not for sale; 《*something*》 for private distribution. ¶ ～《게시》 Not for sale. *or* Not to be sold. *or* Privately Printed 〔Distributed〕.

**비명**(非命) ¶ ～에 죽다〔가다〕 die an unnatural 〔untimely, accidental〕 death; die before *one's* time; die by violence. ◉ ～횡사 an unnatural 〔untimely, accidental〕 death; death by violence.

**비명**(悲鳴) a cry (of distress 〔pain〕); 《갑자기 지르는》 a shriek; 《아픔·공포의》 a scream. ¶ ～을 올리다 cry in distress; utter 〔give〕 a shriek; shriek; scream; let out a scream; cry for help (도와달라고) / 무서워 ～을 지르다 utter a shriek of terror / 아파서 ～을 지르다 give a cry of pain; shriek with pain; scream in pain / 갑자기 날카로운 ～이 적막을 깨뜨렸다 A shrill cry suddenly pierced the stillness. / 주문이 쇄도하여 그들은 즐거운 ～을 지르고 있다 With orders pouring in on them, they are alternating between joy and embarrassment.

**비명**(碑銘) an epitaph; an inscription 《on a grave stone》.

**비모음**(鼻母音) a nasal vowel.

**비목**(費目) an item of expenditure.

**비몽사몽**(非夢似夢) as in a dream; dreamlike; dreamy; dim; vague; faint; indistinct. ～하다 (be) dreamlike; dim; faint. ¶ ～간에 between being asleep and awake; ecstatically.

**비무장**(非武裝) demilitarization. ¶ ～의 unarmed; demilitarized / 도시를 ～화하다 demilitarize a city. ◉ ～도시 an open city. ～중립 unarmed neutrality. ～지대 a demilitarized zone (생략 DMZ). ～화(化) demilitarization.

**비문**(碑文) an epitaph; an epigraph; an 〔a monumental〕 inscription.

**비문명**(非文明) ¶ ～의 uncivilized; unenlightened; barbarous. ◉ ～국 an uncivilized nation.

**비문화적**(非文化的) (being) uncivilized 〔uncultured, unenlightened, preliterate〕.

**비물질론**(非物質論) 〖철학〗 immaterialism.

**비물질적**(非物質的) immaterial; nonmaterial.

**비민주적**(非民主的) undemocratic; nondemocratic 《policy》.

**비밀**(秘密) 《상태》 secrecy; confidentiality; 《내용》 a secret; a mystery; confidence; 《국가 기밀 등》 《미》 classified information; 《사생활의》 privacy. (★ 비밀구분: 1급 비밀 top secret, 2급 비밀 secret, 3급 비밀 confidential). ¶ ～의 secret; confidential; private; hush=hush 《구어》 / ～히 secretly; confidentially; privately; in secrecy; in private 〔confidence〕 / 공공연한 ～ an open secret / 통신의 ～ the privacy 〔confidentiality〕 of correspondence / 잘 지

켜진 ~ a well-kept secret / ~정보 secret 〔confidential, classified〕 information / ~회합 a secret 〔clandestine〕 meeting / ~을 지키다 keep a 〔the〕 secret; observe 〔maintain〕 secrecy / ~로 하다〔해두다〕 make a secret of 《*a matter*》; keep 《*a matter*》 secret 〔private, dark〕; keep 《*a matter*》 to *oneself;* keep 《*a thing*》 from 《*a person*》; keep 《*a thing*》 under wraps / ~로 하지 않다 make no secret 〔mystery〕 of 《*a matter*》 / ~에 싸여 있다 be veiled 〔shrouded〕 in mystery / ~을 드러내다〔폭로하다〕 reveal 〔disclose, lay bare〕 a secret / ~을 누설하다 leak 〔let〕 out a secret; betray a secret; give a secret away; tip of a secret; let the cat out of the bag / ~을 눈치채다 have an inkling of the secret / ~을 유지하다 keep a secret; observe secrecy / ~을 캐다 pry into a secret / ~을 캐내다 ferret 〔worm〕 out a secret / ~을 털어놓다〔밝히다〕 confide 〔reveal, disclose〕 a secret to 《*a person*》; let 《*a person*》 into a secret; take 《*a person*》 into *one's* confidence; spill the beans 《미구어》 / ~을 풀다 unravel a mystery / ~이 누설되다 a secret gets 〔leaks〕 out / ~이 드러났다 The secret came to light. / 이 일은 ~이다 This is under your hat. / 자네, 이 일은 ~을 지켜 줘야 되겠다 I must rely on your secrecy in this matter. / 그 조사는 ~리에 진행되었다 The investigation was conducted in secret. / 아무도 내 ~을 알아챈 사람은 없다 No one has 「found out 〔discovered〕 my secret yet.
◉ ~결사 a secret society; an underground organization. ~결혼 a clandestine marriage. ~경찰 the secret 〔security〕 police; a G-man 《미》; 《구소련의》 the KGB; the Committee of State Security; 《나치의》 the Gestapo. ~계정 a secret account; an off-the-book(s) account. ~계좌 《은행의》 *one's* secret bank account; numbered account. ~공작원 an undercover agent. ~군사 협정 a secret military accord 《between》. ~누설(죄) divulgence 〔leakage〕 of a secret; 《국가 기밀의》 a charge of revealing national security information. ~단체 a secret organization. ~마이크 a hidden 〔concealed〕 microphone; a bug 《미구어》. ~명령 a secret 〔sealed〕 order. ~문서 a classified 〔confidential〕 document. ~병기 a secret weapon. ~선거〔투표〕 secret voting 〔ballot〕. ~수사 (an) undercover investigation: ~ 수사원(搜査員) an undercover investigator 〔man〕. ~외교 secret diplomacy. ~요정 an unlicensed clandestine restaurant. ~적립금 a hidden deposit. ~정보 secret 〔classified 《미》〕 information (군사·정부 등의); an inside story; a tip-off (경마·투기 등의): ~정보원(源) a confidential source. ~조사 a private 〔secret〕 investigation; a confidential inquiry. ~조약 a secret treaty. ~출판 secret publication. ~탐정 a secret (service) agent. ~통로 a secret 〔concealed〕 passage 〔path〕. ~투표 a secret ballot; secret voting. ~회담 a closed-door talk. ~회의 a closed 〔secret〕 meeting 〔conference〕; a secret 〔closed-door〕 session.

**비밀번호**(秘密番號) a personal code number. ¶ ~를 누르시오 Please 「key in 〔enter〕 your code number.

**비바람** rain and wind; a (rain) storm; a driving rain. ¶ ~치다 it storms / ~을 맞다 be exposed to the weather; be weather-beaten / 세찬 ~을 무릅쓰고 가다 go in spite of violent wind and rain.

**비바리**, **비발** a fisher-girl.

**비방**(秘方) ① 《방법》 a secret process 〔method〕. ② 《처방》 a secret recipe 〔formula〕 (of medicine). ¶ ~의 묘약 a proprietary medicine.

**비방**(誹謗) (a) slander; abuse; calumny; a libel; defamation. ~하다 slander; abuse; libel; speak ill of; heap calumny upon; calumniate; defame.

> **용법** **slander** 구두로 하는 비방. **libel** 문서나 그림 등으로 하는 비방. 그러나 실제에 있어서는 위 두 낱말이 혼용되고 있다. 그리고 slander나 libel은 「비방」의 내용이 사실과 상반되는 것이지만, **abuse**는 사실인 경우도 해당된다.

¶ ~을 듣다 be slandered / 그는 나를 직무태만이라고 ~했다 He abused me for my neglect of duty.
◉ ~자 a slanderer; a vilifier.

**비버** 『동물』 a beaver. ⇨ 해리(海狸).

**비번**(非番) being off duty. ¶ ~의 off duty 〔guard〕 / ~날 an off day / ~의 경찰관 an off-duty policeman / ~이다 be 〔go〕 off duty; be off / 내주 수요일 나는 ~이다 I'll be off duty next Wednesday.

**비범**(非凡) extraordinariness; uncommonness; uniqueness. ～하다 (be) 《뛰어난》 extraordinary; 《드물게 보는》 uncommon; 《보통이 아닌》 unusual; 《주목할만한》 remarkable; out of the ordinary; 《놀랄만한》 prodigious; rare; unique. ¶ ～한 사람 a remarkable man; a man of unusual 〔uncommon〕 ability; a prodigy; a man above the common run of humanity / ～한 재주 an unusual gift 〔talent〕 / ～한 솜씨 rare 〔unusual〕 ability 〔skill〕 / 그는 ～한 사람이다 He is 「no ordinary man 〔a prodigy〕. / 그 시인은 어딘가 ～한 데가 있다 There's something extraordinary about that poet. *or* There's something out of the ordinary in that poet.

**비법**(秘法) a secret process 〔method〕; a mystique; mysteries. ¶ 건강의 ～ a secret formula for good health / ～을 전수하다 initiate 《*a person*》 into the mysteries 〔secrets〕 《of》 / ～을 전수받다 be initiated in the mysteries / ～을 터득하다 master the mysteries 《of》.

**비법인**(非法人) ¶ ～의 unincorporated.

**비보**(秘寶) a hidden treasure; a treasured article.

**비보**(悲報) sad news; sad tidings; 《죽음의》 the news of 《*a person's*》 death. ¶ ～에 접하다 hear 〔receive〕 sad news.

**비복**(婢僕) (domestic) servants; domestics; menials.

**비분**(悲憤) indignation; resentment. ～하다 be indignant 《at *a matter,* with *a person*》; be resentful. ¶ ～강개하다 deplore; resent; be indignant 《at, over》 / 공직자 부패에 대해 ～강개하다 deplore 〔be indignant over〕 the corruption among government officials / ～의 눈물을 흘리다 shed tears of indignation.

**비브라폰** 《악기》 a vibraphone. ¶ ～연주자 a vibraphonist.

**비브리오** 《세균》 a vibrio (*pl.* ～s).

**비비**(狒狒) 〖동물〗 a baboon; a dog ape.

**비비꼬다** ① 《꼬다》 braid 〔twist〕 together tight; twist over and over again. ¶ 몸을 ～ twist the body about; twist *oneself;* writhe / 실을 ～ twist thread into string / 비비 꼬이다 get braided 〔twisted〕 together tight; be twisted many times / 넥타이가 비비 꼬여 있다 *one's* necktie gets all twisted up; have *one's* tie twisted up. ② 《말을》 talk ironically; give an indirect cut. ⇨ 비꼬다.

**비비다** ① 《문지르다》 rub; scrub. ¶ 눈을 ～ rub *one's* eyes / 눈을 비벼 잠을 쫓다 rub the sleep out of *one's* eyes / 서로 ～ rub against each other / 손을 ～ rub *one's* hands; 《아첨·난처》 wash *one's* hands in invisible soap / 손을 비벼 녹이다 chafe *one's* hands (together) for warmth / 비벼 꾸깃꾸깃하게 하다 crumple 《a piece of paper soft》; rumple; wrinkle / 옷의 진흙을 비비어 떨다 scrub the dirt 〔scrape the mud〕 off the dress.
② 《송곳을》 drive a gimlet 《into》; drill. ¶ 송곳을 비비어 구멍을 뚫다 bore a hole with a gimlet.
③ 《둥글게》 (make a) roll.
④ 《버무리다》 mix 《food》. ¶ 밥을 ～ make a hash 《with rice》; mix boiled rice with minced meat and other various kind of cooked 〔fresh〕 greens 〔ingredients〕 (and spicy red pepper paste).
⑤ [비유적] push (*oneself*) through a crowd. ¶ 비비고 들어가다 elbow *one's* way forward.

**비비대기** jostling 《with one another》; a jostle; a tussle. ～치다 ① 《붐비다》 jostle one another; hustle and jostle; push and shove; struggle 〔tussle〕 with one another. ② 《부산하다》 run 〔move〕 about busily.

**비비대다** rub repeatedly. 「against.

**비비적거리다** rub and rub; chafe

**비비틀다** twist 〔wrench〕 hard. ¶ 비비 틀리다 get twisted 〔wrenched〕 hard.

**비빈**(妃嬪) the queen and the royal concubine. 「tures.

**비빔국수** noodles with assorted mix-

**비빔밥** boiled rice with assorted mixtures; boiled rice mixed with minced meat and other various kind of cooked 〔fresh〕 greens 〔ingredients〕 (and spicy red pepper paste).

**비사**(秘史) hidden history; a secret 〔an undisclosed〕 history. ¶ 한국전쟁 ～ the secret history of the Korean War.

**비사교적**(非社交的) (being) unsociable; retiring. ¶ ～인 사람 an unsociable person; a bad mixer 《미구어》.

**비산**(飛散) scattering. ～하다 disperse; scatter; fly. ¶ 사방으로 ～하다 fly in all directions.

**비산**(砒酸) 〖화학〗 arsenic acid. ◉ ～납 lead arsenate. ～염 arsenate.

**비상**(非常) ① 《보통이 아님》 extraordinariness; unusualness; uncommonness; excessiveness. ～하다 (be) extraordinary; be out of the ordinary; (be) unusual; uncommon (비범한); remarkable (현저한); exceptional (예외적); excessive (과도한); extreme; immense. ¶ ~하게 extraordinarily; uncommonly; unusually; exceptionally / ~한 재능 remarkable 〔exceptional〕 ability / ~한 솜씨 unusual 〔uncommon, great〕 skill / ~한 관심을 보이다 show 〔display〕 an extreme interest 《in》.

② 《긴급사태》 an emergency; a contingency. ¶ ~용 for emergency; 《게시》 For emergency use only. / ~에 대비하다 provide against emergencies; prepare for the worst / ~이 걸리다 be put on emergency 〔special〕 alertness; be under the emergency duty orders / 그들은 ~ 경계 태세에 들어갔다 They moved to red alert.

◉ ~경계 emergency guard. ~경보 an alarm (signal); an emergency warning: ~ 경보기 《화재의》 a fire alarm. ~계단 an emergency staircase; a fire escape. ~계획 contingency plans. ~관제 emergency control. ~구 an emergency exit 〔door〕; a fire exit. ~국무회의 《call》 an emergency Cabinet meet(ing). ~금 an emergency fund; a nest egg. ~기획 위원회 《국무총리 직속의》 the Emergency Planning Commission. ~나팔 an alarm (call): ~ 나팔을 불다 sound the alarm. ~미(米) emergency rice. ~소집 an emergency call 〔summons〕: 경찰을 ~소집하다 call out the police reserves. ~수단 an emergency 〔exceptional〕 measure: ~ 수단을 쓰다〔강구하다〕 take 〔resort to〕 emergency 〔extreme〕 measures. ~시국 an emergency situation. ~식량 emergency provisions 〔rations〕. ~신호 an alarm call. ~전화 an emergency call; a hurry call 《미》. ~조치 an extraordinary step. ~직통전화 《국가간의》 a hot line. ~착륙 a forced 〔an emergency〕 landing; a crash landing (동체 착륙 따위): ~착륙 훈련 an emergency landing drill / ~착륙을 하다 make an emergency landing. ~콕 an emergency handle.

**비상**(砒霜) arsenic poison.

**비상**(飛翔) a flight; flying; soaring. ~하다 fly; take a flight; soar (up). ¶ 독수리의 ~ the soaring of an eagle.

**비상근**(非常勤) part-time service. ¶ ~의 일 a part-time job; part-time work / ~으로 일하다 work part-time; work on a part-time basis. ◉ ~강사 a part-time teacher 〔instructor〕. ~이사 a part-time director. ~직원 a part-time worker; a part-timer.

**비상사태**(非常事態) a state of emergency. ¶ ~를 선언하다 declare a state of emergency; proclaim an emergency / ~에 있다 be under 〔in〕 a state of emergency / ~에 대비하다 provide against emergencies; be ready 〔prepared〕 for emergencies.

◉ 국가 ~ 선언 a state-of-national-emergency declaration.

**비상선**(非常線) a (police) cordon; a patrol line; 《화재의》 a fire line. ¶ ~을 뚫다 escape 〔break〕 through a cordon / ~을 치다 post 〔form, place, draw〕 a (police) cordon; throw a cordon 《around a building》 / 경찰은 데모대가 미대사관에 접근 못하도록 그 일대에 ~을 쳐서 차단했다 The police cordoned off the area to prevent the demonstrators from reaching the U.S. embassy.

**비상시**(非常時) an emergency; a crisis (위기). ¶ 국가의 ~ a national emergency / ~에 in case of emergency; in an emergency / ~에 대비하다 prepare for an emergency.

**비상식**(非常識) lack of common sense. ¶ ~적인 thoughtless; senseless; absurd / ~적인 소리 하지 마라 Don't be absurd 〔ridiculous〕.

**비상용**(非常用) for emergency. ◉ ~ 사다리 an emergency ladder.

**비상장주**(非上場株) an unlisted stock 〔share 《영》〕; an over-the-counter stock.

**비색계**(比色計) a colorimeter.

**비색증**(鼻塞症) 〖한의〗 occlusion of the nares; stoppage of the nostril.

**비생산**(非生産) unproductivity; nonproductiveness. ¶ ~적(인) unproductive; nonproductive; unfruitful / ~적 노동 unproductive labor / ~적 사업 a nonproductive enterprise / ~적 자본 dead capital / ~적 생각 an unproductive 〔a far from constructive〕 idea.

◉ ~성 투자 investment in unproductive sectors.

**비서**(秘書) ① 《사람》 a (private) secretary. ¶ ~의 일 secretarial work 〔duties〕 / 그녀는 사장 ~이다 She is 〔acts as〕 (a, the) secretary to the president. *or* She is the president's secretary. ② 《책》 a treasured 〔a secret〕 book 〔document〕.

◉ ~과 a secretarial section. ~관 a

secretary: 국무총리 ~관 a secretary to the Prime Minister. ~실 a secretary's office; a secretariat: ~실장 a chief secretary. ~직 secretaryship. ~학과〔학교〕 a secretarial course 〔school〕.

> 참고 (a, the) secretary: 「그녀는 사장의 비서이다」 She is (a, the) secretary to the president.
> 무관사인 경우는 단순히 신분을 말하고, a를 수반하는 경우는 몇 사람의 비서들 중의 한 사람임을, the가 붙는 경우는 특정한 한 사람의 비서임을 뜻한다.

**비석**(砒石) arsenious anhydride.
**비석**(碑石) a tombstone; a gravestone; a stone slab 〔tablet〕; a (stone) monument. ¶ ~을 세우다 erect 〔raise, put up〕 a stone monument 〔tombstone〕; set up a monument 《to the memory of *a person*》.
**비설거지** getting 《a house》 in order for a rain. ~하다 get everything ready for the rain; protect 〔shelter〕 《*a thing*》 from rain.
**비성**(鼻聲) a nasal voice. ⇨ 콧소리.
**비소**(砒素) 〚화학〛 arsenic (기호 As). ¶ ~는 맹독성이다 Arsenic is violently poisonous. ◉ ~제(劑) an arsenic compound. ~중독 arsenic poisoning. ~화물 an arsenide.
**비소수**(非素數) 〚수학〛 a composite number.
**비속**(卑俗) vulgarity; coarseness. ~하다 (be) vulgar; coarse; broad; low 《jokes》. ¶ ~한 사람 a man of low 〔vile〕 character / ~한 취미 (a) bad 〔vulgar〕 taste / 그는 ~한 말을 쓴다 He uses vulgar language 〔expressions〕.
**비속**(卑屬) 〚법〛 a descendant. ¶ 직계〔방계〕~ a lineal 〔collateral〕 descendant.
**비손** ~하다 rub *one's* hands together in supplication to a god.
**비송**(非訟) nonlitigation. ◉ ~사건 a nonlitigation 〔noncontentious〕 case.
**비수**(匕首) a dagger. ⇨ 단도(短刀).
**비수**(悲愁) grief; sorrow; pathos.
**비수기**(非需期) a slack season.
**비수리** 〚식물〛 a sericea (lespedeza).
**비술**(秘術) a secret art; the secrets; the mysteries of an art. ¶ ~을 전수하다 initiate 《*a person*》 into the mysteries 《of》 / ~을 다하여 싸우다 fight to the best of *one's* skill.
**비스듬하다** (be) slightly slanting 〔oblique〕; be a bit askew; be a little off-center. ¶ 비스듬히 obliquely; aslant; askew; diagonally; slant-wise / 비스듬해지다 incline; lean; slant; tilt / 모자를 비스듬히 쓰다 cock *one's* hat; wear a hat tilted to one side / 비스듬하게 하다 tilt; slant; incline / 탑이 한쪽으로 ~ a tower leans on one side / 배가 강을 비스듬히 가로질러 갔다 The boat moved diagonally across the river.
**비스러지다** get a little out of shape; be a bit irregular.
**비스름하다** (be) somewhat similar; be rather alike. ¶ 그들은 성격이 ~ They are somewhat alike in character.
**비스마르크제도**(—諸島) 《서남태평양의》 Bismarck Archipelagos.
**비스무트** 〚화학〛 bismuth (기호 Bi).
**비스코스** 〚화학〛 viscose. ◉ ~사(絲) viscose yarn.
**비스킷** 《미》 a cracker; 《미》 a cookie (단 것); a biscuit 《영》.
**비스타비전** 〚영화〛 Vista Vision (상표명).
**비슥거리다** ① 《일을》 spare *oneself;* do not exert 〔throw〕 *oneself* 《in》; be an unwilling worker. ② 《가까이 않다》 keep away from 《*a person*》; give 《*a person*》 a wide berth; hold back 《from》; hang back; balk.
**비슬거리다** totter; reel; stagger; falter; walk unsteadily. ¶ 한대 얻어 맞고 ~ reel under a heavy blow / 비슬거리며 거리를 걸어가다 totter feebly along the street / 무거운 짐을 지고 ~ stagger under a heavy load / 그는 비슬거리며 길을 건넜다 He crossed the street with unsteady steps.
**비슬비슬** reelingly; totteringly. ¶ ~ 걸어가다 walk with faltering steps; stagger 〔shamble, dodder〕 along / ~ 일어서다 stagger 〔totter〕 to *one's* feet / 그 취객은 ~ 집으로 걸어갔다 The drunk went lurching home.
**비슷비슷하다** be much 〔nearly〕 the same; be of the same sort; 《구어》 be much of a muchness. ¶ 둘이 ~ The two are much the same. *or* They are both of a sort. / 그들의 나이는 ~ They are about the same age. / 둘의 생김새가 ~ The two look alike.
**비슷이**[1] 《같게》 alike; similarly; likely. ¶ ~ 닮다 bear some resemblance to 《*a person*》 / ~ 알아맞히다 nearly guess right / 그의 예언이 ~ 맞았다 By and large, his prediction has turned out to be right.
**비슷이**[2] 《비스듬히》 leaning a bit to one side. ¶ ~ 기울어진 벽 a wall with a

slight lean.

**비슷하다**[1] 《같다》 (be) like; similar 《to》; resembling; analogous; be alike (둘이). ¶ 비슷한 예〔속담〕 a like instance 〔proverb〕 / 그와 비슷한 이야기 a story like that; a similar tale / 길이가 ~ the length is about the same / 두 사람의 얼굴이 ~ the two look alike / 비슷하지 않다 bear no resemblance 《to》; be nothing like / 좀 비슷한 데가 있다 bear some resemblance 《to》; have some similarities 《between》; have something in common 《with》 / 아주 ~ bear a close resemblance 《to》; be 〔look〕 very much like / 그 두 사람의 성격이 ~ The two of them are much alike in character. / 비슷한 것을 본 적이 있다 I have seen the like. / 그와 나는 생각이 ~ He and I think alike. / 그들의 생애는 서로 비슷한 데가 있다 We can trace a parallel between their careers.

**비슷하다**[2] 《비스듬하다》 lean a bit to one side.

**비시지** BCG (vaccine). 〔< *B*acillus *C*almette-*G*uérin〕 ¶ ~를 접종하다 inoculate 《*a person*》 with BCG (vaccine). ◉ ~접종 inoculation of BCG.

**비신** rain shoes.

**비신사적**(非紳士的) (being) ungentlemanlike; ungentlemanly. ¶ ~ 행위 a conduct unbecoming to a gentleman.

**비실비실** ⇨ 비슬비슬.

**비실제적**(非實際的) (being) unpractical; impractical; unrealistic. ¶ ~인 지식 an impractical knowledge.

**비싸다** ① 《값이》 (be) high; expensive; costly; dear. ¶ 기껏 비싸야 at most; at the highest / 비싸게 보이는 expensive-looking / 비싼 옷 expensive clothes / 터무니없이 비싼 가격 a ridiculously high price; an exorbitant price / 비싸게 먹히다〔치이다〕 cost 《*a person*》 「a great deal 〔a lot〕; cost too much; come high; (prove to) be 〔come 《구어》〕 expensive / 비싸게 받다〔부르다〕 charge too much; overcharge / 비싸게 팔다〔사다〕 sell 〔buy〕 at a high price / 값이 (너무) ~ The price is (too) high. *or* It is (too) expensive. / 생각했던 것보다(도) 값이 ~ It costs more than I thought. / 뭐든지 다 비싸졌다 Everything has 「gone up 〔risen〕 in price.
② 《태도가》 (be) proud; haughty; puffed-up; uppish 《구어》. ¶ 비싸게 굴다 assume 「an air of importance 〔a haughty attitude〕; put on airs.

**비쌔다** ① 《돌아내리다》 decline reluctantly; pretend reluctance. ② 《어울리기 싫어하다》 keep aloof; avoid company.

**비아냥거리다** make sarcastic 〔cutting〕 remarks; talk cynically 《about》.

**비아냥스럽다** (be) sarcastic; cynical.

**비아이에스** 《국제 결제 은행》 BIS. 〔< *B*ank for *I*nternational *S*ettlement〕

**비애**(悲哀) sorrow; grief; sadness; pathos. ¶ ~의 sorrowful; sad; pathetic; affecting / 인생의 ~ the sorrows 〔sadness〕 of life / 환멸의 ~ a sad disillusionment; the sorrow of disillusionment / ~를 느끼다 feel sorrow 〔sad〕 / 그녀는 인생의 갖가지 ~를 맛보아 왔다 She has had a great deal of sorrow 〔sadness〕 in her life. ◉ ~감 (a) sense 〔feeling〕 of sorrow.

**비애국적**(非愛國的) (being) unpatriotic.

**비약**(飛躍) ① 《뛰어오름》 a leap; a (flying) jump. ~하다 leap; jump. ② 《활약》 activity. ~하다 be active; play an active part. ¶ 암중 ~하다 be active behind the scene; take a bold leap in the dark. ③ 《진보·향상》 rapid progress; a big 〔great〕 leap. ~하다 make rapid progress. ¶ ~적 발전을 하다 make 〔take〕 great strides; make rapid progress; 《장사가》 grow by leaps and bounds / 매상이 ~적으로 늘었다 There has been a big leap in sales. ④ 《논리의》 ¶ 논리의 ~ a jump of logic; a logical leap / 그의 의견에는 논리의 ~이 있다 There is a jump in the logic of his opinion.

**비약**(秘藥) a secret medicine 〔remedy〕; a nostrum (묘약).

**비어**(卑語·鄙語) ① 《천한 말》 a vulgarism; a vulgar word 〔expression〕; vulgar language; 《외설한 말》 (an) obscenity; obscene language. ② 《낮춤말》 a depreciatory term.

**비어**(蜚語·飛語) a vicious rumor; a false report; a wild 〔flying〕 rumor. ⇨ 유언(流言).

**비어** beer. ⇨ 맥주. ◉ ~가든 a beer garden. ~홀 a beer hall 〔parlor〕; a beer-house; an alehouse 《영》.

**비어지다** ① 《속엣것이》 stick out; protrude; jut out. ¶ 주머니에서 비어져 나오다 stick out of *one's* pocket. ② 《비밀이》 come to light; be revealed; be laid bare.

**비업무용**(非業務用) 《of》 non-business purpose. ¶ ~ 토지를 백만 평이나 소유하다 possess one million p'yŏng of non-business idle land. ◉ ～ 부동산 non-business purpose real estate; idle land.

**비엔나** 《빈》 Vienna. ¶ ～의 Viennese. ◉ ～사람 a Viennese. ～소시지 (a) Vienna sausage; 《미》 (a) wiener. ～왈츠 a Viennese waltz.

**비엔날레** a biennale (It.); a biennial (art show). (★ 2년마다 열리는 국제적 현대 미술 전람회). ◉ ～전(展) a biennial exhibition.

**비역** sodomy; buggery; p(a)ederasty. ⇨ 남색(男色). ～하다 practice 〔commit〕 sodomy.

**비열**(比熱) 〚물리〛 specific heat.

**비열**(卑劣·鄙劣) meanness; baseness. ～하다 (be) mean; base; low; sordid; nasty; shabby; sneaking; cowardly; contemptible; dastardly. ¶ ～한 놈 a sneak; a mean fellow; a reptile; a hound; 《영구어》 a meanie / ～한 수단 a dirty 〔nasty〕 trick / ～한 짓을 하다 play 《*a person*》 foul; hit 〔strike〕 《*a person*》 below the belt / ～한 수단으로 속이다 deceive 《*a person*》 by a 「mean 〔dirty〕 trick / 뒤에서 욕하는 것은 ～한 짓이다 Backbiting is a mean deed.

**비염**(脾炎) 〚한의〛 splenitis.

**비염**(鼻炎) 〚의학〛 nasal catarrh; (a) nasal inflammation; (an) inflammation of the mucous membrane of the nose; rhinitis. ¶ 알레르기성 ～ allergic rhinitis; allergic coryza; 《꽃가루 알레르기》 hay fever.

**비영리**(非營利) nonprofit(-making). ◉ ～단체 a 「nonprofit 〔noncommercial〕 organization. ～법인 a 「nonprofit-making 〔noncommercial〕 corporation. ～사업 a nonprofit enterprise. ～회사 a nonprofit corporation.

**비영비영하다** be thin and haggard 〔wasted away〕 from illness.

**비예술적**(非藝術的) inartistic.

**비오디** 《생화학적 산소요구량》 BOD. [<*b*iochemical *o*xygen *d*emand]

**비오리** 〚조류〛 a merganser; a goosander.

**비오큐** 〚미육군〛 《독신 장교 숙소》 BOQ. [<*b*achelor *o*fficers' *q*uarters]

**비옥**(肥沃) fertility; richness 《of the soil》. ～하다 (be) fertile; rich; productive. ¶ ～한 땅 fertile 〔rich〕 soil / 홍수와 가뭄이 없는 ～한 땅 fertile land free of flood and drought / ～해지다 grow 「fertile 〔rich, productive〕 / 이곳은 땅이 ～하다 The soil here is very productive. ◉ ～토 fertile 〔rich〕 soil.

**비올라** 〚음악〛 a viola. ¶ ～를 켜다 play the viola. ◉ ～연주자 a viola player; a violist.

**비옷** a raincoat; a mackintosh (고무 입힌). ¶ ～을 입다 put on a raincoat.

**비용**(費用) expense(s) (★ expense가 지출·소비 행위를 나타내는 경우는 단수형이며, 지출금·학비 따위를 나타낼 때에는 관용구를 제외하고 흔히 복수형을 씀); expenditure; (a) cost; (an) outlay. ¶ 결혼〔여행〕～ wedding 〔traveling〕 expenses / ～만 헛되이 쓰다 end 〔result〕 in waste of money / 높은 유통 ～ high (physical) distribution costs.

비용이: ～이 드는 costly; expensive / ～이 들지 않는 inexpensive / ～이 무척 들다 cost a great deal; be very expensive / ～이 아무리 들더라도 at any 「cost 〔expense〕 / ～이 겹치다〔누적되다〕 expenses 「pile 〔run〕 up.

비용에: ～에 관계없이 regardless of expense / … ～에 충당하다 cover the expense of….

비용을: 막대한 ～을 들여서 at 「a great 〔a huge, an enormous〕 cost / ～을 부담하다〔내다〕 bear 〔defray〕 the expenses; 《구어》 foot the bill / ～을 부담시키다 let 《*a person*》 defray the expenses / ～을 분담하다 share the expenses / ～을 분담하여 with expenses shared / ～을 아끼다 spare 〔grudge〕 expenses / ～을 줄이다 cut down on expenses; curtail expenditure / ～을 지출하다 meet *one's* expenses.

비용으로: …의 ～으로 at a cost 〔the expense〕 of 《50,000 won》 / 적은 ～으로 at 〔with〕 a small outlay.

¶ ～이 너무 많이〔적게〕 났다 It cost 「too much 〔very little〕. / 결혼은 막대한 ～이 든다 Marriage is a great expense. / ～은 개인 부담으로 여행했다 I traveled at my own expense. / ～은 얼마든지 내겠다 I will go to any expense. / 삼촌은 내가 대학을 마칠 때까지의 ～을 대주었다 My uncle saw me through college. / ～이 절약되었다 It saved the expenses. / 새 집을 짓는 데는 얼마나 ～이 들까요 How much does it cost to build a new house? / ～은 10만원 정도 들 것이다 The expenses will 「amount 〔come〕 to about 100,000 won.

◉ ～절감 cost-cutting〔-saving〕: ～절감 운동〔조치〕 a cost-saving〔-cutting〕 move 〔measure〕.

**비우다** ① 《속엣것을》 empty 《a box, a glass》; clear out 《a cupboard》; exhaust 《the water in a vessel》. ¶ 병

을〔광주리를〕 ～ empty a bottle 〔basket〕/ 물통을 ～ empty (the water out of) a pail / 술잔을 ～ empty *one's* glass 〔cup〕; drain 〔drink off〕 the cup / 호주머니를 ～ empty a pocket of its contents; clear (out) *one's* pocket / 방을 비워두다 reserve a room 《for *a person*》/ 행간에 여백을 ～ leave a space between lines / 간밤에 우리 둘은 위스키 한 병을 비웠다 Last night we killed 〔put away〕 a bottle of whisky between the two of us. ② 《집 따위를》 (**a**) 《외출하여》 leave *one's* house; stay 〔be〕 away 《from home》; be out. ¶ 내가 없는 동안 집을 비우지 마라 While I'm away, don't leave the house. / 그녀가 잠깐 집을 비운 사이에 도둑이 들었다 She was out of the house for a short time and it was robbed 〔broken into〕. *or* Her house was robbed 〔broken into〕 while she was away for a short time. (**b**) 《명도하다》 vacate 〔evacuate〕 《a house》; leave 《a house》 empty. ¶ 집을 이달말까지 비워 주시오 I request you to evacuate the house by the end of this month.

**비우호적**(非友好的) (being) unfriendly. ¶ ～인 관계 unfriendly relations 《with》.

**비운**(悲運) (a) misfortune; ill 〔bad〕 luck; adverse fortune 〔fate〕. ¶ ～을 한탄하다 lament (over) *one's* misfortune. ⇨ 불운(不運).

**비웃** 《청어》 a herring. ◉ ～백숙 boiled herring. ～젓 salted herring.

**비웃다** laugh 《*a person*》 to scorn 〔ridicule〕; laugh at; ridicule; deride; jeer 〔sneer, scoff, mock〕 at; scorn. ¶ 비웃으며 mockingly; scornfully / 남을 ～ sneer 〔laugh〕 at others / 아무의 어리석은 짓을 ～ ridicule *a person's* stupidities / 비웃는 얼굴을 하다 make a face of derision 《at》/ 그들은 그를 비겁하다고 비웃었다 They taunted him for being a coward.

**비웃음** a derisive 〔mocking〕 smile; a scornful laugh; a sneer; a jeer; ridicule. ¶ ～받다 be sneered at; be subjected to ridicule 〔scorn〕/ ～을 사다 incur 〔excite〕 ridicule; bring 〔draw〕 ridicule upon *oneself* / 그는 ～거리가 되었다 He became the target of scorn.

**비웃적거리다** ＝빈정거리다.

**비원**(秘苑) a palace garden; 《창덕궁의》 the Secret Garden.

**비원**(悲願) a merciful Buddhist prayer to save mankind; *one's* earnest prayer 〔wish〕. ¶ ～을 이루다 realize 〔achieve〕 *one's* earnest 〔long-cherished〕 wish; have *one's* earnest wish fulfilled 〔answered〕/ 그의 ～이 이루어졌다 His dearest wish came true.

**비위**(脾胃) ① 《비장과 위》 the spleen and the stomach.
② 《기호》 taste; palate; liking; choice. ¶ ～가 좋다 have a strong stomach / ～에 맞다 suit 〔be to〕 *one's* taste 〔palate〕/ 그 음식은 내 ～에 맞지 않는다 The food goes against my stomach.
③ 《기분》 humor; temper. ¶ ～가 상하다 be nauseated 《by》; be 〔feel〕 disgusted 《at, by, with》/ ～가 틀리다 get out of humor; take umbrage 《at》/ ～를 거스르다〔건드리다〕 offend 《*a person*》; rub 《*a person*》 the wrong way; put 《*a person*》 in(to) a bad humor; hurt 《*a person's*》 feeling; incur 《*a person's*》 displeasure; jar on 《*one's*》 nerves 〔feelings〕/ ～를 맞추다 put 《*a person*》 in good humor; please 《*a person's*》 humor 〔whim〕; 《아첨하여》 fawn upon; flatter; curry favor with 《*a person*》.
④ 《신경이 굵음》 ¶ ～가 좋다 have a nerve; be shameless 〔impudent, brazenfaced〕/ 너 참 ～도 좋구나 You've got a nerve.

**비위생적**(非衛生的) (being) insanitary; unsanitary; unhygienic; unhealthy; unwholesome. ¶ ～ 환경 an insanitary environment / ～인 생활 an unhygienic life / ～이다 be bad for the health; be unhealthy.

**비유**(比喩·譬喩) a figure of speech; a simile (직유); a metaphor (은유); 《우화》 an allegory; a parable. ～하다 compare 《to》; liken 《to》; use a simile 〔metaphor〕; speak figuratively 〔metaphorically〕. ¶ ～적인 표현 a metaphorical 〔figurative〕 expression / ～적으로 metaphorically; figuratively / ～해서 말하면 to use a metaphor / ～로 나타내다 figure; represent by metaphor / 그는 ～를 잘 쓴다 He uses metaphors well. / 그 어구는 ～적인 뜻으로 쓰인다 That phrase is used in a figurative sense.

**비육**(肥育) fatting (up); fattening (up). ～하다 fat 〔fatten〕 up 《cattle》. ◉ ～우(牛) a beef (cow); beef cattle [총칭].

**비육지탄**(髀肉之嘆) a regret at *one's* inactivity. ¶ ～이 있다 fret from forced idleness; *one's* fingers itch to do something; be eager for a fray (간절

히 바라다).
**비율**(比率) (a) ratio; (a) percentage; rate; proportion. ¶ 구성～〚통계〛 a component 〔distribution〕 ratio / 남녀의 ～ females / …의 ～로 at the rate of; in the ratio of / 백 명에 대하여 2명의 ～로 in the proportion of two to a hundred / 3대 1의 ～로 in the ratio of 3 to 1 / 4대 1의 ～을 보이다 show a ratio of four to one / 이 학급의 남녀 ～은 2대 1이다 The ratio of boys and girls in this class is 2 to 1. / 대학에 진학하는 여학생의 ～이 높아지고 있다 The percentage of girl students who go to college is increasing.
**비음**(鼻音) 〚음성〛 a nasal (sound).
◉ ～화 nasalization.
**비익조**(比翼鳥) legendary birds that had only one wing each so that they had to fly in pairs; [비유적] husband and wife; a couple.
**비익하다**(裨益—) benefit; profit 《*a person*》.
**비인간적**(非人間的) (being) inhuman 〔impersonal〕.
**비인도적**(非人道的) (being) inhumane. ¶ ～ 교도소 상태 the inhumane prison condition.
**비인칭**(非人稱) ¶ ～의 〚문법〛 impersonal.
◉ ～구문 an impersonal construction. ～동사 an impersonal verb.
**비일비재**(非一非再) ～하다 be (very, quite) common; be frequent. ¶ ～하게 frequently; often; again and again; over and over again; time and (time) again; repeatedly / 그런 일은 ～하다 There are no end of such cases. / 장갑을 잃어버린 일이 ～하다 I lost my gloves again and again.
**비자**(榧子) 〚한의〛 a Korean nutmeg nut. ◉ ～나무 a Korean nutmeg; *Torreya nucifera* (학명).
**비자** a visa. ⇨ 사증.
**비자금**(秘資金) a slush fund. ¶ ～의 조성 raising a slush fund / ～을 축적하다 build up a slush fund.
**비잔틴** Byzantine. ¶ ～의 Byzantine.
◉ ～미술 Byzantine art. ～식 건축 Byzantine architecture; the Byzantine style of architecture. ～제국〔파〕 the Byzantine Empire 〔school〕.
**비장**(秘藏) storing in secrecy; treasuring; hoard(ing). ～하다 store in secrecy; treasure (up); prize; cherish; keep 《*a thing*》 under lock and key 〔with great care〕. ¶ ～의 treasured; prized; 《좋아하는》《미》 favorite / ～의 수단 *one's* best card; the last resort 〔resource〕 / 아버지는 고려청자 몇 점을 ～하고 있다 Father treasures some pieces of Koryo celadon.
◉ ～서적 *one's* treasured books. ～품 a treasure; a treasured article.
**비장**(脾臟) 〚해부〛 the spleen. ¶ ～은 혈액의 질을 관리한다 The spleen regulates the quality of the blood.
◉ ～병 a disease of the spleen: ～병 환자 a splenetic patient.
**비장**(悲壯) ～하다 (be) pathetic; touching; tragic; heroic; grim. ¶ ～한 각오〔결의〕 a grim resolution 〔determination〕; a heroic resolve; a tragic but brave resolution / ～한 최후를 마치다 die a tragic 〔heroic〕 death; meet (with) a tragic end / 그는 끝까지 싸울 ～한 결심을 했다 He made a heroic resolve to fight to the last.
◉ ～미(美) tragic beauty.
**비재**(菲才·非才) poor talent; lack of ability; want of talent; incapacity; incompetence. ¶ 비록 ～이지만 incapable 〔incompetent〕 as I am / ～를 무릅쓰고〔～의 몸으로〕 그 직을 맡았습니다 I have accepted the appointment though I am incapable 〔in spite of my poor capability〕.
**비적**(匪賊) a bandit; 《떼》 a set 〔gang〕 of bandits; a band of marauders. ¶ ～질 banditry.
**비적비적** protruding 〔coming out〕 here and there.
**비적성**(非敵性) non-hostility.
◉ ～국가 a non-hostile country 〔nation〕: 모든 비동맹 ～ 국가들과의 관계 개선 정책을 추구하다 pursue the policy of improving relations with all the nonaligned non-hostile nations.
**비전**(秘傳) a secret; a recipe; the mysteries. ¶ ～의 묘약 a medicine secretly handed down (in the family) / ～을 전수하다 initiate 《*a person*》 into the secret 〔mysteries〕 《of a craft》.
**비전** vision. ¶ ～이 있는 사람 a man of vision / 위대한 ～을 지닌 정치가 a statesman of great breadth of vision / 그는 대학의 미래에 대한 ～을 갖고 있었다 He had a vision of what a college should be.
**비전략물자**(非戰略物資) nonstrategic goods.
**비전론**(非戰論) (an) antiwar argument; arguments against war; 《미》 pacifi(ci)sm. ¶ ～을 외치다 cry against war; advocate peace. ◉ ～자 a pacifist.
**비전투원**(非戰鬪員) 《군의관 등》 a noncombatant; 《민간인》 a civilian. ¶ ～을

소개시키다 evacuate civilians《from》.

**비전하**(妃殿下) a princess; 《3인칭》 Her (Royal) Highness (생략 H.R.H.); 《2인칭》 Your Royal Highness.

**비접** a change of place (for a sick person); a change of air 〔climate〕. ¶~ 나가다 《환자가》 take 〔get〕 a change of air《for *one's* health》; go to《a place》for a change of air.

**비정**(非情) ~하다《냉혹한》(be) cold=〔hard-, stone-〕hearted; cruel; 《인정 없는》 heartless; unfeeling; inhuman; insensate; 《생명 없는》 inanimate; 《감각 없는》 insentient. ¶~한 아버지 a cold-hearted father.

**비정**(秕政·粃政) misgovernment; misrule; maladministration.

**비정규**(非正規) ¶~의 irregular.
◉ ~군 irregulars; irregular troops.

**비정상**(非正常) anything unusual; abnormality; irregularity. ¶~의 abnormal; unusual; irregular; singular / ~적인 사건들 the out-of-ordinary happenings / 시월 치고는 ~적으로 덥다 It is unusually hot for October. / 생후 2개월된 갓난아기의 이가 나는 것은 ~이다 It is abnormal for a baby to have teeth at the age of two months. ◉ ~아(兒) an abnormal child. ~자 〖심리〗 a deviate.

**비정형**(非定型) ¶~의 atypical. ◉ ~시(詩) free verse.

**비조**(悲調) a plaintive note; a touch of sadness.

**비조**(鼻祖) the founder. ⇨ 시조(始祖).

**비좁다** (be) narrow and close; cramped; confined. ¶비좁은 곳 a confined place / 비좁아서 답답하다 [장소가 주어] be too cramped for comfort; [사람이 주어] feel cramped in a confined space / 이 집은 4인 가족이 살기에는 좀 ~ This house is a little too small for a family four to live in.

**비종교적**(非宗敎的) (being) unreligious; nonreligious. ¶~인 문제 an unreligious question.

**비주룩하다** be sticking out a bit. ¶비주룩이 sticking out a bit.

**비주류**(非主流) a non-mainstream group 〔faction〕; non-mainstreamers; the factions out of power.

**비죽** ① 《입술을》 sticking out *one's* lip(s) to indicate displeasure. ¶~거리다 pout *one's* mouth; screw up *one's* lips; 《울려고》 be going 〔ready〕 to cry; suppress crying. ② 《내밀다》 so that it sticks out 〔protrudes〕. ¶송곳이 주머니 속에서 ~ 나오다 a gimlet sticks out of *one's* bag / 혀를 ~ 내밀다 stick out *one's* tongue.

**비준**(批准) ratification. ~하다 ratify《a treaty》. ¶~이 끝난 ratified / 아직 ~이 안 된 unratified / ~을 기다리다 await ratification / ~을 필요로 하다 be subject to ratifications / 국회는 이번 회기 중에 그 조약을 ~할 예정이다 The National Assembly is expected to ratify the treaty during this session.
◉ ~서 an instrument of ratification; a ratification instrument: ~서를 교환하다 exchange instruments of ratifications.

**비중**(比重) ① 〖물리〗 specific gravity. ¶~을 재다 measure 〔find out〕 the specific gravity《of silver》/ 구리는 철보다 ~이 크다 Copper has a greater specific gravity than iron.
② 《중요성》 relative importance; weight. ¶~을 두다 place「a great deal of weight 〔great weight〕《on》/ 이 문제에 더 ~을 두어야 한다 This problem should be given much more weight. / 예산 전체에서 인건비가 차지하는 ~이 크다 The personnel expenditure is given much weight in the total estimate. / 입학 시험에서는 영어의 ~이 매우 크다 English is given a great deal of weight on the entrance examination.
◉ ~계 a gravimeter; 《액체의》 a hydrometer; an areometer. ~천칭 a hydrostatic balance. ~표 a table of specific gravities.

**비즈니스** business. ◉ ~클래스 《여객기의》 business class.

**비즈니스맨** 《기업인》 a businessman; 《회사원》 an office worker.

**비지** bean-curd refuse; the edible residue left after the production of bean curd. ¶~ 먹은 배는 연약과도 싫다 한다 《속담》 A full stomach is not interested in delicacies.
◉ ~찌개 a casserole of bean-curd dregs, salted shrimp, beef or pork, and kimchi. 비짓국 a coarse soup made from bean-curd dregs: 비짓국 먹고 용트림하다 《속담》 pretend elegance 〔opulence〕.

**비지**(鄙地) my humble place of residence.

**비지땀** heavy sweat; beads of sweat 〔perspiration〕. ¶~을 흘리며 soaked with sweat / ~을 흘리다 sweat 〔perspire〕 heavily 〔copiously〕; drip with sweat; have heavy sweating / ~ 뺐네 I really sweated it out!

**비지떡** "dreg cake"; a cake of bean=

curd dregs. ¶ 싼 것이 ～《속담》 Penny wise and pound foolish. *or* The money spent on cheap merchandise ends up being wasted.

**비질** sweeping (with a broom). ～하다 sweep with a broom. ¶ 마당을 ～하다 sweep the yard.

**비집다** ①《틈내다》 split open; 《벌리다》 pull open; spread apart. ¶ 비집어 열다 wrench〔pry, prize〕 open; break〔force〕 open; jimmy open (지레로) / 상자 뚜껑을 비집어 열다 prize a box open; pry the top off a box. ②《헤치다》 push〔shove, thrust〕 aside; 《끼어들다》 wedge (*oneself*) in(to); force〔edge〕 *one's* way in; break〔cut, shove〕 in《on》. ¶ 사람들을 비집고 나아가다 elbow〔push, work, force〕 *one's* way through the crowd / 만원 버스에 비집고 들어가다 squeeze *oneself* into a crowded bus. ③《눈을》 rub *one's* eyes open.

**비쭉** ⇨ 비죽.

**비참**(悲慘) misery; wretchedness; pitiableness; distress. ～하다 (be) miserable; wretched; tragic; pitiful; pitiable; sorrowful. ¶ ～한 광경 a pitiable scene; a terrible sight / ～한 생활 a miserable〔wretched〕 life / ～한 사건 a tragic〔terrible〕 accident; a tragedy; a disaster / ～한 죽음을 하다 die tragically; meet (with) a tragic death〔end〕 / ～한 처지에 빠지다 be driven into a piteous plight / ～하기 짝이 없다 be in the depths of misery / 선생님은 전쟁의 ～함을 우리에게 이야기해 주셨다 Our teacher told us about the misery of the war.

**비창**(悲愴) sadness; mournfulness; pathos. ～하다 (be) pathetic; sorrowful; sad. ¶ ～ 교향곡 the "Pathetic" Symphony.

**비책**(秘策) a secret plan〔scheme〕; a subtle stratagem; secret measures; a secret《of》. ¶ ～을 짜다 elaborate〔work out〕 a secret plan / ～을 전해주다 give secret measures〔tactics〕 / 그는 신입사원에게 고객을 확보하는 ～을 일러줬다 He initiated the new employee into the secrets of securing customers.

**비척거리다** stagger; totter. ⇨ 비틀거리다.

**비척걸음** a stagger; a staggering walk.

**비천**(卑賤) lowliness; humbleness; obscurity. ～하다 (be) lowly; humble; obscure. ¶ ～한 태생이다 be of humble birth / ～한 신분에서 출세하다 rise from obscurity〔humble origins〕《to》.

**비철**(非一) out of season; off season. ¶ 수박은 지금 ～이다 Watermelons are out of season now.

**비철금속**(非鐵金屬) a nonferrous metal.

**비첩**(婢妾) a slave concubine.

**비추**(悲秋)《가을》 lonely autumn; 《슬퍼함》 grieving over the autumn.

**비추다** ①《빛을》 (***a***)《빛·불빛 등을》 shine on; shed light on; flash on; light (up). ¶ 회중전등을 아무의 얼굴에〔아무에게〕 비추다 flash a torch in *a person's* face〔at *a person*〕/ 회중전등으로 가는 길을 비추다 play *one's* flashlight along *one's* way / (탐조등이) 해상을 ～ (the search light) flash over the sea; play on the sea. (***b***)《빛에》 hold《*a thing*》 to the light. ¶ 사진을 햇빛에 ～ hold a picture up against sunlight / 전등불에 비추어 보다 hold《*a thing*》 before the electric light.
②《반사하다》 (***a***)《거울·수면 등에》 reflect; mirror; image. ¶ 얼굴을 거울에 ～ hold *one's* face up to a mirror; look at *one's* face in the mirror / 거울로 햇빛을 ～ flash sunlight with a mirror / 호수가 산 그림자를 비추고 있다 The lake reflects〔mirrors〕 the mountains. / 자식들은 부모를 비추는 거울이다 Children are a mirror reflecting their parents. (***b***)《그림자를》 project; cast. ¶ 그림자를 ～ cast〔throw〕 a shadow / 영화를 스크린에 ～ project a motion picture on a screen / 그는 요즘 그림자도 비추지 않는다 I have seen nothing of him lately.
③《넌지시》 hint《at》; suggest; drop〔give〕 a hint《of, to》. ¶ 값을 ～ suggest a possible price / 사의(辭意)를 ～ hint at resignation.
④《견주다》 compare《with》; consider; refer《to》. ¶ …에 비추어 in view《of》; in (the) light《of》; according to《the rules》/ 전례에 비추어 in the light of precedents / 법조문에 비추어 사건을 처리하다 decide a case according to the provisions of the law / 이것이 실패로 끝나리란 것은 지난 경험에 비추어 명백하다 In the light of past experience(s) this is bound to fail.

**비추이다, 비취다** be shone; have light shed《on *a thing*》; be lighted (up); get reflected〔mirrored〕.

**비축**(備蓄) saving for emergency. ～하다 save〔store, reserve〕《rice, petroleum》 for emergency. ¶ 식량을 ～하다 store〔lay in〕 provisions / 6개월분의 석유를 ～해 둬야 한다 We have to have a six-month supply of oil stored up. ◉ ~미 reserved rice; rice stored in the public granary.

**비취**(翡翠) green jadeite; jade. ◉ ~ 가락지 a jade ring. ~색〔빛〕 jade green. ~옥 =비취. ~잠(簪) an ornamental jade hairpin.

**비치** 《해변》 a beach. ◉ ~가운 a beach gown. ~발리볼 beach volleyball. ~볼 a beachball. ~웨어 beachwear. ~파라솔 a beach umbrella.

**비치**(備置) furnishing; equipping. ~하다 furnish; provide; equip; 《기계 따위를》 install; fit; keep 《*a thing*》 ready. ¶ 도서관에 책을 ~하다 stock a library with books / (상점이) 갖가지 통조림제품을 ~하다 keep canned goods of various kinds / …이 ~되어 있다 be furnished 〔provided, equipped, fixed〕 with… / 교수실에 ~된 도서 books kept in a professor's office / ~된 약품 emergency remedies / 전화를 ~하다 install a telephone 《in a room》 / 이 교실에는 TV가 ~되어 있다 This classroom is equipped with a TV. / 방마다 전화가 ~되어 있다 A telephone is installed in each room.

**비치다** ① 《햇빛 등이》 shine 《upon, in(to), through》; strike 《on》. ¶ 석양이 비치는 방 a room exposed to the westering sun / 아침해가 지붕을 비치고 있다 The morning sun is shining on the roof. / 이 방은 해가 잘 비친다 This room gets a lot of sunshine. / 구름 사이로 햇빛이 ~ The sunshine breaks through the clouds. ② 《그림자가》 be reflected; be imaged 〔mirrored〕 《on, in》; fall 〔be thrown〕 upon 《the ground, water》. ¶ 장지에 비치는 사람 그림자 the shadows of men falling on the paper sliding door / 거울에 ~ be reflected in a mirror / 나무 그림자가 벽에 비친다 The shadow of the tree falls on the wall. / 구름이 잔잔한 호수에 비쳤다 The clouds were reflected 〔imaged〕 in the still lake. ③ 《속엣것이》 show 《through》; be transparent. ¶ 속살이 비치는 블라우스 a see=through blouse / 인쇄가 뒷면에 비친다 The printing shows through on the other side. / 옷이 얇아서 팔이 비친다 Her arms are seen through her thin dress. ④ 《인상을 주다》 impress; appear 《to》. ¶ 외국인 눈에 비친 한국 Korea as she appears to foreign eyes; Korea as foreigners see it; Korea through a foreigner's eye.

**비칭**(卑稱) 《give》 a humble 〔vulgar〕 term 〔name, title〕.

**비커** 〖화학〗 a beaker.

**비켜나다** step aside (옆으로); step back (뒤로); get out of the way (양보). ¶ 비켜 나서 마차를 통과시키다 step aside to let the cart pass.

**비켜서다** stand aside; stand back. ¶ 그는 뒤로 비켜 서라고 우리에게 손짓을 했다 He motioned us to stand back. / 좀 옆으로 비켜 서라 Move a little aside!

**비키니** 《수영복》 a bikini.

**비키다** ① 《길 따위에서》 get out of the way; make room 《for》; move 〔step〕 aside 《from》; step back (뒤로); 《피하다》 avoid; keep clear of; 《몸을 번드쳐》 dodge; ward off. ¶ 물구덩이를 ~ avoid 〔walk around〕 a puddle / 소를 비켜 가다 go around a cow / 암초를 ~ steer clear of a reef / 차를 ~ dodge a car; 「get out of the way of 〔step aside from〕 a car; make way for a car / 비키지 않고 있다 keep in the way / 비켜라 Make off. *or* Get out of my way. *or* Clear the way. / 그 부인에게 길을 비켜 드려라 Step aside, to make way for the lady.
② 《위치를 옮기다》 move 《*a thing*》 「aside 〔out of the way〕. ¶ 장애물을 ~ clear 《*a thing*》 out of *one's* way; clear the way of obstacles / 의자를 좀 비켜주시겠습니까 Will you please move your chair a little aside?
③ 《좌석에서》 retire; withdraw; stay out. ¶ 자리좀 비켜 주시지 않겠습니까 Would you kindly leave us alone?

**비타민** vitamin(e). ¶ ~ A, vitamin A / ~이 많다 contain 〔be rich in〕 vitamin / ~이 파괴되다 be devitaminized. ◉ ~ 결핍증 a vitamin deficiency disease; 〖의학〗 avitaminosis. ~B 복합체 vitamin B complex. ~정(錠) a vitamin tablet. ~제(劑) a vitamin compound. ~학 vitaminology.

**비타협적**(非妥協的) ¶ ~인 unyielding; uncompromising; intransigent / ~ 태도 intransigence; intransigency / ~ 태도를 취하다 take an unyielding stand.

**비탄**(飛彈) a flying bullet.

**비탄**(悲嘆) grief; sorrow; anguish; lamentation. ~하다 grieve; mourn; sorrow 《over, on》; lament; deplore; bewail. ¶ ~한 나머지 in *one's* 〔overcome with〕 grief 〔sorrow〕 / ~에 빠지다〔잠기다〕 abandon *oneself* to grief; be grieved 《at》; be overcome with sorrow 〔grief〕 《over》; 《구어》 eat *one's* heart out / 그녀는 아이를 잃고 ~에 잠겨 있다 She is greatly grieved over the death of her child. / 그녀는 ~끝에 죽었다 She died of grief.

**비탈** a slope; an incline; 《철도 등의》 a gradient. ¶ 오르막 ~ an upward slope; an ascent 〔acclivity〕; an upgrade / 내리막 ~ a downward slope; a descent 〔declivity〕; a downgrade / ~지다 《오르막》 slope up(ward); 《내리막》 slope down(ward) / ~이 가파르게〔완만하게〕 지다 sharply 〔gradually〕 slope / ~을 올라가다 go up 〔ascend, climb〕 a slope; go uphill / ~을 내려가다 go down 〔descend〕 a slope; go downhill. ◉ ~길 a sloping road; a slope.

**비통**(悲痛) intense 〔bitter〕 grief; bitterness; pathos. ~하다 (be) sad; grievous; sorrowful; bitter; touching; affecting; pathetic. ¶ ~한 외침 a heartrending cry / ~한 표정 a look of sorrow (on *one's* face) / ~한 생각에 잠기다 be filled with deep sadness.

**비트적-** ⇨ 비틀-.

**비트족**(一族) [총칭] the beat generation; the beatniks; 《개인》 a beatnik.

**비틀거리다** stagger; totter; reel. ¶ 비틀거리며 with tottering 〔unsteady, faltering〕 steps / 비틀거리며 걷다 reel 〔stagger〕 along / 비틀거리며 일어서다 stagger to *one's* feet / 비틀거리며 쓰러지다 topple down 〔over〕.

**비틀걸음** tottering 〔faltering, unsteady〕 steps. ¶ ~으로 걷다 walk with tottering steps; stagger 〔shamble, dodder〕 along.

**비틀다** twist; wring; wrench; 《고동 등을》 turn. ¶ 젖은 수건을 비틀어 물을 짜내다 wring water out of the wet towel / 사지를 ~ contort *one's* limbs / 팔을 ~ twist 〔wrench〕 《*a person's*》 arm / 비틀어 끊다 wrench 〔wrest, twist〕 off / 가지에서 열매를 비틀어 따다 wrench a fruit off a branch / 나는 그의 손을 비틀어 그것을 빼앗았다 I twisted it out of his hand.

**비틀리다** = 비틀어지다.

**비틀비틀** staggeringly; totteringly; reelingly; falteringly.

**비틀어지다** ① 《꼬이다》 get twisted; get bent. ② ⇨ 틀어지다 ②.

**비틈하다** (be) oblique; indirect; allusive.

**비틈히** 《say》 in a roundabout way; vaguely; by hinting; indirectly.

**비파**(琵琶) a Korean mandolin 〔lute〕.

**비판**(批判) (a) criticism; (a) comment; (a) critique; (a) forum. ~하다 criticize; comment 《on》; pass judgment 《on》. ¶ ~적(으로) critical(ly) / 통렬한 ~ severe criticism / 자기~ self-criticism / 칸트의 순수 이성 ~ Kant's *Critique of Pure Reason* / ~적 태도를 취하다 assume a critical attitude 《toward》 / 아무를 ~하다 criticize *a person;* form an estimate of *a person* / 세부에 걸쳐 ~하다 go into detailed criticism 《of the editorial》 / ~을 받다 be criticized 《by》; encounter 〔face, run into〕 criticism / ~할 여지가 없다 be above criticism; give no grounds for criticism 〔animadversion〕 / …에 ~적이다 be critical of…; have a poor opinion of… / ~적인 눈으로 보다 look 《at *a thing*》 「critically 〔with a critical eye〕 / 외국인들은 한국 사람을 너무 많은 시간 일한다고 ~한다 Foreigners criticize the Koreans for spending too much time working. ◉ ~력 critical faculty 〔power, ability〕. ~자 a critic. ~철학 critical philosophy.

**비평**(批評) (a) criticism; a critical essay; (a) comment (논평); a review (신간서 등의); a note (단평). ~하다 criticize; comment 《on》; pass criticism 《on》; review 《a book》; 《감상을 말하다》 remark 《that…, on》. ¶ 문명에 대한 ~ criticism on civilization / ~을 받다 receive criticism; get criticized / ~할 가치도 없다 be beneath criticism. ◉ ~가 a critic (문예·미술의); a reviewer. ~사 history of criticism. 문예~ literary criticism.

**비폭력**(非暴力) ahimsa; nonviolence. ¶ ~의 nonviolent / ~ 저항 《put up》 nonviolent resistance. ◉ ~주의 the doctrine of ahimsa.

**비품**(備品) fixtures; furniture; furnishings. ◉ ~목록 a list of fixtures.

**비프** beef. ◉ ~스테이크 (a) beefsteak. ~스튜 beef stew. ~커틀릿 a beef cutlet.

**비하**(卑下) abasement; belittlement; disparagement; humbleness. ~하다 belittle 〔humble, disparage, depreciate〕 *oneself;* speak 〔think〕 depreciatingly of *oneself.* ¶ 지나치게 자신을 ~할 필요는 없다 You don't have to humble yourself too much.

**비하다**(比一) compare 《*one thing*》 with 〔to〕 《*another*》. ⇨ 비교하다. ¶ …에 비해 (as) compared with 〔to〕; by 〔in〕 comparison with 〔to〕 / 비할 수 없을

만큼 beyond (all) comparison / 전에 비해 그는 점잖아졌다 Compared with what he was, he has become gentle. / 그 소년은 나이에 비해 키가 크다 The boy is tall for his age. / 세계에 비할 데가 없다 It stands unchallenged 〔unrivaled〕 in the world. / 그의 영어는 도저히 자네에게 비할 바가 못 되네 He is no match for you in English.

**비학술적**(非學術的) (being) unacademic; unscholarly; unscientific.

**비합리**(非合理) irrationality. ¶ ～인 irrational. ◉ ～주의 irrationalism.

**비합법**(非合法) illegality. ¶ ～적(인) illegal; unlawful; illicit / ～적인 활동 illegal 〔unlawful〕 activities / ～적이다 be out of order / ～화하다 illegalize; outlaw 《a party》; make 《a movement》 illegal.

**비핵화**(非核化) denuclearization. ～하다 denuclearize 《a nation, an area》. ¶ 한반도의 ～ the denuclearization of the Korean Peninsula.

**비행**(非行) wrongdoing; a misdeed; misconduct; a malpractice; delinquency (청소년의); an evil deed. ¶ 청소년 ～의 증가 an increase in juvenile delinquency / ～을 들추어 내다 expose 〔reveal〕 《*a person's*》 misdeeds 〔misconduct〕; bring 〔put〕 《*a person's*》 misconduct 〔crime〕 to light / ～을 저지르다 misconduct *oneself;* commit an irregularity. ◉ ～청소년 a juvenile delinquent.

**비행**(飛行) flight; flying; 《1회의》 a flight; 《항공술》 aviation. ～하다 fly (in the air); make a flight; travel by air. ¶ ～중에 while 「flying 〔in flight〕 / ～금지 구역 the no-fly zone / 세계 일주 ～ a round-the-world flight / 500킬로

[참고] 비행기 여행과 관련된 절차·낱말들

1. 비행기 탑승 절차(check-in)—공항 내 출발 라운지(a departure lounge)에 있는 항공회사(an airline company) 카운터에 가서, 수화물(baggage; luggage)을 맡기고 수화물 영수증(a claim tag)을 받는다. 여권(a passport), 항공권(an air ticket), 출입국 카드(an ED card; Embarkation / Disembarkation)를 제시하고 탑승권 (a boarding pass 〔card〕; a flight coupon)을 받는다. 여기서 좌석 배당 (a seat assignment)이 행해진다. 좌석은 퍼스트 클래스(first class), 비즈니스 클래스(business 〔executive〕 class), 이코노미 클래스(economy 〔coach〕 class)로 나뉘며, 통로측의 좌석(an aisle seat), 창문가의 좌석(a window seat) 따위로 분류된다. 탑승구(a boarding gate)의 번호는 탑승권에 기재되어 있다.

2. 출국 절차(embarkation procedure)

(1) 출국 심사(Emigration; passport control)—여권, 출입국 카드, 탑승권을 제시하고, 여권에 출국 스탬프를 받는다.

(2) 세관(Customs)—고가의 외국 제품을 지참하고 출국할 때에는 휴대 출국 증명 신청서(a custom declaration form)를 함께 제시한다.

(3) 검역(Quarantine)—출국 목적지에 따라서, 예방접종 증명서(a vaccination certification; 《통칭》 a yellow card)가 필요하다.

3. 수화물 검사—비행기 납치(hijack) 사고 예방을 위한 기내 반입 수화물(carry-on 〔hand-carry〕 baggage)의 검사(check)를 받는다. 본인은 위험물 검사 통로(a walk-through gate; a security checkpoint)를 통과하며, 공항에 따라서는 안전 계원(a security officer)에 의한 신체 검사를 받을 수도 있다.

4. 탑승(boarding)—탑승 대합실(a waiting lounge)에서 출발시간까지 기다리며, 그동안 면세품점(a dutyfree shop)에서 선물 따위를 살 수 있다.

5. 입국 지점(the port of entry)에 도착—입국 심사(Immigration)를 받기 위해 여권, 입국 카드를 제시한다. 이때 입국 심사관(an immigration officer)은 예정 체류 기간(intended length of stay)에 관하여 How long are you going to stay in the United States? (미국에서의 체류기간은)이라든가, 또는 Are you on sightseeing or on business? (관광입니까, 상용입니까) 등으로 한 두가지 질문을 하게 된다. 이 때는 Two weeks. 또는 Sightseeing. *or* Business.라고 간단히 대답하면 된다. 다음으로 수화물 받는 곳(a baggage claim area)에 가서, 턴테이블(a turntable; a carrousel)에서 빙빙 돌고 있는 수화물 중에서 자기 것을 찾아들고 세관의 검사대를 통과한 후, 도착 로비(an arrival lounge)로 나온다. 그러나 환승객(a transit passenger)은 환승 라운지(a transit lounge)로 나와 다음 비행기를 기다려야 한다.

의 ～거리 a flight of 500 kilometers / 시험～《make》 a test flight / 장거리〔저공〕～ a long-distance 〔low-altitude〕 flight / 그는 ～ 경력 5,000 시간의 베테랑 조종사이다 He is a veteran pilot with 5,000 hours' flying time. / 강풍으로 ～은 중지되었다 The flight was 「called off 〔canceled〕 because of the strong wind. / 날씨가 ～에 알맞지 않았다 The weather was unfavorable for flying.

◉ ～갑판《항공 모함의》 a flying deck. ～거리 fly; a flight. ～경로 a flight path. ～ 기록장치 a flight recorder: ～자료 기록 장치 a flight data recorder (생략 FDR). ～기지 an air base. ～대 an air corps; a flying corps. ～모 an aviation cap; a flying helmet. ～복 a flying dress 〔suit〕; a flight uniform; an aviation garment. ～속도 (an) air speed; (a) flying speed: ～속도계 an airspeed indicator. ～수당 a flight allowance. ～술 the art of flying; aeronautics. ～시간 《비행기의》 flight time; 《비행사의》 flying hours 〔time〕. ～운 a contrail; a vapor 〔condensation〕 trail. ～접시〔물체〕 a flying saucer 〔disk, object〕. ～정 a flying boat; a seaplane; an aeroboat. ～정보 구역 the 《Korean》 flight information region (생략 FIR). ～통제 구역 the flight restriction area.

**비행가**(飛行家) an aviator; an airman.

**비행기**(飛行機) ① 《항공기》 an airplane; a plane; an aeroplane 《영》; aircraft [총칭]. ¶ 민간～ a commercial plane / 쌍엽～ a biplane / 대형 수송 ～ a sky truck / ～로 가다 go by air; fly 《to Paris, across the Pacific》 / ～를 조종하다 pilot a plane / ～를 타다 board 〔take〕 a plane; have a ride in an airplane; get into 〔get aboard〕 an airplane / ～는 곧 이륙할 것이다 The airplane will soon take off. / ～가 추락했다 The airplane crashed. / ～가 불시착했다 The airplane 「crashlanded 〔made a forced landing〕. / ～가 활주로에 착륙했다 An airplane 「touched down 〔landed〕 on the runway. / 우리는 ～로 서울에서 런던까지 갔다 We went from Seoul to London by plane 〔air〕. ② 《추어올림》 ¶ ～(를) 태우다 praise 《*a person*》 skyhigh; be profuse in *one's* praise.

◉ ～ 격납고 an aviation 〔airplane〕 shed; a hangar. ～멀미 airsickness: ～멀미가 나다 get 〔become〕 airsick. ～사고 《meet *one's* death in》 a plane 〔an air〕 accident 〔crash〕. ～승무원 flight crew. ～여행 an air trip. ～표 an air 〔airline〕 ticket 《to New York》.

**비행사**(飛行士) an aviator; an airman; a flier 〔flyer〕; a pilot. ¶ ～가 되다 take to the air. ◉ 민간 ～ a civilian aviator.

**비행선**(飛行船) an airship; a blimp; a 「dirigible.

**비행장**(飛行場) an airfield; a flying field; an air station; an air depot 《미》; an airdrome 《미》; an aerodrome 《영》; an airport (공항).

**비현실**(非現實) ¶ ～적(인) unrealistic; out of touch with reality; 《실행불가능한》 impracticable; unfeasible; 《실제적이 아닌》 impractical; 《실재하지 않은》 unreal; 《공상적인》 fantastic; imaginary / ～적인 계획 an unfeasible 〔impracticable〕 plan / ～적인 사람 an impractical person / 그의 아이디어는 극히 ～적이다 His idea is far from realistic 〔very fantastic〕. ◉ ～성 unreality.

**비협력**(非協力) ¶ ～적(인) uncooperative.

**비호**(庇護) protection; patronage; aegis. ～하다 protect; shelter; shield; take 《*a person*》 under *one's* wings; 《죄인 등을》 cover; harbor. ¶ …의 ～하에 under the aegis 〔protection, patronage〕 of…; under the wing of…. ◉ ～자 a guardian; a protector; a patron.

**비호**(飛虎) an agile tiger. ¶ ～ 같다 be (as) fast 〔quick〕 as lightning.

**비화**(飛火) ① 《불똥》 flying sparks (of a fire); leaping flames. ～하다 flames 〔sparks〕 leap to 《another house》. ② 《사건의》 an effect felt in unexpected quarters. ～하다 come to involve 《another》; spread repercussions. ¶ 최근 폭로된 사건은 예기치 않은 곳에까지 ～했다 The latest revelations involved people in quite unexpected quarters.

**비화**(秘話) a secret story; an unknown episode; a behind-the-scenes story 《of》.

**비화**(悲話) a sad tale; a tragic story.

**비활성기체** 〖화학〗 rare 〔noble, inert〕 gases.

**비후성비염**(肥厚性鼻炎) hypertrophic 「rhinitis.

**빅딜** 《큰 거래》 a big deal.

**빅뱅** 〖경제〗 《근본적인 개혁》 (the) big bang; 《증권제도의 자유화》 Big Bang; 〖천문〗 《우주 대폭발》 the big bang. ◉ ～이론 《우주 대폭발 생성론》 the big bang theory.

**빅수** ⇨ 비김수.

**빈개념**(賓概念) 〖논리〗 the predicate.

**빈객**(賓客) a guest of honor; an honored guest.

**빈고**(貧苦) the hardships 〔pressure〕 of poverty; pinching poverty. ¶ ～에 시달리다 be poverty-stricken.

**빈곤**(貧困) ① 《가난》 poverty; penury; indigence; 《궁핍》 need; destitution. ～하다 (be) indigent; poor; needy; destitute; poverty-stricken. ¶ ～한 사람들 the poor (and needy) / ～에 빠지다 be reduced to 〔sink into〕 poverty 〔penury〕 / ～에 시달리다 suffer extreme poverty / ～속에서 자라다 be brought up amidst destitution; have a penurious childhood / ～에서 헤어나다 emerge from poverty.
② 《내용의 부족》 shortage; want; lack; poverty; poor. ¶ 사상의 ～ poverty of thought 〔ideas〕 / 그의 비평은 상상력의 ～을 여실히 보여주고 있다 His remarks clearly show a lack of imagination.
◉ ～가정 a poor family.

**빈광**(貧鑛) poor 〔lean, low-grade〕 ore.

**빈궁**(貧窮) destitution; extreme poverty. ～하다 (be) destitute; poverty-stricken; penurious.

**빈궁**(嬪宮) the Crown Princess.

**빈농**(貧農) a poor farmer; a needy peasant.

**빈대** 〖곤충〗 a bedbug; a (house)bug 《영》. ¶ ～ 잡으려고 집에 불놓는다 《속담》 "Burn the barn down to get rid of the mice".

**빈대떡** a mung-bean pancake. ¶ ～을 지지다 make mung-bean pancakes.

**빈도**(頻度) frequency. ¶ 말의 사용 ～ frequency in use of a word / ～가 높은〔낮은〕 high 〔low〕 frequency / 낱말의 사용 ～를 조사하다 check 〔see〕 how frequently a word is used 《in everyday Korean》.
◉ ～수 the frequency (number): ～수가 높은 말 a word of high frequency. ～순 the order of frequency: 사용하는 ～순에 따라 in the order of frequency in use.

**빈둥거리다** idle; lounge; loaf; idle 〔laze, snooze, dawdle〕 *one's* time away; loaf away *one's* time. ¶ 빈둥거리는 자 an idler; a lazybones 《속어》 / 집 안에서 ～ loaf at home / 하는 일 없이 빈둥거리고 있다 fiddle about doing nothing / 일정한 직업 없이 빈둥거리고 있다 be at a loose end.

**빈둥빈둥** idly; lazily; slothfully. ¶ 하루 종일 ～ 지내다 spend a whole day idly / ～ 세월을 보내다 idle 〔loaf〕 away *one's* time 〔days〕; fool around 〔about〕 / 당장은 실직으로 ～ 놀고 있다 be out of employment 〔work〕 at the moment; be unemployed 〔jobless〕 at the moment.

**빈들-** = 빈둥-.

**빈랑**(檳榔) a betel nut; an areca nut.
◉ ～나무 〖식물〗 a betel(-nut) palm.

**빈말** idle talk; empty 〔hollow〕 words; lip homage (마음에도 없는 말); an empty 〔a specious〕 promise. ～하다 talk idly; pay lip service 《to》; make idle promises. ¶ ～이라도 그렇게 말할 수는 없었다 I could not say so even as a joke.

**빈미주룩하다** (be) slightly showing 〔protruding〕.

**빈민**(貧民) poor people; the poor; paupers; the needy. ¶ ～을 구제하다 relieve 〔give aid to〕 the poor 〔needy〕.
◉ ～가 a slum. ⇨ 빈민굴. ～ 구호법 the poor law. ～ 복지사업 settlement work. ～학교 a poor 〔pauper〕 school.

**빈민굴**(貧民窟) a slum; [총칭] the slum quarters; the slums; the gutter. ¶ ～의 slummy / ～의 사람 a slummer / ～을 없애다 clear 〔wipe out〕 slums.

**빈발**(頻發) frequent occurrence. ～하다 occur frequently; happen often. ¶ 철도 사고의 ～ the (high) frequency of train accidents / 교통 사고가 ～하다 traffic accidents occur very often.

**빈방**(一房) 《사람이 없는》 an empty room; 《쓰지 않는》 a vacant room; an unoccupied 〔unused〕 room.

**빈번**(頻繁·頻煩) frequency; bustle. ～하다 (be) frequent; incessant; bustling. ¶ ～히 frequently; at short intervals; very often; incessantly / 왕래가 ～한 거리 a busy 〔bustling〕 street / ～히 일어나는 일 a matter of frequent occurrence / 해마다 이맘때면 화재가 ～하다 Fires are frequent at this time of the year.

**빈병**(一甁) an empty bottle.

**빈부**(貧富) 《가난과 부유》 poverty and wealth; 《가난한 자와 부자》 (the) poor and (the) rich. ¶ ～의 구별없이 rich and poor alike / ～의 격차 the gulf between rich and poor; the gap between haves and have-nots / ～의 격차를 좁히다 narrow the gap between the wealthy and the poor / 중류층의 증가에도 불구하고 부(富)의 ～ 간 격차는 넓어졌다 Despite an expanding middle class, the gap in wealth between the nation's wealthiest and the poorest group of people has widened.

**빈사**(賓辭) 〖논리〗 the predicate.

**빈사**(瀕死) a dying condition; (being on) the brink of death. ¶ ～의 환자 a dying patient; a patient on the verge of death / ～ 상태에 있다 be in a dying condition; hang between life and death; be on the verge of death; 《위독하다》 be critically ill.

**빈삭**(頻數) frequency; oftenness. ～하다 (be) frequent; often.

**빈소**(殯所) a room where a coffin is placed until the funeral day. 「말.

**빈소리** useless 〔pointless〕 words. ⇨빈

**빈속** an empty stomach. ¶ ～에 술을 마시다 drink on an empty stomach.

**빈손** an empty 〔a bare〕 hand. ¶ ～으로 empty-handed; with empty hands; without taking any present (with *one*) / ～으로 돌아오다 return 〔come home〕 empty-handed / ～으로 방문하다 visit 《*a person*》 without taking a present / ～으로 보내다 send 《*a person*》 away empty-handed / 옛 친구를 ～으로 찾아갈 수는 없다 I can not call on my old friend without taking a present for him.

**빈약**(貧弱) scantiness; poorness; meagerness. ～하다 (be) poor; scanty; meager; limited. ¶ 내용이 ～한 《a book》 poor in substance / ～한 식사 a meager 〔scanty〕 meal / ～한 지식 scanty 〔poor〕 knowledge / 풍채가 ～한 사람 an insignificant-〔unimposing-〕looking man / 그의 연설은 내용이 ～했다 His speech 「lacked substance 〔sounded hollow〕.

**빈자**(貧者) a poor man; a pauper; [총칭] the poor 〔needy〕. ¶ ～의 일등(一燈) 〖불교〗 a widow's mite.

**빈자리** ① 《공석》 a vacant 〔an unoccupied〕 seat; room (여지). ¶ ～를 만들다 make room / ～가 없었다 There was no room left. *or* There were no empty seats. ② 《결원》 a vacancy; a vacant position; an opening. ¶ ～가 나다〔생기다〕 cause a vacancy; create a vacancy; a vacancy occurs / ～를 메우다 fill (up) a vacancy / ～를 메우지 않고 그대로 두다 leave a position 「unfilled 〔vacant〕. ③ 《여백》 a space; a blank. ¶ 신청 용지의 ～에 써넣다 fill in 〔《미》 fill out〕 the blanks on an application form.

**빈정거리다** 《비꼬다》 be cynical 〔sarcastic〕 about; make sarcastic 〔ironical〕 remarks; talk cynically; 《비웃다》 mock; 《조롱하다》 make fun of; poke fun at; tease. ¶ 자못 빈정거리는 투로 말하다 say with evident 〔heavy, biting〕 sarcasm / 그는 그녀의 이중인격을 빈정거리곤 한다 He is often cynical about her double personality. / 그의 빈정거리는 말이 비위에 거슬렸다 His sarcastic remark jarred on my nerves.

**빈주먹** an empty hand 〔fist〕. ¶ ～으로 empty-handed; barehanded; [비유적] 《start》 from nothing 〔scratch 《구어》〕; with empty pockets; 《make *one's* fortune》 without anything to start with / ～으로 장사를 시작하다 start a business with practically no capital.

**빈지** 〖건축〗 shutters. ¶ ～를 닫다〔열다〕 put up 〔take down〕 the shutters.

**빈집** a vacant 〔an empty, an unoccupied〕 house. ¶ 그 집은 ～이다 The house is left vacant. ◉ ～털이 《행위》 sneak-thieving; 《사람》 a sneak thief.

**빈차**(一車) an empty car; 《택시의 게시》 Free. 《미》; For hire. 《영》.

**빈촌**(貧村) a poor village.

**빈총**(一銃) 《실탄을 재지 않은》 an unloaded gun; 《공포》 blank charge 〔shot〕. ¶ ～을 놓다 fire a blank.

**빈축**(嚬蹙) a frown; a scowl. ¶ ～살 만한 disdainful; despicable / ～을 사다 be frowned at 〔on〕 by 《*a person*》; incur 《*a person's*》 displeasure / 그녀의 행동은 모든 사람들의 ～을 샀다 Her behavior 「disgusted everyone 〔was frowned on by everybody〕. / 나는 웃어서 그의 ～을 샀다 He frowned at me when I laughed.

**빈치류**(貧齒類) 〖동물〗 Edentata. ¶ ～의 edentate.

**빈탕** ① 《과실의》 an empty nut. ② 《실속없는 것》 something with no substance. 「lot.

**빈터** vacant land; a vacant 〔an empty〕

**빈털터리** a man who is broke; a man without ready money; a man with empty pockets 〔with a flat pocketbook〕; a penniless person. ¶ ～가 되다 become (quite) penniless; go clean 〔stone〕 broke / 나는 ～야 I'm stone broke. / 그는 화재로 ～가 되었다 The fire disaster left him with nothing of his property.

**빈틈** ① 《벌어진 틈》 a gap; a crevice; a crack; an opening; a chink; 《여지》 room; space. ¶ ～없이 closely; compactly; leaving no space between them / ～을 메우다 fill 〔stop〕 a gap /

~없이 들어차다 be packed to the full; be crammed 〔jammed〕 《with people》; be filled to capacity. ② 《불비》 unpreparedness; 《허술한 틈》 an unguarded moment; a blind side; an opening 《for attack》; a weak point (허점). ¶ ~없는 shrewd; sharp; wide-awake; keen; clever; careful; prudent (주의깊은); tactful (재치 있는) / ~없는 이론 close 〔cogent, watertight, sound〕 reasoning / ~없는 사람 an alert 〔a shrewd, a sharp〕 person / 그들은 급습을 당하지 않기 위해 한시도 ~을 보이지 않았다 They were constantly on the alert so as not to be taken by surprise. / 그는 상대방 논점의 ~을 노리고 있었다 He was watching for the slightest weakness in his opponent's argument.

**빈한**(貧寒) poverty. = 빈궁(貧窮).

**빈혈**(貧血) poverty of blood; 〖의학〗 anemia. ¶ ~이 되다 become anemic; be drained of blood / ~을 일으키다 have an attack of anemia.
◉ ~성 an anemic constitution. ~증 〖의학〗 anemia; exsanguinity: ~증이 있는 사람 an anemic person / ~증이 있다 be anemic; suffer from anemia.

**빌다** ① 《구걸·탄원하다》 beg; ask; solicit; plead. ¶ 도움을 ~ beg for help / 밥을 ~ beg *one's* bread; beg food / (살려달라고) 목숨을 ~ ask 〔plead, appeal〕 for *one's* life; beg *one's* life. ② 《기원하다》 pray 《to God》; invoke; supplicate; wish (바라다). ¶ 두손 모아 ~ pray with *one's* hands joined together / (병의) 쾌유를 ~ pray 《to a god》 for 《*a person's*》 recovery / 성공을 빕니다 I wish you success. ③ 《용서를》 ask 〔beg〕 《*a person's*》 pardon; apologize 〔make apology〕 《to *a person*》 for. ¶ 용서를 ~ beg 〔implore〕 forgiveness; ask 〔seek〕 《*a person's*》 forgiveness / 잘못을 ~ apologize 《to *a person*》 for *one's* fault / 무릎을 꿇고 ~ beg 〔implore, supplicate〕 《a *person's*》 pardon on *one's* knees; go down on *one's* knees to beg 《*a person's*》 pardon.

**빌딩** a building (생략 bldg.); an office building. ¶ 고층 ~ a high-rise building / 10층 ~ a ten-story building.
◉ ~가(街) a block 〔street〕 of large buildings; a street lined with large buildings. ~바람 a strong wind blowing along a street of high-rise buildings. ~증후군〔신드롬〕 a building syndrome.

**빌레몬서**(一書) 〖성서〗 (The Epistle of St. Paul to) Philemon (생략 Philem.).

**빌려주다** lend; loan. ⇨ 빌리다 ①, ②.

**빌리다** ① 《대여하다》 lend; loan 《미》; advance 《money》; accommodate 《*a person* with money》 (변통해 주다). ¶ 빌려주는 사람 a lender / 돈을 ~ lend 〔loan〕 money / 손을 ~ lend a (helping) hand 《in, at》; lend *one's* help 《to》 / 지혜를 빌려주다 give advice 〔counsel〕 《to》 / 책을 ~ lend 〔loan〕 a book / 힘을 ~ lend *one's* aid 《to a project》 / (담뱃)불 좀 빌립시다 May I have a light, please?
② 《임대하다》 hire 〔let〕 out; keep 《*a thing*》 on hire; 《집·토지 등을》 let 《*one's* house for the winter》; rent 《a house to *a person*》; rent out; 《토지를》 lease; let out 《land》 on lease. ¶ 2층의 방을 월 5만원에 빌려주고 있다 The room upstairs rents for fifty thousand won a month.

> 참고 lend는 들고 다닐 수 있는 것을 「대여」할 때, 고정된 전화처럼 들고 다닐 수 없는 것을 「대여」할 때는 let 《*a person*》 use 《*one's* telephone》이라고 한다. 집·토지 등을 「대여」할 때, 《미》에서는 rent (out), 《영》에서는 let가 일반적이며, 극히 드물게 rent라고 할 때도 있다. 집·토지 이외의 것을(비교적 단기간) 「대여」할 때, 《미》에서는 rent out, 《영》에서는 hire out라고 한다.

③ 《금품·물건을》 borrow 《*a thing* from *a person*》; have 〔get〕 a loan of 《money》. ¶ 은행에서 돈을 ~ borrow (some money) from a bank / 담보를 잡혀 돈을 ~ borrow money on *one's* property 〔security〕 / 옷을 빌려 입다 wear borrowed clothes.
④ 《도움 등을》 get 《*a person's*》 aid 〔help〕; employ 《*a person's*》 assistance; 《사용하다》 use. ¶ 그의 말을 빌리면 to use 〔borrow〕 his words; in his phrase / 술의 힘을 빌려 with the help of alcohol 〔drink〕 / 돈의 힘을 빌려 by employing *one's* moneyed power; through the influence of money / 남의 손〔힘〕을 ~ get another's help; be helped by another; get assistance from another / 잠시 전화 좀 빌릴까요 May I use your telephone for a moment, please?
⑤ 《임차하다》 hire 《a boat》; rent 《a house, a room》; lease 《land》. ¶ 승용차를 일주일간 ~ hire a car for a

week / 집을 한 채 ~ rent 〔take the lease of〕 a house / 극장을 하룻밤 ~ hire a theater for one evening.

**빌립보서** (—書) 〖성서〗 The Epistle of St. Paul to the Philippians; 《약칭》 Philippians (생략 Phil.).

**빌미** the cause of evil 〔trouble〕; an evil spell; a curse. ¶ ~(가) 붙다 inflict a calamity 〔an evil〕 on; haunt (원귀가).

**빌미잡다** attribute 《a calamity》 to; blame 《the calamity》 (up)on.

**빌붙다** flatter; fawn on; toad (to); play up to; "lick (at) 《*a person's*》 hand 〔heel〕" (to curry favor). ¶ 상관에게 ~ flatter 〔curry favor with, play up to〕 *one's* superior.

**빌어먹다** 《…이》 beg *one's* bread; go (about) begging; live as a beggar; 《…을》 beg for. ¶ 빌어먹는 신세 beggary; mendicancy / 빌어먹는 한이 있더라도 even if *one* would be reduced 〔brought〕 to beggary 〔begging〕 / 빌어먹는 놈이 콩밥을 마다 할까 《속담》 Beggars cannot be choosers.

**빌어먹을** Damn…!; Damn 〔Hang〕 it!; Gosh! 《미》. ¶ 빌어먹을! 비가 오네 Damn the rain!

**빔**[1] ① 《옷을 입음》 dressing up (for a particular occasion). ~하다 dress up 《for a gala》. ② 《옷》 gala dress; fine dress 《worn on the New Year's Day》.

**빔**[2] a beam. ◉ ~안테나 a beam antenna. ~컴퍼스 a beam compass.

**빗** a comb. ¶ 얼레〔참〕빗 a wide-tooth 〔fine-tooth〕 comb / 휴대용 빗 a pocket comb / 빗으로 빗다 comb (down) 《*one's* hair》 / 빗을 꽂다 wear 〔put on〕 a comb.

**빗가다** ⇨ 빗나가다.

**빗각** (—角) 〖수학〗 an oblique angle. ◉ ~기둥〔뿔〕 an oblique prism 〔pyramid〕.

**빗금** a diagonal 〔an oblique〕 line; a slanting line.

**빗기다** ① 《머리를》 comb 《*a person's* hair》. ¶ 개의 털을 ~ comb a dog. ② 《남을 시켜서》 get someone to comb 《*a person's* hair》. ¶ 하녀에게 딸의 머리를 ~ have the maid comb *one's* daughter's hair.

**빗나가다** ① 《목표에서》 miss; go wide 〔astray〕; 《실패하다》 fail; go wrong 〔amiss〕; 《이야기 등이》 deviate 〔diverge〕 《from》; wander 〔digress〕 《from》; 《궤도·중심에서》 run off 《the rails》; stray off 《*one's* course》; 《일기예보 등이》 prove wrong. ¶ 계획이 ~ be baffled in *one's* design / 과녁에서 ~ miss the target; go wide of the mark / 예상이 ~ [사물이 주어] fall short of *one's* expectations; [사람이 주어] be disappointed of *one's* expectations / (이야기가) 딴 데로 ~ wander 〔digress〕 from the subject / 만사가 빗나갔다 Everything went wrong with me. / 인공위성이 지구 궤도에서 빗나갔다 The satellite strayed out of its orbit around the earth. / 일기 예보가 빗나갈 때도 있다 Weather forecasts 「are not always right 〔sometimes prove wrong〕. ② 《행실이》 go astray; be against; be contrary to. ¶ 빗나간 행동 immoral behavior / 규칙에서 ~ be against the rules / 도리에서 ~ be 「contrary to 〔against all〕 reason.

**빗다** comb 《*one's* hair》; pull 〔run〕 a comb through 《*one's* hair》; card (양털을). ¶ 잘 빗은 머리 well-combed hair / 빗지 않은 머리 unkempt 〔uncombed〕 hair.

**빗대다** ① 《에둘러 꼬집다》 have a sly dig 《at》; hint (obliquely) at; make an insinuating remark 《at》; give an indirect cut; insinuate. ¶ 은근히 빗대어 악평하다 have a sly 〔quiet〕 dig 《at *a person*》 / 그것은 나를 두고 빗댄 말이었다 That was a cut at me. *or* That remark was really a dig at me. ② 《틀리게》 make a false statement; misstate; perjure. ¶ 빗대지 말고 바로 대라 Don't perjure yourself, tell the truth.

**빗돌** (碑—) a stone monument; a monumental stone.

**빗듣다** mishear; hear 《it, him》 wrong; be misinformed.

**빗디디다** take 〔make〕 a false step; miss *one's* step; miss 〔lose〕 *one's* footing 《on the stairs》. ¶ 나는 발을 빗디뎌 계단 밑으로 굴러 떨어졌다 I lost my footing and fell down the stairs.

**빗뜨다** 《눈을》 look out of the corner of (*one's* eye); look sidewise; give a sharp sidelong glance 《at》.

**빗맞다** 《맞지 않다》 (***a***) 《표적에》 miss the mark; glance off. ¶ 그는 연방 쏘았으나 모두 빗맞았다 He fired by volley, but all the shots missed. (***b***) 《일이》 go awry 〔wrong, amiss〕; miscarry; "misfire"; "backfire". ¶ 예상이 ~ [사물이 주어] fall short of *one's* expectations; [사람이 주어] be disappointed of *one's* expectations / 모든 계획이 빗맞았다 All my schemes backfired.

**빗먹다** 《a saw》 veer off-line; go in crooked. ¶ 톱이 빗먹는다 The saw goes into the log at the wrong angle.

**빗물** rainwater. ¶ ～이 괸 곳 a rainpool / 길에 ～이 흐르고 있었다 The streets were running with rain.

**빗발** the density of falling rain; streaks of rain; rain. ¶ ～이 굵어지다 the rain becomes heavier / ～이 가늘어지다 the rain slackened to a drizzle.

**빗발치듯** thick and fast (like streaks of rain); in (great) streaks; in rain. ¶ ～하는 탄알〔화살〕 a rain of bullets 〔arrows〕 / ～하는 질문 a volley 〔barrage〕 of questions / (탄알이) ～ 쏟아지다 rain; shower like hail; come thick and fast / 주문이 ～하다 have a flood 〔rush〕 of orders.

**빗방울** a raindrop. ¶ ～ 소리 pattering of raindrops / ～이 듣다 raindrops fall.

**빗변**(―邊) 〖수학〗 an oblique side; 《삼각형의》 a leg; 《직각 삼각형의》 the hypotenuse.

**빗보다** mistake 〔take〕 《A for B》; misjudge. ¶ 사람을 ～ misjudge a person / 신호를 ～ mistake 〔misread〕 a signal.

**빗살** the teeth of a comb.

**빗소리** the sound of raining.

**빗속** 《in》 the midst of rain. ¶ ～을 걷다 walk in the rain.

**빗솔** a brush for cleaning combs.

**빗원기둥**(―圓―) an oblique cylinder.

**빗장** a crossbar; a bolt; a bar. ¶ 문에 ～을 지르다〔벗기다〕 bar 〔unbar〕 the gate.

**빗장고름** a bow-tied ribbon.

**빗장뼈** the collarbone; the clavicle.

**빗접** a comb box; an oilpaper wrap for a comb. ◉ ～고비 a comb cabinet.

**빗줄기** streaks 〔sheets〕 of rain. ¶ ～가 세다 It rains hard. *or* It pours down. *or* "It rains cats and dogs."

**빗질** combing 《*one's* hair》. ～하다 comb 《*one's* hair》.

**빗치개** a kind of pin used for parting the hair and for cleaning combs.

**빙** ① 《한 바퀴 도는 모양》 round; around 《미》. ¶ 공장 안을 한 바퀴 빙 돌다 make a round of the factory / 서울을 한 바퀴 빙 돌다 take a turn around Seoul. ② 《둘러싸거나 앉다》 round; in a circle. ¶ 빙 둘러앉다 sit in a circle 〔ring〕 / 빙 둘러싸다 surround 《*a person*》; close 〔throng〕 around 《*a person*》. ③ 《정신이》 ¶ 머리가 빙 돌다 feel dizzy 〔giddy〕; *one's* head reels 〔spins, swims〕. ④ 《눈물이》 ¶ 눈물이 빙 돌다 be moved to tears.

**빙결**(氷結) freezing; congelation 《of water》. ～하다 freeze; be frozen (over); 《항구 등이》 be icebound; congeal. ¶ ～을 방지하다 keep 《*a thing*》 free of ice; 〖항공〗 deice.

**빙고**(氷庫) a storehouse for ice; an icehouse.

**빙고**(憑考) ～하다 examine; inquire 《into》; investigate; refer to; consult 《a book》.

**빙고** 《놀이》 bingo (game).

**빙과**(氷菓) ices; frozen sweets 〔treats, candies〕; a bar of sherbet (on a stick); 《상표》 a Popsicle; 《英》 an ice 〔iced〕 lolly; (an) ice cream.

**빙괴**(氷塊) a lump 〔block, piece〕 of ice; 《떠도는》 an ice floe.

**빙그레** ⇨ 방그레.

**빙그르르** 《skating, gliding, "whipping"》 around smoothly.

**빙글거리다** smile 《at *a person*》; beam 《upon *a person*》.

**빙글빙글**[1] 《skating, gliding》 around and around smoothly. ¶ 스케이터가 ～ 돌기 시작했다 The skater began to spin on the ice.

**빙글빙글**[2] smilingly; beamingly; with a smile. ¶ ～ 웃는 얼굴 a beaming 〔smiling〕 face; a radiant look.

**빙낭**(氷囊) an ice bag 〔pack〕. ◉ ～걸이 an ice-bag suspender 〔holder〕.

**빙모**(聘母) ＝ 장모(丈母).

**빙벽**(氷壁) an ice ridge.

**빙부**(聘父) ＝ 장인(丈人).

**빙빙** 《spinning, whirling, turning》 round and round. ¶ ～ 돌다 turn round and round; circle.

**빙산**(氷山) an iceberg; a floating mass of ice (유빙); an ice floe (해상의). ¶ ～의 일각 the tip of an iceberg / 이번 밀수 사건은 ～의 일각에 지나지 않는다 This smuggling case is just the tip of the iceberg.

**빙상**(氷上) ¶ ～에서 on the ice. ◉ ～경기 ice sports. ～발레 a ballet on ice. ～쇼 an ice show. 대한 ～ 경기 연맹 the Korea Amateur Skating Union.

**빙설**(氷雪) ice and snow.

**빙수**(氷水) ① 《얼음 물》 iced 〔ice 《미》〕 water. ② 《갈아 만든 얼음 음료》 shaved ice with 《sugar, fruit》 syrup.

**빙실**(氷室) an icehouse; a refrigeratory.

**빙어**(―魚) 〖어류〗 a pond smelt.

**빙원**(氷原) an ice field; 《해상의》 an ice floe.

**빙자**(憑藉) ① 《의지》 dependence; reliance; leaning 《on》. ～하다 depend 〔rely〕 《on》; lean 《on》; be dependent 《upon》; rely 《on *one's* connection》. ¶ 저 친구는 아버지의 세도를 ～하여 언제

나 제멋대로 군다 Taking advantage of his father's influence, he always has his own way.
② 《핑계》 a pretext; a pretense; an excuse; a plea; a cloak. ～하다 make a pretext 〔an excuse〕 《of》; use 《*something*》 as pretext; find an excuse 《in》. ¶ …을 ～하여 under 〔on〕 the pretext 〔plea〕 of; under the cover 〔guise〕 of 《friendship》; under the cloak 〔mask〕 of 《charity》 / 취직 알선을 ～하여 돈을 사취하다 swindle 《*a person*》 out of money under the pretext of finding employment / 그들은 자선을 ～하여 사복(私腹)을 채웠다 They feathered their own nests under the mask of charity.

**빙장석**(氷長石) 〖광물〗 adularia (feld「spar).

**빙점**(氷點) the freezing point. ¶ ～ 이하로 내려가다 fall below (the) freezing point / 온도는 ～하 5도까지 내려갔다 The temperature dropped to「five degrees below (the) freezing point 〔5° below zero〕.

**빙정석**(氷晶石) 〖광물〗 cryolite.

**빙초산**(氷醋酸) 〖화학〗 glacial acetic acid.

**빙충맞다** (be) clumsy; stupid; thick-headed; timid; nervous.

**빙충이** a clumsy 〔nervous〕 person; a big ox; a stupid person; a dolt.

**빙침**(氷枕) an ice pillow. ¶ ～을 베다 rest *one's* head on pillow of ice.

**빙탄**(氷炭) 《얼음과 숯》 ice and charcoal; [비유적] incompatibility; contradiction. ¶ ～ 불상용(不相容)이다 be as irreconcilable as oil and water; agree like cats and dogs; be antagonistic 〔contradictory〕 to each other.

**빙퉁그러지다** 《하는 짓이》 go amiss 〔wrong〕; 《성질이》 be perverted 〔cross=grained〕; have a perverse mind.

**빙판**(氷板) an icy road 〔place〕.

**빙하**(氷河) a glacier. ¶ ～의 glacial / ～ 전기의 preglacial / ～ 후기의 post-glacial. ◉ ～기〔시대〕 the glacial epoch 〔period, era〕; the ice age. ～작용 glaciation; glacial action. ～학 glaciology.

**빙해**(氷海) a frozen sea; icy waters.

**빙해**(氷解) melting away; clearance 《of doubt》. ～하다 《해빙》 melt away; thaw; 《의심 등이》 be cleared 〔dispelled, dissipated〕.

**빚** a debt; a loan; liabilities; what *one* owes. ¶ 막대한 빚 a heap of debts / 이자가 붙지 않는 빚 a passive debt / 빚독촉 a dun; a demand for (the) payment of debt.
빚을: 빚을 독촉하다 dun 《*a person*》 for the payment of a debt; press 《*a person*》 to pay a debt / 빚을 지다 borrow money 《from》; fall 〔run, get〕 into debt; incur debts / 빚을 지지 않다 keep 〔be〕 out of debt; keep *one's* head above water / 빚을 안 지고 살다 pay *one's* (own) way / 빚을 짊어지다 be saddled with a debt / 빚을 갚다 pay 〔clear〕 (off) *one's* debt; discharge 〔repay〕 *one's* debts; pay *one's* score / 빚을 못 갚다 fail to pay (*one's* debt) / 빚을 깨끗이 가리다 get out debt; clear (up) *one's* debts; clear 〔work〕 off *one's* debts / 빚을 떼어먹다 bilk *one's* debt 〔bill〕 / 빚을 갚기 위해 또 다른 빚을 지다 borrow from Peter to pay Paul / 빚을 남기고 죽다 leave debts behind *one* / 남의 빚을 떠맡다 shoulder 〔assume〕 another's debts.
빚이: 빚이 있다 be in debt 《to, with》; owe 《*a person*》 money; have a debt (to pay) / 십만원의 빚이 있다 owe 《*a person*》 100,000 won / 빚이 없다 be free 〔out〕 of debt; be in the clean / 빚이 늘어나다 run up a score 《at》; run up bills 《with》.
빚으로: 빚으로 꼼짝 못 하다 be deeply 〔over head and ears, up to the ears〕 in debt / 많은 빚으로 압박을 받다 be under pressure of heavy debts 《of 20 million won》.

**빚거간**(一居間) ① 《사람》 a loan agent 〔broker〕; 《영업》 a loan agency 〔brokerage〕. ～하다 act as a loan agent. ② ＝빚지시.

**빚꾸러기** a debt-ridden person.

**빚내다** borrow money 《from》; get 〔obtain〕 a loan. ¶ 부동산을 저당으로 은행에서 ～ get a loan from a bank on *one's* real estate.

**빚놀이** money-lending (business); making a loan. ～하다 make a loan 《to》; run money-lending business.

**빚놓다** lend money; loan 《*a person*》 money 《미》. ¶ 고리로 ～ lend money at a high rate of interest.

**빚다** ① 《가루·반죽을》 shape dough for 《rice cakes》; roll into balls 《as dumplings》. ¶ 떡을 ～ shape dough for rice cakes / 만두를〔송편을〕 ～ make dumplings 〔stuffed rice cakes〕. ② 《술을》 brew 《rice wine》; ferment. ③ 《어떤 사태를》 bring about 〔on〕; give rise to; cause; breed. ¶ 가난이 빚은 비극 a tragedy resulting from poverty / 물의를 ～ arouse 〔evoke〕 criticism; cause 〔give rise to〕 public discussion; raise a scandal.

**빚돈** a loan; a debt. ⇨빚.

**빚물이** paying someone else's debts. ～하다 pay 《*a person's*》 debts for *him*.

**빚받이** collecting debts. ～하다 collect (debts).

**빚쟁이** 《채귀(債鬼)》 a dun; 《채권자》 a creditor; 《수금원》 a (bill) collector; 《고리 대금업자》 a loan shark 《구어》; a moneylender; a usurer. ¶ ～에게 시달리다 be hounded by *one's* creditors.

**빚주다** lend money; loan. ¶ 빚주고 뺨맞기 having good repayed with evil.

**빚지다** borrow money 《from》; get 〔run, fall〕 into debt; contract 〔incur〕 a debt. ⇨빚. ¶ 빚지고 도망가다 run away leaving *one's* debt unpaid / 내가 자네에게 빚진 것이 얼마나 되나 How much do I owe you? / 빚진 죄인이라 거북하기 짝이 없다 I am really in a fix—being, as they say, "a criminal in debt" 〔"a prisoner of my debts"〕.

**빚지시** an intermediary party to a loan.

**빛** ① 《광》 (a) light; 《광선》 rays (of light); a ray; a beam; 《광택》 (a) gloss; (a) luster; 《섬광》 a flash; a gleam (어둠 속의); a twinkle (별 등의); 《희미한》 a glimmer; 《빛남》 a glow; (a) shine; brightness; brilliance. ¶ 달빛 the light of the moon; moon-light / 햇빛 the light of the sun; sunshine; sunlight / 개똥벌레의 빛 the glow 〔flimmer〕 of a firefly / 밝은 빛 bright light / 희미한 빛 dim 〔feeble, faint〕 light / 빛의 굴절〔반사〕 refraction 〔reflection〕 of light / 빛의 속도 the speed of light / 빛을 내다 《광택을》 gloss; glaze; bring out the luster; polish up / 빛을 발하다 emit 〔give out〕 light / 빛을 발하는 물체 a luminous body / 빛의 속도는 매초 약 18만 6천 마일이다 The velocity of light is about 186,000 miles per second.
② 《빛깔》 a color; a hue; a tint; a tinge; 《그림물감의》 a color. ¶ 가을 빛 autumnal tints / 밝은〔어두운〕 빛 bright 〔dark〕 colors / 부드러운 빛 a delicate color / 빛의 배합 a color scheme / 빛의 조화 color harmony / 빛을 내다 bring out the color / … 빛을 띠다 be tinted 〔tinged〕 with 《crimson》 / 빛이 변하다 change color / 빛이 짙다〔엷다〕 be of a deep 〔light〕 color / 빛이 바래다 fade; be discolored / 빛좋은 개살구 a gimcrack; a gewgaw; (a) trumpery.
③ 《얼굴빛》 complexion; color; 《기색》 a sign 〔mark〕; a look; an air. ¶ 실망의 빛 a look of disappointment / 우려의 빛 the imprint of anxiety on *one's* face / (얼굴)빛이 흰 fair-〔white-〕complexioned; with a white skin / 싫어하는 빛도 없이 without (any appearance of) reluctance / 성난〔피로의〕 빛을 보이다 show a sign of anger 〔exhaustion〕 / 피로의 빛을 보이지 않다 show no trace of fatigue / 그녀는 얼굴에 수심의 빛을 띠고 있었다 Her countenance assumed a deep cast of dejection. / 그녀의 얼굴에는 후회하는 빛이 없었다 There was no look of remorse on her face.
④ 《광명·희망》 light; hope; a bright future 〔prospect〕. ¶ 장밋빛의 미래 a rosy future / 희망의 빛 a ray 〔gleam〕 of hope / 어둠 속에서 빛을 발견하다 see the silver lining in the dark cloud / 빛은 동방에서 Light from the East.
⑤ 《부류》 a cast; a sort. ¶ 빛 다른 사람 a man of different cast.
⑥ 《기타》 ¶ 빛을 보다 (1) 《실현되다》 see the light of day; 《계획 등이》 be realized; materialized; (2) 《발견되다》 be brought to light / 세상에서 빛을 못 보다 be obscure; be little known in the world; remain obscure 〔unknown〕.

**빛깔** a shade of color; a color; a hue. ⇨빛 ②. ¶ ～을 넣은〔넣어〕 in color(s) / 밝은 ～로 그리다 paint in bright 〔glowing〕 colors / ～이며 디자인이며 다 좋다 The coloring and design are perfect.

**빛나다** ① 《비치다·번쩍이다》 shine; be bright 〔brilliant〕; be radiant; be luminous; glitter (금은 따위가); glisten (반사로); glint; beam; glimmer (희미하게); gleam (어둠 속에서); flash (번득이다); twinkle (별이); sparkle (보석 등이). ¶ 빛나는 눈 bright eyes / 하늘에 빛나는 별 stars twinkling up in the sky / 해가 ～ the sun shines bright(ly) / 보석이 햇빛에 ～ jewels shine in the sun / 기뻐서 눈이 ～ *one's* eyes sparkle with joy / 그녀의 손가락에서 금반지가 빛났다 A gold ring shone on her finger.
② 《영광스럽다》 be glorious; become distinguished. ¶ 빛나는 장래 a bright 〔promising〕 future / 빛나는 최후를 마치다 die a glorious death / 청사에 ～ remain long 〔immortal〕 in history /

그의 이름이 역사에 길이 빛난다 His name shines forth in history.
③《돋보이다》 look better 〔to advantage〕; shine 《among, amid》; be prominent; be outstanding; cut a figure 《among, with》. ¶ 교사로서 ~ shine as a teacher / 그의 작품은 다른 어떤 것보다도 빛나고 있다 His work stands out above all the rest.

**빛내다** make 《*a thing*》 shine; brighten; 《광을 내다》 gloss; glaze; bring out the luster; polish up; 《영광스럽게 하다》 bring glory 〔fame, distinction〕 to; glorify. ¶ 모국을 ~ bring glory to *one's* motherland; glorify the name of *one's* country / 이름을 ~ win fame; immortalize *one's* name.

**빛살** rays of light.

**빛접다** be something to be proud of; (be) shining; glorious.

**빠개다** ①《단단한 것을》 split; cleave. ¶ 장작을 ~ split firewood. ②《일을》 spoil; ruin; wreck. ¶ 계획을 ~ spoil 〔thwart〕《*a person's*》 plan 〔design〕.

**빠개지다** ①《조각나다》 split (apart); cleave. ¶ 머리가 빠개질 듯이 아프다 be racked with a headache; have a splitting headache / 이 나무는 잘 빠개진다 This wood splits nicely. ②《일이》 get ruined; be spoiled; fail; come to naught. ¶ 우리 일이 빠개졌다 Our work came to naught.

**빠그라지다** get broken; be destroyed; be ruined; collapse. ¶ 자금난으로 그의 계획은 빠그라졌다 His plan collapsed due to financial difficulties.

**빠그르르** ⇨ 바그르르.

**빠닥빠닥** crisping. ¶ ~한 지폐 a crisp bank note.

**빠드득-** ⇨ 바드득-.

**빠득빠득하다** ①《언행이》 (be) headstrong; disobedient; perverse; hardheaded. ¶ 아이가 ~ be a perverse child. ②《떫다》 (be) astringent; mouth-puckering; bitter; sour; acrid. ¶ 감이 ~ the persimmon makes *one's* mouth pucker. ③《눈이》 be dry and tired; burn. ¶ 눈이 ~ *one's* eyes are tired; *one's* eyes burn.

**-빠듯** a bit less than; just under; a little short of. ¶ 두 자빠듯 just under two *cha* 〔feet〕 (long).

**빠듯이** ①《겨우》 barely; narrowly; with difficulty; just (barely). ¶ 시간에 ~ 대다 be just 〔barely〕 in time 《for the last train》 / 그는 월급으로 ~지낸다 He barely manages to live on his salary. ②《꼭 끼게》 tightly; closely. ¶ 구두가 ~맞다 the shoes just 〔barely〕 fit.

**빠듯하다** ①《꼭 끼다》 (be) tight; close fitting. ¶ 빠듯한 구두 tight shoes / 그 모자는 너무 ~ The hat is too tight for me. ②《겨우 미치다》 (be) barely enough. ¶ 빠듯한 이익 marginal profits / 천 원은 차표 사기에 ~ 1,000 won will barely pay for the railroad ticket.

**빠뜨리다** ①《떨어뜨리다》 (***a***) 《아래로》 let 《*a thing*》 fall into; drop 《*a thing* in(to)》; 《빠져나가다》 slip out of 〔through〕; miss *one's* hold. ¶ 동전을 흙탕에 ~ drop a coin in the mud / 모자를 강에 ~ let *one's* hat fall into the water. (***b***) 《분실하다》 lose; drop. ¶ 지갑을 ~ drop *one's* wallet; lose *one's* purse. (***c***) 《못받다》 ¶ 공을 ~ miss a ball; fail to catch a ball; muff (일단 받았다가).
②《누락시키다》 omit; miss (out); leave out; 《건너 뛰다》 skip (over) 《a passage》. ¶ 못보고 ~ look over; overlook; pass over 〔by, up〕; fail to notice / 명단에서 이름을 ~ miss *a person's* name out of the list / 두 자를 ~ leave out two letters / 한 줄을 ~miss a line / 한 명도 빠뜨리지 않고 다 잡다 arrest all without exception / 답안지에 수험 번호 쓰는 것을 빠뜨리지 않도록 해라 Take care that you don't forget to write your seat number in your examination paper.
③《함정·계략 등에》 entrap; ensnare; 《유혹에》 tempt; entice; take in. ¶ 곤란에 ~ land 〔plunge〕 《*a person*》 in difficulties; put 《*a person*》 in a fix / 유혹에 ~ allure 〔lead〕 《*a person*》 into temptation / 남을 범죄에 ~trick *a person* into committing a crime / 그는 나를 불리한 입장에 빠뜨렸다 He has taken the wind out of my sails.

**빠르다** ①《신속하다》 (***a***) 《속도가》 (be) fast; quick; rapid; speedy; swift. ¶ 빠른 물살 a rapid 〔swift〕 stream; a torrent / 빠른 열차 a fast train / 발이 ~ be swift of foot; be a good walker / 진보가 ~ make rapid progress / 호흡이 ~ [사람이 주어] breathe hard / (시계가) 2분 ~ be two minutes (too) fast / 하루 5분씩 ~ gain five minutes a day / 빛은 소리보다 ~ Light travels faster than sound. / 세종로에서 갈아타는 것이 ~ It takes less time to change cars at Sejongno. (***b***) 《민첩하다》 (be) brisk; smart; quick; prompt. ¶ 계산이 ~ be quick at accounts 〔figures〕; be ready at figures / 눈치가 ~ be a quick judge of situations; size things up fast / 동작이 ~ be quick in motion; move quickly / 이해가 ~ be quick to understand; catch on fast / 일이 ~ be quick about *one's* work; be a good worker.

② 《시간적으로 이르다》 (be) early; premature a little (시기 상조). ⇨이르다. ¶ 조금 빨리 a little early 〔earlier〕; earlier (than usual); ahead of time / 빠르면 at the earliest date 〔chance〕; 《순조로우면》 if things go well; if nothing unexpected intervenes / 네 결혼은 아직 ~ You are not old enough to get married. / 빠르면 빠를수록 좋다 The sooner, the better.

③ 《손쉽다》 (be) easy; simple; quick. ¶ 외국어를 배우는 가장 빠른〔쉬운〕 길 the shortest 〔easiest〕 way to learn foreign languages.

**빠른걸음** a quick pace. ¶ ~으로 《walk》 fast; at a fast walk; at a quick 〔great, brisk〕 pace; with hurried 〔hasty〕 steps / ~이 되다 quicken 〔mend〕 *one's* pace.

**빠른우편**(―郵便) special 〔express〕 delivery.

**빠이빠이** 《소아어》《안녕》 bye-bye !; bye, bye !; ta-ta !

**빠지다**[1] ① 《물·허방 등에》 fall in(to); sink 〔plunge, slip〕 into; go down; be drowned. ¶ 물에 ~ fall into water 〔a pool, a river, a well〕; fall overboard; drown / 도랑에 ~ be mired in a ditch / 수렁에 ~ bog (down); sink in a bog; be 〔get〕 bogged; [비유적] be bogged 〔mired〕 down; get stuck in a bog / 진창에 ~ be caught 〔stuck〕 in the mud / 물에 빠진 사람 짚이라도 잡는다 《속담》 A drowning man will catch at a straw.

② 《상태에》 fall 〔get〕 into; run into; be led into; lapse into; be thrown into; 《속다》 be cheated; be taken in. ¶ 빠지기 쉬운 죄악 a besetting sin / 계략에 ~ fall into a snare; be entrapped 〔ensnared〕 / 곤경에 ~ be cornered; get into a scrape 〔difficulties〕; be in a sad 〔sorry〕 plight / 나쁜 습관에 ~ fall into 〔take to〕 bad habits / 위독상태에 ~ fall into a critical condition; [병이 주어] take a critical 〔dangerous〕 turn / 위험에 ~ run into danger; be endangered / 위기에 ~ face a crisis; be confronted by a crisis / 유혹에 ~ yield 〔succumb〕 to temptation / 혼수상태에 ~ become unconscious; fall 〔lapse〕 into a coma 〔comatose state〕 / 속임수에 빠졌다 I have been done 〔taken in〕.

③ 《탐닉하다》 indulge 《in》; be addicted 〔given〕 《to》; give *oneself* up 《to》; be immersed 〔steeped〕 《in》; go deep 《into》; 《구어》 be hooked 《on a girl, on gambling》. ¶ 공상에 ~ indulge in reverie / 사치에 ~ revel 〔be lapped〕 in luxury / 여자에 ~ be gone on a girl; be infatuated with a woman / 도박에 ~ be addicted to gambling / 주색에 ~ give *oneself* up to woman and liquor.

④ 《탈락하다》 (***a***) 《누락하다》 be omitted; be missing; get 〔be〕 left out; be excluded; be not included. ¶ 선택에서 ~ be left out of selection; be rejected; be not accepted / 초대에(서) ~ be left out of the invitation / 글자가 두 자 빠져 있다 Two characters are missing. / 명부에 그의 이름이 빠져 있다 His name is not (included) in the list. (***b***) 《붙은 것·끼인 것》 come out 〔off〕; fall 〔slip〕 out 〔off〕; be removed; be taken out 〔off〕 (얼룩 등이); wash off 〔out〕 (때 등이); get out of place; get removed; 《관절이》 be get out of joint; be dislocated. ¶ 머리털이 ~ *one's* hair falls out 〔off〕; *one's* hair thins (out) / 병마개가 ~ a cork comes out / 턱이 ~ get *one's* jaw out of joint / 단추가 빠져 있다 be unbuttoned / 손잡이가 빠져 있다 The handle 〔knob〕 is off. / 아무리 빨아도 얼룩이 빠지지 않는다 The stains will not come out, however hard I may try to wash them off. (***c***) 《색깔 등이》 fade; discolor. ¶ 물이 빠지기 쉬운 fugitive / 물이 빠지지 않는 fadeproof; fadeless; fast; standing / 빨강은 물이 빠지기 쉽다 Red is apt to fade. *or* Red fades easily. / 이 천은 물이 빠지지 않는다 This cloth holds dye well. (***d***) 《칼붙이·그릇 등의 이가》 break (off); be broken (off); chip (off) (그릇의 전이). ¶ 이 빠진 식칼 a kitchen knife with a nicked edge 〔broken blade〕 / 이빠진 술잔 a chipped cup.

⑤ 《물·부기 등이》 subside; abate; fall; ebb; go down; sink; 《배수되다》 drain; flow off; run out; 《바람 등이》 leak out; escape. ¶ 바람 빠진 타이어 a flat tire / 물이 잘 ~ drain well; flow well / 물이 잘 안 ~ drain ill; does not flow well / 부기가 ~ the swelling subsides 〔goes down〕 / (홍수진) 물이 ~ the water 「sinks 〔goes down, subsides〕 /

조수가 ～ the tide subsides / 타이어의 바람이 빠졌다 The tire has gone flat. *or* You have a flat tire.
⑥《몸이》 get lean; become 〔grow〕 thin; lose flesh (병으로); pine away (근심·걱정으로). ¶ 살빠지게 하는 약 a fat-reducer; a flesh-reducer; an antifat remedy 〔cure〕/ 살이 ～ lose (*one's*) weight / 빠져 보이다 look peaked.
⑦《힘·김·냄새 따위가》 be gone; grow weak; be exhausted; get flat; become stale; fail; vanish; disperse; give out. ¶ 김 빠진 맥주 stale 〔flat〕 beer / 힘 빠진 목소리 a faint voice / 맥이 ～ be discouraged 〔disappointed〕; be damped; lose interest / 얼이 ～ be stupefied; be dazed; be abstracted / 정신이 ～ *one's* attention is distracted / 힘이 ～ *one's* strength is gone 〔ebbs〕; [사람이 주어] be exhausted; be spent up.
⑧《불참하다》 be absent《from》; absent *oneself*《from》; do not appear; miss 〔cut〕《*one's* class》. ⇨ 불참하다, 결석하다. ¶ 학교를 ～ stay 〔remain〕 away from school; miss school / 그 모임에는 많은 사람들이 빠졌다 The meeting was poorly attended.
⑨《빠져나가다》 (***a***)《탈출하다》 escape; slip 〔go, get, steal〕 out of; get away; sneak 〔shirk〕 away《from》;《피하다》 evade; dodge; excuse *oneself* from. ¶ 손아귀에서 ～ slip through *one's* fingers / 묶은 밧줄에서 빠져나오다 wriggle out of 〔*oneself* free from〕 *one's* bonds / 위험에서 빠져 나오다 escape danger; find *oneself* way out of danger / 수업을 빼먹고 학교를 빠져 나오다 cut a lesson and beat it《구어》/ 집에서 빠져나갈 틈이 없다 I have no chance to slip out of the house. / 오늘밤 송별회는 빠질 수가 없다 I can't excuse myself from the farewell meeting this evening. (***b***)《통과하다》 go by 〔through〕; pass 〔cut〕 through;《길이 …로》 lead to;《…길로 빠져 나오다》 strike upon; find *oneself*《at, in》. ¶ 비밀 통로로 ～ go by a secret path / 이 길은 바다쪽으로 빠진다 This path leads 〔goes〕 to the sea. / 이 길은 어디로 빠지는가 Where does this street lead? *or* What place does this street run into? / 이 샛길로 빠집시다 Let us go by this lane. (***c***)〖야구〗《공이》 pierce; shoot through. ¶ 3루를 빠지는 안타 a single past third.
⑩《탈퇴·불관여하다》 break off connections《with》; leave; quit; drop out; withdraw 〔secede〕《from》; break 〔pull〕 out of. ¶ 논쟁에서 ～ drop out of contention / 연맹에서 ～ break 〔pull〕 out of federation / 이번에는 나도 빠지겠다 I will drop out this time.
⑪《못하다》 compare unfavorably《with》; be inferior《to》; cannot stand 〔bear〕 comparison《with》; do not come up to; fall 〔lag〕 behind. ¶ 아무에게도 빠지지 않다 yield 〔be second〕 to none; prove *oneself* equal to anyone / 그녀의 옷이 그중 빠졌다 Her dress was the least attractive one there.
⑫《제비 뽑히다》 draw; win《in a lottery》; fall《to *one's* lot》.

**빠지다**[2] [조동사] get 〔become〕《old, rotten, musty, *etc.*》 through and through; [부사적] utterly; quite; thoroughly; to the core; all the way.
¶ 말라빠진 할멈 a withered old woman / 썩어빠진 정치 politics that are rotten to the core / 낡아빠진 옷 well-worn clothes / 요 약아빠진 놈 this shrewd rascal / 게을러빠진 놈 a thoroughly lazy rascal / 그 포도주는 시어빠졌다 The port wine has turned all sour (to the bottom of the bottle).

**빠짐없이** without (any) omission 〔exception〕; wholly; thoroughly; exhaustively; in full; one and all.
¶ 원서에 ～ 기입하다 fill in each item on the application form; fill in all the blanks (without any omission) on the application form / ～ 통지하다 tell《*something*》 to everybody / ～ 투표하다 vote without exception / ～ 조사하다 investigate thoroughly; make a thorough investigation.

**빡빡**[1] ⇨ 박박[2].

**빡빡**[2] ①《담뱃대를 빠는 모양》⇨ 뻑뻑. ②《긁는 모양》⇨ 박박[1].

**빡빡하다** ①《음식이》 (be) dry and hard. ¶ 삶은 달걀이 먹기에 너무 ～ The boiled egg is too dry to eat. / 반찬이 없어서 먹기에 ～ It is hard to swallow the food without (the juice of) side dishes. ②《꼭끼다》 (be) hard; tight. ¶ 빡빡한 일정 a tight schedule / 빡빡하여 열리지 않는 서랍 a tight drawer / 바퀴가 빡빡하게 돈다 The wheels are turning hard. ③《편협》 (be) narrow-minded; stubborn. ¶ 빡빡한 영감 a narrow-minded old man.

**빡작지근하다** ⇨ 뻑적지근하다.

**빤질거리다** ⇨ 반질거리다.

**빤짝** ⇨ 반짝.

**빤하다** ① 《분명하다》 (be) transparent; clear; obvious; evident; plain; blatant; flimsy; patent. ¶ 빤한 사실 an obvious fact; the plain truth / 빤한 거짓말 a transparent 〔an obvious〕 lie; a manifest 〔palpable〕 lie / 빤한 일이다 It is self-evident. *or* It is (as) plain as a pikestaff. / 그가 나를 싫어하는 것이 ∼ It is clear that he dislikes me. *or* He clearly dislikes me. / 아버지의 유산이래야 ∼ My father has left me no property worth mentioning. / 어차피 실패할 것은 ∼ It is doomed to failure.
② 《환하다》 (be) bright; light. ¶ 해가 창에 빤하게 비친다 The sun brightens up the window.
③ 《잠깐 틈이 있다》 odd moments; be free for a moment. ¶ 빤한 틈을 타서 꽃을 가꾸다 use *one's* odd moment to grow flowers.
④ 《병세가》 improve slightly; take a slight turn for the better; get a bit better; show signs of improvement. ¶ 병세가 ∼ a patient gets a bit better.

**빤히** ① 《환히》 bright(ly). ¶ 날이 ∼ 트다 the day dawns bright and clear.
② 《명백히》 clearly; plainly; evidently; obviously; patently. ¶ ∼ 들여다 보이는 거짓말 a transparent lie / ∼ 알면서 understanding clearly; knowing full well; with full knowledge; in full possession of the facts / 그는 비가 올 줄 ∼ 알면서 우산 없이 학교에 갔다 He went to school without his umbrella, while he knew full well it was going to rain.
③ 《보다》 fixedly; hard; intently. ¶ ∼ 쳐다보다 stare at / 남의 얼굴을 ∼ 쳐다보는 것은 실례가 된다 It is rude to stare others in the face.

**빨간** 《온통》 out-and-out; downright; thorough; pure; barefaced; unadorned; unvarnished; utter. ¶ ∼ 거짓말 a barefaced 〔downright〕 lie.

**빨강** red; red color; red dye.

**빨강이** 《물건》 a red-colored thing; a red one.

**빨갛다** (be) red; scarlet; crimson. ¶ 빨간 구두 red shoes / 빨갛게 단 난로 a red-glowing stove / 빨갛게 물든 나뭇잎 red 〔scarlet-tinged〕 leaves.

**빨개지다** turn bright-red; redden. ¶ 내가 그 소녀의 이름을 대니까 그는 얼굴이 빨개졌다 He went red when I mentioned the girl's name.

**빨갱이** 《공산주의자》 a Red; a Commie 《구어》; a communist.

**빨그스름하다** ⇨ 발그스름하다.

**빨다**[1] 《뾰족하다》 (be) tapered; pointed. ¶ 끝이 빤 sharp-pointed / 끝이 빤 손가락 tapered fingers; fingers which come to a point / 턱이 ∼ have a pointed jaw.

**빨다**[2] 《입으로》 suck; suck on 〔at〕; draw 《on》; inhale; take a drag on. ¶ 젖을 ∼ suck the breast / 사탕〔엄지손가락〕을 ∼ suck a piece of candy 〔*one's* thumb〕 / 한가히 담뱃대를 ∼ suck leisurely at *one's* pipe / 아기가 계속 젖병을 빨고 있다 The baby is sucking away at a feeding bottle.

**빨다**[3] 《빨래를》 wash 《clothes》; launder; wash out. ¶ 옷을 ∼ wash *one's* clothes / 빨래를 ∼ do the washing 〔laundry〕; wash the clothes / 빨아도 줄지 않다 be shrinkproof 〔sanforized〕 / 이것은 빨면 준다 This shrinks in washing. / 잉크 얼룩은 빨아도 지지 않는다 The ink stain will not wash out.

**빨대** a (drinking) straw. ¶ ∼로 우유를 먹다 drink milk through a straw / 아무에게 ∼를 대다〔놓다〕 [비유적] suck *a person* of all *his* money; drain *a person* dry; take everything *a person* has.

**빨딱** ⇨ 발딱.

**빨래** ① 《세탁》 a wash; washing 《clothes》; laundering. ∼하다 wash. ¶ ∼(하기)를 싫어하다 dislike doing the wash / ∼가 잘 되다 《clothing, water, soap, *etc.*》 wash well / 이런 종류의 천은 ∼가 잘 안 된다 These kinds of material wash poorly. ② 《세탁물》 clothes washed 〔to wash, to dry〕; [총칭] washing; the wash; the laundry. ¶ ∼를 널어 말리다 hang out the wash to dry / ∼를 빨다 do the wash. ◉ ∼광주리 a laundry basket. ∼집게 a clothespin 《미》; a clothespeg 《영》. ∼터 a wash place; a place for doing the laundry (near a well or stream). ∼통 a washtub. ∼판 a washboard. ∼품(삯) laundry charge; fee 〔charge〕 for washing; laundry bill. 빨랫돌 a flat stone used as a washboard; a laundry stone. 빨랫말미 a spell of dry weather during the wet season. 빨랫방망이 a wooden paddle used in washing clothes; a laundry paddle. 빨랫비누 detergent; laundry soap. 빨랫줄 a clothesline; a washline: 빨랫줄

에 ～를 널다 hang out the wash on a clothesline.

**빨리** 《일찍》 early; 《바로》 soon; immediately; instantly; 《신속》 quickly; fast; rapidly; 《급히》 in haste; 《당장》 promptly; right away. ¶ 될 수 있는 대로 ～ as soon as 「*one* can 〔possible〕 / ～ 대답하다 answer promptly / ～ 가라 Go at once! / ～ 돌아와라 Don't be long! / ～ 해라 Make haste! *or* Hurry up! *or* Be quick 《about your work》! / 너무 ～ 왔다 We arrived too early. / 좀더 ～ 왔으면 좋았는데 You should have come earlier. / 한시라도 ～ 그에게 알리지 않으면 안 된다 We must lose no time to let him know about it. / ～ 해, 아주 급하단 말이야 Don't be long about it, as I'm in a hurry. *or* Make it snappy! We are pressed for time. / ～ 설날이 왔으면 좋겠다 I wish New Year would come soon.

**빨리다**[1] ① 《빪을 당하다》 be sucked. ¶ 카누는 소용돌이 속으로 빨려들어갔다 The canoe was sucked (down) into the whirlpool. ② 《착취당하다》 be squeezed; be extorted 〔exploited〕. ¶ 돈을 ～ be squeezed out of *one's* money.

**빨리다**[2] 《빨게 하다》 let suck; let suckle; nurse with 《milk》. ¶ (아이에게) 젖을 ～ suckle 《a baby》; give the breast to 《a baby》; give 《a baby》 suck; put 《a baby》 to the breast; nurse / 어머니가 애기한테 젖을 빨리었다 The mother gave suck to her baby.

**빨병**(—甁) a water bottle; a canteen; a thermos.

**빨아내다** suck 〔draw〕 out; absorb; 《해면으로》 sponge; 〖의학〗 aspirate (고름 따위를). ¶ 압지로 ～ blot / 해면으로 ～ soak up with sponge.

**빨아들이다** 《기체를》 inhale; breathe 〔draw, take〕 in; 《액체를》 suck in 〔up〕; soak up; absorb. ¶ 연기를 ～ inhale the smoke / 탈지면은 물을 빨아들인다 Absorbent cotton absorbs water.

**빨아먹다** ① 《음식물 따위를》 eat 〔drink〕 by sucking; suck. ¶ 빨대로 우유를 ～ suck milk through a straw / 젖을 ～ suck milk; take breast. ② 《우려내다》 squeeze; exploit. ¶ 아무의 돈을 ～ squeeze money out of *a person*.

**빨아올리다** suck 〔draw〕 up; pump up. ¶ 나무는 땅에서 수분을 빨아 올린다 Plants suck up moisture from the earth.

**빨쪽이** ⇨ 발쪽이.

**빨치산** a partisan 〔partizan〕 (fighter); a guerrilla.

**빨판** 〖동물〗 a sucker; a sucking disk; 《거머리 등의》 an acetabulum.

**빨펌프** a suction 〔lift(ing)〕 pump.

**빳빳이** ① 《단단하고 곧게》 straight(ly); stiffly. ¶ 뱀이 고개를 ～ 세웠다 The snake raised its head straight. / 셔츠에 풀을 너무 ～ 먹였다 They have put too much starch in my shirts. ② 《완강히》 headstrongly; firmly. ¶ ～ 버티다 be unyielding; stand firm.

**빳빳하다** ① 《단단하고 곧다》 (be) straight; stiff. ¶ 빳빳한 머리 wiry hair / 빳빳한 수염 a tough beard / 빳빳한 새 지폐 a crisp bank note; a brand-new bill / 빳빳한 칼라 a stiff collar / 죽어 ～ lie stiff in death / 오래 걸었더니 다리가 ～ I feel stiff after a long walk. ② 《완강하다》 (be) firm; headstrong; unyielding; willful.

**빵**[1] bread (식빵); a bun (햄버거빵). ¶ 빵문제 a bread-and-butter problem; a question of livelihood / 빵부스러기 bread crumbs / 버터 바른 빵 bread and butter / 잼 바른 빵 bread and jam / 건포도빵 raisin 〔plum〕 bread / 고단백빵 high-protein bread / 롤빵 a roll 《of bread》 / 마늘빵 garlic bread / 보리빵 barley bread / 옥수수빵 corn bread 〔pone〕 / 소라빵 a cream horn / 크림빵 a cream bun / 팥빵 a red bean jam bun / 호밀빵 rye bread / 흑빵 brown bread / 흰빵 white bread / 빵 한 조각 a piece 〔slice〕 of bread / 빵 한 덩어리 a loaf of bread / 구운 빵 toast / 빵을 굽다 bake bread 《in an oven》; bake 《flour》 into bread; toast bread (토스트를 만들다) / 빵에 잼을 바르다 spread jam on (the slice of) bread / 빵을 얻기 위해 일하다 [비유적] work for bread 〔*one's* living〕 / 사람은 빵으로만 살 수는 없다 《성서》 Man cannot live by bread alone.

**빵**[2] ① 《소리가》 with an explosion; pop; bang. ¶ (총소리가) 빵 나다 bang; 《guns》 go off with a bang / 고무 풍선이 빵 터졌다 The balloon burst with a pop. / 자동차 타이어가 빵 터졌다 The automobile tire blew out with a bang. ② 《구멍이》 with a hole 〔tear〕 in 《*a thing*》; 《a hole》 glaring; gaping; 《torn》 apart; clean; hollow. ¶ 양말 뒤꿈치에 구멍이 빵 뚫렸다 There is a hole glaring 〔gaping〕 in the heel of my sock.

**빵가게** 《빵 만들어 파는 집》 a bakery.

**빵가루** 《부스러기》 bread crumb; crumbs (of bread).
**빵긋–** ⇨ 방긋–.
**빵빵** ① 《소리》 with explosion after explosion; popping and popping; 《총소리》 bang! bang!; with a bang and a bang. ¶ 총을 ~ 쏘다 fire a gun in rapid succession; blaze away / ~ 총소리가 울렸다 I heard the bang-bang 〔cracking〕 of gunfire. / 그는 옆을 지나가면서 경적을 ~ 울렸다 He honked his horn as he went past. ② 《구멍》 with hole after hole; gaping and gaping. ¶ 오래 신어서 양말에 구멍이 ~ 뚫렸다 I've worn holes in my socks.
**빵집** a bakery; a bakeshop.
**빻다** grind; powder; pulverize. ¶ 곡물을 가루로 ~ grind flour from corn / 커피열매를 ~ grind coffee beans / 후추를 ~ grind pepper / 견과를 빻는 기계 a machine that pulverizes nuts.
**빼** ① 《어린애가》 bawling. ¶ 어린애가 빼운다 The baby is bawling (its head off). ② 《피리 따위가》 whistling; screeching. ¶ 피리를 빼 불다 screech on a reed pipe.
**빼기** 〖수학〗 subtraction.
**빼나다** ⇨ 빼어나다.
**빼내다** ① 《박힌 것을》 pull 〔draw, take〕 out; extract 《*something* stuck or embedded》. ¶ 가시를 ~ pull 〔pick〕 out a thorn / 상처에서 총알을 ~ extract 〔remove, take out〕 a bullet from the wound / 생선의 배알을 ~ remove the guts from a fish; gut a fish.
② 《골라내다》 pick 〔single〕 out; select; point (with pride) to; extract. ¶ 많은 중에서 몇을 ~ select some of the many 〔a few from the lot〕 / 가장 좋은 것을 ~ select 〔pick out〕 the best.
③ 《훔치다》 pilfer 《from》; steal; filch; swipe. ¶ 짐을 ~ pilfer from a load; pilfer baggage / 봉투에서 우편환을 ~ abstract 〔steal〕 a money order from an envelope / 그에게서 그 문제에 관한 정보를 빼냈다 I extracted the information about 〔on〕 the matter out of him.
④ 《갇힌 몸을》 liberate 《*a person*》 from a situation 〔profession〕. ¶ 유치장에서 ~ bail 〔get〕 《*a person*》 out of jail; "spring" 《*a person*》 / 몸값을 치르고 창녀를 ~ ransom a prostitute.
⑤ 《꾀어 내다》 entice away; lure out. ¶ 고용인을 ~ hire 《*a person*》 away 《from another company》.
**빼놓다** 《제외하다》 except 《*something* from the list》; leave 〔count〕 《*a thing, a person*》 out; omit; miss (out); skip; 《골라놓다》 pick 〔single〕 out; select; sort out. ¶ …(을) 빼놓고 omitting; leaving out; except (for); but (for) / 하나도 빼놓지 않고 잡다 arrest all without exception / 큰것만을 ~ select 〔pick out〕 the largest one / 너 빼놓고는 다 준비가 되었다 Everybody is ready except you. / 나만 빼놓고 모두 영화 구경하러 갔다 All went to movies leaving me alone. / 일요일을 빼놓고는 매일 집에 있다 I am always at home except Sunday. / 어려운 부분은 빼놓아도 좋다 You may skip the difficult parts.
**빼다** ① 《뽑아내다》 (***a***) 《박힌 것·속엣 것을》 draw 〔pull, pluck, take〕 out; extract. ¶ 코르크마개를 ~ pull a cork from a bottle; uncork a bottle / (자기가) 이를 ~ extract 〔pull out〕 a tooth; 《남이》 have a tooth (pulled) out / 못을 ~ extract 〔pull out, draw out〕 a nail; unnail 《a box》 / 타이어의 공기를 ~ let air out of a tire; deflate a tire / 칼을 ~ draw 〔unsheathe〕 a sword / 권총을 빼는 솜씨가 빠르다 be quick on the draw / 빼도 박도 못 하다 be in a fix; be in a bind; be in a deep trouble; get bogged down. (***b***) 《발췌하다》 pick out; extract. ¶ 책에서 한 구절을 ~ quote a passage from a book.
② 《물을》 drain (water off). ¶ 밭의 물을 ~ drain (water from) a field; dry 〔drain〕 land / 목욕통의 물을 ~ drain (the water from) the bathtub.
③ 《제거하다》 take away 〔off, out〕; remove. ¶ 때를 ~ remove 〔take out, wash off〕 the stain / 잉크의 얼룩을 ~ remove an ink spot.
④ 《제외하다》 exclude 《from》; omit; eliminate; leave 〔keep〕 out; 《예외로서》 except. ¶ 명부에서 이름을 ~ strike 《*a person's* name》 off a list; omit a name from the list / 그 낱말 앞의 정관사는 빼는 것이 좋다 You had better leave out 〔omit〕 'the' before the word. / 그는 일요일만 빼고 매일 학교에 간다 He goes to school every day except Sunday.
⑤ 《차감·공제하다》 subtract 《from》; take away 〔off〕; deduct 〔subduct, detract〕 《from》. ¶ 10에서 5를 ~ subtract five from ten / 봉급에서 ~ deduct 《a sum》 from *one's* salary; take 《a sum》 off *one's* pay / 10에서 5를 빼면 5가 남는다 5 from 10 leaves 5. *or* Ten

minus five equals five.
⑥ 《힘·기운을》 exhaust; exert. ¶ 어깨의 힘을 ～ relax *one's* shoulders.
⑦ 《꼭닮다》 be just 〔exactly〕 like; be as like as two peas. ¶ 딸은 어머니를 쏙 뺐다 The daughter is the spitting image 〔very picture〕 of her mother.
⑧ 《꾸미다》 affect; assume; put on airs; pose 《as》. ¶ 점잔을 ～ be prudish 〔genteel〕; give *oneself* airs.
⑨ 《회피하다》 evade; shirk; avoid. ¶ 꽁무니를 ～ shirk *one's* responsibility / 발을 ～ wash *one's* hands of 《an affair》; be through with; sever connections 〔relations〕 with.
⑩ 《차려 입다》 dress 〔doll〕 up. ¶ 그는 옷을 쪽 빼 입었다 He is all dressed up. *or* He is dressed in his best.

**빼돌리다** keep secret; hide; hoard secretly; 《선수 등을》 hide 《*a person*》 away; entice. ¶ 빼돌려 둔 돈 pin money; a secret hoard / 아무를 ～ hide 〔entice〕 *a person* away.

**빼뜰다** ⇨ 빼앗다.

**빼먹다** ① 《빠뜨리다》 omit; pass over; miss (out); leave out. ¶ 말을 ～ forget to mention / (뜨개질을) 한 코 ～ drop a stitch / 명부에서 이름을 ～ omit a name out of 〔from〕 the list / 그녀는 "accommodation"을 쓰면서 "m"자 하나를 빼먹었다 She left out an "m" in "accommodation". / 강사는 가장 중요한 점을 빼먹은 것 같았다 The lecturer seemed to pass over the most important point. ② 《훔치다》 steal; swipe; pilfer; ransack. ¶ 짐을 ～ pilfer baggage. ③ 《수업을》 play truant; cut a class 〔lesson〕. ¶ 학교를 ～ play hooky 《미속어》. ④ 《꼬치 따위에서》 take off; gobble off. ¶ 꼬치에서 경단을 허겁지겁 ～ gobble dumplings off a stick.

**빼물다** pout (*one's* lips) in anger. ¶ 입을 ～ make a wry face; pout.

**빼빼** thin; rawboned; skinny; haggard; gaunt; emaciated. ¶ ～ 마른 사람 a bag of bones; a living skeleton / ～ 여위다 be worn to a shadow.

**빼쏘다** be as like as two peas 〔eggs〕; be exactly alike; be the picture 《of *one's* mother》. ¶ 이 아이는 아버지를 꼭 빼쏘았다 This child is the very picture of his father. *or* This child bears a close resemblance to his father.

**빼앗기다** ① 《강탈당하다》 be robbed of 《*a thing*》; have 《*something*》 taken 〔snatched〕 away; 《약탈당하다》 be plundered; 《박탈당하다》 be divested of; be deprived of; 《유린당하다》 be seduced 〔dishonored〕 (정조를); be infringed (인권을). ¶ 권리를〔재산을, 희망을〕 ～ be deprived of *one's* right 〔property, hope〕 / 돈을 ～ be robbed of *one's* money / 시계를 ～ have *one's* watch stolen 〔snatched away〕 / 왕위를 ～ be usurped the throne / 그 사고로 많은 사람이 목숨을 빼앗겼다 The accident took a heavy toll of lives. / 그는 일에 대부분의 시간을 빼앗긴다 Work absorbs most of his time.
② 《정신을》 be absorbed; be engrossed; 《매혹되다》 be fascinated 〔captivated〕 《by》; be enraptured 〔carried away〕 《by》; lose *one's* heart to. ¶ 여자에게 정신을 ～ be fascinated 〔captivated〕 by a woman; be enamored of a woman / 음악에 정신을 ～ be enraptured by music / 그는 손자의 재롱에 정신을 빼앗기고 있었다 He was absorbed 〔engrossed〕 in his grandson's movements.

**빼앗다** ① 《탈취하다》 take (by force); snatch 〔wrest, wrench〕 《*a thing*》 from 《*a person*》; 《약탈하다》 rob 《*a person*》 of 《*a thing*》; plunder; loot; pillage; 《찬탈하다》 usurp; 《박탈하다》 divest 〔deprive〕 《*a person*》 of 《*a thing*》; 《유린하다》 seduce 〔violate, dishonor〕 (정조를); infringe (인권을). ¶ 아무의 권리를〔희망을, 생명을〕 ～ deprive *a person* of *his* rights 〔hope, life〕 / 남의 물건을 ～ take another's property / 손에 쥔 핸드백을 ～ snatch a handbag from 《*a person's*》 hand / (진지를) ～ capture 〔carry〕 a fort / 면허장을 ～ revoke a licence / 생명을 ～ take 《*a person's*》 life / 왕위를 ～ usurp the throne / 정조를 ～ violate 〔seduce, dishonor〕 a woman / 투수로부터 안타 다섯을 ～ collect five hits off the pitcher / 나는 그의 칼을 빼앗았다 I wrested the sword from him.
② 《정신을》 absorb 《*one's*》 attention; engross 《*one's*》 mind; 《매혹하다》 fascinate; charm; captivate. ¶ 관객의 눈길을 ～ fascinate 〔enthrall〕 the audience / 넋을 ～ captivate 《*a person*》.

**빼어나다** (be) outstanding; eminent; preeminent; prominent; distinguished; excel 《as》; surpass others; stand conspicuous; stand head and shoulders above others; cut a splendid figure 《of》. ¶ 빼어난 정치가 an eminent 〔a preeminent〕 statesman / 빼어

난 재주 distinguished 〔unusual〕 ability / 그는 수학에 빼어난 재능이 있다 He has exceptional talent in mathematics. / 그녀는 영어에 특히 ～ She excels in English. / 그는 재능이 남보다 빼어나다 He is above all the rest in ability.

**빼주룩—** ⇨ 비주룩—.

**빼치다** ① 《빠지게》 let 《*a thing*》 get away; let go of 《*a thing*》. ② 《끝이 빨게》 sharpen 〔taper〕 《*a thing*》; put a point on 《*a thing*》.

**빽**[1] 《소리》 with a whistle; with a cry. ¶ 기적이 빽 울다 the steam whistle blows / 빽 소리 지르다 cry at the top of *one's* voice / 기차가 빽 기적을 울리며 역을 떠났다 The train pulled out of the station with a whistle.

**빽**[2] ＝ 빽빽이.

**빽**[3] 《연줄·배경》 favor; patronage; backing; help; pull 《미》; 《후원자》 a patron; a backer; a supporter. ¶ …을 빽으로 하여 backed (up) by / 아무의 빽으로 회사에 들어가다 enter a company 〔obtain a position in the firm〕 through *a person's* influence 〔pull〕 / 그에게는 좋은 빽이 있다 He has a powerful supporter 〔good backing〕.

**빽빽** 《소리》 whistling and whistling; crying and crying.

**빽빽이** packed; compactly; tight(ly); thick(ly); densely. ¶ 나무가 ～ 들어찬 야산 a thickly〔heavily〕-wooded hill / 소나무가 ～ 나다 pine trees grow densely / 집들이 ～ 들어서다 houses stand close together / 그 방에 사람들이 ～ 찼다 The room is packed with people.

**빽빽하다** ① 《촘촘하다》 (be) packed; dense; tight and close. ¶ 방이 사람으로 ～ the room is packed with people. ② 《막혀서》 (be) clogged; be blocked up; be stopped up. ¶ 담뱃대가 빽빽이 막히다 the pipe is clogged / 코가 빽빽이 막히다 *one's* nose is stuffed up. ③ 《소견이》 (be) narrow-minded; intolerant; illiberal. ¶ 그는 앞뒤가 빽빽이 막힌 사람이다 He is a narrow-minded person.

**빽지르다** shout; cry; shriek.

**뺀둥—** ⇨ 빈둥—.

**뺄셈** 〖수학〗 subtraction. ～하다 subtract.

**뺏다** ⇨ 빼앗다.

**뺑뺑** ⇨ 빙빙.

**뺑소니** running away; flight. ⇨ 도망. ◉ ～ 사고 a hit-and-run case 〔accident〕. ～운전사〔차〕 a hit-and-run driver 〔car〕.

**뺑줄** 《연》 intercepting and snatching another person's kite; 《일》 taking a job away from 《*a person*》. ～맞다 have *one's* kite 〔job〕 grabbed. ～치다 grab 《*a person's*》 kite 〔job〕.

**뺨** the cheek(s). ¶ 뺨이 붉은 red〔rosy-〕cheeked / 우묵한〔여윈〕 뺨 sunken 〔hollow〕 cheeks / 뺨(을) 때리다〔치다〕 slap 《*a person*》 on the cheek / 뺨을 꼬집다 pinch *a person's* check / 뺨을 비비다 press *one's* cheek against another's / 뺨을 붉히다 blush 《with shame》; redden / 뺨이 토실토실하다 have chubby cheeks.

**뺨따귀** cheek(s). ⇨ 뺨.

**뺨치다** ① 《뺨을》 box 《*a person's*》 ears; slap 《*a person*》 on the cheek. ② 《못하지 않다》 outdo 〔outshine〕 《*a person*》. ¶ 그는 전문가 뺨칠 정도다 He puts a professional to shame 〔in the shade〕. / 그의 연기는 배우 뺨칠 정도로 훌륭했다 He outshone the professionals with his excellent performance.

**뻐개다** ① 《나무 등을》 split; cleave; rend asunder 〔apart〕; chip; chop. ¶ 나무를 ～ split wood / 장작을 ～ chop wood. ② 《일을》 spoil; ruin; destroy. ¶ 일을 ～ spoil 《*a person's*》 plan; vitiate a program.

**뻐개지다** ① 《물건이》 split; cleave; 《깨지다》 break; be broken. ¶ 머리가 뻐개질 듯이 아프다 have a racking 〔splitting〕 headache. ② 《일 등이》 be spoilt; be ruined; go wrong. 〔destroyed〕.

**뻐걱—** ⇨ 바각—.

**뻐그러지다** get broken; be ruined

**뻐그르르** ⇨ 바그르르.

**뻐근하다** 《거북하다》 be sore all over (from overwork or heavy work); feel a dull pain. ¶ 가슴이 ～ feel heavy in the chest / 어깨가 ～ feel stiff in the shoulders; have a stiff shoulder; *one's* shoulders grow stiff / 등이 ～ feel a soreness in *one's* back.

**뻐기다** be proud; be haughty 〔pompous〕; be stuck 〔puffed〕 up; feel 〔show〕 pride; give *oneself* airs; boast. ¶ 뻐기는 haughty; overbearing; arrogant / 뻐기며 haughtily; overbearingly / 뻐기고 다니다 strut 《about, along》; swagger / 부하들에게 ～ domineer 〔ride roughshod〕 over *one's* inferiors; lord it over *one's* subordinates / 그는 제가 제일인 체 뻐긴다 He is puffed up with his own importance. / 뻐기지 마라 Don't brag!

**뻐꾸기** 〖조류〗 a cuckoo. ¶ ～ 소리 a cuckoo's notes; a cuckoo's song.

**빼꾹** cuckoo. ¶ 빼꾸기가 ~하고 운다 The cuckoo cuckooes. ◉ ~시계 a cuckoo clock.

**빼끔빼끔** ①《구멍》(with) cracks here and there; with many cracks. ~하다 be cracked here and there; have many cracks. ¶ 포탄을 맞은 벽에는 구멍이 ~ 뚫려 있었다 There were gaping holes in the wall where it had been hit by the shells. ②《빨다》puffing. ¶ 담배를 ~ 빨다 puff on a pipe; puff (away) at *one's* pipe〔cigarette〕.

**빼끔하다** (be) cracked; be split apart. ¶ 빼끔히 뚫린 큰 구멍 a large gaping hole / 빼끔히 구멍이 나다 a hole breaks open / 길에는 큰 구멍이 빼끔히 나 있었다 A big hole had opened up in the road.

**빼덕빼덕하다** be stiff〔hard〕. ¶ 가죽이 ~ the leather is stiff.

**빼드러지다** ①《이 따위가》protrude. ②《뻣뻣해지다》stiffen; get stiff; become rigid;《죽다》(stiffen and) die; drop dead.

**빼드렁니** a projecting〔prominent〕front tooth; a bucktooth. ¶ ~의 buck-toothed / ~의 사내 a man with buck-teeth.

**빼드렁이** a person with protruding teeth; a bucktoothed person.

**빼세다** be stiff and tough.

**빼젓하다** ⇨ 버젓하다.

**빽빽**《suck at a pipe》noisely; busily; with puffs. ¶ 담뱃대를 ~ 빨다 suck noisily at *one's* pipe.

**빽빽하다** ⇨ 빡빡하다.

**빽적지근하다** get〔grow, become〕stiff. ¶ 어깨가 ~ have a stiff shoulder; *one's* shoulder is stiff; feel stiff in the shoulder / 몸이 ~ feel pretty strained.

**뺀둥-** ⇨ 빈둥-.

**뺀드르르** ⇨ 반드르르.

**뺀뺀하다, 뺀뺀스럽다** (be) shameless; brazen; impudent; unabashed; brass=nerved《속어》. ¶ 뺀뺀하게 impudently; audaciously; shamelessly / 뺀뺀한 거짓말을 하다 tell a barefaced lie / 뺀뺀한 놈 a cheeky〔brazen-faced〕fellow / 뺀뺀하게도〔스럽게도〕…하다 have the face〔cheek, front〕to *do;* be shameless enough to *do* / 뺀뺀스러운 부탁입니다만 …해 주실 수 없는지요 May I take the liberty to ask you to *do?* / 그는 뺀뺀하게도 그런 말을 한다 He is shameless enough to say that. / 뺀뺀스럽기 짝이 없군 Well, all cheek! / 그는 뺀뺀스럽게도 내게 데이트를 신청해 왔다 He has a lot of nerve. He asked me for date.

**뺀적-** ⇨ 반짝-.

**뺀죽거리다** ⇨ 번죽거리다.

**뺀지르르** ⇨ 반지르르.

**뻔질나게, 뻔찔나게** continuously coming and going; very often; very frequently. ¶ ~ 다니다 visit《a house》frequently; frequent《a house》; pay frequent visits《to》; make repeated calls on《*a person*》.

**뻔하다**[1] ⇨ 빤하다.

**뻔하다**[2]《까딱하면…》be〔come, go〕near《*do*ing》; almost; nearly; well=nigh《*do*》; just barely escape《*do*ing》. ¶ 차에 치일 ~ come near being run over / 죽을 ~ be nearly dead / 물에 빠질 뻔했다 I came very near〔close to〕being drowned. *or* I was nearly〔almost〕drowned. / 그는 못 갈 뻔했다 He nearly didn't go. *or* "The wonder is he went at all." / 그는 갈 뻔했다 He almost went. *or* "The wonder is he didn't go." / 그가 실없이 한 말이 스스로를 망칠 뻔했다 His casual remarks came near ruining him.

**뻔히** ⇨ 빤히.

**뻗다**[1] ①《가지·덩굴 등이》spread; stretch; extend. ¶ 뿌리는 땅속으로 뻗어 나간다 The roots grow down into the soil. / 나뭇가지는 해가 비추는 쪽으로 뻗는다 The boughs〔branches〕of trees reach out toward the sunlight〔in the direction of the sun〕. ②《힘 따위가》extend; spread out; grow; advance; expand. ¶ 해외로 뻗어 나가다 make overseas expansion / 유럽 열강의 세력이 아시아로 뻗었다 The authority of the European powers was extended toward Asia. ③《길·지대가》run; range; spread; extend. ¶ 철도가 그 나라 남단까지 뻗어 있다 The railway line extends to the southern end of the country. / 해안 모래톱이 저 멀리 뻗어 있다 A sandy beach extends far into the distance.

**뻗다**[2]《팔·다리를》stretch out (from a bent position);《죽다》collapse; pass out. ¶ 팔을〔다리를〕~ stretch *one's* arm〔leg〕/ 그 한 방에 그는 뻗어 버렸다 The blow finished him.

**뻗대다** insist on; do not give in; be obstinate〔perverse〕.

**뻗서다** resist; oppose; stand〔rise〕against; face up to. 「person.

**뻗정다리** a stiff leg;《사람》a stiff-legged

**뻗치다** ①《저끝까지》range; extend; lie〔stand, stretch〕in a row. ¶ 그 섬은 남북으로 뻗쳐 있다 The island stretches

〔runs〕 north and south. ②《가지·힘 따위가》 open out; spread 《toward》. ⇨뻗다②. ③《손길·세력 따위를》 stretch; extend; lengthen; spread. ¶ 수재민에게 구원의 손길을 ~ extend a helping hand to the those left homeless by the flood / 국력을 해외에 ~ extend the national power overseas / 세력을 ~ extend *one's* power / 문학에 손을 ~ hold out a hand to literature. ④《팔다리를》 ⇨뻗다².

**뻘건** ⇨빨간.

**뻘겋다** ⇨빨갛다.

**뻘때추니** a girl who is fond of going out just as she pleases; a party girl.

**뻘떡-** ⇨벌떡-.

**뻘뻘** 《sweat》 profusely; dripping. ¶ 땀을 ~ 흘리며 in a sweat; all of a sweat / 땀을 ~ 흘리다 be dripping with sweat / 그는 얼굴에 땀을 ~ 흘리고 있었다 Sweat was pouring down his face. *or* His face was running with sweat.

**뻣뻣하다** 《부드럽지 않다》 (be) hard; stiff; starchy (풀기로); crisp (종이 등이); 《태도가》 (be) firm; tough; headstrong; unyielding; disobedient. ¶ 뻣뻣한 손 horny hands / 뻣뻣한 머리 wiry hair / 뻣뻣한 (새) 지폐 crisp bank notes / 뻣뻣한 털 a bristle; a seta (*pl.* -tae) / 목이 ~ have a stiff neck / 뻣뻣해지다 stiffen; get 〔become〕 stiff / 이 와이셔츠는 풀을 너무 먹여 ~ This shirt is starched too stiff. / 시체는 이미 뻣뻣하게 굳어 있었다 The corps was already stiff.

**뻣세다** (be) stiff and tough; headstrong.

**뻥** ①《거짓말》 a lie; a fib (악의 없는); falsehood; a horn blowing. ¶ 뻥까는 사람 a liar; a horn blower / 뻥까다 tell a lie; horn blow / 그것은 뻥이다 That's a lie. ② =뻥짜. ③《소리》 pop; bang. ¶ 뻥하고 with a pop / 병마개를 뻥하고 뽑다 pop the cork out of a bottle. ④《구멍이》 ¶ 크게 뻥 뚫린 구멍 a large gaping hole / 뻥 뚫어지다 break open.

**뻥놓다** 《비밀을 드러내다》 leak out (a secret); disclose; "spill the beans"; 《거짓말하다》 tell a lie.

**뻥뻥** ①《터지다》 with explosion after explosion; popping and popping. ¶ 샴페인을 ~ 터뜨리다 uncork bottles of champagne one after another. ②《뚫리다》 with hole after hole.

**뻥뻥하다** be at a loss; (be) puzzled. ¶ 나는 뻥뻥하여 대답을 못 했다 I was at my wit's end for an answer. / 시험문제가 어려워서 뻥뻥했다 I was quite overwhelmed by the examination questions.

**뻥뻥히** puzzled; at a loss.

**뻥실-** ⇨방글-.

**뻥짜** a defective, useless thing.

**뻥튀기** popping rice 〔corn〕; 《과자》 popcorn; poprice.

**뼈** ①《사람·동물의》 a bone; 《뼈대》 a skeleton.

¶ (부러진) 뼈를 맞추다 set the (broken) bone / 뼈를 바르다 bone 《a fish》; remove the bones from 《a chicken》 / 뼈를 삐다 sprain a bone / 뼈가 퉁그러지다 be 〔be put〕 out of joint; dislocate / (말라빠져) 뼈만 남다 be reduced to a mere skeleton / 온 몸의 뼈가 쑤시다 feel pain in all *one's* joints / 추위가 뼛속까지 스미다 be chilled 〔frozen〕 to the bone(s); the chill penetrates to the very bone / 뼈에 사무치다 《훈계 따위가》 sting 〔touch〕 《*a person*》 to the quick; sink deep into the mind; come 〔go〕 home to 《*a person*》; strike 《*a person*》 home / 뼈에 사무치게 느끼다 feel in *one's* bones; feel 《*something*》 keenly; fully 〔acutely〕 realize / 뼈빠지게 일하다 work *one's* finger to the bones / 그는 생선을 뼈째 다 먹었다 He ate the fish bones and all. / 그는 창문에서 뛰어내려 양쪽 복사뼈를 삐었다 He sprained his anklebones when he jumped out of the window. / 그에 대한 원한이 뼈에 사무치고 있다 I have a deep grudge against him. / 그는 뼈와 가죽만 남았다 He is all skin and bone. *or* He is a mere skeleton 〔bag of bones〕. / 뼈빠지게 일한 보람이 있다 My pains have been rewarded. *or* It was worth the trouble. / 뼈빠지게 일한 보람이 없었다 All my trouble went for nothing.

②《저의》 an implication; a hidden meaning; the connotation. ¶ 뼈 있는 말 words full of hidden 〔latent〕 meaning; suggestive words.

③《기개》 spirit; grit; backbone. ¶ 뼈 있는 사람 a man of spirit / 뼈 없는 사람 an invertebrate; a spineless 〔poor=spirited〕 person.

> 참고 여러 가지 뼈
> 물렁뼈 cartilage 복사뼈 anklebone 등뼈 backbone 빗장뼈 collarbone 궁둥뼈 hipbone 턱뼈 jawbone 무릎뼈 kneecap 코뼈 nasal bone 갈비뼈 rib 정강이뼈 shinbone 어깨뼈 shoulder blade 머리뼈 skull.

**뼈고도리** an arrowhead made out of bone.

**뼈끝** ①《끝》 the tip of a joint (of a bone). ②《고기》 flesh over the bone.

**뼈다귀** a bone; a piece of bone. ¶ 개는 ～를 좋아한다 Dogs like to gnaw bones.

**뼈대** ①《구조》 framework; structure; the frame; the shell; 《선박의》 the carcass. ¶ 건물의 ～ the framework of a building / 그 다리는 ～가 튼튼해서 아무리 큰물이 져도 떠내려가지 않는다 The bridge's frame is strong, so it won't be carried 〔washed〕 away no matter what flood we have.
②《골격》 a skeleton; (a) build; (a) frame; physique. ¶ 연약한 ～ a delicate frame / ～가 굵은 large-boned; of strong build / ～가 단단한 사람 a man of sturdy 〔strong〕 build; a sturdily built man / ～가 굵어지다 grow bony; 《자라다》 be brought up; be bred / ～가 크다〔작다〕 *one* has a large 〔small〕 frame / 그 운동선수는 ～가 단단하다 The athelete has a sturdy 〔well knit〕 body.
③《대요》 an outline; a general plan. ¶그는 계획의 ～를 간단히 설명해 주었다 He gave me a brief outline of the plan.
④《명문》 ¶ ～ 있는 집안 a good 〔distinguished〕 family.

**뼈들다** ①《일이》 be hard and linger; be difficult and endless. ②《손장난하다》 play 〔fool, fiddle〕 around with a tool.

**뼈들어지다** do not cut well; become dull.

**뼈뜯이** scrapings from the bone.

**뼈마디** the joint of a bone; joints. ¶ ～가 굵은 strong-jointed; large-boned / ～가 시다 have sore joints / ～가 아프다 I feel an ache in my joints.

**뼈물다** ① ＝벼르다. ②《성내다》 show temper readily; be touchy 〔irritable〕. ③《옷치장하다》 dress up; be gaily dressed.

**뼈아프다** ＝뼈저리다.

**뼈오징어** 〖동물〗 a cuttlefish.

**뼈저리다** pierce *one's* heart 〔bone〕; pierce deeply into *one's* mind. ¶ 뼈저린 keen; severe; acute / 뼈저리게 keenly; severely; acutely / 상호 협력의 필요성을 뼈저리게 느끼다 feel 〔realize〕 keenly the necessity of mutual aid / 그의 비난은 뼈저린 것이었다 His reproach cut me to the heart. / 내 어리석은 짓을 뼈저리게 후회하고 있다 I feel (a) bitter regret for my follies.

**뼈지다** ①《속이》 be pressed 〔packed〕 together hard (like a bone); (be) solid. ¶ 그 떡이 ～ That rice cake is quite solid. ②《말이》 (be) sharp; pointed; pithy; piquant. ¶ 그의 말은 ～ His speech cuts to the quick.

**뼘** a span; the span of a hand. ¶ 뼘으로 재다 span / 뼘으로 재니 3피트였다 I made it 3 ft. by spanning it.

**뼘다** measure by the span; span off 《with *one's* hand》. ¶ 길이를 뼘어라 Span off the length! / 그 길이는 뼘어서 두 치다 The length spans at two feet.

**뼘들이로** one after another; in quick succession; consecutively.

**뼛성내다** flare 〔blow〕 up (in anger).

**뽀그르르-** ⇨ 바그르르-.

**뽀도독-** ⇨ 바드득-.

**뽀로통하다** ⇨ 부루퉁하다.

**뽀뽀** 《아기에게》 Kiss-kiss!; Give us a kiss!

**뽀얗다** (be) milky-white. ⇨ 보얗다.

**뽀유스름하다** ⇨ 보유스름하다.

**뽐내다** 《자랑하다》 take pride 《in》; pride *oneself* 《on》; be proud 《of, that》; boast 《of》; 《태도가》 be haughty; be puffed up; give *oneself* airs; put on airs; 《큰소리하다》 talk big; brag. ¶ 뽐내는 haughty; overbearing; arrogant / 뽐내어 domineeringly; overbearingly / 뽐내는 사람 a high-hat 《미구어》 / 뽐내며 걷다 swagger; strut / 그것은 뽐낼 것이 못 된다 That's nothing to boast of. / 그는 항상 저만 잘난 것처럼 뽐낸다 He is always puffed up with self-importance. / 그는 내로라 하고 뽐낸다 He boasts "me! me! me!" as if he had the whole world in his mind. / 성공했다고 뽐내지 마라 You should not allow yourself to be elated by your success! / 그녀는 요리 솜씨를 뽐낸다 She prides herself on her cooking. / 그는 1등상을 탔다고 뽐냈다 He boasted of having won (the) first prize.

**뽑다** ①《빼다》 take 〔draw, pull, pluck〕 out; extract; root up 《a tree》. ¶ 권총〔칼〕을 ～ draw a pistol 〔sword〕 / 닭털을 ～ pluck a chicken / 못을 벽에서 ～ pull a nail out of a wall / 병마개를 ～ open 〔uncork〕 a bottle / 이를 ～ pull out 〔extract〕 a tooth; 《남이》 have a tooth (pulled) out / 나무를 뿌리째 ～ uproot a tree ⇨ 뿌리째 / 제비를 ～ draw 〔cast〕 lots / 아버지는 뜰에서 잡초를 뽑고 있었다 Father was pulling (up) weeds in the garden.
②《근절하다》 eradicate; root 《*a thing*》

out. ⇨ 뿌리뽑다.
③《선발·선거하다》pick 〔single〕 out; select; elect (투표로). ¶ 반장으로 ～ single《*a person*》out as a monitor.
④《모집하다》enlist; enroll;《지원자 등을》invite; collect; raise. ¶ 군인을 ～ conscript 〔enlist〕 soldiers / 사무원을 ～ invite applications for the position of clerk / 학생을 ～ enroll students / 회사는 그를 간부 사원으로 뽑았다 The company enrolled him on their staff. / 지원자 5백 명 중에서 60명만 뽑았다 Only sixty were admitted from among the five hundred candidates.
⑤ 《본전을》 recover. ¶ 본전을 ～ recover *one's* investment; return the original investment; earn *its* cost / 그렇다면 본전도 못 뽑는다 Then I shall be unable to recover the cost.
⑥《실 등을》spin; draw. ¶ 솜에서 실을 ～ spin cotton into yarn.

**-뽑이** a puller; pincers. ¶ 못뽑이 a nail puller / 마개뽑이 a corkscrew.

**뽑히다** ①《빠지다》be taken out; be pulled out; be come off. ¶ 못이 쉽게 뽑힌다 The nail comes out easily. ②《선발되다》be singled out; be admitted; be allowed to enlist. ¶ 반장으로 ～ be elected monitor / 축구 선수로 ～ be singled out as a football player / 국회 의원으로 ～ be elected to the National Assembly / 그는 올림픽 육상 선수로 뽑혔다 He gained a place on the Olympic track team.

**뽕** ⇨ 뽕잎.

**뽕나무** a mulberry (tree). ◉ ～밭 a mulberry field 〔plantation〕. ～ 열매《오디》a mulberry.

**뽕따다** pick mulberry leaves.

**뽕빠지다** ①《결딴나다》be broken; go bankrupt. ¶ 결혼 잔치 치르느라 나는 뽕빠졌다 I went broke after giving the wedding reception. / 그녀와 그렇게 자주 데이트하면 너 뽕빠진다 You will go broke if you date her so often. ②《지치다》be exhausted; be spent; be done up; have a hard time. ¶ 시험 치르기에 나는 뽕빠졌다 I'm done up from exams.

**뽕뽕** ⇨ 뽕뽕[1, 2].

**뽕잎** mulberry leaves. ¶ ～을 따다 pick mulberry leaves / 누에에 ～을 주다 feed mulberry leaves to silkworms / ～은 누에를 치는 데 귀중하다 Mulberry leaves are valuable in breeding silkworms.

**뾰로통하다** (be) sulky; pouty. ¶ 뾰로통한 얼굴 a sulky look / 뾰로통해지다 get sulky 〔peevish〕; pout; sulk / 무엇 때문에 뾰로통한가 What makes you so sulky? / 조금만 야단쳐도 그 아이는 뾰로통해진다 The child gets sulky at the slightest scolding. / 남편이 늦게 귀가하자 아내는 뾰로통해서 말을 안 했다 The wife sulked 〔pouted〕 silently when her husband came home late.

**뾰롱뾰롱하다** ＝ 뾰로통하다.

**뾰루지** a boil; an abscess; an eruption; a skin eruption;《여드름》a pimple; a spot. ¶ 얼굴에 ～가 나다 have 〔break out with〕 pimples / 다리에 ～가 생겼다 I got a boil on my leg.

**뾰조록이** sticking out a bit.

**뾰조록하다** stick out a bit.

**뾰족구두** high heels; high-heeled shoes. ¶ ～를 신다 wear (high) heels.

**뾰족뾰족** all pointed. ～하다 be all pointed. ¶ 침봉(針峰)에는 꽃을 고정시키는 바늘이 ～하게 박혀 있다 A frog has many spikes for holding flowers.

**뾰족이** ⇨ 뾰조록이.

**뾰족집** a building with a spire 〔steeple〕;《성당》a Catholic church.

**뾰족탑**(—塔) a steeple; a spire; a pinnacle.

**뾰족하다** (be) sharp-pointed; pointed. ¶ 뾰족한 연필〔코〕 a pointed pencil 〔nose〕 / 끝이 뾰족한 손가락 fingers with pointed tips / 부리가 뾰족한 구두 (a pair of) pointed shoes; shoes with pointed toes / 입을 뾰족하게 내밀다 pout (out) 〔purse up〕 *one's* lips / 끝이 ～ be sharp-pointed 〔pointed at the end〕; have a sharp point / 연필을 뾰족하게 깎았다 I put a sharp point on my pencil.

**뿌그르르** ⇨ 바그르르.

**뿌글거리다** boil; seethe; be on the boil;《거품이》bubble up; rise in bubbles.

**뿌다구니, 뿌다귀** a part 〔corner〕 sticking out 〔up〕.

**뿌두둑-** ⇨ 바드득-.

**뿌드드하다** ⇨ 부드드하다.

**뿌드득-** ⇨ 바드득-.

**뿌듯하다** ①《꼭 끼다》(be) tight; close. ⇨ 빠듯하다①. ②《가슴이》(be) full. ¶ 가슴 뿌듯한 기쁨 an overflowing joy / 너무나 가슴이 뿌듯해서 아무 말도 못했다 My heart was too full for words. / 그녀는 자긍심으로 가슴이 뿌듯했다 Her heart was full with pride.

**뿌루퉁하다** ⇨ 부루퉁하다.

**뿌리** ①《식물의》a root. ¶ ～를 박다〔내리다〕 strike 〔take〕 root; find roots《in》; take firm hold / 깊이 ～ 박다 strike 〔take〕 root deep《into the soil》/ 땅속에 ～를 내리다 take root in the ground / ~를 뻗다 spread root / 잡초의 ~를 뽑다 root up 〔uproot〕 weeds; pluck up weeds by the roots / 그 개나리 가지는 벌써 ~가 내렸다 The forsythia branch has already struck root. ② 《기부(基部)》 a root; 《근원》 the root(s); the (root) cause. ¶ 혀~ the root of the tongue / 털〔이, 손톱〕 ~ the root of a hair 〔tooth, fingernail〕 / 모든 악의 ~ the root of all evil / 자기의 ~를 찾다 search for *one's* roots. ③ [비유적] getting established 〔settled〕; taking root. ¶ ~ 깊은 습관 an inveterate habit / ~ 깊은 적개심 a deep-rooted animosity / ~를 박다 take root; become established; become settled / 그들은 강원도에 ~박고 산다 They have settled in Kangwondo. / 그의 장사는 ~를 내렸다 He got settled in business. / 민주주의가 한국 땅에 ~를 내렸다 Democracy planted its roots in Korea.

◉ ~등걸 the stump of a tree with its roots. ~줄기 〚식물〛 a rhizome. ~털 the root hair. ~혹 a root nodule 〔tubercle〕: ~혹박테리아 root nodule bacteria.

**뿌리다** ① 《비가》 rain slightly; sprinkle. ¶ 후두두 뿌리는 비 a scatter of rain / 비가 몇 방울 뿌린다 It sprinkles. / 눈이 세차게 오두막 안으로 뿌렸다 Snow drove furiously into the hut.

② 《물 등을》 sprinkle; shower; water; 《흩뿌리다》 scatter (about); spread; 《전단 등을》 hand 〔give〕 out. ¶ 길에 물을 ~ sprinkle the street with water / 잔디에 물을 ~ sprinkle the lawn / 식물에 살충제를 ~ spray an insecticide on plants; spray plants with an insecticide / 눈에 고춧가루를 ~ throw powdered red pepper into 《*a person's*》 eyes / 밭에 재를 ~ spread ashes on the field / 비행기에서 전단을 ~ drop 〔scatter〕 handbills from an airplane / 그는 밭에 비료를 뿌렸다 He spread manure over the field.

③ 《씨를》 sow; scatter. ¶ 씨를 ~ sow 〔scatter〕 seed / 밭에 보리 씨를 ~ sow field with barley / 봄에 옥수수 씨를 ~ sow corn in (the) spring / 불화의 씨를 ~ sow the seeds of strife / 나는 뜰에 해바라기 씨를 뿌렸다 I planted the sunflower seeds in the garden.

④ 《돈을》 spend freely; squander; scatter. ¶ 돈을 ~ spend money freely 〔recklessly〕; scatter *one's* money / 그는 많은 돈을 뿌려 표를 샀다는 소문이다 Rumor has it that he spent freely buying votes.

**뿌리뽑다** root up 〔out〕; uproot; pull 〔dig〕 《a plant》 up by the roots; 《근절하다》 root 〔stamp〕 out; eradicate; exterminate; extirpate. ¶ 뿌리뽑을 수 있는 eradicable; exterminable 《evils》 / 뿌리뽑기 힘든 악폐 ineradicable evils / 사회악을 ~ root 〔stamp〕 out social evils / 사회의 안정과 발전을 저해하는 온갖 불법 행위를 ~ root out all sorts of illegal acts detrimental to social stability and development / 마약 밀매를 뿌리뽑아야 한다 We must eradicate drug traffic, root and branch. / 새 정부는 정치 부패를 뿌리뽑을 결의를 다졌다 The new government is determined to root out political corruption.

**뿌리째** ① 《식물을》 by the roots. ¶ ~ 먹는 채소 vegetables eaten 「with their roots 〔roots and all〕 / 나무를 ~ 뽑다 uproot a tree / 정원의 잡초를 ~ 뽑았다 I pulled up 〔out〕 the weeds in the garden by the roots.

② 《몽땅》 thoroughly; root and branch. ¶ 이들 범죄 조직은 ~ 없애 버려야 한다 These crime syndicates must be destroyed root and branch.

③ 《근본부터》 fundamentally; 《구어》 from the ground up. ¶ ~ 흔들다 rock 〔shake〕 to *its* foundation(s) / 그 대사건은 체제를 ~ 흔들어 놓았다 The serious incident shook (up) the establishment to its foundation. / 그의 학설은 새 학설로 인해 ~ 뒤집혔다 His theory was completely exploded by the new theory. *or* The new theory knocked the bottom out of his theory.

**뿌리치다** ① 《잡은 손을》 shake *oneself* free from 《a grasp》; shake off. ¶ 잡은 손을 ~ shake off 《*a person's*》 hand / 그 아이는 내 손을 뿌리치고 거리로 뛰쳐나갔다 The child shook himself free from my hand and rushed into the street.

② 《물리치다》 refuse; reject 《*a person's* request》; rebuff; wave 《*a person's* objection》 aside. ¶ 유혹을 ~ eschew 〔cast aside〕 temptation / 노동자측은 경영진의 부당한 요구를 뿌리쳤다 The laborers refused 〔rejected〕 the unreasonable demands of the management.

**뿌옇다** ⇨ 보얗다.

**뿌예지다** ⇨ 부예지다.

**뿌장귀** a sharp edge; a projection; a projecting piece.

**뿌지지, 뿌지직** ⇨ 바지지.

**뿐** ①《용언 뒤에서》 nothing but; only. ¶ …할 뿐(만) 아니라, …뿐더러 not only... but (also); both... and...; as well as (★ not only A but (also) B는 B에 중점을 두며, both A and B에서는 양쪽 다 중요도를 보임. 또 B as well as A는 not only A but B와는 순서가 거꾸로 됨에 주의할 것); moreover; furthermore; besides; in addition; on top of that / 한국으로부터 뿐만 아니라 일본으로부터도 not only from Korea, but also from Japan / 하루 종일 울 뿐이다 do nothing but cry all day / 나는 그것을 신문을 통해서 알 뿐이다 I just know it from the newspapers. / 나는 내 의무를 다했을 뿐이다 I have done nothing but my duty. / 그는 학자일 뿐더러 시인이기도 하다 He is a poet as well as a scholar. / 나는 피곤했을 뿐더러 배가 고팠다 I was not only tired but also hungry. / 그는 중국어를 할 뿐 아니라 일본어도 한다 He speaks Japanese as well as Chinese. / 그저 약간 틀렸을 뿐입니다 You made only 〔just〕 a few mistakes. (★ only, just, merely의 위치는 written English에서는 애매성을 피하기 위해서 수식하는 말의 앞에 둠: I want only three.「세 개만 원한다」. 그러나 spoken English에서는 I only want three.도 같은 뜻을 나타냄. 또 spoken English에서는 sentence stress, intonation, rhythm 따위도 의미 결정의 요소가 됨).
②《체언 뒤에서》 only; merely; alone. ¶ 믿을 사람은 너뿐이다 I have no one but you to rely upon. / 이 의견을 가진 사람은 나뿐이 아니다 I am not alone in this opinion. / 내 소지금은 이것뿐이다 This is all (the money) that I have with me. / 그는 아들이 단 하나뿐이다 He has only one son. / 그것을 할 수 있는 사람은 나뿐이다 I am the only one who can do it. / 늦은 사람은 그이뿐이었다 He alone came late. / 그것뿐인가 Is that all? / 회의에 출석하는 것뿐만 아니라 토론에 참가하는 것도 중요하다 It is important not only to attend the meeting but (also) to take part in the discussion. *or* It is important to take part in the discussion as well as to attend the meeting.

**뿔** ①《동물의》 a horn. ¶ 사슴의 뿔 an antler / 뿔이 있는 horned / 뿔이 없는 hornless / 뿔이 돋다 [동물이 주어] sprout horns / 뿔로 받다 butt with *its* horns; horn; 《소가》 gore / 뿔 뺀 쇠 상(相)이다 《속담》 have a position with no power. ②《물건의》 a protrusion.
◉ ～관자(貫子) beads of chin strap made of horn. ～세공 hornwork; antler work. ～싸움 fighting with the horns 〔antlers〕. ～잔 a horn chalice. ～피리 a horn.

**뿔긋뿔긋** ⇨ 발긋발긋.

**뿔끈** ⇨ 발끈.

**뿔매** 〖조류〗 a Hodgson's hawk-eagle.

**뿔면**(一面) 〖수학〗 a conical surface.

**뿔뿔이** 《흩어져》 scatteringly; 《따로따로》 separately; singly; severally. ¶ ～ 흩어진 scattered; dispersed in all directions / ～ 헤어지다〔흩어지다〕 get separated 〔scattered〕; break up / 그들은 ～ 흩어져 도망쳤다 They fled this way and that. / 경찰을 보자 그들은 ～ 흩어졌다 They scattered in all directions when they saw the policeman. / 학교가 파한 후 학생들은 ～ 제 집으로 돌아갔다 After school the students returned to their separate homes. / 전쟁으로 그의 가족은 ～ 흩어졌다 The war broke up his family. *or* His family 「broke up 〔was scattered〕 because of the war.

**뿔체**(一體) 〖수학〗 a conical form.

**뿜다** 《분출하다》 spout (out); spurt (out, up); gush out; 《가스 등을》 blow out 〔up〕; 《연기를》 belch; emit; 《뿌리다》 sprinkle; spray. ¶ 연기를 ～ belch smoke / (화산이) 용암을 ～ vomit 〔spout, spew out〕 lava / 꽃에 물을 뿜어주다 spray flowers / 상처에서 피가 뿜어 나왔다 Blood spurted from the wound. / 분수가 물을 뿜고 있다 The fountain is playing. / 저 봐, 고래가 물을 뿜는다 There a whale blows 〔spouts water〕! / 공장 굴뚝이 뿜어내는 연기가 자연환경을 오염시킨다 The natural environment is polluted by the clouds of smoke sent up by the factory chimneys. / 아내는 구깃구깃한 와이셔츠에 물을 뿜고 다렸다 My wife sprayed water on a wrinkled shirt and ironed it.

**뿡** ⇨ 붕.

**쀼루퉁하다** ⇨ 뾰로통하다.

**쀼주룩이** ⇨ 뾰조록이.

**삐걱거리다** creak; squeak. ¶ 삐걱거리는 소리 a creaking 〔squeaking〕 sound / 마루〔의자〕가 ～ the floor 〔chair〕 creaks / 녹슨 경첩이 ～ the rusty hinge creaks / 이 마룻바닥은 걸으면 삐걱거린다 The floor squeaks when walked upon.

**삐걱빼각** creaking and squeaking.

**삐걱삐걱** creaking; squeaking.

**삐꾸러지다** ⇨ 비꾸러지다.

**삐끗삐끗** ⇨ 배끗배끗.

**삐다**[1] 《괸 물이》 run low; drain. ¶ 괸 물이 삐었다 The stagnant water drained.

**삐다**[2] 《관절을》 sprain; wrench; twist. ¶ 목을 ～ wrick *one's* neck; have a wrick in *one's* neck / 손목을 ～ sprain 〔wrench〕 *one's* wrist / 발목을 ～ sprain 〔wrench〕 *one's* ankle; put *one's* foot out of joint / 그는 무릎을 삐었다 He got his knee dislocated.

**삐대다** make a nuisance of *oneself;* bother people.

**삐드득-** ⇨ 바드득-.

**삐딱-** ⇨ 비딱-.

**삐뚜로** ⇨ 비뚜로.

**삐삐** a beeper; a pager. ¶ ～를 치다 beep; page / 나에게 ～를 쳐라 Beep me. *or* Page me. /「몇 시에 차로 너를 태우러 갈까」—「쇼핑이 끝나면 너에게 ～를 칠게」 "What time should I pick you up?"—"I'll beep you when I've finished shopping."

**삐악** with a peep 〔cheep〕. ¶ ～ 울다 cheep; peep / ～삐악 peep-peep!; cheep-cheep!

**삐죽-** ⇨ 비죽-.

**삐치다**[1] 《글자의 획을》 sweep 〔brush〕 up (leftward).

**삐치다**[2] 《느른해지다》 feel weary 〔spiritless, languid, enervated〕.

**삐치다**[3] 《토라지다》 sulk; pout; get 〔go〕 sulky; have a fit of the sulks. ¶ 응석받이로 자란 아이는 뜻대로 안 되면 곧 삐친다 The spoilt child soon pouts when he doesn't get his own way.

**삐트적-** ⇨ 비틀-.

**삑** ⇨ 빽[1.2].

**삘기살** beef shank.

**삥그르르** ⇨ 빙그르르.

**삥등그리다** show a reluctant gesture twirling *one's* head.

**삥땅** a cut; 《구어》 a kickback; a rake=off. ～하다 take 《1,000 won》 off 《*a person's* wages》; pocket a rake-off 〔kickback〕; take a cut 《off *a person's* wages》.
¶ 회계는 부정하게 회비를 ～했다 The treasurer milked the club fees dishonestly. / 그는 수수료의 5퍼센트를 ～했다 He took a five percent cut of the commission.

**삥삥** ⇨ 빙빙.

**삥삥매다** fluster *oneself;* make much ado; busy *oneself* 《about》; bustle 《about》; go about busily.

**삥실-** ＝방실-.

**사**[1] 《단춧구멍의》 a buttonhole stitch; hemstitching. ⇨ 사뜨다.

**사**[2] 〖음악〗 G; sol (It.). ¶ 사음자리표 a G clef / 올림〔내림〕사 G sharp〔flat〕.

**사**(士) ① 《선비》 an officer; a gentleman; a figure. ② 《장기의》 a chessman in Korean chess〔*changgi*〕.

**사**(巳) 〖민속〗 ① 《십이지의》 the sign of the Snake〔Serpent〕; the 6th of the 12 Earth's Branches. ② ⇨ 사방(巳方). ③ ⇨ 사시(巳時).

**사**(死) ① = 죽음. ¶ 자연사 a natural death. ② 《야구 등의》 out. ¶ 2사 만루 《with》 the bases loaded and two outs.

**사**(私) 《공(公)에 대한》 privateness; privacy; self (자기); 《사리》 self-interest; 《비밀》 secret. ¶ 사가 있는 selfish; self-interested / 사가 없는 unselfish; disinterested / 사를 버리다 sink〔efface〕 self; rise above *oneself*.

**사**(邪) 《악》 evil; vice; wrong; 《부정》 injustice; unrighteousness; 《이단》 heterodoxy. ¶ 사불범정(邪不犯正) The right cannot be beaten by the wrong. *or* Virtue triumphs over vice. *or* Right will prevail (in the end).

**사**(社) 《회사》 a company; a firm; a corporation 《미》; 《사무소》 an office.

**사**(紗) (silk) gauze; thin silk; gossamer.

(-)**사**(辭) ① 《한시의》 a form of Chinese poetical composition. ② 《인사말》 an address; a speech; a message. ¶ 송별사 a parting〔farewell〕 speech〔address〕 / 환영사 an address of welcome / 취임사 an inauguration speech.

**사**(四) four. ¶ 제4 the fourth / 4분의 1 one quarter; one fourth / 4배 four times; fourfold; quadruple / 4배하다 increase fourfold; quadruple / 4차원 the fourth dimension / 제4계급 《신문기자》 the fourth estate; 《근로자》 the proletariat.

-**사**(史) history; 《연대사》 annals; chronicles. ¶ 한국 문학사 A History of Korean Literature (사서) / 현대〔근세, 중세, 고대〕사 contemporary〔modern, medieval, ancient〕 history.

-**사**(寺) a temple. ¶ 봉원사 the Pongwon Temple.

**사가**(史家) a historian.

**사가**(私家) a private house〔residence〕; *one's* home.

**사각**(四角) four corners; a square; a rectangular; a quadrilateral. ¶ ~의 square; four-cornered / ~이다 be square〔four-cornered〕.
◉ ~기둥 a square pillar. ~모(자) a (square) college cap; a mortarboard. ~형 〖수학〗 a quadrilateral; a tetragon; a quadrangle; 《미》 a trapezium (*pl.* ~s, -zia): ~형의 quadrilateral; tetragonal / 정~형 a square; a regular tetragon.

**사각**(死角) 《사격의》 a dead angle; dead ground〔space〕; 《자동차 운전시의》 a blind spot. ¶ ~에 들다 be in the dead angle〔ground〕; be in *one's* blind spot.

**사각**(射角) an angle of fire; an elevation.

**사각**(斜角) 〖수학〗 an oblique angle. ⇨ 빗각.

**사각**(寫角) 〖사진〗 a camera angle. = 카메라 앵글.

**사각거리다** crunch; be crisp〔crunchy〕 (to the teeth); eat crisp. ¶ 이 사과는 사각거린다 This apple is crisp to eat.

**사각사각** with a crunch; crisply. ¶ 무를 ~ 먹다 crunch a radish.

**사갈**(蛇蝎) 《뱀과 전갈》 snakes and scorpions; 《사람》 a malignant person. ¶ ~시(視)하다 hate; abominate 《*a person*》 like a serpent〔viper〕; hate 《*a person*》 like poison; detest; abhor.

**사감**(私憾) a personal spite〔grudge, resentment〕; a bitter feeling; malice. ¶ ~을 품다 bear〔have, hold, nurse〕 a grudge against 《*a person*》; have a rancor against 《*a person*》 / 그 사람에게는 아무 ~도 없네 I have no resentment against him.

**사감**(舍監) 《남자》 a dormitory inspector〔superintendent, dean〕; the supervisor of a dormitory; 《영》 a housemaster; 《여자》 a housemistress; a housemother.

**사개** ① 〖건축〗 a dovetail. ¶ ~를 물리다 (make a) dovetail. ② 《상자의》 the dovetailing on the four corners of a box. ◉ ～다리 legs on the corners of a box 〔chest〕. ～맞춤 a dovetail joint. ～통 a dovetail at the top of a pillar.

**사갱**(斜坑) 《광산의》 an inclined shaft.

**사거**(死去) death; decease; demise; passing. ～하다 die; decease; pass away.

**사거리**(四―) a crossroads. ＝네거리.

**사거리**(射距離) ＝사정(射程).

**사건**(事件) 《일어난 일》 an event; an occurrence; a happening; 《사변》 an incident; 《사고》 an accident; 《문제》 a matter; an affair; 《소송의》 a (legal) case; 《음모》 a plot; 《말썽》 complications; a trouble; 《추문》 a scandal.

> 용법 **event** 어떤 뚜렷한 원인에 의해 일어나는 중요하고 주목할 만한 일, 특히 역사상으로 기록될 수 있는 사건. **incident** 커다란 사건에 부수되어 일어나는 자질구레한 사건. **accident** 돌발적으로 일어나는 불의의 사건, 사고 등. **matter** 문제가 되는 일. **affair** 특정한 사람 또는 사항에 관련되어 일어나는 일, 즉 연애 사건 따위. **case** 법률적 또는 범죄 따위의 사건에 쓰임.

¶ 인류 역사상 획기적 ～들 the epoch-making events in the history of mankind / 사기〔살인〕～ a fraud 〔murder〕 case / 연애 ～ a love affair / ～을 떠맡다 take up a case in hand / ～을 검찰에 송치하다 send a case to the public prosecutor's office / ～을 은폐하다 cover 〔hush〕 up the scandal / 이상한 ～이 일어나다 something strange occurs 〔happens〕/ 그 ～에 관계하다 have a hand in the affair / 경찰은 그 ～을 수사 중에 있다 The police are working on the case. / 그 ～은 어떻게 전개될까 How will the matter develop? / 그 ～은 미궁에 빠졌다 The case has been wrapped in mystery. / 그는 수뢰 ～에 관련된 혐의로 체포되었다 He was arrested for being concerned with the bribery case. / 독립 선언의 서명은 역사상 중대 ～이었다 The signing of the Declaration of Independence was an important historical event. ◉ ～기자 a news reporter on the police beat. ～전모 the whole picture of the incident.

**사격**(射擊) firing; shooting; gunshot; fire. ～하다 shoot; fire at 《*a person*》; fire on 《a fortress》. ¶ ～의 명수 a skillful 〔good〕 marksman; an expert 〔a crack〕 shot / ～을 잘하다 be skilled at shooting; shoot well; be a good shot / ～을 개시하다 start firing; open fire 《on》. ◉ ～교관 a shooting 〔gun〕 instructor. ～교련 rifle drill. ～대회 a shooting match 〔contest〕; a rifle meeting. ～술 marksmanship: ～술 예비 훈련 preliminary rifle instruction (생략 P.R.I.). ～신호 a shooting signal. ～연습 field firing (대포의); shooting 〔target〕 practice. ～장 a rifle range 〔ground〕; a shooting 〔firing〕 range; a shooting gallery (옥내의): 태능 국제 ～장 the T'aenŭng international shooting range. ～지휘 fire direction 〔control〕. 한국～연맹 the Korea Shooting Federation (생략 KSF).

**사견**(私見) *one's* personal 〔private〕 opinion 〔views〕; *one's* point of view. ¶ ～으로는 to my thinking 〔mind〕; in my (personal) opinion 〔view〕/ 이것은 내 ～에 지나지 않는다 This is only my personal 〔private〕 opinion. / 감히 ～을 말씀드리겠습니다 Let me give my humble opinion.

**사견**(邪見) a wrong idea 〔view〕; heretical opinions.

**사경**(四更) 1-3 o'clock a.m.; the small hours (of the morning). ◉ ～추(니) an early cock (crowing).

**사경**(死境) a deadly situation; the brink of death; 《궁경》 miserable circumstances; a sad plight; hard lines; a deadly pass. ¶ ～에 처하다 be at the point of death; 《궁경》 be placed in a sad plight; fall into great straits / ～을 헤매다 hover 〔hang〕 between life and death / ～을 벗어나다 「be saved 〔escape〕 from the jaws of death; 《궁경》 get out of a sad plight.

**사경제**(私經濟) 〖경제〗 private 〔individual〕 economy.

**사경회**(査經會) 〖기독교〗 a Bible class.

**사계**(四季) 《사시》 the four seasons; 《사계삭》 the last month of each season.

**사계**(射界) a field 〔zone〕 of (gun)fire.

**사계**(斯界) this field 〔world〕; the specific field; the line 《of business》; this circle. ¶ ～의 권위자 an authority 「on the subject 〔in the particular field〕.

**사고**(社告) an announcement 〔a public notice〕 《of a firm》.

**사고**(事故) ① 《뜻밖의 사건》 an accident; an incident; an untoward event; 《고장》 a breakdown; a hitch; trouble. ¶ 음주 운전 ～ a "drunken driver" accident / 철도 건널목 ～ an accident

ㅅ

at a train crossing / ～를 내기 쉬운 운전자 an accident-prone driver / 어떤 뜻밖의 ～로 말미암아 in certain contingencies / ～가 나다 an accident happens / ～를 일으키다 cause 〔bring about, give rise to〕 an accident; run into 〔have some〕 trouble / ～를 방지하다〔줄이다〕 prevent 〔reduce〕 accidents / ～ 없이 끝나다 go off without mishap 〔a hitch〕 / 위험한 곳—～다발 지역 《게시》 Dangerous area: frequent accidents. / ～란 나기 쉬운 것이다 Accidents will happen. / ～는 운전 부주의가 원인이었다 The accident was due to careless driving. / 그는 귀가 중에 ～를 당했다 He had 〔met with〕 an accident on his way home. / 그 ～로 30명이 죽었다〔부상당했다〕 Thirty persons were 「killed 〔injured〕 in the accident.

② 《사정·이유》 reasons; circumstances. ¶ 부득이한 ～로 from 〔owing to〕 unavoidable circumstances / 무슨 ～로 오지 못했습니까 What kept you from coming?

◉ ～방지대책 a measure to prevent accidents. ～방지 운동 a "Safety First" movement. ～빈발〔다발〕 지점 a high=accident-frequency location 〔spot〕; a 〔an accident〕 black spot. ～사(死) an accidental death; a death by accident.

**사고**(思考) thinking; thought; consideration. ～하다 think; consider; regard 《*a thing* as》; conceive; intellectualize. ◉ ～력 thinking faculty 〔power〕; the power of thought: 나이가 들수록 ～력이 떨어진다고는 믿지 않는다 I don't believe that our thinking power weakens as we grow old. ～방식 *one's* way of thinking: 구태의연한 ～방식 obsolete way of thinking. ～작용〔과정〕 thought process; process of thinking. ～장애 『의학』 thinking disturbance. 수평〔수직〕～ lateral 〔vertical〕 thinking.

**사고무친**(四顧無親) ～하다 be orphaned and friendless; have no relative to turn to; stand alone and helpless.

**사공**(沙工) a boatman; a waterman; a ferryman (나룻배의). ¶ ～이 많으면 배가 산으로 올라간다 《속담》 Too many cooks spoil the broth 〔soup〕.

**사과**(沙果) an apple. ¶ ～를 깎다 pare 〔peel〕 an apple / 이 ～는 속이 썩었다 This apple is rotten at the core. / ～ 하나 깎아 주시오 Will you please pare an apple for me? ◉ ～나무 an apple tree. ～식초 cider vinegar. ～주 apple wine; cider (★ 우리 나라에서 말하는 사이다(soda pop)와는 다름). ～주스 apple juice. ～참외 a kind of cantaloup(e). ～화채 a punch made of chopped apple soaked in honey.

**사과**(謝過) an apology 《for》; pardon; an excuse. ～하다 apologize; make an apology 〔excuse〕 《for》; beg 〔ask〕 pardon 《of *a person*》; ask 〔beg〕 《*a person's*》 pardon; beg 《*a person's*》 forgiveness 《for》; offer 《*a person*》 an apology; express *one's* regret 《for》.

¶ ～ 편지 a letter of apology / ～를 요구하다 demand an apology 《from》 / ～를 받아들이다 accept an apology / 공개 ～하다 openly apologize 《to》 / 진심으로 ～하다 offer *one's* sincere apology 《for》; tender a heartfelt apology 《for》; make a humble apology 《for》 / 부주의〔무례〕를 ～하다 apologize to 《*a person*》 for *one's* carelessness 〔rudeness〕 / 무릎을 꿇고 ～하다 beg *a person's* pardon on *one's* knees / 남을 대신해서 ～하다 intercede with 《*a person*》 for 〔in behalf of〕 another / 무어라 ～드려야 할지 모르겠군요 I do not know what excuse to offer. *or* I have no words to apologize to you. / 자네에게 ～하지 않으면 안 되겠네 I owe you an apology. / 거듭 ～드립니다 I ask you a thousand pardons 〔apologies〕. / ～할 것 없다 No apology is necessary. / ～할 사람은 네가 아니라 나다 It is not you but I that have to apologize. / 일본 천황은 제2차 세계 대전 중 일본군에 의해 저질러진 고통에 대해 애석하게 여긴다고 말했으나, 많은 중국인들이 바라던 ～는 하지 않았다 The Japanese emperor said (that) he deplored the suffering caused by Imperial troops during World War Ⅱ, but he didn't make the apology sought by many Chinese. ◉ ～문〔장〕 《issue》 an apology statement; a letter of apology; a written apology.

**사관**(士官) an 〔a commissioned〕 officer. ◉ ～생도 a military cadet (육군); a midshipman (해군); an aviation cadet (공군). ～실 the officers' quarters; a wardroom (해군). ～학교 the Military Academy; 《간부 후보생의》 an officers' training school (생략 O.T.S.). ～후보생 an officers' candidate; a cadet (officer).

**사관**(史官) 『역사』 a historiographer; a 「chronicler.

**사관**(史觀) a historical view; a view 〔concept〕 of history.

**사광**(砂鑛) a placer (mine); an alluvial gold mine. ◉ ～권 a placer mining right. ～업 placer mining.

**사교**(邪敎) heresy; a false 〔heretical, perverse〕 religion 〔creed〕; evil doctrines; corrupt teaching; paganism; heathenism. ¶ ～의 pagan. ◉ ～도 a heretic; a pagan; a heathen.

**사교**(社交) social intercourse; social relationships 〔contacts〕; society; social life. ¶ ～상의 예의 social etiquette / ～적인〔상의〕 social; sociable; 《be》 outgoing / ～적이다〔적이 아니다〕 be sociable 〔unsociable〕; be a good 〔bad〕 mixer 《미》 / ～를 좋아하다 be fond of society 〔mixing with people〕; enjoy people's society / 그것은 ～상 부득이한 일이다 That's unavoidable in social life. / 그는 ～적인 인사로 그리 말한 것 뿐이었다 He said so only to be polite. / 그는 매우 ～적이지 못하다 He is very unsociable.
◉ ～가 a sociable person; a good mixer 《구어》; a society man 〔woman〕 (사교계에서 활약 중인 사람): 그는 제법 ～가답다 He is quite a sociable man. ～단체 a social organization 〔group〕. ～댄스 a social 〔ballroom〕 dance: ～댄스를 연습하다〔배우다〕 practice 〔take lessons in〕 social dancing / ～댄스를 추다 dance at a party. ～란 a society column. ～술 the art of social inter-

---

참고 **사과·사죄에 관한 표현들**

사죄·사과에 관한 영어 표현으로 흔히 쓰이는 대표적인 말은 Excuse me. / Sorry. / I am sorry. / Pardon me. / Please accept my (sincere) apology. 등 참으로 다양하다. 이것들을 「실례합니다」, 「미안〔죄송〕합니다」, 「용서를 빕니다」 따위의 하나로 고정시켜서 해석하거나 사용한다면 엉뚱한 오해가 생길 가능성이 많다. 동서양간의 생활 관습·사고 방식이 서로 다르기 때문이다.

1. 자신에게 조그마한 과실이 있어서 「미안〔죄송〕합니다」, 「실례했습니다」라고 사과할 때는 보통, Excuse me. / I am sorry. / Pardon me. 등이 쓰인다. 《미》에서는 Excuse me.가 흔히 쓰이고, I'm sorry.는 사과의 정도가 약간 더 깊은 느낌을 주려고 할 때 쓰이지만, 《영》에서는 I'm sorry.가 더 일반적이다. 흔히 I'm을 생략하고 Sorry.라고 하는 경우도 많다. Pardon me.는 《영》《미》 모두 자주 쓰이는데, 이것은 앞의 두 경우보다 사과의 정도가 더 강한 느낌을 주는 표현이다.

2. 자신에게 실수나 과오가 없더라도 상대방에게 번거로움을 끼치게 될 때, 예를 들면 대화 중에 잠시 자리를 떠야 할 때, 상대의 앞을 지나가야 할 때, 모르는 사람에게 질문을 할 때 따위에 쓰이는 말로, 「실례합니다」 「실례입니다마는…」에 해당되는 영어 표현으로 Excuse me. / Pardon me.가 《영》《미》 모두 가장 일반적이다. 사과를 하는 쪽이 복수인 경우는 Excuse us. 또, 모자를 썼든가 복장 따위로 미안하다고 할 경우는 Please excuse my hat 〔appearance〕.로 표현한다.

3. 낱말에 주어지는 강세에 따라서도 사과·사죄의 표현은 그 뜻이 달라진다. 특히 Excúse me. / Párdon me.라고 발음하면 가벼운 인사치레의 사과가 되지만, Excúse mé. / Párdon mé. 처럼 me에도 강세를 주어 말하면 사과의 뜻이 강해진다. 또 상대의 사과를 받고 나서 「저도 실례를 한 걸요. 뭘.」이라고 대답할 경우도 me에 강세를 주게 된다.

4. 「…을 사과 드립니다」란 뜻의 표현
- 「저의 경솔함을 사과드립니다」 Please excuse (me for) my carelessness.
- 「허락도 없이 당신 편지를 읽은 것을 사과드립니다」 I must apologize (to you) for having read the letter without your permission.
- 「진심으로 사과를 드립니다」 Please accept my sincere apology.
- 「혹시 당신에게 거슬리는 말을 했다면 사과드립니다」 I apologize if I said something that offended you.
- 「저의 경솔한 발언을 매우 유감으로 여기고 있습니다」 I deeply regret my careless remarks.

5. 사과에 대한 응답의 몇가지 예
- 「앗, 방해해서 미안합니다」—「괜찮아요」 "Oh, sorry to disturb you."—"That's all right." or "That's OK."
- 「앗, 저런, 안 다쳤어요」—「아니, 괜찮아요」 "Oh, no! Did I hurt you?"—"No, I'm okay."
- 「미안합니다」—「괜찮아요〔문제될 것 없어요〕」 "I'm sorry."—"No problem."
- 「실례하겠습니다」—「예, 어서 …하세요」 "Excuse me."—"Certainly." (공손한 표현).

course. ～클럽 a social club: ～ 클럽의 회원 a clubman; a clubwoman.

**사교계**(社交界) fashionable society; a fashionable world; society circles. ¶ ～의 명사 a figure in society; a prominent person in the fashionable world; a socialite / ～의 사람들 society people; club people《미》/ ～의 여왕 a society beauty; a queen 〔belle〕 of society / ～의 중심 인물 a society leader; a socialite / ～에 나가다 go 〔get〕 into society; come out; make *one's* debut into society.

**사교성**(社交性) sociality; sociability. ¶ ～이 있다 be sociable; be a good mixer《미》/ ～이 없다 be unsociable; lack sociability; be a bad mixer《미》.

**사구**(四球) 〖야구〗 a base on balls.

**사구**(死球) a hit by pitch. = 데드볼.

**사구**(砂丘) 〖지질〗 a sand dune 〔pile〕; a down《고어》; a sand hill. ◉ ～림(林) a forest on a sand dune. 「-li).

**사구체**(絲球體) 〖생물〗 a glomerulus (*pl.*

**사군자**(士君子) a gentleman; a man of honor; a scholar; the *literati* (L.).

**사군자**(四君子) 〖미술〗 the Four Gracious Plants (*i.e.* plum, orchid, chrysanthemum and bamboo); the four gentlemanly plants.

**사권**(私權) 〖법〗 a private right.

**사귀**(邪鬼) a devil; an imp; an evil spirit; a demon.

**사귀다** 《알게 되다》 get 〔become〕 acquainted《with》; get to know *a person;* make *a person's* acquaintance; make friends《with》; hold intercourse with; mix 〔mingle〕 with. ¶ 친구를 ～ make a friend / 나쁜 사람들과 ～ keep bad company; hang around with the wrong sort / 친하게 ～ be on intimate terms with; form a close friendship with; be great friends with / 대등하게 ～ associate《with *a person*》 on equal terms / 아무와 사귀기를 꺼려하다 be unsociable; prefer *one's* own company / 사귀기 어렵다 be hard to get acquainted with / 사람은 그가 사귀는 친구를 보면 알 수 있다 A man is known by the company he keeps.

**사귐성**(一性) sociability; affinity; affability; companionableness. ¶ ～ 있는 〔없는〕 사람 a person who is easy 〔hard〕 to get along 〔on〕 with; a good 〔bad〕 mixer《미》; a sociable 〔an unsociable〕 person.

**사그라뜨리다** collapse; resolve; make 《a boil》 subside; let《*a thing*》 wither. ¶ 뾰루지를 ～ make a boil subside 〔go down〕; resolve a boil.

**사그라지다** go down; subside; wither; recede; 《썩어서》 decompose; 《녹아서》 melt away; 《종기 따위가》 resolve; be resolved. ¶ 기운이 ～ lose *one's* spirit; lose heart 〔courage〕; get down in the dumps / 불이 ～ the fire 「burns low 〔sinks〕 / 종기가 사그라졌다 The tumor was resolved. 「thing.

**사그랑이** a worn-out 〔threadbare〕

**사그랑주머니** a thing which looks good but is really worn out; a gimcrack; a trumpery; a specious bargain.

**사극**(史劇) a historical drama 〔play〕.

**사근사근하다** ① 《성품이》 (be) docile; compliant; submissive; obedient; sweet and gentle; amiable; agreeable; pleasant; affable. ¶ 사근사근한 사람 an affable person / 사근사근한 여자 a docile woman / 사근사근하게 amiably; affably; pleasantly / 사근사근하게 대하다 make *oneself* agreeable to《*one's* guest》. ② 《입에》 be crisp to 「the teeth 〔eat〕; be fresh. ¶ 이 사과는 ～ This apple is crisp to eat.

**사글세**(一貰) monthly rent 〔rental〕. ¶ 우리는 5만원의 ～를 내고 있다 We pay fifty thousand won for the house every month. / 집주인은 ～를 2만원 올렸다 The landlord has just raised my rent by twenty thousand won a month. ◉ ～방 a rented room. 사글셋집 a rented house.

**사금**(砂金) alluvial 〔placer〕 gold; gold dust. ¶ ～을 채취하다 《모래를 일어》 wash for gold; 《바닥에 구멍 뚫은 냄비로 선광하여》 pan gold.
◉ ～채취 alluvial 〔placer〕 mining: ～채취권 a placer mining right / ～채취선 a placer (gold) mining boat. 「債).

**사금융**(私金融) private loan. ⇨ 사채(私

**사금파리** a potsherd; a crock; chips; a piece 〔fragment〕 of broken china or porcelain. ¶ ～에 손을 베다 cut *one's* hand on a broken piece of porcelain 〔chinaware〕.

**사기**(士氣) morale; fighting 〔martial〕 spirit. ¶ ～ 왕성하다 have high morale; be full of fighting spirit / ～가 떨어지다 be 〔become〕 demoralized / ～를 떨어뜨리다 depress 〔sap〕 the morale 《of the troops》; demoralize 《an army》 / ～를 북돋우다 raise 〔stiffen, stir up〕 the morale 《of the men》; enhance 〔inspire〕 《*a person's*》 spirit;

《사물이》 have an inspiring effect on the morale; give a stimulus to the fighting spirit 《of the men》 / ~에 영향을 주다 affect the morale / 연패로 선수들의 ~는 떨어졌다 The players' morale sagged 〔flagged〕 owing to their successive defeats. / 그 전승의 소식으로 군대의 ~가 올라갔다 Thanks to the news of the victory the morale of the army was greatly raised. 「historical book 〔work〕.

**사기**(史記) a history; a chronicle; a

**사기**(死期) the time 〔hour〕 of *one's* death; *one's* last hour; *one's* time 〔end〕. ¶ ~에 접어들다 be on *one's* deathbed.

**사기**(邪氣) ① 《악의》 malice; wickedness. ② 《독기》 a miasma (늪의); poison; malarial 〔poisonous〕 air; pestilent 〔noxious〕 vapor; an evil influence. ¶ ~를 물리치다 purge 〔clear away〕 noxious vapor; exorcise an evil influence.

**사기**(沙器) porcelain; china(ware); crockery; earthenware; pottery.

◉ ~그릇 ＝사기(沙器). ~전(廛) a china store 〔shop〕; a china(ware) shop. ~접시 porcelain 〔china〕 dishes.

**사기**(社旗) the flag of a company; 《상선의》 a house flag.

**사기**(詐欺) (a) fraud; fraudulence; a swindle; (an) imposture; a trick; trickery. ~하다 commit a fraud 《on》; 《돈을》 swindle 《money out of *a person*》; practice 〔perpetrate〕 a swindle 《on》; defraud 《*a person* of *his* money》. ¶ 670만 달러의 무기 거래 ~ the $6.7 million arms deal fraud / 교묘한 ~ very clever 〔deliberated〕 fraud / 결혼~ a marriage fraud / 법률상의 ~ legal fraud / ~를 당하다 get 〔be〕 swindled; fall a victim to fraud / 그는 나한테서 백만원을 ~했다 He swindled one million won out of me. / 그는 ~를 당해 전재산을 잃었다 He was swindled out of his whole fortune.

◉ ~꾼 a swindler; a defrauder; an impostor; a trickster; a confidence 〔con 《구어》〕 man: 그 노인은 ~꾼에 걸려들어 저금한 모든 돈을 잃었다 The old man lost all his savings to a swindler. ~도박 fraudulent gambling. ~수단 fraudulent means; jugglery; trickery. ~죄 〖법〗 fraud; false pretenses: ~죄로 걸리다 be accused of fraud. ~취재(取財) 〖법〗 swindling: ~취재를 하다 swindle 〔cheat〕 《*a person*》 out of *his* property; obtain 《*another's*》 property by fraud. ~투표 fraudulent voting. ~행위 (an) imposture; fraudulent practices. ~혐의자 a fraudulence suspect.

**사기업**(私企業) 〖경제〗 an individual enterprise; a private(ly owned) company. 「days.

**사나나달** three or four 〔four or five〕

**사나이** a man. ⇨ 사내. ¶ ~ 중의 ~ a man among men.

**사날** 《삼사일》 three or four days; a few days; several days.

**사납금**(社納金) 《택시 기사의》 money which taxi drivers have to turn over to the company out of their daily earning.

**사납다** ① 《성질 등이》 (be) rough; wild; harsh; violent; rude; fierce; ferocious. ¶ 사납게 fiercely; roughly; violently; wildly; rudely; outrageously / 사나운 눈으로 with a fierce look; with glaring eyes / 사나운 개〔짐승〕 a fierce dog 〔animal〕 / 사나운 사람 a rowdy fellow; a roughneck 《미》; a savage / 말투가 ~ use harsh language; be rough in speech / 성질이 ~ have a violent temper / 사납게 덤벼들다 fly out 《at, against》.

② 《나쁘다》 (*a*) 《운수·조짐 등이》 (be) unlucky; bad; ill; evil. ¶ 수 사나운 일 ill luck; an occurrence of evil portent / 운수가 ~ be unlucky; have ill luck. (*b*) 《날씨 등이》 (be) rough; violent; fierce; stormy. ¶ 사나운 물결 stormy 〔rough〕 seas; raging waves / 사납게 부는 바람 a raging 〔fierce〕 wind. (*c*) 《각박하다》 (be) hard; harsh; unkind; unfeeling. ¶ 인심이 ~ be unkind 〔unsympathetic〕; be harsh 〔bitter〕 / 인심 사나운 세상이로다 What a hard 〔tough〕 world we live in!

**사낭**(砂囊) ① 《모래주머니》 a sandbag; 〖군사〗 an earth bag. ② 〖조류〗 a gizzard.

**사내** ① 《남자》 a man; a male; 《구어》 a fellow; a guy. ¶ ~ 대장부 a man; a manly man / ~ 아이 a boy; 《아기》 a baby boy; a boy baby / ~다운 ~ a manly man; a man's man; a he-man / 멋진 ~ a nice fellow 〔guy〕 / ~ 중의 ~ a man among men / ~같은 mannish 《woman》 / ~답지 못한 unmanly / ~답게 굴다 be a man; behave 〔act〕 like a man / ~답게 싸우다 fight in a manly way / 아기는 ~아인가

요 계집아인가요 Is the baby a boy or a girl? / 그는 ~답지 못한 녀석이군 He's not much of a man, is he? ② 《남편》 a husband; *one's* man. ③ 《정부》 a lover; a paramour.

**사내**(社內) ¶ ~의〔에〕 in the firm 〔company〕/ ~에서 within *one's* 〔the〕 firm 〔office, company〕/ 그는 ~에서 평판이 좋다 He has a good reputation 「in the office 〔at work〕. / 그는 ~에서 승진이 가장 빨랐다 He got the quickest promotion in his company. / 그것은 ~에서는 공공연한 비밀이다 It's an open secret in the office. / 미스 홍은 ~에서 가장 예쁘다 Miss Hong is the most charming girl in our company 〔office〕. ◉ ~결혼 an intra-office marriage; a marriage between two employees of the company. ~보(報) a house journal 〔organ〕; an in-house bulletin 〔newspaper〕. ~부채 internal liabilities. ~연수 in-house training. ~유보 internal reserves. ~일동 all the staff of a company: ~일동을 대표하여 in the name of the staff. ~전화 an interoffice telephone. ~조사 an in-house survey.

**사내끼** a landing net; a scoop 〔dip〕 net. ¶ ~로 떠내다 scoop 《fish》 with a landing net.

**사냥** 《조수의》 hunting; shooting (새의); a hunt; a chase. ~하다 hunt; shoot. ¶ 호랑이〔맹수〕~ tiger 〔big game〕 hunting / ~하러 가다 go hunting 〔shooting〕; go on a hunting expedition 〔trip〕/ 여우〔토끼〕를 ~하다 hunt the fox 〔hare〕/ 그는 ~을 아주 잘한다 He is a very good hunter. / 4월부터 10월까지는 ~이 금지된다 Hunting 〔Game〕 is preserved from April to October. / 본 사찰 경내에서 ~을 금함 《게시》 Shooting (is) prohibited within the precincts of the temple.
◉ ~금지 《금렵》 prohibition of hunting: ~금지 기간 a closed season / ~금지 구역 a (game) preserve 〔reserve〕; a 《bird, wildlife》 sanctuary. ~꾼 a hunter; a huntsman; a huntress (여자); a sportsman. ~철 the hunting 〔shooting〕 season; an open season. ~총 a hunting gun; a game rifle. ~터 a hunting ground 〔field〕.

**사냥감** game; a bag; quarry; the spoils of the chase. ¶ ~이 많은 곳 a place rich in game / ~이 많다〔적다〕 have plenty of 〔do not have much〕 game; have a good 〔poor〕 bag.

**사냥개** a gundog; a hunting dog; a hound. ¶ (여우사냥시) ~ 떼 a pack of hounds / ~를 풀어주다 slip a hound from the leash; unleash 〔let loose〕 a gundog / 포인터와 세터는 ~로 키운다 Pointers and setters are kept for hunting 〔shooting〕. ◉ ~자리 〖천문〗 the Hunting Dogs; Canes Venatici.

**사냥질** hunting; a hunt. ⇨ 사냥.

**사념**(邪念) a vicious 〔an evil〕 mind; an evil intention; a wicked 〔an evil, a depraved〕 thought. ¶ ~이 없다 have no depraved thoughts / ~을 버리다 free *oneself* of evil thoughts.

**사념**(思念) thought. = 사려(思慮).

**사농공상**(士農工商) the traditional Four Classes of society (*i.e.* aristocrats, farmers, artisans and tradesmen).

**사느랗다** (be) cool; cold; chill(y). ¶ 사느랗게 되다 get cold; cool down 〔off〕.

**사다** ① 《돈을 주고》 (***a***) 《물품을》 buy; purchase; get; take. ¶ 살 사람 a buyer; a purchaser / 싸게〔비싸게〕 ~ buy cheap 〔for a high price〕; make a good 〔bad〕 bargain / 만원에 ~ buy 〔get〕 《*a thing*》 at 〔for〕 ten thousand won; pay 〔give〕 ten thousand won for 《*a thing*》/ 한 다스〔개〕 천원에 ~ buy 《*something*》 at one thousand won a dozen 〔apiece〕/ 만원에 사겠다고 하다 offer 《*a person*》 10,000 won for 《*a thing*》/ 소매〔도매〕로 ~ buy 《*something*》 retail 〔wholesale〕/ 외상〔현금〕으로 ~ buy 《*a thing*》 on credit 〔for cash〕/ 물건 사러 가다 go (out) shopping 〔marketing〕/ 덮어놓고 물건을 ~ buy a pig in a poke / 사주다 buy 〔get〕 《*something*》 for 《*a person*》/ 돈으로 사랑을 살 수는 없다 Money cannot buy love. / 500만원으로는 좋은 차를 살 수 없다 You cannot get a good car for five million won. / 나는 그녀에게 반지를 사주었다 I bought her a ring. *or* I bought a ring for her. (***b***) 《사람을》 engage; employ; take on 《workers》; hire. ¶ 사람을 ~ hire 〔engage〕 a person.
② 《곡식을》 sell 《grain》 in exchange for money. ¶ 쌀을 ~ sell rice 《in the market》.
③ 《초래하다》 incur; invite; provoke; evoke 《a grievance from *a person*》. ¶ 노여움을 ~ offend 《*a person*》; incur 〔provoke〕 《*a person's*》 anger; provoke 《*a person*》/ 동정을 ~ draw 〔arouse, win〕 《*a person's*》 sympathy / 미움을 ~ incur hatred / (윗사람의) 역

정을 ～ get on the wrong side of《a senior》; incur《*one's* superior's》displeasure / 의심을 ～ bring suspicion upon *oneself* / 환심을 ～ curry favor with《*a person*》; win《*a person's*》favor / 그의 원한을 살 일을 한 적이 없다 I certainly haven't done anything to earn〔incur〕his enmity. / 사서 고생이군 You are making yourself miserable gratuitously, aren't you?
④《인정하다》recognize; appreciate. ¶ 높이 ～ think highly〔well〕of; have a good〔high〕opinion of; hold in high regard / 사장은 그녀를 비서로서 높이 사고 있다 The president thinks highly of her as a secretary.

**사다리** a ladder. ¶ ～의 단 a rung; a round / 고가 ～ (소방차의) an extension〔aerial〕ladder / 비상 ～ an emergency〔a fire〕ladder / 줄～ a rope ladder / ～를 놓다 place〔rest〕a ladder《against the wall》/ ～를 올라가다 climb〔go〕up a ladder / ～를 내려가다 climb〔come〕down a ladder / 내가 ～에 올라 있는 동안 ～를 잡아줘 Steady the ladder while I'm on it.
◉ ～꼴〖수학〗a trapezoid; a trapezium《영》: ～꼴 대형 an echelon formation (군대 편성). ～차 a (hook and) ladder truck; an aerial ladder truck. ～타기《곡예》acrobatic performances on a ladder: ～타기 곡예사 an acrobatic performer on a ladder.

**사다새**〖조류〗a pelican.

**사닥다리** ladder. ⇨ 사다리.

**사단**(社團) a corporation; an association. ◉ ～법인〖법〗a corporate juridical person; a corporation (aggregate); an incorporated body〔association〕.

**사단**(事端) the origin〔cause〕of an affair; (the cause of ) a trouble; the inception; the beginning; an incident. ¶ ～을 일으키다 stir up troubles; give rise to complications.

**사단**(師團)〖군사〗a〔an army〕division. ¶ ～의 divisional / 기갑 ～ an armored division / ～을 편성하다 organize a division / 완전 편성의 제1～ the First Division at full strength. ◉ ～사령부 the division(al) headquarters (생략 D.H.Q.). ～장 a division(al) commander: ～장으로 임명하다 put《a general》over a division; appoint《a general》to take the command of a division.

**사담**(私談) a private conversation〔talk〕; a confidential talk. ～하다 talk privately《with》; have a private〔confidential〕talk with《*a person*》. ¶ ～을 엿듣다 overhear a private talk.

**사당**(私黨) a private party; a faction; 《음모의》a cabal; 《비밀 결사의》a junto.

**사당**(祠堂) an ancestral tablet hall; a sanctuary; a (household) shrine; an ancestral shrine. ¶ ～에 모시다 enshrine; dedicate a shrine to an ancestral mortuary tablet / ～에 제사드리다 offer worship at the ancestral shrine. ◉ ～치레 embellishment of a household shrine; ostentation; display.

**사대**(私大)《사립대학》a private university〔college〕.

**사대**(事大) submission〔subserviency〕to the stronger; worship of the powerful. ～하다 become a toady〔flunk(e)y〕; worship〔serve〕the powerful. ◉ ～근성 slavish submission to power. ～당 a toady〔flunk(e)y〕party; trucklers. ～주의〔사상〕flunkyism; toadyism; worship of the powerful: ～주의자 a truckler; a toady; a flunk(e)y.

**사대부**(士大夫) an illustrious official; a man of noble〔high〕birth; the gentry [총칭].

**사대육신**(四大六身) flesh and bones (of a human being); the whole body.

**사도**(私道) a private road〔path〕.

**사도**(邪道) ①《못된 길》an evil〔a wrong〕course; evil ways; (a) vice. ¶ ～에 빠지다 go wrong〔astray〕; stray from「the right path〔the path of virtue〕; fall into evil courses / ～로 이끌다 pervert〔mislead〕《*a person*》; lead《*a person*》astray (from the right path). ②《사설(邪說)》a heretical doctrine〔teaching〕; heresy; 《이단》heterodoxy.

**사도**(使徒) an apostle; a disciple. ¶ 십이～ the (Twelve) Apostles (신약의) / 평화의 ～ an apostle of peace / ～의 지위 apostolate. ◉ ～신경 the Apostles' Creed. ～행전 the Acts (of the Apostles).

**사도**(師道) the duty of a teacher; teachers' code.

**사도**(斯道) ①《유교의》Confucian morality. ②《각자의》the subject; the line; the art; the craft; the profession.

**사돈**(査頓) relatives by marriage; a member of the family of *one's* daughter-〔son-〕in-law; in-laws《구어》. ¶ ～의 팔촌 a remote〔distant〕relative (who is as good as an utter stranger) /

～간이 되다 get related by marriage 《to》. ◉ ～댁《사람》 the wife of an in-law; 《집》 an esteemed house 〔family〕 of in-laws. ～집 a house 〔family〕 of in-laws: ～집과 뒷간은 멀어야 한다 《속담》 The house of in-laws, like the toilet, should be located at a distance.

**사동**(使童) an errand 〔office〕 boy; a page (boy); a messenger (boy).

**사동사**(使動詞) 〖문법〗 a causative verb.

**사동치마**(四―) a vertically four-color kite.

**사되다**(私―) (be) (preemptorily) private; be to *one's* private 〔selfish〕 advantage. ¶ 사되게 쓰다 put 〔turn〕 《*a thing*》 to personal 〔private〕 use; use 《*a thing*》 for private 〔*one's* own〕 purposes / 사된 일로 외출하다 go out on personal business.

**사두마차**(四頭馬車) a carriage and four; a coach-and-four; a four-horse coach.

**사들이다** buy (in); purchase; 《가게에서 팔기 위해》 lay in 《a stock》; stock. ¶ 대량으로 ～ make a large purchase of 《rice》 / 겨울 준비로 양식과 연탄을 ～ lay in provisions and briquets for the winter.

**사등분**(四等分) ～하다 divide 《*a thing*》 into quarters; quarter. ¶ 그녀는 케이크를 ～했다 She divided 〔cut〕 the cake into four parts.

**사디스트** 《색정광》 a sadist.

**사디즘** 《학대음란증》 sadism.

**사또** 〖고제도〗 a district magistrate; a lord; 《호칭》 my lord. ¶ 신임 ～ the new lord / ～떠난 뒤에 나팔 분다 《속담》 It's too late now. *or* You came a day after 〔too late for〕 the fair.

**사뜨다** buttonhole; work with buttonhole stitch; work close loop stitch 《around a buttonhole》.

**사라사** [<*saraça* (Port.)] printed cotton; chintz; calico 《미》; print 《영》.

**사라센** ¶ ～(사람)의 Saracen; Saracenic. ◉ ～사람 a Saracen.

**사라쌍수**(沙羅雙樹) 〖불교〗 the four pairs of sal trees that surrounded the Buddha when he entered into Nirvana.

**사라지다** ① 《모습 등이》 disappear; vanish; go out of sight; 《빛·소리가》 fade (out, away); die away 〔off, out〕. ¶ 연기로 ～ vanish into smoke / 연기〔거품〕처럼 ～ vanish like smoke 〔a bubble〕 / 화면에서 ～ go 〔get〕 「out of the picture 〔off the screen〕 / 어둠 속으로 ～ disappear 〔be swallowed up〕 in the darkness / 군중 속으로 ～ be lost in a crowd / 형장의 이슬로 ～ end *one's* life 〔days〕 on the gallows / 이 세상에서 ～ go out of the world / 기차 소리는 차츰 멀리 사라져 갔다 The sound of the train gradually faded 〔died〕 away in the distance. / 그것을 보자 그녀의 얼굴에서 미소가 사라졌다 The smile left her face when she saw it. / 페인트 냄새는 다음날까지도 사라지지 않았다 The smell of the paint still hung about 〔still hadn't gone〕 the next day.

② 《인상·희망 등이》 fade out; die out; vanish; wear off; go (아픔 등이). ¶ 사라지지 않는 인상 an indelible impression / 아픔이 사라졌다 The pain has gone. / 그의 모든 희망이 사라졌다 All his hopes evaporated. / 세월이 가면 모든 슬픔도 사라진다 Time heals all sorrows. / 그 일이 마음에서 사라지지 않는다 I cannot put it out of my mind. *or* It is indelibly impressed on my mind. / 그의 이름은 세인의 기억에서 사라졌다 His name faded from the memory of the world. / 둘째가 태어난 후로 맏이를 잃은 슬픔이 조금씩 사라져 갔다 After the birth of our second child, our grief at the death of our son has gradually faded.

**사람** ① 《인류》 man (★ 보통 단수로 관사가 없음); mankind; human beings; humans. ¶ ～은 죽게 마련이다 Man is mortal. *or* All man must die. / ～은 생각한다는 점에서 동물과 다르다 Human beings differ from animals in that they think. / ～은 만물의 영장이다 Man is the soul of the universe. *or* Man is the lord of all creation.

② 《개인》 a man; a person; an individual; one (아무) (★ 「사람」을 뜻하는 총칭으로 one을 쓰는 경우는 격식차린 표현이며, 구어에서는 대체로 we, you, they, people 따위를 씀. 주어로 one이 쓰인 경우, 문장 안에서는 one's (소유격), one (목적격), oneself (재귀대명사)로 받는 것이 일반적이나, 《미》에서는 his, him, himself로 받는 일이 많음: *One* should do *one's* 〔*his*〕 best). ¶ 어떤 ～ a certain person; some people / 두서너 ～ a few people / 그 ～ that man 〔woman〕; he; she / 서울 ～ a Seoulite; the people of Seoul / 시골 ～ country people / 미국 ～ an American; Americans / 스미스라는 ～ one 〔a〕 Smith; a man named Smith / 민씨네 ～ [단수] a Min; a

member of the Min family; [복수] the Mins; the Min family / ~의 일생 a human life / ~은 정직해야 한다 One 〔We, You〕 should be honest. / 그는 정신이 돈 ~처럼 행동하고 있다 He behaves like one who has gone mad. / 많은 ~이 죽었다 Many lives are lost. / 공원에는 ~이라고는 그림자도 없었다 Not a single soul was to be seen in the park. *or* I did not see a soul in the park. / 테니슨은 언제 ~입니까 About when did Tennyson live? / 그는 상당히 중요한 ~인 것 같다 He seems to be somebody rather important. / 자네와 이야기하고 싶어하는 ~이 있네 There is somebody 〔someone〕 who wants to speak to you. / 야구를 좋아하는 ~도 있고 싫어하는 ~도 있다 Some are fond of baseball and others hate it. / 노력하는 ~은 보답 받으리라 Those who make efforts will be rewarded. / 하고많은 ~ 중 하필이면 왜 그를 뽑았느냐 Why did you elect him of all people? / 그는 부산 ~이다 He is (a man) from Pusan. *or* He comes from Pusan. (★ 출신지를 나타내는 경우의 come은 과거형으로 쓰지 않음.) / 네가 없다고 하던 ~을 만났다 I met the man who you said was away. (★ who 대신에 whom을 쓸 수 없음. 이것은 I met the man.과 You said *he* was away.의 두 문장을 관계대명사로 연결시킨 것으로 he에 해당하는 관계대명사는 주격이어야 함.) / ~은 죽어도 이름은 남는다 A man dies, but his name remains. / ~은 누구나 다 결점이 있다 Every man has his fault(s).
③《세인》people; men; the world; 《남들》others; other people. ¶ ~을 깔보는 태도 an insolent 〔arrogant〕 attitude / ~들 앞에서 울다 cry in the presence of others / ~ 접촉을 피하다 shun society / ~들 위에 서다 lead others; play first fiddle / ~들이 뭐라고 할까 What will people say? *or* I wonder what the world will say. / ~들의 입을 막을 수는 없다 People will talk. / 그 추문은 ~의 입에 오르내렸다 The scandal was on everybody's lips.
④《인재》a man of talent; a capable 〔an able, a fine, a competent〕 man; talent [총칭]; the right man (적임자); 《성격·인물》character; personality; disposition; nature. ¶ ~이 좋은〔나쁜〕 good-〔ill-〕natured / 아인슈타인 같은 ~ an Einstein / 자타가 공인하는 ~ a man of recognized ability; an acknowledged authority / ~을 만들다 make a man of *him;* build a fine character; bring up a useful citizen / 유능한 ~을 구하다 get 〔find〕 a competent person 《for a job》/ ~을 보는 눈이 있다〔없다〕 be a good 〔a poor, no〕 judge of character / 윤군은 어떤 ~입니까 What sort of man is Yun? / 그는 거짓말을 할 ~이 아니다 He is not the sort of man to tell a lie. / 그는 ~이 변했다 He is not what he was. *or* He has become another person. / 공업계에 ~이 없다 The industrial field is short of talent. / 김 교수는 철학계에 이름난 ~이다 Prof. Kim is an acknowledged authority on philosophy. / 사귀는 친구를 보면 그 ~을 알 수 있다 Men are known by the company they keep.
⑤《참사람》a true man. ¶ ~이 아니다 be a brute (of a man); be a monster (of cruelty).
⑥《방문자》a visitor; a caller; a guest; company. ¶ 지금 ~이 와 있다 We have a visitor now. / 우리 집에는 좀처럼 ~이 안 온다 We seldom have visitors. / 오늘 저녁 ~이 찾아오기로 돼 있다 We expect company this evening.
⑦《나》I; me. ¶ ~을 깔보지 마라 Don't look down on me. / ~을 뭘로 생각하는 거야 Who do you think I am?
⑧《막연히》¶ 의사를 부르러 ~을 보내다 send for the doctor / 7시에 ~을 만날 약속이 있다 I「have an appointment 〔must meet someone〕 at seven.
⑨《아내》(my) wife. ¶ 우리 집 ~ my wife.

**사람구실** behaving as a person should; living up to *one's* role. ~하다 behave as a person should 〔as befit *one*〕; live up to *one's* role 〔name〕; do a proper job of it; do *one's* bit; be a man about it. ¶ 그는 ~을 못한다 He is not worth his salt. *or* He doesn't pull his weight. / 그는 작년에 대학을 졸업했는데도 아직 ~을 못한다 He cannot take care of himself though he graduated from college last year.

**사람답다** (be) worthy of the name of man; (be) decent; modest; humane; be truly human. ¶ 사람다운 사람 a true 〔decent〕 man; a man of humane feelings / 사람다운 생활을 하다 live decently; live 〔lead〕 a life worthy of man / 그는 사람답지 않다 He is a depraved character.

**사람됨** 《인품》*one's* character 〔personality〕; 《타고남》*one's* nature 〔disposition〕. ¶ ~이 정직하다 be honest by nature / 이 사실은 그의 ~을 나타낸다 This fact is characteristic of him. *or* This fact shows what he is (like).

**사람멀미** being sick of people. ~하다 feel sick from the jostling of a crowd; get sick from overcrowding.

**사랑**[1] love 《for *a person,* of *a thing*》; 《애정》 affection 《for, to *a person*》; 《연정》 tender passion; 《애착》 attachment 《to, for》. (★ love는 자식·친구·이성·신, 때로는 물건에 대한 사랑. affection은 사람에 대한 지속적인 사랑. attachment는 사람·물건·주의에 대한 애착을 말함). ~하다 love; be fond of; have affection 〔a passion〕 for; be attached to. ¶ ~하는 《…을》 loving; affectionate; 《…이》 beloved; dear (★ 수식받는 명사가 의미상 능동적인 역할을 하고 있을 때는 loving, affectionate를, 수동적일 때는 beloved, dear를 씀: my *loving* son = my son who loves me 「나를 사랑하는 아들」; my *beloved* son = my son who is loved by me = my son whom I love 「내가 사랑하는 아들」). / ~하는 아내 *one's* dear 〔beloved〕 wife / ~하는 처녀 a girl in love; 《마음속으로》 a girl after *one's* heart / ~스러운 lovable; lovely (귀여운); amiable (상냥한) / ~이 없는 loveless; coldhearted / 자식에 대한 부모의 ~ parental love 〔affection〕 for their children / 형제〔부부〕의 ~ fraternal 〔conjugal〕 love / 정신적〔육체적〕 ~ platonic 〔physical〕 love / 맹목적 ~ blind love / 친구의 ~ friendly affection / 이웃간의 ~ neighborly love / 자연〔하느님〕에 대한 ~ love of nature 〔God〕 / 하느님의 ~ divine 〔God's〕 love / 조국에 대한 ~ love for *one's* country / 깊은 ~ deep love / 따뜻한 ~ warm love / 변치 않는 ~ steadfast love / 영원한 ~ eternal 〔everlasting〕 love / 참된 ~ true love / ~없는 결혼 a loveless marriage; marriage without love / ~하고 ~받고 싶은 욕망 a desire to love and be loved in return / 나라〔동포〕를 ~하다 love *one's* country 〔*one's* fellow countryman〕.

사랑의: ~의 결정 《아이》 the fruit of love; a pledge of love / ~의 대상 the object of *one's* love 〔affection〕; a love object / ~의 속삭임 《murmur》 sweet nothings; soft whispers of love / ~의 신 the god of love; 〖그神〗 Eros; 〖로神〗 Cupid / ~의 여신 the goddess of love; 〖그神〗 Aphrodite; 〖로神〗 Venus / ~의 증표 a love token; a token of affection / ~의 보금자리를 꾸미다 build a love nest; make a lovers' sweet home / ~의 손길을 뻗치다 extend a helping hand.

사랑에: ~에 굶주리다 「hanker after 〔starve for〕 love / ~에 보답하다 return 《*a person's*》 love / ~에 빠지다 fall in love 《with》 / 자식 ~에 빠지다 dote on *one's* child / ~에 얽매이다 be enchained by affection.

사랑을: ~을 가장하여 under pretense of love; with false love / ~을 고백하다 declare *one's* love 《to》 / ~을 독차지하다 monopolize 《*a person's*》 love / ~을 바치다 devote *one's* love 《to》 / ~을 받다 be loved 《by》; receive 《*a person's*》 love / ~을 받아들이다 accept 《*a person's*》 love / ~을 얻다 win 《*a person's*》 affection; gain 《*a person's*》 heart; earn 《*a person's*》 love / ~을 잃다 lose 〔forfeit〕 《*a person's*》 love / 영원한 ~을 맹세하다 pledge eternal love; promise to love each other forever.

¶ ~하는 형제 자매들이여 My dear friends! / 그들은 서로 ~하고 있다 They are in love (with each other). *or* They love each other. (★ They are loving…. 이라고는 하지 못함. love, want와 같이 상태를 나타내는 동사는 원칙적으로 진행형을 만들 수 없으므로 「…하고 있다」고 할 때는 현재형으로 나타냄). / 그녀는 이제 ~을 알 만한 나이이다 She is old enough to be susceptible to tender sentiment. / 많이 ~해 주십시오 Please honor me with your friendship. / 자식에 대한 어머니의 ~만큼 강한 것은 없다 Nothing is stronger than mother's love for her child. / 그녀는 그의 ~이 넘치는 편지에 감동되었다 She was moved by his affectionate letter. / 이웃 ~하기를 네 몸과 같이 하라 〖성서〗 Thou shalt love thy neighbor as thyself.

◉ ~노래 an amorous 〔a love〕 song. ~싸움 a quarrel between lovers 〔husband and wife〕; a marital dispute 〔quarrel〕.

**사랑**[2] 《임》 *one's* sweetheart; *one's* darling; *one's* beloved; *one's* lover (남자); *one's* love (여자). ¶ 내 ~아 My love 〔darling〕!

**사랑**(舍廊) a reception room for entertaining (male) guests; the male quarters. ◉ ~놀이 entertaining guests; a party. ~양반 your husband; the husband; the master of a house. ~채 a detached building used for a reception room; the men's part of a house.

**사랑니** 〖해부〗 a wisdom tooth. ¶ ~가

나다 cut *one's* wisdom teeth.

**사랑스럽다** (be) lovely; charming; lovable; pretty; sweet; cute《구어》. ¶ 사랑스럽게 charmingly / 사랑스러운 처녀 a lovely girl / 사랑스러운 어린이 a cute child / 그녀의 사랑스러운 입가에 미소가 떠올랐다 A smile played about her lovely lips.

**사래질하다** winnow; fan.

**사략**(史略) an outline history.

**사레** ¶ ～ 들리다 swallow the wrong way; be choked《by, with》; get something caught in *one's* windpipe / 차를 마시다가 ～ 들렸다 His tea choked him. *or* His tea went down in the wrong way.

**사려**(思慮) thought; prudence; discretion; (good) sense; consideration. ¶ ～ 깊은 thoughtful; prudent; deliberate; discreet; sensible; judicious; well-advised / ～ 깊은 사람 a man of discretion 〔prudence〕; a man of good sense / ～ 없는 thoughtless; indiscreet; imprudent; ill-advised / ～가 부족하다 lack prudence 〔discretion〕.

**사력**(死力) desperate 〔frantic〕 efforts; herculean efforts. ¶ ～을 다하다 make frantic 〔desperate〕 efforts; move heaven and earth《to *do*》; make herculean efforts / ～을 다하여 desperately; to the best of *one's* power 〔ability〕 / ～을 다하여 싸우다 fight desperately 〔a desperate fight〕; fight to the death.

**사련**(邪戀) immoral 〔guilty〕 love《for a married woman》.

**사령**(司令) 〖군사〗 ① 《통솔》 (a position of) command; control; 《사람》 a commandant; a commander. ② 《일직·주번의》 a duty 〔an orderly〕 officer.
◉ ～관 a commander; a commandant; a commanding officer: 최고 ～관 a supreme commander; a commander in chief. ～부 the headquarters (생략 HQ); the command: 전투 ～부 a command post / 총～부 general headquarters (생략 GHQ, G.H.Q.). ～선 《우주선의》 the command module (생략 CM). ～탑 《군함의》 a conning tower; 《비행장의》 a control tower.

**사령**(死靈) the spirit of a dead person; a departed soul; a ghost; 《*a person's*》 manes.

**사령**(辭令) ① 《응대말》 words; wording; diction; language. ¶ 외교 ～ diplomatic language. ② 《관직의》 a government order; an official announcement of appointment; a commission (장교 임관의). ¶ 면직〔임명〕 ～ a notice of dismissal 〔appointment〕 / ～을 내리다 issue a government order / ～을 받다 receive an official announcement of appointment.
◉ ～장 a written 〔letter of〕 appointment; a written order.

**사례**(事例) an instance; an example; a case; 《선례》 a precedent. ¶ 그는 구체적인 ～를 몇가지 제시했다 He gave 〔showed〕 us some concrete examples. / 그의 이론을 뒷받침할 ～는 많다 There are a lot of instances which support his theory.
◉ ～연구 a case study.

**사례**(謝禮) 《감사》 thanks; gratitude; appreciation; acknowledgment; 《보수》 a remuneration; a reward; a recompense; 《의사·변호사 등의》 a fee; an honorarium (연사 등에 대한). ～하다 thank; express *one's* gratitude; tender *one's* thanks; 《보수》 remunerate; recompense; (give a) reward; pay a fee to 《*a person*》. ¶ …의 ～로서 in reward for 《*a person's* services》 / ～의 뜻으로서 「as a 〔in〕 token of *one's* thanks 〔gratitude〕 《for》 / 수고에 대해서 ～하다 reward 《*a person*》 for *his* trouble / ～의 뜻으로 그 의사에게 위스키 한 병을 보냈다 I sent the doctor a bottle of whisky in token of my thanks. ◉ ～금 a reward; a fee; a recompense; an honorarium.

**사로자다** sleep with an uneasy mind; sleep uneasily; have a restless sleep. ¶ 잠을 ～ sleep a troubled sleep.

**사로잠그다** lock halfway; leave half unlocked; bolt 《a door》 insecurely.

**사로잡다** 《생포하다》 catch 〔capture, take〕 《an animal》 alive; capture 《*a person*》; take 《*a person*》 prisoner 〔captive〕; 《매혹하다》 captivate; charm; fascinate; bewitch; enthrall.
¶ 곰을 ～ catch 〔capture〕 a bear alive / 적장을 ～ capture the enemy general / 남자의 마음을 ～ captivate 〔fascinate〕 a man / 사람의 마음을 사로잡는 마력이 있다 possess a magical power of charming people.

**사로잡히다** ① 《생포되다》 be taken 〔caught, seized〕 alive; be captured; be taken 〔led〕 prisoner 〔captive〕. ¶ 적군에게 ～ be captured (alive) by the enemy.
② 《마음이》 (*a*) 《매혹되다》 be fascinated 〔captivated, enraptured〕 《by》; be enslaved 《by》; be a slave to. ¶ 여색〔미모〕에 ～ be captivated by 〔fall a

victim to〕 a woman's charms; lose *one's* heart to 〔be captured by〕 womanly beauty / 아름다운 경치에 ~ be impressed by the picturesque scenery. (***b***) 《격렬한 감정에》 be seized 〔stricken〕 《with》; be carried away by 《*one's* feeling》. ¶ 감정에 ~ be swayed by *one's* feelings / 공포에 ~ be seized with panic 〔fear〕; be struck with terror; fall (a) prey to fear.
③ 《얽매이다》 stick 〔adhere〕 to 《a habit, tradition》; be a slave to; be shackled by 《convention》. ¶ 인습〔돈〕에 ~ be a slave to convention 〔money〕 / 인습에 사로잡히지 않다 be 「free from 〔unhampered by〕 conventions / 형식에 ~ stick to forms; adhere to formality / …한 생각에 ~ be prepossessed with the idea that… / 사람은 자칫 선입견에 사로잡히기 쉽다 Men are likely to be possessed by a preconceived idea.

**사론**(史論) a historical essay 〔treatise〕.

**사론**(私論) *one's* private 〔personal〕 opinion 〔view〕. 「tell; inform.

**사뢰다** say 《to an honored person》;

**사료**(史料) historical material 〔records, sources, documents〕; material for history. ¶ 제2차 세계 대전에 관한 ~를 수집하다 collect historical material with regard to World War Ⅱ / 그것은 ~를 어떻게 해석하느냐에 달려 있다 It depends on how you interpret 〔read〕 the historical sources 〔documents〕. ◉ ~편찬 historiography: ~편찬관〔위원〕 a historiographer; an official historian / ~편찬국 the bureau of compilation of historical materials. 「regard; deem; judge.

**사료**(思料) ~하다 consider; think;

**사료**(飼料) (livestock) feed; provender; fodder; forage. ¶ 배합 ~ assorted 〔mixed〕 feed / 양계 ~ feed for poultry / 마른 풀을 ~로 주다 fodder 《a horse》 with hay. ◉ ~가게 a feedstore 《미》. ~곡물 stock feed; feed grains.

**사륙배판**(四六倍判) 〖인쇄〗 a large 〔royal〕 octavo.

**사륙판**(四六判) 〖인쇄〗 twelvemo; duodecimo (생략 12mo, 12°). ¶ ~ 250페이지 250 pages in duodecimo.

**사륜**(四輪) four wheels. ¶ ~의 four=wheel(ed). ◉ ~구동 four-wheel drive (생략 4WD): ~구동 장치 a four-wheel drive system / 이 자동차는 ~구동이다 This car is four-wheel drive. / 새로 개발된 ~구동 장치는 동력을 항시 자동차의 네 바퀴에 곧장 전달할 수가 있다 The newly developed 4WD system can transfer power to four wheels of a vehicle directly at all times. ~차〔마차〕 a four-wheel(ed) vehicle 〔carriage〕.

**사르다**[1] ① 《태워 없애다》 burn (up); commit 《*a thing*》 to the flames; throw into (the) fire. ¶ 편지를 불에 ~ throw a letter into the fire / 휴지를 불에 ~ burn wastepaper. ② 《불붙이다》 make 〔build〕 (up) a fire; kindle. ¶ 아궁이에 불을 ~ make a fire in the fireplace.

**사르다**[2] 《키질하다》 winnow 《from, out, away》. ¶ 곡물을 ~ winnow the chaff from the grain.

**사르르** ⇨스르르.

**사름** the taking root of a transplanted rice-plant; the way a transplanted rice-plant turns out. 「리다.

**사리**[1] 《감은》 a coil 《of noodles》. ⇨사

**사리**[2] 《국수 등의》 a coil. ⇨한사리.

**사리**(私利) self-interest; *one's* own interest; self-profit; personal profit; private gain. ¶ ~를 꾀하다 look to 〔after〕 *one's* (own) interests; try to feather *one's* (own) nest; be self-seeking / ~를 꾀하는 사람 a self-seeking person; a self-seeker / ~만 생각하고 있다 be guided by self-interest / 그는 ~만을 좇고 있다 He is seeking nothing but his own interests.
◉ ~사욕 self-interest and selfish desire: 그는 ~사욕을 위해서라면 무슨 짓이든 한다 He will do anything in his own self-interest.

**사리**(舍利) ① 《불사리》 Buddha's 〔a saint's〕 bones; a relic of the Buddha; *sarira* (Sans.). ② 《경전》 Buddhist scriptures; the Sutras.
◉ ~탑 a (*sarira*) stupa. ~함 a *sarira* case; a reliquary.

**사리**(事理) reason; 《사실》 facts; 《적부》 propriety. ¶ ~에 맞는〔안 맞는〕 reasonable 〔unreasonable〕; logical 〔unlogical〕; coherent 〔incoherent〕 / ~에 맞지 않는 소리를 하다 talk nonsense / ~에 밝다〔를 알다〕 be sensible; have good sense; listen to reason / ~에 어둡다〔를 모르다〕 be unreasonable; be impervious to reason / ~를 깨우치게 하다 make 《*a person*》 see reason / 그는 ~에 밝다〔를 안다〕 He is a man of sense. *or* He is a man with good sense enough to know what's what. / 그런 사람에게 ~를 따져야 헛일이다 You might as well reason with a dummy as with him.

**사리**(射利) seeking profit by hook or by crook. ～하다 seek but profit; aim for gain. ◉ ～심 a mercenary 〔mercantile〕 spirit.

**사리**[3]《인도 민족복》a sari; a saree.

**사리다** ①《포개 감다》coil; wind. ¶ 국수를 ～ wind noodles into a ball / 새끼줄을 ～ wind up a rope in a coil / 뱀이 사리고 있다 A snake is lying in a coil. ②《몸을 아끼다》spare *oneself;*《조심하다》take care to *oneself;* shrink from danger. ¶ 몸을 사리지 않고 일하다 work「without sparing 〔unsparingly〕 *oneself.* ③《못을》clinch (the point of a protruding nail). ¶ 박은 못을 ～ clinch a driven nail.

**사리사리** coil after coil; in nice coils. ¶ 국수를 ～ 사리다 wind the noodles into a lot of nice coils.

**사리풀**〖식물〗a (black) henbane.

**사린**(四隣) the whole neighborhood; the surrounding countries; (on) all sides.

**사린교** ⇨사인교.

**사립**(私立) ¶ ～의 private; nongovernmental / 이 학교는 ～이다 This school is「a private institution 〔under private management〕. ◉ ～대학 a private college 〔university〕. ～탐정 a private detective. ～학교 a private school《미》; a public school《영》; a voluntary 〔nongovernmental〕 school: ～학교법 the Private School Law / ～학교 교원 연금법 the Private School Teachers' Pension Law.

**사립문**(一門) a gate made of branches and twigs; a brushwood door.

**사립짝** one of the two doors of a twig gate.

**사마귀**[1] ①《무사마귀》a wart;〖의학〗a verruca (*pl.* -cae). ¶ ～가 많은 warty; verrucose / ～가 생기다 get 〔have〕 a wart; a wart forms 〔grows〕 / 손가락에 ～가 돋았다 A wart has formed on a finger. ②《검은》a mole; a pigmented nevus; a beauty spot (애교점). ¶ ～를 떼다 remove a mole.

**사마귀**[2]〖곤충〗a (praying) mantis (*pl.* -tises, -tes).

**사마리아**〖지리〗Samaria. ◉ ～사람〖성서〗a Samaritan.

**사막**(沙漠) a desert [dézərt] (★ dessert [dizə́ːrt] 식후의 디저트와 혼동하지 않도록 주의). ¶ 황량한 ～ a bleak desert / 끝없는 ～ a limitless desert / ～의 폭풍 작전 the "Operation Desert Storm." ◉ ～식물〔동물〕 a desert plant 〔animal〕. ～화 desertification: ～화 하다 turn into (a) desert.

**사망**(死亡) death; decease; demise. ～하다 die; pass away; be carried away;《사고 따위로》be killed. ¶ 교통 사고로 ～하다 be killed in a traffic accident / 심장 발작에 의한 ～ death from a heart attack.

◉ ～공고 a death notice. ～기사 an obituary (notice). ～란 an obit column. ～보험 mortality life insurance: ～보험금 a death benefit. ～신고서 a notice of death: ～신고서를 내다 send in a notice of *a person's* death. ～진단(서) a (medical) certificate of death; a death certificate. ～추정 시각 the presumed 〔estimated〕 time of《*a person's*》death. ～통계 mortality statistics. ～통계표〖보험〗a mortality table. ～통지《공고》a death notice; an announcement 〔a notice〕 of《*a person's*》death.

**사망률**(死亡率) mortality (rate); death rate. ¶ 위암 ～ the rate of deaths 〔the mortality〕 from stomach cancer / 유아 ～ infant mortality / ～이 높다〔낮다〕 the death rate is high 〔low〕 / ～이 높은 병 a very murderous disease; a decimating illness.

**사망자**(死亡者) the dead; the deceased;《사고 등에 의한》persons killed; deaths; fatalities. ¶ ～가 많이 나다 cause many deaths; take a heavy toll of lives.

◉ ～명부 a death roll 〔list〕. ～수 the death toll; the number of deaths: 차량사고 ～수 automobile fatalities statistics. ～통계 statistics of mortality; mortality returns.

**사매**(私—) private punishment; illegal flogging; a lynch(ing). ◉ ～질 lynching.

**사면**(四面)《네 면》the four sides;《모든 면》all sides; all directions. ¶ ～팔방에 on all sides; in every direction / ～이 바다로 둘러싸인 나라 a seagirt country; a country encircled 〔isolated, surrounded〕 by water 〔sea, the seas〕 / ～에서 공격을 받다 be attacked on every side. ◉ ～체 a tetrahedron: ～체의 tetrahedral / 정～체 a regular tetrahedron.

**사면**(赦免) (a) pardon; (a) remission; (an) amnesty (대사(大赦)); absolution; indulgence. ～하다 pardon; let《*a person*》off《a penalty》; remit《a punishment》; absolve《*a person* from 〔of〕》; grant clemency to《a prisoner》; 《석방하다》 discharge; liberate. ¶ 일반~ a general pardon / 특별~ a particular 〔special〕 pardon; special amnesty / 죄인의 ~ a pardon for 〔to〕 offenders. ◉ ~장 a (letter of ) pardon. 국제~위원회 the Amnesty International.

**사면**(斜面) a slope; a slant; a slanting 〔sloping〕 surface; an inclined plane. ¶ 완만한〔급한〕 ~ an easy 〔a steep〕 slope. ◉ ~도 an oblique section.

**사면발이** ① 〖곤충〗 a crab 〔pubic〕 louse (*pl.* lice). ② 《사람》 a flatterer; a toady.

**사면초가**(四面楚歌) ¶ ~다 have the world against *one;* be surrounded by foes on all sides; be forsaken by everybody / 아무도 편을 안 들어줘 그는 ~ 속에 있는 느낌이었다 Nobody was on his side and he felt as though he were surrounded by foes on all sides.

**사멸**(死滅) extinction; annihilation; destruction; (a) death. ~하다 die out; become extinct; be annihilated; be extirpated; perish. ¶ ~ 직전에 놓여 있다 be on the verge 〔brink〕 of extinction; be in danger of extinction.

**사명**(社命) an order 〔a directive〕 of the company 〔firm〕. ¶ ~에 의하여 by order of the company / ~으로 해외에 나가다 go abroad under company orders.

**사명**(使命) a mission; a commission; an appointed task. ¶ ~을 띠다 be charged 〔entrusted〕 with a mission / ~을 다하다 fulfill 〔perform, accomplish, execute, carry out〕 *one's* mission / ~을 다하지 못하다 fail in *one's* mission / ~을 맡다 assume 〔take up〕 a mission / 그는 외교상의 중대한 ~을 띠고 워싱턴으로 파견되었다 He was sent to Washington on an important diplomatic mission.
◉ ~감 a sense of mission 〔duty〕: 올바른 교육에 대한 ~감과 책임감 a sense of mission and responsibility for correct education.

**사모**(思慕) ① 《그리워함》 (a) longing; yearning; deep attachment; love. ~하다 long for; yearn after; love dearly; burn with love. ¶ ~하는 마음이 불같다 burn with yearning 《after, for》 / 그는 내 누이 동생을 ~하고 있다 He is deeply attached to my sister.
② 《경모》 admiration; adoration. ~하다 regard 《*a person*》 with love and respect; admire; adore. ¶ 스승의 덕을 ~하다 adore a teacher for his virtue.

**사모**(師母) *one's* teacher's wife. ¶ ~님 Madam; Mrs.

**사모아** 《남태평양의 군도》 Samoa; the Samoan Islands. ◉ ~사람 a Samoan.

**사무**(社務) company business 〔affairs〕.

**사무**(事務) office 〔clerical〕 work; business (matters); affairs; the duties 〔charge〕 of an office. ¶ ~적인 businesslike; practical ⇨ 사무적 / ~가 바빠서 by the pressure of business / ~의 신속한 처리 quick dispatch of business / ~를 보다 do office work; attend 「to the office work; be at *one's* desk / ~를 관리〔관장〕하다 administrate 〔manage, conduct〕 the affairs / ~를 인계하다 transfer 〔hand over〕 business 〔*one's* affairs〕 / ~를 인계받다 take over business 〔the charge of an office〕 《from another》 / ~를 처리하다 manage 〔conduct〕 business / ~에 밝다 be familiar with the routine of the office; be experienced in business 〔office work〕 / ~의 간소화〔신속화〕를 꾀하다 try to simplify 〔expedite〕 business / 그 대학은 컴퓨터로 ~를 처리하고 있다 The university has computerized its procedures. / 일요일에는 ~를 보지 않음 《게시》 On Sunday no business is transacted.
◉ ~가 a man of business; a practical man. ~(계)직원 a clerical worker 〔employee〕; a deskworker. ~계통: ~계통 업무 white-collar work; clerical job. ~관 an assistant junior official; a Grade-5 official. ~관리 office management; charge 〔management〕 of business. ~국 an executive office; a secretariat. ~규정 regulations for business; office regulations. ~담당자 a business manager; a person in charge 《of the business》. ~당국 the authorities (directly) in charge; the officials in charge. ~복 an office uniform 〔suit〕; a working garment. ~비 office expenses. ~소 an office: 법률~소 a lawyer's office. ~실 an office (room). ~용품 office supplies. ~원 a clerk; an office worker 〔man〕. ~인계 handing over 「the work 〔the management of an office〕 《to *one's* successor》. ~인수 taking over 「the work 〔the management of an office〕 《from *one's* predecessor》. ~장 a head official; 《배·비행기의》 a purser. ~차장

a vice 〔deputy〕 secretary-general; the assistant director general. ～총장 a secretary-general.

**사무엘** ◉ ～전서 『성서』 The First Book of Samuel; 《약칭》 I Samuel (생략 I Sam.). ～후서 The Second Book of Samuel; 《약칭》 II Samuel (생략 II Sam.).

**사무자동화**(事務自動化) office automation (생략 OA). ◉ ～기기 the office automated machine.

**사무적**(事務的) (being) businesslike; practical. ¶ ～인 재능 business ability 〔talent〕 / ～으로 《handle an affair》 in a businesslike way 〔manner〕; in a matter-of-fact way.

**사무치다** touch the heart; sink into the mind; penetrate; pierce; come 〔go〕 home to 《*one*》. ¶ 가슴에 ～ pierce 〔touch〕 *one's* heart; sink deep in *one's* mind / 원한이 뼈에 ～ bear 〔harbor〕 a deep grudge against 《*a person*》; be full of rancor 《against》 / 그의 너그러운〔친절한〕 마음씨가 가슴에 사무치게 고마웠다 His generosity 〔kindness〕 touched my heart.

**사문**(死文) a dead letter; a (mere) scrap of paper. ◉ ～화 ending in a scrap of paper: ～화 되다 prove (to be) 〔turn out〕 a dead letter; end up a mere scrap of paper / ～화 된 법률 a law that has become a dead letter.

**사문**(沙門) a Buddhist priest 〔monk〕.

**사문**(査問) inquiry; inquisition; inquest; hearing; interrogation. ～하다 inquire into 《*a matter*》; examine; interrogate 《a suspect》. ◉ ～위원회 an inquiry commission. ～회 a board of inquiry; a court of inquest: ～회를 열다 hold an inquiry 《into *a matter*》; hold an inquest 《on, over》.

**사문서**(私文書) a private document; private papers. ◉ ～위조 forgery of 「private papers 〔a private document〕.

**사문석**(蛇紋石) 『광물』 serpentine (rock); ophiolite.

**사물**(死物) 《생명 없는 물건》 a dead 〔lifeless〕 thing; an inanimate object; 《쓰지 못할 물건》 a useless thing. ¶ ～화 하다 become useless. ◉ ～기생(寄生) 『생물』 saprophytism: ～기생 생물 a saprophyte.

**사물**(私物) *one's* private 〔personal〕 thing 〔property〕; *one's* personal effects. ¶ 이것은 내 ～입니다 This is my 「personal belongings 〔private property, personal effects〕.

**사물**(事物) things; affairs; matters. ¶ 한국의 ～ things Korean.
◉ ～관할 『법』 material jurisdiction.

**사물놀이**(四物―) the (Korean) traditional percussion quartet, *"Samulnori"*; a folk music accompanied by four percussion instruments.

**사뭇** ① 《마음껏·마냥》 at *one's* pleasure; to *one's* satisfaction; to *one's* heart's content; unreservedly; 《그저》 intently; solely; only. ¶ ～ 놀기만 하다 be always playing 〔idle〕; do nothing but play / ～ 울기만 하다 be weeping *one's* heart out. ② 《아주·매우》 wholly; utterly; entirely; quite; very (much); 《훨씬》 by far; far and away. ¶ ～ 다르다 be quite 〔widely〕 different 《from》 / 이쪽이 ～ 좋다 This is far better. ③ 《줄곧》 all through; without a break. ¶ 한 달 내내 ～ 바빴다 I was busy all through the month. ④ 《기타》 ¶ 그들은 ～ 주먹질이라도 할 기세였다 They were on the point of coming to blows.

**사미**(沙彌) 『불교』 a Buddhist acolyte; a novice; a *śrāmanera* (Sans.).
◉ ～니(尼) a novice nun; a *śrāmaneriā* (Sans.).

**사민**(四民) the four classes (*i.e.* the scholars, farmers, artisans, and merchants); the whole nation. ◉ ～평등 the equality of the four classes in the country; equality of man.

**사바나** a savanna(h) (열대의 초원).

**사바사바** paying a bribe. ～하다 bribe an official; buy off an official. ¶ ～해서 건축 청부를 맡다 buy an official to get a building contract.

**사바(세계)**(娑婆(世界)) 『불교』 *sabha* (Sans.); the world of suffering; this world. ¶ ～의 earthly; worldly; mundane.

**사박거리다** crunch softly.

**사박사박** with a soft crunch. ¶ 모래밭을 ～ 걷다 crunch on the sand; walk across the sand with a soft crunch / 사과를 ～ 씹다 munch an apple.

**사박자**(四拍子) 『음악』 quadruple time 〔measure, rhythm〕.

**사반**(死斑) a death spot; 『의학』 a livor.

**사반기**(四半期) a quarter (of the year). ¶ 제일 ～ the first quarter (of the year).

**사반세기**(四半世紀) a quarter of a century.

**사발**(沙鉢) 《그릇》 a porcelain bowl; 《분량》 a bowlful; a bowl 《of》.
◉ ～고의(袴衣) men's (summer) pants which reach to the knee. ～농사 begging; mendicancy: ～농사하다 beg food;

live as a beggar. ～무더기 a bowlful (of something heaped up). ～밥 the rice (served) in a bowl; a bowlful of rice. ～시계 a (bowl-shaped) table 〔desk〕 clock. ～통문 a round robin. 밥～ a rice bowl.

**사방**(巳方) 〖민속〗 the Direction of the Snake (＝southeast-by-south).

**사방**(四方) the four quarters; four sides; all directions.

¶ ～에 on all sides; on every side; in all directions; all around; to all points of the compass / ～에서 from all quarters; from every direction / 2마일 ～(에) (within) 「two miles around 〔a radius of two miles〕/ ～을 돌아보다 look around / ～(팔방)을 찾다 seek every corner 《for *something*》/ ～으로 손을 쓰다 leave no stone unturned / ～ 3피트이다 It is three feet square. / 이 역에서 ～으로 선로가 통하고 있다 The railroad lines radiate from this station. / ～이 고요하다 Everything is quiet. / 우리 마을은 ～이 산으로 둘러싸여 있다 Our village is surrounded on all sides by the mountains. / ～에서 사람들이 모여들었다 People gathered from all quarters. /언덕 위에서는약 10마일 ～을 볼 수 있다 From the top of the hill we can see about ten miles around.

◉ ～등(燈) a square hand-lantern.

**사방**(砂防) erosion control; sandbank fixing; sand arrestation. ◉ ～공사 sand guard; anti-erosion work; sand arrestation work. ～댐 〖토목〗 barrier 〔dam〕 against landslide. ～림 an erosion control forest. ～조림 afforestation for erosion control.

**사방정계**(斜方晶系) 〖광물〗 the rhombic 〔trimetric〕 system. ¶ ～의 prismatic.

**사배**(四倍) four times; fourfold; quadruple. ～하다 multiply by four; quadruple; quadruplicate. ¶ ～의 fourfold; quadruple. ◉ ～체 〖생물〗 a tetraploid.

**사백**(舍伯) (my) eldest brother.

**사범**(事犯) a crime; an offense; an illegality; an illegal action. ¶ 경제 ～ an economic offense / 폭력～ a violent crime / 선거～ election illegalities.

**사범**(師範) 《모범》 a model 〔an example〕 to others; 《교사》 a teacher; a master; a preceptor; an instructor; a coach. ¶ 권투 ～ a boxing master 〔instructor〕/ 펜싱 ～ a fencing master. ◉ ～교육 teacher training; normal 〔normal-school〕 education. ～대학 a college of education. ～학교 a normal school.

**사법**(司法) 〖법〗 the administration of justice; judicature. ¶ ～의 judicial; judiciary / ～적 해결 a judicial settlement.

◉ ～경찰 the judicial police: ～경찰관 〔리〕 a judicial police officer 〔constable〕. ～관 a judicial 〔law〕 official; [총칭] judges and prosecutors; the judiciary; the justice: ～관 시보 a probationary judicial officer. ～관청 the bureau of judicial affairs. ～권 judicial 〔judicatory〕 power 〔rights〕; jurisdiction: ～권을 발동하다 invoke 〔exercise〕 judicial power; exercise jurisdiction / 준～권 《empower》 quasi-judicial power. ～기관 the machinery of law. ～당국 the judiciary authorities. ～보호 judicial protection: ～보호 사업 relief work for ex-convicts. ～부 the judicature. ～시험 a state law 〔legal, bar〕 examination; a judiciary test. ～연수생 a judicial apprentice. ～연수원 the Judicial Research and Training Institute. ～위원 the judiciary committee. ～재판 a judicial trial. ～제도 the judicial system. ～해부 《perform, carry out》 an autopsy 《on the victim》 by order of the court. ～행정 judicial administration. 국제～재판소 the International Court of Justice.

**사법**(私法) private law.

◉ ～인 a private corporation. ～학 (the study of ) private law.

**사변**(四邊) the four sides; all sides. ¶～에 on all sides; all around.

◉ ～형 〖수학〗 a quadrilateral: 평행～형 a parallelogram.

**사변**(事變) ① 《심상치 않은 일》 a mishap; an accident; an untoward event; a disaster 〔calamity〕 (재난). ⇨ 사고. ¶ 예기치 않은～ an unforeseen accident. ② 《변란》 an incident; a trouble; a disturbance; an upheaval; an uprising; 《이변》 an emergency; an exigency. ¶ 나라에 ～이 났을 때 in case of a national emergency.

**사변**(思辨) ① 《분별》 discrimination. ② 〖철학〗 speculation. ¶ ～적 speculative / ～적 방법 a speculative method.

◉ ～철학 speculative philosophy.

**사별**(死別) separation by death; bereavement. ～하다 be bereaved 《of》; be parted 《from *a person*》 by death. ¶ 남편과 ～하다 lose *one's* husband through death; be parted from *one's* husband by death; be bereaved of *one's* husband.

**사병**(士兵) 〖군사〗 a private (soldier); an enlisted man 《미》; the rank and file [총칭]. ¶ 일개 ~에서 장군까지 승진하다 rise from the ranks to be a general.

**사보타주** sabotage. ⇨ 태업(怠業).

**사보텐** 〖식물〗 a cactus (*pl.* -ti, ~es).

**사복**(私服) plain clothes; civilian 〔private〕 clothes; civies 《구어》; mufti (군인 등의). ¶ ~으로 《a police inspector》 in plain clothes; 《a military officer》 in civilian attire 〔clothes〕; in mufti. ◉ ~경찰관 a plain-clothes policeman; a policeman in civilian clothes. ~형사 a plain-clothes man.

**사복**(私腹) *one's* self-interest; *one's* personal end; *one's* selfish ends. ¶ ~을 채우다 stuff 〔enrich, fill, line〕 *one's* (own) pockets; enrich *oneself;* feather *one's* (own) nest; 《공인이》 graft; practice jobbery.

**사복음**(四福音) 〖성서〗 the Four Gospels.

**사본**(寫本) a copy; a duplicate (부본); 《필사본》 a (book in) manuscript (생략 MS., *pl.* MSS.). ¶ ~을 만들다 (make a) copy; get a duplicate 《of》; duplicate 《a letter》.

**사부**(四部) four parts. ◉ ~작 a tetralogy; a 4-part work. ~합주 a quartet. ~합창 a vocal quartet; a chorus in four parts: ~ 합창곡 a 4-part song.

**사부**(師父) ① 《스승과 아버지》 *one's* father and master. ② 《스승》 a (fatherly) master; an esteemed teacher.

**사부**(師傅) ① 《스승》 a teacher; a tutor; a master. ② 《태사·태부》 a tutor to the king's sons 〔grandsons〕; prince's fosterer and tutor.

**사부랑거리다** ⇨ 시부렁거리다.

**사북** 《접부채의》 the pivot.

**사분**(四分) dividing in four. ~하다 divide in four; separate into four parts; quarter. ¶ ~의 1 a quarter; one fourth / ~의 3 three fourths; three quarters. ◉ ~기 a quarter (of the year); a quarter term: 제 1 ~기 the first「quarter 〔three months〕 (of the year). ~면〔원, 의(儀)〕 a quadrant. ~쉼표 a quarter rest; a crotchet rest 《영》. ~음 a quarter tone. ~음표 a quarter note; a crotchet.

**사분**(私憤) personal grudge 〔resentment, enmity, spite〕. ¶ ~을 풀다 vent 〔satisfy〕 *one's* spite.

**사분거리다** ① 《농치며 끈기있게 조르다》 tease 《*a person*》 humorously. ② 《가만가만 지껄이다》 speak in a quiet 〔an equable〕 (tone of) voice.

**사분사분** softly; lightly.

**사분오열**(四分五裂) utter disruption 〔disunion, division, breakup, split, disorganization〕. ~하다 be utterly disrupted 〔disunited, divided〕; be torn apart 〔into pieces, asunder〕; become (totally) disorganized. ¶ 위원회는 ~의 상태이다 The committee is divided against itself. / 데모 행진은 ~ 상태가 됐다 The demonstration parade has fallen into great disorder.

**사붓(사뿟)** with a light-footed step.

**사브르** 《펜싱의》 a *sabre* (F.).

**사비**(私費) private expense; *one's* own expense. ¶ ~로 at private expense; at *one's* own expense; out of *one's* own pocket / 나는 ~로 유학했다 I studied abroad at my own expense 〔cost〕. ◉ ~유학생 a student studying abroad at his own expense.

**사비**(社費) the company's 〔firm's〕 expenses; the upkeep of a company; the outlay(s) of a company (지출). ¶ ~로 여행하다 travel at the company's expenses / 그는 ~로 1개월간 미국에 다녀왔다 He has been to America for a month at the expense of the company.

**사뿐** with a soft 〔muffled〕 step; lightly. ¶ 담에서 땅으로 ~히 뛰어내렸다 jump from the wall and land on the ground lightly 〔with a muffled thud〕.

**사뿐사뿐** with soft steps.

**사사**(私事) a private 〔personal〕 matter; personal 〔private〕 affairs 〔concerns〕.

**사사**(師事) making 《*a person*》 *one's* teacher. ~하다 study under 〔with〕 《*a person*》; look up to 《*a person*》 as *one's* teacher; apprentice *oneself* 《to》; become 《*a person's*》 pupil; receive instruction at 《*a person's*》 feet. ¶ 다년간 그(분)에게 ~했다 I sat at his feet for many years. / 그는 황교수에게 ~하여 2년간 경제학을 공부했다 He studied economics, under Professor Hwang's instruction for two years.

**사사건건**(事事件件) each and every event 〔matter, case, affair〕. ¶ ~ 반대하다 oppose 《*a person*》 in every way; contradict 《*a person*》 at every chance.

**사사기**(士師記) 〖성서〗 (the Book of ) Judges (생략 Judg.).

**사사로이**(私私—) personally; privately; in private; informally.

**사사롭다**(私私—) (be) personal; private. ¶ 사사로운 생활 *one's* private life / 사사로운 접촉이 있다 be in personal contact 《with》 / 사사로운 감정에 끌리다 be swayed by personal feelings / 나는 사사로운 일로 하루 휴가를 얻었다 I took a day off on (my) private affairs 〔business〕. / 사사로운 청이 있어 왔네 I came to ask you a personal favor.

**사사오입**(四捨五入) ⇨ 반올림. ∼하다 round off 《to the nearest whole number》. ¶ 소수점 이하 세자리에서 ∼하다 round 《5.342》 off to two decimal places.

**사산**(死産) (a) stillbirth. ∼하다 have a stillbirth; give birth to a dead child; *one's* baby is born dead. ◉ ∼아 a stillborn baby.

**사살**(射殺) ∼하다 shoot 《*a person*》 dead 〔to death〕. ¶ 그는 호랑이를 그 자리에서 ∼했다 He shot the tiger dead on the spot. / 탈출을 시도하는 자를 발견하면 ∼하라는 명령이 있었다 Our orders were that, if we saw anyone trying to escape, we should shoot to kill.

**사삿일**(私私—) a private matter; private 〔personal〕 affairs. ¶ 남의 ∼에 참견하다 pry into 〔meddle in〕 other's business; put 〔poke〕 *one's* nose into other's private affair.

**사상**(史上) in history. ¶ ∼ 최대의 전쟁 〔참사〕 the greatest war 〔disaster〕 in history / 그것은 ∼ 유례없는 사건이었다 That was a case unparalleled 〔unprecedented〕 in history.

**사상**(死相) the seal 〔sign〕 of death 《on *one's* face》. ¶ 얼굴에 ∼이 나타나다 have the seal of death on *one's* face.

**사상**(死傷) death and injury 〔wounds〕; casualties; loss(es); [형용사적] killed and wounded. ⇨ 사상자. ◉ ∼병 the killed and wounded soldiers; troop casualties.

**사상**(事象) a phenomenon (*pl.* -na); an event; a matter; an aspect; a phase.

**사상**(思想) thought; an idea; 《개념》 a conception; 《이데올로기》 an ideology. ¶ 건전한 ∼ healthy 〔sound〕 thought / 한국 ∼의 주류 the main current of Korean thought / 신구 ∼의 충돌 a conflict between new and old ideas / ∼을 전달하다 communicate *one's* thought 《to》; convey *one's* ideas across 《to》 / ∼을 통제하다 control public thought / ∼을 말로 표현하다 express *one's* thought by means of words / ∼이 풍부〔빈약〕하다 be rich 〔poor〕 in thought / 그의 ∼은 실존주의의 영향을 받고 있다 His ideas are colored by existentialism. / 그의 ∼은 온건〔과격〕하다 He has a sober 〔radical〕 thought. / 한국의 헌법은 ∼의 자유를 보장하고 있다 The Constitution of Korea guarantees freedom of thought. / 그들은 직간접적으로 서구 ∼의 영향을 받고 있었다 They were under the direct or indirect influence of Western thought.
◉ ∼가 a (great) thinker; a man of (profound) thought; a 《political, social》 thinker 〔theorist〕. ∼개조 thought-remolding〔-reform〕. ∼경향 the tendency 〔trend〕 of thought. ∼계 the world 〔realm〕 of thought; the thinking world. ∼극 a problem play. ∼내용 thought content. ∼문제 a thought problem. ∼범 《죄》 a thought 〔political〕 offense; 《사람》 a political offender. ∼선도 (judicious) guidance of public thought. ∼운동 a thought 〔an ideological〕 movement. ∼전 ideological warfare; an ideological battle. ∼통제 thought control; censorship of thought. ∼투쟁 an ideological strife.

**사상**(絲狀) ¶ ∼의 thready; filiform.
◉ ∼균 『식물』 a filamentous fungus; a mold: ∼균상 효모 moldy yeast. ∼체 『의학』 a filament. ∼충 『동물』 a heartworm; a filaria (*pl.* -ae).

**사상**(寫象) an image. ◉ ∼주의 imagism: ∼주의자 an imagist. ∼파 the imagists.

**사상누각**(砂上樓閣) a house of cards 〔on sand〕; 《build》 a castle in Spain 〔the air〕.

**사상자**(死傷者) the killed and the wounded; casualties; losses. ¶ 많은 ∼ heavy 〔serious〕 casualties; a heavy toll of lives / 교통 사고에서 다행히 ∼는 없었다 Fortunately there were no casualties in the traffic accident. / 승객 중 20명의 ∼가 났다 Twenty passengers were either killed or wounded. ◉ ∼명단〔명부〕 a casualty list; a list of casualties. ∼수 losses; (the number of ) casualties; the toll of casualties 《미》.

**사색**(四色) ① 《색》 four colors; four=color. ② 『역사』 the Four Factions (of the middle period of the Chosŏn Dynasty). ◉ ∼당쟁 strife among the Four Factions. ∼판 『인쇄』 four-color printing.

**사색**(死色) deadly 〔ghastly〕 pale look; a cadaverous face. ¶ 얼굴이 ~이 되다 turn ghastly 〔deadly〕 pale.

**사색**(思索) speculation; thinking; cogitation; contemplation; meditation. ~하다 think reflectively; muse 〔meditate, speculate〕 on; contemplate (on); revolve 《a problem》 in *one's* mind. ¶ ~적(인) speculative; meditative / ~적인 생활 a life of meditation / ~에 잠기다 be given to speculation; be lost 〔absorbed, engrossed〕 in contemplation 〔meditation, thought〕 / 인생의 의미에 관해 ~해 보는 것도 때로는 유익하다 It is sometimes good for one to philosophize about the meaning of life.
◉ ~가 a thinker; a thinking person.

**사생**(死生) life and 〔or〕 death. ◉ ~관두(關頭) the brink of death: ~관두에 서다 lie between life and death; be on the verge of death; stand 〔be〕 at the crossroads of a matter of life and death. ~동고(同苦) standing together in life and death.

**사생**(寫生) sketching; drawing 〔painting〕 from nature 〔life〕. ~하다 sketch; paint 〔draw, sketch〕 from nature; make a sketch 《of a view》. ¶ ~의 sketchy / ~하러 가다 go sketching.
◉ ~대회 a sketch contest. ~첩 a sketchbook. ~화 a picture drawn from life 〔nature〕; a sketch: 정물 ~화 a still life; a still-life painting.

**사생결단**(死生決斷) risking *one's* life; fighting it out at the risk of *one's* life. ~하다 risk 〔stake〕 *one's* life; be desperate. ¶ ~하고 at the risk of *one's* life; desperately / ~의 싸움 a life and death struggle.

**사생아**(私生兒) an illegitimate child; a natural 〔love〕 child; a child born out of wedlock; 《경멸》 a bastard. ¶ ~로 태어나다 be of illegitimate birth; be born out of wedlock / ~를 친자로 인지하다 legitimatize 〔recognize〕 a natural child as *one's* issue / 그는 ~다 He was born out of wedlock.
◉ ~인지 bastardization; filiation.

**사생활**(私生活) *one's* private 〔home〕 life; *one's* privacy. ¶ ~에 있어서는 in private life / ~에 간여하다 dig 〔nose〕 into 《*a person's*》 private life.

**사서**(司書) a librarian; a custodian of a library. ◉ ~보(補) a sublibrarian; an assistant librarian.

**사서**(四書) the Four Books (of Ancient China) (*i.e.* the Analects of Confucius, the Works of Mencius, the Doctrine of the Mean and the Great Learning). ◉ ~삼경 the Four Books and the Three Classics.

**사서**(史書) a history book; writings by historians.

**사서**(辭書) a dictionary. ⇨ 사전(辭典).

**사서함**(私書函) a post-office box (생략 P.O. Box, P.O.B., POB); a call box 《미》. ¶ 중앙 우체국 ~ 96호 C.P.O. Box (No.) 96 / 국제 우체국 ~ 225호 I.P.O. Box (No.) 225 / ~ 18호로 회답 바랍니다 Please direct your answer to P.O.B. No. 18.

**사석**(私席) an unofficial 〔an informal, a private〕 occasion. ¶ ~에서 informally; unofficially.

**사석**(捨石) 〚토목〛 a riprap; a rubble mound; 《바둑의》 a sacrificed stone.

**사선**(死線) 《죽을 고비》 a life-or-death crisis; 《교도소 등의》 a deadline. ¶ ~을 넘다 survive a life-or-death crisis / ~을 넘어 across the deadline / 그는 지금까지 여러 번 ~을 넘었다 He has been 「face to face with 〔threatened with〕 death several times.

**사선**(私線) 《통신·철도·선로》 a private 〔nongovernmental〕 telegraphic 〔railroad〕 line.

**사선**(斜線) a diagonal 〔an oblique〕 line; a slanting line; 《and / or 와 같은 경우의》 a (diagonal 〔slanting〕) stroke; solidus (*pl.* -di); a slash (mark).

**사설**(私設) [형용사적] privately established; private. ~하다 establish privately. ¶ 그 철도는 ~이다 The railroad is under private management.
◉ ~강습소〔학원〕 a private 〔proprietary〕 institute 〔school〕. ~묘지 a private cemetery. ~시장 a private market. ~연구기관 a private think tank. ~응원단 a private cheer group. ~철도 a private railroad. ~회사 a private company.

**사설**(邪說) 《교리》 a heretical doctrine; heretical teachings (★ teachings는 보통 복수형); heterodoxy; heresy; 《의견》 corrupt opinions; perverse views.

**사설**(社說) an editorial (article); a leading article 《영》; a leader. ¶ 격렬한 ~ a highly explosive editorial / 경제에 관한 ~ an editorial 〔a leading article〕 on economics / ~에서 논하다 discuss 《*a matter*》 in an editorial; comment editorially 《on》; editorialize 《on》/ 그 문제에 관하여는 각 신문의 ~에서 논평하고 있다 Every paper comments editorially on the subject. *or* Every paper editorializes on the subject. ◉ ~기자 an editorial writer. ~란 the editorial column.

**사설**(辭說) 《노래말》 words; poetic diction; 《이야기》 an account; a telling; a story; 《잔말》 (empty) prattle; tattle; 《불평》 nag; grumble.
◉ ~시조 〖문학〗 a form of *shijo* with unlimited length in the middle verse. ~쟁이 a chatterbox.

**사성**(四姓) 《인도의》 the four castes (of Brahmans (승려), Kshatriyas (무사·귀족), Vaisyas (상민), and Sudras (천민)).

**사성**(四聖) the four greatest sages of the world; the Four Great Sages (*i.e.* Confucius, Buddha, Jesus and Socrates).

**사성**(四聲) the four tones (of Chinese 「characters).

**사성**(賜姓) ~하다 the king bestows 〔confirms〕 a surname 《on》.

**사세**(社勢) the 「influence 〔strength〕 of a company. ¶ ~를 얻다〔만회하다〕 gain 〔regain, win back〕 the 「influence 〔power〕 of a company / ~를 확장하다 extend 〔broaden〕 the power of a company.

**사세**(事勢) the situation; the aspect of affairs; (the state of) things; the way things are. ⇨ 사태(事態). ¶ ~부득이 unavoidably; driven by circumstances; out of sheer necessity / ~가 불리하여 under unfavorable situations.

**사소**(私訴) 〖법〗 a civil suit 〔action〕.

**사소설**(私小說) an autobiographical novel; a novel based on the author's personal life; a novel 〔story〕 depicting the author's private life; a first=person story; an "I" story; an *Ich=roman* (G.).

**사소하다**(些少—) (be) trivial; trifling; petty; small; slight; insignificant. ¶ 사소한 돈 a trifling sum of money / 사소한 일 a (mere) trifle; a trivial 〔trifling〕 matter / 사소한 차이 a slight difference / 사소한 잘못 a trifling 〔minor〕 error; a light 〔an insignificant〕 mistake / 사소한 일로 법석을 떨다 make a fuss about trifles / 사소한 일을 떠벌리다 make much of a trifling matter; exaggerate; overdraw a matter / 사소한 일에 화를 내다 get angry at trifles.

**사수**(死守) a desperate 〔stubborn〕 defense. ~하다 defend to the last 〔death〕; maintain 〔defend〕 desperately 〔stubbornly〕 (필사적으로). ¶ 고지를 ~하다 defend a plateau desperately / 진지를 ~하다 defend a position to the last.

**사수**(射手) a marksman; a shooter; a shot; a rifleman; a gunner; 《활의》 an archer; a bowman. ¶ 명~ 《총의》 a master 〔crack, dead〕 shot; 《활의》 a master bowman.

**사숙**(私淑) ~하다 adore 《*a person*》 (in *one's* heart); take 〔look up to〕 《*a person*》 as 〔for〕 *one's* model; follow in the footsteps 《of》; model *oneself* 《on *a person*》; be strongly influenced 《by》. ¶ 문 박사를 ~하다 be an admirer of Dr. Mun / 그녀는 내가 ~하는 시인 중의 한 사람이다 She is one of the poets I admire.

**사숙**(私塾) a private 〔home〕 school; a private class at *one's* home. ¶ 농촌에 ~을 열다 run 〔keep〕 a private school in the farm village.

**사순절**(四旬節) 〖기독교〗 Lent. ¶ ~의 Lenten / ~의 단식 the Lenten fast.

**사술**(邪術) witchcraft; black magic; the black art; sorcery; an evil trick.

**사슬** a chain; 《개를 매는》 a tether. ¶ ~에 매인 포로 a captive fastened 《to a pole》 with chains; a war prisoner (shackled) in chains / ~로 매다 enchain; chain up; put 《men》 in chains / ~을 풀다 unchain; undo the chain; put out of chain / ~에 매여 있다 《개 따위가》 be 「chained 〔on a chain〕; 《죄수가》 be in chains / ~에서 벗어나다 [비유적] free *oneself* from restraint; cast 〔shake〕 off the yoke / 개는 ~에 매여 있다 The dog is on a chain. ◉ ~고리 a link. ~돈 loose 〔unstrung〕 coins. ~문고리 a chain doorlock.

**사슴** 〖동물〗 a deer (*pl.* ~, 때로 ~s); 《숫사슴》 a stag; 《암사슴》 a doe; a hind; 《새끼》 a fawn. ¶ ~머리 a staghead (벽장식용) / ~가죽 deerskin; buckskin / ~뿔 an antler; a pair of antlers (한 쌍) / ~고기 venison.
◉ ~사냥 deer hunting; deerstalking (몰래 하는). ~사육장 a deer garden.

**사습**(私習) private study; self-teaching. ~하다 study by 〔for〕 *oneself*.

**사시**(巳時) 〖민속〗 the Watch of the Snake: ① the 6th of the 12 double=hours (*i.e.* the period between 9 and 11 a.m.). ② the 11th of the 24 hours (*i.e.* 9:30-10:30 a.m.).

**사시**(四時) 《계절》 the four seasons.
◉ ~사철 [부사적] at 〔in〕 all seasons

(of the year); all the year round.

**사시**(史詩) an epic (poem).

**사시**(斜視) 《시선의 불일치》 a squint; 〖의학〗 strabismus; 《흘겨봄》 looking askance. ¶ ～다 have a squint 〔cast in the eye〕; be squint-eyed 〔cross-eyed (내사시), wall-eyed (외사시)〕/ 아주 심한 ～다 have a fearful squint; squint dreadfully.
◉ ～수술〔교정술〕 〖의학〗 strabotomy.

**사시나무** 〖식물〗 an aspen; a poplar. ¶ ～ 떨듯하다 tremble 〔quiver〕 like an aspen leaf; quiver all over.

**사시장청**(四時長靑) being evergreen. ～하다 (be) evergreen; be green at all seasons 〔the year around〕.

**사시장춘**(四時長春) 《언제나 봄》 everlasting spring; 《안락 생활》 an easy life; a comfortable living.

**사식**(私食) private food sent in to a prisoner.

**사신**(私信) a private message 〔letter, note〕; a private communication.

**사신**(使臣) an envoy; an ambassador (대사); a minister (공사). ¶ 각국의 ～ the foreign representatives 〔envoys〕; 《외교단》 diplomatic corps / ～을 파견하다 dispatch 〔send〕 an envoy 《to》.

**사실**(史實) a historical fact; a matter of history; historical evidence.

**사실**(私室) a private room.

**사실**(事實) ① 《실제의 일》 a fact; an actual fact; 《현실》 a reality; actuality; 《실상》 the case; 〖법〗 a *factum* (*pl.* -ta); 《진실》 the truth.
¶ ～상 ⇨ 사실상 / 명백한〔뚜렷한〕 ～ a broad 〔a palpable, an obvious〕 fact / 부인할〔숨길〕 수 없는 ～ an undeniable 〔indisputable〕 fact / 엄연한 ～ a hard fact / 기정 ～ an established 〔accomplished〕 fact; a solid fact / 적나라한 〔꾸밈 없는〕 ～ the naked 〔plain〕 truth; a straight fact / ～의 은폐 suppression of the truth; *suppresio veri* (L.) / ～로 말하면 to tell the truth / ～에 비추어 in view of these facts; such being the case / ～에 반하다 be contrary to the fact(s) / ～을 근거로 하다 be grounded 〔based, founded〕 on fact; take *one's* stand on fact / ～을 왜곡하다 falsify facts; pervert 〔distort〕 the truth / ～을 인정〔무시〕하다 admit 〔ignore〕 the fact / ～을 조사하다 inquire into the facts (of the case) / ～을 있는 그대로 진술하다 state facts as they are / ～의 뒷받침이 없는 추정을 내리다 draw inferences not authorized by facts / ～은 이렇다 The truth of the matter is this. / ～은 부정할 수 없다 There is no denying the fact. / 그건 ～로서 알려져 있다 That is known 「as a fact 〔to be the truth〕. / 그것이 ～임을 알고 있다 I know it for a fact. / 그것이 ～임은 경험으로써 알 수 있다 Experience shows that such is the case. / 그가 그렇게 말한 것이 ～입니까 Is it a fact that he said so? / 그가 정직하다고들 하는데 ～은 그 반대이다 They say he is honest. In fact, the opposite 〔reverse〕 is the case. / ～은 그렇지 않다 That is not the case. / 예언은 ～이 되었다 The prediction has come true. / 이것은 지어낸 이야기가 아니라 ～이다 This is a real occurrence, not a fictitious anecdote. / 이 소설은 ～을 근거로 하여 쓴 것이다 The novel is founded on fact. ② [부사적으로] 《진실로》 surely; really; truely. ¶ ～ 그 소년은 매우 영리한 아이다 It is true that he is a very bright boy. / ～ 나는 그녀와 거기서 만났다 I really did meet her there.
◉ ～무근 ⇨ 사실 무근. ～문제 a matter 〔question〕 of fact; 《당연한》 the (real) question at issue. ～오인(誤認) 〖법〗 a mistake of fact. ～조사 = 실정 조사.

**사실**(査實) an investigation of the facts; an actual inspection; a survey. ～하다 make 「an investigation 〔a survey〕 《of》; inspect.

**사실**(寫實) representing things as they really are; exact, objective description; realism. ～하다 represent things as they really are; describe graphically; give a graphic 〔realistic〕 description 〔representation〕. ¶ ～적(인) realistic; true to life 〔nature〕; objective; graphic / ～적으로 묘사하다 describe 〔depict〕 graphically 〔realistically〕; give a graphic description 〔representation〕 《of》. ◉ ～소설 a realist(ic) novel: ～소설가 a realistic novelist. ～주의 realism; 〖미술〗 literalism: ～주의자 a realist; a realistic writer; 〖미술〗 a literalist. ～파 the realistic 〔representationalist〕 school.

**사실무근**(事實無根) being groundless. ¶ ～의 groundless; unfounded; absurd; false; entirely contrary to fact / ～이다 be unfounded 〔groundless〕; be false 〔fictitious〕 / 그 보고는 전혀 ～이다 The report is 「entirely false 〔contrary to fact〕. / A군이 우리 클럽을 탈퇴하리라는 소문은 ～으로 밝혀졌다 The rumor that Mr. A would quit our club 〔society〕 proved (to be) unfounded 〔false〕.

**사실상**(事實上) 《실제로》 actually; in reality; 《사실인즉》 as a matter of fact; in point of fact; 《실질적으로》 practically; virtually; to all intents and purposes. ¶ ∼의 factual; actual; real; virtual; practical; what amounted to / ∼의 정부〔승인〕 a *de facto* government 〔recognition〕 / 그는 ∼ 그 회사의 사장이다 He is virtually 〔practically〕 the head of the company. *or* He is the head of the company in all but name. / 전쟁은 ∼ 끝나 있었다 The war was virtually ended. / 그 개정판은 ∼ 또 다른 하나의 새 책이다 The revised edition is to all intents and purposes a new book.

**사심**(邪心) an evil mind; a wicked 〔black〕 heart; a malicious intention; an evil design. ¶ ∼ 있는 wicked; malicious.

**사심**(私心) 《이기심》 selfishness; a selfish motive; self-interest; partiality; 《자기 생각》 *one's* own (humble) mind. ¶ ∼ 없는 unselfish; selfless; disinterested; fair; impartial / ∼ 없이 without prejudice; impartially; unselfishly; fairly / ∼을 버리고 from unselfish 〔disinterested〕 motives; unselfishly; impartially; fairly / ∼을 품다 harbor a selfish motive; have an ax to grind / ∼ 없이 들어 주십시오 Give me a candid hearing.

**사십**(四十) forty. ¶ 제 ∼ the fortieth / ∼대의 사람 a person in his 〔the〕 forties; a quadragenarian / ∼ 전의 under 〔on the sunny side of〕 forty / ∼이 넘은 over 〔on the wrong side of〕 forty / ∼대다 be in *one's* forties / 나이 ∼ 고개를 바라보다 be close 〔hard〕 upon forty; be getting on for 〔to〕 forty / ∼에 첫 버선 doing 《*something*》 for the first time late in life.

**사십구일재**(四十九日齋) the memorial service on the forty-ninth day after *a person's* death.

**사악**(邪惡) wickedness; viciousness; vice; evil. ∼하다 (be) wicked; vicious; malicious; sinister; black-hearted. ¶ ∼한 사람 a wicked man; a godless person; a villain.

**사안**(私案) *one's* private 〔personal〕 plan 〔idea, design〕; *one's* suggestion.

**사안**(事案) 《법률적인》 a case; a matter; an item.

**사암**(砂岩) 〖지질〗 sandstone.

**사약**(賜藥) (the King's) bestowal of poison (as a death penalty). ¶ ∼을 내리다 bestow poison 《to *a person*》 as a death penalty.

**사양**(斜陽) the evening sun(light); the setting 〔declining, sinking〕 sun. ¶ ∼길에 접어들다 be on the decline 〔wane〕; be on the downgrade.
◉ ∼산업 a fading 〔an eclipsed, a declining, a sinking〕 industry. ∼족 the new poor; the upper-class families on the decline; the fallen aristocracy; 《구어》 the has-been (families).

**사양**(飼養) rearing; breeding. ⇨ 사육.

**사양**(辭讓) 《양보·사절》 declining in favor of another; courteous refusal; refusal with appreciation; 《겸손·삼감》 reserve; modesty. ∼하다 《양보·사절하다》 decline in favor of another; refuse courteously; decline with thanks 〔regrets〕; 《겸손하다》 (be) reserved; modest; 《주저하다》 hesitate. ¶ ∼하지 않고 freely; unreservedly; without ceremony 〔reserve〕 / 제의를 ∼하다 decline 《*a person's*》 offer / …하기를 ∼치 않다 be ready 〔be (quite) willing〕 to *do* / 무엇이든지 ∼ 말고 요구하시오 Don't scruple to ask for anything. / 그의 초대는 ∼하고 싶다 I'd like to decline his invitation. / 원하는 것이 있으면 ∼치 말고 말해라 Don't hesitate to ask if you want anything. / ∼하는 할머니에게 자리를 양보했다 I insisted on giving my seat to an elderly lady. / ∼ 말고 음식을 드십시오 Please help yourself to the food without ceremony 〔reserve〕. / 죄송하지만 ∼하겠습니다 I'm sorry, but I can't help declining it. / 그는 총리직을 ∼했다 He declined the post of the premiership.

**사어**(死語) a dead language; an obsolete word (폐어).

**사업**(事業) ① 《일》 an undertaking; a project; an enterprise; activity; work; a task. ¶ 큰〔대〕 ∼ a big undertaking 〔enterprise〕 / 국가 ∼ a state 〔national〕 undertaking / 유엔의 ∼ the workings of the United Nations / 무모〔위험〕한 ∼ a rash 〔dangerous〕 enterprise / 그 상사(商社)의 다각적인 ∼ the many-sided activities of the firm.
사업에: ∼에 관계하고 있다 have an interest in an enterprise / ∼에 성공〔실패〕하다 succeed 〔fail〕 in *one's* undertaking / ∼에 출자하다 finance a commercial undertaking; invest money in an enterprise.
사업을: ∼을 시작하다 start an enter-

prise; set a project on foot; launch a new venture; start a new enterprise / 새 ～을 계획하다 have a new enterprise in view 〔under consideration〕 / ～을 경영해 나갈 수완이 있다 have the capacity to manage enterprise.

② 《실업》 (a line of ) business; a business; an industry (상공업). ¶ 장래성 있는 ～ a business that has a future; a promising enterprise / ～을 하다 carry on 〔engage in〕 business / ～을 시작하다 start a 〔*one's*〕 business; set (*oneself*) up in business; begin 〔go into〕 business / ～을 그만두다 close 〔give up〕 *one's* business / ～을 경영하다 run a business / ～을 떠맡다〔인수하다〕 undertake a business / ～이 잘 되다 have 〔do, enjoy〕 a thriving business / ～에 소질이 있다 have a good head for business / ～에 실패하다 fail in business / ～이 부진하다 have a slump in business; business slackens / ～을 확장〔축소〕하다 extend 〔reduce〕 *one's* business / 무슨 ～을 하십니까 What line of business are you in? / 그 ～에는 생무지입니다 I am not in that line. *or* It is out of my line. / 그건 수지맞는 ～이다 It is a paying business.

③ 《업적》 an achievement; a deed. ¶ 큰 ～을 이룩하다 achieve 〔do〕 a great thing.

◉ ～가 a person of enterprise; an enterpriser; an *enterpreneur* (F.); an industrialist; a businessperson; a worker in…. ～계 the enterprising world; the industrial 〔business〕 world; industrial 〔business〕 circles. ～계획 a plan of operation; a business program. ～공채 an industrial bond. ～부 an operation division; an enterprise department. ～비 working expenses. ～세 the enterprise tax. ～소〔장〕 a place of business; an establishment. ～소득 a business income; an income from an enterprise: ～소득세 the business tax. ～연도 a business year 〔term〕; an accounting period. ～자본〔자금〕 business funds. ～주 a business proprietor. 협력～ a joint enterprise.

**사업화**(事業化) 《공업화》 industrialization; 《상업화》 commercialization. ～하다 industrialize; commercialize; put 《*a thing*》 on a commercial basis.

**사에이치클럽**(四—) a Four-H 〔4-H〕 club (★ 4-H는 head, heart, hands, health를 의미).

**사역**(使役) employment; work; (forced) labor; service; 〖군사〗 a fatigue. ～하다 employ; use 《personnel》; work 《*a person*》 hard; set 《*a person*》 to work 〔a task〕. ¶ 그 영주는 소작인들을 노예처럼 ～했다 The lord set his peasants to work like slaves. ◉ ～동사 〖문법〗 a causative verb.

**사연**(事緣) the origin and circumstances of a matter 〔case〕; the (full) story; matters (as they stand); reasons (이유). ¶ 말 못할 ～이 있어서 for some secret reasons / 어찌 된 ～이냐 What's the story? *or* What's it all about? / ～은 이러하다 This is how it is. / ～을 말해 주시오 Tell me the whole story of it.

**사연**(辭緣) contents (of a letter); the gist; the import.

**사열**(四列) four lines 〔rows〕. ¶ ～종대 a column of four / ～로 서다 《종대로》 form fours; line up four abreast; 《횡대로》 be drawn up four deep / ～로 서서 나아가다 go 〔march〕 four abreast; march by fours.

**사열**(査閱) 〖군사〗 (an) inspection (of troops); a parade; a review. ～하다 inspect troops; review (troops). ¶ ～을 받다 be inspected 《by》; undergo inspection.

◉ ～관 an inspector. ～대 a reviewing stand. ～식 a military inspection 〔reviewing〕; a military review; a parade: ～식을 갖다 hold a military review 〔a grand parade〕. ～장 a parade ground.

**사염화**(四塩化) 〖화학〗 tetrachloride. ◉ ～탄소 carbon tetrachloride.

**사영**(私營) private operation; private management. ◉ ～사업 a private enterprise.

**사영**(射影) 〖수학〗 projection. ～하다 project. ¶ ～의 projective. ◉ ～기하학 projective geometry. 정〔등각〕～ orthogonal 〔isometric〕 projection

**사영**(斜影) a slanting shadow.

**사옥**(社屋) an office building; the building of a company.

**사욕**(私慾) self-interest; a selfish desire. ¶ ～이 없는 unselfish; disinterested / ～을 떠나다〔버리다〕 rise above 〔put aside〕 self-interest / ～을 채우다 satisfy 〔gratify〕 *one's* selfish desires / ～을 추구하다 pursue *one's* own self=interest / ～에 눈이 어두워지다 be blinded by self-interest / ～에 사로잡히다 be the slave of 〔to〕 self-interest / 그녀는 ～으로 그것을 한 것이 아니다 She hasn't done that out of self-interest.

**사욕**(邪慾) 《못된 욕심》 an evil desire; 《육욕》 an evil passion; a carnal desire; a sinful lust.

**사용**(私用) ① 《사사로이 씀》 private 〔personal〕 use; 《공용물의 유용》 (an) appropriation; (a) misappropriation. ～하다 turn 〔divert, put〕 《*a thing*》 to private use; use 《*a thing*》 for private purposes; misappropriate; appropriate; embezzle 《public money》. ¶ 공금을 ～하다 turn public funds to private use / 그는 위탁받은 돈을 ～했다 He appropriated the money entrusted to him.
② 《사삿일》 private 〔personal〕 business. ¶ ～으로 on personal 〔private〕 business / ～ 전화는 삼가 주십시오 Kindly refrain from using the telephone for a private purpose.
◉ ～도로 a private road.

**사용**(社用) company 〔*one's* firm's〕 business. ¶ ～으로 on company business; 《be away in Tokyo》 on business for *one's* firm. ◉ ～족(族) expense-account spenders 〔aristocrats〕; businessmen winning and dining at their firms' expense.

**사용**(使用) use; employment; application (응용). ～하다 use; make use of 《gas》; put to use; employ; apply 《force》. ¶ ～할 수 있는〔없는〕 usable 〔unusable〕; fit 〔unfit〕 for use / …을 ～해서 with 〔by〕…; using…; by the use of…; by means of…; with 〔by〕 the aid of… / 현대 기계의 ～ the use of modern machinery / ～하지 않는 방 an unused room / ～되지 않는 기계 a machine that 「is not in use 〔is lying idle〕 / 아주 유효하게 ～하다 make the best (possible) use of / 자주 ～하다 make frequent use of / …을 마음대로 ～하다 have the free use of…; be at liberty to use… / 널리 ～되고 있다 be widely 〔generally〕 used; be in wide 〔general〕 use / 일상 ～되고 있다〔있지 않다〕 be in 〔out of〕 daily use / ～하게 되다 come into use / ～되지 않게 되다 go 〔drop〕 out of use; fall into disuse / ～을 제한하다 limit the use 《of》 / 오랜 ～에 견디다 stand long use / 시간을 유익하게 ～하다 employ *one's* time profitably / ～을 허락하다〔금하다〕 allow 〔forbid, ban〕 the use 《of firearms》 / 그것은 무엇에 ～됩니까 What is it used for? / 이 표현은 지금 ～되지 않는다 This expression has gone out of use now. / (방 따위의) ～중 《게시》 In Use. *or* Occupied. / 이 기계는 오랫동안 ～되었다〔되지 않았다〕 This machine has long been 「in 〔out of〕 use. / 이 돈은 선생님 마음대로 ～하십시오 This money is entirely at your disposal.
◉ ～가치 utility 〔use〕 value; the value in use. ～권 the right of using; the right to use; the use: 건물의 ～권을 가지다 have the use of a building. ～량 the amount used; the quantity consumed. ～료 a rental fee; the rent; the hire. ～법 how to use; the use 《of》; directions (for use) (약 등의). ～설명서 《기계 등의》 instructions. ～인 an employee; a servant (하인); [총칭] the employed. ～자 a user; a consumer (소비자); an employer (고용주). ～필핵연료 spent nuclear fuel.

**사우**(社友) a friend of a firm; 《동료》 a colleague; an office mate.

**사우나** a sauna. ¶ ～실 a sauna parlor / ～탕 a sauna (bath).

**사우디아라비아** 《왕국》 Saudi Arabia.
◉ ～사람 a Saudi Arabian; a Saudi.

**사우스다코타** 《미국의 주》 South Dakota (생략 S.Dak.; S.D.). ◉ ～사람 a South Dakotan.

**사우스캐롤라이나** 《미국의 주》 South Carolina (생략 S.C.). ◉ ～사람 a South Carolinian.

**사우스포** 〖야구〗 a southpaw (pitcher); 〖권투〗 a southpaw.

**사운**(社運) ¶ ～을 걸고 at the risk of the future of the company / 그 회사는 막대한 비용이 드는 새로운 산업기술(개발)에 ～을 겂으로써 엄청난 도박을 하고 있는 셈이다 The company is taking a huge gamble by staking 〔risking〕 its future on expensive new technology (development).

**사운드** a sound. ◉ ～박스 a sound box. ～카드 a sound card. ～트랙 a sound track.

**사원**(寺院) a (Buddhist) temple. ⇨ 성당, 성원.

**사원**(私怨) private 〔personal〕 grudge 《against》; personal grievances 〔spites〕. ¶ ～으로 from 〔out of〕 personal spite.

**사원**(社員) a member (of the staff); a staff member; an employee 《of a company》; [총칭] the staff 〔personnel〕. ¶ 신입～ a new employee 〔member of the staff〕; an incoming

employee / ～에게 주는 할인 the employees' rate; a staff discount / ～일동을 대표하여 on behalf of the staff / ～이 되다 join the staff 《of》; join 〔enter〕 the service of a company / ～을 줄이다〔늘리다〕 reduce 〔increase〕 the staff 〔personnel〕 / 그는 생명 보험 회사 ～이다 He is on the staff of a life insurance company. *or* He works for a life insurance company. / 그는 정～으로 채용되었다 He was employed as a regular member.
◉ ～명부 the roster 《of a company》. ～식당 the staff canteen.

**사월**(四月) April (생략 Apr.).

**사위** 《딸의 남편》 a son-in-law (*pl.* sons-in-law). ¶ 큰〔만〕～ the oldest son-in-law / 작은〔막내〕～ a younger 〔the youngest〕 son-in-law / ～를 맞다 get a son-in-law; take a husband for *one's* daughter / ～ 사랑은 장모 It is the mother (rather than the father) who loves the son-in-law.
◉ 사윗감 a suitable person for a son-in-law; a likely son-in-law: 사윗감을 고르다 look for a man to marry *one's* daughter to / 사윗감으로 훌륭하다〔시원찮다〕 be a good 〔poor〕 match for *one's* daughter.

**사위**(詐僞) deception; falsehood; beguilement. ～하다 deceive; beguile; betray *one's* conscience.

**사위다** burn up; be burnt out; go out; burn itself out. ¶ 숯불이 거진 다 사위어 간다 The charcoal is nearly burned out.

**사유**(私有) private ownership 〔possession〕. ¶ ～의 privately-owned; private / 토지의 ～ private ownership of land / ～로 하다 possess *oneself* 《of *a thing*》; make 《*a thing*》 *one's* private possession. ◉ ～권 the right of private property; private ownership 〔rights〕. ～림 a private forest. ～물 private possessions 〔property〕. ～재산 private property: ～ 재산제 the private property 〔ownership〕 system. ～지 private land; privately-owned land. ～화(化) privatization: ～화하다 privatize.

**사유**(事由) a reason; a cause; 《근거》 a ground. ⇨ 이유.

**사유**(思惟) thinking; thought. ～하다 ⇨ 「생각하다.

**사육**(飼育) breeding; raising 《of cattle, *etc.*》. ～하다 breed; raise; rear; keep. ¶ 누에의 ～법 the method of rearing silkworms / 그는 목장에서 소를 ～하고 있다 He raises 〔breeds〕 cattle on his ranch. ◉ ～기술 handling and feeding techniques. ～자 a breeder; a rearer; a 《bird》 fancier. ～장 a (horse-)breeding farm; a stud farm (말의); 《목장》 a ranch: 가축〔소〕 ～장 a cattle ranch. ～학 thremmatology.

**사육제**(謝肉祭) the carnival.

**사은**(謝恩) repaying 《*another's*》 kindness; an expression of gratitude. ～하다 repay a kindness; express gratitude; appreciate favors.
◉ ～판매 thank-you sales. ～회 a party given 《by the graduates》 in honor of 《their teachers》; a thank-you party 《for the teachers》; a testimonial dinner: 졸업생들에 의해 ～회가 개최되었다 A thank-you party given by the graduates in honor of their teachers was held.

**사음**(一音) 〖음악〗 G.
◉ ～자리표 a G 〔treble〕 clef.

**사음**(邪淫) adultery; lasciviousness; lewdness; licentiousness; immorality. ～하다 (be) immoral; lewd; lascivious; licentious.

**사의**(謝意) ① 《감사의 뜻》 gratitude; thanks. ¶ ～를 표하다 express *one's* gratitude 〔thanks〕; tender *one's* thanks 《to》 / 미소로써 ～를 표하다 smile *one's* thanks / ～를 표하기 위해 선물을 하다 make a present in token of *one's* gratitude / 그녀는 그에게 머리를 숙여 정중하게 ～를 표하였다 She bowed to him her most profuse thanks. / 여러분의 친절에 대해서 충심으로 ～를 표합니다 I wish to express my hearty appreciation for your kindness. ② 《사과의 뜻》 apology. ¶ ～를 표하다 apologize 《for》; tender an apology 《for》.

**사의**(辭意) 《사퇴의 뜻》 *one's* resolution 〔intention〕 to resign. ¶ ～를 비치다 reveal 〔hint, make known〕 *one's* intention to resign / ～를 굳히다 firmly resolve *one's* intention to resign / ～를 표명〔번복〕하다 announce 〔reconsider〕 *one's* resignation / 그는 좋지 않은 건강을 이유로 ～를 굳혔다 He decided to resign for the reason that he was in poor health.

**사이** ① 《공간적인》 (***a***) 《간격》 an interval; a space; 《거리》 (a) distance; 《틈새》 an opening; a gap. ¶ 일정한 ～를 두고 at regular intervals / ～를 떼다 leave a space; space out; 《행간을》 leave space between the lines / ～를 좁히다 leave no space. (***b***) 《간(間)》 in; 《둘 사이》 between; 《셋 이상》

among; 《한 가운데》 amid (★ 원칙적으로 in의 뒤에는 복수명사·집합명사가 옴). ¶ 3국 ～의 협정 the agreement between the three powers (★ 3자 이상의 경우라도 관계가 개별적인 경우는 between을 씀) / 너와 나와 그와의 ～ between you and he and I (★ 셋 이상이라도 and로 연결되면 between) / 책 ～에 편지를 끼우다 put a letter between the leaves of a book / 톰과 제인 ～에 앉다 sit between Tom and Jane / 그녀는 많은 학생들 ～에서 선발되었다 She was chosen from among many students. / 나는 그들 ～에 끼여 입장이 난처했다 Placed between them, I found my position awkward. / 두 집 ～의 간격이 좁다 There is not enough space between the two houses. / 그녀는 젊은이들 ～에서 인기가 있다 She is popular among 〔with〕 young people.

② 《시간적인》 an interval; time; a while; a space; a period (기간); a span. ¶ ～에 in; for; while; when; during / 눈 깜짝할 ～에 in a blink 〔wink〕; in an instant / 과거 3년 ～에 in the past 〔last〕 three years / 집을 비운 ～에 when 〔while〕 *one* is out; in *one's* absence / 밥 먹을 ～도 없다 have no time even to take a meal / 그녀는 남들이 노는 ～에 열심히 공부했다 She worked 〔studied〕 hard while the others were playing. / 밤～에 비가 왔다 It rained during the night. / 4시와 5시 ～에 오시지요 Please come between four and five o'clock. / 버스가 10분씩 ～를 두고 운행된다 The buses run at 10-minute intervals. / 어느 ～에 어찌 벌써 돌아왔느냐 What are you doing back so soon?

③ 《관계》 relationship; 《사귀는》 relations; terms; a footing. ¶ 정다운 ～ harmonious 〔friendly〕 relations / 아버지와 자식 ～ the relation of 〔between〕 father and son / ～가 좋다〔나쁘다〕 be on good 〔bad, poor〕 terms 《with》 / ～가 가깝다〔멀다〕 be on intimate 〔distant〕 terms / ～가 벌어지다〔멀어지다〕 be estranged from each other / ～를 갈라놓다 come between 《the two》; estrange 《A from B》 / …와는 만나면 인사나 하는 ～다 be on nodding terms with… / …와 친한 ～가 되다 form a friendly 〔familiar〕 terms with… / 그 사람과는 어떤 ～인가 What relation is he to you? *or* How are you related to him? / 나와 그녀와의 ～에는 아무런 관계도 없다 I have nothing to do with her. / 그들 ～가 좋지 않다 They do not get on well with each other. / 돈이 그 둘 ～를 갈라 놓았다 Money came between the two.

**사이다** 《음료》 a soda pop; carbonated drinks (★ cider는 사과주). ◉ ～병 a pop bottle.

**사이드** a side. ◉ ～라이트 (a) sidelight. ～라인 〖스포츠〗 a sideline. ～미러 a sideview mirror; 《영》 a wing mirror. ～스로 〖야구〗 a sidearm delivery 〔throw〕. ～스텝 a side step. ～스트로크 〖수영〗 a side-stroke. ～아웃 〖배구〗 a side out. ～카 a sidecar; 《사이드카가 달린 오토바이》 a motorcycle combination. ～타이틀 a side title. ～테이블 a side table. ～플레이어 〖영화〗 a side player; a by-player.

**사이렌** a siren; a whistle. ¶ ～을 울리다 blow 〔sound〕 a siren / 소방차가 요란스레 ～을 울리며 달려갔다 Fire engines scudded away with sirens wailing. / 경기 개시 ～이 울렸다 The siren signaled the beginning of the game.

**사이버** cyber-(★ 「인터넷에 메시지를 보내기 위해 컴퓨터에 연결된 전자 통신; 가상(假想)」 이란 뜻). ◉ ～쇼핑 《컴퓨터를 통해 상품을 선별·구매할 수 있는 온라인 쇼핑》 cybershopping. ～펑크 cyberpunk (★ 컴퓨터 네트워크가 관리하는 미래 사회를 묘사하는 공상과학 소설 (S.F.)의 한 분야). [< *cyber*netics + *punk*]

**사이버공간**(一空間) ⇨ 사이버스페이스.

**사이버네이션** 《컴퓨터와 자동제어 기기가 결합된 시스템》 cybernation [< *cybernetics* + autom*ation*]

**사이버네틱스** 《인공 두뇌학》 cybernetics.

**사이버스페이스** 《컴퓨터 네트워크 상에서 가상 공간》 cyberspace.

**사이보그** 《인조 인간》 a cyborg.

**사이비**(似而非) pseudo; quasi; would=be; sham; mock; false.
◉ ～군자〔신사〕 a hypocrite; a would=be gentleman. ～기자 a quasi-reporter. ～언론인 a quasi-journalist. ～종교 a pseudo-religion. ～철학 pseudo-philosophy; philosophism. ～학자 a pretended scholar; a charlatan.

**사이사이** ① 《공간》 spaces 《between》; intervals; gaps; distances. ¶ 장미꽃 ～에 백합꽃을 심다 plant lilies among the roses. ② 《시간》 intervals 《of, in, between》; in between times. ¶ 일하는 ～에 in the intervals 〔intermission〕 of work; in *one's* spare moments from *one's* work.

**사이즈** size. ¶ ～가 맞다 fit *one;* be *one's*

size / ～가 안 맞다 be not *one's* size / ～를 재다 take the size 《of》/ ～가 맞나 입어보다 try 《a jacket》 on for size / 와이셔츠 ～가 어떻게 되십니까 What size shirt do you take 〔need〕?

**사이짓기** 〖농업〗 the intercropping.

**사이참**(一站) ① 《휴식》 a break; a respite; a brief rest; a time out. ② 《음식》 a snack between regular meals; between-meals; refreshments. ¶ ～ 먹다 eat between-meals; have a snack / ～으로 감자를 먹다 eat potato between=meals; eat potato for *one's* snack.

**사이코드라마** 《심리극》 a psychodrama.

**사이클** 《기계·전기의》 a cycle; 《주기·순환기》 a 〔the〕 cycle; 《자전거》 a cycle; a bicycle; a bike 《구어》. ◉ ～선수 a bicycle racer.

**사이클로이드** 〖수학〗 a cycloid.

**사이클로트론** 〖물리〗 a cyclotron. ¶ ～의 cyclotronic.

**사이클론** 〖기상〗 a Cyclone.

**사이클링** cycling; bicycling. ¶ ～을 가다 go on a cycling tour; go cycling.

**사이클히트** 〖야구〗 ¶ ～를 치다 hit for the cycle.

**사이키델릭** psychedelic. ◉ ～음악 psychedelic music.

**사이판** 《태평양의 섬》 Saipan (Island).

**사이펀** a siphon; a syphon. ◉ ～기압계 a siphon barometer. ～병 a siphon bottle. ～작용 siphonage; (a) siphon effect.

**사이프러스** Cyprus.

**사인**(死因) the cause of 《*a person's*》 death. ¶ ～이 불명하다 die from some unknown cause / ～을 조사하다 inquire into the cause of 《*a person's*》 death / ～은 …이다 die of…; 《*a person's*》 death is due to… / …의 ～이 되다 be the death of… / ～은 무엇입니까 What was the cause of 《*a person's*》 death? / 그의 ～은 연탄 가스 중독으로 보인다 The cause of his death is believed to be anthracite briquet gas poisoning.
◉ ～통계 statistics of death causes.

**사인**(私人) a private man 〔person〕; a private individual 〔citizen〕. ¶ 일개 ～의 자격으로 as a private person; in *one's* private capacity.

**사인**(私印) a private 〔personal〕 seal. ◉ ～도용 surreptitious use of a private seal. ～위조 forgery of a private seal.

**사인**[1] ① 《신호》 a signal; a sign (암호). ¶ 투수에게 ～을 보내다 signal 〔give signals〕 to the pitcher / 그 투수와 포수는 몰래 ～을 교환했다 The battery stealthily exchanged signals with each other.
② 《서명》 a signature; an autograph (유명인의). ～하다 sign *one's* name 〔autograph〕 《on》; put *one's* signature 《to》; autograph; sign 《a letter》. ¶ ～이 있는 사진〔공〕 an autographed photo 〔ball〕 / ～을 받다 get 《*a person's*》 autograph / 서류〔수표〕에 ～하다 sign 「the papers 〔a check〕 / 저자가 책에 ～을 해주었다 The author autographed a copy of his book for me.
◉ ～공세 storming for autographs: ～공세를 받다 be besieged by 〔plagued with〕 autograph hunters 〔seekers〕. ～첩 an autograph album 〔book〕.

**사인**[2] 〖수학〗 sine (생략 sin). ◉ ～곡선 a sine curve.

**사인교**(四人轎) a sedan chair borne on poles by four men.

**사인승**(四人乘) ◉ ～ 자동차 a four-seater.

**사인조**(四人組) a group 〔team〕 of four people; a quartet; a foursome.

**사일**(巳日) 〖민속〗 the Day of the Snake.

**사일런트** ① 《묵음자》 a silent letter. ② 《무성 영화》 a silent picture 〔movie, film〕.

**사일로** 〖농업〗 a silo.

**사일열**(四日熱) 〖의학〗 quartan (fever, malaria).

**사임**(辭任) resignation; retirement from office; going out of office. ～하다 resign (from *one's* post); leave the service; 「go out of 〔step down from〕 office. ¶ 관직을 ～하다 resign a government office / 강제로 ～시키다 force 《*a person*》 out of office; compel 《*a person*》 to resign (his post).

**사자**(四者) ¶ ～(간)의 quadripartite.
◉ ～회담 a quadripartite meeting; four-party 〔four-country〕 talks: 한반도에서의 영구적인 평화 협정을 위한 ～회담 the four-country talks for a permanent peace arrangement on the Korean Peninsula.

**사자**(死者) a dead person; the deceased; 《사고로 인한》 fatalities; deaths; [총칭] the dead. ⇨ 사망자.

**사자**(使者) ① 《사람》 a messenger; an envoy; a mission. ¶ ～를 보내다 send a messenger 《to》/ ～로서 가다 go on a mission. ② 〖불교〗 the messenger who takes a dead soul to the underworld.

**사자**(嗣子) a successor; an heir (남자).

**사자**(獅子) 〖동물〗 a lion; a lioness (암컷). ¶ ～ 같은 leonine; lionlike / 성난 ～와 같이 like a lion at bay; with lionlike fury. ◉ ～자리 〖천문〗 the Lion; Leo. ～춤 a lion dance; a dance with a lion's mask. ～코 an upturned nose; a pug 〔snub〕 nose. 새끼～ a lion cub.

**사자**(寫字) copying; transcription. ◉ ～생 a copyist; a scribe; an amanuensis.

**사자어금니**(獅子—) an indispensable 「thing 〔person〕.

**사자후**(獅子吼) ① 《사자의》 the roaring of a lion. ② 《열변》 an impassioned 〔inflammatory, eloquent〕 speech. ～하다 make an eloquent 〔impassioned〕 speech.

**사장**(死藏) hoarding; dead storage. ～하다 hoard (up); keep in dead storage; keep 《*a thing*》 idle. ¶ 재물을 ～하다 keep a fortune as a buried treasure / 책을 ～하다 be a mere book hoarder; coffin books.

**사장**(沙場) a sandy beach; a shoal; the 「sands; a sandbar.

**사장**(社長) the president 〔head〕 《of a company》; 《영》 a managing director. ¶ 부～ a vice-president / ～이 되다 become president of a company; assume the presidency of a corporation. ◉ ～실 the president's office.

**사장**(射場) a 「firing 〔target-practice〕 range; an archery ground (활터).

**사재**(私財) private funds 〔assets, means, property, fortune〕. ¶ ～를 털어 out of *one's* own purse 〔pocket〕; at *one's* own expense / 공공 사업에 ～를 털어넣다 use 〔spend, expend〕 *one's* funds upon a public undertaking.

**사재기** hoarding; cornering; a corner. a hoard 《of》. ～하다 hoard (up); stock up 《on》; buy up 《all the coffee in the market》; make a corner 《in wheat》. ¶ ～한 물품 hoardings / 그는 대량의 설탕을 ～했다 He hoarded a large amount of sugar.

**사쟁이** ⇨ 옥사쟁이(獄—).

**사저**(私邸) *one's* private residence 〔man「sion〕.

**사적**(史的) (being) historic(al). ¶ ～ 고찰 historical investigations / ～ 사실 a historical fact / ～ 연구 historical studies. ◉ ～유물론 historical materialism.

**사적**(史蹟) a historical spot 〔site, place〕; a place of historic(al) interest; historic(al) relics 〔remains〕. ¶ ～이 많다 be rich in historic remains / ～을 보존하다 preserve historic remains / ～을 찾다 visit places of historic interest / 이 건물은 ～으로 지정되었다 This building was designated as a place of historic interest. ◉ ～보존회 a society for preservation of historic(al) relics.

**사적**(史籍) a history (book).

**사적**(私的) (being) private; individual; unofficial; personal. ¶ ～으로 privately; individually; unofficially / ～ 감정 personal feeling / ～ 의견 *one's* personal opinion 《on》 / ～ 생활 *one's* private life / ～ 교제가 있다 have 〔be in〕 personal contact 《with》 / 이것은 ～인 일이다 This is something personal. *or* This is a private matter 〔affair〕. / ～ 용무로 하루 휴가를 얻었다 I took a day off for a personal affairs 〔matters〕.

**사적**(事績) an achievement; accomplishments; a deed; an exploit; services; merits. ¶ 위인의 ～ the deeds of a great man / 그의 ～은 길이 역사에 남을 것이다 His achievements will long remain in history.

**사적**(事蹟·事跡) (an) evidence; a vestige; a trace.

**사전**(私田) a private(ly-owned) field.

**사전**(私錢) counterfeit 〔forged〕 money; 《경화》 a false coin. ◉ ～꾼 a counterfeiter; a coiner 《영》.

**사전**(事典) an encyclop(a)edia 《of》.

**사전**(事前) ¶ ～의 before the fact; advance 《warning》; prior 《notice》 / ～에 before the fact; in advance; beforehand / ～에 방지하다 prevent an affair from arising / ～에 통고하다〔알리다〕 notify 〔inform〕 《*a person*》 in advance / ～에 경고하다 give advance warning / ～에 준비하다 prepare in advance; have 《*a thing*》 ready beforehand / 그는 그 결과를 ～에 알고 있었다 He knew the result(s) in advance. ◉ ～검열 precensorship. ～계획 a prearranged plan. ～공작 preparatory operations. ～동의 a prior consent; a consent before the fact. ～ 선거 운동 preelection campaigning; precandidacy propaganda: ～ 선거 운동은 금지되어 있다 Preelection campaigning is prohibited. ～수회(收賄) acceptance of a bribe before an act. ～승인 《obtain *a person's*》 prior approval. ～준비 advance preparations. ～통고 (an) advance notice; (a) previous notice: ～ 통고 없이 without a previous notice. ～행위 an act before the fact. ～협의 preliminary 〔prior〕 consultation.

**사전**(辭典) a dictionary; a wordbook; 《고전어의》 a lexicon; 《용어 풀이》 a glossary; 《동의어의》 a thesaurus (*pl.* ～es, -ri). ¶ 인명〔지명〕～ a biographical 〔geographical〕 dictionary / 학습 ～ a learner's dictionary / ～을 찾다 look

up 《a word》 in a dictionary; consult 〔refer to〕 a dictionary 《for the meaning of a word》 / 이 낱말은 내 ～에 나와 있지 않다 This word is not (given) in my dictionary.
◉ ～편집자 a lexicographer; a compiler of a dictionary. ～학 lexicology.

**사절**(四折) (being) folded in four; fourfold; a quarto; a quarter (사진의).
◉ ～판(判) a quarto (edition); a 4to.

**사절**(使節) 《개인》 an envoy; an ambassador; a delegate; 《일행》 a mission. ¶ ～을 파견하다 send a delegate / 그들은 무역〔친선〕 ～단으로 이탈리아에 갔다 They went on a trade 〔goodwill〕 mission to Italy. ◉ ～단 a mission; a delegation: 교육 ～단 an educational mission / 군사 ～단 a military mission / 문화 ～단 a cultural mission / 경제 ～단을 파견하다 dispatch 〔send〕 an economic mission to.

**사절**(謝絶) refusal; declination. ～하다 refuse; decline; turn down. ¶ 면회를 ～하다 decline to receive 〔see〕 a visitor; be not at home to a visitor / 제의를 ～하다 decline an offer / 면회 ～ 《게시》 No visitors (allowed). / 작업중 면회 ～ 《게시》 Visits 〔Interviews〕 declined during working hours. / 외상 ～ 《게시》 Cash Please. *or* No Credit. / 입장 ～ 《게시》 No Admission. / 미성년자 입장 ～ Adults only. *or* No children. / 화환은 ～합니다 《게시》 We request that no flowers be sent. *or* No flowers.

**사점**(死點) 〖기계〗 a dead point 〔center〕.

**사정**(私情) personal feelings 〔regard, consideration, affection, sentiment〕; a bias. ¶ ～에 매이지 않고 「regardless of 〔unbiased by〕 *one's* personal feelings; impartially / ～에 이끌리다〔좌우되다〕 be swayed 〔influenced〕 by personal feelings / ～을 버리다 set aside *one's* personal feelings.

**사정**(事情) ① 《형편·이유 등》 circumstances; conditions; reasons; 《정세》 the situation; the state of things 〔affairs〕. ¶ 가정 ～ *one's* family circumstances 〔reasons〕 / 교통 ～ traffic conditions / 식량〔주택〕 ～ the food 〔housing〕 situation / 자세한 ～ the details; the whole circumstances.
사정의: ～(의) 여하를 막론하고 regardless of circumstances / 급수 ～의 악화 the worsening of the condition of water supply.
사정에: ～에 몰려 driven by the stress of circumstances / 그 지역의 특수 ～에 비추어 in view of the peculiar circumstances of the region / ～에 어둡다 be ill informed of the circumstances 〔affairs〕 / 정계 ～에 밝다 be well informed on 〔about〕 political affairs.
사정이: ～이 허락하는 한〔허락하면〕 as 〔so〕 far as circumstances permit 〔will allow〕 / ～이 부득이한 경우에는 in case there arise unavoidable circumstances / 어떤 ～이 있더라도 in 〔under〕 any circumstances; in any case; on any account / 특별한 ～이 있는 때에 한해서 only in special circumstances.
사정을: ～을 밝히다 clear up matters; reveal the affair 〔situation〕 / ～을 참작하다〔고려하다〕 make allowance(s) for circumstances.
사정으로: 말 못할 ～으로 for some secret 〔inexpressible〕 reasons / 불가피한 ～으로 from 〔under, compelled by〕 unavoidable circumstances; for some unavoidable reasons / 여러 가지 ～으로 for many reasons combined / 이러한 ～으로 under 〔in〕 these circumstances; such being the case / 지금 ～으로는 in our present circumstances / 가정 ～으로 학교를 그만두다 quit 〔leave〕 school for family reasons.
¶ ～을 말하시오 What's your problem 〔situation〕? / 참 ～이 딱하십니다 It's too bad! / ～이 있어 말할 수 없습니다 There is a certain reason why I cannot speak about it. / ～이 많이 달라졌다 Things have changed greatly.
② 《배려》 consideration; 《관용》 leniency; 《간청》 (an) entreaty; (a) solicitation; an earnest request. ～하다 entreat; implore; solicit 《*one's* special consideration》; ask (leniency); beg (a favor). ¶ 하룻밤 재워 달라고 ～하다 ask for a night's lodging / ～했지만 그는 들은체도 하지 않았다 He did not pay the slightest attention 〔regard〕 to my solicitation. / 그는 남의 ～을 잘 이해한다 He is very considerate of others.

**사정**(査定) 《세금의》 assessment; 《자격의》 screening. ～하다 assess 《taxes》; make an assessment 《of》; screen. ¶ (소득을) 백만 원으로 ～받다 be assessed at 1,000,000 won. ◉ ～가격 an assessed value 〔price〕. ～기관 an assessing organ. ～액 an assessed amount; an assessment: 소득 ～액 an assessed income. ～자 an assessor.

**사정**(射程) a (shooting) range; shot; 〖포술〗 amplitude; scope (화살의). ¶ 유효 ~ the effective range《of a missile》/ 원거리〔근거리〕 ~ a long〔short〕range / ~ 안〔밖〕에 within 〔out of〕 range 〔shot〕《of》/ ~을 정하다 range.
◉ ~거리 a range: 이 대포의 ~거리는 10마일 이상이다 This cannon「ranges over〔has a range of over〕ten miles.

**사정**(射精) 〖생리〗 ejaculation; emission (of semen); seminal emission. ~하다 ejaculate; eject 〔emit, discharge〕 semen. ◉ ~관 an ejaculatory duct.

**사정사정**(事情事情) pleading *one's* case; [부사적] pleadingly; imploringly. ~하다 plead *one's* case; beg《*a person's*》 consideration(s)〔leniency〕; earnestly request 〔ask for〕; implore; entreat. ¶ ~해서 승낙을 얻다 entreat *a person* into consent.

**사정없다**(事情—) (be) merciless; relentless; severe; ruthless; inexorable; unsparing. ¶ 사정없이 mercilessly; ruthlessly; severely; without mercy / 사정없이 때리다 beat《*a person*》 mercilessly〔unsparingly〕/ 사정없이 처벌하다 punish《*a person*》 without mercy / 범법자에 대해서는 조금도 ~ show〔allow〕 no mercy toward the offender.

**사정협의회**(司正協議會) a meeting of ranking officials in charge of audit and inspection; the interministry audit session.

**사제**(司祭) a (Catholic) priest; a celebrant; a pastor (신교의). ◉ ~관(館) a parsonage.

**사제**(私製) private 〔illicit〕 manufacture. ¶ ~의 private; unofficial; privately made. ◉ ~담배 privately made cigarettes. ~엽서 a private 〔an unofficial〕 postcard; a postcard (★ 관제 엽서는 a postal card). ~품 privately made goods; an article of private manufacture.

**사제**(舍弟) ①《자기 아우》 my younger brother. ②《형에게》 me; I who am your younger brother.

**사제**(師弟) teacher and pupil 〔student〕; master and disciple. ¶ ~(지)간 the relationship between teacher and pupil / ~의 도(道)를 무너뜨리다 tear down the teacher-student ethics.

**사제**(瀉劑) a laxative; a purgative.

**사조**(—調) 〖음악〗 (the key of ) G.
◉ 사장조〔단조〕《a sonata in》 G major〔minor〕.

**사조**(思潮) a trend 〔current〕 of thought. ¶ 근대 문예 ~ the trend of modern literature / 시대 ~ the spirit of the times / 현대 ~ contemporary thought 〔ideas〕.

**사족**(四足) ①《네 발》 four feet. ②《사지》 the arms and legs; the limbs. ¶ ~성한 병신 an idler; a wastrel / ~을 못 쓰다 [비유적] be awfully fond of; have a weakness 〔passion〕《for》; be spellbound; be a sucker《for》; be crazy《about》/ 여자라면 ~을 못 쓰다 be crazy 〔mad〕 about a woman / 그는 술이라면 ~을 못 쓴다 He has a weakness for wine. *or* He is simply mad so far as wine is concerned.
◉ ~발이〔백이〕 a horse with all four hooves white. ~수(獸) a four-footed animal; a quadruped.

**사족**(蛇足) (a) superfluity; (a) redundancy; padding. ¶ ~의 superfluous / ~을 달다 make an unnecessary addition《to》; add a fifth wheel; pad (out)《a speech, writing》/ 그것은 ~이다 That's quite unnecessary to add. *or* That's like putting a fifth wheel on a coach. *or* That's superfluous.

**사죄**(死罪) a capital crime 〔offense〕; a crime punishable with death; 〖가톨릭〗 a mortal sin.

**사죄**(赦罪) 《용서·사면》 pardon; remission; absolution; amnesty; 〖가톨릭〗 absolution. ~하다 pardon; remit《a punishment》; absolve《*a person* from 〔of〕》.

**사죄**(謝罪) (an) apology. ~하다 apologize《to *a person* for》; beg《*a person's*》 pardon 〔forgiveness〕《for》; make an apology《for》; express *one's* regret《for》. ¶ ~를 받다 accept an apology / ~를 요구하다 demand an apology《from》/ 무릎을 꿇고 ~하다 beg《*a person's*》 pardon on *one's* knees. ◉ ~광고 a notice of apology: 신문에 ~ 광고를 내다 publish an apology in a newspaper.

**사주**(四柱) 〖민속〗 the "four pillars" for the year, month, day and hour of *one's* birth (which are supposed to have influence upon *one's* fortune). ¶ ~(를) 보다 have *one's* fortune told.
◉ ~단자 a letter to the house of the *fiancée* in which the Four Pillars of the bridegroom-to-be are written. ~쟁이 a fortune teller. ~점 *one's* fortune as determined by the Four Pillars. ~팔자 the Four Pillars and the (cyclic) Eight Characters for the

year, month, day and hour of *one's* birth; 《운수》 *one's* fate 〔destiny, fortune〕; *one's* lot: ～팔자가 좋다〔나쁘다〕 be born under a lucky 〔an unlucky〕 star. ｢the proprietor of a firm.

**사주**(社主) the owner of a company;

**사주**(使嗾) instigation; incitement. ～하다 entice; instigate; incite; abet; egg 〔edge, set〕 《*a person*》 on 《to》; stir up; provoke. ¶ …의 ～를 받고 instigated by 《*a person*》; at 《*a person's*》 instigation / ～하여 …시키다 tempt 〔set on〕 《*a person*》 to *do;* egg 《*a person*》 on to *do* / ～하여 죄를 범하게 하다 abet 《*a person*》 in a crime.
◉ ～자 an instigator. ｢reef.

**사주**(砂洲) a sandbar; a sandbank; a

**사중**(四重) ① 《네 겹》 ¶ ～의 quadruple; quadruplex / ～으로 quadruply. ② 〖불교〗 the Four Major Prohibitions of Buddhism (against killing, stealing, adultery and thoughtless remarks).
◉ ～주 a quartet(te): 현악 ～주(단) a string quartet(te). ～창 a (vocal) quartet(te).

**사증**(査證) a visa. ～하다 visa 《a passport》. ¶ 입국 ～ an entry visa / 외국인 출국 ～ foreigners exit visas / 취업 및 관광 겸용 ～ working holiday visas / ～이 있는 visaed; visa'd / 여권에 ～을 받다 get 〔have〕 a visa on *one's* passport; get *one's* passport visaed / 미국에 입국 ～을 신청하다 apply for an entry visa for the United States / 나는 미국 입국 ～을 받았다 I got 〔was granted〕 a visa to the U.S. / 그는 ～을 받아야 했다 He had to get his passport visaed.
◉ ～료 a visa fee. ～담당관 a visa officer. 상용～ a business visa.

**사지**(四肢) the limbs; the legs and arms; the members. ¶ ～가 묶인 어린 염소 a kid tied by the four legs / ～가 튼튼하다 have stout limbs / ～가 멀쩡하다 have no physical defects / ～를 자르다 dismember a body; cut off the limbs; amputate / ～가 잘리다 have *one's* limbs amputated 〔cut off〕. ◉ ～동물 a four-legged〔-footed〕 animal; a quadruped. ～마비 〖병리〗 quadriplegia.

**사지**(死地) the jaws of death; a fatal position 〔situation〕; the place of death. ¶ ～로 들어가다 go into the jaws of death / ～를 벗어나다 escape from the jaws of death / ～에 빠지다 fall into 〔be in〕 the jaws of death; be at death's doorstep.

**사지**(寺址) a temple site.

**사지**(砂紙) sandpaper. ＝사포(砂布).

**사직**(司直) administration of justice; [총칭] the judicial authorities; the court(s); the bench. ¶ 마침내 ～ 당국이 그 사건에 손을 댔다 The judicial authorities have taken action of that case at last. *or* The arm of the law has reached the affair at last.
◉ ～당국 the judicial authorities.

**사직**(社稷) 《신》 Land God and Grain God; the guardian deities of the State; 《국가》 sovereignty; the State.
◉ ～단(壇) an altar to the State deities. ～지신(之臣) a pillar of the State; a leading statesman.

**사직**(辭職) resignation. ～하다 resign (from) 《*one's* office 〔post〕》; check out (of office) 《미구어》; quit 〔leave〕 office; step down from office. ¶ 권고～ an urged 〔advised〕 resignation / ～을 권고하다 advise 〔urge〕 《*a person*》 to resign / 신병을 이유로 ～하다 resign on the ground of illness 〔for reasons of health〕 / 그는 위원장직을 2주전에 ～했다 He resigned as chairman two weeks ago. / ～한다는 게 정말이냐 Are you in earnest about resigning? / 그에게는 ～하는 길밖에 없다 There is no alternative 〔choice〕 but to resign his post.

**사직서**(辭職書) 《사표》 *one's* resignation; a letter of resignation. ¶ ～를 내다 submit 〔tender, give in, hand in〕 *one's* resignation / ～를 수리하다 accept 《*a person's*》 resignation / 그의 ～는 수리되었다 His resignation was accepted.

**사진**(沙塵) dust; a dust storm; a sandstorm. ¶ ～을 일으키다 raise a cloud of dust.

**사진**(寫眞) a photograph; a picture; a photo 《구어》; 《스냅》 a snapshot; a snap 《구어》. ¶ 단체 ～ a group portrait 〔photograph〕 / 기념 ～ a souvenir photograph / ～이 찍히는 거리 내에(서) within camera range / ～을 찍다 photograph; take a photograph 〔picture, shot〕 《of》; photo; 《남이 자기를》 have 〔get〕 *one's* photograph taken / ～을 현상〔인화〕하다 develop 〔print〕 a film / ～을 확대하다 enlarge a photograph / ～이 실물보다 낫다 look better in a photo / ～ 찍기를 싫어하다 be shy of camera; be camera-shy; be a camera-hater / ～ 찍는 것을 거절하다 refuse to face the camera / 기록

～을 찍다 make a photographic record《of》/ ～이 잘 나왔다 The picture came out well. / 이 ～을 확대〔현상〕해 주십시오 I want this picture enlarged 〔developed〕. / 이 ～을 한 장 더 인화해 주시오 Please make another copy of this picture. / 그녀는 ～을 잘 받〔지 않〕는다 She looks good 〔bad〕 in pictures 〔photos〕. *or* She photographs well 〔badly〕. / 이 카메라로 내 ～을 찍어 주시오 Take my photo with this camera, please.

◉ ～관 a photo studio. ～기 a camera: 망원 ～기 a telephotographic camera / ～기를 어깨에 메고 with a camera slung across *one's* shoulder / ～기에 필름을 넣다 load a camera. ～기술 a photographic technique. ～기자 a (newspaper) cameraman. ～대지(臺紙) a (photograph) mount. ～망원경 a phototelescope. ～반 a photography team; 《반원》 a staff photographer; a (newspaper) cameraman. ～복제 a photographic facsimile. ～부《신문사 등의》 the photo department: ～부장 a photo editor. ～분광기(分光器) a photospectroscope. ～사 a photographer; a cameraman. ～석판 a photolithograph. ～술 photography. ～아연판 a photozincograph. ～작가 a professional photographer; a photo artist. ～전보 a phototelegram. ～제판〖인쇄〗 photomechanical process; photoengraving. ～지도 a photomap. ～집 a collection of photographs 《of nude women》. ～첩 a photo(graph) album. ～촬영 대회 a photographic contest. ～취미 a photo fad 〔hobby〕. ～측량 photogrammetry; photographic surveying 〔measurement〕; (a) photo survey. ～틀 a picture 〔photo〕 frame. ～판 a photo plate; 《철(凸)판》 a phototype; 《요(凹)판》 a photogravure: ～판으로 하다 photograph 《the pages of a book》. ～판정 a photo finish: ～ 판정하다 decide 《the winner》 by (means of) a photo(graph). ～화보 a pictorial (magazine); an illustrated magazine.

**사진식자**(寫眞植字) 《미》 photocomposition; 《미》 phototypesetting; phototypography. ◉ ～기 a photocomposing 〔phototypographic composing〕 machine; a photocomposer.

**사진전송**(寫眞電送) phototelegraphy; telephotography. ～하다 send 〔transmit〕 《a picture》 by telephotography; telephotograph.

**사질**(砂質) ¶ ～의 sandy; psammitic. ◉ ～암 sandstone; psammite. ～토 sandy soil.

**사차**(四次) the fourth (time). ¶ ～의 biquadratic; quartic. ◉ ～방정식 a biquadratic equation. ～식 a quartic.

**사차선도로**(四車線道路) a four-lane road 〔highway〕.

**사차원**(四次元) 《네 개 차원》 four dimensions; 《제4 차원》 the fourth dimension. ¶ ～의 four-dimensional; fourth=dimensional 《world》.

**사찰**(寺刹) a Buddhist temple. ⇨ 절. ¶ ～ 내의〔내에서〕 in the temple; in 〔within〕 the temple precincts.

**사찰**(査察) 《조사》 investigation; (an) inspection; 《사상 관리》 thought control. ～하다 investigate; inspect; make an inspection 《of》. ¶ 공중 ～ an aerial inspection / 특별 ～ a special inspection / 현지 ～ an on-site 〔on-the-spot, on-the-job〕 inspection.

◉ ～계 the Investigation Section (of the police). ～관 an inspector. ～비행 an inspection flight. ～제도 an inspection system.

**사창**(私娼) an unlicensed prostitute; a streetwalker; a woman of the streets. ¶ ～ 생활을 하다 practice clandestine prostitution; be on the street / ～을 두다 keep women for prostitution / ～을 단속하다 repress 〔suppress〕 clandestine prostitution / ～을 근절하다 eradicate 〔uproot〕 unlicensed prostitution. ◉ ～가(街) an unlicensed gay 〔prostitute〕 quarters. ～굴 a brothel; a bawdy 〔whore〕 house; a house of ill fame.

**사채**(私債) a personal loan; (private) moneylending. ¶ ～를 쓰다 use private loans; obtain a private loan / ～를 주다 extend private loans.

◉ ～놀이 《run》 a moneylending business. ～동결 freezing of private loans. ～시장 the private money 〔loan〕 market. ～업자 a private 〔curb〕 moneylender; a money broker; a usurer; 《구어》 a loan shark.

**사채**(社債) a corporate debenture 〔bond〕. ¶ 단기〔장기〕～ a long-〔short=〕term debenture 〔bond〕.

**사천(왕)**(四天(王)) 〖불교〗 the Four Devas; the four heavenly guardians (on each side of Mt. Sumi).

**사철**(四一) ① 《네 계절》 the four seasons. ② [부사적] 《항상》 all the year round; in 〔through〕 all seasons;

throughout the year; always.

**사철**(私鐵) a private 〔privately-owned〕 railroad.

**사철**(砂鐵) iron 〔magnetic〕 sand.

**사철나무**(四—) 〖식물〗 a spindle tree.

**사체**(四體) the limbs; the extremities; members of the body.

**사체**(死體) a (dead) body. ◉ ～부검 an autopsy; a post-mortem.

**사체**(斜體) 《letter in》 italics; italic type; 《필기의》 an oblique hand. ¶ ～의 italicized.

**사초**(莎草) ① 〖식물〗 a sedge; a nut grass 〔sedge〕 (향부자). ② 《잔디》 turf; sod. ～하다 sod 〔turf〕 a grave.

**사촌**(四寸) ① 《친족》 a cousin (on the father's side); a first 〔full〕 cousin; a cousin-german. ¶ 외～ a cousin on the mother's side / ～의 자식 a first cousin once removed / 이웃 ～ 《속담》 A good neighbor is better than a brother 〔relative〕 far off. ② 《네 치》 4 inches. ◉ ～간 cousinship; cousinhood.

**사춘기**(思春期) adolescence; (the age of) puberty. ¶ ～의 adolescent; pubescent / ～의 소년소녀 boys and girls at puberty / ～가 되다 reach 〔arrive at, attain〕 (the age of) puberty.

**사출**(射出) 《쏘아 내보냄》 shooting out; catapulting; emission; 《복사》 radiation. ～하다 shoot out 《flames》; emit 《light》; eject 《the pilot》; catapult 《an airplane》; radiate 《heat, beams》. ◉ ～기(機) a catapult. ～성형(成形) 〖기계〗 injection molding. ～좌석 〖항공〗 an ejection 〔ejector〕 seat.

**사취**(詐取) fraud; a swindle. ～하다 obtain 〔get〕 《*a thing*》 by fraud 〔deception〕; swindle 《out of》; defraud 《*a person*》 of 《*his* property》. ¶ 돈을 ～하다 obtain money by false pretenses; defraud 《*a person*》 of *his* money; swindle 《*a person*》 out of money; swindle money from 《*a person*》.

**사치**(奢侈) (a) luxury; (an) extravagance; lavishness. ～하다 be extravagant 〔luxurious, lavish〕; indulge in luxury. ¶ ～를 좋아하는 luxury-loving / ～성 소비재 luxurious consumer goods / (대규모) ～성 유흥업 a (large-scale) leisure and entertainment business / ～성 재산 luxurious property / ～에 흐르다〔빠지다〕 fall into luxurious 〔lavish〕 habits; be addicted to extravagance / 음식〔옷〕에 ～하다 indulge in luxurious food 〔clothing〕 / ～를 삼가다 deny *oneself* luxury / 그런 ～를 할 여유가 없다 I cannot afford such luxury. / 지금 우리 소득으로 에어컨을 사는 것은 ～다 With our present income, the purchase of an air-conditioner would be an extravagance. ◉ ～관세 duty on luxury imports. ～세 taxes on luxuries; a luxury tax. ～업소 the luxury leisure establishments. ～품 luxury articles; luxuries: 외래 ～품 foreign luxury goods. ～풍조 sumptuous moods; luxurious trends; the extravagance tendency: 최근 사회에 만연되고 있는 ～ 풍조 the extravagance tendency prevailing in society of late.

**사치스럽다**(奢侈—) (be) luxurious; extravagant; lavish; expensive; sumptuous. ¶ 사치스러운 옷 extravagant clothes / 사치스러운 식사 a sumptuous meal; 《keep》 a luxurious table / 사치스러운 생활 a luxurious 〔an extravagant〕 life; high living / 사치스럽게 살다 live in luxury; live a luxurious 〔an extravagant〕 life; live high / 사치스럽게 자라다 be bred in luxury; be brought up in (the lap of) luxury.

**사칙**(四則) 〖수학〗 the four (fundamental) rules of arithmetic.

**사칙**(社則) the company regulations. ¶ ～을 어기다 break a company regulations.

**사친회**(師親會) a parent-teacher association (생략 P.T.A.).

**사칭**(詐稱) false assumption; a false statement. ～하다 assume a false 〔another's〕 name; sail under false colors. ¶ 신분 ～ false personation / 학력 ～ a false statement of *one's* academic career / 이름을 …로 ～하여 under a feigned 〔an assumed〕 name of... / 관명 ～의 혐의로 on a charge of abusing an official title / K라고 ～하고 살다 live under the assumed name of K / 관명을 ～하다 abuse 〔(falsely) assume〕 an official title; represent *oneself* as a government official.

**사카린** 〖화학〗 saccharin(e). ¶ ～의 saccharic.

**사커** soccer; 《영》 (association) football. ◉ ～선수 a soccer player.

**사타구니** the groin. ⇨ 샅.

**사탄** 《마왕》 Satan.

**사탑**(斜塔) ¶ 피사의 ～ the Leaning Tower of Pisa.

**사탕**(砂糖) ① sugar. ⇨ 설탕. ② 《과자》 candy 《미》; sweets 《영》 (★ candy는 드롭스·캐러멜·봉봉 등도 포함); a taffy 〔toffee 《영》〕 (땅콩 등이 든); a lollipop (막대사탕). ◉ ～가게 a candy store. ～단풍 a sugar maple. ～무 a sugar beet. ～밀(蜜) = 당밀. ～수수 a sugar cane. ～야자 a gomuti (palm). ～옥수수 a sorg(h)o; a sweet sorghum. ～장수 a confectioner.

**사탕발림**(砂糖—) sugarcoated 〔honeyed〕 words; flattery; 《구어》 sweet talk; soft soap. ～하다 use fair 〔sweet〕 words; 《미구어》 sweet-talk; 《구어》 butter (up); soft-soap; sugar (up) 《영》; cajole; flatter. ¶ ～에 넘어가다 be taken in by 《*a person's*》 honeyed words; be soft=soaped.

**사태** beef shank (used to make a thick soup).

**사태**(死胎) a dead fetus. ◉ ～분만 a stillbirth.

**사태**(沙汰) ① 《무너짐》 《미》 a landslide; 《영》 a landslip; an avalanche (눈사태). ¶ 눈～ a snowslide; an avalanche (of snow) / 진흙 ～ a mudslide / ～가 나다 landslide; a landslip occurs / ～로 기차가 불통이 되었다 The landslide locked the railway traffic. ② 《많음》 lots 《of》; a flood; a crowd; a multitude 《of》; an avalanche. ¶ 편지 ～ an influx of letters / 사람 ～ lots of people; an avalanche of people / 불경기로 실업자 ～가 났다 Depression has brought forth a mass discharge of employees.

**사태**(事態) the situation; (the state of) things 〔affairs〕. ¶ 비상 ～ a state of emergency / 심상치 않은〔심각한〕 ～ a serious 〔critical〕 situation / ～를 개선하다 improve matters 〔the situation〕 / ～를 관망하다 watch the situation; observe the state of things / ～를 수습〔해결〕하다 save 〔settle, solve〕 the situation / ～를 악화〔완화〕시키다 aggravate 〔ease, relieve〕 the situation / ～가 호전되었다 Things took a favorable turn. / 최악의 ～에 대비하다 prepare 〔be prepared〕 for the worst / 국가 비상 ～를 선포하다 declare a state of national emergency / ～가 악화〔호전〕되고 있다 Things are getting worse 〔better〕.

**사택**(私宅) *one's* private residence; *one's* (own) home.

**사택**(社宅) a company house 《for its employees》; [총칭] company housing; 《기숙사》 a company dormitory; a company flat (아파트식).

**사토**(沙土·砂土) sandy soil.

**사토장이**(莎土匠—) a gravedigger.

**사통**(私通) ① 《연락·편지》 private correspondence. ～하다 keep private correspondence 《with》. ② 《밀통》 illicit intercourse; an illicit liaison; intimacy (완곡히); fornication (미혼자와의); adultery (기혼자와의). ～하다 have improper relations 《with》; establish illicit liaisons 《with》; commit adultery; fornicate 《with》. ◉ ～자 an adulterer; an adulteress (여); a fornicator.

**사통오달**(四通五達) = 사통팔달.

**사통팔달**(四通八達) 《roads》 running 〔stretching〕 in all directions. ～하다 《roads》 run 〔stretch〕 in all directions. ¶ ～한 곳 a key junction; a focus of traffic arteries; a center of traffic / 이 지방은 철도가 ～해 있다 There is a whole network of railroads in this district.

**사퇴**(辭退) 《퇴거》 excusing *oneself* from a senior's presence; taking *one's* leave from elders; 《사직》 resignation; 《사양》 declining; refusing to accept. ～하다 excuse *oneself* from a senior's presence; take *one's* leave from elders; resign 《*one's* position》; decline 《an offer, *a person's* invitation》; refuse to accept. ¶ 자진 ～ voluntary resignation / 공직을 ～하다 resign (from) *one's* office; leave office.

**사투**(死鬪) a desperate struggle; a fight to the death; mortal combat. ～하다 struggle for *one's* life; fight desperately; engage in a fight to the death. ¶ 그들은 적군과 ～를 벌였다 They engaged in a desperate 〔life-and=death〕 battle with the enemy.

**사투**(私鬪) personal 〔private〕 strife. ～하다 struggle personally; fight privately.

**사투리** a dialect; an accent; a provincialism. ¶ 지방 ～ a local 〔provincial〕 dialect 〔accent〕 / 심한 ～를 쓰다 speak with a broad 〔strong〕 dialect / 경상도 ～로 말하다 speak with a Kyŏngsang-do accent / 그녀는 별로 ～를 쓰지 않는다 She doesn't have much of an accent.

**사특**(邪慝) ～하다 (be) vicious; wicked; villainous; sinister.

**사파**(娑婆) ⇨ 사바(세계).

**사파리** 《수렵 여행》 a safari. ◉ ～재킷 a safari jacket. ～파크 a safari 〔wildlife〕 park.

**사파이어** 『광물』 a sapphire. ¶ ～ 반지 a sapphire ring.

**사팔눈** a squint (eye); cross-eye (내사시); walleye (외사시); a cast in the eye; 『의학』 strabismus. ¶ ～의 squinty; squint-eyed / ～이다 have a squint 〔cast in *one's* eye〕; be squint-eyed 〔cross-eyed, walleyed〕.

**사팔뜨기** a squint-〔cross-〕eyed person; a squint-eye; a squinter.
**사포**(砂布) sandpaper; emery paper; glass cloth. ¶ 거친〔고운〕 ~ coarse 〔fine〕 sandpaper / ~로 닦다 polish 《*a thing*》 with sandpaper.
**사표**(師表) a model; a pattern; an example; an ideal; a paragon. ¶ 일세의 ~ a model character; the light of the world / 일세의 ~로서 존경받다 be looked up to as a leader of the age.
**사표**(辭表) a 〔*one's*〕 resignation; a letter of resignation. ¶ ~를 내다 tender 〔send in, hand in, submit〕 *one's* resignation to 《the chief》/ ~를 반려〔수리, 철회〕하다 turn down 〔accept, withdraw〕 《*a person's*》 resignation.
**사뿟** with a light-footed step; lightly.
**사풍**(邪風) reckless words and shocking behavior. ~맞다, ~스럽다 (be) outrageous.
**사풍**(社風) the ways of a company; a company's custom 〔tradition〕.
**사프란** 『식물』 a saffron. ¶ ~색의 saffron; saffron-colored.
**사필귀정**(事必歸正) a corollary. ¶ 법원의 판결을 ~으로 환영하다 welcome the court ruling as a corollary / ~이다 Right will prevail in the end. *or* Truth wins out in the long run.
**사하다**(赦―) pardon; forgive; excuse; absolve 《*a person*》 of 《sins》; grant clemency to 《a prisoner》.
**사하다**(謝―) ① 《감사하다》 thank; express *one's* gratitude; tender *one's* thanks. ⇨ 감사하다. ② 《사과하다》 apologize 《to *a person* for》; make an apology 《for》. ⇨ 사과하다.
**사하라사막**(―砂漠) the Sahara (Desert).
**사하중**(死荷重) the deadweight; the dead load 《of a wagon》.
**사학**(史學) historical science; history; the study of history. ◉ ~과 《학부》 the history department; 《학과》 a history course: ~과 학생 a history student. ~자 a historian.
**사학**(私學) a private school 〔college, university〕. ¶ ~ 출신자 a graduate of a private school 〔college, university〕. ◉ ~보조금 government subsidies to private education institutions 〔schools and universities〕.
**사학**(斯學) this study 〔science, subject, research〕. ¶ ~의 권위자 an authority on the subject.
**사할린** 《러시아의 섬》 Sakhalin.
**사항**(事項) a matter; an item; facts (사실); articles; particulars. ¶ 관련 ~ relevant 〔related〕 facts / 주요 ~ an essential particular; a main point / 주의 ~ a point to notice / 협의〔토의〕~ an agenda; 《미》 a program / …의 ~에 관하여 in matters of / 모든 ~에 관하여 on all matters / 조사를 요하는 ~ a matter for investigation / 과학에 관한 ~ matters in science.
**사해**(四海) 《온 세상》 the whole world. ¶ ~를 평정하다 establish peace and order in the world. ◉ ~동포 universal brotherhood 〔fraternity〕: ~동포주의 cosmopolitanism.
**사해**(死海) 《중동의 염호》 the Dead Sea. ◉ ~문서 the Dead Sea Scrolls.
**사행**(私行) ① 《행위》 a private act; *one's* private conduct. ② 《여행》 a private trip 《of an official》. ~하다 travel 〔make a trip〕 on private business.
**사행**(射倖) speculation; adventure; taking a chance 〔flyer〕. ~하다 speculate; take the chance 〔flyer 《미구어》〕 《in》. ◉ ~심 a speculative 〔gambling〕 spirit: ~심을 조장하다 arouse 〔stir up〕 the passion of gambling. ~행위 단속법 the Speculation Control Law.
**사행**(蛇行) meandering. ~하다 snake along; meander; crawl meanderingly; wind its way 《through》.
**사향**(思鄕) thoughts of home; nostalgia. ~하다 think of *one's* home; yearn 〔long〕 for *one's* home; be homesick. ◉ ~병 homesickness.
**사향**(麝香) musk. ¶ ~ 냄새가 나는 《be》 musky; musk-scented. ◉ ~고양이 a musk 〔civet〕 cat. ~나무 a musk tree. ~노루 a musk deer. ~뒤쥐 a muskrat. ~소 a musk ox (*pl.* musk oxen). ~수(水) musk water 〔scent〕.
**사혈**(死血) impure 〔virulent〕 blood.
**사혈**(瀉血) bloodletting; phlebotomy; venesection. ~하다 phlebotomize; let 〔draw〕 blood 《from a patient》.
**사형**(死刑) capital punishment; the death penalty. ~하다 put 《*a person*》 to death; do to death 《고어》. ¶ ~에 처할만한 죄 a capital offense 〔crime〕; an offense punishable by death / ~에 처하다 put 《*a person*》 to death; send 〔bring〕 《*a person*》 to the scaffold / ~에 처해지다 go to 〔mount〕 the scaffold / ~을 받다 be punished with death / ~을 선고하다 pass a death sentence 《on》; sentence 〔condemn〕 《*a person*》 to death / ~을

집행하다 execute《a criminal》; put《*a person*》to death.

◉ ～선고 a death sentence; a sentence of death. ～수 a condemned criminal;《미》a death-row convict;《미》a convict on death row: ～수 감방 a condemned cell;《미》a death row〔house〕. ～실 a death chamber. ～장 an execution ground. ～죄 a capital offense〔crime〕. ～집행 execution: ～집행인 an executioner;《교수인》a hangman / ～ 집행 유예 a reprieve / ～ 집행 영장 a death warrant / ～ 집행을 연기하다 reprieve. ～폐지 the abolition of capital punishment: ～ 폐지를 주창하다 advocate abolition of capital punishment.

**사형**(私刑) lynching; lynch law; private punishment (outside the law). ～하다 take the law into *one's* own hands; lynch. ¶ ～을 가하다 = ～하다.

**사형**(舍兄)《형》my elder〔big〕brother;《자기의 겸양어》me〔I〕who am your elder brother.

**사화**(士禍) a massacre〔purge〕of scholars; the calamity of *literati.*

◉ 갑자～ the *Kapcha* calamity of savants.

**사화**(史話) a historical story〔tale〕.

**사화**(私和)《송사의》a private settlement; settlement out of court;《화해》reconciliation. ～하다 settle《*a matter*》privately〔out of court〕; reconcile; become reconciled《with》; settle amicably.

**사화**(詞華) flowery language; flowers of speech; rhetorical flourishes.

**사화산**(死火山) an extinct〔a dead〕volcano.

**사환**(使喚) an errand boy; a boy; an「office boy〔girl〕.

**사활**(死活) life and〔or〕death. ¶ ～을 건 투쟁 a life-and〔-or〕-death struggle / 이 기획의 결과에 회사의 ～이 걸려 있다 The issue of this project affects the very existence of the company.

◉ ～문제 a matter of life and death; a life-and-death problem; a question of vital importance: 내게는 그것이 ～의 문제다 To me, it's a life-and-death question.

**사회**(司會)《일》direction of〔directing〕a meeting〔ceremony〕; chairmanship; chairing (a meeting);《사회자》a chairperson. ⇨ 사회자. ～하다 preside at〔over〕《a meeting》; chair《a meeting》; take the chair《at a conference》; conduct〔perform〕the ceremony; act as a master of ceremonies《for》; present《a TV show》. ¶ ～를 보다 = ～하다 / A씨의 ～로《the meeting is opened》with Mr. A in the chair; under the presidency of Mr. A. ◉ ～봉(棒) a gavel: ～봉을 두드리다 rap the gavel.

**사회**(社會) (a) society; a community; the public; the world (at large). ¶ ～적인 social ⇨ 사회적 / 일반 ～ the general public; society at large; the public in general / 시민〔봉건〕 ～ civic〔feudal〕society / ～ 일반의 이익 public interest〔welfare〕/ ～ 규범에 따르다 keep peck(ing) order / 남성 본위의 ～ a male-dominated〔male-centered〕society / 동물 ～《in》the animal world / 꿀벌 ～에서는 in the world of the social honeybee / 예술인〔학자〕들의 ～ the world of artists〔scholars〕.

사회의: ～의 social; communal / ～의 일원 a member of society / ～의 적 a public enemy; an enemy of society / 인류 ～의 진화 the evolution of human society / ～의 풍조《go with》the trend of society.

사회에(서): ～에 공헌하다 contribute to social welfare / ～에 나가다 go out into the world; set out in the world / ～에 해독을 끼치다 do harm〔be harmful〕to society; exert an evil influence on the public mind / ～에 복귀시키다 rehabilitate《*a person*》(in society); enable《*a person*》to return to society / ～에서 은퇴하다 retire from society〔active life〕.

사회를: ～를 위하여 for the good of the public〔society〕; for the welfare of society / ～를 개조하다 remodel society《on a democratic pattern》/ ～를 알다 know the world / ～를 위해 진력하다 labor〔work, exert *oneself*〕for the public good; render services to society.

¶ 그는 ～를 개선하기 위해 일생을 바쳤다 He devoted his life to the improvement of society. / 그녀는 올봄에 대학을 졸업하고 ～에 진출했다 She graduated from the university and went into the world in this spring. / 자넨 ～의 일원으로서의 자각을 가져야 한다 You must realize that you are a member of society. / 거친 ～풍파에 직면해 봐야 비로서 한 사람의 ～인이 되는 것이다 By facing the storms of life one becomes a full-fledged citizen. / 그런 사고 방식은 오늘날의 ～에서는 통용되지 않는다

Such a way of thinking will not do in today's society.
◉ ~ 간접 자본 the social overhead capital. ~개량 social reform: ~개량을 하다 reform 〔improve〕 society. ~개발 social development. ~개혁론 reformism. ~경제 social economy. ~계약설 the theory of social contract. ~계층 a social stratum: 모든 ~계층의 사람 people of all social standings. ~공학 social technology. ~과 social studies 〔subjects〕. ~과학 social science(s): ~과학 대학 a college of social sciences / ~과학 연구소 a social science research institute. ~관 *one's* view of social life. ~관습 social usage. ~교육 social education: ~교육과 the social education department. ~구조〔조직〕 social structure 〔organization〕. ~극 a drama of social problems. ~기구(機構) the framework of society; the social framework. ~기사 《신문의》 a human interest story. ~당(黨) the Socialist Party. ~도덕 social morality. ~도태 social selection; the survival of the fittest (in a society). ~면(面) 《신문의》 the local news page 〔section〕; the city news page. ~민주당 the Social Democratic Party; the Social Democrats. ~민주주의 social democracy. ~보장 social security: ~보장 제도 the social security system / ~보장을 받다 enjoy the benefits of the social security services. ~보험 social insurance. ~복귀 rehabilitation in society 〔the community〕. ~봉사 voluntary social service: ~봉사를 하다 do 〔engage in〕 social 〔public〕 service; work for the public benefit / ~ 자원 봉사 활동 social volunteer-service activities. ~부 《신문사의》 the local news section; the city editor's section 《미》. ~분화 social differentiation. ~사 social history. ~사상 social thought. ~사정 social condition. ~상 phases 〔aspects〕 of life; social conditions 〔phenomena〕: 현 ~상을 잘 반영하고 있다 reflect 〔be a mirror of〕 actual social conditions. ~생물학 sociobiology. ~생태학 ecology. ~성 sociality; social nature. ~소설 a social novel. ~심리학 social psychology. ~아(我) the social self. ~안정 social stability: ~ 안정을 저해시키는 요인 a factor causing social instability. ~운동 a social movement; a public campaign: ~ 운동을 일으키다 start a social movement. ~유기체 a social organism: ~ 유기체론 the organic conception of society. ~윤리 social ethics; social morality; the social code. ~의식 social consciousness. ~인 a member of society 〔the community〕: ~인이 되다 go out into the world; launch forth into life; start *one's* adult life. ~인류학 social anthropology. ~장(葬) 《conduct》 a public funeral 《for》. ~정의 social justice. ~정책 a social policy. ~제도 the social system. ~조사 a social survey 〔research〕. ~진화 social evolution: ~진화론 the theory of social evolution. ~질서 《maintain, observe》 public 〔social〕 order. ~집단 a social group 〔community〕. ~통계학 social statistics. ~통념 a socially accepted idea; an idea commonly 〔generally〕 accepted in the world. ~통제 social control. ~평론가 a social critic 〔commentator〕. ~풍조 the trend 〔drift〕 of public opinion. ~학 sociology: ~학과 the department of sociology / ~학자 a sociologist / 문화 ~학 cultural sociology. ~혁명 a social revolution. ~현상 a social phenomenon 〔phase〕. ~형태 a social form; the form of a society; the type of social system. ~화 socialization: ~화하다 socialize / 의료 기관을 ~화하다 socialize medicine. ~환경 social environment.

**사회기강**(社會紀綱) social discipline. ¶ ~이 해이해지기 쉬운 여름철 summer season during which social discipline is liable to be slack.
◉ ~사범 criminal offenders who disturb the social discipline.

**사회문제**(社會問題) a social problem. ¶ ~가 되다 constitute a public 〔social〕 problem; become an object of public concern / ~를 제기하다 pose a social problem / 사회가 진보함에 따라 갖가지 ~가 야기(惹起)된다 Various social problems arise as a society progresses.

**사회복지**(社會福祉) social welfare. ¶ ~를 꾀하다 take a measure with a view to social welfare / ~를 증진하다 promote social welfare. ◉ ~과(科) 《대학의》 the department of Social Welfare 《of a university》. ~기관〔시설〕 social welfare organs 〔facilities〕; an organization for social welfare.

**사회불안**(社會不安) social unrest. ¶ ~을 낳다 breed 〔cause〕 social unrest / ~

을 빚다〔조성하다〕 ferment 〔create〕 social unrest / ～을 제거하다 dispel 〔remove〕 social unrest.

**사회사업**(社會事業) social work 〔service〕; public welfare service. ¶ ～을 하다 work for the public good; engage in public welfare service.
◉ ～가 a social 〔welfare〕 worker.

**사회생활**(社會生活) social life (★「사교 생활」「남과의 교제」라는 뜻으로도 쓰임); life in society; life as a member of society; community 〔communal〕 life. ¶ ～을 하다 live socially.

**사회악**(社會惡) a social evil; social ills 〔abuses〕. ¶ 우리 사회의 고질인 각종 ～과 부조리를 뿌리 뽑다 root out 〔eradicate〕 the various social ills and irregularities endemic in our society.

**사회자**(司會者) the chairperson; the president; 《연회의》 the toastmaster; 《방송 등의》 the master 〔mistress〕 of ceremonies (생략 m.c., MC., M.C.); the presenter; a program host 〔hostess〕; 《토론 등의》 the moderator; 《의식의》 the officiant; 《미구어》 an emcee; 《영》 a compere. ¶ ～를 맡아보다 act as master of ceremonies 《for》; 《미구어》 emcee 《a show》.

**사회적**(社會的) social; societal. ¶ 반～인 antisocial / ～으로 socially / ～으로 보아 from a social point of view / ～으로 매장되다 be ousted from society; become a social outcast; be ruined socially / 인간은 ～ 동물이다 Man is a social animal.
◉ ～ 감정 social feeling. ～ 긴장 social tension. ～ 명사 a society personage; [총칭] the social elite. ～ 문제 a social problem; a problem of society. ～ 불공정 social injustice. ～ 불공평 social inequality. ～ 생산 기반(설비) (a) social infrastructure: 정부는 고대하던 국가의 ～ 생산 기반 설비 강화 계획을 공개했다 The government unveiled eagerly=awaited schemes to beef up the nation's infrastructure. ～ 세력 social power. ～ 영향 a social influence; an influence on society. ～ 욕구 social wants 〔desire〕. ～ 의무 a social 〔public〕 duty. ～ 제재 social sanctions; social discipline 〔restraints〕. ～ 지위 *one's* station in life; *one's* social position 〔standing〕: ～ 지위가 있는 사람 a person in a public 〔social〕 position. ～ 추방 outlawry; social ostracism. ～ 합의 social consensus.

**사회정세**(社會情勢) social conditions; the state of affairs in a community. ¶ ～의 추이〔변화〕 the drift of 〔a change in〕 the condition of public life / ～의 변화에 부응하다 keep up with the trend of society / ～에 적응하다 adapt 《*oneself*》 to the conditions of changing times / ～를 일변시키다 work out a drastic change in the state of affairs in a community; radically alter the social conditions.

**사회정화**(社會淨化) social purification 〔cleanup〕. ◉ ～운동 a social purification drive; a movement for purification of society. ～위원회 the Social Reform Commission.

**사회주의**(社會主義) socialism. ¶ ～의 socialist(ic) / ～적(인) socialistic.
◉ ～경제학 socialist(ic) economics. ～국가〔단체, 운동, 정책〕 a socialist state 〔organization, movement, policy〕. ～시장경제 a socialist market economy. ～ 인터내셔널 the Socialist International. ～자 a socialist. 국가〔기독교〕～ state 〔Christian〕 socialism. 수정～ revised socialism.

**사후**(死後) ¶ ～에 after *one's* death; posthumously / ～의 after *one's* death 〔decease〕; posthumous 《honors》; post-mortem 《examinations》 / ～세계 the next world; the life 〔world〕 after 〔beyond〕 death / ～ 약방문 "prescription of a drug only after the death of the patient"; the doctor after death / ～의 일을 걱정하다 worry about things after *one's* death / ～의 일을 부탁하다 give 《another》 the charge of the affairs after *one's* death / ～의 일을 생각하다 look beyond the grave; 《유족의 일을》 think of those *one* will leave behind / 시체는 ～ 1주일이 경과된 것으로 추정된다 The man is estimated to have been dead for a week.
◉ ～강직 cadaveric stiffening 〔rigidity〕; *rigor mortis* (L.). ～공명(功名) posthumous fame 〔honors〕; fame after death. ～신탁 a legacy trust.

**사후**(伺候) ～하다 attend; serve; wait upon; make a courtesy call 《on》; pay *one's* respect 《to》.

**사후**(事後) ¶ ～의 after the fact 〔matter〕; *ex post facto* (L.) / ～에 after the fact; *post factum* (L.) / ～ 참고를 위하여 for further reference / 그들은 ～처리를 그르쳤다 They made a mistake in dealing with what had happened.
◉ ～검열 post censorship. ～관리 post management. ～대책 *ex post facto*

measures. ～보고 an *ex post facto* report. ～승낙 an *ex post facto* consent [approval]; the after ratification of an accomplished act: ～ 승낙을 구하다 ask for 《*a person's*》 *ex post facto* consent [approval].

**사흗날** the third (day of the month). ¶ 5월 ～ the third of May.

**사흘** 《3일간》 three days; 《3일째 되는 날》 the third day. ¶ ～ 걸러 every fourth day / ～마다 every three days / ～에 한번 once in every three days / ～이 멀다 않고 almost every other day; very frequently / ～ 굶어 도둑질 안 할 사람 없다 《속담》 Necessity knows no law. ◉ ～돌이 every three days.

**삭갈이** 〚농업〛 a single plowing before transplanting rice plants. ～하다 plow just once before transplanting (rice plants).

**삭감**(削減) (a) reduction; curtailment; retrenchment; a cut. ～하다 curtail; retrench; reduce; cut (down); slash 《미》. ¶ 대(大)～ a drastic reduction / 경비를 ～하다 pare [cut] down expenses / 예산을 ～하다 curtail [slash] the budget.

**삭과**(蒴果) 〚식물〛 a capsule.

**삭구**(索具) rigging. ¶ (배에) ～를 달다 rig 《a ship》.

**삭다** ① 《오래되어》 (***a***) 《낡다》 wear thin [threadbare]; wear [be worn] out [off]; get [become] threadbare. ¶ (옷이) 삭아서 너덜너덜해지다 be worn to rags. (***b***) 《부식되다》 decay; eat 「into [away]; erode; rust; be rusted. ¶ 녹슬어 ～ be eaten away with rust. ② 《음식이》 (***a***) 《유동식·술 등이》 turn bad; ferment; become watery. ¶ 술이 ～ rice wine ferments / 죽이 ～ rice porridge turns bad. (***b***) 《소화되다》 be digested; digest. ¶ (먹은 것이) 잘 ～[삭지 않다] digest well [ill]; be digestible [indigestible]. (***c***) 《익다》 acquire [develop] flavor; mature. ¶ 김치가 ～ the kimchi picks up flavor. ③ 《기운이》 (***a***) 《감정 등이 누그러지다》 be mitigated [alleviated]; calm [cool] down; be softened; abate. ¶ 노여움이 ～ *one's* anger dies down / 아무에 대한 감정이 ～ relent toward *a person*. (***b***) 《염증이》 resolve; be resolved. ¶ 종기는 곧 삭을 게다 The tumor will soon be resolved. (***c***) 《사위다》 be burnt out; go out. ¶ 불이 ～ fire dies.

**삭도**(索道) a cableway; a ropeway. ◉ ～차 a cable car. ～철도 a cable [funicular] railway.

**삭막**(索莫·索漠) ～하다 (be) dim (in *one's* memory); 《광야가》 (be) dreary; bleak; desolate. ¶ ～한 풍경 a dreary [bleak] sight.

**삭망**(朔望) ① 《초하루와 보름》 the first and fifteenth days of the lunar month. ② 《제사》 memorial services held on the first and the fifteenth days of the lunar month.

**삭모**(槊毛) decorative tassels.

**삭발**(削髮) (a) tonsure. ～하다 be tonsured; get [have] *one's* head shaved; take the tonsure. ¶ ～한 tonsured; shaven headed / ～하고 중이 되다 shave *one's* head and become a Buddhist priest.

**삭신** the sinews and joints. ¶ ～이 쑤시다 have an acute pain all over; feel sharp [tingling] pains in the sinews and joints.

**삭은코** a nose that bleeds easily.

**삭이다** ① 《음식을》 digest. ¶ 삭이기 쉽다 [어렵다] be easy [hard] to digest / 음식을 ～ digest food. ② 《분을》 mitigate 《*one's* anger》; appease; quell; calm *oneself*. ¶ 분을 ～ swallow [mitigate, appease] *one's* anger.

**삭정이** 「dead branches [withered twigs] on a tree. ¶ ～를 쳐[잘라] 내다 trim the dead branches off the tree.

**삭제**(削除) elimination; erasure; cancelation; deletion; expurgation; amission; striking out. ～하다 eliminate; erase; cancel; delete; blot [strike, cross] out; expunge; expurgate. ¶ 두 자 ～ two letters crossed out / 명부에서 ～하다 strike 《*a person's* name》 off a list; expunge 《a name》 from a list / 단어 몇 개를 ～하다 cancel [delete, cross out] a few words / 무～판 a complete and unexpurgated edition; an unabridged edition / 편지의 일부를 ～하다 leave out a part of a letter / 마지막 2장(章)을 ～하다 strike off the last two chapters / 법안 중 1항을 ～하다 delete a section in a bill / 다음 여섯 낱말을 본문에서 ～하세요 Please delete [cross out, eliminate] the next six words from the text. / 그 결의는 의사록에서 ～되어 있었다 The resolution was struck (out) from the minutes. / 회비 미납자는 명부에서 ～됩니다 Members in arrears will be crossed off the list. ◉ ～판 an expurgated edition.

**삭치다**(削—) cancel; erase; strike [cross]

out; strike off; offset each other; set off; balance (books). ¶ 주고 받을 것을 ～ wipe the slate clean / 셈을 ～ cancel 〔cross〕 the accounts; consider the accounts as settled.

**삭탈관직**(削奪官職) removing a government official from office; stripping a government official of office 《for misconduct》. ～하다 deprive 〔strip〕 《*a person*》 of *his* office; remove from office.

**삭풍**(朔風) a north 〔piercing〕 wind (of winter).

**삭히다** 《소화》 digest; 《발효》 ferment 《it》; cause 《it》 to ferment; mellow; 《종기 따위를》 resolve.

**삯** ① 《품삯》 wages; pay; hire. ¶ 삯을 받다 receive wages / 하루 팔천 원씩 삯을 받고 일하다 work for a wage of 8,000 won a day. ② 《요금》 fare; charges. ¶ 기차 삯 a railway fare / 전차 삯을 올리다 raise the streetcar fare / 인천까지 찻삯이 얼맙니까 What is the fare to Inch'ŏn?

**삯꾼** a wage earner; a hired man 〔hand〕.

**삯말** a horse for hire; a hack 《영》.

**삯메기** a wage-paying farm job (that does not include meals).

**삯바느질** needlework for pay.

**삯빨래** laundry done for pay; taking in laundry.

**삯일** job work; a job (of work); wage labor; 《하는 대로 버는》 work done by the piece; piecework; an odd job; 《시간제의》 timework. ～하다 do job work 〔piecework〕; do odd jobs; do work at piece rates. ¶ ～하는 사람 a pieceworker; a timeworker; a jobber.

**삯짐** a load carried by a porter. ¶ ～을 지다 carry a load for hire.

**삯팔이** wageworking. ◉ ～꾼 a wageworker; a wage earner.

**삯품** wage labor. ¶ ～(을) 팔다, ～팔이하다 work for wages.

**산**(山) ① 《산악》 a mountain; a mount; a hill (구릉); 《주로 복수형으로》 heights (고지); a peak (봉우리). (★ mountain과 hill의 구별은 절대적인 높이에 의한 것은 아니며 그 지방 풍경에 주는 변화 여하에 따름. 비교적 낮은 산도 평지에 있으면 mountain이라고 하며 높은 산이라도 산지에 있을 경우에는 hill이 됨. 영국에서는 거의 hill로 부름). ¶ 한라산 Mt. Halla / 산이 많은 mountainous; hilly / 산 중턱에 on the mountainside 〔hillside〕 / 산을 따라서 〔타고〕 from mountain to mountain; over the mountains / 산을 넘(어가)다 cross 〔go across〕 a mountain / 산에 오르다, 산을 올라가다 go up 〔climb (up), ascend〕 a mountain 〔hill〕; make an ascent of a mountain / 산을 내려가다〔오다〕 go 〔come, climb〕 down a mountain; descend a mountain / 산같이 우뚝 솟다 tower 〔stand, soar〕 like a mountain / 한국은 산이 많다 Korea is mountainous country. / 신념은 산도 움직일 수 있다 Faith can move mountains. / 산너머 산이라 《속담》 One calamity followed close on the heels of another. *or* Out of the frying pan into the fire. /산에 가야(지) 범을 잡는다 《속담》 Nothing venture, nothing have.
② 《야생의》 wild; wildgrowing. ¶ 산딸기 wild berries; a raspberry.

**산**(酸) 〖화학〗 (an) acid. ¶ 산의 acid / 산과다(증) 〖의학〗 hyperacidity / 산류(類) acids / 산염화물 an acid chloride.

**-산**(産) 《산물》 a product 《of》; manufacture 《of》. ¶ 외국산(의) foreign-made / 국산 쌀 homegrown rice / 외국산의 식물 plants of foreign growth / 캘리포니아산 오렌지 oranges of California growth; oranges grown 〔produced〕 in California / 아랍산 말 an Arab horse.

**산가**(山家) a cottage in a mountain; a mountain lodge 〔hut〕; a chalet (산장). ¶ ～ 생활 mountain life.

**산가지**(算—) primitive counting sticks made of wood 〔bone〕.

**산간**(山間) 《among》 the mountains 〔hills〕; a remote place. ¶ ～에 살다 live among 〔in〕 the mountains 〔hills〕.
◉ ～벽지 a remote and secluded place in 〔among〕 the mountains: ～벽지에서도 even at the most secluded place in the mountains. ～벽촌 a remote mountain village.

**산개**(散開) (military) deployment; extension; development. ～하다 extend; spread 〔fan〕 out; deploy; form in open 〔extended〕 order.
◉ ～대형 《in》 open 〔extended〕 order. ～전 fighting in open 〔extended〕 order; a skirmish.

**산경**(山景) mountain scenery.

**산계**(山系) a mountain system 〔chain, range〕. ¶ 히말라야 ～ the system of the Himalaya.

**산고**(産故) childbirth; delivery.

**산고**(産苦) 《suffer》 labor pains; the pain(s) of childbirth; birth pangs.

**산골**(山—) a mountain district; a secluded place in the mountains.

¶ ~ 사람 mountain 〔hill〕 folks 〔people〕; a hillbilly 《미》/ ~에서 자라나다 be brought up the hills. ◉ ~짜기 a mountain valley; a gorge; a ravine.

**산과**(產科) 《학문》 obstetrics; 《병원의》 the obstetrical department; maternity division. ¶ ~의 obstetrical. ◉ ~병동 a maternity ward. ~병원 a maternity (clinic 〔hospital〕); a lying-in clinic 〔hospital〕. ~의사 an obstetrician. ~학 obstetrics; midwifery.

**산광**(散光) 〖물리〗 diffused 〔scattered〕 light. ◉ ~렌즈 a dispersing lens.

**산굴**(山窟) a mountain cave.

**산굽이**(山—) the bend in the foot of a mountain.

**산금**(產金) gold mining; producing gold. ~하다 produce 〔mine〕 gold. ◉ ~량 gold output. ~업 the gold-mining industry. ~지대 a gold field.

**산기**(產氣) labor pains; travail; labor; pangs of childbirth. ¶ ~가 있다 labor starts; [사람이 주어] begin to labor; have 〔feel〕 labor pains; suffer the pains of childbirth / 갑자기 ~를 느끼다 feel sudden labor pains 《while she is in the car》.

**산기**(產期) the expected time of delivery 〔parturition〕; period 〔term〕 of delivery; *one's* time. ¶ ~가 되다 come to *one's* time (of parturition).

**산기슭**(山—) the foot 〔bottom, base〕 of a mountain. ¶ 우리는 그 ~에서 야영을 했다 We camped at the foot of the mountain.

**산길**(山—) a mountain 「path 〔road, trail, pass〕. ¶ 한 낮에도 어두운 ~ a somber 〔gloomy〕 mountain path even in the daytime / ~을 가다 trudge 〔toil, go〕 along a mountain path.

**산꼭대기**(山—) the summit 〔top〕 of a mountain 〔hill〕; the mountaintop. ¶ 설악산 ~에서 on the top 〔at the summit〕 of Mt. Sŏrak; atop Mt. Sŏrak / 그 ~에 호수가 있다 There is a lake on the top of the mountain.

**산나리**(山—) 〖식물〗 a gold-banded lily.

**산나물**(山—) wild edible greens. ¶ ~을 캐다 pick wild greens.

**산너머**(山—) ¶ ~에(는) across 〔beyond〕 the mountain / ~에서 《come》 from beyond the mountain.

**산놀이**(山—) a mountain excursion 〔picnic, hike〕.

**산놓다**(算—) calculate with sticks 〔on an abacus〕.

**산누에** 〖곤충〗 a wild silkworm; a tussah. ◉ ~고치 tussah cocoons. ~나방 a tussah moth.

**산달**(產—) the month of giving birth.

**산대**(山臺) *sandae;* a makeshift stage for a medieval masked drama. ~하다 put on a medieval masked drama. ◉ ~극〔놀음〕 a masked drama. ~도감 a *sandae* troupe. ~탈 a *sandae* drama mask. ~판 the scene of a *sandae* drama.

**산더미**(山—) a great mass; a huge amount; a mountain; a heap 〔heaps〕 《of》; a large pile 《of》. ¶ ~같이 많은 a mountain of; heaps of; lots of / ~같은 숙제 a ton 〔pile〕 of homework / ~ 같은 파도 mountainous waves / ~같다 be big as a mountain / 걱정이 ~같다 be tormented with no end of anxieties / 빚이 ~ 같다 be head over heels in debt; be over head and ears in debt; have a pile of debts a mile high / ~같이 쌓다 pile 《books》 on 《*one's* desk》/ ~같이 쌓이다 be piled up (mountain-)high; lie in heaps / 일이 ~같이 있다 I have lots of things to do. *or* I've got a million things to do. / 우선 처리해야 할 일이 ~같이 많다 I have a whole stack of work to get through first.

**산도**(產道) 〖의학〗 the parturient 〔obstetric, birth〕 canal.

**산도**(酸度) 〖화학〗 acidity. ◉ ~계 an acidimeter. ~측정 acidimetry.

**산독증**(酸毒症) 〖의학〗 acidosis.

**산돌배**(山—) a wild pear.

**산돼지**(山—) 〖동물〗 a wild boar.

**산드러지다** (be) light; nimble; lively; breezy; vivacious; light-hearted; buoyant; gay; cheerful. ¶ 산드러지게 걷다 walk buoyantly 〔breezily〕 / 산드러지게 웃다 laugh a gay 〔coquettish〕 little laugh.

**산들거리다** blow cool and gentle.

**산들바람** a light 〔gentle〕 breeze; a soft wind; a soft breath of air. ¶ 봄의 ~ a spring breeze / ~이 나뭇잎을 살랑살랑 흔들었다 The breeze 〔light gentle wind〕 stirred the leaves.

**산들산들** 《blow》 gently; softly; in cool ripples. ¶ 아침 바람이 ~ 불고 있었다 A morning breeze was blowing soft and fresh.

**산등성이**(山—) a (mountain) ridge; the ridge 〔spine〕 of a mountain; a spur (옆으로 뻗은 지맥). ¶ ~를 따라서 along the ridges 《of the mountains》/ ~를 타다 go along the ridge.

**산딸기** wild berries; a raspberry.

**산딸나무**(山—) 〖식물〗 a dogwood.

**산뜻하다** 《보기 좋다》 (be) clean; neat; tidy; light; smart; nice; 《선명하다》 (be) fresh; vivid; clear; bright; 《기분이》 (be) crisp; feel refreshed 〔fine〕; 《맛이》 (be) light; plain. ¶ 산뜻하게 clearly; brightly; splendidly; finely / 산뜻한 날씨 a crisp weather / 산뜻한 빛깔 a bright color / 산뜻한 음식 light 〔plain〕 food / 산뜻하게 차려 입다 be neatly dressed.

**산란**(産卵) laying eggs; egg-laying; spawning (어패류의); oviposition (곤충의). ～하다 lay 〔deposit〕 eggs; spawn; oviposit (곤충이); blow (파리가). ¶ 많은 물고기가 바다에서 살다가 ～을 위해 민물을 찾는다 A number of fish live in sea and enter freshwater to spawn. ◉ ～관 《곤충의》 an ovipositor. ～기(期) the breeding 〔spawning〕 season. ～장 an egg-laying site; 《물고기의》 a spawning ground.

**산란**(散亂) dispersion; disorder; confusion. ～하다 get dispersed; be scattered 〔lying〕 about; [장소가 주어] be in disorder; be littered with 《scraps of paper》. ¶ 빛의 ～ disperse of light / 걱정으로 마음이 ～해지다 distract the mind with cares / ～한 마음을 가라앉히다 recover *one's* shattered nerves.

**산령**(山靈) the spirit of a mountain.

**산록**(山麓) the foot 〔base, bottom〕 of a mountain. ¶ ～의 마을 a village at the foot of a mountain. ◉ ～지대 a piedmont (district).

**산류**(酸類) 〖화학〗 (the) acids.

**산릉**(山陵) mountains and hills; 〖왕릉〗 a royal tomb 〔mausoleum〕.

**산림**(山林) 《산과 숲》 mountains and forests; 《산에 있는 숲》 a forest (on a mountain). ¶ ～을 보호하다 conserve forests / ～을 가꾸다〔벌채하다〕 afforest 〔deforest〕 a mountain. ◉ ～감시원 a (forest) ranger. ～남벌 reckless deforestation. ～벌채 deforestation. ～법 the Forest Law. ～보호 forest conservancy 〔protection〕. ～소득 an income from forestry. ～업 the forestry industry. ～조합 a forestry (owners') association. ～지대 forestland. ～청 the Forest Service. ～학 forestry; 《수목학》 dendrology: ～학자 an expert in forest; a dendrologist. ～행정 forest administration.

**산마루**(山—) the top 〔ridge〕 of a mountain.

**산마리노** 《이탈리아 동부의 공화국》 San Marino.

**산막**(山幕) a mountain hut 〔cottage〕.

**산만**(散漫) diffuseness; looseness; desultoriness. ～하다 (be) loose; discursive; desultory; diffuse. ¶ ～한 독서 desultory 〔inattentive〕 reading / 머리가 ～한 사람 a scatter-brained 〔loose-thinking〕 person / ～한 문체로 씌어 있다 be written in a diffuse 〔loose〕 style / 주의력이 ～하다 have little power of concentration.

**산매**(散賣) retailing; retail sale. ⇨ 소매. ¶ ～가격으로 at the retail price.

**산맥**(山脈) a mountain range 〔chain〕; a range 〔chain〕 of mountains. ¶ 태백 ～ the T'aebaek Mountains; the T'aebaek Mountain range / 알프스 ～ the Alps; the Alpine range.

**산멱통** the throat of a living animal.

**산명수려**(山明水麗) scenic beauty. ⇨ 산자수명.

**산모**(産母) a woman delivered of a child; a woman in her confinement. ◉ ～보호 maternity protection. ～사망률 (a) maternal mortality (rate).

**산모퉁이**(山—) the spur of a hill; the corner of a mountain skirts.

**산목숨** *one's* life. ¶ ～을 겨우 이어가다 eke out *one's* living.

**산문**(山門) ① 《절의 문》 the main gate of a Buddhist temple; a temple gate. ② 《산어귀》 the entrance to a mountain. ③ 《절》 a Buddhist temple.

**산문**(産門) the outlet of the birth canal; the vulva.

**산문**(散文) prose (writings). ¶ ～적(으로) prosaic(ally) / ～적인 표현 a prosaic expression; a prosaism / ～으로 쓰다 write in prose / 운문을 ～으로 고치다 turn a verse into prose. ◉ ～시 a prose poem; [총칭] prose poetry. ～(작)가 a prose writer. ～체 prose style.

**산물**(産物) ① 《산출물》 a product; produce (★ 주로 곡물·우유·과일 등 농장에서 산출되는 것의 총칭. 공산물은 products). ¶ 주요 ～ staple products 〔produce〕; a staple / 농〔해〕～ agricultural 〔marine〕 products / 부～ a by-product; a residual product / 이 지역 주요 ～은 과일과 차다 The staple products around this area are fruit and tea. ② 《성과》 a result; an outcome; (the) fruit(s) 〔product, harvest〕 《of *one's* labor》. ¶ 지력의 ～ intellectual products / 시대의 ～ a creature of the day 〔age〕 / 타협의 ～ the result(s) of the compromise 《between A and B》 / 인

간은 환경의 ～이 아니다 Man is not the product of his environment.

**산미**(産米) 《산출미》 rice products; 《해산쌀》 rice for a woman during her confinement.

**산미**(酸味) acidity; sourness; a sour taste. ¶ ～가 있는 sour; acid / ～를 띠다 have an acid taste; taste sour / 이 포도는 ～가 강하다 These grapes taste awfully sour.

**산밑**(山—) the foot 〔bottom, base〕 of a mountain.

**산바람**(山—) a mountain wind 〔breeze〕.

**산발**(散發) sporadic occurrence. ～하다 occur 〔break out〕 sporadically. ¶ ～적(으로) sporadic(ally) / ～적 활동 scattershot operations / ～적 발생 isolated 〔sporadic〕 outbreaks.

◉ ～성 sporadicity: ～성 이질〔적리〕 sporadic dysentery. ～안타 〖야구〗 scattered hits.

**산발**(散髮) disheveled 〔unkempt〕 hair. ～하다 have 〔wear〕 *one's* hair loose 〔disheveled〕. ¶ ～한 여자 a woman with disheveled hair.

**산방꽃차례**(繖房—) 〖식물〗 a corymb. ¶ ～의 corymbose; corymbous.

**산법**(算法) arithmetic.

**산벼락** a horrible experience. ¶ ～ 맞다 undergo a horrible experience.

**산병**(散兵) 《흩어진》 scattered soldiers; skirmishers; 《산개된》 deployed soldiers 〔troopers〕. ～하다 scatter 《troops》; deploy in extended order. ◉ ～교련 skirmish drill. ～선(線) a front line of deployed soldiers. ～호 a trench for deployed troopers.

**산보**(散步) a walk; a stroll. = 산책.

**산복**(山腹) a hillside; a mountainside.

**산봉우리**(山—) a (mountain) peak; the summit 〔top〕 of a mountain.

**산부인과**(産婦人科) obstetrics and gynecology. ◉ ～의사 《산과》 an obstetrician; 《부인과》 a gynecologist.

**산부처** a living Buddha; a virtuous person.

**산불**(山—) a wood fire 《미》; a forest fire. ¶ ～조심 《게시》 Prevent forest fires.

**산비둘기**(山—) 〖조류〗 a collared dove; a ringdove; a turtledove.

**산비탈**(山—) a steep mountain slope.

**산뽕나무**(山—) 〖식물〗 a wild mulberry tree.

**산사**(山寺) a mountain temple; a temple in a mountain.

**산사나무**(山査—) 〖식물〗 a hawthorn.

**산사람**(山—) a wild man 《of the mountains》; a woodsman; a mountaineer.

**산사태**(山沙汰) a landslide; a landslip 《영》; a landfall. ¶ ～가 나기 쉬운 landslide-prone 《ledge》 / ～로 열차가 불통되었다 The landslide blocked the rail=road traffic.

**산삭**(産朔) the month of parturition.

**산산이**(散散—) 《break, fall》 in 〔to〕 pieces; 《scatter》 in all directions. ¶ ～ 부수다 smash 《dishes》 to pieces / ～ 부서지다 be broken to 〔in〕 pieces / ～ 흩어지다 disperse; be scattered / 그 가족은 전쟁으로 ～ 흩어졌다 The family was broken up 〔torn asunder〕 by the war. / 석고가 마루 위에 ～ 부서져 있었다 The plaster was on the floor in pieces. / 차가 콘크리트 벽에 부딪쳐 ～ 부서졌다 The car was smashed to pieces by hitting the concrete wall.

**산산조각**(散散—) broken pieces; bits and pieces; fragments. ¶ ～이 나다 be broken 〔smashed, crushed〕 to 〔into〕 pieces; break into fragments.

**산삼**(山蔘) 〖식물〗 a wild ginseng.

**산상**(山上) ¶ ～의〔에〕 at 〔on〕 the top 〔summit〕 of a mountain. ◉ ～수훈(垂訓) the Sermon on the Mount.

**산새**(山—) a mountain bird.

**산색**(山色) mountain scenery; a hillscape.

**산성**(山城) a mountain fortress wall.

**산성**(酸性) 〖화학〗 acidity. ¶ 토양의 ～ soil acidity / ～의 acid 《soil》 / ～으로 하다 acidify; acidulate / ～이 되다 become acid; acidify. ◉ ～도 acidity. ～반응 (an) acid reaction. ～비 acid rain. ～산화물 an acid oxide. ～시험 an acidity test. ～식품 acid foods. ～염 acid chloride. ～염료 an acid dye. ～증 〖의학〗 acidosis. ～진(塵) acid dust. ～토양 acid soil.

**산세**(山勢) the physical aspect 〔geographical features〕 of a mountain.

**산소**(山所) 《묘》 a grave; a tomb; 《묘소》 an ancestral graveyard.

**산소**(酸素) 〖화학〗 oxygen (기호 O). ¶ 액체～ liquid oxygen (생략 lox) / 공기중의 ～ 농도 the oxygen content of the air / ～로 처리하다 treat with oxygen; oxygenate / ～를 제거하다 deoxidize; deoxygenate / 혈액에 ～를 공급하다 oxygenate the blood.

◉ ～마스크 an oxygen mask. ～부채 〖생리〗 oxygen debt. ～실린더〔봄베〕 an oxygen cylinder 〔bottle〕. ～압축기 an oxygen compressor. ～요법 oxygen treatment. ～용접〔땜〕 oxyacetylene welding. ～천막 an oxygen tent. ～화합물 an oxygen compound; an oxide.

**산소결핍**(酸素缺乏) deficiency of oxygen 《in the air》; 〖의학〗 hypoxia. ¶ ～의

oxygen-poor〔-short〕/ ∼에 시달리다 suffer from oxygen starvation / 물 속의 ∼으로 연못의 물고기가 많이 죽어서 떠올랐다 A lot of dead fish surfaced in the pond owing to the deficiency of oxygen in the water. ◉ ∼증 〖의학〗 anoxia; hypoxia.

**산소흡입**(酸素吸入) oxygen inhalation. ¶ ∼을 받다 be put on oxygen / 환자에게 ∼을 시키다 have 〔make〕 a patient inhale oxygen; administer 〔give〕 oxygen inhalations to a patient.
◉ ∼기 an oxygen inhaler 〔inhalator〕. ∼용 마스크 ⇨ 산소 마스크.

**산속**(山—) the heart 〔recesses〕 of a mountain. ¶ ∼의 마을 a village in 〔among〕 the mountains / ∼에(서) in 〔among〕 the mountains / 깊은 ∼에 deep in the mountains; far up (in) the mountain / 깊은 ∼에 살다 live in the heart of a mountain / ∼에 있는 외딴 집 a solitary house among the mountains 〔in a mountain recess〕 / ∼에서 길을 잃다 lose 〔miss〕 *one's* way in the mountain.

**산송장** a walking 〔living〕 corpse; the living dead. ¶ ∼이나 다름없다 be as good as a living dead.

**산수**(山水) ① 《산과 물》 mountains and water(s); hills and streams. ② 《경치》 landscape; scenery. ¶ ∼의 아름다움 scenic 〔natural〕 beauty / ∼ 명미한 곳이다 be noted for its scenic beauty.
◉ ∼화(법) a (Chinese-style) landscape (painting): ∼화가 a landscape painter; a landscapist.

**산수**(算數) 《계산》 calculation; 《산술》 arithmetic. ¶ ∼를 잘〔못〕하다 be good 〔poor〕 at arithmetic. ◉ ∼문제 an arithmetical problem; a problem in arithmetic; a sum 《to *do*》.

**산수소**(酸水素) 〖화학〗 oxyhydrogen.
◉ ∼불꽃 an oxyhydrogen flame. ∼용접 oxyhydrogen welding. ∼취관(吹管) an oxyhydrogen blowpipe. ∼폭발가스 oxyhydrogen detonating gas.

**산술**(算術) arithmetic. ¶ ∼의 arithmetical / ∼을 잘〔못〕하다 be good 〔poor〕 at sums; have a good 〔poor〕 head for figures / ∼을 하다 do sums; cipher.
◉ ∼계산 arithmetical computation; 《perform》 an arithmetical operation. ∼급수 = 등차급수. ∼평균 the arithmetic(al) mean. 상업∼ commercial arithmetic.

**산스크리트** 〖언어〗 Sanskrit (생략 Skr., Skt., Sans.). ◉ ∼학자 a Sanskritist; a Sanskrit scholar.

**산식**(算式) 〖수학〗 an arithmetic expression; a formula.

**산신**(山神) a mountain god; the guardian spirit of a mountain.
◉ ∼령 = 산신. ∼제 a religious service for the mountain god.

**산실**(産室) a lying-in room 《in a hospital》; a delivery room; a maternity ward (한 병동의).

**산실**(散失) being scattered and lost. ∼하다 get 〔be〕 scattered and lost. ¶ ∼된 기록 a document scattered and lost.

**산아**(産兒) 《해산》 childbirth; 《아이》 a newborn baby. ∼하다 give birth to a baby.

**산아제한**(産兒制限) birth control; 《가족계획》 family planning. ¶ ∼을 하다 practice birth control. ◉ ∼론자 an advocate of birth control. ∼상담소 a birth-control clinic.

**산악**(山嶽·山岳) mountains.
◉ ∼고도계〔기압계〕 an orometer. ∼문학 literature of the mountain. ∼병 mountain sickness. ∼부〔회〕 an alpine society; an alpine 〔a mountaineering〕 club. ∼숭배 mountain worship. ∼지대 a mountain(ous) area. ∼지방 a mountainous 〔hilly〕 region 〔district〕. ∼풍경화 a mountainscape. ∼학 orography; orology. 대한∼연맹 the Korea Alpine Federation.

**산액**(産額) the amount of production; the output 《of gold》; the yield 《of rice》. ¶ ∼을 늘리다 increase output 《of》.

**산야**(山野) fields and mountains; hills and valleys. ¶ ∼를 돌아다니다 roam the countryside; roam over 〔range〕 hill and dale.

**산양**(山羊) a goat; 《영양》 an antelope.

**산언덕**(山—) a hillock; a hill; a mound.

**산업**(産業) (an) industry. ¶ 주요 ∼ the chief 〔key, major〕 industries / 첨단 ∼ the high-tech industry / ∼의 industrial / ∼용의 for industrial use 〔purposes〕 / ∼의 발달 the progress of industry; industrial development / ∼의 합리화 the rationalization of industry / 오늘날의 복잡한 ∼ 사회 today's complex industrial society / 국제시장에서의 ∼ 경쟁력 향상 the enhancement of industrial competitiveness in the international market / ∼을 장려하다 encourage 〔promote〕 industry / 그 나라는 ∼이 번창하고 있다 The country is having a great boom in industry. *or* Industry is flourishing remarkably in the country. / 근래 몇년간 ～의 발달이 두드러졌다 Industrial development has been remarkable for some recent years. / 그 발명으로 새로운 ～이 일어났다 As a result of the invention a new industry sprang up. / ～ 발전은 환경 오염의 확산이란 결과를 낳았다 Industrial development has resulted in the spread of environmental pollution.

◉ ～개발 industrial development. ～계(界) industry; industrial circles; the industrial world. ～공동화(空洞化) deindustrialization. ～공학 industrial engineering. ～공해 industrial pollution. ～교육 industrial education. ～구조 industrial structure. ～국 an industrial nation 〔country〕. ～국유화 the nationalization of industries: ～국유화 정책 a policy of industrial nationalization. ～규격 an industrial standard: 한국～규격 the Korean Industrial Standards (생략 KS). ～금융 채권 industrial finance debenture. ～기술 《cooperation in》 industrial technology: ～기술자〔인〕 an industrial technician. ～기지 an industrial base 〔site〕. ～도로 an industrial road. ～도시 an industrial city. ～동원 industrial mobilization. ～디자인 industrial design. ～물류(物流) 지원 센터 the Industrial Logistics Center (생략 ILC). ～박람회 an industrial exhibition. ～사회 industrial society. ～스파이 an industrial 〔a corporate〕 spy: ～스파이 사건 an industrial espionage case. ～심리학 industrial psychology. ～예비군 an industrial reserve army 〔force〕. ～용 로봇 an industrial robot. ～(용) 컴퓨터 an industrial computer. ～위생 industrial hygiene. ～입국 the establishment of a state on the basis of industries. ～자금 industrial funds. ～자본 industrial capital. ～자원부 the Ministry of Commerce, Industry and Energy. ～재산권 industrial property right. ～재해 industrial disaster: ～ 재해자 an industrial disaster victim / ～ 재해 보상 보험 workmen's accident compensation insurance. ～전사 a soldier of industry. ～전환 industrial conversion. ～정책 an industrial policy: ～ 정책 심의회 the Industrial Policy Screening Meeting. ～조직 industrial organization. ～조합 an industrial guild 〔association〕. ～주의 industrialism. ～지리(학) industrial geography. ～통제 《strengthen》 the control of industry. ～투자 industrial investment. ～폐기물 industrial waste(s). ～혁명 『역사』 the Industrial Revolution. ～화 industrialization: ～화하다 industrialize. ～훈장 the Order of Industrial Service Merit.

한국 ～ 경제 기술 연구원 the Korea Institute for Industrial Economics and Technology (생략 KIET). 한국～기술 정보원 the Korea Institute of Industry and Technology Information (생략 KINITI). 한국～은행 the Korea Development Bank (생략 KDB).

**산업별**(産業別) ◉ ～(노동)조합 an industrial 〔a vertical 《미》〕 union. ～노조회의 《미국의》 the Congress of Industrial Organizations (생략 C.I.O.).

**산역**(山役) construction 〔repair〕 of a tomb; tomb work. ～하다 construct 〔repair〕 a tomb. ◉ ～꾼 men working on a grave; a graveyard worker.

**산욕**(産褥) childbed; confinement. ◉ ～기 a lying-in 〔confinement〕 period. ～부 a lying-in woman. ～열 puerperal 〔childbed〕 fever.

**산울림**(山—) the rumbling of a mountain.

**산울타리** a 《quickset》 hedge; a live 〔quick〕 fence. ¶ ～를 만들다 plant 〔put〕 a hedge 《around》 / ～를 두른 정원 a garden surrounded with 〔by〕 a hedge / ～를 두르다 「put a hedge around 〔hedge in〕 《a garden》.

**산원**(産院) a maternity hospital 〔home〕; a lying-in hospital.

**산월**(産月) the month of delivery 〔parturition〕.

**산유**(産油) oil producing. ◉ ～국 an oil=producing country 〔nations〕.

**산입**(算入) inclusion; calculating in. ～하다 include 〔add〕 in; count 〔reckon〕 in. ¶ 미결 구류의 일수는 본형에 ～될 수 있다 The number of days of detention pending trial may be reckoned into the principal penalty.

**산자수명**(山紫水明) scenic beauty; beautiful landscape. ～하다 (be) scenically beautiful. ¶ ～한 곳 a place of great natural beauty; a scenic spot.

**산장**(山莊) 《별장》 a mountain villa 〔retreat〕; 《오두막》 a mountain hut 〔cottage〕.

**산재**(散在) being scattered; lying here and there. ～하다 [사물이 주어] lie 〔be〕 scattered about; lie here and there;

be found here and there; [장소가 주어] be dotted 〔studded〕 with 《sheep》. ¶ 인가가 ～하는 마을 a straggling village / 남해에는 크고 작은 섬들이 ～해 있다 The southern sea is studded with islands, large and small.

**산재**(散財) waste of money; a wasteful use of money; dissipation; extravagance. ～하다 spend money freely 《on》; waste *one's* money 《on》; dissipate *one's* fortune 《in》; lavish 〔squander〕 money 《on》. ¶ ～케 해서 미안합니다 I'm sorry to have put you to a lot of expense.

**산재**(産災) ⇨ 산업재해. ◉ ～장애인 the disabled by industrial disaster.

**산적**(山賊) a bandit (*pl.* ～s, banditti); a brigand. ¶ ～떼 a gang 〔set〕 of bandits / ～의 소굴 a bandits' den / ～이 출몰하는 곳 a bandit-ridden place / ～을 만나다 fall among bandits. ◉ ～질 banditry; brigandage.

**산적**(山積) a mountainous pile 《of》; piling up (like a mountain). ～하다 pile 〔heap〕 up; lie in a heap 〔in piles〕; make a large pile. ¶ 할 일이 ～해 있다 have a lot of work to do; have lots 〔a heap〕 of things to do / 책상 위에 서류가 ～해 있다 The desk is piled high with documents. / 항구에는 체화가 ～해 있다 Piles of goods lie undelivered at the port.

**산적**(散炙) 《펜》 shish kebab; meat and vegetables broiled on a skewer; 《안펜》 unskewered shish kebab. ◉ ～꼬챙이 a (shish kebab) skewer; a spit: ～ 꼬챙이에 꿰다 spit 《meat》.

**산적도둑**(散炙―) 《미식가》 an epicure; a gourmet; 《딸》 *one's* married daughter.

**산전**(山田) a field in the mountains; a field among hills.

**산전**(産前) before childbirth 〔delivery〕. ¶ ～ 산후의〔에〕 before and after childbirth 〔delivery〕 / ～ 산후 휴가 《take》 a maternity leave.

**산전수전**(山戰水戰) fighting all sorts of hardships; being buffeted by the waves of adversity. ¶ ～을 겪다 go through 「(many) hardships 〔hell and high water〕; taste the bitters and sweets of life / ～ 다 겪은 사람 a person who has tasted the sweets and bitters of life; a man of the world; a crafty old fox (교활한).

**산정**(山亭) an arbor in a mountain.

**산정**(山頂) the top 〔summit〕 of a mountain; a mountaintop. ⇨ 산꼭대기. ¶ ～이 눈에 덮인 산 a snow-capped mountain / 지리산 ～에(서) on the top 〔at the summit〕 of Mt. Chiri.

**산정**(算定) 《계산》 computation; calculation; reckoning; 《평가》 assessment; 《견적》 estimate. ～하다 compute; calculate; reckon; work out; assess; estimate 《the cost at two million won》. ¶ 상환액의 ～ assessment of the amount of redemption / ～을 그르치다 miscalculate; make a mistake in calculation / 피해는 총액 3억원으로 ～되었다 The total amount of the damage was estimated at three hundred million won. ◉ ～가격 estimated price 〔value〕; appraisal.

**산줄기**(山―) a mountain range; a chain 〔line〕 of mountains.

**산중**(山中) ＝산속. ¶ ～의, ～에(서) among the hills; in the mountains.

**산중턱**(山―) a hillside; a mountainside. ¶ ～에 있는 집 a house on a hillside / ～에 있다 It is 〔lies, stands〕 halfway up the hill.

**산증**(疝症) 『한의』 colic. ¶ ～이 나다 suffer from colic.

**산지**(山地) a mountain(ous) district 〔region〕; a hilly district 〔country〕; the highlands.

**산지**(産地) 《산물의》 a producing district 〔area, center〕; a place 〔an area〕 of production 〔origin〕; 《동식물 등의》 the home; the habitat; a growing district (식물의). ¶ 담배의 ～ a tobacco-growing district / 쌀의 ～ a rice-producing district / 유명한 말의 ～ a famous horse-breeding center / ～ 직송의 감자 potatoes direct from 「the farm (where they're grown) / 김포는 쌀의 ～로 유명하다 Kimp'o is famous for its production of rice. *or* Kimp'o is well-known as a rice producing district. 「《묘의》 a grave keeper.

**산지기**(山―) 《산림의》 a forest ranger;

**산지니**(山―) a mountain hawk; a wild 〔an untrained〕 falcon.

**산짐승**(山―) a mountain animal.

**산채**(山菜) wild edible greens; edible mountain herbs. ¶ ～를 캐다 gather mountain herbs.

**산채**(山寨·山砦) 《산속의 성채》 a fort 〔stronghold〕 in the mountains; 《산적의》 a den of mountain bandits.

**산채로** alive. ¶ ～ 잡다 catch 〔capture〕 《a raccoon》 alive / ～ 잡히다〔묻히다〕 be caught 〔buried〕 alive.

**산책**(散策) a walk; walking; a stroll; a

promenade; a turn (한 바퀴 돌기). ~하다 take a walk 〔stroll〕; take the air; take 〔go for〕 a turn; stroll. ¶ 운동을 위한 ~ a walk for exercise / 아침 ~ a morning walk / 한 시간의 ~ an hour's walk / 건강을 위한 ~ a constitutional (walk) / 거리를 ~하다 stroll through a street / 교외로 ~을 가다 take 〔go for〕 a (long) walk in the suburbs / (잠시) ~을 나가다 go out for a (short) walk / 공원을 ~하다 「take a walk 〔take a turn〕 in the park (★ to the park라고 하면 「공원까지 산책하다」의 뜻이 됨) / ~ 나가고 없다 be out for a walk / 나는 아침마다 ~하기로 하고 있다 I make it a rule to take a walk every morning. ◉ ~길 a walk; a promenade (포장된); an esplanade (해변·호숫가의).

**산천**(山川) 《산과 내》 mountains and streams; 《자연》 nature. ¶ 고향 ~ the natural surroundings of *one's* native place. ◉ ~초목 nature; natural scenery; landscape.

**산천어**(山川魚) 〖어류〗 a trout; a coho(e) (salmon); a silver salmon.

**산초**(山椒) Chinese pepper. ◉ ~나무 〖식물〗 a Chinese pepper tree.

**산초어**(山椒魚) 〖동물〗 a salamander. = 도롱뇽.

**산촌**(山村) a mountain village 〔hamlet〕.

**산출**(産出) 《생산》 production; yield; output. ~하다 produce; yield; bring forth. ¶ 좋은 포도를 ~하는 지방 a region producing good grapes / (금을) 많이 ~하는 광산 a productive 〔rich〕 (gold) mine / 그 나라에서는 쌀의 ~이 수요를 웃돈다 The production 〔yield〕 of rice exceeds the demand in that country. / 그 광산은 양질의 광석을 ~한다 The mine yields good ore. / 이 지역은 오래 전부터 석탄을 ~해 왔다 This area has produced coal for a long time. ◉ ~고〔량〕 the (amount of) production; the yield 《of rice》; the output 《of gold》. ~력 producing 〔productive〕 power; productivity. ~물 a product. ⇨ 산물. ~지 a producing center; a place of production.

**산출**(算出) calculation; computation. ~하다 calculate; compute; reckon; work out. ¶ ~된 세액 a calculated tax amount / ~하면 비용이 1인당 20달러가 된다 The cost works out at twenty dollars a head.

**산타마리아** *Santa Maria* (It.); Saint Mary.

**산타클로스** Santa Claus; St. Nicholas; 《영》 Father Christmas. ¶ ~할아버지는 착한 어린이에게 선물을 갖다 주신다 Santa Claus comes to give presents to good little children.

**산탄**(霰彈) a 《lead》 shot; a case shot; a buckshot (굵은); a slug (공기총의). ◉ ~총 a shotgun. ~통 a canister.

**산턱**(山—) the ledge 〔shoulder〕 of a mountainslope.

**산토끼**(山—) a hare; a wild rabbit; a jackrabbit. ◉ ~사냥 hare hunting.

**산토닌** 〖약〗 santonin. ◉ ~정(錠) a santonin tablet.

**산통**(疝痛) 〖의학〗 colic (pains); enteralgia (장의); the gripes.

**산통**(算筒) 《점대의》 a case for bamboo fortune slips; 《산가지의》 a case for counting sticks. ¶ ~ 깨(뜨리)다 spoil; ruin 《a scheme, a plot》; put a spoke in 《*a person's*》 wheel / ~ 깨지다 be spoiled 〔ruined〕; come to naught; fall through; go to pot.

**산파**(産婆) a midwife; a maternity nurse. ◉ ~술 midwifery. ~역 the job of midwife: ~역을 하다 [비유적] assist in 〔serve as midwife to〕 the formation 《of Cabinet》.

**산판**(山坂) a forest preserve. ⇨ 멧갓.

**산패**(酸敗) 〖화학〗 acidification. ~하다 acidify; turn sour. ¶ ~한 rancid; sour. ◉ ~유 sour milk.

**산포**(散布) (a) scattering; (a) sprinkling; spreading; distribution. ~하다 scatter; sprinkle; spread; distribute. ◉ ~도(度) measure of dispersion.

**산포도**(山葡萄) 〖식물〗 ① 《머루》 a wild vine; 《열매》 wild grapes. ② 《담쟁이》 an ivy.

**산표**(散票) scattered votes.

**산하**(山河) mountains and rivers.

**산하**(傘下) ¶ ~의 under the influence 〔protection〕 《of》; affiliated 《unions》; subsidiary 《companies》 / 한국 노총 ~의 노조 labor unions 「affiliated to 〔under the umbrella of〕 the Federation of Korean Trade Union / …~에 들다 join; become an affiliate of... / …~에 모이다 be enlisted under the banner of...; join the banner of.... ◉ ~기관 an affiliated organization. ~기업 affiliated enterprises. ~노조 subordinate labor unions. ~회사 a subsidiary 〔an affiliated〕 company 《of Hyundai》; a subsidiary.

**산학협동**(産學協同) cooperation between industry and the academic world 《in a project, in *do*ing》; academic-industrial collaboration; university-indus-

try cooperation. ◉ ~체 an educational-industrial complex. ⌈and sea.
**산해**(山海) mountains and seas; land
**산해진미**(山海珍味) delicacies〔dainties〕 of all lands and seas; a sumptuous feast〔repast〕. ¶ ~를 대접하다 entertain《*a person*》 with all sorts of delicacies / ~를 먹다 have all sorts of delicacies.
**산허리**(山—)《중턱》 a mountainside; a hillside. ¶ ~에 있는 집 a house on a hillside / 그 호텔은 ~에 있다 The hotel stands halfway up the hill.
**산협**(山峽) ① =두메. ②《골짜기》 a gorge; a ravine; a glen.
**산형꽃차례**(繖形 —) 〚식물〛 an umbel. ¶ ~의 umbellar; umbellate.
**산호**(珊瑚) coral. ¶ ~(빛)의 coral 《brooch》/ ~ 모양의 coralliform / ~질의 coralline / ~를 채집하다 fish (for) coral / ~ 기둥에 호박 주추다 live in a gorgeous house; live in grand style. ◉ ~목걸이 a coral necklace. ~석 corallite. ~섬 a coral island. ~수(樹) a coral formation. ~채취 coral fishing. ~초 a coral reef; an atoll (환초). ~충 a coral insect〔polyp〕. ~해 the Coral Sea.
**산화**(散華) a heroic death in battle 〔action〕. ~하다 die a glorious〔heroic〕 death.
**산화**(酸化) 〚화학〛 oxidation; oxidization. ~하다 oxidize; oxidate; oxygenate. ¶ ~되다 be oxidized / ~하기 쉬운 금속 an easily oxidizable metal / ~란 어떤 물질이 산소와 화합하는 것이다 Oxidation is the combination of a substance with oxygen.
◉ ~구리 oxidized copper. ~납 plumbic oxide. ~망간 manganese oxide. ~물 an oxide (compound); an oxided substance: 중성 ~물 a neutral oxide. ~방지제 an antioxidant. ~수소 oxide of hydrogen. ~알루미늄 an oxide of aluminum. ~염(炎) oxidizing flame. ~염료 oxidation dyestuffs. ~제 an oxidizing agent; an oxidizer. ~철 iron oxide. ~칼슘 calcium oxide.
**산회**(散會) adjournment; closing (a meeting). ~하다 adjourn〔close〕《the meeting》; break up; disperse; rise. ¶ 몇 시에 ~하였나 When did the meeting break up? / 위원회는 오후 8시에 ~하였다 The committee rose at 8 in the evening.
**산후**(産後) ¶ ~의〔에〕 after childbirth 〔parturition〕; postpartum; postpartal / ~의 회복 convalescence after childbirth / ~의 몸조리 postpartum care / ~ 회복이 좋다〔좋지 않다〕 be doing well〔badly〕 after childbirth / 그녀는 ~ 회복이 빠르다 She is gaining quickly after childbirth.
**산휴**(産休) a maternity leave. ¶ ~를 얻다 take a maternity leave.
**살**[1] ① (***a***)《뼈·가죽에 대하여》 flesh; muscles (근육). ¶ 볼의 살 the flesh of the cheeks / 살의 fleshy; sarcous / 살이 찐 fleshy; fat / 살이 단단한 사람 a muscular〔brawny〕 man / 살이 오르다〔찌다〕 put on〔gather, get, gain〕 flesh; grow fleshy; get fat; gain〔put on〕 weight / 살이 쪄 있다 have plenty of flesh on *one* / 살이 내리다〔빠지다〕 lose flesh〔weight〕; get〔become〕 lean 〔thin〕 / 《운동으로》 군살을 빼다 get rid of superfluous flesh; wear〔work〕 off surplus fat / 살이 되다 be nutritious; do《*a person*》 good; [비유적] be beneficial / 자네는 좀더 살이 쪄야 되겠네 You need more flesh on you. (***b***)《사상·조각 등의》 ¶ 살을 붙이다 give body and substance《to》; put flesh《on》; flesh out / 등장 인물에 살을 붙이다 round out *one's* characters.
②《살갗》 the skin;《육체》 the body. ¶ 살빛 skin color / 살을 에는 듯한 바람 a bleak〔nipping〕 wind / 살을 에는듯한 추위 biting〔cutting, piercing〕 cold / 살이 검은 남자 a man of dark skin / 살이 깨끗하다 have a clean〔spotless〕 skin / 그녀는 살이 거칠다〔매끈하다〕 She has a rough〔smooth〕 skin.
③《식용의》 (***a***)《고기》 meat (수육); fish (meat) (생선의); game (사냥한 것의). ¶ 연한 살 tender meat / 질긴 살 tough meat / 살점 a piece〔cut〕 of meat; a chop / 살코기를 썰다 cut 〔carve〕 meat. (***b***)《과일의》 flesh; pulp; 《견과·패각류 등의》 meat. ¶ 게살 crab meat / 호두 살 the meat of a nut.
④ ⇨살붙이. ¶ 살이 살을 먹는다 The brothers are engaged in an internecine feud〔war〕.
**살**[2] ①《뼈대》 (***a***)《장지문 등의》 a frame; a lattice(work). ¶ 장지의 살 the frame of a paper sliding-door / 창살 없는 감옥 a prison without bars. (***b***)《버티는 것》 a rib (뼈대가 되는 부분); a stretcher (우산 등의); a spoke (바퀴 등의); support; a stay; a stick. ¶ 부챗살 the ribs of a fan / 우산살 an umbrella stretcher〔rib〕 / 자전거 바큇살이 하나 부러졌다 One of the spokes in my

bicycle is broken. ② 《빗살》 the teeth (of a comb). ¶ 살이 가는 빗 a fine=tooth comb. ③ 《어살》 a fishing weir.

**살**[3] ① 《화살》 an arrow; a shaft; a dart (던지는). ¶ 살같이 like an arrow / 살같이 빠르다 be as swift as an arrow / 살을 쏘다 shoot an arrow. ② 《기운》 a force like an arrow; 《빛의》 a beam; 《흐름의》 a current. ¶ 햇살 sunbeams / 센 물살 a strong 〔rapid〕 stream 〔current〕. ③ 《옷 등의 구김》 wrinkles; creases; folds. ⇨ 구김살.

**살**[4] 《벌레의》 a sting. ¶ 벌의 살 the sting of a wasp / 살에 쏘이다 get stung.

**살**[5] 《떡살 무늬》 a pattern (pressed on a rice cake). ¶ 떡에 살을 박다 press a pattern into the rice cake.

**살**[6] 《나이》 age; (*one's*) years. ¶ 스무 살 twenty years of age / 다섯 살 난 사내아이 a five-year-old boy; a boy of five (years) / 다섯 살이 될 무렵에는 by the age of five; by the time *one* is five / 그는 스무 살에 죽었다 He died at (the age of) twenty. / 「몇 살입니까」—「20살 입니다」 "How old are you?"—"I am twenty (years old)".

**살**(煞) ① 《악령》 a weird air 〔feeling〕; an evil spirit; baleful influence; plague; the devil's work; an ill-fated 〔unlucky〕 touch; a fatal contact; a kiss of death; a black hand. ¶ 살(이) 낀 날 a fateful 〔an ill-starred〕 day; a day of doom / 살을 풀다 exorcise evil spirits 《from 〔out of〕 *a person* 〔*place*〕》; drive out 〔away〕 evil spirits / 이 여자는 살이 있다〔세다〕 She is plagued (with the devil). *or* She is an ill=starred woman. ② 《나쁜 띠앗》 bad blood; poor relations 〔animosity〕 within a family. ¶ 그 형제들은 살이 세다 There is bad blood between the brothers.

**살가다**(煞—) be damned 〔plagued, sorely beset〕; be under the influence of the devil.

**살가죽** the skin. ⇨ 피부.

**살갈퀴** 〖식물〗 a tare; a vetch.

**살갑다** be larger 〔wider〕 than 《it》 looks; 《다정하다》 (be) kind; warm=hearted; 《속이 너르다》 (be) broad=minded; open; receptive.

**살강** a kitchen shelf. ¶ ～ 밑에서 숟가락 얻었다 《속담》 enjoy a specious windfall 〔a doubtful find〕.

**살갗** the skin (surface). ¶ ～이 거칠다 〔곱다〕 have a rough 〔clear〕 skin.

**살결** grain; (a) texture. ¶ 고운 ～ a smooth skin; a lovely complexion / ～이 검은 사람 a person of dark complexion / ～이 곱다 be of fine 〔delicate〕 texture; have a clear 〔spotless〕 skin / ～이 거칠다 have a rough 〔coarse〕 skin.

**살구** 〖식물〗 an apricot. ◉ ～꽃 apricot blossoms. ～나무 an apricot tree. ～빛 apricot (color). ～씨 an apricot stone.

**살균**(殺菌) sterilization; disinfection; 《저온 살균》 pasteurization. ～하다 sterilize; disinfect; pasteurize. ¶ ～성의 disinfectant. ◉ ～기 a sterilizer. ～력 sterilizing 〔germicidal〕 power: ～력 있는 germicidal. ～법 a germ-killing process; pasteurism. ～온도 a thermal death point. ～우유 sterilized 〔pasteurized〕 milk. ～작용 sterilizing action. ～제 a germicidal agent; a sterilizer; a disinfectant; a germicide; a bactericide.

**살그머니** 《몰래》 secretly; in secret; 《남의 눈을 피하여》 on the quiet 〔sly〕; stealthily; by stealth; 《남의 눈에 띄지 않게》 without letting anyone see; without being seen. ¶ ～ 나가다〔들어오다〕 sneak out 〔into〕 / ～ 다가가다 steal near; sneak 〔stalk〕 《up to》 / ～ 사라지다 slip off; go away 〔leave〕 unobserved / ～ 도망치다 steal away / ～ 돈을 손에 쥐어주다 slip a coin into 《*a person's*》 hands; hand 《*a person*》 the money secretly / ～ 뒤를 밟다 shadow 《*a person*》 stealthily / ～ 쳐다보다 look furtively at 《*a person*》; steal a glance at 《*a person*》 / ～ 핀잔을 주다 get in a sly dig at 《*a person*》; make a snide remark / 그녀는 ～ 자리를 떴다 She left her seat without a sound. / 그의 말에 ～ 화가 치밀었다 At his words I felt indignation swell up in my heart.

**살금살금** surreptitiously; sneakingly; stealthily; secretly; furtively; quietly; covertly; on the sly; ever so furtively; behind 《*a person's*》 back. ¶ ～ 걷다 walk noiselessly 〔stealthily〕 / ～ 다가가다 steal *one's* way 《to》; make a stealthy approach 《to》 / ～ 돌아다니다 skulk 〔sneak〕 about / ～ 훔쳐보다 cast covert 〔sneak〕 glances at 《*a person*》 / ～ 훔치다 swipe 〔steal〕 《it》 when no one is looking; pilfer / 그는 ～ 그녀의 방으로 기어 들어갔다 He stealthily crept into her room.

**살기**(殺氣) an atmosphere 〔a look〕 of menace; bloodthirstiness; thirst for blood; a violent temper; a murderous spirit. ¶ ～에 찬 군중 an excited 〔a bloodthirsty〕 mob 〔crowd〕 / ～를 띠다 reek of murder; look menacing 〔threatening〕; be wildly excited / ～ 등등하다 be bloodthirsty; *one's* blood is up; be thirsty for blood / 그의 눈은 ～에 차 있다 There is danger in his eye. / ～가 가득 차 있었다 Death was in the air.

**살길** 《생활의》 a means to live; a livelihood; 《활로》 a means of escape; a way out (of the difficulty). ¶ ～을 찾다 seek a way to make a living; 《활로를》 find a way out (of the difficulty); find a means of survival / ～을 잃다 lose *one's* livelihood.

**살날** the rest of *one's* life; *one's* remaining days. ¶ 그는 ～이 얼마 안 남았다 His days are numbered. *or* He has but a few days 〔years〕 to live.

**살내리다** get thin; become thinner 〔leaner〕; lose flesh 〔*one's* weight〕; flesh falls off. ¶ 살내리는 약 a reducing drug 〔medicine〕 / 살내리기 위한 운동을 하다 take fat-reducing exercises.

**살내리다**(煞—) have *one's* evil spirit exorcised; 《띠앗》 have *one's* family feud vanished.

**살다**[1] ① 《생존하다》 live; subsist; exist; stay alive; be alive 〔living〕 (살아 있다); survive (살아 남다); revive (소생하다). ¶ 살아 있는 물고기 a live fish / 산 교훈〔증거〕 a living lesson 〔witness, example〕 / 사는 기쁨 the joy of living / 죽느냐 사느냐의 문제 a matter of life and death / 살아 있는 동안에 while *one* lives 〔is alive〕; during *one's* life / 살아 있는 한 so long as *one* lives; as long as *one* has a drop of blood in *one* / 오래 ～ live long; enjoy longevity / 백 살까지 ～ live to be a hundred (years old) / 살아 나가다 live on / 미래에 ～ live in the future / 희망에 ～ live 〔feed〕 on hope / 먹지 않고 ～ live 〔exist〕 on air 〔nothing〕 / 밥을 먹고 ～ live 〔exist, subsist〕 on rice / 세상을 속아 ～ live *one's* life in illusion / 살기 위해 먹다 eat to live; eat so that *one* may live / 살아서 돌아오다 return 〔come back〕 alive / 오래 살아 욕을 보다 outlive *one's* fame / 오래 살면 별꼴을 다 본다 To live long is to outlive much. / 우선 살고 볼 일이다 While there is life, there is help. / 그는 남을 위해서 살았다 He lived for others.

② 《생활하다》 live; make a living; get *one's* living; support 《*oneself*》; get along; get by. ¶ 바쁘게 ～ live a busy life / 행복하게 ～ live happily / 혼자 ～ live alone / 호화롭게 ～ live in luxury; lead a luxurious life / 붓으로 ～ live by *one's* pen / 월급으로 ～ live on *one's* salary / 월 120만원으로 ～ support *oneself* on 1.2 million won a month / 부유〔유복〕하게 ～ be well off; make a good living; be in easy circumstances / 가난하게 ～ make a poor living; lead a miserable life / 살기가 어렵다 be in needy 〔narrow〕 circumstances; find it hard to make both ends meet; be badly off / 겨우〔근근히〕 살아가다 pick up a scant living.

③ 《거주·서식하다》 live 《in, at》; inhabit 《a town》; occupy 《a house》; settle 《in Seoul》; reside; dwell; be domiciled 《at, in》. (★ reside, dwell은 둘 다 문어. 보통은 live를 씀. settle은 「정주하다」의 뜻. inhabit는 타동사로서 쓰임). ¶ 숲에 사는 새 birds living in a wood / 사람이 살지 않는 집 an untenanted 〔an unoccupied, a vacant, a deserted〕 house / 살기에 적당한〔적당치 않은〕 inhabitable 〔uninhabitable〕; fit 〔unfit〕 to live in; livable 〔unlivable〕 / 서울에서 ～ live 〔make *one's* home〕 in Seoul / 아저씨와 같이 ～ live with *one's* uncle / 오래 살던 고장을 떠나다 leave the town where *one* has lived long / 그는 술집에서 살다시피 한다 He spends most of his time at the bar. / 그 집은 살기 좋고 편하다 The house is pleasant and comfortable to live in.

④ 《생동하다》 be enlivened; have life given to 《it》. ¶ 이 초상화는 꼭 살아 있는 듯하다 This portrait 「is full of life 〔is really lifelike〕. / 그의 소설은 대화가 살아 있다 In his novel the conversations are really alive.

⑤ 『바둑』 get permanently secure 〔free from danger〕.

⑥ 『야구』 be safe. ¶ 1루에서 ～ be safe on first base.

**살다**[2] 《벼슬·징역을》 serve 《*one's* term》. ¶ 벼슬을 살고 있다 be in the government service; hold an office in 〔under〕 the government / 5년간 징역을 ～ serve a sentence of five years' penal servitude.

**살담배** cut 〔shredded〕 tobacco.

**살덩어리**, **살덩이** a chunk of meat 〔flesh〕.

**살돈** 《도박의》 gambling money; a stake; 《밑천》 seed money; funds; capital. ¶ ～을 대다 supply 《*a person*》 with funds.

**살뜰하다** 《알뜰하다》 (be) frugal; thrifty. ¶ 살뜰히 frugally; economically / 살뜰한 아내 a devoted wife / 알뜰살뜰한 주부 a frugal house-wife.

**살랑거리다** ① 《바람이》 blow gently (with somewhat chill). ¶ 가을 바람이 살랑거린다 An autumn 〔autumnal〕 breeze blows softly. ② 《걸음걸이가》 (walk) gracefully. ¶ 살랑거리며 걷다 walk like a fashion model.

**살랑살랑** ① 《바람이》 《blow》 gently; softly. ② 《걷는 모양》 《walk》 with a mincing gait; briskly.

**살래살래** waving; wagging. ¶ 고개를 ~ 흔들다 shake *one's* head / 개가 꼬리를 ~ 흔든다 The dog wags its tail.

**살려내다** rescue; save; help 《*a person*》 out of 《a dangerous place》; deliver 《*a person*》 out of 《difficulty》. ¶ 목숨을 ~ save 《*a person*》 from death / 물에 빠진 사람을 ~ save 〔rescue〕 《*a person*》 from drowning / 불속에서 어린 애를 ~ rescue a boy from 〔out of〕 the fire.

**살려주다** save; rescue; spare 《*a person's*》 life. ¶ 목숨을 ~ 《죽이지 않고》 spare 《*a person's*》 life; 《죽게 된 것을》 save 《*a person*》 from death / 목숨만은 살려 주십시오 Spare my life!

**살롱** a salon; a saloon; 《파리의 미술전》 the Salon. ◉ ~음악 salon music.

**살리다** ① 《죽이지 않고》 keep 《an animal, a fish》 alive; let 《*a person*》 live; spare 《*a person, a person's* life》; 《구조하다》 save; rescue; deliver. ¶ 아무의 목숨을 ~ 《죽이지 않고》 spare *a person's* life; 《죽게 된 것을》 save 《*a person*》 from death / 사람 살리라고 외치다 cry, "Help, help"; cry for help / 녀석을 살려둘 수는 없다 We can't let that fellow live. / 그를 살리건 죽이건 당신 마음대로요 He is left at your mercy. *or* His life is wholly in your hands.
② 《소생시키다》 revive; resuscitate; bring 《*a person*》 round; bring 《*a person*》 back to life; restore 《a deleted word》.
③ 《활용하다》 make the most 〔best〕 of 《*one's* opportunities》; make the best use of 《the funds》. ¶ 돈을 살려서 쓰다 spend *one's* money usefully 〔profitably〕; improve *one's* money; make the best use of *one's* money / 여가를 ~ make the most of *one's* spare time / 이곳에서의 경험을 살려 앞으로 한일 친선의 징검다리가 되고자 합니다 I'd like to make use of my experience here to be a bridge between Korea and Japan. / 요리의 비결은 사용되는 재료의 특성을 살리는 것이다 The secret of cooking is to enhance the qualities of the ingredients. / 그 경험을 살린다면 당신은 반드시 성공할 겁니다 If you can use your experience, you will surely succeed.
④ 《생기를 주다》 give life 〔vividness〕 《to》; vivify; put vigor 〔life〕 《into》. ¶ 그림을 ~ give life to the picture / 배역을 ~ sustain *one's* role / 붓을 한 번 더 대어서 그림을 ~ make a picture come to life with one more stroke.

**살리실산**(―酸) 〖화학〗 salicylic acid.

**살림** 〖생계〗 (a) livelihood; (a) living (★ 복수형 불가); 《살림살이》 a household; housekeeping; 《생활》 life. ~하다 keep house; run *one's* household; manage household affairs; make a 〔*one's*〕 living. ¶ ~하는 방식 a way 〔manner, style〕 of living / 분수〔수입〕에 어울리게〔어울리지 않게〕 ~하다 live within 〔beyond〕 *one's* means 〔income〕.
살림에: ~에 찌든 얼굴 a face worn with domestic cares / ~에 드는 비용 living 〔housekeeping〕 expenses / ~에 쪼들리다 find it hard to make a living; live in want ⇨~이 어렵다 / ~에 찌들다 be 〔look〕 worn out by domestic 〔family〕 cares.
살림을: ~을 나다 set up a separate household / ~을 내다 keep a separate house / ~을 차리다 start housekeeping; (get married and) make a new home 《at, in》; make *one's* home 《at》 / ~을 걷어치우다 wind 〔shut〕 up *one's* house; give 〔break〕 up housekeeping / ~을 꾸려나가다 live; make 〔earn, gain〕 a 〔*one's*〕 living 〔livelihood〕; make the pot boil; manage household affairs / 가까스로 ~을 꾸려나가다 make a bare living; earn 〔eke out〕 a scanty livelihood / 월 100만 원으로 ~을 꾸려나가다 cover all the household with one million won a month / ~을 잘하다〔못 하다〕 be a good 〔poor〕 housekeeper 〔housewife〕; be good 〔bad〕 at housekeeping / ~을 맡다 take charge of the household / ~을 맡기다 entrust 《*one's* daughter-in-law》 with household affairs / ~을 조리차하다 cut down *one's* living expenses.
살림이: ~이 넉넉하다〔구차하다〕 be well 〔badly〕 off; be in easy 〔bad〕 circum-

stances; be comfortably 〔poorly〕 off / ～이 어렵다 make a poor living; be badly off; be hard up; be in needy circumstances.
¶ 삼촌은 ～이 그다지 넉넉하지 못하다 My uncle is not a very well-to-do man. / 그녀는 ～살이의 어려움을 모른다 She does not know how hard it is to run a house. / 그는 학교 ～을 혼자 도맡아 하고 있다 He has the entire management of the school. / 그는～이 어려운 것처럼 보인다 It seems he is having trouble (in) getting by. *or* He seems to find it difficult to make both ends meet.
◉ ～꾼 《맡은 이》 the mistress of a house; 《잘 하는 이》 a good housewife. ～도구 household goods 〔necessaries〕. ～방 living quarters; housekeeping rooms. ～살이 ＝살림. ～집 a private home.

**살맛**[1] 《사는 맛》 ¶ ～을 느끼다 find *one's* life worth living / 아이가 없어 ～이 없다 be dull without a child / ～이 없어지다 grow weary 〔get sick〕 of life; lose interest in life; find life a bore.

**살맛**[2] 《육체의》 the touch of skin. ¶ 여자의 ～을 알다 know a woman / 여자 ～을 모르다 have no carnal knowledge of women.

**살맞다**(煞—) 〖민속〗 be struck by illness 〔misfortune〕 after attending a ceremonial rite of some outside family.

**살며시** ① 《가만히》 gently; quietly; lightly; softly; cautiously. ¶ ～ 걷다 walk lightly; tread softly / ～ 자리를 뜨다 leave *one's* seat quietly / ～ 아기를 안다 pick up a baby cautiously / 그녀는 ～ 내 손을 잡았다 She took my hand gently. ② 《남몰래》 stealthily; furtively; secretly; in private. ¶ ～ 도망치다 go away stealthily; slip away / ～ 집을 나가다〔집으로 들어오다〕 「steal out of 〔slip into〕 the house / ～ 엿보다 steal a look 《at》; cast a furtive glance 《at, on》 / ～ 돈을 쥐어 주다 slip money into 《*a person's*》 hand / ～ 웃다 laugh inwardly; laugh in *one's* sleeves.

**살모넬라** 〖생화학〗 *Salmonella* (식중독의 원인이 되는 균). ¶ ～에 의한 식중독 salmonella poisoning; salmonellosis.

**살몽혼**(—朦昏) 〖의학〗 local anesthesia. ¶ ～을 하다 《해받다》 be given a local anesthetic.

**살무사** 〖동물〗 a (kind of ) pit viper.

**살문**(—門) 〖건축〗 a lattice door 〔window〕.

**살밑** 《화살촉》 an arrowhead.

**살바람** ① 《틈바람》 a draft (of air). ¶ ～이 들어오는 방 a drafty room / ～을 막다 cut off 〔prevent〕 drafts / ～이 들어온다 There is a draft here. ② 《봄철의》 a chill (spring) wind. ¶ 초봄의 ～ a chill wind in early spring.

**살박다** press a pattern into a rice cake; decorate a rice cake.

**살받이** the ground around a target; a target board.

**살벌**(殺伐) ～하다 (be) bloody; bloodthirsty; brutal; savage; sanguinary. ¶ ～한 분위기 a brutal atmosphere; an air of imminent violence / 그 때는 폭동 등이 빈번했던 ～한 시대였다 It was a bloody age with many riots and other disturbance.

**살별** 〖천문〗 a comet. ⇨ 혜성(彗星).

**살보시**(—布施) sexual relations with a Buddhist priest. ～하다 have illicit sexual relations with a monk.

**살붙이** ① 《일가》 *one's* relatives 〔relations〕; *one's* kith and kin. ② 《고기》 meat.

**살빛** ① 《피부빛》 the color of the skin; complexion. ¶ ～이 희다 have a fair skin 〔complexion〕; be fair / ～이 검다 have a dark skin; be dark-complexioned / ～ 스타킹 natural-colored stockings. ② 《육색》 the color of (human) flesh; (a) flesh color 〔tint〕.

**살살**[1] 《가만가만》 gently; softly; lightly; slowly (천천히). ¶ ～ 걷다 walk softly / ～ 구워삶다 coax 《*a person*》 round; win 《*a person*》 over; wheedle 〔cajole〕 《*a person* out of 〔into〕》 / 눈이 ～ 녹다 snow melts imperceptibly / 아이를 ～ 달래다 comfort 〔persuade〕 a child gently / 상처를 ～ 만지다 touch a wound lightly / 바람이 ～ 분다 The wind blows softly.

**살살**[2] ① 《기다》 with a brisk crawl. ¶ 아기가 ～ 긴다 A baby crawls around at a lively pace. ② 《흔들다》 with a gentle shake. ¶ ～ 머리를 흔들다 shake *one's* head gently. ③ ¶ 배가 ～ 아프다 have a slight pain in the stomach.

**살살이** a wily 〔tricky〕 one; a schemer; a back scratcher; a boot-licker.

**살상**(殺傷) killing and injuring 〔wounding〕; bloodshed. ～하다 kill and wound; shed blood. ¶ 많은 사람들이 ～되었다 Many people were killed and injured. ◉ ～률 《무기 등의》 the kill rate 《of a weapon》.

**살생**(殺生) the destruction 〔taking〕 of life; butchery; shooting and fishing (사냥). ~하다 destroy 〔take〕 life; kill animals. ¶ 쓸데없는 ~ wanton destruction of life; a useless 〔pointless〕 cruelty / ~을 즐기는 cruel; merciless / ~을 금하다 prohibit killing animals / 무익한 ~을 하지 마라 You should not kill animals needlessly.

**살수**(撒水) water sprinkling; watering. ~하다 sprinkle 《the street》 with water; sprinkle water 《over the garden》. ◉ ~기(器) a sprinkler. ~장치 a sprinkler 〔sprinkling〕 system. ~차 a water 〔motor, street〕 sprinkler; a sprinkler (truck).

**살신성인**(殺身成仁) ~하다 sacrifice *oneself* to preserve *one's* integrity; become a martyr to humanity; do an act of benevolence at the sacrifice of *oneself*.

**살아가다** ① 《생명을 이어가다》 lead a life; live; get along; sustain 〔maintain〕 life; keep on living. ¶ 간신히 ~ manage to keep body and soul together; make a bare living; live at subsistence level; scrape a living / 정직하게 ~ live straight; live an honest 〔decent〕 life; earn an honest living / 사이좋게 ~ live together happily; get along well 《with》 / 살아갈 목표가 있다 have something to live for / 지식만으로는 세상을 살아갈 수 없다 Knowledge alone cannot carry you through life.
② 《살림을 이어가다》 live; make a 〔*one's*〕 living; earn *one's* livelihood 〔bread〕. ¶ 분수에 맞게〔맞지 않게〕 ~ live within 〔beyond〕 *one's* means / 얼마 안 되는 봉급으로 ~ live on a small salary / 살아가기가 매우 어렵다 cannot 〔can hardly〕 manage (to live) on 《*one's* income》; be in needy 〔straitened〕 circumstances.

**살아나다** ① 《소생하다》 revive; recover consciousness; come ｢to *oneself* 〔to *one's* senses〕; be brought (back) to life 〔to *oneself*, to *one's* senses〕; return 〔be restored〕 to life. ¶ 살아나게 하다 bring 《*a person*》 round 《to》; recall 〔restore〕 《*a person*》 to life; revive; resuscitate / 인공 호흡으로 ~ be resuscitated by artificial respiration / 시든 꽃이 다시 ~ a drooping flower comes to life again.
② 《구조되다》 be saved 〔rescued, relieved〕; be spared; survive 《a disaster》; 《모면하다》 escape 《death》; live. ¶ 간신히 ~ have a narrow 〔bare〕 escape; escape by a hair's breath / 기적적으로 ~ have a miraculous escape / 살아날 길을 찾다 see 〔find〕 *one's* way out / 살아날 가망이 없는 것으로 단념하다 give up 《*a person*》 for dead / 살아난 사람들 the survivors; the rescued / 살아난 기분이 들다 feel relieved; have a feeling of relief / 이제 살아났다 What a blessed relief!
③ 《기운이》 (***a***) 《불 따위가》 burn 〔flame up〕 (again). ¶ 숯불이 ~ the charcoal fire glows (again). (***b***) 《세력이 다시》 (make a) rally; come back; make a comeback; recover. ¶ 기세가 ~ pick up 〔regain〕 *one's* strength; rally 《from》.
④ 《형태가》 be restored to (the original form); resume.

**살아생전**(—生前) *one's* lifetime. ¶ ~에 in 〔during〕 *one's* lifetime; while alive 〔in life〕; before *one's* death / ~ 너의 출세를 보고싶다 I hope I may live long enough to see you rise in the world.

**살얼음** thin ice. ¶ ~을 밟는〔딛는〕 것 같다 feel as if (*one* were) treading 〔stepping, skating〕 on thin ice; feel like treading on eggs / 연못에 ~이 얼었다 The pond was frozen over with thin ice. *or* The pond was thinly coated with ice. ◉ ~판 a tricky 〔delicate, touchy〕 situation: ~판을 밟는 듯한 교섭 walk-on-eggs negotiations.

**살오르다** get 〔become〕 fat; gain flesh.

**살오르다**(煞—) an evil influence 〔spirit〕 ascends (within *one*); 《띠앗》 a household is torn with disharmony.

**살육**(殺戮) mass killings; (a) massacre; slaughter; butchery; carnage. ~하다 massacre; slaughter; butcher. ¶ 대량 ~ mass murder; a bloodbath; genocide / 양민족간의 불화는 마침내 비극적인 대량 ~으로 발전했다 The feud between the two peoples escalated into a tragic bloodbath.

**살의**(殺意) murderous intent; intent to murder. ¶ ~를 품다 intend to kill 〔murder〕 《*a person*》 / ~를 품고 with murderous intent; with intent to kill 《*a person*》 / 처음부터 ~가 있었던 것은 아니다 It was not his original intention to kill the man.

**-살이** 《생활》 living; life. ¶ 징역살이 serving *one's* term of imprisonment; penal servitude / 시집살이 living with *one's* husband's parents / 머슴살이 working as a farmhand / 고생살이 leading a hard life.

**살인**(殺人) murder; manslaughter; homicide. ～하다 commit murder 〔homicide〕; kill 〔murder〕《*a person*》.

> (용법) **murder** 살의가 있어서 행해진 살인. 모살(謀殺). **manslaughter** 살의가 없는 상태에서 행해진 살인. 법률상으로는 「과실치사」. **homicide** murder와 manslaughter의 두 뜻을 다 포함.

¶ ～적인 deadly《heat》; hectic《confusion》; terrific《congestion》; cut-throat《competition》/ ～이 나다 have a murder case (happen) / 두 번 ～을 범하다 commit two murders / ～ 혐의를 받다 be suspected of murder / 러시아워의 통근열차는 언제나 ～적인 만원〔혼잡〕상태이다 Commuter trains are always terribly crowded in the rush hour. / 올 여름의 ～적인 더위로 나는 녹초가 되었다 I felt quite enervated by the deadly heat this summer.

◉ ～광 a homicidal maniac. ～광선 a death 〔lethal〕 ray. ～귀〔마〕 a devilish homicide; a bloodthirsty killer. ～미수(未遂) an attempted murder: ～미수자 a would-be murderer. ～범 a murderer; a murderess (여자); a homicide: 금품을 노린 ～범 a murderer for gain. ～사건 a murder case. ～수사반 a homicide squad. ～용의자 a murder suspect. ～청부업자 a (professional, hired) killer; a professional gunman 〔assassin〕. 청부～ murder by contract.

**살인죄**(殺人罪) murder; (felonious) homicide. ¶ ～를 범하다 commit homicide 〔murder〕/ ～로 기소되다 be accused of murder / ～로 잡히다 be arrested on a charge of murder.

**살잡히다** 《구김살이》 be wrinkled 〔crumpled, rumpled〕; become creased; 《살얼음이》 form a thin coat of ice; ice over.

**살점**(―點) a piece of meat.

**살조개** 〖조개류〗 a cockle.

**살지다** ① 《살이》 (be) fleshy; fat. ② 《땅이》 (be) fertile; rich.

**살집** fleshiness. ¶ ～이 좋다 be fleshy 〔plump, stout〕.

**살짝**(**살짝**) ① 《남몰래》 furtively; by stealth; in secret; on the sly 〔quiet〕. ¶ ～ 귀띔해 주다 tell《*a person*》secretly《about *a thing*》/ ～ 훔쳐보다 steal a glance《at》/ ～ 만나다 meet《*a person*》in secret. ② 《손쉽게》 effortlessly; adroitly; easily; skillfully; deftly. ¶ ～ 해치우다 do《*a thing*》cheap. ③ 《가볍게》 lightly; slightly; softly. ¶ ～ 때리다 tap lightly.

**살짝곰보** a slightly pockmarked 〔pitted〕 face 〔person〕.

**살쩍** the hair under the temple.

**살찌다** grow 〔get〕 fat 〔stout〕; gain 〔put on〕 weight; become plump; fatten. ¶ 살찐 fat; plump; stout; corpulent / 살찌게 하다 fatten up / …을 먹고 ～ grow fat on《meat》/ 그녀는 좀더 살쪄야 한다 She needs to fill out. / 그녀는 살찌는 체질이다 She is apt to gain weight. / 자네 요즘 살찐 것 같은데 You've put on a bit of weight recently. / 자네 너무 살찌지 않도록 조심해야겠어 You must guard against overweight.

> (참고) 살찐 사람: 「살찐〔비만형의〕 사람」을 a fat man 〔woman〕이라고 표현하는 것은 매우 실례되는 말. fat 대신 plump (보기 좋게 살찐), stout (튼튼해 보일 정도로 살찐)를 쓰는 것이 좋으나, 더 무난한 표현은 (rather) overweight이다. 「살찌다」란 동사는 put on weight가 가장 무난한 표현이다: (보기) She is on the stout side. (그녀는 좀 살이 찐 편이다).

**살찌우다** make《a pig》fat; fatten; fat 〔feed〕 up. ¶ 돼지를 ～ fatten pigs.

**살창**(―窓) a lattice window.

**살촉**(―鏃) an arrowhead.

**살충**(殺蟲) ～하다 kill 〔destroy〕 insects; destroy worms. ◉ ～등(燈) an insecticidal lamp. ～분무기 an insecticide sprayer; an insect spray. ～제 an insecticide; a vermicide; an insect powder (가루).

**살치다** cross 〔X, mark〕 out; cancel.

**살코기** lean meat; red meat.

**살쾡이** 〖동물〗 a wildcat; a lynx. ◉ ～자리 〖천문〗 the Lynx.

**살팍지다** (be) sinewy; strong and lean; muscular; brawny. ¶ 그는 ～ He is built strong and lean.

**살판나다** strike it rich; come into a fortune; *one's* ship comes in. ¶ 그는 부잣집에 장가 들어 살판났다 His ship came in when he married into a wealthy family.

**살펴보다** look (a)round 〔about〕; look into; have 〔take〕 a good 〔careful〕 look; examine; watch for; observe. ¶ 서류를 ～ examine the papers / 사건

의 원인을 자세히 ~ look into the causes / 형세를 ~ see how the wind blows / 방안을 살펴보았으나 찾지 못했다 I searched all over the room, but I could not find it. / 그는 혹시 누가 보는 사람이 없는가 주변을 살펴보았다 He looked about 〔around〕 him to see if anybody was watching.

**살포**(撒布) (a) scattering; (a) sprinkling; (a) spraying. ~하다 scatter 《seeds》; sprinkle 《water》; spray 《insecticide》; dust 《chemical powder》. ¶ 화학 약품의 ~ chemical spraying / 지금 나무에 살충제를 ~하고 있는 중이다 I'm now dusting 〔sprinkling〕 the trees with insecticide. / 음식물 위에 ~하지 마시오 《게시》 Avoid spraying on foods. ◉ ~기 a sprinkler; a sprayer; a duster. ~약〔제〕 dusting powder.

**살풀이**(煞—) 〖민속〗 *salpuri;* a service 〔ceremony〕 of exorcism (굿); exorcising an evil spirit (행위). ~하다 exorcise; drive out an evil spirit; perform *salpuri.*

**살품** the space between clothes and the chest; the bosom.

**살풍경**(殺風景) ~하다 《무풍류하다》 (be) tasteless; inelegant; unrefined; graceless; inartistic; unromantic; boorish; 《쓸쓸하다》 (be) dreary 《sight》; bleak 《scene》; 《재미없다》 (be) dull; drab. ¶ ~한 경치 rough scenery; a bare landscape; a dreary sight / ~한 뜰 a garden 「lacking in taste 〔of bad taste〕 / ~한 건물 buildings out of taste / 방 안에는 테이블과 의자만 달랑 놓여 있어 ~했다 Only with a table and a chair, the room looked bare.

**살피다** ① 《잘 보다》 see; watch; observe; make an observation 《of》; 《고찰하다》 consider; study; 《조사하다》 examine; inquire 〔look〕 into; inspect closely; 《탐지하다》 spy on; search; feel. ¶ 남의 눈치를 ~ study 〔read〕 《*a person's*》 feelings 〔state of mind〕 / 적정(敵情)을 ~ feel 〔spy on〕 an enemy; watch the movements of the enemy / 여론의 동향을 ~ see 〔watch〕 the trend of public sentiment / 옛 역사를 ~ study ancient history / 주위를 ~ look about; give a look around / 형세를 ~ feel out the situation; see how the wind blows / 문단속이 잘 되었나 ~ see that the door is fastened.
② 《헤아리다》 (***a***) 《판단하다》 judge; gather. ¶ 그의 말하는 품으로 살피건대 as I gather from his words / 남의 마음속을 ~ read 《*a person's*》 mind. (***b***) 《남의 사정 등을》 consider; take into consideration; sympathize with; enter into 《*a person's*》 feelings. ¶ 남의 기분을 살피지 못한다 He lacks consideration for the feeling of others.
③ 《주의하다》 pay 〔give〕 attention 《to》; keep close watch 《on》; take care 〔be careful〕 《of》; 《경계하다》 be cautious 《about》; look out 《for》. ¶ 신호를 잘 ~ look to 〔out for〕 a signal / 건강을 잘 ~ take care of *oneself;* be careful about *one's* health / (화재 예방을 위해) 불을 잘 ~ take care not to start a fire; take precautions against fire / (넘어지지 않도록) 발밑을 살피며 걷다 pick *one's* steps 〔way〕.

**살핏하다** (be) rather loose-woven; gauzelike.

**살해**(殺害) murder; killing. ~하다 murder; kill; put to death; slay; slaughter (학살하다); assassinate (암살하다). ¶ ~할 의도로 with murderous intent / ~를 기도하다 make an attempt on 《*a person's*》 life; attempt 《*a person's*》 life / 경찰은 조지를 ~한 범인을 잡았다 The police arrested the criminal who had killed George. ◉ ~기도 a murderous attempt. ~사건 a case of murder; a murder case. ~자 a murderer; a murderess (여자); an assassin (암살자). ~현장 the spot of murder.

**삶** life; living; existence. ¶ 삶의 쓰라림 bitterness of life / 삶을 위한 투쟁 struggle for life / 삶의 질 the quality of life / 삶을 영위하다 lead a life; live / 삶을 즐기다 enjoy life.

**삶다** ① 《끓이다》 boil; simmer (뭉근한 불로); cook. ¶ 달걀을 ~ boil eggs / 너무 ~ overdo; overboil; boil too much 〔long〕 / 다시 ~ reboil; cook over again / 갓 삶아 낸 hot from the pot / 흐물흐물하도록 ~ boil 《*something*》 to (a) pulp / 생선을 뭉근한 불로 ~ let fish simmer gently. ② 《구슬리다》 win 《*a person*》 over; cajole; coax; wheedle; bribe; corrupt. ¶ 배심원을 ~ fix 〔buy, bribe〕 the jury / 아무를 삶아서 …하게 하다 bribe *a person* to *do;* wheedle *a person* into *do*ing.

**삶아지다** be boiled 〔cooked〕; boil. ¶ 잘 삶아진 감자 well-cooked potatoes / 흐물흐물하게 ~ be boiled to (a) pulp / 너무 ~ be overdone.

**삼**[1] 〖식물〗 flax; flax plant (아마); a hemp (plant) (대마); ramie (저마);

jute (황마); 《섬유》 flax; hemp; jute.

**삼**[2] 《태아의》 the amnion 〔caul〕 and the placenta. ¶ 삼(을) 가르다 cut a navel string 〔an umbilical cord〕.

**삼**[3] 〖의학〗 a leucoma; a white speck. ⇨ 삼눈. ¶ 눈에 삼이 생기다 get a leucoma; have a white speck in *one's* eye.

**삼**(三) three. ¶ 제3, the third / 3분의 1, 「a 〔one〕 third.

**삼**(蔘) (a) ginseng. ⇨ 인삼(人蔘).

**삼가**(三價) 〖화학〗 trivalence; trivalency. ◉ ~원소 a triad. ~탄소 trivalent carbon.

**삼가** respectfully; reverently; humbly. ¶ ~ 아룁니다 I beg to say that…; I have the honor to inform you that … / ~ 감사의 말씀을 드립니다 I respectfully express my thanks to you. / ~ 애도의 뜻을 표합니다 I respectfully express my condolence. / ~ 축하를 드립니다 I offer congratulations in a humble way. / ~ 사죄드립니다 I humbly beg 〔ask〕 your pardon. / ~ 조의(弔意)를 표합니다 Please accept my deepest condolence.

**삼가다** ① 《억제하다》 restrain *oneself;* refrain 〔abstain, keep〕 from; be restrained 《in》; eschew; 《절제하다》 be moderate 《in smoking》. ¶ 담배를 ~ refrain from smoking / 술을 ~ keep off alcohol; be temperate in drinking / 폭음폭식을 삼가라 Don't eat or drink 「too much 〔to excess〕. / 차내에서는 담배를 삼가 주십시오 《게시》 Passengers are requested not to smoke. / 의사는 술과 담배를 삼가라고 말했다 The doctor told me to cut down on my drinking and smoking. ② 《조심하다》 be cautious; caution *oneself* 《against》; be discreet 《in *one's* behavior》; be careful 《about》; be prudent; be circumspect. ¶ 행동을 ~ be circumspect in behavior; behave *oneself* prudently / 말을 ~ be discreet in what *one* says; mind 〔be careful about〕 *one's* language / 언행을 삼가시오 Behave (yourself)! / 말을 삼가시오 You should be more careful what you say. *or* Mind your language.

**삼각**(三角) triangularity; 《삼각형》 a triangle; 《삼각법》 trigonometry. ¶ ~의 triangular; three-cornered / ~으로 triangularly; in a triangular form. ◉ ~건(巾) a triangle (bandage). ~관계 the eternal triangle; a triangular 〔triple〕 love affair; a love triangle. ~근(筋) 〖해부〗 a deltoid (muscle). ~급수 trigonometrical series. ~기(旗) a burgee; a (triangular) pennant. ~기둥 a trigonal 〔triangular〕 prism. ~동맹 a triple 〔triangular〕 alliance. ~돛 〖항해〗 a jib; a staysail. ~모 a three-cornered hat. ~무역 triangular 〔triple〕 trade. ~방정식 a trigonometrical equation. ~법 trigonometry. ~뿔 a trigonal 〔triangular〕 pyramid. ~익(翼) 〖항공〗 a delta wing: ~익의 비행기 a delta-wing(ed) airplane. ~자 a triangle; a set square. ~점 〖측량〗 a triangulation point: ~점의 표석 a stone triangulation marker. ~주(洲) a delta. ~측량 triangulation; triangular surveying. ~파(波) chopping waves. ~함수 〔비〕 trigonometric function 〔ratio〕.

**삼각**(三脚) three legs; a tripod. ¶ ~가(架) a tripod; a tripod mounting / 이인~ 《경기》 a three-legged race. ◉ ~의자 a three-legged stool.

**삼각형** a triangle. ¶ 둔각〔예각〕 ~ an obtuse-〔acute-〕angled triangle / 등변〔부등변〕 ~ an equilateral 〔a scalene〕 triangle / 역~ an inverted triangle / 이등변〔직각, 구면〕 ~ an isosceles 〔a right-angled, a spherical〕 triangle / 정~ a regular triangle / ~의 꼭지점〔높이, 밑변〕 the vertex 〔altitude, base〕 of a triangle.

**삼강**(三綱) the three basic human relations (between sovereign and subject, father and son, husband and wife); the three bonds. ◉ ~오륜(五倫) the three fundamental principles and the five moral disciplines in human relations.

**삼거리**(三―) a junction of three roads; a three-forked road.

**삼겹실**(三―) three-ply thread.

**삼겹살** 《고기》 meat from the sides of a pig usually sliced thin and fried for food; 《요리》 broild *samgyopsal.*

**삼경**(三更) (around) midnight; the dead of night.

**삼경**(三經) the Three Classics (of 「Ancient China).

**삼계탕**(蔘鷄湯) *samgyetang;* chicken broth with ginseng (and other ingredients).

**삼관왕**(三冠王) 〖스포츠〗 a triple crown; a triple gold medalist. ¶ ~이 되다 get 〔win〕 a triple crown (야구에서); become the triple gold medalist.

**삼교**(三校) the third (printer's) proof.

**삼국**(三國) three countries 〔states〕. ◉ ~간섭 〖역사〗 the Triple Intervention. ~동맹 a triple alliance. ~시대

the period 〔age, era〕 of the Three Kingdoms 〔States〕. ～유사(遺事) *Samguk Yusa*, Legends and History of the Three Kingdoms. ～협상 a triple entente. ～협정 a tripartite agreement. 제～ the third「power〔state〕: 제～인 a national of a third country.

**삼군**(三軍) 《전군》 the whole army; 《육해공군의》 three armed services; the armed forces. ¶ ～을 지휘하다 command the whole army.
◉ ～사관학교 the Third Military Academy. ～의장대 the triservice honor guard. ～합동작전 joint operations of the three armed services.

**삼굿** a hemp-steaming pit 〔kiln〕. ～하다 steam hemp to remove the outer covering.

**삼권**(三權) the three powers (of administration, legislation and judicature).
◉ ～분립 respective independence of the three powers (of administration, legislation, and judicature); separation of three powers; the separation of legal, administrative, and judicial powers. 「〖전기〗 a triode.

**삼극**(三極) ¶ ～의 tripolar. ◉ ～(진공)관

**삼년**(三年) three years. ¶ ～생 a 3rd-year (class) student; 《미》 a 3rd-grade student; a third grader; a junior (student) (미국 대학의) / ～마다 triennial; every three years / ～째 햇볕을 못 보고 묵혀 있다 remain buried in obscurity for three long years / ～마다 한 번씩 홍수가 난다 We have a flood every「three years 〔third year〕.
◉ ～상(喪) two-year mourning. ～생식물 a triennial.

**삼노** a hemp rope 〔cord〕. 「(*pl.* -nae).

**삼눈** a phlyctenule; a phlyct(a)ena

**삼다** ① 《…을 —으로 하다》 make; adopt 《*a person*》 as; set up 《*a person*》 as; use 〔have, regard〕 《*a thing*》 as. ¶ 소일 삼아 just to kill time / 장난 삼아 half in fun / 재미 삼아 partly out of sport; partly for fun; by way of amusement / 양자로 ～ adopt 《*a person*》 (as *one's* son); receive 《a nephew》 into *one's* family as a son / 사위로 ～ make 《*a person*》 *one's* son-in-law / …을 구실 삼아 on the pretext 〔plea〕 of; making 《it》 an excuse to... / …을 낙으로 ～ delight in; take pleasure 〔delight〕 in / …을 벗～ make a friend 〔companion〕 of; make friends with / …을 모델로 ～ pattern 〔model〕 after 《*a person*》; follow the model 〔example〕 of 《*a person*》; take 《*someone*》 for a model / …하는 것을 규칙으로 ～ make it a rule to *do* / 문제로 삼지 않다 take no notice 〔account〕 of; make little 〔light〕 of; do not care 《a bit》 / 김선생을 우리들의 대표로 삼자 Let's make Mr. Kim our representative. / 여름은 자연과 벗삼을 좋은 기회다 Summer is a good chance to「commune 〔be in close contact〕 with nature. ② 《짚신을 만들다》 make (a sandal); 《뽑다》 spin 《hemp》. ¶ 짚신을 ～ make straw sandals / 명주실을 ～ spin silk.

**삼단** a bunch of hemp. ¶ ～ 같은 머리 long「thick 〔luxuriant〕 hair; tresses.

**삼단**(三段) three stages; the third stage. ◉ ～기사 《신문의》 a three-column article. ～뛰기 〖스포츠〗 hop, step 〔skip〕, and jump; triple jump. ～로켓 a 3-stage rocket.

**삼단논법**(三段論法) 〖논리〗 a syllogism. ¶ ～적으로 syllogistically / ～으로 논하다 syllogize; argue 〔reason〕 by syllogisms. ◉ 생략～ an enthymeme.

**삼대**(三代) three generations. ¶ ～ (가는) 부자 없다 No fortunes of a family last more than three generations.

**삼도내**(三途—) 〖불교〗 the (River) Styx. ¶ ～를 건너다 cross the Styx; die.

**삼독회**(三讀會) 〖법〗 《pass》 the third reading 《of a bill in the legislature》.

**삼동**(三冬) ① 《겨울의 석달》 the three winter months. ② 《세 겨울》 the winters of three years. 「umvirate.

**삼두정치**(三頭政治) 〖역사〗 triarchy; tri-

**삼등**(三等) the third class 〔rate〕; 《셋째》 the third place. ¶ ～으로 여행하다 travel 〔go〕 third(-class); travel (in the) steerage (배의) / ～이 되다 win the third prize; get (the) third place; 《경주에서》 come in third.
◉ ～객 a third-class passenger (열차의); 《배의》 a steerage passenger. ～국 a third-rate power; a minor country. ～칸 a third-class compartment. ～표〔석〕 a third-class ticket 〔seat〕. ～품 a third-rate article.

**삼등분**(三等分) trisection; dividing into three equal parts. ～하다 divide 〔cut〕 《*a thing*》 into three equal parts; divide equally among the three; 《선·각 따위를》 trisect. ¶ 그 돈은 너희들끼리 ～하여라 Divide the money equally among you three.

**삼라만상**(森羅萬象) Nature; all (things in) nature; the universe; all 〔the whole of〕 creation.

**삼루**(三壘) 〖야구〗 the third base. ¶ ～에 나가다 go 〔advance〕 to third; take third / ～에 도루하다 steal third; steal into the third base / ～를 밟는 데 성공하다 succeed in taking third base.
◉ ～선 the third base line. ～수 a third baseman. ～타 a three-base hit; a triple.

**삼류**(三流) the third rate 〔grade, class, order〕. ¶ ～의 third-rate〔-class〕; of the third order / ～호텔〔가수〕 a third-rate hotel 〔singer〕. ◉ ～인물 a third-rater. ～작가 a third-rate writer; a hack. ～학교 a third-class school.

**삼륜차**(三輪車) 《ride》 a tricycle; 《구어》 a three-wheeler; 《영구어》 a trike; 《세발 자전거》 a velocipede.

**삼림**(森林) a forest; a wood; woods (★ a forest는 사람 손이 별로 가지 않은 자연림. woods, a wood는 보통 마을에서 가까운 숲. 《미》에서는 woods를 많이 씀). ¶ ～이 우거진 지역 a lushly forested region / ～의 경치 woodland scenery.
◉ ～경비원 a forest ranger. ～공원 a forest park. ～관리 forestry management. ～남벌 reckless deforestation. ～대(帶) a forest belt 〔zone〕. ～벌채 deforestation. ～법 the Forest Act. ～보호〔애호〕 conservation 〔conservancy, protection〕 of forests. ～욕(浴) 《take》 a therapeutic walk in the forest 〔woods〕; basking in the woods. ～자원 forest 〔timber〕 resources. ～지대 a wooded country; a wooded 〔timber〕 region; woodland(s); 《미》 timberland. ～철도 a logging railroad 〔railway 《영》〕 (in a forest area). ～학 forestry. ⇨임학(林學). ～행정 forest administration.

**삼매**(三昧) 〖불교〗 concentration; absorption; samadhi; 《삼매경》 the perfect state of spiritual concentration. ¶ 독서 ～에 빠지다 be absorbed in reading / 독서 ～로 날을 보내다 live *one's* days among books; give all *one's* time to reading.

**삼면**(三面) ① 《세 방면》 three sides 〔faces〕. ¶ ～이 산으로 둘러싸이다 be surrounded by hills on all sides but one. ② 《신문의》 the third page 《of a newspaper》. ◉ ～각 a trihedral angle. ～경(鏡) a three-sided 〔triple〕 mirror; a dresser with three mirrors. ～육비(六臂) versatility. ～체 a trihedron (*pl.* ～s, -dra).

**삼모작**(三毛作) 〖농업〗 《raise》 three crops a year.

**삼목**(杉木) 〖식물〗 a Japan(ese) cedar; a cryptomeria.

**삼민주의**(三民主義) 〖정치〗 《쑨 원(孫文)의》 the Three Principles of the People.

**삼바** 《춤·춤곡》 (a) samba. ¶ ～를 추다 (dance the) samba.

**삼박거리다** (*one's* eyes) blink lightly.

**삼박자**(三拍子) ① 〖음악〗 three-part time; (simple) triple time 〔measure〕. ② 《조건》 the three important 〔requisite〕 conditions. ¶ ～를 갖춘 triple-threat; all-(a)round; 《완전한》 ideal; consummate / ～를 갖춘 선수 a triple-threat player; a triple threat(er).

**삼발이** a tripod; a trivet; a spider.

**삼배**(三倍) three times; threefold. ～하다 treble; multiply 《a number》 by three. ¶ ～의 three times as 《many, much, large, *etc.*》 as; treble / 수입을 ～로 늘리다 treble *one's* income / 5의 ～는 15이다 Three times five is fifteen. *or* 5 multiplied by 3 is 15. / 그는 나보다 ～나 많은 책을 가지고 있다 He has three times as many books as I (do 〔have〕).

**삼배**(三拜) bowing thrice.

**삼배체**(三倍體) 〖생물〗 《상태》 triploidy; 《개체》 a triploid.

**삼베** hemp cloth; flax.

**삼복**(三伏) the hottest period of summer; the (three) dog days; midsummer. ◉ ～더위 the midsummer heat; the sultry weather of the dog days.

**삼봉낚시**(三鋒―) a three-prong fishhook; a three-forked fishing hook.

**삼부**(三部) 《3개 부분》 three parts 〔sections〕; 《책의》 three copies 〔volumes〕; 《3개의 부서》 three departments.
◉ ～곡 〖음악〗 a trilogy. ～작 a trilogy. ～합창〔합주〕 a chorus 〔an ensemble〕 of three parts; a trio. ～형식 〖음악〗 (a) ternary 〔three-part〕 form.

**삼분**(三分) dividing into three parts; trisection. ～하다 divide 《*a thing*》 into three (parts); trisect; divide by three. ¶ ～의 1, one 〔a〕 third / ～의 2, two thirds / 출석자의 ～의 2 이상의 다수결을 요한다 It requires a majority vote of two thirds or more of those attending 〔those present〕.

**삼분오열**(三分五裂) ～하다 break 〔tear〕 asunder; be broken 〔torn〕 asunder; be disrupted. ⇨ 사분오열.

**삼불** 《태를 사르는》 the fire to burn an afterbirth.

**삼사**(三思) ～하다 think over and over again; speculate 〔reflect〕 《on, about》.

**삼사분기**(三四分期) 《한 해를 나눈》 《during》 the third quarter of the year.

**삼사월**(三四月) March and 〔or〕 April. ¶ ~ 긴긴 해 the long (sunny) days of March and April (under the lunar calendar).

**삼산화**(三酸化) 〖화학〗 ◉ ~물 a trioxide. ~바나듐 vanadium trioxide.

**삼삼오오**(三三五五) 《떼를 지음》 by twos and threes; in groups 《of twos and threes》. ¶ ~ 떼를 지어 걷다〔역으로 가다〕 walk 〔go to the station〕 by twos and threes.

**삼삼하다** ① 《기억이 또렷하다》 be unforgettably vivid 〔fresh〕. ¶ 그것은 지금도 내 기억에 ~ It is still vivid 〔fresh〕 in my memory. / 죽은 아내의 모습이 베갯머리에 삼삼히 떠오르다 I see by my bedside a vivid image of dead wife. ② 《음식이》 be tasty with slight touch of saltiness. ③ 《난감하다》 be perplexed 〔puzzled〕; be at a loss (as to) what to *do;* be at *one's* wits' end. ¶ 그것 참 삼삼하구나 Well, this leaves me completely at a loss.

**삼색**(三色) three colors; tricolor. ¶ ~의 three-color; tricolor(ed).
◉ ~기 a tricolor (flag). ~무늬 a tricolored pattern. ~판 〖인쇄〗 three=color 〔tricolor, trichromatic〕 printing: ~판 인쇄법 the three-color process.

**삼서다** get a corneal ulcer 〔leucoma〕; have a white speck in *one's* eye.

**삼선**(三選) election for the third term. ¶ ~되다 be (re)elected for the third (consecutive) term / ~을 노리다 seek a third term.

**삼성**(三省) ~하다 reflect upon *oneself* (three times a day); examine *oneself* over and over again; introspect.

**삼성**(三聖) the three holy sages (*i.e.* Buddha, Confucius and Christ); the three greatest saints 《of the world》.

**삼성들리다** ① 《무당이》 eat an exorcism feast greedily. ② 《욕심껏》 stuff *oneself* with food; eat to *one's* heart's content.

**삼세**(三世) ① 〖불교〗 《삼계(三界)》 the three states 〔existence〕 (*i.e.* the past, present and future); the Triple Universe. ② 《삼대》 three generations; 《제삼대》 the third generation; ... the Third. ¶ 재미 교포 ~ a third-generation Korean-American / 헨리 ~ Henry Ⅲ 〔the Third〕.

**삼세번**(三一番) (exactly) three times; thrice.

**삼승**(三乘) ① 〖수학〗 cube. ⇨ 세제곱. ② 〖불교〗 the three conveyances (*i.e.* *Bôdhisattva, Pratyeka,* and Buddha's disciples).

**삼시**(三時) 《식사》 three daily meals; 《현재·과거·미래》 the present, the past and the future; 《세 계절》 the three seasons for farming; spring, summer and autumn. ¶ ~ 세 때를 챙겨 먹다 never miss to take three meals a day.

**삼신**(三神) ① 《삼성》 the legendary three founders of ancient Korea. ② 《신령》 the three gods governing childbirth.

**삼실** hemp yarn; linen thread.

**삼십**(三十) thirty. ¶ 제~ the thirtieth / ~대의 사람 a person in the 〔*one's*〕 thirties / ~을 갓 넘은 in *one's* early thirties; just out of *one's* twenties / ~대에 죽다 die in *one's* thirties.

**삼십육계**(三十六計) running away; flight; decampment. ¶ ~를 놓다 beat a retreat; take to *one's* heels; run away / ~에 줄행랑이 제일 《속담》 The wisest thing to do now is to run away. *or* Discretion is the better part of valor.

**삼십팔도선**(三十八度線) 《위도》 38 degrees north latitude; 《한반도의》 the 38th parallel (dividing Korea). ¶ 여기가 ~입니다 This is on the 38th parallel.

**삼씨** hempseed. ◉ ~기름 hempseed oil.

**삼엄**(森嚴) solemnity. ~하다 (be) solemn; grave; awe-inspiring. ¶ ~한 분위기 awe-inspiring atmosphere / 경찰의 ~한 경계망을 뚫고 도주하다 run away 〔disappeared *oneself*〕 through tightly-guarded police.

**삼엽충**(三葉蟲) 〖고생물〗 a trilobite.

**삼오야**(三五夜) 《십오야》 the fifteenth night of a lunar calendar; a night of full moon. ¶ ~ 밝은 달 a bright full moon (on the fifteenth night).

**삼용**(蔘茸) ginseng and (deer) antler.

**삼우**(三友) three delights (*i.e.* poem, wine and music 〔lute〕); pine, bamboo and plum blossom; mountain and stream, pine and bamboo, lute and wine.

**삼원색**(三原色) (the) three primary colors. ¶ ~을 활용한 trichromatic 〔trichromic〕 《printing, photography》.

**삼월**(三月) March (생략 Mar.).

**삼위일체**(三位一體) 〖성서〗 the Trinity; the Holy 〔Blessed〕 Trinity. ¶ ~의 기독교 교리 the Christian doctrine of the Trinity / ~가 되어 forming a trinity / 연합군은 육해공이 ~가 되어 행동했다 The Allied army, navy and air forces did their work in close cooperation. ◉ ～론 Trinitarianism: ～론자 a Trinitarian.

**삼인조**(三人組) a trio; a triad. ¶ ～(의) 강도 a trio of burglars; a gang of three robbers.

**삼인칭**(三人稱) 〖문법〗 the third person. ◉ ～ 단수〔복수〕 third person singular 〔plural〕.

**삼일**(三日) 《사흘》 three days; 《초사흘》 the third day of the month; 《해산·결혼한 뒤의》 the third day after childbirth 〔marriage〕. ¶ ～동안 for three days / 5월 ～ the third of May / ～ 걸러 every fourth day / ～마다 every three days / ～에 한 번 once (in) every three days / ～이 멀다하게 very frequently; almost every other day. ◉ ～예배 〖기독교〗 Wednesday evening church service. ～장(葬) burial on the third day after death. ～천하 a short-lived rule; a three-day 〔a very brief〕 reign: 그 내각은 ～천하였다 The Cabinet was in power for a very short period of time.

**삼일운동**(三一運動) the 1919 〔*Samil*〕 Independence Movement (of Korea).

**삼일절**(三一節) the anniversary of the Independence Movement of March 1st, 1919. ¶ 오늘은 제75회 ～이다 Today marks the 75th anniversary of the *Samil* 〔the March 1〕 Independence Movement.

**삼자**(三者) ① 《제삼자》 the third party 〔person〕; an outsider. ⇨ 제삼자(第三者). ② 《삼인》 three persons; the three parties. ¶ ～간의 tripartite; triple. ◉ ～범퇴 〖야구〗 All the three batters 「retired in quick order 〔were easily put out〕. ～회담 a tripartite meeting; a tripartite 〔three-way〕 talk.

**삼재**(三災) ① 《운성(運星)》 one of the baleful stars. ② 《재난》 the three disasters 《*i.e.* flood, fire and wind or war, pestilence and famine》.

**삼족**(三族) the three sets of relatives; 《집밖의》 relatives on *one's* father's side, *one's* mother's side and *one's* wife's side; 《집안의》 *one's* parents, *one's* siblings 〔brothers and sisters〕, *one's* wife and children.

**삼종**(三種) three kinds; 《제3종》 the third class. ◉ ～백신 〖의학〗 triple vaccine. ～우편(물) third-class mail.

**삼주기**(三周忌) the second anniversary of 《*a person's*》 death.

**삼중**(三重) triple. ¶ ～의 threefold; treble; triple; triplicate / ～의 목적 a triple purpose / ～으로 trebly. ◉ ～결합 〖화학〗 a triple bond. ～고 a triple handicap (of being blind, deaf, and dumb); triple distress. ～살 〖야구〗 a triple play. ～수소 tritium. ～점 〖물리〗 a triple point. ～주〔창〕 a (musical) trio (*pl.* ～s). ～충돌 a three-way 〔ternary〕 collision. ～탑 a three-storied pagoda.

**삼지사방**(—四方) all directions. ¶ ～으로 도망치다 flee 〔disperse〕 in all directions.

**삼지창**(三枝槍) 《창》 a three-pronged spear; a trident; 《포크》 a fork.

**삼진**(三振) 〖야구〗 a strike-out; three strikes. ¶ ～시키다〔으로 잡다〕 strike 《a batter》 out; fan 《a batter》 《구어》 / ～당하다 be struck out; be fanned out / 그는 ～ 3개를 빼앗았다 He struck out three batters. ◉ 탈～기록 a strike-out record.

**삼짇날**, **삼짇**(三—) the third of the third 「lunar month.

**삼차**(三次) 《세 번》 the third time; 〖수학〗 the third power; cubic. ◉ ～곡선 a cubic (curve). ～근수(根數) a cubic root. ～내각 the third Cabinet. ～방정식 a cubic (equation). ～산업 the tertiary industries. ～식 a cubic expression. ～함수 a cubic. 제～5개년 계획 the third five-year plan.

**삼차신경**(三叉神經) 〖해부〗 the trigeminal 〔trifacial〕 (nerve); the trigeminus (*pl.* -ni). ◉ ～통 trigeminal neuralgia.

**삼차원**(三次元) three dimensions; the third dimension. ¶ ～의 three-dimensional 《space》; third-dimensional; 3-D / ～의 세계 the three-dimensional world; the world of three dimensions.

**삼창**(三唱) three cheers; 《독창의》 reciting 〔singing〕 three times. ～하다 《만세를》 give three cheers 《for》; 《노래를》 sing three times.

**삼척동자**(三尺童子) a (mere) child. ¶ ～도 그것은 안다 Even a mere child knows it.

**삼천리**(三千里) the whole (land) of Korea. ¶ ～ 방방곡곡에 throughout 〔all over〕 the country; in every corner of the land of Korea. ◉ ～강산〔강토〕 all Korea: ～ 강산에 all over 〔throughout〕 Korea.

**삼천세계**(三千世界) 〖불교〗 entire world; the whole universe.

**삼촌**(三寸) ① 《아버지의 형제》 an uncle (on the father's side). ¶ 외～ an uncle on the mother's side / 처～ a

wife's uncle. ② 《세 치》 3 inches.
◉ ~댁《집》 *one's* uncle's (house); 《숙모》 the wife of a paternal uncle; an aunt.

**삼총사**(三銃士) ① 《단짝》 a triumvirate; a trio. ② 《소설 제목》 *The Three Musketeers.*

**삼추**(三秋) ① 《가을의 석 달》 the three autumn months; an autumn of three months. ② 《세 해의 가을》 three autumns; three years. ¶ 일각이 ~ 같다 feel a moment as if it were three years; be dying to see 《*one's* lover》; miss 《*one's* sweetheart》 for a single day as if it were three years.

**삼춘**(三春) ① 《봄의 석 달》 the three spring months; a spring of three months. ② 《세 해의 봄》 three springs; three years.

**삼출**(滲出) exudation; percolation; 〖의학〗 effusion; exosmosis. ~하다 exude; percolate; ooze (out). ◉ ~액 an exudate; a percolate.

**삼층**(三層) 《세 층》 three stories; 《셋째 층》 the third floor 〔story〕; the second floor 《영》. ¶ 내 방은 ~에 있다 My room is on the third floor. ◉ ~집 a three-story 〔three-storied〕 house.

**삼치** 〖어류〗 a mackerel 〔saury〕 pike.

**삼칠**(三七) twenty-one. ◉ ~일 a baby's twenty-first day of life (celebrated with a party): ~일 잔치 a feast in celebration of the 21st day of a newborn child.

**삼키다** ① 《입으로》 swallow; choke down; take 〔get〕 down. ¶ 침을 ~ swallow *one's* saliva; catch 〔hold〕 *one's* breath (긴장 등으로) / (씹지 않고) 그대로 ~ swallow up (without chewing) / 단숨에 ~ swallow 《the pills》 at one gulp / 통째(로) ~ swallow 《a biscuit》 whole / 음식을 너무 급히 ~ swallow *one's* food too quickly.
② 《파도 따위가》 swallow up 〔engulf〕. ¶ 파도가 배를 삼켜 버렸다 The waves engulfed 〔swallowed up〕 the vessel.
③ 《참다》 bear; suppress; keep 〔hold〕 back. ¶ 눈물을 ~ keep 〔hold〕 back *one's* tears; choke 〔gulp〕 down *one's* tear / 하품을 ~ suppress a yawn.
④ 《횡령하다》 make 《*something*》 *one's* own; take 《*something*》 to *oneself;* pocket; appropriate (to *oneself*). ¶ 공금을 ~ divert public money into *one's* own pocket / 남의 것을 ~ take the belongings of another for *oneself.*

**삼태기** a carrier's basket; a pan-shaped dust-basket.

**삼투**(滲透) saturation; infiltration; permeation; 〖화학〗 osmosis. ~하다 saturate; permeate; infiltrate; pass into.
◉ ~계수 an osmotic coefficient. ~성 osmosis; permeability. ~압 osmotic pressure. ~작용 (an) osmotic action.

**삼파전**(三巴戰) a three-cornered〔-way〕 fight; a three-sided contest 〔struggle, battle〕; a triangular contest. ¶ ~을 벌이다 break out 〔engage in〕 a triangular struggle.

**삼판양승**(三—兩勝) a three-game match; a three-bout contest; a rubber. ¶ 브리지를 ~제로 하다 have 〔play〕 a rubber of bridge.

**삼팔선**(三八線) ⇨ 삼십팔도선(三十八度線).

**삼팔륙세대**(386世代) the so-called '386 generation' means those who are in their 30s, attended college in the 80s, and born in the 60s.

**삼포**(蔘圃) a ginseng field.

**삼한사온**(三寒四溫) a cycle of three cold days and four warm days.

**삼할**(三割) 30 percent. ◉ ~타자 〖야구〗 a .300 〔three hundred〕 hitter.

**삼합사**(三合絲) three-ply thread.

**삼항식**(三項式) 〖수학〗 a trinomial (expression).

**삼행광고**(三行廣告) a classified (three-line) advertisement 〔ad〕; 《미구어》 a want ad. ¶ ~란 the classified ad columns; 《미구어》 the want ads.

**삽**(鍤) a shovel; a spade; a scoop (작은). ¶ 모래 한 삽 a shovelful of sand / 삽으로 땅을 파다 spade the soil / 삽으로 푸다 shovel; take up with a shovel.

**삽가래**(鍤—) a 2-man shovel with rope attached to handle.

**삽목**(揷木) a cutting. = 꺾꽂이.

**삽사리, 삽살개** a shaggy dog; a poodle.

**삽상하다**(颯爽—) (cool and) crisp; fresh; refreshing; bracing. ¶ 삽상한 가을바람 a crisp autumn breeze.

**삽시간**(霎時間) a minute; a moment; an instant; a flash; a twinkle. ¶ ~에 in an instant 〔a moment, a flash〕 / 그것은 ~에 일어난 일이었다 It all happened in a moment 〔flash〕.

**삽입**(挿入) insertion; interposition; interpolation. ~하다 insert; put in 〔between〕; interpose; interpolate.
◉ ~구 a parenthesis (*pl.* -ses). ~물 an interposition. ~부 〖음악〗 an episode. ~어 an interpolation. ~화면〔자막〕 〖영화·TV〗 an insert.

**삽지**(鍤紙) 〖인쇄〗 paper-feeding. ~하다

feed paper ⟪to a printing press⟫. ◉ ～공 a (paper-)feeder. ～판 a feed board.

**삽질**(鍤—) spade work; shoveling. ～하다 do the spade work; dig with a spade; shovel.

**삽화**(挿話) an episode. ¶ ～적(인) episodic(al) / 자기 생애 중의 ～적인 사건 an episode in *one's* life.

**삽화**(挿畫) an 〔a cut-in〕 illustration; a cut; a figure. ¶ 원색 ～ a full-color illustration / ～ 설명 a caption / 아름다운 ～가 들어 있는 잡지 a beautifully illustrated magazine / ～를 넣다 illustrate ⟪a book⟫; insert 〔put in〕 an illustration. ◉ ～가 an illustrator.

**삿갓** a conical hat of loosely woven reed 〔bamboo〕. ◉ ～장이 ⟪만드는 사람⟫ a man who makes reed 〔bamboo〕 hats. ～쟁이 ⟪쓴 사람⟫ a man wearing a reed 〔bamboo〕 hat.

**삿대** a pole; a rod. ⇨ 상앗대.

**삿대질** ① ⇨ 상앗대질. ② ⟪상대에게⟫ ～하다 thrust *one's* fist 〔finger〕 in(to) ⟪another's⟫ face; shake *one's* fist at ⟪*a person*⟫; point 〔stick〕 at….

**삿자리** a reed mat. ¶ ～를 깔다 spread a reed mat.

**상**(上) ① ⟪부분⟫ upper; above; ⟪등급⟫ the first (class, grade); the best; the superior. ¶ 상부 the upper part / 상반신 the upper part of ⟪*a person's*⟫ body / 상의 상 the very best; extra fine; superfine / 상중하 fine, medium and poor / 천상(天上)으로부터 from above 〔heaven〕 / 지평선상에 above the horizon / 그의 학교 성적은 상에 속한다 His schoolwork 〔school record〕 is rather good.
② ⟪신분·지위 등의⟫ senior. ¶ 상부의 명령 an order from above / 하극상 a revolt against seniors.
③ ⟪상권⟫ the first volume. ¶ 상중하의 3권 a set of three volumes / 상하 2권(의 소설) a two-decker.
④ ⟪상감⟫ His Majesty.

**상**(床) a table; a desk. ¶ 상을 차리다〔보다〕 lay the cloth; set the table (for dinner) / 상을 치우다 clear the table; remove 〔take away〕 the cloth / (…을) 상에 올려 놓다 serve ⟪fish⟫ at ⟪*a person's*⟫ table / 밥 한 상에 얼마요 How much do you charge for a meal?

**상**(相) ① ⟪인상(人相)⟫ physiognomy; lineaments; ⟪얼굴⟫ countenance; features; ⟪표정⟫ a look; a face. ¶ 악마의 상 a diabolical look / 상을 보다 read 〔judge〕 ⟪*a person's*⟫ character 〔fortune〕 by the face / 상을 찌푸리다〔찡그리다〕 frown; make a grimace 〔a wry face〕; give a scowl / 그의 얼굴을 보니 장수할 상이다 His physiognomy indicates that he will enjoy long life. / 자네 얼굴에는 여난지상이 나타나 있군 You've got the sort of face that suggests you might have trouble with women.
② ⟪상태⟫ an aspect; a phase; a facet. ¶ 사회상 phases of social life; an aspect of society.
③ 〖천문〗 a phase. ¶ 식(蝕)상 the phase of an eclipse / 월(月)상 a phase of the moon.
④ 〖문법〗 (verbal) aspect.
⑤ 〖전기·화학〗 phase. ¶ 단(單)상 single phase / 단상 전동기 a single-phase motor. / 삼(三)상 three phases / 액상 liquid phase.

**상**(商) ① 〖음악〗 the next-to-lowest note of the Korean pentatonic scale.
② 〖수학〗 the quotient.

**상**(喪) ⟪거상⟫ mourning. ¶ 상을 당하다 a death occurs ⟪in *one's* family⟫; be bereaved ⟪of *one's* father⟫ / 상을 입다 go into 〔take to〕 mourning ⟪for *a person*⟫ / 상을 알리다 announce 〔notice〕 ⟪*a person's*⟫ death / 상중(喪中)에 있다 be in mourning ⟪for⟫ / 상을 벗다 the period of mourning expires; be out of mourning.

**상**(想) an idea; a thought; a conception. ¶ 좋은 상이 떠오르다 a bright idea crosses *one's* mind; be struck with a bright idea.

**상**(像) ⟪화상⟫ a picture; a portrait; ⟪조상⟫ an image; a statue; a figure; ⟪우상⟫ an idol; 〖물리〗 an image.
¶ 사자의 상 a figure of a lion / 성모 마리아의 상 an image of the Virgin Mary / 자유의 여신상 the Statue of Liberty / 상을 만들다 make an image ⟪of⟫; mould ⟪clay into a bust⟫; ⟪광선이⟫ throw an image ⟪on a screen⟫ / 상을 세우다 erect 〔set up〕 a statue to ⟪*a person*⟫.

**상**(賞) a prize ⟪for good conduct⟫; an award; a reward (보수). ¶ …의 상으로 as a prize for…; in reward for… / 우등상 an academic prize / 일등상 the first prize / 노벨 평화상 a Nobel prize for peace / 아카데미상 Academy Award / 금년도 퓰리처상 this year's Pulitzer Prize / 상을 타다 win 〔get, gain, obtain〕 a prize / 상을 받다 receive 〔be awarded〕 a prize / 상을 걸다 offer a prize / 상을 주다 present 〔award〕 a prize 《to》; bestow a prize 《on》.

**-상**(上) 《…상으로 보아》 from the viewpoint 〔standpoint〕 of; in terms of…; viewed in the light of; as a matter of. ¶ 교육상 from the educational point of view; educationally / 역사상 historically / 그녀는 경제상의 이유로 학교를 그만두었다 She left school for financial reasons.

**-상**(狀) 《모양》 -like; -shaped; -form; 《상태》 condition; state. ¶ 고체상 a solid state / 구상(球狀)의 globe-shaped.

**-상**(商) 《장사》 business; commerce; trade; 《상인》 a merchant; a dealer. ¶ 도매상 《상점》 a wholesale store 〔firm〕; 《상인》 a wholesale dealer 〔merchant〕; 《장사》 a wholesale trade / 그의 부친은 포목상이다 His father is 「a draper 〔engaged in the draper's trade〕.

**상가**(商家) a store; a shop; a merchant 〔mercantile〕 house.

**상가**(商街) a shopping street 〔center, district〕; a street of stores; 《지붕 있는》 an arcade. ¶ ～에 가다 go to a shopping center. ◉ ～아파트 an apartment house with stores on the ground floor.

**상가**(喪家) a mourner's house; a family in mourning; a house of mourning 〔death〕. ¶ ～에 문상 가다 go to offer *one's* condolences to the family in mourning; go to make a condolatory address to the family in mourning / 상갓집 개 a dog in a house of death; a dog belonging to nobody; [비유적] a lean dispirited person / 상갓집 개 같다 be as miserable as a dog in a house of death; be in a terrible state of neglect; be famished and lean.

**상각**(償却) (a) refunding; (a) repayment; redemption (공사채의); amortization (연부(年賦)로). ～하다 repay 《*one's* debt(s)》; pay 〔clear〕 off 《a loan》; redeem 《a loan》; amortize. ¶ 감가 ～ 기금 a depreciation fund / 감가 ～비 depreciation cost / 미～의 unrepaid; unredeemed; unamortized. ◉ ～자금 a redemption 〔sinking〕 fund. ～자산 depreciable assets.

**상감**(上監) His Majesty; the King.

**상감**(象嵌) inlaid work (세공); mortising; inlay; marquetry. ¶ ～을 하다〔박다〕 inlay 《*a thing* with gold》; damascene 《metal》 / ～의〔박은〕 inlaid. ◉ ～세공 inlaid work: ～세공 하는 사람 an inlayer.

**상갑판**(上甲板) 〖항해〗 an upper 〔a spar, a sun〕 deck. ¶ ～에 나가다 go topside.

**상강**(霜降) 《절기》 *Sanggang;* the frost-falling; the 18th of the 24 seasonal divisions (around 24 Oct.).

**상객**(上客) ① 《주빈》 a guest of honor; a chief guest; a guest of high rank. ② 《후행》 the member of the family who accompanies the bride or groom at a wedding.

**상객**(常客) a regular customer 〔patron〕; a frequenter; a client (단골 손님).

**상거래**(商去來) a commercial 〔business〕 transaction 《with》; 《make》 a business deal 《with》. ¶ 거기는 ～가 활발하다 Business transactions are briskly carried on there.

**상거지**(上—) the most wretched of beggars.

**상견**(相見) interview; meeting 《*a person*》. ～하다 interview; meet 〔see, look at〕 each other; exchange looks. ◉ ～례 the formal exchange of nuptial bows.

**상경**(上京) coming 〔going〕 up to the capital 〔Seoul〕. ～하다 come 〔go〕 up to the capital 〔Seoul〕; leave for Seoul. (★ come은 서울을 중심으로 하여 서울에 올 경우, go는 서울을 향해 갈 경우에 씀). ¶ 그는 취직 시험을 보려고 ～중이다 He is (up) in Seoul to take an examination for employment.

**상계**(上界) 〖불교〗 the upper world; heaven.

**상계**(相計) an offset; a setoff. ～하다 offset; set off; cancel each other. ◉ ～계정 an offset account. ～관세 《impose》 a countervailing duty 《on》.

**상계**(商界) the business world; the world of commerce; business circles.

**상고**(上古) ancient times; remote ages; remote antiquity (★ the Middle Ages 「중고」, the early modern age 「근고」). ¶ ～의 ancient; of remote antiquity 〔ages〕. ◉ ～사 an ancient history.

**상고**(上告) ① 《고함》 telling 〔informing〕 to *one's* superiors. ② 〖법〗 an appeal (to the Supreme Court); a final appeal. ～하다 appeal 〔make an appeal〕 to a final court; make a final appeal 《in a court》; petition 〔present a demand〕 for revision. ¶ ～를 기각하다 dismiss 〔reject〕 a final appeal; put an appeal out of court 《미》 / ～에 대한 심리 결과 하급 법원의 판결은 파기되었다 On final appeal the judgment of the lower court was reversed. ◉ ～기각 dismissal of a final appeal. ～기한 the time for (final) appeal. ～법원 a court of final appeal; a court of last resort; the Supreme Court. ～심 a hearing at the court of final appeal; (a) trial at the Supreme Court. ～이유서 a statement of grounds of the final civil appeal. ～인 an appellant; a demandant; an applicant for revision.

**상고**(詳考) a careful examination [consideration, study]; scrutiny. ～하다 examine carefully; consider thoroughly; think over; scrutinize; consult 《a book》 in detail; refer closely 《to》.

**상고대** a heavy frost on treetops [plants]. ～끼다 be frost-covered.

**상고머리** 《머리깎기의》 a crew cut [haircut]; a square-cut hair; 《머리》 a square-cropped head. ¶ ～로 깎다 dress [cut] *one's* hair square.

**상공**(上空) 《하늘》 the sky; the skies; 《하늘 높은 곳》 the upper air [regions]. ¶ 서울 ～에(서) in the skies of Seoul; over Seoul / 까마득한 ～에(서) far [high] up in the sky [air]; high above / 1,000미터 ～에서 at an altitude [a height] of 1,000 meters; at 1,000 meters (high) in midair / 서울 ～을 날다 fly over Seoul.

**상공**(商工) commerce [trade] and industry. ¶ ～의 commercial and industrial. ◉ ～채권 commercial and industrial bonds. ～회의소 the Chamber of Commerce and Industry: 대한 ～ 회의소 the Korea Chamber of Commerce and Industry (생략 KCCI).

**상공업**(商工業) commerce and industry. ¶ ～의 commercial and industrial. ◉ ～자 merchants and industrialists.

**상과**(商科) a commercial course; a department [school] of business administration. ¶ ～ 학생 a commerce student. ◉ ～대학 a college of commerce; a commercial college.

**상관**(上官) a higher [superior, senior] officer [official]; a chief. ¶ ～의 명령에 복종하다 obey *one's* chief's orders. / ～을 모욕하다 insult *one's* senior (in rank) / ～의 명령을 거역하다 be insubordinate to *one's* superior (officer).

**상관**(相關) ① 《상호 관계》 correlation; interrelation; mutual relation(s). ～하다 be related 《to》; bear on; have an interrelation(ship) 《with》. ¶ ～ 적인 interrelated; mutually related; correlative; interdependent.

② 《관련》 relation; connection; 《관여》 participation. ～하다 《관계가 있다》 have (something) to do 《with》; have relations [connections] 《with》; 《관여하다》 take part 《in》; have [play] a part 《in》; have a hand 《in》; 《말려들다》 be implicated [involved] 《in》; get mixed up 《in》. ¶ 그런 일에 ～하고 싶지 않다 I don't like to be mixed up in such a business.

③ 《간섭》 meddling; (an) interference. ～하다 meddle 《in, with》; interfere 《in, with》; put [poke, thrust] *one's* nose 《into》. ¶ (남의 일에) 쓸데없이 ～하다 make uncalled-for meddling; put *one's* finger in another's pie / 네가 ～할 일이 아니다 It's none of your (nosy) business.

④ 《개의》 concern; care. ～하다 concern [trouble] *oneself* 《about》; care 《about》; mind; have a regard for. ¶ 옷차림에 ～ 않다 be careless about *one's* appearance / 조금도 ～ 않다 do not care a bit 《about》 / 남들이 뭐라고 하든 ～ 않는다 I don't mind what people say of me.

⑤ 《성교》 connection; (sexual) relations [intercourse]. ～하다 have connection [relations] 《with》. ¶ 여자와 ～하다 have relations with a woman.

◉ ～계수 『통계』 a coefficient of correlation. ～관계 (an) interrelation; mutual relation; (a) correlation; (an) interrelationship: 인구 증가와 토지 가격의 상승 사이에는 ～ 관계가 있다 The increase of population and the rise of land prices are mutually related. ～비 (a) correlation ratio. ～성 interrelationship; correlativity; reciprocality. ～작용 (a) correlation; (an) interaction ～접속사 『문법』 a correlative conjunction.

**상관습**(商慣習) business [commercial] usage; normal business [commercial] practice; 『법』 the custom of trade. ¶ 그것이 한국에서의 ～이라고 네가 그를 설득시킬 수는 없을 거라고 생각한다 I don't think you can convince him that it is normal business practice in Korea.

**상관없다**(相關—) ① 《관계없다》 (***a***) 《관련 없다》 have nothing to do 《with》; bear no relation 《to》; be not concerned 《about》; be unrelated 《to》; 《말려들지 않다》 be not involved [mixed up] 《in》. ¶ …에 상관 없이 independent(ly) of; irrespect(ly) of. (***b***) 《무방

하다》 [사람이 주어] may 〔can〕 *do;* be allowed to 《*do*》; [사물이 주어] be justifiable; do (well); be all right. ¶ …라고 말해도 ～ One may safely say that…; It is not too much to say that… / 술담배는 조금 해도 ～ A little liquor or tobacco will do you no harm. / 재미만 있다면 어떤 책이라도 ～ Any book will do, so long as it is interesting. / 「당신 사진을 찍어도 괜찮겠습니까」—「예, 상관 없습니다」 "Do you mind if I take your picture ?"—"No, it's all right with me." ② 《개의치 않다》 do not care 〔mind〕; be indifferent 《to》; 《중요치 않다》 do not matter. ¶ …에 상관 없이 regardless of; without regard to; irrespective of / 남들이야 어떻게 생각하든 상관 없이 no matter 〔without regard to〕 what other people (may) think / 복장 따위는 아무래도 ～ I don't care how I dress. / 어느 쪽이 이기건 상관 없었다 Which of them won was a matter of indifference. / 그건 아무래도 상관 없지 않은가 What does it matter?

**상관적**(相關的) interrelative; correlative; mutually related. ¶ ～으로 interrelatively; correlatively.

**상괭이** 〖동물〗 a porpoise.

**상궁**(尙宮) a court lady.

**상권**(上卷) volume one; book one; the first volume 《of two, three》.

**상권**(商權) commercial power 〔supremacy〕; 〖법〗 commercial rights. ¶ ～을 장악하다 acquire commercial supremacy; dominate the market.

**상궤**(常軌) a beaten track; a normal course of action; a proper course; normality. ¶ ～를 벗어난 abnormal 《leanings》; eccentric 《behavior》; preposterous 《claims》 / ～를 벗어나다 be eccentric 〔abnormal〕; run 〔go〕 off the rails 〔track〕; go beyond 〔outstep〕 the bounds of common sense / 그의 사고 방식은 ～를 완전히 벗어나 있다 His way of thinking is quite eccentric.

**상규**(常規) established rules 〔regulations〕; normal usages.

**상극**(相剋) ① 〖민속〗 being mutually destructive; incompatibility. ¶ 물과 불은 ～이다 Water and fire are mutually destructive. / 그것들은 서로 ～이다 They cannot hit it off together. ② 《충돌》 (a) conflict; (a) rivalry; friction; strife. ¶ (서로) ～이다 struggle 〔vie〕 with 《each other》; be at variance 《with》; conflict 《with》.

**상근**(常勤) full-time employment. ¶ ～의 full-time 《workers》. ◉ ～감사(監事) a standing statutory auditor. ～자 a full-time employee; a full-timer.

**상글거리다** smile gently 〔blandly〕; beam.

**상글방글, 상글상글** beaming; smiling.

**상금**(賞金) prize money; a prize; a (cash) reward; a premium (장려금). ¶ ～을 노리는 사람 a pothunter / ～을 걸다 offer a prize 《for》; set 〔put〕 a prize 《on *a person's* head》 / ～을 주다 award a prize 《to》 / 그는 1등에 당선되어 100만 원의 ～을 탔다 He won the first prize of one million won.

**상급**(上級) 《윗단계·계급》 an upper 〔a higher〕 grade 〔rank〕; 《학교의》 an upper 〔a higher, an advanced〕 class. ¶ ～의 upper(-class); higher(-grade, =rank); superior; senior / ～ 영어 코스 an advanced course in English / ～반이다 be in a higher class. ◉ ～공무원 high-ranking government officials. ～과정〔코스〕 an advanced class 〔course〕. ～관청 superior offices 〔authorities〕. ～법원 a superior 〔higher〕 court. ～생 a senior student; an upperclassman; an upper-class student. ～직 a senior post. ～직원 [총칭] high-ranking personnel. ～학교 an advanced school; a school of higher grade.

**상긋** with a (sudden) smile. ～하다 give a sudden smile.

**상긋거리다** smile; beam; smile blandly.

**상긋방긋, 상긋상긋** smiling; beaming.

**상기**(上記) ＝상술(上述). ¶ ～의 the above; the above-mentioned / ～와 같이 as mentioned 〔stated〕 above; as aforesaid / ～와 같은 이유로 for reasons mentioned above; for above=mentioned reasons.

**상기**(上氣) a rush of blood to the head; dizziness; 《얼굴의》 flushing; a glow. ～하다 have a rush of blood to the head; get 〔feel〕 dizzy; 《얼굴이》 flush (up); 《흥분하다》 get excited. ¶ 상기된 볼 flushed cheeks / 그녀는 기쁨으로 ～되었다 She (was) flushed with joy.

**상기**(詳記) a minute description; a full 〔detailed〕 account. ～하다 describe minutely; state in detail; give a full account 《of 》.

**상기**(想起) remembrance; recollection. ～하다 remember; recollect; recall; call 〔bring〕 《*a thing*》 to mind. ¶ ～되다 [사물이 주어] come back into *one's* mind; come to mind 〔*one's* recollection〕/ ～시키다 remind 《*a person* of *a matter*》; (re)call 《*something*》 to 《*a person's*》 mind.

**상길**(上―) the best quality; top-grade 〔first-class, first-rate〕 merchandise. ¶ ～의 《an article》 of superior 〔fine〕 quality / ～의 담배 the best quality tobacco.

**상납**(上納) payment to the government 〔authorities〕 《in money, in kind》. ～하다 pay to the government; 《뇌물을》 offer a (regular) bribe 《to》. ¶ 매월 백만 원씩 ～받다 take 〔accept〕 one million won monthly (as a bribe) 《from subordinates》. ◉ ～금 money paid as a tax; money offered to *one's* superior. ～미 rice delivered as a tax.

**상냥하다** 《부드러운》 (be) gentle; tender; soft; 《다정한》 (be) affectionate; sweet; nice; 《붙임성 있는》 (be) amiable; affable; 《친절한》 (be) kind; kindly; kind-hearted. ¶ 목소리가 상냥한 sweet-voiced / 상냥하게 gently; kindly; nicely; tenderly; sweetly; affectionately / 상냥하게 굴다 be gentle 〔kind, nice, good, sweet, affectionate〕 to 《*a person*》/ 그 간호사는 언제나 환자들에게 ～ The nurse is always 「gentle with 〔nice to〕 the patients.

**상년**(常―) 《비천한》 a vulgar 〔low〕 woman; a woman of low birth; 《상스런》 a mean woman; 《음란한》 a bitch; a lewd woman.

**상념**(想念) a notion; a conception; an idea. ¶ ～에 잠기다 be lost in (a) conception.

**상노**(床奴) a servant 〔an errand〕 boy.

**상놈**(常―) 《본데없는》 an ill-bred fellow; 《비천한》 a vulgar man; a man of low birth; a lowly fellow; 《상스런》 a mean guy; 《평민》 a plebeian; a common person; 《속물》 a Philistine.

**상늙은이**(上―) the eldest 〔dean, senior〕 of a group of old man 〔woman〕.

**상다리**(床―) table legs. ¶ ～가 휘어지게 차리다 serve all sorts of delicacies on the table.

**상단**(上段) the top 〔upper〕 portion 〔division, paragraph〕; the top 〔upper〕 row 〔seat, tier, step〕. ¶ ～침대 an upper berth(열차의); an upper bunk (2단 침대의) / 검을 ～자세로 잡다 《검도에서》 raise 〔hold〕 *one's* sword over *one's* head.

**상단**(上端) the upper end; the top.

**상달**(上―) the tenth lunar month; Harvest month.

**상달**(上達) a report 《to a superior》. ～하다 report 《to a superior》. ¶ 하의(下意) ～은 바라기 힘든 일이다 Lower-status people find it hard to get their views across to their superiors.

**상담**(相談) (a) consultation; counsel; (a) conference; a talk. ⇨ 상의(相議). ◉ ～란 《신문의》 the consulting column 《of a newspaper》; the consulting department 《of a magazine》. ～역 《회사 등의》 a counselor; a consultant; 《개인의》 an adviser; a consultant: 나에겐 ～역이 없다 I have no one to consult. / 그 건에 관해 그의 ～역이 되어 주십시오 Please give him advice on the subject. ～원 a counselor; a councilor.

**상담**(商談) a business talk; 《교섭》 negotiations; a deal. ～하다 talk business 《with》; have a business talk 《with》; negotiate 《with》. ¶ ～을 매듭짓다 strike 〔close〕 a bargain 《with》; close a deal 《with》/ ～을 추진하다 go ahead with a business talk / ～에 응하다 enter into negotiations / 나는 그 거래에 관해 미국인과 ～중이다 I am negotiating with an American for the deal. / 새 계약에 관한 ～이 이루어졌다 The negotiation of a new contract was settled 〔concluded〕.

**상담소**(相談所) an information 〔consultation〕 office 〔bureau〕; a counselor's office. ¶ 결혼 ～ a marriage bureau / 법률 ～ a legal advice office / 아동 ～ a child guidance clinic / 직업 ～ a vocational clinic.

**상답**(上畓) a productive 〔rich〕 rice field.

**상당**(相當) ¶ ～의 suitable; befitting; corresponding (대응); equivalent (필적) / ～수의 a good many / 지위 ～의 예우로써 with due respect; with the honor suitable to 〔befitting〕 《*a person's*》 rank / 5만 원 ～의 선물 a present worth fifty thousand won / 3 개월 봉급 ～의 상여금 a bonus equivalent to three months' pay.

**상당하다**(相當―) ① 《알맞다》 be due to; be fit 《for, to *do*》; be proper 〔suitable〕 《for》; be suited to 《*a person*》; be proportionate to (걸맞다). ¶ 상당한 보수 a worthy 〔due〕 reward / 능력에 상당하는 급료 a salary proportionate to *one's* ability / 지위에 상당한 수입 an income befitting 《*a person's*》 rank. ② 《어지간하다》 (*a*) 《꽤 …하다》 (be)

considerable; pretty; fair; be (in) no small 《amount》. ¶ 상당한 거리 a good distance / 상당한 교육 a good education / 상당한 금액 a considerable 〔sizable〕 sum of money; a pretty big money / 상당한 사례 a good round fee / 상당한 수입 a handsome income; a fairly big salary / 상당한 재능 fair ability / 상당한 속도로 at a good speed / 상당한 이익을 올리다 make a good profit / 상당한 시간이 걸리다 take a good long time / 그는 재주가 ~ He is a man of considerable talent. / 이 방면에 상당한 경험이 있는 사람이 필요하다 I am in need of a man who has a fair knowledge of this line. (***b***) 《부끄럽지 않다》 (be) decent; respectable. ¶ 상당한 집안 a respectable 〔decent〕 family / 옷차림이 ~ be decently dressed.
③ 《무리 없다》 (be) fair; reasonable; 《충분하다》 (be) sufficient. ¶ 상당한 이유 a sufficient 〔good〕 reason / 상당한 이유 없이 without a plausible 〔convincing〕 reason.
④ 《맞먹다》 be equal 〔equivalent〕 《to》; be worth; be worthy of; correspond 〔answer〕 to. ¶ 이 말에 상당하는 영어는 없다 There is no English equivalent for the word. / 1달러는 천이백 원에 상당하다 A dollar is equivalent to 1,200 won.

**상당히**(相當—) fairly; pretty; rather; quite; considerably; decently; tolerably; to no small degree 〔extent〕. ¶ ~ 큰 집 a pretty big house / ~ 비싼 값 a pretty high price / ~ 오랫동안 (for) quite a long time 〔a while〕 / ~ 먼 rather far / ~ 많은 quite a few / ~ 잘 살다 be pretty well off; make a decent living / ~ 춥다 be pretty cold / 영어를 ~ 잘 하다 speak fairly good English; speak English pretty well / 책을 ~ 갖고 있다 have a good many books / 밤이 ~ 깊었다 The night was fairly advanced.

**상대**(相對) ① 《대면》 facing 〔confronting〕 each other; an interview. ~하다 face 〔confront, see〕 each other.
② 《놀이·이야기·공부 따위의》 a companion; a mate; a fellow; 《미》 a date (남녀 교제의); a partner; a pal. ~하다 keep company 《with》; make a companion of; keep 〔bear〕 《*a person*》 company; deal with; entertain (손님을). ¶ 놀이 ~ a playmate / 술 ~ a boon companion / 이야기〔말〕 ~ a (talking) companion; someone to talk to / 의논 ~ a person to consult with; an adviser 〔advisor〕; a confidant; 《전문적》 a counselor; a consultant / …을 ~로 with… as a companion 〔partner〕; in the companionship of… / 술 ~를 하다 bear 《*a person*》 company in drinking / ~하지 않다 refuse to deal 〔do anything〕 《with》; ignore; take no notice 《of》; have nothing to do 《with》; do not care 《for》 / …을 ~로 영어 연습을 하다 practice *one's* English on 《*a person*》 / 그는 그녀의 훌륭한 결혼 ~이다 He is a good match for her. / 그는 ~를 가리지 않고 바른 말을 한다 He speaks straightforward to anybody. / 사람들은 그런 인간을 ~하려 들지 않는다 People will have no dealings with a man of his type.
③ 《상대방》 the other man 〔person〕; the other 〔opposite〕 party; a counterpart; 《적수》 an opponent; a rival; an adversary; an antagonist; 《겨룰 자》 a match; an equal. ~하다 deal with; contend 《with》; play (against) 《*a person*》; take 《*a person*》 on 《at golf》; 《도전을 받다》 accept the challenge. ¶ 아무를 ~로 in opposition to *a person;* with *a person* for a counterpart / 체스 ~를 하다 play opposite 〔against〕 《*a person*》 at the game of chess / ~가 안 되다 be no match for; be unrivaled / 좋은 ~다 be a good match for 《*one*》; find a good match in 《*a person*》 / 아무를 ~로 소송을 제기하다 bring a suit 〔an action〕 against *a person* / 나는 그의 ~가 못 된다 I am not a match for him. / 아무나 나와라, 내가 ~하마 Let any one come, I am his man.
④ 《대상》 the object. ¶ 연애 ~ the object of *one's* love / 학생 ~의 잡지 a magazine for students; a student=oriented magazine / 학생 ~의 다방 a tearoom with students for customers / …을 ~로 장사를 하다 do business with… as customers / 말도 ~를 잘 가려서 해야지 Is that the way you talk to me? *or* You must know whom you are talking to.
⑤ 〖철학〗 relativity; reciprocity. ¶ ~적 (으로) relative(ly); correlative(ly).
◉ ~가격 a relative price. ~개념 a relative concept. ~분산도(分散度) 〖물리〗 relative dispersion. ~빈도 〖통계〗 relative frequency. ~습도〔속도〕 relative humidity 〔velocity〕. ~운동 a

relative motion. ~적 평가 〖교육〗 relative evaluation. ~주의 relativism.

**상대성**(相對性) relativity.
◉ ~이론〔원리〕〖물리〗 the theory 〔principle〕 of relativity; the Einstein theory: 일반〔특수〕~ 이론 the general 〔special〕 theory of relativity.

**상대역**(相對役) the player of an opposite 〔a secondary〕 role; 《춤의》 a partner. ¶ ~을 하다 play 《a part》 opposite (to) 《an actor》.

**상도**(常道) the normal 〔proper, regular〕 course; an ordinary way; a beaten track; a common way 〔path〕; a universal law. ⇨ 상궤.

**상도덕**(商道德) business 〔commercial〕 morality 〔ethics〕. ◉ ~앙양 enhancement of business morality.

**상도의**(商道義) = 상도덕.

**상동**(相同) homology. ¶ ~의 homologous; homogenous. ◉ ~기관 a homologous organ; a homologue. ~염색체 a homologous chromosome.

**상되다**(常—) (be) vulgar; base; mean; ignoble. ¶ 상된 말 vulgar words / 상된 사람 a low fellow.

**상등**(上等) superiority; excellence. ¶ ~의 first-class〔-rate〕; very good 〔nice〕; of superior grade; excellent; superior; fine; up to grade / 최~의 of the highest 〔finest〕 quality; of prime 〔top〕 quality; the best. ◉ ~석 the first-class seat. ~품 a first-class article; a top-grade article; a superior 〔choice〕 article; an article of excellent quality; good stuff; quality goods.

**상등**(相等) equality. ~하다 (be) equal; be equivalent 《to》; be as good as.

**상란**(上欄) 《위의 난》 the top column; 《앞의 난》 the preceding column. ¶ ~에 기재한 바와 같이 as stated in the preceding column.

**상략**(商略) a commercial 〔business〕 policy.

**상량**(上樑) putting up the ridge beam; setting up the framework. ~하다 raise 〔set up〕 the framework 《of a house》; raise a ridgepole. ◉ ~식 the ceremony of putting up the ridgepole 〔ridgebeam〕 of a new house; a framework-raising ceremony.

**상련**(相連) linking; connecting 《with》. ~하다 be linked; link 《with》; connect 《with》; (ad)join.

**상련**(相憐) mutual sympathy. ¶ 동병(同病)~ Grief is best pleased with grief's company. *or* Fellow sufferers pity 〔sympathize with〕 one another.

**상례**(常例) a common 〔an established〕 usage; a custom; a usual practice; convention. ¶ ~의 customary; usual conventional / ~에 따라 in accordance with the usage 〔custom〕; as usual; in *one's* usual way / ~를 따르다〔좇다〕 follow 〔observe〕 the conventional practice; follow the usage 〔custom〕 / ~에 구애받다 stick to the usage / ~에 따르지 않다 be contrary to usage / ~를 어기다 act contrary to 〔be against〕 the custom / ~를 존중〔무시〕하다 respect 〔defy〕 customary practice.

**상례**(喪禮) funeral rites.

**상록**(常綠) ¶ ~의 evergreen; indeciduous. ◉ ~수 an evergreen 〔indeciduous〕 tree; evergreens [총칭].

**상론**(詳論) full discussion 〔treatment〕; a detailed explanation. ~하다 discuss 《a subject》 in detail 〔at (full) length〕; treat 《a subject》 in detail; dwell 〔expatiate〕 (up)on; enter 〔go〕 into details.

**상류**(上流) ① 《강의》 the upper stream 〔course; reaches〕. ¶ ~의〔에〕 upstream; upriver / …강 ~에 《build a dam》 up the 《Han》 river / 10 마일~ 쪽에 10 miles above 〔up〕 the river / 배를 ~로 저어가다 row the boat 「upstream 〔up the stream〕 / 이 강의 ~는 폭이 매우 좁다 The upper reaches of this river are very narrow. / 이 다리 ~ 5킬로 지점에 폭포가 있다 There is a waterfall 5 kilometers above the bridge.
② 《사회의》 the higher 〔upper〕 classes; polite 〔high〕 society; high circles. ¶ ~(층) 사람들 upper-class people; the elite of society; people of high birth / ~(가정) 출신이다 be of high birth; be born with a silver spoon in *one's* mouth.
◉ ~계급 the upper classes. ~부인 a woman 〔lady〕 of the upper classes; a lady of fashion; a society woman. ~사회 high society; the upper classes; the cream of society. ~생활 high 〔fashionable〕 life. ~인사 (people of) gentility; gentlefolks; society people. ~지역〔지방〕 an upriver district.

**상륙**(上陸) landing; disembarkation. ~하다 go ashore 《at Inch'ŏn》; land 《in a country, at a port》; disembark; make 〔effect〕 a landing (군대 등이); strike 〔hit〕 (태풍 등이) (★ 단순히 육지에 오른다는 표현이 go ashore. 목적지에 도착해서 상륙한다는 뜻이 land. 출입국 관리·교

통 기관 등의 정식 용어가 disembark). ¶ ～해 있다 be「ashore (on shore) / ～을 허락하다 grant《a sailor》shore leave / ～을 금지하다《선객에게》forbid disembarkation;《선원에게》withhold shore leave / 무사히 ～하다 come safe to land / ～시키다 put《*a person*》on shore / 도중에 기항하여 ～하다 land at a port of call on the way / 적전 ～을 하다 effect a landing in the face of the enemy / 남제주 지방에 태풍이 ～했다 The typhoon struck (hit) the southern part of Cheju. ◉ ～거점 a beachhead. ～금지 stoppage of leave. ～부대 a landing force (party); landing troops. ～용 주정 a landing craft; a landing ship tank (생략 LST). ～인원 men on leave. ～일《해군의》a liberty day. ～작전 landing operations. ～지점 a landing spot; a point of disembarkation. ～허가 (a) shore leave.

**상리**(常理) a matter of course; the nature of things; the natural (proper) course to take.

**상말**(常—) ①《쌍말》a vulgar word (expression); a vulgarism; (an) indecent talk; vulgar (foul) language; a four-letter word. ¶ ～을 쓰다(하다) use vulgar (abusive) language / ～로 …이라고 하다 be vulgarly (commonly) called…. ②《속담》a proverb; a (common) saying.

**상머리**(床—) the table side. ¶ ～에 앉다 sit at the table side; sit down to table.

**상머슴**(上—) a heavy-duty (seasoned, full-fledged) farmhand.

**상면**(上面) the top side; the upper side; the upside; the surface. ¶ ～에 over (on)《*a thing*》.

**상면**(相面) seeing each other; meeting; an interview. ～하다 see (each other); meet《with》; be acquainted《with》; have an interview《with》; meet for the first time. ¶ 20년만에 ～하다 meet after twenty years' separation / 유명한 학자와 ～했다 I had an interview with a famous scholar.

**상무**(尙武) militarism. ～하다 encourage militarism; pursue the policy of militarism. ¶ ～의 기상 the martial (militaristic) spirit.

**상무**(常務)《업무》regular business; daily (routine) work; daily routine;《직위》《미》a managing (an executive) director (★《영》에서는 a managing director는「사장」을 뜻함). ◉ ～위원 a member of a standing committee. ～이사 a standing director.

**상무**(商務) commercial (business) affairs. ◉ ～관(官) a commercial attaché (agent). ～부《미》the Department of Commerce. ～장관《미》the Secretary of Commerce.

**상문**(上聞) informing the King; bringing to the Royal ear (attention). ¶ ～에 달하다 reach the King's ears; become known to the sovereign.

**상문**(尙文) encouragement of learning.

**상문**(喪門)〖민속〗a baleful direction. ¶ ～풀이하다 have (perform, undergo) an exorcism…. ◉ ～살(煞)〖민속〗the evil influence emanating from a place where someone has died.

**상미**(上米) first-class rice; best quality of rice; grade-A rice.

**상미**(賞味) appreciation. ～하다 relish; taste (eat) with relish (gusto, pleasure); appreciate.

**상미**(賞美) ～하다 praise; admire; applaud; appreciate (the beauty of).

**상민**(常民) a commoner; the common people [총칭].

**상박**(上膊) the upper arm; the brachium (*pl.* -chia). ¶ ～의 brachial. ◉ ～골 a humerus (*pl.* -ri). ～근 a brachial muscle. ～동맥 a brachial artery. ～부 the humeral region.

**상반**(上半) the first (upper) half《of》. ◉ ～기 the first half of the year; the first half of a term: ～기 결산 보고 the statement of accounts for the first half year.

**상반**(相反) being contrary to《each other》; conflicting with each other. ～하다 be contrary to《each other》; run counter to《each other》; disagree (conflict) with《each other》. ¶ ～된 개념 directly-opposed ideas; antithetic(al) concepts / 우리들의 이해는 서로 ～된다 Our interests run counter to (conflict with) each other. / 그의 설명은 사실과 ～된다 His explanation disagrees with the facts. / 이론과 실제는 흔히 ～되는 경우가 있다 Theory and practice often conflict. ◉ ～곡선〖수학〗a reciprocal curve. ～교배〖생물〗reciprocal crossing. ～력 repugnant forces.

**상반신**(上半身) the upper half (part) of *one's* body; the bust. ¶ ～을 벗은 채로 naked from the waist up; stripped (down) to the waist / ～ 사진을 찍다 take a picture of《*a person*》from

the waist up / ～을 쑥 내밀다 lean 〔bend *oneself*〕 forward.
◉ ～사진 a photograph of the upper half of the body; a bust shot.

**상밥**(床—) a meal on an individual table; a set dinner (served at an eating house).

**상방**(上方) the upper part. ¶ ～에 above; upward.

**상배**(喪配) the death of *one's* wife. ～하다 lose 〔be bereaved of〕 *one's* wife.

**상배**(賞盃) a prize cup; a trophy.

**상벌**(賞罰) reward and punishment; prizes and penalties. ¶ ～ 없음 《이력서에서》 No reward and no punishment. / ～을 주다 mete out justice 〔reward and punishment〕 《to》.

**상법**(商法) commercial 〔mercantile〕 law; the Commercial Code (육법의).

**상병**(上兵) a corporal (육군·해병); a Petty Officer 3rd Class (해군); an airman 1st class (공군).

**상병**(傷兵) a wounded soldier; [총칭] the wounded.

**상병**(傷病) the sick and wounded.
◉ ～포로 sick and wounded prisoners of war.

**상보**(床褓) a tablecloth; a meal cloth; a cloth that covers a prepared meal. ¶ ～를 덮다 put a cloth over a meal.

**상보**(詳報) a detailed 〔full〕 report. ～하다 report in full 〔detail〕; make a full report 《on, of》; give particulars 〔a full account〕 《of》. ¶ 사고의 ～ a full account of the accident.

**상보다**(床—) set 〔lay, prepare〕 the table 《for dinner》.

**상보다**(相—) tell 《*a person's*》 fortune by physiognomy; read 《*a person's*》 physiognomy.

**상복**(喪服) (a) mourning dress 〔clothes〕. ¶ 미망인의 ～ widow's weeds / ～을 입고 있다 wear 〔be in〕 mourning (dress, clothes); be in (mourning) black.

**상복부**(上腹部) 〖해부〗 the epigastrium; the upper part of the belly.

**상봉**(相逢) meeting (each other); reunion (재회). ～하다 meet 〔see〕 (each other); reunite (재회하다). ¶ 이산 가족의 ～ a reunion of the dispersed 〔separated〕 family members.

**상부**(上部) ① 《부분》 the upper part; the top 〔head〕 《of》; the upside. ¶ ～의 upper / 나의 이름은 명단 ～에 있다 My name is at the top 〔head〕 of the list. ② 《직위·관청》 the superior office 〔authorities〕. ¶ ～의 명령 an order from above / ～의 지시가 있을 때까지 기다리다 wait for further instructions from the superior authority. ◉ ～구조 a superstructure.

**상부**(喪夫) being widowed; losing *one's* husband. ～하다 have *one's* husband die; lose 〔be bereaved of〕 *one's* husband. ◉ ～살(煞) 〖민속〗 evil influence bringing about widowhood.

**상부**(孀婦) a young widow.

**상부상조**(相扶相助) mutual help 〔aid〕; interdependence. ～하다 help 〔aid〕 each other; be interdependent; cooperate. ¶ ～의 정신 a spirit of mutual help.

**상비**(常備) preparedness; reservation. ～하다 《예비하다》 reserve 《*something*》 for 《a sudden need》; 《준비해 두다》 always have 《*something*》 ready 〔available, on hand〕; 《마련해 두다》 be provided with 《*something*》. ¶ ～의 standing; permanent; regular / 우리 집에는 소화기가 ～되어 있다 Our house is provided with a fire extinguisher.
◉ ～군 a standing 〔standby〕 army; ready troops. ～병력 a standing force. ～약: 가정 ～약 a household medicine.

**상사**(上士) a master sergeant (육군); a senior master sergeant (공군); a senior chief petty officer (해군); a master gunnery sergeant (해병대).

**상사**(上司) a higher office; *one's* superior(s); *one's* boss(es); 《구어》 *one's* chief; the higher-ups in *one's* firm 〔office〕. ¶ 직속 ～ *one's* immediate boss 〔superior〕 / ～를 수행하여 in attendance upon *one's* boss; in a higher official's suite of / 그는 나의 ～이다 He is my boss. / 회사에 돌아가 ～와 의논하겠습니다 I'll go back to the office and consult my superiors.

**상사**(相似) (a) resemblance; (a) similarity; (a) similitude; 〖생물〗 (an) analogy. ～하다 (be) similar 《to》; analogous 《to》; be alike; resemble.
◉ ～기관 〖생물〗 analogous organs. ～물 an analogy. ～형 ⇨ 닮은꼴.

**상사**(相思) mutual love; reciprocal affection; pining for each other. ～하다 be in love with each other; pine 〔long, languish〕 for each other.
◉ ～병 lovesickness: ～병이 나다, ～병에 걸리다 be lovesick 〔lovelorn〕; languish with love 《for》; suffer from lovesickness.

**상사**(商社) a business 〔commercial〕

company 〔firm〕; 《무역의》 a trading company 〔firm〕; a business 〔trading〕 concern. ¶ 외국 ~ a foreign firm / 종합 ~ a general trading firm / 전자기기 전문 ~ a trading company specializing in electronic products 〔goods〕.

**상사**(商事) business affairs; commercial matters. ◉ ~계약 a commercial contract. ~회사 a commercial 〔trading〕 firm 〔company〕.

**상사**(常事) an affair of common 〔everyday〕 occurrence. ¶ ~의 usual; ordinary / ~가 아닌 unusual; uncommon.

**상사**(喪事) (an occasion for) mourning. ¶ ~가 나다 have mourning.

**상사람**(常—) a commoner; a plebeian; [총칭] the common people; the populace.

**상상**(想像) imagination; (a) fancy; 《가정》 (a) supposition; 《추측》 (a) conjecture; (a) surmise; (a) guess. ~하다 imagine; fancy; suppose; picture 〔figure〕 to *oneself;* 《추측하다》 guess; surmise; conjecture.
¶ ~의 세계 a dream world; an imaginary world 〔society〕; a Utopia / ~적(인) imaginary; imaginative; fancy / ~할 수 있는 imaginable; conceivable; thinkable / ~할 수 없는 unimaginable; unthinkable; inconceivable; beyond conception / 아무리 ~해 보아도 by any stretch of (the) imagination / 우리가 ~조차 할 수 없는 괴로움 such sufferings as we cannot even imagine / ~하기 어렵다 be beyond conception 〔imagination〕 / ~하기 어렵지 않다 you may easily imagine that…; it can readily be imagined that… / 단지 ~에 의거하다 be based on mere supposition / 멋진 미래를 ~하다 draw a fine picture of *one's* future / ~의 날개를 펴다 give full play 〔scope〕 to *one's* imagination / 그 절차의 복잡함이란 도저히 ~도 할 수 없을 정도였다 The complexity of the formalities is far beyond imagination. / 그가 범인이라고는 ~도 할 수 없었다 It was impossible to imagine that he was the criminal. / 이것은 ~할 수 없는 위력을 가진 무기다 This is a weapon of unimaginable power. / 나머지는 너의 ~에 맡긴다 I leave the rest to your imagination. / 한국에 오기 전에 한국은 어떤 나라라고 ~하셨습니까 What sort of country did you think 〔imagine〕 Korea was before you came here?
◉ ~임신 imaginary 〔false, phantom〕 pregnancy. ~화(畫) an imaginary 〔a fancy〕 picture.

**상상력**(想像力) imaginative power 〔faculty〕; (power of) imagination. ¶ ~을 발휘하다 exercise *one's* imagination; give *one's* imagination full play / ~이 풍부하다〔부족하다〕 be imaginative 〔unimaginative〕; have a vigorous 〔little〕 imagination.

**상상봉**(上上峰) the highest peak 〔summit〕.

**상서**(上書) writing 〔sending〕 a letter to *one's* senior 〔elders〕. ~하다 write 〔send〕 a letter to *one's* senior 〔parents〕.

**상서**(祥瑞) a lucky 〔propitious, good〕 omen; a happy augury. ~롭다 be of good omen; (be) felicitous; auspicious; lucky; propitious. ¶ ~로운 일 an auspicious 〔a happy〕 event.

**상석**(上席) 《상좌》 the upper 〔highest〕 seat; the top seat; the head (식탁의); 《주빈석》 the seat 〔place〕 of honor; 《석차》 seniority; precedence. ¶ ~을 차지하다 take the 「seat of honor 〔top seat〕 / ~에 앉히다 give 《a guest》 a seat of honor / 아무의 ~에 있다 rank above *a person.*
◉ ~자 a superior official; a senior.

**상석**(床石) the stone offertory table in front of a tomb.

**상선**(商船) a merchant ship 〔vessel〕; a trading vessel; a trader; a merchantman (*pl.* -men); [총칭] the merchant marine 《of a nation》.
◉ ~기(旗) a merchant flag. ~대(隊) a merchant fleet.

**상설**(常設) ~하다 establish… permanently. ¶ ~의 standing 《committees of the National Assembly》; permanent 《facilities》. ◉ ~경제협력기구 《establish》 a standing economic cooperation organization. ~국제사법재판소 The Permanent Court of International Justice. ~영화관 a (regular) movie house; a cinema 《영》.

**상설**(詳說) a detailed 〔full〕 explanation 〔account〕; expatiation. ~하다 explain 〔state〕 in detail 〔full〕; give a detailed 〔full〕 account 《of》; expatiate. ¶ 자기 소신을 갖가지 예를 들어 ~하다 explain *one's* statement in detail 〔full〕 with various examples.

**상세**(詳細) details; particulars. ~하다 (be) minute; detailed; particular; full; circumstantial; be in detail.

¶ ～한 보고 a detailed report 〔statement〕/ ～히 in detail; minutely; at length; at large; fully / ～히 보고〔설명〕하다 report 〔explain〕 in detail; make a detailed report 〔explanation〕/ ～히 보도하다 report 《of 〔on〕 *a matter*》 in full 〔in detail, at length〕; make a full report 《on》/ ～한 것은 K 씨에게 문의하시오 Apply to K for further particulars. / 그는 회담에 관해 ～한 보고서를 준비했다 He prepared a detailed 〔an in-depth〕 report on the conference. / 목격자는 사건에 관해 ～히 진술했다 The eyewitness gave a full account of the incident. / 세법에 관해 ～히 알고 있는 회계사를 채용했다 We hired a new accountant who knows the ins and outs of the tax laws.

**상소**(上疏) (presenting) a memorial to the King. ～하다 present a memorial to the King; memorialize the King. ◉ ～문 a memorial to the Throne.

**상소**(上訴) 〖법〗 an appeal; a recourse. ～하다 appeal 《to a higher court》. ¶ ～를 취하하다 withdraw an appeal / ～를 포기하다 waive an appeal. ◉ ～관할권 an appellate jurisdiction. ～권 the right of appeal. ～인 an appellant.

**상속**(相續) succession; inheritance. ～하다 succeed 〔be heir〕 to 《*one's* father's estate》; inherit. ¶ 유산 ～ succession to property; inheritance / 공동 ～ joint inheritance 〔succession〕/ ～의 승인〔포기〕 acceptance 〔refusal〕 of succession / 그녀의 자식들은 모두 공평하게 ～받을 것이다 All her children will inherit equally. / 그 건물과 토지는 ～에 의해 그의 것이 되었다 The building and the land came to him by inheritance. / 그 소녀는 조부로부터 막대한 유산을 ～받았다 The girl inherited a huge fortune from her grandfather.
◉ ～권 heirship; 《claim》 the (right of) succession; *one's* inheritance rights: 공동(共同) ～권 joint heirship; (co)parcenary. ～동산 an heirloom. ～법 the law of inheritance. ～분쟁 a dispute about 〔a quarrel over〕 the succession. ～세 an inheritance 〔a succession〕 tax; a death duty 《영》. ～인〔자〕 a successor; 《남자》 an heir; 《여자》 an heiress: 법정 ～인 a legal heir; an heir-at-law / 추정 ～인 an heir presumptive / 공동 ～자 a joint heir; a coheir; a coinheritor; a (co)parcener (토지의). ～재산 an inheritance; inherited property. ～증여세 an inheritance and gift tax.

**상쇄**(相殺) an offset; canceling 〔balancing〕 each other; a counterbalance. ～하다 offset 〔cancel〕 each other; set 《the advantages》 off 《against the disadvantages》; counterbalance. ¶ 국내 회사가 올린 이윤은 해외 부문에서 생긴 손실로 ～되곤 한다 The losses of our overseas section cancel out the profits made by the company at home. / 인플레는 증산으로 ～시킬 수 있다 Inflation can be offset by increased production. / 그 손실은 이들 이익이 ～해 줄 것이다 These gains will compensate for the loss.

**상쇠**(上—) 〖민속〗 a first gong-player in a folk band.

**상수**(上手) 《사람》 a good 〔better〕 hand 《at *something*》; an expert; an adept; *one's* superior 《in *something*》; 《솜씨가》 upper skill; dexterity. ¶ …보다 ～이다 be better 《at *a thing*》 than 《*a person*》; be superior 《to》; be more skillful 《than》; surpass / ～로 두다 《바둑·장기에서》 play as a superior player; have a handicap 《of two stones in game of *paduk*》/ 조금 ～다 《구어》 be a cut above 《*a person*》.

**상수**(常數) ① 《운명》 the natural course of things; fatality; destiny; fate. ② 〖수학〗 a constant; an invariable (number).

**상수도**(上水道) tap 〔piped〕 water; 《설비》 waterworks; water service 〔supply〕. ⇨수도. ¶ 서울 시청은 총 2,500km에 달하는 시의 녹슨 ～관을 교체하기로 결정하였다 The Seoul City government decided to replace the city's rusted tap water pipeline totaling 2,500km. ◉ ～시설 water-works; water supply facilities.

**상수리** 〖식물〗 an acorn. ◉ ～나무 an oak (tree). ～쌀 ground acorns.

**상순**(上旬) the first ten days 〔the early part〕 《of the month》. ¶ 3월 ～에 early in March; at the beginning of March / 내달 ～에 early next month. ⇨초순.

**상술**(上述) preceding descriptions 〔explanations〕; the above statements. ～하다 state 〔say, mention〕 above. ¶ ～한 the above(-stated); the above-mentioned; the aforesaid; the said 《company》/ ～한 바와 같이 as mentioned 〔stated〕 above; as aforesaid.

**상술**(商術) 《요령》 a trick of the trade; 《상재》 business ability 〔talent〕; 《영업 정책》 a business policy. ¶ ~에 능하다 have a good head for business; have a shrewd business acumen.

**상술**(詳述) a detailed 〔full〕 explanation 〔account〕. ~하다 explain 〔state〕 in full 〔detail〕; make 〔give〕 a detailed explanation 《of》; give a full account 《of》; dwell 〔enlarge〕 《on a subject》. ¶ ~하면 to be more particular.

**상스럽다**(常—) (be) vulgar; low; base; mean; indecent. ¶ 상스러운 사람 a vulgar 〔mean〕 person / 상스러운 이야기 indecent talk / 상스러운 말을 하다 talk vulgar; use vulgar language / 하는 짓이 ~ be coarse in manners / 그의 행위는 ~ His behavior is in bad taste. / 그녀의 태도는 숙녀로서는 너무나 ~ Her manners are too gross for a lady.

**상습**(常習) 《사회의》 a convention; a common 〔an established〕 practice; a usage; a regular custom; 《개인의》 a habitual practice; a habit; an inveterate habit. ¶ ~적(인) habitual; customary; confirmed; regular / ~적으로 habitually / ~적으로 …하다 be in the habit of *doing* / 그는 도둑질을 ~적으로 한다 He has thieving ways.
◉ ~범 《사람》 a habitual 〔confirmed〕 criminal; a habitual 〔repeated〕 offender 《of the rules》; a recidivist; 《구어》 a jailbird; 《죄》 a habitual crime; recidivism: ~범(형벌) 가중죄 cumulative punishment / 소매치기 ~범 a confirmed pickpocket. ~사기 《charge of》 habitual fraud. ~자 an addict: 도박 ~자 a regular 〔confirmed〕 gambler / 마약 ~자 a drug addict / 음주 ~자 a habitual drunkard.

**상승**(上昇) a rise 《in temperature》; the ascent 《of a balloon》; ascension; 《경향》 upward tendency; a rising trend; an upturn. ~하다 go up; rise; ascend; soar; climb; assume an upward curve. ¶ ~하는 ascending / 물가가 꾸준히 ~하고 있다 Prices are rising 〔going up〕 steadily.
◉ ~곡선 a rising 〔an upward〕 curve. ~기류 an updraft; a rising current of air; an ascending (air) current; 〖항공〗 a bump; 〖기상〗 《온난 기류》 a thermal: ~ 기류를 타다 ride an up-current of air; ride updrafts. ~력 climbing power. ~속도 the rate of climb. ~시세 a bull market. ~음계 〖음악〗 an ascending scale. ~한도 〖항공〗 the (flight) ceiling: 절대〔실용〕 ~한도 an absolute 〔a service〕 ceiling.
급~ a sudden rise 《of prices》; skyrocketing; 〖항공〗 zooming; a zoom: 급~하다 rise suddenly; skyrocket; 〖항공〗 zoom; chandelle.

**상승**(常勝) ¶ ~의 ever-victorious; invincible.

**상승**(相乘) 〖수학〗 multiplication. ~하다 involve; multiply. ◉ ~법 a multiplication method. ~비(比) a geometrical ratio. ~작용 synergism. ~적(積) the product of 《A》 multiplied by 《B》. ~평균 a geometrical mean. =기하평균. ~효과 〖약〗 the synergistic effect; 〖경제〗 the multiplier effect.

**상시**(常時) ordinary 〔normal〕 times; at all times; always. ¶ ~에 at ordinary 〔normal〕 times.

**상식**(上食) offering of meals to a departed soul; sacrificial meals offered to the deceased.

**상식**(常食) staple 〔daily〕 food; a diet. ~하다 live 〔diet〕 on 《rice》. ¶ 아시아인 대부분이 주로 쌀을 ~한다 Most Asians live chiefly on rice. / 양은 풀을 ~한다 Sheep feed on grass.

**상식**(常識) common sense; practical sense 〔wisdom〕; good sense (양식); common knowledge; horse sense 《미구어》. ¶ ~적(인) commonsense; sensible; matter-of-fact; practical; 《보통의》 ordinary; normal / ~적으로 sensibly; in a practical manner / ~적으로 생각하여 in the name of common sense; from a commonsense point of view / ~적인 견해 a commonsense view / ~적인 문제 a matter of common sense; a sensible question / ~에 벗어〔어긋〕나다 be eccentric; be against common sense / …은 ~이다 it is 「obvious 〔common knowledge〕 that…; it goes without saying that…; it is taken for granted that….
상식이: ~이 있다 have common 〔good〕 sense; be sensible / ~이 있는 사람 a man of common sense; a person of (good) sense / ~이 없다 lack 〔have no〕 common sense / ~이 되다 become general 〔common〕 knowledge / ~이 풍부하다 have plenty 〔a good deal〕 of sense; be very sensible.
상식으로: ~으로 판단하다 judge by 〔from〕 common sense / …(임)은 ~으로 알 수 있다 common sense tells us that….

¶ 그만한 일은 ~적으로 알 수 있을 텐데 You ought to have enough common sense to know it. *or* Common sense ought to tell you as much. / 오늘날 그것은 ~에 속하는 일이다 It is a matter of common 〔general〕 knowledge today. *or* Everybody knows that nowadays / 나는 방사능에 관해 ~ 정도의 지식은 있다 I have a layman's knowledge of radioactivity.

◉ ~가 a sensible person. ~시험 a general information 〔knowledge〕 test.

**상신**(上申) a report《to a superior 〔higher〕 official》. ~하다 report 〔state〕《to a superior 〔higher〕 official》; submit a report《to *one's* chief》; lay a report before《the authorities》.

◉ ~서 a written report 〔statement〕. ~자 a reporter.

**상실**(喪失) loss; forfeiture. ~하다 lose; forfeit; be deprived《of sight》; divest *oneself*《of》; be bereft《of》. ¶ 권리 ~ the loss 〔forfeiture, lapse〕 of *one's* right / 기억 ~ the loss of memory / 자격을 ~하다 be disqualified from 〔for〕.

**상심**(喪心)《망연》absent-mindedness; distraction; stupor; trance; abstraction; stupefaction;《낙담》dejection; dispiritedness. ~하다 be absent-minded; be stupefied; fall into trance; be abstracted; be depressed; be dejected; be cast down.

**상심**(傷心) a broken heart; heartbreak; grief; sorrow; distress. ~하다 grieve; sorrow; be grieved《at, over》; be distressed. ¶ ~한 broken-hearted; heartbroken; grief-stricken / 아내를 여의고 ~하다 be grieved over the loss of *one's* wife.

**상아**(象牙) an elephant tusk;《공예 재료》ivory. ¶ 모조〔인조〕 ~ imitation 〔artificial〕 ivory / 상앗빛의 ivory=white; ivory《skin》.

◉ ~도장 an ivory seal. ~세공 ivory work: ~ 세공사 an ivory turner. ~제품 ivory products; ivory goods;《구어》ivories. ~조각 ivory carving. ~질《치아》dentin(e).

**상아탑**(象牙塔) an ivory tower; a tower of ivory. ¶ ~에 묻혀 살다 live in 〔keep to〕 an ivory tower; lead a scholastic life detached from the world.

**상악**(上顎)〖해부〗an upper jaw. ◉ ~골 an upper jawbone; a maxillary bone.

**상앗대** a boat(man's) pole. ¶ ~로 밀다 pole off; shore《a boat》with a pole / ~로 배를 밀어 나아가다 pole a boat; propel a boat with a pole.

**상앗대질** poling; punting. ~하다 pole 〔punt〕《a boat》; propel《a boat》with a pole. ¶ ~하는 사람 a punter; a poler.

**상약**(常藥) a folk remedy 〔medicine〕.

**상어**〖어류〗a shark. ¶ ~ 지느러미 요리 shark's fin chop suey / ~밥이 되다 fall a prey to a shark. ◉ ~가죽 sharkskin; shagreen; fishskin; sea leather. ~기름 shark oil.

**상업**(商業) commerce; trade; business. ~하다 engage 〔be engaged〕 in commerce; carry on business 〔trade〕; conduct a business. ¶ ~적〔의〕 commercial; business; mercantile / ~상 commercially; from the commercial point of view / ~의 중심지 the center of commerce; a business 〔commercial〕 center / ~이 침체하다 commerce stagnates / 그는 ~에 종사하고 있다 He is engaged in business. / 생산량이 아직 ~적인 규모가 아니다 It is not yet being produced「in commercial quantities 〔on a commercial scale〕.

◉ ~거래 a commercial 〔business〕 transaction. ~계 the commercial 〔business〕 world; business circles. ~고등학교 a commercial high school. ~광고 a commercial (message). ~교육 commercial education. ~국 a mercantile nation. ~금융 commercial finance. ~대요(大要)〔통론〕 an introduction to commercial science. ~도덕 commercial morality. ~도시 a commercial 〔merchant〕 town 〔city〕. ~디자인 a commercial design. ~란《신문의》《미》a commercial 〔financial〕 column;《영》city articles. ~미술 commercial art. ~부기 commercial bookkeeping. ~송장 a commercial invoice. ~어음 a commercial 〔mercantile〕 bill; commercial paper [총칭]: ~ 어음의 할인 the discount of commercial bills. ~영어 business 〔commercial〕 English. ~용어 business terms; commercialism. ~은행 a commercial bank. ~자본 a trading 〔business, commercial〕 capital. ~정책 a commercial policy. ~조합 a trade association; a guild. ~주의 commercialism. ~지리학 commercial geography. ~지역 the business area 〔sections, districts〕. ~통신(문) commercial 〔business〕 correspondence; business letters.

**상업방송**(商業放送) commercial broadcasting; 《1회의》 a commercial 〔sponsored〕 broadcast 〔telecast〕; 《프로》 a commercial radio 〔TV〕 program. ¶ ~을 개시하다 begin broadcasting 〔telecasting〕 on a commercial basis. ◉ ~국 a commercial radio 〔TV〕 station.

**상업화**(商業化) commercialization. ~하다 commercialize; put on a commercial basis. ¶ 크리스마스는 많은 나라에서 ~되고 있다 Christmas has been commercialized in many countries.

**상없다**(常—) (be) unreasonable; irrational; absurd.

**상여**(喪輿) a (funeral) bier. ¶ ~를 메다 bear a bier; shoulder a bier. ◉ ~꾼 a pallbearer; bierbearers. 상엿소리 a pallbearers' dirge. 상엿집 a funeral equipment shed.

**상여금**(賞與金) a bonus; a reward; a prize. ¶ 연말 ~ a year-end bonus / ~을 주다 give 《*a person*》 a bonus.

**상연**(上演) presentation 〔staging〕 《of a play》; performance. ~하다 put 〔present〕 《a play》 on the stage; mount 〔get up〕 《a play》; perform; stage 《a drama》. ¶ ~을 금하다 ban a play / 「햄릿」을 ~하다 give (a performance of) *Hamlet* / 신극을 ~하다 present a new play / 연극이 ~중이다 The play is on 〔is being presented〕. / 그의 신작극은 국립 극장에서 ~ 되었다 His new play was staged at the National Theater. / 우리는 다음달에 「오셀로」를 ~할 예정이다 We are going to stage *Othello* next month. / 무단 ~ 금지 All rights reserved. *or* No performance may be given without written permission. ◉ ~권 performing 〔acting〕 rights. ~물 a play; a piece; a number.

**상영**(上映) screening; showing. ~하다 screen; show; put 《a movie》 on the screen; run off. ¶ 현재 ~중인 영화 a picture 〔movie〕 now 〔currently〕 showing 〔on show, on view, running〕 / 근일 ~할 영화 the forthcoming film / 영화를 ~하다 show a movie / H극장에서는 지금 무엇을 ~하고 있습니까 What's on at the H Theater ? / 다음 차례 ~ 《게시》 Next attraction / 근일 ~ 《게시》 Coming soon. ◉ ~시간 the running time 《of a movie》: 이 영화의 ~ 시간은 2시간이다 This film runs two hours. ~중 《게시》 Now showing. 절찬~중 《게시》 Smash hit.

**상오**(上午) the forenoon. ⇨ 오전(午前).

**상오리**(常—) 〖조류〗 a teal.

**상온**(常溫) the normal temperature.

**상왕**(上王) the abdicated king; an ex-king〔-emperor〕.

**상용**(常用) common 〔habitual, constant, ordinary〕 use; daily 〔everyday〕 use; addiction. ~하다 use habitually 〔regularly, commonly〕; make regular 〔habitual〕 use of 《a medicine》. ¶ ~의 in common 〔ordinary, everyday〕 use / 마약을 ~하다 be addicted to narcotics / 나는 이 수면제를 ~하고 있다 I take this sleeping drug habitually. / 이 약은 ~해야 효과가 있다 This medicine has to be taken regularly to be effective. ◉ ~로그〔대수(對數)〕 common logarithms. ~어 commonly used words; common words 〔vocabulary〕; words in common 〔daily〕 use. ~자 a habitual 〔constant〕 user 《of》; an 《opium》 addict: 마약 ~자 a drug addict.

**상용**(商用) (commercial) business. ¶ ~으로 방문하다 pay a business call 〔visit〕 《to》; make a business call 《on *a person*》 / 아버지는 ~으로 부산에 가셨다 My father went to Pusan on business. ◉ ~문 commercial correspondence; a business letter. ~어 a commercial 〔business〕 term. ~여행 a business trip.

**상운**(祥運) good luck. ⇨ 길운.

**상원**(上元) 〖민속〗 January fifteenth of the lunar calendar.

**상원**(上院) the Upper House; the House of Lords 《영》; the Senate (미국 등의). ◉ ~의원 a member of the Upper House; a Senator 《미》. ~인준 청문회 the Senate confirmation hearing.

**상위**(上位) a high position; a higher 〔superior〕 rank; precedence. ¶ 세계의 ~ 50대 회사 the world's fifty largest corporations / ~를 차지하다 hold a high rank; rank high; 《우선하다》 take 〔have〕 (the) precedence 《over 〔of〕 others》 / …보다 ~에 있다 rank higher than 《another》; be 《another's》 senior in rank; outrank 《another》 / …의 ~에 놓이다 be placed above 《another》 / 오늘날은 여성 ~ 시대이다 Women are placed above men today. ◉ ~개념 〖논리〗 a superordinate concept. ~입상자 a prize winner.

**상위**(相違) (a) difference; (a) disparity; disagreement; (a) discrepancy; a gap; a contrast (대조). ⇨ 차이(差異). ～하다 differ《from》; be different 《from》; vary《from》; disagree《with》; be at variance《with》; be contrary to 《the fact》. ¶ 의견의 ～ a difference of opinion / 그 기사는 사실과 ～하다 The account is at variance with the facts. / 위와 같이 ～ 없음《이력서 따위에서》I affirm the above to be true (and correct) in every particular 〔respect〕. *or* I hereby certify the above statement to be true and correct in every detail. ◉ ～점 a point of difference.

**상응**(相應) ① 《대응》 correspondence. ～하다 correspond《to》; answer《to》. ¶ 힘에 의한 ～ 보복 조치 a corresponding retaliation in strength / 능력에 ～하는 급료 a salary proportionate to *one's* ability. ② 《적합》 suitability; fitness. ～하다 be suitable《for, to》; be suited《to》; suit; 《어울리다》 become; befit; be proper《for》.

**상의**(上衣) a coat; a jacket; an upper garment; a tunic (군복의); a blouse; a shirtwaist《미》; outerwear [총칭]. ¶ ～를 입다〔벗다〕 put on 〔take off〕 *one's* coat / ～를 벗고 with *one's* jacket off; in *one's* shirt sleeves / ～를 입혀〔벗겨〕 주다 help《*a person*》on 〔off〕 with *his* coat.

**상의**(上意) the will 〔intention, wish〕 of the sovereign 〔*one's* superior〕. ¶ ～하달 the transmission of the wishes of those in authority to their subordinates; communications from the top down / ～하달하다 transmit《policy decisions》down「the hierarchy 〔the chain of command〕; 《구어》 pass the word down.

**상의**(相議) ① 《의논》 (a) consultation; a talk; (a) conference; 《구어》 a confab; 《구어》 a powwow. ～하다 talk 《with *a person* over *a matter*》; consult《*a person*, with *a person* about *a matter*》; have a talk 〔hold a consultation〕《with》; discuss《*a matter* with *a person*》. ¶ ～해서 by mutual agreement 〔consent〕 / ～한 뒤(에) after consultation《with *a person*》/ ～중이다 be in consultation 〔negotiation〕 / 이마를 맞대고 ～하다 lay 〔put〕 their 〔our〕 heads together《about *a matter*》/ 아내는 나와 ～없이 차를 샀다 My wife bought a car「without letting me know about it 〔over my head〕. / 과장님과 ～해보죠 I'll have a conference with the chief. ② 《조언을 구함》 ～하다 consult《a lawyer》; ask 〔seek〕《*a person's*》 advice; take counsel《with 〔of〕 *a person*》. ¶ ～에 응하다 take part in a consultation; give advice 〔counsel〕 《to》; 《도와주다》 give 〔lend〕 a helping hand《to》/ ～를 받다 be consulted by《*a person* about *a matter*》/ 신상 문제를 ～하다 consult《*a person*》〔seek 《*a person's*》 advice〕 about *one's* personal affairs / ～하러 가다 go to seek 《*a person's*》 advice; go to《*a person*》 for advice / 나는 무슨 일이나 아버지와 ～한다 I ask my father's advice on everything. / 이 건에 관해서는 변호사에게 ～하시는 것이 좋겠습니다 As far as this matter is concerned, I think you should go to see a lawyer for legal advice.

**상이군인**(傷痍軍人) a wounded soldier; a disabled veteran 〔ex-serviceman〕; [총칭] the war disabled. ◉ ～회 the Wounded Soldiers'〔Disabled Veterans'〕 Association.

**상인**(商人) a merchant; a trader; a dealer《in》; a tradesman; a shopkeeper (가게의); tradespeople [총칭]. ¶ 모피 ～ a fur trader; a trader in furs / 저 녀석은 ～ 근성이 너무 지나쳐서 싫다 I don't like him; he is too mercenary. ◉ ～근성 a commercial 〔mercenary〕 spirit.

**상인방**(上引枋) 〖건축〗 the upper lintel.

**상일** physical 〔muscular, manual〕 labor 〔work〕. ¶ ～을 하다 do physical labor. ◉ ～꾼 a manual laborer.

**상임**(常任) ¶ ～의 standing; permanent; regular. ◉ ～고문 a standing advisor 《for》. ～위원 a member of the standing 〔permanent〕 committee: ～위원회 a standing 〔permanent〕 committee. ～이사 an executive director: (비)～이사국《유엔의》a (non-)permanent member of the UN Security Council. ～지휘자 a permanent (orchestra) conductor.

**상자**(箱子) a box; a case; a chest; a packing case; a casket (작은). ¶ ～모양의 box-shaped / ～에 든 cased / ～뚜껑 the lid of a box; a boxtop / 한 ～가득 a boxful / 사과 한 ～ a box of apples / 포도주 한 ～ a case of wine / 빈 ～ an empty box 〔case〕 / ～에 넣다 put 〔pack〕《*a thing*》 in a box 〔case〕; encase / ～로 사다 buy《*a thing*》 by the box / ～를 열다 unpack a case.

**상잔**(相殘) struggling with each other. ～하다 struggle〔fight〕with each other; devour〔prey on〕one another. ◉ 골육〔동족〕～ a family quarrel; an internal〔internecine〕strife〔struggle, feud〕; a domestic dissension: 골육〔동족〕～하다 engage in an internecine feud〔war〕.

**상장**(上場) 〘증권〙 ～하다 list《stocks on the stock market》. ¶ ～되다 be listed《on the stock exchange》. ◉ ～기업〔법인, 회사〕 an enterprise〔a corporation, a company〕 listed on the stock exchange. ～절차 listing procedures. ～주(株) listed stocks〔shares〕: 비(非)～주(株) unlisted〔outside〕 stocks〔shares〕. ～폐지 delisting. 한국 ～회사 협의회 the Association of the Listed Firms of Korea.

**상장**(喪章) a mourning badge〔band〕; a crape (band). ¶ ～을 달다《팔에》 wear a crape〔mourning band〕 on *one's* sleeve;《가슴에》 wear a mourning badge on *one's* breast.

**상장**(賞狀) 《award》 a certificate〔diploma〕 of merit;《honor with》 a testimonial; a letter of commendation; a letter of appreciation. ¶ 우등～ a diploma of honors; an honors diploma / 우등～을 받다 receive〔be awarded〕 an honor prize《for excellence in history》/ 정부는 그녀에게 ～을 수여했다 She was granted a certificate of commendation from the government.

**상재**(商才) business ability〔capacity, acumen〕. ¶ 그는 ～가 뛰어나다 He is a shrewd〔an astute〕 businessman.

**상쟁**(相爭) a dispute; a strife〔struggle, conflict〕 with each other. ～하다 have a dispute; struggle〔quarrel, wrangle〕 with each other. ⇨ 상잔.

**상적**(相敵) ～하다 match; be a match for each other; equal; rival.

**상적**(商敵) a rival in trade; a commercial rival; a business competitor.

**상전**(上典) *one's* lord and master;《고용주》 the employer;《상관》 *one's* higher〔superior〕 officer〔official〕; *one's* senior. ¶ ～을 충실히 모시다 serve *one's* master faithfully.

**상전**(相傳) inheritance; transmission《from father to son》. ～하다 inherit; transmit; hand down.

**상전**(相戰) a fight; a quarrel; argument. ～하다 quarrel; fight; argue《with》; compete《with》.

**상전벽해**(桑田碧海) convulsions of nature; violent changes in nature; the changeableness of things. ¶ ～가 되다 Naught may endure but mutability. *or* The world is a scene of changes, and to be constant in nature is inconstancy.

**상점**(商店) 《미》 a store;《영》 a shop. ¶ ～을 열다〔닫다〕 open〔close〕 the store / 역 주변에 많은 ～이 모여 있다 Many stores are clustered around the station. ◉ ～가 a shopping street〔district, center〕: 역전의 ～가 a shopping area near the station. ～주인《미》 a storekeeper; a store owner;《영》 a shopkeeper.

> 참고 **shop**과 **store**
> 일반적으로 「상점」을《미》에서는 store,《영》에서는 shop이라고 한다.《미》에서 shop은 전문점, 서비스 센터 따위를 가리키고,《영》에서는 stores라고 하면 백화점을 뜻한다.

**상접**(相接) contact. ～하다 come in contact〔touch〕 with each other; be contiguous to each other. ¶ 피골이 ～하다 be reduced to a (mere) skeleton; be all〔waste away to〕 skin and bones; be worn to a shadow.

**상정**(上程) laying before the National Assembly; presentation《of a bill》. ～하다《일정에》 introduce〔present, put〕《a bill》 on the agenda;《의회에》 lay《a bill》 before the National Assembly;《토의에》 bring up《a bill》 for discussion. ¶ 의안은 ～되었다 The bill came up for debate. *or* The bill was on the table. / 정부는 이번 국회 회기 중에 추가 예산안을 ～할 것이다 The government will put a supplementary budget bill on the agenda of the coming session of the National Assembly.

**상정**(常情) 《인정》 human feelings;《인성》 human nature; humanity. ¶ 쾌락을 추구하는 것은 인지～이다 The desire to pursue pleasure is but natural to the human nature.

**상정**(想定) a hypothesis (*pl.* -ses); (a) supposition; (an) assumption. ～하다 suppose; imagine; assume; estimate (어림하다). ¶ ～적(인) imaginary; hypothetic(al);《어림한》 estimated / 우리는 화재가 일어났다고 ～하고 방화 훈련을 했다 We conducted a fire drill on the assumption that a fire occured. / 이렇게 ～하고 토의를 시작하자 Let's start our discussion with this hypothesis. ◉ ～량 an estimated volume.

**상제**(上帝) God. ⇨ 하느님.

**상제**(喪制) ① 《사람》 a person in mourning; a mourner. ¶ 맏～ a chief mourner / ～가 되다 be bereft of *one's* parents. ② 《제도》 the mourning practice 〔custom〕; the ritual of mourning.

**상조**(尙早) prematurity. ¶ ～의 premature; too early 〔soon〕 / 시기 ～이다 Time is not mature 〔ripe〕 for it yet.

**상조**(相助) mutual aid 〔assistance, help〕; interdependence; cooperation. ～하다 aid 〔assist, help〕 each other 〔one another〕; cooperate 《with》. ¶ ～적(인) cooperative; friendly / ～정신 a spirit of cooperation; (a spirit of) mutual helpfulness. ◉ ～회 a mutual aid society; a benefit 〔friendly〕 society; a fraternal society 〔order〕.

**상존**(尙存) ～하다 be still in existence; still exist; 《잔존하다》 remain.

**상종**(相從) intercourse; association; company; friendship; acquaintanceship. ～하다 associate 《with》; hold intercourse 《with》; keep company 《with》; mix 《with》. ¶ ～하지 않다 refuse to deal with; sever acquaintance with; break off friendship with / 유유～ Like attracts like. / 그런 자들하고는 ～하지 않는다 I avoid keeping company with such people.

**상종가**(上終價) 〖증권〗 《hit》 the daily permissible ceiling.

**상좌**(上佐) 〖불교〗 a monk who is first in line to succeed his master 〔teacher〕.

**상좌**(上座) the top seat. ⇨ 상석(上席).

**상주**(上奏) a report 〔an address〕 to the Throne. ⇨ 상소(上疏). ～하다 report to the Throne 〔His or Her Majesty〕; submit 《*a matter*》 to the Throne.

**상주**(常住) ～하다 reside 《in, at》. ¶ 한국에 ～하는 외국인 the foreign residents in Korea. ◉ ～불멸 〖불교〗 immortality and indestructibility: ～ 불멸하다 live forever; be immortal and indestructible; be eternal. ～인구 a settled population. ～자 (habitual) residents 《in this city》.

**상주**(常駐) ～하다 be permanently stationed 《at》; stay permanently 《at》. ¶ 수비대를 그곳에 ～시키기로 결정했다 It was decided that a garrison should be (permanently) stationed there. ◉ ～대사관 《open》 a resident embassy 《in》. ～특파원 a permanently stationed correspondent.

**상주**(喪主) the chief 〔principal〕 mourner.

**상주**(詳註) detailed 〔copious〕 notes.

**상중**(喪中) the period of mourning; in mourning. ¶ 나는 아버님 ～에 있다 I am in mourning for my father. / 나는 ～이라 경축모임에 참석하는 것을 삼가고 있다 Since I'm in mourning, I am refraining from attending celebratory gatherings.

**상중하**(上中下) 《3단계》 the first, the second, and the third classes 〔grades〕; 《품질·능력 등의》 good, better, and the best; the three grades of quality—good, fair, and poor. ¶ ～ 3권〔한 질〕 a set of three volumes; a three-decker.

**상지**(上肢) 〖해부〗 the upper limbs; the arms.

**상지상**(上之上) the best (of the best); 「the very best.

**상질**(上質) the best quality. ⇨ 상길(上一).

**상징**(象徵) a symbol; an emblem; 《모양으로 나타내기》 symbolic representation. ～하다 symbolize; emblematize; stand as a symbol 《for》; be symbolic 〔emblematic〕 《of》. ¶ ～적(인) symbolic(al) / ～적 의미 a symbolic meaning / 국가의 ～ the symbol of the State / 비둘기는 평화의 ～이다 The dove is the symbol of peace / 그것은 ～적인 사건이었다 It was a symbolic event. ◉ ～극 a symbolic play 〔drama〕. ～시 symbolical poetry [총칭]. ～주의 symbolism: ～주의자 a symbolist. ～파 the symbolic 〔symbolist〕 school; the symbolists.

**상찬**(賞讚) admiration; praise. ⇨ 칭찬.

**상찰**(詳察) full 〔detailed〕 consideration; minute 〔close〕 observation; careful inspection. ～하다 consider fully 〔in detail〕; observe carefully 〔closely〕.

**상책**(上策) a good 〔capital〕 plan 〔idea〕; the best plan; the best policy 〔scheme〕; the wisest thing 《to *do*》. ¶ 그렇게 하는 것이 ～은 아니다 It is not advisable to do so.

**상처**(喪妻) the death 〔loss〕 of *one's* wife; bereavement of *one's* wife. ～하다 lose 〔be bereaved of〕 *one's* wife by death. ¶ ～한 사람 a widower.

**상처**(傷處) ① 《부상》 a wound; an injury; a hurt; a cut; a scratch; a slash; a gash; a bruise; a scrape. ¶ 가벼운〔심한〕 ～ slight 〔serious〕 injury / ～를 입다 get 〔be〕 hurt; be

injured; be wounded; get a cut / ~를 입히다 injure; hurt; inflict an injury 〔a wound〕 on 《*a person*》/ ~를 입지 않고 피하다 escape unhurt; get away with a whole skin / ~를 치료하다 treat a wound / 그는 온몸이 ~투성이였다 He was wounded all over. *or* He was black and blue all over / ~때문에 밤새도록 잠을 이루지 못했다 My wound kept me awake all night.
② 《흉터》 a scar. ¶ 이마에 ~가 있다 have a scar on *one's* forehead; *one's* forehead is scared 〔bears a scar〕.
③ [비유적] ¶ 전쟁의 ~ the scars of the war / (마음의) ~를 입다 be hurt / 감정〔명성〕에 ~를 입히다 hurt *a person's* feelings 〔reputation〕/ 육체의 ~는 빨리 아물지만 마음의 ~는 오래간다 Bodily injury soon heals, but emotional injury takes (much) longer.

> 용법 **wound** 무기·흉기 따위에 의해 (의식적으로) 가해진 상처. **injury** 사고 따위와 같이 우연한 일에 의해 입은 상처. **hurt** injury의 스스럼없는 쉬운 말로, 다음의 여러 낱말 대신으로 쓸 수 있다. **cut** 피부에 입은 베인 상처. **slash** 칼 따위로 기다랗게 베인 상처. 특히 길고 깊은 상처는 **gash**라고 한다. **bruise** 타박상. **scratch** 끝이 날카로운 것으로 할퀴어서 생긴 상처. **scrape** 잦은 마찰에 의해 생긴 상처.

**상체**(上體) the upper (part of the) body.
**상초**(上焦) 〖한의〗 the upper chest.
**상추** 〖식물〗 (a) lettuce. ◉ ~쌈 lettuce-wrapped rice.
**상춘**(常春) everlasting spring. ¶ ~의 나라 a land of everlasting spring.
**상춘**(賞春) admiring spring scenery; enjoying 〔appreciating〕 spring. ~하다 admire spring scenery; enjoy 〔appreciate〕 spring. ◉ ~객 springtime merrymakers; springtime picnickers.
**상층**(上層) 《지층 따위의》 an upper layer 〔stratum〕; 《하늘의》 the upper regions 〔air〕; 《건물의》 the upper stories 〔floors〕; 《사회의》 the upper classes 〔social strata〕; a higher stratum of society. ¶ 정부의 ~부 the high government circle; the leading members of the government / 하늘의 ~은 공기가 희박하다 The air is rare in the upper regions. ◉ ~계급 the upper classes; the high circles. ~기류 the upper air currents. ~부 topsiders. ~운 high 〔upper〕 clouds.
**상치**(上—) top-quality stuff; the best (of its kind); an article of superior quality.
**상치**(相馳) a conflict; a collision; discord. ~하다 conflict 《with》; collide 〔clash〕 《with》; be contrary 《to》. ¶ 서로 ~되는 개념 directly-opposed concepts 〔ideas〕/ 두 사람의 의견은 서로 ~된다 The opinions of the two are「contrary to 〔in conflict with〕 each other.
**상치**(常置) ~하다 keep 〔maintain〕 permanently. ¶ ~하는 permanent; standing. ◉ ~신호기 《철도》 a fixed signal.
**상침**(上針) 《바늘》 a needle of superior quality; a good needle; 《바느질》 decorative saddle stitching 《on clothes》. ¶ ~놓다 saddle-stitch.
**상쾌**(爽快) ~하다 (be) refreshing; exhilarating; invigorating; bracing; crisp. ¶ ~한 바람 a refreshing breeze / ~한 아침 a crisp 〔nice and cool〕 morning / 기분이 ~해지다 feel 〔be〕 refreshed / 심신을 ~하게 하다 refresh *one* in mind and body / 하룻밤을 푹 잤더니 오늘 아침은 기분이 ~하다 I'm feeling bright this morning after a good night's sleep.
**상타다**(賞—) win 〔gain, obtain, get〕 a prize; bear 〔carry〕 away a prize; receive 〔be awarded〕 a prize. ¶ 국제관계에 관한 논문으로 상(을) 타다 win a prize for an article on international relations.
**상탄**(賞嘆) admiration; praise; applause.
**상태**(狀態) the state 《of things》; a condition; a situation; 《외관·국면》 an aspect.

> 용법 **state** 「상태」를 나타내는 가장 일반적인 말. **condition** 환경·원인과의 관계를 암시하는 말. **situation** 주위와의 상호관계를 뜻하는 말. **aspect** 사물의 「외관·국면·정세」 따위를 뜻하는 말.

¶ 재정 ~ the financial standing 〔showing〕/ 경제 ~ economic conditions / 정신 ~ a mental state / 전시 ~에서는 on 〔under〕 war conditions / 어떤 기후 ~에서도 under all climate conditions / 이런 ~로 가면 if things go at this rate / 한국인의 영양 ~ the nutrition situation of the Korean people / 무방비 ~의 도시 a city in defenseless state / 말도 못 할 지독한 ~ a very rotten condition / 한심한 ~ a lamentable state / 빈사 ~에 있다 be in a dying condition / 전쟁 ~를 종결하다 end 〔terminate〕 a state of war / 당시 산업은 침체 ~였다 The industry was then in a state of doldrums. / 내 건강 ~는 양호하다 The state 〔condition〕 of my health is good. / 그 원고는 아직도 거의 완전한 ~로 남아있다 The manuscripts are still in almost perfect condition today. / 현재 ~로는 이 작품의 연내 완성은 무리다 Under the present circumstances, it is impossible to complete this work within the year.

**상태**(常態) a normal state 〔condition〕; an ordinary 〔a usual〕 state; normality; normalcy.

**상통**(相—) a face; a (cast of) countenance; 《구어》 a phiz; a mug. ¶ ~을 찡그리다 frown; scowl; grimace / 이 ~아 You clumsy idiot! *or* You stupid fool!

**상통**(相通) 《의사 소통》 mutual understanding; 《서로 통함》 communication; 《공통》 commonness. ~하다 understand each other; communicate 《with》; have *something* in common. ¶ 의사가 ~하다 understand each other; come to a mutual (good) understanding / 기맥이 ~하다 have a tacit understanding with / …와 일맥 ~하는 바가 있다 have something in common 《with》….

**상투** a topknot (of hair). ¶ ~를 틀다 tie 〔wear〕 a topknot; wear *one's* hair in a knot. ◉ ~쟁이 a person with a topknot. 상툿바람 《with》 a bare topknot; bareheaded; hatless.

**상투**(常套) conventionality; commonplaceness. ¶ ~적(인) commonplace; conventional; hackneyed (진부한); the same old / ~적인 말을 쓰다 use hackneyed words. ◉ ~어 a hackneyed 〔stereotyped〕 expression 〔phrase〕; a stock phrase; *cliché* (F.): 「선처하겠습니다」는 정치가들이 사용하는 하나의 ~어구이다 "We'll take proper measures" is one of the stock 〔hackneyed〕 phrases politicians usually use.

**상투수단**(常套手段) a well-worn device; an old trick 〔《구어》 ploy〕; stereotyped 〔worn-out〕 measures; *one's* usual 〔hackneyed〕 practice. ¶ ~을 쓰다 use *one's* old 〔favorite〕 trick / 그것은 그의 ~이다 That's the same old trick of his. *or* That's the way he usually does it.

**상파울루** 《브라질의 도시》 São Paulo.

**상판대기**(相—) a face; a cast of countenance; 《구어》 a phiz; a mug.

**상팔자**(上八字) good fortune; a happy lot; high living. ¶ ~를 타고 나다 be born under a lucky star / ~로 지내다 live in clover 〔comfort〕.

**상패**(賞牌) a medal; a medallion; a wooden 〔brass, plastic〕 plaque stating the achievement of the owner. ¶ ~가 수여되다 win 〔be awarded〕 a medal. ◉ ~수령자 a medalist.

**상편**(上篇) the first volume (of a book in two or three volumes).

**상포**(喪布) cloth for funeral use.

**상표**(商標) a trademark; a brand. ¶ 등록~ a registered trademark / 외국 ~의 도입 the introduction of foreign trademarks / 유명 ~ a renowned brand 〔trademark〕 / ~를 등록하다 register a trademark; trademark / ~를 붙이다 put 〔affix〕 a trademark 《on》; trademark; brand / ~를 도용하다 pirate the trademark 《of》.
◉ ~권 the trademark right: ~권 침해 piracy of a trademark; (a) trademark infringement / ~권을 침해하다 infringe upon a trademark. ~도용(盜用) trademark piracy. ~등록필 《표시》 Registered. ~명 a trade 〔brand〕 name.

**상품**(上品) ① 《일등품》 a first-class 〔choice〕 article; a superior article. ② 〖불교〗 the Land of Supreme Happiness.

**상품**(商品) a commodity; an item on 〔for〕 sale; a product; [집합적] goods; wares; commodities; merchandise.

> (용법) **goods** 주로 소매상에서 취급하는 상품. **merchandise**는 도매상 등에서 취급하는 상품. **product** 제품, 생산품이란 뜻에서의 상품.
> 「상품」에 관련된 몇가지 단어들을 열거하면 다음과 같다. 「우연히 찾아낸 진귀한〔값싼〕 상품」 a lucky find; a good buy / 「아주 싸게 산 상품」 a bargain / 「상점에서 손님을 끌기 위해 싸게 파는 상품」 a come-on; a loss leader / 「수입 상품」 imported goods / 「비매품」 (an article) not for sale.

¶ 주요 ~ staple 〔major〕 goods / ~이 많다〔적다〕 《종류》 keep a rich 〔limited〕 assortment of goods; 《수량》 have a large 〔small〕 stock of goods / (점포에서) ~을 사들이다〔들여놓다〕 lay in a stock 《of goods》 / ~을 처분하다 dis-

pose of goods / 각종 ~을 취급하다 deal in various lines of commodities / 5백만 원어치의 ~ 재고가 있다 carry a five million won stock / ~화하다 produce 《an article》 on a commercial scale 〔basis〕; commercialize / 이 물건은 ~이 될 수 없다 This article is unmarketable. / 그런~은 취급하지 않습니다 We don't carry such items. *or* We don't deal in such a line of goods.
◉ ~가치 commercial value: ~ 가치가 있는 marketable; salable; 《chemical compound》 of commercial value. ~거래소 a commodity exchange. ~견본 a trade sample; 《우편물의 표기》 Samples: ~견본시 a trade fair / ~견본장(帳) a sample card. ~권 a gift 「certificate 〔token〕. ~매입〔매출〕 대장 a 「purchase 〔sales〕 book. ~명 a brand 〔trade〕 name. ~목록 a catalog(ue); 《재고의》 an inventory. ~반입구 《백화점 따위의》 a goods entrance. ~시장 a commodity market. ~이미지 the brand image. ~재고 the amount of stock: ~재고 대장 a stock book. ~진열관 a commodity museum. ~진열실〔진열장, 진열창〕 a 「showroom 〔showcase, show=window〕. ~차관 commodity loans. ~창고 a merchandise warehouse. ~테스트 a quality test of merchandise. ~학 the study of merchandising. ~화 계획 《마케팅》 a merchandising. ~회전율 merchandize turnover ratio.

**상품**(賞品) a prize; a trophy; a pot. ¶ ~을 건네주다 hand out a prize 《to》 / ~을 타다 win 〔take, gain, be awarded〕 a prize / ~을 수여하다 award 《*a person*》 a prize; bestow a prize 《on》. ◉ ~수여식 a prize-awarding ceremony.

**상피**(上皮) 〖해부·생물〗 the epithelium (*pl.* ~s, -lia); the epidermis. ¶ ~의 epidermal; epithelial. ◉ ~세포 an epithelial cell.

**상피**(相避) incest. ¶ ~붙다 commit 「incest.

**상피병**(象皮病) 〖의학〗 elephantiasis.

**상하**(上下) ① 《위와 아래》 top and bottom; the upper and lower sides 〔parts〕. ¶ ~의 up-and-down / ~로 《move》 up and down; upward and downward; 《높게 낮게》 high and low / ~ 좌우에 in every direction.
② 《귀천》 the upper and lower classes; superiors and inferiors; high and low. ¶ ~ 구별 없이 irrespective of 「rank 〔standing〕; without distinction of social standing; high and low alike / ~가 단결하여 all classes being unanimous.
③ 《짝을 이루는 것》 ¶ ~ 2권의 책 a book in two volumes; two-volume books / 신사복 ~ a suit of clothes; a 《business》 suit.
④ 《왕래의》 going up and coming down; ups and downs.
⑤ 《변동》 rise and fall; fluctuations. ¶ 증권 시세의 ~ 변동 fluctuations in share quotations.
◉ ~동(動) an up-and-down motion; 《지진의》 a vertical shock. ~수도 water supply and drainage.

**상하**(常夏) everlasting summer. ¶ ~의 나라 a land of 「everlasting 〔continual〕 summer.

**상하다**(傷—) ① 《물건을〔이〕》 damage; be damaged; injure; be injured; hurt; be 〔get〕 hurt; 《마손》 wear 〔be worn〕 out (헐다); flaw 〔crack, be bruised〕 (상처나다); become deteriorated (나빠지다); 《음식이》 rot; go bad; spoil; be spoiled; turn sour (우유 따위가); be stale (생선 따위가). ¶ 상하기 쉬운 물건 《깨지기 쉬운》 a fragile article; a delicate thing; 《썩기 쉬운》 perishable goods; perishables / 상한 고기 tainted 〔stale〕 meat / 상한〔상하지 않은〕 사과 a 「bruised 〔sound〕 apple / 상한 토마토 a rotten tomato / 음식이 ~ food is spoiled; food has gone bad / 심한 서리로 곡식이 ~ the crop is damaged by a heavy frost / 짐이 운반중에 상했다 My baggage was damaged in transit.
② 《마음·기분 등을〔이〕》 hurt; get 〔be〕 hurt; injure; be injured; harm; impair; grieve; be grieved 《at》; worry; be worried about; be 「distressed 〔troubled〕 《with》. ¶ 감정을 상하게 하다 hurt 〔injure〕 《*a person's*》 feelings; hurt 〔offend〕 《*a person*》 / 속이 ~ feel bad; be grieved at heart; be 「worried 〔anxious, dejected〕 / 어머니의 속을 상하게 하다 worry 〔grieve〕 *one's* mother / 나는 그의 기분을 많이 상하게 했다 I happened to injure his feelings not a little. / 속상해 죽겠다 I am worried to death. / 그 소식을 듣고 나는 몹시 마음이 상했다 The news pained me a great deal.
③ 《몸을〔이〕》 grow haggard; become thin; be emaciated; be broken 《in health》. ¶ 건강을 ~ impair 〔injure〕 *one's* health; ruin 〔lose〕 *one's* health / 그녀는 과로로 얼굴이 몹시 상해 보인다

She looks haggard from overwork. / 어머니는 오랜 병으로 모습이 볼품없이 상하셨다 My mother is worn to a shadow on account of a long illness

**상학**(上學) the opening 〔beginning〕 of school. ～하다 begin; take up. ◉ ～시간 the hour at which school begins: ～시간은 8시다 School begins at eight. ～종 the opening bell.

**상학**(商學) commercial science.

**상한**(上限) 《put, set》 an upper limit 《on 〔to〕 the size》; a maximum; 〚수학〛 the supremum; the least upper bound (생략 lub). ◉ ～선 the top 〔highest〕 limit; a ceiling; the maximum: ～선을 두다〔정하다〕 put a ceiling on; set 〔fix〕 an upper limit.

**상한**(象限) 〚수학〛 a quadrant. ⇨ 사분면.

**상항**(上項) the above item 〔provision〕.

**상항**(商港) a mercantile 〔trading〕 port; a commercial harbor.

**상해**(傷害) (an) injury; bodily harm. ～하다 injure; do 《*a person*》 an injury; inflict an injury upon 《*a person*》. ◉ ～보험 accident insurance. ～사건 an injury case. ～죄 a charge of injuring another: ～죄로 구속되다 be arrested on a charge of injuring 《*a person*》. ～치사(죄) (a) bodily injury resulting in death.

**상해**(詳解) a detailed 〔minute〕 explanation 《of》; a full commentary 《on》. ～하다 explain minutely 〔in detail〕; give 〔make〕 a detailed explanation 《of》; give a full commentary 《on》.

**상해**(霜害) frost damage; damage from 〔by〕 frost. ¶ ～를 입다 suffer from frost.

**상행**(上行) going up; going toward Seoul. ～하다 go up; go toward Seoul. ◉ ～선 《고속도로의》 the upbound lane of a highway. ～열차〔선〕 an up train 〔line〕.

**상행위**(商行爲) a commercial 〔business〕 transaction.

**상향**(上向) ¶ ～의 upward / 은행 금리의 ～ 조정 the upward readjustment to bank interest rates / (시세가) ～세를 보이다 show a rising 〔an upward〕 tendency; tend upward. ◉ ～선(線) an upswing: 꾸준히 ～선을 그리다 be steadily on the upswing / 매출액은 ～선을 그렸다 The sales figures have risen in a curve. ～시세 an advancing 〔a bull〕 market.

**상현**(上弦) the first quarter of the moon. ◉ ～달 a young 〔waxing〕 moon. 「hieroglyphic (character).

**상형문자**(象形文字) a pictograph; a

**상호**(相互) reciprocity; mutuality. ¶ ～의 mutual; reciprocal / ～간에 mutually; reciprocally; 《help》 each other; one another (셋 이상) / ～의 이익을 위하여 《work》 for the mutual benefit 《of》 / ～협조하여 in cooperation 〔concert〕 with each other / 회원 ～간의 친목과 복지를 도모하다 promote amity and welfare among the members. ◉ ～계약 a mutual contract. ～관계 mutual 〔reciprocal〕 relation; interrelationship. ～교수법 a mutual teaching system. ～무역 two-way trade. ～방위조약 a mutual defense treaty 〔pact〕. ～보험 mutual insurance. ～부금 a mutual savings account. ～불간섭주의 the principles of mutual noninterference. ～불신 mutual suspicion 〔distrust〕. ～사찰 mutual inspections. ～신용금고 a mutual savings and finance company. ～안전보장조약 a mutual security pact 〔treaty〕. ～원조 조약 a mutual assistance pact 〔treaty〕. ～유도 〚전기〛 mutual induction. ～의존 interdependence; mutual dependence. ～이해 mutual understanding. ～작용 (a) reciprocal action; (an) interaction. ～참조 cross 〔reciprocal〕 reference. ～출자 mutual investment. ～협력 mutual cooperation: ～ 협력 증진 방안 avenues for beefing up bilateral collaboration.

**상호**(商號) a firm 〔trade〕 name.

**상호부조**(相互扶助) mutual aid 〔assistance, help〕. ～하다 aid 〔assist, help〕 mutually. ¶ ～론 mutualism / ～제도〔조직〕 a cooperative 〔mutual aid〕 system.

**상혼**(商魂) a commercial 〔an enterprising〕 spirit 〔enthusiasm〕; (aggressive) salesmanship. ¶ ～이 악착같다 be aggressive in salesmanship; be a keen 〔sharp〕 businessman; be a shrewd merchant.

**상환**(相換) exchange; change. ～하다 exchange; change. ¶ 현금 ～으로 물품을 인도하다 hand over the goods in exchange for cash; deliver an article against a receipt. ◉ ～권 an exchange ticket; a coupon. ～증 a receipt; an exchange; a check 〔bond〕. 대금～인도 cash on delivery (생략 c.o.d.).

**상환**(償還) repayment; refundment; redemption; amortization (분할에 의한). ～하다 repay; refund; redeem;

amortize. ¶ 2005년 ～ 채권 a bond redeemable in 2005 / 외채를 ～하다 redeem 〔refund, retire〕 a foreign loan / 장기 국채는 10년 후에 ～된다 Long-term government bonds are redeemable in ten years.

◉ ～계산서 a recourse account. ～금 money repaid; repayments. ～기금 a fund for redemption; a redemption fund. ～기한 the term of redemption; maturity (만기): ～ 기한이 되다 be due for redemption. ～만기일 the date of maturity. ～의무자 a recourse debtor. ～주식 a callable stock. ～차익 profits from redemption. ～청구권 (the right of) recourse. 만기전～ prior redemption.

**상황**(狀況) the state of things 〔affairs〕; conditions; a situation; circumstances; the context. ¶ 현재 ～으로는 as matters stand; as things go; in the present situation; under the existing conditions; under these circumstances / ～을 알다〔파악하다〕 know how matters stand; get the bearings of the situation / ～을 조사하다 inquire into the state of things / ～에 따라 판단하다 judge from 〔by〕 the existing state of things / ～은 호전되고 있다 The situation has been improving. / ～은 악화되었다 The situation grew worse. / 이 곳의 ～은 아직 아무런 변화도 없다 The condition of affairs here remains unchanged. / 그곳 ～을 알려 주십시오 Please let me know how matters stand in your town.

◉ ～설명 a briefing. ～실 the briefing room. ～증거 〖법〗 circumstantial 〔indirect, presumptive〕 evidence. ～판단 circumstantial judgment; *one's* assessment of the situation.

**상황**(商況) commercial 〔trade, business, market〕 conditions; the market (situation). ¶ ～이 부진〔활발〕하다 The market is dull 〔brisk〕. ◉ ～보고 a market report 〔bulletin〕. ～시찰 a market survey. 해외～ commercial conditions abroad.

**상회**(上廻) ～하다 top; be more than; exceed; be in excess of. ⇨ 웃돌다. ¶ 2천만섬을 ～하는 수확 a crop rising twenty million *sŏm* / 원가를 ～하는 이익 the gain over the cost 《of...》 / 수출이 수입을 대폭 ～했다 Export exceeded import by a great margin.

**상회**(商會) a commercial firm 〔concern〕; a trading company.

**상훈**(賞勳) citation of merit.

**상흔**(傷痕) a scar; a cicatrix (*pl.* -trices, -trixes); a cicatrice. ⇨ 흉터. ¶ ～을 남기다 leave a scar / ～이 남다 a scar still remains.

**샅** ① the crotch; the inside of the thigh; the groin. ② 《틈》 a fork(ing); a crotch.

**샅바** 《씨름》 a wrestler's thigh band; 《죄인의》 a leg-band 《for a prisoner》. ¶ ～ 채우다 bind the legs of 《a prisoner》.

**샅샅이** all over; in every nook and cranny 〔corner〕; everywhere; throughout. ¶ ～ 찾다 look in every nook and cranny; leave no corner unsearched 〔no stone unturned〕; search every corner 〔cranny〕 《of a place for *something*》; rummage; ransack; comb 《*a place* for a criminal》 / 집안을 ～ 뒤지다 look all over the house 《for *a thing*》; search the house high and low / 방안을 ～ 뒤졌으나 시계를 찾지 못했다 I searched all over the room, but I could not find my watch.

**새**[1] ① 〖식물〗 cogongrasses, eulalias and other gramineous plants. ② ⇨ 억새. ③ = 이엉.

**새**[2] 〖조류〗 a bird; a feathered 〔winged〕 creature; 《참새》 a sparrow; a fowl (★「새」는 bird가 가장 일반적인 말. fowl은 닭·오리·칠면조 따위를 말하나, 앞에 수식어구를 수반하여 「조류」란 집합적인 뜻이 되기도 함: waterfowl (물새)). ¶ 새 소리 a bird-call 〔birdsong〕; the wood-notes / 새 파는 가게 a bird shop / 장속의 새 a caged bird / 새의 보금자리 a bird-nest; a nest of a bird / 새 까먹은 소리 《속담》 spreading false rumors / 새발의 피 practically nothing; a mere smidgen / 새가 울다 a bird chirps / 새를 기르다 keep 〔breed〕 a (caged) bird / 새에게 모이를 주다 feed a bird 《on》 / 새 중에는 날 수 없는 것도 있다 Not all birds can fly. /새도 가지를 가려서 앉는다 《속담》 Choose your companions well. / 일찍 일어나는 새가 벌레를 잡는다 《속담》 The early bird catches the worm. / 새도 앉는 곳마다 깃이 떨어진다 《속담》 You lose some of your possessions whenever you move.

**새**[3] an opening; an interval. ⇨ 사이.

**새**[4] 《새로운》 new; 《신기한》 novel; 《신선한》 fresh; 《최근의》 recent; latest; up-to-date. ¶ 새 사상 up-to-date ideas / 새 생활 a new life / 새 책〔집〕 a new book 〔house, home〕 / 새 차 a brand=new car / 얼마 안 있으면 새 학기가 시작된다 A 〔The〕 new school term will soon begin.

**새-** 《짙은》 vivid; deep; intense. ¶ 새까맣다 be jet black / 새하얗다 be snow white / 새파랗다 be deep blue.

**새가슴** a pigeon 〔chicken〕 breast. ¶ ~의 pigeon-〔chicken-〕breasted.

**새것** a new thing 〔one, brand〕. ¶ ~이나 다름없다 look brand-new; be 〔look〕 as good as new.

**새겨듣다** 《주의해서》 listen carefully 〔attentively〕 to; pay attention to; 《되씹어서》 appreciate 〔catch〕 the meaning (of what is said); hear 〔listen to〕 reason. ¶ 선생님의 말을 새겨 들어라 Listen carefully to what your teacher tells you.

**새경** the annual salary given to a 「farm servant.

**새꼬막** 〖조개류〗 an ark shell.

**새그물** a fowler's 〔fowling〕 net.

**새근거리다**[1] 《숨을》 breathe quick and hard; be short-winded; become short=breathed; gasp 〔pant〕 (for breath). ¶ 성이 나서 ~ breathe quick and hard with anger.

**새근거리다**[2] 《뼈마디가》 feel a slight pain 《in *one's* joints》; feel a slight twitch of arthritis. ¶ 뼈마디가 ~ feel a dull pain in *one's* joints.

**새근새근** short of breath; with gentle gasps; 《sleep》 calmly; quietly; peacefully. ¶ 아기는 ~ 자고 있다 The baby is sleeping calmly 〔quietly, peacefully〕.

**새근하다** be slightly painful; have a bit tight. ¶ 뼈마디가 ~ My joints feel a bit tight.

**새금하다** (be) sour; acid; tart. ¶ 이 사과는 ~ This apple tastes a bit sour.

**새기다**[1] ① 《파다》 carve 《in, on, out of》; engrave; sculpt; chisel; cut; inscribe (비문 등). ¶ 나무에 이름을 ~ carve *one's* name on a tree / 도장을 ~ engrave a seal / 책상에 이름의 머리글자를 ~ cut *one's* initials in a desk / 돌에다 부처를 ~ carve a Buddha out of stone. ② 《마음에》 engrave; impress; stamp; inscribe 《in, on》; take 《*something*》 to heart. ¶ 기억에 ~ keep 〔register〕 《*something*》 in *one's* memory / 마음속에 ~ bear 〔keep〕 《*something*》 in mind; take 《the advice》 to heart; have 《*something*》 stamped 〔engraved〕 on *one's* mind / 그녀의 아름다운 모습들은 내 기억에 뚜렷이 새겨져 있다 Her beautiful images are strongly impressed on my memory. / 나는 아버지의 말씀을 마음 속 깊이 새겨 두고 있다 My father's words are graven on my heart. / 그의 말이 마음깊이 새겨졌다 His remarks sank deep in my mind.

**새기다**[2] 《해석하다》 interpret; explain; construe; translate. ¶ 시를 ~ interpret a poem / 한문을 ~ translate classical Chinese into Korea / 올바로〔잘못〕 ~ interpret rightly 〔falsely〕 / 여러 가지로 ~ interpret variously.

**새기다**[3] 《반추하다》 chew the cud; ruminate. ¶ 소가 먹은 것을 새기고 있다 The cow is chewing its cud.

**새김** ① 《해석》 paraphrase; interpretation; 《번역》 translation; 《한자의 뜻》 the Korean tag translation of a Chinese character. ¶ 이 구절은 사람에 따라 ~이 다르다 This passage is variously interpreted by different people. ② 《조각》 carving; engraving; sculpture. ③ 《윷놀이》 an extra play gained by making *one's* point in *yut*. ◉ ~질[1] = 새김 ②. ~칼 a graver; a burin; a chisel.

**새김질**[2] 《반추》 chewing the cud; rumination. ~하다 = 새기다[3].

**새까맣다** ① 《빛깔이》 (be) deep-black; jet-〔coal-〕black. ¶ 새까만 머리 jet=black hair; raven hair / 새까맣게 타다 《불에》 be scorched 〔burned〕 black; 《볕에》 be tanned almost black; be brown as a berry / 사람들이 새까맣게 꾀어들다 people gather 《before, round》; be crowded with people. ② 《연륜·능력 등》 be far superior 〔inferior, behind〕. ¶ 새까만 선배이다 be *one's* senior by many years.

**새끼**[1] 《줄》 a (coarse) straw rope. ¶ ~를 꼬다 make 〔twist〕 a rope / ~를 치다 stretch a rope 《around a place》; rope off 〔out〕 《a place》.

**새끼**[2] ① 《동물의》 the young [총칭]; 《한 마리》 a young; a youngling; 《소의》 a calf (*pl.* calves, calfs); 《말·사슴의》 a colt; 《고양이의》 a kitty; 《개·여우·이리의》 a pup; a puppy; 《양의》 a lamb; 《염소의》 a kid; 《곰·사자·이리·호랑이·고래의》 a cub; 《물고기의》 fry [단복수 같음]; 《닭》 a chick. ¶ 한 배 ~ a litter / ~를 배다 be with young / ~를 낳다 〔치다〕 bring forth 《its》 young; litter; cub; lamb (양); pup (개); kitten (고양이); calf (소) / (고양이가) ~ 다섯마리를 낳다 have a litter of five kittens.

② 《자식》 a child; a son (아들); a daughter (딸).
③ 《욕》 a fellow; a guy; a brat. ¶ 개 ~(같은 놈) You son of a bitch! *or* You dog! / 저 ~ that fellow 〔chap, swine〕/ 이 바보 ~야 You fool!
④ 《이자》 interest. ¶ ~를 치다 bear 〔yield〕 interest 《at five percent》.
◉ ~발가락 a little toe. ~발톱 a little toenail. ~손가락 a little 〔small〕 finger. ~손톱 a little fingernail. ~집 the womb (of an animal).

**새날** a new day; 《시기》 a new era 〔stage, epoch〕.

**새너토리엄** 《요양소》 a sanitarium 《미》; 《결핵의》 a (T.B.) sanatorium.

**새다** ① 《날이》 dawn; break; grow light; turn gray. ¶ 날이 ~ it 〔day〕 dawns; the day breaks / 날이 새기 전에 before light / 날이 샐 무렵에 at the crack 〔peep〕 of dawn; toward daybreak.
② 《밖으로》 (***a***) 《기체·액체 등이》 leak (out); escape; get 〔find〕 vent; run out; 《빛 등이》 shine 〔break, come〕 through. ¶ 새는 데 a vent (hole); a leak / 새는 곳을 막다 stop 〔plug〕 the leak / 지붕이 ~ the roof leaks / 가스가 관에서 ~ gas escapes from the pipe / (그릇이) 물이 새지 않다 hold water; be watertight / 문틈으로 불빛이 새어 나왔다 The light showed 〔streamed〕 through the chinks of the doors. (***b***) 《말소리가》 be heard outside. ¶ 그들의 말소리가 창밖으로 새어나왔다 Their talk was heard outside the window. (***c***) 《비밀 등이》 leak out; get 〔slip〕 out; be disclosed 〔divulged〕. ¶ 비밀이 ~ a secret leaks 〔gets〕 out / 정보가 밖으로 ~ the information leaks out. (***d***) 《말·감정 등이》 find vent 〔expression〕; escape. ¶ 입에서 (말이) ~ pass 〔escape〕 *one's* lips / 입에서 고통스러운 신음 소리가 새어 나오다 a painful moan escapes 「from *one's* lips 〔*a person*〕.
③ 《빠져 나오다》 slip 〔get〕 out of; sneak away from. ¶ (학교) 수업중 가로 ~ cut a lesson and beat it.

**새달** next month; the month ahead 〔after〕; the coming month. ¶ ~ 초하루 the first (day) of next month.

**새댁**(―宅) ① = 새집¹. ② = 새색시.

**새되다** (be) shrill-voiced; high-pitched; shrill. ¶ 새된 소리로 in a shrill voice; with a shriek / 새된 소리를 내다 give a shrill cry; shriek.

**새둥주리** a bird('s) nest.

**새득새득** slightly dry 〔withered〕. ~하다 be somewhat dry 〔withered, wizened〕.

**새뜨다** 《공간적으로》 (be) separated; be at a distance; be spaced (at intervals); 《시간적으로》 (be) slow; be few and far between; 《관계가》 (be) estranged 〔alienated〕 《from》.

**새뜻하다** 《빛깔이》 (be) fresh and bright; 《차림새 등이》 neat and clean; tidy; trim. ¶ 새뜻한 빛깔 bright color / 새뜻하게 차려입고 있다 be neatly dressed.

**새로** new(ly); anew; afresh. ¶ ~ 생긴 가게 a newly opened store / ~ 지은 집 a newly built house / ~ 온 사람 a newcomer; a freshman / ~ 오신 선생님 a new teacher / ~ 시작하다 begin afresh / ~ 출발하다 make a new 〔fresh〕 start / 문에 ~ 칠을 했다 The gate has been newly painted.

**새로에** 《…은 커녕》 anything but; far from 《*doing*》; instead of 《*doing*》; on the contrary; 《말할 것도 없고》 not to speak of; to say nothing of; let alone. ¶ 폭풍우가 자기는~ 더 심해 간다 The storm, far from abating, increased in its fury. / 그는 술은~ 맥주도 안 마신다 He does not drink beer, to say nothing of wine.

**새로이** newly; anew; afresh. ⇨ 새로. ¶ 결의를 ~ 하다 make a fresh determination.

**새록새록** in succession; with one (new) thing popping up after another.

**새롭다** (be) new; novel (신기하다); original (독창적); 《신선·생생하다》 (be) fresh; 《최신이다》 (be) recent; latest; hot; 《현대적이다》 (be) up-to-date; modern. ¶ 아주 새로운 brand-new; up-to-the-minute / 새롭게 newly; freshly; anew; afresh. ⇨ 새로(이) / 새로운 뉴스 hot news / 새로운 사상 new ideas; a new thought; up-to-date ideas / 새로운 시도〔출발〕 a new attempt 〔departure〕/ 새로워지다 be renewed 〔renovated〕/ 아직도 기억이 ~ be (still) fresh in *one's* memory / 새로운 맛을 주다 add a new note / 새로운 맛이 없다 lack freshness / 새로운 장을 열다 open a new chapter 《in》/ 그 정보는 내 귀에 ~ That bit of information is news to my ears. / 고향으로부터 새로운 소식이라도 들었습니까 Have you got any fresh news from home?

**새롱거리다** 《야불야불 지껄이다》 talk glibly 〔volubly〕; chatter; prattle; prate; 《희

룽대다》 flirt 〔sport, dally, fondle〕 with 《*a person,* each other》; be jolly with 《a girl》. ¶ 그들은 신나게 새롱거리고 있었다 They rattled on gaily.

**새롱새롱** 《지껄이는 모양》 glibly; volubly; rattlingly; 《희롱대는 모양》 flirtingly; dallyingly.

**새마을** a new community; a *Saemaul.* ◉ ～공장〔금고〕 a *Saemaul* factory 〔finance firm〕. ～사업 a *Saemaul* 〔New Community〕 project. ～운동 the *Saemaul* 〔New Community〕 Movement. ～정신 *Saemaul* spirit. ～지도자 a *Saemaul* leader. ～훈장 the Order of *Saemaul* Service Merit.

**새맛** freshness; novelty. ¶ ～을 내다 display originality 《in》.

**새매** 〖조류〗 a 〔an Asiatic〕 sparrow hawk.

**새물** ① 《과일·생선의》 the first (product) of the season; the first supply 《of》. ¶ ～의 early / ～ 사과 early apples / ～ 딸기를 먹다 eat early strawberries. ② 《옷의》 freshly 〔newly〕 washed clothes. ¶ ～ 셔츠를 입다 wear a newly washed shirt. ◉ ～내 a fresh-washed smell (of clothes). ～청어 《청어》 the first herring on the market; 《사람》 a new 〔green, raw〕 hand; a freshman.

**새밭** a field (full) of eulalia.

**새벽**[1] 《아침》 dawn; daybreak; the break of the day. ¶ ～에 at dawn 〔daybreak〕; at break of dawn; before dawn 〔daybreak〕; toward daybreak / ～부터 해거름까지 from dawn till dusk; from sunup to sundown 《미》 / ～같이 so early in the morning; before sunrise / ～같이 일어나다 rise with the sun; get up at daybreak / 그는 이른 ～에 마을을 떠났다 He left the village before dawn 〔daybreak〕.
◉ ～녘 the peep of dawn 〔day〕; toward daybreak. ～동자 cooking at dawn: ～동자하다 cook 《the rice》 at dawn. ～바람 a morning breeze. ～밥 breakfast at dawn. ～일 early-morning chores. ～잠 a sound 〔heavy, deep, fast〕 sleep at dawn: ～잠이 들다 fall fast asleep at dawn. ～종 the daybreak 〔dawn〕 bell. ～하늘 the dawning sky.

**새벽**[2] 〖건축〗 loam; loamy plaster. ¶ 벽에 ～을 바르다 plaster a wall with loam. ◉ ～질 《do》 plastering with loam.

**새보다** chase birds away from crops; watch for 〔against〕 birds.

**새봄** 《이른 봄》 early spring; 《오는 봄》 next 〔the coming〕 spring. ¶ 새소리는 ～의 전령이라 한다 The song of birds is said to herald the coming of spring.

**새빨갛다** ① 《색이》 (be) bright 〔deep〕 red; crimson. ¶ 새빨갛게 단 난로 a red-glowing stove / 새빨갛게 단 쇠막대 a red-hot iron rod / 새빨갛게 달다 be red-hot / 석양이 서쪽 하늘을 새빨갛게 물들였다 The setting sun fired the western sky. ② 《거짓말이》 (be) downright. ¶ 새빨간 거짓말 a downright 〔barefaced〕 lie / 새빨간 거짓말을 하다 tell a palpable lie.

**새빨개지다** turn 〔go〕 red 〔crimson〕; 《상기하여》 flush deeply; 《부끄러워》 blush scarlet 〔crimson〕 《for shame》. ¶ 성이 나서 ～ be 〔go〕 red with rage 〔anger〕.

**새사냥** bird shooting 〔hunting〕; fowling. ～하다 go fowling 〔bird hunting〕. ◉ ～꾼 a fowler.

**새사람** ① 《앓고 난》 someone just recovered from a serious illness; a convalescent. ② 《신부》 a (recent) bride. ③ 《신인》 a new man 〔figure〕; a newcomer. ④ 《갱생한》 a reborn 〔reformed, new〕 man. ¶ ～이 되다 turn over a new leaf; become a new man / 그는 아주 ～이 되었다 He is quite another man now.

**새살** proud flesh; (a) granulation (tissue); new skin. ¶ ～이 나다 granulate.

**새살거리다** talk 〔chat〕 pleasantly; talk on smilingly.

**새살궂다** (be) light and chatty 〔talkative〕; very flippant.

**새살림** a new home. ¶ ～을 차리다 make a new home; set up house.

**새살스럽다** (be) light and chatty 〔talkative〕; flippant. ¶ 새살스런 여자 a talkative woman.

**새삼** 〖식물〗 a dodder; a love vine.

**새삼스럽다** (be) abrupt; sudden and unexpected; feel anew. ¶ 새삼스럽게 anew; afresh; 《다시》 again; 《특히》 specially; 《이제 와서》 now; after so long a time; abruptly at this belated time / 새삼스러운 말 a remark unnecessary to say anew 〔again〕 / 새삼스럽게 말할 필요도 없이〔없지만〕 Needless to say…; It is nothing new to say that…; It is hardly necessary to say that… / 새삼스럽게 잊은 일을 꺼내다 go out of *one's* way to bring up a matter long forgotten / 새삼스럽게 상식의 필요성을 느꼈다 I felt all the more keenly the importance of common sense. / 새삼스럽게 말할 필요도 없다 It is too well known to be mentioned here. / 새삼스레 이제 와서 무슨 말이냐 You should have said something earlier.

**새새틈틈** ①《장소·공간》 every nook and corner. ¶ ~ 찾다 look in every nook and corner. ②《시간》 at intervals; at *one's* odd moments. ¶ ~ 공부하다 study *one's* lessons at odd moments.

**새색시** a bride; a newly married 〔wedded〕 woman.

**새생활**(—生活) a new life; a new career. ¶ ~에 들어가다 begin 〔start〕 a new life; turn over a new leaf.

**새서방**(—書房) a bridegroom; a new ⌈husband.

**새소리** a birdcall; the song 〔note, call〕 of a bird; a chirp.

**새시** 《창틀》 a sash. ◉ 알루미늄~ an ⌈aluminium sash.

**새시대**(—時代) a new age 〔era, epoch〕. ¶ ~의 정치상(像) a new political image; a new image of politics / ~를 여는 epoch-making 〔epochal〕《discoveries》/ ~를 여는 사람 an epoch-maker / 그 이론은 물리학의 ~를 열었다 The theory made an epoch in physics.

**새싹** a shoot; a sprout; a bud. ¶ ~이 나다 bud; sprout; shoot forth / 지난 주에 심은 화초가 ~이 돋기 시작했다 The flowers that I planted last week have started to sprout 〔put out sprouts〕.

**새아기** *one's* new daughter-in-law.

**새알** a bird's 〔sparrow's〕 egg. ¶ ~ 꼽재기만 하다 be very small. ◉ ~심 a small dumpling in redbean gruel.

**새앙** 〖식물〗 a ginger. ⇨ 생강.
◉ ~뿔《생강뿔》 ginger stumps; 《소뿔의》 stumps of a bull's 〔cow's〕 horns. ~손이 a person with stumps of fingers (because of amputation).

**새앙머리** a kind of hairdo worn by maids-in-waiting; *one's* hair done up to two locks.

**새옷** a new suit 〔dress〕; new clothes. ¶ 맞춘 ~을 입다 put *one's* new tailor-made suit on.

**새옹** a small brass kettle.

**새옹지마**(塞翁之馬) the irony of fate. ¶ 인간 만사 ~ Inscrutable are the ways of Heaven. *or* An evil may sometimes turn out to be a blessing in disguise.

**새우** 〖동물〗 a shrimp (작은); a prawn (보리새우); a lobster (바닷가재).
¶ ~로 잉어를 낚다 throw a sprat to catch a whale; give an egg to gain an ox / 고래 싸움에 ~등 터진다《속담》 An innocent bystander ⌈gets hurt 〔suffers a side blow〕 in a fight.
◉ ~덮밥 rice topped with deep-fried prawns. ~등 a bent 〔rounded〕 back; a stoop; round 〔stooped〕 shoulders / 나이가 들어 ~등이 되다 *one's* back is bent with age. ~볶음 braised shrimp. ~완자튀김 deep-fried minced shrimp balls. ~젓 salted 〔pickled〕 shrimps. ~탕면 noodle soup with shrimps.

**새우다** 《밤을》 stay 〔sit〕 up all night; keep 〔remain〕 awake all night; keep vigil 《over》. ¶ 공부로 밤을 ~ study all night long; sit 〔stay〕 up all night for study / 밤을 새워 간호하다 sit up with 《an invalid》 all night; keep all-night vigil 《over》/ 밤을 새워 끝내다 finish 《*something*》 by working all night (through) / 밤을 새워 마시다 drink all night long; drink the night away / 밤을 새워가며 회의하다 have an all-night conference / 이야기로 밤을 ~ talk the night away / 한밤을 울며 ~ pass a whole night in tears; weep all night.

**새우잠** sleeping all curled up (in fetal position). ¶ ~을 자다 sleep 〔lie〕 curled up; lie huddled up in bed; curl up 《on the sofa》.

**새장**(—欌) a birdcage. ¶ ~에 갇힌 새 a caged bird / 새를 ~에서 기르다〔에 넣다〕 keep 〔put〕 a bird in a cage.

**새조개** 〖조개류〗 a cockle; a cockleshell.

**새중간**(—中間) the very middle. ⇨ 중간.

**새지식**(—知識) new 〔up-to-date〕 knowledge 〔information〕. ⇨ 신지식(新知識).

**새집**[1] ①《신축한》 a newly-built 〔new〕 house; 《이사 온》 *one's* new house. ¶ ~을 짓다 build a new house / ~으로 이사하다 move (in)to a new house. ②《사돈집》 the house of a new relative by marriage.

**새집**[2] 《새의》 a bird('s) nest; a birdhouse (인공의). ¶ 나무에 ~을 달아주다 put up a birdhouse in a tree.

**새짬** 《공간의》 an opening 〔an aperture, a crack, a chink〕 between; 《시간의》 a break 《between tasks》; a spare moment.

**새창** the lower intestine of an ox.

**새척지근하다** (be) sourish.

**새총**(—銃) ①《공기총》 an air rifle 〔gun〕; 《엽총》 a fowling piece. ②《고무총》 a slingshot; a catapult 《영》.

**새출발**(—出發) a fresh start 〔departure〕. ~하다 make a fresh start 〔a new beginning〕; set out anew. ¶ 인생의 ~ a fresh start of the path of *one's* life.

**새치** prematurely gray(ing) hair; white 〔gray〕 hair in youth. ¶ ～가 나다 have gray hair appear while (*one* is still) young.

**새치기** ① 《차례 등의》 cutting in. ～하다 break 〔cut, shove〕 in. ¶ 줄선 틈바구니에 ～하다 break 〔cut〕 into the line; cut 〔push〕 in front of others; jump the queue 《영》 / 줄에 ～하지 마시오 Don't 「jump 〔cut in〕 the line. / 다른 차가 우리 앞에 ～못하게 해라 Don't let another car in front of us. ② ～하다 《본업 이외의 일을 하다》 do an odd job; take an extra 〔another〕 job; moonlight 《구어》.

**새치름하다** ① 《쌀쌀하게 시치미 떼다》 (be) prim and proper; cold and indifferent; standoffish; aloof; [서술적] assume 〔put on〕 a prim air. ¶ 새치름한 태도〔여자〕 a cold and prim attitude 〔girl〕 / 그녀는 새치름해서 게임에 끼어들지 않았다 She was too prim to join in our game. / 그녀는 언제나 ～ She is always prim and proper. ② 《불만으로》 (be) disgruntled; displeased; be not quite happy; be put out. ¶ 그녀는 사달라는 옷을 그가 안 사준다고 새치름해 있다 She is put out that he will not buy her the clothes she asks for.

**새치부리다** pretend to be disinclined; behave *oneself* with reserve; pretend diffidence; keep saying "no thank you". ¶ 새치부리지 말고 술 좀 마셔라 Can't I twist your arm into having a little more to drink?

**새침데기** a smug-looking 〔an affected〕 person; a prim-looking girl; a prim.

**새침하다** ⇨ 새치름하다.

**새카맣다** ⇨ 시커멓다.

**새콤-** ⇨ 새금-.

**새털** a feather; a plume; plumage [총칭]; 《솜털》 down. ◉ ～구름 a cirrus (*pl.* cirri) (cloud).

**새퉁스럽다** (be) absurd; ridiculous; silly.

**새퉁이** a flippant 〔silly〕 person 〔act〕. ¶ ～ 부리다 act silly.

**새파랗다** ① 《매우 파랗다》 (be) vivid 〔deep〕 blue; indigo; [비유적] (be) deadly 〔ghastly〕 pale; as white as a sheet. ¶ 새파란 하늘 the deep blue sky / 새파랗게 질리다 《*one's* face》 turn deadly pale 〔as white as a sheet〕 《with fright》 / 추워서 손이 새파랗게 얼었다 My hands are blue with cold. ② 《썩 젊다》 (be) young; green; [비유적] (be) inexperienced. ¶ 새파란 젊은이 a green youth; an inexperienced young fellow / 새파란 애송이가 무엇을 할 수 있단 말인가 What can a greenhorn do?

**새하얗다** (be) dazzling white; snow-white; pure-white. ¶ 새하얀 웨딩드레스 a pure-white wedding dress / 산은 눈으로 ～ The hills are white with snow. / 그녀의 피부는 눈처럼 ～ Her skin is as white as snow.

**새해** the New Year; a new year. ¶ ～를 맞이하다 see the new year in; greet the New Year / 묵은 해를 보내고 ～를 맞이하다 see the old year out and the new year in / ～에 복 많이 받으십시오 I wish you a happy New Year. *or* (A) Happy New Year!
◉ ～문안 New Year's greetings 〔wishes〕. ～전갈 sending New Year's greetings through a messenger to *one's* relatives. ～차례 an ancestor-memorial service on New Year's Day.

**새호리기** 〖조류〗 a hobby; a falcon.

**색**(色) ① 《빛깔》 (a) color; 《색조》 a hue; a tint; a tinge; a shade.

> **용법** **color**는 색을 나타내는 가장 일반적인 말. **hue**는 「색조」를 뜻하는 시적인 말. **tint**는 「미묘한 색조」. **shade**는 주로 「검은색의 농담의 정도」를 나타내는데, hue나 tint의 뜻으로도 쓰임.

¶ 색의 배합 a color scheme / 색의 조화 color harmony / 무지개의 색 the colors of the rainbow / 밝은 색 a bright color / 부드러운 색 a delicate color / 우중충한 색 a dark 〔sordid〕 color / 차분한 색 a subdued hue / 색이 진하다〔엷다〕 be of a deep 〔light〕 color; be deep-〔light-〕colored / 색을 내다 bring out the color / 색을 맞추다 match colors / 색이 날다〔바래다〕 be discolored; the color fades 〔runs〕 / 색이 변하다 change color; discolor / 색이 빠지다〔벗겨지다〕 the color comes off 〔out〕 / … 색을 띠다 be tinted 〔tinged〕 with 《red》 / 색을 입히다 color; tint; tinge / 개는 색을 분간 못한다 Dogs cannot see colors 〔see in color〕.
② 《그림물감의》 a color. ¶ 색을 바르다〔칠하다〕 color; paint; daub 《a wall》 with 《paint》.
③ 《정욕》 lust; sexual passion; sensual pleasure. ¶ 색을 좋아하다 be amorous 〔lustful〕; be lascivious; be sensual / 색에 빠지다 be lost in lust;

indulge in *one's* sexual desires. ◉ 색감각 〖물리·생리〗 color sensation. 색견본 a color sample; colorings. 색분해 〖물리〗 color separation.

**색** 《자루》 a sack; 《케이스》 a case; 《피임구》 a condom; a rubber 《속어》; 《손가락용》 a fingerstall; a thumbstall (엄지의). ¶ 색 드레스〔코트〕 a sack dress 〔coat〕.

**색각**(色覺) (a) color sense; color vision. ¶ ~ 이상(異常) dyschromatopsia.

**색갈다**(色—) make a change in; diversify; variegate; spread out.

**색감**(色感) the impression of a color (느낌); the color sense (감각); color vision. ⇨ 색각. ¶ ~이 날카롭다 have (very) keen color sense / 디자인과 ~이 다 좋다 It's good in both design and coloring.

**색골**(色骨) a lewd 〔lecherous〕 person; a sensual person; a satyr; a lecher.

**색광**(色光) 〖사진〗 colored light.

**색광**(色狂) a sex-crazed person; a sex maniac 〔fiend〕; an erotomaniac; a nymphomaniac (여자); a satyr (남자). ◉ ~증 sex(ual) mania 〔craze〕; erotomania.

**색깔**(色—) color. ⇨ 빛깔. ¶ 그 대회는 정치적 ~이 짙다 The rally has a strong political tinge.

**색다르다**(色—) be of a different cast 〔mold, pattern, appearance〕; (be) out of the ordinary; novel; different; unusual; strange; odd. ¶ 색다른 맛이 없는 common; commonplace; ordinary; stale / 색다른 것 a novelty; something out of the ordinary / 색다른 사람 a man of a different mold / 색다른 디자인 a novel design / 색다르게 보이다 look queer 〔strange〕 / 그녀는 색다른 복장을 하고 있었다 She (was) dressed in a singular fashion.

**색덕**(色德) (a lady's) beauty and virtue. ¶ ~을 갖추다 combine 〔have both〕 beauty and virtue.

**색도**(色度) chromaticity; 〖조명〗 chroma. ◉ ~도(圖) a chromaticity diagram. ~측정 colorimetry.

**색동**(色—) rainbow-striped cloth. ◉ ~옷 a rainbow-striped garment for children. ~저고리 a jacket with sleeves of many-colored stripes.

**색떡**(色—) colored rice cake.

**색마**(色魔) a sex maniac 〔fiend〕; a woman-hunter.

**색맹**(色盲) color blindness; achromatopsia. ¶ 적 ~ red blindness / 적록 ~ red-green (color) blindness; Daltonism / 전~ total color blindness; achromatopsia / 그는 ~이다 He is color-blind. ◉ ~검사 a color blindness test.

**색사진**(色寫眞) a color picture 〔photograph〕.

**색상**(色相) the tone of color; a color 「tone; a hue.

**색상**(色傷) 〖의학〗 illness resulting from the excesses of sex.

**색색** 《breathe》 in light little gasps. ¶ ~거리다 breathe lightly 〔softly〕 / ~잠을 자다 sleep sweetly 〔calmly, peacefully〕.

**색색이**(色色—) with 〔in〕 various 〔divers〕 colors. ¶ ~ 물들이다 dye 《cloth》 in various colors.

**색소**(色素) coloring matter; 〖생물〗 (a) pigment. ¶ ~의 pigmental; pigmentary / 식용 ~ food colors. ◉ ~결핍증 〖의학〗 albinism. ~세포 〖생물〗 a pigment 〔pigmentary〕 cell; a chromatophore. ~체 〖생물〗 a plastid: ~체

참고 **주요 색의 이미지와 그 어구들**

검은색 black: 슬픔·악·절망·어둠 따위
black art 악마술, black money 부당이익, a black sheep 골칫거리, blackout 정전, black-hearted 사악한.

흰색 white: 청순·공정·순진·항복 따위
a white lie 악의없는 거짓말, a white day 좋은 날, a white flag 백기.

적색 red: 정열·축하·위험·좌익 따위
red-hot 흥분한, see red 화내다, a red-letter day 축일, a red idea 좌익 사상, He was treated to the red carpet. (그는 성대한 환영을 받았다.)

청색 blue: 희망·최우수·우울 따위
a blue blood 고귀한 태생, a blue chip 우량주, the blues (음악의) 블루스, He looks blue today. (그는 오늘 우울해 보인다.)

녹색 green: 젊음·안전·질투 따위
a greenhorn 풋내기, a green light 청신호, green-eyed 질투심에 찬.

자주색 purple: 고귀·미사여구·격노 따위
He married a woman who was born to the purple. (신분이 높은 집안의 여자와 결혼했다.)

분홍색 pink: 건강·활력 따위
She is in the pink (of health). (그녀는 매우 건강하다.)

유전 plastid inheritance / ～체 유전자 plastogene. ～층 〖해부〗 a pigment layer.

**색소폰** 《악기》 a saxophone. ◉ ～주자 a saxophonist; a saxophone player.

**색수차**(色收差) 〖광학〗 chromatic aberration; chromatism.

**색스혼** 〖악기〗 a saxhorn.

**색시** ① 《처녀》 a maiden; a girl; an unmarried woman. ② 《새색시》 a bride. ¶ ～를 얻다 take 〔get〕 a wife; get married. ③ 《접대부》 a hostess; a waitress; a barmaid.
◉ 색싯감 a likely 〔prospective〕 bride.

**색신검사**(色神檢査) an examination of the color sense; 《have》 a color test.

**색실**(色—) colored thread.

**색심**(色心) ① 《정욕의》 sensual 〔sexual〕 desire; a lustful soul. ② 〖불교〗 Matter and Mind.

**색쓰다**(色—) ① 《성교하다》 have sex 〔sexual relations〕; 《교태짓다》 sex up; play the coquette. ② ＝사정하다.

**색안경**(色眼鏡) 《a pair of》 colored glasses; sunglasses; shades 《속어》; [비유적] unfairly prejudiced 〔biased〕 view. ¶ ～을 쓰다 wear colored glasses / ～을 쓰고 보다 look on 《*things*》 「with a jaundiced eye 〔from a biased viewpoint〕.

**색약**(色弱) 〖의학〗 color weakness; dyschromatopsia. ¶ ～이다 be color=weak.

**색연필**(色鉛筆) a colored pencil; a grease pencil.

**색욕**(色慾) sexual appetite; sexual 〔carnal〕 desire; lust; a craving for sex. ¶ ～이 일어나다 be seized with sexual passion / ～을 만족시키다 gratify *one's* lust / ～을 삼가다 keep down *one's* carnal desire.

**색유리**(色琉璃) stained 〔colored〕 glass.

**색인**(索引) an index (*pl.* ～es, -dices). ¶ 카드식〔ABC순〕 ～ a card 〔an alphabetical〕 index / ～이 있는〔없는〕 책 an indexed 〔unindexed, indexless〕 book / ～을 달다 index 《a book》; provide 《book》 with an index / 이 책은 ～이 잘 되어 있다 This book is well 〔fully〕 indexed. ◉ ～카드 an index card.

**색전증**(塞栓症) 〖의학〗 embolism.

**색정**(色情) sexual urge(s); sexual passion; sexual 〔carnal, lustful〕 desire; lust. ¶ ～적인 소설 a suggestive 〔lascivious〕 novel / ～을 도발〔자극〕하다 excite 〔provoke, stimulate〕 *one's* sexual desire. ◉ ～광 ＝색광(色狂). ～탐닉 sexual indulgence.

**색조**(色調) the tone of color; a color tone; shade; 〖미술〗 tonality. ¶ 차가운〔선명한, 밝은, 칙칙한〕 ～ a cool 〔vivid, light, dull〕 tone / 침침한 ～의 그림 a picture painted in low key / 갖가지 ～의 파란 색 various shades of blue / 나는 이 그림의 부드러운 초록 ～가 좋다 I like the soft green tone of this painting.

**색종이**(色—) colored paper. ¶ ～접기 folding colored paper into various figures.

**색주가**(色酒家) ① 《창녀》 a loose barmaid; a prostitute. ② 《술집》 a shady bar 〔saloon〕; a bar-whorehouse combinaton.

**색채**(色彩) a color; a tint; a hue; coloring; 《기미》 a tinge; a tincture. ¶ 현란한〔야한〕 ～ flamboyant 〔loud〕 colors / 지방적 ～ a local color / 공산주의의 ～를 띤 with a communistic leaning; with a tendency to communism / 정치적 ～가 있는 politically=tinged 《trade》; 《a decision》 with political overtones 〔implications〕 / 정치적 ～가 없는 《a club》 with no political affiliations / ～가 풍부하다 be full of colors; be colorful / ～를 가하다 color; give coloring 《to》 / … ～를 띠고 있다 be tinged 〔tinctured〕 with... / ～를 띠다 take 〔put〕 on color 〔tints〕 / ～를 강하게〔약하게〕 하다 heighten 〔dull〕 the color / 그 풍속에는 종교적 ～가 있다 The custom has a religious color. / 그 시장은 정당 ～가 짙다 The mayor has a strong party coloring.
◉ ～감각 color sensation; 《심미안》 (a) color sense. ～파 the colorists. ～학 chromatics; chromatology. ～효과 a color effect.

**색출**(索出) ～하다 search 〔seek, ferret〕 out; hunt up; detect. ¶ 도망자를 ～하다 ferret out a fugitive / 경찰은 범인을 ～했다 The police ferreted out the criminal.

**색칠**(色漆) coloring; painting. ～하다 color; paint. ¶ 지도를〔그림을〕 ～하다 color a map 〔picture〕.

**색탐**(色貪) lust; lewd 〔lecherous〕 desire. ～하다 lust (for sex).

**색향**(色香) 《색과 향》 color and scent; 《미색》 the beauty 〔charms〕 of a woman.

**샌님** ① 《생원》 ⇨생원(生員). ② 《얌전한 사람》 a meek 〔prudish〕 fellow; [비유적] a weak-kneed and bigoted person; 《보수적인 사람》 a person with conservative views.

**샌드** 《모래》 sand. ◉ ～백 a sandbag. ～스톰 〖기상〗 a sandstorm. ～페이퍼 《a piece of》 sandpaper.

**샌드위치** sandwiches. ¶ 햄～ ham sandwiches. ◉ ～맨 a sandwich man: ～맨의 광고판 sandwich boards.

**샌들** 《a pair of》 sandals; sandal shoes. ¶ ～을 신은 사람 a sandaled person.

**샌디에이고** 《미국의 항구》 San Diego.

**샌프란시스코** 《미국의 도시》 San Francisco(생략 Frisco). ◉ ～시민 a San Franciscan.

**샐러드** (a) salad. ¶ 야채〔닭고기〕～ a vegetable 〔chicken〕 salad / 햄～ ham and salad / ～를 만들다 make 〔prepare〕 a salad. ◉ ～그릇 a salad bowl. ～드레싱 salad dressing. ～유 salad oil.

**샐러리** a salary (★ 한달이나 그 이상 정기적으로 지급되는 봉급). ¶ 월 백만원의 ～를 받다 draw 〔get, receive〕 a salary of one million won a month. ◉ ～맨 a salaried man (★ a salary man은 오용); an office worker; a white-collar worker: ～맨 계층 the salaried class; the salariate.

**샐비어** 〖식물〗 a salvia; a (scarlet) sage.

**샘**[1] ① 《물이 솟는》 a spring; a fountain. ¶ 지식의 샘 a font 〔fount〕 of knowledge / 콸콸 내솟는 샘 a gushing spring / 샘이 콸콸 솟고 있다 A fountain is gushing out. /샘이 말랐다 The spring has run dry. ② 〖해부〗 a gland. ¶ 눈물샘 a lachrymal gland. ◉ 샘물 spring water: 샘물 줄기 a stream of spring water.

**샘**[2] 《시기》 jealousy; (green) envy. ～하다 envy 《another》; be jealous 〔envious〕 《of another's success》; feel envy 《of *a person*》. ¶ 샘 많은 envious; jealous / 샘이 나서 from 〔out of 〕 jealousy / 샘이 나다 feel 〔become〕 jealous / 샘을 내다 show jealousy ⇨ 샘하다 / 샘을 받다 be envied; become an object of jealousy / 샘이 나서 못 견디다 be burning with jealousy / 그녀는 친구의 행운에 샘이 났다 She was jealous of her friend's good fortune.
◉ 샘바리 a jealous 〔an envious〕 person.

**샘**[3] 《지대공 미사일》 SAM. 〔< *s*urface-to=*a*ir *m*issile〕

**샘솟다** gush 〔spring〕 out 〔forth〕; well up. ¶ 샘솟듯 흘러 나오다 gush out like a spring / 눈물이 ～ tears well up in *one's* eyes / 찬물이 바위 틈에서 샘솟고 있었다 Cold water was gushing out between rocks.

**샘터** a fountain(-site). ¶ ～에서 빨래하다 do *one's* washing at the fountain.

**샘플** a sample; a specimen. ¶ ～대로 나오다 come up to sample / 당신 회사 제품의 ～을 몇 개 가져오시오 Bring some samples of your firm's product. ◉ ～케이스 a sample case.

**샘플링** 《견본의》 sampling. ◉ ～검사 sampling (inspection).

**샛-** 《빛깔이》 vivid; deep; intense. ¶ 샛노랗다 (be) deep-yellow.

**샛강**(―江) a tributary (stream); a branch. ¶ 한강의 ～ a branch 〔tributary〕 of the Han river.

**샛길** a byway; a byroad; a by-path; a narrow path. ¶ 이 ～로 가면 30분 단축된다 If you take this byroad, you can save 30 minutes.

**샛문**(門―) a side gate 〔door〕.

**샛바람** an east(erly) wind.

**샛밥** ① 《곁두리》 snack (for farmhands). ② 《끼니 외의》 a snack; a meal taken at an irregular time.

**샛별** the morning star; Lucifer; Venus.

**샛서방**(―書房) a paramour; a (woman's) secret lover. ¶ ～을 보다 cuckold 〔be unfaithful to〕 *one's* husband.

**생**(生) ① 《생명·삶》 living; life; existence. ¶ 생과 사(死) life and death / 생에 집착하다 cling to life / 조용히 생을 마감하다 end *one's* life in peace. ② 《교정용어》 stet (생략 st.).

**생-**(生) ① 《조리하지 않은》 raw 《fish》; uncooked; 《안 익은》 green; unripe; 《설익은》 underdone; half-boiled; rare; 《가공하지 않은》 crude; unprocessed; natural; wild; 《신선한》 fresh 《vegetables》. ¶ 생것 raw food / 생고기 raw meat / 생고무 crude 〔raw〕 rubber / 생굴 a raw oyster / 생과실 unripe 〔green〕 fruits / 생우유 raw milk / 생필름 raw film. ② 《살아 있는》 live; living; alive. ¶ 생나무 a live tree; green wood / 생지옥 a hell on earth / 생매장 당하다 be buried alive. ③ 《엉뚱한》 unreasonable; irrational; arbitrary; forced. ¶ 생돈 money spent to no purpose / 생벼락 unreasonable scolding; undeserved misfortune / 생트집 a false charge 〔accusation〕 / 생사람 잡다 inflict injury upon an innocent person. ④ 《녹화·녹음이 아닌》 live. ¶ 생방송 live broadcasting. ⇨ 생방송.

**-생**(生) ① 《청년》 young man's title. ¶ 김생 young Mr. Kim. ② 《학생》 a student 《of》…. ¶ 의학생 a medical student. ③《생년의》 born in《a year》. ④《식물의》 ¶ 일년생〔다년생〕 식물 an annual 〔a perennial〕 plant.

**생가**(生家) the house of *one's* birth; the house where *one* was born; *one's* paternal 〔parents'〕 home.

**생가슴**(生—) a needlessly troubled breast 〔soul〕. ¶～ 앓다, ～ 뜯다, ～ 태우다 be needlessly troubled 〔upset〕.

**생가죽**(生—) rawhide; undressed hide; raw pelt.

**생가지**(生—) a live branch 〔twig〕.

**생각** ①《사고》 thinking; 《사상》 (a) thought; ideas; 《심사·숙고》 deliberation; meditation; reflection. ¶ ～ 끝에 on reflection / 진보적인 ～ progressive ideas / 가슴속 깊이 간직한 ～ *one's* intimate thoughts / ～에 잠기다 be lost 〔buried, sunk〕 in (*one's*) thought; be in deep thought / 아무와 ～을 같이하다 think with 《*a person*》 / ～을 메모해 두다 put *one's* thoughts on paper / ～을 고치다 revise *one's* thinking / ～을 전하다 convey *one's* thoughts 《to》 / ～을 정리하다 collect *one's* thoughts; put *one's* ideas into shape; shape up *one's* ideas / ～이 상대에게 통하다 have *one's* ideas communicated to another; get *one's* ideas across / ～만 해도 지겹다 It makes me sick to think of it. / ～만 해도 오싹해진다 My flesh crawls to think of it. *or* I shudder at the very thought of it.

②《관념·착상》 an idea; a notion; a conception; a thought; 《계획》 a plan; 《창의》 initiative. ¶ 멋진〔좋은〕 ～ a capital 〔bright, happy〕 idea; a happy thought / 묘한〔색다른〕 ～ a queer notion 〔idea〕 / 어리석은 ～ a foolish idea; a silly notion / 잘못된 ～ an erroneous 〔a false, a wrong〕 idea; a mistaken notion / …이라는 ～은 일체 물리치다 reject any thought that... / ～을 고치다 modify *one's* idea / ～이 떠오르다 come 〔flit, flash〕 across 〔into〕 *one's* mind; come into *one's* head; occur to *one* / 자신의 ～으로 하다 do 《*something*》 upon *one's* own initiative / …하다는 ～을 품다 foster 〔harbor〕 the idea that...; have a notion that... / 좋은 ～이 떠올랐다 A bright idea occurred to me. *or* I hit upon a capital idea.

③《…하려는》 (***a***) 《의도》 an intention; a design; an idea; a view; an aim; a motive (동기). ¶ 아무 ～ 없이 with no definite idea / …할 ～으로 with a view to 《*do*ing》; with the intention of 《*do*ing》 / 군인이 될 ～ the idea of becoming a soldier / ～을 품다 cherish an intention; conceive an idea / ～을 실행에 옮기다 carry out *one's* intention; translate *one's* thought into action / 사직할 ～은 없다 I have 「no intention to resign 〔no thought of resigning〕.

(***b***) 《마음》 mind; sense; heart; 《기분·감정》 feelings; (a) sentiment. ¶ ～이 들다 feel; have a feeling 《that...》 / …하고 싶은 ～이 들다 feel inclined to *do* 《*something*》; feel like 《*do*ing》 / ～이 바뀌다 change 〔alter〕 *one's* mind / 사과 ～이 나다 feel like (having) an apple / …하려는 ～을 일으키다 think of 《*do*ing》; take it into *one's* head to 《*do*》 / …할 ～이 있다 have a mind 《to *do*》; have an idea of 《*do*ing》 / 그렇게 할 ～은 없다 have no mind to do so / 품은 ～은 입으로 나온다 What the heart thinks, mouth speaks.

④《의견》 an opinion; a view; *one's* point of view; 《신념》 a belief; 《인상》 an impression; 《제안》 a suggestion. ¶ 내 ～으로는 in my opinion 〔view〕; to my mind 〔thinking〕 / 인생에 대한 ～ *one's* view 〔philosophy〕 of life / 그 일에 대한 나의～ my opinion 〔thought〕 of the matter / ～을 말하다 express 〔give〕 *one's* opinion 〔views〕; make a suggestion / ～을 바꾸다 change *one's* point of view; view 《*a thing*》 from another 〔a different〕 angle / 자네 ～은 어떤가 What is your opinion? *or* What do you say to that? / 나는 네 ～과 다르다〔같다〕 I have 「a different opinion from yours 〔the same opinion as you〕. / 내 ～은 그렇지 않다 I think otherwise. / 그에게는 그 나름대로의 ～이 있을 것이다 He may have an opinion of his own.

⑤《사려·분별》 discretion; prudence; 《판단》 (good) judgment. ¶ ～ 있는 thoughtful; discreet; prudent / ～ 없는 thoughtless; indiscreet; imprudent / (앞뒤) ～ 없이 thoughtlessly; recklessly; rashly / ～없이 일을 하다 do 《*something*》 thoughtlessly / 자기 ～에 따라 행동하다 act on *one's* own discretion / 이 일은 네 ～대로 해라 I leave this matter to your discretion 〔good judgment〕. / 내 혼자 ～으로 결정할 수가 없다 I can't decide it (either way) at my own discretion.

⑥《예상》 expectation; hope; 《소원》

(a) wish; desire; 《그리움》 longing. ¶ ~대로 as *one* likes 〔pleases, thinks fit, desires, wishes〕; in *one's* own way; after *one's* own heart / ~밖의〔지 않은〕 unexpected; least expected; unforeseen; unanticipated; unlooked=for; casual; accidental / ~지 않은 사람 an unexpected person / ~지 않은 일 an unexpected happening; an unforeseen occurrence / 임 ~이 나다 long for *one's* sweetheart / ~대로 되다 meet *one's* expectation; come 〔measure〕 up to *one's* expectation; turn out as *one* has figured / ~이 이루어지다 realize 〔fulfill〕 *one's* wishes; have 〔get〕 *one's* wish (realized); attain *one's* desire / 결과가 ~대로 되었다 The results turned out just as I expected. ⑦ 《상상》 imagination; fancy (공상); supposition (가정); a guess (추측). ¶ ~도 할 수 없는 unimaginable; unthinkable / 엉뚱한 ~ an extravagant flight of fancy / ~이 맞다〔틀리다〕 guess right 〔wrong〕 / 그런 일은 꿈에도 ~하지 못했다 I never dreamed of it. ⑧ 《기억·회상》 memory; recollection; remembrance. ¶ ~이 나다 remember; recall; have the recollection / 옛 ~을 더듬다 trace back in memory / 어릴 때의 ~이 아직도 뚜렷이 남아 있다 I still have a clear 〔vivid〕 memory of my boyhood 〔childhood〕. / 그 노래를 들으니 옛 ~이 난다 The song carries me back to the old days. ⑨ 《고려》 consideration; thought; regard; 《참작》 allowance. ¶ ~이 깊은 considerate; thoughtful / …에 대하여 ~을 하지 않다 do not take 《*something*》 into consideration; take no account of 《*something*》 / 이것에 대해 ~해 주십시오 Please take this into consideration. ⑩ 《각오·결의》 a resolution; *one's* mind. ¶ ~을 정하다 decide 《to *do*》; make up *one's* mind 《to *do,* to an act》 / 네가 그렇게 나온다면 이쪽에도 ~이 있다 Two can play at that game. *or* That's a game that two can play.

**생각건대** in my opinion; to my mind 〔thinking〕; I think that…; It seems to me that…. ¶ ~ 그들은 실패할 것이다 In my opinion they will fail. / ~ 인생이란 꿈에 불과하다 When we think of it, life is nothing but a dream.

**생각나다** [사물이 주어] come to mind 〔*one's* recollection〕; occur to *one* 〔*one's* mind〕; be reminded of; [사람이 주어] call 〔bring〕 to mind; think of; 《생각이 떠오르다》 hit upon 《an new idea》; flash on. ¶ 생각나게 하다 remind 《*a person*》 of 《*something*》; suggest 《an idea》 to 《*a person*》; be suggestive of; recall 《*a thing*》 to 《*a person's*》 mind / 어린 시절이 ~ be reminded of *one's* childhood / 그의 이름이 생각나지 않는다 His name does not come to mind. / 너를 보니 내 동생이 생각난다 You remind me 〔put me in mind〕 of my brother.

**생각다못해** at *one's* wit's 〔wits'〕 end; at the end of *one's* tether. ¶ ~ 그는 아버지에게 진실을 털어놓았다 He told his father the truth because he was at his wit's end.

**생각되다** ① 《…으로 보이다》 look; seem 《to be》; appear 《to be》; 《…으로 들리다》 sound; 《인상을 주다》 strike 〔impress〕 《*a person*》 as. ¶ 비가 올 것 같이 생각된다 It looks 〔seems〕 like rain. / 정말이라고 생각된다 It certainly looks true. ② 《여겨지다》 be thought of 《as》; be supposed; be considered (as); 《간주되다》 be regarded 《as》. ¶ 좋게〔나쁘게〕 ~ be well 〔ill〕 thought of 《by others》.

**생각하다** ① 《사고하다》 think 《of, on, about, over》; consider; give (a) thought to; 《…이 아닌가 하고》 suspect; 《…은 아닐 것으로》 doubt. ¶ 생각할 수 있는 thinkable; conceivable / 생각할 수 없는 unthinkable; inconceivable / 생각해야할 일 something to think about / 잘 ~ think well of / 잘못 ~ think badly 〔ill〕 of / 아무리 생각해 보아도 however hard I may think; by any reckoning / 얼핏 생각하면 at first thought; on a moment's thought / 앞일을 ~ think of 〔about〕 the future / 천천히 ~ take time to think / 혼자〔마음속으로〕 ~ think 〔say〕 to *oneself* / 생각해 보다 give 《it》 a thought / 무언가 생각하고 있다 have something on *one's* mind / 나 역시 그렇게 생각한다 I think so, too. / 좀 생각해 보렴 Just 〔Only〕 think about it. / 네 말이 옳다고 생각한다 I think you are right. / 대답하기 전에 생각 좀 하게 해주시오 Let me ｢think over 〔sleep on〕 the matter before giving my answer. / 나는 그가 사기꾼이 아닌가 생각했다 I suspected that he might be an imposter. / 그것은 생각하기도 싫다 I dislike the very thought of it. / 그가 정직하다고 생각한다 I think 〔consider〕 him (to be) honest 〔an

honest man]. / 생각하면 할수록 더 모르겠다 The more I think, the more puzzled I am. / 나는 미국 유학을 생각하고 있다 I am thinking about studying in America.
② 《숙고하다》 consider; think 〔ponder〕 over 《*a matter*》; deliberate on; weigh (비교 검토해서); meditate; muse on. ¶ 곰곰이 ~ think seriously; give 《*a matter*》 much thought / 잘 생각해서 결정하다 weigh well before deciding / 잘 생각하고 말해야 한다 Consider carefully before you speak. *or* You must weigh your words.
③ 《의도하다》 intend to 《*do*》; think of 《*doing*》; have 《*something*》 in mind; plan to 《*do*》. ¶ 내년에 미국에 가려고 생각한다 I intend to go 〔I am thinking of going〕 to America next year. / 아버지는 나를 화가로 만들려고 생각한다 Father intends me to be a painter.
④ 《의견·견해를 갖다》 view 《*a thing*》; be of (the) opinion 《that...》. ¶ 내가 생각하기로는 in my view / 일을 깊이〔겉면만〕 ~ have a deep 〔superficial〕 view of things / 그 문제는 여러 가지로 생각할 수 있다 The subject may be viewed in different ways. / 나는 그들이 실패할 것이라고 생각한다 I am of the opinion that they will fail.
⑤ 《판단하다》 judge; conclude figure; 《오인하다》 take 〔mistake〕 for. ¶ 그의 말로써 생각해 보면 judging from his statement / 아무리 생각해도 to the best of *one's* judgment / …라고 ~ it is my judgment that... / 나는 그를 정직한 사람이라고 생각한다 I judge 〔figure〕 him to be an honest man. / 처음에 나는 그녀를 미국 사람이라고 생각했다 At first I took 〔mistook〕 her for an American. / 첫눈에 나는 그를 사기꾼으로 생각했다 At a glance I concluded him to be a swindler.
⑥ 《믿다》 believe; hold; be convinced; be sure 《of, that》. ¶ 옳다고 ~ believe 《it》 to be right / 신이 존재한다고 생각합니까 Do you believe in God? / 그는 꼭 올 것이라고 생각한다 I'm sure that he will come.
⑦ 《예기하다》 expect; anticipate; hope (for). ¶ 생각한 대로 as *one* expected 〔feared〕 / 생각지 않은 unexpected; unlooked-for / 생각지 않은 실수를 하다 meet with an unexpected failure / 생각했던 것보다 일이 쉬웠다 The work was easier than I had expected. / 결과는 생각한 대로였다 The result met my expectation. / 그는 우리가 생각했던 대로 최선을 다했다 He did the best we could hope for.
⑧ 《바라다》 wish 《that...》; desire 《to *do*, that...》; want 《to *do*》. ¶ 생각한 대로 as *one* wishes; to *one's* satisfaction / 일이 생각하는 대로 되지 않는다 Things do not 「turn out 〔go〕 as I wish. / 그는 늘 큰 집을 가졌으면 하고 생각했다 He always wanted to have a large house.
⑨ 《고려하다》 consider; consult 《*one's* own interests, convenience》; take 《*a matter*》 into consideration 〔account〕; 《참작하다》 make allowance for. ¶ 남을 ~ consider others / 비용을 ~ take the expenses into consideration / 이것들은 특별히 생각해야 할 점이다 These are the points to be specially considered. / 그가 아직 젊다는 것을 생각해 주어야 한다 You must make allowance for his youth. / 그건 생각해 볼 문제다 It is a matter for consideration.
⑩ 《염려하다》 fear; be afraid 《of》; 《걱정하다》 concern *oneself* about; worry (*oneself*) about. ¶ 먼 훗날의 일까지 ~ concern *oneself* about the distant future / 오후에 비가 오지 않을까 생각한다 I'm afraid it will rain this afternoon. / 내 건강을 생각해 주어 고맙다 Thank you for your concern about my health.
⑪ 《상상·추측하다》 imagine; picture 《to *oneself*》; think; suppose; fancy; guess. ¶ 생각할 수 없는 unimaginable; unthinkable / 생각하는 바와 같이 as *one* suppose / 아무리 생각해 보아도 by any stretch of the imagination / 좀 생각해 봐라 Just imagine! / 나는 그가 나이를 훨씬 더 먹었을 것이라고 생각했다 I imagined him to be much older. / 나는 그가 집에 있을 것이라고 생각했다 I supposed he was at home.
⑫ 《기억·회상하다》 recall; remember; recollect; look back upon 《the past》; 《반성하다》 reflect (up)on 《*one's* deed》; reconsider. ¶ 그녀는 전쟁 전 시절을 생각했다 She looked back upon the days before the war. / 그를 어디서인가 만났던 것으로 생각한다 I remember seeing him somewhere. / 요즈음은 종종 고향 마을을 생각한다 These days my mind often travels back to my native village.
⑬ 《각오·준비하다》 be prepared for; be ready 《for, to *do*》; provide against.

¶ 최악의 경우를 ~ prepare for the worst / 그는 장래의 일을 생각하여 돈을 저축하고 있다 He is saving money for the future.

⑭ 《간주하다》 regard 〔deem〕 《as》; take 《*a thing* as 〔for〕》; look (up)on 《as》; consider 《*a person* to be》; reckon 《*a person* to be》; count 《as》. ¶ 아무를 좋게〔나쁘게〕 ~ think well 〔ill〕 of *a person* / 그것을 명예로 ~ regard it as an honor / 나는 그를 은인으로 생각한다 I regard him as my benefactor.

⑮ 《염두에 두다》 think of; be interested in. ¶ 아무렇지도 않게 ~ do not care a bit 〔straw〕 《about》; pay no attention 《to》; do not feel for 《*a person*》 at all / 그는 고향에 두고 온 자식을 생각했다 He thought of the child he had left at home.

⑯ 《그리워하다》 yearn after 〔to, for〕; long for; 《사랑하다》 love; care for. ¶ 고향을 ~ yearn for *one's* home / 그는 그녀를 진심으로 생각한다 He loves her in his heart. / 세상에 자식을 생각하지 않는 부모가 있습니까 Are there any parents in the world who don't love their children?

⑰ 《느끼다》 feel; feel like. ¶ 행복하다고〔슬프다고〕 ~ feel happy 〔sad〕 / 잘못 대답하고 나는 바보가 아닌가 생각했다 I felt like an idiot when I answered wrong.

⑱ 《반성하다》 reconsider; reflect (up) on. ¶ 네가 한 짓을 생각해 보아라 Reflect upon 〔Reconsider〕 what you have done. / 생각해보니 내가 역시 잘못했다 On reflection, I must admit I was wrong.

**생각해내다** ① 《안출하다》 think out 《a plan》; think of 《an idea》; devise 《new products》; contrive 《a thing》; think up 《an excuse》; work out 《a scheme》; invent. ¶ 도망칠 방법을 ~ contrive a way to escape / 일을 할 방법을 ~ think out a way of doing the work.
② 《상기(想起)하다》 remember; recall; recollect; be reminded of.

**생강**(生薑) 〚식물〛 a ginger plant; 《향신료》 ginger. ◉ ~빵 ginger bread. ~즙 ginger juice. ~차 ginger tea.

**생거름**(生—) raw manure; unmixed fertilizer.

**생것**(生—) raw food. ⇨ 날것.

**생견**(生絹) raw silk.

**생경**(生硬) ~하다 (be) raw; crude; immature; unrefined; stiff. ¶ ~한 문장 a crude piece of writing / ~한 번역 an unrefined 〔unpolished〕 translation.

**생계**(生計) livelihood; living. ¶ ~가 막연하다 have no means of livelihood / ~를 돕다 contribute to 《*a person's*》 support / ~를 세우다 make *one's* living 《by》; get a living / 그녀는 부업으로 부모님의 ~를 돕고 있다 She helps her parents with their living expenses by working part-time.
◉ ~비 living costs; living expenses; the cost of living: ~비 수당 a cost-of-living allowance / ~비 지수 an index of living costs; a cost-of-living index. ~수단 a means of living. ~유지자 a family supporter; the bread earner; the breadwinner.

**생고무**(生—) raw 〔crude〕 rubber.

**생과부**(生寡婦) a divorced 〔neglected, separated〕 wife; a grass widow.

**생과실**(生果實) unripe fruit; raw fruit.

**생과자**(生菓子) (a) cake; (a) pastry.

**생굴**(生—) a raw 〔fresh〕 oyster.

**생글거리다** smile gently 〔affably〕.

**생긋** ¶ ~ 웃다 smile sweetly 《at》; grin.

**생기**(生氣) animation; (vivid) life; vitality; vigor; spirit. ¶ ~ 없는 얼굴 a face 「with no 〔lacking in, devoid of〕 animation / ~가 있다 be animated 〔vital, lively, spirited〕; 《문장이》 be crisp / ~가 없다 be lifeless 〔spiritless, dull, inanimate〕 / ~발랄하다 be energetic 〔vigorous, vivacious, full of life〕 / ~를 주다 invigorate; give life 〔animation〕 《to》; put 〔infuse〕 life 《into》; enliven; vitalize / ~를 되찾다 come to life; be revitalized.

**생기다** ① 《없던 것이》 come into being 〔existence〕; spring (up); 《형성되다》 form; take shape. ¶ 좋은〔나쁜〕 습관이 ~ form good 〔bad〕 habits / 전쟁 후 새로운 국가가 많이 생겼다 A lot of new nations 「came into existence 〔were born〕 after the war. / 용기는 신념에서 생긴다 Courage springs from conviction. / 비가 와서 군데군데 웅덩이가 생겼다 Pools were formed at places owing to the rain. / 무에서 유는 생기지 않는다 Nothing comes out of nothing.
② 《발생하다》 (***a***) 《일어나다》 happen; occur; take place; come about 〔up〕; 《전쟁·화재 등이》 break out. ¶ 무슨 일이 생기더라도 whatever may happen; no matter what happen / (무슨 일이) 생길 것 같다 be likely (to happen); be in 〔on〕 the cards / 그에게 무슨 일이 생겼는가 Did anything happen to

him? / 결원이 생겼다 A vacancy occurred. / 그들간에 알력이 생겼다 Quarrels broke out among them. / 무슨 일이 생기면 나에게 알려 주시오 If anything happens, please let me know. (**b**) 《기인하다》 arise 〔stem〕 《from》; result 《from》; originate 《in》. ¶ 홍수로 생긴 피해 the damage resulting from the flood / 오해에서 생긴 불화 a discord which originated in a misunderstanding / 인플레이션으로 인해 생기는 여러 문제 various issues stemming from the inflation / 과로로 병이 ~ get ill by overwork; fall ill from overwork / 그 병은 여러 가지 원인으로 생긴다 The disease arises from various causes. (**c**) 《이자 등이》 accrue 《from》. ¶ 땅에서 생기는 이익 profits accruing from landed property.
③ 《얻다》 obtain; get; come by. ¶ 일거리가 ~ get 〔find〕 a job / 돈이 ~ come into money.
④ 《친구가》 make 《a friend》; 《애인이》 have 《a girl friend》. ¶ 나쁜 친구가 ~ get into bad company / 그녀는 애인이 생긴 것 같다 She seems to have found a lover.
⑤ 《아기가》 be born; have 《a baby》. ¶ 아기가 ~ 《임신하다》 get pregnant; 《낳다》 have a new baby / 둘 사이에 아이가 생겼다 A child was born to them.
⑥ 《얼굴·모습이》 look; have looks 〔appearance〕. ¶ 잘〔못〕~ have good 〔bad, plain〕 looks / 정직하게〔이상하게〕 ~ look honest 〔funny〕 / 그 사람이 어떻게 생겼나 What is he like?

**생김새** 《용모》 features; looks; 《겉모양》 (an) appearance; 《형상》 (a) form; (a) shape. ¶ ~가 좋은 well-shaped / ~가 사내답다 look manly / ~가 좋다 〔흉하다〕 have nice 〔ugly〕 looks / 그는 얼굴 ~가 반듯하다 He has regular features.

**생나무**(生—) 《살아 있는》 a live tree; 《설마른》 unseasoned timber 〔wood〕; 《생목》 green wood; wet fagot 〔wood〕. ¶ ~를 베다 cut down a live tree.

**생남**(生男) the birth of a son; delivery of a boy. ~하다 give birth to a son; beget 〔be delivered of〕 a boy. ◉ ~턱 〔례〕 celebration of the birth of *one's* son; "handing out cigars".

**생녀**(生女) the birth of a daughter; delivery of a daughter 〔girl〕. ~하다 give birth to a daughter; be delivered of a girl.

**생년**(生年) the year of *one's* birth. ◉ ~월일(시) the date (and hour) of *one's* birth: ~월일을 쓰다 put down the date of *one's* birth.

**생니**(生—) a healthy 〔good〕 tooth.

**생담배**(生—) a lighted cigarette left lying in the ash tray; a burning cigarette.

**생도**(生徒) =학생. ¶ 사관~ a cadet; 《해군의》 a midshipman.

**생돈**(生—) money spent to no purpose. ¶ ~을 쓰다〔날리다〕 waste 〔throw away〕 *one's* money 《on》.

**생동**(生動) being full of life; animation; lifelikeness; vividness. ~하다 be full of life; be animated; be lifelike 〔vivid〕. ¶ 봄에는 만물이 ~한다 In spring everything is fresh and vivid. / 이 초상화는 ~하는 것 같다 This portrait looks so lifelike.

**생동**(生銅) unrefined copper; native copper.

**생득**(生得) ¶ ~의 inborn; innate 《talent》. ◉ ~관념 〖철학〗 innate ideas. ~권 *one's* birthright. ~설 〖철학〗 nativism.

**생때같다**(生—) (be) healthy; robust; fine and dandy; be spanking 《구어》.

**생떼**(生—) insistent 〔perverse〕 asking; obduracy; perversity. ¶ ~를 쓰다 stubbornly persist 《in》; stick to 《it》 doggedly; act perversely.

**생략**(省略) (an) omission; 〖문법〗 (an) ellipsis (*pl.* -ses); 《간략화》 (an) abbreviation; (an) abridgment. ~하다 omit 〔leave out〕 《the chapter》; 《줄이다》 abbreviate; abridge; shorten.

> 용법 **omission** 어구 따위의 문자를 생략하여 짧게 하는 것. **ellipsis** 문법적인 용어: if it is possible → if possible 로 하는 따위. **abbreviation** 책·이야기·낱말 따위의 내용을 바꾸지 않고 요약하는 것: 'Sept' is an abbreviation of 'September.' **abridgment** 흔히 가산명사로는 책·각본 따위의 「간약판·초록·적요 등」의 뜻. 불가산 명사로는 축소·요약 하는 행위.

¶ ~할 수 있는 omissible / ~하여 in abbreviated form; for short / ~하지 않고 in full; without abridgment / 이하 ~ The rest is omitted. / 1998년을 ~하여 '98이라고 쓴다 The year 1998 is abbreviated as '98.
◉ ~문 an elliptical sentence. ~법 〖문법〗 ellipsis. ~부호 an apostrophe. ~어 a clipped word; an abbreviation.

**생령**(生靈) 《백성》 people; 《생명》 life; 《살아 있는 영혼》 a wraith; an apparition of a living person.

**생리**(生理) ①《생리 기능·현상》 physiology. ¶ ～적(인) physiological; 《육체적》 physical / ～적 결함 a physiological defect / ～적 요구 the needs of the body / ～적 욕구 a physical desire / ～적 현상 a physiological phenomenon / 나는 그와 ～적으로 맞지 않는다 I have an instinctive dislike for him. ②《월경》 menstruation; *one's* period. ¶ ～중에 있다 be having *one's* period / ～가 시작되었다 My period has started.
◉ ～대(帶) a hygienic band; a sanitary napkin 〔towel, belt〕. ～용품 sanitary items. ～위생 physiology and hygienics. ～일(日) *one's* menstrual 〔catamenial〕 period; *one's* monthly days. ～작용 a physiological function. ～통 period pains; menstrual pains 〔cramps 《미》〕. ～화학 physiological chemistry. ～휴가 a monthly physiologic leave; a special monthly leave for women.

**생리학**(生理學) physiology. ¶ ～적인〔상의〕 physiological / ～상 physiologically; from the physiological point of view.
◉ ～자 a physiologist. 정신～ psycho=physiology.

**생매장**(生埋葬) burying alive. ～하다 bury 《*a person*》 alive; [비유적] oust 《*a person*》 from society; ostracize; blackball. ¶ ～되다 be buried 〔entombed〕 alive; be ostracized from society (사회적으로) / 산사태로 세 사람이 ～되었다 Three people were buried alive in a landslide.

**생맥주**(生麥酒) draft 〔draught 《영》〕 beer; beer on draft 〔tap〕. ¶ ～를 한 잔 마시다 have a glass of draft beer. ◉ 생맥줏집 a beer house; a draft house.

**생면**(生面) 《첫 대면》 *one's* first meeting 〔interview, introduction〕 《with》; 《사람》 a stranger (whom *one* has just met 〔introduced〕); a new acquaintance. ～하다 meet 〔interview, be introduced to〕 《*a person*》 for the first time. ◉ ～부지(不知) having never seen before; a perfect 〔total〕 stranger.

**생명**(生命) ①《목숨》 life. ⇨ 목숨. ¶ ～의 은인 the preserver 〔savior〕 of *one's* life / ～의 기원 the origin of life / ～에 관계되는 fatal 《disease》; mortal 《wound》 / ～이 있는 living; live; alive (★ live는 한정적, alive는 흔히 서술적: a live fish / The man was still alive.) / ～이 없는 lifeless / ～의 위험을 느끼다 be in terror of *one's* life / 그는 내 ～의 은인이다 I owe him my life. / 그는 그 사고로 ～을 잃었다 He lost his life in the accident. ②《한 분야에서의 활동》 (the) life. ¶ 그의 정치 ～도 이것으로 끝이다 His political life 〔career〕 is finished 〔over〕. / 한국의 대중 가수들은 대체로 ～이 짧다 Korean pop singers are, in general, short-lived as such. ③《가장 소중한 것》 the life; the soul. ¶ 명료함이 연설의 ～이다 Clarity is the life 〔soul〕 of a speech.
◉ ～감 a feeling of vitality; the sense of being alive. ～공학 biotechnology; biotech. ～과학 life science. ～선 a lifeline; 《손금의》 the Lifeline: ～선을 지키다 guard *one's* lifeline. ～수 life=giving〔-restoring〕 water; the water of life. ～유지장치 life-sustaining equipment; a life-support system (생략 LSS). ～주기모형 〖컴퓨터〗 a life cycle model. ～징후 a vital sign. ～표 a life chart.

**생명력**(生命力) life force; survival power 〔ability〕; *one's* 〔*its*〕 hold on life; vitality; vital force. ¶ ～이 있는 viable / 잡초는 강한 ～이 있어서 좀처럼 근절시킬 수가 없다 The weeds are difficult to eradicate owing to their strong hold on life.

**생명보험**(生命保險) life insurance 〔assurance 《영》〕. ¶ ～에 들다 insure *one's* life 《for ten million》; have *one's* life insured / ～에 들어 있다 have a policy with a life insurance company. ◉ ～배당금 a life insurance bonus. ～증서 a life insurance policy. ～회사 a life insurance company. 종신～ straight 〔whole〕 life insurance.

**생모**(生母) *one's* real mother.

**생모시**(生—) unbleached cambric.

**생목**(生—) regurgitated food. ¶ ～이 오르다 (have food) regurgitate.

**생목**(生木) 《무명》 unbleached cloth.

**생목숨**(生—) ① 《살아 있는》 life; body and soul; living and breathing. ② 《죄 없는》 an innocent 〔a blameless〕 life.

**생무지**(生—) an utterly inexperienced person; a greenhorn; a green 〔untrained〕 hand; a beginner. ¶ ～의 눈에는 to an inexperienced eye / 목공 일에는 ～다 be a greenhorn in carpentry.

**생물**(生物) a living thing 〔being〕; a creature; an organism; a life form; [총칭] life. ¶ 고등～ a higher 「organism 〔form of life〕 / ～이 있는 행성 a

life-bearing planet / 숲속의 ～ the life of a forest / ～을 죽이다 kill some living animals; destroy life / ～의 다양성 biodiversity / 북극에는 ～이 거의 없다 There is little life in the Arctic.
◉ ～경제학 bioeconomics. ～계 the biological world. ～공학 bionics; biotechnology. ～권 the biosphere. ～물리학 biophysics. ～발생설 (the theory of) biogenesis. ～분포학 chorology. ～산업 bioindustry. ～상(相) a biota. ～생태학 bioecology. ～의학공학 biomedical engineering. ～전기 bioelectricity: ～ 전기학 electrobiology. ～지리학 biogeography; biological geography. ～진화 biological evolution. ～체 an organism. ～체 연료 biofuel. ～화학 biochemistry: ～화학자 a biochemist. ～화학 병기 biological weapons.

**생물학**(生物學) biology. ¶ ～적(인)〔상의〕 biologic(al) / ～상〔적으로〕 biologically / ～적 요인 〖사회〗 a biological factor. ◉ ～자 a biologist. ～적 산소요구량 biochemical oxygen demand (생략 BOD). ～적 요법 biotherapy.

**생민**(生民) 《백성》 the people; the public; the populace; 《민생》 public welfare.

**생밤**(生―) a raw chestnut.

**생방송**(生放送) live broadcasting; 《1회의》 a live broadcast 〔telecast〕. (★ telecast는 TV의). ～하다 cover 〔carry〕 《an event》 live 《on radio, television》; broadcast 〔televise〕 《an event》 live. ¶ 현장으로부터의 ～ live broadcasting from the scene / 텔레비전으로 ～되다 be televised live; carry 〔cover〕 《a night game》 live on television.

**생배앓다** be 〔feel〕 jealous 《of *another's* success》; be sick with envy.

**생백신**(生―) 〖의학〗 live vaccine.

**생베**(生―) unbleached hemp cloth.

**생벼락**(生―) 《꾸지람》 an unreasonable scolding 〔reproof〕; 《재앙》 an unexpected disaster; an undeserved misfortune; a sudden calamity. ＝날벼락. ¶ ～이 떨어지다 get an unreasonable scolding / ～을 맞다 meet a sudden calamity; meet an unexpected stroke of misfortune / 이번 일은 뜻밖의 ～이다 It is some thing like a bolt from the blue.

**생병**(生病) a (nervous) breakdown; sickness (caused by overwork 〔anxiety〕). ¶ ～이 날 지경이다 be on the point 〔edge〕 of a nervous breakdown.

**생부**(生父) *one's* real father.

**생부모**(生父母) *one's* real parents.

**생불**(生佛) a living Buddha; an incarnation of Buddha; a saintly person.

**생사**(生死) life and 〔or〕 death; *one's* safety (안부); *one's* fate (운명). ¶ ～의 문제 a matter of life and 〔or〕 death; a vital question / ～ 불명인 사람들 persons whose fate is unknown; missing persons / 친척의 ～ 확인 the confirmation of the life or death of relatives / ～(지)경을 헤매다 wander 〔hover〕 between life and death; linger on the verge 〔brink〕 of death / ～를 같이하다 share *one's* fate 《with》; throw 〔cast〕 in *one's* lot 《with》 / 이것은 그의 ～가 걸린 중대한 문제다 This is a matter of life or death to him.

**생사**(生絲) raw silk. ¶ 고치에서 ～를 뽑다 reel off raw silk from cocoons. ◉ ～검사소 a silk conditioning house. ～업 the sericultural industry.

**생사람**(生―) ① 《죄 없는》 an innocent person 〔party〕. ¶ ～을 잡다 arrest an innocent man (체포하다); kill an innocent person (죽이다); inflict injury upon an innocent person (모함하다). ② 《관계없는》 an unconnected 〔unrelated〕 person; an outsider; a disinterested person. ③ 《생때같은》 a vigorous 〔robust〕 person.

**생산**(生産) ① 〖경제〗 production. ～하다 produce; make; turn 〔put〕 out; manufacture (대량으로). ¶ ～적(인) productive / ～적 노동〔사업〕 productive labor 〔industry〕 / …의 기록적 ～ the record production of... / ～을 시작하다 bring 〔put〕 《radios》 into production / ～을 촉진하다〔확대하다〕 step up 〔build up, increase, boost〕 the production 《of》 / ～을 줄이다〔늘리다〕 curtail 〔increase〕 the production 《of》 / 석탄 ～이 크게 감퇴됐다 Coal production is lagging. / 이 공장은 하루 천 대의 자동차를 ～한다 This factory produces 〔turns out, manufactures〕 one thousand cars a day. / 이 상품은 대량 ～되므로 값이 비교적 싸다 This goods are not so expensive because they are mass-produced. / ～을 높이려면 기구를 능률화해야 한다 In order to increase production, we must have a more efficient system. ② a childbirth; a delivery. ⇨ 출산(出産).
◉ ～가격 cost(s) of production; production cost. ～가치 productive value. ～계수 the coefficient of production. ～계획 output schedule. ～고 ＝생산량. ～공장 a manufacturing plant 〔fac-

tory]. ～공학 production engineering. ～과잉 overproduction; excessive [surplus] production. ～관리 production control. ～기술 manufacturing technique(s) [know-how]; industrial technology. ～능률 《increase》 production efficiency. ～력 production [manufacturing] capacity [power]: ～력 확충 increase [expansion] of production capacity / 1일 4,300대의 자동차 ～력 the production capacity of 4,300 cars a day. ～물 a product; 《농산물》 produce [총칭]. ～방식 a production method. ～부족 underproduction. ～설비 production [productive] facilities; plants and equipment. ～수단 means of production. ～실적 an actual output [yield]. ～액 =생산량. ～업 《제조업》 the manufacturing industry; 《광업·농업·어업 등의》 the extractive industry. ～연도 a production year. ～율 rate of production; production rate. ～의욕 the will to produce; zeal [enthusiasm] for industrial production. ～자 a producer; a manufacturer; a maker: ～자 가격 a producer('s) price / ～자 미가(米價) the producer rice price. ～자본 capital for production; productive capital. ～재(財) producers' [capital] goods. ～재료 production material. ～제한 production curtailment; restriction of output. ～제휴 collaboration in production. ～조정 an [the] adjustment of production: ～조정을 하다 adjust production. ～조합 a producers' guild; an industrial guild [association]. ～지 a producing district [center]: 사과 ～지 an apple-producing district. ～지수[함수, 곡선] a production index [function, curve]. ～카르텔 a producer's cartel. ～할당 a production quota. ～확장[증가] expansion [increase] of production. 국내～ domestic production. 대규모～ large-scale production.

**생산규모**(生產規模) production scale; scale of production. ¶ ～를 확대하다 expand [enlarge] the production scale; bring production on a larger scale.

**생산량**(生產量) an output; a yield; an outturn. ¶ 1인당 ～ production per man / ～을 늘리다 increase [extend] the output 《of》 / ～을 제한하다[줄이다] limit [reduce] the output 《of... to...》. ◉ 공업～ an industrial output. 총～ the total [gross] output [production].

**생산목표**(生產目標) a goal of production; an output goal; a production target. ¶ ～를 달성하다 attain [reach, come up to] the goal of production / ～에 미달하다 fall short of [fail to attain] the goal of production.

**생산비**(生產費) the cost of production; production cost. ¶ ～를 절감하다 curtail [cut down] the cost of production. ◉ 한계[평균, 총]～ the marginal [average, total] cost of production.

**생산성**(生產性) productivity. ¶ 노동 ～ productivity of labor / 높은[낮은] ～ high [low] productivity / ～을 높이다 promote [increase, raise] productivity / ～ 향상에 힘을 기울여야 한다 We must direct our energies toward higher productivity. *or* Our energies must be directed toward higher productivity. ◉ ～가능 시험 《유전 개발 등에서》 a Drill Stem Test(생략 DST). ～향상 운동 a movement for higher productivity; a productivity movement. 아시아 ～기구 Asian Productivity Organization(생략 APO). 한국 ～본부 Korea Productivity Center (생략 KPC).

**생살**(生—) 《성한 살》 healthy flesh; 《새살》 proud flesh. ¶ 피부가 벗겨진 (빨간) ～ raw flesh (looking red) with the skin taken off.

**생살**(生殺) life and death; sparing life and [or] taking it; letting live or killing. ◉ ～여탈권 《hold》 the power of life and death 《over *a person*》.

**생색**(生色) face-saving patronage [benevolence]; a favorable impression; a credit. ¶ ～나는 선물 a gift that impresses / ～을 내다 pose as a benefactor 《to》; emphasize the favor done to 《*a person*》; take credit to *oneself;* place 《*a person*》 under obligation 《for》 / 그렇게 했으면 너도 ～이 났을 것이다 If you did so, it must have reflected credit on you. / 자네 그 하찮은 선물로 ～내려 드네그려 You are doing yourself proud by giving me this small present, aren't you?

**생생이** taking 《*a person's*》 money by cheating in gambling.

**생생하다**(生生—) (be) fresh (신선한); lively (기운찬); animated (활기찬); vivid (선명한); lifelike (살아 있는 것 같은); active (활발한); [서술적] be full of life. ¶ 생생히 vividly; lively; graphically; full of life; true to life / 생생한 기억 a fresh memory [recollection] 《of》; a memory still fresh in *one's* mind / 벽에 남은 생생한 총알 자국 a fresh bullet mark in the wall / 생생하게 묘사하다〔그리다〕 describe 〔show〕 vividly 〔graphically〕; give a graphic 〔vivid〕 description 〔picture〕 of / 그녀의 생생한 묘사는 인상적이었다 Her vivid description was impressive. / 그 광경은 지금도 내 마음속에 생생하게 남아 있다 The sight is still vivid in my mind.

**생석회**(生石灰) quicklime.

**생선**(生鮮) raw 〔fresh〕 fish; (a) fish. ¶ ~뼈 a fish bone / ~을 굽다 broil fish / ~을 날로 먹다 eat fish raw.
◉ ~가게 a fish store 〔market, shop 《영》〕. ~구이 roast 〔broiled〕 fish. ~매운탕 hot fish stew. ~묵 boiled fish paste. ~장수 a fish dealer; 《영》 fishmonger; a fish peddler (행상인). ~전 pan-fried fish fillet. ~조림 fish stew seasoned with soy sauce. ~초밥 vinegared rice balls topped with sliced raw fish. ~회 *sashimi;* sliced 〔slices of〕 raw fish; assorted raw fish slices: ~회를 치다 slice raw fish; prepare sliced raw fish.

**생성**(生成) coming into being; creation; formation; generation. ~하다 come into being; be created 〔formed, generated〕. ¶ 우주의 ~ the formation of the universe. ◉ ~문법 『언어』 generative grammar. ~물 『화학』 a product.

**생소**(生疎) ① 《낯설음》 unfamiliarity; alienation. ~하다 be unfamiliar 〔unacquainted〕 《with》; be a stranger 《to》. ¶ ~한 곳 an unfamiliar place / ~한 땅 a land *one* isn't familiar with; a strange 〔foreign, an alien〕 land / ~한 사람 a stranger; an unacquainted man / 나는 시골에서 올라와 서울은 아주 ~합니다 As I am fresh from the country, I am an utter stranger in Seoul.
② 《서투름》 lack of skill 〔experience〕; inexperience. ~하다 be lacking in skill 〔experience〕; (be) bad 〔poor〕 《at》; inexperienced; unskillful; unaccustomed 《to》. ¶ ~한 일 a job *one* isn't good at / 그들은 이러한 일에 ~하다 They are unaccustomed 〔new〕 to this kind of business.

**생소리**(生—) groundless 〔preposterous〕 remarks; a lie; a fabrication; an absurdity. ~하다 say something preposterous 〔far-fetched〕; 《구어》 talk through *one's* hat; make an unreasonable 〔a groundless〕 remark.

**생손** a whitlow; a felon. ⇨ 생인손.

**생수**(生水) natural 〔spring〕 water; 《음료용의》 bottled natural water. ¶ ~의 자동화된 병 주입 절차〔방법〕 the automatized procedure of bottling natural water. ◉ ~받이 a rice field irrigated with spring water. ~시장 (the nation's) bottled water market.

**생시**(生時) 《난 시간》 the time 〔hour〕 of *one's* birth; 《살아 있을 때》 *one's* lifetime; 《깨어 있을 때》 *one's* waking hours. ¶ 꿈에도 ~에도 그는 그녀를 잊을 수 없었다 Awake or asleep, he couldn't forget her.

**생식**(生食) ~하다 eat uncooked food; eat 《*something*》 raw. ¶ ~용 굴 oysters for eating raw.

**생식**(生殖) reproduction; procreation; generation. ~하다 reproduce; generate; procreate.
◉ ~기(期) the mating season; a period of reproduction. ~기능〔작용〕 reproductive 〔generative〕 function; reproduction. ~력 generative power; fecundity (여성의); virility (남성의): ~력이 있는 generative; reproductive; progenitive. ~불능 impotence: ~불능자 an impotent; 『법』 a spado. ~선(腺) a genital 〔sex(ual)〕 gland; a gonad. ~세포 a reproductive 〔generative, germ〕 cell. ~욕 the reproductive urge.

**생식기**(生殖器) the organs of generation 〔reproduction〕; the genital 〔reproductive, sexual〕 organs; genitals.
◉ ~숭배 phallicism; phallic worship 〔cult〕. ~장애 a genital trouble 〔disorder〕.

**생신**(生辰) birthday. = 생일(生日).

**생쌀**(生—) raw 〔uncooked〕 rice.

**생애**(生涯) 《일생》 a life; a lifetime; a career; 《평생》 all *one's* life. ¶ 행복〔비참〕한 ~ a happy 〔miserable〕 life / 정치가로서의 ~ *one's* career as a politician / ~를 마치다 end *one's* life 〔days〕; close *one's* career / ~를 보내다 live 〔lead〕 a 《happy》 life / 암 연구에 ~를 바치다 devote *one's* life to cancer research.

**생약**(生藥) a herb medicine; a crude drug. ◉ ~학(學) pharmacognosy; pharmacognosia.

**생억지**(生—) irrational insistence on having *one's* own way; arbitrariness; stubbornness. ¶ ~를 쓰다 demand *one's* own way; say extremely unreasonable things; stick to *one's* unjust opinion; act unreasonably 〔perversely〕.

**생업**(生業) an occupation; a calling; a profession; a trade; a business. ¶ …을 ~으로 하다 make a living by《*doing*》. ◉ ~자금 a rehabilitation fund; a fund for operating business.

**생우유**(生牛乳) raw milk.

**생울타리**(生—) a hedge. ⇨ 산울타리.

**생원**(生員) 〖역사〗 a person who had passed the minor state examination; 《존칭》 Mister…; Mr. …; … Esquire (생략 Esq.).

**생육**(生肉) raw meat.

**생육**(生育) 《발육》 growth; development; 《나서 자람》 birth and breeding. ~하다 《키우다》 grow; raise; 《자라다》 grow (up); be born and bred 〔brought up〕; vegetate (식물이). ◉ ~기 〖식물〗 the growing period 〔season〕. ~지 〖생물〗 the habitat.

**생으로**(生—) ① 《날로》 raw; fresh; uncooked; *au naturel* (F.). ¶ 달걀을 ~ 먹다 eat an egg raw. ② 《부당히》 unreasonably; irrationally; arbitrarily; wrongfully; without any reason; 《억지로》 forcibly; by forces; willy-nilly; against *one's* will. ¶ ~ 때리다 hit 《*a person*》 on no provocation.

**생이** 〖동물〗 a caridean shrimp.

**생이별**(生離別) separation (forced) by circumstances. ~하다 be separated from 《*one's* spouse》 by adverse circumstances. ¶ 그들은 전쟁으로 ~했다 They were separated by the war.

**생이지지**(生而知之) ~하다 know from birth 〔without being taught〕; know intuitively.

**생인발** 〖의학〗 a boil on the tip of toe; a sore toe.

**생인손** 〖의학〗 a whitlow; felon; (a) paronychia; a sore finger.

**생일**(生日) a birthday; *one's* natal day. ¶ ~을 맞이하다 reach *one's* 《thirtieth》 birthday / ~을 축하하다 celebrate 《*a person's*》 birthday / 내 ~은 8월 15일이다 My birthday is (on) August 15. / ~을 축하합니다 Happy birthday to you! *or* I wish you many happy returns of the day.
◉ ~선물 a birthday gift: ~ 선물을 하다 send 〔present〕 a gift 《to *a person*》 in celebration of the birth. ~잔치 《give》 a birthday party.

**생자**(生者) 《사람》 a living person; 《만물》 a living thing 〔being〕; a (living) creature; [집합적] life 《on Earth》.
◉ ~필멸(必滅) 〖불교〗 A living being is mortal. *or* Man is mortal.

**생장**(生長) growth; increment. ⇨ 성장.

**생전**(生前) *one's* life(time). ¶ ~에 during 〔in〕 *one's* lifetime; while *one* was alive; in life; before *one's* death / ~ 처음 for the first time in *one's* life / ~의 공로에 의하여 in recognition of the services done in *one's* lifetime / 서울에는 ~ 처음이다 This is my first visit to Seoul. / 부모님 ~에 효도하다 Be obedient 〔dutiful, devoted〕 to your parents in their lifetime.

**생존**(生存) existence; being; life; subsistence; survival (살아남음). ~하다 exist; live; 《살아남다》 survive; outlive. ¶ 적자 ~ the survival of the fittest / ~의 목적 the aim of life / ~ 중에 in *one's* lifetime; in life / ~을 유지하다 maintain *one's* existence / ~해 있다 be alive; be in existence / 우리의 ~과 안녕을 파괴하다 destroy our well-being and even our survival / 이 섬에는 생물이 ~하고 있지 않다 No living things exist on the island.
◉ ~권 the right to live 〔life〕: ~권을 위협하다 menace 《*a person's*》 right to live. ~능력 viability. ~본능 survival instincts. ~욕(慾) the desire for existence; the will to live. ~율 a survival rate.

**생존경쟁**(生存競爭) a struggle for existence. ¶ 치열한 ~ a hard 〔fierce〕 struggle for existence / ~을 하다 have 〔experience〕 a struggle for existence / ~에 지다 be down and out in the struggle for existence.

**생존자**(生存者) a survivor. ¶ 조난선의 유일한 ~ the sole survivor from 〔of〕 the shipwreck / ~는 불과 3명이었다 Only three persons saved alive. *or* Only three survived.

**생죽음**(生—) a violent death. ~하다 die a violent death; meet a tragic 〔an unnatural, an accidental〕 death.

**생쥐** 〖동물〗 a (house) mouse (*pl.* mice). ¶ 물에 빠진 ~가 되다 be 〔get〕 drenched 〔wet, soaked〕 to the skin; get wet through; be thoroughly drenched.

**생지옥**(生地獄) a hell on earth. ¶ 그 광경은 문자 그대로 ~이었다 The sight was literally a hell on earth.

**생질**(甥姪) *one's* sister's son; a nephew.
◉ ~녀 *one's* sister's daughter; a niece.

**생짜**(生—) unripe fruit; uncooked stuff.

**생채**(生菜) raw 〔uncooked〕 vegetables;

a (vegetable) salad; a lettuce. ¶ 무〔오이〕 ~ a radish 〔cucumber〕 salad.

**생채**(生彩) brilliance; vividness; life; vitality. ¶ ~ 없는 그림 a lifeless 〔drab〕 painting.

**생채기** a 《nail》 scratch. ¶ ~가 나다 get 「a scratch 《on》.

**생철**(一鐵) tin plate; latten; white iron. ◉ ~지붕 a tin 〔zinc〕 roof. ~통 a tin; a can 《미》; a zinc bucket. ~판 a tinplate sheet; tinned sheet iron.

**생청**(生淸) unrefined 〔raw〕 honey.

**생청스럽다** (be) preposterous; unreasonable; being far-fetched.

**생체**(生體) a living body; an organism. ¶ ~ 현미경 검사 biomicroscopy. ◉ ~간이식 a liver transplant from a living donor. ~공학 bionics; bioengineering. ~막 a biomembrane. ~반응 the reaction of a living body. ~실험 medical experimentation 〔a medical experiment〕 on a living body. ~자기제어 biofeedback. ~전기 bioelectricity. ~조직검사 a biopsy. ~학 somatology: ~학적(인) somatological / ~학자 a somatologist. ~해부 vivisection: ~해부를 하다 vivisect. ~해부(론)자 a vivisectionist.

**생탈**(生頉) deliberately caused trouble.

**생태**(生態) a mode of life; ecology. ¶ 곤충의 ~ the ecology of an insect / 낙엽수의 ~ the botany of deciduous trees / 현대 여성의 ~ the mode of life of today's women. ◉ ~계 an ecosystem; an ecological system. ~변화 ecological adaptation. ~피라미드 《먹이 사슬》 ecological pyramid. ~형(型) an ecotype.

**생태학**(生態學) 《animal, plant》 ecology; bionomics. ¶ ~적(인)〔상의〕 ecological; bionomic(al). ◉ 각개~ autecology. 군집~ synecology.

**생트집**(生—) picking fault; a false charge 〔accusation〕; unreasonable 〔malicious〕 faultfinding. ¶ ~을 잡다 provoke; find fault 《with》; pick holes 〔flaws〕 《in》; make a false charge; make up a pretext for a fight 《with *a person*》; nag; ride 〔rag〕 《*a person*》 / ~을 잡지 마라 Stop riding me!

**생파리** 《파리》 a lively fly; 《사람》 a cool and distant person; 《구어》 a cold fish. ¶ ~ 잡아떼듯한다 stoutly maintain *one's* ignorance; deny stubbornly 〔stiffly〕 / 그녀는 ~같다 She is 「snobbish 〔stuck up〕. *or* She looks prim 〔prissy〕.

**생판**(生板) 《터없이》 groundlessly; unjustly; unreasonably; outrageously; 《전연》 entirely; utterly; completely; wholly. ¶ ~ 모르는 사람 a total 〔complete〕 stranger; an utter stranger / ~ 다르다 be quite 〔entirely〕 different 《from》; differ entirely 《from》 / 그를 ~ 모른다 I don't know him at all.

**생포**(生捕) capturing 〔catching〕 alive. ~하다 capture; take 〔make〕 《*a person*》 prisoner; 《동물을》 capture 〔catch〕 《an animal》 alive.

**생피**(生皮) rawhide.

**생핀잔**(生—) undeserved shame. ¶ ~을 주다 reprove 《*a person*》 without any cause; have no call to put 《*a person*》 to such shame.

**생필름**(生—) raw film.

**생혈**(生血) fresh blood; the blood of living man 〔animal〕; lifeblood. ¶ ~을 빨다 suck the lifeblood 《of》.

**생호령**(生號令) a wrong reprimand; an unjust scolding. ~하다 scold 《*a person*》 unreasonably.

**생화**(生花) a natural flower; a real 「〔fresh〕 flower.

**생화학**(生化學) biochemistry; chemicobiology. ¶ ~적(인) biochemical / ~적으로 biochemically. ◉ ~무기 chemical and biological weapons (생략 CBW). ~자 a biochemist. ~적 산소요구량 the biochemical oxygen demand (생략 BOD).

**생환**(生還) returning alive 〔safe〕; 《야구에서》 reaching the home plate. ~하다 come back 〔return〕 alive 〔safe〕; 《야구에서》 reach 〔cross〕 the home plate. ¶ 주자를 ~시키다 bring home the runner / 그는 2루타로 주자를 ~시켰다 He scored a run on a double. *or* The runner reached home on his double. / 그 우주 비행사는 우주선에서 지구를 두 바퀴 돌고 무사히 ~ 하였다 The astronaut have 「returned safely 〔made a safe return〕 after two orbits of the earth in the spaceship. ◉ ~자 a survivor: ~자는 겨우 두 명이었다 Only two came back alive.

**생활**(生活) (a) life; an existence; 《생계》 (a) living; livelihood; subsistence. ~하다 live; exist; 《생계를 세워가다》 make a living; subsist; support *oneself*. ¶ 규칙적〔불규칙적〕인 ~ a regular 〔desultory〕 life / 불안정한 ~ a precarious life / 가치 있는 ~ a life worth living / 충실한〔풍족한〕 ~ a full 〔rich〕 life / 평범한 ~ a mediocre life / ~을

위해 for a livelihood / ～을 보장하다 guarantee 《*a person's*》 living / 월급으로 ～하다 live on *one's* salary / ～을 안정시키다 stabilize *one's* livelihood 〔living〕 / 월 100만 원으로 ～하다 support *oneself* on a million won a month / ～을 해나가다 get 〔earn〕 *one's* living; live 《on, by》 / ～의 안정을 얻다 secure *one's* living 〔livelihood〕 / ～이 어렵다 find it difficult to make both ends meet; be badly off / 비참한 ～을 하다 make a poor living; lead a dog's life / 겨우 ～해 나가다 barely manage to eke out a living; pick up a scanty 〔bare〕 livelihood / 빚으로 ～하다 live on credit / 분수에 맞는〔넘친〕 ～을 하다 live within 〔beyond〕 *one's* means / 거지 ～을 하다 follow 〔pursue〕 the life of a beggar / 고생을 모르는 ～을 하다 live free from care / 해마다 서민의 ～이 향상되고 있다 The people have a better life each year. / 그녀는 이웃 아이들에게 영어를 가르치며 ～하고 있다 She makes a living by teaching English to some neighbor's children. / 물은 일상 ～에 없어서는 안 되는 것이다 Water is essential to daily 〔everyday〕 life. / 그는 도시 ～에 적응할 수 없었다 He could not adapt himself to urban life.

◉ ～간소화 the simplification of life. ～감정 life feeling; the mood of the people: 현대 한국인의 ～ 감정 the mood of contemporary Korean people. ～개선 (운동) (a movement for) the improvement of living conditions. ～고 hardships of life; economic distress. ～공간 living space. ～교육 practical education; education for living. ～권(圈) a zone 〔sphere〕 of life; *one's* (daily) milieu: ～ 기능권 a living sphere / 전국을 5개의 ～ 기능권으로 나누다 divide the country into five living spheres. ～권(權) living rights; the right to life. ～극빈자 a needy person; 〔집합적〕 the (poor and) needy. ～급 pay 〔wages〕 calculated 〔paid〕 on the basis of need. ～기능 vital functions. ～기록 a human 〔life〕 document; an account 〔a record〕 of *one's* life. ～물자 subsistence goods; daily commodities. ～반응(反應) 〖생리〗 (a) vital reaction. ～보호 livelihood protection 〔assistance〕: ～ 보호법 the Livelihood Protection Law / ～보호 세대 a household on welfare / 그는 ～ 보호를 받고 있다 He is on welfare 《미》 〔on social security 《영》〕. ～불안 economic insecurity. ～상태 living conditions. ～설계 a design of *one's* life; life planning; plans for the future: ～설계사 《보험 회사의》 a life planner. ～수단 a means of making a living; a means of living. ～안정 the stabilization of livelihood. ～양식 a way of life; a life-style; a mode of living: 미국풍의 ～ 양식 the American way of life. ～연령 *one's* chronological age. ～자금 money to live on. ～전선 a battle of life. ～정도 ⇨ 생활 수준. ～조건 living conditions. ～ 지도 《교육상의》 educational guidance. ～체험 experience in actual life. ～필수품 the necessaries 〔necessities〕 of life; daily necessaries. ～환경 *one's* living environment: 보다 나은 ～환경 better living circumstances. 사치～ lavish life; high living: 사치～을 하다 eat high on the hog. 사회〔일상, 정신〕～ social 〔everyday, spiritual〕 life. 원시～ a primitive life. 절약～ frugal life; thrifty living. 종합～ 기록부 《학생의》 (the) comprehensive (high) school records: 종합～ 기록부에는 학업 성적뿐만 아니라 학생의 그룹 활동, 자원 봉사, 교외 콘테스트의 성적들이 반영될 것이다 Comprehensive school records will reflect students' group activities, volunteer work and results of outside-school contests as well as academic performances.

**생활난**(生活難) hard living; living difficulties; economic distress. ¶ ～과 싸우다 struggle against hard life.

**생활력**(生活力) *one's* earning power; *one's* ability to make 〔earn〕 *one's* living; 《활력》 《full of》 vitality. ¶ ～이 없는 남자 a man of no ability to make a living / ～이 강하다 be full of vitality; have high earning power / 그는 ～이 없다 He isn't able to make a living.

**생활비**(生活費) living expenses; the cost of living. ¶ 높은〔낮은〕 ～ the high 〔low〕 cost of living / ～를 벌기 위해서 일하다 work for *one's* keep / 서울은 ～가 많이 드는 도시이다 Seoul is an expensive city to live in.

**생활수준**(生活水準) a standard of living; a living standard. ¶ ～의 향상〔저하〕 a rise 〔decline〕 in the standard 〔scale〕 of living / ～을 높이다〔낮추다〕 raise 〔lower〕 the standard of living.

**생회**(生灰) quicklime. ⇨ 생석회.

**생후**(生後) [부사적] after 〔since〕 *one's* birth. ¶ ~ 3개월 된 아기 a three-month-old baby / ~ 일주일만에 죽다 die a week after (*its*) birth.

**생흙**(生—) fresh 〔uncultivated〕 soil.

**샤머니즘** shamanism. ¶ ~의 shamanistic; shamanic. 「ic; shaman.

**샤먼** a shaman (*pl.* ~s). ¶ ~의 shaman-

**샤시** 《차대(車臺)》 a chassis (*pl.* ~(es)).

**샤워** a shower (bath). ¶ ~를 하다 take 〔have〕 a shower (bath); shower. ◉ ~실 a shower stall 〔room〕.

**샤프** ① 《날카로움》 being sharp. ~하다 (be) sharp. ② 〖음악〗 a sharp (기호 #). ◉ ~펜슬 a mechanical 〔an automatic, 《영》 a propelling〕 pencil.

**샤프롱** a chaperon(e). 「crankshaft.

**샤프트** 〖기계〗 a shaft. ¶ 크랭크~ a

**샴** 《태국의 옛이름》 Siam. ¶ 샴의 Siamese / 샴말 Siamese / 샴사람 a Siamese (*pl.* ~); the Siamese [총칭].

**샴페인** champagne; fizz. ¶ ~ 병을 펑하고 따다 pop open a champagne bottle / ~ 잔을 치켜들고 축하하다 drink champagne in honor 〔celebration〕 of 《the event》. ◉ ~사이다 a carbonated soft drink.

**샴푸** 《세발》 a shampoo; 《세발제》 shampoo. ¶ ~로 머리를 감다 shampoo 《*one's* hair》; have a shampoo.

**샹들리에** a chandelier; 《전등의》 a 〔an electric〕 chandelier.

**샹송** 〖음악〗 a *chanson* (F.). ◉ ~가수 a *chanson* singer.

**섀미가죽** chamois (leather); shammy.

**서**(西) west (생략 W). ¶ 서의 west; western; westerly / 서풍 the west wind / 서향 집 a house facing west.

**서**(序) 《서문》 a preface; a foreword.

**서**(書) 《글씨》 writing(s); 《서적》 a book; 《서간》 a letter; an epistle; 《필적》 handwriting; 《서도》 calligraphy.

**서**(署) an office; a station; 《경찰서》 a police station. ¶ 서로 연행하다 walk 〔take〕 《a suspect》 to a police station.

**서**[1] 《셋》 three. ¶ 서 돈 three (Korean) ounces / 서 되 three (Korean) quarts.

**서**[2] [조사] ① [명사에 붙어] ¶ 혼자서 by *oneself* / 미국서 오다 come from America / 서울서 살다 live in Seoul / 여기서 일하다 work here. ② [동사·형용사에 붙어] ¶ 걸어서 가다 go on foot 《to》 / 병이 나서 자리 보전하다 be ill in bed / 추워서 떨다 shiver with cold / 가서 보고 오다 go and have a look at 《it》.

**서가**(書架) a bookshelf (*pl.* -shelves); a bookcase; a (book) stack.

**서가**(書家) a calligrapher; a calligraphist; a penman.

**서각**(犀角) rhinoceros horn.

**서간**(書簡) a letter; an epistle; a note (외교상의); correspondence [총칭]. ◉ ~문 an epistolary style. ~문학 epistolary literature. ~전 letter paper; a writing pad (철해져 있는). ~집 a collection of letters; collected letters. ~체 an epistolary style: ~체로 쓰다 write in an epistolary style.

**서거**(逝去) death; passing away. ~하다 die; pass away.

**서걱-** ⇨ 사각-.

**서경**(西經) 〖지리〗 the west longitude. ¶ ~ 50 도 longitude 50 degrees west.

**서경**(敍景) description of scenery; a scenery sketch. ◉ ~시 a poem describing scenery. 「서관의).

**서고**(書庫) a library; a stack room (도

**서곡**(序曲) 〖음악〗 a prelude 《to》; an overture 《to》; a prolog(ue). ¶ 대전의 ~ a prelude to a great war / ~을 연주하다 play an overture; prelude.

**서관**(書館) 《서점》 a bookstore; a bookshop; 《출판사》 a book 〔publishing〕 firm.

**서광**(曙光) the first streak of daylight; dawn; 《희망·기대》 hope; prospects. ¶ 문명의 ~ the dawn of civilization / 성공의 ~ a gleam of success; prospects of success / 희망의 ~ a ray 〔gleam, flash〕 of hope / 해결의 ~ the first ray of hope for the settlement 《of *a matter*》.

**서구**(西歐) 《서부 유럽》 West(ern) Europe; 《서양》 Europe; the West; the Occident. ¶ ~적 European; Western. ◉ ~문명〔문화〕 Western civilization 〔culture〕. ~사상 Western ideas. ~연합 the Western European Union (생략 WEU). ~제국(諸國) the West European countries; the Western nations.

**서구화**(西歐化) Westernization; Europeanization. ~하다 westernize. ¶ ~되다 be westernized / ~의 영향 a westernizing influence.

**서근서근하다** ⇨ 사근사근하다.

**서글서글하다** 《허물없다》 (be) free and easy; 《너그럽다》 (be) open-hearted; magnanimous; broad-minded; 《상냥하다》 (be) amiable; affable; sociable. ¶ 서글서글한 사람 a man of magnanimous disposition; an affable person.

**서글프다** (be) sad; sorrowful; melancholy; lonesome; lonely; [서술적] be touched 〔moved〕 《to tears》. ¶ 서글픈 노래 a touching 〔plaintive〕 song / 서

글퍼지다 feel somewhat 〔little, rather〕 sad; feel lonely / 어쩐지 ~ I am so sad, I know not why.

**서기**(西紀) the year of grace 〔Christ〕; the dominical year; the Christian Era; *Anno Domini* (생략 A.D.). ¶ ~ 1998년에 in A.D. 1998; in the year of our Lord 1998; in 1998 A.D.

**서기**(書記) a clerk; a secretary; a clerical staff. ¶ 법원 ~ a clerk of a court. ◉ ~관 a fourth grade official; a secretary: 1등 ~관 a first secretary / 주한 미 대사관 3등 ~관 a third secretary at the U.S. Embassy in Seoul. ~보(補) an assistant clerk; a probationary secretary. ~장 a head 〔chief〕 secretary; 《정당의》 a secretary-general.

**서기**(瑞氣) auspicious signs; a good omen.

**서까래** 〖건축〗 a (common) rafter. ¶ 서까랫감 raftering (material).

**서껀** 《함께 다》 together with; and so on 〔forth〕; and the like; and others; et cetera (생략 etc.). ¶ 술~ 떡~ 많이 먹었다 I had lots to eat and drink— cakes, wine and so on.

**서남**(西南) the southwest. ¶ ~의 southwestern; southwesterly / ~에 in 〔to, on〕 the southwest 《of》 / ~으로 southwestward. ◉ ~단(端) the southwestern end 〔extremity〕. ~서 west-southwest (생략 WSW). ~풍 a southwesterly wind; a southwester. ~향 《having》 a southwest aspect; facing southwest.

**서낭** 〖민속〗 《서낭신》 a tutelary deity; a *genius loci* (L.); 《나무》 a tree where a tutelary deity dwells. ¶ ~에 나다 disaster strikes. ◉ ~단(壇)〔당(堂)〕 the altar 〔shrine〕 for a tutelary deity. ~신 a tutelary deity; a local god. ~제(祭) the festival of the local god.

**서너** about three; three or four; a few 《of》. ¶ ~ 번 three or four times; several times / ~ 개 a few pieces / ~ 친구를 만나다 meet a few of *one's* friends.

**서너너덧** about three or four; from three to five; a few 《of》.

**서넛** about three; three or four; a few 《of》. ¶ 일꾼 ~이 필요하다 I need three or four hands.

**서녀**(庶女) a daughter born of a concubine; an illegitimate daughter.

**서녘**(西—) the western direction; the west. ¶ ~ 하늘이 노을로 불타는 듯하다 The western sky is glowing with the setting sun.

**서늘하다** ① 《날씨·온도가》 (be) cool; refreshing. ¶ 서늘한 바람 a cool breeze / 서늘한 곳에 두다 keep 《*a thing*》 in a cool place / 서늘해지다 get 〔become〕 cool. ② 《마음이》 (be) chilled; feel 〔have〕 a chill. ¶ 간담을 서늘하게 하다 [사물이 주어] strike terror into *one's* heart; make *one's* blood run cold / 간담이 서늘해지다 be struck with terror; have a thrill of horror; be scared 〔frightened〕; be amazed 《at, with》 / 놀라서 가슴이 서늘했다 I was chilled with fright.

**서다** ① 《사람이》 stand; take a stand 《at》; 《일어서다》 stand up; rise; get on 〔rise to〕 *one's* feet; draw *oneself* up. ¶ 거울 앞에 ~ stand before a mirror / 산꼭대기에 ~ stand at the top 〔summit〕 of a mountain / 연단에 ~ take 〔stand on〕 the rostrum 〔platform〕 / 창문 옆에 ~ stand beside a window / 막아 ~ stand in 《*a person's*》 way; 《떡 버티고》 stand with *one's* legs wide apart / 벌떡 일어~ spring up; start 〔spring, jump〕 to *one's* feet / 일렬로 줄지어 (늘어) ~ stand in a line 〔row〕; queue up (줄서서 기다리며); line (up) / 서 있다 be standing; 《착석 않고》 be on *one's* feet; be standing up / 줄곧 서 있다 keep standing; keep on *one's* legs / 하루 종일 서 있다 keep standing all day long / 가만히 서 있다 stand still.

② 《물건이》 stand erect. ¶ 팻말이 서 있다 There is a bulletin board put up there. / 높은 나무가 집 앞에 서 있다 A tall tree stands in front of my house.

③ 《건조물이》 stand; be built 〔erected〕; be set up. ¶ 건물이 설 곳 the building site 《for》 / 우리 집 주변에 주택들이 자꾸 (들어)선다 Houses are springing up all over my neighborhood. / 공원 한가운데에 임금의 동상이 서 있다 In the center of the park stands 〔is, is set up〕 a statue of the king.

④ 《수립·설립되다》 be established 〔founded〕; 《대책·계획 등이》 be formed 〔laid〕; be worked out. ¶ 계획이 ~ a plan is worked out / 새 정부가 ~ a new government is established / 학교가 ~ a school is established 〔set up〕.

⑤ 《위치·처지에》 be placed in 《a position》; stand 《as》; serve 《as》; 《입각하다》 be based 〔grounded, founded〕

on; take *one's* ground on. ¶ 교단에 ~ engage in education; teach / 들러리를 ~ serve as a best man 〔bridesmaid〕/ 보증을 ~ stand security 〔guarantee〕; go bond 《for *a person*》/ 보초를 ~ stand 〔keep〕 sentinel; be on sentry (duty) / 수세에 ~ take the defensive; stand 〔be〕 on the defensive / 우위에 ~ be 〔stand〕 at advantage 《over》; have an advantage 《over》/ 중간에 ~ act as intermediary; go 〔get〕 between 《the two parties》; 《중매하다》 act as (a) go-between / 증인을 ~ stand witness for 《*a person*》; testify 《to》; bear witness to 《a fact》/ 증인석에 ~ take 〔go on〕 the (witness) stand / 인간 평등의 입장에 ~ take a stand for the equality.

⑥ 《정지하다》 stop; halt; come to a stop 〔stand(still), halt〕; draw 〔pull〕 up (말·차 등이); heave to (배가); run down (동력 등이). ¶ 시계가 ~ a watch stops 〔runs down〕/ 팽이가 ~ a top sleeps / 갑자기 ~ stop short 〔suddenly〕; make 〔come to〕 a sudden stop 〔halt〕/ 딱 멈춰 ~ stop dead / 서 있다 be at a stop 〔standstill〕; stand still / (열차가) 정거장에 ~ stop at a station / (열차 등이) 도중에 서지 않고 달리다 run without stopping 〔a stop〕; run past 《a stop》/ 이 버스는 정류소마다 선다 This bus stops at all stops. / 차는 우리 집 앞에서 섰다 The car pulled up in front of my house.

⑦ 《장이》 open; be held. ¶ 장이 서는 도시 a market town / 장이 섰다 A fair is opened 〔held〕. / 장이 서는 날〔장날〕이다 This is the day for the fair. *or* It is market day today.

⑧ 《날이》 be sharpened; be edged; be sharp; stand out (sharply). ¶ 날이 ~ have a keen 〔sharp〕 edge / 칼날이 잘 ~ take a nice edge.

⑨ 《핏대가》 a vein stands out; turn purple 《with rage》; 《핏발이》 become bloodshot. ¶ 핏발이 선 눈 bloodshot eyes / 이마에 핏줄이 ~ veins stand out on *one's* forehead.

⑩ 《명령·규율이》 be obeyed 〔followed〕; be carried out. ¶ 명령이 ~ orders have 〔carry〕 authority / 규율이 서 있다 be orderly 〔well-disciplined〕/ 명령이 잘 서지 않는다 The orders are being ignored. / 학교 규율이 서 있지 않다 School discipline is not as it should be.

⑪ 《조리가》 hold good; hold water; 《명분·이유가》 be just; be justifiable; be admissible. ¶ 조리가 서지 않는 illogical; unjustifiable; unreasonable / 이유가 ~ 〔서지 않는다〕 *one's* reasoning holds good 〔no good〕; stand to reason 〔no reason〕/ 명분이 서지 않다 cannot be justified; be hardly justifiable / 조리가 서지 않는 말을 하다 talk incoherently; make disjointed remarks / 그것은 조리가 선 결론이다 That is a logical conclusion.

⑫ 《면목·체면·권위 등이》 hold. ¶ 체면이 ~ save *one's* face; save the honor; keep *one's* appearances / 부하들에게 권위가 서지 않다 have no authority over *one's* subordinates / 자네 체면이 설 수 있도록 어떤 방법을 모색해 보겠다 I'll try to find a way to save your face.

⑬ 《아이가》 conceive; become pregnant; get with child.

⑭ 《결심이》 make up *one's* mind; make a resolve 〔resolution〕. ¶ 결심이 안 ~ be irresolute; be undecided 《about》.

⑮ 《무지개가》 span 〔hang in〕 (the sky); appear 〔rise〕 《against》. ¶ 무지개가 ~ a rainbow spans the sky.

⑯ 《발기하다》 have an erection 〔a hard-on 《속어》〕.

**서당**(書堂) a village schoolhouse; a private school (for the study of Chinese classics). ¶ ~ 개 삼년에 풍월한다 《속담》 A saint's maid quotes Latin. *or* The sparrows near a school sing the primer.

**서대기** 〖어류〗 a sole.

**서덜** ① 《물가의》 a stony 〔pebbly〕 riverside. ② 《생선의》 the bones of a fish (with the meat gone).

**서도**(西道) the northwestern provinces of Korea.

**서도**(書道) penmanship; calligraphy. ⇨ 「서예(書藝).

**서두**(序頭) the beginning; the outset; the start; the opening 《of a composition, speech》. ¶ ~에 싣다 give 《an article》 at the beginning / 그는 ~를 이끌어내는 데 능하다 He knows when and how to broach a subject.

**서두**(書頭) 《첫머리》 the introduction 〔opening〕 of a book.

**서두르다** 《빨리》 hasten; hurry (up); nip; make haste; rush; make time; step on it 《구어》; get a move on 《구어》; press; urge; 《조급해 하다》 be impatient; be impetuous; 《걸음을》 walk 〔go〕 fast.

¶ 서둘러 in a hurry; in haste; hastily; hurriedly; quick(ly); without delay ⇨급히 / 서둘러 돌아오다 hurry back; 《집으로》 hurry 〔hasten〕 home / 서둘러 가버리다 hurry off 〔away〕 / 서둘러 나가다 hurry out / 서두른 나머지 in *one's* hurry / 서두르는 기색도 없이 calmly; serenely; in a suave and graceful manner / 일을 ~ speed 〔hurry〕 up *one's* work / 서두르고 있다 be in haste 〔a hurry〕; 《구어》 be in a rush / 서두르는 바람에 이것저것 다 잊다 forget everything in *one's* hurry / 될 수 있는 대로 ~ hurry as much as *one* can; make as much haste as possible / 서두를 것 없다 There is no need for haste. *or* There's no hurry. / 우리는 늦지 않도록 서둘렀다 We hurried so as not to be late. / 서두를 일일수록 천천히 하라 《속담》 More haste, less speed; Make haste slowly. / 늦지 않으려면 빨리 서두르는 것이 좋다 If you don't want to be late, you had better hasten there at once. / 서두르지 않으면 기차를 놓친다 Hurry up, or you will miss the train. / 왜 그리 서두르십니까 Why are you in such a hurry? *or* What's your 〔the〕 rush? / 그렇게 서두르지 마라 Don't be in such a hurry. *or* Don't hurry. (★「서두르지 마라」는 Don't be in haste. 로 쓰지 않으며, 이것은「당황하지 마라」의 뜻임).

**서둘다** ⇨서두르다.

**서든데스** 〖경기〗 《연장전에서》 sudden death.

**서랍** a drawer. ¶ ~ 속 깊숙이 in the back of a drawer / ~을 열다〔빼다〕 open 〔pull out, draw out〕 a drawer / ~을 닫다 shut 〔close, pull in〕 a drawer / 그는 책상 ~을 꼭 자물쇠로 채운다 He never fails to lock his desk drawer.

**서러움** ⇨설움.

**서러워하다** grieve 《at, over》; be grieved 《at, over》; be sad 《at》; feel sad unhappy〕 《about》; feel sorrow 《for》; have a heavy 〔broken〕 heart; 《애통하다》 deplore; lament 《*a person's* death》; mourn 《for, over》; regret. ¶ 서러워하여 in sorrow; sorrowfully / 서러워하는 얼굴 a sad look 〔face〕.

**서럽다** (be) sad; sorry; sorrowful; mournful; grievous. ¶ 서러운 나머지 in *one's* sorrow 〔grief〕 / 그 말을 들으니 ~ His remarks make me sad.

**서력**(西曆) ◉ ~기원 = 서기(西紀).

**서로** mutually; reciprocally; (with) each other; together; 《셋 이상》 (with) one another. ¶ ~의 mutual; reciprocal; each other's; one another's / ~ 합의하여 by mutual consent / ~ 돕다 help each other 〔one another〕 / ~ 사랑하다 love each other / ~ 상대의 얼굴을 바라보다 look at each other 〔each other's faces〕 / ~ 싸움하다 fight with each other / ~ 욕하다 call each other names / ~ 헐뜯다 find fault with each other / ~의 이익을 꾀하다 consult mutual interests / 그들은 ~ 존경하고 있다 They respect each other. *or* They have mutual respect.

**서론**(序論·緖論) an introduction; introductory 〔prefatory〕 remarks; a proem. ¶ ~으로(서) by way of introduction; as an introduction 《to *one's* story》.

**서류**(書類) a document; papers. ¶ 선적 ~ shipping documents / 중요 ~ important papers / ~를 작성하다 draw up 〔write out〕 documents / ~를 제출하다 submit 〔send in〕 papers / ~를 정리하다 set the papers in order; file the papers / 관계 ~를 자세히 살펴보아 주십시오 I would like you to go carefully over the relevant documents. / 「이 ~ 취급에는 주의를 다하시오」—「기밀 ~인가요」 "Please treat this document carefully."—"Is it confidential?" ◉ ~가방 a briefcase; an attaché case. ~철 《문방구》 a file; a folder (책표지 모양의). ~함 a filing cabinet.

**서류송청**(書類送廳) ~하다 send the papers pertaining to a criminal case to the Public Prosecutors Office.

**서류전형**(書類銓衡) ~하다 draw up a (short) list on the basis of the candidates' documents 〔records〕; screen candidates by examining their papers.

**서른** thirty. ◉ ~번째 the thirtieth. ~살 thirty years of age.

**서름(서름)하다** 《친하지 않다》 (be) distant; estranged 《from》; standoffish; lacking in intimacy; 《거북하다》 feel unpleasant 〔awkward〕; 《익숙지 않다》 be unfamiliar 〔unacquainted〕 《with》. ¶ 서름서름하게 대하다 treat 《*a person*》 like a stranger / 두 사람 사이가 서름서름해졌다 They don't get on so well as before.

**서리**[1] ① 〖기상〗 frost; white 〔hoary〕 frost. ¶ 된~ a heavy frost; [비유적] a great 〔hard〕 blow / 무~ an early frost / 첫~ the first frost of the season / ~ 내리는 날씨 a frosty sky; frosty weather / ~가 내리다 frost forms; it frosts (up) / ~ 내린 아침 a frosty morning / ~를 막다 protect 〔shelter〕 《a plant》 from (the) frost /

～를 없애다 defrost 《a refrigerator》/ 풀밭에 ～가 내렸다 There is frost on the grass. ② 《타격》 a blow; damage; harm; 《손실》 a loss. ⇨ 서리맞다.
◉ ～병아리 a chicken born in late autumn; a weakling; a runt. ～제거장치 a defrosting device; a defroster. ～피해 damage by frost; frost damage: ～ 피해를 입다 suffer from 〔be nipped by〕 frost. 서릿바람 a frosty 〔chilly〕 wind.

**서리**[2] 《훔치기》 stealing 《fruits, chickens, *etc.*》 in a band (out of a mischievous motive); a group raid on 《another's melon field》; a children's poaching party. ～하다 make a raid on 《another's melon field》; steal out of mischievous motive. ◉ 닭〔참외〕～ a raid on 《*a person's*》 「chickens 〔melon patch〕.

**서리**[3] 《무더기》 a mass; a pile; a group. ¶ 나무 ～a pile of wood.

**서리**(署理) 《사람》 a deputy (official); a proxy; an acting director; a locum tenens(특히 의사·목사의); 《일》 administering as an acting director; procuration; proxy; attorneyship. ～하다 administer 《affairs》 as an acting director. ¶ 교장～ an acting principal; the acting director 《of the school》/ 국무총리 ～ the acting premier / 의장～ a deputy chairperson / ～를 보다 act for; act in place 〔behalf〕 of; stand proxy for.

**서리다**[1] ① 《김이》 get steamed; steam up; (become) dim; be clouded; fog up (안개가); collect moisture 〔get misted〕 (렌즈·유리 등이); become smoked (up) (등피 등이). ¶ 유리창에 김이 ～ the window is steamed up; the windowpane is clouded up with steam / 숨 때문에 안경에 김이 서렸다 My breath fogged my glasses. ② 《어리다》 be filled 《with》. ¶ 위엄이 서린 얼굴 a dignified look / 노여움이 ～ look angry. ③ 《가슴에》 be harbored 〔cherished, nursed〕. ¶ 오랫동안 가슴속에 서린 원한 a long-cherished grudge / 원한이 서려 있다 have old scores to settle 《with》. ④ 《줄이》 be 〔get〕 entangled 〔coiled〕. ⑤ 《기가 꺾이다》 get 《*one's* ego》 deflated; lose heart 〔courage〕.

**서리다**[2] ⇨사리다①.

**서리맞다** be frosted 《over》; be touched 〔nipped〕 by frost; [비유적] suffer a blow; receive a setback; be (hard) hit; be frustrated. ¶ 꽃이 서리맞았다 The flower is nipped by frost. / 면업계는 그로 인해 서리를 맞았다 The cotton industry was hard hit by it.

**서림**(書林) 《서점》 a bookshop; a bookstore 《미》.

**서릿발** ① 《서리의》 ice needles 〔columns〕; frost columns 〔crystals〕. ¶ 오늘 아침에 ～이 섰다 Frost columns formed on the ground this morning. ② 《엄함》 being rigorous; sternness; relentlessness. ¶ ～ 같은 논고 a most relentless argument 《against》/ ～ 같은 명령 a stern 〔relentless〕 order.

**서막**(序幕) ① 《연극의》 the opening 〔first〕 act 〔scene〕; the curtain raiser. ② 《시초》 a prelude; a beginning. ¶ 그 주가 폭락은 거품 경제 붕괴의 ～이었다 The sharp decline in stock prices proved to be the prelude to the collapse of bubble economy.

**서머** summer. ◉ ～스쿨 a summer school. ～타임 daylight saving time (생략 DST); summer time 《영》 (생략 S.T.). ～하우스 a summer house.

**서머(서머)하다** [서술적] be ashamed 《of *oneself*》; be 〔feel〕 abashed; be unable to face 《others》. ¶ 서머하게 하다 put 《*a person*》 out of countenance 〔to the blush〕; take 〔bring〕 《*a person*》 down a peg / 서머해서 고개를 숙이다 hang *one's* head with shame.

**서먹(서먹)하다** 《관계가》 (be) distant; estranged; cold; reserved; 《거북하다》 [서술적] feel awkward 〔out of place, nervous〕 《before an audience》; feel small 〔cheap, embarrassed〕 《in company》; feel ill at ease; be not at home; 《익숙지 않다》 (be) unfamiliar 《with》. ¶ 서먹서먹하게 awkwardly; shyly / 서먹서먹한 사람 an unfamiliar person / 서먹서먹해 하다 be reserved; stand on ceremony 《toward *a person*》/ 둘 사이가 서먹서먹해졌다 The two became estranged. *or* Some coldness came between them. / 여기 있기가 서먹서먹하다 I feel out of place here. / 파티에 가면 서먹서먹한 게, 나는 비사교적이야 I don't feel at ease at a party. I'm a bad mixer.

**서면**(書面) 《편지》 a letter; 《문서》 a document. ¶ ～으로 by letter; in writing / 본인이나 혹은 ～으로 personally or by mail / 구두나 ～으로 orally or in writing / ～으로 하다 put 《*something*》 in writing; commit 《*something*》 to writing / ～으로 신청〔탄원〕하다 submit

〔send in〕 a written application 〔petition〕《to》/ ~으로 알리다 let《a person》know by letter.
◉ ~결의 a documentary resolution 〔decision〕. ~심리《법원의》(a) documentary examination; (an) examination by means of documents. ~주문 a written order.

**서명**(書名) the title 〔name〕 of a book. ◉ ~목록 a title catalog(ue).

**서명**(署名) a signature; an autograph (자기 사진·작품 등에 하는);《서명하기》signing; autographing. ~하다 sign 〔write (down)〕 *one's* name; sign《a treaty》; affix 〔attach, put〕 *one's* signature《to a document》; subscribe *one's* name《to a document》.
¶ ~한〔이 있는〕 signed《by the author》; autographed《photo》; carrying 〔bearing〕《*a person's*》signature / ~ 날인한《a bond》under《*a person's*》hand and seal / ~이 없는 편지 an unsigned letter / ~이 있는 사진 an autographed photo / ~이 있는 그림 a picture signed by the artist / 청원서에 ~을 (사람에게서) 받다 collect signatures on a petition / 서류에 ~ 날인하다 sign and seal a document; affix *one's* signature and seal to a paper / 조약〔계약〕에 ~하다 sign a treaty 〔contract〕/ 여기에 ~해 주십시오 Sign here, please. / 저자는 그 책에 자필로 ~했다 The author signed his autograph in the book.
◉~국《조약 등의》a signatory (power). ~기사(記事) a signed article; a byline(d) article. ~운동 a signature-collecting campaign 〔drive〕: ~운동을 벌이다 launch a signature-collecting drive. ~자 a signer; the undersigned 〔over-signed〕(문서에서 지칭하는).

**서모**(庶母) *one's* father's concubine.

**서목**(書目)《목차》the list of contents (attached to a document);《도서 목록》a catalog(ue) of books.

**서무**(庶務) general affairs. ◉ ~계 a general affairs clerk. ~과 the general affairs section. ~규정 office routine regulations.

**서문**(序文)《머리말》a preface 〔foreword〕《to》; an introduction《to》. ¶ ~을 쓰다 preface《a book》; write a preface to 〔prepare a preface for〕《a book》.

**서미남**(西微南) west by south (생략 WbS).

**서미북**(西微北) west by north (생략 WbN).

**서민**(庶民) the (common) people;《미》common 〔ordinary〕 folks 〔folk《영》〕; the populace; the commonality; the commonalty [총칭];《대중》the masses;《평균적인》the man in the street;《개인》a commoner. ¶ ~적인 popular《music》; everyday《dishes》; folksy《humor》/ 물가 상승은 ~의 살림에 바로 영향을 미친다 A rise in prices directly affects the lives of the people.
◉ ~계급 the mass of (the) people; the masses 〔populace〕; working classes. ~금고 a people's bank. ~금융 petty loans for the working classes; small-loan finance. ~사회 democratic 〔demotic, popular〕 society. ~아파트 an apartment for the low income bracket.

**서바이벌 게임** a survival game.

**서반구**(西半球) the western hemisphere.

**서반아**(西班牙) Spain. =스페인.

**서방**(西方) ①《서쪽》the west. ②《지방》western districts;《나라》western countries;《동서 양진영의》the West. ③〚불교〛=서방정토.
◉ ~정토〚불교〛the Western Paradise; the Buddhist Elysium. ~측 (the side of) the West; the Western Powers: ~측 진영 the Western camp 〔bloc〕.

**서방**(書房) ①《남편》*one's* husband; *one's* old man《구어》; *one's* hubby《구어》. ¶ ~(을) 맞다 get married to a man; marry. ②《호칭》Mr. ¶ 김~ Mr. Kim. ③《하인에게》¶ 박~ Old Park.

**서방질**(書房―) (a married woman's) adultery; cuckolding. ~하다 cuckold 〔deceive〕 *one's* husband; have a lover; commit adultery with.

**서버**《테니스 등의》a server.

**서벅돌** a friable 〔crumbly〕 stone.

**서법**(書法) penmanship; calligraphy.

**서변**(西邊) the west; the western side.

**서부**(西部) the western part(s); the west;《미국의》the West. ¶ ~의 western. ◉ ~극 a horse opera;《영화》a western (film); a cowboy picture. ~음악 western music;《민속적인》country (music). ~지방 the western district 〔provinces〕; the West《미》.

**서북**(西北) ①《방향》the northwest (생략 NW);《서와 북》west and north. ¶ ~의 northwestern; northwesterly / ~에 (to the) northwest《of》/ ~으로 northwestward. ②《지방》the northwestern provinces of Korea.
◉ ~서 west-northwest (생략 WNW). ~풍 a northwestern 〔northwesterly〕 wind. ~항로 a northwest service 〔line,

run〕. ~향 facing the northwest.

**서브** a serve; a service. ¶ ~(를) 넣다 serve 《a ball》/ ~를 받다 receive the serve 〔service〕/ ~를 잘〔못〕 넣다 have a good 〔poor〕 serve / 누가 ~할 차례냐 Whose service is it? ◉ ~권(權) 《*one's*》 serve: ~권을 얻다 get the serve.

**서브루틴** 〖컴퓨터〗 a subroutine.

**서브타이틀** 《부제목·영화 자막》 a subtitle. ¶ ~을 붙이다 subtitle 《a book》.

**서비스** ① 《봉사》 service. ~하다 give *one's* service; attend on 《a customer》; 《무료로》 「provide 《*a thing*》 extra 〔throw 《*a thing*》 in〕 free of charge. ¶ ~가 좋다〔나쁘다〕 They give good 〔poor〕 service (in that store). / 이것은 ~입니다 I'll throw this in (free of charge). *or* This is on the house. ② 《테니스·탁구에서》 a service. ⇨ 서브. ◉ ~개선 improvement of services. ~라인 the service line. ~료 a service charge; 《식당·요정 등의》 a cover charge: ~료는 안 받습니다 We don't charge for service. ~부문 the service sector. ~스테이션 《주유소》 a service 〔gas 《미》, petrol 《영》〕 station. ~업 a service industry 〔job〕; services. ~에어리어 《방송국·고속도로 등의》 a service area. ~에이스 〖테니스〗 an 〔a service〕 ace. ~코트 〖테니스〗 the service court.

**서사**(敍事) description of deeds 〔incidents〕. ~하다 describe; narrate. ¶ ~적(인) descriptive; narrative. ◉ ~문 a description; a narrative. ~시 an epic (poem); [총칭] epic poetry: ~시 시대 the age of epic poetry / 영웅 ~시 a heroic epic.

**서사**(書寫) transcription; copying. ~하다 transcribe; copy. ◉ ~료 a copying fee.

**서사모아**(西―) Western Samoa.

**서산**(西山) the western mountain 〔hill〕.

**서생**(書生) ① 《유생》 a student (of Chinese classics); a (young, budding) Confucianist. ② 《남의 집의》 a student dependent; a student servant 〔houseboy〕.

**서서히**(徐徐―) slow(ly); gradually; little by little; by degrees. ⇨ 천천히. ¶ 그는 ~ 공부에 흥미를 느끼게 되었다 He became more and more interested in his studies.

**서설**(序說) an introduction.

**서설**(瑞雪) auspicious 〔propitious〕 snow.

**서성거리다** walk up and down restlessly; hang about 〔around〕 《a house》. ¶ 나는 마음을 가라앉히려고 방안을 서성거렸다 I walked up and down the room trying to compose myself. / 이 근처에 서성거리지 마라 Don't loiter round 〔hang about〕 here!

**서성서성** pacing back and forth restlessly.

**서속**(黍粟) 〖식물〗 millet.

**서수**(序數) 〖수학〗 an ordinal (number). ◉ ~사(詞) ordinal numerals.

**서술**(敍述) (a) description; (a) depiction; an account; (a) delineation; (a) narration. ~하다 describe; delineate; narrate; give an account 《of》. ¶ ~적인 descriptive; narrative; 〖문법〗 predicative / ~에 뛰어난 문장가 a descriptive writer / ~을 잘하다 excel in description. ◉ ~부〔어〕 〖문법〗 the predicate (of a sentence). ~자 a narrator; a depictor. ~형용사 〖문법〗 a predicative adjective; an adjective used predicatively.

**서스펜스** suspense. ¶ ~가 넘치는 영화 a suspenseful film; a film full of suspense.

**서슬** 《날붙이의》 a burnished blade; the edge 〔sharpness〕 of a blade; 《기세》 the brunt 《of an attack, argument》; impetuosity; *one's* looks; an attitude; *one's* mettle 〔spirit〕. ¶ ~이 푸르다 《날이》 be sharp 〔glittering〕; 《기세가》 have a threatening 〔menacing〕 look 〔attitude〕/ ~이 시퍼런 칼 a glittering sword / 그는 자못 ~이 시퍼래져서 우리 방으로 뛰어 들어왔다 He stormed 〔burst〕 into our room with a ferocious expression on his face.

**서슴거리다** hesitate; waver; be hesitant. ¶ 서슴거리며 hesitatingly; with hesitation; irresolutely / 가기를 ~ hesitate about going. ⇨ 서슴다.

**서슴다** hesitate 《at, about》; scruple 《at》; waver; vacillate; falter; shilly=shally; be irresolute 〔hesitant〕; think twice 《about》; 《두려워 꺼리다》 be afraid 〔shy〕 of.

¶ 서슴지 않고 without hesitation; unhesitatingly; without scruples 〔wavering〕/ …하기를 서슴지 않다 be ready 〔willing〕 to *do* / (능히) …도 서슴지 않다 stick at nothing; make no scruple to *do* 〔of *do*ing〕; be capable of 《any crime》/ 죽음도 서슴지 않다 do not hesitate even to die / 무슨 짓이라도 서슴지 않을 놈이다 He may go to any extreme. / 그는 넉넉지 못한 처지임에도 가난한 사람들에게 베풀기를 서슴지 않았다 He never hesitated to give things away to the poor despite his own poverty.

**서슴없다** (be) unhesitating; be not hesitant; have no scruples about; make no scruple of; do not stick at. ¶ 서슴없이 without (a moment's) hesitation; unhesitatingly; without scruple 〔reserve, wavering〕/ 서슴없이 말하다 speak without hesitation / 그는 서슴없이 소신을 말했다 Without hesitation he gave utterance to what he believed.

**서식**(書式) a (due, fixed, prescribed) form; 《컴퓨터·문서의》 a format. ¶ ～대로 in due 〔the proper〕 form; in accordance with 〔according to〕 the form prescribed / 일정한 ～ a prescribed 〔due〕 form / ～에 기입하다 fill out 〔in, up〕 a form / 원서는 ～에 따라서 써 주시오 The application should be written「in due form 〔according to the form prescribed〕.

**서식**(棲息) (in)habitation. ～하다 live 《in, at》; be native 《to》; inhabit 《the earth》. ¶ ～에 적합한 (in)habitable / 물 속에 ～하다 live in the water / 숲에 ～하다 inhabit a forest; be forest-dwelling. ◉ ～지 a habitat; the home 《of the tiger》.

**서신**(書信) 《편지왕래》 correspondence; communication; 《편지》 a letter; a note; a missive; a message. ¶ ～ 왕래가 있다 be in correspondence with 《*a person*》; keep in touch with each other by letter / …에게 ～을 내다 write a letter to 《*a person*》; send 〔address〕 a letter to 《*a person*》/ …와 ～ 왕래가 끊이지 않다 be in constant correspondence with….

**서안**(西岸) the west coast.

**서약**(誓約) an oath; a vow; a (solemn) pledge; a covenant; 〖법〗 recognizance. ～하다 swear; vow; pledge; take 〔make, swear〕 an oath 《that》; give *one's* pledge 〔word〕 《that》; pledge 〔commit〕 *oneself* 《to *do*》. ¶ ～대로 faithful 〔true〕 to *one's* vow; in conformity with *one's* promise 〔pledge〕/ ～을 실행하다 put *one's* pledge into effect; discharge 〔fulfill〕 *one's* vow / ～을 지키다 keep *one's* pledge 〔vow, word〕/ ～을 어기다 break *one's* oath 〔vow〕; violate *one's* pledge. ◉ ～서 a written oath 〔pledge, promise〕: ～서를 쓰다 write a pledge. ～자 a party to a covenant; a recognizor.

**서양**(西洋) the West; the Occident; Europe (and America). ¶ ～의 Occidental; Western; European / ～화하다 westernize; Europeanize / ～물이 들어 있다 be touched 〔imbued〕 with Occidentalism; be Europeanized; be under Western influence / 서양이란 말은 미국·캐나다와 서유럽·남유럽 및 북유럽 제국을 가리키는데 쓰이고 있다 The West is used to refer to the United States, Canada and the countries of Western, Northern and Southern Europe. ◉ ～문명〔사상〕 Western civilization 〔ideas〕. ～문학 Western literature; European literature. ～사 European 〔Occidental〕 history. ～식 Western style 〔ways〕; Occidental 〔European〕 manner: ～식으로 after 〔in〕 European fashion; in Western style / ～식 사고방식 the Western way of thinking. ～요리 Western food 〔dishes〕. ⇨ 양식(洋食). ～음악 Western music. ～인 a Westerner; an Occidental; a European or an American. ～제국(諸國) the Western countries 〔nations〕. ～풍 = ～식. ～화 (a) Western 〔Occidental〕 painting; (an) oil painting (유화). ⇨ 양화(洋畫). ～화가 an artist of Western painting; an oil painter (유화의).

**서언**(序言·緖言) a foreword; a preface; an introduction; an introductory remark.

**서역**(西域) the countries to the west「of China.

**서열**(序列) rank; ranking; order 《of precedence》; 《구어》 peck(ing) order (사회적인). ¶ ～에 따라 in order of importance / ～이 Y 다음이다 stand next to Y in line / 당～ 제3위를 차지하다 rank No. 3 in the party hierarchy.

**서예**(書藝) calligraphy; penmanship. ¶ ～의 대가 a master 〔great〕 calligrapher.

**서운**(瑞雲) propitious 〔auspicious〕 clouds; clouds of good omen. ¶ ～이 서려 있다 auspicious clouds hang over 《a place》.

**서운하다** ① 《사람이》 (be) sorry; sad; reluctant; regrettable; [서술적] leave a sensible void. ¶ 아들이 없어 ～ I miss my son. / 그를 보지 못해 ～ I am sorry to have missed seeing him. / 그녀가 없으면 몹시 서운할 것이다 She will be badly missed. ② 《일·처사 등이》 (be) displeasing; unfair; unjust; unkind. ¶ 서운한 대접 unfair treatment / 서운하게 대하다 treat 《*a person*》 in a displeasing way 〔with unkindness〕; behave unfairly toward 《*a person*》.

**서운해하다** be sorry; be saddened by; miss; 《…을》 be displeased at; feel mistreated 〔hurt〕 at; feel the unfairness of; consider 《*a thing*》 unkind 〔unjust, unfair〕. ¶ 그 처사를 ~ consider the treatment unfair.

**서울** ① 《수도》 a capital. ¶ 영국의 ~ 런던 London, the capital of England. ② 《한국의》 Seoul. ¶ ~식 요리 a dish in the Seoul style / ~로 가다 go 〔come〕 up to Seoul.
◉ ~깍쟁이 the shrewd Seoulite; a Seoulite. ~내기 a trueborn Seoulite; a (native) Seoulite. ~대공원 the Seoul Grand Park. ~대학교 Seoul National University: ~대학교 보건 대학원 the Seoul National University Graduate School of Health. ~시민 a citizen of Seoul; a Seoulite. ~시장 the Mayor of Seoul: ~ 시장 후보 a Seoul mayoral candidate. ~시청 the City Hall of Seoul; the Seoul Metropolitan Government (office): ~시청 출입 기자단 the press corps of the Seoul City government. ~ 외국인 학교 Seoul Foreign School. ~장안 《in》 all Seoul. ~ 지방 경찰청 the Seoul Metropolitan Police Agency: ~ 지방 경찰청장 the Commissioner of the Seoul Metropolitan Police Agency. ~특별시 《주소로 사용시》 Seoul City; 《기관 명칭》 Seoul Metropolitan City.

**서원**(書院) ① 《강론하는 곳》 a lecture hall; an auditorium. ② 《제사하는 곳》 a memorial hall for the great scholars and loyal subjects of the past.

**서원**(署員) (a member of) the 《police》 staff 〔force〕. ¶ 마포 경찰~ a member of the Map'o Police Station / 세무~ a tax(-office) clerk / 소방~ a fireman.

**서원**(誓願) a vow; a pledge; an oath. ~하다 vow; swear (an oath); take 〔make〕 a vow; pledge *oneself* 《to *do*》; pronounce a vow 《to god》.

**서인도**(西印度) West(ern) India. ◉ ~제도(諸島) the West Indies: ~제도의 West Indian.

**서임**(敍任) appointment; installation; investiture. ~하다 appoint; install; invest 《in an office》.

**서자**(庶子) 《첩의》 a child born of a concubine; 《사생아》 a child born out of wedlock; an illegitimate child.

**서작**(敍爵) conferment of a peerage; ennoblement. ~하다 confer a peerage 《on *a person*》; raise 《*a person*》 to the peerage; ennoble.

**서장**(書狀) 《편지》 a letter; a note.

**서장**(署長) the head 〔chief, superintendent〕 《of a police 〔fire〕 station》; a 《town, fire》 marshal (경찰·소방서의).

**서재**(書齋) a study; a library. ¶ ~에 틀어박히다 be confined 〔shut *oneself* up〕 in *one's* study. ◉ ~인 a person of the study; an academic person.

**서적**(書籍) books; publications (출판물). ◉ ~광 bibliomania; 《사람》 a lover of books; a bibliophile; a bibliomaniac. ~목록 a book catalog; a catalog of books. ~상 《사람》 a bookseller; 《가게》 ⇨ 서점. ~상조합 a booksellers' association. ~출판업 the publishing business. ~판매업 the bookselling business.

**서전**(緖戰) the beginning 〔an early stage〕 of a war 〔game〕. ¶ ~을 승리로 장식하다 win the first match 〔game〕; 《전쟁에서》 win battle in the early stages of a war.

**서점**(書店) a bookseller's; a bookstore 《미》; a bookshop 《영》.

**서정**(庶政) civil services; general administrative affairs 《of state》. ¶ ~을 쇄신하다 purify officialdom; enforce official discipline.

**서정**(敍情·抒情) delineation 〔description〕 of feeling; lyricism. ¶ ~적(인) lyric(al) / ~적으로 lyrically / 그의 단편 소설은 매우 ~적이고, 장편 소설보다 작품성이 우수하다 His short stories are full of lyricism and more excellent than his novels. ◉ ~문 lyric writing. ~시 a lyric (poem); lyric poetry [총칭]. ~시인 a lyric poet; a lyricist.

**서조**(瑞兆) a good omen; an auspicious sign.

**서주**(序奏) 〖음악〗 an introduction. ◉ ~곡 an entree; an overture; a prelude.

**서지**(書誌) a bibliography. ◉ ~학 bibliography: ~학자 a bibliographer.

**서지** serge (cloth). ¶ 감색 ~ blue serge / 순모~ woolen serge / 얇은 ~ sergette / ~옷 a serge suit. 「문진.

**서진**(書鎭) a paperweight; a weight. =

**서쪽**(西—) the west (생략 W). ¶ ~의 west; western; westerly / ~에 in 〔to, on〕 the west 《of》 / 시의 ~에 (to the) west of the city / ~으로 가다〔향하다〕 go 〔proceed〕 west(ward).

**서책**(書册) books. =서적.

**서첩**(書帖) a scrapbook (of writings

and pictures).

**서체**(書體) (a style of) handwriting; a calligraphic style; a style of penmanship; 《활자의》 a style of type.

**서출**(庶出) an offspring of a concubine. ¶ ~의 born of a concubine.

**서치라이트** a searchlight. ¶ ~로 비추다 turn 〔flash, play〕 a searchlight 《on》.

**서캐** a nit. ¶ ~ 훑듯 하다 leave no stone unturned (in a search); scour 〔comb〕 《a place for something》.

**서커스** a circus (show). ¶ ~ 곡예사 a circus performer / ~를 흥행하다 run 〔put on〕 a circus. ◉ ~단 a circus troupe. ~단장 a circus master.

**서클** a circle. ⇨ 동아리.

**서킷** 《자동차 경주의》 a (racing) circuit; 《전기 회로》 a circuit.

**서킷트레이닝** 〖스포츠〗 circuit training.

**서투르다** 《솜씨가》 (be) unskillful; inexpert; poor; awkward; clumsy; unhandy; bungling; 《익숙하지 않아》 (be) unfamiliar 《with》; unaccustomed 〔unused〕 《to》; ignorant 《of》; strange; new 《to, at》; [서술적] be not at home 《in》.
¶ 서투른 솜씨로 with a clumsy hand / 서투르게 clumsily; awkwardly; in a clumsy way / 서투른 그림〔번역〕 a poor picture 〔translation〕 / 서투른 사람 a poor hand 《at》; a bungler / 서투른 솜씨 a clumsy workmanship / 서투른 표현 a clumsy expression / …이 ~ be bad 〔not good, a bad hand〕 at / 계산이 ~ be bad 〔poor〕 at figures / 글씨가 ~ write a poor hand / 바느질이 ~ be clumsy with *one's* sewing / 미국 생활방식에는 ~ be unfamiliar with the American way of living / 서투른 바둑을 두다 play a poor game of *paduk* 《with》 / 서투른 영어를 하다 speak in poor 〔broken〕 English / 서투른 짓을 하다 make a blunder; make a mess of it; bungle; 《어리석은 짓을》 act foolishly / 서투른 무당이 장구만 나무란다 《속담》 A bad workman quarrels with his tools. / 서투른 풍수 집안만 망친다 《속담》 A little knowledge is a dangerous thing.

**서평**(書評) a book review. ¶ ~을 하다 review a book. ◉ ~가 a book reviewer. ~란(欄) the book-review columns.

**서표**(書標) a bookmark(er).

**서푼**(一分) 《돈》 three *p'un;* a farthing; [형용사적] of little worth. ¶ 그것은 ~짜리도 안된다 It is not worth a penny 〔fig, straw〕.

**서품**(敍品) 〖가톨릭〗 ordination. ~하다 ordain. ◉ ~식 the ceremony 〔rite〕 of ordination.

**서풍**(西風) a west 〔westerly〕 wind; Zephyr.

**서풍**(書風) a style of calligraphy 〔penmanship〕.

**서핑** surfing; surfriding. ~하다 surf; ride a surfboard. ¶ ~하는 사람 a surfer / ~을 하러 가다 go surfing.

**서한**(書翰) a letter; an epistle; [총칭] correspondence. = 편지.

**서해**(西海) the western sea; 《황해》 the Yellow Sea. ◉ ~안 the west coast: ~안 간선도로 the west coast highway.

**서행**(徐行) going slowly; 《게시》 Go slow. *or* Slow. *or* Drive slow 《speed limit 10 km/h.》. ~하다 go slowly; slow down 〔up〕; go 〔drive〕 at a slow speed; proceed at reduced speed; 《기선이》 steam along slowly; 《점차로》 slow down 〔up, off〕. ¶ 열차를 ~시키다 slow down a train / ~중인 차 a slow-moving vehicle / 차는 ~했다 The car drove slow 〔slowly〕. / 커브에서는 ~토록 하여라 Slow down at the curve. ◉ ~속도 (a) low speed.

**서향**(西向) (having) a western exposure; facing west; looking toward (the) west. ¶ 창은 ~이다 The windows face west. ◉ ~집 a house facing (the) west; a house with a western exposure; a house open to the west.

**서향**(瑞香) 〖식물〗 a daphne.

**서혜**(鼠蹊) 〖해부〗 the groin. ¶ ~의 inguinal. ◉ ~부 the groin 〔inguinal〕 region. ~헤르니아 〖의학〗 an inguinal hernia.

**서화**(書畫) paintings 〔pictures〕 and calligraphic works. ◉ ~골동 《deal in》 objects of art and curios. ~상 a dealer in pictures and calligraphic works. ~전람회 an exhibition of pictures and calligraphic works. ~첩 an album of paintings and calligraphic works.

**서훈**(敍勳) (conferment of a) decoration; bestowal of an order. ~하다 confer a decoration 《on *a person*》; invest 《*a person*》 with a decoration; decorate. ¶ ~을 신청하다 recommend 《*a person*》 for a decoration.

**석**(石) a *sŏk.* = 섬[1].

**석** three. ¶ 석 달 three months / 석 장 three sheets of paper.

**-석**(石) 《시계의》 ¶ 18석의 시계 a 18-jewel watch; a watch of 18 jewels.

**–석**(席) a seat; a place. ¶ 부인석 the ladies' seats / 마부석 the driver's seat on a carriage / 예약〔지정〕석 a reserved seat / 《극장 따위의》 귀빈석 a royal box.
**석가**(釋迦) S(h)akyamuni; Gautama; the Buddha. ◉ ∼모니(牟尼) ⇨석가. ∼여래 S(h)akyamuni Tathagata. ∼탄신일 the Buddha's Birthday. ∼탑 the pagoda of S(h)akyamuni.
**석가산**(石假山) an artificial 〔a miniature〕 hill 〔mountain〕《in a landscape garden》. ¶ ∼을 만들다 build 〔heap up〕 a mound; build an artificial hill; make a rock garden.
**석각**(石刻) stone carving; a carved stone. ∼하다 carve stone 《for a statue》; carve 《a statue》 out of stone.
**석간**(夕刊) evening publication; an evening paper; the evening edition 《of a paper》; 《구어》 an afternooner. ◉ ∼신문 an evening paper.
**석경**(石鏡) a mirror; a looking glass.
**석고**(石膏) 〖광물〗 gypsum; gyps; plaster. ◉ ∼모형 a plaster cast. ∼붕대 a plaster-of-Paris bandage. ∼상 a plaster figure 〔bust〕. ∼세공 plaster work; plastering: ∼세공인 a plasterer. ∼조각 gypsography.
**석공**(石工) 《석수》 a (stone)mason; a stonecutter; 《석공업》 masonry.
**석관**(石棺) a stone coffin; a sarcophagus; 〖고고학〗 a cist.
**석굴**(石窟) a rocky cavern; a stone cave; a grotto. ◉ ∼암(庵) Sŏkkuram cave 〔grotto〕.
**석권**(席卷) ∼하다 《휩쓸다》 carry everything before *one;* sweep 《over, across》; overwhelm; 《정복하다》 make a conquest of; conquer. ¶ 전유럽을 ∼하다 sweep 〔pour〕 over the whole of Europe / 외국 자본이 국내 시장을 ∼하고 있다 Foreign capital is overwhelming our market(s).
**석기**(石器) stoneware; stonework; 〖고고학〗 a stone implement 〔tool〕. ¶ 뗀〔타제〕∼ a chipped stone tool / 간〔마제〕 ∼ a polished stone tool. ◉ ∼시대 the Stone Age: 신∼ 시대 the neolithic age; the New Stone Age / 구∼ 시대 the palaeolithic age 〔era〕; the Old Stone Age.
**석남**(石南) 〖식물〗 a rhododendron; an alpine rose. 「= 돌계집.
**석녀**(石女) a barren 〔sterile〕 woman.
**석뇌유**(石腦油) 〖화학〗 naphtha.
**석다** 《눈이》 melt; thaw; 《양조물이》 mellow.
**석등**(石燈) a stone lantern.
**석랍**(石蠟) coal oil; paraffin.
**석류**(石榴) 〖식물〗 a pomegranate. ◉ ∼나무 a pomegranate tree.
**석류석**(石榴石) 〖광물〗 garnet.
**석면**(石綿) 〖광물〗 asbestos; amiantus. ◉ ∼섬유〔슬레이트〕 asbestos fiber 〔slate〕. ∼침착증 〖의학〗 asbestosis.
**석명**(釋明) (an) explanation; elucidation; explication; an apology; (a) vindication (변명). ∼하다 explain; elucidate; explicate; vindicate 《*oneself*》; clear up; apologize 《for》.
**석묵**(石墨) 〖광물〗 graphite. = 흑연(黑鉛).
**석방**(釋放) release; discharge; liberation; (an) acquittal. ∼하다 release; let off; turn loose; set free; let 《*a person*》 out of prison; acquit. ¶ 조건부 ∼ conditional release / ∼을 위해 교섭하다 negotiate for 《*a person's*》 release / ∼을 간청〔탄원〕하다 plead for the release of 《*a person*》 / 교도소에서 ∼되다 be released from prison; be let out of prison. 「cliff.
**석벽**(石壁) 《벽》 a stone wall; 《절벽》 a
**석별**(惜別) parting with regrets; unwillingness to part; reluctance to leave. ∼하다 part with regrets; be unwilling 〔sorry, loath〕 to part 《from *one's* friend》; be reluctant to leave 《*a person*》. ¶ ∼의 눈물 tears at parting / ∼의 정을 말하다〔표하다〕 express *one's* sorrow at parting. ◉ ∼연 a farewell party 〔banquet〕; a send-off
**석부**(石斧) a stone ax. 〔dinner.
**석불**(石佛) a stone Buddhist image.
**석비**(石碑) a stone monument.
**석빙고**(石氷庫) an ice storage house; an earthen-covered stone construction for ice storage in ancient times.
**석사**(碩士) 《선비》 a worthy scholar (holding no office); 《칭호》 Mister; 《학위》 Master. ¶ 문학 ∼ Master of Arts (생략 M.A.) / 이학 ∼ Master of Science (생략 M.S., M.Sc.). ◉ ∼과정 the master's course 《in》. ∼논문 a master's thesis 《in》. ∼학위 《get》 a master's degree 《in》.
**석산**(石山) a stony 〔rocky〕 mountain.
**석산**(石蒜) 〖식물〗 a cluster-amaryllis.
**석삼년**(一三年) nine years; [비유적] many 〔several〕 years; a long time.
**석상**(石像) a stone image 〔statue〕.
**석상**(席上) ¶ ∼에서 at the meeting 〔assembly〕; in public / 회의 ∼에서 발언하다 speak at a conference.
**석송**(石松) 〖식물〗 a club moss; a buck

grass; a coral evergreen; a ground pine.
**석쇠** a gridiron; a grill.
**석수**(石手) a (stone)mason; a stone-cutter. ◉ ～질 masonry (work).
**석수**(汐水) the evening tide.
**석순**(石筍) 〖광물〗 stalagmite.
**석순**(席順) = 석차(席次).
**석실**(石室) a stone chamber 〔hut〕.
**석양**(夕陽) the evening 〔setting, declining〕 sun. ¶ 서쪽 하늘이 ～을 받아 붉게 빛나고 있다 The western skies are aglow with the setting sun. ◉ ～녘 sunset. ～볕 the warmth 〔heat〕 of the setting sun. ～빛 the light of the setting sun.
**석연하다**(釋然―) [사람이 주어] be satisfied 《with the explanation》; be relieved from doubt; feel free from doubt; [사물이 주어] (be) satisfactory. ¶ 석연치 않다 be unsatisfactory 〔unconvincing, ununderstandable〕; be (still) in doubt 《of, about》; be dubious 《of, about》; be not quite satisfied 〔happy〕 《with the explanation》 / 석연치 않은 인물 a doubtful character / 무언가 석연치 않은 데가 있다 There is something inexplicable in the matter. *or* There is something to be clarified.
**석염**(石鹽) 〖광물〗 rock salt. = 암염.
**석영**(石英) 〖광물〗 quartz.
◉ ～반암(斑岩) quartz porphyry. ～사 quartz sand. ～암 quartzite. ～유리 quartz glass. ～조면암(粗面岩) quartz trachyte. 녹(綠)～ prase. 유(乳)～ milky quartz.
**석유**(石油) oil; 《중유 등》 petroleum; 《등유》 《미》 kerosene; coal oil 《미》; paraffin 《영》. ¶ ～의 petrolic / ～를 함유한 oil bearing / ～를 찾아내다 hit 〔strike〕 oil / ～를 연료로 하다 use oil for fuel / ～탐사를 시작하다 launch a search for oil 《in》.
◉ ～가격 oil price: ～ 공시 가격 posted oil price. ～가스 petroleum gas: 액화 ～ 가스 liquefied petroleum gas(생략 LPG). ～갱 a petroleum 〔an oil〕 well. ～공업 the petroleum 〔oil〕 industry. ～관련제품 petroleum-based products. ～광상(鑛床) an oil deposit. ～기지 an oil camp. ～난로 an oil 〔a kerosene 《미》, a paraffin 《영》〕 heater 〔stove〕. ～등 an oil 〔a kerosene 《미》〕 lamp 〔lantern〕. ～매장량 (an estimated amount of) oil deposits. ～발동기 an internal-combustion engine (내연기관). ～비축(備蓄) petroleum reserves; oil stock: ～ 비축기지 an oil stockpiling base. ～사업법 the Petroleum Business Law. ～산업 the oil industry. ～수송관 an oil pipe(line). ～수출국 기구 the Organization of Petroleum Exporting Countries (생략 OPEC). ～식품 petrofood; food produced from petroleum. ～안정기금 the Petroleum Stability 〔Stabilization〕 Fund. ～업자 an oilman. ～연료 petroleum fuels. ～위기〔파동〕 an oil crisis 〔shock, squeeze, pinch〕. ～유제 petroleum emulsion. ～자원 petroleum 〔oil〕 resources; oil reserves: ～자원을 개발하다 develop 〔exploit〕 petroleum resources. ～정제 a petroleum refining. ～정제소 an oil 〔a petroleum〕 refinery. ～제품 petroleum 〔oil〕 products. ～ 채굴 oil (well) drilling: ～채굴권 an oil concession; oil-drilling rights / ～ 채굴 업자 an oil driller. ～탐사작업 an oil-hunt〔-search〕 operation. ～탱크 an oil tank. ～통 an oil-can; a kerosene tin 《영》. ～회사 an oil company. 세계～회의 the World Petroleum Congress (생략 WPC). 한국 ～ 개발 공사 Korea Petroleum Development Corp (생략 PEDCO).
**석유화학**(石油化學) petrochemistry.
◉ ～공업 the petrochemical industry. ～공장 a petrochemical plant. ～제품 a petrochemical (product). ～콤비나트 a petrochemical 〔an oil〕 complex.
**석이다** 《녹게 함》 cause 《snow》 to thaw; thaw; 《양조물이》 cause 《a brew》 to mellow; ferment. ⇨ 석다.
**석인**(石人) a stone statue 〔image, figure〕 of a man.
**석일**(昔日) old 〔former〕 times. = 옛날.
**석자** an iron-scoop net.
**석장**(錫杖) 〖불교〗 a monk's staff.
**석재**(石材) (building) stone. ◉ ～상 《사람》 a stone dealer; 《가게》 a stone dealer's (shop).
**석전**(石戰) a rock(-throwing) fight; a battle with stones.
**석전**(釋典) 〖불교〗 Buddhist scriptures. 「= 불경(佛經).
**석전**(釋奠) a festival held twice a year to honor Confucius. ◉ ～제 = 석전.
**석조**(石造) stone construction. ¶ ～의 stone-built 《houses》; built of stone.
◉ ～건물 a stone house 〔building〕.
**석존**(釋尊) 〖불교〗 S(h)akyamuni; the Buddha.
**석종유**(石鍾乳) 〖광물〗 stalactite.
**석주**(石柱) a stone pillar.

**석죽**(石竹) 〖식물〗 a pink; a China pink.

**석차**(席次) 《학교의》 the class order; the order of seats 〔places〕; the seating order; 《의식 등의》 the order of precedence; ranking. ¶ ~가 오르다 go up 《two places》 in class 〔in the class order〕 / 학기말에는 그의 ~가 뚝 떨어졌다 At the end of the term his name was very low down on the list. / 그의 ~는 반에서 세 번째다 He ranks third in his class. ◉ ~다툼 a quarrel over precedence; 《학교에서의》 a competition for higher class order. 졸업~ *one's* graduation standing.

**석창포**(石菖蒲) 〖식물〗 a sweet flag 〔rush〕.

**석축**(石築) stonework; masonry. ¶ ~의 《a house》 built of stone; stone-built. ◉ ~제방 a stone embankment; a sheath.

**석출**(析出) 〖화학〗 eduction; extraction. ~하다 educe; extract.

**석탄**(石炭) coal. ¶ 타고 있는〔이글거리는〕 ~ live 〔red-hot〕 coals / ~을 때다 burn coal / ~을 싣다 bunker 〔take (in)〕 coal; ship coal / ~을 지피다 put coal(s) on 《the fire》; feed 《a stove》 with coal / ~을 캐다 mine 〔dig out〕 coal / ~을 연료로 하다 use coal for fuel / ~을 삽으로 퍼 넣다 shovel coal(s). ◉ ~가루 coal dust. ~가스 coal gas. ~건류 coal carbonization. ~계 〖지질〗 the Carboniferous system: ~계의 Carboniferous. ~고 《저장소》 a coal depot; 《배의》 a (coal) bunker; 《지하의》 a coal hole. ~광 a coal mine. ~광부 a coal miner. ~광업권 a coal mining right. ~기 〖지질〗 the Carboniferous period. ~매장량 (the estimated amount of ) coal deposits; coal reserves. ~보급지 a coal base. ~분쇄기 a coal breaker 〔crusher〕. ~산 〖화학〗 ⇨ 페놀. ~산지 a coalfield. ~선 《운반용의》 a collier; a coal ship. ~액화 coal liquefaction 〔benginization〕; liquefaction of coal. ~운반부 a coal heaver; a coal-whipper. ~재〔찌끼〕 coal cinders. ~저장소 a coalbin. ⇨ ~고. ~적재 coaling; bunkering: ~적재항〔부두〕 a coaling port 〔wharf〕. ~차 《철도·광산의》 a coal car. ~체 a coal screen. ~층 a coal seam 〔bed〕. ~통 a coal scuttle; a coalbox. ~포대〔부대〕 a coal sack. 대한~공사 the Dai Han Coal Corporation.

**석탑**(石塔) a stone pagoda 〔stupa, tower〕.

**석판**(石版) 〖인쇄〗 lithography (석판술); a lithograph (석판화). ¶ ~(인쇄)의 lithographic. ◉ ~용지 lithographic paper. ~인쇄 lithography; lithographic print(ing): ~인쇄를 하다 lithograph. ~화 a lithograph. 사진~술 photolithography.

**석패**(惜敗) a defeat by a narrow margin; a regrettable defeat. ~하다 be defeated 〔lose a game〕 by a narrow margin; lose by a whisker.

**석필**(石筆) a slate pencil; a stylus.

**석학**(碩學) a great 〔distinguished〕 scholar; a man of erudition 〔profound learning〕; a savant (F.).

**석화**(石火) 《불꽃》 a flint fire 〔spark〕; 《몹시 빠름》 flash. ¶ 전광 ~같이 (as) quick as lightning; with lightning speed 〔swiftness〕.

**석회**(石灰) lime. ¶ 소(消)~ slaked 〔slack, dead〕 lime / ~성의 〖동물·해부〗 calcific / ~분이 많은 토양 soil rich in lime / ~를 뿌리다 sprinkle lime 《over》. ◉ ~동 a lime grotto; a limestone cave. ~모르타르 lime mortar. ~분(粉) lime powder. ~비료 lime fertilizer. ~석〔암〕 limestone. ~수 limewater. ~유 milk 〔cream〕 of lime. ~질 calcium: ~질의 calcareous; calcic. ~질소(窒素) calcium cyanamide; nitrolime. ~침착 〖의학〗 calcium 〔lime〕 deposit; calcification. ~화(華) calcareous sinter; flowers of lime. ~화(化) calcification.

**섞갈리다** be confusing; be mixed up; get confused 〔tangled, complicated〕. ¶ 셈이 ~ get confused in calculation / 이야기가 섞갈린다 The story gets entangled.

**섞다** mix; admix; mingle; blend; compound 《this and that》; 《불순물을》 adulterate 《with》. ¶ 물을 ~ dilute 《a solution》 with water / 술에 물을 ~ adulterate liquor with water; add water to liquor / 시멘트에 모래를 ~ mix cement with sand / 약품에 다른 약품을 ~ incorporate a chemical substance with others / 물을 기름에 섞기는 어렵다 You can hardly mix oil with water. /파랑과 노랑을 섞으면 녹색이 된다 If you blend 〔combine〕 blue and yellow, you'll get green.

**섞바꾸다** alternate (with each other); interchange regularly with 《*something*》.

**섞바뀌다** be alternated; alternate; be interchanged regularly with 《*something*》.

**섞사귀다** mix with a person of different social standing.

**섞음질** adulteration; mixing. ～하다 adulterate 《*sul*》 with 《water》; mix 《*something*》 with 《another》; doctor. ¶ ～하지 않은 unadulterated; pure / ～한 것 a mixture; an adulteration; impurities.

**섞이다** ① 《혼합되다》 be 〔get〕 mixed; be mingled 〔blended〕; mix. ¶ 유머가 섞인 연설 a speech seasoned with humor / 기름과 물은 섞이지 않는다 Oil and water will not mix. / 그에게는 외국인의 피가 섞여 있다 He has racially mixed blood. ② 《남들과》 mix 《with》; mingle 《with》; join. ¶ 군중 속에 ～ mingle with the crowd / 나도 그들 속에 섞여 있었다 I was among 〔one of〕 them.

**섟**[1] 《감정》 a sudden feeling (of doubt 〔anger〕); a (passing) doubt; a (moment of) suspicion; (a fit of) anger.

**섟**[2] 《물가의》 a good place to tie up a boat.

**섟삭다** 《의심이》 be resolved; be dispelled 〔dissipated〕; 《노여움이》 be allayed; [사람이 주어] relent 《toward *a person*》.

**선** a meeting 〔an interview〕 preliminary with a view to marriage; a marriage meeting; 《첫 등장》 *one's* debut. ⇨선보다.

**선**(先) ① 《차례》 precedence; the first. ② 《바둑·장기의》 the first move; 《화투·카드놀이의》 (the) lead; a dealer. ¶ 선을 하다[두다] make 〔have〕 the first move 《in a game of *paduk*》 / 누가 선이냐 Whose deal 〔lead〕 is it? ③ 《고인》 (the) deceased. ¶ 선대인 your late father.

**선**(善) the good; goodness; virtue; 《선행》 a good deed. ¶ 최고의 선 the highest good / 선과 악 good and evil / 선을 행하다 do good; practice virtue / 악을 선으로 갚는 것은 훌륭한 일이다 It is noble to return good for evil.

**선**(腺) 〖해부〗 a gland. ¶ 선 분비물 glandular secretions; excreta / 림프선 a lymph(atic) gland.

**선**(線) ① (***a***) 《가는 줄》 a line; 〖광물·해부〗 a stria (*pl.* -ae). ¶ 교차〔평행〕선 a cross 〔parallel〕 line / 가는〔굵은〕선 a fine 〔thick〕 line / 선을 긋다 draw a line / 우리들은 공과 사에 선을 그어야 한다 We should draw a line between public and private business 〔affairs〕. (***b***) 《씨줄·날줄》 ¶ 삼팔선 the 38th parallel / 자오선 the meridian line. ② 《철도·항로》 a line; a track (궤도); a route (노선); a course. ¶ 2번선 Track Two; the second track; platform (No.) 2 / 경인선 《on》 the Kyŏng-in line / 상행〔하행〕선 an up 〔a down〕 line. ③ 《수준》 a level. ¶ 지출을 그 선에서 억제하다 hold down expenses to that level. ④ 《전선》 a wire; a line. ¶ 전선 an electric wire 〔cord〕; a cable; a power line / 전화선 telephone lines / 송전선 transmission lines. ⑤ 《광선》 a beam of light. ¶ 엑스선 an X-ray.

**선**(縇) an edge; a frill; a border; trim(ming). ¶ 선을 두르다 sew on a frill; put a border on 《an apron》; edge.

**선**(選) (a) selection; (a) choice; 《편집의》 compilation; editing. ¶ 명작선 a selection of masterpieces 〔famous literary works〕 / 선에 들다 be chosen; be selected; be accepted / 선에 들지 못하다 be rejected; be not accepted; be left out.

**선**(禪) 〖불교〗 dhyana (Sans.); 《한국》 *Sŏn;* 《중국》 *Ch'an;* 《일본》 *Zen;* (religious) meditation.

**선-** 《덜됨》 untrained; unskilled; immature; green; new; novice; clumsy. ¶ 선무당 an inexperienced 〔a new〕 shaman / 선머슴 a wild 〔naughty, mischievous〕 boy.

**-선**(船) a ship; a vessel. ¶ 외국선 a foreign ship / 운송선 a transport ship.

**선가**(船價) boat fare; passage (fare, money); ferriage (나룻배의); 《화물의》 freight (rates); freightage; shipping charges; boatage.

**선가**(禪家) 〖불교〗 the dhyana 〔*Zen, Ch'an*〕 sect of Buddhism; a dhyana 〔*Zen, Ch'an*〕 temple 〔priest〕.

**선각**(先覺) ～하다 see 〔perceive〕 in advance; foresee; foreknow.

**선각자**(先覺者) a man of foresight; a pathfinder; a pioneer; a forerunner; a leading spirit. ¶ 시대의 ～이다 be ahead of *one's* times / 그는 한국 교육의 ～였다 He was one of the pioneers of Korean education.

**선개교**(旋開橋) 〖토목〗 a swing 〔swivel, turn〕 bridge.

**선객**(先客) a preceding 〔an earlier〕 visitor 〔guest〕. ¶ ～이 있어 잠시 기다리고 있었다 I waited for some time, because there was already a visitor before me.

**선객**(船客) a passenger. ¶ 1〔2〕등 ～ a first-〔second-〕class passenger / 3등 ～ a third-class passenger; a steerage passenger; [총칭] the steerage. ◉ ～명부 a passenger list. ～실 the passenger quarters.

**선거**(船渠) a dock. ◉ 건～ a dry dock. 습(濕)～ a wet dock.

**선거**(選擧) (an) election. ～하다 elect; vote for; return 《영》. ¶ ～ 전의 pre-election 《campaign》 / 공명～ a clean election / 타락～ a corrupt election / 대통령 ～ a presidential election / ～의 종반전 the last-stage (election) campaign / ～를 (실시)하다 hold 〔have〕 an election / ～에 간섭하다 intervene in an election / ～에 나서다〔출마하다〕 run for election / ～에 이기다 win an election / ～에 지다 lose an election; be defeated in an election / ～를 참관하다 be (a) witness at the polls / ～하러 가다 go to the polls / ～감시단을 편성하다 form an election-watch group / ～에 압승하다 win a landslide victory in an election / 그는 대통령 ～에 출마했다 He ran for President. / 이 ～에 우리는 반드시 이겨야 한다 We must win this election by all means. ◉ ～간섭 《the government》 interference 〔intervention〕 in an election. ～공보 the official gazette for elections. ～공약 an electoral commitment; a campaign 〔an election〕 pledge 〔promise〕. ～공영 public management of election. ～대책 위원회 an election polling committee. ～방송 a 《radio, TV》 broadcast for election campaign. ～방해 election obstruction. ～부정 election malpractice. ～분위기 an election atmosphere: 공명 ～ 분위기를 해치는 행위 an activity detrimental to a fair election atmosphere. ～비용 election expenses; expenses for an election campaign. ～사범 election crimes. ～소송 an election case 〔lawsuit〕. ～속보 a prompt report of election returns. ～연설 a campaign speech; an election address: ～지원 연설 a vote-getting speech / 합동 ～ 연설회 a joint stumping rally. ～위반 election irregularities 〔offenses; frauds〕; an election (law) violation. ～유세 an electioneering 〔a canvassing, a stumping 《미》〕 tour: ～ 유세를 하다 go canvassing; take 〔go on〕 the stump 《미》. ～일 (the) election 〔polling〕 day. ～자금 an election campaign fund. ～전(戰) an election 〔electoral〕 campaign 〔fight〕: 대통령 ～전 a presidential race; a race for presidency. ～제도 an election system. ～참관인 a witness (at the polls); 《영》 a scrutineer (개표의). ～참모 a campaign strategist 〔manager〕. ～포스터 a campaign poster. ～학(學) psephology.

**선거관리**(選擧管理) election administration. ◉ 중앙～위원회 the Central Election Management Committee (생략 CEMC).

**선거구**(選擧區) an electoral 〔an election〕 district 〔zone〕; a constituency; a precinct 《미》. ¶ 대〔중, 소〕～제 the major 〔medium, minor〕 constituency 〔electorate〕 system / 한 ～의 인구수 an electoral district's population / ～의 조정 rezoning of electoral districts / (의회에서) ～를 대표하다 sit for a constituency.

**선거권**(選擧權) the (voting, elective) franchise; the suffrage; the right to vote; voting rights. ¶ ～을 주다 enfranchise; give the franchise 《to》 / ～을 박탈하다 deprive 《*a person*》 of the right of casting the ballot; disfranchise / ～을 행사하다 exercise *one's* franchise; exercise the ballot / ～이 없다 be voteless; have no voting rights. ◉ ～자 an electorate; an elector; a voter.

**선거법**(選擧法) election 〔electoral〕 law. ◉ ～ 개정 (an) electoral reform; (a) revision of the election law: ～개정안 an election law revision bill. ～ 위반 (a) violation of election law; an election law violation: ～위반자 an election law breaker 〔violator〕.

**선거사무**(選擧事務) election campaign business. ◉ ～소 an electioneering 〔a campaign〕 office. ～장 a campaign manager.

**선거운동**(選擧運動) an election campaign; electioneering; canvassing (주로 호별 방문). ¶ 사전 ～ preelection campaigning; precandidacy propaganda / ～을 하다 stage 〔deploy〕 a campaign; electioneer; canvass for an election. ◉ ～비〔자금〕 campaign 〔electioneering〕 expenses 〔funds〕. ～원 an election campaigner; an electioneer(er); a canvasser.

**선거위원**(選擧委員) an election committeeman. ◉ ～장 a campaign chairman. ～회 an election committee.

**선거인**(選擧人) an elector; a voter; a constituent; [총칭] the electorate. ◉ ～단 the electoral college 《미》. ～

명부 a pollbook; a voters' list; a register of electors 《미》: ~ 명부에서 누락되다 be left off the voters' list. ~ 자격 electorship; the qualification of an elector.

**선견**(先遣) ~하다 send forward 〔in advance〕. ◉ ~대원 an advance man. ~부대 advance troops; an advance party; the first contingent.

**선견지명**(先見之明) the wisdom and power to see into the future; farseeing wisdom; foresight. ¶ ~이 있는 farseeing; foresighted; farsighted; long-sighted / ~이 없는 short-sighted; lacking foresight / ~이 있는〔없는〕 사람 a farsighted 〔shortsighted〕 person; 「a man of foresight 〔a bad prophet〕/ 그는 ~이 있다 He has foresight. *or* He is far-sighted. / 그에겐 ~이 없었다 He lacked 〔was lacking in〕 foresight.

**선결**(先決) a previous decision; prior settlement. ~하다 decide 〔settle〕 beforehand. ¶ 장소의 확보가 ~이다 How to get the place is the first problem to be settled. *or* We must get the place first of all. ◉ ~요건 a prerequisite 《to》.

**선결문제**(先決問題) a matter claiming prior settlement; a problem requiring an urgent solution; the first consideration. ¶ 이것이 ~이다 This is the matter to be settled first. / 어떻게 그녀의 허락을 얻느냐가 ~다 How to get her permission is the first consideration. / 비용이 ~이다 The question of expenses takes precedence over all others.

**선경**(仙境) 《신선이 사는》 a land of wizards; a fairyland; an elf land; 《속세를 떠난》 an enchanted land.

**선고**(先考) *one's* deceased 〔late〕 father.

**선고**(宣告) 《공표》 pronouncement; announcement; 《재판의》 a (juridical) sentence; adjudication; condemnation. ~하다 pronounce; announce; 《형을》 sentence; condemn; adjudge; pass a sentence on 《*a person*》.
¶ 무죄를 ~하다 judge 《*a person*》 not guilty; acquit 《the prisoner》 of the charge 《of murder》/ 유죄를 ~하다 convict 《*a person*》 of a crime / 사형을 ~하다 sentence 〔condemn〕《*a person*》 to death / 유죄〔무죄〕를 ~받다 be convicted 〔be acquitted (of the charge)〕/ 파산을 ~하다 adjudicate 《*a person*》 to be bankrupt / 5년 징역의 ~를 받다 be sentenced to five years' servitude / (의사한테) 불치라는 ~를 받다 be pronounced incurable. 「衡).

**선고**(選考) selection; choice. ⇨ 전형(銓

**선곡**(選曲) selection of music. ¶ 김씨 ~ Music selected by Mr. Kim. / 이 음악 프로 전용의 라디오 방송국은 ~이 참 좋다 This music station plays great selections.

**선공**(先攻) ~하다 attack first; 〖야구〗 (go to) bat first. ¶ 그 야구 경기는 A팀의 ~으로 시작되었다 The baseball game began, A-team going to bat first. *or* The baseball game started with the A-team batting first.

**선광**(選鑛) concentration 〔separation〕 of ore; ore dressing. ~하다 dress (ore); concentrate ore. ¶ 비중〔부유, 자력〕 ~ ore dressing by gravity separation 〔floatation, magnetic separation〕. ◉ ~기 an ore separator. ~소 a dressing plant.

**선광**(旋光) polarization. ⇨ 편광(偏光).

**선교**(宣教) missionary work; missions. ~하다 propagate 《its faith》; preach religion; do missionary work. ◉ ~단체 a mission. ~사 a missionary: ~사단 a mission / ~사로 일하다 be a missionary; engage in mission work.

**선교**(禪教) 〖불교〗 the *Zen* sect and Doctrinism of Buddhism.

**선교**(船橋) 《배다리》 a pontoon 〔floating〕 bridge; 《배의 갑판의》 a bridge.

**선구**(先驅) ① 《앞섬》 the lead; the initiative. ¶ ~적인 pioneering 《works》; pioneer 《physicists》/ ~가 되다 be the first 《to do *something*》; take the lead 《in》; lead the way 《in》. ② ⇨ 선구자. ③ 《차·말의》 an outrider; a pilot car.

**선구**(船具) rigging; gearing; tackle; (ship's) fittings; [총칭] ship chandlery. ◉ ~상 a ship chandler; a ship-outfitter('s).

**선구안**(選球眼) 〖야구〗 the batting eye. ¶ ~이 좋다〔나쁘다〕 have a good 〔bad〕 batting eye.

**선구자**(先驅者) a pioneer; a forerunner; a precursor; a harbinger. ¶ ~가 되다 be ahead of *one's* times; take the lead; be in the vanguard 《of》/ K박사야말로 심장 이식의 ~이다 Heart=transplant surgery was pioneered by Dr. K.

**선굿** an exorcism rite performed by a shaman in standing position.

**선그래프**(線—) a line graph.

**선글라스** 《a pair of》 sunglasses; 《wear》

dark glasses.

**선금**(先金) a prepayment; a payment in advance; an advance payment. ⇨ 선불(先拂). ¶ ～을 치르다 pay 《the rent》 in advance.

**선급**(先給) payment in advance; advance payment; prepayment 《of wages》; cash before delivery (생략 C.B.D.). ～하다 pay 〔disburse〕 in advance; advance 《money》; make an advance 《on a contract》; prepay 《of wages》. ¶ ～(의) 조건으로 on condition of advance payment.
◉ ～금 money paid in advance; an amount prepaid; an advance; a prepayment. 우편료～ postage prepaid. 운임～ freight prepaid 〔included〕; carriage forward 〔prepaid〕.

**선급**(船級) (ship's) classification 〔class〕. ◉ ～증서 a classification certificate. ～협회 a classification society.

**선남선녀**(善男善女) righteous people 〔men and women〕; pious people 〔folk〕; 《불교도》 (good) Buddhists.

**선납**(先納) prepayment; payment in advance; advance payment. ～하다 pay in advance; prepay.

**선녀**(仙女) a fairy; a nymph.

**선다형**(選多型) a multiple-choice method. ◉ ～문제 a multiple-choice question. ～시험 a multiple-choice test.

**선단** a vertical 〔an up-and-down〕 hem.

**선단**(船團) a fleet (of vessels). ¶ 수송 ～ a convoy of transport ships (호위함이 딸린) / 출어～ a fishing fleet / 포경～ a fleet of whalers / ～식 경영 《재벌회사의》 the "fleet-style" operation 〔management〕.

**선대**(先代) 《앞 시대》 the previous age; 《앞 세대》 the previous 〔last〕 generation; 《선조》 the predecessor (in the family line).

**선대**(船隊) a fleet (of ships). ⇨ 선단(船團). ¶ 상(商)～ a commercial fleet.

**선도**(先渡) 〖상업〗 forward 〔future〕 delivery.

**선도**(先導) guidance; leadership. ～하다 guide; conduct; (take the) lead; lead the way; precede. ¶ 관광 안내원의 ～로 led 〔preceded〕 by a guide / 유행에 관해 말하면 그녀가 언제나 우리 서클을 ～해 왔다 When it comes to fashion she has always led our circle. ◉ ～자 a guide; a leader. ～차 a leading car; 《경찰의》 a (police) pilot car.

**선도**(鮮度) 《싱싱함》 (the degree of) freshness. ⇨ 신선도. ¶ 이 오징어는 ～가 떨어지기 시작했다 This cuttlefish has started to lose its freshness.

**선도**(善導) proper 〔judicious〕 guidance. ～하다 lead 〔guide〕 properly; guide aright; lead 《*a person*》 to the path of virtue; lead 《people》 into the right path. ¶ 비행 청소년을 ～하다 guide a juvenile delinquent 「onto the right path 〔in the right direction〕. ◉ ～책(策) measures for proper guidance: 청소년의 ～책이 시급히 요청된다 Establishment of measures for proper juvenile guidance is urgently called for.

**선돌** 〖역사〗 a menhir.

**선동**(煽動) agitation; instigation; abetment; (an) incitement; demagogy (민중 선동). ～하다 instigate; abet; incite; stir up; agitate; set 〔egg〕 on; fan. ¶ ～적(인) inflammatory; incendiary; agitative; seditious; demagogic(al) / ～할 목적으로 for agitative 〔demagogic〕 purposes / 누군가의 ～을 받아 at someone's instigation / 민중을 ～하여 난동을 일으키다 instigate 〔incite, excite〕 people to violence.
◉ ～연설 an inflammatory harangue; a seditious speech: ～ 연설가 a stump orator; an agitator; a demagog(ue). ～자 an agitator; an instigator; a provocateur; 〖법〗 an abettor. ～정치 the politics of demagoguery: ～정치가 a demagogic politician; a demagog(ue); a political agitator. ～죄 sedition; abetment.

**선두**(先頭) the front (position); the head; the top; the lead; the van; the first; the forefront. ¶ 아무를 ～에 세우고 headed by *a person;* with *a person* in the lead / ～에 나서다 lead (the way); take the lead; top; head / ～에 서다 be at the head 《of》; be in the forefront 〔van〕 《of a parade》; take 〔gain〕 the lead 《in》; take 〔lead〕 the van; head / ～를 지키기 위해 나는 많은 노력을 해야만 했다 I had to work hard to keep on the lead. / 학생들이 공해 반대 운동의 ～에 섰다 Students took the lead in the campaign against pollution.
◉ ～부대 the van; the leading troop. ～주자 a front-running man; a forerunner; a front runner (주로 선거에서): 개발 도상국의 ～ 주자로 부상하다 emerge as a forerunner among the developing countries. ～타자 〖야구〗 a lead-off man 〔batter〕; 《그 회(回)의》 the first batter.

**선두르다**(縇—) hem 《a handkerchief》; rim; sew on a frill 〔a border, some edging, some trimming〕. ¶ 상보에 ~ trim a tablecloth with frills.

**선두리** 〖곤충〗 a water beetle.

**선둥이**(先—) the firstborn of twins.

**선드러지다** (be) buoyant; gay; cheerful; lighthearted. ¶ 선드러지게 걷다 sail; walk breezily 〔with sprightly steps〕.

**선득거리다** 《추워서》 feel chilly; feel a chill; 《놀라서》 shudder 《at》; be horrified; have a thrill of horror.

**선들바람** a cool 〔refreshing〕 breeze.

**선떡** a half-steamed〔-boiled〕 rice cake. ¶ ~ 받듯이 with lukewarm pleasure; unenthusiastically.

**선똥** half-digested excrement.

**선뜩** with a sudden chill. ~하다 (be) chilly; [서술적] have a chill 《of horror》. ~거리다 have 〔feel〕 chills running up and down *one's* spine.

**선뜻** 《가볍게》 lightly; 《쾌히》 readily; willingly; with pleasure; with a good grace; 《빨리》 at short notice; at *one's* bidding; offhand (즉석에서). ¶ ~ 승낙하다〔응하다〕 readily 〔willingly〕 consent 《to it》; comply willingly 〔with a good grace〕; give a ready consent 《to》 / 부탁을 ~ 들어주다 comply with 《*a person's*》 request with a good grace / 돈을 ~ 빌려주다 lend money with a good grace / 나는 그 계획에 ~ 동의할 수가 없다 I can't readily agree upon the plan.

**선량**(善良) goodness. ~하다 (be) good; virtuous; honest. ¶ ~한 시민 a good 〔law-abiding〕 citizen.

**선량**(選良) ① 《엘리트》 an elite; the nation's 〔people's〕 choice. ② 《국회 의원》 a member of「the National Assembly 〔Congress〕.

**선령**(船齡) the age of a vessel. ¶ ~ 25년 이상의 배 ships over 25 years old.

**선례**(先例) 《전례》 a precedent; a previous instance; a former example; 〖법〗 prejudication.

선례가: ~가 있다 [사람이 주어] have precedents 《for》 / ~가 되다 become 〔form〕 a precedent / ~가 없다 be without precedent; be unprecedented; be beyond (all) precedents; there is no precedent 《for》 / ~가 없는 일 an unprecedented matter / …의 ~가 되다 give precedent for….

선례에: ~에 따라(서) according to precedent / ~에 따르다 follow「a precedent 〔suit〕 / ~에 어그러지다〔어긋나다〕「depart from 〔be contrary to〕 precedent.

선례를: ~를 깨(뜨리)다 break with precedent / ~를 어기고 against precedent / ~를 만들다 set 〔make, establish, create〕 a precedent.

선례로: ~로 삼다〔하다〕 take 《*a thing*》 as a precedent.

¶ 이것에는 ~가 전혀 없다 There is no precedent for this. / 이것이 ~가 된다는 것은 생각해 볼 문제이다 It would not be wise for us to allow this to become a precedent.

**선로**(線路) a railroad 〔railway 《영》〕 track; a track; a (railroad) line. ¶ ~를 놓다〔깔다〕 lay a line 〔railroad〕; lay a track / ~를 건너다 cross a line 〔track〕 / ~를 따라 걷다 follow 〔walk along〕 the track / ~ 안에 들어가지 마시오 《게시》 Keep off the track. ◉ ~공 a lineman; a trackman; 《미》 a section hand 〔man〕; [총칭] 《미》 the section crew 〔gang〕. ~공사 railroad 〔line〕 construction; 《선로 부설》 track laying; 《보수·수리》 track maintenance. ~반 a track-maintenance gang. ~표지 a track indicator.

**선린**(善隣) good neighborhood 〔neighborliness〕; neighborly friendship. ◉ ~관계 good neighborly relations 《with》. ~(우호)정책 a good neighbor policy. ~정신 the spirit of good-neighborliness.

**선망**(羨望) envy. ~하다 envy; feel envy 《at》; be envious 《of》; regard 《*a person*》 with envy; look enviously 《at》. ¶ 그녀는 학급 전원의 ~의 대상이 되었다 She has become an object of envy among all her classmates.

**선매**(先賣) selling in advance; an advance sale. ~하다 sell in advance; sell ahead 〔beforehand〕. ¶ ~ 후급의 사회 the buy-now-pay-later society. ◉ 입도(立稻)~ preharvest sale of rice crop.

**선매권**(先買權) (the right of) preemption. ¶ ~을 얻다 preempt.

**선머리**(先—) the head; the van. ⇨ 선두.

**선머슴** a mischievous 〔naughty, roguish〕 boy; an urchin; an imp.

**선명**(宣明) proclamation; declaration. ~하다 proclaim; announce; declare; promulgate; enunciate.

**선명**(鮮明) clearness; distinctness; lucidity; vividness. ~하다 (be) clear; clear-〔sharp-〕cut; distinct; vivid.

¶ ~하게 clearly; distinctly; vividly / ~한 영상 《텔레비전의》 a clear 〔distinct〕 picture / ~한 윤곽 a sharp outline / ~한 색채 vivid colors / ~한 사진 a clear photograph / ~하지 않다 lack clearness; 《인쇄 등이》 do not come out well; be dim / 태도를 ~히 하다 assume a definite attitude; make *one's* attitude clear / 인쇄가 ~하다 The print is clear. / 여러 기억들이 그의 마음에 ~히 되살아났다 The memories came vividly back to his mind.

◉ ~도 《TV·렌즈 등의》 definition; distinction. ~야당 a clear-cut opposition party.

**선모**(腺毛) 〖생물〗 a tentacle; a glandular hair.

**선모충**(旋毛蟲) a trichina (*pl.* ~e, ~s). ¶ ~의 trichinal. ◉ ~병 〖병리〗 trichinosis.

**선묘**(線描) (line) drawing. ~하다 draw in lines.

**선무**(宣撫) pacification; placation.

◉ ~공작 pacification work 〔activity〕. ~반 a placation 〔win-over〕 squad; a pacification unit.

**선무당**(—巫堂) a new 〔green, novice〕 shaman. ¶ ~이 사람 잡는다 《속담》 A little knowledge is a dangerous thing. / ~이 장구 탓한다 《속담》 A bad workman quarrels with his tools.

**선물**(先物) ① = 맏물. ② 〖증권〗 《buy, deal in》 futures. ¶ ~을 사다〔거래하다〕 deal in futures / ~로 팔다 sell for futures delivery; sell forward.

◉ ~가격 future price. ~거래 trading 〔dealing〕 in futures; futures deals: 한국 ~거래소 the Korea Futures Exchange. ~매매 a forward bargain; arrival sales. ~매입 purchase of futures; forward buying. ~시세 futures quotations. ~시장 a futures market.

**선물**(膳物) a present; a gift; a souvenir (기념품). ~하다 give 〔make〕 《*a person*》 a present; make a gift 《to *a person*》; present.

> 용법 **present**는 친한 사람끼리 주고받는 선물로서, 가장 일반적인 말. 생일·크리스마스 선물 등이 이에 해당됨. 그러나 실제에 있어서는 엄밀한 구분 없이 말하는 사람의 기호에 따라 혼용되는 경우가 더 많음. **gift**는 present보다 격식을 갖춘 말로, 의례적인 선물의 뜻. 큰 액수의 돈·귀중품이나 결혼·이별의 선물 따위에 흔히 쓰임. **souvenir**는 추억이 되는 기념품으로서의 선물이란 뜻이지만, 남에게 선물하지 않고 자기의 추억으로서 간직하는 것도 포함됨.

¶ 새해의 ~ a New Year's gift / ~ 포장용 리본 a gift-wrapping ribbon / 해외여행의 ~ a souvenir of *one's* trip abroad / ~을 주다 = ~하다 / ~을 받다 take 〔accept〕 a present; receive a gift 《from *a person*》 / ~을 보내다 send a gift (over) to 《*a person*》 / 시계를 ~로 주다 present 《*a person*》 with a watch; present a watch to 《*a person*》; give 〔offer〕 《*a person*》 a watch as a gift / 애들에게 줄 ~을 가지고 집에 돌아오다 take 《*something*》 home to *one's* children / 훌륭한 ~을 주셔서 대단히 고맙습니다 Thank you very much for your nice present.

◉ ~교환 an exchange of presents. 연말~ a year-end present.

**선미**(船尾) the stern; the buttock(s); the poop. ¶ ~에 in the stern 《of a boat》; astern; aft. ◉ ~갑판 a quarter deck. ~재(材) a sternpost.

**선민**(選民) 〖성서〗 the chosen (people); the elect. ◉ ~사상 the idea of God's elect. ~의식 elitism.

**선박**(船舶) a vessel; a ship; a bottom; [총칭] shipping; craft. = 배. ¶ 항내 ~ vessels in port; shipping in port 〔the harbor〕 / ~의 출입 the entry and clearance of ships; the movements of shipping.

◉ ~검사증 a ship inspection certificate. ~과 the marine section. ~관리료 husbandage. ~국적증명서 the certificate of a ship's nationality. ~등급〔적재량〕 ship's classification 〔burden〕. ~등기부 the shipping register. ~무선국 a ship's radio station. ~법 the Ships Act; the marine act. ~보증 ship's warrant. ~사용료 charterage. ~설계 ship design. ~세 the shipping tax. ~소유자 a shipowner. ~수리 shiprepairing. ~수송업자 a shipping agent. ~업 the shipping industry 〔business〕: ~업자 a shipper; a shipping man; the shipping interests [총칭]. ~용 기관〔기압계〕 a marine engine 〔barometer〕. ~용 로프 marine rope. ~용품 ship's stores. ~입항〔출항〕신고 a ship's clearance inward 〔outward〕; a ship's entry 〔clearance〕. ~주(株) shippings; shipping stocks. ~중개인 a ship broker. ~채권자 a ship's creditor. ~톤수 [총칭] shipping. ~해상보험 hull insurance. ~해체 shipbreaking. ~회사 a shipping company.

**선반** a shelf (*pl.* shelves); 《벽에서 돌출한》 a ledge; 《그물·격자 모양의》 a rack.

¶ ~을 매다〔달다〕 make 〔put up〕 a shelf; fix a shelf 《to》/ ~ 위에 두다〔얹다〕 put 〔place〕 《*a thing*》 on a shelf; shelve. ◉ ~받이 a bracket; a shelf support. ~턱 an extra board attached to the edge of a shelf.

**선반**(旋盤) a lathe. ¶ ~으로 깎다 lathe 《*a thing*》. ◉ ~공 a turner; a lathe-man: ~공으로 일하다 work on the lathe. ~공장 a turnery. ~대(臺) a lathe bed. 자동~ an automatic lathe.

**선발**(先發) starting 〔leaving〕 in advance; getting 〔taking〕 a head start. ~하다 start 〔go〕 in advance 《of others》; go ahead 《of》; get 〔take〕 a head start; start first; precede 《another》. ◉ ~견본 an advance sample. ~대 an advance party 〔force, element, group, team〕; an advanced contingent; a forward party 〔outfit, group〕. ~투수 『야구』 a starting pitcher; a starter.

**선발**(選拔) selection; choice; picking out. ~하다 select; choose; mark out 《for》; pick 〔single〕 out; draft. ¶ ~된 selected; chosen: picked / 팀의 ~에서 누락되다 be not picked for the team / 지원자 5백 명 중에서 ~하다 single out of 500 applicants / 20명의 지원자 중에서 그녀 한 사람이 ~되었다 She was alone selected from among the twenty applicants. ◉ ~경기 an elimination match; a tryout. ~군〔팀〕 a picked 〔pickup〕 team; 《all-star》 selections. ~시험 a selective examination; a selection examination 〔test〕. ~위원회 a selection committee.

**선방**(善防) a good defense. ~하다 put up a good defense; defend well.

**선배**(先輩) an elder; a senior; a superior; a predecessor; an old-timer 《구어》. ¶ 대~ a big senior / ~인 체하다 pose 〔give *oneself* airs〕 as a senior / 그는 나의 대학교 2년 ~이다 He is my senior by two years at the university.

**선법**(旋法) 『음악』 a mode. ◉ 장〔단〕~ a major 〔minor〕 mode.

**선변**(先邊) interest paid in advance.

**선별**(選別) sorting; selection; 《광석의》 concentration; dressing. ~하다 sort; select; concentrate; dress. ¶ 크기에 따라 ~하다 sort according to size / 불량품을 ~하다 sort out defective articles. ◉ ~기 a sorter; a grader; a classifier; a selector; a concentrator: 우편물 ~기 a mail 〔postal〕 sorter. ~융자 selective lending.

**선병**(腺病) 『의학』 scrofulosis; strumosis; a gland disease 〔disorder〕. ¶ ~의 lymphatic; scrofulous. ◉ ~질 scrofulousness; the scrofulous tendency (of body).

**선보다** pay a preliminary visit to the prospective bride(groom); 《맞선을》 meet each other with a view to marriage; have an interview with a prospective bride(groom). ¶ 선보고 하는 결혼 an arranged marriage; a marriage by arrangement / 선뵈이는 사진 a photo to be given to *one's* prospective bride 〔bridegroom〕.

**선복**(船腹) the bottom (of a ship); 《선박》 bottoms; [총칭] shipping; tonnage; 《짐 싣는 곳》 space; freight space. ¶ ~의 과잉 an excess of bottoms / ~의 부족 the scarcity 〔shortage〕 of bottoms. ◉ ~량 gross tonnage (생략 GT). ~신청서 an application for space. ~예약〔할당〕 space booking 〔allotment〕.

**선봉**(先鋒) the van; the vanguard; the advance guard; the spearhead; the scouting line. ¶ ~에 서서 in the van 《of the attack on...》/ ~이 되다 be in the van 《of the attack》; spearhead 《an operation》; become the spearhead of an advance 〔attack〕/ 그는 사회 개혁 운동의 ~이다 He is in the vanguard 〔van〕 of the social reform movement.

**선분**(線分) 『수학』 a segment (of a line).

**선불**(先拂) payment in advance; advance payment; prepayment 《of wages》; cash before delivery (생략 C.B.D.). ⇨ 선급(先給). ¶ 대금은 ~입니다 The price is「payable 〔to be paid〕 in advance. / 주문은 ~로 해 주십시오 Please pay for your order in advance.

**선비** 《학자》 a classical scholar; a learned man; 《덕이 있는 사람》 a man of virtue; a gentleman.

**선비**(先妣) *one's* deceased 〔late〕 mother.

**선사** 《선물》 presentation; giving a present. ~하다 make 〔give〕 《*a person*》 a present; send 《*a person*》 a gift. ¶ ~를 받다 receive a present / 자네에게 그것을 ~하지 I will make a present of it to you.

**선사**(先史) prehistory. ¶ ~의 prehistoric(al). ◉ ~시대 the prehistoric age: ~시대 유적 prehistoric remains. ~학 prehistory.

**선사**(善事) ① 《공양》 an offering; an oblation. ~하다 offer (up). ¶ 절에서 부

처님께 ～하다 make an 〔a monetary〕 offering to Buddha at a temple. ② 《좋은 일》 a good thing; 《선행》 a good deed.

**선사**(禪師) 〖불교〗 a Zen master 〔priest〕; an esteemed priest; the Reverend 〔Rev.〕....

**선산**(先山) *one's* ancestral burial ground; *one's* family graveyard.

**선상**(船上) ¶ ～에(서) on board (a ship); aboard. ◉ ～난민 boat people (베트남의). ～생활 life on board 〔shipboard〕.

**선상지**(扇狀地) 〖지질〗 a fan; an alluvial fan; a fan delta (삼각주).

**선생**(先生) ① 《교사》 a teacher; an instructor; a master. ¶ 영어 ～ a teacher of English; an English teacher / 학교 ～ a schoolteacher / 엄한 ～(님) a stern teacher; a taskmaster / ～이 되다 become a teacher; take to teaching / ～님 Sir! ; 《여선생에게》 Ma'am! ② 《존칭》 Mister (생략 Mr.); sir; 《의사》 a doctor. ¶ 김 ～ 안녕하십니까 How are you, Mr. Kim? ③ 《당신》 you. ¶ ～도 그렇게 생각하십니까 Do you think so, too?

**선서**(宣誓) an oath; parole. ～하다 swear; take 〔make〕 an oath; pledge *one's* word of honor. ¶ ～를 어기다 break *one's* parole / ～시키다 administer an oath to 《*a person*》; attest; swear; put 《*a person*》 on (*his*) oath / 복종할 것을 ～하다 swear allegiance 〔fidelity〕 《to》 / 대통령 취임 ～를 하다 take a presidential oath / 법정에서 그는 진실을 말하겠다고 ～했다 In court he swore an oath to tell the truth. ◉ ～문 a deposition; an affidavit; a written oath. ～식 administering of an oath; a swearing-in ceremony. ～증언 a deposition; sworn testimony. ～증인 a deponent.

**선선하다** ① 《날씨가》 (be) cool; refreshing. ¶ 선선한 바람 a cool 〔refreshing〕 breeze / 날이 ～ It is cool today. / 여기는 선선해서 좋다 It is nice and cool here. ② 《사람·태도가》 (be) candid; frank; unreserved; openhearted; 《동작이》 (be) active; brisk; spirited.

**선선히** candidly; frankly; openly; cheerfully; 《기꺼이》 readily; willingly; with a good grace. ¶ ～ 기부하다 donate readily 《to》 / ～ 승낙하다 readily consent 《to it》; give a ready consent 《to》 / ～ 자백하다 make a manly confession / ～ 자기 잘못을 인정하다 acknowledge *one's* fault with a good grace / 돈을 ～ 내놓지 않다 grudge money / 부탁을 ～ 들어주다 comply with another's request with a good grace.

**선세**(先貰) 〖법〗 advanced payment 〔prepayment〕 of rent; prepaid rent. ¶ ～를 내다 pay rent in advance; prepay the rent.

**선소리** foolish 〔silly〕 talk; rubbish; an absurd remark. ¶ ～를 하다 make an absurd remark; talk foolishly 〔nonsense〕.

**선손질**(先—) striking the first blow; starting a fight. ～하다 strike the first blow; start a fight. ¶ ～ 후방망이 《속담》 "He who sows the wind shall reap the whirlwind."

**선수**(先手) ① 《바둑》 placing the first stone; 《장기》 moving first. ¶ ～를 두다 have 〔make〕 the first move. ② 《기선》 forestalling. ¶ ～를 치다〔쓰다〕 take 〔seize, obtain〕 the initiative 《from *a person* in *something*》; forestall; get the start 《of》; anticipate 《*a person* in doing *something*》 / ～를 빼앗기다 be forestalled; lose the initiative.

**선수**(船首) the bow; the head. = 이물.

**선수**(選手) 《경기자》 a 《baseball》 player; an athlete; a representative player (대표 선수).

> **용법** 대개의 경우, 영어에서는 「선수」를 동사에 -er를 붙여 a runner, a swimmer, a skier 등으로 표현함. 단, 게임에 임한 선수를 칭할 때는 player를 써서 a baseball 〔tennis〕 player라고 하지만, 어느 경우에나 다 그런 것은 아님. a golfer 따위가 그러한 경우임.

¶ 프로 야구 ～ a professional baseball player / ～가 되다 become a player / 그는 대학에서 야구 ～였다 He played baseball for his university. *or* He was on the baseball team of his university. ◉ ～단 a team; a squad. ～선서 an athletes' oath: 참가 ～들을 대표해서 ～ 선서를 하다 take an athletes' oath on behalf of the participating athletes. ～촌 an athletes' village; athletes' quarters 〔dormitories〕: 태능 ～촌 the T'aenŭng Training Center / ～촌 숙박소 the athletes' hostel. 후보～ a substitute; an alternate; 《야구의》 a bench polisher.

**선수권**(選手權) a championship; a title; the crown. ¶ ～을 다투다 play 〔contend〕 for the championship 〔title〕 /

～을 방어하다 defend the title / ～을 보유하다 keep *one's* title; hold 〔retain〕 the championship / ～을 빼앗다 wrest the championship 《from》/ ～을 잃다 〔따다〕 lose 〔win, gain〕 the championship. ◉ ～경기 a title match 〔bout〕. ～대회 a championship series; a championship tournament. ～보유자 a titleholder: 세계 ～ 보유자 a world champion. 전국～ the national championship 〔title〕.

**선술집** a (stand) bar; a (drinking) tavern; a public house (with no seating facilities); a groggery 《미》; a grogshop 《영》; a pub 《영구어》.

**선승**(先勝) ～하다 win the first game; score the first point.

**선신세**(鮮新世) 〖지질〗 the Pliocene (epoch). ⇨ 플라이오세.

**선실**(船室) a (ship's) cabin; a stateroom (특실); [총칭] the passenger's quarters. ¶ 1등～ a first-class cabin; a saloon / 2등 ～ a second-class cabin / 3등 ～ the steerage / ～을 예약하다 reserve a passage; book a berth. ◉ ～배당표 a berth list.

**선심**(善心) 《착한 마음》 virtue; conscience; virtuous mind; kind heart; 《자비심》 mercy; a mercyful heart; kindness; benevolence; 《너그러운 마음》 generosity; liberality. ¶ ～을 쓰다 do a kindness 《for *a person*》; do something nice 《for *a person*》; display 〔show〕 *one's* liberality; have mercy on 《*a person*》. ◉ ～공세 pork-barreling; the use of patronage for political advantage.

**선심**(線審) 《구기에서》 a linesman.

**선악**(善惡) good and 〔or〕 evil; virtue and vice; goodness and badness; right and wrong. ¶ ～을 구별하다 distinguish good from bad; know good from evil; distinguish 〔discern〕 right from wrong. ◉ ～과(果) 〖성서〗 the fruit of the Tree of Knowledge (of Good and Evil).

**선약**(仙藥) a wonderful 〔miraculous〕 remedy 〔medicine〕; the elixir of life.

**선약**(先約) a previous engagement 〔appointment〕. ¶ ～순으로 in the sequence of the orders received; on the first-come-first-served basis / 죄송합니다 ～이 있습니다 I'm sorry I have a previous engagement.

**선양**(宣揚) enhancement; increase. ～하다 enhance; raise; increase; exalt; heighten. ◉ 국위～ enhancement of national prestige: 국위를 ～하다 promote the national glory; enhance the prestige of the country.

**선어**(鮮魚) fresh 〔raw〕 fish. ◉ ～운반선 a fresh-fish carrier.

**선언**(宣言) a declaration; a proclamation; a profession; a pronouncement; an announcement; a statement; a manifesto (*pl.* ～(e)s). ～하다 declare; make a declaration 《of》; pronounce; profess; proclaim; announce. ¶ (의장이) 개회를 ～하다 call a meeting to order / 출마를 ～하다 announce *one's* candidacy / 엄숙히 ～하다 make a solemn declaration / 정부는 긴급 사태를 ～했다 The government proclaimed a state of emergency. / 사람들은 그의 폭탄 ～에 놀랐다 People were surprised at his bombshell declaration. ◉ 독립 ～ the declaration of independence.

**선언**(選言) 〖논리〗 disjunction. ◉ ～명제 a disjunctive (proposition); a disjunction.

**선언서**(宣言書) a (written) declaration; a manifesto (*pl.* ～(e)s); a statement. ¶ ～를 발표하다 issue 〔give out〕 a declaration / ～를 작성하다 draw up a declaration.

**선열**(先烈) patriotic forefathers; previous martyrs.

**선염**(腺炎) 〖의학〗 adenitis.

**선왕**(先王) the late 〔preceding〕 king.

**선외**(選外) ¶ ～의 left out of selection 〔choice〕; rejected / ～가 되다 be left out of selection; fail to be selected 〔accepted〕; be rejected. ◉ ～가작(佳作) a good work left out of the final selection: ～ 가작이 되다 receive 〔win〕 an honorable mention.

**선용**(善用) good use. ～하다 make good use of; put 《money》 to a good use; turn 《spare time》 to good account; employ 《time》 well 〔wisely〕. ¶ 책 읽는 데에 여가를 ～해라 Make good use of your leisure time by reading books.

**선웃음** a forced 〔a feigned, an affected〕 laugh 〔smile〕. ¶ ～을 치다 force 〔affect, feign〕 a smile 〔laugh〕; smile a forced smile; simper.

**선원**(船員) [총칭] the crew; a ship's company; [개인] one 〔a member〕 of the crew; a crewman; a seaman; a mariner; a sailor. ¶ 고급 ～ a (ship's) officer; the quarter-deck [총칭] / 하급 ～ a sailor; a seaman; a jack-tar 《구어》; the sailor [총칭] / ～이 되다 become a sailor; go to sea. ◉ ～법 the Seamen Act. ～보험 seamen's insurance. ～생활 a sailor's life; a seafaring. ～수첩 a seaman's pocket ledger. ～실 the crew's quarters; the crew space. ～용어 nautical terms; sea-terms. ～위생 the hygiene of seafarers.

**선위**(禪位) abdication (of the throne). =양위. ～하다 abdicate; vacate the throne.

**선유**(船遊) a boating (excursion). =뱃놀이.

**선율**(旋律) 『음악』 (a) melody. ¶～적 melodious; tuneful / 감미로운 ～ a sweet melody. ◉ ～법〔학〕 melodics.

**선의**(船醫) a ship's doctor 〔surgeon〕.

**선의**(善意) 《좋은 뜻》 a favorable sense; 《좋은 의도》 good intentions; good will; 『법』 good faith; *bona fides* (L.). ¶～의 well-meaning; well-intentioned; well-meant / ～로 with good intentions; in good faith / ～로 한 일 a well-meant〔-intentioned〕 attempt; a well-intended act 〔deed〕 / ～의 경쟁 competition in good faith / ～의 사람 a man of good will / ～의 조언 well-meant advice / ～의 제삼자 『법』 a third party (acting) in good faith / ～로 해석하다 take 《it》 in a favorable sense; take 《*a person's* reproof》 kindly; put a good construction on 《*a person's* action》; 《의심스러울 경우》 give 《*a person,* a story》 the benefit of the doubt.

**선의권**(先議權) the right to prior deliberation 〔consideration〕 《on a bill》.

**선이자**(先利子) interest (rates) paid in advance. ◉ ～지급 payment of interest (rates) in advance.

**선인**(先人) ① =선친(先親). ② 《전대의 사람》 *one's* predecessors; 《선구자》 a forerunners; a pioneer. ¶～ 미답(의) untrodden; unexplored / ～의 발자취를 더듬다 tread the beaten track; follow in the footsteps of *one's* predecessors.

**선인**(善人) a virtuous person; a good man. ¶～과 악인 (the) good and (the) bad; [비유적] the sheep and the goats / ～은 흥하고 악인은 망한다 《격언》 A virtuous man triumphs over the vice.

**선인선과**(善因善果) 『불교』 the results of good deeds; the rewards of virtue.

**선인장**(仙人掌) 『식물』 a cactus; an opuntia.

**선임**(先任) 《전임》 seniority; 《전임자》 a predecessor. ¶～의 senior; elder. ◉ ～권 the seniority right. ～자 a senior member. ～장교 a senior officer.

**선임**(船賃) passage (fare). ⇨ 뱃삯.

**선임**(選任) election; assignment; nomination (지명). ～하다 select and appoint; elect; nominate; assign 《*a person* to a post》. ¶ 변호인의 ～ designation of counsels / 그는 재차 위원장에 ～되었다 He was elected chairman for the second time.

**선입감**(先入感) ⇨ 선입견.

**선입견**(先入見) a preconception; a prepossession; a preconceived idea; a preoccupation; 《편견》 a prejudice; a bias. ¶～을 가지다 have a preconceived idea 〔opinion〕 / ～을 깨뜨리다 destroy a preconceived notion / ～을 버리다 divest *oneself* of prejudice; get rid of *one's* prejudice 〔preconceived notion〕 《against》 / 그에 대한 잘못된 ～을 버려야 한다 You should discard the prejudice against him.

**선입관**(先入觀) ⇨ 선입견.

**선입선출**(先入先出) first-in first-out 〔(FIFO)〕.

**선잠** a light sleep; a broken 〔short〕 sleep; an uneasy sleep; dogsleep; a catnap. ¶～을 자다 take 〔have〕 a (little) nap 〔catnap〕; have a short 〔poor〕 sleep.

**선장**(船長) a (ship's, sea) captain; the master (of a ship); a master mariner; a commander; 《작은 상선·어선의》 a skipper; 《연락선의》 a ferry master. ◉ ～면허증 a master's certificate of competence; a master's license. ～실 the captain's cabin. ～직 mastership; captaincy.

**선재**(船材) 『조선』 timber.

**선저**(船底) the bottom of a ship. ◉ ～도료 bottom paint.

**선적**(船積) 《발송》 shipment; shipping; 《적하》 loading; lading. ～하다 ship 《a cargo》; load 《a ship》 with a cargo; make a shipment 《of textiles to Singapore》. ¶～ 계원 a shipping clerk / 부산에서 ～된 영국행 화물 goods shipped from Busan for England. ◉ ～가격 a free on board price; an F.O.B. price. ～계약 a shipment 〔loading〕 contract. ～불 cash on shipment (생략 C.O.S.). ～비용 shipping expenses 〔charges〕. ～서류 shipping documents 〔papers〕. ～송장 a shipping invoice. ～안내서 a shipping note. ～완료 completion of shipment. ～인 a shipper. ～지시서 a shipping order. ～통지서 a shipping advice; (a) notice of shipment; (an) advice of dispatch. ～항 a port of loading 〔lading, shipment〕. ～화물 cargo; shipping goods. 부분～ part(ial) shipment. 분할～ split shipment; shipment by installments.

**선적**(船籍) the nationality of a ship; a ship's flag. ¶ 미국 ～의 배 a ship of American nationality 〔registry〕; a ship sailing under the American flag / ～ 불명의 배 a vessel of unknown nationality / ～을 등록하다 register a ship. ◉ ～기호 a nationality mark. ～증명(서) a certificate of 《a ship's》 nationality. ～항 the port of registry.

**선전**(宣傳) propaganda; publicity; propagandism; 《광고》 advertisement. ～하다 propagate; publicize; give publicity 《to》; propagandize; make 〔conduct〕 propaganda; disseminate; play up 《미구어》; 《광고하다》 advertise; give publicity 《to》.
¶ 자기 ～ self-advertisement / ～을 위해〔목적으로〕 for propaganda purposes / ～을 개시하다 institute 〔launch〕 a propaganda / ～을 잘하다 be good at publicity; be an able publicity man / 대대적으로 ～하다 carry on propaganda on a large scale / 요란하게〔야단스럽게〕 ～하다 make much propaganda 《of》; propagandize 〔advertise〕 extensively; carry on 〔out〕 an active 〔a vigorous〕 propaganda / 과대하게 ～하다 advertise 《*a thing*》 with exaggerated praise / ～에 넘어가다 swallow the propaganda / 자기 ～을 하다 advertise *oneself* / ～하여 일꾼을 모으다 advertise for workers / 지금은 ～ 시대다 This is the age of advertisement. / 이 행사는 회사의 좋은 ～이 되었다 This event was good publicity for the company. / 그 회사는 TV에서 활발히 새 차 ～을 하고 있다 The company is promoting a new car on TV. ◉ ～가치 propaganda 〔promotional〕 value. ～공세 propaganda offensive; a propaganda 〔an advertising〕 onslaught; a propaganda attack. ～공작 propaganda maneuvers 〔efforts〕. ～극 a propaganda drama. ～기관 a propaganda machine(ry); a medium of publicity. ～기사 a publicity article. ～문구 an advertisement; a sales message; an advertising statement. ～방송 an advertisement broadcast; a commercial. ～부 the publicity department: ～부원 a publicity man / ～부장 the publicity manager. ～비 advertising 〔publicity〕 expenses. ～사진 a promotion picture. ～업 the publicity business: ～업자 a publicity agent. ～영화 a propaganda film. ～운동 a propaganda 〔publicity〕 campaign. ～전 a propaganda war(fare); a propaganda contest 〔campaign, battle〕; an advertising 〔a publicity〕 campaign. ～전단 a propaganda bill 〔leaflet〕; a (propaganda) handbill: ～전단을 뿌리다 distribute leaflets. ～차 an advertising van; a loudspeaker car; a sound truck 〔car〕. ～포스터 a propaganda 〔publicity〕 poster. ～활동 propaganda activity. ～효과 (a) propaganda effect; a propaganda impact. 과대～ an exaggerated 〔extravagant〕 advertisement; a dazzling ad; a puff: 과대 ～을 하다 give a big build-up to; 《미구어》 ballyhoo. 가두 ～원 a town=crier; an advertisement man.

**선전**(善戰) a good fight 〔battle〕. ～하다 fight a good battle; put up a good fight; fight bravely 〔well〕. ¶ 한정된 자금으로 그는 ～하고 있다 Despite a limited fund, he is putting up a good fight. / 우리 팀은 ～에도 불구하고 6-4로 패했다 Our team did its best, but lost the game by a score of 6 to 4.

**선전포고**(宣戰布告) a declaration 〔proclamation〕 of war. ～하다 declare 〔proclaim〕 war 《(up)on, against》. ¶ ～나 다름없는 중대한 도발 행위 a grave and serious provocation tantamount to a declaration of war 《against》.

**선점**(先占) prior occupation. ◉ ～(권)자 an occupant. ～취득 acquisition by occupancy.

**선정**(善政) good government 〔administration〕; just 〔benevolent〕 rule. ¶ ～을 베풀다 govern well; rule wisely.

**선정**(煽情) ¶ ～적(인) inflammatory; voluptuous; sensational; sultry; suggestive; lascivious / 그 잡지는 ～적인 기사를 특집으로 다루고 있다 The magazine features sensational articles.
◉ ～소설 a sultry novel; a suggestive story. ～적 저널리즘 yellow journalism.

**선정**(選定) selection; choice. ～하다 select; choose; make a selection 〔choice〕 《of》. ¶ ～도서목록 a reading list; a reference (reading) list / 교과서를 ～하다 adopt a textbook. ◉ ～기준 a basis of selection; criteria for selection.

**선제**(先制) leading off; 《경기 따위의》 a head start. ¶ ～점을 올리다 score the first points 〔runs〕 / ～ 홈런을 치다 start the scoring by hitting a homer 〔home run〕.

**선제공격**(先制攻擊) a containment offensive; a preemptive strike 〔attack〕. ～하다 open the first strike; attack 《the enemy》 first; carry out a preemptive strike 《against》; take the initiative in an attack.

**선조**(先祖) an ancestor; a forefather; a progenitor; a predecessor. ¶ ～ 대대의 묘 a family tomb / ～ 전래의 가보 an ancestral 〔hereditary〕 treasure / 그의 집은 ～ 대대로 농가였다 His family has engaged in farming for generations.

**선종**(腺腫) 『의학』 an adenoma (*pl.* ～s, -mata).

**선종**(禪宗) 『불교』 the Zen 〔Dhyāna〕 sect; Zen Buddhism.

**선주**(船主) a shipowner. ◉ ～협회 a shipowners' association.

**선지** 《동물의》 blood from a slaughtered animal. ◉ ～피 fresh animal blood. 선짓국 ox-blood soup. 선짓덩이 (a lump of ) clotted blood.

**선지자**(先知者) a prophet; a seer; a predictor.

**선진**(先陣) the van (of an army); the advance guard; the vanguard. ¶ ～이 되다 lead the van.

**선진**(先進) 《앞섬》 being advanced; 《선구자》 a pioneer; a precursor; a farsighted leader; a pathfinder; 《선배》 a senior; a superior; an elder. ¶ ～의 advanced; developed; senior. ◉ ～국 an advanced nation; a developed country: 공업 ～국 an industrially advanced nation / ～국 수뇌회담 the Summit Conference of the Leading Industrialized Nations / ～국 대열에 끼이다 join the ranks 〔columns〕 of advanced countries. ～기술 advanced technology: ～ 기술의 도입 the introduction of advanced technology.

**선집**(選集) a selection; selected works; an anthology 《of modern poetry》. ¶ ～으로 엮다 anthologize 《modern poetry》.

**선착**(先着) ① 《먼저 도착》 first arrival. ～하다 arrive 〔come〕 first 〔beforehand〕. ¶ ～순으로 in (the) order of arrival 〔receipt〕; on a "first-come-first-served" basis / ～순 20명에 한해 초대권을 드립니다 Complimentary tickets will be given to the first twenty arrivals. / ～순 500명까지, 학생 무료 입장 Admission free to the first 500 students only. ② 《먼저 착수》 undertaking first; taking the first hand; 《선편(先鞭)》 getting the first chance. ～하다 undertake first. ◉ ～자 the first comer; the first to arrive.

**선착장**(船着場) 《부두》 a wharf (*pl.* ～s, wharves); a harbor.

**선창**(先唱) leading 《in chorus》; [비유적] advocacy; initiation. ～하다 lead the chorus 〔cheer〕; [비유적] take the lead; play first violin; call the tune. ¶ Y씨의 ～으로 만세삼창을 했다 Three cheers were given at the call of Mr. Y. *or* They gave three cheers led by Mr. Y. ◉ ～자 《노래의》 a chorus leader; 《주창자》 a leader.

**선창**(船倉) the hold (of a ship). ¶ 화물을 ～에 싣다 stow 〔load〕 cargo in the hold.

**선창**(船窓) a porthole.

**선창**(船艙) a wharf (*pl.* ～s, wharves); a quay; a (landing) pier. ¶ 배를 ～에 대다 bring a boat alongside the pier / ～까지 전송하다 see 《*a person*》 off at the pier. ◉ ～사용료 wharfage; pier dues; pierage; quayage.

**선책**(善策) a good plan; a fine scheme; a capital plan; a good policy.

**선처**(善處) the adequate 〔appropriate〕 steps; proper dealing. ～하다 take the appropriate steps 《in 〔concerning〕 a matter》; make the best of 《*one's* adverse circumstances》; take proper measures 《against》; cope with 《a difficult problem》; deal wisely 《with》. ¶ ～를 부탁드립니다 I beg you will manage it all right. / ～해 드리죠 I will 「see to it 〔make it, fix it〕 all right.

**선천론**(先天論) 『철학』 nativism; apriorism. ¶ ～자 a nativist.

**선천병**(先天病) a congenital 〔hereditary〕 disease.

**선천성**(先天性) apriority. ¶ ～ 매독 congenital 〔hereditary〕 syphillis.

**선천적**(先天的) inborn; innate; native; congenital; 《유전적》 inherent; hereditary; 『철학』 a priori. ¶ ～으로 by nature; innately; naturally; 《병 따위가》 congenitally; inherently / ～ 백치 a congenital idiot / ～ 불구 a congenital deformity / 그는 음악에 ～인 재주가 있다 He is a born musician. *or* He was born with a talent for music.

**선철**(先哲) ancient sages; wise 〔learned〕 men of the past; the sages of old.

**선철**(銑鐵) pig iron; pig.

**선체**(船體) the hull; a ship (배). ¶ ～가 두 동강이 났다 The ship was broken in two. ◉ ～강재(鋼材) ship steel. ～구조 hull construction. ～보험 hull insurance.

**선출**(選出) election. ~하다 elect; return 《영》. ¶ 서울에서 ~된 국회 의원 a member of the National Assembly for 〔(elected) from〕 Seoul / 종로에서 ~되다 be 「elected from 〔returned for〕 Chongno / 우리는 그를 의장으로 ~했다 We elected him the chairperson.

**선충**(線蟲) 〖동물〗 an eelworm; a nematode (worm). ◉ ~구제약 a nematocide. ~류 *Nematoda* (학명).

**선취**(先取) taking 〔occupying〕 first; preoccupation. ~하다 take first; preempt; preoccupy. ¶ 한 점을 ~하다 score the first one point 〔run (야구에서)〕; score a point in advance. ◉ ~(득)점 points 〔marks〕 obtained first; 〖야구〗 runs scored first: ~점을 올리다 score first points 〔runs〕.

**선취특권**(先取特權) a preferential 〔prior, priority〕 right; (the right of) priority; priority of claim; a (prior) lien. ¶ ~이 있는 preferential; preferred / ~이 있다 have the prior right 《to》; have a priority right 《over》 〔claim 《on》〕. ◉ ~자 a lien holder.

**선측**(船側) the side of a ship; a ship's side. ◉ ~인도(引渡) 《적하》 free alongside (ship) (생략 F.A.S. f.a.s.); 《양륙》 ex ship.

**선친**(先親) my deceased 〔late〕 father.

**선태**(蘚苔) 〖식물〗 moss(es). ◉ ~류〔식물〕 a bryophyte. ~학 bryology.

**선택**(選擇) selection; choice; option. ~하다 select; choose; pick up; make *one's* choice; make *one's* option. ¶ 인위〔자연〕 ~ 〖생물〗 artificial 〔natural〕 selection / ~의 자유 the liberty of choice / ~적인 selective / ~을 잘〔잘못〕하다 make a good 〔bad〕 choice; choose the good 〔wrong〕 one / ~을 망설이다 be at a loss which to choose / …의 ~에 맡기다 leave the choice to 《*a person*》; leave 《*a matter*》 to 《*a person's*》 choice / ~하기가 어렵다 find difficulty in *one's* choice / ~은 네 자유다 You have a free choice. ◉ ~과목 an elective (course) 《미》; an option 《영》; an optional course: ~ 과목으로 화학을 택했다 I minored in chemistry. ~권 option; the right of choice: ~권이 있다 have the right of choice; have *one's* 〔the〕 pick 《of》. ~법 a method of selection. ~지(肢) 《다항식 선택법의》 《six》 choices. ~투표 preferential voting. ~형 문제 a multiple-choice question(naire).

**선팽창**(線膨脹) 〖물리〗 linear expansion. ◉ ~률〔계수〕 the coefficient of linear expansion.

**선편**(船便) (a) shipping service; 《우편》 surface 〔sea〕 mail. ¶ ~으로 by ship 〔sea, water〕; 《우편으로》 by surface 〔sea〕 mail / 나는 그에게 ~으로 책을 부쳤다 I sent him a book by surface 〔sea〕 mail.

**선평**(選評) selection and criticism. ~하다 select and criticize.

**선포**(宣布) proclamation; promulgation. ~하다 proclaim; promulgate. ¶ 계엄령을 ~하다 proclaim martial law.

**선표**(船票) a (ship) passenger ticket; a boat ticket.

**선풍**(旋風) a whirlwind; a cyclone; a tornado (*pl.* ~(e)s); a twister. ¶ ~적인 sensational / 검거~ a wholesale arrest; a sweeping roundup / ~이 일어나다 a whirlwind springs up / ~에 휩쓸리다 be caught up in a cyclone / (일대) ~을 일으키다 《인기면에서》 create a great sensation; cause a sensation; make 〔cut〕 a splash 《구어》 / 그의 소설은 문단에 일대 ~을 일으켰다 His novel 「caused a great sensation 〔made quite a splash〕 in literary circles.

**선풍기**(扇風機) an electric fan; 《천장에 설치한》 a ceiling fan. ¶ ~ 바람 the draft 〔breeze〕 from an electric fan / ~를 틀다 set an electric fan in motion; turn 〔switch〕 on an electric fan / ~를 끄다 turn 〔switch〕 off an electric fan.

**선하**(船荷) a (ship's) cargo. ⇨ 선화(船貨).

**선하다** (be) vivid; fresh 《before *one's* eyes》; live vividly in *one's* memory. ¶ 눈에 ~ be fresh 〔live〕 in *one's* memory; linger 〔stay〕 before *one's* eyes / 그 광경이 아직도 눈에 ~ The scene is still lingering in my eyes. / 그의 모습이 아직도 눈에 ~ The memory of his visage still haunts me. ⇨ 선히.

**선하다**(善―) = 착하다.

**선하품** 《억지의》 a forced yawn; 《소화불량시의》 a yawn caused by indigestion. ¶ ~을 하다 force a yawn; feign a yawn.

**선행**(先行) preceding; going first; walking ahead. ~하다 go first; go 〔walk〕 ahead 《of》; precede. ¶ 시대에 ~하다 be ahead of the times. ◉ ~권 《도로 교통의》 《have》 (the) right of way. ~사 〖문법〗 an antecedent. ~조건 a condition precedent; an essential prerequisite. ～지수 a leading composite index (생략 CI). ～지표 a leading [an early] indicator.

**선행**(善行) good conduct; a good [praiseworthy] deed. ¶ ～을 쌓다 keep on doing good (deeds) / ～을 표창하다 (officially) recognize [show appreciation] of 《*a person's*》 good conduct / 그는 ～으로 당국의 표창을 받았다 He won official commendation for his good deeds. ◉ ～상(賞) a prize for good conduct.

**선향**(線香) a joss stick; an incense rod [stick]. ¶ ～을 피우다 burn incense.

**선험**(先驗) 〖철학〗 ¶ ～적 transcendental; *a priori*. ◉ ～론 transcendentalism. ～적 인식 transcendental cognition. ～적 확률 *a priori* probability. ～철학 transcendental philosophy; transcendentalism.

**선헤엄** treading water; standing stroke. ¶ ～을 치다 tread water.

**선현**(先賢) ancient sages. = 선철(先哲).

**선혈**(鮮血) (fresh) blood; lifeblood. ¶ ～이 낭자하다 be covered [dripping] with blood.

**선형**(扇形) a fan shape; 〖기하〗 a sector.

**선형**(船型) the type [class] of a ship.

**선형**(線形) ¶ ～의 linear. ◉ ～도시 a linear city. ～디자인 linear design.

**선호**(選好) preference. ～하다 prefer 《to》. ¶ 유동성 ～ 〖경제〗 liquidity preference / 남아 ～ 사상 a notion of preferring a son to a daughter / 그들은 커피보다 녹차를 ～한다 They like better green tea than coffee. *or* They have a liking [preference] for green tea to coffee.

**선홍색**(鮮紅色) scarlet (color).

**선화**(線畫) a (line) drawing; line-work.

**선화**(船貨) a (ship's) cargo; a freight; a lading. ◉ ～주 the shipper. ～증권 《issue》 a bill of lading (생략 B/L).

**선화지**(仙花紙) reclaimed paper.

**선회**(旋回) (a) revolution; (a) turn (-ing); (a) rotation; circling; gyration. ～하다 turn; revolve; rotate; circle [whirl, swing] round; wheel; gyrate. ¶ 한 마리의 독수리가 상공에서 ～하고 있다 A vulture is circling overhead.
◉ ～비행 《make》 a circular flight. ～운동 a turning [gyrating, rotating] movement. ～축 a pivot.

**선후**(先後) 《앞뒤》 front and rear; beginning and end; 《순서》 order; sequence. ¶ ～가 뒤죽박죽이 되다 be topsy-turvy; be out of order; be inverted. ◉ ～도착(倒錯) reversing the proper order; putting the cart before the horse.

**선후책**(善後策) remedial [relief] measures; remedies. ¶ ～을 강구하다 devise [work out] remedial measures; consider the remedies how to cope with the situation.

**선히** freshly; vividly; distinctly; graphically. ¶ 베갯머리에 돌아가신 어머니 모습이 ～ 보였다 I saw by my bedside a vivid image of my dead mother.

**섣달** the twelfth month of lunar calendar; the last month of the year; December. ◉ ～그믐 New Year's Eve.

**섣부르다** 《어설프다》 (be) awkward; clumsy; unskillful; tactless; 《경솔하다》 (be) careless; thoughtless; heedless; rash; indiscreet; hasty. ¶ 섣부른 일 a hazardous thing [undertaking] / 섣부른 짓을 하다 do a rash thing; act foolishly [unwisely] / 섣부른 짓 하다간 큰 코 다친다 When you play with fire you are apt to get burned.

**섣불리** awkwardly; clumsily; tactlessly; 《경솔히》 thoughtlessly; heedlessly; rashly; indiscreetly. ¶ ～ 입 밖에 내다 let slip [drop] an offhand remark; give away 《a secret》 through carelessness / ～ 손을 댈 수 없는 일이군 This is certainly a matter not to be lightly handled.

**설** 《정초》 the New Year (season); 《설날》 New Year's (Day). ¶ 설음식 the dishes for the New Year / 설 연휴 the New Year's holidays / 설(을) 쇠다 celebrate the New Year; observe the New Year's day / 설맞이하다 greet the New Year.

**설**(說) ① 《의견》 an opinion; a view. ¶ 설을 굽히다[굽히지 않다] change [stick to] *one's* view(s) / 그것에 관해서는 구구한 설이 있다 There are many different opinions about it. / 그들은 지구가 편평하다는 설을 고집했다 They persisted in the view that the earth was flat.
② 《학설·신조》 a theory; a doctrine. ¶ 맬서스의 설 the Malthusian theory [doctrine] / 새로운 설을 확립하다 establish [put forward] a new theory.
③ 《풍설》 a rumor; a talk; a report; 《해석》 a version. ¶ 일설에는 …라고 한다 One version says [has it] that… / 그 정치가는 범죄 단체와 연관이 있다는 설이 있다 There's a report that the politician has links with a criminal organization.

**설-** insufficient; half-done; not enough; imperfect; under; barely; hardly. ¶ 설익은 half-cooked〔-done, -boiled〕; underdone / 설익히다 parboil.

**설거지** dishwashing; washing-up 《영》. ∼하다 do 〔wash〕 the dishes; 《영》 wash up. ◉ ∼물 dishwater. ∼통 a sink; a dishpan; a washing-up bowl.

**설겅거리다** chew hard; taste lumpy; be half-done and indigestible. ¶ 콩이 덜 익어서 설겅거린다 These beans are not well done so they are hard to eat.

**설겅설겅** hard-chewing; lumpy-tasting.

**설경**(雪景) a snow(-covered) scene 〔view〕; a snowscape.

**설계**(設計) a plan 《for》; a design 《for》. ∼하다 plan; design; make a plan 《for》; work out a design 《for》; 《도면을》 lay out; draw up a plan; project. ¶ ∼중(인) in the planning 〔design〕 stage; 《a rocket》 under design / 도시 ∼ city planning / 생활 ∼ life planning / 미래를 ∼하다 map out *one's* future / 정원을 ∼하다 lay out a garden / 이 주택은 ∼가 잘〔잘못〕 되어 있다 This is a well-〔ill-〕planned house. / 이 집은 Y씨의 ∼로 지어졌다 This house was built from the design of Mr. Y. ◉ ∼도 a plan; a draft; a blueprint; a design drawing. ∼명세서 specifications. ∼자 a designer 〔planner, projector〕.

**설교**(說敎) ① 《성직자의》 a sermon; preaching. ∼하다 preach (a sermon); deliver 《*a person*》 a sermon; 《단상에서》 occupy the pulpit. ¶ ∼를 듣다 hear 〔listen to〕 a sermon / 가두(街頭)에서 ∼하다 preach on the streets / 신도들에게 하느님 말씀을 ∼하다 preach the congregation the word of God. ② 《훈계》 a moralizing lecture 〔discourse〕; 《잔소리》 scolding; remonstrance; admonition; a talking-to. ∼하다 lecture 《*a person*》; scold; admonish 《*a person* for *something*》; give 《*a person*》 a (good) talking-to. ¶ ∼를 듣다 be scolded; be lectured 《on *one's* conduct》; be given 〔get〕 a scolding; get a talking-to / 아버지의 ∼는 이젠 딱 질색이다 I have had quite enough of a lecture from my father. ◉ ∼단 a pulpit. ∼사 a preacher; [경멸적] a pulpiteer.

**설기** 《떡》 steamed rice cake.

**설날** New Year's (Day); the first of the year.

**설늙은이** a person prematurely aged.

**설다** ① 《덜 익다》 be unripe 〔immature, half-boiled, half-done〕. ¶ 선 과일 unripened fruits / 밥이 ∼ Rice is undercooked. ② 《술·김치 등이》 be not thoroughly fermented; be not fully pickled. ③ 《잠이》 be light; be not sound enough. ④ 《익숙지 않다》 (be) unfamiliar 《with》; unaccustomed 《to》; unpracticed; new 《to, at》; green. ¶ 낯이 ∼ be unfamiliar 〔strange〕 / 낯이 선 사람 a stranger. ⑤ ⇨ 서럽다.

**설다루다** do a poor job 《of it》; handle carelessly; do a halfway job. ¶ 개를 설다루면 물린다 If you don't handle the dog carefully you will get bitten.

**설득**(說得) persuasion. ∼하다 persuade; prevail (up)on 《*a person* to *do*》; talk 《*a person*》 into compliance; talk 〔win〕 《*a person*》 over; bring 《*a person*》 around. ¶ ∼하여 by 〔through, with〕 persuasion / ∼하여 …시키다 persuade 《*a person*》 to *do;* reason 〔talk〕 《*a person*》 into *do*ing / ∼하여 그만두게 하다 reason 《*a person*》 from *do*ing / 나는 동생이 엉뚱한 생각을 버리도록 ∼했다 I talked my brother out of his foolish idea. ◉ ∼대표 an explainer; an explaining representative. ∼력 persuasive 〔reasoning〕 power; 《*one's*》 powers of persuasion: ∼력이 있는 연설 a persuasive speech / 자기 견해를 ∼력 있게 말하다 give *one's* view in a way that carries conviction; speak convincingly.

**설듣다** half-hear; mishear; pay no attention 《to *a person's* talk》.

**설렁거리다** 《바람이》 blow gently; 《걷는 꼴》 walk briskly. ¶ 봄바람이 설렁거린다 There's a gentle spring breeze.

**설렁설렁** 《바람이》 《blow》 gently; softly; 《걸음을》 《walk》 with brisk steps. ¶ 바람이 ∼ 분다 The wind blows gently. *or* There is a gentle breeze.

**설렁탕**(一湯) *sŏllŏngt'ang;* cow bone and tripe 〔internals〕 soup with rice.

**설렁하다** be a bit chilly; be slightly cold. ¶ 방이 ∼ I feel slightly cold in my room.

**설레다** throb; palpitate; flutter; beat high 《with the hope of》; 《불안·흥분으로》 feel uneasy; fidget; be restless. ¶ 가슴이 ∼ *one's* heart goes pit-a-pat 《with fright》; feel uneasy 〔nervous〕; have 〔feel〕 a presentiment; be in a flutter / 설레는 가슴을 가라앉히다 calm *one's* agitated mind / 내 가슴은 기대감

에 설레었다 My heart fluttered 〔beat fast〕 in anticipation.

**설레설레** ⇨ 살래살래.

**설령**(設令) even if; (even) though; although; granting 〔admitting, supposing〕 that…. ¶ ~ 그렇다 해도〔치더라도〕 even if it were so; granting that it is so / ~ 어떠한 일이 있더라도 whatever 〔no matter what〕 may happen; come what may / ~ 네 말이 사실이라 할지라도 그것은 변명이 되지 못한다 Granted 〔Granting〕 that what you say is true, it's no excuse.

**설립**(設立) foundation; establishment; setting up; institution; 《회사들의》 incorporation; flotation; organization. ~하다 establish; found; institute; set up; organize; incorporate.

> (용법) **foundation** 기초를 놓는 것. **establishment** foundation 보다 뜻이 강하며, 영속적인 존재로 설립하는 것. **institution** 위의 두 낱말보다 범위가 넓으며, 영속적이 아닌 것에도 쓰임.

¶ 학교를 ~하다 found 〔establish〕 a school / ~을 허가하다 charter 《a bank》/ 새로운 상사를 ~하다 found a new business company / 본교가 설립된지 80년이 되었다 It has been 80 years since our school was founded 〔established〕. *or* Our school was founded 〔established〕 80 years ago. ◉ ~등기 registration of incorporation. ~발기인 a promoter. ~비용 organization expenses. ~위원회 an establishment committee. ~자 a founder; an organizer; an institutor. ~절차 formalities of incorporation. ~취지서 a prospectus.

**설마** surely (not); (not) possibly 〔by any possibility〕; it is not 〔least〕 likely 《that…》; by no means; hardly; never; on no account. ¶ ~(하니) Impossible! *or* That can't be true! *or* You don't say so! *or* No kidding? 《구어》/ ~ 그럴라구 It is not at all likely. / ~그런 일은 없을 테지 I don't think it possible. *or* That is highly impossible 〔hardly possible〕. / ~그가 나를 잊었으랴 He would hardly have forgotten me! / ~ 너 혼자 가는 건 아닐 테지 Surely you are not going alone? / ~ 그가 도둑질을 하랴 He would be the last man in the world to steal things. / ~ 그러리라고는 생각 못 했다 That's the last thing I expected. / ~ 오늘 비는 안 오겠지 It is hardly going to rain today. / ~ 그런 일은 없으리라고 생각했다 I never thought it possible. / ~ 그녀가 가수로 성공하리라고는 생각조차 못했다 It never occurred to me that she would be a successful singer. /「그이가 날 때리려고 했어요」—「~ 그럴리가」 "He was going to strike me."—"Oh you're kidding!"

**설맞다** receive a flesh wound. ¶ 너 매를 아직 설맞았다. 좀더 맞아야겠다 You have just had a taste of the beating you deserve, you need a little more.

**설면하다** ① 《소원》 (be) estranged; alienated; distant. ② 《정답지 않다》 be on cold terms with; want in familiarity.

**설명**(說明) (an) explanation; (an) exposition; an account; (an) interpretation; (an) elucidation; a caption (삽화나 사진의). ~하다 explain; give an explanation 《of》; account 《for》; interpret; elucidate; make clear; expound; illustrate; outline (대체적으로); demonstrate (작동 등을 실지로).

> (용법) **explain** 이해하기 쉽도록 말이나 문장으로 해설한다는 뜻의 일반적인 말. **account for** 납득하기에 충분한 이유나 원인을 들어 설명한다는 뜻. **interpret** 시나 연극 따위의 예술 작품이나 추상적인 사항, 외국의 작품·문화 따위에 관하여 「뜻을 말하다」, 「해설, 설명하다」란 뜻. **illustrate** …을 실례를 들어 설명하거나 이론 따위를 예시하며 설명하다. **demonstrate** 실물이나 실험 따위로 사용법, 효과 따위를 설명하다.

¶ ~할 수 있는〔없는〕 explainable 〔unexplainable〕; explicable 〔inexplicable〕/ …의 ~으로서 in explanation of… / ~조로 in a recitative tone / ~을 요하지 않다 be self-explanatory; be self-evident; need no explanation / ~을 요구하다 demand an explanation 《of》/ 외교 정책을 ~하다 elucidate the country's foreign policy / 이론을 ~하다 expound a theory / 대충 ~하다 explain roughly 〔briefly〕; give a brief explanation / 자세히 ~하다 explain at length 〔at large, in details〕/ 내가 그 사건에 관하여 ~하겠다 I will render 〔give〕 an account of the incident. / 나는 그들에게 새로운 규칙을 ~했다 I explained the new rules to them. (★

explain은 2중 목적어를 취하지 않는다. 따라서 I explained them the new rules. 는 잘못된 문장임.) / 나는 어째서 그런 실수가 일어났는지 설명할 수 없다 I can't 「account for 〔explain〕 the mistake.
◉ ~도 a diagram. ~문 an explanation; an explanatory note. ~서 an explanatory (leaflet); an explanation; an exposition; a description (제품의); 《기계 조작법 등의 사용 설명서》 an operating manual; an instruction book; operating instructions. ~어 the predicate (of a sentence). ~자 an explainer; an elucidator; an expositor; 《학설 등의》 an exponent. ~회 a briefing session; an explanatory meeting.

**설문**(設問) a question. ~하다 「make up 〔pose〕 a question(naire). ¶ 다음 ~에 답하시오 Answer the following question(s).

**설법**(說法) 《불교에서》 a Buddhist sermon; preaching. ~하다 preach (a sermon). ¶ 부처에게 ~하다 《속담》 Preaching Buddhism to Buddha. *or* Don't try to teach your grandmother (how) to suck eggs.

**설보다** see unclearly or wrongly.

**설복**(說服) persuasion. ⇨ 설득(說得).

**설봉**(舌鋒) ¶ 날카로운 ~으로 in most cutting terms; with an incisive tongue; 《criticize》 sharply / ~이 날카롭다 have an incisive 〔trenchant〕 tongue.

**설비**(設備) equipment; an installation; arrangements; appointments; conveniences; facilities (시설); accommodation(s) (수용 설비). ⇨ 시설. ~하다 equip 〔provide, furnish〕 《with》; install; accommodate; arrange.
¶ 근대적인 ~ modern conveniences / 기술적인 ~ technical installations / ~가 빈약한 poorly-equipped; poorly-appointed / ~가 좋은 방 a well-furnished room / ~가 좋은 호텔 a well-appointed hotel / …의 ~가 되어 있다 be equipped 〔provided, furnished, installed〕 with… / 난방 ~가 되어 있다 have a heating system / 숙박 ~가 없다 have no sleeping accommodations / 그 호텔에는 온갖 근대적 ~가 갖춰져 있다 The hotel is equipped 〔fitted〕 with all modern comforts and conveniences. / 그 호텔은 ~가 좋다〔나쁘다〕 The hotel has admirable 〔poor〕 accommodations. / 그 빌딩은 자가 발전 ~가 있다 The building has its own (electric) power plant.
◉ ~비 the cost of equipment. ~수출 plant export. ~자금 an equipment fund. ~투자 plant investment; investment in plant and equipment; equipment 〔facility〕 investment. 과잉~ excessive facilities.

**설빔** the New Year's best (clothes); a fine 〔gala〕 dress worn on New Year's Day. ~하다 dress up for New Year's.

**설사**(泄瀉) loose bowel movement; 〖의학〗 diarrhea. ~하다 have loose bowel movement; suffer from diarrhea. ¶ 물 같은 ~ explosive 〔watery〕 diarrhea / 심한 ~ violent purging / ~를 막다 stop diarrhea; bind the bowels / ~를 하고 있다 be loose in the bowel movement. ◉ ~약 a diarrhea remedy; a binding medicine; a paregoric (소아용).

**설사**(設使) even if. ⇨ 비록, 설령.

**설산**(雪山) a snow-covered mountain.

**설상**(舌狀) ¶ ~의 tongue-shaped; lingulate. ◉ ~기관 a lingua; a tongue-like organ. ~돌기 〖해부〗 a lingula (*pl.* -lae). ~판(瓣) 〖식물〗 a ligula; a ligule. ~화 〖식물〗 a lingulate flower.

**설상가상**(雪上加霜) ¶ ~으로 to make things 〔matters〕 worse; (and) what is worse; to add to *one's* troubles 〔miseries〕; as if to rub salt in the wound / ~으로 비까지 오기 시작했다 To make us more miserable, it began to rain.

**설선**(雪線) 〖지리〗 a snow line 〔limit〕.

**설설**[1] 《끓는 모양》 gently; softly; lightly; warmly. ¶ 물이 ~ 끓다 water simmers.

**설설**[2] 《기다》 with a brisk crawl; 《무서워서》 with fear; timidly; nervously; with restrainedly; 《고개를》 with a shake of the head. ¶ 아내 앞에서 ~ 기는 남편 a henpecked husband / 아버지 앞에서 ~ 기다 cringe before *one's* father; keep *one's* head low 〔be awe-struck〕 before *one's* father / 고개를 ~ 내젓다 shake *one's* head / 그의 무서운 눈초리에 비서가 ~ 긴다 The secretary cowers before his stern gaze. / 그의 아내는 그 앞에서 ~ 긴다 His wife cannot hold up her head before him. *or* His wife is completely under his thumb.

**설암**(舌癌) 〖의학〗 cancer of the tongue.

**설야**(雪夜) a snowy night.

**설염**(舌炎) 〖의학〗 glossitis.

**설왕설래**(說往說來) arguing back and forth; bandying words; argument. ~

하다 argue back and forth; wrangle; bandy words 《with》.

**설욕**(雪辱) ① 《치욕 등의》 vindication of *one's* honor. ～하다 vindicate *one's* honor; clear *oneself* of a disgrace; wipe out *one's* shame. ② 《패배의》 revenge. ～하다 get revenge for *one's* defeat; have *one's* revenge; settle 〔square〕 accounts 《with》; 《경기에서》 get even 《with》; redeem *oneself.* ¶ 지난번의 패배를 ～하다 revenge a former defeat; wipe out the stain of a former defeat. ◉ ～전 a return match 〔game〕: ～전에 응하다 give 《*a person*》 *his* revenge.

**설움** sadness; sorrow; grief; distress; woe; lamentation; mourning. ¶ 복받치는 ～ the sorrow welling up within *one* / ～이 복받쳐 in (the excess of) *one's* grief 〔sorrow〕 / 집없는 ～을 겪다 be in a miserable plight as a houseless person / ～을 겪다〔당하다〕 come to grief 〔misery〕; be looked down (up)on 《for》; be treated with contempt 《for》; be held in contempt / ～을 못 이기다 be overcome with sorrow; be overwhelmed with grief / ～이 복받쳐 울다 fall to crying in (the excess of) *one's* sorrow 〔grief〕.

**설원**(雪原) a snowfield; a frozen waste.

**설원**(雪寃) vindication; exoneration. ～하다 clear *oneself* 《of a false charge》; exonerate 〔vindicate〕 *oneself* 《from guilt》; prove *one's* innocence.

**설유**(說諭) (an) admonition; (a) exhortation; (a) reproof. ～하다 admonish; exhort; reprove.

**설음**(舌音) 〖음성〗 a lingual (sound). ¶ ～화하다 lingualize.

**설익다** 《음식이》 get 〔be〕 half-done〔-cooked, -boiled〕; 《과일이》 be unripe 〔immature, green〕. ¶ 설익은 half=cooked; underdone / 설익은 과일 unripe 〔green〕 fruits.

**설인**(雪人) 《히말라야의》 a 〔an Abominable〕 Snowman; a yeti.

**설자다** sleep fitfully 〔poorly〕.

**설잡다** hold 《*a thing*》 loosely; half=hold.

**설전**(舌戰) a verbal battle 〔contest, war〕; a hot 〔heated〕 discussion; a war of words; a wordy battle. ～하다 have 〔engage in〕 a wordy war 〔a heated discussion〕 《with》; fight verbally; argue. ¶ 두 대통령 후보는 TV토론에서 ～을 벌였다 The two presidential candidates had a heated discussion in a TV debate.

**설정**(設定) establishment; creation; institution; fixing; setting up. ～하다 establish; create; institute; set up; fix. ¶ 저당권 ～ settlement of mortgage / 기금(基金)을 ～하다 set up a fund.

**설죽다** be half-killed〔-dead〕; be nearly killed.

**설중**(雪中) ¶ ～의〔에〕 in the snow / ～행군을 하다 march through the snow.

**설차림** preparing the New Year's festive dishes.

**설철**(屑鐵) scrap iron; iron scraps.

**설측음**(舌側音) 〖음성〗 a lateral (sound).

**설치**(設置) establishment; foundation; institution; installation. ～하다 establish; institute; set up; found; install; organize. ¶ 영사관을 ～하다 set up a consulate / 위원회를 ～하다 organize 〔set up〕 a committee.

**설치다** ① 《중도에 그만두다》 leave 《*a thing*》 half-done; stop 《work》 halfway; 《잠을》 sleep badly; fail to get to sleep (enough); be sleepless. ¶ 간밤에는 잠을 설쳤다 I slept badly last night. *or* I had a disturbed sleep last night. ② 《날뛰다》 thrive; overrun; be rampant; run wild 〔riot, amuck〕; rave 〔rage, ramp〕 about; infest; be unruly. ¶ 소매치기들이 설치는 거리 a street infested with pickpockets / 거리를 설치고 다니다 storm through the street.

**설치류**(齧齒類) 〖동물〗 rodents. ¶ ～의 rodential.

**설탕**(雪糖) sugar. ¶ ～ 한 파운드 a pound of sugar / ～을 넣은 sugared; sweetened with sugar / ～으로 조린 candied 《fruits》 / ～을 치다〔넣다〕 put sugar in 《*one's* coffee》; sugar; sweeten with sugar / ～에 절이다 preserve in sugar / ～을 입히다 coat with sugar; ice; frost / ～을 넣어 드릴까요 Do you take sugar 《in your tea》?
◉ ～가루 powdered 〔granulated〕 sugar. ～그릇 《식탁용》 a sugar bowl; a sugar basin 《영》. ～물 sugared water. ～조림 food preserved in sugar. 입자형～ granulated 〔crystallized〕 sugar.

**설태**(舌苔) 〖의학〗 fur (on *one's* tongue); "tongue fur 〔fuzz〕." ¶ ～가 낀 혀 a coated 〔furred〕 tongue.

**설파**(說破) 《밝혀 말함》 clear statement; elucidation; exposure; 《논파》 refutation; confutation. ～하다 《밝혀 말하다》 state plainly; express 〔point out〕 clearly; elucidate; 《논파하다》 refute 《an argument》; confute 《*one's* opponent》; disprove. ¶ 진리를 ～하다 give an expression to the truth.

**설편**(雪片) a snowflake. ＝눈송이.

**설피다** (be) loose-〔coarse-〕woven; rough; coarse.

**설핏하다** (be) rather loose-woven; gauzelike; somewhat coarse.

**설하선**(舌下腺) 〖해부〗 the sublingual gland. ＝혀밑샘.

**설한**(雪寒) the cold following a snowfall. ⇨ 엄동.

**설해**(雪害) snow damage; damage 「from 〔caused by〕 snow 〔a snowfall〕.

**설형**(楔形)¶ ～의 wedge-shaped; cuneiform; sphenoid(al). ◉ ～문자 a cuneiform (character); a sphenogram.

**설혹**(設或) even if. ⇨ 설령(設令).

**설화**(舌禍) trouble brought on by a slip of the tongue. ¶ ～를 자초하다 be criticized for what *one* said carelessly. ◉ ～사건 trouble caused by 「*one's* unfortunate statement 〔*one's* incriminating utterance (in public)〕.

**설화**(雪花·雪華) 《눈송이》 snowflakes; 《나뭇가지의》 snow on the branches; silver thaw. ◉ ～석고(石膏) alabaster.

**설화**(說話) a tale; a story; a narrative; a fable. ◉ ～문학 narrative 〔legendary〕 literature. ～체 a narrative style: ～체의 소설 a novel in narrative form.

**섧다** ⇨ 서럽다.

**섬**[1] ① 《멱서리》 a bag; a bale; a straw sack. ¶ 쌀 섬 a rice bag. ② 《용량》 a *sŏm* (＝5.12 U.S. bushels; 47.6 U.S. gallons).

**섬**[2] 《도서》 an island; an isle; an islet (작은). ¶ 섬의 insular / 외딴 섬 a solitary 〔an isolated〕 island / 섬사람 an islander; an inhabitant of an island / 섬을 돌아보다 make a tour of islands; go (a)round an island / 그녀는 섬에 살고 있다 She lives on an island.

**섬광**(閃光) a flash; a glint 〔sudden gleam〕 of light; 〖천문〗 scintillation. ¶ ～을 내다〔발하다〕 flash.
◉ ～경보기 a flashlight crossing signal. ～계(計) a flash meter. ～계수기 〖물리〗 a scintillometer. ～기 a flashing apparatus. ～등 a flashlight. ～사진 flashlight photography. ～신호 a flashing light signal. ～전구 a flash bulb 〔lamp〕; a photoflash lamp.

**섬기다** serve 《*one's* master》; be in 《*a person's*》 service; work under 〔for〕 《*a person*》; attend 〔wait〕 on 《*a person*》. ¶ 남편을 ～ be attentive 〔devoted〕 to *one's* husband / 부모를 ～ be 「devoted to 〔dutiful toward〕 *one's* parents; take care of *one's* parents / 어른을 ～ serve elders; show respect to elders / 신을 ～ serve God / 그녀는 병약한 남편을 정성껏 섬겼다 She 「devoted herself to 〔waited on〕 her sick husband.

**섬나라** an island 〔a seagirt〕 country; an insular nation. ◉ ～근성 the islander mentality; insularity; an insular spirit; insularism.

**섬돌** stone steps; a flight of stone steps.

**섬뜩하다** (be) frightened; horrified; startled; [서술적] have a fright 〔scare〕; be taken aback. ¶ 섬뜩하게 하다 take 《*a person's*》 breath away; startle; make 《*a person's*》 hair stand on end.

**섬멸**(殲滅) annihilation; extermination; total 〔complete〕 destruction. ～하다 annihilate; destroy totally; wipe 〔stamp〕 out; exterminate. ◉ ～전 an exterminatory war.

**섬모**(纖毛) ① 〖동물〗 a cilium (*pl.* ～s, -ia); [총칭] ciliation. ¶ ～의 ciliary / ～가 있는 ciliate(d); ciliolate. ② ＝섬유(纖維). ◉ ～반(盤) 〖동물〗 a ciliary disc. ～운동 ciliary movement. ～충 a ciliate.

**섬섬옥수**(纖纖玉手) a slender 〔delicate〕 hand.

**섬세**(纖細) delicacy; fineness; daintiness. ～하다 (be) delicate; fine; subtle; (fine and) slender; exquisite 《designs》. ¶ ～한 감정 delicate feeling 〔sentiment〕 / ～한 손가락 slender 〔delicate〕 fingers / ～하고 율동적인 움직임 a delicate rhythmical move / ～한 디자인〔모양〕 an exquisite design / 음악에 대한 감각이 ～하다 have a delicate 〔exquisite〕 ear 〔sense〕 for music.

**섬약**(纖弱) delicacy; frailty. ～하다 (be) weak; feeble; frail; fragile; delicate.

**섬유**(纖維) a fiber; a strand; textiles. ¶ ～성의 fibrous (섬유가 많은); fibroid (섬유로 이루어진) / ～상(狀)의 fibriform / 천연 ～ a natural fiber / 동물〔식물〕성 ～ an animal 〔a vegetable〕 fiber / 이 로프는 질긴 ～로 만들어졌다 This rope is made from strong fibers.
◉ ～공업 the textile 〔fiber〕 industry. ～공장 a textile mill. ～기계 textile machinery. ～상(狀) 물질 a fibrous material. ～석고 satin gypsum. ～세포 〖식물〗 a fibrous cell. ～소(素) roughage (음식물의); 〖동물〗 fibrin; 〖식물·화학〗 cellulose: 천연 ～소 natural cellulose. ～속(束) 〖해부〗 a fascicle; fascicular

fibers. ~유리 fiberglass; spun glass. ~작물 a fiber crop. ~제품 textile goods. ~조직 〖식물〗 fibrous tissue. ~종(腫) 〖의학〗 a fibroma (*pl.* ~s, -mata); a fibrous tumor. ~증 〖의학〗 fibrosis. ~질 fibroid material: ~질 식품 fibrous food; food with a lot of (dietary) fiber. ~층 〖해부〗 a fibrous layer. ~ 형성질 fibrinoplastin.

다국〔다자〕간 ~ 협정 the Multinational 〔Multilateral〕 Fiber Agreement (생략 MFA).

**섬지기** 〖농업〗 a rice-field requiring a *sŏm* of seed (about one hectare, 10,000 square meters).

**섬질** planing off 〔away〕 the side of a board. ~하다 plane off the side 《of》.

**섬참새** 〖조류〗 a russet sparrow.

**섭금류**(涉禽類) 〖조류〗 wading birds.

**섭렵**(涉獵) extensive reading. ~하다 read extensively 〔widely〕. ¶ 널리 문헌을 ~하다 「range extensively over 〔dig deeply into〕 the literature.

**섭리**(攝理) ① 《병조리》 taking care of *one's* ill health. ~하다 take care of *one's* ill health; recuperate *oneself.* ② 《하느님의》 providence; dispensation; 〖신학〗 economy. ¶ 신의 ~ divine providence 〔disposal〕; the Providence of God / 자연의 오묘한 ~ a happy dispensation of Nature / 하늘의 ~ the wise providence of Heaven / 신의 ~에 맡기다 trust in Providence.

**섭새기다** emboss; carve in relief 〔openwork〕.

**섭생**(攝生) ⇨ 양생(養生)①.

**섭섭하다** ① 《서운하다》 (be) sorry; sad; reluctant; regretful. ¶ 섭섭한 듯이 wistfully; reluctantly; lingeringly; with a regretful glance / 헤어지기가 ~ be sorry 〔sad〕 to part from 《*a person*》; be reluctant 〔feel loath〕 to leave 《a place》; feel the sorrow of parting / 그는 섭섭한 듯이 떠나갔다 He went his way with lingering steps.

② 《애석하다·유감스럽다》 (be) sorry; regrettable; regretful; 《원망스럽다》 (be) disappointing; reproachful. ¶ 섭섭한 듯이 with regret; regretfully; ruefully / 섭섭하게도 to *one's* regret 〔disappointment〕 / 섭섭하지만 I am sorry (to say); I regret (to say) / 섭섭하게 여기다 be sorry 《for》; (feel) regret; miss (없어서); 《원망스럽게》 be disappointed 《at》; have a grudge 《against》 / 섭섭하지만 참석 못 한다는 편지를 보내다 send a letter regretting that *one* is unable to attend 《a meeting》 / 섭섭하지만 사실이다 It is only too true. / 뵙지 못해 섭섭했습니다 I was sorry to miss you. / 그가 그런 적은 돈도 빌려 주지 않겠다고 하니 ~ I am disappointed to hear that he will not lend me such a trivial sum.

> 용법 **sorry** 불행·불운에 대한 슬픈 감정을 나타내는 일반적이고 구어적인 말. **regret** 특히 후회하는 마음이나 어찌 할 수 없는 것에 대한 유감스러운 심사를 나타내는 말. **repent** 회개하는 마음을 내포하는 격조 있는 말.

**섭섭히** with regret; to *one's* regret; unfortunately. ¶ ~ 여기다 be sorry for; be regretful; have a grudge 《against》 / 떠나는 것을 ~ 여기다 regret to leave; leave with regret / ~ 생각되는 것은 하나도 없다 I have no regrets.

**섭씨**(攝氏) centigrade (생략 C., C, c, Cent., cent.); Celsius (생략 C., Cels). ¶ ~ 25도 2분 《at》 25.2° C (★ twenty-five point two degrees centigrade라고 읽음) / ~ 10도의 물 water at 10° C. ◉ ~ 온도계 a centigrade thermometer; a Celsius (thermometer).

**섭외**(涉外) 《연락》 liaison; 《행사 등의》 arrangements; 《대외 관계》 public relations (생략 P.R.). ¶ 이 행사에서 ~를 좀 맡아 줄 수 없겠습니까 Could you be in of the arrangements for this event? ◉ ~계원〔담당자〕 a public relations man 〔agent〕; a liaison clerk 〔officer〕. ~과〔부〕 the public relations 〔liaison〕 section 〔division〕. ~사무 public relations business; liaison business.

**섭정**(攝政) 《일》 regency; 《사람》 a regent. ~하다 rule as regent. ¶~을 두다 set up regency; appoint a regent. ◉ ~왕세자 the Prince Regent.

**섭조개** 〖조개류〗 a blue mussel.

**섭취**(攝取) intake; intussusception; adoption; ingestion. ~하다 take (in); absorb; ingest (영양을); assimilate (동화하다). ¶ 단백질의 ~ the intake of protein / 영양을 ~하다 take nutrition. ◉ ~물 ingesta. ~량: 칼로리 ~량 a 〔*one's*〕 caloric intake.

**섯등** 《염전의》 an implement used to filter seawater in making salt.

**섰다** a kind of Korean card game.

**성** 《노염》 anger; rage; displeasure; indignation; wrath. ⇨성나다, 성내다. ¶ 성이 나게 하다 make 《*a person*》 angry 〔mad 《미속어》〕; anger; stir to anger; offend; outrage; 《벌컥》 rouse 《*a person*》 to anger; set 《*a person's*》 blood on fire / 성을 잘 내다 be quick to take offense; be liable to fits of temper; be inflammable / 벌컥 성을 내다 flare up; flash up; be roused to anger; fly into a (great) rage / 성이 나서 얼굴이 벌개지다 be red 〔flushed〕 with anger / 성을 가라앉히다 quell 〔appease〕 *one's* anger; calm 〔appease〕 《*a person's*》 anger.

**성**(姓) a family name; a surname; *one's* last name 《미》. ¶ 성과 이름 《give》 *one's* full name.

**성**(性) ① 《본성》 nature. ¶ 인간의 성은 선하다 Man is naturally good. *or* All men are born good. ② 〖문법〗 gender. ¶ 남〔여, 중〕성 the masculine 〔feminine, neuter〕 gender. ③ 〖철학〗 an attribute; a nature. ④ 《남녀의 성별》 (a) sex; *one's* sex; 《성적 본능》 sex. ¶ 연령, 성별에 관계 없이 regardless of age or sex / 성적 매력 sex appeal / 성적 욕구 a sexual desire / 성적인 sexual / 성적으로 조숙한 sexually precocious / 성의 해방 liberation of sex / 성문제 a sex problem / 성체험 sexual experience / 성혁명 the sex revolution / 성본능 sex(ual) instinct / 성 억제 sex control / 성의 자각 the sexual awakening / 성에 눈뜨다 become conscious of sex; be(come) sexually awakened; begin to feel the urge of sex / 성을 의식하고 있다 have a sexual awareness.

◉ 성결정 유전자 a sex determinating gene. 성지식 knowledge about sex; 《구어》 the facts of life; the 「birds and bees 〔bees and the flowers〕 (어린이가 배우는). 성호르몬 sex hormone.

**성**(省) 《내각의》 a ministry; an office; a department 《미·영》; 《중국의 행정 구획》 a province. ¶ 성의 ministerial; departmental); official / 산둥성 Shantung Province.

**성**(城) a castle; 《요새》 a fortress; a citadel; 《성벽》 a wall; (castle) walls. ¶ 성을 쌓다 build a castle / 성을 빼앗다 take 〔capture〕 a castle / 성을 포위하다 besiege 〔lay siege to〕 a castle.

**성**(聖) 《성인》 a sage; a saint; 《그 방면에 걸출한 인물》 a great master. ¶ 성바울 St. Paul / 악성 베토벤 the great composer Beethoven.

**성가**(成家) ～하다 《학문의 체계를》 establish *oneself* as a master; develop a style of *one's* own; make a name (for *oneself*); 《집을》 establish *one's* own household; succeed in life; make a fortune of *one's* own. ¶ 자수 ～하다 make 《a fortune》 by *one's* own efforts.

**성가**(聖歌) a sacred song; a hymn; 《크리스마스의》 a carol. ◉ ～대 a choir: ～대원 a chanter; a chorister (특히 소년). ～집 a hymnal; a hymnbook.

**성가**(聲價) (a) reputation; repute; fame (명성); popularity (인기). ¶ ～가 높아지다 *one's* reputation 「goes up 〔is enhanced〕 / ～가 떨어지다 fall in public 〔popular〕 estimation; lose *one's* reputation 〔credit, popularity〕 / ～를 높이다 enhance *one's* reputation / ～를 얻다 win a reputation; gain popularity / ～를 유지하다 maintain 〔keep up〕 *one's* reputation; retain 〔keep〕 *one's* prestige / 그는 그 영화로 감독으로서의 ～가 높아졌다 That film raised his reputation as a movie director.

**성가시다** 《귀찮다》 (be) troublesome; annoying; bothersome; harassing; burdensome; irksome; vexatious; cumbrous (주체스러워서); 《끈덕지다》 (be) pertinacious; inquisitive (자꾸 캐물어서); importune (졸라대서). ¶ 성가신 아이 a troublesome child / 성가신 사람 a nuisance / 성가신 일 an irksome task / 성가신 질문 a troublesome 〔pestilent〕 question / 성가신 듯이 with an annoyed look 〔air〕 / 성가시게 annoyingly; tiresomely; importunately / 성가시게 조르다〔보채다〕 pester 《*a person*》 into 《*doing*》; importune 《*a person*》 「to 《*do*》 〔for 《*a thing*》〕; ask importunately for 《money》 / 성가셔 하다 find 〔consider〕 《*a thing*》 troublesome; regard 〔look upon〕 《*a thing*》 as a nuisance / 성가시게 묻지 마라 Don't bother 〔harass, pester〕 me with questions. / 그 때문에 성가시게 될 걸세 It will get you into trouble.

**성가족**(聖家族) the Holy Family.

**성감**(性感) sexual feeling 〔excitement〕. ¶ ～을 높이다 [사물이 주어] promote 〔work up〕 *one's* sexual feeling.
◉ ～대(帶) a sexually sensitive area; an erogenous zone.

**성검사**(性檢査) a sex check; a feminity control; a gender verification (여성 경기 종목에서 경기 전에 하는 성별 검사).

**성게** 〖동물〗 a sea urchin 〔chestnut〕; an echinoid.

**성격**(性格) ① 《사람의》 character; personality. ¶ ～적인 characteristic / ～상의 결점 a flaw 〔defect〕 in *one's* character / ∼의 차이 dissimilarity 〔disparity〕 in character / ∼이 강인한〔나약한〕 사람 a man of strong 〔weak〕 character 〔personality〕; a strong 〔weak〕 character / ∼이 좋은 사람 a good-natured person; an agreeable character / ∼이 침착한 사람 an even tempered person; a person of even temper / 솔직한 ∼ a straightforward character / 매력적인 ∼ an attractive personality / 밝은〔어두운〕 ∼ a cheerful 〔gloomy〕 disposition 〔personality〕 / ∼에 맞다 be congenial to 《*one*》; suit *one's* nature / ∼에 맞지 않다 be uncongenial to 《*one*》; be not in *one's* line; do not suit *one's* nature / 좋은 ∼을 가지다 bear 〔possess, have〕 a good character / ∼이 맞다〔맞지 않다〕 be similar 〔dissimilar〕 in character; be agreeable 〔disagreeable〕 to each other / ∼을 묘사하다 delineate 〔describe〕 《*a person's*》 character / ∼을 만들다 《환경 따위가》 shape 《*a person's*》 character / 그의 ∼은 내 성격과 정반대다 His character is diametrically opposed to mine. / 그들은 ∼이 맞는다 They hit it off with each other. / 그와는 ∼이 전혀 맞지 않는다 He is totally different in cast from me. / 형제이지만 ∼은 전혀 다르다 Though brothers, they have quite different characters. / 그것은 그의 타고난 ∼이다 It is his own nature.

② 《사물의 고유 성질》 character; nature. ¶ 문제의 ∼ the nature of the problem / …의 ∼을 띠다 take on the character of 《ritual》 / 이 두 문제는 ∼을 달리하고 있다 These two problems are of a different character 〔nature〕.

◉ ∼검사 a personality test. ∼극 a character drama. ∼묘사 characterization; character drawing 〔delineation, description, portrayal〕. ∼배우 a character actor 〔actress〕. ∼장애 a personality disorder: ∼장애자 an abnormal character; a screwball 《미속어》. ∼학(學) characterology. ∼형성 character formation.

**성결**(性—) (a) nature; (a) disposition; personality; (a) temper. ¶ ∼이 곱다 have a sweet temper; be of gentle disposition.

**성결**(聖潔) holiness and purity. ∼하다 (be) holy and pure. ◉ ∼교회 the Holiness Church.

**성경**(聖經) a holy book; the (Holy) Bible; the Scriptures; the Holy Writ. ¶ ∼의 Biblical; scriptural / ∼의 인용 a Biblical quotation.

◉ ∼구절 a Biblical expression; a scriptural phrase. ∼낭독 a scripture reading; Bible lesson. ∼문학 Biblical literature. ∼연구회 a Bible class; a Biblestudy group. ∼용어 biblical language. ∼이야기 a Bible story. ∼인용(문) a biblical quotation. ∼학자 a Biblicist. ∼해석학 hermeneutics. ∼협회 a Bible society.

신〔구〕약∼ the New 〔Old〕 Testament.

**성공**(成功) ① 《잘 됨》 (a) success; 《히트》 a hit; a coup; 《성취》 achievement. ∼하다 [사물이 주어] succeed; come out well; go well; [사람이 주어] succeed 《in》; be successful 《in》; do well; make good; make *one's* mark 《as a writer》; 《구어》 make a go of 《*one's* attempt》. ¶ ∼적으로 successfully; with success / 사업에 ∼하다 succeed in *one's* undertaking / ∼으로 끝나다 result 〔end〕 in success; be crowned with success.

성공의〔할〕: ∼할 가망 the chances 〔prospects〕 of success / ∼할 가망이 충분히 있다 stand 〔have〕 a good chance of success.

성공을: ∼을 갈망하다 be too eager for success / ∼을 기대할 만하다 have a chance of success; be expected to success / ∼을 거두다 achieve 〔win, gain〕 success; make 〔pull off〕 a coup / ∼을 축하하다 congratulate 《*a person*》 on *his* success / 사업의 ∼을 위해 축배하다 toast the success of the enterprise.

¶ 네가 ∼할 가망은 거의 없다 There is a slim chance of your success. / 이만하면 ∼했다고 볼 수 있다 This result may fairly be called a success. / 그의 연설은 대∼이었다 His speech was a great success.

② 《출세》 success in life 〔the world〕; 《번영》 prosperity. ∼하다 succeed 〔rise〕 in the world; get on in life 〔in the world〕; get ahead; 《번영하다》 prosper; thrive. ¶ ∼담 a success story / ∼법 how to get on in life / ∼의 비결 the secret of 〔key to〕 success / 그는 하는 일마다 ∼했다 Everything he did prospered with him. / 노력한 보람이 있어, 그는 ∼했다 His efforts were rewarded with success.

**성공회**(聖公會) the Anglican Church 《영》; the Episcopal Church 《미》.

◉ ∼원 an Anglican 《영》; an

Episcopalian 《미》.

**성과**(成果) a result; a product; a fruit; an outcome. ¶ 노력의 ~ the fruit 〔product, result〕 of *one's* labor 〔efforts〕 / ~를 거두다〔올리다〕 **[사물이 주어]** obtain 〔get〕 good results; be rewarded with good fruits; be crowned with great success / 소기(所期)의 ~를 못 거두다 fail to realize the anticipated result; the result fall short of *one's* expectation / ~는 기대 이상이었다 The result was better than we had expected. / 이 논문은 그의 오랜 연구의 ~이다 This essay is the fruit of his long study.

**성과급**(成果給) piece rate. ¶ ~ 근로자 a pieceworker / ~ 방식의 일 piecework.

**성과학**(性科學) sexology. ¶ ~적(인) sexological / ~자(者) a sexologist.

**성곽**(城郭) 《성》 a castle; a citadel; 《성채》 a fortress; a stronghold; 《성벽》 castle walls. ◉ ~도시 a walled city.

**성교**(性交) sexual intercourse 〔connection, union〕; coitus; coition. ~하다 have (sexual) intercourse 《with》; 《구어》 have sex 《with》; sleep 《with》; make love 《to》 (완곡하게 표현하여). ◉ ~불능 impotence; impotency: ~ 불능자 an impotent person.

**성교육**(性教育) 《give》 sex education 〔information〕.

**성구**(成句) a set phrase; an idiomatic phrase 〔expression〕.

**성구**(聖具) a sacred utensil.

**성군**(星群) 〖천문〗 a cluster of stars; an asterism.

**성군**(聖君) a sage king.

**성군작당**(成群作黨) ~하다 form a faction 〔clique〕; band together; conspire 《with》; 《구어》 gang up.

**성극**(聖劇) a Biblical drama; a scriptural play.

**성금**(誠金) a donation; a contribution; a gift of money; a subscription. ¶ ~을 내다 contribute; donate; subscribe to 《a fund》 / 아무리 적은 ~이라도 감사히 받음 《게시》 The smallest contribution thankfully received. ◉ 불우이웃돕기~ a donation for the needy.

**성급하다**(性急—) (be) hasty; quick-tempered; impetuous; rash. ¶ 성급하게 impatiently; impetuously; hastily / 성급한 사람 a man of quick temper; a person of impetuous disposition; a hotheaded man; a hotspur / 성급한 기질 a hasty temper; an impetuous disposition / 성급하게 행동하다 act rashly 〔on impulse〕; rush *one's* fences.

**성기**(性器) the sexual 〔genital〕 organs; genitals.

**성기**(聖器) 〖기독교〗 a consecrated 〔holy, sacred〕 vessel.

**성기다** 《사이가 배지 않다》 (be) sparse; thin; scattered; loose. ¶ 성긴 수염 a thin mustache / 성긴 옷감 loose fabric / 성긴 체 a wire sieve of large meshes / 성기게 난 풀 a thin growth of herbage / 머리털이 ~ be thinly haired 〔covered with hair〕 / 나무를 성기게 심다 put in plants at considerable distance from each other / 활자를 성기게 짜다 set type leaving spaces between / 성기어지다 become sparse 〔thin〕.

**성깃성깃** thinly; scatteringly; sparsely; loosely; here and there.

**성깃하다** (be) sparse; thin; loose; be somewhat far apart; be rather sparsely spaced; be a bit separated. ¶ 성깃하게 뜨다 knit with large stitches; make 《a net》 with large meshes.

**성깔(머리)** a sharp temper; an irritable disposition; a fierce 〔crabby〕 temperament. ¶ 성깔이 있는 사람 a man of violent 〔impetuous〕 temper; a quick-〔hot-, short-〕tempered person.

**성나다** ① 《화나다》 get 〔become, grow, be〕 angry 《with *a person*, at 〔about〕 *something*》; be angered 〔enraged, furious〕 《by》; be offended 《at》; get mad 《with, at》 《미》; take offense; fly into a fury; be in a fume 〔huff〕. ¶ 성(이) 나서 angrily; in *one's* anger; in a fit of rage / 몹시 ~ fret 〔fuss〕 and fume; blow *one's* top; get hopping mad; 《불처럼》 be hot with anger 〔rage〕; boil with rage / 성나 있다 be angry 《with, at》; be in a bad temper; be in fury; be mad 《미구어》 / 성난 기색을 보이다 betray *one's* anger / 성나는 것을 눌러 참다 restrain 〔contain, hold in〕 *one's* anger; repress 〔suppress, keep down〕 *one's* wrath / 성나 바위 차기 beating *one's* head against a stone wall.
② 《거칠어지다》 get 〔become〕 rough; rough (up); rage. ¶ 성난 파도 raging 〔angry〕 waves; high 〔heavy〕 seas.
③ 《덧나다》 get worse; fester (곪다). ¶ 종기가 성났다 A boil got worse.

**성내**(城內) inside a fortress 〔a city wall, a castle〕; within the city.

**성내다** ⇨성나다. ¶ 사소한 일에 ~ get angry on the slightest provocation; get angry at 〔about〕 trifles / 벌컥〔발

끈〕 ～ flare up; blow *one's* top; fly into rage; burst with anger.

**성냥** a match. ¶ ～ 한 갑 a box 〔pack (-et)〕 of matches / ～을 긋다 strike 〔scratch〕 a match / ～을 켜다 light a match; scrape a match into flame; strike a light. ◉ ～갑 a matchbox: ～갑 같은 집 a house like a matchbox. ～개비 a match (-stick). ～불 a match flame. 안전～ a safety match. 종이～ a matchfolder; a matchbook.

**성냥일** blacksmithing. ⇨ 대장일.

**성냥하다** 《쇠를 달구다》 heat 《metals》; forge; harden; anneal; temper.

**성녀**(聖女) 〖가톨릭〗 a holy woman; a woman saint; a saintess.

**성년**(成年) (legal) majority; full 〔adult, lawful〕 age; man's 〔woman's〕 estate. ¶ ～에 달하다 come of age; attain 〔reach〕 *one's* majority; arrive at manhood 〔womanhood〕; reach full age / ～에 미달하다 be under age. ◉ ～식 a coming-of-age ceremony; an initiation 「ceremony 〔rite (미개 사회의)〕. ～의 날 Coming-of-Age Day. ～자 an adult; a major; a person of legal age: 미～자 a minor.

**성능**(性能) capacity; power; efficiency; 《기계의》 performance; 《특질》 a property. ¶ 고～ 카메라 a highly efficient camera / ～이 좋은 《a car》 with a good 〔high〕 performance; highly efficient; high-power(ed) / …보다 ～이 뛰어나다 outperform 《the other machine》 / ～을 높이다〔개량하다〕 improve the performance / 그들은 그 엔진의～을 검사했다 They tested the capability of the engine. / GK사 제품의 ～을 어떻게 생각하십니까 What do you think of the performance of the GK Company's products?
◉ ～계수 quality factor. ～곡선 a performance curve. ～시험〔검사〕 an efficiency 〔a performance〕 test: 기계의 ～ 검사를 하다 put the machine to a performance test.

**성단**(星團) a group 〔cluster〕 of stars.

**성단**(聖壇) a pulpit; an altar; a shrine.

**성당**(聖堂) a 《Catholic》 church; a sanctuary.

**성대** 〖어류〗 a gurnard; a sea robin.

**성대**(聖代) an age of sage rules; a glorious reign. ¶ 태평 ～ a peaceful reign.

**성대**(盛大) ～하다 《장려한》 (be) grand; splendid; magnificent; pompous; 《번영하는》 prosperous; flourishing; thrive; 《성공적인》 successful. ¶ ～히 splendidly; pompously; with splendor; with pomp; in grand style; on a large scale / ～한 의식 a grand ceremony; an impressive ceremony with a large attendance / ～한 환영 a very warm welcome 〔reception〕 / 식이 끝난 뒤에 ～한 연회가 있었다 After the ceremony a splendid banquet was given.

**성대**(聲帶) the vocal cords 〔bands〕.
◉ ～모사 imitation of another's voice; vocal mimicry: ～모사를 하다 mimic 〔imitate〕 another's voice 〔way of speaking, way of singing〕.

**성덕**(盛德) flourishing 〔illustrious〕 virtue(s).

**성덕**(聖德) 《성인의》 saints' 〔saintly〕 virtues; 《왕의》 royal virtues; royal favor.

**성도**(成道) 《예술 따위의》 attainment of perfection; mastering 《of the art》; 〖불교〗 Buddha's attainment of Great Wisdom; mastering the secrets 《of religion》. ～하다 attain perfection; become expert 《as a writer》; be a master 《of the art》; attain Buddhahood.

**성도**(星圖) 〖천문〗 a celestial 〔star〕 map.

**성도**(聖徒) 《성인》 a (Christian) saint; 《사도》 an apostle; a disciple of Christ. ◉ ～전 a hagiology; the lives of saints.

**성도**(聖都) the Holy City (예루살렘).

**성도덕**(性道德) sexual morality.

**성도착**(性倒錯) sexual perversion 〔inversion〕. ¶ ～자 a (sexual) pervert.

**성량**(聲量) the volume of (*one's*) voice. ¶ ～이 풍부하다 have a full 〔rich, powerful〕 voice; have a voice of great volume / ～이 부족하다 be wanting in the volume of voice; have a weak voice.

**성령**(聖靈) the Holy Ghost 〔Spirit〕; the Spirit of the Lord. ◉ ～강림절 Whitsunday; Pentecost: ～강림절 주간 Whitsuntide; the season of Pentecost.

**성례**(成禮) a marriage 〔wedding〕 ceremony. ⇨ 혼례. ～하다 hold 〔solemnize〕 a wedding.

**성루**(城壘) a fort; a fortress; ramparts (성벽). ¶ ～를 지키다 take *one's* stand in a fortress; guard the ramparts.

**성리**(性理) human nature and natural laws; the rule of Heaven. ◉ ～학 《송학(宋學)》 Sung Confucianism; the doctrines 〔teachings〕 of Chu-tzŭ.

**성립**(成立) ① 《생겨남》 coming into being 〔existence〕; 《실현》 materialization; realization. ～하다 come 〔be brought〕 into being 〔existence〕; materialize; be materialized 〔realized〕. ¶ ～시키다 bring 〔call〕 into existence 〔being〕; 《실현시키다》 materialize; effect(uate); bring about / 그 계획은 ～되지 않았다 The project failed to materialize. ② 《조직·구성됨》 formation; organization. ～하다 be formed 〔organized〕; 《…로 이루어지다》 be composed 〔made〕 of; consist of. ¶ ～시키다 form; organize / 연립 내각이 ～되었다 A coalition cabinet was formed. ③ 《협정·약정 등의》 conclusion. ～하다 be concluded; be effected. ¶ 계약이 ～했다 The contract has been concluded. / 양가 사이에 약혼이 ～되었다 A marriage has been arranged between the two families. / 양국간에 조약이 ～되었다 A treaty was concluded between the two nations.

**성마르다**(性—) (be) narrow-minded and hot-tempered; short-〔quick-〕tempered; impatient; impetuous. ¶ 성마른 사람 a quick-〔hot-〕tempered person; a hotspur.

**성망**(聲望) reputation; fame; popularity. ⇨ 인망.

**성명**(姓名) *one's* family name and given name; a full name. ¶ ～ 미상의 unidentified; unknown / ～을 사칭하다 assume a false name.

**성명**(聲明) (a) (public) declaration; a statement; (an) announcement; (a) proclamation. ～하다 declare; announce; issue a statement 《on》; proclaim. ¶ 공동 ～ a joint statement 〔communiqué〕 / 공식 ～을 발표하다 deliver 〔issue〕 an official statement / 항의 ～을 전달하다 hand 《*a person*》 a statement of protest / 지지 ～을 내다 declare *one's* support 《for》 / 반대〔찬성〕 ～을 하다 declare *oneself* against 〔for〕 《the plan》 / 정부는 내일 중대～을 발표할 예정이다 The Government is going to issue an important statement tomorrow.
◉ ～서 a (public) statement; a manifesto (*pl.* -(e)s). ～전 an exchange of charges and countercharges.

**성모**(聖母) the Holy Mother; Our Lady; the Virgin Mary. ¶ ～의 원죄 없으신 잉태 the Immaculate Conception. ◉ ～마리아 the Virgin 〔Holy Mother〕 Mary. ～병원 the St. Mary's Hospital. ～승천 the Assumption (of the Virgin Mary). ～찬가 〖음악〗 Ave Maria.

**성묘**(省墓) a visit to *one's* ancestral graves 〔tombs〕. ～하다 visit *one's* ancestral graves 〔tombs〕; pay a visit to *one's* ancestor's grave. ¶ ～를 위해 귀향하다 return home to visit the family graves. ◉ ～행렬 queues of visitors to their ancestral tombs.

**성문**(成文) ◉ ～계약 a written contract. ～법 a statute law; a written law; a *lex scripta* (L.); a *jus scriptum* (L.). ～헌법 a written constitution. ～화 codification; legalization: ～화하다 codify; put in statutory form.

**성문**(城門) a city 〔castle〕 gate.

**성문**(聲門) 〖해부〗 the glottis (*pl.* ～es, -tides); the vocal chink.

**성문**(聲紋) a voiceprint.

**성미**(性味) nature; disposition; 《기질》 temperament; temper; 《성격》 character. ¶ ～가 좋은〔고약한〕 good-〔ill-〕natured / ～가 급한 사람 a hot-〔quick-, short-〕tempered person / ～가 급하다 be short-〔quick-〕tempered; be hasty 〔rash〕 / ～가 까다롭다 [사람이 주어] be hard to please / ～가 맞지 않다 cannot get along together; do not agree 〔hit it off〕 with 《*a person*》 / 그는 흥분하기 쉬운 ～의 사람이다 He gets excited easily. / 그들은 ～가 안맞는다 They are not suited to each other. / 그는 ～가 까다롭다 He is a particular 〔fastidious〕 person.

**성범죄**(性犯罪) 《commit》 a sex(ual) offense 〔crime〕.

**성벽**(性癖) *one's* natural disposition; an inclination; a propensity; a proclivity; a mental habit; a characteristic. ¶ 과장하는 ～ a tendency 〔propensity〕 to exaggerate / 그에겐 이상한 ～이 있다 He has a curious habit.

**성벽**(城壁) a castle wall; a rampart; a circumvallation; 《city》 walls. ¶ ～으로 둘러싸인 도시 a walled city / ～을 쌓다 build a rampart; wall 《a castle》 / ～을 두르다 surround 《a castle》 with a rampart; wall 《a town》; circumvallate 《a town》.

**성별**(性別) the distinction of sex. ¶ ～에 관계없이 irrespective 〔without distinction〕 of sex / 등록 카드에 ～을 기재하시오 Please enter your sex on the registration card.

**성병**(性病) a venereal disease (생략 V.D., VD); a social disease 《미》. ¶ ～의 예방 prevention of venereal disease / ～에 걸리다 catch 〔have〕 (a) venereal disease. ◉ ～감염 venereal infection. ～전문병원 《구어》 a VD clinic. ～학 venereology. ～환자 a person venereally infected.

**성복**(成服) 《상복을 입음》 wearing mourning. ～하다 wear 〔put on〕 mourning; go into 〔take to〕 mourning 《for *a person*》; be in mourning 〔black〕.

**성부**(聖父) 〚성서〛 the Father.

**성분**(成分) 《혼합물의》 an ingredient; 《단일물의》 a component; a constituent; an element (요소). ¶ 부(副)～ an accessory ingredient / 주(요)～ the main 〔chief, principal〕 ingredients 《of》. 공기〔약〕의 ～ the composition of air 〔a medicine〕 / ～을 분석하다 analyze the components 〔constituent〕 / 화학 조미료의 ～은 무엇입니까 What are the ingredients of the chemical seasoning? / 산소와 수소는 물의 ～이다 Oxygen and hydrogen are the elements of water.

◉ ～시험 a chemical experiment 〔test〕. ～표시 an ingredients label.

**성불**(成佛) attaining Buddhahood; entering Nirvana. ～하다 attain Buddhahood; enter Nirvana; become a Buddha; 《죽다》 pass away; die.

**성사**(成事) 《성취》 accomplishment; achievement; attainment; 《실현》 realization; 《성공》 success. ～하다 succeed; accomplish 〔achieve〕 《*a thing*》; attain; realize. ¶ 모사 재인(在人)이요 ～ 재천(在天)이라 Man proposes, God disposes. *or* Do your best and leave the rest to Providence.

**성사**(盛事) a splendid enterprise; a grand event. ¶ 이 ～를 함께 기뻐하자 Let us rejoice together on this great occasion.

**성사**(聖事) divine service; 〚가톨릭〛 the sacraments; a sacrament.

**성산**(成算) confidence 〔hope, chances〕 of success; prospects of sure success. ¶ ～이 있다〔없다〕 be confident 〔have little hope〕 of success / ～이 없더라도 해보겠다 Though I have little hope of success, I will try.

**성상**(星霜) years; time. ¶ 10개 ～ ten years' time; a space 〔period〕 of ten years; a 10-year period / 5개 ～이 흘렀다 Five years passed 〔elapsed〕.

**성상**(聖上) (His Majesty) the King.

**성상**(聖像) a sacred image 〔portrait〕; an icon.

**성생활**(性生活) sex(ual) life.

**성서**(聖書) ＝성경(聖經).

**성선**(性腺) 〚해부〛 a sex gland; a gonad. ⇨ 생식선.

**성선설**(性善說) 〚윤리〛 the ethical doctrine that man's inborn nature is good; the view of human nature as fundamentally good.

**성성이**(猩猩―) 〚동물〛 an orangutan; a pongo (*pl.* ～es).

**성성하다**(星星―) (be) hoar(y); gray; grizzled; gray-streaked. ¶ 백발이 성성한 머리 gray-white〔-flecked〕 hair; grizzled 〔frosty〕 hair; hair streaked with gray.

**성세**(盛世) a prosperous 〔glorious〕 age; an era of prosperity.

**성소**(聖所) 〚성서〛 the holy place; sanctum. ¶ 지(至)～ the holy of holies; sanctum sanctorum.

**성쇠**(盛衰) ups and downs; rise and fall; prosperity and decline; vicissitudes. ¶ 인생의 ～「the vicissitudes 〔the ups and downs〕 of life / 국력의 ～ the rise and fall of national power.

**성수**(星宿) 〚천문〛 the stars; the various constellations.

**성수**(聖水) 〚가톨릭〛 holy water.

**성수기**(盛需期) a high-demand season. ¶ ～를 맞이한 상품 goods most in demand / ～를 맞이하다 be much in demand; be in great 〔high〕 demand.

**성수품**(盛需品) commodities in high 《seasonal》 demand; highly-demanded 《industrial》 products.

**성숙**(成熟) ① 《잘 익음》 ripeness; maturity. ～하다 ripen; be 〔get〕 ripe. ② 《충분한 발육》 full 〔complete〕 growth; maturation. ～하다 attain 〔reach〕 full growth; grow into adulthood. ¶ ～한 처녀 a mature 〔marriageable〕 girl / 성적으로 ～하다 reach sexual maturity. ③ 《기회·시기 등의》 maturity; ripeness. ～하다 mature; ripen; attain 〔come to〕 maturity. ¶ 국민의 정치적 ～도 political maturity of the people / 때가 ～하기를 기다리자 Let us wait till the time is ripe.

**성숙기**(成熟期) 《때의》 (the period of) maturity; 《사춘기》 adolescence; puberty. ¶ ～에 달하다 arrive at puberty; reach adolescence; attain (to) maturity.

**성스럽다**(聖―) 《신성하다》 (be) holy; sacred; divine; 《숭고하다》 (be) sublime; solemn. ¶ 성스러운 생활 a holy life / 성스러운 곳 a holy 〔sacred〕 place; a spot of sanctity.

**성시**(成市) opening a fair 〔market〕. ～

하다 open 〔keep〕 a fair. ¶ 문전 ～하다 be crowded with visitors 〔callers, customers〕; have a constant stream of visitors.

**성시**(城市) a walled city.

**성신**(星辰) the stars; heavenly bodies.

**성신**(聖神) ＝성령.

**성실**(誠實) sincerity; faithfulness; honesty; devotion. ～하다 (be) sincere; faithful; truthful; honest; devoted. ¶ ～한 친구 a loyal friend / ～하게 sincerely; faithfully; honestly; with sincerity; in good faith; devotedly / ～성이 없다 lack sincerity / ～하게 일하다 work faithfully; do *one's* work with sincerity / 그는 ～한 사람이다 He is a man of integrity 〔sincerity〕.

**성심**(聖心) the Sacred Heart.

**성심**(誠心) sincerity; good faith. ¶ ～껏 〔으로〕 sincerely; wholeheartedly; devotedly; from (the bottom of) *one's* heart / ～껏 일을 보다〔하다〕 deal with 《*a matter*》 in all sincerity; go heart and soul into 《*a thing*》; do 《*a matter*》 with *one's* whole heart.

**성싶다** seem; look (like); appear; be likely 《to *do*》. ¶ 눈이 올 ～ It seems likely to snow. *or* It looks as though it were going to snow. / 그를 한번 본 ～ It seems to me that I have met him before. / 그 계획은 좋을 ～ The plan appears to be a good one. / 그는 올성싶지 않다 It is not likely that he will come. *or* He is not likely to come.

**성씨**(姓氏) your 〔his〕 esteemed surname 〔family name〕.

**성악**(聲樂) vocal music; singing. ¶ ～을 배우다 take vocal lessons 《from》. ◉ ～가 a vocalist; a singer. ～과 a vocal music course.

**성악설**(性惡說) 〖윤리〗 the ethical view that human nature is fundamentally evil; the view of human nature as fundamentally depraved.

**성안**(成案) a definite plan 〔scheme〕; a concrete program. ～하다 form a definite plan; map out a concrete program.

**성안**(城―) ＝성내(城內).

**성애**(性愛) sexual love.

**성어**(成魚) an adult fish; a full-grown fish.

**성어**(成語) ① 《숙어》 a (set) phrase; an idiom; an idiomatic phrase. ② 《말을 이룸》 forming 「a word 〔a set phrase〕.

**성업**(盛業) a thriving business. ¶ ～중인 상점 a store with lots of business; a thriving store / ～중이다 be doing a flourishing business 〔trade〕 / ～을 축하합니다 I congratulate you on 〔upon〕 your success in business.

**성에** ① 《얼어붙은》 (a layer of) frost. ¶ ～가 낀 유리창 a frosted windowpane / (냉장고의) ～를 제거하다 defrost 《a refrigerator》. ② 《성엣장》 ice drifts; drifting 〔floating〕 ice; a floe. ◉ ～제거장치 《냉장고의》 a defroster.

**성역**(聖域) sacred 〔holy〕 precincts; a consecrated ground; a sanctuary.

**성역**(聲域) 〖음악〗 a range of voice; a register.

**성염색체**(性染色體) a sex chromosome.

**성영**(聖嬰) 〖가톨릭〗 the Holy Child; the infant Christ.

**성외**(城外) outside the walls 《of a castle, a city》; beyond the wall.

**성욕**(性慾) sexual desire; sexual 〔carnal〕 appetite; libido; lust (육욕). ¶ 변태 ～ abnormal sexuality / ～이 강한 strongly-〔highly-〕sexed / ～을 자극하다 arouse 〔stimulate〕 *a person's* sexual desire / ～을 만족시키다 satisfy 〔satiate〕 *one's* carnal appetite 〔desire〕. ◉ ～결핍 sexual disinclination 〔apathy〕. ～앙진 aphrodisia; morbid sexual excitement. ～이상 《남자의》 sex mania; erotomania; 《여자의》 nymphomania.

**성우**(聲優) a radio actor 〔actress〕; a dubbing artist.

**성운**(星雲) 〖천문〗 a nebula (*pl.* -lae, ～s); a nebulosity. ¶ 소용돌이 꼴〔와상(渦狀)〕 ～ a spiral nebula / 가스 ～ a gaseous nebula / 환상(環狀)～ an annular nebula; a ring nebula. ◉ ～설 the nebular hypothesis 〔theory〕.

**성원**(成員) ① 《조직원》 a member. ¶ 사회의 ～ a member of society. ② 《필요한 인원》 (one of) a quorum; a constituent (member). ¶ ～이 되다 constitute 〔form〕 a quorum. ◉ ～미달 lack of a quorum.

**성원**(聖院) 《회교의》 a mosque.

**성원**(聲援) ① 《기운을 북돋움》 a shout of encouragement; 《경기에서의》 cheering; rooting 《미구어》. ～하다 shout encouragement 《for》; 《경기에서》 cheer 《a team (on) to victory》; root 《for a team》 《미구어》. ¶ 팬들은 그들이 좋아하는 농구팀에게 ～을 보냈다 The fans cheered their favorite basketball team. ② 《도움》 support. ～하다 support; give *one's* support 《to》. ¶ 당신의 각별한 ～을 부탁드립니다 I hope to have your full support. ◉ ～자 a cheerer; a rooter (응원의); a supporter (후원의). 「chrism.

**성유**(聖油) 〖가톨릭〗 consecrated oil;

**성윤리**(性倫理) ethics on sex.

**성은**(聖恩) 《왕의》 Royal favor 〔grace, benevolence〕; 《신의》 divine favor; heavenly blessings.

**성음**(聲音) a vocal sound. ◉ ～문자 a phonogram. ～학 phonetics.

**성읍**(城邑) a (castle) town.

**성의**(誠意) sincerity; good faith. ¶ ～있는 sincere; true; faithful; honest / ～(가) 없는 insincere; false; fickle / ～를 가지고 in good faith; with sincerity / ～를 보이다 show *one's* good faith / ～를 의심하다 doubt 〔question〕 《*a person's*》 sincerity.

**성인**(成人) an adult; a grown-up (person). ¶ ～이 되다 grow up (to be a man 〔woman〕); attain 〔arrive at〕 adulthood 〔manhood, womanhood〕; become an adult / 입장료는 ～ 1인당 1,000원이다 The admission is one thousand won per adult. ◉ ～교육 adult education. ～병 adult diseases; geriatric diseases. ～영화 an adult 〔X-rated〕 film 〔movie〕; a movie for adults only. ～학교 an adults' school.

**성인**(聖人) a sage; a saint; a holy man. ¶ ～같은 saintly; saintlike / 옛～ a sage of old / 나는 ～군자는 아니지만 그런 비열한 짓은 하지 않는다 I'm no saint, but I would never play such a dirty trick on you.

**성자**(聖子) 〖성서〗 the Son (of God).

**성자**(聖者) ＝성인(聖人).

**성장**(成長) growth. ～하다 grow (up); be brought up. ¶ 연차 경제～ 목표 an annual economic growth target / (다)～한 grown-up; full-grown; matured; adult / ～함에 따라 as *one* grows older / 성인으로 ～하다 grow into a man 〔woman〕; grow up to be a man 〔woman〕 / (한창) ～하는 growing 《children》 / ～이 빠르다 grow quickly 〔rapidly〕; be fast-growing / ～이 늦다〔더디다〕 grow slowly; be of tardy growth / ～이 멈추다 stop growing / ～을 돕다 foster 〔help〕 the growth 《of》 / ～을 방해하다 check 〔hamper〕 the growth 《of》 / ～을 촉진하다 promote 〔stimulate〕 the growth 《of》; accelerate the growth 《of》 / 그의 지적 ～은 실로 놀랄만했다 His mental development was truly remarkable. ◉ ～곡선 a growth curve. ～기간〔과정〕 a growth period 〔process〕. ～산업 a growth industry. ～요인 a growth factor. ～점 〖식물〗 a growing point. ～주(株) a growth stock. ～호르몬 a growth hormone.

**성장**(盛裝) full dress; a gala costume; beautiful attire. ～하다 dress *oneself* handsomely; be finely 〔richly〕 dressed; be dressed in *one's* (Sunday) best; be all dressed up; be in gala costume; wear 〔be in〕 full dress. ¶ ～하여 in gala dress; in *one's* (Sunday) best / ～시키다 dress up 〔deck out〕 《*one's* daughter》 / 그녀는 ～을 하고 외출했다 She went out in her Sunday best.

**성장률**(成長率) a growth rate; a rate of growth. ¶ 경제 ～ the rate of economic growth. ◉ 실질～ the real growth rate.

**성적**(成績) 《학업 등의 결과》 a result; a record; 《평점》 a grade 《미》; a mark 《영》; 《사업 등의》 a result; a showing; a record; merit (개인의); 《시험의》 score. ¶ 학교 ～ *one's* school record / 시험 ～ 《publish》 the results of an examination / 영업 ～ 《improve *one's*》 business showings / ～이 좋은 학생 a high-achieving pupil / 3승 2패의 ～ a three-to-two record; a record of three victories to two defeats / ～이 좋다〔나쁘다〕 do well 〔poorly〕 《at school》; make 〔get〕 good 〔poor〕 grades 《in *one's* studies》; show good 〔poor〕 《business》 results 〔showings〕 / 좋은 ～을 올리다 [사물이 주어] obtain 〔bring about〕 good 〔satisfactory〕 results; [사람이 주어] make a good record 〔showing〕 / 뛰어난〔상당한〕 ～을 올리다 make a wonderful 〔fair〕 showing / 좋은 ～을 유지하다 keep *one's* grades high / ～이 나아졌다〔떨어졌다〕 *one's* grades improved 〔fell, dropped〕 / 승진은 ～에 달렸다 Promotion goes by merit. / 시험 ～이 어찌 되었나 How did you make out in the exam? / 이번 학기의 영어 ～은 올라갔다〔내려갔다〕 I have got a better 〔worse〕 grade 〔mark〕 in English this term. / 그는 학교 ～이 좋다 He has a fine record at school. / 그녀의 ～은 학급의 3분의1 이상에 속한다 She stands among the upper a third of her class in respect of achievement. ◉ ～증명서 a transcript 《미》. ～표 《전체의》 (a list of) students' records; 《개인의》 a report card; a grade transcript; an academic record; 《경기의》 scorecard.

**성적**(性的) (being) sexual. ¶ ～으로 조

숙하다〔늦되다〕 be sexually precocious 〔backward〕; know the sex early 〔lately〕/ ~인 관계를 갖다 have sexual relations 《with》/ ~ 흥분을 느끼게 되다 become sexually excited 〔aroused〕. ◉ ~대상 a sex object. ~ 매력 《have》 sex appeal; it 《미속어》: ~매력이 있는 여자 a woman with 《strong》 sex appeal; a sexpot / ~ 매력이 있다〔없다〕 have a lot of 〔have not〕 sex appeal; be 〔be not〕 sexually attractive. ~ 욕망 sexual appetite 〔desire〕. ~ 지식 knowledge of sexual matters. ~ 차별 sexual discrimination; sexism. ~ 충동 a sex urge 〔drive〕. ~ 특징 sex 〔sexual〕 characteristics.

**성적순**(成績順) the order of merit 《at school》. ¶ ~으로 뽑다 select by the order of merit / ~으로 앉다 sit in the order of merit 〔the achieved performance records〕.

**성전**(性典) a book on sex; a cyclopedia of sex.

**성전**(聖殿) a sacred shrine 〔hall〕; a sanctuary.

**성전**(聖戰) a holy war; a crusade.

**성전환**(性轉換) a sex change; the change of sex; sex transformation. ◉ ~수술 a sex-change 〔transsexual〕 operation. ~자 a transsexual.

**성정**(性情) *one's* character 〔nature, disposition, temper〕. ◉ ~머리 =성정.

**성조기**(星條旗) the Stars and Stripes; the Star-Spangled Banner.

**성좌**(星座) a constellation. ⇨ 별자리.

**성주** 〖민속〗 the guardian god of a homesite; a hearth god; a tutelary deity. ¶ ~받이 a shaman rite to induce the homesite god to enter 〔reenter〕 the house / ~ 받다, ~받이하다 have a shaman rite to propitiate the homesite god.

**성주**(城主) the lord of a castle; a feudal lord.

**성지**(城址) = 성터(城—).

**성지**(聖旨) the Royal will 〔wish〕; the Royal decree. ¶ ~를 받들어 in obedience to His Majesty's pleasure.

**성지**(聖地) a sacred ground; a holy place; the Holy Land. ◉ ~순례 a pilgrimage to the Holy Land.

**성직**(聖職) (holy) orders; the ministry. ¶ ~에 있다 be in (holy) orders. ◉ ~자 a churchman; a minister; a clergyman; a man of the cloth: ~자가 되다 take (holy) orders; be ordained (priest).

**성질**(性質) ① 《천성》 (a) nature; (a) disposition; 《기질》 (a) temper; (a) temperament; 《성격》 character; a make-up (★ 보통 단수 취급).

> **용법** **nature** 사람·동물·사물 따위의 타고난 성질, 천성을 뜻함. **disposition** 타고난 성질뿐만이 아니라, 그 사람의 기질, 인품, 성벽, 자연적 경향 따위를 뜻함: a crooked disposition(삐뚤어진 성격). **temper** 감정적으로 본 성질. **temperament** 생각, 행동, 정서에 바탕을 둔 기질. **character** 정신적·도덕적으로 본 성격. **make-up** 여러 가지 특성의 합성으로서 본 성질의 뜻.

¶ ~이 좋은〔나쁜〕 사람 a good-natured 〔an ill-natured〕 person / 온화한〔난폭한〕 ~의 사람 a person of (a) mild 〔rough〕 disposition / ~이 비슷하다〔다르다〕 be alike 〔different〕 in character / ~이 완고하다 be stubborn by nature / ~을 내다〔부리다〕 get 〔become〕 angry 《with, at》/ 사람의 ~은 행동에 나타난다 One's character finds expression in *one's* conduct.

② 《특질》 a property; 《소질》 a quality. ¶ 석탄의 ~ the properties of coal / 비누는 때를 없애는 ~이 있다 Soap has the property of removing dirt.

③ 《사물의》 character; nature. ¶ 일의 ~ the nature of a job / 문제의 ~상 from the nature of the matter / 그 두 문제는 ~이 다르다 The two questions are of different character. / 그런 ~의 돈은 받을 수 없다 I cannot accept money of that nature.

**성징**(性徵) 〖생물〗 a sex 〔sexual〕 character. ¶ 1차〔2차〕 ~ a primary 〔secondary〕 sex character.

**성차**(性差) differences between the sexes; a gender gap (정신면의).

**성차별**(性差別) sexual 〔gender〕 discrimination; sexism. ¶ 아직도 여성은 직장에서 ~을 받는 경우가 많다 It is still common for women to be discriminated against at work because of their sex.

**성찬**(盛饌) a feast; a sumptuous 〔capital, grand〕 dinner; a good table; a groaning board; dainty dishes. ¶ ~을 대접하다 give 《*a person*》 a capital dinner / ~을 차리다 set a good table 《for》.

**성찬**(聖餐) 〖기독교〗 (Holy) Communion; the Lord's Supper; the Eucharist. ¶ ~(식)에 참석하다 take 〔go to〕 Communion. ◉ ~식 = 성찬.

**성찰**(省察) self-examination; self-reflection; reflection; introspection. ～하다 reflect on; introspect; examine *oneself.*

**성채**(城砦) a fortress (and a stockade); a fort; a stronghold; a citadel. ¶ ～를 지키다〔점령하다〕 hold 〔take〕 a fortress.

**성체**(成體) 〚생물〛 an imago (*pl.* ～es, imagines); an adult.

**성체**(聖體) ① 《왕의》 the person of a king. ② 〚가톨릭〛 the body (of Christ); the holy bread; the Eucharist (성찬); the Host. ¶ ～를 받다 receive Communion. ◉ ～강복식 Benediction. ～공존(共存) consubstantiation. ～봉헌(식) Oblation. ～성사 (the Sacrament of) the Eucharist; (Holy) Communion.

**성추행**(性醜行) disgraceful 〔shameful, scandalous〕 conduct 《to a woman》; sexual infamies. ⇨ 성희롱, 성폭행.

**성충**(成蟲) 〚곤충〛 an imago (*pl.* ～es, imagines); an adult (insect). ¶ ～의 imaginal. ◉ ～기 the imago stage.

**성취**(成娶) ～하다 marry 〔espouse〕 《a woman》; take 《a woman》 to wife; take 《a woman》 in marriage.

**성취**(成就) 《달성》 accomplishment; attainment; achievement; fulfillment; 《완성》 completion; 《실현》 realization; 《성공》 success. ～하다 accomplish 《*one's* purpose, an undertaking》; achieve 《an end》; attain 《*one's* object》; fulfill; realize 《*one's* wishes》; succeed 《in an enterprise》; work out 《*one's* invention》. ¶ 사업을 ～하다 accomplish 〔achieve〕 an undertaking / 소원을 ～하다 realize *one's* wishes; have *one's* desire fulfilled; have *one's* wish realized / 모든 숙원이 ～됐다 All our cherished aims 〔desires〕 have been fulfilled.

**성층**(成層) 〚지질〛 bedding; stratification. ◉ ～광상(鑛床) a stratified ore deposit. ～암 (a) stratified rock; (a) sedimentary rock (퇴적암). ～화산 a stratovolcano.

**성층권**(成層圈) 〚기상〛 the stratosphere. ¶ ～의 stratospheric / ～을 비행하다 fly through the stratosphere. ◉ ～ 비행 a stratosphere 〔stratospheric〕 flight. ～비행기 a stratoplane; a stratoliner.

**성큼**(성큼) with big 〔long〕 strides; briskly; light-footedly; lightly. ¶ (기일 등이) 성큼 다가오다 draw near 〔up, on〕; be close at hand; approach / 성큼성큼 걷다 walk briskly; walk with long strides.

**성탄**(聖誕) ① 《왕·성자의》 the birth of a saint 〔king〕. ② 〚기독교〛 ⇨ 성탄절. ◉ ～절 Christmas (Day); Xmas.

**성터**(城—) 《자리》 the site of an ancient castle; a fortress site; 《유적》 the ruins 〔remains〕 of a castle.

**성토**(盛土) 《일》 raising the ground level; 《흙》 earth laid on the ground; 〚토목〛 banking. ～하다 lay earth on the ground; raise the ground level.

**성토**(聲討) censure; impeachment; denunciation. ～하다 censure; denounce; impeach. ¶ 굴욕 외교를 ～하다 censure the humiliating diplomacy. ◉ ～대회 《stage》 a rally; an indignation meeting.

**성패**(成敗) success and 〔or〕 failure; hit or miss. ¶ 일의 ～ success or failure of a matter / ～에 관계없이 whether successful or not; sink or swim / ～를 떠나 해보다 run the risk; try *one's* chance / ～는 시운에 달려있다 Success depends on chance.

**성폭행**(性暴行) sexual violence; a sexual assault 〔abuse〕; a rape. ¶ ～하다 attack 〔assault〕 《a woman》; rape; do (sexual) violence to.

**성품**(性品) 《천품》 nature; disposition; 《기질》 temper; temperament; 《품격》 (a) character. ¶ ～이 상냥하다 be of gentle disposition / ～에 맞지 않다 be uncongenial to *one;* go against the grain with *one.*

**성하**(盛夏) high summer; midsummer. ◉ ～염열(炎熱) the extreme heat of midsummer.

**성하**(聖下) His 〔Your〕 Holiness. ¶ 요한 바오로 2세 교황 ～ His 〔Your〕 Holiness Pope John Paul II.

**성하다** ① 《온전하다》 (be) good; whole; undamaged; unimpaired; flawless; spotless; intact; sound. ¶ 성한 과일 sound fruit / 집에는 성한 접시가 하나도 없다 There isn't a whole plate in the house. ② 《탈없다》 (be) healthy; sound; be in good condition. ¶ 성한 몸 a sound body / 몸성히 있다 be in good condition; be doing quite well.

**성하다**(盛—) ① 《초목이》 (be) dense; thick; luxuriant; rampant. ⇨ 무성하다. ② 《기운·세력 등이》 (be) prosperous; flourishing; thriving; active; lively; vigorous. ¶ 성해지다 prosper; thrive; flourish; become active; 《득세하다》 gain force / 전염병이 ～ an epidemic is raging / 그 지방에서는 농업이 ～ Agriculture is extensively carried on in that district.

**성함**(姓銜) your 〔his〕 esteemed name; *one's* (honored) name. ¶ ~이 어떻게 되십니까 May I ask your name?

**성행**(性行) character and conduct.

**성행**(盛行) prevalence; vogue; a rage. ~하다 prevail; be prevalent 〔rampant, fashionable〕; be much in fashion; be very popular. ¶ 도박 풍습이 ~하다 the gamblings are prevalent habits / 빈민가에는 질병과 악덕 행위가 ~하고 있다 Disease and vice are rampant at the slums.

**성행위**(性行爲) (sexual) intercourse; sex; a sex(ual) act. ¶ ~를 하다 have (sexual) intercourse 《with》; 《구어》 have sex 《with》; make love 《to》.

**성향**(性向) an inclination; a disposition; a propensity. ¶ 소비〔저축〕 ~ the propensity to consume 〔save〕.

**성현**(聖賢) saints; sages. ¶ ~의 가르침 the teaching of the sages; the words of the wise. 「Jesus).

**성혈**(聖血) 〖기독교〗 sacred blood (of

**성형**(成形) ① 〖생물〗 an adult form. ② 〖의학〗 correction of deformities; 《얼굴의》 face-lifting. ◉ ~수술 《have, undergo》 a plastic operation. ~외과 plastic surgery: ~ 외과의(醫) a plastic surgeon / 미용 ~ 외과 cosmetic surgery.

**성호르몬**(性—) a sex hormone. 「결혼.

**성혼**(成婚) a wedding; a marriage. ⇨

**성홍열**(猩紅熱) scarlet fever; scarlatina. ◉ 악성~ scarlatina maligna.

**성화**(成火) worry; annoyance; irritation; a bother; a torment. ¶ ~(가) 나다 be irritated; be vexed; become impatient 〔nervous〕 / ~부리다〔대다〕 annoy; pester 《*one's* mother》 for 《money》. ◉ ~거리 a source 〔cause〕 of irritation; a bother; a nuisance.

**성화**(星火) ① = 운성(隕星). ② 《별똥빛》 the light of a shooting star 〔meteor〕. ③ 《불티》 sparks (of fire).

**성화**(聖火) the sacred fire 〔flame〕; a sacred torch. ¶ 올림픽의 ~ the Olympic Flame; 《릴레이의》 the Olympic Torch / 올림픽 ~의 최종 주자 the last runner of the Olympic sacred-fire relay. ◉ ~대 the platform 〔structure〕 bearing the Olympic flame. ~봉송 the sacred-fire〔-torch〕 relay; the Olympic torch relay. ~주자 a flame-bearer.

**성화**(聖畫) a holy 〔sacred, religious〕 picture.

**성화같다**(星火—) (be) urgent; pressing; impatient; importunate. ¶ 성화같이 urgently; impatiently; importunately / 성화같이 재촉〔독촉〕하다 make an urgent request 《for》; press 《*a person*》 hard 《for》.

**성황**(盛況) 《번성》 prosperity; 《활황》 a boom; 《성공》 a success. ¶ ~을 이루다 be a great success; be well attended / 전람회는 대단한 ~이었다 The exhibition was a great success. *or* There was a great turnout (of people) at the exhibition. / 그 영화는 대 ~이었다 The film made a lucky hit.

**성황당**(城隍堂) ⇨ 서낭당.

**성훈**(聖訓) the teachings of 「a wise man 〔a saint〕; the instructions of a king.

**성희롱**(性戲弄) sexual harassment. ¶ 사무실에서의 ~ sexual harassment in the office / 그녀는 상사를 ~으로 고소했다 She accused her superior of sexual harassment.

**성히** in good condition. ⇨ 성하다.

**섶**[1] 《섶나무》 brushwood; firewood. ¶ 섶을 지고 불로 들어가는 격이다 It is a case of a summer insect flying into a flame to death.

**섶**[2] 《꼬챙이》 a support; a stay; a prop; 《누에의》 cocoon holders. ¶ 섶으로 어린 나무를 받치다 support a young plant with a stick. 「gusset; a gore.

**섶**[3] 《깃헝겊》 outer collar of a coat; a

**세**(貰) 《임대·임차》 lease; tenancy (부동산의); hire; hiring (물건의); charter (선박의); 《사용료》 (a) rent; hire; charterage (선박의). ⇨ 세내다. ¶ 방〔집〕세 a room 〔house〕 rent / 세가 오르다〔내리다〕 the rent rises 〔falls〕 / 세를 들다〔얻다〕 rent 〔hire, engage〕 a room; take a room 《with *a person's* family》 / 세를 물다〔내다〕 pay the rent 《on the house》; pay for 《a room》 / 세를 주다 lease; hire ⇨ 세주다 / 방을 세놓다 rent rooms 《미》. ⇨ 세놓다 / 방을 월 5만원에 세들다 rent a room at 50,000 won a month.

**세**(稅) 《세금》 a tax; a duty 《on goods》; dues; rates (지방세 등); a toll (통행세); 《과세》 taxation. ¶ 세의 부담 a tax burden 〔load〕.

**세**(勢) power (권력); influence (권세); strength (힘). ⇨ 세력(勢力).

**세** 《셋의》 three. ¶ 세 남자 three men / 세 살적 버릇이 여든까지 간다 《속담》 As a boy, so the man. *or* What is learned in the cradle is carried to the grave.

**-세**(世) ① 《대·시대》 a generation; an

age. ¶ 재미교포 2세 a Korean American; an American-born Korean / 헨리 8세 Henry Ⅷ 〔the Eighth〕. ② 〖지질〗 an epoch. ¶ 홍적세 the diluvial epoch.

**-세** let's. ⇨ -자 ①. ¶ 가세 Let's go.

**세가**(勢家) 《사람》 an influential person; 《집안》 a powerful family.

**세가락도요새** 〖조류〗 a sanderling.

**세가락딱따구리** 〖조류〗 a Korean three-toed woodpecker.

**세가락메추라기** 〖조류〗 a Burmese button-quail.

**세간** 《살림 도구》 household furniture and utensils; household effects 〔goods, necessaries, stuffs〕. ¶ 그 집은 ~이 많다 The house is well furnished.

**세간**(世間) ① ＝세상. ② 〖불교〗 the mundane world.

**세간나다** set up housekeeping on *one's* own; start a branch family. ¶ 장가 들어 ~ get married and set up housekeeping on *one's* own.

**세간내다** set up a separate home 《for》. ¶ 아들을 ~ set up a separate home for *one's* son.

**세간치장**(—治粧) interior decorating; fastidious taste in household goods; furnishing. ~하다 do the interior decorating of a house; have fastidious taste in *one's* household effects; furnish a home.

**세게** 《강하게》 strongly; stoutly; powerfully; firmly; intensely; 《세차게》 hard; severely; violently; keenly (느낌); impressively (인상); 《강조하여》 with emphasis; 〖음악〗 *forte* (It.)(생략 *f.*). ¶ (태도가) ~ 나오다 show a bold 〔unyielding〕 front; go strong; take the high hand with 《*a person*》 / ~ 때리다 hit 〔strike〕 hard 〔vigorously〕 / ~ 하다 strengthen; make strong 〔vigorous〕; intensify; invigorate / 그는 기둥에 머리를 ~ 부딪쳤다 He hit his head hard against the pillar.

**세계**(世界) ① [일반적] the world; 《지구》 the earth; the globe. ¶ ~에서 in the world; on earth / ~의 끝까지 to the end(s) of the earth / ~ 각지로부터 from all parts of the world; from the four corners of the world / 온 ~에〔의〕 all over the world; in all 〔throughout〕 the world / ~에 유례가 없는 unique in the world / ~ 제일의 부호 the richest man in the world / 전 ~에 명성을 떨치다 *one's* fame resounds all over the world / 영어는 온 ~에서 쓰이고 있다 English is spoken all over the world. / 에베레스트산은 ~에서 가장 높은 산이다 Mt. Everest is the highest mountain in the world.
② 《우주》 the universe; the cosmos; 《그 일부》 a world. ¶ 달〔별〕의 ~ the lunar 〔stellar〕 world.
③ 《세상》 the world. ¶ 그런 바보는 어느 ~에도 없다 He is the biggest fool on earth.
④ 《특수 사회》 a world; a society; circles; 《영역》 a realm. ¶ 꿈의 ~ the realm of dreams; dreamland / 상상〔공상〕의 ~ the world of imagination 〔fantasy〕 / 어린이의 ~ the world of children / 밤의 ~ night 〔nocturnal〕 life / 사후(死後) ~ a life after death / 이상 ~ an ideal world / 음악 ~ the world of music; music circles.
◉ ~경제 international 〔world〕 economy: ~경제 공황 the world economic crisis (1929년). ~관 a view of 〔an outlook on〕 the world; a world view 〔outlook〕. ~국가 the World State. ~기상 기구 the World Meteorological Organization (생략 WMO). ~노동조합연맹 the World Federation of Trade Unions (생략 WFTU). ~대전 the World War: 제1〔2〕차 ~ 대전 World War Ⅰ 〔Ⅱ〕; the First 〔Second〕 World War. ~력(曆) the World Calendar. ~무역기구 the World Trade Organization (생략 WTO). ~문제 a world-wide question; an international problem 〔issue〕. ~박람회 an international exhibition; a world's fair. ~보건 기구 the World Health Organization (생략 WHO). ~사 world history; the history of the world. ~사조 the current thoughts of the world. ~선수권 a world 〔an international〕 championship 〔title〕. ~시(時) world standard time; universal time; Greenwich (Mean) Time. ~식량계획 the World Food Plan (생략 WFP). ~어 a world 〔an international〕 language. ~연방 the World Federation of Nations: ~ 연방주의 World Federalism. ~유산 a world 〔cultural, natural〕 heritage. ~은행 the World Bank; 《정식명》 the International Bank for Reconstruction and Development (생략 IBRD). ~인 a citizen of the world; a cosmopolitan. ~인권 선언 the Universal Declaration of Human Rights. ~저작권 협약 the Universal Copyright Convention (생략 UCC). ~정세 the world situation. ~정신 the world spirit 〔soul〕. ~정책 a world 〔global〕 policy. ~제패 domi-

nation of the world; world hegemony. ~주의 cosmopolitanism: ~주의자 a cosmopolitan. ~지도 a map of the world. ~지적 재산권 기구 the World Intellectual Property Organization (생략 WIPO). ~평화 world peace; the peace of the world.

**세계기록**(世界記錄) a world record. ¶ ~을 세우다 establish 〔make, set (up)〕 a world record 《in》. ◉ ~보유자 a world record holder.

**세계일주**(世界一周) a tour round the world; a round-the-world trip; a world cruise (여객선에 의한). ~하다 go 〔trip〕 around the world; travel (all over) the world; make a round=the-world trip; go on a world cruise.

**세계적**(世界的) world; worldwide; universal; global; international. ¶ ~ 문제 an international problem 〔issue〕 / ~ 불경기 a worldwide depression / ~인 인물 a world figure; a person of world=wide fame / ~으로 유명한 world=famous〔-renowned〕 / ~으로 알려져 있다 《His fame》 be known all over the world; enjoy worldwide fame.

**세계화**(世界化) globalization; internationalization (국제화); *segyehwa* (한국의). ~하다 globalize. ¶ 세계화의 성취는 선언만으로는 결코 오지 않는다 The achievement of globalization never comes only through a declaration. ◉ ~구상 globalization vision. ~운동 a globalization campaign. ~정책 globalizing policy.

**세공**(細工) work; workmanship; craftsmanship. ~하다 《…으로》 work 《in》; 《…에》 work 《on》 (★ 이 뜻으로는 종종 불규칙 변화); craft. ¶ 그물 ~ netting; network / 놋쇠 ~의 worked 〔wrought〕 in brass / ~이 훌륭하다〔엉성하다〕 be superbly 〔poorly〕 worked; be of excellent 〔poor〕 workmanship / 보석에 ~하다 work on precious stone / 정교하게 ~되어 있다 be cunningly wrought.
◉ ~인 a worker; a craftsman; an artisan. ~품 a (piece of) work; a handiwork; ware: 미술 ~품 an art object; an *object d'art* (F.).

**세관**(稅關) a custom(s)house; the customs. ¶ ~ 검사 (a) customs inspection 〔examination〕 / ~ 감시선 a customs inspection boat; a revenue cutter / ~에 소지품을 신고하다 declare *one's* things / ~에 관세를 납부하다 clear goods / ~을 통과하다 get through 〔pass〕 the customs / ~에서 흉기의 소지 여부를 검사받았다 We were inspected at the customs whether or not we carried dangerous weapons. / 김포 ~은 절차를 완화하였다 The Kimp'o Customs Office eased customs procedures 〔formalities〕.
◉ ~명세서 a customs specification. ~법규 customs regulations. ~송장 a customs invoice. ~수수료 a customs 〔an entry〕 fee. ~신고서 a customs declaration. ~압수품 customhouse seizures. ~원 a customhouse officer; a customs officer 〔inspector〕; a customs agent. ~장 the superintendent 〔director〕 of customhouse; a custom director. ~창고 a customs shed.

**세광**(洗鑛) 〖광산〗 ore washing. ~하다 wash 《ore》; scrub 《ore》. ◉ ~반(盤) a frame. ~조(槽) a buddle; a hutch.

**세궁역진**(勢窮力盡) ~하다 be reduced 〔driven〕 to the last extremity; be faint with exhaustion 〔fatigue〕.

**세균**(細菌) a bacillus (*pl.* bacilli); a bacterium (*pl.* -ria); a germ; a microbe. ¶ ~의 bacterial; bacillar; bacillary / ~을 죽이다 destroy 〔kill〕 germs; sterilize / 노출되어 있는 상처는 ~에 감염되기 쉽다 The open wounds are apt to become infected.
◉ ~검사 a bacteriological examination; bacilloscopy: ~ 검사를 하다 carry out a bacteriological examination 《on》. ~바이러스 a bacterial virus. ~배양 germiculture; bacterial culture. ~병기 a bacteriological weapon. ~성 간경변 bacterial cirrhosis. ~성 이질 bacillary dysentery. ~성 질병 a germ disease; a bacterially caused disease. ~여과기 a bacterial filter. ~요법 bacteriotherapy; bacillotherapy. ~전 bacteriological 〔germ〕 warfare. ~탄 a germ 〔microbe〕 bomb. ~학 bacteriology; microbiology: ~학자 a bacteriologist.

**세금**(稅金) a tax; 《지방세》 a local tax; 《관세》 a duty 《on》; 《통행세》 a toll; dues (수수료). ¶ ~ 포함 가격 the price 「before (deduction of) 〔plus, including〕 tax / ~의 입회 조사 on-the-spot tax investigation.
세금을: ~을 내다〔납부하다〕 pay a tax 〔duty〕 《on》 / ~을 부과하다 impose 〔lay〕 a duty 《on an article》; levy a tax 《on *a person*》 / ~을 속이다 defraud a tax; cheat on taxes / ~을 징수하다 collect 〔draw〕 taxes 《from》 / ~을 체납하다 let taxes fall in arrears; fail to pay a tax on the due date / ~

을 포탈하다 evade a tax.
세금이: ～이 붙다 be dutiable 〔taxable〕; be subject to duty 〔taxation〕/ ～이 면제되다 be exempted from taxation 〔a tax〕; be free of duty; be duty=〔tax-〕free.
◉ ～공제 the personal tax deduction: ～공제 가격 the price after (deduction of) tax / ～ 공제 급료 take-home pay; pay after (deduction of) tax; pay with tax excluded. ～부담 a tax burden 〔load〕: 임금 생활자의 ～ 부담을 줄이다 lighten the tax burden of wage earners. ～체납 tax arrearage; tax delinquency. ～포탈 tax evasion. ～혜택 a tax favor: ～ 혜택을 주다 give a tax favor 《to》.

**세기**(世紀) a century. ¶ 금～ this 〔the present〕 century / 20～ the twentieth 〔20th〕 century / ～의 대사건 the salient event of the century / ～의 비극 the tragedy of century / 18 ～ 초〔중, 후〕엽에 in the early 〔mid-, late〕 eighteenth century / 컴퓨터는 금～의 대발명품이다 Computers are the great invention of this century.

**세기말**(世紀末) the end of a century; the *fin de siècle* (F.) (19세기의). ¶ ～적인 *fin-de-siècle;* decadent.

**세끼** three (regular) meals (a day); daily meals.

**세나다**[1] 《덧나다》 《a wound, rash or swelling》 get worse; grow.

**세나다**[2] 《잘 팔리다》 sell well; enjoy a good demand; be much in demand; be much sought after. ¶ 요새 달걀이 세난다 Eggs are selling well these days.

**세나절** taking entirely too long 《to do *something*》.

**세내다**(貰―) rent; hire; lease (계약으로); charter (탈것을); pay to use. ¶ 배를 ～ hire 〔charter〕 a boat / 자동차를 ～ rent 〔hire〕 a car / 집을 5년 계약으로 ～ take a house on a lease of five years.

**세네갈** 《아프리카의 공화국》 Senegal. ¶ ～의 Senegalese. ◉ ～말 Senegalese. ～사람 a Senegalese.

**세놓다**(貰―) let out (on hire); hire out; rent 《to》; lease. ¶ 자동차를 시간제로 ～ hire out a car by the hour / 자전거를 ～ let bicycles out on hire / 집〔방〕을 ～ rent a house 〔room〕 《to》/ 세놓습니다 《게시》 For rent 《미》; To let 《영》.

**세뇌**(洗腦) brainwashing; brainwash; indoctrination. ～하다 brainwash 《*a person*》; indoctrinate forcibly. ¶ 그는 교도소에서 ～당했다 He was brainwashed in prison. ◉ ～공작 brainwashing. ～교육 《undergo》 forcible indoctrination education.

**세다**[1] ① 《강하다》 (***a***) 《힘이》 (be) strong; powerful; mighty; vigorous (기력이); muscular; robust (강건하다). ¶ 힘이 센 사람 a strong 〔powerful〕 man; a brawny man / 세어 보이는 strong=looking / 기운〔힘〕이 무척 ～ be as strong as a horse; have the strength of a lion / 세어지다 become 〔grow〕 powerful 〔strong, stout〕. (***b***) 《마음이》 (be) tough; firm; stubborn (완강하다). ¶ 고집이 ～ be stubborn 〔obstinate〕 / 배짱이 ～ have pluck 〔mettle〕; have iron nerves. (***c***) 《세차다》 (be) strong; forcible; intense; violent; hard; severe; keen; rough. ¶ 센 물살 a swift 〔strong〕 current; rapids / 센 바람 a strong 〔heavy, violent〕 wind / 센 빛 a strong 〔an intense〕 light / 물결이 ～ the waves are high; the sea is rough / 바람이 ～ it is blowing hard; [바람이 주어] blow hard 《against》; [장소가 주어] be windy / 화력이 ～ have strong caloric force / 불길이 세어지다 the fire gathers strength / 빛이 너무 ～ The light is too strong. (***d***) 《잘하다》 [서술적] be good 《at》; be strong 《in》. ¶ 바둑이 ～ be a good player of *paduk* / 술이 ～ be a heavy drinker.
② 《물이》 (be) hard; 《풀기가》 (be) stiff. ¶ 센 물 hard water / 풀기가 너무 ～ be starched too stiff.
③ 《팔자가》 (be) ill-omened; unlucky. ¶ 팔자가 ～ be ill-starred 〔unlucky〕; be born under an unlucky star / 터가 ～ a site is ill-omened; [집이 주어] have an unlucky aspect.

**세다**[2] 《머리털이》 turn gray 〔white〕; become grizzled 〔grizzly〕. ¶ 머리가 ～ *one's* hair turns gray.

**세다**[3] 《수를》 count; reckon; calculate; number; enumerate (열거하다). ¶ 다시 ～ recount; count (all over) again; count over / 잘못 ～ count wrong; miscalculate; miscount / 하나에서 열까지 ～ count from one to ten / 돈을 ～ count the money / 대충 세어 …이 되다 be roughly estimated at… / 출석자〔결석자〕의 수를 ～ count the number of people present 〔absent〕/ (돈 따위를) 세어서 내다 count out 《10 five-dollar bills》/ 셀 수 없이 많은 numberless;

countless; innumerable / 하늘에는 별이 셀 수 없을 만큼 많다 There are too numerous stars to count in the sky.

**세단** 《자동차》 a sedan; a saloon (car) 《영》.

**세대**(世代) a generation. ¶ 차～ the next 〔coming〕 generation / 새로운 ～ the new generation / 젊은 ～ the rising 〔younger〕 generation / 다음 ～를 짊어지다 be destined to lead the next generation / 아버지와 자식 사이에는 ～ 차이가 있다 There is a generation gap between the father and his son. ◉ ～교번(交番) 〖생물〗 alternation of generations; heterogenesis; digenesis. ～교체 a change of generation; generational change; a shift 〔transfer〕 in generation: ～교체를 부르짖다 call for a shift in generation.

**세대**(世帶) 《사회적인 단위로》 a household; 《가정》 a home; 《가족》 a family. ¶ 12 ～가 그 아파트에 살고 있다 Twelve families live in the apartment. / 그 화재로 4～ 15명이 집을 잃었다 Fifteen people of four households lost their homes in that fire. / 그는 20세 때에 이미 한 ～의 가장이 되었다 He had already become the head of a household 〔family〕 at the age of twenty. ◉ ～수 the number of households. ～주 a householder; the head of a household 〔family〕.

**세도**(世道) public morals. ◉ ～인심 public morals and popular attitudes 〔sentiments〕.

**세도**(勢道) power; (political) influence 〔authority〕; (holding) the reign of government. ¶ ～를 부리다 wield 〔exercise〕 power 《over》. ◉ ～가 《사람》 a man of power 〔influence〕; 《집안》 a family in power.

**세도막형식**(一形式) 〖음악〗 (a) ternary 〔three-part〕 form.

**세뚜리** ① 《식사》 three persons dining together. ② 《나눔》 dividing (a crock of pickled shrimp or the like) into three portions.

**세레나데** 〖음악〗 a serenade.

**세력**(勢力) ① 《지배력》 influence; power; might; strength; sway. ¶ 자기 ～의 확대 self-aggrandizement / ～의 균형 balance of power / 극동의 안정 ～ the main prop and stay of the Far East. 세력이: ～이 늘다 increase in power; gain in influence / ～이 있다 be influential 〔powerful〕; 《미치다》 exercise 〔have〕 influence 《over, with》; carry weight 《with, among》 / ～이 백중하다 be almost equal in power / ～이 있는 influential; powerful; mighty / ～이 없는 uninfluential; powerless; with 〔having〕 no influence. 세력을: ～을 꺾다 break 《*a person's*》 power; destroy 〔undermine〕 《*a person's*》 influence / ～을 떨치다 wield power 〔influence〕; hold 〔bear〕 sway; dominate / ～을 늘리다〔펴다〕 promote 〔increase〕 *one's* influence / ～을 만회하다 regain 〔win back〕 *one's* power 〔strength〕 / ～을 얻다 acquire 〔gain〕 influence; become powerful 〔influential〕 / ～을 잃다 lose *one's* power; forfeit *one's* influence / ～을 확립하다 establish 〔fix〕 *one's* influence / ～을 확대하다 extend 〔broaden〕 *one's* power 〔influence〕.
¶ 그는 부내에서 ～이 당당하다 He wields much influence in the Ministry. / 신문은 사회에서 하나의 ～이다 The press is a power in society. / 그는 재계에 상당한 ～을 가지고 있다 He has considerable power in business circles.
② 《물리적인 힘》 force; energy. ¶ 태풍은 점차 ～을 더해가고 있다 The typhoon is increasing in strength.
◉ ～가 an influential person. ～권(圈) ＝ ～범위: ～권을 넓히다 extend *one's* territory; enlarge *one's* beat / ～권을 침범하다 intrude 〔break〕 into 《*a person's*》 domain; encroach 〔trespass〕 on 《*a person's*》 territory. ～균형 the balance of power: ～ 균형을 유지하다〔깨뜨리다〕 maintain 〔break〕 the balance of power. ～다툼 a struggle 〔scramble〕 for power; a power grab. ～범위 a sphere 〔scope〕 of influence 〔power〕; 《깡패 등의》 *one's* domain 〔beat〕; *one's* territory: ～ 범위를 다투다 quarrel over 《their》 sphere of influence / ～ 범위 내에 있다 be within *one's* territory 〔sphere of influence〕.

**세련**(洗練) polishing; refinement. ～하다 polish (up); refine; finish. ～되다 be polished 〔refined, finished, elegant〕. ¶ ～된 문체 a polished 〔an elegant〕 style / ～된 숙녀 a polished 〔refined〕 lady / ～된 표현〔말〕 well=polished phrases / ～된 태도〔매너〕 *one's* refined 〔elegant〕 manners / 태도가 ～되다 have polished manners / 말을 ～되게 하다 refine (on, upon) *one's* language / 그는 ～된 사람이다 He is a person of refinement.

**세례**(洗禮) baptism; christening. ¶ ～를

베풀다〔주다〕 administer baptism《to》; baptize / ～를 받다 receive baptism; be baptized / 포탄 ～를 받다 receive a volley of gun fire; undergo *one's* baptism of fire / 주먹 ～를 퍼붓다 hail blows upon《*a person*》.

◉ ～명 a baptismal 〔Christian〕 name. ～식 (a) baptism; a baptismal ceremony; (a) baptismal service. ～요한 John the Baptist. ～자 a baptist. 침수〔관수〕～ baptism by immersion 〔effusion〕.

**세로** [명사]《길이》length;《높이》height; [부사적] perpendicularly; vertically; lengthwise; endwise. ¶ ～ 넉자다 measure 4 *ja* in length; be four *ja* long / ～로 베다 cut lengthwise; sliver / ～로 쓰다 write vertically. ◉ ～줄무늬 vertical stripes. ～쓰기=종서(縱書). ～줄 a perpendicular 〔vertical〕 line; a (longitudinal) stripe: ～줄을 긋다 draw a perpendicular 〔vertical〕 line.

**세로지**(一紙)《종이결》paper grain that runs lengthwise;《긴 조각》slip of paper 〔cloth〕.

**세로축**(一軸) a vertical 〔longitudinal〕 axis; 〖수학〗 the axis of ordinates.

**세론**(世論) public opinion. =여론(輿論).

**세론**(細論) a detailed discussion. ～하다 discuss in detail.

**세류**(細流) a streamlet; a brooklet.

**세륨**〖화학〗 cerium (기호 Ce).

**세리**(稅吏) a revenue officer; a tax collector.

**세말**(歲末) =세밑.

**세면**(洗面) washing *one's* face. ～하다 wash *one's* face; have a wash;《미》wash up. ◉ ～기 a washbowl《미》; a washbasin《영》;《붙어 있는》a lavatory. ～대 a washstand; a washhand stand《영》. ～도구 toilet articles. ～소 a lavatory; a toilet room《미》; a washroom (공공건물의).

**세모** (having) three corners; (being) triangular; triangularity; a triangular thing. ⇨삼각. ¶ ～가 나다 have three corners; be three cornered / ～난 모자 a three-cornered hat.

◉ ～기둥 a trigonal prism. ～꼴 a triangle. ～끌 a triangular file. ～송곳 a triangle drill.

**세모**(歲暮) the close 〔end〕 of the year; the year-end. ⇨세밑. ¶ ～선물 a year-end gift 〔present〕 / 거리의 ～ 풍경 a year-end scene of the street.

**세모시**(細一) ramie cloth of fine texture.

**세목**(細目) details; particulars; (specified) items; specifications. ¶ ～으로 나누다 itemize; specify / ～에 이르다 enter into details; go into particulars. ◉ 교수～ a detailed plan for instruction; a (teaching) syllabus (*pl.* ～es, -bi).

**세목**(稅目) items 〔headings〕 of a tariff; items of taxation; tax items.

**세무**(世務)《be well versed in》public 〔worldly〕 affairs.

**세무**(稅務) taxation business; tax matters. ◉ ～공무원 a revenue officer 〔official〕; a tax collector. ～사 a licensed tax accountant. ～사찰〔조사〕 a tax investigation 〔surveillance〕; a tax probe: 정밀 ～조사 an intensive tax investigation. ～상담소 a tax information office. ～행정 tax administration. ～회계 tax accounting.

**세무서**(稅務署) a tax(ation) office; a revenue office. ◉ ～원 a tax-office clerk; a tax collector 〔man〕. ～장 the superintendent of a revenue office.

**세물**(貰物) an object for hire 〔rent〕. ◉ ～전(廛) a renter's store: ～전 영감이다 be well-informed.

**세미나** a seminar. ¶ ～를 개최하다 conduct 〔hold〕 a seminar《on international relations》.

**세미다큐멘터리**〖영화〗 a semidocumentary (film).

**세미콜론** a semicolon (;). ¶ ～을 찍다 put a semicolon《to》.

**세미파이널**《준결승》semifinals.

**세미프로**《사람》a semiprofessional; a semipro《구어》. ¶ ～의 semiprofessional; semipro.

**세밀**(細密) minuteness; elaborateness. ～하다 (be) minute [mainjú:t] (★ a minute [mínit]는 「분」.); detailed; fine; close; elaborate. ¶ ～한 검사 close 〔minute〕 examination / ～한 주의 close attention; meticulous care;《지시》detailed instructions / ～히 조사하다 inquire minutely into《*a matter*》.

◉ ～화(畫) a miniature.

**세밑**(歲一) the end 〔close〕 of the year; the year-end.

**세발**(洗髮) washing of the hair; a shampoo. ～하다 wash the hair; have *one's* hair shampooed (남이 감겨주다).

◉ ～제 a hair wash; (a) shampoo.

**세배**(歲拜) a formal bow of respect to *one's* elders on New Year's Day;《정초인사》the New Year's greeting. ～하다 perform a New Year's bow. ¶ ～를 가다 pay a visit of respect on New Year's Day; make a New Year's call / ～ 다니다 make a round of New Year's calls. ◉ ～꾼 a New Year's caller 〔visitor〕. ～상 the New Year's feast (served to visitors): ～상을 차리다 prepare the New Year's feast. 세뱃돈 the New Year's gift of money given to *one's* juniors; "bow money": 세뱃돈을 주다 give 《a child》 a New Year's gift (of money).

**세법**(稅法) the tax law; 《과세 방법》 a system 〔scheme〕 of taxation.

**세별**(細別) subdivision. ～하다 subdivide; itemize.

**세보**(世譜) a genealogy; a family tree.

**세부**(細部) details; particulars. ¶ ～에 걸쳐 조사하다 go into details 〔particulars〕.

**세부득이**(勢不得已) by force of circumstances; by an unavoidable circumstance. ～하다 (be) unavoidable.

**세분**(細分) fractionation; subdivision. ～하다 fractionate; fraction(al)ize; subdivide; break into parts; itemize. ¶ 다섯 조로 ～하다 subdivide into five sets; itemize 《*things*》 into five.

**세비**(歲費) 《지출》 annual expenditure; 《연간 경비》 yearly pay; an annual allowance 〔salary〕.

**세사**(世事) worldly affairs; mundane matters; the business 〔ways〕 of the world. ⇨ 세상 물정. ¶ ～에 밝은 사람 a man of the world; a worldly-wise man / ～에 어두운 사람 a person unaccustomed to the ways of the world.

**세살** three years of age. ¶ ～적 버릇 여든까지 간다 《속담》 As a boy, so the man. *or* The child is father of the man.

**세살**(細—) 《부채·문 따위의》 slender ribs 〔frames〕; fine 《wooden》 strips. ◉ ～문 a crude window with a small frame. ～부채 a narrow-ribbed fan; a fan with fine ribs. ～창 a window with a frame of slender pieces.

**세상**(世上) ① 《세간》 the world; (a) society (사회); the public (사람들); 《인생·생애》 life. ¶ 이 ～ this world 〔life〕 / 저 ～ the next world; the world beyond / ～과의 인연을 끊다 shut *oneself* up from the world; renounce the world.

세상의: ～의 도움이 되다 benefit mankind 〔the world〕; do the world good / ～의 물의를 일으키다 give birth to public controversy; bring on the censure of the public / ～의 쓴맛단맛을 다 맛보다 taste the sweets and bitters of life / ～의 웃음거리가 되다 be made a laughingstock of the public; be held up to public ridicule / ～의 주목을 끌게 되다 come into the limelight.

세상에: ～에 드문 rare; 《*a person*》 rarely to be met with (in the world) / ～에 (태어) 나다 be born into the world; see the light (of day) / ～에 나오다〔나서다〕 go out into 〔set out in〕 the world; begin the world 〔*one's* career〕; launch in life / ～에 내보내다 《자식 등을》 send out to the world; place out in life; 《사물을》 give 《a book》 to the public 〔world〕 / (못된 일이) ～에 드러나다 get abroad; come to light; become public / ～에 알리다 bring to light; make public / ～에 잘 알려진 well-known; widely known; famous; notorious (악명이) / ～에 알려지지 않은 obscure; unknown; nameless; little known (in the world).

세상에서: ～에서 버림받다 be rejected 〔forsaken〕 by the world; be shut 〔cast〕 out of society / ～에서 잊혀지다 be buried in oblivion; be forgotten by the world.

세상을: ～(눈)을 꺼리다 shun public notice; avoid the eyes of the world / ～을 놀라게 하다 create 〔make〕 a stir; astonish the world; 《깜짝》 take the world by surprise / ～을 덧없어 하다 feel 〔realize〕 the vanity of the human life / ～을 떠나다 leave this world; pass away / ～을 버리다 forsake the world; hide *oneself* from the world; 《자살하다》 kill *oneself;* commit suicide; end *one's* own life / ～을 살아가다 live; pass through life; make *one's* way 〔get, go〕 through the world / ～을 알고 있다 know the world; have seen much of life / ～을 모르다 be ignorant of the world; have seen (but) little of the world.

세상이: ～이 싫어지다 be 〔get〕 sick (and tired) of the world.

¶ ～이 다 안다 All the world knows it. / ～이 뭐라고들 할까 What will people say? / ～이란 (바로) 그런 것이다 That's the way 「things are 〔it goes〕. *or* That is the way of the world.

② 《시대》 the age 〔era〕; the days; the times. ¶ ～의 변천 the change of the times; the march of times / 이처럼 날로 진보해 가는 ～에 in this rapidly advancing 〔ever-progressing〕 age / ～에 뒤지다 fall 〔lag, get〕 behind the times; get out of touch with the world / ~에 뒤지지 않도록 하다 keep up with the times; keep abreast 〔pace〕 of 〔with〕 the times / 지금은 정보화 ~이라고 해도 지나친 말이 아니다 It is surely no exaggeration to say that this is the age of information. ③《독무대》¶ …의 ~이다 be *one's* own master 〔boss〕; have *one's* own way / 그가 없어졌으니 이젠 우리들 ~이다 Now that he is gone, we are our own masters. / 여기는 내 ~이다 Here I am absolutely my own boss.

**세상맛**(世上—) the sweets and bitters of life. ¶ ~을 알다 know what the world is like.

**세상물정**(世上物情) (the condition of) the world; the ways of the world; worldly matters. ¶ ~에 밝다 know much of the world; be a man of the world / ~에 어둡다 know little 〔be ignorant〕 of the world; be out of touch with the world.

**세상사**(世上事) worldly affairs. ⇨ 세상물정.

**세상살이**(世上—) way of living; mode of life; living. ~하다 go 〔walk〕 through the world; go on in the world; lead a life.

**세상없어도**(世上—) 《반드시》 under 〔in〕 any circumstances; whatever may happen; by all means; 《절대로》《not》 for all the world; for the life of *one;* on no account; under no condition. ¶ ~ 이 일은 해야 한다 Nothing shall hinder me from accomplishing my purpose. / ~ 그것은 안 하겠다 I would not do it for all the world. / ~ 말 못 하겠다 Come what may, I can't tell you.

**세상없이**(世上—) ever so; beyond words; beyond comparison; utterly.

**세상에**(世上—) 《how, what, why》 in the world 〔on earth〕; in God's name. ¶ ~ 이게 무슨 일이냐 What in the world is it? / 참 ~ 별일 다 보겠군 Of all things! *or* Never in my life have I seen anything like that!

**세세하다**(細細—) ① 《미세하다》 (be) small; fine; minute. ② 《상세하다》 (be) detailed; minute; circumstantial; 《정밀하다》 (be) close. ¶ 극히 세세한 점에 이르기까지 to the remotest particulars 〔minutest details〕 / 세세한 데까지 미치다 《주의가》 be attentive to details; be very careful; 《배려가》 be thoughtful; be considerate.

**세세히**(細細—) minutely; circumstantially; with particulars; in detail; to the smallest detail. ¶ ~ 기록하다 write down the full particulars / ~ 이야기하다 tell 〔go into〕 all the details; give a full account.

**세속**(世俗) 《세상의 풍습》 common 〔popular, vulgar〕 customs; 《세상》 the (mundane, secular) world. ¶ ~의 common; worldly; mundane; secular; popular; vulgar; 《구어》 lowbrow / ~에서 말하는 in common 〔vulgar〕 parlance; as is commonly said / ~적으로 말하면 as the world goes; as men go; talking in a worldly way / ~적 명성 worldly fame / ~에 영합하다 curry favor with the hoi polloi; cater 〔play down〕 to the popular taste / ~을 초월하다 stand aloof of 〔rise above〕 the trivialities of life; be free from the trammels of ordinary life. ◉ ~주의 secularism. ~화 secularization.

**세수**(洗手) face washing; washing up. ~하다 wash (*one's* face); have a wash; wash up. ¶ 식사 전에 ~하다 wash up before a meal. ◉ ~간 a washroom. ~수건 a (hand) towel. 세숫대야 a wash basin. 세숫물 water for washing up. 세숫비누 toilet soap.

**세수**(稅收) tax revenue(s) 〔yields〕. ¶ ~증가〔감소〕 an increase 〔a drop〕 in tax revenue(s).

**세슘** 〖화학〗 cesium (기호 Cs).

**세습**(世襲) (transmission by) heredity; descent. ~하다 transmit from generation to generation. ¶ ~적인 hereditary; patrimonial. ◉ ~권 a hereditary right 《to》. ~귀족 a hereditary peer. ~재산 hereditary property 〔estate〕; a heritage; a patrimony.

**세시**(歲時) ① 《새해》 the beginning of the year; the New Year. ② 《때때》 times and seasons. ◉ ~기(記) an almanac.

**세심**(細心) carefulness; prudence; circumspection; scrupulosity. ~하다 (be) very careful; prudent; circumspect; scrupulous. ¶ ~하게 with the greatest care; with meticulous care; most carefully; prudently; scrupulously / ~한 주의 scrupulous care; careful attention / ~한 주의를 하다 pay close attention 《to》.

**세안**(洗眼) eyewashing. ~하다 wash *one's* eyes; have *one's* eyes washed.

**세액**(稅額) the amount of (a) tax; the tax amount; tax liability. ¶ ~의 산정

(a) tax assessment / 결정～ the settled tax amount.
◉ ～공제 tax deduction 〔credit〕. ～조정 settlement of a tax.

**세업**(世業) hereditary occupation.

**세우**(細雨) a drizzle; a fine 〔misty〕 rain.

**세우다** ① 《서게 하다》 (***a***) 《일으키다》 stand 《a candle》; make 《*a thing*》 stand; erect; raise; set up; put up; set 《a book》 on edge 〔end〕; stand 《*a* long *thing*》 on end; plant (기둥 등을); prick (up) 《*one's* ears》. ¶ 기둥을 ～ plant a pillar; erect 〔set up〕 a post / 옷깃을 ～ turn 〔pull〕 up the collar / 팻말을 ～ set 〔put〕 up a bulletin board / 아무를 일으켜 ～ make *a person* stand (up); 《부축해서》 set 〔get〕 *a person* on *his* legs; help *a person* (back) up to *his* feet / 상자를 세워 놓다 place a box on end / 귀를 쫑긋 세우고 듣다 prick *one's* ears and listen / 세워 놓을 것 《게시》 To be kept upright. (***b***) 《사람을》 form 〔draw up〕 《*persons*》 in a line; place 《men》 in a row. ¶ 사람을 두 줄로 ～ draw up people in two lines.
② 《건조물을》 build; construct; 《동상·기념비를》 erect; set 〔put〕 up; raise 《an edifice》. ¶ 동상을 ～ erect 〔set up〕 a bronze (statue) / 기념비를 ～ erect a monument 《of a war》; erect a memorial 《to *a person*》 / 새로 집을 ～ have a new house built; build *oneself* a new house.

> 용법 아래 열거된 단어는 모두 「세우다」란 뜻으로 쓰이나, 내포되어 있는 뜻의 차이는 아래와 같음. **build** 여러 부품을 조립하여 하나의 건조물을 세우는 것. **construct** 일정한 계획에 따라 건조물을 세우는 과정을 강조하며, 특히 대규모 건설 공사를 뜻하는 말. **erect** 본래는 높은 것을 세운다는 뜻으로 쓰여졌으나 지금은 단순히 건립한다는 뜻으로도 널리 쓰여지며, 과정보다는 건립〔건설〕되는 사실에 중점을 둠. **put up** 「세우다」란 뜻의 구어적인 표현.

③ 《수립하다》 (***a***) 《설립·조직하다》 establish; create; found; form; organize; set up; institute. ¶ 정부〔학교·회사〕를 ～ establish 〔set up〕 a government 〔a school, a firm〕 / 좋은 전통을 ～ form 〔establish〕 a good tradition 《of》. (***b***) 《계획을》 make 〔form, lay〕 《a plan》; shape; lay (down) 《*one's* course》; map out 《a program》; make a blueprint 《미》. ¶ 계획을 ～ lay a plan; devise 〔formulate, work out〕 a plan / 인생의 방침을 ～ lay down the course of *one's* life. (***c***) 《이론·학설·원칙 등을》 advance; set up; set forth; put forward; lay down; formulate; frame; develop. ¶ 원칙을 ～ formulate 〔lay down〕 a principle / 이론을 ～ formulate 〔develop〕 a theory; theorize / 새 학설을 ～ advance 〔set up, formulate〕 a new theory.
④ 《정하다》 lay down; establish; enact. ¶ 규칙을 ～ lay down rules; establish regulations / 법률을 ～ enact a law.
⑤ 《차·말을》 stop; put a stop to; bring to a stop 〔halt, standstill〕; hold up 〔on〕. ¶ 말을 ～ pull up 〔rein in〕 a horse; bring *one's* horse to a stop / 차를 ～ bring a car to a halt; 《불러서》 call a halt; 《주차시키다》 park a car / 택시를 ～ 《손을 들어》 stop 〔hold up〕 a cab / 차를 문 앞에 세워 주시오 Pull the car up at the gate.
⑥ 《날을 날카롭게》 put 〔forge〕 an edge 《on》; sharpen; set. ¶ 칼날을 날카롭게 ～ put a sharp edge on a knife / 톱날을 ～ set (the teeth of ) a saw.
⑦ 《뜻을》 set an aim in life; have 《an object》 in view; be determined 《to *do*》; have a fixed purpose 《in life》. ¶ 음악가가 되고자 뜻을 ～ aspire to be a musician.
⑧ 《예산을》 make 〔form, draw up〕 a budget 〔an estimate〕; forecast budget for 《the coming year》.
⑨ 《생계를》 support 〔maintain〕 *oneself;* earn *one's* living 〔livelihood〕; make a 〔*one's*〕 living; make the pot boil.
⑩ 《공을》 render 《distinguished services》; perform 《meritorious deeds》. ¶ 공을 ～ perform a feat; do a meritorious deed / 업적을 ～ produce achievements.
⑪ 《기대놓다》 put 〔rest, lean〕 《*a thing*》 against. ¶ 우산을〔사다리를〕 벽에 ～ stand an umbrella 〔a ladder〕 against the wall.
⑫ 《체면을》 save *one's* face 〔honor〕; keep up 《appearances》.
⑬ 《어떤 위치에》 put up; set; have 《*a person*》 over (추대하다). ¶ 두목으로 ～ place 《*a person*》 at the head / 보증인을 ～ give 〔find〕 surety 〔security〕 《for》 / 왕으로 ～ set 《*a person*》 on the throne / 후보를 ～ put up a candi-

date; have《*a person*》stand for《the House》.
⑭《기타》¶ 기강을 ～ enforce 〔maintain〕 discipline / 고집을 ～ be obstinate 〔stubborn〕; have *one's* own way; stick to《*one's* position》doggedly / 명분을 ～ justify *oneself* 〔*one's* conduct〕 / (말의) 조리를 ～ make《*one's* story》consistent; make《it》coherent / 위엄을 ～ show 〔get on〕 *one's* dignity; keep *one's* dignity.

**세워총**(一銃)〖군사〗《구령》Order arms! ～하다 order arms.

**세원**(稅源) a source of 「tax revenue 〔taxation〕; 《과세 대상》 an object of taxation.

**세월**(歲月) ①《시일》 time (and tide). ¶ ～이 감에 따라서 with the lapse of time; as time passes by; as days 〔the years〕 go by / ～을 헛되이 보내다 pass time idly; idle 〔dawdle〕 *one's* time away / 바쁜 ～을 보내다 have a busy time / ～이 유수 같다 Time flies. / ～은 사람을 기다리지 않는다 Time and tide wait for no man.
②《시세·경기》 (the) times; things; business; the market; conditions. ¶ ～이 좋다〔나쁘다〕 Times are good 〔bad〕. / 요즘 ～이 어떻습니까 How goes it with you? *or* How is your business these days? / ～이 별로 없습니다 Business is kind of slow. *or* Business 〔The market〕 is dull. *or* Trade is bad.

**세율**(稅率) tax rates; the rate of taxation; a tariff (관세의). ¶ ～ 변경 the modification of the tax rates / 고정〔보통, 단일, 협정, 특혜, 호혜〕 ～ a statutory 〔general, single, conventional, preferential, reciprocal〕 tariff / ～을 올리다〔내리다〕 raise 〔lower〕 the tax rates 〔the tariff (관세의)〕 / ～을 정하다 tariff《goods》. ◉ ～표 a table of tax rates; a tariff. 수입～ the import rates of duty.

**세이레**〖민속〗《삼칠일》 the 21st day after a baby's birth.

**세이프**〖야구〗 safe. ¶ 3루에서 간신히 ～되다 be narrowly safe at third (base) / 심판은 ～를 선언했다 The umpire declared safe.

**세인**(世人) people; the world; the (general) public. ¶ ～의 이목을 피하다 avoid public notice; slip from the sight of the world / 이 사건은 ～을 놀라게 했다 The incident surprised the world.

**세인트루이스**《미국의 도시》 Saint Louis.

**세인트헬레나** 《아프리카 서안(西岸)의 섬》 Saint Helena.

**세일** a sale. ¶ 바겐～ a bargain sale.

**세일러복**(一服) a sailor 〔middy〕 blouse; a sailor suit. ¶ ～을 입은 소녀 a girl in a sailor blouse.

**세일즈맨** a salesman; 《지방으로 도는》 a traveling salesman; a commercial traveler; 《호별 방문의》 a house-to-house salesman.

**세입**(稅入) tax revenues 〔yields〕.

**세입**(歲入) 《국가의》 revenue; 《개인의》 an annual income. ◉ ～세출 revenue and expenditure. ～예산 명세서 a detailed statement of estimated revenue. ～예산안 a revenue bill. ～예산액 an estimated amount of revenue; estimated revenue. ～위원회 《영·미국 하원의》 the Committee on 〔of 《영》〕 Ways and Means.

**세자**(世子) the Crown Prince.

**세자**(細字) small type; small characters 〔letters〕; fine print.

**세전**(世傳) ～하다 hand down from generation to generation. ¶ ～지물 things handed down from generation to generation; heirlooms.

**세전**(歲前) ¶ ～에 before the New Year.

**세정**(世情) the state of society. ⇨ 물정.

**세정**(洗淨) washing; cleansing. ＝ 세척.

**세정**(稅政) tax administration. ¶ ～ 방향 the direction of tax administration.

**세제**(洗劑) a cleanser; cleaning material; a detergent; a detersive. ¶ 중성〔합성, 연성〕 ～ a neutral 〔synthetic, soft〕 detergent.

**세제**(稅制) the tax 〔taxation〕 system. ¶ ～의 합리화 rationalization of tax system. ◉ ～개혁 a tax reform 〔revision〕. ～혜택 a tax favor 〔privilege〕: 각종 ～ 혜택을 주다 give various tax favors《to》.

**세제곱**〖수학〗 cubing; cube. ～하다 cube; raise《a number》to the third power; multiply《a number》「by its square 〔twice by itself〕. ¶ 3의 ～은 27이다 The cube of 3 is 27. ◉ ～근 a cube root: ～근풀이 extraction of the cubic root. ～비 a triple ratio.

**세존**(世尊) Buddha. ⇨ 석가.

**세종문화회관**(世宗文化會館) the Sejong Cultural Center.

**세주다**(貰一) hire (out); let out (on hire); 《집을》 rent《a house to *a person*》《미》; let《영》; 《토지를》 lease 《the land》. ¶ 배를 시간제로 ～ hire out a boat by the hour / 방을 ～ take in roomers 〔lodgers〕; rent a room 《미》; let a room 《영》.

**세차**(洗車) car washing. ~하다 wash a car. ◉ ~장〔업〕 a car wash.

**세차다** (be) powerful; mighty; violent; vigorous; energetic. ¶ 세찬 물결 rough waves / 바람이 세차게 분다 The wind blows hard.

**세차(운동)**(歲差(運動)) 〖천문〗 precession (of the equinoxes). ¶ ~의 precessional.

**세찬**(歲饌) ① 《음식》 food for treating New Year's guests. ② 《선물》 New Year's gifts.

**세척**(洗滌) washing; cleansing; rinsing; 〖의학〗 irrigation; lavage; 《수술 후의》 toilet. ~하다 wash; rinse out 《impurities》; deterge; 〖외과〗 irrigate; syringe. ¶ 위(胃)를 ~하다 carry out a lavage of *a person's* stomach; wash out *one's* stomach; administer a stomach pump 《to *a person*》.
◉ ~기 a cleansing device; a syringe; a washer. ~제 a wash; a lotion; a cleanser; an abstergent; a detergent.

**세출**(歲出) annual expenditure(s).
◉ ~예산액 estimated expenditures. ~ 외 자금 nonappropriated funds. ~ 위원회 《미국 하원의》 the House Appropriation Committee.

**세칙**(細則) detailed rules 〔regulations〕; 「bylaws.

**세칭**(世稱) the so-called; what is known as; what is called; what you 〔they, people〕 call. ¶ ~ 일류대학 a so-called prestige university.

**세컨드** ① 〖야구〗 《2루》 (the) second (base); 《2루수》 a second baseman. ② 〖권투〗 a second. ③ 《시간의 초》 a second. ④ 《첩》 *one's* secondary wife; a (kept) mistress.

**세탁**(洗濯) wash; washing; laundry; cleaning. ~하다 wash; launder; clean; do *one's* washing 〔wash〕. ¶ ~에 견디다 wash; be washable 〔washfast〕; stand 〔bear〕 washing / ~하러 보내다 send on 〔out〕 《*one's* clothes》 for laundry / ~해도 줄지 않다 do not shrink in the wash / 그는 하루 걸러 ~한다 He does the washing every other day. ◉ ~기 a washing machine. ~물 wash; washing; laundry. ~비 laundry charges. ~비누 laundry 〔washing〕 soap. ~소 a laundry; a launderette (빨래방); a cleaner's. ~업자 a laundryman; a washerman.

**세태**(世態) a phase 〔an aspect〕 of life; a sign of the times; social conditions; the way 〔order〕 of the world. ¶ TV드라마에서 요즘 ~의 한 단면을 볼 수 있다 A present aspect of life can be 「seen 〔watched〕 on television play. / 대중 가요는 ~를 반영한다 Popular songs reflect the social conditions (of the day). ◉ ~인정(人情) the manners 〔ways〕 of the world.

**세터** 《사냥개》 a setter; 〖배구〗 a setter.

**세톱**(細―) a fine-tooth saw.

**세트** ① 《한 벌》 a set 《of》. ¶ 응접 ~ a drawing-room suite / 커피 ~ a coffee set; a coffee service / 세 개 한 ~ a three-piece set 〔suite (가구)〕. ② 《장치》 a setting; 《영화의》 a (film) set; a studio set. ③ 《수신기》 a receiving set. ¶ 텔레비전 ~ a television set. ④ 《퍼머넌트의》 a (wave) set. ~하다 get 〔give〕 a permanent wave; apply a wave set to the hair. ¶ 머리를 ~하다 set *a person's* 〔*one's*〕 hair. ⑤ 《테니스 등의》 a set. ¶ ~포인트 a set point / 3 ~의 경기 a three-set match. ◉ ~디자인 set design.

**세트포지션** 〖야구〗 the (pitcher's) set 「position.

**세파**(世波) the rough-and-tumble of life. ¶ ~에 시달리다 be buffeted about by the storms of life; be tossed about in the storms of life; go through the hardships of life; meet with the rough dealings of the world / 모진 ~를 견디어 나가다 stand up under the wear and tear of the world.

**세평**(世評) public opinion; popular judgment 〔verdict〕; popularity; hearsay; rumor (소문). ¶ ~에 의하면 according to public opinion; People 〔They〕 say that...; Rumor has it that...; It is said 〔reported〕 that... / ~에 오르다 get 〔be〕 talked about; be the talk of the town; become common talk / ~을 두려워하다 be afraid of what people say; be shy of popular judgment / ~을 무시하다 be indifferent 「to praise or censure 〔to public opinion〕; do not care about what people say / ~이 좋다〔나쁘다〕 have a good 〔bad, poor〕 reputation; be well 〔ill〕 spoken of.

**세포**(細胞) ① 〖생물〗 a cell. ¶ ~의 cellular. ② 《조직·단체의》 a cell. ¶ 공산당 ~ a Communist cell 〔fraction〕 / 지하 ~ an underground cell / ~를 조직하다 organize a cell.
◉ ~막 cell membrane. ~병리학 cytopathology. ~분열 cell division. ~유전학 cytogenetics. ~조직 (the) cel-

lular tissue. ～질 protoplasm; cytoplasm: ～질의 cytoplasmic; cellular. ～체 a cell body. ～학 cytology: ～학자 a cytologist. ～핵 a (cell) nucleus (*pl.* -clei, ～es). ～형성〔발생〕 cytogenesis.

**섹션** 《부분·구역》 a section.

**섹스** sex. ¶ ～의 산업화 sexploitation / ～하다 have sex 《with》; make love 《to》. ◉ ～심볼 a sex symbol. ～어필 sex appeal; sexual attractiveness; it 《구어》: ～ 어필하다 have (a lot of) sex appeal; be sexually attractive.

**섹시하다** (be) sexy; sexually attractive 〔appealing〕. ¶ 섹시한 여자 a sexy 〔glamour〕 girl; a sexpot 《구어》.

**섹트주의**(—主義) sectarianism. ◉ ～자 a sectarian.

**센말** 〖언어〗 an intensive 〔emphatic〕 variant of a word.

**센머리** gray hair (반백); white 〔hoary〕 hair (순백). ¶ ～가 나다 [머리가 주어] *one's* hair turns 〔goes〕 gray 〔white〕; [사람이 주어] go gray 〔white〕.

**센물** 《경수(硬水)》 hard water.

**센서** 《감지기》 a sensor.

**센서스** 《국세 조사》 《take》 a census.

**센세이션** sensation. ¶ 일대 ～을 불러일으키다 create 〔cause〕 a great sensation 〔stir〕 《in the medical world》.

**센스** a sense; perception. ¶ ～가 있다〔없다〕 have good 〔no, poor〕 sense / ～가 빠르다〔무디다〕 have a quick 〔slow〕 perception; be sharp 〔dull〕 / 음악에 ～가 있다〔없다〕 have 「a good 〔no〕 musical sense; have an 〔no〕 ear for music.

**센터** ① 〖야구〗 (the) center field; 《사람》 a center fielder (중견수). ② 《중심지·시설》 a center 《of trade, business, *etc.*》. ◉ ～포워드〔하프〕 〖축구〗 a center forward 〔half(back)〕.

**센터플라이** 〖야구〗 a fly ball to center; a center fly ball. ¶ ～를 치다〔쳐서 잡히다〕 fly 〔fly out〕 to center.

**센털** ① 《희어진 털》 gray fur; white 〔hoary〕 hair 〔fur〕. ② 《빳빳한》 a bristle; a stiff hair.

**센트** a cent (생략 c.; 기호 ¢). ¶ 1달러 14～ one dollar and fourteen cents.

**센티** 《미터법의》 centi-; 《센티미터》 a centimeter (생략 cm). ◉ ～그램 a centigram (생략 cg). ～리터 a centiliter (생략 cl).

**센티멘털리즘** 《감상주의》 sentimentalism.

**센티멘털하다** be sentimental. ¶ 센티멘털해지다 become sentimental.

**셀러리** 〖식물〗 celery.

**셀로판** cellophane. ◉ ～지(紙) cellophane paper. ～테이프 cellophane adhesive tape; 《상표명》 Cellotape; Scotch tape.

**셀룰로오스** 〖화학〗 cellulose.

**셀룰로이드** 〖화학〗 celluloid. ◉ ～판 sheet celluloid.

**셀프서비스** self-service. ¶ ～식 가게 a self-service store / 우리는 ～ 식당에서 점심을 먹는다 We have lunch at a self-service restaurant 〔a cafeteria〕.

**셀프타이머** 〖사진〗 a self-timer; an auto-timer. ¶ ～가 장치된 카메라 a camera with a built-in self-timer.

**셈** ① 《계산》 calculation; computation; counting; reckoning. ⇨ 셈하다①. ¶ 셈이 바른 calculating / 셈에 넣다 figure in; 《고려하다》 take 《*a thing*》 into consideration 〔account〕 / 셈에 넣지 않다 leave 《*a thing*》 out of account; count 〔reckon〕 without 《*something*》 / 셈을 잘하다〔잘못하다〕 be good 〔poor〕 at figures 〔sums, reckoning〕 / 셈이 맞다 the figures add up; the accounts tally / 셈이 빠르다〔느리다〕 be quick 〔slow〕 at figures 〔accounts〕 / 셈이 틀리다 make an error 〔a mistake〕 in calculation / 셈은 셈이다 Business is business. / 요금은 거리로 셈한다 Fares are reckoned by the distance.

② 《지불》 settlement of accounts; payment of bills. ⇨ 셈하다②. ¶ 셈을 치르다 pay a bill; settle *one's* accounts / 셈을 미루다 postpone 〔put off, delay〕 payment / 셈을 치르고 호텔을 나오다 pay *one's* bill at a hotel and leave; check out 《미》 / 셈이 불어나다 *one's* bills run up / 셈해 주세요 My check 〔bill 《영》〕 please! / 셈이 틀린 것 같군요 I am afraid there is a mistake in the bill. / 셈이 모두 얼마나 되나요 How much does the whole account come to? *or* How much will they be altogether? *or* How much is my bill? *or* How much do I owe you? / 셈은 현금으로 하십니까 Are you paying (in) cash?

③ 《셈판》 the situation; the matter; reason; cause. ⇨ 셈판. ¶ 어찌된 셈인지 for what reason; somehow; why.

④ 《속셈·작정》 an intention; a design; an idea; 《동기》 a motive; 《예기》 an expectation. ¶ …할 셈으로 with the intention 〔aim, idea〕 of…; with a view to; from 〔through〕 motives / 그가 어쩔 셈인지 도무지 모르겠다 I cannot quite see 〔understand〕 his motive 〔idea〕. / 나는 오전중으로 돌아올 셈입니

다 I expect to come back before noon. / 자네 그럴 셈이었나 Is that what you intended?
⑤ 《분별》 sense; discretion; judgment. ⇨ 셈나다. ¶ 셈이 없다 have no sense / 나이가 들어야 셈이 난다 Sense comes with age.

**셈나다** grow sensible; acquire common sense; mature. ¶ 인제야 셈(이)났구나 You are a man 〔young lady〕 now. / 그는 아직도 셈이 나지 않았다 He is still wet behind the ears.

**셈들다** = 셈나다.

**셈본** arithmetic. ¶ ~의 arithmetic(al).

**셈속** ① 《속 내용》 the inside details 〔story〕; the real state of things. ② 《속뜻》 an ulterior 〔underlying〕 motive; a hidden intention; a secret intention 〔desire〕; a personal interest. ¶ ~이 있다 have a secret intention / 무언가 ~이 있어서 for some hidden object / 그의 ~을 모르겠다 I do not know what he has in mind. / 그에게는 ~이 있다 He has 「an ulterior motive 〔a secret intention〕.

**셈치다** 《가정》 suppose; assume; grant (that...). ¶ 자네가 오는 셈치고 준비하겠네 I am preparing on the supposition that you will come. / 저녁 한끼 잘 먹은 셈치고 적십자사에 20,000원을 기부했다 I donated 20,000 won to the Red Cross, pretending to myself that I had eaten a nice dinner with the money. / 죽을 셈치고 휴전선을 넘었다 I crossed the armistice line at the risk of my life. / 그것은 잃어버린 셈치자 Let us suppose that we lost it.

**셈판** 《형편》 the situation; circumstances; the matter; the case; 《까닭》 reason; cause. ⇨ 셈 ③. ¶ 무슨 ~인지 모르겠다 I don't know how the matter stands. *or* I cannot make head or tail of it. / 그가 오지 않으니 무슨 ~일까 What's the matter with him that he doesn't come?

**셈평펴이다** become better off; see easier days; live in ease 〔comfort, plenty〕; be well to do; have *one's* prospects improve. ¶ 셈평펴일 날이 없다 I have no chance to get on in the world.

**셈하다** ① 《계산을》 count; reckon; calculate; do 〔work〕 a sum 〔sums〕. ¶ 손가락을 꼽아 ~ count on *one's* fingers / 주판으로 ~ reckon on the abacus / 이자를 ~ compute interest.
② 《치르다》 pay 〔make out〕 a bill; settle *one's* account; settle 〔square〕 accounts 《with *a person*》.

**셋** three.

**셋돈**(貰—) rent (money). ¶ ~을 내다 pay *one's* rent.

**셋방**(貰房) a room 「for rent 《미》 〔to let 《영》〕; a rented room (세든). ¶ ~ 있음 《게시》 Rooms 「for rent 〔to let 《영》〕. *or* Vacancy. / ~ 구함 《광고》 Room wanted. / ~을 얻다 take 〔rent〕 a room; find 〔take〕 lodgings; 《미》 room 《in *a person's* house》. ◉ **~살이** a living in a rented room: ~살이를 하다 live in a rented room; live in lodgings.

**셋붙이** 《셋갖춤》 a three-piece suit; a suit of clothes (신사복의).

**셋집**(貰—) a house 「for rent 《미》 〔to let 《영》〕; a rented house; 《빈민들의》 a tenement (house). ¶ ~을 구하다 hunt 〔look〕 for a house 「for rent 〔to let〕 / ~을 얻다 rent a house / ~에 살다 live in a rented house / ~ 있음 《게시》 For rent. 《미》 *or* To let. 《영》

**셋째** the third.

**셍기다** ① 《말을》 talk away; rattle on 〔off〕; say in rapid-fire order; 《구어》 talk *one's* head off. ② 《일거리를》 provide; supply (continuously); feed 《work, jobs, tasks》 to 《*a person*》; keep 《*a person*》 hopping with one 《job》 after another.

**셔링** 《장식 주름》 shirring.

**셔츠** 《속옷》 an undershirt; 《와이셔츠》 a shirt; a dress shirt. ¶ ~ 바람으로 in *one's* shirt-sleeves 〔undershirt〕.

**셔터** ① 《사진기의》 a shutter; a shutter release button. ¶ ~를 누르다 release the shutter; press the shutter release button. ② 《문》 a shutter. ¶ ~를 내리다 pull down a shutter.
◉ 자동~ an automatic shutter.

**셧아웃** 〖야구〗 a shutout (game). ¶ ~시키다 shut out 《the opposing team》 / ~당하다 get a shutout.

**셰르파** 《티베트계 네팔인》 a Sherpa (*pl.* ~(s)).

**셰리** 《포도주》 sherry.

**셰익스피어** 《영국의 극작가·시인》 William Shakespeare (1564-1616). ¶ ~의 Shakespearian / ~ 전집 the Complete Works of Shakespeare.

**셰퍼드** 《미》 a German shepherd (dog); 《영》 an Alsatian.

**소**[1] 〖동물〗 [집합적] cattle; a bull (황소); a cow (암소); 《거세한》 an ox (*pl.* oxen); a bullock; a steer (식용). ¶ 소 100마리 a hundred head of cattle (★

head는 단·복수 동형) / 소를 기르다[치다] keep cows; raise cattle / 소걸음으로 걷다 walk at a snail's pace / 소처럼 먹다 eat like a horse / 소처럼 부리다 use《*a person*》like a beast of burden / 덴 소 날치듯 하다 make a great fuss [uproar] / 소 닭 보듯 닭 소 보듯 하다 stare vacantly (with no interest) / 소 잃고 외양간 고친다《속담》To lock the stable door after the horse has bolted. *or* After death, the doctor. / 소꼬리보다 닭머리《속담》Better be the head of a dog than the tail of a lion.
◉ 소도둑 a rustler《구어》; a cattle thief. 소떼 a herd of cattle. 수입소 imported cattle.

**소**[2]《만두·떡의》dressing; stuffing. ¶ 팥소 bean jam / 만두[빵]에 소를 넣다 stuff a dumpling [bun].

**소**(小) [형용사적] small; little; minor; lesser; miniature. ¶ 소도시 a small town / 소위원회 a subcommittee / 소를 죽이고 대(大)를 살리다 amputate a limb to save the body; kill a few to save the many.

**소**(沼) a swamp; a marsh; a bog. ¶ 소가 많다 be marshy; be swampy; be boggy.

**소가족**(小家族) a small family. ◉ ～제도 the small-family system.

**소가지**《심지》nature; disposition; temperament. ¶ ～가 나쁘다 be ill-natured.

**소각**(燒却) destruction by fire; incineration. ～하다 destroy《*a thing*》by fire; incinerate; burn (up); commit《*a thing*》to the flames; throw《*a thing*》into the fire; reduce to ashes.
◉ ～기[로(爐)] an incinerator; a trash burner.

**소간사**(所幹事)《볼일》business; affairs.
◉ 일상～ the daily routine.

**소갈머리** = 소가지.

**소갈증**(消渴症) 〖한의학〗 a disease symptomized by thirst.

**소감**(所感) *one's* impressions [thoughts, opinions]. ¶ ～을 말하다 give *one's* impressions《of》; give [express] *one's* opinion [view]《on》/ 이 일에 관해서 몇 마디 ～을 말씀 드리겠습니다 Let me say a few words about this.

**소강**(小康) a (temporary) lull; a breathing space; a brief period of tranquility; 《have, enjoy》a (brief) respite《from the enemy's》attacks.
¶ ～ 상태가 되다 come to a (state of) lull / 증권 시장은 ～ 상태에 있다 The stock market is having 「a temporary lull [a breathing space]. / 중동 정세는 ～ 상태에 있다 The Middle East is going through a brief period of tranquility.

**소개**(紹介) ①《알게 함》(an) introduction. ～하다 introduce; present. ¶ …의 ～로 on the introduction of…; with an introduction from… / 정식으로 ～하다 make a formal introduction; introduce《Miss A》formally to《Mr. B》/ 일동에게 ～하다 introduce《*a person*》all around / …한테 ～를 청하다 seek an introduction from… / ～받다 have the honor [pleasure] of being introduced / …라고 자기 ～를 하다 introduce *oneself* as… / 내 친구 김군을 ～하겠습니다 Let me [Allow me to] introduce [present] my friend Mr. Kim. *or* I'd like you to meet my friend Mr. Kim. / 방금 ～받은 김입니다 My name is Kim as has been mentioned in my introduction. *or* I am Kim who has had the honor of being introduced to you.
②《주선》good [kind] offices; references (직업의); 《추천》recommendation; 《중개》mediation; agency. ～하다 use [exercise, lend] *one's* good offices; use *one's* influence; recommend; 《중개하다》mediate《between》; intercede《with A for B》; act as an agent. ¶ …의 ～로 by [through] the good offices of《Mr. A》; through the agency of《a broker》/ 일자리를 ～하다 get [find]《*a person*》a job.
◉ ～료 brokerage; a commission. ～업 brokerage; commission agency; go=between business: ～업자 an (employment) agent. ～자 an introducer; 《주선인》a go-between; 《추천인》a recommender.

**소개**(疏開)《퇴거》(an) evacuation; 《산개》dispersal; deployment (군대의); 《철거》removal. ～하다《물러나다》evacuate; be evacuated (전쟁 등으로); move [flee] to《a place》for safety; 《흩다》disperse; 《제거하다》remove; thin out. ¶ 집단 ～ an evacuation in a group [body] / 시골로 ～하다 evacuate into the country / 공장을 ～하다 dismantle a plant [mill].
◉ ～자 an evacuee. ～지 *one's* place of refuge. 강제～ forced removal; compulsory evacuation.

**소개념**(小槪念) 〖논리〗 minor (term).

**소개장**(紹介狀) a letter of introduction.
¶ ～을 받다 get a letter of introduc-

tion《to》/ ～을 써주다 write a letter of introduction《for *a person*》.

**소거**(消去) ①〖수학〗elimination. ～하다 eliminate. ②《말소》erasure. ～하다 erase.

**소견**(所見) *one's* view〔opinion〕; *one's* impressions. ¶ ～을 말하다 give〔set forth〕*one's* view〔opinion〕《on》; express *one's* impressions《of》/ ～을 묻다 ask for《*a person's*》opinion / 이 문제에 대한 ～을 여쭙고 싶습니다 Please let me know what you think〔feel〕about this issue. ◉ ～표 a school report; a report on a student's record. 진단～ a diagnostic view; *one's* diagonosis and observations《entered on a patient's clinical record card》.

**소결절**(小結節)〖병리·식물〗a nodule.

**소경** ①《맹인》a blind〔sightless〕person; [총칭] the blind. ¶ ～의 blind; sightless; eyeless / ～이 되다 become〔go〕blind; lose *one's* (eye)sight / ～단청 구경 be a wasted〔unappreciated〕sight / ～ 매질하듯 doing a slipshod job of it. ②《문맹자》an illiterate;《무식자》an ignorant person.

**소계**(小計) a subtotal. ¶ ～를 내다 subtotal; do a partial sum / ～ 1만 원이다 It subtotals ten thousand won.

**소고**(小鼓) a small hand drum; a tabor. ◉ ～잡이 a tabor〔small-drum〕player.

**소고**(小考) a short article; a study〔poetry〕; a sketch.

**소곡**(小曲) a short piece of music

**소곳이** with *one's* head drooped. ¶ 머리를 ～ 숙이다 lower *one's* head《with shame, modesty》.

**소관**(所管) jurisdiction; control; competency. ¶ 교육부 ～ 사항 matters under the jurisdiction of the Education Ministry /…의 ～에 속하다 fall under the jurisdiction of...; be under the control of...; belong in the competance of... (법정의) /…의 ～ 밖이다 be beyond〔outside〕the jurisdiction of... / 이 사건은 우리 ～ 밖이다 This matter doesn't come within our jurisdiction. *or* This case is beyond our competence. (법정의) ◉ ～관청 the competent〔proper〕authorities; the authorities concerned.

**소관**(所關) what is concerned; matters concerned. ◉ ～사(事) *one's* business; *one's* concern.

**소구**〖악기〗a tabor. ⇨ 소고.

**소국**(小國) a small〔minor〕country; a weak nation; a lesser〔minor〕power.

**소굴**(巢窟) a den; a haunt; a nest; a hotbed; a hangout《미구어》. ¶ 도둑의 ～ a den〔haunt〕of robbers / 범죄의 ～ a hotbed of crime.

**소권**(訴權)〖법〗the right to bring an action in a court《against *a person* for *a matter*》.

**소규모**(小規模) a small scale. ¶ ～의 small-scale; on a small scale;《a project》of small dimensions / ～로 on a small scale; in a small way / 그의 사업은 ～로 운영되고 있다 His business is operated on a small scale.

**소극**(消極) ¶ ～적(인) negative; passive / ～적 정책 a negative policy / ～적 전법 passive tactics / ～적 저항 a passive resistance / ～적으로 negatively; passively / ～적인 태도를 취하다 take a negative attitude; act passively / 그녀는 매사에 ～적이다 She is passive in every affairs.

◉ ～성 passivity; passiveness. ～주의 negativism: ～주의자 a negativist.

**소극**(笑劇) a farce.

**소극장**(小劇場) a little theater.

**소금** salt. ¶ ～에 절이다 salt (down); preserve〔pickle〕《vegetables》in〔with〕salt / ～에 절인 salted; pickled〔preserved〕with salt / ～을 넣지 않은 unsalted《butter》/ ～을 뿌리다 scatter a pinch of salt; throw out some salt (액막이로) / (음식에) ～을 치다 sprinkle salt on《fish》; sprinkle《fish》with salt / ～을 찍어 먹다 eat《*a thing*》with salt.

◉ ～기 a salty taste; saltiness: ～기 있는 물 brackish water. ～물 salt water: ～물로 입안을 가시다 rinse (out)〔gargle〕*one's* mouth with salt water / ～물에 담그다 soak〔steep〕in brine. ～버캐 salt incrustation. ～엣밥 a poor meal; plain fare〔food〕. ～쩍 lumps of salt in a substance.

**소금구이** ¶ ～로 하다 broil《fish》with salt.

**소금쟁이**〖곤충〗a pond skater; a water strider.

**소급**(遡及) going back《to the past》; retroactivity; retroaction. ～하다 go〔trace〕back《to the past》; retroact《to》; be retroactive《to》; retrospect《to》. ¶ ～해서 retroactively / 법률을 ～해서 적용하다 apply a law retroactive to《March 1》/ 새 급여는 5월 1일로 ～하여 지급된다 The new pay scales are retroactive to May 1st. / 본법은 5월 1일자로 ～하여 효력을 갖는다 This law is effective retroactive to May 1.

◉ ～력 retroactive〔retrospective〕

power; retroactivity: ~력을 가진 retroactive. ~법 a retrospective 〔retroactive〕 law.

**소기**(所期) ¶ ~의 expected; anticipated; hoped-for / ~한 바와 같이 as *one* expected; as was expected; as might have been expected / ~의 목적을 달성하다 realize the object *one* had in mind; attain the desired end / ~의 성적을 올리다 achieve the expected results / 인내하지 않으면 ~의 목적을 달성할 수 없다 You'll never get what you want unless you persevere.

**소꿉** toy flatware 〔kitchenware〕; a toy used in playing house. ◉ ~놀이〔장난〕= 소꿉질. ~동무 a friend of *one's* early childhood; a childhood playmate.

**소꿉질** playing house; playing at housekeeping. ~하다 play (at) house; play at housekeeping.

**소나기** a shower; a passing rain; a squall (열대의). ¶ 큰 ~ a heavy shower / ~가 오다 it showers / ~가 지나가다 a shower passes / ~를 만나다 be caught in 〔overtaken by〕 a shower / ~가 쏟아질 것 같다 It looks like a shower. / 대체로 흐리고 가끔 ~가 오겠다 It is cloudy with occasional showers. ◉ ~구름 a shower cloud; a cumulonimbus. ~밥 sudden overeating (by someone of a usually modest appetite). ~술 sudden overdrinking (of liquor by an unlikely person).

**소나무** 『식물』 a pine (tree). ◉ ~숲 a pine grove. ~잎 《솔잎》 pine needles.

**소나타** 『음악』 a sonata. ¶ ~ 형식으로 in sonata form.

**소낭**(嗉囊) a crop. ⇨ 멀떠구니.

**소네트** a sonnet. ◉ ~시인 a sonneteer.

**소녀**(少女) a (young) girl; a maiden. ¶ ~다운 girlish; maidenly; maidenlike / 10대 ~ a girl in her teens; a teenage(d) girl.
◉ ~단 the Girl Scouts 〔Guides 《영》〕: ~단원 a girl scout; a girl guide 《영》. ~시절 *one's* young girlhood (days). ~취미 (school)girlish tastes.

**소년**(少年) a boy; a lad. ¶ ~다운 boyish 《ardor》 / ~ 소녀 가장 a young family head; children 〔juvenile〕 family heads / 불량 ~ a bad 〔delinquent〕 boy / 비행 ~ a juvenile delinquent / ~은 늙기 쉽고 학문은 이루기 어렵다 Do as much learning as possible while you are young, for memory soon grows feeble.
◉ ~단 the Boy Scouts: ~단원 a boy scout. ~범죄 juvenile crime 〔delinquency〕: ~범죄자 a juvenile delinquent 〔offender〕. ~법 the Juvenile Act. ~보호 juvenile protection: ~ 보호소 a juvenile detention home. ~소녀 (young) boys and girls; [총칭] young people. ~시절 《in》 *one's* boyhood. ~원 a juvenile reformatory; a training school; an approved school 《영》. ~잡지 a children's magazine.

**소농**(小農) a small 〔petty〕 farmer; a peasant; [총칭] peasantry. ◉ ~가 a small farmer's household; a small farmer. ~제도 the peasant-proprietor 〔small-farm〕 system.

**소뇌**(小腦) 『해부』 the cerebellum (*pl.* ~s, -la).

**소닉붐** 《음속 돌파음》 a sonic boom.

**소다** soda. ◉ ~공업 the alkali manufacture. ~수 soda water 〔pop〕; a soda (pop) (한 잔). ~크래커 a soda cracker. ~회(灰) soda ash.

**소달구지** an oxcart.

**소담**(小膽) cowardice; timidity. ~하다 (be) cowardly; timid; fainthearted.

**소담스럽다** (be) appetizing; juicy 〔tasty〕 looking; delicious; look nice and ripe.

**소담하다** (be) pleasantly plump; buxom; big and beautiful; full; juicy; tasty; nice and ripe. ¶ 소담한 복숭아 a fat juicy peach / 소담한 꽃송이 a full=petaled flower / 소담하게 차린 식탁 a table with appetizing dishes.

**소대**(小隊) a platoon. ◉ ~장 a platoon leader 〔commander〕. 비행~ an element.

**소댕** a kettle cover 〔lid〕. ◉ ~꼭지 the handle of a kettle cover.

**소도**(小島) an islet; a small island.

**소도둑놈** ① 《도둑》 a cattle thief 〔rustler〕. ② 《욕심쟁이》 a greedy and bad-tempered person.

**소도록하다** ⇨ 수두룩하다.

**소도시**(小都市) a small(er) town.

**소독**(消毒) disinfection; sterilization; 《우유 따위의》 pasteurization; 《훈증으로》 fumigation. ~하다 disinfect 《a room》; sterilize; pasteurize; fumigate; sanitize. ¶ ~된 disinfected; sterilized; pasteurized / ~이 된 병 a sterilized bottle / 일광으로 ~하다 disinfect 《*a thing*》 by sunning 〔the sun's rays〕 / 끓는 물로 ~하다 sterilize in boiling water / 상처를 ~하다 disinfect the wound / 의사들은 기구를 사용한 후에는 매번 ~한다 Doctors sterilize their

instruments after each use. / 이 타월은 이미 ~되었다 This towel has already been sterilized.
◉ ~기 a sterilizer; a disinfector. ~력 the disinfective 〔sterilizing〕 power. ~붕대 sterilized bandages. ~수 an antiseptic solution. ~실 a disinfecting 〔sterilizing〕 room. ~약〔제〕 a disinfectant; an antiseptic. ~의〔복〕 a disinfected overgarment. ~저 sanitary 〔disposable, sterilized〕 chopsticks. 유황~ sulfur disinfection.

**소동**(騷動) 《법석》 (a) disturbance; (an) agitation; (an) uproar; an upheaval; 《혼란》 confusion; disorder; a row; a tumult; a commotion; 《분쟁》 a strife; a dispute; a trouble; 《폭동》 a riot; a rising; an uprising; 《싸움》 a quarrel; a brawl; a ruckus 《미》; 《사건》 an affair. ¶ ~이 일어나다〔벌어지다〕 a riot arises 〔breaks out〕 / ~을 일으키다〔벌이다〕 raise 〔make, create, cause〕 a disturbance 〔an uproar〕; start a riot; stir up「troubles 〔a riot〕; 《어떤 일이》 create a commotion; cause a stir / ~을 가라앉히다 quiet 〔suppress〕 a disturbance; quell 〔put down〕 a riot / 그는 학교에서 ~을 일으켰다 He stirred up trouble at school. / 그의 발언으로 정계에 ~이 일어날 것 같다 His remark may create a disturbance in the political world.

**소두**(小斗) a half-*mal* measure. 「륨.

**소듐** 〖화학〗 sodium (기호 Na). ⇨ 나트

**소득**(所得) 《수입》 (an) income; 《수익》 earnings; profits; gain. ¶ ~의 균형 분배 a balanced distribution of income / ~ 재분배 income redistribution / 그는 연 3,000만 원의 ~이 있다 He has a yearly income of thirty million won. /「그의 ~은 얼마나 될까」—「월 200만 원 정도일거야」 "How much 〔What〕 is his income ?"—"I guess he makes 〔gets, earns〕 about two million won a month." ◉ ~격차 the income disparity 《between》; the income gap. ~계층 the income bracket. ~공제 (a) deduction (from *one's* income); income deduction (to reduce tax): ~공제액 a tax deduction; an amount deducted from *one's* income. ~배증안(倍增案) the income-doubling program. ~분배 income distribution. ~수준 an income level 〔standard〕 《of the nation》. ~위장 분산 camouflaged diversion of income earnings (for tax evasion). ~자 an income earner 〔obtainer〕: 고〔저〕~자 a large 〔small〕 income earner 〔obtainer〕; people in the upper 〔lower〕 income brackets. ~정책 an incomes policy. ~층 an income group: 고(高)~층 the high-income brackets.

**소득세**(所得稅) an income tax. ◉ ~법 the Income Tax Law. ~액 the amount of *one's* income tax. 개인~ the individual income tax. 초과~ an excess income tax.

**소득액**(所得額) (the amount of) *one's* income. ¶ ~의 사정(査定) assessment of *one's* income / ~을 신고하다 make 〔file〕 income tax returns.

**소등**(消燈) ~하다 put 〔turn〕 out the lights; switch the lights off. ◉ ~나팔 《sound》 taps (흔히 단수 취급). ~시간 the hour for putting out lights; lights-out: ~ 시간은 12시다 Lights-out is twelve o'clock. *or* Lights go out at twelve. / 그는 ~시간 후에 기숙사에서 몰래 빠져 나갔다 After lights-out he tiptoed out of our dormitory.

**소띠** the characteristics of (*one* born under the sign of) the Ox.

**소라** ① 〖조개〗 a turban 〔wreath〕 shell; a turbo (*pl.* turbines, ~s). ② 〖악기〗 a trumpet shell; a conch horn. ¶ ~를 불다 blow a trumpet shell. ◉ ~게 〖동물〗 a hermit 〔soldier〕 crab; a pagurian. ~고둥 〖조개류〗 a conch; a trumpet shell. ~딱지 the shell of a turbo. ~젓 salted turbos.

**소락소락하다** (be) frivolous; light.

**소란**(騷亂) 《소동》 a disturbance; a commotion; (a) disorder; 《분쟁》 troubles; 《폭동》 a riot; fuss; bustle; stir; 《시끄러움》 (a) noise; (an) uproar. ~하다, ~스럽다 (be) disturbing; noisy. ¶ ~한 교실 a noisy classroom / ~을 피우다 make a noise; 《사건으로》 create a public commotion; raise 〔create〕 a disturbance / 술에 취해 ~을 피우다 make a commotion under alcoholic influence / 민심을 ~케 하다 stir up public sentiment / 경찰은 ~을 가라앉혔다 The police quieted 〔put down〕 the disorder. / ~ 피우지 마라 Don't make a scene. 《미》 / 이런 일로 동네를 ~케 해서 미안합니다 I am sorry this has caused such anxiety to my neighbors. ◉ ~죄 the crime of riot. ⇨ 소요죄.

**소략하다**(疎略―) (be) rough; careless; negligent; inattentive; cursory.

**소량**(少量) a small quantity 〔amount,

portion, dose〕; a little; a bit; a dash. ¶ ～ 거래 transactions in small lots / ～ 주문 a petty order / 물에 ～의 브랜디를 타다 put a dash of brandy in the water.

**소련**(蘇聯) 《독립 국가 연합 이전의》 the Soviet Union; Soviet Russia; the U.S.S.R. [<the *U*nion of *S*oviet *S*ocialist *R*epublics]

**소령**(少領) 〖육군〗 a major; 〖해군〗 a lieutenant commander; 〖공군〗 a major 《미》.

**소로**(小路) a (narrow) path; an alley; ⌈a lane; a trail.

**소론**(所論) *one's* view 〔opinion〕; what *one* holds (as an opinion); the view *one* holds.

**소르르** ① 《풀리는 모양》 《untangle》 easily; smoothly; readily. ¶ (허리띠가) ～ 풀어지다 slip off / 엉힌 실이 토리에서 ～ 풀리다 the threads of a tangled skein unravel easily. ② 《바람이 부는 모양》 gently; softly. ¶ 바람이 ～ 불다 a breeze blows softly. ③ 《졸음이 오는 모양》 ¶ 잠이 ～ 오다 sleep steals 《upon *a person*》.

**소름** goose pimples 〔bumps 《미》〕; gooseflesh. ¶ ～(이) 끼치는 hair-raising; bloodcurdling; horrible / ～이 끼치다 have 〔feel, get〕 goose pimples 〔bumps〕 / ～ 끼치게 하다 make *one's* blood run cold; make *one's* hair stand on end; curdle 〔chill〕 *one's* blood; give *one* goose pimples 〔cold shivers〕 / 생각만 해도 ～이 끼치다 shudder 〔be horrified〕 at the mere thought 〔idea〕 《of》 / ～ 끼치는 이야기다 The story makes my hair stand on end. *or* The story gives me goose pimples. / 이 끔찍한 광경에 그는 ～이 끼쳤다 His hair bristled at this dire sight.

**소리** ① 《음향》 (a) sound; 《소음》 a noise; a din; a report (총 따위의); a roar (굉음); clamor (계속되는 소음).

★ 영어에는 의성어가 꽤 많음 : a clatter 「접시·기계 따위의 소리」 / a crash 「깨지는 소리」 / a bang 「문 따위의 쾅 하는 소리」 / a splash 「물 튀기는 소리」 / a crack 「채찍 따위의 소리」 / a patter 「비 따위가 후두두후두두 내리는 소리」 / the creaking of shoes 「구둣소리」 / the babbling of a brook 「시냇물 소리」 / the boom of a gun 「대포 소리」 / a bump 「쿵하고 부딪는 소리」 / a thud 「쿵하고 떨어지는 소리」.

¶ 나팔〔북〕 ～ the sound of a trumpet 〔drum〕 / 맑은 ～ a clean and serene sound / (뱃 속의) 꾸루룩 ～ the rumbling of the stomach / 벨 ～ the ring of a bell / 파도 ～ the roar of the sea 〔waves〕 / 해변에 철썩거리는 파도 ～ the lapping of the waves / 폭포 ～ the roar 〔sound〕 of cataracts / 피아노 ～ notes of a piano / 나뭇잎의 살랑거리는 ～ a rustle of leaves; a murmur / 바이올린의 감미로운 소리 the sweet tones of a violin / 비가 지붕을 때리는 ～ the patter of rain on the roof / 천둥 ～에 놀라다 be frightened at (the sound of) thunder.

소리의: ～의 높이 pitch / ～의 세기 loudness.

소리가: ～가 안 나는 엔진 a silent 〔noiseless〕 engine / ～가 안 나는 자동차 a noiseless car / ～가 들리는 곳에서 within the sound 《of》 / ～가 나다 ⇨ ～를 내다 / ～가 듣기 싫다〔좋다〕 sound stiff 〔sweet, well〕.

소리를: ～를 내다 produce a sound; make a sound 〔noise〕; set up a noise / ～를 내는 물건 a noisemaker / ～를 내며 noisily; with a crash; with a (great) noise / ～를 내지 않고 silently; quietly; softly / ～를 죽이고 noiselessly; softly; quietly; stealthily / 큰 ～를 내며 폭발하다 explode with a loud report / …(의) ～를 듣고 at the sound of… / ～를 없애다 arrest 〔absorb〕 the noise 〔sound〕 / ～를 작게 하다 lower the volume 《of a stereo》; tone down 《a transistor》.

¶ 그 종은 깨진 ～가 난다 The bell sounds cracked. / ～가 전혀 들리지 않았다 Not a sound was heard. / 그는 ～없이 몰래 방으로 들어왔다 He stole into the room.

② 《목소리》 a voice; a tone (of voice); 《외치는 소리》 a cry; an outcry; 《새·벌레의》 notes; call; chirp; a song. ⇨ 목소리. ¶ 큰〔굵은, 가는, 낭랑한, 목쉰, 맑은〕 ～ a loud 〔deep, thin, sonorous, husky, clear〕 voice / 큰 ～로 in a loud voice; loudly / 작은 ～로 in whispers; in a low 〔small〕 voice / 쩌렁쩌렁 울리는 ～ a penetrating voice / 뻐꾸기 ～ a cuckoo's notes / ～(를) 지르다 cry; shout; yell out / ～ 내어 읽다 read aloud / 새된 ～를 지르다 give a shrill cry; shrill; shriek; give a scream / 날카로운 ～를 내다 utter a piercing shriek.

③ 《노래》 a folk song; a ballad. ¶ ～를 잘 하다 sing (a tune) well.

④ 《말》 talk; words. ¶ 이상한 ～ 같지만 it may sound strange, but… / 듣기 좋

은 ~를 하다 say pleasant things / 그게 무슨 ~냐 What do you mean? / 별 ~ 다 한다 The things you say! / 너 큰 ~ 치는구나 You talk big! / 그 녀석은 개~ 쇠~ 다 한다 He says all sorts of stupid 〔nasty〕 things.
⑤《소문》 a rumor; a report; news; an account. ¶ 그것은 터무니없는 ~다 The report is unfounded.
◉ ~굽쇠 〖물리〗 a tuning fork. ~글자 a phonetic symbol. ~꾼〔쟁이〕 a (ballad) singer. ~판 a record.

**소리**(小利) a small profit; a little gain. ¶ 목전의 ~에 눈이 어두워지다 be blinded by a small immediate profit.

**소리소리** ¶ ~ 지르다 yell; shout; bawl; holler.

**소리지르다** ＝소리치다.

**소리치다** cry; shout; bawl; holler; yell; give 〔utter〕 a cry; let out a yell. ¶ 성이 나서 ~ roar with anger / 도와 달라고 ~ cry 〔scream〕 for help / "도둑이야" 하고 ~ cry "Thief!" / 나는 귀머거리가 아니니 소리칠 것 없네 I'm not deaf, you needn't shout.

**소립자**(素粒子) 〖물리〗 an elementary particle. ◉ ~론 the theory of elementary particles. ~물리학 elementary particle physics.

**소말리아**《아프리카의 공화국》 Somalia. ¶ ~의 Somalian. ◉ ~사람 a Somali.

**소망**(所望) (a) desire; a wish; a request; 《기대》 hope; expectation. ~하다 desire; wish for; ask for; hope for; expect. ¶ ~에 따라 at 〔in compliance with〕 《*a person's*》 request; by request from 《*a person*》 / 간절한 ~ an ardent desire; an earnest wish / 오랜 ~ a long-cherished desire / ~을 이루다 realize *one's* desire 〔wishes〕; attain *one's* object; have *one's* wishes fulfilled.

**소망**(素望) *one's* long cherished wish; *one's* heart's desire; *one's* dream of dreams.

**소매** a sleeve; an arm (양복의). ¶ ~가 넓은 loose-〔full-〕sleeved / 긴〔짧은〕 ~ a long 〔short〕 sleeve / ~를 걷(어 올리)다 turn 〔roll, tuck〕 *one's* sleeves up; bare *one's* arms; 《양복》 turn 〔roll〕 up *one's* cuffs / ~를 잡다 hold 《*a person*》 by the sleeve; 《만류하다》 buttonhole 《*a person*》 / ~를 끌(어 당기)다 pull 《*a person*》 by the sleeve; solicit (창녀가) / ~에 매달리다 cling to 〔hang on〕 《*a person's*》 sleeve; 《애원하다》 implore 《*a person* to *do*》; appeal to 《*a person*》 for mercy / 눈물로 ~를 적시다 wet *one's* sleeves with tears / ~가 길면 춤을 잘 추고 돈이 많으면 장사를 잘 한다 《속담》 You can't get something for nothing. *or* It takes money to make money.
◉ ~길이 the length of a sleeve. ~통 the width of a sleeve. 소맷부리 a sleeve band; a cuff: 소맷부리를 뿌리치고 가다 tear *oneself* away. 소맷자락 the edges of a sleeve.

**소매**(小賣) retail(ing); retail sale. ~하다 retail; sell at 〔by 《영》〕 retail. ¶ ~로 at 〔by〕 retail / ~로 1파운드에 천 원이다 be a thousand won a pound at retail / 그들은 그것을 ~로는 결코 팔지 않는다 They never sell it at retail. / ~사절 《게시》 Wholesale 〔Trade (sales) 《영》〕 only.
◉ ~가격 the retail price. ~물가 지수 a retail price index. ~부 the retail section. ~시장 a retail market. ~업 retail trade. ~점 a retail store 〔shop〕.

**소매상**(小賣商) 《일》 retail trade; 《사람》 a retail dealer; a retailer. ¶ ~을 하다 carry on retail trade; run a retail business.

**소매치기** 《사람》 a pickpocket; 《행위》 pocket-picking. ~하다 pick 《*a person's*》 pocket. ¶ ~당하다 have *one's* pocket picked / ~ 조심 《게시》 Beware of 〔Look out for〕 pickpockets. / 현금을 인출할 때는 ~, 날치기를 조심하세요 When you draw cash, beware of pickpockets and snatchers.

**소맥**(小麥) wheat; corn 《영》.

**소면**(素麵) plain noodles.

**소멸**(消滅) 《절멸》 extinction; 《소실》 disappearance; expiation (죄의); 《실효》 extinguishment; nullification; termination; lapse (권리 불행사로 생기는). ~하다 become extinct; cease to exist 〔be〕; 《소실하다》 disappear; vanish; 《실효하다》 become null 〔void〕; be nullified 〔extinguished, expired〕; lapse; 《죄가》 be expiated.
¶ 계약의 ~ the discharge of a contract / 권리의 ~ lapse of *one's* rights / ~시키다 extinguish 《a mortgage》; nullify 《a contract, a right》 / 이 조약은 오는 6월 5일에 ~된다 This treaty will terminate on the 5th June.
◉ ~시효 extinctive prescription. 공유권~ extinguishment of common property. 자연~ natural extinction: 자연~하다 cease to exist as a matter of course; die out of itself.

**소멸**(燒滅) destruction by fire. ～하다 《…을》 destroy 《*a thing*》 by fire; reduce to ashes; 《…이》 be destroyed by fire; be reduced to ashes.

**소명**(召命) 《왕의 명》 a royal summons; 《신의 부름》 calling. ¶ ～을 내리다 call; summon.

**소명반**(燒明礬) 〖화학〗 burnt alum.

**소모**(消耗) consumption (소비); exhaustion (소진); dissipation; waste (낭비); wear and tear; 《체력의》 emaciation; 〖의학〗 《소모증》 marasmus. ～하다 consume; exhaust; dissipate; waste; use up. ¶ 정력을 ～하다 waste 〔dissipate〕 *one's* energy / 장거리 수영으로 체력을 ～했다 I was exhausted by a long-distance swim.
◉ ～비 wear and tear expenses. ～성 질환 a wasting disease. ～열(熱) a hectic fever. ～율 the attrition rate. ～전 a war of attrition. ～품 articles for consumption; consumer goods; (expendable) supplies; expendables; 《사무용품》 office supplies.

**소모**(梳毛) combed wool; 《작업》 combing 〔carding〕 wool. ◉ ～기 a carding machine; a (wool) comber. ～사 worsted (yarn).

**소목**(小木) 《소목장이》 a joiner; a cabinetmaker.

**소몰이** 《일》 cattle droving; 《사람》 a cattle drover.

**소묘**(素描) 〖미술〗 a (rough) sketch; rough drawing; a *dessin* (F.).

**소문**(所聞) (a) rumor; (a) report; hearsay; (a) gossip; news; talk; scuttlebutt 《미구어》. ¶ 근거 없는 ～ a groundless rumor; an unfounded report; a *canard* (F.) (신문 등의 허보) / 헛～ an idle rumor / ～으로 듣다 hear of; know by hearsay / ～이 나다 become the talk 《of》; be talked 〔gossiped〕 about / ～을 쉬쉬하다 hush up 〔stifle〕 a rumor / ～을 퍼뜨리다〔내다〕 spread 〔start, circulate〕 a rumor; set a rumor afloat / …라는 ～을 듣다 get wind of 《the affair》 / …라는 ～이다 rumor has it that…; there is a rumor 〔story〕 going around that…; word has spread 〔got around〕 that…; they say 〔I hear, I am told〕 that…; it is said 〔rumored, reported〕 that… / ～으로 알고 있을 뿐이다 I know it only from 〔by〕 hearsay. / ～이 자자하다 Word has been spreading 〔getting around〕. / 그는 ～처럼 그리 나쁜 사람은 아니다 He is not so black as he is painted. / 나쁜 ～이 나겠다 You'll get a bad reputation.

**소문자**(小文字) a small letter.

**소박**(素朴) simplicity; naivety; *naïveté* (F.); artlessness. ～하다 (be) simple; artless; plain; naive; unsophisticated. ¶ ～한 시골 사람들 simple villagers.

**소박**(疏薄·疎薄) maltreatment; mistreatment; abuse; desertion 《of *one's* wife》. ～하다 maltreat 《*one's* wife》; desert; abandon. ¶ 아내를 ～하다 abuse 〔desert〕 *one's* wife. ◉ ～데기 a mistreated 〔an abused〕 wife; a deserted 〔an abandoned〕 wife.

**소박맞다**(疏薄―) be mistreated 〔abused〕; get deserted. ¶ 소박맞은 여자 a deserted woman.

**소박이** ① 《오이의》 stuffed-cucumber kimchi. ② 《음식》 any stuffed food.

**소반**(小盤) 《상》 a small dining table.

**소방**(消防) fire fighting. ～하다 fight a fire; put out (a fire); extinguish; arrest the flames; get a fire under control; prevent a fire.
◉ ～관 a fire fighter; a fireman; a fire officer. ～기구〔용구〕 fire fighting equipment 〔apparatus, appliances〕. ～대 a fire brigade; a fire band; a fire company 《미》: 의용 ～대 a volunteer fire brigade. ～모 a smoke helmet. ～비상선 a fire line. ～사닥다리 a fire ladder; 《신축식》 an extension ladder. ～서 《미》 a firehouse; 《영》 a fire station: ～서장 a fire marshal 〔chief〕. ～(자동)차 a fire engine. ～정 a fireboat. ～펌프 a fire(-engine) pump. ～훈련 a fire drill.

**소변**(小便) urine; 《비어》 piss; pee 《소아어》. ¶ ～을 누다〔보다〕 urinate; pass 〔discharge〕 urine; make 〔pass〕 water; empty *one's* bladder; do *one's* needs; piss 《비어》; pee / ～을 참다 contain *one's* urine; retain *one's* water / ～이 잦다 have frequent calls of nature; be frequently called by nature / ～을 보고 싶다〔마렵다〕 Nature calls (me). / ～ 금지 《게시》 No Urinating. *or* Decency forbids. *or* No nuisance (here).
◉ ～검사 urinalysis; urine analysis. ～기 a urinal (receptacle). ～소 a urinal.

**소별**(小別) (a) subdivision. ⇨ 소분.

**소복**(素服) white clothes; 《상복》 (white) mourning clothes. ～하다 wear white clothes. ¶ ～한 여인 a woman in white.

**소분**(小分) a subdivision. ～하다 subdivide 《into》; 《세분하다》 itemize. ¶ 각 장(章)은 더 작은 절(節)로 ～된다 Each chapter is subdivided into smaller sections.

**소비**(消費) 《물자의》 consumption; 《돈·시간의》 spending; expenditure. ～하다 consume; spend; 《시간·노력을》 expend. ¶ 돈을 ～하다 spend money 《on》 / 시간을 ～하다 spend time 《in *do*ing *something*》 / 건전한 ～ 풍토를 해치다 hamper the sound consumption climate / 그 일에 막대한 정력과 시간을 ～하다 expend enormous energy and time on the work / 석유 ～는 여름보다 겨울이 훨씬 많다 Oil consumption is much greater in winter than in summer.
◉ ～감퇴(減退) decrease of consumption; underconsumption. ～경제 consumer economy. ～규제 readjustment of consumption. ～단위 a consumption unit. ～도시 a consuming city. ～량 the consumption 《of electricity 〔gasoline〕》; the volume 〔amount〕 of consumption. ～물자 consumption goods; consumables: 가정용 ～ 물자 goods for household consumption. ～사회 (a) consumer 〔consuming〕 society. ～생활 *one's* daily life as a consumer. ～성향 the propensity to consume. ～세 (a) consumption tax: 특별 ～세 (a) special excise tax. ～수준 the level of consumption. ～액 the amount of consumption. ～율 the rate of consumption 〔usage〕. ～인구 consuming population. ～인플레 consumption inflation. ～자본 a consumption capital. ～재 consumer(s') 〔consumption〕 goods: 기본 ～재 vital consumption goods / 내구(耐久) ～재 durable consumer goods. ～절약 economy in consumption. ～제한 restriction on consumption. ～조합 a consumers' cooperative society; a consumers' cooperation: ～ 조합 매점 a cooperative store. ～혁명 a consumer revolution. 자가 ～ self-consumption.

**소비자**(消費者) a consumer. ¶ 일반 ～ the consuming public. ◉ ～가격〔물가〕 the consumers' price: ～ 가격〔물가〕 지수 the consumer(s') price index (생략 CPI, c.p.i.). ～금융 consumer credit. ～단체 a consumer('s) group 〔organization〕. ～대표 consumer representatives. ～만족 customer('s) satisfaction (생략 CS). ～보호법 the Consumer's Protection Law. ～보호(운동) consumerism. ～보호원 the Consumer Protection Board. ～보호협회 a consumer protection organization. ～신뢰지수 the index of consumer confidence. ～심리 consumer sentiment. ～운동 a consumer campaign. ～조합 a consumer(s') union. 국제 ～기구 the International Organization of Consumers Union (생략 IOCU).

**소사**(小史) a short 〔brief〕 history.

**소사**(小辭) 〖논리〗 a minor term.

**소사**(掃射) machine-gunning; strafe. ～하다 sweep 〔rake〕 《the enemy's position》 with fire; mow 《the enemy》 down; machine-gun; strafe. ¶ 무장 헬리콥터가 군용열차에 기총～를 퍼부었다 An armed helicopter raked the troop train with machine-gun fire.

**소사**(燒死) death by fire. ～하다 be burnt to death; perish in the fire 〔flames〕. ◉ ～자 a person burnt to death; [총칭] the dead in a fire. ～체 a charred body.

**소산**(所産) a product; an outcome; a result; fruit(s); an outgrowth. ¶ 다년간에 걸친 노력의 ～ the fruits of *one's* many years' labors.

**소산**(消散) disappearance; vanishing; dispersion; dissipation; 《열·질환 따위의》 lysis; resolution (종기의). ～하다 disappear; vanish; disperse; dissipate; evanesce; evaporate (증발하다); lift (안개 따위가).

**소살**(燒殺) destruction 〔killing〕 by fire. ～하다 burn 《*a person*》 to death; burn 《*a person*》 alive.

**소상**(小祥) the first anniversary of 《*a person's*》 death.

**소상**(昭詳) ～하다 (be) full; detailed; minute. ¶ ～히 minutely; in detail; fully; at length / ～히 설명하다 explain 《*a matter*》 in detail.

**소상**(塑像) a plastic 〔plaster〕 image; a clay figure.

**소상인**(小商人) a small trader 〔businessman〕; a small scale retailer.

**소생**(小生) I; me; myself.

**소생**(所生) *one's* children 〔offspring〕; progeny. ¶ ～이 많다 have many children / ～이 없다 have no children; be childless.

**소생**(蘇生·甦生) revival; resuscitation. ～하다 be restored 〔recalled, brought back〕 to life; come to (*oneself* 〔*one's* senses〕); regain 〔recover〕 consciousness; revive; resuscitate. ¶ ～시키다 bring 《*a person*》 back to life; bring 《*a person*》 around; restore 《*a person*》 to consciousness; revive 《*a per-*

*son*》; resuscitate / ～한 기분이다 feel greatly relieved; breathe freely (again).

**소서**(小暑) 11th of the 24 seasonal divisions (around 7 July).

**-소서** please *do;* I beg you to *do.* ¶ 백세 천세 누리소서 Long may you live! / 용서하소서 I beg you to forgive me.

**소석고**(燒石膏) 〖화학〗 burnt 〔oxidized〕 plaster; plaster of Paris.

**소석회**(消石灰) 〖화학〗《수산화칼슘》 calcium hydroxide; slaked lime.

**소선거구**(小選擧區) a small electoral district; 《1구 1인의》 a single-member constituency. ◉ ～제 the minor 〔a small〕 constituency system; the single-member electorate 〔constituency〕 system.

**소설**(小雪) 20th of the 24 seasonal divisions (around Nov. 22).

**소설**(小說) a novel(장편); a story; a tale; a romance; [총칭] fiction (★ 보통 a novel 은 18세기 무렵부터 생긴 새로운 소설. a story는 이야기체로 된 소설이나 비교적 짧은 소설. a romance는 전기 소설, 공상 소설, 또는 18세기까지의 옛 형식의 소설). ¶ 과학～ science fiction (생략 SF) / 단편～ a short story; a brief tale; a novelette / 대하～ a saga (novel); an epic (novel) / 모험～ a story of adventures / 문제～ a problem novel / 연재～ a serial story (in a newspaper) / 역사～ a historical novel / 연애～ a romance; a love story / 유머～ a humorous story / 장편～ a (full-length) novel / 중편～ a short novel; a medium-length 〔a long short〕 story / 추리～ a mystery 〔detective〕 story / 통속～ a popular 〔lowbrow〕 story / ～적인 romantic; fictitious / ～을 쓰다 write a novel / ～화하다 write a novel out of 《*a person's* life》; fictionize; novelize.

◉ ～가 a novelist; a fiction 〔story〕 writer; a fictionist. ～문학 novel literature. ～책 a storybook; a novel; a book of fiction.

**소성**(小成) a small (measure of) success. ¶ ～에 만족하다 be contented with *one's* small success.

**소성**(塑性) 〖물리〗 plasticity. ¶ ～이 있다 be plastic.

**소셜 덤핑** 〖경제〗《해외에서 부당한 덤핑》 social dumping.

**소소리바람** 《이른 봄의 찬 바람》 a bleak 〔desolate〕 wind (in the early spring); 《회오리바람》 a whirlwind.

**소소리패** frivolous youngsters.

**소소하다**(小小—) (be) trivial; small; insignificant.

**소속**(所屬) *one's* position 〔post, place〕; an *attaché* (F.). ～하다 belong 《to》; be attached 《to》; affiliate *oneself* 《with》; be under the command 〔control〕 《of》. ¶ ～의 attached 〔belonging〕 to / ～ 미정(未定)의, 무～의 unassigned; unattached / ～시키다 attach 《to》; assign 《to》; put 《*a person*》 under the command 〔control〕 《of》 / 민주당 ～의원 a House member 「of 〔belonging to, affiliated with〕 the Democratic Party / 그는 그 위원회에 ～해 있다 He is a member of the committee. ◉ ～부대 *one's* regiment 〔unit〕.

**소송**(訴訟) a lawsuit; a suit; an action (at law); litigation. ～하다 bring an action 〔a suit〕 《against *a person* for *something*》; sue 《*a person* for *something*》; go to law 《with 〔against〕 *a person* over *something*》. ¶ 민사〔형사〕～ a civil 〔criminal〕 suit / 민사〔형사〕～법 the code of civil 〔criminal〕 procedure / 이혼 ～ a suit 〔an action〕 for divorce / 행정 ～ administrative litigation / ～중이다 be at law; be in litigation; be in the courts.

소송에: ～에 이기다 win 〔gain〕 a lawsuit 〔*one's* case〕 / ～에 지다 lose a lawsuit 〔*one's* case〕.

소송을: ～을 제기하다 institute 〔start, raise〕 a lawsuit 《against》; take 〔file, bring, institute〕 an action 《against》 / ～을 기각하다 dismiss an action 〔a case〕 / ～을 취하하다 drop 〔discontinue〕 the suit; abandon an action.

¶ 그는 손해 배상 청구 ～을 제기했다 He started a suit to collect damages for his injuries / 그는 명예훼손으로 그 신문사를 상대로 ～을 제기했다 He started a libel suit against the newspaper company.

◉ ～관계인 a litigant; [총칭] the litigants. ～기각 dismissal of a case. ～기록 the records of a lawsuit. ～능력 litigation capacity. ～당사자 the parties (in 〔to〕 a lawsuit); the litigants (in a lawsuit). ～대리인 a counsel; a process attorney. ～물 the object of a lawsuit. ～법 the code of legal procedure. ～비용 the costs of a lawsuit; court costs. ～위임장 a warrant of attorney. ～의뢰인 a client; [총칭] clientele. ～인 a plaintiff; a suitor; a litigator; 《당사자》 a (party) litigant; [총칭] the parties litigant. ～행위 an act of litigating; litigation.

반대～ a cross-suit; a cross action. 손해 배상～ the action for damages.

**소송사건**(訴訟事件) a case in litigation; a legal 〔law〕 case; a lawsuit. ¶ (변호사가) ～을 맡다 take a brief.

**소송절차**(訴訟節次) legal procedure; legal 〔judicial〕 proceedings. ¶ ～를 밟다 take 〔institute〕 legal 〔judicial〕 proceedings; go through (due) legal process; proceed against 《*a person*》.

**소수**(小數) 〖수학〗 a decimal (fraction). ¶ 무한〔유한〕～ an infinite 〔a finite〕 decimal. ◉ ～점 a (decimal) point: ～점 이하 셋째 자리까지 계산하다 calculate down to three places of decimals.

**소수**(少數) a small number; a minority. ¶ ～의 사람들 a small number of people; a few persons; a handful of people / ～의 사람만이 회의에 참석했다 Only a small number of people attended the meeting.
◉ ～당(黨) the minority; a minority party 〔group〕. ～민족 a minority race. ～의견 the opinion of the minority; a minority opinion. ～정예 the elect 〔select〕 few: 우리 회사 인사 방침은 ～정예주의다 Our personnel policy is "Small numbers-exceptional talent." ～투표 the minor vote. ～파 a minority faction; the minority.

**소수**(素數) 〖수학〗 a prime (number).

**소스** sauce; gravy. ¶ 화이트～ white sauce / ～를 치다 put sauce 《on》; pour sauce 《over》; sauce 《meat》.
◉ ～병 a sauce pot; 《배 모양의》 a sauceboat. 살사 ～ salsa (sauce).

**소스** 〖컴퓨터〗 《원본 자료》 a source.
◉ ～디스크 a source disk. ～컴퓨터 a source computer.

**소스라치다** be frightened 〔astonished, startled〕; start (with fright); be taken aback. ¶ 비명 소리에 ～ be startled at a shriek.

**소슬**(蕭瑟) ～하다 (be) bleak; chilly; lonely and desolate. ¶ ～한 가을바람 a sobbing autumnal wind 〔blast〕.

**소승**(小乘) 〖불교〗 Hinayana; the Lesser Vehicle. ¶ ～적 견지 a narrow view; a narrow point of view. ◉ ～불교 Hinayana Buddhism.

**소시민**(小市民) a petty 〔a petit〕 bourgeois; the lower middle class.

**소시지** (a) sausage. ◉ 비엔나～ Vienna sausage; wienerwurst 《미》. 프랑크 푸르트 ～ frankfurter 《미》. 햄～ ham sausage.

**소식**(小食) light eating. ～하다 eat little. ◉ ～가 a light 〔small〕 eater.

**소식**(素食) a meatless meal; plain fare.

**소식**(消息) 《기별》 news; tidings; word; 《정보》 information; 《서신 왕래》 communication; correspondence; 《편지》 a letter; 《통지》 notice; a message; 《동정》 movements. ¶ ～을 듣다 hear 〔learn〕 the news of 《*a person*》 / ～을 듣지 못하다 hear nothing of / ～을 전하다 bring 〔bear〕 the news 《of *a person*》 to 《another》; write (a letter) 《to》; drop a line / ～이 있다 hear from; get a letter from; get word from / ～이 없다 hear nothing 〔have no news, receive no word〕 from / ～에 정통하다 be well-informed 《about, on》; be familiar 〔conversant〕 《with》; be fully primed 《with》 / 오랫동안 ～을 전하지 않다 keep silent for a long time / 그 후 그에게서 ～이 없다 He has not been heard from since. *or* I have not heard from him since. / 가끔 ～이나 전해 주십시오 Drop 〔Write〕 me a line once in a while. *or* Let me have some news from you every so often. / 그로부터 ～이 뚝 끊어졌다 He dropped his correspondence with me. / 무～이 희～ 《속담》 No news is good news.
◉ ～통 《계통》 well-informed circles 〔quarters, sources〕; a source; a channel; 《사람》 a well-informed person; a person in the know; an insider: 외교계의 ～통 the informed diplomatic sources / 그는 정계의 ～통이다 He is a political expert.

**소식자**(消息子) 〖의학〗 a probe; a sound.

**소신**(所信) *one's* belief 〔conviction〕; *one's* opinion 〔view〕. ¶ ～을 말하다 express 〔give〕 *one's* opinion 〔belief〕 《about》; voice *one's* conviction / ～을 굽히지 않다 be firm 〔unshaken〕 in *one's* convictions; stick 〔hold fast〕 to *one's* view 〔belief〕 / ～대로 밀고 나가다 force 〔push〕 *one's* decision through; carry through 〔out〕 what *one* has decided; act according to *one's* belief.

**소실**(小室) a (kept) mistress; a concubine. ◉ ～자식 a child by a concubine.

**소실**(消失) disappearance; loss; vanishing; vanishment. ～하다 《…이》 disappear; vanish; die away; 《…을》 lose.

**소실**(燒失) destruction 〔loss〕 by fire. ～하다 《…이》 be destroyed 〔consumed〕 by fire; burn 〔be burnt〕 down; go up in fire 〔flames〕; be reduced to ashes; 《…을》 lose by fire; have 《*a thing*》 destroyed by fire. ¶ 가재 도구를 몽땅 ～하다 lose all *one's* house-hold goods in the fire / ～을 면하다 escape the fire. ◉ ～가옥 burnt houses; houses destroyed by fire.

**소심**(小心) 《겁많음》 timidity; cowardice; faintheartedness; 《주의 깊음》 prudence. ～하다 (be) timid; cowardly; timorous; fainthearted; chicken 《속어》; 《주의 깊다》 (be) cautious; prudent. ¶ ～한 사람 a coward; a chicken-hearted person.

**소싯적**(少時―) (the time of) *one's* boyhood 〔*one's* youth〕. ¶ ～에 in *one's* youth 〔early days〕.

**소아**(小兒) a baby; a young 〔little〕 child; an infant. ◉ ～과 〖의학〗 pediatrics; pediatry: ～과 의(사) a children's doctor; a pediatrician; a child specialist / ～과 병원 a children's hospital. ～마비 infantile paralysis; polio(myelitis). ～병 a children's 〔an infantile〕 disease; [비유적] infantilism: ～병적(인) infantilistic. ～외과 pediatric surgery. ～정신과 pediatric psychiatry.

**소아**(小我) the self; the ego.

**소아시아**(小―) Asia Minor.

**소액**(少額) a small 〔petty〕 sum 〔amount〕. ¶ ～의 돈 a small 〔petty〕 sum of money.

◉ ～대부 a petty loan. ～보험 petty=sum insurance. ～심판 a small-sum civil suit. ～지폐 a note 〔bill〕 of small denomination. ～화폐 a fractional coin. ～환(換) a postal order (생략 P.O.); a postal note 《미》: 만 원짜리 ～환 a postal order for 10,000 won.

**소야곡**(小夜曲) 〖음악〗 a serenade.

**소양**(素養) 《기초》 a grounding 《in》; 《지식》 (a) knowledge 《of》; acquirements; attainments; 《교양》 culture; accomplishments; 《훈련》 training. ¶ ～이 있는 cultured; cultivated; trained / 어학의 ～ linguistic attainments / 경제학에 ～이 없는 학생 students untrained 〔with no training〕 in economics / ～이 있다 be well grounded 《in》; have a grounding 《in》; have some knowledge 《of》 / ～이 없다 be ill 〔poorly〕 grounded 《in》; have no knowledge 《of》 / 그녀에겐 문학에 대한 ～이 있다 She has learned a good deal of literature.

**소양증**(搔痒症) 〖의학〗 pruritus; itching.

**소연**(小宴) a small feast; an informal dinner 〔party〕; a little dinner; a collation.

**소연**(騷然) ～하다 (be) noisy; clamorous; confused; disturbed; agitated; uproarious; tumultuous; turbulent. ¶ ～해지다 be thrown into a commotion 〔an uproar〕. 「(agent).

**소염제**(消炎劑) 〖약〗 an antiphlogistic

**소엽**(小葉) 〖식물〗 a foliole; a leaflet; 〖해부〗 a lobule; a lobelet. 「hut.

**소옥**(小屋) a small house; a cottage; a

**소외**(疏外·疎外) (an) estrangement; alienation. ～하다 estrange; avoid 〔shun〕 《*a person's*》 company; keep 《*a person*》 at a distance; be cool 《toward》. ¶ 그는 모두에게 ～당한 느낌이었다 He felt that he was「left out of the group 〔neglected by all〕.
◉ ～감 feelings 〔a sense〕 of alienation: 학급내의 아무도 그에게 말을 걸지 않았기 때문에 그녀는 ～감을 느꼈다 Since nobody in the class talked to her, she felt alienated. 인간～ the alienation of「man 〔human beings〕.

**소요**(所要) what is needed 〔required〕; the need; requirement. ¶ ～의 necessary; 《articles》 needed; required.
◉ ～시간 the time required 〔needed〕; the necessary time: ～ 시간은 2시간이다 It takes two hours.

**소요**(逍遙) a ramble; a saunter. ～하다 walk leisurely; stroll; saunter; ramble. ◉ ～학파 〖철학〗 the Peripatetic school.

**소요**(騷擾) (a) disturbance; a commotion; an agitation; a riot; a sedition; an uprising. ¶ ～를 일으키다 cause 〔raise〕 a disturbance 〔riot〕. ◉ ～죄 a crime of rioting 〔riotous assembly〕: ～죄로 기소되다 be indicted for rioting / ～죄를 적용하다 apply 〔invoke〕 the anti-riot law 《against extremist rioters》 / 그 대학생은 ～죄로 체포되었다 The university student was arrested on a charge of staging a riot.

**소용**(所用) 《유용성》 use; usefulness; service; 《쓰임》 what is used; the use; 《필요》 necessaries; 《경비》 expenses.
¶ ～되다 be used; be needed; be in need 〔want〕 of; be necessary 〔required〕 / ～ 있다 be useful; be of use 〔service〕 / ～없다 be useless; be of no use 〔avail〕; be needless 〔unnecessary〕 / ～에 닿다 serve the purpose; be useful 〔serviceable〕 / ～없는 걱정을 하다 feel needless anxiety / 그런 것은 ～없다 I don't want it. / 이제 그런

소리해 봤자 ~없다 It is (of) no use 「to say 〔saying〕 such a thing now. (★ of 없는 것은 구어적) / 그런 여자에게 부탁을 해 봤자 아무 ~이 없다 What is the good of asking a favor of her? / 상의해 봤지만 ~이 없었다 We consulted with 《*him*》 about the matter but it was a waste of time. *or* Nothing came out of the discussion. *or* The discussion came to nothing.

**소용돌이** a whirlpool; a swirl; an eddy (작은); a vortex. ~치다 eddy; wind; whirl 《around》; flow in whirls; swirl (흐르는 물이). ¶ ~치는 물〔급류〕 swirling waters 〔torrents〕 / 전란의 ~ 속에 in the vortex of war / ~ 속에 휩쓸리다 be drawn into a whirlpool 〔vortex〕; [비유적] be drawn into the maelstrom 〔vortex〕 of 《war》. ◉ ~무늬 a scroll.

**소우주**(小宇宙) 〖철학〗 a microcosm(os); a miniature universe. 「자리.

**소웅좌**(小熊座) the Little Bear. = 작은곰

**소원**(所願) *one's* desire 〔wish〕. ¶ ~대로 as *one* wishes; according to *one's* desire / 제발 ~이니 for God's sake; for mercy's sake / ~대로 되다 things turn out as *one* wishes / ~을 들어주다 grant 〔comply with〕 《*a person's*》 request / ~을 이루다〔성취하다〕 have 〔get〕 *one's* wish; have *one's* wish granted; have *one's* (cherished) wishes realized 〔fulfilled〕; *one's* wish comes true / ~을 들어주지 않다 refuse 〔turn down〕 《*a person's*》 request / ~이 이루어지지 않다 be unable to get 〔have〕 *one's* wish / ~을 있는대로 다 말해봐라 Make all the wishes you want. / 파리에 가서 그림 공부를 하고 싶다는 그의 오랜 ~이 이루어졌다 His long-cherished desire to go to Paris for the study of painting was fulfilled.

**소원**(疏遠·疎遠) (an) estrangement; alienation; 《격조》 a long silence. ~하다 (be) estranged; alienated. ¶ ~해지다 become estranged 〔alienated〕 《from》 / 둘은 차츰 더 ~해졌다 They drifted farther and farther apart.

**소원**(訴願) a petition; an appeal. ~하다 petition 《for》; appeal 《to the authorities》; lodge 〔file, submit, hand in〕 a petition 《to》. ¶ 당국에 ~하다 present a petition before the authorities 《for》; appeal to the authorities 《for》. ◉ ~심의회 the Petition Committee. ~인 an appellant; a petitioner.

**소위**(少尉) 〖육군〗 a second lieutenant; 〖해군〗 an ensign 《미》; an acting sublieutenant 《영》; 〖공군〗 a second lieutenant 《미》; a pilot officer 《영》. ¶ 총 221명의 사관학교 생도들이 ~로 임관되었다 A total of 221 cadets were given the commission of second lieutenant.

**소위**(所爲) 《하는 짓〔일〕》 *one's* conduct; an act; a deed; *one's* doing 〔work〕; what *one* does.

**소위**(所謂) the so-called; what is called; what you 〔we, they〕 call. ¶ ~ 운명이라는 것은 사람이 스스로 친 거미줄이다 What a man calls fate is a web of his own weaving.

**소위원회**(小委員會) a subcommittee.

**소유**(所有) 《상태》 ownership; possession; 《물건》 ⇨ 소유물. ~하다 have; own; possess; hold; be the owner of; be in possession of. ¶ Y씨 ~의 《*a thing*》 owned by 〔belonging to〕 Mr. Y / …의 ~가 되다 [사물이 주어] come 〔fall〕 into *one's* hands; pass into *one's* possession; be in the possession of 《John》; [사람이 주어] come into possession of 《*something*》 / 그는 많은 토지를 ~하고 있었다 He possessed a lot of land. / 이 집은 누구의 ~입니까 Who owns this house? *or* Who(m) does this house belong to? ◉ ~격 〖문법〗 the possessive 〔genitive〕 case. ~물 *one's* possessions 〔belongings〕; *one's* property: 이것은 K씨 ~물이다 This belongs to Mr. K. / 이 가판(街販) 시설은 서울 특별시 ~물입니다 《게시》 This kiosk is the property of Seoul City. ~욕 a desire for possession: ~욕이 강한 possessive; grasping; covetous. ~주 an owner; a possessor: ~주가 없는 ownerless / ~주가 바뀌다 shift its proprietor. ~지(地) *one's* land 〔estate〕. 개인〔공동〕~ individual 〔joint〕 ownership.

**소유권**(所有權) (the right of) ownership 〔proprietorship〕; proprietary rights; a right 〔title〕 《to *a thing*》; 《땅의》 dominium; dominion. ¶ ~을 갖고 있다 have 〔hold〕 the ownership 《of》 / ~을 이전하다 transfer the ownership 《of a house from A to B》. ◉ ~이전 (a) transfer of the ownership. ~자 an owner. ~침해 (an) infringement of 《*a person's*》 ownership.

**소음**(騷音) (a) noise; (a) din. ¶ 도시의 ~ the din and bustle of a town; city sounds; street noises / 귀청이 찢어질 것 같은 ~ a deafening 〔earsplitting〕

noise / ～을 줄이다 reduce noise / 굉장한 ～을 내다 produce [generate, make] a tremendous noise / 우리는 갖가지 ～에 시달리고 있다 We are greatly harassed by noise of various kinds.
◉ ～계 a noise [sound-level] meter. ～공해 noise damage [pollution]. ～방지 prevention of noise; sound suppression: ～ 방지법 the Anti-Noise Act.

**소음기**(消音器) 《권총의》 a silencer; 《자동차의》 a muffler; 《영》 a silencer. ¶ ～를 장착한 총 a gun fitted with a silencer; a silenced gun.

**소읍**(小邑) a small town.

**소이**(所以) a reason; (the reason) why 「….

**소이탄**(燒夷彈) an incendiary (bomb [shell]); a fire bomb.

**소인**(小人) 《어린이》 a minor; a child; a little one; 《난쟁이》 a little man; a pigmy; a dwarf; 《소인물》 a mean [stingy, petty] person; an insignificant [a worthless] person; a small mind; 《겸칭》 I; me; myself.
◉ ～국 a land of pigmies; Lilliput. ～배(輩) small fry 《구어》.

**소인**(素人) an amateur. ◉ ～극 amateur theatricals.

**소인**(素因) a (causative) factor; a primary cause; a principle; 〖의학〗 a (pre)disposition. ◉ ～수(數) 〖수학〗 a prime factor.

**소인**(消印) a postmark; a (postal) canceling [cancellation] mark. ～하다 postmark; cancel (with a stamp). ¶ 런던의 ～이 찍힌 편지 a letter 「postmarked from London [bearing the London postmark] / 편지에 ～을 찍다 imprint a postmark on a letter.

**소일**(消日) whiling away [killing, passing] time. ～하다 pass [spend] *one's* time [days]; while away [kill] time. ¶ 빈둥빈둥 ～하다 idle [dawdle] *one's* time away / 독서로 ～하다 spend *one's* time (in) reading. ◉ ～거리 a time-killer; a pastime.

**소임**(所任) ① 《직》 a post; a position; *one's* office; 《책임》 a duty; responsibility; 《임무》 a task; 《사명》 a mission. ¶ ～을 맡다 take up *one's* duties [post]; take office; take charge 《of》 / ～을 다하다 fulfill *one's* duties; perform *one's* office; carry out *one's* mission. ② 《하급 직원》 an underling.

**소자**(小子) 《부모에게》 I; me.

**소자**(素子) 〖전자공학〗 an element; a device.

**소자본**(小資本) a small capital.

**소작**(小作) (farm) tenancy; tenant farming; sharecropping 《미》. ～하다 farm 《land》 as a tenant.
◉ ～권 a tenant right. ～농 tenant farming (일); a tenant farmer (사람). ～료 rent (paid by a tenant farmer). ～인(人) a tenant (farmer); a sharecropper 《미》; [총칭] tenantry. ～쟁의 a dispute between landowners and tenant farmers; a tenancy dispute [trouble]. ～제도 the tenant system.

**소작**(燒灼) 〖의학〗 cautery. ～하다 cauterize. ◉ ～기 a cautery; a cauter. ～제(劑) a cauterant.

**소장**(小腸) 〖해부〗 the small intestine.
◉ ～염(炎) enteritis.

**소장**(少壯) vigorous youth; the young. ¶ 전도가 유망한 ～ 실업가 a promising young businessman.
◉ ～파 the young group [faction]. ～학파 the young school.

**소장**(少將) 〖육군·해병대〗 a major general; 〖해군〗 a rear admiral; 〖공군〗 a major general 《미》; an air vice-marshal 《영》.

**소장**(所長) the head [chief, manager] 《of an office, a factory》.

**소장**(所藏) *one's* possession. ¶ 민 박사 ～ 《*a thing*》 owned by Dr. Min / …～의 골동품 *one's* collection of curios; curios in *one's* possession / 김 박사가 ～한 그림이 곧 이 미술관에 기증될 것이다 The pictures owned by Dr. Kim will soon be presented to this art gallery.

**소장**(消長) prosperity and decline; rise and fall; ups and downs; ebb and flow. ～하다 prosper and decline; rise and fall; have ups and downs.

**소장**(訴狀) 〖법〗 a (written) complaint; a bill of complaint; a brief; pleadings; 《진정서》 a petition. ¶ ～을 제출하다 present [submit] a petition 《to》; lodge [file] a complaint 《with》.

**소재**(所在) 《사람의》 *one's* whereabouts; where a person is; 《사물의》 (the place) where 《*a thing*》 is (kept); 《건물 등의》 the site; 《위치》 the position; the situation; the location. ¶ ～를 감추다 conceal *one's* whereabouts; disappear; hide *oneself;* go into hiding / ～를 모르다, ～ 불명이다 *a person's* whereabouts is unknown; be missing / ～를 찾아[알아]내다 discover [find out] 《*a person's*》 whereabouts; locate 《the enemy's camp》 / 보물의 ～

를 묻다 ask where the treasure is kept / 책임 ~를 밝히다 find out where the responsibility lies; find out who is responsible 《for》. ◉ ~지 the location; the site; the seat: 도청 ~지 the seat of a provincial office / 그 호텔의 ~지를 알려 주시겠습니까 Can you tell me where that hotel is?

**소재**(素材) (raw) material; 《for *one's* book》 a theme; a subject matter; 《신문 기사 따위의》 copy. ¶ ~를 모으다 gather 〔collect〕 material 〔data〕 《for》. ◉ ~산업 basic materials industries; industrial materials manufacturing: 석유화학공업은 ~ 산업의 중요한 부분을 이룬다 The petrochemical industry forms a vital sector in the manufacture of industrial materials. 집필 ~ writing material (★ writing materi- ⌊als「필기구」).

**소저**(小姐) a young lady.

**소전**(小傳) a short 〔brief〕 biography; a biographical sketch 〔profile〕.

**소전제**(小前提) 〖논리〗 a minor premise.

**소절**(小節) 《예절》 minor matters of etiquette 〔protocol〕; 《절조》 minor points of honor; trifles; 〖음악〗 a bar; a measure.

**소정**(所定) ¶ ~의 fixed 〔appointed〕 《place, time》; prescribed; stated 《hours》; established; designated; set / ~의 사항 designated items / ~의 용지 a prescribed form / ~의 학과 the prescribed course of study / ~의 과정을 마치다 complete a required course / ~의 절차를 밟다 go through the regular course 〔the prescribed〕 formalities.

**소조**(小潮) the neap (tide).

**소조**(塑造) modeling; molding. ◉ ~예술 plastic arts.

**소주**(燒酒) *soju;* (cheap) distilled spirits; (distilled) liquor; hard liquor. ◉ 막~ crude 〔low-grade〕 *soju.*

**소중**(所重) ~하다 《중요하다》 (be) important; weighty; significant; momentous; 《귀중하다》 (be) valuable; precious; dear to *one.* ¶ ~한 물건 a valuable article; [총칭] valuables; treasures / 목숨만큼이나 ~한 것 a thing as dear as life itself / ~히 seriously; carefully; with (much) care; with caution / ~히 간직하다 treasure (up); prize; keep 〔hold〕 《*things*》 with jealous 〔greatest〕 care / ~히 하다〔여기다〕 prize; treasure; think 〔make〕 much of 《*a person, a thing*》 / 목숨보다도 명예를 ~히 여기다 hold *one's* honor dearer than *one's* life; put *one's* honor above *one's* life / 무엇보다 건강이 ~하다 Health comes before everything else.

**소증**(素症) ① 《고기 먹고 싶음》 a craving for meat. ¶ ~이 나다 crave meat; have a craving for meat. ② 〖의학〗 protein deficiency.

**소지**(所持) possession. ~하다 possess; own; have 《in *one's* possession》; have 《money》 about 〔with, on〕 *one;* bear; carry. ¶ 마약의 불법 ~ illegal possession of drugs. ◉ ~금 money 〔cash〕 carried in *one's* pocket 〔on *one's* purse〕. ~자 the owner; a possessor; a holder; a bearer. ~품 *one's* things 〔belongings〕; *one's* personal effects: ~품 검사 (body) search; frisk(ing) / ~품을 조사하다 examine 〔check up on〕 《*a person's*》 things / 시체의 신원을 그의 ~품에서 알아냈다 The body was identified by his personal effects 〔belonging's〕.

**소지**(素地) 《소질(素質)》 the making; an aptitude 《for》; 《기초·토대》 groundwork; a foundation. ¶ ~를 마련하다 lay the foundation 《for》.

**소지**(燒紙) 〖민속〗 sacrificial paper (burned to departed spirits). ¶ ~(를) 올리다 《the shaman》 burn the sacrificial paper.

**소진**(消盡) vanishing completely. ~하다 totally vanish; disappear altogether; exhaust; use up; consume.

**소진**(燒盡) reduction to ashes; total destruction by fire. ~하다 《건물이》 be burnt down; be reduced to ashes; be razed to the ground; 《연료가》 be burnt out; be exhausted. ¶ 화재로 모든 것이 ~되었다 The fire burnt out everything.

**소질**(素質) 《자질》 the makings; temperament; character; (a) nature; fiber; composition; 《체질》 constitution; make-up; predisposition 《to diabetes》 (병에 걸리기 쉬운); 《경향》 a tendency 《to, toward》. ¶ 암에 걸리기 쉬운 ~ a hereditary predisposition to cancer / 유전적 범죄 ~ inherited criminal tendencies / 문학적 ~이 있는 사람 a person of a literary turn (of mind) / 소설가〔지도자〕가 될 ~이 있다 have the making of a novelist 〔leader〕 / 어학 ~이 있다 have a natural aptitude for languages / 나는 음악에는 ~이 없다 I am not cut out「for music 〔to be a musician〕.

**소집**(召集) a call; a summons; 《군대의》 a muster; a levy; a call-up; 《미》 a draft; 《회의의》 convocation. ~하다 《회의를》 call 《a committee》 (into session); convene; convoke; summon; 《군대를》 levy; muster; call up 〔out〕; 《군대에》 call 《*a person*》 into the army; draft 《*a person*》 (for service) 《미》. ¶ 임시〔정기〕 국회를 ~하다 convene 〔summon〕 a special 〔regular〕 session of the National Assembly / 군대에 ~되다 be called into the army; be summoned to the colors; be called up for (military) service; 《예비역이》 be called to active duty / 회의를 ~하다 call 〔convene〕 a meeting; call a meeting into a session.
◉ ~나팔 a bugle call. ~령 《issue》 a draft (call): 미육군은 5 만명에게 ~령을 내렸다 The U.S. Army issued a draft call for 50,000 men. ~영장 a call-up papers 《영》; a draft card 《미》; a summons to the colors. ~해제 demobilization: ~ 해제가 되다 be demobilized; be demobbed 《영구어》. 연습~ a maneuver levy.

**소쩍새** 〖조류〗 a (common, little) cuckoo.

**소차**(小差) a small 〔slight〕 difference; 《차》 a narrow 〔slim〕 margin; a short lead.

**소찬**(素饌) a plain dinner; a simple vegetable dinner (without meat or fish).

**소채**(蔬菜) vegetables; greens. ⇨ 채소.

**소책자**(小冊子) a booklet; a pamphlet; a leaflet; a brochure; a tract.

**소철**(蘇鐵) 〖식물〗 a cycad; a sago palm.

**소청**(所請) a request. ¶ ~이 있다 have a favor to ask of 《*a person*》 / ~을 들어주다 comply with 〔accede to〕 《*a person's*》 request; grant a request; do 《*a person*》 a favor / ~을 물리치다 〔거절하다〕 turn down 〔refuse〕 《*a person's*》 request.

**소총**(小銃) a rifle; [총칭] small arms.
◉ ~탄알 a bullet; a rifleshot. 엠십육 ~ an M-16 (rifle). 카빈~ a carbine.

**소추**(訴追) 《형사상의》 prosecution; indictment; accusation. ~하다 prosecute 〔indict〕 《*a person* for a crime》; accuse 《*a person* of a crime》; bring a legal action 《against *a person* for *something*》.

**소출**(所出) crops; yield(s); products. ¶ ~이 많은 heavily 〔highly〕 productive 《farm》.

**소치**(所致) what is brought 〔caused〕 by; the result. ¶ 성적이 좋지 않은 것은 네가 게으른 ~다 Your poor school records come 〔stem〕 from your laziness. / 모두 제 부덕한 ~입니다 I am solely to blame for it. *or* All is due to my lack of discretion.

**소침**(消沈) depression; gloom. ⇨ 의기소침.

**소켓** a socket; a receptacle 《미》. ¶ ~에 끼다 fit 〔screw〕 《a light bulb》 into the socket; socket / ~을 달다 fix a socket. ◉ 쌍~ a two-way socket.

**소쿠리** a wicker 〔bamboo〕 basket.

**소크라테스** 《그리스의 철학자》 Socrates (470?-399 B.C.).

**소크백신** 〖의학〗 salk vaccine.

**소탈**(疏脫) informality; unceremoniousness; lack of ceremony. ~하다 (be) informal; free and easy; open-hearted; unceremonious; offhand; bohemian. ¶ 그는 대범하고 ~한 사람이다 He is a carefree and open-hearted person.

**소탐대실**(小貪大失) incurring a great loss by pursuing a small profit. ~하다 suffer a big loss in going after a small gain.

**소탕**(掃蕩) sweeping; clearing; a sweep; 《잔적 등의》 mopping up; a mop-up; a cleanup. ~하다 sweep; drive; clear; stamp 〔wipe〕 out; get rid of; 《잔적 등을》 mop up; clean up; clear out. ¶ 적을 ~하다 clear 〔sweep〕 《the area》 of the enemy / 잔적을 ~하다 mop up the remnants of the enemy. ◉ ~작전 a cleanup 〔mopping-up〕 operation.

**소태** 〖식물〗 《나무》 a kind of sumac; 《껍질》 sumac bark. ¶ ~ 같다 be as bitter as gall.

**소택**(沼澤) a swamp; a marsh; a bog.
◉ ~지 marshy ground; marshland: ~지의 식물 swamp plants.

**소통**(疏通) 《의사의》 mutual understanding; communication. ~하다 have 〔enjoy〕 mutual 〔good〕 understanding. ¶ 의사의 ~ mutual understanding / 서로 의사가 ~되다 be understood 《by》; come to a mutual understanding 《about *a matter*》; come to understand each other / 의사를 ~시키다 get (*oneself*) across; communicate 《*one's* thoughts clearly》; make *oneself* fully understood 《by》 / 의사 ~이 안 되다 lack understanding; be at odds 《with *a person*》 / 의사 ~을 꾀하다 try to bring about a better understanding 《between》/ 외국에 나가면 의사 ~의 어려움을 통감한다 In a foreign country I keenly realize how difficult it is to make *myself* understood.

**소파**(搔爬) 『의학』 curettage. ~하다 curet(te); remove the fetus by scraping the uretus; perform 〔do〕 a D and C (★ D and C는 dilation and curettage의 생략). ¶ ~ 수술을 받다 undergo curettage.

**소파** a sofa. ¶ ~에 앉다 sit on a sofa.

**소편**(小片) a bit; a fragment; a small piece; a splinter.

**소포**(小包) a parcel; a package; a packet. ⇨ 소포 우편. ¶ ~가 왔다 A package has come by parcel post. / ~ 찾는 곳 2층 후문 《개시》 To pick up parcels, use rear entrance on the second floor. ◉ ~우송료 postage rates for parcels. 국내〔국제〕~ domestic 〔international〕 parcels. 보험~ insured parcels.

**소포우편**(小包郵便) 《제도》 parcel(s) post; (생략 P.P., p.p.); 《우편물》 a (postal) parcel; a (postal) package. ¶ ~으로 보내다 send 《a book》 by parcel post 《to》; mail a package 《미》/ ~으로 하다 have 《*something*》 sent by parcel post. ◉ ~료 parcel post postage 〔charge, rates〕. ~(취급)창구 a parcel post window.

**소폭**(小幅) 《폭》 single breadth; 《범위》 narrow range; narrow limits. ¶ (증권 시세 등의) ~ 등락 fluctuations of a narrow range / ~의 변동을 보이다 move within narrow limits.

**소품**(小品) 《문장》 a literary sketch; a pastel; a short piece of composition; 《그림·조각》 a small piece of painting 〔sculpture〕; 『연극』 (stage) properties; props 《속어》. ◉ ~곡 a short piece of music; a musical sketch. ~담당 a prop(erty) man 〔master〕. ~실 a stage properties room; a props storeroom. ~집(集) a sketch book.

**소풍**(逍風) 《산책》 an outing; 《피크닉》 a picnic; a hike; a walking tour; a holiday expedition; an excursion. ~하다 take a walk; go for an outing; go on an excursion 〔outing〕. ¶ 학교 ~ a school excursion / 교외로 ~ 나가다 take a walk in the suburbs. ◉ ~객 an excursionist; a holidaymaker.

**소프라노** 『음악』 soprano; 《가수》 a soprano; a soprano singer. ¶ ~로 노래하다 sing in soprano.

**소프트** soft. ◉ ~볼 《play》 softball; 《공》 a softball. ~ 아이스크림 (a) soft ice cream. ~웨어 『컴퓨터』 software.

**소피**(所避) urination; relieving *oneself*. ~보다 urinate; pass 〔discharge〕 urine; make 〔pass〕 water.

**소하어**(遡河魚) an anadromous fish.

**소한**(小寒) the 23d of the 24 seasonal divisions (around 6 January).

**소해**(掃海) 『군사』 sea clearing; mine sweeping 〔dragging〕. ~하다 sweep 〔drag〕 the sea for mines; sweep up mines; clear the sea.
◉ ~작업 sea-clearing 〔minesweeping〕 operations; minesweeping. ~정(艇) a minesweeper.

**소행**(所行) *a person's* doing 〔work〕; an act; a deed; 《the Devil's》 handiwork. ¶ 미치광이의 ~ the work of an insane man / ~이 사납다 be ill-behaved / 이건 도대체 어느 녀석의 ~이냐 Who the devil did it 〔this〕? / 이건 그의 ~임에 틀림없다 It must be his doing.

**소행**(素行) conduct; behavior; *one's* natural character. ¶ ~ 나쁜 사람 a man of 「bad conduct 〔loose morals〕/ ~이 나쁘다 conduct *oneself* improperly; be dissolute / ~을 조사하다 examine into 《*a person's*》 private character.

**소형**(小型) a small size; a pocket size. ¶ ~의 small-sized; small; miniature; pocket 《dictionaries》; portable (휴대용의); midget.
◉ ~권총 a pocket pistol. ~비행기 a cub 〔midget〕 plane; a light plane; light aircraft [총칭]. ~승용차 a minicar; a compact 〔small〕 car. ~카메라 a miniature camera. ~트럭 a light (delivery) truck; a pickup (truck). ~판(判) a miniature 〔pocket〕 edition.

**소형화**(小型化) miniaturization. ~하다 miniaturize. ¶ 초~ microminiaturization.

**소호** SOHO. [<*S*mall *O*ffice *H*ome 「*O*ffice]

**소홀**(疏忽) indifference; negligence; carelessness. ~하다 (be) negligent; remiss; careless; inattentive; indifferent. ¶ ~히 indifferently; rudely; roughly; negligently; carelessly; inattentively / ~히 하다 neglect; be negligent 〔neglectful〕 of; pay no attention to; slight; be indifferent to / 일〔건강〕을 ~히 하다 neglect 〔slight, scamp〕 *one's* 「work 〔health〕/ ~히 하지 않다 pay careful attention to; think a great deal of / 공부를 ~히 하지 않도록 해라 You shouldn't neglect your studies.

**소화**(笑話) a funny 〔humorous〕 story.

**소화**(消火) fire extinguishing 〔fighting〕. ～하다 put out 〔extinguish, fight〕 a fire. ¶ ～용의〔으로〕 for fire-extinguishing〔-fighting〕 purposes / ～에 임하다 fight a fire / 초기 ～에 실패하다 fail to bring the fire under control 「at an early stage 〔in its early stages〕.
◉ ～기 a fire extinguisher. ～용수 water (available) for fire-fighting. ～전 a fireplug (생략 F.P.); a (fire) hydrant. ～호스〔펌프〕 a fire hose 〔pump〕.

**소화**(消化) ① 《음식의》 digestion. ～하다 digest. ¶ ～가 잘 안되는 음식 indigestible 〔heavy〕 food / ～가 빠르다〔더디다〕 be quick 〔slow〕 of digestion / ～가 잘 되다〔안되다〕 digest well 〔poorly, ill〕 / ～하기(가) 쉽다〔힘들다〕 be easy 〔hard〕 to digest; be digestible 〔indigestible〕 / ～를 돕다 aid 〔help, promote〕 the 〔*one's*〕 digestion / ～를 방해하다 disturb 〔upset, impair〕 the digestion.
② 《이해·동화》 assimilation; digestion. ～하다 assimilate; digest. ¶ ～를 제대로 못한 지식〔사상〕 ill-digested knowledge 〔thought〕 / 배운 것을 잘 ～하다 assimilate 〔digest〕 what *one* has learned / 이 책은 어려워서 나로서는 ～할 수 없다 This book is too difficult for me to assimilate.
③ 《소비》 absorption; consumption; 《작업 따위의》 finishing. ～하다 《상품을》 absorb; consume; 《작업을》 finish. ¶ 국채의 ～ absorption of government bonds / 국내 시장만으로는 도저히 이 상품을 ～시킬 수 없다 The home market alone cannot consume all these goods. *or* It is impossible for the domestic market alone to consume all these goods.
◉ ～관(管) 〖해부〗 an alimentary canal 〔tract〕. ～기(器) 〖해부〗 a digestive organ: ～기 계통 the digestive 〔alimentary〕 system / ～기 계통의 병 an alimentary disease; a gastrointestinal disease / ～기 장애 (a) digestive trouble. ～력 digestive power. ～불량 《suffer from, have an attack of》 indigestion 〔dyspepsia〕: 더위가 심해서 ～불량이 생겼다 The severe heat has given me indigestion. ～선(腺) 〖해부〗 a peptic gland. ～액 digestive fluid 〔juice〕. ～작용 a digestive process. ～제 an anti-indigestion tablet 〔powder〕; a digestive; a digester; a peptic. ～효소 digestive enzymes.

**소화물**(小貨物) a parcel; a packet; a package 《미》. ¶ ～로 보내다 《우편으로》 send 〔forward〕 《*something*》 by mail; 《철도편으로》 consign 《*something*》 as a parcel 《미》. ◉ ～담당자 a checkman. ～차 a parcels 〔luggage〕 van; an express car 《미》. ～취급소 a parcels office.

**소환**(召喚) 〖법〗 a summons (*pl.* ～es); a call. ～하다 call; summon; cite; subp(o)ena; demand. ¶ ～을 받다 receive a summons; be served with a subp(o)ena / 법정에 ～되다 be summoned to (appear before) the court / ～에 응하다 answer 〔obey〕 a summons / 증인으로 ～되다 be summoned as a witness; be called in testimony.
◉ ～장 a (writ of ) summons; 《벌칙이 따른》 a subp(o)ena; a citation: ～장을 내다 issue a summons 《against *a person*》.

**소환**(召還) the recall (★ 복수형은 쓰지 않음). ～하다 recall; call 〔order〕 back; summon to return. ¶ 대사를 ～하다 recall an ambassador / 본국에 ～되다 be summoned 〔recalled, ordered〕 home. ◉ ～제도 the recall system.

**소회**(所懷) *one's* intimate impressions 〔thoughts〕. ⇨ 소감.

**속** ① 《안》 the inside; the interior 《of *a thing*》; the inner part; 《깊숙한》 the innermost 〔inmost〕 recess; the heart. ¶ 산 속 the heart of a mountain / 서랍〔봉투〕 속 the inside of a drawer 〔an envelope〕/ 그림 속의 꽃 the flowers in the picture / 말 속의 숨은 뜻 the hidden meaning of words / 물 속 깊이 deep in the water; at the bottom of the sea / 숲 속을 지나가다 pass 〔go〕 through a wood / 숲 속으로 들어가다 take to the woods.
속에: 속에 in; into; within; inside; inward; 《많은 것의》 among / 빈곤 속에서 in poverty / 서랍 속에서 꺼내다 take 《*something*》 out of a drawer / 굴 속에서 살다 live in a cave / 붐비는 인파 속에서 놓치다 lose sight of 《*a person*》 in the crowd.
¶ 배는 바닷속에 가라앉았다 The ship sank down to the bottom of the sea.
② 《마음·이면》 the depth; the bottom; the heart; inner workings (장사의). ¶ 속이 검은 black-hearted; scheming / (마음)속으로는 at bottom 〔heart〕; in *one's* heart of hearts / 속을 알 수 없는

사람 a mysterious character; an enigmatic person; a sphinx / 속으로 걱정하다 be secretly worried 《about》/ 속으로 웃다 laugh in *one's* sleeve; grin inside / 속을 떠보다 sound 《*a person*》 on 〔about〕; probe 《*a person's*》 intention; throw out a feeler / 속을 빤히 들여다 보다 see through 《*a person's*》 intention; see through 《*a person's*》 heart; read another's inmost thoughts / 속을 썩이다 worry *oneself* 〔be worried〕 《about, over》/ 속을 털어 놓다 unbosom 〔unburden〕 *oneself* 《to》; speak (out) *one's* mind / 속이 들여다 보이다 be easily seen through / 속이 빤히 들여다 보이는 거짓말 a transparent 〔an obvious〕 lie / 속이 들여다 보이는 짓을 하다 resort to a shallow trick; make a hollow imposture / 가슴 속에 비밀을 품다 keep a secret in *one's* bosom / 속 각각 말 각각 do not mean what *one* says / 그는 속이 넓은 사람이다 He is large-hearted. / 그는 장사 속을 잘 안다 He knows the business inside out.

③ 《속엣것》 contents (내용); substance (실질); stuff (이불·박제 표본 따위의). ¶ 연필속 lead / 매트리스에 속을 넣다 stuff the mattress / 그릇 속의 것을 비우다 drain a vessel of its contents / 지갑 속을 털다 empty *one's* purse / 상자 속의 것은 무엇입니까 What is there in the box?

④ 《중심·핵》 a heart; a core (과일의); a pith (초목의); 《뼛속》 the marrow. ¶ 사과 속을 도려내다 core an apple / 배추 속 the heart of a Chinese cabbage / 속속들이 썩다 be rotten to the core / 추위가 뼛속까지 스며들다 be chilled to the marrow 〔bone〕.

⑤ 《뱃속》 insides; stomach. ¶ 빈 속 empty stomach / 속이 비다 get 〔feel〕 hungry / 속이 좋지 않다 《느글거리다》 feel sick 〔nausea〕; be sick at the stomach; 《배탈이 나서》 get *one's* bowels out of order; 《얹혀서》 be heavy 〔stodgy〕; oppress the stomach.

⑥ 《한창 …하는 가운데》 ¶ 쏟아지는 빗속을 《go out》 in the (pouring) rain / 그들은 폭풍우 속에서 출항했다 They left in the middle of the storm.

**속**(屬) 〖생물〗 a genus. ¶ 속의 generic.

**속**(束) 《묶음》 a bundle 《of dried laver》.

**속**(續) a second series; a sequel; (a) continuation 《of》. ¶ 속편 a supplementary volume; a follow-up; a sequel to a preceding volume.

**속가**(俗歌) a popular 〔folk〕 song; a ditty; a ballad.

**속가죽** the inner part 〔layer〕 of hide 〔skin〕.

**속간**(續刊) continuation of publication. ～하다 continue to publish; continue the publication 《of the magazine》.

**속개**(續開) resumption; continuation. ～하다 resume; continue. ¶ 회의는 내일 ～된다 The conference will resume its session tomorrow.

**속객**(俗客) 〖불교〗 the laity; a layman; 《멋없는 사람》 a crass person.

**속격**(屬格) 〖문법〗 the genitive (case).

**속결**(速決) ＝즉결(卽決).

**속계**(俗界) the (mundane) world; the earthly 〔secular〕 world. ⇨ 속세.

**속고**(續稿) remaining manuscripts; manuscripts continued 《from》; the sequence 《of manuscripts》.

**속고갱이** the heart; the very heart 〔core〕. ¶ 배추의 ～ the heart of a cabbage.

**속곳** a slip; a petticoat; underwear. ¶ ～ 바람으로 with nothing on but a slip.

**속공**(速攻) a quick attack. ～하다 launch a swift attack on 〔against〕 《the enemy》. ¶ (경기에서) 다양한 ～을 펼치다 charge 《the Japanese team》 with varied types of quick attacks.

**속구**(速球) 〖야구〗 《throw》 a speed 〔fast〕 ball. ◉ ～투수 a fast-ball pitcher; a speedballer 《미속어》.

**속국**(屬國) a dependency; a subject 〔vassal〕 state 〔country〕; a tributary (state). ¶ 영국의 ～이다 be subject to England / ～이 되다 come 〔pass〕 under the sway 〔rule〕 of 《another state》; become (a) tributary to 《some power》.

**속궁리**(一窮理) reflecting to *oneself;* considering. ～하다 reflect 《on》; cast about in *one's* mind 《for》; mull 《over》.

**속기**(俗氣) vulgarity; worldliness; worldly ambition. ¶ ～가 있다 be vulgar 〔worldly〕.

**속기**(速記) ① 《속필》 quick 〔prompt〕 writing. ～하다 note down fast; take rapid notes 《of》. ② 《속기법》 shorthand (writing); stenography. ～하다 write 〔take〕 down in shorthand; take stenographic notes 《of》; stenograph. ¶ ～를 배우다 learn shorthand; take lessons in stenography / 연설을 ～하다 take down a speech in shorthand. ◉ ～록 a stenographic record; shorthand notes. ～문자 a stenographic character. ～법〔술〕 stenography; shorthand. ～사 a stenographer; a shorthand writer. ～학교 a shorthand school.

**속꺼풀** the inner layer of the outer cover.

**속껍데기**, **속껍질** the inner layer of skin 〔cover〕; 〖동물·식물〗 the endoderm; 〖해부〗 the endothelium (*pl.* -lia).

**속끓이다** worry 《about》; suffer anxiety; be overanxious.

**속내** 《내부 사정》 the real state 《of affairs》; the internal conditions; the inside (facts); concealed 〔undisclosed〕 circumstances; the inside story; 《장사의》 inner workings. ¶ ～를 들여다보다 see behind the scenes / ～를 알고 있다 have an inside knowledge 《of》; have the low-down 《on》; be in the know / ～를 알아보다 inquire into the real state.

**속념**(俗念) vulgar 〔secular〕 thoughts; worldly considerations 〔thoughts〕; earthly desires 〔ambitions〕; worldliness. ¶ ～을 버리다 free *oneself* from earthly desires.

**속눈뜨다** peer 〔peek〕 through half-closed eyes.

**속눈썹** eyelashes; lashes; winkers 《구어》. ¶ 긴 ～ long lashes. ◉ 인조～ false eyelashes.

**속다** get deceived; be cheated 〔defrauded, fooled〕; be imposed (up)on; be taken in. ¶ 잘 속는 gullible; credulous / 잘 속는 사람 a credulous person; a dupe; a gull; a sucker / 감쪽같이 ～ be nicely 〔fairly〕 taken in; fall an easy victim to 《*another's*》 trick / 속아서 돈을 빼앗기다 get cheated out of money; be swindled / 물건을 속아 사다 get gypped in buying 《*a thing*》; get stung; buy a lemon 《구어》/ 세상을 속아 살다 live *one's* life in illusion 〔under illusions〕 / 그녀의 얌전한 태도에 속았다 Her quiet manner deceived 〔fooled〕 me. / 나는 그 녀석한테 감쪽같이 속았어 I was completely 〔fairly〕 taken in by him. / 그에게 속아 넘어갔다 He has made a dupe of me. / 그런 달콤한 말에 나는 안 속는다 I won't fall for your sweet words. / 그런 수단에 속을 줄 아느냐 Is there any green in my eye? / 아 속았구나 Alas! I've been duped! / 너한테 속지 않는다 You can't fool me. / 그 집을 속아서 샀다 I got stung when I bought that house. / 속는 셈 치고 이 약을 한 번 먹어보게 Just trust me this once and try this medicine.

**속닥-** ⇨ 숙덕-.

**속단**(速斷) ① 《빠른 단정》 a hasty conclusion. ～하다 make 〔draw, form〕 a hasty conclusion; jump to a conclusion; decide rashly 〔hastily〕; run away with the idea 《that…》. ¶ 성공이 틀림없다고 ～하다 jump to the conclusion that this will ensure *one's* success / 그가 우리에게 한 말이 거짓말이라고 ～해서는 안 된다 You should not jump to the conclusion that what he told us is a lie. ② 《빠른 판단》 an immediate judgment; a prompt decision. ～하다 pass 〔form〕 an immediate judgment 《on》; be prompt in deciding 《that》.

**속달**(速達) special delivery 《미》; express delivery 《영》. ～하다 deliver by express. ¶ ～로 보내다 send 《a letter》 by express 〔special delivery〕; express 《a parcel》 / ～로 보내려면 요금이 얼마나 듭니까 How much does it cost if I send it (by) express?
◉ ～료 a special-delivery fee; an express-delivery charge. ～소포 a special-delivery package 〔parcel〕. ～우편 special delivery mail 《미》; express delivery post 《영》. 국내 항공～ domestic air mail express.

**속달다** be anxious 〔eager〕 《to *do*, for》; be impatient 《to *do*, for》; worry 《about》; bother (*oneself*) 《about》; be nervous 《about》; be all hot and bothered 《to *do*》; jitter 《about》; go 〔get〕 into a stew 《about》 《구어》. ¶ 결과를 알고싶어 ～ be anxious to know the result / 속달게 하다 fidget; fret 《*a person's*》 heart; 《불안으로》 keep 〔hold〕 《*a person*》 in suspense / 그렇게 속달아 할 것 없다 Don't fret yourself like that.

**속담**(俗談) a proverb; a (common) saying. ¶ ～에 있듯이 as the proverb goes 〔runs〕.

**속대**[1] 《채소의》 the heart 《of vegetables》. ◉ ～쌈 rice wrapped in cabbage hearts. 속댓국 cabbage-heart soup.

**속대**[2] 《댓개비의》 bamboo pith.

**속대중** *one's* personal estimate; a rough guess based on *one's* feelings.

**속도**(速度) (a) speed; (a) rate; (a) velocity; a pace; 〖음악〗 (a) tempo. ¶ 최고～ 《at》 maximum 〔top〕 speed / 고속도로에서의 최저 ～ the minimum speed on the expressway / 고〔저〕～로 at high 〔low〕 speed / 경제～로 at an economic speed / 무서운 ～로 at breakneck speed / ～가 빠르다〔느리다〕 be high-〔low-〕speed; be fast 〔slow〕 / ～가 붙다〔줄다〕 gain 〔lose〕 in speed / ～를 내다 increase 〔gather, put on〕 the speed; speed up; 《자동차의》 step on the gas 《미구어》 / ～를 줄이다〔늦추다〕 slow down; decrease 〔reduce〕 speed / ～를 조절하다 regulate 〔control〕 the speed 《of》 / ～를 줄이시오 《게시》 Reduce speed. *or* Slow down. / 나는 시속 60km의 ～로 차를 달렸다 I drove at (a speed of) 60 kilometers per 〔an〕 hour. / 태풍이 시속 200km의 ～로 접근하고 있다 A typhoon is approaching at a velocity of 200km per hour. / 나는 언제나 제한 ～를 지키고 있다 I always obey the speed limit. ◉ ～계 a speedometer; a speed indicator; 《자동차 따위의》 an autometer. ～시험 a speed test. ～조절기 a speed regulator; a governor.

**속도위반**(速度違反) going over 〔exceeding〕 the speed limit; speeding; violation of the speed regulations. ¶ ～단속 경찰(관) a speed cop / ～으로 벌금을 물다 be fined 《30,000 won》 for speeding / ～을 하다 break 〔violate〕 the speed law. ◉ ～자 a violator of the speed regulations; a speeder.

**속도제한**(速度制限) a speed limit. ¶ ～을 하다 set 〔place〕 a speed limit 《on》; enforce speed regulations / ～시속 30마일 《게시》 Speed limit: 30 mph. ◉ ～장치 a speed-limiting device. ～표지 a speed-limit sign.

**속독**(速讀) rapid 〔fast, quick〕 reading. ～하다 read 《a book》 rapidly 〔fast〕.

**속되다**(俗—) 《비속하다》 (be) vulgar; low; base; 《통속적이다》 (be) common; popular; 《세속적이다》 (be) worldly; secular; mundane. ¶ 속된 사람들 worldly people / 속된 취미 vulgar 〔low〕 tastes / 속된 말로 하면 to use a common word 〔phrase〕; in everyday language / 속된 마음을 버리다 free *oneself* from earthly desires.

**속등**(續騰) a continued advance; a further rise; spiraling. ～하다 continue to advance 〔rise〕; spiral upward.

**속뜻** inner meaning.

**속락**(續落) a continued fall 〔drop〕; a further decline; sagging; sliding. ～하다 continue to fall 〔drop〕; keep declining; fall persistently.

**속량**(贖良) emancipation of slaves; freeing slaves. ～하다 emancipate; free 《slaves》.

**속력**(速力) (a) speed; (a) velocity; (a) rate. ⇨ 속도. ¶ 전～으로 at full 〔top〕 speed; (at) full tilt / 놀라운 ～으로 with (a) surprising speed.

**속령**(屬領) 《영토》 a territory; a possession; 《속국》 a dependency; a dependent domain 〔territory〕; a subject province.

**속례**(俗例) convention; a (popular) custom; a (common) usage; a common way.

**속론**(俗論) conventional views; conventionalism; vulgar opinion. ¶ ～에 따르다 bow to people's opinion; 《시류를 좇다》 swim with the current.

**속류**(俗流) the common 〔ordinary〕 run of men; the vulgar masses.

**속립**(粟粒) a millet seed. ¶ ～ 모양의 miliary; granular. ◉ ～결절〔포진〕 『의학』 a milium (*pl.* -lia). ～결핵 miliary tuberculosis.

**속마음** *one's* innermost feelings; *one's* inmost heart; *one's* heart of hearts; the bottom of *one's* heart; *one's* real intention 〔motive〕; 《엉큼한》 a secret intention 〔desire〕. ¶ ～을 알아차리다 see through 《*a person's*》 underlying motive / ～을 털어놓다 reveal *one's* real intention; unbosom *oneself;* lay bare *one's* heart / 서로 ～을 잘 아는 사이다 be close friends; be well used to each other's ways / 그는 겉으론 그런 말을 하지만 ～은 다르다 He may talk that way on the surface, but deep down inside he's thinking something else. / 그것이 과연 그의 ～에서 나온 말일까 I wonder if he really meant what he said.

**속말** a confidential 〔private〕 talk; a confidence. ¶ 친구에게 ～을 하다 confide a secret to a friend; take a friend into *one's* confidence.

**속명**(俗名) ① 《통속적인》 a popular 〔familiar〕 name; a common 〔vernacular〕 name (속칭); 『불교』 a secular name. ② 《속된 명성》 worldly fame 〔reputation〕.

**속명**(屬名) 『생물』 a generic name.

**속무**(俗務) worldly affairs; down-to=earth matters; everyday business; daily routine. ¶ ～에 쫓기다 be 〔find *oneself*〕 busy with routine work.

**속문학**(俗文學) vulgar literature.

**속물**(俗物) a snob; a philistine; a vulgar person; a worldling. ¶ 그는 보기보다 더 ～이다 He is more snobbish

than he looks.
◉ ～근성 snobbery; Philistinism.
**속바지** underpants; drawers.
**속박**(束縛) (a) restraint; (a) restriction; shackles; trammels; fetters; a yoke. ～하다 restrain; restrict; put restraints 〔restrictions〕《on》; place 〔lay〕《*a person*》 under restraint; trammel; shackle; enchain; fetter; bind; put under the yoke. ¶ 공무의 ～ official trammels / 도덕적 ～ moral restraints / 자유를 ～하다 restrain 《*a person*》 of *his* liberty; restrict 《*a person's*》 freedom / ～을 받다 be subject to restraint; be placed under restraint; be fettered 《by》 / ～을 받지 않다 be free from restraint; be untrammeled 〔untethered〕 / 행동을 ～당하다 be restricted in *one's* movements / 언론의 자유를 ～하다 「place a gag on 〔restrict〕 freedom of speech / ～을 벗어나다 free *oneself* from restraint; break away from the yoke 《of》 / 규정이나 규칙으로 아무를 ～하다 restrain 《*a person*》 with rules and regulations.
**속발**(續發) successive 〔frequent〕 occurrence; a succession 〔series〕 《of events》. ～하다 happen 〔occur〕 in succession; come out 〔crop up〕 one after another. ¶ ～하는 사건 a rash 〔close sequence〕 of events / 최근 교통 사고가 ～하고 있다 There has been a series of traffic accidents recently. / 이 부근에서는 날치기 사건이 ～하고 있다 There has been a succession of purse-snatching incidents around here.
**속버선** double-layer inner socks worn under the heavy cotton-padded outer socks.
**속벌** a set of underwear.
**속병**(―病) a chronic internal disease; a gastroenteric disorder; an intestinal disease.
**속보**(速步) 《사람의》 a quick pace; quicksteps; 『군사』 a quick march; 《말의》 a trot. ¶ ～로 at a 「quick pace 〔trot〕 / ～로 걷다 《말이》 trot; 《사람이》 walk fast / 매일 ～로 2km를 걷다 walk at a brisk pace for two kilometers every day.
**속보**(速報) a prompt 〔quick〕 report 〔announcement〕; 《라디오·텔리비전 따위의》 a news flash; spot news. ～하다 report promptly; announce quickly; make a quick report 《on》. ¶ 선거 ～ prompt 〔hour-by-hour〕 reports of the election returns 〔results〕 / 뉴스 ～로 그 사고를 알게 되었다 I learned of the accident from a news flash. / 개표 결과의 ～가 있었다 There was a news flash of the results of the votecount. ◉ ～판(板) a bulletin 〔flash〕 board; a newsboard 《주로 영》.
**속보**(續報) a continued 〔follow-up〕 report; a follow-up; further news; further 〔additional〕 particulars. ¶ 현지에서의 사건 ～ 《receive》 a follow-up spot report.
**속보이다** be easily seen through; be transparent; be conjecturable. ¶ 속보이는 짓을 하다 resort to a shallow trick.
**속사**(俗事) worldly 〔mundane, secular〕 affairs 〔matters〕; common(place) business; daily affairs 〔routine〕. ¶ ～에 쫓기다 be busy with routine work; be engrossed in daily affairs / ～에 얽매이지 않다 rise 〔be〕 above the world; stand aloof from mundane affairs.
**속사**(速射) firing in rapid succession; rapid fire. ～하다 fire quickly 〔in rapid succession〕; machinegun.
◉ ～포(砲) a quick-firing gun; a rapid-fire gun.
**속사**(速寫) 《빨리 베낌》 quick copying; 『사진』 snapshooting; snapshotting. ～하다 copy quickly; snapshoot; take a snapshot 《of》; snap. ◉ ～카메라 a snapshot 〔candid〕 camera.
**속사정**(―事情) the inside 〔unrevealed〕 circumstances.
**속삭거리다** whisper. ⇨ 속삭이다.
**속삭속삭** in whispers; under *one's* breath.
**속삭이다** whisper; talk 〔say〕 in whispers; speak under *one's* breath; 《시냇물·바람 따위가》 murmur; ripple. ¶ 사랑의 속삭임 soft nothings; sweet whispers of love / 귀에 (대고) ～ whisper in 《*a person's*》 ear / 서로 ～ exchange whispers; whisper to each other.
**속산**(速算) 《do, make》 a rapid calculation.
**속살** ① 《옷 속의》 parts of the body ordinarily covered by clothing; *one's* nakedness. ¶ ～이 내비치는 블라우스 a see-through blouse. ② 《고기의》 the inner meat of 《a lobster》; 《쇠고기의》 the meat in the cow's mouth.
**속살찌다** ① 《살찌다》 (be) fat; plumper than 《he》 looks; solidly fleshy. ② 《실속 있다》 (be) substantial; solid; rich.
**속상하다**(―傷―) [주어는 it] be distress-

ing 〔worrisome, annoying, exasperating〕; get on *one's* nerves; [주어는 I] be distressed 〔worried, annoyed, exasperated, vexed, harassed, troubled〕. ¶ 속상하게 굴다 vex; harass; annoy; get on 《*a person's*》 nerves; "get 《*a person's*》 goat" / 비가 늘 와서 속상해 죽겠다 This constant raining 「gives me the willies 〔is making me a nervous wreck〕. *or* Drat this rain! / 기차를 놓쳐서 ～ I am mad at missing the train.

**속상해하다** 《…이》 《you, he》 be distressed 〔worried, annoyed, exasperated, harassed, troubled〕; 《…을》 be annoyed at 〔vexed by, worried over, exasperated at〕.

**속생각** inward thoughts; thinking to *oneself*. ～하다 think to *oneself*.

**속설**(俗說) a common 〔popular〕 saying; a common talk; a popular version; 《전설》 folklore; a legend. ¶ ～에 의하면 it is traditionally said that…; according to a popular tradition…; the popular account is that….

**속성**(俗姓) *one's* secular surname.

**속성**(速成) 《단기 양성》 an intensive training 《in》; short-course instruction 《in》; 《조기 완성》 rapid completion. ～하다 train 《*a person*》 quickly; give 《*a person*》 an intensive training 《in English》; complete rapidly. ¶ ～으로 프랑스 말을 배우다 learn French by hasty cramming. ◉ ～과(科) a short 〔an intensive〕 course 《in French》: 영어 회화 ～과 《간판》 A short, intensive course in English Conversation. ～법 a shortcut 〔royal road〕 《to》; a quick (-mastery) method 〔way〕.

**속성**(屬性) 〖논리〗 an attribute; a property; 〖생물〗 a generic character.

**속세**(俗世) this world; mundane life; earthly existence. ¶ ～를 버리다 renounce 〔retire from〕 the world; go to live in seclusion.

**속세간**(俗世間) this world. ⇨ 속세.

**속셈** ① 《심산》 a secret intention; private intentions; inner thoughts; an ulterior motive. ¶ 무언가 ～이 있어서 for some hidden object / ～이 있다 have a plot in mind; have a secret design 〔intention〕; have some private end in view; have something up *one's* sleeve / ～을 꿰뚫어 보다 penetrate 〔see through〕 the designs of … / ～을 드러내다 reveal *one's* secret intention / 그의 ～을 모르겠다 I don't know what he has in mind. / 그의 ～은 뻔하다 I can see through his intentions. / 그의 ～은 우리와 사뭇 다르다 His true intentions are quite different from ours.

② 《암산》 mental arithmetic 〔calculation〕. ～하다 calculate mentally; do (*one's*) sums in *one's* head.

**속셔츠** an underwear shirt; an undershirt; next-to-skin wear. ¶ ～만 입고 있다 have nothing on but an undershirt / ～ 바람으로 일하다 work in *one's* undershirt.

**속속**(續續) one after another; successively; in (close, rapid) succession; one upon the heels of another. ¶ ～ 밀려들다 rush on 《a place》 / ～ 탈당하다 leave the party one after another / 주문이 ～ 들어왔다 Orders poured in. *or* We were flooded with orders.

**속속곳** women's underwear; *lingerie* (F.) (worn under slip).

**속속들이** to the core; thoroughly; inside out. ¶ ～ 썩다 be rotten to the core / ～ 젖다 be drenched 〔wet〕 to the skin; 《옷이》 get dripping wet / 사람의 마음을 ～ 알다 know a man through and through / 그 장사는 내가 ～다 안다 I know the business inside out.

**속손톱** the half-moon 〔lunule, root〕 of 「a fingernail.

**속수무책**(束手無策) helplessness; resourcelessness; being at a loss; being at *one's* wit's 〔wits'〕 end. ¶ ～이다 be (quite) at a loss what to do; be at *one's* wit's end / ～이군 Nothing can be done about it. *or* What else could be done? *or* There's no help for it.

**속썩다** feel sick at heart; be worried 〔troubled〕 《about》; worry 〔trouble〕 *oneself* 《about》.

**속씨식물**(一植物) an angiosperm.

**속아넘어가다** be deceived; be cheated; be fooled. ¶ 감쪽같이 ～ be nicely 〔fairly, completely〕 taken in 《by》; be caught in a trap; fall for a trick; be nicely deceived.

**속악**(俗惡) vulgarity; inelegance; coarseness. ～하다 (be) vulgar; low(brow); coarse.

**속안**(俗眼) a layman's eye 《속어》; a lay opinion 〔view〕; a popular view.

**속어**(俗語) a slang word 〔expression〕; [총칭] 《a piece of》 slang. ¶ ～를 쓰다 use slang / ～를 쓰기 좋아하다 be fond of using slang; be addicted to slang / 「빵간」은 「감방」의 ～이다 "Pen"

is slang for "prison".
**속어림** *one's* guess; a conjecture; *one's* personal 〔mental〕 estimation. ¶ ～으로 by guess(work); in *one's* estimation 〔thought〕. 「talk.
**속언**(俗言) a vulgar saying; common
**속언**(俗諺) a common 〔popular〕 saying; an old saw; a proverb.
**속없다** 《실속 없다》 (be) unsubstantial; empty; 《줏대 없다》 (be) spineless; spiritless; 《악의 없다》 (be) innocent; harmless. ¶ 속없는 말 idle talk / 속없는 사람 an easygoing person; a shallow person; a spineless person / 속없이 한 말이다 I meant no harm 〔offense〕. 「속이다.
**속여먹다, 속여넘기다** cheat; deceive. ⇨
**속연**(續演) the continuation of a show. ～하다 continue to stage 〔put on〕 《a play》; run 《a show》 consecutively 《for three months》.
**속열매껍질** 『식물』 an endocarp.
**속영**(續映) a continued run 《of a film》. ～하다 continue to show 《a movie》; run 《for three months》.
**속옷** underwear; underclothes; undergarments. ¶ ～을 갈아입다 change *one's* underlinen. 「ballad; a ditty.
**속요**(俗謠) a popular 〔folk〕 song; a
**속요량**(一料量) conjecturing to *oneself;* making a private estimate. ～하다 conjecture to *oneself;* privately estimate.
**속음**(俗音) a popular pronunciation 〔reading〕 of a Chinese character.
**속이다** ① 《기만하다》 deceive; cheat; dupe; swindle; fool; impose on 《*a person*》; take 《*a person*》 in; defraud; play 《*a person*》 false 〔a trick〕. ¶ 속이기〔잘 속기〕 쉬운 gullible; credulous / 속이기 쉬운〔잘 속는〕 사람 a dupe; a gull; a sucker 《미속어》 / 근량을〔저울눈을〕 ～ give short 〔light〕 weights; shortweight / (남의) 눈을 ～ hoodwink 《*a person*》; pull 〔draw〕 the wool over 《*a person's*》 eyes / 놀음에서 ～ cheat in gambling / 자신을 ～ deceive *oneself* / 속여서 빼앗다 defraud 〔hoax〕 《*a person*》 of 《*something*》; cheat 〔bilk〕 《*a person*》 (out) of 《*something*》; swindle 〔wheedle, trick, do, cajole〕 《*a person*》 out of 《*something*》; cajole 《*something*》 out of 《*a person*》 / 속여서 …하게 하다 trick 〔deceive〕 《*a person*》 into *do*ing / 물건을 속여 팔다 sell a thing fraudulently.
② 《거짓말·허위 따위로》 lie; tell a lie; fake; falsify; misrepresent; 《가장하다》 feign; pretend; dissemble. ¶ 나이를〔사실을〕 ～ misrepresent *one's* age 〔a fact〕 / 대학생이라고 ～ feign 〔pretend to be〕 a university student; pass 〔palm〕 *oneself* off as a university student / 아프다고 ～ feign illness; pretend to be ill / 이름을 ～ assume 〔give〕 a false name.
③ 《잔재주를 피워》 cook (up); doctor; tamper with; 《일시적으로 넘기다》 temporize; patch up 《*things*》. ¶ 가스 계량기를 ～ tamper with the gas meter / 장부를 ～ juggle the accounts; cook up 〔doctor〕 the accounts / 청구서를 ～ cook up 〔fudge〕 a bill.
**속인**(俗人) 《평신도》 a layman; [총칭] the laity; 《세속인》 a common person; a worldling; a vulgar 〔materialistic, unrefined〕 person.
**속인주의**(屬人主義) 『법』 the personal 〔nationality〕 principle; the principle of personal (privilege for) jurisdiction.
**속임수** (a piece of) trickery; a (fraudulent) trick; cheat(ing); a sly artifice. ¶ ～를 쓰다 practice deception on 《*a person*》; resort to tricks; play 〔serve〕 《*a person*》 a (deceitful) trick; play a trick on 《*a person*》 / ～에 걸리다〔넘어가다〕 be taken in; be tricked; fall a victim to fraud / 그 ～에는 안 넘어간다 That trick won't work with me.
**속잎** inner leaves (of a vegetable).
**속자**(俗字) the popular (simplified) form of a Chinese character.
**속잠방이** short underpants.
**속장** 《책의》 the inside pages.
**속적삼** an undershirt; underwear.
**속전속결**(速戰速決) an intensive 〔all=out〕 surprise attack 〔offensive〕; a *blitzkrieg* (G.). ¶ ～ 방식으로 하다 act decisively on the basis of a quick decision. ◉ ～전법 blitz tactics.
**속절없다** 《어쩔 수 없다》 (be) hopeless; (quite) helpless; cannot help 《it》; 《it》 cannot be helped; 《불가피하다》 (be) inevitable; unavoidable; inescapable. ¶ 속절없이 helplessly; unavoidably; inevitably / 속절없이 굶다 starve helplessly / 속절없이 붙잡히다 be held 〔arrested〕 with no way out / 모든 일이 ～ All is vanity.
**속죄**(贖罪) atonement for 〔expiation of〕 *one's* sin(s); redemption. ～하다 「make amends 〔atone〕 for *one's* sin(s); expiate *one's* sin(s). ¶ 그리스

도의 ~ the (Vicarious) Atonement; the Redemption / 죽음으로써 ~하다 expiate a crime with death.
◉ ~론 the doctrine of atonement. ~양 a scapegoat.

**속주다** speak *one's* mind; take 《*a person*》 into *one's* confidence; open *one's* heart 《to *a person*》; let 《*a person*》 know *one's* mind.

**속지주의**(屬地主義) 『법』 the territorial principle; the principle of territorial for jurisdiction.

**속진**(俗塵) the world; earthly 〔mundane〕 affairs. ¶ ~을 떠나다 keep away from the crowd 〔earthly things〕; live secluded from the world.

**속짐작** *one's* (mental) estimation; a guess; a conjecture; a surmise.

**속창** a shoe liner; an inner sole. ¶ 신에 ~을 깔다 put liners in shoes.

**속출**(續出) successive 〔frequent〕 occurrence 〔appearance〕. ~하다 appear 〔come out〕 one after another; occur in succession. ¶ 부상자가 ~하였다 One person after another got wounded. / 비행기 사고가 ~했다 Air accidents occurred in succession.

**속치레** interior decoration. ¶ ~를 하다 decorate the interior.

**속치마** an underskirt; a slip; a chemise; a petticoat.

**속치장**(—治裝) interior decoration 〔design〕.

**속칭**(俗稱) a popular 〔familiar〕 name; 《학명에 대해》 a common 〔vernacular〕 name. ~하다 call 〔name〕 popularly; be popularly 〔better〕 known as. ¶ ~ …라 하다 be commonly called…; be popularly known as….

**속타다** be worried 《about》; feel 〔be〕 uneasy 〔anxious, nervous〕 《about》; be vexed 〔harassed, annoyed〕; fret (and fume); be all hot and bothered. ¶ 속타는 일 sources of worry; worries; anguish; agony / 근심 걱정으로 ~ be tormented with cares and anxieties / 속(이) 타서 병이 나다 worry *oneself* ill.

**속탈**(—頉) a stomach upset 〔trouble, disorder〕. ¶ ~이 나다 get *one's* bowels out of order; have stomach trouble.

**속태우다** ① 《자신을》 worry 〔bother〕 (*oneself*) 《about》; be anxious 《about》; be distressed 〔upset, anxious, bothered〕; feel nervous. ¶ 쓸데없는 일에 ~ worry over trifles / 아이 때문에 어머니가 속(을) 태운다 The mother is worried about the child. ② 《남의 속을》 worry; cause worry 〔anxiety〕 to; upset; distress; make nervous; bother; keep 《*a person*》 in suspense; put 《*a person*》 in a ruffle. ¶ 아이가 어머니를 속태운다 The child worries the mother. / 속태우지 말고 빨리 가르쳐 줘 Don't keep me in suspense.—Tell me right away.

**속편**(續編) a sequel 《of, to》; a continuation 《of》; a follow-up; a supplementary 〔second〕 volume.

**속표지**(—表紙) a title page; the front page; the title leaf.

**속필**(速筆) quick writing; a hasty scribble; a fast hand (with pen or brush).

**속하다**(速—) (be) fast; quick; swift; rapid; speedy. ⇨ 빠르다 ① (***a***).

**속하다**(屬—) 《소속하다》 belong 《to》; appertain 《to》; be affiliated with 《the party》; 《분류상》 come 〔fall〕 under 《a category》. ¶ 가옥과 그에 속한 모든 물건 the house and all that goes with it / 세균은 식물계에 속한다 Bacteria belongs to the vegetable kingdom. / 그 문제의 연구는 본래 심리학 영역에 속한다 The study of that subject belongs properly to the domain of psychology. / 그는 민주당에 속해 있다 He is affiliated to the Democratic Party. / 괌은 미국에 속한 섬이다 Guam is an island (which is) subject to the United States. / 거부권은 대통령 권한에 속한다 The veto power is invested in the President.

**속항하다**(續航—) continue the voyage; [배가 주어] keep the sea.

**속행**(速行) ~하다 go 〔walk〕 quickly; carry out speedily; take prompt action.

**속행**(續行) continuation; continuance. ~하다 proceed 〔go ahead〕 《with》; continue 《to *do*, with the work》; go 〔carry〕 on 《with》; keep on 《*do*ing》; pursue; 《재개하다》 resume. ¶ 경기를 ~하다 continue 〔proceed with〕 a game / 토의〔회의〕를 ~하다 continue 〔proceed with〕 debates 〔its session〕 / 교섭은 아직 ~ 중이다 The negotiations are still going on.

**속화**(俗化) vulgarization; popularization; secularization. ~하다 《…을》 vulgarize; popularize; secularize; 《…이》 get vulgarized; become vulgar; be secularized.

**속회**(續會) resumption of a meeting. ~하다 resume a meeting.

**속효**(速效) an immediate 〔a quick〕 effect. ⇨ 즉효(卽效).

**속히**(速—) rapidly; swiftly; speedily;

quickly; promptly. ¶ ～ 대답(을) 하다 make a prompt reply / ～ 말해라 Speak up!

**솎다** thin 〔cull〕 (out); weed out. ¶ 양파를 ～ thin out the onion plants / 무는 알맞게 솎아 줘야 굵어진다 The radishes won't grow unless you thin out the seedlings properly.

**솎음(질)** 《일》 thinning out; weeding out. ～(질)하다 thin 〔weed〕 out.

**손**[1] ① 《사람·동물의》 the hand; the arm (팔). ¶ 손 하나 까딱 않다 be a perfect lazybones; be laziness itself; do not lift a finger.

손이: 손이 닿다 《can》 reach 《the ceiling》/ 손이 닿는〔미치는〕 곳에 있다 be within *one's* reach 〔grasp〕; be within (the reach of) *one's* hands / 손이 닿지 않는 곳에 있다 be beyond *one's* reach; be out of *one's* grasp / 손이 닳도록 빌다 apologize abjectly; be bowing with *one's* hands on the floor; humbly beg 《*a person's*》 pardon.

손에: 손에 땀을 쥐고 in breathless suspense / 손에 건네다〔넘기다〕 give 《*a thing*》 into another's hand; hand over 《*a thing* to *a person*》; place 《*a thing*》 in 《*a person's*》 hands / 손에 손을 잡고 걷다 walk hand in hand / 책을 손에 들고 산책하다 take a walk, book in hand 〔with a book in *one's* hand〕.

손으로: 손으로 만들다 make by hand / 손으로 만든 것 a handmade article.

손을: 손을 내밀다 hold 〔stretch〕 out *one's* hands; offer *one's* hands / 손을 주머니에 넣고 with *one's* hands in the pocket / (잡았던) 손을 놓치다 loose *one's* hold of 〔on, over〕/ (잡았던) 손을 놓다 let go *one's* hold; unhand 《*a thing, a person*》/ 손을 놓고 with *one's* hands free / 손을 묶이다 have *one's* hands tied / 손을 들다 raise 〔lift〕 a 〔*one's*〕 hand / 손을 들고 with *one's* hands up; 《stand》 with upraised hand / 손을 벌리다 《팔을》 spread *one's* arms; 《쥐었던 손을》 open *one's* hand 〔fist〕; spread (out) the palm of *one's* hand / 손을 뻗(치)다 stretch (out) *one's* hand; put out *one's* hand; reach out 《to》; reach for 《a book》/ 손을 비비다 rub 〔chafe〕 *one's* hands / 두 손을 모으다 fold 〔clasp〕 *one's* hands / 손을 잡다〔쥐다〕 take 〔seize〕 《*a person's*》 hand; grasp another's hand; 《악수하다》 shake hands; clasp hands 《with》; shake 《*a person*》 by the hand / 손을 흔들다 wave *one's* hand; give a wave of *one's* hand / 두 손(을) 모아 빌다 pray with *one's* hands pressed together / 그는 넘어지면서 손을 짚었다 He stumbled and fell on hand. / 군중은 승리자에게 환성을 지르며 손을 흔들었다 The crowd cheered and waved to the winner.

② 《수중》 the hands 《of》; possession. ¶ 손에 넣다 get; obtain; win; take 〔gain〕 possession of; get 〔come〕 at; come by; secure / 손에 들어오다 come into *one's* possession; come to 〔fall into〕 *one's* hands / …의 손에 넘기다 hand over 《*a thing* to *a person*》/ 남의 손에 넘어가다 pass 〔fall〕 into another's hands / 그의 생사는 내 손에 달려 있다 His fate lies in my hands.

③ 《일손》 a hand; a man; a worker; an agency; 《도움》 a (helping) hand; a help. ¶ 여러 사람의 손으로 된 번역 a translation by various hands / …손을 거치다 pass through 《*a person's*》 hands / 손이 모자라다 be short of hands; be shorthanded; be undermanned / 손이 비다 have no work on hand; be disengaged; be at leisure / 손을 빌다 ask for help; ask 《*a person*》 a (helping) hand; call in the aid of / 손을 빌리다 give 〔lend〕 a hand; give 〔lend〕 《*a person*》 a helping hand / 일이 손에 안 잡히다 cannot go about *one's* work; have no heart for the work; be in no mood for work / 손에 익히다 get into practice; get *one's* hand 《in》/ 이 일은 여러 사람의 손이 필요하다 This work requires 〔calls for〕 many hands. / 나는 지금 손을 뗄 수 없는데, 네가 좀 해 주겠느냐 Would you do that for me? I'm tied up at the moment.

④ 《손질》 trouble; labor; care (돌봄). ¶ 손이 많이 가는 일 laborious 〔troublesome〕 work; a piece of work requiring great care / 손이 많이 가다 take much trouble; require much work; take a lot of care; be troublesome / 손을 덜다 save trouble.

⑤ 《관계·교제》 connection; meddling. ¶ 손을 대다 ⇨ 손대다 ② / 손을 끊다 ⇨ 손끊다 / 손을 떼다 ⇨ 손떼다 / 손을 쓰다 ⇨ 손쓰다 / 손을 잡다 join hands with 《*a person*》; tie 〔link〕 up with 《*a person*》.

⑥ 《때림》 a blow; strike. ⇨ 손대다 ③.

⑦ 《활수》 generosity. ⇨ 손크다.

⑧ 《수단·방법》 a way; a means. ⇨ 손쓰다 ¶ 이제와서는 더 손을 쓸 수가 없다

There's nothing more we can do now.
⑨《수완·잔꾀》a trick; an artifice; a trap; a snare; an art. ¶ …의 손에 걸리다 fall into 《*another's*》 hand; fall into a trap 〔snare〕 of. ＝수(手) ②.

**손**[2] ①《손님》a guest; a visitor; a caller; a customer; a traveler (길손). ②〖민속〗a wandering evil spirit.

**손**(損) loss; damage; disadvantage; harm. ⇨ 손해, 손실. ¶ 손을 보다 lose; suffer a loss / 손을 보는 것이 이득이 되다 gain by losing; sow loss and reap gain.

**손**[3]《가정·양보》(supposing) that. ¶ …손 치더라도 if we suppose that / …손 치자 let us suppose that / 네가 잘못했다손 치더라도 even supposing you to be in the wrong.

**손가락** a finger (★ 보통, 엄지손가락은 finger에 포함이 안됨). ¶ 엄지～ the thumb / 집게～ the forefinger; the index 〔first〕 finger / 가운뎃〔약, 새끼〕～ the middle 〔ring, little〕 finger / ～을 꼽아 세다 count on the fingers / ～에 끼다 put 〔wear〕 《a ring》 on *one's* finger / ～을 빨다 suck *one's* thumb 〔fingers〕 / ～을 딱딱 꺾다 crack *one's* finger joints / ～ 하나 까딱하기 싫다 do not want to lift a finger / ～ 하나(도) 건드리지 못하게 하다 do not allow 《*a person*》 to touch even with a finger; keep 《*something*》 inviolate 〔absolutely intact〕 / 그가 지금껏 제시간에 대어온 횟수는 열～으로 셀 수 있을 정도다 I could count the number of times he's been on time on the fingers of two hands.

**손가락자국** a finger mark; a fingerprint (지문).

**손가락질**《지시》pointing *one's* finger 《at》;《비난》shunning; scorning; treating with contempt. ～하다 point at 〔to〕; indicate;《비난하다》shun; scorn. ¶ ～을 받다 be pointed at 〔talked about〕 with scorn; be an object of social contempt / 남을 ～하는 것은 결례다 It is bad manners to point at a person. / 나는 절대로 남의 ～ 받을 일은 안 한다 I will never do anything which will bring contempt upon me.

**손가방** a briefcase; a portfolio; a valise; a handbag (여자용).

**손거스러미** a hangnail; an agnail. ¶ ～가 생기다 have a hangnail 《at》.

**손거울** a hand glass.

**손거칠다**《도벽이 있다》(be) light-fingered; thievish; [서술적] have sticky fingers. ¶ 그 아이는 손이 거칠다 The boy has sticky fingers 〔thievish habits〕.

**손겪다**《대접하다》entertain a guest.

**손결** the texture 〔skin〕 of the hand. ¶ 그녀는 ～이 곱다 She has soft hands.

**손곱다**《*one's* hands》be numb 〔stiff〕 with cold; [서술적] have numb hands. ¶ 손이 곱아 펜을 쥘 수가 없다 My fingers are so contracted by cold that I cannot hold a pen.

**손금** the lines of the palm. ¶ ～을 보다 read 《*a person's*》 palm 〔hand〕; tell 《*a person's*》 fortune by the lines on *his* palm;《남에게 보게 하다》have *one's* palm read 《by》; consult a palmist / ～이 좋다 have lucky lines in *one's* hand. ◉ ～쟁이 a palm reader; a palmist.

**손금**(損金) losing money; pecuniary loss.

**손길** an outstretched hand. ¶ ～(을) 잡다 join 〔clasp〕 hands / 따뜻한 구호의 ～을 뻗(치)다 extend a warm helping hand 《to *a person*》.

**손꼽다** count on *one's* fingers. ¶ 손꼽는 실업가 a leading businessman / 손꼽아 수를 세다 count numbers using *one's* fingers / 손꼽아 기다리다 look forward to; anticipate; wait eagerly for / 그는 그 고을에서 손꼽히는 재산가의 한 사람이다 He is one of the richest men in the town.

**손꼽아치다** be counted 《among》; rank; count 《among》; be eminent 〔ranking, leading, prominent, outstanding〕.

**손끊다**《관계를》break with; break away from; sever (*one's*) connection with; cut *oneself* free of. ¶ 그런 사람하고는 손끊어라 You should cut all your connections with that man. *or* Break it off with him.

**손끝** ①《손가락 끝》a fingertip. ¶ ～을 칼에 다치다 cut the tip of *one's* finger / ～이 닳도록 일하다 work *one's* fingers to the bone. ②《일 솜씨》manual dexterity. ¶ ～이 여물다 be clever at handicraft; be cleverhanded; be deft-fingered; be dexterous; be smart with *one's* hand. ③《모진 결과》an evil-working touch of *one's* fingers; an evil hand. ¶ ～(이) 맵다 have an evil hand; have a contaminating touch / 그는 모든 일에 ～이 맵다 He fouls up everything he touches. ④《기타》¶ ～(을) 맺다 remain idle; look on with folded arms.

**손녀**(孫女) a granddaughter.

**손놀림** ¶ 어색한〔서투른〕 ~으로 with clumsy hands; clumsily; awkwardly.

**손놓다** 《중단하다》 stop 《*do*ing》; cease from 《*do*ing》; leave off; discontinue 《*do*ing》; 《포기하다》 give up 《*do*ing》.

**손누비** quilting by hand. ◉ ~버선 hand-quilted bootees 〔socks〕.

**손님** ① 《방문객》 a caller; a visitor; a guest (초대객); company [총칭]. ¶ ~을 맞다 receive 〔see〕 a caller / ~이 있다 have a visitor / ~을 접대하다 entertain a guest / 결혼식에 ~을 청하다 invite guests to a wedding / 귀한 ~도 사흘 묵으면 귀찮다 《속담》 Fish and guests smell at three days old.
② 《구매자》 a customer; a patron (단골); custom [총칭]; trade; 《극장의》 an audience; 《승객》 a passenger; 《투숙객》 a guest. ¶ 현금으로 구매하는 ~ a satisfied customer / 단골~ regular customers / ~을 끌다 attract custom(-ers); draw custom 〔trade〕; 《유객꾼이》 tout; solicit customers / ~이 많다 have many customers; have a large custom / ~이 없다 have no customer / ~이 적다 have few customers; attract few customers; do little business / ~이 줄다 lose customers; be less patronized than before / 상점에 ~이 많다 a store enjoys wide patronage; a store has 〔attracts〕 a lot of customers / ~ 접대가 좋다〔나쁘다〕 be hospitable 〔inhospitable〕; 《가게 따위에서》 give good 〔bad〕 service / ~은 왕이다 The customer is king 〔is always right〕.
③ 《천연두》 『의학』 smallpox.

**손대다** ① 《손을 대다》 touch; lay *one's* hands 《on》. ¶ 진열품에 ~ touch exhibits / 남의 돈에 ~ make free with 〔dip into〕 another's money / 손대지 못하게 하다 keep 《*a thing*》 absolutely intact / 음식에 손대지 않다 leave food untouched / 손대지 않고 그대로 두다 leave 《*a thing*》 untouched 〔alone〕 / 저금에 손대지 않다 leave the savings intact / 손대지 마시오 《게시》 Hands off 《미》. *or* Please don't touch. / 마지막 문제는 손도 대지 못했다 I couldn't touch the last question.
② 《관여하다》 meddle with; have a finger 〔a hand, an oar〕 in; get 〔be〕 involved 《in》; put 〔turn, set〕 *one's* hand to 《a task》; attempt; 《착수하다》 start; set about; take up 《golf》; 《여자에게》 become intimate with 《a girl》; have carnal connection with. ¶ 정치에 손을 대다 dabble in politics / 사업에 ~ have a hand in 《a business》; concern *oneself* 《with》; embark on / 여자에게 ~ make advances to 〔make a pass at〕 a woman / 이런 일에 손대 본 적 있는가 Have you ever tried your hand in this kind of job? / 모르는 일에 손대지 마라 Don't get into things you don't understand.
③ 《때리다》 strike; hit; take a fist 〔give a blow〕 to. ¶ 먼저 ~ strike the first blow / 누가 먼저 손을 댔느냐 Who started the fight?

**손대야** a handbasin; a washbowl 《미》.

**손대중** measuring 〔weighing〕 by hand; hefting. ¶ ~으로 재다 measure by hand; heft 《*something*》 / 그의 ~은 꽤 정확하다 He measures by hand fairly accurately.

**손도끼** a hand ax; a hatchet.

**손도장**(一圖章) a thumb impression; a thumbmark; a thumbprint. ¶ ~을 찍다 seal 《a document》 with *one's* thumb.

**손독**(一毒) a hand-borne infection. ¶ ~(이) 오르다 be infected by touching with *one's* hands / 상처를 만지지 마라, ~이 오를라 Don't touch the wound, or it will get infected.

**손동작**(一動作) hand movement(s); manual activity.

**손들다** ① 《손을 들다》 raise 〔hold up〕 *one's* hand; lift *one's* hand 《against》 (때리려고). ¶ 손들어 Hands 〔Hold〕 up! ② 《지다》 be beaten 〔defeated〕; 《항복하다》 yield 《to》; give in; throw up *one's* hand. ¶손들었다 I'm beaten. ③ 《애를 먹다》 be 〔get〕 floored; be annoyed 《at, by, with》. ¶ 그 시험 문제에는 손들었다 I was stumped by the examination. / 그 바보 녀석에겐 손들었다 I don't know what to do with that fool.

**손등** the back of the hand.

**손때** dirt from the hands; thumbstains; finger marks; soiling by hand. ¶ ~ 묻은 책 a well-thumbed book / ~ 묻다 become hand-stained / ~ 묻히다 soil 《*a thing*》 with 〔by〕 the hand.

**손떼다** ① 《끝내다》 finish; complete; clear up. ¶ 일에서 ~ finish *one's* work; get work off *one's* hands. ② 《관계를 끊다》 finish with; get 《*something*》 off *one's* hands; sever *one's* connection with; break off 〔sever〕 *one's* relationship 〔connections〕 with 《*a person*》; wash *one's* hands of; pull out of; withdraw *oneself* from; be through with. ¶ 정치에서 손을 떼다 withdraw *oneself* from politics; put an end to *one's* political life / 그와는 손을 뗐다 I am through with him.

**손료**(損料) (a) rent (fee); hire. ¶ ～를 물다 pay for the hire 《of》.

**손모**(損耗) wear and tear; loss; wearing out. ¶ 기계의 ～가 매우 심하다 Wear on the machine is very severe.

**손목** a wrist; 〖해부〗 a carpus (*pl.* -pi). ¶ ～을 잡다 take 《*a person*》 by the wrist; catch 《*a person's*》 wrist; 《쥐다》 grasp 〔grab, grip〕 《*a person*》 by the wrist / ～이 가늘다 be slim-wristed. ◉ ～시계 a wristwatch; a watch.

**손바느질** sewing by hand; needlework. ¶ 고운 ～ fine needlework / ～한 hand-sewn.

**손바닥** the palm 〔flat〕 of the hand. ¶ ～만한 땅 a strip of land; a bit of ground / ～만한 마당 a miniature garden / ～으로 때리다 slap; give a slap; strike with the palm of *one's* hand / ～을 들여다보듯 환하다 know 《*a thing*》 like the palm of *one's* hand / 그것은 ～을 뒤집듯이 쉬운 일이다 It is as easy as turning the hand.

**손바람** the swish 〔swing〕 of a hand. ¶ 일에 ～이 나다 get into the swing of *one's* work.

**손발** hands and feet; hand and foot; 《사지》 the limbs. ¶ ～을 노출한 bare=limbed / ～이 크다 be big-limbed / ～을 묶다 bind 《*a person*》 hand and foot / ～을 못쓰게 되다 lose the use of *one's* limbs / 남의 ～이 되어 일하다 serve *a person* like a tool.

**손버릇** any habitual action of the hands; a thievish habit (도벽). ¶ ～이 나쁘다〔사납다〕 be light-fingered; have sticky fingers; be thievish.

**손보다** 《보살피다》 care for; take care of; see to it that there are no defects; 《수리하다》 repair 《a house》; mend; fix 《미구어》; put 《*something*》 in repair; service 《a car》; 《원고 따위를》 improve 《*one's* essay》; correct 《a manuscript》; touch up. ¶ 크게 ～ make 〔do〕 thorough 〔large〕 repairs 《on》 / 자네 만화는 조금 손보면 아주 좋아질 것이다 Your cartoons will be much better if you touch them up a little.

**손봐주다** 《도와주다》 give 〔lend〕 a (helping) hand; help 《in》; 《고쳐주다》 fix 〔repair〕 《*a thing*》 for 《*a person*》. ¶ 숙제를 ～ help 《a child》 with 《*his*》 homework / 이 라디오를 손봐 주시오 I want to have this radio repaired 〔fixed〕.

**손부**(孫婦) the wife of *one's* grandson.

**손부끄럽다** be embarrassed (by nonfulfillment of a request for which *one* has extended *one's* hand). ¶ 그가 돈을 꿔주지 않아서 손부끄러웠다 I was embarrassed by his inability to lend me money.

**손붙이다** set *one's* hand 《to》. ⇨ 착수하다.

**손빌리다** have 〔receive〕 help 《from》; be helped by; get 〔procure〕 assistance 《from》. ¶ 친구의 손을 빌려 with the help of a friend / …의 손을 빌리다 enlist 〔receive〕 the aid of….

**손뼉** the palm 〔flat〕 of *one's* hand. ¶ ～(을) 치다 clap *one's* hands (in applause); 《칭찬》 give 《*a person*》 a clap; cheer and clap (갈채) / 훌륭한 연주에 ～을 치다 applaud a fine performance.

**손상**(損傷) (an) injury; damage. ～하다 《…을》 damage; injure; damnify. ¶ 신체 내부의 ～ an internal injury / ～되다 get damaged; be injured; sustain an injury; suffer a loss / 명예를 ～시키다 disgrace 〔injure〕 *one's* reputation; cast a slur on *a person's* name / 인명을 ～하다 destroy life / 뇌에 ～을 입다 suffer brain damage / ～을 면하다 escape damage.

**손색**(遜色) inferiority. ¶ ～이 없다 bear 〔stand〕 comparison 《with》; be equal 《to》; compare favorably 《with》; suffer nothing by comparison 《with》; be by no means inferior 《to》.

**손서**(孫壻) the husband of *one's* granddaughter.

**손서투르다, 손설다** (be) poor; awkward; clumsy; unskilled; unfamiliar 《with》; unaccustomed 《to》; [서술적] be bad 〔no good, poor〕 at 《carpentry》; be a poor 《writing》; be weak 《in mathematics》; be all thumbs. ¶ 손서투른 사람 a poor hand 《at》; a bungler; a lubber; a dub 《미속어》 / 일이 ～ do a job clumsily.

**손수** 《직접, 스스로》 in person; with *one's* own hands; personally; 《do it》 *oneself.* ¶ ～ 만든 homemade; of *one's* own making / 이것을 ～ 만드셨습니까 Is this your own make? 「kie 《구어》.

**손수건**(—手巾) a handkerchief; a han-

**손수레** a handcart.
**손숫물** water for washing hands.
**손쉽다** (be) easy; simple. ¶ 손쉽게 easily; with ease; without difficulty 〔effort〕; readily / 손쉬운 일 an easy job 〔task〕/ 성공하기에 손쉬운 길 a shortcut to success / 돈을 손쉽게 벌다 make「easy money 〔an easy gain〕/ 손쉽게 생각하다 take 《*a matter*》 easy / 손쉽게 이기다 win easily; win an easy victory 《over》; have a walkover / 그는 손쉽게 그 일을 했다 He did it with ease. / 그는 큰 돈을 손쉽게 벌었다 He earned a lot of money with wet fingers. / 그것이 가장 손쉬운 방법이라고 나는 생각한다 I think that is the easiest way to do it.
**손시**(巽時) 〖민속〗 the 10th of the 24 hour periods (=8:30-9:30 a.m.).
**손시늉** hand gestures 〔mimicry〕. ~하다 gesture; make gestures. ¶ ~으로 알리다 make signs 〔a sign〕/ ~으로 말하다 talk by signs 〔in sign language〕.
**손실**(損失) (a) loss; damage (손해). ~하다 lose; suffer 〔incur〕 a loss 《of》. ¶ 적은 ~ a small 〔little, trifling〕 loss / 인명과 재산의 ~ a loss of life and property / 회복할 수 없는 ~ an irreparable loss / ~의 분담 share of loss; sharing the loss / 국가적 ~ a national loss; a loss to the country / ~을 메우다 cover 〔make up〕 the loss; recoup 〔compensate for〕 the loss / ~을 입다 suffer 〔sustain, have〕 a loss / ~을 입히다 inflict 〔entail〕 a loss 《on》; cause a loss 《to》/ 네가 그만두면 우리한테는 큰 ~이다 If you leave, it will be a great loss to us. / 그의 죽음은 사학계에 큰 ~이다 His death is a serious loss to the world of historical scholarship. ◉ ~보상 compensation for a loss. ~액 the (amount of ) loss. 인명~ casualties.
**손심부름** a petty errand. 「dexterous.
**손싸다** (be) nimble; quick; agile; deft;
**손쓰다** exert *oneself;* make every effort; take a step; take measures; adopt 〔resort to〕 a measure; take action; make a move. ¶ 이리저리 ~ try every (possible) means / 어떻게 손쓸 수가 없다 be in a deadlock; be at *one's* wit's 〔wits'〕 end / 미리 ~ take preventive measures 《against》/ 위험을 피하려면 무언가 손을 써야 한다 We must do something to avert the danger.
**손아귀** the space between the thumb and the fingers; the (power of *one's*) grip. ¶ ~에 in *one's* hands; within *one's* grasp / ~가 세다 have a strong grip / ~에 넣다 have 《*a person*》 under *one's* thumb 〔control〕; have 《*a person*》 well in hand; keep 《*a person*》 under control / ~에 쥐다 take 〔get〕 hold of.
**손아래** juniority; being younger 〔subordinate〕. ¶ ~의 younger; junior; subordinate / ~ 남동생 a younger brother / 그는 나보다 2년 ~다 He is two years my junior 〔two years younger than me〕. ◉ 손아랫사람 *one's* junior 〔inferior〕; *one's* subordinate.
**손어림** measuring roughly with *one's* hands. ~하다 measure 〔weigh〕 roughly by (the) hand; use *one's* hands to make a rough estimate 《of》; heft; span.
**손위** seniority. ¶ ~의 누이 an older sister / 그는 나보다 두 살 ~다 He is my senior by two years. ◉ 손윗사람 《respect》 *one's* senior; *one's* elder; *one's* superior.
**손익**(損益) profit and loss; loss and gain. ¶ ~을 맞추다 balance profit and loss 〔loss and gain〕; balance the gain against the loss / ~ 없음 The losses and gains are on a par. ◉ ~계산서 income statement; a profit=and-loss statement (생략 P / L). ~계정 the profit-and-loss account. ~분기점 the break-even point.
**손익다** get 〔be〕 familiar 《with》; get skillful 〔be at home〕 《in》; get accustomed 《to》; become 〔be〕 a good 〔practiced〕 hand 《at》; be used to. ¶ 손익은 일 an accustomed work.
**손일** manual work; handwork; handicraft; a trade. ¶ ~을 하다 do manual work; work with *one's* hands.
**손자**(孫子) a grandchild; a grandson.
**손자귀** a hand-adz(e).
**손잡기다** have *one's* hands full; be busy; be engaged. ¶ 일에 손잡겨 지금 나갈 수 없다 I have my hands too full to go out now.
**손잡다** ① 《쥐다》 grasp another's hand; take 《*a person*》 by the hand. ② 《제휴·합작하다》 join hands 《with》; cooperate 《with》; tie up 《with》; go hand in hand 《with》; be aligned 《with》; 《동맹하다》 combine 《with》; ally *oneself* 《with》. ¶ …와 손잡고 《work》 in concert 〔cooperation〕 with.
**손잡이** a handle; a grip; a knob (문

의); a pull (서랍의); an ear (주전자의); a hilt (칼 따위의). ¶ 지팡이의 ~ the handle of a stick / 문의 ~ a door knob / ~를 달다 knob; furnish a knob; fix a handle / ~가 떨어져 있다 The handle [knob] is off. ◉ ~끈 《버스 따위의》 a strap: ~끈을 잡다 hang on to [from] a strap.

**손장난** toying with *one's* hands; trifling; fumbling; fidgeting; fiddling. ~하다 trifle; fumble; fidget; fiddle 《with》. ¶ ~이 심하다 fidget incessantly / 만년필을 가지고 ~하다 toy with a fountain pen.

**손장단**(—長短) ¶ ~을 치다 beat time with the hands; keep time 《to the music》 with hand-clapping / 우리는 ~에 맞추어 민요를 불렀다 We sang folk songs beating time with the hands.

**손재간**(—才幹) = 손재주.

**손재수**(損財數) the doom [forthcoming fate] to lose *one's* possessions.

**손재주** hand skill; dexterity; finesse; 《솜씨》 workmanship; craftsmanship. ¶ ~가 있다[많다] be dexterous; be skillful with *one's* fingers; be deft-fingered[-handed]; be clever [smart] with *one's* hands / ~ 있는 사람 a clever-fingered man; a man of deft hand; a handy man / ~ 없는 사람 a bungler / 바느질에 ~가 있다 be clever at sewing.

**손전등**(—電燈) a flashlight 《미》; an electric torch 《영》.

**손질** ① 《매만짐》 handling; care; trimming (나무·정원·머리칼을). ~하다 care for; take care of; tend; trim 《a tree》. ¶ ~이 잘 된[안 된] 정원 a well-kept [ill-kept] garden / ~이 잘 된[안 된] 머리칼 well-groomed [unkempt] hair / ~을 잘 하다 take a good care of / 수염을 매일 아침 ~하다 trim *one's* beard every morning / 손톱 ~을 하다 do *one's* nails. ② 《수리》 repair; mending; remodeling; 《정비》 maintenance. ~하다 repair 《a house》; mend 《shoes》; remodel; maintain 《a car》. ¶ ~이 잘 되어 있다 be in a good state of repair; be well-kept / ~이 안 되어 있다 be out of repair. ③ 《정정》 correction; retouch. ~하다 correct; touch up; improve 《*one's* essay》.

**손짓** a gesture (of *one's* hand); signs; dumbshow. ~하다 motion; gesture; make signs; make a gesture. ¶ ~으로 가라고 하다 motion 《*a person*》 away / ~하여 부르다 beckon 《to *a person*》 / 앉으라고 ~하다 motion 《*a person*》 to (take) a seat / ~으로 말하다 talk in sign language.

**손찌검** a blow; striking; hitting; beating. ~하다 strike; hit; beat; slap; give [deal] a blow. ¶ 누가 먼저 ~했느냐? Who struck the first blow?

**손치다**[1] 《여관에서》 take in lodgers; put up 《*a person*》.

**손치다**[2] ① 《바로잡다》 smooth; put in order (with *one's* hand); put *one's* hand to 《smoothing, ordering》. ② 《어지르다》 get mussed up [messed up, scattered, out of order].

**손치르다** entertain *one's* guests; play host 《to》.

**손크다** ① 《활수하다》 (be) big-[liberal-]handed; generous; liberal. ¶ 손큰 사람 a liberal giver; an open-handed [a generous] man / 손크게 돈을 쓰다 be free with *one's* money; dip into *one's* pocket / 그는 손크게도 아들에게 모든 여행 경비를 대주었다 He generously paid all the travel expenses for his son. ② 《수단이 많다》 (be) resourceful.

**손타다** 《도둑맞다》 have 《*one's* rice》 stolen little by little.

**손톱** a fingernail; a nail. ¶ ~만큼도 《not》 a bit [whit]; 《not》 in the least / ~ 밑의 때 the dirt in [under] the nails / ~에 때가 끼다 have dirty nails / ~을 기르다 let *one's* nails grow long / ~을 깎다 trim [cut, pare] *one's* nails / ~을 바싹 깎다 pare a nail to the quick / ~을 다듬다 do *one's* nails / ~을 씹다 bite [gnaw] *one's* nails / ~을 빨갛게 칠하다 paint *one's* nails red [with red polish] / ~이 길다 wear *one's* fingernails long / ~이 자라다 *one's* fingernails grow / ~으로 할퀴다 scratch with *one's* nails / 거짓말은 ~만큼도 안 한다 I'm not lying for a minute [for one minute]. / 그는 양심이라고는 ~만큼도 없다 He has not an ounce [atom] of conscience in him. ◉ ~깎이 nail scissors; a nail clipper [nipper]. ~자국 a nail mark; 《상처》 a scratch: ~자국을 내다 mark with *one's* nails. ~줄 a nail file; an emery board. 엄지~ a thumbnail.

**손틀** 《손재봉틀》 a hand-operated sewing machine.

**손풀무** a hand(-operated) bellows.

**손풍금**(—風琴) an accordion; a concertina; a melodeon.

**손해**(損害) 《손상》 damage; (an) injury (★ 흔히 damage는 무생물에, injury는 생물에 쓰임); harm; 《손실》 (a) loss; 《상해》

casualties.
¶ 물적 ~ property damage; material loss(es) / 인적(人的) ~ casualties; personnel loss(es) / 200만 원의 ~ a loss 〔damage〕 to the extent of 〔amounting to〕 two million won / 막대한 ~ great 〔serious〕 damage / 경미한 ~ slight damage / (…에) ~를 주다〔입히다〕 damage; injure; cause damage 〔losses〕 《to》; do harm 《to》; inflict a loss 〔damage〕 《on》 / ~를 입다〔보다〕 suffer 〔receive〕 damage; suffer 〔sustain〕 a loss / ~를 보고 팔다 sell 《*something*》 at a loss / ~를 메우다 cover 〔make good (for)〕 the loss; balance a loss / ~를 배상하다 recompense 〔compensate for〕 the damage; repair the loss / ~에 대한 책임이 있다 be liable for damage / 그 ~ 부담은 내가 지겠네 I'll stand the damage. / 태풍으로 작물은 큰 ~를 입었다 The typhoon did 〔caused〕 much damage to the crops. / ~는 약 6천만 원으로 추정되었다 The damage 〔loss〕 is 「estimated 〔put〕 at about sixty million won.
◉ ~보험 nonlife 〔property〕 insurance: 그는 1만 달러의 ~ 보험에 들어 있다 He has $10,000 worth of property insurance. ~액 the amount of the damage; the damage 〔loss〕: 추정된 ~액 the estimated damage 〔loss〕 / ~액은 2천만원이다 The damage comes 〔amounts〕 to twenty million won.

**손해배상**(損害賠償) (a) compensation for damage 〔the loss〕; reparation for injury; indemnity (for damage done). ~하다 compensate 《*a person*》 for damages; indemnify 《*a person*》 for the loss; pay damages 《to》. ¶ ~ 소송을 제기하다 go to law 《against *a person*》 for damages; sue 《*a person*》 for damages / ~을 청구하다 demand reparation for injury; claim 〔demand〕 damages 《against》. ◉ ~금 《obtain》 damages. ~청구 a claim for damage.

**솔**[1] 〖식물〗 a pine; a pine tree. ¶ 솔 심어 정자라 《속담》 Count *one's* chickens before they are hatched.

**솔**[2] ⇨ 솔기.

**솔**[3] 《브러시》 a brush. ¶ 옷〔구둣〕솔 a clothes 〔shoe〕 brush / 솔로 털다 brush 《*one's* clothes》; brush off 〔away〕 《dust》.

**솔**[4] 〖음악〗 sol.

**솔가리** fallen pine needles; pine twigs. ¶ ~를 긁다 rake pine needles.

**솔가지** pine twigs 《for fuel》.

**솔개** 〖조류〗 a (black) kite.

**솔기** 《옷의》 a seam. ¶ ~가 있는 seamy / ~ 없는 seamless / ~가 터지다 a seam opens 〔runs〕 / 바지의 뒷~를 터서 내다 let the pants out.

**솔깃하다** be interested 《in》; be enthusiastic 《about》. ¶ 이야기에 귀가 ~ be interested in 《*a person's*》 talk / 귀가 솔깃해서 듣다 listen to 《*a person*》 with enthusiasm 〔interest〕; bend an ear 《to》 / 그거 귀가 솔깃해지는 이야기군 That's a tempting offer. *or* That sounds inviting.

**솔다**[1] 《가렵고 아프다》 (be) itchy and sore; irritating; 《좁다·죄다》 (be) narrow; cramped; small. ¶ 저고리 품이 ~ The jacket is skimpy.

**솔다**[2] ① 《귀가》 get 〔be〕 sick of hearing; hear more than enough of; have sore ears. ¶ 시끄러워 귀가 ~ the noise is nerve-racking. ② 《단단히 굳다》 dry up; tighten up 〔contract〕 with dryness. ③ 《무솔다》 《a vegetable》 decay from the damp; molder. ④ 《물결이》 foam; surge.

**솔딱새** 〖조류〗 a Siberian flycatcher.

**솔로** 〖음악〗 a solo (*pl.* ~s, soli). ¶ ~로 노래하다 sing a solo / ~를 하다 《악기로》 play a solo. ◉ ~가수〔연주자〕 a soloist. ~홈런 〖야구〗 a solo homer. 피아노~ a piano solo.

**솔로몬제도**(—諸島) 《남태평양의》 the Solomon Islands.

**솔뮤직** 《흑인 영가의 요소를 가미한 대중음악》 soul music.

**솔발**(鉢鈸) 《놋쇠 방울》 a small brass handbell. ¶ ~ 놓다 ring a handbell; 《소문내다》 spread a rumor.

**솔방울** a pinecone; a cone.

**솔밭** a pine grove; a pine forest.

**솔봉이** a countrified 〔boorish〕 young person; a young rustic 〔clodhopper〕; a young (country) bumpkin.

**솔부엉이** 〖조류〗 a brown hawk-owl.

**솔불** a fire set to pine knots; a pine torch.

**솔뿌리** a pine root.

**솔새** 〖조류〗 a Swinhoe's willow warbler.

**솔선**(率先) ~하다 take the lead 〔initiative〕 《in》; take up the running. ¶ ~해서 on *one's* own initiative / ~해서 …하다 be the first to 《*do*》; take the lead 〔initiative〕 in 《*doing*》; act as pioneer in 《*doing*》 / ~수범하다 set 〔give〕 an example 《of moderation to others》 / ~해서 담배를 끊다 be the first to give up smoking; set an example by giving up smoking.

**솔솔** soft-flowing; softly; gently; smoothly; effortlessly; easily; readily; nicely. ¶ 바람이 ~ 불다 the wind blows softly / 밀가루가 자루에서 ~ 새다 a tiny stream of flour leaks out of the bag / 이슬비가 ~ 내리다 it drizzles lightly / 영어를 ~ 하다 speak English fluently.

**솔송나무** 〖식물〗 a Japanese hemlock.

**솔수펑이, 솔숲** a pine wood 〔forest〕; a pinery.

**솔이끼** 〖식물〗 hair 〔haircap〕 moss.

**솔잎** pine needles. ◉ ~상투 a topknot braided out of short hair.

**솔잣새** 〖조류〗 a Korean crossbill.

**솔직**(率直) plainness; frankness; straightforwardness; honesty. ~하다 (be) honest; frank; candid; outspoken; plain; openhearted; straightforward. ¶ ~하게 honestly; frankly; plainly; candidly; outspokenly / ~한 대답 a straight 〔downright〕 answer / ~한 사람 a plain-spoken person / ~히 말하면 frankly 〔plainly〕 (speaking); in plain words 〔terms〕; to put it bluntly; to speak honestly; to be frank 〔plain, honest〕 with you / ~히 말하다 speak plainly (and frankly); call a spade a spade / ~히 대답하다 give a straightforward answer / 그는 자기의 부주의를 ~히 인정했다 He frankly admitted of his carelessness. / ~히 말해서 너의 제안은 비현실적이다 To be frank, I don't think your proposal is practical. / 그는 태도가 ~하다 He is frank in manner.

**솔질** brushing. ~하다 brush 《a hat》; give a brush(ing) 《to》. ¶ 옷을 ~하다 give *one's* clothes a brushing.

**솔트** 《전략 무기 제한 협정》 SALT. [<the *S*trategic *A*rms *L*imitation *T*alks]

**솔포기** a small pine tree with thick branches.

**솜** cotton (wool); 《옷의》 wadding. ¶ 솜 같은 구름 fleecy 〔wooly〕 clouds / 솜을 두다 wad 《a gown》; stuff 《a cushion》 with cotton; pad 《bedclothes》 with cotton / 솜을 타다 whip 〔willow〕 cotton / 귀를 솜으로 틀어막다 stop *one's* ears with cotton; put cotton in *one's* ears.

**솜대** 〖식물〗 a black bamboo.

**솜돗** a willowing mat (for cotton).

**솜몽둥이** a cotton-tipped stick (used as a dauber).

**솜뭉치** a wad of cotton.

**솜바지** padded trousers.

**솜버선** cotton-padded socks.

**솜붙이** padded clothes.

**솜사탕**(—砂糖) cotton candy; spun sugar.

**솜씨** 《손재주》 skill; dexterity; finesse; deftness; knack; 《만듦새》 performance; make; hand; workmanship; 《수완》 ability; capacity; 《교제상의》 tact. ¶ ~ 있게 skillfully; neatly; expertly; finely; cleverly; tactfully; 《말씨를》 with felicity; in fine style / 멋진 ~로 with great adroitness; with a deft hand / 서투른 ~로 with clumsy hands; clumsily; awkwardly / ~ 있는 사람 a handy man; a clever-fingered man / 훌륭한 ~ a splendid 〔creditable〕 performance; a superb skill / ~가 좋다 〔나쁘다〕 perform well 〔ill〕; be skillful 〔awkward〕 《in *doing something*》; be clever 〔clumsy〕 《at *something*》; do a good 〔poor〕 job 《of *something*》; [사물이 주어] be finely 〔poorly〕 executed; be of excellent 〔inferior〕 workmanship / ~를 겨루다 try *one's* skill with 《*a person*》 / ~를 보이다 show 〔display〕 *one's* skill 〔dexterity, ability〕 《in》 / 훌륭한 ~를 보이다 acquit *oneself* to *one's* credit; do a top job 《of》 / ~를 자랑하다 plume *oneself* on *one's* skill 《at》; be proud of *one's* prowess 《in》 / ~를 (갈고) 닦다 improve 〔cultivate, develop〕 *one's* skill 〔art, talent, ability〕 / ~를 마음껏 발휘하다 give full play to *one's* power 〔talent〕 《in》; do ample justice to *one's* skill; strut *one's* stuff / 요리 ~가 있다 be a clever cook; be handy in the kitchen / ~ 있게 말하다 talk skillfully; speak very well; have the gift of gab; have a way with words / ~ 있게 일을 처리하다 manage the matter skillfully / 참 멋진 ~다 It's a splendid performance. *or* Well done!

**솜옷** padded clothes.

**솜저고리** a padded jacket.

**솜채** a cotton-beating 〔willowing〕 stick.

**솜털** downy 〔fine soft〕 hair 《of a baby》; 《새의》 down; fluff. ¶ ~이 난 downy.

**솜틀** a cotton gin; a willowing machine; a willow(er).

**솜화약**(—火藥) cotton powder; guncotton.

**솟고라지다** 《끓어오르다》 boil up; 《솟구쳐오르다》 leap up.

**솟구다** raise; make rise; jump up. ¶ 몸을 ~ spring 〔leap, jump〕 up.

**솟구치다** raise quickly; make a quick rise; 《불길이》 blaze 〔flame〕 up. ¶ 불길이 ~ burst into flame.

**솟국**(素—) 《고기 없이 끓인 국》 vegetable soup.

**솟다** ① 《용솟음치다》 gush out 〔forth〕; spring 〔flow〕 out 〔forth〕; well up; spout; spurt; break forth 《from》. ¶ 솟아 나오는 샘물 a gushing 〔live〕 spring / 수정 같은 물이 솟는 샘 a fountain welling forth its crystalline waters / 피가 ～ blood spurts 〔gushes out〕 / 용기가 ～ take heart; be encouraged 《at, by》; feel reassured / 힘이 ～ gain (in) strength; gather strength; revive; be invigorated.
② 《높이》 rise; tower; soar. ¶ 해가 ～ the sun rises 〔comes up〕 / 구름 위로 ～ rise 〔tower〕 above the clouds / 하늘 높이 솟아 오르다 soar 〔go up〕 in the air; rise 〔soar〕 to the sky 〔skyward〕 / 백두산은 하늘높이 솟아 있다 Mt. Paektu rises high in the sky.
③ 《불길이》 burst into flame; flame 〔blaze〕 up.

**솟대** ① 〖고제도〗 a stick with a dragon 〔fish〕 made out of cloth and attached to its tip, standing in a village in honor of those passing a civilservice examination. ② 〖민속〗 a big stick with a sack of rice attached to it, standing beside a farm house; the pole upon which a masked acrobat climbs to perform his tricks.
◉ ～쟁이 a masked acrobat who climbs a pole to perform his tricks.

**솟아나다** well up; spring 〔gush〕 out 〔forth〕; spout; spurt. ¶ 눈물이 ～ tears well up in *one's* eyes / 샘이 ～ a spring wells 〔gushes〕 forth / 그들의 가슴에는 새로운 희망이 솟아났다 Hope sprang afresh in their breasts.

**솟을대문**(―大門) a tall gate; a house gate taller than the *haengnang* on either side.

**솟을무늬** embossed pattern on a cloth.

**송**(頌) a panegyric; a eulogy; an encomium.

**송가**(頌歌) a hymn; an anthem.

**송골매**(松鶻―) 〖조류〗 a Siberian peregrine falcon; a duck hawk.

**송골송골** 《sweat, goose pimples appearing》 in profuse beads.

**송곳** 《도래송곳》 a gimlet; 《타래송곳》 a screw auger; 《작은 구멍 뚫는》 an awl; 《쇠·돌을 뚫는》 a drill. ¶ ～ 자루 a drill stock / ～의 끝 a drill bit / ～으로 구멍을 뚫다 bore a hole 《in *something*》 with a gimlet 〔an awl〕; drill a hole 《in a metal plate》 / ～을 돌리다 drive a gimlet 《into》 / ～도 끝부터 들어간다 《속담》 You have to start at the bottom to climb a ladder.
◉ ～칼 a combination knife-drill.

**송곳니** a canine tooth; a cuspid.

**송구**(送球) ① 《던짐》 passing a ball. ～하다 pass 〔throw, toss〕 a ball 《to》. ② 〖스포츠〗 handball. ⇨ 핸드볼.

**송구스럽다**(悚懼―) ① 《감사해서》 be 〔feel〕 much obliged 《to》; be grateful 〔thankful〕 to 《*a person*》 for. ¶ 이것 참 송구스럽습니다 Many thanks for your kindness. ② 《부끄럽다》 feel ashamed 《of》; feel small; feel embarrassed. ¶ 칭찬해 주시니 오히려 송구스럽습니다 Your praises put me to shame. ③ 《미안하다》 be sorry for; regret. ¶ 대단히 송구스럽습니다만… I am very sorry to trouble you, but … / 공부를 방해해서 참 송구스럽습니다 I am very sorry to trouble your studies.

**송구영신**(送舊迎新) ～하다 ring out the old and ring in the new; see the old year out and the new year in.

**송금**(送金) (a) remittance. ～하다 remit 〔send〕 money 《to *a person*》; make (a) remittance 《to》.
¶ 대금을 온라인으로 ～하다 remit 〔send〕 payment on the on-line system / 우편환으로 10만 원을 ～하다 remit 〔make remittance of〕 one hundred thousand won by a postal money order / ～을 끊다 stop sending money to 《*a person*》 / 그녀는 매월 어머니에게 30만 원을 ～한다 She remits 〔sends〕 three hundreds thousand won to her mother every month. / 매월 집에서 오는 ～이 끊어졌다 Monthly remittances from home have stopped. / 청구 금액을 수표로 ～해 주십시오 Please remit the amount of your bill by check. / ～하신 것이 아직 도착하지 않은 것 같습니다 The remittance doesn't seem to have arrived yet.
◉ ～수수료 a remittance charge 〔fee〕. ～수취인 the remittee. ～수표 a remittance check. ～액 the amount of remittance. ～어음 a remittance draft. ～인 the remitter. 국내〔외국〕～ a domestic 〔foreign〕 remittance.

**송기**(松肌) pine endodermis. ◉ ～떡 a rice cake flavored with pine endodermis.

**송년**(送年) bidding the old year out. ～하다 see the old year out (and the new year in). ◉ ～회 a year-end party.

**송달**(送達) conveyance; delivery. ～하다 send; deliver; dispatch; forward; convey. ¶ 영장을 ～하다 serve a writ on 《*a person*》; serve 《*a person*》 with a writ. ◉ ～부 a chitbook; a delivery book.

**송당송당** 《cut 〔chop〕 *a thing*》 in haste 〔at random〕 letting the knife 〔needle〕 fall where it may. ¶ 칼로 오이를 ～ 썰다 chop a cucumber at random / ～ 바느질하다 sew roughly.

**송덕**(頌德) eulogy. ～하다 eulogize; commend (for) virtue. ◉ ～문 a eulogy; an encomium; a panegyric. ～비 a monument (erected) in honor of 《*a person*》; a monument in eulogy of 《*a person's*》 virtuous deeds.

**송독**(誦讀) recitation. ～하다 recite; recite from memory.

**송두리째** root and all 〔branch〕; all; completely; entirely; thoroughly; in its entirety. ¶ ～ 파〔뽑아〕내다 dig 〔pluck〕 up 《a tree》 by the roots; uproot / 노름으로 재산을 ～날리다 gamble away all *one's* property.

**송로**(松露) ① 《이슬》 dew on pine needles. ② 《버섯》 a truffle; an earthnut.

**송료**(送料) 《우편의》 postage; 《화물의》 carriage; transportation 《미》; shipping charge. ¶ ～ 포함 5천 원 5,000 won postage 〔carriage〕 included / ～를 선급하다 prepay the postage 〔carriage〕 / 이 책의 ～는 얼마입니까 What is the postage on this book? / 이것은 ～ 포함 가격입니다 This is the price including postage.
◉ ～무료 Postage free; Carriage free. ～선급 carriage prepaid.

**송림**(松林) a pine forest 〔wood, grove〕.

**송백**(松柏) the pine and the nut pine.
◉ ～과 *Coniferae:* ～과 식물 a conifer; a coniferous plant 〔tree〕.

**송별**(送別) a farewell; a send-off. ～하다 bid 《*a person*》 farewell; give 《*a person*》 a send-off.
◉ ～사 a farewell speech 〔address〕: 그가 대표로 ～사를 했다 He made a farewell speech on behalf of the groups. ～연 a farewell dinner. ～회 a farewell party 〔meeting〕: 우리는 브라운 씨의 ～회를 열었다 We gave a farewell party 「for 〔in honor of〕 Mr. Brown.

**송부**(送付) sending; forwarding; remittance (돈의). ～하다 send; forward; remit.

**송사**(訟事) a lawsuit; a suit; litigation; legal proceedings 〔steps〕. ～하다 sue; file suit; take legal proceedings 《against》.

**송사**(頌辭) a laudatory address; a memorial; a eulogy; a panegyric.

**송사리** ① 『어류』 a cyprinodont; a minnow. ② 《하찮은 사람》 small 〔lesser〕 fry. ¶ 거물급은 놓아 주고 ～만 들볶는 이유가 뭘까? Why are they hitting the small fry while letting the big ones go free?

**송송** ① 《썰다》 《chop》 into small pieces; finely. ¶ 파를 ～ 썰다 chop scallion into small pieces. ② 《구멍이》 full of small holes; perforated. ¶ 냄비 바닥에 구멍이 ～ 뚫려 있다 The pan has holes all over the bottom.

**송수**(送水) water supply; water conveyance. ～하다 convey water 《to》; 《공급하다》 supply water 《to》; supply 《a town》 with water. ◉ ～관 a water pipe. ～본관 a water 〔service〕 main.

**송수**(送受) ◉ ～신기 《라디오의》 a transceiver. ～화기 《전화의》 a handset.

**송신**(送信) transmission of a message 〔picture〕. ～하다 transmit 〔dispatch〕 a message 〔picture〕 《to》; send a letter. ¶ 뉴스는 즉시 서울로 ～되었다 The news was transmitted 〔dispatched〕 to Seoul at once.
◉ ～국〔탑〕 a transmitting station 〔tower〕. ～기 a transmitter; a transmitting set: 무전 ～기 a radio 〔wireless〕 transmitter. ～자 the sender; the transmitter.

**송아리** a small bunch 《of flowers, fruit》.

**송아지** a calf (*pl.* calves). ¶ 수～ a male calf; a bullcalf / ～를 낳다 calve.
◉ ～가죽 calfskin; calf (leather). ～고기 veal.

**송알송알** ① 《땀이》 in profuse drops. ¶ ～ 땀이 나다 perspire profusely / 그의 이마에는 땀이 ～ 맺혀 있었다 Beads of sweat stood on his forehead. ② 《술·간장이 괴어》 fermenting; bubbling. ¶ ～ 괴다 ferment; undergo fermentation.

**송액**(松液) 《송진》 rosin; pine resin.

**송어**(松魚) 『어류』 a trout (★ 단·복수 동형); a salmon trout.

**송연하다**(悚然—) (be) fearful; timorous. ¶ 송연히 fearfully; timorously / 모골이 송연해지는 hair-raising; horrible; frightful; gruesome / 모골이 송연해졌다 My hair stood on end (with horror).

**송영**(送迎) welcome and send-off; greeting and farewell; seeing off and welcoming back. ～하다 《보내고 맞다》 welcome and send off; 《송구 영신》

see the old year out and the new year in. ¶ 공항은 ~객으로 붐볐다 The airport was crowded 〔alive〕 with people that had come to meet friends or see them off.

**송영**(誦詠) recitation 《of a poem》. ~하다 recite 《a poem》.

**송유**(送油) oil supply; sending oil. ◉ ~관 an oil pipe(line).

**송이** ① 《과일의》 a cluster; a bunch 《of fruit》; 《꽃의》 a blossom; a flower. ¶ 꽃 한 ~ a flower / 포도 한 ~ a bunch 〔cluster〕 of grapes / ~로 피다 bloom in clusters. ② 《눈의》 a flake 《of snow》. ¶ 눈~ a snowflake. ③ 《방울》 a seed cone. ¶ 잣~ a pine cone.

**송이**(松栮) a *song-i* mushroom. ¶ ~를 캐다 gather *song-i* mushrooms / ~ 캐러 가다 go mushroom-gathering 《on Sunday》. ◉ ~누름적 *song-i* mushroom coated with egg and then broiled on a skewer. ~전골 『요리』 pine mushroom and beef in a pot. 양~ a mushroom; a champignon.

**송이송이** in clusters; in bunches.

**송장** a dead body; a corpse; a cadaver. ⇨ 시체. ¶ ~에 매질하다 speak ill of the dead / 그는 산~이다 He is a living corpse.

**송장**(送狀) an invoice. ¶ ~ 변경 reconsignment / ~을 보내다 send an invoice / ~을 작성하다 invoice 《a shipment of goods》; make out an invoice. ◉ ~금액 invoice value. 견적~ a pro-forma invoice. 내국〔외국〕~ an inland 〔a foreign〕 invoice. 본선도(渡)〔선측도〕~ an F.O.B. 〔F.A.S.〕 invoice. 세관〔영사〕~ a custom 〔consular〕 invoice. 수출〔수입〕~ an export 〔import〕 invoice. 약식~ an abstract invoice. 운임〔운임·보험료〕포함~ a C.&F. 〔C.I.F.〕 invoice. 정정(訂正)~ a corrected invoice.

**송장개구리** a ranid; a true frog.

**송장벌레** a burying beetle; a gravedigger.

**송장헤엄** the backstroke. ⇨ 배영(背泳). ¶ ~치다 do the backstroke; swim backstroke.

**송전**(送電) transmission of electricity; power 〔electric〕 transmission; electric 〔power〕 supply. ~하다 transmit electricity 《from... to...》; supply electric power 《to》. ¶ ~을 끊다 cut 〔shut〕 off the power supply 《to》. ◉ ~력 carrying 〔transmission〕 capacity. ~선 a power-transmission line 〔wire〕; a power cable (고압선). ~탑〔소〕 a (power-)transmission tower 〔site〕.

**송죽**(松竹) pine and bamboo.

**송진**(松津) (pine) resin; pitch.

**송채**(送綵) 『민속』 sending red and blue silk from the bridegroom's family to the bride's (after setting the date for the wedding).

**송청**(送廳) ~하다 《서류를》 send 《the papers pertaining to a case》 to the public prosecutor's office; 《범인을》 commit 《a culprit》 for trial.

**송축**(頌祝) blessing; commendation and benediction; a eulogy. ~하다 bless; eulogize.

**송충이**(松蟲—) 『곤충』 a pine caterpillar. ¶ ~를 근절하다 exterminate pine caterpillars / ~를 대하듯 싫어하다 hate 《*a person*》 like a serpent 〔viper〕 / ~가 갈잎을 먹으면 떨어진다 《속담》 The cobbler should stick to his last.

**송충나방**(松蟲—) 『곤충』 an eggar 〔egger〕.

**송치**(送致) sending; forwarding; dispatch; commitment. ~하다 send; forward; dispatch; remand; commit 《to》. ¶ 용의자를 ~하다 remand a suspect.

**송판**(松板) a pine board; a deal.

**송편**(松—) *songpyŏn;* a half-moon-shaped rice cake steamed on a layer of pine needles.

**송풍**(松風) 《바람》 the wind passing through the pine trees; 《소리》 the soughing of the wind in the pines.

**송풍**(送風) ventilation. ~하다 ventilate 《a room》; send air 《to》. ◉ ~관 a blastpipe. ~기 a ventilator; a blower; a fan.

**송화**(送話) transmission. ~하다 transmit. ◉ ~구 a mouthpiece. ~기 a transmitter. ~선 a transmitting line.

**송환**(送還) sending back; 《추방》 deportation; 《포로 따위》 repatriation. ~하다 send 《*a person*》 back; 《본국으로》 send 《*a person*》 home; repatriate; 《외국인을 국외로》 deport. ¶ 강제~ compulsory repatriation; deportation / 포로를 본국으로 ~하다 send war prisoners home 〔back〕; repatriate prisoners of war / ~되다 be sent back home / 한국에 불법 입국하려 했기 때문에 그녀는 본국으로 ~되었다 Since she tried to enter Korea illegally, she was deported (back) to her own country. ◉ ~자 《본국으로》 a returnee; (one of) the repatriated; 《강제 추방으로》 a deportee.

**솥** a pot; a kettle. ¶ 밥솥 a rice-cook-

er; a pot 〔cooker〕 for boiling rice / 솥을 걸다 install a kettle 《in a fireplace》/ 한 솥 밥을 먹다 live under the same roof 《with》; eat at the same mess; be a messmate 《with》.
◉ 전기밥솥 an electric rice-cooker. 증기솥 《요리용》 a steam cooker.

**솥땜장이** a tinker.

**솥뚜껑** the lid 〔cover〕 of a kettle.

**솥발** the tripod base of a kettle; kettle legs.

**솥솔** a pot brush; a scouring brush.

**솥전**(一廛) a kitchen-hardware shop.

**솨** 《소리》 with a cool gust; briskly. ¶ 바람이 솨 분다 The wind blows briskly. / 비가 솨 쏟아졌다 The rain came lashing down.

**솰솰** with a great flow; in torrents; briskly. ¶ 시냇물이 ~ 흐르다 a stream rushes past / 머리를 ~ 빗다 comb *one's* hair briskly.

**쇄골**(鎖骨) 『해부』 the collarbone; the clavicle.

**쇄광**(碎鑛) 『광산』 crushing ore. ◉ ~기 an ore crusher; a stamp(ing) mill.

**쇄국**(鎖國) (national) isolation; seclusion. ~하다 close the country; close the door 《to foreigners》. ◉ ~정책 a policy of seclusion; a national isolation policy. ~주의 seclusionism; (national) isolationism.

**쇄도**(殺到) a rush; a flood; a stampede. ~하다 rush 〔pour〕 in 《to the bargain floor》; throng 《a place》; rush to 《a place》; swoop down on 《the enemy》; flood 《into》 (홍수처럼). ¶ 주문〔신청〕이 ~하다 have a rush 〔flood〕 of orders 〔applications〕; be flooded 〔deluged〕 with orders 〔applications〕/ 항의 편지가 ~하다 be inundated with letters of protest / 군중이 출구로 ~했다 The crowd rushed to the exit. / 사람들이 후보자의 선거연설을 듣기 위해 홀에 ~했다 People thronged into the hall to hear the candidate's stump speech.

**쇄빙**(碎氷) crushing ice; ice breaking. ~하다 break 〔crush〕 ice.
◉ ~기 an ice crusher. ~선 an icebreaker; an iceboat.

**쇄석**(碎石) rubble; broken stones; debris; 《포장용의》 macadam. ~하다 break stone. ¶ (길에) ~을 깔다 macadamize 《a road》.

**쇄신**(刷新) (a) reform; (a) renovation; (an) innovation. ~하다 reform; innovate; renovate. ¶ 정계의 ~ a political reform 〔cleanup〕/ 공직 사회의 기강을 ~하다 renovate the discipline in bureaucracy / 일대 ~을 단행하다 carry out a radical reform / 인사(人事)를 ~하다 carry out a personnel reshuffle 〔shake-up〕.

**쇄편**(碎片) a fragment; a broken piece; a splinter.

**쇄항**(鎖港) ~하다 close the ports; exclude foreigners from the ports.

**쇠** ① 《철》 iron; metal (쇠붙이). ¶ 쇠로 만든 iron; (made) of iron / 쇠를 함유하다 contain iron. ② 《지남철》 a compass. ③ 《여잠그는》 a key (열쇠); a lock (자물쇠). ④ 《경첩》 a hinge.

**쇠-**[1] 《작은 종류》 a small one. ¶ 쇠고래 a small whale; a gray whale.

**쇠-**[2] 《소의》 of cattle; ox-. ¶ 쇠고기 beef.

**쇠가죽** oxhide; cowhide. ¶ ~ 무릅쓰다 《낯이 두껍다》 have the cheek to *do*.

**쇠갈고리** an iron hook.

**쇠고기** beef. ◉ 수입~ the imported beef.

**쇠고랑** handcuffs; manacles. ¶ ~을 찬 죄수 a handcuffed prisoner / ~을 차다 be arrested 《for》; be in irons / ~을 채우다 handcuff; manacle; put 《*a person*》 in irons.

**쇠고리** an iron ring; a clasp.

**쇠골** cow's brains; ox-brain (식용의).

**쇠공이** 《절구의》 an iron pestle 〔pounder〕.

**쇠귀** cow's ears; ox-ear. ¶ ~에 경읽기 preaching to deaf ears / 아무리 충고해도 ~에 경읽기였다 All my advice fell on deaf ears.

**쇠귀나물** 『식물』 an arrowhead.

**쇠기름** (beef) tallow.

**쇠기침** a chronic cough.

**쇠꼬리** 《소의 꼬리》 a cow's tail; (an) oxtail.

**쇠꼬챙이** an iron skewer; a steel spit.

**쇠다**[1] ① 《야채가》 become tough and stringy. ¶ 시금치가 쇠었다 Spinach is tough and stringy. ② 《병 따위가 덧나다》 get worse; grow chronic. ¶ 기침이 ~ *one's* cough becomes worse.

**쇠다**[2] 《명절을》 keep 《*one's* birthday, *etc.*》; celebrate; observe. ¶ 명절을 ~ celebrate a festival day / 설을 ~ keep the New Year's Day.

**쇠다리** a cow's leg; the leg 〔shank〕 of beef.

**쇠달구** an iron pile-driver 〔rammer〕.

**쇠도리깨** an iron frail.

**쇠똥**[1] 《쇠의 부스러기》 iron slag; dross; scoria.

**쇠똥**[2] 《소의》 cattle dung.

**쇠뜨기** 『식물』 a field horsetail.

**쇠막대기** an iron bar; a metal rod.

**쇠망**(衰亡) a decline; ruin; a fall; a downfall. ~하다 《멸망하다》 go to ruin; be ruined; fall; go down; 《쇠퇴하다》

decline; decay; fall into decay. ¶ 로마 제국의 ~ the decline and fall of the Roman Empire.

**쇠망치** an iron hammer.

**쇠머리** a cow's head; 《쇠머릿살》 ox-head (meat).

**쇠먹이** cattle feed; fodder.

**쇠못** an iron nail; a nail.

**쇠몽둥이** an iron bar; an iron rod.

**쇠몽치** a small metal bar; a billet.

**쇠문**(一門) an iron gate 〔door〕.

**쇠물닭** 〖조류〗 an Indian water hen; a moorhen.

**쇠물푸레나무** 〖식물〗 an ash tree.

**쇠뭉치** a mass of iron; a pig; pig iron.

**쇠미**(衰微) a decline; decay; eclipse; wane. ~하다 decline; decay; wane; sink 〔fall〕 into decay.

**쇠백장** a butcher.

**쇠버짐** a kind of ringworm. ⇨버짐.

**쇠붙이** ironware; hardware; metal (things).

**쇠비름** 〖식물〗 a purslane.

**쇠뼈** cow 〔ox〕 bones.

**쇠뿔** a cow's horn; an oxhorn. ¶ ~에 받히다 be gored by a bull; be horned 《by》; take a goring / ~도 단김에 빼랬다 《속담》 Strike the iron while it's hot.

**쇠사다리** a metal ladder.

**쇠사슬** a chain; a metal 〔an iron〕 chain; 《개를 매는》 a tether. ¶ ~에 매인 개 a dog on a chain / ~에 매인 죄수들 prisoners (shackled) in chains / ~로 매다 enchain; chain up; chain 《*a person*》 down; put 《men》 in chains.

**쇠스랑** 〖농업〗 a rake; a forked rake.

**쇠시리** 〖건축〗 molding.

**쇠심** beef 〔ox〕 tendon.

**쇠약**(衰弱) weakness; weakening; feebleness; debility; prostration; (a) breakdown; enervation; asthenia; 〖의학〗 hyposthenia; emaciation. ~하다 (be) weak; enfeebled; emaciated; [서술적] be in poor health. ¶ ~해지다 become 〔grow〕 weak; weaken; become feeble 〔low〕; sink; be debilitated 〔enervated〕; be worn out / 몸이 ~해지다 decline 〔be broken〕 in health; fall in *one's* health / 병으로 ~해지다 grow weak from illness; be enfeebled by ill health / ~하게 하다 weaken; enfeeble; waste; enervate; prostrate; emaciate. ◉ ~증 a wasting 〔consumptive〕 disease. 신경~ (a) nervous breakdown; neurasthenia. 전신~ general prostration.

**쇠운**(衰運) *one's* declining fortune(s). ¶ ~의 극에 달하다 be at the nadir of *one's* fortune(s); reach 《*its*》 lowest ebb / ~이 들다 begin to sink 〔decline, wane〕; be going downhill; be on the wane 〔decline〕 / ~을 만회하다 retrieve *one's* fortunes; recover 〔regain〕 *one's* former prosperity.

**쇠자루** a metal handle 〔grip〕.

**쇠잔**(衰殘) failing; decaying. ~하다 decline; fail; decay; be feeble 〔weak〕. ¶ 오랜 병으로 그의 몸은 많이 ~해졌다 Because of a long illness, his health conditions are remarkably declined.

**쇠잡이** 《꽹과리치는 사람》 a gong beater.

**쇠족**(一足) ox-hoof.

**쇠죽**(一粥) boiled cattle feed. ◉ ~가마 a large kettle to cook cattle feed in. ~바가지 a cattle-feed dipper. ~통 a boiled-fodder tub.

**쇠줄** (iron) wire; metal wire; a cable; a chain.

**쇠지레** a crowbar; a crow; a jimmy.

**쇠진**(衰盡) decay; exhaustion. ~하다 decay; be exhausted.

**쇠창살**(一窓一) an iron window bar; a grating; a grate; a grill(e).

**쇠천** 《동전》 a small copper coin. ¶ ~ 샐 닢도 없다 be penniless; have not a penny 〔red cent〕 in the world; be utterly broke 《미》.

**쇠코뚜레** a cow's nose ring.

**쇠테** an iron 〔a metal〕 frame 〔rim〕.

**쇠톱** a hacksaw.

**쇠퇴**(衰退·衰頹) decline; decay. ~하다 fall off 〔away〕; decay; fail; decline; go downhill; ebb (away); 《기운 따위가》 sink; wane. ¶ ~할 줄 모르는 정력 《with》 unflagging energy / ~기에 있다 be on the decline 〔wane〕; be on the downgrade; be at the low ebb / 나이를 먹으면 기억력이 ~한다 Age dims our memory. *or* Our memory deteriorates 〔declines〕 with age.

**쇠파리** 〖곤충〗 a warble fly; a gadfly.

**쇠푼** a small 〔petty〕 sum of money. ¶ 그는 ~깨나 모았다 He made a small fortune.

**쇠하다**(衰一) 《쇠약해지다》 become 〔grow, get〕 weak; fail; lose vigor; waste away; be enfeebled; 《시들다》 wither; fade; 《쇠퇴하다》 decline; decay; wane. ¶ 기력이 ~ lose *one's* vigor 〔energy〕 / 운이 ~ be down on *one's* luck / 그녀는 요즈음 눈에 띄게 쇠하였다 She has lost a great deal of her vigor lately.

**쇠혀** 《소의 혀》 a cow's tongue; 《식용의》 beef 〔neat's〕 tongue.

**쇤네** I; me; your humble servant.

**쇳내** smelling of rust; a metallic taste. ¶ ～가 나다 smell metallic; 《맛이》 taste metallic; give a taste of iron.

**쇳덩이** a lump of metal.

**쇳독**(一毒) metallic poison(ing).

**쇳물** a metallic stain 〔spot〕. ¶ 내 셔츠에 ～이 묻었다 I have a rust spot on my shirt.

**쇳소리** a metallic sound; 《목소리》 a piercing 〔shrill〕 voice. ¶ ～가 나다 sound like something metallic.

**쇳조각** an iron piece; a scrap of iron.

**쇳줄** 《광맥》 a mineral vein; a vein of ore.

**쇼** a show. ¶ 쇼를 보러가다 go to see a show. ◉ 쇼걸 a show girl.

**쇼맨십** showmanship.

**쇼비니즘** 《맹목적 애국주의》 chauvinism.

**쇼윈도** 《진열장》 a show window; a display window; a shopwindow. ¶ ～에 진열되어 있다 be on display in a (show) window.

**쇼케이스** 《진열장》 a showcase.

**쇼크** 《충격》 a shock. ¶ ～를 느끼다 feel a shock / ～를 받다 be 《greatly》 shocked 《at》; receive a shock / ～를 주다 give 《*a person*》 a shock; shock. ◉ ～사(死) (a) death from shock: 페니실린에 의한 ～사 (a) shock death from penicillin injection. ～요법 shock therapy 〔treatment〕.

**쇼트** ① 〖야구〗《유격수의 수비 위치》 a shortstop. ¶ ～를 보다 play shortstop. ② 《단편》 a short (소설·영화의). ③ 〖전자〗 a short circuit. 「《미》.

**쇼트닝** 《과자용 우지 따위》 shortening

**쇼트케이크** a 《strawberry》 shortcake.

**쇼트트랙** short track. ◉ ～ 스피드 스케이팅 short track speed skating.

**쇼트팬츠** 《a pair of》 shorts.

**쇼핑** shopping. ～하다 do *one's* 〔the〕 shopping; make a purchase. ¶ ～하러 가다 go shopping. ◉ ～몰 《보행자 전용 상점가》《미》 a shopping mall. ～백 a shopping bag. ～센터 a shopping center.

**숄** a shawl. ¶ ～을 걸치다〔걸치고 있다〕 put on 〔wear〕 *one's* shawl.

**숄더백** a shoulder(-strap) bag.

**수**[1] 《수컷》 a male; a he. ¶ 수나귀 a jackass / 수염소 a he-goat / 수참새 a cock sparrow / 수캐 a male dog / 수코양이 a he-cat; a tomcat / 수퇘지 a boar.

**수**(手) ① 《손》 a hand. ② 《바둑·장기의》 a move; 《씨름 등의》 a trick; 《수단》 a means; 《꾀·계략》 a trick; an artifice; resourcefulness. ¶ 나쁜 수 a bad move / (장기의) 수가 높다 be a better man than 《*a person*》 / 수가 없다〔막히다〕 have no good move to make; be at a loss what move to make / 묘수를 놓다 《장기에서》 make a fine 〔clever〕 move / 한 수 위다 [사람이 주어] be a cut 〔stroke〕 above 《*a person* in》; be more than a match for 《*a person*》; be more skillful 《than》; be superior 《to》; be a better hand 《at *something*》 / 세 수에 너를 이길 수 있다 I can beat you in three moves. / 또 그 수로군 You are up to your old trick, aren't you? *or* The same old game! / 두 번 다시 그런 수에는 안 넘어가겠네 I won't have the same trick played on me again.

**수**(秀) 《학업 성적의》 Excellent; 《미》 A. ¶ 전과목 수 straight A's / 수를 받다 get an "Excellent" 《in *one's* composition》.

**수**(數) ① 《운수》 luck; fortune. ⇨ 운수. ¶ 수가 좋은 fortunate; lucky; happy / 수가 좋아서 fortunately; luckily; by a piece of good luck / 수가 좋으면 if *one* is lucky (enough); if fortune smiles upon *one* / 수가 나다 run into a piece of good luck; hit the jackpot / 수가 좋다〔나쁘다〕 have good 〔bad〕 fortune / 수가 사납다 be unlucky 〔unfortunate〕; be out of luck / 수가 트이다 be in luck's way; *one's* circumstances change for the better way.
② 《수효》 a number; a figure. ⇨ 수효. ¶ 수많은 사람들 a large number of people / 수 없이 많은 별들 innumerable stars / 수가 적다〔많다〕 be few 〔many〕; be small 〔large〕 in number / 수가 증가하다 increase in number / 요새 실업자의 수가 많이 늘었다 The number of the unemployed has increased greatly.
③ 《몇》 a few; several. ¶ 수일 several 〔a few〕 days / 십 수일 over ten days.
④ 《…의 수》 the number of. ¶ 권수 the number of books.

**수**(壽) ① 《연령》 *one's* age. ¶ 수가 몇이나 되시는지요 May I know your age? ② 《장수》 (a) long life; longevity; 《수명》 *one's* (natural) life. ⇨ 수하다. ¶ 수를 누리다 enjoy a long life; live long / 수를 늘리다 lengthen *one's* span of life / 수를 다하고 죽다 die a natural death / 수가 짧다 be shortlived; have only a short life / 그는 수가 짧았다 He had a short life.

**수**(繡) embroidery. ¶ 꽃을 수놓은 옷 a

dress embroidered with flowers / 수(를) 놓다 embroider / 비단에 꽃을 수놓다 embroider flowers on silk.

◉ 수실 embroidery thread. 수틀 an embroidery frame; a taboret.

**수**[2] ①《도리·방법》 a way; a measure; a means; a step; a remedy; a resource; help.

¶ 무슨 수를 써서라도 by all means; by fair means or foul; by hook or by crook; at any cost 〔price, risk〕; on all accounts; in any case / 온갖 수를 써서 by one means or another / 온갖 수를 다 쓰다 use 〔try〕 all conceivable means / 하는 수 없이 helplessly; reluctantly; against *one's* will / 하는 수밖에 없다 there is nothing for it but to *do;* cannot help *do*ing; have no choice but to *do* / 어찌할 수가 없다 There is no way out. *or* There is no help for it. *or* Nothing can be done. / 위험을 면하기 위해 무슨 수를 써야 겠다 We must do something to avert the danger.

②《경우·가능》 an occasion; a possible occasion; a possibility; a likelihood; 《능력》 ability; capability.

¶ 있을 수 있는 일 a possibility; a probability / …수 있다 it may be…; there is the possibility of… / 바랄 수 없는 일을 바라다 hope against hope 《that…》; cry 〔ask, wish〕 for the moon / 참을〔견딜〕 수 없다 [사람이 주어] cannot bear 〔stand〕; [사물이 주어] be intolerable 〔unbearable〕 《to *one*》; be beyond bearing; be too much 〔bad〕 《for *one*》 / 그럴 수 있다〔없다〕 It may 〔cannot possibly〕 be so. *or* Such things do 〔don't〕 happen. / 그건 있을 수 없는 일이다 It is impossible. *or* It is out of the bounds of possibility. / 이른 봄에 서리가 내릴 수도 있다 There is the possibility of frost in early spring.

**수**(首) ①《시의》 a poem; a piece. ¶ 시 한 수를 짓다 compose a poem / 시 한 수를 읊다 recite a poem. ②《마리》 ¶ 닭 20수 twenty chickens.

**수가**(酬價) ¶ 의료 ～ a medical charge 〔fee〕; a doctor's bill 〔fee〕; medical treatment charges.

**수간**(樹幹) a (tree) trunk; a shaft.

**수간**(獸姦) bestiality.

**수감**(收監) confinement; imprisonment. ～하다 imprison; confine 〔put〕 《*a person*》 in prison. ¶ ～돼 있다 be (held 〔confined〕) in prison 〔jail〕; be behind (the) bars.

◉ ～자 a prisoner; a prison inmate.

**수갑**(手匣) (a pair of) handcuffs; cuffs 《구어》. ¶ ～을 채우다 handcuff; slip 〔put, place〕 handcuffs on 《*a person*》 / 그는 ～이 채워져 있었다 He was in handcuffs. / 그녀의 손목에 ～이 찰칵 채워졌다 Handcuffs were slipped 〔snapped〕 onto her wrists.

**수강**(受講) taking a course; attending a lecture. ～하다 attend a lecture 〔class〕; take a course; 《실기 연습을》 take part 〔participate〕 in a training session. ¶ 제가 두 과목을 ～할 수 있습니까 Do you think I can take two courses? ◉ ～료 tuition; a tuition fee. ～생 a member 《of a class》; a trainee; a participant. ～신청 an application for attending the lecture.

**수개**(數箇) several (items); a few (pieces). ¶ ～월 several months / 지난 ～월 동안 for months past.

**수갱**(竪坑) 〖광산〗 a shaft; a pit. ¶ ～을 파다 sink 〔put down〕 a shaft.

**수거**(收去) ～하다 take away; remove; collect. ¶ 불온 선전물 ～함 a subversive publications collection box.

◉ 분뇨 ～차 a dung cart; a honey wagon 《미속어》. 쓰레기 ～차 a refuse cart; a garbage wagon 〔truck〕.

**수건**(手巾) a towel. ¶ ～으로 손을 닦다 wipe 〔dry〕 *one's* hands with 〔on〕 a towel / ～을 짜다 wring a wet towel / ～을 적시다 moisten a towel.

◉ ～걸이 a towel-hanger.

**수검**(受檢) ～하다 undergo 〔go through〕 an examination; be inspected; be subjected to inspection. ◉ ～자 an examinee.

**수결**(手決) *one's* signature. ¶ (…에) ～(을) 두다〔쓰다〕 sign; put 〔affix〕 *one's* signature to.

**수경**(水耕) hydroponics.

◉ ～농장 a hydroponic farm. ～법〔재배〕 hydroponic 〔soilless〕 (plant) culture; water culture; tank farming; aquiculture; hydroponics.

**수경성**(水硬性) 〖화학〗 hydraulicity.

◉ ～시멘트 hydraulic cement.

**수계**(水系) a water 〔river〕 system; the drainage pattern 《of》.

**수계**(水界) the hydrosphere. ＝수권(水圈).

**수고** trouble(s); labor; toil; pains; efforts; services. ～하다 take pains 《to *do,* in *do*ing》; make an effort 《to *do*》; exert *oneself* 《to *do*》; take trouble 《to *do*》; put *oneself* out 《to *do*》;

do 《*a person*》 a service; render services 《to》. ¶ 헛～ vain efforts; a waste of labor ⇨헛수고 / ～가 들다 take 〔require〕 (much) trouble 〔labor〕; be troublesome / ～를 끼치다 give 《*a person*》 trouble; put 《*a person*》 to trouble 〔bother〕; trouble 《*a person*》 / ～를 덜다 save 《*a person*》 trouble / ～를 아끼다 be sparing of *oneself;* be stingy of labor; spare *oneself* trouble / ～를 아끼지〔마다하지〕 않다 spare no pains 〔efforts, trouble〕 to 《*do*》; do not spare *oneself* / 아이 기르기에 ～가 많다 go through many hardships to raise the children / ～좀 해 주십시오 Please do me a favor. / ～를 끼쳐 미안합니다 I am sorry for the trouble I have caused you. / ～하셨습니다〔해주셔서 고맙습니다〕 Thanks for your trouble. *or* I appreciate what you have done. / ～했지만 결과는 실망스러웠다 I worked hard but the result was disappointing. / ～한 보람이 없었다 All the efforts were in vain. / ～한 보람이 있었다 It was worth the trouble. ◉ ～비 a gift for services rendered; a recompense 〔compensation〕 for *one's* services; the charge 〔wages〕 for *one's* labor.

**수고롭다, 수고스럽다** (be) troublesome; toilsome; laborious; tiresome; painstaking. ¶ 수고로운 일 a heavy 〔hard, painstaking, laborious, backbreaking〕 job; an uphill task / 수고롭지 않은 일 an easy task; a soft job / 수고롭겠지만… I hate 〔am sorry〕 to trouble you, but...; May I trouble you to 《*do*》?; Would you mind 《*doing*》? / 아이 기르기는 ～ Children are a lot of trouble to raise. / 수고스러우시겠지만 함께 가 주실 수 있을까요 May I trouble you to come with me? 「cat.

**수고양이** a tomcat; a he-cat; a male

**수공**(水攻) inundation tactics. ¶ ～을 당하다 have 《the castle》 inundated; 《물 보급이 끊기다》 have the water supply cut off.

**수공**(手工) manual work 〔arts〕; handiwork; handicraft. ¶ ～품 handiwork / ～이 들다 take much trouble; involve much labor; be laborious. ◉ ～업 handicraft; handicraft manufacturing 〔industry〕: ～업자 a handicraftsman.

**수공예**(手工藝) handicrafts and manual arts. ◉ ～품 a piece of handicraft work. 「『동물』 a siphon.

**수관**(水管) a water pipe 〔line, tube〕;

**수괴**(首魁) the ringleader; the leader.

**수교**(手交) ～하다 hand (over); place 《*a thing*》 in 《*a person's*》 hand; deliver 〔hand〕 《*a thing*》 personally 〔in person〕 《to》. ¶ 각서를 ～하다 hand a memorandum; deliver a note / 이 편지를 그녀에게 ～해 주시오 Please hand her this letter yourself.

**수교**(修交) amity; friendship; friendly relations. ～하다 form a friendly relationship. ◉ ～조약 a treaty of amity 〔friendship〕: ～조약을 맺다 conclude 〔sign〕 a treaty of amity 《with》. ～훈장 《confer》 the Order of Diplomatic Service Merit 《Grand Kwanghwa Medal》.

**수구**(水球) 『스포츠』 water polo.

**수구**(守舊) 《보수》 adherence to traditional customs; conservatism. ～하다 adhere to traditional customs; be conservative. ◉ ～세력 the conservative force. ～파 the conservatives; the old liners.

**수구**(壽具) a shroud and its accessories; cerements; graveclothes.

**수국**(水菊) 『식물』 a hydrangea.

**수군**(水軍) the naval forces.

**수군거리다** whisper; exchange whispers; whisper to each other; speak under *one's* breath; talk in whispers; hold a whispered conversation. ¶ 귀에 대고 ～ whisper in 《another's》 ear / 그 두 사람은 무엇인가를 수군거렸다 Those two were whispering about something.

**수군수군** whispering; in whispers; in an undertone; 《가만히》 secretly; in secret; between 〔among〕 themselves.

**수굿이** drooping 〔hanging〕 low.

**수굿하다** be drooping 〔hanging〕 low; be bowed 〔lowered〕.

**수권**(水圈) the hydrosphere.

**수권**(授權) authorization; delegation of legal power. ～하다 give authority 《to *a person*》; authorize 〔empower〕 《*a person* to *do*》. ◉ ～대리인 an authorized agent. ～자본 『경제』 authorized capital.

**수그러지다** ① 《머리가》 become low; lower; drop; sink. ¶ 그의 고귀한 인품에 저절로 머리가 수그러진다 His dignified presence commands one's respect. ② 《기세 따위가》 be softened; become mild 〔less severe〕; moderate; go 〔die, calm〕 down; subside; abate. ¶바람이 수그러졌다 The wind abated 〔subsided〕. / 추위가 수그러졌다 The cold has decreased in severity.

**수그리다** bend *oneself.* ⇨ 숙이다.

**수금**(水禽) a waterfowl; a water 〔an aquatic〕 bird. ◉ ~류 Natatores; swimmers.

**수금**(囚禁) imprisonment; confinement. ~하다 imprison; put in jail; lock up.

**수금**(收金) collection of money; bill collecting. ~하다 collect money 〔bills〕. ¶ ~하러 다니다 make a round of calls to collect bills; go *one's* round and collect bills / ~이 잘 안 되었다 The result of bill collection was far from satisfactory. ◉ ~원 a bill 〔money〕 collector.

**수급**(首級) a decapitated head 《of the enemy》.

**수급**(需給) supply and demand. ¶ ~의 균형을 유지하다〔조정하다〕 adjust supply and demand; keep supply and demand in balance / 장기 에너지 ~ 정책을 마련하다 work out a long-term policy on the demand and supply of energy. ◉ ~갭 《fill》 the supply=demand gap. ~계획 a demand-supply program 《of》. ~관계 supply-demand relation; the relation between supply and demand; the supply-demand relationship. ~상태 《adjust》 the supply-demand situation. ~조절 adjustment of demand and supply.

**수긍**(首肯) assent; consent; a nod; understanding. ~하다 《동의하다》 consent 《to》; assent 《to》; nod *one's* assent 《to》; 《납득하다》 be convinced 〔persuaded〕 《of, that...》. ¶ ~이 가는 〔가지 않는〕 convincing 〔unconvincing〕 / ~이 가게 하다 win 《*a person's*》 consent; convince 〔persuade〕 《*a person* of *something,* that...》 / ~이 가도록 설명하다 give 《*a person*》 a satisfactory explanation 《of》 / 이렇게 설명하면 쉽게 ~할 수 있을 것이다 I think this explanation is sufficiently convincing. / 그의 말을 들으니 ~이 간다 I was convinced by his story. / 그의 설명에는 ~이 가지 않는데가 있다 His explanation fails to convince us in some particulars.

**수기**(手記) a note; a memorandum (*pl.* ~s, -da); a memo (*pl.* ~s) 《구어》; memoirs (회상록). ~하다 note 〔take, put〕 down; take notes 《of》. ¶ ~를 쓰다 write down *one's* memories.

**수기**(手旗) a flag; a signal(ing) flag. ¶ ~로 신호하다 signal with a flag. ◉ ~신호 flag signaling; semaphore.

**수꽃** 〖식물〗 a male 〔sterile, staminate〕 flower.

**수꿩** a male pheasant; a cock-pheasant.

**수나다**(數—) hit the jackpot; have a stroke of luck; have unexpected luck.

**수나사**(—螺絲) a male screw.

**수난**(水難) 《익사》 drowning; being 〔getting〕 drowned; 《해난》 a disaster at sea; a shipwreck; 《수해》 a flood; an inundation. ¶ ~을 당하다 《익사하다》 be 〔get〕 drowned; 《난선하다》 be shipwrecked; 《수해를 당하다》 suffer from 〔be damaged by〕 a flood.

**수난**(受難) ordeals; a severe trial; sufferings. ~하다 suffer. ¶ 예수의 ~ the sufferings of Christ (on the cross); the (Savior's) Passion / 과거의 민족적 ~과 오욕의 사슬에서 벗어나다 liberate from the chains of national ordeals and disgrace in the past. ◉ ~곡 Passion music. ~극 a Passion play. ~상(像) a crucifix. ~일 Good Friday. ~주(간) Passion Week.

**수납**(收納) 《금전의》 receipt. ~하다 receive. ◉ ~계원 a receiver; a receiving teller (은행의). ~액 the amount received. ~장 an account book. ~전표 a receiving slip. 국고 ~금 money taken into the Treasury.

**수납**(受納) receipt; acceptance. ~하다 accept; receive. ◉ ~자 a recipient.

**수냉식**(水冷式) water cooling. ¶ ~의 water-cooled. ◉ ~엔진 a water=cooled engine.

**수녀**(修女) a nun; a sister (of the Catholic church). ¶ ~가 되다 enter 〔go into〕 a convent; take the veil. ◉ ~원 a nunnery; a convent: ~원장 an abbess.

**수년**(數年) several 〔some〕 years; a few years. ¶ ~간 for 〔over〕 (several) years; 《앞으로》 for some years ahead 〔to come〕 / ~전 a few years ago / ~래 for several years now / 그한테서 ~동안 소식이 없다 I haven't heard from him for (some) years.

**수놈** a male (animal). ⇨ 수컷.

**수놓다**(繡—) embroider 《a figure on a handkerchief, a handkerchief with figure》; do 〔lay〕 embroidery 《on》.

**수뇌**(首腦) a head; a leader; [집합적] the brains; the core; the soul. ¶ 군의 ~ the brains of the armed forces / 정당의 ~ the chief executive of a political party; the soul of a party / ~가 되다 head 《a group》; take the lead; play the leading part 《in》 / 당의

～들이 여러 파로 분열되어 있다 The leaders of the party split into several factions.
◉ ～부 《회사의》 the chief 〔top-level〕 executives 〔management〕 of a company; 《정당 따위의》 the governing body; the administration; 《정부의》 the leading members of the government. ～회담 a summit 〔top-level〕 conference 〔meeting〕: 한미 ～ 회담 a summit conference 〔meeting〕 between Korea and the United States.

**수뇌**(髓腦) 〖해부〗 the myelencephalon.

**수뇨관**(輸尿管) 〖해부〗 the ureter.

**수다** chattering. ¶ ～(를) 부리다〔피우다, 떨다, 늘어놓다〕 chatter; chat; have a chat; gossip 《with, about》. ◉ ～쟁이 a chatterbox; a talkative person; a tattler; a prattler; a non-stop talker.

**수다스럽다** (be) talkative; chatty; gossipy; loquacious; wordy; talk too much. ¶ 수다스런 계집아이 a talkative girl; a talk-box chick 《속어》.

**수다하다**(數多—) 《다수》 (be) many; (be) large in number; numerous. ¶ 수다한 가족 a large family.

**수단**(手段) a means (단·복수 동형); a way; a measure; a step; 《궁리》 a device; a contrivance; 《편법》 an expedient; a shift; a resource.
¶ 목적을 위한 ～ a means to an end / 일시적 ～ a makeshift; an expedient / 부정한 ～ a foul means; an unjust step / 안전한〔틀림없는〕 ～ a safe 〔sure〕 step / ～을 안 가리고 by fair means or foul; by hook or by crook / 최후 ～으로 as a 〔in the〕 last resort / 다른 ～을 쓰다 resort to other means; try some other means; play another trick upon / 과격한〔극단적인〕 ～을 쓰다 take 〔resort to〕 drastic 〔extreme〕 measures / 모든〔온갖〕 ～을 다 쓰다 try every means available; take all possible steps; leave no stone unturned; exhaust *one's* resources / ～ 방법을 가리지 않다 be indiscreet in employing means 《to》 / ～이 다하다 exhaust every means; be at *one's* wit's 〔tether's〕 end / 부정한 ～으로 돈을 벌다 make money via unfair means / 그는 ～이 좋다 He is resourceful. / 그는 목적을 위해서는 ～ 방법을 안 가린다 He will stop at nothing to gain his end. *or* He will do it by fair means or foul. / 목적은 ～을 정당화한다 The end justifies the means. / 전화는 통신의 한 ～이다 The telephone is one means of communication. / 온갖 ～을 다 써봤지만 돈을 빌릴 수 없었다 I tried all possible means, but I couldn't borrow money.
◉ ～가 a man of ability; an able 〔a capable〕 man; an enterprising man; a tactician.

**수단** 《아프리카의》 the Sudan. ¶ ～의 Sudanese. ◉ ～사람 a Sudanese.

**수단추** a male snap 〔fastener〕; a stud.

**수달**(水獺) 〖동물〗 an otter. ◉ ～피 an otter skin 〔fur〕.

**수답**(水畓) 《논》 a paddy 〔wet〕 field.

**수당**(手當) 《보수로서의》 an allowance; a stipend; a pension (연금); a compensation 《미》; 《기본급의》 an allowance; (a) benefit. ¶ ～을 주다 give an allowance; recompense 《*a person*》 for / ～을 타다 draw an allowance 《from》 / 월 8만 원의 ～을 지급하다 allow 《*a person*》 eighty thousand won a month / 월급 외로 가족 ～과 별도의 야근 ～이 지급된다 Besides the basic salary you will be given a family allowance and extra pay for night work. ◉ 광열～ an allowance for light and heat. 연말～ a year-end bonus. 피복～ a clothing 〔dress〕 allowance.

**수더분하다** 《순박한》 (be) simple and unaffected; good-natured; be not particular (까다롭지 않은); be not fussy. ¶ 수더분한 사람 an easygoing person.

**수도**(水道) ① 《물》 piped 〔city, tap〕 water; 《설비》 waterworks; (a) water supply 〔service〕. ¶ ～를 놓다〔끌다〕 have water pipes laid; have water supplied 〔laid on〕; lay on water / ～를 틀다〔잠그다〕 turn on 〔off〕 the tap / ～를 끊다 shut off the water / 이 일대는 수돗물 사정이 좋다 We have a good supply of water in this vicinity. / 우리 집은 ～가 잘 나온다〔나오지 않는다〕 The water pressure in our house is good 〔poor〕. / 공사로 인해 내일 아침 5시부터 8시까지 ～가 나오지 않습니다 Due to construction work, the water supply will be cut off from 5:00 o'clock until 8:00 tomorrow morning. ② 《수로》 a water-way; a water course; 《해협》 a channel; a gut; 《도수로》 an aqueduct; a water conduit.
◉ ～공사 waterworks. ～관 a water 〔service〕 pipe; a water main (본관). ～교 a raised aqueduct. ～국 《시의》 the Waterworks Bureau. ～꼭지 a tap;

《미》 a faucet; a hydrant (소화전): ~꼭지를 틀어 놓다 leave a tap open. ~료〔요금〕 water rates 〔charges〕; tap water charges. ~사업소 a waterworks office. 수돗물 city 〔tap, piped〕 water; running water: 수돗물이 달려 고생하다 suffer from a short water supply.
한려~ the *Hallyŏ* Waterway.

**수도**(水稻) 《논벼》 lowland 〔paddy〕 rice.

**수도**(受渡) (a) delivery; (a) transfer. ~하다 deliver 《goods》; transfer 《property》; hand over.

**수도**(首都) a capital (city); a national capital; a metropolis. ¶ ~의 metropolitan / 서울은 한국의 ~이다 Seoul is the capital 〔metropolis〕 of Korea.
◉ ~경비사(령부) the Army Capital Garrison Command; the Capital Defense Command.

**수도**(修道) religious austerities; an ascetic practice 〔penance〕. ~하다 do penance; practice asceticism; search for truth. ◉ ~사 a monk; a friar; an ascetic. ~생활 an ascetic life; monasticism; a monastic life. ~승 a Buddhist monk. ~원 a religious house; an abbey (큰것); a priory (작은 것); a monastery; a cloister; a convent (주로 수녀의); a nunnery (수녀의): ~원장 a superior; 《남자》 an abbot; a prior; 《여자》 an abbess; a prioress. ~회 an order (of religious regulations).

**수도권**(首都圈) the metropolitan area; the capital region. ¶ ~ 방위 태세 the nation's defense posture in the metropolitan area / ~의 교통인구를 분산시키다 disperse traffic population in the metropolitan area.
◉ ~개발 심의위원회 the Metropolitan Area Development Deliberation Committee. ~고속도로 the Metropolitan-Area Expressway. ~재개발 redevelopment of the capital region. ~재정비안 the metropolitan rearrange program: ~ 재정비안을 마련하다 work out a master plan for rearrangement of the metropolitan region.

**수동**(手動) ¶ ~의 hand-powered; hand-operated〔-worked〕; manually operated / ~ 기계 a hand-powered machine / ~(조종)으로 전환하다 go 「on (to) 〔over to〕 manual / ~ 조종장치 manual control(s) / 보조 ~ 조종장치 a back-up manual system. ◉ ~변속장치 《a car with》 (a) manual transmission. ~브레이크 a hand brake. ~펌프 a hand 〔manual〕 pump.

**수동**(受動) passivity; passiveness. ¶ ~적인 passive / ~적으로 passively / ~적인 태도를 취하다 take a passive attitude; 《공격에》 stand on the defensive. ◉ ~태 〖문법〗 the passive (voice): 다음 문장을 ~태로 고치시오 Put the following sentence into the passive.

**수두**(水痘) 〖의학〗 varicella; chicken pox.

**수두룩하다** 《많다》 (be) numerous; plentiful; abundant. ¶ 수두룩이 plentifully; abundantly; commonly / 나는 할 일이 ~ I have a heap of work to do. / 그는 자식들이 ~ He has a great many children. / 상점에 물건이 ~ The stores are loaded with merchandise. / 그런 사람들이 ~ There are lots 〔plenty〕 of people like that.

**수들수들** dried up partially. ~하다 be partially dried up; be (a bit) withered. ¶ ~ 마르다 wither (a bit).

**수때우다**(數—) forestall predicted bad luck by deliberately undergoing a lesser hardship beforehand.

**수땜**(數—) forestalling predicted bad luck by deliberately undergoing a lesser hardship beforehand. ¶ ~을 한 셈치고 체념합시다 We will take it as the price for our escape from misfortune.

**수라**(水剌) 《왕의 식사》 a royal meal; the king's dinner. ◉ ~간〔상〕 a royal kitchen 〔table〕.

**수라장**(修羅場) a pandemonium; a shambles; a scene of violence 〔bloodshed, utter confusion〕. ¶ ~이 되다 become a scene of carnage; be turned into a shambles; become chaotic.

**수락**(受諾) acceptance; consent (승낙). ~하다 accept 《an offer》; agree to 《the conditions》; assent 〔give *one's* assent〕 to 《the terms offered》. ¶ 정식 ~ formal acceptance / 신청을 ~하다 accept a proposal / 요청을 ~하다 comply with the request / 취임을 ~하다 accept the post 《of chairperson》 / 누가 뭐라 하든 그 사람은 ~하지 않을 것이다 He'll be against it, whatever others may say. / 그것은 이의 없이 ~되었다 It was accepted with unanimity.

**수란**(水卵) a poached egg. ¶ ~을 뜨다 poach an egg. ◉ ~짜 an egg poacher; a poacher.

**수란관**(輸卵管) 〖해부〗 an oviduct. ⇨ 나팔관.

**수량**(水量) the quantity 〔volume〕 of

water. ¶ 그 강은 ~이 풍부하다 The river has a great volume of water. / 비로 강의 ~이 불었다 The river has risen 〔has swollen〕 after the rain. *or* The river is in flood after the rain. ◉ ~계 a water gauge 〔meter〕.

**수량**(數量) (a) quantity; (an) amount; volume. ¶ ~이 늘다 increase 〔gain, grow〕 in quantity 〔volume〕 / ~이 줄다 decrease 〔diminish〕 in quantity 〔volume〕.

**수렁** a bog; a slough; a (quag)mire; a morass; a marsh. ¶ ~에 빠지다 bog (down); sink in a bog; be 〔get〕 bogged / ~에 빠져들다 [비유적] be bogged 〔mired〕 down; be driven into a quagmire; mire *oneself* 《in a war》/ ~에서 빠져 나오다 find a way out of the swamp. ◉ ~논 a swampy rice field. ~배미 a strip of swampy rice field.

**수레** a wagon; a cart; a van; 《손수레》 a handcart; 《타는》 a carriage (마차); a vehicle. ¶ ~에 싣다 load a cart 〔wagon〕 《with goods》/ ~를 끌다 pull 〔draw〕 a cart.
◉ ~바퀴 a (wagon) wheel.

**수려**(秀麗) grace; beauty. ~하다 (be) graceful; beautiful; handsome. ¶ 이목이 ~한 청년 a very handsome young man.

**수력**(水力) water 〔hydraulic〕 power. ¶ ~으로 움직이는 water-powered; hydraulic / ~을 이용하다 make use of water 〔hydraulic〕 power.
◉ ~발전 water-power 〔hydroelectric power〕 generation: ~ 발전소 a hydroelectric power plant 〔station〕. ~자원 water-power resources. ~전기 hydroelectricity; water-powered electricity: ~전기의 hydroelectric. ~학 hydraulics.

**수련**(修鍊) practice; training; exercise; discipline; drilling. ~하다 practice 〔train, drill〕 《at》. ◉ ~생 a trainee. ~의(醫) an apprentice doctor; an intern; a resident (doctor).

**수련**(睡蓮) 〖식물〗 a water 〔pond〕 lily.

**수렴**(收斂) ① 《세금 따위의》 levying and collecting of taxes. ~하다 exact taxes 《from》; collect taxes.
② 《수축》 〖의학〗 astriction; 〖물리·수학〗 convergence. ~하다 be astringent; be astrictive; converge. ¶ ~성의 astringent; astrictive; convergent.
③ 《여론 따위의》 collecting; (a) reflection. ~하다 collect. ¶ 여론을 ~하다 collect the public opinions / 각계의 폭넓은 의견을 ~하다 collect extensive opinions from all walks of life; take opinions from various strata of society into consideration. ◉ ~급수〔렌즈〕 a convergent series 〔lens〕. ~제 an astringent; an astrictive.

**수렴청정**(垂簾聽政) 〖역사〗 administering state affairs from behind the veil 〔curtain〕.

**수렵**(狩獵) hunting; shooting; the chase. ⇨ 사냥. ¶ ~하러 가다 go shooting 〔hunting〕.
◉ ~가 a hunter; a sportsman. ~기 the hunting 〔open〕 season: ~ 금지기 the closed 〔close《영》〕 season. ~면허증 a shooting 〔hunting〕 license. ~법 the game law. ~조 a game fowl. ~지 a hunting ground.

**수령**(守令) 〖고제도〗 a provincial mandarin; a magistrate.

**수령**(受領) receipt. ~하다 receive; accept; be in receipt 《of》. ¶ 틀림없이 ~했습니다 Received with thanks.

**수령**(首領) a chieftain; a chief; a (ring)leader; a boss. ¶ ~이 되다 assume 〔take〕 the leadership 《of a group》; lead 《others in *something*》.

**수령**(樹齡) the age of a tree. ¶ 이 나무는 ~ 200년이다 The tree is two hundred years old.

**수로**(水路) a waterway; a watercourse; 《항해로》 a lane; a fairway (항구의). ¶ ~로 가다 go to 《Pusan》 by sea 〔water, ship〕. ◉ ~관측소 a hydrographic observatory. ~도 a hydrographic map. ~측량 a hydrographical survey. ~표지 a beacon; a channel mark. ~학 hydrography. 관개~ an irrigation canal 〔ditch〕. 국제~ international waterways.

**수로안내**(水路案內) pilotage; piloting; 《사람》 a pilot. ~하다 pilot 《a boat》.
◉ ~료 pilotage (dues): 입항〔출항〕~료 inward 〔toward〕 pilotage. ~선(船) a pilot boat.

**수록**(收錄) ~하다 ① 《기재하다》 put 《*a person's* letters》 (together) 《in a book》; mention; contain; 《기록하다》 record. ¶ 이 사전에는 약 15만 표제어가 ~되어 있다 This dictionary contains about 150,000 entries. ② 《녹음·녹화하다》 record 《a speech on tape, a scene on video tape》.

**수뢰**(水雷) a torpedo (*pl.* ~es); a naval mine. ⇨ 어뢰, 기뢰. ¶ ~를 발사하다 fire a torpedo. ◉ ~방어망 torpedo netting. ~정 a torpedo boat.

**수뢰**(受賂) accepting a bribe. ⇨ 수회(收賄). ～하다 take 〔accept〕 a bribe; take graft《미》.

**수료**(修了) completion《of a course》. ～하다 complete; finish《courses of study》. ¶ 전과정을 ～하다 complete the whole course of study / 3학년을 ～하다 finish the third-year course / … 과정을 ～했음을 증명함 This is to certify that《*a person*》has completed the course of…. ◉ ～증 a certificate (of completion of a course).

**수류**(水流) a (water) current; a stream (of water); a watercourse; a flow.

**수류탄**(手榴彈) a hand grenade; a pineapple《군사속어》. ¶ ～을 던지다 throw a hand grenade.

**수륙**(水陸) land and water 〔sea〕. ¶ ～양용의 amphibian; amphibious. ◉ ～공동작전 amphibious operations. ～양서동물 an amphibian; an amphibious animal. ～양용 비행기 an amphibian (plane). ～양용 전차 an amphibious tank. ～양용차 an amphibian 〔amphibious〕 car 〔vehicle〕.

**수리**〖조류〗 an eagle. ¶ ～의 aquiline. ◉ ～둥지 an aerie; an eyrie. ～부엉이 an eagle owl.

**수리**(水利) utilization of water; 《급수》 water supply; 《관개》 irrigation; 《수운》 water transportation; water carriage. ◉ ～공사 irrigation works. ～권 water rights. ～사업 irrigation works 〔projects〕. ～시설 irrigation facilities. ～조합 an irrigation association. ～학 hydrography.

**수리**(受理) acceptance. ～하다 accept; take up; receive. ¶ 고소〔상고〕를 ～하다 take up a charge 〔an appeal〕 / 사표를 ～하다 accept《*a person's*》resignation / 청원서를 ～하다 accept a petition.

**수리**(修理) repair(s); mending; a refit (특히 배의); service. ～하다 repair《a TV set》; make repairs on《a house》; mend《a watch》; refit《a ship》; fix (up)《a machine》; service《a motorcar》. ¶ 자동차 ～ automobile repairs / ～중이다 be under repair / 대～를 하다 make 〔do〕 thorough 〔large〕 repairs《on》/ ～시키다 have 〔get〕《*one's* watch》repaired 〔mended〕《by》/ ～할 수가 없다 be beyond 〔past〕 repair / ～를 요하다 be in need of repair; need repairs 〔repairing〕 / ～가 잘돼 〔안 되어〕 있다 be in good 〔bad〕 repair; be in 〔out of〕 repair / 내부 ～중—휴업《게시》 Closed for alterations. ◉ ～공 a repairman; a repairer. ～비 repairing charges; the cost of repairing; repair expenses. ～점《전기 기구·라디오의》 a service station.

**수리**(數理) a mathematical principle. ¶ ～적(인) mathematical / ～에 밝다 be strong in mathematics. ◉ ～경제〔물리, 통계〕학 mathematical economics 〔physics, statistics〕.

**수리수리하다** (be) dim; misty. ¶ 나이를 먹으면 눈이 수리수리해진다 Our sight grows dim 〔misty〕 with age.

**수림**(樹林) a wood; a forest; a grove.

**수립**(樹立) establishment; founding; setting-up. ～하다 establish; found; set up. ¶ 계획을 ～하다 devise 〔work out, formulate〕 a plan / 국교를 ～하다 establish 〔enter into〕 diplomatic relations《with》/ 신정부를 ～하다 establish 〔set up〕 a new government / 외교 정책을 ～하다 formulate a foreign policy / 그는 또 세계 신기록을 ～했다 He made 〔established, set〕 another new world record.

**수마**(水魔) a disastrous flood; an inundation; angry flood waters. ¶ ～가 덮치다 be struck by a disastrous flood.

**수마**(睡魔) (the arms of ) Morpheus (그리스 신화의); 《졸음》 drowsiness; sleepiness; 《옛이야기의》 the sandman. ¶ ～가 덮치다 become 〔get, feel〕 sleepy; be overcome by drowsiness / ～와 싸우다 try not to fall asleep.

**수마트라**《인도네시아의 섬》 Sumatra.

**수만**(數萬) tens 〔scores〕 of thousands. ¶ ～의 관객〔인파〕 scores of thousands of 「spectators 〔a (surging) crowd〕.

**수많다**(數—) ¶ 수많은 a large number 〔quantity〕 of; a great many; a lot of; numerous; countless; a great deal of; immense; vast / 수많은 돈 oceans of money / 수많은 사람들 a great number of 〔a great many〕 people; numbers 〔scores, crowds〕 of people / 수많은 인파에 부대끼다 be jostled among 〔in, by〕 the crowd.

**수말** a male horse.

**수매**(收買) (a) purchase; buying; 《정부의》 procurement. ～하다 purchase; buy (out). ¶ 정부의 쌀 ～가 the Government's purchasing price of rice.

**수맥**(水脈) 《땅 속의 물줄기》 a water vein; 《뱃길》 a water route. ¶ ～을 찾아내다 strike 〔hit〕 (a vein of ) water.

**수면**(水面) 《on》 the surface of the

water; the water surface. ¶ ~에 뜨다 float on the surface (of the water) / ~에 떠오르다 rise 〔come up〕 to the surface; break (the) surface; surface / ~에서 3미터 위〔아래〕 three meters above 〔below〕 the water.

**수면**(睡眠) (a) sleep; (a) slumber. ¶ ~을 충분히 취하다 sleep well; have 〔take, get〕 a good sleep (1회의) / ~을 방해하다 disturb 〔interrupt〕《*a person's*》 sleep. ◉ ~병 sleeping sickness. ~시간 sleeping hours; hours of sleep. ~제 a sleeping drug 〔pill〕; a narcotic; a soporific.

**수면부족**(睡眠不足) lack 〔shortage〕 of sleep; insufficient sleep. ¶ 너는 ~이다 You are short of sleep. / ~으로 신경이 날카로워져 있었다 My nerves were on edge from lack of sleep.

**수명**(壽命) the span of life; *one's* life (span); the length of *one's* days; 〖보험〗 life expectancy (생존 확률); 《물건의》 wear; durability; life. ¶ 평균~ the average span of (human) life / 자동차의 ~ the expected life span of motorcars / ~이 길다〔짧다〕 have 〔enjoy〕 a long 〔short〕 life; be long-〔short-〕lived; 《물건이》 wear well 〔badly〕; be 〔be not〕 durable / ~을 늘이다〔줄이다〕 lengthen 〔shorten〕 *one's* life / ~을 다하고 죽다 die a natural death / 저 선수는 선수 ~이 길다 The player has a long career. / 이 건전지는 ~이 거의 다 됐다 This battery is almost dead. / 현 내각의 ~도 이제 얼마 안 남았다 The present Cabinet's days are numbered.

**수모**(受侮) scorn; disdain; slight. ~하다 be insulted 〔humiliated, despised, abused〕. ¶ ~를 받다 be held in contempt; suffer an insult; be insulted 〔humiliated, despised, abused〕 / 나는 온갖 ~를 다 참아야 했다 I had to pocket not a few insults.

**수목**(樹木) a tree; 〔총칭〕 trees (and shrubs). ¶ ~이 없는 treeless; bare of trees / ~이 울창한 woody; wooded 《mountain》; tree-covered. ◉ ~숭배 dendrolatry. ~원 a tree garden; an arboretum. ~학 dendrology.

**수몰**(水沒) submergence. ~하다 be submerged 《in》; be flooded 〔inundated〕 (with water); go under water. ◉ ~지역 submerged districts; an area (to be) underwater.

**수묵**(水墨) India ink. ¶ ~(이) 지다 get smudged / ~(을) 치다 cover up; gloss over 《a mistake》. ◉ ~화 a painting in India ink.

**수문**(水門) a floodgate; a sluice (gate); a water gate; a lock gate (운하의).

**수문**(守門) keeping 〔guarding〕 a gate. ◉ ~군 sentries; guards. ~장 the chief of gatekeepers.

**수미**(首尾) the beginning and the end of a matter; the whole particulars; from beginning to end. ¶ ~ 상접하다 run in unbroken succession; be continuous.

**수미**(愁眉) knitted (eye)brows; a worried look. ¶ ~를 펴다 feel relieved; breathe freely 〔again〕.

**수밀**(水密) ¶ ~의 watertight. ◉ ~시험 a watertight test.

**수밀도**(水蜜桃) a peach.

**수박** a watermelon. ¶ 씨 없는 ~ a seedless watermelon / ~ 겉핥기 지식 superficial 〔half, shallow〕 knowledge; a smattering 《of Latin》.

**수반**(水盤) a (flower) tray.

**수반**(首班) the head. ¶ 내각의 ~ the head of a cabinet; a premier; a prime minister / 정부의 ~ the head of government 〔state〕 / 정부의 ~이 되다 assume 〔take over〕 the reigns of government; head the cabinet / 내각 ~으로 지명하다 name 〔designate〕《*a person*》 as premier.

**수반**(隨伴) accompaniment; concomitance. ~하다, ~되다 accompany; go 〔come〕 with; be concomitant 〔attended〕 with; attend on. ¶ …에 ~하는 폐해 the evil effects attendant upon… / 어려움이 ~되다 be attended 〔beset〕 with 〔by〕 difficulties; bring difficulties in its train.

**수방**(水防) flood control; prevention of floods. ◉ ~공사 anti-flood construction. ~대책 a measure to prevent floods; an anti-flood measure; a flood control measure.

**수배**(手配) 《준비》 arrangement(s); preparations; 《배치》 disposition (of men); 《경찰의》 (a) search. ~하다 make arrangements 〔preparations〕; arrange 〔prepare〕 for; take (the necessary) steps 《for, to *do*》; 《경찰이》 begin 〔institute〕 a search 《for》; spread a search 《for》; cast a dragnet 《for》. ¶ ~중인 범죄자 a wanted man; a person wanted 〔sought〕 by the police; a fugitive from justice / 지명~ arrangements for the search of an identified criminal / 요소요소에 ~해 놓다 make dispositions at important points / 경찰은 그 사나이를 전국에 지명 ~했다 The police put the man on the wanted list throughout the country. / 그는 경찰의 ~를 받고 있다 He is wanted by the police. ◉ ~자 사진 a wanted person's photo; a mug shot 《속어》.

**수배**(數倍) several 〔a number of〕 times as large 〔many, long, deep, *etc.*〕 as....

**수배자**(受配者) ① 《배급 받는 사람》 a recipient of rations 〔distribution, a dividend〕. ② 《경찰 수배를 받는 사람》 a wanted criminal; a person wanted by the police.

**수백**(數百) hundreds; several 〔a few〕 hundred. ¶ ~ 명 several hundred men; hundreds of people / ~ 킬로미터 a few hundred kilometers. ◉ ~만 millions: ~만 명〔년〕 millions of people 〔years〕.

**수벌** a male bee; a drone.

**수범** a (male) tiger.

**수범**(垂範) setting an example. ~하다 set 〔give〕 an example 《of abstinence》 to 《others》. ¶ 솔선~하다 take the initiative and set an example.

**수법**(手法) a technique; a style; a way 《of *do*ing *something*》; a method; a trick. ¶ 똑같은 ~ the same old trick 〔game〕 / 범죄~ a method employed in a crime / 흔히 볼 수 있는 사기~ a classic swindling gambit / 새 ~의 사기 a swindle of a new type / 너와는~이 다르지 I do it in a way different from yours.

**수병**(水兵) a navy enlisted man; a seaman; a sailor; a bluejacket.

**수보다**(數—) get lucky; have a run-in with luck; hit the jackpot; come into a fortune.

**수복**(收復) reclamation; recovery. ~하다 recover; reclaim; win back. ¶ 영토를 ~하다 recover territory.
◉ ~민 inhabitants of the recovered area. ~지구 a recovered area.

**수복**(修復) ① 《복원》 restoration (to the original state). ~하다 be restored 〔restore 《*a thing*》〕 to *its* original state. ② 《답장》 writing a reply. ~하다 reply.

**수복**(壽福) long life and happiness.
◉ ~강녕 health, longevity, happiness and peace.

**수부**(水夫) a mariner. ⇨ 선원.

**수북수북** in heaps. ~하다 be heaped up.

**수북이** high; in a heap 〔pile〕; in heaps. ¶ 사발에 밥을 ~ 담다 fill a bowl heaping full of rice; heap rice on *one's* bowl; heap up in *one's* bowl with rice / ~ 달아주다 give a heaping measure.

**수북하다** be heaped up; be heaping full. ¶ 할 일이 ~ have a heap of work to do / 접시에 포도가 ~ Grapes are heaped up on the plate.

**수분**(水分) water; moisture; humidity; 《즙》 juice; 《나무의》 sap. ¶ ~이 많은 watery; moist; humid; succulent 《plant》; juicy 《fruit》 / ~을 보급하다 restore moisture 《to》; rehydrate / ~을 빼다〔없애다〕 remove water 〔moisture〕 《from》; dehydrate; anhydrate (특히 식품 가공시에); 《건조시키다》 desiccate; dry (up) / ~을 흡수하다 absorb 〔suck up〕 water.

**수분**(受粉) 〖식물〗 pollination. ~하다 be pollinated. ¶ ~시키다 pollinate.

**수불**(受拂) receipt(s) and disbursement(s); collection(s) and payment(s). ~하다 take in and pay out.
◉ ~금 incomes and outgoes; receipts and disbursements.

**수비**(守備) ① 《방어》 (a) defense; garrisoning; defensive measures. ~하다 defend; guard; assume the defensive; take up 〔be on〕 garrison duty. ¶ ~를 강화하다 strengthen the defense. ② 《야구의》 fielding. ~하다 field; play field. ¶ ~가 엉성한 선수 a butterfingers / 철통같은 ~ airtight fielding / ~를 보다 take to the field / ~를 잘하다〔못하다〕 be good 〔poor〕 at fielding; be a good 〔poor〕 fielder.
◉ ~대 a garrison; guards: 국경 ~대 the border guards. ~병 a (member of the) garrison; guards. ~율 〖야구〗 fielding average. ~전 a defensive war 〔fight〕. ~측 〖야구〗 the defensive team; the team in the field.

**수비둘기** a cock-dove; a male pigeon.

**수사**(手寫) copying by hand; a hand copy. ~하다 copy by hand; make a hand copy of. ◉ ~본 a book copied by hand.

**수사**(修士) a monk; a friar.

**수사**(修辭) a figure of speech; rhetoric. ¶ ~적 기교 a rhetorical device.
◉ ~학 rhetoric: ~학자 a rhetorician.

**수사**(搜査) (a) criminal investigation 《by police, by prosecutors》; 《수색》 a search; 《미》 a manhunt (범인의). ~하다 investigate 《a case》; conduct 〔make〕 an investigation 《into, of》;

《수색하다》 search 〔make a search〕 《for》. ¶ 범죄 ~ (a) criminal investigation / 과학적 범죄 ~ scientific crime detection / ~에 착수하다 start 〔institute〕 a search / ~를 포기〔중단〕하다 give up 〔abandon〕 the search 《for》/ ~를 계속하다 pursue 〔carry on〕 an investigation 《of, into》/ 경찰은 그 범죄 사건의 원인을 ~중이다 The police are investigating the cause of the crime. ◉ ~과 the (criminal) investigation section 〔division〕. ~관 an investigator. ~능력 《strive to raise》 *one's* investigation capability. ~당국 the investigating authorities. ~반〔진〕 a crime 〔criminal investigation〕 squad: 합동 ~반 the joint investigation team / ~반장 the chief investigator. ~본부 the investigation headquarters. ~선 the network of police search: ~선상에 오르다 appear on the network of police search. ~주임 the chief investigator (lieutenant). ~진(陣) a criminal investigation squad 〔team〕. ~카드 a 'wanted' card. 국립 과학~ 연구소 the National Institute of Scientific Investigation (생략 NISI).

**수사**(數詞) 〖문법〗 a numeral.

**수사납다**(數—) (be) unlucky; unfortunate. ¶ 수사납게도 기차를 놓치다 have the bad luck to miss a train.

**수사망**(搜査網) the police dragnet. ¶ ~에 걸려들다 be caught in 〔by〕 the police dragnet / ~을 펴다 spread 〔drop〕 the dragnet.

**수산**(水産) ⇨ 수산물. ◉ ~가공품 processed marine products. ~대학〔학교〕 a fisheries college 〔school〕. ~물 《be rich in》 marine 〔aquatic〕 products. ~시험장 a fisheries experiment station; a marine laboratory. ~식품 seafood. ~업 fisheries; marine product industries: ~업 협동조합 Fisheries Cooperatives / ~업 협동조합 중앙회 National Federation of Fisheries Cooperatives (생략 NFFC). ~학 fishery science.

**수산**(蓚酸) 〖화학〗 oxalic acid.

**수산화**(水酸化) 〖화학〗 hydration. ◉ ~나트륨 sodium hydroxide. ~물 a hydroxid(e). ~바륨 barium hydroxide. ~아연〔마그네슘, 칼슘〕 zinc 〔magnesium, calcium〕 hydroxide. ~암모늄 ammonium hydroxide. ~철 hydrated iron. ~칼륨 potassium hydroxide.

**수삼**(水蔘) fresh 〔green, undried〕 ginseng.

**수삼차**(數三次) a couple of times; several times.

**수상**(水上) ¶ ~의 water-surface; aquatic / ~에(서) on (the surface of) the water / ~ 식당에서 식사하다 have dinner on a floating restaurant. ◉ ~가옥 a house built on stilts over the water. ~경기 water 〔aquatic〕 sports: ~ 경기대회 a swimming meet; an aquatic competition. ~경찰 the water 〔harbor, marine〕 police. ~목 timber carried down river on floats. ~(비행)기 a seaplane. ~생활 aquatic life; life on the water. ~스키 water skiing; 《용구》 water skis: ~스키를 하다 water-ski. ~운동 aquatic sports 〔exercise〕. ~운송 water(-borne) transport; shipping by water.

**수상**(手相) = 손금. ◉ ~술 palmistry; chiromancy.

**수상**(首相) the Premier; the Prime Minister; the Chancellor (독일의); 《영구어》 the PM. ¶ 전(前) ~ an expremier; a former prime minister / ~이 되다 hold (the) premiership; head a Cabinet. ◉ ~관저 the official residence of the Prime Minister. ~대리〔서리〕 the acting prime minister. ~직 premiership.

**수상**(受像) ~하다 receive (television) pictures; televise. ¶ 이 화면은 위성 중계로 ~된 것이다 This screen received television images with a satellite telecast. ◉ ~관 a picture 〔an image-receiving〕 tube. ~기 a television receiver 〔set〕; a TV set. ~면 the television screen; the telescreen.

**수상**(受賞) ~하다 receive a prize 〔an award〕; win 〔be awarded〕 a prize. ◉ ~자 a prize 〔medal〕 winner: ~자 명단 a (prize) winners' list / 노벨상 ~자 a Nobel-prize winner; a Nobel laureate. ~작 a prize-〔an award-〕 winning work. ~작가 an award-winning writer.

**수상**(殊常) suspiciousness. ~하다〔스럽다, 쩍다〕 (be) suspicious; doubtful-looking; odd; peculiar; 《구어》 fishy; questionable; dubious. ¶ ~한 사람 a (man of) suspicious character; 《보기에》 a suspicious-looking man / 거동이 ~한 자 a prowler; a loiterer / ~히 여기다 suspect; feel suspicious 《about》/ 놈이 ~하다 I suspect him. / 그는 거동이 ~하다 He acts suspiciously. /그의 하는 짓이 ~스러웠다 His action aroused suspicion.

**수상**(授賞) awarding a prize; recognition. ~하다 award 〔give〕 a prize 《to *a person*》; recognize. ◉ ~식 an award ceremony.

**수상**(樹上) ¶ ~의〔에(서)〕 on a tree / ~생활의 arboreal; tree-dwelling. ◉ ~가옥 an arboreal hut. ~동물 arboreal animals.

**수상**(隨想) 《생각》 occasional 〔random, stray〕 thoughts. ◉ ~록 essays; stray notes; jottings.

**수색**(搜索) a search; (a) quest; (an) investigation; a manhunt (범인의). ~하다 search 〔look, hunt〕 《for》; make a search 《for》; rummage 《a house for *a thing*》; 《강을》 drag 《a river for a dead body》; 《소지품을》 frisk 《*a person* for a gun》 《구어》. ¶ 범인을 ~하다 search for a criminal / 철저히 ~하다 search thoroughly 《for》; comb 《a region for *a person*》 / 경찰은 범인을 ~ 중에 있다 The police are after the culprit. / 폭설로 인해 그들은 ~을 포기할 수밖에 없었다 Because of the snowstorm, they had no choice but to give up the search.
◉ ~기 a search(ing) plane. ~대 a search(ing) party. ~선 a search ship. ~ 영장 a search warrant: 가택 ~ 영장 a warrant to search the house. ~원 an application to the police to search for a missing person: ~원을 내다 ask the police to search 《*a person*》. ~작전 a search operation.

**수색**(愁色) a melancholy 〔gloomy〕 air; a worried 〔an anxious〕 look; the traces of sorrow. ¶ ~을 띠다 wear a worried look.

**수서**(水棲) ¶ ~의 aquatic; 《plants》 living in the water; water-dwelling.
◉ ~동물 an aquatic (animal). ~생물 [총칭] aquatic life; water creatures. ~식물 an aquatic 〔a water〕 plant; a hydrophyte.

**수석**(首席) the chief; the head; 《석차·지위》 the top 〔head〕 seat. ¶ …을 ~으로 하는 대표단 the delegation headed by… / ~으로 졸업하다 graduate first on the list / 학급의 ~을 차지하다 be at the top 〔head〕 of the class; lead *one's* class / ~을 다투다 contend for the top seat 〔place〕 / 그는 시험에 ~으로 합격했다 He topped the list at the examination. ◉ ~대표 the chief delegate; the head of the delegation. ~판사 the chief judge.

**수선** noise; fuss; bustle; (an) uproar; (a) clamor. ¶ ~부리다 = 수선떨다.
◉ ~쟁이 a fussbudget; a chatterbox.

**수선**(垂線) 〚수학〛 a perpendicular (line). ¶ ~을 내리긋다 draw a perpendicular.

**수선**(修繕) repair(s); mending. ~하다 repair; mend; make repairs; fix (up). ¶ ~이 안된다 be beyond repair / ~하러 보내다 send 《*a thing*》 for repair(s) / 시계를 ~시키다 have 〔get〕 a watch mended / 구두를 ~해야겠다 My shoes need repairing.
◉ ~공 a repairman. ~비 repair(ing) expenses. 응급~ emergency repair.

**수선거리다** make a noise; make 〔raise〕 a fuss. ¶ 옆방에서 수선거리는 말소리가 들려왔다 From the next room I could hear the buzz of conversation.

**수선떨다, 수선피우다** make 〔raise〕 a fuss 《over》; fuss 《about》. ¶ 하찮은 일에 수선을 떨다 make a fuss about trifles; make a great ado 〔to-do〕 about nothing; make a mountain out of a molehill.

**수선스럽다** (be) unquiet; noisy; turbulent; tumultuous; troubled; disturbed; boisterous. ⇨ 어수선하다.

**수선화**(水仙花) 〚식물〛 a narcissus (*pl.* ~es, -cissi). ◉ 나팔~ a daffodil.

**수성**(水成) ¶ (바위가) ~인 hydrogenous. ◉ ~암 aqueous 〔sedimentary〕 rock.

**수성**(水性) ¶ ~의 aqueous. ◉ ~가스 water gas. ~도료 emulsion (paint); water paint.

**수성**(水星) 〚천문〛 Mercury. ¶ ~의 Mercurial.

**수성**(獸性) 《man's》 brutal 〔animal〕 nature; the brute 〔beast〕 《in man》; brutishness.

**수세**(水洗) rinsing; washing (by water); a flushing. ◉ ~(식) 변소 a flush toilet; a water closet (생략 W.C.): ~식 변소로 개조하다 convert the lavatory into a flush toilet.

**수세**(水勢) the force of water 〔current〕.

**수세**(守勢) a defensive attitude 〔position〕; the defensive. ¶ ~의 defensive; passive / ~를 취하다〔에 서다〕 assume 〔go on, take〕 the defensive; stand 〔be, act〕 on the defensive / ~를 벗어나다 get off the defensive / ~로 몰아넣다 put 《the union》 on the defensive.

**수세**(收稅) tax gathering; collection of taxes.

**수세미** a (pot) scourer; a vegetable sponge; a pot cleaner. ◉ ~외 〚식물〛 a dishcloth gourd; a sponge cucumber 〔gourd〕.

**수소** a bull; 《불깐》 a steer; an ox.
**수소**(水素) 『화학』 hydrogen. ¶ ~의 hydrogenous; hydric / ~와 화합시키다 combine with hydrogen; hydrogenate; hydrogenize / ~를 제거하다 remove hydrogen 《from》; dehydrogenize.
◉ ~가스 hydrogen gas. ~산 hydracid. ~이온 a hydrogen ion: ~ 이온농도 hydrogen ion concentration. ~화물(化物) a hydrid(e).
**수소문**(搜所聞) ~하다 inquire into rumors; ask around. ¶ ~해서 잃은 아이를 찾다 search for a lost child by tracing rumors.
**수소폭탄**(水素爆彈) a hydrogen bomb; an H-bomb 《미》; a hell-bomb; a city-buster. ◉ ~실험 an H-bomb [a thermonuclear] test. ~탄두 a hydrogen [an H-bomb] war head.
**수송**(輸送) transport; transportation; transit; conveyance. ~하다 transport; convey; carry. ¶ 육상[해상] ~ transport by land [sea]; land [marine] transportation [carriage] / 철도 ~ railroad transport / 항공 ~ air transport; an airlift / 대량 ~ 수단 a large-scale transportation means / ~중이다 be in transit; be on the way / 그 배는 원료를 중국으로부터 ~하고 있다 The ship transports raw materials from China. / 상품이 ~중에 파손[분실]되었다 The goods were damaged [lost] in transit. / 공장에서 상점까지 트럭으로 물건들을 ~한다 Goods are transported from factories to stores by trucks. / 그 도시는 남부 지방에서 육상 ~의 요지이다 The city is a key center for land transport [transportation] in the southern districts.
◉ ~기 a transport plane. ~난 transport difficulties. ~대 『군사』 a transportation unit. ~량 (the volume of) traffic; carloadings (화물의). ~력 transport(ation) [carrying] capacity; carrying [transit] power. ~로(路) a transport route. ~비 the cost of transportation; transporting expenses. ~선(線) a line of transportation. ~선(船) a transport ship. ~시설 transportation facilities. ~열차 a transport train: 군대 ~열차 a troop train.
**수송기관**(輸送機關) a means of transportation.
**수쇠** ① 《돌쩌귀의》 the male [protruding] part of a hinge. ② 《자물쇠의》 the tumblers [serrations] of a lock. ③ 《맷돌의》 the pivot [a metal protrusion on the bottom plate] of a mill.
**수수** 『식물』 an African [Indian] millet; durra; a kaoliang; a sorghum.
◉ ~깡 a kaoliang [millet] stalk. ~쌀 grains of kaoliang.
**수수**(授受) giving and receiving; transfer; delivery. ~하다 give and receive; transfer; deliver. ¶ "금전의 ~는 없었다"고 그는 밝혔다 He declared that no money had changed hands.
**수수께끼** a riddle; a conundrum; a puzzle; an enigma; a mystery (불가해한 일). ¶ ~같은 enigmatic; mysterious; puzzling / ~같은 이야기 an enigmatic story; a puzzling story / ~같은 사람 a mystery man; a sphinx (*pl.* ~es, sphinges) / 우주의 ~ the mystery of the universe / 풀기 어려운 ~ a hopeless puzzle; 《난문》 a poser; 《구어》 a hard nut to crack; a crux (*pl.* ~es, cruces) / ~를 내놓다 ask [set, give] 《*a person*》 a riddle [puzzle] to guess [make out]; propose [put] a riddle to 《*a person*》 / ~를 풀다[맞히다] solve [guess, find out, undo] a riddle; answer [work out, make out] a puzzle; solve [untangle] a mystery / ~ 놀이를 하다 play riddles; exchange riddles 《with》 / 풀리지 않는 ~로 남다 remain an unsolved mystery / ~에 싸여 있다 be wrapped up in (a) mystery / 그가 왜 사직했는지 아직도 ~다 It is still a mystery to me why he resigned. / 이집트의 피라미드 축조술 중 몇 가지는 아직까지도 ~로 남아있다 Some of the Egyptian pyramid-building techniques still remain mysteries. / 그는 ~같은 말을 했다 He said something mysterious.
**수수돌** 『광물』 calcite which contains gold dust.
**수수료**(手數料) 《구전》 a commission; a percentage; brokerage (소개의); 《요금》 a charge (for trouble); a fee. ¶ 판매 ~ a selling commission / ~를 (5백원) 받다 charge 《*a person*》 a (500 won) commission / ~를 내다 allow [give] a commission / ~를 징수하다 levy a charge (for trouble) / 이것은 ~가 없습니다 This is free of charge. / 나는 그에게 20%의 ~를 지불했다 I paid him twenty percent commission. / 송금 ~는 2,000원입니다 The remittance charge is two thousand won. *or* It costs 2,000 won to make a bank transfer.

**수수방관**(袖手傍觀) ～하다 look on with folded arms; stand by in complete passivity; look unconcernedly on 《another's distress》; be 〔remain〕 an idle spectator 〔onlooker〕. ¶ 지금은 ～하고 있을 때가 아니다 This is no time (for us) to stand by idly.

**수수하다** 《모양·차림새가》 (be) ordinary looking; be of average appearance; 《검소하다》 (be) plain; simple; quiet; unpretentious (삼가는). ¶ 수수한 옷 a quiet dress / 수수한 빛깔 a sober color / 인물이 수수한 여자 a woman of average beauty; a woman passable in appearance / 수수하게 살다 lead a plain living; live in a quiet way / (옷을) 수수하게 차리다 be soberly 〔quietly〕 dressed 〔attired〕; be dressed unpretentiously / 그녀는 수수하게 생겼다 She has average looks.

**수술** 〖식물〗 a stamen (*pl.* ～s, -mina); an androecium (*pl.* -cia).

**수술**(手術) a surgical operation; an operation; surgery. ～하다 operate 《on》; perform 〔conduct〕 an operation 《on》. ¶ 대～ a major operation / 복부～ an operation on the abdomen 《of a patient》 / 외과～ a surgical operation / ～을 받다 undergo 〔have, go through〕 an operation 《for gastric ulcer》; be operated (up)on 《for appendicitis》; go under the knife / 맹장을 ～하다 perform an appendectomy; operate on a patient for appendicitis / ～을 두려워 하다 「be afraid 〔have a horror〕 of the knife 〔operation〕 / 그는 김 박사의 ～을 받았다 He was operated on by Dr. Kim. *or* He had an operation under Dr. Kim. / 어려운 ～을 하다 perform delicate surgery 《on the eye》 / ～은 성공이었다〔실패였다〕 The operation was a success 〔failure〕. / ～하기에는 너무 늦다 It is too late to operate. / 그의 ～ 후의 경과는 매우 좋다 His postoperative recovery is good and speedy. / 그는 ～ 중에 사망했다 He died on the operation table. / ～중 《게시》 operation in progress. ◉ ～담당 의사 an operating surgeon. ～대〔실〕 an operating table 〔room〕. ～비〔료〕 charges for an operation. ～복 an operating gown.

**수습**(收拾) 《제어》 control; 《해결》 settlement; solution. ～하다 settle; get *a thing* under control; deal 〔cope〕 with; manage; control; save; handle. ¶ 난국을 ～하다 save 〔settle, straighten out〕 a difficult situation / 사태를 ～하다 save 〔cope with〕 the situation; have the situation in hand / 혼란을 ～하다 unsnarl 〔disentangle〕 the chaos / 원만히 ～하다 reach a peaceful settlement; come to a perfect understanding / 회의가 ～할 수 없게 되었다 The conference was thrown into confusion 〔got out of control〕. / 마침내 사태가 ～되었다 The situation was settled at last. / 일이 너무 복잡해져서 우리로선 ～할 수가 없다 The affair has become too (much) complicated for us to manage.

**수습**(修習) apprenticeship; probation. ～하다 receive training; practice *oneself* 《in a trade》; learn 《the business routine of an office》.
◉ ～간호사 a student nurse; 《영》 a probationer nurse. ～공, ～생 an apprentice (student); a probationer; a trainee. ～기간 the probationary period; the period of apprenticeship. ～기자 a cub 〔junior〕 reporter. ～사원 a probationary employee. ～제도 a apprenticeship training system.

**수시**(隨時) ¶ ～로 (at) any time; at all times; 《필요에 따라》 on demand; as occasion calls 〔arises, demands〕; 《때때로》 from time to time / 본교는 ～로 학생의 입학을 허가한다 Students are admitted at any time into this school.

**수식**(水蝕) 〖지질〗 erosion (by the action of water).

**수식**(修飾) (a) decoration; ornamentation; (an) adornment; (an) embellishment; 《특히 문장의》 a rhetorical flourish; 〖문법〗 modification. ～하다 decorate; adorn; ornament; 〖음악〗 figure; 《윤색하다》 embellish; polish up 《a sentence》; 〖문법〗 modify.
◉ ～어 a modifier; a qualifier.

**수식**(數式) a numerical formula 〔expression〕.

**수신**(水神) the water god; a naiad (물의 요정).

**수신**(受信) the receipt of a message; reception. ～하다 receive a message 〔letter〕; receive. ¶ 배로부터 긴급 메시지를 ～하다 receive an urgent message from a ship / 산악지대에서는 텔레비전의 ～상태가 좋지 않다 Television reception is poor in mountainous regions.
◉ ～국〔소〕 a receiving station 〔office〕. ～기 a receiver; a receiving apparatus; a telegraph 〔radio〕 receiver. ～료 a (radio, TV) license fee; a subscrip-

tion fee. ～부(簿) a letter and telegram register. ～안테나 a receiving antenna. ～장치 a receiving apparatus 〔set〕. ～함 a letter box; 《미》 a mail box (각집의). ～회로 a receiving circuit.

**수신**(修身) moral training 〔culture〕. ～하다 practice morals. ◉ ～제가(齊家) moral training and home management: ～제가하다 cultivate *one's* moral culture and manage *one's* family.

**수신인**(受信人) an addressee; a recipient. ¶ ～ 불명의 편지 a blind letter / ～ 불명으로 되돌아오다 be sent back labeled "blind" / 겉봉에 ～ 주소 성명을 쓰다 address 〔direct〕 an envelope 《to *a person*》.

**수심**(水深) the depth of water; (the) water depth; soundings (측량한 깊이). ¶ ～을 재다 sound 〔measure〕 the depth of water / ～이 20미터다 The water is 20 meters 「deep 〔in depth〕. / 우리는 ～ 40미터 되는 곳에서 침몰선을 발견했다 We found a sunken ship at a depth of forty meters. / 위험— ～ 2미터 《게시》 Danger: water 2 meters deep. ◉ ～측량 sounding; plumbing: ～측량기 a depth-sounding apparatus.

**수심**(垂心) 〖수학〗 an orthocenter.

**수심**(愁心) anxiety; grief; melancholy; sadness; pensiveness. ¶ ～에 잠기다 be in a state of deep anxiety; be lost in apprehension 〔pensive mood〕; be sunk in grief / ～을 띠다 look sorrowful; appear disconsolate mind from care. 「mind.

**수심**(獸心) a brutal heart; a bestial

**수십**(數十) (several) tens 《of》; scores 〔dozens〕 《of》. ¶ ～ 년 scores of years / ～만 명 hundreds of thousands of people / 사람이 ～ 명 왔다 People came in scores.

**수압**(水壓) water 〔hydraulic〕 pressure. ¶ ～이 높다〔낮다〕 the hydraulic 〔water〕 pressure is high 〔low〕.
◉ ～계 a water-pressure gauge; a piezometer. ～관 a hydraulic pipe. ～기관 a hydromotor. ～력 hydraulic power. ～시험 a hydraulic test.

**수액**(樹液) (tree) sap; milk (야자수·고무나무 등의). ¶ ～이 많은 sapful; sappy / ～이 없는 sapless / ～을 채취하다 sap 《a rubber tree》.

**수양**(收養) fostering; adoption 《of children》. ～하다 foster; adopt 《children》. ◉ ～딸〔아들〕 a foster daughter 〔son〕. ～아버지〔어머니〕 a foster father 〔mother〕.

**수양**(修養) moral 〔mental〕 culture; (the) cultivation of the mind (정신의 교화); moral training (도덕적인 훈련); character-building (인격 형성). ～하다 cultivate *one's* mind; improve *oneself.* ¶ 정신 ～ moral 〔spiritual〕 culture / ～을 쌓은 사람 a cultured mind; a well-cultivated mind / ～이 없는 uncultured / ～을 쌓다 build up *one's* moral character / 자네는 아직 ～이 부족해 You have still room for moral training. *or* You should learn to exercise self-control. *or* You ought to have more self-discipline.
◉ ～법 a method of moral culture; how to cultivate *one's* mind. 「low.

**수양버들**(垂楊—) 〖식물〗 a weeping wil-

**수업**(授業) teaching; instruction; (school) lessons; school(work); classwork; (a) class. ～하다 teach; instruct; give lessons; give classes. ¶ 과외 ～ extra classes; the out-of-school teaching / ～을 받다 take a lesson 《in English》 / ～중이다 be now in *one's* class / ～에 들어가다 《선생이》 「go to 〔teach〕 *one's* class; 《학생이》 attend 「school 〔a class〕 / ～을 끝내다 dismiss a class; 《학교가》 dismiss school / ～을 빼먹다 dodge 〔skip, cut〕 a lesson; play truant; play hooky 《미》 / 우리 ～ 시간은 50분이다 Our classes last 50 minutes. / ～은 몇 시에 시작하고 몇 시에 끝나느냐 What time does school begin 〔start〕 and end 〔finish〕? / 오늘은 ～이 없다 We have no school today. / ～중에는 잡담하지 마라 No talking in class. / ～중에 졸지 마라 Don't nod off during the 「class 〔lesson〕. / 자, 오늘 ～을 시작하자 Let's begin our lesson for today. / 오늘 ～은 이것으로 끝 So much for today. *or* That's all for today. / 우리는 일주일에 세 번 영어 ～을 받는다 We take English classes three times a week.
◉ ～계획 syllabus planning. ～료 school 〔tuition〕 fees. ～시간 school 〔lesson〕 hours. ～일수 the number of school days.

**수업**(修業) pursuit of knowledge; study; training (단련); 《수료》 completion of a course. ～하다 study; pursue *one's* studies; train *oneself* 《in》; complete a course. ◉ ～연한 the years required for graduation from a school; the years required for completing *one's* course of study: 본교의 ～ 연한은 3년

이다 The course of study in our school spreads 〔extends〕 over three years. ~증서 a certificate of study.

**수 없다** 《수단·방법이》 have no way to *do* 《it》; cannot *do* 《it》. ¶ 하는 수 없이 helplessly; reluctantly / 계획 변경은 하는 수 없었다 The change 「of our plan 〔in our plans〕 was unavoidable.

**수없다**[1](數一) 《운수가》 lack 〔have no〕 luck; (be) unlucky.

**수없다**[2](數一) (be) countless; numberless; innumerable. ¶ 수없이 innumerably; countlessly; beyond 〔out of〕 count / 수없이 많은 too many 《stars》 to count / 예를 수없이 들다 give no end of examples.

**수에즈운하**(一運河) the Suez Canal.

**수여**(授與) 《상의》 awarding; 《증서 등의》 conferment; presentation. ~하다 award 《a medal to a winner》; confer 《a degree on *a person*》; decorate 《*a person* with an order》; grant 《a license》; present 《*a thing* to *a person*》. ¶ 졸업 증서를 ~하다 grant 〔issue, present〕 a diploma 《to》 / 학위를 ~하다 confer a degree on 《*a person*》 / 상품을 ~하다 award prizes 《to》 / 그에게 노벨 평화상이 ~되었다 He was awarded the Nobel Peace Prize.

**수여리** 〖곤충〗 a female honeybee; a queen bee.

**수여식**(授與式) a conferment ceremony; an awarding ceremony. ¶ 상품 ~ awarding 〔distribution〕 of prizes / 졸업증서 ~ a graduation ceremony; commencement exercises 《미》.

**수역**(水域) 《in》 the water area 《of, around》; 《in Korean》 waters; river basin (강의). ¶ 경제~ economic sea zone / 배타적 경제 ~ an exclusive economic zone (생략 EEZ) / 200해리(海里) 어로 ~ the 200-mile fishing zone / 어로 전관(專管) ~ the exclusive fishing zone 〔waters〕 / 한강 상류 ~ the upper reaches of the Han River. ◉ 공동 규제 ~ a jointly controlled waters 〔fishing zone〕. 중립~ neutral waters.

**수연**(水鉛) 〖화학〗 molybdenum.

**수연**(水煙) water spray 〔mist〕.

**수연**(壽宴) a birthday feast for an old 「man.

**수열**(數列) 〖수학〗 a series; (a) (numerical) progression. ¶ 등비〔등차〕 ~ a geometrical 〔an arithmetical〕 progression 〔series〕.

**수염**(鬚髥) 《사람의》 a mustache (콧수염); a beard (턱수염); whiskers (구레나룻); sideburns 《미》 〔sideboards 《영》〕 (살쩍); 《동식물의》 whiskers (고양이·염소·범 따위의); a barbel (물고기의); a hair (식물의 잎·줄기의); an awn (보리의); (corn) silk (옥수수의). ¶ 염소~ a goatee / 황제~ an imperial / ~이 있는〔난〕 bearded; mustached; 《면도를 안 해서》 unshaven / ~이 없는 beardless; 《면도해서》 clean=shaven / ~을 기르다 grow 〔cultivate〕 a mustache 〔beard〕; 《기르고 있다》 have 〔wear〕 a mustache 〔beard〕 / ~을 깎다 shave (*oneself*); shave off *one's* mustache; 《이발소 등에서》 have 〔get, take〕 a shave; get shaved; have *one's* mustache 〔beard〕 cropped / ~을 쓰다듬다 stroke *one's* beard / 가짜 ~을 달고 변장하다 disguise *oneself* with a false mustache 〔beard〕 / 두주 동안이나 ~을 안 깎다 have a two week's beard on *one's* chin / ~이 빨리 자란다 My beard grows quickly. / 그는 ~을 깨끗이 깎았다 He is clean-shaven 〔well shaven〕. / ~을 깎아 주십시오 Give me a shave, please. / ~이 대 자라도 먹어야 양반 《속담》 Fine manners are no cure for an empty stomach. *or* Even a gentleman has to eat. ◉ ~수세 the density of beard.

**수영** 〖식물〗 a (sour) sorrel.

**수영**(水泳) swimming; bathing; a swim; a bathe 《영》. ~하다 swim; 《영》 bathe 《in the sea》; have a swim 〔bathe 《영》〕. ¶ ~의 명수 an expert swimmer / ~하러 가다 go swimming 〔for a swim〕; go bathing 〔for a bathe〕 《영》 / ~을 잘〔잘못〕하다 be a good 〔poor〕 swimmer / ~을 전혀 못하다 can't swim a stroke / ~을 배우다 learn how to swim; take lessons in swimming.

◉ ~경기 (the sport of ) swimming; a swimming match 〔race〕. ~대회 a swimming meet. ~모 a swimming 〔bathing〕 cap. ~복 a swimming suit; swimwear; 《상하가 붙은 여성용의》 a swimsuit. ~선수 a swimmer. ~장 a swimming pool 〔place〕. ~팬츠 bathing drawers; swim(ming) trunks. 한국 ~연맹 the Amateur Swimming Federation of Korea.

**수예**(手藝) handicraft; manual arts.

◉ ~품 fancy works; handicraft articles: ~품 전시회 an exhibition of fancy works.

**수온**(水溫) water temperature.

**수완**(手腕) ability; capability; capacity; skill; competence; talent. ¶ ~이 있는

able; capable; talented / ～이 없는 incapable; incompetent / ～이 있는〔없는〕 사람 a man of 〔of no〕 ability / 외교적 ～ diplomatic ability / ～을 발휘하다 show 〔exhibit, display〕 *one's* ability; 《충분히》 give full play 〔scope〕 to *one's* ability / ～을 부리다 exercise *one's* ability 〔skill〕 / 굉장한 ～을 발휘하다 show remarkable ability / 그의 정치적 ～은 모두가 높이 평가하고 있다 The public has a high opinion of his political ability. ◉ ～가 a man of ability 〔skill〕; an able man; a go=getter.

**수요**(需要) demand; request; want. ¶ 가(假)～ disguised demand; speculative demand (투기성의); temporary demand (일시적인) / 유효～ effective demand / 잠재～ potential demand / ～가 있다 be in demand; be wanted / …에 대한 ～ demand 〔call〕 for… / 꾸준한 ～ steady demand 《for》 / ～의 탄력성 elasticity of demand / 가장 ～가 많은 것 things most in demand / ～가 많다 be much in demand 〔request〕; be in great demand; be greatly wanted; [사람이 주어] have 〔find〕 a great demand 〔call〕 《for》 / ～가 적다 there is little demand 《for》; be unmarketable / ～를 채우다〔충족시키다〕 supply 〔meet〕 the demand / 국내 ～를 채우다 fulfill 〔meet〕 domestic needs / 가격을 올려 ～를 억제하다 discourage demand with higher prices / ～가 급격히 늘어났다 There was a sharp rise in demand. / ～가 공급을 웃돈다 The demand exceeds the supply. *or* Supply cannot catch up with demand. / 한국에서는 이 제품의 ～가 큰가요 Is there a big demand for this product in Korea? / 이것이 그 상품의 ～를 촉진시킬 것이다 This will create 〔cause〕 a big demand for the product. / 생산고가 일반의 ～를 충족하기에는 부족하다 The output is not large enough to meet the demand from the public.
◉ ～감소 reduced 〔decreased, decreasing, lesser〕 demand. ～공급 supply and demand: ～공급의 법칙 the law of supply and demand / ～ 공급의 일치 the meeting of supply and demand. ～과잉 인플레 demand-pull inflation. ～독점 monopsony. ～억제 demand restraint. ～자 a consumer; a prospective customer 〔buyer〕: ～자 금융 the customer's finance system. ～조작 demand management: ～ 조작으로 총수요를 억제하다 suppress 〔repress〕 total demand through demand management. ～증가 increased 〔increasing, greater〕 demand.

**수요일**(水曜日) Wednesday (생략 Wed.).

**수욕**(水浴) bathing. ～하다 take a bathe 《in a river》; bathe in water.

**수욕**(受辱) suffering insult; humiliation. ～하다 get humiliated; suffer insult; be insulted; be disgraced.

**수욕**(獸慾) a bestial desire; animal appetites 〔desire(s), passion(s)〕; carnal desires; lust. ¶ ～을 채우다 satisfy *one's* carnal desires.

**수용**(收用) expropriation. ～하다 expropriate *a thing* 〔*a person*〕 「from *a person* 〔of *a thing*〕. ¶ ～한 토지에 대한 보상 compensation for expropriated land / 시당국은 쓰레기 처리시설 건립을 위해 그 토지를 ～했다 The city authorities expropriated the land for the construction of waste disposal systems.
◉ 토지～ land expropriation: 토지 ～권 (the right of) eminent domain / 토지 ～법 the Compulsory Purchase of Land Act; the Land Expropriation Law; the Eminent Domain Law.

**수용**(收容) accommodation; reception; admission; seating; housing; picking up (구조된 선원 등의); a picking. ～하다 accommodate 《travelers》; admit 《students to a school》; seat 《so many persons》; receive 〔take in〕 《a patient》; intern 〔impound〕 《prisoners》; house 《sufferers》; evacuate 《the wounded from a post》. ¶ 이 호텔은 약 1,500명을 ～할 수 있다 This hotel holds 〔can accommodate, has accommodation(s) for〕 about 1,500 guests. / 강당은 천명을 ～한다 The hall seats 1,000. *or* The auditorium has a seating capacity of one thousand. / 부상자는 인근 병원에 ～되었다 The injured were taken to the nearby hospital. / 홍수에 의한 이재민들은 학교에 ～되었다 The flood victims were lodged in the schoolhouse.
◉ ～(능)력 a seating capacity 《of 400》 (극장 등의); sleeping accommodation(s) 《for 300 persons》 (호텔 등의): 이 음악당의 ～능력은 2천명이다 This concert hall has a seating capacity of 2,000. ～소 a home; a camp; an asylum; a POW camp (포로의); a (concentration) camp (강제수용소); a detention house (불법입국

자 등의); a repatriates reception center (귀환자의): 북한의 강제 ~소 경비병 한 사람이 제 3 국을 통해 한국으로 귀순해 왔다 A North Korean concentration camp guard has defected to South Korea via a third country. ~인원 the number of persons to be admitted. ~자 inmates (양로원 등의); 《civilian》 internees (적국인 수용소 등의); inpatients (병원의).

**수용**(受容) reception; acceptance. ~하다 accept 《new ideas》; receive; be receptive 《to others' opinions》. ¶ ~적인 receptive; recipient 《mind》 / 외국 문화의 ~ adoption of foreign civilization.

◉ ~성〔력〕 receptive capacity; receptivity; receptiveness: ~력이 있다 be 《highly》 receptive 《to new ideas》. ~태세 preparedness 〔readiness〕 to receive; a reception setup 《for immigrants》: ~ 태세를 갖추다 get ready to receive; prepare for (receiving).

**수용**(需用) consumption. ◉ ~자 a consumer.

**수용성**(水溶性) solubility in water. ¶ ~의 water-soluble / ~ 비료 water-soluble manure.

**수용액**(水溶液) an aqueous 〔a water〕 「solution.

**수운**(水運) water transport; transportation by water; water traffic. ¶ ~의 편의가 좋다 have 〔enjoy〕 good water transportation facilities.

**수원**(水源) 《강의》 the source 《of a stream》; a riverhead; a fountainhead; a headspring; 《수도의》 the source of water supply; a reservoir (저수지). ¶ 강의 ~을 찾다 trace a river 「to 〔as far as〕 its source / 서울의 상수도 ~은 한강이다 Seoul depends on the Han River for its water supply. ◉ ~지 the catchment area 〔basin〕.

**수원**(受援) receipt of (foreign) assistance. ◉ ~국 a recipient country.

**수월래놀이** 〖민속〗 singing and dancing the *kang-kang-suwollae.*

**수월찮다** 《일이》 (be) not easy; hard; difficult; 《수·양이》 (be) not a few 〔little〕; no small; many; much; considerable. ¶ 수월찮은 큰 수입 a handsome 〔good, tidy〕 income / 수월찮이 돈이 들다 cost fairly much of money.

**수월하다** (be) easy; simple; be no trouble; be a pushover 〔snap, cinch〕. ¶ 수월한 일 an easy 〔a light〕 task; a soft job / 하기가 ~ it is no trouble to do; have no difficulty in doing / 수월하지 않다 be no pushover; be some trouble / 자금 문제만 해결되면 그 나머지는 ~ Once the problem of financing has been solved, the rest is plain sailing.

**수월히** easily; readily; handily; with ease 〔facility〕; without difficulty 〔trouble, effort〕. ¶ ~ 이기다 win easily; win an easy victory 《over》 / ~ 할 수가 있다 be easy to do; be easily done / ~ 돈을 벌다 make an easy gain.

**수위**(水位) water level. ¶ ~가 높다〔낮다〕 The water level is high 〔low〕. / 댐의 ~가 10미터 올라갔다〔내려갔다〕 The water level in the dam rose 〔fell〕 (by) ten meters.

◉ ~계 a water gauge; a hydrograph. ~표 a watermark. 위험~ the dangerous water level.

**수위**(守衛) guard(ing) (지키는 일); a (security) guard (경비원); a sergeant (at arms) (의회·법정 등의); 《문지기》 a doorkeeper; a gatekeeper; a porter; a janitor. ~하다 guard. ¶ ~를 보다 keep guard 《over》. ◉ ~실 a guard office (경비실); a (porter's) lodge (건물 입구의). ~장 the chief guard.

**수위**(首位) the premier 〔first, top〕 place; the leading 〔foremost〕 position; primacy. ¶ ~를 다투다 struggle for primacy / ~를 차지하다 occupy 〔win〕 (the) first place; be at the head 〔top〕 《of》; head 〔top〕 the list 《of》; stand 〔rank〕 first 《in》 / ~의 자리를 지키다 keep 〔hold〕 the first rank / 그 백화점은 매상에서 ~를 점하고 있다 The department store stands 〔ranks〕 first in 「the sales 〔the amount sold〕. ◉ ~타자 〖야구〗 the leading hitter.

**수유**(授乳) nursing; breast-feeding; suckling; lactation. ~하다 nurse; feed; suckle 《a baby》; give the breast 《to a baby》; 《모유로》 breast-feed 《a baby》. ◉ ~기 the (period of) lactation.

**수육** boiled 〔cooked〕 beef.

**수육**(獸肉) flesh of animals; meat (식용 「의).

**수은**(水銀) 〖화학〗 mercury; quicksilver; hydrargyrum (기호 Hg).

◉ ~광(鑛) mercurial ore. ~기압계 a mercury barometer. ~농약 an agricultural chemical containing mercury. ~등 a mercury(-vapor) lamp 〔light, tube〕. ~압력계 a mercury manometer. ~연고 mercury ointment.

～오염 mercury contamination. ～온도계 a mercury thermometer. ～전지 a mercury battery. ～제 a mercurial (preparation). ～주 a mercurial column. ～중독 mercury poisoning; mercurialism. 유기～ (화합물) an organic mercury (compound).

**수은**(受恩) reception of favors. ～하다 receive favor 〔kindness〕.

**수음**(手淫) masturbation; self-abuse; onanism. ～하다 practice masturbation; masturbate.

**수의**(壽衣) garment for the dead; a shroud.

**수의**(隨意) voluntariness; option; pleasure. ¶ ～의 optional; free / ～로 voluntarily; freely; at will; as *one* pleases / 복장은 ～임 《안내장·게시》 Dress optional. ◉ ～계약 a private 〔free〕 contract; a contract *ad libitum* (L.). ～과목 an optional 〔elective〕 course 〔subject〕. ～근(筋) 〚해부〛 a voluntary muscle. ～선택 *one's* free 〔optional〕 choice. ～판단 discretion.

**수의**(獸醫) a veterinary (surgeon); a veterinarian; a vet 《구어》.
◉ ～과 the veterinary faculty: ～과 대학 a college of veterinary medicine; the veterinary college. ～사(師)＝수의(獸醫). ～학 veterinary science 〔medicine〕: ～학과 the department of veterinary science.

**수익**(收益) earnings; gain(ing)s; proceeds; returns; a profit. ¶ 평균〔순, 총, 예정〕～ average 〔net, gross, estimated〕 earnings / ～이 있는 장사 a profitable 〔lucrative〕 business / ～을 올리다 realize 〔make, turn out〕 a profit; make 〔fetch〕 《a million won》 / 전람회의 ～은 전부 이 대학에 기부된다 All the proceeds from the exhibition will be donated to this college.
◉ ～금 earnings; gains; proceeds; profits. ～력 earning power. ～률 an earning rate; 《주식의》 price-earnings rate. ～세 the profit tax. ～자 《신탁 따위의》 a beneficiary; 《이득자》 a person enriched. ～자산 live assets. ～체감(遞減)의 법칙 the law of diminishing returns.

**수익**(受益) ～하다 benefit 《by an investment》; receive benefits 《from a project》. ◉ ～자 〚경제〛 a beneficiary: ～자 부담의 요금 beneficial rates / ～자 부담의 원칙 the benefit principle. ～증권 a beneficiary certificate.

**수익다**(手—) get used to 《the ways of *doing something*》; get familiar 《with》.

**수인**(囚人) a prisoner; a convict; a jailbird.

**수인**(數人) a few people; several persons.

**수인성**(水因性) ¶ ～의 waterborne. ◉ ～전염병 waterborne contagious diseases.

**수일**(數日) 《for》 a few 〔several〕 days. ¶ ～ 내에 in a matter of days; in several 〔a few〕 days / 그는 서울에서 ～간 머물렀다 He stayed in Seoul for a few 〔several〕 days. / 지난 ～ 동안 날씨가 좋았다 We have had good weather for 「the last few 〔several〕 days.

**수임**(受任) acceptance of an appointment 〔a nomination〕. ～하다 be nominated; accept an appointment 〔office〕; take office 《as dean》.
◉ ～자 an appointee; a nominee.

**수입**(收入) an income (개인의); earnings (법인·국가의); revenue (세입); proceeds (매상); takings; receipts (입금). ¶ 고정〔일정한〕 ～ a fixed income / 일정치 않은 ～ a fluctuating income / 실～ a net income; take-home 〔after-tax〕 pay (급료의) / 잡～ miscellaneous earnings; sundry receipts / 총～ a total 〔gross〕 income / ～과 지출 incomings and outgoings; receipts and expenses; revenue and expenditure (국가의) / 월 백만원 ～ an income of one million won a month / ～이 좋은 직업 a gainful occupation / ～이 많은〔적은〕 사람 a man of large 〔small〕 income / ～이 많다〔적다〕 have 〔earn, draw〕 a large 〔small〕 income / …의 ～이 있다 have 〔earn, enjoy, gain, draw〕 an income 《of》 / ～을 올릴 방법을 궁리하다 think out a means of gaining some money / ～의 길이 막히다 lose sources of *one's* income / ～을 얻다 earn 〔gain〕 an income 《of》; derive 〔draw〕 *one's* income 《from》 / ～에 맞는〔한도내에서, 이상으로〕 생활하다 live on 〔within, beyond〕 *one's* income / 새로운 ～원을 찾다 look for a new source of revenue / ～이 늘었다〔줄었다〕 My income has increased 〔decreased〕. / 지난 달에는 지출이 ～을 상회했다 The outgo was more than the income last month.
◉ ～계정 revenue account. ～인지 a revenue 〔fiscal〕 stamp.

**수입**(輸入) import; importation; 《제도·문물의》 introduction. ～하다 import; introduce 《foreign civilization》.
¶ 간접〔직접〕 ～ indirect 〔direct〕 import / 밀～ smuggling; contraband

(trade) / ～할 수 있는 importable / ～된 imported; introduced / ～의 장벽을 높이다 step up import barriers 《against》/ ～의 문호를 좀 더 개방하다 open *one's* import market more widely / ～을 제한하다〔금지하다〕 limit〔prohibit〕 the import 《of》/ 그들은 원료를 ～하고 완제품을 수출한다 They import the raw materials and export the finished product. / 그 나라는 원유 소요량의 50퍼센트를 ～하고 있다 The country imports 50 percent of its crude oil from abroad.

◉ ～가격 an import price. ～감시품목 the import surveillance items. ～결제어음 an import settlement bill. ～계약 an import contract. ～과징금 an import surcharge. ～관세 import duties. ～국 an importing country. ～금지 an import prohibition: ～을 금지하다 prohibit the importation of 《*a thing*》. ～담보율 the import deposit〔mortgage〕 rate. ～대리점 an import agent. ～대체산업 import substitute〔replacing, saving〕 industry. ～량 import volume. ～면장 an import license. ～무역 import trade. ～상〔업자〕 an importer; an import trader. ～상사 an import firm〔house〕. ～성향(性向) the propensity of import. ～세 an import tax; import duties. ～쇠고기 the imported beef. ～신고(서) an import declaration. ～신용장 an import (letter of ) credit. ～신청서《세관에의》 an import entry. ～액 the amount of imports. ～어음 an import bill. ～억제〔금지〕품목 import-restricted〔-banned〕 items. ～의존도 the rate of dependence on imports. ～자유화 the import liberalization; the liberalization of imports. ～절차 the process of import; import(ation) procedure〔formalities〕. ～제한 import restrictions; a curb on imports; an import relief (국내 산업보호를 위한): ～제한 품목 import-restricted items. ～품 imports; imported goods〔articles〕; imports from abroad; an import item: 밀～품 smuggled goods / 주요～품의 일람표 a list of main imports. ～할당 an import (allotment) quota (생략 IQ): ～ 할당 제도 the (import) quota system. ～항 a port of entry. ～허가제 the import licensing system. ～허가증 a import license〔permit〕.

**수입규제**(輸入規制) import regulations 《imposed by advanced nations》; import restraints〔restrictions curbs〕. ¶ 한국 상품에 대한 ～《enforce》 import restrictions against Korean products / ～의 완화를 요구하다 ask for relaxation of import restraints.

**수입초과**(輸入超過) an excess of imports (over exports); an unfavorable balance of trade; the deficit in the balance of trade; the balance of trade against a country. ¶ ～이다 Imports exceeds exports. *or* There is an adverse〔unfavorable〕 balance of trade. / 외국 무역은 40억 달러의 ～를 기록하고 있다 The balance of foreign trade shows an excess of imports of 4 billion dollars. *or* The total of foreign trade shows an unfavorable balance of 4 billion dollars.

**수있다**《수단·방법이》 can *do* 《it》; have a way to *do* 《it》; be able to *do*. ⇨ -ㄹ 수 있다.

**수있다**(數—) 《재수가》 be lucky; have luck.

**수자원**(水資源) water resources. ¶ ～의 적극적인 개발 positive exploitation of water resources / ～의 최대 이용 the maximum utilization of water resources. ◉ ～개발 the development of water resources. 한국 ～ 공사 the Korea Water Resources Corporation.

**수작**(秀作) an excellent〔outstanding〕 work〔piece〕《of art》; a masterpiece.

**수작**(授爵) elevation to the peerage; ennoblement. ～하다 elevate to the peerage; make 《*a person*》 a peer.

**수작**(酬酌) 《술잔을》 exchanging wine cups; 《말을》 exchanging words. ～하다 exchange cups; exchange words. ¶ 허튼～을 하다 talk nonsense; say silly things. 「퓨터〕 handling time.

**수작업**(手作業) handwork. ◉ ～시간〚컴

**수잠** a light sleep. ¶ ～ 들다 doze off.

**수장**(水葬) burial at sea〔in the sea〕; water burial. ～하다 bury at sea.

**수장**(收藏) garnering 《agricultural produce》; storage. ～하다 garner (up); keep〔put〕《*a thing*》 in storage; house 《a collection of Renoir's paintings》. ◉ ～고(庫) a repository.

**수재**(水災) a flood disaster. ¶ 이 지역은 매년 여름에 ～를 당한다 This district suffers from a flood (disaster) every summer. ◉ ～민 flood sufferers〔victims〕: ～민 구호 물자 relief goods to flood victims. ～의연금 a relief fund for flood victims.

**수재**(秀才) 《뛰어난 재주》 great ability;

《사람》 a talented person; a bright 〔brilliant〕 boy; an able student. ¶ 전교 제일의 ～ the brightest student in the whole school / 그는 천하의 ～다 He is a genius of nationwide fame. ◉ ～교육 education of 〔for〕 「gifted children 〔bright young intellectuals〕.

**수저** a spoon and (a pair of) chopsticks; 《순가락》 a spoon. ¶ ～ 한 벌 a set of spoon and chopsticks / ～를 상에 놓다 place spoons and chopsticks on the table. ◉ ～통 a spoon stand. 수젓집 a spoon bag.

**수적**(數的) numerical. ¶ ～으로 numerically; in number / ～ 우세 numerical superiority 《over》 / ～으로 우세하다 be numerically superior 《to》; exceed 《the enemy》 in number / ～으로 열세하다 be inferior in number.

**수전**(水田) a wet field; a rice paddy.

**수전**(水電) hydroelectricity. 「⇨논.

**수전**(水戰) a battle on the water; water warfare. ⇨ 해전(海戰).

**수전노**(守錢奴) a miser; a stingy man; a skinflint; a penny pincher.

**수전증**(手顫症) 〖한의〗 tremor of the hand; palsy in the hand.

**수절**(守節) maintaining *one's* chastity; faithfulness. ～하다 《절의를 지키다》 adhere 〔stick, keep, be turn〕 to *one's* principles; remain faithful to *one's* cause; 《정절을 지키다》 remain faithful to *one's* deceased husband; remain chaste 〔a widow〕.

**수정**(水晶) (rock) crystal; crystallized quartz. ¶ 자(紫)～ amethyst / 연(煙)～ smoky 〔veined〕 quartz / ～같은 crystalline; crystal-clear 《water》 / 이 연못은 ～처럼 맑다 This pond is crystal=clear. ◉ ～궁(宮) the Crystal Palace. ～석 cryolite. ～세공 crystal ware. ～시계 a crystal 〔quartz〕 clock 〔chronometer〕. ～점 crystalgazing: ～점쟁이 a crystal gazer. ～체 〖해부〗 the crystalline lens; the eye lens: ～체염(炎) lentitis; crystallitis.

**수정**(受精) 〖생물〗 fertilization; insemination; 〖식물〗 pollination. ～하다 be 〔get〕 fertilized 〔inseminated〕; be pollinated. ¶ 인공～ artificial insemination 〔impregnation〕 / 배우자간〔비배우자간〕 인공～ artificial insemination by husband 〔donor〕 / 체내〔체외〕 ～ internal 〔external〕 fertilization. ◉ ～능력 fertility. ～란(卵) a fertilized egg.

**수정**(修正) 《법안·조문 등의》 (an) amendment; (a) revision; (a) modification; 《잘못의》 (a) correction; (a) rectification. ～하다 amend; revise; modify; revamp; make a revision 《of》; correct. ¶ 다소 ～하여 in a modified form / 자구(字句)를 ～하다 alter 〔modify, make some changes in〕 the wording / 의안을 ～하다 amend a bill / ～되다 be revised; undergo revision / (인공 위성 따위가) 궤도를 ～하다 correct an orbit / 원고를 ～하다 correct a manuscript / 예산안을 ～하다 revise a budget bill / 상향〔하향〕으로 ～되다 be revised upward 〔downward〕 / 계획은 약간의 ～이 필요하다 The plan requires slight modification. ◉ ～액 《미》 whiteout; 《영》 correction fluid. ～예산 a revised budget. ～용 파일 〖컴퓨터〗 an amendment file. ～자본주의 revised capitalism. ～주의 revisionism: ～주의적인 revisionist(ic) / ～주의자 a revisionist / ～주의 노선을 걷다 take 〔follow〕 the revisionist course. ～취소 〖컴퓨터〗 de-updating.

**수정**(修整) 《고쳐 정돈함》 adjustment; regulation; 〖사진〗 retouching; a retouch. ～하다 adjust; regulate; retouch; touch up (손질을 가하다). ¶ 텔레비전 화상의 ～ the adjustment of the picture on the TV screen / 사진 원판을 ～하다 retouch a negative / 이 사진은 좀 ～한 것 같다 This photograph appears to have been slightly retouched.

**수정**(授精) 〖생물〗 fertilization; insemination. ～하다 fertilize; inseminate; 〖식물〗 pollinate. ¶ 인공적으로 ～하다 artificially fertilize 《eggs》. ⇨ 수정(受精).

**수정과**(水正果) cinnamon flavored persimmon punch; sweet cinnamon punch.

**수정관**(輸精管) 〖해부〗 the deferent duct 〔canal〕; the seminal canal; the spermatic duct.

**수정안**(修正案) 《초안》 a draft amendment; a proposed amendment 〔revision〕; 《수정된 의안》 an amended 〔a revised〕 bill; an amendment. ¶ ～을 제출하다 propose 〔put forward〕 an amendment 《to a bill》.

**수제**(手製) ¶ ～의 《손으로 만든》 handmade; made by hand; 《스스로 만든》 homemade; made by *oneself;* of *one's* own making. ◉ ～폭탄 a handmade bomb. ～품 a handmade article; a handiwork.

**수제비** flour dumplings served in soup; soup with dough flakes. ¶ ～를 뜨다

put dough flakes into soup.

**수제자**(首弟子) the best pupil 〔disciple〕《of》.

**수조**(水槽) a water tank; a cistern.

**수족**(手足) hands and feet; the limbs. ¶ ~이 크다 be large-limbed / ~을 결박하다 bind 《*a person*》 hand and foot / ~을 못쓰게 되다 lose the use of *one's* limbs / ~처럼 일하다 move at 《another's》 beck and call; work for 《*a person*》 most devotedly; serve 《*a person*》 like *his* tool / 그는 아버지의 ~이 되어 일했다 He helped his father with all his work.

**수족**(水族) aquatic animals; the finny race 〔tribe〕; sea creatures; water life. ◉ ~관 an aquarium (*pl.* ~s, -ria): 해양 ~관 an oceanarium (*pl.* ~s, -ria).

**수족**(垂足) 〖수학〗 a pedal. ◉ ~곡선 a pedal curve.

**수종**(水腫) 〖의학〗 dropsy. ◉ ~다리 dropsical legs. ⇨ 수중다리.

**수종**(隨從) ① 《하인》 an attendant; a servant. ② ⇨ 시중.

**수종**(樹種) species of trees. ◉ ~개량 improvement of species of trees: ~개량을 하고 더 많은 경제림을 심다 improve the species of trees and plant more lucrative trees.

**수주**(受注) acceptance 〔receiving〕 an order; booking. ~하다 receive 〔accept〕 an order; book. ¶ ~하는 즉시 upon receipt of *one's* order / 그 부품의 ~가 있었다 We accepted an order of those parts. / 엔고(円高) 때문에 해외로부터의 ~가 격증하고 있다 Orders from overseas 〔Overseas orders〕 have increased sharply because of the appreciation of the yen. ◉ ~고〔액〕 the amount 〔volume〕 of orders received; order awarded. ~산업 an industry which produces on orders: 조선(造船)은 ~산업이다 Shipbuilding industry produces on orders. ~잔고 the order backlogs: ~잔고가 기록적 수준이다 The order backlogs are at a record high.

**수준**(水準) 《수평면》 water level; 《표준》 a level; a standard. ¶ 지적 ~ an intellectual level / 문화 ~ a cultural level / 최고 ~ the highest level; the high-water mark 《of》 / …와 같은 ~이다 be on the same 〔at a〕 level with …; be on a par with… / ~ 이상이다 be above the (common) level / 그들의 문화 ~은 높았다 They had a high level of culture.

수준이: 지적 ~이 높은〔낮은〕 사람 a person (who stands) on 〔at〕 a high 〔low〕 intellectual level / ~이 높다〔낮다〕 the level 〔standard〕 is high 〔low〕; be 〔stand〕 on 〔at〕 a high 〔low〕 level / ~이 높아지다 attain 〔reach〕 a higher level / 이 나라는 생활 ~이 높다 This country has a high standard of living.

수준에: ~에 달하다〔미치다〕 reach 〔attain〕 the level; come up to the standard; be up to par / ~에 달하지〔미치지〕 못하다, ~ 이하이다 be below the level 〔standard〕; fall short of the standard; be below par / 그의 연구는 세계적 ~에 달해 있다 He has attained the world level in his research.

수준을: ~을 높이다 raise 〔elevate, improve〕 the level 〔standard〕 / 생활 ~을 낮추다 lower the standard of living / ~을 유지하다 maintain a standard (of…) / ~을 정하다 set a standard (of…).

◉ ~기 a (water) level: ~기로 재다 level. ~선〔면〕 a level line 〔surface〕. ~의(儀) a leveling instrument; a surveyor's level. ~점 a bench mark (생략 BM). ~측량 leveling.

**수줍다** (be) shy; bashful; timid; 《여자가》 (be) coy. ¶ 수줍어서 bashfully; shyly / 수줍은 남자 a timid 〔shy〕 man / 수줍은 얼굴 bashful looks / 수줍은 얼굴을 하다 look shy 〔abashed〕 / 수줍어서 말도 못하다 be coy of speech / 그녀는 너무 수줍어서 낯선 사람을 만나지 못한다 She is too bashful to meet strangers.

**수줍어하다** be 〔feel〕 shy; be coy; be bashful 〔abashed〕; look abashed; be self-conscious. ¶ 그 소녀는 내 앞에서 수줍어했다 The girl was abashed before me.

**수줍음** bashfulness; shyness; diffidence; self-consciousness; timidity. ¶ 남의 앞에서 ~을 타다 be shy and timid in another's presence.

**수중**(水中) ¶ ~의 underwater / ~을 항해하다 cruise underwater / ~에 in the water; under water / ~에 가라앉다 sink under water; be submerged / ~에서 구조해 내다 help 《*a person*》 out of the water / ~에서 건져〔끌어〕 올리다 draw 〔pull〕 up 《*a thing*》 from the water / ~에서 작업하다 work underwater / ~으로 뛰어들다 jump 〔plunge〕 into the water; 《배에서》 leap overboard.

◉ ~발레 synchronized swimming. ~발사관 a submerged tube. ~속력 an underwater 〔a submerged〕 speed 《of 25 knots》. ~안경 a hydroscope; a water glass; 《잠수용》 diving goggles; 《수영용》 swimming goggles. ~전파탐지기 a sonar 《미》; an asdic 《영》. ~청음기 a hydrophone; an underwater sound detector. ~총(銃) a spear gun. ~촬영 underwater photography. ~탐색 요원 an underwater investigator (of the navy). ~(텔레비전) 카메라 an underwater (Television) camera. ~폐 a scuba. ~폭발 an underwater explosion 〔detonation〕. ~폭탄〔폭뢰〕 a submarine bomb; a depth charge.

**수중**(手中) ¶ ~의 in *one's* hands; within *one's* power / ~의 돈 money on hand; ready money / …의 ~에 있다 be in the possession of…; be in 《*a person's*》 hands; be at the mercy of… / ~에 넣다 get; come by; get 〔come〕 at; secure; win; take 〔get, gain〕 possession of / ~에 들어오다 come into *one's* possession; come to 〔fall into〕 *one's* hands / 아무의 ~으로 돌아가다 fall into *a person's* hands / 재산은 채권자의 ~에 있었다 The property was in the creditors' hands. / 적군의 운명은 이제 아군의 ~에 있다 The hostile armies are now at our mercy.

**수중다리** 〖의학〗 dropsical legs.

**수중보**(水中洑) sluice gates under a bridge.

**수중익**(水中翼) a hydrofoil. ◉ ~선(船) a hydrofoil (craft 〔boat〕).

**수증기**(水蒸氣) (aqueous, water) vapor (자연 상태에서 나는); steam (열을 가할 때 나는). ¶ ~로 되어 증발하다 pass off 〔vanish〕 in vapor; evaporate / ~를 내다 emit vapor.

**수지**(收支) income and outgo; earnings and expenses; 《국가의》 revenue and expenditure.

¶ ~가 맞다 have a balanced income and outgo; 《장사가》 be on a paying basis; pay (well); pay off 《미》; be profitable; be in the black; [사람이 주어] find *one's* account in 《it》; find 《it》 pay / ~ 맞는 장사 a paying 〔profitable〕 business / ~가 안 맞다 income does not cover 〔meet〕 the expenses; 《거래 등이》 do not pay (off); be not a paying business / ~를 맞추다 make (both) ends meet; balance the budget; make 《it》 pay / 그 일은 ~가 안 맞는다 The work does not pay. / 한국의 무역〔국제〕 ~는 흑자〔적자〕이다 Korea's balance of trade 〔balance of payments〕 is in the black 〔red〕. / 한국은 국제 ~의 적자를 줄이지 않으면 안 된다 Korea has to reduce her balance-of-payment deficit.

◉ ~결산 settlement of accounts: ~결산을 하다 settle accounts 《with》; strike a balance. ~균형 the balance 〔equilibrium〕 between incomings and outgoings: ~ 균형을 유지하다 maintain equilibrium between incomings and outgoings. ~일람표 a balance sheet.

**수지**(樹脂) 《유동체》 resin (끈끈한); rosin (고체). ¶ ~의〔가 많은〕 resinous / ~를 바르다 resin 《*a thing*》. ◉ ~가공 plasticization: ~ 가공하다 resin; resinate; resin treatment. ~광택 resinous luster. ~비누 resin soap. ~성 물질 resinoid. 고무~ gum resin. 고형(固型)~ galipot. 열가소성 ~ thermoplastic resin.

**수지**(獸脂) animal fat; grease; tallow.

**수지니**(手—) a (hand-)trained falcon.

**수직**(手織) handweaving. ¶ ~의 woven by hand; handwoven; handloomed; homespun. ◉ ~기 a handloom.

**수직**(垂直) perpendicularity; verticality. ¶ ~의 perpendicular; vertical; plumb / ~으로 perpendicularly; vertically; at right angles 《to》 / ~으로 만나는 두 직선 two lines crossing at right angles / …에 ~으로 선을 긋다 draw a line perpendicular 〔at right angles〕 to 《a given line》 / ~이 아니다 be out of plumb / 헬리콥터는 수직으로 이륙할 수 있다 A helicopter can take off vertically.

◉ ~강하 〖항공〗 a vertical descent; a nose-dive. ~경사 〖광산〗 underlay (of ore). ~사고 〖철학〗 vertical thinking. ~선〔면〕 a perpendicular 〔vertical〕 line 〔plane〕. ~안정판 〖항공〗 a (tail) fin. ~운동 a vertical movement. ~이동 〖컴퓨터〗 vertical feed. ~이착륙기 a vertical takeoff and landing craft (생략 VTOL [víːtɔl]); a VTOL plane. ~적 국제분업 〖경제〗 vertical international specialization. ~중복검사 〖컴퓨터〗 vertical redundancy checking (생략 VRC). ~처리기 〖컴퓨터〗 vertical processor. ~축 ordinate. ~형식 〖컴퓨터〗 a vertical format.

**수질**(水質) the quality 〔purity〕 of water; the water quality. ◉ ~검사 (an) examination of water; 《분석》 (a) water analysis: ~ 검사하다 analyze 〔examine〕 the water 《of a well》. ~관리 water-purity control. ~오염 water contamination 〔pollution〕: ~ 오염 방지법 the Water Pollution Prevention Act. 「collect; gather.

**수집**(收集) collection; gathering. ~하다

**수집**(蒐集) (a) collection; (an) accumulation. ~하다 collect; gather; accumulate 《data》; make a collection of 《stamps》. ¶ 정보를 ~하다 collect 〔glean〕 information / 각계 각층의 의견을 ~하다 collect various opinions of every stratum of society / 그녀의 취미는 나비~이다 Her hobby is 「collecting butterflies 〔butterfly collecting〕. ◉ ~가 a collector: 미술품 ~가 an art collector. ~벽 a mania for 《stamp》 collecting; a collecting mania.

**수쪽** the right half of a transaction paper; the right half (stub) of an IOU 〔of a check〕.

**수차**(水車) 《물레방아》 a water mill 〔wheel〕; 《터빈》 a water 〔hydraulic〕 turbine.

**수차**(收差) 〚물리〛 aberration. ¶ 구면(球面)~ spherical aberration.

**수차**(數次) several 〔a number of〕 times; time and again. ¶ ~ 시도하다 make several attempts / ~에 걸쳐 게재하다 publish serially 〔in serial form〕; serialize / 그 잡지는 환경문제를 ~에 걸쳐 실었다 The magazine ran a series of articles on environmental issues. / 나는 ~ 충고했으나 그는 받아들이지 않았다 My repeated warnings were lost on him.

**수찬**(修撰) ~하다 edit; redact.

**수찰**(手札) a letter; a note; an epistle.

**수창**(首唱) ~하다 advocate; promote; be first to 《*do*》; pioneer in. ◉ ~자 an advocate; a pioneer.

**수채** a sewer; a drain; a sink (부엌의); a draining floor (목욕탕 등의). ¶ ~를 놓다 lay out a drainage system / ~를 쳐내다 clean 〔scour〕 a sewer 〔drain〕 / ~가 막혔다 The sewer is clogged up. *or* The drain is stopped up. ◉ ~통 a drainpipe. 수챗구멍 a drainage vent 〔outlet〕; a drain.

**수채화**(水彩畫) a watercolor painting; a watercolor. ¶ 그녀는 ~로 꽃을 그렸다 She painted flowers with watercolors. ◉ ~가 a watercolor painter; a watercolorist. ~물감 watercolors.

**수척**(瘦瘠) emaciation. ~하다 (be) emaciated; haggard; gaunt; wasted. ¶ ~한 얼굴〔모습〕 a haggard face 〔figure〕; an emaciated 〔a worn-out〕 look / ~해지다 get 〔become〕 lean 〔thin, haggard〕; get emaciated 〔gaunt〕; be worn out; waste 〔fall〕 away / 옛 모습을 찾아 볼 수 없을 정도로 ~해지다 be a mere shadow of *one's* former self / 그녀는 걱정 때문에 ~해졌다 She was worn to a shadow with anxiety.

**수천**(數千) (several) thousands. ¶ ~명 thousands of people (★ 수사 뒤에 오는 thousand 복수형은 s를 붙이지 않음: three thousand) / ~만 billions 《of stars》; countless numbers.

**수첩**(手帖) a pocket notebook; a reminder 〔memorandum〕 book; a pocketbook. ¶ ~에 적어 두다 write 〔take, jot, put〕 down 《*a person's* address》 in *one's* pocketbook; make 〔take〕 a note of.

**수청**(守廳) ~들다 《a *kisaeng*》 give her bed service to the local magistrate; serve *one's* magistrate.

**수축**(收縮) contraction; shrinking; shrinkage; constriction. ~하다 contract (금속·근육 등이); shrink (천 등이); be constricted (압축되어 좁아지다); deflate (공기가 빠져). ¶ 통화 ~ deflation / 담배가 혈관 ~의 원인이 된다 Tobacco causes the blood vessels to contract. / 철은 가열하면 팽창하고 식히면 ~한다 Iron expands when heated and contracts when cooled. ◉ ~계수 a coefficient of contraction. ~근(筋) 〚해부〛 a contractile muscle. ~력 contractile force 〔power〕. ~성 contractibility: ~성이 있는 contractile. ~한계 shrinkage limit.

**수축**(修築) repairs 《of a building》; mending. ~하다 repair; mend. ¶ 저 낡은 건물은 ~중이다 That old building is under repairs.

**수출**(輸出) export; exportation. ~하다 export; ship abroad. ¶ ~할 수 있는, ~용의 exportable 《commodities》 / 무형 ~ invisible exports / 기아(飢餓) ~ hunger export / 플랜트 ~ export of plants / 녹다운 ~ knockdown export / ~을 금하다 place 〔lay, put〕 an embargo on the export 《of》; forbid 〔prohibit, ban〕 the export 《of》 / ~을 장려하다 encourage the export 《of》 / ~을 늘리다 raise exports; increase the amount of export 《of》 / ~ 촉진을 위한 종합적인 조치 comprehensive steps to expedite exports / ~ 주도의 경제 an export-oriented economy / 우리 나라의 ~은 증가 일로에 있다 Our exports are increasing. / 그 회사는 제품의 70퍼센트를 ~하고 있다 The firm exports 70 percent of its production.

◉ ~가격 an export price. ~가득율 the rate of net exchange earning from exports. ~견본 an export sample. ~경기 an export boom: ~ 경기 회복세 the export recovery trend. ~경쟁력 competitiveness in exports. ~공업 단지 the export industrial complex 〔estate〕. ~국(國) an exporting country; an exporter (country). ~규제 restrictions on exports: ~자율〔자주〕 규제 voluntary export restrictions; self-restraint in exports. ~금융 export financing. ~면장 an export permit. ~목표 export target 〔goal〕: ~목표액 《surpass》 the target amount of exports 《by 10%》. ~무역 export trade. ~보험 export insurance. ~부진 a slump in exports. ~산업 an export industry: 한국 ~산업 공단 Korea Export Industrial Corp. ~상 =~업자. ~상사 an export 〔a shipping〕 house. ~세 export duties. ~송장(送狀) an export invoice. ~승인서 an export license. ~승인제 the export licensing system. ~신고서 a declaration for exportation; an export declaration. ~신고필(畢) entered outward. ~신용 보험 export credit insurance. ~신용장 an export letter of credit. ~실적 the export performance; the actual exports. ~액 exports; the amount of export (in terms of money): 총 ~액 the total export / 1999년의 한국 ~액 Korea's exports in 1999. ~어음 an export bill: ~ 어음 인수 trade acceptance. ~업 export business: ~업자 an export trader; an exporter / ~업에 종사하다 be engaged in export (business). ~원서 an export entry; an entry outward 〔for export〕. ~의 날 the Export Day. ~인수신용장 an export acceptance credit. ~자유지역 the free export zone: 마산 ~ 자유 지역 관리청 the Office of Masan Free Export Zone Administration. ~장려 encouragement of export trade: ~장려금 an export bounty; a bounty on exports / ~장려 정책 export targeting policy. ~장벽 export barrier. ~절차 export formalities 〔procedure〕. ~정보 센터 a trade information center. ~정보 체계 the system to facilitate export information exchanges. ~주문 an export order. ~진흥 정책 an export promotion policy. ~통관 절차 customs clearing procedure for exports. ~할당 an export (allotment) quota: ~ 할당제 the export quota system. ~항(港) an export(ing) port; an outport. ~허가서 《세관의》 an export permit. ~환(換) export exchange.

**수출금지**(輸出禁止) an export ban; an embargo (*pl.* ~es). ~하다 put 〔place, lay〕 an embargo 《on》; forbid 〔ban, prohibit〕 the export 《of》. ¶ 금〔무기〕의 ~ an embargo on (the export of) gold 〔arms〕 / ~를 해제하다 lift 〔remove, take off〕 the embargo 《on》.

**수출시장**(輸出市場) an export market. ¶ ~의 다변화 diversification of export markets / 새로운~ 개척을 위하여 노력을 배가하다 double *one's* efforts to explore new export market.

**수출입**(輸出入) import and export; exportation and importation; import-export. ¶ ~의 차액 the balance of trade / ~의 격차 a trade gap.

◉ ~업 the export-import business 〔trade〕: 그들은 ~업으로 큰 돈을 벌었다 They made a fortune in the export-import business 〔trade〕. ~은행 an export-import bank; 《한국의》 the Export-Import Bank (생략 Ex-Im). ~품 the imports and exports; import-export goods: ~금지품 a contraband.

**수출초과**(輸出超過) an excess of exports (over imports); a favorable balance of trade. ¶~는 10억 달러다 Export exceeds import by 〔The total of foreign trade shows a favorable balance of〕 one billion dollars.

**수출품**(輸出品) export(ed) goods 〔commodities, articles〕; exports. ¶ 주요 ~ important 〔principal, staple〕 exports; chief export items.

◉ ~명세표 a shipping list 〔bill〕. ~전시회 an exports exhibition.

**수취**(受取) receiving. ~하다 receive; bear. ¶ 소포를 ~했다 I have received a package. / 물품을 ~하는 즉시 대금을 보내겠다 I will send you the payment as soon as I receive the goods.

◉ ~인 a receiver; a recipient; a payee (어음의); a consignee (화물의); an addressee (우편물의); a beneficiary (보험의): 이 선적 화물의 ~인은 우리 회사의 외국 무역부이다 The consignee of the shipment is the foreign trade department of our company. / 이 수표의 ~인은 나의 숙모이다 My aunt is the payee of this check. *or* This check is payable to my aunt. / ~인불(拂) 《전화의》 a collect call.

**수치**(羞恥) (a) shame; (a) disgrace; (a) dishonor. ~스럽다 (be) shameful; disgraceful; dishonorable.
¶ ~스러운 행위 disgraceful 〔shameful〕 behavior / 나라의 ~ the shame of a nation; a national disgrace / ~를 당하다 disgrace 〔humiliate〕 *oneself;* be put to shame; be insulted / …을 ~로 알다 think it a shame to *do;* disdain *do*ing 〔to *do*〕 / …의 ~이다 be a disgrace 〔discredit〕 to…; bring disgrace 〔dishonor〕 on… / 가문의 ~다 be a disgrace to *one's* family / ~를 알다 have a sense of honor / ~를 모르다 be shameless; be dead 〔lost〕 to (all sense of ) shame; have no sense of shame / ~를 씻다 wipe away disgrace; clear *one's* name / 청빈은 결코 ~가 아니다 Honest poverty is no disgrace. / 묻는 것은 일시적인 ~요 모르는 것은 일생의 ~다 To ask may be a moment's shame, indeed, but not to ask and to remain ignorant must be a lifelong shame. ◉ ~심 a sense of shame: 그는 전혀 ~심이 없는 사내다 He is quite a shameless man.

**수치**(數値) numerical value. ¶ ~를 구하다 evaluate / ~로 나타내다 express 《the result》 numerically. ◉ ~데이터 〖컴퓨터〗 numeric data. ~연산보조처리기 〖컴퓨터〗 a math coprocessor. ~연산용 칩 a math chip. ~예보 〖기상〗 numeral weather forcasting. ~제어 〖컴퓨터〗 numerical control (생략 NC): ~제어기계 NC machine. ~처리 〖컴퓨터〗 number crunching. ~해석 〖수학·통계〗 numerical analysis.

**수치질**(―痔疾) 〖의학〗 external hemorrhoids; blind piles.

**수칙**(守則) rules; regulations; 《지시》 directions; instructions. ¶ 학생~ rules for students.

**수캉아지** a male pup; a he-puppy.

**수캐** a male dog; a he-dog.

**수컷** a male (animal); a cock (새의); a bull (고래·물소·코끼리 등의); a he.
¶ 그것은 ~이냐 암컷이냐 Is it a male or a female?

**수키와** a convex (roofing) tile. ¶ ~와 암키와 convex and concave (roofing) tiles.

**수탁**(受託) trust. ~하다 be entrusted 《with *a thing*》; be given in trust; take charge of 《*a thing*》. ¶ 공증인은 그의 유서를 ~했다 The notary took charge of his will.
◉ ~금 trust money; money given in trust 〔charge〕. ~료(料) a depository. ~물 a thing put under 〔in〕 *one's* custody; a thing entrusted. ~법원 a court of requisition. ~자 a trustee; 《상품의》 a consignee; 《권리 등의》 an assignee; a fiduciary: ~자의 자격으로 in a fiduciary capacity. ~판사 a commissioned 〔requisitioned〕 judge.

**수탈**(收奪) plundering; exploitation. ~하다 plunder; wrest; usurp; exploit.
¶ 재화를 ~하다 plunder 〔despoil〕 *a person* of *his* goods / 원주민들은 그들의 토지를 백인에게 ~당했다 The original inhabitants had their land seized from them by the white men.

**수탉** a rooster 《주로 미》; a cock.

**수태**(受胎) conception; impregnation; 〖생물〗 fecundation; fertilization. ~하다 get 〔become〕 pregnant; conceive 《a child》; get fecundated 〔fertilized〕.
◉ ~고지(告知) 〖기독교〗 the Annunciation. ~(능)력 fertility; conceiving power. ~연령 〖의학〗 conceptual age. ~조절 conception 〔birth〕 control. ~현상 〖생물〗 fertilization; fecundation; impregnation.

**수톨쩌귀** the male joint of a hinge.

**수통**(水桶) a water pail; a (water) bucket. = 물통.

**수통**(水筒) a (water) flask; a canteen; a water bottle 《영》.

**수통**(水筩) ① 《관》 a water pipe 〔tube〕. ② 《수도전》 a hydrant; a tap.

**수퇘지** a (male) hog; a boar(-pig).

**수틀**(繡―) a tambour (for embroidering); an embroidery hoop 〔ring, frame〕. ¶ ~에 헝겊을 끼다 stretch a piece of cloth over a tambour / ~에 수를 놓다 embroider on a hoop; tambour.

**수평**(水平) horizontality. ¶ ~의 level; even; horizontal / ~으로 horizontally; on a level 《with》 / 지면과 ~으로 even 〔level〕 with the ground / ~이 아니다 be out of the horizontal / …와 ~을 이루다 be level with… / ~이 되게 하다 make 《a surface》 level.
◉ ~각〔거리〕 a horizontal angle 〔distance〕. ~기 a level. ~동(動) a horizontal movement. ~면 a horizontal level 〔plane〕; a level surface.

~무역 〖경제〗 horizontal trade. ~비행 a level flight. ~이동〔분포〕〖생물〗 horizontal migration 〔distribution〕. ~적 국제 분업 〖경제〗 horizontal international specialization. ~축 〖수학〗 abscissa.

**수평(아리)** a male chick.

**수평선**(水平線) 《물과 하늘의 경계》 the horizon; 《수평한 선》 a horizontal line. ¶ ~상에 나타나다 rise 〔appear〕 above the horizon / ~ 밑으로 지다 sink 〔disappear〕 below the horizon / 멀리 ~까지 뻗어 있다 stretch as far as the horizon.

**수포**(水泡) ① 《거품》 a foam; a bubble. ② 《헛된 결과》 naught; nothing. ¶ ~로 돌아가다 end 〔go up〕 in smoke; end 〔result〕 in (a) failure; come 〔be brought〕 to naught 〔nothing〕; be in vain / 그의 다년간의 노력도 ~로 돌아갔다 His many year's hard work has come to nothing. / 우리들의 노력은 모두 ~로 끝났다 All our efforts ended in failure.

**수포**(水疱) 〖의학〗 a (water) blister; a vesicle (작은); a bulla (큰). ◉ ~진 〖의학〗 vesicular exanthema.

**수폭**(水爆) ⇨ 수소폭탄.

**수표**(手票) a check 《미》; a cheque 《영》. ¶ 100만원 짜리 ~ a check for one million won; one million-won check / ~를 떼다〔끊다, 발행하다〕 draw 〔issue, make out〕 a check / ~로 지급하다 pay by check; 《미》 check out 《a deposit》 / ~를 현금으로 바꾸다 cash a check / 「~를 누구 앞으로 써드릴까요」—「김씨 자동차 정비소 앞으로요」 "Who do I make out a check to?"—"Kim's Auto Repair, please." / 내일 ~로 당신 계좌에 넣어 드리겠습니다 I'll pay it to your account by check tomorrow. ◉ ~발행인 the issuer of a check; a check drawer 〔writer 《미》〕. ~책〔장〕 a checkbook 《미》; a chequebook 《영》. 분실~ a lost check. 자기앞~ a cashier's check; a bank 〔banker's〕 check.

**수표**(數表) a numeration table.

**수풀** 《숲》 a wood; a forest; a grove; 《덤불》 a thicket; a bush; a coppice. ¶ 공이 정원 ~ 속으로 굴러 들어갔다 A ball rolled into a thicket of the garden.

**수프** soup. ¶ 야채 ~ vegetable soup / 맑은 ~ consommé; clear soup / 진한 〔묽은〕 ~ a thick 〔thin〕 soup / ~를 먹다 eat 〔take〕 soup / ~를 먹을 때는 소리를 내지 마라 Don't slurp when you eat soup. ◉ ~접시 a soup plate; a soup tureen (뚜껑 있는).

**수피**(樹皮) tree bark; cortex. ¶ ~를 벗기다 bark 《a tree》.

**수피**(獸皮) a 〔an animal〕 skin; a hide; a fell; a fur (모피).

**수필**(隨筆) an essay; literary jottings; miscellaneous writings; a miscellany. ◉ ~가 an essayist; a miscellaneous writer. ~란 a miscellany column; a column for literary jottings. ~문학 essay literature. ~집 a collection of essays 〔literary jottings〕.

**수하**(手下) ① 《손아래》 *one's* junior. ¶ ~의 younger; junior. ② 《부하》 a follower; a subordinate; [총칭] *one's* men; a following. ¶ ~가 많다 have a large following / ~가 되어 일하다 work under *a person.*

**수하**(誰何) ① 《누구》 who (and what); anyone. ¶ ~를 막론하고 anyone; regardless of who it may be; irrespective of persons. ② 《검문》 a challenge. ~하다 challenge. ¶ 보초에게 ~를 받다 be challenged by a guard / 「누구냐」하고 초병이 ~했다 "Who goes there?" challenged a soldier on guard.

**수하다**(壽—) enjoy longevity 〔a long life〕; live long; live to a great age.

**수학**(修學) pursuit of knowledge; learning; study. ~하다 pursue knowledge; study; get *one's* education 《from》. ◉ ~능력시험(能力試驗) a scholastic aptitude test 《미》 (생략 SAT); the national scholastic achievement test (for the college entrance); a proficiency test for college education. ~여행 a school excursion 〔trip〕; a trip for educational purposes: ~ 여행 가다 go on a school excursion 〔a study tour, an educational trip〕.

**수학**(數學) mathematics (★ 학과목은 단수 취급); math 《구어》. ¶ 응용〔순수〕~ applied 〔pure〕 mathematics / ~적 정확성으로 with mathematical precision / ~을 잘하다 be good at math; have a head for 〔be clever at〕 mathematics. ◉ ~문제 a math(ematical) problem. ~자 a mathematician.

**수해**(水害) 《손해》 damage by 〔from〕 a flood; flood damage; 《재해》 a flood disaster. ¶ ~를 입다 suffer from flooding 〔a flood〕; be damaged by a flood; have a flood disaster / 이 지역은 해마다 다소의 ~를 입는다 This district suffers more or less from floods

every year. / 큰 태풍으로 많은 집들이 ～를 당했다 A lot of houses were flooded by a big typhoon.
◉ ～구제 flood relief. ～대책 《방지의》 a flood-control measure; anti-flood measures; 《구제의》 a relief measure for flood sufferers. ～방지 prevention of floods; flood control. ～이재민 flood victims 〔sufferers〕; sufferers from a flood. ～지 a flooded 〔flood-stricken〕 district.

**수해**(樹海) a broad expanse of dense woodland; a sea of trees 〔leaves, foliage〕.

**수행**(修行) 《종교적》 ascetic practices; self-discipline; self-improvement〔-cultivation〕; 《수련》 practice; training. ～하다 discipline 〔train〕 *oneself;* work (at self-improvement); 《종교적》 practice asceticism. ¶ ～을 쌓다 get a thorough training; be well trained / ～중이다 《스님이》 be in *one's* novitiate. ◉ ～자 a trainee; an ascetic; a disciplinant.

**수행**(遂行) achievement; accomplishment; effectuation; execution; performance. ～하다 achieve; accomplish; effect(uate); execute; perform; fulfill; carry out 《a plan》; carry 《a plan》 into execution. ¶ …의 효과적인 ～을 위해 for the efficient conduct of… / 그는 직무 ～중 순직했다 He died in the discharge 〔line〕 of his duties. / 그는 훌륭하게 임무를 ～했다 He carried out 〔executed, performed〕 his duties very competently.

**수행**(隨行) attendance 〔accompaniment〕 (on a journey). ～하다 attend 《*a person* on a journey》; tag along with 《*a person* on a tour》; accompany; follow. ¶ …를 ～하여 in attendance upon 《*a person*》; accompanying 《*a person*》; in the suite of… / 그는 무역 사절단을 ～하여 일본에 갔다 He accompanied the trade mission to Japan. / 그는 총리를 ～하여 워싱턴에 갔다 He went to Washington, D.C. in the Prime Minister's retinue.
◉ ～원〔자〕 an attendant; a member of 《*a person's*》 suite; 《수행단》 a suite; a retinue; (a train of) attendants; an entourage (측근): 공식 ～원 an official entourage member / 장관 및 ～원 the Minister and (his) suite.

**수험**(受驗) undergoing 〔going through〕 an examination. ～하다 take a test; take 〔undergo, go through〕 an examination; sit 〔go in〕 for the entrance examination 《for A University》. ¶ ～준비〔공부〕를 하다 prepare (*oneself*) for an (entrance) examination.
◉ ～과목 subjects of examination. ～료 an examination fee. ～번호 an examinee's (seat) number. ～생 (1) 《수험준비 중인》 a student preparing *himself* for an examination. (2) ＝수험자. (3) 《학원에 다니는》 a prep 《미구어》. ～자 an examinee; a candidate for an examination; a testee: ～자의 평균 득점 the average scores of examinees. ～자격 qualifications of candidacy for an examination: ～자격이 있다 be qualified for an examination. ～지옥 the ordeal of examination. ～참고서 a reference book 〔manual〕 for entrance examinations; a crammer, a cram-book. ～표 a certificate 〔an admission ticket〕 for an examination.

**수혈**(輸血) (a) blood transfusion. ～하다 give a blood transfusion 《to *a person*》; transfuse 《*a person's*》 blood 《into a patient》. ¶ ～ 받는 사람 a blood recipient / ～을 받다 receive a (blood) transfusion / O형의 피를 ～하다 give a transfusion of Type O blood 《to a patient》 / ～해 달라고 부탁 받다 be asked to give *one's* blood to 《a friend》 / 그는 ～로 살아났다 A blood transfusion saved his life.

**수형**(受刑) being under sentence. ～하다 serve time 《for swindling》. ◉ ～자 a convict; a convicted prisoner.

**수호**(守護) protection; guard; safeguard. ～하다 protect; guard; keep guard 《over, round》; keep 《a place》 safe 《from》; defend. ¶ 신의 ～ divine protection. ◉ ～성인 『가톨릭』 a patron saint. ～신 a guardian 〔protecting〕 deity 〔god〕; a tutelary god 〔spirit〕. ～자 a protector; a guardian. ～천사 a guardian angel.

**수호**(修好) amity; friendship; friendly relations. ～하다 get along amicably.
◉ ～조약 a friendship pact 〔treaty〕; a treaty of amity 〔friendship〕: ～조약을 맺다 conclude 〔sign〕 a treaty of amity 《with》.

**수화**(水化·水和) 『화학』 hydration. ～하다〔시키다〕 hydrate. ⇨ 수산화.

**수화**(手話) sign 〔finger〕 language. ～하다 use 〔talk in〕 sign language; talk with the hands 〔fingers〕. ¶ ～를 사용하는 뉴스캐스터를 텔레비전에서 보았다 I have seen a newscaster using sign

language on TV.
◉ ～법 chirology; dactylology.

**수화**(繡畫) an embroidered picture.

**수화기**(受話器) a (telephone) receiver; an earpiece; a headpiece; 《송수화기》 a handset; 《무전의》 radio earphones; a receiving set. ¶ ～를 들다 take 〔pick〕 up the receiver / ～를 놓다 hang up 〔put back〕 the receiver / ～를 제자리에 놓지않다 leave the phone 〔receiver〕 off the rest 〔cradle〕 / ～를 귀에 대다 put 〔apply〕 the earphone to *one's* ear / ～는 사용 후 제자리에 놓아 주시오 《게시》 After using the phone, please hang up the receiver.

**수화물**(手貨物) (hand) baggage 《미》; (personal) luggage (★ luggage와 baggage는 bag, suitcase, trunk 등의 총칭이며 집합적으로 쓰이기 때문에 낱낱을 말할 때는 a piece 〔two pieces〕 of baggage 〔luggage〕처럼 말한다); 《소지품》 personal effects; traps 《구어》. ¶ 제한외 ～ excess 〔overweight〕 baggage / 휴대 ～ a hand-carry baggage; hand baggage 〔luggage 《영》〕 / 많은 ～ much 〔a lot of〕 baggage / ～을 맡기다 have *one's* baggage 〔luggage 《영》〕 checked; check *one's* baggage / ～을 역에 맡기다 register 〔book〕 *one's* baggage to a station / ～을 포터에게 맡기다 leave *one's* baggage with a redcap 〔porter〕 / ～을 몇개 가지고 있습니까 How much baggage do you have (with you)? / ～은 이 곳에 맡기십시오 《게시》 Small parcels checked here. / 이것은 20킬로그램 중량 범위내의 ～로 취급할 수 없습니다 This cannot be counted as part of the 20-kilogram baggage allowance. / 「기내 반입 ～은 한 개 뿐 입니다」—「이 인형은 유리 케이스 안에 있어서 그런데, 특별히 (추가로) 좀 봐 줄 수 없겠습니까」 "Will you please take only one piece of baggage onto the aircraft?"—"This doll is in a glass case, so would you kindly allow me to bring this one too?"
◉ ～계원 a baggage 〔luggage 《영》〕 clerk; a baggageman. ～꼬리표 a baggage 〔luggage 《영》〕 label. ～물표〔쪽지〕 a luggage ticket; a baggage(=claim) check 《미》; ～보관소 《미》 a parcels room; a checkroom; 《영》 a cloak-room. ～운반인 a baggage 〔luggage〕 man. ～차 a luggage van. a baggage car 《미》; ～취급소 a baggage room 〔office〕 《미》; a luggage office; ～표 《공항의》 a claim tag.

**수확**(收穫) 《일》 harvesting; 《수확물》 a harvest; a crop; a yield; [비유적] the fruit 《of labor》. ～하다 gather (in) a harvest; harvest; reap; gather in.

> 용법 **crop** 곡물이나 그 밖의 농작물을 수확한 것 또는 자라고 있는 작물. **harvest** 곡물의 수확 과정·시기를 강조하며, crop과는 달리 비유적으로도 쓰임. **yield** crop의 양이나 액수.

¶ 기록적인 ～ a record crop 〔harvest〕 / 올해의 보리 ～ this year's barley harvest; the yield of barley this year / ～이 많다〔적다〕 have a good 〔bad, poor〕 harvest 〔crop〕 / 척박한 땅에서는 ～이 적다 Poor soil produces a small crops. / 올해의 ～은 평년작 이하로 예상된다 This year's harvest is estimated to be below the average.
◉ ～기(期) the harvesting season; the harvest time. ～기(機) a reaping machine; a reaper; a harvester. ～량〔고〕 the yield; the crop: 예상 ～량〔고〕 the estimated crop 〔harvest〕. ～연도 a crop year. ～예상 harvest prospects; a harvest 〔crop〕 estimate. ～체감 diminishing returns: ～체감의 법칙 the law of diminishing returns.

**수회**(收賄) acceptance of a bribe; corruption; graft 《미》. ～하다 take 〔accept〕 a bribe; take graft 《미》. ¶ ～ 혐의로 on the charge of taking a bribe; on bribery charges / 그는 ～죄로 기소되었다 He was prosecuted for taking bribes 《from trading companies》.
◉ ～관리 a corrupt official. ～사건 a bribery case 〔affair〕; a graft scandal 《미》. ～자 a recipient of a bribe; a bribee; a grafter 《미》. ～죄 bribery.

**수회**(數回) a number of times; several times. ¶ ～에 걸쳐 several times; on several occasions; repeatedly.

**수효**(數爻) a number; a figure; an amount. ¶ 사람 ～ the number of people / ～가 많다〔적다〕 be many 〔few〕; be large 〔small〕 in number / ～가 늘다 grow 〔increase〕 in number / ～를 세다 (count the) number; count; take count of / ～를 늘리다〔줄이다〕 increase 〔decrease〕 the number 《of》 / ～를 채우다 make up the number / ～를 틀리다 count wrong; miscount / ～에 넣다 count in 〔among〕 the number 《of》; include in the number; take into account / ～에 넣지

않다 be not counted 《among》; be not included; be excluded / 그들이 우리보다 ～가 많다 They exceed us in number.

**수훈**(垂訓) (giving) teachings; a precept. ～하다 teach; instruct 《in》. ¶ 산상～ 『성서』 the Sermon on the Mount.

**수훈**(殊勳) distinguished 〔conspicuous〕 service(s); meritorious deed(s). ¶ 최고 ～ 선수 『야구』 the most valuable player (생략 MVP) / ～을 세우다 render distinguished service(s); distinguish *oneself* 《in a battle》; fight 〔play〕 with distinction. ◉ ～상 《운동 경기 등의》 the outstanding performance prize 〔award〕; a most-valuable-player prize (야구 등의). ～자 a person of distinguished service.

**숙고**(熟考) (mature, due) consideration; deliberation; mature reflection. ～하다 think over 《*a matter*》; mull over; ponder on 〔over〕 《a problem》; consider 《*a matter*》 carefully; reflect upon 《a problem》; deliberate; chew the cud. ¶ ～한 끝에 after due 〔mature〕 consideration; after mature reflection; on second thought(s) / 우리는 지금 그 문제를 ～하고 있다 We now have the matter under consideration. / 심사 ～ 끝에 나는 그 제의에 응했다 After much consideration, I accepted the offer.

**숙녀**(淑女) a lady; a gentlewoman; a well-bred woman. ¶ ～다운 ladylike / 전혀 ～답지 않은 utterly unbecoming (to) a lady of gentle birth.

**숙달**(熟達) proficiency; mastery; skill. ～하다 master 《English》; get a mastery 《of the piano》; attain proficiency 《in》; get 〔become〕 proficient 〔skillful, skilled〕 《at, in》; acquire skill 《at》. ¶ ～한 proficient; skilled; expert; adept / 외국어에 ～하다 acquire 〔get〕 a mastery of a foreign language / …에 ～해 있다 be proficient 〔accomplished〕 in 《flower-arrangement》; be a master 〔have a mastery〕 of 《the piano》; be versed 〔well up〕 in 《Chinese》; be at home in 《English》; be skilled 〔adept〕 in 《drawing》; be an expert in 〔at〕 《figures》 / 1년 정도로는 영어에 ～할 수 없다 You cannot master English in only a year or so.

**숙당**(肅黨) ～하다 purge 〔eliminate〕 disloyal elements from the party.

**숙덕**(淑德) womanly graces; feminine virtues. ¶ ～이 높은 부인 a lady of eminent virtues.

**숙덕거리다** whisper; talk in whispers; exchange subdued remarks; hold a whispered conversation. ¶ 나를 가지고 ～ pick me for the topic of their whispers / 숙덕거리지 말고 의견이 다르면 당당히 말해라 Please stop whispering. If you disagree, speak your mind clearly.

**숙덕숙덕** 《얘기를》 in whispers; under *one's* breath. ¶ ～ 이야기하다 talk in whispers.

**숙독**(熟讀) careful reading; perusal. ～하다 read 「carefully 〔with care, through and through〕; peruse. ¶ 이 책은 ～할 가치가 있다 This book is well worth careful reading.

**숙려**(熟慮) careful 〔mature〕 deliberation. ⇨ 숙고(熟考).

**숙련**(熟練) skill; dexterity; mastery; expertness. ¶ ～된 skilled (훈련 등으로 기술을 습득한); skillful; trained; experienced; practiced; expert / 미～의 unskilled; inexperienced / ～을 요하는 delicate; ticklish 《affairs》 / ～을 요하다 require great skill / 그는 ～된 외과의사다 He is an expert surgeon. / 그것은 대단한 ～을 필요로 한다 It requires a great amount of skill. ◉ ～자 a skilled hand; an expert; a man of experience. ～공 a skilled worker 〔laborer, craftsman〕; a trained hand 〔workman〕; [총칭] skilled 〔trained〕 labor.

**숙맥**(菽麥) 《콩과 보리》 beans and barley; 《사람》 a foolish man; a stupid person.

**숙면**(熟眠) a sound 〔deep, profound, heavy〕 sleep. ～하다 sleep well 〔heavily, soundly〕; fall into a deep slumber; have a good sleep. ¶ 나는 ～을 못한다 I am a bad 〔light〕 sleeper.

**숙명**(宿命) fate; destiny; 『불교·힌두교』 karma; predestination. ¶ ～적인 fatal; predestined / ～적으로 fatally / ～으로 정해져 있다 be ordained by fate / ～이다 be fated 〔destined〕 《to *do*》; be predestined 《for a teacher》 / 이렇게 되는 것이 내 ～이다 This is my destiny. *or* I'm destined to come to this pass. ◉ ～론 fatalism; necessitarianism: ～론적(인) fatalistic / ～론자 a fatalist.

**숙모**(叔母) the wife of *one's* father's younger brother; an aunt.

**숙박**(宿泊) (a) lodging; a stay. ～하다 lodge 《in, at》; put up 〔stay, stop〕 《at》; register 〔take a room〕 《at a hotel》; 《미》 check in 《at a hotel》; 《군대가》 be billeted 〔quartered〕 《on》. ¶ 분산 ～하다 put up separately 《at different hotels》 / 민가에 ～하다 be billeted in private homes 《of a town》 / 호텔에 ～을 예약하다 make reservation at a hotel / ～시키다 lodge 《*a person*》; put up 《*a person*》; provide accommodation 〔quarters〕 《for》 / 친구 집에서 ～하다 stop 〔stay〕 with *one's* friend / 하룻밤 ～하다 stop overnight; pass the night / 이 도시에서 여행객은 비교적 싼 요금으로 ～할 수 있다 Travelers can find accommodation at moderate rates in this town.
◉ ～료, ～비 lodging 〔hotel〕 charges 〔expenses〕; a hotel bill: ～료를 치르다 pay a hotel bill / ～비를 떼어먹다 jump *one's* hotel bills / 하루 ～비가 얼마입니까 What is the charge for a day? ～부 a hotel register 〔book〕; a guest book: ～부에 적다 register 《*one's* name》 in the hotel book. ～산업 lodging industry. ～설비 accommodation(s) (★ 미국에서는 복수형, 영국에서는 불가산명사로 쓴다). ～소 *one's* lodgings 〔quarters〕; an inn: 간이 ～소 a cheap lodging 〔rooming〕 house; a flophouse 《미구어》 / 무료 ～소 a free lodging house. ～인 a hotel guest; a lodger; a boarder (하숙의).

**숙변**(宿便) feces contained for a long time in the intestines; 《suffer from》 retention of feces.

**숙부**(叔父) *one's* father's younger brother; an uncle.

**숙부드럽다** (be) gentle; quiet; meek; modest; reserved; submissive. ¶ 숙부드러운 여자 a modest girl.

**숙사**(宿舍) a lodging house; lodgings; quarters; a billet (군대의). ¶ ～의 설비 accommodation(s) / ～를 할당하다 assign 〔allot〕 quarters 《to》; billet 《troops in private homes》 / 참가 선수에게 ～를 제공하다 provide accommodation for the participants.

**숙성**(夙成) precocity. ⇨ 조숙(早熟). ～하다 (be) precocious; [서술적] be ahead of *one's* years; be big for *one's* age (of children). ¶ ～한 아이 a precocious 〔forward〕 child / 아이가 참 ～합니다 Your boy is big for his age.

**숙성**(熟成) ripening; maturing; maturation. ～하다 ripen; mature; get mellow. ¶ ～한 포도주〔치즈〕 ripe wine 〔cheese〕 / 통 속의 위스키가 ～할 때까지 기다리다 wait for the whisky to mature in the cask. ◉ ～온도 the ripening temperature.

**숙소**(宿所) *one's* (place of) abode; *one's* quarters; 《여관》 an inn; a hotel. ¶ ～를 잡다 take up *one's* quarters 《in》; stay 〔put up〕 at 《an inn, a hotel》 / ～를 옮기다 change *one's* lodging 〔quarters〕 《to》 / 나는 그의 ～를 안다 I know where he stays. *or* I have his address.

**숙수**(熟手) a (fancy) cook; a caterer.

**숙식**(宿食) lodging and boarding; room and board; board and lodging. ～하다 board and lodge. ◉ ～비 the charge for board and lodging: 한 달 ～비는 얼마나 됩니까 What 〔How much〕 do you charge a month for room and board? / ～비는 주당 50달러 《광고》 Board and lodging $50 weekly.

**숙신산**(一酸) 〖화학〗 succinic acid.

**숙어**(熟語) a phrase; 《관용구》 an idiomatic 〔a set〕 phrase; an idiom; a compound word (복합어). ◉ ～집 an idiom list; a phrase book; a dictionary of phrases.

**숙어지다** 《기울어지다》 hang (down); droop; be bowed; 《줄다》 become less severe; be alleviated. ⇨ 수그러지다. ¶ 졸려서 머리가 ～ *one's* head hangs heavy with sleep.

**숙연하다**(肅然一) (be) solemn; reverential; silent. ¶ 숙연히 《엄숙히》 solemnly; reverently; in reverence; 《조용히》 silently; quietly / 숙연해져서 옷깃을 여미다 be struck with awe 〔reverence〕; assume a reverential attitude 《toward》. / 그는 숙연히 관속에 누워있는 주검을 내려다 보았다 He gazed reverently down at the body in the coffin.

**숙영**(宿營) billeting; quartering; 《막사》 military quarters; billets. ～하다 be quartered 〔billeted〕 《in》; camp; quarter. ◉ ～지 a billeting area 〔place〕.

**숙원**(宿怨) an old 〔a deep-seated〕 grudge 〔enmity〕; a long-harbored resentment 〔enmity〕. ¶ ～을 풀다 work off an old grudge; pay off old scores 《with》 / 그는 나에게 ～을 품고 있다 He has an old grudge against me.

**숙원**(宿願) *one's* heart's desire; a long-cherished desire. ¶ ～을 이루다 realize *one's* heart's desire / 미국에 가는 것은 나의 오랜 ～이었다 I have long been wishing to go to America.

**숙의**(熟議) due deliberation; careful consultation; exhaustive discussion. ~하다 deliberate 《on》; discuss fully; talk 《*a matter*》 over; consult carefully. ¶ ~한 끝에 after careful discussion / 그 문제에 대해서 ~를 거듭하다 fully discuss 〔deliberate on〕 the question; mull the matter over.

**숙이다** lower 《*one's* head》; drop; hang; droop; bow. ¶ 머리를 숙이고 with *one's* head down; 《공손히》 respectfully; 《애원하듯》 imploringly / 머리를 숙이고 기도하다 bow *one's* head in prayer.

**숙적**(宿敵) an old enemy 〔foe〕; a long-standing 〔an inveterate〕 foe 〔rival〕. ¶ 테니스 코트에서는 ~이었지만 우리는 아주 가까운 친구였다 Though we were long-standing rivals on the tennis court, we were the closest of friends.

**숙정**(肅正) 《단속》 regulation; enforcement 《of discipline》; purification (정화). ~하다 regulate; enforce. ¶ 관기를 ~하다 enforce discipline among government officials. ◉ ~작업 a cleanup campaign: 공무원 ~작업 a cleanup drive in officialdom.

**숙제**(宿題) ① 《학교의》 homework; a home task; an assignment 《미》. ¶ ~를 내다 set 《pupils》 a home task; give 《pupils》 homework / ~를 돌봐주다 help 《*a person*》 with *his* homework / ~를 하다 do *one's* homework / ~가 많다 I have lots of homework to do. / ~는 다 했니 Have you done your homework? ② 《현안》 a pending 〔an open〕 question. ¶ 오랜 ~ a question of long standing / ~로 남겨 두다 leave 《*a matter*》 open 〔in abeyance〕; reserve 《*a matter*》 for future discussion / ~를 해결하다 settle a pending question / ~를 떠맡다 take over the unfinished task 《of reforming the election system》. / 그 법안이 국회를 통과할지는 ~로 남아 있다 Whether the bill will pass the Assembly remains open to question. ◉ ~장 a homework notebook. 방학 ~ a holiday task.

**숙주**(宿主) 〚생물〛 a host. ¶ 중간~ an intermediary host.

**숙주**(나물) green-bean sprouts.

**숙지**(熟知) full knowledge; familiarity. ~하다 know well 〔fully, thoroughly〕; have thorough knowledge of; be well aware 《of》; be well acquainted 《with》. ¶ 그는 정계의 사정에 대해 ~하고 있다 He is familiar with political affairs.

**숙직**(宿直) (*one's* turn for) night duty; (a) night watch. ~하다 keep night watch; be on night duty. ¶ 오늘 ~은 누구냐 Who is on duty tonight? / 나는 어젯밤 ~이었다 I was on duty last night. / 그가 ~일 때 그 사건이 일어났다 The accident occurred when he was on night duty. ◉ ~교사 a teacher on night duty; a night-duty teacher. ~비 a night-watch allowance. ~실 a night-duty room; a night custodian's room. ~원 a person on night duty; a night watchman.

**숙질**(叔姪) an uncle and his nephew 〔niece〕.

**숙청**(肅淸) a cleanup; a purge; liquidation. ~하다 clean up; purge; liquidate. ¶ ~당한 사람 a purgee / ~을 시작하다 begin a housecleaning / 국회는 부패한 의원을 ~해야 한다 The National Assembly must be purged of its corrupt members.

**숙체**(宿滯) 〚한의〛 chronic indigestion 〔dyspepsia〕.

**숙취**(宿醉) lingering intoxication (from drinking the night before); the after-effects of the night's drink; a hangover 《미》. ~하다 have 〔suffer from〕 a hangover; suffer from the aftereffect of drink.

**숙친**(熟親) a very close relationship; intimacy. ~하다 (be) intimate; close; well-acquainted; familiar.

**숙환**(宿患) a chronic 〔an inveterate〕 disease. ¶ ~으로 자리 보존하다 be confined to bed by an attack of a chronic disease / ~으로 쓰러지다 fall a prey to *one's* chronic disease.

**순**(旬) ① 《열흘간》 a period of ten days; a third of a month. ¶ 상〔중, 하〕순 the first 〔middle, last〕 part of a month. ② 《십년》 ten years; a decade. ¶ 칠순 노인 a person of seventy years old / 팔순이 넘다 be over eighty years 〔eight decades〕 old.

**순**(筍) a sprout; a shoot; a bud. ¶ 대순 a bamboo shoot / 순이 나다 bud out; sprout / 순을 치다 cut 〔nip〕 off extra sprouts; trim off sprouts.

**순** 《욕할 때의 말》 very; true; real; downright. ¶ 순 못된 놈 a bad man through and through / 순 악질 a thorough-paced villian 〔wicked fellow〕 / 순 거짓말쟁이 a downright lier.

**순**(純) 《순수한》 pure; genuine; 《순전한》 sheer; utter; 《진짜의》 genuine; unalloyed; unadulterated; unmixed; 《이익의》 net; clear. ¶ 순 문학 pure literature / 순모 all [pure] wool / 순 서울내기 a trueborn Seoulite; a Seoulite to the very marrow / 순 이익 net profit / 순 이론적 문제 a purely theoretical question / 순 한국식 정원 a garden in a purely [of entirely] Korean style / 순 우리식이다 It is purely our style.

**-순**(順) 《순서》 order; 《차례》 a turn. ¶ 번호순 numerical order / 가나다순 《in》 alphabetical order / 선착[접수]순 《by》 order of receipt / 연령순 《in》 order of age / 신청순으로 in the order of application / 크기순으로 according to size / 성적순으로 앉다 sit in the order of merit [the achieved performance records] / 키순으로 서다 stand in order of height.

**순간**(旬刊) ¶ ~의 《a magazine》 published [issued] every ten days.

**순간**(瞬間) an instant; a second; a moment. ¶ ~적인[의] momentary; instantaneous / ~적으로 instantaneously; in an instant; in a moment; in the twinkling of an eye; in a flash / ~적 쾌락 the mere pleasures of the moment / ~적인 재치 quick [ready] wit / 극적인~ a dramatic moment / 그것을 들은 ~ the moment [instant] I heard it / 한 ~도 지체할 수 없다 There is not a moment to lose. / 방문을 여는 ~ 전화 벨이 울렸다 The moment I opened the door, the telephone rang. / ~적으로 일어난 일이라 나는 어찌 할 바를 몰랐다 As it happened in a flash, I didn't know what to do. ◉ ~온수기 an instantaneous water heater. ~접착제 《a tube of》 instant glue. ~ 최대 풍속 the maximum instantaneous wind velocity.

**순견**(純絹) pure [neat] silk; all-silk. ¶ ~의 pure-silk; all-silk. ◉ ~양말 sheer silk [pure-silk] stockings.

**순결**(純潔) 《순수》 purity; integrity; 《결백》 innocence; immaculacy; 《동정》 chastity; virginal purity. ~하다 (be) pure; clean; immaculate; unspotted; 《성적으로》 (be) chaste; vestal. ¶ ~한 사랑 pure [platonic] love / ~한 처녀 a chaste maiden; a virgin / 마음이 ~한 사람 a purehearted person; a person pure in heart / ~을 더럽히다 sully [stain] the purity 《of a woman》; deflower 《a maiden》 / ~을 빼앗기다 be deprived of *one's* virginity. ◉ ~교육 education in [on] sexual morality.

**순경**(巡警) 《순찰》 patrol(ling); 《경찰관》 a policeman.

**순계**(純系) 〖생물〗 a pure line.

**순교**(殉教) (religious) martyrdom. ~하다 be martyred; die a martyr (for *one's* faith); suffer martyrdom. ◉ ~사(史) a martyrology. ~자 a martyr (남자); a martyress (여자).

**순국**(殉國) patriotic martyrdom; dying for *one's* country. ~하다 die for *one's* country. ◉ ~선열 a (patriotic) martyr. ~정신 the spirit of 「martyrdom [self-sacrifice for *one's* country].

**순국산**(純國産) ¶ ~의 entirely home=produced[-manufactured]; wholly domestic; 《한국산의》 of entirely Korean make; all-Korean / ~ 피아노 a piano of purely Korean make. ◉ ~품 《한국의》 an all-Korean product.

**순금**(純金) solid [pure] gold. ¶ ~의 pure-gold; all-gold / ~ 반지 a pure=gold ring.

**순대** *sundae;* a sausage made of bean curd, mung-bean sprouts and pig's blood stuffed in pig intestine. ◉ 순댓국 pork soup mixed with sliced *sundae.*

**순도**(純度) (degree of) purity; 《금·은의》 fineness. ¶ ~ 높은 플루토늄 plutonium of high purity / ~를 검사하다 test the purity 《of》.

**순동**(純銅) pure copper.

**순두부**(―豆腐) *sundubu;* uncurdled bean 「curd.

**순라**(巡邏) 〖고제도〗 a patrol; a round; 《사람》 a patrolman; a watchman. ◉ ~꾼 a patrolman; a patrol.

**순량**(純量) net weight.

**순량**(順良) ~하다 (be) good and obedient; gentle; peaceable. ¶ ~한 백성 (a) law-abiding people.

**순력**(巡歷) a tour (rounding); 《순시》 an inspection tour. ~하다 (make a) tour 《of, through Europe》 (round); travel about [through].

**순례**(巡禮) a pilgrimage. ~하다 make [go on] a pilgrimage 《to》. ¶ 그들은 예루살렘으로 ~의 길을 떠났다 They went on [made] a pilgrimage to Jerusalem. ◉ ~자 a pilgrim; a palmer: ~자의 옷차림으로 in a pilgrim's garb. ~지 a place of pilgrimage; a pilgrimage resort.

**순록**(馴鹿) 〖동물〗 a reindeer.

**순리**(純理) pure reason; scientific principles. ◉ ~론(論) rationalism: ~론자 a rationalist.

**순리**(順理) submission to reason; reasonableness. ¶ ～적(인) reasonable; rational; right; proper / ～적으로 reasonably; rationally; in a rational manner / ～적으로 해결하다 solve 《*matters*》 with reason / ～이다 stand to reason; be reasonable / ～가 아니다 be unreasonable; be against 〔contrary to〕 reason / 차근차근 ～대로 해나가다 carry out step by step what we can do as water flows / 그렇게 되는 것이 ～다 It is natural that it should be so.

**순막**(瞬膜) 『동물』 a nictating membrane; a haw.

**순면**(純綿) pure cotton; all cotton. ¶ ～의 pure-cotton; all-cotton. ◉ ～제품 all-cotton stuff 〔fabrics〕.

**순모**(純毛) pure 〔all〕 wool. ¶ ～의 pure-wool; all-wool. ◉ ～셔츠 an all-wool 〔a 100% wool〕 shirt. ～제품 all-wool goods 〔fabrics〕.

**순무** 『식물』 a turnip.

**순문학**(純文學) pure 〔polite〕 literature 〔letters〕; *belles lettres* (F.). ¶ ～의 belletristic / ～파 a belletrist.

**순박**(淳朴·醇朴) simplicity; homeliness; lack of sophistication 〔guile〕. ～하다 《기질이》 (be) simple and honest; simple-hearted; unsophisticated; unspoilt; naive; 《풍속이》 (be) homely; simple-mannered. ¶ ～한 시골 노인 an old countryman, simple and honest by nature.

**순발력**(瞬發力) ability to react instantly 〔momentarily〕; instantaneous reactionary force 〔ability〕 《of *one's* muscle》.

**순방**(巡訪) a round of visits 〔calls〕. ～하다 make a round of calls; visit one after another. ¶ 여러 나라를 ～하다 make a tour of various countries / 명사들을 ～하다 visit one man of distinction after another.

**순배**(巡杯) passing the wine cup around. ～하다 pass 《a wine cup》 around. ¶ 한 ～ a round of drinks / 술잔이 한 ～ 돌다 a wine cup goes round every member of the party.

**순백**(純白) pure 〔snow〕 white; sheer white. ¶ ～의 pure-〔snow-〕white; white as snow; immaculate / ～색의 셔츠〔웨딩드레스〕 a pure-white shirt 〔wedding dress〕.

**순번**(順番) order (순서); turn (차례). ¶ ～으로 in due 〔regular〕 order; in turn; by turns; by rotation / ～을 기다리다 await 〔wait (for)〕 *one's* turn; 《이발소 등에서》 wait for attention / ～이 돌아오다〔되다〕 *one's* turn comes round / 이 번호표를 가지고 ～을 기다리시오 Take this number and wait your turn, please.

**순보**(旬報) a ten-day report.

**순분**(純分) fineness; 《금의》 carat; karat.

**순사**(殉死) ① 《자결》 suicide committed for *one's* country; patriotic suicide. ～하다 die for *one's* country. ② 《따라 죽음》 self-immolation; 《과부의》 suttee. ～하다 immolate *oneself* 《on the death of *one's* lord, *etc.*》.

**순산**(順産) an easy delivery 〔childbirth〕; a smooth delivery. ～하다 have an easy delivery; give an easy birth to. ¶ 그녀는 아들을 ～했다 She gave an easy birth to a boy. / 아내는 ～이었다 My wife was fortunate in her confinement.

**순색**(純色) solid color; 《of》 one color; unmixed shade.

**순서**(順序) 《차례》 (sequent) order; (a) sequence; 《절차》 procedure; 《방법》 a system 〔method〕; 《계획》 a program 《of events》. ¶ ～ 있는 orderly; methodical; systematic / ～ 없는 disorderly; out of order; irregular; unsystematic; unmethodical / 정해진 ～대로 하다 follow the procedure; go through due formalities.

순서가: ～가 엉망이다 be out of order 〔turn〕 / ～가 틀리다 be in wrong order.

순서로: 여느 ～로 in the usual order / 그 크기의 ～로 in the order of their size / 나이 ～로 앉다 sit in order of seniority.

순서를: ～를 거꾸로 하다 reverse 〔invert〕 the order / ～를 어기다 follow the wrong order; fail to follow the right order / ～를 기다리다 wait for *one's* turn; 《점포 등에서》 await attention / 줄을 서서 ～를 기다리는 사람들 people standing in queues awaiting their turn / ～를 당기다 move up 《*something*》 in order / ～를 뒤엎다 disturb 〔upset, disarrange〕 the order / ～를 바꾸다 change the order / ～를 바로잡다 correct the order / ～를 짜다 form 〔put together〕 a program.

¶ ～는 아무래도 좋으니까 이 책들을 정리해라 Arrange these books in any order. / 일에는 ～가 있다 There is an order in doing everything. / 무슨 일이든 ～를 제대로 밟아서 해라 No matter what you do, you must follow the correct order. / 우선 그의 의향을 물어보는 것이 ～일 게다 We ought to ask his intention before anything else.

**순소득**(純所得) net income. ¶ 그는 연간 ～이 2천만원 이다 He has a yearly 〔an annual〕 net income of twenty million won.

**순손**(純損) a dead 〔net〕 loss.

**순수**(巡狩) a royal tour 〔trip, progress〕. ～하다 make a royal tour. ◉ 진흥왕 ～비 the monument commemorating King Chinhŭng's tour.

**순수**(純粹) purity; genuineness. ～하다 (be) pure; genuine; real; 《섞이지 않은》 (be) unalloyed; unmixed; unadulterated; undiluted; 《순혈의》 (be) full=blooded; trueborn.

¶ ～한 사랑 pure 〔genuine〕 love / ～한 광물질 a mineral substance in a pure state / ～한 동기 pure motives / ～한 켈트 민족 a genuine Celtic people / ～한 테리어 a pedigreed terrier; a terrier of pure stock / ～한 서울내기 a Seoulite born and bred; a trueborn Seoulite / 한국어의 ～성을 보존하다 preserve the pure well of Korean undefiled.

◉ ～과학 pure science. ～논리학〔수학〕 pure logic 〔mathematics〕. ～배양 pure culture: ～배양하다 cultivate a pure culture 《of an organism》. ～시 pure poetry. ～이성비판 《칸트의》 the Critique of Pure Reason. ～주의 〖미술〗 purism. ～철학 metaphysics.

**순수입**(純收入) net income 〔earnings〕.

**순순하다**(順順—) (be) gentle; docile; obedient; submissive.

¶ 순순히 tamely; quietly; smoothly; without trouble 〔resistance〕; obediently / 순순히 명령에 따르다 obey 〔submit to〕 an order meekly / 순순히 (죄를) 자백하다 confess (the crime) frankly; make a frank confession (of the crime) / 순순히 충고를 받아들이다 accept *a person's* advice at once 〔without argument〕 / 순순히 포박당하다 surrender tamely; suffer *oneself* to be bound; be arrested without resistance / 그녀는 어머니의 말을 순순히 들었다 She listened to her mother without objecting.

**순순하다**(諄諄—) be kind and gentle 《in admonishing》. ¶ 순순히 gently; patiently / 순순히 타이르다 inculcate 〔exhort, admonish〕 gently.

**순시**(巡視) a round of inspection 〔visits〕. ～하다 make a tour 〔go a round〕 of inspection; inspect; 《담당구역을》 patrol; walk *one's* beat.

¶ 공장 안을 ～하다 inspect 〔go over〕 a factory / 피난민 수용소를 ～하다 make a tour of refugee camps.

◉ ～선 a patrol boat. ～자 a patrolman (순찰자); a floorwalker (판매장의 감독); a supervisor (감독자). 연두～ the new year inspection tour.

**순시**(瞬時) a moment; an instant; a short while. ¶ ～에 in a moment; in a twinkling.

**순식간**(瞬息間) a brief instant. ¶ ～에 in a twinkling; in the twinkling of an eye; in a blink 〔wink〕; in an instant; in a flash / ～에 먹어치우다 eat 〔devour〕 in an instant / ～에 목조 건물에 불이 붙었다 In a flash the wooden building caught fire. / 이 모두가 실로 ～에 생긴 일이었다 All this happened in an instant. / 제트기는 ～에 날아가버렸다 The jet plane flew away 「in a twinkling 〔in the twinkling of an eye〕.

**순양**(巡洋) cruising; a cruise. ～하다 cruise the sea. ◉ ～전함 a battle cruiser. ～함 a cruiser: 경〔중〕～함 a light 〔heavy〕 cruiser / 보조 ～함 an auxiliary cruiser.

**순여**(旬餘) ten days or so; over 〔more than〕 ten days.

**순연**(順延) postponement; deferment. ～하다 put off; defer; postpone. ¶ 우천시 ～ 《게시》 In case of rain to be postponed till the next fine day 〔till the first fine day following〕.

**순열**(順列) 〖수학〗 (a) permutation; (a) linear arrangement. ¶ ～과 조합 permutations and combinations.

**순위**(順位) order; rank(ing); standing; placing; precedence. ¶ 최우선 ～ top priority / ～를 다투다 quarrel about precedence; contend 〔compete〕 for (the order of) precedence / ～를 정하다 rank; decide ranking / 경제 정책은 물가 안정에 최우선 ～를 두고 있다 Economic policy places top priority on price stability. ◉ ～결정전 《경기 따위의》 a play-off. ～표 a graded 〔ranking〕 list: ～표를 만들다 make a graded list 《of》.

**순유**(巡遊) a (pleasure) tour; an itinera(n)cy. ～하다 make 〔go on〕 a tour; travel 《through, about》; itinerate. ¶ 그들은 유럽을 ～했다 They went on a tour of Europe.

**순육**(馴育) taming. ～하다 tame; domesticate.

**순은**(純銀) pure 〔solid〕 silver. ¶ ～의 of pure 〔solid〕 silver; all-silver. ◉ ～숟가락 a silver spoon.

**순음**(脣音) 〖언어〗 a labial (sound).

**순응**(順應) adaptation; accommodation; adjustment. ~하다 adapt 〔accommodate, adjust, acclimate《미》〕 *oneself* 《to the new environment》. ¶ …에 ~하여 in sympathy with… / 시대〔시류〕에 ~하다 go 〔swim〕 with the times 〔tide〕 / 대세에 ~하다 accept the logic of events. ◉ ~성 adaptability.

**순이익**(純利益) a net 〔neat, clean, pure〕 profit 〔gain〕; net proceeds. ¶ 2만원의 ~이 나다 have a net gain of 20,000 won / 거래에서 백만원의 ~을 올리다 make a net profit of one million won on the deal / 연(年) 3할의 ~을 올리다 net a 30 per cent a year.

**순익**(純益) = 순이익.

**순일**(純一) purity; genuineness; homogeneity; uniformity. ~하다 (be) pure (and simple); sheer; unalloyed; unmixed; genuine; uniform.

**순장**(旬葬) burial on the tenth day after death.

**순장**(殉葬) 〖고제도〗 burial of the living with the dead (as servants with their dead master). ~하다 bury alive with the dead.

**순전**(純全) ~하다 (be) pure; spotless; genuine; true; utter; sheer; absolute; downright; out-and-out. ¶ ~히 wholly; purely; completely / ~한 거짓말〔사기〕 a downright lie 〔swindle〕 / ~한 오해 a sheer misunderstanding / ~한 개인 문제 a purely personal matter / 그것은 ~히 내 잘못이다 It is clearly my mistake.

**순절**(殉節) dying in defense of *one's* chastity 〔integrity, loyalty〕. ~하다 die for *one's* chastity.

**순정**(純正) ~하다 (be) pure; genuine; real. ¶ ~과학 pure science / ~부품 genuine 〔real〕 parts. / ~식품 natural food(s).

**순정**(純情) a pure heart 〔mind〕; pure-minded feeling 《for *a person*》. ¶ ~의 pure-hearted; unspoilt; unsophisticated / ~ 어린 loving; affectionate; tender / ~을 바치다 give all *one's* love 《to》. ◉ ~소설 a boy-meets-girl story.

**순조**(順調) a favorable 〔normal, unimpeded〕 condition; favorableness; smoothness; 《날씨의》 seasonableness. ~롭다 (be) favorable; smooth; go 〔run, progress〕 smoothly 〔without trouble, with no hitch〕; 《날씨가》 (be) seasonable.
¶ ~롭게, ~로이 smoothly; satisfactorily; well; without trouble 〔a hitch〕; [비유적] in smooth water(s); before the wind / ~로운 날씨 seasonable 〔favorable〕 weather / 만사 ~로우면 if every thing goes 〔comes out〕 well / ~로운 경과를 보이다 follow a normal course / ~로이 진행되다〔나아가다〕 go smoothly 〔well, with a swing〕; go 〔be〕 well along; progress satisfactorily; proceed favorably / ~롭게 팔리다 enjoy a steady sale / ~롭게 되지 않다 go wrong 〔amiss〕; be unsatisfactorily / ~로워지다 take a favorable turn; improve / 무역이 다시 ~로워졌다 Trade has got back to normal. / 계획은 ~롭다 Our plans are going all right 〔shaping well〕. / 모든 일이 ~롭게 풀렸다 Everything has been going smoothly with me.

**순종**(純種) unmixed breed; a thoroughbred; a full 〔pure〕 blood.
¶ ~의 full-〔pure-〕blooded; thoroughbred; purebred 《dog》; 《a dog》 of unmixed bred / ~의 말 a blood horse. ◉ ~교배 purebred breeding.

**순종**(順從) obedience; submissiveness; compliance. ~하다 follow 《*a person*》 obediently; obey 《*a person*》 meekly; yield 〔give in, submit〕 《to》. ¶ 어른에게 ~하다 obey *one's* elders.

**순직**(純直) simplicity and uprightness. ~하다 (be) simple(-minded) and upright.

**순직**(殉職) dying at *one's* post of duty. ~하다 die at *one's* post (of duty); die in the line of duty; be killed at work; die in harness; 《구어》 die with *one's* boots on. ¶ 소방대원 세 명이 ~했다 Three firemen died 〔were killed〕 in the performance of their duties.
◉ ~경찰관 a policeman who died on duty 〔in harness〕. ~자 a victim to his post (of duty); a martyr to duty.

**순진**(純眞) innocence; naivety; simplicity 《of mind》; purity. ~하다 (be) innocent; naive; genuine; pure; guileless. ¶ ~한 마음 a pure and simple heart / ~한 생각 a simple 〔an unsophisticated〕 idea / ~한 어린이 a child pure in heart; an innocent child / ~하게 웃다 laugh an innocent laugh / 마음이 ~하다 be pure in heart.

**순차**(順次) order; turn. ¶ ~적으로 in (serial, consecutive) order; successively; in due sequence; in regular succession 〔sequence, series〕 / 일을 ~적으로 처리하다 dispose of matters in due order; settle things one by one.

**순찰**(巡察) a round of inspection; a patrol. ~하다 make 〔go〕 a round of inspection; patrol; go 〔walk〕 the 〔*one's*〕 round(s) 《of the barracks》. ¶ ~ 나가다 set out on a round of official calls / 공장 안을 ~하다 inspect 〔go over〕 a factory.
◉ ~구역 a beat; rounds. ~대 a patrol party: ~대원 a patrolman. ~장교 an officer on patrol. ~차 a (police) patrol car; a squad car.

**순치**(馴致) ①《길들임》 domestication; taming. ~하다 domesticate; tame. ②《초래》 bringing about; giving rise to. ~하다 gradually lead 《to》; bring about gradually; give rise to; pave the way for.

**순치음**(脣齒音) 〖음성〗 a labiodental 〔dentilabial〕 sound.

**순탄**(順坦) ~하다 《길이》 (be) even; level; smooth; 《성질이》 (be) gentle; mild; be not fastidious; 《순조롭다》 (be) uneventful; peaceful. ¶ ~한 생활 an uneventful life; an even tenor of life / ~하게 자라다 be bred in favorable circumstances / 그녀의 생애 마지막 10년은 ~했다 The last ten years of her life were quite uneventful.

**순풍**(淳風) a good custom. ◉ ~미속 good morals and manners.

**순풍**(順風) a favorable 〔fair〕 wind; a tailwind. ¶ ~에 돛을 달다 sail before 〔with〕 the wind (★ 비유적으로도 쓰임) / ~을 받고 달리다 《a ship》 run before the 〔a fair〕 wind; square away / 인생은 ~에 돛단 듯 평온 무사한 것이 아니다 Life is by no means smooth 〔plain〕 sailing.

**순하다**(順—) ①《온순하다》 (be) gentle; docile; meek; dovelike; obedient; amiable. ¶ 순한 아이 a gentle 〔docile〕 child / 성질이 ~ be mild in disposition. ②《맛이》 (be) mild; light; smooth. ¶ 순한 담배 mild cigarettes / 이 술은 ~ This wine is light. ③《일이》 (be) smooth; simple; easy. ¶ 만사가 순하게 풀려 갔다 Everything went smoothly.

**순항**(巡航) a cruise; cruising; cruise flight (비행기의). ~하다 cruise 〔make a cruise〕 《on the Pacific》. ¶ ~ 중이다 be on a cruise / 연안을 ~하다 cruise on the coast. ◉ ~고도 (a) cruising altitude: ~고도에 달하다 reach 〔climb to〕 cruising altitude. ~미사일 a cruise missile. ~선 a cruiser. ~속도 (a) cruising speed: 최대 ~속도로 《sail》 at full cruising speed.

**순행**(巡行) a patrol; a round; a tour. ~하다 go round; go the round of 《the district》; 《담당 구역을》 go 〔make〕 *one's* rounds; go on patrol.

**순행운동**(順行運動) 〖천문〗 direct motion.

**순혈**(純血) pure blood 〔breed〕. ⇨ 순종.

**순화**(純化) purification. ~하다 purify.

**순화**(醇化) refinement; sublimation. ~하다 refine; purify; sublimate. ¶ 우리 말을 ~하다 purify 〔refine〕 our language.

**순화**(馴化) acclimation; acclimatization. ~하다 acclimate 〔acclimatize〕 《to》; get acclimated 〔acclimatized〕 《to new surroundings》. ¶ 그 식물은 한국 풍토에 ~되지 않았다 The plant is not acclimated to Korea.

**순환**(循環) circulation; rotation; cycle; 《혈액의》 the circulation of blood. ~하다 circulate 《through》; rotate; go in circles 〔cycles〕. ¶ ~적인 circular; circulatory; cyclic; recurring / 경기 ~ a business 〔trade 《영》〕 cycle / 빈곤의 악~ the vicious circle of poverty / 혈액 ~을 좋게 하다 improve the circulation of blood / 혈액은 체내를 ~한다 The blood circulates in the body.
◉ ~계(통) the circulating system (of the blood): ~계 질환 a circulatory illness 〔troubles, ailments〕. ~곡선 a recurring curve. ~급수 〖수학〗 recurring series. ~기(期) a cycle. ~기(器) a circulatory organ. ~논법 〖논리〗 a circular argument; 〖논리〗 a vicious circle. ~도로 a circular road; a beltway; a belt highway: 남산 ~도로 the Namsan Circular Road / 교통 사고로 ~도로 전체가 막히고 말았다 The entire beltway is congested because of the traffic accident. ~반응 circular reaction. ~버스 a belt-line bus; a bus on a circular route. ~선(線) 《철도의》 a loop 〔belt 《미》〕 line: 교외 ~선 the suburbs loop line. ~소수(小數) 〖수학〗 circulating decimals; a circulator.

**순회**(巡廻) a round; a patrol; a tour. ~하다 go 〔walk〕 round; go *one's* rounds; make a tour; patrol.
¶ 지방 ~ a provincial tour 《of professional wrestlers》 / 담당 구역을 ~하다 make the round of *one's* assigned block 〔beat〕 / 경찰이 ~ 중이다 The policeman is on patrol.
◉ ~강연 a lecturing 〔lecture〕 tour. ~공연 a provincial 〔local〕 perfor-

mance; a show on tour; a road show. ～구역 *one's* beat 〔round〕. ～극단 a touring company. ～대사 a roving ambassador; an ambassador=at-large. ～도서관〔문고〕 an itinerant 〔a traveling〕 library; a library on wheels. ～재판 assizes: ～ 재판소 a circuit court. ～진료소 a traveling clinic.

**순후하다**(醇厚—) (be) pure-minded; 「warm-hearted.

**숟가락** a spoon. ¶ 밥 한 ～ a spoonful of rice / 찻～ a teaspoon / 설탕 한〔두〕 ～ a spoonful 〔two spoonfuls〕 of sugar / ～으로 뜨다 spoon up 〔out〕 《soup》 / ～으로 젓다 stir with a spoon. ◉ ～총 the handle of a spoon.

**술**[1] 《주류》 rice wine (약주 등); liquor; alcoholic drink 〔beverage〕; an intoxicant; booze 《구어》; wine (포도주). ¶ 감칠맛이 있는 술 wine of good body / 독한〔약한〕 술 a strong 〔weak〕 wine; a hard 〔light〕 liquor / 술냄새를 풍기는 입김 breath reeking of liquor / 술만 들어가면 when *one* drinks; when in wine / 술의 힘을 빌어 fortified 〔emboldened〕 by liquor; on the (false) courage of alcohol / 술 상대를 하다 keep company in drinking / 술 한 병을 돌려가며 마시다 pass around a battle of whisky 〔liquor〕.

술이: 술이 들어가면 잘 우는 사람 a maudlin drinker / 술이 세다 be a heavy 〔hard〕 drinker / 술이 약하다 be a small 〔poor〕 drinker.

술로: 술로 슬픔을 달래다 drown *one's* grief in drink; drink sorrow down / 술로 시름을 달래다 drown care in wine bowl; drink down *one's* cares / 술로 몸을 녹이다 keep warm on liquor / 술로 밤을 지새우다 drink all night long; drink the night away.

술에: 술에 취해 일어난 말다툼 a drunken brawl / 술에 취하다 get drunk; become intoxicated / 술에 얼큰히 취하다 be dazed by liquor / 술에 물을 타다 water wine / 술에 빠지다 indulge in wine; give *oneself* up to drinking; be addicted to drinking / 술에 젖다 be steeped in liquor; be soaked in drink.

술을: 술을 좋아하는 사람 a thirsty soul; a drinker / 술을 마시다 drink; take wine; 《한잔하다》 have a drink / 술을 데우다 warm up wine in a bottle; heat wine / 술을 데워 마시다 drink wine hot 〔warm〕 / 술을 마시며 이야기하다 talk over a glass 〔bottle〕 / 술을 마시고 자다 drink *oneself* asleep / 술을 대접하다 offer 《a guest》 a drink / 술을 따르다 serve 《*a person*》 with wine; pour out wine 《for *a person*》; fill 《*a person's*》 cup; fill 《a glass》 with liquor / 술을 벌떡벌떡 들이키다 guzzle; drink like a fish / 술을 빚다 brew rice wine / 술을 끊다 give up 〔quit, knock off 《구어》〕 drinking; become a total abstainer; cut out wine / 술을 삼가다 refrain 〔abstain〕 from drinking / 술을 과하게 마시다 drink heavily / 술을 좋아하게 되다 take to drinking 〔the bottle〕 / 술을 억지로 권하다 press 〔force〕 wine upon 《*a person*》; make 《*a person*》 drink / 술을 너무 즐기다 be too fond of drink / 술을 한 모금도 못 하다 do not touch alcohol; be a teetotaler 《by nature》; be a total abstainer.

¶ 술은 백약(百藥)의 으뜸 Good wine makes good blood. / 그의 입에서는 술냄새가 풍겼다 I could smell liquor on his breath. / 아이구 술냄새 You smell of wine! / 그는 술만 들어가면 딴사람처럼 된다 He looks quite another man when the wine is in. / 술이라면 사족을 못 쓴다 He is simply mad so far as wine is concerned. / 술 기운이 오르기 시작했다 The wine began to take effect. / 술 기운에 한 말입니다 I said so under the influence of liquor. / 「무슨 술을 드시겠습니까」—「아닙니다. 술을 마시지 않습니다」 "What are you drinking?"—"Oh, no thanks, I don't drink."

**술**[2] 《분량》 a spoonful. ¶ 다음에는 소금을 세 큰 술 넣으세요 Next add three tablespoonfuls 〔tablespoons〕 of salt.

**술**[3] 《쟁기의》 the blade-guard of a Korean plow 〔plough 《영》〕.

**술**[4] 《장식용의》 a tassel; a tuft; a fringe. ¶ 술 달린 목도리 a shawl with fringed ends / 술 달린 기 a tasselled flag.

**술**[5] 〖식물〗 the pistil(s) and stamens of a flower. ¶ 수술 a stamen / 암술 a pistil.

**술**[6] 《책 따위의 부피》 the thickness of a book, paper, or cloth bolt. ¶ 술 두꺼운 책 a bulky 〔massive, thick〕 volume.

**술**(戌) 〖민속〗 ① 《십이지의》 the Sign of the Dog (＝11th of the 12 Earth's Branches). ¶ 술년(戌年) the Year of the Dog / 술일(戌日) the Day of the Dog. ② ⇨술시.

**술값** 《술 먹은 대금》 (a) drink charge; 《술먹을 돈》 drink money. ¶ ～을 요구

하다 demand drink money / ～을 떼어 먹다 do not pay for *one's* drink; leave *one's* bar bill unpaid / 그가 버는 돈은 모두 ～으로 나간다 All the money he earns goes for drink.

**술고래** a strong 〔heavy, hard〕 drinker; a tippler; 《미속어》 a lush; 《구어》 a boozer. ¶ 그는 ～다 He drinks like a fish.

**술국** broth prepared to be taken with liquor; broth to wash the liquor down.

**술기**(一氣) 《취기》 intoxication; tipsiness. ¶ ～를 띠고 있다 be drunk; be under the influence of liquor; have had one 〔a few〕 too many 《구어》; have had one over the eight.

**술기운** the influence of wine. ¶ ～이 돌다 become 〔get, grow〕 drunk 〔tipsy〕; show signs of intoxication; feel high 《구어》 / ～이 깨다 sober up; get 〔become〕 sober.

**술김** the influence of liquor. ¶ ～에 under the influence of liquor 〔alcohol〕; emboldened by liquor; in a drunken fit / ～에 하는 싸움 a drunken brawl / ～에 부리는 객기 Dutch courage / ～에 싸우다 quarrel under the influence of liquor.

**술꾼** a (heavy) drinker; a tippler; 《애주가》 a thirsty soul.

**술내** the smell 〔odor〕 of liquor; an alcoholic smell. ¶ ～가 나다 smell of liquor; reek of wine; have an alcoholic breath.

**술대** 『음악』 a plectrum 〔pick〕 used in playing a *kŏmun-go* harp.

**술도가**(一都家) a brewery; a distillery.

**술독** ① 《항아리》 a liquor jug. ② 《술고래》 a sot; a tippler.

**술독**(一毒) alcohol poisoning. ＝주독(酒毒).

**술래** a tagger; it. ¶ 네가 ～다 You're it.

**술래잡기** tag; tig; touch-last; 《숨바꼭질》 hide-and-seek; hy-spy; I-spy. ～하다 play tag 〔tig〕; play hide-and-seek.

**술렁거리다** be disturbed 〔perturbed〕; be uneasy 〔upset〕; be in a commotion; (make a) stir; be all abuzz. ¶ 그 소식에 온 서울 장안이 술렁거렸다 The whole Seoul buzzed 〔was astir〕 with the news. / 그가 단상에 오르자 청중이 술렁거렸다 When he appeared on the platform, a stir ran through the audience.

**술렁술렁** disturbed; perturbed; uneasy; upset; in a commotion; all abuzz.

**술맛** the taste 〔flavor〕 of wine. ¶ ～을 보다 taste wine.

**술망나니** a confirmed drunkard; a sot.

**술먹은개** a drunkard; a drunken person.

**술밥** 《지에밥》 steamed rice for making wine; 《주반》 rice boiled with wine, soysauce and sugar.

**술버릇** ¶ ～이 나쁜 사람 a person who gets nasty when drunk / ～이 나쁘다 be quarrelsome in *one's* cups; be a bad drunk; 《몹시》 be a terrible 〔vicious〕 drunk / ～이 좋다 be a good drunk.

**술법**(術法) magical tricks; conjury; magic; mysteries; 《복술》 the art of divination; fortunetelling. ¶ ～을 쓰다 practice 〔use〕 magic.

**술병**(一病) an alcoholic disorder. ¶ ～이 나다 drink *oneself* ill; be sick from drink.

**술병**(一甁) a liquor bottle.

**술부**(述部) 『문법』 the predicate.

**술부대**(一負袋) a hard 〔heavy〕 drinker. ＝술고래.

**술살** fat put on by habitual drinking. ¶ ～이 오르다 get fat from alcohol.

**술상**(一床) a drinking table. ¶ ～을 차리다 prepare dishes for drink; set a drinking table.

**술수**(術數) ① ＝술법(術法). ② 《술책》 an artifice; a trick; tactics; an intrigue. ¶ ～를 쓰다 resort to tricks; 《권모술수를》 resort to trickery 〔wiles〕.

**술술** ① 《새는 모양》 soft-flowing; smoothly; effortlessly; easily; readily; nicely. ¶ 물이 솥에서 ～ 샌다 Water is leaking from the kettle in a steady stream. ② 《유창히》 fluently; expertly; 《어려움 없이》 without any trouble. ¶ 영어를 ～ 말하다 speak English fluently / 어려운 문제를 ～ 풀다 solve hard problems without any trouble at all. ③ 《막힘없이》 smoothly; easily; nicely. ¶ 계획이 ～ 진척되고 있다 The project is going ahead smoothly. / 이 만년필은 ～ 써진다 I can write easily with this fountain pen. / 실이 ～ 풀리다 the tangled thread straightens out nicely. ④ 《비·바람이》 gently; softly; lightly. ¶ 바람이 ～ 불고 있었다 The wind was blowing gently. / 비가 아침부터 ～ 내리고 있다 It has been 「drizzling 〔raining softly〕 since this morning.

**술시**(戌時) 『민속』 the 11th of the 12 double-hours (＝the period between 7 and 9 p.m.).

**술안주**(一按酒) a 「tidbit 〔relish〕 (taken with alcoholic drinks); snack (eaten with wine); a side dish 《for wine》. ¶ ～가 아무 것도 없다 There is nothing good to take with wine. / 이것은 ～로는 그만이다 This goes very well with wine. / 그들은 사장에 대한 욕을 ～삼아 술을 마셨다 They badmouthed their boss to give added zest to their drinking.

**술어**(述語) the predicate. ¶ ～적 predicative 《use》. ◉ ～동사 a predicate verb.

**술자리** a drinking party; a banquet. ¶ ～를 마련하다 give a drinking party; hold a banquet / ～에서 싸움이 벌어지다 get into a fight while drinking.

**술잔**(—盞) a wine cup; a liquor glass. ¶ ～을 돌리다 pass the cup round; circulate the wine cup; offer a cup in return (반배하다) / ～을채우다 fill a cup / ～을 비우다 drain 〔drink off〕 the cup; drink the cup dry / ～을 부딪치다 touch cups 《with *a person*》/ ～을 주다〔받다〕 offer 〔accept〕 a cup / ～을 주고받다 exchange drinking cups / 이별의 ～을 나누다 drink a parting cup; have a parting drink.

**술잔치** a drinking party 〔bout〕; a feast; a carousal. ¶ ～를 벌리다 have a drinking bout; carouse.

**술장사** the liquor(-selling) business.

**술장수** a liquor dealer; a wine seller.

**술집** a drinking house; a tavern; a grogshop; a bar(room); a saloon 《미》; a public house 《영》; a pub 《영》. ¶ ～을 돌아다니며 마시다 loaf around saloons; barhop; do 〔make〕 a pub crawl; go pub-crawling / 어젯밤 친구와 ～을 돌아다니며 마셨다 I went barhopping with a friend of mine last night. ◉ ～여자〔호스티스〕 a barmaid; a B-girl 《미속어》. ～주인 a barkeep(er); a saloon keeper.

**술책**(術策) an artifice; a stratagem; a trick; wiles; an intrigue; tactics. ¶ ～에 능한 사람 a man of resources; a tactician / ～을 부리다 resort to tricks / ～에 넘어가다〔빠지다〕 walk into 〔fall for〕 a trap 《set by *a person*》; play into the hands 《of》; be entrapped 《by》.

**술추렴** ～하다 ① 《분담하다》 pool the expenses for a drinking party; have everyone chip in for a drinking party. ② 《돌아가며 내다》 《everyone》 give a drinking party by turns.

**술친구**(—親舊) a boon 〔drinking〕 companion; a drinking 〔boozing〕 pal.

**술타령**(—打令) ～하다 ask for 〔suggest〕 nothing but liquor; think only of liquor. ¶ 그는 ～만 한다 He has nothing but drinking on his mind.

**술탈**(—頉) an upset 〔accident〕 due to drinking.

**술통**(—桶) a wine barrel 〔cask, keg〕.

**술파** 〖화학〗 sulfa; sulpha. ◉ ～제 sulfa drugs; sulfas: ～제의 sulfa.

**술판** 《hold, have》 a drinking party 「〔bout〕.

**술회**(述懷) an effusion of *one's* thoughts (and feelings); reminiscence(s); recollection(s). ～하다 relate *one's* thoughts and feelings; reminisce; recollect. ¶ 지난 날을 ～하다 recall the past; speak about 〔give reminiscences of〕 *one's* old days / 그는 당시에 관해서 다음과 같이 ～했다 Reminiscing about those days, he spoke as follows:….

**숨** ① 《호흡》 a breath; breathing; respiration. ¶ 숨을 쉬다 breathe; respire; take breath; draw (*one's*) breath / 숨을 내쉬다 breathe out 〔forth〕; give out breath; exhale / 숨을 들이쉬다 breathe in; take in breath; inhale / 숨을 쉬기가 어렵다 breathe with difficulty / 숨을 돌리다 ⇨ 숨돌리다 / 숨을 거두다 die; breathe 〔gasp〕 *one's* last / 숨을 죽이다 hold 〔catch, bate〕 *one's* breath; stay with bated breath / 숨을 죽이고 with bated breath; in breathless suspense / 숨을 죽이고(서) 듣다 〔지켜보다〕 listen 〔watch〕 with breathless attention / 숨을 헐떡이다 gasp; pant (for breath); become short 〔out〕 of breath / 숨이 답답하다 be choky 〔stuffy〕/ 숨이 막히다 ⇨ 숨막히다 / 숨이 차다 ⇨ 숨차다 / 그녀는 숨도 안 쉬고 계속 지껄였다 She talked on and on without pausing for breath. / 그들은 숨을 죽이고 그것을 기다렸다 They held their breath in expectation of it. / 깊이 숨을 들이쉬고 난 다음에 내쉬어라 Breathe in 〔Inhale〕 deeply and then breathe out 〔exhale〕. / 그녀는 청중 앞에서 잠시 숨을 돌린 후 말문을 열었다 She began to talk to the audience after a little pause.
② 《채소의》 the crispness 《of fresh vegetables》. ¶ 숨이 죽다 a vegetable wilts 〔loses its crispness〕/ 배추가 숨이 죽었다 The cabbage has lost its crispness.

**숨가쁘다** (be) gasping; panting; be short 〔out〕 of breath. ¶ 숨가쁘게 out of breath; gaspingly; breathlessly / 뛰어와서 ～ I came running here, so it's hard to breathe.

**숨결** breathing; respiration. ¶ ~이 거칠다 breathe hard 〔short, heavily〕; be gasping / 이미 시골에서는 봄의 ~을 느낄 수 있다 We already feel the breath of spring in the countryside. 「(延髓).

**숨골** the medulla (oblongata). ⇨ 연수

**숨구멍** ① 《숨통》 the windpipe; the trachea. ② 〖동물·식물〗 a pore; a stoma (*pl.* -mata) (식물의); a stigma (*pl.* -mata) (동물의). ③ 〖해부〗 《숫구멍》 the fontanel(le).

**숨기**(—氣) signs of breathing; the breath. ¶ ~가 없다 show no sign of life / 아직 ~가 있다 show signs of life; be still breathing.

**숨기다** 《모습·물건 등을》 hide 《*one's* face》; conceal 《*one's* money》; ensconce 《*oneself*》; secrete 《stolen goods》; 《덮어 가리다》 cover 《a fact》; veil 《*one's* displeasure》; draw 〔throw〕 a veil over 《a fact》; cloak 《*one's* ignorance》; 《차폐하다》 screen; obstruct; 《안 보이게 하다》 put 《*a thing*》 out of sight; keep 《*a thing*》 from sight; 《비밀로》 keep 《*a matter*》 secret 〔back〕 《from》; 《감정 등을》 pocket 《*one's* feelings》; dissimulate; 《사람을》 give 〔provide〕 shelter to; shield 〔protect, shelter〕 《*a person* from》.

¶ 나이를 ~ conceal 〔make a secret of〕 *one's* age / 범죄를 ~ cover *one's* crime / 몸을 ~ hide (*oneself*) 《behind, under, in》; shelter *oneself* 《under, beneath, behind》; be in hiding / 본색을 ~ wear 〔put on〕 a mask; disguise *oneself* / 사실을 ~ repress 〔cover up〕 a fact / 놀라움〔슬픔, 기쁨, 낙담〕을 ~ hide 〔conceal〕 *one's* surprise 〔sorrow, joy, disappointment〕 / 얼굴을 ~ hide *one's* face 《in *one's* handkerchief》; screen *one's* face 《with *one's* umbrella》 / 자기 재능을 ~ hide *one's* light 〔candle〕 under a bushel / 숨기지 않고 말하다 tell the truth; speak candidly; hold nothing back / 자동차 키를 의자 밑에 ~ conceal the car keys under the seat / 보이지 않는 곳에 ~ conceal 《*a thing*》 from view / 숨기지 않다 have no secret 《of *a matter* from *a person*》; keep nothing (a secret) 《from》; be frank 〔open〕 / 이름을 숨기고 신문에 투서하다 write to a newspaper 〔the editor〕 anonymously / 그는 자기 계획을 내게 숨기고 있었다 He concealed from me what his plans were. / 이것은 그의 숨겨진 일면을 나타내는 것이다 This shows a hidden part of his character. / 너는 나에게 무언가 숨기고 있다 You are keeping 〔hiding〕 something from me.

**숨김** concealment; keeping 《*a matter*》 secret. ¶ ~ 없는 frank; open (and aboveboard) / ~없이 without concealing; straightforwardly; frankly; openly; unreservedly / ~없이 말하다 speak (straight) out; make a clean breast of 《a fact》 / 이것에 관해서 하나도 ~없이 말하겠다 I'll tell you everything I know about this. / 나는 당신에게 하나도 ~이 없습니다 I am not holding anything back from you. *or* I have told you all I know. 「die.

**숨넘어가다** breathe *one's* last; expire;

**숨다** ① 《안 보이게》 hide; hide 〔conceal〕 *oneself;* take cover; lurk in; be in hiding; 《사라지다》 disappear; 《피신》 take 〔seek〕 refuge 〔shelter〕 《in, under, behind, with》. ¶ 숨어서 《keep》 out of sight; secretly; by stealth; under cover / 숨은 hidden; unseen; 《알려지지 않은》 unknown; 《익명의》 anonymous / 숨은 뜻 《look for》 a hidden 〔an inner〕 meaning / 숨은 천재〔인재〕 an unknown genius 〔man of talent〕 / 숨은 자선가 an anonymous philanthropist / 숨은 재주 *one's* hidden talents / 나무 뒤에 ~ conceal *oneself* 〔lie concealed〕 behind a tree; hide 〔cover〕 *oneself* behind a tree / 문 뒤에 ~ hide behind the door / 이웃집에 ~ seek refuge 〔hole up〕 with a neighbor / 서울에 숨어 있다 be in hiding in Seoul / 여우가 바위 뒤에 숨어 있다 A fox is lurking behind the rock. ② 《은둔하다》 retire 《from the world》; live in seclusion. ¶ 그는 산에 숨어 살고 있다 He has retired among the mountains. *or* He lives in the mountains, keeping his seclusion from the world.

**숨돌리다** take 〔gather〕 breath; fetch 〔recover〕 *one's* breath; come to *oneself* 〔life (again)〕; 《휴식》 take 〔have〕 a breather; pause for breath; take (a) pause. ¶ 숨돌릴 틈도 없다 have scarcely time to breathe; have hardly a breathing spell / 바빠서 숨돌릴 겨를도 없다 I'm so busy (that) I don't have time to rest for a moment.

**숨막히다** be suffocated; be choked. ¶ 숨막히는 choking; oppressive 《silence》; breathtaking; suffocating / 숨막히는 더위 suffocating heat / 숨막힐 듯한 침묵

an oppressive silence / 더워서 숨막힐 지경이었다 We were almost stifled by the heat.

**숨바꼭질, 숨박질** hide-and-seek; I-spy; hy-spy. ～하다 play hide-and-seek.

**숨소리** the sound of breathing. ¶ ～를 죽이다 hold *one's* breath.

**숨숨하다** (be) pockmarked.

**숨쉬다** breathe; respire; take breath. ¶ 숨쉴 사이 없이 바쁘다 I am so busy that I haven't had a chance to catch my breath.

**숨어들다** get in by stealth; sneak 〔steal〕 into《a place》; smuggle *oneself* into. ¶ 지하로 ～ go underground.

**숨지다** breathe *one's* last; expire; die. ¶ 그녀는 어젯밤에 숨졌다 She died 〔breathed her last〕 last night. / 내가 도착했을 때 병자는 이미 숨져 있었다 When I arrived, the sick person had already stopped breathing.

**숨차다** be out of breath; be short of breath 〔wind〕; be breathless; be short-winded. ¶ 숨차지 않다 have a long wind / 약간의 비탈을 올라가는 데도 숨이 차다 I pant for breath even when going up a gentle slope.

**숨통**(—筒) the windpipe; (the breath of ) life. ¶ ～을 끊다 put an end to《*a person's*》life; give《*a person*》*his* quietus.

**숨표**(—標) 〖음악〗 a breathing mark.

**숫—** pure; unspoiled; spotless; undefiled; innocent. ¶ 숫총각 an innocent bachelor / 숫처녀 an immaculate virgin.

**숫구멍** the fontanel(le).

**숫기**(—氣) manly openness; boldness. ¶ ～ 좋다 be unashamed 〔unabashed, bold, outgoing〕 / ～가 없다 be 〔feel〕 shy 〔bashful〕; be coy (소녀가); 《낯을 가리다》 be shy of strangers; be self=conscious / ～가 없어서 말도 못하다 be too shy to speak / ～ 좋게 말하다 speak out unabashed 〔unreservedly〕.

**숫돌** a whetstone; a grindstone; 《면도칼용》 a hone. ¶ ～에 갈다 sharpen《a knife》 on a whetstone; whet 〔grind〕 《a knife》.

**숫되다** (be) naive; artless; unaffected; unsophisticated; simple; unspoiled. ¶ 숫된 아가씨 역에는 저 여배우를 따를 사람이 없다 The actress is unrivaled in ingénue role.

**숫보기** a naive 〔simple, guileless〕 person.

**숫사람** 《숫된 사람》 a simple 〔an unsophisticated〕 person.

**숫실**(繡—) embroidery thread.

**숫자**(數字) a numeral (letter); a figure. ¶ 아라비아〔로마〕 ～ Arabic 〔Roman〕 numerals / 막대한 ～ enormous 〔huge, stupendous〕 figures / 정확한 ～ exact 〔precise〕 figures / 천문학적 ～ astronomical figures / 두 자리 ～의 물가 상승률 a double-digit inflation rate / ～상으로 numerically; in figures / 두〔세〕 자리 ～ double 〔three〕 figures / ～상의 착오 a numerical error / ～를 들다 give 〔cite〕 figures / ～로 나타내다 express 〔state〕 in figures / 그는 ～에 강하다〔약하다〕 He is good 〔bad〕 at figures 〔numbers〕. / 번호판에는 ～와 문자가 씌어 있다 A license plate has both letters and numbers 〔numerals〕. ◉ ～기보법(記譜法) 〖음악〗 numerical notation.

**숫접다** (be) pure; innocent; chaste; sincere; modest. ¶ 숫저운 색시 an innocent girl.

**숫제** ① 《진실하게》 sincerely; wholeheartedly. ¶ ～ 얘기해 주는 것이 약이 된다 A straight talking-to will do him good. ② 《아예》 rather; preferably; from the first 〔beginning〕; 《not》 at all. ¶ ～ 상대도 않다 refuse to deal with 《us》 at all / 그가 오리라고는 ～ 기대하지도 않았다 I did not expect at all that he would come.

**숫지다** (be) simple; simple-hearted; naive; homely. ¶ 숫진 농부 a simple=hearted peasant.

**숫처녀**(—處女) an immaculate 〔undefiled〕 virgin.

**숫총각**(—總角) an innocent bachelor.

**숭고**(崇高) sublimity; loftiness. ～하다 (be) sublime; noble; lofty. ¶ ～한 이상 a lofty idea.

**숭굴숭굴하다** ① 《생김새가》 (be) chubby; plump; happy-looking. ¶ 숭굴숭굴한 얼굴 a chubby face. ② 《성질이》 (be) affable; amiable; open; friendly; pleasant; easy-going; be easy to get along with. ¶ 숭굴숭굴한 사람 an amiable person / 숭굴숭굴한 태도 smooth 〔bland〕 manners.

**숭늉** water boiled in a kettle where rice has been steamed; "scorched=rice water".

**숭덩숭덩** ⇨송당송당.

**숭배**(崇拜) worship; adoration; admiration. ～하다 worship; venerate; adore; admire; regard 《*a person*》 with deep respect; 《우상처럼》 make an idol of. ¶ 우상 ～ idol worship; idolatry / 조상 ～ ancestor worship / ～의 대상 an object of veneration / …을 맹목적으로

~하다 make a fetish of ⟪*a person*⟫; be a blind adorer 〔devotee〕 of ⟪*a person*⟫ / 나는 진심으로 이 순신 장군을 ~하고 있다 I am an ardent admirer of Admiral Yi Sunshin. / 세계의 많은 사람들이 슈바이처 박사를 ~하고 있다 Many people in the world worship Dr. Schweitzer. ◉ ~자 a worshiper; an adorer; an admirer.

**숭상**(崇尙) respect ⟪for learning, *etc.*⟫. ~하다 respect; honor; revere; esteem; set a high value on; look up to; think much of. ¶ 무(武)를 ~하다 pursue the policy of militarism.

**숭숭** ⇨ 송송.

**숭어** 〖어류〗 a gray mullet.

**숭엄**(崇嚴) solemnity; sublimity; majesty. ~하다 (be) solemn; sublime; majestic.

**숯** charcoal. ¶ 숯가루 charcoal powder / 숯검정 charcoal soot / 숯덩이 a lump of charcoal / 숯섬 a charcoal sack / 숯장수 a charcoal dealer / 숯장이 a charcoal maker / 숯을 굽다 burn 〔make〕 charcoal / 숯이 되다 become charcoal 〔carbonized〕; char; be charred / 숯이 검정 나무란다 ⟪속담⟫ The pot calls the kettle black.

**숯가마** a charcoal kiln; a charcoal pit.

**숯내** smell of burning charcoal; fumes issuing from burning charcoal. ¶ ~(가) 나다 smell burning charcoal / ~ 맡다 get poisoned by charcoal fumes.

**숯등걸** charcoal cinders; half-burned charcoal.

**숯머리** a headache from inhaling charcoal fumes. ¶ ~를 앓다 be poisoned by charcoal fumes.

**숯불** charcoal fire. ¶ 생선 ~구이 charcoal-broiled 〔charbroiled〕 fish / ~을 피우다 make 〔build〕 fire with charcoal.

**숱** quantity; thickness; density; richness (especially of hair). ¶ 숱이 많은 머리 thick hair / 머리 숱이 많다〔적다〕 have thick 〔thin〕 hair; be thick-〔thin-〕haired / 머리 숱을 치다 thin *one's* hair out.

**숱하다** ⟪풍부⟫ (be) plentiful; thick; dense; rich; ⟪양⟫ (be) much; considerable; ⟪수⟫ (be) many; numerous. ¶ 숱하게 많다 abound in 〔with〕; be abundant 〔rich〕 ⟪in *things*⟫; be plentiful; [사람이 주어] have plenty of / 이 호수에는 물고기가 숱하게 많다 This lake abounds with fish. / 숱한 별들이 갠 밤하늘에 빛나고 있었다 Millions of stars were twinkling in the clear night sky.

**숲** ⟪큰⟫ a forest; ⟪작은⟫ a wood; woods ⟪미⟫; a grove; ⟪잡목숲⟫ a copse; ⟪밀림⟫ a jungle. ¶ 소나무 숲 a pine wood; a grove of pine trees / 숲에 사는 동물 a forester / 굴뚝의 숲 [비유적] a forest of chimneys / 지향없이 숲 속을 헤매다 stray aimlessly through the wood / 나무는 보고 숲을 보지 못하다 cannot see the wood for the trees.

**숲길** a forest path 〔road〕.

**쉬(이)** Shoo! ¶ 쉬(이)하고 참새를 쫓다 shoo the sparrows away.

**쉬**[1] ⟪파리알⟫ eggs of a fly; flyblows. ¶ 파리가 쉬를 슬다 a fly blows eggs ⟪upon meat⟫.

**쉬**[2] ⇨ 쉬이.

**쉬**[3] ① ⟪제지하는 소리⟫ Hush!; Sh! ¶ 쉬 조용히 해라 Hush! Be quiet! ② ⟪쉬야⟫ Weewee!; Pee!; Piddle!; Piss!; Tinkle-tinkle! ⇨ 쉬하다. ¶ 바지에 쉬하다 wet *one's* pants.

**쉬다**[1] ⟪음식이⟫ go bad; turn sour; spoil; become putrid. ¶ 쉰 밥 spoiled rice / 쉰내 a stale 〔musty, sourish〕 smell / 장마철에는 밥이 쉬기 쉽다 Boiled rice easily goes bad in the rainy season.

**쉬다**[2] ⟪목이⟫ become hoarse; hoarsen; get 〔go, grow〕 hoarse 〔husky〕. ¶ 쉰 목소리 a hoarse voice; a husky voice / 감기가 들어 목이 ~ *one's* voice is hoarse from a cold / 축구 경기 응원 때문에 우리는 목이 쉬었다 We got hoarse from cheering at the soccer match.

**쉬다**[3] ① ⟪휴식⟫ rest (up); repose 〔rest〕 (*oneself*); have 〔take〕 a rest; take time off; take a break (잠깐 쉬다); relax (느긋하게 쉬다). ¶ 쉬는 시간 a break; a recess; an intermission / 쉬지 않고 without rest 〔a break〕 / 잠시 ~ take a (brief) rest; refresh *oneself;* take breath / 쉬지 않고 일하다 keep at work (without letup) / 쉴 사이도 없다 have no time to rest / 쉴새 없이 손님이 오다 have callers one right after another / 두세 시간 쉬면 괜찮아질 것이다 A few hours' rest will set you right. / 잠깐 쉽시다 Let's have a break. / 열중 쉬어 ⟪구령⟫ Parade rest! / 편히 쉬어 ⟪구령⟫ At ease! *or* Stand at ease!
② ⟪일을⟫ knock off 〔drop〕 ⟪work⟫; rest from ⟪*one's* work⟫; give *oneself* rest; ⟪결석·결근⟫ be absent 〔absent *oneself*〕 ⟪from⟫; stay 〔keep〕 away

《from》; 《휴가를 얻어서》 take「a 《few days》 holiday 〔a day off〕. ¶ 병으로 ~ be laid aside by illness / 학교를 ~ stay away 〔absent *oneself*〕 from school / 감기로 어제 하루 쉬었다 I took yesterday off on account of a cold. / 그는 3일간 일을 쉬고 있다 He has stayed away from work for three days. ③ 《중단》 suspend 《business》; discontinue; halt; close. ¶ 여름방학 동안 학교가 ~ school is closed for the summer vacation / 파업으로 공장이 ~ a factory suspends operations because of a strike / 이 가게는 월요일은 쉰다 The shop does not open on Mondays. / 이 장사는 겨울에는 쉰다 This business closes down in winter. / 불경기로 인해 많은 공장들이 작업을 쉬고 있다 Many factories have suspended operations owing to the recession. ④ 《자다》 go to bed; retire; sleep; rest. ¶ 하룻밤 푹 ~ get a good night's rest.

**쉬다**[4] 《숨을》 draw (a breath); heave. ¶ 깊이 숨을 ~ draw a deep breath / 한숨을 ~ heave 〔fetch〕 a sigh; sigh / 숨을 쉴 틈도 없다 do not have time to breathe; be very busy / 그녀는 안도의 숨을 내쉬었다 The woman heaved a sigh of relief.

**쉬르레알리스트** 《초현실주의자》 a surrealist.

**쉬르레알리슴** 《초현실주의》 surrealism; superrealism. ¶ ~의 surrealistic.

**쉬쉬하다** (hush-)hush. ¶ 사건을 ~ hush 〔cover, smother〕 up a matter / 쉬쉬하며 말하다 talk hush-hush.

**쉬엄쉬엄** with frequent rests; intermittently; in easy stages; off and on. ¶ ~ 일하다 work taking frequent breaks; do a job in easy stages / ~ 가다 go resting at frequent intervals; travel by easy stages / 우리는~ 산에 올랐다 We climbed the mountain resting at several intervals.

**쉬이** ① 《쉽게》 easily; readily; lightly; with ease. ¶ ~ 풀 수 있는 문제 a problem easy to solve / ~ 풀다 solve 《a riddle》 in no time 〔like nothing〕 / ~ 믿어지지가 않다 find 《*something*》 hard to believe / ~ 받아들이다 accept 《an offer》 readily. ② 《곧》 soon; before long; one of these days. ¶ ~ 또 찾아뵙겠습니다 I will call on you again before long. / ~ 더워지는 방이 ~ 식는다 《속담》 Soon hot, soon cold.

**쉬지근하다** 《음식 등이》 (be) rather stale-smelling 〔musty, sourish〕.

**쉬척지근하다** (be) quite stale-smelling 〔sourish, musty〕.

**쉬파리** a blowfly; a bluebottle (fly).

**쉬하다** weewee; piddle; pee 《구어》; have 〔take〕 a pee.

**쉰** fifty. ¶ 쉰 살 fifty years of age / 쉰 고개를 넘은 남자 a man over fifty years of age / 나이 쉰을 바라보다 be close upon fifty; be getting on for 〔to〕 fifty.「years of age.

**쉰둥이** a child born to a person 50

**쉴새없이** incessantly; continuously; continually; unceasingly; ceaselessly; without (a) letup; without a break. ¶ ~ 지껄이다 talk without ceasing 〔a pause〕; chatter ceaselessly; have no end of talk / ~ 사람이 드나들었다 People were constantly coming and going. / 그는 온종일 거의 ~ 담배를 피운다 He smokes almost without a break all day.

**쉼표**(一標) 『음악』 a rest; a pause. ¶ 온 〔2분, 4분〕 ~ a whole 〔half, quarter〕 rest.

**쉽다** ① 《용이》 (be) easy; simple; light; plain; 《…하기가》 be easy to 《*do*》. ¶ 쉽게 easily; with ease; without difficulty 〔trouble〕; readily / 쉬운 일〔문제〕 an easy job 〔question〕 / 사용자가 이해하기 쉽게 만든 설명서 a user-friendly manual / 쉬운 글로 쓰다 write in plain 〔simple, easy〕 language / 읽기 ~ be easy to read / 부서지기 ~ be easy to break; break easily; be fragile / 쉽게 문제를 해결하다 solve a problem easily / 이 문제는 내게는 너무 ~ This question is too easy for me. / 말하기는 쉬우나 행하기는 어렵다 It's easier 〔Easier〕 said than done. / 쉽게 얻는 것은 잃기도 ~ 《속담》 Easy come, easy go. / 외국어를 마스터하기란 쉬운 일이 아니다 It is no easy job 〔not easy〕 to master a foreign language.
② 《경향》 be apt to; be prone to; be liable to; be ready to; be likely to. ¶ 감기에 걸리기 ~ be liable to catch cold; be susceptible to a cold / 잘못을 저지르기 ~ be open to errors; be liable to err / 이른 봄에는 날씨가 변하기 ~ The weather「tends to change often 〔is changeable〕 in early spring. / 남을 나쁘게 생각하기 ~ We are apt to think ill of others.

**쉽사리** easily; with ease; readily; without trouble 〔effort〕. ¶ ~ 허락을 얻다

get ready permission / ~ 돈을 벌다 make an easy gain / ~ 대답할 수 없다 cannot give an offhand answer / 그가 ~ 승낙할 것 같지 않다 I am afraid he will not consent readily. / 그는 그 큰 돌을 ~ 들어올렸다 He lifted the big stone very easily 〔with great ease〕.

**슈미즈** a chemise; 《메리야스제》 a vest.

**슈샤인** shoeshine. ◉ ~보이 a shoeshine boy.

**슈크림** [<*chou à la crème* (F.)] a cream puff.

**슈타이크아이젠** [<*Steigeisen* (G.)] 〖등산〗 climbing irons; crampons.

**슈트** a suit. ◉ ~케이스 a suitcase.

**슈퍼** super(-). ◉ ~마켓 a supermarket: 손님이 북적거리는 ~마켓 a busy supermarket / ~마켓에 쇼핑하러 가다 go shopping at a supermarket. ~맨 a superman. ~ 301조 《미국의》 the Super 301 trade provision of the U.S. Omnibus Trade Act. ~소닉 《초음속의》 supersonic 《speed》. ~스타 《대스타》 a superstar. ~제트 《초음속 제트기》 a superjet. ~컨덕터 《초전도체》 a superconductor. ~컴퓨터 a supercomputer. ~탱커 《초대형 유조선》 a supertanker. ~하이웨이 《고속도로》 《미》 a superhighway.

**슈피리어호**(一湖) 《미국·캐나다 사이의》 the Lake Superior.

**슛** shooting; a shot. ~하다 shoot 《a ball》. ¶ 롱슛 a long shot / 정확한 중거리슛 an accurate medium-range shot / 골밑슛 an under-the-basket shot.

**스낵** 《have, eat》 a snack. ◉ ~바〔코너〕 a snack bar 〔counter, stand〕.

**스냅** ① 《야구》 a snap. ② 《사진》 a snapshot. ¶ ~ 사진을 찍다 snapshot; snap 《*a person*》 / 너 ~ 사진 찍어 줄게 I will take snapshot of you.

**스님** ① 《사승(師僧)》 a teacher 〔master〕 of a Buddhist priest. ② 《중》 a priest; 《경칭》 (the) Reverend (생략 Rev.).

**스라소니** 〖동물〗 a lynx.

**스란치마** a long skirt (that hides the feet).

**스러지다** vanish; disappear. ⇨사라지다.

**-스럽다** be (like); seem; look (like). ¶ 보배스럽다 be precious; be valuable / 극성스럽다 be vigorous / 변덕스럽다 be capricious / 신비스럽다 be mysterious.

**스르르** gently; softly; easily; of itself. ¶ 눈을 ~ 감다 softly close *one's* eyes / 입에서 ~ 녹다 melt away in the mouth / (허리띠가) ~ 풀리다 slip off.

**-스름하다** ① 《빛깔》 be '-ish'; be slightly colored 〔tinged〕 with. ¶ 푸르스름하다 be bluish. ② 《형상》 be '-ish'; be slightly characterized by. ¶ 가느스름하다 be thinnish.

**스리랑카** Sri Lanka.

**스릴** 《전율》 a thrill. ¶ ~ 있는 thrilling; adventuresome 《life》 / ~을 느끼다 have a kick 〔thrill〕 《from》; be thrilled 《by》 / 그 영화는 ~ 만점이었다 The movie was full of thrills. *or* The movie was really thrilling.

**스릴러** 《공포 영화·소설 등》 a thriller.

**스마트하다** (be) smart; stylish; chic; 《옷차림이》 (be) smartly dressed; 《풍채가》 have a smart appearance.

**스매시** 〖테니스·탁구〗 smashing; a smash. ~하다 smash 《a ball》; hit 《a ball》 with a smash.

**스멀거리다** itch; feel creepy 〔itchy, crawly〕. ¶ 등이 ~ *one's* back itches / 온몸이 스멀거린다 I feel itchy all over.

**스멀스멀** itchy; creepy; crawly.

**스모그** smog. ¶ ~ 경보 a smog warning 〔alert〕 / ~가 심한 smoggy; smog-laden 《city》 / ~로 뒤덮인 smog-bound 《Seoul》 / 광화학 ~ photo-chemical smog.

**스무** twenty. ¶ ~번째 the twentieth / ~날 twenty days; the 20th day / 사과 ~개 twenty apples; a score of apples / ~살 된 청년 a young man twenty years old; a young man of twenty. ◉ ~고개 (the game of) "Twenty Questions".

**스무드하다** (be) smooth. ¶ (일이) 스무드하게 되어 나가다 go on smoothly 〔without a hitch〕.

**스물** twenty; a score; 《스무살》 twenty years of age. ¶ ~ 하나 twenty-one / 아직 ~ 안짝이다 I am still in my teens.

**스미다** soak in 〔into, through〕; sink in(to); infiltrate 《into, through》; permeate 《the soil》. ¶ 스며들다 《액체·냄새 등이》 soak 〔sink, seep〕 into; infiltrate into; 《사상·감정이》 be impressed 《on *one's* mind》; sink into 《*one's* mind》; penetrate; 《추위 등이》 be biting; be piercing / 천천히 스며들다 soak into 《*a thing*》 bit by bit / 물이 스며들지 않다 do not let in water; be watertight 〔waterproof〕 / 스며나오다 soak out; ooze 〔seep〕 out; exude; transude / 땀이 셔츠에 ~ the perspiration soaks through *one's* shirt; *one's* shirt is wet with perspiration / 추위가 뼛속까지 스며들다 The cold pierces to the marrow of my bones. / 물은 땅에 스며든다 Water permeates the soil. / 편지에는 딸에 대한 그의 깊은 애정이 스며 있었다 His deep affection for his daughter permeated his letter. / 그녀의 말이 내 가슴에 스며들었다 Her words penetrated my mind.

**스미스소니언박물관** the Smithsonian national museum.

**스스럼없다** feel at (*one's*) ease 《in *a person's* presence》; be self-assured; act naturally; do not worry 《about》. ¶ 스스럼없이 without constraint 〔reserve〕; unreservedly; freely; without hesitation / 스스럼없는 사이 《on》 frank 〔intimate〕 terms 《with…》/ 스스럼없는 태도 an unconstrained manner / 스스럼없이 이야기하다 talk in a familiar way; speak without restraint 〔reserve〕.

**스스럽다** (be) diffident; reserved; shy; feel「constrained 〔ill at ease, uneasy〕; have scruples 《about *doing*》; have regard 《*a person's* feeling》.
¶ 스스럽지 않은 친구 a candid 〔an intimate〕 friend; a friend on frank terms / 스스러워하는 태도 a constrained manner 〔air〕; an air of constraint / 스스러워하지 않다 feel at (*one's*) ease; act naturally; have no regard 《for *a person's* feeling》; have no scruples 《about *doing*》/ 그녀는 선배를 대하면 늘 스스러워한다 She always feels ill at ease with her seniors. / 그는 누구에게나 스스럽지 않게 군다 He is free and easy with everybody. / 필요하신 것은 스스러워 마시고 말씀하십시오 Don't scruple to ask for anything you want.

**스스로** ① 《저절로》 naturally; spontaneously; of its own accord; of 〔by〕 itself; automatically (자동적으로). ¶ 문이 ~ 열렸다 The door opened all by itself 〔automatically〕. / 충치 하나가 ~ 빠졌다 A decayed tooth has come out of itself.
② 《몸소》 (for) *oneself;* in person; personally; 《자발적》 of *one's* own accord 〔free will, choice〕; on *one's* own initiative. ¶ ~ 하다 do it *oneself* / ~ 돌아(다)보다 reflect on *oneself* 〔*one's* own conduct〕/ ~ 소개하다 introduce *oneself* / 그건 그가 ~ 부른 재앙이다 He has brought the calamity on himself. / 네가 ~ 갈 필요는 없다 You don't have to go yourself 〔in person〕. / 그녀는 ~ 퇴학했다 She left school of her own accord.
③ 《혼자서》 alone; for 〔by〕 *oneself;* by *one's* own efforts 〔account〕; single-handed(ly); unaided. ¶ ~ 하다 do 《*a thing*》 single-handed; go it alone / ~ 결정하다 decide 《*a matter*》 for *oneself* / ~ 연구하다 study 《it》 for *oneself* / 자기 일은 ~ 해라 Do your work (by) yourself.
④ [명사적] *oneself.* ¶ 내 ~ 말하기는 이상하지만 though I say it myself / ~를 괴롭히다 torture *oneself* / ~를 이기다 control *oneself;* conquer (*one*)*self;* be master of *oneself* / ~를 잊다 get carried away; forget *oneself;* go beyond *oneself* / ~(에게) 묻다 ask *oneself* / ~를 알라 Know thyself. / 하늘은 ~ 돕는 자를 돕는다 《속담》 Heaven 〔God〕 helps those who help themselves.

**스승** a teacher; a master. ¶ ~의 날 the Teachers' Day / ~의 은혜 the favors of *one's* teacher / ~과 제자 master and disciple; teacher and pupil / ~ 밑에서 배우다 study under 《*a person*》; take lessons 《in *Kayagŭm* from *a person*》/ ~으로 받들다〔섬기다〕 look up to 《*a person*》 as *one's* mentor 〔preceptor〕.

**스와질란드** 《나라 이름》 (the Kingdom of ) Swaziland. ¶ ~(사람)의 Swazi.
◉ ~사람 a Swazi (*pl.* ~(s)).

**스와프** 《교환》《구어》 swap. ~하다 do a swap; swap 《with》. ◉ ~거래 〖경제〗 a swap transaction. ~협정 〖경제〗 a swap arrangement.

**스웨덴** (the Kingdom of) Sweden. ¶ ~(사람)의 Swedish. ◉ ~말 Swedish. ~사람 a Swede. ~ 체조 Swedish gymnastics.

**스웨터** a sweater; a pullover (머리로 부터 입는). ¶ ~를 뜨다 knit a sweater.

**스위스** [<*Suisse* (F.)] Switzerland. ¶ ~의 Swiss / ~제의 《a watch》 of Swiss make; Swiss-made. ◉ ~사람 a Swiss. ~ 연방 공화국 the Swiss Confederation.

**스위치** a switch; a light switch (전등의). ¶ ~를 넣다〔끄다〕 switch 〔turn〕 《the light》 on 〔off〕/ 전등 ~를 끄다 switch 〔turn〕 off an electric light / 이것은 저절로 ~가 꺼지게 되어 있다 It switches itself off. ◉ ~히터 〖야구〗 a switch-hitter.

**스위트룸** 《호텔 따위의》 a suite of rooms.

**스위퍼** 〖축구〗 a sweeper.

**스윙** 〖음악〗 swing (music); 〖스포츠〗 a 《long》 swing.

**스쳐보다** look askance 〔sideways〕 at 《*a person*》; give 《*a person*》 a sidelong look; glance sideways 《at》; cast 〔look with〕 a sidelong glance 《at》. ¶ 그녀는 나를 스쳐보기만 하고 그냥 지나갔다 She passed by with only a side glance at me.

**스치다** graze; flit (생각 등이); 《스쳐 지나가다》 go past by 《*a person*》; brush past 《*a person*》; 《마찰하다》 rub 〔chafe, scrape〕 《against》; be rubbed; 《수면 등을》 skim; scud.
¶ 나뭇잎이 스치는 소리 rustling 〔a rustle〕 of leaves / (탄알이) 어깨를 ～ go 〔whiz〕 past *one's* shoulder / 스칠 듯이 close to 《the rocks》; 《pass》 by a (close) shave / 소녀는 스쳐 지나가며 나에게 미소를 지었다 The girl smiled at me as we passed each other. / 새가 물을 스칠 듯이 날아갔다 A bird skimmed over the water. / 의심스런 생각이 그의 뇌리를 스쳤다 A suspicion flitted across his mind. / 그는 피부가 스쳐서 벗겨졌다 He has rubbed the skin off. / 옷깃만 스치는 것도 전생의 인연 Even a chance meeting is due to the Karma in a previous life.

**스카시** 〖컴퓨터〗 SCSI. 〔<*S*mall *C*omputer *S*ystem *I*nterface〕 (컴퓨터 주변 장치를 연결할 때 사용되는 고속의 병렬 인터페이스).

**스카우트** a scout. ～하다 scout (for) 《a promising player》; recruit 《new members》. ¶ 코치는 유망한 선수를 ～하러 다녔다 The coach scouted around for a promising player. / 그들은 젊은 인재들을 ～하려고 기를 쓰고 있다 They are eager to scout 「young talented people 〔young talent〕. (★ talent는 「재능있는 사람들」이라는 뜻의 집합명사).

**스카이** the sky. ◉ ～다이버 a skydiver. ～다이빙 skydiving: ～다이빙하다 skydive. ～라운지 a sky lounge. ～라인 a skyline (하늘을 배경으로 한 건물 등의 윤곽선). ～블루 sky blue. ～웨이 a skyway; a (scenic) mountain highway.

**스카치** 《위스키》 Scotch whiskey; 《모직》 tweed 《suit》; 《옷》 《in》 (Scotch) tweeds; 《털실》 (Scotch) woolen.
◉ ～테리어 〖동물〗 a Scotch 〔Scottish〕 terrier. ～테이프 Scotch tape (상표 이름); cellophane tape.

**스카프** 《장식·방한용의 얇은 천》 a scarf.

**스칸디나비아** Scandinavia. ¶ ～의 Scandinavian. ◉ ～반도 the Scandinavian Peninsula. ～사람 a Scandinavian.

**스칼러십** a scholarship. ¶ ～을 받다 receive a scholarship / ～을 받아 대학에 다니다 attend a university on a scholarship.

**스캐너** 〖컴퓨터〗 a scanner.

**스캔들** 《추문》 a scandal. ¶ ～을 무마하다 cover up a scandal / ～에 말려들다 get involved in a scandal / 그 ～은 세상에 쫙 퍼졌다 The scandal was noised abroad. / 정계의 ～을 폭로하다 expose the scandal in the political circles.

**스커드 미사일** 〖군사〗 a scud missile.

**스커트** a skirt. ¶ 롱〔타이트, 플레어, 플리트〕 ～ a long 〔tight, flared, pleated〕 skirt / 미니 ～ a miniskirt / ～의 주름 a pleat 〔gather〕 on a skirt / ～를 길게〔짧게〕 하다 make the skirt longer 〔shorter〕 / ～를 입다〔벗다〕 put on 〔take off, remove〕 *one's* skirt / 유행이 변함에 따라 ～ 길이가 짧아지기도 하고 길어지기도 한다 When fashions change, hemlines are raised or lower.

**스컹크** 〖동물〗 a skunk.

**스케이트** (a pair of ) skates. ¶ 스피드 ～ 선수권 대회 a speed skating championship / ～를 잘〔못〕타다 be good 〔no good, poor〕 at skating / ～ 타러 가다 go skating / ～를 타다 skate 《on the ice》; do skating. ◉ ～보드 a skateboard. ～장 a skating 〔an ice〕 rink; 《경기용》 an ice arena 《미》. ～화 《put on》 skates.

**스케일** a scale (규모); a caliber (도량). ¶ ～이 큰〔작은〕 large-〔small-〕scale 《plans》 / ～이 큰〔작은〕 사람 a man of large 〔small〕 caliber / 그는 ～이 큰 경영자이다 He is a high-caliber manager. / ～이 큰 그들의 구상에는 놀라지 않을 수 없었다 The huge scale of their project simply filled me with admiration.

**스케줄** a schedule; a plan; a program. ¶ 꽉 찬〔빡빡한〕 ～ a crowded 〔crammed, heavy, tight〕 schedule / ～대로 as scheduled; on schedule / ～을 짜다 make 〔map, lay〕 out a schedule 《for, of 》/ ～을 고치다 reschedule / ～대로 진행하다 proceed in accordance with the schedule; go by *one's* schedule / 나의 ～은 아주 빡빡했다 My schedule was very tight. / 그는 우리를 환영하기 위해 ～에 쫓기는 바쁜 생활에서 시간을 짜냈다 He squeezed time out of his schedule-chasing life to welcome us.

**스케치** sketching (사생); a sketch (사

생화). ～하다 sketch; make a sketch of《*a thing*》. ¶ ～풍의 sketchy / ～하러 가다 go sketching. ◉ ～북 a sketchbook.

**스코어** a score. ¶ ～를 기록하다 keep the score《of》/ ～를 따다 score up; record the score / 3대 2의 ～로 우리 팀이 이겼다 Our team won by a score of 3 to 2. / 2대 2의 타이 ～다 The score is tied at 2 to 2. ◉ ～보드 a scoreboard. ～북 a scorebook.

**스코틀랜드** Scotland. ¶ ～의 Scottish; Scotch. ◉ ～말 Scotch. ～사람 a Scotchman; a Scot; the Scotch [총칭].

**스콜**〖기상〗a squall.

**스콜라철학**(―哲學) Scholasticism; Scholastic philosophy. ◉ ～자 a Scholastic; a Schoolman.

**스쿠너**《종범식 범선》a schooner.

**스쿠버**《수중 호흡기》a scuba. [<*s*elf=*c*ontained *u*nderwater *b*reathing *a*pparatus] ◉ ～다이빙 scuba diving.

**스쿠터** a (motor) scooter. ¶ ～를 타다 take 〔have〕 a ride on a (motor) scooter.

**스쿠프**《특종》a scoop; a beat《미》. ～하다 scoop《news, a rival paper》. ¶ 뇌물사건을 ～하여 다른 신문들을 앞지르다 scoop 〔beat〕 all the other papers with a payoff scandal.

**스쿨** a school. ◉ ～버스 a school bus.

**스쿼시**《음료》《lemon》squash;《운동》squash tennis.

**스퀘어댄스** a square dance. ¶ ～를 추다 dance 〔perform, have〕 a square dance.

**스퀴즈(플레이)**〖야구〗a squeeze (play). ～하다 run 〔try〕 a squeeze.

**스크래치 파일**〖컴퓨터〗a scratch file.

**스크랩** ①《신문·잡지 따위의》(a) scrap; a clipping《미》; a cutting《영》. ¶ ～(을) 하다 clip (out)《an article》. ②《폐물》scrap. ¶ ～으로 만들다 scrap《an old car》/ ～으로 팔다 sell《a dismantled ship》as 〔for〕 scrap. ◉ ～북 a scrapbook.

**스크럼**《럭비》a scrum; a scrimmage《주로 미》; a scrummage《영》. ¶ ～을 짜다 form 〔line up for〕 a scrummage; scrimmage / ～을 풀다 break up a scrummage.

**스크루**《배의》a screw (propeller);《나사》a screw. ◉ ～드라이버《공구》a screwdriver;《칵테일》(a glass of) screwdriver.

**스크린**《영사막》a screen;《영화계》the screen. ¶ ～에 나오다 appear on the screen; play for the screen. ◉ ～쿼터 screen quota. ～테스트 a screen test. ～플레이〖농구〗a screen-play.

**스크립터**〖영화〗a continuity clerk 〔man, girl〕(★「스크립터」는 잘못 쓰인 영어. 영어의 scriptwriter는「시나리오 작가」).

**스크립트** a《TV》script. ◉ ～걸 a script 〔continuity〕 girl.

**스키**《스포츠》(snow) skiing;《기구》(a pair of) skis. ¶ ～하러 가다 go skiing / ～를 타다〔하다〕 go 〔slide〕 on skis; ski / ～를 타고 산을 내려오다 ski down a hill / ～를 신다 put on skis. ◉ ～경기 a skiing match. ～교사 a ski instructor. ～구두〔화〕《a pair of》ski boots. ～대회 a ski competition. ～리프트 a ski 〔chair〕 lift. ～모자 a ski cap. ～복 a ski suit 〔outfit〕. ～부대〖군사〗a ski-borne troop. ～장 a skiing ground; a ski area 〔slope〕. ～점프 a ski jump. 노르딕～ nordic skiing. 알파인～ alpine skiing.

**스키트**《사격의》skeet shooting.

**스킨** skin. ◉ ～로션 skin lotion. ～크림 skin cream.

**스킨다이빙** skin diving. ～하다 skin-dive.

**스타** a (movie) star. ¶ 영화 ～ a film 〔movie〕 star / 인기 ～ a box-office star / ～ 총출연의 star-studded / ～가 되다 become a star; be starred; rise to stardom. ◉ ～시스템 the star system. ～플레이어 a star player.

**스타덤** stardom. ¶ ～에 오르다 enter 〔achieve, jump to〕 stardom.

**스타디움** a stadium (*pl.* ～s, -dia).

**스타우트**《흑맥주》stout.

**스타워스**〖군사〗Star Wars 〔미국의 전력 방위 구상(Strategic Defence Initiative의 별칭)〕.

**스타인벡**《미국의 소설가》John Ernest Steinbeck (1902-1968).

**스타일**《몸매》a form; *one's* figure;《양식·복장 따위의》a 〔*one's*〕 style; a mode;《문체》a writing style. ¶ 최신 유행의 ～ the latest style 〔pattern〕/ ～ 구기다 get 〔look〕 out of shape; be put out of countenance / 그녀는 ～이 좋다〔나쁘다〕 She has a good 〔poor〕 figure. / 그의 문장 ～은 간단명료하다 His writing style is clear and explicit. ◉ ～리스트《문장의》a stylist; a stylish writer;《복장의》a dandy; a stylish dresser (멋쟁이); a stylist (디자이너 등). ～북 a stylebook.

**스타카토**〖음악〗*staccato* (It.).

**스타킹** (a pair of) stockings. ¶ 팬티 ～ (a pair of) panty hose; tights《영》/

심레스~ seamless stockings / 나일론 ~ nylon stockings / ~을 신다[벗다] pull stockings on [off].
**스타터** 《출발 신호인》 a starter; 《자동차의》 a (self-)starter.
**스타트** a start; point of departure (출발점); a getaway (경마·자동차 등의). ~하다 start; make a start; get started. ¶ ~에서 골인 지점까지 from start to finish / ~가 좋다[나쁘다] start well [poorly]; start quick [slow]; make a good [poor] start / ~를 끊다 (make a) start; get off the mark / ~를 잘못하다 make a wrong [bad] start / 남보다 ~가 빠르다 have a good start of others / 이번 계획은 ~가 좋았다 The plan this time has gotten a good start. ◉ ~대 《수영 경기의》 a starting box. ~라인 a starting line: ~ 라인에 서다 toe the line [mark, scratch]. ~신호 a starting signal.
**스타팅** starting. ◉ ~게이트 《승마 등의》 a starting gate. ~멤버 a starting member [line-up]. ~블록 《육상의》 a starting block.
**스태그플레이션** 〖경제〗 stagflation. [< *stag*nation+in*flation*]
**스태미나** stamina; staying power. ¶ ~가 있다[없다] have [lack] stamina / ~를 기르다 develop [build up] *one's* stamina. ◉ ~식(食) sustaining food.
**스태프** the staff. ¶ ~ 일동 all the members of the staff / ~의 일원이다 be on the staff 《of》.
**스탠더드** a standard. ¶ ~를 정하다 fix [set up] a standard. ◉ ~넘버 〖음악〗 a standard number.
**스탠드** ① 《관람석》 the stands; 《지붕 없는》 the bleachers 《미》. ¶ ~를 메운 관중 spectators filling the stand to capacity. ② 《대(臺)》 a stand. ¶ 잉크~ an inkstand. ③ 《탁상등》 a desk lamp; a bedside lamp; a floor lamp (바닥에 놓는). ④ 《간이 식당》 a food stand; a snack bar. ⑤ 《판매장》 a 《fruit》 stand; a booth. ⑥ 《주유소》 a gas [filling] station. ◉ ~플레이 a grandstand play: ~ 플레이를 하다 play to the grandstands.
**스탠스** 〖야구·골프〗 a stance.
**스탬프** a stamp; 《날짜 도장》 a datemark; 《우편의 소인》 a postmark. ¶ ~를 찍다 stamp 《a card》; affix a stamp 《on a card》; 《소인을》 post stamp. ◉ ~잉크 stamp ink.
**스턴트맨** 《영화에서 위험한 장면의 대역》 a stunt man. (★ 여성은 a stunt woman [girl] 이라고 함).
**스테레오**(-) 《음향장치》 a stereo (*pl.* ~s); a stereo set; 《방식》 the stereophonic sound (reproduction) system. ¶ ~로 듣다 listen to 《a recording of a symphony》 on stereo. ◉ ~녹음 stereo(phonic) recording. ~레코드 a stereo(phonic) record [disk]. ~음향 stereophony. ~재생 장치 a stereophonic sound reproduction system. ~전축 a stereophonic [stereo] phonograph. ~테이프 a stereo tape.
**스테레오판**(—版) 〖인쇄〗 stereo(type).
**스테로이드** 〖생화학〗 steroid (호르몬제의 일종).
**스테아린** 〖화학〗 stearin(e).
**스테이션** a (railroad) station. ¶ 우주~ a space station. ◉ ~왜건 a station wagon.
**스테이지** a stage. ⇨ 무대. ¶ ~를 밟다 [떠나다] go on [off] the stage. ◉ ~댄스 a stage dance. ~매니저 a stage manager. ~세트 a stage set.
**스테이크** a (grilled) steak; a beefsteak. ◉ ~소스 (a) steak sauce.
**스테이플** a staple. ¶ ~을 찍다 staple 《sheets of paper》 together.
**스테이플파이버** staple fiber; rayon staple. ¶ ~가 섞인 mixed with staple fiber.
**스테인드글라스** stained glass.
**스테인리스(강**(鋼)) stainless steel. ¶ ~제(製)의 《a gas range》 of stainless steel; stainless-steel 《knife》.
**스텐실** a stencil. ◉ ~판 a stencil plate. ~ 페이퍼 stencil paper.
**스텔스** 〖군사〗 stealth. ◉ ~기능 stealth function. ~전투기 a stealth fighter. ~전함 a stealth battleship. ~폭격기 a stealth bomber. ~효과 a stealth effect.
**스텝** ① 《춤의》 a step. ¶ ~을 밟다 do [perform] dance steps; dance 《a waltz》. ② 《초원》 a steppe.
**스토브** a stove; a heater. ¶ 가스 ~ a gas heater [stove] / 석유[전기] ~ an oil [electric] heater / ~를 피우다 make a fire in the stove; light a stove [heater]. ◉ ~리그 〖야구〗 the trading of players in the off season.
**스토아** ¶ ~주의 [철학] Stoicism / ~학파 the Stoic school.
**스토어** a store; a shop 《영》.
**스토커** 《비행을 목적으로 하는 미행자》 a stalker; a criminal who follows 《*a woman*》 over a period of time 《in order to...》.

**스토킹** 《사람을 미행하는 행위》 stalking.
**스톡** 《재고》 a stock. ¶ 재료의 ~이 많다 keep a large stock of materials on hand.
**스톱** a stop. ~하다 stop. ¶ 이 열차는 각역마다 다 ~한다 This train stops at every station. ◉ ~워치 a stopwatch: ~ 워치를 누르다 start a stopwatch.
**스튜** 〖요리〗 (a) stew. ¶ 비프 ~ beef stew; stewed beef. ◉ ~냄비 a saucepan; a stewpan 《영》.
**스튜던트파워** student power.
**스튜디오** a studio (*pl.* ~s). ◉ 영화~ a film studio; a movie lot 《미》.
**스튜어디스** a stewardess; an air-hostess; a flight attendant.
**스트라이크** ① 《파업》 a strike; a walkout. ~하다 strike; go on (a) strike; walk out. ¶ ~ 중지 명령 a stop-strike order / ~중이다 be on (a) strike; a strike is on / ~를 중지하다 halt 〔call off〕 a strike. ② 〖야구·볼링〗 a strike. ¶ ~가 되다 score a strike / 제3구는 ~ The third ball scored a strike. / 카운트는 원 ~ 투 볼 The (batter's) count is two (balls), one (strike). (★ 어순에 주의할 것).
◉ ~존 the strike zone.
**스트럭아웃** 〖야구〗 a strikeout. ¶ ~이 되다 be 〔get〕 struck out / ~을 먹이다 〔시키다〕 strike 《the batter》 out.
**스트레스** 〖의학〗 stress. ¶ ~가 많은 stressful 《situations》 / ~에 의한 궤양 a stress ulcer / ~를 해소하다 get rid of stress 《by engaging in sports》; dispel a stress / ~가 쌓인다 Stress is building up. / 나는 많은 ~를 받아 왔다 I've been under so much stress. / 그의 위장병은 ~가 원인이다 His stomach disorder results from emotional stress. / 탁구라도 치면서 ~를 풀자 Let's play pingpong to relax. (★ relax는 「긴장을 풀다」의 뜻). ◉ ~산업 stress industry. ~요인 a stressor; a cause of stress. ~학설 the stress theory.
**스트레이트** ① 《운동 경기의》 a straight (victory); 〖야구〗 a straight ball 〔pitch〕; 〖권투〗 《give》 a straight punch 《on》. ¶ ~로 이기다 win a straight victory 《over》; win in straight sets / ~로 지다 suffer a straight defeat 《from》; lose in straight sets. ② 《술 따위》 straight 《미》; neat 《영》. ¶ 위스키를 ~로 마시다 drink whiskey straight.
**스트렙토마이신** 〖약〗 streptomycin.
**스트로** a straw; a sipper (종이로 만든). ¶ ~로 빨다 suck 《milk》 through a straw 〔sipper〕.
**스트로보** 〖사진〗 a stroboscope; a strobe. ◉ ~전구 a strobo light. ~촬영 speed light photography. ~플래시 a strobo flash.
**스트로크** 《골프·테니스·수영의》 a stroke. ¶ 원 ~의 차로 이기다〔지다〕 win 〔lose〕 《the race, competition》 by a stroke. ◉ ~플레이 stroke play.
**스트론튬** 〖화학〗 strontium (기호 Sr). ◉ ~석 strontianite.
**스트리크닌** 〖약〗 strychnin(e); strychnia.
**스트리킹** streaking.
**스트리퍼** a stripper; a stripteaser.
**스트립쇼** a strip show; a striptease.
**스티로폼** 《상표명》 Styrofoam.
**스티커** a sticker; a 〔an adhesive〕 label. ¶ ~를 차체에 붙이다 put a sticker on the body of a car.
**스틱** a (walking) stick; a cane; 《하키의》 a hockey stick.
**스틸** ① 《강철》 steel. ② 〖야구〗 a steal. ¶ 홈 ~하다 steal home. ③ 〖영화〗 a still (picture).
**스팀** steam. ¶ ~이 들어오다 be steam=heated; be heated by steam / ~으로 방을 덥게 하다 heat a room by steam. ◉ ~난방〔설비〕 steam heating; 《장치》 a steam heater.
**스파게티** spaghetti.
**스파르타** Sparta. ¶ ~식의 Spartan. ◉ ~사람 a Spartan. ~(식) 교육 Spartan training 〔education〕.
**스파링** 〖권투〗 sparring. ◉ ~파트너 *one's* sparring partner.
**스파이** a spy; a secret 〔an espionage〕 agent. ⇨ 간첩, 첩보원. ¶ 이중 ~ a double (secret) agent / 산업 ~ an industry spy; industrial espionage (행위) / ~ 임무를 띠고 on a spy mission / ~ 노릇을 하다 spy; act as spy / ~ 혐의로 체포되다 be arrested under suspicion of being a spy.
◉ ~단 a spy ring. ~망 an espionage chain; a network of spies. ~비행 a spy 〔an espionage〕 flight; an intelligence flight. ~소설 a spy novel. ~영화 an espionage movie; a spy film. ~위성 a spy satellite. ~행위 spying; espionage. ~활동 espionage activities.
**스파이크** 《구두의》 a spike; 〖야구〗 spiking; 《배구의》 spiking; a spike. ~하다 spike 《the first baseman》; 《배구에서》 spike (the ball). ◉ ~구두〔화〕 spiked shoes.

**스파크** 〖전기〗 a spark. ～하다 spark. ¶ ～가 가스를 점화시켰다 A spark ignited the gas.
**스패너** a wrench 《미》; a spanner 《영》. ◉ 멍키〔자재〕 ～ a monkey wrench 〔spanner〕; a screw wrench.
**스퍼트** 〖스포츠〗 a spurt. ～하다 spurt; make 〔put on〕 a spurt. ¶ 라스트 ～ 《put on》 the last spurt.
**스펀지** (a) sponge. ⇨ 해면. ¶ ～로 몸을 닦다 wash *oneself* with sponge.
◉ ～고무 sponge rubber. ～볼 a sponge ball. ～케이크 sponge cake.
**스페어** a spare; spare parts. ◉ ～타이어 a spare tire.
**스페이드** a spade. ¶ ～ 에이스 an ace of spades.
**스페이스** 《공간》 (a) space; room; 《행간·자간》 (a) space. ¶ ～를 남기다〔두다〕 space (out) 《letters, words》; make room 《for》 / 여기에는 책상을 놓을 ～가 없다 There's no room 〔space〕 to put a desk in here. / 더블 ～로 타이프를 쳐 주시오 Please type double-spaced. / 한 사람 더 들어갈 ～가 있을까 Is there space for one more person? / 사과나무는 10m의 ～를 두고 심어져 있다 The apple trees are spaced out 10 meters apart.
**스페이스 셔틀** a space shuttle.
**스페인** Spain. ¶ ～의 Spanish. ◉ ～말 Spanish; the Spanish language. ～사람 a Spaniard; the Spanish [총칭].
**스펙터클** a spectacle. ◉ ～영화 a film full of spectacles; a spectacular film.
**스펙트럼** a spectrum (*pl.* ～s, -tra).
◉ ～분석 〖광학〗 spectrum analysis. ～사진 a spectrogram. ～선 a spectral line.
**스펠(링)** spelling. ⇨ 철자(綴字). ¶ ～은 d, o, g입니다 It is spelt d-o-g.
**스포이트** [< *spuit* (D.)] 《만년필의》 a fountainpen filler.
**스포츠** sports (전체); a sport (하나의). ¶ ～를 좋아하는 sports-minded / ～를 하다 practice 〔go in for〕 a sport; enjoy 〔take part in〕 sports / 너는 무슨 ～를 좋아하느냐 What sports do you 「like 〔go in for〕? / 너는 어떤 ～를할 줄 아느냐 Do you play any sports? / 그는 보는 ～가 아니라 하는 ～를 좋아한다 He is a lover of participant sports, not of spectator sports.
◉ ～계 the sporting world; sportsdom 《미》. ～과학 연구소 the Sports Science Institute. ～기자 a sportswriter. ～난 a sports section 〔column〕. ～뉴스 (a piece of) sports news. ～드링크 a sports drink. ～맨 a sportsman; an athlete: ～맨십 sportsmanship / ～맨다운〔답지않은〕 sportsmanlike 〔unsportsmanlike〕. ～면 《신문의》 a sports page. ～방송 sportscasting; a sportscast (1회의): ～ 방송을 하다 broadcast a sports event. ～센터 a sports center. ～셔츠 a sports shirt. ～신문 a sports (news) paper 〔journal〕. ～아나운서 a sports announcer; a sportscaster. ～용어 sporting terms; sports jargon. ～용품 sports equipment; sporting goods. ～웨어 [집합적] sportswear. ～의학 sports medicine. ～잡지 a sports magazine. ～정신 sportsmanship; (the) sporting spirit. ～카 a sports car. ～평론가 a sports commentator 〔columnist〕. ～하이라이트 sports highlights. ～화 sports shoes. ～활동 sporting activities.
**스포크** 《바퀴살》 a radius; a spoke.
**스포크스맨** a spokesman. ⇨ 대변인.
**스포트라이트** a spotlight. ¶ ～를 비추다 direct 〔turn, focus〕 a spotlight 《on》 / ～를 받고 있다 be in the spotlight.
**스포티하다** (be) sporty. ¶ 스포티한 차림으로 in sporty outfits.
**스폰서** a sponsor. ¶ 라디오〔TV〕 프로의 ～ a radio 〔TV〕 program sponsor / ～가 되다 sponsor 《a TV program》.
**스폿** a spot. ◉ ～광고 spot advertising. ～뉴스 spot news. ～방송 (a) spot announcement.
**스푼** a spoon. ¶ ～으로 하나 a spoonful 《of salt》 / ～으로 뜨다 spoon up 〔out〕 《soup》. ◉ ～레이스 an egg-and-spoon race.
**스프레이** 《분무기》 a spray. ¶ ～통 a spray (can) / ～를 뿌리다 put spray on 《*one's* hair》.
**스프롤 현상**(—現象) 《도시의》 sprawling; urban sprawl.
**스프린터** 〖스포츠〗 a sprinter.
**스프링** ① 《용수철》 a spring. ¶ ～ 침대 a spring bed. ② 《봄》 spring(time).
◉ ～보드 《수영》 a springboard. ～코트 a topcoat; a light overcoat.
**스프링클러** 《자동살수장치》 a sprinkler.
**스피드** speed. ⇨ 속도(速度). ¶ ～가 빠른 speedy / 보통 ～로 at an ordinary speed / 풀～로 at full speed / 굉장한 ～로 at a terrific 〔furious, breakneck〕 speed / 시속 50마일의 ～ 50 m.p.h. speed / ～를 올리다〔내다〕 speed up; increase 〔gather, pick up〕 speed;

put on 〔get up〕 speed / ～를 떨어뜨리다〔낮추다〕 decrease 〔reduce〕 speed; slow down 〔up〕 / 더 ～를 내라고 말하다 ask 〔tell〕《the driver》 to drive faster / 시속 200킬로의 ～를 내다 get up to 〔develop〕(a speed of) 200 kilometers an hour / 일에 좀더 ～를 내라 Put a little more speed in your work.
◉ ～건 a speed gun. ～광 a speed maniac 〔fiend《미》〕. ～레이스 a speed race. ～볼 〖야구〗 a speed 〔fast〕 ball. ～스케이팅 speed skating: ～ 스케이팅 선수권 대회 a speed skating championship meet. ～시대 the age of speed. ～업 speeding up; a speed-up: ～업하다 speed up. ～제한 speed regulation; a speed limit.

**스피디하다** (be) speedy. ¶ 스피디한 주자 a speedy runner.

**스피로헤타** 《파상균》 a spiroch(a)ete.

**스피츠** 〖동물〗 a spitz (dog).

**스피치** a speech. ¶ 테이블 ～ an after-dinner speech / ～를 하다 make 〔deliver〕 a speech. ◉ ～콘테스트 a speech contest.

**스피커** 《확성기》 a (loud)speaker; 《라디오의》 a radio speaker. ¶ 고음용 ～ a tweeter / 저음용 ～ a woofer / ～로 방송하다 announce through a loudspeaker.

**스핑크스** a sphinx (*pl.* ～es, sphinges).

**슬개골**(膝蓋骨) 〖해부〗 the kneepan; the kneecap; the patella (*pl.* -lae).

**슬그머니** ⇨ 살그머니.

**슬금슬금** ⇨ 살금살금. ¶ ～ 달아나다 run away stealthily; slip away; sneak off 〔away〕 / ～뒤를 밟다 shadow《*a person*》 stealthily / ～ 훔쳐보다 steal a glance 《at》; look 〔glance〕 furtively 《at》; cast 〔throw〕 a furtive 〔surreptitious〕 glance 《at》.

**슬기** intelligence; sagacity; wisdom; prudence; sense. ¶ ～가 있다 have (good) sense; be intelligent.

**슬기롭다** (be) intelligent; sagacious; wise; bright; prudent; sensible. ¶ 슬기로운 사람 a man of wisdom 〔resources〕 / 슬기롭게 굴다 act wisely 〔sensibly〕 / 슬기롭지 못하다 be unwise 〔unintelligent〕; be injudicious 〔inadvisable〕; be dull / 정말이지 슬기롭지 못한 놈이군 What a senseless fellow he is!

**슬다**[1] ① 《없어지다》 disappear; break; be gone; vanish; wither. ¶ 땀띠〔뾰루지〕가 ～ the heat rash 〔the boil〕 disappears. ② 《채소가》 wither; wilt.

**슬다**[2] ① 《알을》 lay 《eggs》; blow (파리가 쉬를); spawn (물고기가). ¶ 파리가 쉬를 ～ a fly blows eggs. ② 《녹이》 gather 〔form〕 rust; rust; be rusted; get rusty. ¶ 녹슨 칼 a rusty sword / 쓰지 않아서 녹이 ～ rust from disuse.

**슬다**[3] 《풀기를 죽이다》 soften 《starched cloth》; get the stiffness out of.

**슬라브** Slav. ◉ ～말 Slavic: ～말의 Slavic. ～ 민족 the Slavs: ～ 민족의 Slavic. ～사람 a Slav; a Slavonian.

**슬라이더** 〖야구〗 a slider.

**슬라이드**[1] 《영사용》 a (lantern) slide; a transparency; 《현미경의》 a slide; 《계산척》 a slide rule. ¶ ～를 끼우다 slide down a slide / 컬러 ～를 스크린에 영사하다 project color slides on the screen / ～를 사용하며 강연하다 illustrate a lecture with slides. ◉ ～글라스 a slide. ～영사기 a slide 〔film-strip〕 projector.

**슬라이드**[2] 〖경제〗 《물가 변동에 따라 임금 등을 조절하는 일》 ¶ 임금을 물가 변동에 따라 ～시키다 Wages are 「indexed to the cost of living 〔index-linked〕. ◉ ～제(制) 〖경제〗 a sliding-scale (system): 우리 급료는 물가 ～제이다 We are paid on a sliding-scale.

**슬라이딩** 〖야구〗 sliding. ◉ ～태클 〖축구〗 a sliding tackle.

**슬랄롬** 〖스키〗 slalom.

**슬래그** 〖광물〗 slag.

**슬래브** a slab. ◉ ～지붕 a slab roof.

**슬랙스** 《a pair of》 slacks. ¶ ～를 입은 《a girl》 in slacks.

**슬램덩크** 〖농구〗 a slam dunk.

**슬랭** a slang word 〔expression〕; a word of slang; [총칭] slang.

**슬러거** 〖야구〗 a slugger; a hard hitter.

**슬럼** a slum. ¶ ～화하다 turn into slums. ◉ ～가(街) the slum quarters 〔areas〕; the slums.

**슬럼프** a slump. ¶ ～에 빠지다 hit 〔be in〕 a slump / ～에서 헤어나다 get 〔come〕 out of a slump.

**슬레이트** a slate. ¶ ～ 지붕 a slate roof / ～ 지붕의 slate-roofed 《house》 / ～로 지붕을 이다 slate a roof; 「cover a roof 〔roof a house〕 with slates.

**슬로건** a slogan; a motto (*pl.* ～(e)s). ¶ …라는 ～을 내걸고 under the slogan of… / ～을 내세우다 publish a slogan.

**슬로모션** slow motion. ¶ ～의 장면 a scene in slow motion / ～으로 《shoot the motions of a swimmer》 in slow motion. ◉ ～영화 a slow-motion picture 〔film〕.

**슬로바키아** 《국가 이름》 Slovakia.

**슬로베니아** 《유고연방의》 Slovenia. ◉ ~공화국 the Republic of Slovenia. ~인 a Slovenian.

**슬로프** a slope. ¶ ~를 미끄러져 내리다 slide down a slope.

**슬롯머신** a slot machine.

**슬리퍼** (a pair of) slippers; backless slippers; scuffs; mules. ¶ ~로 바꿔 신다 change into slippers / ~를 신다 have *one's* slippers on.

**슬립** ① 《여자 속옷》 a slip; an underslip. ② 《미끄러짐》 a slip. ~하다 slip; skid (옆으로). ¶ ~ 방지가 된 타이어 a skidproof tire. ◉ ~다운 〖권투〗 slip down.

**슬며시** ⇨ 살며시, 슬그머니.

**슬슬** ① 《천천히》 slowly; leisurely; 《조금씩》 gradually; bit by bit; little by little. ¶ ~ 일하다 work leisurely / ~ 걷다〔가다〕 walk 〔go along〕 at a snail's pace / 날씨가 ~ 추워지고 있다 It's getting colder and colder.
② 《달래다·꾀다》 《soothe》 gently; nicely; soothingly; artfully. ¶ 우는 아이를 ~ 달래다 soothe a crying baby gently / 아이를 ~ 달래어 약을 먹이다 coax a child to take its medicine / ~속여 먹다 swindle 《*a person*》 nicely / 그는 ~ 구슬리면 말을 잘 듣는다 Properly treated, he is perfectly easy to handle.
③ 《부드럽게》 《blow》 gently; softly; lightly. ¶ 봄바람이 ~불어 소풍가기에 아주 좋은 날씨다 There's a gentle spring breeze, and the weather is perfect for a picnic. / 상처를 ~문지르다 rub the wound lightly.
④ 《모르는 사이에》 unconsciously; unperceptibly. ¶ 식사를 잘하고 나니 그들의 마음이 ~ 풀리기 시작했다 After a good dinner, they began to thaw. / 눈이 ~ 녹아버렸다 The snow unconsciously melted away.

**슬쩍(슬쩍)** ⇨ 살짝(살짝). ¶ 일을 ~ 해치우다 make short work of 《*a thing*》 / 몸을 ~ 피하다 dodge 《it》 as quick as lightning; elude 《it》 nimbly.

**슬퍼하다** 《…을》 grieve 《at the news, over a friend's death》; be sad 《at》; be grieved 《at, over》; feel sad 《about》; feel sorrow 《for》; 《한탄하다》 deplore; lament; mourn 《for, over》; be distressed 《over》. ¶ 아무의 불행을 ~ feel sorry for 《*a person's*》 misfortune / 죽음을 ~ mourn 〔lament〕 《*a person's*》 death / 마음속으로 ~ be sad (and sorry) in *one's* heart / 자신의 불행〔불운〕을 ~ grieve about *one's* misfortunes; bewail *one's* ill fortune; sorrow over *one's* hard fate / 뭣 때문에 그는 슬퍼하고 있나 What is the reason for his sadness? / 그는 친구의 불행을 슬퍼하고 있다 He is sad at 〔with〕 his friend's mishap. / 그저 슬퍼만 하고 있을 때가 아니다 This is no time to give way simply to sorrow.

**슬프다** (be) sad; distressed; grieved; tearful; saddening; sorrowful; mournful; doleful; distressing; 《애처로운》 touching; pathetic; plaintive (목소리·음조 따위가).
¶ 슬픈 이야기 a sad tale 〔story〕; a pathetic story / 슬픈 소식 (a piece of) sad news / 슬픈 노래 an elegiac 〔a plaintive〕 song / 슬픈 목소리로 in a sad 〔plaintive〕 voice / 슬픈 나머지 in (the excess of) *one's* sorrow 〔grief〕 / 즐거울 때나 슬플 때나 in joy and in sorrow / 슬픈 얼굴을 하다 look sad 〔unhappy, sorrowful〕; have a sad look on *one's* face / 슬픈 경험을 하다 have a sad experience / 슬프도다 Alas! *or* Woe is me! / 그것을 생각하면 ~ It is sad to think of it. / 그를 생각하면 슬퍼진다 It makes me feel sorrow when I think of him. / 너무 슬퍼서 눈물도 안 나온다 My grief is too deep for tears.

**슬픔** sadness; sorrow; woe; 《비애》 grief; distress; 《비탄》 lament(ation); mourning. ¶ ~에 잠기다 be woebegone; be grief-stricken; be in deep grief / ~속에 살다 live in sorrow / ~에 겹다 be overwhelmed with grief; be overcome with sorrow / ~을 술로 달래다 drown *one's* sorrow in drink / ~과 기쁨이 엇갈리다 have a mingled feeling of joy and sorrow / 그녀는 자식을 잃고 ~에 잠겨 있다 She is greatly grieved over the death of her child. / 그녀는 ~이 지나쳐 병이 났다 She became ill through too much sorrow.

**슬피** sadly; sorrowfully; mournfully; plaintively; dolefully. ¶ ~ 울다 cry in a mournful manner.

**슬하**(膝下) the care 〔protection〕 of *one's* parents. ¶ 부모 ~에서 자라다 grow up under *one's* parents' wing(s) 〔*one's* parental care〕 / 부모 ~를 떠나다 leave home; live away from *one's* parents; leave 〔bid farewell to〕 *one's* parental roof.

**슴베** the handle end 《of a knife, plow

or hoe blade》; a tang; a fang.

**습격**(襲擊) an attack; an assault; a raid; a storm; a charge; an onslaught. ～하다 attack; make an attack 〔onset, a raid〕 on; raid; assault; swoop down 《upon》; fall 《on》. ¶ 불시에 ～하다 make a surprise attack 《on》; take 《the enemy》 by surprise / 집단으로 ～하다 gang up on / ～해서 점령하다 take 《a town》 by assault 〔storm〕. ◉ ～대 an attacking 〔a raid〕 force; a storming party.

**습관**(習慣) a habit (습성); a custom (관습); a practice (상습); (a) usage (관용); a convention (인습).

> 용법 **habit** 개인이 무의식적으로 반복하는 버릇. 종종, 바람직스럽지 못한 버릇을 뜻함. **custom** 장기간에 걸쳐 행해져 내려와 정착된 하나의 사회·단체의 관습. 또 개인에게 있어서는 거의 고정되다시피 한 습관. **practice** 개인적으로는 의식적으로 지속하는 버릇, 사회적으로는 관습, 관행 등에 두루 쓰인다.

¶ ～적 habitual; usual; customary; conventional / ～적으로 habitually; from habit; through 〔by〕 custom / ～(의 힘)으로 from 〔out of, by force of〕 habit / 평소의 ～ *one's* habitual ways / 일찍 일어나는〔담배 피우는〕 ～ the habit of 「early rising 〔smoking〕 / 예로부터의 ～ an old custom.

습관이: ～이 붙다 acquire 〔contract, form, pick up, take on〕 a habit; a habit grows upon *one* / 못된 ～이 붙다 contract 〔take to〕 a bad habit / …하는 ～이 있다 have 〔be in〕 the habit of 《*do*ing》.

습관에: ～에 따라(서) according to 〔in accordance with〕 custom / ～에 반하여 against 〔contrary to〕 custom / 전부터의 ～에 따르다 follow 〔conform to〕 the traditional custom.

습관을: ～을 붙이다〔기르다〕 form 〔cultivate, build up〕 a habit / ～을 버리다 discard 〔abandon, give up, throw aside〕 a habit; break (off) 〔shake off〕 a habit / 못된 ～을 고치다 《자신의》 get over 〔get rid of〕 the bad habit; break 〔cure〕 *oneself* of a bad habit; 《남의》 wean 《*a person*》 from a bad habit; break 〔cure〕 《*a person*》 of a bad habit.

¶ 악수하는 ～을 외국인에게서 배우다 pick up 〔catch〕 the habit of shaking hands from foreigners / ～은 제2의 천성이다 Habit is second nature. / ～이 되어 버렸다 It's getting to be a habit. 《미》 / 그는 못된 ～이 붙었다 He has fallen 〔got〕 into bad habit. / 아침식사를 하며 신문을 읽는 것이 그의 ～이었다 He was wont to read the paper at breakfast.

◉ ～성 tendency; habituation: ～성이 있는 habit-forming / ～성 의약품의 판매를 금지하다 ban sales of habit-forming medicines / 이 약은 ～성이 될 수 있다 This drug can be addictive.

**습기**(濕氣) moisture; damp(ness); humidity. ¶ ～ 있는〔많은〕 wet; moist; damp; soggy; humid / ～없는 dry; free from moisture / ～가 끼다〔차다〕 get damp; dampen; moisten; become damp 〔wet〕 / ～찬 공기 damp air / ～찬 장소 a damp place / ～없는 곳에 두다 keep 《*a thing*》 「in a dry place 〔free from moisture〕 / 오늘은 ～가 많다 It is so humid today. / ～가 많은 기후는 류머티스에 좋지않다 A humid 〔damp〕 climate is bad for rheumatism. / ～ 조심 《게시》 Guard against damp. / 서적 재중(在中) ― ～주의 《표시》 Books—to be kept perfectly dry.

**습도**(濕度) humidity. ¶ ～를 재다 measure the humidity 《of the atmosphere》 / ～가 높다 show a high percentage of humidity. ◉ ～계 a hygrometer: 자기(自記) ～계 a hygrograph.

**습득**(拾得) picking up; finding. ～하다 pick up; find 《lost property》. ◉ ～물 a find; a found article; findings; 《게시》 Lost and Found. ～자 a finder.

**습득**(習得) learning; acquirement. ～하다 master; learn; acquire 《an art》. ¶ 3개 국어를 ～하다 master three languages / 그는 불과 한달만에 자동차 운전기술을 ～했다 He mastered how to drive (a car) in only one month.

**습랭**(濕冷) 〘한의〙 rheumatism in the lower part of *one's* body.

**습성**(習性) an acquired habit; second nature; one's way(s). ⇨ 버릇, 습관. ¶ ～이 되다 become a habit; grow into a habit; [사람이 주어] contract a habit of / 나방은 빛 주위에 모이는 ～이 있다 Moths have the habit of gathering around the light.

**습성**(濕性) wetness; wet (in quality). ◉ ～늑막염 wet 〔moist〕 pleurisy; pleurisy with effusion. ～천식 humid asthma.

**습윤**(濕潤) moisture; dampness. ～하다

(be) wet; moist; damp.
**습자**(習字) penmanship; handwriting; 《붓글씨》 calligraphy. ～하다 practice 〔learn〕 handwriting 〔calligraphy〕.
◉ ～지 writing paper. ～책 a copy book; a writing book. 영어～ English penmanship.
**습작**(習作) a study; an *étude* (F.). ～하다 study.
**습전지**(濕電池) a galvanic battery.
**습종**(濕腫) 〖한의〗 abscesses and ulcers on the leg.
**습증**(濕症) rheumatism.
**습지**(濕地) 《습한 땅》 swampy land; damp 〔boggy〕 ground; marsh. ◉ ～대(帶) a damp area; marshy areas; wetlands.
**습진**(濕疹) 〖의학〗 eczema; moist 〔humid〕 tetter.
**습포**(濕布) a wet compress 〔pack, pad cloth〕; 〖의학〗 a poultice (약바른); a cataplasm. ～하다 apply a poultice 《to》; put a (wet) compress 《on》. ¶ 목에 ～하다 pack *one's* throat; apply a wet compress to *one's* throat.
◉ ～제 poultice (medicine). 냉～ a cold compress 〔pad〕. 온～ a hot compress.
**습하다**(濕―) (be) damp; moist; wet; soggy. ¶ 습한 공기 damp 〔moisture=laden〕 air / 약이 습하지 않도록 병 뚜껑을 닫아라 Cap the bottle so the medicine won't get damp.
**승**(乘) 〖수학〗 multiplication. ⇨ 곱, 제곱.
**승**(勝) a victory; a win. ¶ 7승 3패의 성적으로 with 7 victories and 3 defeats / 3승하다 win three games.
**승**(僧) a monk. ⇨ 중, 승려.
**-승**(乘) 《탈것의》 riding; a ride. ¶ 2인〔1인〕승 비행기 a two-〔single-〕seater plane / 5인승 자동차 a five-passenger car; a five-seater automobile.
**승강**(昇降) 《오르내림》 ascent and descent; 《아래위로》 rise and fall; 《변동》 fluctuation; vacillation. ～하다 ascend and descend; go up and down; rise and fall; fluctuate.
◉ ～구 an entrance; 《배의》 a hatch (-way); a companionway (계단). ～기 an elevator 《미》; a lift 《영》. ～타(舵) 〖항공〗 an elevator.
**승강**(乘降) getting on 〔in〕 and off 〔out〕 《a car》; boarding and alighting. ◉ ～장 a platform.
**승강이**(昇降―) a petty quarrel; wrangling; altercating. ～하다 have a petty quarrel 《with》; wrangle 《with》. ¶ 서로 ～를 벌이다 wrangle against each other.
**승객**(乘客) a passenger; 《유료의》 (a) fare (택시 등의). ¶ 기차〔일등석〕 ～ train 〔first-class〕 passengers / ～을 태우다 take on passengers; take passengers on board (배에) / ～의 편의를 도모하다 consult the convenience of passengers / 이 택시는 ～ 네 명을 태운다 This taxi carries four passengers. / 이 기선은 1,500명의 ～을 태울 수 있다 This steamer can accommodate 1,500 passengers. ◉ ～명부 a register 〔list〕 of passengers; a passenger list. ～안내소 an information 〔inquiry〕 office (for passengers).
**승격**(昇格) the elevation 〔raising〕 of status; promotion in status. ～하다 rise in status; be promoted 〔raised, elevated〕 to a higher status.
¶ 대학교로 ～하다 be raised to the status of university / 공사관을 대사관으로 ～시키다 raise a legation to the status of embassy / 외교 관계를 영사급에서 대사급으로 ～시키다 upgrade the diplomatic relations from the consul general to ambassadorial level.
**승계**(承繼) succession. ⇨ 계승(繼承).
**승급**(昇級) promotion to a higher grade; advance(ment); preferment. ～하다 obtain 〔win〕 promotion; get promoted; be promoted 〔advanced〕 《to》; rise in rank. ¶ ～이 빠르다 obtain 〔win〕 quick promotion / ～시키다 promote; advance 《*a person*》.
**승급**(昇給) a rise 〔an increase〕 in 〔of〕 salary; a raise in pay; a pay raise 〔boost, hike, increase〕. ～하다 get a raise 〔rise〕 in *one's* salary 〔pay〕; have *one's* salary raised. ¶ 정기 ～ a set annual pay raise / 5퍼센트 ～하다 get a five percent pay raise / 공적에 의한 ～ a pay raise by merit / ～시키다 increase 〔raise〕 《*a person's*》 salary / 이제 ～할 때쯤 됐다 It is about time I got a rise in my salary.
**승기**(勝機) a chance of victory 〔winning〕. ¶ ～를 잡다〔놓치다〕 seize 〔miss〕 a chance of victory.
**승낙**(承諾) consent; assent; compliance; acceptance; agreement. ～하다 consent 〔assent, agree〕 《to》; give *one's* consent 〔assent〕 《to》; comply 《with》; say yes 《to》; accept.
¶ 구두〔서면〕 ～ a verbal 〔written〕 acceptance / 사전 ～ a previous consent / ～없이 without permission; without leave / ～을 얻어〔얻지 않고〕 with 〔without〕 《*a person's*》 consent 〔permission〕 / ～을 구하다 ask 《*a per-*

*son's*》 consent 《to》/ ~을 얻다 obtain 〔win〕 《*a person's*》 consent 〔assent〕; secure 《*a person's*》 compliance / 억지로 ~시키다 force 〔impose〕 *one's* will upon 《another》/ 그 자리에서〔쾌히, 마지못해〕 ~하다 give a ready 〔willing, reluctant〕 consent 《to》/ 조건부로 ~하다 accept on condition of 〔that〕... / 그녀는 아버지께 결혼 ~을 얻었다 She obtained her father's consent to her marriage. / 그는 아버지의 ~도 없이 학교를 중퇴했다 He left school halfway without his father's consent. / 누구의 ~을 받고 한 짓이냐 On whose authority did you do that? / 이 가격이면 그들의 ~을 받을 수 있을 것 같다 These prices just might win their approval. ◉ ~서 a written consent 〔acceptance〕. 「《미》.

**승냥이** 〖동물〗 a Korean wolf; a coyote

**승니**(僧尼) Buddhist priests and nuns.

**승당**(僧堂) a Buddhist monastery.

**승도**(僧徒) priests; monks.

**승도복숭아**(僧桃—) 〖식물〗 a nectarine.

**승려**(僧侶) a (Buddhist) monk 〔priest〕. ¶ ~가 되다 become a bonze; enter the priesthood.

**승률**(勝率) the percentage of victories (to the total number of matches).

**승리**(勝利) (a) victory; (a) triumph; winning; 《경기의》 a win; (a) success. ~하다 take 〔have, win〕 the victory. ¶ ~의 여신 the goddess of victory; 〖그神〗 Nike; 〖로神〗 Victoria / 현대 과학의 ~ the triumph of modern science / 정의의 ~ the triumph of justice / 대~ a great 〔glorious, sweeping〕 victory / 힘들여 얻은 ~ a hard-earned victory 〔triumph〕 / ~를 거두다〔얻다〕 win 《the war, the match》; gain 〔win, score〕 a victory 《over》; clinch victory 《over the Giants》/ ~를 다투다 strive for victory / …의 ~로 돌아가다 end in a victory for... / ~의 영관을 차지하다 carry 〔bear〕 away the garland 〔bell〕 / 팀을 ~로 이끌다 lead the team to victory / 선거에서 압도적인 ~를 거두다 win a sweeping victory in the election / ~는 우리의 것이다 The day is ours. *or* The victory is on our side. / 브라운 투수는 이번 시즌 15번째의 ~를 기록했다 Pitcher Brown scored 〔posted〕 his 15th win 〔victory〕 of the season. / 참는 자가 최후의 ~를 얻는다 Perseverance will prevail in the long run. / 3대 2로 그의 ~였다 The score was 3 to 2 in his favor. / 그것은 외교상의 ~였다 It was a diplomatic triumph.
◉ ~자 a victor; 《경기의》 a winner: 사랑의 ~자 a successful lover. ~타점 〖야구〗 game winning runs batted in. ~투수 the winning pitcher.

**승마**(乘馬) 《말타기》 horse(back) riding; riding; horsemanship; 《말》 a riding horse. ~하다 ride 〔mount〕 a horse; take horse. ¶ ~하러 가다 go horse-riding; go for a ride / ~를 잘하다〔못하다〕 be a good 〔poor〕 rider.
◉ ~바지 riding breeches. ~복 a riding dress 〔suit〕; a riding habit (여자용). ~술 horsemanship. ~연습 a riding exercise: ~ 연습을 하다 take riding lessons. ~클럽 a riding club. ~학교〔훈련소〕 a riding school 〔academy〕. ~화 riding boots.

**승무**(僧舞) a dance in Buddhist attire; a Buddhist dance.

**승무원**(乘務員) a flight attendant (비행기의); a member of the crew 《on ship, train, plane》; a crewman; the crew [총칭]; 《열차의》 a trainman; a train crew [총칭]. ¶ (비행기의) 여자 ~ a stewardess; an air hostess / (비행기·배의) 남자~ a steward / 배에 ~을 배치하다 man a ship 〔boat〕 / 그 비행기에는 10명의 ~이 타고 있었다 Ten crewmen were aboard the plane.
◉ ~명부 a crew list. 「Buddhism.

**승문**(僧門) the Buddhist priesthood;

**승방**(僧房) a Buddhist nunnery; nuns' living quarters. 「monk.

**승병**(僧兵) a monk soldier; a warrior-

**승복**(承服) ① 《동의》 consent; 《받아들임》 acceptance. ~하다 consent 〔assent〕 《to》; accept. ¶ ~할 수 없는 조건 unacceptable conditions 〔terms〕 / 너의 의견에 ~할 수 없다 I can't 「consent to 〔accept〕 your opinion. ② 《고백》 confession of a crime. ~하다 confess 《a crime》. 「garb.

**승복**(僧服) a priest's robe; a clerical

**승부**(勝負) 《승패》 victory or defeat; 《시합》 a contest; a game; a match. 《권투의》; a bout; a round. ¶ ~의 세계 the world where might rules / 무~ a drawn 〔tie〕 game; a draw; 《경주에서》 a dead heat / ~를 도외시하고 regardless of whether *one* will win or lose; win or lose / ~를 다투다 contend for victory; compete; vie 《in, with》; contest / ~를 짓다〔내다〕 fight to the finish; fight it out; settle the day; decide a contest / ~에 이기다〔지다〕

win 〔lose〕 a game / 좀처럼 ~가 나지 않았다 It was a close game 〔contest〕. / 정정당당하게 ~하자 Let's play fair.
◉ ~차기 〖축구〗 spot kicks after a tie; a (penalty) shoot-out (to decide the winner when both teams have the same score at the end of a game): ~차기에서 이라크 팀을 5대 4로 누르다 beat the Iraqi team 5-4 on spot kicks after a tie.

**승산**(勝算) prospects of victory; a plan that is certain to succeed; a chance of victory 〔success〕.
¶ ~없는 전쟁 a hopeless war / ~이 있다 be confident of victory 〔success〕; stand 〔have〕 a good 〔fair〕 chance of winning; the odds are in *one's* favor / ~이 없다 stand no chance 《against》; have no prospect 〔show〕 of winning; the odds are against *one;* have little hope of success / 내겐 ~이 없다 The chances are against me. / 나의 ~은 반반이다 I have a fifty-fifty 〔an even〕 chance of winning. *or* My chance of winning is evens 〔even odds 《미》〕. / 나는 처음부터 ~이 없었다 It was a lost cause from the start. / ~이 없는 상황이 될 것 같다 This seems to be a no-win situation.

**승선**(乘船) embarkation; boarding. ~하다 embark 《in a ship》; go 〔get〕 on board 〔aboard〕 《a ship》; take (a) ship 〔boat〕 《at Pusan for Japan》. ¶ ~ 예약을 하다 book 〔engage〕 *one's* passage 《on a steamer》/ ~시키다 take 《*a person*》 on board / 우리는 미국 가는 배에 ~했다 We went on board a ship bound for America. / 그들은 부산에서 ~ 하여 하와이로 향했다 They boarded a ship at Pusan bound for Hawaii. / 승객 여러분은 9시까지 모두 ~해 주십시오 The passengers are requested to be on board by 9 o'clock. ◉ ~권 a passage ticket.

**승소**(勝訴) winning a lawsuit. ~하다 [사람이 주어] win 〔gain〕 a case 〔*one's* suit〕; [사건이 주어] result 〔be decided〕 in favor of *a person.*

**승수**(乘數) 〖수학〗 a multiplier. ◉ ~이론 the theory of multiplier. ~효과 a multiplier effect. 피~ a multiplicand.

**승승장구**(乘勝長驅) ~하다 make a long drive taking advantage of victory; press hard on the heels of the enemy. ¶ ~하여 driving on without a stop; availing *oneself* of the gathered momentum.

**승압**(昇壓) 〖전기〗 ~하다 boost 〔raise〕 the voltage 《of》. ◉ ~기 a step-up 〔boosting〕 transformer; a booster.

**승용**(乘用) ¶ ~의 for riding / ~으로 쓰다 use 《a horse》 in riding. ◉ ~마 a riding horse; a saddle horse; a mount. ~차 a (passenger) car: 고급 ~차 a deluxe motorcar.

**승원**(僧院) a monastry (수도원); a temple (절).

**승인**(承認) ① 《인가·찬성》 approval; 《미구어》 an O.K. 〔okay〕 (*pl.* O.K.'s). ~하다 approve; give (*one's*) approval 《to》; endorse; O.K. 〔OK, okay〕 (★ 과거형 및 진행형은 각기 O.K.'d, O.K.'ing이 되지만 okayed, okaying으로 쓰는 일이 많음). ¶ ~을 얻어 with 《*a person's*》 approval / ~을 구하다〔요청하다〕 ask for 《*a person's*》 approval / ~을 얻다 obtain 〔gain〕 《*a person's*》 approval; get an O.K. 《on》 / 정식으로 ~하다 give official approval 《to》 / ~하지 않다 disapprove of 《*a person's* intentions》 / 국회는 예산안을 ~했다 The National Assembly approved the budget. / 당신 상사의 ~을 얻어 주십시오 Please obtain the approval of your boss. / 그 의안은 과반수의 ~을 필요로 한다 The bill requires approval by a majority.
② 《승낙》 consent; agreement; assent. ~하다 consent 《to》; give *one's* consent 〔assent〕 《to》; agree 〔assent〕 《to》. ¶ ~장 a letter of assent / 동의(動議)가 ~되었다 The motion was passed. / 전원이 그의 제안을 ~했다 Everybody consented to his proposal. / 각의에서 ~되었다 It was endorsed by the Cabinet.
③ 《인정》 admission; recognition; acknowledgment. ~하다 admit; recognize; accord 〔grant〕 recognition 《to》; acknowledge. ¶ ~서 a written acknowledgment / 사실상의 ~ a *de facto* recognition / 정식 ~ a *de jure* recognition / 독립을 ~하다 recognize the independence 《of a country》 / 사실을 ~하다 admit a fact.

**승인**(勝因) the cause of the victory.

**승자**(勝者) a victor; a winner. ¶ ~없는 전쟁 a no-win war.

**승적**(僧籍) the priesthood; the holy orders. ¶ ~에 들다 become a bonze 〔priest〕; enter the priesthood; take holy orders / ~을 떠나다 leave holy orders.

**승전**(承前) a continuation 《of》. ~하다 be continued from; continue.

**승전**(勝戰) a victory; a successful war 〔battle〕. ～하다 win a war 〔battle〕.
◉ ～고(鼓) the (battle-)drum of victory.

**승제**(乘除) 〖수학〗 multiplication and division. ¶ 가감～ addition, substraction, multiplication and division; the four operations 〔rules〕 of arithmatic.

**승직**(僧職) priesthood.

**승진**(昇進·陞進) promotion; advancement; a rise in rank; preferment. ～하다 get 〔obtain, win〕 promotion; get 〔be〕 promoted 〔advanced〕 《to manager, to the position of manager》; rise (in rank); move up 《to》.
¶ ～이 빠르다 obtain 〔win〕 quick promotion / ～이 늦다 be slow in promotion / ～시키다 raise; promote; advance / ～의 길을 막다 block the way of promotion / ～의 길을 트다 open up the way of promotion 《for》 / 교수〔육군 중위〕로 ～하다 be promoted to professor 〔lieutenant〕 / 그는 선임인 나를 앞질러서 ～했다 He was promoted over my head. / 그는 과장〔중역〕으로 ～했다 He was promoted to 「section chief 〔director〕.

**승차**(乘車) taking a train 〔car, taxi〕; getting on a car; entrainment. ～하다 board a train 〔bus〕 《미》; take a train 〔tram, car, taxi〕; get on a train 〔bus〕; get in a car. ¶ (택시가) ～를 거부하다 refuse (to accept) passengers 〔customers〕 / 모두 ～해 주십시오 All aboard! / 우리는 서울역에서 ～했다 We boarded 〔get aboard〕 the train at Seoul Station.
◉ ～구 the entrance (to the platform); 《게시》 Way in. ～규정 rules for passengers. ～역 the 〔*one's*〕 entraining point 〔station〕. ～제한 restriction on railway travel.

**승차권**(乘車券) a (railway, tramcar) ticket; passenger ticket; a book 〔sheet〕 of ticket (회수권); a commutation 〔commuter〕 ticket (정기권). ¶ 급행〔무임〕 ～ an express 〔a free〕 ticket / 우대 ～ a complimentary pass / 좌석〔입석〕 ～ 발매중 《게시》 Tickets for seat 〔standing〕 available / 정기·회수 ～ 파는 곳 《게시》 Commuter passes and ticket booklets.
◉ ～매표소〔발매소〕 a ticket window 〔booth〕; a booking office 《영》. ～예매 the advanced sale of tickets for passengers. ～자동판매기 a ticket (vending) machine.

**승천**(昇天) the Ascension (예수의); the Assumption (성모 마리아의); ascension (to heaven); death (죽음). ～하다 rise 〔go, ascend〕 to heaven; die. ¶ ～입지(入地)하다 "rise to heaven and descend into the earth"; disappear.
◉ ～일 〖기독교〗 Ascension Day.

**승패**(勝敗) victory and 〔or〕 defeat; the final consequence; the issue 《of a battle》; the outcome. ¶ ～를 겨루다 contend for victory / ～를 결(決)하다 fight to the last 〔finish〕; fight it out / 그 ～는 결판이 나기 어려울 것 같았다 The issue 《of battle》 did not seem to be decided. / ～를 떠나서 최선을 다해 싸울 작정이다 Win or lose, I mean to fight as well as I can.

**승하**(昇遐) the death of a king. ～하다 《a king》 die; demise; pass away.

**승하다**(乘—) = 곱하다 ②.

**승함**(乘艦) ～하다 go on board a warship; embark; 《승무원이》 join *one's* ship.

**승홍**(昇汞) 〖화학〗 corrosive sublimate; mercuric bichloride; bichloride of mercury. ◉ ～수 a solution of corrosive sublimate.

**승화**(昇華) 〖화학·심리〗 sublimation. ～하다 sublimate; sublime. ¶ ～시키다 sublime; sublimate / 그는 성욕을 예술적 창작에까지 ～시킬 줄 알았다 He knew how to sublimate his sexual desire into artistic production.
◉ ～물 a sublimate.

**시**(市) ① 《행정 단위》 a city; a town; 《자치체》 a municipality (★ 영국에서는 city란 말을 별로 안 쓰고 town을 쓰나, 미국에서는 city, town을 거의 같은 뜻으로 쓰되, 좀 큰 도시는 거의 city로 씀). ¶ 시 당국 the municipal authorities / 서울시 the city of Seoul; Seoul city / 시로 승격되다 be raised to the status of a city / 이 도시는 6월 1일에 시가 되었다 The town gained city status on June 1. ② 《시장》 a market; a fair. ¶ 견본(見本)시 a sample fair / 야시 a night fair.

**시**(時) 《시각》 o'clock; time; 《시간》 hour (★ o'clock은 two o'clock처럼 우수리 없는 시각에 쓰며, five past two 따위와 같은 경우에는 보통 o'clock은 안 붙임).
¶ 두 시 two o'clock / 6시 반 열차로 by 〔on 《미》〕 the 6:30 train / 오전〔오후〕 9시에 at nine (o'clock) in the morning 〔afternoon〕; at 9 a.m. 〔p.m.〕 / 지금 몇 시입니까 What time is it now? / 2시 20분입니다 It is twenty minutes past 〔after 《미》〕 two. *or* It is two

twenty. / 5시 5분 전이다 It is five minutes to 〔of《미》〕 five. / 내일 몇 시에 올까요 At what time shall I come tomorrow? / 이 약은 공복시에 마셔라 Drink this medicine when your stomach is empty.

**시**(詩) [총칭] poetry; verse (운문); a poem (한 편의 시); an ode (짧은 시); lines (시구(詩句)); (a) rhyme (압운시). ¶ 서사〔서정〕시 epic 〔lyric〕 poetry / 시와 산문 poetry and prose / 시적인 풍경 poetic scenery / 시로 만들다 versify; write 〔express〕 in verse; describe 〔depict〕《a scene》 in poetry / 시를 짓다 write 〔compose〕 a poem; write poetry / 시를 이해하다 have a poetic sense / 시를 낭독하다 recite a poem / 시를 음미하다 appreciate a poem / 감동을 시로 표현하다 make *one's* impression into a poem.

**시**[1] 〚음악〛 si; ti; B.

**시**[2] [감탄사] Pshaw!; Huh!; Hmph!; 「Damn!

**시-** vivid; deep; intense. ¶ 시꺼멓다 be jet-〔deep-〕black; be very black.

**시-**(媤) 《a sister》 of the husband; 《an in-law》 on the husband's side.

**시가**(市街) the streets (거리); city (시); town. ¶ 서울 ~ the streets of Seoul. ◉ ~전 street(-to-street) fighting. ~지 an urban district 〔area〕: ~지 개발 urban development. ~행진 a street march 〔parade〕: ~ 행진을 하다 march 〔parade〕 along the street. 신〔구〕~ a new 〔the old〕 section of a city.

**시가**(市價) the market price 〔value〕. ¶ ~ 기준 the market level / ~ 변동 market fluctuations; fluctuations of prices / ~의 2할 할인으로 at a discount of 20 percent below the market price / ~로 팔다 sell at the market price / 그것은 ~ 20만원짜리다 It has a market value of two hundred thousand won.

**시가**(時價) the current price; the running price; quotations 《for》. ¶ ~로 쳐서 (estimated) in current prices; in today's money / 그 땅은 ~ 이상으로 팔렸다 The lot was sold above the current price.

**시가**(媤家) the family of *one's* husband.

**시가**(詩歌) poems and songs; songs and lyrics; poetry; a poetical composition. ◉ ~선집 an anthology.

**시가** a cigar. ¶ ~를 입에 물고 신문을 보다 read a newspaper with a cigar in ⌊*one's* mouth.

**시가레트** a cigarette.

**시각**(時刻) the hour and minute; time; hour; a short time. ¶ 이 ~에 at this time of day / 제 ~에 punctually; on time 《미》 / ~을 다투는 문제 a problem that needs a speedy solution; a burning question / 지금 ~은 2시 30분입니다 The hour is 2:30. / 그것은 ~을 다투는 급한 일이다 The matter doesn't allow a moment's delay. ◉ ~측정(법) chronometry. ~표 《열차의》 a timetable; 《미》 a (train) schedule.

**시각**(視角) 〚물리〛 the visual 〔optic〕 angle; an angle of view; 《견지》 a point of view; a viewpoint.

**시각**(視覺) (the sense of) sight; vision; eyesight. ¶ ~을 잃다 lose *one's* eyesight / ~을 끌다〔에 호소하다〕 appeal visually 《to》 / ~을 통해 배우다 learn by sight. ◉ ~공해 visual pollution. ~교육 visual education: ~ 교육 교재 visual aids. ~기관 an organ of vision. ~예술 visual arts. ~중추 the visual center. ~형(型) the visual type.

**시간**(時間) an hour: 《시각》 time; 《학교의》 an hour; a period; a class. ¶ 한 ~ one hour / 영어 ~ an English lesson / 약속~ the appointed time 〔hour〕 / 정확한 ~ the correct 〔right〕 time / 규정된 ~ regular 〔prescribed〕 hours / 배당된 ~ time assigned / 제 ~에 punctually; on time; at the appointed 〔fixed〕 time (정시에) / ~으로 《hire a car》 by the hour.

시간이: ~이 지남에 따라 as time goes by; with the lapse of time; in process 〔in the course〕 of time / ~이 걸리다 take 〔require〕 (a lot of) time / ~이 많다 have plenty of time before *one;* find *oneself* in plenty of time / ~이 모자라다 have not enough time 《for, to *do*》 / 책 읽을 ~이 없다 have no time for reading / ~(이) 가는 줄 모르다 be unaware 〔unconscious〕 of the passage of time.

시간에: 일정한 ~에 at a certain 〔given〕 hour of the day / 역사 ~에 during a history lesson 〔the history class〕 / ~에 늦다 be behind the appointed time; be late for *one's* appointment / (제) ~에 대다 be in time for 《the train》; 《일 따위를》 get 《*a thing*》 ready 〔done〕 by the time appointed / ~에 매이다 be restricted by time / ~에 매이지 않고 with no restrictions on how I spend my time / ~에 쫓기다 be pressed 〔pushed〕 for time; be racing against time.

시간을: ~을 어기지 않고 punctually;

on time; in good time / ~을 잡아먹는 time-consuming 《task》/ ~을 마련하다 arrange hours; manage to find time / ~을 맞추다 set *one's* watch (aright) by 《the radio time signal》/ ~을 묻다 ask the time / ~을 벌다 play for time; gain 〔earn, buy, spare for〕 time / ~을 보내다 pass 〔while〕 away time; kill time (무료하게) / ~을 소비하다 spend time / ~을 보다 glance at the time / ~을 낭비〔절약〕하다 waste 〔save〕 time / ~을 아끼다 economize time; be economic 〔sparing〕 of time / ~을 지키다 be punctual / ~을 쪼개다 find time to ... / ~을 …에 할애〔책정〕하다 devote *one's* time to 〔assign *one's* time for〕《a task》/ 그것에 많은 ~을 들이다 put many hours in it.

¶ ~은 돈이다 Time is money. / 그는 두 ~ 동안 계속 이야기했다 He spoke for two solid hours without stopping. / 여기서 정거장까지 얼마나 ~이 걸리나 How long does it take from here to the station? / 카드놀이로 ~을 보냈다 We killed time playing cards. / 잠깐 ~을 내주시겠습니까 I wonder if I might have a few minutes of your time. / 별로 ~이 걸리지 않는다 It won't be long. / 이 시계는 ~이 잘 맞는다〔맞지 않는다〕 This watch keeps good 〔bad〕 time. / 이제 잘 ~이다 It is time you went to bed. *or* It's time to go to bed. (★ 'you went'는 「현재 그렇지 않지만 당연히 그래야 한다」는 뜻에서 가정법 과거를 쓴 것임. It is time we *were* leaving. 「이제 작별할 시간이다」도 마찬가지) / 열차는 제 ~에 도착하였다 The train arrived on schedule 〔time〕. / 그들은 ~ 관념이 없다 They have no idea of time. *or* They take no thought of time. / ~이 좀 걸려도 상관 없다 You may take your (own) time. / 그는 ~을 주체 못하고 있다 Time hangs heavy upon his hands. / 근무~중 면회 사절《게시》 No interviews are allowed during business hours. / 지금 어려운 문제를 안고 있지만, ~이 해결해 줄 것이다 We now have difficult problems, but I'm sure time is on our side. / 나머지는 ~이 해결해 줄거다 Time will take care of the rest.

◉ ~강사 a part-time lecturer 〔teacher〕. ~급(給) payment by the hour; time wages: 우리는 ~급이다 We are paid by the hour. ~기록기 a time clock 〔recorder, register〕. ~문제 a question 〔matter〕 of time 〔of the hour〕: ~ 문제(에 불과하)다 be only a question of time. ~엄수 punctuality. ~예술 arts based on tempo. ~제한 a time limit. ~차(差) a time lag: ~차 공격 《배구의》 delayed spiking; the time differential attacks. ~표(表) 《학교의》 a 《classroom, teaching》 schedule; 《열차의》 a timetable.

**시간급수**(時間給水) water rationing; an hour restricted supply of water. ◉ 수도 ~제 an hour-restricted water supply system; water rationing.

**시간대**(時間帶) a time zone; a period of time; a time period. ¶ 광고주(主)는 특정 ~를 방송국과 계약한다 The advertiser contracts with a broadcasting station for specified periods of time.

**시간외**(時間外) ¶ ~의〔에〕 overtime; outside 〔after〕 the business 〔office〕 hours; 《학교의》 outside the school hours; after school (방과후). ◉ ~근무 overtime work: ~ 근무를 하다 work overtime 〔extra hours, after usual hours〕 / ~ 근무 시간 overtime; extra time / ~ 근무 수당 overtime pay 〔allowance〕.

**시간제**(時間制) ¶ ~의 일 timework / ~로 일하다 work by the hour. ◉ ~임금제 the pay-by-the-hour fare system.

**시거에** 《우선》 for the moment; hastily; 《곧》 at once; immediately; precipitously.

**시건방지다** (be) saucy and pert. ¶ 시건방진 태도 an impudent manner / 그녀는 시건방지게 나를 촌놈이라고 했다 She was impudent enough to call me a bumpkin.

**시경**(詩經) the Book of Odes 〔Poetry〕; the Shih Ching.

**시경찰국**(市警察局) ⇨ 경찰청.

**시계**(時計) a timepiece; 《벽시계》 a clock; 《손목 시계》 a (wrist) watch; 《회중 시계》 a (pocket) watch; 《자명종》 an alarm clock.

¶ ~를 고치다 mend 〔repair〕 a watch; have *one's* watch mended / ~를 더가게〔빠르게〕하다 put 〔set〕 a watch fast 〔on〕《ten minutes》; advance 〔set ahead〕 a clock / ~를 덜 가게 하다〔늦추다〕 put 〔set〕 a watch slow 〔back〕; turn back a clock / ~를 보다 look at 〔consult, refer to〕 *one's* watch / ~의 태엽을 감다 wind (up) a watch 〔clock〕 / ~를 맞추다 set right the watch; put a clock in order / ~를 시보에 맞추다 set the watch by the 《radio》 time signal; check up *one's* watch with the time signal / ~를 3시

로 해 놓다 put the clock to three / ~를 분해 청소하다〔고치다〕 have *one's* watch cleaned 〔mended〕 / ~가 서다 a watch stops / 이 ~는 빠르다〔늦다〕 This watch gains 〔loses〕. / 이 ~는 10분 빠르다〔늦다〕 This clock is ten minutes fast 〔slow〕. / ~가 지금 10시를 쳤다 It 〔The clock〕 has just struck ten. / 네 ~로는 몇 시냐 What time is it by your watch? *or* What time do you make it? / 그의 ~는 오전 1시를 가리켰다 His watch showed 〔gave〕 the time as 1 a.m. / 내 ~는 정확하다 My watch keeps good time.

◉ ~방 a watch store; a watchmaker's; a clockmaker's 《영》: ~방 주인 《미》 a jeweler; 《영》 a watchmaker; a clockmaker. ~방향: ~방향의 right-handed; clockwise / ~반대방향의 counterclockwise. ~소리 ticking of a clock; ticktack. ~수리공 a watch mender. ~장치 clockwork. ~탑 a clock tower. ~포 a watch repair shop. 시곗바늘 the hands: 시곗바늘을 더 가게〔덜 가게〕 돌리다 set 〔put〕 the hands forward 〔back〕 《five minutes》. 시곗줄 a watch chain 〔guard〕.

뻐꾹~ a cuckoo clock. 야광~ a glow 〔luminous〕 watch. 자동~ a self-winding watch. 전기~ an electric clock. 전자 ~ an electronic watch. 진자〔추〕~ a pendulum clock. 탁상~ a table clock. 탑~ a tower clock.

**시계**(視界) the field 〔range〕 of vision. ⇨ 시야. ◉ ~비행 visual flying; a visual flight: 계기 비행에서 ~비행으로 전환하다 shift from instrument to visual flight. ~비행규칙 visual flight rules (생략 VFR).

**시고모**(媤姑母) an aunt on *one's* husband's side. ◉ ~부(夫) the husband of an aunt on *one's* husband's side.

**시골** ① 《지방》 a countryside; the country; the provinces; a rural district; a remote area; the backwoods; the sticks. ¶ ~에서 자란 country-bred; rustic / ~ 태생의 country-born / ~서 갓 올라온 fresh from the country / ~에 가다 go into the country / ~에서 살다 live in the country / ~티가 나다 have 〔bear〕 a rural air 〔appearance〕; wear a rustic 〔countrified〕 air; look rustic / 가친께서는 서울을 떠나 아주 ~로 내려가셨다 My father left Seoul and retired into the country.

② 《고향》 *one's* native 〔birth〕 place; *one's* home 〔native village〕. ¶ ~에 계신 부모 *one's* parents at home / ~에 편지를 쓰다 write home / ~에 내려가다 go home; go back to *one's* old home / ~을 다녀 오다 pay a visit to *one's* native place / 그는 휴가를 얻어 ~에 내려가 있다 He is now home for the holidays. / 노모께서는 지금도 ~에 혼자 살고 계시다 My old mother still lives alone in my hometown.

◉ ~구석 a remote village; a secluded place: ~ 구석에서 자라나다 be brought up in some little country village. ~길 a country lane 〔road〕. ~내기〔사람〕 a country person; a rustic; rural folk [총칭]. ~뜨기 a country bumpkin; a hick; a rube; a clodhopper. ~말〔사투리〕 a rustic 〔provincial, local〕 dialect; a rustic tongue; a localism. ~살림〔생활〕 country 〔rural, rustic〕 life. ~색시 a country girl. ~집 a country house; a cottage. ~풍경 rural scenery. ~풍습 country fashion; rural manners.

**시공**(施工) carrying out 《construction work》; execution 《of work》. ~하다 carry out 〔undertake〕 construction; construct 《a building》. ¶ 우리는 그 건축 공사를 ~하고 있다 We are executing the construction work. ◉ ~도(圖) a working drawing. ~자 a (main) constructor.

**시공**(時空) 〖물리〗 space-time. ¶ ~의 spatiotemporal / ~ 연속체 a space-time continuum (4차원).

**시구**(市區) a municipal district; a borough. ◉ ~개편 town 〔city〕 replanning; street improvement.

**시구**(始球) opening of a ball game. ¶ 국무총리의 ~로 경기가 시작되었다 The game was started with the first ball thrown 〔tossed〕 by the Premier.

◉ ~식 opening ceremony of a ball game.

**시구**(詩句) a verse; a stanza; a stave.

**시국**(時局) the state of affairs 〔things〕; the situation. ¶ 비상~ an emergency; a crisis / 중대 ~ a critical juncture / ~의 추이 changes in 〔development of〕 the situation / 혼란한 현~ these turbulent times / ~에 관한 의견 *one's* view on the situation / ~을 논하다 discuss the present 〔existing, current〕 situation / ~의 진상을 간파하다 see the position as it really stands / ~에 대처하다 deal 〔cope〕 with the situation / 어려운 ~을 수습하다 settle 〔sort out, straighten out〕 a difficult situation / 현 ～에 비추어 볼 때, 경찰은 …하여야 한다 Considering 〔In view of〕 the current situation, the police need to *do*…. ◉ ～간담회〔강연회〕 a consultation 〔lecture〕 meeting on the current situation.

**시굴**(試掘) prospecting; (a) trial digging 〔boring〕. ～하다 prospect 《a mine》; drill 〔bore〕 for 《oil》; drill an experimental 《oil, gas》 well. ◉ ～갱 a test 〔trial〕 pit. ～권 a prospecting right. ～원 an application for prospecting. ～자 a prospector.

**시궁** a cesspool. ◉ ～구멍 the opening of a cesspool. ～쥐 a Norway 〔brown〕 rat. ～창 a cesspool (물이 고인 곳); a ditch (도랑); 《하수도》 a gutter; a drain; a sewer: ～창물 filthy 〔dirty, ditch〕 water; sewage / ～창에 빠지다 fall into a ditch / ～창을 치다 clear a ditch.

**시그널** 《신호》 a signal. ¶ ～을 보내다 signal (to) *a person* 《to *do*, that…》 / 교통 ～이 빨강으로 바뀌었다 The traffic signal 〔sign〕 turned red.

**시그러지다** fade; vanish; become enervated; lose *one's* vigor. ¶ 시그러질 줄 모르는 정력(으로) (with) unflagging 〔undiminished〕 energy.

**시극**(詩劇) a poetical drama; a play 〔drama〕 in verse; a verse play 〔drama〕; 《극시》 dramatic poem.

**시근거리다**[1] 《숨을》 breathe hard; gasp; pant; heave. ¶ 시근거리며 말하다 gasp 〔pant, puff〕 out / 시근거리며 달려오다 run up all out of breath.

**시근거리다**[2] 《관절이》 feel a "sour" 〔an arthritic〕 pain 《in *one's* joints》; feel a slight twitch of arthritis.

**시근시근**[1] 《숨을》 short of breath; with heavy gasps.

**시근시근**[2] 《관절이》 with a "sour" 〔an arthritic〕 pain in *one's* joints. ～하다 《a joint》 be very sore; feel a dull pain 《in *one's* ankle》.

**시글시글** 《우글우글》 swarming; wiggling. ～하다 [장소가 주어] (be) swarming. ¶ 저 오두막은 도마뱀과 벌레가 ～하다 That hut is crawling with lizards and insects. / 물탱크에 모기 유충들이 ～하다 The water tank teams with mosquito larvae.

**시금**(試金) assaying; an assay. ～하다 assay; make an assay of. ◉ ～술 the art of assaying. ～천칭 an assay balance.

**시금떨떨하다** (be) sour and puckery.

**시금석**(試金石) ① 《돌》 a touchstone; a Lydian stone. ② [비유적] a test; a touch; a test case. ¶ 가난은 그에게 ～이 될 것이다 Poverty will be a test 〔touchstone〕 of his character. / 이 일은 그의 능력을 시험해보는 ～이다 This work is the touchstone of his ability.

**시금시금하다** (be) all rather sour.

**시금씁쓸하다** (be) rather sour and bitter.

**시금치** 〖식물〗 a spinach. ¶ ～국 spinach soup / ～ 한 다발 a bunch of spinach.

**시금하다** (be) a bit sour; taste sour.

**시급하다**(時急—) (be) pressing; urgent; exigent; immediate; imminent. ¶ 시급한 문제 urgent questions / 시급히 urgently; at once / 문제를 시급히 해결하다 settle 《*a matter*》 without a moment's delay / 시급한 용무가 생겼다 Some urgent business has turned up.

**시기**(時期) 《때》 time; a period; 《계절》 season; the time of (the) year. ¶ 시험 ～ examination times / 여행하기에 적당한 ～ a favorable time to travel / 매년 이 ～에는 at this time every year / ～가 좋다〔나쁘다〕 be 「favorable time for 〔adverse time to〕 / ～가 절박하다 Time presses. / 수영하기에는 아직 ～가 이르다 It is too early to go swimming. / 공부하는 데는 지금이 가장 좋은 ～다 Now is the best time for study.

**시기**(時機) an opportunity; a chance; time; the (proper) moment; 《경우》 an occasion. ¶ ～에 적합한 opportune; timely; well-timed; appropriate / ～에 맞지 않는 untimely / ～를 보아 …하다 take occasion to 《*do*》 / ～를 기다리다 wait for the right moment 〔a ripe opportunity〕 / ～를 놓치다 miss an opportunity; let a chance slip by; slip a 〔lose *one's*〕 chance / ～를 엿보다 watch for a chance / ～를 포착하다 seize the opportunity / ～를 타다 take advantage of an opportunity / 무엇에나 ～가 있다 There is a time for everything. / 지금이 절호의 ～다 This is the time of all times. / ～를 놓치지 마라 《속담》 Strike while the iron is hot. / 아직 그 ～가 아니다 The time is not quite ripe for it.

**시기**(猜忌) jealousy; green envy. ～하다 be envious 《of *a person's* popularity》; be jealous 《of *a person's* beauty》; envy 《*a person* of *his* good luck》. ¶ ～하여 from 〔out of〕 jealousy

〔envy〕/ ～가 많다 be jealous《of》/ 남을 ～하다 be jealous of another / 그는 너의 명성을 ～하고 있다 He is jealous of your good name. ◉ ～심 jealousy; envy: ～심을 일으키다 feel 〔become〕 jealous《of》.

**시기상조**(時機尙早) being too early to 《*do*》. ¶ 투자하기에는 ～다 The time is not yet ripe for investment. / 그 안을 실행하기에는 ～다 The time is not quite mature for taking action on the plan.

**시꺼멓다** 《색깔이》 (be) deep-(jet=) black; 《마음이》 (be) black-hearted; evil-disposed〔-minded〕; crafty. ¶ 시꺼멓게 더러워진 stained black as coal / 시꺼멓게 타다 be burned black; 《햇볕에》 be tanned almost black (by the sun).

**시끄럽다** ① 《소란하다》 (be) noisy; boisterous; clamorous; uproarious. ¶ 시끄러운 거리 a noisy street / 시끄러운 소리 disturbing 〔annoying〕 noise; din / 시끄럽게 noisily; boisterously; uproariously; clamorously / 시끄럽게 떠들다 make clamor / 이웃을 시끄럽게 하다 disturb the neighborhood; raise a storm in a teacup / 어린아이들이 ～ the children are noisy / 왜 이렇게 시끄러워 What a noise! *or* What an uproar! / 교실이 시끄러워 내 목소리가 안 들렸다 My voice was drowned in the noise in the class. / 시끄러워 Be quiet! *or* Hold your tongue! / 라디오 소리가 시끄러워 잘 수가 없다 The radio is so loud (that) I can't get to sleep. ② 《여론이》 be much discussed; be (much) bruited about. ¶ 시끄러운 세상〔시기〕 troublous world 〔times〕/ 시끄러운 문제가 되다 become 〔come to be〕 much discussed 〔talked of〕; become the subject of much discussion / 이 문제로 세상이 ～ Public excitement runs high about this question. / 토지 문제가 다시 시끄러워졌다 The land question is again to the fore. / 대학 교육 개혁의 목소리가 ～ There are loud cries raised for the reform of university education. / 이 문제에 관해선 아직도 여론이 ～ This problem is still in public controversy.

**시끈가오리** 〖어류〗 an electric ray (fish); a numbfish; a crampfish.

**시나리오** a scenario (*pl.* ～s); a (film) script; a screenplay. ◉ ～라이터〔작가〕 a scenario writer; a scenarist; a screenwriter.

**시나브로** ① 《조금씩》 by imperceptible degrees; little by little; bit by bit. ② 《사이사이에》 in between other jobs; at odd moments.

**시나이반도**(一半島) 〖지리〗 Sinai Peninsula.

**시내** a brook(let); a rivulet; a stream (-let). ◉ 시냇가 the bank of a stream.

**시내**(市內) the city; (the area) within the city limits (시의 행정 구획 안). ¶ ～에(서) in 〔within, inside〕 the city; within the city limits / ～에서 살다 live in the city / ～를 구경하다 see 〔do〕 (the sights of) the city / ～는 무료 배달한다 Delivery within the city (limits) is free.
◉ ～거주자 city residents. ～버스 an urban bus; an intracity bus: ～버스 요금 intracity bus fares. ～전차 a (city) streetcar 《미》; an urban tramcar 《영》. ～통화 a local call.

**시냇물** the waters of a brook; a stream. ¶ 급히 흐르는 ～ a swiftly flowing stream / ～이 바위 틈으로 흘러 내리고 있었다 A small stream was running down among the rocks.

**시너** 〖화학〗 thinner.

**시너지** 《상승 작용》 synergy. ¶ ～효과 the synergy effect.

**시네라마** 《상표명》 a Cinerama.

**시네마** a movie; a kinema; a cinema.

**시네마스코프** 《상표명》 a CinemaScope.

**시녀**(侍女) a waiting woman 〔maid〕; 《궁녀》 a lady-in-waiting; 《귀부인의》 a lady's maid.

**시누이**(媤—) *one's* husband's sister; a sister-in-law. ◉ ～올케 the sister of *one's* husband and the wife of *one's* brother.

**시늉** mimicry; imitation; apery; aping; 《흉내》 a take-off; 《체하기》 show; pretension. ～하다 mimic; ape; imitate; 《체하다》 pretend; feign (★ mimicry, mimic은 종종 까불거리는 경우에 쓰임).
¶ ～말 onomatopoeia / 귀먹은 ～을 하다 assume to be deaf; play deaf / 놀란 ～을 하다 put on a surprised air / 우는 ～을 하다 pretend to be weeping; shed false tears / 죽은 ～을 하다 sham 〔feign〕 death / 앓는 ～을 하다 feign *oneself* to be sick / 그녀는 미친 ～을 하고 있다 She is pretending to be mad.

**시니컬하다** (be) cynical. ¶ 시니컬한 말을 하다 make a cynical remark.

**시다** ① 《맛이》 (be) sour; acid; tart. ¶ 신 사과 a sour apple / 맛이 ～ it tastes sour / 시어지다 turn sour. ② 《관절이》 (be) painful; feel a dull pain. ¶ 발목이 ～ feel a dull pain in *one's* ankle.

③《하는 짓이》(be) unseemly and unpleasant; intolerable; be beyond forbearance. ¶ 하는 짓이 눈꼴 ~ hate to see 《*a person*》 putting on airs. ④《눈이》(be) dazzling; glaring; blinding. ¶ 눈이 시어서 뜰 수가 없다 My eyes are so dazzled that I cannot keep them open.

**시단**(詩壇) poetry 〔poetical〕 circles; (the society of) poets; the poetry world.

**시달**(示達) 《문서의》 written instructions; directions; 《공문》 an official notice; a notification. ~하다 instruct; issue an official notice 《to》; inform 〔notify〕 《*a person* of *something*》. ¶ 당국의 ~을 받다 receive a government notice 《from》; be notified by the government.

**시달리다** be harassed 〔vexed〕 《with》; be annoyed 《by》; be troubled 〔afflicted〕 《with》; be worried 《about》; suffer 《from》.
¶ 가난에 ~ be poverty-stricken / 거리 소음에 ~ be annoyed by the noises in the streets / 남편에게 ~ be mistreated by *one's* husband / 더위〔뱃멀미〕에 ~ suffer from heat 〔seasickness〕 / 빚에 ~ be harassed with debts; be embarrassed by debts / 빚쟁이에게 ~ be pressed by creditors; be dunned / 생활고에 ~ be in distress for *one's* livelihood / 과중한 세금에 ~ groan under heavy taxation / 모진 세상 풍파에 ~ be buffeted about in the world; be tossed about in the storms of life; suffer hardships of life / 아이들에게 ~ be worn to a frazzle by *one's* children / 몹시 ~ be put to great annoyance 《by》; be sorely tried 《by》 / 만원 버스 안에서 ~ be jostled 〔tossed about〕 in a crowded bus / 밤새 모기에 시달렸다 Mosquitoes kept annoying me all night.

**시담**(示談) a private settlement 〔arrangement〕. ~하다 settle privately; compromise.

**시답지않다** be unsatisfied; [사물이 주어] be not quite 〔entirely〕 satisfactory; be unsatisfactory; go against the grain; be not to 《*a person's*》 liking. ¶ 시답지 않은 소리를 하다 say something offensive.

**시대**(時代) 《시기》 a time; a period; an epoch; 《연대》 an age; an era; 《세대》 a generation; 《시세(時世)》 the times.
¶ 반항의 ~ a rebellious period (성장과 정의) / 우주 여행 ~ the age of space travel / 원자력 ~ the age of nuclear 〔atomic〕 energy / 컴퓨터 ~ the computer age / 내 아버지 ~에는 in my father's days / 지금과 같은 국제 협력 ~에 in these days of international cooperation / ~에 뒤진〔뒤떨어진〕 behind the time; out-of-date; old-fashioned / ~에 뒤떨어진 사람 《구어》 a has-been; a back number / ~의 변천에 따라 with the changes of the times / ~에 앞서다〔뒤떨어지다〕 be ahead of 〔behind〕 the times / ~에 역행하다 swim against the current; put the clock back / ~에 순응하다 avail *oneself* of the times / ~의 요구에 응하다 meet the demands 〔needs〕 of the times / 새로운 ~의 첨단을 가다 be in the van(guard) 〔forefront〕 of the new era / …의 ~는 지났다 the day of … is over 〔past〕 / …와 ~가 같다 be contemporary with… / 지금은 실력의 ~다 We live in an age where ability wins. / 그 ~에는 텔레비전이 없었다 At that date television was unknown. / ~에 뒤지지 않도록 해야 한다 We must keep up with the times. / 그는 그녀와 같은 ~의 사람이다 He was (a) contemporary with her. / ~가 변했다 Times 〔The times〕 have changed. / 인터넷은 인류 발달에 새로운 ~를 가져 왔다 The Internet introduced a new era in the advancement of mankind.
◉ ~감각 the sense of the times. ~고증(考證) background research. ~구분 the division 《of history》 into periods; periodization 《in history》. ~극 a historical drama; a costume play. ~사조 the current thought of the times. ~상(相) phases of the times. ~소설 a period novel. ~정신 the spirit of the times: ~정신이 그의 저작 속에 구현돼 있다 The spirit of the age is embodied in his writings. ~착오 anachronism: ~착오의 anachronistic.

**시댁**(媤宅) the esteemed family of your 〔her〕 husband; the esteemed house of the father-in-law (of a woman).

**시도**(示度) a reading; registered 〔recorded〕 degree. ¶ 기압의 중심 ~는 1,350 밀리바였다 The central pressure showed 1,350 milibars. / 온도계의 ~는 영하 12도다 The thermometer shows a reading of 12 degrees below zero.

**시도**(視度) visibility. ¶ 수평방향의 ~ the

horizontal visibility.

**시도**(試圖) a try; a trial; an attempt (기도); an experiment (실험). ～하다 try; make 〔have〕 a trial 《of》; make 〔have〕 a try; (make an) attempt 《at, to *do*》. ¶ 새로운〔첫〕 ～ a new 〔first〕 attempt / 한번 ～해 보시오 Just try it. / 그 ～는 실패로 돌아갔다 The attempt turned out fruitless. / 나는 온실에서 난 재배를 ～했다 I tried growing orchiards under glass. / 그는 세 번째 ～에서 성공했다 He succeeded on his third try 〔attempt〕.

**시동**(始動) starting. ¶ ～을 걸다 set 〔start〕 a machine / 엔진은 큰 소리를 내며 ～이 걸렸다 The engine started (up) with a roar. ◉ ～기(機) a starter; a starting engine. ～장치 a starting device 〔system〕.

**시동생**(媤同生) *one's* husband's younger brother.

**시드** ～하다 〖스포츠〗 seed 《a player》. ¶ ～되지 않은 선수 an unseeded player. ◉ ～교(校) a seeded school team. ～머니 seed money. ～선수 a 《top-, second-》 seeded player 〔competitor〕.

**시들다** ① 《초목이》 wither; wilt; droop; be emaciated; be haggard; be thin. ¶ 시든 채소 wilted vegetables / 꽃이 시들어 버렸다 The flowers are all wilted. / 서리를 맞아도 이 꽃들은 시들지 않는다 Frost won't kill 〔blight〕 these flowers. ② 《활력이》 become weak; lose vigor; wither; fade; shrivel up. ¶ 아름다운 용모가 ～ lose *one's* looks 〔charms〕 / 인기가 ～ lose popularity; *one's* popularity declines / 젊음이 시들어 버렸다 The youthfulness has faded 〔died out〕. / 피부는 나이와 더불어 시든다 The skin shrivels with age.

**시들부들**, **시들시들** slightly wilted 〔withered〕. ～하다 (be) slightly wilted; have withered a little. ¶ 꽃이 시들시들 시들었다 The flower withered somewhat.

**시들하다** ① 《탐탁지 않다》 (be) unsatisfying; unsatisfactory; dissatisfied; discontented; be not gratified; leave 《*something*》 to be desired. ¶ 시들한 이야기 a dull story / 이제는 명예도 돈도 ～ Fame and money have lost their taste for me now. / 그런 생활은 그녀에게는 시들했다 Such a life was unsatisfactory for her. ② 《내키지 않다》 (be) reluctant 《to *do*》; disinclined; indisposed 《to *do*》; unwilling; halfhearted; uninterested 《in》; [서술적] be in no mood 《to *do*》. ¶ 극장 구경 가기가 ～ be not in the mood to go to a show / 시들한 대답을 하다 give a halfhearted 〔dry〕 answer / 얘기해 보았으나 그는 시들해 했다 I did not find him very responsive when I talked about it. ③ 《하찮다》 (be) trivial; trifling; be of no account 〔value〕. ¶ 시들한 일 a poor job / 어른의 말을 시들하게 여기다 make light of an elder's remarks / 아무의 이야기를 시들하게 듣다 listen to 《*a person*》 apathetically / 이번 일은 시들히 여겨서는 안 된다 It is inadvisable for you to take little account of the matter.

**시디**[1] ① a CD; certificates of deposits (양도성 예금 증서). ② a cash dispenser (현금 자동 지급기).

**시디**[2] a CD; a compact disc. ◉ ～롬 a CD-ROM. ～플레이어 a CD player (생략 CDP).

**시디시다** be sour as sour can be.

**시래기** dried radish leaves. ¶ ～국 soup cooked with dried radish leaves.

**시럽** sirup 《미》; syrup 《영》.

**시렁** a wall shelf. ◉ ～가래 crosspoles used as a shelf.

**시력**(視力) eyesight; sight; vision; eye strength. ¶ ～이 약하다 be weak-eyed; be weak in sight; have weak vision; have poor sight / ～을 잃다〔회복하다〕 lose 〔recover〕 *one's* eyesight / ～이 약해지다 *one's* sight is failing; *one's* eyesight fails / 그녀는 ～도 청각도 예민하다 She has keen sight and hearing / 저이는 ～이 약해서 지금은 장님이나 마찬가지다 His sight is now so weakened that he is almost blind. / 새는 개보다 ～이 좋다 Birds have better sight than dogs. ◉ ～감퇴 amblyopia. ～검사 an eye test: ～검사표 a sight-testing chart; an eye test chart / ～검사를 하다 test *a person's* eyesight 〔vision〕. ～검안사(檢眼士) an optometrist; an oculist (안과의사). ～계〔측정 장치〕 an optometer.

**시련**(試鍊) a trial; a test; an ordeal. ¶ 가혹한 ～ severe 〔bitter〕 trials; trying ordeals / ～을 겪은 tried; tested / 모진 ～을 겪고 있다 be in the crucible / ～을 극복하다 rise above hardships; overcome all hardships. / ～에 견디다 endure 〔stand〕 the trials 《of life》 / 지금이 나에게는 ～의 시기다 It 〔This〕 is a time of trial for me.

**시론**(時論) ① 《여론》 a current trend of opinion; a current 〔contemporary〕 view; public sentiments (of the day).

¶ ～에 귀를 기울이다 give 〔pay〕 careful attention to the trends of public opinion. ② 《시평》 comments upon current events.

**시론**(試論) an essay 《on》; a sketch 「《of》.

**시론**(詩論) poetics; a criticism of poems; an essay on poetry.

**시료**(施療) free medical care 〔treatment〕. ～하다 treat without charge; give 《*a person*》 free medical treatment. ¶ ～를 받다 be treated free of charge. ◉ ～병원 a dispensary; a public 〔free〕 clinic; a charity hospital. ～환자 a charity 〔free〕 patient.

**시료**(試料) 《실험용의》 a sample; materials for experiment; a sample ore (광석의).

**시루** an earthenware steamer. ¶ ～에 물(퍼)붓기 《속담》 (like) pouring water into a sieve; waste labor 〔effort〕. ◉ ～떡 steamed rice cake. 시룻방석 a steamer mat-cover. 시룻번 dough used to fill the gap between a steamer and a cauldron.

**시류**(時流) 《풍조》 the trend 〔current〕 of the times; the general drift of affairs; 《시대》 the times; 《유행》 the fashion of the day. ¶ ～에 순응〔역행〕하다 go with 〔against〕 the stream; swim with 〔against〕 the current / ～를 초월하다 stand aloof from the crowd / ～에 따르다 《풍조를》 follow the fashion (of the day); 《대세를》 go with the current of the times; swim 〔go〕 with the tide; keep up 〔abreast〕 with the times / ～에 영합하다 curry favor with the public / 그는 ～를 잘 탄다 He knows well how to swim with the tide.

**시르죽다** 《기운 없다》 (be) disheartened; dispirited; dejected; downcast; blue; 《기를 못 펴다》 feel ill at ease; feel constrained.

**시름** anxiety; worry; care; trouble; grief; sorrow. ～하다 be anxious 《about》; be worried 〔troubled〕 《about》; be ill at ease. ¶ ～이 많다 be full of troubles 〔cares〕; be care=laden / ～을 놓다〔덜다〕 feel relieved; unload *one's* mind; set *one's* cares aside / 술로 ～을 달래다 drown *one's* cares 〔sorrows〕 in wine / 그 소식에 한 ～ 놓았다 The news took a weight off my mind.

**시름시름** lingeringly. ¶ ～ 앓는 병 a lingering illness 〔disease〕 / ～ 앓다 have a long drawn-out 〔persistent〕 illness; suffer from a lingering disease / ～ 앓다가 죽다 die after a lingering illness.

**시름없다** 《걱정되다》 (be) worried; anxious; 《멍하다》 (be) absentminded; blank; be devoid of thoughts.

**시름없이** 《근심·걱정으로》 worriedly; depressedly; dispiritedly; dishearteneldy; 《멍하니》 inadvertently; carelessly; unintentionally; absentmindedly; vacantly. ¶ ～ 한 말 a desultory remark / ～ 창 밖을 내다보다 look out the window absentmindedly.

**시리다** 《몸의 어떤 부분이》 (be) cold. ¶ 귀가〔손이〕 ～ *one's* ears 〔hands〕 are cold / 차디찬 바람에 뼛속까지 시렸다 The icy wind chilled us to the bone.

**시리아** 《나라 이름》 Syria. ¶ ～의 Syrian. ◉ ～ 사람 a Syrian.

**시리즈** a series. ¶ ～로 출판하다 publish in a serial form. ◉ ～물 a serial.

**시립**(市立) [형용사적] municipal; city=established. ¶ 이 학교는 ～이다 This school is under municipal management. / 이 병원은 ～이다 The hospital is maintained at municipal expense. ◉ ～도서관 a city library. ～병원 a municipal hospital.

**시말**(始末) the beginning and the end; facts of a case; the particulars; circumstances. ¶ 일의 ～은 이렇다 This is how it happened. ◉ ～서 a written explanation 《of a case》; a written apology: ～서를 쓰게 되다 be asked to give a written explanation.

**시맥**(翅脈) 〚곤충〛 a vein; a nerve; nervure.

**시멘트** cement. ¶ ～를 바르다 cement. ◉ ～공사 cement work. ～공장 a cement plant 〔factory〕. ～기와 a cement tile. ～믹서 a cement mixer.

**시목**(市木) the official tree of a city. ¶ 서울시 당국은 은행나무를 서울의 ～으로 지정하였다 The Seoul municipal government designated Ginkgo "the official tree" of Seoul.

**시무**(始務) the opening of government offices for the year; reopening of office business after the New Year holidays. ～하다 resume 〔reopen〕 office business after the New Year recess. ◉ ～식 the opening ceremony (for the year).

**시무룩하다** (be) sulky; sullen; peevish; glum; moody; be in one of *one's* moods. ¶ 시무룩한 얼굴 a sullen 〔grim〕 look / 시무룩해서 말이 없다 keep a sullen silence / 그녀는 그의 말을 듣고 시무룩해졌다 She got 〔became〕 sulky 〔sullen〕 at 〔over〕 his remark.

**시문**(時文) contemporary writings; current literature. ◉ ～체 current style of writing.

**시문**(詩文) poetry and prose. ◉ ～선 a selection of 《English》 prose and poetry.

**시문**(試問) a question; an examination; a test; an interview. ～하다 question 〔interview〕 《*a person*》; put a question 《to *a person*》; examine.

**시뮬레이션** 《모의 실험》 (a) simulation.

**시민**(市民) the citizens; the townsmen; the populace; civilians; 《개인》 a citizen. ¶ 서울 ～ the citizens of Seoul [총칭] / (한 사람의) 미국 ～ an American citizen / ～ 경제 정의 연합회 the Citizens' Coalition for Economic Justice. ◉ ～계급 *bourgeoisie* (F.). ～대학 a college open to the public. ～대회 a mass meeting of citizens. ～사회 civil society. ～생활 《regulate》 the civic life. ～운동 a citizens' campaign 《for》. ～윤리 a civic ethics: 건전한 ～ 윤리의 확립 the establishment of a sound civil ethics. ～회관 a civic center.

**시민권**(市民權) (the right of ) citizenship; civil 〔civic, citizens〕 right. ¶ ～을 부여하다 grant citizenship to 《*a person*》; citizenize 《미》 / 미국 ～을 얻다 acquire citizenship in the United States.

**시반**(屍斑) a death spot; 〖의학〗 a livor.

**시발**(始發) the first departure; the start. ¶ 서울 ～ 부산행 열차 a train bound for Pusan from Seoul / ～ 전차 a first streetcar 〔tramcar 《영》〕 / ～은 오전 4시 30분이다 The first train starts at 4:30 a.m. ◉ ～역 the station of origin; the departure terminal; the starting station.

**시방서**(示方書) 《meet》 specifications 《for construction work》; 《명세서》 a detailed account 〔statement〕. ¶ 새로운 교량은 엄격한 정부 ～에 따라서 건설되었다 The new bridge has been built according to strict government specifications.

**시범**(示範) setting an example; a model for others. ～하다 set 〔give, offer〕 an example 《to》. ◉ ～경기 an exhibition game 〔match〕. ～농장〔학교〕 a model farm 〔school〕. ～지역 a model area.

**시베리아** Siberia. ¶ ～의 Siberian. ◉ ～사람 a Siberian. ～철도 the Siberian Railway.

**시보**(時報) ① 《보도》 a news sheet; a gazette; a bulletin; a review (평론). ② 《방송의》 announcement of the time; a time signal; timecast 《미》. ¶ 시계를 라디오 ～에 맞추다 set *one's* watch by the radio time signal.

**시보**(試補) a probationer.

**시보레** a Chevrolet (car). ¶ 85년형 ～ a 85 Chevrolet.

**시복**(諡福) 〖가톨릭〗 beatification. ～하다 beatify 《*a person*》. ◉ ～식 a beatification.

**시부렁거리다** prattle; chatter; talk nonsense 〔pointlessly〕.

**시부모**(媤父母) a woman's parents-in-law; the parents of *one's* husband.

**시부저기** effortlessly; easily; "without lifting a finger".

**시비**(市費) municipal expenses; city expenditure (경비). ¶ ～로 at municipal expenses; at the expense of the city.

**시비**(侍婢) a maid.

**시비**(是非) ① 《잘잘못》 right and wrong. ¶ ～를 논하다 discuss the rights and wrongs 《of》 / ～를 가리다 discriminate 〔distinguish〕 between right and wrong / 그는 이제 ～를 판단할 수 있는 나이다 He is old enough to tell 〔know〕 right from wrong. ② 《논쟁》 a dispute; a quarrel; a wrangle; an argument; a fight. ～하다 quarrel 《with》; have a quarrel 〔dispute〕 《with》; dispute 《with *a person* about *something*》. ¶ ～를 걸다 provoke 《*a person* to》 a quarrel; pick a fight with 《*a person*》 / ～조로 나오다 put *oneself* into a fighting attitude; assume 〔take〕 a defiant attitude; show fight / 그들은 무슨 구실로든 ～를 걸 것이다 They will pick quarrel with you on some pretext or other. ◉ ～곡직 the right and the wrong; the crooked 〔twisted〕 and the straight.

**시비**(施肥) manuring; fertilizing. ～하다 apply manure; fertilize; manure.

**시뻘겋다** (be) deep red; crimson; be a vivid red. ¶ 시뻘겋게 단 난로 a red-glowing stove / 시뻘겋게 타다 get 〔become〕 red-hot / 석양이 서쪽 하늘을 시뻘겋게 물들였다 The setting sun fired the western sky. / 불타는 듯한 시뻘건 저녁 노을의 아름다움은 말로 표현할 수 없다 The beauty of a flaming sunset is indescribable.

**시사**(示唆) (a) suggestion. ～하다 suggest; be suggestive of; give 〔offer〕 《*a* *person*》 suggestions 《as to》; hint (at). ¶ ～적(인) suggestive / ～하는 바가 크다 be (very) suggestive; be full of suggestions.

**시사**(時事) current events 〔affairs, questions〕; the events of the day. ¶～를 논하다 discuss 〔talk of〕 current events / ～에 밝다 be well acquainted with current affairs; keep up with 〔follow〕 the news; be in touch with the times / ～에 어둡다 be ignorant of current events; be out of touch with the times. ◉ ～소설 a current-affair novel. ～영어 current English. ～잡지 a magazine for current affairs. ～평론 comments on contemporary topics.

**시사**(試射) test-firing; trial firing. ～하다 testfire 《a gun》; test 《a weapon》. ◉ ～장 a (test)firing range: 로켓 ～장 a rocket range. ～탄 a trial shot.

**시사**(試寫) a preview; a private showing; a trade première 〔show〕 (영화 관계자에게만 하는). ～하다 preview; give 〔hold〕 a preview of a film. ◉ ～실 a projection room. ～회 a cinema 〔movie〕 preview; a trade show: ～회를 열다 give 〔hold〕 a preview 《of》.

**시사문제**(時事問題) a current question; issues of the day; question of the day 〔times〕; current topics. ¶ ～에 관한 기사 topical articles; articles on current events / ～를 해설하다 comment on questions of the day.

**시사해설**(時事解說) comments on current topics; news commentary. ◉ ～자〔가〕 a commentator on current events; a news commentator; a (radio) commentator.

**시산**(試算) a trial (calculation). ～하다 try 《calculation》; make a trial balance. ◉ ～표 a trial balance (sheet).

**시살**(弑殺) murdering a superior; assassination. ～하다 kill; murder; assassinate.

**시삼촌**(媤三寸) an uncle of *one's* husband. ◉ ～댁 the wife of an uncle of *one's* husband.

**시상**(施賞) awarding (a prize). ～하다 award 〔give〕 a prize. ◉ ～대 《stand on》 the winner's podium; an honor platform. ～식 a ceremony of awarding prizes.

**시상**(視床) 『해부』 a thalamus (*pl.* -mi); an optic thalamus.

**시상**(詩想) 《시적 감정》 a poetic(al) sentiment; sentiment expressed in poem; 《시적 착상·영감》 a poetical imagination 〔inspiration, idea〕. ¶ 좀처럼 ～이 떠오르지 않는다 Poetical thoughts would not flash upon me.

**시새** fine sand.

**시새(우)다** ① 《질투하다》 be terribly jealous of; be green with envy of. ¶ 남을 ～ be awfully jealous of others. ② 《다투다》 compete 《with》. ¶ 두 학생은 시새워 공부했다 The two students competed with each other in their studies.

**시생**(侍生) I; me; your humble servant.

**시생대**(始生代) 『지질』 the Arch(a)eozoic (era).

**시서늘하다** 《음식이》 get cold; cool off; (become) cool.

**시선**(視線) *one's* gaze; *one's* eye(s). ¶ 그들의 ～이 마주치면 when 〔as〕 their eyes meet / ～을 모으다 attract public gaze / ～을 피하다 avoid 《*a person's*》 eye; escape 《another's》 gaze / ～을 딴데로 돌리다 avert 〔turn〕 *one's* eyes 《from, off》; look away / 모든 사람의 ～이 그에게로 쏠렸다 Everyone looked at him. *or* All eyes were turned upon him.

**시선**(詩仙) a divine poet; a great poet.

**시선**(詩選) selected poems; an anthology; a selection of poems.

**시설**(柿雪) bloom. ¶ 곶감에 ～이 앉았다 The dried persimmons have bloom on them.

**시설**(施設) an institution; an establishment; 《설비》 equipment; facilities; setup; 《고아·노인 등의》 a home; an asylum. ～하다 provide 〔equip, furnish〕 《with》; establish.
¶ 군사 ～ military installations / ～이 좋은 well-equipped; well-furnished / ～에 수용하다 receive 《an orphan》 into a home; send 《a foundling》 to an asylum; institutionalize 《the aged》 / 이 공장은 ～이 완전하다 This factory is perfectly equipped. / 그 방에는 전등 ～이 없다 No electric lights are installed in the room. / 저 아파트는 ～이 좋다 That apartment house has a nice setup. / 우리 마을에는 오락 ～이 부족하다 Our town needs more facilities for recreation 〔entertainment〕. / 이 호텔은 2백 명을 수용할 ～이 되어 있다 This hotel has accommodations for 200 guests. / 이 배는 무전 ～이 되어 있다 This ship is fitted with a wireless apparatus. / 이 도시에는 고아를 위한 ～이 있다 There is an institution 〔a home〕 for orphans in

this city. / ~물에 손대지 마시오《게시》 Don't touch equipment.
◉ ~비 the cost of equipment. ~자금 facility funds: ~자금의 출처를 캐다 ferret out the sources of facility funds. ~투자 facility investment; investment in equipment. ~확장 facility expansion.
공군~ air installations. 산업~ industrial facilities. 상점~ the fittings of a store. 세탁〔조리〕~ arrangements for washing〔cooking〕. 오락〔위락〕~ recreation(al)〔amusement〕facilities. 지상~ ground facilities. 탁아~ public day-care facilities《for infants》. 하수〔위생〕~ drainage〔sanitary〕arrangements. 호텔~ hotel accommodations; hotel appointments.

**시성**(詩聖) a great poet; a celebrated〔master〕poet.

**시성**(諡聖)〚가톨릭〛canonization (of a martyr as a saint). ~하다 canonize《*a person*》for a saint;《the pope》proclaim a martyr's sainthood. ¶한국 복자(福者) 103 위의 ~을 거행하다 perform the canonization of the 103 blessed Korean martyrs.

**시성식**(示性式)〚화학〛a rational formula.

**시세**(市稅) a municipal tax〔rate〕.

**시세**(市勢) ①〚경제〛market condition. ②《시정 상태》the conditions of municipal life; the state of city affairs. ◉ ~조사《take》a municipal census.

**시세**(時世) the times; the era; the age. ⇨시대. ¶~의 진보 the advancement of the age; contemporary progress.

**시세**(時勢) ①《세상 형편》the signs of the times; the drift of the times; the situation; conditions; the times. ¶험악한 ~ troublous times / ~를 탓하다 blame it on the times / ~가 이롭다 the times are favorable; the situation is opportune / ~를 타고 나다 be born under a lucky star / 그 계획을 실행하기에는 ~가 불리하다 Conditions are unfavorable for carrying out the plan.
②《시가(時價)》the current price; the market price;《경기》the market; business conditions. ¶쌀~ the rice market; market quotation on rice / 달러 ~ the exchange rate of the dollar / 주식 ~ stock quotations / ~의 변동 fluctuations in the market / ~가 오르다〔내리다〕rise〔fall〕in price; prices rise〔fall〕/ 오늘의 주식 ~는 어떠합니까 What are today's quotations of shares? / 그 땅은 ~ 이상으로 팔렸다 The lot was sold above the current price〔market value〕. / ~는 약세입니다 The market is weak. / 요새 ~가 없다 Business is dull〔off〕these days.

**시세닿다**(時勢―) reach a good price; come up with a fair price; get *one's* price. ¶시세가 닿기를 기다리다 wait for a good price / 시세가 닿아서 땅을 팔았다 When I got my price, I sold the land.

**시세폭**(時勢幅) a price range; price changes〔fluctuations〕. ¶큰〔작은〕~ a wide〔narrow〕range of prices.

**시소** a seesaw. ¶~를 타고 놀다 play (at) seesaw. ◉ ~게임 a seesaw game.

**시속**(時俗) the customs of the age〔times〕.

**시속**(時速) speed per hour;《풍속》velocity per hour. ¶~600 마일 six hundred miles an〔per〕hour; 600 mph / 태풍이 ~ 160 킬로미터로 이동하고 있다 The typhoon is moving at a velocity of 160 kilometers an hour.

**시숙**(媤叔) brothers of *one's* husband.

**시술**(施術) a surgical operation. ~하다 operate; perform an operation.

**시스템** (a) system. ¶~화하다 systematize. ◉ ~공학 systems engineering. ~분석 system analysis. ~엔지니어 a system engineer.

**시승**(試乘) a trial ride. ~하다 test《a vehicle》; try out; have〔make〕a trial ride in. ◉ ~차 a demonstrator.

**시시각각**(時時刻刻) hourly; every moment; momentarily; constantly; repeatedly; from moment to moment. ¶~으로 변하다 change momentarily〔every moment〕/ ~으로 변하는 광경 an ever-changing scene / ~으로 증가하다 increase by the minute / 위험이 ~ 다가오고 있다 The danger is coming nearer every moment. / 재해 상황이 ~으로 보고되었다 The news of the disaster was sent moment by moment.

**시시덕거리다** chat and giggle; flirt. ¶그녀는 잘 생긴 남자만보면 시시덕거린다 She flirts with every handsome man she meets.

**시시때때로**(時時―) ⇨ 때때로.

**시시부지하다** drop into oblivion; drift into obscurity; vanish; go up in smoke; evaporate. ¶시시부지되다〔끝나다〕be dropped; become hazy; end in smoke / 사건은 시시부지되었다 The affair ended in nothing. / 한달이 지나자 그 살인 사건은 시시부지해졌다 After one month, the murder case was forgotten. / 노사간의 대화는 시시부지하게 끝났다 The talk between labor and management yielded no definite results.

**시시비비**(是是非非) 《공평한 판단》 "calling what's right, right, and what's wrong, wrong"; rendering an impartial decision; handing down a judgment; reaching a decision on the merits of a dispute. ～하다 call a spade a spade; render an impartial decision; hand down a judgment. ¶ 정부는 이 문제에 대하여 ～의 태도를 견지해야 한다 In this matter the government should hold firm to an impartial policy. ◉ ～주의 a free and unbias(s)ed policy; a clear-cut principle; the principle of being fair and just.

**시시콜콜** inquisitively. ¶ ～ 캐묻다 inquire of 《*a person*》 about every detail of 《*a matter*》; catechize 《*a person*》 to the last detail about 《*a matter*》; be inquisitive about 《*a matter*》.

**시시티브이** 《폐쇄 회로 텔레비전》 a CCTV. [<*c*losed-*c*ircuit *t*ele*v*ision]

**시시하다** 《흥미 없다》 (be) dull and flat; uninteresting; jejune (무미건조한); 《미미하다》 (be) insignificant; 《무가치하다》 (be) worthless; be of no value; 《어리석다》 (be) silly; stupid; 《사소하다》 (be) trifling; trivial; petty; 《쓸모없다》 be of no use; (be) useless. ¶ 시시한 일 a matter of no importance [consequence]; a trifling affair; a trifle; a triviality; unattractive work (재미없는); unprofitable work (이득 없는) / 시시한 경기 a dull [joyless] game / 시시한 놈 a poor [a worthless, an insignificant] fellow; a bore; a nobody / 시시한 배우 a poor actor / 시시한 책 a stupid [worthless, boring] book / 시시한 소설 a trashy novel; a dime novel / 시시한 강연 a tedious speech; a dull lecture; a tiresome talk / 시시한 듯이 with a bore look; with a disappointed look / 시시한 소리를 하다 talk nonsense [rot]; say silly things / 시시한 일에 화를 내다 take offense at trifles / 시시한 이야기였다 It was such a boring talk. / 정말 시시했다 We were bored to death. / 두 사람은 시시한 일로 종종 싸운다 The two often quarrel over a trifle. / 그녀는 시시한 친구와 결혼했다 She has married a nobody. (★ nobody의 반대말은 somebody 「상당한 인물」임).

**시식**(試食) food-tasting; sampling. ～하다 taste; try; sample 《the cake》. ¶ 그 과자를 ～해 보았더니 아주 맛있었다 We sampled the cake and found it very nice. ◉ ～회 a sampling party.

**시신**(侍臣) an official in attendance; an attendant.

**시신**(屍身) a dead body; a corpse.

**시신경**(視神經) 〖해부〗 the optic [visual] nerve. ◉ ～상(床) the optic thalamus (*pl.* -mi). ～염 optic neuritis.

**시심**(詩心) poetic sentiment [instinct].

**시아버님**(媤—) 《your, my, her》 esteemed father-in-law.

**시아버지**(媤—) a woman's father-in-law; *one's* husband's father.

**시아이디** 《범죄 수사대》 CID. [<*C*riminal *I*nvestigation *D*etachment]

**시아이시** 《방첩대》 CIC. [<*C*ounter *I*ntelligence *C*orps]

**시아이에스** 《독립국가연합》 CIS. [<the *C*ommonwealth of *I*ndependent *S*tates]

**시아이에이** 《미국 중앙 정보국》 CIA. [<the *C*entral *I*ntelligence *A*gency]

**시아이에프** 《운임·보험료 포함 가격》 CIF; C.I.F.; c.i.f. [<cost, insurance & freight]

**시아주버니**(媤—) *one's* husband's older brother.

**시안**(試案) a tentative plan [proposal, draft]; a (tentative) outline; a draft policy. ¶ ～을 작성하다 draw up [make out, formulate] a tentative plan.

**시안** 〖화학〗 cyanogen. ◉ ～화물(化物) a cyanide.

**시앗** a concubine of *one's* husband. ¶ ～을 보다 see *one's* husband take a mistress.

**시애틀** 《미국의 항구도시》 Seattle.

**시야**(視野) a visual field; the field [range] of vision; (a field of) view; [비유적] *one's* mental vision; *one's* view. ¶ ～를 가리다 obstruct [close] the view / ～를 넓히다 broaden *one's* outlook 《on》; widen *one's* mental horizon / ～에 들어오다 come within the range [sweep] 《of a telescope》; come into view; come [appear] in sight / ～에서 멀어지다 get [go, pass] out of sight / ～가 넓다[좁다] *one's* mental vision is broad [narrow]; have a broad [narrow] view of things / 해외 여행을 하여 그는 크게 ～를 넓혔다 Traveling abroad greatly widened his horizons.

**시약**(施藥) free dispensing of medicine (약을 줌); medicine dispensed free (약). ～하다 dispense [serve out] medicine (free) 《to the poor》.

**시약**(試藥) 〖화학〗 a reagent; a test. ◉ ～병 a reagent bottle.

**시어**(詩語) poetic language [diction] [총칭]; a poetic word.

**시어머니**(媤―) *one's* husband's mother; a woman's mother-in-law.

**시어머님**(媤―) 《your, my, her》 esteemed mother-in-law.

**시업**(始業) commencement of work; opening; inauguration. ～하다 start [commence] (work); begin; open; reopen (휴일 다음에). ¶ ～(을 알리는) 벨 the beginning bell / 학교는[사무실은] ～이 오전 9시, 종업은 오후 4시이다 School [The office] opens at 9 a.m. and closes at 4 p.m. ◉ ～시간 the opening hour 《of a school, of a firm》. ～식 an inaugural [opening] ceremony.

**시에라리온** 《나라 이름》 Sierra Leone.

**시에이티브이** 《공동시청 안테나 TV》 CATV. [<*c*ommunity *a*ntenna *t*elevision]

**시에프** 《상업 광고용 필름》 a CF. [<commercial film]

**시엔디** 《핵무장 금지 운동》 C.N.D. [<*C*ampaign for *N*uclear *D*isarmament]

**시엔시** 《컴퓨터 수치 제어》 CNC. [<*c*omputer *n*umerical *c*ontrol]

**시엔엔** 《미국의 유선 뉴스 방송망》 CNN. [<the Cable News Network]

**시엠** 《광고용 방송》 a CM. [<commercial message] ◉ ～송 a CM song.

**시역**(市域) the city limit(s); the municipal area.

**시역**(視域) 〖물리〗 field. ¶ 망원경의 ～ the field of a telescope. ◉ ～렌즈 field lens [glass].

**시역**(弑逆) the murder of *one's* lord [parent]. = 시살.

**시연**(試演) a trial performance 《of a play》; a demonstration; a preview; a rehearsal. ～하다 rehearse (publicly); preview; give a trial performance 《of an opera》. ◉ 공개～ a public demonstration [rehearsal].

**시영**(市營) city [municipal] operation [management]. ¶ ～의 city-operated; city-run; municipal; city / 가스·수도 사업의 ～ municipal trading [enterprise] in gas and water; municipal supply of gas and water service / 이 지하철은 ～이다 This subway is operated by the city. ◉ ～버스 a city [municipal] bus. ～주택 a municipal dwelling house. ～화 municipalization: ～화하다 municipalize.

**시오니즘** 《유태 민족운동》 Zionism.

**시외**(市外) the outskirts of a city; the suburbs. ¶ ～에 살다 live in the suburbs 《of Seoul》 / ～ 부탁합니다 《전화》 I want a long-distance call 《미》. *or* Give me trunks 《영》. ◉ ～거주자 an out-of-towner. ～버스 a cross-country bus. ～전차 a suburban streetcar. ～통화 an out-of-town call.

**시외가**(媤外家) *one's* husband's mother's house [family].

**시외삼촌**(媤外三寸) *one's* husband's maternal uncle; the brother of the mother of a woman's husband.

**시외전화**(市外電話) 《선》 a toll line; a trunk line 《영》; 《통화》 a toll [a long-distance, an out-of-town] call. ¶ ～를 걸다 make a long-distance call. ◉ ～교환대 a toll (switch) board. ～국번 a long-distance number [code]; an area code.

**시용**(試用) using as a trial; a trial; a test. ～하다 try out; use as a trial; make (a) trial of; put 《*a thing*》 to trial. ¶ 신제품을 ～하다 try out the new product.

**시운**(時運) propitiousness of the times; luck; fortune. ¶ ～ 성쇠 the fluctuation of fortune / ～이 바뀌어 at the turn of the wheel / ～이 나쁘다 The condition is unfavorable to us. / ～이 형통하다 The luck is good. / ～이 우리에게 불리하다 The times are against us.

**시운전**(試運轉) 《차의》 a trial run [trip, drive, voyage]; a trial operation; 《기계의》 test working; a test; 《배의》 a test cruise; a cruise test. ～하다 take 《a vehicle》 on a trial run; make a trial run 《of a train》; try out 《a machine, a car》. ¶ 엔진 ～ a test run of an engine / 지하철 ～ a subway trial run / ～ 결과는 매우 만족할 만했다 The result of the test-working was very satisfactory. /배는 ～을 받았다 The ship underwent a test cruise. / 새 기계는 ～중이다 The new machine is 「being tested [given a trial run].

**시원섭섭하다** feel mixed emotions of joy and sorrow. ¶ 딸을 시집보내고 나니 ～ feel relieved but sad at marrying off *one's* daughter.

**시원스럽다** 《성격이》 (be) frank; open-

hearted; unreserved; 《동작이》 (be) brisk; spirited; active; quick; 《말이》 (be) clear; flowing; outspoken.
¶ 시원스런 눈 large, bright eyes / 시원스런 성격(의 사람) (a person of) a frank disposition; (a man of) a free and frank nature / 문제를 시원스럽게 풀다 solve the question quite easily / 시원스럽지 못한 사람 a self-contained 〔reserved〕 man; a shilly-shallying person / 시원스럽게 처리하다 dispose of 《*a matter*》 lightly; dismiss 《*a matter*》 summarily / 시원스럽게 일하다 work with alacrity 〔in a brisk way〕 / 시원스럽게 말하다 speak briskly; give a satisfactory account / 나는 시원스러운 남자가 좋다 I like a frank 〔an open-hearted〕 man.

**시원시원하다** (be) clear and quick; be sparkling 〔bubbling〕 with life; (be) bright; animated; lively; exciting; inspiring. ¶ 시원시원한 어조로 in a clear 〔a distinct, an articulate〕 tone / 일하는 것이 ~ be a brisk 〔lively〕 worker / 시원시원하게 대답하다 give a straightforward 〔a frank, an unreserved〕 answer / 그의 시원시원한 대답이 나에게는 인상적이었다 His crisp repartee was very impressive to me.

**시원찮다** (be) unsatisfying; unsatisfactory; lacking; wanting; lack briskness 〔liveliness, freshness〕; (be) uninspiring; dull; disappointing.
¶ 시원찮은 대답 an answer that leaves something to be desired; an unsatisfactory answer / 시원찮은 수입 a scanty 〔meager, small〕 income / 시원찮은 상품 goods of poor quality / 결과가 별로 ~ I am not quite satisfied with the result. *or* The result is not much to my mind. / 그는 건강이 ~ He is not in the best of health. / 사업이 ~ The business is not doing very well. *or* The business is hard-pressed.

**시원하다** ① 《상쾌하다》 (be) refreshing; invigorating; inspiring; reviving; fresh; cool (서늘하다); brisk; 《만족스럽다》 (be) gratifying; pleasing; satisfactory; satisfying. ¶ 시원한 아침 a fresh morning / 시원한 바람 a refreshing breeze (★ a fresh breeze는 「질풍」이란 기상용어) / 시원한 음료 a refreshing drink / 기분이 ~ feel refreshed / 시원한 곳에 두다 keep 《*a thing*》 in a cool place / 여기는 시원해서 기분이 좋다 It is pleasantly cool here. / 소다수를 마시니 시원했다 I took soda water and it soothed my stomach. / 목욕하고 나면 시원해질 거야 You will feel refreshed after a bath. ② 《후련하다》 be a relief; feel good; feel relieved. ¶ (속)시원하게도 … to *one's* relief; it feels good to… / 할말을 다 해서 속이 ~ Now that I have had my say, I feel better. / 빚을 다 갚고 나니 ~ The load is off my mind now that I have cleared off my debts. ③ 《행동·말 따위가》 ⇨ 시원스럽다, 시원시원하다

**시월**(十月) October (생략 Oct.). ◉ ~막사리 around the end of October. ~상달 October the Harvest Month.

**시위** 《활의》 a bowstring. ¶ ~를 메우다 string a bow.

**시위**(示威) demonstration; display; showing. ~하다 demonstrate; display; show off. ¶ ~적(인) demonstrative; threatening; intimidating / 가두 ~ a street demonstration / 반전 ~ an anti-war demonstration / 근로자들이 생활비 상승에 항의하는 ~로 시가 행진을 했다 The workers marched through the streets to demonstrate against the rising cost of living.
◉ ~운동 a demonstration: ~ 운동자 a demonstrator / ~ 운동을 하다 have 〔hold, stage〕 a demonstration 《against》. ~진압 장비 riot control equipment. ~행진 a demonstration parade.

**시위**(侍衛) the Royal Body Guards. ~하다 guard; serve as attendant to 《the king》.

**시유**(市有) city 〔municipal〕 ownership; [형용사적] city-owned; municipal. ¶ 공장 이전 후에 당국은 그 자리를 ~화했다 After the move of the factory the authorities municipalized the site.
◉ ~림 a municipal 〔city-owned〕 forest. ~재산 municipal property. ~지 city land.

**시음**(試飮) sampling a beverage. ~하다 sample 《a beverage》; try 《a glass of bourbon》; test 《beverage》 by tasting. ¶ 이 포도주가 입에 맞으실는지 ~해 보십시오 Please taste 〔try〕 this wine to see if you like it.

**시읍면**(市邑面) cities, towns and villages; municipalities. ◉ ~장 the mayor of a city or town or the headman of a village.

**시의**(侍醫) the king's physician; a court physician.

**시의**(時宜) the right time; the right occasion; circumstances. ¶ ~에 맞지 않는 untimely; inopportune / ~를 얻

은 말 a word in season; a timely remark.

**시의**(猜疑) 《시기》 jealousy; 《의심》 suspicion. ～하다 《시기하다》 be jealous of 《*a person*》; 《의심하다》 be suspicious of 《*a person*》; suspect; doubt. ¶ ～의 눈으로 보다 look upon 《*a person*》 with suspicious eyes; suspect.
◉ ～심 suspicious mind: ～심이 강하다 be extremely jealous 〔suspicious〕 of 《*a person*》.

**시의회**(市議會) a city 〔municipal〕 assembly; a city 〔local〕 council.
◉ ～의사당 a municipal assembly hall. ～의원 a member of a municipal assembly; a municipal assemblyman; 《미》 a city councilman (★ 여성은 a councilwoman); an alderman; 《영》 a city councillor: ～ 의원 선거 a municipal election. ～의장 the president of a city assembly.

**시인**(是認) 《승인》 approval; endorsement; admission (허용); 《인정》 recognition; acknowledgment. ～하다 approve; endorse; 《구어》 OK; okay; admit 《a fact》; acknowledge 《*one's* fault》; concede 《that…》; own 《*oneself* guilty》. ¶ 비공식적으로 ～하다 give an unofficial endorsement 《to》 / 피고는 죄를 ～했다 The accused man admitted his guilt. / 자기의 잘못을 ～하다 admit 〔acknowledge〕 *one's* mistake / 그는 돈 훔친 것을 ～했다 He admitted to stealing money. / 내가 잘못이었다는 것을 ～한다 I do admit that I was wrong.

**시인**(詩人) a poet; a poetess (여자). ¶ 엉터리 ～ a poetaster; a versemonger / ～기질이 있다 have a poetic turn (of mind); have something of the poet 《in her》.

**시일**(時日) 《날짜》 the date; the day 《of》; 《때》 time; days; hours. ¶ ～과 장소 time and place / ～의 경과 the passage of time / ～이 경과함에 따라 as time passes 〔goes by〕; as the days go by / ～이 촉박하므로 as we are pressed for time / ～이 지나면 with the lapse 〔passage〕 of time / ～을 정하다 fix the date; choose the day; appoint the day / ～이 걸리다 take 〔require〕 (much) time; take long 〔many〕 days / ～이 얼마 없다 have little time left / 그것은 ～ 문제다 It is a question of time. / ～이 지나면 알게 된다 Time will tell 〔show〕 you. / 회합 ～은 아직 정해지지 않았다 The date has not yet been fixed for the meeting.

**시작**(始作) 《최초·개시》 the beginning; the first; the opening; the commencement; 《발단》 the start; the outset; 《기원》 the origin; the early stage (초기). ～하다 begin; commence; open 《the meeting》; 《장사 따위를》 set up「shop 〔business〕; open 〔start〕 《a store》; start 〔set up〕 《in business》; 《일 따위를》 set about 《*one's* work》; start 《on a job》; go 〔get down〕 to work; set 《a plan》 on foot (손대다). ¶ ～되다 begin; open; commence; start; date from (어느 날부터); be open (거래 따위가); break out (전쟁 따위가); set in (계절이); 《일어나다》 happen; arise 《from》; 《기인하다》 originate 《from 〔in〕 *a thing*》; originate 《with 〔from〕 *a person*》 / 역사가 ～된 이래 from the (earliest) dawn of history / ～부터 끝까지 from beginning to end / ～을 잘하다 make a good start / ～을 그르치다 begin at the wrong end; make a false start / 일을 ～하다 begin 〔set, start〕 to work; begin 〔start〕 working; set about *one's* work / 웃기 ～하다 begin to laugh / 영어 공부를 ～하다 begin learning 〔to learn〕 English / 정치 생활을 ～하다 enter upon a political career / 논쟁을 ～하다 start 〔launch into〕 an argument / 처음부터 다시〔새로〕 ～하다 begin again; make a new 〔fresh〕 start; do 《*a thing*》 over again / 5페이지에서 ～하다 begin on 〔at〕 page 5 / 제1장부터 ～하다 begin with the first chapter / 식당을 ～하다 open a restaurant / 학교는 8시〔3월 1일〕부터 ～한다 School begins at eight 〔on March 1st〕. / 장마철이 ～되었다 The rainy season has set in. / 무엇부터 ～할까요 What shall I 〔we〕 begin with? / 그녀는 양장점을 ～했다 She set up in business as a dressmaker. / 고유 명사는 대문자로 ～해야 한다 You must commence a proper noun with a capital letter. / 매사 ～이 어렵다 Everything is hard at the beginning. / 그때 벌써 수업은 ～되고 있었다 School was going on then. / ～한 것은 끝까지 해라 Stick to what you have started. / 질투에서 싸움이 ～됐다 The quarrel originated in jealousy. / 영화는 몇 시에 ～합니까 What time does the show start? / 회합은 7시에 ～될 것이다 The meeting will begin at seven o'clock. / 그녀는 현기증을 느

끼기 ~했다 She began to feel dizzy. / 비가 내리기 ~했다 It started raining. / 요즈음 ~된 이야기가 아니다 That is an old story. / 이것은 근대에 이르러 ~된 것이다 This is of modern origin. / ~이 반이다 《속담》 A good start is half the battle. *or* A good beginning is half done. / 시합은 제시간에 ~되었다 The game kick off on time.

**시작**(試作) trial manufacture 〔production〕; manufacture for trial; 《재배》 trial growing; 《문예》 a (creative) study; an *étuae* (F.). ~하다 manufacture 〔create〕 for trial; produce by way of trial 〔experiment〕; 《작품을》 compose 〔write, sculpture, *etc.*〕 as an experiment. ◉ ~전시회 a study exhibition.

**시작**(詩作) composition of poems; versification; poem writing; verse-making. ~하다 write 〔compose〕 poems; versify. ¶ ~에 골몰하다 devote *oneself* to the composition of poems.

**시장** hunger. ~하다 (be) hungry; feel empty; (be) famished 《미》. ¶ 몹시 ~하다 be (as) hungry as a hunter; be savagely hungry / ~해서 죽겠다 I am dying with hunger. / ~이 반찬 《속담》 Hunger is the best sauce.

**시장**(市長) a mayor; a mayoress (여시장). ¶ 서울 ~ the Mayor of Seoul / 런던 ~ the Lord Mayor (of London).
◉ ~관사 a mayor's mansion. ~부인 the wife of a mayor; a mayoress 《영》. ~선거 a mayoral(ty) election. ~임기 mayoralty. ~직 mayorship.

**시장**(市場) 《정기적으로 열리는》 a market; a market place (시장터); 《상설의》 a shopping center 〔precinct〕.
¶ 어(魚)~ a fish market / 청과 ~ a vegetable market / 과점 ~ an oligopolistic market / 자본~ the capital market / 지방~ a local market / 외국〔해외〕 ~ a foreign 〔an overseas〕 market / 국내 ~ the home 〔domestic〕 market / 중앙 도매 ~ the central wholesale market / 공개 ~ 조작 an open market operation / 증권 ~의 폭락 the stock market crash / ~에 내놓다 bring 《commodities》 to the market; put 〔place〕 on the market / ~에 나오다 come into 〔appear in〕 the market / ~에 나와 있다 be on 〔in〕 the market / 세계 ~에서 경쟁하다 compete in the world 〔global〕 marketplace / ~에 …을 공급하다 provide 〔supply〕 a market with … / ~을 장악〔지배〕하다 hold 〔control〕 a market / ~을 개척하다 open up 〔cultivate〕 a market / ~을 구축하다 build up a market 《for》 / ~을 독점하다 engross 〔swipe〕 the market / ~을 조종하다 manipulate the market / ~을 확장하다 extend 〔develop〕 a market / 새로운 ~을 획득하다 acquire 〔capture〕 a new market / ~의 동향을 살피다 read the market / 새로운 상품을 ~에 내놓다 introduce a new product into a market / ~은 강세다 The market is firm 〔strong〕. / ~이 불황이다〔약세다〕 The market is flat 〔stagnant, weak〕. / 우리는 새로운 외국 ~을 찾고 있다 We are seeking a new foreign market. / 신제품은 곧 중국 ~에서 판로를 찾아낼 것이다 The new products will soon find their way into the Chinese market.
◉ ~가격 market prices; a market rate. ~가치 market value. ~경제 the market economy. ~다변화 market diversification. ~분석 a market analysis: ~ 분석가 a market analyst. ~붕괴 (a) market meltdown. ~생산 production for markets. ~시세 a market price; quotations. ~점유율 a (market) share. ~조사 a market survey; market surveying 〔research〕: ~ 조사를 하다 conduct a market survey. ~조작 market manipulation 〔operations〕.

**시장개발**(市場開發) market development; opening up new markets 〔the market〕.

**시장개방**(市場開放) opening 《Korea's》 markets 《to the world》. ¶ ~ 압력 market-opening pressure / 쌀 ~ 반대 캠페인 a campaign against rice market opening / 외국으로부터 ~ 요구가 거세지고 있다 There are growing foreign demands that we open our markets. ◉ ~책(策) market-opening measures 〔policies〕.

**시장기**(一氣) hungriness. ¶ ~가 심하다 be terribly hungry / ~를 느끼다 feel empty 〔hungry〕 / 차 한 잔으로 ~를 달래다 allay hunger with a cup of tea.

**시장성**(市場性) marketability. ¶ ~이 있는 marketable / ~이 없는 유가 증권 unmarketable 〔nonnegotiable〕 securities.

**시재**(詩才) poetic talent 〔genius〕. ¶ ~가 있다 have a genius for poetry; be endowed with poetic genius / ~를 발휘하다 display 〔show, exhibit〕 *one's* poetic genius.

**시재**(詩材) a subject for a poem; verse

material; material for poetry.

**시적**(詩的) poetic(al) (★ '시의'의 뜻으로는 보통 poetical, '시적인'의 뜻으로는 보통 poetic을 씀). ¶ ~인 아름다움 poetic beauty / 이 광경은 아주 ~이군 The scene is a fit subject for a poem. / 그녀의 편지에는 ~인 표현이 넘친다 Her letter is full of poetic expressions. ◉ ~감흥(이 솟아나다) (have) a poetic inspiration.

**시적거리다** do reluctantly 〔listlessly, sluggishly〕.

**시적시적** listlessly; sluggishly; without enthusiasm; with little spirit.

**시절**(時節) ① 《계절》 the season; the time of the year. ¶ 꽃피는 ~ the flower season / ~에 맞는 seasonable / ~에 맞지 않는 out of season; unseasonable / 백합꽃이 피는 ~에 at lily time / 해마다 이 ~에는 늘 바람이 세차다 It generally blows hard at this time of the year. ② 《시기》 time; an occasion; an opportunity. ¶ 살기 힘든 ~ hard times / 그 ~에(는) in those days; at that time; then / 학생 ~에 in *one's* school days / 소년 ~에 when *one* was a boy; in *one's* boyhood 〔childhood〕 / 청년〔젊은〕 ~에 in *one's* youth; while (*one* is) young / 좋은 ~을 기다리다 wait for a 「ripe opportunity 〔better chance〕 / 그 ~에는 인쇄술이 없었다 Printing was yet unknown in those days. / 옛 ~이 그립다 How well I recall the good old days!

**시점**(時點) a point of 〔in〕 time. ¶ 이 ~에서 at 〔from〕 this point of time / 오늘의 ~에서 as of today / 현~까지 up to the present / 그 ~에서는 모든 것이 잘되고 있었다 Everything went well at that time.

**시점**(視點) a visual point; 《관점》 a point of view. ¶ 사물을 여러 ~에서 보다 see things from various points of view / 정치적 ~에서 보다 consider from a political point of view.

**시접** a margin 「to sew up 〔to seam〕; a tuck.

**시정**(市井) ① 《시가》 a street; streets; a town. ¶ ~의 일들 events in 〔on〕 the streets / ~사람〔인〕 a man in 〔on〕 the street. ② 《시정아치》 a market tradesman 〔merchant〕; townsmen.

**시정**(市政) municipal 〔city〕 administration 〔government〕. ¶ ~의 civic; municipal / ~을 개혁하다 reform municipal government; make a civic 〔municipal〕 reform.

**시정**(是正) correction; rectification; revision (수정). ~하다 correct; rectify; set right; put to right; revise. ¶ 못된 버릇을 ~하다 correct a bad habit; break *oneself* of an evil habit / 잘못을 ~하다 correct errors / 폐단을 ~하다 put down abuses; redress evils / 선거제도를 ~하다 revise the election system / 불공평을 ~하다 correct 〔rectify〕 (the) inequities / 이 제도는 ~할 필요가 있다 This system must be improved upon. / ~해야 할 점이 몇 가지 있다 There are some points to be 「improved upon 〔straightened out〕. / 이러한 점들은 ~할 필요가 있다 It is necessary to straighten out these points.

**시정**(施政) administration; statesmanship; government. ~하다 administer 〔govern〕 《a land properly》. ◉ ~권 an administrative authority. ~방침 an administrative policy; 《정당의》 party lines: ~방침을 정하다〔발표하다〕 decide upon 〔announce, make a declaration of〕 an administrative policy. ~연설 a policy speech on state affairs; a speech on *one's* administrative policies.

**시정**(詩情) poetic sentiment 〔feeling〕.

**시제**(市制) municipal system 〔organization〕. ¶ ~를 실시하다 reorganize 《a town》 as a city 〔municipality〕; municipalize 《a town》.

**시제**(時制) 〖문법〗 the tense. ¶ 현재〔과거, 미래〕 ~ the present 〔past, future〕 tense / ~의 일치 the sequence of tenses.

**시제**(時祭) ancestor-memorial services performed in each season of the year.

**시제**(詩題) a subject 〔theme〕 for a poem.

**시조**(始祖) the founder 《of a family, a dynasty, *etc.*》; the originator; the progenitor; the father. ¶ 인류의 ~ the progenitor of the human race / 노동운동의 ~ the father of labor movement / 우리 나라 서양 의학의 ~ the father of Western medical science in our country. ◉ ~새 〖고생물〗 an archaeopteryx (*pl.* -es).

**시조**(時調) a *shijo* (= a kind of short lyric poem). ¶ ~를 읊다 recite a *shijo* / ~를 짓다 compose 〔write〕 a *shijo*.

**시종**(始終) [명사적] beginning and end; [부사적] from start to finish; throughout; all through; all the way 〔time〕. ¶ ~일관 consistently / ~여일하다 be the same from beginning to end; be consistent / 경기는 ~ 일방적이었다 The game was one-sided from start to finish. / 그녀는 ~ 찡그리고〔툴툴대고〕 있다 She is always frowning 〔grumbling〕. / 그는 ~ 묵묵히 그들의 논쟁을 듣고 있었다 He remained silent from first to last listening to their discussion.

**시종**(侍從) a chamberlain; a lord 〔gentleman〕 in waiting《영》. ◉ ~무관 an officer in attendance on His Majesty. ~장(長) the Grand Chamberlain.

**시주**(施主)〖불교〗《사람》 a benefactor; a donor; a donator; an offerer;《행위》 almsgiving (to a priest 〔temple〕); donation; offering;《금품》 alms; an offering. ~하다 give alms (to a temple). ¶ 감사의 ~ a thanksgiving offering to a temple《for》/ 절에 ~하다 make an 〔a monetary〕 offering to a temple.

**시준**(視準)〖물리〗 collimation. ~하다 collimate《a telescope》. ◉ ~기 a mercury collimator. ~오차 a collimation error.

**시중** personal attention; attendance; service; waiting on; care; trouble. ~하다 attend; wait on; serve; take care of. ~하다〔들다〕 help《*a person* with *his* work》; lend a (helping) hand《to》; wait (up)on《*a person*》; attend (on); take care of; care for; look 〔see〕 after《*a person*》; see to.
¶ 병자를 ~하다 attend (on) the sick; tend 〔care for〕 the sick / 부모를 ~하다 take care of *one's* parents / 식사 ~을 들다 wait on《*a person*》 at table; wait (on) table / ~ 좀 들어 다오 I need your help.

**시중**(市中) ①《도시의 안》《in》 the city; the street; [형용사적] urban. ②〖금융〗《시장》 the open market. ◉ ~금리 the open market interest rate. ~시세 the open market price. ~은행 a city 〔commercial〕 bank.

**시즌** a season. ¶ 야구〔수영〕~ the baseball 〔bathing〕 season.

**시지에스단위**(一單位) C.G.S. 〔c.g.s., cgs〕 system. [< *c*entimeter, *g*ram, *s*econd]

**시진**(視診)〖의학〗 an ocular inspection. ¶ ~만으로도 …로 진단하다 make an ocular inspection of《a patient》 and diagnose *his* illness as《neurosis》.

**시집**(媤—) *one's* husband's home 〔family〕. ¶ ~도 가기 전에 기저귀 마련한다《속담》 Count *one's* chickens before they are hatched. / ~에서 쫓겨나다 be compelled to leave her husband's home.

**시집**(詩集) a collection 〔an anthology〕 of poems; poetical works. ¶ 근대 ~ a book of modern verse; an anthology of modern poetry / 바이런 ~ (a collection of) Byron's poetical works.

**시집가다**(媤—) marry《a man》; be 〔get〕 married《to *a person,* into a family》; take a husband. ¶ 시집간 married / 시집갈 준비를 하다 prepare for marriage / 시집갈 나이이다 be old enough to be 〔get〕 married; be of a marriageable age / 그녀는 시집갈 나이가 지났다 She is past marriageable age.

**시집보내다**(媤—) marry《*one's* daughter》(off)《to *a person*》; give《*one's* daughter》(away) in marriage. ¶ 딸을 의사에게 ~ marry *one's* daughter to a doctor.

**시집살이**(媤—) married life 〔housekeeping〕 in the home of the husband's parents. ¶ ~에 고생하다 lead a hard married life (in *one's* parents-in-law's home).

**시차**(時差) a time difference 〔differential〕; (a) difference in time;〖천문〗 the equation of time. ¶ 서울과 뉴욕은 14 시간의 ~가 있다 There is a fourteen-hour time difference between Seoul and New York. / ~로 인한 피로를 회복하는 데 이틀 정도 걸렸다 It took a couple of days to recover from jet lag.
◉ ~계 an equation timepiece. ~제 staggering work-hour system: ~제 출근《adopt, enforce》 staggered working 〔office, commuting〕 hours.

**시차**(視差)〖천문〗 (a) parallax. ¶ ~의 〔에 의한〕 parallactic《motion》/ 두 눈〔태양〕의 ~ binocular 〔solar〕 parallax.

**시찰**(視察) (an) inspection; observation. ~하다 inspect; observe; make an inspection of; visit. ¶ 현장을 ~하다 take a view of the scene / 현지를 ~하다 make an on-site inspection《of》/ 여러 학교를 ~하다 inspect 〔make an inspection of〕 various schools / 일선을 ~하러 가다 go on an observation trip to 〔at〕 the front / 장관은 지금 수재 지역을 ~중이다 The Minister is on an inspection tour of the flood-stricken area.
◉ ~단 an inspection party; a group

of inspectors; 《사업의》 a business mission 《to the U.S.》; 《군사 시설 등의》 an observation team. ~여행 an inspection tour; a tour of inspection; an observation trip.

**시채**(市債) a municipal 〔city〕 loan 〔debt〕; a municipal bond (채권). ¶ ~를 모집〔발행〕하다 raise 〔issue〕 a municipal loan.

**시책**(施策) a measure; a policy; 《시행》 enforcement of policies. ~하다 enforce 〔execute〕 a policy. ¶ 나라의 ~ state measures / ~을 강구하다 consider how to cope with 《the situation》; take measure to meet 《the situation》 / ~을 그르치다 take a wrong step 〔measure〕 / 정부는 폭동을 진압하기 위한 ~을 강구했다 The Government has taken measures 〔steps〕 to put down the riot.

**시척지근하다** be sourish (by being 「partly spoiled).

**시청**(市廳) a municipal 〔city〕 office; 《청사》 a city hall; the municipal building.

**시청**(視聽) looking and listening. ~하다 look and listen. ¶ 텔레비전을 ~하다 watch television. ◉ (텔레비전) ~료 television 〔TV〕 subscription fee.

**시청**(試聽) an audition 《of new recordings》. ~하다 give an audition 《to》; audition. ◉ ~실 an audition room.

**시청각**(視聽覺) the visual and auditory senses; (the senses of) sight and hearing. ◉ ~교육 audio-visual teaching 〔education〕. ~교재 audio-visual materials 〔aids〕. ~실(室) an audio-visual room.

**시청률**(視聽率) 〖TV〗 a program 〔an audience〕 rating; a (popularity) rating; a viewing rate. ¶ ~이 제일 높은 TV프로 the top-rated TV program / ~을 높이다 improve the audience ratings. ◉ ~조사 《make》 an audience rating survey.

**시청자**(視聽者) 〖TV〗 a (TV) (tele)viewer; the TV audience [총칭]. ◉ ~상담실 viewers' consultation room. ~여론조사 the audience response rating. ~참가프로 a participation program 〔show〕; 《전화에 의한》 a phone-in; a call-in 《미》.

**시체**(屍體) a (dead) body; a corpse; a cadaver (해부용의); a carcass (동물의). ¶ ~의〔같은〕 cadaverous / ~를 유기〔발굴〕하다 abandon 〔exhume〕 a dead body / ~ 발굴 exhume of a dead body / 타살~ the body of a murdered person / ~를 발견하다 find 〔recover〕 a body / ~로 발견되다 be found dead / ~를 안치하다 lay the remains in state / ~를 인도하다 hand *a person's* body over 《to》 / ~의 인수자가 없다 No one has claimed the body. ◉ ~검사 an inquest (on the body of). ~안치소 a morgue; a mortuary; a dead house. ~유기 abandonment of a dead body: ~유기죄 《be accused of》 (the crime of) abandoning a dead body. ~해부 dissection of a dead body; necrotomy; 《검시를 위한》 an autopsy; a postmortem (examination).

**시초**(始初) the beginning; the inception; the opening; the start; 《발단》 the outset; 《기원》 the origin. ⇨처음.

**시추**(試錐) drilling (for exploratory wells); boring. ~하다 drill; bore. ¶ 석유 ~ oil(-well) drilling. ◉ ~공(孔) a wildcat; an exploratory hole. ~기 a drill; a drilling 〔boring〕 machine. ~선〔장비〕 an oil drilling ship 〔rig〕.

**시취**(屍臭) the smell of a dead body; a putrid smell.

**시취**(詩趣) poetical interest 〔feeling, sentiment〕. ¶ ~가 있다 be poetic(al) / ~가 없다 have no 〔hardly any〕 poetry 《in it》; be prosaic.

**시치다** tack; baste. ¶ 주름을 ~ tack down a fold.

**시치름하다** ⇨ 새치름하다.

**시치미** 《말·짓》 feigned ignorance; assumed innocense; false pretense; dissimulation. ¶ ~를 뚝 뗀 얼굴 표정 《have》 a blank look; 《make》 a poker face / ~를 떼고 with an air of innocence; with a straight face; boldly / ~를 떼다 play (the) innocent; feign 〔pretend〕 ignorance; pretend not to know / ~를 떼고 물어보았다 I asked him about it as if I did not know. / 그는 ~를 떼고 모른다고 했다 With 「feigned ignorance 〔an air of innocence〕, he said, "I know nothing about it." / ~ 떼지 마라, 네가 무슨 짓을 저질렀는지 잘 알 텐데 Don't play innocent. You know very well what you've done. 「(It.).

**시칠리아** 《이탈리아의 섬》 Sicily; *Sicilia*

**시침** ① ⇨ 시침질. ② ⇨ 시치미.

**시침**(時針) the hour 〔short〕 hand (of a timepiece). 「baste.

**시침질** tacking; basting. ~하다 tack;

**시카고** 《미국의 도시》 Chicago. ◉ ~시민 a Chicagoan.

**시커멀다** (be) deep-〔jet-〕black; raven; 《속셈이》 (be) wicked. ¶ 마음이 ~ be blackhearted 〔evilhearted, wicked〕.

**시케이디 제도**(CKD 制度) 《부품 수출, 현지 조립 판매 방식》 the Complete Knock Down system.

**시큰둥하다** (be) pert; impudent; fresh; sassy; smart-alecky; be full of back-talk. ¶ 시큰둥한 대답 a pert answer; a saucy reply / 시큰둥한 소리를 하다 say saucy things / 그 시큰둥한 소리 좀 집어쳐 Don't be saucy.

**시클라멘** 〖식물〗 a cyclamen.

**시큼-** ⇨ 시금-.

(-)**시키다** 《강제하다》 force 〔compel〕 《*a person* to *do*》; make 《*a person do*》; 《허가·방임하다》 let 《*a person do*》; allow 《*a person* to *do*》; 《주문하다》 order 《*something* from *a person, a person* to *do something*》; 《의뢰·부탁하다》 get 《*a person* to *do*》; have 《*a person do*》. (★ 이들 동사를 사역 동사(causative verb)라 함. 그 가운데 어느 것은 뒤에 원형 부정사(root-infinitive)가 계속되고, 어떤 것은 뒤에 to 있는 부정사(to-infinitive)가 계속됨. 앞의 것으로는 make, let, bid, have가 있고 뒤의 것으로는 order, ask, cause, allow, get 등이 있음).
¶ 아무에게 일을 ~ make *a person* work; put *a person* to work / 딸에게 노래를 ~ have *one's* daughter sing a song; ask *one's* daughter to sing / 피자를 ~ order a pizza / 사직~ force 《*a person*》 to resign; dismiss 《*a person*》 / 아들을 공부~ give *one's* son education; educate *one's* son / 서울 구경을 ~ show 《*a person*》 round Seoul / 싸움을 ~ get a fight started; get 《*a person*》 to fight / 아무에게 극장 구경을 ~ treat *a person* to a show / 웨이터에게 식사 준비를 ~ have the waiter prepare the table / 학생을 유학 ~ arrange for a student to study abroad / 시키는 대로 하다 do as *one* is told 《to *do*》 / 아무를 시켜서 의사를 부르다 send *a person* out for a doctor / 아버지가 (나를) 졸업시켰다 My father made me graduate. / 그 애에게 말(을) 시켜 보세요 Try to get the child to talk. / 나는 그들에게 그 방의 청소를 시켰다 I had 〔made〕 them clean the room. *or* I got them to clean the room. / 그것은 일반에게 구경시키지 않는다 They don't let the public see it. / 그 일은 저에게 시켜 주십시오 Let me do it, please. / 네게 그런 일을 시키려고 했던 것은 아니다 I didn't mean you to do anything of the sort. / 나는 구두 수선을 시켰다 I had 〔got〕 my shoes mended. (★ 이 경우에는 had나 got에 악센트가 있음. 그러나 I had my father killed. 「아버지가 피살되었다」의 경우는 사역이 아니고 피동이므로 had에 악센트가 없음).

**시토** SEATO. [<the *S*outh*e*ast *A*sia *T*reaty *O*rganization]

**시퉁스럽다** (be) impertinent; impudent; cheeky; fresh. ¶ 시퉁스러운 말투 a cheeky 〔impertinent〕 way of talking 〔speaking〕.

**시트** ① 《자리》 a seat. ¶ 그 자동차의 뒤쪽 ~는 세 사람이 앉을 만큼 넓다 The back seat of the car is wide enough for three people. ② 《우표의》 a sheet; 《침대의》 a (bed) sheet. ¶ 침대에 ~를 갈다 change the sheets on *one's* bed.

**시트론** ① 〖식물〗 a citron. ② 《음료수》 citron water.

**시트콤** (a) situation comedy; 《구어》 (a) sitcom.

**시틋하다** (be) disinclined; unwilling; languid; weary; [서술적] be tired of.

**시판**(市販) marketing; sale at a market. ~하다 market; put 《goods》 「on the market 〔on sale〕; sell over the counter. ¶ ~ 가능성 marketability / ~되고 있다 be on the market / 이 제품은 어제부터 ~되기 시작했다 This product came onto the market only yesterday. ◉ ~품 goods on the market. 공동~ joint marketing.

**시판**(試販) 《상품의》 an adventure. ◉ ~품 goods on trial sale.

**시퍼렇다** ① (be) deep blue; [서술적] be a vivid blackish blue. ¶ 시퍼렇게 멍들도록 때리다 beat 《*a person*》 black and blue. ② 《안색이》 (be) pallid; [서술적] be deadly 〔ghastly〕 pale. ③ 《날붙이 서슬이》 (be) sharp; sharp-edged. ¶ 서슬이 시퍼런 날 a well-sharpened 〔sharply honed〕 blade. ④ 《위풍·권세가》 (be) powerful; influential; stately. ¶ 권세가 ~ be very powerful 〔influential〕 / 그는 서슬도 시퍼렇게 나에게 대들었다 He turned on me 「with an angry look 〔threateningly〕.

**시편**(詩篇) 〖성서〗 the Book of Psalms; 《약칭》 the Psalm (생략 Ps., Psa.).

**시평**(時評) comments on current events 〔topics〕; comments on the day's problem. ◉ ~가 a (news) commentator. ~란(欄) a column on current events. 문예~ comments on current literature.

**시폐**(時弊) evils of the times; abuses

of the age; existing evils. ¶ ～를 바로잡다 remedy 〔correct〕 the (prevailing) evils of the time / ～에 물들다 be 「tainted 〔stained, infected〕 with evils of the times.

**시풍**(詩風) a poetical style.

**시프트** 〖컴퓨터〗 shift. ◉ ～레지스터 a shift register. ～섹터 a shift sector. ～아웃〔인〕 shift-out〔-in〕. ～키 a shift key.

**시필**(試筆) writing for trial. ～하다 write for trial. ◉ 신년～ the New Year's writing.

**시하**(侍下) a person supporting *one's* parents 〔grandparents〕.

**시하**(時下) [부사적] at present; at this time. ¶ ～ 엄동에 in this season of cold winter.

**시학**(詩學) study of poetry; poetics; 「prosody (운율학).

**시한**(時限) a time limit; a limit of time; a deadline. ¶ 법적 ～ the legal deadline / 다행히 ～에는 댈 수 있어서 문제되지 않았다 Fortunately I was able to meet the deadline and didn't cause any trouble at all.
◉ ～부 동맹 파업 a strike for a limited number of hours; a time-limited strike. ～부 인생 《lead》 a time-limited life: 그녀는 자주 ～부 인생을 살고 있는, 죽음을 목전에 둔 환자들을 방문한다 She often visits patients who are leading time-limited life and face death. ～부 환자 《take care of》 a terminally ill patient. ～장치 a time device: ～장치는 오후 2시에 맞추어졌다 The time device 「was set at 〔had been timed for〕 2 p.m. ～폭탄 a time bomb.

**시할머니**(媤—) *one's* husband's grandmother.

**시할아버지**(媤—) *one's* husband's grand「father.

**시합**(試合) a match; a contest; a game; a bout; 《행위》 play(ing). ⇨ 경기.

**시행**(施行) carrying out; enforcement; operation. ～하다 carry out; enforce; put in force; put 《a law》 into operation 〔effect〕; carry into effect; give effect 《to》. ¶ ～되다 take 〔go into〕 effect; be put in force; become effective; come into force 〔operation〕 / ～되고 있다 be in force 〔operation〕 / 이 법률은 2001년 3월 1일 이후 ～된다 The law will 「take effect 〔go into operation〕 on and after March 1, 2001.
◉ ～규칙 enforcement regulations. ～기간 a period of effectiveness. ～기일 the date of enforcement. ～령 an enforcement ordinance. ～세칙 detailed regulations for the application of a law.

**시행착오**(試行錯誤) 〖심리·컴퓨터〗 trial and error. ¶ 인간은 ～로 많은 기술을 습득한다 A man acquires a lot of skills by trial and error. / 인생은 ～의 연속이다 Life is the repetition of trial and error. ◉ ～법 a trial-and-error method 〔technique〕; the rule 〔method〕 of trial and error.

**시허옇다** (be) snow-white.

**시험**(試驗) ① 《지식·능력의》 an examination; a test; a quiz (*pl.* ～zes) 《미》 (간단하고 비공식의); an exam 《구어》. ～하다 examine *somebody* 《in chemistry, on *his* knowledge of English》; hold 〔conduct〕 an examination 《in》; give *somebody* an exam 〔a test〕 《in》; test *somebody* 《on》.
¶ 무～으로 without examination / 모의 ～ a sham examination; a mock exam / 수학〔영어〕 ～ an examination in mathematics 〔English〕 / 어려운 ～ a stiff examination / ～을 보다〔치르다〕 take 〔undergo, sit for, go in for〕 an examination / ～ 감독을 하다 supervise 〔proctor 《미》, invigilate 《영》〕 an exam / 학생에게 영어를 ～하다 examine students in English; test the students English / ～에 떨어지다〔실패하다〕 fail in an examination; flunk a test 〔quiz〕 (★ 미어에서는 fail an examination이라고도 함) / ～에 합격하다 succeed 〔be successful〕 in an examination; pass an examination / ～을 보고〔보지않고〕 입학하다 enter a school through 〔without〕 an examination / (문제가) ～에 나오다 be asked 〔given〕 in an examination / 남에게 대리 ～을 치게 하다 get another to sit for the examination for *one* / ～중이다 The examination is going on now. / 내일 ～이 있다 I have an exam coming up tomorrow. / ～ 채점에 바쁘다 I am busy looking over the examination papers. / 이건 ～에 나올 듯한 문제다 This question seems likely to be asked in the examination. / 이번 ～은 잘 봐야만 한다 I've got to do well in the coming exam. / 그 문제는 지난 ～에 나왔었다 The same question was 「asked in the last examination 〔appeared on the last test〕. / ～ 잘 쳤느냐? How have you fared in your exam?
② 《실험》 an experiment; a trial. ～하다 experiment 《on》; do 〔conduct〕 an

experiment 〔a test〕《on, in》; test《a new car》; make a trial of; put《*a thing*》to the test.
¶ ~적(인) tentative; experimental;《제조 등의》pilot《production, medicine》/ ~적으로 in a tentative way 〔manner〕; tentatively; experimentally; on a trial basis / ~삼아 ⇨ 시험삼아 / 이미 ~이 끝난 tried and tested 〔trusted〕/ 기술을 ~해 보다 test《*a person's*》skill / 새 라디오를 ~하다 try out a new radio / 인물을 ~하다 put *a person's* character to the test / 마이크 ~중입니다 Testing, testing, testing, One, two, three—testing.
◉ ~감독《일》the proctoring of an exam; an invigilation《영》;《사람》a proctor; an invigilator《영》. ~공부 preparation 〔cramming (벼락 공부)〕 for an examination: ~ 공부하다 prepare 〔cram〕 for an exam; slog 〔grind〕 (away) at examination subjects. ~공장 a pilot plant. ~과목 a subject for 〔of〕 examination. ~관(官) an examiner. ~기간《새 방식 따위의》a test (-ing) period; a term of trial. ~기일 the date of an examination. ~단계 the testing stage. ~답안지 an examination 〔a test《미》〕 paper 〔sheet〕; a blue book《미》. ~문제 exam(ination) questions; questions for an examination. ~발사 test-firing: ~ 발사하다 test-fire. ~방법 a method of exam(ination). ~비행 a test 〔trial〕 flight: ~비행하다 test《an airplane》 in flight; flight-test / ~비행사 a test pilot. ~생산 pilot production. ~소 = 시험장. ~실 a test room; a laboratory. ~위원 an examiner; an examination board [총칭]. ~제도 the examination system. ~지《시험 용지》an examination paper;〖화학〗a litmus paper. ~지옥 the ordeal of (entrance) exams. ~필《게시》Tried.
강도〔내구성〕~ a strength 〔durability〕 test. 검정~ a certificate 〔license〕 examination. 자격~ a qualifying examination. 학년말~ a year-end exam (-ination). 학력~ an achievement test; an examination to test scholastic ability.

**시험관**(試驗管) a test tube. ¶ ~ 배양 a (test-)tube culture. ◉ ~내 수정《체외 수정》in vitro fertilization (생략 I.V.F.). ~아기 a test-tube baby; a tubebaby

**시험삼아**(試驗—) by way of experiment 〔trial〕; on 〔for〕 trial; tentatively; as a test 〔an experiment〕. ¶ ~ 해보다 try; have a try《at》; make an attempt; give《*a thing*》a trial; do《*something*》on trial; try *one's* hand 《at》; take chances《with》/ ~ 고용하다 employ《*a person*》「by way of experiment 〔on a trial basis〕; hire 《*a person*》tentatively / 한 달간 ~ 써보다 give《*a person*》a month's trial.

**시험장**(試驗場)《입시 따위의》an examination room 〔hall〕;《실험실·연구실 따위》a《hygienic》laboratory; an《agricultural》experiment station;《무기·농법 따위의》a testing 〔proving〕 ground. ¶ 농업 ~ an agricultural experiment station.

**시험준비**(試驗準備) preparation for an examination. ¶ ~를 하다 prepare for an examination; cram for an exam.

**시현**(示現) revelation (by a divinity).

**시형**(詩形) a verse 〔poetic〕 form. ◉ ~학 prosody.

**시호**(諡號) a posthumous title (granted by the king to an eminent scholar or to an outstanding statesman).

**시화법**(視話法) visible speech.

**시화전**(詩畫展) an exhibition of illustrated poems《by》.

**시황**(市況) the tone 〔state, movement〕 of the market; market conditions; the market. ¶ ~의 전망 the market outlook 〔prospect〕/ ~이 활발〔한산〕하다 The market is brisk 〔quiet〕. / ~은 정상 상태를 되찾았다 The market has come to a normal trade condition. ◉ ~보고 a market report. ~산업 a cyclical business; market-driven industry: 섬유 산업은 ~ 산업이다 Textile industry is market-oriented. 증권~ the stock market; stock exchange quotations.

**시회**(詩會) a poetry club.

**시효**(時效)〖법〗prescription; the statute of limitations. ¶ 소멸〔취득〕~ negative 〔positive〕 prescription / ~에 걸리다 be barred 〔extinguished〕 by prescription; lapse / ~가 끝나다 the 《ten-year》statute of limitations runs out / ~에 의한 권리를 주장하다 prescribe《for, to》/ ~를 취득했다 The prescription has been acquired.
◉ ~기간 the period of prescription. ~정지〔중단〕 suspension 〔interruption〕 of prescription.

**시후**(時候) the season;《일기》weather. ◉ ~문안 compliments of the season.

**시흥**(詩興) poetic inspiration. ¶ ~이 샘솟다 be inspired「to make up〔to compose〕a poem; have poetical inspiration.

(-)**식**(式) ①《식전》a ceremony; rites; rituals. ¶ 장례식 the funeral〔burial〕rites / 결혼식 a wedding ceremony / 세례식 rites of baptism / 식을 거행하다〔올리다〕hold〔have, perform〕a ceremony; celebrate《a wedding》.
②《양식》a form; an established form; formality; style. ¶ 식을 따르다 conform to forms / 식을 갖추어 딸을 혼인시키다 marry *one's* daughter in proper style.
③《형》a mode; a style; a type; a fashion; a plan;《방식》a method; a system; a way; a manner. ¶ 존스식 발음 기호 the Jones's system of phonetic notation〔symbols〕/ 신식 영어 교수법 a new method of teaching English / 한국식(의) (of) Korean style〔fashion〕/ 서양식으로 집을 짓다 build a house in western style / 나는 내 식으로 일한다 I have my own way of doing things. / 저런 식으로 하면 그는 실패할 것이 틀림없다 If he does it (in) that way, he must fail. (★ way가 this, that 등의 말과 함께 쓰이면 구어체에서는 전치사가 생략되어 부사적으로 쓰임: Do〔Have〕it (in) your own way.) / 편지는 이런 식으로 쓰는 것이다 This is the way to write a letter. (★ the way how〔in which〕대신 the way나 how만을 씀).
④〖수학〗an expression;〖화학〗a formula (*pl.* ~s, -lae). ¶ 대수식 an algebraic expression / 이항식 a binomial expression / 화학식 a chemical formula / 물의 분자〔구조〕식 the molecular〔structural〕formula for water / 식으로 나타내다 formulate《a theorem》;「put into〔express in〕formula; formularize.

**식**(蝕)〖천문〗an eclipse; occultation.

**식간**(食間)〔부사적〕between meals. ¶ ~에 약을 먹다 take *one's* medicine between meals.

**식객**(食客) a retainer; a hanger-on (*pl.* hangers-on); a parasite; a dependent; a sponger. ¶ ~생활 parasitism / ~노릇을 하다 be a dependent《on》; live〔sponge〕《on》.

**식견**(識見)《판단력》knowledge; experience; insight; discernment;《의견》views; an opinion. ¶ ~이 높은 of exalted ideas / ~이 높은 사람 a man of exalted ideas; a man of broad views and high intelligence / ~이 있다《제 의견을 갖고 있다》have an opinion of *one's* own;《안식이 있다》have an eye《for paintings》; have considerable insight.

**식경**(食頃)〔부사적〕for the period of a single meal; for a while.

**식곤증**(食困症) languor〔drowsiness〕after a meal.

**식구**(食口) members of a family; a family; mouths to feed. ¶ ~ 수 the number of mouths to feed; the number of dependents / ~가 많다〔적다〕have a large〔small〕family (★ have many families로는 할 수 없음); have many〔few〕mouths to feed / ~를 부양하다 support *one's* family / 우리 집은 다섯 ~다 We are a family of five. / 그는 나를 한 ~처럼 대한다 He treats me like〔as〕one of the family. / 우리 집 ~들은 일찍 일어난다 My family are early risers.

**식권**(食券) a meal ticket〔coupon〕;《영》a luncheon voucher (직원에게 지급되는).

**식균작용**(食菌作用)〖동물〗《백혈구의》「phagocytosis.

**식기**(食器)《그릇》tableware; a dinner set; a table service;《주발》a bowl. ¶ 전자식 ~ 세척기《접시 따위의》an electronic dishwasher. ◉ ~건조기 a dish dryer. ~세척기 a dish washer. ~장 a pantry; a cupboard.

**식다** ①《온도가》get cold; cool off; (become) cool. ¶ 다 식은 커피 stone-cold coffee / 식은 땀 a cold sweat / 식지 않도록 하다 keep《*something*》hot / 저녁이 식기 전에 먹다 eat before dinner gets cold / 커피가 식겠습니다 Your coffee will get cold. / 식기 전에 먹어라 Eat〔Take〕it before it gets cold.
②《열이》abate; subside; lapse back〔away〕;《열의·애정 등이》flag; be dampened; cool down〔off〕. ¶ 열의(熱意)가 ~〔사람이 주어〕lose interest《in》; grow less enthusiastic / (몸의) 열이 식었다 The fever has broken〔dropped〕. / 그녀에 대한 그의 애정이 차츰 식어 갔다 His affection for her gradually cooled. / 그의 개혁에 대한 열의는 식어버렸다 His enthusiasm for reform has cooled (down). / 식은 죽 먹기다《속담》It's an easy task〔job〕. *or* That's as easy as pie. / 쉬 덥는 방이 쉬 식는다《속담》Soon hot, soon cold.

**식단**(食單) a menu; a bill of fare. ¶ ~을 짜다 make out a menu. ◉ 주문 ~

제 *a la carte* system at restaurants.

**식당**(食堂) a dining room 〔hall〕; 《군대·공장 따위의》 a mess hall; 《역·극장 등의》 a refreshment room; 《대학·교회 등의》 a refectory; 《음식점》 a restaurant; an eating house (작은); a lunch counter, a lunchroom (간이 식당); a cafeteria (셀프서비스식). ◉ ~차 a dining 〔restaurant〕 car; a diner; a dining coach 《영》; a buffet car.

**식대**(食代) 《음식점의》 the charge for food; 《식비》 food expense 〔cost〕.

**식도**(食刀) a kitchen knife. =식칼.

**식도**(食道) 〖해부〗 the gullet; the esophagus. ◉ ~경 an esophagoscope. ~암 〖의학〗 cancer of the esophagus. ~염 〖의학〗 esophagitis. ~협착 stricture of the esophagus.

**식도락**(食道樂) epicurism; gourmandism. ◉ ~가 an epicure; a gourmet; a gourmand.

**식량**(食糧) food; provisions; foodstuffs; 〖군사〗 rations. ¶ 하루치의 ~ a day's provisions; 《병사나 등산가 등이 휴대하는》 a day's ration(s) / 비상 ~ emergency rations / ~의 자급자족 self-sufficiency in food / ~을 공급하다 provide 〔supply〕 《*a person*》 with food; provide food 《for *a person*》; provision 《a district》 / ~을 비축하다 lay 〔store〕 up provisions / ~을 사들이다 lay in provisions / ~을 확보하다 secure foodstuffs / ~ 부족으로 죽다 die for want of food / ~이 떨어졌다〔부족해졌다〕 We have run 「out 〔short〕 of food. / 그들은 1주일분의 ~을 갖고 여행을 떠났다 They took a week's provisions on their trip. ◉ ~관리〔통제〕 food control. ~난 the difficulty of obtaining food. ~농업 기구 《유엔의》 the Food and Agriculture Organization (생략 F.A.O.). ~대책〔정책〕 a food policy; food measures. ~문제 the food problem. ~배급 (food) rationing. ~부족 a shortage of provisions; a food shortage. ~사정 the food situation: ~ 사정의 악화 aggravation of the food situation. ~생산 food production. ~원조 food assistance 〔aid〕: 최근 북한은 U.N.에, 다른 구제 계획에 앞서, ~ 원조를 제공해 달라고 요청했다 North Korea has recently asked the U.N. for the provision of food assistance ahead of other relief programs. ~위기 a food crisis: 북한의 ~ 위기는 지금 평양 주민들이 공원으로 나물을 찾아다닐 만큼 악화되고 있다고, 한 유엔 관리는 말했다 North Korea's food crisis is worsening with residents of Pyongyang now scouring parks for grass to eat, a U.N. official said. ~자급률 the degree of self-sufficiency in food. ~정책 a food policy. ~조기 경보 시스템 the global information and early warning of food and agriculture. ~혁명 the green revolution. 예비~ a reserve of provisions. 세계~계획 the World Food Program (생략 WFP).

**식료**(食料) food; foodstuffs. ¶ 죽순은 좋은 ~가 된다 Bamboo shoots make good eating. ◉ ~품 《an article of》 food; a foodstuff; [총칭] groceries; eatables; foodstuffs; provisions: ~품상 a dealer in food-stuffs; a provisions dealer; a grocer / ~품점 a grocery (store) 《미》; a grocer's (shop) 《영》.

**식림**(植林) afforestation; tree planting; reforestation (재식림). ~하다 plant trees; reforest 《land》 with trees; afforest. ◉ ~계획 an afforestation 〔a reforestation〕 project. ~사업 a reforestation project. ~지(地) a plantation.

**식모**(植毛) a hair transplant.

**식모**(食母) a kitchenmaid; 《하녀》 a maidservant; a (house)maid; a domestic (help). ⇨ 가정부. ◉ ~살이 domestic service: ~살이하다 be in domestic service.

**식목**(植木) planting trees; forestation. ~하다 plant trees; do planting. ¶ 산에 ~하다 reforest a mountain. ◉ ~일 Arbor Day 《미》 (★ 미국 각 주에서는 4, 5월인데 날짜는 일정치 않음). ~행사 a tree-planting event.

**식물**(食物) food; provisions.

**식물**(植物) a plant; [총칭] plant life; vegetation; a flora (*pl.* ~s, -rae); the botany 《of Korea》. ¶ 고산〔열대〕~ an alpine 〔a tropical〕 plant / 귀화~ a naturalized plant / 기생~ a parasitic plant; a phytoparasite / 다년생〔1년생〕~ a perennial 〔an annual〕 plant / ~분포 a geographical distribution of plants / ~ 명패 a plant marker / ~을 채집하다 collect plants; botanize; herborize / 한국의 ~을 연구하다 study the botany of Korea / ~의 성장에는 햇빛이 필요하다 Sunlight is needed for plant growth.
◉ ~계(界) the vegetable 〔plant〕 kingdom. ~구계(區界) a flora. ~군락(群落) a plant community. ~대(帶) a floral 〔vegetation〕 zone; a zone of

vegetation. ~병리학 plant pathology; phytopathology. ~분류학 systematic botany; plant taxonomy. ~상(相) a flora (*pl.* ~s, -rae). ~생리학 plant physiology; physiological botany. ~생태학〔조직학〕 plant ecology 〔histology〕; ecological 〔structural〕 botany. ~섬유 (a) vegetable fiber. ~성 플랑크톤 phyto-plankton. ~세포(細胞) a vegetable cell: ~ 세포학(學) plant cytology. ~염기(塩基) a plant 〔vegetable〕 base. ~원(園) botanical gardens. ~인간 a person in a vegetative state; a vegetative existence; a (human) vegetable 《구어》; a gork 《속어》: ~인간으로 살(아가)다 《구어》 live as a cabbage 〔vegetable〕; keep alive at a vegetable level. ~지(誌) a flora (*pl.* ~s, -rae); a herbal: 한국 ~지 《책이름》 *the Flora of Korea.* ~지리학 geographical botany; plant geography. ~질(質) vegetable matter 〔material〕: ~질의 vegetable. ~표본 a botanical specimen; [총칭] a herbarium (*pl.* ~s, -ria). ~해부학 phytotomy; plant anatomy. ~형태학 plant morphology; morphological botany. ~호르몬 a plant hormone; a phytohormone. ~화학 plant chemistry; phytochemistry.
양지〔음지〕~ a sun 〔shade〕 plant. 한국~ 도감 a pictorial 〔an illustrated〕 book of the Korean flora.

**식물성**(植物性) vegetability; vegetable property. ¶ ~의 vegetable / ~ 식품 plant 〔vegetable〕 foods. ◉ ~기름〔버터〕 vegetable oil 〔butter〕. ~단백질 vegetable albumin; phytalbumin.

**식물채집**(植物採集) plant collecting; botanization; herborization. ¶ ~가 a herborist 〔herbalist〕; a plant collector / ~함(函) a vasculum (*pl.* -la, ~s) / ~하러 가다 go botanizing 〔herborizing, plant collecting〕 《in, at》.

**식물학**(植物學) botany; phytology. ¶ ~상〔적으로〕 botanically; from the botanical point of view. ◉ ~자 a botanist.

**식민**(植民) colonization; settlement. ~하다 colonize 《in a land》; plant a colony 《in》; settle 《in》. ◉ ~사업 colonization. ~시대 the colonial period. ~자 a colonizer (식민지 개설자). ~주의 colonialism.

**식민지**(植民地) a colony; a settlement. ¶ ~의 colonial / ~ 총독 a proconsul / 해외 ~ an overseas settlement / ~ 정책 a colonial policy / 반~주의 anti=colonialism / ~ 보유국 a colonial power / 반~ 투쟁 anticolonial struggle / ~화 colonialization / ~화하다 colonialize.

**식별**(識別) discernment; discrimination. ~하다 discriminate 《A from B, between A and B》; tell 《A from B》; discern; distinguish 《between》; 《감별·인식하다》 identify; recognize. ¶ 빛깔의 ~ color vision / ~할 수 있는〔없는〕 distinguishable 〔indistinguishable〕; recognizable 〔unrecognizable〕 / ~하기 어렵다 be hard 〔difficult〕 to tell apart; be almost 〔virtually〕 indistinguishable / ~ 못할 정도로 beyond 〔out of 〕 recognition / 진위를 ~하다 winnow the false from the true; winnow truth from falsehood / 어둠 속에서 사람들의 얼굴을 ~하다 distinguish people's faces in the dark. ◉ ~력 discrimination; the power of discernment; discerning power. ~역(閾) 〚심리·생리〛 the threshold of difference.

**식복**(食福) the blessing 〔good fortune〕 of having things to eat. ¶ ~이 있다 be blessed with (good) things to eat.

**식부**(植付) planting; setting out. ~하다 do the planting; plant; set out. ¶ 대량 ~ a heavy planting 《of corn》.
◉ ~면적 acreage under crop; the planted area.

**식분**(蝕分) 〚천문〛 a phase of an eclipse.

**식비**(食費) price of a meal; food expenses; 《하숙의》 (the charges for) board. ¶ ~로 만 원을 내다 pay 10,000 won for board / ~로 얼마씩 내고 있느냐 How much do you pay for your board? / 매달의 예산 중 ~가 제일 많이 든다 Food is the most expensive item in my monthly budget. / 우리 집 ~는 매달 50만 원이 든다 Our food expenses come to 500,000 won a month.

**식빵**(食—) (plain) bread; table bread. ¶ ~ 한 덩어리〔조각〕 a loaf of bread / ~에 잼을 바르다 spread jam on bread; spread bread with jam.

**식사**(式辭) a formal address (in a ceremony); a congratulatory address (축사). ¶ ~를 읽다〔하다〕 read 〔give〕 an address.

**식사**(食事) a meal; a repast; eating. ~하다 take 〔have〕 a meal; dine; eat. ¶ 간단한〔가벼운〕 ~ a light meal; a simple repast / 충분한 ~ a good 〔big, square, substantial〕 meal / 규칙적으로 ~하다 have *one's* meals regularly / 정

해진 시간에 ~를 하다 have regular mealtimes / 밖에서 ~하다 dine 〔eat〕 out / ~ 준비를 하다 prepare a meal; set 〔fix 《미》〕 the table 《for dinner》 (식탁의); get a meal ready (요리의) / ~를 거르다 miss 〔《구어》 skip, do not take〕 a meal / ~를 제한하다 put 《a patient》 on a (restricted) diet / ~ 대접을 하다 serve a meal / ~를 함께 하다 dine 〔take dinner〕 with 《*a person*》 / 급히 ~를 하다 「make a hasty 〔have a hurried〕 meal / ~를 들면서 이야기하다 talk at table / ~ 뒤에 상〔식탁〕을 치우다 clear the table / ~중이다 be at (the) table; be having a meal 〔lunch, dinner〕 / ~에 초대받다 be invited 〔asked〕 to dinner / 오셔서 ~를 같이 하셨으면 영광이겠습니다 It would give us a great pleasure if you would come and dine with us. / ~중에 말을 많이 하지 마라 Don't talk much at meal. / ~하러 나감 《게시》 Out to lunch. ◉ ~시간 a mealtime: ~ 시간이다 It is time for dinner. ~예법 table manners.

**식산**(殖産) 《증산》 increase of productions; 《축재》 making money; accumulation of wealth.

**식상**(食傷) 《식중독》 food poisoning; 《배탈》 indigestion (from overeating); a stomach upset; 《물림》 surfeit; glut. ~하다 be poisoned by food; 《물리다》 have had enough 《of》; be surfeited 〔satiated, cloyed〕 《with》; be fed up with *something;* be sick of. ¶ 그는 뭔가를 잘못 먹어 ~한 것 같다 Something he ate seems to have disagreed with him. / 이제 그런 경기라면 ~해 있다 I am fed up with that sort of game.

**식생활**(食生活) dietary 〔food〕 life. ¶ ~의 변화 a change of diet; a change in *one's* eating 〔dietary〕 habit / ~을 개선하다 improve *one's* diet 〔dietary life〕 / ~을 보다 즐겁게 하다 enhance the pleasure of the table.

**식성**(食性) likes and dislikes in food; (*one's*) taste. ¶ ~에 맞다 suit *one's* taste 〔palate〕; be to *one's* taste / ~이 까다롭다 have a delicate taste; be particular about food.

**식솔**(食率) mouths to feed; a family. ⇨식구.

**식수**(食水) drinking 〔potable〕 water. ¶ 이 우물의 물은 ~로 할 수 없다 The water from 〔in〕 this well is not 「fit to drink 〔drinkable〕. ◉ ~난 a drinking water shortage: ~난에 시달리다 suffer from a drinking water shortage.

**식수**(植樹) tree planting. ⇨식목.

**식순**(式順) the order 〔program〕 of a ceremony.

**식식** in heavy gasps; heavily.

**식식거리다** breathe heavily 〔hard〕.

**식언**(食言) breaking 〔retracting〕 a promise. ~하다 eat *one's* words; go back on *one's* word; break 〔retract, take back〕 *one's* promise.

**식염**(食塩) (table) salt; common 〔culinary〕 salt. ◉ ~수 a solution of salt; a saline solution. ~주사 (a) salt 〔saline〕 injection.

**식욕**(食慾) (an) appetite; desire to eat. ¶ ~을 돋우다 stimulate 〔heighten, boost, sharpen, whet, arouse, excite〕 *one's* appetite / ~을 채우다 satisfy *one's* appetite / ~이 나다 feel an appetite; *one's* appetite improves 〔increases, develops〕 / ~이 있다〔없다〕 have a good 〔poor〕 appetite / ~이 왕성하다 have 〔get〕 a healthy desire for food / ~이 없어지다, ~을 잃다 *one's* appetite fails; [사람이 주어] lose *one's* appetite / 굉장한 ~을 보이다 eat with a heavy appetite / ~을 감퇴〔증진〕시키다 diminish 〔increase〕 *one's* appetite / 가을에는 누구나 ~이 난다 Everybody has a good appetite in autumn. ◉ ~감퇴 a decrease 〔falling-off〕 of appetite; a poor 〔dull, feeble〕 appetite; loss of appetite. ~부진 lack 〔loss〕 of appetite; in appetence; anorexia. ~억제제 an appetite suppressant. ~증진 improvement 〔promotion〕 of appetite: ~증진제 an appetizer.

**식용**(食用) edibility. ¶ ~의 edible; eatable; (used) for food / ~으로 쓰다〔재배하다, 사육하다〕 use 〔grow, raise〕 《*a thing*》 for food / ~에 적합하다 be good to eat; be edible. ◉ ~개구리 an edible frog; a bullfrog. ~근 edible roots. ~기름 edible 〔cooking〕 oil; (vegetable) cooking fat. ~버섯 edible mushrooms. ~색소 food coloring. ~식물 esculent plants; plants for food. ~품 an article of food; edibles; food(stuff).

**식육**(食肉) 《먹음》 meat-eating; 《고기》 (edible) meat. ~하다 eat meat; be carnivorous. ◉ ~가공업자 a meat processor. ~류 meat-eating 〔carnivorous〕 animals; the Carnivora. ~소 [총칭] beef cattle.

**식은땀** (a) cold sweat. ¶ ~을 흘리다 「be in 〔break into〕 a cold sweat; have cold drops come out on *one's* skin / ~이 이마에 나다 cold sweat stands upon *one's* brow / 몸이 떨리며 ~이 났다 I trembled and broke into a cold sweat.

**식은죽**(―粥) cold gruel 〔porridge〕. ¶ 그런 것은 ~ 먹기다 Nothing is easier. *or* That's (as) easy as pie. *or* That's a cinch 《미속어》.

**식음**(食飮) eating and drinking. ¶ ~을 전폐하다 give up eating and drinking; fast.

**식이**(食餌) a diet; food. ◉ ~성 중독진(中毒疹) alimentary toxic-exanthema.

**식이요법**(食餌療法) a diet(ary) cure; a dietetic treatment. ¶ ~을 하다 be 〔go〕 on a (restricted) diet / ~을 시키다 put 《a patient》 on a diet; diet 《*a person*》.

**식인**(食人) eating people; cannibalism. ◉ ~귀 a cannibal demon. ~종 a cannibal race; cannibals; man-eaters; [비유적] wild 〔unruly〕 people.

**식자**(植字) typesetting; composition. ~하다 compose 〔set〕 type. ◉ ~공 a typesetter 《주로 미》; a compositor. ~대 a composing stand 〔frame〕. ~판 a galley. (자동) ~기 a typesetting 〔composing〕 machine; a typesetter.

**식자**(識者) well-informed〔-intelligent〕 people; the wise; men of good sense; thoughtful 〔thinking〕 people. ◉ ~층 the literate stratum (of society).

**식자우환**(識者憂患) Ignorance is bliss.

**식장**(式場) the place where a ceremony is held; a hall of ceremony; a ceremonial hall. ¶ ~이 어딥니까 Where is the 《wedding》 ceremony to be held?

**식전**(式典) a ceremony. ⇨ 의식(儀式).

**식전**(食前) [부사적] ① 《식사 전》 before meals. ¶ ~ 복용 《약을》 To be taken before meals. ② 《이른 아침》 before breakfast; early morning.
◉ ~바람 before breakfast (time); on an empty 〔unbreakfasted〕 stomach. ~참(站) the early morning (before breakfast); a stopping place reached before breakfast.

**식중독**(食中毒) food poisoning. ¶ ~에 걸리다 get 〔suffer from〕 food poisoning; [음식이 주어] disagree with 《*a person*》 / 무엇엔가 ~이 된 것 같다 I may have eaten something that has disagreed with me.

**식체**(食滯) indigestion; dyspepsia.

**식초**(食醋) (table) vinegar. ¶ ~를 치다 vinegar 《food》.

**식충**(食蟲) insect-eating; 《생물》 an insect-eater; an insectivore; [비유적] a glutton; a gourmand.
◉ ~류 『동물』 the insectivora. ~식물〔동물〕 an insectivorous plant 〔animal〕. ~이 a glutton; a gourmand.

**식칼**(食―) a kitchen knife; 《정육점의》 a butcher's knife; a cleaver. ¶ ~질하다 carve 〔cut〕 《meat》 with a kitchen knife; chop with a cleaver.

**식탁**(食卓) a dining table. ¶ ~용의 table 《knife, spoon》; for table use / ~에 앉다 sit at 〔down to〕 table; be at table (앉아 있다) / ~을 치우다 clear the table / (음식이) ~에 오르다 be served at table. ◉ ~보 a (table-) cloth. ~염 table salt.

**식탈**(食頉) a stomach upset caused by 「overeating.

**식품**(食品) food(s); foodstuffs; groceries. ¶ 주요~ staple foods; staples / 감량~ low-calorie food; diet food / 냉동~ frozen food / 불량~ illegal 〔unsanitory〕 foodstuff; substandard food / 인스턴트~ convenience food; precooked food; instant / 가공 ~ processed food.
◉ ~가공 food processing: ~가공업 food processing industry / ~가공업자 a food processor. ~공업 the food industry. ~공학 food engineering: ~공학과 the department of food engineering. ~과학 food science. ~관리 food control: ~관리법 the Staple Food Control Law. ~영양학과 the department of food and nutrition. ~위생 food sanitation 〔hygiene〕: ~ 위생법 the Food Sanitation 〔Hygiene〕 Act. ~의약품 안전청 the Food and Drug Administration. ~점 a grocer's (shop) 《영》; a grocery (store) 《미》. ~중독 foodstuff poisoning. ~첨가물 a food additive; a food reservative (보존용). ~학 sitology. ~화학 food chemistry.

**식피**(植皮) skin graft(ing); transplantation of skin. ~하다 graft skin.
◉ ~술 『의학』 a skin-grafting operation.

**식혜**(食醯) fermented rice punch; rice 「nectar.

**식후**(食後) [부사적] after a meal; after dinner. ¶ ~의 휴식 《have, take》 a short recess 〔brief rest〕 after the meal / ~ 30분에 복용 To be taken 30 minutes after each meal.

**식히다** ① 《차게 하다》 cool; chill; ice (얼음으로); refrigerate (냉장고에서); let 《*a thing*》 cool. ¶ 식힌 cooled; chilled / 식혀 두다 Keep 《*a thing*》 cool / 뜨거운

물을 ～ let hot water cool / 얼음주머니로 머리를 ～ cool *one's* head with an ice bag / 뜨거운 차를 불어서 ～ blow on hot tea to cool it / 뜨거우면 식혀서 드세요 If it's too hot, let it cool down before you drink it.
② 《냉정해지다》 cool 〔calm〕 down. ¶ 머리를 식히고 생각을 다시 해보세요 Calm down and think it over again.
③ 《열의를》 dampen 《*one's* eagerness》; put a damper on 《*one's* enthusiasm》.

**신**[1] 《신발》 footgear; footwear; shoes. ¶ 갖신 Korean leather shoes / 신 한 켤레 a pair of shoes / 신을 신고 《walk》 in *one's* shoes / 신을 신은 채로 《enter a room》 with *one's* shoes 〔clogs〕 on / 신을 신다 put on *one's* shoes; wear shoes / 신을 신고 있다 be in *one's* shoes / 신을 벗다 take off *one's* shoes / 신을 신기다 put shoes on 《*a person*》; have 《*a person*》 put on *his* shoes / 신을 닦다 polish 〔black, shine 《미》〕 *one's* 〔another's〕 shoes / 이 방에서는 신을 신고 있어도 괜찮다 You may keep your shoes on in this room. / 그는 다 떨어진 신을 신고 있었다 He was in worn-out shoes. / 어떤 사이즈의 신을 신으십니까 What size shoes do you wear? / 신을 벗으시오 《게시》 Kindly take off your shoes. *or* Remove shoes.

**신**[2] 《신명》 enthusiasm; excitement; warmth; heart; fervor. ¶ 신이 나다 become enthusiastic; get excited; be elated 《by, with》; warm (up) 《to》 / 신이 나서 이야기하다 speak with great fervor / 정치 이야기가 나오기만 하면 그는 신이 난다 All you have to do is mention politics and he gets excited.

**신**(申) 〖민속〗 ① 《십이지의》 the sign of the Monkey (= the 9th of the 12 Earth's Branches). ② ⇨ 신방(申方). ③ ⇨ 신시(申時).

**신**(辛) 〖민속〗 ① 《십간의》 the 8th of the 10 Heaven's stems. ② ⇨ 신방(辛方). ③ ⇨ 신시(辛時).

**신**(臣) ① 《신하》 a statesman. ② 《임금에게》 I; me; Your Majesty's servant.

**신**(信) ① 《성실》 faith; fidelity; sincerity; trust; reliance. ② 《소식》 news; tidings.

**신**(神) 《일신교의》 God; the Almighty (전능자); Providence; the Supreme Being; the Lord (천주); the Creator (조물주); the Father (하느님 아버지); Allah (회교의); 《다신교의》 a deity; a god; a goddess (여신); a demon (귀신); a spirit (신령); a genie. ¶ 그리스의 신들 the gods of the Greece / 신의 은총 the grace of God / 신의 조화 divine work; work of God; an act of God / 신의 뜻 God's 〔the divine〕 will / 신의 가호 divine protection / 신이 내린 무당 an inspired 〔a possessed〕 shaman / …을 신에게 빌다 pray to God for … / 신을 믿다 believe in God / 신을 공경하다 revere God / …을 ～으로 받들다 worship 〔*a person, something*〕 as a god; deify.

**신**(腎) ① 《음경》 the penis. ② 《신장》 the kidney.

**신** a scene. ¶ 라스트～ the last scene / 러브 ～ a love 〔romantic〕 scene / 극적인 ～을 전개하다 develop a dramatic scene.

**신-**(新) new; modern (현대적); up-to-date (신식); latest (최신의); novel; neo-. ¶ 신무기 a modern device of war / 신발명 a new invention / 신대통령 the new President; 《미취임의》 the President elect; the incoming President / 신내각 the new Cabinet / 신유행 the latest fashion / 신여성 the new 〔modern〕 woman.

**신간**(新刊) a new publication; a newly-published 〔new〕 book; a recent release. ¶ ～의 newly-published 〔=issued〕; new. ◉ ～목록 a catalog 〔list〕 of new publications. ～서적 new books; a new publication: ～ 서적 안내 《신문 등의》 a book notice. ～소개 a book review: ～소개를 하다 review a book 《for a newspaper》. ～예고 an advertisement 〔announcement〕 of forthcoming books 〔publications〕.

**신갈나무** 〖식물〗 a Mongolian oak.

**신개발**(新開發) ¶ ～의 newly-opened; newly-developed. ◉ ～주택지 a newly-developed residential area.

**신개척지**(新開拓地) a newly-reclaimed 〔=opened〕 land. ⇨ 신개발.

**신건이** a nonsensical character; a silly fool; a dull 〔stupid〕 person.

**신격**(神格) divinity; godhead. ◉ ～화 deification 《of Muhammad》: ～화하다 deify; apotheosize.

**신결석**(腎結石) 〖의학〗 a renal calculus; a nephrolith; 《병》 nephrolithiasis.

**신경**(信經) 〖종교〗 a creed. ◉ 니케아 〔아타나시오〕 ～ the Nicene 〔Athanasian〕 Creed. 사도～ the Apostles' creed.

**신경**(神經) ① 〖해부〗 a nerve. ¶ ～의 nerval; neural; nervine / ～성의 nervous 《fever》; neural 《paralysis》 / 구심성 ～ an afferent nerve / 반사 ～ 《develop good》 reflexes / ～이 없는 nerveless / ～을 죽이다 kill 〔deaden〕 a nerve. ② 《감각·의식》 *one's* nerves; sensitivity; 《걱정·관심·배려》 care; concern; consideration. ¶ ～의 피로 〔과로〕 nerve strain.

신경이: ～이 날카로운 nervous; sensitive; sensible; susceptible; touchy; edgy / ～이 둔한〔무딘〕 insensitive; insensible; dull; thick-skinned / ～이 곤두서다 be jittery 〔nervy〕 《미구어》; *one's* nerves are on edge / ～이 곤두서 있다 be nervous; 《구어》 be edgy 〔on *one's* edge, nervy 《영》〕 / ～을 곤두서게 하다 set 《*a person's*》 nerves on edge; make 《*a person*》 jittery 〔irritable, touchy〕 / ～이 굵다 《뻔뻔함》 have plenty 〔a lot〕 of nerve 《미》; 《두려움을 모름》 be fearless 〔undaunted〕 / ～이 날카로워지다 *one's* nerves become edgy; [사람이 주어] become excited 〔jittery, touchy〕; be highly strung; be nervous; 〔nervy 《미구어》〕 / ～이 쓰이다 [사물이 주어] get on *one's* nerves; weigh 《*a person's*》 mind; [사람이 주어] feel uneasy about; be anxious about.

신경에: ～에 거슬리다 jar 〔get, work〕 on *one's* nerves; irritate *one's* nerves / ～에 무리를〔부담을〕 주다 ⇨ 신경을 자극하다.

신경을: ～을 건드리다 get 〔jar〕 on *one's* nerves; irritate *one's* nerves; make 《*a person*》 jittery 〔irritable〕 / ～을 가라앉히다 soothe 〔quiet, tranquilize〕 *one's* nerves / ～을 자극하다 be a 《great》 strain on *one's* nerves; be trying to nerves / ～을 쓰다 strain *one's* nerves; mind; care 《about》; 「concern *oneself* 〔be concerned〕 《about》; worry (*oneself*) 《about》; be careful; be thoughtful of 《*one's* reputation》; be sensitive 《about *one's* appearance》 / ～을 쓰지 않다 do not mind; be indifferent to 《*one's* looks》; take 《*a thing*》 easy; care nothing for 《*one's* appearance》; 《조금도》 do not care a bit 〔feather〕 / 치아의 ～을 마취시키다 anesthetize the nerve of a tooth.

¶ 그건 ～ 탓이겠지 I suppose it is a touch of nerves. / 그는 ～이 극도로 날카로워져 있다 His nerves are highly strung. *or* He is all worked up. / 네 병은 순전히 ～ 탓이야 Your sickness is purely imaginary. / 저에게 일부러 ～ 쓰지 마십시오 Don't bother 〔mind〕 about me. / 세상의 소문 따위에는 ～ 쓰지 말게 Don't mind what the world says (about you). / 그는 가난 따위에는 별로 ～을 쓰지 않는다 He is rather indifferent to his poverty. / 자네의 말 한마디 한마디에 ～이 쓰인다 Every little thing you say gets on my nerves.

◉ ～가스 〖군사〗 nerve gas. ～계(통) a nervous 〔neural〕 system: 자율〔중추〕 ～계 the automatic 〔central〕 nervous system / 말초 ～계 the peripheral nervous system / 알코올은 ～계통에 영향을 미친다 Alcohol 「acts on 〔affects〕 the nervous system. ～과 《병원의》 the department of neurology: ～과 의사 a neurologist. ～말단 《이빨의》 a nerve pulp. ～망 a nerve network. ～병 a nervous disease 〔disorder〕; neurosis (*pl.* -ses): ～병학 neurology / ～병 환자 a neuropath; a neurotic. ～병리학 neuropathology: ～병리학자 a neuropathologist. ～분포 innervation. ～섬유 a nerve fiber. ～세포 a nerve cell; a neuron(e). ～안정제〔진정제〕 a nervous sedative; a nervine. ～염 neuritis. ～외과 neurological surgery: ～외과학 neurosurgery. ～장애 neuropathy. ～전 psychological warfare; a war of nerves. ～절 a (nerve) ganglion (*pl.* ～s, -glia). ～절제 neurotomy. ～정신병 neuropsychosis. ～정신 의학 neuropsychiatry. ～조직 nervous tissues. ～주위염 perineuritis. ～중추 the nerve center. ～증 neurosis: ～증의 neurotic / ～증 환자 a neurotic (patient). ～지배 innervation. ～초(鞘) a nerve sheath; a neurilemma. ～통 neuralgia: ～통의 neuralgic / ～통을 앓다 suffer from neuralgia / ～통으로 고통받고 있다 I am tormented with 〔by〕 neuralgia. ～학 neurology: ～학자 a neurologist.

**신경과민**(神經過敏) nervousness; oversensitiveness; morbid sensitiveness. ¶ ～의 nervous; oversensitive; nervy; 《구어》 touchy / ～이 되다 get nervous; suffer from nerves / 건강에 ～이 되다 worry about *one's* health / 그는 지나치게 ～이다 He is all nerves 〔oversensitive, hypersensitive〕.

**신경쇠약**(神經衰弱) 〖의학〗 a nervous breakdown; nervous prostration; neurasthenia. ¶ ～자 a neurasthenic / ～에 걸리다 suffer from 「nervous prostration 〔a nervous breakdown〕; suffer from nervous prostration of the worst kind (극도의); 《걸려 있다》 have a nervous breakdown.

**신경지**(新境地) a new land 〔frontier, world〕. ¶ ～를 개척하다 break new ground; open up a new ground 《in the sphere of art》; open a new field 《of art》.

**신경질**(神經質) a nervous temperament; nervousness. ¶ ～의 (highly) sensitive; delicate; nervous; jittery 《미구어》 / ～적인 사람 a man of highly nervous temperament / ～을 부리다 show nervousness / ～이 나게 하다 get on 《*a person's*》 nerves; make 《*a person*》 nervous / 그는 ～을 너무 부린다 He is too nervous.

**신경향**(新傾向) a new tendency 〔trend〕. ¶ ～을 보이다 display 〔show〕 a new tendency. ◉ ～파 the Anti-Conventional School 《of Korean literature》.

**신고**(申告) a (legal) report; a statement (주장의); a notification; a notice; filing; 《세관에서의》 a declaration; 《수입·매상고 등의》 a return. ～하다 report; state; declare; notify; file; make 〔file〕 a return of 《*one's* income》; 《등록》 register. ¶ ～를 게을리하다 neglect to (make a) report / 관청에 ～하다 report to an office / 부친의 사망 ～를 하다 report *one's* father's death / 소득세 ～를 하다 declare 《*one's* earnings》 for income tax; make 〔file out〕 *one's* income tax return / 경찰에 도난 ～를 하다 report a theft to the police / (습득물을) 경찰에 ～하다 report (a find) to the police / 세관에 ～하다 make a declaration at the customhouse / 소득금액을 ～하다 declare 〔make a return of〕 *one's* income; report the amount of *one's* income / 그는 소득 금액을 허위 ～했다 He falsified 〔fiddled 《구어》〕 his (income) tax return. *or* He made a false return of his income. / 그는 지난해의 소득을 과소 ～했다 He underreported his income for last year.

◉ ～가격 a reported price. ～납세 tax payment by self-assessment: ～납세자 a self-assessed taxpayer. ～마감 날짜 the final day for filing. ～용지 a return blank 〔form〕. ～자 a reporter; a filer; a declarer. ～제 《세금의》 the report 〔return〕 system; 《관세 등의》 the declaration system. 사망～ a notice of death. 세관～ a customs declaration. 소득세～ an income tax return. 예정〔확정〕～ a provisional 〔final〕 return.

**신고**(辛苦) hardship(s); trials; trouble; suffering. ～하다 go through hardships; take pains; suffer hardships; undergo privations; have bitter experiences. ¶ 그의 성공은 오랜 ～ 끝에 이루어진 결과다 His success is born out of a long period of hardship.

**신고서**(申告書) a (written) report; a notice; a declaration; a statement; a tax return (세금).

◉ 소득세～ an income tax return. 원산지～ a declaration of origin. 입고〔선적, 재선적〕～ a declaration for warehousing 〔shipping, reshipment〕.

**신고안**(新考案) a new device; a novel contrivance; a new gadget.

**신곡**(神曲) 《단테의》 The Divine Comedy; *Divina Commedia* (It.).

**신곡**(新曲) a new musical composition; a new tune 〔piece〕.

**신곡**(新穀) a new crop of rice; new grain. ◉ ～머리 a harvest time.

**신골** a shoemaker's last. ◉ ～방망이 a shoemaker's hammer.

**신관**(信管) the fuse (of an explosive charge). ¶ ～을 끊다 〔장치하다〕 cut 〔set〕 a fuse / ～을 제거하다 remove the fuse 《from a bomb》; defuse 《a bomb》. ◉ 격발～ a percussion fuse. 시한～ a time 〔clockwork〕 fuse.

**신관**(新官) a newly-appointed official; a new appointee. ¶ ～ 사또 the newly= appointed governor 〔magistrate〕.

**신관**(新館) a new building; 《증축한, 별관》 an annex; an extension 《미》. ¶ 호텔의 ～ a hotel annex.

**신교**(信教) religious belief; faith in religion. ¶ ～의 자유 religious freedom 〔liberty〕; freedom of religion 〔worship〕 (★ freedom의 성구에는 보통 관사를 붙이지 않음) / ～의 자유를 보장하다 guarantee freedom of religion / ～의 자유를 침해하다 violate freedom of religion.

**신교**(新教) Protestantism. ¶ ～의 선교사 a Protestant missionary. ◉ ～도 a Protestant.

**신구**(新舊) the old and the new (★ 신과 구의 어순의 반대가 됨에 주의). ¶ ～의 old and new; incoming and outgoing 《minister》 / ～서적 old and new books / ～약 〖성서〗 the Old and New Testaments / ～ 사상의 충돌 a collision between old and new ideas / 지금은 ～ 교체의 과도기다 We are now in a period of transition, the old giving way to the new.

**신국면**(新局面) a new aspect 〔phase〕. ¶ ～을 전개하다 take on a new aspect / ～에 접어들다 enter (up)on a new phase / 사건은 ～을 맞이했다 The case is beginning to assume a new aspect. *or* The case is beginning to enter a new phase.

**신권**(神權) divine right. ◉ ～정치 theocracy.

**신규**(新規) a new regulation; a new project. ¶ ～의 new; fresh / ～로 anew; newly; afresh / ～로 사람을 채용하다 hire 〔employ〕 a new hand. ◉ ～계정〔예금〕 anew account 〔deposit〕. ～모집 recruitment. ～사업 a new enterprise 〔business, undertaking〕.

**신극**(新劇) a new drama 〔play〕; modern drama utilizing Western stage techniques; a new school of acting (연출상의). ◉ ～여배우 an actress of the new drama. ～운동 a new-drama movement.

**신근**(伸筋) a protractor; an extensor (muscle).

**신기**(神技) a superb 〔wonderful〕 performance; a marvelous trick 〔act, deed〕; an exquisite skill; a superhuman feat.

**신기**(神奇) being marvelous. ～하다 (be) marvelous; miraculous; supernatural. ¶ ～한 일 a mystery; a wonder / ～하게 marvelously; strangely; mysteriously / ～한 듯이 with curiosity; in wonder (경탄하여) / ～하게 여기다 wonder; marvel 《at》 / (일이) 참으로 ～하기도 하구나 It is nothing short of a miracle.

**신기**(神氣) vigor; vitality; spirit; the mind. ¶ ～가 상쾌하다 be refreshed; feel refreshed and serene / ～가 혼탁하다 the mind is confused and turbid.

**신기**(新奇) novelty; originality. ～하다 (be) novel; original; new. ¶ ～한 방법으로 in a novel way / ～한 것을 좋아하다 be fond of novelty / 비행기 여행도 이제는 그리 ～한 것이 아니다 Traveling by air has lost much of its novelty now.

**신기다** put 《footwear》 on 《*a person*》; get 《*a person*》 to put on 《footwear》. ¶ 아이에게 양말〔신〕을 ～ put a child's socks 〔shoes〕 on him; have a child put his socks 〔shoes〕 on.

**신기록**(新記錄) a new record 〔mark〕. ¶ ～을 세우다 establish 〔make, set〕 a new record. ◉ 세계～ a new world record. 한국～ a new Korean record: 그는 200미터 평영에서 한국 ～을 세웠다 He established 〔made〕 a new Korean record in the 200-meter breast stroke.

**신기료장수** a shoe repairer; a cobbler.

**신기루**(蜃氣樓) a mirage. ¶ ～가 나타나다 a mirage appears.

**신기원**(新紀元) a new era 〔epoch〕. ¶ ～을 이루는 사건 an epoch-making 〔an epochal〕 event / ～을 짓다〔이룩하다〕 mark 〔make〕 an epoch 《in》.

**신기축**(新機軸) a new departure 〔device〕; a novel contrivance. ¶ ～을 이루다 make 〔mark〕 a new departure; set up a new milestone.

**신나다** get in high spirits; get elated; feel on top of the world. ¶ 신나는 이야기 a highly amusing story; a very interesting 〔entertaining〕 talk / 비행기를 타고 가면 신날 거야 It will be jolly 〔fine, capital〕 fun if we go by airplane.

**신나무** 〖식물〗 the Amur maple.

**신내리다**(神—) 《a shaman》 fall into a trance; be possessed by a spirit.

**신녀**(信女) 〖불교〗 a female believer.

**신년**(申年) the Year of the Monkey.

**신년**(新年) a new year; the New Year. ¶ 근하～ A Happy New Year! / ～초에 at the beginning of the new year / 묵은 해를 보내고 ～을 맞다 see the old year out and the new year in; 《제야의 종소리와 함께》 ring out the old (year) and ring in the new. ◉ ～호《잡지의》 a New Year issue. ～회 a New Year's (dinner) party.

**신념**(信念) belief; faith; (a) conviction (확신). ¶ ～을 가지고 with a strong will / ～의 사나이 a man of strong conviction / ～이 강한〔약한〕 사람 a man of strong 〔weak〕 faith / 정치적 ～ *one's* political creed / 굳은 ～ 《have》 a firm 〔strong〕 faith; a sturdy faith / 흔들리지 않는 ～ an unshaken 〔unshakable, impregnable〕 faith / …라는 ～으로 with 〔in〕 the belief that… / ～을 가지다 have 〔hold〕 faith 〔belief〕 《in》 / ～을 관철하다 carry through *one's* faith; maintain *one's* conviction to the end / ～을 굳히다 strengthen *one's* faith 〔belief〕; [사물이 주어] confirm 〔corroborate〕 *one's* belief / ～을 버리다 relinquish 〔discard, give up〕 *one's* belief / ～을 잃다 lose *one's* faith 〔belief〕 《in》 / …하다는 ～을 품다 entertain 〔cherish〕 the belief that… / ～이 없다 lack faith 《in》/ ～에 따라 행동하다 act up to *one's* belief / 그에게는 확고한 ～이 없다 He is not a man of unshaken faith. / 그는 ～을 굽히지 않는다 He sticks to his conviction. / 그녀는 사랑은 모든 것을 극복한다는 ～을 가지고 있다 It is her belief that love conquers all. / 그 말을 듣고 그는 ～이 흔들렸다 His faith wavered 〔was shaken〕 when he heard that.

**신다** put 〔have〕 on; wear 《footgear》 (★ put on은 신는 동작, have on과 wear는 신고 있는 상태를 나타냄).
¶ 신을 신고 《walk》 in *one's* shoes / 신을 안 신고 barefoot(ed) / 신을 신은 채 with *one's* shoes on / 구두를〔양말을〕 ～ put on *one's* shoes 〔socks〕 / 구두를 신어 보다 try the shoes on; try on a pair of shoes / 스타킹을 신고 있다 have stockings on / 양말을 갈아 ～ change *one's* socks / 그는 장화를 신고 있다 He has long boots on. / 이 신은 더 신을 수 있다 These shoes are still good to wear. / 그는 신을 신고 있는 중이다 He is putting (his) shoes on. / 너 새 신 신었구나 You have new shoes on, don't you?

**신당**(新黨) a new political party. ¶ ～을 결성하다 form 〔organize〕 a new political party.

**신대륙**(新大陸) the New Continent; the New World.

**신도**(信徒) a believer; a devotee; an adherent; a follower; 《교회 전체의》 the congregation; the flock; the faithful [총칭]. ¶ 기독교～ a Christian / 불교～ a Buddhist.

**신도시**(新都市) a new town.

**신동**(神童) a (child) prodigy; a wonder child; an infant genius 〔prodigy, phenomenon〕; a whiz kid 《구어》; a *wunderkind* (G.). ¶ 그 아이는 정말 ～이다 The child is really a marvel 〔wonder, phenomenon〕.

**신뒤축** a shoe heel. ¶ ～이 높다 have high heels; be high-heeled / ～이 닳다 the heels are worn (down); 《the shoes》 be down at the heels.

**신드롬** 〖의학〗《증후군》 a syndrome.

**신디케이트** 〖경제〗 a syndicate. ¶ ～를 조직하다 form a syndicate.

**신딸**(神―) the young apprentice of an aging *mudang*.

**신랄하다**(辛辣―) (be) sharp; biting; bitter; severe; acid; cutting; poignant; pungent. ¶ 신랄하게 poignantly; scathingly; severely; incisively; acrimoniously / 신랄한 말로 in acid language; 《어조》 in acrid tones / 신랄한 풍자 a pungent satire / 신랄한 필치 an acrimonious pen / 신랄한 언사를 쓰다 say a cutting thing; make a cutting remark / 신랄하게 비평하다 make a severe 〔a vitriolic, an incisive, a sharp〕 criticism.

**신랑**(新郞) a bridegroom; a newlywed husband. ◉ ～감 a likely 〔suitable〕 bridegroom. ～들러리 the best man. ～신부 the bride and bridegroom; the new 〔newly-married〕 couple; the newlyweds.

**신령**(神靈) 《신》 a divine spirit; spirits; the gods; 《망령》 a soul. ¶ ～의 가호 divine protection.

**신록**(新綠) fresh verdure; tender green; fresh green. ¶ ～의 계절 the season of fresh verdure 〔green〕 / ～으로 덮이다 be covered with fresh green 〔verdant vegetation〕.

**신뢰**(信賴) trust 《in》; reliance 《on》; dependence 《on》; confidence 《in》. ～하다 trust (in); rely on; depend 《upon》; confide in; put confidence in; put faith in; place reliance on.
¶ ～할 수 있는 trustworthy; reliable; dependable / ～할 수 없는 untrustworthy; unreliable / ～를 받고 있다 enjoy the confidence of 《*a person*》 / ～를 배반하다〔어기다〕 betray 《*a person's*》 trust 〔confidence〕; 《구어》 let 《*a person*》 down / ～에 보답하다 prove worthy of 《*a person's*》 trust; live up to 《*a person's*》 expectations / 잘못하여 …를 ～하다 misplace *one's* confidence 《in》 / 국민의 ～를 회복하다 restore the people's confidence / 국민의 ～와 사랑을 받는 경찰상(像)을 만들어 내다 create a police image which will enjoy the people's confidence and love / 그는 ～할 수 없다 He is not a man to be trusted 〔relied upon〕. / 그는 ～할 수 있는 사나이다 He is someone 〔a man〕 we can trust. *or* He is a reliable man. / 그는 사장으로부터 전폭적인 ～를 받고 있다 He enjoys the fullest confidence of the president.
◉ ～관계 a relationship of mutual trust; 〖법〗 (a) fiduciary relation. ～사회 a trustworthy society.

**신망**(信望) confidence and popularity; prestige. ¶ ～이 있다 enjoy 〔possess〕 the confidence 《of》; be popular 《with》; have 〔enjoy〕 prestige 《in the community》 / ～을 잃다 lose 〔forfeit〕 the confidence 《of》; lose 〔suffer a loss of〕 prestige《in the town》/ 세인의 ~을 얻다 win〔gain, obtain〕 public confidence.

**신명**(身命) *one's* life. ¶ ~을 걸고 at the risk of *one's* life; sacrificing *oneself* / ~을 바치다 sacrifice〔lay down〕 *one's* life.

**신명**(神明) a (shining) deity; a divinity; a god. ¶ 천지~에 맹세코 그 일을 하지 않았다 I swear by heaven and earth I did not do it.

**신명기**(申命記)〖성서〗The Book of Deuteronomy;《약칭》Deuteronomy (생략 Deut.).

**신명나다** get enthusiastic《about》; be enraptured《over, at》; get excited《at, by》; warm (up)《to *one's* work》; enter into the spirit《of *things*》.

**신묘**(辛卯)〖민속〗the 28th binary term of the sexagenary cycle.

**신묘**(神妙) being mysterious and marvelous. ~하다 (be) mysterious; marvelous; wondrous.

**신문**(訊問) (judicial) questioning; cross-examination; interrogation; an inquest. ~하다 question; (cross-)examine; interrogate; press《*a person*》 with questions. ¶ 준엄한 ~을 받다 be subjected to〔be put through〕 a severe cross-examination; be grilled《미구어》. ◉ ~자 an examiner. ~조서 an interrogatory. 반대~ a cross-question.

**신문**(新聞) a newspaper; a paper; a journal; the news (in the papers); the press [총칭].

¶ ~의 newspaper; press; journalistic / ~에(서) in a newspaper; in the papers; in the press / 일간 ~ a daily (newspaper); the daily press [총칭] / 철한 ~ filed newspapers; newspapers on file / 헌 ~ an old newspaper / 시카고 ~의 조간〔석간〕 the morning〔evening〕 edition of the *Chicago* / ~의 여론 환기 캠페인 a press campaign / ~에 의하면 according to the newspapers / ~에 내다〔싣다〕 give《*a matter*》 to the press; carry《an article》 in the paper / ~에 나다 appear in the papers; get into the papers / ~에 나지 않게 하다 keep《*a matter*》 out of papers / ~에 논설을 쓰다 write an article for a newspaper / ~에 투고하다 write to《the *Dong-A*》/ ~에서 대서특필하다 give front-page prominence《to》; devote much space to; write up (칭찬하여) / ~에서 가볍게 다루다 relegate to inside pages; have only a small space《for, to》/ ~에서 보다 see〔read〕《*something*》 in the papers / ~에서 공격하다 open a newspaper campaign against / ~에서 얻어맞다 be attacked〔criticized〕 in the press; be written down / ~에서 호평을 받다 have〔enjoy〕 a good〔favorable〕 press; be favorably noticed by the press / ~에서 악평을 받다 get〔receive, be given〕 a bad press / ~을 발행하다 publish〔issue〕 a newspaper / ~을 편집하다 edit a newspaper / ~을 발송하다 distribute papers / ~을 배달하다 deliver newspapers / ~을 보다《구독하다》take (in) a newspaper; subscribe to a paper;《읽다》read a newspaper / ~을 접다 fold up a newspaper / ~을 창간하다 launch a newspaper / ~을 펼치다 spread a newspaper《on a seat》/ ~에 …이라고 나 있다 It says〔is reported〕 in the paper that….; The paper says that…. / 그의 이름을 ~에서 보았다 I saw his name in the paper. / 그 뉴스는 ~에 크게 났다 The news went into headlines. / 우리는 그날 그날 세상 돌아가는 일을 ~을 통해서 안다 We depend upon newspapers for the daily news. *or* We learn from the newspapers what is going on in the world. / 이런 작은 사건은 ~에 나지 않을 게다 Such a minor incident is unlikely to find its way into the papers〔the press〕. / 무슨 ~을 보십니까 What paper do you take?

◉ ~값 the《monthly》 charge for the newspaper. ~광고 newspaper advertising; a newspaper advertisement; an ad (in the paper);《구어》classified ads (항목별 광고란의). ~구독료 the subscription to a newspaper. ~구독자 a (newspaper) reader; a subscriber to a newspaper. ~논조 the tone of the press; press comments《on》. ~발표《issue》a press release〔handout (인쇄된)〕. ~발행인 a newspaper publisher《미》; a newspaper proprietor《영》. ~방송학과 the department of mass communication. ~보급소 a newspaper agency: ~보급소장 a newsagent《영》; a newsdealer《미》. ~소설 a serial novel〔story〕 in a newspaper. ~스크랩 newspaper clippings《미》; newspaper cuttings《영》. ~업 the newspaper industry; journalism. ~열람실 a news room. ~용지

newsprint. ~ 윤리 강령 the Press Moral Code. ~자동판매기 a newspaper vendor; a honor box 《미》. ~주간 Newspaper Week. ~지 newspaper (★ 무관사); the newspaper itself. ~판매대 a news stand; 《영》 a news stall. ~판매점 《미》 a newsdealer's shop; 《영》 a newsagent's shop. ~팔이 a newsboy; a news vendor. ~편집국 the editorial office: ~ 편집국원 the editorial staff (전원). ~학 (the study of) journalism: ~학과 《대학의》 a journalism course. 주간~ a weekly newspaper. 세계~협회 The World Association of Newspapers. 한국 ~ 방송 편집인 협회 The Korea News Editors' Association. 한국 ~ 협회 The Korean Newspapers Association. 한국 ~ 회관 the Press Center of Korea.

**신문기사**(新聞記事) a news (item); an article (in a newspaper); a write-up (in the paper); a newspaper account 〔story, article, report〕. ¶ 신문기삿거리 a news matter 〔item〕; news / 신문기삿거리가 되다 become a good topic for the newspapers.

**신문기자**(新聞記者) a newsman; a newspaperman; a journalist; a (newspaper) pressman 〔reporter〕 《영》. ◉ ~단 a press corps: ~단 회견 a press interview 〔conference (정식의)〕. ~석 the press gallery 〔box, section〕. ~클럽 a press club.

**신문배달**(新聞配達) 《사람》 a newsboy; a newspaper delivery man; a (news) paper boy; 《일》 delivering newspaper. ¶ ~을 하다 deliver newspapers; take a paper route; have 〔be carrying〕 a paper route.

**신문사**(新聞社) a newspaper publishing company; a newspaper office. ¶ ~에 근무하다 be on (the staff of) a newspaper.

**신물** water brash. ¶ ~이 올라오다 have (a fit of) water brash / ~(이) 나다 [비유적] get sick and tired 《of》; become (quite) disgusted 《with》; get sick (to death) 《of》; have had enough 《of》; 《구어》 be fed up 《with》; be bored 《with, by》 / ~이 날 정도로 to a sickening extreme 〔disgusting degree〕; (L.) *ad nauseam* / 그의 강의라면 ~이 난다 I am bored to death with his lecture. / 그 놈의 얼굴만 봐도 ~이 난다 The very sight of him is loathsome 〔makes me sick〕. *or* It makes me sick even to look at him.

**신미**(辛未) 〖민속〗 the 8th binary term of the sexagenary cycle.

**신민**(臣民) the officials and the people; a subject.

**신바닥** the bottom of *one's* shoes; a shoe sole. ¶ ~을 갈다 resole shoes.

**신바람** high 〔exulted〕 spirits; elation; excitement.

**신발** footwear; footgear; shoes. ⇨ 신[1]. ¶ ~을 닦으시오〔터시오〕 《게시》 Please use mat. *or* Clean shoes before entering. ◉ ~가게 a footwear store 〔shop 《영》〕. ~장수 a footwear dealer. ~제조업자 footwear makers 〔manufacturers〕. ~주머니 a shoes-keeping sack.

**신발견**(新發見) a new 〔fresh, recent〕 discovery 〔find〕; a discovery. ~하다 make a new discovery.

**신발명**(新發明) a new invention. ~하다 newly invent. ¶ ~의 newly-invented; of recent invention.

**신발족**(新發足) a new 〔fresh〕 start. ~하다 make a new 〔fresh〕 start; start afresh.

**신방**(申方) 〖민속〗 the Direction of the Monkey (= southwest-by-west).

**신방**(新房) a bridal room; a bride-chamber. ¶ ~에 들다 consummate a marriage; get into the bridal bed.

**신벌**(神罰) divine punishment 〔judgment, retribution〕.

**신법**(新法) ① 《법률》 new regulations; a new law. ② 《방법》 a new method; newly discovered methods.

**신변**(身邊) *one's* person; *one's* side. ¶ ~의 위험 *one's* personal danger; uncertainty of *one's* position / ~을 경계하다 watch over 《*a person*》 to protect 《*him*》 from danger / ~을 염려〔걱정〕하다 worry 〔be anxious, be apprehensive〕 about *a person's* (personal) safety / ~을 정리하다 put *one's* affairs in order; arrange *one's* affairs / ~이 위험하다 be in personal danger / ~에 두다 keep *something* by *one's* side / ~에 호위를 붙이다 keep *one's* body guards about 《*one*》 / 그는 ~을 정리한 뒤 자수했다 He gave himself up to police authorities after arranging his affairs. ◉ ~경호 personal protection. ~소설 a personal novel; a novel depicting the author's personal life. ~잡기 *one's* memoirs; memoirs 〔jettings〕 on *one's* private life.

**신병**(身病) bodily illness; sickness 《미》. ¶ ~으로 on account of sickness; owing to ill health / ~으로 드러

눕다 be laid up (with sickness).

**신병**(新兵) a (fresh 〔raw〕) recruit; a newly-enlisted soldier; a new conscript; a (fresh) draftee; a rookie《구어》. ◉ ～훈련 boot 〔recruit〕 training: ～ 훈련소 a recruit training center; a boot camp《미구어》.

**신볼** the width of a shoe. ¶ ～이 좁다 the shoes are tight across the instep.

**신봉**(信奉) belief; faith. ～하다 adhere《to》; believe 〔have faith〕《in》; follow. ◉ ～자 a believer《in》; an adherent《of》; a devotee《of》.

**신부**(神父) a Catholic priest; a (holy) Father. ¶ 홍 ～ Father 〔Fr.〕 Hong / ～가 되다 be ordained a priest.

**신부**(新婦) a bride; a newlywed wife; a recent bride. ¶ ～감을 고르다 look for a bride; search for a wife. ◉ ～들러리 a maid-of-honor; a bridesmaid. ～의상 a bridal costume 〔dress〕; a bride's outfit. ～학교 a finishing school; a school for domestic training.

**신분**(身分)《사회적 지위》(*one's*) status; *one's* social position 〔standing〕; *one's* station in life; *one's* position in society;《위계》a rank;《신원》*one's* identity; origin; birth;《분수》*one's* means. ¶ ～이 높은 사람 a person of high standing 〔rank〕/ ～이 낮은 사람 a lowly person; a person of low birth 〔lower classes, low station, humble condition〕/ ～에 걸맞지 않는 행동 activities incompatible with *one's* status / ～의 차이 (a) difference in《*their*》social position 〔rank〕/ ～ 차이가 나는 결혼 a misalliance / ～ 여하를 막론하고 regardless of *one's* position; whatever position *one* may hold / ～이 높다 be of high standing; be of a high social level / ～이 다르다 differ in social standing / ～을 밝히다 〔감추다〕 reveal 〔hide〕 *one's* identity; disclose 〔conceal〕 *one's* origin / ～에 어울리게〔어울리지 않게〕 살다 live within 〔beyond〕 *one's* means / 인간의 가치를 ～에 따라 판단해서는 안 된다 You should not judge a man's worth by his social standing 〔status〕. / 그는 대학교수 ～을 버리고 작가로서 살아갈 결심을 했다 He decided to give up his position as college professor and live as a writer. ◉ ～보장 (a) guarantee of *a person's* status. ～제 a status system. ～증명 identification: ～증명서 an identification 〔ID〕 card / ～증명을 요구하다 demand identification《from》.

**신불**(神佛) gods and Buddha; shamanism and Buddhism. ¶ 그들은 ～의 가호를 빌었다 They prayed for divine protection.

**신비**(神秘) (a) mystery. ～하다, ～롭다 (be) mysterious; mystic(al). ¶ 생명의 ～ the mystery of life / 자연의 ～ the mysteries of nature / ～에 싸여 있다 be wrapped 〔shrouded〕 in mystery / ～를 풀다 unravel 〔solve〕 a mystery / ～를 탐색하다 explore a mystery / ～의 베일을 벗기다 strip *something* of its aura of mystery; demystify. ◉ ～경(境) a land of mystery. ～극 a mystery drama 〔play〕. ～성〔감〕 a mystique. ～소설 a mystery story. ～주의 mysticism: ～주의자 a mystic; an occultist. ～철학 esoterics; mystic philosophy.

**신빙**(信憑) trust; reliance; credence. ～하다 trust; rely on. ◉ ～성 reliability; credibility; authenticity: ～성이 있다〔없다〕 be reliable 〔unreliable〕; be credible 〔incredible〕; be authentic 〔unauthentic〕.

**신사**(辛巳)〖민속〗the 18th binary term of the sexagenary cycle.

**신사**(紳士) a gentleman; a man of honor; [총칭] (the) gentry;《미》gentlefolk(s). ¶ ～적인, ～다운 gentlemanly; gentlemanlike / 비～적인 ungentlemanly / ～적으로 in a gentlemanly way 〔manner〕/ ～연하다 play the gentleman; pose as 〔set up for〕 a gentleman / ～의 체면에 관계되는 문제다 be beneath《*a person's*》dignity as a gentleman / 그는 전형적인 ～이다 He is a typical gentleman. / 그런 짓을 하면 ～의 체면이 깎일 것이다 That would be beneath your dignity as a gentleman. / 그는 도저히 ～라곤 할 수 없다 He is hardly a gentleman. / ～숙녀 여러분《호칭》Ladies and Gentlemen! (★ 여성이 한 명이라도 이렇게 말함) / 그는 ～적으로 행동했다 He acted as a gentleman. ◉ ～도 gentlemanship; the code of a gentleman. ～록 a Who's Who; a social register《미》. ～복 men's suit; a sack 〔business〕 suit; a lounge suit《영》. ～협정 a gentlemen's agreement. ～화(靴) men's shoes.

**신산**(辛酸) hardships; sufferings; bitterness. ¶ 갖은 ～을 맛보다 taste the bitters of life; suffer 〔undergo〕 many hardships.

**신상**(身上)《몸》*one's* body;《처지》*one's*

situation 〔circumstances〕; the conditions of *one's* life. ¶ (아무의) ~을 걱정하다 feel concerned about 《*a person's*》 welfare 〔safety〕; wonder 〔be anxious to know〕 how 《*a person*》 is doing. ◉ ~문제 *one's* personal affairs: ~문제를 의논하다 consult 《*a person*》 〔seek *another's* advice〕 about *one's* personal affairs. ~상담란 a personal advice 〔home council, 《영》 an agony〕 column; a human-relation column; the problem page. ~조사서 〔명세서〕 a report card on *one's* family.

**신상필벌**(信賞必罰) sure penalty and certain reward. ~하다 never fail to reward a meritorious service or let a fault go unpunished. ¶ ~주의로 on the principle that good work will be rewarded and bad work punished.

**신색**(神色) complexion; expression; looks. ¶ ~이 좋다〔나쁘다〕 look well 〔pale〕.

**신생**(新生) a new birth; [형용사적] newborn; renascent (재생의). ◉ ~국 a newly emerging nation. ~대 〖지질〗 the Cenozoic 〔Cainozoic〕 era.

**신생물**(新生物) 〖병리〗 a neoplasm.

**신생아**(新生兒) a newborn baby; 〖의학〗 a neonate. ¶ ~기의 neonatal / ~의 사망 neonatal death. ◉ ~용품 baby goods. ~학 neonatology: ~학자 a neonatologist. ~황달 jaundice of the newborn (babies).

**신생활**(新生活) a new life. ¶ ~로 들어가다 begin 〔start〕 a new life; turn over a new leaf. ◉ ~운동 a new-life 〔life-reform〕 movement.

**신서**(信書) a letter; (personal) correspondence [총칭]. ⇨ 편지. ¶ ~의 비밀을 침해하다 violate the privacy of (personal) correspondence.

**신서**(新書) a newly-published book; a new book 〔publication〕. 「장 결석.

**신석**(腎石) 〖의학〗 a renal calculus. = 신

**신석기**(新石器) 〖고고학〗 a neolith; a neolithic stone implement.

◉ ~시대 the Neolithic era 〔age〕; the New Stone Age.

**신선**(神仙) a Taoist hermit with supernatural powers; 《은자》 a hermit; an ascetic; 《세속을 벗어난 사람》 an unworldly man. ◉ ~경 a fairyland; an enchanted place.

**신선**(新鮮) freshness. ~하다 (be) fresh. ¶ ~한 공기 fresh air / ~한 채소 fresh vegetables / ~하게 하다 make fresh; freshen; refresh / 이 레몬은 ~해 보인다 This lemon looks fresh. / 밖으로 나가 ~한 공기를 마시자 Let's go out and get a breath of fresh air. / 국무총리의 연설에 ~한 것은 아무것도 없었다 We found nothing novel in the Prime Minister's speech. / 그 그림은 참으로 ~한 인상을 주었다 The picture made quite a new impression on me.

**신선도**(新鮮度) (the degree of) freshness. ¶ ~가 높은〔좋은〕 very fresh; lively / ~가 떨어지다 lose (some of) 《its》 freshness.

**신선로**(神仙爐) a brass chafing dish; vegetables, meat and sea foods in a chafing-dish; *shinsŏllo.*

**신선미**(新鮮味) freshness. ¶ ~가 없다 lack freshness / ~를 느낄 수 없다 find nothing fresh 《in the work》.

**신설**(新設) (new) establishment; founding; creation. ~하다 establish 〔organize〕 newly; create; found. ¶ ~의 newly-formed〔-established, -organized〕; new / 우체국을 ~하다 set up a new post office 《at》; open a post office / 학교를 ~하다 establish 〔found〕 a school / 역 근처에 파출소가 ~되었다 A new police box has been set up near the station. ◉ ~학교〔공장〕 a newly-founded school 〔factory〕. ~회사 a newly-established〔-organized〕 company; a new company.

**신설**(新說) 《학설》 a new theory 〔doctrine〕; 《견해》 a new light 〔view〕; 《해석》 a new interpretation. ¶ ~을 제기하다 propound 〔advance, put forward〕 a new theory.

**신성**(神性) divine nature; divinity; godhead. ¶ ~을 띠다〔지니다〕 be touched by 〔with〕 divinity.

**신성**(神聖) sacredness; sanctity; holiness. ~하다 (be) holy; sacred; consecrated; divine; sanctified.

> **용법** **holy** 근본적으로 종교에 관련되며, 종교적으로 깊이 존경받는 정신적인 순수함을 뜻한다. **sacred** 계율이나 단체 따위에 의해 종교적인 의미가 주어진 성스러운 것으로 신에게 바쳐지는 것이란 뜻이 있다. **divine** 「신성(神性)을 가진, 신에게서 나오는, 신에 관계하는」이란 뜻으로, 초인간적인 힘 즉 최고의 위대함을 나타낸다.

¶ ~한 sacred; holy; divine / ~화하다 sanctify; consecrate; hallow / ~시하다 hold 《*a thing*》 sacred / ~ 불가침의 sacred and inviolable; sacrosanct / ~

을 더럽히다〔모독하다〕 violate 〔defile〕 the sanctity《of》; desecrate; profane / …을 ～한 의무로 여기다 regard 《*a thing*》 as a sacred duty.
◉ ～동맹 〖역사〗 the Holy Alliance. ～로마제국 the Holy Roman Empire.

**신성**(新星) 〖천문〗 a nova (*pl.* ～s, -vae); a new star. ¶ 영화〔가요〕계의 ～ a new film 〔pop song〕 star.

**신세** moral indebtedness; an obligation; a debt of gratitude.
¶ ～를 지다 be indebted 〔obliged〕 to 《*a person*》; owe 《*a person*》 a debt of gratitude; be under indebtedness to 《*a person*》; 《도움을 받다》 receive assistance; be under the care of; 《짐이 되다》 be a burden to; live at 《*a person's*》 expense; live with 〔on〕 《*a person*》 / ～를 갚다 repay 〔return〕 《*a person's*》 favor 〔help〕; show *one's* gratitude to *a person* / ～를 끼치다 trouble 《*a person*》; give 《*a person*》 trouble; put 《*a person*》 to trouble / 남의 ～를 지지 않다 take care of *oneself;* look after *oneself;* manage *one's* own affairs; be self-reliant / 정말 ～졌습니다 Thank you for your kind help. *or* I am very much obliged to you (for your kindness). *or* Many thanks for your trouble. / 그에게 많은 ～를 졌다 He has done me various acts of kindness.

**신세**(身世) *one's* lot; *one's* circumstances; *one's* personal affairs. ¶ 딱한 ～ adverse circumstances; a sad lot / ～타령하다 bewail *one's* lot 〔ill fortune〕; grieve about *one's* misfortune / 거지 ～가 되다 be reduced to beggary / 그는 부랑자 ～로 전락했다 He fell so low as to become a tramp.

**신세계**(新世界) a new world; 《아메리카 대륙》 the New World.

**신세대**(新世代) the new generation.

**신소리**[1] 《말장난》 a game of rhymings; a play on words; a pun. ～하다 play upon words; make puns. ¶ ～마라 None of your lip!

**신소리**[2] 《신발의》 the echo of footsteps; sound of walking shoes.

**신속**(迅速) quickness; rapidity; swiftness; promptitude. ～하다 (be) quick; rapid; swift; speedy; prompt. ¶ ～히 quickly; swiftly; promptly; rapidly / 아무의 ～한 회복을 바라다 wish *a person* speedy recovery from illness / 그는 일을 ～히 해치운다 He quickly carries out his business. ◉ ～대응부대 a rapid reaction unit.

**신수**(身手) *one's* bearing; *one's* air; *one's* appearance 〔looks〕. ¶ ～가 훤하다 have a fine appearance 〔presence〕; cut a fine figure; have a good bearing; carry *oneself* splendidly.

**신수**(身數) *one's* luck; *one's* fortune. ¶ ～가 펴이다 fortune turns in *one's* favor; be in luck's way / ～를 보아 주다 tell 〔read〕 《*a person's*》 fortune / ～를 보다 consult a fortuneteller; have *one's* fortune told / 금년에는 ～가 나쁘다 This is an unlucky year for me.

**신승**(辛勝) ～하다 win 《a game》 by a narrow 〔small〕 margin; carry 〔win〕 the day after a hard struggle 〔fight〕; nose 〔edge〕 out 《구어》.

**신시**(申時) the 9th of the 12 double=hours (= 3-5 p.m.); the 17th of the 24 hours (= 3:30-4:30 p.m.).

**신시**(辛時) 〖민속〗 the 20th of the 24 hours period (= 6:30-7:30 p.m.).

**신시**(新詩) 《새로 지은》 a new poem; 《신체시》 a modern poem.

**신시내티** 《미국의 도시》 Cincinnati.

**신시대**(新時代) a new age 〔era, epoch〕. ¶ ～를 여는 epoch-making; epochal.

**신식**(新式) 《새양식·신형》 a new type 〔style〕; a new mode; 《조직》 a new system; 《방법》 a new method. ¶ ～의 new; new-style〔-type, -pattern〕; 《현대적》 up-to-date; new-fashioned; modern / ～으로 하다 modernize / 이것은 아주 ～의 언어교수법이다 This is quite a new method of language teaching. ◉ ～생활 a new mode of living; modern living. ～총 a new-type gun.

**신신당부**(申申當付) an explicit entrusting; an explicit 〔repeated〕 request 〔solicitation〕. ～하다 explicitly 〔repeatedly〕 request 〔solicit〕.

**신실**(信實) sincerity; honesty; faithfulness. ～하다 (be) sincere; faithful; truthful. ¶ ～한 말 sincere words.

**신심**(信心) faith; piety; devotion. ¶ ～이 깊다 be devout; be pious; be (deeply) religious.

**신안**(新案) a new idea; a new device; a new design 〔mode〕; a novelty. ¶ ～의 newly-devised; newly-designed; novel / 실용 ～특허를 신청하다 apply for a utility model patent.

**신앙**(信仰) (religious) faith; belief; a creed. ～하다 believe 〔have faith〕 in 《God》. ¶ 기독교 ～ the Christian belief / ～의 자유 religious liberty; freedom of religion 〔faith〕 / ～(심)이 없는 impious; infidel; unbelieving; 《*a person*》 with no religious belief 〔faith〕 / ～을 버리다 discard 〔give up, abjure, abandon, forsake〕 *one's* faith 〔religion〕 / ～이 두텁다 be devout; be pious; be deeply religious / ～을 간직하다 keep the faith / 기독교～을 갖게 된 동기는 무엇이냐 What motivated you to have faith in Christianity? / 그는 신흥 종교를 ～하고 있다 He believes in a newly-risen religion.

◉ ～고백 a confession of faith; the profession 《of Christianity》: ～고백자 a professor of religion. ～생활 a religious life; a life of faith: ～ 생활을 하다 lead a religious life. ～신조(信條) the articles of faith 〔belief〕; a creed. ～심 (religious) piety; faith. ～요법 the faith cure. ～인 a believer; a devotee.

**신약**(神藥) a wonder 〔miracle〕 drug; a wonder-working remedy. ⇨ 영약.

**신약**(新約) 〖성서〗 the New Testament (생략 NT, N.T.).

◉ ～성서 ＝신약. ～시대 New Testament times.

**신약**(新藥) 《develop》 a new medicine 〔drug〕 《for》.

**신어**(新語) a new word (교과서 등의); a newly-coined word (신조어); a neologism. ¶ ～를 만들다 coin new words.

◉ ～사용 neologism.

**신여성**(新女性) the modern girl; the new woman.

**신역**(新譯) a new translation; a new version (of translation); [형용사적] newly translated. ～하다 translate anew; give a new translation.

**신열**(身熱) a (body) temperature; (a) fever. ¶ ～이 있다 have (a) fever; be feverish / ～이 높다 have 〔run〕 a high fever / ～이 나다 develop 〔run〕 a fever; become feverish / ～이 좀 내리다 *one's* fever goes down a little / ～을 재다 take *one's* temperature.

**신염**(腎炎) 〖의학〗 nephritis.

**신예**(新銳) new and superior. ¶ ～의 new and powerful 《weapon》; fresh 《troops》 / 최～의 전자 장비 the state-of-the-art electronics.

◉ ～기(機) a newly produced war plane. ～무기 new (powerful) weapons.

**신용**(信用) 《신임》 confidence; trust; faith; reliance (신뢰); 《거래상의》 credit; 《평판》 *one's* reputation. ～하다 trust; put (*one's*) trust 〔faith〕 in; place confidence 〔credence〕 in; rely on; give credit to; accept 《*something*》 as true.

> 용법 **confidence** 확실한 증거나 유력한 이유가 있어서 사람이나 물건을 신용하는 것. **trust** 염려 없을 거라고 생각하며 믿는 것으로, 무조건적 신뢰를 뜻함. **faith** 전연 증거가 없더라도 무언가를 믿는 것으로, 맹목적인 신뢰를 뜻함.

¶ ～ 있는 사람 a person of good credit; a person of established reputation; a reliable person; 《약속을 지키는 사람》 a man of his word / ～할 수 있는 trusty; trustworthy; reliable; credible; creditable / ～할 수 없는 untrustworthy; unworthy of trust; unreliable / …에게 ～이 있다 be trusted 〔credited〕 《by》; have 〔enjoy〕 《*a person's*》 confidence / ～이 없다 have no credit 〔enjoy little credit〕 with; lack 《*a person's*》 trust / ～을 얻다 win 《*a person's*》 confidence; gain credit 《with *a person*》 / ～을 잃다〔떨어뜨리다〕 lose *one's* credit; lose 《*a person's*》 confidence; lose credit 《with another》; fall into disrepute 〔discredit〕 《with》 / ～을 되찾다 regain the confidence 《of》 / ～을 유지하다 maintain *one's* reputation 〔credit〕 / ～을 손상하다 injure 〔impair〕 *one's* credit; stain *one's* reputation; bring discredit on... / ～에 관계되다 [원인이 주어] reflect (badly) on *one's* trustworthiness; affect people's confidence in *one;* damage 〔affect〕 *one's* standing 〔credit〕 / 신문 기사를 ～하다 give credence to a newspaper account / 아무의 말을 ～하다 believe what *a person* says; take *a person* at *his* word (액면 그대로) / 그의 말이면 다 ～한다 I have confidence in whatever he says. / 그는 주인한테 ～이 있다 He has his master's confidence. / 그는 ～할 만한 사람이 못된다 He is not a man to be trusted 〔relied upon〕. / 신문 기사를 너무 ～하지 마라 Don't put too much confidence in what the newspaper say. / 그 사람의 말을 어디까지 ～해야 할지 모르겠다 I don't know how far we should believe him. / 그런 일을 하면 세상에서 ～을 완전히 잃을거다 That'll discredit you hopelessly with the public. / 나 같으면 그 사람보다 그녀의 말을 더 ～했을 텐데 I would have taken her word against his. / 타회사

와 거래를 시작하려면 그 회사의 ~ 상태를 점검할 필요가 있다 In case we open an account with a certain firm, we'll need to check their credit standing. ◉ ~관리 기금 the Credit Management Fund. ~금고 a credit union 〔association〕; a savings and loan association. ~기관 an organ of credit. ~보증 기금 the trust guarantee funds. ~보험 《대손(貸損)에 대한》 credit insurance; 《고용인 등에 대한》 fidelity insurance. ~사기 a confidence trick 〔game 《미》〕; a con game. ~정보 회사 a credit information company. ~조사 an inquiry 〔investigation〕 into 〔concerning〕 the financial status 〔credit standing〕 《of》; 《조회》 a credit inquiry 〔research〕. ~조합 a credit union 〔association〕. ~증권 credit paper; an instrument of credit. ~카드 a credit card: ~카드 받습니다 《게시》 Credit cards (are) accepted here. ~판매 selling on credit. ~한도 a credit limit. 무담보~ clean credit. 상업~ commercial 〔trade〕 credit. 국가~등급 《uprade》 soverign credit ratings.

**신용거래**(信用去來) dealings 〔sales〕 on credit; credit dealing 〔transactions〕; 『증권』 margin trading. ¶ ~를 하다 sell 〔buy〕 on credit; do 〔carry on〕 credit transactions 《with》 / ~로 10만 주를 사다 buy 100,000 shares on the margin. ◉ ~처 a credit 〔charge〕 customer.

**신용대출**(信用貸出) a credit loan; a loan on credit; a charter loan. ~하다 give 〔extend, grant〕 《*a person*》 (a) credit 《for 1,000,000 won to *a person*》. ¶ ~로 on trust 〔credit〕. ◉ 장기〔단기〕~ a long 〔short〕 credit.

**신용도**(信用度) credit rating. ¶ 그의 ~는 높다〔낮다〕 He is a good 〔poor, bad〕 credit risk.

**신용상태**(信用狀態) *one's* financial 〔credit〕 status 〔standing〕. ¶ 회사의 ~ the credit status of a firm / ~를 조사하다 inquire into 〔make sure of〕 《*a person's*》 financial status.

**신용장**(信用狀) a letter of credit (생략 L/C); a bill of credit; a credit. ¶ ~의 발행〔양도, 분할, 갱신〕 issuance 〔transfer, division, renewal〕 of a credit / ~을 개설하다 open 〔establish〕 an L/C 《with a bank, by cable, for a sum》 / ~을 발행〔확인〕하다 issue 〔confirm〕 an L/C. ◉ ~개설〔발행, 매입, 확인〕 은행 an L/C opening 〔issuing, negotiating, confirming〕 bank. ~발행자 an accrediting party; an opener of L/C. 내국~ a local L/C.

**신우**(腎盂) 『해부』 the pelvis of the kidney. ◉ ~염 『의학』 pyelitis.

**신원**(身元) 《본인》 *one's* identity; 《경력》 *one's* career 〔antecedents〕; 《지위》 *one's* social position; 《내력》 *one's* origin; *one's* background (배경). ¶ ~ 불명의 unidentified / ~을 밝히다 《남의》 prove 〔recognize〕 《*a person's*》 identity; 《자기의》 disclose *one's* identity; identify *oneself* 《as》 / ~을 숨기다 conceal 〔sink〕 *one's* identity / ~을 조사하다 inquire 〔look〕 into 《*a person's*》 (family and social) background 〔antecedents〕; check 《*a person's*》 record; 《고용주 등이》 inquire into 《*a person's*》 reliability / ~을 조회하다 refer to 《a company》 for 《*a person's*》 character / ~을 증명하다 prove *one's* identity; 《스스로》 identify *oneself* 《as》 / ~이 밝혀지다 be identified; *one's* identity is established / ~이 밝혀지지 않다 be unidentified / 시체의 ~을 확인하다 establish the identity of the corpse / 경찰은 그의 ~을 캐고 있다 The police are looking into his background. / 비행기 추락 사고의 희생자 ~이 판명되기까지 꼬박 1주일이 걸렸다 It took a whole week to identify the victims of the plane crash. / 그 남자는 소지품으로 ~이 판명되었다 The man was identified by his things. ◉ ~인수인 a guarantee. ~조사 police clearance. ~조회처 a reference. ~증명서 identity papers; an identification 〔ID〕 card.

**신원**(伸冤) redressing a grievance 〔wrong〕. ~하다 redress a grievance.

**신원보증**(身元保證) personal reference; a certificate of good character. ¶ 전 고용주의 확실한 ~ excellent references from former employer / ~을 요함 A good reference (is) necessary. ◉ ~금 caution money; security; a bond for good conduct. ~인 a surety; a reference; a guarantee; 《보석의》 a bail: ~인이 되다 stand surety for; go bail for.

**신위**(神位) an ancestral tablet.

**신유**(辛酉) 『민속』 the 58th binary term of the sexagenary cycle.

**신음**(呻吟) a groan; a moan. ~하다 groan 《under the heavy tax burden》; moan; give a groan 〔moan〕 languish 《in prison》. ¶ 고통으로 ~하

다 moan 〔groan〕 with pain / 병상에서 ~하다 be confined to bed / 부상자들이 고통으로 ~하는 소리가 밤새도록 들려왔다 I heard the wounded people groaning with pain all night.

**신의**(信義) faithfulness; fidelity; loyalty; truthfulness. ¶ ~가 있다 be faithful / ~가 없다 be perfidious 〔faithless, insincere〕 / ~를 지키다 keep faith 《with *a person*》; observe fidelity; be true to *one's* word / ~를 저버리다〔어기다〕 break faith 《with *a person*》 / ~에 어긋나는 짓이다 be an act running counter to good faith / ~를 중히 여기는 사람 a man of honor. 「Providence.

**신의**(神意) the divine will; God's will;

**신의**(神醫) a wonderful physician.

**신인**(神人) ① 《신 같은 사람》 a divine person; a godlike person; a man of god; a god man. ② 《신과 사람》 god and man; the gods and men. ¶ ~공노하다 god and men are angry alike. ③ 〖기독교〗 God in Man. ◉ ~동형 anthropomorphism. ~상통 communication between god(s) and men.

**신인**(新人) a new man; a new figure; a recruit; 《신진》 a rising man; 《영화 등의》 a new face; a new star; 《스포츠의》 a rookie 《미구어》. ¶ 시단(詩壇)의 ~ a new figure in poetry / 야구의 ~왕 the rookie king / 정계의 ~ a new political figure; 《신참자》 a novice in politics. ◉ ~가수 a new singer. ~상 the Rookie of the Year award. ~선수 《야구의》 a rookie. ~왕전 〖권투〗 the fight of the 《1999》 Rookie King Pro Boxing Championships. ~작가 a budding writer.

**신임**(信任) confidence; trust; credence. ~하다 trust; place confidence 〔*one's* trust〕 in 《*a person*》; confide in; put trust in; 《내각을》 give a vote of confidence to 《the government》. ¶ ~이 두터운 trusted / ~을 얻다 win 〔gain〕 the confidence 《of》; be trusted 《by》 / ~을 얻고 있다 have 〔enjoy〕 the confidence 《of *one's* boss》 / 상사의 ~을 잃다 fall into discredit with *one's* superiors / 국민에게 ~을 묻다 make an appeal to the confidence of the whole nation. ◉ ~안 a confidence motion.

**신임**(新任) new appointment. ~하다 newly appoint to office. ¶ ~의 newly= appointed; new / ~인사를 하다 make an inaugural address.
◉ ~교수 a newly appointed professor. ~교장 the new principal. ~자 a new appointee. ~지 *one's* new post; a new post of duty.

**신임장**(信任狀) credentials; a letter of credence. ¶ ~을 제정〔제출〕하다 present *one's* credentials. ◉ ~제정 credentials presentation.

**신임투표**(信任投票) a vote of confidence. ¶ ~에서 이기다〔지다〕 win 〔lose〕 the vote of confidence 《on a policy》.

**신입**(新入) (newly) entering; incoming; new. ◉ ~사원 a new 〔newly-hired〕 employee. ~자 a newcomer; a new face; a novice; a new bird (교도소의).

**신입생**(新入生) a new pupil (초등학교·중학교의); a new 〔newly-enrolled〕 student; a freshman 《미》 (★ freshman은 여성에게도 쓰임). ¶ ~ 환영회 a welcome meeting for the freshmen.

**신자**(信者) a believer 《in Christianity》; a devotee; an adherent 《of》; a follower 《of》; [총칭] the faithful. ¶ 불교 ~ a believer in Buddhism / 기독교 ~가 되다 turn 〔become a〕 Christian; 《개종하다》 be converted to Christianity / 그는 기독교 ~다 He is a believer in Christianity. *or* He is of the Christian persuasion.

**신작**(新作) a new work; a new production 〔composition〕. ¶ ~을 발표하다 publish a new (piece of) work; give the first public performance 《of a new piece of music》.

**신작로**(新作路) a newly constructed road; a new highway.

**신장**(—欌) a shoes 〔footgear〕 cabinet 〔chest〕; a boot cupboard.

**신장**(身長) stature; height. ¶ ~이 크다〔작다〕 be tall 〔short〕; be high 〔short, small〕 in stature / ~순으로 《line up, stand》 in order of height / ~이 작은 short of stature / ~을 재다 take 〔measure〕 《*a person's*》 height / ~이 6피트이다 stand six feet (high); be six feet tall 〔in stature, in height〕 / ~이 커지다 grow 〔advance, increase〕 in stature; become 〔grow〕 taller / ~이 190센티에 달하다 attain a stature of 190 centimeters / ~이 얼마나 됩니까 What is your height? *or* How tall are you? / 그는 ~이 나보다 1센티가 크다 He is one centimeter taller than me.

**신장**(伸張) extension; elongation; expansion. ~하다 extend; expand; elongate; lengthen; stretch. ¶ 세력 ~ extension of *one's* influence / 수출을

～하다 increase 〔expand〕 exports / 국위를 해외로 ～하다 extend the national prestige overseas.
◉ ～성 expansibility; stretch property: ～성이 없다 have no stretch.

**신장**(神將) ① 《장수》 a general of divine 〔exceptional〕 ability. ② 《귀신》 a powerful spirit. ◉ ～대 a shaman's wand (used to invoke spirits); a spirit medium's staff.

**신장**(新裝) 《차림새》 a new dress; new attire 〔look〕; 《설비·장식》 new equipment; new decoration(s); new furnishing(s); 《책의》 new binding. ～하다 attire *oneself* in a new dress; newly decorate; provide with new equipment; remodel 《a building, *etc.*》; redecorate. ¶ ～한 newly-decorated / 공들여 ～하다 give a new look 《to》; refurbish; redecorate; remodel (개조하다) / 4월 5일 ～ 개업 《게시》 Completely remodeled. Reopening Apr. 5.

**신장**(腎臟) 〚해부〛 the kidney. ¶ ～이 나쁘다 have a kidney trouble. ◉ ～결석 a kidney stone; a nephrolith; a renal calculus (*pl.* -li); 〚의학〛 nephrolithiasis. ～병 a kidney 〔renal〕 disease 〔trouble〕. ～염 nephritis. ～이식 a kidney transplant. ～적출 〚외과〛 (a) nephrectomy. ～투석(透析) kidney dialysis. 인공～ a kidney machine.

**신저**(新著) a new work 《of a writer》; 《신간》 a new publication.

**신전**(神前) ¶ ～에서 before God 〔gods〕.

**신전**(神殿) a shrine; a sanctuary; a tabernacle; a temple.

**신접**(新接) 《새살림》 setting up a new home; 《이사하여 삶》 taking up *one's* abode (in a new place).
◉ ～살이 life in a new home; starting housekeeping: ～살이를 차리다 make a new home; set up house.

**신정**(神政) theocracy; thearchy.

**신정**(新正) the first 〔opening〕 day of the New Year; the New Year's day.

**신정**(新訂) a new revision; newly revised. ～하다 newly revise. ◉ ～판 a newly revised 〔new and revised〕 edition.

**신정권**(新政權) a new regime.

**신정책**(新政策) a new policy.

**신제**(新製) ¶ ～의 new; newly-made.

**신제도**(新制度) a new system. ¶ 이 ～는 미국의 현행 제도를 따라 만들어졌다 The new system was modeled on that in use in America.

**신제품**(新製品) a new product; an article newly manufactured 〔produced〕 《by》. ¶ 폐사 ～에 대한 설명을 드릴 기회가 있었으면 좋겠습니다 We'd like to ask for an opportunity to make a presentation of our new product.

**신조**(神助) god's help; divine grace 〔aid〕; providence. ⇨ 천우신조. ¶ 천우～로 by the grace of God 〔Heaven〕.

**신조**(信條) 《종교의》 an article of faith; a creed; a credo (*pl.* ～s); 《신념》 a principle; a belief; a creed. ¶ ～를 지키다 keep *one's* creed; be true to *one's* creed / 오직 정직 하나를 ～로 삼다 carry through with *one's* only weapon of honesty. ◉ 생활～ *one's* principles (of life).

**신조**(新造) new construction. ～하다 construct 〔build〕 anew; lay down; 《신어를》 coin. ¶ ～한 newly-built 〔=made〕; 《말 따위를》 new(ly)-coined / 배를 ～하다 build a ship. ◉ ～선(船) a new 〔newly-built〕 ship 〔boat〕. ～어(語) a new 〔newly-coined〕 word; a neologism.

**신종**(新種) 《종자》 a new species; 《신발견의》 a newly-discovered species 《of orchard》; 《변종》 a new variety 《of tulip》; 《신형》 a new type. ¶ ～사기 a new type of swindling.

**신주**(神主) a mortuary tablet; an ancestral tablet. ¶ ～를 모시다 enshrine *one's* ancestral tablet.

**신주**(新株) new stocks 〔shares 《영》〕. ¶ ～를 배당하다 allot new stocks / ～를 공모하다 offer new stocks for public subscription. ◉ ～락(落) 《권리락》 ex rights; ex allotment. ～발행비 stock issue costs. ～부(付) cum rights. ～인수권 preemptive rights.

**신중**(愼重) prudence; discretion; circumspection; caution; care. ～하다 (be) cautious; careful; circumspect; prudent; discreet; deliberate.
¶ ～히 carefully; circumspectly; cautiously; deliberately; discreetly; with caution; prudently / ～해지다 be discreet; be cautious / ～한 회답을 하다 give a guarded answer / ～한 태도를 취하다 take 〔assume〕 a prudent 〔cautious〕 attitude 《in》; tread warily 《in》; go easy on *something* / ～하지 않다 be careless; be incautious; be imprudent / ～히 고려하다 consider 《*a matter*》 seriously; give 《*a matter*》 a serious consideration 〔thought〕 / ～히 심의하다 give careful consideration to 《*a matter*》; deliberate on 《*a matter*》 / ～히 행동하다 act with pru-

dence 〔discretion〕; move with circumspection / ~히 말을 가려서 발언하다 speak in measured words / 무엇을 하는 데 ~을 기하다 be wary 〔circumspect, deliberate〕 in *do*ing; use discretion 《in》; handle *something* with kid gloves / 그 사람은 ~함이 없다 He lacks prudence. *or* He is careless 〔imprudent〕 《in his action》. / 그는 보기보다 ~한 사람이다 He is a more discreet person than he appears to be.

**신지식**(新知識) up-to-date knowledge 〔information〕; new 〔advanced〕 knowledge 〔idea〕. ¶ ~의 소유자 a man with up-to-date knowledge.

**신지피다**(神—) 〚민속〛 know much as the result of a mystical union with a god; a divine 〔shamanic〕 spirit enter into 《*a person*》. ¶ 신지핀 divinely inspired.

**신진**(新進) ¶ ~의 rising; coming forth / ~기예의 young and energetic; up=and-coming. ◉ ~작가 a rising 〔coming〕 novelist; a young writer.

**신진대사**(新陳代謝) 《신구 교체》 assimilation of the new and excretion of the old; replacing the old with the new; regeneration; 〚생물〛 metabolism; metastasis. ¶ ~의 metabolic / 인체의 ~ body metabolism / ~를 하다 replace the old with the new / ~가 되다 be renewed; be replaced; be regenerated / ~시키다 metabolize; subject to metabolism; change by metabolism / ~가 심하다〔완만하다〕 have a high 〔low〕 metabolism 〔metabolic rate〕 / 몸은 끊임없이 반복되는 ~를 한다 The human body is subject to constant metabolism. / ~는 자연의 법칙이다 It is the law of nature that the old give place to the new 〔the new take the place of the old〕. / 저 회사에서는 ~가 활발하다 The staff of the company is constantly changing.

**신짝** a shoe; an odd shoe (of a pair). ¶ 헌~처럼 버리다 reject 《*a thing*》 as worthless; cast 《*a thing*》 away like dirt.

**신착**(新着) new arrival; 《새로 도착한 물건》 a new arrival. ~하다 newly arrive; be a new arrival. ¶ ~의 newly=arrived; newly-received / ~의 양서 newly-imported foreign books.
◉ ~품(品) newly arrived 〔received, imported〕 goods; new arrivals.

**신찬**(新撰) new compilation; [형용사적] newly compiled 〔selected, edited〕. ~하다 newly compile 〔select, edit〕.

**신참**(新參) 《관리의》 a newly appointed official's first visit to his office; 《신참자》 a new official; a newcomer; 《미숙한 사람》 a new 〔green〕 hand; a greenhorn. ~하다 attend the office newly; arrive newly.

**신창** a shoe sole. ¶ ~을 갈다 resole shoes; have *one's* shoes resoled 《by》.

**신천옹**(信天翁) 〚조류〛 an albatross; a gooney bird.

**신천지**(新天地) a new world. ¶ ~를 개척하다 open up a new field of activity; break new ground.

**신청**(申請) 《출원·응모》 (an) application; 《청원》 a petition; 《참가의》 an entry; 《주식 등의》 subscription; 《요구》 a request; 《예약》 booking; reservation. ~하다 《출원하다》 apply 〔make (an) application〕 《to *a person* for *a thing*》; petition 《for》; 《제의하다》 propose 《marriage to》; 《참가를》 enter for 《a contest》; 《예약하다》 book 《a seat》; reserve; subscribe 《for the new stocks》; 《요구하다》 request 《an interview》; 《제기하다》 offer; make an offer; raise 《an objection》; 〚법〛 move 《for》. ¶ ~하는 대로 on application 〔request〕 / 법원에 ~하다 move the court 《for *a thing*》 / ~을 거절하다〔수락하다〕 decline 〔accept〕 an offer / ~을 접수하다 receive 〔accept〕 applications 〔subscriptions〕 / 변호인의 ~을 기각하다 reject a lawyer's motion / 입회를 ~하다 apply for membership in a society / 건축 허가를 ~하다 apply for the building permit 《to》 / 수험을 ~하다 enter for an examination / 대학에 입학을 ~하다 apply for admission to 〔into〕 a university / 클럽에 입회를 ~하다 apply for membership in a club / 잡지의 구독을 ~하다 subscribe to a magazine; send a subscription to a magazine / 취직의 ~을 하다 apply for a job / ~에 응하다 accept a request / 많은 ~이 있다 have a large number of applications / ~은 …로 《게시》 Apply to…; Applications received at…. / ~이 쇄도하고 있다 Applications are pouring in. *or* There are many applications. / 30건의 응모 ~이 있었다 We have received thirty applications. / 그 마라톤 경주에는 200명의 참가 ~이 있었다 There were two hundred entries for the marathon race. *or* Two hundred people entered 〔signed up for〕 the marathon

race. / 나는 그로부터 결혼 ~을 받았다 I received 〔have had〕 a proposal (of marriage) from him. / 나는 학생 비자를 ~하고 싶습니다 I'd like to apply for a student visa. / 서면이나 구두로 ~해 주십시오 Apply either in writing or in person.
◉ ~기한〔마감〕 the deadline for making application《for》; a time limit for application(s). ~료 application fee 〔money〕. ~서 a letter of application; an 〔a written〕 application; a petition; 《용지》 an application form 〔blank〕: 당국에 ~서를 제출하다 file an application with the authorities / ~서에 필요 사항을 기입하다 fill out an application blank; fill in an application form. ~순 the order of applications received: ~순으로 in order of application. ~인〔자〕 an applicant; a petitioner; a proposer; 《신문·주식 따위의》 a subscriber. ~접수처 a place for application. 여권~ an application for a passport: 여권~ 서류 papers for passport application.

**신체**(身體) the body; the person; 《체격》 the physique; 《체질》 the constitution. ¶ ~의 bodily; physical / ~의 구조〔발육〕 the bodily structure 〔development〕 / ~의 결함 physical defect / ~의 자유 personal liberty / ~의 과도한 노출 excessive bodily exposure / ~를 단련하다 build up a healthy body / ~가 튼튼하다 have a strong constitution / ~가 건전하다 be sound in body / 건전한 ~에 건전한 정신이 깃든다《격언》 A sound mind in a sound body. / ~적으로는 아무 이상이 없습니다 You are physically all right.
◉ ~각부 the parts of the body. ~언어 body language. ~요법 somatotherapy. ~활동 physical 〔body〕 activity.

**신체**(新體) new forms 《of literature, *etc.*》. ◉ ~시 the new-style of poetry; 《한 편》 a new-style poem.

**신체검사**(身體檢査) a physical examination; a physical checkup 《미》; 《소지품 검사》 a body search; frisk; 《공항에서의》 security check. ¶ ~를 하다 hold a physical checkup 〔examination〕; 《소지품의》 search a person / ~를 받다 《건강의》 have 〔undergo〕 a physical 〔medical〕 examination 〔checkup〕; 《소지품의》 have *one's* person searched; be searched 〔frisked〕.

**신체장애**(身體障礙) 《suffer from》 a disability.

**신체장애인**(身體障礙人) a physically handicapped person; a disabled person; [총칭] the disabled. ¶ 직업 훈련을 확충함으로써 ~들이 자립할 수 있도록 돕다 help handicapped people stand on their own feet by expanding vocational training / ~을 사회에서 수용할 방법을 강구해야 한다 The certain ways should be decided to accept physically handicapped people into society. ◉ ~복지법 the Disabled Persons Welfare Law. ~시설 facilities for the (physically) handicapped. ~연금 the pension for the physically handicapped.

**신체제**(新體制) a new structure 〔system, order〕. ¶ ~로 개편하다 reorganize 《the economic structure or political system》 for new system.

**신축**(辛丑) 〖민속〗 the 38th binary term of the sexagenary cycle.

**신축**(伸縮) expansion and contraction; 《탄성》 elasticity; flexibility. ~하다 expand and contract; be elastic. ¶ ~자재(自在)의 elastic; flexible.
◉ ~관세 a flexible tariff 《미》. ~성 elasticity; flexibility: ~성이 없는 lack elasticity / ~성을 주다 give elasticity to 《*a thing*》 / ~성이 뛰어나다 be extremely elastic.

**신축**(新築) new construction. ~하다 newly build; construct. ¶ ~한 집 a new(ly)-built 〔new〕 house / ~중인 집 a house under 〔in course of〕 construction. ◉ ~건물 a new building. ~건물 낙성식 the celebration of the completion of a new building. ~계획 a building program.

**신춘**(新春) 《새봄》 early spring; the new 〔fresh〕 spring; 《새해》 the New Year. ◉ ~문예 a literary contest in spring. ~휘호(揮毫) the first writing of the year; the New Year's writing.

**신출귀몰**(神出鬼沒) elusiveness; sudden appearance and disappearance; elusive movements. ~하다 suddenly appear and suddenly disappear; appear in unexpected places 〔at unexpected moments〕; be elusive; be of preternatural agility. ¶ ~하는 강도 a protean burglar; a Proteus / 행동이 ~하다 be elusive in *one's* movements.

**신출내기**(新出—) a newcomer; a greenhorn; a novice; a Johnny-come=lately 《미구어》. ¶ ~기자 a cub reporter.

**신코** the toe 〔tip〕 of a shoe; a toe (-cap).

**신탁**(信託) trust; committing (to the care of); entrusting. ~하다 trust 《*a person*》 with 《*a thing*》; entrust 《*a thing*》 to 《*a person*》 〔《*a person*》 with 《*a thing*》〕; leave 《*one's* property》 in trust with 《a bank》. ¶ ~의 fiduciary / ~을 받다 hold 《*a thing*》 in trust / 재산을 ~하다 leave *one's* property in trust / 유언으로 그는 자식들을 위해 재산을 ~하였다 By his will he created trusts for his children.
◉ ~계약 a trust agreement. ~관리인 a trust executor 〔administrator〕. ~대출 trust lending. ~료 a trust fee. ~물 a trust. ~부 《은행의》 a trust department. ~수익자 a beneficiary. ~업 trust business: ~업법 the Trust Business Law. ~업무 trust work. ~은행 a trust bank. ~자 a truster: 피~자 a trustee. ~재산 an estate in trust; a trust estate; fiduciary estates. ~증권 a trust instrument. ~증서 a trust deed 〔certificate〕; an indenture 《미》. ~투자 trust investment. ~해제 cancelation of trust. ~회사 a trust company. 개인~ a personal trust. 공익~ a charitable trust. 대출~ a loan trust. 명목 ~ a nominal trust. 수익~ a beneficial trust. 물품 ~부 a safety deposit department.

**신탁**(神託) a divine message 〔revelation〕; an oracle. ¶ 크리서스에게 「너는 대제국을 멸망시킬 것이다」라는 델포이의 ~이 있었다 The Delphic oracle told Croesus that he would destroy a great empire.

**신탁기금**(信託基金) a trust fund. ¶ ~을 설정하다 establish 〔create, set up〕 a trust fund.

**신탁예금**(信託預金) a trust deposit 〔fund〕. ¶ 백만 원을 ~하다 leave 1,000,000 won in trust 《with bank》.

**신탁통치**(信託統治) trusteeship. ¶ ~이사회 the Trusteeship Council / ~령(領) 〔지역〕 a trust territory / 유엔의 ~아래 두다 put 〔place〕 《an island》 under the UN trusteeship.

**신토불이**(身土不二) *shintoburi, one's* body and soil are inseparable each other; The domestic farm products are the best. ¶ ~운동 Buy Korean Farm= Products 「Campaign 〔Movement〕.

**신통**(神通) the supernatural; the occult; miraculous skill. ~하다 (be) wonderful; marvelous; remarkable; admirable; extraordinary. ¶ ~한 아이 a wonder 〔an extraordinary〕 child / 《약이》 ~하게 잘 듣다 be most efficacious; work wonders. ◉ ~력 an occult 〔a supernatural〕 power; a divine power.

**신트림** belching up a bit of sour vomit. ~하다 belch 〔eruct〕 an acid fluid.

**신파**(新派) ① 《유파》 a new school. ② =~극. ◉ ~극 a new-school play 〔drama〕. ~배우 an actor of the new school; a new-school (play) actor.

**신판**(新版) 《개정판》 a new edition 〔version〕; 《신간》 a new publication. ¶ ~의 newly-edited〔-published〕.

**신편**(新編) a new edition.

**신품**(新品) a new 〔brand-new〕 article. ¶ ~구입시 따라오는 부품 original equipment / ~이나 다름없다 look brand-new; be 〔look〕 as good as new; be virtually new.

**신풍**(新風) 《새로운 풍조》 a new phase.

**신하**(臣下) a subject; 《가신》 a retainer; a vassal. ¶ ~로서의 예를 취하다 pay homage to 《*a person*》.

**신학**(神學) theology; divinity. ◉ ~교 a divinity 〔theological〕 school; a seminary. ~박사 《칭호》 Doctor of Divinity (생략 D.D.); 《사람》 a doctor of divinity. ~생 a theological 〔divinity〕 student. ~자 a theologian: 해방 ~자 a liberation theologist.

**신학기**(新學期) a new (school) term; the new semester.

**신학문**(新學問) the new learning; modern sciences.

**신항원**(新抗原) 〖의학〗 a neoantigen.

**신해**(辛亥) 〖민속〗 the 48th binary term of the sexagenary cycle.

**신허**(腎虛) 〖한의〗 loss of virility; impotence.

**신형**(新型) a new style 〔fashion〕; the latest model 〔design〕; a novelty. ¶ 최~ 컴퓨터 a computer of the latest model / 모두 다 ~입니다 These are all in the latest style. ◉ ~자동차 a new= model car; a motorcar of the latest model: 그 공장은 ~자동차 생산용으로 설비를 변경했다 The factory is retooled for the new-model car.

**신호**(信號) a signal; 《교통 신호》 traffic light(s); lights; 《일·동작》 signaling. ~하다 signal 《*a person*》 to *do;* make 〔give〕 a signal.
¶ 위험〔주의〕~ a danger 〔caution〕 signal / 호출 ~ 《통신》 a call signal 〔sign〕 / ~를 무시하고 길을 건너는 사람 a jaywalker 《미》 / ~를 무시하고 길을

건너다 jaywalk《미》/ ～로 알리다〔를 보내다〕 signal; send (out) a signal / ～에 답하다 return a signal / ～에 주의하다 look「to 〔out for〕 a singal / ～를 기다리다 wait for the signal; 《교통 신호를》 wait for the traffic light(s) to change / ～를 올리다 put up 〔raise, hoist〕 a signal / ～로 구조를 청하다 signal for rescue 〔help〕 / ～를 못 보다 fail to notice a signal / ～를 지키다 observe a 《traffic》 signal / ～를 무시하다 ignore the red light; 《구어》 jump the lights (운전자가) / 잘못 ～하다 make a wrong signal / ～를 잘못 보다 mistake 〔misread〕 a signal / 발차 ～를 하다 give 〔show, indicate〕 a starting signal; 《손을 들어》 raise a hand as a signal for starting / ～에 따르시오 《게시》 Obey signal. / 선원들은 낮에는 수기로, 밤에는 등불로 ～한다 Sailors signal with flags by day and with lights at night. / 빨간 등은 흔히 위험 ～이다 A red light is usually a signal of danger. / ～가 녹색불로 바뀔 때까지 기다려야 한다 You must wait until the (red) light changes to green. / 녹색 ～로 바뀌면 가도 좋다 You may go when the light turns green.
◉ ～기(旗) a signal flag; 〚해양〛 a cornet; a code flag. ～기(機) a signal (apparatus); 《철도의》 a railroad signal; a semaphore: 자동 폐쇄 ～기 《열차의》 an automatic block signal. ～법 signal code. ～변환기〔처리기〕 〚컴퓨터〛 a signal converter 〔processor〕. ～소 a signal station; 《철도의》 a signal box. ～수 a signalman; a flagman 《미》; a buzzer 《군사속어》. ～수신기 〚통신〛 a signal receiver. ～전파 〚항공〛 beam: ～전파를 벗어나〔타고〕 off 〔on〕 the beam. ～탑 a signal tower. 무선～ a wireless signal. 음향～ an audible signal. 자동～ an automatic signal.

**신호등**(信號燈) a signal lamp 〔light〕; a blinker (점멸). ¶ 교통규칙을 위반하고 빨간 ～에 길을 건너다 cross the road on the red light against the traffic regulations / 빨간 ～이 켜졌다 《교차로에서》 The signal is against us. / 주의—전방(에) ～《게시》 Caution: signal light ahead.

**신혼**(新婚) a new marriage 〔wedding〕. ◉ ～부부 a newly-married couple; the newlyweds 《미구어》: 이 집은 ～부부에게는 안성맞춤이다 This house is ideal for「newlyweds 〔a newly-married couple〕. ～생활 newly-married life; newlywed life.

**신혼여행**(新婚旅行) a honeymoon. ¶ ～자 a honeymoon couple; honeymooners / ～을 하다 honeymoon 《in, at》 / ～을 떠나다 go (off) on a honeymoon / ～은 어디로 떠날 예정입니까 Where are you going on 〔for〕 your honeymoon? / ～은 하와이로 갈 생각입니다 We are planning to go Hawaii for our honeymoon.

**신화**(神化) 《신으로 화함》 deification. ～하다 deify; get deified; become a god.

**신화**(神話) a myth; a mythological story; mythology [총칭]. ¶ ～의 mythical; mythological; fabulous / ～적 영웅들 mythical heroes / ～와 전설로 유명하다 be famous in myth and legend / 한국의 ～에 의하면… according to Korean myth; Korean mythology has it that…. ◉ ～극 a mythological play. ～시대 the mythological 〔fabulous, legendary〕 age. ～학 mythology: ～학자 a mythologist. 건국～ the birth myth of nation.

**신화사**(新華社) the New China News Agency (생략 NCNA).

**신효**(神效) a remarkable efficaciousness 《of medicines》. ～하다 (be) wonderfully efficacious.

**신흥**(新興) newly rising 〔emerging〕. ～하다 newly rise. ¶ ～의 rising; new. ◉ ～계급 a newly-risen class 《of real estate owners》; a newly emerging 〔an up-and-coming〕 class. ～공업 경제 지역 Newly Industrializing Economies (생략 NIEs.). ～공업국 newly industrialized 〔industrializing〕 countries (생략 NICs). ～국 an emerging 〔a developing〕 nation 〔country〕. ～도시 a boom 〔new〕 town. ～부유 계급 the new rich class. ～산업 a new 〔burgeoning〕 industry. ～세력 the growing power; the new emerging forces. ～아프리카제국(諸國) the emergent countries of Africa. ～재벌 a newly-rising business tycoon. ～종교 a newly-risen〔-emerging〕 religion. ～주택지 a newly-developed residential area.

**싣다** ① 《적재하다》 load 《a truck with goods》; 《배에》 ship; put 〔place〕 《a cargo》 on board; [배가 주어] take 《a cargo》 on board. ¶ 트럭에 목재를 ～ load a truck with lumber; load lumber on a truck / 말에 짐을 ～ pack a load on a horse / 화물차에 석탄을 ～ load a freight car with coal / 선창에

화물을 ～ stow a cargo in the hold; stow the hold with cargo / 배는 원면(原綿)을 실었다 The ship took on a cargo of raw cotton. / 그 배는 인천행의 짐을 싣고 있다 The ship is loading for Inch'ŏn.
② 《기록·게재하다》 record; put in; carry 《an article》. ¶ 광고를 ～ insert 〔put〕 an advertisement 《in a newspaper》 / 기사를 ～ print news 《for》; carry news 《in a daily》 / 신문〔잡지〕에 소설을 ～ publish a novel in a newspaper 〔magazine〕.
③ 《논 따위에 물을》 store (water in a reservoir or paddy field).

**실**[1] ① 《바느질용》 thread; 《옷감 짜는》 yarn. ¶ 무명〔비단〕 실 (a piece of) cotton 〔silk〕 thread / 실처럼 가는 as thin as a thread / 실을 감다 quill; 《실패에》 spool; reel / 실을 꼬다 twist thread / 실을 잣다 spin thread 〔yarn〕 / 엉클어진 실을 풀다 unloose 〔unravel〕 tangled thread / 바늘에 실을 꿰다 thread a needle / 실을 뽑다 《수술 후에》 take out the stitches. ② [비유적] a thin fine thing; a long narrow thing. ¶ 실골목 a narrow alley 〔lane, path〕. ◉ 실뭉치 a ball of thread.

**실**(失) (a) loss. ⇨ 손실.

**실**(室) a room; a chamber; a compartment. ¶ 6호실 room (number) six / (호텔 등의) 704호실에 있습니다 I'm in room 704. (★ 숫자는 seven 0 four로 읽음).

**실**(實) truth; sincerity; (real) substance. ¶ 실은 really; in fact; as a matter of fact; The truth is that...; To tell the truth... / 실은 이렇다 I'll tell you what. *or* The truth is this.

**실**[2] a seal. ¶ 크리스마스 ～ a Christmas seal / ～을 붙이다 seal up; put a seal 《upon》.

**실가**(實價) ① 《진가》 intrinsic 〔true〕 value; sterling worth. ② 《실제의 값》 actual 〔real〕 price. ③ 《원가》 the cost (price). ¶ ～로 at the cost price / ～의 반액으로 at half its value.

**실각**(失脚) ① 《헛디딤》 a slip of the foot; losing *one's* footing. ～하다 slip; lose *one's* footing. ② 《몰락》 loss of *one's* position; a downfall. ～하다 lose *one's* position; fall from power; be ruined 〔overthrown〕. ¶ ～한 정치가 a knock-out politician / ～시키다 bring about 《*a person's*》 downfall / 그의 ～은 도박과 술 때문이었다 His downfall was caused by gambling and drink.

**실감**(實感) actual feeling; solid sense; *one's* sense of reality; 《체득》 realization. ～하다 feel actually; 《체득》 realize; 《경험》 experience. ¶ ～이 나다 appeal to *one's* sense of reality; be realistic; be true to nature; make 《*a person*》 feel as if it were real / ～나게 시를 낭독하다 read a poem aloud with feelings / 이 그림은 ～이 나지 않는다 This picture is not true to nature 〔life〕. / 나는 자유의 여신상을 보았을 때 미국에 있다는 것을 ～했다 I realized I was in America when I saw the Statue of Liberty. / 복권에서 300만원이 당첨됐는데 아직도 ～이 나지 않는다 I won three million won in a public lottery, but I still don't feel like it. ◉ ～온도 『의학』 effective temperature.

**실감개** a spool; a bobbin; a reel. ¶ ～에 실을 감다 wind thread on a spool; spool; reel.

**실개천** a streamlet; a brooklet; a thin ribbon of a stream.

**실격**(失格) disqualification; elimination. ～하다 be disqualified 《for a post, from *doing*, *etc.*》; be eliminated 《out of, from》; 《규칙에 따라》 be ruled out; 《국회 의원 등이》 be unseated 《for treating》. ¶ ～시키다 disqualify; scratch / 달리기에서 ～되다 be put out of the race / 선수는 반칙 다섯 번이면 ～된다 The players will be disqualified for five fouls. / 그는 교사로서는 ～이다 He is a failure as a teacher. ◉ ～경기자 a suspended player. ～자 a disqualified person; a nonqualifier (경기의).

**실경**(實景) the actual view 〔scene〕. ¶ 이 그림은 ～을 그린 것이다 This picture is drawn from nature.

**실고추** threaded 〔shredded〕 red pepper.

**실과**(實果) (a) fruit. ＝과실(果實).

**실과**(實科) a practical course.

**실국수** thin 〔thread-like〕 noodles.

**실권**(失權) loss of authority and power; loss of *one's* rights; disfranchisement. ～하다 lose *one's* rights 〔authority power〕; be disfranchised.

**실권**(實權) real power(s) 《of government, *etc.*》. ¶ ～이 없는 사장 a president in name only / ～을 장악하다 hold 〔take〕 the reins of 《government》; 《지배》 hold 〔seize〕 the (real) power 《over》 / 이 회사의 ～은 그에게 있다 He is the virtual manager of this company. / 한국의 주부들은 가정의 ～을 쥐고 있다 Korean wives wear the pants in their family. / 그가 정부의 ~을 잡고 있다 He holds the real power in the government. ◉ ~자 the person in authority.

**실금** a fine crack; a threadlike fissure. ¶ 찻잔에 ~이 갔다 The tea cup got a fine crack in it. 「urine》.

**실금**(失禁) 『의학』 incontinence 《of

**실긋거리다** shift from side to side; wobble; be unsteady; be unbalanced.

**실긋실긋** shifting from side to side; wobbling; unsteady; unbalanced.

**실긋하다** be out of shape [balance]; (be) distorted; pushed-out; unsteady; wobbly; unbalanced.

**실기**(失期) ~하다 fail to keep an appointed time.

**실기**(失機) ~하다 miss [lose, overlook] an opportunity; lose the chance; let a chance slip away.

**실기**(實技) 《이론에 대한 기술》 practical skill [talent]; 《실습》 practice; an exercise; a training. ¶ 체육 ~ physical training. ◉ ~시간[수업] a practical class [lesson]. ~시험 practical (talent) examination; driving test (운전의); skill test: 미술[성악] ~ 시험 「fine arts [vocal music] talent test.

**실꾸리** a ball [skein] of yarn [thread].

**실낱** a (single) thread; a strand; a ply. ¶ ~ 같은 목소리 a thin strand of a voice / ~ 같은 목숨 a life hanging by a thread / ~ 같은 희망 《there is》 a ray of hope.

**실내**(室內) the (interior of a) room. ¶ ~의 indoor / ~에서 indoors; in [inside, within] the room; within / ~에서 놀다 play in the room / ~에 들어박히다 stay [keep] indoors / ~를 장식하다 decorate [dress up] a room 《with pictures》; 《커튼·가구 등으로》 upholster a room / ~온도는 섭씨 25도이다 The temperature reads [stands at] 25 degrees centigrade indoors. ◉ ~게임 an indoor game [amusement (오락)]. ~(관현)악단 a chamber orchestra. ~노동 indoor labor. ~디자인 interior design. ~복 a housedress; a dressing gown [robe]. ~수영장[풀] an indoor swimming pool. ~안테나 an indoor antenna. ~운동 indoor exercise. ~(음)악 chamber music. ~전화 an interphone. ~조명 interior illumination. ~체육관 a gymnasium (*pl.* ~s, -sia); a gym. ~화 indoor [house] shoes; slippers.

**실내장식**(室內裝飾) interior [house] decoration; upholstery. ◉ ~가 an interior decorator; an upholsterer.

**실농**(失農) ~하다 miss the season for farming.

**실눈** narrow (slit) eyes. ¶ ~을 뜨다 narrow *one's* eyes / ~을 뜨고 보다 look through half-closed eyes; look at 《*a thing*》 with *one's* eyes slightly opened.

**실답다**(實—) (be) sincere; trustworthy; faithful. ¶ 실다운 청년 a trustworthy young man.

**실답지 않다**(實—) (be) untrustworthy; unreliable; insincere; untrue.

**실덕**(失德) loss of virtue. ~하다 meet dishonor; lose *one's* virtue [reputation].

**실떡거리다** prattle; chatter; say silly things. 「game.

**실뜨기** 《play》 cat's cradle; a string

**실랑이(질)** bothering 《*a person*》. ~하다 bother [pester] 《*a person*》.

**실력**(實力) ① 《능력》 real ability [power]; capability; merit; efficiency. ¶ ~이 있다 be capable; be talented; be able; be efficient / 영어 ~이 있다 [없다] be proficient [weak, poor] in English / ~있는 선생 a competent [an able] teacher / ~ 있는 사람 a man of ability [merit, real worth]; an able [a capable] man / ~에 따라 최선을 다하다 do *one's* best according to *one's* ability [merits] / ~을 기르다 cultivate *one's* ability; improve *oneself* 《in》; make *oneself* proficient 《in》; foster real ability / ~을 충분히 발휘하다 do *oneself* justice 《in》; give full play to *one's* ability / ~을 보이다 prove *oneself* really capable / ~으로 이기다 win on *one's* merits / 영어 ~이 붙다 become proficient in English / ~으로 출세하다 rise through ability; succeed by sheer talent / ~ 이상으로 해내다 surpass *oneself* / 결국은 ~이 이긴다 Real ability will win in the long run. / 나는 학위보다도 ~을 존중한다 I esteem [value] real ability more than academic titles [honors]. / 그는 사람들의 지도자가 될 만한 ~을 갖고 있다 He has it in him to be a leader of men. / 지금이야말로 너의 숨은 ~을 보여 줄 좋은 기회다 Now is a good chance for you to display your hidden ability.
② 《행동》 action; 《폭력》 force; arms. ¶ ~을 행사하다 take action; use force; appeal to arms; go on a strike (파업하다).

◉ ～자 a strong man《in the government》; a man of influence《in the political world》; an influential person; a big wheel〔shot〕. ～주의 the merit system. ～파 a competent group. ～행사 use of force;《파업》a strike: ～ 행사를 중지하다 call off a strike.

**실례**(失禮) discourtesy; impoliteness; rudeness; bad manners〔form〕; a lapse《in etiquette》; a breach of etiquette. ～하다 commit a discourtesy; be impolite; be rude《to *a person*》. ¶ ～되는 impolite; rude; discourteous; impudent / ～를 무릅쓰고 …하다 take the liberty〔freedom〕of *do*ing〔to *do*〕/ ～의 말을 하다 say rude things; make rude remarks / ～(이)지만 Excuse〔Pardon〕me, but…;《부탁할 때》May I ask…?; I'm sorry to trouble you but… / ～지만 몇 시입니까 Excuse me, can you tell me the time? / ～지만 무슨 일로 오셨습니까 May I ask what your business is? / 식사중에 담배를 피우는 것은 ～다 It is against etiquette〔bad manners〕to smoke at table. / ～지만 혹시 한 선생님이 아니십니까 Excuse me, but aren't you Mr. Han? / ～합니다 (1) Sorry! *or* I am Sorry! (2)《남의 옆을 통과할 때》Excuse me. (3)《남의 집에 찾아가서》May I come in? (4)《자리를 뜰 때》Excuse me (for) a minute. / 먼저 ～합니다 Please excuse me my leaving earlier. / 이만 ～ 하겠습니다 (Well,) I must be going now. *or* (I am afraid) I must say good=by(e). / ～했습니다 (1) I am sorry to have bothered you. *or* I beg your pardon. *or* Pardon me. (2)《작별할 때》Thank you, good-bye. / ～합니다 저는 이런 사람입니다《명함을 줄 때》Allow me to give you my card. / 지난번에 오셨을 때에는 출타 중이어서 ～했습니다 I am sorry I was out when I have missed your call the other day. / ～지만 이것 좀 김선생님께 건네주십시오 I am sorry to trouble you, but please hand this to Mr. Kim.

**실례**(實例) an (actual) example; an instance; a concrete case;《적례》a case in point;《예증》an illustration;《선례》a precedent. ¶ 아직까지 ～가 없는 unprecedented; unexampled / ～를 들면 for example; for instance / ～를 들다 give〔cite〕an example〔instance〕/ ～를 들어 설명하다 illustrate《*something*》by an example; exemplify / 이것은 많은 것 중의 한 ～에 지나지 않는다 This is only one instance out of many. / 그 낱말의 용법에 관한 ～를 2, 3개 드시오 Give two or three illustrations of the use of the word. / 부자라고 해서 반드시 행복한 것은 아니라는 것을 보이는 ～는 세상에 드물지 않다 There are any number of instances which show that the rich are not always happy.

**실로**(實—) in truth; truly; really; indeed;《실지로》in fact;《대단히》very much;《확실히》surely. ¶ 그는 ～ 비범한 사람이다 He is indeed a remarkable man. / ～ 30년만의 재회였다 We had this reunion for the first time, indeed, in thirty years. / 나는 ～ 어리석은 짓을 했다 I did something very foolish.

**실로폰**〖악기〗a xylophone. ◉ ～연주자 a xylophonist.

**실록**(實錄) an authentic〔a true, a faithful〕record〔history, story, account〕; chronicles.

**실루엣** a silhouette. ¶ ～의 옆모습 a profile in silhouette.

**실룩거리다** twitch (and twitch); jerk; quiver. ¶ 입이 ～ *one's* mouth twitches〔quivers〕/ 눈을 ～ twitch *one's* eye; wink / 그녀의 얼굴은 고통으로 실룩거렸다 Her face twitched with pain.

**실룩실룩** with repeated twitching〔winking, quivering〕.

**실리**(失利) (financial) loss. ～하다 suffer (financial) loss.

**실리**(實利) utility; (an actual) profit; material gain〔interests〕; benefit. ¶ ～적인 practical; utilitarian / ～가 있다 be useful; be profitable. ◉ ～주의 utilitarianism;《영리주의》commercialism: ～주의자 a utilitarian; a materialist.

**실리다** ①《기재되다》be recorded; be carried; get into《a newspaper》; be given; appear《in a magazine》. ¶ 논설이 신문에 ～ an article is carried in a newspaper / 그 말은 사전에 실려 있지 않다 That word is not given in the dictionary. ②《싣게 하다》get《*something*》loaded; load. ¶ 화물을 트럭에 ～ have *one's* goods loaded on a truck; load *one's* goods on a truck.

**실리카**《규토》silica.

**실리콘**〖화학〗silicone. ⇨ 규소.

**실리콘밸리**《미국 Santa Clara의 속칭》Silicon Valley.

**실린더**〖기계〗a cylinder.

**실링**《영국의 옛 화폐》 a shilling (생략 s.). ¶ 3～ 6펜스 three (shillings) and six (pence) (생략 3s. 6d.).

**실마리** a beginning; a start; the first step; the impetus; a clue《to》. ¶ …의 ～를 찾다〔놓치다〕 find〔lose〕 a〔the〕 clue to… / ～가 되다 lead to《success》; be a clue to《discover》/ 문제 해결의 ～를 잡다 get a clue to (the solution of) a problem / 아직 문제 해결의 ～를 못찾고 있다 No clue has yet been found which might lead to a solution of the problem. / 이것이 그의 출세의 ～가 되었다 This was the first step of his success in the world. / 지문이 범인 체포의 ～가 되었다 The fingerprints gave a clue that led to the arrest of the culprit.

**실망**(失望) disappointment; discouragement;《절망》 despair. ～하다 get〔be〕 disappointed《at, in, of, with》; be disheartened; despair《of》; lose heart. ¶ ～하여 disappointedly; in despair / ～시키다 disappoint《*a person*》〔《*a person's*》 hopes〕; let《*a person*》 down; dash《*a person's*》 hope / ～한 나머지 …하다 despair drives《*a person*》 to *do* / 그 결과에〔그 사람에게, 그것을 듣고〕 ～하다 be disappointed at the result〔in *a person,* to hear it〕/ ～의 빛을 나타내다 look disappointed / 그 사람은 너를 ～시키지 않을 게다 He will never let you down. / ～하기에는 아직 이르다 It's too early to give up all hopes. / 그는 ～한 나머지 자살했다 Despair drove him to commit suicide. / 내게는 그것이 큰～이었다 It was a bitter disappointment to me. / 데이트의 상대가 오지 않아 그는 ～하고 돌아왔다 He returned home in disappointment because his date didn't turn up.

**실명**(失名) name unknown; anonymity. ～하다 be unknown (as to name). ◉ ～씨《무명씨》 an unknown〔an anonymous, a nameless〕 person.

**실명**(失明) loss of eyesight. ～하다 lose *one's* eyesight; go blind; become sightless. ¶ 두 눈다 ～하다 lose the sight of both eyes. ◉ ～자 a sightless〔blind〕 person; the blind [총칭].

**실명**(實名) *one's* real name. ¶ ～제 = 금융거래 실명제. ◉ ～거래 real-name financial transaction. ～계좌 real-name accounts.

**실무**(實務) (practical) business〔affairs〕; actual affairs; business practice. ¶ ～적 businesslike; practical / ～급 관리 a working-level official / ～에 재능이 있는 사람 a person of business talent〔ability〕/ ～를 배우다〔익히다〕 receive a training〔train *oneself*〕 in practical business; study〔get a training in〕 the practice of business / ～에 경험이 있다 be experienced in business; have business experiences / ～에 숙달하다 become experienced〔versed〕 in business / ～에 어둡다 be not familiar with office routine; be out of touch with the world / ～에 종사하다 engage in〔go into〕 business. ◉ ～가 a man of business〔affairs〕. ～경험 hands-on-background. ～(담당)자 a clerk〔a person, an official〕 in charge《of》. ～연수 in-service training. ～자(급) 접촉 the working-level contact. ～자(급) 회담 a working-level talk〔meeting, conference〕. ～작업단 a working-level task forces.

**실물**(實物) the real thing; the (actual) object;《진짜》 a genuine article〔thing〕;《그림에 대해서》 life;《사진에 대해서》 the original. ¶ ～같이 보이다 look like a real one; be lifelike / ～보다 사진이 더 낫다 look better in a photo〔the picture〕/ ～을 그리다 draw〔paint〕 from〔after〕 (the) life / ～을 보고 실망했다 I was disappointed when I saw it with my own eyes. / ～을 보기 전에는 확실한 것을 말할 수 없다 I cannot tell for certain unless I see it with my own eyes. / 이 사진은 ～만 못하다 This photo does not do her justice. / 이 조화는 ～처럼 보인다 This artificial flower looks just like a real〔natural〕 one. ◉ ～거래 (a) spot〔cash〕 transaction. ～경제 object economy. ～광고 an object advertisement. ～교수 an object lesson; object teaching. ～묘사 model drawing. ～크기《painting》 actual size; the size of the original: ～크기의 as large as life; full-size(d); life-size(d) / ～ 크기 모형 a full-size model; a mock-up / ～크기로 확대한 사진 a life-size enlargement of a photograph.

**실물대**(實物大) actual size. = 실물 크기.

**실바람** a slight air; a light breeze.

**실밥** ①《뜯은 보무라지》 bits of thread. ¶ 치마에 ～이 묻다 have a (bit of) thread on *one's* skirt. ②《솔기》 the spacing of stitches; a stitch; a seam.

¶ ～을 뽑다 undo a seam; cut a seam open / ～이 풀리다 a seam starts.

**실뱀** a small thin snake.

**실뱀장어**(一長魚) a small eel; an elver.

**실버** silver. ⇨ 은(銀). ◉ ～산업 the industry [business] aimed for the aged. ～스크린 《영화계》 the silver screen. ～웨딩 《은혼식》 a silver wedding (결혼 25주년). ～타운 a town for the aged.

**실버들** a slender weeping willow.

**실보무라지** a bit of thread; waste thread.

**실비**(實費) 《실제로 쓴》 actual expenses; 《원가》 (real) cost price; prime cost. ¶ ～ 500원 cost five hundred won / ～만 받는 진료소 a clinic operated at cost / ～로 팔다[제공하다] sell [offer] 《*a thing*》 at cost / 5천원에 파니까 ～는 3천원쯤 될 겁니다 It sells for 5,000 won, so its cost (price) will be about 3,000 won. ◉ ～제공 a cost sale. 생산～ the cost of production.

**실사**(實査) an on-the-spot survey; an actual inspection; a working survey; an (actual) investigation. ～하다 survey; investigate; inspect actually; make a survey of; conduct an actual investigation 《into》.

**실사**(實寫) a photograph taken from life [on the spot]. ～하다 take a photograph on the spot; film an event on the spot.

**실사회**(實社會) the real [actual] world; the everyday [workaday, sober] world; realities of life. ¶ ～에 나가다 launch forth into the world; go (out) into the world; (get a) start in life [the world].

**실상**(實狀) the actual circumstances; the real state of things; a real condition [situation]; [부사적] truly; verily; in reality; in fact. ¶ ～을 말하면 to tell the truth; the fact is; in fact / 나는 ～을 조사하여 보겠다 I'll find out how things stand.

**실상**(實相) the (real) facts 《of a case》; reality; actual circumstances; the real aspects [state, condition] 《of affairs》. ¶ 사회의 ～ a true picture of life / ～은 이러하다 The fact is this.

**실상**(實像) 『물리』 a real image.

**실색**(失色) changing color [countenance]. ～하다 change [lose] color; change countenance; turn [go] pale. ¶ 그는 그 소식을 듣자 ～했다 Color left his face when he heard the news.

**실생활**(實生活) real [actual] life; practical life; (the realities of) life. ¶ ～에서 취재한 이야기 a tale taken from real life / ～에 소용이 안 되다 be useless in life / 지식을 ～에 살리다[이용하다] apply *one's* knowledge in *one's* real life / 학교에서 배우는 대부분의 것은 그다지 ～에 도움이 되지 않는다 The greater part of school learning is not of much use in actual life.

**실선**(實線) a solid line.

**실성**(失性) mental derangement; distraction; insanity; madness. ～하다 become insane; go mad; lose *one's* mind [wit, reason]; be out of *one's* mind [head]. ¶ ～한 mad; insane; crazy / ～한 사람 a mad [an insane] person / ～한 사람처럼 frantically; madly / 그런 짓을 하다니 ～했나 보다 He must be mad to do such a thing. / 슬픈 나머지 그녀는 ～했다 Grief drove her mad. *or* Grief has turned her brain.

**실세**(失勢) loss of power [influence]. ～하다 lose power [influence].

**실세**(實勢) actual influence [power]; 《실력자》 a powerful [dominant] figure; a 《political》 strong man.

**실소**(失笑) sudden uncontrollable laughter. ～하다 laugh 《at》; burst into laughter. ¶ ～를 금치 못하다 cannot help laughing 《at *a person, etc.*》.

**실속**(實一) substantiality; substance; content; real worth; solidity. ¶ ～있는 substantial; solid / ～있는 장사 a solid business / ～없는 연설 an empty speech / 겉보다 ～을 택하다 prefer substance to appearance; choose real achievement rather than empty reputation.

**실속**(失速) 《항공기의》 a stall. ～하다 stall; be stalled; go into a stall. ¶ 공중제비를 할 때 제트기는 돌연 ～하여 추락했다 When it had looped the loop, the jet plane suddenly stalled and crashed into the ground.

**실수**(失手) a mistake; 《과실》 a blunder; 《사소한》 a slip. ～하다 make a mistake [slip]; commit a blunder; botch; goof 《속어》. ¶ 말을 ～하다 make a slip of the tongue / 일을 ～하다 botch a job / 그가 하는 일엔 ～가 없다 He does everything perfectly. / 그건 내 ～다 It is an oversight on my part. *or* I am to blame for it. / 그런 사람의 말을 들은 것이 나의 ～였다 It was my mistake to have listened to such a man.

**실수**(實收) real〔actual, net〕income; actual receipts;《실수 급료》take-home pay〔wages〕《미》;《수확》actual yield. ¶ 2만원의 ～를 얻다 realize 20,000 won《from》/ 금년 ～는 예상보다 많다 The actual receipts for this year are greater than I expected. (★ receipts는 보통 복수 취급함) / 이 일은 세금을 공제하고 월(月) ～ 70만원이 된다 This job will bring〔fetch〕you 700,000 won net a month after tax.

**실수**(實數) ①〖수학〗a real number〔quantity〕;《피승수》a multiplicand. ②《실제의 수》an actual number.

**실수요**(實需要) actual demand; consumptive demand. ◉ ～자 an end user.

**실수익**(實收益) actual gain.

**실습**(實習) practice《in》; (a practical) exercise; (practical) training; (a) drill. ～하다 practice《nursing》; have (practical) training in; intern in. ◉ ～교(校)《사범 학생의》a school where a student teacher practices teaching. ～생 a student apprentice; an apprentice; a trainee;《병원의》an intern. ～시간 practice hours.

**실시**(實施) practical application; enforcement; execution. ～하다 enforce; put〔carry〕《a law》into effect; give effect to; put in〔into〕force; put〔bring〕《a system》in〔into〕operation〔practice〕. ¶ ～되다 be enforced; come into force〔operation〕; take effect / ～되어 있다 be in force〔effect〕/ 신체 검사는 내일 ～된다 Physical examination will be held tomorrow. / 그것은 계획대로 ～될 것이다 It will be carried out as planned. ◉ ～안(案) a working plan.

**실신**(失神)《기절》a swoon; a faint; fainting;《정신나감》trance; abstraction. ～하다 faint〔swoon〕(away); fall into a faint〔swoon〕; fall unconscious;《정신나가다》be in trance. ¶ ～한 사람처럼 like a man in a trance / ～상태에 있다 be in a swoon〔faint〕; be in a trance / 그녀는 ～한 것 같다 She looks faint. / 그는 ～할 만큼 놀랐다 He was frightened out of his wits.

**실실** with a silly snicker. ¶ ～ 웃다 snicker; giggle.

**실안개** a thin mist.

**실액**(實額) actual amount of money.

**실어증**(失語症) loss of speech;〖의학〗aphasia. ◉ ～환자 an aphasiac.

**실언**(失言) a slip〔lapse〕of the tongue; an improper remark; misstatement;《불온한 언사》improper〔indiscreet〕language. ～하다 make a slip of the tongue; use improper language〔words〕; commit an impropriety in speech; make an improper remark; put *one's* foot in it〔in *one's* mouth《구어》〕. ¶ ～을 사과하다 apologize for *one's* slip of the tongue / ～을 취소하다 retract〔take back, withdraw〕「*one's* words〔what *one* said〕/ …이라고 말한 것은 그의 ～이었다 He made a mistake in saying that….

**실업**(失業) unemployment; joblessness. ～하다 lose *one's* work〔job, employment, place〕; be (thrown) out of work〔employment, job〕; become unemployed〔jobless〕. ¶ 그는 현재 ～중이다 He is「unemployed〔out of work〕now. ◉ ～대책 an unemployment policy; a measure against unemployment; a relief measure for the unemployed: ～대책 사업 relief program〔work〕for the unemployed / ～대책의 하나로 실시되는 도로 보수 계획 a make-work road repair program. ～률 the unemployment rate. ～문제 the unemployment problem. ～보험 unemployment insurance. ～수당 an unemployment allowance〔benefit〕: ～ 수당을 타다〔타고 있다〕get〔be getting〕unemployment benefit; go〔be〕on the dole《영구어》. ～조사 an investigation of the unemployment situation;《실업자 조사》an unemployment census. 계절적 ～ seasonal unemployment. 구조적 ～ structural unemployment. 만성적 ～ chronic unemployment. 잠재～ latent unemployment; potential〔disguised〕unemployment.

**실업**(實業)《산업》industry;《상업》business. ¶ ～의《산업의》industrial;《상업의》business; commercial / ～에 종사하다 be (engaged) in business; go into〔take to〕business. ◉ ～가 a man of business; a businessman;《산업가》an industrialist. ～계 the business〔industrial〕world〔circles〕: ～계에 발을 들여놓다 enter the business world; go into business. ～(고등)학교 a vocational〔technical, business〕(high) school. ～교육 vocational training〔education〕. ～단체 a business corporation. ～팀 a business《baseball》team.

**실업자**(失業者) a person out of work

〔employment〕; an unemployed person; [총칭] the unemployed; the jobless. ¶ ～를 구제하다 relieve the unemployed / ～가 많다 Many people are out of work. / ～가 늘고 있다 Unemployment is on the increase. / 거리에는 ～가 우글거린다 Unemployed workers fill the streets. *or* Workers are out of work all over the town.

**실없다** (be) untrustworthy; insincere; unreliable; idle; vain; silly. ¶ 실없는 사람 an untrustworthy person; a silly person / 실없는 말 idle talk / 실없는 소리 마라 Don't talk rubbish 〔rot〕! *or* Stop 〔None of〕 your nonsense 〔jokes〕!

**실없이** frivolously; nonsensically; rubbishly; uselessly; flippantly. ¶ ～ 말하다 make idle 〔flippant〕 remarks.

**실연**(失戀) the loss of *one's* sweetheart 〔lover, beloved〕; 《짝사랑》 unrequited love; disappointed 〔unreturned〕 love; a broken heart. ～하다 be crossed 〔disappointed〕 in love 《for *a person*》; be lovelorn; have *one's* heart broken; lose 《*a person's*》 love. ¶ ～한 lovelorn; broken-hearted / 그는 젊어서 ～했다 He was disappointed in love as a young man. / 그녀는 ～해서 투신 자살했다 She drowned herself out of disappointment in love.

**실연**(實演) 《무대에서의》 (a) stage performance; actual performance; a stage 〔live〕 show; 《실험·수업 따위의》 a (public) demonstration 〔presentation〕. ～하다 act 〔perform, present〕 on the stage; give a (public) demonstration 《of》.

**실오리** a piece of thread 〔string〕. ¶ ～ 같은 희망 a shadowy hope / (몸에) ～ 하나 걸치지 않고 stark-naked; with nothing on; in *one's* bare skin.

**실온**(室溫) 《at》 room temperature.

**실외**(室外) ¶ ～의 outdoor / ～에(서) outside the room; outside; outdoor(s); without doors; out of doors / ～에 내놓다 put 《*a thing*》 out of the room.

**실용**(實用) practical use; utility. ～하다 put to practical use. ¶ ～과 장식을 겸하다 answer the purpose of both utility and decoration; be both useful 〔practical〕 and decorative / ～화하다 make 《a process》 practicable; make 《*a thing*》 fit for practical use. ◉ ～가구 utility furniture. ～단위 『물리』 a practical unit. ～성 practicality; utility: ～성이 있는 useful; of practical use / ～성이 없는 of no practical use / ～성이 없다 have no practical use. ～신안 a utility model: ～ 신안 특허를 신청하다 apply for a utility model patent. ～영어〔수학〕 practical English 〔mathematics〕. ～주의 『철학』 pragmatism: ～주의자 a pragmatist. ～품 a utility article; a useful article; utility goods; 《필수품》 (daily) necessaries; 《바늘·실·핀 따위》 notions.

**실용적**(實用的) (intended) for practical 〔actual〕 use; practical. ¶ ～이다 be of practical use / 정말 ～이다 It is of great utility. / 그것은 ～이지 않다 It is of no practical use.

**실은**(實—) really; in truth; in fact; as a matter of fact; in reality; the truth is (that...); to tell the truth; to be frank with you. ¶ ～ 이렇다 I'll tell you what. *or* The truth is this. / ～ 전혀 반대다 In point of fact, the reverse is the case. / ～ 나도 잘 모른다 I must confess I am hardly better informed. / ～ 그 이야기는 거짓말이었다 The truth is (that) the story was a lie. (★ 《구어》에서 that은 흔히 생략됨) / ～ 나는 그 책을 아직 읽지 않았네 As a matter of fact, I haven't read the book yet.

**실의**(失意) 《실망》 disappointment; despair; a broken heart. ～하다 be disappointed; be disheartened; be thrown into despair; despair. ¶ ～의 시절 *one's* dark days; *one's* period of adversity / ～에 잠긴〔빠진〕 사람 a disappointed man / ～의 구렁텅이에 빠져 있다 be in the depths of despair / 그는 ～에 잠겨 죽었다 He died a broken-hearted man.

**실익**(實益) 《실수익》 an actual 〔a net〕 profit; 《실리》 practical use; benefit; material gain; utility; 《유용》 real service. ¶ ～이 있다 be useful; be (actually) profitable; have a net gain of 《50,000 won》 / 취미와 ～을 겸하고 있다 It combines profit with a hobby. / 그런 것이 과연 ～이 있을지 의심스럽다 I doubt if such a thing would be of any practical use.

**실장**(室長) 《연구실의》 the head of a laboratory 〔an office〕; 《부·국 등의》 a section chief; 《기숙사 따위의》 a senior roommate.

**실재**(實在) real existence; actual being 〔existence〕; reality. ～하다 (really) exist; be in (actual) existence. ¶ ～하는〔의〕 actual; existent; real / ～하지 않는 unreal; nonexistent; imaginary /

유형적 ～ corporeal entities / 절대적〔물질적, 영적, 잠재적〕 ～ absolute 〔material, spiritual, potential〕 being / ～적 관념론 real idealism / 그가 ～ 인물이었음에는 의심의 여지가 없다 There is no doubt that he was a real person. / 나는 신의 ～를 믿는다 I believe in the existence of God.
◉ ～론 realism; externalism: 관념적 ～론 ideal realism / ～론자 a realist.

**실적**(實績) (actual) results; past records; *one's* record (of performance); solid results; achievements. ¶ ～을 올리다 give actual 〔satisfactory〕 results; bear fruit; bring about good results / 이 일은 아직 ～이 없다 The work has not yet borne fruit. / 아무런 ～도 못 올렸다 Nothing has come out of it. / ～이 오르지 않아 그들은 애를 먹었다 Since the work did not bear fruit, they had a hard time. / 우리 회사에서 입사 1년의 영업사원으로 이만큼의 ～을 올린 자는 없다 No one ever produced such excellent results as a salesman as he did in his first year with our company. ◉ ～제 the merit system 《미》.

**실전**(實戰) actual fighting 〔warfare〕; real warfare; a battle; active service. ¶ 많은 ～ 경험을 쌓은 노병 a veteran of considerable combat experience / ～과 같은 맹연습 a vigorous maneuver just like actual fighting / ～에 임하다 〔참가하다〕 be in action 〔actual combat〕; take part in actual fighting; be in the field; see battle.

**실점**(失點) points 〔runs〕 *one* allows *one's* opponent in a game. ～하다 lose a point; allow the 〔*one's*〕 opponent to gain a point. ¶ 우리 팀은 그 시합에서 ～을 되풀이했다 Our team allowed the opponent to gain successive points.

**실정**(失政) misgovernment; maladministration; misrule. ¶ 오랜 ～에 시달리다 suffer years of misrule 《under a weak president》.

**실정**(實情) the actual circumstances; the real state of affairs; the real condition(s); the facts of the case; the real situation; the true state 〔facts〕; the realities. ¶ ～은 as things 〔matters〕 stand; the fact is 《that...》.
실정에: ～에 밝다 be in the swim / ～에 어둡다 be out of touch with things as they are; be not well up in the actual situation 《of》.
실정을: ～을 알다 know the actual circumstances; know how the matter (really) stands / ～을 이야기하다 tell 《*a person*》 how things stand 《in the North Korea》 / ～을 조사하다 investigate the actual circumstances / ～을 털어놓다 confide the real state of things 《to *a person*》; take 《*a person*》 into *one's* confidence / ～을 호소하다 tell 《*a person*》 the true story / ～을 그대로 진술하다 state just how things stand; represent things as they are.
¶ ～은 이렇다 The fact is that.... / ～을 알아보겠다 I will find out how things stand. / 그는 중국 ～에 훤하다 He is familiar with the actual 〔real〕 state of affairs in China. / 그것이 대략의 ～이다 That's about the size of it.

**실정법**(實定法) 〖법〗 the positive law.

**실정조사**(實情調査) fact-finding. ◉ ～기관 a fact-finding agency. ～단 a fact-finding party. ～위원 a fact-finder: ～위원회 a fact-finding committee.

**실제**(實際) 《사실》 the (exact) truth; a fact; 《실정》 an actual state; the actual condition of things; 《실지》 practice; 《현실》 reality; actuality. ¶ ～의〔적인〕 practical; actual; real; 《구체적》 concrete; down-to-earth / ～가치 real 〔actual〕 value / ～(적인) 의견 a practical view / 이론과 ～ theory and practice / ～적으로 in a practical manner / ～로 있었던 일 an actual occurrence / ～로 practically; in reality; in effect; in practice; virtually; 《정말로》 in fact; as a matter of fact; actually; to tell the truth; as it is (★ to tell the truth는 항상 이 형태로 쓰이는 부정사(不定詞)의 독립 용법. as it is는 글 첫머리에 오면 가상했던 것과 다르다는 뜻으로, in reality는 「실정은」의 의미, 글 가운데 오면 「현상태로는」의 뜻, 글 끝에 오면 「있는 그대로」의 뜻임) / ～로 그렇게 생각한다 I do think so. / ～로 그렇다 It's a fact. / 상상과 ～는 딴판이었다 I found the reality quite different from what I had imagined. / ～로 일어난 대로 이야기해 주시오 Tell me exactly as it happened. / 그를 위대하다고들 하는데 ～로 그렇더라 He is said to be great as indeed he is. / 이 두 가지는 ～ 동일한 것이다 The two are practically 〔virtually〕 the same. / ～로 나는 그것을 보았다 I saw it with my own eyes. *or* I actually saw it. (★ actually에는 「믿을 수 없겠지만, 실제로」란 뜻이 있음) / 모든 일은

～로 당해 봐야 안다 We cannot learn anything without having practical experience of it. / 이 그림은 ～를 그린 것이다 This picture is drawn from life. / 사진에서는 ～보다 크게 보인다 It looks larger than life in the picture. ◉ ～가 a practical man. ～교육 practical instruction. ～문제 a practical question.

**실조**(失調) (a) malfunction; 〖의학〗 asynergia; ataxia. ◉ 영양～ malnutrition; undernourishment; unbalanced nutrition.

**실족**(失足) 《잘못 디딤》 a false step; a misstep; 《행동을 잘못함》 a misdeed; an evil deed. ～하다 《발을》 slip; miss *one's* foot 〔step〕; lose *one's* footing; make 〔take〕 a false step; misbehave; do (*something*) wrong. ¶ 계단에서 ～하다 miss *one's* footing on the stairs / ～하여 추락사하다 lose *one's* footing and fall to death.

**실존**(實存) existence. ～하다 exist. ◉ ～주의 existentialism: ～주의자 an existentialist. ～철학 existential philosophy.

**실종**(失踪) disappearance; absconding (특히 범죄 용의자의); missing; 《군인의》 missing in action (생략 MIA). ～하다 disappear; abscond; drop from sight; 《행방 불명》 be missing. ¶ A씨 ～ 사건 the disappearance of Mr. A / 약 2만명의 한국 군인들이 한국전쟁 중에 ～되었다 About 20,000 South Korean soldiers were missing in action following the Korean War. ◉ ～신고〔선고〕 a report 〔the adjudication〕 of 《*a person's*》 disappearance. ～자 a missing person; an absconder.

**실주**(實株) a real stock; a spot share.

**실증**(實證) an actual 〔empirical〕 proof; corroborative evidence; verification. ～하다 show by means of evidence 《that...》 prove 《*a person's* guilt, that *a person* is guilty》; establish 《a fact》 (by proof); verify; corroborate 《a statement》; demonstrate; substantiate. ¶ ～적(으로) positive(ly); empirical(ly) / ～을 잡고 있다 hold the actual proof 《of》 / ～을 들다 give an actual proof 《of *a thing*》 / ～에 의해 확신을 얻다 corroborate *one's* belief / 사건의 보고서는 목격자에 의해 ～되었다 The report of the accident was verified by eye-witnesses. / 그의 머리가 좋다는 것이 ～되었다 It has been proved that he is bright.

◉ ～론〔주의〕 positivism: ～주의자 a positivist / 논리적 ～주의 logical positivism. ～철학 positive philosophy.

**실지**(失地) a lost territory. ¶ ～를 회복하다 recover the lost territory. ◉ ～회복 the recovery of the lost territory.

**실지**(實地) practice; actuality; reality. ¶ ～의 practical; real; actual / ～로 practically; for practical purposes; in practice; personally / ～로 경험하다 have practical experience 《in》 / ～로 응용하다 apply to practice / ～로 행하다 carry 〔put〕 《a theory》 into practice; carry out / ～는 이론처럼 쉽지 않다 It isn't so 〔as〕 easy in practice as in theory. / 나는 ～ 경험을 이야기하고 있는 것이다 I speak from (my own) experience. / 이 도구는 ～로 쓸모가 있었다 This tool turned out to be useful in practice.

◉ ～검증 an inspection on the scene; ⇨ 현장 검증. ～경험 practical experience: 그는 아직 교사로서의 ～ 경험이 없다 He has no personal experience in teaching as yet. ～관찰 actual observation. ～답사 an actual survey. ～시험 a practical 〔field〕 test. ～연습 practical exercises; practice; a trial practice. ～응용 a practical application. ～조사 an actual 〔on-the-spot, on-site〕 survey. ～지도 practical guidance. ～체험 actual experience. ～훈련 on-the-job 〔practical〕 training.

**실직**(失職) unemployment. ⇨ 실업. ～하다 lose *one's* employment 〔job, position〕; be thrown out of work 〔employment〕; become workless 〔jobless〕; 《공무원이》 be out of office; 《실직중이다》 be out of work.

◉ ～자 an unemployed person; a jobless 〔displaced〕 person; an unemployed; [총칭] the unemployed; the jobless.

**실질**(實質) 《재료》 (a) material; 《본질》 substance; essence (중요한 부분); 《소질》 quality. ¶ ～적(으로) substantial(ly); essential(ly); material(ly); virtual(ly) / ～적인 원조 substantial aid / ～적인 진보 substantial progress / ～적이 아닌 unsubstantial; empty / 외견뿐 아니라 ～에 있어서 in essence as well as in outward form / ～적인 합의 substantial agreement / ～적인 경제 유대 substantial economic ties / ～은 형식보다 중요하다 Substance is more important than form. / 양자간에는 ～적으로 차이가 없다

There is no practical difference between the two. / 매출은 증대했으나 ~적으로는 아직 적자다 The sales have improved, but we are still virtually in the red. / 겉보기보다 ~을 택하라 Prefer substance to appearance [shadow]. ◉ ~ 경제성장 real economic growth. ~구매력 real purchasing power. ~국민소득 the real national income. ~소득[임금] real income [wages]: 공무원의 ~ 소득을 올릴 방안을 연구하다 study measures to raise government officials' real income.

**실쭉거리다** distort; move at a bad angle [in a misshapen way]; sulk.

**실쭉하다** ① = 씰그러지다. ② 《불만으로》 be displeased; be dissatisfied; be discontented; look glum [sullen]. ¶ 실쭉해서 입술을 내밀다 push *one's* lips out in discontent.

**실책**(失策) a faulty policy; a blunder; a slip; a bungle; a stumble; an error; a mistake; 〚야구〛 a misplay. ¶ 큰 ~ a gross mistake; a serious blunder / ~을 저지르다 do 《*a matter*》 amiss; make a mistake [slip] 《in *doing*》; commit an error [a blunder]; bungle; fall into an error / 1루수의 ~으로 세이프가 되다 be safe on an error by the first baseman / 그런 사람을 신용한 것이 내 ~이었다 I made a mistake in trusting such a man.

**실천**(實踐) practice. ~하다 practice; put 《a theory》 into practice. ¶ ~적(으로) practical(ly) / 남에게 권하는 것을 자기 스스로도 ~하여라 Practice what you preach. / 말[이론]보다는 ~ An ounce of practice is worth a pound of theory. / 그는 자신의 주장을 ~으로 옮겼다 He practiced what he had advocated.
◉ ~계획 an action plan. ~도덕[이성, 철학] practical morality [reason, philosophy]. ~윤리(학) practical ethics. ~주의 activism.

**실천력**(實踐力) power of execution; executive faculty [ability]; action. ¶ ~이 있는 사람 a person [man] of action / 그는 계획은 잔뜩 있으나 ~이 없다 He has a full of schemes, but lacks the power of execution.

**실체**(實體) substance; subject; an entity; 《본성》 the true nature 《of》. ¶ ~의 substantial; noumenal; essential / ~가 있는 substantial; solid / ~가 없는 unsubstantial; incorporeal; impalpable 《forms and figures》 / ~화하다 make 《*something*》 substantial; give substance 《to *something*》; substantiate / 사물의 ~를 파악하다 grasp the facts of a case; get at the heart of things / ~를 잘 모르다 do not know what 《it》 really is; the actualities are yet to be ascertained [are still unknown].
◉ ~경(鏡) a stereoscope. ~관측 〚토목〛 stereoscopic measurement. ~론 ontology; substantialism. ~법 a substantial law. ~사진 a stereoscopic photograph: ~사진 측량 stereophotogrammetry. ~상(像) 〚토목〛 a stereoscopic model. ~설 the substantiality theory; substantialism. ~성 substantiality.

**실추**(失墜) loss. ~하다 《떨어지다》 fall 《in public estimation》; sink; 《잃다》 lose 《*one's* credit with》; forfeit 《*a person's* confidence》. ¶ 신용의 ~ loss of *one's* credit / 권력을 ~하다 fall from power / 위신을 ~하다 lose *one's* prestige / 미국의 위신은 크게 ~되었다 The prestige of the United States suffered a severe downgrading.

**실측**(實測) (a) survey; (an) actual survey; (a) survey on the spot [ground]; actual measurement. ~하다 make a survey of; survey; measure.
◉ ~도 a surveyed map; an ordinance map 《영》: 5만분의 1 ~도 a 50,000 scale [1 / 50,000th] map.

**실컷** *one's* fill; to *one's* heart's content; to *one's* complete satisfaction; as much as *one* likes; more than enough. ¶ ~ 먹다[마시다] eat [drink] *one's* fill; have plenty of 《food and drink》 / ~ 울다 cry *oneself* sick; cry *one's* eyes out / 인생을 ~ 즐기다 enjoy life to the full / 노래를 ~ 부르다 sing as many songs as *one* likes / ~ 놀게 내버려 둬라 Let him have his fling!

**실크로드** 〚역사〛 the Silk Road.

**실크해트** a silk hat; a top hat; a chimney pot hat 《영구어》.

**실큼하다** be somewhat disliked; be rather unpleasant.

**실탄**(實彈) 《총탄》 a ball [live, loaded] cartridge; 《포탄》 a loaded shell; a live shell; a solid shot. ¶ ~을 발사하다 fire with live 「shells [bullets]. ◉ ~사격 firing with live ammunition; 《소총의》 ball-firing; 《대포의》 target practice with live shells: 중국은 지난 화요일 대만 해협에서 ~ 사격 군사 훈련을 시작했다 China started live-fire military exercises on the last Tuesday in the Taiwan Strait.

**실태**(失態) 《창피》 disgrace; ignominy; 《실수》 a blunder; an error; a fault; a failure (실패). ¶ ～를 부리다 commit a blunder 〔an indiscretion〕; disgrace *oneself;* expose *oneself* to ridicule; make a scene (추태); goof 《구어》.

**실태**(實態) the actual conditions; the realities; a real picture 《of》. ¶ 부실 기업의 ～를 조사하다 investigate the actual conditions of insolvent enterprises / 실업자의 ～를 조사하다 investigate the actual conditions of 〔among〕 the unemployed. ◉ ～조사 research on the actual state; survey of actual condition; an investigation into the actual condition; 《회계의》 audit: ～조사위원회 a fact-finding committee 〔agency〕 / 투자 목적을 위한 ～ 조사 사절단 a fact-finding mission for investment purposes.

**실터** the narrow empty area between one house and the next.

**실토**(實吐) a true confession; telling the whole truth; speaking with sincerity. ～하다 confess; spit out the truth; tell the whole truth. ¶ 모든 것을 ～하다 make a clean breast of 《the secrets》; own up / ～해라 Own up! *or* Come clean! 《구어》.

**실톱** a kind of jigsaw; a fret saw.

**실톳** thread wound on a spool; a spool(ful) of thread.

**실투**(失投) 〖야구〗 a careless pitch 〔throw〕. ～하다 deliver 〔throw〕 a ball carelessly; make a careless pitch. ¶ 그의 홈런은 투수가 ～한 탓이다 It was because the pitcher delivered a careless ball that he swatted a homer.

**실파** a small green onion.

**실팍지다** ⇨ 실팍하다.

**실팍하다** (be) strongly built; sturdy; hard; firm; solid; substantial. ¶ 실팍한 사람 a person of sturdy physique / 이 책상은 ～ This desk is strongly built.

**실패** a flat piece of wood for winding thread; a spool; a bobbin; a reel. ¶ ～에 실을 감다 (wind thread on a) spool; reel.

**실패**(失敗) (a) failure; miscarriage; a flop 《구어》; a washout 《구어》; 《과실》 a miss; a blunder; 《실책》 a bungle. ～하다 [사람이 주어] fail 《in》; be unsuccessful 《in》; [사물이 주어] end 〔result〕 in failure; 《계획 등이》 go wrong; fall through; be a failure. ¶ 대(大)～ a complete 〔an utter〕 failure; a fiasco (*pl.* ～(e)s) / ～로 돌아가다〔끝나다〕 end in failure; meet with failure; be 〔turn out〕 a failure; come to grief; be brought to naught / 사업〔시험〕에 ～하다 fail in *one's* business 〔an examination〕 / 사사건건 ～하다 fail at every step; everything goes wrong with *one* / 계획이 ～하다 *one's* plan fails 〔goes wrong〕; [사람이 주어] fail in *one's* attempt; be bulked 〔frustrated〕 in *one's* plan / 국회 의원 재선에 ～하다 fail to get reelected to the National Assembly / 이런 유(類)의 사업은 ～할 위험이 없다 This kind of business is free from risks. / 그는 정치가로서는 ～였다 He was a failure as a statesman. / 그의 시도는 모조리 ～로 끝났다 Everything he has tried 〔attempted〕 has ended in failure. *or* All his attempts have proved abortive. / 여러번 ～한 끝에 성공했다 Success came after many failures. / 그 신극은 큰 ～작이었다 The new play was a pathetic fiasco. / ～는 성공의 어머니 《속담》 Failure is but a stepping stone to success. ◉ ～자 a failure; 《낙오자》 a social failure. ～작 a failure; a flop (책·연극의); an article of poor workmanship.

**실하다**(實—) ① 《건강》 (be) healthy; sturdy; strongly built; solid; substantial. ¶ 몸이 실한 사람 a person of solid build. ② 《재산이》 (be) wealthy; well-to-do; solid; substantial. ¶ 실한 장사꾼 a solid businessman. ③ 《믿을 만하다》 (be) trustworthy; reliable; solid; substantial. ¶ 실한 친구 a solid friend. ④ 《내용이》 be rich in content; (be) full; substantial. ¶ 실하지 않은 이야기 an empty talk.

**실학**(實學) practical science. ◉ ～파 a realistic 〔positive〕 school 〔group, faction〕.

**실행**(實行) 《실천》 practice; action; deed; 《수행》 execution; performance; 《이행》 fulfillment; 《실시》 enforcement; operation. ～하다 carry into effect; carry out 《a plan》; practice 《what *one* preaches》; put 《*one's* ideas》 into practice 〔effect, operation〕; execute 《a plan》; perform; fulfill; enforce. ¶ ～가능〔불가능한〕 계획 a practicable 〔an impracticable〕 plan / 경작이 ～가능한〔불가능한〕 토지 land feasible 〔unfeasible〕 for cultivation / ～상 practically; in practice / ～상의 곤란 a practical difficulty; a difficulty in fulfilling 〔putting into effect〕 / ～에 옮기다 put 《an idea》 in(to) practice; give effect to 《an idea》; get 《a plan》 under way / 계약을 ～하다 execute a contract / 약속을 ～하다 fulfill 〔keep, carry out〕 *one's* promise / 신념을 ～하다 act up to *one's* principle / 말뿐이지 ～하지 않다 be all talk and no action; be a man of words and not of deeds / 우리들에게 필요한 것은 말이 아니라 ～이다 What we need is not words but deeds. ◉ ～가 a man of deeds 〔action〕. ～기관 an executive organ. ～력 power of execution; executive ability: ～력이 있다 have executive talent / ～력이 있는 사람 a person of action. ～예산 the operating 〔working〕 budget. ～위원회 an executive committee 〔commission〕.

**실험**(實驗) (an) experimentation; 《실험실에서의》 laboratory work; 《1회의》 an experiment; a test. ～하다 experiment 《on, in》; make 〔do, conduct〕 an experiment 《on, in》; 《성능 등을》 put 《*a thing*》 to the test. ¶ ～적으로 experimentally; by way of experiment; on an experimental basis / 화학 ～을 하다 make 〔conduct〕 a chemical experiment / (여러 가지 방법으로) 동물 ～을 하다 experiment on animals (in various methods) / ～중이다 be under experiment; be in an experimental stage / ～을 통해서 가르치다 demonstrate; teach by the help of experiments / 그는 생물공학에 관해서 ～을 하고 있다 He is making 〔doing〕 experiment in biotechnology. / ～은 잘 되지 않았다 The experiment 〔test〕 didn't work well. / 그는 동물에 그 약을 ～했다 He tested the drug on animals. / 그 안전성은 많은 동물 ～으로 입증돼 있다 Its safety has been proved through many animal experiments. ◉ ～공장 a pilot 〔demonstration〕 plant. ～과학 an experimental science. ～극장〔무대〕 an experimental theater. ～농장 a pilot 〔an experimental〕 farm. ～단계 the mock-up 〔experimental〕 stage: 그 계획은 아직 ～단계에 있다 The plan is still in the experimental stage. ～대(臺) a testing bench; an experiment stand. ～대상 an experimental object. ～동물 an experimental animal. ～론 『철학』 positivism. ～목장 an experimental livestock farm. ～소 an experimental station; a laboratory. ～소설 an experimental romance. ～식(式) an empirical formula. ～실 a laboratory. ～심리학 experimental psychology. ～자 an experimenter; a tester. ～자료 (a) material for experiments; [비유적] a guinea pig; a laboratory rabbit. ～장〔지역〕 《신무기 등의》 a testing ground 〔area〕. ～장치 an experimental device; experimental equipment. ～주의 『철학』 experimentalism: ～주의자 an experimentalist. ～철학 empirical philosophy.

**실현**(實現) realization; attainment; actualization; materialization. ～하다 realize 《*one's* ideal》; attain 《*one's* aim to》; put 《*a plan*》 into practice; turn 《the dream of flight》 into reality; make 《a dream》 come true; materialize; come true (소원 등이). ¶ ～ (불)가능한〔의〕 (un)realizable; (un)feasible / ～ 가능한 계획 a feasible scheme / ～되다 be materialized; come to pass; become a reality; be realized; take shape / 이상을 ～하다 realize *one's* ideal / 꿈을 ～하다 make a dream an actuality / 그의 오랜 야망은 드디어 ～되었다 His long-cherished ambition has finally been materialized. / 언젠가 당신의 희망〔꿈〕이 ～되기를 빕니다 I hope your wish 〔dream〕 will come true someday. / 우주 여행은 곧 ～될 것이다 Manned space navigation will soon become an accomplished fact. / 그의 이상은 ～될 것 같지 않다 His ideal is unlikely to be realized 〔to be translated into reality〕. / 현재의 사정으로는 이 계획을 가까운 장래에 ～시키기가 사실상 불가능하다 In present circumstances, it seems to be practically impossible for us to realize this plan in the near future.

**실형**(實兄) an older blood brother.

**실형**(實刑) imprisonment; a prison 〔jail〕 sentence.

**실화**(失火) an accidental fire. ～하다 take fire by accident. ¶ 그 화재의 원인은 ～인가, 방화인가 Was the fire accidental or deliberate? / 그의 집은 ～로 소실되었다 His house was destroyed by an accidental fire. / 그 화재는 ～가 아니고 방화였다 The fire was not accidental, but incendiary.

**실화**(實話) a real(-life) story; a true story; an authentic account 《of》. ¶ …의 ～를 쓰다 write a true story of... / 이 이야기는 ～입니다 The tale is taken from real life. ◉ 범죄～ a factual account of crime.

**실황**(實況) 《실정》 the actual 〔real〕 situation 〔state of things〕; 《광경》 the actual scene. ¶ ～을 시찰하다 inspect actual conditions / ～을 목격하다 witness the scene / 행진 ～을 전해 드리겠습니다 I am now going to bring you a word picture of the parade. ◉ ～녹음 (a) live recording: ～녹음 음반 a recording of an actual performance. ～중계 a relay from the spot 〔scene〕.

**실황방송**(實況放送) an on-the-spot 〔a live〕 broadcast; an outside broadcast 〔telecast (TV의)〕; a running commentary; a ball-by-ball 〔play-by-play 《미》〕 commentary 〔account〕 《of a sporting event》. ¶ ～자 a commentator / ～을 하다 broadcast on the spot; keep up a running commentary 《on》.

**실효**(失效) invalidation; a lapse. ～하다 lose effect; become (null and) void; get 〔become〕 invalid(ated); lapse. ¶ 조약의 ～ the lapsing of a treaty / 법률상의 권리가 행사되지 않으면, 그 권리는 몇년 후에는 ～된다 If a legal claim is not enforced, it lapses after a certain number of years. / 운전 면허증 갱신을 하지 않으면 ～한다 Your driver's license will be invalid if you fail to renew it.

**실효**(實效) 《효과》 practical effect; 《능률》 efficiency; 《약 따위의》 efficacy. ¶ ～가 있다 be effective 〔efficacious〕 / ～가 없다 be ineffective / ～를 거두다 do good work; give satisfactory results / ～를 나타내다 prove (to be) effective (in practice); produce material results.
◉ ～가격 〖경제〗 the effective price 《of a commodity》. ～금리 〖경제〗 the effective 〔real〕 interest rate. ～성 effectiveness. ～습도 〖기상〗 effective humidity. ～치〔값〕 〖전기〗 virtual 〔effective〕 value.

**싫건좋건** whether *one* will 〔likes it〕 or not; whether willing or not; willy-nilly. ¶ ～ 가야 한다 I have no choice but to go. *or* I have to go whether I like it or not.

**싫다** 《불쾌》 (be) unpleasant; disagreeable; distasteful; loathsome; 《혐오》 dislike; loathe; hate; be unwilling 〔loath, reluctant〕 《to *do*》.
¶ 싫은 일 distasteful 〔unpleasant, undesirable〕 work / 보기 싫은 놈 an odious 〔a disgusting〕 fellow / 싫은 얼굴을 하다 frown; make a wry face; look offended 〔displeased〕 / 싫어지다 be 〔become, get〕 disgusted 《with》; be 〔become, get〕 sick 《of》; get tired of; grow weary of; come to dislike / 그를 도와 주기가 ～ I am reluctant to help him. *or* I hate to help him. / 나는 사탕이 ～ I have no taste for sweets. / 나는 ～ I don't like it. *or* I won't do so. / 거저 줘도 ～ I would not have it (even) as a gift. / 뱀은 아주 ～ I have a strong dislike for snakes. / 보기 ～ I don't like you! / 그는 보기도 ～ The very sight of him is disgusting. / 그런 말 듣기 ～ I don't want to hear about it! / 그는 살기가 싫어졌다 He grew tired of life. / 싫으면 가지 않아도 좋다 You do not have to go there if you do not want do.

**싫어하다** dislike; hate; detest; loathe; have a distaste for; abhor; 《내키지 않다》 be unwilling 〔reluctant〕 《to *do*》; be prejudiced 《against》; be averse 《to *a thing*, to *do*ing》. ¶ 싫어하는 것 what *one* does not like; an abomination / 담배 냄새를 ～ abhor the smell of tobacco / 수학을 ～ dislike mathematics / 가기(를) ～ be unwilling to go / 이웃 사람들은 모두 그를 싫어한다 He is a nuisance to all the neighborhood. / 왜 밥 먹기를 싫어하는지 모르겠다 I don't see why he refuses to eat. / 그들은 그에게 싫어하는 술을 억지로 먹였다 They made him drink against his will. / 나는 거짓말하기를 싫어한다 I hate to lie. (★ I hate lying.이면 「자기든 남이든 거짓말 하는 것을 싫어한다」는 뜻이 됨) / 그들은 결혼하기 싫어하는 딸을 시집보냈다 They married off their daughter against her will.

**싫증**(─症) repugnance; dislike; disgust; aversion. ¶ ～이 나다 feel a repugnance 《toward》; get disgusted 《with》; become weary 《of》; be bored 《with》; get 〔grow〕 tired 〔weary〕 of 《a task》; lose interest in / ～나는 이야기 a boring story; a tedious tale / 공부에 ～이 나다 be sick and tired of studying / 그는 무엇을 하든 곧 ～을 낸다 He sticks to nothing. / 그의 장광설에 청중은 ～이 났다 The audience became 「bored by 〔tired of〕 his long speech. / 그의 아첨에 ～이 났다 I was disgusted with his flattery.

**심** a sinew. ＝심줄.

**심**(心) ①《나무의》 the heart; the pith; 《핵심》 the core; the inside. ¶ 이 나무는 심까지 썩었다 This tree is rotten to the heart 〔core〕. ②《줄기》 a string. ¶ 순무에 심이 있다 a turnip is stringy. ③《연필의》 the lead. ④《심지》 a padding (옷 따위의); a wick (초·램프 등의); a wick sponge (외과용의). ¶ 심을 넣다 pad (a sash); interline / 이 공은 심이 납으로 되어 있다 This ball is padded with lead. ⑤《새알심》 a dumpling. ⑥《마음》 heart; feeling; emotion; sense; mind; psyche. ¶ 심적(인) mental; psychological / 애국심 patriotism / 충성심 sense of loyalty / 자부심 self-confidence. 「first trial.

**심**(審) a trial; a hearing. ¶ 제1심 the

**심각**(深刻) ～하다 (be) serious; severe; grave; keen; acute; poignant; deep. ¶ ～한 인생 문제 a serious problem in *one's* life / ～한 불황 a deep depression / ～히 seriously; gravely; soberly; intensely; deeply / ～히 생각하다 think deeply 〔seriously, profoundly〕 / ～해지다 become intensified 〔aggravated〕; get 〔become〕 more strained 〔acute〕 / ～한 얼굴을 하다 look serious 〔grave〕 / 날로 ～해지는 교통문제의 해결을 위한 방안을 마련하다 work out a plan to solve the ever-serious traffic problems / 생활난은 점점 더 ～해져 가고 있다 It is getting more and more difficult to 「make 〔manage〕 a living.

**심경**(心境) a frame 〔state〕 of mind; a mental state 〔attitude〕; *one's* mind. ¶ 현재의 ～ *one's* present state of mind / 평온한 ～ a serene mind / ～의 변화를 가져오다 undergo a change of mind; change *one's* mind / ～을 말〔토로〕하다 speak 〔tell〕 *one's* mind 《to》; open *one's* heart; unbosom *oneself* 《to》 / 그분의 그러한 ～에는 동정이 간다 I sympathize with him in his mental attitude. / 현재의 ～을 말씀해 주시겠습니까 Will you please tell me how you feel now 〔at present〕?
◉ ～소설 a mental-life 〔psychological〕 novel.

**심경**(深耕) deep plowing 〔ploughing 《영》〕. ～하다 plow deep. 「⇨ 심야.

**심경**(深更) the dead 〔middle〕 of night.

**심계항진**(心悸亢進) 〖의학〗 palpitations; heart acceleration; tachycardia.

**심근**(心筋) 〖해부〗 the myocardium (*pl.* -dia); the heart muscle. ◉ ～경색 myocardial infarction: 급성 ～경색 acute myocardial infarction. ～경화증 cardiosclerosis. ～염 myocarditis. ～운동도(圖) a myocardiogram.

**심금**(心琴) heartstrings; the deepest emotions. ¶ ～을 울리다 touch 〔pull at, tug at〕《*a person's*》 heartstrings; touch a cord 〔string〕 in 《*a person's*》 heart; touch the lute strings of 《*a person's*》 heart / 독자의 ～을 울리다 awake a responsive cord in the hearts of the readers.

**심기**(心氣) the mind; mood; sentiment. ¶ ～전환을 위하여 in order to distract 〔divert〕 *one's* mind / ～가 상쾌하다 feel (greatly) freshed / ～가 불편하다 be in an ill 〔a bad〕 temper 〔mood〕; be out of humor 〔temper〕; be displeased.

**심기**(心機) mental activity; the mind. ¶ ～일전하다 *one's* mind takes a new turn; turn over a new leaf; become a new man; change *one's* mind.

**심기다** ①《사역》 cause to plant; have 《*a person*》 plant. ②《피동》 get planted; be planted.

**심난하다**(甚難—) (be) extremely difficult. 「-dia).

**심낭**(心囊) 〖해부〗 the pericardium (*pl.*

**심내막**(心內膜) 〖해부〗 an endocardium. ◉ ～염 〖의학〗 endocarditis.

**심다** plant; sow; 《재배》 grow; raise; 《잔디를》 sod; 《마음에》 implant. ¶ 뜰에 국화를 ～ plant a garden with chrysanthemums; plant chrysanthemums in the garden / 국민에게 자신감과 희망을 심어주다 implant self-confidence and hope in the people / 거리에 나무를 심자 Let's plant trees in the streets. *or* Let's plant the street with trees. / 건강이 무엇보다 중요하다는 것을 그녀의 머릿속에 단단히 심어 주었다 I have got it firmly into her head that health is more important than anything else.

**심대하다**(甚大—) (be) very great; immense; enormous; tremendous; serious; heavy. ¶ 심대한 영향 a profound influence / 심대한 손해 serious damage; a heavy loss / 심대한 해를 입히다〔끼치다〕 do a great deal of harm 《to》 / 심대한 피해를 당하다 suffer great 〔immense〕 damage.

**심덕**(心德) virtue; uprightness of heart.

**심도**(深度) (degree of) depth. ¶ ～를 재다 measure the depth 《of》; sound 《the sea》; take soundings 《in》 / ～있는〔깊은〕 연구 《do》 an in-depth study. ◉ ～계 a depth gauge.

**심드렁하다** 《썩 내키지 않다》 be rather uninterested 《in》; be unwilling 《to *do*》; take little interest 《in》; 《움직임·병세 따위가》 be slow moving; drag; linger 《on》; hang on.

**심란**(心亂) confusion 〔disturbance, disorder〕 of mind. ～하다 be confused in mind; (be) upset; disturbed; be in mental turmoil.

**심려**(心慮) uneasiness of heart; (an) anxiety; (a) worry; cares; concern; apprehensions. ～하다 worry about 〔over〕; worry *oneself* about; be anxious 〔concerned〕 《about》; apprehend. ¶ ～를 끼치다 cause anxiety 《to》; give 《*a person*》 trouble; trouble 《*a person*》 / 여러 가지로 ～를 끼쳐 죄송합니다 I am sorry to have occasioned you (so) much anxiety.

**심령**(心靈) spirit. ¶ ～적(인) spiritual; psychic(al). ◉ ～연구 psychical research; psychicism: ～연구회 a psychical research society. ～학 psychics; spiritism; 《심령술》 spiritualism: ～학자 a psychicist. ～현상 a spiritual 〔psychic〕 phenomenon.

**심로**(心勞) cares; anxiety; worries; mental fatigue.

**심록**(深綠) deep 〔dark〕 green.

**심리**(心理) a mental state; mentality; psychology; the mind. ¶ 어린이의 ～ children's psychology 〔mentalities〕 / 범죄자의 ～ the psychology of criminals / ～적(으로) mental(ly); psychological(ly) / ～적으로 나쁜 영향을 주다 be bad 〔harmful〕 in 《its》 psychological effect 《on a child》 / 그의 ～를 알 수가 없다 I have no idea of his real state of mind. / 이것은 보통 미국 사람의 ～를 잘 나타내고 있다 This speaks eloquently of the mentality of an average American.
◉ ～극 『정신요법』 (a) psychodrama. ～묘사 (a) psychological description. ～사회학 psychosociology. ～상태 a 〔*one's*〕 mental state; mentality. ～소설 a psychological novel. ～요법 psychotherapy. ～작용 a mental process; psychosis. ～작전 psychological tactics. ～전(쟁) psychological warfare. ～현상 a psychological phenomenon. 부패～ corrupt mentality.

**심리**(審理) (a) trial; (an) examination; (an) inquiry; 《형사 사건의》 (a) (legal) hearing. ～하다 try 《a case》; examine 〔inquire into〕 《a case》; sit in judgment 《on trial》. ¶ ～를 받다 be under at the bar / ～중이다 be under 〔on〕 trial; be under 〔on〕 discussion; be pending; 『법』 be subjudice / ～중인 사건에 대한 신문의 논평은 바람직하지 못한 일이다 Newspaper comments on cases under trial are undesirable.

**심리학**(心理學) psychology. ¶ 일반〔행동〕～ general 〔behavioristic〕 psychology / ～상 psychologically / ～상의 psychological / ～을 연구하다 psychologize. ◉ ～자 a psychologist. 게슈탈트～ Gestalt psychology. 기술(記述)～ psychography.

**심마니** mountain hermits who collect wild ginseng; a wild-ginseng digger. ◉ ～말 the ginseng-digger jargon.

**심메** gathering wild ginseng. ¶ ～(를) 보다 engage in wild-ginseng gathering.

**심문**(審問) a trial; an inquiry; an examination; a hearing. ～하다 try; hear 〔examine, inquire into〕 《a case》. ¶ 증인 ～ examination of a witness / ～을 받다 be examined; be tried / 그는 그 사건으로 ～을 받고 있다 He is on trial. *or* His case is being heard.

**심미**(審美) appreciation of the beautiful; (a)esthetics. ¶ ～적 esthetic(al). ◉ ～가 an esthete. ～감 a sense of beauty; esthetic sense 〔feeling〕. ～안 an eye for the beautiful; an esthetic sense; esthetic appreciation: ～안이 있다 have 「an eye for 〔a good sense of〕 the beautiful; have a sense of beauty. ～주의 estheticism. ～파 an esthetic school. ～학 esthetics.

**심박**(心搏) 『의학』 a heartbeat. ¶ ～수(數) 《an increase in》 *one's* 〔the〕 heart rate / ～은 아주 정상입니다 Your heartbeat is quite normal. ◉ ～정지 『의학』 (a) cardiac arrest.

**심방**(心房) 『해부』 an atrium (*pl.* -ria). ¶ 우〔좌〕～ the right 〔left〕 atrium.

**심방**(尋訪) a visit; a call. ～하다 visit; make a call; go and see 《*a person*》.

**심벌** a symbol; an emblem. ¶ 평화의 ～ a symbol of peace / 올리브 가지는 평화의 ～이다 The olive branch stands for peace. ◉ ～리즘 symbolism. ～마크 a symbol; a logo; a logotype.

**심벌즈** 『음악』 cymbals.

**심병**(心病) ① 《근심》 anxiety; sickness at heart; worry; suffering. ② 『의학』 syncope; a fainting fit.

**심보**(心―) nature. ⇨ 마음보.

**심복**(心服) hearty submission 〔obedience〕. ～하다 be obedient 〔devoted〕

《to》; 《존경하다》 have a high regard for 《*a person*》; hold 《*a person*》 in high esteem.

**심복**(心腹) ① 《가슴과 배》 the heart and the stomach. ② 《긴요한 것》 the indispensable; the necessary; a *sine qua non* (L.). ③ 《사람》 *one's* right=hand man; *one's* confidant; *one's* second self. ¶ 그때 이래로 줄곧 그는 K 씨의 ~이 되어 있다 He has been Mr. K's confidant 〔right-hand man〕 ever since.

**심부**(深部) a deep part; a depth.

**심부름** an errand; a message. ~하다 do 〔run〕 an errand. ¶ ~ 보내다 send 《*a person*》 on an errand / ~을 가다 go 〔run〕 on an errand / ~ 좀 해줄래 Can you do a little errand for me? / ~할 일이 있다 I have an errand to do. / 그녀는 슈퍼에 ~을 갔다 She has gone on an 〔some〕 errand to the supermarket. ◉ ~값 a tip for a messenger; an errand charge. ~꾼 an errand boy; a messenger; an office boy: ~꾼을 보내느니 자네가 직접 가서 그에게 얘기하는 것이 좋겠다 You should go and talk to him in person instead of sending a messenger.

**심부전**(心不全) 〖의학〗 cardiac insufficiency 〔arrest〕; insufficiency of the heart; heart failure.

**심사**(心事) (a) thought; mind; cares; concerns.

**심사**(心思) ill will; malicious intention; malice; malevolence. ¶ ~가 나쁘다 〔사납다〕 be malicious; be ill-natured; be evil-minded; be spiteful; be malevolent / ~가 나다 get cross; bear malice / ~가 나서 아무를 비방하다 disparage *a person* 「out of 〔from〕 spite / ~를 부리다 thwart; disturb; get in the way; cross 《*a person's*》 path; put a spoke in 《*a person's*》 wheel / 그가 ~를 부려서 계획이 망쳐졌다 Our plan was spoiled by him and his ways.

**심사**(深謝) 《감사》 sincere 〔cordial, hearty〕 thanks; deep 〔heartfelt〕 gratitude; 《사죄》 a sincere apology. ~하다 thank 《*a person*》 heartily; express 〔extend, present〕 *one's* heartfelt gratitude; 《사죄》 make a sincere apology; offer 〔tender, express〕 *one's* heartfelt apologies.

**심사**(審査) 《판정》 judging; 《조사》 (an) examination; (an) investigation; 《검사》 (an) inspection; 《선발》 screening. ~하다 judge; examine; inspect; investigate; screen (사람을). ¶ 최종 ~ final screening / ~중이다 be under examination / ~에 합격하다, ~를 통과하다 be accepted; pass inspection; be found eligible / ~ 결과를 보고하다 report *one's* findings / 자세한 ~로 그것이 허위로 판명되었다 On closer inspection it proved to be false. ◉ ~관〔원, 위원〕 a judge; an examiner; a juror (콩쿠르 등의); 〔총칭〕 a panel of judges. ~위원장 the president of the board of examiners; the chairman of the screening 〔awarding〕 committee. ~위원회 a judging 〔screening〕 committee.

**심사숙고**(深思熟考) (serious) consideration; contemplation; deliberation; hard thinking. ~하다 consider 《*a matter*》 carefully; give deep thought; think 《it》 over; contemplate; ponder 《on, over》; deliberate; give a careful consideration. ¶ ~ 끝에 after due 〔mature〕 consideration / 그 문제는 ~를 필요로 한다 The subject demands 〔requires〕 careful consideration.

**심산**(心算) an intention; design; calculation. ¶ …할 ~으로 with the intention 〔object, aim〕 of *do*ing; with a view to 〔of〕 *do*ing; expecting 〔believing〕 that… / …할 ~이다 intend to *do;* will *do;* mean 〔expect〕 to *do;* have a mind to *do;* be going to *do;* think of *do*ing / 그의 ~을 전혀 모르겠다 I cannot quite see 〔understand〕 his motive 〔idea〕. / 무슨 ~으로 그런 소리를 하느냐 What do you mean by (saying) that? / 그런 ~으로 한 것은 아니다 I didn't mean that at all. / 그는 친구를 도울 ~으로 그렇게 한 것이다 He did so by way of helping his friend. / 그녀는 그것을 농담으로 말할 ~이었는데, 많은 사람들은 그것을 곧이 곧대로 받아들였다 She intended it as a joke, but a lot of people took her seriously.

**심산**(深山) a mountain recess; deep 〔remote〕 mountains. ◉ ~궁곡〔유곡〕 steep mountains and deep valleys; a remote mountainous region; high mountains and secluded valleys: ~유곡에(서) 《lead an ascetic life》 deep in the mountains / ~유곡에 깊숙이 들어가다 go 〔push (*one's* way)〕 deep into the mountains.

**심상**(心像) 〖심리〗 a mental image; an image.

**심상**(尋常) 〔형용사적〕 ordinary; commonplace; usual. ~하다 《보통의》 (be) ordinary; common; usual; average (평균적); 《평범》 commonplace; mediocre. ¶ ～히 matter-of-factly; commonly; ordinarily / ～치 않은 unusual; uncommon; serious; extraordinary / ～치 않은 소리 《hear》 an alarming sound / ～치 않은 사태 a grave 〔critical, serious〕 situation / (일이) ～치 않게 되다 grow 〔become〕 serious 〔grave〕; [사물이 주어] take a serious turn / ～치 않은 일이다 It is no ordinary 〔trivial〕 matter.

**심성**(心性) nature; disposition; temper; 《심정》 mentality.

**심성암**(深成岩) 『광물』 plutonic rocks; 「hypogene rock.

**심술**(心術) cross temper; ill nature; perverseness. ¶ ～궂다 be cross(-minded); be ill-tempered〔-natured〕; be cantankerous; be perverse; be pigheaded; be nasty / ～을 부리다〔내다, 피우다〕 act surly 〔cross〕; behave perversely; give vent to *one's* cross temper; get 〔grow〕 cross 〔perverse〕 / 그는 ～궂은 말을 했다 He said spiteful things. / ～ 부리지 말고 밥 먹어라 Don't be so cross, but eat your dinner. ◉ ～쟁이〔통이, 꾸러기〕 a crosspatch; a dog in the manger; an ill-natured person. ～패기 a cross child; a perverse youngster.

**심신**(心身) mind and body; body and soul (★ mind and body는 body and mind라고 말할 수 있지만, soul을 쓰면 body and soul이 영어의 관용(慣用)이며 soul and body라고는 하지 않음). ¶ ～의 피로〔휴양〕 mental and physical exhaustion 〔rest〕 / ～을 단련하다 cultivate 〔train〕 *one's* body and mind / ～이 모두 건전하다 be sound 〔healthy〕 in mind and body; be mentally and physically sound / ～이 상쾌해지다 feel refreshed 〔bright〕 in body and mind / 그녀는 ～이 모두 지쳐 있었다 She was mentally and physically exhausted. ◉ ～장애자 the (mentally and physically) handicapped: ～장애자 복지법 the Mentally and Physically Disabled Persons' Welfare Act. ～증 (a) psychosomatic disease: ～증 환자 a psychosomatic patient.

**심신**(心神) mind; mentality. ¶ ～이 산란하다 be deranged; be unhinged in mind / ～상실 상태에 있다 『법』 (L.) be *non compos* (*mentis*) (★ *non compos*는 항상 보어로서 쓰임); be not of sound mind. ◉ ～장애자 a weak-〔feeble-〕 minded person.

**심실**(心室) 『해부』 the ventricle(s) of the heart. ◉ 우〔좌〕～ the right 〔left〕 ventricle.

**심심소일**(一消日) = 심심풀이.

**심심파적**(一破寂) = 심심풀이.

**심심풀이** killing time; whiling away the hours; beguilement; (a) diversion; a pastime; a timekiller; a way to kill time. ～하다 kill time; while the time away; beguile *one's* hours; divert *oneself;* pass the time (away). ¶ ～로 to kill time; by way of killing time; to while away the time / ～로 책을 읽다 read to kill time / ～로 장기를 두다 play *changgi* to pass the time / 낚시질은 좋은 ～다 Fishing is a good timekiller.

**심심하다**[1] 《일없어》 be bored; feel weary; have a dull time. ¶ 심심해 보이다 look bored; wear a bored look / 심심해 죽겠다 be bored to death / 할 일이 없어 ～ be weary of having nothing to do / 너무 심심해서 책을 읽다 read from sheer boredom.

**심심하다**[2] 《맛이》 be 〔taste〕 slightly flat.

**심악**(甚惡) being harsh 〔cruel〕. ～스럽다, ～하다 (be) harsh; cruel; merciless.

**심안**(心眼) *one's* mind's eye; mental perception 〔vision〕. ¶ ～을 뜨다 open *one's* mind's eye / ～에 비치다 be visible to the eye of the mind / ～으로 보다 see in 〔with〕 *one's* mind's eye.

**심야**(深夜) the middle 〔dead〕 of night; midnight. ¶ ～에 at 〔in the〕 dead of night; late at night / ～까지 till late at night; far 〔deep〕 into the night / 그녀는 ～까지 스테레오를 듣고 있었다 She was listening to stereos far into the night. ◉ ～방송 late-night 〔all-night〕 broadcasting; 《프로》 a midnight(time) TV 〔radio〕 program. ～영업 late-night operation: ～영업의 식당 an eating house kept open late at night / ～영업을 하다 keep the door open till late at night; be open at late hours / ～영업을 하는 술집은 한 군데도 없다 There are no bars 〔saloons〕 which are open till late at night. ～요금 a late-night rate.

**심약**(心弱) feeble-mindedness; weak-mindedness. ～하다 (be) feeble-minded; weak-minded; irresolute.

**심연**(深淵) a deep swamp; [비유적] a gulf (*pl.* ～s); an abyss.

**심오**(深奧) profundity; abstruseness. ～하다 (be) profound; abstruse; esoteric. ¶ ～한 지식 (a) deep 〔profound〕 knowledge 《of art》 / ～한 종교 사상

profound religious thought.

**심원**(心願) *one's* heart's desire; *one's* heartfelt wish; *one's* dearest wish. ¶ ～성취 the realization 〔fulfillment〕 of *one's* earnest wish.

**심원**(深怨) deep resentment 〔grudge〕. ¶ ～을 품다 bear *a person* a deep grudge; have 〔bear〕 a grudge against *a person;* deeply resent.

**심원**(深遠) profundity; depth. ～하다 (be) profound; deep; abstruse; unfathomable. ¶ ～한 교리 an esoteric 〔a recondite〕 doctrine.

**심음**(心音) 〚의학〛 cardiac 〔heart〕 sound. ◉ ～기록계 a phonocardiograph. ～기록도 a phonocardiogram.

**심의**(審議) consideration; deliberation; 《논의》 (a) discussion; 《조사》 (an) investigation; a going-over (철저한). ～하다 deliberate 《on *a matter*》; consider; discuss; 《조사》 investigate; examine. ¶ ～를 거듭한 끝에 after much deliberation; after due consideration / ～중이다 [사물이 주어] be under consideration; be on the carpet 〔*tapis*〕; [회의가 주어] be discussing 《a proposal》; be sitting 《on a bill》 / ～에 부치다 refer 《*a matter*》 to 《a committee》 / ～에 부쳐지다 come on the *tapis* / 축조(逐條) ～하다 discuss article by article / 그 법안은 오늘 ～를 위해 상정(上程)돼 있다 The bill is up for consideration today.
◉ ～권 the right to deliberate. ～기관 an organ of consultation. ～회 a (deliberative) council; an inquiry commission: 교육 ～회 an educational council.

**심이**(心耳) 〚해부〛 the auricles of the heart. ◉ 우〔좌〕～ the right 〔left〕 auricle.

**심장**(心臟) ① 〚해부〛 the heart; the ticker 《속어》. ¶ ～의 cardiac / ～의 고동 the beating 〔palpitation〕 of the heart; a heartbeat / ～의 기능 the function of the heart / ～ 고동의 멎음 cardiac arrest; a heart stoppage / ～이 약하다〔나쁘다〕 have 〔suffer from〕 a weak 〔bad〕 heart; have heart trouble / 그 소식을 듣고 ～이 마구 뛰었다 My heart beat fast at the news. / 그의 ～ 고동이 멎었다 His heart stopped beating.
② 《배짱》 nerve; cheek; guts 《미구어》. ¶ ～이 약한 사람 a nerveless fellow / ～이 강하다 be bold; be impudent; be cheeky; have much nerve; be brazen-faced / ～이 약하다 be timid 〔shy, fainthearted〕 / 그는 ～이 강한 사나이다 He has a lot of nerve. / 정말이지 강 ～이구먼 What a nerve he's got! *or* What (a) cheek! / 그에게 그런 말을 하다니 자네 ～도 어지간하군 The nerve of you to say such a thing to him! *or* What nerve you have to say such a thing to him!
◉ ～마비 a heart attack; cardiac paralysis; heart 〔cardiac〕 failure: 그녀는 ～마비로 죽었다 She died of heart failure. ～마사지 《do》 (a) heart massage. ～발작 《have》 a heart attack 〔stroke〕. ～병 a heart disease; heart trouble: ～병 약 a cardiac remedy / ～병 환자 a cardiac (patient); a heart patient / 선천성 ～병 a congenital heart trouble 〔cardiopathy〕. ～부 the heart 〔core〕 《of a city》. ～비대(증) hypertrophy of the heart; cardiac hypertrophy. ～수축 contraction of the heart; systole. ～염 inflammation of the heart; carditis. ～외과 cardiosurgery; heart 〔cardiac〕 surgery. ～이식(수술) a heart transplant (operation). ～장애 heart trouble. ～전문의 a heart specialist. ～절개(수)술 an open-heart operation; cardiotomy. ～질환 a cardiac disorder. ～천식 cardiac asthma; cardiasthma. ～파열 rupture of the heart. ～판막 valves of the heart: ～판막증 a valvular disease of the heart. ～학 cardiology.

**심장**(深長) deep and far-reaching. ～하다 (be) deep; profound. ¶ 의미 ～하다 be profound in meaning; be deeply significant; be full of meaning; have a deep meaning; be of profound significance.

**심적**(心的) mental; psychological. ¶ ～경향 《have》 an inclination 《to *do*》; a tendency. ◉ ～상태 a mental state; mentality. ～작용〔결함〕 a mental action 〔defect〕. ～태도 mental attitude. ～현상 a mental phenomenon.

**심전계**(心電計) 〚의학〛 an electrocardiograph.

**심전도**(心電圖) 〚의학〛 an electrocardiogram (생략 ECG).

**심정**(心情) the heart; *one's* feeling. ¶ 아무의 ～을 이해하다〔헤아리다〕 understand 〔know〕 how *a person* feels; enter into *a person's* feelings; 《동정하다》 sympathize with *a person;* feel for *a person* / 울고 싶은 ～이다 I feel like crying.

**심줄** a sinew; a tendon. ¶ ～이 많다 《the meat》 be tough.

**심중**(心中) the mind; the heart; *one's* inmost thoughts; *one's* true motive. ¶ ～에 품다 keep 《a secret》 in *one's* heart / ～을 털어놓다 lay bare *one's* heart; unbosom 〔unburden〕 *oneself* 《to *a person*》; take 《*a person*》 into *one's* confidence / ～을 헤아리다 enter into 〔share〕 《*a person's*》 feelings; sympathize with 《*a person*》 in *his* feelings; read 《*a person's*》 thoughts; feel for 《*a person*》.

**심중**(深重) prudence; discretion; caution. ～하다 (be) prudent; discreet; circumspect.

**심증**(心證) ① 〖법〗 《확신》 a strong belief; a conviction. ¶ ～을 갖다 have a strong belief 《that》 / ～을 굳히다 be confirmed in *one's* belief that… / ～이 가다 gain a confident belief / 재판관의 ～을 흐리게 하다 injure the conviction of a judge / 검사는 피고가 진범이 아니라는 ～을 가졌다 The prosecutor had a firm belief 〔was convinced〕 that the accused was not the real culprit. ② 《인상》 an impression. ¶ ～을 해치다 give 《*a person*》 an unfavorable impression; hurt 《*a person's*》 feelings.

**심지**(心—) ① 《등잔·초 따위의》 a wick. ¶ ～를 자르다 《초의》 snuff a candle; 《등잔의》 trim a wick / (램프의) ～를 돋우다〔낮추다〕 turn up 〔down〕 the wick. ② 《상처의》 a piece of gauze inserted in a wound to drain it; a wick sponge. ¶ 짼 상처에 ～를 박다 insert a wick sponge in an incised wound.

**심지**(心地) 《마음바탕》 nature; temper; disposition; character. ¶ ～가 곱다 have a lovely disposition / ～가 사납다 be perverse; be crooked.

**심지**(心志) mind; intention; purpose; the will.

**심지어**(甚之於) what is more 〔worse〕; on top of that; worst of all; 《not》 so much as. ¶ ～ 그녀는 결혼 반지까지 팔았다 She went so far as to sell her wedding ring. / ～ 눈까지 오기 시작했다 What was worse, it started to snow. / 그는 ～ 제 이름조차 쓸 줄 모른다 He cannot even write his own name.

**심축**(心祝) earnest congratulations 〔good wishes, blessings〕. ～하다 offer hearty congratulations 《to》; bless from the bottom of *one's* heart.

**심취**(心醉) fascination; infatuation; absorption; a mania 《for *a thing*》. ～하다 adore; worship; be an admirer of; idolize; come under the spell of 《*a person*》; be fascinated 《by, with》; be infatuated 〔charmed〕 《with》. ¶ 미술에 ～하다 be fascinated with art / 서양 문명에 ～하다 be infatuated with occidental civilization. ◉ ～자 an adorer; an ardent 〔a devoted〕 admirer; a fan; an idolater; a devotee.

**심층**(深層) the depths 《of *one's* consciousness》. ¶ ～의 in-depth. ◉ ～구조 〖언어〗 deep structure. ～기사 an in-depth story: ～기사를 쓰다 do an in-depth story 《on》. ～심리학 depth psychology.

**심통**(心—) bad disposition. ¶ ～이 사납다 be perverse; be crooked.

**심통**(心痛) mental suffering 〔agony, anguish〕; heartache; concern; worry; distress. ～하다 be troubled (in mind); be worried about. ¶ 그녀는 지나친 ～으로 병이 났다 She became ill with worry.

**심판**(審判) 《재판의》 judgment; 《심판원》 a referee (럭비·권투 등); an umpire (야구 경기의); a judge (경기·토론의). ～하다 judge; referee 《a game》; umpire 《a baseball game》. ¶ 최후의 ～ the Last Judgment; the Great Assize / 최후 ～의 날 (the) Judgment Day; doomsday / ～을 보다 judge; act as umpire 〔referee〕 / K씨의 ～으로 오후에 두 경기가 있었다 Two games were held in the afternoon with Mr. K as umpire 〔referee〕. / ～결정에 항의해도 소용없다 It is no use objecting 〔kicking at〕 an umpire's decision. ◉ ～원 a referee; an umpire; a judge.

**심포니** a symphony. ⇨ 교향곡. ◉ ～오케스트라 a symphony orchestra.

**심포지엄** a symposium (*pl.* -sia).

**심피**(心皮) 〖식물〗 a carpel.

**심하다**(甚—) ① 《지나치다》 (be) severe; intense; violent; extreme; excessive; harsh. ¶ 심한 바람 violent wind / 심한 추위 a bitter cold / 심한 노동 hard labor / 심한 감기 a nasty cold / 근시가 심한 사람 a very nearsighted person / 심하게 말하면 if I push the matter to extremes / 심하게 다치다 be badly hurt; get a serious injury / 그 사업은 경쟁이 ～ There is keen competition in that business. / 농담이 너무 ～ You carry your joke too far. / 기침〔열〕이 ～ I have a bad cough 〔an awful

fever〕. / 그의 병은 ~ His illness is a serious one. / 당시에는 취직난이 지금보다 심했다 The difficulty of securing employment was felt more keenly than now.
② 《엄하다·가혹하다》 (be) strict; stern; severe; relentless; harsh. ¶ 심하게 굴다 be severe 〔stick〕 with 《*a person*》; be hard on 《*a person*》 / 독촉이 ~ press hard for 《*a thing*》 / 심한 소리를 하다 use strong language / 그건 너무 ~ It's too cruel of you. *or* Don't be so hard on me. / 그런 짓을 하다니 너도 참 심하구나 It is heartless of you to do such a thing.

**심해**(深海) the deep sea; deep waters; 《대양의》 ocean depths; an abyss. ¶ 그들은 ~를 탐사했다 They explored the deep sea 〔ocean depths〕. ◉ ~어 a deep-sea fish. ~어업 deep-sea fishery 〔fishing〕. ~측심(測深) deep sea sounding. ~탐사선 a bathyscaphe.

**심혈**(心血) the heart's blood; [비유적] heart and soul; *one's* whole energy. ¶ ~을 기울이다 put 〔pour〕 *one's* heart (and soul) 《into》; give *one's* whole mind 《to》; devote *oneself* 《to》; do *one's* utmost / ~을 기울인 작품 a work of great devotion; *one's* most laborious work / ~을 기울여 with all *one's* heart.

**심호흡**(深呼吸) deep breathing 〔respiration〕; a deep breath. ~하다 breathe deeply; do deep breathing exercises; draw 〔take〕 a deep 〔full〕 breath.

**심혼**(心魂) *one's* heart 〔soul〕. ¶ 일에 ~을 기울이다 put *one's* heart 〔soul〕 into a job 〔*one's* task〕; devote all *one's* energy 《to *do*ing》.

**심홍**(深紅) deep red; crimson.

**심화**(心火) heartburn(ing); anger; passion. ¶ ~가 나다 burn with wrath / ~가 끓어 오르다 be infuriated 〔enraged〕; be filled with rage.

**심화**(深化) deepening. ~하다 deepen; intensify 《*one's* hatred at 〔for〕》; heighten. ¶ 관계가 ~되다 get more deeply involved.

**심황**(一黃) 『식물』 a turmeric; a curcuma.

**심히**(甚一) severely; intensely; gravely; harshly; extremely; exceedingly; greatly; excessively; very much; badly. ¶ ~ 춥다 be bitterly cold / 아이에게 ~ 굴다 be strict with 〔be hard on〕 a child.

**십**(十) ten; X. ¶ 제십 the tenth / 십 원 ten won / 십 일 《열흘》 ten days; 《날짜》 the tenth day / 십 주년 the 10th anniversary / 십 배 ten times; tenfold / ~분의 1, one-tenth; a tenth.

**십각**(十角) (having) ten angles; [형용사적] ten-angled. ◉ ~형 a decagon.

**십각**(十脚) (having) ten legs; [형용사적] ten-legged. ◉ ~류 『동물』 decapods.

**십계명**(十誡命) 『성서』 the Decalog(ue); the Ten Commandments.

**십구**(十九) nineteen; XIX. ¶ 제~ the nineteenth / ~ 세기 the nineteenth century / ~분의 1, one-nineteenth.

**십년**(十年) ten years; a decade.
¶ ~마다 every ten years; decennially / 수~ 동안 for several decades / 앞으로 수~ the next few decades / ~을 하루같이 without a break for long years / ~ 감수하다 be scared to death; have a hard time (of it) / ~공부 나무아미타불, ~공부 도로아미타불 《속담》 Fail to reap the fruits of one's long exertion by grudging a little effort at the last stage. / ~이면 강산〔산천〕도 변한다 《속담》 Ten years can bring a lot of changes. ◉ ~일득 a success once in a blue moon. ~지계 plans for ten years; a ten-year plan. ~지기 an old acquaintance; a friend of long standing.

**십대**(十代) 《be in》 *one's* teens. ¶ ~ 소년〔소녀〕 a teen-ager; teen-age boys 〔girls〕; boys 〔girls〕 in their teens (★ teens, teenager로 표현되는 「십대」는 13-19세를 말함) / ~를 갓 넘어 서다 be just out of *one's* teens / ~에 이미 그의 이름이 알려져 있었다 His name was known even in his teens.

**십만**(十萬) a hundred thousand. ¶ 수~ hundreds of thousands.

**십면체**(十面體) a decahedron.

**십분**(十分) ① 《시간》 ten minutes. ¶ 두 시 ~ ten minutes after two. ② 《십등분》 division in ten. ~하다 devide into ten. ¶ ~의 1, one-tenth; tithe(s) / ~의 9, nine-tenths. ③ 《충분히》 fully; sufficiently; plentifully; in plenty; to the full; well; enough. ¶ ~ 믿을 만하다 can place full confidence 《in *a person*》; have good 〔every〕 reason to believe / 실력을 ~ 발휘하다 give full play to *one's* ability.

**십사**(十四) fourteen; XIV. ¶ 제~ the fourteenth. ◉ ~처(處) 『가톨릭』 the stations of the cross. ~행시 fourteen-line verse; a sonnet.

**십삼**(十三) thirteen; XIII. ¶ 제~ the thirteenth / ~일의 금요일 Friday that falls on the thirteenth day; Black Friday / ～이라는 숫자는 서양에서 불길하게 여긴다 The number of thirteen is regarded as ill-omened in Western countries.

**십상** ① 《제격》 just right; just; the (right) thing 《for》; excellent; admirable; just the way it ought to be; perfectly. ¶ 그 모자가 너에게는 ～이다 That hat was made for you! / 재떨이로 쓰기에 ～ 좋다 It makes an admirable ashtray. ② 《자칫 …하는 경향》 ¶ (자칫) …하기 ～이다 be given to *doing*; be apt 〔liable〕 《to *do*》 / 아침에는 마음이 움직이기 ～이다 be susceptible to flattery / 생선은 날씨가 더우면 상하기 ～이다 Fish soon goes bad in hot weather.

**십시일반**(十匙一飯) making a united effort to help a person.

**십억**(十億) a billion 《미》; a thousand million 《영》; a *milliard* (F.).

**십오**(十五) fifteen; XV. ¶ 제～ the fifteenth / ～분 fifteen minutes (시간); a quarter (of an hour) / 1시간 ～분 an hour and a quarter / ～분의 1, one 〔a〕 fifteenth / ～주년 기념일 a 15th anniversary; a quindecennial. ◉ ～야 the fifteenth night (of a lunar month); a night with a full moon: ～야의 달 a full moon; the harvest moon (추분경의).

**십육**(十六) sixteen; XVI. ¶ 제～ the sixteenth. ◉ ～밀리 (영화) a 16mm (sound movie) film. ～분 쉼표 〖음악〗 a semiquaver 〔sixteenth〕 rest. ～분음표 〖음악〗 a semiquaver; a sixteenth note 《미》.

**십이**(十二) twelve; a dozen; XII. ¶ 제～ the twelfth / ～층 건물 a twelve-storied building. ◉ ～각형 a dodecagon. ～궁 the Twelve Houses; zodiacal constellations. ～면체 a dodecahedron. ～사도 〖기독교〗 the Twelve Apostles. ～십이〔12·12〕 사건 the Dec. 12, 1979, Military Incident. ～지(支) 〖민속〗 the 12 Earth's Branches; the twelve horary signs.

**십이월**(十二月) December (생략 Dec.).

**십이지장**(十二指腸) 〖해부〗 the duodenum (*pl.* ～s, -na). ◉ ～ 궤양 a duodenal ulcer. ～염 duodenitis; inflammation of the duodenum. ～충(蟲) 〖동물〗 an ancylostome; a hookworm: ～충병 hookworm disease; ancylostomiasis.

**십인십색**(十人十色) So many men, so many minds. ⇨ 각인각색.

**십일**(十一) eleven; XI. ¶ 제～ the eleventh.

**십일월**(十一月) November (생략 Nov.).

**십일조**(十一租) tithes. ¶ ～를 부과하다 〔바치다〕 tithe.

**십자**(十字) (the figure of) a cross; an upright cross (sign); a plus (sign). ¶ 적～ the Red Cross / (열)～로 〔부사〕 crosswise / (열)～형의 cross-shaped; cruciform / ～(성호)를 긋다 cross *oneself;* make the sign of the cross on *one's* breast. ◉ ～낱말풀이 a cross-word puzzle.

**십자가**(十字架) a cross; 〖가톨릭〗《십자가상》 a crucifix; 〖기독교〗 the Holy Rood. ¶ ～에 못 박다 crucify; put 《*a person*》 on the cross / ～에 못 박히다 be nailed to a cross; be crucified / ～를 지다 bear 〔carry〕 *one's* cross.

**십자군**(十字軍) a crusade; the crusaders. ¶ ～ 전사 a crusader.

**십자로**(十字路) a crossroads (★ 보통 단수 취급); X-roads. ¶ ～에 서다 be 〔stand〕 at a crossroads.

**십자매**(十姉妹) 〖조류〗 a society finch; a Bengalee; a Bengalese.

**십자수**(十字繡) a cross-stitch. ¶ ～를 놓다 cross-stitch.

**십자포화**(十字砲火) crossfire. ¶ 적에 ～를 퍼붓다 catch the enemy in a crossfire; pour crossfire on the enemy / ～를 받다 be caught in a crossfire; draw a crossfire.

**십자형**(十字形) a cross (shape). ¶ ～의 cross-shaped / ～으로 crosswise.

**십장**(什長) the chief workman; a foreman; a boss.

**십종경기**(十種競技) the decathlon. ◉ ～선수 a decathlonist; a decathlete.

**십주희**(十柱戱) tenpins. ＝볼링.

**십중팔구**(十中八九) 〔부사적〕 in nine cases out of ten; ten to one; most likely; (most) probably; in all probability. ¶ 그는 ～ 실패할 것이다 Ten to one, he will fail. / ～ 잘 될 것이다 In nine cases out of ten 〔Most likely〕 it will be successful. / ～ 내일은 비가 올 것이다 It will probably rain tomorrow. *or* It is likely to rain tomorrow.

**십진**(十進) progressing by tens; 〔형용사적〕 decimal. ◉ ～급수 decimal scale. ～법 the decimal system; the denary scale 〔notation〕. ～분류법 《도서의》 the Dewey (decimal) classification: 한국 ～ 분류법 the Korean Decimal Classification (생략 KDC).

**십철**(十哲) ¶ 공자 문하의 ～ the ten leading disciples of Confucius.

**십칠**(十七) seventeen; XVII. ¶ 제～ the seventeenth / 방년 ～세의 소녀 a girl of (sweet) seventeen.

**십팔**(十八) eighteen; XVIII. ¶ 제～ the eighteenth. ◉ ～금 18-karat gold; gold 18-karat fine. ～번 *one's* forte 〔specialty〕; *one's* favorite trick: 그 노래가 그의 ～번 이다 That is his favorite song.

**십팔기**(十八技) 18 martial arts.

**싯누렇다** (be) a vivid 〔bright, golden〕 yellow.

**싱가포르** 《동남아의 공화국》 Singapore.

**싱겁다** ① 《간이》 be not properly salted; 《맛이 없다》 (be) flat; tasteless; insipid; 《술·담배 따위》 (be) weak; mild; watery 〔thin〕 《liquor》. ¶ 싱거운 술 flat rice-wine / 맛이 ～ taste flat; be flat to the taste / 이 국은 ～ This soup needs a bit of salt. ② 《언행이》 (be) flat; dull; pointless; tedious; boring; irksome. ¶ 싱거운 이야기 a dull story; a silly talk / 싱거운 사람 a boring 〔wishy-washy〕 person / 싱겁게 굴지 마라 Don't be so dull!

**싱그레** with a gentle smile. ¶ ～ 웃다 smile a gentle smile; beam 《upon *a person*》; smile 《at *a person*》.

**싱글** 《양복》 a single-breasted coat; 《객실》 a single(-bedded) room; 《탁구 등의》 《a match of》 singles. ¶ 남자 ～ 결승전 the men's singles final (match) / ～경기를 하다 play singles / 여자 ～에서 우승하다 win in the women's singles. ◉ ～베드 a single bed. ～코트 〖테니스〗 a single court. ～히트 〖야구〗 a single (hit); a base hit: ～히트를 치다 make a base hit.

**싱글벙글** smilingly; with a (broad) smile; beamingly. ～하다 smile 《at》; beam 《upon》; be all smiles; look happy.

**싱글싱글** grinningly. ¶ ～ 웃다 grin; give a broad grin; smile sweetly.

**싱둥싱둥하다** be still lively 〔vigorous〕.

**싱숭생숭하다** scatter; wander; (be) distracted. ¶ 봄에는 마음이 ～ My mind wanders during the springtime.

**싱싱하다** (be) fresh; lively; 《젊음 따위가》 (be) young and fresh; fresh-looking; new; be full of life. ¶ 싱싱한 생선 a fresh fish; fish fresh from the water / 싱싱한 푸성귀 fresh vegetables / 꽃이 ～ The flowers are fresh.

**싱커** 〖야구〗 a sinker (ball).

**싱크대**(—臺) 《부엌의》 a sink.

**싱크로** 〖사진〗 a synchroflash.

**싱크로나이즈드스위밍** 《수중발레》 synchronized swimming.

**싱크로트론** 〖물리〗 a synchrotron.

**싱크탱크** 《두뇌집단》 a think tank.

**싶다** ① 《욕구》 《I》 want 《to》; wish 《to》; be desirous of 《*do*ing》; feel like 《*do*ing》; would 〔should〕 like to (★ would 〔should〕 like는 want보다 공손한 말씨로, would like는 모든 인칭에, should like는 주로 《영》에서 1인칭에 사용함); [부정문·의문문에서] care 《for *a thing*, to *do*》. ¶ 꼭 …하고 ～ be anxious 〔eager, dying〕 to *do* / …하고 싶은 마음이 들다 feel inclined to *do;* feel like 《*do*ing, a walk》; feel moved to *do* / …하고 싶은 마음이 없다 do not feel like 《*do*ing》; be in no mood 〔humor〕 《for, to *do*》 / 제 하고 싶은 대로 내버려 두다 let *a person* have *his* own way / 가고 싶지 않다 I don't want to go. *or* I don't feel like going. / 집에 돌아가고 ～ I want 〔wish〕 to go home. *or* I would 〔should〕 like to go home. / 울고 ～ I feel like crying. / 직장을 그만두고 ～ I intend to quit my job 〔post〕. / 그를 만나고 싶구나 I wish I could see him! / 차를 마시고 ～ I should 〔would〕 like some tea. / 차 한 잔 마시고 싶으냐 Would you like a cup of tea? / 새 자동차를 가지고 ～ I want a new car. / 콧노래라도 부르고 싶은 기분이다 I feel like humming. / 뭐 꼭 그렇게 하고 ～는 것은 아니다 I don't particularly want to do it.
② 《추측》 look; seem; appear; be likely to. ¶ 비가 올 듯～ It looks like rain. *or* It is likely to rain. / 그는 올 성싶지 않다 He is not likely to come.

**싶어하다** want 〔wish, desire〕 《to *do*》; be desirous 《of *do*ing》; feel like 《*do*ing》; would like 《to *do*》; be eager 〔anxious, impatient, long〕 《to *do*》. ¶ 몹시 …하고 ～ become eager to *do* / …와 교제를 하고 ～ long for *a person's* companionship / …하고 싶어하지 않다 be unwilling 〔reluctant, disinclined, loath〕 to *do;* hate *do*ing 〔to *do*〕 / 그 아이는 캔디를 먹고 싶어한다 The child is eager to have some candy. / 그는 몹시 여행을 하고 싶어한다 He has his heart set on taking a trip.

**싸개** wrapping paper; a wrapper; cover material; a (slip) cover. ◉ ～장이 an upholsterer. ～질 upholstering. ～통

a crowded quarrel; a squabble; 《욕먹기》 a kangaroo court.

**싸고돌다** ① 《추종하다》 form a small clique 〔an inside group, an intimate circle〕 around. ¶ 그들이 사장을 싸고도는 사람들이다 They are the ones who are close to the head of the firm. ② 《두둔하다》 shield; protect; stand by; cover up for 《*a person*》; take 《*a person*》 under *one's* protection 〔*one's* wings〕. ¶ 아들을 ~ shield *one's* son / 내가 큰 실수를 할 때면 어머니가 싸고 도셨다 When I made a blunder, my mother never failed to 「back me up 〔speak up for me〕.

**싸구려** cheap stuff 〔things〕. ¶ ~로 cheaply; on the cheap / ~를 찾아 헤매다 look 〔hunt〕 for a bargain 〔cheap article〕. ◉ ~판 selling 《*things*》 at any price.

**싸늘하다** ① 《온도가》 (be) chilly; icy. ¶ 싸늘한 바람 a chilly 〔cold〕 wind / 싸늘해지다 get cold; cool down 〔off〕 / 날씨가 ~ the weather is chilly. ② 《태도가》 (be) cool; cold; unfriendly. ¶ 요즘 그녀의 태도가 싸늘해졌다 Her attitude towards me has lately got indifferent. ③ 《시신 같은 것이》 be cold in death; die. ¶ 병원으로 달려갔을 때 아버지는 이미 싸늘한 시신으로 변해 있었다 When I arrived at the hospital, my father was already dead and cold.

**싸다**[1] ① 《값이》 (be) cheap; inexpensive; low-priced. ¶ 싸게 cheap; at a low price; at a bargain / 싼 집세 a low rent / 싼 의복 cheap clothes / 싼 주(株) low-priced stocks / 싸지다 《물건이》 become cheaper; go down 《in price》; 《값이》 fall / 아주 ~ be dirt cheap; be dog-cheap / 싸게 치이다 come 〔prove〕 inexpensive; be economical / 물건을 싸게 팔다〔사다〕 sell 〔buy, get〕 a thing cheap / 저 가게는 물건(값)이 아주 ~ They sell very cheap at that store. / 더 싼 것은 없습니까 Can you show me cheaper one? / 다른 곳에선 더 싸게 살 수 있다 We can get them cheaper elsewhere. / 물가가 ~ Prices are low. / 싼 것이 비지떡 《속담》 "Penny-wise and pound-foolish."
② 《마땅하다》 be well deserved; be none too little. ¶ 욕먹어 ~ deserve censure; need to be scolded / 그래 ~ It serves you right!

**싸다**[2] ① 《동작이》 (be) swift; quick; agile; nimble. ¶ 걸음이 ~ be quick of foot; have a quick step / 동작이 ~ move swiftly 〔with alacrity〕. ② 《입이 가볍다》 (be) talkative; flippant; be a blabbermouth 《구어》. ¶ 그녀는 입이 ~ She can't keep a secret. ③ 《불이》 burn fast. ¶ 불이 ~ The fire burns briskly.

**싸다**[3] 《포장하다》 wrap (up); 《짐을》 pack (up); 《덮다》 cover 《with》; bundle 《clothes》. ¶ 보자기〔손수건〕에 ~ wrap 〔tie〕 up 《*a thing*》 in a cloth 〔handkerchief〕 / 한데 ~ put 《*things*》 into one parcel / 단단히 ~ make a neat parcel 《of》; tie 〔do〕 up neatly / 책을 종이에 ~ wrap 〔do〕 books in paper / 물건을 신문지로 ~ wrap a thing up in newspaper / 아기를 담요로 ~ wrap a baby in a blanket / 짐을 ~ pack things; pack up / 고쳐〔다시〕 ~ wrap 《*a thing*》 over again / 도시락을 ~ prepare a boxlunch; pack 〔fill〕 a lunch box; put up a lunch / 짐을 다 쌌느냐 Have you packed (up)? / 싸 드릴까요 Shall I wrap 《them》 up? / 선물은 예쁜 종이에 싸여 있었다 The present was wrapped up in beautiful paper.

**싸다**[4] 《대·소변을》 void; discharge; excrete 《urine, feces》. ¶ 똥을 ~ have a bowel movement; [비유적] be hard put to it; have a hard time of it / 오줌을 ~ urinate; make 〔pass〕 water; piss; 《실수로》 wet *one's* 〔the〕 bed 〔pants〕 (at night).

**싸다니다** walk around; gad 〔wander, loiter, traipse〕 about; hang about 〔around〕; bum around 《미구어》. ¶ 잘 싸다니는 사람 a regular gadabout / 잘 ~ be always on the gad / 싸다니기를 좋아하다 have a roving foot / 하루 종일 ~ wander about all day long / 시험이 다가오는데도 그는 매일 밤 싸다닌다 He is out on the town every night even though the test is drawing near. / 이 밤중에 어딜 싸다니고 있었느냐 Where have you been hanging 〔fooling, roaming〕 around at this time of night?

**싸데려가다** 《신랑이》 the groom side 「provides the dowry.

**싸라기** ① 《쌀의》 broken (bits of) rice; crushed rice. ② = 싸락눈.

**싸락눈** small pellets of dry snow; hail; 「graupel.

**싸리(나무)** 〖식물〗 a bush clover.

**싸리버섯** 〖식물〗 an edible fungus of the family *Clavariaceae.*

**싸매다** (wrap and) tie up. ¶ 수건으로 머리를 싸매고 with a towel worn 〔tied〕 round *one's* head.

**싸우다** ① 《말다툼하다》 (have a) quarrel; dispute 《with》; wrangle; have words 《with》; 《불화》 fall out 《with》; be at variance 〔discord〕 《with》; be at issue 〔odds〕 《with》; 《투쟁하다》 fight; scuffle; come to blows. ¶ 싸우게 하다 set 《*a person*》 to fight 《with another》; make 《*a person*》 fight 《with 〔against〕 another》; pit 《a dog》 against 《another》 / 사소한 일로 아무와 ~ quarrel with *a person* about 〔over〕 trifles / 법정에서 ~ go to 〔contend at〕 law / 조국을〔자유를〕 위해서 ~ fight for *one's* country 〔liberty〕 / 도둑들은 장물의 분배를 놓고 서로 싸웠다 The thieves quarreled with one another about how to divide the loot.

② 《전쟁하다》 make war 《on》; wage 〔go to〕 war 《on, against, with》; 《전투하다》 fight 《with, against》; fight a battle; join 〔engage in, do〕 battle 《with》; 《1대 1로》 do combat 《with》. ¶ 잘 ~ fight a good battle / 필사적으로 ~ fight desperately / 끝까지 ~ fight 〔battle, struggle〕 on to the end; fight it out / 싸우지 않고 이기다 conquer without bloodshed / 아군은 그 고지를 점령하고자 적군과 싸웠다 Our troops contended with enemy for the hill. / 영국은 프랑스에 가담해서 독일과 싸웠다 England fought for France against Germany.

③ 《경기하다》 play a game 《with》. ¶ 정정당당히 ~ play a fair game / 우승을 걸고 ~ challenge for championship; play for a title.

④ 《곤란·운명 등과》 struggle 《against》; grapple 〔contend〕 《with》; strive 《against fate》; battle 〔war〕 《against inequality》. ¶ 곤란과 ~ contend with 〔combat with, fight against〕 difficulties / 유혹과 ~ struggle 〔wrestle〕 with temptation; resist (a) temptation / 더위와 ~ stand against the heat / 빈곤과 ~ struggle against poverty / 탐험대는 추위와 싸우며 앞으로 나아갔다 The expedition party marched on, struggling against the cold.

**싸움** 《말다툼》 a quarrel; a dispute; a brawl; a squabble; 《난투》 a fight; a scuffle; 《불화》 disagreement; dissension; 《전투》 a fight; a battle; 《교전》 an engagement; 《격투》 a combat; 《전쟁》 a war; 《투쟁》 a struggle; a conflict; strife; 《시합》 a contest; a race; a game. ~하다 = 싸우다.

¶ 치열한 ~ a severe battle / 빈곤과의 ~ the 〔a〕 struggle against poverty / 영혼과 육신의 ~ a struggle 〔conflict〕 between the spirit and the flesh / 암과의 ~ 《개인의》 a battle against cancer; 《의학계 전체의》 the war against cancer / ~에 이기다〔지다〕 win 〔lose〕 a fight 〔war, battle〕; gain a victory 〔be defeated in a war〕 / ~을 뜯어 말리다 draw the combatants apart / ~을 말리다 make people stop quarreling; smooth over a quarrel / ~을 그만두다 put down a fight / ~을 선포하다 declare war 《on, against》 / ~이 일어나다 a dispute 〔quarrel〕 arises 《among, between》; [사람이 주어] have a dispute 〔quarrel〕 《about, over, on》; 《전쟁》 a war breaks out / ~을 걸다 pick 〔provoke〕 a quarrel 〔fight〕 《with *a person*》; egg 《*a person*》 on to a quarrel; 《전쟁》 challenge (to battle); provoke war / 그것이 원인이 되어 ~이 벌어졌다 It gave rise to a quarrel. / 그들은 ~ 끝에 화해했다 They made up their quarrel. / ~은 이제부터다 The real war has not begun yet 〔is yet to come〕. *or* [비유적] The real struggle 〔battle〕 hasn't started yet. / 경찰과 몇몇 시위자들 사이에 ~이 벌어졌다 There was a scuffle between the police and some demonstrators.

◉ ~꾼 a man of combative spirit; a fire-eater. ~패 a gang of roughs; a hooligan; a rowdy; a hoodlum 《미》.

**싸움터** a battleground; a battlefield. ¶ ~에 나가다 go to war; go to the front; take the field.

**싸움판** the scene of a quarrel 〔fight〕. ¶ ~이 벌어지다 a fight takes place.

**싸이다** 《둘러싸이다》 get 〔be〕 wrapped 〔covered〕. ¶ 수수께끼에 ~ be shrouded in mystery / 그 문제는 신비에 싸여 있다 The subject is enveloped 〔veiled〕 in mystery. / 그 집은 삽시간에 불길에 싸였다 The house was enveloped in flames in a moment. / 산들이 안개에 싸였다 The hills are veiled in mist.

**싸잡다** round up; lump things together. ¶ 싸잡아(서) in the lump; wholesale / 싸잡아 비난하다 make a sweeping criticism 〔denunciation〕 / 많은 사람들이 요즘의 한국 소설을 싸잡아 재미없다고 한다 Many people complain that Korean stories nowadays are all alike in being boring.

**싸전**(—廛) a rice store 〔shop〕. ◉ ~쟁이 a rice dealer.

**싸하다** 《맛이》 taste mentholated; (be) piquant; (pepper)minty; tingling;

"sharp"; "cool"; tongue-biting; "tingly"; fizzy.

**싹**[1] ①《싹눈》 a bud; a sprout; a shoot; 《어린 싹》 a germ; 《감자의》 an eye. ¶ 싹이 트다 bud; sprout; shoot; come out the bud / 싹을 따다 pull the buds off / 나무에 싹이 트기 시작했다 The trees have begun to bud. / 식물은 봄이 되면 새싹이 튼다 Plants push out new shoots in spring. / 범죄의 싹은 일찍 잘라 버려야 한다 We must nip a crime in the bud. / 계속된 비로 보리에 싹이 텄다 The continuous wet weather has sprouted the barley. ② ⇨싹수.

**싹**[2] ①《단번에》 with one clean stroke. ¶ 종이를 싹 베다 cut paper with one stroke. ②《완전히》 with clean sweep; completely; entirely; clean; neat. ¶ 도둑이 물건을 싹 쓸어갔다 The thief swept the house clean. / 그녀는 그 후 사람이 싹 달라져 명랑해졌다 Her character changed completely since that time and became cheerful.

**싹독** ¶ ~ 자르다〔베다〕 snip (off).

**싹독거리다** slice; mince; chop; snip.

**싹독싹독** chop-chop; snip-snip; slice=slice. ¶ 종이를 ~ 자르다 cut paper up snip-snip-snip! / 이발사는 내 뒷머리를 몇 번 ~ 잘랐다 The barber made a few snips at the back of my head.

**싹수** a good omen; promise; hope. ¶ ~가 있다〔없다〕 show 〔show no〕 promise of success / ~가 노랗다《속어》 There is not a dog's 〔cat's〕 chance. / 올해 농사는 ~가 틀렸다 There is no hope for this year's crops.

**싹싹**[1]《빌다》 imploringly (as if rubbing *one's* hands up and down in supplication). ¶ 잘못했다고 눈물을 흘리며 ~ 빌다 beg for forgiveness with tears in *one's* eyes / 살려 달라고 ~ 빌다 beg 〔plead〕 for *one's* life.

**싹싹**[2] ①《베다》 with clean strokes (one after another). ¶ ~ 베다 cut off with clean strokes. ②《쓸다》 (with) one clean sweep after another.

**싹싹하다** (be) friendly; pleasant; affable; sociable; amiable; good-humored.

**싹트다** ①《초목의 싹이》 sprout; bud; put forth shoots. ②《일이》 begin to develop 〔grow〕. ¶ 사랑이 ~ love develops 〔sets in, starts to bloom〕 / 두 사람 사이에 사랑이 싹트기 시작했다 Tender feelings 〔Love〕 began to grow in the hearts of the two.

**싼값** a cheap price; a low price 〔rate, figure〕; a 《record》 low; 『상업』 a low level. ¶ ~에 사다 buy 《*a thing*》 cheap; make a good bargain / ~에 팔다 sell cheap; sell at a reduced 〔low〕 price; sell at a bargain 〔sacrifice〕; 《파격적으로》 sell at an exceptionally low price; sell dirt 〔dog〕 price (똥값에) / (다른 데보다) ~에 팔다〔~을 매기다〕 undersell 〔underquote〕 《*one's* competitors》.

**싼거리** a bargain; a good buy; 《물건》 cheap goods; a cheapie 《구어》. ¶ ~를 사다 get a bargain.

**싼흥정** buying 〔selling〕 at a bargain price. ¶ ~으로 사다 get a bargain; buy cheap / ~으로 팔다 make a sacrifice 《of》; sacrifice; sell cheap.

**쌀** ①《미곡》 (raw, uncooked) rice. ¶ 쌀생산지 a rice-producing district / 쌀생산비 rice production cost / 쌀시세 the price of rice / 쌀을 일다〔씻다〕 wash rice / 쌀로 밥을 짓다 cook rice / 쌀을 안치다 prepare rice for boiling / 쌀농사를 짓다 grow 〔raise〕 rice / 쌀을 주식으로 하다 《Most Asians》 live chiefly on rice. ②《알곡》 any hulled grain.
◉ 쌀 시장 개방(一開放) the opening of the domestic rice market to foreign suppliers: 쌀 시장 개방 반대 운동 a campaign against rice market opening. 쌀 자급(자족) rice self-sufficiency: 점증하는 농지의 전환은 쌀 자급자족을 위협하고 있다 The ever increasing conversion of farm fields 《to roads, housing and other facilities》 is threatening self-sufficiency in rice supply.

**쌀가게** a rice store 〔shop〕.

**쌀가루** rice flour.

**쌀가마니** a straw rice bag 〔sack〕.

**쌀값** the price of rice; the rice price. ¶ ~이 오르다〔내리다〕 Rice rises 〔falls〕 in price. / 정부는 ~의 안정세가 당분간 지속될 것으로 내다보고 있다 The Government forecast the rice price would remain stable for the time being.

**쌀겨** rice bran.

**쌀농사**(一農事) 《재배》 cultivation of rice; rice growing; 《수확》 rice crop 〔harvest〕. ¶ ~가 잘〔잘 안〕 되다 have a good 〔poor〕 crop of rice.

**쌀눈** an embryo bud (of rice).

**쌀뜨물** the waste water left over from washing rice; unboiled rice water.

**쌀밥** boiled 〔cooked〕 rice.

**쌀벌레** ①《바구미》 a rice weevil. ②《밥벌레》 an idler; a good-for-nothing; a ne'er-do-well.

**쌀보리** 『식물』 rye.

**쌀부대**(一負袋) a rice bag.
**쌀쌀**[1] ⇨ 살살[2].
**쌀쌀**[2] 《복통》 with a slight pain in the 〔*one's*〕 stomach. ¶ 배가 ~아프다 have a slight pain in the bowels; have a slight stomachache.
**쌀쌀맞다** 《냉담하다》 (be) cold; frigid; unfriendly; 《퉁명스럽다》 (be) blunt; curt; short; flat; point-blank. ¶ 쌀쌀맞은 대답 a curt answer; a brusque reply / 쌀쌀맞은 소리를 하다 say a harsh thing; speak heartlessly / 그녀가 왜 내게 쌀쌀맞게 구는지 알 수가 없다 I don't know why she is cool toward me.
**쌀쌀하다** ① 《날씨가》 (be) chilly; rather cold; [서술적] feel chilly. ¶ 쌀쌀한 날씨 chilly weather / 날로 쌀쌀해집니다 It is getting cooler day by day. ② 《태도가》 (be) cold; cold-hearted; chilly; unfriendly; unkind; frigid; 《퉁명스럽다》 (be) short; brusque; curt. ¶ 쌀쌀한 태도 a cold 〔a cool, an unfriendly〕 attitude; a distant manner 〔air〕 / 쌀쌀하게 in a chilly 〔frigid〕 manner; coldly / 쌀쌀하게 거절당하다 meet with a curt 〔flat〕 refusal / 쌀쌀하게 대하다〔굴다〕 turn 〔give, show〕 the cold shoulder 《to *a person*》; be short 《with *a person*》; give a cold reception 《to》 / (태도가) 쌀쌀해지다 cool off 《toward *one's* lover》 / 그녀는 쌀쌀하게 대답했다 She gave me a cold reply. / 그녀는 나를 쌀쌀하게 맞이했다 She gave me a cold welcome.
**쌀알** ① 《쌀의 알》 a grain of rice. ② 《모든 알곡의》 a grain of any hulled cereal.
**쌀장사** dealing in rice.
**쌀장수** a rice dealer.
**쌈** ① 《음식》 rice wrapped in leaves 《of lettuce, seaweed, *etc.*》; stuffed leaves. ¶ 상추쌈 lettuce-wrapped rice. ② 《바늘 등의》 a pack 《of needles》; a bundle 《of cloth》; 100 taels of gold.
**쌈노** a cord used in fastening pieces of wood together.
**쌈지** a tobacco pouch.
**쌈질** fighting; quarreling. ~하다 fight; quarrel.
**쌉쌀하다** (be) slightly bitter; taste bitterish.
**쌍**(雙) a pair; a couple; a brace; twins. ¶ 꿩 한 쌍 a brace of pheasants / 한 쌍의 젊은 부부 a young (married) couple / 쌍을 이루다 make a pair; pair up.
**쌍가마**(雙—) a double vortex of hair on the crown of *one's* head.
**쌍가지소켓**(雙—) a two-way socket.
**쌍갈랫길**(雙—) a forked road; a crossroad(s).
**쌍갈지다** divide 〔fall〕 into two parts; fork. ¶ 쌍갈진 가지 twin branches / 이 길은 여기서 쌍갈(이)진다 This road forks 〔branches (off)〕 here.
**쌍견**(雙肩) both shoulders; *one's* shoulders. ⇨ 양어깨.
**쌍고치**(雙—) a cocoon made by two silkworms; a double cocoon.
**쌍곡선**(雙曲線) 〖수학〗 a hyperbola (*pl.* ~s, -lae); a hyperbolic curve. ¶ ~의 hyperbolic / ~을 그리다 describe 〔draw〕 a hyperbolic curve. ◉ ~공간 hyperbolic space. ~함수 a hyperbolic function.
**쌍구균**(雙球菌) a diplococcus (*pl.* -ci).
**쌍극**(雙極) ◉ ~안테나 a dipole antenna. ~자 〖물리〗 a dipole.
**쌍꺼풀**(雙—) a double eyelid. ~지다 acquire 〔have〕 a double eyelid.
**쌍끌이어업** double-boat dragnet fishing.
**쌍날**(雙—) a double blade; a double edge. ◉ ~칼 a double-edged sword.
**쌍두**(雙頭) a pair (of animals); two head(s). ¶ ~의 뱀 a double-headed snake. ◉ ~마차 a carriage and pair. ~정치 dyarchy.
**쌍둥이**(雙—) twins; twin children; twin sons 〔daughters〕; twin brothers 〔sisters〕; 《그 중의 한 사람》 a twin. ¶ 남녀(의) ~ mixed twins; a pigeon pair; twin boy and girl / 남자〔여자〕 ~ boy 〔girl〕 twins; twin brothers 〔sisters〕 / 그의 ~형〔아우〕 his twin brother / ~형제 twin brothers / ~를 낳다 give birth to twins / ~로 태어나다 be born twins; be twinborn. ◉ 자리 〖천문〗 Gemini. 세~ triplets.
**쌍떡잎**(雙—) 〖식물〗 a double seed-leaf; a dual cotyledon; [형용사적] dicotyledonous. ◉ ~식물 a dicotyledon; a dicotyledonous plant.
**쌍말** a vulgar word 〔expression〕. ⇨ 상말.
**쌍무**(雙務) ¶ ~적 bilateral; reciprocal. ◉ ~계약 a bilateral 〔reciprocal〕 contract. ~조약 a bilateral treaty. ~협정 a bilateral 〔reciprocal, two-way〕 agreement.
**쌍무지개**(雙—) a double rainbow.
**쌍발**(雙發) 《엔진의》 (having) twin engines 〔motors〕; 《총의》 (having) double shots. ¶ ~의 〖항공〗 twin-engine(d). ◉ ~(비행)기 a twin-motor plane; a twin-engine(d) plane; a bimotored airplane. ~총 a double-barreled gun.

**쌍방**(雙方) both; both parties; both sides; either party (★ both는 복수 명사, either는 단수 명사 앞에 옴); 《부정》 neither. ¶ ～의 both; mutual; two-way (양쪽으로부터의); bilateral (쌍무적인) / ～을 위하여 for mutual interests; in the interest of both parties; in 《their》 mutual interests / ～의 이익〔의무〕 mutual interest 〔obligation〕 / ～의 양보 mutual concessions / 노사 ～의 주장〔요구〕 the claims of both labor and capital / ～의 동의로〔합의에 따라〕 by mutual consent 〔agreement〕 / ～이 모두 나쁘다 They are both to blame. / ～이 다 양보하려 하지 않는다 Neither will give in. / ～이 다 불행하다 Neither (of them) is 〔are 《구어》〕 happy. / ～이 다 불행한 것은 아니다 《한쪽만 불행》 Both of them are not unhappy. / ～을 다 안다 I know both of them. *or* I know them both. / ～다 모른다 I don't know either of them. *or* I know neither of them. (★ I don't know both of them.하면 한쪽은 안다는 뜻임).

**쌍벌**(雙罰) punishing both sides; dual punishment. ◉ ～규정 provisions of dual punishment. ～죄 a crime of dual punishment. ～주의 the principle 〔theory〕 of dual punishment.

**쌍벽**(雙璧) a pair of jewels; 《사람》 the two greatest masters 〔authorities〕; the matchless twin stars. ¶ 한국 시단(詩壇)의 ～ the two great poets of Korea.

**쌍봉낙타**(雙峰駱駝) 〖동물〗 a Bactrian camel; a two-humped camel.

**쌍분**(雙墳) twin graves.

**쌍생아**(雙生兒) = 쌍둥이. ◉ 일란성〔이란성〕～ identical 〔fraternal〕 twins.

**쌍수**(雙手) both hands. ¶ ～를 들어 찬성하다 raise both hands in agreement; give *one's* hearty support 《to》; support with all *one's* heart / ～를 들어 환영하다 receive 《*a person*》 with open arms; extend open arms of welcome 《to》.

**쌍시류**(雙翅類) 〖곤충〗 Diptera. ¶ ～의 곤충 a dipteron (*pl.* -ra).

**쌍심지**(雙—) a double wick. ¶ 눈에 ～를 켜고 with glaring eyes / ～(가) 나다 get 〔have〕 fire in *one's* eyes (from rage); burn with anger; flare up / 눈에 ～를 켜다 raise *one's* angry eyebrows; glare at.

**쌍십절**(雙十節) 《중국의》 the Double Tenth (Festival).

**쌍쌍이**(雙雙—) by twos; in pairs; two by two; in couples. ¶ 학생들은 ～ 나갔다 The students went off in pairs.

**쌍안**(雙眼) two eyes; both eyes; a pair of eyes; binocular. ◉ ～리플렉스 카메라 a twin reflex camera. ～현미경 a binocular microscope.

**쌍안경**(雙眼鏡) (a pair of) binoculars; 《야외·육군용》 field glasses; 《해군용》 marine glasses; 《극장용》 an opera glass. ¶ ～으로 보다 look through field glasses.

**쌍알**(雙—) an egg with a double yolk. ¶ ～(이) 지다 《어떤 날·일이 겹치다》 coincide 〔clash〕 《with》; overlap 《with》; fall on 《Sunday》 / 토요일에 두 모임이 ～(이) 졌다 On Saturday two meetings coincided. / 시험과 ～이 져서 모임에 나갈 수 없었다 The meeting clashed with my examinations, so I could not attend it.

**쌍자엽**(雙子葉) = 쌍떡잎.

**쌍지팡이**(雙—) (a pair of) crutches. ¶ 남의 일에 ～를 짚고 나서다 interfere in 〔meddle with〕 other's affairs; 《구어》 poke *one's* nose into other's business.

**쌍칼잡이**(雙—) a two-sword fencer.

**쌍태**(雙胎) twin embryos 〔fetuses〕. ¶ ～낳은 호랑이 하루살이 하나 먹은 셈 《속담》 The food is too little to satisfy *one's* appetite.

**쌓다** ① 《포개다》 pile up; heap up; lay; stack 《boxes》; put one upon another. ¶ 쌓아 올리다 heap up; pile up; pile in heaps; stack (up) / 책상에 책을 ～ heap a desk with books / 돌을 ～ heap up stones / 벽돌을 ～ lay bricks / 장작을 산같이 ～ pile firewood mountain-high / 쓰레기장에는 낡은 타이어가 산더미처럼 쌓여 있었다 Old tires were piled up high in the garbage dump.

② 《구축하다》 build; erect; raise. ¶ 담을 ～ build 〔set up〕 a wall / 탑을 ～ erect a tower / 토대〔기초〕를 ～ lay a foundation / 한강에 제방을 ～ build 〔construct〕 an embankment along the Han River / 그는 착실하게 사업 기반을 쌓았다 He has built up a firm basis of business.

③ 《축적하다》 gain; acquire; accumulate; store; amass. ¶ 경험을 ～ acquire 〔accumulate〕 experience (by degrees) / 경험을 쌓음에 따라 as *one's* experience enlarges 〔widens〕 / 덕을 ～ cultivate (religious) virtue; strive after virtue / 엄청난 부를 ～ amass a big fortune / 학식〔지식〕을 ～ accumulate a store of knowledge / 기량을 더 쌓을 필요가 있다 You need to acquire more skills. / 그건 오랜 훈련을 쌓은 다음에야 얻을 수 있는 기술이다 That is a skill one can attain only after many years' intensive training. / 좋은 교사가 되기 위해서는 여러 가지 경험을 쌓아야 한다 Being a good teacher requires various experiences.

**쌓이다** be piled up; get 〔be〕 accumulated; 《눈·먼지 따위가》 lie 《on》.
¶ 쌓이고 쌓인 원한 growing hatred; a long series of hatred; deep-rooted rancor 《against》 / 상위에 그릇이 ～ dishes are piled up on the table / 눈이 땅 위에 ～ snow piles up on the ground / 할 일이 태산같이 쌓였다 I have stacks of work to do. / 눈이 3센티나 쌓였다 The snow lay three centimeters deep. / 테이블 위에 먼지가 잔뜩 쌓여 있었다 The table was thickly covered with dust. / 방은 쓸지 않으면 곧 먼지가 쌓인다 Dust soon accumulates if the rooms are not swept.

**쌔근–** ⇨ 새근–.

**쌔비다** 《훔치다》 swipe; steal; make free with 《another's possessions》.

**쌨다** (be) plentiful; abundant; commonplace; [서술적: 장소가 주어] be full of; be strewn 《with》; [사물이 주어] be lying about (all over the place). ¶ 시장에 물건이 ～ There are plenty of goods on the market. / 그런 물건은 쌔고 ～ You can find that sort of thing anywhere.

**쌩** whistling; whizzing; ping.

**써내다** write and submit 〔hand in〕; turn out 《written material》; write. ¶ 답안을 ～ hand in *one's* paper / 원서를 ～ submit the application.

**써넣다** write in; make an entry 《into》; 《용지에》 fill out the blank 《미》; fill up 〔in〕 the form 《with *one's* name》 《영》; insert (by writing).

**써늘하다** (be) cool; refreshing. ⇨ 서늘「하다.

**써다** ebb; flow back; 《줄다》 subside.

**써레** 〖농업〗 a harrow. ◉ ～질 harrowing a field: ～질하다 harrow a field; harrow. 써렛발 the prongs 〔pegs, spikes, tines, teeth〕 of a harrow.

**써리다** 〖농업〗 harrow. ¶ 밭을 ～ harrow a field.

**써먹다** use; make use of. ¶ 써먹을 만하다 be useful; be of use / 써먹을 데가 없다 be useless; be of no use; be unfit for any employment.

**썩** ① 《매우》 very (much); greatly; exceedingly. ¶ 썩 좋은 기회 a very lucky opportunity / 그는 노래를 썩 잘 부른다 He sings very well. ② 《즉시》 right away; immediately. ¶ 썩 꺼져(버려) Get lost! *or* Get out (of here)!

**썩다** ① 《부패하다》 go bad 〔rotten〕; rot; decay; putrefy (고기가); turn 〔go〕 sour (우유가); stale (생선 따위가); addle (달걀이); corrode (부식하다); corrupt (부패·타락하다). ¶ 썩은 bad; rotten; stale; corrupt(ed); spoiled / 썩은 이빨 a decayed tooth / 썩은 과일 a rotten fruit / 썩은 달걀 addled 〔bad, rotten〕 eggs / 썩지 않은 목재 sound timber / 우유가 ～ milk turns (sour) / 썩기 쉽다 spoil 〔go bad〕 easily 〔quickly〕; soon go bad; be perishable / 생선이 썩었다 The fish spoiled. / 기둥이 썩어 간다 The post is going to rot. / 그 정부는 썩었다 The government is corrupt. / 썩어도 준치 《속담》 An old eagle is better than a young crow.
② 《활용 안되다》 gather dust; get rusty. ¶ 이 학교에서 나의 음악 재주가 썩는다 My musical ability is going to waste in this school. / 도서관에서 책이 썩는다 The books are gathering dust on the library shelves.
③ 《마음이》 become heavy; feel depressed 〔blue〕; break. ¶ 못된 아들 때문에 어머니의 속이 썩는다 The mother's heart is heavy because of her wayward son.

**썩둑–** ⇨ 싹독–.

**썩어빠지다** rot 〔decay〕 completely; rot away; be utterly rotten.

**썩이다** 《속을》 eat *one's* heart out 《with》; make *one* sick at heart; make *one's* heart break. ¶ 걱정으로 속을 ～ eat *one's* heart out with anxiety / 불효자는 부모의 속을 썩일 것이다 A bad 〔An undutiful〕 son will break his parents' hearts. / 그는 취직을 못해 속을 썩였다 His failure to find work made him sick at heart.

**썩정이** something rotten 〔decayed〕.

**썩히다** ① 《부패시키다》 rot; spoil; allow 《meat》 to spoil 〔rot, putrefy〕; addle (달걀을); corrode (금속을); let 《*a thing*》 decay 〔rot〕. ¶ 우유를 ～ let milk spoil / 습기는 재목을 썩인다 Moisture rots lumber. ② 《안쓰다》 leave 《an asset》 unemployed; keep 《*something*》 idle; let 《*something*》 go to waste. ¶ 돈을 ～ let *one's* money stay unemployed; do not put *one's* money to work / 책을 ~ let *one's* books gather dust / 지식을 ~ 「do not use 〔waste〕 *one's* knowledge.

**썰다** chop; mince; dice; slice; cut up. ¶ 오이를 ~ slice cucumbers / 얇게 ~ cut 《*something*》 in(to) slices 〔thin pieces〕 / 잘게 ~ chop 《onion》 fine; mince 《garlic, onions together》 / 그는 고기를 큼직큼직하게 썰었다 He cut meat into thick pieces.

**썰렁-** ⇨ 설렁-.

**썰매** a sled; a sleigh (대형의); a sledge (개 따위가 끄는); a toboggan (미국·캐나다의); 《경기용》 a bobsleigh; a bobsled. ¶ ~를 타다 ride in a sleigh 〔on a sled〕; be sledding; sled 〔sledge, sleigh〕 《along》 / ~를 끄는 개 a sled dog. ◉ ~놀이〔타기〕 sledding; sleighing; sleigh riding.

**썰물** an ebb(ing) tide; low water 〔tide〕. ¶ ~ 때에 at low tide 〔water〕 / 지금은 ~이다 The tide is ebbing 〔on the ebb〕. / 오늘은 아침 다섯시에 ~이 된다 The tide will begin to ebb at five today.

**썸벅** 《cutting》 with one light stroke; easily. ~하다 make a light stroke with a knife. ¶ 무를 ~ 베다 slice a radish.

**쏘가리** 『어류』 a mandarin fish.

**쏘개질** taletelling. ~하다 tell tales 《about, against, upon》 *a person*.

**쏘다** ① 《벌레가》 sting; bite. ¶ 벌이 내 팔을 쏘았다 A bee stung me on the arm. *or* A bee stung my arm.
② 《화살을》 shoot 《an arrow》; 《겨냥하여》 shoot 《at》; 《발사》 fire; shoot; discharge 《a gun》. ¶ 과녁을 향해 ~ shoot at a target / 과녁을 쏘아 맞히다 hit the target / 총을 ~ shoot; fire; take a shot 《at》 / 몸을 숨기고 총을 ~ shoot from ambush; snipe 《away, at》 / 화살로 새를 ~ shoot a bird with an arrow / 계속해서 5발을 ~ fire 〔let go〕 five shots successively / 무턱대고 ~ shoot without aim; fire blindly; try a shot in the dark / 마구 쏘아대다 fire 〔blaze〕 away 《at the enemy》; fire 《guns》 by volleys (일제 사격에서) / 쏘아죽이다 shoot 《*a person*》 dead / 탄알을 다 쏘아 없애다 shoot away all *one's* ammunition / 쏘아 관통하다 pierce; penetrate.
③ 《맛이》 be burning; be hot 〔spicy〕; 《냄새가》 stink; be offensive to the nose. ¶ 혀를 톡 쏘는 요리 spicy food / 마늘 냄새가 톡 ~ stink of garlic.
④ 《말로》 make cutting remarks; make a sharp 〔harsh〕 retort; attack bitterly.
⑤ 《쑤시다》 throb 〔smart〕 with pain; feel a smarting pain. ¶ 이가 ~ a tooth stings; have a toothache.

**쏘다니다** run around; gad 〔roam, wander〕 about. ¶ 일자리를 구하러 ~ pound the pavement 〔sidewalks〕 looking for a job / 이 시간까지 어디를 ~ 왔느냐 Where have you been roaming about until this time? / 쏘다니지 마라 Stop 「running around 〔gadding about〕 so much!

**쏘삭거리다** ① 《꼬드기다》 incite *a person* 《to an act, to *do*》; instigate; induce; egg *a person* on 《to *do*, to *something*》; stir up. ¶ 아무를 쏘삭거려서 싸우게 하다 get *a person* to quarrel 《with *another*》; stir up a fight / 누군가 뒤에서 쏘삭거리고 있음에 틀림없다 Someone must be at the bottom of the affair. ② 《무엇을 찾으려고》 rummage 《for》. ¶ 서류를 ~ rummage among the papers 《on *one's* desk》.

**쏘시개** ⇨ 불쏘시개.

**쏘아보다** stare 〔glare〕 《at》; give 《*a person*》 a fierce look; scowl (fiercely) 《at》; look daggers 《at》. ¶ 그는 나를 쏘아보았다 He gave me a fierce look. *or* He scowled fiercely at me.

**쏘아붙이다** speak daggers to; make cutting remarks.

**쏘아올리다** 《하늘에》 shoot up; send up; set off; let off; launch (인공 위성을). ¶ 불꽃을 ~ display 〔set off〕 fireworks / 인공 위성을 ~ put 〔get, fire〕 an artificial satellite into the sky.

**쏘이다** be stung. ¶ 벌에게 ~ get 〔be〕 stung by a wasp / 팔을 ~ be stung on the arm / 벌레에 쏘인 자리가 부었다 The sting of an insect has swollen up.

**쏙, 쏙쏙** ⇨ 쏙[3], 쑥쑥.

**쏙닥-** ⇨ 숙덕-.

**쏙독새** 『조류』 a Korean goatsucker; a nightjar.

**쏜살** a shot arrow. ¶ ~ 같다 be as swift as an arrow / ~같이 as swift as an arrow; like an arrow; with lightning speed; lickety-split 《구어》 / ~같이 달리다 run like a bullet shot out of a gun / 그는 ~같이 방에서 뛰어나갔다 He flew out of the room like greased lightning 〔like a house on fire, like a bat out of hell〕.

**쏟다** ① (*a*) 《붓다》 pour 《into, out》; empty 《liquid, grain》. ¶ 통의 물을 독에 ~ pour water from a bucket into a jar; empty a bucket into a jar / 설거지물을 쏟아 버리다 throw out dishwater / 쌀을 자루에 쏟아 넣다 pour rice in a bag. (**b**) 《엎지르다》 spill; drop; shed (눈물을). ¶ 소파에 커피를 ～ spill coffee on the sofa / 책상에 잉크를 쏟고 말았다 I spilled some ink on the desk. ② 《집중》 concentrate 《on》; devote 《to》. ¶ 애정을 ～ give 《*a person*》 great affection / 정력을 ～ concentrate *one's* energies 《on》; devote *oneself* to; do *one's* best 〔utmost〕 / …에 마음을 ～ give *one's* mind to 《*a thing*》; concentrate *one's* mind upon; direct 〔pay〕 *one's* attention to / 일에 전력을 ～ focus 〔concentrate〕 *one's* efforts on a task; apply 〔bend, devote, direct〕 (all) *one's* energies to a task.

**쏟뜨리다** spill; slop. ¶ 차를 테이블 위에 ～ spill tea on the table / 쌀알을 땅에 ～ spill rice on the ground.

**쏟아지다** pour 《in, out, down》; 《용솟음치다》 gush out; spout; spurt. ¶ 돈이 ～ money pours in / 비가 ～ the rain pours / 쏟아지는 빗속을 in (the) pouring rain; in a downpour / 쏟아져 내리는 눈속을 in a heavy snowstorm / 쏟아지는 비를 무릅쓰고 in spite of pouring rain / 새 유정에서 쏟아져 나오는 석유 oil gushing from a new well / 선물이 쏟아져 들어왔다 Gifts poured in from all quarters. / 그녀의 볼에 눈물이 쏟아져 흘렀다 Tears were pouring down her cheeks. / 상처에서 피가 쏟아져 나왔다 Blood gushed 〔spouted〕 out of his wound. / 눈이 쏟아지고 있었다 The snow was falling thick and fast.

**쏠다** gnaw; chew; bite. ¶ 쥐가 찬장문을 ～ a mouse gnaws on a pantry door / 쥐가 상보를 쏠아 구멍을 냈다 The mice have chewed a hole in the tablecloth.

**쏠리다** 《기울다》 lean 《to》; incline 《towards》; 《집중》 concentrate 《on》; center 《on, around》. ¶ 한쪽으로 ～ tend to 〔toward〕 one side / 모든 사람의 눈이 그에게 쏠렸다 All eyes were turned on him. / 동정〔비난〕이 그에게 쏠렸다 He became the object of public sympathy 〔criticism〕. / 그 여자한테 마음이 쏠린다 I am attracted by her. / 배가 한쪽으로 쏠린다 The boat heels 〔lists, careens〕 to one side.

**쐐기**[1] 《틈새에 박는》 a wedge. ¶ ～ 모양의 wedge-shaped / ～를 박다 drive a wedge in; [비유적] make sure; confirm. ◉ ～문자 cuneiform characters.

**쐐기**[2] 〖곤충〗 a caterpillar.

**쐐기풀** 〖식물〗 a nettle (hemp).

**쐬다** 《햇볕·바람 따위에〔를〕》 expose; be exposed to; air. ¶ 햇볕에〔을〕 ～ expose *something* to the sun / 바람을 ～《물건을》 expose *something* to the air; 《사람이》 expose *oneself* to the wind; 《바깥 공기를》 air *oneself;* take the air 〔a walk〕 / 저녁 바람을 ～ air *oneself* in the evening; enjoy the cool of the evening / 이부자리를 햇볕에 ～ let the bedding get some sun / 바람을 쐬어 잘 말리다 air *something* well; give *something* a good airing / 담요를 바람에 ～ air the blanket; give the blanket airing.

**쑤군-** ⇨ 수군-.

**쑤다** cook 《hot cereal, porridge》; prepare; make. ¶ 죽을 ～ make gruel; boil rice into gruel / 풀을 ～ prepare paste.

**쑤석거리다** ① 《찾기 위해》 ransack 《a room》; rummage 《to》. ¶ 서랍속을 ～ rummage in the drawer / 그들은 중요 서류를 찾으려고 방안을 쑤석거렸다 They ransacked the room trying to find the vital document. ② 《부추기다》 incite; instigate; egg 《*a person*》 on 《to *do*》; put 《*a person*》 up to…. ¶ 그녀는 그를 쑤석거려 그 돈을 훔치게 했다 She egged him on to steal the money.

**쑤셔넣다** push 〔shove, squeeze, cram, jam〕 *something* 《into》. ¶ 서류를 가방 속에 ～ shove 〔cram〕 the papers into *one's* briefcase.

**쑤시개** a poke; a pick. ¶ 굴뚝 ～ a chimney poke / 이 ～ a toothpick.

**쑤시다**[1] ① 《틈을》 pick; poke. ¶ 이〔귀, 코〕를 ～ pick *one's* teeth 〔ears, nose〕 / 쑤시개로 막힌 파이프를 ～ poke a clogged pipe with a pipe cleaner / 벽을 쑤셔 구멍을 내다 poke a hole in a wall. ② 《선동하다》 incite; instigate; egg 〔set〕 *a person* on 《to *do,* to *a thing*》; urge. ¶ 아무를 들쑤셔 나쁜 짓을 하게 하다 set *a person* on to evil deeds.

**쑤시다**[2] 《아프다》 feel sharp pains; be sore; tingle; throb 〔smart〕 with pain. ¶ 다리가 ～ have a twinge in *one's* leg / 귀가 ～ have a sore ear / 이가 ～ have a toothache; a tooth stings / 머리가 ～ have a splitting headache / 옆구리가 쑤신다 I have a stitch in my side. / 온 몸이 쑤신다 I feel sharp pains all over my body. / 다친 등허리가 쑤시고 아팠다 My wounded back throbbed with pain.

**쑥**[1] 〖식물〗 wormwood; mugwort.

**쑥**[2] 《못난이》 a soft-headed 〔stupid〕 person; a fool. ¶ 어이구 이 쑥아 You silly blockhead!

**쑥**[3] ① 《들어감·내밂》 (protruded) way out; (sunken) way in. ¶ 쑥 들어간 눈 deep-set eyes / 쑥 나온 눈 protruding eyes; goggle eyes / 혀를 쑥 내밀다 stick *one's* tongue out / 개구리의 눈알은 머리에서 쑥 튀어나온 것 같았다 The frog's eyes seemed to be goggling out of its head. / 그는 배가 쑥 나왔다 He is potbellied. ② 《뽑는 모양》 《pull out》 with a jerk. ¶ 말뚝을 땅에서 쑥 뽑다 jerk 〔yank 《구어》〕 a stake out of the ground / 나무를 쑥 뽑다 uproot a tree. ③ 《불쑥》 abruptly; bluntly; brusquely; roughly.

**쑥갓** 〖식물〗 a crown daisy; *Chrysanthemum coronarium* (학명).

**쑥대** a wormwood 〔mugwort〕 stalk. ◉ ~밭 《쑥이 우거진》 a plot 〔patch〕 of wormwood; a field overgrown with mugwort; 《폐허》 ruins; a wasteland (황무지): ~밭을 만들다 lay waste; devastate 《land》; ruin; turn 《a place》 into ruins / ~밭이 되다 be ruined 〔devastated〕; go to ruin; fall into ruins; be reduced to complete ruin.

**쑥대강이** disheveled 〔unkempt〕 hair. ¶ 네 머리는 ~다 Your hair 「is a mess 〔is a "rat's nest"〕.

**쑥덕공론**(一公論) secret talks; a secret conference; a caucus. ~하다 discuss things under *one's* breath; hold (a) secret discussion; caucus. ¶ ~으로 계획을 세우다 plan 《*a thing*》 through secret talks.

**쑥떡** a cake made of rice flour and artemisia 〔wormwood〕 paste.

**쑥밭** ⇨ 쑥대밭.

**쑥버무리** steamed rice cake mixed with mugwort.

**쑥부쟁이** 〖식물〗 an aster; a starwort.

**쑥스럽다** ① 《격에 안 맞다》 (be) unseemly; improper; ugly; indecent. ¶ 쑥스럽게 굴다 behave unseemly; cut a ridiculous figure. ② 《겸연쩍다》 feel 〔be〕 awkward; be embarrassed; be 〔feel〕 abashed. ¶ 쑥스러운 듯이 bashfully; self-consciously; in 〔with〕 some embarrassment / 지나친 칭찬을 받아 ~ be embarrassed 〔be made to feel self-conscious〕 by overmuch 〔an excess of〕 praise / 대중 앞에서 연설하기는 ~ It's embarrassing to make a speech in public.

**쑥쑥** ① 《들어감·내밂》 all (protruded) way out; all (sunken) way in. ② 《뽑는 모양》 jerking out 〔yanking 《구어》〕 repeatedly. ¶ 무를 ~ 뽑다 pull out radishes one after another. ③ 《쑤심》 pricking; tingling. ¶ ~ 쑤시다 prick; tingle; hurt / 팔이 ~ 쑤신다 I have a twinge in my arm. ④ 《자라는 모양》 very fast; quickly; rapidly. ¶ ~ 자라다 grow very fast.

**쑬쑬하다** be so-so; be all right I guess but nothing much to brag about. ¶ 쑬쑬히 so-so.

**쓰개** a headgear; a headdress. ◉ ~치마 an old-fashioned woman shawl once used to cover the head and upper body when going out.

**쓰다**[1] 《글씨를》 write 《in ink, with a pen, in English, about 〔on〕 *a thing,* a letter to》; 《적다》 put 〔write, note〕 down; 《글을》 compose; describe. ¶ 책을〔이름을, 편지를〕 ~ write a book 〔*one's* name, a letter〕 / 글을 ~ write; write an essay 〔a paper, an article〕 / 영수증을 ~ write 〔make〕 out a receipt / 글씨를 잘〔서투르게〕 ~ write a good 〔poor〕 hand / 잡지에 글을 ~ write for a magazine / 책에 주를 써넣다 write notes in a book / 제 이름도 못 ~ cannot even write 〔spell〕 *one's* own name; be quite illiterate / 갈겨 ~ scrawl; dash 〔scribble〕 off 〔down, out〕 / 다시 ~ rewrite; write over again; write afresh 〔anew〕; 《정서》 make a fair copy 《of》; write out / 편지에 …라고 써 있다 the letter says 〔it says in the letter〕 that… / 편지에는 그렇게〔이렇게〕 써 있다 The letter reads 〔runs〕 so 〔as follows〕. *or* The letter goes like this. / 그 책에는 무엇이라 써 있느냐 What does the book say? / 그는 시를 조금 쓴다 He is a bit of a poet. / 이 펜은 잘 안 써진다 This pen does not write well. / 대학을 나와도 편지 하나 제대로 쓰지 못하는 사람이 있다 There are some university graduates who cannot write a decent letter. / 그는 지금 새로운 소설을 쓰고 있다 He is working 〔at work〕 on a new novel. / 이 낱말은 어떻게 쓰죠 How do you spell this word? *or* What is the spelling of this word? / 그녀는 답장을 쓰기 위하여 마음을 가다듬었다 She composed herself to answer the letter. / 이 책을 쓴 박씨는 원래 신문기자였다 Mr. Park, the author of this book used to be a newspaperman.

**쓰다**[2] ① 《고용하다》 employ; take 《*a person*》 into *one's* service 〔office〕; hire; keep 《a servant》; keep 《*a person*》 in *one's* employ 〔service, pay〕. ¶ (시험삼아) 써 보다 give 《*a person*》 a trial; take 《*a person*》 on trial / 가정부를 ~ keep a housemaid / 역사 선생으로 ~ employ 《*a person*》 as a history teacher / 중책에 쓰이다 be given an important position / 그 일에 나를 써 주십시오 Use me for the work. / 그는 쓸 만한 사람이다 He is quite useful. / 당신 가게에서는 몇 사람을 쓰고 있습니까 How many people are employed in your shop?

② 《소비하다》 spend 《money, time》; consume; use (소모품을). ¶ 다 써버리다 use up (★ up은 종결·완결을 나타내는 부사); exhaust; drain; deplete; spend all 《*one's* money》; go 〔run〕 through 《*one's* fortune》 / 돈을 물같이 ~ spend money like water / 책〔옷〕에 많은 돈을 ~ spend a lot of money on books 〔for clothes〕 (★「돈을 쓰다」의 뜻으로는 on이 가장 보편적으로 쓰이며, 목적의 의미를 강조할 경우에는 for를 써도 무방함. in은 음식 또는 동명사 및 그와 유사한 행위를 나타내는 명사 앞에 쓰이는 수가 많음. 따라서 in book이라고는 할 수 없음). / 한 달에 석탄 한 톤을 ~ use a ton of coal a month / 자원을 다 ~ drain 《a country》 of 《its》 resources / 체력을 다 써버렸다 I am absolutely played out. *or* 《미》 I am quite exhausted. / 돈을 다 써버렸다 All my money is gone. *or* I used up 〔ran through〕 all my money. / 그 돈은 마음대로 쓰십시오 The money is at your disposal. / 종이를 몽땅 다 써버렸다 The paper has been all used up. / 쓸데없는 일에 돈을 쓰지 말도록 (하시오) Don't spend money on useless things. / 헛된 시간만 써버린 셈이군요 You have wasted time, haven't you?

③ 《착복·유용하다》 embezzle; peculate; appropriate to *one's* own use. ¶ 주인의 돈을 ~ appropriate 〔embezzle〕 *one's* master's money to *one's* own use / 공금을 ~ embezzle public funds.

④ 《힘·능력을》 exert; exercise; use; put forth. ¶ 힘을〔애를〕 ~ exert *oneself;* make 〔bend *one's*〕 efforts; use *one's* strength 〔energy〕; endeavor; take pains / 머리를 ~ use *one's* head; exercise 〔rack〕 *one's* brains; do brain work; 《머리를 짜내다》 cudgel *one's* brains / 머리를 너무 ~ overwork 〔overtax〕 *one's* brains / 폭력을 ~ use 〔employ〕 violence 〔force〕 《on *a person*》 / 언론 자유를 위해 힘을 ~ strive for free speech / 출세하려고 애를 ~ endeavor to achieve eminence / 그는 사회를 개선하기에 온갖 힘을 썼다 He made every attempt to improve society.

⑤ 《사용하다》 use 《as, for》; make use of; put to use; employ; utilize; 《다루다》 work 《a machine》; handle 《a tool》; manipulate 《an instrument》. ¶ 쓰지 않는 방 an unused room / 거의 쓸 수 없는 물건 things practically no use / 쓰다 남은 것 the remnant; the remainder; the leftover 《미》; 《종이·헝겊 등을》 scraps / 쓰다 남은 remnant; leftover / 쓸 수 없는〔있는〕 unusable 〔usable〕; unfit 〔fit〕 for use / ~ 남기다 leave *something* unused; 《돈을》 leave money unspent / 사전을 써서 with the help of a dictionary / 써 버릇하다 get accustomed to using 《*a thing*》 / 쓰게 하다 allow 〔give〕 the use 《of》 / 자유로이〔마음대로〕 ~ have the free use 《of》; be at liberty to use / 한번 쓰고 버리다 discard 《*a thing*》 after a single use / 자주〔유효하게〕 ~ make frequent 〔good, fruitful〕 use 《of》 / 되도록 유효하게 ~ make the best (possible) use 《of》 / 오래 쓸 수 있다 stand long use / 가스를 ~ use 〔consume〕 gas; make use of gas / 재봉틀을 ~ work a sewing-machine / 구두 만드는 데 가죽을 ~ use leather for making shoes / 학교를 사령부로 ~ use a school as headquarters / 배운 것을 실제로 ~ put what one has learned to practical use / 이 칼은 고기를 자르는 데 쓴다 We use this knife to cut meat. / 마음대로 쓰시오 You are welcome to the use of it. / 이것은 무엇에 쓰(이)느냐 What is this used for? / 공손한 말을 올바르게 쓴다는 것은 어렵다 It is difficult to use polite expressions properly. / 시간을 잘 활용해서 쓰도록 해라 Try to make the most of your time. / 이 솔은 너무 오래 써서 못 쓰게 됐다 This brush has been worn out by long use. / 아직 얼마든지 더 쓸 수 있다 There is plenty of wear in it yet. / 그건 이제 쓸 수가 없다 It is past use. / 이 만년필은 못 쓰겠다 This fountain pen is no good. / 지레를 써서 이 돌을 들어올릴 수 있다 We can lift this stone by using 〔making use of〕 a lever. *or* This stone can be lifted by

means of a lever.
⑥《채택하다》 adopt; take. ¶ 그들은 새 방법을 쓰기로 의견 일치를 보았다 They agreed that they would adopt the new method.
⑦《말하다》 speak; hold. ¶ 거만한 말씨를 ~ use haughty language / 문자를 ~ talk like a book / 스위스에서는 어떤 말을 쓰고 있는가 What language do they speak 〔use〕 in Switzerland? *or* What language is spoken 〔used〕 in Switzerland? / 무슨 뜻으로 그 말을 썼느냐 In what sense did you use the word?
⑧《술법·수를》 practice; do; deal in; play; take; resort《to》. ¶ 요술을 ~ practice magic; do conjuring tricks / 수단을 ~ take 〔resort to〕 a measure / 속임수를 ~ resort to tricks / 우리는 그 문제에 대해 조속히 손을 써야 한다 We must take prompt measures on the matter.
⑨《행사하다》 circulate; pass; utter. ¶ 가짜 돈을 ~ pass counterfeit money.
⑩《색을》 ¶ 색을 ~ have sex; copulate.
⑪《약을》 administer《medicine》; dose; use; apply. ¶ 병자에게 약을 ~ administer medicine to a patient / 이 약을 써서 감기를 뗐다 I got rid of my cold with a dose of this medicine.
⑫《대접하다》 treat *a person* to《*something*》; stand 〔buy〕 *a person*《a dinner》. ¶ 비프스테이크를 한턱 ~ treat *a person* to a steak.
⑬《장기 따위》 ¶ 말을 ~ move a piece; make a move.

**쓰다**[3] ①《착용하다》 wear《a crown》; put on; have on (★ put on은 동작, have on은 상태에 대하여 쓰임. on은 어느 경우나 adverb이며, 따라서 종종 목적어 다음에 놓이는 수가 있음. 특히 목적어가 it인 경우에는 반드시 put 〔have〕 it on이 됨); cover《*one's* head with a towel》. ¶ 우정〔자선〕의 가면을 쓰고 under the mask 〔cloak〕 of friendship 〔charity〕 / 모자를 ~ put on a hat; have a hat on; wear a hat / 모자를 고쳐 ~ adjust *one's* hat / 가면〔탈〕을 ~ wear a mask; dissemble (감정);《변장》 disguise *oneself*《as》;《위장》 play the hypocrite / 너울을 쓰(고 있)다 be veiled; wear 〔be in〕 a veil / 안경을 ~ put on 〔wear〕 (a pair of) spectacles / 모자를 써보다 try a hat on / 모자도 쓰지 않고 외출하다 go out 「without *one's* 〔without a, with no〕 hat on / 그는 모자를 쓴 채 서 있다 He is standing with a hat on. / 나는 햇볕에 한 시간이나 모자를 안 쓰고 서 있었다 I was standing bareheaded in the sun for an hour.
②《우산을》 hold 〔put〕 up《an umbrella》; hold《an umbrella》 over *one's* head. ¶ 우산을 쓰고 under an umbrella.
③《뒤집어쓰다》 pour water on *oneself* (물을); be covered with dust (먼지를); pull 〔draw〕 over (이불을). ¶ 이불을 뒤집어 ~ pull the quilt over *one's* head.
④《죄를》 be wrongfully charged《with》; be accused of wrongfully 〔falsely〕. ¶ 남의 죄를 ~ take upon *oneself* another's fault 〔guilt〕 / 누명을 ~ be stigmatized; be branded with infamy; incur 〔suffer〕 disgrace《for》; bring disgrace on《*one's* own head》.

**쓰다**[4]《뫼를》 choose the site of a grave by geomancy. ¶ 뫼를 ~ set up a grave (at a site chosen by geomancy).

**쓰다**[5]《맛이》 (be) bitter; taste bitter. ¶ 쓴 경험〔맛〕 a bitter experience 〔taste〕 / 쓴 약 a bitter medicine 〔pill〕 / 소태같이 ~ be bitter as gall / 입맛이 ~ taste bitter; frown《at》; be disgusted《with》/ 인생의 쓴맛 단맛을 다 보다 taste the sweets and bitters of life / ~ 달다 말이 없다 say nothing at all; keep silent《about》; make no response whatever / 그 소식에 입맛이 썼다 I was bitter to hear the news.

**쓰다듬다** ①《어루만지다》 stroke; smooth; caress; pass *one's* hand《over, across》. ¶ 수염을〔머리를〕 ~ stroke *one's* beard 〔hair〕 / 턱을 ~ rub 〔touch〕 *one's* chin / 어린아이를 ~ caress a child / 대머리를 ~ pass *one's* hand over *one's* bald head. ②《달래다》 soothe; allay; pacify; caress; stroke. ¶ 우는 아기를 ~ soothe a crying baby.

**쓰디쓰다** be bitter as bitter can be.

**쓰라리다**《상처가》 smart; (be) sore;《괴롭다》 bitter; hard; trying. ¶ 쓰라린 경험 a bitter experience / 쓰라린 경험을 하다 go through hardships; have bitter 〔hard, trying〕 experiences; have a hard time (of it) (★ 이 it는 별 뜻이 없는 관용적 표현임. 보기: 「빼도 박도 못하게 됐다」 We are in for *it.* / 「하룻밤 진탕 마시자」 Let's make an evening of *it.*) / 가슴이 ~ have heartburn; it wrings *one's* heart / 할퀸 상처가 아직도 ~ The scratch still smarts.

**쓰라림**《상처의》 soreness; smartness;《괴로움》 pain; bitterness; sorrow. ¶

이별의 ~ the pain of parting / 가난의 ~을 알다 know what it means to be poor.

**쓰러뜨리다** ① 《서 있는 것을》 bring 〔throw, knock〕 *something* down; blow *something* down (바람이); 《농작물을》 lodge; lay; 《베어넘기다》 cut 《a tree》 down; fell; 《철거하다》 pull down; demolish; 《지진 등이》 destroy; 《사람을》 throw 《*a person*》 to the ground; get 《*a person*》 down; floor 《*a person*》; knock down; trip up (발을 걸어). ¶ 집을 ~ demolish 〔destroy, pull down〕 a house / 그는 어퍼컷으로 챔피언을 쓰러뜨렸다 He floored the champion with an uppercut.
② 《정권 등을》 overthrow; subvert; ruin; undermine. ¶ 정부를 ~ overthrow 〔overturn, unseat, topple〕 the government; give the government the bum's rush / 폭군을 ~ bring down 〔depose〕 a tyrant.
③ 《경기에서》 defeat; beat; 《죽이다》 kill.

**쓰러지다** ① 《물건이》 fall (down); tumble 〔come〕 down; collapse; 《전복되다》 be overturned; bite the dust 《구어》; 《사람이》 fall; drop; go over; sink to the ground. ¶ 쓰러진 fallen 《trees》 / 쓰러져 가는 tottering 《towers》 / 쓰러져 가고 있다 be on the point of falling / 푹 ~ fall with a crash 〔thud〕; drop like a log; fall all of a heap / 앞으로 〔뒤로, 옆으로〕 ~ fall forward 〔backward, sideways〕 / 굴뚝이 바람에 ~ a chimney topples in the wind / 총알에 맞아 ~ fall hit by a bullet / 벼가 바람에 ~ rice plants are beaten down 〔laid low〕 by the wind / 술에 취해 ~ collapse 〔fall down〕 dead-drunk / 이 기둥이 있어서 집이 쓰러지지 않는 것이다 This post is all that keeps the house from falling down. / 바람에 나무가 많이 쓰러졌다 The wind brought 〔blew〕 down a large number of trees. / 그녀는 그 소식을 듣자 쓰러졌다 She collapsed on hearing the news. / 그는 쓰러져 죽었다 He dropped down dead.
② 《병·피로 따위로》 break down 《from overwork》; be down 《with a cold》; give way 〔succumb〕 《to a disease》; 《죽다》 fall a victim 《to》; die 《of, from》. ¶ 더위에 ~ collapse from the heat; have a heat stroke / 배가 고파 쓰러질 것 같다 sink 〔be faint〕 with hunger / 기진맥진하여 ~ break down from exhaustion / 쓰러질 때까지 싸우다 fight to the death; fight to the last / …의 손에 ~ fall at the hand of…; be assassinated by … / 암으로 ~ die of 〔fall victim to〕 cancer; be carried off by cancer / 전장에서 ~ be killed in action; fall in battle.
③ 《도산·몰락하다》 be ruined; go to ruin; go 〔become〕 bankrupt (파산). ¶ 쓰러져 가는 은행 a bank on the verge of bankruptcy / 회사가 ~ a company goes bankrupt / 내각이 쓰러졌다 The Cabinet has collapsed. / 불경기로 많은 중소 기업이 쓰러지고 말았다 Because of depression a lot of small and medium-sized enterprises have become bankrupt 〔failed〕.

**쓰레기** sweepings; refuse; rubbish; trash; waste. ¶ ~를 버리다 throw 〔chuck〕 garbage away; throw away household waste (가정의) / ~를 치우다 dispose of trash / 이 곳에 ~를 버리지 마시오 《게시》 Don't throw trash here. *or* No litter. (공원 등지에서) *or* No dumping (here). / ~를 줄이자 Let's cut down garbage. / ~는 태울 수 있는 것, 태울 수 없는 것, 부엌 ~로 분리하여 버립시다 Please sort out trash into combustibles, incombustibles and garbage before you dump it.
◉ ~더미 a trash 〔rubbish〕 heap. ~분리 수거 separate garbage collection. ~장 a dumping ground 〔place〕; 《미》 a garbage dump; 《영》 a rubbish tip. ~종량제 the volume-rate garbage disposal system: ~종량제 봉투 a standard plastic garbage bag. ~차 a dust cart; a garbage truck. ~처리장 waste disposal sites; 《매립장》 a landfill: ~의 처리, 특히 산업 ~의 처리는 ~처리장〔매립장〕의 부족으로 점점 더 어려워지고 있다 Disposing of trash, particularly industrial waste, is growing more difficult because of the lack of landfills. ~통 a garbage 〔trash, an ash〕 can; a dustbin 《영》. 부엌 ~ kitchen refuse; garbage 《미》. 인간 ~ the dregs of mankind; the scum of society. 재활용 ~ recyclable 〔recurrent〕 wastes: 비재활용 ~ nonrecurrent wastes. 음식물 전용 ~ 봉투 a 'food-waste-only' garbage bag.

**쓰레받기** a dustpan. ¶ ~에 쓸어 담다 sweep into a dustpan.

**쓰레질** sweeping (and cleaning). ~하다 sweep (and clean).

**쓰르라미** 〖곤충〗 a clear-toned 〔green=colored〕 cicada; an evening cicada.

¶ ～가 울다 a cicada sings.

**쓰르람쓰르람** chirping (of a cicada). ～하다 chirp.

**쓰리다** tingle; smart; burn; (be) tingling. ⇨쓰라리다. ¶ 속이 ～ have a burning feeling in *one's* stomach; have a sour stomach.

**쓰이다**[1] ① 《써지다》 write; be written 《with》. ¶ 이 만년필은 잘 쓰인다 This fountain pen writes well. / 이 종이에 글씨가 잘 쓰인다 This paper writes well. ② 《쓰게 하다》 get 《*a person*》 to write 《a letter》; have 《a letter》 written. ¶ 아들에게 편지를 ～ have *one's* son write a letter.

**쓰이다**[2] ① 《소용되다》 be spent; be consumed; take; cost; need; want. ¶ 집에 돈이 많이 ～a house costs a lot of money / 겨울에 석탄이 많이 쓰인다 A great deal of coal is consumed during the winter.
② 《사용되다》 be used; be utilized; be in use; be made use of; be employed. ¶ 널리 쓰이는 말 a word in general use / 쓰이게 되다 come to be used; come into use / 쓰이지 않게 되다 go 〔drop〕 out of use; fall into disuse / 맥주 만드는 데 홉이 쓰인다 Hops are used in brewing beer. / 그것은 오래 쓰이지 않았다 It has long been out of use. / 이 교과서는 널리 쓰이고 있다 The text book is in general use. / 그것은 식탁으로도 쓰인다 It 「does the duty of 〔serves as〕 a table. / 망치는 못을 박는 데 쓰인다 The hammer is used for driving in nails. / 이 (낱)말은 현재 쓰이지 않는다 The word is now out of use.

**쓰적거리다** ① 《비벼지다》 rub 《against》. ¶ 바람에 나뭇가지가 창에 ～ twigs rub against the window in the wind. ② 《대강 쓸다》 sweep lackadaisically 〔roughly〕.

**쓱** quietly 《slipping away》; 《vanishing》 under *one's* eyes; 《running out, bolting》 abruptly; 《passing by》 rapidly; 《rubbing》 lightly. ¶ 방문을 쓱 열다 open the door quietly.

**쓱싹거리다** emit a rasping sound; make a grating sound; rasp; grate.

**쓱싹쓱싹** with a rasping 〔grating〕 sound.

**쓱싹하다** ① 《착복하다》 misappropriate; embezzle; pocket. ¶ 공금을 ～ embezzle public funds / 여비의 나머지를 자기들끼리 ～ pocket the rest of the travel money among themselves. ② 《잘못을》 cover 〔hush〕 up 《the misdeeds of *one's* ingroup》. ③ 《셈을》 offset 《each other》; settle; square. ¶ 그는 며칠 일해주고 그의 빚을 쓱싹해 달라고 했다 He asked to square the debt by working a few days.

**쓱쓱** 《비비는 모양》 rubbing; scrubbing; 《일 따위를》 easily; with ease. ¶ 두 손을 ～ 비비다 rub *one's* hands / 머리를 ～ 쓰다듬다 smooth (down) *one's* hair / 일을 ～ 해치우다 do *one's* work 「with ease 〔without difficulty〕.

**쓴맛단맛** the bitter and the sweet; prosperity and adversity. ¶ 인생의 ～을 다 맛보다 taste the sweets and bitters of life.

**쓴술** ① 《맛이》 bitter wine. ② 《멥쌀술》 wine made from nonglutinous rice.

**쓴웃음** a bitter 〔grim, wry〕 smile; a forced smile (억지웃음). ¶ ～을 짓다 smile 〔give〕 a bitter 〔wry, sour〕 smile; force a smile.

**쓸개** the gall(bladder). ¶ ～ 빠진 사람 a white-livered person; a spiritless man. ◉ ～머리 beef from the top of the gallbladder. ～즙 bile; gall.

**쓸다**[1] ① 《쓰레질하다》 sweep (up, away, off); 《전염병이》 spread; sweep; 《판돈을》 sweep the (gambling) board. ¶ 방을 ～ sweep a room / 방에서 먼지를 쓸어내다 sweep the dust out of a room / 비로 ～ sweep with a broom / 마루를 깨끗이 ～ sweep up the floor / 쓸어 모으다 sweep together; sweep 《rubbish》 into a heap / 판돈을 ～ win all the money / 전염병이 한 마을을 ～ an epidemic sweeps a village.
② 《제 앞일만》 attend to *one's* own interests; show no concern for another. ¶ 제 앞만 ～ look to *one's* own interest only.

**쓸다**[2] 《줄로》 rasp; file. ¶ 줄로 ～ file / 쓸어서 매끈하게 하다 file away roughness.

**쓸데** a use; usefulness; (to some) purpose. ¶ ～가 많다 have various uses; be useful 〔utilized〕 for various 〔a variety of〕 purposes / ～〔쓰일 데〕가 있다 be useful 〔serviceable, of use〕 《for》 / 모든 것은 각기 ～가 있는 법이다 Everything has its use 〔is useful in its own way〕.

**쓸데없다** 《필요없다》 (be) needless; unnecessary; 《쓸모없다》 (be) useless; be of no use; 《사람이》 be a good-for-nothing fellow; 《군더더기》 (be) superfluous; redundant; 《원하지 않다》 (be) uncalled-for; unwanted.

¶ 쓸데없는 사람 a useless fellow / 쓸데없는 이야기 a useless 〔an idle〕 talk; gossip; air / 쓸데없이 to no purpose; in vain; unreasonably; wastefully / 쓸데없는 말을 하다 say uncalled-for things / 쓸데없는 걱정을 하다 feel 〔give *oneself*〕 needless anxiety; worry (*oneself*) 《about *something*》 unnecessarily / 쓸데없는 참견을 하다 poke *one's* nose into *a person's* affairs / 돈을 쓸데없이 쓰다 waste 〔squander〕 *one's* money 《on》 / 애써 보았으나 쓸데없었다 I have labored in vain. / 울어도 ~ It is (of) no use crying. / 후회해야 ~ It is no use crying over spilt milk. / 쓸데없는 참견 말게 That is not your business. *or* Mind your own business.

**쓸리다**[1] 《쓰레질을 당하다》 (be) swept; get swept. ¶ 눈이 바람에 ~ snow is swept by the wind.

**쓸리다**[2] ① 《거친 줄에》 get rasped 〔filed〕. ② 《기울어지다》 be leaning; be tottering.

**쓸모** use; usefulness; utility. ¶ ~ 없는 사람 a good-for-nothing / ~가 많다 be of extensive use; be very useful / 그것은 ~가 없어졌다 It has lost its usefulness.

**쓸쓸하다** ① 《적적하다》 (be) lonely; lonesome; 《황량하다》 (be) desolate; dreary; 《고독하다》 (be) solitary; forlorn. ¶ 쓸쓸히 lonesomely; solitarily / 쓸쓸한 거리 a lonely street; a deserted street / 쓸쓸한 얼굴 a cheerless countenance / 쓸쓸한 웃음 a sad 〔melancholy〕 smile / 쓸쓸하게 지내다 lead a lonely life / 말동무가 없어 ~ feel lonely having no one to talk to. ② 《날씨가》 (be) dreary; dismal; gloomy. ¶ 날씨가 ~ The weather is gloomy.

**쓸어들이다** sweep in; rake in. ¶ 돈을 ~ shovel up 〔in〕 money.

**쓸어버리다** sweep out 〔away〕; brush up.

**쓿다** polish 《gain》. ¶ 쌀을 ~ polish rice.

**씀바귀** 『식물』 a lettuce. ◉ ~나물 (a salad of) lettuce greens.

**씀씀이** expense; expenditure. ¶ ~가 크다 have large expenditures; spend money liberally / ~가 적다 be modest in expenditure; spend little / ~가 헤프다 spend money wastefully 〔lavishly〕; throw *one's* money around 〔about〕; be too free 〔generous〕 with *one's* money; spend money like water.

**씁쓰레하다** be 〔taste〕 a bit bitter.

**씁쓸하다** be 〔taste〕 rather bitter.

**씌다** 《귀신이》 be possessed by some evil spirit; be obsessed by 〔with〕 a demon. ¶ 마치 무엇이 씐 것같이 행동하다 act like a man possessed.

**씌우다** ① 《머리에》 put 《a hat》 on. ¶ 아이에게 모자를 ~ put a cap on a child. ② 《덮다》 plate 《*a thing*》 with 《gold》; cover. ¶ 이에 금을 ~ put a gold crown on a tooth; crown a tooth with gold / 뚜껑을 ~ put the lid on / 테이블에 하얀 보자기를 ~ cover a table with a white cloth. ③ 《죄를》 impute 《a guilt to》; charge 《*a person*》 with 《a blame》; put 〔throw〕 《a crime on *a person*》; pin 《a fault》 on 《*a person*》. ¶ 죄를 아무에게 ~ impute a fault to *a person;* lay a blame on *a person* / 아무에게 누명을 ~ put a slur on *a person* / 남에게 책임을 씌우려 들지 마라 Don't try to shuffle off your responsibility on another's shoulder.

**씨**[1] ① 《종자》 a seed; a kernel (과실의 핵); a stone (매실 따위); a pit (복숭아 따위의) 《미》; a pip (사과 따위의). ¶ 씨가 많은 seedy / 씨 없는 포도 seedless grapes / 씨를 뿌리다 sow 〔plant〕 seed (★ sow seed는 흩뿌림의 뜻, plant seed는 한알 한알 집어서 뿌린다는 뜻); seed 《a garden with...》 / 뜰에 씨를 뿌리다 plant seeds in the garden / 밭에 보리 씨를 뿌리다 seed 〔sow〕 the field with barley; seed 〔sow〕 barley in the field / 씨를 받다 gather (the) seeds / 씨를 빼다〔발라내다〕 remove the seeds 《from a fruit》; seed 《a watermelon》 / 씨가 생기다 seed; bear seeds; go 〔run〕 to seed / 이 씨로 재배한 수박은 맛이 좋다 The watermelons raised from this seed are sweet. / 꽃이 (시들고) 씨를 맺었다 The flowers ran 〔went〕 to seed. ② 《혈통·품종》 (a) breed (종류); a stock (혈통); a lineage; a descent. ¶ (마소가) 씨가 좋다 be of (a) good stock; be of a fine breed / 씨 좋은 말 horses of a fine 〔good〕 breed 〔stock〕; a thoroughbred / 씨를 받다 breed 《from》.
③ 《사람의》 paternal blood. ¶ 불륜의 씨 a child born in sin; a child born out of wedlock / 씨 다른 형제〔자매〕 half brothers 〔sisters〕 / 아무의 씨를 배다 be with child by *a person;* be pregnant by *a person* / 씨는 같지만 배가 다르다 They are of the same father but of different mothers.
④ 《근원》 a source; a cause; the origin. ¶ 눈물의 씨 a cause of tears

〔sorrow〕/불평의 씨 a source of complaint/불화의 씨를 뿌리다 sow (the seeds of) trouble; sow discord.
**씨**[2] 《피륙의》 woof; weft; the widthwise threads. ¶ 씨와 날 woof and warf.
**씨**[3] 〖언어〗 a part of speech. ⇨ 품사. ¶ 움직씨 a verb.
**씨**(氏) ① 《남자의 경칭》 Mr. (★ Mister의 간약형. 성이나 성명 앞에 붙여씀: Mr. An 「안 씨」 Mister An으로는 쓰지 않음/Mr. Kyŏngsu Han 「한 경수씨」); Messrs. (★ Mr.의 복수. Messrs. A and B 「A, B 양씨」); Esq. 《영》 (★ Esquire의 간약형. Edward Smith, Esq.처럼 성명 뒤에 붙임. 미국에서는 변호사 등의 경칭 등으로만 쓰임).
② 《여자의 경칭》 Miss (양); Mrs. (부인) (★ Miss, Mrs. 모두 Mistress의 간약형); Misses (★ Miss의 복수형); Mmes. (★ Mrs.의 복수형). ★ 미혼의 자매를 함께 부를 때는 the 「Miss Browns 〔Misses Brown〕이라 하고 개별적으로는 Miss Brown (장녀), 차녀 이하는 Miss *Mary* Brown이라고 구별함.
③ 《씨족》 a family; a clan; a lineage. ¶ 안동 김씨 the Kims of Andong.
④ [대명사] the gentleman; he. ¶ 씨에 의하면 according to him; in his opinion/씨의 요절은 참으로 애석한 일이다 His premature death is really lamentable.
**씨감자** seed potatoes.
**씨눈** 〖식물〗 the germinal disk; an embryo; 〖동물〗 a fetus.
**씨닭** a chicken raised for breeding.
**씨도리**(배추) a cabbage left in the field for seed.
**씨돼지** a breeding pig.
**씨름** ① *ssirŭm;* Korean wrestling; a wrestling match. ～하다 wrestle 《with》. ¶ ～의 수 a *ssirŭm* trick/～을 한 판 하다 have a *ssirŭm* match/～에 이기다 〔지다〕 win 〔lose〕 a *ssirŭm* match/～대회를 열다 hold public *ssirŭm* matches.
② 《문제 따위와》 ～하다 wrestle with 〔tackle〕 《a task》; cope with 《a problem》. ¶ 어려운 문제와 ～하다 tackle 〔grapple with, come to grips with〕 a difficult problem/사전과 씨름하며 책을 읽다 go through a book by thumbing a dictionary.
◉ ～꾼 a *ssirŭm* player. ～판 a wrestling match. 발～ ankle 〔shin〕 wrestling. 팔～ arm wrestling.
**씨말** a breeding horse; a stud(horse); a stallion.
**씨받이** 《대리모》 a surrogate mother.
**씨방**(―房) 〖식물〗 an ovary.
**씨뿌리기** sowing; seeding.
**씨소** a breeding ox; a seed bull.
**씨아** a cotton gin. ¶ ～로 목화의 씨를 빼다 gin cotton. ◉ ～손 the handle of a cotton gin.
**씨알** ① 《종란》 an egg for breeding. ② 〖광산〗 a tiny nugget.
**씨알머리** a bad seed; a rogue; a nasty fellow. ¶ ～ 없다 be nasty.
**씨암탉** a brood hen; a breeder. ◉ ～걸음 waddling (like a fat hen).
**씨앗** seeds 《of grain, vegetable》. ¶ 배추 ～ cabbage seeds/밭에 ～을 뿌리다 sow a field. ◉ ～장수 a seed(s)man.
**씨억씨억** firmly and briskly; energetically. ～하다 (be) energetic.
**씨젖** 〖식물〗 endosperm; 《배유》 albumen.
**씨족**(氏族) a family; a clan. ◉ ～사회 a clan society. ～제도 the clan system.
**씨주머니** 〖식물〗 a seedbag; 《자낭》 an ascus.
**씨줄** 《위선》 (a line of) latitude; 《피륙의》 the woof; the weft.
**씩** with a quick smile. ¶ 씩 웃다 give a quick smile; grin.
**-씩** each; respectively; apiece. ¶ 하나씩 one by one/조금씩 little by little; bit by bit; piece by piece; inch by inch/두〔한〕 사람씩 two 〔one〕 by two 〔one〕; two 〔one〕 at a time/두세 사람씩 by twos and threes/하루에 3번씩 three times a day/3사람에게 3개씩 three to every three persons/반씩 내서 사다 buy 《*a thing*》 each paying half 〔by joint purchase〕/날마다 여덟 시간씩 일하다 work 8 hours every day/각각 사과 한 개씩을 사다 each buys one apple apiece/사람이 둘씩 셋씩 온다 People come by twos and threes./똑같이 열 개씩 가져라 You each get ten./편지는 하루에 두 번씩 배달된다 Mail is delivered twice a day./이것들은 얼마씩입니까 How much are these apiece?/적군은 셋씩 짝지어 시내를 순찰했다 Enemy troops patrolled the streets in threes./이 구두들은 한 켤레에 얼마씩이나 합니까 About how much does a pair of these shoes?/조금씩 마셔라 Drink a little at a time./그는 좌우 양 옆에 아이 하나씩을 데리고 앉아 있었다 He was sitting with a child on each side of him./하나에 1달러씩이다 They cost a dollar each./오렌지는 한 개에 5백원씩이다 The oranges are 500 won each./선생님은 각 학생에게 수학 문제를 하나씩 내주었다 The teacher gave one math question to each student.

**씩둑거리다** talk idly; prattle; chatter.

**씩둑씩둑** 《talk》 idly; chattering; prattling.

**씩씩하다** (be) manly; valiant; brave; gallant; strong. ¶ 씩씩한 남자 a fine strapping fellow; a dashing fellow / 씩씩한 기상 a brave 〔valiant〕 spirit / 일을 씩씩하게 하다 do a job energetically; do a magnificent job / 씩씩하게 싸우다 fight gallantly 〔heroically〕.

**씰그러지다** get out of shape 〔balance〕; get distorted; be pushed out of shape; wobble.

**씹** ① 《음문》 the vulva. ② 《성교》 copulation; sexual intercourse.

**씹다** chew; masticate. ¶ 씹는 담배 chewing tobacco; a plug / 껌을 ~ chew gum / 음식을 잘 ~ chew *one's* food well / 씹어 뱉듯이 말하다 speak as if in disgust; speak snappishly 〔curtly, disgustedly〕 / 음식을 삼키기 전에 잘 씹어라 Chew your food well before you swallow it.

**씹히다** ① 《…이》 be chewed; be masticated. ¶ 잘 씹히지 않다 be hard to chew; 《질겨서》 be tough / 밥에 돌이 ~ bite on a grit in the rice. ② 《…을》 let 《*a person*》 chew 〔masticate〕 《on》. ¶ 어린 아이에게 밤을 ~ give a child a chestnut to chew on.

**씻가시다** wash and rinse.

**씻개** something to wipe with; a wiper. ◉ 밑~ toilet paper.

**씻기다** ① 《…을》 let 〔have〕 《*a person*》 wash. ¶ 딸에게 그릇을 ~ have *one's* daughter wash dishes. ② 《…이》 wash; be washed. ¶ 잘 ~ be washed well 〔easily〕; wash well / 그릇이 잘 씻기지 않다 a dish does not wash well.

**씻김굿** 〚민속〛 a *kut* 〔shaman ritual〕 for cleaning dead person's soul.

**씻다** ① 《물로》 wash; cleanse (세척); 《박박 비벼서》 rub; scour; bathe 《a cut》 (상처 따위를). ¶ 손〔몸, 그릇〕을 ~ wash *one's* hands 〔*oneself*, dishes〕 / 때를 ~ wash off the dirt / 잘 ~ 《물건을》 give 《*a thing*》 a good wash / 더운 물로 눈을 ~ bathe *one's* eyes in warm water / 구두에 묻은 흙을 씻어내다 wipe the mud off *one's* shoes / 더러운 스튜 냄비를 잘 ~ give a dirty saucepan a good scour.
② 《누명을》 clear *oneself* 《from》; wipe out. ¶ 씻을 수 없는 치욕 an indelible disgrace / 누명을 ~ clear *oneself* of a false charge / 그 행동으로 그는 이전의 불명예를 씻었다 By that act he blotted out all his former disgraces.
③ 《물기를 닦아내다》 wipe (off). ¶ 입을 ~ wipe *one's* mouth off / 이마의 땀을 ~ wipe the sweat off *one's* brow / 물묻은 손을 행주치마에 ~ wipe 〔dry〕 *one's* hands on *one's* apron / 눈물을 씻어 버리다 wipe *one's* tears away.

**씻부시다** wash 《dishes》 clean; cleanse; clean.

**씻은듯이** clean(ly); completely; entirely; thoroughly; once (and) for all. ¶ 병이 ~ 낫다 recover completely / 종기가 ~ 낫다 a boil is all healed up / 하늘이 ~ 맑다 The sky is as clear as can be.

**씽** whistling; singing; whiz; hiss. ¶ 바람이 씽 불다 the wind is singing.

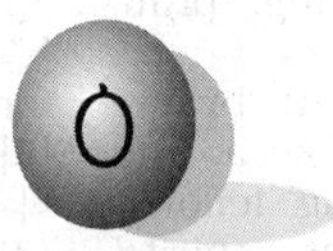


**아**(亞) 《아시아》 Asia; Asian. ¶ 구아(歐亞)대륙 the Eurasian continent.

**아**(阿) Africa; African. ¶ 아아(阿亞) 블록 the Afro-Asian bloc.

**아**[1] ① 《감탄》 Ah!; Oh!; 《놀람》 O dear!; Oh!; Dear me!; Good gracious!; (Good) heavens!; Oh, my 「goodness [gracious]! (여성이); God bless me!; Why! ¶ 아, 큰일났군 Heavens! / 아, 아버지 Oh, father! / 아, 깜짝이야 Oh, what a surprise! / 아, 지갑을 안 갖고 왔다 Dear me! I forgot my purse. / 아, 알겠다 Oh, I see. / 아, 참 반갑습니다 Oh, what a nice surprise to see you! / 아, 참 아름답군 Oh, how beautiful! / 아, 그럴리가 Why, that can't be so!
② 《비탄·실망》 Ah!; Alas! ¶ 아, 불쌍한 것 Ah, poor thing! / 아, 그것 고민인데 Ah! That's the trouble! / 아, 이제 그는 가고 없구나 Alas! He is no more. *or* Alas, he is dead and gone! / 아, 정말로 슬프도다 What a sad thing it is!
③ 《가벼운 감정》 Oh!; Well. ¶ 아, 드디어 왔다 Well, here we are at last. / 「어제 그 여자를 만났지」—「아, 그래요」 "I saw her yesterday."—"Oh, did you?" / 「그녀는 영어를 잘 합니다」—「아, 그렇습니까」 "She is good at English." —"Oh, is she?" (★ 맞장구칠 때엔 상대의 말을 되풀이함) / 아, 이제 생각 나는군 Oh, I remember it now.
④ 《말을 걸 때》 Oh; I say; Say; Look (here); 《대답》 Yes (긍정); No (부정); Well (글쎄). ¶ 아, 여보세요 Hello! *or* I say! / 아, 이 사람아 Say [I say], you! *or* Hey, you! / 아, 저기 그가 있다 Look! There he is. / 아, 지금 간다 Yes, I'm coming. (★ I'm going.은 「나는 밖에 나간다」의 뜻) / 아, 그래요 Really? *or* Oh, is that so? (맞장구).

**아**[2] 《받침 있는 명사 뒤에》 Hey!; O(h)!; Say! ¶ 복순아, 이리 오너라 Come here, Poksun. / 밝은 달아 O shining moon!

**아**-(亞) 《다음가는》 second; sub-; near-. ¶ 아류 an (inferior) imitator; a follower 《of》; an epigone / 아열대 지방 the subtropics.

**아가** = 아기.

**아가**(雅歌) 『성서』 the Songs of Solomon 「(생략 Solom.).

**아가리** ① 《사람·동물의》 《속어》 a mouth; a muzzle; a snout; a beak (거북의). ¶ ~ 닥쳐 Shut up (your mouth)! *or* Hold your tongue! / ~를 크게 벌리다 open *one's* mouth wide.
② 《그릇 등의》 a mouth. ¶ 병 ~를 열다 open the mouth of a bottle.
◉ ~질 talking; a wrangle; 《욕》 abusive language.

**아가미** the gill(s) 《of a fish》; the branchia. ⇨ 아감. ◉ ~호흡 branchial respiration.

**아가씨** 《처녀》 Miss; a young lady [girl]; a Maid(en); a damsel; 《구어》 a missy; 《부를 때》 you; Miss; Young lady! ¶ 귀여운 ~ a lovely little girl / 그 ~는 누구지요 Who is the young lady? / ~는 어디서 오셨나요 Where are you from, Miss?

**아가위** the fruit of a hawthorn; a haw. ◉ ~나무 『식물』 a hawthorn; a May tree.

**아가페** 《신의 인간에 대한 사랑》 agape (G).

**아감** 《아가미》 the gill(s) 《of a fish》. ◉ ~구멍 a 「branchial [gill] cleft. ~딱지 an operculum (*pl.* ~s, -la); a gill cover. ~뼈 branchial bones. ~젓 salted fish-gills.

**아강**(亞綱) 『생물』 a subclass.

**아교**(阿膠) glue (made from oxhide). ¶ ~질의 gluey; glutinous; colloid; gelatinoid; gelatiniform / ~로 붙이다 glue 《one thing》 to 《another》; fasten 《*a thing*》 with glue.

**아구창**(鵝口瘡) 『한의』 thrush; aphtha.

**아국**(我國) our 「country [land, nation].

**아군**(我軍) our 「forces [troops, army]; 《우군》 friendly forces.

**아궁이** a fireplace; a fuel hole.

**아귀**[1] ① 《갈라진 곳》 a crotch; a fork. ¶ 입~ the corners of the mouth.
② 《옷의 터놓은 곳》 side slits 《on an overcoat》 (like slash pockets). ¶ 두루마기에 ~를 트다 provide a Korean overcoat with side slits.
③ 《씨의》 that part of a seed through which it sprouts. ¶ 씨가 ~트다 a seed sprouts up [puts forth].
④ 《활의》 the curved-in part of an

archer's bow. 「toad.

**아귀**[2] 〖어류〗 an angler(fish); a sea

**아귀**(餓鬼) 〖불교〗 a hungry ghost; a famished 「devil 〔demon〕; 《사람》 a greedy person; a person of voracious appetite. ¶ ～ 같은 greedy; gluttonous. ◉ ～다툼 《속어》 a quarrel; a bickering; a spat.

**아귀맞추다** round out the number; make it come out 「even 〔as it should〕; bring it up to the proper amount.

**아귀세다** ① 《굳세다》 (be) strong; firm; tough; strong-minded. ¶ 아귀센 아이 a tough boy. ② 《쥘힘이》 have a strong grip.

**아귀아귀** greedily; ravenously; with avidity. ¶ ～ 먹다 eat greedily; gobble 〔wolf, devour〕 *one's* food; shovel 《food》 into *one's* mouth.

**아그레망** an *agrément* (F.); approval; acceptance. ¶ ～을 요청하다 ask for an *agrément* / ～을 주다 give an *agrément* 《to》 / 김 박사의 대사 임명에 대해 영국 정부에 ～을 요청하다 ask for the British Government's *agrément* to the appointment of Dr. Kim as ambassador.

**아그배** 〖식물〗 a toringo crabapple. ◉ ～나무 *Malus sieboldii* (학명).

**아긋아긋** a bit 「open 〔ajar, apart〕; not quite fitting (together).

**아긋하다** (be) a bit 「open 〔ajar, apart〕; do not quite fit; be not quite together.

**아기** ① a baby; an infant; a child; a babe 《시어》. ¶ ～가 사내입니까 계집애입니까 Is 「your baby 〔it〕 a boy or a girl? ② 《딸·며느리》 *one's* 「dear 〔darling〕; a pet. 「totter; waddle.

**아기똥거리다** walk with a strut; toddle;

**아기똥아기똥** struttingly; mincingly; toddlingly; totteringly. 「puffed up.

**아기똥하다** (be) haughty; arrogant; be

**아기서다** become 〔get〕 pregnant; conceive 《a baby》.

**아기자기하다** ① 《잘 어울려 예쁘다》 (be) sweet 〔charming; fascinating〕 in harmony with 《surroundings; others》; (be) harmoniously charming; 《취미 등이》 (be) tasteful; various; diverse. ¶ 아기자기하게 꾸민 방 a charmingly decorated room / 아기자기하게 잘 조화된 예쁜 색깔 fascinating colors in complete harmony / 그는 정원을 아기자기하게 꾸며 놓았다 He laid out a tasteful garden.
② 《재미있다》 (be) juicy; amusing; interesting; be full of interest. ¶ 아기자기한 이야기 a juicy story / 아기자기한 결혼 생활을 하다 lead a very 「happy 〔juicy〕 married life.

**아기작거리다** toddle; totter; waddle.

**아기집** 〖해부〗 the womb; the uterus (*pl.* -ri). ⇨ 자궁.

**아까** a (little) while ago; some time ago; a moment ago; just now. ¶ ～부터 for some time; since a while ago / ～ 말씀드린 그 분 the man of whom I spoke a little while ago / ～ 무엇이라고 말했느냐 What did you say a while ago? / ～부터 너를 기다리고 있었다 I have been waiting for you quite a while.

**아깝다** ① 《서운하다》 (be) regrettable; pitiful; [사람이 주어] (be) sorry. ¶ 아깝게도 regrettably; lamentably; sad to say / 아깝게 지다 be defeated by a narrow margin / 참 ～ That's a pity! *or* That's too bad. / 그가 그렇게 일찍 죽다니 참 ～ It is sad that he should have died so young. / 그가 이런 절호의 기회를 놓치다니 ～ It is a pity that he should miss such a golden opportunity.
② 《소중하다》 (be) precious; dear; valuable; worthy. ¶ 아까운 목숨 *one's* precious life / 아까운 사람을 잃었다 His death is a great loss to us. *or* We lost a very promising person. / 누구나 목숨은 아까운 법이다 Life is dear to everybody. / 나라를 위해서는 목숨도 아깝지 않다 I would give my life itself for my country. / 시험이 끝날 때까진 한 시간이라도 ～ I grudge even one hour until the examination is over.
③ 《애석·과분하다》 (be) wasteful; be too good 《for》. ¶ 아까운 듯이 grudgingly; reluctantly; unwillingly / 버리기는 아깝다 It is wasteful to throw it away. *or* It's too good to be thrown away. / 그에겐 아까울 정도의 아내다 She is really almost too good a wife for him.

**아끼다** ① 《절약하다》 spare; grudge; be sparing of 《*oneself*》 (노고 등을); be saving of (돈 등을); be frugal (알뜰하다); 《인색하다》 be miserly; be stingy. ¶ 돈을 ～ begrudge money; be frugal with *one's* money / 물을 ～ economize water; use water sparingly / 수고를〔비용을〕 ～ spare 「trouble 〔expense〕 / 시간을 ～ economize time; be 「economic 〔sparing〕 of time / 아끼지 않다 《물건을》 be 「liberal 〔lavish, prodigal, profuse〕

of 《*anything*》; be generous with 《*one's* possessions》; 《수고·노력을》 do not spare *oneself* 〔*one's* efforts〕; spare no efforts to 《*do*》; 《비용을》 spare no expense / 돈〔시간〕을 아끼어 쓰다 use *one's* money 〔time〕 sparingly / 푼돈을 아끼다가 천냥을 잃는다 Penny wise and pound foolish.
② 《소중히 하다》 hold 《*a thing*》 dear; value; prize; 《돌보다》 care for; take (good) care of; do well by 《*a person*》; make 〔think〕 much of. ¶ 눈을 ~ take good care of *one's* sight; save *one's* eyes / 목숨을 ~ hold *one's* life dear / 몸을 ~ take (good) care of *oneself* / 부하를 ~ treat *one's* subordinates kindly / 사람을 ~ make much of a person.

**아낌없이** unsparingly; with unsparing hand; ungrudgingly; without stint 〔reluctance〕; freely; liberally; generously; lavishly.
¶ ~ 돈을 쓰다 spend money lavishly; be lavish with 〔of〕 *one's* money / ~ 주다 give away freely; be liberal in giving / 저 사람은 자선사업에 많은 돈을 ~ 내놓았다 That man gave a lot of money freely to charities.

**아나** ① 《아이에게》 Hey!; Hey there! ② 《고양이 부르는 소리》 Here puss!; Kitty-kitty!

**아나나스** 〖식물〗 an ananas; a pineapple.

**아나운서** a (radio, TV) announcer. ◉ 스포츠~ a sportscaster. 여자~ a lady 〔woman〕 announcer.

**아나운스먼트** 《발표·성명》 an announcement.

**아나크로니즘** anachronism (시대 착오).

**아나키** 《무정부》 anarchy. ◉ 아나키스트 an anarchist. 아나키즘 anarchism.

**아낙** ① 《내간》 a woman's room 〔quarters〕; a boudoir (F.). ② ⇨ 아낙네.
◉ ~ 군수(郡守) a person who stays at home all the time; a stay-at-home; a homebody. ~네 a woman; a wife: ~네들 the women-folk; women.

**아날로그** an analog(ue). ◉ ~시계 an analog watch 〔clock〕. ~컴퓨터 an analog computer.

**아내** a wife (*pl.* wives); *one's* better-half 《구어》; 〖법〗 a spouse (배우자).
¶ 사랑하는 ~ *one's* beloved 〔darling〕 wife / 내연의 ~ a common-law wife / ~의 할 일 《do》 wifely duties / ~를 얻다 take 〔get〕 a wife; marry / ~로 삼다 take 《a woman》 to wife; make 《a woman》 *one's* wife; get married to 《a girl》 / 그녀는 훌륭한 ~가 되었다 She made a good wife. / 나에겐 ~가 없다 《미혼이다》 I'm not married.

**아네모네** 〖식물〗 an anemone; a windflower.

**아녀자**(兒女子) children and women; 《여자》 a woman; a skirt 《속어》.

**아늑하다** (be) cozy; snug. ¶ 아늑히 cozily; snugly / 그는 나를 따뜻하고 아늑한 방으로 안내했다 He showed me into a warm and cozy room.

**아는체하다** pretend to know; pretend as if *one* knew; assume an air of wisdom; speak in a knowing manner; have a knowing look; act knowing.
¶ 아는 체하는 사람 a knowing fellow; a pedant; a wiseacre; a know-it-all 《구어》.

**아니** ① 〔부사적〕 not. ¶ ~ 가다 do not go / ~ 땐 굴뚝에 연기 날까 《속담》 Where there is smoke, there is fire. *or* (There is) no smoke without fire.
② 《대답》 no; nay; "nope"; yes (긍정).
¶ ~라고 대답하다 say no; answer in the negative / 「그의 이름을 모릅니까」—「~ 압니다」 "Don't you know his name?"—"Yes, I do." (「예 모릅니다」는 No, I don't.) / ~ 천만에요 Not at all. *or* You are welcome. 《미》 / 「하나 더 드시지요」—「~ 많이 들었습니다」 "Won't you have another one?"—"No more 〔I have had enough already〕, thank you" / 「올거니」—「~안 갈래」 "Will you come?"—"No, I won't." / 「편지를 썼니」—「~ 나중에 쓸거야」 "Have you written the letter?"—"No, I am going to write it later." / 「돼지고기를 싫어하십니까」—「~ 좋아합니다」 "Don't you like pork?" — "Yes, I do."
③ 《놀람·의심》 why; what; dear me; good heavens. ¶ ~ 웬 일이냐 Why, what happened? / ~ 또 늦었니 What! Are you late again?

**아니꼽다** ① 《메스껍다》 (be) sick; nauseated; 〔서술적〕 feel sick 〔queasy, nausea〕; be sick at the stomach. ¶ 보기만 해도 ~ make *one* 〔feel〕 sick at the mere sight 《of》. ② 《불쾌하다》 (be) disagreeable; sickening; revolting; offensive; repulsive; detestable; disgusting. ¶ 아니꼬운 자식 a disgusting 〔disagreeable〕 fellow; a snob / 아니꼽다는 (말)투로 in an injured tone / 하는 짓이 ~ 《*a person's*》 behavior is disgusting / 별 아니꼬운 말 다 듣겠네 What a revolting thing to say!

**아니나다를까** (just) as *one* expected 〔thought〕; (just) as expected; as was expected; as might have been expected; as feared; sure enough 《구

어》. ¶ ~ 그는 거기 있었다 Sure enough, I found him there. / ~ 그는 나타나지 않았다 As was 〔might have been〕 expected, he failed to turn 〔show〕 up. / ~ 그는 입시에 실패했다 He failed in the entrance examination, as I feared he would.

**아니다** (be) not; no. ¶ (만일) …이 아니라면 without…; were it not for… / …이 아니었더라면 had it not been for … / …도 아니고 ―도 ~ neither… nor ― / 나는 그것에 대해 찬성도 반대도 ~ I'm neither for nor against it. / 그는 학생이 ~ He is not a student. / 그것은 그런 것이 ~ It is not so. / 그는 갈 마음이 전혀 없는 것도 ~ He is not entirely unwilling 〔reluctant〕 to go. / 이것은 상상이 아니고 사실이다 This is not imagination but reality. / 바보가 아닌 이상 그런 짓은 하지 않을 것이다 None but a fool would do such a thing. / 기적이 아니라면 그녀는 살아나지 못했을 게다 Nothing short of a miracle could have saved her. / 「이것이 시청인가요」―「아니요, 문화 회관입니다」 "Is this the City Hall?"—"No, it's the Culture Center." / 그는 거짓말할 사람이 ~ He is above telling a lie.

**아니라고** 《say》 that it is not; saying that it is not. ¶ 그는 그것이 자기 것이 ~ 주지 않았다 He wouldn't give it to me saying that it was not his (own).

**아니라도** even if 〔though〕 (you say) it is not. ¶ 설사 자기 것이 ~ 낭비하는 것은 나쁘다 It is bad for anyone to waste things even if they are not his own.

**아니라면** if (you say) it is not.

**아니면** either… or―; 《그렇지 않으면》 otherwise; else; or (else). ¶ 자네가 ~ 내가 잘못이지 Either you or I am wrong. (★ either… or로 이어지는 주어에 계속되는 동사의 수·인칭은 or 다음 주어나 오는 말에 일치함) / 자유가 ~ 죽음을 달라 Give me liberty, or give me death.

**아니스** 〖식물〗 anise (*pl.* ~(s)).

**아니오** no; yes; nay 《문어》. (★ 영어의 yes, no는 대답의 내용이 긍정이면 yes, 부정이면 no를 씀. 따라서 우리말의 「예」「아니오」와는 다름). ¶ 「이것은 네 것이냐」―「~ 그것은 한군의 것입니다」 "Is this yours?"—"No, it is Mr. Han's." / 「자넨 학생이 아니지」―「~ 학생입니다」 "You are not a student, are you?"—"Yes, I am (a student)."

**아니참** Oh!; Uh!; Well!; That reminds me.; I just thought of something.

**아니하다** do not. ⇨ 않다.

**아닌게아니라** sure enough; just as *one* thought; indeed; really. ¶ ~ 그렇다 Certainly it is. / ~ 네 말이 옳다 To be sure, what you say is right. / ~ 그녀는 미인이다 Sure enough she is a beauty.

**아닌밤중**(一中) ¶ ~에 at midnight; at dead of night; in the dead 〔depth〕 of the night; suddenly; unexpectedly; abruptly / ~에 홍두깨로 abruptly; unexpectedly; all of a sudden; like a bolt from the blue / ~에 이 웬 소란이냐 What is all this noise in this dead of the night?

**아닐린** 〖화학〗 aniline. ◉ ~염료〔색소〕 aniline dyes 〔colors〕.

**아다지오** 〖음악〗 an *adagio* (It.).

**아담** 〖성서〗 Adam.

**아담**(雅淡) ~하다, ~스럽다 《조촐하다》 (be) nice; refined; neat; tidy; trim; 《우아하다》 (be) graceful; noble; elegant; 《아늑하다》 (be) cozy; snug. ¶ ~한 가구 a piece of elegant furniture / ~한 방 a snug 〔cozy〕 room / ~한 집 tidy 〔trim〕 house.

**아데노이드** 〖의학〗 adenoids. ¶ ~의 절제 수술 adenoidectomy.

**아동**(兒童) a child; a juvenile; [총칭] children; boys and girls; pupils (학동). ¶ ~용(用)의 juvenile; 《books》 for young children / 취학 전의 ~ preschool children; a preschooler / 초등 학교 ~ elementary 〔primary〕 school children. ◉ ~교육 juvenile education; the education of children. ~극 juvenile drama; 《개별적으로》 a play for children. ~기(期) (*one's*) childhood. ~도서관 a juvenile 〔children's〕 library. ~문학 juvenile 〔children's〕 literature; literature for children: ~ 문학가 a writer of juvenile stories. ~병원 a children's hospital. ~보호 사업 juvenile protection work. ~복 children's wear 〔clothes〕. ~복지(사업) child welfare (work): ~ 복지법 the Child Welfare Law / ~ 복지 시설 a child welfare institution. ~상담소 a child consultation center; child-guidance clinics. ~심리학 child 〔juvenile〕 psychology: ~ 심리학자 a child psychologist. ~연구 the study of children: ~ 연구소 a child research institute. ~학 pedology. ~학대 child abuse. ~화(靴) children's shoes.

**아둔패기** a stupid person; a dolt; a fool.

**아둔하다** (be) stupid; dull; slow; 《구

어》 dim-witted; [서술적] be thick 〔fat〕 in head. ¶ 그는 아둔해서 늘 속는다 He is so stupid that he is always taken in.

**아듀** an *adieu* (F.); goodby(e); so long.

**아드님** (your, his) esteemed son.

**아드득아드득** ¶ ~ 깨물다 crunch / ~ 이를 갈다〔윽물다〕 grind 〔gnash〕 *one's* teeth.

**아드레날린** 〖생화학〗 adrenalin(e).

**아드리아해**(—海) the Adriatic Sea.

**아득하다** ①《거리가》(be) far; faraway; far-off; remote. ¶ 아득히 먼 내 고향 my faraway 〔remote〕 native country / 갈 길이 ~ have a long way to go / 섬이 저 멀리 아득하게 보인다 An island can be seen far in the distance.

②《시간이》(be) a long time ago; long ago; remote; far-off; far back. ¶ 아득한 옛날에 far back in the past / 내가 런던에 간 것은 아득한 옛날 일이다 It is a long time ago that I went to London.

③《정신이》(be) vague; dim; hazy; fuzzy. ¶ 아득한 기억을 더듬다 trace *one's* vague memory back / 나의 아득한 기억이 남아 있는 한 as far as my dim memory goes / 기억이 ~ be dim in *one's* memory.

**아들** a son; a boy. ¶ 대를 이을 ~ *one's* son and heir / ~답다 be filial; be a worthy 〔good〕 son / 훌륭한 ~을 갖다 be blessed with a good son.

◉ ~놈〔아이, 자식〕 my son; my boy. ~딸 son(s) and daughter(s).

**아따** Gosh !; (Oh) Boy !; My !; My goodness !; Gee !; Whiz !; Good lord !; Damn !; Dammit !; Damn it ! ¶ ~, 그 사람 키도 크다 Gee 〔Jesus〕, what a tall man he is ! / ~, 걱정도 많다 Dammit—don't worry so much. / ~, 말도 많이 한다 Oh boy, you are really talkative !

**아뜩(아뜩)하다** (be) suddenly dizzy; giddy; dazed; stunned; stupefied. ¶ 그 소식에 정신이 ~ be stunned by the news / 머리를 얻어맞아 ~ be dazed by a blow on the head.

**아라베스크** 〖미술·음악〗 an arabesque.

**아라비아** Arabia. ¶ ~의 Arabian; Arabic. ◉ ~ 고무 gum arabic. ~ 낙타 an Arabian camel. ~말 an Arab (horse). ~ 문자 Arabic characters. ~ 문화 Arabic culture. ~ 반도 the Arabian Peninsula. ~ 사람 an Arabian; an Arab: ~ 사람의 Arabian; Arabic. ~ 사막 the Arabian Desert. ~ 숫자 Arabic numerals 〔figures〕. ~어 Arabic: ~어의 Arabic. ~해 the Arabian Sea.

**아라비안 나이트** 《책이름》 *The Arabian Nights' Entertainments; The Thousand and one Nights; The Arabian Nights* (천일야화).

**아 라 카르트** 《일품요리》 *à la carte* (F.). ¶ ~ 요리 the *à la carte* dinner.

**아람** 《밤·상수리 등의》 fully ripened nuts. ◉ 밤~ fully ripened chestnuts.

**아랍** Arab. ¶ ~화하다 Arabize; Arabicize. ◉ ~게릴라 an Arab guerilla. ~국가 the Arab States. ~민족주의 Arab nationalism. ~ 석유 수출국 기구 the Organization of Arab Petroleum Exporting Countries (생략 OAPEC). ~ 에미리트 연방 the United Arab Emirates (생략 UAE). ~연맹 the Arab League. ~연합 the United Arab States. ~제국(諸國) Arab countries. 통일 ~ 공화국 the United Arab Republic (생략 U.A.R.).

**아랑곳** ①《개의》 concern; interest. ~하다 be concern about; concern oneself with; take an interest in. ¶ 그것은 네가 ~할 바가 아니다 That's none of your concern. / 그것이 네게 무슨 ~할 일이냐 What concern is it of yours?

②《유의》 attention; heed; notice; regard. ~하다 give attention 〔heed〕 to; take notice of. ¶ ~하지 않다 do not care 〔mind〕; be indifferent 《to》; give no attention 〔heed〕 to; be heedless of 《others》; care nothing 《about》 / 그는 나의 충고 따위는 ~하지 않는다 He doesn't care my advice. *or* He gives no heed 〔attention〕 to my advice. / 위험 따위는 ~하지 않는다 Dangers are indifferent to me. / 그는 남의 기분 따위는 ~하지 않고 하고 싶은 대로 한다 He does what he likes regardless of other people's feelings.

③《간섭》 meddling; interference. ~하다 meddle in 〔with〕; interfere in 〔with〕. ¶ 남의 일에 ~하다 interfere with *a person* in *his* affairs / 그의 일에 아랑곳하지 말라 Don't interfere with him in his affairs.

**아랑곳없다** be no concern of; have no interest in; have no concern with. ¶ …에도 아랑곳 없이 in the teeth of…; in defiance 〔spite〕 of… / 그것은 나에게는 아랑곳 없는 일이다 It's no concern of mine. / 그들은 나의 성공에는 ~ They have no concern with my success.

**아래** ①《아랫부분·아래쪽》 the lower part; the bottom; the foot; the base.

¶ ～의 under; lower; downstair(s) (아래층) / ～에(서) under; below; beneath; underneath (바로 아래); downstairs (아래층) / ～(쪽으)로 down; downward(s) (★ down은 동작을 나타내는 동사와 더불어 쓰이는 경우가 많음: come down 「아래로 내려오다」. beneath는 다분히 시적인 말인데, 반대말인 on만큼 많이 안 쓰임: a fly walking on the ceiling 「천장을 기어 다니는 파리」의 경우 시각적으로는 beneath가 타당하지만 「표면」이란 뜻으로 on이 사용되는 경우가 많음. 단, 열등한 것을 뜻하는 beneath는 많이 쓰임) / 나무 ～에서 under a tree / 다리 ～에 under 〔beneath〕 a bridge (★ below a bridge는 「다리의 하류」) / 눈 ～에 below *one's* eyes (★ under를 쓰면 눈 앞에 「before *one's* eyes」를 뜻함) / 층계〔언덕, 산〕 ～에서 at the foot of stairs 〔a slope, a mountain〕 / 침대 ～에 underneath a bed / ～에서 다섯째 줄 the fifth line from the bottom / 아랫방 a downstair(s) room / 저 ～ 사람 the people down there / 강 ～ 마을 a village down the river / ～에 놓다 lay 〔put, set〕 down / ～로 내려가다 go 〔come〕 down 〔downstairs (아래층으로)〕 / ～로 떨어지다 fall down; fall to the ground (지상에) / 지평선 ～로 지다 sink below the horizon / ～를 보다 look down / 눈을 ～로 내리깔다 lower *one's* eyes / 다리 ～를 빠져나가다 pass under a bridge / ～에서 받치다 support 《*a thing*》 from below / 하늘 ～ 새로운 것은 없다 There is nothing new under the sun. / 그림의 왼쪽 ～에 원이 그려져 있다 There is a circle drawn at the bottom left-hand corner of the picture.

② 《지위·연령이》 under. ¶ ～의 lower; subordinate; inferior / ～에 below; under; beneath (★ 보통 below는 지위가 아래, under는 예속을, beneath는 열등을 뜻함) / 왕으로부터 ～로는 백성에 이르기까지 from the king down to the peasant / …의 ～서 일하다 work under 《*a person*》 / ～급으로 떨어지다 be demoted to a lower rank / 그의 지위는 나보다 ～다 He stands below me in rank. / 그는 나보다 두 살 ～다 He is two years my junior 〔younger than I〕.

③ 《기준보다》 ¶ 평균보다 ～ below the average / 스무 살 ～의 사람들 persons under twenty years old / 천원 ～로는 팔 수 없다 We can't sell under 〔at less than〕 a thousand won.

④ 《다음》 below. ¶ ～와 같다 be as follows / ～의 통계표를 보라 See the statistics in the chart(s) below.

⑤ 《압박》 under 《a load》; bearing. ¶ 무거운 짐 ～ 쓰러지다 sink under a heavy load / …의 폭정 ～ 신음하다 groan under the tyranny of….

⑥ 《영향·인도·관할》 under 《the influence, the guidance, the direction, the sponsorship, *etc.*》. ¶ 이러한 정세 ～서 under such a situation.

⑦ 《하체》 the lower part of the body; 《음부》 the genitalia; private parts. ¶ ～를 주무르다 massage the lower part of the body.

**아래옷** lower garment; bottom piece; the bottom(s) of a garment.

**아래위** the lower and upper parts; up and down; top and bottom; above and below. ¶ ～로 움직이다 move up and down / 아무를 ～로 훑어보다 look *a person* up and down.
◉ ～턱 distinction between seniors and juniors 〔superiors and inferiors, right and wrong〕.

**아래윗막이** ① 《막은 부분》 end pieces; top and bottom pieces. ② 《옷》 upper and lower (garments); top(s) and bottom(s). 「an *ensemble* (F.).

**아래윗벌** a suit 《of clothes》; an outfit;

**아래짝** the lower one 《of a pair set》; the lower piece 《of a 2-part object》; the bottom member.

**아래쪽** ① 《아래 방향》 down; lower position 〔direction〕. ¶ ～으로 downward(s); down / ～을 보다 look down / 강의 6백미터 ～에 다리가 있다 There is a bridge 600 meters down 〔below〕 the river. ② 《남쪽》 the south.

**아래채** an outhouse (near the gate).

**아래층**(―層) the downstairs. ¶ ～방 a downstairs room / ～으로 내려가다 go downstairs / ～에서 기다리다 wait downstairs.

**아래턱** the lower jaw; the underjaw. ¶ ～을 쓰다듬다 stroke *one's* chin.

**아래통** the girth of the lower part. ¶ ～이 가늘다 have a slender waist.

**아랫길** ① 《길》 the low(er) road; the way below. ② 《품질》 inferior quality; poorer grade.

**아랫녘** 《영남·호남 지방》 the southern part of Korea, especially the Kyŏngsang, Chŏlla Province; 《남쪽》 the south.

**아랫눈썹** the lower eyelashes.

**아랫니** the lower teeth.

**아랫대**(―代) later generations.

**아랫도리** 《하체》 the lower half of the

body; [부사적] from the waist down; 《옷》 lower garment(s); bottom(s).

**아랫동아리** ① the lower part 《of *a thing*》. ¶ 나무의 ~ the base of a tree. ② = 아랫도리.

**아랫막이** ① 《막은 부분》 bottom end-piece; bottom piece. ② 《옷》 bottom (garment); bottoms.

**아랫머리** the bottom end; the bottom (of two similar ends).

**아랫목** the place on the *ondol* floor near to the fireplace; the warmer part of an *ondol* floor.

**아랫반**(一班) a lower 「class 〔grade〕.

**아랫방**(房) a room of outhouse; a detached room.

**아랫배** the underbelly; the abdomen; the stomach. ¶ ~가 아프다 have 〔feel〕 pain in the abdomen / ~에 힘을 주다 put *one's* whole strength in the abdomen.

**아랫벌** the lower garment.

**아랫사람** ① 《손아래》 *one's* junior. ② 《지위의》 *one's* inferior; a subordinate; an underling. ¶ ~이 되어 일하다 work under 《*a person*》. 「outhouse.

**아랫사랑**(一舍廊) a guest room in the

**아랫수염**(一鬚髥) a beard 《on *one's* chin》; a goatee. ⇨턱수염. ¶ ~을 기르다 have 〔wear〕 a beard.

**아랫입술** the lower lip. ¶ ~을 깨물다 bite *one's* lower lip.

**아랫잇몸** the lower gum.

**아랫자리** ① 《하위자의 자리》 the seats for *one's* juniors 〔subordinates〕; 《아래에 있는 자리》 the seat below. ② 〖수학〗 one position down; the next decimal position.

**아랫집** the house just below.

**아량**(雅量) tolerance; generosity; magnanimity; broad-mindedness. ¶ ~이 있는 magnanimous; generous 《to》; broad-minded / ~이 없는 intolerant; narrow-minded / ~을 보이다 show *oneself* to be magnanimous 〔generous〕.

**아련하다** (be) dim; vague; faint; hazy; indistinct. ¶ 아련하게 dimly; vaguely; faintly; hazily; indistinctly / 기억이 ~ remember dimly; have a dim memory 《of》; have a 「faint 〔hazy〕 recollection 《of》 / 아련한 기억을 더듬다 trace back a vague memory / 나무들 사이로 저멀리 바다가 아련히 보였다 We could glimpse the distant ocean through the trees. / 멀리 송악산이 아련히 보인다 Mt. Songak can be seen dimly in the distance.

**아령**(啞鈴) 《a pair of》 dumbbells. ◉ ~체조 exercise with dumbbells.

**아로새기다** engrave 〔carve〕 elaborately; make an elaborate bas-relief. ¶ 마음에 ~ bear 〔keep〕 《*something*》 in mind; take 《the advice》 to heart; have 《*something*》 stamped 〔engraved〕 on *one's* mind / 그것은 내 마음에 깊이 아로새겨져 있다 It is written indelibly on my heart. *or* It is 「engraved 〔etched〕 on my mind.

**아롱다롱하다** (be) spotted; dotted; speckled. ¶ 무늬가 아롱다롱한 천 cloth speckled with designs.

**아롱아롱하다** (be) variegated; mottled.

**아롱지다** (be) variegated; mottled.

**아뢰다** tell 〔inform〕 a superior.

**아류**(亞流) 《추종하는 사람》 a follower; an adherent; 《모방자》 an (inferior) imitator; a bad second; an epigon(e).

**아르** 《면적의 단위》 an are (=100 sq. meters).

**아르누보** [< *art nouveau* (F.)] New Art.

**아르바이트** [< *Arbeit* (G.)] a side job; a part-time job; work 〔a job〕 on the side; 《구어》 moonlighting (학생 이외의). ~하다 do a side job; work at a part-time; 《자기의 직업 이외에》 take on 「another 〔an extra〕 job; moonlight 《구어》. ¶ ~하는 사람 a part-timer / ~를 하고 있다 have a job on the side / ~자리를 찾다 find 〔get〕 a job (on the side) / ~로 학비를 벌다 work for *one's* school expenses / ~를 해서 번 돈으로 금강산 여행을 가다 go on a trip to Mt. Geumgang with the money *one* has earned by working part-time / 나는 식당에서 ~를 하고 있다 I'm working part-time at the restaurant. / 그는 ~를 하여 대학을 마쳤다 He has worked his way through college. / 그녀는 여름방학에 백화점에서 ~를 했다 She worked 「at 〔in〕 a department store during the summer vacation.

◉ ~학생 a working student; a student worker: ~ 학생을 고용하다 employ a student worker.

**아르에이치** Rh (★ rhesus의 생략). ¶ ~식 혈액형 (blood types of) Rh groups. ◉ ~마이너스 Rh negative(생략 Rh−). ~인자 〖의학〗 an Rh 〔a rhesus〕 factor; Rh antigen. ~플러스 Rh positive(생략 Rh+).

**아르오티시** 《학생 군사 교육단》 R.O.T.C. [< *R*eserve *O*fficers' *T*raining *C*orps]

**아르키메데스** 《수학자·물리학자》 Archimedes (287?-212 B.C.). ¶ ～의 원리 the Archimedean 〔Archimedes'〕 principle.

**아르헨티나** Argentina; the Argentine. ¶ ～의 Argentine. ◉ ～공화국 the Argentine Republic. ～사람 an Argentine; an Argentinean.

**아른거리다** ⇨어른거리다.

**아름** the span of both arms; an armstretch. ¶ 한 ～의 책 an armful of books / 이 나무는 세 ～이 된다 This tree measures three spans of a man's arms around.

**아름다움** beauty. ⇨미(美). ¶ …의 ～에 매료되다 be struck by the beauty of…; fall under the spell of 《*a person's*》 charm.

**아름답다** (be) beautiful; pretty; 《경치가》 (be) picturesque; 《사랑스럽다》 (be) charming; lovely; 《훌륭하다》 (be) fine; 《용모가》 (be) handsome; good-looking. ¶ 아름다운 마음 a pure heart / 아름다운 목소리 《in》 a sweet voice / 아름다운 곳 a beautiful place; a place of great beauty / 아름다운 여자 a beautiful girl / 아름다운 이야기 a beautiful story / 아름다운 인정 human kindness / 아름다운 행실 exemplary conduct / 모양이 아름다운 shapely; well-formed / 마음이 ～ have a heart of gold; be noble-minded 〔sweet-natured〕 (★ 주로 여성에게 쓰임); be pure in 〔of〕 heart / 아름답게 beautifully; charmingly / 아름답게 하다 beautify; make 《*a thing*》 beautiful 〔pretty〕 / 아름답게 보이다 look pretty 〔beautiful〕 / 아름답게 차려입다 dress *oneself* colorfully / 그 산은 경치가 ～ That hill has 〔commands〕 a fine view. / 그 꽃 정말이지 아름답기도 하다 What a beautiful 〔lovely〕 flower (this is)! / 그 도시는 경치가 아름다워서 유명하다 The town is famous for its scenic beauty.

**아름드리** an armful. ◉ ～나무 a tree measuring more than an arm's span around.

**아리다** ① 《상처 등이》 smart; tingle; burn; hurt; (be) smarting; prickly. ¶ 목이 ～ *one's* throat tingles / 상처가 ～ have a tingling pain / 연기로 눈이 ～ *one's* eyes smart from the smoke / 상처가 아직도 ～ The wound still smarts. ② 《맛이》 (be) pungent; acrid; sharp; [서술적] be biting to the taste. ¶ 맛이 ～ taste sharp 〔acrid〕; have a tingling 〔biting, burning〕 taste.

**아리땁다** 《여자가》 (be) lovely; charming; attractive; fair. ¶ 아리따운 처녀 a charming young lady.

**아리송하다** 《분간할 수 없다》 (be) indistinct; indistinguishable; [서술적] be not clear; do not know what's what; 《모호하다》 (be) ambiguous; equivocal; vague. ¶ 아리송한 대답을 하다 give an equivocal 〔a vague〕 answer; give a noncommital answer / 그는 생각을 분명히 나타내고 있어 그의 의도에 아리송한 점은 없다 He expresses himself clearly and leaves no uncertainty about his intentions.

**아리아** 〖음악〗 an aria.

**아리안** 《인종》 Aryan. ◉ ～족〔인종〕 the Aryan races; the Aryans.

**아릿하다** (be) acrid; pungent; biting; sharp; tasting; tingling; [서술적] sting the tip of *one's* tongue. ¶ 아릿한 맛이 나다 taste acrid; be biting 〔tingling〕 to the tongue.

**아마**(亞麻) 〖식물〗 flax. ¶ ～의 flaxen. ◉ ～실 flax yarn 〔line〕. ～인 flaxseed; linseed. ～(인)유 linseed oil. ～포 linen.

**아마**[1] ⇨아마추어.

**아마**[2] 《대개》 perhaps; maybe; probably; (very 〔most〕) likely; possibly; as likely as not; 《십중팔구》 in all likelihood 〔probability〕; ten to one; 《걱정되어》 I am afraid; I fear; 《의심될 때》 I suspect. (★ maybe 영국에서는 좀처럼 자주 쓰이지 않지만, 미국 구어에서는 흔히 쓰임. perhaps와 더불어 가능성이 적을 때 씀. probably는 가능성이 많을 때, possibly는 perhaps보다 가망이 더 적을 때 씀.)

¶ ～ 그럴테죠 Maybe so. *or* I suppose so. / ～ 그럴지도 모른다 It may perhaps be so. / ～ 그는 영국인인가 보다 Perhaps he is English. / ～ 그는 못 올 겁니다 He probably won't be able to come. / ～ 그는 20살쯤일 거다 My guess is (that) he's about twenty. / ～ (자네한테) 갈 수 없을 걸세 I am afraid I shall not come. / 그는 ～ 떠났을지도 모른다 He may have started. *or* It may be that he has already started. / ～ 그는 지금쯤은 집에 닿았을 게다 He must have arrived home by now. / ～ 그는 실패할 게다 The chances 〔odds〕 are that he will fail. / ～ 그는 다음 열차로 오겠지 He'd probably come by the next train. / ～ 그는 내일은 돌아올 겁니다 He will very 〔most〕 likely come back tomorrow. / ～ 그사람은 그걸 알아채지 못하고 있을 테지 Most probably he is unaware of it. / ~ 그 여자에겐 무죄판결이 내려질 테죠 In all likelihood she will be found innocent. / 그 여자는 ~ 동의하지 않을 걸세 There is little likelihood of her giving consent to it. / ~ 이것은 이런 종류의 것으로는 최상의 것일 게다 This is the best of the kind, I dare say. / ~ 그의 짓일 테죠 He did it, I suspect. / 그것은 ~ 지난달 17일이었을 거야 If I remember rightly 〔As I recall〕, it was on the 17th of last month.

**아마도** perhaps; indeed; quite probably 〔likely〕; like as not.

**아마릴리스** 〖식물〗 an amaryllis.

**아마존** an Amazon. ¶ ~(유역)의 Amazonian. ◉ ~강 the Amazon (River).

**아마추어** an amateur; a dabbler; a nonprofessional; the inexperienced. ¶ ~다운 amateurish / ~의 수준을 벗어나다 [일이 주어] be free from amateurishness; be far from amateurish; be as good as professional; [사람이 주어] have more than amateur's skill / 그는 ~에 지나지 않다 He is just 〔only〕 an amateur.

◉ ~규정 requirements for amateurship. ~무선국 an amateur radio station. ~무선사 a radio amateur; a (radio) ham. ~선수 an amateur 《tennis》 player. ~스포츠 amateur sports. ~정신 (the spirit of ) amateurism. ~화가 a Sunday painter (일요화가).

**아말감** 〖화학〗 amalgam. ◉ ~법 the amalgamation process. ~은 silver amalgam.

**아메리카** America; the United States (of America) (생략 U.S.A.). ⇨ 미국.

◉ ~주〔대륙〕 the American continent.

**아메리칸** American. ◉ ~리그 the American League. ~인디언 American Indians; the Red Indians; Native Americans. ~풋볼 (American) football.

**아메바** 〖동물〗 an amoeba 〔《미》 ameba〕 (*pl.* ~s, -bae). ◉ ~성 이질 amoebic dysentery. ~운동 amoeboid movement.

**아멘** 〖기독교〗 Amen!; So be it!

**아명**(兒名) *one's* baby 〔childhood〕 name.

**아모스서**(—書) 〖성서〗 the Book of Amos; 《약칭》 Amos.

**아목**(亞目) 〖동물〗 (biological) suborder.

**아무** ① 《누구》 any person; anyone; anybody; 《부정》 no one; nobody; none. ¶ ~라도 할 수 있다 Anyone can do it. / ~나 보러 와도 좋다 Anybody may come and see it. / ~한테도 말하면 안 돼 You must not tell anybody. / ~도 모른다 Nobody knows that. *or* No one can tell. / 나는 조수 한 사람이 필요하다. ~라도 좋다 I want an assistant. Anyone will do. / 너처럼 노래를 잘 하는 사람은 ~도 없다 Nobody else can sing so well as you. / ~도 그를 도와 주려는 사람은 없었다 Nobody would offer to help him. / 그는 수학에서는 ~한테도 뒤지지 않는다 He is second to none in mathematics. / ~도 오지 않았다 No one came. *or* Not a single person came. / 그 집에는 ~도 없었다 There was nobody in the house. / ~도 그곳에 가지 않았다 No one 〔Nobody〕 went there. (★ 윗 문장을 Anybody did not go there. 라고는 할 수 없음: 영어에서는 한 절 속에서 any ... not의 어순은 취할 수 없음: I did not think anyone could solve the problem.「아무도 그 문제를 풀 수 없었다고 생각했다」라고는 할 수 있음) / ~도 출석지 않았다 There were none present. (★ *none*은 복수형으로서 흔히 쓰임: None were 〔was〕 of any help to me.「누구 하나 내게 도움이 안 되었다」. 그러나 "not one"의 뜻을 명시해야만 할 경우에는 단수형 동사를 씀: There were three of us in the car, but *none* was injured.「차 안에는 3명이 있었는데 한 명도 다치지 않았다」/ There is none to help me.「나를 도와 주는 사람은 단 한 사람도 없다」).

② [명사 앞에서] any; "any old"; 《부정》 not at all; no. ¶ ~ 것(도) anything (at all); "any old thing" / ~ 것도 않고 without doing anything / ~ 생각 없이 unintentionally / ~ 까닭 없이 for nothing; without any reason / ~ 어려움도 없이 without any difficulty / ~ 것도 아닌 일 a trifling matter / ~짝에도 못 쓸 놈 a good-for-nothing (fellow) / ~ 상관도 없다 have no relation 〔connection〕 whatever 《with》; have nothing to do 《with》; 《미》 be through 《with》 / ~ 때나 오십시오 Come and see me any time. / 그런 일은 알고 있어도 ~ 소용이 없다 It is no use learning such a thing. / 차린 것은 ~ 것도 없습니다 There is not much of a dinner. / 그는 ~ 말도 하지 않았다 He didn't utter a single word. / 그녀는 나의 애인도 ~도 아니다 She is anything but my lover.

③ 《아무개》 So-and-so; Something-or-other. ¶ 김 ~라는 사람 a man called something-or-other Kim.

**아무개** ① 《누구》 any person; anybody.

② 《어떤 사람》 a certain person; Mr. So-and-so; Mr. X; Mr.—(★ Mr.—는 Mr. So-and-so로 읽는 것이 보통이나 Mr. Blank, Mr. Something으로 읽어도 됨. 여성인 경우는 Mr. 대신 Ms., Mrs.를 사용); John Doe. ¶ 김 ～라는 사람 a (certain) Mr. Kim / ～가 그렇게 말했다 Mr. So-and-so said so.

**아무데** [아무 곳] any place; anywhere. ¶ ～도 [부정] nowhere; not… anywhere / ～라도 좋다 Any place will do. / ～나 가도 좋다 You may go anywhere (you like). *or* You may go wherever you like. / 그것은 ～나 있다 Everywhere you go, you will find it. / ～나 앉으십시오 Sit wherever you like. / ～도 안 간다 I am not going anywhere. *or* I am going nowhere.

**아무때** 《어느 때》 (at) any time; any day (날을 가리지 않고); 《항상》 always; all the time; 《…할 때는 언제나》 whenever. ¶ 날씨가 좋으면 ～나 whenever the weather permits / ～고 좋다 Any time will do. / 우리는 ～나 출발할 수 있다 We are ready to start any time [at a moment's notice]. / ～나 오십시오 Come (at) any time you please. *or* You are welcome at any time. / ～고 힘이 되어 드리죠 I'm ready to help you. / ～고 그는 그 곳에 있습니다 He will be there at any moment.

**아무래도** ① 《어떻든》 anyhow; anyway; no matter what (*one* may do); come what may. ¶ ～ 내가 가야겠다 I have no choice but to go. *or* I have to go whether I like it or not. / ～ 그것은 해야 한다 I must [am bound to] do it anyhow. / ～ 이건 좀 크다 No matter what you do, it's a little too big.

② 《불가피하게》 surely; inevitably; infallibly; by all (manner of) means; somehow or other. ¶ ～ 5만 원은 있어야겠다 I must have 50,000 won. *or* I simply have to get 50,000 won. / 그 계획은 ～ 실패다 The enterprise is doomed to failure.

③ 《아무리 …해도》 for anything; for all the world; by any means; on any account; never. ¶ 그 일을 하는 것은 ～ 싫다 I wouldn't do that on any account [for anything in the world]. / ～ 그 돈은 못 받겠다 I can't bring myself to accept the money. / 그는 ～ 회복될 것 같지 않다 His recovery is beyond hope. / 그의 의도를 ～ 알 수 없다 I cannot, for the life of me, understand his intention.

④ 《결국》 eventually; in the long run; in the end; after all. ¶ ～ 실력이 이긴다 Real ability will win in the end. / 이치상으로 따지면 ～ 이렇게 된다 This is the only logical conclusion. / ～ 싼 물건이 언제나 가장 비싸게 먹힌다 Cheap things always prove the most expensive in the long run.

⑤ 《아무리 보아도》 any way you look at it; in every [all] respect; to all appearance(s). ¶ 그는 ～ 삼십 이상이다 He must be over thirty. / ～ 부부라고 밖에 볼 수 없다 They are, to all appearance, man and wife.

⑥ 《무관심》 in any way; anyhow. ¶ ～ 좋은 일 a matter of no consequence [of indifference]; a trivial matter; a trifle / ～ 좋다는 태도를 취하다 take an indifferent attitude 《toward》; be devil-may-care 《about》 / 그런 일은 ～ 좋다 I don't care a fig for it. *or* That does not matter. / 돈[명성] 따위는 ～ 좋다 I don't care for money [fame]. / 몸차림 따위는 ～ 좋다 I don't care a bit [damn] how I look [dress]. / 성공을 하건 말건 ～ 좋다 Success or failure makes no difference [odds] to me.

**아무러면** ① 《결코·설마》 surely 《not》; cannot 《be, *do*》; 《not》 in any case; 《not》 by any means; It is unlikely [impossible] that…. ¶ ～ 그가 거짓말을 할까 Surely he would not tell a lie! / ～ 그럴 수 있을까 It is not at all likely. / ～ 그가 그런 일을 했을까 Why, he is the last person in the world who would have done such a thing!

② 《아무런들》 (no matter, it makes no difference) whatever it is; however it is; whoever says it; whatever you [anybody] may say. ¶ 옷이야 ～ 어떠냐 It doesn't matter how your clothes look. *or* Don't mind what you wear. *or* Don't bother to dress up. / 사람들이 ～ 어떠냐 Don't mind what people say.

**아무런** any sort of; any; no; whatever; 《not》 in any way. ¶ ～ 사고 없이 without any accident / ～ 생각 없이 unwittingly; unintentionally; unconsciously / ～ 까닭[이유]도 없이 without any reason; for naught [nothing] / ～ 관계도 없다 have no relation [connection] whatever 《with》; have nothing to do 《with》; be not in any way related 《with》 / ～ 소용도 없다 be of no use; be no good; be good for nothing; be utterly useless.

**아무렇거나** anyhow; anyway; at any rate; in any case. ¶ ~ 해 보세 Anyhow, let us try. / ~ 즉시 집으로 돌아가는 것이 좋을 게다 In any case, you had better go home right away.

**아무렇게나** 《되는 대로》 in any manner *one* pleases; carelessly; in a slovenly way; at random; halfheartedly. ¶ ~ 말하다 talk at random; say irresponsible things / 일을 ~ 하다 do things by halves; do *one's* job in a halfhearted way; scamp *one's* work; slight 〔slapdash〕 *one's* work / ~ 다루다 handle roughly; treat 《*a person*》 with neglect / ~ 글을 쓰다 write carelessly; dash off / ~ 말하는 게 아니란다 Don't talk at random 〔wildly〕. / 아버지는 무슨 일이건 ~ 해두는 것을 싫어하신다 My father hates leaving anything half done.

**아무렇게도** in any 〔no〕 way; 《무관심》 nothing; not at all; not a bit. ¶ ~ 생각 안 하다 《우습게 여기다》 make little 〔nothing, light〕 of; 《서슴지 않다》 do not hesitate; 《개의치 않다》 do not care a bit 《about》; be quite indifferent 《to》 / 욕을 먹는 것쯤 ~ 생각 않는다 I am quite indifferent to abuse. / 그는 학교의 규칙 따위는 ~ 여기지 않는다 He pays no attention to the school regulations. / 나는 영어를 할 때 실수하는 것을 ~ 생각지 않는다 I don't care a bit about mistakes in speaking English.

**아무렇든지** no matter what; in any case 〔event〕; anyway; at any rate; at all events. ¶ ~ 이 계획을 포기할 수는 없다 We must stick to this plan, whether or no. / ~ 해보는 것이 좋겠다 At all events you had better try.

**아무려면** certainly; surely (not); under any 〔no〕 circumstances. ¶ ~ 그럴까 You don't say!? *or* How could it possibly be? / ~ 그렇지 Indeed it is! *or* Certainly!

**아무렴** of course; surely; certainly; to be sure. ⇨ 아무려면. ¶ 「그것이 사실입니까」—「~」 "Is that true?"—"Of course!" / 「저하고 가시겠어요」—「~ 같이가지」 "Will you go with me?"—"To be sure, I will."

**아무르강**(一江) 《흑룡강》 the Amur River.

**아무리** however (much); no matter how. ¶ ~ 돈이 많아도 no matter how rich a man may be; however rich a man may be / ~ 열심히 일해도 however hard *one* may work; no matter how hard *one* may work / ~ 보아도 to all apearance(s); in every respect; in all probability / ~ 감사를 드려도 오히려 부족한 느낌이 듭니다 I feel I cannot thank you enough. / 그는 ~ 보아도 군인이다 He is every inch a soldier. / 그는 ~ 보아도 20 세 미만이다 He is, to all appearance, under twenty. / 그는 ~ 보아도 학자는 아니다 He is anything but a scholar. / ~ 해도 그녀 이름이 생각 나지 않는다 For the life of me, I can't remember her name. / ~ 늦어도 다섯 시까지는 집에 돌아가야 한다 I've got to be home by five o'clock at latest. / ~ 힘이 세도 그것은 못 한다 Even the strongest cannot do it. / 그 사람은 ~ 칭찬을 해도 모자란다 We cannot praise him too much. / ~ 생각해 봐도 이 일은 성공하지 못한다 I have 〔There is〕 every reason to believe that this will not work out. / ~ 자네가 내 친구지만 그건 옳지 않아 It is not fair, even though you are my friend. / ~ 설명해도 그녀는 못 알아들었다 No matter how much I explained she couldn't understand.

**아무말** (not) any word. ¶ ~ 없이 without (saying) a word; not uttering a single word; 《허가 없이》 without *one's* permission 〔knowledge and consent〕 / ~ 도 없었다 Not a word was said. / ~ 도 할 것이 없다 I have nothing to say. / ~ 도 듣기 싫다 Not another word out of you! / 이 일에 대해서 사람들에겐 ~ 도 하지 마라 Keep mum about this affair.

**아무아무** certain persons; such-and=such persons. ⇨ 아무. ¶ ~ 가 그 여자를 죽였다고 그는 경찰에 고발했다 He informed the police that such-and=such men killed the woman.

**아무일** something; anything; 《부정》 nothing. ¶ ~ 없이 without incident 〔accident, mishap〕; without a hitch; quietly; uneventfully / 하루종일 ~ 없었다 The day passed peacefully. *or* Nothing happened all day. / 그는 ~ 도 없었다는 듯이 자리에 앉았다 He sat down as if nothing had happened.

**아무짝** any use. ¶ ~ 에도 못 쓸 인간 a good-for-nothing (fellow); a no-good 《미》 / ~ 에도 못 쓰다 be good for nothing; be utterly useless / ~ 에도 못 쓰겠다 It is of no use whatsoever.

**아무쪼록** as much as *one* can; to the best of *one's* ability; by all means.

¶ ～ 그렇게 해 보겠다 I'll try my best to do so. / ～ 빨리 오십시오 Please come as quickly as you can. / ～ 몸 조심하십시오 I hope you will take good care of yourself. *or* Take the best possible care of yourself. / ～ 그이가 무사히 돌아오시기를 May he return in safety! / ～ 그렇게 해 주세요 Will you kindly do so? *or* Do so, if you please. / ～ 조속한 회답을 주시기 바랍니다 Let me have your answer as soon as「possible〔you can〕.

**아물거리다** ① 《가물거리다》 keep coming in and out of sight; be glimpsed now and then (in the distance); be dim〔hazy〕. ¶ 아물거리는 기억 a dim memory / 등대가 멀리 아물거린다 A lighthouse is glimpsed now and then in the distance. ② ⇨ 어물거리다.

**아물다** heal (up); be healed. ¶ 상처가 ～ a wound heals up; be healed of *one's* wound / (상처가) 저절로 ～ heal of itself / 상처가 아무는 데 생각보다 오래 걸렸다 The wound took longer to heal than it should.

**아물리다** ① 《아물게 하다》 treat 《a wound》; make〔help〕《a wound》 heal. ¶ 연고로 상처를 ～ help heal a wound with an ointment. ② 《일을》 finish up; conclude; wind up. ¶ 일을 ～ finish up *one's* work; bring *one's* work to a conclusion.

**아물아물** 《가물가물》 (be seen) now and then in the distance; barely; dimly; vaguely. ¶ ～한 윤곽 a vague outline / ～ 보이다 come in and out of sight.

**아미**(蛾眉) arched eyebrows; eyebrows of a beautiful woman.

**아미노** 〖화학〗 amino. ◉ ～기 the amino group〔radical〕. ～산 an amino acid: 필수 ～산 the essential amino acids.

**아미타불**(阿彌陀佛) 〖불교〗 Amitabha.

**아바마마**(―媽媽) my father the King.

**아방가르드** 《예술의 전위파》 [< *avant=garde* (F.)] the vanguard.

**아방게르** 《예술의 전전파》 [< *avant-guerre* (F.)] prewar; before the war.

**아방튀르** 《모험성을 띤 (연애)사건》 [< *aventure* (F.)] an amorous adventure; a love affair.

**아버님** 《경칭》 father. ⇨ 아버지.

**아버지** a father; 《어린이 말》 papa; daddy; dad; 《하나님》 Father. ¶ ～다운 fatherly; fatherlike; paternal / ～답지 않은 unfatherly / ～쪽의 (친척) (a relative) on the father's〔paternal〕 side / ～로서의 자격 fatherhood; paternity / ～의 사랑 paternal affection〔love〕/ ～의 유산 patrimony / ～ 없는 아이 a fatherless child; 《사생아》 an illegitimate〔a love〕 child; a bastard (경멸적) / ～를 닮다 take after *one's* father / ～를 여의다 be left fatherless / ～처럼 돌보다 father 《*a person*》/ 그 ～에 그 아들 Like father, like son. / 호머는 서사시의 ～다 Homer is the father of epic poetry. / 그녀는 ～뻘이나 되는 남자와 결혼했다 She married a man who was old enough to her father.

**아범** ① 《비칭》 father; 《며느리가》 my husband; 《어른이》 your〔his〕 father. ② 《하인》 an elderly manservant.

**아베마리아** an Ave (Maria); (a) Hail Mary.

**아베크** [< *avec* (F.)] a couple〔lovers〕 on a date; a pair of sweethearts; 《밀회하는》 a rendezvousing couple; 《밀회》 a rendezvous; a date 《미》. ～하다 have a date 《with》; go on a date; rendezvous. ¶ ～로 《두 사람이》 together; 《go for a walk》 with *one's* boyfriend〔girlfriend〕; 《미》 with *one's* date; 《몇 쌍씩》 in couples; in pairs.

**아부**(阿附) flattery; adulation; sycophancy. ～하다 flatter (and toady); curry favor with 《*one's* superior》; cringe〔tuckle〕 to 《*a person*》; play up to; butter 《*a person*》 up 《구어》.

**아비규환**(阿鼻叫喚) ① 〖불교〗 *Avici* and *Raurava* (Sans.); two of the eight burning hells according to Buddhism. ② 《참상》 agonizing cries; pandemonium; "all hell"; appalling confusion. ¶ ～의 소리 agonizing cries / ～의 참상 an agonizing〔a heart-rending〕 scene; a terrible scene of confusion / ～의 수라장 the veriest hell; a sheer hell; a scene of utter confusion / 그 소식이 전해지자 시내는 순식간에 ～의 수라장으로 변했다 Pandemonium reigned in the town the moment the news reached them.

**아비산**(亞砒酸) 〖화학〗 arsenious acid; arsenic. ◉ ～염 arsenite. ～해독제 an arsenic antidote. 무수～ arsenic trioxide; arsenious oxide; white arsenic.

**아빠** papa; daddy; dad; pop 《미구어》.

**아뿔싸** Oops!; Oh my!; Darn〔Dash〕 it!; Hang it!; Shucks!; Good gracious!; Gosh!; Damn! ¶ ～ 노트를 안 가져왔네 Gosh! I forgot to bring my notebook with me. / ～ 그녀와 도서관에서 만나기로 돼 있었는데 Gosh! I was supposed to meet her in the library.

**아사**(餓死) (death by) starvation; death from hunger. ～하다 starve to death; die of 〔from〕 hunger; be starved 〔famished〕 to death. ¶ ～시키다 starve 《*a person*》 to death; starve out 《*a person*》/ ～ 직전에 있다 be close to starvation; be nearly dying from starvation / 혹한으로 넓은 지역에 걸쳐 야생 동물들이 ～하였다 The severe winter starved wild animals (to death) over a large area.

**아삭** 《깨물 때 나는 소리》 with a crisp 〔crunch〕; 《씹히는 소리》 with a hard bite. ～하다 《…이》 crunch; 《…을》 crunch 《it》.

**아삭거리다** 《…을》 crunch 《it》; 《…이》 crunch; taste crips; be crispy. ¶ 이 과자는 아삭거린다 This cracker eats crisp.

**아삭아삭** crunching. ～하다 《사과 따위가》 (be) crisp; crispy; crunchy; [서술적] eat crisp. ¶ ～한 사과 a crispy apple / 사과를 ～ 씹다 crunch an apple.

**아산화물**(亞酸化物) 〖화학〗 a suboxide.

**아서라** 《금지》 (Oh) No!; Ugh!; Gee!; Gosh!; Quit!; Stop!; "Cut it out!"; "Knock it off!"; Now now!; Come come!; Come now! ¶ ～ 남을 욕하지 마라 Now now! Don't run other people down. / ～ 그 쯤 해둬라 That's enough. / ～ 그래야 마찬가지다 Don't! It won't do any good.

**아성**(牙城) the inner citadel; the stronghold; the bastion; an impenetrable fortress. ¶ 보수주의의 ～ the stronghold of conservatism / 적의 ～에 육박하다 march on 〔press on to〕 the enemy's citadel.

**아성층권**(亞成層圈) the substratosphere. ¶ ～의 substratospheric / ～을 비행하다 fly in the substratosphere. ◉ ～비행 a substratospheric flight.

**아세안** 《동남아 국가 연합》 ASEAN. [<the *A*ssociation of *S*outh*e*ast *A*sian *N*ations] ◉ ～ 각료회의 the ministerial meeting of the ASEAN. ～ 자유 무역 지대 the ASEAN Free Trade Area (생략 AFTA).

**아세테이트** 〖화학〗 acetate. ◉ ～견사 acetate rayon 〔silk〕; cellulose acetate fiber.

**아세톤** 〖화학〗 acetone. ¶ ～의 acetonic.

**아세트산**(―酸) 〖화학〗 acetic acid. ◉ ～균 mother (of vinegar). ～나트륨 sodium acetate. ～메틸 metyle acetate. ～비닐 vinyl acetate. ～섬유(소) cellulose acetate. ～염(塩) an acetate. ～용액 acetum.

**아세틸** 〖화학〗 acetyl.

**아세틸렌** 〖화학〗 acetylene. ◉ ～가스 acetylene gas. ～램프 an acetylene torch. ～발생기 an acetylene (gas) generator. ～ 용접 장비 acetylene welding equipment.

**아셈** 《아시아 유럽 정상회의》 ASEM. [<the *A*sia-*E*urope *M*eeting]

**아수라**(阿修羅) 〖불교〗 *Asura* (Sans.); a battling giant demon of Buddhism. ¶ ～(와) 같은 with berserk(er) fury 〔rage〕; 《go》 berserk; like fury / ～같이 싸우다 fight like a demon (in a fury). ◉ ～왕 the King of the *Asuras*.

**아쉬움** (a) regret; attachment (애착). ¶ 이별의 ～ the sorrow of parting / 아직 ～이 남아 있다 be unable to put *something* 〔*somebody*〕 out of *one's* mind; be still attached 《to》.

**아쉬워하다** 《없어서》 miss; feel the lack of; be inconvenienced by not having; 《섭섭해하다》 be unwilling 〔reluctant〕; be loath. ¶ 이별을 ～ be reluctant 〔grudge〕 to part 《from *a person*》; be unwilling 〔feel loath〕 to part 《from *one's* friend, with *one's* pet dog》.

**아쉰대로** lacking anything better; inconvenient though it is; such as it is; as a temporary makeshift; anyway; making do with what *one* has; *faute de mieux* (F.). ¶ ～ 이만큼 있으면 당분간 쓸 수 있다 We can do with this amount for the time being. / 칼을 잊어버리고 와서 안 됐지만 ～ 이것을 쓰자 It's too bad we forgot to bring a knife with us, but let's make do with this as best we can.

**아쉽다** miss; feel the lack of; be inconvenienced by not having. ¶ 아쉬운 것 없이 지내다 live in comfort; be comfortably 〔well〕 off / 아쉬운 감이 들다 feel something wanting 〔lacking〕; have an unsatisfied feeling; miss something / 아쉬움을 참다 put up with inconvenience / 응접실이 없어서 ～ It is inconvenient not to have a drawing room. / 어딘지 아쉬운 데가 있다 It leaves 〔has〕 something to be desired. / (이것이) 없어서 ～ I feel at a loss without (this). / 이런 때 칼이 없어서 ～ I miss having a knife at a time like this. / 시계가 없어져서 ～ I really miss having my watch. / 아무 것도 아쉬운 것이 없도록 해주마 You shall want for nothing.

**아스라이** far; far off 〔away〕; in the distance; a long way off; 《희미하게》 dimly; faintly; vaguely. ¶ ~ 보이다 be seen dimly 〔at a dim distance〕/ 한라산이 저 멀리 ~ 보이다 see Mt. Halla is dimly visible in the distance / 나는 그 일을 ~ 기억하고 있다 I have a 「faint recollection 〔dim memory〕 of it.

**아스라하다** (be) far-off; 《어렴풋하다》 (be) dim; faint; indistinct.

**아스러지다** ① 《덩어리가》 crumble. ② 《살이》 be abraded; get rubbed raw.

**아스트린젠트** 《화장수》 an astringent.

**아스파라거스** 〖식물〗 an asparagus.

**아스팍** ASPAC. ⇨ 아시아 태평양 각료 이사회.

**아스팔트** asphalt. ¶ ~ 포장(의) asphalt=paved / ~를 깔다 asphalt 《streets》; pave 《streets》 with asphalt. ◉ ~길 an asphalt(-paved) road; a blacktop road.

**아스피린** 〖약〗 (an) aspirin. ¶ ~을 두 알 먹다 take two aspirins.

**아슬아슬하다** (be) dangerous; nervous; thrilling; risky; critical.
¶ 아슬아슬하게 narrowly; by hair-breadth / 아슬아슬한 때에 in the nick of time; at the eleventh hour; at the critical moment; within a hair's-breadth / 아슬아슬한 고비 a fateful 〔critical〕 moment / 아슬아슬한 승부 a close game; a tight match / 아슬아슬하게 이기다 win by a narrow margin / 아슬아슬하게 (죽음을) 면하다〔살아나다〕 escape narrowly 〔by a hair's=breadth〕; have a narrow escape / 아슬아슬하게 졌다 I only lost by a neck. / 그는 아슬아슬하게 당선됐다 He was elected by a narrow majority. / 그는 아슬아슬한 득표차로 선거에 이겼다 He won election by razor-thin margin.

**아습** a nine-year-old 《ox, horse》.

**아시리아** 〖역사〗 Assyria. ¶ ~의 Assyrian.

**아시아** Asia. ¶ ~(사람)의 Asian; Asiatic / ~는 모든 대륙중에서 제일 크다 Asia is the largest of all the continents of the world.
◉ ~ 개발 은행 the Asian Development Bank (생략 ADB). ~ 경기 대회 the Asian Games; the Asiad: 서울 ~ 경기 대회 조직 위원회 the Seoul Asian Games Organizing Committee (생략 SAGOC). ~ 경제 협력 기구 the Organization for Asian Economic Cooperation (생략 OAEC). ~ 극동 경제 위원회 the Economic Commission for Asia and the Far East (생략 ECAFE). ~ 대륙 the Asian Continent; the Continent of Asia. ~ 문제 연구소 the Asian Research Center 《of Korea University》. ~민족 Asian people; the Asian races; an Asian nation. ~ 사람 an Asian; an Asiatic. ~ 생산성 기구 the Asian Productivity Organization. ~ 신문 재단 the Press Foundation of Asia (생략 PFA). ~ 야구 선수권 대회 the Asian Baseball Championship Series. ~ 영화제 the Asian Film Festival. ~ 인종 the Asian race. ~주 Asia. ~ 지역 위성 텔레비전 Satellite Television Asia Region (생략 STAR). ~ 콜레라 《진성 콜레라》 the Asiatic cholera. ~ 탁구 연맹 the Asia Table Tennis Union (생략 ATTU). ~ 태평양 각료 이사회 Asian and Pacific Council (생략 ASPAC). ~ 태평양 경제 사회 이사회 the Economic and Social Commission of Asia and Pacific (생략 ESCAP). ~ 태평양 경제 협력 기구 the Asia-Pacific Economic Cooperation (생략 APEC). ~ 태평양 방송 연합 the Asian-Pacific Broadcasting Union (생략 ABU). ~ 태평양 시대 《the opening of》 an Asia-Pacific era. ~ 태평양 의원 연맹 the Asia-Pacific Parliamentarians Union (생략 APPU). ~ 태평양 지역 정보통신 기반 구조 the Asia-Pacific Information Infrastructure (생략 APII).
동북 ~ Northeast Asia. 동~ 경제회의 the East Asia Economic Caucus (생략 EAEC).

**아시아·아프리카** Africa and Asia; Afro=Asian; Afro-Asiatic. ◉ ~ 법률 자문 위원회 the Asian-African Legal Consultative Committee (생략 AALCC). ~ 블록 the Afro-Asian bloc. ~ 회의〔그룹〕 the Asian-African 〔Afro-Asian〕 Conference 〔Group〕.

**아식축구**(一式蹴球) association football; soccer. ⇨ 축구.

**아씨** 《경칭》 madam; 《호칭》 your (good) lady; Mrs. ...; 《하인의》 mistress; madam.

**아아** 《일이 잘못된 때》 oh-oh!

**아악**(雅樂) (classical) court 〔ceremonial〕 music. ¶ ~을 연주하다 play ceremonial music.

**아야** ouch. ¶ ~ 아프다 Ouch, it hurts!

**아얌** a fur cap worn by women in winter.

**아양** coquetry; flirtation; winsomeness. ¶ ~을 부리다〔떨다〕 play the coquette 《with》; flirt 《with》; make up to 《*a* *person*》; purr at 《*one's* lover》/ ～(을) 떠는 여자 a coquette; a coquettish woman / 돈을 보고 ～ 떨다 flatter for money / ～ 떨며 말하다 speak in a coquettish tone / 어린 딸이 아버지에게 ～을 부린다 The little girl is making up to her father.

**아어**(雅語) a refined diction 〔speech〕; an elegant word; a genteelism.

**아역**(兒役) 〖연극〗 a child's part 《in a play》; a juvenile part; 《사람》 a child actor 〔actress〕.

**아연**(亞鉛) 〖광물〗 zinc (기호 Zn). ¶ ～을 입힌 coated with zinc; galvanized / ～을 입히다 zinc; zincify; coat with zinc.
◉ ～광 zinc ore. ～도금 zinc galvanizing; galvanization. ～철 galvanized iron. ～철판(凸版) 〖인쇄〗 anastatic printing; photozincography; 《원판》 an anastatic plate. ～판(板) a zinc plate 〔sheet〕. ～판(版) zincography; 《인쇄판·인쇄물》 a zincograph; a zincotype. ～화(華) zinc flowers; zinc oxide: ～화 연고 zinc ointment.

**아연**(俄然) [부사적] suddenly; (all) of a sudden; abruptly. ¶ ～ 활기를 띠다 begin to show sign of activity suddenly / ～ 긴장하다 be strained all of a sudden / 흉기의 발견으로 경찰은 ～활기를 띠었다 All of a sudden, new enthusiasm was breathed into the police by the discovery of the weapon.

**아연**(啞然) ～하다 《*one's* mouth》 be stunned 《by》; be dumbfounded; be struck dumb with astonishment; stand aghast 《at》; be tongue-tied. ¶ ～(하여) agape (with wonder); in mute 〔utter〕 amazement; in open-mouthed surprise / ～케 하다 strike 《*a person*》 dumb 〔speechless〕; dumbfound; knock 《*a person*》 all of a heap; take 《*a person*》 aback / ～ 실색하다 turn pale with surprise 〔fright〕/ 그 광경에 ～했다 The sight struck me dumb.

**아열대**(亞熱帶) the subtropics; the subtropical zones 〔regions〕. ¶ ～의 subtropic(al); near-tropical. ◉ ～기후〔식물〕 a subtropical climate 〔plant〕.

**아예** from the (very) first 〔start, beginning〕; (not) by any means; (not) on any account; altogether; never; at all. ¶ 거짓말은 ～ 하지 마라 Never tell a lie. / ～ 선생 노릇을 할 생각일랑 말게 Never intend to be a teacher.

**아옹** a miaow; with a miaow; mew. ～하다[1] 《고양이가》 miaow; meow; mew.

**아옹거리다** 《서로》 quarrel 〔dispute, wrangle〕 《with》; bicker with each other; 《불화·반목》 feud 〔be at feud〕 《with》; be at loggerheads 〔daggers drawn〕 《with》; be at outs 〔odds〕 《with》.

**아옹하다**[2] ① 《굴·구멍 등이》 (be) sunken; hollow-looking. ② 《속이 좁아》 (be) disgruntled; griped; be complaining 〔griping〕 to *oneself*.

**아우** ① 《동생》 a man's younger brother; a woman's younger sister. ¶ ～보다 get 〔have〕 a younger brother 〔sister〕. ② 《나이 적은 이》 a junior 《in age》; a junior colleague.

**아우르다** put 〔join〕 together; unite. ⇨ 「어우르다.

**아우성** shouting; a hubbub; a clamor. ¶ ～을 치다 shout; bawl out; raise a hubbub; set up a shout 〔clamor〕; make an outcry; 《불만으로》 let out a squawk.

**아우타다** 《젖먹이가》 (a child) get thin from premature weaning (as a result of the mother's new pregnancy).

**아우타르키** 〖경제〗 《국가의 경제적 자급 자족》 autarchy; autarky.

**아우토반** 《고속도로》 an autobahn; a superhighway. [＜*Autobahn* (G.)]

**아우트라인** an outline; a sketch. ¶ 계획의 ～ an outline of a scheme / ～을 말하다〔보이다〕 give an outline 《of》; outline 〔sketch (out)〕 《a plan》; give a rough idea 《of》.

**아욱** 〖식물〗 a mallow; a hollyhock.

**아울러** (joining) together. ¶ ～ 가지다 possess together 《with》; possess 《*a thing*》 in addition 《to》; have both 《A》 and 《B》; combine 《A》 with 《B》.

**아웃** ① 《구기에서》 out; a put-out (생략 PO). ¶ ～이 되다 be put 〔thrown〕 out; go down / ～으로 하다 get 〔put〕 《a player》 out; make a put-out 《on a throw to first》; retire 《a runner》/ ～을 선언하다 call 〔give〕 《a runner》 out / 라이트플라이로 ～이 되다 go 〔be〕 out on a fly to right / 홈베이스로 볼을 던져 ～을 시키다 throw 《a runner》 out at the plate / 쳐서 ～이 되다 hit into an out. ② out(side).
◉ ～도어 outdoor(s). ～드롭 an outdrop. ～카운트 the number of outs 〔batters out〕. ～커브 an outcurve. ～코너 the outside (corner): ～ 코너 볼 an outside ball. ～ 파이팅 〖권투〗 outfighting. ～포커스 《영화에서》 out of focus.

**아웃소싱** 〖경제〗《외부용역으로의 대치》 outsourcing.

**아웃코스** 《트랙의》 an outside lane. ¶ (야구에서) ～로 직구를 던지다 deliver a straight ball over the far side of the plate (from the batter).

**아이** ① 《어린애》 a child (*pl.* children); a youngster; a little one; a kid(dy) 《구어》; a boy (남아); a girl (여아); 《아가》 a baby; an infant; [총칭] little ones 〔fellows〕; a family. ¶ ～의 child; child's; juvenile / ～ 같은 childlike; baby 《act》; 《유치한》 childish 《trick》; 《아이다운》 becoming a child / ～를 못 낳는 barren (of children); sterile / 사내 ～ a boy(-child) / 계집 ～ a girl (-child) / 어린 ～ a (preschool) child; a baby / 여섯 살 된 ～ a child of six / 뱃속의 ～ an expected 〔a coming〕 child / 자기 ～ a child 〔fruit〕 of *one's* loins / ～를 돌보다 nurse 《a baby》; tend a child; look after a baby; baby-sit 《미》 / ～ 보는 여자 a (dry) nurse; a nursemaid; a baby-sitter 《미》 / ～를 가지다〔배다〕, ～가 생기다 《임신하다》 get pregnant; be with child; conceive a child / ～가 많다 have many 〔lots of〕 kids; have a large family 《to provide for》 / ～ 많은 부부 a couple with many children / ～가 없다 be childless; be without issue / ～들을 좋아하다 be fond 〔a lover〕 of children / ～같이 굴다 behave childishly / 그녀는 곧 ～를 가질거다 She is going to have a baby before long. *or* She is expecting. / 늙으면 ～가 된다 An old man is twice a boy.
② 《자식》 *one's* (own) child.
③ 《젊은이》 a young man 〔fellow〕; a lad; a youth; the young [총칭].
◉ ～방 a nursery. ～ 아버지 the father of (the) children; *one's* husband. ～ 어머니 the mother of (the) children.

**아이고(머니)** ① 《아플 때나 힘들 때》 Oh!; Ah!; Dear me!; Oh my!; My goodness!; Good heavens!; Good lord!; Ouch!; Woe is me! ¶ 아이고 머리야 Oh, how my head aches! / 아이고 귀찮다 Good lord, how annoying! / 아이고머니 시계를 잃어버렸다 Heavens! I have lost my watch. / 아이고 죽겠다 Oh, I am dying! / 아이고 가엾어라 Poor creature! / 아이고 아파라 Ouch! How it hurts!
② 《경탄·놀랄 때》 Oh; Why; Good gracious!; Dear me! ¶ 아이고 어머니 Oh, mother! / 아이고 깜짝이야 Good lord, what a scare you gave me! *or* Ah, what a surprise!
③ 《반갑거나 좋을 때》 Ah!; Oh! ¶ 아이고 고마워라 Thank you very much. / 아이고 좋아라 What a delight! *or* Oh! How glad I am!
④ 《뒤늦게 깨달을때》 Well!; Well now!; Ah well. ¶ 아이고 가봐야겠다 Well, I guess I'll have to be going now.

**아이누** 《사람》 an Ainu; 《종족》 the Ainus; 《말》 Ainu.

**아이다호** 《미국의 주》 Idaho (생략 I., Id., Ida.).

**아이디** 《신원을 증명하는 것》 ID; I.D.; 〖컴퓨터〗《개인 식별 기호》 ID; I.D. [<identification; identifier] ◉ ～카드 《신분증명서》 an identity card; an ID card.

**아이디어** an idea. ¶ ～가 풍부한 사람 a man of ideas / ～를 모집하다 ask for 〔invite〕 new ideas. ◉ ～맨 a man of ideas; an idea(s)man. ～상품 a novelty.

**아이러니** irony. ¶ 소크라테스적 ～ Socratic irony (무지를 가장해서 역으로 상대의 무지를 깨우치게 하는 방법).

**아이로니컬하다** (be) ironical. ¶ 아이로니컬하게도 through the irony of chance; by the irony of fate; ironically (enough).

**아이론** ① 《다리미》 an iron. ⇨ 다리미.
② 《머리용》 a curling iron.

**아이보리코스트** 《나라 이름》 Ivory Coast.

**아이비리그** 《미국 동부의 8개 명문 대학》 the Ivy league. ¶ ～ 학생〔졸업생〕 an Ivy Leaguer.

**아이비아르디** 《세계은행》 I.B.R.D. [<the *I*nternational *B*ank for *R*econstruction and *D*evelopment]

**아이비에프** IBF. [<*I*nternational *B*oxing *F*ederation]

**아이비엠** 《미국의 전산기 회사》 I.B.M. [<*I*nternational *B*usiness *M*achines Corporation]; 《기계》 an IBM computer 〔machine〕.

**아이빔** 〖건축·토목〗 an I-beam.

**아이섀도** eye shadow. ¶ ～를 바르다 apply 〔put on〕 eye shadow; wear eye shadow.

**아이소토프** 〖화학〗 an isotope. ◉ ～요법 isotope therapy.

**아이소톤** 〖물리〗 an isotone.

**아이스** ice. ◉ ～댄싱 ice dancing. ～링크 an ice rink. ～박스 《냉장고》 an icebox; an ice chest 《미》. ～쇼 an ice show. ～캔디 a Popsicle 《미》; an ice lolly 《영》. ～커피 iced coffee. ～케이크 a Popsicle 《미》. ～큐브 an ice cube. ～크림 (an) ice cream; an ice 《영》:

～크림 제조기 an ice-cream freezer. ～폴 〖등산〗 an icefall. ～하키 ice hockey; 《미》 hockey: ～하키 선수 an ice hockey player.

**아이슬란드** Iceland. ¶ ～(사람, 말)의 Icelandic. ◉ ～말 Icelandic. ～ 사람 an Icelander. 「circuit]

**아이시** 《집적 회로》 an IC. [< *i*ntegrated

**아이시비엠** 《대륙간 탄도탄》 ICBM. [< *I*nter*c*ontinental *B*allistic *M*issile]

**아이시에이** 《국제 협조처》 I.C.A. [< the *I*nternational *C*o-operation *A*dministration]

**아이시에이오** ICAO. [< the *I*nternational *C*ivil *A*viation *O*rganization]

**아이아르** 《정보검색》 IR. [< *i*nformation *r*etrieval]

**아이아르비엠** 《중거리 탄도탄》 IRBM. [< *I*ntermediate *R*ange *B*allistic *M*issile]

**아이아르에이** 《아일랜드 공화국군》 IRA. [< the *I*rish *R*epublican *A*rmy]

**아이언클럽** 〖골프〗 an iron (club). ¶ 5번 ～ a five-iron.

**아이에스디엔** 〖컴퓨터〗 《종합 정보 통신망》 ISDN. [< *I*ntegrated *S*ervices *D*igital *N*etwork]

**아이에스비엔** 《국제 표준 도서번호》 ISBN. [< the *I*nternational *S*tandard *B*ook *N*umber]

**아이엔에스** 《고도 정보 통신 시스템》 INS. [< the *I*nformation *N*etwork *S*ystem]

**아이엘오** 《국제노동기구》 I.L.O. [< the *I*nternational *L*abor *O*rganization]

**아이엠에프** 《국제통화기금》 IMF. [< the *I*nternational *M*onetary *F*und] ¶ ～8조국(條國) an IMF Article 8 nation / ～시대 the so-called IMF era / 지역적 금융 위기로 초래된 ～ 긴급구제 금융 계획은 한국에서의 종신 고용이란 신화를 산산조각냈다 The IMF bailout program brought on by the regional financial crises has shattered the myth of lifelong employment in Korea.

**아이오시** 《국제 올림픽 위원회》 IOC. [< the *I*nternational *O*lympic *C*ommittee]

**아이오와** 《미국의 주》 Iowa (생략 Ia.).

**아이오유** 《차용증》 an I.O.U. [< I owe you]

**아이이에이** 《국제 에너지 기구》 IEA. [< the *I*nternational *E*nergy *A*gency]

**아이젠** [< *Steigeisen* (G.)] climbing irons; 《등산용》 crampons; a cramper.

**아이지다** have a miscarriage; have a stillborn baby 〔a stillbirth〕.

**아이쿠** Oh!; Ouch! 「quotient]

**아이큐** 《지능지수》 I.Q. [< *i*ntelligence

**아이티** 《Hispaniola섬의 옛 이름, 나라 이름》 Haiti. ¶ ～의 Haitian. ◉ ～말 Haitian. ～ 사람 a Haitian.

**아이피유** 《국제 의회 연맹》 IPU. [< *I*nter-*P*arliamentary *U*nion]

**아인슈타인** 《물리학자》 Albert Einstein (1879-1955). ¶ ～의 상대성이론 Einstein's theory of relativity.

**아일랜드** 《영국 서부의 섬》 (the Republic of) Ireland. ◉ ～말 Irish; the Irish language. ～사람 an Irishman; an Irishwoman.

**아잇적** childhood days; when a child.

**아장아장** with toddling steps; with mincing 〔short〕 steps; at a trot. ¶ (어린애가) ～ 걷다 toddle 〔waddle〕 along 〔about〕; make *one's* unsteady steps / ～걷는 아이 a toddler; a toddling child.

**아재** 《아저씨》 an uncle; 《아주버니》 *one's* husband's brother; a brother-in-law.

**아쟁**(牙箏) 〖악기〗 《7현의》 a bowed seven-stringed instrument.

**아저씨** ① 《삼촌》 an uncle. ② 《부모 또래》 a man (of *one's* parents' age).

**아전**(衙前) 〖역사〗 a petty town official.

**아전인수**(我田引水) drawing water to *one's* own mill; seeking 〔promoting〕 *one's* own interests; arguing from a self-centered angle. ¶ ～의 selfish; self-seeking; self-centered / ～격인 견해 a selfish view / 그것은 ～격이다 You feather your own nest. / ～도 정도껏 해라 Don't be so self-seeking.

**아제** ① ＝아저씨 ①. ② 《자매의 남편》 the husband of a girl's 〔woman's〕 sister. 「subspecific.

**아종**(亞種) 〖생물〗 a subspecies. ¶ ～의

**아주** ① 《썩·영영》 quite; entirely; utterly; completely; altogether; (not) at all; very (much); extremely. ¶ ～ 기분이 좋다 feel quite well / ～ 예쁘다 be very pretty / ～ 피곤하다 be dead tired; be utterly exhausted / ～ 기뻐하다 be hugely 〔immensely〕 delighted / ～ 관계를 끊다 break off entirely 《with》; sever *one's* connections 《with》; 《미》 be entirely through 《with》 / 그는 ～ 상식이 없다 He doesn't have a grain of common sense. / 그는 ～ 가버렸다 He has gone for good. / 그는 ～ 바보는 아니다 He is not altogether a fool. / 그녀는 꾸벅꾸벅 졸았으나 ～잠들지는 않았다 She drowsed, but did not quite fall asleep. ② 《꼭》 just like; 《매우·몹시》 very; awfully. ¶ 그는 아버지와 ～ 같다 He is the very image 〔picture〕 of his father. ③ 《비웃는 말》

You think so!; Oh really!

**아주**(亞洲) the Continent of Asia.

**아주**(阿洲) the Continent of Africa.

**아주까리** a castor-bean plant; 《씨》 a castor(-oil) bean. ◉ ～기름 castor oil.

**아주머니** 《숙모》 an aunt; 《아줌마》 an auntie 〔aunty〕; 《일반 부인》 a lady.

**아주버니** *one's* husband's older 〔younger〕 brother.

**아지랑이** (heat) haze; the shimmer of the air; heat waves; shimmer(ing air). ¶ ～가 일고 있다 The air is shimmering. *or* Heat waves are shimmering. *or* The heat is waving the air. ◉ ～ 현상 〖물리〗 schlieren.

**아지작** with a crunch.

**아지작거리다** crunch; munch; crush.

**아지작아지작** 《깨물 때·씹을 때》 crunching; crushing; champing. ¶ 사탕수수 깡을 ～ 씹다 crunch on a stalk of sugar cane / 과자를 ～ 씹어 먹다 munch candies.

**아지트** 《거점》 a secret base of operations 《for communists》; an agitating point; 《은신처》 a hideout 《미구어》.

**아직** ① 《아직도》 (not) yet; still; 《지금까지도》 as yet; even now; so far. ¶ 그는 ～ 오지 않았다 He has not come yet. / ～ 모자란다 This isn't enough yet. / 그는 ～도 살아 있다 He's still alive. / 집에서 편지가 ～도 없다 There are still no letters from home. / 나의 의문은 ～ 풀리지 않고 있다 My doubt is still unsolved. / 페인트칠이 ～ 마르지 않았다 The paint is still wet. / ～끝나지 않았다 It is not finished yet. / 비는 ～도 내리고 있다 It is still raining. / 휴가까지는 ～ 열흘이 남았다 There are still 〔We still have〕 ten days before the vacation begins. / ～ 그를 만나본 적이 없다 I haven't met him as yet. / 그 사람 ～도 노여움이 안 풀렸는가 Is he still angry? / 그는 ～도 어린애다 He is still a mere child. / 갈 길이 ～ 3마일 남았다 We have still three more miles to go. / ～ 할 일이 많다 There is a lot of work yet to be done. / 이 냉장고는 ～껏 고장난 적이 없다 This fridge has never been out of order.

② 《그/이 밖에 또·더》 besides; more. ¶ 사과는 ～ 더 있습니까 Have you any more apples? *or* Have you any apples left? / 너에게 이야기할 것이 ～ 더 있다 I have something more to tell you.

③ 《겨우》 only; still. ¶ 결혼한 지 ～ 반년 밖에 안된다 It is only six months since we were married. / 그 대지진이 일어난 것은 내가 ～ 중학생 무렵이었다 That great earthquake occurred while I was still in junior high school.

**아직까지** 《지금까지》 up to now; till now; so far; as yet. ¶ 그한테서 ～ 소식이 없다 I've heard nothing from him as yet. / ～ 아무런 보고도 받지 못했다 No report has been received so far. / ～ 그것은 꿈에 지나지 않는다 So far, it is only a dream.

**아질산**(亞窒酸) 〖화학〗 nitrous acid. ◉ ～염 nitrate. ～칼리 potassium nitrite.

**아집**(我執) egoistic attachment; egotism. ¶ ～이 센 사람 an egoistic man / ～을 버리다 get rid of 〔rid *oneself* of *one's*〕 selfishness.

**아찔하다** (be) dizzy; feel giddy; *one's* head swims; faint (away); swoon; fall senseless.

**아차(차)** Dear me!; Tsk!; Darn it!; Gee!; Shucks!; Damn!; O my!; Gosh!; Hang it! ¶ 아차 우산을 두고 왔군 Shucks, I left my umbrella behind. / 아차 또 속았구나 O my! I have been fooled again!

**아첨**(阿諂) flattery; adulation; sycophancy. ～하다 flatter 《*a person*》; toady 《to》; fawn on; curry favor 《with *a person*》; soft-soap 《*a person*》; butter *a person* up 《구어》; play up to. ¶～에 넘어가다 be taken in by flattery / ～을 잘 하다 be adept in flattery / 그는 우리에게 무척 ～했다 He gave us lots of soft soap. / ～을 잘 하시는군요 You flatter me. *or* Don't flatter me. ◉ ～꾼〔쟁이〕 a toady; a sycophant; a flatterer; an apple-polisher.

**아청**(鴉靑) a dark 〔Prussian〕 blue (color).

**아취**(雅趣) elegance; tastefulness; artistry; refinement. ¶ ～ 있는 tasteful; elegant; graceful; refined / ～ 없는 tasteless; commonplace; flat / ～ 있는 사람 a man of (refined) taste / ～ 있는 생활을 하다 lead a tasteful life.

**아치**(雅致) good taste; elegance; grace; artistry; artistic effect; gusto. ¶ ～ 있는 elegant; graceful; refined; tasteful; artistic / ～ 있는 별장 a tasteful cottage.

**아치** an arch; a green arch 《of welcome》; 〖야구〗 a home run; a homer. ¶ ～형의 arch-shaped; arched / (야구에서) 높이 ～를 그리다 swat a high-flying homer 《over the left field wall》.

**-아치** ¶ 벼슬아치, 벗아치 an official; a public official.

**아침** ① 《때》 morning; morn 《시어》.

¶～ (나절)에 in the morning / ～내 from early morning till breakfast time / ～ 일찍이 early in the morning; in the early morning / ～ 아홉 시에 at nine in the morning / ～부터 저녁까지 from morning till evening; all day (long) / 3일날 ～에 on the morning of the 3rd / 월요일 ～에 on Monday morning / 내일 ～에 tomorrow morning / 어느 여름날 ～ one summer morning / 화창한 ～에 on a fine morning / ～ 늦게〔일찍〕 일어나다 rise late 〔early〕/ ～이 되다 morning breaks / 조용한 ～의 나라 the Land of Morning Calm / 인생은 ～ 이슬과 같다 Men's life vanishes like the dew. *or* Life is but a span.
② 《끼니》 breakfast; the morning meal. ¶～ 겸 점심, 늦은 ～밥 brunch 《구어》/ ～식사 때에 at breakfast / ～(밥)을 먹다 have breakfast; breakfast 《on bread and coffee》/ ～(밥)을 끝내다 finish *one's* breakfast / 하루에 ～ 점심 저녁 세끼 식사를 하다 have three meals a day, in the morning, at noon and in the evening / ～ 잡수셨습니까 Have you had breakfast? / ～부터 줄곧 비가 오고 있다 It has been raining since morning.
◉ ～거리 breakfast makings; foodstuff for breakfast. ～결 the forenoon. ～기도 a morning prayer; matins (교회의). ～나절 the forenoon; the first half of the day between breakfast and lunch. ～놀 the morning glow; the glow of sunrise in the sky. ～바람 the morning breeze. ～상 a breakfast table 〔tray〕. ～선반 time off for breakfast and a rest (on the job). ～술 wine drunk early in the morning. ～안개 (the) morning mist 〔fog〕. ～이슬 morning dew: ～ 이슬 같은 인생 transient life. ～잠 a morning nap. ～참 a breakfast break (in work); a breakfast stop (on a journey). ～해 the morning sun; the rising sun; 《아침 햇살》 morning sunshine: ～햇빛을 받다 be bathed in the morning sunshine / ～ 해가 뜬다 The sun rises.

**아침저녁** morning and evening. ¶～으로 서늘하다 We have cooler mornings and evenings now. *or* It is quite chilly in the mornings and evenings.

**아카데미** an academy. ◉ ～상 〖영화〗 the Academy Award 〔Prize〕; the Oscar: ～상 수상 배우〔여배우〕 the Oscar actor 〔actress〕. ～즘 academism.

**아카시아** 〖식물〗 an acacia. 「곡).

**아카펠라** 〖음악〗 a cappella (무반주 합창

**아칸소** 《미국의 주》 Arkansas (생략 Ark.).

**아케이드** 《지붕이 있는 상점가》 an arcade.

**아코디언** 〖악기〗 an accordion. ◉ ～도어 an accordion door. ～ 연주자 an accordionist.

**아퀴** 《끝매듭》 the final touches; finish; settlement. ¶ 일의 ～를 짓다 wind up *one's* work; finish *one's* work; bring a matter to a conclusion 〔to an end〕; put an end to; give the final touches to the job.

**아크등**(―燈) an arc light 〔lamp〕.

**아크로바트** 《사람》 an acrobat; 《재주》 acrobatics. ◉ 아크로바틱 댄스 an acrobatic dance.

**아크로폴리스** 《고대 그리스의》 an acropolis; 《아테네의》 the Acropolis.

**아킬레스** Achilles. ◉ ～건(腱) 〖해부〗 the Achilles' tendon; [비유적] a vulnerable point; *one's* Achilles' heel: 그는 연습중에 ～건이 끊겼다 He tore his Achilles' tendon while training.

**아탄**(亞炭) lignite; brown coal.

**아태국가**(亞太國家) the Asian and Oceanic countries 〔nations〕.

**아테네** 《그리스의 수도》 Athens.

**아토니** 〖의학〗 atony.

**아톰** 〖물리〗 《원자》 an atom.

**아트로핀** 〖화학〗 atropine; atropia. ◉ ～중독 atropism; atropinism.

**아트지**(―紙) 《종이》 coated paper 《미》; art paper 《영》; slick 〔glossy〕 paper.

**아틀리에** an *atelier* (F.); a studio (*pl.* ～s); 《일터》 a workshop.

**아파치** 《미국 인디언의 한 부족》 an Apache. ◉ ～족 the Apache people.

**아파트** an apartment house 《미》; a block of flats 《영》; 《방》 an apartment 《미》; a flat 《영》. ¶～를 빌리다 rent an apartment / 역 가까이 있는 ～를 구하다 look for an apartment near the station / 그는 ～에 살고 있다 He lives in an apartment.
◉ ～관리비 the maintenance cost 〔charge〕 of an apartment house. ～관리인 the superintendent of an apartment house. ～단지 an apartment complex. ～채권(債券) 입찰제 the bond-accompanied apartment bidding system. ～형 공장 an apartment-type factory.
고층～ a high-rise apartment (building). 분양〔호화〕～ a lot-sold 〔luxury〕 apartment. 정부 고시 ～ 건설 가격 the Government-set apartment building

cost.

**아파하다** express 〔show〕 pain; complain of pain; say 〔complain〕《it》 hurts.

**아펜니노산맥**(—山脈) 《이탈리아의》 the Apennino Mountains; the Apennines.

**아편**(阿片·鴉片) opium; dope 《미구어》. ¶ ~을 피우다 smoke 〔eat〕 opium. ◉ ~굴 an opium den. ~매매 opium traffic. ~분말 powdered opium. ~상 an opium peddler. ~연(煙) opium tobacco; opium smoke. ~쟁이 = ~중독자. ~전쟁 the Opium War. ~제 an opiate; opium products. ~중독 opiumism; opium poisoning; opium addiction: ~ 중독자 an opium addict 〔eater, smoker〕; an opium fiend; a hophead / 그는 ~중독자다 He is addicted to opium.

**아포스테리오리** 〖철학〗 *a posteriori* (L.).

**아폴로** 《그리스·로마 신화의》 Apollo. ¶ ~ 계획 the Apollo Project.

**아프가니스탄** 《나라이름》 Afghanistan. ¶ ~의 Afghan. ◉ ~말 Afghan. ~사람 an Afghan.

**아프다** ① 《신체·상처 따위가》 (be) painful; sore; 《욱신욱신》 (be) smart; feel 〔have, suffer from〕 a pain 《in *one's* back》; ache; pain. ¶ 아픈 상처 a sore wound / 아픈 이 an aching tooth / 목〔발〕이 ~ have a sore throat 〔foot〕 / 머리〔배〕가 ~ feel 〔have〕 a pain in *one's* head 〔stomach〕; have a headache 〔stomachache〕 / 아파서 울다 cry with pain / 아파서 얼굴을 찡그리다 twist *one's* face in pain / 아픈 데를 건드리다 touch 《*a person*》 on a sore place ⇨ 아픈데 / 건드리면 ~ [환부가 주어] be sore to the touch / 아이고 ~ Ouch! How it hurts (me)! / 걸으면 ~ It hurts me to walk. / 상처가 아파서 못 견디겠다 My wound is paining terribly. / 머리가 빠개질 듯이 ~ I have a splitting headache. / 어느 이가 아픕니까 Which tooth hurts 〔pains〕 you? / 어디가 아픕니까 Where do you feel the pain? *or* Where does it hurt? / 조금도 아프지 않다 It doesn't hurt at all. / 피로 때문에 온 몸이 ~ My whole body aches with weariness. / 그 떠드는 소리를 들으니 골치가 ~ The noise causes my head to ring.
② [비유적] ¶ 마음이 ~ be sore at heart; grieve / 배가 ~ be green with envy; be jealous / 배가 아파서 in envy 《of》; out of 〔from〕 envy / 골치가 ~ be annoyed 〔harassed, pestered〕 / 골치 아픈 일 a cause of headache; "a headache" / 좀 아픈 맛을 보여주다 make 《*a person*》 smart 〔sweat〕 for it; give 《*a person*》 gyp 《구어》 / 자네 말은 내 아픈 곳을 찔렀네 You touch me on a sore point. / 그들의 모습을 보니 마음이 아팠다 It cut me to the quick to see them. / 아들의 말에 가슴이 아팠다 My son's remark broke my heart. / 그녀의 심한 말에 그의 마음은 몹시 아팠다 Her harsh words caused 〔gave〕 him a lot of pain. / 어머니가 얼마나 괴로우셨을까 생각하면 가슴이 ~ It pains me to think of how much my mother suffered. / 속이 쓰리고 아팠으나 어쩔 수 없이 5백만원을 지불해야만 했다 I had to pay five million won, though it broke my heart (to do it).

**아프레** 《제1·2차 세계대전 후》 *après* (F.). ◉ ~게르 *après-guerre* (F.); postwar.

**아프리카** Africa. ¶ ~의 African / …을 ~화하다 Africanize / 남~ 태생의 백인 an Afrikander; an Afrikaner; a Boer. ◉ ~대륙 the African Continent. ~민족회의 the African National Congress. (생략 ANC). ~사람 an African. ~주 the African Continent. ~통일 기구 the Organization of African Unity (생략 OAU).

**아프트** Abt. ◉ ~식 철도 an Abt-system railroad; a cog 〔rack〕 railway.

**아픈 데, 아픈 곳** 《약점》 *one's* weak point; *one's* sore 〔sensitive〕 spot. ¶ ~를 찌르다 strike 〔poke〕 *a person* at *his* most vulnerable point / 자네의 말은 내 ~를 찔렀네그려 You've got me there! *or* You've found my weak point, haven't you?

**아플리케** 〖자수〗 *appliqué* (F.).

**아픔** (a) pain; an ache; 《쑤시는》 a smart; 《마음의》 (mental) pain; 《슬픔》 grief; sorrow. ¶ 가슴〔위(胃)〕의 ~ a pain in the breast 〔stomach〕 / 상처의 ~ the smart of a wound / 이별의 ~ the pain of parting / 격심한 ~ a severe 〔sharp, bad〕 pain / ~을 느끼다 feel pain / ~을 참다 stand 〔bear, endure〕 the pain / ~을 진정시키다 relieve 〔ease〕 pain / ~이 가셨다 The pain has 「gone 〔left me〕.

**아하** Oh!; Dear me!; My goodness!; Well!; What-do-you-know! ¶ ~, 그것을 깜박 잊었구나 Oh my goodness!—it slipped right out of my mind.

**아하하** 《조소》 Ha-ha!; Hmmph!.

**아한대**(亞寒帶) 《북반구의》 the subarctic zone; 《남반구의》 the subantarctic zone.

**아호**(雅號) a pen 〔literary〕 name; a *nom de plume* (F.); a pseudonym. ¶ …란 ~로 쓰다 write under the pen name of….

**아홉** nine. ¶ ~째(의) the ninth / ~째로 ninthly. ◉ ~수 numbers ending in 9.

**아황산**(亞黃酸) 〖화학〗 sulfurous acid. ◉ ~가스 sulfurous acid gas. ~나트륨〔소다〕 sodium sulfite. ~염(塩) sulfite.

**아흐레** ①《아홉 날》 nine days. ② ⇨ 아흐렛날.

**아흐렛날**《제9일》 the ninth day;《그 달의》 the ninth day of the month.

**아흔** ninety. ¶ ~째(의) the ninetieth.

**악**[1]《모질게 쓰는 기운》 desperate 〔frantic〕 efforts; stick-to-itiveness; desperation (자포자기);《노한 감정》 the fury of *one's* passion; wild rage; violent anger. ¶ 악이 바치다 become 〔grow〕 desperate 〔reckless〕; be excited 〔enraged〕; go mad / 악에 바쳐 desperately; in desperation; recklessly; in 〔out of〕 despair;《구어》 like mad 〔hell〕 / 악을 쓰다 shout; cry; shriek ⇨ 악쓰다 / 악이 오르다 get mad / 남편에게 악쓰(며 대들)다 bawl at *one's* husband / 악에 바쳐 술을 마시다 take to drink out of desperation / 사람은 악에 바치면 무슨 일이든 저지른다 A desperate man will go to any lengths.

**악**[2]《몹시 놀랄 때》 Oh!; Dear me! ¶ 악, 뱀이 있다 Oh, there's a snake!

**악**(惡) badness; (an) evil; wickedness; (a) vice. ¶ 선과 악 good and evil / 사회악 the social evil / 악의 소굴 criminal quarters; the underworld / 악에 이기다〔지다〕 conquer 〔fall into〕 vice / 악에 물들다 be steeped in vice; sink into vice / 악에 빠지다 fall into evil ways; be given to evil ways; take to an evil course; abandon *oneself* to evil / 악을 거듭하다 repeat malpractices 〔acts of wickedness〕 / 악을 응징하다 punish the wicked / 악을 선으로 갚다 return good for evil / 악에 강한 자는 선에도 강하다 Extremes in wickedness make for extremes in goodness. / 그는 선에도 악에도 강하다 He has a great capacity for either good or evil.

**악감(정)**(惡感(情)) ill feeling; animosity; an unfavorable impression; a grudge. ¶ 국제간의 ~ international animosities / ~을 품다 have 〔bear, harbor, entertain〕 an ill feeling《against, toward》; bear《*a person*》 a grudge 〔an ill-will〕; be ill disposed《toward》/ ~을 주다〔사다〕 make an unfavorable impression《on another's mind》; impress《*a person*》 unfavorably; offend《*a person*》/ 그는 나에게 ~을 품고 있는 것 같다 He seems to dislike me.

**악계**(樂界) the world of music; musical circles.

**악곡**(樂曲) a musical piece 〔composition〕; a piece of music; a tune.

**악골**(顎骨) 〖해부〗 a jawbone; a maxilla (*pl.* ~s, -lae). ◉ ~동맥 a maxillary artery.

**악공**(樂工) a court musician.

**악구**(惡球) 〖야구〗《throw, hit》 a wild pitch 〔ball〕.

**악귀**(惡鬼) a demon; a devil; an evil spirit. ¶ ~ 같은 fiendish; demoniac(al) / ~가 들리다 be possessed of a demon.

**악극**(樂劇) a musical (drama); a play with music. ◉ ~단 a musical troupe.

**악기**(樂器) a musical instrument. ¶ ~를 연주하다 play on a musical instrument / ~에 맞도록 편곡하다 arrange《music》 for instruments; instrument / ~를 다룰 줄 아느냐 Can you play an instrument?
◉ ~반주 instrumental accompaniment. ~점 a musical instruments' store 〔shop〕; a music shop.

**악기류**(惡氣流) air turbulence; turbulent air; a treacherous air current.

**악녀**(惡女) a wicked woman; a virago; a witch;《용모의》 an ugly woman.

**악다구니** a name-calling quarrel; bickerings; mud-flinging〔-slinging〕; a brawl; an altercation. ~하다 brawl; engage in mud-flinging at each other; fling 〔throw〕 mud《at》; wrangle.

**악단**(樂團) an orchestra; a band. ¶ ~의 반주 an orchestral accompaniment. ◉ ~연주 a band concert. ~원 a member of an orchestra. ~장 a bandmaster.

**악단**(樂壇) the musical world; musical circles.

**악담**(惡談) a curse; a malediction; abusive 〔offensive, foul〕 language; abuse;《중상》 slander. ~하다 curse; swear at; call《*a person*》 (bad) names; revile; speak ill of. ¶ 아무를 ~하다 curse *a person;* speak ill of *a person* / 안 보는 데서 아무를 ~하다 backbite *a person;* speak ill of *a person* behind *his* back / ~을 퍼붓다 heap abuses on《*a person*》; call《*a person*》 all sorts of (bad) names.

**악당**(惡黨) a scoundrel; a rascal; a villain; a ruffian; 《깡패》 a hooligan; a hoodlum 《미구어》.

**악대**(樂隊) a (musical) band; 《취주악단》 a brass band; 《관현악단》 an orchestra. ¶ ～의 연주회 a band concert / ～를 선두로 행진했다 We marched on with the band at the head.
◉ ～원 a bandsman. ～음악 band music. ～장 a bandmaster.

**악덕**(惡德) (a) vice; immorality; evil conduct; 《타락》 corruption. ～하다 (be) vicious; vice-ridden; depraved. ¶ ～을 쌓다 commit a series of vicious acts; commit one vice after another.
◉ ～기업주 a vicious entrepreneur. ～기자 a corrupt newspaperman. ～변호사 a fixer 《미구어》; a shyster 《미구어》. ～상인〔업자〕 a wicked 〔dishonest, crooked 《구어》〕 dealers 〔traders〕. ～신문 a yellow newspaper (저속하고 선정적인); the corrupt press [총칭]. ～정치가 a corrupt politician.

**악도리** a bad 〔tough〕 guy; a roughneck; a ruffian; a rowdy.

**악독**(惡毒) viciousness; spitefulness; venom; perversity; harshness. ～하다 (be) vicious; spiteful; venomous; harsh. ¶ ～한 행위 infernal deed; vicious practices.

**악동**(惡童) a bad 〔naughty, mischievous〕 boy.

**악랄**(惡辣) viciousness; spitefulness; knavishness. ～하다 (be) vicious; spiteful; knavish; nasty; unscrupulous. ¶ ～한 수법 a mean 〔knavish〕 trick; a foul means / ～한 수법으로 번 돈 money acquired by unscrupulous means; ill-gotten gains / ～한 짓을 하다 do a nasty thing; play a mean trick; resort to knavish tricks; 《상습적으로》 be given to sharp practices.

**악력**(握力) grasping power; grip. ¶ ～이 세다〔약하다〕 have a strong 〔weak〕 grip / 오른손의 ～은 약 70킬로다 be able to exert a right-handed squeeze of 70 kilograms or so. ◉ ～계 a (squeeze) dynamometer; 《유희장의》 a try-your-grip machine.

**악령**(惡靈) an evil spirit. ¶ ～에 들려〔씌어〕 있다 be possessed by an evil spirit / ～을 내쫓다 drive out demons.

**악례**(惡例) a bad example; an evil precedent. ¶ ～를 남기다〔만들다〕 set 〔establish〕 a bad precedent.

**악리**(樂理) the theory of music.

**악마**(惡魔) an evil spirit; a devil; a demon; a fiend; 《마왕》 Satan; Lucifer. ¶ ～의, ～적인 satanic 〔Satanic〕 《influence》; demonic 《power》; diabolical 《laughter》 / ～ 같은 devilish; fiendish; demoniac(al); diabolic / ～같이 devilishly; fiendishly; demoniacally; diabolically / ～에 들려〔씌어〕 있다 be possessed by a devil; be occupied by an evil spirit / ～를 물리치다 exorcise 〔drive out, drive away〕 evil spirits 《from *a person*》 / (주문으로) ～를 불러내다 raise the devil.
◉ ～주의 Satanism; diabolism. ～파 the Diabolists; the Satanic school.

**악머구리** a "croaker"; a leopard frog. ¶ ～ 끓듯하다 make a lot of noise.

**악명**(惡名) a bad name; an evil reputation; an ill repute; notoriety. ¶ ～(이) 높은 infamous; notorious 《for his goings-on》 / ～이 높아지다 become notorious / ～이 높다 be notorious 《for》; be infamous / ～을 덮어쓰다 be given a bad name.

**악몽**(惡夢) a bad 〔an evil〕 dream; a hideous 〔terrible〕 dream; a nightmare. ¶ ～ 같은 nightmarish / ～을 꾸다 have a bad 〔torturing〕 dream; 《가위눌림》 have a nightmare / ～에서 깨어나다 awake from a nightmare; [비유적] come to *one's* senses / 매일 밤 그는 ～에 시달렸다 Night after night he was oppressed by a nightmare. / ～과도 같은 하루였다 It was 〔has been〕 a nightmarish day.

**악물다** 《이를》 clench 《*one's* teeth》; set 《*one's* jaw》; compress 《*one's* lips》. ¶ 이를 악물고 with *one's* teeth set / 이를 악물고 고통을 참다 endure the pain by clenching *one's* teeth / 이를 악물고 일하다 clench *one's* teeth and dig into the job; work with firm determination / 이를 악물고 싸우다 fight bitterly 〔fiercely〕 / 모진 고통에도 이를 악물고 참아내는 그녀의 모습은 너무나 마음 아팠다 It was painful to watch her, gritting her teeth to bear the agony she was suffering.

**악바리** 《모진 사람》 a harsh tough person; 《영악한 사람》 a hard shrewd person.

**악법**(惡法) a bad law. ¶ 비록 ～이라도 법은 법이다 A law is a law, however undesirable it may be.

**악벽**(惡癖) a bad habit; a vice; a vicious 〔pernicious〕 habit. ¶ ～을 고치다 《남의》 cure *a person* of a bad habit; 《자기의》 break *oneself* of 〔get over, kick《구어》] a bad habit.

**악보**(樂譜) a music; a (musical) score (총보(總譜)); a music book (악보집); [집합적] 《read》 music. ¶ ~를 보다 read music / ~ 없이 연주하다 play 「without music [by ear, from memory] / ~를 보며 즉석에서 연주하다 sight-read music; play at sight.
◉ ~대(臺) a music stand [rack]. ~집 a music book. 관현~ a full [an orchestral] score. 단행(單行)~ a sheet music.

**악사**(惡事) [일반적] an evil [a wicked] deed; a misdeed; 《범죄 행위》 a crime. ¶ ~를 꾀하다 plot evil / ~를 저지르다 do wrong [evil] / ~천리 Ill news runs apace [fast].

**악사**(樂士) a band(s)man; a musician.
◉ ~장 the chief music master.

**악상**(樂想) 『음악』 a theme; a melodic subject; a motif. ¶ ~이 떠오르다 a musical motif comes into *one's* mind.

**악서**(惡書) a harmful [bad] book; undesirable publications. ¶ ~를 추방하다 put harmful books out of circulation; get rid of undesirable books.

**악선전**(惡宣傳) 《악질의》 vile [pernicious] propaganda; 《악의에 찬》 malicious propaganda; 《거짓》 false propaganda. ~하다 launch false propaganda 《about》; make [spread] a bad [malicious, sinister] rumor 《about》. ¶ ~에 현혹되다 be misled by pernicious propaganda.

**악설**(惡舌·惡說) abusive language; slander; backbiting; curse; malediction. ~하다 speak ill; abuse; curse.

**악성**(惡性) malignancy; malignity; viciousness. ¶ ~의 malignant 《cancer》; virulent 《disease》; vicious / ~의 질병 a malignant disease.
◉ ~감기 a bad [nasty] cold: 그는 ~감기에 걸려 있다 He has a bad [nasty] cold. ~빈혈 pernicious anemia. ~인플레이션 vicious [spiraling, runaway] inflation. ~ 종양 a malignant [vicious] tumor.

**악성**(樂聖) a celebrated [master] musician; a great musical artist. ¶ ~ 베토벤 Beethoven, the great musician.

**악센트** (an) accent; (a) stress; 《억양》 a tone; accentuation. ¶ ~가 있는 accented; stressed / ~ 없는 unaccented; unstressed / ~를 붙이다 accent 《a word on the second syllable》; stress [lay, put (the) stress on] 《the first syllable》 / 첫째 음절(音節)에 ~가 있다 The stress falls on the first syllable.

**악송구**(惡送球) 《야구에서》 a wild ball [pitch]. ~하다 throw a wild ball; make a bad throw 《to》.

**악수**(握手) handshaking; a handshake; 《화해》 reconciliation; making-up 《구어》. ~하다 shake hands 《with》; shake 《*a person*》 by the hand; [비유적] make peace 《with》; make up 《구어》; join hands 《with》. ¶ ~를 청하다 offer *a person one's* hand / ~를 나누다 exchange a handclasp; shake hands with each other; shake each other by the hand / 모두와 ~를 나누다 shake hands all around / ~로써 맞이하다 greet 《*a person*》 with a handshake / 그는 따뜻한 손길로 ~했다 He gave my hand a warm clasp. / 두 사람은 굳은 ~를 나눈 후 헤어졌다 They parted after exchanging a firm handshake. / 과거는 씻어버리고 ~를 하여라 You should forget the past and be friends.

**악수**(惡手) 《바둑 등의》 《make》 a bad move [play] 《at chess》.

**악순환**(惡循環) 《form》 a vicious circle [cycle]. ¶ 가난의 ~ a vicious circle of poverty / 물가(物價)와 임금(賃金)의 ~ a vicious cycle [spiral] of prices and wages; a wage-price [price-wage] spiral / ~에 빠지다 be caught [locked] in a vicious circle / ~을 일으키다 cause [start] a vicious circle / 군비 경쟁의 ~을 끊지 않으면 안 된다 We should break the vicious circle of the armaments race.

**악습**(惡習) 《못된 버릇》 a bad habit [custom]; a vicious [pernicious] habit; evil ways; 《악폐》 an evil practice; an abuse; a vice. ¶ 음주(飮酒)의 ~ the vice of intemperance / ~에 물들다 contract a bad habit / ~에 빠지다 give *oneself* up [abandon *oneself*] to a vice; indulge in a vice / ~을 없애다 《자기의》 get rid [break *oneself*] of a bad habit; 《악폐를》 do away with [wipe out] a bad custom [abuses] / (사회의) ~을 일소하다 extirpate evil practices.

**악식**(惡食) 《나쁜 음식》 poor fare; plain food; coarse [gross] food; 《먹기》 gross feeding; (eating) repulsive food; 《승려의 육식》 eating meat (despite Buddhist teachings). ~하다 be a gross feeder; live on plain food; eat repulsive food.

**악심**(惡心) an evil mind 〔intention, thought〕; a malicious intent; a sinister motive. ¶ ～을 품다 become evilly inclined; be tempted 《to *do*》.

**악쓰다** ① 《소리치다》 yell in anger 〔protest〕; bawl out; shout; cry; shriek. ¶ 남편에게 ～ bawl at *one's* husband. ② 《기쓰다》 try hard; be out 《to *do*, for》; struggle; go all out 《미구어》.

**악아** 《아기》 baby!; 《딸》 daughter!; 《며느리》 daughter-in-law!

**악어**(鰐魚) 〖동물〗 a crocodile (아프리카산); an alligator (북아메리카산); a cayman (라틴아메리카산); a gavial (인도산). ¶ ～의〔같은〕 crocodilian.
◉ ～가죽 alligator 〔crocodile〕 leather 〔skin〕. ～(핸드)백 an alligator(-skin) handbag; a handbag of alligator.

**악언**(惡言) bad language; evil speech; abuse. ～하다 speak ill of; abuse; call names; backbite.

**악업**(惡業) 〖불교〗 evildoing in *one's* former existence; 《악행》 a sinful deed; a misdeed; a wicked act. ¶ 전세의 ～은 피할 수 없다 There is no escape from the redemption of evil deeds *one* committed in *one's* previous life.

**악역**(惡役) a villain's part 〔character〕; (the role of) the villain; a heavy. ¶ ～을 맡(아 하)다 play the villain 〔a villain's part〕 《in a film》.

**악역**(惡疫) a plague; a pestilence; an epidemic; an infectious disease. ¶ ～이 만연한 곳 a plague spot; a pestilence stricken district / ～이 만연 중이다 A pestilence is prevalent.

**악연**(惡緣) 《불행한》 an evil connection 〔destiny〕; an unfortunate affinity 〔relation〕; 《끊을 수 없는》 an unhappy and inseparable relation; fatal bonds 〔ties〕 (특히 남녀의). ¶ 끊을 수 없는 ～으로 알고 단념하다 give up hope of breaking off *one's* relations 《with *a person*》.

**악연**(愕然) ～하다 (be) aghast; appalled; amazed; shocked; startled. ¶ ～하여 in amazement 〔astonishment〕 / ～케 하다 strike 《*a person*》 with terror; frighten; shock; amaze; astonish; startle / ～실색하다 turn pale with consternation; be terror-stricken / 소식을 듣고 ～해하다 be astonished to hear the news / 나는 믿었던 친구의 배신에 ～했다 I was absolutely flabbergasted at being deceived by my trusted friend. / 아내가 연속살인범이었음을 알고 ～했다 I was horrified to discover that my wife was a serial killer.

**악영향**(惡影響) a bad 〔a baneful, an evil〕 influence; a ill 〔an adverse〕 effect. ¶ ～을 미치기 쉬운 infectious / ～을 미치다 have 〔exert〕 a bad 〔harmful〕 influence 《on》 / …의 ～을 받다 receive a bad influence from…; be adversely affected by… / 그 텔레비전 프로는 청소년에게 ～을 끼쳤다 The television program had a bad influence on the younger generation.

**악용**(惡用) (an) abuse; (a) misuse; (an) improper use. ～하다 make bad 〔wrong〕 use 《of》; abuse; misuse; put 〔turn〕 《*something*》 to evil ends; use 《*something*》 for the wrong 〔an evil〕 purpose. ¶ 금전을 ～하다 put money to a bad use / 권력을〔지위를, 힘을〕 ～하다 abuse *one's* authority 〔position, power〕 / 남의 이름을 ～하다 use another's name for evil purpose; make an illicit use of another's name.

**악우**(惡友) a bad 〔an evil〕 friend 〔companion〕; [총칭] bad company. ¶ ～와 어울리다 keep bad company / ～가 생기다 get 〔fall〕 into bad company / ～를 피하다 「keep from 〔avoid〕 bad companions; keep out of bad company.

**악운**(惡運) the devil's luck; bad 〔adverse〕 fortune; ill luck 〔fate〕. ¶ ～이 세다 have the devil's (own) luck; thrive in spite of *one's* evil courses / ～이 다하다 come to the end of *one's* devil's luck.

**악음**(樂音) a musical tone 〔sound〕.

**악의**(惡意) malice; ill will; an evil intention; a malicious intent; a sinister motive. ¶ ～ 있는 ill-intentioned; evil-minded; malicious; spiteful / ～ 없는 innocent; harmless / ～로〔에서〕 maliciously; out of spite 〔malice〕; 《일부러》 with malicious intent / ～를 품다 bear ill will 《against》; bear 《*a person*》 malice 〔ill will〕; harbor malice 《to, toward》 / ～로 해석하다 take 《*a thing*》 ill 〔amiss, in ill part〕 / 그가 한 말에는 조금도 ～가 없었다 There was no malice in what he said. / 그는 내게 아무 ～도 품고 있지 않다 He bears no malice to me. / ～로 한 것은 아니다 He meant no harm. / 그는 ～(가) 없는 사람이다 He is a good-natured fellow.

**악의악식**(惡衣惡食) poor clothing and

poor food; a plain dress and a poor meal. ～하다 be ill clad and poorly fed. ¶ ～에 만족하다 be content「with coarse clothing and poor food [with a simple life].

**악인**(惡人) a bad [wicked] man; a villain; a wrongdoer. ¶ 그는 소문만큼의 ～은 아니다 He is not so black as he is painted.

**악장**(樂長) a conductor; a music director; a bandmaster; an orchestra leader.

**악장**(樂章) a movement (of music); a chapter. ¶ 제1 ～ the 1st movement.

**악전고투**(惡戰苦鬪) a desperate struggle; a hard fight; 《경기》 a hard game; 《경쟁》 a stiff contest. ～하다 fight desperately; fight against great odds; fight with *one's* back to the wall; struggle hard 《against, with》. ¶ 선거에서 ～하다 have a close contest in the election / 우리는 ～ 끝에 시합에서 이겼다 We finally won the game after a tough fight.

**악절**(樂節) 〖음악〗 a passage.

**악정**(惡政) misgovernment; misrule. ⇨ 비정(秕政).

**악조건**(惡條件) adverse [unfavorable] conditions [factors]; a bad condition; a handicap. ¶ ～을 무릅쓰고 in spite of unfavorable conditions / 심한 ～ 하에(서) under a severe handicap / ～ 하에서의 전투 a hardy combat / ～을 극복하다「get over [surmount] a handicap / ～하에서 뛰어난 성과를 올리다 achieve excellent results under unfavorable conditions / 이와 같은 ～하에서는 연구를 계속할 수 없다 We can't continue the study any longer under these bad conditions.

**악조증**(惡阻症) morning sickness; 〖의학〗 *hyperemesis gravidarum.* ⇨ 입덧.

**악종**(惡種) a bad seed; a wicked fellow; a villain.

**악증**(惡症) 《병(病)》 a malignant disease; a violent disorder; 《못된 짓》 a wicked act; bad conduct; evil ways.

**악질**(惡疾) a malignant [bad, foul, virulent] disease. ¶ ～에 걸리다 be seized with a malignant disease.

**악질**(惡質) 《성질》 bad [inferior] quality; evil nature; wickedness; 《사람》 a wicked fellow. ¶ ～의 vicious; bad; wicked 《lies》; 《열등》 inferior; 《병》 malignant 《tumors》 / ～적인 장난 malicious mischief / 가장 ～적인 반동주의자 a reactionary of the worst type / ～적인 선거법위반 a flagrant violation of the Election Law.

◉ ～범죄 a flagrant offense. ～분자 bad elements; undesirables. ～선전 pernicious propaganda. ～업자 a wicked dealer [trader].

**악처**(惡妻) a bad [wicked] wife; a Xanthippe. ¶ ～는 평생 골치다 A bad wife is the shipwreck [ruin] of her husband.

**악천후**(惡天候) inclement [bad, unfavorable, rough, nasty] weather. ¶ ～를 무릅쓰고 in spite of bad [nasty] weather; braving adverse weather conditions / ～로 인해 우리는 출발할 수가 없었다 Nasty [Bad] weather prevented us from setting out.

**악취**(惡臭) a bad [foul, nasty] smell; an offensive odor; a stench; a stink. ¶ ～를 풍기는 ill-[bad-]smelling; stinking; stenchy / ～를 풍기다 emit an offensive odor; give out [off] a bad smell; smell bad; stink; reek 《of》 / ～를 막다 destroy a foul odor; deodorize / ～를 없애다 remove a bad smell; deodorize / ～가 코를 찌른다 An offensive smell assails *one's* nostrils. / 생선이 ～를 풍긴다 The fish stinks.

**악취미**(惡趣味) vulgar [bad] taste. ¶ 심한 ～ execrable taste.

**악티늄** 〖화학〗 actinium (기호 Ac.).

**악패듯** harshly; relentlessly; ruthlessly.

**악평**(惡評) 《평판》 a bad reputation; ill fame [repute]; 《비난》 unfavorable criticism. ～하다 speak ill of; run down; talk scandal 《about》; make malicious remarks 《about》; criticize unfavorably [severely]; "blast". ¶ ～이 있는 사람 a person of ill repute / ～을 받다 be criticized (unfavorably); 《구어》 get a bad press (신문 따위에서); 《평판》 be spoken ill of / ～을 퍼뜨리다 circulate scandal 《about *a person*》 / 그녀를 너무 호되게 ～하지 마라 Don't criticize her too severely.

**악폐**(惡弊) an evil; an abuse; a vicious [corrupt, wrong] practice. ¶ ～를 일소하다 do away with abuses [evils]; stamp out evils; sweep away [wipe out] abuses; clear society of its evils / ～를 바로잡다 remedy [correct] evils / ～를 근절[일소]하다 uproot [extirpate] evil practices; wipe [stamp] out evils / 그들은 오랫동안 지속되어 온 ～에 애를 먹고 있다 They are helpless against long existing abuses.

**악풍**(惡風) a bad habit [custom]; vicious manners; evil ways 〔practices〕. ¶ 세상의 ~에 물들다 be led astray 〔infected〕 with the evil ways of the world / ~을 타파하다 do away with a bad custom.

**악필**(惡筆) bad (hand)writing; a poor 〔bad〕 hand; a villainous scrawl. ¶ ~이다 write a bad 〔poor〕 hand; be a bad penman / ~은 일생의 손해다 Bad writing is a lifelong disadvantage 〔loss〕. ◉ ~가(家) a poor 〔bad〕 penman; a scrawler 〔scribbler〕.

**악하다**(惡—) 《도덕적으로》 (be) bad; immoral; wrong; 《사악하다》 (be) evil; wicked; malicious. ¶ 악한 사람 a wicked man; a rascal / 성질이 ~ be ill-natured / 악한 짓을 하다 do 《*something*》 wrong; commit a sin 〔crime〕.

**악한**(惡漢) a wicked fellow; a bad man; a rascal; a villain.

**악행**(惡行) evil conduct; wrongdoing; an evil deed; a wicked act; a misdeed; misdoings.

**악형**(惡刑) a cruel 〔severe〕 punishment; torture. ¶ ~을 가하다 punish 〔inflict〕 a cruel punishment 《on a *person*》.

**악화**(惡化) 《형세·상태의》 a change for the worse; an aggravation; 《품질 따위의》 deterioration; 《풍속 따위의》 degeneration; corruption. ~하다 grow 〔get, become〕 worse; go from bad to worse; 《병이》 take a turn for the worse; 《사태가》 grow more serious; get complicated 〔entangled〕; aggravate; deteriorate. ¶ ~시키다 make 《*something*》 worse; aggravate / 그만두시오 도리어 사태를 더 ~시킬 따름이오 Don't do it. It will only make matters worse. / 그 나라의 경제 상태는 더욱 ~되고 있다 The economic situation in the country is getting 「increasingly worse 〔more serious〕. *or* That country's economic situation is going 〔growing〕 from bad to worse.

**악화**(惡貨) a bad coin; bad 〔invalid〕 money; worthless currency. ¶ ~는 양화를 구축한다 Bad money drives out good (money).

**안**[1] ① 《내부》 the interior; the inside. ¶ 집〔차〕안에 in 「the house 〔a car〕 / 안에(서) within; inside; indoors / 안의 사정 the internal affairs / 안으로부터 from within; from the inside / 안으로 모시다 let 〔show〕 《*a person*》 in / 공을 상자 안에 넣다 put a ball into the box / 안으로 들어가다 go 〔come, get, step, walk〕 in (★ 위의 「안에 들어가다〔모시다〕」 등에 있어서 in은 부사적인 용법으로 전치사의 in 보다도 힘줌말임: [부사] He went in.; [전치사] He went in 〔into〕 the house.) / 안에서 놀다 play indoors / 집안에서 나오다 come from within the house / 집안에 들어박혀 있다 stay indoors; be confined to *one's* house; stick 「at home 〔in the house〕 / 집안은 모든 것이 뒤죽박죽이었다 There was a great hubbub inside the house. *or* All was confusion within the house. / 문이 안에서 열렸다 The door opened from within. / 그의 장래는 내 손안에 있다 I have his future in my hands.
② 《미만》 inside of; within; less 〔not more〕 than; during (…중에). ¶ 일주일 안에 within 〔in less than, inside of 《미》〕 a week / 그 날 안으로 in the course of the day / 기한 안에 within the time limit / 한 시간 안에 회답하겠습니다 I will give you my answer in an hour.
③ 《뒷면》 the back; the wrong side; the reverse side; the other side; the under surface (아래쪽); the inside (내면). ¶ 천의 안쪽 the wrong side of the cloth / 안을 뒤집다 turn inside out.

**안**[2] 《옷의》 the lining 《of a coat》. ¶ 안을 대지 않은 unlined / 안을 대다 line 《a coat with fur》 / 드레스의 안감은 푸른색 비단으로 하시는 것이 어떻습니까 Why don't you use blue silk to line the dress ? / 그 옷은 안이 비단이다 The dress has a silk lining.

**안**[3] ① 《내실》 a boudoir; an inner room; the women's part of the house. ¶ 어머니는 안에 계시다 Mother is in back. ② 《아내》 *one's* wife.

**안**[4] 《여자》 females; womenfolk. ¶ 안주인 a mistress / 안손님 a lady visitor.

**안**(案) ① 《제안》 a proposition 《미》; a proposal; a suggestion (시사). ¶ 안을 제출하다 make a proposal; advance a suggestion / 안을 철회하다 withdraw the proposal. ② 《계획》 a plan; a program; a project; a scheme. ¶ 안을 세우다 set up 〔make, map out〕 a plan; work out a program / 안을 다듬다 elaborate a plan / 정부의 안은 많은 외국 자본과 선진 기술을 국내로 유치하는데 목적을 두고 있다 The government program is aimed at attracting much foreign capital and advanced technology into Korea. ③ 《고안》 an idea; a design; a device. ¶ 명안 a good idea. ④《의안》 a bill; a measure; a draft (초안). ¶ 증세(增稅)안 a tax increase bill / 안을 짜다 make 〔work out〕 a draft / 안을 국회에 제출하다 submit a bill to the National Assembly / 안을 통과시키다 pass a bill.

**안간힘** ¶ 분을 참느라고 ～을 쓰다 try hard to restrain *one's* indignation. / 사업에 성공하려고 ～을 쓰다 struggle to succeed in business / 그는 아들을 구하려고 ～을 썼다 He made a desperate effort to rescue his son.

**안감** 《옷의》 lining (material); cloth for lining.

**안강**(安康) comfortable circumstances and good health. ～하다 (be) well; healthy; safe and sound.

**안갚음** repaying *one's* indebtedness to *one's* parents. ～하다 show *one's* appreciation of *one's* parents; repay *one's* parents for taking care of *one* as a child.

**안개** (a) mist; 《짙은》 (a) fog. (★ a fog, fogs가 되는 까닭—안개라는 현상을 일반적으로 말할 때에는 관사가 안 붙지만, 보통 a London fog처럼 셀 수 있는 말로 봄. 따라서 몇 번인가의 안개는 fogs가 됨). ¶ 짙은 ～ a heavy 〔thick, dense〕 fog / 옅은 ～ a thin 〔light〕 fog / ～에 싸인 산 hills veiled in mist / ～에 싸인〔～가 자욱한〕 골짜기 a mist-hung〔-filled〕 gorge / ～ 낀 아침 a misty morning / ～가 짙은 날 a foggy day / ～에 싸이다 be shrouded by fog; be enveloped 〔wrapped〕 in a fog / ～가 끼다 the fog gathers; a fog sets in; a mist settles / ～가 걷히다 the mist clears up; the fog lifts 〔disperses〕 / 짙은 ～에 싸여 있다 be wrapped 〔enveloped〕 in a dense fog; lie deep in fog / ～가 짙어진다 The fog thickens. / 런던은 겨울에 ～가 심하다 London has bad fogs in winter. / 공항은 온통 짙은 ～에 싸여 있었다 The airport was shrouded in dense fog. / 공항이 짙은 ～에 갇혀서 항공편이 재개될 때까지 두 시간이나 기다려야 했다 The airport was fog-bound, so we had to wait two hours for flights to restart.
◉ ～구름 stratus (clouds). ～상자 〖물리〗 a cloud chamber. ～속 [비유적] 《미궁(迷宮)》 mystery; a maze; a labyrinth: ～속에 싸이다 be in a fog 〔maze〕; be mystified; be shrouded in mystery.

**안거**(安居) a peaceful 〔tranquil, quiet〕 life. ～하다 lead a peaceful life; live in peace; live quietly.

**안건**(案件) an item; a matter; a case; 《의안》 a bill. ¶ 중요 ～ an important item 《on the agenda》.

**안걸이** 《씨름에서》 an inside foot-trip.

**안경**(眼鏡) (a pair of) glasses; eyeglasses; spectacles; specs 《구어》; 《코안경》 a *pince-nez* (F.); 《먼지막이·비행사용》 goggles. (★ 두 개의 렌즈로 만들어진 안경은 복수형을 쓰지만 동사나 대명사는 단수형으로 함. 셀 때에는 a pair of ～, two pairs of ～의 꼴을 취함). ¶ 뿔테 ～ tortoiseshell 〔horn-rimmed〕 spectacles / 테 없는 ～ rimless glasses / 도수가 높은 ～ powerful spectacles; thick 〔strong〕 glasses / 원시〔근시〕용 ～ spectacles for a far-sighted 〔near-sighted〕 person / 원근(遠近)양용의 ～ bifocals; bifocal glasses / ～을 쓰다 put *one's* glasses 〔spectacles〕 on / ～을 쓰고 있다 wear 〔be in〕 glasses / ～을 쓰고 with glasses on / ～을 벗다〔닦다〕 take off 〔wipe〕 *one's* glasses / ～너머로 보다 look over (the edge of) *one's* glasses / ～을 코끝에 걸고 있다 wear *one's* glasses low 〔right〕 down on *one's* nose / ～을 쓰게 되다 take to wearing glasses / 「당신 ～의 도수는 몇 도입니까」—「7도입니다」 "How strong are your glasses?"—"It is 7 (degrees)." / 이 ～은 도수가 맞지 않는다 The glasses aren't the right strength for my eyes. / 그는 ～ 없이도 책을 읽는다 He can read without glasses.
◉ ～다리 the temples 〔sides《영》〕 of a pair of spectacles. ～알 a spectacle lens. ～자국 imprints (on the skin) from wearing glasses. ～쟁이 a (be-) spectacled person; a glasses-wearer; a four-eyes 《구어》. ～점 an optician's shop. ～집 a spectacle case. ～테 the rim 〔frame〕 of a pair of spectacles. 독서용～ reading glasses.

**안계**(眼界) 《시야》 the range 〔field〕 of vision; view; (eye)sight; mental view; outlook. ⇨ 시계(視界).

**안고름** the inside tie-string on a Korean coat.

**안고지다** boomerang; be entrapped by *one's* own trick. ¶ 그는 남을 해치려다가 도리어 안고졌다 He planned to do harm to others but the scheme boomeranged on him.

**안공**(眼孔) 〖해부〗 an eyehole; the eye socket; the orbit of an eye; an eyepit.

**안과**(眼科) 《학문》 ophthalmology; eye specialty; 《병원의》 the department of ophthalmology.
◉ ～병원 an ophthalmic clinic. ～의사 an oculist; an eye doctor [specialist]; an ophthalmologist. ～학(學) (the study of) ophthalmology.

**안광**(眼光) 《안채》 the glitter of *one's* eyes; the light in *one's* eye(s); 《보는 힘》 insight; vision. ¶ ～이 날카롭다 be sharp-[eagle-]eyed; have piercing [sharp] eyes.

**안구**(眼球) 《눈알》 an eyeball. ◉ ～염 ophthalmitis; ophthalmia. ～은행 an eye bank. ～적출(술) (an) ophthalmectomy.

**안구**(鞍具) saddlery; saddle gear; horse gear; harness; tack.

**안기다**[1] 《품 속에 들다》 (come and) nestle in 《*a person's*》 arms; go [move] into 《*a person's*》 arms; throw *oneself* in 《*a person's*》 arms; cuddle; [피동] be embraced; be in 《*a person's*》 arms. ¶ 엄마 품에 안겨 있는 어린애 an infant nestling in its mother's bosom / 아기가 엄마 품에 ～ a baby cuddles up to its mother's bosom / 자연의 품에 ～ be (nestled) in the bosom of nature / 안기어 자다 sleep in 《*a person's*》 arms [bosom].

**안기다**[2] ① 《안도록 하다》 let [have] 《*someone*》 hold in the arms. ¶ 어머니한테 아기를 ～ give the baby to the mother; put the baby in its mother's arms.
② 《죄·책임 등을》 fix 《responsibility》 upon 《*a person*》; put 《responsibility》 on 《*a person's*》 shoulders; charge 《*a person* with a duty》; lay 《the blame》 on 《*a person*》. ¶ 친구에게 책임을 ～ give a friend the responsibility / 빚을 ～ hold 《*a person*》 liable for the debt / 비용을 ～ charge 《*a person*》 with the expenses.
③ 《물건을》 trust [intrude] an article upon 《*a person*》; 《강매》 force a sale on 《*a person*》; 《가짜를》 palm off a fake on 《*a person*》; pass [foist, impose] 《*a thing*》 (up)on 《*a person*》. ¶ 가짜를 ～ pass a false article for a genuine one / 나쁜 물건을 ～ palm off [impose] a bad article upon 《*a person*》 / 선물을 ～ press a gift on 《*a person*》 / 그녀는 관광객에게 가짜 다이아몬드를 떠안겼다 She palmed off an imitation diamond on the tourist.
④ 《알을》 make 《a hen》 sit on 《eggs》. ¶ 닭에게 알을 ～ set the hen (*on* the eggs).
⑤ 《치다》 lodge a blow. ¶ 한 대 ～ give [deal] 《*a person*》 a blow; let 《*a person*》 have it / 귀싸대기를 한 대 ～ slap *a person* [give *a person* a slap] on the cheek.

**안남**(安南) Annam. ¶ ～(사람)의 Annamese. ◉ ～말 Annamese. ～미(米) Annam rice. ～사람 an Annamese; an Annamite.

**안내**(案內) 《인도》 guidance; conduct; lead; 《통지》 information; (a) notice. ～하다 《인도하다》 guide; act as a guide; lead the way 《to》; show 《*a person*》 over [around]; usher [show, conduct] 《*a person*》 in(to) 《a room》; 《초대하다》 invite; ask; 《통지하다》 notify [inform] 《*a person* of, that...》. ¶ 길～ 《일》 guidance; 《사람》 a guide / 연예 ～ 《신문 따위의》 an entertainment guide / 아무의 ～로 under the guidance of *a person*; accompanied by *a person* / 응접실로 ～하다 show 《*a person*》 into the drawing room / 그 부인을 2층으로 ～하시오 Ask the lady upstairs. / 그녀는 우리에게 시내를 ～해 주었다 She took us around the city. / 우리는 그의 ～로 연구소 안을 견학했다 We went around the research institute under the guidance of [guided by] him. / 그녀는 나를 일부러 병원까지 ～해 주었다 She took the trouble to conduct me to the hospital. / 직원의 ～를 받으십시오 《게시》 Escort required. / 나를 ～해 주실 수 없을까요 Would you be so kind as to act as my guide? / 그 소녀는 나를 내 좌석으로 ～했다 The girl ushered me to my seat (in a cinema). / 이 곳 명승지를 구경하고 싶은데 ～해 주실 수 있겠습니까 I want to visit places of interest here. Would you please act as my guide? / ～말씀 드립니다 《공항 따위에서》 Attention, please.
◉ ～(계)원 《호텔 따위의》 a clerk at the information desk; the information desk [booth]; 《백화점의》 a floorwalker; a floorman. ～광고 classified [want] ad. ～도(圖) a guide map; a road map. ～서 a guide(book); a roadbook; a handbook. ～소 an inquiry office 《영》; an information bureau [desk, booth] 《미》; 《게시》 Information. ～원실 《극장 등의》 an usherettes room. ～인[자] a guide; an attendant; 《관광 따위의》 a cicerone;

《극장 따위의》 an usher; an usherette (여자). ～장 an invitation; a card 〔letter〕 of invitation; 《상업용》 a letter of advice. ～표(標) a direction sign.

**안녕**(安寧) ① 《평안》 (public) peace; tranquility; 《복지》 welfare; well-being; 《건강》 good health. ～하다 be in good 〔sound〕 health; (be) well; uneventful; live in peace. ¶「어머님께서는 ～하시나」—「예, ～하십니다」 "How is your mother?"—"Thank you, she is fine."

② 《인사》 ¶ ～하십니까 How are you? *or* How do you do? *or* Good morning 〔day, afternoon, evening〕. (★ How do you do?는 「처음 뵙겠습니다.」의 뜻의 초대면 인사. 종종 How d'ye do? 심하게는 Howdy [háudi]?처럼 발음됨. How are you?는 「건강은 어떻습니까?」란 뜻. are에 stress를 두어 발음됨. 병자에게는 How do you feel?을 씀) / ～하셨습니까 How have you been?

③ 《작별 인사》 good-by(e) (★ 격식을 따지지 않을 때는 goodby(e)로도 씀); (I'll) see you again 〔later〕.; 《친구 사이에서》 so long!; 《여행 때》 farewell; I hope you'll have a pleasant journey 〔voyage〕.; *Bon voyage!* (F.). ～하다 say good-by; bid 《*a person*》 farewell. ¶ ～히 가십시오, ～히 계십시오 Good-bye!; Adieu!; Farewell!; So long!; See you later. (★ 작별할 때 쓰이는 「안녕」이란 인사에는 시간에 따라 Good morning.; Good day.; Good afternoon.; Good evening.; Good night. 따위도 쓰이는데, 이 경우는 반드시 말끝을 올려서 발음함. 말끝을 내리면 만났을 때의 인사가 됨).

◉ ～질서 peace and order: 나라의 ～질서를 유지〔교란〕하다 maintain 〔disturb〕 peace and order in the country.

**안노인**(—老人) 《집안의》 an old woman 〔lady〕 《of the household》.

**안다** ① 《팔·품에》 hold 〔take, carry〕 《a baby》 in *one's* arms; hug; embrace. ¶ 우는 아이를 ～ hug a crying child / 안고 있다 have 《a baby》 in *one's* arms / 안아 올리다 lift 《a girl》 up in *one's* arms / 안아 일으키다 raise 〔lift up〕 《*a person*》 in *one's* arms; help 《*a person* to sit》 up 《in bed》 / (서로) 껴〔부둥켜〕～ embrace 〔hug〕 each other; 《남녀가》 neck (with one another) 《구어》 / 어머니는 여동생을 부둥켜안고 급히 의사에게 달려갔다 Mother hurried to the doctor's carrying my sister in her arms. / 잠깐 아기를 안아 주세요 Hold the baby in your arms a minute please.

② 《생각으로 지니다》 ⇨ 품다 ②.

③ 《불행을》 suffer; encounter 《misfortune》. ¶ 손해를 ～ suffer a loss.

④ 《바람을》 go in the face 〔teeth〕 of. ¶ 바람을 안고(서) 가다 go against 〔in the teeth of〕 the wind.

⑤ 《남의 책임을》 undertake another's responsibility; shoulder; answer 〔hold *oneself* responsible〕 for; take charge of. ¶ 빚을 ～ 《남의》 shoulder another's debt; 《자신의》 hold *oneself* liable for a debt.

⑥ 《새가 알을》 sit on 《eggs》; brood 《eggs》. ¶ 암탉이 알을 ～ a hen sits on her eggs.

**안다미** shouldering another's responsibility. ¶ ～ 씌우다 shift 〔shuffle〕 the responsibility 《for *something*》 on to 《*a person*》; pass the buck to 《*a person*》.

**안단테** 〖음악〗 *andante* (It.).

**안단티노** 〖음악〗 *andantino* (It.).

**안달** fretting; irritation; vexation; impatience. ～(복달)하다 fret 〔worry〕 *oneself* 《about》; be vexed; become impatient; be anxious 《to, about》; be impatient 〔overanxious, nervous〕; be in a fidget 〔stew〕. ¶ ～복달하며 살다 fret away *one's* life / ～하여 병이 나다 fret 〔worry〕 *oneself* ill / 가지 못해 ～하다 be anxious to go; "be champing at the bit" / 그는 결과를 알지 못해 ～이 났다 He is anxious to know the result. / ～나게 하지말고 어서 말하시오 You are trying my patience, tell me at once. / 무엇 때문에 ～하느냐 What are you fretting over?

◉ ～(뱅)이 a fretful person; a worry-wart; a hasty-pants.

**안대**(眼帶) an eyepatch; an eye bandage. ¶ ～를 하다 have *one's* eye in bandage.

**안댁**(—宅) 《your, his》 esteemed wife; Madam; Mrs. ….

**안데스산맥**(—山脈) 〖지명〗 the Andes Mountains.

**안도**(安堵) relief; reassurance. ～하다 be 〔feel〕 relieved 〔reassured〕; feel at ease; breathe easy 〔again〕. ¶ ～의 한숨을 쉬다 heave 〔give〕 a sigh of relief; feel greatly relieved; breathe again freely / 네가 무사히 도착했다는 말을 듣고 ～했다 We were relieved to hear that you had arrived safely. ◉ ～감(感) a relieved feeling; a feeling of relief.

**안되다** ① 《끝나지 않다》 be 〔have〕 not finished; 《잘 되지 않다》 do not go

〔come off〕 well; go wrong 〔amiss〕. ¶ 그의 계획은 잘 안 되었다 His plans have gone amuck. / 그렇게는 안 될걸 《네 생각대로는》 You're not getting away with that!; 《결과가》 It won't work out that way. / 그런 방식으론 잘 안 될 게다 You won't get very far, doing it that way.
② 《금지》 must 〔should〕 not *do;* ought not to *do* (★ must, ought는 다같이 조동사를 취하지 않음. [부정의 명령문] do not...; do not allowed to *do;* be forbidden to *do;* be prohibited from *do*ing. [주어가 2인칭·3인칭·평서문] shall not). ¶ 들어가면 안 됩니까 May I not 〔Can't I〕 come in? / 떠들면 안 된다 Do not make any noise. *or* You must not be noisy. / 더 이상 전쟁을 해서는 안 된다 There must be no more war. / 거짓말을 해서는 안 된다 You must not tell a lie. / 이 차에 개를 태우면 안 된다 Dogs are not allowed in this car. / 그것을 허락하면 안 된다 It ought not to be allowed.
③ 《쓸모없다》 be of no use; won't 〔will not〕 *do* 〔work〕. ¶「이 연필이면 됩니까」—「안 됩니다」 "Will this pencil do?"—"No, it won't." / 이것으론 안 된다 This will not do. / 그 정도의 돈으론 안 된다 That amount of money will not do. / 이 기계는 작동이 안 된다 This machine does not work.
④ 《필요》 be necessary for; need to 《*do*》; 《실패》 be a failure; be unsuccessful; fail. ¶ 되든 안 되든 간에 whether successful or not / 그는 우리 학교에서 없어서는 안 될 선생님이다 He is an indispensable teacher at our school. / 소금은 우리 몸에 없어서는 안 된다 Salt is necessary for our bodies.
⑤ 《조심》 ¶ …하면 안 되니까 lest...; for fear that *one* should *do;* in case...; so as not to *do;* so that... may not... (★ lest, for fear는 문어적. 또 lest, for fear, in case절에서는 영국에서는 should를 쓰고, 미국에서는 should 대신 동사의 원형을 씀: He tried his best *lest* 〔for fear 〔that〕〕 he (*should*) ruin his own reputation.) / 잃어버리면 안 되니까 이 돈은 내가 맡아 두겠다 I shall keep this money, lest you should lose it. / 비에 젖으면 안 되니까 우산을 가지고 가시오 Take an umbrella with you lest 〔in case〕 you should get wet. *or* It might rain so you had better take an umbrella with you. (★ might는 may보다 좀더 부드러운 표현).
⑥ 《…해야만 한다》 ¶ …않으면 ～ must *do;* need *do*ing; ought to *do* / 6시까지 돌아오지 않으면 안 된다 You must be back by six. / 이 책은 내일까지 돌려주지 않으면 안 됩니다 You must return this book by tomorrow. / 이 집은 수리하지 않으면 안 된다 This house needs repairing. / 그녀는 누군가가 도와 주지 않으면 안 된다 She is in need of help.
⑦ 《부족·미달》 be short of. ¶ 2마일이 안 되는 a little short of two miles / 여덟살이 안 되는 어린이 child under eight years of age / 급료는 백만원이 채 안 된다 My pay 〔salary〕 is less than 1,000,000 won. / 2년도 안 되어 영어 회화를 마스터한다는 것은 무리다 It is impossible to master conversational English in less than two years. / 그것은 버스값도 안 된다 That is not even enough for a bus fare.
⑧ [형용사] 《유감이다·딱하다》 be 〔feel〕 sorry 《for, to hear that...》; (be) regrettable; be a pity; take pity 《on》; sympathize 《with》 (동정). ¶ 보기에 안됐다 be pitiful to see / 아프다니 안됐구나 You are ill? That's too bad. / 몸이 편치 못하다니 안됐습니다 It is too bad that you are not feeling well. / 그것 참 안됐군요 I am very sorry for you (to hear that). *or* That's a pity. / 그가 불행하다고 들으니 안됐다 I regret to hear of his ill luck.

**안드로겐** 〖생화학〗 an androgen.

**안드로메다** 《별자리》 the Andromeda.

**안뜰** the front yard of the inner wing of a house.

**안락**(安樂) ease; comfort. ～하다 (be) comfortable; cozy; easy. ¶ ～한 생활 a comfortable life / ～하게 comfortably; in (ease and) comfort / ～하게 살다 live in (ease and) comfort; lead an easy life; live on a bed of roses 〔flowers〕 / 노후를 마음 편히 ～하게 보내다 spend *one's* remaining years in peace and confort.
◉ ～의자 an armchair; an easy chair.

**안락사**(安樂死) an easy and painless death; mercy killing; euthanasia. ¶ 바티칸 당국은 ～를 조건부로 인정한다고 발표했다 Vatican authorities said they would accept euthanasia, but with some conditions. / 그는 ～를 원했다 He asked for (an) easy death. / 의사는 그녀를 ～시키는 것을 거부했다 The doctor refused to administer euthanasia to her. *or* The doctor refused to put her to (an) easy death. / ～는 의사에게 심각한 윤리상의 문제를 제기하고 있다 Euthanasia poses a serious ethical problem for physicians.

**안력**(眼力) ① 《관찰력》 power(s) of observation; perception; penetration; insight. ¶ 날카로운 ～ an acute 〔a sharp〕 insight; acute observation. ② ＝시력(視力).

**안료**(顔料) ① 《화장품》 cosmetics; face-paints. ② 《도료》 a color; a paint; 《색소》 (a) pigment.

**안마**(按摩) massage. ～하다 massage 《*a person, a person's* back》. ¶ ～를 받다 have 〔get〕 a massage; have *oneself* 〔*one's* shoulders〕 massaged. ◉ ～기(器) a kneader. ～사 a massagist 〔massager〕; a masseur (남자); a masseuse (여자): ～사를 불러들이다 call in a massagist. ～시술소 a massage parlor. ～치료 a massage treatment; chiropractic; osteopathy.

**안마**(鞍馬) 『체조』 《기구》 a pommel horse; 《미》 a side horse; 《종목》 the pommel 〔side〕 horse.

**안면**(安眠) a peaceful slumber; a calm rest; a quiet 〔sound, good〕 sleep; a comfortable sleep. ～하다 sleep quietly 〔well, in peace〕; have a quiet sleep; sleep soundly. ¶ ～을 방해하다 disturb *a person's* (quiet) sleep / ～을 못 하다 have a troubled 〔bad〕 sleep; cannot get a quiet night's sleep; have 〔pass〕 a bad night / 이 약을 먹으면 ～을 취할 수 있네 This dose will give you a quiet sleep. / 그 스테레오 좀 꺼줘. ～을 취할 수 없어 Turn off the stereo. It's keeping me awake 〔I can't sleep〕. ◉ ～방해 disturbance of sleep; nuisance at night.

**안면**(顔面) ① 《얼굴》 the face. ¶ ～의 facial. ② 《친분》 acquaintance. ¶ ～이 있다 be acquainted with 《*a person*》; know 《*a person*》 / ～ 있는 사람 an acquaintance / 서로 ～이 있다 know each other by sight; have met before 〔previously〕 / ～이 넓다 have a wide acquaintance; have a large 〔wide〕 circle of acquaintances; be widely known / ～ 박대하다 slight (an acquaintance); treat meanly / 나는 그와 ～은 있으나 아직 이야기는 나누어 보지 못했다 I know him by sight, but I have never spoken to him. / 나는 그 모임에 ～이 적다 I have few acquaintances in that circle. ◉ ～각 the facial angle. ～경련 a histrionic spasm; facial tics 〔spasm〕. ～계수 the facial index. ～골〔근, 동맥〕 the facial bone 〔muscle, artery〕. ～신경 the facial nerve: ～ 신경 마비 『의학』 facial paralysis / ～신경통 『의학』 face-ache; facial neuralgia.

**안면부지**(顔面不知) ¶ ～의 strange; unfamiliar; unknown / ～의 사람 a stranger; an utter 〔a total, a perfect〕 stranger; a man whom one has never met / ～이다 have no (personal) acquaintance 《with *a person*》; be a total stranger to 《*one*》.

**안목** inside 〔interior〕 dimensions; inside measurements 《of a room 〔bowl〕》. ¶ ～으로 (재어) in the clear / ～이 두 자이다 It measures 2 *cha* 「in the clear 〔on the inside〕.

**안목**(眼目) ① 《견식》 an appreciative 〔a discerning〕 eye; a sense of discrimination; appreciation; judgment; an eye 《for》. ¶ 전문가의 ～ an expert's eye / ～이 있다 have an eye 《for works of art》 / 골동품에 대한 ～이 있다 have an eye for 〔be a connoisseur of〕 curios / 예술가로서의 ～을 기르다 train 〔develop〕 artistic judgment 〔discrimination〕 / 최고급 진주를 고르시는 것을 보니 꽤 ～이 있으십니다 It was very discerning of you to choose a pearl of such high quality. ② 《주안(主眼)》 the main object; the point; the gist.

**안무**(按舞) the arrangement of a dance; dance composition; 《발레의》 choreography. ～하다 design the dances 〔movements〕 《for a singing group》; arrange a dance; compose 〔undertake〕 the choreography 《of》. ◉ ～가 a choreographer; a dance director.

**안문**(—門) the inner door 〔gate〕; the door to the inner part of the house.

**안반**(짝) a dough board.

**안방**(—房) the main 〔the women's〕 living room; the women's quarters.

**안배**(按排·按配) 《배치》 arrangement; disposition; 《배분》 distribution; assignment. ～하다 arrange; distribute; assign; set in order.

**안벽**(—壁) the inner wall.

**안벽**(岸壁) a quay (wall); 《부두》 a wharf; 《방파제》 a breakwater. ¶ ～에 배를 대다 bring 〔moor〕 a boat alongside the quay.

**안보**(安保) national security. ¶ 국가의 ～ 문제 national security problems /

물샐틈없는 ~ 태세 the water-tight security posture / 고위급 ~회의 a high-level security meeting.

◉ ~무임승차 a security free ride. ~외교 diplomacy for national security. ~의식 sense of national security: 국민들의 ~ 의식 the public perception of security. ~이사회 《유엔의》 the Security Council. ~ 정세 보고회 a national security briefing session. ~조약 the 《Korea-U.S.》 Security Treaty. ~협의회 the Security Consultative Meeting (생략 SCM). 한미 연례 ~회의 the annual ROK-U.S. Security Consultative Meeting.

**안부**(安否) ① 《무사 여부》 safety; welfare; well-being; 《소식》 news; tidings; a letter. ~하다 inquire after 《*a person*》. ¶ ~를 묻다 inquire after 〔ask about〕 《*a person's*》 health 〔safety〕 / ~를 걱정하다 worry about 《*a person's*》 safety / 아무에게 ~를 알리다 let *a person* know how *one* is / 그 분의 ~를 모르겠다 I don't know how he is getting along. / 나는 그의 ~를 묻는 전보를 쳤다 I sent him a telegram inquiring after his safety.

② 《특히 편지에서의 인사말》 ¶ …에게도 아무쪼록 ~전해주세요 please remember me to 《*a person*》; give my (best 〔kind〕) regards to 《*a person*》; 《육친·친한 친구에게》 give my love to 《*a person*》 / 김 선생에게 ~ 전해 주십시오 Remember me kindly to Mr. Kim. / 춘부장께도 ~ 전해 주십시오 Give my cordial 〔best, kindest, affectionate〕 regards to your father. / 가끔 ~를 전해 주십시오 Please write to me 〔Drop me a line〕 from time to time 〔once in a while〕 and let me know how you are. / 그 분이 당신에게 ~합디다 He sends his regards to you.

**안부**(鞍部) 《산의》 a col; a saddle.

**안부모**(―父母) *one's* female parent; *one's* mother.

**안부인**(―夫人) 《your, his》 esteemed wife; madam.

**안분**(按分) ~하다 divide 〔distribute〕 proportionally 《among》; divide 《*things*》 in proportion. ◉ ~비례 proportional distribution: ~ 비례로 나누다 divide 《*things*》 in proportion.

**안빈낙도**(安貧樂道) ~하다 be content amid poverty and take delight in the (Taoist) Way.

**안사돈**(―査頓) a daughter's mother-in-law; a daughter-in-law's mother.

**안사람** *one's* wife.

**안산암**(安山岩) 〖지질〗 andesite.

**안살림** home 〔household〕 management; housekeeping.

**안색**(顔色) ① 《얼굴빛》 a 〔*one's*〕 complexion; color of the face. ¶ ~이 희다 〔검다〕 have a fair 〔dark〕 complexion / ~이 좋다〔나쁘다〕 look fine 〔bad, ill〕; look well 〔unwell, pale, sick〕/ ~이 좋아지다〔나빠지다〕 look better 〔worse〕; regain 〔lose〕 color. / ~이 변하다 a change comes over *one's* face.

② 《표정》 a look; a countenance; an expression. ¶ ~에 나타내다〔나타나다〕 betray 《anger》; show / ~을 고치다〔부드럽게 하다〕 compose 〔soften〕 *one's* countenance / 아무의 ~을 살피다 try to gauge 〔judge〕 *a person's* feelings 〔state of mind〕 (from *his* expression); read 〔study, search〕 *a person's* face 〔expression〕 / 불안한 ~을 하다 look uneasy; have a concerned look / 그것을 본 순간 그는 ~이 변했다 The color left his face the instant he saw it. / ~으로 그가 성난 것을 알았다 I read 〔saw〕 anger in his countenance. / 나쁜 소식을 듣고서도 그는 ~하나 바꾸지 않았다 Even on hearing the bad news he retained all his customary composure. *or* He received the bad news unblinkingly.

**안성맞춤**(安城―) the very thing; the very 〔right〕 thing wanted 〔one wants, desired〕; just the thing. ¶ ~의 suitable 〔fit〕 《for》; the most suitable; ideal / ~의 날씨 ideal weather 《for fishing》 / ~의 물건 the most suitable thing; the very 〔right〕 thing 《for》; a thing exceedingly happy 《for》 / 그에게 ~의 일 《be》 just the job for him; the work he is best fitted to undertake / 그 사람은 그 일에 ~이다 He is just the man for the work. *or* He is cut out for the job.

**안섶** an in-turned *chŏgori* collar.

**안손님** a woman caller; a lady visitor; a guest of *one's* wife.

**안수**(按手) 〖기독교〗 the imposition of hands; the laying on of hands (in prayer). ~하다 impose hands 《on *a person*》; confirm 《*a person*》.

◉ ~례 the (order 〔rite〕 of) confirmation; the ordination (성직 수임의).

**안식**(安息) rest; repose; doing no labor. ~하다 rest; repose.

◉ ~교(敎) the Seventh-Day Adventist Church. ~년 a sabbatical year. ~일 the Sabbath; a Sabbath day; the

Lord's day: ～일을 지키다 keep 〔observe〕 the Sabbath / ～일을 안 지키다 break the Sabbath. ～처 a place to rest; a resting place; a refuge; a place to find peace: 종교에 ～처를 구하다 seek refuge 〔solace, peace〕 in religion; find relief in religion.

**안식**(眼識) a critical 〔discerning〕 eye; discernment. ⇨ 안목.

**안식구**(—食口) the female members of a family; *one's* wife.

**안식향**(安息香) 〖식물〗 a benzoin; 〖화학〗 benzoin; gum benjamin 〔benzoin〕.
◉ ～산(酸) 〖화학〗 benzoic acid.

**안심** 《쇠고기의》 lean meat of short ribs.

**안심**(安心) ① 《평안》 peace of mind; freedom from care 〔anxiety〕; relief; ease; assurance; reassurance. ～하다 feel easy 《about》; feel at ease; 《안도하다》 feel relieved (마음놓다); 《걱정없다고 여기다》 feel no anxiety; 《틀림없다고 여기다》 feel reassured; be confident 《of, that...》; be 〔rest〕 assured. ¶ ～하고 at (*one's*) ease; free from care; without (any) anxiety / ～하고 죽다 die in peace / ～이 되다 feel relief; be reassured / ～이 안 되다 feel uneasy 《about》; be anxious 《about》; fear / ～시키다 put *a person* at *his* ease; ease *a person's* mind; relieve 《*a person*》 of *his* anxiety 〔fear〕 / 그가 그렇게 말하니 ～이 된다 I am reassured by his saying so. / 그 소식에 ～이 됐다 I was relieved at the news. / 마침내 그가 와서 누구나 크게 ～했다 At last he arrived to the great relief of everybody. / 그 점은 ～하십시오 Put 〔Set〕 your mind at rest 〔ease〕 about that 〔on that score〕. / 만사가 잘 될 것이니 ～해라 I can assure you that things will go well with you.
② 《안전》 security; safety. ¶ ～할 수 없는 병세 a serious 〔dangerous, critical〕 condition / ～하고 살다 live in security / 환자는 아직 ～이 안 된다 The patient is still in serious condition. / 환자는 이제 ～이다 The patient is out of danger now.
③ 《신뢰》 confidence; trust. ～하다 《확신하다》 feel safe 〔confident〕. ¶ ～하고 《자신을 갖고》 with confidence / ～할 수 있는〔없는〕 사람 a reliable 〔an unreliable〕 man / ～하고 그를 믿을 수 없다 We cannot safely unbend with him. / 그 사람이면 ～하고 일을 맡길 수 있을거다 You may trust him to do the work for you. / 틀림없이 합격할테니 ～해라 I can assure that you will pass the exam.

**안심부름** errands around the house; household chores.

**안심찮다**(安心—) ① 《안심 안 되다》 (be) uneasy; anxious; uncertain; insecure; precarious; be ill at ease. ¶ 안심찮게 여기다 feel uneasy; be anxious 《about》; be uncertain 《over》; have misgivings 《about》; be in suspense / 안심찮은 기색이다 look anxious.
② 《꺼림하다》 be sorry. ¶ 폐를 끼치어서 안심찮습니다 I am sorry for all the trouble I am causing you.

**안쓰럽다** be sorry for troubling 《*a person*》 worse off than *oneself*. ¶ 이런 폐를 끼치게 되니 안쓰럽기 짝이 없네 I am so sorry to cause you this kind of trouble.

**안아맡다** bear 〔assume, accept, shoulder, undertake〕 《*another's* responsibility》. ¶ 남의 빚을 ～ shoulder another's debt.

**안아일으키다** raise 〔lift〕 《*a person*》 in *one's* arms; help 《*a person*》 get to *his* feet; help 《*a person*》 (to) sit up in bed. ¶ 그는 노모를 안아일으켰다 He helped his old mother (get) to her feet.

**안압**(眼壓) 〖의학〗 intraocular pressure.

**안약**(眼藥) (an) eyewash; (an) eyewater; (an) eye lotion; eyedrops; medicine for the eyes; an eye salve (연고). ¶ ～을 넣다 apply eyewash 〔eye lotion〕; put drops in *one's* eyes.

**안염**(眼炎) 〖의학〗 inflammation of the eyes; ophthalmia.

**안온**(安穩) peace; tranquility; quiet; calmness. ～하다 (be) tranquil; peaceful; quiet; calm; [서술적] be at ease. ¶ ～하게 peacefully; quietly; tranquilly; calmly / ～한 생활 a placid life / ～한 세상 peaceful 〔tranquil〕 times / 집에서 ～하게 살다 remain quietly at home.

**안올리다** color the inside of; paint the 「inner surface 《of a dish》.

**안와**(眼窩) 〖해부〗 the eye socket; the orbit (of the eye). 「⇨ 청음.

**안울림소리** 〖언어〗 a clear voice 〔note〕.

**안위**(安危) safety and 〔or〕 danger; welfare; security; fate. ¶ 국가의 ～ a national crisis / 국가 ～에 관계되는 문제 a matter affecting the security of the nation; an issue on which the fate of the nation depends / 그는 자신의 ～도 아랑곳 않고 물에 빠져 허우적거리는 소년을 구출했다 Disregarding his own safety, he rescued a drowning boy.

**안이하다**(安易—) (be) easy; easygoing. ¶ 안이하게 easily; 《편하게》 at ease; at *one's* ease / 안이한 생각 an easygoing 〔happy-go-lucky〕 way of thinking / 안이한 생활 an easy life / 안이하게 생각하다 take things too easy / 안이하게 타협하다 make an easy compromise / 그건 지나치게 안이한 사고 방식이다 It is too easygoing a way of thinking.

**안일** housework; women's work. ～하다 do housework.

**안일**(安逸) (idle) ease; idleness; indolence; sloth. ～하다 (be) idle; indolent. ¶ ～한 생활 a life of (idle) ease / ～을 탐하다 live at ease; live in idleness; lead an idle life; idle away *one's* time. ◉ 무사～주의 a peace-at=any-price principle.

**안잠자기** 《가정부》 a (sleeping-in, resident) housemaid. ¶ ～를 두다 keep a housemaid.

**안잠자다** (a maidservant) sleeps 〔lives〕 in (her employer's house).

**안장**(安葬) burial; interment. ～하다 bury; inter; lay to rest; commit to the earth. ¶ 그는 이곳에 ～되었다 He was laid to rest here. ◉ ～지 a burial ground.

**안장**(鞍裝) a saddle. ¶ ～을 지우다 saddle 《a horse》; put on a saddle / ～을 풀다 unsaddle 《a horse》/ ～ 없이 말을 타다 ride bareback. ◉ ～코 a nose with a sunken bridge; a flat 〔pug, snub〕 nose; a person with such a nose.

**안저**(眼底) 〖해부〗 the fundus (of the eye); the eyeground. ◉ ～검사(법) 〖의학〗 funduscopy. ～출혈 〖의학〗 (a) hemorrhage in the eyeground. ～혈압계 an ophthalmodynamometer.

**안전**(安全) safety; security. ～하다 (be) safe; secure; be free from danger. ¶ ～하게 safely; securely; in 〔with〕 safety / ～한 방법 a safe method 〔way〕 / ～한 장소 a place 〔zone〕 of safety / ～한 투자 a sound investment / 생명과 재산의 ～ security of life and property / 작업의 ～ safety in work operations / ～하게 하다 secure; make safe 《against》/ 일신의 ～을 도모하다 look to 〔seek〕 *one's* own safety; play safe / ～을 위협하다 threaten the security 《of》; compromise the safety 《of》/ ～을 유지하다 maintain the safety / 국가의 ～을 위태롭게 하다 endanger national security / ～한 장소에 두다 keep 《*a thing*》 out of harm's way / ～을 위하여 그것을 은행에 맡겨라 For the sake of safety, deposit it in the bank. / 기차로 가는 것이 ～하다 It is safe(r) to take a train. / ～ 거리 유지 《게시》 Keep safe distance. / 여기 있으면 ～하다 You are safe here. *or* We are out of danger here. / ～상의 이유로 창문에 창살을 설치했다 For security reasons we had railings put on the windows. / ～을 확인한 다음 길을 건너도록 해라 Make sure that it's in safe before you cross the road. / 이 집은 어떤 지진에도 ～하다 This house is secure in any earthquakes.
◉ ～감 a sense of security. ～관리 safety supervision: ～ 관리자 a safety supervisor. ～기(器) 《전기의》 a circuit breaker; a cut-out switch. ～등 《광산용의》 a safety lamp. ～띠 a safety belt: ～띠를 매어 주십시오 《게시》 Fasten safety belts.; 《좌석의》 Please fasten your seat belt. ～면도(날) a safety razor (blade). ～모(帽) a crash helmet. ～성(性) safety. ～수칙 《observe》 safety regulations; safety rules. ～운동 safety campaign. ～유리 safety glass. ～율(率) a safety factor; the factor of safety. ～장교 a safety officer. ～장치 a safety device 〔appliance〕; 《총포의》 a safety bolt 〔lock, catch, lever〕; a safety 《구어》: (총에) ～ 장치를 하다 put 《a gun》 on safety; put the safety catch on / (총의) ～장치를 풀다 put off the safety (catch). ～점검 《launch》 a safety check-up 《of》. ～제일 Safety First: ～제일주의로 나가다 act on the principle 〔basis〕 of safety first. ～조업 safety operation. ～주간 Safety Week. ～지대 a safety zone; 《도로의》 an island; a traffic 〔safety 《미》〕 island; 《영》 a refuge. ～책 a safe measure; a safe plan: ～책을 취하다 take precautions 〔safe measures〕; 《구어》 play it safe. ～ 통신 전술 a safety communication tactics. ～판 a safety valve. ～핀 a safety pin: ～핀을 꽂다 fasten 《a crape to *one's* sleeve》. 교통～ traffic 〔road〕 safety: 아이들에게 교통～에 관해서 가르치는 일은 매우 중요하다 It's very important to teach children about road safety.

**안전권**(安全圈) 《지대》 a safety zone; 《선거·경쟁 등에서의》 a safe lead. ¶ (경쟁에서) ～에 들다 get 〔secure〕 a safe lead / (선거에서) K씨는 ～에 들어 있다

Mr. K is safe to win the seat. *or* 《구어》 Mr. K is home free. *or* 《구어》 Mr. K is home and dry.

**안전기준**(安全基準) safety standards. ¶ 방사능이 원자력 위원회에서 정한 ~을 웃돌았다 The radioactivity rose above the safety levels established by the Atomic Energy Commission.

**안전벨트**(安全—) a safety belt. =안전띠.

**안전보장** security. ¶ 집단 ~ collective security. ◉ ~조약 a security pact. ~이사회 《유엔의》 the Security Council. 국가~ 회의 the National Security Council. 집단~협정 the Collective Security Arrangement.

**안전시설**(安全施設) safety facilities.

**안전운전**(安全運轉) safe 〔careful〕 driving. ¶ (자동차의) ~ 규칙 road safety rules / ~을 하다 drive safely 〔carefully〕 / ~을 하도록 하여라 Drive safely 〔safe〕.

**안절부절못하다** "be on pins and needles"; be restless; be anxious; be agitated 〔nervous〕; be impatient; be 〔get〕 irritated; be in a fidget; fret (and fume). ¶ 안절부절 못하여 restlessly; nervously; uneasily; impatiently; irritatingly; in a fret / 안절부절 못하는 사람 a restless person; a fidget / 안절부절 못하게 하다 vex; fret; give 《*a person*》 the fidgets / 네가 좀처럼 오지 않아(서) 안절부절 못했다 I was irritated at your delay.

**안정**(安定) stability; stabilization; steadiness. ~하다 (be) stable; stabilized; settled; become steady; 《변동이 없는 상태》 level off. ¶ 물가〔경제, 통화〕의 ~ price 〔economic, currency〕 stabilization / 생활의 ~ security of living 〔*one's* livelihood〕 / ~이 결여하다 be unsettled; lack stability / ~을 유지하다〔잃다〕 keep 〔lose〕 *its* 〔*one's*〕 balance 〔equilibrium〕; maintain 〔lose〕 *its* 〔*one's*〕 stability / 생활의 ~을 얻다 secure *one's* livelihood; find a sure means of living / (경제를) ~시키다 stabilize (economy) / 국민 생활을 ~시키다 stabilize national life / ~되다 be stabilized / ~ 속에 발전을 바라는 대다수의 국민 the majority of the people in wish of progress amid stability / ~된 다수 a stable majority / ~ 속의 개혁 reforms amid stability / 나라의 정치적 ~ the nation's political stability / 정국은 ~되어 있다 The political situation is stable. / 그녀는 정서가 불~하다 She is emotionally unstable. ◉ ~감 a sense of stability: ~감이 있는〔없는〕 stable 〔unstable〕; secure 〔insecure〕. ~경제 a stable economy. ~고용 steady 〔stable, safe, secure〕 employment 〔job〕. ~공황 a stabilization crisis. ~기금〔자금〕 safety 〔stabilization〕 fund: 농가 ~ 기금 farming safety fund. ~도〔성〕 stability. ~성장 『경제』 a stabilized 〔stable〕 growth: 경제의 ~ 성장기 a period of stable economic growth. ~세력 a stabilizing force 〔power〕. ~ 인구 a stable population. ~의(儀) a ship stabilizer. ~장치 a stabilizer; an equilibrator. ~정권 a stabilizing government. ~주주 a strong stockholder. ~책 stabilization measures. ~통화〔화폐〕 stabilized money; a stable currency. ~판(板) 《비행기의》 a stabilizer: 수직 ~판 a (vertical) fin; a vertical stabilizer / 수평~판 a horizontal stabilizer.

**안정**(安靜) rest; quiet; peace; repose. ~하다 (be) tranquil; quiet; peaceful; be at ease. ¶ ~하게 quietly; in quiet / ~을 요하다 [병·환자가 주어] require rest in bed / ~을 유지하다 keep quiet; lie quietly; 《병상에서》 stay in 〔keep to *one's*〕 bed / ~시키다 set at ease; quiet; relieve / 의사는 그에게 절대 ~을 명했다 The doctor prescribed 「an absolute 〔a complete〕 rest for him. ◉ ~요법 a rest cure 〔therapy〕.

**안정**(眼睛) the pupil 〔apple〕 of the eye. ◉ ~피로 『의학』 asthenopia; eyestrain; fatigue of the eyes.

**안주**(安住) peaceful living; a comfortable life; a serene life. ~하다 live peacefully; lead 「a comfortable life 〔a peaceful living〕. ¶ ~할 땅을 찾다 seek a place where *one* can live in peace / 현재의 지위에 ~하고 있다 be content with *one's* present position.

**안주**(按酒) a 「side dish 〔tidbit〕 taken with alcoholic drinks; a relish taken with wine; a dish eaten with wine. ¶ 안줏감 side-dish 〔tidbit〕 makings / 술과 ~ wine and some eatables / 술 ~로 as a side dish for wine / 이것은 술~에 좋습니다 This goes very well with wine. / ~는 무엇이 있습니까 What eatables do you have with your wine? / 술~가 아무 것도 없습니다 I have nothing to take with wine. / ~는 별로 없지만, 많이 드십시오 I'm sorry I don't have much to go with wine, but please drink heartily. / 상사에 대한 험담을 ~ 삼아 술을 마셨다 We gossiped about our boss to give added zest to our drinking.

**안주머니** an inside pocket. ¶ ～에 넣어 두다 keep 《*a thing*》 in one of *one's* inside pockets.

**안주인**(一主人) the lady of the house; the wife; the landlady; the hostess; the mistress.

**안중**(眼中) ① 《눈 속》 inside of the eye; in the eye. ② 《마음 속》 attention; notice; mind; heart. ¶ ～에 없다 be out of *one's* account 〔consideration〕 / ～에 두지 않다 take no notice of; be of no concern; pay no attention to; think 〔make〕 nothing 《of》; disregard / ～에 사람이 없다 think of none but *oneself* / …은 ～에 두지 않다 take no regard 〔account, thought, notice〕 of... / 그의 ～에는 돈밖에 없다 He thinks nothing but money. / 그 같은 사람은 ～에도 없다 I take no notice of such a fellow (as he). *or* Such a man is beneath the notice.

**안질**(眼疾) an eye disease 〔complaint, trouble, disorder〕; sore eyes; an ophthalmic ailment 〔case〕. ¶ ～에 고춧가루 a very annoying thing / ～에 노랑 수건 something kept close at hand for use; an intimate; a constant companion / ～을 앓다 suffer from an eye trouble; be afflicted with an eye disease.

**안집** 《안채》 an inner building 〔wing〕; the main building (of a house).

**안짝** ① 《…내》 within; inside a limit; less 〔not more〕 than. ¶ 천원 ～의 금액 a sum not exceeding a thousand won / 백만원 ～의 수입 an income short of one million won / 1마일 ～ a short mile; a distance short of a mile / 1주일 ～에 within 〔in less than, inside of 《미》〕 a week / 그는 나이가 기껏해야 20세 ～이다 He is twenty at the most. / 만 원 ～으론 팔 수 없다 I won't sell under 〔for less than〕 10,000 won. ② 〖문학〗 the first line (of a couplet).

**안짱다리** a bowlegged person. ¶ ～의 bowlegged / ～로 걷다 walk intoed 〔pigeon-toed〕; walk with *one's* toes turned in 〔inward〕.

**안쪽** the inside; the interior; the inner part. ¶ ～의 inside; inner / ～에 inside; within / ～에서 열다 open from within / ～에서 자물쇠를 채우다 lock from 〔on〕 the inside; bar from within / ～에서 잠겨 있다 be locked on the inside 〔from within〕 / ～으로만 열리다 open only inward / 바깥쪽은 녹색이고 ～은 황색이다 It is green without and yellow within.

**안쫑잡다** ① 《마음 속에》 keep in mind. ② 《대중잡다》 grasp; take in; roughly understand; get the general idea; make a rough estimate 《of》.

**안찝** ① 《옷의》 the lining of a garment; (cloth for) lining. ② 《내장》 the viscera 〔guts〕 of an animal. ③ 《관》 a coffin.

**안차다** (be) bold; daring; fearless; dauntless. ¶ 안찬 사람 a bold man.

**안착**(安着) safe arrival; 《물품의》 safe receipt. ～하다 arrive safe 〔safely, in safety〕; reach 《London》 safe and sound; 《물건이》 duly reach; reach in good condition. ¶ ～을 알리다 inform 《*a person*》 of *one's* safe arrival.

**안창** a shoe liner; an inner sole. ¶ 구두에 ～을 깔다 put liners in shoes.

**안채** the main building (of a house).

**안채**(眼彩) the brightness of the eyes; the glitter of the eyes.

**안출**(案出) contrivance; invention. ～하다 contrive 《a plan》; devise; think 〔make, work, strike〕 out 《a plan》; invent; originate; study out. ◉ ～자 a contriver; an inventor; an originator.

**안치**(安置) ① 《불상 따위를》 enshrinement; installation; 《관을》 laying in state. ～하다 install; enshrine; lay in state. ¶ 절에 ～된 불상 the Buddhist image enshrined in the temple / 유해를 ～하다 lay 《*a person's*》 remains in state 〔mortuary〕 / 그 절에는 작은 불상이 ～되어 있다 There is a little Buddhist image enshrined in the temple. ② 《죄인을》 confining an exile in his place of exile.

**안치다**[1] 《솥에》 get 《rice》 ready to cook; prepare 《rice》 for cooking 〔boiling〕.

**안치다**[2] 《어려운 일이》 press upon *one;* threaten; 《절박하다》 be imminent; lie ahead; impend; be in the offing.

**안타**(安打) 〖야구〗 a hit; a base 〔safe〕 hit; 《단타》 a single (hit). ¶ 깨끗한 ～ a clean hit / 3루를 뚫는 ～ a hit through third / 투수의 머리 위를 빠지는 ～ a hit over the pitcher's head / ～를 치다 hit; make 〔get〕 a (safe) hit / (투수가) 타자에게 ～를 허용하다 allow a hit to the batter / 6～를 빼앗다 collect six hits 《off the pitcher》 / 2～로 막다 hold 《the opposing team》 to two hits / ～ 넷으로 3점을 올

리다 score three runs on four hits / 무~로 봉쇄하다 keep 《the opposing team》 hitless. ◉ 우전〔좌전, 중전〕~ a hit to right 〔left, center〕.

**안타까워하다** ① 《애태우다》 "be all hot and bothered"; be anxious about 〔over〕; be 〔feel〕 impatient 《at, for, of》; be irritated 《at, by, with》; be tantalized 《at》; be annoyed by; be nervous 〔upset, agitated〕 about; be vexed at. ¶ 정치의 부패를 ~ deplore the corruption of politics / 시간이 더디 가는 것을 ~ be impatient for the time to pass; feel that time drags by too slow / 너무 안타까워 말게, 내일이면 결과를 알게 되니 Don't be so impatient, we will know the result tomorrow. ② 《마음 아파하다》 be heartbroken 《at》; be distressed 〔devastated〕 《by》; 《딱하게 여기다》 feel 〔be〕 sorry 《for *a person*》; pity. ¶ 남의 불행을 ~ feel sorry for another's misfortune.

**안타깝다** ① 《애타다》 it is frustrating 〔tantalizing, upsetting〕; it is annoying; it gets on *one's* nerves; it bothers 〔upsets〕 *one;* it makes *one* anxious 〔impatient〕; it gets *one* "all hot and bothered". ¶ 미국에 못가서 ~ be anxious to go to America / 방학을 안타깝게 기다리다 wait impatiently for the school vacation / 보기만 하고 만지지 못하니 ~ It is tantalizing to see it but not to touch it. / 참 안타깝구나 How vexing 〔provoking〕! *or* You try my patience. *or* I am losing my patience with you. / 시간가는 것이 안타까웠다 Times hung heavy on my hands.
② 《마음 아프다》 (be) pitiful; pitiable; poor; it is distressing 〔heartbreaking〕; it makes *one* feel bad 〔sorry〕. ¶ 안타까운 처지 a 「pitiable 〔poor〕 condition / 안타깝게 여기다 feel pity for 《*a person*》; take 〔have〕 pity on 《*a thing*》 / 그가 그렇게 젊어서 죽다니 ~ It is heartbreaking that he should have died so young.

**안타깝이** an impatient person; a nervous 〔"jumpy"〕 person; an anxious person; a "worry-wart".

**안타깨비** a coarse silk woven from broken threads.

**안타다** ride in front of 《*a person*》 (on a horse or a sedan chair).

**안택**(安宅) 〖민속〗 calming the household god for the peace of the household. ~하다 bring peace to the home by offering sacrifice to the household god. ◉ ~경 scriptures read in the shamanistic rites for the household god. ~굿 the shaman rite for the household god.

**안테나** 〖라디오·TV〗 an antenna 《미》; an aerial (wire) 《영》. ¶ 접시형(型) ~ a dish antenna; a (radio) dish / 실내~ an indoor antenna / ~를 세우다 set 〔put〕 up an antenna; stretch 〔prop〕 an antenna / 집집마다 지붕에 TV ~가 세워져 있다 TV antennas are sticking up high on the roofs of the houses. ◉ ~회로〔버팀대〕 an antenna circuit 〔support〕. 자동차용~ an auto antenna. 지향〔송신〕~ a directive 〔sending〕 antenna.

**안티모니, 안티몬** 〖화학〗 antimony; stibium (기호 Sb). ◉ ~산 antimonic acid: ~산염 antimonate.

**안티피린** 〖약〗 antipyrin(e).

**안팎** ① 《안과 밖》 the inside and outside; obverse and reverse; the ins and outs. ¶ ~의 internal and external; home and foreign / ~의 정세 the internal and external state of affairs/ ~으로 within and without; inside and outside 《a house》; in and out; 《국내외로》 at home and abroad / ~으로 다난한 해 an eventful year both at home and abroad / 옷의 ~을 뒤집다 turn a dress inside out / 집의 ~이 깨끗하다 The house is spick and span inside and out.
② 《표리》 two sides; the right and wrong sides. ¶ ~이 있는 double-dealing / ~이 있는 사람 a double-dealer; 《고용인 따위의》 an eye server / ~이 없는 single-hearted〔-minded〕 / 그는 ~이 다르다 He plays a double game. *or* He is two-faced. / 사람이 ~이 있어서는 못 쓴다 You must not deal with a double game.
③ 《내외》 husband and wife; man and wife. ¶ ~이 금실좋게 살다 have a happy married life; live happily together as man and wife.
④ 《대략》 more or less; around 《미》; about; some; or so; thereabouts; approximately. ¶ 열흘 ~ ten days or so / 5 백 원 ~ five hundred won or so; around 〔about〕 500 won / 1주일 ~으로 in a week or so; in about a week / 비용은 백만원 ~이 들겠다 The cost will be about a million won.
◉ ~벽(—壁) inner and outer walls. ~심부름 inside and outside chores. ~일 inside and outside work. ~채 inner and outer buildings.

**안팎곱사등이** a person with a hump-back and a protruding chest.

**안팎노자**(一路資) the round-trip fare. ¶ 인천까지 ~가 얼마입니까 How much is it round-trip to Inch'ŏn?

**안편지**(一便紙) 《내간》 a letter from a woman to a woman.

**안표**(眼標) a sign; a mark; an ear-mark. ~하다 make 〔leave, put〕 a mark 《on》; (ear)mark. ¶ 빨간 리본을 ~로 달다 put a red ribbon as a mark / ~로 책장의 모서리를 접다 fold down the corner of a page to mark the place. 「sue paper.

**안피지**(雁皮紙) unsized silk paper; tis-

**안하**(眼下) under *one's* (very) eyes; (right) beneath the eyes. ¶ ~에 내려다보다 《경멸하다》 look down upon 《*a person*》 / ~무인이다 be too proud to have an eye for anyone; be haughty 〔stuck-up, supercilious〕 / ~무인의 overbearing; arrogant; audacious; outrageous; insolent; defiant / ~무인으로 audaciously; outrageously; insolently; overbearingly; 《고자세로》 high=handedly / ~무인의 거동 insolent behavior / 그는 하는 짓이 ~무인이다 He behaves audaciously.

**안한**(安閑) leisure; idleness. ~하다 be at leisure; be at peace; (be) idle. ¶ ~히 idly; lazily; in idleness / ~히 지내다 pass *one's* time in idleness.

**앉다** ① 《자리에》 sit (down); take 〔have〕 a seat; seat *oneself;* 《쭈그리고》 squat (down). ¶ 단정히 ~ sit straight (up); sit in the correct manner 《on》 / 책상다리하고 ~ sit crosslegged / 의자 위에 ~ sit down on a chair / 피아노를 향해 ~ sit down on a piano / 책상을 향해 ~ sit at a desk / …와 등을 맞대고 ~ sit back to back with... / 무릎을 꿇고 ~ sit on *one's* heels 〔knees〕 / 편히 ~ sit at *one's* ease / 앉아 있다 be seated / 털썩 ~ sink 〔drop〕 into 《a chair》 / 잠시도 앉아 있을 새가 없다 be too busy to sit down (for a rest) / 벤치에 네 사람은 넉넉히 앉을 수 있다 The bench can accommodate four persons easily. / 앉으십시오 Please take a seat. *or* Won't you sit down 〔have a seat〕, please? / 직업상 앉아만 있는 사람에게는 이것이 좋은 운동이 된다 This is good exercise for people in sedentary occupation.

② 《지위에》 take (up) *one's* office; assume 〔come into〕 office 《as》; be installed 《in an office》. ¶ 권좌에 앉은 사람들 men in the saddle; those in (position of) power / 국무장관 지위에 ~ take office as the Secretary of State / 선생 자리에 ~ take up a post as a teacher / 후임으로 ~ succeed *a person* 《as manager, in *his* post》; take *a person's* place; step into *a person's* shoes / 자네가 그 자리에 앉은 것을 보니 기쁘네 I am glad to see you installed in that chair.

③ 《새 따위가》 alight 〔light, perch, sit, settle〕 《on》; roost (홰에). ¶ 새가 나뭇가지에 앉아 있다 A bird perchs on a twig. / 자네 왼발에 모기가 앉았네 There is a mosquito on your left leg. / 나비가 내 손등에 앉았다 A butterfly settled on the back of my hand.

④ 《먼지 따위가》 gather; accumulate. ¶ 책상에 먼지가 앉았다 Dust gathered on the table.

**앉아서** from *one's* seat 〔place〕; at *one's* home; without traveling 〔stirring〕. ¶ ~ 세계 일주를 하다 take an arm-chair tour of the earth / ~ 설악산을 볼 수가 있다 can enjoy a view of Mt. Sŏrak from *one's* own room; can stay home and see Mt. Sŏrak.

**앉은걸음** ¶ ~으로 다가가다 crawl up 《to a place》 on *one's* knees; sidle 〔edge〕 up 《to》.

**앉은검정** 《솥 밑에 붙은》 the soot on the bottom of a kettle; kettle-black.

**앉은뱅이** a cripple who can only move on *his* (hand's and) knees (★ cripple은 영어에서도 차별어이므로 피해야 함); a wheel-chair case. ¶ 그는 ~이다 He is crippled 《with rheumatism》. / ~ 용쓴다 《속담》 barking at 〔against〕 the moon 《미》. ◉ ~저울 a platform scale.

**앉은부채** 〖식물〗 a skunk cabbage.

**앉은일** a sedentary job; seated work; bench work. ¶ ~을 하다 have a sedentary job / ~을 하는 사람 a sedentary.

**앉은자리** a seat which has been taken; *one's* seat 〔sitting〕. ¶ ~에서 there and then; immediately; on the spot; impromptu; off the cuff 《구어》; at a sitting / ~에서 만들다 make 《*a thing*》 on the spot / ~에서 시를 짓다 improvise a poem; compose a poem extempore / ~에서 의견을 말하다 give an offhand opinion 《on *a person*》 / ~에서 맥주 여섯 병을 마시다 finish up half a dozen bottles of beer at a stretch / 그 건(件)에 관해서는 ~에서 답변 드리기 어렵습니다 About that matter, I don't think I can give you an answer right away.

**앉은장사** keeping a shop (as contrasted with an itinerant trade). ¶ ～를 하다 keep a shop.

**앉은차례**(一次例) the seating order; the order of seats.

**앉은키** *one's* sitting height. ¶ ～가 작은 short-bodied / ～를 재다 measure 《*a person's*》 sitting height.

**앉을깨** ① 《베틀의》 the seat of a loom. ② 《걸터앉는》 a straddle seat.

**앉을자리** a place to sit. ¶ ～를 가리키다 motion to a seat.

**앉음새** the way *one* sits; *one's* seated posture. ¶ ～로 미루어 인격까지도 짐작할 수 있다 You can figure out a person's character from the way he sits.

**앉히다** ① 《앉게 하다》 seat; place 《*a person*》 in a seat; have 《a *person*》 sit down. ¶ 안락 의자에 ～ seat 《a *person*》 〔have 《*a person*》 sit〕 in an armchair / 상좌에 ～ give 《a guest》 the seat of honor; seat 《*a person*》 at the head 〔top〕 of the table. ② 《지위에》 place 〔install〕 《*a person* in a position》. ¶ 시장 자리에 ～ appoint 《*a person*》 to the post of mayor / 왕위에 ～ set 《*a person*》 on the throne. ③ 《버릇을》 teach 《manners》; discipline. ④ 《따로 잡아 기록하다》 transfer an item 《into a record》.

**않다** be not; do not...; have not. ¶ 조금도 …～ not... at all; not... in the least / …하지도 —하지도 ～ neither... nor— / 누구에게도 지지 ～ be unbeatable; can stand up to anybody / 조금도 노력을 ～ do not lift a hand / 집이 크지 ～ The house is not large. / 덥지도 춥지도 ～ It is neither hot nor cold. / 나는 돈을 갖고 있지 ～ I have no money with 〔about〕 me. / 그 여자는 예쁘지 ～ She is not pretty. / 그 사람은 모자를 쓰지 않는다 He does not wear a hat. / 그런 짓은 하지 않겠다 I won't do such a thing. / 인천에 같이 가지 않겠니 Won't you come with me to Inch'ŏn? / 그는 이틀이나 아무것도 먹지 않고 지냈다 He went without food for two days.

**않을 수 없다** be compelled 〔forced, obliged〕 to 《*do*》; be under the necessity of 《*do*ing》; be driven by dire 〔sheer〕 necessity to 《*do*》. ¶ …하지 ～ 《어쩔 수 없이》 have to *do;* must *do;* have no choice but to *do;* be forced 〔compelled〕 to *do;* 《안하려고 해도》 cannot help *do*ing; cannot but *do;* cannot help but *do* / 최후 수단을 쓰지 ～ be driven 〔impelled〕 to extreme measure / 나는 그를 존경하지 ～ I cannot but respect him. / 나는 그가 무죄라고 생각지 ～ I cannot help believing that he is innocent. / 긴급한 일이라고 해서 즉시 가지 않을 수 없었다 I had to go straightaway because they said it was urgent. / 나머지는 운에 맡기지 않을 수 없었다 I had no choice but to leave the rest to chance.

**알**[1] ① 《새의》 an egg; 《물고기·개구리의》 spawn. ¶ 새알 a bird's egg / 생선 알 fish eggs; spawn; roe (몸 안의) / 갓 낳은 알 a new-laid egg / 알을 낳다 lay an egg; 《물고기가》 spawn; discharge its spawn / 알을 품다 sit on eggs; brood / 알을 품게 하다 set 《a hen》 on eggs / 알을 까다 hatch an egg / 알을 깨다 break 〔open〕 an egg 《into a bowl》.
② 《달걀》 a chicken egg.
③ 《작고 둥근 것》 any small round object; a bead. ¶ 눈알 an eyeball / 안경알 a spectacle lens / 탄알 a ball; 《포탄》 a shell; 《산탄》 a shot; 《소총탄》 a bullet / 콩알만 하다 be no bigger than a bean / 이 포도는 알이 잘다 In this bunch, the grapes are small.
④ 《낟알·알맹이》 a grain; a berry. ¶ 쌀알 a grain of rice / 모래알 a grain of sand / 알이 들다 go 〔run〕 to seed; grow ripe; ripen / 이 쌀은 알이 고르다 This rice is even-grained.

**알**[2] ⇨ 아래. ¶ 알로 내려가거라 Go on down!

**알–** bare; naked; stripped (down to essentials); uncovered; out-and-out; bald; essential; important; core; net; real; true-to-life; sure-enough; down-to-earth; thorough; complete; whole. ¶ 알몸 a naked body / 알부피 net bulk.

**알갱이** a kernel; a grain; a berry; 《작은》 a granule.

**알거지** a man with no property but his own body; a person as poor as a crow 〔church mouse〕. ¶ ～가 되다 become (quite) penniless; lose everything *one* has 〔in *one's* possession〕.

**알겨먹다** trick a weaker person out of some small thing. ¶ 불쌍한 소녀의 돈을 ～ defraud 〔cheat〕 a poor girl of her money.

**알겯다** 《암탉이》 cluck for a rooster (to mate with).

**알곡**(一穀) ① 《알곡식》 pure grain with no grit in it. ② 《깍지 벗긴》 husked grain.

**알과녁** a (target) bull's-eye.

**알깍쟁이** 《지독한 노랑이》 a real tightwad; a real "stinker".

**알다** ① [일반적] know; have (good) knowledge 《of》; be familiar 《with》; find out; get knowledge 《of》. ¶ 이미 알고 있는 known / 잘 아시는 바와 같이 (as) you know; as you are well aware / 내가 알기에는 as far as I know; for all I know; to (the best of) my knowledge / 알 권리 the 《public's》 right to know; the right to free access to information / …할 줄 ~ know how to…; can… / …인 것을 ~, …인 줄로 ~ know 〔find out〕 that… / 헤엄을 칠 줄 ~ know how to swim / 그가 폐병임을 ~ know that he is a consumptive / 알게 되다 come to *one's* knowledge / 자기를 ~ know *oneself* / 미국을 잘 ~ have first-hand knowledge of America / 독일어를 좀 ~ have some knowledge of German / 속속들이 ~ have a thorough knowledge 《of》; be very much in the know 《about》; understand fully / 전혀 알지 못하다 have not the least 〔slightest〕 idea 《of》; be utterly 〔completely〕 ignorant 〔unaware〕 《of》 / 아는 체하다 pretend to know; speak knowingly; have a knowing look / 잘 알고 있습니다 I know it very well. / 어떤 일이 일어날지 아무도 알 수 없다 No one knows 〔can tell〕 what will happen. *or* There is no saying 〔telling, knowing〕 what may happen. / 모두가 그 사실을 알고 있다 Everybody knows the fact. *or* The fact is known to everybody. (★ The fact is known *by* everybody는 틀림. known은 형용사처럼 생각할 수 있으므로 be familiar to와 마찬가지로 to를 취함. by는 보통 A man is known *by* the company he keeps.「친구를 보면 그 사람의 사람됨을 알 수 있다」와 같이 딴 뜻으로 쓰임) / 내가 알기에는 그 문제를 다룬 책이 없다 To (the best of) my knowledge, there are no books on the subject. / 아는 것이 병 《속담》 Ignorance is bliss. / 이럴 줄 알았다면 오지 않았을 텐데 If I had known how it would be, I would not have come.

② 《이해하다》 understand; know; see; grasp; 《구어》 get; catch; follow; make out; take in. ¶ 어린이를 ~ understand children / 전기의 사용법을 알고 있다 understand how to use electricity / 말이 너무 빨라서 무슨 말을 하는 건지 알 수가 없네 You speak so fast that I can't follow you. / 그 이유를 알 수 없다 I fail to understand the reason. / 그가 왜 왔는지 알지 못하겠다 I can't understand why he came. / 그가 말하는 것을 알지 못하겠다 I cannot understand 〔make out〕 what he says. /「내 말을 알겠습니까」—「압니다」"Do you understand me?"—"I understand." / 아시겠습니까 Do you get it? / 알았다 I see. / 저자의 뜻하는 바를 아시겠습니까 Can you make sense of what the author says?

③ 《인식·인지하다》 realize; recognize; be convinced 《of》. ¶ 자기 잘못을 ~ be convinced of *one's* (own) error; realize *one's* error / 중요성을 ~ recognize the importance 《of》 / 못 알아볼 만큼 자라다 grow out of recognition / 그것이 진실인 것을 알 때가 있으리다 There will be time when you will be convinced of its truth. / 그의 얼굴 표정으로 나를 싫어하는 걸 알았다 From the expression on his face I realized he didn't like me at all. / 대번에 그것이 위조 지폐임을 알았다 At (the) first glance I noticed that it was a false note.

④ 《면식·사귀다》 be acquainted 《with》; get to know. ¶ 잘 아는 familiar / 아는 사람을 만나다 find a familiar face; meet an acquaintance / 아무를 알게 되다 become acquainted with 〔get to know〕 *a person* / 이름〔얼굴〕만은 알고 있다 know 《*a person*》 by 「name 〔appearance, sight〕 only / 친구는 아니고 그저 아는 사이다 He is not a friend, but an acquaintance. (★ acquaintance가 「안면」이란 뜻일 때는 무관사. friend보다 교제가 덜 깊은 사람을 뜻하며, 집합적으로도 쓰임: I have many acquaintances 〔a large acquaintance〕.「나는 아는 사람이 많다」) / 그와는 여러 해 동안 알고 지냅니다 I have been acquainted with him for many years. / 나는 이 곳에는 아는 사람이 없다 I am a stranger here. / 그를 어떻게 알게 됐느냐 How did you come to know him? (★ I know him.과 I know of him.의 차이—know him은 「직접적으로 알고 있다」, know of him은 「간접적으로 알고 있다」는 뜻) / 대개는 내가 알지 못하는 사람들이었다 Most of them were strangers to me.

⑤ 《깨닫다》 find; notice; become aware 《of》; be conscious 《of》; get 〔come〕 to know; perceive; sense; realize. ¶ 알지 못하는 사이에 unconsciously; before *one* knows 〔is aware〕; without *one's* knowledge; unnoticed / 시계가 없어진 것을 ~ find *one's* watch gone / 그 아이가 정직한 것

을 알았다 I found him an honest boy. / 내가 잘못된 것을 알았다 I found that I was mistaken. / 그렇게 하는 것이 어렵다는 것을 알았다 I found it difficult to do so.

⑥《느껴 알다》be sensible《to, of》; feel; be sensitive《to》; be aware《of》. ¶ 부끄러움을 ～ feel shame / 은혜를 ～ be aware of *one's* indebtedness.

⑦《미루어 알다》guess; gather; infer; tell. ¶ 그의 말로 그가 학자인 것을 알았다 I gathered from his speech that he is a scholar. / 옷을 보아 그 여자가 가난한 것을 알 수 있다 From her dress you can tell she is a poor woman. / 나머지는 알 만하다 The rest may be inferred〔imagined〕.

⑧《들어서 알다》know《of》; have heard《of》; learn. ¶ 그 일은 친구에게 들어서 알고 있다 I have learned of it from my friend.

⑨《경험》have experience《with》; have been exposed《to》; know. ¶ 슬픔〔가난〕을 ～ know sorrow〔poverty〕/ 남자를 알지 못하다 have no carnal knowledge of men; be a virgin; know no man / 그 아가씨는 이미 남자를 안다 The girl「has been around〔is no virgin〕.

⑩《관여》be concerned《with》; have to do《with》. ¶ 네가 알 바가 아니다 It is no concern of yours. *or* It's none of your business. *or* It's not your affair. / 내가 알 바 아니다 It is no concern of mine〔my own〕. *or* It's nothing to do with me. *or* It's none of my business. / 그녀석이 어떻게 되든 내 알 바 아니다 I don't「give〔care〕a damn what becomes of him.

⑪《좋음·고마움을》appreciate; know. ¶ 그림〔음악〕을 ～ have an eye〔ear〕for pictures〔music〕; be a good judge of pictures〔music〕/ 건강의 고마움을 ～ appreciate the blessing〔importance〕of health; know what a good thing it is to keep *oneself* fit.

⑫《…으로 보다》regard《as》; take; consider. ¶ 잘못 ～ take〔mistake〕《A》for《B》/ 어떤 사람을 다른 사람으로 잘못 ～ mistake one person for another / 나를 무엇으로 알아 What do you take me for? / 그를 사복 형사로 알았다 I took him for a plainclothes man.

**알데히드**〖화학〗an aldehyde. ◉ ～수화물(水化物) an aldehyde hydrate.

**알땅** naked〔unprotected, unvegetated〕land.

**알뚝배기** a small unglazed pottery bowl.

**알뜰이** a crab with spawn removed.

**알뜰살뜰하다** (be) extremely frugal〔thrifty, prudent, provident〕. ¶ 아무리 알뜰살뜰히 해도 한 달에 10만 원 가지고는 못 산다 I cannot keep body and soul together on less than 100,000 won a month, even if I practice severe economy.

**알뜰하다**《규모가》(be) frugal; thrifty; prudent; provident《of》;《정성스럽다》(be) wholehearted; earnest; assiduous. ⇨ 알뜰히. ¶ 알뜰한 성질《of》an economical turn of mind;《of》a frugal mind / 알뜰한 살림 a decent living; a frugal life / 알뜰한 주부 a thrifty housewife / 그 여자는 알뜰한 생활을 보내고 있다 She leads a frugal life.

**알뜰히** ①《규모 있게》frugally; sparingly; economically; carefully. ¶ ～ 살다〔지내다〕live frugally〔close〕; lead a frugal life; live in a small way / ～ 하다 practice〔use〕economy; be careful (with *one's* money) / ～ 돈을 모으다 save money frugally / 그녀는 ～ 하여 돈을 모았다 She has enriched herself by being provident with her money. / 그녀는 살림을 ～ 한다 She manages her household frugally.

②《정성껏》eagerly; earnestly; wholeheartedly. ¶ 남편을 ～ 보살피다 be devoted〔attentive〕to *one's* husband; be〔make〕a good wife.

**알라**《이슬람교의 신》Allah.

**알락** ⇨얼룩. ◉ ～꼽등이〖곤충〗a camel〔cave〕cricket. ～도요〖조류〗a wood=sandpiper. ～뜸부기〖조류〗a swinhoe's crake. ～할미새〖조류〗a white=faced wagtail.

**알랑거리다** cajole; coax; flatter; toady; cringe《to》; fawn《on, upon》; court favor; curry favor《with *a person*》; wheedle. ¶ 윗사람에게 ～ fawn upon a superior / 아무에게 알랑거려 …하게 하다 coax *a person* to *do*〔into *doing*〕/ 아무에게 알랑거려서 돈을 우려내다 cajole *a person* out of money / 그의 알랑거리는 소리에 넘어갔다 I was caught〔seduced, trapped〕by his sweet=talk. / 윗사람에게 알랑거리는 사람은 아랫사람에게는 거만한 법이다 Those who fawn upon their superiors are apt to be arrogant toward their inferiors. / 윗사람에게 알랑거려서까지 출세하고 싶지는 않다 I don't want to be promoted if it involves fawning on my superiors.

**알랑쇠** a flatterer; a sycophant; a toady; a sweet-talker; an apple-polisher 《구어》.

**알랑수** resort to flattery; a bit 〔piece〕 of flattery.

**알랑알랑** (allure, tempt) cunningly; craftily; artfully; with flattery. ¶ ～ 여자를 꾀다 seduce a girl cunningly.

**알래스카** 《미국의 주》 Alaska (생략 Alas.). ¶ ～의 Alaskan. ◉ ～공로(公路) Alaskan 〔Alcan〕 Highway. ～사람 an Alaskan.

**알량하다** 《비꼬는 투》 (be) just "fine" 〔"dandy, ducky, grand"〕. ¶ 알량한 놈 a good-for-nothing / 알량한 소리를 하다 talk rot / 넌 참 알량한 친구다 A fine friend you have been! / 그 알량한 책을 가지고 야단도 한다 Why are you making such a big fuss over that "precious" book of yours?

**알레그로** 〖음악〗 allegro.

**알레르기** 〔<*Allergie* (G.)〕 〖의학〗 (an) allergy. ¶ ～성의 allergic 《to *a thing*》 / ～를 일으키는 allergenic 《food》 / ～를 일으키지 않는 hypoallergic 《cosmetics》 / ～를 일으키다 develop an allergy 《to》 / 나는 꽃가루 ～다 I am allergenic to pollen. *or* I have an allergy to pollen. ◉ ～반응 (an) allergic reaction. ～성 비염(鼻炎) allergic rhinitis. ～성 질환 allergic diseases. ～전문의 an allergist.

**알렉산더대왕** 《마케도니아의 왕》 Alexander the Great (356-323 B.C.).

**알려지다** become known 《to》. ＝알리어지다.

**알력**(軋轢) friction; (a) conflict; (a) collision; discord; a clash; strife. ¶ ～이 있다 be in conflict / ～을 초래하다 produce 〔lead to〕 friction / ～을 피하다 avoid friction / 당원 사이에 ～이 생기다 friction arises among the party members / 그들 사이에는 언제나 ～이 있다 They are always in discord. / 그 문제로 인해서 회사 내에 많은 ～이 생겼다 A good deal of discord has arisen in the company over the question.

**알로까다** 《몹시 약다》 (be) cocky; shrewd; astute; be wide-awake (to *one's* own interests); be a sharp customer. ¶ 그는 알로깐 녀석이다 He is as sharp as a needle. *or* He's nobody's fool. / 저렇게 알로깐 놈에게서 돈을 뜯다니 어림없다 It's hopeless to try to get money out of such a sharp customer.

**알로에** 〖식물〗 aloe.

**알로하셔츠** an aloha shirt.

**알록점**(—點) a diversifying spot or blotch of color; mottles; dapples; speckles; polka dots.

**알루미나** 〖화학〗 alumina; aluminium oxide.

**알루미늄** aluminum (기호 Al.). ◉ ～새시 an aluminum sash. ～제품 aluminum ware. ～합금 aluminum alloy.

**알류샨열도**(—列島) the Aleutian Islands; the Aleutians.

**알리다** let 《*a person*》 know; tell 《*a person* about *something*》; inform 〔notify〕 《*a person* of *something*》; send 〔bring〕 word 《to》; report 《*something* to *a person*》; give notice 《of, that...》; give *a person* the news 《that...》; let *a person* in on *something* 《구어》; get 《a fact》 across to *a person;* blow the whistle 《미》.

¶ 이미 알려 드린 바와 같이 《보도 따위에서》 as 「previously 〔already〕 announced 〔reported〕 / 일어난 일을 아무에게 ～ let *a person* know what has happened / 넌지시 ～ suggest; hint; intimate / 미리 ～ give *a person* (previous) notice; warn 〔forewarn〕 《*a person* about *something*》 / 일주일 전에 ～ give 《*a person*》 a week's notice / 적기의 내습을 ～ give warning of an air raid / 전화로 ～ let 《*a person*》 know by 〔through the〕 telephone; telephone 《*a person* that...》 / 편지로 ～ inform 《*a person*》 of 《*something*》 by letter; write to 《*a person*》 / (나쁜) 소식을 ～ break the news 《to *a person*》 / (시계가) 시각을 ～ strike 《three》 / 알리지 않다 leave *a person* uninformed 《about *something*》; keep 《*a matter*》 (secret) from 《*a person*》; keep 《*a matter*》 to *oneself* / 새벽을 알리는 절의 종소리 the temple-bell telling the hour of dawn / 떠날 뜻을 ～ signify *one's* intention of leaving / 그는 그것을 내게 알리지 않고 했다 He did it without my knowledge. / 알려 드리지 못한 점 사과드리겠습니다 I owe you an apology for not informing you. / 될 수 있는 대로 빨리 알려 다오 Send me word as soon as possible. / 그 사건을 알려 드리겠소 I will let you know about the incident. / 이 사건을 경찰에 알렸다 I put police wise about the case. / 그는 자신의 결혼을 아무에게도 알리지 않았다 He kept his marriage from everybody. / 그것은 알리지 않고 놔두는 것이 좋겠다 You had better leave it unsaid.

**알리바이** 《현장 부재 증명》 an alibi. ¶ ～가 있다〔없다〕 have an 〔no〕 alibi / ～를 세우다 set up 〔establish〕 an alibi;

make 〔fix〕 an alibi / ~를 조작하다 concoct 〔frame, fake〕 an alibi / ~를 입증하다 prove *a person's* alibi / ~를 깨뜨리다 break *a person's* alibi / 그에겐 문제의 그 시각에 완벽한 ~가 있다 He has an watertight 〔a cast-iron〕 alibi for the time in question. / 나는 그녀의 ~를 세워 주었다 I established alibis for her.

**알리어지다** ① 《알게 되다》 get 〔be, become〕 known 《to》; come to *a person's* knowledge. ¶ 세상에 ~ become generally known; be known to the general public; gain publicity / 그것은 널리 알려져 있다 It is of common knowledge. *or* It is a matter of universal knowledge. / 그 일이 어머니에게 알려졌다 The affair has come to the knowledge of my mother. / 그 이야기는 신문을 통해 세상에 알려졌다 The story got out through the papers.
② 《유명해지다》 become well known; become famous; win 〔acquire, come to〕 fame. ¶ 세상에 알려지지 않은 unknown; obscure; nameless / 널리 알려진 음악가 a renowned musician / 세상에 알려지지 않은 천재 an unknown genius / 그는 세계적으로 알려진 학자이다 He is a scholar of world-wide fame. / 그는 정치가로서보다도, 시인으로서 더 알려져 있다 He is better known as a poet than as a statesman.

**알맞다** 《어울리다》 (be) becoming; matching; fitting; 《적당하다》 (be) proper; appropriate; adequate; be fit 〔adapted〕 for; be suited 〔suitable〕 to 〔for〕; 《적임이다》 (be) competent 〔qualified〕 《for, to *do*》; 《시기에》 (be) timely; opportune; seasonable.
¶ 신분에 알맞은 befitting *one's* station / 알맞게 suitably; properly; adequately; moderately / 알맞은 거리에 at a proper distance / 알맞은 때에 at a 〔the〕 proper time 〔season〕 / 알맞은 가격 a moderate price / 시국에 알맞은 연설 a speech appropriate to the situation / 알맞은 운동 moderate 〔a proper amount of〕 exercise / 사과 재배에 알맞은 기후 a climate suited to the cultivation of apples / 달리 알맞은 말이 없어서 for want of a better word / 알맞은 조건으로 on fair 〔reasonable〕 terms / 알맞게 …하다 be moderate in *do*ing; use moderation in... / 그 자리에 알맞은 사람 a man fit for the post / (음식을) 알맞게 먹다 eat moderately / 땅이 …의 재배에 ~ The soil is suited to the cultivation of.... / 그 모자에는 그 리본이 ~ That ribbon 「goes 〔matches〕 well with your hat. / 저널리즘이 그에겐 ~ Journalism is the right thing for him. / 술도 알맞게 마시면 약이 된다 When it is taken in moderation, wine has medicinal qualities.

**알맹이** ① 《과실 속》 a kernel; a grain. ¶ 땅콩의 ~ kernels of peanuts.
② 《내용》 substance; matter; content(s). ¶ ~ 없는 meager in contents; poor in substance; unsubstantial; empty / ~ 없는 강연 an empty 〔unsubstantial〕 speech / ~ 없는 책 a book poor in substance.

**알몸(뚱이)** ① 《나체》 a naked body; a nude (미술품 따위의); stark-nakedness. ¶ ~의 naked; bare; nude / ~로 with nothing on; in the nude; in the altogether 《구어》; stark-naked; in *one's* bare skin / ~가 되다 undress; become 〔strip *oneself*〕 naked 〔bare, stark-naked〕; strip *one's* clothes off; take off all *one's* clothes; 《강제로 알몸이 되다》 be stripped naked / 더워서 ~가 되다 strip because of the heat / ~로 만들다 strip 《*a person*》 naked 〔to the skin, of *his* clothes〕; undress 《a baby》.
② 《빈털터리》 pennilessness. ¶ ~가 되다 go broke; become penniless; lose the shirt off *one's* back; be stripped of all *one's* possessions / ~로 시작하다 start business with practically nothing / 딸을 ~로 시집보내다 marry off a daughter with no dowry provided / 그는 ~로 미국에 왔다 He came to America with little more than the shirt on his back. / 집에 불이 나서 ~가 되었다 I lost everything in the fire we had.

**알바니아** Albania. ¶ ~의 Albanian.
◉ ~ 사람 an Albanian.

**알밤** ① 《밤톨》 a (shelled) chestnut. ② =아람.

**알배기** 《알 든 생선》 a fish full of roe.

**알부랑자**(一浮浪者) a barefaced rascal 〔scoundrel〕; a regular rogue.

**알부민** 〚생화학〛 albumin; albumen.
◉ ~지(紙) albumin paper. 독성~ toxalbumin.

**알사탕**(一砂糖) toffees; toffies.

**알선**(斡旋) 《주선》 arrangement; management; services; good 〔kind〕 offices; recommendation (추천); 《중재》 mediation; conciliation (쟁의 해결의). ~하다 arrange; act as (an) intermediary

between 《A and B》; do good offices; use *one's* good offices 〔*one's* influence〕; put in a good word 《for *a person*》; mediate 〔go〕 between; conciliate. ¶ 김 선생의 ~으로 by 〔through〕 the good offices of Mr. Kim / 일자리를 ~해 주다 help 《*a person*》 (to) find a job / 남에게 ~(해 줄 것)을 부탁하다 ask *another* to act as (a) go-between; ask for *another's* 「recommendation 〔mediation, good offices〕 / ~하겠다고 나서다 offer *one's* good offices 《to settle a dispute》 / 나는 아저씨 ~으로 취직했다 Through my uncle's good offices I have got a job.
◉ ~수뢰(收賂) taking a bribe for a favor given; influence peddling: 그는 재직중의 ~수뢰죄로 기소되었다 He was indicted for peddling influence while in office. ~자 a go-between; a mediator; an intermediary.

**알선**(一線) 〖전기〗 a naked electric wire.

**알섬** a small uninhabited island.

**알속** 《비밀 내용》 the substance of a secret; 《실속》 the actual content; 《정미》 the real 〔net〕 amount 〔weight, distance, bulk, *etc.*〕. ~하다 reveal 《secret, information》. ¶ ~무게 the net weight.

**알슬다** 《물고기가》 spawn; discharge *its* spawn; 《벌레가》 lay eggs; deposit; oviposit; 《파리가》 blow.

**알심** 《동정》 hidden sympathy; 《힘》 hidden strength.

**알싸하다** ① 《혀·콧속이》 tingle (from a pungent sensation). ¶ 음식이 좀 매워서 혀가 ~ The food is a bit spicy—it makes my tongue tingle. ② 《톡 쏘다》 have a spicy taste 〔smell〕; (be) sharp; hot; strong. ¶ 그 음식이 알싸해서 눈물이 난다 The food is so sharp (that) it brings tears to my eyes.

**알쏭달쏭하다** ① 《줄·무늬가》 be spotty and variegated in designs; be diversified in designs; (be) motley; jumbled; intricated. ¶ 알쏭달쏭한 무늬 a bewildering 〔puzzling, jumbled, mixed〕 pattern / 무늬가 알쏭달쏭한 천 cloth with varied designs.
② 《뜻이》 (be) vague; ambiguous; slippery; indefinite; obscure; hazy; doubtful; equivocal; evasive. ¶ 알쏭달쏭한 문제 a perplexing problem / 알쏭달쏭한 말을 하다 evade the point; speak 《of *a matter*》 in general terms / 알쏭달쏭한 태도를 취하다 maintain an ambiguous 〔uncertain〕 attitude 《toward》; take 〔assume〕 a noncommittal 〔dubious〕 attitude 《toward》 / 말의 진의가 ~ The real meaning of the word is slippery. / 뭐가 뭔지 ~ I cannot make any sense of it. *or* I cannot make neither head nor tail.

**알씬거리다** hand around in 《*a person's*》 presence (to curry his favor); flatter; fawn 《upon *a person*》.

**알아내다** find out; discover; 《위치·소재·원인을》 detect; locate; pinpoint (정확히); 《신원 따위를》 identify; 《뜻 따위를》 make out. ¶ 남의 비밀을 ~ find out another's secret / 인용구의 출처를 ~ dig up the source of a quotation / 소문의 출처를 ~ trace the origin of a rumor / 고장난 곳〔아픈 원인〕을 ~ locate a trouble 〔the source of a pain〕 / 글귀의 뜻을 ~ understand 〔make out, grasp〕 the meaning of a passage / 병원체(病原體)를 ~ identify the virus / 아무의 소재를 ~ find out 〔locate〕 *a person's* whereabouts / (애를 써서) 답을 ~ find 〔work out〕 an answer 〔solution〕 to a problem / 경찰은 테러범들의 아지트를 알아냈다 The police found the house which was used as a hideout by the terrorists. / 그들의 은신처를 알아내는 데 한 주일이나 걸렸다 It took us a week to locate 〔discover〕 their hideaway 〔hiding place〕.

**알아듣다** 《이해하다》 comprehend; understand; get 〔catch〕 the meaning; 《사리를》 listen to 〔hear〕 reason; be reasonable; 《구별하다》 recognize 《*a person's* voice》; tell 《the difference》 by hearing.
¶ 알아들을 수 없는 inaudible / 알아듣게 말하다 convince 《*a person*》; persuade 《*a person*》 / 알아듣도록 설명하다 explain convincingly; explain to *one's* satisfaction / 농담을 ~ see a joke / 잘못 ~ hear *a person* 〔*something*〕 wrong 〔amiss〕; mishear; 《오해하다》 misunderstand 《what *a person* says》 / 알아듣기 힘들다 be difficult 〔hard〕 to hear; 《분명하지 않다》 be indistinct / 아무의 말을 ~ understand 〔get the gist of〕 what *a person* says / 제 말을 알아듣겠습니까 Do you understand 〔follow〕 me? *or* Are you following me? / 자네 말은 무슨 소린지 도무지 알아들을 수가 없네 What you say is all Greek to me. *or* I can make nothing of what you say. / 그는 내 말을 알아듣지 못했다 He didn't understand what

I said.

**알아맞히다** guess right; make a good guess. ¶ 못 ~ guess amiss 〔wrong〕; miss *one's* guess; make a wrong guess / 그녀는 내가 무엇을 걱정하는지 정확히 알아맞혔다 She guessed exactly what I was worried. / 어디 누가 알아맞추나 보자 Let us see who guesses right.

**알아보다** ① 《조사·문의하다》 inquire 《of *a person,* about *a matter*》; make inquiries; look into; check 《on, upon》; investigate; examine. ¶ 아무의 이름을 ~ inquire *a person's* name / 호텔에 방이 있나 ~ inquire for a room in a hotel / 원인을 ~ inquire into the cause / 취직 자리를 ~ look out for a job / 아무의 전력(前歷)을 ~ probe into *a person's* past; trace *a person's* career / A씨의 품성에 관하여 전 회사에 ~ refer to Mr. A's former company for his character / 그는 날마다 일자리를 알아보러 다닌다 He goes out every day to hunt for a job. / 사무실에 알아보세요 Please inquire at the office. / 나는 범죄 심리에 관한 문헌이 있는지 사서한테 알아보았다 I inquired of the librarian if he had any literature on criminal psychology. / 공보과에 기자를 보내서 그 사건을 알아보게 했다 I sent a reporter to the Department of Information and had him look into that. / 알아보니 그것은 오보였다 On inquiry, it turned out to be a false report.
② 《확인하다》 ascertain 《*a person's* attitude》; 《넌지시 마음을》 probe (into) 《*a person's* mind》; sound *a person* (out) 《on *a matter*》; tap 〔fathom〕 《*a person's* opinion》; feel out 《*a person's* view》. ¶ 보도의 사실 여부를 ~ ascertain whether 〔if〕 a piece of news is true / 그녀가 무엇을 생각하고 있는지 속마음을 알아보려 했으나 허사였다 He tried, but with no success to probe into her mind to find out what she was thinking.
③ 《기억하다》 remember; 《식별·인식하다》 recognize; know 《*a person*》 by sight; 《감별하다》 identify 《plants》. ¶ 알아볼 수 없을 만큼 변하다 change out of (all) recognition; be altered 〔transformed〕 beyond recognition / 이 아이는 벌써 엄마 얼굴을 알아본다 The baby already recognizes its mother's face. / 나를 알아보시겠습니까 Do you recognize 「me 〔who I am〕?

**알아주다** 《이해하다》 understand; feel 《for》; sympathize 《with》; 《인정하다》 appreciate; recognize; acknowledge; 《높이》 think highly 〔well〕 of. ¶ 알아주는 noted; well-known; leading; prominent / 아무의 진가를 ~ appreciate *a person's* real worth / 남의 공로를 ~ recognize another's services / 알아 주지 않다 think little 〔poorly〕 of; do not think much of / 그는 한국에서 알아주는 사업가이다 He is a leading businessman in Korea. / 그의 성실성은 알아주어야 한다 We must give him a due credit for his good faith. / 그들은 그의 학설을 그다지 알아주지 않는다 They don't think much of his theory. / 제 어려움을 알아 주십시오 Try to understand my difficulties.

**알아차리다** ① realize in advance; anticipate (in *one's* mind); be (mentally) prepared for. ② become aware of.

**알아채다** become aware 〔conscious〕 of; see (through); notice; sense; perceive; realize; grasp; get scent 〔wind〕 of; have 〔get〕 an inkling of 《the intrigue》; be suspicious of; 《수상쩍음을》 smell a rat.
¶ 알아채이다 be suspected 《by》; be smelled out / 대번에 상황을 ~ take in the situation at a glance / 비밀을 ~ smell 〔ferret〕 out a secret / 음모를 ~ penetrate (into) a plot / 얼굴 빛으로 그가 성난 것을 알아챘다 I read anger in his face. / 나는 그의 계획을 알아챘다 I saw through his trick. / 그가 주모자임을 단번에 알아챘다 I immediately spotted him as the ring-leader. / 아내는 이미 남편이 바람피우고 있음을 알아채고 있었다 The wife was already aware that her husband was 「having an affair 〔playing around 《구어》〕. / 위험이 닥쳐 오고 있음을 알아챘다 I sensed the danger that was coming upon me. / 그가 일찍 떠난 것을 알아챘다 I noticed that he left early.

**알아하다** do 「at *one's* discretion 〔as *one* thinks fit〕; do with care. ¶ 알아하도록 각자에게 맡기다 leave 《*a matter*》 to individual discretion / …은 아무가 알아할 일이다 It is within *one's* discretion to *do*. / 너 좋을 대로 알아서 해라 Do as you please. *or* Take your own way. *or* Do as you think fit. / 그것은 네가 알아할 일이다 You can suit yourself. *or* It's up to you. / 그 일은 네 판단하에 알아서 해라 I leave the matter to your discretion. / 이 일 처리는 너에게 맡기니 알아서 해라 The disposition of this work is at your discretion.

**알알이** egg after 〔by〕 egg; grain after 〔by〕 grain; berry after 〔by〕 berry.

**알알하다** 《상처 따위가》 smart; tingle; (be) prickly; 《맵다》 bite; burn; (be) piquant; pungent. ¶ 혀가 ~ *one's* tongue smarts 〔stings, burns〕.

**알약**(—藥) a tablet; a tabloid. ¶ 두 개의 아스피린 ~ two tablets of aspirin.

**알은체** ① 《남의 일에》 concern; interest. ~하다 show concern; show interest. ¶ ~ 안하다 look unconcerned / 그는 그 일에 ~ 안한다 He shows no interest in that matter. ② 《사람을 보고》 (a show, gesture of) recognition. ~하다 recognize; notice. ¶ (…를 보고도) ~(도) 하지 않다 cut *a person* dead; pretend not to recognize *a person* / 그는 나를 보고 ~했다 He nodded at me in recognition. / 그는 길에서 나를 ~도 하지 않았다 He cut 〔snubbed〕 me on the street.

**알음** ① 《안면》 acquaintance(ship). ¶ 우연한 ~ a casual acquaintance / 사업상의 ~ a business acquaintance / ~이 있다〔없다〕 have 〔have no〕 acquaintance with / 그와는 아무 ~이 없다 I have no personal acquaintance with him. *or* He is quite a stranger to me. ② 《이해》 understanding; knowing. ③ 《능력 범위》 *one's* purview; *one's* area of competence. ④ 《신의 보호》 the kind influence 〔protection〕 of a god.

**알음알음** 《아는 관계》 mutual acquaintance; 《친분》 shared intimacy. ¶ ~으로 through some acquaintance(s) / ~으로 취직하다 get a job through pull.

**알음알이** ① 《아는 사람》 an acquaintance(ship); a person *one* knows. ¶ ~가 많다 have a wide 〔large〕 circle of acquaintances. ② 《꾀바른 수단》 cleverness; knowledge; know-how. ③ 《자라나는 재주》 the gradually developing 〔growing〕 knowledge 〔talent〕 of a child.

**알음장** letting 《*a person*》 know with a look 〔wink〕. ~하다 give a significant look 〔wink〕.

**알자리** a nest for laying eggs.

**알젓** salted 〔seasoned, pickled〕 roe 〔spawn〕.

**알제리** 《나라 이름》 Algeria.

**알주머니** an ovisac; the spawn sac of a fish; 《가오리·상어 등의》 a sea purse.

**알짜** the best thing 〔part〕; the cream; the pick; the choice; a choice one; 《정수》 the essence; the quintessence; the pith; 《진수》 the gist; the genius. ¶ …의 ~ 부분 the pith and marrow of… / ~를 뽑아 내다 choose 〔select〕 《a book》 from among many; get the cream 《of》; take 〔extract〕 the essence 《of》 / 도둑이 ~만 가져갔다 The thief took 「the best of everything 〔all the best ones〕.

**알짝지근하다** have a bit sharp taste; be rather hot 〔spicy, peppery, pepperminty〕.

**알짱거리다** 《알랑거리다》 go around hoodwinking people with flattery; scrounge around; 《돌아다니다》 loaf around idly.

**알짱알짱** 《속이는 모양》 going around hoodwinking people with flattery; 《돌아다니는 모양》 loafing around idly.

**알츠하이머병**(—病) 〖의학〗 (an) Alzheimer's disease.

**알칼로이드** 〖생화학〗 an alkaloid. ¶ ~의 alkaloidal.

**알칼리** 〖화학〗 (an) alkali (*pl.* ~(e)s). ¶ ~금속 alkali metals / ~성〔도〕 alkalinity / ~성의 alkaline / ~성 반응 an alkaline reaction / ~성 식품 alkaline foods / ~성 토양 alkaline soil / ~화하다 alkalify; alkalize. ◉ ~전지 an alkaline cell. ~중화제 an antalkali; an antalkaline (agent). ~천(泉) an alkalispring. ~토류(土類) alkaline earth.

**알코올** 〖화학〗 alcohol; spirits. ¶ ~(성)의 alcoholic / 음용〔약용〕~ potable 〔medicinal〕 alcohol / ~에 담그다 preserve 《*a thing*》 in spirits; alcoholize / ~류는 일체 입에 대지 않다 「abstain from all 〔do not touch〕 alcoholic drinks / ~로 상처를 소독하다 disinfect an wound with alcohol.
◉ ~램프 an alcohol 〔a spirit〕 lamp. ~량 측정기 《불어서》 《미》 a drunkometer; 《영》 a breathalyzer (상표명에서). ~분(分) alcoholic content 〔strength〕. ~(비중)계 an alcoholometer. ~온도계 an alcohol thermometer. ~음료 a 〔an alcoholic〕 drink. ~의존증 (morbid) dependence on alcohol. ~정량(定量) alcoholometry. ~중독 alcoholism; alcoholic poisoning: ~ 중독자 an alcoholic / ~ 중독자 갱생회 Alcoholic Anonymous (생략 AA) / ~ 중독이 되다 suffer from alcoholism; be addicted to alcohol; be an alcoholic. 공업용~ industrial alcohol. 에틸〔메틸〕~ ethyl 〔methyl〕 alcohol. 혈중~ 농도 Blood Alcohol Concentration (생략 BAC).

**알타이** Altai(c). ¶ ～의 Altaic. ◉ ～말 Altaic. ～산맥 the Altai Mountains. ～어족 the Altaic language family.
**알탄**(一炭) an oval 〔egg-shaped〕 briquet(te).
**알토** 〖음악〗 Alto. ◉ ～가수 an alto 「(singer).
**알통** 《근육의》 flexed muscles; (well-developed) biceps. ¶ ～을 만들다 flex *one's* muscles; show *one's* biceps; make a muscular knob.
**알파** alpha; *α*. ¶ ～와 오메가 alpha and omega; beginning and end / ～로 이기다 〖야구〗 win a game with (part of) the last inning left / 봉급 2개월분 플러스 ～의 보너스 a bonus equivalent to two months' pay plus something. ◉ ～선 〖물리〗 alpha rays. ～입자 〖물리〗 an alpha particle.
**알파벳** the alphabet. ¶ ～순 《in》 alphabetical order / ～순으로 늘어놓다 arrange alphabetically 〔in alphabetical order〕.
**알파인** ¶ ～의 Alpine / ～종목〔경기〕 the Alpine events. ◉ ～스키 Alpine skiing.
**알파카** 〖동물〗 an alpaca; 《직물》 alpaca. ¶ ～코트 an alpaca coat.
**알프스** the Alps. ¶ ～의 Alpine. ◉ ～산맥 the Alps.
**알피니스트** an Alpinist.
**알현**(謁見) having 〔enjoying〕 an audience 《with the king》. ～하다 have an audience 《with a king》; be received in audience 《by a king》; be presented 《to》. ¶ 교황은 그에게 ～을 허락했다 The Pope granted him an audience.
**앎** knowledge; information; wisdom. ¶ 앎이 많다 be well-informed; know a lot 《of things》; have seen much of life.
**앓는소리** moaning; groaning; 《우는 소리》 a complaint. ～하다 moan; groan; 《우는 소리를》 complain 《about, of》; make complaints to *a person* about 《*something*》. ¶ 그는 언제나 ～를 한다 He always draws in his horns.
**앓다** ① 《병을》 《영》 be ill 《with》; 《미》 be sick 《with》; 《…에 걸리다》 be taken ill; suffer from 《illness》; be afflicted 〔affected〕 《with》; ail 《from》. ¶ 눈을 ～ have eye trouble 〔trouble with *one's* eyes〕; suffer from eye disease / 감기를 ～ suffer from cold / 배를 ～ have a stomachache / 이를 ～ have a toothache / 머리를 ～ be sick in the head; have a head 〔brain〕 ailment / 가슴을 ～ have a complaint in the chest / 폐를 ～ suffer from tuberculosis 〔T.B.〕; have lung trouble / 폐렴을 앓아 위독하다 be critically sick with pneumonia / 치질을 앓고 있다 be ill 〔ailing〕 with piles / 병을 심하게 ～ be seriously ill; suffer from a grave illness.
② [비유적] be afflicted 〔distressed, troubled〕 《with》; feel annoyed 《at》. ¶ 골치를 ～ puzzle *one's* head 〔brains〕 《about, over》; 《걱정으로》 be worried 《about, over》 / 많은 빚 때문에 골치를 ～ be afflicted with a heavy load of debts / 앓던 이 빠진 것 같다 feel sudden relief / 아들 때문에 어머니는 늘 골머리를 앓고 있다 The son is a chronic headache to his mother.
**-앓이** ache; sickness. ¶ 가슴앓이 a pain in the chest / 귀앓이 an earache / 배앓이 a stomachache / 이앓이 a toothache.
**암**[1] ① 《암컷》 a female; a she. ¶ 암캐 a bitch / 암컷 a female / 암코끼리 a cow elephant / 암곰 a female bear / 암토끼 a doe rabbit / 암늑대 a bitch 〔she-〕 wolf / 암염소 a nanny goat; a she-goat / 물고기의 암놈 a female fish / 암수를 구별하다 tell its sex; sex 《a chicken》. ② 《기와 따위의》 concave; internal.
**암**(癌) ① 〖의학〗 (a) cancer. ¶ 암의 cancerous / 발암물질 carcinogen / 암세포 a cancer(ous) cell / 직장암 a cancer of the rectum / 폐암 lung cancer; cancer of the lung / 위〔유방〕암 stomach 〔breast〕 cancer / 암조직 cancer tissue / 암의 조기 발견 early detection of cancer / 암의 치료 a cure for cancer / 목〔후두〕에 암이 생기다 get 〔develop〕 cancer of the throat; get a cancer in the throat / 암으로 죽다 die of cancer / 암의 검진을 받다 undergo an examination for cancer / 식도〔혀〕에 암이 생겼다 A cancer has grown on my gullet 〔tongue〕. / 그는 암에 걸렸다 He has cancer. / 암이 그의 온몸에 퍼졌다 The cancer has spread to his whole body. / 암은 조기 발견, 조기 치료를 하면 낫는다 Cancers are curable if they are 「found 〔detected〕 and treated at an early stage.
② 《폐단·장애》 a cancer; a curse; an evil; the root of evil 〔trouble〕; a stumbling block. ¶ 민주 정치의 암 a curse to democracy / 시정(市政)의 암 a scourge 〔curse, cancer〕 in the municipal administration / 그는 교육계의 암이다 He is 「the rotten apple

of the education world 〔a cancer in the world of education〕.
◉ 암센터 a cancer center. 암환자 a cancer patient. 국제 암 연구 기관 the International Agency for Research on Cancer (생략 IARC).

**암²** 《아무려면》 surely; certainly; of course; to be sure; naturally; no doubt; why not? ¶ 암 그렇지 Why of course! *or* But definitely! /「가느냐고」—「암 가고 말고」 "Will I go, you say?"—"Sure, I will." /「학교는 재미있느냐」—「암 재미있지」 "Do you enjoy school?"—"Why, certainly. 〔Why not?〕" /「괜찮을까요」—「암 괜찮고 말고」 "Is it safe?"—"Oh, it's safe enough."

**암갈색**(暗褐色) dark brown; umber; dun. ¶ ～의 dark-brown; dun-colored.

**암거**(暗渠) an underdrain; a culvert. ◉ ～배수 drainage by culvert; underdrainage.

**암거래**(暗去來) black-marketeering; black-market 〔underground〕 dealings; illegal「trade 〔business transactions〕; transactions on the black market; 《물밑 교섭》 secret dealings; an undercover 〔a secret〕 arrangement. ～하다 sell 〔buy〕 《goods》「on the black market 〔through an illegal channel〕; black-marketeer; black=market 《goods》; do illicit transactions; handle a black-market business. ¶ ～를 단속하다 police the black market / 그는 그들과 무언가 ～를 하고 있는 것 같다 I suspect he is having some underhand business with them.
◉ ～망〔루트〕 《through》 illegal channels. ～시세 a black-market price 〔rate〕. ～시장 a black market; 《상점》 a black-market stall. ～인(人) a black marketeer. ～품 black-market 〔bootleg〕 goods. ～행위 an illegal act; a black-market deal.

**암구다** make a match; set animals to copulating; mate.

**암굴**(岩窟) a cave; a (rocky) cavern; a「grotto.

**암글** ① 《활용 못하는 지식》 knowledge that *one* is unable to put to practical use; (mere) "booklearning"; unproductive or impractical scholarship. ② 《낮춤말》 *Hangul* script.

**암기**(暗記) learning by heart; memorizing. ～하다 memorize 《미》; learn 〔get, know〕 《*a thing*》 by heart; commit 《*a thing*》 to memory. ¶ 영어 단어의 ～법 how to learn 〔memorize〕 English words / 기계적인 ～ rote memorization; learning by rote / 무턱대고 ～하다 cram / ～하고 있다 know 〔have got〕 《*a thing*》 by heart / 그는 무엇이든지 ～하고 있다 He commits everything to memory. *or* He learns everything by heart. / 그는 ～를 잘 한다 He excels in memory work.
◉ ～력 (*one's* powers of) memory; retentive power: ～력이 좋다〔나쁘다〕 have a good 〔bad, poor〕 memory.

**암꽃** 〖식물〗 a female 〔pistillate〕 flower.

**암꽃술** 〖식물〗 a pistil.

**암꿩** 《까투리》 a hen pheasant.

**암나사**(—螺絲) a female 〔an internal〕「screw.

**암내** ① 《발정 냄새》 the odor of a female animal in heat 〔estrus〕. ¶ ～ 내다 be in 〔on, at〕 rut 〔heat〕 / ～ 나다 《수컷이》 rut; go 〔come〕 into rut; 《암컷이》 go 〔come〕 into 〔《영》 on〕 heat / 개가 ～를 내다 A dog is in rut 〔heat〕. ② 《겨드랑이의》 the (strong) smell of armpits; underarm odor; 《체취》 body odor (생략 B.O.). ¶ 그한테서 ～가 난다 His body smells bad.

**암녹색**(暗綠色) dark green; bottle green.

**암단추** a female button 〔snap〕.

**암달러**(暗—) a black-market dollar. ¶ ～ 거래 a black-market dollar transaction / ～ 시장 the dollar black market. ◉ ～상(商) an illegal dollar dealer; a foreign exchange black-marketeer.

**암담**(暗澹) gloominess; the gloom; the dismal. ～하다 (be) dark; gloomy; dismal. ¶ ～한 전도 gloomy prospects / 전도가 ～하다 The future looks gloomy 〔grey〕. *or* The outlook is black.

**암띠다** ① 《비밀 기질》 be a person who loves secrets. ② 《숫접다》 be easily embarrassed.

**암루**(暗淚) silent tears. ¶ ～를 흘리다 shed 〔be moved to〕 silent tears; weep in silence.

**암류**(暗流) an undercurrent (★ 비유적으로도 쓸 수 있음); a hidden drift 〔tendency〕. ¶ ～가 흐르고 있다 An undercurrent runs. / 그 조합은 겉으로는 평화로우나 만만찮은 ～가 흐르고 있다 Peaceful as it outwardly appears, that association has in it a pretty strong hidden agitation.

**암만해도** ＝ 아무래도.

**암말** a mare; a female horse.

**암매매**(暗賣買) ⇨ 암거래.

**암매상**(暗賣商) a black-market dealer; a black-marketeer; a secret 〔an illegal〕 dealer; a smuggler; 《주류의》 a bootlegger.

**암매장**(暗埋葬) secret burial. ⇨ 암장(暗葬).
**암모늄** 〚화학〛 ammonium (기호 $NH_4$). ¶ 염화~ ammonium chloride.
**암모니아** 〚화학〛 ammonia (기호 $NH_3$). ◉ ~냉동법 ammonia refrigerating. ~비료 ammonite. ~수 ammonia water; aqueous ammonia. 액체~ liquid ammonia.
**암묵**(暗默) silence; tacit(ness); unspoken(ness); withholding of comment. ¶ ~리에 tacitly; by a tacit consent 〔understanding〕 / ~의 양해 a tacit consent 〔understanding〕 / ~의 승낙을 하다 give a tacit 〔an implicit〕 permission / 두 사람 사이에는 ~의 양해가 성립돼 있었다 There was 「an unspoken agreement 〔a tacit understanding〕 between the two of them.
**암반**(岩盤) bedrock; a rock bed; solid rock.
**암벌** 《수여리》 a female bee; a queen bee.
**암범** a tigress.
**암벽**(岩壁) a rockwall; a rock face. ¶ 필사적으로 ~을 기어오르다 clamber frantically up the rockwall.
◉ ~등반 rock-climbing. ~화(畫) 〚고고학〛 a graffito.
**암산**(暗算) mental arithmetic 〔calculation, figuring〕. ~하다 figure 《it》 out 〔do a sum〕 in *one's* head; do (sums in) mental arithmetic; make a mental count 《of》. ¶ ~으로 in mental arithmetic.
**암살**(暗殺) (an) assassination. ~하다 assassinate. ¶ ~을 기도하다 plan to assassinate *a person;* make an attempt on 《*a person's*》 life / ~당하다 get assassinated / 그들은 총리의 ~을 기도했다 They designed to assassinate the prime minister. ◉ ~계획 a plot against the life of 《*a person*》. ~단 a hit team. ~미수 an attempted assassination; an unsuccessful attempt at assassination. ~자 an assassin.
**암상** jealousy; (green) envy. ~궂다, ~스럽다 (be) jealous; envious; look cross 〔displeased〕 out of jealousy. ¶ ~떨다, ~내다 = 암상부리다 / ~하다 = ~궂다 / ~이 많다 be jealous.
◉ ~꾸러기 a jealous person.
**암상부리다** nurse jealousy; have 〔feel〕 envy; show *one's* jealousy 〔get sulky〕 out of spite.
**암새** a female bird.
**암석**(岩石) (a) rock; a crag 《hill》. ¶ ~이 많은 rocky; craggy. ◉ ~층 a rock layer 〔stratum〕. ~학 petrology; the study of rocks.
**암소** a cow.
**암송**(暗誦) recitation; recital; memorization. ~하다 recite 《a poem》; repeat 《a passage》 from memory; give a recitation; say by rote 〔heart〕.
**암쇠** ① 《열쇠·자물쇠 등의》 a keyhole plate. ② 《맷돌의》 the bottom 〔pounding〕 plate of a mill; the gudgeon or rynd of a millstone.
**암수** female and male.
**암수**(暗數) 《속임수》 a trick; a means of deception. ¶ ~를 쓰다 play 《*a person*》 a trick / ~에 걸리다 fall into a trick. ◉ ~거리 fraud; deception; trickery; double-dealing.
**암순응**(暗順應) 〚심리〛 dark adaption.
**암술** 〚식물〛 a pistil. ¶ ~이 없는 꽃 a barren flower.
**암술대** 〚식물〛 the style (of a flower).
**암시**(暗示) a hint; a suggestion; an allusion; an intimation. ~하다 hint 《at》; suggest; allude 《to》; give 〔drop〕 a hint. ¶ ~적인 suggestive / ~가 풍부한 full of suggestions; thought-provoking / ~를 주다 give 〔drop〕 《*a person*》 a hint 〔clue〕 / ~를 얻다 receive a hint 〔suggestion〕 《from》 / ~에 걸리다 be subjected to (hypnotical) suggestion; respond to suggestion / ~에 걸리기 쉽다 《최면술에서》 be easily influenced by suggestion; be susceptible 〔amenable〕 to suggestion / 나는 최면술 ~에 걸렸다 I was subjected to (hypnotical) suggestion. / 그는 그 비밀을 알고 있음을 ~했다 He hinted that he knew the secret. / 이 사건에서 ~를 얻어 그는 소설을 썼다 This event 「gave him the idea 〔suggested the plot〕 for his novel. ◉ ~요법 suggestive medicine 〔therapy〕. 피~성 suggestibility.
**암시세**(暗時勢) a black-market price; off-the-books quotations.
**암시장**(暗市場) a black market.
**암시장치**(暗視裝置) night-vision equipment; a nightviewer; noctovision.
**암실**(暗室) a (photo) darkroom.
¶ ~용 램프 a darkroom lamp.
**암암리**(暗暗裡) tacitness; implicitness. ¶ ~에 tacitly; implicitly; 《남몰래》 secretly; in secret / ~에 가리키다 allude 《to》; hint 《at *a matter*》 / ~에 승낙하다 give a tacit consent 《to *a person's* marriage》 / 그는 ~에 돈을 요구했다 He 「made an indirect request 〔indirectly asked〕 for money.

**암야**(暗夜) a (pitch-)dark 〔moonless〕 night. ¶ ～를 틈타 under (the) cover of night 〔darkness〕. ◉ ～공포증 nyctophobia.

**암약**(暗躍) activity 〔maneuvering〕 behind the scenes; underground activities; secret machinations 〔maneuvers〕. ～하다 get about in secret; be active 〔maneuver〕 behind the scenes; engage in secret machinations 〔maneuvers〕.

**암염**(岩塩) 〖광물〗 rock salt; halite. ¶ ～을 채굴하다 mine (rock) salt. ◉ ～갱 a salt mine.

**암영**(暗影) 《그림자》 a (dark) shadow; a gloom; 《장애·어려움》 an obstruction; an obstacle; a hindrance; a shadow in *one's* path. ¶ …의 전도에 ～을 던지다 cast a gloom 〔shadow〕 over the future of….

**암운**(暗雲) 《먹구름》 dark 〔murky〕 clouds. (★ 복수형으로 쓰임). ¶ ～이 감돌다 dark clouds are hanging 《on the horizon, over the political world》.

**암울**(暗鬱) gloominess. ⇨ 음울.

**암유**(暗喩) (a) metaphor. ⇨ 은유.

**암자**(庵子) a small Buddhist temple; a Buddhist hermitage 〔retreat〕; a hermit's cell 〔cottage〕. ¶ ～를 짓다 build a hermitage / ～에 은거하다 live in a hermitage 《in, at》; 《은둔하다》 seclude *oneself* 《in, at》.

**암자색**(暗紫色) dark purple.

**암장**(暗葬) secret burial. ～하다 bury secretly.

**암적색**(暗赤色) dark red.

**암전**(暗轉) 〖연극〗 a dark change 《of scenery》; changing sets during a stage black-out.

**암종**(癌腫) 〖의학〗 a carcinoma (*pl.* ～s, -mata); cancer; a cancerous growth. ¶ ～의 carcinomatous. ◉ ～증 carcinomatosis (*pl.* -ses).

**암죽**(一粥) thin rice gruel (as baby food).

**암중**(暗中) darkness; in the dark. ◉ ～모색 groping in the dark: ～모색하다 grope (blindly) in the dark; be at sea; be at a loss 《(as to) what to do》. ～비약 secret maneuvers: ～비약하다 be active behind the scenes; engage in secret maneuvers; move stealthily.

**암초**(暗礁) a sunken 〔submerged〕 rock; an unknown reef; a reef; a cay. ¶ ～에 걸리다 strike a rock; go 〔run〕 on a reef; be stranded; [비유적] hit a snag; come to 〔reach〕 a deadlock (계획 따위가) / 배가 ～에 걸려 난파했다 The ship grounded and was wrecked. *or* The ship was wrecked on a rock. / 교섭은 ～에 부딪혔다 The negotiations are deadlocked.

**암치질**(一痔疾) 〖의학〗 internal hemorrhoids.

**암캉아지** a female puppy; a she-puppy.

**암캐** a female dog; a she-dog; a bitch.

**암컷** a female (animal); a she; 《새의》 a hen-bird. ¶ 그것은 ～이냐 수컷이냐 Is it a she 〔female〕 or a he 〔male〕? *or* What is the sex? / ～인지 수컷인지 모르겠다 I can't tell its sex.

**암키와** a concave 〔an upturned〕 roof-tile.

**암탉** a hen; 《햇닭》 a pullet. ¶ ～이 울면 집안이 망한다 《속담》 It goes ill in the house where the hen sings and the cock is silent.

**암톨쩌귀** the knuckle 《of a hinge》; a gudgeon.

**암퇘지** a female hog; a sow.

**암투**(暗鬪) an undercover struggle; a secret strife 〔feud〕; veiled enmity. ～하다 struggle under cover; feud silently. ¶ 그들 사이에는 끊임없는 ～가 벌어지고 있다 There is constantly veiled enmity among them.

**암팡스럽다** 《몸집 작은 사람이》 (be) aggressive; cocky; spunky; scrappy; intrepid; energetic; [서술적] be strong 〔plucky, active〕 for *one's* size. ¶ 암팡스럽게 싸우다 fight ferociously; put up quite a scrap / 암팡스럽게 밥을 먹다 eat heartily; eat a big meal for such a little person.

**암팡지다** ＝암팡스럽다.

**암페어** 〖물리〗 an ampere; an amp. ◉ ～계(計) an amperemeter; an ammeter. ～수(數) amperage. ～시 an ampere-hour.

**암표상**(暗票商) an illegal ticket-broker; a (ticket) scalper; a speculator 《미》.

**암행**(暗行) travelling in secret 〔in disguise〕; being undercover. ～하다 travel in secret 〔in disguise, incognito〕. ◉ ～어사 〖역사〗 a secret royal inspector; an undercover emissary 〔agent〕 of the king.

**암호**(暗號) 《군호》 a password; a watchword; a countersign; a sign; 《전신용》 a cipher (비밀 암호); a code (주로 상업용). ¶ ～로 in cipher / ～를 풀다〔해독하다〕 decode 〔decipher〕 《a message》; 《적의 통신 따위의》 break 〔crack〕 a code / ～로 적다 encode; encipher; write in code; put in cipher / ～로 통신을 보내다 send a message in code. ◉ ～문 a coded message; a cryptogram. ～문자 a cipher; a code=word. ～(작성)법 cryptography. ～장(帳) a code book. ～전신부 a cipher code. ～통신 the signal; cryptography. ～해독 cryptanalysis; codebreaking: ～해독관 《대사관의》 a cipher officer. ～화 encryption: ～화하다 code; encode. 문자～ a letter code. 숫자～ a figure code. 데이터 ～화 기준 Data Encryption Standard (생략 DES).

**암호전보**(暗號電報) a code 〔cipher〕 telegram. ¶ ～를 치다 send a code(d) telegram; wire *a person* in code / ～를 풀다 decipher a code telegram / 그는 나에게 ～를 쳤다 He sent me a telegram in cipher. ◉ 해외～ a cablegram in code; a code(d) cable.

**암흑**(暗黑) darkness; blackness. ¶ ～의 dark; pitch-dark〔-black〕; black; gloomy / 불이 다 나가서 우리는 ～ 속에 있었다 All the lights went out and we were left in the dark.
◉ ～가 the dark quarters; the underworld; gangland. ～계 the underworld. ～대륙 〖역사〗 the Dark Continent. ～면 the dark 〔gloomy〕 side 《of society》; the seamy side 《of life》. ～색 a pitch-dark〔-black〕 color. ～시대 a dark age; a black period; 《중세 유럽의》 the Dark Ages.

**압각**(壓覺) 〖심리〗 pressure sensation.

**압권**(壓卷) 《가장 뛰어난 것》 the masterpiece; the best (part) 《of a book》; the highlight 《of the day》; 《최고조》 《reach》 the 〔its〕 climax 《of the drama》. ¶ 현대시의 ～ the greatest masterpiece of modern poetry.

**압도**(壓倒) overwhelming; overcoming; surpassing. ～하다 overwhelm; overpower; surpass. ¶ ～적(으로) overwhelming(ly); overpowering(ly) / ～적 세력 an overwhelming 〔irresistible〕 force / ～적 승리를 거두다 win an overwhelming 〔a sweeping〕 victory 《over》; 《선거에서의》 a landslide (victory) 《미》/ ～적 다수로 당선되다 be elected 《president》 by an overwhelming majority / 품질에서 다른 물건을 단연 ～하다 be far superior to others in quality / 다수에 ～당하다 be overwhelmed by superior numbers / 우리 팀은 그들을 ～했다 Our team overpowered them. / 적은 숫적으로 우리를 ～했다 The enemy exceeded us in number. / 그 법안은 ～적 다수로 가결되었다 The bill was passed by an overwhelming majority. / 이 부문에서는 한국제품이 일본 제품을 시장에서 ～하고 있다 In this sector, articles made in Korea are driving Japanese goods out of the market. / 그녀의 아름다움에 그 자리의 사람들은 모두 ～당하고 말았다 All those present were overpowered by her beauty.

**압력**(壓力) pressure; stress. ¶ 군사 및 경제적 ～ the big stick / ～을 넣다 《물건에》 press; give 〔apply〕 pressure 《to》; 《사람에게》 put pressure on *a person* 《to *do*》; 《미》 pressure *a person* 《to *do* 〔into *do*ing〕》; turn the screw / ～을 넣어 …하게 하다 〔하지 않게 하다〕 pressure 《*a person*》 into 〔out of〕 《an act, *do*ing *something*》/ ～을 받다 be 〔come〕 under pressure 《to *do*》; be pressured 〔pressurized〕 《to *do* 〔into *do*ing〕》/ ～을 완화하다 relax 〔reduce〕 the pressure 《on》/ 증기의 ～을 올리다 get up a head of steam / ～에 굴하다 bow 〔bend〕 to 《*another's*》 pressure / 타이어의 ～이 정상인가 살펴보다 see that the tire pressure is right / 그가 의견을 바꾸도록 ～이 가해졌다 Pressure was brought to bear on him to make him change his opinion. / 한국은 미국으로부터 수입량을 더 늘리도록 ～을 받고 있다 Korea is being pressurized to increase her imports from the U.S.A.
◉ ～계 a manometer; a pressure gauge. ～단체 a pressure group. ～솥 a pressure cooker. ～시험 a pressure test. ～저항 pressure resistance. 대기～ atmospheric pressure. 외부～ outside pressure. 절대〔총〕～ absolute 〔total〕 pressure.

**압록강**(鴨綠江) *Amnokkang;* the Yalu (River).

**압류**(押留) 〖법〗 (a) seizure; (an) attachment; distraint; distress. ～하다 seize 〔attach, distrain〕 《*a person's* property for a debt》; place under distraint; sequestrate; confiscate. ¶ 재산을 ～하다 attach 〔levy on〕 《*a person's*》 property / 물품을 ～하다 seizure 〔distrain upon〕 《*a person's*》 goods / ～당하다 have 《*one's* property》 attached / ～중에 있다 be under attachment 〔distraint〕 / ～딱지를 붙이다 paste distraint paper on goods / ～를 해제하다 release 〔relieve〕 《*a person's* property》 from attachment / 가～하다 seize 〔attach〕 *another's* property provisionally; sequester; sequestrate.
◉ ～물 a seized article; seized property. ～영장 a warrant 〔writ〕 of

seizure 〔attachment〕; an attachment; a seizure note. ～인 a seizor; a distrainer; a sequestrator: 피～인 a distrainee. 저당물～ foreclosure of a mortgage《on a house》.

**압박**(壓迫) pressure; oppression; persecution; 《압제》 tyranny; 《강제》 coercion. ⇨ 탄압. ～하다 《압력을 가하다》 press; 《탄압하다》 oppress《the poor》; suppress; tyrannize (압제); bear 〔grind〕 down (꺾어누름); persecute (박해); 《강제하다》 coerce《*a matter, a person*》. ¶ 일상 생활의 ～ the stress 〔pressure〕 of daily life / ～을 받다 be pressed 〔pressured〕; be subjected to 〔come under〕 pressure / ～을 받고 under the pressure《of》/ 가난하고 약한 사람을 ～하다 oppress the poor and the weak / 언론의 자유를 ～하다 suppress the freedom of speech 〔the press〕 / …에 ～을 가하다 put 〔exert〕 pressure on…; bring pressure (to bear) on… / 여론의 ～으로 정부는 증세 계획을 포기했다 The Government gave up its plans to raise taxes under the pressure of public opinion. / 물가 상승이 가계를 ～하고 있다 The rise in prices strains our family budget. / 당국은 그들을 끊임없이 ～하고 있다 The authorities are constantly 「putting 〔exerting〕 pressure on them.
◉ ～감 an oppressive feeling; a sense of being oppressed. ～민족 an oppressing race: 피～ 민족 an oppressed people. ～붕대 a compress. ～자 an oppressor; a tyrant.

**압사**(壓死) death from pressure. ～하다 be crushed 〔pressed, squeezed〕 to death. ¶ 그는 불행히도 낙석에 깔려 ～했다 He had the misfortune of being crushed to death under falling rocks. / 담이 무너져 두 소녀가 ～했다 Two girls were crushed to death by a falling wall.

**압살**(壓殺) 《눌러 죽임》 killing by pressing 〔squeezing〕. ～하다 crush 〔press, squeeze〕《*a person*》 to death. ¶ 국민의 언론자유를 ～하다 suppress 〔snuff out〕 the people's freedom of speech; gag the people.

**압송**(押送) 〖법〗 sending《a criminal》 in custody. ～하다 transfer《a convict》 to《a different》 prison; send《*a person*》 in custody.

**압수**(押收) 〖법〗 (a) confiscation; (a) seizure. ～하다 seize《smuggled goods》; confiscate; impound; take over; take (legal) possession of《*a person's* property》. ¶ 서류를 ～하다 capture 〔retain〕 papers / 면허증을 ～당하다 be confiscated *one's* license / 경찰은 밀수입된 향수를 ～했다 The police confiscated the smuggled perfume. ◉ ～물 a confiscated article; seized property; confiscated goods. ～수색 영장 a seizure and search warrant. ～ 영장 a confiscation warrant.

**압승**(壓勝) an overwhelming 〔a sweeping〕 victory; a landslide (victory). ～하다 win an overwhelming victory《over》; swamp; capture a sweeping victory. ¶ 총선거에서 K당은 ～했다 The K Party won 〔scored〕 an overwhelming 〔a landslide〕 victory in the general election. / 타이거스는 라이온스에 10대 1로 ～했다 The Tigers smashed the Lions 10 to 1.

**압연**(壓延) rolling. ～하다 roll. ◉ ～강(鋼) rolled steel. ～공장 a rolling mill. ～관(管) a rolled tube. ～기 a rolling machine. ～박판(薄板) rolling strip. ～알루미늄 합금 rolled aluminum alloy. ～장치 a rolling 〔roll〕 mill. 열〔냉〕간 ～ hot 〔cold〕 rolling.

**압운**(押韻) rhyming; rhyme. ～하다 rhyme; rime《미》. ◉ ～시(詩) rhymed verse; (a) rhyme; a rhymed poem. ～형식 a rhyme scheme.

**압정**(押釘) a (thumb) tack; a push pin; 《제도용》 a drawing pin. ¶ ～으로 고정시키다 tack down《a carpet》/ 게시를 벽에 ～으로 고정시키다 tack a notice to the wall.

**압제**(壓制) 《압박》 oppression; 《강제》 coercion; 《학정》 tyranny; 《전제》 despotism. ～하다 oppress; treat《the populace》 highhandedly; 《학정》 tyrannize《over》. ¶ ～적(인) oppressive; tyrannical; highhanded / ～의 희생자 victims of oppression / ～를 가하다 oppress; tyrannize《over》; treat with a high hand; rule with an iron hand; tread on the neck《of》/ ～를 벗어나다 be freed from tyranny 〔oppression〕 / ～에 시달리다〔신음하다〕 suffer from 〔groan under〕 tyranny / 국민은 ～에 신음했다 The people groaned under tyranny. ◉ ～력 despotic power. ～자 an oppressor; a despot; a tyrant. ～정치 despotism.

**압지**(壓紙) blotting paper; a blotter.

**압착**(壓搾) compression; pressure. ～하다 compress; press. ◉ ～가스 compressed gas. ～공기 compressed air:

~ 공기관 a compression tube / ~ 공기판 a compression tap 〔valve〕. ~기 a compressor; a press. ~식 여과기 a filter press.

**압축**(壓縮) compression; constriction; condensation; 〖컴퓨터〗 pack; compaction. ~하다 compress 《air》; constrict; condense. ¶ 의견의 ~ compression of ideas / ~할 수 있는, ~성의 compressible / 내용물이 ~되어 있음 《게시》 Contents under pressure. / 이 보고서를 3페이지로 ~해다오 Condense this report into three pages, will you? ◉ ~가스〔공기〕 compressed gas 〔air〕. ~계 a piezometer. ~기 a compressor. ~냉동기 a compression refrigerator. ~성〔률〕 compressibility. ~시험기 a compression tester. ~압력계 a compression pressure gauge. ~지(紙) pressboard. ~천연가스 compressed natural gas (생략 CNG). ~펌프 a compressor.

**압출**(壓出) pressure. ~하다 press out; extrude 《plastics》. ◉ ~기 an extruder; an extrusion press.

**앗** 《위급할 때·놀랄 때》 O dear!; Oh!; Dear me!; (Good) heavens!; Oh, my goodness 〔gracious〕!; Why! ¶ 앗 큰일났군 Heavens! / 앗 비행기가 날고 있다 Look, there's an airplane flying! / 앗 지갑이 없다 My god, my purse is gone! / 앗 김군이다 Why, it is Kim! / 앗 아파 Ouch!

**앗기다** ⇨ 빼앗기다.

**앗다** ① ⇨ 빼앗다. ② 《씨를 빼다》 peel and seed 《fruit》; gin 《cotton》. ③ 《품을》 pay for labor in kind. ¶ 품을 ~ exchange labor.

**앗아가다** snatch 〔wrest〕 《*a thing*》 (away) from 《*a person*》; rob 〔deprive〕 《*a person*》 of 《*a thing*》. ¶ 그는 내 손에서 와락 편지를 앗아갔다 He snatched the letter out of my hand. / 그 전염병은 수많은 인명을 앗아갔다 The plague carried off thousands of people.

**앙가발이** ① 《사람》 a short bowlegged person. ② 《찰거머리》 a persistently sticky person; a leech.

**앙가슴** the middle of the chest 〔bosom〕.

**앙감질** hopping (on one leg). ~하다 hop on one foot 〔leg〕.

**앙갚음** 《보복》 taking out *one's* spite 〔ill-will〕 on 《*a person*》; getting back at 〔getting even with〕 《*a person*》; revenge; retaliation; tit for tat; requital. ~하다 take out *one's* spite 《on》; get even 〔square accounts〕 《with *a person*》; give 〔pay〕 tit for tat; avenge; revenge *oneself* 〔be revenged〕 on 《*a person* for *a thing*》; retaliate on 〔against〕 《*a person*》; pay off old scores; repay. ¶ ~으로 out of spite; from ill-will / (상대와) 같은 수법으로 ~하다 pay 《*a person*》 in 《*his*》 own coin; serve 《*a person*》 with the same sauce / ~으로 아무를 죽이다 kill *a person* 「for revenge 〔out of spite〕 / 불공평한 처사〔모욕〕에 대하여 ~하다 revenge an injustice 〔insult〕 / 그에게 ~하겠다 I will pay him off 〔out〕. / 이 ~은 꼭 하고야 말 테다 I will pay you back 〔I will get my own back〕 for this. / ~으로 다른 소년의 발목을 찼다 He retaliated by kicking the other boy on the ankle.

**앙고라** Angora. ◉ ~토끼 an Angora rabbit.

**앙골라** 《나라이름》 Angola.

**앙괭이** 〖민속〗 a witch who is supposed to visit houses on New Year's night in search of children's shoes to fit her feet.

**앙괭이그리다** blacken *one's* face; daub 「black on *one's* face.

**앙구다** ① 《음식을 묻어두다》 keep 《food》 warm. ② 《곁들이다》 put 《several kinds of food》 on the same plate. ③ 《사람을》 accompany or see 《*a person*》 on *his* way.

**앙그러지다** ① 《음식이》 (be) well prepared; nicely seasoned; 《먹음직스럽다》 (be) delicious-looking; appetizing; tempting. ¶ 음식을 앙그러지게 만들다 prepare food nicely. ② 《어울리다》 (be) nice; shapely; orderly. ¶ 앙그러지게 일(을)하다 do a job in good shape.

**앙글방글** ① 《a child smiles》 sweetly; beamingly. ¶ 그 아기가 ~ 웃는 것이 귀엽기도 하다 What a lovely smile the baby has! ② 《선웃음》 with a smirk; with an insincere 〔a deceptive〕 smile. ¶ 그녀는 ~ 웃으면서 빤한 거짓말을 했다 She told an out-and-out lie, wearing a smile on her face all the while.

**앙금** 《침전물》 a deposit; a sediment; settlings; 《술 따위의》 dregs; lees; 《커피 따위의》 grounds. ¶ ~이 앉다 dregs settle; be deposited; settle (out) / ~을 앉히다 settle dregs / ~까지 다 마시다 drink 〔drain〕 *something* to the dregs 〔lees〕 (★ 비유적으로도 쓰임) / ~이 앉아 술이 맑아졌다 The dregs settled and the wine became clear. / ~이 앉았다 Dregs are deposited at the bottom.

**앙금앙금** 《baby》 crawling; creeping; sprawling. ¶ ~ 기다 crawl; go on all fours.

**앙등**(昻騰) 《물가 따위》 a rise; an advance; 《화폐 가치 따위》 appreciation. ~하다 rise (suddenly); soar; go up; take a jump; shoot up. ¶ ~하는 생활비 the rising cost of living / 달러의 ~ the appreciation of the dollar / 지가(地價)〔집세〕의 ~ the rise of the land value 〔house rent〕/ 쌀값이 ~한다 Rice soars in price. / 물가가 ~했다 Prices have gone up. / 물가가 놀랄 만큼 ~하고 있다 The prices are staggeringly high. *or* Prices are skyrocketting. / 지가의 ~은 내집 마련의 꿈을 무산시켰다 The soaring 〔skyrocketing〕 land prices have ended our dream of having our own house.

**앙망**(仰望) looking up to with hope; 《우러러 봄》 looking up to 《*a person*》. ~하다 look up to with hope; expect; hope; wish. ¶ 곧 답장해 주시기를 ~하나이다 Kindly favor me with an early answer. / 참석해 주시기를 ~하나이다 A cordial invitation is extended to you. *or* You are cordially invited.

**앙모**(仰慕) ~하다 look up to with respect; long for; admire; adore. ¶ 스승으로 ~하다 look up to 《*a person*》 as *one's* teacher.

**앙바틈하다** (be) short and broad; fat and short; stocky; chunky 《미》.

**앙버티다** resist to the (bitter) end; hold 〔stand, stick〕 it out. ¶ 앙버티고 꼼짝않다 hold out to the last.

**앙살** ~하다〔부리다, 피우다〕 fuss (and grumble) in opposition; balk.

**앙상궂다** (be) terribly gaunt 〔haggard〕.

**앙상블** an *ensemble* (F.).

**앙상하다** (be) gaunt; haggard; thin; spare; sparse; be a mere skeleton; be skin and bones. ¶ 몸골이 앙상한 사람 a person of spare frame; a skinny person; a bag of bones / 잎이 떨어져 앙상한 나뭇가지 bare 〔naked〕 branches / 말라서 뼈만 ~ be wasted 〔reduced〕 to a skeleton; be reduced to skin and bones; be nothing but skin and bones / 잎이 떨어져서 나무가 앙상하게 보인다 The trees look thin with most of their leaves fallen.

**앙세다** 《보기보다 다부지다》 be weak-looking but have hidden strength.

**앙숙**(怏宿) ¶ ~이다 be on bad terms 《with》; 《특히 부부가》 lead a cat-and-dog life / 두 사람은 서로 ~이다 They are at daggers drawn with each other.

**앙심**(怏心) grudge; ill will; spite; rancor. ¶ ~을 품은 (re)vengeful; vindictive; spiteful; implacable (화해할 수 없는) / ~ 품은 여자 a vindictive woman / ~을 품다 harbor a grudge 〔bear ill-will〕 toward 《*a person*》/ 아무에게 잔뜩 ~을 품다 bear *a person* a deep-rooted grudge / 그는 나에게 ~을 품고 있다 He has a grudge against me.

**앙앙**(怏怏) ~하다 (be) displeased 〔unhappy〕; discontented; dissatisfied; dispirited; dejected; disheartened. ¶ ~불락(不樂)하다 be disconsolate; be discontented / 마음이 ~하다 be unhappy at heart.

**앙양**(昻揚) exaltation; enhancement; uplift. ~하다 exalt; enhance; uplift; whip up 《war spirit》. ¶ 국민 정신의 ~ the upsurging of national sentiment / 국민 도의를 ~하다 raise the standard of the national morals / 국민 정신을 ~하다 uplift the national spirit / 국위를 ~하다 heighten 〔raise, enhance〕 national prestige / 자유 민권 사상을 ~하다 promote the ideal of civil liberties.

**앙증하다**, **앙증스럽다** (be) disproportionately 〔extraordinarily〕 small 〔tiny, little〕. ¶ 그 개는 앙증스럽다 The dog is extraordinarily small.

**앙짜** ① 《점잔 빼》 putting on 〔giving *oneself*〕 airs; acting prim. ¶ ~ 빼지 마라 Stop acting so prim. ② 《암상스런 사람》 an irritatingly jealous person.

**앙천대소**(仰天大笑) ~하다 have a hearty 〔good〕 laugh; laugh loudly; burst out laughing. ¶ 우리들 모두는 이 일로 ~했다 We all had a good laugh about it.

**앙칼스럽다**, **앙칼지다** 《성질이》 (be) aggressive; fierce; sharp; furious; vehement. ¶ 앙칼스러운 여자 an aggressive woman / 앙칼진 말을 하다 make blistering 〔spiteful〕 remarks / 앙칼스럽게 일에 달려들다 tackle *one's* work savagely / 그녀는 앙칼지게 그에게 달려들었다 She sprang at him furiously. / 그녀는 앙칼지게 쏘 붙였다 She retorted with a sharp remark.

**앙케트** [<*enquête* (F.)] an opinionnaire; a questionnaire; an inquiry; an investigation. ¶ ~조사를 하다 send out 〔obtain information through〕 a questionnaire / 그 정보는 50명의 대학

생을 대상으로 한 ~를 바탕으로 얻어졌다 The information was obtained through questionnaires sent to fifty university students.

**앙코르** an encore. ¶ 세 번 ~를 받아 노래하다 sing three encores / ~를 청하다〔받다〕 call for 〔receive, get〕 an encore / 파바로티의 공연은 우뢰와 같은 ~를 받았다 Pavarotti's performance, greeted by roars of "Encore!"

**앙큼상큼** with short steps. ¶~ 걷다 walk with 〔take〕 short steps.

**앙탈** scheming to disobey; trying to avoid what is right; grumbling. ~하다, ~부리다 scheme to disobey; try to avoid what is right; grumble angrily; 《대들다》 turn 〔round〕 on 《*a person*》; nag; fuss. ¶ 공연히 ~하다 make a big fuss over nothing; grumble at nothing / 그녀는 발끈해서 남편에게 ~을 부렸다 She turned on her husband in a fury. / 그는 그 일을 하지 않으려고 ~했다 He tried frantically to get out of the job.

**앙혼**(仰婚) a morganatic marriage; marriage with 《*a person*》 of higher status. ~하다 marry above *one;* marry into a higher status.

**앙화**(殃禍) divine wrath; (a) misfortune; calamities (재난); woe(s). ¶~ 입은 cursed; ill-fated / ~(를) 입다〔당하다〕 be punished by Heaven; suffer Heaven's displeasure; meet with (a) misfortune 〔disaster〕 / ~를 초래하다 incur divine wrath; bring (an) evil upon *oneself;* invite disaster 《by *one's* conduct》.

**앞**[1] ① 《전면》 the front; the fore part; 《전방》 ahead; beyond; off; away. ¶ 앞에(서) in front (of); before / 바로 앞에 just 〔right〕 in front (of) / 수마일 앞에 several miles ahead 〔away〕 / 집 앞에 in front of the house / 50미터쯤 앞에 about 50 meters along 〔ahead〕 / 뜰 앞 the front part of a garden / 앞줄 the front row / 앞자리 a front seat / 집의 앞뒷문 the front and the back door of a house / 앞집 《맞은편 집》 the opposite house / (열차의) 앞에서 두번째의 차량 the second car from the front 《of the train》 / 앞에 앉다 sit in front; take a front seat / 곧장 앞으로 가다 go straight ahead / 우리 앞에 칠판이 있다 In front of us is the blackboard. / 3시에 도서관 앞에서 기다리겠습니다 I'll be waiting for you in front of the library at three. / 그는 우리의 몇 발짝 앞에서 걷고 있었다 He was walking a few steps ahead of us. / 그의 머리는 앞쪽이 하얗게 세어 있다 His hair is white at the front. / 캄캄하여 한 발짝 앞도 볼 수 없었다 It was pitch-dark and I could not see one foot ahead. / 앞이 막혀 있다 《길이》 It is blocked ahead.

② 《선두》 the front; the head; the foremost; the lead. ¶ 행렬의 앞 the head of a procession / 맨 앞 부대 the foremost troop of an army / 앞에 서다 be at the head; be in the front 〔van〕 《of the parade》; take the lead; lead the way; act as leader 《to》 / 앞을 다투다 strive to be the foremost; try to be first; rival *a person* for priority / 앞 다투어 …하다 try to get ahead of others in *doing*; struggle to *do* / 앞을 다투어 도망치다 run away in confusion / 앞을 다투어 자리를 차지하다 scramble for seats / 그들은 앞을 다투어 밖으로 나가려 했다 They made a rush all at once for the door. / 그의 이름이 명단 맨 앞에 나와 있다 His name leads the list. / 나는 도무지 남보다 앞서서 그런 일을 할 마음이 들지는 않았다 I was in no mood to take the lead in an attempt like that. *or* I wouldn't be the first to do a thing like that for anything. / 그 점에서 그는 훨씬 시대를 앞서갔다 He was far ahead of his times in that respect.

③ 《면전·대중 앞》 the public; company; the presence 《of *a person*》. ¶ 남의 앞에서 in public 〔company〕; in the presence of others; in *a person's* face 〔presence〕; before 〔around〕 people / 남의 앞도 꺼리지 않고 without any regard to decency / 아버지 앞에 불려가다 be called before *one's* father / 그는 바로 내 눈앞에서 그런 짓을 했다 He did it before my very eyes. / 법 앞에서는 만인이 평등하다 All men are equal before the law. / 숙녀 앞에서 상스러운 말을 하면 못 쓴다 Don't talk about indecent things in the presence of ladies. / 사람들 앞에서 남의 욕을 해서는 안 된다 Don't abuse 〔speak ill of〕 others in public 〔company〕. / 사람들 앞에서 말할 수 없다 It is not to be said in public. / 그는 여자들 앞에서 부끄러워 한다 He feels bashful around women.

④ 《장래》 the future. ¶ 앞으로 2, 3일 for some days to come; for the next few days; for a few days ahead / 앞으

로 5년 (동안) for the next 〔coming〕 five years; for the five years to come / 앞을 내다보는 long-sighted; far-sighted / 선거일을 2주일 앞두고 with the election day two weeks off 〔ahead〕 / 앞을 내다보다 look into the future; look ahead 〔to the future〕 / 앞을 내다보고 with an eye to the future / 앞으로 값이 오를 것으로 기대하고 in expectation 〔anticipation〕 of a rise in price / 앞을 생각하다 think of the future / 앞으로의 계획을 세우다 make plans for the future; plan ahead / 앞 일이 캄캄하다 《전망할 수 없다》 I cannot tell with any certainty how things will turn out. *or* 《전망은 절망적》 There is absolutely no hope for the future. *or* The future looks black. / 앞으로 그런 일은 다시는 하지 않겠습니다 I won't ever do it again. / 앞으로 어떻게 살아나갈 작정인가 How are you getting along in future?
⑤ 《몫》 a share; a portion; a quota. ¶ 학생 한 사람 앞에 연필 두 자루씩 주었다 I gave the pupils two pencils each 〔apiece〕. *or* I gave two pencils to each pupil. / 그의 재산 대부분이 맏아들 앞으로 갔다 Most of his estate went to the oldest son. / 그는 제 앞만 차린다 He is out for his own interest only.
⑥ 《시간적·순차상의》 the foregoing 〔preceding〕 part. ¶ 앞(서)의 former; ex-; one-time; 《최근의》 recent; late / 앞페이지 the preceding page / 앞에서 말한 바와 같이 as mentioned earlier; as previously stated; as we have said above; as aforementioned / 이 문제에 관해서는 앞에서 간단히 언급했다 I have touched on this subject briefly above.
⑦ 《눈앞》 what is in front of *one's* eyes; 《시력·시각》 eyesight; sight. ¶ 앞을 못보게 되다 lose *one's* sight; become blind / 그는 앞을 못 본다 He is blind.

**앞**[2] ① 《편지 따위의》 addressed 〔directed〕 to 《*a person*》. ¶ 김씨 앞으로 된 편지〔소포〕 a letter 〔parcel〕 addressed 〔directed〕 to Mr. Kim / 네 앞으로 편지가 왔다 There is a letter for you. ② 《어음 따위의》 drawn in *one's* favor. ¶ C은행 앞으로의 수표 a check drawn upon C Bank / 홍씨 앞으로 어음을 발행하다 draw a bill 「for 〔in favor of〕 Mr. Hong.

**앞가림** having just enough education to get by. ~하다 have just enough education to get by.

**앞가슴** the breast; the chest 《of the body, of a garment》.

**앞갈이** 〖농업〗 ① 《애벌갈이》 the first plowing 〔ploughing 《영》〕 of a rice field. ② 《보리갈이》 the first of the annual crops.

**앞길** ① 《갈 길》 the road ahead; the way yet to go; the distance yet to cover; the journey before *one*. ¶ 아직 ~이 멀다 [사람이 주어] have a long way to go; [사물이 주어] be a long way off 〔in the future〕 / ~을 가로막다 block 《*a person's*》 path; stand in 《*a person's*》 way / 우리 ~에 숲이 있다 There lies a wood in our way.
② 《전정·전망》 the 〔*one's*〕 future; *one's* prospects; (an) outlook. ¶ ~을 그르치다 [사물이 주어] ruin 〔wreck〕 *one's* career 〔future〕 / ~을 비관하다 despair of *one's* future / ~에 가로놓이다 lie ahead of *one* / 나의 ~은 암담하다 My prospects are gloomy. / 당시 한국의 ~은 참으로 암담했다 The outlook for Korea at that time looked black indeed. / 나는 저 애의 ~이 걱정된다 I am anxious about that child's future. / 그의 ~은 창창하다 He has the world before him. / 우리의 ~에는 수많은 어려움이 가로놓여 있다 There are a number of difficulties in store for us. / 그에게는 창창한 ~이 열려 있다 A great career is open to him. / 그의 ~이 걱정된다 It's a bad lookout for him.

**앞날** the days ahead 〔to come〕; the future; remaining years 〔days〕; 《여생》 the rest 〔remainder〕 of *one's* life. ¶ ~의 즐거움 pleasure to come; expectation / ~을 생각하다 think ahead 〔of the future〕; look ahead 〔to the future〕 / ~을 위해서 돈을 모으다 save money for the future / 먼 ~의 일까지 생각하다 think of the distant future / 아무의 ~을 걱정하다 be 〔feel〕 anxious about *a person's* future / 그의 ~이 멀지 않았다 He is not long for this world. *or* His days are numbered. / 그는 ~에 크게 되겠다 He promises to achieve great things. / 나는 아들놈의 ~이 걱정된다 I have misgiving about my son's future. / ~은 언제나 불확실한 것이다 The future must always be uncertain.

**앞니** a front tooth; a foretooth; an incisor. ¶ ~ 세 개가 부러지다 have three of *one's* front teeth broken / 내 아기의 ~가 났다 My baby cut his front teeth.

**앞다리** ①《네발짐승의》 a foreleg;《발톱 있는 짐승의》 a paw. ②《집》 a 〔*one's*〕 new house 〔residence〕 (to move into). ¶ ～를 정해 놓고 집을 팔다 sell *one's* house after *one* has procured a new one. ③《중개인》 an intermediary; a go-between; an agent; a third party. ¶ ～를 놓다 use a go-between / ～를 놓아서 그를 알아보았다 I investigated him through a third party. ④《베틀의》 the beam stand of a hand loom.

**앞당기다** 《시일을》 move 〔carry〕 《a date》 up; advance 《a date》; make 《*anything*》 earlier. ¶ 시일을 이틀 ～ push two days ahead; advance 〔move up〕 the date by two days / 결혼 날짜를 사흘 ～ advance the wedding date three days; shift the wedding date three days ahead / 다섯째 시간의 영어 시간을 셋째 시간으로 ～ move up the English lesson from the fifth hour to the third / (회의 등을) 앞당겨 열다 hold 《a meeting》 ahead of schedule / 예정 시일보다 두 달이나 앞당겨 완성되다 be completed two months ahead of schedule.

**앞두다** have 《a period, a distance》 ahead or to face 〔go〕; be close 〔near〕 at hand; be just around the corner. ¶ 열흘(을) ～ have ten days to go 〔run〕 / 십 마일(을) ～ have ten miles ahead (to cover) / 곧 선거를 앞두고 있다 The election is close at hand. / 시험을 앞두고 학생들은 몹시 바쁜 것 같다 The students seem to be very busy with the examination coming soon.

**앞뒤** ①《위치》 the fore and the back; the front and the rear. ¶ ～로 before and behind; in front and in (the) rear / ～를 둘러보다 look around 《*one*》; look in both direction / ～로 움직이다 move 《*a thing*》 back and forth / ～로 적의 공격을 받다 be attacked both in the front and in the rear; be attacked from both sides / 우리는 ～로 적을 습격했다 We attacked the enemy front and rear.
②《일관성·분별》 consistency; sequence; consequence. ¶ ～가 맞지 않는 변명 a lame excuse 〔apology〕 / ～ 생각 없이 thoughtlessly; without thought; regardless 〔reckless〕 of the consequences / ～를 가리다〔재다〕 be prudent; reflect on the consequences / ～가 맞다 be consistent; be coherent; hang together / ～가 맞지 않다 be self=contradictory; be inconsistent; be incoherent / (말·이야기의) ～를 맞추려고 하다 try to make 《*one's* story》 sound plausible / 네 말은 ～가 맞지 않는다 You talk incoherently.

**앞뒷집** houses in front and in (the) rear; the surrounding 〔neighboring〕 houses; the neighbors. ¶ ～에 살다 be 〔live〕 next door to each other.

**앞뜰** the front yard.

**앞머리** ①《앞쪽 머리》 the forehead; the sinciput. ②《물건의》 the front end. ③《선두》 the vanguard; the van; (the) front.

**앞메꾼** the blacksmith wielding the large hammer.

**앞못보다** ①《보지 못하다》 be blind; can't see what is going on. ②《무식하다》 be ignorant 〔illiterate〕.

**앞문**(―門) the front door 〔gate〕; the front 〔main〕 entrance.

**앞바다** coastal and off-shore areas; the offing; the open sea.

**앞바닥** the forepart of a sole.

**앞바람** ①《마파람》 a southerly 〔south〕 wind. ②《역풍》 a head wind.

**앞바퀴** a front 〔fore〕 wheel.

**앞발** 《소·말 따위의》 a forefoot; a front leg; a fore leg; 《개·고양이의》 a (fore-) paw. ◉ ～질 kicking with the forefeet.

**앞산**(―山) the mountain in front (of a house).

**앞서거니 뒤서거니** now ahead and now behind. ¶ ～하다 pass or go ahead of one another in turn / 개는 ～ 나를 따라왔다 The dog followed me, now ahead and now behind.

**앞서다** go first; go before 《*a person*》; go 〔be〕 ahead 《of》; go in advance 《of》; precede; lead 《others》; take the lead 《in》; 《문화·산업 기술 등이》 be advanced; 《우선하다》 take precedence. ¶ 앞서서 걷다 walk at the head of a procession 〔ahead of 《others》〕 / 앞선 기술 advanced technology / 경주에서 ～ get the lead in a race / 경제 문제가 무엇보다도 앞선다 The economic problem takes precedence over everything else. / 무엇보다 앞서는 것은 돈이다 Money is the first consideration for anything. *or* Money is what we need 〔one needs〕 first of all. / 한국은 이 기술 분야에서는 세계에서 가장 앞선 나라이다 Korea leads the world in this field of technology.

**앞서(서)** ①《전에·지난번》 previously; before; earlier; 《일전에》 the other day; some time ago; several 〔a few〕 days ago; 《최근의》 lately; recently. ¶

앞서 말한 바와 같이 as previously stated / 앞서 편지로 말한 바와 같이 as I have stated in my previous letter / 이에 앞서 prior 〔previous〕 to this; before this / 사용하기에 앞서 before using 《it》/ 출발에 앞서 before *one* starts 〔leaves〕/ 그것에 관해서는 앞서 자네한테 말하지 않았던가 Haven't I told you about it on the former 〔an earlier〕 occasion ?
② 《먼저》 ahead 《of》; in advance 《of》; earlier (than); prior to. ¶ 정한 시간보다 앞서 before 〔prior to〕 a designated hour / 예정 시간보다 앞서 출발하다 start 〔leave〕 earlier than the fixed 〔scheduled〕 time / 남보다 ～ 가다 go ahead of others / 앞서가십시오 Go ahead, please. / 내가 너보다 앞서 왔다 I came 「ahead of 〔earlier than〕 you. *or* I got before you. / 출발에 앞서 그녀에게 감사의 편지를 썼다 I wrote a letter of appreciation to her 「prior to 〔preceding, before〕 my departure.

**앞세우다** ① 《앞서게 하다》 make 〔let〕 《*a person*》 go ahead; make 〔let〕 《*a person*》 lead 〔precede〕; set 《*a person*》 at the head; 《우선시키다》 give priority to. ¶ 국기를 앞세우고 with the national flag at the head 《of》/ 행렬에 악대를 ～ place a band at the head of a procession / 학생들이 김군을 앞세우고 총장을 만나러 왔다 Led by Kim 〔With Kim in the lead〕 the students came to see president. / 정치 문제보다 경제 문제를 앞세워야 한다 We must give priority to economic problems over political ones. ② 《먼저 여의다》 survive; outlive. ¶ 아들을 ～ survive 〔outlive〕 *one's* son; be left behind by *one's* son.

**앞앞이** for 〔to〕 each one 〔person〕; individually; respectively; severally; separately. ¶ ～ 하나씩 one piece each; one apiece / 그 애들은 ～ 방이 있다 Each of the children has his own room.

**앞이마** the (front) forehead.

**앞일** things to come; the future. ¶ ～을 생각하다 think ahead 〔of the future〕; look ahead 〔to the future〕/ ～에 대비하다 provide for the future / ～을 예언하다 predict 〔forecast〕 the future / ～은 알 수 없다 I don't know what is coming in the future. *or* We never can tell what the future has in store for us. / 네가 게을러서 네 ～이 걱정된다 Your idleness makes me worry about your future. / 내 ～을 생각하니 맥빠진다 It is discouraging to think of my future.

**앞자락** the front part 〔ends〕 《of a garment》.

**앞잡이** ① 《길잡이》 a guide; a leader. ¶ 길 ～ a guide / ～가 되다 lead 《a party》; act as a guide. ② 《끄나풀》 an agent; a tool; a cat's-paw. ¶ 경찰의 ～ a stool pigeon; a police spy 〔agent〕; a paid informer of the police / ～로 부리다 make a cat's-paw 〔tool〕 of 《*a person*》; use 《*a person*》 as a tool 〔an agent〕/ ～가 되다 be made a cat's-paw 《of *a person*》/ act as an agent 《for》; work 《*a person's*》 instrument / 다른 패들은 단순히 그의 ～에 지나지 않는다 The others are merely his instruments.

**앞장** 《선두》 the lead; the head; the van(guard). ¶ ～(을) 서다 lead (the van of); stand at the head 《of》; be in the lead; act as leader 《to》/ ～ 서서 …하다 be the first 《in, to *do*》; take the lead 〔initiative〕 in / ～ 서서 걷다 walk at the head 《of》/ 행렬의 ～을 서다 be at the head of a procession / 유행에 ～ 서다 lead 〔set〕 the fashion / 노동 운동의 ～을 서다 take the initiative in a labor movement / 새마을 운동의 ～을 서다 stand in the vanguard of the New Community Movement / 민 선생은 이 계획을 착수하는 데 ～ 섰다 Mr. Min took the lead in getting this program started.

**앞정강이** the (fore-)shin. ⇨정강이.

**앞지르다** get ahead of 《another》; steal 〔get〕 a march on 《the other》; leave 《another》 behind; 《능가하다》 outdo; surpass 《another in school work》; 《달리어》 pass 《another in the race》; outrun; outstrip; 《훨씬》 outdistance; 《배가》 outsail; outsteam. ¶ 남의 이야기를 ～ get ahead of 〔anticipate〕 《*a person*》 telling a story / 훨씬 ～ get far ahead of 《*a person*》; outdistance / 다른 차를 ～ pass another car ahead / 앞지름을 당하다 《전문 분야에서》 be outdone by another; be beaten in *one's* own field / 그녀를 앞질러 교회에 갔다 I went to church ahead of her. / (회사에서) 적지 않은 후배들이 그를 앞질렀다 He has been outstripped by quite a few men younger than him. / 어휘력을 늘린다면 영어에서 경쟁자를 앞지를 수가 있다 You will get a start on your rivals in English if you increase your vocabulary.

**앞집** the house in front.

**앞차**(―車) an earlier departing car 〔train〕; the car 〔train〕 ahead.

**앞창** a half sole. ¶ ～을 대다 half-sole; 《수리시키다》 have *one's* shoes resoled.

**앞채** ① 《집》 the front wing of a house. ② 《가마·상여의》 the front carrying-pole of a sedan chair. ③ 《앞마구리》 the front end-board of a saddle-rack.

**앞치마** an apron; a pinafore (유아의). ¶ ～를 입다 put on 〔wear〕 an apron.

**애**[1] ① 《수고로움》 pain; trouble; effort. ¶ 애를 쓰다 take pains; exert *oneself;* make efforts. ② 《초조한 마음속》 impatience; worry; anxiety; trouble. ¶ 애가 타다 be anxious 《to》; be nervous 〔worried〕 《about》; worry 〔bother〕 *oneself* 《about》; be agitated 〔disturbed〕.

**애**[2] a child. ⇨ 아이.

**애–** 《어린》 the very young; a tiny 〔baby〕 one; 《앳된》 green; raw; immature; inexperienced; 《첫》 the very first. ¶ 애송이 a greenhorn; a novice / 애호박 a zucchini / 애순 a fresh sprout.

**애가**(哀歌) a sad 〔doleful, plaintive〕 song; an elegy; a dirge; a jeremiad; 『성서』 The Lamentations (of Jeremiah).

**애간장**(―肝腸) [비유적] ¶ 그녀는 아들의 일로 ～을 태우고 있다 She worries very much about her son. *or* Her heart bleeds for her son. / 그녀는 아들이 죽었을 때 ～이 끊어지는 느낌이었다 She was heartbroken when her son died. / 그 소식을 듣고 ～을 태웠다 The news has rent 〔wrung〕 my heart.

**애개**(개) 《아뿔사》 My !; Gosh !; Golly !; 《몹시 작을 때》 How skimpy 〔puny, little〕! ¶ ～ 이렇게 조금만 주니 My, you give me so little. / ～ 저 자동차 작기도 하다 Look, what a tiny car it is !

**애걸**(哀乞) an entreaty; imploring; supplication. ～하다 entreat; implore; supplicate; beg 《to *do*》. ¶ ～복걸하다 beg earnestly; implore / 자기들을 처벌하지 말아달라고 ～했다 They implored 〔begged〕 us not to punish them.

**애견**(愛犬) *one's* pet 〔favorite〕 dog. ◉ ～가 a dog-lover; a lover of dogs; a dog-fancier.

**애고**(愛顧) patronage; custom; favor. ～하다 patronize; favor; love and think of; take care of. ¶ …의 ～를 입다 be patronized 《by another》; receive favors 《from another》; enjoy the patronage of… / 아무의 ～에 보답하다 be worthy of *a person's* patronage / 평소의 ～에 감사합니다 Thank you for your patronage. / 계속 ～해 주시기를 바랍니다 We hope you will continue to patronize us.

**애고대고** crying and wailing. ～하다 cry and wail.

**애곡**(哀哭) bitter weeping; mourning; lamentation; grief; wailing. ～하다 mourn 《for, over》; lament 《for》; grieve 《at, over》; wail.

**애교**(愛嬌) winsomeness; 《매력》 attractiveness; charm(s); amiability; 《상인들의》 courtesy. ¶ ～(가) 있는 charming; pleasing; attractive; winsome; amiable / ～ 없는 unattractive; 《용모》 sour; 《태도》 blunt; 《대답이》 curt / ～ 있는 웃음 a winning 〔bland〕 smile / ～가 넘쳐 흐르다 be overflowing with smiles / ～ 부리다〔떨다〕 behave *oneself* attractively 〔delightfully〕 《to》; display *one's* charm; make *oneself* pleasant 《to》; be all smiles 《to》 / 그녀는 꽤 ～가 있다 She's very charming. *or* She has an attractive personality. / 그녀는 그곳에 있는 모든 사람에게 ～를 떨었다 She turned on her charm for everyone who was there.

**애교심**(愛校心) love of 〔attachment to〕 *one's* school 〔alma matar〕.

**애교점** a beauty spot; a patch.

**애구** Oh !; Oh, my goodness !

**애국**(愛國) patriotism; love of 〔for〕 *one's* country. ¶ ～적인〔의〕 patriotic. ◉ ～가 a patriotic song; 《국가》 a national anthem: 여러분, ～가 제창입니다 Ladies and gentlemen, our national anthem. ～단체 a patriotic society 〔organization〕. ～선열 deceased patriots. ～애족 devotion to *one's* country and people. ～운동 a patriotic movement. ～자 a patriot. ～정신 patriotism.

**애국심**(愛國心) patriotism; patriotic sentiment 〔feeling, spirit〕; nationalism. ¶ ～에 불타는 마음 *one's* heart burning 〔glowing〕 with patriotism / ～이 강하다 be very patriotic / ～이 있다 be patriotic; have a love for *one's* country / ～을 앙양하다 arouse patriotism / 그는 젊은이들에게 ～을 고취했다 He inspired young men with the spirit of patriotism.

**애긍**(哀矜) compassion; pity. ～하다 be pitiable 〔piteous, pathetic〕.

**애기** a baby; an infant. ⇨ 아기.

**애기잠** the first dormant period of the

silkworm.

**애꾸** 《눈》 a blind eye; 《사람》 a one-eyed person. ¶ ~눈의 one-eyed / ~가 되다 lose an eye; lose the sight of one eye / ~(눈이)다 be blind of 〔in〕 one eye.

**애꿎다** be undeservedly mistreated; (be) innocent; blameless. ¶ 애꿎은 사람 an innocent 〔a blameless〕 person / 애꿎은 그녀의 동생에게 화풀이 하다 vent *one's* anger on *her* innocent younger brother.

**애끊다** feel *one's* heart torn 〔rent〕 to pieces; *one's* heart bleeds; feel as if *one's* heart would break. ¶ 애끊는 슬픔 heartrending 〔heartbreaking〕 grief / 그 소식을 듣고 나의 가슴은 애끊는 듯했다 My heart broke when I heard the news. *or* My heart bled to hear the news.

**애끓다** be all roiled 〔"riled"〕 up; be upset; be anxious 〔worried, impatient, nervous〕; fret 〔worry〕 *oneself* 《about》; be in a fidget 〔stew〕 《구어》.

**애늙은이** a young person who looks 〔behaves〕 like an old person; 《성질》 a young person with an old man's mind 〔heart〕.

**애니메이션** 《만화영화》 an animated cartoon; an animation.

**애니미즘** 〖종교〗 《영혼 신앙》 animism.

**애달다** be anxious 《to》; be impatient 《at》; worry 《over》; feel worried 《about》. ¶ 그는 내가 꾸물거리는 데 애달고 있다 He is impatient at my slowness. / 그는 장사가 잘 안 되어 애달아한다 He is worrying over his slow business. / 그는 너를 만나고 싶어 애달아 했다 He was anxious to meet you.

**애달프다** (be) heartbreaking; heartrending; anguishing; heartbroken; painful; distressing; pathetic; be sore at heart. ¶ 애달픈 소식 heartbreaking news / 그가 죽었다니 정말 애달픈 일이다 It is truly heartbreaking to hear that he is dead.

**애닯다** ⇨ 애달프다.

**애당심**(愛黨心) party 〔partisan〕 spirit.

**애당초**(一當初) the very first time. ⇨ 애초.

**애도**(哀悼) the deepest regret 〔sympathy〕; lamentation; grief; condolence. ~하다 grieve 《for》; lament; regret; mourn 《over *a person's* death, for the dead》. ¶ ~의 뜻을 표하다 express *one's* regret 〔deep sorrow〕 《over the death of...》; 《유족 등에게》 express 〔present, offer〕 *one's* condolence(s) 《to》 / ~의 뜻을 표하며 in token of respect to the memory 《of》 / 충심으로 ~의 뜻을 표합니다 Please accept my sincere condolences. ◉ ~사 a condolatory address; a funeral oration. ~자 a condoler; a mourner.

**애독**(愛讀) love of reading; reading (for pleasure). ~하다 read 《a book》 with pleasure 〔keen interest〕; like to read; be fond of reading; read 《a magazine》 regularly. ¶ 나는 디킨스의 책을 ~하고 있다 I love to read Dickens's work. *or* Dickens is my favorite author. / 이 책은 아이들에게 ~된다 This book is 「very popular 〔a great favorite〕 with 〔among〕 children. / 너만할 때, 나는 늘 만화 잡지를 ~했다 I used to read comic magazines with pleasure when I was your age. ◉ ~서〔작가〕 *one's* favorite book 〔author〕.

**애독자**(愛讀者) an avid reader 《of a book》; an admirer 《of an author》; 《예약 구독자》 a subscriber 《to a magazine》; 《신문 따위의》 a regular reader 《of The Times》. ¶ 이 잡지는 ~가 많다 This magazine has a large circle of readers.

**애동대동하다** (be) very young; [서술적] be still a boy.

**애드** an ad(vertisement); advertising. ◉ ~맨 an ad-man.

**애드벌룬** an advertising balloon; an ad-balloon. ¶ ~을 띄우다〔내리다〕 float 〔pull down〕 advertising balloon.

**애디슨병**(一病) Addison's disease.

**애락**(哀樂) grief and joy; sadness and pleasure.

**애련**(哀憐) pity; compassion. ~하다 (be) piteous 〔pitiable, pathetic, touching〕. ¶ ~의 정(情)을 금치 못하다 be overwhelmed with pity 《for》; be greatly moved with compassion 《for》; have 〔take〕 great compassion 《on》.

**애로**(隘路) ① 《좁은 길》 a narrow path; 《산간의》 a defile. ② 《장애·어려움》 a bottleneck. ¶ ~를 타개하다 break (through) the bottleneck 《in production》 / ~가 되다 cause a bottleneck; form 〔be〕 a bottleneck 《in *something*》 / 그 계획의 전도에는 잇따른 ~가 있다 There are a series of bottlenecks to the way of the program. / 자금 부족이 생산의 ~가 되고 있다 Lack of capital is a bottleneck to production.

**애리조나** 《미국의 주》 Arizona (생략 Ariz.).

**애림**(愛林) loving 〔cherishing, protecting〕 the forests; forest conservation. ◉ ~녹화(綠化)《게시》 "Keep the Trees Green"; "Save the Trees": ~녹화하다 take care of trees 〔forests〕 and make the land green. ~사상 interest in forest conservation. ~주간 the Arbor Week.

**애마**(愛馬) a horse *one* keeps with tender care; *one's* cherished mount.

**애매**(曖昧) obscurity; ambiguity; vagueness. ~하다 《모호함》 (be) vague; 《뜻이》 (be) ambiguous; obscure; equivocal; 《발음 따위가》 indistinct; 《의심스럽다》 (be) dubious; suspicious; 《진술 따위가》 (be) noncommittal; evasive; 《불확실》 (be) uncertain; indefinite.

> 용법 **vague** 기억·의미 따위가 분명치 않아, 「막연하다」란 뜻. **ambiguous** 여러 가지 의미로 해석된다는 뜻. 「막연하다」는 의미는 없음. **equivocal** 「두 가지 뜻으로 해석되는」이란 뜻. **noncommittal** 「언질을 잡히지 않는」이란 뜻. **evasive** 「회피적인」이란 뜻.

¶ ~한 기사 news of doubtful authority / ~한 말 weasel words / ~한 대답 an equivocal 〔a vague〕 answer 〔reply〕 (막연한); an evasive answer (회피적인); a noncommittal answer (이도저도 아닌) / ~한 변명을 하다 give a vague 〔an equivocal〕 explanation / ~하게 말하다 speak ambiguously; equivocate / ~한 말〔진술〕을 하다 make an ambiguous remark 〔statement〕 / ~한 태도를 취하다 maintain an uncertain 〔a dubious〕 attitude 《toward》; do not commit *oneself;* sit 〔stand〕 on the fence / 이 글은 뜻이 ~하다 The meaning of this sentence is ambiguous. / 이 규칙에는 ~한 점이 많다 These regulations are full of ambiguities. / 그는 이 일에 관해서 ~한 태도를 취하고 있다 He is taking an uncertain attitude in this matter. / 이 계약서는 ~하게 되어 있다 This written contract is ambiguously worded. / 이 구절에서 ~한 데를 분명하게 하자 Let's clear up the ambiguity in this paragraph.

**애매하다** be unjustly treated; be unjustly convicted 《of a forgery charge》; be falsely 〔wrongly, unjustly〕 accused 《of》; be under a false charge; be unjustly suspected 《of a guilt》; (be) innocent. ¶ 애매한 사람을 죽이다 kill an innocent person / 애매하게 도둑 누명을 쓰다 be falsely accused of stealing / 애매하게 꾸중을 듣다 get an unwarranted scolding / 그는 애매한 죄로 고소당했다 He was charged with a crime he had not committed. / 그가 ~는 이의 신청은 기각되었다 His plea for innocence was turned down.

**애먹다** have much trouble 《with》; be a bad hand at; be at 〔be driven to〕 *one's* wit's end; be put out 《with》; find 《*a person, a thing*》 unmanageable; have a hard time 《with》; [사물이 주어] be more than *one* can manage; be too much for *one.* ¶ 그는 그 일에 애먹었다 He was a bad hand at the business. *or* He had much trouble with the business. / 교사는 그 학생을 다루는 데 무척 애먹고 있다 The teacher is having a lot of trouble handling that student. / 자네 사무실 찾느라 무척 애먹었네 I had quite a hard 〔rough〕 time locating your office.

**애먹이다** put 《*a person*》 out; put 〔bring, drive〕 《*a person*》 to *his* wit's end; give 《*a person*》 much trouble. ¶ 우리 집 아이들은 때때로 나를 애먹인다 My children sometimes embarrass me 〔give me a lot of trouble〕.

**애먼** ① 《엉뚱한》 far-fetched; unlikely. ② 《죄 없는》 innocent; uninvolved; wrongly accused. ¶ ~ 사람 잡지 마라 Don't get the wrong man for your culprit.

**애면글면** struggling with all *one's* might; doing *one's* feeble best. ~하다 do *one's* feeble best.

**애모**(愛慕) affection; attachment; love. ~하다 be attached to; love; long 〔yearn, pine〕 for. ¶ ~를 받다 be beloved by 〔of〕 / 그들은 깊은 ~의 정으로 맺어져 있다 They are deeply attached to each other.

**애무**(愛撫) a caress; caressing; petting; endearment; stroking fondly. ~하다 caress; pet; love; fondle. ¶ 그는 그녀의 얼굴을 사랑스러운 듯이 ~했다 His hands caressed her face lovingly.

**애물** ① 《애태우는 것》 a (cause of) worry; a source of anxiety. ② 《죽은 자식》 a son 〔daughter〕 who died young.

**애바르다** be alive to *one's* interests; be wide-awake to *one's* own interests; be keen on money matters; (be) money-mad. ¶ 돈벌이에 ~ be alert to money-making; be a shrewd man of business / 어떻게 저토록 애바를 수가 있

을까 How on earth can he be money=mad? ⌈skinflint.

**애바리** a money-grubber; a miser; a

**애벌** ①《대충 만진 것》 a rough 〔tentative, temporary, superficial〕 job of it. ② [부사적] roughly; tentatively. ③ = 초벌 ①. ¶ ~ 찌다 give 《food》 its first 〔preliminary〕 steaming; steam 《food》 for the first time. ◉ ~갈이 〖농업〗 a first 〔rough, preliminary〕 plowing. ~김 〖농업〗 rough weeding. ~빨래 a first laundering; rough washing. ~일 a rough job; spadework.

**애벌레** 〖곤충〗 a larva (*pl.* -vae); a green caterpillar.

**애벌칠**(漆) 《페인트 등의》 undercoating; an undercoat; the first 〔ground〕 coat. ¶ ~을 하다 put 〔lay〕 the undercoat(ing) 《on》; give the first 〔ground〕 coat 《of paint to the wall》.

**애사**(哀史) a sad 〔pathetic, tragic〕 story 〔history〕 《of *Tanjong*》.

**애사정신**(愛社精神) loyalty 〔devotion〕 to *one's* company; company loyalty.

**애살스럽다** (be) stingy; tight; tight=fisted; miserly; penny-pinching.

**애서**(愛書) *one's* favorite books; a fondness 〔liking〕 for books; bibliophilism. ◉ ~가 a bibliophile; a booklover. ~광 a madness 〔craze〕 for books; bibliomania; 《사람》 a bibliomaniac; an insatiable collector of books.

**애서다** 《임신하다》 get 〔become〕 pregnant; conceive 《a child》.

**애석**(哀惜) 《슬픔》 lamentation; grief; sorrow; 《유감》 regret; a pity. ~하다 (be) sad; lamentable; regrettable; pitiful. ¶ ~한 마음을 전하다 express 〔present〕 *one's* condolences / ~해 하다 mourn over; lament 《*a person's* death》; regret 《being unable to come》/ …이라니 참 ~한 일이다 It is a pity that… / 참 ~하다 What a pity! / 그가 죽었다는 말을 듣고 ~한 마음을 금할 수 없다 The news of his death fills me with sorrow.

**애소**(哀訴) an entreaty; a plea; an appeal; begging. ~하다 entreat 〔implore〕 《*a person* to *do*》; appeal 《to *a person* for help》; make an appeal 《to》; plead 〔beg〕 for.

**애솔** a young pine tree.
◉ ~밭 a grove of young pines.

**애송**(愛誦) love of reading 《a poem》; reciting with pleasure. ~하다 love to recite 〔read〕 《a poem》; recite 〔read〕 with pleasure. ¶ 그는 곧잘 괴테의 시를 ~한다 He often recites Goethe's poems admiringly. ◉ ~시 *one's* favorite poems. ~시집 a collection 〔an anthology〕 of *one's* favorite poems.

**애송아지** a young calf; a newborn calf.

**애송이** an immature 〔a green, a callow〕 youth; a greenhorn; a novice. ¶ ~인 주제에 그렇게 시건방진 소리 좀 하지 마라 Don't talk so impudently, you greenhorn.

**애수**(哀愁) sadness; sorrow; grief; pathos. ¶ ~를 띤 노랫소리 a plaintive singing voice / ~에 잠기다 be overcome with sorrow; be merged in sentiment of sadness / ~를 느끼다 feel sad 〔sorrowful〕; be grief-stricken / ~를 자아내다 make 《*a person*》 feel sad; excite 《*a person's*》 grief; induce sadness in 《*a person*》/ 가을이면 ~를 느끼는 일이 종종 있다 We often feel sad in autumn. / 이 샹송 가수가 부르면 노래는 일종의 ~를 띤다 Songs, when sung by this chanson singer, take on a peculiar pathetic note.

**애순**(一筍) a fresh sprout; a (young) bud; a shoot.

**애쓰다** ①《힘쓰다》 take pains 〔trouble〕 《to *do*》; make ⌈an effort 〔efforts〕; try (hard); exert *oneself* 《to *do*》; endeavor; strive 《for victory》; put *oneself* out 《to *do, do*ing》. ¶ 애쓴 보람도 없이 for all *one's* pains; for all 〔in spite of〕 the efforts / 목적을 이루려고 ~ endeavor to attain *one's* object / 영어를 배우려고 ~ make an effort to learn English / 애써 공부하다 study hard / 애쓴 보람이 없다 labor in vain 〔for nothing〕; beat the air / 애쓴 보람이 없었네 I gained nothing for all my trouble. *or* All my efforts ⌈ended in vain 〔ended in a waste of labor, bore no fruit〕. / 애쓰지 않으면 얻는 것이 없다 Nothing can be obtained without effort. / 애쓰고 경만 쳤다 I got a thrashing for my pains. / 애쓴 보람이 있었다 It was worth the trouble I took. *or* My efforts have been rewarded (with success). / 그는 애쓰지 않고 돈을 벌려고 한다 He wants to make money without efforts. / 이 저작에는 애쓴 흔적이 많이 보인다 The author seems to have taken great pains over this work.
②《힘을 바치다》 do 《*a person*》 a service; render service. ¶ 나라를 위해 ~ serve *one's* country / 세계 평화를 위해

～ labor for world peace / (여러 모로) 애써 주셔서 고맙습니다 Thank you 〔I am grateful to you〕 for your trouble.

**애애하다**(靄靄―) ①《안개가》(be) hazy; misty; foggy; cloudy; dark. ②《화기가》(be) peaceful; harmonious; happy. ¶ 화기 ～ be peaceful 〔harmonious, happy〕 / 화기애애한 가정 a happy home / 화기애애한 분위기 속에 회담은 진행되었다 The conference proceeded in a most friendly atmosphere.

**애연가**(愛煙家) a regular 〔habitual〕 smoker; a person who indulges in 〔enjoys〕 tobacco. ¶ 대단한 ～ a heavy smoker.

**애오라지**《겨우》 to some extent 〔degree〕; somewhat; rather; quite; but; only; just; but... somewhat. ¶ ～ 독서가 유일한 위안이다 Reading is my sole 〔only〕 consolation.

**애옥살이**《궁핍한 생활》 a poor 〔miserable, indigent〕 life 〔home〕; a grubby 〔shabby, slummy〕 way to live. ～하다 live in poverty; lead an indigent life; be in narrow circumstances.

**애옥하다**《살림이 구차하다》(be) poor; shabby; slummy; grubby; miserable.

**애완**(愛玩) love《of *one's* pet, of a prized possession, *etc.*》. ～하다 love; pet; make a pet of; fancy; 《소중히 아끼다》 prize; treasure; value. ◉ ～가(家) a lover; 《개·새 따위의》 a fancier. ～동물 *one's* pet (animal). ～물(物) 《동물》 *one's* pet; 《물건》 *one's* prized article; *one's* treasured possession.

**애욕**(愛慾) love and lust; sexual desire; (sexual) passion. ¶ ～의 노예가 되다 become a slave of (amorous) passion; fall a prey to passion.

**애용**(愛用) *one's* favorite 〔habitual〕 use. ～하다 use「habitually 〔regularly〕; make habitual use of; 《상품을》 patronize. ¶ ～하는 *one's* favorite 《cigars》 / ～하는 만년필 *one's* favorite fountain pen / ～하는 약 *one's* favorite medicine; the medicine *one* regularly takes / 국산품을 ～하다 patronize home production / 더욱 국산품을 ～해야 한다 We should use 〔buy〕 more domestic products. ◉ ～가 a habitual 〔regular〕 user 《of》; a patron; a person who favors 《the products of our company》.

**애원**(哀願) (an) entreaty; an appeal; supplication. ～하다 entreat 〔implore〕 《*a person* to *do*》; appeal 《to *a person* for help》; beg 〔plead〕 《for》; supplicate 《*a person* for pardon》. ¶ ～하듯이 imploringly; with a look of entreaty / 아무에게 자비를 베풀기를 ～하다 entreat *a person* to show mercy / 자기를 도와달라고 친구에게 ～하다 implore a friend to help *one* / 그는 아버지에게 재정적 지원을 ～했다 He appealed to his father for financial help. / 그녀는 한 주일만 기다려 달라고 그에게 필사적으로 ～했다 She implored him frantically for a week's grace. / 그녀의 ～도 그에게는 전혀 통하지 않았다 Her entreaties fell on his deaf ear. ◉ ～자 an implorer; a suppliant.

**애육**(愛育) ～하다 bring up 〔nurse, foster〕 《a child》 with tender care; protect; coddle up; cosset; pamper (up).

**애음**(愛飮) fondness of drinking.

**애인**(愛人) 《남자》 *one's* lover 〔boyfriend〕; 《주로 여자》 *one's* sweetheart; 《여자》 *one's* love 〔girlfriend〕; a beloved; a dear heart; a mistress 《시어》; *one's* (best) girl 《미》; *one's* steady 《미구어》. ¶ ～이 생기다 get a girlfriend 〔boyfriend〕 / 그녀는 미스터 김의 ～이다 She's Mr. Kim's girl.

**애자**(哀子) I who am the chief mourner.

**애자**(碍子) 『전기』 an insulator.

**애자**(愛子) *one's* (beloved) son; 《사랑》 love for *one's* son.

**애잔하다**《아주 약하다》(be) very weak; frail; delicate; fragile; 《애처롭다》(be) touching; pathetic; plaintive.

**애장**(愛藏) ～하다 treasure; cherish. ¶ ～하는 골동품 *one's* treasured antiques. ◉ ～서(書) *one's* treasured 〔cherished〕 book.

**애저**(―猪) suckling pig. ◉ ～구이 roast of suckling pig.

**애절하다**(哀切―·哀絶―) ⇨ 애처롭다.

**애정**(哀情) sadness; (a feeling of) sorrow; grief; pity. ¶ ～을 느끼다 feel sad / ～을 자아내다 make *one* feel sad; excite *one's* grief.

**애정**(愛情) affection; love; attachment; 《다정》 tenderness; a tender feeling; 《애착》 devotion. ¶ ～이 있는 loving; affectionate; warm-hearted; tender(=hearted) / ～이 없는 cold(-hearted); loveless; unfeeling / ～이 넘치게 affectionately; lovingly / ～에 굶주린 love=starved 《children》 / ～이 넘치는 편지 an affectionate letter / ～이 넘치는 말 affectionate words / ～이 없는 결혼 a loveless marriage 〔match〕 / ～이 없는 사람 a stone-hearted person / ～이 깊은 사람 a person of strong affection / ～을 바치다 give (all) *one's* love 《to》; devote *one's* affection 《on another》 / ～을 보이다 show affection 〔*one's* love〕 《for》 / ～을 쏟다 give 《*a person*》 great affection / ～을 얻다 win another's affection 〔love〕; gain 〔steal〕 another's heart / ～을 품다〔가지다〕 have 〔cherish〕 affection 《for》; feel affection 〔tender〕 《toward》; have a tender feeling 《for》 / ～이 식다 lose affection 《for》 / 그 아이는 부모의 ～에 굶주리고 있다 The child is starving for its parental affection. / 그는 자신의 일에 ～을 가지고 있다 He is attached to his own work. / 편지에는 그에 대한 ～이 넘쳐 있었다 The letter was full of affection for him. / 딸에 대한 따뜻한 ～이 여느 때처럼 편지에 스며 있었다 His tender affection for his daughter permeated his letter as usual.

**애조**(哀調) 《가락》 a plaintive 〔sad, sorrowful〕 tone 〔song〕; 《곡》 a mournful 〔sad〕 melody. ¶ ～를 띤 mournful; plaintive; sentimentally sad / ～를 띤 노래 an elegiac 〔a plaintive〕 song / ～를 띤 멜로디 a sad melody.

**애조**(愛鳥) *one's* pet bird. ◉ ～가(家) a lover of birds; a bird fancier 〔lover〕.

**애족**(愛族) loving *one's* people.

**애주**(愛酒) love of wine. ～하다 be fond of drinking; love wine; drink wine 〔liquor〕 regularly. ◉ ～가(家) a habitual 〔regular〕 drinker.

**애중**(愛重) ⇨ 애지중지(愛之重之).

**애증**(愛憎) love and hatred 〔hate〕; likes and dislikes; preference(s) and aversion(s). ¶ ～이 뒤얽힌 관계 a love=hate relationship / ～의 념(念)이 강하다 have a strong partiality / ～은 근본을 따져보면 같은 것이다 Love and hatred are 「one and the same thing 〔one in the final analysis〕. *or* Love and hate spring from the same source.

**애지중지**(愛之重之) ～하다 love and prize; prize 〔value〕 highly; keep 《*a thing*》 as the apple of *one's* eye; treasure; think 〔make〕 much of 《*a person, a thing*》; set a high value 《upon》. ¶ ～하는 딸 *one's* loving daughter; *one's* favorite 〔pet, dear〕 daughter / ～하는 책 a treasured book / 손자를 ～하다 dote on *one's* grandchild; love (and foster) *one's* grandchild as the apple of *one's* eyes.

**애착**(愛着) fondness; attachment; devotion; affection; love. ¶ 향토에 대한 ～심 attachment to *one's* native place / (…에) ～을 가지다 be attached 《to》; be fond 《of》 / ～이 없다 be not (particularly) attached 《to》 / ～을 느끼게 되다 become attached 《to》 / 나는 이 직업에 아무런 ～도 느끼지 않는다 I am not attached to this job at all. / 오래 써서 길든 만년필에는 누구나 ～을 느끼는 법이다 Everybody is strongly attached to the fountain pen he has used for a long time.

**애창**(愛唱) ～하다 love to sing 《a song》. ◉ ～가(歌) *one's* favorite song: ～가집 a songbook.

**애처**(愛妻) *one's* (beloved, dearest) wife. ◉ ～가 a devoted 〔an uxorious〕 husband.

**애처롭다** (be) pitiful; sorrowful; pathetic; touching. ¶ 애처로운 이야기 a sad 〔touching〕 story 〔tale〕 / 애처로운 광경 a touching 〔pathetic〕 sight / 애처롭게 여기다 be touched with pity; feel compassion 〔pity〕 《for an orphan》; take 〔have〕 pity 《on *a person*》 / 어린아이가 추위에 떠는 것을 보니 애처로웠다 It was a pitiful sight to see a child shivering with cold. / 부모도 없는 아이고 보니 더더욱 애처롭게 느껴진다 I pity the child the more because he is an orphan.

**애첩**(愛妾) *one's* (favorite) concubine; 「*one's* mistress.

**애초** the very first time; the very beginning; the start; the outset. ¶ ～의 《최초의》 the first; the primary; 《본래의》 the original / ～의 의도〔계획〕 the 〔*one's*〕 original intention 〔plan〕 / ～의 목적 the 〔*one's*〕 primary object / ～에는 at first; in 〔at〕 the beginning; 《본래는》 originally / ～에 in the first place; at the outset 〔start, beginning〕; (at) first; to begin 〔start〕 with / ～부터 from the first 〔start, beginning〕 / ～에는 회원이 열밖에 없었다 We had only ten members to start with.

**애칭**(愛稱) a pet name; a terms of endearment; 《별명》 a nickname. ¶ ～으로 부르다 call 《*a person*》 by *his* pet name / 그들은 그를 허리란 ～으로 불렀다 They nicknamed him Hurry. / 윌리엄의 ～은 빌이다 "Bill" is a name of endearment for William. / 버니는 토끼의 ～이다 "Bunny" is a pet name for a rabbit. / 존은 아내를 슈거라는 ～으로 부른다 John's pet name for his wife is "Sugar." *or* John calls his wife by the pet name of "Sugar."

**애타**(愛他) loving others; altruism. ¶ ～적(的) altruistic / ～정신의 함양은

교육의 중요한 일부이다 To foster altruistic spirit is an essential part of education. ◉ ∼심 an altruistic spirit. ∼주의 altruism: ∼주의자 an altruist.

**애타다** feel uneasy; be anxious 《for, about》; be 「nervous 〔much worried〕 《about》; worry *oneself* (sick) 《about》; bother *oneself* 《about》; be in a stew; have the jitters. ¶ 어린아이의 병이 낫지 않아서 ∼ be in anguish on account of *one's* child's protracted sickness / 그는 일이 뜻대로 되지 않아서 애가 탔다 He was all hot and bothered that things didn't turn out the way he wanted. / 딸이 자정이 넘도록 귀가를 하지 않아서 그녀는 애가 탔다 She was beside herself with worry when her daughter didn't come home until past midnight.

**애태우다** agonize; torture; annoy; worry; bother; irritate; vex; tantalize; keep 《*a person*》 in suspense. ¶ 부모를 ∼ worry 〔grieve〕 *one's* parents / 돌아오기를 애태우며 기다리다 wait in anxious suspense for 《*a person's*》 arrival / 근심 걱정으로 몹시 ∼ tortured with anxiety / 그런 일로 애태우지 마라 Don't let that worry you.

**애통**(哀痛) 《슬픔》 sorrow; grief; sadness; heartache; 《비탄》 lamentation. ∼하다 grieve 〔sorrow〕 《at, over》; lament 《for *a person's* death》; 《울며 슬퍼하다》 weep 〔mourn〕 《over》; 《유감》 regret; be heart-stricken. ¶ ∼한 sad; lamentable; deplorable / ∼한 나머지 in (the excess of) *one's* grief 〔sorrow〕 / 어머니의 죽음을 ∼해 하다 mourn 〔lament〕 *one's* mother's death.

**애틋하다** 《애가 타는 듯하다》 (be) worried; troubled; vexed; anxious; 《슬픈 듯하다》 (be) sad; plaintive; pathetic; melancholy. ¶ 애틋한 심정이 되게 하다 [사물이 주어] bring on feelings of melancholy.

**애티** childishness; puerility; puerilism; juvenilities; juvenile behavior. ¶ ∼가 있다 be childish 〔puerile〕 / ∼를 벗다 leave childhood behind; grow up.

**애팔래치아산맥**(—山脈) 《미국 동부의》 the Appalachian Mountains.

**애프터서비스** after-sales service; 《automobile repair》 service; servicing 《on goods sold to customers》; guarantee 《주로 미》. (★ 애프터서비스는 한국식 영어). ∼하다 give service (on the article sold); provide servicing 〔maintenance〕 《for》. ¶ ∼를 해주지 않다 neglect after-sales service / 이 TV는 1년간의 ∼가 보장됩니다 We guarantee this TV set for one year. *or* This TV set has a one-year guarantee. / 작은 상점이 ∼가 더 좋다 Small stores offer better after-sales service. / 저 상점은 ∼가 나쁘다는 평판이 있다 That store has a reputation for poor servicing. ◉ ∼담당원 《기계 따위의》 a service repairman 〔engineer〕.

**아프터케어** 《병후의 치료》 aftercare.

**애플** 《사과》 an apple. ◉ ∼소스 applesauce. ∼주스 apple Juice. ∼파이 (an) apple pie.

**애해** Well!; Eh!; Pshaw!; Oh yeah!

**애햄** hem; ahem. ∼하다 hem; clear *one's* throat.

**애향**(愛鄕) love of 〔for〕 *one's* home 〔native place〕. ∼하다 love *one's* native place; be devoted to *one's* hometown. ◉ ∼심 love of *one's* province 〔hometown〕.

**애호**(愛好) love 《for, of》; a liking 《for》. ∼하다 love; be fond of; care for 《music, *etc.*》; have a liking for; be devoted 〔addicted〕 to 《music》. ¶ 한국 사람은 평화를 ∼하는 국민이다 The Koreans are a peace-loving people. ◉ ∼가〔자〕 a devotee; a lover 《of music, literature, *etc.*》; an amateur; a 《movie, sports》 fan; a dilettante; a connoisseur; fancier (동식물의).

**애호**(愛護) protection; kind treatment; tender 〔loving〕 care. ∼하다 treat 《an animal》 kindly; be kind 《to animals》. ¶ 동물 ∼ 정신 kindness to animals / 동물 ∼ 주간 Be-kind-to-Animals Week / 동물 ∼협회 the Society for the Prevention of Cruelty to Animals (생략 S.P.C.A.)

**애호박** a young 〔green〕 pumpkin.

**애화**(哀話) a sad 〔pathetic〕 story 〔episode〕.

**애환**(哀歡) the joys and sorrows 《of 「life》.

**애휼**(愛恤) charity; compassion; sympathy; pity. ∼하다 show sympathy for; take compassion on; pity and help. ◉ ∼운동 a charity campaign.

**액**(厄) woes; a calamity; a disaster; (a) misfortune; ill luck; an evil. ¶ 액을 막다 keep 〔ward〕 off evil fortune / 액을 모면하다 escape a disaster / 액을 물리치다 drive out an evil spirit; exorcise / 액을 때우다 take the edge off a calamity by undergoing one of lesser degree / 액을 피하기 위해 그런 일을 한다 They do such things to avoid bad luck.

**액**(液)《액체》liquid; fluid (유동체);《즙액》juice (과즙); sap (수액); (a) liquor (알코올성(의)); secretion (분비액); (a) solution (용액). ¶ 액을 짜다 squeeze juice《from fruit》.

**-액**(額)《금액》an amount; a sum《of money》;《양》a quantity; a volume. ¶ 생산액 the amount of production 〔output〕; the volume of manufacture / 소비액 the amount consumed / 거액에 달하다 reach a colossal amount; amount 〔come up〕 to big figures.

**액년**(厄年) an ill-fated 〔a bad, an unlucky, an evil〕 year 〔age〕; a critical year 〔age〕 (for *one*); a climacteric year. ¶ 작년이 내 ~이었다 Last year was an unlucky year for me. / 42세는 남자의 ~이라고들 한다 Forty-two is said to be a critical age for a man.

**액달**(厄—) an evil 〔an unlucky, an ill-fated, a bad〕 month; a critical month. ¶ 이 달은 나에게 ~이다 This is an unlucky month for me.

**액때움, 액땜**(厄—) forestalling an impending misfortune by undergoing one of lesser degree. ~하다 take the edge off a evil fortune《by》. ¶ 그것을 ~으로 알고 단념하겠다 We will take it as the price for our escape from a misfortune of greater degree.

**액량**(液量) liquid measure. ◉ ~계(計) a dosimeter; a drop meter.

**액막이**(厄—)〖민속〗preventing 〔forestalling〕 misfortune; warding off evil; exorcism. ~하다 prevent 〔ward off, take steps against〕 misfortune; drive away 〔get rid of〕 *one's* evils; exorcize. ¶ 이것을 갖고 있으면 ~가 된다 This will protect you from evils 〔dangers〕. ◉ ~굿 a yearly exorcism by a shaman. ~부적 a talisman against evils.

**액면**(液面) the surface (of a liquid).

**액면**(額面) face value; par (value);《채권의》a denomination. ¶ ~ 이상으로〔이하로〕 above 〔below〕 par; at a premium 〔discount〕 / ~에 달하다 reach par / 말을 ~ 그대로 받아들이다 accept《*a person's*》word at (its) face value / 소문을 ~대로 받아들이다 take a report 〔rumor〕 at (its) face value / ~가로 (주식을) 1,000주 사다 buy one thousand shares at par / 그 말을 ~대로 받아들여서는 안 되네 You must take the story with a grain of salt. / 채권이 ~ 이상으로 팔렸다 The bonds were sold at a premium. ◉ ~가격 face 〔par〕 value: ~ 가격으로 at par. ~금액 nominal value. ~상환《채권의》redemption at par value. ~주 (a) par value stock.

**액모**(腋毛) underarm 〔axillary〕 hair; the hair of the armpit.

**액비**(液肥) liquid manure; a liquefied fertilizer.

**액사**(縊死) death by hanging; hanging *oneself*. ~하다 die by hanging; hang *oneself*《on a tree》; strangle *oneself*《with a cord》.

**액살**(縊殺) murder by strangling; strangulation. ~하다 strangle《*a person*》to death; murder《*a person*》by strangulation. ◉ ~시체 the body of a strangled man 〔woman〕.

**액상**(液狀) ¶ ~의 liquid; liquefied / ~단백질 liquid protein / ~막(膜) liquid membrane / ~을 유지하다 keep 〔remain〕 liquefied.

**액세서리** accessories; accessaries;《보석류의 장신구》jewelry. ¶ ~를 하다〔달다〕 wear accessaries (★ 복수형이 보통); wear trimmings《on the suit》.

**액세스**〖컴퓨터〗access. ¶ ~타임 access time / 랜덤〔임의〕 ~ random access.

**액셀러레이터** an accelerator. ¶ ~를 밟다 step on 〔press〕 the accelerator 〔gas pedal《미》〕; push down the gas; tread on the gas / ~에서 발을 떼다 take *one's* foot off the gas / ~에서 발을 서서히 떼다 ease 〔let《구어》〕 up on the accelerator.

**액션** action. ◉ ~영화 an action film 〔movie〕.

**액수**(額數) the amount (of money); the sum. ¶ ~로 백만 원쯤 about one million won in value / 큰〔적은〕 ~ a large 〔small〕 amount of money / 상당한 ~ a good sum of money; a sizable amount of money; a considerable sum of money《미》/ 전체는 엄청난 ~에 달한다 The whole comes to an enormous sum.

**액운**(厄運) a hapless 〔an untoward〕 fate; misfortune; adverse fortune; bad luck. ¶ ~을 만나다 fall on evil days; meet with a reverse.

**액자**(額子) a (picture) frame. ¶ ~에 끼우다 set 〔put〕《a picture》in frame; frame《a picture》.

**액자**(額字) letters written on a signboard.

**액정**(液晶)〖화학〗liquid crystal. ¶ ~(표시) 전자계산기 an LCD electronic calculator. ◉ ~소자〔표시(기)〕 liquid crystal display 〔diode〕 (생략 LCD). ~ 프린터

〖컴퓨터〗 an LCD printer.

**액제**(液劑) 〖약〗 a liquid medicine.

**액즙**(液汁) juice; sap. ¶ 포도나무를 자르면 ~이 나온다 A grapevine bleeds when cut.

**액체**(液體) (a) liquid; (a) fluid (유동체). ¶ ~의 liquid / 투명한 ~ a clear liquid. ◉ ~공기 liquid air. ~동역학 hydrodynamics. ~비중계 a hydrometer; an areometer; a spindle. ~ 비중 측정법 hydrometry; areometry. ~산소 liquid oxygen. ~압력 hydraulic pressure (수압). ~연료 liquid fuel. ~열량계(計) a liquid calorimeter. ~온도계 a liquid thermometer. ~유막(油膜) liquid membrane. ~정역학 hydrostatics. ~탄산 liquid carbon dioxide.

**액취**(腋臭) underarm 〔axillary〕 odor; the (strong) smell of the armpit.

**액화**(液化) liquefaction. ~하다 turn to liquid; 《액체가 되다》 become liquid; liquefy 《coal》; be liquefied. ¶ 암모니아가 ~된다 Ammonia is changed into a liquid. ◉ ~가스 liquefied gas. ~기 a liquefier. ~석유 가스 liquefied petroleum gas (생략 LPG). ~제 liquefacient. ~천연가스 liquefied natural gas (생략 LNG).

「(agent).

**앤티노크** 《내폭제(耐爆劑)》 an antiknock

**앨라배마** 《미국의 주》 Alabama (생략 Ala.).

**앨범** ① 《사진·우표 따위의》 an album. ¶ 사진 ~ a photograph 〔photo〕 album / 접착식 ~ a paste-in album / 포켓식 ~ a slip-in album / ~에 붙이다 paste 〔fix, stick〕 《a picture》 in an album / ~에 끼우다 slip 《a picture》 in an album. ② 《음반》 an album.

**앰뷸런스** 《구급차》 an ambulance. ¶ ~를 부르다 call an ambulance / 환자를 ~로 운반하다 carry a sick man by ambulance.

**앰풀** an ampoule; an ampul(e).

**앰프, 앰플리파이어** 《증폭기》 an amplifier. ¶ ~를 단 기타 an amplified guitar / 그곳에서는 ~로 볼륨을 잔뜩 올린 록밴드가 연주를 하고 있었다 A rock band was playing there, with amplifiers at full volume 〔full on〕.

**앳되다** look young 〔new, childish〕.

**앵**[1] 《소리》 《with》 a buzz; a hum; a drone; a whiz; a zoom. ¶ 모기가 앵 소리를 내며 날아다닌다 Mosquitoes are buzzing about.

**앵**[2] 《불쾌할 때》 Humph!; Huh!; Pooh!

**앵글** ① 《각도》 an angle; 《관점》 an angle; a viewpoint. ¶ 카메라 ~ a camera angle. ② 《철재》 an angle bar.

**앵글로색슨** Anglo-Saxon. ◉ ~ (민)족 the Anglo-Saxon race; the Anglo-Saxons.

**앵돌아지다** sulk; pout; turn about completely; make a volte-face; get 〔be〕 sulky 〔cross, sore〕. ¶ 그녀는 그 사건 때문에 나에게 앵돌아졌다 She turned her back on me because of the incident.

**앵두** 〖식물〗 *Prunus tomentosa* (학명). ¶ ~ 같은 입술 lips red as a cherry; rosy lips / ~ 따다 《울다》 cry; weep.

**앵무**(鸚鵡) 《앵무새》 a parrot; a parakeet; a macaw. ¶ ~새처럼 남의 말을 되뇌다 echo 〔repeat〕 *a person's* words (mechanically). ◉ ~병 〖의학〗 parrot fever 〔disease〕; psittacosis. ~조개 a (pearly) nautilus (*pl.* ~es, -li).

「poppy (flower).

**앵속**(罌粟) 〖식물〗 a poppy. ◉ ~화 a

**앵앵** buzzing; humming; droning. ~하다, ~거리다 buzz; hum; drone. ¶ 벌들이 꽃속에서 ~거린다 The bees are buzzing among the flowers.

**앵초**(櫻草) 〖식물〗 a primrose.

**앵커리지** 《알래스카의 항구》 Anchorage.

**앵커** ① 《닻》 an anchor. ② 《뉴스 프로의》 the anchor man 〔woman〕; the presenter; 《릴레이의 최종 선수》 the anchor (man) 《in a relay team》. ¶ ~를 맡아하다 anchor 《a relay team》 / (경영에서) ~인 홍선수가 물속으로 뛰어들었다 Hong, the anchor man, dived in for the last lap.

**앵하다** be chagrined 《at》; (be) offended; miffed; resentful; take umbrage; feel bitter 《about》. ¶ 손해를 봐서 ~ feel bitter about *one's* loss.

**야** ① 《놀람》 Oh!; Good heavens 〔gracious〕!; Gosh!; Dear me!; My goodness! ¶ 야 큰일났다 Good heavens, now this is serious! / 야 이건 너무했다 By heavens, this is really too much! / 야 김군이다 Hey! Here's Kim. ② 《부름》 Hey (you)!; Hey there!; Hullo!; Hello!; 《미》 Hi! ¶ 야 너는 누구냐 Hey there—who are you? / 야 김형 오래간만이군 Hullo, Kim! I haven't seen you for a long time 〔for ages〕.

**야**(野) 《야당》 an opposition party; the opposition. ¶ 야에 있다 be in private life; 《야당》 be in opposition / 야로 물러나다 《개인이》 leave the government service; retire from public office; 《정당이》 go out of power / 그는 야에 있은 지 이미 5년이나 된다 He has been five years out of government service.

**야간**(夜間) night; nighttime. ¶ ~에(는)

at 〔by, in the〕 night; during the nighttime / ～ 외출은 금지합니다 Going out at night is prohibited. / 미성년자는 ～에 이런 곳에서 일할 수 없다 A minor is not allowed to work in such a place at night. / ～영업 《게시》 Open evenings. *or* Staying open.
◉ ～경기 a night game. ～경비원 a night guard 〔watchman〕. ～근무 night duty; a night shift. ～당직 a night watch 〔duty〕. ～부 a night class; the evening 〔night〕 class 〔session〕 《of a school》: ～부 학생 a night=school student. ～비행 a night flight. ～연습 a night practice 〔operation〕. ～촬영 photographing at night. ～통행금지 a curfew. ～폭격 night bombing. ～학교 an evening 〔a night〕 school: ～학교에 다니다 attend an evening school.

**야경**(夜景) a night view 〔scene〕. ¶ 서울의 ～ a night view of Seoul. ◉ ～화(畵) a night piece 〔scene〕; a nocturne.

**야경**(夜警) night watch. ～하다 keep (the) night watch. ¶ ～ 돌다 make the round 《of a district》 at night; go on *one's* rounds at night / ～(을) 서다 stand 〔be〕 on night duty 〔watch〕.
◉ ～꾼 a night watchman.

**야고보서**(—書) 〖성서〗 The General Epistle of St. James (생략 Jam.).

**야곡**(夜曲) 〖음악〗 a serenade; 《야상곡》 a nocturne.

**야광**(夜光) noctilucence. ¶ ～의 noctilucent. ◉ ～도료 a luminous paint. ～시계 a glow 〔luminous〕 watch; a watch with a luminous dial. ～주(珠) a gem that emits light at night. ～충(蟲) a noctiluca (*pl.* -cae).

**야구**(野球) baseball. ¶ ～경기 a baseball game / ～를 하다 play baseball / ～경기를 하다 hold 〔have, play〕 a baseball game; cross bats 《with》 / ～(경기)를 보러가다 go to see a baseball game / ～경기를 TV로 보다 enjoy a baseball game on television.
◉ ～계 the baseball world: ～계의 스타 a star player in the baseball world. ～공 a baseball. ～광〔팬〕 a baseball buff 〔fan〕. ～ 담당기자 a baseball writer 〔reporter〕. ～부 a baseball club: ～부장 the president of a baseball club / ～부 주장 the captain of a baseball team. ～선수 a baseball player; a ballplayer; 《선수 전체》 the nine: 프로～선수 a professional baseball player. ～연맹 a baseball league. ～열 baseball fever; a mania of baseball. ～장 a diamond; a baseball ground; a ballpark 《미》. ～팀 a baseball team; the 《Seoul》 nine. 미국 프로～ 선수권 경기 World Series. 한국 ～위원회 the Korean Baseball Organization (생략 KBO).

**야근**(夜勤) night duty; 《주야 교대의》 a night shift; 《야업》 night work. ～하다 be on night work 〔shift〕; take night duty. ¶ ～ 간호사 a night nurse / ～중이다 be at *one's* night work; be on night duty / ～이 끝나다 come off the night duty 〔shift〕 / 오늘밤 그는 ～이다 He is on duty tonight. / 나는 한 달에 몇 번씩 ～을 한다 I take night duty 〔shift〕 several times a month.
◉ ～수당 a night-work allowance; 《시간외 수당》 an overtime pay. ～시간 night shift; night-work hours.

**야금**(冶金) metallurgy. ¶ ～의 metallurgical. ◉ ～술 (technique, art of) metallurgy. ～업 metallurgical industry 〔enterprise〕. ～학 (the science of) metallurgy: ～학자 a metallurgist.

**야금**(野禽) a wild bird; a wild fowl.

**야금거리다** take repeated little bites.

**야금야금** bit by bit; bite by bite; little by little. ¶ ～ 먹다 eat by bits / ～ 먹어 들어가다 eat into little by little; 《침입》 invade gradually.

**야긋야긋** jagged; with an indented 〔a ragged〕 edge; having teeth. ～하다 (be) notched; indented; jagged; have teeth.

**야기**(夜氣) 《공기》 night air; nocturnal atmosphere; 《냉기》 the cool 〔chill〕 of the night.

**야기부리다** ① 《꾸짖어 호통치다》 give a good scolding 《to》; haul 《*a person*》 on the carpet; bawl out; berate. ② 《불만으로 소란떨다》 make 〔kick up〕 a great fuss 《about *something* dissatisfied》; take out *one's* complaints on 《*a person*》; raise a clamor.

**야기하다**(惹起—) cause; occasion; bring about 〔on〕; raise 《a question》; create 《a trouble》; give rise 〔birth〕 to; lead to. ⇨ 일으키다 ②. ¶ 물의를 ～ lead to controversy / 분쟁을 ～ cause 〔trigger〕 a dispute / 전쟁을 ～ bring about 〔bring on〕 a war / 그것이 중대한 문제를 야기할지도 모른다 It may give rise to a serious trouble. / 운전자의 순간적인 부주의가 대사고를 야기한다 A moment of carelessness by a driver 「can cause 〔lead to, bring about, trigger〕

a disaster. / (배심원의) 평결은 거리의 폭동을 야기시켰다 The verdict led to riots in the streets. / 그 연설은 대소동을 야기했다 The speech gave rise to great commotions.

**야뇨증**(夜尿症) 『의학』 (nocturnal) enuresis; bed-wetting.

**야단**(惹端) ① 《소동·격동》 an uproar; a clamor; a row; a commotion. ～하다 make a row; raise a 「clamor 〔disturbance〕; raise 〔make〕 an uproar; make a scene; fuss about; shout; yell. ～스럽다 (be) noisy; uproarious; clamorous; fussing; 《야하다》 (be) showy; gaudy; gay 《color, garments》; noisy; flashy. ¶ ～ 나다 a commotion breaks out; a great stir is created; be uproarious; be clamorous; be in commotion / 시시한 일을 가지고 ～이다 make a great fuss over trifles; make much ado about nothing / 임금을 올리라고 ～이다 clamor for a higher wage / ～스럽게 차려 입다 dress *oneself* showily; be 「gaudily 〔flashily〕 dressed.

② 《꾸짖음》 a scolding; a chiding; a rebuke; a lecture. ～하다〔치다〕 blow 《*a person*》 up; take 《*a person*》 roundly to task; give 《*a person*》 a good scolding; storm at 《*a person*》; bawl out; haul 《*a person*》 on the carpet; rebuke; berate; read a lecture to; raise hell with. ¶ 게으르다고 아들을 ～ 치다 berate *one's* son for his laziness / ～을 맞다 be scolded roundly; be lectured 「sharply 〔severely〕; catch it (hot) 《구어》; be hauled on the carpet / 아무 말 없이 외출했다고 ～을 맞았다 I was told off for going out without permission. / 지각하여 선생님께 ～을 맞았다 The teacher gave me a sharp scolding for being late for school. / 들키면 ～ 맞는다 You will catch it if you're found out.

③ 《큰일남·낭패》 a predicament; a quandary; a trouble; a plight; a pickle; a (disagreeable) situation; a fix; a pass. ¶ ～ 나다 be 「in a quandary 〔at a loss〕 (what to do); be 「up a tree 〔out on a limb, stumped, in trouble〕; be in a 「fix 〔pickle, dilemma〕 / 참 ～났다 Well, what 「a pretty pickle 〔a fine fix〕 this is! *or* Things have come to a pretty pass! / 별안간에 시험을 보게 되어 ～ 났다 That shotgun quiz really knocked me for a loop. / 비가 쉬 안오면 ～ 나겠는데 If it doesn't rain soon, we'll be in a hell of a fix.

**야단법석**(惹端—) a boisterous merry-making; a spree; a racket. ～하다 have high jinks 《구어》; go 〔be〕 on the 「spree 〔loose〕. ¶ 아무 일도 아닌데 왜 이 ～이냐 Why do you make such a fuss 「about 〔over, of〕 nothing? *or* What a lot of excitement over nothing!

**야담**(野談) a historical romance; an unofficial historical 「story 〔tale〕.
◉ ～가 a (professional) historical storyteller. ～책 a historical storybook.

**야당**(野黨) an opposition party; a party 「out of 〔not in〕 power; a nongovernment party; the outs; the Opposition.
◉ ～공세 an offensive (move) taken by the outs against the government. ～기관지〔당수〕 an Opposition 「organ 〔leader〕. ～연합 a combination of parties out of power; coalition between nongovernment parties. ～의석 the opposition benches. ～의원 a member of the Opposition. ～통합 merger of the opposition parties.

**야독**(夜讀) reading at night; night study. ～하다 read in the night; study till late at night.

**야드** a yard (생략 yd.).
◉ ～자 a yard measure; a yardstick.

**야들야들하다** (be) soft and delicate; soft and shiny. ¶ 야들야들한 비단 fine soft silk / 아기 손이 ～ The baby has soft delicate little hands.

**야료**(惹鬧) disturbance; violence. ¶ ～를 부리다 behave rampageously; make a fuss.

**야릇하다** (be) strange; odd; queer; peculiar; eccentric; mysterious; out of the ordinary. ¶ 야릇한 사람 a queer 「bird 〔duck, guy〕 / 야릇한 세상 this treacherous life / 야릇한 운명 a strange fate; a 「curious 〔strange〕 irony of fate / 그와 그녀의 야릇한 관계 「an odd 〔a funny〕 relationship between him and her / 야릇하게 굴다 behave oddly; be particular / 야릇한 경험을 하다 have an odd experience / 야릇한 기분이 들다 feel strange; have a strange sensation / 운명이란 ～ Fate plays strange tricks.

**야마** 『동물』 a l(l)ama.

**야만**(野蠻) savagery; savageness; barbarism; barbarity. ～하다 (be) barbarous; savage; uncivilized; wild. ¶ ～적 풍습 uncivilized manners; a barbarous custom / ～시(視)하다 stigmatize 〔look upon〕《their customs》 as barbarous.

◉ ～국 a savage country; an uncivilized land 〔country, nation〕. ～시대 an age of barbarism 〔savagery〕; barbarous days. ～인 a barbarian; a savage; barbarous people; a wild 〔an uncivilized〕 man. ～행위 a barbarous act; (acts of) barbarity.

**야말로** indeed; precisely; exactly; just; really; none other than. ¶ 그～ indeed... / 이거～ 우리가 찾던 책이다 This is the very book that we have been looking for. / 저～ 사과를 드려야 할 것입니다 It is I, not you, that must apologize. / 영어～ 세계에서 가장 어려운 말이다 English is really the most difficult language in the world. / 그 사람이～ 그 일의 적임자다 He is the very man 〔just the man〕 for the job. / 이번이～ 잘 해야 할 텐데 I must succeed this time or never. / 이제～ 우리가 궐기할 때다 Now is the time for us to rouse ourselves to action.

**야망**(野望) 《대망》 (an) ambition; (an) aspiration (★ ambition은 개인적인 욕망을 포함하는 야망, aspiration은 숭고한 목적에 수반되는 대망); pretension; 《모반심》 treachery; a treasonous design. ¶ ～있는 ambitious; treacherous / ～을 품다 be (highly) ambitious 《of, for, to *do*》; entertain 〔harbor〕 an ambition 《for *doing*》; be treacherous / ～을 실현하다 realize 〔fulfill〕 *one's* ambition; have *one's* ambition realized / 위대한 가수가 되는 것이 나의 ～이다 It is my ambition to be a great singer. / 그는 그 자리에 ～이 있다 He has his eye on that position. / 그의 시도는 ～이 지나쳐서 결국 실패로 끝나고 말았다 His attempt was over-ambitious and ended in failure.

**야맹증**(夜盲症) night 〔moon〕 blindness; 〖의학〗 nyctalopia. ¶ ～의 night=〔moon-〕blind; moon-eyed; nyctalopic.

**야멸스럽다, 야멸치다** (be) cold(-hearted); hard-hearted; heartless; inhuman(e); callous; unsympathetic; inconsiderate. ¶ 야멸치게 in a chilly manner; coldly; 《일언지하에》 bluntly; flatly; pointblank / 야멸치게 거절하다 refuse 〔reject〕 flatly 〔pointblank〕; turn 《*a person*》 down flat; give 《*a person*》 a flat refusal / 야멸스런 말을 하다 speak cruelly; say a harsh 〔mean〕 thing / 야멸스러운 짓을 하다 behave callously 〔in a heartless manner〕 / 그들은 야멸친 사람이다 They are people without feelings.

**야무지다** be short but vigorous; be a "regular little ball of fire"; be "a little bundle of energy"; (be) hard; strong; solid; tough; firm. ¶ 야무진 사람 a man of firm character / 솜씨가 ～ be dexterous; be deft-handed; be clever with *one's* hands.

**야물거리다** chew with *its* gums; mumble.

**야물다** ① 《씨 따위가》 get 〔grow, become〕 ripe; ripen; mature. ¶ 야문 씨 ripe seeds / (열매가) 따도 될 만큼 잘 ～ be ripe enough to be picked. ② 《일·성질 따위가》 (be) sound; solid; steady; 《솜씨가》 (be) skillful; clever; dexterous; deft-handed. ¶ 손끝이 ～ be clever with the hands.

**야바위** trickery; swindle; fraud; imposition; imposture; deception; camouflage. ¶ ～ 치다 play a trick upon 《*a person*》; cheat 〔swindle, fool, deceive〕 《*a person*》; pull the wool over 《*a person's*》 eyes; 《미끼를 쓰다》 employ a decoy / ～에 걸리다 be imposed upon; be cheated; be taken in; become a victim of a deception. ◉ ～꾼 a swindler; an impostor; a cheat.

**야박**(野薄) unfeelingness; heartlessness; stinginess. ～하다 (be) unfeeling; ungenerous; stingy; cold-hearted; heartless; pitiless; hard. ¶ ～한 세상 a hard 〔rough〕 world; hard 〔stern〕 life / ～하게 굴다 treat 《*a person*》 cruelly; be hard on 《*a person*》 / ～한 세상이다 This is a rough 〔hard〕 world we are living in. *or* These are hard times. *or* What a hard world we are (living) in!

**야반**(夜半) midnight; late at night; the middle of the night. ¶ ～에 at midnight; in the middle of the night; at 〔in the〕 dead of night / ～이 되도록 공부〔일〕하다 burn the midnight oil; study 〔work〕 till ⌈late in the night 〔far into the night〕. ◉ ～도주 flight by night: ～ 도주자 a fly-by-night / ～도주하다 flee by night; run away under cover of night.

**야번**(夜番) night watch; night guard; duty at night; night sentry; 《사람》 a night watchman 〔guard〕; a night watcher.

**야비**(野卑) vulgarity; meanness; boorishness; bad taste. ～하다 (be) vulgar; base; unrefined; coarse; mean;

boorish; gross. ¶ ~한 근성 a mean mind; *one's* baser self / ~한 말《use》 vulgar〔coarse〕language; vulgarism / ~한 사람 a vulgar〔low〕person; 《교양이 없는》 an uncultured person; 《본데없는》 an ill-bred person / ~한 취미 unrefined〔boorish, vulgar〕tastes / ~한 태도 a boorish〔low〕manner / ~한 마음에서 from base〔sordid〕motives / 행동이 ~하다 be guilty of base〔low〕conduct / 그는 말씨가 ~하다 He is vulgar in his language. / 그것은 ~한 짓이다 It is bad taste to do such a thing. / 그런 ~한 짓은 그만둬라 You mustn't stoop so low as to do a thing like that.

**야사**(野史) an unofficial〔unauthorized〕history〔chronicle〕.

**야산**(野山) a hillock; a hill on a plain.

**야살** peevishness; perverseness; crabbedness; impertinence; impudence. ¶ ~ 떨다[부리다] behave in a hypocritical〔deceitful〕way; do《*a thing*》crabbed. ◉ ~(쟁)이 a peevish〔cross〕person; a crab; a saucy fellow.

**야살스럽다** (be) peevish; cross(-grained); perverse; crabbed; impertinent; impudent.

**야상곡**(夜想曲)〖음악〗a nocturne.

**야생**(野生) growing in the wild. ~하다 grow (in the) wild; be found wild; live in the wild state (특히 동물이). ¶ ~의 wild; feral; undomesticated; uncultivated / ~의 상태에서는 in the〔a〕wild state; in the wild / 이 식물은 ~한다 These plants grow wild. ◉ ~과일 wild fruit. ~동물 wild〔feral〕animals. ~상태〖동식물〗state of nature; feral state. ~생물 [총칭] wildlife. ~식물 a wild plant; a wilding. ~화(花) a wild flower.

**야성**(野性) wild〔savage, unpolished〕nature; brutal nature. ¶ ~적(인) wild; rude; rough; boorish / ~을 발휘하다 《동물이》 run wild; 《사람이》 give vent to *one's* savage instinct; commit barbarity / ~적인 성질을 잃다 lose *its* wild nature / ~화(化)하다 go wild / 그는 어딘지 ~적인 데가 있다 There is something rough and wild about him. ◉ ~미(美) unpolished beauty.

**야속하다**(野俗—) (be) inhospitable; unkind; unfriendly; hard; unsympathetic; inconsiderate. ¶ 야속하게 여기다 feel bitter《against *a person*》/ 야속하게도 그는 내 청을 들어주지 않았다 He was so unkind as to refuse my request.

**야수**(野手)〖야구〗a fielder; a glove man. ¶ 내~ an infielder; a baseman; [총칭] the infielder / 외~ an outfielder; a fielder. ◉ ~선택《become safe on》a fielder's choice.

**야수**(野獸) a wild〔feral〕beast; a wild animal. ¶ ~같은 brutal; beastly; bestial; beast-like / ~와 같은 사나이 a brutal〔beastly〕man; a beast. ◉ ~성 brutality; bestiality; the brute: ~성을 발휘하다 display *one's* brutality. ~파(派)〖미술〗Fauvism(주의); a Fauvist (사람): ~파의 Fauvist《paintings》.

**야스락거리다, 야슬거리다** talk profusely; be verbose; be prolix; perorate; harangue.

**야습**(夜襲) a night attack〔raid, assault〕; a nocturnal assault; an attack〔a surprise〕by night. ~하다 make〔attempt〕a night attack〔raid〕《on the enemy》; make an attack at night; attack《the enemy》under cover of the night. ¶ ~을 당하다 be attacked at night / 우리는 적에게 ~을 감행했다 We made an attack on the enemy under cover of the night.

**야시(장)**(夜市(場)) a night market〔fair〕.

**야식**(夜食) a midnight〔late-night〕snack. ~하다 have a midnight snack〔meal〕《of noodles》.

**야심**(夜深) being late at night. ~하다 be late at night. ¶ ~할 때까지 일하다 work「far into the night〔till late at night〕; burn the midnight oil.

**야심**(野心)《대망》(an) ambition; a strong desire《to make a name for *oneself*》; (an) aspiration; 《흉계》 an evil design; ill designs. ¶ ~ 있는 ambitious; designing / 엉뚱한 ~ an inordinate ambition / 영토적 ~ territorial ambition / ~을 품고 with a design / ~을 품다 be ambitious《of, for, to *do*》; entertain〔have, harbor〕an ambition《for *do*ing》/ ~을 이루다 realize *one's* ambition; have *one's* ambition realized / ~만만하다 burn with〔be burning with, be full of〕ambition; be highly ambitious / 그는 그 지위에 ~이 있다 He has his eye on that position. / 그는 아무런 정치적 ~도 없다고 말했다 He disavows any political ambitions on his part. ◉ ~가 an ambitious〔enterprising〕person; a man of ambition. 그는 ~가이다 He is「ambitious〔an ambitious man〕. ~작 an ambitious work.

**야업**(夜業) night work; 《교대일의》 a nightshift. ⇨ 야근. ～하다 work at 〔by〕 night; do night work; work into the night (밤까지); 《야근으로》 work on the nightshift; 《잔업으로》 work overtime; 《공장이》 operate at night. ◉ ～수당 an allowance for night work; a night-work allowance; an overtime pay.

**야영**(野營) camping (out); military encampment「in the country 〔in the open air〕; bivouac. ～하다 camp (out); make camp; encamp; bivouac; pitch camp. ¶ ～을 철거하다 strike 〔break up〕 camp. ◉ ～지 a camping ground; bivouac area.

**야옹** Meow! ¶ ～하고 울다 mew; miaow.

**야외**(野外) 《들》 the field; 《옥외》 the open air. ¶ ～의 field; open-air; outdoor / ～에(서) out in the field; in the open (air); out of doors; outdoors / ～로 산책나가다 take a stroll out of town / 야생 동물을 관찰하기 위해 ～로 나가다 go out into the field to observe wild animals.
◉ ～강연 a field 〔an open-air〕 lecture. ～경기 field 〔outdoor〕 games. ～극 an outdoor play; a pageant. ～극장 an open-air 〔outdoor〕 theater. ～사생 outdoor sketching. ～연습 field exercise; field work 〔drill〕. ～연주회 an open-air concert. ～요리 outdoor cooking; a cookout. ～운동 an outdoor sport; outdoor exercises. ～음악당 the outdoor music hall. ～음악회 an open air concert. ～작업 field work. ～조사 〔연구〕 field research 〔work〕. ～촬영 location.

**야위다** get 〔become〕 thin 〔lean, haggard, gaunt, emaciated〕 《from》; be worn out. ⇨ 여위다. ¶ 야윈 얼굴 a haggard 〔worn〕 face / 고생〔근심〕으로 ～ be careworn / 병으로 몹시 ～ become worn out from illness; be pulled down by *one's* illness / 열병으로 ～ be consumed by fever.

**야유**(野遊) a picnic; an excursion; an outing. ◉ ～회 a picnic: ～회를 가다 go on a picnic 〔an excursion〕.

**야유**(揶揄) raillery; banter; ridicule; hooting; jeering; 《극장에서의》 catcalling; 《의회에서의》 heckling. ～하다 ridicule; make fun 〔sport〕 of; banter 《with *a person*》; chaff; rally; hoot; hiss. ¶ 연사를 ～하여 하단시키다 hoot 〔hiss〕 a speaker down / 그의 말에 ～가 터져 나왔다 His remark was greeted by boos and hisses. / 그는 연설을 하려고 일어섰으나 청중의 ～로 물러났다 He stood up to speak, but his audience cried him down.

**야음**(夜陰) the darkness of night. ¶ ～을 타서 under cover 〔the cloak〕 of darkness 〔night〕; under the screen of night; taking advantage 〔availing *oneself*〕 of darkness.

**야인**(野人) ① 《시골사람》 a country 〔rustic〕 person; a farmer; a rustic. ② 《조야한》 a man with rough and simple tastes; an uncultured 〔boorish〕 person; a boor; a bumpkin. ③ 《벼슬 않는》 a person without 〔out of 〕 official position. ¶ ～이 되다 leave the government service; retire from public office / 그는 은퇴를 하고난 후에는 일개의 ～으로서 지냈다 After retirement he lived as a private citizen.

**야자**(椰子) 〖식물〗 a palm (tree); a palmetto. ◉ ～수 the coconut palm. ～열매 a coconut. ～유 palm 〔coconut〕 oil.

**야적**(野積) open-air storage 《of freight 〔goods〕》. ¶ 많은 폐 타이어가 ～되어 있다 A lot of used tires are piled up out in the open.
◉ ～장 an open storage yard 《for》.

**야전**(夜戰) a night battle 〔operation〕. ～하다 engage in a night operation.

**야전**(野戰) field warfare; field operations 〔battles〕; a plain 〔an open〕 battle. ～하다 engage in field warfare. ◉ ～군 field army. ～병원 a field hospital. ～우체국 a field post office. ～우편 mail 〔post〕 for the field. ～잠바 a field jacket. ～장비 field equipment. ～통신〔전화〕 the field telegraph 〔telephone〕. ～포병 field artillery: ～포병중대 a field battery. 「칭〕.

**야조**(野鳥) a wild bird; wild fowl 〔총

**야차**(夜叉) 〖불교〗 a *yaks*(*h*)*a* (Sans.); a (female) demon; a (she-)devil. ¶ 보살 같은 모습에 ～ 같은 마음 An angel without, a devil within.

**야찬**(夜餐) 《밤참》 a midnight 〔late-night〕 snack.

**야채**(野菜) (green) vegetables; greens; 《미》 garden stuff 〔truck〕. ¶ ～를 가꾸다 grow 〔raise〕 vegetables; 《시장 상대로》 grow garden stuff 〔truck〕 / ～를 곁들이다 add some greens 《to a meat dish》 / 농장에서 ～를 가꾸고 있다 We grow 〔raise〕 vegetables on the farm. ◉ ～가게 a greengrocery. ～밭 《가정의》 a kitchen 〔vegetable〕 garden; 《시장

상대의》《미》 a truck farm 〔garden〕; 《영》 a market garden. ～샐러드 vegetable salad. ～수프 vegetable soup. ～요리 greens; a vegetable dish. ～장수 a greengrocer; 《행상》 a vegetable peddler. ～탕면 noodle soup with vegetables. 모듬～볶음 braise mixed vegetables.

**야취**(野趣) rural beauty; rusticity.

**야코죽다** feel small; be overawed.

**야코죽이다** overawe; score off.

**야틈하다** be rather shallow 〔low〕.

**야포**(野砲) a field gun; a fieldpiece; field artillery [총칭]. ◉ ～대 a field=artillery corps; 《중대》 a field battery.

**야하다**(冶·野—) ① 《난하다》 (be) gaudy; flashy; gorgeous; showy; loud 《color》; garish; tawdry. ¶ 야한 옷 gaudy clothes / 야한 취미 poor taste / 야한 화장을 한 thickly painted / 옷차림이 ～ be loudly 〔gaudily, showily, colorfully〕 dressed / 이 옷은 내겐 너무 ～ This dress is too showy 〔gay〕 for me. ② 《속되다》 (be) vulgar; mean; low; coarse.

**야학**(夜學) an evening 〔a night〕 class 〔school〕. ¶ ～에 다니다 attend 〔go to〕 a night school 〔class〕 / ～에서 가르치다 teach a night school 〔class〕 / 나는 ～에서 공부했다 I studied at a night school. ◉ ～생 an evening 〔a night〕 school student.

**야합**(野合) ① 《남녀간의》 an illicit relationship 〔union〕 (불륜); a common=law marriage (내연 관계). ～하다 form an illicit union; have illicit intercourse; misconduct *oneself* 《with》. ② 《정당간의》 a 〔an unprincipled〕 coalition between political parties (formed with a sole view to seizing (political) power).

**야행**(夜行) nocturnal travel; a night trip; an afterdark journey. ～하다 travel 〔go〕 by night.
◉ ～성 『동물』 the nocturnal habits: ～성 동물 a nocturnal animal.

**야화**(夜話) an anecdote. ◉ 천일 ～《아라비안나이트》 the *Arabian Nights' Entertainments.*

**야회**(夜會) an evening party; a *soirée* (F.); a ball (무도회). ¶ ～를 열다 hold an evening party; give a ball. ◉ ～복 an evening dress 〔suit〕; 《남자의》 a dress coat; a soup-and-fish 《속어》; 《여자의》 a dress suit; an evening gown.

**약**(葯) 『식물』 an anther.

**약**(藥) ① 《약제》 (a) medicine (조제된 내복약); a drug (조제 안 된); a pill (환약); a tablet (정제); a remedy; an ointment (연고); a liquid medicine (물약); a decoction (달인 한약 따위).

> (용법) **medicine** 의료용으로 쓰이는 약의 총칭. 주로 조제된 내복약을 지칭하는 경우가 많음. **drug** 약의 재료가 되는 약물. 즉, 조제 안 된 약재를 말함. 또 「마약·독」이란 뜻으로도 쓰임. **pill, tablet** medicine을 대신하는 일상어로 흔히 쓰임. pill은 「환약」, tablet는 「정제」란 개념이 내포되어 있음. **remedy** 특정 질환의 치료약을 말할 때, 병명과 함께 쓰임: a headache remedy (두통약). 그러나 remedy는 「개선법·구제법」이란 비유적인 뜻으로 쓰이는 경우가 더 많음.

¶ 약 1회분 a dose of medicine / 엉터리약 a quack medicine 〔remedy〕 / 감기약 a cold cure 〔tablet〕 / 잠오는 약 a sleeping drug 〔pill〕 / 위장약 a stomach remedy / 약을 조제〔처방〕하다 compound 〔prescribe〕 a medicine 《for *a person*》 / 약을 쓰다 administer a medicine 《to *a person*》 / 약을 바르다 apply an ointment 《to》 / 약을 먹다 take medicine(s) / 이 약은 감기에 좋다 This medicine is good for cold. / 이 약은 두통에 잘 듣는다 This medicine is effective against headache. / 이 약은 먹기 쉽다 This medicine is agreeable. / 이 약은 써서 먹기가 나쁘다 This medicine is too bitter for me to take. / 약 받는 곳 《게시》 Pick up medication here. / 이것은 어디에 먹는 약이냐 What is this medicine good for? / 이 약은 조금도 효력이 없다 This medicine does not work at all. / 그는 이 약 저 약 다 먹어 보았다 He tried all sorts of drugs.

② 《화공약》 chemicals; chemical products; 《제약 원료》 pharmaceuticals; pharmaceutical products.

③ 《유약(釉藥)》 (a) glaze; (an) enamel. ¶ 약을 바르지 않은 unglazed 《earthware》.

④ 《도움·유익한 것》 a medicine; (a) benefit; good. ¶ 약이 되다 be good 《for》; do *one* good / 모르는 게 약 Ignorance is bliss. / 적당한 운동은 몸에 약이 된다 Moderate exercise 「will do you good 〔is good for the health〕. / 신선한 공기와 햇빛은 건강에 가장 좋은 약이다 Fresh air and sun-

shine「are the best things for your health 〔are the best of all medicines〕. / 좋은 약은 입에 쓰나 몸에 이롭다 A good medicine is bitter to the mouth but of value for the body. / 실패가 오히려 약이 됐다 The failure was a lesson to him. / 그에게 친절 같은 것은 약에 쓰려고 해도 없다 He has not a spark of kindness in him. *or* He has no dose of kindness.
⑤《뇌물》a bribe. ¶ 약을 쓰다 oil 〔grease〕《*a person's*》palm; cross《*a person's*》palm《with silver》.

**약**(約) about; some; nearly; … or so; almost; in round numbers; around《미》; approximately.

> 용법 **about** 수·양·시간 등에 관해 쓰이는 가장 일반적, 일상적인 말. **some** 약간 격식을 갖춘 말로서, 수사 앞에서만 쓰임. **nearly** 꼭 필요로 하는 수에는 미치지 못하지만 조금만 더 있으면 족하다는 것을 나타내는, 차이가 매우 작음을 강조하는 말. … **or so** 수량 등을 나타내는 명사 뒤에 붙여서, 「…정도」라는 뜻이 되는 구어적인 표현. **almost** 꼭 필요로 하는 수에 약간 미치지 않는다는 것을 강조하는 말. **approximately** 대강 정확하면서, 일치하지 않는 점이 있더라도 그것이 그다지 문제가 되지 않거나 중요하지 않다는 것을 암암리에 뜻하는 약간 격식을 차린 말.

¶ 약 이십 분 about twenty minutes; twenty minutes or so / 약 백 명, 100 persons or so / 약 5마일 about 〔nearly〕 five miles / 약 1만, 10,000 in round numbers / 약 3천 명의 청중 an audience estimated at three thousand.

**-약**(弱) a little less than 〔short of〕; a little under.

**약가**(藥價) ⇨ 약값. ◉ ∼기준 price standards for medicine.

**약가심**(藥—) chasing the aftertaste of a medicine. ∼하다 chase 〔cut, take off〕 the aftertaste of a medicine. ¶ ∼으로 사과를 먹다 eat an apple to chase 〔cut〕 the aftertaste of a medicine.

**약간**(若干) some; somewhat;《양》some quantity of; a little;《수》a few; a number of. ¶ ∼의 돈〔책〕 some money 〔books〕 / ∼의 설탕 some quantity of sugar / 군인 ∼명 a number of soldiers / 그것은 ∼ 어렵다 It is somewhat difficult.

**약값**(藥—) the price of 〔the charge for a〕 medicine; drug 〔medical〕 fee(s); a doctor's 〔pharmacy's〕 bill. ¶ ∼을 치르다 pay the charge for 〔the price of〕 a medicine; pay the doctor's bill.

**약골**(弱骨) a weak 〔feeble, delicate〕 constitution;《사람》a weakling. ¶ ∼이다 be of delicate health.

**약과**(藥果) ①《과줄》a round fried cake made from wheatflour, oil and honey; honey cookies. ②《어렵지 않음》a cinch《구어》; an easy thing; "duck soup". ¶ 그것은 ∼다 It's 〔That's〕 an easy task. *or* It's a mere child's play. *or* That's nothing 〔a cinch〕.

**약관**(約款)《협약》an agreement;《조항》a stipulation; a provision; an article; a clause.

**약관**(弱冠) a youth of twenty; a young man. ¶ ∼에 at the age of twenty; in *one's* twentieth year / 그는 ∼에 명성을 얻었다 He made himself a name while in youth.

**약국**(藥局)《약방》a pharmacy; a drugstore《미》; a chemist's 〔pharmacist's〕 (shop)《영》;《개업의의》a medicine room;《병원의》a dispensary; a pharmacist's office.

> 참고 영미의 약국: 영미의 약국에서는 약뿐만 아니라 비누·치약 따위 잡화류도 팔고 있다. 특히 미국의 drugstore에서는 팔고 있는 잡화류의 종류가 다양하게 많다. 화장품·문방구·잡지·서적 등도 있고 간단한 식사도 할 수 있는 곳이 있다. 따라서 약국을 drugstore로 번역하면 다소의 뉘앙스 차이가 생기는 점에 주의해야 한다. 또 영미의 약국에서는 의사의 처방전(prescription)이 없으면 약을 거의 살 수 없다는 것도 알아둘 필요가 있다.

◉ ∼방《약전》a pharmacopeia.

**약기**(略記) a brief 〔short, rough〕 sketch; an outline; a quick write-up. ∼하다 make a short sketch《of》; give a rough sketch; outline; sketch (out); describe in outline; jot down.

**약다** (be) shrewd; smart; clever; sharp; wide-awake; keen; prudent; tactful. ¶ 약은 아이 a clever child / 약은 사람 a shrewd 〔sharp〕 fellow; a cute chap / 약은 수법 a shrewd way《of handling business》/ 약은 개 a smart dog / 약게 굴다 act smartly; be tactful / 그는 너무 약아서 제 꾀에 속는다 He outsmarts himself.

**약대**(藥大) a college of pharmacy.

**약대접**(藥—) a bowl to drink a herbal medicine.

**약도**(略圖) 《지도의》 a「route 〔sketch〕 map 《of》; an outline map; a rough sketch 《of》; 《건축에서》 a rough plan 《of》. ¶ …의 ~를 그리다 draw a rough sketch of… / 여기서 집까지의 ~를 그려라 Please make a sketch map showing the way to your house from here.

**약동**(躍動) a lively motion; a stir; a throb; a palpitation. ~하다 move in a lively way; be「quick 〔"hop"〕 with life; be full of life; be in full play. ¶ 생기가 ~하다 be vibrant with life; be full of life (and energy); be overflowing with youth and vigor / 봄이 되면 만물이 ~한다 Everything moves lively in spring.

**약력**(略歷) *one's* brief personal「record 〔history〕; a sketch of *one's* life; a brief survey of *one's* career; an outline of *one's*「career 〔life〕; 《죽은 사람의》 a memoir.

**약령(시)**(藥令(市)) a herb market (held in the cities of Daegu, Cheongju, Gongju, Daejeon and Jeonju each spring and fall).

**약리**(藥理) ◉ ~유전학 pharmacogenetics. ~작용 a medical action. ~학 pharmacology: ~학자 a pharmacologist.

**약물**(藥—) ① 《약수》 medicinal waters; mineral waters. ② 《탕약 달일 물》 water for a medicinal decoction. ③ 《우린 물, 탄 물》 water in which medicine has been dissolved.

◉ ~꾼 a spa visitor. ~터 《약수터》 a mineral spring; a spa.

**약물**(藥物) (a) medicine; drugs; medication; medicament; medicinal substances; materia *medica* (L.). ¶ ~에 의한 치료 medicinal treatment. ◉ ~검사 examination by medicine; doping test. ~사용 《운동 선수의 금지 약물 사용》 doping. ~ 생체 반응학 pharmaco kinetics. ~요법 medication; medical therapy. ~의존 drug dependence. ~중독 medicinal poisoning. ~학 pharmacology: ~학자 a pharmacologist.

**약밥**(藥—) sweet steamed rice; steamed glutinous rice flavored with honey, dates, chestnuts, *etc.*

**약방**(藥房) a pharmacy. ⇨ 약국. ¶ ~에 감초 ⇨ 감초(甘草).

**약방문**(藥方文) a prescription (slip); a recipe. ¶ 사후 ~ the doctor after death / ~을 쓰다 write「out 〔give〕 a prescription; prescribe / ~에 따라 약을 짓다 make「up 〔fill〕 a prescription.

**약변화**(弱變化) 〚문법〛 weak conjugation (동사의). ◉ ~동사 weak verbs.

**약병**(藥甁) a medicine bottle; a vial; a phial; a bottle of medicine.

**약복**(略服) an「ordinary 〔everyday, informal〕 dress. ¶ ~을 입고 있다 be in「informal 〔casual〕 dress.

**약봉지**(藥封紙) a paper packet of medicine.

**약분**(約分) 〚수학〛 abbreviation; reduction of a fraction (to its lowest terms). ~하다 reduce 《a fraction》; abbreviate; cancel. ¶ ~할 수 없는 irreducible / $\frac{3}{9}$을 $\frac{1}{3}$로 ~하다 reduce $\frac{3}{9}$ to $\frac{1}{3}$.

**약빠르다** (be) shrewd; sharp; smart; tactful; cunning; quick-〔ready-〕witted; have quick wits. ¶ 약빠른 사람 a quick-witted person; a smart guy 《미》 / 약빠르게 굴다 use *one's* brains 〔head〕; use 〔exercise〕 tact; act sensibly / 그는 대단히 ~ He has a nimble wit. *or* He has all his wits about him.

**약사**(略史)「an abbreviated 〔a short, an abridged〕 history; a historical sketch; an outline history. ¶ 한국 ~「an outlined 〔a shortened〕 history of Korea.

**약사**(藥師) a pharmacist; 《미》 a druggist; 《영》 a (pharmaceutical 〔dispensing〕) chemist.

◉ ~ 국가시험 a state examination for pharmaceutical chemist. 대한 ~회 the Korean Pharmaceutical Association (생략 KPA).

**약사발**(藥沙鉢) 《탕약 사발》 a bowl of decoction; 《사약 그릇》 a bowl of poison offered 《*a person*》 as an honorable execution; a hemlock bowl. ¶ ~을 받다 be given a hemlock bowl / ~을 내리다 offer 《*a person*》 a hemlock bowl.

**약사법**(藥事法) the pharmaceutical affairs law; the Drugs, Cosmetics and Medical Instruments Law.

**약삭빠르다, 약삭스럽다** = 약빠르다.

**약상자**(藥箱子) a medicine「chest 〔cabinet〕.

**약석**(藥石) medicine and acupuncture; medicines. ¶ ~의 보람 없이 죽다 die in spite of careful medical treatment.

**약설**(略說) a brief explanation; summarization; *résumé* (F.). ~하다 give an outline 〔a sketch〕《of》; summarize; abridge; sum up; epitomize; resume.

**약세**(弱勢) 〖증권〗 bears; shorts; bearish trend 〔sentiment〕. ¶ 원자재 가격이 국제 시장에서 ~를 유지하고 있다 Raw material prices remain in a bearish trend in the international market. ◉ ~매도 〖증권〗 stop-loss selling. ~시장 〖증권〗 a weak 〔bear〕 market.

**약소**(弱小) the weak and small; the weak; the minor; the lesser. ~하다 (be) small and weak.
◉ ~국(가) a lesser 〔minor, weak〕 power; a small nation. ~민족 the people of a small and weak power.

**약소하다**(略少—) 《적다》 (be) few; little; scanty; 《보잘것 없다》 (be) insignificant; negligible; trivial; trifling. ¶ 약소한 돈 a little money.

**약속**(約束) ① 《언약》 a promise; 《회합·출연·결혼 등의》 an engagement; 《계약》 a contract; 《협정》 an agreement; an understanding; 《만날》 an appointment; 《남녀간의》 a date 《미》; 《매매의》 a bargain; 《조건》 a condition. ~하다 (make a) promise; give 〔pass〕 *one's* word; make an appointment 《with》; make a date 《for dinner with》 《미》; agree 《upon *something* with *a person*》; pledge *oneself* 《to *do*》. ¶ ~의, ~한 promised; agreed; appointed / ~ 시간에〔까지〕 at 〔by〕 the appointed time / ~한 대로 as promised; true to *one's* word 〔promise〕 / …이란 ~으로 on the promise that…; under agreement that…; under promise to *do;* 《조건으로》 on condition that… / (미리) ~이나 한 듯이 as if prearranged; as if by common consent; as if by previous arrangement; as if agreed beforehand / ~한 시간 the time agreed upon; the appointed time; the hour named / ~을 잘 지키는 사람 a man of *one's* word / 거짓~ a mere 〔false〕 promise / ~을 지키다〔이행하다〕 keep 〔live up to〕 *one's* word; keep 〔honor, abide by, act up to〕 *one's* promise; fulfill 〔carry out〕 *one's* engagement / ~을 어기다 break *one's* promise 〔word〕; 《회합·만남의》 break an appointment 〔a date〕 《with》 / 만날 ~을 잊다 forget an appointment / ~을 취소하다 withdraw *one's* promise; call off *one's* engagement / 매매 ~을 하다 strike 〔make〕 a bargain / 굳게 ~하다 make a solemn promise; give *one's* word of honor / 여섯시에 여자 친구와 만날 ~이 있다 I have a date with my girl friend at six o'clock. / 그는 ~한 곳에 오지 않았다 He did not show up at the place we had agreed upon. / 내일 무슨 ~이 있습니까 Do you have any appointment tomorrow? / 별다른 ~도 없습니다 I have no particular engagement. / ~은 ~이다 A bargain is a bargain. / 그렇다면 처음의 ~과 다르다 If so, it doesn't agree with the original arrangement. / 그는 꼭 ~을 지킨다 He never fails to keep his word. *or* He is always as good as his word. / 너의 ~은 휴지나 마찬가지다 Your promises are like piecrust. / 그 여자는 그와 결혼을 ~하고 있다 She is engaged to him. / 너는 우리에게 ~했잖아 You gave us your word, didn't you? / 그는 원조를 ~했다 He promised (me) to help me. *or* He promised me that he would help me. / 1주일에 6시간 그에게 영어를 가르칠 ~이었다 I was under contract to teach him English six hours a week. / 모두 ~이나 한 듯이 침묵했다 All fell dumb as if with one accord. / 그런 ~은 하지 않았다 I didn't bargain for that.
② 《가능성·운명》 a promise; a prospect. ¶ 네게는 훌륭한 장래가 ~되어 있다 A great future is reserved for you. / 그 성공은 더욱 빛나는 미래를 그녀에게 ~하는 듯이 보였다 The success seemed to augur a brighter future for her.
③ 《관례》 (a) convention; a rule (규칙). ¶ 무대 위에서의 ~ stage conventions.
◉ ~어음 《issue》 a promissory 〔contract 《영》〕 note: ~어음 발행인 a promisor / 그는 은행 앞으로 100만 원의 ~어음을 발행했다 He drew a promissory note on a bank for a million won. ~의 땅 〖성서〗 the Promised Land; the Land of Promise.

**약손**(藥—) ① ⇨ 약손가락. ② 《만지면 낫는》 a soothing touch of the hand; a comforting hand.

**약손가락**(藥—) the medical 〔medicinal〕 finger; the third finger; the ring finger.

**약솜**(藥—) surgical cotton; absorbent 〔sanitary〕 cotton; cotton wool 《영》.

**약수**(約數) 〖수학〗 a (exact) divisor; a measure.

**약수**(藥水) ＝약물(藥—) ①.

**약수터**(藥水—) a mineral spring resort; a spa.

**약술**(略述) a brief 〔short, rough〕 sketch; a brief 〔summary〕 account; a succinct 〔terse〕 mention; a sketch; an outline. ～하다 give a rough sketch 《of》; make a short sketch 《of》; outline; 《the political background》; sketch 《out》; describe in outline.

**약술**(藥—) medicinal wine.

**약시**(弱視) weak 〔poor〕 eyesight; 『의학』 amblyopia. ¶ ～의 《*a person*》 with weak eyes; weak-eyed〔-sighted〕; amblyopic.

**약시중**(藥—) administering medicine 《to a patient》. ～하다 administer medicine.

**약식**(略式) informality. ¶ ～의 informal; summary / ～으로 informally; in an informal way; without formality; without circumstances.
◉ ～기소 a summary indictment. ～명령 a summary order. ～복장 ordinary 〔everyday, informal, casual〕 clothes 〔dress〕. ～재판 a summary trial. ～절차 『법』 informal proceedings. ～처분 summary disposition.

**약식**(藥食) ＝약밥(藥—).

**약실**(藥室) ① 《총의》 a cartridge 〔powder〕 chamber. ② ⇨약국.

**약어**(略語) an abbreviation; an abbreviated 〔a shortened〕 word; an acronym; a contraction.
◉ ～풀이 a key to an abbreviation.

**약언**(略言) a brief statement; a summary; an outline; an epitome. ～하다 summarize; state briefly; epitomize; outline; sum up. ¶ ～하면 in short 〔brief〕; in a word; to be brief; to make a long story short.

**약연**(藥碾) a druggist's 〔chemist's〕 mortar.

**약오르다** ① 《고추·담배 따위가》 ripen to its full flavor. ② 《골나다》 chafe 《at, under》; be nettled 《at, by, with》 feel 〔be〕 vexed 〔offended〕 《at, by》; get 〔be, become〕 angry 《with *a person*, at *a thing*》; be exasperated. ¶ 약오르는 말 a provoking remark / 약올라 있다 be in a bad temper; be out of temper / 그는 내 말에 약이 올라 있다 He is「exasperated 〔offended, vexed〕 at 〔by〕 my remarks.

**약올리다** provoke; exasperate; nettle; ruffle; madden; make anger; displease; offend; give offense 《to》; grate on 《*a person's*》 nerves. ¶ 욕을 해서 ～ provoke 《*a person*》 with abuse.

**약용**(藥用) 《for》 medical use; 〔형용사적〕 medicinal 《use》. ～하다 use medicinally; use 《*a thing*》 for medicinal purposes. ¶ 이 식물은 ～이 된다 This plant is used for medicinal purposes. ◉ ～비누 medicated soap. ～식물 a medicinal 〔curative〕 plant 〔herb〕. ～크림 medicated cream. ～포도주 medical wine.

**약육강식**(弱肉強食) the law of the jungle; the survival of the fittest. ～하다 the stronger prey upon the weaker; the weak fall a prey to the strong. ¶ ～의 세계 a world where the weak are victims of the strong; a world where the law of the jungle prevails / ～은 자연의 법칙이다 It is a rule of nature that the strong prey upon the weak.

**약음기**(弱音器) 『음악』 a mute; a damper; a *sordino* (It.). ¶ 현에 ～를 달고 with muted strings.

**약자**(弱者) the weak; a weak person; the underdog. ¶ ～의 보호 protection of the weak / ～의 편을 들다 stand by 〔side with〕 the weak / 강자에 대해 ～를 돕다〔옹호하다〕 help 〔champion〕 the weak against the strong.

**약자**(略字) 《한자의》 a simplified (Chinese) character; an abbreviated 〔a simpler〕 form (of a Chinese character); 《약어》 an abbreviation; 《약호》 a logogram (★ $, & 따위). ¶ …의 ～이다 be the simpler form for… / I.O.C.는 무엇의 ～입니까 What does the I.O.C. stand for? *or* What is the I.O.C. short for?

**약장**(略章) a miniature decoration 〔medal〕; a (service) ribbon. ¶ ～을 달고 있다 wear a (service) ribbon.

**약장**(藥欌) a medicine cabinet 〔chest〕.

**약재**(藥材) medicinal stuff; *materia medica* (L.); a drug.

**약저울**(藥—) pharmacy scales.

**약전**(弱電) a weak (electric) current.
◉ ～기기(器機) a light electric appliance: ～기기 메이커 light electrical appliance manufacturers.

**약전**(略傳) a short 〔brief〕 biography; a biographical sketch.

**약전**(藥典) a pharmacopoeia. ◉ 대한～ the Korean Pharmacopoeia.

**약점**(弱點) a weak 〔vulnerable〕 point; a weakness; a foible; a drawback; 《결점》 shortcomings; a flaw; a defect;

《불리한 점》 a disadvantage; *one's* blind side; 《급소》 a sore spot 〔place〕; *one's* Achilles' heel. ¶ ~을 지니고 있다 have a weakness 《for women》; have a weak point / ~을 찔리다 be struck at *one's* most vulnerable point / ~을 잡히다 give a handle 《to the enemy》 / ~을 틈타다 take advantage of 《*a person's*》 weak spot; avail *oneself* of 《*a person's*》 disadvantage / ~을 드러내다 betray *one's* weak point; show the white feather / 아무의 ~을 건드리다 touch *a person* on the raw / 아무의 ~을 발견하다 spot *a person's* weakness / 자기의 ~을 극복하다 conquer *one's* shortcomings / 나는 그의 ~을 쥐고 있다 I have got his sore spot. *or* I have a hold on him.

**약정**(約定) a promise; 《협정》 an agreement; an arrangement; 《규정》 a stipulation; 《계약》 a contract; 《매매의》 a bargain. ~하다 agree to 《*do*》; agree on 《*something*》; contract; engage; promise; make a contract. ¶ ~의 promissory; contracted; agreed; stipulated / ~에 의해서 by agreement 〔arrangement〕 / …라는 ~으로 under agreement 〔contract〕 that…; on the understanding that…. ◉ ~기한 the stipulated time. ~서 a written agreement; a (written) contract; a pact. ~이율 the agreed rate of interest.

**약제**(藥劑) a medicine; a drug; a remedy. ◉ ~사 a pharmacist. ~실 a pharmacy; a pharmacist's office.

**약조**(約條) an agreement; a promise; a condition. ~하다 agree; promise. ¶ 우리는 시간당 얼마로 ~하고 보트를 빌렸다 We hired a boat by the hour.
◉ ~금 a contract deposit.

**약졸**(弱卒) a cowardly 〔weak〕 soldier; a poltroon. ¶ 용장 밑에 ~ 없다 Brave soldiers under a brave general.

**약종**(藥種) medicinal stuff; drugs; *materia medica* (L.); pharmacopoeia.
◉ ~상 a seller of *materia medica;* an apothecary; a drug merchant.

**약주**(藥酒) 《청주》 strained rice wine; 《약술》 a medicinal wine.

**약진**(弱震) 〖지학〗 a slight earthquake shock; an 〔a faint〕 earth tremor. ¶ ~이 있었다 There was an earth tremor. *or* A slight earthquake was felt.

**약진**(躍進) rapid progress 〔advance〕; a 《great》 leap forward; great 〔rapid〕 strides. ~하다 make rapid progress 〔advance〕; make great strides; bound 〔leap〕 forward; progress 〔advance〕 rapidly. ¶ 한국의 경제적 ~ the rapid 〔remarkable〕 economic advance of Korea / ~에 약진을 거듭하다 advance leaps and bounds / 5위에서 1위로 ~하다 jump from the fifth place to the top / 한국의 화학 공업은 최근 대~을 이루었다 Chemical industry in Korea has recently made a remarkable development.

**약질**(弱質) 《체질》 a weak 〔delicate〕 constitution; 《사람》 a weak person; a weakling.

**약체**(弱體) a weak body. ¶ ~의 weak; effete / ~화하다 weaken; become weak 〔effete〕; become weakened.
◉ ~내각 a weak 〔frail〕 Cabinet. ~보험 substandard 〔maximum-risk〕 life insurance. ~정부 a weak government.

**약초**(藥草) a medical plant; a (medicinal) herb; herbage [총칭]. ◉ ~상 a herbalist. ~원(園) a herb garden; a herbary. ~학 medical botany: ~학자 a medical botanist; a herbalist.

**약칭**(略稱) an abbreviation; an abbreviated title; an acronym. ¶ ~을 …라고 하다 be called … for short; be abbreviated to… / FBI는 연방수사국의 ~이다 FBI is short for the Federal Bureau of Investigation. / 국제 연합을 보통 유엔이라고 ~한다 The United Nations is commonly called the UN for short.

**약탈**(掠奪) plunder; pillage; a sack. ~하다 plunder; pillage; loot; despoil; 《점령군이 도시를》 sack. ¶ 마을을 ~하다 plunder 〔pillage〕 a village / 재화를 ~하다 despoil 〔plunder〕 《*a person*》 of 《*his* goods》 / 그들은 그 도시에서 닥치는 대로 모든 것을 ~했다 They plundered the city of everything they could lay hands on.
◉ ~농업 plunder farming; a slash=and-burn method of agriculture. ~자 a plunderer; a looter; a despoiler. ~자산 a looted property. ~품 spoil(s); loot; plunder; booty.

**약탕관**(藥湯罐) a clay pot in which a decoction is prepared.

**약포**(藥包) ① 《약 싸는》 a chartula (*pl.* ~e). ② 《화포의》 a (live) cartridge.

**약포**(藥圃) 《약초밭》 a herb garden.

**약품**(藥品) medicines 《미》; drugs; 《화학 약품》 chemicals. ◉ ~명 drug names.

**약하다**(弱—) ① 《힘·세력이》 weak; feeble; infirm; 《연약하다》 frail; 《소리·빛

등이》 faint 《sound》; feeble 《light》; 《술 등이》 weak; light 《beer》; mild 《tobacco》; 《바람 등이》 light; gentle. ¶ 약한 목소리 a weak 〔faint〕 voice / 도수가 약한 망원경 a low-powered telescope / 약해지다 weaken ⇨ 약해지다 / 시력이 ~ have bad sight; be weak in sight / 그녀의 맥박이 점점 약해졌다 Her pulse became fainter (and fainter). / 이 안경은 도수가 ~ These glasses 〔spectacles〕 are weak.

> 용법 **weak** strong의 반대어로, 체력·의지·능력에 있어서 「약하다」는 뜻의 가장 일반적인 말. **feeble** powerful의 반대어로, 형편없이 「힘이 없고 약하다」의 뜻. weak보다 뜻이 셈. **infirm** 늙거나 병으로 약하다는 뜻의 말. feeble과 거의 같은 뜻으로 쓰임. **frail** 원래 체질이 병 따위에 저항력이 없고 연약·허약하다는 뜻.

② 《허약하다》 weak; weakly; infirm; delicate (섬약하다). ¶ 마음이 약한 faint=hearted; timid; timorous / 의지가 약한 사람 a man of weak will; a weak=willed person / 몸이 ~《체질적으로》 be delicate; have a weak 〔delicate〕 constitution; 《건강치 않다》 be in delicate 〔poor〕 health / 심장이 ~ have a weak heart; be weak in the heart; [비유적] be timid 〔shy, chicken-hearted〕 / 약한 자를 괴롭히다 bully 〔tyrannize〕 the weak / 그녀는 다리가 ~ She is weak in the legs. / 그렇게 마음이 약해서야 쓰나 Such faint heart won't do. *or* Nerve yourself!
③ 《잘하지 못하다》 poor 《at》; weak 《in》. ¶ 수학에 ~ be poor at 〔weak in〕 mathematics / 바둑이 ~ be a poor hand at *paduk;* be a poor *paduk* player / 나는 숫자에 ~ I am poor at numbers. *or* I have 「no 〔a poor〕 head for numbers.
④ 《저항력이》 be easily affected 《by》; be sensitive 《to》. ¶ 술에 ~ easily get drunk; cannot hold 〔take〕 *his* drink / 배〔비행기〕에 ~ easily get seasick 〔airsick〕 / 추위에 ~ be sensitive to cold / 열에 ~ be easily affected by heat / 지진에 ~ be vulnerable to earthquakes / 이 세균은 햇빛에 ~ This germ has a low (degree of) tolerance to sunlight.
⑤ 《유혹 등에》 be vulnerable 〔susceptible〕 《to》. ¶ 뇌물〔유혹〕에 ~ be vulnerable to bribery 〔temptation〕 / 아첨에 ~ be susceptible to flattery / 그는 여자에게 ~ He has a weak spot for women. *or* He has a weakness for women.

**약하다**(略—) ① 《줄이다》 abridge (요약하다); abbreviate; 《길이를》 shorten; cut (short); curtail. ¶ 약하여 for short / 약하지 않고 말하다 tell 《*a matter*》 in full / 한자를 약해서 쓰다 write a Chinese character in a simpler 〔an abbreviated〕 form / (이름 등을) 약하지 않고 쓰다 write in full / 엘리자베스를 약하여 베티라고 부른다 Elizabeth is called Betty for short. *or* We call Elizabeth Betty for short.
② 《생략하다》 omit; leave out; 《…없이 하다》 do without; dispense with. ¶ 허례를 ~ omit 〔cut〕 the protocol; dispense with empty formalities / 인사는 일체 약합시다 Let us do without formal greetings. / 보고문 낭독은 지루하니 약하기로 합니다 To spare you tedium, we will dispense with (reading) the reports.

**약학**(藥學) pharmacy; pharmaceutics. ◉ ~과 the pharmaceutical department; the department of pharmacy. ~대학 a college of pharmacy. ~사〔박사〕《학위》 Bachelor 〔Doctor〕 of Pharmacy (생략 Phar. B. 〔D.〕). ~자 a pharmacologist.

**약해**(藥害) 《suffer from》 harmful effects of a medicine; 《농약의》 damage from agricultural chemicals.

**약해지다**(弱—) get 〔grow, become〕 weak(er); weaken; 《소리 등이》 grow fainter; die down; 《바람 등이》 abate. ¶ 몸이 ~ fail 〔decline〕 in health / 불길은 곧 약해졌다 The fire died down in a short time.

**약협**(藥莢) a cartridge (case).

**약호**(略號) 《전신의》 a cable 〔code〕 address; a code.

**약혼**(約婚) an engagement; a betrothal. ~하다 be 〔get〕 engaged 《to *a person*》; get engaged 《to *a person,* to marry *a person*》; be betrothed 《to》. ¶ ~한 여자 *one's* intended wife; 《his》 intended / A양과 B씨의 ~ the engagement of Miss A to Mr. B / ~을 발표하다 announce the engagement 《of *one's* daughter to a man》 / A와 B 사이에 ~이 이루어졌다 A marriage has been arranged between A and B. / 그는 딸을 부자와 ~시켰다 He betrothed his daughter to a rich man. / 나는 그녀와의 ~을 파기했다 I broke off my

engagement to her. / 그들 두 사람은 ~한 사이이다 They are engaged to be married.
◉ ~기간 an engagement period. ~반지 an engagement ring. ~선물 betrothal presents 〔gifts〕: ~ 선물을 교환하다 exchange betrothal presents. ~식 an engagement party 〔ceremony〕. ~자 an engaged person; *one's* betrothed; 《남자》 *one's* fiancé (F.); 《여자》 *one's* fiancée (F.). ~파기 〔파약〕 a breach of promise of marriage. ~피로연 a betrothal party.

**약화**(弱化) weakening; enfeeblement. ~하다 be 〔become〕 weakened; weaken; grow weak; be enfeebled; get feeble. ¶ ~시키다 weaken; enfeeble; make 《*a thing*》 weak 〔feeble〕; 《화력을》 turn down / 고열이 환자를 ~시켰다 A high fever made the patient feeble.

**약화**(略畫) a (rough) sketch. ¶ ~를 그리다 draw a sketch; make a rough sketch 《of》.

**약효**(藥效) the effect 〔virtue, good, efficacy〕 of a medicine. ¶ ~가 있는 effective; efficacious; good 《for》 / ~가 없는 ineffective; 《be》 no good; useless / ~를 나타내다 tell 《on》; take effect work; prove efficacious / 이것은 두통에 신통한 ~가 있다 This medicine works wonders on a headache.

**얄궂다** 《짓궂다》 (be) perverse; treacherous; nasty; provoking; aggravating; 《기이하다》 quaint; queer; odd; curious; 《얄망궂다》 (be) eccentric; erratic. ¶ 얄궂게도 miraculously; strange enough; by a curious coincidence / 얄궂은 날씨 nasty weather / 얄궂은 사람 an aggravating person; a provoking person / 얄궂은 심사 a perverse state of mind / 얄궂은 운명 the curious irony of fate / 얄궂게 웃으면서 말하다 talk with a nasty smirk.

**얄긋거리다** quiver; shake; be quivery; be shaky; be unsteady; be rickety. ¶ 탁자 다리가 좀 얄긋거린다 The legs of the table are a bit shaky.

**얄기죽거리다** sway *one's* hips.

**얄망궂다, 얄망스럽다** (be) erratic. ¶ 얄망궂게 굴다 behave erratically.

**얄밉다** (be) hateful; detestable; disgusting; spiteful; provoking; mean (and nasty); 《뻔뻔스럽다》 (be) saucy; cheeky. ¶ 얄미운 말 nasty 〔ugly〕 words / 얄미운 소리를 하다 say spiteful things / 얄밉게 굴다 behave meanly 〔provokingly〕 / 얄미울 정도로 침착하다 remain provokingly calm 〔cool〕 / 그녀는 얄미울 정도로 노래를 잘 한다 She is an enviously good singer.

**얄밉상스럽다** (be) rather hateful.

**얄브스름하다** (be) rather thin.

**얄찍하다** be a bit thin.

**얄타** 《흑해안의 항구 도시》 Yalta. ◉ ~협정〔회담〕 the Yalta Pact 〔Conference〕.

**얄팍하다** ① 《두께가》 (be) thin; flimsy. ¶ 얄팍한 방석 a thin cushion / 이 책은 얄팍한데도 값은 비싸다 For such a thin book it's very expensive. ② 《생각이》 shallow; superficial. ¶ 얄팍한 생각 a shallow idea; a superficial way of thinking / 얄팍한 교양 a thin veneer of education / 그의 문학 지식은 ~ His knowledge of literature is shallow.

**얇다** (be) thin; lack thickness. ¶ 얇은 판자〔옷〕 thin board 〔clothes〕 / 창이 얇은 구두 thin-soled shoes / 얇은 이부자리 thinly stuffed bedding / 얇게 썬 빵 a thin slice of bread / 입술이 ~ have thin lips / 고기를 얇게 썰다 slice meat thin / 얇아지다 get 〔become〕 thin 〔thinner〕 / 사전에는 보통 얇은 종이를 사용한다 Thin paper is usually used for a dictionary.

**얌생이** ¶ ~ 몰다 sneak; pilfer; steal. ◉ ~꾼 a sneak; a pilferer; a filcher.

**얌심** mean jealousy; spite. ¶ ~스럽다 be mean and jealous; be spiteful / ~부리다〔피우다〕 show *one's* spite.
◉ ~꾸러기〔데기〕 a mean and jealous person; a spiteful person.

**얌전떨다, 얌전부리다** behave nicely; be prudish.

**얌전하다** ① 《차분·단정하다》 (be) gentle; modest; polite; graceful; 《주로 여성이》 (be) genteel; 《품행이》 (be) well-behaved〔-mannered〕; charming; nice; pleasant. ¶ 얌전한 색시 a modest girl / 몸가짐이 ~ behave nicely; be modest 〔graceful〕 in *one's* manner / 얌전히 굴다 behave *oneself;* act as *one* should *do;* be a good child (어린아이가) / 얌전히 포승을 받다 surrender tamely; suffer *oneself* to be arrested / 이 애는 참 얌전하구나 How quiet 〔meek〕 this child is! / 얌전히 굴지 않으면 아무데도 데려가지 않을 테야 If you don't behave (yourself), I won't take you anywhere. ② 《솜씨·모양이》 (be) nice; clean; neat; pleasing. ¶ 일을 얌전하게 하다 do a nice job / 글을 얌전하게 쓰다 write neatly / 옷을 얌전하게 입다 dress nicely / 바느질이 ~ She does a nice job of sewing.

**얌체** a selfish person; a shameless person.

**양**(羊) 〖동물〗 a sheep (*pl.* ～); a ram (수컷); a ewe (암컷); a wether (불깐); a lamb (새끼). ¶ 양가죽 sheepskin; 《제본용》 a roan / 양고기 mutton; 《새끼의》 lamb / 양떼 a flock of sheep / 양의 우리 a sheepfold; a sheepcot(e) / 양치는 사람 a shepherd / 양 지키는 개 a sheep dog / 길 잃은 양 a lost 〔stray〕 lamb / 양의 가죽을 쓴 늑대 a wolf in sheep's clothing / 양털을 깎다 shear a sheep / 양이 울다 A sheep bleats. / 그는 양같이 온순하다 He is as gentle as a lamb. ◉ ～자리 〖천문〗 Aries

**양**(良) 《성적·등급》 minimum passing; "D" 《미》. ¶ 영어에서 양을 받다 get a D in English.

**양**(䏡) 《소의》 tripe.

**양**(量) ① 《분량》 (a) quantity; (an) amount; volume. ¶ 양적(인) quantitative / 양의 증가 an increase in quantity / 양이 많다〔적다〕 be large 〔small〕 in quantity / 양이 늘다〔줄다〕 gain 〔diminish〕 in quantity 〔volume〕 / 양보다는 질 Quality before 〔matters more than〕 quantity. / 양이 많아지면 질이 떨어진다 What we gain in quantity we lose in quality.
② 《먹는》 capacity for eating; appetite. ¶ 양이 크다 be a great eater; have a great capacity for eating / 양이 적다 eat a small amount of food; do not eat much / 양이 큰 사람 a great eater; a heavy feeder / 양껏 먹다〔마시다〕 eat 〔drink〕 *one's* fill 〔to *one's* heart's content, as much as *one* likes〕 / 양이 과하다 take too much 《wine》; 《약의》 have an overdose 《of》 / 술〔담배〕의 양을 줄이다 reduce drinking 〔smoking〕 / 식사의 양을 줄이다 reduce *one's* diet / 양껏 먹었다 I have had enough.
③ 《국량(局量)》 capacity; caliber.

**양**(陽) 〖철학〗 Yang; the male 〔positive〕 principle in nature; 〖수학〗 positive. ¶ 양의 수 a positive number / 양과 음 the positive and the negative; the male and the female.

**양**(兩) ① 《옛 화폐 단위》 an ancient Korean monetary unit. ② 《무게 단위》 a unit of weight; a tael.

**양-**(兩) 《둘》 a pair; a couple; both; two. ¶ 양국 both countries / 양끝 both ends.

**양-**(洋) imported; foreign; Western; European; American; modern. ¶ 양담배 imported tobacco; American cigarettes / 양요리 foreign 〔Western〕 food 〔dishes〕.

**양-**(養) 《수양》 adopted; adopting; foster. ¶ 양아들 an adopted 〔a foster〕 son / 양아버지 a foster father.

**-양**(孃) 《처녀》 Miss. ¶ 김양 Miss Kim.

**양가**(良家) a respectable family. ¶ ～자녀 sons and daughters 「of good families 〔of respectable parentage〕 / ～태생이다 be well-born; come of a good family.

**양가**(兩家) two 〔both〕 houses; two 〔both〕 families.

**양가**(養家) an adoptive family. ¶ ～의 부모 *one's* adoptive parents.

**양각**(陽刻) engraving in relief; embossed 〔raised〕 carving; (bas-)relief. ～하다 carve in relief; emboss. ◉ ～세공 relief (work); embossed work.

**양갈보**(洋—) a whore 〔prostitute〕 for foreigners; 《기지촌의》 a Korean girl caters to American soldiers.

**양감**(量感) (a feeling of) massiveness. ¶ ～이 있다 be massive; be voluminous; bulky (크기가); heavy (무게가) / 그 그림에는 놀라운 ～이 있다 There is a wonderful feeling of massiveness in the painting.

**양갱**(羊羹) (a bar of) sweet red-bean paste.

**양견**(兩肩) *one's* shoulders. ⇨ 쌍견(雙肩).

**양계**(養鷄) poultry farming 〔raising〕; chicken raising 〔rearing〕. ～하다 raise poultry 〔chickens〕. ◉ ～업 poultry (farming); poultry 〔egg〕 industry: ～업자 a poultryman; a chicken-farmer; an egg-man. ～장 a poultry 〔chicken〕 farm.

**양곡**(糧穀) (food) grain; rice; cereals; corn 《영》. ¶ ～을 운반하다 haul grain 《미》; carry corn 《영》 / 정부 ～의 방출가격 the selling prices of staple grains held by the government.
◉ ～거래소 the grain exchange center. ～ 관리 기금 a grain management fund. ～관리법 the Grain Management Law. ～도입 imports 〔importation〕 of grain. ～ 수급 계획 a plan for demand and supply of grain. ～ 중개인 a grain broker 《미》. ～증권 grain bonds. ～증산 increased production 〔output〕 of grain: ～증산 계획 a program for increasing the output of grain. ～창고 a granary; a grain elevator 《미》. ～총소비량 total grain consumption; the nation's entire consumption of grain.

**양과자**(洋菓子) (a) cake; confections; confectionery [총칭]. ◉ ～점 a confectionery; a confectioner's (store).

**양관**(洋館) ① 《서양식 집》 a house built in Western style; a Western-style house; a European-style building. ② 《공관》 a legation of the Western country.

**양국**(兩國) two 〔both〕 countries. ¶ 경기 후 한일 ~의 선수들은 우호적으로 악수를 나누었다 After the game (was over), both Korean and Japanese players shook hands in a friendly way.

**양군**(兩軍) two 〔both〕 armies; 《양편 팀》 「two 〔both〕 teams.

**양궁**(洋弓) Western-style archery (궁술); Western-style bow (활). ¶ 세계 ~ 선수권 대회 the World Archery Championships.

**양귀비**(楊貴妃) 『식물』 the poppy. ¶ ~씨 「a poppy seed.

**양극**(兩極) 《남북극의》 both 〔the two〕 poles; the north and south poles; 《음양 양극》 the positive and negative poles. ¶ ~의 bipolar / (의견 따위가) 서로 ~이다 be poles apart 《in their opinions》. ◉ ~성 polarity. ~지방 the polar circles 〔areas〕.

**양극**(陽極) 『물리』 the positive pole 〔terminal〕; the anode; the plus terminal.

**양극단**(兩極端) both 〔the two〕 extremes. ¶ ~은 일치한다 Extremes meet. / 정치적으로 두 사람은 ~이다 Politically they are poles apart.

**양금**(洋琴) 『악기』 a dulcimer.
◉ ~채 light, small hammers (for striking a dulcimer): ~채 같다 be fine and delicate; 《목소리가》 be sweet / ~채 같은 목소리 a sweet voice.

**양기**(陽氣) ① 《만물 생성의》 the male 〔positive〕 element in nature. ② 《남자의》 virility; vigor; vitality; energy. ¶ ~를 보하다 increase *one's* virility. ③ 《햇볕의》 sunlight; brightness.

**양끝**(兩―) both ends 〔extremes〕. ¶ ~을 끊다 cut 《a stick》 at both ends.

**양날톱**(兩―) a double-edged saw.

**양녀**(洋女) a Western 〔an European, an American〕 woman.

**양녀**(養女) an adopted 〔a foster〕 「daughter.

**양념** spice(s); flavor; condiments; (a) seasoning. ¶ ~을 치다 spice 〔flavor, season〕 《a dish》 / 고기를 ~에 무치다 season meat with spices / 국에 ~을 넣다 put spices into soup; season soup / ~을 더 하면 맛이 더 좋아진다 If you make it more spicy, it will taste better. ◉ ~병 a cruet; a caster.

**양다리**(兩―) ＝두 다리. ¶ ~ 걸치기 double-dealing / ~ 걸치는 사람 a double-dealer; a timeserver / ~ 걸치다 try to have 〔play〕 《it》 both ways; play (a) double (game); sit on the fence.

**양단**(兩端) both ends; both extremes. ¶ 다리 ~에 at both ends 〔either end〕 of the bridge.

**양단**(兩斷) bisection. ~하다 cut 〔break, split〕 《*a thing*》 in two; bisect. ¶ ~되다 get split in two; be bisected / 국토는 ~되고 말았다 The country has broken 〔split〕 in half 〔two〕.

**양단**(洋緞) brocade.

**양단간**(兩端間) one or the other; between two alternatives; anyhow; anyway; at any rate; in any case; at all events; somehow or other. ¶ ~ 해야 할 일이다 I must do it anyhow. / ~에 손해는 없다 We shall not be a loser whichever way the matter ends.

**양달**(陽―) a sunny place 〔spot〕. ¶ ~에 내놓다 keep 《*a thing*》 in the sun / ~에 말리다 dry 《*a thing*》 in the sun / ~에 빨래를 널다 hang the wash out in a sunny spot / ~에서 볕을 쬐다 bask 〔bathe〕 in the sun; sun *oneself*. ◉ ~쪽 the sunny side.

**양담배**(洋―) imported tobacco; American 〔foreign〕 cigarettes.

**양당**(兩黨) the two 〔both〕 political parties. ◉ ~외교 bipartisan diplomacy. ~정치〔제도〕 two-party politics 〔system〕.

**양도**(兩刀) two swords; a sword in either hand. ◉ ~논법 dilemma.

**양도**(糧道) a supply line (of provisions). ¶ 적의 ~를 끊다 cut off the enemy's supplies 〔lines of supply〕.

**양도**(讓渡) 『법』 transfer; conveyance; alienation (재산권의); assignment (권리·재산의); 《영토의》 cession; 《어음의》 negotiation. ~하다 alienate; transfer 《to》; turn 〔make, hand〕 over 《*one's* property to *a person*》; 『법』 assign; convey 《*a thing*》 to 《*a person*》 by deed 《영》; deed 《*a thing*》 to 《미》; cede. ¶ 재산의 ~ alienation of property / ~할 수 있는 transferable; alienable; 《어음의》 negotiable / 권리를 ~하다 transfer *one's* right 《to *a person*》 / ~ 불능의 untransferable; 《어음이》 unnegotiable.
◉ ~가격 transfer 〔sale〕 price. ~성 예금 a negotiable deposit: ~성 예금증서 a negotiable certificate of deposit. ~소득 income from the transfer of *one's* property: ~소득세 a transfer income tax. ~인 a transferer; a

grantor; an assignor; an alien(at)or: 재산 ~인 a settlor / 피~인 a transferee; an assignee. ~증서 a (deed of) transfer; a conveyance.

**양도체**(良導體)〖물리〗a good conductor《of heat》.

**양돈**(養豚)《미》hog raising;《영》pig breeding 〔farming〕. ~하다 raise 〔breed〕 hogs; raise pigs. ◉ ~가 a hog raiser《미》; a pig breeder 〔farmer〕《영》; a hog-farmer. ~업 the hog raising industry. ~장 a piggery; a hog yard; a hog 〔pig〕 farm.

**양동이**(洋—) a (metal) pail; (a metal) bucket. ¶ ~로 물을 긷다 draw water with a bucket / ~에 물을 붓다 pour water into a metal bucket.

**양동작전**(陽動作戰) a feint operation; diversionary activities. ¶ ~으로 나오다 make a feint operation 〔sham attack〕.

**양돼지**(洋—) a pig of a Western breed; a Western pig 〔hog〕.

**양두**(兩頭) two heads; 〔형용사적〕 double-headed; dicephalous; bicephalous. ◉ ~사(蛇) an amphisbaena (*pl.* ~s, -nae). ~정치 diarchy; dyarchy.

**양두구육**(羊頭狗肉) ~하다 cry wine and sell vinegar; use a better name to sell inferior goods; make an extravagant advertisement.

**양딸**(養—) an adopted daughter.

**양딸기**(洋—)〖식물〗a (Chilean) strawberry.

**양떼**(羊—) a herd of sheep. ◉ ~구름 〖기상〗a cumulocirrus (cloud).

**양력**(揚力)〖물리〗(dynamic) lift. ◉ ~계수 a lift coefficient.

**양력**(陽曆) the solar 〔Julian〕 calendar. ¶ ~ 3월 1일 March 1 by the solar calendar.

**양로**(養老)《대비》provision for old age; 《보살핌》 taking care of the aged. ◉ ~보험 old-age insurance; endowment insurance. ~시설 an institution for the aged. ~연금 an old-age pension; an endowment annuity: ~연금제 an old-age annuity system / ~연금을 받다 draw an old-age pension. ~원 an asylum 〔a home〕 for the aged; an old folks' 〔people's〕 home: 유료 ~원 a paid home for old folks 〔senior citizens〕.

**양론**(兩論) both arguments; both sides of the argument.

**양륙**(揚陸)《상륙》landing;《선화의》unloading 《of cargo》. ~하다 land 《goods》; unload goods 《from a ship》; discharge 《cargoes》. ◉ ~비(費) landing charges. ~선 a lighter; a barge. ~인부 a dock hand; a docker; a stevedore; a longshoreman. ~장(場) a landing place 〔platform〕; a wharf. ~절차 landing formalities. ~지(地) a designated landing place. ~항(港) a port of discharge; an unloading port.

**양립**(兩立) coexistence; standing together; compatibility. ~하다 coexist 《with》; stand together; be consistent 〔compatible〕《with》. ¶ ~시키다 cope with both…; manage both… / ~할 수 없다 be incompatible 〔inconsistent〕《with》/ 이 사상은 우리 나라의 전통과 ~하지 않는다 This idea is inconsistent with the tradition of our country. / 이 두 가치관은 결코 ~할 수가 없다 These two sets of values are never compatible.

**양막**(羊膜)〖해부〗the amnion (*pl.* ~s, -nia). ◉ ~강(腔)〔습(褶)〕 an amniotic cavity 〔fold〕. ~염(炎) amnionitis.

**양말**(洋襪)《짧은》socks;《긴》stockings; 《양말류》 hose; hosiery. ¶ 나일론 ~ nylon socks / 순모 ~ all-wool socks / 신사용 ~ socks for gentlemen; men's socks / ~ 한 켤레 a pair of socks 〔stockings〕 / ~ 짜는 기계 a hosiery knitting machine / ~을 신다 wear 〔put on〕 socks; pull 〔have〕 on stockings / ~을 벗다 pull 〔take, peel〕 off *one's* socks 〔stockings〕. ◉ ~대님 garters《미》; sock-suspenders《영》.

**양면**(兩面) two 〔both〕 faces 〔sides〕. ¶ ~의 double-faced〔-sided〕; two-sided / 레코드판의 ~ both sides of a record / 인생의 어둡고 밝은 ~을 보다 look on both the bright and dark sides of life / 물심 ~으로 도와주다 support 《*a person*》 both spiritually and materially / 모든 사물에는 앞뒤 ~이 있다 There are two sides to every matter. ◉ ~날염(捺染) duplex printing. ~레코드 a double-faced record. ~인쇄 printing on both sides 《of the paper》. ~작전 operations 〔a strategy〕 on two fronts. ~정책 a two-pronged policy.

**양명**(揚名) fame; renown. ~하다 make a name; rise to fame; gain renown; make *oneself* famous. ¶ 입신 ~하다 rise in the world and win 〔achieve〕 fame.

**양명학**(陽明學) the philosophy 〔doctrines, teachings〕 of Wang Yang-ming.

**양모**(養母) a foster 〔an adoptive〕 mother.

**양모**(羊毛) (sheep's) wool. ¶ ~의 woolen 《blanket》/ ~같은 woolly 《nylon》/ 금년의 ~ 생산고 the wool clip for this year; this year's cut of wool / ~를 깎다 shear 〔fleece〕 sheep.
◉ ~공업 the woolen and worsted industry. ~상(商) a wool merchant 〔stapler〕; a woolman. ~제품 woolen goods; 《의류》 woolens. ~지(脂) wool fat 〔grease〕; yolk; lanolin(e). ~직 woolen fabric 〔textiles〕.

**양모제**(養毛劑) a hair tonic.

**양미**(糧米) rice; provisions.

**양미간**(兩眉間) the middle of the forehead; the brow. ¶ ~을 찌푸리다 knit 〔gather〕 *one's* brows; frown 《at, on》.

**양민**(良民) a law-abiding 〔good〕 citizen; [총칭] good citizenry.
◉ ~학살 massacre 〔slaughter〕 of the innocent people.

**양반**(兩班) 『고제도』 (the) *yangban*. ① 《동반·서반》 the two upper classes of old Korea; 《계급》 the aristocratic class; the nobility. ¶ ~으로 태어나다 be of noble birth. ② 《사람》 an aristocrat; a nobleman; a gentleman; a man; 《남편》 *one's* husband. ¶ 우리집 ~ *one's* old man 《구어》/ 주인 ~ the master 《of a house》/ 정거장 가는 길은 저 ~한테 물으시오 Ask the gentleman the way to the station.

**양방**(兩方) both; both sides 〔directions〕; both parties; the two; 《부정》 neither. ⇨ 양쪽. ¶ 그렇게 하면 ~ 모두 만족한다 That will satisfy both parties.

**양배추**(洋—) (a) cabbage. ◉ ~밭 a cabbage patch.

**양버들**(洋—) a poplar.

**양병**(養兵) building up 〔maintaining〕 an army. ~하다 build up 〔maintain, train〕 an army.

**양병**(養病) ① 《병 조리》 care of health. ~하다 take care of *one's* health. ¶ ~에 소홀하다 be careless of *one's* health. ② 《병의 악화》 getting worse of *one's* illness. ~하다 get complicated; grow 〔get〕 worse. ¶ 감기가 폐렴으로 ~되었다 The cold developed into pneumonia.

**양보**(讓步) (a) concession; (a) compromise. ~하다 concede 《to》; make a concession; compromise; give way to 《*a person*》; meet 《*a person*》 halfway. ¶ 조금도 ~하지 않다 make no concession at all; do not yield an inch / ~를 얻어내다 get 〔win, obtain, wrest〕 concessions from 《*a person*》/ ~해서 그의 요구를 받아들이다 concede 〔make a concession, give way〕 to his demands / 서로 ~해서 by mutual concession / 노인에게 자리를 ~하다 offer *one's* seat to an old man / 최대한의〔굴욕적인〕 ~를 하다 make 「the maximum 〔a humiliating〕 concession 《to their demand》/ 우리는 서로 ~해서 합의했다 We reached an agreement through concession. / 이 점은 도저히 ~할 수 없다 We can't concede 〔compromise on, give ground on〕 this point.
◉ ~절(節) 『문법』 a concessive clause.

**양복**(洋服) a suit (of clothes); a dress; 《한복에 대하여》 Western clothes. ¶ ~을 입은 《a young man》 wearing 〔in〕 a suit; 《a lady》 in a dress; 《a gentleman》 dressed in Western style / ~을 입다〔벗다〕 put on 〔take off〕 *one's* clothes / ~을 한 벌 맞추다 have 〔get〕 a suit made / 너에게는 한복보다 ~이 더 잘 어울린다 Western dresses suit you better than traditional Korean ones. ◉ ~감〔지〕 cloth 〔material〕 (for Western clothes). ~걸이 a coat hanger. ~장(欌) a wardrobe. ~장이 《만드는 사람》 a tailor. ~쟁이 《입은 사람》 a man attired in Western clothes. ~점 a tailor's (shop).

**양봉**(養蜂) beekeeping; bee culture 〔raising〕; apiculture. ~하다 keep 〔culture〕 bees. ¶ ~의 apirarian / ~에 종사하다 engage in apiculture; keep bees. ◉ ~가 a beekeeper; an apiculturist; an apiarist. ~업 bee-farming. ~장 a bee farm 〔yard〕; an apiary. ~통 a (wooden) beehive; a (movable) comb hive.

**양부**(良否) 《좋고 나쁨》 goodness and 〔or〕 badness; whether good or bad; 《질》 (relative) quality. ¶ ~를 알아내다 ascertain the quality 《of *a thing*》/ 물건의 ~를 조사하다 examine the quality of an article; examine an article to see whether it is good or bad.

**양부**(養父) a foster 〔an adoptive〕 father. ¶ ~모 foster parents.

**양부인**(洋婦人) a foreign lady; 《양갈보》 a whore 〔prostitute〕 for foreigners.

**양분**(兩分) bisection. ~하다 cut in two; bisect; halve; divide 《*a thing*》 into two parts; cut 〔break〕 《*a thing*》 into halves.

**양분**(養分) nourishment; nutriment. ¶ ～이 있다 be nourishing 〔nutritious〕; contain nourishment / ～이 많다〔적다〕 be rich 〔poor〕 in nutritional content / ～을 흡수하다 《plants》 take nourishment 《from its roots》 / ～을 주다 nourish. ◉ ～비(比) nutrient ratio.

**양산**(量産) mass production. ～하다 mass-produce 《cars》; produce in large quantities. ¶ ～체제로 들어가다 enter into mass production / 지금은 마이크로 컴퓨터까지 ～되고 있다 Even micro-computers are being mass=produced now. / 자동차 ～을 개시하기까지 2년은 걸릴 것이다 It will take two years to start producing cars in volume. ◉ ～계획 a plan for the mass production 《of》. ～태세: ～ 태세에 들어가다 [제품이 주어] be put into commercial production; [사람이 주어] go into quantity production.

**양산**(陽傘) a parasol; a sunshade. ¶ ～을 받다〔펴다, 접다〕 put up 〔open, close〕 a parasol / ～이 바람에 뒤집혔다 I had my parasol blown inside out.

**양상**(樣相) an aspect; a phase; a condition. ¶ 새로운 ～을 띠다 take on a new aspect; enter upon a new phase / ～을 일변시키다 change the whole situation / 심상치 않은 ～을 보이다 take on 〔assume〕 a serious aspect / 사태는 비극적인 ～을 나타내기 시작했다 Things began to take on a tragic aspect.

**양상군자**(梁上君子) 《도둑》 a thief; a burglar; 《쥐》 a rat.

**양생**(養生) ① 《건강을 위한》 care 〔preservation〕 of *one's* health; 《병후의》 recuperation. ～하다 take care 〔be careful〕 of *one's* health; improve 〔promote〕 (*one's*) health; recuperate 〔recruit〕 *oneself* (병후에). ¶ ～하러 온천에 가다 go to a hot spring resort to improve *one's* health. ② 《콘크리트 따위의》 cure. ¶ 콘크리트를 ～하다 cure the concreted surface. ◉ ～법 a regimen; rules for healthy living.

**양서**(良書) a good book. ¶ ～를 구하다〔고르다〕 seek 〔choose〕 good books.

**양서**(兩棲) (being) amphibious. ◉ ～동물 an amphibian (animal). ～류 *Amphibia:* ～류의 동물 a batrachian / ～류의 amphibian; batrachian.

**양서**(洋書) a foreign 〔Western〕 book. ◉ ～목록 a catalog of foreign books.

**양성**(良性) 〖의학〗 ¶ ～의 benign / ～종양이니 걱정하지 마라 Don't worry, it's just a benign tumor.

**양성**(兩性) the two sexes; both sexes. ◉ ～생식 amphigony; gamogenesis; bisexual reproduction. ～체 〖생물〗 a bisexual. ～화(花) a bisexual 〔an androgynous〕 flower.

**양성**(陽性) 〖의학〗 positivity; 《성질》 a positive 〔an extrovert, a cheerful, a sunny〕 disposition. ¶ ～의 positive; 〖식물〗 plus / ～이다 prove positive / ～으로 전화(轉化)하다 turn positive / 나의 투베르클린 반응은 ～이었다 My reaction to the tuberculin test proved positive. *or* I showed a positive reaction to the T.B. test. ◉ ～반응 (a) positive reaction. ～원소 a positive element. ～화(化) bringing 〔coming〕 into the open: 무허가 건물의 ～화 licensing unauthorized shacks / 정치 자금을 ～화하다 bring out into the open sources of political funds; make public the sources of political funds.

**양성**(養成) training; education; cultivation. ～하다 train; educate; cultivate; rear; bring up. ¶ 인재를 ～하다 cultivate men of talent 〔ability〕 / 인내력을 ～하다 cultivate *one's* patience / 간부를 ～하다 train some members of the staff to be leaders / 간호사를 ～하다 train hospital nurses / 그 학교에서는 기술자를 ～하고 있다 They train technicians at that school. ◉ ～기간 a training period; the period of apprenticeship. ～소 a training school 〔center〕: 교원〔기술자〕 ～소 a training school 〔center〕 for teachers 〔technicians〕.

**양성자**(陽性子) 〖물리〗 a proton.

**양소매책상**(兩―冊床) a kneehole desk.

**양속**(良俗) a good 〔fine〕 custom 〔morals〕. ¶ 미풍〔공서〕 ～ good morals 〔public order〕 and beautiful customs / ～에 반(反)하다 be prejudicial to public morals.

**양손**(兩―) both hands. ¶ ～ 가득한 금화 a double handful of gold coins / ～을 다 쓰는 ambidextrouse; able to use both hands with equal ease / ～에 쥐다 hold 《*a thing*》 in both hands.

**양수**(羊水) 〖생리〗 amniotic fluid; 《통속적으로》 the waters. ¶ ～가 터지다 the waters break.

**양수**(兩手) 《양손》 both hands; two hands; 《양팔》 both arms. ◉ ～걸이 《일 따위의》 playing (a) double (game); 《장기 등의》 = ～잡이

(1). ～겸장(兼將)《announce》a double check; a fork (서양 장기의). ～잡이 (1)《장기 등의》scoring a double point with a single move. (2)《사람》an ambidexter;《솜씨》ambidexterity.

**양수**(揚水) pumping up; pumping water. ～하다 pump (up) water. ◉ ～기 a water pump. ～장 a pumping station. ～장치 pumping equipment.

**양수**(讓受) (acquisition by) transfer; inheritance; taking over. ～하다 obtain 《*a thing*》 by transfer; take over; inherit; succeed《to a fortune》. ¶ 사업을 ～하다 take over a business / 부모의 재산을 ～하다 inherit 〔succeed to〕 *one's* parents' property. ◉ ～인《권리·재산 등의》a grantee; a transferee; an assignee. ～증 a (certificate of) receipt; a receipt form.

**양수기**(量水器) a water meter 〔gauge〕.

**양순**(良順) gentleness; meekness; docility. ～하다 (be) gentle; good; docile; meek. ¶ ～하게 gently; meekly; docilely / ～한 백성 law-abiding 〔obedient〕 people / ～하게 말을 듣다 do as told without objection.

**양식**(良識) good 〔common〕 sense. ¶ ～ 있는 사람 a sensible person; a person with good sense / ～을 의심하다 doubt *a person's* good senses / ～ 있는 행동을 기대하다 expect *a person* to act sensibly.

**양식**(洋式) Western style. ¶ ～의 방 a room furnished in Western style.

**양식**(洋食) Western(-style) food 〔dishes〕; Western cooking. ¶ ～ 식사법 Western table manners.
◉ ～기(器) Western tableware. ～당〔집〕 a restaurant (serving foreign dishes). ～요리법 Western cooking.

**양식**(樣式) 《정해진 형식》a form; 《예술의 표현 형태》a mode; a style; 《공통의 방식》a pattern. ¶ 건축 ～ a style of building / 일정한 ～ a fixed form / ～화하다 stylize; conventionalize / 옛날 ～의 가구 old-style furniture / 법률 문서의 ～ the form of legal documents / 행동 ～ patterns of behavior / 소정의 ～으로 원서를 제출하다 submit *one's* application in the proper 〔prescribed〕 form / 과학의 진보는 우리들의 생활 ～을 바꿔놓았다 The progress of science has changed our mode 〔style〕 of living.

**양식**(養殖) raising; culture; farming; cultivation; breeding. ～하다 raise; cultivate; culture; breed. ¶ 이 지역은 굴～으로 유명하다 This area is famous for its oyster farming.
◉ ～어(魚) hatchery fish. ～업 cultivating 〔breeding〕 industry; 《어업》 the fish-raising industry. ～장 a nursery; a farm: 굴～장 an oyster bed 〔farm〕 / 진주 ～장 a pearl farm. ～진주 a cultured pearl.

**양식**(糧食) food (supplies); provisions. ⇨ 식량. ¶ 생명의 ～ the bread of life / 마음의 ～ spiritual 〔mental〕 food / ～이 떨어지다〔부족하다〕 provisions 「give out 〔run short〕; 〔사람이 주어〕 run 「out 〔short〕 of provisions / 3일 분의 ～을 휴대하다 take a three-day supply of food.

**양실**(洋室) a European-〔Western-〕style room; a room furnished in European=〔Western-〕style.

**양심**(良心) (a) conscience. ¶ ～적(으로) conscientious(ly) / ～상 for conscience(') sake; for the sake of *one's* conscience / 비～적인 unconscientious / 학자적 ～ academic 〔scientific〕 honesty; a scholarly conscience / ～적 참전〔병역〕 거부자 a conscientious objector (생략 C.O.).

양심의: ～의 가책 the pangs 〔qualms, pricks〕 of conscience; a sting of conscience / ～의 소리 the voice of conscience / ～의 가책을 받다 be conscience-stricken; be stung by *one's* conscience; suffer from a guilty conscience; feel the qualms 〔stings, pricks〕 of conscience / ～의 가책으로 괴로워하다 be tormented by a guilty conscience.

양심에: ～에 따라 행동하다 act according to *one's* conscience / ～에 부끄럽다〔부끄럽지 않다〕 have a guilty 〔clear〕 conscience / ～에 걸리다 lie heavy on *one's* conscience / ～에 어긋나다 betray *one's* conscience; go against 〔run counter to〕 *one's* conscience / ～에 비추어 보다 consult *one's* conscience / ～에 호소하다 address 〔appeal〕 to 《*a person's*》 conscience.

양심이: ～이 있다 be conscientious / ～이 없다 have no conscience; be without a conscience; be unscrupulous / ～이 없는 conscienceless / ～이 있는〔없는〕 사람 a man of 〔without〕 conscience / ～이 명하는 바에 따르다 follow 〔obey〕 the dictates of *one's* conscience; do what conscience dictates. ¶ ～에 찔린다 My conscience smites

〔pricks〕 me. / ~에 걸려서 그런 일은 할 수 없다 I cannot, in all conscience, do such a thing. / 그 일로 나는 ~의 가책을 받았다 My conscience was burdened with it. / 어떻게 하든 자네 ~에 맡기겠네 I leave《it》to your conscience. / 그 문제가 그의 ~을 괴롭혔다 The matter weighed upon his conscience. / 자네 ~에 물어보게 Listen to what your conscience tells you. / 당신이 용서해 주더라도 내 ~이 용서치 않습니다 You may forgive me, but my conscience won't. / 그는 ~이라곤 손톱만큼도 없다 He has not an ounce of conscience. / 그는 ~의 가책에 견딜 수 없어 죄를 자백했다 He was driven to admit 〔confess〕 his guilt by the pangs of conscience. / 우리는 그것을 ~적으로 다루어야 한다 We must make it a matter of conscience.
◉ ~선언 a declaration of conscience. ~수(囚) a conscientious prisoner.

**양아들**(養—) an adopted 〔a foster〕 son.

**양아버지**(養—) a foster 〔an adoptive〕 father.

**양아치** a ragpicker; a ragman.

**양악**(洋樂) Western 〔European〕 music. ◉ ~가(家) a musician 〔player〕 of Western music.

**양안**(兩岸) both banks; either bank. ¶ ~에 on either bank 〔both banks〕《of the river》/ ~에는 버드나무가 줄지어 서 있었다 The river was lined on either bank with willows.

**양안**(兩眼) both eyes. ¶ ~이 다 멀다 be blind in both eyes.

**양약**(良藥) an efficacious 〔a good〕 medicine. ¶ ~은 입에 쓰다 Good medicine tastes bitter. *or* Good advice is seldom to swallow.

**양약**(洋藥) Western 〔European〕 medicines; foreign 〔imported〕 drugs.

**양양**(洋洋) ~하다《바다 등이》(be) vast (in expanse); boundless; wide;《장래가》(be) bright; promising; rosy. ¶ ~한 대해 a boundless 〔broad expanse of〕 ocean / 너의 앞길은 ~하다 You have a bright 〔great〕 future before you. *or* A rosy future is smiling on you. / 그는 전도가 ~하다 He has a great 〔bright, rosy〕 future before him.

**양양하다**(揚揚—) (be) exultant; elated; triumphant. ⇨ 의기양양. ¶ 승리로 의기가 ~ exult in *one's* victory / 그들은 의기도 양양하게 행진했다 They marched on proudly and triumphantly.

**양어**(養魚) fish farming 〔breeding, cultivation〕. ~하다 breed 〔raise〕 fish. ◉ ~가 a fish farmer 〔breeder〕. ~장 a fish farm. ~조(槽) a fish-rearing tank. ~지(池) a fish-breeding pond.

**양어깨**(兩—) (*one's*) both shoulders. ¶ 국가의 운명을 ~에 짊어지다 bear the destiny of the nation on *one's* shoulders / 한국의 장래는 제군의 ~에 달려 있다 Korea's future rests on your shoulders.

**양어머니**(養—) a foster 〔an adoptive〕 mother.

**양어버이**(養—) foster 〔adoptive〕 parents.

**양여**(讓與) concession《of a privilege, of a right》;《영토의》cession;《양도》transfer; conveyance. ⇨ 양도. ~하다 concede《a privilege to *a person*》; hand 〔make〕 over《*one's* property to *one's* son》; cede《a territory》; transfer《*a thing* to *a person*》. ¶ 그녀는 전 재산을 딸에게 ~했다 She handed over the whole of her property to her daughter.

**양옥**(洋屋) a Western-style house.

**양요**(洋擾)〖역사〗an invasion of Korea by a Western power.

**양요리**(洋料理) Western food 〔dishes, cuisine〕; Western cookery 〔cooking〕. ◉ ~점 a Western-style restaurant.

**양용**(兩用)《for》double use. ◉ 수륙 ~ 비행기〔전차〕 an amphibious plane 〔tank〕.

**양원**(兩院) both 〔the two〕 Houses. ¶ ~ 일치의 의결 a concurrent vote of both Houses / ~을 통과하다 pass both Houses / 그 법안은 ~에서 검토되었다 The bill was considered in the two Houses. ◉ ~제도 a bicameral system. ~협의회 a joint conference of the two Houses. 상하~ the Houses of Representatives and Councilors; the Houses of Commons and Lords《영》; the House and Senate《미》.

**양위**(讓位) abdication (of the throne); demise of the Crown. ~하다 abdicate the Crown 〔throne〕《in favor of *a person*》; demise the throne.

**양육**(羊肉) mutton;《새끼의》lamb.

**양육**(養育) bringing 〔rearing〕 up; fostering. ~하다 bring up; foster; rear; raise. ⇨ 기르다. ¶ 그녀는 어렸을 때 할머니에게 ~되었다 She was brought up by her grandmother when she was a little child.
◉ ~법 the method 〔way〕 of bringing up children. ~비 the expense 〔cost〕 of bringing up a child. ~원《고아원》

an orphanage; an orphan asylum [home]; 《기아의》 a foundling hospital: ～원에 수용하다 take 《a child》 into an orphanage. ～자 a fosterer; a rearer; a breeder.

**양은**(洋銀) albata; German [nickel] silver. ◉ ～그릇 nickel silver ware.

**양의**(良醫) a good [skilled] physician [doctor].

**양의**(洋醫) a Western physician; a Western (medical) doctor.

**양이**(攘夷) exclusion [expulsion] of foreigners. ◉ ～론 exclusionism; anti=alienism: ～론자 an antialienist.

**양이온**(陽—) 〖물리〗 a positive ion.

**양익**(兩翼) ① 《날개》 both wings. ¶ ～을 펼치다[접다] spread [fold] both wings. ② 《전투 대형의》 both flanks. ¶ ～을 공격하다 attack both flanks 《of the enemy line》. ③ 《야구·축구의》 left and right fields [wings].

**양인**(兩人) both 《of us [you, them]》; a couple. ¶ ～의 행복을 빌다 wish both of them great happiness.

**양인**(洋人) a Westerner; an Occidental; a European.

**양일**(兩日) two days; a couple of days. ¶ ～간(에) during [for] two days; (within) two days.

**양자**(兩者) both; the two; both [the two] parties (소송·계약 등의). ¶ ～합의하에 by mutual consent [agreement]. ◉ ～택일 selecting one alternative: ～ 택일하다 select one alternative; choose between the two.

**양자**(陽子) 〖물리〗 ⇨ 양성자.

**양자**(量子) 〖물리〗 a quantum (*pl.* -ta) (생략 q). ◉ ～론 the quantum theory. ～물리학 quantum physics. ～역학 quantum dynamics [mechanics].

**양자**(養子) an adopted son [child]. ¶ ～가다, ～들다 get [be] adopted 《into a family, as *a person's* son》; become 《*a person's*》 adopted child / ～로 삼다 adopt 《a child》 (as *one's* son) / ～ 보내다 give *one's* child to 《*a person*》 as an adopted son. ◉ ～결연 adoption.

**양자강**(揚子江) the Yangtze River.

**양잠**(養蠶) sericulture; silkworm culture; keeping [raising] silkworms. ～하다 raise [rear, breed] silkworms. ◉ ～가 a sericulturist; a silk grower [raiser]. ～ 농가 a silk-raising farmer; a silkfarmer. ～소 a cocoonery. ～업 the sericultural [silk-raising] industry.

**양장**(羊腸) ① 《창자》 the entrails of a goat; sheep's intestines. ② 《길》 a winding [twisting, tortuous] path; a narrow meandering road.

**양장**(洋裝) ① 《옷》 Western-style clothes. ～하다 dress in Western-style clothes; be dressed in Occidental attire (Western-style); wear Western clothes. ¶ ～한 숙녀 a lady in a Western dress; a lady dressed in Western style / 그녀는 ～이 더 어울린다 She looks better in Western dress. ② 《제본》 binding 《a book》 in Occidental style. ～하다 bind 《a book》 in Occidental style. ¶ ～한 책 a book bound in Western style. ◉ ～점 a dressmaking shop; a boutique.

**양재**(良材) 《재료》 good material; 《재목》 good [excellent] timber; 《인재》 a man of ability; a gifted man; (a) talent.

**양재**(洋裁) (foreign-style) dressmaking; couture. ¶ ～를 배우다 take lessons in dressmaking. ◉ ～사 a dressmaker. ～점 a dressmaker's shop. ～학원 a dressmaking [dressmakers'] school.

**양재기**(洋—) an enamelware.

**양잿물**(洋—) caustic soda; lye; alkaline solution.

**양적**(量的) quantitative. ¶ ～으로 quantitatively.

**양전기**(陽電氣) 〖물리〗 positive [plus] electricity. ¶ ～의 electropositive.

**양전자**(陽電子) 〖물리〗 a positron. ¶ ～ 방사 단층 촬영법[술] positron emission tomography (생략 PET).

**양정**(量定) appreciation; 〖법〗 determination. ¶ 형(刑)의 ～이 부당하다 The penalty has been meted out unjustly [improperly].

**양정**(糧政) 《행정》 food administration; 《정책》 a food policy.

**양젖**(羊—) goat('s) milk; sheep('s) milk.

**양조**(釀造) 《맥주·청주 등의》 brewing; brewage; 《소주·위스키 등의》 distillation. ～하다 brew 《beer》; distill 《whisky》. ¶ 맥주는 보리로 ～한다 Beer is brewed from barley. ◉ ～법 the method of brewing; brewage. ～세 tax on brewage. ～시험소 a brewing laboratory. ～업 the brewery business; the brewing industry. ～(업)자 a brewer; a distiller; a wine-maker. ～장 a brewery (맥주 등의); a distillery (위스키 등의). ～주 brewage; a liquor made by fermentation. ～학 zymurgy.

**양종**(洋種) Western kinds or seeds; a

foreign breed. ¶ ～의 imported; foreign. ◉ ～닭 a chicken of foreign stock.

**양주**(洋酒) Western liquors; whisky and wine; wines and spirits.

**양지**(良知) intuitive knowledge; intuition.

**양지**(洋紙) (machine-made) paper; Western paper.

**양지**(陽地) 《볕이 잘 드는 곳》 a sunny spot 〔place〕; 《햇볕》 sunshine. ¶ ～가 음지(陰地)되고 음지가 ～된다 Life is full of vicissitudes 〔ups and downs〕.

**양지**(諒知) understanding; appreciation. ～하다 understand; appreciate; know; be aware 〔conscious〕 of. ¶ ～하시는 바와 같이 as you see 〔are aware〕 / 이상 ～하시기 바랍니다 We beg to inform you that….

**양지꽃**(陽地—) 〖식물〗 a cinquefoil.

**양지머리** the brisket of beef; beef ribs. ◉ ～뼈 the ribs of an ox 〔a beef〕.

**양지바르다**(陽地—) (be) sunny; be full of sunshine. ¶ 양지바른 곳에 집을 짓다 build a house in a sunny place / 이 방은 ～ It's a sunny room. *or* This room gets much sun.

**양지쪽**(陽地—) the sunny side; a sunny spot. ¶ ～에 나가 놀아라 Go out and play in the sunny side.

**양진영**(兩陣營) both camps 〔parties〕; the two opposing sides.

**양질**(良質) good quality. ¶ ～의 of good 〔fine, superior〕 quality; good 〔high〕 quality.

**양짝**(兩—) both (of a pair); both counterparts; the two of them; the two mates.

**양쪽**(兩—) both; both sides 〔parties〕; either side; the two sides; each of the two; 《부정》 neither. ¶ ～에 on both sides; on either side / 'A' 'B' ～ both A and B / 길의 ～ both sides of the street / ～ 다 나쁘다 They are both to blame. / ～ 다 양보 안 한다 Neither will give in. / ～ 다 알고 있다 I know them both. / ～ 다 모른다 I don't know either of them. *or* I know neither of them. (★ I don't know both of them. 이라고 하면 「양쪽은 모르나 한 쪽은 알고 있다」의 뜻이 됨) / ～ 다 불행한 것은 아니다 《한 쪽만이 불행》 Both of them are not unhappy. / ～ 다 불행하다 Neither (of them) are happy. / ～ 다 내 것이 아니다 Neither (of them) is mine. (★ *a*) either, neither, each 따위는 단수동사를 수반함. *b*) neither =not either이나 either … not의 어순으로는 안 됨. 따라서 Either is not mine.은 틀림) / ～의 말을 들은 후에야 그들을 판단할 수 있다 You cannot judge them until you hear what both parties have to say.

**양찰**(諒察) sympathetic understanding 〔consideration〕. ～하다 consider; take into consideration 〔account〕; enter into 《*a person's*》 feeling; sympathize with. ¶ 제 입장을 ～하시기 바랍니다 I beg you to understand my position. / 이러한 사정이오니 ～하시기 바랍니다 Such being the case, I beg you will kindly excuse me.

**양책**(良策) a good scheme 〔plan〕; a well-advised 〔wise〕 policy; a good 〔fine, happy〕 idea.

**양처**(良妻) a good wife. ¶ ～가 되다 make a good wife. ◉ 현모～ a good 〔faithful〕 wife and wise mother.

**양철**(兩凸) double-convex. ◉ ～렌즈 a biconvex lens.

**양철**(洋鐵) 《아연을 입힌》 galvanized iron (sheet); 《주석을 입힌》 tinned iron; a tin plate. ◉ ～가위 (a pair of) snips. ～공 a tinman; a tinner; a tinsmith. ～제품 tinware. ～지붕 a tin roof. ～집 a tin-roofed house. ～통 a tin pail; a metal bucket.

**양초**(洋—) a (foreign-made) candle; 《가는》 a taper. ¶ ～를 켜다〔끄다〕 light 〔put out, blow out〕 a candle / ～가 타고 있다〔다 타들어가고 있다〕 A candle is burning 〔burning low〕. / ～가 바람에 꺼질 것 같다 The candle is in danger of being blown out.
◉ ～심지 the wick (of a candle); a candlewick. 양촛대 a candlestick; a candleholder. 양초동강 a candle ends.

**양춘**(陽春) ① 《음력 정월》 January (of the lunar calendar). ② 《봄》 spring; the springtime; the spring tide. ¶ ～ 3월에 in March, when spring comes round with its warm sunshine.
◉ ～가절 the pleasant springtime.

**양측**(兩側) both sides; the two sides; either side. ¶ 길 ～에 on 「both sides 〔either side〕 of the street. (★ either는 each of the two와 one of the two의 두 가지 뜻을 가짐. 따라서 either side는「한 쪽」의 뜻으로도 쓰임) / ～의 사상자 casualties on both sides / ～의 말을 듣다 hear both sides.

**양치**(養齒) 《이 닦기》 brushing *one's* teeth; 《입안을 가심》 rinsing (out) *one's* mouth; gargling. ～하다 brush *one's* teeth; rinse (out) the mouth; gargle (the throat). ¶ 소금물로 ～하다 rinse out *one's* mouth with salt and water.

◉ ∼그릇 a gargling bowl. 양칫소금 salt for cleaning teeth; dentifrice salt. 양칫물 gargling water; mouth wash; 《약》 a gargle.

**양치기**(羊—) sheep-raising; 《사람》 a shepherd.

**양치류**(羊齒類) 〖식물〗 the ferns.

**양친**(兩親) (*one's*) parents. ⇨ 부모.

**양코**(洋—) a large protruding nose; a Westerner('s nose). ¶ ∼배기 a Westerner; a Yankee (미국인).

**양키** a Yankee; a Yank 《구어》. ◉ ∼기질 Yankeeism. ∼본드 a Yankee bond.

**양탄자**(洋—) a rug; a carpet; carpeting [총칭]. ¶ 두꺼운 ∼가 깔린 마루 a thick-carpeted floor / ∼를 깔다 spread a carpet; carpet 《a floor》 / 층계〔방〕에 ∼를 깔다 carpet the stairs 〔a room〕.

**양털**(羊—) wool; sheep's hair. ＝양모.

**양토**(養兎) rabbit raising 〔rearing, farming〕. ∼하다 raise 〔breed〕 rabbits. ◉ ∼장 a rabbitry; a rabbit farm.

**양파**(洋—) an onion. ¶ ∼껍질 the skin of an onion.

**양팔**(兩—) two 〔both〕 arms. ¶ ∼을 뻗다 extend 〔outstretch〕 *one's* arms.

**양편**(兩便) two 〔both〕 sides; either side; both parties. ¶ 길 ∼에 on both sides 〔either side〕 of the street / 길 ∼에 은행나무가 죽 서 있다 On either side of the road grows a long line of gingko trees. / 그렇게 하면 ∼이 다 만족하겠다 That will satisfy both parties. / ∼ 말을 다 듣고 판단하라 One man's story is no story, hear both sides. / ∼에 다 할 말이 있다 Much may be said on both sides.

**양푼** a large brass bowl 〔basin〕.

**양품**(洋品) imported 〔foreign-made〕 goods; fancy goods; 《미》 haberdashery. ◉ ∼점 a foreign-goods shop 〔store〕; a fancy (goods) shop; a haberdasher's (shop); a haberdashery.

**양풍**(良風) a good 〔praiseworthy, fine〕 custom. ◉ ∼미속(美俗) a good and beautiful custom. ＝미풍 양속.

**양풍**(洋風) Occidental custom(s); foreign manner(s); European 〔Western, American〕 style.

**양피**(羊皮) sheepskin; goatskin (털이 붙어 있는); 《제본용》 roan. ◉ ∼구두 sheepskin 〔goatskin〕 shoes. ∼지 parchment; 《특히 표지용》 for(r)el.

**양학**(洋學) Western 〔European〕 learning. ¶ ∼을 배우다 study Western science. ◉ ∼자 a scholar of Western learning.

**양항**(良港) a good 〔fine〕 harbor.

**양해**(諒解) understanding; comprehension; consent (동의); agreement (승낙); approval (찬성). ∼하다 understand; comprehend. ¶ ∼할 수 있는 understandable; comprehensible / ∼하기 어려운 incomprehensible; beyond 〔above〕 *one's* comprehension / 상호 ∼하에 by mutual agreement / 이것을 ∼하고 with 〔on〕 this understanding / 아무의 ∼를 얻어 with *a person's* consent / 우리가 ∼하는 바로는 as we understand; as far as we know / ∼가 이루어지다 come to 〔arrive at〕 an understanding 〔an agreement〕 《with》 / ∼를 얻다〔구하다〕 seek 〔obtain〕 《*a person's*》 understanding; obtain 〔ask for〕 《*a person's*》 consent. ◉ ∼각서 a memorandum of understanding. ∼사항 agreed items; items of understanding.

**양행**(洋行) ① 《외국행》 going 〔traveling〕 abroad. ∼하다 go 〔travel〕 abroad; make a trip abroad; go on a foreign tour. ② 《회사》 a foreign business firm; a hong (중국의).

**양형**(量刑) the assessment of the culpability 《of》; a question of law. ¶ ∼은 재판장이 결정한다 Question of law are for the judge.

**양호**(良好) good; satisfactory. ∼하다 (be) good; favorable; fine; successful; satisfactory. ¶ 성적이 ∼하다 show a good result; the results are excellent / 경과가 ∼하다 be steadily getting better; make satisfactory progress.

**양호**(養護) protective care (of children); protection; nursing. ∼하다 give protective care; take 《*a person*》 under *one's* protection; protect. ◉ ∼교사 a nurse-teacher; a school nurse. ∼시설 a protective institution; a home for dependent. ∼아동 a weak boy 〔girl〕 for protection.

**양호유환**(養虎遺患) nourishing a serpent in *one's* bosom.

**양홍**(洋紅) 《물감》 red dyes; carmine; crimson. ¶ ∼색의 carmine; crimson.

**양화**(良貨) good 〔worthy, valid〕 money. ¶ 악화(惡貨)는 ∼를 구축한다 Bad money drives out good.

**양화**(洋畫) (a) Western 〔European〕 painting; (an) oil painting (유화); 《영화》 a foreign movie 〔film〕. ◉ ∼가(家) an oil painter; an artist of Western painting.

**양화**(洋靴) ＝구두. ◉ ∼공(工) a shoemaker. ~점 a shoe store; a shoemaker's: ~점 주인 a shoemaker; a shoe dealer.

**양화**(陽畫) 『사진』 a positive (picture).

**양회**(洋灰) cement. =시멘트.

**얕다** ① 《깊이 따위가》 (be) shallow. ¶ 얕은 개울〔연못, 그릇〕 a shallow stream 〔pond, dish〕/물이 얕은 곳 a shoal; a shallow / 얕은 상처 a slight 〔flesh〕 wound / 얕은 상처를 입다 be slightly wounded / 얕은 곳에서 헤엄쳐야 한다 You should swim in shallow water. / 얕은 내도 깊게 건너라 《속담》 One cannot use too much caution. *or* Much caution does no harm. *or* It is best to be cautious.
② 《생각·지식·정도 따위가》 (be) superficial; shallow; imprudent. ¶ 얕은 꾀 transparent subterfuge 〔guile〕 / 얕은 생각 a shallow idea; a superficial way of thinking / 얕은 지혜 a shallow wit / 영문학에 대해 얕은 지식밖에 없다 have only a superficial knowledge of English literature / 그는 장사 경험이 아직 ~ He has little experience in business. / 의사와 결혼하면 잘 살거라는 얕은 생각에서 그녀는 그와 결혼했다 She married him with the shallow notion that marriage with a doctor would bring her an easy living.
③ 《높이·지위가》 (be) low; [비유적] (be) humble; lowly; mean (비천하다). ¶ 지붕이 얕은 집 a house with a low roof / 얕은 지위 a humble position / 신분이 ~ be of low 「birth 〔social position〕 / 지위가 ~ be low in position; be placed low.

**얕보다** look down on 〔upon〕; have a low opinion of; 《경시하다》 make light of; make little of; think lightly 〔meanly〕 of 《*a person*》; hold 《*a person*》 cheap; disregard; slight; belittle; contempt; despise. ¶ 얕볼 수 없는 not to be despised; formidable 《enemy》/ 사람을 얕보는 태도로 with a superior air / 상대를 사뭇 ~ 「make light 〔think nothing〕 of *one's* adversary / 남의 학식을 ~ belittle another's learning / 그의 법률 지식은 얕볼 게 아니다 His knowledge of the law is not to be made light of. / 그는 사람을 얕보는 버릇이 있다 He has a way of looking down upon people. / 사람을 얕보지 말라구 Who do you think I am?

**얕잡다** make a low estimate of; hold 《*a person, a thing*》 in contempt; belittle. ⇨ 얕보다. ¶ 남을 얕잡아 보면 안 된다 You ought not to hold people cheap. / 사람 얕잡아 보지 말게 I am not so cheap a fellow as you think me. / 나이 어리다고 얕잡아 보지 마시오 Though young, I am not a man to be made a fool of.

**얘** ① 《이 애》 this child 〔boy, girl〕; he; she; it. ② 《부를 때》 Sonny; My boy; You (there)!; Hey!; I say!; Come!; Here!; There. ¶ 얘, 잠깐 기다려 Hey, just a minute! / 얘, 가까이 오지 마 Hey, hey, stay away from here. / 얘야, 어디 가니 Hey you, where are you headed for? / 얘가 왜 이래 What's the matter with you? / 얘, 네 선생님이 오신다 Look, there is your teacher on his way here now.

**어** 《감탄》 Oh!; Well!; Why! ⇨ 어럽쇼.

**-어**(語) 《낱말》 a word; 《전문어》 a term; 《언어》 a language. ¶ 법률어 legal terms / 속어 a slang / 비어 a vulgarism.

**어가**(御駕) a royal carriage.

**어간** 《넓은 사이》 an interval; a gap; a space.

**어간**(語幹) the stem (of a word).

**어감**(語感) 《사람이 느끼는》 sensitivity to words; 《낱말이 주는》 a nuance; (a) tinge; connotation. ¶ (말의) 미묘한 ~ (a) subtle nuance / ~이 좋다〔나쁘다〕 sound well 〔bad, jarring〕 / ~을 키우다 develop a feeling for language / ~이 날카롭다 《her remarks》 have a keen sense of language.

**어개**(魚介) 《어류·조개》 fish and shellfishes; 《해산물》 marine products.

**어거하다**(馭車—) 《소·말을 몰다》 drive 《the ox or horse》; 《제어하다》 manage; handle; control; govern; rule; reign. ¶ 어거하기 쉬운 manageable; easy to manage 〔control, handle〕 / 어거하기 어려운 unmanageable; unruly; intractable / 어거할 수 없는 사람 a tough man; a holy terror 《구어》 / 어거하기 쉬운 사람 an easy man to deal with / 어거하기 어렵다 be out of hand 〔control〕; get out of hand 《구어》 / 여자를 마음대로 ~ control a woman at will.

**어구**(語句) words and phrases. ¶ ~의 용법 phraseology / ~의 적절한 사용으로 문장이 살아난다 Good wording gives life to a composition. / 법률 ~에 너무 구애되어 그 정신을 망각하기 쉽다 We are apt to observe the letter, and not the spirit of the law.

**어구**(漁具) fishing implements; [총칭] fishing tackle 〔gear〕.

**어구**(漁區) a fishing zone. ⇨ 어장(漁場).

**어군**(魚群) a shoal 〔school〕 of fish. ◉ ～탐지기 a fish finder; a fish detector. ～탐지선 a fish-detector vessel.

**어군**(語群) 〖문법〗 a word group.

**어귀** an entrance; an entry; an approach; a mouth. ¶ 강의 ～ an estuary; a river-mouth / 동네의 ～ an entrance to a village / 항구의 ～ the mouth of a harbor / 터널 ～ the approach to a tunnel.

**어귀어귀** ravenously; voraciously; greedily. ¶ ～ 먹다 eat ravenously 〔"like a horse"〕 / 음식을 ～ 씹다 chaw on food; mouth food; eat with a stuffed mouth.

**어귀차다** (be) strong; firm; strong=minded.

**어그러지다** ① 《법·약속·기대에》 be 〔go〕 against 《the rule, *a person*》; go wrong with 《*a person*》; run counter 《to》; transgress; violate; deviate 〔depart, swerve, differ〕 《from》; be contrary to 《reason》. ¶ 예의에 ～ violate propriety; be a lapse of etiquette; be bad manners / 예상이 ～ guess wrong / 기대에 ～ be contrary to *one's* expectation(s); fall short of 〔do not come up to〕 *one's* expectation(s); disappoint 《*one*》 / 법에 ～ be against the law / 그의 기대는 어그러졌다 It didn't come up to his expectation. / 기대에 어그러지지 않도록 최선을 다하겠습니다 I will do my best to act up your expectation. / 그것은 약속에 어그러지는 일이다 That runs counter to what was promised. / 모든 일이 내 생각과 어그러지게 되었다 Nothing worked out as I expected. / 만사가 다 어그러졌다 I was disappointed at every turn. *or* Everything went against me.
② 《사이가》 go badly; become strained; become estranged 〔alienated〕 《from》. ¶ 친구와 사이가 ～ be estranged from a friend / 친한 두 친구 사이가 어그러졌다 The two old friends became estranged.

**어근**(語根) the root of a word.

**어근버근** 《사개가》 not dovetailing; not meshing; not fitting into each other properly; 《사람 사이가》 not getting along smoothly; not harmonizing. ～하다 do not dovetail 〔fit together, mesh〕; do not get along 〔harmonize〕.

**어금니** a back 〔cheek〕 tooth; a molar (tooth); 《구어》 grinder.

**어금막히다** lie crisscross 〔crosswise〕.

**어금지금하다** be all rather even; be all much alike; show (but) little divergence; be of little difference; be much the same. ¶ 모두 ～ There is not much to choose between them. / 그들은 둘 다 ～ They are both much of a muchness.

**어긋나다** 《길이》 pass 〔cross〕 each other; 《엇갈리다》 go amiss 〔awry, wrong〕; run 〔be〕 contrary 《to》; run off 《the rails》; stray off 《*one's* course》. ¶ 예상이 ～ guess wrong / 계획이 ～ be baffled in *one's* design / 모든 일이 어긋난다 Everything goes wrong with me. / 네 말은 그의 말과 어긋난다 Your statement conflicts with his. / 그 결과는 우리 기대에 어긋났다 The results turned out at variance with our expectations. / 길이 어긋나서 우리는 서로 만나지 못했다 We took different routes, so we missed seeing each other. *or* We weren't able to meet, we seemed to have crossed each other somewhere on the way.

**어긋놓다** stack them crisscross 〔at angles〕 (so they will not meet).

**어긋맞다** be at odd angles from each other; be crisscross.

**어긋매끼다** alternate 《with》; stack 〔insert〕 in alternation. ¶ 검은 줄과 흰 줄을 ～ alternate white lines with black / 흰 종이와 빨간 종이를 어긋매끼어 놓다 stack papers, alternating the white with the red.

**어긋물리다** join; engage; dovetail; fit 〔secure, fasten〕 together. ¶ 어긋물린 톱니바퀴 a skew gear / 사개를 ～ join a tenon and mortise; dovetail / 톱니바퀴를 ～ engage 〔enmesh〕 gears; put it in gear.

**어긋버긋하다** be all out of joint (with each other); (be) loose; uneven.

**어긋하다** be a bit out of joint; be (a bit) off.

**어기**(漁期) a fishing 〔an open〕 season. ¶ 연어의 ～가 시작되었다 The salmon (fishing) season has opened 〔begun〕. / 송어는 지금이 ～이다 Trout are now in season.

**어기다** 《지켜야 할 일을》 go against; offend against; violate; infringe; break; transgress; trespass against; disregard; ignore; forget; lapse from. ¶ 부모의 뜻을 어기어 against *one's* parents' wishes / 규칙을 ～ violate the rule / 맹세를 ～ break a vow / 예정을 ～ depart from the original plan / 뜻을 ～ resist 《*a person's*》 will; act against 《*a person's*》 wishes / 부모님의 분부를 ～ disobey *one's* parents' orders / 약속을 ～ break a promise 〔*one's* word〕 / 약속 시간을 ～ fail to arrive on time; be late / 법을 ～ break 〔violate, infringe〕 the law / 명령을 ～ go 〔act〕 against orders; disregard 〔ignore〕 a command / 그는 일 분도 어기지 아니하고 그 모임에 왔다 He appeared on the dot at the time set for the meeting. / 그는 약속을 어겨본 적이 없다 He has never failed to keep his word.

**어기대다** oppose; go against; contradict; disobey; act contrary to; be insubordinate to. ¶ 어기대지 말고 하란 대로 해라 Don't talk back; just do what you are told.

**어기뚱거리다** shuffle along; waddle; walk *one's* body swaying.

**어기뚱하다** 《태도가》 (be) haughty; audacious; impertinent; be puffed up; 《틈이》 (be) cracked; loose.

**어기적거리다** walk listlessly; walk in an awkward way; shuffle along; waddle.

**어기적어기적** listlessly; with tottering 〔unsteady〕 steps. ¶ ～ 걷다 shuffle along.

**어기중**(於其中) (being) in the middle; within; among; between. ～하다 be in the middle; be middling; be medium. ¶ 그의 성적은 ～하다 His school record is not so bad. *or* He is medium in scholastic standing.

**어기차다** (be) headstrong; determined; willful; stouthearted; dauntless. ¶ 어기찬 아이 a headstrong child.

**어김** 《어기는 일》 a breach; violation; failure. ¶ ～없는 unerring; infallible / ～없이 without fail; surely; certainly / ～없이 …하다 do not fail 〔forget〕 to *do* / ～없이 9시에 와 주십시오 Be sure to come here at nine. *or* Don't forget 〔fail〕 to come here at nine.

**어깨** ① the shoulder. ¶ 처진 ～ sloping shoulders / ～가 딱 벌어진 square= 〔broad-〕shouldered / 총을 ～에 메고 with a gun on *one's* shoulder / ～ 너머로 over *one's* 〔*a person's*〕 shoulder / ～에 메다 shoulder 《*a thing*》; bear 〔carry〕 《*a thing*》 on the shoulder / ～를 으쓱거리다 shrug 〔raise〕 *one's* shoulders / ～를 펴다 pull *one's* shoulders back; square 〔open〕 *one's* shoulders / ～를 다치다 《투수가》 *one's* arm becomes crockery / 아무의 ～를 두드리다 pat 〔tap〕 *a person* 〔give *a person* a tap〕 on the shoulder / …와 ～를 나란히 하다 stand shoulder to shoulder with… / ～가 빠근하다 have a stiff shoulders; feel stiff in *one's* shoulders / ～가 넓다〔좁다〕 be broad= 〔narrow-〕shouldered; have broad 〔narrow〕 shoulders / ～에 손을 얹다 lay a hand on *one's* shoulder / 사진기를 ～에 메다 sling a camera over *one's* shoulder / 내 ～ 좀 주물러 다오 Give me a shoulder massage. / 안마사에게 ～를 주무르게 했다 I had a masseur 〔masseuse (여)〕 massage my shoulders. / 그 소식을 듣자 그는 ～를 축 늘어뜨렸다 His shoulders sagged when he heard the news.
② 《소매와 깃 사이》 the shoulders 《of a coat》; the edges where two parts of a sliding partition of a garment meet.
③ [비유적] ¶ ～를 겨루다〔나란히 하다〕 can compare 〔compete〕 《with》; equal 《*a person* in *a thing*》; rank with 《another》; be on a par with / ～의 힘을 빼다 relax; 《구어》 take it easy / 이런 점에서 이 책과 ～를 겨룰 만한 책은 없다 In this respect there is no book that can compete with this.
④ 《책임》 (a) responsibility; a mission. ¶ ～가 무겁다 be burdensome; be too much 《for *one*》 / ～가 가벼워지다 be 〔feel〕 relieved of responsibility / ～가 가벼워진 것 같다 feel a load off *one's* mind; feel a sense of relief / ～에 지다 bear 《the responsibility》 on *one's* shoulders.
⑤ 《불량배》 a ruffian; a scoundrel; a rogue; a street gangster; a hooligan; a hoodlum 《미》; a rowdy.
◉ ～걸이 a shawl. ～받이 a shoulder= pad. ～벨트 《자동차의》 a shoulder strap.

**어깨너멋글** piggy-back learning (by preschool children); casual acquisition of bits of knowledge; odd pieces of information acquired by overhearing other persons learning their lessons; picked-up knowledge. ¶ ～로 배우다 pick up bits of knowledge casually.

**어깨동무** ① 《친구》 an old playmate; a school chum; a childhood friend. ② 《서로 팔을 얹음》 putting arms around each other's shoulders. ～하다 put arms around each other's shoulders.

**어깨뼈** a shoulder blade; a bladebone; a scapula (*pl.* ～s, -lae) (L.). ¶ ～가 부러지다 get *one's* bladebone broken.

**어깨총**(一銃) 《총을 멤》 shouldering

*one's* rifle; 《구령》 Shoulder arms! ～하다 shoulder 〔slope〕 arms. ¶ ～의 자세를 취하다 come to the shoulder 〔slope〕/ 우〔좌〕로 ～《구령》 Right 〔Left〕 shoulder arms!

**어깨춤** a shoulder dance; moving *one's* shoulders up and down. ¶ ～을 추다 dance with *one's* shoulders moving up and down.

**어깨통** the circumference of *one's* shoulders; *one's* shoulder measurements.

**어깻바람** 《신바람》 wiggling *one's* shoulders with delight 〔elation, exultation〕; 《뽐냄》 swaggering; keeping *one's* nose in the air; being a stuffed shirt. ¶ ～이 나서 in high spirits / ～이 세다 swagger; be elated / ～을 내며 걷다 walk with a sway of the body; strut 〔swagger〕 about / 그 사람 요사이 돈 좀 벌더니 ～이 대단하다 He made a little money recently and has been unbearable ever since.

**어깻숨** a shoulder-heaving breath. ¶ ～쉬다 breathe hard; pant.

**어깻죽지** the shoulder joint.

**어깻짓** moving *one's* shoulders.

**어꾸수하다** ⇨ 엇구수하다.

**어눌하다**(語訥—) be slow of speech; (be) inarticulate; stammer; stutter. ¶ 그의 말이 ～ He stammers.

**어느** ① 《의문》 which; what (one). ¶ ～책〔사람, 날〕 which book 〔person, day〕/ ～것 which one; which / ～ 길로 갈까 Which way shall we go? / ～ 차를 타십니까 Which car will you take? / ～ 김씨 말야, 큰 김씨야 작은 김씨야 Which Mr. Kim do you mean, the older or the younger? / 이 중에서 ～것을 가지고 싶은가 Which of these do you want? / 홍차와 커피 중 ～것을 좋아하십니까 Which do you like better 〔prefer〕, tea ⤴ or coffee ⤵? (★ tea ⤴ or coffee ⤴ 로 끝을 올림조로 발음하면 「홍차와 커피 어느쪽도 좋아하지 않는다면 그 밖에 무엇을 좋아하시는 게 있습니까」의 뜻이 됨) / ～ 요일이 좋으시겠습니까 What day of the week will it be convenient to you?

② 《한》 a; one; 《어떤》 (a) certain; some (... or other) (★ certain은 이름을 알지만 일부러 말하지 않는 경우. some은 이름을 전혀 모르는 경우). ¶ ～ 날 some day; one (fine) day (★ one fine...은 다음에 무슨 일이 일어날 경우 쓰임. fine에는 뜻이 없음. 「어느 갠 날」이면 a fine day) / ～ 날 아침 one morning / ～ 곳에서 at a (certain) place; somewhere / ～ 경우에는 on some occasion; in some cases; sometimes / ～ 의미로는 in a sense; in a way; in a manner / ～ 한 가지 일에 전심해라 Devote yourself to some one subject. / ～ 경우에는 그 규칙이 들어맞지 않는다 That rule does not apply in some cases.

③ 《그 중의 어느…》 whichever; any (one). ¶ ～…도 any; every; whichever; 《부정》 none; neither / ～것이나 whichever; any one / ～것보다도 more than anything else / ～모로 보나 from every point of view; however you look at it; to all appearance; in every respect; every inch / ～ 색이나 다 좋다 either 〔any〕 of these colors will do / 「～것을 먼저 할까요」—「～것이라도 좋다」 "Which shall I begin with?" —"You may do with any one." / ～ 책을 사더라도 값은 한가지다 Whichever book you may buy, the price is the same. / ～것도 그의 마음에 들지 않는다 None of them satisfy him. *or* He does not like any of them. / ～ 아이도 대답을 못했다 None of the children could answer. / ～쪽도 모릅니다 《둘인 경우》 I know neither of them. *or* 《셋 이상인 경우》 I know none of them. / 그와 나 ～쪽도 틀리지 않는다 Neither he nor I am wrong. (★ 복수 동사의 are를 쓸 때도 있으나 대개 동사에 가까운 주어와 일치함) / 그는 ～ 모로 보나 훌륭한 신사다 He is every inch a fine gentleman. *or* He is a fine gentleman from every point of view. / ～ 길로 가도 같은 데에 이른다 Whichever road you take, you will come to the same place.

**어느 겨를에** when with so little time to spare? ¶ 공부하면서 ～ 그림을 그렸느냐 How did you ever find time to paint a picture in the midst of your school work? / ～ 독일어를 배울 수 있어 Where can I find the time to learn German?

**어느덧** 《어느새》 in no time (at all); so soon; before *one* knows 〔realizes, notices〕 it; before *one* is aware; unawares; without knowing it; without *one's* knowledge; unnoticed.

¶ ～ 해가 서산에 기울었다 Before we were aware of it, the sun was going down in the west. / ～ 봄이 왔다 Spring slipped up on us unawares. *or* The spring has stolen over 〔on〕 us. / ～ 내 나이 사십이 되었다 Here I am forty years old without quite realizing it. /

～ 목적지에 닿았다 We arrived at our journey's end before we were aware of it. / ～ 내 청춘이 지나갔다 My youth has stolen by. / ～ 여름 방학이 다 갔다 The summer vacation has passed all too soon 〔has simply flown by〕. / ～ 성탄절이 왔다 Christmas has stolen up on us.

**어느때** (at) what time; when. ¶ ～든지〔나〕any time; whenever; always / ～고 any time; whenever; some time (or other); some day; sooner or later / ～고 좋을 때 오십시오 Come (at) any time 〔whenever〕 you like. / ～고 떠날 채비가 되어 있다 We are ready for departure. / 시작 시간은 ～고 좋다 It does not matter to me when we begin. / 금강산 구경은 ～가 제일 좋습니까 What season of the year is it best to see Mount 〔Mt.〕 *Kŭmgang*? / ～고 후회할 때가 있을 게다 You will be sorry for it sooner or later.

**어느새** ＝어느덧.

**어느 정도**(一程度) (in) some measure; (to) some degree; (to) some 〔a certain〕 extent; somewhat; more or less; partly. ¶ 내 생각은 ～ 네 의견에 기울고 있다 I rather lean to your view. / 사나운 폭풍우도 ～ 가라앉았다 The violence of the storm lulled to some extent. / 나도 그 문제에 ～ 책임이 있다 I am partly responsible for the problem.

**어느쪽** ①《의문》 which (side); any (side). ¶ ～이 마음에 드십니까 Which one do you prefer? / 커피와 홍차 ～을 드시겠어요 Would you prefer a cup of coffee or black tea?
②《무엇이든》 whichever. ¶ ～이든지 네가 원하는 것을 가져라 Take whichever you want. / ～이 이기든지 나는 만족이다 Whichever side wins, I shall be satisfied.
③《선택》 either ... or; neither ... nor. ¶ ～이냐 하면 if (it has to be) one or the other; if anything; if I have to say 〔choose〕; rather; rather than otherwise / ～이냐 하면 여기 있고 싶다 I would rather stay here (than otherwise).
④《두 쪽 다》 both; either; neither (부정). ¶ 양자중 ～ either of the two / ～이든간에 in either case; either way; anyhow; anyway / ～도 못하지 않은 equally competent; well-matched / ～이라도 좋다 Either will do. / 나로서는 ～이든 좋다 It's all the same to me. / 나는 둘중 ～도 모른다 I know neither 〔do not know either〕 of the two (people).
⑤《방향》 what direction 〔side〕.

**어느틈에** ＝어느 겨를에.

**어는점** 〖화학〗 a freezing point. ＝빙점.

**-어도** ①《양보》 though; although; even though; notwithstanding; but; however. ¶ 돈이 없어도 though I am poor / 적어도 at least / 늦어도 다섯 시까지는 와야 한다 You must be here by five at latest. / 싫어도 해야 한다 Though you do not like it, you must do it. / 굶어죽어도 그런 짓은 안 한다 Even though I were starving, I would not do such a thing. / 그것은 있어도 좋고 없어도 좋다 It doesn't make any difference whether I have it or not.
②《승낙·양해》 ¶ 먹어도 되겠습니까 May I 〔Is it all right to〕 eat it? / 먹어도 좋다 You may 〔It is all right to〕 eat it.

**어두커니** in the morning twilight.

**어두컴컴하다** (be) dark. ¶ 어두컴컴한 밤 a dark night; a moonless night / 어두컴컴한 길〔숲〕 a darkish path 〔wood〕.

**어둑새벽** the dusk at dawn; the dark before the dawn.

**어둑어둑하다** (be) rather dark; dusky. ¶ 날이 ～ It gets dark. / 날이 어둑어둑해서 그가 왔다 He came at dark.

**어둑하다** be a bit dark; get dark; 《어수룩하다》 (be) simple; simple-hearted.

**어둔하다**(語鈍―) be slow of speech; (be) tongue-tied.

**어둠** darkness; the dark. ¶ ～ 속에서 in the dark / 밤의 ～ the shadows 〔darkness〕 of night / ～을 틈타서 (도망하다) (escape, make *one's* escape) 「under cover of darkness 〔in the dark〕 / ～ 속으로 사라지다 vanish 〔disappear〕 into darkness / ～ 속에서 덮치다 attack 《*a person*》 in the dark / ～ 속에서 길을 더듬어가다 feel 〔grope〕 *one's* way in the dark / ～ 속을 가다 go darkling / ～ 속을 헤매다 wander in darkness 〔the dark〕 / 현장에 ～이 다가왔다 Night closed upon the scene. / ～이 깔린다 〔깃든다〕 Darkness falls 〔sets in〕.
◉ ～길 a dark road. ～별《금성》 the evening star; Venus. ～상자 a dark box.

**어둠침침하다** (be) gloomy; dark and dismal; somber; dim. ¶ 어둠침침한 불빛 dim light / 어둠침침한 방 a dimly-lit room / 어둠침침한 겨울 저녁 a gloomy winter evening / 어둠침침한 데서 책을 읽다 read a book in the twilight 〔a poor light〕 / 전등이 ～ The electric light is dim.

**어둡다** ① 《밝지 않다》 (be) dark; obscure (불명료); dim (희미); gloomy. ¶ 어둡기 전에 before (it is) dark / 어두워진 뒤에 after dark / 어두운 길을 걷다 go along a dark road / 어둡게 하다 darken; make dim; dim 〔lower〕 《the light》 / 어두워지다 get 〔become〕 dark 〔dim〕 / 바깥은 어두웠다 It was dark outside. / 달 없는 어두운 밤이었다 It was a dark moonless night. / 불빛이 ~ The light is bad. *or* The lamp gives a poor light. / 너무 어두워서 잘 볼 수 없다 It is too dark to see properly.
② 《좋지 않다》 (be) gloomy; dismal; shady; shadowy. ¶ 어두운 과거가 있는 사나이 a man with a shadowy past / 얼굴에 어두운 그림자가 스쳤다 His face clouded. *or* A cloud passed over his face. / 그의 전도는 ~ His future is not going to be bright. *or* Prospects are gloomy for him.
③ 《사물에》 be ignorant 《of》; be a stranger 《to》; be poorly acquainted 《with》; be not well informed 《on》; be blank (when it comes to); be in the dark; be unfamiliar 《with the subject》; know but 〔only〕 little of. ¶ 세상 물정에 ~ know little of the world / 나는 그 사정에 ~ I am ignorant of the circumstances. / 나는 이 부근 지리에 ~ I am not well acquainted with this locality. *or* I am a stranger here.
④ 《약하다》 be weak 《in sight, in hearing》. ¶ 눈이 ~ have bad eyes 〔weak vision, failing sight〕 / 귀가 ~ be hard 〔thick〕 of hearing / 늙으면 눈이 어두워진다 Our sight grows dim 〔misty〕 with age.

**어디**[1] ① 《의문》 what place 〔part〕; where. ¶ ~까지 《거리》 how far; 《정도》 to what extent / ~(에)서 from where; whence 《문어》 / 내 신발이 ~ 있니 Where are my shoes? / 「~ 가니」—「종로에 간다」 "Where are you going?"—"I'm going to Chongno." / ~까지 가십니까 How far are you going? / ~가 아프니 Where do you feel the pain? / 여기가 어딥니까 Where 「are we 〔am I〕 now? *or* What place is this? / 그는 대체 ~ 갔나 Wherever is he gone? / 그가 ~ 갔는지 아무도 모른다 Nobody knows where he has gone. / 자네 이제까지 ~ 있었나 Where have you been all this while? / 자넨 ~서 왔는가 Where did you come from? / 자넨 ~ 출신인가 Where do you hail 〔come〕 from? *or* Where are you from? (★ 출신지를 말할 때는 보통 현재형) / 이것은 다른 것과 ~가 다르냐 Where(in) does this differ from the other? / 그런 버릇을 ~서 배웠느냐 Where did you get such manners? / 그런 남자의 ~가 좋은가 What (good) do you see in such a man? / 그녀의 ~가 예쁜지 모르겠다 I don't see where she is so pretty. *or* I see nothing pretty about her. / 이 소설의 ~가 좋은지 모르겠다 I fail to see anything good in this novel. / 그를 ~까지 믿어야 할지 모르겠다 I don't know how far I can trust him. / 지난번에 ~까지 했던가 《교실에서》 How far did we go last time?
② 《어딘가》 somehow; in some way; 《장소》 somewhere; elsewhere; some=place. ¶ 어딘가(에) somewhere; in some respects 〔points〕; 《의문문에》 anywhere / 어딘지 모르게 somehow; something / 여기 ~에 somewhere about here; near here / 분명히 ~서 본 얼굴인데 ~서 보았는지 생각이 안 난다 I'm sure I've seen him somewhere, but I can't remember where. / 그는 인천 어딘가에 살고 있다 He lives somewhere in 〔near〕 Inch'ŏn. / 이 근처 ~에 우체국이 있습니까 Is there a post office about here? / 그는 이 근처 어딘가에 산다 〔있을 게다〕 He lives 〔must be〕 somewhere around here. / 어딘지 이상하다 Somehow 〔For no special reason〕, it seems strange. / 그 사람에겐 어딘가 천한〔고상한〕 데가 있다 There is something vulgar 〔refined〕 about him. / 그녀에겐 어딘지 모르게 애교가 있다 There is a certain charm about her. / 그는 ~에 내놓아도 부끄럽지 않은 영어 교사다 He is certainly a creditable English teacher. / 장갑을 ~엔가 두고 왔다 I have left my gloves somewhere. / 그는 ~엔가 나갔나 봅니다 He seems to have gone somewhere else. / 그는 충주 ~에서 왔다 He came from Ch'ungju or thereabouts. / 그가 ~에선가 나타났다 He appeared from 〔out of〕 nowhere.
③ 《개괄적으로》 any place; every place; anywhere; everywhere; 《부정》 nowhere; noplace. ¶ ~나, ~든지 anywhere at all; in any place; wherever / ~에(라)도 everywhere; (not) anywhere; 《부정》 nowhere / ~까지나 through and through; 《철두철미》 every inch; out and out; to the (bitter) end 〔last〕; all the way / ~를 가

더라도 wherever you may go / 나는 ~까지나 너를 지지하겠다 I will stand by you to the last. / 인심은 ~나 마찬가지다 Human nature is the same everywhere. *or* People are people all over. / 그는 ~까지나 신문 기자다 He is every inch 〔bit〕 a newspaperman.

**어디²** 《감탄사》 well; well now; now; just; let me see. ¶ ~ 산보나 할까 Let's see now, shall we take a walk? / ~ 두고 보자 He shall 〔You'll〕 pay for it. / ~ 영어 한번해 보아라 Well now, let me hear you speak some English. / ~ 시험삼아서 이 약을 먹어 보자 Well, I guess I might as well try this medicine. / 우리 ~ 그렇게 하여 보자 Let's just try it that way.

**어떠하다** ① 《성질·모양·상태》 be how; be like what. ¶ 오늘은 몸이 어떠하십니까 《환자에게》 How do you feel today? / 요새 어떠하십니까 How have you been? / 위스키 한 잔 어떻습니까 「May I offer you 〔How about〕 a glass of whisky? / 커피 한 잔 어떻습니까 Would you like a cup of coffee? / 영화 구경은 어떻습니까 Wouldn't you like to see the movies? *or* What about going to the movies? (★ What about…, How about… 둘 다 구어이나 후자는 미국에서 많이 쓰임. 또, about 다음에는 명사·대명사·동명사가 오는 것이 보통이나 문장이 올 경우도 있음) / 해운대 여행은 어떠했습니까 How did you enjoy your trip to Haeundae? / 내일은 어떻습니까 How about tomorrow? / 산책 나가시는 게 어떻습니까 《권유》 What do you say to our going out for a walk? *or* How about taking a walk? / 이건 어떻습니까, 아주머니 《점원의 말》 How do you like this, madam? / 이 모자가 나한테 어떻습니까 How does this hat look on me? / 내일 떠나는 것이 어떠냐 How about starting tomorrow? / 오늘 쌀값은 어떤가 How much is rice today? / 그 연극은 (평이) 어떻던가 How did the play go? / 요새 서울이 어떻습니까 How are things in Seoul these days? / 가난하면 어떻단 말이냐 What if you are poor? ② 《지정해 말함》 be somehow; be a certain way; be any 〔every〕 which way. ¶ ~고 말하기 힘든 이상한 음악 a weird and indescribable music / 어떻다고 말할 수 없다 Nothing definite can be said on it. *or* It cannot be described.

**어떠한, 어떤** ① 《무슨·여하한》 what kind 〔sort〕 of; like what. ¶ ~ 이유로 for some reason or other / ~ 일이 있어도 whatever 〔no matter what〕 may happen; under any circumstances; for the world / ~ 일을 치르더라도 at all costs 〔hazards〕 / ~ 가게도 열려 있지 않다 No store is 〔None of the stores are〕 open. (★ none은 흔히 복수 취급: None *were* present. / No one *was* present.) / 그는 ~ 사람이냐 What kind 〔sort〕 of (a) man is he? *or* What is he like? / ~ 책을 지금 읽고 있습니까 What book are you reading now? / 원자탄이란 것이 ~ 것이냐 What is an atomic bomb like? / ~ 일이 있든지 자네 계획은 바꾸지 말게 Don't change your plans, whatever happens. / 당신을 위해서라면 ~ 일이라도 하겠소 「I'm quite willing 〔I'll spare no pains〕 to do anything for you. / ~ 일이 있어도 그것은 못 하겠다 I won't do it, come what may. *or* I would not do it for anything. / 그것이 잘 된다면 ~ 일이든지 하겠다 I would give anything to succeed in it. / ~ 일이 있더라도 책임을 완수하겠습니다 Nothing shall prevent me from doing my duty.
② 《어느》 some; a certain; one; a.

> **용법** **some** 잘 모르는 사람이나 사물에 대해서 쓰며 [sʌm]으로 발음함. **a certain** 알고는 있으나 밝히고 싶지 않은 때에 씀. **one** a certain을 가볍게 줄인 느낌의 말. 과거의 한 때를 지칭하기도 함.

¶ ~ 사람 a certain person; someone; Mr. So-and-so / ~ 것 something / ~ 여름날 밤 one summer night / ~ 의미에서 in a sense / 옛날옛날 ~ 곳에 할아버지와 할머니가 살고 있었습니다 Once upon a time there lived an old man and an old woman in a certain place.

**어떻게** ① 《어떠하게》 how; in what; what manner. ¶ ~ 지내느냐 How are you getting on 〔along〕? / 그녀는 ~ 옷을 입었더냐 How was she dressed? / 대체 그 일이 ~ 일어났는가 How on earth did it happen? / 나는 그것을 ~ 만드는지 모른다 I don't know how they make it. / ~ 여기 왔는가 How is it that you are here? / 자넨 이 계획을 ~ 생각하나 What do you think of this plan? (★ 이 글을 How do you think …? 로 해서는 안 됨. How를 쓰면 생각하는 방법을 묻는 것이 되며, 따라서 I think with my mind.라고나 대답해야 될지. 다만, like를 써서 How do you like that plan?이면 됨: How do you like 〔find〕 the new

house?) / 신문은 그것에 관해서 ~ 말하고 있습니까 What do the papers say about it?
② 《몹시》 how; what; so; to what extent. ¶ 그녀가 ~ 예쁜지 모르겠다 What a beautiful woman she is! / ~나 비가 오는지 앞이 보이지 않는다 It's raining so hard, somehow I can't see in front of me at all.
③ 《어떻게든》 ¶ 5만 원이 필요한데 ~ 안 되겠습니까 I want fifty thousand won. Could you find some means to raise it? / ~ 되도록 해봅시다 I will see what I can do for you. / ~ 될 테지 Somehow it will come out all right. / ~ 좀 나아질 것으로 생각한다 I think it might be improved somehow.

**어떻게 되다** ① 《사람·일이》 how it becomes 〔turns out〕. ¶ 그이가 어떻게 되었을까 I wonder what has become of him. / 그 일이 어떻게 될지 모르겠다 I don't know how things will turn out. / 그 영화는 결국 어떻게 되었나 How did that movie come out? / 어떻게 된 거냐 안색이 나쁜데 What's the matter (with you)? You don't look too well.
② 《그럭저럭》 turn out somehow or other; take care of itself (자연히); be managed (one way or another). ¶ 어떻게 될 테지 Things will turn out one way or the other. *or* It will come out somehow or other. / 여비는 어떻게 될 것 같다 I think I can take care of my travel expenses somehow. / 어떻게 될 수 있다면 부탁하러 오지 않을 텐데 I wouldn't ask your favor if I could help it.

**어떻게든** somehow or other; by some means (or other). ⇨어떻게 하다. ¶ ~ 거기 가겠다 I will get there somehow or other.

**어떻게 하다** do 〔manage〕 by some means or other; do somehow (at whatever risk or cost); manage to do; devise some means; try and manage 《*a matter*》. ¶ 어떻게 해서든 그것을 꼭 찾아내겠다 I will find it out by all means. / 어떻게 해서든 그 법안을 통과시켜서는 안 된다 The bill must not be passed at any cost. / 이 편지를 어떻게 할까요 What shall I do with this letter? / 이 돈을 어떻게 하겠는가 What do you do with this money? / 어떻게 할 생각인가 What would you do? *or* What do you want to do?

**어떻든지** anyhow; anyway; in any case; at any rate; at all events; regardless; whether or not. ¶ 그것은 ~ be that as it may; no matter what it may be / 시비곡직은 ~ whether it is true or not / 비용 문제는 ~ apart from the question of expense / 옳고 그름은 ~ 그것은 사실이다 It may be right or wrong, but it is a fact.

**어뜩** suddenly in passing; by chance; for an instant. ¶ ~ 그 말을 들었다 I happened to hear about it.

**어뜩비뜩** ~하다 (be) fidgety; indecent; improper; unsuitable. ¶ ~한 행동 improper behavior / ~한 언사를 쓰다 use improper words / ~한 태도로 나오다 behave in a disorderly manner; take a threatening attitude.

**어뜩하다** feel (physically) dizzy 〔giddy, faint〕. ¶ 어뜩어뜩하다 = 어뜩하다 / 정신이 ~ feel dizzy 〔faint〕; *one's* head swims 〔reels〕 / 피곤해서 정신이 ~ I'm so tired I think I'll faint.

**-어라** ① 《명령》 Do! ¶ 이것을 먹어라 Eat this. / 여기 있어라 Stay here. / 손을 씻어라 Wash your hands. ② 《감탄》 be indeed! ¶ 아이고, 가엾어라 O, what a pity!

**어란**(魚卵) fish eggs; spawn (산란한); roe (몸 안의).

**어람**(御覽) his majesty's inspection; royal inspection.

**어런더런** hustling and bustling; people going and coming.

**어럽쇼** Oh!; Heavens!; My goodness!; I say!; Gee! 《미구어》. ¶ ~ 내 우산은 어디 갔지 Where is my umbrella, I wonder? / ~ 벌써 10시네 Why! It is ten.

**어레미** a coarse sieve; a riddle. ¶ ~질하다 riddle.

**어려움** 《곤란》 hardship; difficulty; 《곤경》 distress; misery; adversity; 《성가심》 trouble; 《고뇌》 affliction; suffering(s); 《시련》 a trial; an ordeal. ¶ 가난으로 ~을 겪다 be poverty-stricken; be hard up (for money) / ~을 견디다 endure *one's* trouble / ~을 극복하다 get 〔tide〕 over a difficulty.

**어려워하다** feel constraint 《in *a person's* presence》; have a regard for 《*a person's*》 feeling; hold 《*a person*》 in fear; show deference 〔reserve〕; be ill at ease. ¶ 어려워하는 기색 a constrained manner 〔air〕; an air of constraint / 어려워하지 않고 without reserve / 어려워하지 않다 make *oneself* free and easy; make *oneself* at home / 그는 나를 어려워하는 빛이 있다 There is something reserved in his manner toward me. / 그녀는 그를 어려

위해서 말을 안 했다 She kept silence out of deference to him. / 어려워하지 말고 편히 앉으시오 Make yourself at home and sit comfortably.

**어련무던하다** (be) satisfactory; nice; [서술적] be not so bad; be free of faults; 《언동 등이》 (be) harmless and inoffensive. ¶ 어련무던한 소리를 하다 make harmless remark.

**어련하다** (be) infallible; certain; proper; natural; reliable; (be) reasonable; it stands to reason. ¶ 그가 하는데 어련하려고 We may trust him. He knows how to deal with it. /「난 이 일 때문에 무척 애를 썼네」—「어련하시겠습니까」 "I took much pain to do this."—"I can easily imagine."

**어련히** naturally; certainly; undoubtedly; surely; infallibly; as a natural consequence; in the natural course of events; as a matter of course; as expected. ¶ 내버려 둬, ~ 알아서 할라고 Let him alone. He will take care of himself.

**어렴성**(一性) social reserve; constraint; deference. ¶ ~ 없는 unreserved; frank; free (from constraint) / ~ 없이 without reserve 〔hesitation〕; freely; openly / ~ 없는 태도 unconstrained manner / ~ 없이 말하다 speak without reserve; speak freely; open up / ~ 없이 굴다 「make free 〔take liberties〕 with 《*a person*》.

**어렴풋이** dimly; faintly; vaguely; indistinctly; hazily. ¶ ~ 들리는 음악 소리 a distant sound of music / ~ 기억하고 있다 remember dimly 〔vaguely〕; have a faint 〔dim, hazy〕 recollection 〔memory〕 《of》 / ~ 보이다 be seen dimly 〔at a dim distance〕 / 어렸을 때 일어난 일을 ~ 기억하다 have a vague memory of what happened in childhood / 그가 그렇게 말한 것이 ~ 생각난다 I dimly remember hearing him say that. / 불빛이 저 멀리 ~ 보인다 A light glimmers in the distance. / 가로등이 안개 속에 ~ 비쳤다 The street lights shone dimly through the mist. / 종소리가 ~ 들렸다 A sound of a bell is faintly heard.

**어렴풋하다** (be) dim; faint; vague; indistinct; hazy; misty; fuzzy. ¶ 어렴풋한 소리 an indistinct sound / 어렴풋한 빛 a dim 〔feeble〕 light / 어렴풋한 기억을 더듬다 trace back a dim 〔vague, faint〕 memory / 나무가 안개에 싸여 ~ The trees fade into the mist.

**어렵**(漁獵) fishing and hunting; 《어업》 fishing; fishery.

**어렵게** in a hard 〔a difficult, an awkward〕 way.

**어렵다** ① 《힘들다》 (be) hard; difficult; 《구어》 tough; stiff.

> **용법** **hard** 어렵다는 뜻으로 difficult 보다 일반적인 말. 특히 많은 노고나 노력이 필요할 만큼 「어려운」. **difficult** hard 보다 딱딱한 말로서, 복잡한 기술이 필요할 만큼 「어려운」.

¶ 어려운 문제 a hard 〔tough〕 question / 어려운 시험 a difficult 〔stiff〕 examination / 어려운 일 a hard task 〔job〕 / 배우기 어려운 말 a language hard to learn / 비위맞추기 어려운 사람 a person hard to please / 일자리 구하기가 ~ have difficulty in finding a job / 라틴어는 배우기 ~ Latin is difficult to learn. / 그 책은 내게 너무 ~ The book is too difficult for me. / 그의 회복은 ~ His recovery is doubtful. / 그 문제는 대답하기 좀 어려웠다 I found some difficulty in answering the question. / 이것은 참기 ~ This is intolerable. *or* This is unbearable. / 참 어려운 세상이다. 물가는 오르기만 하니 말야 These are hard times. Prices keep going up.
② 《까다롭다》 (be) awkward; embarrassing; vexatious; troublesome; delicate; difficult; trying. ¶ 어려운 사태 a difficult 〔an awkward〕 situation / 풀기 어려운 문제 a knotty problem; a question hard to solve / 다루기 어려운 연장 an awkward tool / 어려운 지경에 빠지다 fall into a difficult 〔trying〕 situation / 요새 국제 정세가 점점 어려워진다 The international situation is getting very delicate these days. / 어려우시겠지만…, 어렵겠지만… I hate to bother you (but…); I'm sorry (but …); Pardon 〔Excuse〕 me, but…; Might I ask you to….
③ 《가난하다》 (be) poor; needy; indigent; destitute. ¶ 집안이 ~ *one's* family is poor / 살림이 ~ be in needy 〔reduced〕 circumstances; be badly off / 어렵게 지내다 live in bad 〔poor〕 circumstances 〔in poverty〕; have a hard 〔trying〕 time of it / 어려울 때의 친구가 참된 친구다 A friend in need is a friend indeed.

**어렵사리** with difficulty; barely. ¶ ~ 번 돈 hard-earned money / ~ 시험에 합격하다 pass an examination with difficulty / 그는 ~ 목적을 달성했다 He barely achieved 〔managed to achieve〕 his object.

**어렵지 않게** easily; readily; facilely; without difficulty 〔trouble〕; with ease; hands-down. ¶ ~ 이기다 beat 〔win over〕 《*a person*》 hands down; win a hands-down victory; gain an easy victory 《over》.

**어렴칙하다** (be) faint; dim; vague. ¶ 어렴칙이 faintly; dimly; vaguely / 기억이 ~ have a vague memory.

**어로**(漁撈) fishing; fishery. ◉ ~과(科) the fishery course. ~금지구역 a restrictive fisheries zone. ~선(線) a fishery conservation line. ~수역 a fishery zone. ~작업 =어로. ~장 a fishing ground: 공동 ~장 joint fishing grounds. ~저지선 the fishing restriction line. ~협정 a fisheries agreement. 공동~ 지역 joint fishing grounds.

**어록**(語錄) analects; sayings. ¶ 처칠 ~ Quotations from Winston Churchill.

**어뢰**(魚雷) a torpedo (*pl.* ~es). ¶ ~를 발사하다 fire 〔launch〕 a torpedo 《at》/ ~에 맞다 take a torpedo hit. ◉ ~공격 a torpedo attack. ~발사관 a torpedo tube; a launching tube. ~정 a torpedo 〔PT(쾌속)〕 boat.

**어루꾀다** lure 〔seduce〕 with flattery; cajole; wheedle; dupe; coax; fool 《*a person*》. ¶ 어루꾀어 만 원을 우려내다 wheedle 《*a person*》 out of 10,000 won.

**어루더듬다** fumble 〔grope〕 around for; feel about for. ¶ 성냥을 어루더듬어 찾다 grope 〔fumble, feel〕 for the matches.

**어루러기** 〖의학〗 leucoderma; vitiligo; a piebald skin.

**어루만지다** ① 《쓰다듬다》 stroke; pat 《a child on the head》; pass *one's* hand over 〔across〕 《*one's* face》; smooth down 《*one's* hair》; feel; 《애무하다》 caress; pet. ¶ 상처를~ feel the wound / 어린아이의 턱을 ~ chuck a child under the chin / 그 아이는 고양이를 어루만지기를 좋아한다 The child loves stroking a cat. ② 《달래다》 placate; pacify; quiet; mollify; console; soothe; appease. ¶ 아랫사람을 ~ placate *one's* subordinates / 성난 아내를 어루만져 주다 humor 〔appease〕 an angry wife.

**어룽(이)** mottled spots; mottled pattern; a mottled thing 〔animal〕; mottling.

**어룽거리다** be dappled 〔spotted, variegated〕. ¶ 오솔길은 나무 사이로 비치는 햇빛에 어룽거렸다 The lane was mottled with the sunbeams filtering through the leaves.

**어룽지다** (be) variegated; mottled. ¶ 햇빛과 그늘로 어룽진 잔디밭 a lawn checkered with sunlight and shade.

**어류**(魚類) fishes; the finny tribe; [총칭] the Pisces (★ 단수 취급). ◉ ~학 ichthyology: ~학상의 ichthyological / ~학자 an ichthyologist.

**어르다** fondle; dandle; nurse; humor 《a baby》; pacify (우는 아기를); try to please 《a baby》; play with 《a baby》; pet. ¶ 아기를 안아서 ~ dandle 〔fondle〕 a baby in the arms / 우는 아이를 ~ humor a crying baby / 아기를 얼러 웃기다 coax a baby to smile / 아이를 얼러 키우다 bring up a child indulgently / 어르고 뺨치기 a smiler with a knife / 어르고 뺨치는 사람 a Job's comforter / 어린애가 우는구나, 잠깐 얼러 줘라 Play with the baby a while—it's crying.

**어르신네** ① 《남의 아버지》 your 〔his, *etc.*〕 (esteemed) father. ¶ ~께서 집에 계시나 Is your father at home? ② 《노인·연장자》 an esteemed elder; sir. ¶ ~께서는 그 사람을 어떻게 생각하십니까 Sir, what do you think of the man?

**어른** ① 《윗사람·노인》 *one's* elder(s); an older 〔elderly〕 person; a senior. ¶ 마을의 ~들 village elders 〔seniors〕; elders of the village / 집안의 ~ the head of a family / ~을 공경하라 Respect your elders. / ~ 앞에서 그런 말을 하면 못쓴다 You should not talk like that in the presence of your elders. ② 《성인》 a grown-up (person); an adult; a man. ¶ ~답지 않은 unworthy of a man; childish; puerile / ~이 되다 become 〔grow into〕 a man 〔woman〕; grow up 《to be a man》; reach manhood; come of age / ~ 티가 나다 look like a grown-up person / ~ 몫의 품삯을 받다 receive a full-rate pay / 그 아이는 ~같이 말한다 The child talks like a man. / 그녀는 이제 아주 ~이 되었다 She has quite grown up.

**어른거리다** ① 《눈·마음에》 flicker; flit; glimmer; waver; be dazzled (눈이); haunt 《*a person*》 (마음에). ¶ 어른거리는 그림자 wavering shadows / 그림자가 불빛에 어른거렸다 The shadows flickered in the light. / 그의 모습이 아직도 눈 앞에 어른거린다 His image still flits before my eyes. *or* The memory of his face still haunts me. / 눈이 어른거려서 잘 보이지 않았다 I was dazzled and could not see very well. / 의혹의 빛이 그의 얼굴에 어른거렸다 An expression of doubt flitted across his face. ② 《어리대다》 hang 〔loaf〕 around. ¶ 여기서 어른거리지 말고 나가거라 Stop hanging around here—scram!

**어른스럽다** look like a grown-up; 《조숙하다》 (be) precocious. ¶ 어른스러운 말투 a precocious way of talking / 어른스럽게 말하다 (try to) talk like a grown-up / 어른스럽게 굴다 「behave like 〔assume an air of〕 a grown-up (person).

**어른어른** flickering(ly); glimmering(ly); fluttering(ly). ¶ 눈이 ~하다 be dazzled; be dazed.

**어름** ① 《끝이 맞닿는 점》 a point of contact which both ends meet. ② 《한가운데》 right in the middle; the very middle.

**어름거리다** ① 《언행을》 do 〔say〕 ambiguously; mumble. ¶ 말을 ~ say an ambiguous thing; speak ambiguously; make a vague remark; equivocate / 대답을 ~ give 「an equivocal 〔a vague, a noncommittal〕 answer; equivocate in replying / 태도를 ~ maintain 「an uncertain 〔a dubious〕 attitude 《toward》 / 어름거리지 말고 무엇을 원하는지 똑똑히 말해라 Stop beating around the bush and tell me clearly what it is you want. ② 《일을》 scamp 〔skimp〕 《*one's* work》; do a slapdash 《work》.

**어름어름** 《불분명》 ambiguously; vaguely; equivocally; 《엉터리로》 carelessly and hastily; sloppily.

**어리광** a child's winning ways; playing the baby. ~떨다, ~부리다 display winning ways; play the baby; behave like a spoilt child. ¶ ~ 떠는 아이 a wheedling child; a mama's child / 엄마에게 ~ 떨다 seek a lot of affection from *one's* mother; play the baby to *one's* mother / (여자가) ~조로 말하다 speak in a coquettish tone; coo 《at》 / 우리집 애는 너무 ~이 심하다 My child has got quite spoilt. / ~ 부리지 마라 Don't act like a baby. / 선생님께 너무 ~ 떨면 안 된다 You shouldn't depend too much on your teacher's kindness.

**어리굴젓** salted oysters with hot pepper; fermented oysters salted with hot pepper.

**어리다**[1] ① 《나이가》 (be) (very) young; infant; juvenile. ¶ 어리지만 child as it is; though young; young as *one* is / 어릴 때부터 from 〔(ever) since〕 *one's* childhood 〔early days〕 / 어린 나무 a young plant 〔tree〕 / 어린 마음 a 〔*one's*〕 childish mind / 어릴 때 동무 a friend of *one's* early childhood; a childhood playmate / 어릴 때 모습을 간직하다 retain *one's* infant features / 나는 어렸을 때 자주 거기에 가곤 했다 I used to go there 「in my childhood 〔when I was a child〕. / 그는 나보다 두 살 ~ He is two years younger than I. / 우리는 어릴 때부터 아는 사이다 We have known each other since our childhood. / 그는 어린 시절에 부모를 여의었다 He lost his parents very early in life. / 어린 마음에도 슬퍼서 눈물이 나왔다 Though I was a child, I felt very sad and shed tears. / 그는 어렸을 때 미국에 건너갔다 He went over to the United States at an early age. ② 《미숙하다》 (be) immature; green; 《유치하다》 childish; infantile. ¶ 어린 생각 a childish idea / 생각이 ~ have immature ideas / 이 일을 하기에는 그는 아직 ~ He is still green at this job.

**어리다**[2] ① 《눈물이》 《tears》 gather in the eyes. ¶ 눈물 어린 눈 moist eyes; eyes moist with tears / 눈물 어린 눈으로 with tears in *one's* eyes; with tearful eyes / 그녀의 눈에 눈물이 어리었다 Tears stood 〔gathered, formed〕 in her eyes. / 그 이야기를 할 때 그의 눈에는 눈물이 어리었다 Telling the story brought tears to his eyes. ② 《엉기다》 coagulate; congeal; curdle (우유가); clot (피가). ¶ 수프 표면에 기름기가 어리었다 The fat congealed on (the) top of the soup. ③ 《깃들다》 be filled 《with》. ¶ 애정(이) 어린 편지 an affectionate letter 《to》 / 정성어린 선물 a gift from 《*a person*》 with 《*his*》 best wishes.

**어리대다** 《얼씬대다》 hang 〔loiter, linger〕 about 〔around〕 《a place》. ¶ 수상한 사나이가 집 앞에서 어리대고 있다 A suspicious-looking man is hanging around the house.

**어리둥절하다** (be) dazed; stupefied; stunned; bewildered; embarrassed; perplexed; puzzled; confused; be at a loss. ¶ 어리둥절한 표정으로 with a perplexed look 〔air〕 / 어리둥절케 하다 embarrass 〔puzzle〕 《*a person* with difficult questions》/ 어리둥절해서 어찌 할 바를 모르다 be quite at a loss what to do / 그 급보를 받고 나는 어리둥절했다 I was struck dumb with astonishment at the sudden news. / 그의 갑작스런 키스에 그녀는 어리둥절해서 그 자리에 서 있었다 She stood there in dumb surprise when he suddenly kissed her.

**어리마리** drowsily. ～하다 (be) sleepy-headed; half-asleep; drowsing.

**어리벙벙하다** (be) bewildered; dazed; confounded; muddled; confused. ¶ 어리벙벙하게 하다 strike 《*a person*》 speechless 〔dumb〕; bewilder / 어리벙벙해지다 be struck dumb with surprise; be dumbfounded / 어리벙벙해서 어찌할 줄을 모르다 be so bewildered that *one* does not know what to do / 뜻밖의 질문에 나는 어리벙벙했다 I got confused because I was asked an unexpected question. / 새 일을 맡고 보니 모든 것이 ～ I feel out of myself in this new line of business.

**어리보기** 《얼뜬 사람》 a dimwit; a half-wit; a stupid person.

**어리석다** (be) foolish; stupid; silly. ¶ 어리석게도 foolishly enough / 어리석은 사람〔생각〕 a foolish person 〔idea〕 / 어리석은 짓을 하다 play 〔act〕 the fool; act foolishly; play the ass; make an ass of *oneself* / 그런 사람을 믿다니 자네 참 어리석군 How foolish of you to trust such a man! / 어리석게도 나는 승낙했다 Foolishly enough, I said yes. / 어리석은 짓 작작해라 Don't make yourself ridiculous. / 그런 짓을 할 만큼 어리석지는 않다 I am not 「such a fool 〔so foolish〕 as to do such a thing. / 어리석게도 그는 그런 거짓말을 했다 It was stupid of him to tell such a lie. / 그에게서 돈을 꾸다니 어리석기도 했다 I was fool enough to borrow money from him. (★ be fool enough to...는 It was foolish of me to...의 뜻이며, fool이 형용사적으로 쓰이고 있음).

**어리숭하다** ① 《분명치 않다》 ⇨ 아리송하다. ② 《어리석은 듯하다》 [서술적] look a little foolish; be a bit foolish. ¶ 그 아이는 어리숭해 뵈지만 재주는 대단하다 The boy looks foolish but he has quite a bit of talent.

**어리어리하다** (be) dim, hazy, indistinct, vague; dazzled. ¶ 눈이 ～ My eyes are dazzled.

**어리치다** swoon; faint (away); get fuzzy.

**어리칙칙하다** 《어리석은 체하다》 (be) pretending to be stupid; (be) putting on a "dumb" act.

**어린것** a little 〔young〕 one; a youngster; a kid. ¶ (집에) ～이 많다 have a lot of kids (in *one's* family).

**어린 녀석** a little chap; a brat; an urchin.

**어린아이, 어린애** a child (*pl.* children); a little one; a youngster; an infant (유아); a baby; 《구어》 a kid; little ones [총칭].

> [용법] **child** 부모·자식 관계에서는 연령에 관계없이 「자식→어린애」를 가리키지만, 일반적으로는 남녀 구별 없이 약 14세 이하의 어린애를 뜻함. **infant** 법률에서는 20세 미만의 미성년자를 가리키지만, 일반적으로는 7세 미만의 어린애를 뜻함. 미국에서는 baby와 같은 뜻으로 쓰이나 약간 고풍의 딱딱한 표현임. **baby** 보통 2세 미만으로 혼자 걷지 못하는 갓난아기를 칭하는 말. **kid** child와 대응할 수 있는 구어. 미국에서는 「젊은이」를 뜻하는 구어로 쓰임: college kids (대학생).

¶ ～(와) 같은〔다운〕 childlike; childish; infantile (★ childlike는 좋은 뜻으로 쓰이며 childish는 어린애에게 쓸 때에는 「어린애다운」, 어른에 대해 쓸 때에는 「어린애처럼 유치한」이 되어 경멸적이 됨. infantile은 「어린애처럼 유치한」이란 나쁜 뜻으로 흔히 쓰임.) / ～ 같은 수작〔짓〕 childish remarks 〔behavior〕 / ～ 같은 소리를 하다 talk like a child; say childish things / ～가 없다 be childless; have no children of *one's* own / ～를 낳다 give birth to 《a child》 / ～를 배다, ～가 생기다 be pregnant 《with baby》 / ～가 젖을 먹다 a baby 「sucks 〔takes *one's*〕 milk; a baby sucks its mother's breast / ～한테 젖을 먹이다 suckle a baby; give the breast to a child; put a baby to the breast / ～를 업다 carry a child on *one's* back / ～를 어르다 dandle a child / ～를 좋아하다 be fond of children / ～ 취급을 하다 treat 《*a person*》 like a child; make a baby 〔fool〕 of 《*a person*》; baby 《*a person*》 / ～같은 짓은 그만둬라 Don't behave so childishly. / 그는 아직도 ～다 He is a mere child. / ～라도 그것쯤은 안다 A mere child knows it. / 그는 라디오를 갖게 되어 ～처럼 기뻐하고 있다 He is as pleased as a little boy with a radio set. / 그녀에겐 곧 ～가 생긴다 She is going to have a baby before long.

**어린이** a child. ⇨ 어린아이.

¶ ～의 juvenile; of a child / ～를 위한 방송 〔책〕 juvenile 〔children's〕 broadcasts 〔books〕; broadcasts 〔books〕 for children / ～ 보호 구역 《게시》 Children playing.

◉ ～공원 a children's garden 〔park〕: ～대공원 the Children's Grand Park. ～교육 child education. ～날 Children's Day. ～놀이터 a playground for children. ～방 a children's room; a nursery. ～시간 《라디오·텔레비전의》 the children's hour. ～신문 a children's newspaper. ～영화 a film for children. ～옷 children's clothing 〔garments〕; 《유아의》 smallclothes; shortclothes. ～은행 a children's 〔juvenile〕 bank. ～헌장 the Children's Charter. ～회관 a children's hall.

**어림** an approximation; a rough guess 〔estimate〕. ～하다 ＝～잡다. ¶ ～으로 〔잡아〕 at a rough estimate; roughly; by guesswork / ～잡다 estimate 〔calculate〕 roughly; make a rough estimate 《of》/ 비용은 ～잡아 다음과 같다 The expenses are roughly estimated as follows. ◉ ～셈 a rough calculation 〔estimate〕; a rough computation: ～셈으로 at a rough estimate; roughly; approximately. ～수 a rough number 〔figure〕; round numbers; approximate figures.

**어림없다** (be) wide of the mark; (be) far from it; 《수작·행동이》 (be) preposterous; absurd; nonsensical; 《가능성이》 be hardly possible 《to》; be beyond…; 《능력이》 be not nearly so good as…; be no match for; 《…는 커녕》 be anything but….

¶ 어림없는 수작〔요구〕 preposterous remarks 〔demand〕; a damned silly remark 〔demand〕/ 그녀가 미인이라니 ～ She is anything but beautiful. / 수학에서는 나는 그에게 ～ I am not nearly so strong in mathematics as he. / 이 일은 내 힘으로는 ～ This work is far beyond my capacity. *or* I am nowhere near up to the job. / 어림없지 그 따위 속임수에는 안 넘어간단 말야 None of your tricks with me. *or* You can't fool me so easily. / 그 물건을 사는 데 천원 가지고는 ～ What could be more absurd than to think of buying the thing with 1,000 won? / 어림없는 소리 마라 What a thing to say! *or* Far from it ! / 네가 그걸 하겠다고, ～ You say you will do that? Impossible, indeed !

**어림짐작** a rough 〔random〕 guess; a (mere) conjecture; guesswork. ～하다 guess 《at》; make a shot 《at》; make a (random) guess. ¶ ～으로 by 〔at a〕 guess; by guesswork; as a shot / ～으로 맞히다 make a good shot 《at》; guess right / ～일 뿐이다 It's mere guesswork.

**어릿거리다, 어릿대다** 《둔하고 생기 없다》 (be) dull; unlively; spiritless; sluggish. ¶ 어릿거리는〔어릿어릿한〕 사람 a dullard / 말을 ～ talk dull / 어릿어릿하게 굴다 act dull.

**어릿광대** a clown; a buffoon.

**어릿하다** 《혀끝이》 sting the tip of *one's* tongue; (be) tongue-stinging; biting.

**어마** O my!; Dear me!; Oh dear!; Good heavens! ¶ ～ 예쁘기도 하다 O my, but how lovely! / ～이게 뭐야 Oh, my! What is this? / ～ 당신이 그런 일을 하다니 Fancy your doing that! / ～ 이게 누구야 Good heavens, it is certainly a surprise to see you!

**어마어마하다** ① 《장대하다》 (be) awe-inspiring; magnificent; majestic; grand; imposing; stately. ¶ 어마어마한 고층 건물 an imposing skyscraper / 어마어마하게 큰 성당 a magnificent cathedral / 어마어마한 행렬 a stately procession. ② 《엄청나다》 (be) tremendous; terrific; colossal; immense; enormous. ¶ 어마어마한 부자 a man of colossal wealth / 어마어마한 비용이 들다 cost a tremendous amount / 키가 어마어마하게 크다 He is terribly tall. ③ [과장적] (be) ostentatious; pompous; pretentious; (high-)sounding. ¶ 어마어마한 직함 an ostentatious 〔a grandiose〕 title / 어마어마하게 말하다 exaggerate; say extravagantly; make too much of 《*a matter*》/ 어마어마하게 차려입다 dress *oneself* showily; be loudly 〔gaudily〕 dressed.

**어망**(漁網·魚網) a fishing net.

**어머나** Oh!; Oh my (goodness)!; Dear me!; Good gracious!

**어머니** ① a mother; 《소아어》 mam(m)a; 《미구어》 mom; 《영구어》 mummy (주로 여성·아이들이 사용). ¶ ～의, ～다운 motherly; motherlike; maternal / ～ 없는 motherless / ～의 사랑 mother's love; maternal affection 〔love〕/ ～ 쪽의 친척 a relative on the mother's side / 친～같이 대하다 act like *one's* real mother / ～를 여의다 lose *one's* mother; be left motherless / 그 형제는

~가 다르다 They are brothers by different mothers. / 그녀는 이제 삼남매의 ~가 되었다 She is now the mother of three children.
② 《근원》 origin; source; (the) cause; the mother 《of》. ¶ 대지는 살아있는 만물의 ~다 The earth is the mother of all things alive. / 필요는 발명의 ~다 Necessity is the mother of invention. ◉ ~날 Mother's Day. ~회 《조직》 a mother's association; 《모임》 a mother's meeting.

**어멈** ① 《하녀》 a housemaid; an amah; a maid(servant). ② 《어머니의 낮춤말》 a 〔*one's*〕 mother.

**어명**(御命) 《issue》 a Royal 〔King's〕 command 〔order〕.

**어묵**(魚—) boiled fish paste.

**어물**(魚物) 《생선》 fishes; 《건어물》 dried 〔cured〕 fish; stockfish. ◉ ~상(商)〔장수〕 《사람》 a fishmonger; a fish dealer 〔peddler (행상)〕. ~전 a fish store 〔shop〕; a driedfish shop 〔store〕.

**어물거리다** 《모호하게 하다》 talk 〔act〕 ambiguously; equivocate; prevaricate; do not make *oneself* clear; take an indecisive attitude. ¶ 말을 ~ say an ambiguous thing / 대답을 ~ give a vague answer / 결단을 못 내리고 ~ waver in *one's* determination / ~가 기회를 놓치다 dally away *one's* opportunity / 집세 이야기만 꺼내면 그는 늘 어물거린다 Whenever I remind him of the rent, he starts to prevaricate.

**어물다** (be) immature; undeveloped. ¶ 어물어 빠졌다 be utterly immature.

**어물어물** 《모호하게》 equivocally; ambiguously; vaguely; indefinitely. ¶ ~ 말하다 equivocate; prevaricate / 일을 ~하다 scamp 〔skimp〕 the work; do a slapdash 〔sloppy〕 job / 요점을 ~ 흐리다 evade the point; quibble / 태도를 ~하다 do not commit *oneself;* take an irresolute attitude / ~ 넘길 게 아니야, 우리는 확답을 바라고 있어 Don't use such evasive words. We want a definite answer.

**어물쩍** evasively; ambiguously; equivocally. ~하다 evade; dodge; equivocate; prevaricate; pass off; shuffle. ¶ 질문을 ~ 넘기다 turn a question off; evade 〔dodge〕 a question / 일을 ~ 해치우다 finish the work sloppily / 그는 대답을 ~ 피했다 He escaped answering indirectly. / 그는 화제를 바꾸어 핵심을 교묘하게 ~해 버렸다 He changed the topic and skillfully evaded the point.

**어물쩍거리다** mystify; equivocate; prevaricate; quibble; shuffle. ¶ 대답을 ~ equivocate in replying; give a vague answer / 태도를 ~ maintain an uncertain attitude 《toward》 / 어물쩍거리지 말고 똑똑히 대답해라 Don't shuffle, give a clear answer. / 어물쩍거리며 사람을 속이다 take people in with a bit of hocus-pocus.

**어미** ① 《동물의》 a mother animal; a dam (가축의). ¶ ~개〔고양이, 새〕 a mother 〔parent〕 dog 〔cat, bird〕. ② 《어머니의 낮춤말》 a mother.

**어미**(語尾) the ending 《of a word》. ◉ ~변화 inflection; declension: 라틴어는 ~변화가 많다 Latin is a highly inflected language.

**어민**(漁民) fishermen; fishing people; fisherfolk.

**어버이** parents. ¶ ~의 parental / ~다운 parentlike; parental / 친 ~ *one's* real 〔true〕 parents / ~를 공경하다 be respectful towards *one's* parents / ~ 말씀을 따르다 「obey *one's* 〔be obedient to〕 parents / ~를 잃다 loss *one's* parents / ~에게 효도하다 serve *one's* parents devotedly / ~에게 불효하다 be unkind to *one's* parents; ill-treat *one's* parents. ◉ ~날 the Parents Day.

**어벌쩡하다** (be) evasive; cajoling; wheedling; deceitful; tricky; explain away. ¶ 어벌쩡한 대답 an evasive answer / 어벌쩡하여 남의 것을 빼앗다 cajole *a person* out of a thing.

**어법**(語法) (a mode of) expression; usage (of language); wording; phraseology; diction; grammar (문법). ¶ 한국말의 ~ Korean usage 〔grammar〕 / ~에 어긋나다 be solecistic; make a grammar slip. ◉ ~위반 a breach of syntax; a solecism; a slip in grammar.

**어보**(魚譜) an atlas of fish.

**어복**(魚腹) the belly of fish. ¶ ~에 장사지내다 become food for fishes; find a watery grave.

**어부**(漁夫) a fisherman. ¶ ~지리를 얻다 make profit out of two contestants; gain the third party's profit.

**어부바** "up we go!" ~하다 ⇨ 업다.

**어분**(魚粉) fish meal.

**어불성설**(語不成說) lack of logic; illogicality. ¶ ~이다 be illogical 〔unreasonable〕; lack logic; 《*one's* argument》 do not hold water.

**어비**(魚肥) fish manure; fish fertilizer.

**어사**(御史) 『고제도』 a royal emissary; a royal inspector 〔censor〕 (who travels incognito to check on local government).

**어사리**(魚—) fishing with a moored net. ～하다 fish with a moored net.

**어살**(魚—) a (fish) weir; a fish trap; a fishpound.

**어상반하다**(於相半—) be much the same; be nearly alike; be almost equal. ¶ 그와 나는 키가 ～ He is about as tall as I. / 두 물건의 질이 ～ There is not much difference in quality between the two.

**어새**(御璽) the Royal seal; the Privy ｢Seal.

**어색하다**(語塞—) ① 《말이 막히다》｢be stuck for 〔stumble over〕 words; be at a loss for a word; (be) silenced. ② 《겸연쩍다·거북하다》 feel awkward; be 〔feel〕 embarrassed; be ashamed 〔abashed〕; feel 〔be〕 ill at ease. ¶ 여자들하고 같이 있기가 ～ feel ill at ease in the presence of ladies / 어색한 침묵을 지키다 keep awkward 〔strained〕 silence / 어색한 입장에 있다 be in an awkward situation / 사람들 앞에서 연설하기가 어색했다 It was embarrassing to make a speech in public. ③ 《서투르다》 (be) awkward; clumsy; crude; 《부자연스럽다》 (be) unnatural; stiff; constrained. ¶ 어색한 동작 stiff 〔awkward, constrained〕 manners / 어색한 웃음 a forced 〔an artificial〕 smile / 어색한 문장을 쓰다 write in ｢a stiff 〔an awkward〕 style / 일하는 것이 ～ be awkward in doing a thing / 외국 관광객들은 식탁에서 어색한 손놀림으로 젓가락을 사용하고 있었다 The foreign tourists were using chopsticks ｢clumsily 〔with clumsy hands〕 at the table.

**어서** ① 《빨리》 quick(ly); fast; promptly; without delay 〔hesitation〕. ¶ ～ 오너라 Come quick. / ～ 대답해라 Answer promptly. / ～ 일을 해 치웁시다 Let's be quick and get our work done. ② 《부디》 please; kindly; right; without hesitation; by all means. ¶ ～ 들어오십시오 Come right in, please. / ～ 이쪽으로 오시지요 This way, please. / ～ 많이 드시지요 Please help yourself. / ～ 오십시오 Welcome!; 《호객시에》 Walk up!; 《점포에서》 Good morning 〔afternoon, evening〕, sir 〔madam〕. What can ｢I do for you 〔I show you〕?

**-어서** and so; and then; so as to; (go) for; to. ¶ 너무 적어서 나누기가 어렵다 be too little to divide / 이렇게 멀리서 와 주시어서 대단히 고맙습니다 Thank you for coming such a distance. / 이렇게 늦어서 미안합니다 I'm sorry to be so late.

**-어서가** not... that... (but...). ¶ 돈이 없어서가 아닙니다 It is not that 〔because〕 I haven't got the money. / 일이 싫어서가 아니고 일을 감당할 수 없기 때문입니다 Not that I dislike the task, but I am unequal to it.

**-어서도** ① =-어도. ② 《또한》 ¶ 디자인은 물론 품질에 있어서도 우리 제품이 제일이다 Our product comes the first in quality as well as design.

**-어서야** if; even 〔only〕 if; when; even 〔only〕 when; not until. ¶ 인제 나이가 들어서야 only now that I've grown older / 지금 이렇게 늦어서야 어떻게 가나 How can we go when it's so late now? / 밤이 늦어서야 비로소 그가 왔다 He didn't come till late at night.

**어선**(漁船) a fishing boat 〔vessel, craft〕; a fisher boat; 《활어조(活魚槽)를 갖춘》 a smack. ◉ ～단〔대〕 a fishing fleet.

**어설프다** 《성기다》 (be) coarse; rough; loose; 《탐탁찮다》 (be) poor; untidy; slovenly; careless; sloppy; clumsy. ¶ 어설픈 지식 a smattering of 《Latin》; a superficial 〔half〕 knowledge / 일하는 것이 ～ be a sloppy worker / 어설프게 일(을)하다 do a slovenly job.

**어설피** 《성기게》 coarsely; roughly; loosely; 《탐탁찮게》 poorly; in a slovenly 〔sloppy, careless, clumsy〕 way. ¶ 그물을 ～ 뜨다 make a net with large meshes / ～ 지은 집 a poorly built house.

**어세**(語勢) stress 《on a word》; emphasis; (dynamic, stress) accent; a tone 《of voice》. ¶ ～를 높이다 emphasize; lay stress 〔emphasis〕 on 《a word》 / ～를 높여 말하다 speak emphatically.

**어수룩하다** ① 《성질이》 (be) naive; simple; unsophisticated; innocent; unspoiled. ¶ 어수룩한 성격 an unsophisticated 〔unaffected〕 character. ② 《물정에 어둡다》 (be) ignorant 《of》; do not know much about 《the world》. ¶ 어수룩한 사람 a person who ｢does not know 〔has not seen〕 much of the world; a person who is ignorant of the ways of the world / 넌 아주 어수룩하구나 You know nothing of the world.

**어수선하다** ① 《난잡·혼란하다》 be ｢in disorder 〔in confusion, in a muddle, in a mess〕; (be) jumbled; chaotic. ¶ 어수선하게 disorderly; in disorder; in confusion / 어수선한 머리 disheveled 〔unkempt〕 hair / 어수선한 시대 troubled 〔unsettled〕 times / 어수선해지다 fall into disorder 〔confusion〕; get confused / 방이 ~ The room is a shambles 〔in a mess〕. / 테이블을 어수선하게 하지 마라 Don't litter up your table. / 그 당시 나라가 대단히 어수선했다 At that time the country was in turbulent disorder. ② 《산란하다》 (be) distracted; troubled; disturbed; deranged; confused. ¶ 앓는 아이 때문에 그 집안은 매우 ~ The family is much troubled over their sick boy. / 그 소식을 듣고 마음이 어수선했다 My mind was disturbed at the news.

**어순**(語順) 〖문법〗 word order. ¶ ~을 틀리게 하다 make an error in the arrangement of words.

**어스러지다** 《말·풍채가》 become 〔get〕 abnormal 〔queer, eccentric, aberrant, erratic〕; 《어슷하게 되다》 be distorted 〔contorted, crooked〕. ¶ 그 사람은 좀 어스러진 성품이다 He is a queer sort of fellow.

**어스레하다** (be) dusky; dim; gloomy. ¶ 어스레하게 hazily; dimly; indistinctly / 어스레한 빛 《in》 dim 〔feeble, faint〕 light / 어스레한 저녁 a dusky evening / 어스레해지다 become rather dark.

**어스름** 《땅거미》 dusk; 《희미한 빛》 dim 〔faint, feeble〕 light. ~하다 (be) dusky. ¶ ~달 a clouded 〔dusky, hazy, dim〕 moon / ~달밤 a misty moonlit 〔moonlight〕 night; a night with a hazy 〔misty〕 moon.

**어슬렁거리다** stroll 〔ramble〕 about; saunter 〔loiter〕 along; hang 〔hover, linger〕 about 〔around〕; lounge about 〔along, off〕; (take a) prowl; rove 《over》. ¶ 공원을 ~ saunter about a park / 밤에 어슬렁거리며 걷다 prowl (around) at night / 바닷가를 ~ take a stroll on the beach / 수상한 사람 둘이 그 집 부근을 어슬렁거리는 것이 보였다 Two suspicious-looking men were seen prowling about the house.

**어슬렁어슬렁** ¶ ~걷다 stroll 〔ramble〕 about; saunter 〔lounge〕 along; walk at a leisurely pace; prowl; rove.

**어슴새벽** murky 〔early〕 dawn; daybreak. ¶ ~에 towards morning 〔daybreak〕; at peep of dawn / ~부터 일하다 work from early dawn.

**어슴푸레하다** (be) dim; gloomy; faint; dusky; hazy; misty; vague. ⇨ 어렴풋하다. ¶ 어슴푸레한 램프 빛 the dim light of a lamp.

**어슷비슷하다** be much 〔nearly〕 the same; be much of a muchness; be almost similar to; be virtually the same (as); be six of one and half a dozen of the other. ¶ 한국과 유타 주는 크기가 ~ Korea is about the same size as Utah. / 두 모자가 다 ~ You can hardly tell the two hats apart. / 두 사람의 처지가 ~ There is little to choose between the two persons in their circumstances. / 두 사람의 경력은 ~ There is a parallel point in their careers.

**어슷하다** (be) slant; oblique; diagonal. ¶ 어슷하게 aslant; slantwise; obliquely; diagonally on the slant / 어슷하게 자르다 cut diagonally / 어슷하게 나아가다 advance obliquely.

**어시장**(魚市場) a fish market.

**어안**(魚眼) ¶ ~ 렌즈 a fisheye lens / ~석 a fisheye stone.

**어안이 벙벙하다** (be) dumbfounded; dazed; [서술적] be struck dumb; be bowled over. ¶ 어안이 벙벙하여 in blank 〔mute〕 amazement; dumbfounded; in speechless wonder; with a vacant look of astonishment / 어안이 벙벙해서 말도 못 하다 be (struck) dumb with amazement; stare in wonder / 어안이 벙벙해서 서로 얼굴만 쳐다보았다 We all gazed at each other in blank dismay. / 그 대답에 어안이 벙벙했다 I was dumbfounded by 〔at〕 the answer.

**-어야** ① 《당연·조건》 only to the extent that... can 〔do〕 *one*...; if you don't... you can't...; it's by *do*ing that you...; you have to... in order to...; only when 〔if〕 you... do you.... ¶ 그것을 했어야 했다 You should have 〔ought to have〕 done it. / 그렇게 하셔야 해요 That's what you have (got) to do. / 그렇게 하셨어야 했어요 That's what you should have done. / 만 원이 있어야 들어간다 You have to have ten thousand won to get in. / 돈이 있어야 미국에 간다 It takes money to go to America.

② 《제 아무리 …해도》 however (much) *one* may 〔might〕; to whatever extent. ¶ 네가 먹어야 얼마나 먹겠니 You can't possibly eat very much. / 날아야 파리요 뛰어야 벼룩이다 You can fly no farther than a fly and jump no higher than a flea.

**-어야지** 《놀람·실망》 must; don't-you=

see. ¶ 힘이 있어야지 I would have to have the strength. But I haven't got the strength! / 음식을 그만저만 먹어야지 You've got to eat reasonably, you know. *or* How can I afford to feed such a glutton!

**어어** 《의외의 말》 Oh-oh; Oh dear!; Why! ¶ ~ 이상하다, 틀림없이 여기다 두었는데 Why, that's strange. I'm sure I put it here.

**어언간**(於焉間) before *one* is aware of the lapse of time; without *one's* knowledge; all too soon. ¶ ~ 세월이 흘렀다 Years came and out. / ~ 3년이 지났다 So three years glided away. / 겨울 방학도 ~ 지나가 버렸다 The winter vacation has passed all too soon.

**어업**(漁業) fishery; the fishing industry. ¶ 연안〔원양〕 ~ coastal 〔deep-sea〕 fishery / ~에 종사하다 be engaged in fishery. ⇨ 수산(水産).

◉ ~권 fishery 〔fishing〕 rights. ~수역 fishing ground 〔zone, area〕. ~ 전관수역 an exclusive fishing zone: fishing waters; a fishing zone: 200해리 ~ 전관수역 《Korea's》 200-mile fishing zone; (the area within) 《Canada's》 200=mile fishing limits. ~협정 a fisheries agreement: 한일 ~협정 the Korean=Japanese Fisheries Agreement.

**어여차** 《힘을 합하는 소리》 Yo-ho! (Yo) heave-ho! ¶ ~ 어여차 짐을 나르다 carry a load with the cry of heave-ho.

**어연번듯하다** (be) honorable; respectable; decent; good. ⇨ 어엿하다.

**어엿하다** (be) respectable; decent; honorable; good. ¶ 어엿하게 stately; in a dignified manner / 어엿한 사람〔집안〕 a respectable person 〔family〕 / 어엿한 풍채 a stately appearance / 어엿한 신사 an honorable 〔a decent〕 gentleman / 그의 행동은 ~ His conduct is above reproach. / 그는 이제 어엿한 가장이다 He is now a full-fledged head of his own house.

**어옹**(漁翁) an old fisherman.

**어용**(御用) official business; government service. ¶ 현 노조를 경영자측의 ~ 단체로 몰아붙이다 whack existing labor unions for being patronized by 〔for being sycophant to〕 the management side. ◉ ~기자 a journalist in government pay. ~신문 a ministerial paper; a government mouthpiece; the kept press. ~조합 a company 〔kept〕 union. ~학자 a government patronized scholar; a scholar kept by the government.

**어우러지다** get put 〔joined〕 together; harmonize; unite. ¶ 뜰에는 온갖 꽃이 어우러져 피어 있다 The garden is bright with all sorts of flowers blooming. / 나는 어린이들과 어우러져 놀이를 했다 I joined in the children's game.

**어우르다** put together; unite; combine; join together. ¶ 힘을 어울러서 by united effort; in cooperation 《with》 / 힘을 ~ join forces 《with》; unite 《our》 efforts; cooperate 《with》 / 각 파를 어울러서 하나의 당을 만들다 combine the factions into a party.

**어울리다** ① 《한데 섞이다》 join; mix with; mingle with. ¶ 한데 ~ join in a group; get together / 외국 사람과 ~ mix with foreigners / 어린아이와 어울려 놀다 join the children at play / 나쁜 아이들과 어울려 돌아다니다 loaf around in the company of a group of bad boys / 그는 남과 어울리지 않는다 He doesn't mix with others. *or* He keeps to himself.

② 《조화되다》 become; befit; be suitable 《for》; match well; suit 《with》; be in keeping 《with》; go 《with》; 《적절하다》 be proper 〔adequate〕; be appropriate. ¶ 어울리지 않는 unsuitable 《for》; unbecoming 《to, of, for》; unworthy 《of》; ill-matched; improper 《for》; inappropriate 《to》 / 어울리지 않게 큰 disproportionately large / 잘 어울리는〔어울리지 않는〕 부부 a well-matched 〔an ill-matched〕 couple / 학자로서 어울리지 않는 말 words unbecoming to a scholar / 옷과 잘 어울리는 모자 a hat which goes well with *one's* suit / 그 경우에 어울리는 연설 a speech appropriate to the occasion / 그 이름에 어울리는 시인 a poet worthy of the name / (옷 등이) 아무에게 ~ 〔어울리지 않다〕 become 〔do not become〕 *a person*; suit well 〔ill〕 on *a person* / 이 갈색 양복에 잘 어울리는 넥타이를 사고 싶다 I want to get a tie to go (well) with this brown suit. / 이 모자가 나에게 어울립니까 Does this hat suit 〔fit〕 me? / 그녀는 그 파티에 잘 어울리는 옷을 입고 있다 She is suitably dressed for the party. / 그 옷은 너한테 어울린다 That dress looks nice on you. / 양탄자와 커튼이 잘 어울린다 The carpet and curtain are a good match. / 그것은 그에게 어울리는 일이다 It is the kind of job that suits him perfectly. / 그런 일

은 내게 어울리지 않는다 I am not fit for such work. *or* Such work is not in my line. / 저 청년은 우리 딸에겐 어울리지 않는다 That young man is not a good match for our daughter. / 그 그림은 방에 어울리지 않는다 The picture does not suit the room. / 선생 노릇은 너한테 어울리지 않는 것 같다 Your being a teacher doesn't seem right to me somehow. / 그런 일을 하다니 너에게 어울리지 않는다 It's not like you to do a thing like that.

**어웅하다** (be) sunken; hollow-looking. ¶ 어웅한 눈 hollow eyes / 땅에 구멍이 어웅하게 뚫리었다 A big hole is gaping in the ground.

**어원**(語源) 〖언어〗 the derivation 〔origin〕 of a word; etymology. ¶ ~(상)의 etymological / ~을 설명하다 explain the origin《of a word》/ ~을 조사하다 trace a word to its origin; study the etymology《of》/ 말을 ~적으로 연구하다 make an etymological study of words / 이 말의 ~은 미상이다 The origin of the word is unknown. / 이 말들은 ~이 같다 These words have the same pedigree 〔origin〕.
◉ ~사전 an etymological dictionary. ~학 etymology: ~학자 an etymologist.

**어유**(魚油) fish oil.

**어육**(魚肉) 《생선의 고기》 fish (meat); 《생선과 짐승의 고기》 fish and meat. ¶ ~을 많이 먹다 eat much fish (meat).

**어음** 〖경제〗 a bill; a draft; a note. ¶ 기한부 ~ a term bill; usance (bill) / 단독 ~ a sole bill / 기업〔상업〕 ~ a commercial paper (생략 CP) / 부도 ~ a dishonored bill 〔draft〕 / 약속 ~ a promissory note / 지급〔수취〕 ~ a bill payable 〔receivable〕 / ~을 발행하다 draw a bill《for 2,000,000 won on *a person*》; give a promissory note (약속어음을) / ~으로 지급하다 pay by draft / ~을 인수〔거절〕하다 accept 〔repudiate〕 a bill / ~을 현금으로 바꾸다 cash a bill; have a bill cashed / ~을 할인하다 discount a bill; get a bill discounted / ~을 결제하다〔부도내다〕 honor 〔dishonor〕 a bill / ~이 만기가 되다 the bill falls due / ~을 개서하다 renew a bill / 이 ~은 30일간 유효하다 This bill has thirty days to run. / 내달 지급될 ~을 받았다 I received a draft payable next month.
◉ ~계원 a note-teller; a bill clerk. ~교환 bill clearing; (bill) clearance: ~교환고 the total of cleared bills; clearings / ~교환소 a clearing house. ~발행 drawing a bill: ~발행인 the drawer (of a bill 〔draft〕). ~부도 dishonor; nonpayment: ~부도율 the ratio of dishonored bills. ~수취인 the payee (of a bill). ~유통기간 the currency of a bill. ~인수 bill acceptance: ~인수인 an acceptor of a bill. ~재할인 a rediscount. ~중개인 a bill broker. ~할인 a discount (on a bill): ~할인율 a discount rate.

**어의**(語義) the meaning of a word. ¶ 일반적인 ~로는 in the common acceptation of the word; in the sense in which the word is generally understood / ~를 분명히 하다 define 〔clarify the meaning of〕 a word.

**어의**(御醫) the royal physician.

**어이**[1] 《어찌》 why; how. ⇨ 어찌. ¶ ~ 알았으리오, 그 사람이 바로 그가 찾고 있던 그의 아저씨인 줄을 How should we know that the man was his very uncle he was looking for. / 당신이 모르는데 내가 ~ 알겠소 How should I know if you do not?

**어이**[2] 《부를 때》 Hello!; Hullo! 《영》; Hey! ¶ ~ 기다려 Hey, wait!

**어이구** Oh!; Ouch! ⇨ 아이고(머니).

**어이어이** 《울 때》 wailing of mourners; Alas!; Woe! ¶ ~ 울다 cry bitterly; cry *one's* heart out.

**어이없다** be struck dumb; (be) dumbfounded; exorbitant; extravagant; preposterous; absurd; monstrous. ¶ 어이없는 거짓말 a whopping lie / 어이없는 말을 하다 make absurd remarks; talk wild / 어이없이 지다 be beaten too easily; suffer a disappointing defeat / 어이없이 계략에 빠졌다 fall an easy victim to a scheme / 어이없어 서로 얼굴만 쳐다 볼 뿐이었다 We all gazed at each other in blank dismay.

**어이쿠** [감탄사] Oh!; Ouch!

**어장**(漁場) a fishing ground 〔spot, place〕; a fishery. ¶ 근해〔원해〕 ~ an inshore 〔offshore〕 fishery.

**어적거리다** munch; crunch; champ.

**어적어적** with a munching 〔crunching〕. ¶ 무를 ~ 씹다 munch (at) a radish.

**어전**(御前) the Royal presence. ¶ ~에서 in the presence of the King / ~에 나가다〔에서 물러나다〕 come into 〔leave〕 the Royal presence.
◉ ~회의 a council in the Royal presence; the Privy Council.

**어정거리다** walk leisurely along; stroll; ramble; saunter. ¶ 공원을 ~ saunter about a park / 이 밤중에 어디를 어정거리고 있었나 Where have you been hanging 〔fooling〕 around at this time of night? 「py.

**어정뜨다** (be) negligent; careless; slop-

**어정뱅이** ① 《갑자기 잘된 사람》 an upstart; a parvenu; 《구어》 a jumped-up person. ② 《어정대는 사람》 a negligent 〔sloppy, lackadaisical〕 person; a person who never learns anything very well.

**어정버정** walking leisurely; sauntering; rambling. ¶ ~걷다, ~하다 stroll; ramble; saunter / ~하지 말고 어서 가거라 What are you all loitering about over there for? Be off this moment.

**어정쩡하다** (be) suspect; suspicious; questionable; dubious; problematic; unlikely; 《애매하다》 (be) ambiguous; evasive. ¶ 어정쩡한 대답 noncommittal 〔an evasive〕 answer / 어정쩡한 기분으로 with mixed feelings; in a hesitating mind; halfheartedly / 어정쩡한 태도를 취하다 take an equivocal attitude.

**어제** yesterday. ¶ ~아침 yesterday morning / ~신문 yesterday's newspaper / ~부터 병이 났다 I have been sick since yesterday. / 한국을 떠난 것이 ~ 같다 It seems only yesterday since I left Korea. / 그것은 마치 ~ 일처럼 기억에 생생하다 I sticks in my mind as though it were yesterday. / 그를 만난 것은 바로 ~다 It was only yesterday that I met him. / 그것은 ~ 오늘의 일이 아니다 That isn't something that happened yesterday. *or* That didn't just happen recently, you know.

**어조**(語調) the tone of the voice; an accent; a note; a strain. ¶ 진지한〔흥분한〕 ~로 in an earnest 〔an excited〕 tone / 딱딱한 ~로 in a very formal 〔bookish, pedantic〕 way (of expression) / 슬픈 ~로 in a sad tone / ~를 높이다 tone up / ~를 낮추다 tone down; soften *one's* voice; speak in a gentle voice / ~를 부드럽게 하다 soften *one's* voice; modify *one's* tone; tone down / 이 문장은 ~가 좋다 This sentence is euphonic. / 그는 아주 진지한 ~로 말했다 His tone was very earnest. / 그녀는 슬픈 ~로 이야기했다 She spoke in a sad tone.

**어조사**(語助辭) 〖언어〗 a particle (in classical Chinese). 「Pisces.

**어족**(魚族) fishes; the finny tribe; the

**어족**(語族) 〖언어〗 a family of languages; a language 〔linguistic〕 family. ¶ 우랄 알타이 ~ the Ural-Altaic (family of) languages / 인도 유럽 ~ the Indo-European languages.

**어좌**(御座) 《옥좌》 the King's chair; 《왕위》 the royal throne.

**어줍다** 《언어·동작이》 (be) vague; dubious; irresolute; half-hearted; indecisive; lukewarm; noncommittal; 《솜씨가》 (be) unskillful; clumsy; awkward. ¶ 어줍은 사람 an indecisive character; an irresolute person / 어줍은 대답 a noncommittal reply; a vague reply / 바느질 솜씨가 ~ be clumsy with *one's* sewing.

**어중간하다**(於中間—) 《중간》 be about halfway 〔midway〕; half-finished; 《엉거주춤》 (be) indecisive; irresolute; noncommittal. ¶ 어중간하게 half; partially / 어중간한 태도 a lukewarm attitude / 일을 어중간히 하다 do by halves; leave something half-done / 어중간히 그만두려거든 처음부터 하지 마라 You leave it undone than leave it half=done 〔halfway〕.

**어중되다**(於中—) be either too small 〔little, short〕 or too big 〔much, long〕; be unsuitable either way; be insufficient either way; be not fit.

**어중이떠중이** all sorts and conditions of men; (anybody and) everybody; every Tom, Dick, and Harry; the ruck; the rabble. ¶ ~ 다 미국식만 따른다 Everybody goes after stateside fashion. / 모임에는 ~ 다 몰려 왔다 All sorts of people swarmed to the meeting.

**어지간하다** (be) considerable; tolerable; passable; quite. ¶ 어지간한 미인 quite a beauty / 어지간한 수입 a handsome income / 어지간한 재산 a tidy 〔snug〕 fortune / 어지간한 돈 a considerable sum of money / 오늘은 더위가 ~ It is quite warm today. / 그의 영어는 ~ His English is fairly good.

**어지간히** considerably; fairly; passably; tolerably; quite. ¶ ~ 지내다 be comfortably 〔fairly well〕 off; make a decent living / ~ 춥다 be quite cold / 그는 불어를 ~ 잘 한다 He speaks French pretty well. / 여기서 ~ 멀다 It is a good distance from here. / 밤도 ~ 깊었다 The night was fairly advanced. / 그녀는 테니스도 ~ 한다 She is not half bad at tennis. / 그 일에 관해서 ~ 생각해 보았다 I have given considerable thought to the matter.

**어지러뜨리다** 《여기저기》 scatter about; 《어수선하게》 put 《a room》 in disorder 〔confusion〕; disarrange. ¶ 방을 ~ leave a room untidy 〔in disorder〕 / 방안에 종잇조각을 ~ litter a room with scraps of paper.

**어지러이** dizzily; giddily; 《어수선하게》 disorderly; in disorder; in a mess.

**어지럼** dizziness; giddiness; the whirl of the brain; 〚의학〛 vertigo (*pl.* ~(e)s). ¶ ~을 타다 be subject to dizziness, feel 〔get〕 dizzy.

**어지럽다** ① 《눈·정신이》 (be) dizzy; feel giddy; *one's* brain reels; *one's* head swims 〔eyes swim〕. ¶ 어지러울 정도의 높이〔속도〕 a dizzying height 〔speed〕 / 어지럽게 변천하는 세상 the giddy whirl of modern life; the bustling world / 자주 ~ have frequent dizzy spells; be subject to attacks of vertigo / 안 하던 운동으로 어지러웠다 I felt giddy from the unaccustomed exercise.
② 《어수선하다》 be in disorder; (be) disarranged; disturbed; troubled; chaotic. ¶ 어지러운 방 a disorderly room / 어지러운 시대 wild 〔troubled, stormy〕 times / 방바닥에는 책이나 서류들이 어지럽게 흩어져 있었다 Floor was littered all over with books and papers. *or* Books and papers were lying (scattered) about the floor.

**어지럽히다** 《난잡히 하다》 put out of orders; put 〔throw〕 into disorder 〔confusion〕; disarrange; scatter (about) (어지르다); 《교란》 disturb 《peace》; agitate 《the world》; corrupt 《public morals》; derange 〔distract〕 《*one's* mind》. ¶ 가정의 화목을 ~ disturb *one's* domestic peace / 경제 질서를 어지럽히는 불법 사업 활동 unlawful business activities disrupting the economic order.

**어지르다** disarrange; break up; scatter about; litter 《a room with scraps of paper》; put 《a room》 in disorder 〔out of order〕. ¶ 장난감으로 방을 ~ litter a room with toys / 어질러 놓다 leave 《*things*》 lying about / 그는 방을 어질러 놓았다 He left the room in disorder. / 매일 어린애가 방을 어지른다 A child tracks up the room everyday. / 방을 어지른 채 그대로 두면 안 된다 Don't leave your room untidy 〔in a mess〕. / 부엌을 어질러 놓지 마라 Don't litter up the kitchen. / 어지르지 마시오 《게시》 No litter.

**어진**(御眞) the portrait of a king.

**어질다** (be) gentle; kindhearted; considerate; wise; benevolent. ¶ 어진 마음 a compassionate heart; benevolence / 어진 어머니〔사람〕 a gentle mother 〔person〕 / 어진 임금 a benevolent ruler; a gracious lord.

**어질어질** giddily; dizzily; in a whirl. ~하다 feel dizzy 〔giddy〕. ¶ 머리가 ~하다 *one's* head swims; feel dizzy / 수면 부족 때문인지 ~하다 My head swims perhaps from lack of sleep.

**어째** ① 《왜》 why; for what reason; how is it that. ¶ ~서냐 하면 because; for; The reason is... / ~ 그러냐 How so? / ~ 왔느냐 How is that you are here? / 그는 ~ 그 모양이야 How can he be like that? / ~ 그런지 모르겠다 I cannot tell you why. / 그가 ~ 늦는지 모르겠다 I wonder why he is late. / ~ 나를 쳐다보느냐 What are you looking at me for? / ~ 그렇게 생각하느냐 Why do you think so? *or* What makes you think so? / ~ 웃느냐 What makes you laugh? / 아기가 ~ 우느냐 What makes the baby cry?
② 《웬일인지》 somehow; without knowing why; in some way; for some reasons or other; vaguely. ¶ ~ 울고 싶은 마음이다 Somehow I feel like crying.

**어쨌든(지)** 《하여튼·어떻든》 anyhow; anyway; in any case 〔event〕; at any rate; at all events; somehow or other. ¶ 그것은 ~ be that as it may; you may well say so, but...; leaving 〔setting〕 it aside; apart from the matter; meanwhile / ~ 나는 여기 머물러 있겠다 I will stay here at any rate. / 비가 올지도 모르지만 ~ 나가봐야겠다 It may rain, but anyhow I shall go out. / ~ 그를 한 시간 더 기다려 봅시다 At any rate, let's wait for him another hour. / ~ 그는 죄를 면할 수 없다 He is guilty, one way or the other. / ~ 저 친구는 좋은 사람이다 Altogether he is a very nice fellow. / 돈이야 ~ 그는 훌륭한 남편감이다 Setting money aside, he will make a suitable husband. / 그가 어느 방향으로 갔는지 모르나, ~ 이미 돌아갔을 것이다 I don't know which way he went, but in any case it is time he went back.

**어쩌다(가)** ① 《우연히》 by chance; by accident; casually; unexpectedly; by a freak of chance. ¶ ~ 손가락을 베다 cut *one's* finger by accident / 나는 ~ 그의 집 옆을 지났다 I happened to pass by his house. / ~ 그를 길에서 만났다 I met him by accident on the street. / ~ 두 사람은 같은 열차를 탔다 As it happened [chanced], they took the same train. / 되는 대로 쓴 답안이 ~ 맞았다 The answer I wrote at random turned out to be right.

② 《가끔》 once in a while; occasionally; sometimes; at times. ¶ ~ 오는 손님 a casual visitor / ~ 있는 일 a rare occurrence [instance] / ~ 술을 마시다 take a drink once in a while / 그는 ~ 놀러 온다 He comes and sees us once in a while. / 손님은 ~ 있을 뿐이다 We rarely have visitors. / ~ 오는 때도 있지만 그는 좀처럼 오지 않는다 He seldom comes, if ever. / ~ 그를 찾아갔는데 그는 집에 없었다 I could not find him at house, a rare thing as it is to make a call on him. / 누구라도 ~ 잘못하는 수가 있다 All men are liable to err.

**어쩌면** ① [감탄사적] how; what. ¶ ~ 이렇게 추울까 How cold it is! / ~ 새색시가 그렇게 예쁠까 How beautiful the bride is! / ~ 저렇게 뻔뻔할까 What an impudence! / ~ 사람이 저럴까 How can he be like that?

② 《아마》 possibly; maybe; by some possibility; perhaps. ¶ ~ 내일 아침에 못 갈는지도 모르겠다 It may happen that I shall not come tomorrow morning. / ~ 그럴는지도 모르지 It may perhaps be so. / ~ 그는 성공할는지도 모른다 He may possibly succeed. *or* 《가능성 농후》 Probably he will succeed. / ~ 그가 옳을지도 모른다 He is perhaps [probably] right. *or* He may be right. *or* Maybe he is right. / ~ 그는 살아 돌아올는지 모른다 There is a chance that he may come home alive.

**어쩐지** ① 《웬일인지》 without knowing why; for some reason or other; somehow or other; somewhat. ¶ ~ 즐겁다 have a vague feeling of joy / ~ 슬프다 Somehow I feel sad. / 저 사람은 ~ 무섭다 I have a vague [an uncountable] fear of him. *or* I fear him without knowing why. / ~ 울고 싶은 기분이다 Somehow I feel like crying. / ~ 중대한 일이 일어날 것만 같다 Something tells me [I have a presentiment] that a serious matter would happen. / ~ 그가 처음부터 의심스러웠다 I don't know why but somehow I suspected him from the first. / ~ 그 사람은 믿을 수가 없다 Somehow I can't trust him.

② 《왜 그런지》 so that's why; no wonder. ¶ ~ 기쁜 얼굴을 하고 있더라 That explains his happy look. / ~ 그녀가 오전 내내 무척 좋아하더라 No wonder that she was the happiest girl all that long morning. / ~ 네가 그를 변호하더라 No wonder you spoke in favor of him. / 창이 열려 있었구나 — ~ 춥더라 The window was left open — so that's why I've felt cold.

**어쩔수없다** cannot help 《it》; 《it》 cannot be helped; cannot choose but 《*do*》; 《피할 수 없다》 be inevitable [unavoidable]. ¶ 어쩔 수 없는 사정 unavoidable circumstances / 어쩔 수 없는 일 what cannot be helped [avoided]; an unavoidable [inescapable] thing / 어쩔 수 없다고 단념하다 abide by the inevitable; resign *oneself* to fate / 그것은 어쩔 수 없는 일이다 It can't be helped.

**어쭙지않다** (be) pert; perky; fresh; frisky; conceited; condescending. ¶ 어쭙지않게 말하다 talk fresh / 어쭙지않게 그가 남을 설교하다니 I am tickled at the idea of his preaching to others.

**어찌** ① 《왜》 why; for what reason. ¶ ~ 늦었느냐 Why were you late? / ~ 된 일이냐 What is the matter (with you)? (★ What is the matter?는 일상적으로 널리 쓰이는 데 대하여 What is the matter with you?는 상대편이 아프다거나 슬퍼하거나 화내고 있을 경우에 그 까닭을 묻는 데 쓰는 말임) / ~ 왔느냐 How is it that you are here? / ~ 그런 일을 했느냐 What did you do that for? / ~ 사람이 그러냐 How can he be like that?

② 《어떻게》 how; in what way; by what means. ¶ ~ 할 수 없는 경우엔 at a pinch; in case of emergency / 그는 ~ 되었을까 What has become of him? / ~ 해야 좋을지 모르겠다 I don't know what to do. / 그녀는 ~ 할 바를 모르고 있었다 She was at her wits' end. / ~ 살아 돌아오기를 기약하겠소 How should I expect to come back alive? / ~해서 일이 이렇게 되었느냐 How have things come to such a pass?

③ ⇨ 어찌나.

**어찌나** how; what; too; so; very; quite. ¶ ~ 기쁜지 in (the excess of) *one's* joy; be so glad that... / ~ 슬픈지 in *one's* grief; in a passion of grief / 그녀가 ~ 예쁘던지 She was such a beautiful lady. / 오늘은 날이 ~ 더운지 It is such a hot day today! / 이 책은 내가 읽기에 ~ 어려운지 This book is too difficult for me to read. / ~ 우스운지 한동안 대답을 못 했다 I could not answer him at all for a while, I was laughing so.

어찔하다 (be) dizzy; giddy; have vertigo. ⇨ 아찔하다.

어차피(於此彼) anyway; anyhow; at any rate; in any case; 《결국》 after all; 《꼭》 at all. ¶ ~ 언젠가 죽을 몸이다 We shall all die some day, anyhow. / ~ 돈을 갚아야 한다 You have to pay the money back, one way or another. / ~ 그것은 해야 한다 I must 〔am bound to〕 do it anyhow. / ~ 해야 한다면 잘 해라 If you do it at all, do it well. / ~ 늦을 바에야 내일 가도록 합시다 Let's go tomorrow if we're going to be late anyway. / ~ 헤어질 바엔 기분 좋게 헤어지자 Let's part friends, if we must part. / ~ 살아날 가망이 없다면 그가 좋아하는 것을 먹도록 해 주자 Let him eat what he likes, if there is no hope for his life 〔recovery〕.

어처구니없다 be taken aback; (be) dumbfounded; egregious; preposterous; absurd; monstrous; amazing. ¶ 어처구니없는 값 an unreasonable 〔an absurd, a staggering〕 price / 어처구니없는 친구 a horrible 〔disgusting〕 fellow / 어처구니없는 거짓말 an egregious lie / 어처구니없어 말문이 막히다 be speechless with amazement; be dumbfounded 《at, by》.

어초(漁礁) 《build》 a fish-breeding ground 〔reef〕; a breeding ground 〔reef〕 for fish.

어촌(漁村) a fishing village 〔hamlet〕; a sea village.

어치 〖조류〗 a jay.

-어치 worth. ¶ 백만 원어치의 상품 a million won's worth of goods / 눈치라고는 한푼어치도 없다 haven't a penny's worth of sense.

어탁(魚拓) a fish print; an ink rubbing of a fish.

어투(語套) the way *one* talks; *one's* way of talking. ⇨ 말투.

어퍼컷 〖권투〗 an uppercut. ¶ ~을 먹이다 deal 〔land〕 《*a person*》 an uppercut; deliver an uppercut 《to the jaw》.

어폐(語弊) a faulty 〔misleading〕 expression; defects in expression. ¶ ~가 있다 be misleading; be liable to be misunderstood / …라고 말하면 ~가 있을지 모르지만 I wonder if I am right in saying…; I doubt the propriety of the word, but….

어포(魚脯) dried slices of fish seasoned with spices.

어프로치 《접근》 approach; 《길·입문》 an approach.

어필 《호소·항의》 an appeal. ~하다 appeal 《to the masses》. ¶ 섹스 ~ sex appeal / 심판의 판정에 ~하다 make appeal to the referee's decision.

어필(御筆) His Majesty's autograph.

어하다 indulge; spoil; pamper; 《구어》 mollycoddle. ¶ 아이를 너무 어해서 기르다 bring up a child indulgently.

어학(語學) language study; philology; 《언어학》 linguistics. ¶ ~의 linguistic / ~의 천재 a born linguist / ~에〔의〕 재능이 있다〔없다〕 have considerable 〔no〕 linguistic talent; have an 〔no〕 aptitude for (foreign) languages / ~을 잘 하다 be proficient in languages; be a good 〔clever〕 linguist.
◉ ~교사 a language teacher. ~교육 language teaching 〔education〕. ~능력 language ability. ~실습실 a language laboratory. ~자 a linguist; a philologist. ~지식 linguistic knowledge.

어항(魚缸) a fish basin; 《유리의》 a fish bowl 〔globe (둥근)〕; an aquarium (큰 것).

어항(漁港) a fishing port.

어허 《문득 깨달았을 때》 Why!; Oh ! ¶ ~ 큰일났군 Good Heavens ! *or* Gosh ! / ~ 참 그렇군 Why, to be sure ! *or* Oh, I see !

어험 Hem !; Ahem !; Hum hum !. ¶ ~하고 기침을 하다 hem; clear *one's* throat.

어혈(瘀血) 〖한의〗 extravasated blood.

어형(語形) 〖언어〗 a word form; the form of a word. ◉ ~론 〖문법〗 accidence. ~변화 〖문법〗 inflection. ~변화표 〖문법〗 a paradigm.

어획(漁獲) fishery; 《어획고》 a 《big》 haul; a 《good》 catch. ¶ ~이 많다 get 〔make〕 a good catch; the catches are large / 이 앞바다에서는 고등어의 ~이 많다 Mackerels are caught in large quantities off this coast. ◉ ~고〔량〕 a haul 〔catch〕 《of fish》. ~기 fishing season. ~물 fish; catch. ~할당량 fishing 〔catch〕 quota: 연어 ~할당량 《Korea's》 salmon catch quota.

어휘(語彙) a vocabulary; a glossary; *one's* stock of words; lexicon (특정 작가 등의). ¶ 풍부한 ~ an abundant 〔extensive〕 vocabulary; a copious vocabulary / ~가 풍부〔빈약〕하다 have a rich 〔poor〕 vocabulary / ~를 풍부하게 하다 enrich 〔enlarge〕 *one's* vocabulary / 이 사전은 ~가 많다 This dictionary includes an extensive vocabulary. / 어떠한 사전도 ~ 전부를 수록할 수는 없다 No dictionary could list the whole vocabulary of a language. ◉ ~론 lexicology. ~목록 a lexicon. ~집 a word-book; a vocabulary. ~통계 lexical 〔vocabulary〕 statistics. ~항목 a lexical item.

**억**(億) one hundred million. ¶ 10억 a billion 《미》; a thousand million 《영》.

**억겁**(億劫) 〖불교〗 eternity; perpetuity.

**억누르다** press 〔hold〕 down; force down; 《압박》 oppress; 《진압·억압》 suppress 《the rebellion》; put down; repress; 《억제》 restrain; control; check; master; keep down.
¶ 억누를 수 없는 uncontrollable; irrepressible; irresistible / 노염을 ~ master 〔bottle up〕 *one's* anger / 눈물을 ~ repress 〔keep back〕 *one's* tears / 웃음을 ~ stifle a laugh; repress a smile / 감정을 ~ restrain *one's* feelings; stifle 〔suppress〕 *one's* emotions / 언론의 자유를 ~ suppress freedom of speech / 치미는 분노를 억눌렀다 I suppressed my rising passion. / 그는 자존심을 억누르고 아무 말도 하지 않았다 He pocketed his pride and said nothing.

**억눌리다** get forced down; be overpowered; be repressed.

**억단**(臆斷) a conjecture; guesswork; a (random) guess. ~하다 guess; make a (random) guess; hazard a conjecture.

**억류**(抑留) detention; internment. ~하다 detain; intern; keep 《*a person*》 「by force 〔in custody〕. ¶ ~된 배 an interned ship / ~중의〔인〕 under detention / ~되다 be detained; go into internment / 그녀는 간첩 혐의로 ~되어 있다 She is being held on spy charges. / 경찰은 더 심문하기 위해 그를 ~했다 The police detained the man to make further inquiries. ◉ ~소 a detention 〔a concentration, an internment〕 camp. ~어부 a detained fisherman. ~자(者) a detainee; a detained person; an internee.

**억만**(億萬) 《억》 one 〔a〕 hundred million; 《무수함》 myriads; countless numbers. ◉ ~금 millions of money; countless money. ~년 countless years. ~장자 a billionaire; a multimillionaire. ~창생 myriad(s) of people.

**억병** a large drinking capacity. ¶ ~으로 마시다 drink heavily 〔hard〕 / ~으로 취해 있다 be beastly 〔dead〕 drunk.

**억보** a headstrong person; a bullhead; a bigot; a stubborn person.

**억새** 〖식물〗 a eulalia. ◉ ~반지기 a firewood mixture largely consisting of eulalia.

**억설**(臆說) 《억측의 말》 a notion without foundation; a conjecture; a surmise; 《가정》 an assumption; a hypothesis. ¶ 그 일에 관하여 갖가지 ~이 난무했다 Various conjectures about the matter were flying about.

**억세다** ① 《체격·마음이》 (be) strong; tough; firm; stout; tenacious; persistent; pushy; unyielding; resolute; 《근육이》 (be) sinewy; brawny. ¶ 억세게 stubbornly; doggedly; stiffly; stoutly; unbendingly / 마음이 억센 사람 a man of strong heart; a hardheaded person / 손아귀 힘이 ~ have a strong grip / 억세게 밀고 나가는 수밖에 없다 There is no other way than push forward.
② 《뻣뻣하다》 (be) tough; hard; stiff. ¶ 억센 머리털 wiry hair / 억센 수염 a tough beard / 이 배추는 ~ This is a tough cabbage.

**억수** a pouring 〔driving, heavy〕 rain; a downpour (of rain). ¶ ~같이 쏟아지는 비 a rain falling in sheets / 비가 ~같이 쏟아진다 It's raining in torrents. *or* It rains a solid sheet. *or* It rains cats and dogs. / 비가 오기만 하면 으레 ~로 퍼붓는다 It never rains but it pours. ◉ ~장마(가 들다) a steady heavy rain (sets in).

**억압**(抑壓) suppression; oppression; repression; a check. ~하다 suppress; oppress; hold down; repress; check; restrain. ¶ ~된 감정 pent-up feelings / 부당한 ~을 가하다 bring undue pressure upon 《*a person*》 / 언론의 자유를 ~하다 repress freedom of speech / ~된 욕망이 이상한 행동의 원인이 될 경우가 있다 It sometimes happens that suppressed desires lead people into abnormal behavior.

**억양**(抑揚) 〖언어〗 intonation; modulation; (pitch) accent; inflection (of the voice). ¶ ~ 있는 modulated; intoned / ~ 없는 목소리 a monotonous voice / ~을 붙여서 with a certain intonation / ~을 붙이다 modulate; intone; intonate / 의문문은 마지막에 ~이 올라간다 Questions end on a rising intonation.
◉ ~부호 the circumflex.

**억울하다**(抑鬱—) feel pent-up 〔mistreated, victimized]; suffer unfairness. ¶ 억울하게 under a false accusation; on a false charge / 억울한 조처 unfair treatment / 억울한 죄로 on a false charge; under a false accusation / 억울한 죄를 씌우다 charge 《*a person*》 falsely 《with》 / 억울한 죄를 쓰다 be falsely charged 《with》; be falsely accused 《of》 / 억울한 책망을 듣다 get an undeserved scolding / 아무를 억울하게 하다 give *a person* a feeling of being mistreated; give *a person* cause for grievance / 억울해 죽겠다 I am mortified at being mistreated. / 그렇게 말하면 내가 억울합니다 You are being unfair to me when you say that. / 억울한 마음을 참을 수 없었다 I couldn't get over the feeling of being mistreated. / 억울한 사정이 있어 왔습니다 I came to see you to talk about my grievance.

**억제**(抑制) control; restraint; suppression; holdback; constraint; 〖심리〗 (an) inhibition. ～하다 control; repress; constrain; restrain; suppress; lay restraints upon; keep 《*one's* passion》 under control; keep within bounds; put a curb on; (hold in) check; 〖심리〗 inhibit. ¶ ～와 균형 《정치》 checks and balances / ～할 수 없는 uncontrollable; irresistible / 감정을 ～하다 suppress 〔smother〕 *one's* feelings; keep *one's* feelings under control / 노여움을 ～하다 suppress 〔constrain, control〕 *one's* anger / 정욕을 ～하다 keep the passion under control; restrain *one's* sexual desires / 공무원 수의 증가를 ～하다 curb the increase in number of officials / 나는 감정을 ～할 수 없었다 I wasn't able to control myself. *or* I wasn't able to suppress 〔restrain〕 my feelings. / 정부는 휘발유 가격을 ～했다 The government held down gasoline prices.
◉ ～력 restraint; control. ～작용 inhibitory 〔inhibitive〕 action.

**억조**(億兆) ① 《수》 one 〔a〕 hundred million and a trillion. ② 《무수》 myriads; numberless. ¶ 몇 ～ zillion.
◉ ～창생 myriads of people; the people; the masses.

**억지** stubbornness; obstinacy; obduracy; unreasonableness; compulsion; difficulty. ¶ ～(를) 부리다, ～쓰다 insist on having *one's* own way; persist 〔insist〕 stubbornly; 《무리한 요구》 make an unreasonable demand 《of *a person*》 / ～(가) 세다 be stubborn; be obstinate; be headstrong; be self=opinionated / 아들놈이 자동차를 사달라고 ～를 쓴다 The way my son keeps after me to buy him a car, it's out of all reason. ◉ ～웃음 a forced smile. ～해석 forced interpretation.

**억지**(抑止) deterrence. ⇨ 억제(抑制). ～하다 check; deter. ◉ ～력 《전쟁·범죄 따위의》 a deterrent (power) 《to an all-out war》; restraining 〔inhibitive〕 power: 핵무기가 전쟁 ～력으로서 작용한다고 믿고 있는 사람이 아직 많다 A lot of people still believe that the nuclear weapons act as a deterrent.

**억지로** ① 《무리하게》 by force; against *one's* will; under compulsion; under pressure; under coercion; under duress; unwillingly; unreasonably. ¶ ～ 꾸며낸 far-fetched; forced / ～ …(을) 하게 하다 press upon 《*a person*》; force; compel / 술을 ～ 권하다 press wine upon 《*a person*》 / ～ 먹이다 force 《*a person*》 to eat / ～ 웃다 force a smile / ～ 승낙시키다 force 《*a person*》 to consent / ～결혼시키다 make 《*a person*》 marry against his 〔her〕 will; force 《*a person*》 into marriage / 부모는 딸을 ～ 그 남자한테 시집보냈다 The parents coerced their daughter into marrying the man. ② 《간신히》 with difficulty; with much effort. ¶ ～ 살아가다 eke out a living; grub along / 돈을 ～ 마련하다 scrape together a sum of money.

**억지스럽다** 《고집스럽다》 (be) high=handed; willful; demanding; stubborn; insistent; persistent; 《불합리하다》 (be) unreasonable; 《부당하다》 (be) unjustifiable; 《부자연스럽다》 (be) unnatural.

**억지춘향이**(―春香―) doing against *one's* will; compulsion; coercion; compelling; forcing. ¶ ～로 by force; against *one's* will; under compulsion.

**억척** being unyielding 〔unwieldy〕; toughness; stiffness; stubbornness. ～스럽다 (be) stubborn; tough; unyielding; unrelenting; dogged; unbending; obstinate. ¶ ～같다 be unyielding 〔unwieldy, stout-hearted, tough〕 / ～같은 여자 a tough woman / ～ 부리다 show toughness 〔stubbornness〕; be dogged. ◉ ～꾸러기〔보두〕 a tough 〔hard-headed〕 person; an unrelenting 〔indefatigable〕 person. ～빼기 a tough stubborn child.

**억측**(臆測) a random guess; a conjecture; speculation; a surmise; a supposition; an inference. ～하다 (make a) guess; suppose; conjecture; speculate 《on, upon, about》; surmise. ¶ 당치 않은 ～ a wrong guess / ～에 지나지 않다 be a mere conjecture 〔guesswork〕 / ～이 빗맞다 guess wide 〔wrong〕; do not hit the truth; be wide of the mark / 현 단계에 있어서는 갖가지 ～이 있을 수 있다 At this stage one guess is as good as another.

**억판** extremely strained circumstances; dire poverty; indigence. ¶ 사는 것이 ～이다 live in dire poverty.

**억패듯** harshly; relentlessly; ruthlessly; violently. ¶ ～ 사람을 부리다 drive 〔work〕 a person hard; sweat 《*one's* employees》.

**억하심정**(抑何心情) It is hard to understand why…. ¶ 무슨 ～으로 …하느냐 Why 〔How〕 in the world… ? / 무슨 ～으로 그런 짓을 했을까 What made him do such a thing, I wonder?

**언감생심**(焉敢生心) How can you dare! ¶ ～ …하느냐 How dare you…? ! / ～ 내 앞에서 그런 말을 하느냐 How dare you say such a thing in spite of my presence?

**언급**(言及) reference; allusion. ～하다 refer to; mention; make reference to; allude 〔refer〕 to; touch on (짧게); make 《no》 mention of (★ make mention of는 보통 부정문에서 쓰임). ¶ 앞서 ～한 above-mentioned; above alluded to; as stated above / …에 ～하여 referring to… / 문제에 ～하다 refer 〔allude〕 to a question / 잠깐 ～하다 devote only passing attention 《to》 / ～하지 않다 make no mention of; leave 《*a matter*》 untouched 〔alone〕; steer clear of 《a question》 / 그 일에 관해서 ～을 회피했다 He evaded making his comment on it. / 그 책은 주로 공해 문제에 관해 ～하고 있다 The book mainly refers to the pollution problem. / 그것은 몇 가지 보기를 ～하는 것으로 충분할 것이다 It will be sufficient to refer to a few examples.

**언니** an older sibling of the same sex; an older brother (of a boy); an older sister (of a girl). 「underline.

**언더라인** an underline. ¶ ～을 긋다

**언더셔츠** an undershirt; underwear; a vest 《영》.

**언더스로** 『야구』 an underhand 〔underarm〕 throw 〔delivery〕; underhand 〔underarm〕 pitching. ¶ ～로 던지다 throw 《the ball》 underhand 〔underarm〕.

**언더웨어** underwear; underclothing.

**언더파** 『골프』 under par. ¶ 그는 1～71 타로 그 라운드를 끝냈다 He finished the round one stroke under par at 71.

**언덕** 《나지막한 산》 a hill; a hillock; a knoll; a height; 《비탈》 a rising ground; a slope; an incline. ¶ 가파른 ～ a steep ascent 〔slope〕 / ～ 위〔아래〕에 on 〔at〕 the head 〔foot〕 of a slope / ～을 올라가다 go up 〔ascend, climb〕 a slope 〔hill〕; go uphill / ～을 내려가다 go down 〔descend〕 a slope; go downhill / ～ 지다 be hilly; be sloping 〔inclined〕.

◉ ～길 a slope; a sloping 〔an ascending, an uphill〕 road. ～밥 rice cooked partly soft and partly hard (by sloping the raw rice in the pot). ～배기 the top of a hill; a hill; a hilltop.

**언도**(言渡) a sentence. ⇨ 선고(宣告).

**언동**(言動) speech and behavior. ⇨ 언행.

**언뜻** 《얼른》 in an instant; in a flash; quickly; immediately; 《우연》 by chance; unexpectedly. ¶ ～ 듣다 overhear; hear by chance; happen to hear / ～ 보다 glance at 《*a thing*》; catch 〔get, have〕 a (fleeting) glimpse of / …이 ～ 눈에 띄다 catch sight of / ～ 생각나다 occur to 《*one*》; flash across *one's* mind / 그의 뒷모습이 ～ 보였다 I caught a glimpse of his back. / ～ 보아 가짜임을 알 수 있었다 One glance was enough to show that it was an imitation. / 그 소식을 귓결에 ～ 들었다 I overheard the news by chance.

**언론**(言論) speech; discussion; views. ¶ ～의 자유 freedom of speech 〔opinion〕; freedom of the press (출판의); the right of free discussion / ～의 탄압 pressure on discussion 〔public opinion〕 / ～의 통제 control of speech / ～의 힘 power of speech / ～을 단속〔압박〕하다 control 〔shackle〕 speech and writing / ～의 자유를 속박하다 place a gag on free speech / ～의 자유를 침해하다 infringe on the freedom of the press / ～의 자유를 행사하다 exercise freedom of speech / ～의 자유는 헌법으로 보장되어 있다 Freedom of speech is guaranteed by the Constitution.

◉ ～계(界) the press; journalism. ～기관 an organ of expression 〔public opinion]; the (mass) media. ～전(戰) wordy warfare; a verbal clash [battle]; a war of words. ～중재 위원회 the Press Arbitration Commission. 한국 ～노동조합 연맹 the Korean Federation of Press Unions. 한국 ～연구원 the Korea Press Institute. 한국 ～인 금고 the Korea Journalists Fund.

**언명**(言明) declaration; announcement; assertion; statement. ～하다 declare; state; affirm; assert; proclaim; make a definite statement [an assertion]. ¶ 대통령의 ～에 따르면 according to the President's declaration / ～을 피하다 make no comment 《on》/ 사직을 ～하다 pledge *oneself* to resign / 그는 그 문제에 관하여 명확한 ～을 피했다 He avoided making any definite statement on the subject.

**언문일치**(言文一致) unification of the written and spoken language. ¶ ～로 쓰다 write in colloquial style [the spoken language] / ～를 실현하다 weld written and spoken language into an identity.

**언밸런스** unbalance; imbalance. ⇨ 불균형. ¶ ～의 unbalanced.

**언변**(言辯) eloquence; oratorical power. ¶ ～이 좋다 be a glib talker; be glib= [silver-]tongued; have a ready [glib] tongue / ～이 좋은 glib-tongued; talkative; eloquent; fluent / ～이 없는 사람 a poor speaker.

**언비천리**(言飛千里) 《소문이 빠름》 a word flies [travels, spreads] fast.

**언사**(言辭) words; speech; language; expression. ¶ 외교적 ～ diplomatic language / ～가 불손하다 speak disrespectfully; talk insolently.

**언성**(言聲) a (tone of) voice. ¶ ～을 높이다 raise *one's* voice / ～을 높여 loudly; aloud; in a rough [hard] voice; roughly; harshly; in a harsh tone / ～을 높여 말하다 speak loudly [aloud, emphatically]; talk loud.

**언약**(言約) a verbal promise; *one's* word; a pledge; a vow; a plight; an appointment. ⇨ 약속. ～하다 (make a verbal) promise; give *one's* word; pledge *oneself*. ¶ 부부의 ～을 맺다 plight *one's* troth; be pledged to 《*a person*》/ ～을 지키다[어기다] keep [break] *one's* promise [word].

**언어**(言語) (a) language; speech; words. ¶ ～의 verbal / ～의 불명료 inarticulation / ～가 통하다 a language is used [understood]; make *oneself* understood / ～로 표현할 수 없다 be beyond description; defy [baffle, beggar] description / 미국에서 ～가 통하지 않아 고생했다 Because of trouble with the language I had a hard time in the States. / 우리들은 사상을 ～로 표현한다 We express our thoughts through language. / 인간만이 ～를 가지고 있다 Man alone has the gift of speech.
◉ ～감각 a linguistic sense. ～교육 language education. ～교정 speech clinic. ～기능 speech function. ～능력 language [linguistic] ability [abilities, competence]. ～불통 difficulty of communication; difficulty in making *oneself* understood. ～사회학 sociolinguistics. ～상통 facility of communication. ～습관 speech [linguistic] habits. ～심리학 linguistic psychology; psycholinguistics. ～예술 language arts; literature. ～요법(療法) speech therapy. ～장애 〖의학〗 aphasia (실어증); a speech disorder [impediment, defect]: ～ 장애자 an aphasic; a person who has difficulty in speaking. ～중추 the speech center; the center of speech. ～지리학 dialect geography; linguistic geography; geographical linguistics. ～철학 philosophy of language. ～프로세서 〖컴퓨터〗 language processor (언어 번역 프로그램). ～형태학 morphology. ～활동 speech function.

**언어도단**(言語道斷) ¶ ～의 《말할 수 없는》 unspeakable, unutterable; 《용납할 수 없는》 outrageous; abominable; 《어처구니없는》 absurd; preposterous / ～의 요구 a preposterous [an absurd] demand / ～의 조치 an outrageous measure / ～이다 be beyond expression; be unutterable [unspeakable, egregious, abominable, preposterous, absurd] / 그의 행동은 ～이다 His conduct cannot be too severely criticized. / 그들의 잔인한 행위는 ～이다 The atrocities they committed are unspeakable [unpardonable].

**언어학**(言語學) linguistics; philology. ¶ ～적, ～상의 philological; linguistic (-al) / ～상(上) philologically; linguistically / ～적 연구 a philological study.
◉ ～과 the department of linguistics; the philological department. ～자 a linguist; a philologist. ～회 a linguistic society. 심리～ psycholinguistics.

**언어행동**(言語行動) words and actions; speech and behavior. ¶ ～을 삼가다 be careful in *one's* speech and 「behavior 〔conduct〕/ 감정을 ～에 나타내다 betray (*one's* emotions) in speech and action.

**언외**(言外) ¶ ～의 implied; unexpressed / ～의 뜻을 파악하다 catch the implied meaning《of》; read between the lines.

**언재**(言才) oratorical 「talent 〔skill〕; the gift of gab; eloquence. ¶ ～가 있다 have the gift of the gab; be eloquent / ～가 없다 be awkward in speaking; be a poor speaker.

**언쟁**(言爭) a quarrel; a (verbal) dispute; a squabble (사소한 것에 대한). ～하다 quarrel《with *a person,* about 〔over〕 *something*》; dispute《with *a person* on *a matter*》; have (high) words《with》; cross swords《with *a person*》; squabble《with *a person* about *a thing*》. ¶ 그들은 사소한 일로 ～을 했다 A dispute arose between them over a trifle. *or* They began to quarrel over a trifle.

**언저리** the edge; the rim; the brim; bounds; limits. ¶ 접시 ～ the brim of a dish / 입 ～에 about *one's* mouth.

**언제** ① [의문] when; (at) what time; how soon; what 「date 〔day〕; whenever. ¶ ～부터 since when; how long; from what time / 서울엔 ～ 왔나 When did you come to Seoul? / 시험은 ～ 시작됩니까 When does the examination begin? / ～ 찾아 뵐까요 When shall I call on you? / ～가 좋을까요 What 「time 〔day〕 will be convenient for you? / ～부터 병이 났습니까 How long have you been sick? / 그가 ～ 올지 모르겠다 I don't know when he will come. *or* I am expecting him to arrive any minute now. / 그가 ～ 오리라고 생각합니까 When do you think he will come? / 그건 ～ 됩니까 How soon I get it ready?

② [미래] some day; some time;《언제 한번》some other 「day 〔time〕; in the near future; one of these days;《조만간》sooner or later; sometime or other. ¶ ～ 한번 다시 뵙고 싶습니다 I 「would 〔should〕 like to see more of you some time. *or* I hope I can see you again soon. / ～고 진상은 알게 될 테죠 You will learn the whole truth sooner or later. / ～ 한번 (놀러) 오너라 Come and see me one of these days.

③ [과거] once; the other day. ¶ ～인지도 모를 때부터 from time unknown / ～ 한번 그를 만난 기억이 난다 I remember seeing him once. / 그런 일이 ～ 있었는지 알 수가 없다 I do not know when such a thing happened.

④《언제든지》any time; at a moment's notice; all the time; always. ¶ ～고 오시고 싶은 때 오십시오 Please come (at) 「any time 〔whenever〕 you like. / 계산은 ～라도 좋습니다 You may take your own time for payment. / 바다는 ～ 보아도 좋군요 I never get tired of looking out over the sea.

**언제까지** how long; till when; by what time; how soon. ¶ ～고 as long as *one* likes; forever《미》; for ever《영》/ ～ 체류(滯留)하십니까 How long are you going to stay? / ～ 해드리면 되겠습니까 How soon do you want it to be done? / 전쟁은 ～ 계속될 것인지 How long will this war last? *or* When will this war end? / ～고 원하시는 대로 계십시오 You may stay as long as you like. / 이 행복이 ～나 계속되기를 빕니다 I wish this blessing would last forever. / 이 책을 ～ 돌려 드리면 되겠습니까 By what time shall I have to return this book to you?

**언제나**《항상》always; all the time;《평소》usually;《습관적으로》habitually;《…할 때마다》whenever; every time. ¶ 그는 ～ 학교 성적이 좋다 He is always doing very well at school. / 저 녀석은 ～ 불평만 늘어놓는다 That fellow is grumbling all the time. / 그는 ～ 학교에 지각한다 He is habitually late for school. / 둘은 만나면 ～ 싸웠다 「Whenever 〔Every time〕 the two met, they quarreled. / 그녀는 ～ 약속을 지키지 않는다 She never keeps her word. / 나는 ～ 아침 7시에 일어난다 I usually get up at seven in the morning.

**언제든지**《어느 때라도》(at) any time;《항상》always; all the time; at all times; ever; whenever. ¶ 마음이 내킬 때는 ～ whenever you 「like 〔please〕 / 날씨만 좋으면 ～ Whenever the weather permits, .... / ～ 좋습니다 Any time will do. / ～ 형편 닿는 대로 오십시오 Please come at any time that suits you. *or* Feel free to come to see me any time. / ～ 출발할 준비가 되어 있다 We are ready to start at a moment's notice. / ～ 전화하세요 Please feel free to call me anytime.

**언제부터** from what time; since when; how long. ¶ ～ 기다리고 있었느냐 How long have you been waiting? / ～ 영어를 배우고 있느냐 「When did you start 〔How long have you been〕 learning

English?

**언젠가** 《미래의》 some time; some day; one day; one of these days; 《과거의》 once; at one time; before; the other day. ¶ ~는 some time or other / ~ 또 찾아뵙겠습니다 I shall see you some time again. / 이것이 ~ 너에게 이야기한 책이다 This is the book (which) I spoke of to you the other day 〔some time ago〕. / 저분이 ~ 말씀하신 분입니까 Is he the person you spoke of the other day? / 저 사람은 ~ 만나본 일이 있는 것 같다 I think I have met him once. (★ I have once met him.으로 하면 「한번 만난 일이 있다」의 뜻이 됨).

**언죽번죽** brazen-faced; unabashed; impudently.

**언중유골**(言中有骨) a hidden 〔an implied〕 meaning; an expression with hidden meanings.

**언질**(言質) a pledge; a promise; a commitment. ¶ ~을 잡다〔받다〕 take 〔get〕 《*a person's*》 pledge; exact a promise 《from *a person* that...》 / ~을 주다 give a pledge; give 〔pledge〕 *one's* word 《to *do*, that》; commit *oneself* 《on *a matter*, to *do*》; place *oneself* on the record / (확실한) ~을 주지 않다 make no (firm) commitment 《for》.

**언짢다** ① 《불길하다·흉하다》 (be) bad; ill; unlucky; unfavorable; sinister; disastrous; untoward. ¶ 언짢은 소식 a bad news; a sad news / 언짢은 징조 unfavorable symptoms / 언짢은 말을 하다 say ominous things / 일진이 ~ be an unlucky day.
② 《해롭다》 (be) bad; harmful; injurious; detrimental. ¶ 몸에 언짢은 습관 habits injurious to health / 농사에 언짢은 날씨 weather bad for the crops / 눈에 ~ be bad for the eyes.
③ 《속이·안색이》 (be) ill; feel unwell 〔bad, sick〕. ¶ 속이 ~ *one's* stomach feels uneasy; be sick at *one's* stomach / 너 어디가 언짢으냐 Is anything wrong with you? *or* Aren't you feeling well?
④ 《마음이》 feel bad 〔unhappy, sad, sorrowful〕; (be) disagreeable; unpleasant; down in the mouth. ¶ 기분이 ~ feel unwell 〔out of sorts〕; feel mean; be in an ill humor; be in a pet; be out of temper 〔humor〕; be in the blues 〔dumps〕 / 마음을 언짢게 하다 make 《*a person*》 unhappy / 언짢은 얼굴을 하다 look displeased 〔cross, moody, blue〕 / 그는 기분이 언짢은 모양이다 He looks displeased. / 언짢게 생각하지 말게 No hard feelings.
⑤ 《못되다》 (be) bad; ill; evil; wrong. ¶ 언짢은 일을 하다 do wrong / 아무를 언짢게 말하다 speak ill of *a person* / 내 말을 언짢게 여기지 말게 Don't feel bad about what I said. *or* Don't take what I said too hard.
⑥ 《열등》 (be) bad; inferior; be of low grade.

**언책**(言責) ① 《책망》 a verbal reprimand; verbal reproof. ② 《책임》 responsibility for a statement. ¶ ~을 지다 be responsible 〔bear the responsibility〕 for a statement; answer 《for》.

**언청이** (a person with) a harelip; a split lip; a cleft lip. ¶ ~의 harelipped / ~다 be harelipped; have a split lip / ~ 아니면 일색 have only one fault, but what a fault it is.

**언턱** a raised part; a hump; a ridge. ¶ ~지다 be bumpy; be uneven. ◉ 문~ a doorsill; a threshold.

**언턱거리** an excuse; a pretext; grounds; a charge. ¶ ~를 잡다 find a pretext 《to accuse》; invent an excuse 《for》; make a false charge 《against》; pick a quarrel 《with》 / 사소한 일에 ~를 잡다 trump up charges on the slightest pretext / ~를 주다 give 《*a person*》 an excuse 《to accuse》.

**언필칭**(言必稱) in *one's* favorite phrase; as *one* always 〔habitually, invariably〕 says; with *one's* routine comment. ¶ ~ 남녀 동등을 외치다 「be always harping on 〔talk of nothing but〕 the equality of the sexs / ~ 자식 자랑이다 He never opens his mouth without boasting of his son.

**언해**(諺解) Korean annotation of Chinese classics. ~하다 annotate (a Chinese classic) in Korean.

**언행**(言行) words and deeds; speech and action 〔conduct〕. ¶ ~의 불일치 discordance between *one's* words and actions / ~이 일치하다 *one's* deeds correspond with *one's* words; live up to *one's* word / ~을 삼가다 be careful in speech and behavior 〔deeds〕; be circumspect / ~을 일치시키다 act up to what *one* says; correspond actions to words; suit *one's* action to *one's* word / 그는 ~이 일치하지 않는다 His deeds do not agree with his words. *or* He says one thing and does another. ◉ ~록 memoirs; a chronicle of *one's* sayings and doings. ~일치

consistency of speech and action; acting up to *one's* words.

**얹다** put on top; place 〔put, set, lay〕 《*a thing*》 on; place above. ¶ 냄비를 선반에 ~ place a pan on a shelf; shelve a pan / 불 위에 주전자를 ~ put a kettle on the fire / 지붕에 기와를 ~ tile a roof / 가슴에 손을 얹고 생각하다 ponder over 《*a matter*》.

**얹어주다** 《덤으로 더 주다》 give an extra; throw 《*something*》 in (for good measure). ¶ 돈을 조금 ~ pay a little extra 《to *a person*》.

**얹혀살다** be a dependent on 《*a person*》; feed 〔live, sponge〕 on 《*a person*》; live at the expense of 《*one's* daughter》.

**얹히다**[1] ① 《위에》 be put on top; be placed above. ¶ 그릇이 선반에 얹혀 있다 The dishes are put on the shelf. ② 《얹게 하다》 make 〔let〕 《*a person*》 put on top 〔above〕.

**얹히다**[2] ① 《먹은 것이》 《pizzas》 sit heavy on *one's* stomach; have indigestion; have an upset stomach. ¶ 먹은 음식이 얹힌 것이 틀림 없네 Something you ate must have disagreed with you. ② = 얹혀살다. ③ 《좌초되다》 run aground 〔ashore〕; be stranded. ¶ 암초에 ~ run on a sunken rock; go 〔be〕 ashore on a reef / 배가 모래톱에 ~ a ship hits a sandbar; a ship strikes a shoal.

**얻다** ① 《획득하다》 get; obtain; acquire; secure; win; gain; receive. ¶ 권세를 〔명성을〕 ~ rise to power 〔fame〕 / 면허를 ~ obtain 〔secure〕 a license / 신용을 ~ secure 《*a person's*》 confidence / 과반수의 투표를 ~ obtain a majority vote / 인가를 ~ obtain 〔get, secure〕 sanction 〔authorization〕 《from》; obtain a permit 《from》 / 인기를 ~ win 〔attain, gain〕 popularity; find favor with the public / 재정 원조를 ~ receive financial assistance 《from》 / 자신을 ~ gain confidence / 좋은 점수를 ~ get 〔obtain〕 good marks / 지식을 ~ acquire knowledge / 찬성을 ~ be given approval 《by》 / 허가를 ~ get 〔obtain〕 permission / 얻는 것이 많다 gain much 《from, by》; be much benefited 《by》; 《배움》 learn a great deal 《from》 / 자리를 얻어 두다 book a seat / 그의 강연에서 얻은 것이 하나도 없다 I got nothing at all out of his lecture. / 나는 유럽 여행에서 얻은 바가 많았다 I have gained much from my trip to Europe. / 잃는 것은 많고 얻는 것은 적다 The gain is outweighed by the loss. / 그것은 그가 경험에서 얻은 교훈이다 That is a lesson he learned from experience.
② 《줍다》 find 《a book》; pick up. ¶ 길에서 지갑을 ~ pick up a wallet on the road / 테이블 밑에서 돈을 ~ find some money under a table.
③ 《결혼》 marry 《a woman》. ¶ 아내를 ~ take a wife.
④ 《병을》 fall 〔be taken〕 ill; catch 《measles》; get 《cancer》; suffer from 《arthritis》; contract 《mumps》. ¶ 병을 얻어 자리에 누웠다 I got sick and stayed in bed.

**얻어듣다** hear 〔learn〕 casually; pick up 《information》 by hearsay; have an inkling 《of the secret》; get wind of 《the rumor》. ¶ 얻어들은 풍월〔지식〕 knowledge acquired along the way; a smattering (of knowledge) / 친구들로부터 ~ get 《it》 out of a friend / 얻어들은 지식이 많다 have a lot of smattering knowledge.

**얻어맞다** ① 《매를》 get a blow; be beaten; be struck 〔hit〕 on. ¶ 매를 ~ be thrashed; be lashed 〔beaten〕 / 머리를 ~ be struck 〔hit〕 on the head / 뺨을 ~ get slapped / 그런 짓을 하면 얻어 맞는다 If you do such a thing, you will get licked. / 또 얻어맞고 싶으냐 Do you want another thrashing. / 머리를 호되게 얻어맞았다 I received a hard blow on the head. *or* I got a good lick over the head. ② 《공격 받다》 be criticized; denounced; be spoken against. ¶ 신문에서 ~ be attacked 〔severely criticized〕 in the newspaper.

**얻어먹다** ① 《음식 등을》 beg (구걸); get treated to (대접 받다); 《얹혀살다》 rely 《on *a person*》 for 《*one's* food》; live off 《*a person*》. ¶ 밥을 ~ beg *one's* food / 친척한테서 ~ live off *one's* relatives / 얻어먹는 주제에 찬밥 더운 밥 가리랴 A begger should not be a chooser. / 친구의 술을 얻어먹었다 I got treated to drinks by a friend of mine. ② 《욕을》 get called (names); suffer (harsh words); be blamed 〔censured〕 《for》; incur blame. ¶ 욕을 ~ get called names; catch a scolding; be spoken ill of.

**얼**[1] 《흠》 a scratch; a crack. ¶ 얼이 가다 get scratched / 항아리에 얼이 갔다 The jar has a scratch on it.

**얼²** 《정신》 spirit; mind. ⇨ 얼빠지다, 얼빠다. ¶ 독립의 얼 the spirit of independence / 한국의 얼 the spirit of Korea.

**얼간** ① 《절임간》 salting lightly (주로 생선). ② 《사람》 a half-wit; a dolt; a stupid fellow. ¶ ~이다 be a regular stick. ◉ ~고등어 lightly salted mackerel. ~구이 broiled salted fish. ~쌈 cabbage heart that is preserved in salt to be eaten in the winter.

**얼간이, 얼간망둥이** ⇨ 얼간 ②.

**얼갈이** ① 《논밭의》 winter plowing. ② 《푸성귀의》 growing vegetables in the wintertime; early vegetables of the year which were grown in the wintertime. ◉ ~김치 kimchi made with winter-grown cabbage.

**얼개** structure; framework; makeup.

**얼굴** ① 《용모》 a face; a visage; 《이목구비》 *one's* looks (★ 아름다운 용모); *one's* features. ¶ ~의 facial / 무표정~ a poker face / 예쁜〔못생긴, 여윈, 둥근〕 ~ a lovely 〔an ugly, a haggard, a round〕 face / 때벗은 ~ a refined face; a high-class face / ~ 생김새 features; looks / 귀여운 ~의 소녀 a girl with a lovely face; a cute(-looking) girl / ~을 돌리다 look away 〔the other way〕 《from》; turn 〔look〕 aside / ~을 맞대다 meet 《*a person*》 in the face; meet face to face 《with》 / ~을 맞대고 앉다 sit facing each other / ~을 마주 보다 look at each other; 《눈길을》 exchange glances / ~을 보이다 《창 따위에서》 show *one's* face / ~을 내밀다 《나타나다》 show 〔turn〕 up; appear; 《방문》 call on 《*a person*》 / 그저 마지못해〔의례적으로〕 ~을 내밀다 make a token appearance / ~을 쳐들다 look up; lift *one's* face / ~을 뚫어지게 보다 look hard at 《*a person*》 in the face / ~을 씻다 wash *oneself;* have a wash; wash up / ~을 못들다 be ashamed of *oneself* 《toward *a person*》; dare not show *one's* face in public; cannot face 《*a person*》 / ~을 붉히다 flush 《with anger》; blush 《with shame》 / ~을 찡그리다 make grimaces; mop and mow; make a wry face; frown / 부끄러워서 ~을 가리다 hide *one's* face with shame / 두 손에 ~을 묻다 bury *one's* face in *one's* hands / 겁이 나서 ~이 파랗게 질리다 turn pale with fear / ~이 뻔뻔하다 be brazen-faced / 네가 무슨 짓을 했는지 ~에 써 있다 Your telltale face shows what you have done. / 그녀는 ~값을 한다 She is full of her own beauty. *or* She exploits her beauty. / 요샌 그의 ~을 볼 수 없다 I don't see much of him these days. ② 《표정·모습》 a look; a countenance; an expression. ¶ 놀란 ~(을 하다) (take on) a look of surprise / 슬픈〔온화한, 웃는〕 ~ a sad 〔mild, smiling〕 countenance / 험악한〔성난〕 ~ a wild 〔an angry〕 look / 실망한 ~ a disappointed look / ~이 험상궂은 녀석 an ill-looking fellow / 심각한〔슬픈〕 ~을 하다 look grave 〔sad〕 / 불안한 ~을 하다 look uneasy; have a concerned look / ~에 드러내다 betray 《anger》; show / 그녀는 비웃는 ~로 나를 보았다 She threw a look of contempt at me. / 그녀는 근심스러운 ~이다 She wears a troubled look. / 그는 ~과는 딴판으로 정직하다 He is more honest than he looks. *or* He may not look it, but he is honest. ③ 《체면》 *one's* honor; (*one's*) face; prestige. ¶ 내 ~을 보아서 for my sake / ~에 똥칠을 하다 cause 《*a person*》 to lose face; disgrace 〔shame〕 《*a person*》 / ~이 서다 save *one's* face / ~을 깎이다 be put out of countenance; lose face. ④ 《관용적 표현》 acquaintance (면식); influence (영향력); 《구어》 clout. ¶ 그녀는 이곳에서 꽤 ~이 통한다 She's got a lot of influence around here. / 이 도시에서는 그녀의 ~을 모르는 사람이 거의 없다 She has a wide circle of acquaintances in this town. / 그 모임에는 시장도 ~을 내밀었다 The Mayor turned up at the meeting. / 그는 학계에서 꽤 ~이 알려져 있다 He is well=known in the academic world.

**얼굴빛** complexion; color; countenance; looks. ⇨ 안색.

**얼근하다** ① 《맛이》 (be) rather hot 〔peppery, highly seasoned〕. ¶ 음식이 ~ food tastes rather hot. ② 《술이》 (be) rather tipsy. ¶ 얼근하게 취하다 be slightly drunk 〔intoxicated〕; become tipsy.

**얼기설기** in disorder; entangled. ¶ ~ 얽히다 《실 따위가》 get 〔become〕 entangled; 《문제가》 be intricated; get complicated 〔involved〕 / ~ 얽힌 complicated; entangled / 실이 ~ 얽혔다 The thread is raveled. *or* The thread has got entangled. / 이 문제에는 갖가지 사정이 ~ 얽혀 있다 Various circumstances are involved in this matter.

**얼김에** on the spur 〔in the heat〕 of

the moment; under the impulse 《of》; in spite of *oneself.* ¶ ~ 말해 버리다 say on the spur of the moment; let slip 《a secret》 through carelessness / 무서워서 ~ 방에서 뛰어 나갔다 I ran out of the room confused by fear. / 그는 ~ 그렇게 말했다 He said so on the spur of the moment.

**얼넘기다** scamp 《*one's* work》; hush up 《*a matter*》; gloss 〔smooth〕 over; slur over (말을). ¶ 그들은 그 스캔들을 얼넘기려 했다 They tried to hush up 〔hugger-mugger〕 the scandal.

**얼다** ① 《추워서》 freeze; be frozen; congeal; ice; be benumbed. ¶ …에 얼음이 ~ become 〔be〕 covered with ice; ice is formed on / 추워서 손이 ~ *one's* hands are benumbed with cold / 얼어 죽다 freeze to death / 꽁꽁 ~ 《빨래 따위가》 be frozen hard 〔stiff〕 / 고기가 얼어서 딴딴하다 The meat is frozen to a block of ice. / 수도가 얼었다 The water pipe has frozen (up). / 연못에 얼음이 얼었다 Ice froze on the pond. *or* The pond iced over. / 추위로 몸이 얼었다 I am almost frozen with cold.
② 《기가 죽다》 cower; be cowed; lose heart 〔*one's* nerve〕; feel timid 〔small〕; 《무대 등에서》 get stage fright; get nervous 《on the stage》.

**얼떨결** the confusion of the moment; a moment of bewilderment. ¶ ~에 in the confusion of the moment; in a moment of bewilderment; in an unguarded moment; on the spur of the moment / ~에 그것을 깜빡 잊었다 I clean forgot about it in my confusion. / 그는 ~에 그렇게 말해 버렸다 He said so in his bewilderment.

**얼떨떨하다** (be) dazed; stupefied; bewildered; perplexed; puzzled; embarrassed; confused. ¶ 얼떨떨한 기색 marks of confusion / 얼떨떨하여 in a flurried; in confusion; in embarrassment / 얼떨떨한 얼굴로 with a perplexed look 〔air〕 / 느닷없는 질문에 잠시 얼떨떨했다 I felt dazed for a moment at the sudden question. / 잠을 못 자서 정신이 ~ I feel groggy 〔stupefied〕 from lack of sleep. / 그는 그 백화점에 사람이 너무 많아 얼떨떨했다 He was bewildered by the big crowds in the department store.

**얼떨하다** 《바빠서》 (be) flurried; confused; disconcerted; 《머리가》 (be) dizzy; giddy. ¶ 얼떨해 하다 fluster *oneself;* be all in a flurry; be confused; be disconcerted / 머리가 ~ My head buzzes. *or* My head aches. *or* I feel dizzy. / 뜻밖의 질문을 받고 얼떨했다 I got confused at the unexpected question.

**얼뜨기** a half-wit; a dimwit; a stupid person. ¶ 그는 ~다 He is a regular stick.

**얼뜨다** 《어리석다》 (be) slow-witted; dimwitted; silly; 《겁이 많다》 (be) cowardly; timid; retiring; hesitant. ¶ 얼뜬 사람 a dimwit; a timid person / 얼뜬 얼굴 a stupid-looking face / 그것을 믿을 만큼 얼뜨지 않다 I am not so simple as to believe that.

**얼러맞추다** play up to; humor; please 《*one's* master》; please 《*a person's*》 whim; fawn upon; flatter. ¶ 얼러맞추기 힘들다 be hard to please / 잘 얼러맞추면 그를 마음대로 할 수 있다 If you just humor him right, you can easily sway him.

**얼러먹다** eat together; share 《in》.

**얼러붙다** come to close quarters; grapple 《with *a person*》. ¶ 얼러붙어 싸우다 fight hand to hand; fight a close fight; come to grapples 《with》.

**얼러치다** ① 《때리다》 strike 〔hit, score〕 two or more at one time; lump 《*things*》 together. ② 《셈을》 make a combined price 《for the pair, for the lot》.

**얼렁뚱땅하다** ① 《엉터리로》 befuddle; behave evasively; beat around the bush. ¶ 얼렁뚱땅하여 돈을 빼앗다 bamboozle 《*a person*》 out of money / 얼렁뚱땅하지 말고 어서 거스름돈을 내놔라 Stop beating around the bush, give me the change at once. ② 《일을》 do a slapdash job; shuffle along. ¶ 얼렁뚱땅하지 말고 정신차려서 일해라 Don't be so sloppy, pay more attention to your work.

**얼레** a reel; a spool; a bobbin. ¶ ~에 실을 감다 spool; reel; wind thread on a reel / ~에서 실을 풀다 unwind thread from a reel.

**얼레빗** a coarse comb.

**얼루기** ① 《동물》 a spotted 〔speckled, mottled, dappled, brindled〕 animal. ② 《점》 patches; spots; specks.

**얼룩** ① 《더러워진 자국》 a stain; a spot; a blot; a smear; a smudge; a blotch; 《반점》 a speck; dapples.
¶ 잉크 ~ an ink spot / 커피 ~ a coffee stain / 젖어서 생긴 ~ a patch of damp / ~이 있는 stained; spotted; smeared / ~이 없는 stainless; spot-

less; immacurate / ~투성이의 covered with stains 〔blots〕; blotchy / ~이 지지 않는 stain-resistant 《carpets》 / ~이 지게 하다 stain; spot; smear / ~을 없애다 remove 〔take out, wash 〔wipe〕 out〕 a stain 《from》 / ~을 남기다 leave a stain / 옷에 ~이 가다 *one's* clothes get spotted (and stained) / 옷에 ~이 가지〔지지〕 않게 하다 save 〔keep〕 *one's* clothes from spots and stains / 이 ~은 빨아도 안 빠진다 This stain will not wash out. / 비를 맞아 흰 저고리에 ~이 졌다 I got spots on my white coat from the rain. / 비가 새서 천장에 ~이 져 있었다 There were patches of damp on the ceiling. *or* The ceiling was patched with damp.

> 용법 **stain**, **spot** 일반적으로 이물질에 의해 변색된 얼룩. spot은 상처·병으로 인해 변색된 부분도 가리킴. **blot** 잉크 등에 의해 생긴 얼룩. **smear** 기름이나 점성(粘性) 물질 등에 의해 생긴 얼룩. **smudge** 문지르거나 비벼서 색깔이 변해 생긴 얼룩. **speck** 작은 얼룩. **blotch** 얼굴·피부 따위에 생긴 얼룩, 검버섯 등을 가리킴.

② 《치욕》 a disgrace; a stain. ¶ 이름에 ~이 지다 get a stain on *one's* name / 그는 가명(家名)에 ~이 지게 했다 He brought disgrace to 〔on〕 his family.
◉ ~고양이 a tabby (cat). ~말 a zebra; a piebald horse; a horse of more than two colors. ~소 a brindled cow 〔ox〕.

**얼룩덜룩하다** (be) mottled; dappled; polka-dotted; variegated; parti-colored; spotted; stained. ¶ 얼룩덜룩한 옷감 variegated cloth / 얼룩덜룩한 욕의(浴衣) a dappled 〔variegated〕 bathrobe.

**얼룩지다** be stained; be smudged; become stained. ¶ 옷에 얼룩이 지지 않도록 주의하다 be careful so as not to get *one's* clothes stained with spots and stains / 이 옷감은 얼룩지기 쉽다 This material spots easily.

**얼룽덜룽하다** (be) spotted; dappled; mottled; motley; speckled; 《짐승이》 (be) brindled; piebald (흑백으로).

**얼른** quickly; fast; rapidly; promptly; hastily; immediately; swiftly; at once. ¶ ~ 가거라 Go at once! / ~ 대답해라 Answer promptly. / ~ 해라 Hurry it up. *or* Be quick 《about your work》! / 그의 이름이 ~ 떠오르지 않는다 I can't think of his name offhand. / ~ 대답할 수 없었다 I was at a loss for a ready answer.

**얼리다**[1] 《얼게 하다》 freeze 〔congeal〕 《*a thing*》; refrigerate; make (ice). ¶ 얼린 야채 frozen vegetables / 물을 ~ turn water into ice; make ice / 생선을 냉동기에서 ~ freeze 〔refrigerate〕 the fish in the freezer.

**얼리다**[2] ① ⇨어울리다. ② =어우르다.

**얼마** ① 《값》 what price; what sum of money; how much; a certain price; some amount; 《not》 much; any amount. ¶ 이것은 ~입니까 How much is this? *or* What is the price 〔charge, fare, fee, *etc.*〕? / 달걀 값이 ~냐 How much are eggs? / 모두 ~입니까 What do they come up to altogether? *or* What does the bill amount to? / 집세가 ~냐 How much is the rent? / 사과는 ~에 팝니까 How much do you sell your apples for? / ~에 파시겠습니까 What do you ask for it? / ~에 샀습니까 How much did you pay for it?
② 《동안》 how long; a while; some 〔any〕 length of time; 《not》 very long. ¶ ~ 아니하여 before very long; soon; in no time / 그는 결혼한 지 ~ 되지 않는다 It is not long since he got married. / 그는 ~ 있다가 말했다 He spoke after a while. / 그한테서 ~ 동안 소식이 없다 I haven't heard from him for a while. / ~ 안 가서 쌀값이 떨어지겠다 It will not be long before the price of rice goes down. / 그 정부는 ~ 못 간다 That government won't last long. / 아버지가 돌아가신 지 ~ 안 된다 It is only a short time since my father died. / 여기에 ~ 동안 있겠나 How long will you be here? / 학교가 설립된 지 ~ 안 된다 It is not long since our school was founded.
③ 《수·양·정도》 what number; what quantity; how much; how many; some (quantity); a few; a bit; 《not》 many 〔much〕; any (quantity). ¶ ~든지 ever so many 〔much〕 / ~든지 있다 be available as many 〔much〕 as *one* wishes; be a dime-a-dozen / 돈이 이제 ~ 남지 않았다 I have not much money left now. / 물은 이제 ~ 남아 있지 않다 There is not much water left now.
④ 《무게·높이·깊이》 what weight; what measure; how much; some weight 〔measure〕; 《not》 very much; any weight 〔measure〕 at all. ¶ 몸무게가 ~냐 What is your weight? / 그의 키가

~냐 How tall is he?
⑤《거리》 what distance; how far; some distance; 《not》 far; any distance at all. ¶ 서울에서 인천까지 거리가 ~냐 How far is it from Seoul to Inch'ŏn? / 여기서 학교까지는 ~ 안 된다 It is but a step from here to the school. / 여기서 ~ 안 가서 정거장이 있다 The station is not far from here.
⑥《나이》 what age; how old. ¶ 네 나이가 ~냐 How old are you?
⑦《비율》 by. ¶ 한 다스 ~씩으로 팔다 sell 《*things*》 by the dozen / 하루 ~씩 일하다 work at 〔for〕 so much per 〔a〕 day; work so much by the day.
⑧《다소》 some; something; 《일부》 a part. ¶ 비용 중의 ~를 부담하다 bear (a) part of the expense / 수입에서 ~를 저축하다 save something from *one's* income.

**얼마나** ①《값》 (about) how much; (about) what price. ¶ 그 양복은 ~ 주었느냐 How much did you pay for your suit? / 모두 해서 ~ 됩니까 What does it come 〔amount〕 to?
②《동안》 (about) how long. ¶ 중국어를 공부한 지 ~ 됩니까 How long have you been studying Chinese? / 그곳에 ~ 계셨나요 How long did you stay there?
③《수·양》 about what quantity; (about) how many 〔much〕. ¶ 이 도서관에 책이 ~ 있는지 모르겠다 I don't know how many books this library has. / 돈을 ~ 갖고 계십니까 How much money do you have now? / 회합에 사람이 ~ 왔더냐 How many people were present at the meeting? / 상자에 배가 ~ 남았느냐 How many pears are left in the box?
④《무게·깊이·높이·넓이》 about what weight 〔measure〕; how.... ¶ ~ 크냐 How big? / ~ 깊은가 How deep? / ~ 넓으냐 How wide? / ~ 무거우냐 How heavy? / ~ 두꺼우냐 How thick? / 몸무게가 ~ 나갑니까 How much do you weigh? *or* What is your weight? (★ 체중을 물을 때 How heavy를 써서는 안 됨) / 한강 길이가 ~ 되는지 아는가 Can you guess how long the Han river is? / 이 산 높이는 해발 ~ 됩니까 How high 〔What height〕 is this mountain above sea level?
⑤《거리》 about what distance; (about) how far. ¶ 여기서 ~ 머냐 What is the distance 〔How far is it〕 from here?
⑥《나이》 about what age; (about) how old. ¶ 그의 나이가 ~ 되어 보이더냐 Do you have any idea how old he looked?
⑦《정도》 about what degree 〔extent〕; how (much); to what extent. ¶ ~ 추우냐 How cold? / ~ 쓴가 How bitter? / ~ 빠르냐 How fast? / 네가 ~ 안다고 그런 말을 해 What makes you think you know so much you can say that? / 그가 ~ 열심히 일했던지 이루 다 말할 수는 없다 I can hardly describe how hard he worked. / 이것을 들으면 그가 ~ 기뻐할까 How glad he will be to hear it! / 그가 ~ 고생했을까 What he has suffered! / 그 영화에 ~ 감동했는지 모르겠다 I can't tell you how impressed I was with the film.

**얼마든지** 《한없이》 without limit; ever so many 〔much〕; 《원하는 만큼》 as much 〔many〕 as (*one* likes); any amount 〔number〕 of; any sum (금액). ¶ ~ 원하는 대로 주겠습니다 You shall have 〔I will give you〕 as much 〔many〕 as you want. / ~ 부르는 값으로 드리겠습니다 You may have it for any price you offer 〔for your price〕. / 그는 돈이 ~ 있다 He has no end of money. / 아직 ~ 있다 There are ever so many more. / 교통 사고로 죽은 사람은 ~ 있다 Many a man has been killed in traffic accidents. / 시간은 ~ 있다 I have all the time in the world.

**얼마큼** ① = 얼마나. ②《어느 정도》 to some extent; in some degree; some; a little; in part; somewhat; more or less. ¶ ~이라도 있는 것은 없는 것보다 낫다 Something is better than nothing. / 나도 그 일에는 ~ 책임이 있다 I am partly responsible for the problem. / 책 살 돈이 ~ 있다 I have some money to buy a book with. / 기분이 ~ 나아졌다 I feel a bit better.

**얼멍덜멍하다, 얼멍얼멍하다** (be) lumpy; be full of lumps 〔bumps〕. ¶ 죽이 얼멍덜멍하다 The gruel has lumps in it.

**얼바람둥이** a silly 〔absurd〕 person; a crackpot.

**얼바람맞다** act half crazy 〔silly〕; behave as if half out of *one's* mind.

**얼버무리다** ①《말을》 speak ambiguously 〔evasively〕; prevaricate; quibble; equivocate; shuffle. ¶ 대답을 ~ give a vague 〔a noncommittal, an evasive〕 answer / 다른 화제로 얼버무려 넘기다

put off by referring to other things; draw a red herring across the path. ②《잘 씹지 않고》bolt [swallow] 《food》 (down). ¶ 음식을 급히 얼버무려 삼키다 bolt [swallow] *one's* food (down) in a hurry. ③《나물 따위를》mix.

**얼보다** can't see straight [clearly]; see blurred [incorrectly].

**얼보이다** be seen distortedly; be distorted; be blurred. ¶ 거울의 그림자가 얼보인다 My reflection in the mirror is distorted. / 글자가 얼보여서 읽기 어렵다 The writing is blurred and difficult to read.

**얼빠지다** lose *one's* senses; come to lack sense; get absentminded; be stupefied; be abstracted. ¶ 얼빠진 silly; half-witted; stupid; foolish / 얼빠진 사람 a stupid person; a half-wit / 얼빠진 얼굴(로) (with) a stupid look / 얼빠진 수작을 하다 talk nonsense; say stupid things / 얼빠진 짓을 하다 do a silly things / 얼빠진 놈이다 be a regular stick / 슬픔으로 ~ be stupefied with grief.

**얼빼다** make 《*a person*》 senseless; stupefy; stun; daze; drive 《*a person*》 out of *his* mind. ¶ 소란을 피워 ~ stupefy 《*a person*》 with a clamor / 고함을 쳐서 ~ stupefy 《*a person*》 [drive 《*a person*》 out of *his* mind] with *one's* shouting.

**얼싸** 《흥겨울 때》 Yippee!; Whoopee!; Goody-goody!; Oh boy!; Hurrah!; Hurray! ¶ ~ 좋구나 Yippee — hurray!

**얼싸안다** embrace [hug] 《*a person*》 closely [hard]; give a tight hug; hold [clasp] 《*a person*》 in *one's* arms; clasp to *one's* bosom. ¶ 목을 ~ throw [lock, fold] *one's* arms around [about] 《*another's*》 neck / 어린애를 ~ hold a baby fondly in *one's* arms / 그는 그녀를 얼싸안았다 He gave her a squeeze. / 기뻐서 그 둘은 얼싸안고 춤을 추었다 The two danced with joy in each other's arms.

**얼쑹덜쑹하다, 얼쑹얼쑹하다** 《줄·점이》 (be) intricate; confusing; mixed-up; motley; jumbled; eye-troubling; bewildering. ¶ 얼쑹덜쑹한 무늬 a bewildering [puzzling, mixed] pattern.

**얼씨구** Yippee!; Whoopee!; Goody-goody!; Oh boy!; Hurrah!; Hurray! ¶ ~ 좋구나 What a delight!

**얼씬거리다** keep coming around [showing up]; haunt; hang around; make frequent appearance; frequent. ¶ 너 이 근처에는 얼씬거리지도 마라 We don't want to see you hanging around. / 그는 요새 우리 집에 얼씬거리지도 않는다 He no longer visits us at all.

**얼씬못하다** dare not come round [show up]; cannot appear before 《*one's*》 eyes at all. ¶ 집에 얼씬못하게 하다 forbid 《*a person's*》 access to the house; turn 《*a person*》 from *one's* doors. ⇨ 얼씬하다.

**얼씬없다** do not show up; do not appear for even a moment.

**얼씬하다** make [put in] *one's* appearance; show [turn] up; appear briefly. ¶ 얼씬 하지 않다 do not appear for even a moment / 개미새끼 한 마리 얼씬 하지 못할 경계 태세이다 be closely guarded / 그는 요새 얼씬도 하지 않는다 I have seen nothing of him lately. / 그가 다시는 내 집에 얼씬하지 못할 게다 He will never dare to enter my house again.

**얼어붙다** freeze; be frozen (over); freeze (on) to 《*something*》; be frozen hard [fast] 《to》. ¶ 얼어붙은 길 a frozen street / 얼어붙은 파이프 a frozen pipe / 얼어붙을 듯이 춥다 It is freezing cold. / 그 기별을 듣고 전신의 피가 얼어붙는 것 같았다 The news made my blood curdle. / 강이 얼어붙었다 The river is frozen over.

**얼얼하다** 《아파서》 smart; sting; tingle; 《매워서》 bite; taste hot; burn 《the tongue》; (be) piquant; pungent. ¶ 추위로 살이 ~ the cold makes the skin smart / 혀가 ~ *one's* tongue stings [burns] / 화상이 아직 ~ The burn still smarts.

**얼없다** (be) correct; certain; exact; just alike; exactly the same.

**얼요기**(—療飢) a partial meal; an insufficient snack. ~하다 eat just a bite 《of food》.

**얼음** ice. ¶ ~의, ~ 같은 ice; icy; glacial / ~이 언 frozen 《lakes》; ice-covered 《rivers》; ice-bound 《harbor》 / ~이 얼다 ice freezed [forms]; it freezes; be frozen / ~이 녹다 ice melts / ~을 깨뜨리다 crush ice / ~에 갇히다 《배가》 be iced up / ~에 발이 묶이다 be ice-bound / ~이 꺼져 (물에) 빠지다 break through the ice / ~으로 차게 하다 ice 《*a thing*》; cool 《*a thing*》 with ice / 생선을 ~에 채우다 pack fish in ice / ~은 화씨 32°에서 녹는다 Ice melts at 32° Fahrenheit. / ~에 스카치 위스키를 넣어 주게 《술집 등에서》 I'll have a Scotch on the rocks. / 오늘밤에는 ～이 얼겠다 It will freeze tonight. ◉ ～가게 an ice shop. ～경치 an icescape. ～과자 a popsicle; flavored ice on stick. ～덩이 a block of ice. ～물 iced 〔ice《미》〕 water. ～베개 an ice pillow. ～사탕 crystal 〔rock〕 sugar; sugar candy. ～장 a layer 〔coat〕 of ice; a block 〔sheet〕 of ice. ～장수 an ice dealer; 《미》 an iceman. ～조각 (an) ice sculpture: ～조각가 an ice sculptor. ～주머니 an ice bag 〔cap, pack〕. ～집게 ice tongs. ～찜(질) an application of an ice bag. ～창고 an icehouse. ～통 an ice pail 〔bucket〕.

**얼음박이다** [부위가 주어] become frostbitten (심하게); be affected with chilblains (가볍게); [사람이 주어] have chilblains. ¶ 얼음박힌 발가락 frostbitten 〔chilblained〕 toes / 귀에 ～ get 〔have〕 *one's* ears frostbitten.

**얼음지치다** slide on the ice; skate. ¶ 얼음지치러 연못으로 가다 go skating on a pond.

**얼음판** an icy 〔iced〕 ground; the ice. ¶ ～에서 얼음지치다 skate on the ice.

**얼입다** suffer undeservedly in place of another; take the rap 《for》; be left holding the bag; be struck by a chance blow.

**얼쩍지근하다** ① 《살이》 tingle; smart; burn; (be) smarting; pricking; prickling. ¶ 따귀를 맞아서 뺨이 얼쩍지근했다 My cheek smarted from the slap. ② 《맵다》 be a bit spicy; (be) hot-tasting. ¶ 맛이 ～ have a bit hot 〔spicy, peppery〕 taste. ③ 《술이 거나하다》 (be) tipsy; be slightly drunk.

**얼쭝거리다** cajole; coax; flatter; fawn upon 《*a person*》; curry favor with 《*one's* superior》; play up to. ¶ 얼쭝거리는 바람에 속아넘어가다 be imposed upon by flattery.

**얼쭝얼쭝** by honeyed tongue; with fair words; with 〔by〕 cajoling 〔coaxing〕. ¶ ～ 아무를 속이다 impose upon *a person* by flattery.

**얼쯤얼쯤** hesitant(ly); reluctant(ly). ～하다 hesitate; waver.

**얼추** nearly; almost; practically; well-nigh. ¶ 일이 ～ 다되다 the work is nearly finished / ～ 정오가 다되어 간다 It is getting on toward noon.

**얼추잡다** make a rough estimate; make a draft; outline; sketch. ¶ 비용을 ～ make a rough estimate of the expense / 계획을 ～ outline a plan.

**얼치기** 《사물》 something 「half-done 〔half-finished〕; an in-between thing; something half-and-half; a thing of double aspect; odds and ends; 《사람》 a half-trained 〔an inexperienced, unskilled, immature〕 person. ¶ 일을 ～로 하다 do things by halves / 그녀가 하는 짓이란 모두가 다 ～다 She leaves everything 「unfinished 〔half-done〕. / ～로 아는 것 보다는 아무것도 모르는 것이 낫다 One may as well know nothing than know things by halves.

**얼크러지다** tangle; get entangled 〔involved, complicated, messed up〕. ¶ 얼크러진 머리 tangled hair.

**얼큰하다** 《술이》 (be) slightly intoxicated; be tipsy; 《맛이》 be a bit spicy; have a hot 〔spicy, peppery〕 taste. ¶ 그는 얼큰히 취했다 He is tipsy 〔slightly intoxicated〕. *or* He is mellow with wine.

**얼토당토않다** ① 《관련성이 없다》 be (quite) irrelevant 《to》; have no relevance 《to, for》; have 〔bear〕 no relation 《to》; have nothing to do with; be wide of the mark. ¶ 그는 자주 얼토당토않은 말을 한다 What he says is often wide of the mark. / 자네 질문은 당면한 문제와는 얼토당토않은 것이다 Your question has no relevance to the matter we are facing now. ② 《가당찮다》 (be) absurd; preposterous; nonsensical; unreasonable; outrageous; exorbitant. ¶ 얼토당토않은 값 an outrageous 〔exorbitant〕 price / 얼토당토않은 생각 an absurd idea / 얼토당토않은 사람 an incongruous 〔a wrong〕 man for 《the job》 / 얼토당토 않은 비교 a far-fetched comparison / 그녀는 얼토당토않은 요구를 했다 She made an unreasonable 〔preposterous〕 demand. / 자네는 얼토당토 않은 불평을 하는군 You complain at the wrong door.

**얽다**[1] 《없는 사실을》 fabricate; frame 〔make, cook〕 up; 《묶다》 bind; tie 〔truss〕 up. ¶ 밧줄로 얽어매다 bind 《*a thing*》 with a rope / 짐을 ～ tie up goods.

**얽다**[2] ① 《얼굴이》 get 〔be〕 pockmarked; be pitted with smallpox. ¶ 얽은 자국 smallpox marks; pockmarks / 얼굴이 ～ *one's* face is pockmarked. ② 《거죽이》 (be) flawed; cracked; bruised. ¶ 이 꽃병에는 얽은 곳이 있다 There is a small flaw 〔crack〕 in this vase.

**얽동이다** tie 〔bind〕 up; truss up. ¶ 단단히 ~ tie fast 〔hard〕 / 상자를 끈으로 ~ bind (up) a box with a cord / 짐짝을 새끼로 ~ tie up a packing case with straw rope.

**얽둑얽둑** covered with pocks; pocky. ~하다 (be) pockmarked; pitted; pocky. ¶ ~ 얽은 사람 a person with a pocky face / 얼굴이 ~ 얽다 *one's* face is pocky.

**얽매다** 《끈 따위로》 bind 《*a thing*》 (up); tie 《*a thing*》 《with string》; fasten; 《속박하다》 bind; restrict; fetter; tie (일 따위에). ¶ 단단히 ~ tie fast 〔hard〕 / 규칙으로 ~ restrict 《*a person*》 by rule.

**얽매이다** be bound; be tied down; be fettered 〔shackled〕; be restricted. ¶ 규칙에 ~ be bound by a rule; be screwed down to a rule / 시간에 얽매여 있다 be restricted by time; have very little time to call *one's* own / 인습에 ~ be fettered by tradition; be a slave to tradition / 일에 ~ be chained 〔tied down, fettered〕 to *one's* business 〔work〕; be tied up in *one's* business; have *one's* hands full; be hogtied to business / 정에 ~ be overcome by *one's* affection; be tied to 《*a person*》 by affection / 계약 조건에 ~ be bound down by the terms of the contract / 의리에 ~ be fettered by the bonds of obligation / 나는 무슨 일에도 얽매이기를 싫어한다 I can't stand being tied down. *or* I am impatient of any restriction.

**얽빼기** a pockmarked person.

**얽어매다** bind up; tie up. ¶ 한데 ~ tie 《*things*》 into a bundle / 범인의 손발을 포승으로 ~ tie a criminal hand and foot with rope.

**얽이** 《얽는 일》 tying 〔trussing, binding〕 up securely; 《일의 순서·배치》 (getting) an overall picture 〔an outline, a rough idea〕 of things.

**얽이치다** tie crisscross.

**얽적얽적** lightly pockmarked. ~하다 (be) lightly pockmarked.

**얽죽얽죽** heavily pockmarked. ~하다 (be) heavily pockmarked.

**얽히다** 《줄에》 get bound up; be tied; 《감기다》 twine 〔coil〕 round; get coiled round; twist about; 《뒤얽히다》 be 〔get〕 entangled; 《얽혀 들다》 be involved in. ¶ 얽힌 것을 풀다 disentangle; unravel; untie / 삼각관계로 ~ get involved in a love triangle / 밧줄이 발에 얽혔다 My feet were caught in the rope. / 실이 얽혔다 The thread has got entangled. / 낚싯줄이 해초에 얽혔다 My fishing line got entangled in some seaweed. / 이 일에는 여러 가지의 복잡한 사정이 얽혀 있다 Various circumstances are involved in this matter.

**엄격**(嚴格) strictness; sternness; severity; rigor; austerity. ~하다 (be) strict; severe; stern; rigorous.

> 용법 **strict** 규칙 등을 충실히 지키도록 하며 타협을 용납하지 않는. **severe** 사람이나 사물에 널리 쓰이며, 기존의 딱딱한 수준이나 높은 이상에 충실하여 부드러움이나 느슨함이 없는. **stern** severe와 같은 뜻으로 쓰이는데, 굽히지 않는 엄정함이 태도나 용모에 풍기며 인정 사정 없는. **rigorous** severe보다 뜻이 세며, 타협이나 융통성 없이 고통이나 고생을 강요하여 긴장감을 주는.

¶ ~한 아버지 a stern father / ~한 사람 a stern man; a puritan (종교·도덕적으로) / ~한 규율 strict 〔rigid〕 discipline / ~한 선생 a strict 〔severe〕 teacher / ~한 가정 a strict 〔sternly moral〕 family / ~한 구별 a sharp distinction 《between》 / ~하게 strictly; sternly; severely; rigorously / ~하게 기르다 bring up 《a child》 rigorously / 학생들에게 ~하다 be severe 〔stern〕 with students / ~하기는 했지만 자애로운 아버지였다 Stern as he was, our father was full of affection.

**엄금**(嚴禁) strict prohibition; a ban; an interdict. ~하다 prohibit 〔forbid〕 strictly; interdict; place 《*a thing*》 under a ban; ban. ¶ 외출을 ~하다 strictly forbid 《*a person*》 to go out / 기내에서 흡연은 ~되어 있다 Smoking is strictly prohibited on the plane. / 도박은 ~이었다 Gambling was utterly taboo. / 소변 ~ 《게시》 "Commit no nuisance." *or* "Decency forbids." / 화기 ~ 《게시》 Caution: Flammable(s).

**엄나무** 〖식물〗 a kalopanax.

**엄니** a tusk (코끼리·멧돼지 등의); a fang (개·이리 등의). ¶ ~를 드러내고 으르렁대다 snarl; growl 《at》.

**엄닉**(掩匿) concealment; hiding. ~하다 hide; conceal; cover 《over, up》.

**엄단**(嚴斷) ~하다 take stern legal action 《against》; punish 《an offender》 severely.

**엄동**(嚴冬) (a) rigorous 〔hard, severe〕 winter; the midwinter. ◉ ~설한 the coldest period of snowy winter.

**엄두** the very thought 《of *doing*》; daring. ¶ ～를 못 내다 cannot even conceive the idea 《of *doing*》; be 「inconceivable 〔unthinkable, unimaginable〕 / 그들은 올 ～도 못 냈다 They did not dare to come. / 유럽은 ～도 못 내지만 하다못해 일본에라도 가고 싶다 I cannot hope to visit Europe, but at least I wish to see Japan. / 그녀와의 결혼은 나로선 ～도 못낼 일이다 I cannot see myself marrying her. / 그런 일은 ～도 못냈다 I never dreamed of it. / 저항 따위는 ～도 낼 수 없었다 Resistance was 「inconceivable 〔out of the question〕. / 그녀에게 그것을 알릴 ～가 나지 않는다 I don't have the heart to let her know it.

**엄마** mam(m)a; mammy; mummy; 《미구어》 mom; 《영구어》 mum. ¶ 우리 ～와 아빠 my mammy and daddy; my mom and dad.

**엄명**(嚴命) a strict order 〔command〕; a rigid 〔stringent〕 instruction. ～하다 give strict orders 《to *do*》; give stringent instructions. ¶ 지휘관의 ～에 의하여 under a strict order of a commanding officer / ～을 받다 receive strict orders 《to *do*》.

**엄밀**(嚴密) 《자세·정확》 strictness; exactness; closeness; rigidity; 《비밀》 strict secrecy. ～하다 (be) strict; exact; rigid; close; 《비밀》 (be) strictly secret. ¶ ～한 검사 a close 〔rigid, narrow〕 examination / 사회주의에 대한 ～한 고찰 a strict examination of socialism / ～히 strictly; exactly; closely; rigidly; in strict secrecy / ～히 말하면〔말하여〕 strictly speaking / ～한 의미에서 in the strict sense of the word / ～히 조사하다 make a close examination 《of *a matter*》; investigate 《a case》 closely.

**엄벌**(嚴罰) a severe 〔heavy〕 punishment. ～하다 punish 《*a person*》 severely; inflict a severe punishment 《on *a person*》. ¶ ～에 처하다 = ～하다 / ～을 받다 be punished severely; suffer a severe punishment. ◉ ～주의 a severe punishment policy: ～주의로 임하다 adopt a severe punishment policy; go on the principle of martinetism.

**엄범부렁하다** (be) bulky but loose.

**엄법**(罨法) 〖한의〗 fomentation. ⇨ 찜질.

**엄벙덤벙** carelessly; heedlessy; at random; slapdash; sloppily. ～하다 go at it carelessly 〔sloppily〕.

**엄벙하다** ① 《일하는 품이》 (be) sloppy; slack; loose; slovenly. ¶ 일하는 것이 ～ be slack in *one's* work. ② 《언행이》 (be) frivolous.

**엄부**(嚴父) a stern 〔strict〕 father.

**엄부렁하다** ⇨ 엄범부렁하다.

**엄비**(嚴秘) strict secrecy; a carefully guarded 〔closely kept〕 secret. ⇨ 극비.

**엄살** exaggeration 〔pretension〕 of pain 〔hardship〕; much ado 〔a great fuss〕 about nothing; feigned dismay. ～하다 = 엄살부리다. ¶ ～을 떨다 pretend to be 「ill 〔hard〕; make much ado about nothing. ◉ ～꾸러기 a crybaby; a fussbudget; a fusspot.

**엄살부리다** exaggerate 〔pretend〕 pain 〔hardship〕; make 「much ado 〔a great fuss〕 about trifles 〔nothing〕. ¶ 어렵다고 ～ complain too much about the difficulties / 작은 찰과상을 가지고 크게 ～ make a great fuss about a small scratch / 돈 좀 꾸어 달랬더니 그는 한 푼 없다고 엄살을 부렸다 When I asked him for some money, he turned me down with some song-and-dance about not having any.

**엄선**(嚴選) careful selection. ～하다 select 〔screen〕 carefully; choose with care; handpick 《구어》. ¶ ～한 choice 《goods》; select 《members》 / ～된 carefully screened 《students》; hand-picked 《drivers》 / 구직자를 ～하다 carefully screen job applicants.

**엄수**(嚴守) strict observance; rigid adherence 《to rules》. ～하다 observe 《a rule》 strictly; keep 《a secret, *one's* promise》 strictly; rigidly adhere to. ¶ 명령을 ～하다 obey a command to the letter / 시간을 ～하다 be very punctual.

**엄숙**(嚴肅) seriousness; solemnity; gravity; rigor. ～하다 (be) grave; serious; solemn; somber (표정·음색 따위가). ¶ ～한 말투 a solemn tone / ～한 표정 a somber expression 〔look〕 / ～한 분위기 a solemn atmosphere / ～한 기분이 되다 be inspired with awe; be awe-struck / ～히 gravely; seriously; solemnly / ～히 말하다 speak gravely / 진실을 말할 것을 ～히 맹세합니까 Do you solemnly swear to tell the truth? / 식은 매우 ～히 거행되었다 The ceremony was conducted with great solemnity.

**엄습**(掩襲) a surprise 〔sudden〕 attack. ～하다 make a surprise 〔sudden〕 attack on; swoop down on; 《재난 따위

가》 hit; strike; visit. ¶ ～당하다 be attacked; be visited 〔hit〕《by》/ 폭풍우의 ～을 받다 [장소가 주어] be visited 〔hit〕 by a storm; [사람이 주어] be caught in 〔overtaken by〕 a storm / 갑자기 추위가 ～해 왔다 The cold weather took the people by surprise.

**엄시하**(嚴侍下) having only *one's* father alive to serve.

**엄연하다**(儼然―) 《엄숙하다》 (be) dignified; solemn; stern; 《명확하다》 be (as) clear as day. ¶ 엄연한 사실 a stern reality; an undeniable fact / 엄연한 증거 a positive proof / 엄연히 solemnly; sternly; with dignity / 주택부족이라는 엄연한 사실 the stark 〔hard〕 fact of housing shortage / 이 도덕률은 아직도 엄연히 존재한다 This moral law is still in full force.

**엄전하다** (be) gentle; mild; good-tempered; obedient; modest. ¶ 엄전한 여자 a modest woman.

**엄정**(嚴正) exactness; strictness; rigidness; strict fairness. ～하다 (be) exact; strictly fair; impartial; unprejudiced. ¶ ～한 비판(批判) impartial criticism / ～히 strictly; rigorously; fairly; impartially / ～하게 다스리다 deal stringently with… / 작품들을 ～히 심사하다 judge the works fairly.
◉ ～중립 《observe》 strict neutrality.

**엄중하다**(嚴重―) (be) strict; stringent; severe; stern; rigorous. ¶ 엄중한 검사 a severe 〔close〕 inspection / 엄중한 규칙 a strict 〔rigorous〕 rule / 엄중한 문초 〔조사〕 a close examination; a searching investigation / 엄중히 strictly; severely; rigidly; sternly; rigorously; closely / 엄중히 처벌하다 punish 《*a person*》 severely / 엄중한 경고를 하다 give a solemn warning / 엄중히 감시하다 guard closely; keep a close watch 《over》 / 엄중히 단속하다 exercise strict control 《on, over》 / 엄중히 항의하다 make a strong protest.

**엄지** 《엄지가락》 a thumb; a big finger 〔toe〕. ◉ ～머리총각 a lifelong bachelor. ～발가락 a big toe. ～발톱 a big toenail. ～벌레 an imago (*pl.* ～es, imagines). ～손가락 a thumb. ～손톱 a thumbnail.

**엄징**(嚴懲) severe punishment. ～하다 deal with severely.

**엄책**(嚴責) a harsh reproof. ～하다 scold 〔reprimand〕 harshly; reprove sternly.

**엄처시하**(嚴妻侍下) a henpecked husband; petticoat government. ¶ ～에 살다 be tied to *one's* wife's apron strings.

**엄청나다** (be) exorbitant; preposterous; absurd; whacking; wild. ¶ 엄청난 값 an exorbitant price / 엄청난 숫자 an enormous 〔a colossal, a stupendous〕 number / 엄청난 득표 a whacking chunk of votes / 엄청난 요구 a preposterous demand / 엄청나게 excessively; extravagantly / 엄청나게 큰 very big; huge; monstrous; gigantic; enormous / 엄청난 소리를 하다 say extravagant things / 엄청나게 싸게 사다 buy dirt-cheap / 엄청나게 비싸다 It is ridiculously high. / 키가 엄청나게 크다 He is quite tall. / 그 개구리 엄청나게 큰데 What a monster of a frog that is! / 그는 무슨 엄청난 짓을 할 게다 He is sure to set the world on fire.

**엄친**(嚴親) *one's* own father; my father.

**엄탐**(嚴探) a strict search 〔inquiry〕. ～하다 search rigorously 〔intently, closely〕; be on a sharp lookout 《for》; investigate closely. ¶ 범인을 ～중이다 A strict search is being made for the offender. *or* The police are hot on the trail of the culprit.

**엄파이어** an umpire. ¶ ～를 보다 act as umpire 《in a game》; umpire 《a game》.

**엄펑소니** a trick; a sharper's trade; a swindle. ¶ ～를 쓰다 trick 〔swindle〕 《*a person*》; take 《*a person*》 in.

**엄펑스럽다** (be) swindling; crooked; cheating; fraudulent; deceitful.

**엄폐**(掩蔽) concealment; cover. ～하다 cover up; conceal; mask. ¶ 범죄의 흔적을 ～하다 cover up the traces of a crime. ◉ ～물 a cover; a shelter. ～호 a covered trench; an entrenchment; a bunker.

**엄포** (a) bluff; an empty threat 〔menace〕; an idle threat; a claptrap. ¶ ～놓다 utter empty threats 《against》; use empty menaces 《to》; bluster 《out》; speak claptrap / ～를 놓아 그를 찍소리 못하게 했다 I blustered him into silence. / 그건 단순한 ～에 지나지 않는다 That's nothing but a bluff. / 그런 ～는 겁나지 않아 I won't be intimidated by such a bluff. / 그런 ～에 내가 넘어갈 줄 아느냐 Do you really think such a bluff will work with me?

**엄하다**(嚴―) (be) severe; strict; stern; rigid; rigorous; razor-sharp; 《가혹하다》

stringent; harsh; exacting. ¶ 엄한 법〔규칙〕 stringent laws 〔regulations〕/ 엄한 규율 strict 〔rigid〕 discipline / 엄한 부모〔선생〕 strict parents 〔teachers〕/ 엄한 얼굴 a stern face / 어린애들한테 ~ be stern 「to 〔with *one's*〕 children / 엄하게 strictly; severely; sternly; rigorously; rigidly / 엄하게 꾸짖다〔벌하다〕 scold 〔punish〕 《*a person*》 severely / 애들을 엄하게 기르다 bring children up strictly / 학생에 대해 ~ be strict with students / 그 학교는 규율이 ~ That school keeps the students under rigorous discipline.

**엄한**(嚴寒) the intense 〔severe〕 cold; the rigor of winter.

**엄형**(嚴刑) severe 〔heavy, harsh〕 punishment.

**엄호**(掩護) cover(ing); protection; backing. ~하다 back (up); give support 《to》; cover; protect; shelter. ¶ 측면〔퇴각〕을 ~하다 cover the flank 〔retreat〕/ 포병의 ~하에 싸우다 fight under covering fire from artillery. ◉ ~부대 the covering forces 〔unit〕. ~사격 covering fire 〔barrage (탄막)〕; a curtain fire. ~진지 a covering position. ~포화 a wall 〔cover〕 of fire; a barrage.

**업**(業) ① 《직업》 work; a profession (전문적인); an occupation; a calling (천직의); a (line of) business; a trade (상업 등의). ⇨ 직업. ¶ 업으로 하다 make a profession 〔business〕 of / 의술을 업으로 하다 practice medicine; be a physician by profession / 문필을 업으로 삼다 adopt writing as a profession. ② 〖불교〗 *karma* (Sans.); *one's* deed as a determinant factor in *one's* future life. ¶ 이것은 모두 너의 전생의 업이다 This is entirely due to your deeds in your previous existence.

**업계**(業界) business circles 〔quarters, world〕; the industry; the trade. ¶ ~의 거물 a bigwig 〔a leading figure〕 in the world of business / 버스 ~의 사람들 people in the bus trade / ~의 강력한 반대에 부딪히다 be faced with strong opposition of the business world / 그 신상품은 ~의 화제가 되어 있다 The new product is the talk of the trade. ◉ ~지(紙) a trade paper 〔magazine〕. 석유~ the oil industry. 출판~ publishing circles.

**업다** ① 《등에》 carry 《*a person*, a pack》 on the back. ¶ 애기를 (등에) ~ carry a baby on *one's* back. ② 《끌고 들어가다》 implicate; involve in. ¶ 그는 죄를 혼자 지지 않고 친구들을 업고 들어갔다 Refusing to take the guilt upon himself alone, he dragged his friends into it too. ③ 《교미하다》 copulate.

**업둥이** a foster child 「that has come to *one* by chance 〔that has been left on *one's* doorstep〕.

**업무**(業務) business; service; duty; operation; work; affairs.
¶ ~용(의) for business use 〔purposes〕/ ~ 외의 nonoccupational / ~가 다망하여 in the press of business / ~상의 질병이나 부상 sickness or injuries due to occupational cases 〔arising out of duty〕/ ~상의 비밀 trade secrets / ~상의 전화 business calls / ~ 담당 사원 an active 〔a managing〕 partner / 수송 ~ transportation service / ~용의 차 a car for business use / ~를 감독하다 superintend operations / ~를 방해하다 impede 〔interfere with〕 《*a person's*》 business / ~를 처리하다 conduct 〔carry on〕 business / ~를 확장하다 expand 《its》 operations / ~에 힘쓰다 apply *oneself* to *one's* work; attend to *one's* business with diligence; work hard at *one's* business / ~를 게을리 하다 neglect *one's* business / 주요 ~ 계획을 보고받다 be briefed 〔receive a briefing〕 from 《*a person*》 on *his* major business / ~ 확장에 따라 당사는 영업소를 신설하였습니다 Our company opened a new sales office to accomodate business expansion. / 지점은 10월부터 ~를 개시한다 The branch office will open (for business) in October.
◉ ~감사 audit. ~관리 business management 〔control〕. ~명령 a business order. ~방해 interference with *a person's* duties. ~보고 a report on operation(s); a business 〔an operational〕 report. ~부 the Operation 〔Business〕 Department. ~분담표 a work responsibility schedule. ~사원 a member of management department. ~상 과실 (professional) negligence: ~상 과실 치사(죄) (a charge of ) professional negligence resulting in death / ~상 과실 치사상(致死傷)으로 기소되다 be prosecuted for professional negligence resulting in injury and 〔or〕 death. ~상 횡령 embezzlement of corporate funds. ~시간 office 〔business〕 hours. ~일지 a business log. ~제휴 a business tie-up. ~집행 the management 〔conduct〕 of business; the execution of *one's* duty: ~

집행 대리인 a managing agent / ～ 집행 방해 interference in the execution of *a person's* duty.

**업보**(業報) 〖불교〗 retribution for the deeds of 「a former life 〔a previous incarnation〕; *karma* effects.

**업신여기다** despise; make light of 《*a person*》; look down on 《*a person*》; hold 《*a person*》 in contempt; disdain. ¶ 업신여기는 태도〔표정〕 a contemptuous air 〔look〕 / 부모를 ～ slight *one's* parents / 사람을 업신여기는 버릇이 있다 have a habit of looking down upon people / 그는 너를 업신여긴다 He looks down upon you. / 그의 실력을 업신여겨서는 안 된다 You mustn't make light of his ability. / 가난하다고 사람을 업신여겨서는 안 된다 You shouldn't despise a man because he is poor.

**업신여김** contempt; scorn; disdain; slighting. ¶ ～을 당하다〔받다〕 be slighted; be taken lightly; be held in contempt / 나는 네 생각처럼 그렇게 ～을 당할 사람이 아니다 I am not so cheap a fellow as you think me.

**업어치기** 〖유도〗 a back 〔shoulder〕 throw; throwing over *one's* shoulder; 〖레슬링〗 a (cross-)buttock.

**업자**(業者) 《상인》 a trader; a dealer; 《제조업자》 a manufacturer; 《실업가》 a businessman; [총칭] the trade. ¶ 관련 ～ traders 〔manufactures〕 concerned / 악덕 ～ a crooked dealer / 관련 ～를 초청하다 call in traders concerned / ～간의 경쟁을 더욱 활발케 하는 것이 좋다 Competition among the manufacturers should be further stimulated. / 우리는 단골 ～에게 기계 조립을 부탁했다 We asked our regular manufacturer to build a machine.
◉ ～단체 a trade association.

**업적**(業績) 《개인의》 work; achievements; results; contributions; 《회사 등의》 (business) result(s). ¶ 물리학상의 ～ *one's* achievements in physics / 뛰어난 ～을 올리다 get 〔achieve〕 good 《business》 results; produce brilliant 《scientific》 achievements / 그의 학문적 ～은 크게 인정을 받았다 His academic achievements has been widely recognized. / 이 달의 우리 회사 ～은 좋다〔나쁘다〕 Our business this month has been good 〔poor〕. / 사원 전체의 노력으로 회사의 ～은 크게 올라갔다 Our company has achieved much better results because of the great efforts made by all the employees.
◉ ～보고 《회사 등의》 a business report.

**업종**(業種) types of business 〔industry, enterprise〕; a category of business 〔trade〕.
◉ ～별 industrial classification; classification by industry: ～별 전화 번호부 a telephone directory classified by 「the types of business 〔industry〕 / ～별 임금 prevailing wages by industry / ～별로 분류하다 classify by industry.

**업체**(業體) a (business) enterprise.
◉ 민간〔개인〕 ～ a private enterprise. 부실 ～ a 'hole-in-the-wall' enterprise. 생산〔수출〕 ～ a production 〔an export〕 enterprise.

**업태**(業態) business conditions 〔status〕.
◉ ～조사 an inquiry into the business status; a business conditions survey.

**업히다** ① 《등에》 get 〔ride〕 on 《*a person's*》 back; be carried on 《*a person's*》 back; ride piggyback 〔pickaback〕 on 《*a person*》. ¶ 업혀 가다 be carried on 《*a person's*》 back / 어린애가 엄마 등에 ～ A child gets on its mother's back. ② 《…위에》 lie upon another; be piled on another.

**없다** ① 《존재하지 않다》 there is no …; do not exist. ¶ …이 없는 경우에는 in the absence 〔in default〕 of 《the article》 / …이 없으면〔없었다면〕 if there were no …; were it not for; had it not been for; but for / 내가 없는 동안에 during my absence; while I am away / 없는 말을 퍼뜨리다 spread a false rumor / 없는 것이나 매한가지다 be next to nothing / 거기에는 아무도 ～ There is no one there. / 그것을 모르는 사람은 ～ There is no one who doesn't know it. / 유령 따위는 ～ Ghost do not exist. / 있는 것이 없는 것보다 낫다 Something is better than nothing.
② 《소유하지 않다》 have no…; do not have; have not (got); be without; 《결여하다》 want; lack; be wanting 〔lacking〕 in; be devoid of. ¶ …이 없어서 for want of 《a better word》; in the absence of 《further information》 / 돈이 ～ have no money; be out of money; be broke 《구어》 / 용기가 ～ lack 〔be wanting in〕 courage / 의리가 ～ fail to carry out *one's* duty 〔obligations〕 / 재수가 ～ be unlucky / 흥미가 ～ [사물이 주어] be devoid of interest; be uninteresting; [사람이 주어]

be not interested 《in》/ 할 일이 ~ have nothing to do / 그녀에겐 자식이 ~ She has no children. *or* She is childless. / 이 방에는 창문이 ~ This room has no windows. / 우리에게는 자금이 ~ We lack [are out of] funds. / 찾아 뵐 틈이 없습니다 I have no time to call on you. / 그는 그 계획을 실행할 힘이 ~ He lacks the power to carry out the plan.
③ 《있던 것이》 be gone; be lost; be absent; 《눈에 띄지 않다》 be missing; cannot be found. ¶ 그는 오른팔이 ~ He has lost his right arm. / 방금 책상 위에 둔 책이 ~ I cannot find the book that I just put on the table. / 아무리 찾아도 없습니다 It is nowhere to be found. *or* I can't find it anywhere.
④ 《없어지다》 run out [short] 《of》; be out 《of》; be exhausted [used up, consumed]. ¶ 우물에 물이 ~ The well has run dry. / 가솔린이[현금이] ~ We have run out of gas [cash].
⑤ 《결점·장애 따위가》 be free from; be clear of [from]. ¶ 불순물이 없는 물 water free of impurities / 혐의가 ~ be clear from suspicion / 결점이 ~ be free from faults; be faultless / 속박이 ~ be free from fetters / 앞길에 걸릴 것이 ~ There is nothing standing in my way.
⑥ 《죽고 없다》 be deceased; be defunct. ¶ 부모 없는 아이 an orphan / 아버지가 ~ *one's* father is deceased; have no father.
⑦ 《가난하다》 poor; needy; impoverished. ¶ 없는 사람들 the poor; poor people / 없는 살림 a living in poverty / 그는 없는 집안에서 태어났다 He was born of poor parents.
⑧ 《오지 않다》 ¶ 그에게서 전화가 아직 ~ I haven't had a telephone call from him yet. / 왜 그에게서 편지가 없을까 I wonder why he doesn't write.
⑨ 《기타》 ¶ 나는 웃을 수밖에 없었다 I could not help laughing. / 어찌할 수 ~ I can't help it. / 물은 생활에 없어서는 안될 물질이다 Water is something there could be no life without. / 그는 책 읽기에 정신이 ~ He is absorbed in a book.

**없애다** ① 《제거하다》 take off; remove; exclude (배제); omit (생략); leave out; get rid of; exterminate; eliminate. ¶ 나쁜 습관을 ~ get rid of a bad habit / 뜰의 잡초를 ~ clear the garden of the weeds / 명부에서 이름을 ~ strike 《*a person's*》 name off a list / 빈민굴을 ~ clear slums / 장애물을 ~ clear [remove] obstacles / 해충을 ~ exterminate harmful insects. ② 《폐지하다》 do away with; abolish. ¶ 허례를 ~ do away with meaningless formalities / 노예[사형] 제도를 ~ abolish 「slavery [capital punishment]. ③ 《낭비하다》 waste; throw away; 《잃다》 lose; 《써버리다》 spend; use up; exhaust; run out of. ¶ 시간을 ~ spend time / 옷에 많은 돈을 ~ spend a lot of money on clothes / 그는 경마로 돈을 없앴다 He lost his money betting on horses. ④ 《죽이다》 kill; murder; make [do] away with; dispatch; rub out 《속어》. ¶ 방해자들을 ~ kill those who were in *one's* way.

**없어지다** ① 《잃다》 be [get] lost; be missing; be gone. ¶ 없어진 시계 a lost [missing] watch / 모자가 없어졌다 My hat is missing. *or* I have lost my hat. ② 《고갈되다》 be dried up; be used up; be exhausted; be depleted; be drained. ¶ 전쟁으로 이 나라의 자원은 다 없어졌다 The war exhausted the resources of this country. *or* The war was a great drain upon this country's resources. ③ 《사라지다》 disappear; vanish; be gone. ¶ 이제는 없어진 정당 a party now defunct / 희망이 ~ become hopeless / 모든 희망이 없어졌다 All hopes have vanished [gone]. / 흔적이 ~ There is nothing [not a trace] left (of).

**없이** without; not having. ¶ 예외 ~ without exceptions / 그지~ endlessly; infinitely / 맥~ listlessly; dejectedly / 정신~ absent-mindedly / 의심[틀림]~ without doubt [fail] / 할 수 ~ unavoidably; of necessity; out of sheer necessity / 돈 ~ 여행하다 go on a trip without money / 그 여자 ~는 살 수가 없다 I cannot live without her.

**엇-** crooked; curved; diagonal; (a)slant; deviate; wrong; crosswise; mutual; almost; not quite.

**엇가다** go astray; go contrary to reason; deviate; be perverse. ¶ 엇가는 행동 a perverse act. ⇨엇나가다.

**엇각**(—角) 〖수학〗 alternate angles.

**엇갈리다** pass [cross] 《each other》; miss each other on the way; 《letters》 cross in the mail. ¶ 마음에 희비가 ~ joy and grief alternate in *one's* heart / 그를 만나려 하였으나 길이 엇갈

렸다 I wished to see him, but it so happened that we missed (each other) on the way. / 자네 편지와 내 편지가 중도에 엇갈렸다 Your letter has crossed mine. *or* Our letters have crossed in the mail.

**엇걸다** cross 《each other》; make a diagonal loop; stack (총을). ¶ 총을 ~ stack rifles / 국기를 ~ cross 〔inter-wine〕 national flags / 상자를 리본으로 엇걸어 매다 put the ribbon around the box in a diagonal loop.

**엇걸리다** be crossed; be made in a diagonal loop; be stacked.

**엇결** 《나무의》 cross-grain (of timber).

**엇구수하다** ① 《음식이》 (be) rather tasty. ② 《애기가》 (be) rather humorous 〔amusing〕.

**엇나가다** 《방향이》 turn aside 〔away〕; 《이야기 따위가》 stray 〔deviate, digress〕 《from》; 《마음이》 grow crooked; become 〔grow, get〕 perverse; be 〔get〕 distorted 〔twisted, warped〕; 《행동·일이》 go astray 〔wild, wrong〕. ¶ 어제는 만사가 엇나가는 날이었던 모양이다 Everything seemed to be going wrong 〔amiss〕 yesterday. / 이 나이의 소녀들은 엇나가기가 쉽다 Girls at this age are apt to go astray.

**엇대다** ① 《조각을》 fix 〔put〕 askew 〔cockeyed, crooked〕. ¶ 옷에 헝겊을 ~ put a patch on *one's* clothes cockeyed / 책상을 고칠 때 다리를 엇댔다 In repairing the table I put the leg on crooked. ② 《비꼬다》 make an insinuating remark 《at》.

**엇되다** 《건방지다》 (be) snobbish; stuck=up; self-important; uppity. ¶ 엇된 놈 a snob. 「a squinter. ⇨ 사팔뜨기.

**엇뜨기** a cross-〔squint-〕eyed person;

**엇뜨다** squint (*one's* eyes).

**엇먹다** ① 《톱이》 《a blade》 cut at an angle; cut crooked. ② 《비꼬다》 insinuate; distort (remarks); twist (words).

**엇메다** strap under one arm and over the other shoulder (across *one's* chest). ¶ 가방을 ~ sling a satchel from the shoulder across *one's* chest.

**엇바꾸다** exchange 《books》 with each other; interchange.

**엇베다** cut crooked 〔at an angle〕; make an oblique cut. ¶ 종이를 ~ cut paper crooked.

**엇비슷하다** be about alike; be nearly the same; be almost similar. ¶ 값이 ~ the prices are much the same / 그와 나는 키가 ~ He is about as tall as I am.

**엇섞다** mix in alternation.

**-었겠다** 《추측》 ¶ 그의 나이 스물은 넘었겠다 I bet he'll never see twenty again.

**-었느냐** 《의문》 ¶ 너 어디 있었느냐, 하루 종일 보이지 않으니 Where have you been that I haven't seen you all day long?

**-었는지** 《불확실》 whether it was 〔did〕. ¶ 누구였는지 아십니까 Do you know who it was? / 그이가 살았는지 죽었는지 아무도 모른다 Nobody knows whether he is alive or dead. / 그가 정말 그런 말을 했었는지 기억하십니까 Do you remember whether he really said that?

**-었으나** ¶ 처음엔 꽤 문제가 되었으나 이젠 순조로이 진행된다 At first it was quite a problem, but now it's going smoothly.

**엉거주춤하다** ① 《자세가》 half-stand half-sit; half-rise. ¶ 엉거주춤한 자세로 in a half-rising〔-sitting〕 posture / 엉거주춤하지 말고 서든지 앉든지 해라 Either stand up or sit down—stop hovering about! ② 《망설이다》 hover; hesitate; waver 《between》. ¶ 엉거주춤하는 사람 a man on the fence / 엉거주춤하지 말고 결정해라 Get off the fence and make up your mind. / 그는 갈까 말까 잠시 엉거주춤했다 He hovered for a while, unable to make up his mind whether he should go or not.

**엉겁** stickiness; a sticky covering 《of *something*》. ¶ 손에 엿이 ~을 했다 The hands were all sticky with taffy.

**엉겁결에** unexpectedly; unconsciously; without realizing it; (all) unawares; 《의지에 반하여》 in spite of *oneself*. ¶ ~ 웃다 laugh in spite of *oneself* / ~ 그런 말이 튀어 나왔다 The words just escaped my lips.

**엉겅퀴** 〖식물〗 a thistle.

**엉구다** 《주선하다》 form 《a plan》 out; work out; get 《a plan》 ready.

**엉금엉금** crawling; creeping; sprawling. ¶ ~ 기어가다 go on all fours; creep 〔crawl〕 to 〔toward〕.

**엉기다** ① 《뭉치다》 curdle; coagulate; clot; congeal. ¶ 엉긴 피 clotted blood / 우유가 ~ milk curdles. ② 《일이》 be all tangled up 〔snarled up〕; be enmeshed. ¶ 일이 ~ be all tangled up in *one's* work. ③ 《기어가다》 crawl with difficulty 〔effort〕; creep.

**엉기정기** 《무질서하게》 pell-mell; in confusion; in disorder.

**엉너리** bamboozlements to ingratiate

*oneself*. ～치다 try all sorts of tricks to win favor. ◉ 엉너릿손 the skill of ingratiating *oneself*.

**엉덩방아** a fall on *one's* backside 〔buttocks〕; pratfall 《미속어》. ¶～ 찧다 fall (heavily) on *one's* buttocks 〔backside〕; land on *one's* rear; 《미속어》 take a pratfall.

**엉덩이** the buttocks; the hips; the bottom; the rump (새·짐승 따위의); the fanny 《미구어》; the ass 《비어》. ¶～가 큰 여자 a wide-〔broad-〕hipped woman / ～가 무겁다 《자리뜰 줄 모르다》 stay too long; overstay *one's* welcome; 《게으르다》 be sluggish 〔indolent, lazy, slow〕 / ～가 가볍다 do not stay long 《in a place》; 《경박하다》 be flighty 〔imprudent〕 / 아이의 ～를 때리다 spank a child; smack a child's bottom (★ spank는 여러번, smack는 한 번) / ～를 걷어차다 kick *a person's* butt / 여자의 ～를 쫓아다니다 chase after 〔hang about〕 a girl.

**엉덩잇바람** swaying *one's* hips (as *one* walks).

**엉덩잇짓** hip movements; swaying *one's* hips; grinding *one's* hips. ～하다 make hip movements; sway *one's* hips; grind *one's* hips.

**엉덩춤** a hip dance; a hula (하와이의 훌라춤).

**엉덩판** ⇨엉덩이. ¶～이 크다 have big hips.

**엉두덜거리다** 《투덜거리다》 be muttering and grumbling; complain; murmur with discontent.

**엉뚱하다** 《터무니없다》 (be) extraordinary; fantastic; extravagant; preposterous; 《뜻밖이다》 (be) unexpected; 《무모하다》 (be) wild; farfetched; 《사리에 안맞다》 (be) absurd; inconsistent; 《관계없다》 (be) irrelevant; impertinent; 《틀리다》 (be) wrong 《direction》; different.

¶엉뚱한 값 a preposterous price / 엉뚱한 계획 a farfetched scheme; a fantastic plan / 엉뚱한 사람 a wild (-eyed) person (무모한 사람); a different person (다른 사람); a person not related (관계없는 사람) / 엉뚱한 생각 an idea way out of line; an extravagant notion / 엉뚱한 요구 an unreasonable 〔inordinate〕 demand / 엉뚱한 대답 an irrelevant 〔impertinent〕 answer / 엉뚱한 질문을 하다 ask an unexpected question / 엉뚱한 주장을 하다 keep arguing at cross-purpose / 엉뚱한 짓을 하다 《무모한 짓》 act recklessly; take headlong action; 《뜻밖의 짓》 do quite an unexpected thing / 이야기가 엉뚱해서 그가 좀 의심스러웠다 His story was so fantastic that I was somewhat suspicious of him.

**엉망** mess; 《in》 bad shape; ruin; wreck. ¶～이 되다 get out of shape; be spoiled 〔ruined〕 / ～을 만들다 spoil; make a mess 《of》; upset / 일을 ～으로 만들다 mess up matters / 내 모자가 ～이다 My hat is in bad shape. *or* My hat was crushed out of shape. / 폭발 사고 현장은 ～이었다 The scene of the explosion was in turmoil. / 장마로 꽃이 ～이 되었다 The flowers have been ruined by the long rain.

**엉성하다** ① 《짜임새가 없다》 (be) loose; thin; sparse (성기다); coarse (조잡하다). ¶엉성한 번역 a loose translation / 엉성하게 짜다 knit with large stitches / 편집이 ～ be carelessly compiled. ② 《탐탁찮다》 (be) unsatisfactory; 《일 따위가》 (be) slipshod; slovenly; poor. ¶엉성한 결과 an unsatisfactory result / 일솜씨가 ～ be of bad (slovenly) workmanship / 솜씨가 엉성한 unskillful; clumsy.

**엉엉** bawling; squalling. ¶～ 울다 cry bitterly 〔loudly〕; cry *one's* heart out.

**엉엉거리다** ① 《울다》 ⇨ 엉엉. ② 《하소연하다》 complain of 《*one's* hard life》; whine about 《*one's* work》.

**엉정벙정** with superfluous things scattered about. ～하다 be all cluttered up 《with》; leave 《odds and ends》 lying about.

**엉클다** tangle; mix up. ¶고양이가 내 털실 뭉치를 엉클어 놓았다 The cat has made a tangle of my ball of yarn.

**엉클어지다** get tangled; be entangled; be matted. ¶엉클어진 머리 matted 〔tangled〕 hair / 엉클어진 실을 풀다 straighten tangled thread out.

**엉큼성큼, 엉큼엉큼** with long strides. ⇨성큼(성큼). ¶～ 걷다 stride; stalk.

**엉큼하다** 《교활하다》 (be) wily; insidious; treacherous; wicked; 《속이 검다》 (be) blackhearted; deep 《구어》; 《책략을 쓰다》 (be) scheming. ¶엉큼한 사람 an insidious man; 《구어》 a deep one / 엉큼한 속셈 a wily scheme / 엉큼한 눈짓 〔미소〕 a treacherous glance 〔smile〕 / 그는 엉큼한 놈이어서 무슨 짓을 꾸미는지 모른다 He is a wicked and crafty fellow; you never know what he's up to.

**엉키다** ⇨엉클어지다.

**엉터리** ① 《미덥지 못한 사람〔것〕》 a fake; a sham; a gyp; a clip; 《하찮은 물건》

something cheap and shabby; junk; cheap stuff; 《굴퉁이》 a gimcrack; a trumpery; a gewgaw. ¶ ～ 시인 a「poor 〔wretched〕 poet / ～ 의사 a quack (doctor) / ～ 회사 a bogus concern 《미》/ 그는 ～라서 하는 말을 믿어서는 안 된다 He is a fake, you can't believe a word he says. / 그는 일을 ～로 한다 He does a slapdash job.
② 《대강의 윤곽》 framework; general plan; layout. ¶ 일의 ～가 잡히다 the general plan of a job is「drawn up 〔laid out〕; the framework of a project is set up.
③ 《터무니》 a ground; a foundation. ¶ ～없는 수작 groundless 〔baseless, unfounded〕 remarks / ～없는 짓 a foolish act / ～없는 거짓말 a whopping lie.

**엊그저께, 엊그제** a few days ago.

**엊저녁** yesterday evening; last evening 〔night〕.

**엎다** 《뒤집다》 turn 〔lay〕 upside down; turn down; turn over; tip over; 《타도하다》 overthrow. ¶ 책을 엎어놓다 put a book face down / 찻잔을 엎어놓다 put teacups bottom-side up / 성이 나서 밥상을 ～ throw a table over in anger / 사나운 물결이 배를 ～ raging waves capsize a boat / 정부를 ～ overthrow the government.

**엎드러지다** fall on *one's* face; fall down. ¶ 문지방에 걸려서 ～ trip 〔fall〕 over the threshold.

**엎드려쏴** 〖군사〗 firing from a「prone 〔lying-down〕 position; prone fire. ◉ ～자세 prone position.

**엎드려팔굽혀펴기** a push-up 《미》; a press-up 《영》. ¶ 다섯번 ～를 하다 do five push-ups.

**엎드리다** lie on *one's* face; lie flat 《on the ground》; prostrate *oneself;* throw *oneself* flat (on *one's* stomach); lie prone. ¶ 임금 앞에 ～ prostrate *oneself* before the king / 엎드려 자다 sleep on *one's* face / 땅에 납작 ～ lie flat on the ground / 엎드려 바랍니다 I beg you will kindly oblige me. *or* I must humbly ask you 《to *do*》.

**엎어놓다** put 《*a thing*》 face 〔top〕 down.

**엎어누르다** press down; oppress; sup「press.

**엎어지다** ① 《넘어지다》 fall on *one's*「face 〔breast, nose〕; fall 〔tumble, pitch〕 forward; fall down. ¶ 엎어지면 코 닿을 곳에 있다 be within「hail 〔call〕; be at stones throw 《from》/ 그는 발을 헛디뎌 앞으로 엎어졌다 He lost his footing and fell on his face. ② 《뒤집히다》 (***a***) 《위아래가 거꾸로》 be turned upsidedown. (***b***) 《전복되다》 be turned over; be upset; be overthrown; capsize. ¶ 현정부가 ～ the present government is overthrown / 계획이 ～ *one's* plan is upset / 꽃병이 엎어졌다 The vase has been upset. / 배가 엎어져 많은 사람이 죽었다 The boat capsized and many were drowned.

**엎지르다** spill; slop. ¶ 엎지른 물 spilt water / 컵의 우유를 ～ spill milk from a cup / 상에 물을 ～ spill water upon a table / 엎지른 물은 다시 담지 못 한다 《속담》 It is no use crying over spilt milk.

**엎치다** turn upside down. ⇨ 엎다.

**엎치락뒤치락** turning over and over; up-and-down; up-again. ～하다 turn over and over; toss「about 〔roll〕 《in bed》; 《경기 등이》 the「lead 〔advantage〕 shifts rapidly from one contestant to another; be nip and tuck; 《호각》 be neck and neck. ¶ ～하는 대열전 a nip-and-tuck game / ～하는 경기 a seesaw game; a dingdong contest / 그는 잠이 오지 않아 자리에서 ～했다 He tossed about on the bed unable to get to sleep.

**엎친 데 덮치다** add to *one's* troubles; make things worse. ¶ 엎친 데 덮치기로 to make things worse; to add to *one's* miseries; what is worse / 불행이 ～ have one misfortune on top of another / 엎친 데 덮치기로 비까지 왔다 To make matters worse, it started to rain.

**에**[1] [감탄사] well; well now; let me see; uh. ¶ 에, 제가 한입니다 Well, let me introduce myself to you. I am Han.

**에**[2] [조사] ① 《때·시간》 at; in; on (★ at는 시각·때의 한 시점을, in은 오전·오후·주 등 비교적 짧은 기간 뿐 아니라 달·계절·년·세기·시대 등의 긴 기간을, on은 날·요일이나 특정한 아침·오전·오후 등을 나타낼 때 쓰임. at는 보통 the를 수반하지 아니함). ¶ 아침 〔오전, 오후, 저녁〕에 in the「morning 〔forenoon, afternoon, evening〕/ 밤에 at night / 그 전〔후〕에 before 〔after〕 that / 두 시 (15분)에 at (a quarter after) two / 일요일 (아침)에 on Sunday (morning) / 제 시간에 in time / 3월〔봄〕에 in「March 〔spring〕/ 2년에 한 번 once in two years.
② 《나이》 at. ¶ 일곱 살에 학교에 가다 go to school at the age of seven.

③ 《장소》 at; in; on (★ 「좁은 곳」에는 at, 「넓은 곳」에는 in을 쓰는 것이 보통이나 그 넓고 좁은 것은 말하는 사람의 주관에 따라 결정됨. 또한 말하는 사람의 거주지(대도시가 아니라도)에는 in을, 대도시라도 단순히 한 지점으로 보는 경우에는 at을 씀). ¶ 대문에 at the gate / 방에 in the room / 남북에 north and south; from the north to the south / 책상 위에 on the table / 천장에 붙은 파리떼 flies on the ceiling / 물 위에 떠 있는 floating on the water / 10페이지에 on page 10 / 양쪽에 on both sides 〔either side〕 (★ 각기 side의 「수」에 주의할 것) / 서울에 도착하다 arrive in Seoul / 아파트에 살다 live in an apartment / 칠판에 글을 쓰다 write on the blackboard / 봉투에 우표를 붙이다 stick a stamp on the envelope / 입에 담뱃대를 물다 have a pipe in *one's* mouth / 브로드웨이에 살다 live on Broadway 《미》 / 파크레인에 살다 live in Park Lane 《영》 (★ 「…가(街)에」의 경우 영·미에서 전치사가 다름).

④ 《방향》 to; for; on; in; into. ¶ 상자에 넣다 put 《*a thing*》 in 〔into〕 the box / 벽에 기대다 lean against the wall / 학교에 가다 go to (the) school / 집에 들어가다 enter 〔go into〕 the house / 전쟁에 나가다 go to war / 땅에 떨어지다 fall to the ground.

⑤ [비인칭 간접목적] to. ¶ 은행에 보내다 send it to the bank / 대학교에 편지를 쓰다 write a letter to the university / 도서관에 책을 기증하다 donate a book to the library.

⑥ 《비율·꼴》 at; in; for; by; per. ¶ 한 사람에 10발의 탄약, 10 rounds of ammunition per man / 하루에 두 번 twice a day / 10년에 한 번 once in ten years / 한 개 10원에 팔다 sell 《an article》 at ten won a piece / 1년에 얼마로 집을 세내다 rent a house by the year / 1파운드에 6실링씩 지불하다 pay 6 shillings per pound / 그 모자를 얼마에 사셨습니까 How much did you pay for the hat? / 철자를 바르게 댄 아이는 열에 하나꼴도 안 되었다 Not one in ten of the boys could spell well.

⑦ 《…에 대해·관계》 for; to; in; of. ¶ 각 방면에 in every way / 그 사람에 관해서 concerning that person / 아무의 친절에 감사하다 be thankful for *one's* kindness / 건강에 좋다 be good for health / 질문에 대답하다 answer a question / 여행에 5만원을 쓰다 spend 50,000 won on traveling / 어떤 일에 관계하다 be connected with a certain matter / 공부하기에 바쁘다 be busy (with *one's*) studying.

⑧ 《…으로, …에 의해》 by; with. ¶ 비에 젖다 get wet with rain / 눈에 덮이다 be covered with snow / 총알에 맞다 be hit by a bullet / 그의 박학에 놀랐다 I marveled at his profound scholarship.

⑨ 《원인》 with; for; at; because; since. ¶ 그러기 (때문)에 such being the case / 분노에 떨다 tremble with rage / 그 소식에 놀랐다 I was surprised at 〔by〕 the news. / 추위에 감각을 잃었다 I was numb from 〔with〕 the cold. / 서두르는 바람에 책을 가져오는 것을 잊어버렸다 In my hurry I forgot to bring the book.

⑩ 《열거》 and; and all that; and what not; and the like. ¶ 술에 고기에 잘 먹었다 I have had enough drinks, meat and the like.

⑪ 《대조》 against; on; with; and; in contrast 《with》. ¶ 하얀 바탕에 금무늬 a gold figure on 〔against〕 a white background / 그녀는 노란 저고리에 분홍 치마를 입었다 She wore a yellow coat and a pink skirt.

⑫ 《기타》 ¶ 감기에 걸리다 catch a cold / 그 시계에 맞추시오 Set your watch by the clock.

**에게** [여격조사] to; at; for; by 《*a person*》. ¶ 아들~ 돈을 주다 give money to *one's* son; give *one's* son money (★ to를 써서 고쳐쓸 수 있는 동사는 이 밖에 write, tell, pass 따위가 있음) / 우리~ 편지를 쓰다 write us a letter / 사장~ 그것을 말하다 tell that to the boss / 학생~ 책을 보이다 show the book to the student / 누군가 다른 사람~ 일을 하게 하다 get someone else to do the work / 아이~ 밥을 먹이다 feed the child (food) / 아무~ 돈을 먹히다 have *one's* money eaten up 〔swindled away〕 by *a person* / 그~ 차 한 대를 사주다 buy him a car; buy a car for him (★ for를 써서 고쳐쓸 수 있는 동사는 find, get, make, choose 따위가 있음).

**에게는** [조사] to; with; for. ¶ 그~ 술이 약이다 To him wine is a medicine. / 그것이 나~ 편리하다 That is convenient for me.

**에게도** [조사] to 〔at, for, by〕 《*a person*》 also 〔even〕. ¶ 한씨와 홍씨~ 편지를 쓰다 write letters both to Mr. Han and to Mr. Hong / 병난 사람~ 일을 하게 하다 make even the sick people work.

**에게로** [조사] toward 〔to〕《*a person*》. ¶ 아들～ 온 편지 a letter that has come to 〔for〕 my son / 그 허물이 누구～ 돌아갈까 Who(m) does that mistake go back to?

**에게서** [탈격조사] from《*a person*》. ¶ 아들～ 편지가 오다 get a letter from *one's* son / 아버지～도 편지가 없었다 I didn't get a letter from my father either. / 이 돈이 누구～ 나왔느냐 Who(m) did this money come from? / (그 말을) 친구～ 들었다 I heard that from a friend.

**에게해**(―海) the Aegean Sea.

**에고** ego; self. ◉ 에고이스트 an egoist; a selfish 〔self-centered〕 person; an egocentric person. 에고이즘 egoism; selfishness. 에고티스트 an egotist. 에고티즘 egotism.

**에구구** Oh oh!; Oh dear! ¶ ～ 이거 웬 일이야 Oh dear, what's the matter?

**에구데구** 《우는 꼴》 crying and wailing.

**에구(머니), 에그(머니)** ⇨ 아이고(머니).

**에그그** Oh my!; Dear me! ⇨ 에끄.

**에끄** Oh!; Oh my goodness!; Good heavens! ¶ ～ 바위 밑에 뱀이 있네 Goodness—there is a snake under the rock!

**에끼** Oh no!; Fie!; Ugh!; Oo!; How could you!; Come, come! ¶ ～ 나쁜 놈 Ugh—what a dreadful person you are! / ～ 그런 말 하지 마라 Oh no! Don't say such a thing.

**에끼다** 《상쇄하다》 offset 〔cancel〕 each other; mutually cancel; count as even; reckon one for the other. ¶ 우리 빚을 서로 에낍시다 Let's cancel our debts to each other.

**에나멜** enamel. ¶ ～을 입히다 enamel. ◉ ～구두 enameled shoes; patent 〔enameled〕 (leather) shoes. ～질(質) enamel. ～페인트 enamel paint.

**에너지** 〖물리〗 energy. ¶ 핵～ nuclear energy / 태양 ～ the solar 〔sun's〕 energy / …에 ～를 주다 energize / ～를 절약합시다 Conserve energy. ◉ ～량 energy content (of cosmic rays). ～문제 an energy problem. ～보존〔불멸〕 법칙 the principle of the conservation of energy. ～사정 the energy situation. ～산업 energy industry. ～수요 the demand for energy; energy needs. ～양자(量子) 〖물리〗 an energy quantum. ～원(源) an energy source; a source of energy. ～위기 an energy crisis. ～자원 energy resources. ～ 절약운동 an energy conservation drive; energy-saving drives. ～정책 an energy policy. ～혁명 an energy revolution; a revolutionary change in the use of energy. ～효율 an energy efficiency. 결합～ binding energy. 열～ heat energy. 운동～ kinetic 〔motive〕 energy; energy of motion. 잠재～ latent 〔potential〕 energy. 전기～ electrical energy. 한국 ～ 관리공단 Korea Energy Management Corporation (생략 KEMCO). 한국 ～연구소 Korea Advanced Energy Research Institute. 한반도 ～ 개발기구 the Korean Peninsula Energy Development Organization (생략 KEDO).

**에누리** ① 《더 부르는 값》 an inflated 〔a fancy〕 price. ～하다 ask an inflated price (to leave scope for haggling 〔for reducing the price later〕). ¶ ～를 하지 않다 ask only one price; do not overcharge / ～없이 얼마요 Tell me your lowest price. / ～는 일체 없습니다 All our prices are the lowest possible. *or* 《게시》 All prices net. ② 《값을 깎음》 (request for) discount. ～하다 ask a discount; reduce; bid low; take off 《500 won》. ¶ 이야기를 ～해서 듣다 [비유적] discount 《*a person's*》 story; take 《*a person's*》 story with a grain of salt / 10원도 ～ 못 합니다 I can't take off ten won. / 그렇게 ～하지 마십시오 Don't bid so low. / 그녀의 이야기는 ～해서 들어야 한다 [비유적] Her story shouldn't be accepted at face value. ③ 《과장》 (an) exaggeration. ～하다 exaggerate. ¶ ～없이 말하다 state things 〔the facts〕 as they are; 《구어》 call a spade a spade; give *one's* honest opinion 《about》 / 좀 ～해서 말하면 if I may be allowed a little exaggeration.

**에는** [조사] as for; to; at; in. ¶ 내가 보기～, 내 생각～ in my opinion / 일요일 ～ on Sunday / 그래 미국～ 언제 갈 예정인가 Well, when are you leaving for America? / 연극～ 두 가지 종류가 있다 There are two kinds of drama.

**에다**[1] 《도려 내다》 gouge (out); scrape out; hollow out; dig out; cut out. ¶ 에는 듯한 아픔 poignant 〔lancinating〕 pain / 바가지 속을 ～ hollow out a gourd / 통나무를 에어 카누를 만들다 hollow a canoe out of a log / 살을 에는 듯이 춥다 One feels chilled to the bone. *or* It is biting cold.

**에다**[2] [조사] at; in; on. ¶ 개～ 돌을 던지다 throw a stone at a dog / 벽～ 걸다

hang 《*a thing*》 on the wall / 소금～ 절이다 preserve in salt. 「of Eden.

**에덴** 〖성서〗 Eden. ◉ ～동산 the Garden

**에델바이스** 〖식물〗 an edelweiss.

**에도** [조사] also; too; as well; to 〔at, in〕... also 〔either, even〕. ¶ 유럽～ 가다 go to Europe too / 밤～ 못 자다 can't 〔don't〕 sleep 「at night either 〔even at night〕 / 일요일엔 극장～ 간다 on Sunday go to the theater too (as well as other places) / 서울～ 부산에도 있다 They have 《them》 both in Seoul and in Pusan. / 부산～ 서울에도 없다 They have 《them》 neither in Pusan nor in Seoul. / 7월～ 그곳은 춥다 It is cold there even in July.

**에돌다** hovor around shy; linger hesitantly; hang around without doing anything. ¶ 에돌지만 말고 일 좀 해라 Stop hanging around empty-handed —do something! / 아이들은 식탁 근처를 에돌았다 Children hovered about the table.

**에두르다** ① 《둘러막다》 encircle; surround; enclose. ¶ 집을 울타리로 ～ enclose the house with a fence. ② 《말을》 hint 《at》; make a roundabout statement; resort to circumlocution. ¶ 말을 에둘러 하다 talk 〔say〕 in a roundabout way; drop 《*a person*》 a hint; beat about 〔around〕 the bush.

**에듀넷** 《교육 정보망》 Edunet.

**에디슨** 《미국의 발명가》 Thomas Alva Edison (1847-1931). 「of my skin)!

**에뜨거라** Oh (I thought I'd jump out

**에라** ① 《체념·실망》 Oh well!; All right!; Oh my!; Shucks!; Gee!; Gosh! ¶ ～ 그럼 극장에나 가자 All right then, let's go to the show. / ～ 일이 다 틀렸다 Oh my! Everything went wrong. ② 《못하게 할 때》 Don't!; Stop!

**에러** an error; a fumble (야구에서 공을 헛 잡음). ¶ 야수(野手)의 ～ a fielder's error / 투수〔포수〕의 ～ a battery error / ～를 범하다 make an error; fumble.

**에로** 《에로티시즘》 eroticism; [형용사적] erotic; obscene 《books, pictures》. ◉ ～문학 erotic 〔obscene〕 literature; pornography. ～영화 a pornographic 〔an erotic〕 film; a purple 〔sex〕 film. ～잡지 a yellow journal; a dirty magazine. ～책 an obscene 〔a dirty, a pornographic〕 book.

**에로스** 〖그神〗 Eros; 《관능적 사랑》 eros.

**에로틱** ～하다 (be) erotic; sexy; lewd;

**에루화** Oh, what fun! 「sensual.

**에르그** 〖물리〗 an erg.

**에르븀** 〖화학〗 erbium (기호 Er).

**에만** ① 《장소》 just 〔only〕 to 〔at, in〕. ¶ 그는 다방～ 드나든다 He does nothing but visit teahouses. ② 《사물》 only; simply; ... alone. ¶ 그는 한 가지 일～ 열중하고 있다 He is absorbed in only one thing.

**에메랄드** 〖광물〗 emerald.

**에멜무지로** ① 《시험삼아》 on trial; as a sample; as an experiment; to see (how it is). ¶ ～ 써 보다 give 《*a thing*》 a trial. ② 《느슨하게》 《tied》 loosely.

**에베레스트** 《히말라야의》 Mt. Everest.

**에베소서**(—書) 〖성서〗 the Ephesians

**에보나이트** ebonite. 「(생략 Eph.).

**에볼라 바이러스** 〖의학〗 the Ebola virus.

**에비** 《어린애를 무섭게 할 때》 Look out!; Mustn't touch!; Naughty-naughty!

**에서** [조사] ① 《장소》 at; on; in 《a place》. ¶ 한국～ in Korea / 종로～ in 〔on〕 Chongno / 대학교～ 공부하다 study at the university / 집～ 일하다 work at home / 공원～ 산책하다 take a walk in the park / 나는 서울～ 태어나 서울～ 자랐다 I was born and grew up in Seoul.

② 《…부터》 from 《a place, a position, a status, a group, a number》; out of (★ from은 to에 대한 말로서 기점을 나타내고 out of는 into에 대한 말로 「안에서 밖으로」의 뜻); through (바람·빛 따위); at; in; off. ¶ 고향～ 온 편지 a letter from home / 10살～ 15살까지의 소년 boys (ranging) from 10 to 15 years / 바다 저편～ from beyond the sea / 서울～ 평양까지 from Seoul to P'yŏngyang / 기차～ 내리다 get off 〔down from〕 the train / 방～ 나오다 come out of the room / 말〔지붕〕～ 떨어지다 fall off a horse 〔roof〕 / 10쪽～ 시작하다 begin at page ten / 해외～ 돌아오다 return from abroad / 태양은 동쪽～ 떠오른다 The sun rises in the east.

③ 《시간》 from. ¶ 3시 ～ 5시까지 from 3 to 5 o'clock.

④ [비인칭 주어] ¶ 회사～ 나에게 시계를 주었다 The company gave me a watch.

⑤ 《보다》 than. ¶ 이～ 더 큰 사랑은 없느니라 There is no greater love than this.

⑥ 《원인·이유·동기》 from; (out) of. ¶ 호기심～ out of curiosity / 책임감～ …하다 do 《*something*》 from a sense of duty / 숭고한 동기～ 행동하다 act from noble motives.

⑦ 《근거·견지》 from; by. ¶ 사회적 견지

～ 보면 from a social point of view.

**에서도** [조사] even 〔also〕 at 〔from, in〕. ¶ 한국～ 생산되다 be produced also in Korea / 한국～ 유행하지 않게 되다 go out of fashion even in Korea.

**에서만** only 〔just〕 in 〔at, from〕. ¶ 서울～ 팔리다 sell only in Seoul / 오염된 물～ 검출되다 be detected only from the contaminated water.

**에세이** an essay.

**에센스** 《정수》 essence.

**에스** ① 《알파벳》 the letter "S". ② 《동성애의》 a lesbian schoolsister.

**에스겔서**(—書) 〖성서〗 (The Book of) Ezekiel (생략 Ezek.).

**에스더서**(—書) 〖성서〗 (The Book of) Esther (생략 Esth.).

**에스라서**(—書) 〖성서〗 (The Book of) Ezra.

**에스램** 〖컴퓨터〗 《정적 램》 SRAM. [<static RAM]

**에스에프** 《공상 과학 소설》 science fiction (생략 s.f., sf, SF); 《구어》 sci-fi.

**에스오시** 《사회 간접 자본》 SOC. [<Social Overhead Capital]

**에스오에스** 《조난 신호》 an SOS (call); a signal of distress. ¶ ～를 발하다〔수신하다〕 send out 〔pick up〕 an SOS (call).

**에스캅** 《아시아 태평양 경제 사회 이사회》 ESCAP. [<*E*conomic and *S*ocial *C*ommission for *A*sia and *P*acific] (★ 1974년 개편된 에카페(ECAFE) 후신).

**에스컬레이션** (an) escalation.

**에스컬레이터** an escalator; a moving staircase.

**에스코트** escort; 《사람》 an escort. ～하다 escort.

**에스키모** an Eskimo (*pl.* ～, ～(e)s); an Esquimau (*pl.* ～x). ¶ ～의 Eskimo.

**에스토니아** 《발트해 연안 공화국》 Estonia; Esthonia.

**에스파냐** España. = 스페인.

**에스페란토** 〖언어〗 Esperanto. ◉ ～주의자, ～사용자 an Esperantist.

**에스프리** *esprit* (F.); spirit.

**에야디야** 《힘을 합칠 때》 Yo-ho!; Yo-heave-ho!

**에어** air. ◉ ～라인 an air line 〔route〕 (항공로); an airlines (항공 회사). ～백 an air bag. ～브레이크 an air 〔a pneumatic〕 brake (★ 단, 단수형으로 쓰일 경우는 매우 드묾). ～셔틀 an air shuttle. ～쇼 an air show. ～커튼 an air curtain; an air door. ～컴프레서 an air compressor. ～클리너 an air cleaner. ～터미널 an air terminal. ～포켓 an air pocket. ～포트 an airport.

**에어로빅스** 《do》 aerobics (단수 취급). ¶ 에어로빅 댄스 an aerobic dance / 에어로빅 댄싱을 하다 do aerobic dancing.

**에어메일** 《항공 우편》 airmail. ¶ 편지를 ～로 보내다 send a letter by airmail.

**에어버스** 《제트 여객기》 an airbus.

**에어컨(디셔너)** an air conditioner. ¶ ～이〔가〕 설치된 방 an air-conditioned room / ～이〔가〕 고장났다 The air conditioner is out of order.

**에우다** ① 《에워싸다》 encircle; surround. ② 《지우다》 cross out; strike off; eliminate. ¶ 계약서에서 한 조목을 ～ cross an item off a written contract.

**에움길** 《굽은 길》 a roundabout way; a long way round. ¶ ～로 가다 go a roundabout way; take a long way around.

**에워가다** ① 《둘러가다》 go a long way around. ¶ 길을 ～ go a long way around; take a long 〔roundabout〕 way. ② 《지워 나가다》 strike out 《an entry in a ledger》.

**에워싸다** surround; 《사람이》 crowd round; close 〔cluster, throng〕 around 《*a person*》; 《담 따위로》 enclose; encircle; hem 〔edge〕 in 〔round〕; 《적을》 besiege; lay siege to; invest. ¶ 집에 담을 ～ enclose a house with a wall / 적을 멀리 ～ surround the enemy at a distance; close in 〔round〕 on the enemy / 겹겹이 ～ 《성을》 besiege 《a castle》 thick and fast; 《사람을》 a thick wall of people surrounds 《*a person*》 / 사람들이 영화 배우를 ～ people crowded round a movie actor.

**에의** [조사] 《the invitation》 to; at; in. ¶ 성공～ 길 the road to success.

**에이레** 《아일랜드 공화국의 구칭》 Eire.

**에이비시** ① 《알파벳》 the alphabet; 《초보》 ABC; the first step; the elements; the fundamentals. ② 《화생방 무기》 ABC [<*a*tomic, *b*iological, and *c*hemical] armaments. ③ 《기구》 《미》 ABC. [<*A*udit *B*urea of *C*irculation]

**에이스** ① 〖야구〗 an ace pitcher. ② 《카드 놀이》 an ace.

**에이에프케이엔** 《주한 미군 방송망》 AFKN. [<the *A*merican *F*orces *K*orea *N*etwork]

**에이에프피** 《프랑스 통신사》 AFP. [<*A*gence *F*rance *P*resse]

**에이엠방송**(—放送) AM broadcasting (★ AM, A.M., Am., am [<*a*mplitude *m*odulation]).

**에이전트** 《대리인》 an agent.

**에이즈** 〖의학〗 《후천성 면역 결핍증》 AIDS. [<*A*cquired *I*mmune *D*eficiency *S*yndrome] ¶ ～환자 people with AIDS (생략 PWA); an AIDS patient / ～ 바

이러스 the AIDS virus / ～ 바이러스 감염자 HIV-positive. [<*H*uman *I*mmuno-deficiency *V*irus-positive]
**에이치디티브이** 《고선명도〔고화질〕 텔레비전》 HDTV. [<*H*igh-*D*efinition TV]
**에이커** an acre. ¶ 하이드 파크는 몇 ～냐 What is the acreage of Hyde Park?
**에이티엠** 《현금 자동 인출기》 ATM. [<*A*utomated *T*eller *M*achine]
**에이펙** 《아시아 태평양 경제 협력체》 APEC. [<*A*sia-*P*acific *E*conomic *C*ooperation]
**에이프런** 《앞치마》 an apron; a kitchen apron; 《비행장의》 an apron. ¶ ～을 걸치다 wear an apron. ◉ ～ 스테이지 《극장의》 an apron stage.
**에이피** 《미국 연합 통신사》 AP, A.P. [<the *A*ssociated *P*ress]
**에인절피시** 〖어류〗 an angelfish.
**에일** ale (맥주의 일종). ¶ 진저～ ginger ale.
**에잇** Darn it 〔me, you〕!; Damn!
**에참** Shuck!; Damn!; Darn! ¶ ～ 가기 싫다 Gee whiz—I hate to go.
**에칭** 《작품》 an etching; 《기법》 etching.
**에코** ① 〖그神〗 《숲의 요정》 Echo. ② 《메아리》 an echo.
**에콰도르** 《남아메리카의 공화국》 Ecuador. ◉ ～ 사람 an Ecuadorian.
**에크** 《놀람》 Oh!; Dear me!; Heavens!; Gosh! ¶ ～ 큰일이다 Heavens! *or* Dear me!
**에테르** 〖물리·화학〗 ether.
**에토스** 〖철학〗 ethos.
**에튀드** 〖음악〗 an *étude* (F.); a study.
**에트랑제** an *étranger* (F.); a stranger; a foreigner; an outsider.
**에티오피아** 《아프리카의 국가》 Ethiopia. ¶ ～의 Ethiopian. ◉ ～ 사람 an Ethiopian.
**에티켓** etiquette; good manners. ¶ 식사의 ～ table manners / ～을 알다〔지키다〕 know 〔observe〕 the rules of etiquette / …하는 것은 ～에 어긋난다 It is not good etiquette to *do*. *or* It is a breach of etiquette to *do*. / …하는 것이 ～이다 It is 「good manners 〔proper etiquette〕 to *do*.
**에틸** 〖화학〗 ethyl. ¶ ～ 알코올 ethyl 「〔grain〕 alcohol.
**에페** 《펜싱 종목》 an *épée* (F.).
**에펠탑**(―塔) the Eiffel Tower.
**에폭** an epoch. ◉ ～메이커 an epoch 「maker.
**에폭시수지**(―樹脂) epoxy resins.
**에프비아이** 《미국 연방 수사국》 FBI. [<*F*ederal *B*ureau of *I*nvestigation]
**에프엠방송**(―放送) FM broadcasting (★ FM, F.M., f-m, f.m. [<*f*requency *m*odulation]). ◉ ～국 an FM station.
**에프티에이** (FTA) 《자유무역협정》 Free Trade Agreement.
**에피소드** 《삽화》 an episode; 《일화》 an anecdote. ¶ 그에게는 많은 ～가 있다 There are many episodes told of him.
**에필로그** 《끝맺음말》 an epilogue.
**에헴** Ahem!; Hem! ⇨ 애햄.
**엑스** ① 《미지·미정의 것》 "X"; an unknown quantity 〔factor, entity〕. ② 〖약〗 an extract 〔essence〕 《of beef》. ◉ ～세대(世代) the "X Generation."
**엑스선**(―線) X-ray(s); Roentgen 〔Röntgen〕 rays. ¶ ～을 비추다 X-ray. ◉ ～검사 an X-ray examination; X-ray inspection. ～사진 X-ray photograph. ～요법 〖의학〗 X-ray therapy. ～진공관 an X-ray tube.
**엑스트라** an extra; a supernumerary; 《구어》 a super. ¶ ～ 노릇을 하다 play an extra part 《in a movie》 / ～를 고용하다 hire extra hands 《for a movie》.
**엑스퍼트** 《전문가》 an expert 《at, in》.
**엑스포** 《(만국)박람회》 an Expo.
**엔** 《일본 화폐》 a *yen* (기호 ¥). ¶ 천 엔 지폐 a thousand-*yen* note 〔bill〕.
**엔간하다** 《적당하다》 (be) proper; suitable; 《상당하다》 (be) considerable; tolerable; fair. ¶ 엔간히 큰 돈 a considerable sum of money; a good deal of money / 엔간한 여관 a decent hotel / 엔간한 수입 a handsome income / 그는 엔간한 작가와는 다르다 He is no ordinary writer. / 엔간한 운동은 건강에 좋다 Moderate exercise is good for the health. / 그는 엔간하게 살고 있다 He is making a decent living. / 엔간히 좀 해라 That's enough. Stop it!
**엔고**(―高) 《엔화의 높은 시세》 a strong *yen;* a high exchange rate of the *yen;* 《엔화의 상승》 a rise in the exchange rate of the *yen.* [<えんだか(円高)(日)] ¶ ～와 약세 달러 a strong *yen* and a weak dollar / 요즈음 한 동안 ～가 계속되고 있다 The *yen* has been strong for some time now. / 미국 및 EU 여러 나라는 급격한 ～를 초래케 한 일본의 무역 흑자를 줄여야 한다고 요구하기 시작했다 The U.S. and the EU nations have begun to demand that Japan should reduce her trade surplus which has resulted in a steep appreciation of the *yen.* ◉ ～차익 a profit accruing from a rise in the exchange rate of the *yen.*
**엔도르핀** 〖생화학〗 endorphin.
**엔들** even; also; too. ¶ 그만 것이야 우리 집～ 없으라 What makes you think we wouldn't have such a thing at our house too? / 필요하다면 어디～ 못 가랴 I would go any place if (it is)

necessary.

**엔비시**《미국의 방송 회사》NBC. [<the *N*ational *B*roadcasting *C*ompany]

**엔비에이**《미국 농구 협회》NBA. [<the *N*ational *B*asketball *A*ssociation];《미국 권투 협회》NBA. [<the *N*ational *B*oxer's *A*ssociation]

**엔시엔디**〖매스컴〗《긍정도 부정도 않음》NCND. [<*n*either *c*onfirm *n*or *d*eny]

**엔저**(一低)《엔화의 낮은 시세》a weak *yen;* a low exchange rate of the *yen;* 《엔화 하락》a fall in the exchange rate of the *yen.* [<えんやす(円安)(日)]

**엔조이** ~하다 enjoy《life》.

**엔지**〖영화〗n.g.; N.G. [<*no good*]; 《영》a take-out;《재촬영》a retake. ¶~를 내다 spoil〔ruin〕a sequence.

**엔지니어** an engineer.

**엔지오**《비정부 기구》NGO. [<the *N*on=*g*overnmental *O*rganization]

**엔진** an engine. ¶~을 걸다〔시동하다〕start an engine; set an engine going〔at work〕;《크랭크를 돌려》crank up an engine / ~을 멈추다 stop an engine / ~이 고장나다 have some engine trouble / ~이 걸렸다 The engine caught. / ~이 이상해졌다 Something went wrong with the engine.
◉ ~실《항공기 등의》a nacelle. 가스터빈~ a gasturbine engine. 로터리~ a rotary engine. 선박용~ a marine engine. 스팀~ a steam engine. 오일~ an oil engine. 항공~ an aeroengine.

**엔터테이너**《예능인》an entertainer.

**엔트로피**〖물리〗an entropy.

**엔트리**《참가》an entry. ¶~의 절차를 마치다 enter《for a contest》.

**엘니뇨** El Niño. ¶~현상 an El Niño phenomenon.

**엘레지**《애가》an elegy.

**엘렉트라콤플렉스**〖정신분석〗the Electra complex.

**엘리베이터** an elevator;《영》a lift;《화물용》a hoist; a freight elevator《미》. ¶손수 운전하는~ self-service elevator / ~의 버튼 the up〔down〕button / 각층 운행〔급행〕~ a local〔an express〕elevator / ~가 있는〔없는〕아파트 an elevator〔a walk-up〕apartment house / ~를 타고 올라가다〔내려가다〕go「up〔down〕in an elevator.
◉ ~ 운전원 an elevator operator.

**엘리트** [총칭] the elite《of society》; the chosen (few); an elite group;《개인》a member of the elite; an elitist. ¶~중의 ~ the best and the brightest 《of》/ 파워 ~ the power elite《inside the government》.
◉ ~사원 an elite employee. ~의식 elitism; elite consciousness: 그는 ~의식이 강하다 He has a strong sense of being one〔a member〕of the elite. ~주의 elitism: ~주의의 교육제도 an elitist education system. ~코스 the elitist course: ~코스를 밟다 be on course for membership of the elite.

**엘살바도르**《중앙 아메리카의 공화국》El Salvador.

**엘시디**《액정 표시 장치》an LCD. [<a *l*iquid-*c*rystal *d*isplay]

**엘엔지**《액화 천연 가스》LNG. [<*l*iquefied *n*atural *g*as] ¶~가스 터미널 an LNG gas terminal.

**엘피지**《액화 석유 가스》LPG. [<*l*iquefied *p*etroleum *g*as]

**엘피판** an L.P. record. [<a *l*ong=*p*laying record]

**엠브이피**《최우수 선수》MVP. [<the *m*ost *v*aluable *p*layer]

**엠시**《(TV 방송 등의) 사회자》MC [<a *m*aster of *c*eremonies]; an emcee.

**엠아이에스**《경영 정보 시스템》MIS. [<*m*anagement *i*nformation *s*ystem]

**엠엔드에이**〖경제〗《기업의 합병과 매수》M & A. [<*m*erger and *a*cquisition]

**엠피**《헌병》an M.P. [<*m*ilitary *p*olice]

**엠티** (MT)《회원의 훈련》(a) membership training.

**엥**《짜증·성남·딱할 때》Oof!; Oh!; Hmph!

**엥겔**《독일 통계학자》Ernest Engel (1821-96). ◉ ~계수 Engel's Coefficient. ~법칙 Engel's law.

**-여**(餘)《이상》more than; over; and more; in excess of; odd (우수리의). ¶백여 명 a hundred and some men / 이십여 년 more than twenty years; twenty odd years / 2천여 원, 2,000 won odd.

**여가**(餘暇) leisure; spare time; time on *one's* hands; (*one's*) free time. ¶업무의 ~에 in spare moments from *one's* business; in the intervals of business / ~에 독서하다 read in *one's* leisure hours / ~를 이용하다 make use of *one's* spare moments / ~가 나면 언제든 오시오 Come and see me at anytime you get time on your hands. / 가르치느라 책 쓰느라 ~가 없다 Between teaching and writing, I have little time to spare. / 운동할 ~가 없다 I have no leisure for sport.

**여각**(餘角) the complementary angle.

**여간**(如干) some; a little. ¶~일이 아니다 be no easy matter〔task〕/ 그는~일에는 성내지 않는다 He never gets angry over trifles. / 그를 거기서 보고

나는 ～ 놀라지 않았다 I was not a little surprised to see him there.

**여간내기**(如干—) = 보통내기.

**여간 아니다**(如干—) (be) uncommon; unusual; extraordinary; remarkable. ¶ 여간 아닌 미인 a rare beauty / 여간 아닌 학자 a prodigy of learning / 여간 아닌 노력을 하다 make a supreme efforts 《to *do*》 / 오늘 추위는 ～ It is terribly cold today. / 그의 재주가 ～ He has a rare talent. / 그의 고생이 여간 아니었을 게다 It must have been a hard strain for him 《to finish it》.

**여객**(旅客) 《승객》 a passenger; 《여행자》 a traveler; a tourist.
◉ ～기 a passenger plane; an airliner: 초음속 ～기 a supersonic transport (생략 SST). ～명단 a passenger list; a list of passengers. ～선 a passenger ship; a liner. ～수화물(手貨物) traveler's baggage 《미》 〔luggage 《영》〕: ～ 수화물 보관소 a baggage room; a cloakroom 《영》. ～안내소 a travel bureau; an inquiry office 《영》. ～열차 a passenger train. ～운송 passenger transport. ～운임 passenger's fares. ～전무 a train master; a passenger guard; a conductor 《미》.

**여건**(與件) a given condition 〔circumstance〕; postulate. ¶ ～이 허락하는 한 나는 지금의 일을 계속할 것이다 I will go on with my present work as far as circumstances permit.

**여걸**(女傑) a heroine; a brave 〔heroic〕 woman; an Amazon.

**여겨듣다** listen carefully 〔closely〕 《to》. ¶ 선생님 말씀을 ～ listen attentively to what our teacher says / 내가 말하는 것을 여겨들으시오 You mark what I'm telling you.

**여겨보다** see closely; watch (carefully); have 〔take〕 a careful look 《at》.

**여격**(與格) 〖문법〗 the dative (case).
◉ ～동사 a dative verb. 「cop 《구어》.

**여경**(女警) a policewoman; a woman

**여계**(女系) the female line.

**여고**(女高) ⇨ 여자고등학교.

**여공**(女工) a factory girl; a woman worker; a workwoman. ¶ ～을 모집하다 advertise for mill girls.

**여과**(濾過) 〖물리〗 filtration; filtering; percolation. ～하다 filter; filtrate; pass 《a liquid》 through a filter. ¶ 불순물을 ～ 해내다 filter out impurities.
◉ ～기 a filter: ～기로 물을 맑게 하다 purify water by a filter. ～성 filterability: ～성 병원체 a (filterable) virus. ～액 filtrate. ～지(池) a filter bed. ～지(紙) filter paper. ～층 a filter layer. ～통 a filter box.

**여관**(女官) 〖고제도〗 a court lady; a lady-in-waiting; a maid of honor.

**여관**(旅館) a Korean-style hotel 〔inn〕. ¶ ～에 들다〔묵다〕 put up 〔stay〕 at a hotel; check in / ～에서 나가다 check out / ～을 경영하다 run 〔keep〕 a hotel 〔an inn〕 / 나는 어젯밤 시내의 ～에서 묵었다 I stayed 〔put up〕 at a hotel in the city last night. ◉ ～비 lodging expenses; hotel bills. ～업 the hotel business. ～주인 a hotelier; a hotelkeeper; an innkeeper; the proprietor of a hotel.

**여광**(餘光) ① 《빛》 afterglow; lingering 〔remaining〕 light. ② 《여덕》 the reward (for virtue); the influence (of virtue).

**여광**(濾光) filtering light. ◉ ～기〔판〕 〖사진〗 a light filter.

**여교사**(女敎師) a schoolmistress; a woman 〔female, lady〕 teacher.

**여군**(女軍) a woman soldier; Women's Army Corps (여군부대).

**여권**(女權) women's 〔woman's〕 rights; 《여성 참정권》 woman 〔female〕 suffrage. ◉ ～론〔주의〕 feminism: ～론자 a feminist; a suffragist; a suffragette (여자). ～신장〔확장〕 the extension of women's rights: ～신장론자 a feminist. ～운동 the women's rights movement.

**여권**(旅券) a passport. ¶ 관용～ an official passport / 단수～ a single passport / 복수～ a multiple passport / 외교관～ a diplomat's passport / 일반～ an ordinary passport / ～을 신청하다 apply for a passport / ～을 교부하다 issue a passport 《for》 / ～을 교부받다 obtain 〔get〕 a passport; have a passport issued / ～에 비자를 받다 have *one's* passport visaed / 오늘 ～에 사증을 받으러 간다 I'm going to get my visa today. ◉ ～법 Passport Control Law. ～사증 a passport visa.

**여급**(女給) 《급사》 a waitress; 《바의》 a barmaid.

**여기** here; this point 〔place, spot〕. ¶ ～에(서) here; in 〔at〕 this place / ～부터 from here; from this place 〔point〕 / ～까지 (up) to this place; thus 〔so〕 far; as far as here / ～쯤에 hereabouts; about 〔around〕 here; in this neighborhood / ～가 어디입니까 What place is this? *or* Where 「am I 〔are we〕? / ～다 Here we are. *or* This is the place. / ～ 있다 Here it is. *or* Here you are. / ～ 있어라 Stay right where you are! / ～서 멉니까 Is it far from here? / 오늘은 ～까지 합시다 《교실에서》 So much for today. *or* That's all for today. *or* Let us leave off here. / 너는 ～가 틀렸다 You are wrong on this point.

**여기**(餘技) a hobby; an avocation. ¶ ～로 그림을 그리다 take up painting as a hobby.

**여기다** think; hold; consider 《as》; 《간주하다》 regard 《as》; treat 《as》; take 《as》; 《의아하게》 wonder; suspect; 《느끼다》 feel. ¶ 나쁘게 ～ think ill of 《*a person*》; take 《*a thing*》 amiss / 좋게 ～ think well of 《*a person*》; think a lot of 《*a person*》 / 심각하게 ～ take 《it》 seriously / 행복하게〔슬프게〕 ～ feel happy 〔sad〕 / 아무를 귀엽게 ～ hold *a person* dear / 돈을 천하게 ～ treat money cheap / 아무를 바보로 ～ consider *a person* as a fool / 나는 그것을 불행으로 여기지 않는다 I don't regard it as a misfortune.

**여기자**(女記者) a woman reporter; a newspaperwoman 《미》; a news-woman.

**여기저기** here and there; from place to place; 《곳곳에》 in places; 《이리저리》 back and forth 《미》; to and fro 《영》; up and down; 《모든 곳》 everywhere; in all directions. ¶ ～에서〔로 부터〕 《come》 from different 〔various〕 quarters; 《flock》 from far and near / ～ 돌아다니다 wander 〔tramp〕 from place to place / ～ 빚이 있다 have several (different) debts / ～ 찾다 look for 《*a thing*》 here and there; search everywhere 〔far and wide〕.

**여난**(女難) 《get into》 troubles 〔misfortunes〕 with women. ¶ 자네에겐 ～상(相)이 있네 그려 You have the sort of looks that ask for trouble in the way of women.

**여남은** some ten odd; somewhat over 〔more than〕 ten. ¶ 연필 ～ 자루 a dozen pencils / ～ 사람 a dozen men.

**여념**(餘念) ¶ ～이 없다 be intent 《on》; be absorbed 《in》; be deeply occupied 《with》; be devoted 《to》; give undivided attention 《to》; busy *oneself* 《in a task》 / ～없이 earnestly; eagerly; absorbedly; with *one's* whole heart / 공부에 ～이 없다 study 〔work〕 with *one's* whole heart; devote 〔apply〕 *oneself* (closely) to *one's* studies / 독서에 ～이 없다 be absorbed in 〔wholly occupied by〕 reading.

**여느** ① 《보통의》 commonplace; ordinary. ¶ ～ 사람 an ordinary man; an average mortal; a common being; [총칭] the common run of people / ～ 일 an ordinary affair; a matter of common 〔everybody〕 occurrence / ～ 날은 on ordinary days / ～ 사람과 다르다 be out of the common run; be extraordinary / 그에게는 어딘가 ～ 사람과는 다른 데가 있다 There is something extraordinary about him. ② 《그 밖의 다른》 other; different.

**여느때** ordinary times. ¶ ～의 《평상의》 usual; 《매일의》 everyday; 《보통의》 common; 《습관적》 habitual / ～와 같이 as usual; in *one's* 〔the〕 usual way / ～ 같으면 in ordinary times; ordinarily / ～와는 달리 unusually; contrary to *one's* 〔the〕 normal custom 〔habit〕 / 그는 ～보다 일찍 나왔다 He came earlier than usual. / 그는 ～와 다른 데가 없었다 There was 〔I saw〕 nothing unusual about him.

**여단**(旅團) 〖군사〗 a brigade. ¶ 보병 ～ an infantry brigade / ～으로 편성하다 form into a brigade; brigade. ◉ ～사령부 the brigade headquarters. ～장 a brigade commander; a brigadier.

**여닫이** ① 《열고 닫음》 opening and shutting 〔closing〕. ② 《미닫이》 sliding doors; 《내리닫이》 a sash window.

**여담**(餘談) a digression; a by-talk. ¶ ～을 하다 digress; wander from the subject / ～이지만 in this connection I may add that… / ～은 그만하고 to return to the subject; to cut short the digression.

**여당**(與黨) the Government 〔ruling〕 party; the party in power 〔office〕. ◉ ～의원 a Member of the Government party.

**여대**(女大) a women's college 〔university〕. ◉ ～생 a student at a women's college; a college woman; 《구어》 a co-ed (남녀 공학의).

**여덟** eight. ¶ ～번 eight times / ～시 eight o'clock / ～째 the eighth. ◉ ～달반 an idiot; a stupid.

**여덟팔자**(一八字) ¶ 이마에 ～를 그리다 knit *one's* brows; frown / ～ 걸음을 걷다 toe out; walk with the toes turned out 〔outward〕.

**여독**(旅毒) the fatigue of travel. ＝노독「(路毒).

**여독**(餘毒) the aftereffect of a poison 〔a sickness〕.

**여동생**(女同生) a younger sister. ¶ 막내

～ *one's* youngest sister.

**여드레** eight days; 《초여드레》 the eighth (day of a month). ¶ 5월 여드렛날 May 8(th); the eighth of May.

**여드름** a pimple; an acne; a comedo (*pl.* -dones); 《끝이 검어진》 a blackhead. ¶ ～자국 an acne scar / ～이 나다 pimples break 〔come〕 out on 〔in〕 *one's* face; have acne / ～난 얼굴 a pimpled 〔pimply〕 face; a face covered with acne / ～을 짜다 squeeze a blackhead.

**여든** eighty. ¶ ～째 the eightieth / ～이 넘다 be over eighty / ～에 둥둥이 a person lacking initiative; a namby=pamby.

**여듭** an eight-year-old horse 〔ox〕.

**여래**(如來) 〖불교〗 Buddha; a *tathagata* (Sans.); a person who has attained Buddhahood.

**여러** several; many; various; diverse; all sorts of. ¶ ～ 사람 several people; all sorts of people / ～ 학교 many 〔various〕 schools / ～날 비가오다 it rains several 〔many〕 days running / ～달째 행방불명이다 be missing for many 〔several〕 months / ～대를 서울에서 살았다 We have lived in Seoul for generations.

**여러가지** all sorts 《of》; various kinds 《of》; several varieties. ¶ ～ 이유로 for various reasons / ～ 상품 goods of different kinds / ～ 물건 all sorts of things / ～로 시도해 보다 try every possible means / ～로 위로하다 console 《*a person*》 in every way / ～ 이야기하고 싶은 것이 많다 I have so many things to tell you. / ～로 해석할 수 있다 It can 〔may〕 be construed 〔interpreted〕 in many ways. / 장미꽃에는 ～가 있다 There are many varieties of roses. / 그는 ～로 애를 써 주었다 He has done all sorts of things for me. / 그분에게는 ～로 신세를 졌다 I have had so many kindnesses shown (to) me by him. / 모자, 넥타이 기타 ～를 샀다 I bought a hat, a tie and what not.

**여러모로** in various 〔many〕 ways. ¶ ～ 생각한 끝에 사임하기로 했다 Taking various considerations into account 〔Taking everything into consideration〕, I decided to resign. / ～ 감사합니다 Thank you very much for everything.

**여러번**(一番) several 〔many〕 times; often; frequently; repeatedly. ¶ ～ 시도하였으나 실패했다 I tried and tried, but did not succeed. / ～ 일본에 가 본 일이 있다 I have been to Japan a number of times. / 그를 ～ 만났다 I saw him often. / 그한테 ～ 말했다 I told him over and over again. ◉ ～인쇄 〖컴퓨터〗 multiple-pass printing.

**여러분** all of you; hello, everybody; ladies and gentlemen. ¶ 신사숙녀 ～ Ladies and Gentlemen ! (★ 청중 중에 여자가 단 한 사람이라도 있으면 이렇게 말함) / ～ 안녕하십니까 Good morning, everybody. *or* 《선생이》 Good morning, class.

**여러해** many 〔several〕 years. ¶ ～동안 (for) a long time; for many years / ～동안 그를 만나지 못했다 I haven't seen him for years.

**여러해살이**(풀) 〖식물〗 a perennial 「(plant).

**여럿** a large number; many; many people. ¶ 그렇게 생각하는 사람이 ～이다 There are many who think so. / ～이 그 시험에 낙방했다 Many failed in the examination.

**여력**(餘力) remaining power 〔strength, energy〕; a reserve of energy; 《돈의》 money to spare. ¶ ～이 충분히 있다 have enough energy 〔strength, money〕 to spare 《for》 / ～을 비축해 두다 keep much in reserve / ～을 아끼다 save *one's* energy / 나에게는 차를 살 ～이 없다 I have no money to spare for a car. / 그에게는 계속해서 달릴 ～이 있었다 He still had the energy left to keep on running.

**여로**(旅路) a journey. ¶ 먼 ～ a long journey / (인생의) ～ 끝에 at *one's* journey's end.

**여론**(輿論) public 〔general〕 opinion; the prevailing view; the popular voice; 《일반 감정》 public sentiment. ¶ 국제 ～ international 〔world〕 opinion / ～의 동향 the trend of public opinion; the swing of the pendulum / ～에 귀를 기울이다 give 〔pay〕 careful attention to the trends of public opinion; have 〔keep〕 an 〔*one's*〕 ear to the ground / ～에 호소하다 appeal to public opinion / ～을 무시〔존중〕하다 defy 〔have a regard for〕 public opinion / ～의 추세를 살피다 find out the trend of public opinion; see how the wind blows / ～을 좇다, ～에 따르다 obey the dictates of public opinion; act in accordance with public opinion / ～을 불러일으키다 arouse 〔stir up〕 public opinion 〔popular sentiment〕 / ～

은 그 정책에 반대〔찬성〕하고 있다 Public opinion is against 〔for〕 the policy. / 신문은 ～을 반영하여야 한다 Newspapers should reflect public opinion. / 그 기사는 이 문제에 관한 ～의 일치를 나타내고 있다 The article expressed the consensus of opinion about this problem.
◉ ～비판 the forum of public opinion. ～연구소 an institute of public opinion. ～함 a suggestion box.

**여론조사**(輿論調査) a survey of public opinion; a public-opinion census 〔poll〕; opinion research; 《비공식의》 a straw poll 《미》. ¶ ～를 받는 자 a pollee / ～를 하다 take 〔conduct〕 a public-opinion poll; poll the public.
◉ ～원 a pollster; a polltaker.

**여류**(女流) women in general; the fair sex; womankind; [형용사적] woman (★ 복수명사 수식 때는 women); lady.
◉ ～문학 literary works by women writers: ～문학가 a lady of letters; a literary women; a bluestocking. ～비행사 a woman aviator; an aviatress; an aviatrix (*pl.* -trices). ～시인 a woman 〔lady〕 poet; a poetess. ～ 작가 a woman 〔lady〕 writer; an authoress.

**여름** summer; (the) summertime. ¶ ～내 through 〔throughout〕 the summer / ～용의 for summer use 〔wear〕 / ～에 in summer; in the summertime / 초〔늦〕～《in》 early 〔late〕 summer / 어느 ～날 one summer day; one day in summer / ～다운 summerlike / ～을 나다 pass 〔spend〕 the summer / ～엔 해가 길다 In summer the days are long. / 지독히 더운 ～이었다 It's been an unusually hot summer. / ～에는 장사가 잘 안된다 Our business slackens in summer. *or* We do very little business in the summer time.
◉ ～감기 a summer cold. ～방학〔휴가〕 the summer vacation 〔holidays〕; the summer recess: ～방학 숙제〔책〕 an assignment 〔a workbook〕 for the summer vacation. ～새 a summer bird. ～옷 summer clothes 〔wear〕; a summer suit. ～철 summer time; the summer season. ～학교〔캠프〕 a summer school 〔camp〕.

**여름타다** be susceptible to the summer heat; lose weight in the summer; suffer from 〔succumb to〕 the summer heat. ¶ 그는 여름을 타지 않는다 The hot weather never bothers him. / 여름을 타서 식욕이 없다 I have lost my appetite because of the summer heat.

**여리꾼** a tout; a barker; a puller-in.

**여리다** ① 《연하다》 (be) soft; delicate; tender; 《약하다》 weak; frail; fragile. ¶ 여린 빛 a light 〔soft〕 color / 여린 살결〔가슴〕 a tender skin 〔heart〕. ② 《모자라다》 (be) short; insufficient. ¶ 옷 한 벌 짓는 데 감이 좀 ～ The material is a little short to make a suit of clothes.

**여망**(輿望) confidence; trust; esteem; popularity; reputation. ¶ 국민의 ～에 부응하다 meet the confidence of the whole nation.

**여명**(餘命) the remainder 〔rest〕 of *one's* life; *one's* remaining days. ¶ 평균 ～ life expectancy; 〖보험〗 average future lifetime / ～이 얼마 남지 않다 have but a few years 〔days〕 to live; have one foot in the grave; *one's* days 〔years〕 are numbered.

**여명**(黎明) dawn; daybreak; the gray of the morning. ¶ ～에 at dawn.
◉ ～기 the dawn(ing): 새 시대의 ～기 the dawn(ing) of a new age / 문예 부흥의 ～기 the dawning of the Renaissance / 우리는 이제 우주 시대의 ～기에 들어서 있다 We now stand at the dawn of the Space Age. ～문학 literature at the dawn of a new era.

**여물** 《마소의》 chaff; (cattle) feed; fodder; forage. ¶ ～을 주다 fodder 《cattle》; put out feed for 《a horse》 / ～을 썰다 cut straw 〔hay〕 finely.
◉ ～죽 boiled cattle feed. ～통 a manger; a crib.

**여물다** get 〔become〕 ripe; ripen; mature. ¶ 벼〔보리〕가 ～ rice 〔barley〕 ripens.

**여미다** adjust; straighten (up). ¶ 옷깃을 ～ adjust *one's* dress; adjust 〔straighten〕 *oneself.*

**여반장**(如反掌) being very easy. ¶ ～이다 be a very 〔quite an〕 easy job / 저런 일쯤은 ～이다 That's duck soup for me. *or* That's nothing. *or* 《구어》 That's a piece of cake.

**여배우**(女俳優) an actress. ¶ 영화～ a film actress / 최우수 ～상 the Best Actress award / ～가 되다 become an actress. ◉ ～지망자 a would-be 〔prospective〕 actress.

**여백**(餘白) a blank; (a) space; margin; a (blank) space. ¶ ～을 남기다 〔채우다〕 leave 〔fill in〕 a space / 이하 ～ No more statement 〔detail〕 hereafter. /

그 책의 ～마다 그녀의 메모가 가득 적혀 있었다 Every blank space of the book was filled with her jottings.

**여벌**(餘―) remainings; remnants; surplus; spare. ¶ ～의 reserved; spare / 인쇄물을 얼마만큼 ～로 두다 save some mimeographed sheets for later use / ～이 하나 있다 There is an extra. / 나는 ～ 옷이 한 벌도 없다 I haven't got a spare suit of clothes.

**여병**(餘病) a complication; a secondary disease. ⇨ 합병증(合併症).

**여보** ① 《여보게》 Hello !; Hey there !; Say !; Look here !; I say 《미》; (If you) please. Excuse me. ② 《부부간의》 Dear !; Darling !; Honey !

**여보세요** ① ＝여보①. ¶ ～ 말씀 좀 묻겠습니다 Please, sir. I want to ask you something. / ～ 물건을 떨어뜨렸습니다 I say, you have dropped something. ② 《전화에서》 Hello !; Hallo !; Are you there ? ¶ 「～ 누구시죠」―「명자예요」 《전화에서》 "Hello, 「who's speaking 〔who is this (speaking)〕?"―"This is Myŏngja (speaking)." / ～ 614번 부탁합니다 Give me 614 〔six one four〕, please.

**여복**(女服) women's dresses; ladies' clothes; female attire.

**여봐란듯이** ostentatiously; for show; to show off. ¶ 그는 비싼 외제차를 ～ 몰고 다닌다 He drives an expensive foreign car ostentatiously.

**여부**(與否) yes or no; whether or not. ¶ 수락 ～ acceptance or rejection / 그 사실 ～는 모르겠다 I don't know whether it is true or not. / 성공 ～는 네 자신의 노력에 달려 있다 Success depends upon your efforts.

**여부없다**(與否―) (be) sure; certain; unquestionable; [서술적] there is no question about it; it is a matter of course. ¶ 「한 손으로 이 돌을 들겠니」―「여부없지」 "Can you lift this stone with one hand ?"―"Of course !"

**여북** not to any small degree; to no small degree; very much; greatly. ～하다 be not to any small degree. ¶ 그의 설움이 ～하겠니 He must be very sorrowful. / 너 배가 ～ 고프겠니 You must be very hungry. / 그가 이것을 들으면 ～ 좋아할까 How glad he will be to hear it !

**여분**(餘分) a surplus; an excess; an extra; a spare; redundancy. ¶ ～의 extra; spare; excessive; surplus; superfluous; redundant / ～이 없다 have no surplus / ～의 돈을 가지고 있다 I have some money to spare.
◉ ～비트 〖컴퓨터〗 a redundant bit. ～코드 〖컴퓨터〗 a redundant code.

**여불비례**(餘不備禮) 《편지의 맺음말》 Yours truly 〔faithfully〕; Sincerely yours; Yours sincerely; With kind regards.

**여비**(旅費) travel(ing) expenses. ¶ ～를 지급하다 allow 〔pay〕 《*a person*》 traveling expenses; grant a travel allowance 《to *a person*》 / 미국까지의 왕복 ～는 얼마입니까 What does it cost to make a trip to America and back ? / ～는 각자 부담이다 You must pay your own traveling expenses.

**여사**(女史) ① 《명망 있는》 a learned woman; 《이름에 붙여》 Mrs.; Madame (기혼); Miss (미혼). ¶ 김～ Mrs. 〔Miss., Ms.〕 Kim. ② ＝부인.

**여사무원**(女事務員) an office girl; a woman clerk.

**여상**(女商) 《여자 상업 고등학교》 a girls' commercial high school.

**여색**(女色) 《미색》 a woman's beauty; feminine charms; 《색욕》 sexual 〔carnal〕 desire; lust. ¶ ～에 홀리다〔제정신을 잃다〕 be in fatuated with a woman; be captivated 〔captured〕 by a girl's beauty / ～에 빠지다 be engrossed in fleshly love; lead a life of debauchery / ～을 삼가다 keep away from women / ～을 좋아하다 be lecherous 〔licentious〕; be a womanizer.

**여생**(餘生) the rest 〔remainder〕 of *one's* life 〔days〕; *one's* remaining years 〔days〕. ¶ ～을 교육에 바치다 devote the remainder of *one's* life to education / 조용히 ～을 보내다 live a quiet life for the rest of *one's* days.

**여섯** six. ¶ ～째 the sixth / ～ 꽃잎의 six-petaled 《flower》.

**여성**(女性) a woman (*pl.* women); 《여성들》 womenfolk; [총칭] women in general; womankind; feminity; the gentle 〔fair〕 sex; womanhood; 〖문법〗 the feminine gender. ¶ 현대 ～ modern women; women of today / ～적 womanly; womanlike; feminine; womanish; 《연약한》 effeminate / 사모하는 ～ a lady 〔girl〕 of *one's* heart / ～적인 남자 a womanish 〔an effeminate〕 fellow; a sissy / 기혼 ～ a married woman / 미혼 ～ a maiden 〔an unmarried〕 woman / ～들만의 모임 a hen party / 정말 ～다운 여성 a truly womanly woman / ～의 사회적 지위를 높이고 사회 활동과 고용의 기회를 넓히다 upgrade women's status in society

and expand the opportunity of women for social activities and employments / 그는 ～들에게 인기가 좋다 He is a great favorite with the ladies. / 그녀는 기름 투성이의 작업복을 걸치고는 있었으나 ～다움은 잃지 않고 있었다 She kept her feminity even in greasy overalls.
◉ ～공포증 gynephobia. ～관 a view of womanhood. ～교육 the education of women 〔girls〕. ～란 the ladies' columns. ～명사 a feminine noun. ～문제 the women's problem. ～미 womanly 〔feminine〕 beauty. ～복 a woman's dress. ～상위 female dominance: ～상위 사회 a female-dominated society. ～어 feminine expressions 〔words〕; female language. ～잡지 a women('s) 〔the ladies'〕 magazine. ～전화 상담 Women's Call. ～차별 discrimination against women; sexism. ～찬미자 an admirer of the fair sex. ～참정권 woman suffrage. ～특별위원회 the Presidential Commission on Women's Affairs. ～학 women's studies. ～해방 women's liberation; the liberation of women: ～해방론 feminism / ～해방 운동 the women's liberation 〔lib 《구어》〕 movement; the feminist movement. ～호르몬 the female (sex) hormone. ～화 feminization: ～화하다 feminize. 한국 ～개발원 the Korean Women's Development Institute.

**여성**(女聲) a female voice. ◉ ～합창 a women's 〔female〕 chorus.

**여성용**(女性用) ¶ ～의 ladies' 《watches》; women's 《sweaters》; for ladies' use.
◉ ～장신구 women's accessories. ～화장실 a ladies' toilet; a women's room; 《게시》 (For) Ladies; WOMEN.

**여세**(餘勢) surplus power 〔energy〕; reserve energy; momentum. ¶ 승리의 ～를 몰다 follow up a victory; push on encouraged by *one's* victory.

**여송연**(呂宋煙) a cigar. ¶ ～을 피우다 smoke a cigar.

**여수**(女囚) a female prisoner 〔convict〕.

**여수**(旅愁) melancholy 〔ennui〕 felt while on a journey; a traveler's melancholy. ¶ ～에 젖다 be in a pensive mood while on a journey / ～를 달래다 relieve *one's* loneliness on a journey; beguile the ennui of *one's* journey.

**여수**(餘數) remainder; the remaining 〔leftover〕 number.

**여습** a six-year-old horse 〔ox〕.

**여습**(餘習) traces of old customs. ¶ 봉건 시대의 ～ customs handed down from the feudal days.

**여승**(女僧) a Buddhist nun 〔priestess〕. ¶ ～이 되다 become a Buddhist nun.

**여식**(女息) a 〔*one's*〕 daughter.

**여신**(女神) a goddess. ¶ 사랑의 ～ the goddess of love; Venus / 자유의 ～상 the Statue of Liberty (미국의).

**여신**(與信) giving 〔extending〕 credit; a credit loan; a loan on credit. ¶ 은행의 주 업무는 ～과 수신이다 The main business of a bank is extending and receiving credit.
◉ ～공급량 the amount of a loan. ～관리 credit management: ～관리국 the credit supervision department / ～관리를 받다 be under credit control / 보다 엄격한 ～ 관리를 받게 하다 place 《the money borrowers》 under stricter credit control. ～규제 credit controls. ～등급 credit rating. ～상태 credit condition. ～업무 a loan business. ～한도 a credit line 〔limit, ceiling〕; a line of credit: ～ 한도를 늘리다 extend credit limits.

**여신**(餘燼) embers; cinders; 《화재 때의》 a smoldering fire.

**여실**(如實) ～하다 be like real; (be) vivid; realistic. ¶ ～히 《사실적으로》 realistically; true to life; as things really are; 《생생히》 vividly; graphically / 인생을 ～히 그리다 depict life just as it is / ～히 이야기하다 give a vivid 〔true, graphic〕 account 《of》 / 인물을 ～히 그리다 portray *a person's* characters to the life / 그 이야기는 1990년대의 서울을 ～히 묘사하고 있다 The story gives a vivid picture of Seoul in the 1990's.

**여심**(女心) a woman's heart. ¶ ～을 알아주지 않는 남자 a man who does not understand the female mind 〔psychology〕.

**여아**(女兒) a girl; a little 〔baby〕 girl; daughter (딸). ¶ ～를 분만하다 give birth to a girl.

**여압**(與壓) pressurization. ◉ ～복 a pressurized 〔pressure〕 suit. ～실 a pressurized cabin 〔chamber〕.

**여액**(餘額) the balance; a remainder.

**여야**(與野) the Government party and the Opposition party; the ins and the outs; the in party and the out party.

**여열**(餘熱) remaining 〔residual〕 heat; 《신열》 lingering fever. ¶ 그녀는 다리미의 ～을 이용해서 몇 장의 손수건을 다렸

다 She ironed several handkerchiefs using the heat still in the iron.

**여염**(餘炎) 《불》 lingering flames; burning cinders; 《더위》 lingering summer heat.

**여염**(閭閻) 《서민 사회》 a middle-class community; 《백성》 respectable citizenry. ◉ ～집 a middle-class home; a respectable home 〔family〕: ～집 부녀 wives and daughters of respectable citizens.

**여왕**(女王) a queen; a queen regnant (군주); [비유적] a belle (최고 미인). ¶ ～ 같은 queenlike; queenly / 엘리자베스 2세 ～ Queen Elizabeth II / 영국 ～ 빅토리아 Victoria, Queen of England / 무도회의 ～ the belle of the ball / 사교계의 ～ a queen of 〔in〕 society. ◉ ～개미 a queen ant. ～국 a queendom. ～벌 a queen bee 〔wasp〕.

**여우** a fox; a vixen (암컷). ¶ ～ 꼬리 a fox brush / ～ 모피 (a) fox fur / ～같다 be foxy; be vulpine / ～같이 얄밉다 be hateful as a sneaky fox; be hatefully sneaky / ～가 울다 bark; yelp / ～에 홀리다 be bewitched by a fox / 마치 ～에 홀린 듯하다 I am puzzled 〔mystified〕. *or* I am greatly bewitched and bewildered.
◉ ～굴 a fox burrow. ～볕 brief sunshine on a cloudy day; fitful 〔intermittent〕 sunshine: ～볕이 나다 the sun comes out for a few minutes on a cloudy day. ～비 a shower when the sun is shining; intermittent showers. ～사냥 fox hunting. ～털 목도리 a fox-fur muffler.

**여우**(女優) an actress. ⇨여배우(女俳優).

**여운**(餘韻) ① 《악기 따위의》 a trailing note; a lingering sound; 《종소리 등의》 reverberations; echoes. ¶ 길게 ～을 남기는 퉁소 소리 the trailing notes of a bamboo flute / 연주가 끝난 후에 그 음악의 ～이 마음 속에 남았다 I felt the music lingering on in my mind after the performance was over. ② 《뒤에 남는 운치》 an aftertaste; an aftereffect; 《시문 등의》 suggestiveness. ¶ 이 시는 ～이 풍부하다 This poem is full of suggestion.

**여울** 《얕은》 shallows; a shoal; a ford; 《물살이 센》 rapids 《in a river》. ¶ ～을 건너다 cross 「a ford 〔the rapids〕; ford (over). ◉ ～목 the neck of the rapids.

**여위다** ① 《몸이》 get 〔become〕 thin 〔haggard〕; be worn out; become emaciated 〔gaunt〕 《from illness》; waste away. ¶ 여윈 얼굴 a haggard face / 여윈 볼 hollow 〔sunken〕 cheeks / 근심으로 ～ be careworn / 병후라 여위어 보이다 look thin after an illness / 여위어서 뼈만 남다 be wasted to mere skeleton / 그녀는 과로로 여위어 보인다 She 「looks haggard from 〔is worn out with〕 overwork. / 아버지는 오랜 병으로 형편없이 여위셨다 My father is worn to a shadow on account of a long illness.
② 《살림이》 become 〔get〕 impoverished; become poor 〔needy〕. ¶ 여윈 살림을 하다 make a poor 〔bare〕 living.

**여유**(餘裕) ① 《여지》 room; space; scope; 《시간·돈·체력의》 time 〔money, energy〕 to spare 《for》; a margin 《for》 money 〔time, energy〕; 《잉여》 (a) surplus; a reserve (예비). ¶ ～있는 생활을 하다 live 「in comfort 〔a comfortable life〕; be well 〔comfortably〕 off / ～없는 생활을 하다 make a bare living / 식량의 ～가 많다 have lots of food in reserve / 활동할 충분한 ～를 주다 allow plenty of scope for 《*a person's*》 activities / 나는 생활의 ～가 거의 없다 I have very little to live on. / 여행을 갈 ～가 없다 I can't afford (to take) 〔the money for〕 a trip. / 버스가 떠나기까지는 아직 30분의 ～가 있다 We have thirty minutes left before the bus leaves. / 바빠서 휴가를 가질 ～도 없다 I am too busy to take holidays. / 차에는 한 사람이 더 탈 ～가 있다 We have enough room for one more in the car.
② 《마음의》 composure; calmness. ¶ ～를 잃다 lose *one's* composure 〔presence of mind〕 / 항상 마음의 ～를 가지시오 Always keep your composure. / 그는 ～ 작작하다 He is calm and at ease.
◉ ～자금 extra funds.

**여의**(如意) ～하다 turn out as *one* wishes; be to *one's* desire. ¶ ～하게 as *one* pleases 〔expected〕; to *one's* heart's content / ～치 않다 go contrary to *one's* wishes; go wrong 〔amiss〕; fall short of *one's* expectations.

**여의다** ① 《잃다·죽다》 lose 《*a person*》; be bereaved 〔bereft〕 of. ¶ 아버지를 ～ lose *one's* father; be bereft of *one's* father / 어려서 어머니를 ～ lose 〔be bereaved of〕 *one's* mother in *one's* childhood / 자식을 ～ survive 〔lose〕 *one's* son; be left behind by *one's* son. ② 《멀리 보내다》 send 《*a person*》 far away; 《시집보내다》 marry 《*one's* daughter》 off 《to *a person*》. ¶ 딸을 멀리 ~ marry off *one's* daughter 《to *a person*》 far away.

**여의사**(女醫師) a lady 〔female〕 doctor; a woman doctor (★ 복수형은 women doctors, lady 〔female〕 doctors).

**여의주**(如意珠) 〖불교〗 *cintámani* (Sans.); a magic pearl that bestows omnipotence on *a person* who acquires it.

**여인**(女人) a woman. ¶ ~ 출입금지 being closed to women; 《게시》 No admittance to women: 그 절은 ~ 금제(禁制)이다 The temple is closed to women. ◉ ~천하 petticoat government.

**여인숙**(旅人宿) an inn; a tavern; a hostelry. ¶ ~주인 an innkeeper; a landlady (여자) / 싸구려 ~ a flophouse 《미》; a doss house 《영속어》.

**여일**(如一) constancy; consistency; being unchanged 〔constant〕. ~하다 (be) constant; unchanged; be just the same. ¶ 시종 ~하게 consistently / 시종 ~하다 be consistent; be the same from first to last / 시종 ~하게 충성을 다하다 remain faithful 《to the Emperor》 to the last.

**여자**(女子) ① 《여성》 a woman; a girl; a lady; a female; [총칭] woman; the fair 〔gentle, weaker〕 sex.

> 용법 **a woman** 「한 사람의 여자」를 나타내는 가장 일반적인 말. 복수형은 women [wímin]. **a girl** 본래 「소녀」를 뜻하나, 《구어》에서는 연령에 관계없이 애인처럼 친밀한 사이의 「여자」를 뜻함. **a lady** woman의 공손한 말씨. 「교양 있고 신분 높은 귀부인」을 뜻하기도 했으나 요즘은 이 뜻으로 별로 쓰이지 않게 되었음. **a female** 성별을 강조할 때 쓰이는 말. **woman** 「여성 전체」를 뜻하는 말, 관사없이 단수형으로만 쓰임.
> 참고 남자와 여자를 구별하는 어형(語形)은 대체로 세 가지가 있다. (1) 별개의 낱말을 씀: a boy—a girl. (2) 어미에 -ess를 덧붙여 여자를 나타냄: an actor—an actress. (3) 남자 또는 여자를 뜻하는 말을 덧붙임: a female cousin; a manservant—a maidservant; a washerman—a washerwoman.

¶ ~의 woman; female; feminine / ~ 같은 effeminate; womanish / ~다운 womanly; ladylike; feminine / ~답지 않은 unwomanly; unladylike / ~만의 모임 《구어》 a hen party / 성적 매력이 있는 ~ a sexpot 《미구어》 / 매력적인 ~ an attractive 〔a charming〕 woman 〔girl〕 / ~의 권리 woman's 〔women's〕 rights / (성장하여) 한 사람의 ~가 되다 grow into a woman; reach 〔attain〕 womanhood / ~에 무르다〔약하다〕 have a weakness for women / ~를 싫어하다 have an aversion for women; be a woman hater / ~용의 ladies' 《wear》; 《clothes》 for ladies' use / 그녀는 마음씨가 고운 ~다운 소녀다 She is a tender-hearted, womanly girl. / 그녀에겐 ~다운 데가 없다 She isn't very feminine. / 그는 아직 ~를 모른다 He still hasn't had a woman. *or* He's still a virgin. / 그녀는 35세란 한창 때의 ~다 She is 35 years old and in the prime of womanhood. / ~는 남자보다 오래 산다 Women live longer than men. / 약한 자여 그대 이름은 ~이니라 Frailty, thy name is woman! ② 《정부(情婦)》 a 〔*one's*〕 mistress; 《애인》 *one's* woman; a sweetheart. ¶ 그에게는 ~가 있다 He has a lover 〔mistress〕. / 남편이 ~를 얻어 그녀는 몹시 고통을 받고 있다 She has been suffering agony since her husband took a mistress.

◉ ~감독 《공장의》 a forewoman; 《영화의》 a female director. ~고등학교 a girls' (senior) high school; a girls' upper secondary school: ~고등학교 학생 a (senior) high-school girl. ~교육 the education of women 〔girls〕; female education. ~기숙사 a women's 〔girls'〕 dormitory. ~대학 a women's college 〔university〕. ~사무원 a female clerk; woman office worker. ~손님 a lady 〔woman〕 visitor 〔guest〕; a woman customer (상점의). ~역 a female role 〔part〕. ~주인 《주부》 a mistress; 《요릿집 따위》 a landlady; a hostess. ~중학교 a girls' junior high 〔lower secondary〕 school. ~친구 a girl 〔woman〕 friend. ~호주 the female head of a family 〔household〕.

**여장**(女裝) 《복장》 a female dress; female attire 〔costume〕; 《분장》 woman's disguise. ~하다 put on 〔wear〕 a female dress; disguise *oneself* as a woman. ¶ ~한 남자 a man in woman's disguise / 살인범은 ~을 하고 도망쳤다 The murderer made his escape disguised as a woman.

**여장**(旅裝) a traveling outfit 〔kit〕. ¶ ~을 꾸리다 make (*one's*) preparations for a journey; equip *oneself* for a journey / ～을 풀다 take off *one's* traveling attire; stop 〔put up〕 at 《a hotel》 (숙박하다).

**여전하다**(如前―) be as before 〔usual〕; be as it used to be; be 〔remain〕 unchanged. ¶ 여전히 as usual 〔ever〕; still; as… as ever; as (it was) before; as (it) used to be; as of old / 여전히 게으르다 be as idle as ever / 그 노인은 기력이 아직도 ～ The old man is still going strong as usual. /「요새 어떻게 지내십니까」―「여전합니다」"How are you getting along these days?"―"The same as usual." / 그는 여전히 가난하다 He is 〔remains〕 as poor as ever. / 이 계약은 여전히 유효하다 This contract holds good even now.

**여점원**(女店員) a saleswoman; a salesgirl; a shopgirl 《영》.

**여정**(旅情) the weary thoughts 〔heart〕 of a traveler. ⇨ 여수(旅愁).

**여정**(旅程) 《거리》 the distance to be covered; 《여행 일정》 an itinerary; the plan 〔schedule〕 for *one's* journey. ¶ 하루의 ～ a day's journey / ～을 짜다 make travel plans; plan an 〔*one's*〕 itinerary / 그들은 상세한 ～을 세웠다 They made up the exact plan of their journey. / 레이건은 "이제 나는 내 인생의 일몰로 가는 ～을 시작합니다"라고 고별사에서 말했다 "I now begin the journey that will lead me into the sunset of my life," Reagan said in his farewell address.

**여제**(女帝) an empress (regnant); a 「queen.

**여존남비**(女尊男卑) respect for woman at the expense of man; putting women above men. ¶ 여권 신장을 ～라고 해석하는 사람도 있다 Putting women above men is sometimes interpreted as feminism.

**여종**(女―) a woman slave 〔servant〕.

**여죄**(餘罪) other 〔further, additional〕 crimes 〔charges〕. ¶ ～를 추궁하다 make further inquiries about further crimes suspected.

**여주** 〖식물〗 a balsam pear.

**여주인공**(女主人公) a heroine.

**여중**(女中) ⇨ 여자 중학교.

**여지**(荔枝) 〖식물〗 a litchi 〔lichee〕.

**여지**(餘地) room; a margin; a scope; space. ¶ 발전의 ～ room 〔margin〕 for development / 말할 ～가 없다 admit of no argument 〔comment〕; be evident / 타협의 ～가 있다〔없다〕 admit of compromise 〔no compromise〕; leave room 〔no room〕 for compromise / ～없이 패하다 suffer 〔sustain〕 a crushing defeat; be beaten utterly 〔all hollow〕 / 논쟁의 ～가 있다 There is enough ground for controversy. / 개선의 ～가 있다 There is room for improvement. / 의심할 ～가 없다 There is no room for doubt. / 변명의 ～가 없다 There is not the slightest excuse. / 이 점에 대해서는 검토할 ～가 있다 The point in question is open to further discussion.

**여진**(餘震) an aftershock; an after tremor. ¶ ～이 있다 feel 〔have〕 an aftershock.

**여질**(女姪) a niece.

**여짓거리다** keep hesitating to speak. ¶ 여짓거리며 hesitatingly; nervously; uneasily.

**여쭈다** ① 《말씀드리다》 tell 《to a superior》; say; inform; state. ¶ 여러분께 여쭙겠습니다 Can 〔May〕 I have your attention, please! ② 《문의하다》 ask 《*a person* about》; inquire 《of *a person* about》. ¶ 좀 여쭤 보겠는데요… Excuse me, but will you tell me…. / 또 한 가지 여쭤 볼 일이 있습니다 I have one more question to ask you.

**여차**(如此) (being) like this. ～하다 be like this; be in this manner 〔way〕; be such; be of this kind. ¶ ～한 사람 such a man; a person like this / ～여차하다 be so and so; be such and such / ～여차한 이유로 for such and such reasons; such being the case; under these circumstances / ～여차하게 말하다 say 〔tell〕 so and so / 사건의 발단이 ～여차하다고 그는 설명했다 He explained that the incident had happened for such-and-such a reason.

**여차장**(女車掌) a female 〔girl〕 conductor; a conductress.

**여차하면** in case 〔time, the hour〕 of need 〔emergency〕; if need be; at a pinch 〔push〕. ¶ ～ 부동산을 팔아치울 생각이다 I am ready to sell my estate at a pinch.

**여체**(女體) the body of (a) woman.

**여축**(餘蓄) savings; (a) stock; reserve; supplies. ～하다 save; stock; reserve; set 〔put〕 aside. ¶ ～이 좀 있다 have some savings / 상당한 ～이 있다 have a nice nest egg / 한푼의 ～도 없다 have not a penny 「saved 〔laid by〕.

**여치** 〖곤충〗 a (long-horned) grasshopper.

**여탈**(與奪) giving and depriving. ◉ ～

권 the power to give and to take away: 생살 ～권을 쥐다 hold the power of life and death《over *a person*》.

**여탕**(女湯) the ladies' section (of a public bathhouse).

**여태(껏)** up to now; till 〔until〕 now; (as) yet; up to date; hitherto. ¶ ～까지 = 여태(껏) / ～ 없었던 사건 an unprecedented incident / ～ 그런 사람은 만난 일이 없다 I have never met such a man in my life. / ～ 편지를 쓰고 있었다 I have been writing a letter (until now). / 그에게서 ～ 소식이 없다 I have heard nothing from him as yet. / ～ 어디 갔었니 Where have you been all this while? / 이런 일은 ～ 없었던 일이다 Such a thing has never happened. *or* This is an unprecedented affair.

**여투다** hoard up; put 〔lay〕 aside; save《money》. ¶ 후일을 위해 여퉈 두다 put aside for future use.

**여파**(餘波) ①《태풍 등의》 a trail; high waves (after a typhoon). ¶ 태풍의 ～로 파도가 높다 The sea is running high on account of a typhoon passing near. ②《영향》 an aftereffect; an aftermath; a side effect. ¶ 경제 공황의 ～ the secondary effect 〔the aftermath〕 of an economic panic / 지진의 ～ the aftereffects of an earthquake / …의 ～를 받다 be under the influence of…; be affected by the sequel of… / 경기 후퇴의 ～로 많은 기업들이 파산했다 Large numbers of businesses went bankrupt in the aftermath of「the recession 〔the business setback〕.

**여편네** a married woman; 《아내》 *one's* wife.

**여피**《도시의 젊은 엘리트족의 한 사람》 a yuppie; a yuppy.

**여필종부**(女必從夫) A wife should follow the lead set by her husband. *or* Wives should be submissive to their husbands.

**여하**(如何) how; what. ～하다 be how; be like what. ¶ ～한 이유로 for what reason; why / …의 ～를 불문하고 regardless 〔irrespective〕 of《whether…》/ ～한 희생을〔대가를〕 치르더라도 at any cost 〔price, sacrifice〕/ ～한 부자라도 no matter how rich a man may be / ～한 경우라도 in any case; under any circumstances; whatever may happen / 사정 ～에 달리다 depend upon circumstances / 성공은 네 노력 ～에 달렸다 Success depends on your efforts. / 가느냐 안 가느냐는 날씨 ～에 따른다 Whether we go or not depends on the weather.

**여하튼**(如何—) anyway; anyhow; at any rate; in any case; at all events. ¶ ～ 그는 위대한 인물이다 He is a great man, after all 〔at all events〕. / ～ 해보겠다 At any rate I'll try. / ～ 처분하겠다 I will dispose it in some way or other. / ～ 전쟁은 이겨야 한다 A war must be won at any cost. / 비가 올지도 모르나, ～ 나가겠다 It may rain, but anyhow I shall go out.

**여학교**(女學校) a girls' school.

**여학생**(女學生) a girl student; a schoolgirl; 《남녀 공학의》 a co-ed 《미》.

**여한**(餘恨) a smoldering 〔lingering〕 grudge 〔regret〕. ¶ ～을 품고 있다 hold a smoldering grudge against《*a person*》/ ～을 풀다 pay off *one's* old scores; be revenged《on *a person* for *something*》.

**여한**(餘寒) the lingering cold (of early spring). ¶ ～이 아직 가시지 않다 the cold still lingers.

**여행**(旅行) traveling; a travel; a journey (긴여행); a trip (짧은); a tour (관광); a voyage (해상); an excursion (유람). ～하다 make a trip 〔voyage, tour〕; travel; journey; tour.

> 용법 **trip** 여행을 뜻하는 일반적인 말로 여행의 장단·수단·목적에 구애받지 않고 두루 쓸 수 있는 말. **travel** 흔히 복수형을 써서 해외 먼곳으로 가는 여행 등에 씀. **tour** 계획된 관광 여행, 두루 돌아다니는 유람 여행 등에 씀. **excursion** 업자·학교 등의 계획에 따라, 단체로 행해지는 하루의 짧은 여행. **journey** 장거리의 느긋한, 주로 육지에서 행해지는 여행. **voyage** journey와 같은 뜻이나 주로 해로(海路)의 여행을 뜻함.

¶ 해외～ a trip abroad; foreign travel / 수학～ a school excursion 〔trip〕/ 버스〔기차〕～ a bus 〔train〕 trip / 관광 ～ a (sightseeing) tour / 주말 ～ a weekend trip / 출장〔업무〕 ～ a business trip / 신혼～ a honeymoon; a wedding tour / 단체～ a group tour / ～의 계절 a tourist season / ～중이다 be on a journey / 각지를 ～하다 travel from place to place / 도보로 ～하다 travel on foot / 배로 ～하다 travel by water / 미국으로 ～가다 make a trip to America / 세계를 ～하다 travel around the world; make a world tour / ～을 떠나다 start on *one's* travels; set out on a trip / ~에서 돌아오다 return from *one's* journey; be back from *one's* travels / ~에 지치다 be tired after *one's* journey; be travel-worn / 그는 ~을 좋아한다 He is fond of traveling. *or* He likes traveling. / 그는 ~ 중이어서 집에 없다 He is away on a trip. / 즐거운 ~을 하시기를 《인사》 Have a nice 〔pleasant〕 trip.

◉ ~가 a traveler; a tourist (유람자). ~가방 a luggage 《미》; a traveling 〔traveler's〕 bag; a suitcase; 《대형의》 a trunk; 《단기용》 an overnight bag. ~기 a book of travels; [총칭] travel literature: ~기 애독자 an armchair traveler. ~담 an account of *one's* travels; a travelog(ue). ~비 traveling expenses. ~사 a travel 〔tourist〕 agency. ~상해 보험 travel accident insurance. ~안내 a traveler's guide; guidance to travelers: ~안내서 a travelers' guidebook; a guidebook for tourist / ~안내소 a tourist bureau. ~일정 an itinerary; a plan for travel; *one's* travel schedule. ~자 a tourist; a traveler: ~자 수표 a traveler's check / ~자 불만 고발 센터 a Tourist Complaint Center. ~지 《목적지》 *one's* destination; 《체재지》 the place where *one* is staying. 세계일주~ a round-the-world trip.

**여호수아서**(一書) 〖성서〗 (The Book of) Joshua (생략 Josh.).

**여호와** 〖성서〗 Jehovah. ¶ ~의 증인 Jehovah's Witnesses.

**여흥**(餘興) 《남은 흥》 unexhausted merriment 〔fun〕; 《연예·오락》 an entertainment; a side show. ¶ ~으로 by way of entertainment; as a side show; for an amusement / ~으로 들어가다 pass 〔proceed〕 on to entertainments / ~으로 춤과 노래가 있었다 For entertainment, dances and songs were presented.

**여히**(如一) as...; like.... ¶ 하기〔상기〕와 ~ as follows 〔above〕; as in the following 〔preceding〕.

**역**(逆) the contrary; the opposite; 〖수학〗 converse; reverse; inverse. ¶ 역의 contrary; opposite; reverse / 역으로 conversely; inversely; on the contrary / 우리의 예상과는 역으로 contrary to our expectation(s) / 역으로 하다 reverse 《the order》; turn 《*a thing*》 upside down (상하를); turn 《*a thing*》 inside out (겉과 속을) / 역도 진(眞)이다 The reverse is also true. / 역이 반드시 진(眞)은 아니다 Converses are not always true.

**역**(閾) 〖심리〗 a threshold.

**역**(驛) a (railroad) station; a depot 《미》. ¶ 서울역 Seoul Station / 출발〔도착〕역 a departure 〔an arrival〕 station / 종착역 《미》 a terminal (station); 《영》 a terminus (*pl.* -mini, ~es) / 역무원 a station employee; [총칭] the station staff / 역앞 광장 a station square 〔plaza〕 / 역에서 사람을 전송〔마중〕하다 see off 〔meet〕 *a person* at the station / 시청에 가려면 어느 역에서 내려야 합니까 At what stop 〔station〕 should I get off if I want to go to City Hall?

**역**(役) 《배역》 a role; a part. ¶ 춘향의 역 the role of Ch'unhyang / …의 역을 하다 play 〔act〕 the part 〔role〕 of 《Hamlet》 / 역을 맡기다 cast 《*a person*》 for 《Hamlet》; cast a part to 《*a person*》 / 맡은 역을 잘 해내다 act 〔play〕 *one's* part well.

**역**(譯) (a) translation. =번역.

**역가**(力價) 〖화학〗 titer.

**역겹다**(逆一) 《메스껍다》 feel sick 〔queasy〕; feel nausea; have a sick stomach; 《혐오스럽다》 be nauseated 〔disgusted〕 《by》; be intolerable 〔detestable〕; be offensive. ¶ 역겨운 냄새 a sickening 〔an offensive〕 smell / 역겨운 광경 a sickening 〔nauseating〕 sight / 보기만해도 ~ Even looking at it displeases me.

**역경**(易經) *the Book of Changes;* the Yi-King. ⇨ 주역(周易).

**역경**(逆境) adversity; an adverse situation 〔fortune〕; adverse 〔unfavorable〕 circumstances. ¶ ~에 처한 사람 a man in adversity; a man with whom the world has not gone well / ~을 극복하다 tide over a difficult situation / ~에 처하다 be in adversity; be in 〔under〕 adverse circumstances / ~에 빠지다 fall into adversity; fall on bad days / ~과 싸우다 struggle 〔wrestle〕 against adversity / ~에서 단련되다 be schooled in adversity / ~에 잘 대처하다 make the best of *one's* ill fortune / ~에 굴하지 않고 without being discouraged by adversity / 그는 ~속에서 자랐다 He grew up in unfavorable circumstances.

**역광선**(逆光線) backlight; 〖물리〗 counterlight. ¶ ~으로 사진을 찍다 take a picture against 〔into〕 the light 〔sun〕.

**역군**(役軍) a laborer; an able worker

[man]; a pillar. ¶ 사회의 ～ a pillar of society.

**역기**(力器) 『스포츠』 a barbell; the weight. ¶ ～를 들다 lift the weight 《in the press》; exercise a barbell.

**역내**(域內) ¶ ～에서 within the area.
◉ ～무역 intra-trade. 「[civil] year.

**역년**(曆年) 《책력의 일년》 a calendar

**역단층**(逆斷層) 『지질』 a reverse fault.

**역담보**(逆擔保) (a) counter-security.

**역대**(歷代) generation after generation; successive generations. ¶ ～의 왕 successive kings; kings of many generations / ～내각 successive cabinets.

**역도**(力道) weight lifting.
◉ ～선수 a weight lifter. 대한 ～ 연맹 the Korea Weight-lifting Federation.

**역도**(逆徒) (a group of) rebels; traitors; insurgents. ⇨ 역적.

**역두**(驛頭) the front of a railroad station. ⇨ 역전(驛前).

**역량**(力量) (a) capacity; capability; (a) talent; ability. ¶ ～ 있는 인물 a man of ability [talent]; an able man / ～ 있는 정치가 an able [a capable, a competent] statesman / ～을 발휘하다 display *one's* ability / ～을 시험하다 try [test] *one's* ability / …할 ～이 없다 have no capacity to *do* [of *do*ing] / 그 일을 할 만한 ～이 있다 be equal to the task / 자기의 ～을 알다 find *one's* feet; know *one's* limitations.

**역력**(歷歷) ～하다 (be) clear; vivid; obvious; plain. ¶ ～하게 clearly; plainly vividly; unmistakably / ～한 사실 an obvious truth [fact] / 증거가 ～하다 The proof is manifest. / 그의 얼굴에 ～히 나타나 있다 It can be plainly seen on his face.

**역류**(逆流) flowing backward; a backward flow; a back current; an upstream current; going against the current; 《조수의》 an adverse [a back=flowing] tide. ～하다 flow upstream [backward]; surge back; go against 《the times》. ¶ 물이 ～하고 있다 The water is flowing backward. / 우리는 물길을 ～해 올라갔다 We rowed against the current.

**역리**(疫痢) 『의학』 children's dysentery; infant diarrhea.

**역리**(逆理) (what is) contrary to rationality; irrationality; a paradox. ¶ ～의 irrational; unreasonable; absurd.

**역링크제**(逆一制) 『경제』 a counterlink system.

**역마**(驛馬) 『고제도』 a post horse.

**역마살**(驛馬煞) ¶ ～이 끼었다 have itchy feet / ～이 끼었는지 또 어딘가 가고 싶다 I must have itchy feet, I want to go on a trip again.

**역마을, 역말**(驛一) a post town.

**역마차**(驛馬車) a stagecoach.

**역모**(逆謀) a plot of treason; a conspiracy. ～하다 plot treason; conspire to rise in revolt.

**역무원**(驛務員) a station employee; the station staff [총칭].

**역문**(譯文) a translation; a version; a translated sentence. 「tion.

**역반응**(逆反應) 『물리』 an inverse reac-

**역방**(歷訪) a round of visits [calls]. ～하다 make a round of visits 《to》.

**역법**(曆法) the 《Roman》 calendar.

**역병**(疫病) 《유행병》 an epidemic; a plague; a pestilence (악질의). ¶ ～이 발생하다 an epidemic breaks out / ～이 유행하고 있다 The plague is prevalent.

**역부족**(力不足) want of ability. ¶ ～이다 be wanting in ability; be incapable; [사물이 주어] be beyond *one's* capacity / 나는 나의 ～임을 잘 안다 I am well aware of my lack of ability.

**역분사**(逆噴射) retrofiring 《of a rocket》.

**역불급**(力不及) (being) beyond *one's* capacity [ability]. ～하다 be beyond *one's* ability; above *one's* ability.

**역비**(逆比) 『수학』 an inverse ratio. ⇨ 반비례. 「muscle man.

**역사**(力士) a strong [powerful] man; a

**역사**(役事) construction work; public works. ～하다 do construction work.

**역사**(歷史) ① history; 《연대기·역대기》 a chronicle; annals. ¶ ～적인[상의] historic(al) / ～ 이전의 prehistoric / ～적으로 historically / 한국[동양, 서양]～ Korean [Oriental, Occidental] history / ～가 시작된 이래 since the dawn of history / ～적(인) 사건[사실, 인물] a historical event [fact, figure] / ～적인 발명 a historic invention / ～에 관한 자료 historical materials [documents] / ～상 유명한 곳 a place of historic interest / ～상 최대의 인물 the greatest man in history / 두 나라 사이의 올바른 ～ 인식에 관한 논쟁 a controversy over the "correct perception of history" between the two countries / 세계 ～에 영향을 미치다 affect 「world history [the history of the world] / 세계 ～에 유례가 없다 be unparalleled in the annals of the world history / ～를 장식하다 adorn the history of... / 한국 기독교의 ～를 더

듬다 trace the history of Christianity in Korea / ~에 길이 남다 remain long in history / ~에 기록되다「be recorded 〔go down〕 in history / ~에 이름을 남기다 leave *one's* mark on history / ~는 되풀이 된다 History repeats itself. ② 《내력》 history; tradition (전통). ¶ ~있는 대학 an old university; a university with a long history / 우리 은행은 50년의 ~를 가지고 있다 Our bank has a history of fifty years.
◉ ~가 a historian. ~관 historical view. ~극 a historical play. ~서 a history (book). ~소설 a historical novel. ~시대 《early》 historic times. ~연표 a chronological table of 《Korean》 history; 《학교용》 a history chart. ~의식 historical consciousness. ~주의 historicism. ~지리 historical geography. ~철학 philosophy of history. ~학 history; historical science. ~학파 〖경제·법학〗 the historical school. ~화 a historical painting.

**역사**(轢死) ~하다 be (run over and) killed by a car 〔train〕.
◉ ~자 a person run over and killed.

**역산**(逆産) ① 〖의학〗 breech birth 〔delivery, presentation〕. ② 《재산》 property of a traitor.

**역산**(逆算) reverse 〔inverse〕 operation. = 역연산(逆演算). ~하다 count 〔reckon〕 backward; calculate back 《to》.

**역서**(曆書) an almanac; a calendar.

**역서**(譯書) a translated book 〔version〕 《of》; a translation.

**역선전**(逆宣傳) counterpropaganda. ~하다 carry out 〔make〕 counterpropaganda; counterpropagandize.

**역설**(力說) assertion. ~하다 emphasize; put 〔lay〕 stress 〔emphasis〕 on 《*a thing*》; stress; urge 《upon *a person* the need of》. ¶ 저금의 필요성을 ~하다 emphasize the necessity of saving money / 직업 교육의 필요성을 ~하다 be very emphatic about the necessity of vocational education / 나는 여러분에게 이 안의 중요성을 ~하고자 합니다 Let me urge upon you the importance of this measure. / 그는 공해 방지 대책의 필요를 ~했다 He stressed the need for antipollution measures.

**역설**(逆說) a paradox. ~하다 state paradoxically. ¶ ~적인 paradoxical / ~적으로 말하면 paradoxically speaking / ~적으로 들릴는지 모르지만 운동이 건강에 해로울 수도 있다 It may sound paradoxical, but exercise can harm our health.

**역성** favoritism; partiality. ~하다, ~들다 show favoritism 〔partiality〕 《toward》; be partial 《to》; treat 《*a person*》 with undue favor. ¶ ~드는 unfair; partial / ~들지 마시오 Please treat us fairly. *or* Please be fair to us. / 그는 그 학생에게 ~들었다 He showed undue favor to the student. / 선생은 어느 학생만 ~들어서는 안된다 A teacher must not be partial to any of his 〔her〕 students.

**역성**(逆成) 〖언어〗 back-formation.
◉ ~어 a back-formation.

**역수**(逆數) 〖수학〗 a reciprocal (number).

**역수입**(逆輸入) reimport; reimportation. ~하다 reimport.「~하다 reexport.

**역수출**(逆輸出) reexport; reexportation.

**역술**(譯述) translation. ~하다 translate.

**역습**(逆襲) a counterattack; a counteroffensive. ~하다 counterattack; make 〔launch〕 a counterattack 〔counteroffensive〕 《on, against》; 《받아치다》 counter; 《말로》 retort 《that...》. ¶ ~을 받다 meet with a reverse / 상대의 말을 받아 ~하다「make a retort to what 《*a person*》 said; come back at 《*a person*》 for what he said / 경기 후반에 ~으로 나가다 stage a counterattack in the second half of the game.

**역시**(譯詩) a translated poem; a poem in translation.

**역시**(亦是) ① 《또한》 too; also; as well; likewise; 《not》 either. ¶ 그 계획에는 나 ~ 반대입니다 I am against the plan, too. / 그도 ~ 그렇다 So is 〔does, *etc.*〕 he. / 나(도) ~ 그것을 좋아하지 않는다 I don't like it, either.
② 《아직도》 still; all the same; after all (결국). ¶ ~ 그건 정말이었다 It turned out to be true after all.
③ 《그래도》 but (then); nevertheless; notwithstanding; in spite of; none the less; with 〔for〕 all 《*one's* faults》. ¶ 결점은 많지만 ~ 그를 좋아한다 I do not love him the less for all his faults. *or* He has many faults, but I like him none the less.
④ 《예상대로》 as (was) expected; true to *one's* expectations; as is usual 《with》; like the rest. ¶ ~ 그는 실패했다 He failed as I feared.

**역신**(疫神) 〖민속〗 the spirit 〔animus〕 of smallpox.

**역암**(礫岩) 〖지질〗 (a) conglomerate.

**역어**(譯語) words 〔terms〕 used in a

translation; translated words [terms]; an 《English》 equivalent. ¶ ~를 고르다 choose appropriate words for translation / 이 영어의 우리말 ~를 찾을 수 없다 I cannot find a Korean equivalent for this English word.

**역연하다**(歷然—) (be) obvious; clear. ⇨ 역력(歷歷)하다.

**역영**(力泳) ~하다 swim with powerful strokes; swim with might and main.

**역외**(域外) ◉ ~구매 an offshore purchase. ~조달 offshore procurement.

**역용**(逆用) a reverse use. ~하다 make a reverse use of; turn 《the enemy's propaganda》 to *one's* own advantage; take advantage of 《*a person's* kindness》. ¶ 사장은 종업원의 선량함을 ~했다 The president turned the good nature of the employees to his advantage.

**역원**(役員) 《단체의》 an official; 《회사의》 an executive; a director. ⇨ 임원(任員).

**역원**(驛員) ⇨ 역무원.

**역이용**(逆利用) ⇨ 역용(逆用).

**역일**(曆日) a calendar [civil] day.

**역임**(歷任) successive holding of various posts. ~하다 hold various posts in succession; successively fill [hold] various posts. ¶ 그는 대학 총장을 ~하였다 He was consecutively occupied the chair of the university president. / 그는 국회의원, 총리를 ~했다 He was consecutively Member of the National Assembly and Prime Minister.

**역자**(譯者) a translator.

**역작**(力作) a laborous work; a work of great labor; 《걸작》 a masterpiece. ~하다 work strenuously on. ¶ 그건 임교수의 ~이다 Prof. Yim took great pains with that work. ◉ ~품 a masterpiece.

**역작용**(逆作用) an adverse effect; (a) reaction; (a) reverse action.

**역장**(驛長) a stationmaster 《at Seoul》; a station agent 《미》. ◉ ~실 the stationmaster's office.

**역저**(力著) a strenuous [laborous] literary work.

**역적**(逆賊) a rebellious subject; a rebel; a traitor. ¶ ~으로 몰리다 be branded as a traitor [rebel] / ~모의하다 conspire to rise in revolt 《against》. ◉ ~질 rebellion; (an act of) treason: ~질로 처형되다 be executed for treason.

**역전**(力戰) a hard fight. ~하다 fight hard; put up a good fight. ¶ ~했으나 그녀는 패했다 She lost the game though she fought well.

**역전**(逆轉) (a) reversal; 《구어》 a turnabout; 〖기상〗 (an) inversion. ~하다 reverse (itself); go into reverse; be reversed; turn about; 〖기상〗 be inverted. ¶ 전황을 ~시키다 roll back the tide of war / …에 대해 형세를 ~시키다 turn the table on 《*a person*》/ 일타(一打) ~의 찬스다 〖야구〗 A hit will turn the tide in the game. / 형세는 우리에게 유리[불리]하게 ~되었다 The situation turned out favorable [unfavorable] for us.
◉ ~승 「a come-from-behind [an upset] victory: ~승하다 win a losing game; win a come-from-behind victory 《over》; come from behind and win; win 《a game》 after defeat seems certain. ~장치 a reversing device [gear]; a reverse. ~층 〖기상〗 an inversion layer. ~패(敗): ~패하다 suffer a reversal; lose 《a game》 after the victory seems certain.

**역전**(歷戰) a long record of active service. ¶ ~의 용사 a veteran; an experienced warrior; a battle-tested veteran.

**역전**(驛前) the station front. ¶ ~ 거리 a station road; a depot street 《미》/ ~파출소 a police box near the station. ◉ ~광장 a station square [plaza].

**역전경주**(驛傳競走) a long-distance relay road race. ¶ 제5회 국제 여자 ~ the fifth international women's long-distance relay road race.

**역점**(力點) ① 《강조》 emphasis; stress. ¶ …에 ~을 두다 lay [put, place] emphasis 《on》; emphasize; attach importance 《to》. ② 〖물리〗 the point of a lever where force is applied.

**역정**(逆情) anger. ¶ ~(이) 나다, ~(을) 내다 get angry.

**역조**(逆潮) weather tide; an adverse current; a counter [head] tide.

**역조**(逆調) an adverse [unfavorable] condition. ¶ 무역 ~ a trade imbalance unfavorable to 《Korea》; an adverse [unfavorable] balance of trade; import excess.

**역종**(役種) the classification of service status.

**역주**(譯註) translation and annotation; translation with notes. ¶ B교수 ~의 「햄릿」 *Hamlet* translated and annoted by Prof. B. ◉ ~서 a copy of translation with notes.

**역주하다**(力走—) run as hard [fast] as *one* can; make a spurt. ¶ 그녀는 골인

지점에서 힘껏 역주했다 She made a tremendous spurt at the finish.
**역진**(力盡) exhaustion (of strength). ～하다 use up *one's* strength; *one's* strength is exhausted.
**역질**(疫疾) 〖의학〗 smallpox.
**역청**(瀝青) 〖광물〗 (mineral) pitch; bitumen; asphalt. ¶ ～질의 bituminous. ◉ ～암 pitchstone. ～탄 bituminous coal.
**역추진로켓**(逆推進—) a retrorocket. ¶ ～에 점화하다 retrofire / ～에 점화하여 속도를 늦추다 ignite a retrorocket to decelerate / ～엔진 a retro-engine.
**역코스**(逆—) the reverse course. ¶ ～를 취하다 take the reverse course; go in the opposite direction.
**역투**(力鬪) a mighty struggle; a hard fight. ～하다 fight ｢hard 〔with might and main〕.
**역투하다**(力投—) 〖야구〗 pitch hard; pitch 〔hurl〕 with might and main.
**역풍**(逆風) an adverse 〔a head, an unfavorable〕 wind. ¶ ～을 거스르고 나아가다 go in the teeth of the wind; sail against the unfavorable wind / 바람은 ～이었다 The wind was unfavorable 〔against us〕.
**역하다**(逆—) (be) repulsive; repellent; disgusting; offensive; rank. ¶ 역한 냄새 a repulsive smell / 그의 말이 역했다 I was repelled by his remarks.
**역학**(力學) 〖물리〗 dynamics; mechanics. ¶ ～적(으로) dynamic(ally).
**역학**(易學) the science of divination; fortune-telling lore.
**역학**(疫學) epidemiology. ¶ ～의 epidemiological. ◉ ～조사 the search into the causes, distribution of diseases and other factors relating to health: 전염병을 ～조사하다 search ｢for 〔after〕 the causes, distribution of an epidemic disease 《prevaling throughout the region》.
**역할**(役割) a role; a part; 《임무》 a duty; function(s). ¶ ～을 정하다 allot 〔assign〕 a part 〔role〕 《to *a person*》 / ～을 다하다 discharge 〔fulfill〕 *one's* duties / 중대한 ～을 하다 play an important part 〔role〕 / 결정적인 ～을 하다 play a decisive role / 이것은 침대 ～을 한다 This serves as 〔for〕 a bed. / 그는 자기의 ～을 훌륭히 해냈다 He performed his part most effectively. / 쌍방을 조정하는 것이 내 ～이다 My function is to mediate between the two parties.
**역해**(譯解) translation with commentary notes; [형용사적] translated and annotated; 《암호의》 decoding. ～하다 translate with commentary notes; decode.
**역행**(力行) strenuous efforts 〔endeavor〕; exertion. ～하다 make strenuous efforts; exert 〔apply〕 *oneself* 《to》; endeavor.
**역행**(逆行) reverse movement; retrogression; reversion; countermarch. ～하다 go back; move backward; retrogress; revert; run counter 《to》. ¶ ～적 retrogressive / 원시시대로 ～하다 revert 〔return〕 to the primitive age / 시대에 ～하다 go against the times; go 〔swim〕 against the stream / 민주주의에 ～하다 run counter to democracy. ｢of age.
**역혼**(逆婚) marriage in reverse order
**역효과**(逆效果) a counter result; a contrary 〔opposite, reverse〕 effect. ¶ ～를 내다 〔가져오다〕 have a reverse 〔an adverse〕 effect 《on》; bring about a contrary 〔boomerang〕 effect; produce a contrary result.
**엮다** ① 《얽어 만들다》 plait; weave. ¶ 자리를 ～ plait a straw mat / 대로 발을 ～ weave a blind out of bamboo. ② 《꾸미다》 weave; 《집필하다》 write; 《편집하다》 compile; edit. ¶ 엮은이 《저자》 a writer; 《편자》 a compiler / 이야기를 ～ weave a story / 역사를〔책을〕 ～ write 〔compile〕 a history 〔a book〕.
**엮음** ① 《엮는 일》 weaving; 《엮은 물건》 a piece of weaving; a woven thing. ② 《편찬》 compiling (일); a compilation (책); [형용사적] compiled by.
**연**(年) a year. ⇨ 년(年). ¶ 연수입 an annual 〔a yearly〕 income / 연 1회 once a year / 연 1할의 이자 10 percent interest per annum / 연평균 yearly mean 〔average〕 / 연 2회 상여금을 〔보너스를〕 받다 receive biannual bonuses.
**연**(延) 《총계》 the total; the aggregate. ¶ 입장자는 연 2,000명이었다 The total number of spectators was two thousand. / 이 일은 연 15일이 걸렸다 This job took a total of 15 days. / 그녀의 비행 시간은 연 100시간이다 She has logged a total of 100 hours flying time.
**연**(鉛) 《납》 lead; 〖화학〗 plumbum.
**연**(鳶) a kite. ¶ 연날리기 kite-flying; flying a kite / 연 싸움 kite-fighting / 연을 날리다 fly a kite / 연을 올렸다 내렸다 하다 let out and draw in *one's* kite.

**연**(蓮) 〖식물〗 a lotus. ¶ 연꽃 a lotus flower.

**연-**(連-) 《계속》 continuing; continuous; in succession. ¶ 연사흘 three days running / 연닷새나 for five days running; for five consecutive 〔straight〕 days.

**연가**(戀歌) a love song 〔poem〕.

**연간**(年刊) 《간행물》 ¶ ~의 published once a year; yearly 《magazines》; annual 《bulletins》.

**연간**(年間) [부사적] during the course of a year; for a year; p.a. 《per annum》. ¶ ~외형 거래액 turnovers worth 《500 million won》 a year in doing business / ~ 매상 백만 달러다 Our yearly turnover amounts to a million dollars. / 그 나라의 ~ 무역흑자는 1999년에 200억 달러에 달했다 The country's yearly trade surplus reached $20 billion in 1999.
◉ ~계획 《make》 a program 〔schedule〕 for the year; a one-year plan. ~생산고 a yearly 〔an annual〕 output. ~생산 능력 annual production capacity. ~소득〔수익〕 an annual income 〔profit〕: 그의 ~ 수익은 2천만 원 정도다 His annual profit amounts to about twenty million won.

**연감**(年鑑) a yearbook; an almanac. ¶ 경제~ an economic yearbook / 통계 ~ a statistical yearbook. 「mon.

**연감**(軟—) 《연시》 a soft 〔ripe〕 persim-

**연갑**(年甲) a person of about *one's* own age; a contemporary. ¶ 그는 내 ~이다 He is about my age.

**연강**(軟鋼) mild steel.

**연거푸**(連—) successively; in succession; consecutively; in a row. ¶ ~ 질문하다 fire questions in rapid succession / ~ 다섯 번 이기다 win five consecutive victories / 맥주를 ~ 석 잔 마시다 drink three glasses of beer one after another 〔in (quick) succession〕 / ~치다 hit again and again; strike repeatedly.

**연건평**(延建坪) total floor space (in *p'yŏng*). ¶ ~ 천평의 10층 건물 a ten-story building having the total floor space of 1,000 *p'yŏng*.

**연결**(連結) connection; coupling; linking. ~하다 connect; join; couple; link. ¶ 15량을 ~한 열차 a 15-car train / 객차를 ~하다 couple cars / 식당차를 ~하다 couple 〔attach〕 a dining car 《to a train》/ A와 B를 ~해서 생각하다 consider A in 「relation to 〔connection with〕 B / 김씨, (수화기를) 잠시 들고 계세요. 남씨에게 ~해 드리겠습니다 《전화에서》 Please hold the line, Mr. Kim. I'll put you through to Mr. Nam. ◉ ~결산 consolidated accounts. ~기(器) 《차량의》 a coupler. ~동사 〖문법〗 a linking verb. ~장치 a coupling device.

**연계**(連繫) connection; contact; liaison; touch. ¶ ~가 있다 be (closely) connected 《with》; be linked 《with》/ 경찰은 이 두 사건을 ~하는 단서를 발견했다 The police found a clue linking these two incidents together.

**연고**(軟膏) (an) ointment; salve. ¶ 페니실린 ~ a penicillin ointment / 생채기에 ~를 바르다 apply ointment to a scratch.

**연고**(緣故) 《사유》 a reason; a cause; 《관계》 relation; (a) connection; a tie-in; a pull 《구어》. ¶ ~를 통해 through *one's* friends 〔relatives〕 / 우리 아버지는 그 회사에 많은 ~가 있다 My father has plenty of pull in that company. / 나는 그 회사와 아무런 ~가 없다 I have no connection with that firm. / 너는 ~를 찾아 취직하는 것이 좋겠다 You'd better get a job through your connections.
◉ ~권 preemptive rights: ~권을 인정하다 give 《*a person*》 preemptive rights. ~자 a relative; a relation. ~채용 hiring 《*a person*》 through personal connections: ~ 채용으로 입사하다 get a post in a company through *one's* personal connections.

**연고로**(然故—) for that reason; because of that; therefore.

**연골**(軟骨) 〖해부〗 cartilage; gristle (식용의); 《사람》 a young 〔an immature〕 person. ¶ 갑상 ~ the thyroid cartilage / ~화하다 chondrify.
◉ ~막 a perichondrium. ~세포 a cartilage cell; a chondrocyte. ~조직 cartilaginous tissue. ~한(漢) a weak character; a spineless fellow.

**연공**(年功) 《근속》 long service; 《경험》 years' 〔long〕 experience. ¶ ~으로 through *one's* long experience 〔service〕 / ~을 쌓다 serve long; have long experience 《in》/ 그 회사에서는 공로보다 ~서열로 승진된다 In the company they are promoted by seniority, not by merit. / 이 회사에서는 지위나 급여가 ~에 의해 정해진다 An employee's rank and salary in this company are based on length of service.

◉ ～가봉(加俸) a long-service allowance; a good service pension; an additional salary for long service; 〖미군〗 a longevity pay. ～규정 seniority provisions. ～서열 임금 the seniority wage system. ～(서열)제도 the seniority system 〔rule〕.

**연공**(年貢) 《pay》 a yearly 〔an annual〕 tribute 《to》. ¶ ～을 징수하다〔바치다〕 collect 〔pay〕 an annual tribute.

**연관**(鉛管) a lead pipe 〔tube〕. ◉ ～공 a plumber. ～공사 plumbing.

**연관**(聯關) = 관련(關聯).

**연광**(鉛鑛) 《광산》 a lead mine; lead deposits; 《광석》 a lead ore.

**연교차**(年較差) 〖기상〗 the annual range.

**연구**(硏究) study; research(es); investigation; inquiry. ～하다 study; make a study 《of》; make researches 《in》; 《조사》 investigate; inquire 《into》. ¶ ～결과를 발표하다 publish the results of *one's* research work 《in a bulletin》; 《구두로》 read *one's* paper / ～를 쌓다 make progress in *one's* studies; make a wider and deeper study 《of》 / ～에 종사하다 be engaged in research (work); pursue 〔follow, carry on〕 *one's* studies; conduct researches 《in》 / (…을) 깊이 ～하다 go deep into the study 《of》; make a profound study 《of》 / (…을) 전문으로 ～하다 make a special study 《of》; specialize 《in》 / 김 교수 지도 밑에서 고대 한국사를 ～하다 study the ancient history of Korea under the guidance of Prof. Kim / ～를 끝내다 complete 〔conclude〕 *one's* studies / ～를 지도하다 direct study 〔research〕 / 그것은 재미있는 ～ 재료다 It forms an interesting study. / 그 문제는 신중히 ～하고 있는 중이다 The problem is receiving careful study.

◉ ～가〔자〕 a student 〔scholar〕 《of》; an investigator. ～개발 research and development (생략 R & D): ～ 개발비 research and development expenditures / ～ 개발 자금 research and development funds. ～과제 a research task. ～교수 a research professor. ～논문 a research paper 《on》; a study 《on》; a treatise (학술 논문); a dissertation (학위 논문); a monograph (단일 소논문). ～단지 a research complex: 대덕(大德) ～ 단지 the Taedŏk Science Town. ～단체 a research body 〔organization〕. ～발표회 a meeting for reading research papers. ～방법 research methods; a method of study 〔research〕. ～보고 a report of research; a research paper (보고서). ～보조금 a research grant. ～비 research expenses 〔funds〕. ～생 a research student. ～소 an 〔a research〕 institute; a (research) laboratory: 어학 ～소 the Language Research Institute / 유전공학 ～소 the Research Institute for Molecular Biology and Genetics. ～수당 the research allowances. ～시설 a research installation. ～실 a study; an office (교수 개인의); a laboratory (화학 등의); a lab 《구어》. ～심 the spirit of inquiry; the love of study; an inquiring mind: ～심이 왕성하다 be highly studious 《about》; show fiery zeal in *one's* studies. ～영역 an area of study 〔investigation〕; a research area. ～원 a research worker; a researcher. ～자료 materials 〔data〕 for *one's* research; research materials. ～제목 a subject for study 〔inquiry〕; a laboratory subject. ～활동 research activities. ～회 a society for the study of 《English literature》.

**연구**(軟球) a softball; a rubber ball.

**연구개**(軟口蓋) 〖해부〗 the soft palate; the velum (*pl.* -la). ¶ ～의 velar.

◉ ～음 〖음성학〗 a velar (sound).

**연극**(演劇) ① 《예술》 a play; a drama; 《무대의》 a theatrical 〔dramatic〕 performance; theatricals. ¶ ～상의 dramatic(al); theatrical / ～에 미친 stage=struck〔-mad〕 / ～을 구경가다 go to (see) plays; go to the theater / ～을 상연하다 put 〔stage〕 on a play; give 〔present〕 a play; run a play / (대학에서) ～을 전공하다 major in theater 〔drama〕 / ～조로 말하다 talk theatrically / ～을 하다 perform a play; give 〔present, put on〕 a play / ～으로 꾸미다 dramatize 《an event》; make a play of 《*something*》; form 《a novel》 into a drama / 소설을 ～으로 꾸미다 dramatize a novel / 그 ～은 성공했다 The play has been successful 〔become a big hit〕.

② 《꾸며하는 행위》 play-acting; a fake; 《구어》 a put-up job. ¶ ～을 하다 put on an act; play a trick; put up a false show / 그녀는 진짜 우는 것이 아니야, ～이야 She's not really crying. She's only acting.

◉ ～계 the theatrical world; the theatrical circles. ～광 a crazy for playgoing. ~부 a drama club; a dramatic society. ~인 a man of the theater. ~비평가 a drama critic. ~애호가 a playgoer; a theatergoer. ~학 dramatics. ~학교 a drama school.

**연근**(蓮根) a lotus root.

**연금**(年金) an annuity; a pension. ¶ 국민 ~ the National Pension / ~으로 생활하다 live on *one's* pension / ~을 타다 receive a pension; draw *one's* pension / ~을 받게 되다 become entitled to a pension / ~혜택을 받다 benefit from the pension system 《after retirement》/ ~을 주어 퇴직시키다 pension 《*a person*》 off / ~을 받고 퇴직하다 retire on a pension.
◉ ~수령자 a pensioner; an annuitant. ~제도 the pension system. ~증서 an annuity bond. ~지급금 benefit(s). 양로~ an old-age pension. 종신 ~ a life annuity.

**연금**(軟禁) informal confinement; house arrest. ~하다 confine 《*a person*》 in 《a room》; keep 《*a person*》 in *his* own custody; place 〔put〕 《*a person*》 under house arrest. ¶ ~ 상태에 놓이다 be placed under the state of house arrest / 자택에 ~되어 있다 be confined in *one's* own house; be (placed) under house arrest.

**연금술**(鍊金術) alchemy. ◉ ~사 an alchemist.

**연급**(年給) an annual salary. ⇨ 연봉(年俸).

**연기**(年期) a term; a fixed period (of years).

**연기**(延期) (a) postponement; deferment; adjournment. ~하다 postpone; put off; defer 《payment, *etc.*》; adjourn 《a meeting》; suspend 《judgment》. ¶ 처형의 ~ a stay of execution / ~되다 be postponed 〔put off, deferred〕 / 무기 ~되다 be postponed indefinitely / 기한을 ~하다 extend 〔prolong〕 the term / 일주일간의 ~를 요청하다 ask for a postponement of a week / 출발을 다음 주로 ~하다 put off *one's* departure until next week / 그 회의는 일주일간 ~되었다 The meeting was adjourned for a week. / 그 날에 비가 올 경우는 운동회를 ~한다 In case it rains on that day, the athletic meeting will be put off.

**연기**(連記) writing down together; 《투표의》 plural entry. ~하다 write down. ¶ (투표에서) 2명 ~하다 write 〔put〕 down two names on a ballot.
◉ ~제 the plural ballot system. ~투표 cumulative voting; a vote with plural entry: 무기명 ~ 투표 a secret vote with plural entry.

**연기**(煙氣) smoke. ¶ ~(가) 나는 smoking; smoky / 담배 ~ cigarette smoke / 한 줄기의 ~ a wisp of smoke / 자욱한 ~ clouds of smoke / ~처럼 사라지다 vanish into thin air; go up in smoke / ~에 숨이 막히다 be choked 〔stifled〕 by smoke / ~를 뿜다 emit smoke; give off 〔out〕 smoke / 굴뚝에서 ~가 난다 Smoke is rising from the chimney. / 방 안에 ~가 자욱하다 The air in the room is thick with smoke. / 아니 땐 굴뚝에 ~날까 《속담》 There is no smoke without fire. *or* Out of nothing, nothing comes.

**연기**(演技) performance; acting. ~하다 act 《well》; perform 《skillfully》. ¶ ~파 여배우 an actress who relies on her acting skills / ~를 지시하다 direct the action 《of an actress》/ 과장되게 ~하다 overact; overplay 《a part》; ham up 《구어》/ 훌륭한 ~를 보이다 show no mean dramatic power; put in splendid acting; perform *one's* part with brilliance / 그는 ~를 잘〔못〕한다 He is a good 〔poor〕 actor.
◉ ~력 acting ability. ~자 a performer.

**연내**(年內) ¶ ~에 before the end of the 〔this〕 year; within the 〔this〕 year; before the year is out / 신축 교사는 ~에 완공될 예정이다 The new schoolhouse is to be completed before the end of the year.

**연년**(年年) every year; year after 〔to, by〕 year; yearly; annually.

**연년**(連年) successive years; 《for》 a series of years. ◉ ~생(生) sibling children born within a year of each other: 그들 자매는 ~생이다 They are sisters born in two successive 〔consecutive〕 years.

**연년익수**(延年益壽) prolonging life. ~하다 prolong life; live long.

**연놈** 《욕》 the man and woman; the husband and wife; a chap and a bitch 《구어》.

**연단**(演壇) a platform; a rostrum (*pl.* ~s, -ra); a pulpit (설교단). ¶ ~에 서다〔오르다〕 stand on 〔step onto〕 the platform; take the rostrum 〔platform〕 / ~에 뛰어 오르다 jump up to the rostrum / ~에서 내리다 leave the platform.

**연달**(練達·鍊達) skill; dexterity. ~하다

be「skilled〔experienced, versed〕《in》.

**연달다**(連—) continue; keep on; add a continuation〔an installment〕to; keep《*a thing*》going; cap. ¶ 이야기를 ～ cap a story《with another》/ 불행한 일이 ～ have a run of ill luck; misfortune comes one after another / 뒤에 사람이 연달리다 be followed by people in a long queue.

**연달아**(連—) continuously; without a break; one after another; successively; consecutively; in sequence; on end; in a row; keep on《*do*ing》(계속…하다). ¶ 두 시간 ～ for two hours running〔in succession, at a stretch〕/ 그날부터 ～ from that day on / ～ 이야기하다 talk continuously; keep on talking; talk on and on / 세 번 ～ 지다 be beaten three times running〔in succession〕/ 그 챔피언은 세 번 ～ 이겼다 The champion won three successive games.

**연대**(年代)《시대》an age; a period; an era; an epoch;《시기》the date《of a battle》. ¶ ～순의 chronological / ～순(으로) (in) chronological order / 1980～(에) (in) the 1980's / ～를 측정하다 date《the fossils》/ ～를 사정(査定)〔정〕하다 assess〔establish〕the date《of》/ 이들 화석의 ～는 에오세로 거슬러 올라간다 These fossils date back〔go back chronologically〕to the Eocene. ◉ ～사, ～기 a chronicle; annals. ～표 a chronological table〔chart〕. ～학 chronology; (the study of) scientific dating: ～학자 a chronologist.

**연대**(連帶) solidarity. ～하다 assume jointly; be jointly and severally with …. ¶ 사회～ social solidarity / ～하여 jointly (and severally) / ～로 돈을 빌리다 borrow money under joint signature〔on joint and several responsibility〕; contract a joint debt / ～로 책임을 지다 be jointly and severally responsible《to *a person* for *a thing*》/ 그들은 ～로 손해 배상의 책임을 져야 한다 They are jointly and severally liable to make compensation for the damage. ◉ ～감 a sense of solidarity. ～채무 joint obligation〔debt〕: ～ 채무자 joint debtors / ～채무 증서 a joint bond. ～책임 joint liability; collective responsibility;〖법〗joint and several liability《for》: ～책임으로 on joint responsibility / ～책임을 지다 be jointly and severally responsible《to *a person* for *a thing*》.

**연대**(聯隊)〖군사〗a regiment. ¶ ～의 regimental / 보병～ an infantry regiment. ◉ ～기 the regimental colors〔standard〕. ～병력 a regimental force〔strength〕. ～본부 the regimental headquarters. ～장 a regimental commander; the commanding officer of a regiment.

**연대보증**(連帶保證) joint and several liability on guarantee. ◉ ～인〖법〗a surety jointly and severally liable《for》: ～인이 되다 stand〔go〕joint and several surety《for the loan of ten million won which A receives from B》; hold joint and several liability《for the debt of ten million won that A owes to B》.

**연도**(年度) a year; a period; a term. ¶ ～별의《a financial report》by year / 사업 ～ a business year / 회계 ～가 바뀔 때에 at the change of the fiscal year / 1999 회계 ～ the 1999 fiscal year; fiscal 1999 / 1999년도 예산 the budget for fiscal 1999 / 1999년도 졸업생 a graduate of the year 1999 / 회계 ～초〔말〕에 at the beginning〔end〕of the fiscal year / 잔고 500만원은 내년도로 이월된다 The balance of ₩5,000,000 will be carried over to the next fiscal year. / 그는 1998년도 A대학의 졸업생이다 He is a graduate of A university in the class of 1998. ◉ ～보고 an annual report.

**연도**(沿道) area along the way〔en route〕; the wayside; the roadside. ¶ ～의〔에〕along the road〔route〕; by〔on〕the roadside / ～는 구경꾼으로 붐볐다 Either side of the street was crowded with spectators.

**연독**(鉛毒) lead poisoning. ¶ ～에 걸리다 suffer from lead poisoning.

**연동**(聯動·連動) gear(ing); linkage. ～하다 be connected〔linked, coupled〕《with》. ◉ ～기 a clutch. ～장치 an interlocker; an interlocking device; a gear《of a machine》. ～전환장치 a gearshift.

**연동**(蠕動) writhing; vermiculation; a peristalsis (*pl.* -ses). ～하다 writhe; move in a wormlike manner;《장이》move in a peristaltic motion.

**연두**(年頭) the beginning〔start〕of the year. ◉ ～교서 the President's annual State of the Union address〔message〕to Congress (미국의); the State of the National Message (한국의). ～사 the New Year's address〔message〕.

**연두**(軟豆) yellowish 〔light〕 green.

◉ ～색, 연둣빛 = 연두(軟豆).

**연락**(連絡·聯絡) ① 《관계》 (a) connection; 《접촉》 (a) contact; liaison; 《연결》 junction; 《우호관계》 affiliation; 『군사』 《본부 등과의》 communication. ～하다 connect; contact; be connected 《with》; make contact with; communicate 《*a thing*》 to 《*a person*》; notify 〔inform〕 《*a person* of *a thing*》; let 《*a person*》 know. ¶ 긴밀한 ～ a close contact / 경찰과 ～하다 contact the police; make contact with the police.

연락이: …와 ～이 있다 have connection with…; be connected 〔linked〕 with…; be in contact 〔touch〕 with … / ～이 끊기다 lose contact 《with》.

연락을: ～을 취하다 get in touch 《with》; effect liaison 《with》 / …와 ～을 취하여 행동하다 act in concert 〔conjunction〕 with… / ～을 강화하다 strengthen the contact 《with the police》 / ～을 유지하다 keep in contact 〔touch〕 《with》; maintain contact 《with》.

¶ 그 사건에 관해서는 끊임없이 경찰과 ～을 취하고 있었다 We were in constant contact with the police about the case. / 기지와의 ～이 끊어졌다 We've been cut off from the base. *or* We have lost contact with the base. / 그녀와 ～이 취해졌느냐 Did you get in touch with her? / 가급적 빨리 내게 ～을 주게 Let me know it as soon as you can. / 곧 ～ 드리겠습니다 I'll be in touch with you in a short time. / 그에게서 아직 아무런 ～도 없다 There is still no contact from him. / 자세히 알고 싶으시면 2층에 있는 연회 예약 사무실로 ～하십시오 For further information, please contact our catering office on the second floor.

② 《통신》 communication; correspondence. ～하다 communicate 《*a matter*》 to; inform 《*a person*》 of 〔that…〕; notify 《*a person* that…》; let 《*a person*》 know. ¶ 전화로 ～하다 contact 《*a person*》 by phone; speak to 《*a person*》 over the telephone / 편지로 ～하다 write 《to》 / 무전으로 ～을 유지하다 maintain radio contact 《with an astronaut》 / …로부터 ～을 받다 receive a communication from… / ～을 끊다 cut off 〔sever〕 communications / …와 ～중이다 be in communication with … / 외부와 ～이 끊겨 있다 be held incommunicado / …와 ～을 취하다 get into communication with… / …와 긴밀한 ～을 유지하고 있다 be in close communication with… / 유람선은 태평양 한가운데서 ～이 두절됐다 The cruiser 「lost 〔went out of〕 communication in the midst of the Pacific Ocean. / 그 배는 떠난 지 3일 만에 ～을 끊었다 The ship ceased communication three days after its departure.

③ 《교통편의 접속》 connection; joining. ～하다 connect with; join; meet. ¶ …에서 본선과 ～되다 join the main line at… / 그 섬은 본토와 기선 ～이 있다 The island is connected by a steamer service with the mainland. / 이 열차는 배와 ～이 됩니까 Does this train connect with the boat?

◉ ～기 a liaison aircraft. ～기관 a liaison organ. ～선 a connecting line. ～장교〔사무소〕 a liaison officer 〔office〕. ～처 a 〔*one's*〕 contact address. ～회의 liaison conference.

**연락선**(連絡船) a ferryboat; a ferry steamer. ¶ 부산·시모노세키 간 ～ a cross-channel liner between Busan and Shimonoseki.

**연래**(年來) ① 《오래된》 for (some) years (past); over the years; over a long period of years; long-standing. ¶ ～의 long-cherished 《hopes》; long-held 《beliefs》 / ～의 습관 a custom of long standing / ～의 현안 a long-pending problem / 우리는 20년래의 친구이다 We have been friends for twenty years. ② 《…년 이래의》 for …years now. ¶ 40년래의 풍작 the richest harvest (that we have had) in the past forty years / 어제 10년래에 큰 눈이 왔다 Yesterday we had the heaviest snowfall in ten years.

**연령**(年齡) age; years. ⇨ 나이. ¶ ～의 차 disparity 〔discrepancy〕 of age / ～에 비하여 for *one's* age / ～순으로 in (descending) order of age / ～에 상관없이 irrespective of age.

◉ ～제한 the age limit. ～층 an age group 〔bracket〕: 그와 같은 ～층의 사람들 people in his age bracket. 생활～ 『심리』 chronological age (생략 CA).

**연례**(年例) yearly (custom). ¶ ～의 yearly; annual. ◉ ～보고 an annual report. ～(총)회 an annual (general) meeting. ～행사 an annual event.

**연로**(年老) old age. ～하다 (be) aged; old; elderly. ¶ ～하여 허리가 굽다 be bent with the weight of years / ～한

부모를 모시고 있다 have *one's* old parents to support.

**연료**(燃料) fuel. ¶ 고〔기, 액〕체 ~ solid 〔gaseous, liquid〕 fuel / 핵~ nuclear fuel / ~가 떨어지다 run out of fuel / ~를 보급하다 refuel 《a plane》 / ~가 떨어져 가고 있다 We are running short of petrol. *or* We are low on gas. / 비행기는 ~가 떨어져 불시착했다 The airplane was out of fuel and made an emergency landing.
◉ ~보급 supply of fuel; refueling. ~보급소 a fueling station. ~봉 《원자로의》 a (nuclear) fuel rod: 사용이 끝난 ~봉 a spent 〔depleted〕 fuel rod. ~부족 lack 〔dearth〕 of fuel. ~비 cost of fuel; fuel expenses: ~비가 적게 먹히는 차 an economical car / ~ 효율이 좋은 엔진 a fuel-efficient engine / ~비가 많이 드는 대형차 a gas-guzzler 《미》 / 내 차는 ~비가 아주 적게 든다 My car is very economical on gas. ~유〔가스, 탄〕 fuel oil 〔gas, coal〕. ~전지 a fuel cell. ~탱크 a fuel tank. ~펌프 fuel pump. ~효율 fuel efficiency. ~화석 fossil fuel.

**연루**(連累) involvement; implication; complicity. ~하다 be involved in 《the crime》; be implicated in 《an affair》. ¶ 뇌물 사건에 ~되다 be implicated 〔involved〕 in the bribery case.
◉ ~자 an accomplice; a confederate 《in》; a person involved 〔concerned〕. 범죄~ complicity with another in a crime.

**연륜**(年輪) ① 《나무의》 an annual ring 〔layer〕 《of a tree》; a growth ring. ¶ 나무의 ~을 세다 count the (growth) rings of a tree. ② 《쌓인 경험·숙련도 따위》 ¶ 두 사람간 ~의 차는 현저하다 There is a marked difference between them in experience and intelligence. / ~이 말을 한다 Experience will tell. *or* That comes from the wisdom of age.

**연리**(年利) 〖경제〗 (an) annual interest (rate). ¶ ~ 6푼으로 은행에서 돈을 빌리다 get a loan from the bank of an annual interest rate of six percent.

**연립**(聯立) (an) alliance; (a) coalition; (a) union. ~하다 be allied; be united 〔combined〕; unite.
◉ ~내각 a coalition cabinet. ~방정식 〖수학〗 simultaneous equations. ~정부〔정권〕 a coalition government; a fusion administration. ~주택 a tenement house; row houses.

**연마**(硏磨) 《갈고 닦음》 grinding; abrasion; polishing. ~하다 grind; polish; whet. ◉ ~기 a grinder; a grinding machine; an abrasive machine; a polisher (렌즈 따위의). ~제 an abradant; an abrasive. ~지 sandpaper; emery paper.

**연마**(練磨) 《기술·정신 등의》 drilling; training; practice; improvement; cultivation; 《학문의》 study; research. ~하다 drill; train; practice; improve; cultivate; 《학문 등의》 make a study of; research. ¶ 다년간의 ~에 의해 by virtue of many years' training / 기술을 ~하다 practice an art; improve *one's* skill / 정신을 ~하다 cultivate 〔train〕 *one's* mind.

**연막**(煙幕) a smoke screen. ¶ ~을 치다 lay (down) a smoke screen. ◉ ~전술 smoke-screen tactics. ~탄 a smoke shell.

**연만**(年滿) being full of years; well advanced in years; being aged. ~하다 be full of years; be old (enough).

**연말**(年末) the year-end; the end 〔close〕 of the year. ¶ ~에 at the end of the year / ~까지 by year's end. ◉ ~대매출 a year-end (bargain) sale: 저 백화점에서는 ~대매출을 하고 있다 That department store is having a year-end (bargain) sale. ~상여금 a year-end bonus. ~정산 《세금의》 the year-end tax adjustment.

**연맥**(燕麥) 〖식물〗 oats.

**연맹**(聯盟) a league; a union; a federation; a confederation; alliance. ¶ …와 ~하여 in league with… / ~에 가입하다〔에서 탈퇴하다〕 join 〔resign from〕 a league / ~을 조직하다 form a league. ◉ ~국 allied countries. ~이사회 the League Council.

**연면**(連綿) consecutiveness; continuity; being uninterrupted 〔unbroken〕. ~하다 (be) continuous; successive; consecutive; unbroken; run continuous 〔successive〕. ¶ ~히 consecutively; continuously.

**연명**(延命) just managing to live; barely maintaining *one's* livelihood; survival. ~하다 barely manage to live; eke out an existence; survive. ¶ ~책을 강구하다 make plans for prolonging *one's* life / 간신히 ~하다 keep body and soul together; eke out a precarious living 〔a scant livelihood〕 / 자네 경우는 운동이 유일한 ~책이다 In your case exercise is the only way of prolonging your life.

**연명**(連名) a joint signature. ～하다 sign jointly. ¶ ～으로 선물을 하다 give 《*a person*》 a present jointly / ～으로 초대장을〔진정서를〕 내다 send an invitation 〔a petition〕 under joint signature. ◉ ～상소 a joint petition to the ruler. ～진정서 a joint petition. ～투표 a joint ballot.

**연모** 《도구와 재료》 tools and materials; a tool; an instrument. ¶ 원시인도 이미 ～를 사용하고 있었다 The earliest-man was already using tools.

**연모**(軟毛) soft 〔downy〕 hairs; down.

**연모**(戀慕) love and yearning; sentimental attachment. ～하다 love (and yearn after); become attached to. ¶ ～를 받다 be loved; be yearned for.

**연목**(軟木) softwood; soft timber.

**연목**(椽木) 〖건축〗 a rafter. ⇨ 서까래.

**연목구어**(緣木求魚) seeking「a fish from a tree 〔the impossible〕. ～하다 try to get a fish from a tree; attempt 〔try to do〕 the impossible.

**연못**(蓮―) a lotus pond; a pond.

**연무**(烟霧·煙霧) smoke and fog; mist and fog; smog (도시의); haze.

**연무**(演武) practice 〔(an) exercise〕 of the martial arts. ～하다 practice the martial arts 〔fencing, taekwondo〕. ◉ ～장 a practice 〔drill〕 hall.

**연무**(鍊武) the martial arts discipline 〔drill, train〕. ～하다 discipline 〔drill, train〕 the martial arts.

**연문**(戀文) a love letter.

**연문학**(軟文學) tender 〔sweet〕 pieces 〔compositions〕 (as poems or the like); light 〔amatory, erotic〕 literature. 「tailcoat; an evening coat.

**연미복**(燕尾服) a swallow-tailed coat; a

**연민**(憐憫) compassion; pity; mercy; commiseration. ¶ ～의 정을 느끼다 feel pity 《for》; be touched with compassion 《for》; be seized with a great pity 《for》 / ～의 정을 일으키게 하다 excite compassion 〔pity〕 《for》.

**연발**(延發) delayed departure. ～하다 start late.

**연발**(連發) ～하다 fire in rapid succession; fire in volley. ¶ ～식의 quick-firing 《guns》; automatic (자동식의) / 소총의 ～ a rapid rifle fire / 질문을 ～하다 fire questions at 《*a person*》 (in succession); assail 《*a person*》 with one question after another; ask one question right after another. ◉ ～총 a magazine rifle: 6～총 a six-shooter; a six-shot〔-chambered〕 revolver.

**연방** ⇨ 연해(連―). ¶ 자동차가 ～ 지나간다 There is a constant stream of motor vehicles.

**연방**(聯邦) a confederation; a federation; a union (of nations); a federal union.

> 용법 **confederation** 독립된 복수의 주(states)가 조약에 따라 하나의 정부를 만들고, 각각의 대표자들로 하여금 공통의 외부 문제에 즉응해서 공동 행동을 취하게 하는 동맹국. **federation** 몇 개의 주(states, provinces), 식민지(colonies)가 연합하여 중앙〔연방〕 정부를 만들어 외교·국방을 맡기고, 내정자치에 관하여는 각각의 주(states)나 식민지가 담당하는 연방국. **union** 연합국가의 뜻.

¶ ～의 federal; confederal / 영 ～ the British Commonwealth of Nations / 러시아 ～ the Russian Federation / 캐나다 ～ the Dominion of Canada. ◉ ～ 공개시장 위원회 《미》 the Federal Open Market Committee (생략 FOMC). ～ 비상사태 관리국 《미》 the Federal Emergency Management Agency (생략 FEMA). ～수사국 《미》 the Federal Bureau of Investigation (생략 FBI). ～이민국 《미》 the Immigration and Naturalization Service (생략 INS). ～재판소 a federal court: ～ 최고재판소 the Supreme Court (of the United States). ～정부 the Federal Government (미국의). ～제, ～제도 a federal system; federalism. ～준비은행 the Federal Reserve Bank. ～회의 a federal council.

**연배**(年輩) 《나이》 similar age(s); 《사람》 a person nearly the same age as another; a contemporary; a coeval. ¶ 동～의 of 〔about〕 the same age / 그들은 모두 같은 ～이다 They are all (of) an age. (★ of는 속성(屬性)을 나타냄. of가 없을 경우에는, 「기술(記述)의 대격(對格)」이라 칭하며, 구어체에 많이 사용됨).

**연백**(鉛白) 〖화학〗 white lead; lead foil.

**연번호**(連番號) a serial number.

**연변**(年邊) annual interest. ⇨ 연리.

**연변**(沿邊) the area along 《a river, a railline, a border》. ¶ 철도 ～의 집들 houses on 〔along〕 a railroad.

**연병**(練兵) a military drill. ～하다 drill; have a drill. ◉ ～장 a drill 〔parade〕 ground 〔field〕.

**연보**(年報) an annual report 〔bulletin〕.

**연보**(年譜) a chronological record 《of

*a person's* career, of the development of an event》. ¶ 셰익스피어 희곡의 ～ a chronological list of Shakespeare's plays.

**연보**(捐補) contributions to help others; church offerings. ～하다 make contributions. ◉ ～금, 연봇돈 money contributed 〔offered〕. ～함 an offertory box.

**연보라**(軟—) light purple; lilac.

**연봉**(年俸) an annual salary; a yearly stipend. ¶ ～ 10만 달러로 at (a salary of) one hundred thousand dollars a year / 그녀는 ～이 8,000만 원이다 Her salary is eighty million won a year. *or* She draws a salary of eighty million won a year. ◉ ～제 annual 〔yearly〕 pay system 〔structure〕.

**연봉**(連峰) a chain 〔series〕 of mountains; a mountain chain 〔range〕. ◉ 알프스～ the Alps range.

**연부**(年賦) a yearly 〔an annual〕 installment. ¶ ～로 by yearly installments; in annual payments / 5년 ～로 지급하다 pay by 〔in〕 yearly installments over a period of five years. ◉ ～상환 redemption by annual installments.

**연분**(緣分) a preordained tie; a predestined bond; fate; connection; relationship; affinity. ¶ 묘한 ～으로 by curious 〔happy〕 chance / ～을 끊다 cut connections 《with》; break off 《from》; break with / ～을 맺다 form a connection 《with》/ 부부의 ～을 맺다 tie the nuptial 〔marriage〕 knot; get married / ～이 있어 두 사람은 부부가 되었다 Fate made the two, man and wife. / 그들은 천생 ～이다 They are a well-matched couple.

**연분홍**(軟粉紅) light 〔soft〕 pink.

**연불**(延拂) deferred payment. ◉ ～방식 deferred payment basis. ～수출 exporting on a 「easy-payment term 〔deferred-payment basis〕.

**연비**(連比) 〖수학〗 a continued ratio.

**연비**(燃比) (gas) mileage; fuel efficiency. ¶ ～ 시험 a mileage test / 1리터당 24.10km라는 가장 효율적인 ～ the most efficient mileage of 24.10km/*l* / 나의 새 차는 ～가 높다 My new car gives very high mileage. / 당신 차의 ～는 어떻게 됩니까 What kind of gas mileage do you get?

**연비**(燃費) fuel expenses. ⇨ 연료비.

**연비례**(連比例) 〖수학〗 a continued proportion.

**연뿌리**(蓮—) a lotus root.

**연사**(演士) a lecturer; a (public) speaker. ¶ 초청 ～ a guest speaker.

**연사**(撚絲) twisted thread 〔yarn〕; twine. ◉ ～공 a twister; a throwster. 견～ twisted silk yarn; thrown silk.

**연삭**(研削) grinding. ◉ ～기 a grinder; a grinding machine. = 연마기.

**연산**(年産) a yearly 〔an annual〕 output; annual production. ◉ ～능력 annual capacity of production.

**연산**(連山) a chain 〔range〕 of mountains; mountain ranges. ¶ 남북으로 뻗친 ～ a range of mountains running north and south.

**연산**(演算) 〖수학〗 operation. ◉ ～제어장치 〖컴퓨터〗 an arithmetic and control unit.

**연상**(年上) seniority in age. ¶ ～의 older; elder; senior / ～의 아내 a wife older than her husband / …보다 5살 ～이다 be five years older than 《*a person*》; be 《*a person's*》 senior by five years.

**연상**(聯想) association (of ideas). ～하다 associate (one thing with another); be reminded of. ¶ …을 ～시키다 suggest 《*something*》 to 《*a person's*》 mind; remind 《*a person*》 of...; bring up the image of / 그를 보면 죽은 아들이 ～된다 He reminds me of my dead son. / 우리는 진화론하면 자연스레 다윈의 이름이 ～된다 We naturally associate the name of Darwin with the theory of evolution. ◉ ～개념 an associate. ～심리학 associationism. 근접〔대비, 유사〕～ association by contiguity 〔contrast, similarity〕.

**연서**(連署) a joint signature. ～하다 sign jointly; affix *one's* signature 《to a deed》 jointly 《with》. ¶ 100명 ～의 청원서 a petition signed by 100 persons / 보증인 ～로 under the joint signature of the surety. ◉ ～국 the cosignatory Powers; cosignatories. ～인 a cosignatory; a joint signer; a cosigner.

**연석**(宴席) (*one's* seat in) a banquet hall. ¶ ～을 베풀다 give a dinner party; hold a banquet / ～에 참석하다 attend a banquet.

**연석**(連席) sitting together; attendance; presence. ～하다 attend; be present at; sit at; be in attendance at. ¶ …의 ～하에 with... in attendance at / 회의에 ～하다 attend a meeting; sit as a member at the meeting. ◉ ～자 attendants. ～회의 a joint meeting. 정부여당 ～회의 a government-ruling party joint conference.

**연선**(沿線) the area 〔district, country〕 along the line. ¶ ～의〔에〕 along a railroad line.

**연설**(演說) a (public) speech; an address; 《학술적인》 a lecture; 《식사》 an oration; a spiel 《구어》. ～하다 make 〔deliver〕 a speech; speak (in public); address 《an audience》; 《가두에서》 soapbox.
¶ 준비된 ～ a prepared speech / ～을 시작하다 open a speech / ～을 방해하다 interrupt 《*a person*》 in *his* speech; 《선거에서》 heckle / ～을 부탁받다 be called upon to make a speech / ～을 잘하다〔못하다〕 be a good 〔bad, poor〕 speaker / ～을 중단시키다 cut short the speaker / ～을 속기하다 take down a speech in shorthand / ～에 익숙하다 be accustomed to speaking to an audience / ～ 조로 이야기하다 speak in a declamatory 〔an oratorical〕 tone / 금주에 관해서 ～하다 speak on temperance / 지루하게 ～하다 give a long-winded speech / 대중 앞에서 ～하다 speak at a large gathering 〔audience〕 / 메모를 보고 ～하다 make a speech 「from 〔referring to〕 notes / 텔레비전을 통해 국민에게 ～하다 address the nation over TV / 그는 무슨 제목으로 ～하였는가 What did he speak on?
◉ ～가 an orator; a (public) speaker; 《거리의》 a soapbox orator. ～회 an oratorical 〔a speech〕 meeting: ～회장 a meeting hall.
추도～ a memorial address.

**연성**(延性) 〖물리〗 ductility; malleability. ¶ ～의 ductile; malleable.

**연성**(軟性) soft(ness); mild(ness).
◉ ～세제 a soft detergent. ～하감(下疳) 〖의학〗 soft chancre; chancroid.

**연세**(年歲) age. ⇨ 나이.

**연소**(年少) youth; being minor 〔juvenile〕. ～하다 (be) young; underage; juvenile. ¶ ～한 아이 a young child / ～기예의 full of youthful ardor; young and spirited / ～하기 때문에 on account of *one's* tender age.
◉ ～자 a youth; young people; minors; underage people; juveniles: ～자 입장 금지 《게시》 No admittance to children. *or* Adults only. *or* No minors.

**연소**(燃燒) burning; combustion. ～하다 《it》 burn. ¶ 완전〔불완전〕 ～ complete 〔imperfect〕 combustion / ～성의 combustible; flammable. ◉ ～강 burnt steel. ～기 a 《gas》 burner. ～로〔실〕 a combustion 「furnace 〔chamber〕. ～물 combustibles. ～성 combustibility; inflammability. ～시간 burning time. ～효율 combustion efficiency.

**연속**(連續) continuity; continuance; succession; a series; a sequence. ～하다 continue; be continuous; last; occur in succession; follow one after another. ¶ ～적(인) continual; continuous; consecutive; successive; serial.

> **용법** **continual** 단속적으로 되풀이해서 장기적으로 일어난다는 뜻으로, 때로는 짧은 시간적 간격을 두고 일어나는 것도 말함. **continuous** 시간적·공간적으로 끊기지 않고 이어짐을 말함. **consecutive** 일정한 순서에 따라 연속됨을 말함. **successive** 순서·간격과 관계없이 다만 연속됨을 말함.

¶ 24시간 ～의 round-the-clock / ～해서 in succession; consecutively; one after another; continuously / 불행의～ a series of misfortunes / 연극의 6개월 ～상연 six months' run of a play / 괴상한 사건의 ～ a mysterious and inexplicable chain of events / ～ 3주간 for three weeks running; for three consecutive weeks / 그들은 3회에서～ 두 개의 홈런을 때렸다 They whacked out two consecutive homers 〔two home runs back-to-back〕 in the third inning. / 그의 일생은 찬란한 모험의 ～이었다 His life was a series of most brilliant adventures.
◉ ～강연 a series of lectures. ～만화 a comic strip. ～물 a serial. ～(방송)극 a serial radio 〔TV〕 drama. ～사진 sequence photographs. ～상영 consecutive 〔continuative〕 showing of a film. ～성 continuity. ～소설 a serial story. ～안타 〖야구〗 a swat parade: ～3안타 three consecutive hits. ～체 〖철학·수학〗 a continum (*pl.* -tinue, ～s). ～호머〔홈런〕 〖야구〗 《two》 consecutive homers. 일일〔주간〕 ～극 a daily 〔weekly〕 serial drama.

**연쇄**(連鎖) a chain; links; a series; connection. ¶ ～살인 사건 the consecutive 〔serial〕 murder incidents / ～살인의 피해자 가족들 family members of the victims of the chain-homicide / 어제 고속 버스 4대의 ～ 충돌로 2명이 죽고 50명이 부상했다 Two persons were killed and 50 others injured yesterday in a chain collision of four express buses.

◉ ～극 a combination play; a screen=and-stage play. ～도산 chain reaction bankruptcies. ～반응 (a) chain reaction: ～ 반응을 일으키다 cause 〔trigger, set off, touch off〕 a chain reaction. ～법 〖논리〗 a sorites; 〖수학〗 the chain rule. ～상구균(狀球菌) a streptococcus. ～점 a chain store; a multiple shop 《영》. ～충돌 a chain collision.

**연수**(年收) an annual 〔a yearly〕 income. ¶ 그의 ～는 1,000만 원이다 His income is ten million won a year.

**연수**(年數) (the number of) years. ¶ ～를 지난 old; aged. ◉ ～가산 an additional grant per number of years.

**연수**(延髓) 〖해부〗 the metencephalon; *medulla*(L.); the afterbrain; the hindbrain. ¶ ～의 bulbar.

**연수**(硏修) research study; study and training. ～하다 study; pursue the study 《of》; take 〔get〕 training 《in》. ◉ ～생 a trainee. ～원 a training institute: 사법 ～원 the Judicial Research and Training Institute. ～회 a workshop. 해외～ overseas training.

**연수**(軟水) soft water. ¶ (경수를) ～로 만들다 soften water.

**연수정**(煙水晶) smoky quartz; morion (거무스름한).

**연숙**(鍊熟) dexterity through practice 〔drill, training〕. ～하다 (be) skilled; trained, practiced; be good 《at》.

**연습**(演習) 《익힘》 practice; an exercise; (a) drill; 《군사 연습》 (drill) maneuvers; exercises; field practice; 《대학의》 a seminar. ～하다 practice; carry out exercises; hold 〔carry out〕 maneuvers. ¶ 사격 ～ rifle 〔target〕 practice / 예행 ～ a rehearsal; a preliminary exercise 〔training〕.
◉ ～림 an experimental plantation. ～장 maneuvering ground.

**연습**(練習) practice; training; (a) drill; (an) exercise; a workout; a warming-up (경기 전의); (a) rehearsal (연극의). ～하다 practice; drill; exercise; train; rehearse 《a play》; do *one's* exercise (학과의); tune up 《미》.
¶ 조금 ～하면 with a little training 〔practice〕 / ～을 시작하다 go into training / ～이 부족하다 be half=trained; be 〔get〕 out of practice; lack training 〔practice〕; be not sufficiently trained / 사격을 ～하다 practice shooting 〔marksmanship〕 / 타자를 ～하다 practice typewriting / 피아노를 ～하다 practice (on) the piano; take lessons on the piano / 맹～을 하다 have hard practice 〔training〕 / 학생들에게 영어(의) 발음을 ～시키다 drill pupils in the pronunciation of English / …의 ～이 되어 있다 be well drilled 〔trained, practiced〕 in… / ～하면 향상된다 You will improve by practice.

> **용법** **practice, drill, exercise** 같은 뜻으로도 쓰이지만, practice는 기술을 더욱 갈고 닦기 위해 거의 습관이 될 정도로 반복해서 연습한다는 뜻. drill은 교실에서의 발음 연습이나 군사 훈련처럼 한 집단이 지도자의 지시에 따라 연습을 되풀이함으로써 머리와 몸에 배도록 가르친다는 뜻. exercise는 머리·기술·몸·근육 등을 조직적인 반복 운동 또는 연습을 통해서 훈련한다는 뜻. **train** 사람이나 동물을 어떤 목적이나 직업에 맞도록 훈련하거나 양성한다는 뜻이며, 한편으로는 운동 경기에서 겨룰 수 있게 훈련한다는 뜻도 있음. **rehearse** 공연을 위해 음악이나 연극의 예행 연습을 한다는 뜻.

◉ ～경기〔시합〕 a practice 〔tune-up〕 game; a workout. ～곡 an *étude* (F.). ～기 a training plane. ～량 the amount of practice 《*one* can put in》. ～문제 exercises; a practice problem: ～문제를 하다 do exercises 《in algebra》. ～문제집 an exercise 〔a drill〕 book. ～부족 lack of training. ～비행 a training flight. ～사격 gunnery exercise; target practice. ～생 a trainee; a student. ～선 a school 〔training〕 ship. ～시간 《lack of》 rehearsal time (공연 준비의). ～장(場) 《육상 경기 등의》 a practice 〔training〕 field 〔track〕. ～장(帳) an exercise book; a workbook. ～함〔함대〕 a training ship 〔squadron〕. 영어문법 ～ a drill in English grammar.

**연승**(連乘) 〖수학〗 continual multiplication. ～하다 multiply continually.

**연승**(連勝) victories in a row; straight 〔consecutive, successive〕 victories; a series of victories; victory after victory. ～하다 win time after time; gain 〔win〕 consecutive victories; win every battle 〔victory after victory〕. ¶ 4～하다 win four consecutive victories 《over》; win four games in a row / 연전 ～하다 win every battle 〔game〕 / 가을 리그전에서 B대학이 ～했

다 B University won consecutive victories in autumn's league series. / A팀은 B팀에게 ～을 거두었다 The A team chalked their consecutive victory over the B team. ◉ ～복식《경마의》 the quinella;《영》 the dual forecast.

**연시**(年始)《해의 시작》 the beginning 〔start〕 of the year;《설날》 New Year's Day.

**연시**(軟柿) a soft 〔ripe〕 persimmon.

**연시간**(延時間) the total number of hours; the total man-hours. ¶ ～ 이백, 200 man-hours.

**연식**(軟式) nonrigid 〔soft〕 type.
◉ ～야구《play》 softball 〔rubber-ball〕 baseball. ～정구《play》 softball tennis.

**연실**(鳶—) a kite string. ¶ ～을 감다 draw 〔reel〕 in the string of a kite / ～을 풀다 let out the string of a kite.

**연실**(蓮實) a lotus pip.

**연안**(沿岸) the coast; the shore. ¶ ～의 〔에〕 on 〔along〕 the shore; on 〔along〕 the coast; coastal / ～을 항해하다 sail along the coast / 시애틀은 태평양 ～에 있다 Seattle is on the shore 〔coast〕 of the Pacific.
◉ ～경비대 the coast guard. ～류 a littoral current. ～무역 coastal 〔coastwise〕 trade. ～방비 coast(al) defense. ～선 a coastline. ～어업 coastal 〔inshore〕 fishery. ～지방〔평야〕 a coastal region 〔plain〕: 미국의 대서양 ～ 지방 the Atlantic seaboard of the United States / 지중해 ～ 지방 the Mediterranean littoral. ～항 a coastal port. ～항로 a coastwise 〔coastal〕 route. ～항해 coastal 〔coastwise〕 navigation: ～ 항해선 a coasting vessel; a coaster.

**연알**(碾—) a metal ball for grinding medicine in a druggist's mortar.

**연애**(戀愛) love; amour. ～하다 fall 〔be〕 in love《with a girl》; make love《to》. ¶ 자유～ free love / 순결한 ～ pure love / 정신적(인) ～ platonic love / ～를 걸다 make love《to》/ ～는 신성하다 Love is sacred. / 자넨 ～ 경험이 없지 You've never been in love, have you?
◉ ～결혼 a love marriage 〔match〕: ～결혼을 하다 marry for love / 자넨 ～ 결혼했는가 Did you marry for love? ～대장 a Don Juan; a great lover. ～문학 erotic literature. ～사건 a love affair. ～소설〔시〕 a love story 〔poem〕. ～지상주의 love for love's sake. ～편지 a love letter.

**연액**(年額) an annual sum; a yearly amount; [부사적] yearly; a year; per annum. ¶ ～ 100만 원 one million won per annum / ～ 2억 원에 달하다 amount to 200 million won a year.
◉ ～보장 임금제 the guaranteed annual wage system.

**연야**(連夜) night after 〔by〕 night; every night. ¶ ～의 nightly.

**연약**(軟弱) tenderness 〔mildness〕 and weakness. ～하다 (be) tender; mild; gentle; weak; weakly; feeble;《지반 따위가》 soft. ¶ ～한 지반 the soft ground / ～한 사내 an effeminate man; a sissy《구어》/ ～한 외교 weak-kneed diplomacy / ～한 여자의 손으로 with the weak hands of a woman / ～해지다 weaken; (grow) effeminate / ～한 여자의 몸으로는 어떻게도 할 수 없었다 Frail woman as she was, she was utterly helpless. / 그는 의지가 ～하다 He has a weak will.

**연어**(連語) (a) collocation;《복합어》 a compound word;《구》 a phrase.

**연어**(鰱魚) 〚어류〛 a salmon (*pl.* ～(s)). ¶ 소금에 절인 ～ salted salmon / 훈제 ～ smoked salmon. ◉ ～새끼 a young salmon; a parr. ～통조림 canned salmon.

**연역**(演繹) 〚논리〛 deduction. ～하다 deduce《from》; evolve. ¶ ～적 deductive / ～적으로 deductively / ～적(인) 추리 deductive reasoning 〔inference〕.
◉ ～법 the deductive method 〔logic〕.

**연연**(戀戀) strong attachment 〔affection〕. ～하다 be ardently attached《to》; be very「attached to 〔fond of〕《a girl》; cling to《*one's* post》. ¶ 지위에 ～하다 retain a lingering desire for the position; be reluctant to give up *one's* position / (아직도) ～해 하다 be still attached《to》; have a lingering affection 〔love〕《for》/ 그는 아직도 자기를 떠난 여자에 대해 ～한 정을 품고 있다 He still retains a lingering love for the girl who left him. / 그는 현재의 지위에 ～해 할 사람이 아니다 He is not a man who is reluctant to give up his present position.

**연연하다**(娟娟—) (be) light and beautiful.

**연예**(演藝) a performance;《dramatic, musical》 entertainments; a variety show;《미》 vaudeville. ～하다 perform; entertain; put on entertainment.
◉ ～계 the entertainment world. ～기자 an entertainments reporter. ～란

the entertainments 〔amusements〕 column 〔section〕 (of a newspaper). ～방송 a theatrical broadcast; an amusement (radio) program. ～인 a performer; an entertainer; an artiste: 인기 ～인 a star 〔principal〕 performer 〔artiste〕; a headliner 《미》. ～장 an entertainment hall; a music hall; a variety theater; a vaudeville theater.

**연옥**(軟玉) 〖광물〗 kidney stone.

**연옥**(煉獄) 〖가톨릭〗 Purgatory. ¶ ～의 purgatorial 《sufferings》 / ～의 고통을 겪다 go through purgatory.

**연옥색**(軟玉色) a light bluish green.

**연와**(煉瓦) a brick. ⇨ 벽돌.

**연운**(年運) the fortune of the year.

**연원**(淵源) an origin; a source; a fountainhead. ¶ …의 ～을 더듬다 trace the origin of…; trace 《*a thing*》 to its source.

**연월**(煙月·烟月) ① 《달빛》 misty moonlight. ② 《시절》 peaceful times.

**연월일**(年月日) a date. ¶ ～이 없는 undated / ～을 기입하다 date 《a letter》; affix 〔attach, put〕 a date 《to》 / ～순으로 철하다 file in close chronological order.

**연유**(緣由) 《사유》 a reason; a ground; a cause; 《유래》 origin; derivation; source. ～하다 originate 《in》; be derived 《from》; be caused 《by》; be due to. ¶ 그 관습은 중국에서 ～한 것이다 The custom is of Chinese origin.

**연유**(煉乳) condensed milk.

**연율**(年率) the annual rate; per annum (생략 p.a.).

**연음**(延音) a prolonged 〔held, lengthened〕 sound; a long vowel 〔syllable〕. ◉ ～기호 〖음악〗 a long mark; a length mark.

**연의**(演義) an exposition; a commentary; an adaptation; a popular version. ～하다 expound; adapt. ¶ 삼국지 ～ a popular version of the historical novel "*Samgukji*".

**연이나**(然―) however; be that as it may; but; and yet; still; nevertheless.

**연이율**(年利率) an annual rate of interest.

**연익**(年益) an annual profit. 「署).

**연인**(連印) a joint signature. ⇨ 연서(連

**연인**(戀人) 《남자》 a lover; *one's* man 〔boy〕; 《여자》 a sweetheart; a love; *one's* girl. ¶ 한 쌍의 행복한 ～ a pair of happy lovers / ～이 생기다 《여자에게》 get her man / 그녀는 나의 ～이다 She is my girl.

**연인원**(延人員) the total number of man-days. ¶ ～ 3만 명이 넘는 대공사 a huge construction project requiring over 30,000 man-days.

**연일**(連日) (for) several days in succession; day after day; every day. ¶ ～연야(連夜) day(s) and night(s) / ～ 내리는 비 a long spell of rainy weather / ～ 비가 오다 it rains day in and day out / ～의 병구완으로 그는 완전히 지쳤다 He is done up with the continuous nursing of several days. / 그 극장은 ～ 만원이다 The theater is drawing a full house every day.

**연일수**(延日數) the total number of working days.

**연임**(連任) reappointment; reelection (재선). ～하다 be reappointed 〔reelected〕.

**연잇다**(連―) join (one thing to another); piece together; put together. ¶ 3일간 연이어 for three consecutive 〔successive〕 days / 두 종이를 ～ join two pieces of paper together / 연이어서 continuously; successively; consecutively; in sequence / 닷새 동안이나 연이어서 비가 왔다 It has rained for five days running.

**연잎**(蓮―) a lotus leaf.

**연자매**(硏子―) a millstone worked by horse 〔ox〕; a horse 〔an ox〕 mill. ◉ 연자맷간 a horse 〔an ox〕 mill.

**연작**(連作) 《작물의》 repeated cultivation. ～하다 plant 《a field》 with the same crop over and over.

**연작**(燕雀) swallows and sparrows. ¶ ～이 어찌 홍곡의 뜻을 알까보냐 Only a hero can understand a hero. ◉ ～류 〖조류〗 Passerine.

**연장** a tool; a utensil; an implement; an instrument. ¶ 농사에 쓰는 ～ a farming tool; farm implements / 목수의 ～ a carpenter's tool. ◉ ～궤 a toolbox. ～자루 a toolbag.

**연장**(年長) seniority. ¶ ～의 older; elder; senior / ～이란 이유로 on the score of seniority / 그는 나보다 일곱 살 ～이다 He is seven years older than I. *or* He is my senior by seven years. ◉ ～자 a senior; an elder: 일행 중〔집안〕의 최～자 the oldest (man) in the party 〔a family〕.

**연장**(延長) ① 《길이의》 extension. ～하다 extend 《a railroad line》; lengthen 《a line》; make 《*a thing*》 longer. ¶ 선을 ～하는 코드 an extension cord / 3피

트 ～하다 make ⟪*a thing*⟫ three feet longer; extend ⟪*a thing*⟫ by three feet / 수명을 ～하다 lengthen *one's* span of life / 철도가〔버스 노선이〕다음 도시까지 ～되었다 The railroad 〔bus〕 line was extended to the next town. / 이 도로는 곧 원주시까지 ～된다 This road is soon to be extended 「as far as 〔to〕 the city of Wonju.
② ⟪기간의⟫ extension; prolongation. ～하다 extend ⟪the session⟫; prolong ⟪a meeting⟫; renew ⟪the contract⟫. ¶ 체재를 1주일간 ～하다 prolong *one's* stay a week / 그에게 2일간의 휴가를 ～해 주다 give 〔allow〕 him a two-day extension to his holidays / 대출 기한을 ～하다 extend the term of the loan / 국회의 회기가 20일간 ～되었다 The session of the National Assembly was extended 〔prolonged〕 another twenty days.
③ ⟪전체 길이⟫ length. ¶ 아마존강은 ～ 6,300킬로미터에 이른다 The total length of the Amazon is 6,300 kilometers.
④ ⟪연장·확대⟫ an extension. ¶ 지역사회는 가족의 ～이라고 생각할 수 있을 것이다 A community may be considered to be an extension of a family.
◉ ～공사 extension work: 지하철 ～공사로 교통이 불통되었다 Traffic was disrupted by work on a subway extension. ～선 an extension (line); a prolongation; 〚수학〛 a production. ～전 an extended game; ⟪축구의⟫ extra time; ⟪야구의⟫ an extra inning game: ～전을 하다 play extra innings / 결승전은 ～전으로 들어갔다 The final game went into extra 〔extended〕 innings.

**연재**(連載) serialization; serial publication. ～하다 publish serially 〔in serial form〕; serialize. ¶ 잡지〔신문〕의 ～물 a magazine 〔newspaper〕 serial / 동아일보에 ～되는 만화 comic strips appearing regularly in Tong-a Ilbo / ～되다 appear 〔be published〕 serially ⟪in a magazine⟫; be serialized ⟪in a newspaper⟫ / 그 신문은 희곡을 ～하고 있다 The newspaper runs a play in daily installments. / 그녀는 신문에 문예 평론을 ～하고 있다 She is writing a series of articles on literary criticism for a newspaper.
◉ ～만화 comic strips; (serial) comics. ～물 a serial: ～물을 5회에 걸쳐서 싣다 ⟪신문이⟫ run a serial in five parts. ～소설 a serial novel 〔story〕.

**연적**(硯滴) a water dropper (for preparing ink).

**연적**(戀敵) a love rival; a rival 「suitor 〔in love〕.

**연전**(年前) ¶ ～에 two or three 〔a couple of 〕 years ago; some 〔several, a few〕 years before 〔earlier〕.

**연전**(連戰) a series of battles. ～하다 fight a series of battles.
◉ ～연승 a series of wins; successive 〔unbroken〕 victories: ～연승하다 win consecutive victories; gain a series of victories; win battle after battle / 아군은 ～연승의 기세로 진격했다 Our army marched on carrying everything before them. ～연패 a series of defeats; successive 〔unbroken〕 defeats: ～연패하다 lose every battle; lose battle after battle 〔game after game〕.

**연접**(連接) connection. ～하다 connect; interlock. ◉ ～봉 〚기계〛 a connecting rod.

**연정**(戀情) tender passion 〔feeling〕; attachment; love. ¶ 불타는 ～ burning passion / ～에 불타다 burn 〔be consumed〕 with love ⟪for⟫ / ～을 고백하다 declare 〔confess〕 *one's* love / ～을 느끼다 feel attached ⟪to⟫ / ～을 품다 fall in love with ⟪*a person*⟫.

**연제**(演題) the subject of an address 〔a speech, a lecture〕; the theme. ¶ 브라운 박사는 「민주주의와 자유」란 ～로 강연했다 Dr. Brown lectured on the subject of 'Democracy and Freedom'.
◉ ～미정 the subject undecided; the theme to be decided.

**연좌**(連坐) ⟪연루⟫ implication; involvement; ⟪앉음⟫ sitting down in a row. ～하다 be implicated in ⟪a crime⟫; be involved in ⟪an affair⟫; sit down in a row. ¶ 부정사건에 ～되다 be involved 〔implicated〕 in a scandal (case); link *one's* name with a scandal.
◉ ～데모 a sit-in〔-down〕 demonstration: ～ 데모하다 stage a sit-in. ～스트라이크 a sit-down strike. ～전술 sit-down tactics: ～ 전술을 취하다 resort to sit-down tactics. ～제(도) the guilt-by-association system; the involvement system.

**연주**(演奏) a (musical) performance; ⟪독주⟫ a recital. ～하다 perform; play; give a recital 〔performance〕. ¶ 피아노를 ～하다 play the piano; present a piano recital / 처음 ～하다 give *one's* first performance / 즉흥적으로 ～하다

ad-lib / 피아노로 베토벤곡을 ～하다 play Beethoven on the piano / 미국 군악대가 행진곡을 ～하였다 An American military band played a march. / 오늘 밤 그는 어디서 바이올린을 ～합니까 Where is he going to give his violin recital tonight? / 그녀의 피아노 ～는 매우 훌륭했다 Her piano recital 〔rendering〕 was excellent.
◉ ～가 a performing musician. ～곡목《전체》 a (musical) program; a repertoire. ～기술 technical skill; technique. ～여행 a concert 〔recital〕 tour. ～자 a performer; a player. ～회 a concert 〔recital〕 (★ a concert는 많은 연주자에 의한 것): 피아노 ～회 a piano recital / ～회를 열다 hold 〔give〕 a concert 〔recital〕 / ～회에 가다 go to 〔attend〕 a concert / ～회에는 청중이 많았다 There was a good attendance at the concert.

**연주창**(連珠瘡) 〖한의〗 scrofula. ¶ ～의 scrofulous.

**연줄**(緣—) connections; contacts; (a) pull; (a) relation; good offices (알선). ¶ ～을 찾다 hunt up some connections / 아무의 ～로 그 회사에 들어가다 get *one's* job in the company through *a person's* 「influence 〔good offices, connections, pull〕 / 아무하고 ～이 있다 have connections 〔be connected〕 with *a person* / 좋은 ～이 있다 have a good pull 〔backing〕 / 그는 ～로 그 직장을 얻었다 He has got that job through his connections. / ～을 통해 그 일을 알아보았다 I inquired into that through my acquaintances. / 그런 사람은 ～이 없어도 출세한다 Such a person will be promoted even if he has no pull.

**연중**(年中) the whole year; all (the) year round; throughout the year; year in year out; 《항상》 all the time; always. ¶ ～ 바쁘다 be always busy / 그 산꼭대기에는 눈이 ～ 있다 There lies snow on the summit of that mountain all the year round. /농부들은 ～ 내내 죽도록 일해야 했다 Farmers had to work very hard all through the year. ◉ ～무휴《게시》 Open throughout the year; Always open. ～행사 regular annual events; annual functions 〔observances〕; the year's celebrations.

**연지**(臙脂) rouge; (a) lipstick. ¶ ～가 묻은 lipstick-stained / 뺨에 ～를 바르다 rouge *one's* cheeks; put rouge on *one's* cheeks / 입술에 ～를 진하게 바르다 rouge 〔paint〕 thickly *one's* lips. ◉ ～분 rouge and face powder; toilet articles; beauty aids. ～색 deep red.

**연직**(鉛直) perpendicularity; verticality. ⇨ 수직(垂直). ◉ ～각 a vertical angle.

**연차**(年次) order by year 〔age〕. ¶ ～로 by age 〔year〕 / ～의 annual; yearly / ～적으로 chronologically; year by 〔after〕 year. ◉ ～계획 a yearly 〔an annual〕 program: 1999년도 ～계획 a program for fiscal 1999. ～대회《정당의》 an annual convention. ～보고 an annual report. ～유급 휴가 an annual 〔a yearly〕 paid holiday 〔vacation〕. ～총회 an annual general meeting (생략 AGM). ～휴가 an annual leave 〔vacation〕.

**연착**(延着) delayed 〔late〕 arrival; delay (in arrival); (a) delay in delivery. ～하다 be delayed; arrive late; be overdue. ¶ 많은 눈으로 기차는 한 시간 ～했다 The train was an hour behind time 〔arrived an hour late〕 because of the heavy snowfall.

**연착륙**(軟着陸) (a) soft landing. ～하다 make a soft landing 《on the moon》; soft-land 《on》. ¶ 우주선의 달 ～ a soft landing of a spacecraft on the moon / 정책의 최고 우선 순위는 물가 안정과 경제의 ～을 이루는 데 두어질 것이다 The top policy priority would be placed on attaining price stability and an economic soft landing.

**연천하다**(年淺—) be short in years 〔time, age〕. ¶ 우리 회사는 창립된지 아직 ～ It's not (very) long since our firm was established.

**연철**(軟鐵) 〖야금〗 soft iron.

**연철**(鍊鐵) 〖야금〗 wrought iron.

**연체**(延滯) delay; procrastination; arrears; arrearage. ～하다 delay; procrastinate; be delayed; 《지급 따위가》 be overdue; be in arrear(s). ¶ (지급이) ～돼 있다 be back (in *one's* payments); be overdue (어음의) / 그는 집세가 ～되어 있다 He is in arrears with his rent. *or* His rent is in arrears. / 나는 가스 대금이 ～되어 있다 I'm behind 〔late〕 in paying of my gas bill. / 그녀는 집 수리할 때 진 빚의 상환이 ～되어 있다 She is overdue in paying the debt for repairs to her house. ◉ ～금 arrears; money in arrears. ～ 대출금 overdue loans. ～료 late fee. ～이자 overdue interest; interest on arrears. ～일수 days in arrears. ～자 a delinquent. 「[총칭].

**연체동물**(軟體動物) a mollusk; *Mollusca*

**연초**(年初) 《at》 the beginning of the year.

**연초**(煙草) tobacco. ⇨ 담배.

**연출**(演出) direction; production; presentation. ～하다 direct; produce; present; stage. ¶ A씨 ～의 produced 〔directed〕 by Mr. A / 이 극은 유명한 극작가가 ～하였다 This play was produced by a famous playwright. ◉ ～가 a producer; a director 《미》. ～대본 an acting copy 〔script〕. ～법 a dramaturgy. ～효과 stage effect.

**연충**(蠕蟲) a worm; 《기생충》 helminth.

**연타**(連打) ～하다 《종 따위를》 clang 〔ring〕 《a bell》 repeatedly; 《구타》 deliver a shower of blows 《on *a person*》; hit 〔strike〕 《*a person*》 repeatedly. ¶ 그는 좌우 ～로 상대방을 녹아웃시켰다 He knocked out the opponent with left and right hand barrages. /투수는 ～를 당해 3회에서 교체되었다 The pitcher was relieved after three innings of continuous hits.

**연탄**(煉炭) a briquet(te). ¶ ～을 갈아 넣다 change 〔replace〕 a briquet. ◉ ～가스 coal 〔briquet〕 gas: ～ 가스 중독으로 죽다 die from briquet gas poisoning. ～공장 a briquet manufactory. ～난로 a briquet stove. ～불 briquet fire. ～재 a used briquet. ～제조기 a briquet pressing machine.

**연통**(煙筒) a chimney; a stovepipe (난로의); a smokestack (공장의); a funnel (기관차·기선의). ⇨ 굴뚝.

**연투하다**(連投—) 〖야구〗 take the (pitcher's) mound in 《three》 successive games.

**연판**(連判) joint signatures (and seals). ～하다 sign seal jointly. ¶ ～으로 under joint signatures. ◉ ～자 a cosignatory. ～장 a compact 〔covenant〕 under joint signatures.

**연판**(鉛版) 〖인쇄〗 a stereotype; a stereo (*pl.* ～s). ¶ ～으로 인쇄하다 stereotype / ～을 뜨다 make a stereotype 《of 》. ◉ ～공 a stereotyper. ～인쇄 stereotypography.

**연패**(連敗) consecutive 〔successive〕 defeats; a series 〔sequence〕 of defeats. ～하다 lose time after time; suffer successive defeats. ¶ 다섯 차례나 ～하다 lose five games in a row; lose five successive games / 선거에 ～하다 suffer successive defeats in the election.

**연패**(連覇) winning the competition 〔championship〕 for 《three》 consecutive years. ～하다 win first place for 《five》 years in a row 〔for 《five》 straight years〕.

**연평수**(延坪數) the total floor space 《of a building》. ¶ 그는 ～가 500평이 되는 건물을 신축한다 He constructs a new building which has the total floor space of 500 *p'yŏng*.

**연표**(年表) a chronological table; a chronology. ¶ 세계사 ～ a chronological table of world history.

**연풍**(軟風) a gentle breeze; a soft 〔light〕 wind; a zephyr 《시어》.

**연필**(鉛筆) a (lead) pencil. ¶ HB ～ an HB pencil / 지우개 달린 ～ a pencil with an eraser-tip / 끝이 뭉툭해진 ～ a blunt pencil / 색～ a colored pencil / ～끝 a pencil point / ～심 the lead of a pencil / ～을 깎다 sharpen a pencil / ～로 선을 긋다 draw a pencil line / ～로 쓰다 write with a pencil / ～로 쓰지 마십시오 Do not use pencil. ◉ ～깎이 a pencil sharpener. ～통 a pencil case. ～화 a pencil sketch 〔drawing〕.

**연하**(年下) juniority. ¶ ～의 younger; junior / 창호는 나보다 두 살 ～이다 Changho is two years my junior 〔two years younger than me〕.

**연하**(年賀) the New Year('s) greetings; 《연하장에서》 (A) Happy New Year. ◉ ～객 a New Year's caller. ～우편 New Year's mail. ～장 a New Year's card: ～장을 보내다 send 《*a person*》 a New Year's card.

**연하다**(連—) adjoin; be connected 《to》. ¶ 한국과 중국은 연해 있다 Korea and China adjoin each other.

**연하다**(軟—) ① 《질기지 않다》 (be) soft; tender. ¶ 연한 고기 tender meat / 연하게 하다 soften; tenderize / 연해지다 become soft 〔tender〕; soften. ② 《빛이》 (be) soft; mild; light; pale. ¶ 연하게 lightly; faintly / 연한 초록빛 a light green / 빛깔을 연하게 하다 lighten the color / 연하게 화장하다 put on light make-up. ③ 《독하지 않다》 weak; mild. ¶ 연한 커피 weak coffee / 차는 연하게 해 주시오 I like my tea weak.

**-연하다**(然—) pretend to be; act as if 《*one* were》. ¶ 학자연하는 사람 a pedantic scholar / 대가(大家)연하다 put on the airs of an authority.

**연한**(年限) a fixed period (of years); a term. ¶ 재직 ～ *one's* term of office / 벌써 ～이 찼다 The term has already expired.

**연합**(聯合) union; league; alliance; concert; coalition; combination. ～하다 combine 《with》; unite 《with》; league 《with》; ally *oneself* 《with》; coalesce 《with》; merge 《with》. ¶ ～의 combined; joint; concerted; allied; united / ～해서 in combination; in concert; in league; unitedly; in one united body / ～하여 적에 대항하다 unite in the struggle against an enemy / 미국 식민지는 ～하여 영국에 대항하였다 The American colonies formed a union against England. / 여러 교회가 ～해서 예배를 보았다 Many of the churches held joint services.
◉ ～고사 unified entrance examination. ～국 the allied nations 〔powers〕; the Allies. ～군 the allied forces; the Allies. ～단체〔회〕 a federation. ～작전 combined 〔joint〕 operations. ～전선 the united front. ～통신사 《한국의》 The Yonhap News Agency; 《미국의》 the Associated Press (생략 AP). ～함대 a combined fleet.

**연해**(沿海) the sea along the coast. ¶ ～의 inshore; coast(al) / ～어 littoral fish / ～의 한촌 a lonely village on the coast.
◉ ～경비 coastal defense. ～도시 coast cities. ～무역 coastal 〔coasting〕 trade. ～선(船) a coasting vessel; a coastal trader. ～어업 coastal 〔inshore〕 fishery. ～지대 the littoral zone. ～항로 a coastal line 〔route〕.

**연해**(煙害) smoke pollution; injury 〔damage〕 from smoke.

**연해**(連—) continuously; uninterruptedly; successively. ¶ ～ 비가 온다 It keeps on raining. / ～ 손님들이 온다 Visitors come one after another. / ～ 불행이 잇따랐다 One misfortune followed another.

**연해안**(沿海岸) the coast; the shore. ¶ ～의 coastal; inshore. ◉ ～지대 coastland.

**연해주**(沿海州) 〚지리〛 the Maritime 〔Littoral〕 Province (of Siberia).

**연행**(連行) ～하다 haul 〔bring〕 《*a person*》 before 《the police authorities》; take 〔walk〕 《*a person*》 to 《a police station》. ¶ 경찰에 ～되다 be taken to the police (station) / 경찰관은 그 용의자를 경찰서로 ～했다 The policeman took the suspect to a police station.

**연혁**(沿革) the history 《of》; the development 《of》; changes (변천). ¶ 학교의 ～ the history of 《our》 school.

**연호**(年號) the name of an era.

**연화**(軟化) softening; mollification; weakening. ～하다 soften; mollify; become soft; go soft (사람이). ¶ 센물을 ～하다 soften hard water / 그들의 태도가 갑작스레 ～했다 Their attitude suddenly became conciliatory. ◉ ～증: 골～증 softening of the bones; osteomalacia.

**연화**(軟貨) soft money 〔currency〕; a banknote (지폐).

**연화**(蓮花·蓮華) a lotus flower.

**연회**(年會) an annual meeting 〔convention, assembly〕.

**연회**(宴會) a dinner (party); a social dinner; a banquet (공식의); a feast (축연). ¶ 신년 ～ a New Year banquet 〔party〕 / ～를 열다 give 〔have〕 a dinner (party); hold 〔give〕 a banquet.
◉ ～장 a banquet hall.

**연후**(然後) ¶ ～에 after that; afterwards.

**연휴**(連休) consecutive holidays; holidays in a row. ¶ 징검다리 ～ a series of holidays separated by one or two workdays (in between) / 이틀 ～ two consecutive work-free days / 하루 거른 ～ sandwiched holidays / ～를 즐기다 enjoy straight holidays / ～를 이용해서 여행가다 go on a trip during the consecutive holidays.

**열**(列) a line; a row; 《횡렬》 a rank; 《종렬》 a column; a file; 《행렬》 a procession; 《차례를 기다리는》 a line; a queue 《영》. ¶ 2열 횡대 a double line / 전〔후〕 열 the front 〔rear〕 rank / 제1〔제2〕 열의 좌석 a seat in the front 〔the second〕 row / 열 밖으로 out of the ranks 〔line〕 / 1열로 in a line 〔row〕 / (새치기로) 열에 끼어들다 cut into the line; 《영》 jump the queue / 열을 이탈하다 drop out of line / 열을 짓다 form a line 〔file, row〕 / 2열 종대로 서다 line up in a double file / 열지어 행진하다 march in files; parade in columns / 극장 앞에 사람들이 열을 지었다 People formed a queue in front of the theater.

**열**(熱) ① 《열기》 heat; warmth. ¶ 열의 thermic; thermal / 내열의 heatproof; heat-resistant / 열을 가하다 apply heat 《to》; heat / 열을 발생하다 generate heat / 열을 전달하다 conduct 〔transfer〕 heat / 열을 발산〔복사, 흡수〕하다 give off 〔radiate, absorb〕 heat.
② 《체온》 (a) temperature; (a) fever. ¶ 열이 나다 develop a fever; become

feverish / 열이 내리다 *one's* temperature falls 〔goes down〕; *one's* fever subsides 〔abates, breaks〕 / 열이 높다 〔조금 있다〕 have a high 〔slight〕 fever / 열이 있다 have a temperature 〔fever〕; be feverish / 열을 내리다 bring down the fever; lower the temperature / 환자의 열을 재다 take a patient's temperature / 감기로 열이 났다 My cold has brought on a fever. / 환자의 열은 39도 8분이었다 The temperature of the patient was thirty-nine point eight degrees. / 아침에는 열이 없어지나 오후에는 다시 난다 The fever leaves me in the morning but in the afternoon it comes back.

③ 《열의》 enthusiasm; zeal; passion; ardor; 《열광》 a mania 《for》; a craze 《for》; a fever; a rage. ¶ 금광열 gold fever / 문학열 a craze 〔mania〕 for literature / 축구열 enthusiasm for football / 부동산 투기열 speculative fever on real estate / 열이 식게 하다 cool 《*a person's*》 ardor 〔enthusiasm〕 《for》 / 멋대로 열을 올려 떠들다 talk away as *one* likes 〔pleases〕; give rein to *one's* tongue / …에 부쩍 열을 올리다 have a craze for 《dancing》; be gone on 《a girl》 《구어》 / 전국에 축구열이 갑작스레 확산되었다 Soccer fever gripped the whole country.

④ 《격정·노기》 passion; anger; rage; offence; heat; wrath; fury. ¶ 열이 나다 be heated (with passion); be offended 《by》; get angry / 열이 나서 아무를 때리다 strike *a person* in passion.

◉ 열공해 heat pollution. 열교환기 a heat exchanger. 열기관 a heat engine; a thermomoter. 열기구 a hot=air balloon. 열소비량 heat consumption. 열에너지 thermal energy. 열효율 thermal efficiency.

**열** ten. ¶ 열번째 the tenth / 열 사람 ten people 〔persons〕 / 열 시 ten o'clock / 그 사람의 명령을 하나에서 열까지 복종할 수 없다 I cannot obey him in every particular. / 그 수는 열을 넘지 않는다 They might be counted on the fingers. / 그는 열이면 아홉은 실패할 게다 He will fail in nine cases out of ten. *or* Ten to one, he will fail. / 열 길 물 속은 알아도 한 길 사람 속은 모른다 《속담》 You can sound water ten fathoms deep, but you cannot sound the human heart a single fathom. / 현자는 하나를 들어 열을 안다 [비유적] A word to the wise is enough. / 열 번 찍어 안 넘어가는 나무 없다 《속담》 The repeated stroke will fell the oak.

**열가소성**(熱可塑性) 〖물리〗 thermoplasticity. ¶ ~의 thermoplastic. ◉ ~재료 thermoplastic material(s).

**열각**(劣角) 〖수학〗 a minor angle.

**열강**(列強) the (Great) Powers; the world powers.

**열거**(列擧) enumeration. ~하다 enumerate; list; go through the list 《of》. ¶ 일일이 ~할 수가 없다 be too manifold to enumerate / 그는 그 계획의 단점을 ~했다 He enumerated the disadvantages of the plan.

**열경화성**(熱硬化性) 〖물리〗 a thermosetting 〔thermohardening〕 property. ◉ ~ 수지 thermosetting resin.

**열관리**(熱管理) control of heat; heat control. ◉ ~사 a heat controller.

**열광**(熱狂) wild enthusiasm; frenzy; fanaticism; mania. ~하다 be wildly excited 《at, over, by》; go 〔get〕 wild with enthusiasm 〔excitement〕 《over》; go crazy 《over, for》; run mad 《after》. ¶ ~적 excited; enthusiastic; frantic / ~하여 frantically; with wild 〔feverish〕 excitement / ~적 환영을 받다 be given an enthusiastic welcome / ~시키다 thrill 〔excite〕 《*a person*》; excite 〔stir up〕 《*a person's*》 enthusiasm / 청중을 ~시키다 rouse *one's* audience to enthusiasm / 그의 묘기는 팬들을 ~케 했다 His fine play enraptured the fans.

**열국**(列國) 《열강》 the (world) powers; the nations of the world; all countries. ¶ 유럽 ~ the European powers / ~의 간섭 foreign intervention.

**열기**(列記) enumeration; listing. ~하다 enumerate; list.

**열기**(熱氣) ① 《더운 공기》 heat; hot air; 《열광적 기분》 fevered air; a heated atmosphere. ¶ ~가 식다 cool down / ~를 뿜다 give off 〔radiate〕 heat / 흥분의 ~에 휩싸이다 be filled with feverish excitement. ② 《신열》 temperature; fever. ⇨ 열(熱).

**열김**(熱—) ① 《열중·흥분으로 인한》 ardor; enthusiasm; fervor; heat; excitement. ¶ 토론 중 ~에 그렇게 말했다 I spoke like that in the heat of discussion. ② 《홧김》 anger; indignation; fury. ¶ 그는 ~에 자리에서 벌떡 일어났다 He started from his seat in indignation.

**열나다**(熱—) ① 《신열이》 become feverish; develop a fever; come to have fever. ¶ 저녁마다 ~ have a fever every evening. ② 《열중하다》 become enthusiastic 《in, about》; be mad 〔crazy〕 《about, over》; be keen 〔intent〕 《on》. ¶ 돈 모으기에 열내다 be intent on making money / 열나게 공부하다 study ardently 〔feverishly〕. ③ 《화나다》 get 〔become, grow〕 angry; be heated with passion. ¶ 열나서 out of resentment.

**열나절** a very long time.

**열넷** fourteen. ¶ ~째 the fourteenth.

**열녀**(烈女) a virtuous woman.

**열다**[1] ① 《닫힌·덮인 것을》 open; unlock 《a door》; uncover; lift (뚜껑을). ¶ 당겨서 〔밀어서〕 ~ pull 〔push〕 《the door》 open / 대문〔문, 창문, 입〕을 ~ open a gate 〔door, window, *one's* mouth〕 / 문을 억지로 ~ open a door by force; force a door (open) / 서랍을 ~ open a drawer / 냄비 뚜껑을 ~ take the lid off a pan / 문을 열어 놓다 leave the door open / 열쇠로 열다 unlock 《the door》 / 창을 열어 두다 keep a window open.

② 《개시·개장하다》 open 《a shop》; start; set up; establish. ¶ 가게를 ~ open 〔start〕 a shop / 새 사무소를 ~ set up 〔establish〕 a new office / 도서관은 여덟 시에 문을 연다 The library opens at 8 o'clock.

③ 《길·땅 따위를》 open (up); clear 《land》; develop 《a country》; break 《the road》; make way 《for *a person*》; clear a path 〔passage〕 《for *a person*》. ¶ 길을 ~ build 〔open〕 a road / 후진에게 길을 열어 주다 give younger generation a chance; open the way of promotion for *one's* juniors.

④ 《모임을》 hold 《a meeting》; give 《a party》; open 《a conference》. ¶ 만찬회를 ~ give a dinner (party) / 잔치를 ~ give 〔throw〕 a banquet / 회의를 ~ hold a meeting / 동양화 전시회를 ~ hold an exhibit of oriental pictures.

**열다**[2] 《열매가》 bear (fruit); fruit. ¶ 열매가 ~ bear fruit / 열매가 잔뜩 연 나무 a tree laden with 〔full of〕 fruits / 열매가 열지 않게 된 나무 a tree past bearing / 열매가 주렁주렁 ~ grow in clusters.

**열다섯** fifteen. ¶ ~째 the fifteenth.

**열대**(熱帶) 〖지리〗 the tropics; the torrid zone. ¶ ~의 tropic(al) / ~기후 a tropical climate / ~ 과일 tropical fruit / ~의 뜨거운 공기 the hot air of the tropics / ~에 살다 live in the tropics.
◉ ~기단(氣團) 〖기상〗 a tropical air mass. ~병 a tropical disease. ~성 저기압〔폭풍〕 a tropical cyclone 〔storm〕. ~식물 a tropical plant; tropical flora [총칭]. ~야(夜) a sweltering 〔tropical〕 night. ~어 a tropical fish. ~우림 a tropical rain forest. ~지방 tropical regions; the tropics.

**열댓** about fifteen. ¶ ~ 살의 소녀 a girl about fifteen years old / ~ 사람 about 〔some〕 fifteen people.

**열도**(列島) a chain of islands; an archipelago (군도(群島)). ¶ 일본 ~ the Japanese Islands.

**열도**(熱度) degree of heat 〔temperature (온도)〕; (relative) heat; fever; 《열심의 도》 degree of enthusiasm.

**열둘** twelve. ¶ 열두째 the twelfth.

**열등**(劣等) inferiority; a low class 〔grade〕; low-grade; poor. ~하다 (be) inferior; poor. ¶ 이 담배는 품질이 ~하다 This tobacco is of inferior quality. / 어느 점에선 남자가 여자보다 ~하다 Man is inferior to woman in some respects. ◉ ~감〔의식〕 a sense of inferiority; an inferiority complex: ~감에 시달리다 suffer from an inferiority complex. ~생 a backward pupil; a poor student. ~품 low-grade goods; an article of inferior quality.

**열띠다**(熱—) grow 〔get〕 excited; 《의론 등이》 become heated; hot up 《영》. ¶ 열띤 경기 hot fighting; a close contest 〔game〕 / 열띤 논쟁〔토론〕 heated controversy 〔discussion〕 / 열띤 환영을 받다 be received with the greatest enthusiasm.

**열락**(悅樂) joy; pleasure; mirth; gaiety. ~하다 take pleasure 〔delight〕 《in》 rejoice 《at, in》; enjoy *oneself*.

**열람**(閱覽) perusal; reading. ~하다 peruse; read. ¶ 도서를 ~하다 read 〔use〕 books 《in a library》 / 도서를 일반 ~에 제공하다 offer 〔provide〕 books for public perusal. ◉ ~권 a library admission ticket. ~료 an admission fee (of a library). ~실 a reading room. ~자〔인〕 a reader; a visitor (in a library). ~표 a call slip.

**열량**(熱量) the amount 〔quantity〕 of heat; 《칼로리》 (a) calorie; calory; 《발열량》 calorific power; heat value. ¶ ~이 많다〔적다〕 be high 〔low〕 in calorie(s) / 그 음식은 2천 칼로리의 ~이 있다 The diet represents a heat value of 2,000 calories.
◉ ~가치 calorific value. ~계 calori-

meter. ～단위 a unit of heat; a thermal unit. ～측정(법) calorimetry.

**열렬하다**(熱烈—) (be) fiery; ardent; fervent; passionate. ¶ 열렬한 사랑 a passionate 〔fiery〕 love / 열렬한 기독교 신자 a devoted 〔fanatic〕 Christian / 열렬한 음악 애호가 a great fan of music / 금주 운동의 열렬한 후원자 an ardent supporter of the temperance cause / 열렬한 어조로 말하다 speak in a fiery tone / 열렬한 환영을 받다 be received with great enthusiasm / 이렇게 열렬한 환영을 받을 줄은 몰랐다 Little did I think of being so warmly welcomed.

**열렬히**(熱烈—) ardently; fervently; passionately. ¶ ～ 사랑하다 love passionately (with all *one's* soul); be madly in love 《with》.

**열루**(熱淚) 《shed》 hot 〔burning〕 tears.

**열리다** ① 《문·뚜껑 따위가》 open; be opened; 《자물쇠가》 be unlocked; be open (★ be open은 「열려 있다」라는 상태를 가리키며 이 때의 open은 형용사. be opened는 「열려지다」란 수동의 동작을 보이며 opened는 동사의 과거분사). ¶ (문이) 확 ～ 《the door》 fly open; be flung open / 문이 안으로 열린다 The door opens inward. / 문이 조금 열려 있다 The door is「ajar 〔slightly open〕. / 서랍이 잘 열리지 않는다 The drawer is tight. / 창문이 (아무리 하여도) 열리지 않는다 The window will not open.
② 《상점·모임 등이》 open; begin; start; be held; take place. ¶ …의 주최로 ～ 《a seminar》 be held under the auspices of… / 은행은 아홉 시에 열린다 The bank opens at nine o'clock. / 전람회는 내일 열린다 The exhibition opens tomorrow.
③ 《문물이》 be 〔become〕 civilized; be enlightened. ¶ 열린 나라 a civilized 〔an advanced〕 country / 그 나라는 1차 대전 후 크게 열렸다 The nation has been greatly enlightened since World War I.
④ 《열매가》 bear fruit; fruit. ⇨ 열다[2].

**열망**(熱望) an ardent wish; a fervent hope; a burning 〔an eager〕 desire; a yen 《구어》; a longing. ～하다 desire eagerly 〔earnestly〕; be anxious 〔eager〕 《for, to *do*》; be zealous 《for》; long 《for, to *do*》. ¶ 그들은 자유를 ～하고 있다 They have intense aspirations toward liberty. / 우리는 평화를 ～한다 We are longing for peace. / 그녀는 여배우가 되기를 ～하고 있었다 She had aspirations to be an actress. / 돌아가기를 ～하고 있다 I am dying to get back. / 참석해 주시기를 우리 모두가 ～하고 있습니다 We are all anxious for your presence (at the party).

**열매** (a) fruit; a berry (장과); a nut (견과). ¶ ～가 많은 fruitful / ～가 없는 fruitless / ～가 익다 grow ripe; ripen / ～를 맺다 bear fruit; (go to) seed; produce seeds; [비유적] bear fruit; produce a result; come to fruition / 이 나무는 ～가 많이〔적게〕 열린다 This tree is a good 〔poor〕 bearer. *or* This tree produce「a lot of 〔little〕 fruit. / 저 귤나무는 ～가 너무 많이 열려서 가지가 부러질 것 같다 That tangerine tree is weighed down with fruit and the bough is about to break. / 「자네의 노력이 언젠가는 ～를 맺을 걸세」—「저도 그러기를 바랍니다」 "Your efforts will bear fruit in time."—"I hope so, too."

**열목어** 〖어류〗 a fresh-water salmon.

**열무** a young radish. ◉ ～김치 young radish kimchi.

**열반**(涅槃) 〖불교〗 ① 《입적》 death of a Buddhist priest. ② 《해탈》 Nirvana (=the state of complete absence of sensation). ¶ ～에 들다 enter 〔pass into〕 Nirvana; attain「Buddhahood 〔supreme enlightenment〕.

**열변**(熱辯) a fiery 〔a vehement, an impassioned, a fervent〕 speech; passionate eloquence. ¶ ～을 토하다 deliver 〔spit out〕 a fiery speech; speak with fervor; deliver 〔make〕 a fervent speech; harangue 〔declaim〕 《against, for》.

**열병**(閱兵) a review; an inspection of「troops. ⇨ 사열(査閱).

**열병**(熱病) a fever; a febrile disease; pyrexia. ¶ ～에 걸리다 catch 〔suffer from〕 a fever.

**열분해**(熱分解) 〖화학〗 pyrolysis. ～하다 pyrolyze. ¶ ～의〔로 생기는〕 pyrolytic.

**열비**(劣比) 〖수학〗 a ratio of lesser inequality; a minor ratio.

**열사**(烈士) a man of fervid loyalty; a patriot; a hero. ◉ 순국～ a 〔an ardent〕 patriot who laid down *one's* life for *his* country; a martyr.

**열사병**(熱射病) 〖의학〗 heatstroke; heat prostration 〔apoplexy〕. ¶ ～에 걸리다 suffer from 〔be affected by〕 heatstroke.

**열상**(裂傷) a lacerated wound; a laceration. ¶ ～을 입다 have 《*one's* face》 lacerated 《by》.

**열생학**(劣生學) 〖생물〗 dysgenics.

**열석**(列席) presence ⟪at a meeting⟫; attendance. ⇨출석.

**열선**(熱線) 〚물리〛 heat 〔thermic〕 rays; infrared rays (적외선); a hot wire.
◉ ～전류계 a hot-wire ammeter.

**열성**(劣性)(genetic) recessiveness; inferiority. ¶ ～의 recessive. ◉ ～유전 recessive heredity: ～유전자 a recessive (gene). ～형질(形質) a recessive (character).

**열성**(列聖) ⟪왕⟫ successive kings; ⟪성인⟫ a number of saints. ◉ ～조(朝) successive reigns.

**열성**(熱誠) earnestness; devotion; ardor; enthusiasm; zeal. ～스럽다 (be) enthusiastic; earnest; ardent; zealous; devoted. ¶ ～적 (being) ardent; zealous / ～을 다해서 with zeal; enthusiastically; heart and soul / ～을 다해서 나라에 이바지하다 serve *one's* country with ardent zeal / ～이 넘쳐흐르다 overflow with enthusiasm / 그의 말 한 마디 한 마디에 ～이 어려 있었다 Every word of his speech reflected his earnestness.
◉ ～가 an enthusiast; a devotee; ⟪열광자⟫ a zealot. ～분자 earnest 〔enthusiastic, devoted〕 elements ⟪of a party⟫.

**열세**(劣勢) numerical inferiority; inferiority in strength 〔numbers〕. ～하다 be inferior in numbers 〔strength〕. ¶ ～의 inferior in strength 〔numbers〕 / ～를 만회하다 turn the tables; rally from an inferior position; regain *one's* strength / 적(敵)은 수적으로 우리보다 ～였다 The enemy was inferior to us in number.

**열셋** thirteen. ¶ ～째 the thirteenth.

**열쇠** ① ⟪자물쇠의⟫ a key. ¶ 현관의 ～ a key to the front door / ～ 꾸러미 a bunch of keys / ～로 (자물쇠를) 열다 unlock 〔open a lock〕 with a key / ～를 잘 잠그어 ⟪keep *a thing*⟫ under lock and key / ～로 잠그다 turn a key on; lock up ⟪a house, a trunk⟫ / ～를 돌리다 turn a key / 자물쇠에 ～를 꽂다 fit a key to a lock; insert a key in a lock.
② ⟪해결의⟫ a clue; a solution; a key. ¶ 미스터리를 푸는 ～ a key to the mystery / 문제(해결)의 ～ a key to the question; the crux of the problem / 문제 해결의 ～를 쥐다 hold the key to the solution of the problem.
③ ⟪요긴한 것⟫ a key. ¶ 성공의 ～ the key to the 〔*one's*〕 success / 교육이 장래 번영의 ～를 쥐고 있다 Education holds the key to our future prosperity.
◉ ～고리 a key ring. ～구멍 a keyhole. ～제조업자〔상〕 a locksmith; a keysmith.

**열심**(熱心) enthusiasm; zeal; eagerness; earnestness; keenness; fervor; ardor; zeal. ¶ ～이다 be eager ⟪about, for, to *do*⟫; be intent 〔keen〕 ⟪on⟫; be devoted ⟪to⟫; be enthusiastic ⟪in⟫; be zealous ⟪for⟫ / 일에 ～이다 be devoted to 〔be intent on〕 *one's* task / 공부에 ～이다 be earnest in *one's* studies / 스포츠에 ～이다 be keen on sports.

**열심히**(熱心―) eagerly; zealously; enthusiastically; ardently; fervently; earnestly; assiduously. ¶ ～ 공부하다 work 〔study〕 hard; apply *oneself* closely to *one's* studies / ～ 듣다 listen intently 〔attentively〕 ⟪to⟫ / 그는 ～ 기도를 드렸다 He prayed fervently. / 그는 ～ 일한다 He works hard 〔diligently〕.

**열십자**(—十字) a cross. ¶ ～꼴의 cross=shaped; cruciform / ～로 crosswise / ～로 매다 tie in a cross / ～를 긋다 cross *oneself;* make (the sign of the) cross ⟪on *one's* breast⟫.

**열씨**(列氏) Réaumur. ¶ ～ 80도 80° 〔eighty degrees〕 R. ◉ ～온도계 a Réaumur thermometer.

**열아홉** nineteen. ¶ ～째 the nineteenth.

**열악**(劣惡) ～하다 (be) inferior; poor; coarse; deteriorated. ¶ ～한 환경에서 살다 live in poor surroundings.

**열애**(熱愛) ardent 〔passionate〕 love; devotion ⟪to a woman⟫. ～하다 love madly 〔passionately〕; be madly in love ⟪with⟫; be devoted to ⟪a woman⟫. ¶ 그는 그녀를 ～하고 있다 He is passionately devoted to her.

**열어젖뜨리다, 열어젖히다** swing 〔push, fling〕 ⟪a door⟫ open. ¶ 문을 ～ fling a door open / 잠긴 문을 ～ force the locked door open.

**열없다** ① ＝열적다①. ¶ 열없어 하다 feel abashed; feel small; be self-conscious. ② ⟪소심하다⟫ (be) soft; timid; fainthearted. ¶ 열없는 사람 a fainthearted; a softy ⟪구어⟫.

**열여덟** eighteen. ¶ ～째 the eighteenth.

**열여섯** sixteen. ¶ ～째 the sixteenth.

**열역학**(熱力學) 〚물리〛 thermodynamics.

**열연**(熱演) an impassioned performance. ～하다 perform 〔play〕 enthusiastically; give an impassioned performance. ¶ 배우는 모두 ～했다 Every actor played his part enthusiasti-

cally 〔with enthusiasm〕.
**열왕기**(列王記) 〚성서〛 the Books of Kings; [약칭] the Kings. 「pacity.
**열용량**(熱容量) 〚물리〛 heat 〔thermal〕 ca-
**열원**(熱源) a heat source 〔reservoir〕.
**열의**(熱意) zeal; enthusiasm. ¶ ～ 있는 zealous; enthusiastic / ～ 없는 unzealous; unenthusiastic / ～가 없어서 for lack of enthusiasm / ～를 보이다 show 〔manifest〕 zeal 《for》; display much enthusiasm 《for》/ 그들은 그 일에 대한 ～가 대단하다 They have a great deal of interest 〔enthusiasm〕 in the undertaking.
**열이온**(熱—) 〚물리〛 a thermion. ◉ ～관〔검파기〕 a thermionic tube 〔detector〕. ～방사 thermionic emission. ～전류 a thermionic current.
**열일곱** seventeen. ¶ ～째 the seventeenth.
**열자기**(熱磁氣) 〚물리〛 thermomagnetism. ◉ ～ 효과 thermomagnetic effect.
**열적다** ① 《멋쩍다》 (be, feel) shy; abashed; awkward; [서술적] become self-conscious; be 〔feel〕 ill at ease. ¶ 여자 앞에서는 열적어 말을 못 한다 I am too shy to speak in front of girls. ② = 싱겁다 ②. ③ 《무료하다》 (be) bored; suffer from ennui.
**열전**(列傳) a series of biographies.
**열전**(熱戰) a hard 〔fierce〕 fight; 《냉전에 대한》 a hot 〔an active〕 war; 《경기의》 a hotly contested match 〔game〕; a close game 〔match〕. ¶ ～을 벌이다 put up a hard fight 《with》; run a neck-and-neck race 《with》/ ～이 벌어지고 있다 A close game is going on.
**열전기**(熱電氣) 〚물리〛 thermoelectricity. ¶ ～의 thermoelectric. ◉ ～온도계 a thermoelectric thermometer.
**열전도**(熱傳導) thermal conduction. ◉ ～율 thermal conductivity.
**열전류**(熱電流) a thermoelectric current; a thermocurrent.
**열전효과**(熱電效果) 〚컴퓨터〛 thermal=electric effect.
**열정**(劣情) low 〔animal〕 passions; carnal desire; lust. ¶ ～을 북돋는 소설 a suggestive novel / ～을 도발하다 rouse 〔stir up〕 low passions.
**열정**(熱情) ardor; fervor; passion. ¶ ～적 passionate; impassioned; ardent / ～적 사랑 ardent love / ～어린 말 impassioned language / 애국의 ～ patriotic ardor / ～을 담아 호소하다 make an impassioned appeal. ◉ ～가 an ardent 〔a passionate〕 person.
**열중하다**(熱中—) have a zeal 《for》; be absorbed 〔engrossed, immersed〕 《in》; be keen 《on》; be enthusiastic 〔mad, crazy〕 《about, for, over》; devoted 《to》; be intent 〔bent〕 《on》. ¶ 열중하는 사람 an enthusiast / 열중하는 성격의 enthusiastic; ardent; earnest / 여자에 ～ be infatuated with a woman / 놀이〔공부〕에 ～ be absorbed in play 〔*one's* studies〕/ 독서에 ～ pore over 〔be very deep in〕 a book / 돈벌이에 ～ be bent 〔intent〕 on money=making / 음악에 ～ have a passion for music / 테니스에 ～ be much given to tennis / 그는 춤에 열중하고 있다 He is so mad on dancing. / 그는 무엇에든 열중하는 기질이다 He goes heart and soul into anything.
**열증**(熱症) 〚의학〛 a fever (case); a febrile disease; pyrexia.
**열차**(列車) a train. ¶ 목포행 ～ a train (bound) for Mokpo / 야간 ～ a night train / 오후 8시 도착 예정의 부산발 ～ a train from Pusan due (to arrive) at 8 p.m. / ～를 운행하다 run trains / ～에 타다 take 〔board 《미》〕 a train / ～에서 내리다 get off a train / 임시 ～를 내다 put on a special train / ～를 전복시키다 wreck a train / 오후 4시 15분 ～로 떠나다 leave 《Seoul》 by the 4:15 〔four fifteen〕 p.m. train / 그 ～는 몇 시에 출발합니까 What time does the train leave 〔go〕? / 2시 45분 열차로 도착할테니 역까지 마중 나와 주시오 Please meet the 2:45 train at the station. ◉ ～강도 a train robber. ～방해 train 〔railroad〕 obstruction. ～사고 a train 〔railroad〕 accident. ～시간표 a train timetable 〔schedule〕. ～운행 train service; train operation: ～운행표 a schedule; a diagram. ～자동 운전 automatic train operation (생략 ATO). ～자동 정지 (장치) automatic train stop (device) (생략 ATS). ～중앙 집중 제어 centralized train control (생략 CTC). ～차장 a passenger conductor.
**열창**(熱唱) passionate 〔fervid, ardent〕 singing. ～하다 sing a song in a passionate tone.
**열처리**(熱處理) heat treatment. ～하다 treat with heat; heat-treat. ◉ ～장치 a heat treatment equipment.
**열탕**(熱湯) boiling 〔hot〕 water. ¶ ～에 데다 be scalded with boiling water / ～ 소독을 하다 disinfect 《a dish》 in boiling water.

**열통적다** (be) rude; boorish; rustic; coarse; crude. ¶ 열통적은 말 a coarse speech / 거동이 ～ be rude-mannered.
**열파**(熱波) a heat wave.
**열패**(劣敗) getting bested; getting defeated through *one's* inferiority. ～하다 be bested; be defeated (through inferiority).
**열팽창**(熱膨脹) thermal expansion. ◉ ～률 a coefficient of thermal expansion.
**열풍**(烈風) a strong 〔high, heavy〕 wind; ⌈a (violent) gale.
**열풍**(熱風) a hot wind 〔blast〕; (a blast of) hot air; 《사막의》 a sirocco (*pl.* -s); a simoom (모래 폭풍).
**열하루** 《열 한 날》 eleven days; 《열 하루째》 the eleventh (day). ¶ 4월 ～ April 11th; the eleventh of April.
**열학**(熱學) 〖물리〗 thermotics; calorifics.
**열한째** the eleventh.
**열핵**(熱核) thermonuclear. ◉ ～무기〔탄두〕 a thermonuclear weapon 〔warhead〕. ～반응〔동력, 융합〕 thermonuclear reaction 〔power, fusion〕. ～전쟁〔실험〕 a thermonuclear war 〔test〕. ～폭발 a thermonuclear explosion. ～폭탄 a themonuclear bomb.
**열혈**(熱血) hot blood; 《열정》 fervent zeal; fieriness. ◉ ～한(漢) a hot=blooded man.
**열호**(劣弧) 〖수학〗 a minor arc.
**열화**(烈火·熱火) a blazing 〔raging〕 fire; furious flames. ¶ ～같이 노하다 flare up; be red with anger; fly into a rage.
**열화학**(熱化學) thermochemistry.
**열확산**(熱擴散) 〖물리〗 thermal diffusion; thermodiffusion. ◉ ～율 thermal diffusivity.
**열흘** 《10일간》 ten days; 《열흘날》 the tenth day (of the month). ¶ ～도 못 되어 in less than ten days.
**엷다** ① 《두께가》 (be) thin; lack thickness. ¶ 엷게 thinly / 엷은 담요 a thin blanket. ② 《빛이》 (be) light; weak; thin. ¶ 엷은 빛 a light color. ③ 《언행이》 (be) shallow; slight. ¶ 속이 엷은 사람 a shallow fellow.
**엷붉다** (be) light red.
**염**(殮) ⇨ 염습(殮襲).
**염가**(廉價) a cheap 〔low〕 price. ¶ ～로 at low 〔moderate〕 prices; at a bargain; cheap / ～로 팔다 sell 《*a thing*》 cheap 〔at a low price, at a bargain〕/ ～로 사다 buy 《*a thing*》 at a bargain rate. ◉ ～(대)판매 a bargain 〔clearance, special〕 sale; 《재고 정리》 clearance sales: 헌 책 ～ 판매 《광고》 Second-hand books sold cheap. *or* Bargain-priced used books. ～(보급)판 a cheap 〔popular〕 edition. ～품 popular-priced 〔low-priced〕 goods.
**염갱**(塩坑) a salt 〔brine〕 pit.
**염광**(塩鑛) a salt mine 〔quarry〕.
**염교** 〖식물〗 a shallot; a scallion.
**염기**(塩基) 〖화학〗 a (chemical) base. ¶ ～성의 basic; positive / ～화하다 basify. ◉ ～성 반응 basic reaction. ～성 산화물 a basic oxide. ～성암 a basic rock. ～성염 a basic salt. ～성 염료 basic dyestuffs. ～성 탄산염 ceruse. 유기～ an organic base.
**염기**(厭忌) abhorrence; detestation. ～하다 abhor; detest; loathe.
**염낭**(—囊) a (money) pouch; a purse.
**염도**(塩度) salinity.
**염두**(念頭) mind; thought; *one's* attention. ¶ ～를 떠나지 않다 [사람이 주어] be unable to forget; cannot put *something* out of *one's* mind; [사물이 주어] be always in *one's* mind 〔thoughts〕/ ～에 있다 be in *one's* thought 〔mind〕/ ～에 두다 give *one's* mind 〔a thought〕 《to》; keep 〔bear〕 《*something*》 in mind / ～에 두지 않다 do not care 《about》; give no thought 〔heed〕 《to》; take no heed 《of》; leave 《*something*》 out of consideration / ～에 떠오르다 occur to *one* 〔*one's* mind〕; flash 〔come〕 across *one's* mind.
**염라**(閻羅) 〖불교〗 《인도 신화》 *Yama* (of the Hindus); the King of Hell. ◉ ～국 Hades; Hell; the Underworld. ～대왕 the King of Hell.
**염려**(念慮) worry; care; trouble; anxiety; apprehension; fear; uneasiness. ～하다 feel anxiety; be anxious 〔apprehensive, worried〕; worry 《about》. ¶ 아들의 건강을 ～하다 be anxious about *one's* son's health / ～를 끼치다 give trouble 《to》; cause 《*a person*》 anxiety / ～가 되다 be anxious 《about》; worry 《over》; be apprehensive / ～ 마십시오, 다 잘 될 테니 Don't worry! Everything will be all right. / 그 점에 대해서는 ～ 마십시오 You may put your mind at rest on that point. / ～하실 것 없습니다 You have nothing to worry about. / 너무 ～를 끼쳐서 죄송합니다 I am sorry to have caused you so much worry. / 아들이 낙방할까 ～했다 I had misgivings that my son might fail in the examination.
**염력**(念力) 《의지의 힘》 the power of the will; will; 《초능력》 psychokinesis.

**염료**(染料) dyestuffs; dyes; colors; stain. ⇨물감. ◉ ～공업 the dye industry. ～제조 dye making 〔manufacture〕. 인조〔합성〕～ artificial (synthetic) dyes. 천연～ natural dyes. 황화〔산성, 질산염〕～ sulphite 〔acid, nitro〕 dyes.

**염류**(塩類) salts.

**염매**(廉賣) bargain sale; discount 〔cut-rate〕 merchandising. ～하다 sell cheap 〔at a reduced price〕; go cheap. ◉ ～점 a cut-rate 〔discount〕 store. ～품 bargain-〔low-〕priced goods.

**염모**(染毛) hair-dyeing. ◉ ～제 a hair=dye.

**염문**(艶文) a love letter. ＝염서(艶書).

**염문**(艶聞) gossip about *one's* love affair; an episode of love; a romance. ¶ ～이 있다 be associated with a love affair / 그의 ～이 자자하다 His love affair gave rise to scandal.

**염병**(染病) 《장티푸스》 typhoid fever; enteric fever; 《전염병》 an epidemic; a contagious 〔an infectious〕 disease. ¶ ～에 걸리다 catch typhoid fever / ～할 Go to hell !; Curse ! / ～할 자식 Devil take you !

**염복**(艶福) good fortune in love. ◉ ～가 a beau; a ladies man.

**염분**(塩分) salt; salt content; salinity. ¶ ～이 있는 saline; salty / ～을 많이 함유하다 contain much salt / 바닷물에는 다량의 ～이 있다 Sea-water holds much salt in solution.

**염불**(念佛) 〖불교〗 repetition of the sacred name of Amitabha; a Buddhist invocation; a prayer to Amida Buddha. ～하다 pray to Amitabha 〔Amida Buddha〕; say 〔chant〕 a prayer to the Buddha; recite Namu Amida Bul. ¶ 그녀에게 담배는 건강에 해롭다는 것을 이해시키려 했으나 쇠귀에 ～하는 격이었다 I've tried to make her understand that smoking is a danger to health, but it's like talking to a statue in the park.

**염산**(塩酸) hydrochloric acid. ◉ ～가스 hydrochloric acid gas. ～칼륨 potassium chlorate.

**염색**(染色) dyeing; 《현미경용》 staining. ～하다 dye. ◉ ～공 a dyer. ～공장 a dye works; a dyeing house. ～기 a dyeing range 〔machine〕. ～법 a process of dyeing; 《현미경용》 staining techniques 〔procedures〕. ～분체(分體) 〖생물〗 a chromatid. ～질 chromatin; karyotin. ～체 〖생물〗 a chromosome: ～체 입자 a chromiole / 성～체 a sex chromosome / ～체의 구성 chromosomal composition 《of male and female body cells》. 머리 ～약 a hairdye.

**염서**(炎暑) intense heat; the scorching heat of summer. ¶ ～지절(之節) the hot weather; (at this) time of hot summer days.

**염서**(艶書) a love letter; a *billet-doux* 「(F.).

**염세**(厭世) being weary of life 〔the world〕; pessimism; world-weariness. ～하다 be sick of life 〔weary of the world〕; be pessimistic. ¶ 그녀는 ～적이 되었다 She got sick of life. / 그는 ～적인 기질이다 He is pessimistic. ◉ ～가 a pessimist; a misanthrope. ～관 a pessimistic view of life; pessimism. ～자살: ～자살하다 despair of life and kill *oneself;* kill *oneself* in despair; commit suicide out of despair. ～주의 pessimism: ～주의자 a pessimist. ～철학 pessimistic philosophy.

**염소** a goat. ¶ ～의 caprine / ～가 울다 a goat bleats. ◉ ～가죽 goatskin; kid (새끼 염소의): ～ 가죽 장갑 kid gloves. ～새끼 a kid; a young goat; a goatling. ～수염 a goatee. ～자리 〖천문〗 the Goat: Capricorn; Caprincornus. 숫〔암〕～ a he-〔she-〕goat.

**염소**(塩素) 〖화학〗 chlorine (기호 Cl). ¶ ～의 chlorine; chlorous / ～로 살균하다 chlorinate 《the water》. ◉ ～가스 chlorine gas. ～산칼륨 potassium chlorate. ～살균〔처리〕 chlorination. ～수 chlorine water.

**염수**(塩水) brine; salt water. ◉ ～선(選) brine assortment. ～호(湖) a salt=water lake (함수호).

**염습**(殮襲) dressing the deceased for burial; washing and clothing the dead; undertaking 《영》. ～하다 dress the deceased; shroud; wash and clothe a corpse.

**염열**(炎熱) the extreme 〔intense〕 heat (of summer); sultriness.

**염오**(厭惡) loathing; abhorrence. ～하다 detest; loathe; abhor. ¶ ～할〔스러운〕 disgusting; detestable; loathsome / ～감을 품다 have an abhorance of 《*a person*》.

**염원**(念願) *one's* heart's desire; *one's* dearest wish; *one's* prayer 〔wish, solicitude〕. ～하다 desire; wish 《for》. ¶ 오랜 ～ *one's* long-cherished desire / 평화적인 통일에 대한 온 한국인들의 ～ the cherished desire of the whole of the Korean people for peaceful reunification / 우리의 간절한 ~이 성취되었다 Our dearest wish has been answered.

**염의없다** have no sense of honor; be lost to shame; be shameless.

**염장**(塩藏) ~하다 preserve with 〔in〕 salt; salt (down).

**염쟁이**(殮—) an undertaker; a mortician.

**염전**(捻轉) twisting; torsion. ¶ 장~ volvulus; torsion of the intestine.

**염전**(厭戰) war-weariness. ¶ ~ 무드 war-weary mood 《songs》/ ~적이 되다 get weary 〔tired〕 of war.

**염전**(塩田) a saltpan; a salt field 〔farm〕.

**염접** trimming 〔folding over〕 the edges of cloth 〔paper〕 to make them even. ~하다 even up the edges of cloth 〔paper〕 by folding 〔trimming〕.

**염좌**(捻挫) a sprain. ~하다 sprain 《*one's* ankle》; have a sprain 《in *one's* wrist》.

**염주**(念珠) ① 〖불교〗 a (Buddhist) rosary; prayer beads. ¶ ~를 굴리다 count 〔tell〕 *one's* beads (of a rosary). ② 〖식물〗 Job's-tears. ¶ ~ 모양의 torose; torous. ◉ ~나무 a kind of linden. ~알 《한 개》 a bead; 《한 묶음》 the beads of a rosary.

**염증**(炎症) 〖의학〗 inflammation. ¶ ~을 일으키다 become inflamed.

**염증**(厭症) an aversion; a dislike; disgust; a repugnance. ¶ ~이 나다 be weary 《of》; be disgusted 《with》; be tired 〔sick〕 《of》; feel a repugnance 《toward》/ 같은 일에 ~이 나다 be tired of doing the same things.

**염직**(染織) dyeing (and weaving). ~하다 dye (and weave). ◉ ~공장 dye works.

**염천**(炎天) 《날씨》 hot 〔broiling, blistering〕 weather; the blazing 〔scorching〕 sun; 《하늘》 the southern sky. ¶ ~하에 under the burning 〔scorching〕 sun.

**염천**(塩泉) a brine 〔saline〕 spring.

**염출하다**(捻出—) 《생각을》 contrive; devise; work 〔think〕 out 《a plan》; 《돈을》 (manage to) raise 《money》. ¶ 새로운 재원을 ~ hit on a new source of revenue / 채무 변상의 새 방법을 ~ work out a new plan for financing *one's* obligations.

**염치**(廉恥) a sense of shame 〔honor〕. ¶ ~가 있다 have a sense of honor / ~가 없다 have no sense of honor; be lost to shame; be shameless / ~없는 사람 a shameless fellow / ~ 불구하고 …하다 stoop to *do*.

**염탐**(廉探) spying 《upon》; making secret observations. ~하다 spy upon 《the enemy's movements》; feel out 《the situation》; make secret observations. ◉ ~꾼 a spy; a secret agent.

**염통** the heart. = 심장(心臟).

**염포**(殮布) hemp-cloth for shrouding the deceased.

**염해**(塩害) damage from sea wind 〔water〕.

**염화**(塩化) 〖화학〗 chloridation. ~하다 chloridize. ◉ ~납〔연〕 lead chloride. ~물 a chloride: ~물로 처리하다 chloridate. ~수소 hydrogen chloride. ~은〔비닐〕 silver 〔vinyl〕 chloride. ~철 iron chloride. ~칼슘〔나트륨〕 calcium 〔sodium〕 chloride.

**엽견**(獵犬) a hunting dog; a hound.

**엽관운동**(獵官運動) seeking a government post; office hunting 〔seeking〕. ¶ ~을 하는 사람 an office seeker 〔hunter〕; a spoilsman 《미》/ ~을 하다 hunt 〔run〕 for office.

**엽궐련**(葉—) a cigar. ¶ ~을 물고 with a cigar in *one's* mouth 〔between *one's* teeth〕/ ~을 피우다 smoke a cigar; puff at *one's* cigar.

**엽기**(獵奇) hunting bizarrerie 〔the bizarre〕; seeking the strange and different. ~하다 seek 〔hunt〕 the bizarre. ¶ ~적 curiosity-seeking; bizarrerie-seeking / ~적인 살인 사건 a grotesque murder case. ◉ ~문학 bizarre literature. ~소설 a bizarre story. ~심 curiosity. ~취미 a taste for the bizarre.

**엽기**(獵期) the hunting 〔shooting〕 season. = 사냥철.

**엽록소**(葉綠素) 〖식물〗 chlorophyl(l). ¶ ~의 chlorophyllous.

**엽록체**(葉綠體) 〖식물〗 a chloroplast.

**엽상**(葉狀) ¶ ~의 leaf-like; foliated; 〖식물〗 foliaceous; foliar; phylloid. ◉ ~식물 a thallophyte. ~조직 phyllome. ~체 a thallus (*pl.* -es, -li); a frond; phyllome.

**엽색**(獵色) philandering; lechery. ¶ ~꾼 a philanderer; a lecher; a debauchee.

**엽서**(葉書) 《사제》 a postcard; 《관제》 a postal card (★ 영국에서는 관제·사제를 다 같이 postcard라 함). ¶ ~로 by postcard / ~를 내다 send 〔drop〕 a postcard 《to》/ ~로 답하다 answer 〔reply〕 by postcard.

**엽전**(葉錢) 《옛날 화폐》 a brass coin.

**엽조**(獵鳥) a game bird 〔fowl〕.

**엽차**(葉茶) coarse (green) tea.

**엽초**(葉草) leaf-tobacco. 「sheath.

**엽초**(葉鞘) 『식물』 a vagina; a (leaf)

**엽총**(獵銃) a hunting 〔sporting〕 gun; a shotgun; 《새잡이용》 a fowling piece.

**엿** (a) taffy; wheat-gluten. ¶ 엿장수 a taffy seller / 엿가래〔엿가락〕 a stick 〔piece〕 of taffy / 엿을 빨다 suck wheat-gluten / 선로가 엿가락처럼 휘어져 있었다 The rails lay bent and twisted out of shape like taffy. ◉ 엿치기 a taffy-breaking game.

**엿** six. ¶ 엿새 six days; the sixth day of the month (여섯째 날).

**엿기름** dried barley sprouts (used for making taffy); malt. ¶ ～을 만들다 malt. ◉ ～가루 powdered malt.

**엿듣다** listen secretly 《to》; overhear; eavesdrop. ¶ 엿듣는 사람 an eavesdropper / 남의 이야기를 ～ overhear another's talk; eavesdrop on the conversation / 전화를 ～ tap wires / 벽너머로 ～ hear 《another's talk》 over the wall / 엿보거나 엿들어서는 안 된다 You must not peep or overhear.

**엿물** taffy liquid (to be boiled).

**엿밥** lees left after taffy water has been strained; taffy dregs.

**엿보다** steal a glance 《at》; sneak a look 《at》; look 〔glance〕 furtively 《at》; watch on the sly 〔with a furtive eye〕; spy on; watch for; 《틈으로》 peep 〔peek〕 through 〔into, out of〕; take a peep 〔peek〕 《at》; get a peep 《at》; 《미루어 알다》 infer; gather. ¶ 기회를 ～ watch 〔wait〕 for a chance 〔opportunity〕 / 지위를 ～ aspire to the position 《of》 / 아무의 눈치를 ～ study *a person's* face on the sly; cast a furtive glance at *a person* to read *his* mind / 빈틈을 ～ try to catch 《*a person*》 off *his* guard / 도망갈 기회를 ～ watch for an opportunity to run away / 그는 집안을 엿보러 왔다 He came to look the house over. / 그의 말에서 무엇을 엿보았느냐 What did you infer 〔gather〕 from his remarks? / 그의 연설에서 깊은 학식이 엿보였다 His speech evinced great learning.

**영** 《산뜻한 기운》 a clean bright atmosphere 《in a house 〔room〕》. ¶ 영이 돌다 have a clean bright atmosphere about it.

**영**(令) ① an order. ⇨ 명령(命令). ② an ordinance; a law; a decree. ⇨ 법령(法令). ③ ⇨ 약령(藥令).

**영**(零) (a) zero (*pl.* ～s, ～es); a cipher; (a) naught; nothing. ¶ 영점 a zero mark / 106 번 《전화 번호》 one-o=〔zero-, naught-〕six / 3 대 0 으로 이기다 win by three to nothing / 시험에 영점을 받다 get zero 〔no marks〕 in an examination.

**영**(靈) ① 《신령》 a divine 〔hallowed〕 spirit. ② 《영혼》 the spirit; the soul. ¶ 영적 spiritual 《life》 / 영과 육 the spirit and the flesh; body and soul / 죽은 사람의 영을 모시다 worship the departed soul of a dead person.

**영가**(靈歌) a spiritual. ¶ 흑인 ～ Negro spirituals.

**영감**(令監) ① 《노인》 an old 〔elderly〕 man. ¶ 고집쟁이 ～ a stiffnecked old man. ② 《남편》 *one's* husband. ¶ 여보 ～ My dear. ③ 《지체 높은 양반》 lord; sir.

**영감**(靈感) (an) inspiration; 《시인 등의》 afflatus. ¶ ～이 번뜩이다 have an 〔a sudden〕 inspiration / ～을 받다 be inspired 《by》; get 〔draw〕 inspiration 《from》; have a brain wave 《구어》 / ～을 주다 inspire 《*a person*》 / 그에게 갑자기 ～이 떠올랐다 An inspiration burst upon him.

**영걸**(英傑) 《사람》 a great man; a hero; a mastermind; a giant; 《성질》 heroic qualities; heroic character.

**영검**(靈—) God's response to *one's* prayer; miraculous efficacy. ～하다, ～스럽다 (be) miraculous; wonder=working. ¶ 그 신은 ～스럽다는 평판이 자자하다 The god is renowned for his ability to fulfill the wishes of worshippers.

**영겁**(永劫) eternity; perpetuity. ¶ ～ 불변의 eternal; lasting; everlasting.

**영결**(永訣) the last parting; the final farewell; separation by death. ～하다 part forever; bid *one's* last farewell to (the dead). ◉ ～식 a funeral ceremony 〔service〕.

**영계**(—鷄) a spring chicken. ◉ ～백숙 boiled chicken with rice.

**영계**(靈界) the spiritual 〔psychical〕 world; the spiritual realm. ¶ (영매(靈媒)로) ～와 교통하다 communicate with the spirit world.

**영고(성쇠)**(榮枯(盛衰)) rise and fall; prosperity and decline; 「ups and downs 〔vicissitudes〕 of life. ¶ 로마 제국의 ～ the rise and fall of the Roman Empire / ～는 인간 상사다 Every life has its ups and downs.

**영공**(領空) territorial air 〔sky〕; 《a country's》 airspace. ¶ 한국의 ～을 침범하다

violate 「the Korean airspace 〔the territorial sky of Korea〕/ 국적 불명의 비행기가 우리 나라 ～을 비행하고 있다 An unidentified plane is flying over our territory. ◉ ～권 《a country's》 airspace; territorial sky 〔air〕. ～침범 the violation of the territorial sky; an intrusion of 《a country's》 airspace.

**영관**(領官) 〖육군〗 a field 〔field-grade〕 officer. ◉ ～급 the field grade: ～급 장교 a field-grade officer.

> 참고 미국·영국의 영관급 명칭: 「영관(급)」은 소령, 중령, 대령을 뜻하나, 군에 따라 그 호칭이 약간씩 다르다. 「위관급」은 company grade라고 한다.
> ① 미국의 영관: 《육군》 colonel (대령); lieutenant colonel (중령); major (소령); 《해군》 captain (대령); commander (중령); lieutenant commander (소령); 《공군》 colonel (대령); lieutenant colonel (중령); major (소령); 《해병》 육군과 동일.
> ② 영국의 영관: 《육군》 미국과 동일; 《해군》 미국과 동일; 《공군》 group captain (대령); wing commander (중령); squadron leader (소령); 《해병》 미국과 동일.

**영관**(榮冠) the laurels; the crown (of glory); the palm. ¶ 승리의 ～을 쓰다 win the laurels; be crowned with victory.

**영광**(榮光) glory; honor. ～스럽다 (be) glorious; honored; honorable; [서술적] be an honor 《to》.
¶ 신의 ～ the glory of God / ～의 나날들 glory days / ～스럽게도 it is my privilege 《to》/ ～스러운 고립(孤立) a splendid isolation (★ 19세기 영국의 외교 정책) / ～이다〔으로 알다〕 feel honored / ～에 빛나다 be covered in glory; be crowned with glory / 승리의 ～에 빛나다 win a great victory / …할 ～을 누리다 have the honor of 《*do*ing》; have the pleasure 〔honor〕 to 《*do*》/ ～을 가득 안다 be loaded with honors; be covered with glory; hold the distinction of being 《a member》/ …해 주시면 ～이겠습니다 I deem 〔esteem〕 it an honor 〔a favor〕 if you will …. / …하는 것은 내가 ～으로 아는 바이다 it is a great pleasure for me to 《*do*》/ ～입니다 I am honored. *or* You do me proud. / 분에 넘치는 ～입니다 The honor is more than I deserve. / 그와 이야기를 나누는 것만도 ～이다 To converse with him is itself a privilege. / 왕림해 주셔서 ～입니다 I take your visit as a great honor 〔compliment〕. / 여러분에게 말씀드리게 된 것을 큰 ～으로 여깁니다 I deem it a great honor for me to address you. / 이 모임에 참석하게 된 것을 ～으로 생각합니다 I feel honored to attend this meeting. / 내일 보잘것 없는 모임에 참석해 주시면 더없는 ～이겠습니다 The honor would be entirely mine, if you would attend my little party tomorrow.

**영교**(靈交) spiritual communion 《with》. ◉ ～술 spiritualism.

**영구**(永久) lastingness; permanence; eternity. ～하다 (be) lasting; everlasting; permanent; eternal. ¶ ～적 lasting; permanent / ～히 permanently; eternally; everlastingly; for good 《영》; forever; for keeps 《구어》/ ～ 불변의 everlasting / 반～적인 semipermanent 《equipment》/ ～히 한국을 떠나다 leave Korea for good (and all) / ～ 불변하게 남다 remain unchanged forever / ～적인 정책을 세우다 form a permanent policy.
◉ ～성 permanency: ～성이 있는 permanent. ～운동 a perpetual motion. ～자석 a permanent magnet. ～치(齒) *one's* permanent 〔second〕 teeth.

**영구**(靈柩) a coffin; a casket 《미》. ◉ ～차 a (motor) hearse; a funeral car 〔coach〕.

**영국**(英國) England; (Great) Britain; the United Kingdom (생략 U.K.); 《공식명》 the United Kingdom of Great Britain and Northern Ireland (연합왕국); 《영연방》 the British Commonwealth (of Nations); 《대영제국》 the British Empire; 《영국의 여러 섬》 the British Isles. ¶ ～의 English; 《특히 영국 전국토의》 British / ～제의 made in England; English-made; of English make / ～특유의 어(구) a Briticism.
◉ ～국교회 the Church of England; the Anglican Church. ～국기 the Union Jack; the British flag; the Union flag. ～국왕〔여왕〕 the King 〔Queen〕 of England. ～ 방송 협회 the British Broadcasting Corporation (생략 BBC). ～사람 an Englishman; an Englishwoman; 《미》 a Britisher; 《별명》 John Bull; the English [총칭]: ～사람 기질 John-Bullism. ～사투리 Britishism; a British accent. ～왕세자 the Prince of Wales. ～정부 the British Government; Downing Street.

～톤 a British ton; a gross 〔long〕 ton. ～풍 Anglicism; Britishism: ～풍으로 하다 Anglicize. ～항공 British Airways (생략 BA).

> 참고 영국의 여러 명칭: **England** 원래 Great Britain에서 Scotland와 Wales를 제외시킨 부분이지만, 영국 전체를 가리키는 뜻으로도 쓰임. **(Great) Britain** England, Scotland 그리고 Wales를 합친 총칭. **the United Kingdom (of Great Britain and Northern Ireland)** (Great) Britain에다 북아일랜드를 포함시킨 공식 명칭으로서 U.K.로 생략. 이 밖에 the Commonwealth (of Nations) (영연방), the British Empire (영제국—자치령이나 보호령을 포함한 영연방의 별명), the British Isles (영국 제도—U.K.의 지리적 명칭) 등의 호칭이 있음.

**영금** 《곤욕》 bitter humiliation. ¶ ～을 당하다 undergo bitter humiliation.

**영남**(嶺南) Yŏngnam district 〔area〕; Kyŏngsang-do provinces; the southeastern part 〔section〕 of Korea.

**영내**(營內) 〖군사〗 inside barracks. ¶ ～의 within barracks. ◉ ～거주 living in barracks. ～근무 service in barracks. ～생활 a barrack life.

**영내**(領內) the domains; the territory. ¶ ～에(서) within the territory.

**영년**(永年) a long time; many 〔long〕 years; [부사적] for many years; for ages; for a long time.

**영농**(營農) engaging in agriculture; farming. ～하다 farm; work on a farm; be engaged in agriculture. ¶ ～의 기계화 mechanization 「in farming 〔of farm methods〕 / 마을의 청년들은 모여서 ～의 경험에 관해 이야기하였다 The young people of the village got together and talked about their experience of farming. ◉ ～가 an agriculturist; a farmer. ～자금 farming funds 〔loans〕: ～자금을 방출하다 release 《the 550 billion won of》 farming loans. 과학～ scientific farming.

**영단**(英斷) 《결단》 a decisive judgment; a wise decision; a firm resolution; 《최종적인》 a final decision; 《조치》 a drastic measure; a resolute step. ¶ ～을 내리다 take 「a decisive step 〔a drastic measure〕 / 당신의 ～을 바라오 The decision rests with you. *or* It is up to you to decide. / 이 일은 총리의 ～을 필요로 한다 This matter calls for a final decision 〔judgment〕 by the prime minister.

**영단**(營團) a corporation; a management group 〔organization〕.

**영달**(榮達) distinction; advancement; rise (in the world). ¶ ～을 바라다 「hanker after 〔aim at〕 distinction; aspire to 〔after〕 high honors / 재능이 있으면 ～의 길이 있다 All honors are open to talent.

**영당**(影堂) 〖불교〗 《영정을 모신》 a shrine 〔hall〕 where the portrait 〔memorial tablet〕 of a founder of a religious sect or a high priest is being worshiped.

**영대**(永代) eternal generations; generations unto eternity; perpetuity. ◉ ～소유권 perpetual ownership; perpetuity. ～재산 perpetuity. ～차지(借地) a perpetual leasehold; a fee farm 《영》: ～차지권 a perpetual lease / ～차지인 a perpetual leasee; a life tenant.

**영도**(零度) zero (degrees); (the) freezing point. ¶ ～ 이하의 기후 sub-zero weather / ～ 이상으로 올라가다 rise above zero / ～ 이하로 내려가다 drop 〔fall〕 below zero.

**영도**(領導) leading; guidance; direction. ～하다 take the lead; lead. ¶ …의 ～하에 under the leadership of… / ～적 역할을 하다 play the part of the leader; take the lead; play a leading part 《in》 / 그는 정계에서 ～적 역할을 하고 있다 He plays a leading role 〔part〕 in the political world. ◉ ～자 a leader. ～정신 a leading spirit; a governing principle.

**영동**(嶺東) Yŏngdong district 〔area〕; Kangwŏn-do provinces; the middle=eastern part 〔section〕 of Korea.

**영락**(零落) ruin; downfall. ～하다 come down in the world; go to ruin; be ruined; lose *one's* fortune; fall low; be in reduced circumstances; be reduced to poverty 〔want〕. ¶ ～한 생활 a wretched life / ～한 사람 a ruined man 〔person〕; a man of broken fortunes / ～한 일가(一家) a family now fallen on evil days / ～되어 있다 be down on *one's* luck; be in very low circumstances; live in poverty / 그는 아주 ～한 몸이다 He is a mere wreck of his former self. / 내 비록 ～은 했지만 그래도 염치는 안다 I have fallen pretty low, but still I am a man of honor.

**영락없다**(零落—) be invariably right; (be) infallible; unfailing. ¶ 영락없이 without any slip; without fail; infallibly; for sure / 계산이 ～ be no mistake in *one's* account / 그는 영락없이 과녁을 맞힌다 He never misses the target / 네 모습을 보니 영락없는 거지로 구나 You look like a begger, every inch of you.

**영령**(英領) British territory 〔possession, colony〕; 《직할 식민지》 a Crown Colony; 《자치령》 a British Dominion. ¶ 구～ an ex-British 〔an former British〕 territory / ～버진 제도 the British Virgin Islands.

**영령**(英靈) the「spirit 〔soul〕 of the departed; 《군인의》 souls of the departed war heroes; the spirits of the war dead; 《애국 지사의》 the fallen patriots. ¶～이여 고이 잠드소서 May your noble soul rest in peace !

**영롱**(玲瓏) ～하다 (be) clear and bright; lucid; serene. ¶ ～한 보석 a clear and bright gem.

**영리**(營利) profit; gain; profit-making; money making. ¶ ～적인 profit-〔money-〕making / ～를 도외시하고 without any thought of「gain 〔profit〕/ ～를 생각하지 않다 have no thought of gain / ～에 급급하다 be intent on gain; be engrossed in money-making / 우리는 단지 ～만을 위해 사업을 하고 있는 것은 아니다 We are not in business only for commercial gain.
◉ ～단체 a profit-making organization: 비～단체 a nonprofit organization. ～법인 a profit-making corporation. ～사업 a profit-making enterprise; a commercial enterprise. ～자본 lucrative capital. ～주의 commercialism. ～회사 a commercial company.

**영리하다**(怜悧—) (be) clever; bright; wise; intelligent; smart.

> 용법 **clever** 모든 것을 배우고 이해하는 능력면에서 뛰어나며, 머리의 회전이 빠름. 인격면이 아니라 지능면만을 칭찬하는 뉘앙스를 풍김. 손발이나 몸을 재치 있게 놀린다는 뜻으로도 쓰임. **bright** 이해나 반응하는 작용이 빠르며 똘똘한 어린이나 손아랫사람에 대해서 씀. **wise** 사려·영민한 지혜·판단력 등을 갖춘 총명함을 가리키는 격조 높고 정중한 말. **intelligent** 교육·지식이 없어도 천부적으로 지성이 높고 이해력이 있다는 뜻. **smart** 약빠르고 빈틈없는 실무 능력이 있다는 뜻.

¶ 영리해 보이는 intelligent-looking / 영리한 아이 a bright child / 영리한 체하는 사람 a knowing chap / 영리한 체하다 try to be smart / 영리해지다 grow wise; gain in wisdom / 그는 영리하지 못하다 He lacks sense. / 그는 영리해서 그런일은 하지 않는다 He is too wise to do such things.

**영림**(營林) forest「administration 〔management〕; afforestation; forestry.
◉ ～사업 a forestry enterprise. ～서(署) a local forestry office.

**영마루**(嶺—) the top of a mountain pass.

**영매**(靈媒) a (spirit, psychic) medium.

**영매하다**(英邁—) (be) brave and sagacious; wise and masterful.
¶ 영매한 군주 a great monarch; an illustrious「sovereign 〔lord〕.

**영면**(永眠) eternal「sleep 〔rest〕; death. ～하다 pass away; die; sleep the long sleep; take *one's* last sleep; rest in the grave.

**영명**(令名) a「fair 〔good, respectable, celebrated〕 name; good repute; fame. ¶ ～ 높은 highly renowned; celebrated; noted; famous / 석학(碩學)으로서 ～이 높다 be「well-known 〔distinguished〕 as a great scholar.

**영묘**(靈廟) a mausoleum (*pl.* ～s, -lea); 「a shrine.

**영묘하다**(靈妙—) (be) ethereal; miraculous; mysterious: exquisite; inexplicable (설명할 수 없는). ¶ 영묘한 가락 an exquisite piece of music.

**영문** 《이유·원인》 (a) reason; (a) cause (원인); 《근거》 grounds; a ground; 《형편》 circumstances; the case. ¶ 무슨 ～으로 Why... ?; Why〔How〕 is it (that)... ? ; On what grounds... ? ; What...for ? ; 《구어》 How come... ? / 무슨〔어떤〕 ～인지 for some (unknown) reason; somehow (or other) / ～ 모를 이야기를 지껄이다 talk「nonsense 〔rubbish〕/ 왜 그런 짓을 했는지 그 ～을 말하여라 Tell me why you did such a thing ? / 대체 무슨 ～으로 그것이 잘못되었다고 말하는거냐 On what grounds do you say that it is wrong ? / 무슨 ～인지 어디 이야기 좀 해 봐라 Tell me what the circumstances are. / 무슨 ～으로 참석자들이 이리 적을까 Why are there so few people present ? / 무슨 ～인지도 모르고 그를 따라갔다 I followed him, not knowing exactly why. / 그가 안 오는 것은 무슨 ～일까 What's the matter with him that he doesn't come ?

**영문**(英文) 《영어》 English; 《영어 문장》 an English sentence. ¶ ~으로 쓰다 write 《a letter》 in English / ~으로 읽다 read 《a story》 in English / ~을 한글로 번역하다 translate English into Korean / 그녀는 ~을 잘 쓴다 She writes good English. *or* Her written English is very good. ◉ ~기자 a writer of English (on the editorial staff). ~소설 a novel 〔story〕 in English; an English novel. ~타자 typing in English. ~편지 a letter in English. ~한역(韓譯) translation from English into Korean; (an) English-Korean translation. ~해석 interpreting an English text.

**영문**(營門) the (main) gate of a barracks 〔camp〕.

**영문법**(英文法) English grammar. ¶ 내가 사용했던 ~책 중에서 가장 좋은 것 the best English grammar book I've ever used.

**영문학**(英文學) English literature. ¶ ~을 전공하다 specialize 〔major 《미》〕 in English literature. ◉ ~과 the department of English (language and) literature; 《과정》 the English (language and) literature course. ~자〔사〕 a scholar 〔a history〕 of English literature.

**영물**(靈物) a spiritual 〔sacred〕 being. ◉ ~학 pneumatology.

**영미**(英美) England and America; Britain and the United States. ¶ ~의 English 〔British〕 and American; British-American; Anglo-American. ◉ ~법 Anglo-American law. ~인 the English and the American.

**영민**(英敏) ~하다 (be) bright; clever; intelligent. ¶ ~한 두뇌 a clear head; a keen intellect / 머리가 ~한 사람 a nimble-witted person.

**영법**(泳法) a swimming style 〔form〕.

**영봉**(靈峰) a sacred mountain.

**영부인**(令夫人) 《your, his》 esteemed wife. ¶ 김 박사와 ~ Dr. and Mrs. Kim.

**영빈관**(迎賓館) a guest house for VIPs from abroad; the (State) Guest House.

**영사**(映寫) projection (on a screen). ~하다 project 〔show, throw〕 《a picture》 on the screen. ◉ ~기 a (film) projector. ~기사 a projectionist. ~막 a (projection) screen. ~시간 the running time 《for a film》. ~실 a projection room 〔booth〕.

**영사**(領事) a consul. ¶ ~의 consular / 카이로 주재 한국 ~ the Korean Consul at Cairo / 그는 L.A.주재 한국 총~가 되었다 He has been appointed Korean consul general (stationed) in L.A. ◉ ~관 a consulate: ~관원 a consular official; the staff of a consulate 〔총칭〕. ~재판(권) consular-jurisdiction. ~조약 a consular agreement. ~(증명) 송장(送狀) 〖무역〗 a consular invoice. 대리~ an acting consul. 명예~ an honorary consul. 부~ a vice-consul.

**영상**(映像) an image; a reflection; 〖TV〗 a picture; 《그림자》 a silhouette; 《거울·수면 상의》 a reflection. ¶ 흐린 ~ a blurred image; a picture out of focus / 선명한 ~ a clear image 〔picture〕 / 레이더에 비치는 ~ a blip on the radar screen / TV의 선명한 ~ a clear picture on a TV screen. ◉ ~회의 a videoconferencing. 국립 ~ 제작소 the National Film Production Center.

**영상**(零上) above zero. ¶ ~ 5도, 5 degrees above zero.

**영상**(領相) 〖고제도〗 the Premier; the Prime Minister.

**영생**(永生) eternal life; immortality. ~하다 live eternally; enjoy immortality.

**영선**(營繕) building and repairs. ~하다 build and repair. ◉ ~과 the building and repairs section. ~비 building and repairing 〔maintenance〕 expenses.

**영성**(靈性) divine nature; divinity; spirituality.

**영성체**(領聖體) 〖가톨릭〗 (Holy) Communion. ◉ ~송(頌) a communion antiphon.

**영세**(永世) eternity; everlasting; permanence. ⇨ 영원. ¶ ~의 permanent; eternal; everlasting. ◉ ~중립 permanent neutrality: ~ 중립국 a permanent neutral state 〔country〕.

**영세**(領洗) 〖가톨릭〗 baptism; christening. ⇨ 세례. ¶ ~를 베풀다 baptize / ~를 받다 accept 〔receive〕 baptism; be baptized 〔christened〕.

**영세**(零細) being small 〔petty〕. ~하다 (be) small; trifling; petty. ¶ ~한 자금으로는 그들과 경쟁할 수 없다 Having only small funds we can't compete with them. ◉ ~가정 a poor family. ~기업 a small business; a small-scale enterprise. ~농가 a petty farmer; a small-income farmer. ~민 the poor (and needy); the destitute 〔indigent〕; the poverty-stricken people: 도시 ~민 the low-income citizens / ~민을 돕다 relieve the poor; give aid the poor. ~어민 a poorly-equipped 〔destitute〕 fisherman. ~업자 a small-scale businessman.

**영속**(永續) everlastingness; long continuance; perpetuation; long duration; imperishableness (불멸의). ~하다 last long; remain permanently; continue forever. ¶ ~적, ~성 있는 lasting; permanent; perpetual / ~하지 않다 be of short duration; be short-lived / 이 장사는 ~성이 없다 This business will not last 〔prosper〕 long.

**영송**(迎送) meeting and farewell. ~하다 meet and send off.

**영수**(領收) receipt. ~하다 receive. ¶ 일금 만 원을 틀림없이 ~하였습니다 I acknowledge receipt of ₩10,000. *or* 《증서에》 Received 《from 〔of〕 *a person*》 the sum of 10,000 won.

◉ ~인 a receiver; a recipient. ~증 a receipt; a voucher: ~증 주고 받기 운동 a receipt-giving-and-taking drive / ~증 보관함 a box for receipts / ~증을 받다 get a receipt (made out) / ~증을 써주다 give 《*a person*》 a receipt 《for》; make out a receipt 《for the money》. ~필 《표기》 Received. *or* Paid.

**영수**(領袖) a leader; a chief; a head. ¶ 정당〔파벌〕의 ~ a leader of a political party 〔faction〕.

**영시**(英詩) English poetry 〔verse〕 [총칭]; an English poem; a poem in English.

**영시**(零時) 《자정》 (twelve o'clock) midnight; 《정오》 noon (★ 하루 24시간제를 사용하는 군대 등에서는 오전 영시를 0000이라 쓰고 zero hours라고 읽음). ¶ ~ 30분 twelve thirty / 오전 ~에 at (twelve o'clock) midnight; at zero hours.

**영식**(令息) 《your, his, her》 esteemed son.

**영아**(嬰兒) an infant; a baby; a new-born child. ◉ ~사망률 (rate of) infant mortality; the death rate of infants. ~살해 infanticide: ~ 살해범 an infanticide; a child murderer.

**영악하다** (be) smart; sharp; shrewd. ¶ 영악한 아이 a smart child.

**영악하다**(獰惡—) (be) fierce; ferocious; cruel; tough. ¶ 영악한 동물 a fierce animal.

**영안실**(靈安室) a mortuary (of a hospital); a hospital's mortuary. ¶ 병원 ~에 안치하다 place a dead body in a mortuary of a hospital.

**영애**(令愛) 《your, his, her》 esteemed daughter. ¶ A씨의 ~ Mr. A's daughter.

**영약**(靈藥) a miraculous medicine; a wonder drug 《미》; a sovereign 〔marvelous〕 remedy.

**영양**(令孃) = 영애(令愛).

**영양**(羚羊) 『동물』 an antelope; a goral.

**영양**(營養) nutrition; nourishment. ¶ ~이 있는〔없는〕 식품 food rich 〔lacking〕 in nutrition; nourishing 〔unnourishing〕 food / ~이 고르게 들어 있는 식사 nutritionally balanced diet / ~이 좋다 be nutritious 〔nourishing〕; be well-fed〔-nourished〕 / ~이 나쁘다 be ill-fed 〔unnourished〕 / 충분한 ~의 섭취는 건강에 매우 중요하다 Good nutrition is important for good health. / 이 음식은 너에게 필요한 모든 ~을 공급하도록 되어 있다 This food is supposed to provide all the nutrition you need.

◉ ~가(價) nutritive 〔nutritional〕 value; 《be low in》 food value: ~가가 높은 of high nutritive value; highly nutritious / ~가가 적은 음식 food of poor nutritive value. ~과다 supernutrition; overnourishment. ~물〔분〕 a nutritious 〔nourishing〕 substance; a nutriment. ~사(士) a nutrition technician; a nutritionist; a dietitian; a dietician. ~상태 nutritive conditions. ~섭취량 (a) caloric intake. ~소 a nutrient. ~식 a nourishing meal 〔food〕. ~연구소 a dietetic laboratory. ~요법 a dietary cure. ~장애 nutrition lesion 〔disorder〕. ~제 a medicine for promoting nutrition; a tonic; a nutrient. ~지수 an index of nutrition. ~학 the science of nutrition; dietetics.

**영양부족**(營養不足) undernourishment; insufficient 〔low, imperfect〕 nutrition. ¶ ~의 ill-fed; poorly fed; undernourished 〔underfed〕 《babies》 / ~으로 인해 through lack of nourishment.

**영양실조**(營養失調) unbalanced nutrition; malnutrition. ¶ ~의 underfed / ~에 빠지다 suffer from malnutrition.

**영어**(英語) the English language; English; an English word (단어). ¶ 고대〔중세, 근대〕 ~ Old 〔Middle, Modern〕 English / 현대 ~ current 〔present-day〕 English / 표준 ~ standard English / 일상 ~ everyday English / 실용〔시사〕 ~ practical 〔current〕 English / 상업 ~ business 〔commercial〕 English / 미국〔영국〕~ American 〔British〕 English / ~(권) 국민 an English-speaking people / ~의 English / ~ 실력 *one's* knowledge of English / 산 ~ living English / 영어다운 ~ idiomatic English / 뉴욕 억양의 ~ English with a New York accent / ~의 조기 교육 early-childhood

English education 〔teaching〕 / ～가 늘다 improve in *one's* English / ～로 쓰다〔말하다〕 write 〔speak〕 in English / ～를 잘 하다〔가 서투르다〕 be a good 〔poor〕 speaker of English (회화에서); be good 〔poor〕 at English / ～를 다시 공부하다 brush up *one's* English / ～를 유창하게 말하다 speak 「English fluently 〔fluent English〕 / 개는 ～로 무어라 하는가 What is in English for "*kae*"? / 이것을 ～로 무엇이라고 합니까 What do you call this in English? / ～를 할 줄 압니까 Do you speak English? *or* Can you speak English? / ～ 수업은 주 6 시간이다 We have six English lessons 〔classes〕 a week.

◉ ～강습 a (short) course of English; an English class. ～교육 the teaching of English; English(-language) teaching: ～ 교육법 a method of teaching English. ～권 the English-speaking world 〔community〕: ～권의 사람들 English-speaking people. ～극 a theatrical performance given in English. ～서한 a letter (written) in English. ～선생 a teacher of English (language); an English teacher (★ 「영어 선생」은 an Énglish teacher이고, an English téacher는 「영국인 선생」의 뜻). ～소설 an English novel; a novel in English. ～시험 an examination in English. ～연설 an English speech. ～잡지〔신문〕 an English magazine 〔journal, newspaper〕 ～학 English philology 〔linguistics〕. ～학과 the department of English language. ～회화 English conversation: 그녀는 ～ 회화를 잘 한다 She is good at English conversation. / ～ 회화 학교 an English conversation school.

> 참고 영어 교육에 관련된 말로 TOEFL, TOEIC 등과 같은 약어를 자주 듣게 된다. 참고로 몇 개를 아래에 열거한다.
> • **TOEFL** [tóufl] *T*est *of E*nglish as a *F*oreign *L*anguage (미국 유학생을 위한 영어 학력 테스트).
> • **TOEIC** [tóuik] *T*est *of E*nglish for *I*nternational *C*ommunication (국제 커뮤니케이션 영어 능력 테스트).
> • **TESL** [tésl] *T*eaching *E*nglish as a *S*econd *L*anguage (제2 언어로서의 영어 교육법).
> • **TESOL** [tíːsɔl, tésl] *T*eachers of *E*nglish to *S*peakers of *O*ther *L*anguages (타국 언어 사용자에게 영어를 가르치는 교사).

**영업**(營業) 《업무》 business; 《장사》 trade; 《판매》 sales; 《운영》 operation(s). ～하다 do 〔carry on〕 business; run 《a liquor store》; trade 〔deal〕 in 《cotton》; 《업으로 삼다》 make a business of 《photography》.

¶ ～상의 비밀 a trade secret / ～을 하고 있다 be in business; be open for business / ～을 시작하다 open 〔commence〕 business / ～을 쉬다 suspend business; close *one's* store / ～을 허가하다 authorize 《*a person*》 to carry on the business / ～중 《게시》 Open. *or* We're open. / 정상 ～중 《게시》 Business as usual. / 저 사람은 무슨 ～을 하고 있나요 What line of business is he in? / ～ 허가가 나지 않았다 No license was granted 〔given〕 for the business. / 그 가게는 ～을 하고 있는가 Is the store open? / 저 가게는 일요일엔 ～하지 않는다 That store is closed on Sundays. / 일요일에는 ～하지 않습니다 We don't open on Sundays. (상점인 경우) *or* We don't do business on Sundays. (회사인 경우) / 그 회사는 심각한 ～ 부진 상태에 빠져 있다 The company is caught up in a serious business slump. / 「토요일에는 몇 시까지 ～합니까」—「10시까지 ～합니다」 "How late are you open on Saturday?"—"We're open until 10."

◉ ～감찰 a business 〔trade〕 license. ～금지 prohibition of business. ～방침 a business policy: 회사의 ～방침을 정하다 set company policies. ～방해 obstructing 《*a person's*》 business; interference with 《*a person's*》 business: ～을 방해하다 obstruct 〔interfere with〕 《*a person's*》 business / 거기 주차하지 마시오. ～방해가 됩니다 Don't park your car there. It's in our way. ～보고〔연도〕 a business report 〔year〕. ～부 the business 〔sales〕 department: ～부장 a sales 〔business〕 manager. ～비 working 〔operating, running, business〕 expenses. ～성적〔실적〕 business 〔trading〕 results 〔performance〕: 우리 회사의 후반기 ～ 성적은 매우 양호하였다 Our company has done very good business during the last half year. ～세 a business tax. ～소 a place of business; a business office: 임시 ～소 a temporary office 〔place of business〕. ～소득 operating income. ～시간 business 〔office〕 hours: ～시간 오전 9시부터 오후 7시까지 《게시》 Open from 9 a.m. to 7 p.m. *or* Operation hours: 9:00−19:00. ∼안내 a business guide; a catalog 〔pamphlet〕 (describing *one's* business). ∼외 손익 incidental profit and loss. ∼외 수입 a non-operating income. ∼이윤 operating profit. ∼자 a business manager; a trader. ∼자본 a working capital. ∼자산 stock-in-trade. ∼장소 a business site; a place of business. ∼종목 the line 〔kind〕 of business. ∼주 a business proprietor. ∼허가 a commercial permit 〔license〕; a business license: ∼ 허가원(願) application for a business license / ∼허가를 받다 secure a license to operate. ∼활동 business activities.

**영업권**(營業權) right of trade 〔business〕; goodwill. ¶ 가게의 ∼을 넘기다 transfer the goodwill of *one's* store / ∼을 팔다 sell out *one's* business; sell the goodwill 《of a shop》.

**영업용**(營業用) ¶ ∼ 기물 office furniture / ∼ 자산 operating assets / ∼ 자동차 cars kept for business (purposes) / 이런 종류의 용기는 이미 ∼으로 사용되고 있다 Containers of this kind are already in commercial use.

**영업정지**(營業停止) suspension of business; business suspension. ∼하다 suspend business; close down. ¶ 15일에서 3개월간의 ∼ business suspension ranging from 15 days to three months / ∼가 되다 be ordered to suspend business; be temporarily closed down.

**영역**(英譯) an English translation 〔version〕. ∼하다 translate 〔put, render〕 into English. ¶ …의 ∼ an English translation 〔version〕 of… / 이것은 박경리 소설의 ∼이다 This is an English translation 〔version〕 of a novel by Pak Kyŏngri. / 다음 글을 ∼하라 Put 〔Translate〕 the following sentences into English. ◉ ∼자 a translator (of Korean) into English. 국문∼ translation from Korean into English; Korean-English translation.

**영역**(領域) 《영토》 a territory; a domain; 《학문·활동 등의》 a field; a sphere; a realm; a line (전문의); a province. ¶ 과학의 ∼ the domain 〔sphere, realm〕 of science / ∼을 넘다〔밖이다〕 「be beyond 〔lie outside〕 the province 《of》; be out of the sphere 〔domain〕 《of》 / ∼을 정하다 fix the territory 〔domain〕 / 아무의 ∼을 침해하다 encroach 〔infringe〕 on *a person's* province / 그는 이 ∼의 전문가이다 He is an expert in this field. / 이것은 전문가의 ∼이다 This is in the province of the specialist. / 그 비행기는 타국의 ∼을 침범했다 The plane has violated 〔intruded into〕 the territory of another country. / 그것은 내 (전문) ∼이 아니다 That is not 「my field 〔in my line〕. *or* That's outside my field 〔sphere〕. *or* That's out of my domain.

**영역**(靈域) sacred ground; holy precincts; a holy district 〔area〕.

**영영**(永永) for good (and all); forever; perpetually; permanently; eternally; 《부정》 at all; utterly; in the least. ¶ 고국을 ∼ 떠나다 leave *one's* homeland for good / 그한테서 ∼ 소식이 없다 I have heard nothing from him.

**영예**(榮譽) 《명예》 honor; glory; 《명성》 fame; renown. ∼롭다, ∼스럽다 (be) honorable; glorious. ¶ ∼로운 날 a glorious 〔splendid〕 day / 국가의 ∼ the glory of a nation / …을 ∼로 여기다 feel 〔consider〕 《it》 an honor to *do* / 그는 ∼를 독차지하였다 Honors were showered upon him. / 이보다 더 큰 ∼는 없을 것이다 No greater glory could be gained than this. / 그것은 저로서는 크나큰 ∼입니다 It's a great honor 〔privilege〕 for me. / 다년간에 걸친 노력의 결과 그는 오늘의 ∼로운 지위를 얻었다 By dint of many years' strenuous effort, he has won the honorable position he now occupies.

**영외**(營外) outside barracks. ¶ ∼ 거주하다 take *one's* lodgings outside barracks.

**영욕**(榮辱) glory and 〔or〕 shame; honor 「and 〔or〕 disgrace.

**영웅**(英雄) a hero (*pl.* ∼es); a great man. ¶ ∼적 heroic / ∼답게 like a hero; heroically / ∼적 행위 a heroic deed; an act of heroism / 국민적 ∼ a national hero / …을 ∼화하다 make a hero of… / 그는 ∼다운 기질이 있다 He is cast in heroic mold. / ∼은 색을 좋아한다 All great men are also great lovers 〔womanizers〕. / 그는 ∼답게 죽었다 He died a hero 〔a hero's death〕. ◉ ∼담〔전〕 an epic; the story of hero. ∼숭배 hero worship. ∼주의 heroism.

**영원**(永遠) eternity; permanence; perpetuity; immortality (불멸). ∼하다 (be) eternal; permanent; everlasting; immortal; perpetual. ¶ ∼히 eternally; perpetually; forever; permanently; for good / ∼한 평화 a permanent peace / ∼한 사랑 everlasting love / ∼한 생명

〔진리〕 eternal life 〔truth〕 / ∼한 계획을 세우다 form 〔make〕 a permanent plan / ∼히 사라지다 leave 《a place》 never to return / 이름을 ∼히 남기다 perpetuate 〔immortalize〕 *one's* name / 예술은 ∼하다 Art is eternal. / 그녀는 ∼히 잠들었다 She passed away. *or* She went to her eternal rest. ◉ ∼성 eternal nature; eternity; perpetuity.

**영위**(營爲) management; operation; running. ∼하다 run; operate; manage; carry on; conduct. ¶ 정직한 생활을 ∼하다 lead an honest life; live honestly.

**영유**(領有) possession. ∼하다 possess; get 〔be in〕 possession of. ¶ …의 ∼로 되다 fall into 《*a person's*》 hands; be annexed to / 그 섬은 전승국이 ∼하게 되었다 That island was annexed to the victorious nation. ◉ ∼권 dominium. ∼지〔물〕 a possession.

**영육**(靈肉) spirit and flesh; body and soul. ¶ ∼의 싸움 a conflict between soul 〔spirit〕 and body.
◉ ∼일치 the unity 〔oneness, harmony〕 of body and soul; the union of body and soul.

**영의정**(領議政) 〖고제도〗 a prime minister 《of the Choson Dynasty》.

**영이별**(永離別) a lifelong separation 〔parting〕. ∼하다 part for life 〔forever〕; part 《from *a person*》 never to meet again. ¶ 이것이 ∼이 될지도 모른다 This may be our last meeting.

**영인**(影印) a photographic reproduction; 《인쇄물》 phototypography. ∼하다 photoprint; print 〔reproduce〕 by phototypography. ◉ ∼본 a photographic edition.

**영일**(寧日) a quiet 〔peaceful〕 day.
¶ ∼이 없다 Not a single day passes quietly. / 공무로 다망하여 ∼이 없다 Pressed by official business, I have hardly a moment to call my own.

**영자**(英字) a letter of the English alphabet; an English letter. ◉ ∼신문 a newspaper in English; an English (=language) paper.

**영작문**(英作文) 《학과목》 English composition; 《쓴 것》 an English composition; an essay (written) in English. ¶ ∼을 쓰다 write an English composition; make a composition in English. ◉ 자유∼ free English composition.

**영장**(令狀) a warrant; a writ; a capias. ¶ 구속∼ a warrant of arrest / 소집∼ a call-up paper 〔card〕 / 소환∼ a writ of summons / 수색∼ a search warrant / ∼에 의해 구속되다 be arrested on a warrant / ∼을 발부하다〔청구하다〕 issue 〔request〕 a warrant 《for *a person's* arrest》 / ∼을 집행하다 serve a warrant 〔writ〕 on 《*a person*》 / ∼ 없이는 가택 수색을 못합니다 You can't search my house without a warrant.
◉ ∼집행 the execution of a warrant.

**영장**(靈長) a supreme creature; the lord of (all) creature. ¶ 인간은 만물의 ∼이다 Man is the lord of (all) creation. ◉ ∼류 〖동물〗 Primates.

**영재**(英才) 《재능》 talent; genius; 《사람》 a brilliant 〔gifted〕 person; a man of talent; a talent; a genius (*pl.* ∼es).
¶ 그 학교는 많은 ∼를 배출했다 That school has turned out 「a lot of 〔many〕 talented men.
◉ ∼교육 special education for the gifted; the talent education.

**영적**(靈的) spiritual; incorporeal.
¶ ∼ 교류 spiritual sympathy / ∼ 생활 the spiritual 〔inner〕 life / ∼ 교감 spiritual communion.

**영전**(榮轉) a promotional transfer; promotion; preferment. ∼하다 get 〔be〕 promoted to 《a higher post》; 「be transferred 〔get a transfer〕 to higher post. ¶ 본사로 ∼되다 be transferred to the head office on promotion / ∼을 축하 드립니다 Let me congratulate you on your promotion. / 그는 뉴욕 지점장으로 ∼되었다 He was promoted to the head of the New York office.

**영전**(靈前) ¶ ∼에 before the spirit of the departed 〔deceased〕 / ∼에 바치다 offer 《a wreath》 to the spirit of the departed / ∼에 머리 숙여 기도하다 bow before the deceased and pray.

**영점**(零點) ① 《무득점》 (a) zero; nothing; no marks; no point. ¶ 답안지에 ∼을 주다 put (a) zero on 《a student's》 paper / 수학에 ∼을 받다 get zero in mathematics / 경기에 ∼으로 지다 lose a game without a single point. ② 《빙점》 freezing point. ③ 《무능·무성과》 nothing; nought; a failure. ¶ 그는 실업가로서는 ∼이다 As a businessman he is a failure.

**영접**(迎接) welcome; reception; meeting. ∼하다 welcome; receive; meet.
¶ ∼을 받다 be met 〔greeted, received〕 《at the airport》 / ∼하러 나가다 go out to meet 《*a person*》.

**영정**(影幀) a (scroll of ) portrait.

**영조**(營造) construction; building. ∼하

다 construct; build.
◉ ~물 an establishment; a building; a structure; [총칭] public works.

**영조**(靈鳥) a sacred bird.

**영존**(永存) remaining forever; existing permanently. ~하다 remain 〔last〕 forever; exist permanently.

**영주**(永住) permanent residence. ~하다 settle down 《in》; reside 〔settle〕 permanently 《in》; make *one's* permanent home 《at, in》. ¶ ~의 settled; resident / 그는 브라질에 ~하였다 He made Brazil his permanent home. / 그들은 장차 미국에 ~할 생각이다 They are planning to settle down in America in the future.
◉ ~권 denizenship; permanent residentship; the right of permanent residence: ~권을 얻다 be denizened; obtain permanent residentship. ~민 permanent residents; settlers. ~자 a permanent resident; a denizen. ~지 *one's* permanent home; a place of permanent residence; a permanent domicile.

**영주**(英主) a wise ruler; an illustrious monarch.

**영주**(領主) a (feudal) lord; 《장원주》 the lord of manor.

**영지**(領地) ① = 영토. ② 《봉토》 a fief; a feud; feudal territory.

**영지**(靈地) a sacred place; a holy ground.

**영진**(榮進) (achieving) promotion. ~하다 achieve promotion; be promoted.

**영창**(映窓) 《한옥의 미닫이》 a paper window; window slides.

**영창**(詠唱) 〖음악〗 an aria.

**영창**(營倉) 〖군사〗 a guardhouse; (a) detention barrack; a military jail 〔cell〕. ¶ 3일간 ~에 갇히다 be confined in the guardhouse for three days.

**영천**(靈泉) a magical fountain; 《온천》 a hot-spring with miraculous efficacy. ¶ 불로불사의 ~ a fountain of (eternal) youth.

**영철**(英哲) 《성질》 great discernment; wisdom; perspicacity; 《사람》 a man of great discernment; a wizard. ~하다 (be) wise and great; sagacious; perspicacious.

**영치**(領置) provisional holding; keeping in custody. ~하다 detain; place in the custody 《of the prison officer》.
◉ ~물 money and personal belongings deposited by inmates.

**영탄**(詠嘆) 《읊조림》 recitation; recital; 《감탄》 exclamation; admiration. ~하다 recite 《a poem》; exclaim; admire.

**영토**(領土) (a) territory; (a) dominion; (a) domain. ¶ ~의 territorial / 한국 ~에서 on Korean soil; in Korean territory / 우리의 ~ 내에서 within our territory / ~적 야심을 품다 have 〔harbor〕 territorial ambitions / ~를 획득〔점령〕하다 acquire 〔seize〕 territory / 타국의 ~를 침범하다 encroach upon the territory of another country / ~를 확장〔할양〕하다 extend 〔cede〕 *one's* territory / 우리는 어떠한 나라도 우리 ~를 침범하지 못하게 할 것이다 No country shall violate 〔invade〕 our soil.
◉ ~권 territorial rights. ~문제 the territorial problems. ~보전 maintenance of the territorial integrity. ~분쟁 a territorial dispute. ~주권 territorial sovereignty; sovereignty upon land. ~침범 encroachment upon the territory of another country. ~확장 expansion of territory; territorial aggrandizement; territorial expansion: ~확장주의 expansionism. ~획득 aquisition of territory.

**영특**(英特) ~하다 (be) wise; sagacious; perspicacious; outstanding. ¶ ~한 아이 a wise child.

**영판** ① 《길흉을 맞힘》 true 〔accurate, inspired〕 fortunetelling. ¶ 내가 올해 장가들 것이라더니 ~이었다 He foretold that I would marry this year, and how true it was! ② 《아주》 just; exactly; quite. ¶ ~ 같다 [쌍방이 주어] be exactly alike; be like two peas in a pod; [한쪽이 주어] be *one's* double; be the picture 《of *one's* father》/ ~ 다르다 be quite different 《from》.

**영패**(零敗) a shut-out; a skunk; not scoring; a whitewash 《구어》. ~하다 be shut out; fail to score; be whitewashed; be skunked 〔blanked〕《미구어》. ¶ ~시키다 whitewash; skunk 《구어》; shut 〔nose〕 out; hold 《an opponent》 scoreless; blank 《미》; 《투수가》 pitch a shutout / 간신히 ~를 면하다 barely miss being shut out.

**영하**(零下) below zero; sub-zero. ¶ ~의 기온 a sub-zero temperature / (기온이) ~ 5도로 내려가다 fall 〔drop〕 to 5 degrees 「below zero 〔below the freezing point, 《영》 of frost〕.

**영한**(英韓) England 〔Britain〕 and Korea; English-Korean; Anglo-Korean. ¶ ~ 양문으로 in English and Korean / ~ 대역의 책 an English book with Korean translation. ◉ ~사전 an English-Korean dictionary.

**영합하다**(迎合―) cater to 《*a person's*》 wishes 〔feelings〕; alter 〔adjust〕 *one's* opinions and behavior to please 《*a person*》; pander to; ingratiate 〔accommodate〕 *oneself* with 《*a person*》.
¶ 관중에 ～ play to the gallery / 일시적인 인기에 ～ seek temporary public popularity / 시대 풍조에 ～ go with the current of the times / 타인의 견해에 ～하다 echo another's opinion. ◉ 영합주의 opportunism; time-serving: ～주의자 a timeserver; an opportunist.

**영해**(領海) territorial waters.
¶ 한국 ～ 내〔외〕에서 within 〔outside of〕 Korean (territorial) waters / 여러 척의 국적 불명 어선이 한국의 ～ 내에서 조업하고 있는 것이 발견되었다 Several vessels of unknown nationality were found fishing within the territorial waters of Korea.
◉ ～선(線) a territorial water line: 12마일의 ～선 안〔밖〕에서 within 〔outside〕 the 12-mile limit of territorial waters. ～침범 violation of territorial waters.

**영향**(影響) (an) influence; 《효과》 (an) effect; 《충격》 an impact 《on》; 《파급적인》 repercussions; consequences.
¶ 외국의 ～ a foreign influence / 원폭의 ～ the effects of the atomic bomb / 불교의 ～ the influence of Buddhism / …의 ～으로 under the influence of…; owing to… / ～을 주다 influence; affect; have 〔exert〕 an effect 〔influence〕 《on》; have 〔produce〕 an effect 《on》; act 〔tell〕 on… / … ～을 받다 be affected 〔influenced〕 by…; come under the influence 《of》 / ～을 미치지〔주지〕 않다 have no effect on / 그것은 나의 이해(利害)에 어떤 ～을 주는가 How does it affect my interests? / 음주는 기억에 ～을 미친다 Drinking tells on the memory. / 환경은 사람의 성격에 ～을 준다 Man is affected in character by his environment. / 출판계는 불황의 ～을 심하게 받았다 The publishing business was hard hit by the depression. / 서울 지방은 오늘 저녁 태풍의 ～을 받게 될 것이다 The Seoul area will feel the effect of the typhoon this evening. / 이런 잡지는 아이들에게 나쁜〔좋은〕 ～을 준다 Such a magazine has a bad 〔good〕 influence 〔effect〕 on children. / 이 문제는 우리 회사에 중대한 ～을 미칠 것이다 This matter will have a big 〔tremendous〕 impact on our firm. / 그녀의 회사는 금리 인상의 ～을 심하게 받았다 Her company was 「seriously affected 〔heavily hit〕 by rising interest rates. / 내가 영어를 좋아하게 된 것은 선생님의 ～이 크다 It is largely because of my teacher that I have come to like English.
◉ ～력 influence: ～력을 행사하다 exercise *one's* influence over / 그는 정부에 대해 상당한 ～력을 가지고 있다 He has considerable influence upon 〔over〕 the Government.

**영험**(靈驗) miraculous efficacy. = 영검.

**영현**(英顯) the spirit of revered memory; 《전사자의》 the souls of the departed war heroes; the spirits of the war dead.

**영혼**(靈魂) the spirit; the soul. ◉ ～불멸(설) (the doctrine of) the immortality of the soul.

**영화**(英貨) British money 〔currency〕; sterling. ¶ ～ 100 파운드, 100 pounds sterling (★ £ 100 s. 〔stg.〕로 생략) / ～로 10파운드 ten pounds 〔£10〕 in English money / ～로 환산하다 convert 《dollars》 into English currency.

**영화**(映畫) a picture; a film; 《미》 a motion picture; 《미》 a movie; [총칭] 《미》 the movies; 《영》 the cinema.
¶ 외국 ～ a foreign movie 〔film〕 / …을 ～에서 보다 see 《it》 in a picture 〔movie〕 / ～를 보다 watch a film 〔movie〕 / ～구경을 가다 go to 「a movie 〔the movies〕; 《영》 go to the cinema 〔pictures〕 / ～를 상영하다 show a movie 〔film〕 / ～를 방영하다 project 《a movie》 (on the screen) / ～를 제작하다〔촬영하다〕 produce 〔shoot〕 a film / ～에 출연하다 play 〔be〕 in a movie; star in a film / 그 ～는 그 극장에서 아직 상영중이다 The picture is still showing 〔on (show)〕 at the theater. / 이 ～는 성인용이다 This movie is intended for adults. / 그 프랑스 ～는 며칠 전에 TV에서 방영되었다 The French movie was shown on television the other day. / 그 ～는 큰 히트를 쳤다 The film was a 「great hit 〔box-office smash〕. *or* The film drew large audience.
◉ ～각본 a scenario (*pl.* ～s); a (film) script: ～ 각본 작자 a scenario writer; a scenarist. ～감독 a movie 〔film〕 director. ～검열 film censorship. ～계 the motion picture 〔movie〕 world; 《영》 film world; movie circles; 《미》 the movies; 《영》 the cinema: ～계에 들어가다 enter the movie world; go

into the movies / 그녀는 1990년에 ～계에서 은퇴했다 She ended her movie career in 1990. ～배급회사 a film distributing agency. ～배우 a movie 〔film, screen, cinema〕 actor 〔actress〕. ～법 the Film Law. ～사업〔산업〕 the movie 〔motion picture, film〕 industry. ～상영권 film rights. ～스타 a film 〔movie〕 star. ～제 a film festival: 아시아 ～제 the Asian Film Festival. ～음악 film music. ～제작 film production: ～ 제작자(製作者) a film producer / ～ 제작 회사 a film producing company. ～제작소 a movie 〔cinema〕 studio; a lot 《미》. ～ 조감독 an assistant director. ～촬영소 = ～ 제작소. ～촬영용 카메라 a motion-picture camera; a cinecamera. ～팬 a film 〔movie〕 fan; a moviegoer 〔a filmgoer 《영》〕 《구어》. ～편집 a film editing 〔cutting〕. ～평론가 a film 〔movie〕 critic. ～회사 a movie company.

**영화**(榮華) glory; splendor; pomp; prosperity; luxury; extravagance; sumptuousness. ～롭다 (be) glorious; pompous; prosperous; sumptuous.
¶ 잠깐 동안의 ～ a brief span of prosperity / ～를 한껏 누리다 live in splendor; be at the height of *one's* prosperity; attain the height of prosperity / ～에 도취하다 revel in prosperity.

**영화관**(映畫館) 《미》 a movie 〔motion picture〕 theater 〔house〕; 《영》 a cinema. ¶ 그 ～에서는 지금 무엇을 상영하고 있지 What's on now at the movie theater?

**영화화**(映畫化) cinematization; filming; picturization. ～하다 make a screen version of 《a novel》; make 《a novel》 into a movie 〔film〕. ¶ 그 소설은 그에 의해 ～되었다 The novel was 「filmed 〔made into a movie〕 by him. *or* He brought the novel to the screen.

**옅다** ① ⇨ 얕다. ② 《빛이》 (be) light; pale. ¶ 옅은 푸른 빛 a light blue.

**옆** the side; the flank. ⇨곁.
¶ 옆의 nearby; neighboring; adjacent; next 《to》 / 옆에 by the side 《of》; by; beside; aside; near; close to; next to / 바로 옆에 near 〔close〕 by / 길 옆의 집 a house by the road / 옆에 가다 come 〔draw〕 near 《to》 / 옆에 가까이 가서 보다 take a nearer view 《of *a thing*》 / 옆을 지나다 pass by 《*a person, a thing*》 / 문 옆에 서다 stand by the gate / 어머니 옆에 앉다 sit beside *one's* mother / 옆으로 비키다 step aside / 길 양옆에는 나무들이 늘어서 있다 The street is lined with trees on either side. / 그는 우연히 옆에 있었다 He happened to be by. / 옆으로 눕힐 것 《지시》 Keep flat. *or* Stow level. / 옆으로 눕히지 말 것 《지시》 Never lay flat. *or* Not to be laid flat.

**옆구리** 《사람의》 *one's* side; 《특히 동물의》 the flank.
¶ 오른쪽 ～ the right side; 《말 따위의》 the right flank / ～를 쿡쿡 찌르다 poke 〔nudge〕 《*a person*》 in the ribs / ～를 차다 kick 《*a person*》 on the side / ～가 아프다 I feel 〔have〕 a pain in my 《right》 side.

**옆길** 《작은 길》 a byroad; a sideroad; a byway; 《잘못된 방향》 the wrong way; 《의론 등의》 digression. ¶ ～로 빠지다 deviate from the right way; 《이야기가》 wander 〔digress〕 from the main subject / ～로 가니 작은 과수원이 나왔다 A bypath led to a small orchard.

**옆막이** things blocking 〔obstructing〕 both sides.

**옆면**(一面) a side; sides.

**옆모습** a profile; a face in profile; a face as seen from the side.
¶ ～을 그리다 draw in profile; draw a profile 《of》 / ～이 아름답다 have a good 〔fine〕 profile; be fine in profile.

**옆문**(一門) a side entrance 〔door〕. ¶ ～을 이용하시오 《게시》 Side entrance. *or* Use next door.

**옆바람** a side wind; 《항해·비행》 a cross-「wind.

**옆방**(一房) the next 〔adjoining〕 room.

**옆자리** the next seat; a side seat (버스 등의) 「(측선).

**옆줄** a side line; 《어류의》 a lateral line

**옆집** the adjacent house; the (house) next door. ¶ ～의 next (to *one*); next-door; neighboring; adjoining / 오른〔왼〕쪽 ～ the next-door house on the right 〔left〕 / ～에 살다 live next door to 《*a person*》 / 한 집 건너 ～에 살다 live next door but one to *one's* house; live two door away from *one's* house / 불은 ～에서 발생했다 The fire broke out in the next door. / 김 선생은 우리 ～에 산다 Mr. Kim lives next door to us. / 그들은 서로 ～에 산다 They are next door neighbors.
◉ ～사람 *one's* next-door neighbor.

**예**[1] 《옛적》 old 〔ancient〕 times; old 〔olden〕 days; days gone by; bygone 〔past〕 days; the (remote) past; former years. ¶ 예로부터 from ancient times / 예나 지금이나 in all ages / 예나

지금이나 다름이 없다 It is the same now as it was in the days gone by.

**예**(例) ①《본보기》 an instance; a case; an example; an illustration. ¶ 예를 들면 for instance 〔example〕/ 예가 되다 serve as an example / 예를 들다 take 〔give〕 an example; cite an instance / 한국을 예로 들다 take Korea as an example; take the case of Korea / 이것은 좋은 예다 This is a good example. *or* This is a case in point. / 한국도 또한 이 예에서 벗어나지 못한다 Korea is no exception to the rule.

② 《전례》 a precedent. ¶ 예에 의해서 according to precedent / 예에 없는 일 an unprecedented event / 예가 되다 become a precedent / 예를 만들다 establish a (new) precedent / 예를 깨(뜨리)다 break the precedent / 그런 예는 여태까지 없었다 There is no precedent for this. *or* This case is unprecedented. *or* There has never been a case like this (before).

③《관례》 a custom; (a) usage. ¶ 예의 《여느 때와 같은》 usual; customary; habitual / 예와 같이, 예에 의해서 as usual; as is usually the case 《with *a person*》/ 예에 없이 unusually / 그는 그날 밤 예에 없이 늦게 돌아왔다 That night he came back much later than usual. / 그는 예에 없는 짓을 했다 He did an unusual thing. / 그는 예의 수법으로 나를 속이려고 했다 He tried the old trick on me.

④《알고 있는 것을 지칭》 ¶ 예의 그 사나이 the man in question; that man.

**예**(禮) ①《의식》 ceremony; the code of ceremonies. ¶ 혼례 a wedding ceremony / 예를 제정하다 build up a code of ceremonies. ②《경례》 a salute; a salutation; a bow. ¶ 예를 하다 make a bow; salute. ③《예법》 decorum; etiquette; propriety; courtesy; manner. ⇨ 예의(禮儀). ¶ 그는 어른을 대접하는 예를 모른다 He does not know how to behave toward his seniors.

**예**[2] ①《대답》 yes; no (부정 의문에 대한 답으로); 《출석했을 때》 Yes, sir 〔madam〕; Here 〔Present〕 sir 〔madam〕; 《알았습니다》 Certainly; 《좋습니다》 All right; OK; Sure. ¶ 예 알았습니다 I see. *or* That's all right. / 「야구를 좋아하느냐」—「예, 좋아합니다」 "Do you like baseball?"—"Yes, I do." / 「너 헤엄 못 치니」—「예, 못 칩니다」 "Can't you swim?"—"No, I can't." / 「다시 거기에 가서는 안 된다」—「예, 안 가겠습니다」 "Don't go there again."—"No, I won't." ②《재우쳐 물음》 eh? ¶ 예, 그렇습니까 Is that so? *or* Really?

**예각**(鋭角) 〚수학〛 an acute angle. ¶ …와 ~을 이루다 make an acute angle with….

**예감**(豫感) a premonition; a presentiment; a presage; a foreboding; a hunch 《미구어》. ~하다 feel 〔have〕 a foreboding 《of, that…》; have a hunch 《that…》; feel a premonition 〔presentiment〕 《of, that…》. ¶ 불길한 ~ a gloomy 〔an ominous〕 foreboding; a previous sense 〔prior feeling〕 of misfortune / 죽음을 ~하다 have a premonition of death / ~이 들다 = ~하다 / 어떤 재난이 닥칠 것 같은 ~이 들었다 I felt in my bones that some disaster was impending. / 네가 올 것 같은 ~이 들었다 I had a hunch that you would come.

**예견**(豫見) foresight; prognostication. ~하다 foresee; prognosticate. ¶ …을 예견하고 in anticipation of… / 이렇게 끊임없이 변화하는 세상에서는 1년 앞 일을 예견할 수 없다 We cannot foresee what will happen a year hence, as we are in such an ever-changing world.

**예고**(豫告) an advance 〔a previous〕 notice; a preliminary 〔prior〕 announcement; 《영화·TV의 광고 포스터에 의한》 advance billing; 《경고》 (a) warning. ~하다 notify 〔announce, inform〕 beforehand 〔previously〕; warn 《*a person* of》; give advance notice. ¶ ~대로 as previously 〔already〕 announced / ~ 없이 without (previous) warning 〔notice〕; 《come》 unannounced / ~ 없는 방문 a surprise 〔an unannounced〕 visit / 1주일 전에 ~하다 give a week's notice 《to》/ 1개월 전에 해고를 ~하다 give 《*a person*》 a month's notice of dismissal / 그는 ~ 없이 해고당했다 He was dismissed without (previous) notice. ◉ ~장치 〚컴퓨터〛 an annunciator. ~편 《영화의》 a (film) trailer; 《영화·TV의》 a preview.

**예과**(豫科) a prep(aratory) school; a preparatory department; the preparatory course 〔class, department〕 《for college》. ¶ ~를 수료하다 complete the preparatory course.

**예광탄**(曳光彈) 〚군사〛 a tracer shell; a light 〔flame〕 tracer; a flare bomb.

**예규**(例規) an established rule 〔regulation〕. ¶ ~에 따라 처리하다 dispose of 《*a matter*》 in accordance with the established regulations.

**예금**(預金) 〖경제〗 deposit; money on deposit; a bank account; savings (저금). ~하다 deposit ⟪money in a bank⟫; make a deposit ⟪in a bank⟫; bank ⟪100,000 won⟫; place ⟪money⟫ on deposit ⟪in a bank⟫. ¶ ~이 늘다 *one's* bank account grows / ~을 찾다 draw 〔withdraw〕 *one's* money 〔deposit〕 ⟪from the bank⟫ / (은행이) ~을 받아들이다 accept a deposit; receive money in a customer's account / (은행이) ~을 내어주다 repay a deposit / 월 5만 원씩 ~하다 deposit fifty thousand won a month / 그는 은행에 ~이 500만 원 있다 He has five million won on deposit in the bank. / 나는 아직 은행에 ~ 잔고가 있다 I still have a balance at my bank.

◉ ~계 the deposit section 〔department〕; ⟪사람⟫ a deposit teller. ~계좌 a bank 〔deposit〕 account; a savings account ⟪미⟫. ~금리 deposit (interest) rate. ~담당대리 an assistant manager in charge of savings deposits. ~대출 a deposit loan. ~보호기금 a fund for the protection of bank depositors. ~액(額) the deposited amount. ~유치능력 *one's* deposit-attracting ability. ~이자 interest on deposits: ~이자세 taxes on deposits. ~자 a depositor. ~증서 a deposit receipt 〔certificate〕. ~지급 유보 the payment suspension of deposited money. ~지급 준비 a reserve for deposit. ~지급준비율 the reserve requirement ratio. ~청구서 a deposit withdrawal slip 〔form〕. ~통장 a deposit passbook; a bankbook.

**예기**(銳氣) (animated) spirit; dash; mettle; ardor; ⟪원기⟫ energy; vigor. ¶ ~에 찬 spirited; mettlesome; in high spirits / ~를 기르다 recreate *oneself;* store up *one's* energy / ~를 꺾다 break 〔shake〕 ⟪*a person's*⟫ spirits(★ 자만·실망 따위 감정을 나타내는 spirit는 복수형을 씀).

**예기**(豫期) expectation(s); (an) anticipation. ~하다 expect; anticipate; look for. ¶ ~치 않은 unexpected; unlooked-for; unforeseen / ~한 대로 as (was) expected / ~에 반하여 contrary to *one's* expectation / ~ 이상으로 beyond *one's* expectation(s) / …을 ~하여 in expectation 〔anticipation〕 of... / ~한 대로 되다 「come up to 〔meet〕 *one's* expectation(s) / ~한 것보다 훨씬 더 좋았다 It was far better than was anticipated.

**예기, 예끼** ⟪나무랄 때⟫ Damn it!; Damn you! ¶ ~ 나쁜 놈 You rascal!

**예납**(豫納) 〖세법〗 prepayment; payment in advance; advance payment. ~하다 pay in advance; prepay.

**예년**(例年) ⟪평년⟫ the average 〔normal, ordinary〕 year; [부사적] every year; annually. ¶ ~의 ⟪평년⟫ normal; usual; ⟪매년⟫ of 〔in〕 the average year; annual / ~의 행사 an annual event / ~대로 as in other years; as usual / ~에 비해서 compared with other years / ~에 없이 unusually / 올 겨울은 ~에 없이 춥다 This winter is 「severer than usual 〔unusually cold〕.

**예능**(藝能) art; the arts; artistic accomplishments; ⟪연예의⟫ performing arts; public entertainments. ⇨ 연예(演藝).

◉ ~과 the art course. ~교육 art education.

**예니레** six or seven days.

**예닐곱** six or seven.

**예단**(豫斷) (a) presupposition; (a) prediction; (a) prophecy. ~하다 presuppose; predict; guess; prognosticate; anticipate. ¶ ~을 불허하다 be unpredictable; be beyond prophecy; there is no knowing 〔predicting〕.

**예답다**(禮—) (be) courteous; ceremonious.

**예대**(禮待) (a) honorable 〔courteous〕 treatment; (a) cordial reception. ~하다 treat ⟪*a person*⟫ with respect; receive cordially 〔courteously〕.

**예도**(藝道) an art; accomplishments. ¶ ~에 정진하다 devote *oneself* to the refinement of *one's* art.

**예라** ① ⟪그만둬라·비켜라⟫ Stop!; Cut it out!; Be off! ¶ ~ 그런 말 하지 마라 Stop talking like that! / ~ 저리 가거라 Away with you! ② ⟪결심·체념⟫ all right; good; well then. ¶ ~ 네가 못 하겠으면 내가 하겠다 You say you can't do it? All right, I will take it on. / ~ 이젠 모르겠다 Well then, I'll have nothing more to do with it.

**예레미야서**(—書) 〖성서〗 the Book of Jeremiah; ⟪약칭⟫ Jeremiah (생략 Jer.).

**예루살렘** ⟪이스라엘의 수도⟫ Jerusalem.

**예리**(銳利) sharpness; keenness. ~하다 (be) sharp; keen. ¶ 날이 ~한 칼 a knife with a keen edge / 그녀는 ~한 두뇌의 소유자다 She has a sharp mind.

**예매**(豫買) advance purchase; (prior) subscription. ~하다 purchase in advance; subscribe to 〔for〕.

**예매**(豫賣) advance sale; ⟪표의⟫ booking; advance subscription(-taking).

～하다 sell in advance; 《표를》 book; take advance subscriptions for. ¶ 추석 고속 버스 승차권 ～ advance sale of express bus tickets for the *Ch'usŏk* holidays / 좌석권의 ～를 하고 있다 They are selling tickets for the reserved seats in advance. / 오늘부터 표의 ～가 시작된다 The advance sale of tickets begins today. ◉ ～권 an advance tickets; a ticket sold in advance: ～권을 여기서 살 수 있습니까 Can I get an advance ticket here?

**예멘** 《나라 이름》 Yemen. ¶ ～의 Yemeni. ◉ ～사람 a Yemeni.

**예명**(藝名) a stage 〔screen〕 name. ¶ …란 ～의 여배우 an actress professionally known as….

**예모**(禮帽) 《예복에 갖추는》 a ceremonial hat; 《실크 모자》 a silk hat; a top hat.

**예모**(禮貌) good manners; etiquette. ¶ ～가 있다〔없다〕 be well-〔ill-〕mannered / ～를 지키다 observe the rules of etiquette / ～에 어긋나다 be not proper; be against etiquette.

**예문**(例文) an example (sentence); an illustrative sentence. ¶ ～이 많은 한영사전 a Korean-English dictionary with a lot of example sentences.

**예물**(禮物) ① 《선물·답례물》 a present; a gift; a thank-you present. ¶ ～을 보내다〔주다〕 make a present 《to *a person*》. ② 《결혼의》 wedding presents from a mother-in-law to a bride; symbolic gifts exchanged between bride and groom. ¶ ～을 주고 받다 exchange wedding presents 〔gifts〕.

**예민**(銳敏) sharpness; keenness; acuteness. ～하다 (be) sharp; keen; acute; sensitive; 《지력의》 (be) quick-witted; shrewd. ¶ ～한 감각 keen 〔quick〕 senses / ～한 두뇌의 소유자 a sharp=witted person; a person 〔possessor〕 of keen intellect / 귀〔코〕가 ～하다 have 「a sharp ear 〔a keen nose〕 / 개는 후각이 ～하다 A dog has an acute sense of smell.

**예바르다**(禮—) (be) courteous; properly behaved; proper; well-bred; refined. ¶ 그는 ～ He is well-mannered. *or* He has good manners.

**예방**(禮訪) a courtesy call; a visit of courtesy. ～하다 pay 〔make〕 a courtesy call on 《*a person*》; pay a courtesy visit 《to》.

**예방**(豫防) prevention 《of》; protection 《from, against》; 〖의학〗 (a) prophylaxis; 《조심》 (a) precaution. ～하다 prevent; ward 〔keep〕 off; protect 《from, against》; protect *oneself* 《against》; take precautions 《against》; take preventive measures 《against》.
¶ ～의 preventive; precautionary / ～할 수 있는 preventable / 질병의 ～ prevention against disease; disease prevention / 화재 ～ 주간 Fire Prevention Week / ～선을 치다 「take precautions 〔set a guard〕 《against》; forestall / 전염(병)을 ～하다 prevent 「infection 〔the plague from spreading〕 / ～은 치료보다 낫다 Prevention is better than cure. / 콜레라 ～을 위해 검역을 실시하고 있다 They are enforcing quarantine to prevent the spread of cholera.
◉ ～약 a preventive 《of, for, against》; a prophylactic (medicine) 《against》. ～위생 preventive hygiene 〔sanitation〕. ～의학 preventive medicine. ～전쟁 a preventive war. ～접종 a vaccination 〔an inoculation〕 《against, for》: ～접종 증명서 a quarantine certificate; a health certificate; a yellow card 〔book〕 / ～접종을 받다 be inoculated 〔vaccinated〕 《against diphtheria》. ～조치〔책(策)〕 《take》 preventive 〔precautionary〕 measures 〔steps〕; precautions: ～ 조치를 강구하다 take preventive measures 《against》 / 전염병～에 대하여 갖가지 ～ 조치가 취해졌다 Various preventive measures 〔precautions〕 are taken against epidemics.

**예방주사**(豫防注射) a preventive injection 〔shot〕; (an) inoculation. ¶ 장티푸스 ～를 맞다 be inoculated against typhoid.

**예배**(禮拜) worship; 《교회의》 church 〔divine〕 service. ～하다 worship. ¶ ～를 보다 worship 《God》 / 교회에서 ～중이다 be at church / ～에 참석하다 attend 〔go to〕 church; attend divine service / 아침 ～(식)을 거행하다 hold morning service / ～ 후에 그녀를 방문하다 visit her after 「church 〔the service〕 (is over) / ～는 10시에 시작한다 Church 〔Divine service〕 begins at ten o'clock. / 그는 오랜만에 저녁 ～에 참석했다 He attended evening service after a long interval. ◉ ～당 a church; a chapel. ～식 (a) service. ～자 《숭배자》 a worshiper; 《순례자》 a pilgrim. 아침～ morning service.

**예법**(禮法) manners; etiquette; good form; decorum; the proprieties. ¶ 식탁의 ～ table manners / 가정에서의 ～ the etiquette in the home / ～을

지키다 observe 「the proprieties 〔proper decorum〕/ ～에 벗어나지 않다〔벗어나다〕「conform to 〔go against〕 etiquette / ～을 배우다 learn good manners / 그는 ～을 모른다 He has no manners. *or* He is ill-mannerd.

**예보**(豫報) a forecast; (a) prediction. ～하다 forecast; predict. ¶ ～한 대로 as (was) previously reported / 일기를 ～하다 forecast the weather / 지진이 있을 것이라고 ～하다 predict that there will be an earthquake / ～가 맞았다〔맞지 않았다〕 The forecast was accurate 〔wrong〕.
◉ 일기～ a weather forecast: 일기～원 a weather forecaster / 장기〔수치〕 일기 ～ a long-range 〔numerical〕 weather forecast / 비가 온다는 일기 ～다 The weather forecast predicts rain.

**예복**(禮服) a ceremonial dress; full 〔formal〕 dress; a dress suit; 《군인용》 a dress uniform; 《야회용》 an evening dress. ¶ ～을 입(고 있)다 wear 〔be in〕 full dress / 이 모임에 ～은 필요 없다 This is not a dress-up affair. / 모두가 ～을 입고 있었다 All were in full dress. / ～ 착용 요망〔불요〕 《초대장 등의 글》 Dress formal 〔informal〕.
◉ 궁중～ a court suit.

**예봉**(銳鋒) a sharp 〔keen〕 point; the brunt 《of an argument 〔attack〕》; trenchant argument. ¶ ～을 꺾다 break the brunt of 《the enemy's attack》/ ～에 맞서다 bear the brunt of 《an attack》.

**예불**(禮佛) 〖불교〗 worship before the image of Buddha. ～하다 hold worship in front of Buddha; pay homage to Buddha.

**예비**(豫備) preparation; a reserve; a spare (비치한 것). ～하다 prepare 《for》; provide 《for》; reserve. ¶ ～의 《비치한》 reserve; spare; 《사전의》 preparatory; preliminary / ～연료 reserve fuel / 만일을 위한 ～ a standby reserve / ～로 갖다 hold 《*a thing*》 in reserve / 나는 약간의 돈을 ～로 갖고 있었다 I had a little money in reserve. / ～식량이 바닥이 나고 있다 Our stock of food is running out.
◉ ～검사〔점검〕 (a) preliminary examination 〔inspection〕; a reconnaissance: ～검사를 하다 examine 〔inspect〕 beforehand; make a preliminary examination 〔inspection〕 《of》; make a reconnaissance 《of》. ～계획 a plan in reserve. ～공작 spadework; preliminaries. ～교 a prep(aratory) school. ～교섭 a preliminary negotiation. ～금〔비〕 a reserve (fund); money in reserve. ～병 a reservist. ～병력 the effective strength of the reserves. ～부품 spare parts. ～사단 〖군사〗 a reserve division. ～선거 《미국의》 a primary election. ～시험 a preliminary examination. ～조사 a preliminary investigation. ～지식 preliminary 〔background〕 knowledge 《of a subject》. ～타이어 a spare tire. ～판사 a reserve judge. ～품 spares; spare stores 〔stocks〕; reserve supply. ～회담 a preliminary 〔preparatory〕 conference.

**예비군**(豫備軍) the reserves; a reserve army; reserve troops 〔forces〕; armed reserve. ¶ 직장〔지역〕 ～ workplace 〔regional〕 reserve forces / 향토 ～ the local reserve 〔defense〕 forces / 향토 ～ 중대본부 the company headquarters of regional reserve forces / 산업 ～ an industrial reserve army / ～을 소집하다 call up the reserve(s).
◉ ～훈련 reserve forces training.

**예비역**(豫備役) (service in) the 《first》 reserve. ¶ ～ 장교 a reserve officer / ～대령 a colonel in the reserve(s) / ～에 편입되다 be placed on the reserve list; be transferred to the 《first》 reserve.

**예쁘다** (be) pretty; lovely; sweet; cute; fair; comely; good-looking. ¶ 예쁜 목소리로 in a sweet voice / 예쁜 꽃 a sweet 〔pretty, lovely〕 flower / 예쁜 여자 a lovely girl / 예쁘게 prettily; finely; sweetly / 옷을 예쁘게 입다 dress *oneself* beautifully / 장미가 예쁘게 피었다 The roses are in beautiful bloom.

**예쁘장하다** (be) lovely; comely; good=looking; [서술적] be on the pretty side. ¶ 예쁘장한 인형 a cute doll.

**예사**(例事) ① 《보통》 a common practice; custom; (a) usage. ¶ ～의 customary; usual / ～가 아닌 unusual; extraordinary; uncommon / ～로 여기다 《망설이지 않다》 do not hesitate 《to *do*》; make no scruple of 《*do*ing》; 《태연하다》 make little 〔nothing〕 of; think nothing of; 《무관심하다》 be indifferent 《to》/ …을 ～로 여기게 되다 become inured 〔get accustomed〕 to 《*a thing*》/ 예삿일이 아니다 It is no 「common case 〔trivial matter〕. *or* Something unusual must have happened. / 그는 실패해도 ～로 안다 He is

none the worse for his failure. / 그는 목적을 위해서는 무슨 일이든지 ～로 한다 He would stop 〔stick〕 at nothing to achieve his objectives. / 그는 ～로 사람을 때린다 He has a way of going around hitting people.
② 《일상사》 an everyday occurrence; a usual affair. ¶ 이런 무력 혁명은 그 나라에서는 ～다 Such an armed revolt is an everyday occurrence in that country.

**예사롭다** (例事―) (be) common; ordinary; usual; run-of-the-mill; commonplace; humdrum; be of no consequence; be as usual. ¶ 예사로운 일 an everyday occurrence; a matter of no consequence; the usual sort of thing / 예사롭게 unconcernedly; indifferently / 그는 정부를 비난하는 것쯤 예사롭게 생각한다 He makes no bones about criticizing the Government.

**예산** (豫算) 《견적》 an estimate 《for, of》; 《수지의 예정》 a budget. ～하다 estimate 《the cost of》; budget 《for the coming year》.
¶ 내년도 ～ the budget for the 「coming 〔fiscal〕 year / 국가 ～ a State budget / 잠정〔수정, 추가, 총〕～ the 「provisional 〔revised, supplementary, total〕 budget / ～의 작성 budget=making / ～규모의 축소 (a) budget squeeze / ～의, ～에 관한 budgetary 《requests, measures》 / ～을 세우다〔짜다〕 make 〔form, draw up〕 「a budget 〔an estimate〕; budget 《for the coming year》 / ～에 계상하다〔넣다〕 include 〔plan〕 《the expenditure for a project》 in the budget; budget for 《the new city hall》 / 실제 경비보다 많은 ～을 세우다 budget for more than *one* spends / ～을 좀더 타내려고 기를 쓰다 campaign for a bigger slice of the budget / ～을 초과하다 go beyond the estimate; go over 〔exceed〕 the budget / ～을 충분히 확보하다 secure an ample budget / ～의 균형을 잡다 balance the budget / ～이 없다 have no budget 《for》 / 공사비 ～은 1천만 원이다 The cost of construction is estimated at ten million won. / ～의 범위 내에서는 그것을 할 수 없다 We cannot do it within the limits of the budget. / ～이 한정되어 있어 충분한 활동을 할 수 없다 With a limited budget we are handicapped in our operations. / 금년도 ～이 승인되었다 The budget for this year was approved. / 우리는 20만 원의 ～으로 여행 떠날 계획을 하고 있다 We are planning to travel on a budget of two hundred thousand won. / ～을 어느 정도로 하고 계십니까 《매매 거래 등에서》 May I ask what price you have in mind?
◉ ～결산특별위원회 a special budget=settlement committee. ～결손〔부족〕 a budgetary 〔budget〕 deficit. ～삭감 a curtailment 〔reduction〕 in the budget. ～성립 coming into force of the budget. ～심의권 《국회의》 the budget deliberation right; the right to deliberate government budget. ～연도 a budget year. ～위원회 a budget committee. ～제출권 a right to present the budget bill to the National Assembly. ～조처 《take》 budgetary measures. ～집행 execution of the budget. ～초과 an excess over the estimates. ～편성 compilation 〔drafting〕 of the budget. ～할당 budgetary allocations. ～항목 a budget item 〔account〕.

**예산안** (豫算案) a draft budget; a budget bill. ¶ 세출 ～ a bill of estimated expenditure / ～을 국회에 제출하다 submit a budget (bill) to the National Assembly / ～을 심의하다 discuss the budget bill. ◉ ～ 심의 deliberation on the budget.

**예산외** (豫算外) ¶ ～의 outside the budget; not included in the budget.
◉ ～수입 receipts outside of the budget. ～지출 extraordinary disbursements; defrayment unprovided for in the budget; unbudgeted outlays.

**예상** (豫想) 《예기》 expectation; anticipation; 《예측》 a forecast; a prospective view; 《추측》 a surmise; a conjecture; 《가상》 supposition. ～하다 expect; anticipate; forecast; surmise; guess; predict; estimate.

> 용법 **expect** 어떤 일이 일어나는 것이 확실하다고 생각하며 기대하고 있다는 뜻. **anticipate** expect와 거의 같은 뜻으로 쓰이나, 미리 장래에 대비한다는 뜻을 함유하는 문어적인 말. **forecast** 데이터 따위를 분석·검토하여 무슨 일이 일어나기 전에 이를 사람들에게 알린다는 뜻. **surmise, guess** 확증은 없지만 정황을 살펴 합리적으로 추측한다는 뜻. **predict** 지식이나 경험에 의해 앞으로 일어날 일들을 예측한다는 뜻.

¶ ～에 어긋난 against 〔contrary to〕 *one's* expectations / ～대로 as expect-

ed / ～대로 되다 come 〔measure〕 up to *one's* expectation(s); meet 〔answer〕 *one's* expectation(s) / …을 ～하여(서) in expectation 〔anticipation, prospect〕 of / ～ 이상이다 exceed 〔be beyond, be ahead of〕 *one's* expectation / ～이 어긋나다 fall short of *one's* expectations; be disappointed of *one's* expectations / 장래를 ～하다 forecast 〔anticipate〕 the future / 결과가 ～대로 되었다 The results came up to my expectations. *or* My guess about the result was right. / 어떤 결과가 될지 ～이 되지 않는다 How the result may turn out is beyond imagination. / 이번 선거에서는 ～을 뒤엎은 일이 많았다 The late election was full of surprise. *or* The late election has had many upsets. / 매상은 ～처럼 오르지 않았다 The sale did not「come 〔measure〕 up to our expectations. / 그가 성공하리라고는 아무도 ～하지 않았다 No one foresaw that he would succeed. / 앞으로 무슨 일이 일어날지 아무도 ～할 수 없다 No one can foresee 〔tell〕 what will happen in the future. / 결과는 ～ 이상이었다 The result surpassed my expectations. *or* The result was better than I had expected.
◉ ～수확량 the estimated crop 〔production〕 《for this year》: 올해의 쌀～수확량 this year's estimated rice crop 〔yield〕. ～액 estimates; an estimated amount: 피해 ～액 estimated damage. ～이익 an imaginary 〔estimated〕 profit.

**예상사**(例常事) an ordinary affair; a matter of common occurrence. ⇨ 예사(例事).

**예상외**(豫想外) ¶ ～의 unexpected; unforeseen; unlooked-for; unhoped-for / ～로 beyond *one's* expectation(s); unexpectedly; contrary to 〔against〕 (*one's*) expectation(s) / 성적이 ～로 좋다〔나쁘다〕 The result is better 〔worse〕 than I expected. / 우리 계획은 ～로 난항을 겪고 있다 We are unexpectedly facing difficulties with our plan.

**예서**(隷書) ornamental seal characters; the scribes' style of writing Chinese characters.

**예선**(豫選) ① 《선거의》 a provisional selection 〔election〕; a preliminary election; a preelection; a primary (election) 《미》. ～하다 elect 〔select〕 in the preliminary 〔primary〕; preelect.
② 《경기·경연 등의》 a preliminary (contest 〔heat, round〕); an elimination 〔eliminating〕 match 〔contest〕; a trial game 〔contest〕; a qualifying test 〔event〕. ～하다 hold a preliminary (contest). ¶ 1차 ～ the first elimination round / 백미터 ～ the 100-meter preliminary; the trial heat of the 100-meters / ～을 통과하다 qualify 《for the semifinal》 / ～에서 떨어지다 be eliminated 《from the tournament》 / 미인 선발 대회에서 5명이 ～에 통과했다 Five girls passed the preliminary stage of the beauty contest.
◉ ～통과자 a qualifier.

**예속**(隷屬) subordination. ～하다 be subordinate 〔subject〕 《to》; be 〔come〕 under the rule 《of》. ¶ ～적 지위 a subordinate position / A를 B에 ～시키다 subordinate A to B. ◉ ～국 a subject nation; a dependency.

**예수** Jesus (Christ). ◉ ～교 Christianity: ～교도, ～교인 a Christian. ～그리스도 Jesus Christ.

**예순** sixty; threescore. ¶ ～의 sexagenary / ～살이다 be sixty years old.

**예술**(藝術) (an) art; the (fine) arts (미술). ¶ ～적인 artistic / 비～적 inartistic / ～을 위한 예술 art for art's sake (예술 지상 주의) / ～화하다 translate into art / ～적 가치가 크다 have 〔show〕 much artistic merit / 그는 ～을 모른다 He cannot appreciate art. / 그녀의 무용은 하나의 ～이다 Her dance is an art. (★ 특별한 한 분야를 말할 때는 관사가 붙음) / ～은 길고 인생은 짧다 Art is long, life is short. / 문학은 언어의 ～이다 Literature is the art of words.
◉ ～가 an artist: 그에게는 ～가 기질이 있다 He has an artistic temperament. ～계 the world of art; artistic circles. ～대학 an art college. ～본능 art instinct. ～비평 criticism of art: ～비평가 an art critic. ～사진 an artistic photograph. ～영화 an art film. ～원 the Art Academy; the National Academy of Arts: ～원상 an Art Academy prize 〔award〕. ～작품 a work of art. ～제 an art festival. ～지상파 the art-for-art school. ～철학 the philosophy of art. ～품 a work 〔an object〕 of art. ～활동 artistic activities.

**예스** yes. ¶ ～냐 노냐의 결정 a yes-no decision. ◉ ～맨 a yes-man.

**예스럽다** (be) antiquated; archaic.
¶ 예스럽게 archaically / 예스런 말〔표현〕 an archaic word 〔expression〕 / 예스런

습관 old customs.

**예습**(豫習) preparation (of *one's* lessons). ～하다 prepare *one's* lessons. ¶ ～하지 않고 학교에 가다 go to school without doing *one's* preparation / 내일 학과의 ～을 하다 prepare *one's* lessons for tomorrow.

**예시**(例示) illustration; exemplification. ～하다 illustrate 《by example》; exemplify.

**예시**(豫示) adumbration; foreshadowing; indication. ～하다 adumbrate; foreshadow; indicate beforehand.

**예식**(例式) an established form.

**예식**(禮式) 《예법》 rules 〔forms〕 of etiquette; 《의식》 a rite; a ceremony; 《결혼식》 a wedding (ceremony). ◉ ～장 a ceremony 〔wedding〕 hall.

**예심**(豫審) 〖법〗 a preliminary examination 〔hearing〕; a pretrial hearing 〔examination〕. ¶ ～ 중이다 be under preliminary examination.
◉ ～법정 the preliminary court of inquiry. ～조서 the minutes 〔records〕 of preliminary examination. ～판사 a preliminary 〔an examining〕 judge.

**예약**(豫約) 《좌석·방 등의》 booking; reservation; 《출판물의》 subscription; 《상품의》 an advance order; 《의사·미용실 등의》 an appointment. ～하다 book 《tickets》; reserve 《a seat》; have 《a room》 reserved; make a 《sleeper》 reservation; make an appointment 《with *one's* hairdresser》; subscribe to 〔for〕 《a magazine》.
¶ ～하고 나타나지 않는 사람 a no-show / 좌석을 ～하다 have a seat reserved; reserve 〔book〕 a seat / 호텔에 방을 ～하다 make reservation at a hotel / 내일의 ～을 변경〔취소〕하다 《병원·미장원 따위의》 change 〔cancel〕 *one's* appointment for tomorrow / B잡지의 1년간 구독을 ～하다 make a subscription to B magazine for a year / 그녀는 5월 10일 오후의 파리행 비행기 좌석 둘을 ～했다 She has reserved 〔booked〕 two seats on an afternoon flight for Paris on May 10. / 그 치과 의사는 ～제로 환자를 받는다 The dentist sees patients by appointment only. / 방은 ～을 해야 합니까 Do I need a reservation of the room? / 오늘 저녁 8시에 세 사람 ～을 하고 싶은데요 《식당에》 I'd like to reserve a table for three at eight this evening. / 이 좌석은 ～되어 있습니다 This table 〔seat〕 is reserved. / 12월 1일부터 ～을 받습니다 We take reservations beginning on December 1. / ～하셨습니까 《호텔·식당 따위에서》 Do you have a reservation? / ～을 취소하고 싶습니다 I'd like to cancel my reservation. / 당일의 ～ 취소에는 위약금을 받습니다 Cancelation of the reservation on the day will incur a cancelation charge.
◉ ～금 a deposit. ～기간 the period 〔term〕 of subscription. ～담당직원 《호텔 등의》 a reservation clerk. ～독자 a subscriber. ～마감일 the last day for subscription. ～모집 invitation for subscription. ～변경 a reservation change; a change of reservation. ～석 a reserved 〔booked〕 seat; 《게시》 Reserved. ～신청서 a subscription form. ～접수처 a reservation desk 《of an airline》. ～제 《on》 a subscription basis: ～제로 판매하다 sell 《an encyclopedia》 by subscription 〔on a subscription basis〕. ～주문 《receive》 an advance order. ～출판 publication by subscription. ～판매 sale by subscription.

**예언**(豫言) (a) prophecy; (a) prediction; a forecast. ～하다 predict; prophesy; foretell; make a prediction; say that *something* will take place. ¶ ～적 prophetic / ～할 수 있는 predictable / ～이 틀리다〔맞다〕 A prophecy fails 〔comes true〕. / 그의 ～은 적중하였다 His prediction has come true.
◉ ～자 a prophet; 《여자》 a prophetess; a soothsayer; a predictor.

**예외**(例外) an exception. ¶ ～적인 exceptional / ～ 없이 without exception / ～적으로 exceptionally / …은 ～로 하고 except(ing)…; with the exception of …; except for… / 한 사람의 ～도 없이 nobody excepted / ～로 하다 make an exception of; except / ～를 인정치 않다 allow 〔admit (of)〕 no exceptions / 모든 규칙에는 ～가 있다 Every rule has its exceptions. / 이것은 ～다 This is an unusual case. / 이 규칙에는 하나의 ～가 있다 There is one exception to this rule.

**예우**(禮遇) honorable 〔courteous〕 treatment; a cordial reception. ～하다 treat 《*a person*》 with respect; receive cordially 〔courteously〕. ¶ ～를 받다 be cordially 〔warmly〕 received; meet with a cordial reception. ◉ ～정지 《의원·외교관 등의》 suspension of the privileges.

**예의**(銳意) [부사적] zealously; diligently;

earnestly; assiduously. ¶ ~ 검토하다 inquire into 《*a matter*》 assiduously; examine 《*a matter*》 in earnest / ~ 주시하다 watch intently; keep a very close watch 《on》.

**예의**(禮儀) courtesy; (good) manners; decorum(s); etiquette; propriety. ¶ ~ 바른 well-mannered; courteous; polite / ~를 모르는 ill-mannered; ill=bred / ~ 바르게 courteously; politely; with due courtesy / ~로 보아 according to etiquette / ~상 by courtesy; out of courtesy [politeness]; as a matter of courtesy / 형식적 ~ outward decorum; sham courtesy / ~를 지키다 observe the decorums [proprieties] / ~를 무시하다 disregard etiquette / ~를 소홀히 하다 forget *one's* manners; ignore decorum; lose *one's* decorum / 그는 ~를 모른다 He has no manners. *or* He is an ill-mannered person. / ~상 그녀의 청을 거절할 수 없었다 For courtesy's sake I couldn't refuse her offer. / 그런 질문은 ~에 어긋난다 It is 「impolite [bad manners] to ask such a question. / 그는 윗사람에 대한 ~를 모른다 He does not know how to behave toward his superiors. / 그렇게 하면 ~에 벗어난다 It is against etiquette to do so. / 친한 사이에도 ~가 있어야 한다 There should be courtesy even between close friends.
◉ ~범절 (the rules of ) etiquette: 부친께서는 ~범절에 까다로운 분이셨다 My father was very particular about manners.

**예인**(藝人) an artiste; a professional entertainer; an entertainer.

**예인선**(曳引船) a tugboat; a towboat. ¶ 그 난파선은 해군 ~에 끌려 왔다 The wrecked boat was towed by a Navy tugboat.

**예장**(禮狀) a letter of thanks [appreciation]; a thank-you letter. ¶ ~을 보내다 send 《*a person*》 a letter of thanks [appreciation].

**예장**(禮裝) ⇨ 예복(禮服). ~하다 wear ceremonial dress; be in full dress. ¶ ~을 하고 in full [ceremonial] dress.

**예전** 《옛날》 old [bygone] days [times]; 《이전》 former days [times]. ¶ ~대로 as of old; as usual / ~부터 from old times; for a long time; from of old / ~에는 formerly; of old / ~의 old; ancient; one-time; past; former; bygone / ~의 그 (사람) his former self; what he used to be / 그것은 ~부터 행해지고 있다 It's an old practice. / 모든 것이 ~과 달라졌다 Things are not what they used to be.

**예절**(禮節) 《예의범절》 courtesy; etiquette; (good) manners; decorums; the proprieties. ¶ ~을 중시하다 think much of the proprieties / ~을 모르다 have no sense of propriety / ~을 닦다 cultivate manners / ~을 지키다 observe the proprieties / 의식(衣食)이 족해야 ~을 안다 One must be well fed before one can be well bred. *or* Well fed, well bred.

**예정**(豫定) a program; a plan; a schedule; 《사전 준비》 (a) previous arrangements; 《예상》 expectation. ~하다 schedule 《to *do*》; plan [intend] 《to *do*》; expect; arrange 「in advance [beforehand]; prearrange; make a plan [program].
¶ ~의 prearranged; scheduled; appointed; intended; expected / ~대로 as scheduled [arranged]; according to schedule / ~보다 2일 빨리[늦게] two days before [behind] time / ~시간에 on scheduled time; at the appointed time; at the hour arranged / …할 ~으로 with the plan [project, schedule, intention] to *do* / …할 ~이다 plan [intend] to *do* [*do*ing]; expect to *do* [that...]; be scheduled [expected] to *do;* be going to *do;* be thinking of *do*ing / 그곳에 이틀 체재할 ~이다 I plan to stay there two days. / 그는 3시까지는 올 ~으로 되어 있다 He is expected to be here by three (o'clock). / 그는 어제 떠날 ~이었다 He was to leave yesterday. / 열차는 몇 시에 도착할 ~인가 When is the train due? / 그가 갑자기 찾아오는 바람에 내 ~이 틀어졌다 His unexpected visit upset my schedule. / 그것은 그녀의 ~된 행동이었다 It was her prearranged course of action. / 나는 그 일을 ~된 시간에 끝내지 못했다 I couldn't finish the job on schedule. / 비행기는 ~보다 30분 일찍[늦게] 도착했다 The plane arrived thirty minutes 「ahead of [behind] 「schedule [time]. / 배는 4월 10일 떠날 ~이다 The ship is scheduled to sail on April 10th.
◉ ~신고 《file》 a provisional return. ~액 an estimated amount. ~일 a prearranged date; the scheduled date: 출산 ~일 *one's* expected date of confinement; *one's* time / 도착 ~일 the estimated date of arrival. ~자 an

expectant: 입후보 ～자 an expectant candidate / 졸업 ～자 an expectant graduate. ～지점 《soft-land on》 a preset 〔predetermined〕 area. ～표 a schedule; a program; a timetable. ～행동 개시 시각 〖군사〗 the zero hour.

**예제** 《여기저기》 this place and that (place); here and there; everywhere.

**예제**(例題) an exercise. ¶ 장(章) 끝에 있는 ～를 풀다 do the exercises at the end of each chapter.

**예조**(禮曹) 〖고제도〗 the Ceremonies 〔Protocol〕 Board; the Ministry of Culture and Education.

**예증**(例證) an example; an illustration; an instance. ～하다 exemplify; illustrate. ¶ ～할 수 있는 exemplifiable / ～으로서 by way of illustration; as an example / ～을 들다 give 〔cite〕 an instance 〔example〕 / 여러 ～을 들다 multiply illustrations / ～이 되다 illustrate; be illustrative of; serve as an example of.

**예지**(叡智) wisdom; clear-mindedness and mental alertness; intelligence.

**예지**(豫知) foreknowledge; foreboding. ～하다 foreknow; know beforehand; foresee; foretell. ¶ 무슨 일이 일어날지를 ～하다 foresee what will happen.

**예진**(豫診) 〖의학〗 (a) medical preexamination. ～하다 make a diagnosis in advance.

**예진**(豫震) a foreshock; a preliminary tremor.

**예찬**(禮讚) praise; admiration; eulogy; high compliment. ～하다 praise; admire; eulogize; glorify; adore. ¶ 모성애의 ～ glorification of motherhood / 미의 ～ a beauty cult; the glorification of beauty.
◉ ～자 an adorer; an admirer.

**예측**(豫測) an estimate; (a) prospect; a forecast; presupposition. ～하다 make an estimate 《of》; forecast; presuppose. ¶ ～을 그르치다 make a wrong estimate 〔forecast〕; err in *one's* estimate 《of》 / 정확히 ～하다 make an accurate estimate 《of》 / 전투의 승패를 ～할 수 없다 The fate of a battle cannot be foreseen. / 어떻게 될지 아무도 ～할 수 없다 How it will turn out is anybody's guess.

**예탁**(預託) depositing; deposition. ～하다 deposit 《money in a bank》.
◉ ～금 a deposit; deposit money. ～자 a depositor. ～증서 a deposit receipt; a certificate of deposit.

**예탐**(豫探) preliminary investigation; spying. ～하다 spy 《upon》; inquire beforehand; sound out. ¶ 적정을 ～하다 spy upon the enemy's movements.
◉ ～꾼 a spy; a secret agent.

**예편**(豫編) ～하다 transfer to the 《first》 reserve; place on the reserve list; 《제대하다》 be discharged from military service.

**예포**(禮砲) a salute; a salvo (일제 발사). ¶ 21발의 ～ a salute of 21 guns; 《fire》 a 21-gun salute / ～를 쏘다 fire 〔give〕 a salute 〔salvo〕; salute with cannon.

**예풍**(藝風) 《개인의》 the style 〔characteristics〕 《of *one's* performance 〔acting〕》; *one's* (personal) technique; 《전통》 the artistic tradition 《of》.

**예하**(猊下) His Eminence (추기경); His Grace (대주교); His Excellency (영어권 이외의 주교·대주교) (★ 호칭의 경우는 His 대신에 Yours를 씀).

**예항**(曳航) towing. ～하다 take 《a ship》 in tow; tow.

**예해**(例解) an example; an illustration; an exemplification. ～하다 exemplify; illustrate.

**예행**(豫行) a rehearsal; a preliminary performance 《of》. ～하다 rehearse; have a rehearsal. ¶ 개회식을 ～하다 have 〔go through〕 a rehearsal of the opening ceremony. ◉ ～연습 a rehearsal; a preliminary drill: ～연습을 하다 ＝ ～하다.

**예회**(例會) a regular 〔stated〕 meeting. ¶ 추계(秋季) ～ the regular autumn meeting.

**예후**(豫後) a prognosis (*pl.* -ses); convalescence; recuperation. ¶ 그는 ～가 좋다 He is convalescing satisfactorily.

**옌장** 《실망의 소리》 Darn!; Damn!; Pshaw!; Gee whiz!; Goodness!

**옐로카드** 〖축구〗 a yellow card (주심이 경고로 내보이는 카드).

**옛** 《지나간》 old; olden; ancient. ¶ 옛 싸움터 an old 〔ancient〕 battlefield.

**옛글** ancient writings.

**옛길** an old road.

**옛날** 《고대》 ancient 〔old〕 time; antiquity; 《지난날》 old 〔bygone〕 days; old 〔olden〕 times. ¶ ～에는 in ancient 〔old〕 times; 《이전에는》 formerly; in former days / ～옛적에 long, long ago; once upon a time / 먼 ～부터 from old 〔ancient〕 times; since early times; from time immemorial / ～의 old; ancient; one-time; earlier; past; former; bygone / ～풍속 an old custom; a long-established custom / 그리

운 ～《sigh for》 the good old days / ～에는 이 곳에 절이 있었다 There used to be a temple here. / 저것을 보니 ～ 생각이 난다 That reminds me of the past. / ～에 심청이라는 소녀가 있었다 Once upon a time there was a girl named Shimch'ŏng. / 그 상점은 ～과 다름없이 번창하고 있다 The store continues to flourish as of old. / ～에는 태양이 지구 둘레를 돈다고 믿고 있었다 In old times people used to believe that the sun went round the earth.

**옛말** ①《고어》 an archaic 〔obsolete〕 word. ②《격언》 an old proverb 〔saying〕. ¶ "옥도 닦지 않으면 빛이 안 난다" 라는 ～이 있다 "An uncut gem does not sparkle," as the proverb says. ③《지난일》 ¶ 그 마을의 번영도 이미 ～이 되었다 The prosperity of the town is now a thing of the past.

**옛모습** traces; remains; vestiges. ¶ ～을 찾을 수 없다《사람》 be a mere shadow of *one's* former self; 《도시 따위》 be a mere shadow of its former prosperity / 현재 서울에서는 조선 왕조 시대의 ～은 거의 찾아볼 수가 없다 Almost no trace of the Dynasty of Chosŏn are retained in Seoul today.

**옛사람** ancient people; men of old 〔former days〕. ¶ ～이 되다 die; pass away.

**옛사랑** a bygone love; 《애인》 *one's* old lover.

**옛상처**(―傷處) an old wound; a scar. ¶ ～를 건드리다 [비유적] reopen (*a person's*) old scares; rake up 《*a person's*》 past misdeeds 〔scandals〕.

**옛식**(―式) an old 〔an ancient, a time-honored〕 rite 〔custom, style〕. ¶ ～을 따라 in accordance with the old 〔time-honored〕 rite 〔custom〕.

**옛이야기** an old story. ¶ 이젠 그것도 다 ～가 되었다 It is now an old story.

**옛일** bygones; a past (event); a thing of the past. ¶ ～을 생각하다 think of *one's* past / 그것도 이제는 ～이 되었다 It is now a thing of the past. / ～은 ～이다 Let bygones be bygones.

**옛적** old 〔olden〕 times. ⇨ 옛날.

**옛정**(―情) the sentiment 〔affection〕 of former days; 《친구간의》 old friendship.

**옛집** *one's* former house; *one's* old home 〔house〕; 《보금자리》 an old nest; *one's* old place 〔haunt〕. ¶ ～으로 돌아오다 revisit *one's* former haunt / ～이 그립다 have a longing for *one's* old home.

**옛추억**(―追憶) the memory of old days; old memories. ¶ ～을 더듬다 think of the good old days.

**옛친구**(―親舊) an old friend.

**옜다** 《여기 있다》 Here (it is)! ¶ ～ 이것 가져라 Here, take this.

**오**(五) five. ¶ 5분의 일 one fifth / 5원 five won / 제5 the fifth / 5배(의) five times; fivefold; quintuple.

**오**(午) 『민속』 ①《십이지의》 the Sign of the Horse(＝the 7th of the 12 Earth's Branches). ② ⇨ 오방(午方). ③ ⇨ 오시(午時).

**오**(伍) 《대오》 a file; a line.

**오** ①《아》 Oh!; O dear!; Ah! (★ 흔히 O의 다음에는 콤마를 붙이지 않으며, Oh 뒤에는 붙임); Look!; Dear me!; Good gracious!; (Good) Heavens!; 《의외》 Why! ¶ 오, 슬프다 Alas! *or* Woe is me. / 오, 하느님 구해 주옵소서 O God, save us! ②《대답》 Yes; Oh. ¶ 오, 그러나 Oh, indeed? / 오, 이제 알겠다 Oh, now I understand.

**오가다** come and go; keep coming and going. ¶ 오가는 사람이 없어지다 [길이 주어] be deserted / 이 거리는 오가는 사람으로 북적댄다 This street is bustling with passersby.

**오가리** ①《말린 것》 dried slices of pumpkin. ② [형용사적] all dried-up (of leaves); shriveled; pushed-in; dented. ¶ ～솥 a dented pot.

**오각형**(五角形) a pentagon. ¶ ～의 5-angled; pentagonal.

**오갈들다** ①《말라서》 dry up; shrivel; wither. ②《두려워》 feel ill at ease; feel timid; cower.

**오감**(五感) the (five) senses.

**오감스럽다** 《경망스럽다》 (be) flippant; frivolous.

**오감하다** 《만족하다》 (be) satisfactory; enough.

**오거리**(五―) a five-way crossing.

**오계**(五戒) 『불교』 the five Buddhist commandments (against murder, theft, adultery, falsehood, and intemperance).

**오계**(誤計) a wrong plan 〔scheme〕; miscalculation.

**오고가다** ⇨ 오가다. ¶ 오고가는 사람들 passersby; streams of people going and coming; the busy coming and going of people.

**오곡**(五穀) 《곡식》 the five grains (i.e. rice, millet, beans, barley, foxtail millet); [총칭] (important) grains; staple cereals. ◉ ～밥 cooked rice mixed with four other cereals.

**오관**(五官) the five sensory organs (of

hearing, seeing, tasting, smelling, and feeling).

**오구**(烏口) 《제도용의》 drawing 〔ruling〕 pen.

**오그라들다** curl up; contract; wither; shrivel. ¶ 손이 ~ *one's* hands contract 〔shrivel〕 / 구두가 ~ shoes get tight 〔curl up〕 / 목재는 마르면 오그라든다 Woods contracts as it dries. / 서리가 와서 잎들이 오그라들었다 The frost made the leaves curl up. / 이 천은 세탁해도 오그라들지 않는다 This cloth won't shrink in the wash.

**오그라지다** ① 《오그라들다》 get curled 〔rolled〕 up; shrivel 《up》; contract. ¶ 나뭇잎이 ~ the leaves curl 〔shrivel〕 up 《in the hot sun》. ② 《찌그러지다》 dent; become indented. ¶ 오그라진 냄비 a dented pan.

**오그랑이** 《물건》 a shriveled-up 〔curled〕 things; 《사람》 a crooked 〔perverse〕 person.

**오그랑장사** 《밑지는》 an enterprise whose capital has dwindled; a failing business.

**오그랑하다** be somewhat shriveled 〔curled〕 up; be slightly dented.

**오그르르** 《물이》 simmering; hubble-bubble; 《벌레가》 swarming; in swarms. ~하다 simmer; swarm.

**오그리다** ① 《몸·발·팔을》 curl 《*one's* body》 up; crouch; draw up 〔in〕; double up. ¶ 다리를 ~ draw in *one's* legs / 몸을 오그리고 자다 sleep curled up / 방 한 구석에 몸을 오그리고 앉다 crouch in a corner of a room / 아파서 몸을 ~ double up with pain / 손을 ~ cup *one's* hand. ② 《물건을》 bend 〔squeeze〕 out of shape; batter. ¶ 빈 깡통을 밟아 ~ make a dent in an empty can by stamping on it / 철사를 둥글게 ~ bend a wire into a circle.

**오글거리다** ① 《물이》 boil in bubbles; simmer. ② 《벌레가》 be thronged; swarm. ¶ 개미가 ~ ants swarm.

**오글보글** 《물·찌개가》 bubbling; simmering; hubble-bubble. ~하다 bubble; simmer.

**오글오글** 《물이》 simmering; 《벌레가》 in swarms. ¶ 물이 ~ 끓다 water simmers / 벌레가 ~ 끓다 worms wriggle about in a swarm.

**오글쪼글** ~하다 (be) wrinkled; withered; shriveled; crinkled; crumpled; rumpled. ¶ ~한 손 a shriveled hand / ~ 늙은 사람 a withered old person / 내 옷에 주름이 ~ 갔다 My clothes have gotten quite wrinkled. / 사과가 시들어 ~하다 The apple is all shriveled up.

**오금** ① 《무릎·팔의》 the crook 〔hollow, inside curve〕 of the knee 〔elbow〕. ¶ ~을 펴다 stretch *one's* knees / ~을 못 쓰다 be unable to move around / [비유적] be daunted; cower; be under 《*a person's*》 thumb; shrink inside *oneself* / 그는 부인 앞에 ~을 못 쓴다 He is under his wife's thumb. ② ⇨ 한오금.

**오금뜨다** gad about; be always on the move.

**오금박다** catch 《*a person*》 in *his* contradiction; trap 〔corner〕 《*a person*》 with *his* own words; squelch. ¶ 오금박히다 be caught in *one's* contradiction; be trapped 〔cornered〕 with *one's* own words / 아무를 꼼짝 못 하게 ~ corner *a person* with *his* own words and leaves *him* with no comeback.

**오금팽이** the inner side of a bend 〔curve〕.

**오긋하다** be somewhat dented 〔indented〕; be pressed in slightly. ¶ 냄비 밑이 오긋하게 들어갔다 The pan has a dent on its bottom.

**오기**(誤記) an error in writing; a clerical error; a miswriting; a slip of the pen; a pen-slip. ~하다 miswrite; make a pen-slip; write incorrectly; misspell 《a word》. ¶ 이 장부에는 ~가 많다 There are a lot of clerical errors in this account book.

**오기**(傲氣) 《오만》 pride; a proud temper; 《지기 싫어하는》 an unyielding spirit. ¶ ~가 나서 in a spirit of rivalry / ~(를) 부리다 try to rival 《another》; refuse to yield 《to》 / ~가 세다 be reluctant 〔unwilling〕 to admit *one's* defeat.

**오나가나** always; all the time; everywhere (you turn); wherever *one* goes. ¶ 그는 ~ 사람들을 속인다 He always takes people in. / 그는 ~ 아들 자랑이다 He always boasts about his son.

**오냐** 《대답》 yes; yea; 《동의》 all right; O.K. ¶ ~알았다 Yes, I see.

**오너** an owner 《of a professional basketball team》. ¶ 이 식당의 ~ the owner of this restaurant. ◉ ~ 드라이버 an owner-driver.

**오년**(午年) 『민속』 the Year of the Horse.

**오뇌**(懊惱) agony; anguish; worry. ~하다 be agonized; be in agony 〔anguish〕; be worried 〔troubled〕. ¶ 몹시 ~하고 있다 be immensely troubled in mind.

**오누이** brother and sister; siblings.

**오뉴월**(五六月) May and June. ¶ ～ 쇠불알 떨어지기만 기다리다《속담》 expect the impossible.

**오는** coming; next; forthcoming. ¶ ～ 토요일(에) next Saturday; on Saturday next / ～ 20일에 on the 20th (of this month).

**오늘** today; this day. ¶ 바로 ～ this very day / ～따라 today of all days / ～부터 from today; from now on / ～까지 till 〔until〕 this day; up to this day / ～ 안에 sometime 〔in the course of 〕 today / ～부터 일주일간 a week from today / ～ 신문 today's newspaper / ～ 오후〔아침〕 this afternoon 〔morning〕/ 내년〔작년〕의 ～ today 〔this day〕 year; a year after 〔ago〕 today / 내월〔지난달〕의 ～ this day month; this day next 〔last〕 month / ～은 무슨 요일〔몇일〕인가 What day of the week 〔month〕 is this? / ～은 일요일〔내 생일〕이다 Today is Sunday 〔my birthday〕. / ～은 4월 3일이다 Today 〔This〕 is the third of April. / ～ 그를 만났다 I saw him today. / ～ 내일 중에 끝마치겠습니다 I'll finish it in「a day or two 〔a couple of days〕.

**오늘날** today; these days 〔times〕; the present day 〔time〕. ¶ ～의 한국 the Korea of today / ～에는 nowadays; at present; these days / ～에 이르기까지 until 〔to〕 the present; up to now; to this day / 원자력 시대인 ～ in this age of atomic energy / ～ 한국에는 문맹이 거의 없다 There is hardly any illiteracy in Korea today.

**오늘밤** this evening; tonight. ¶ ～중에〔안으로〕 in the course of the night / ～은 여기에서 묵자 Let's stay here for the night. / 환자는 ～을 넘기기 힘들 거다 The patient will not live through the night.

**오늬** the notch of an arrow; the nock. ¶ ～를 시위에 걸다 fit an arrow on the string; nock an arrow.

**오다** ① [일반적] come; visit. ¶ 왔다 have come; be here; be arrived 〔come〕/ 왔었다 was 〔were〕 here (and left); came (and went) / 이리 오너라 Come here. *or* Come this way. / 잘 오셨습니다 I'm very glad to see you. *or* You are welcome. / 그녀는 종종 나를 만나러 온다 She often comes to see me. / 많은 사람들이 박물관에 온다 Many people visit the museum. / 서울로 꼭 놀러 오십시오 You must come to see me in Seoul. / 무슨 일로 왔느냐 What has brought you here?
② 《도착하다》 come; reach; arrive 《at, in》. ¶ 미국에서 방금 온 사람 a person (who has) just arrived from America / 기차가 올 때까지 till the train comes in / 가지러〔데리러〕 ～ come 〔call〕 for 《*a thing, a person*》/ 그는 오늘은 오지 않는다 He is not coming today. *or* He won't be here today. / 편지가 왔느냐 Has the mail come yet? / 너한테 전화가 왔다 You are wanted on the phone. / 버스가 온다 Here comes our bus! / 전투중 증원군이 왔다 In the middle of the battle help came. / 선생님께서 아직 안 오셨다 The teacher hasn't showed up yet. / 지난달 주문한 물품이 아직 오지 않았다 The article I ordered last month has not reached me yet.
③ 《계절·시간이》 come round; set in; draw 〔come〕 near. ¶ 좀 있으면 여름 방학이 온다 The summer vacation is just around the corner. / 어느새 봄이 왔다 Spring has come before I knew it. / 시험이 곧 다가온다 The examination is at hand. / 장마철이 왔다 The rainy season has set in.
④ 《전깃불·비·눈 따위가》 come on; drop; precipitate; rain; snow. ¶ 불이 〔전기가〕 ～ the light comes on; the lights come on / 비가〔눈이〕 ～ it rains 〔snows〕 / 서리가 ～ it frosts / 소나기가 ～ it shower.
⑤ 《유래·전래하다》 come from; be introduced from; derive from. ¶ 미국에서 온 정치 사상 political ideas introduced from America / 중국어에서 온 말 a word derived from Chinese; a word of Chinese origin / 미국서 온 춤 a dance of American origin / 그 습관은 불교에서 왔다 The custom can be traced (back) to Buddhism.
⑥ 《말미암다》 come of 〔from〕; be caused by; be due to; arise from. ¶ 연습에서 오는 손재주 skill that comes from practice / 과식에서 오는 병 sickness arising from overeating / 결국 올 것이 ～ reach an inevitable consequence / 가난은 전쟁에서 온다 Poverty stems from war. / 이 병은 대개 과로와 수면 부족에서 온다 This disease is, in most cases, caused by overwork and lack of sleep.
⑦ [조동사] gradually (come in *do*ing); become; grow. ¶ 떠날 날이 자꾸 가까워 온다 The day is drawing near when we are to leave.

**오다가다** 《이따금》 occasionally; at times; now and then; once in a while; 《어쩌다가》 on rare occasions; casually. ¶ ~ 들르는 손님 a casual 〔stray〕 customer (가게의) / ~ 있는 일 rare occurrence; a thing of infrequent occurrence / ~ 들르다 drop in every now and then (집 따위에) / 그녀로부터 ~ 소식이 있다 I hear from her once in a while.
**오달지다** 《여무지다》 (be) solid; compact; 《피륙이》 (be) tight and strong; have a fine weave; 《사람이》 (be) solidly built; firm.
**오대양**(五大洋) the Five Oceans.
**오대주**(五大洲) the Five Continents.
**오더** an order. ⇨주문.
**오도**(誤導) misguidance. ~하다 misguide; mislead; lead 《*a person*》 astray. ¶ 이런 논리는 젊은이들을 ~할 우려가 있다 This logic might lead young people astray.
**오도**(悟道) 〖불교〗 《깨달음》 the attainment of supreme wisdom; spiritual enlightenment. ~하다 attain (the) supreme wisdom; be spiritually enlightened.
**오도독** with a crunching sound. ~거리다 crunch. ¶ ~오도독 crunching; munching / ~오도독 깨물다 champ; crunch 《food》. ◉ ~뼈 cartilage; gristle.
**오도방정** flightiness; giddiness; frivolity; flippancy. ¶ ~을 떨다 act frivolously; behave in a giddy way.
**오도카니** 《멍하니》 absent-mindedly; blankly; vacantly; 《외롭게》 lonely; alone; solitarily.
**오독**(誤讀) misreading; misinterpretation. ~하다 read 〔interpret〕 《a passage》 wrongly; misread; misinterpret. ¶ 암호 전보를 ~하다 misinterpret a telegram in code.
**오돌오돌** ~하다 《표면이》 (be) hard and lumpy; 《씹기가》 (be) somewhat hard to chew; 《잘 삶아지지 않은》 (be) half=boiled.
**오동나무**(梧桐—) 〖식물〗 a paulownia (tree).
**오동통하다** (be) (short and) chubby; plump. ¶ 오동통한 뺨 the plump cheeks / 오동통한 소년 a chubby 〔plump〕 boy.
**오두막(집)** (—幕(—)) a hut; a cabin; a shed; a cottage (시골의 작은 집). ¶ 숲속의 ~ a hut in the wood / ~을 짓다 「put up 〔build〕 a 「shanty 〔shed〕.

> 용법 **hut** 통나무로 만들어 일시적인 숙박에 사용하는 오두막. **cabin** (아메리카 초기의 개척자들이 살았던) 지붕이 낮은 통나무집. 사냥·낚시하러 가는 사람들이나 여행자 등이 묵는 오두막. **shed** 창고나 작업장으로 사용되는 임시 또는 독립된 정·측면이 터져 있는 오두막.

**오들오들** shivering; trembling. ¶ ~ 떨게 하다 strike terror into 《*a person*》; terrify / ~ 떨다 tremble; shiver; quiver / 추워서 ~ 떨다 shiver all over with 〔from〕 cold / 무서워서 ~ 떨다 tremble with 〔for〕 fear; be terrified.
**오등**(吾等) we; us.
**오디** the fruit of the mulberry; mulberries.
**오디션** 〖영화·라디오〗 an audition. ¶ 나는 그 역의 ~을 받았다 I auditioned for the part. / 신인 배우의 ~을 했다 We auditioned 〔gave an audition to〕 a new actor.
**오디오** audio; 《장치》 a stereo 〔audio〕 system; stereo components. ◉ ~비주얼 audio-visual 《education, aids》. ~애호가 an audiophile; an audio fan. ~테이프 audiotape.
**오뚝이** a tumbling doll; a tumbler; a self-righting toy.
**오라** 《포승》 a rope for binding a criminal. ¶ 죄인을 ~로 묶다 bind 〔tie up〕 a criminal; arrest 《a criminal》 / 한 오랏줄로 묶다 tie 《*persons*》 in a row; rope 〔link〕 《*persons*》 together.
**오라기** a bit 〔piece, scrap〕 《of thread, cloth, paper》. ¶ 헝겊 ~ a piece 〔scrap〕 of cloth / 실 ~ 하나 걸치지 않고 stark=naked; without anything on 《*one*》 / 옷에 실 ~가 묻다 have bits of thread on *one's* clothes.
**오라버니** a girl's 〔woman's〕 elder brother. ◉ ~댁 the wife of a girl's 〔woman's〕 elder brother.
**오라지다** be trussed up; have *one's* arms bound behind *one's* back.
**오락**(娛樂) amusement(s); (an) entertainment; (a) recreation; (a) pastime.

> 용법 **amusement** 즐겁고 재미있는 것을 보거나 듣는 폭넓은 뜻의 낱말. **entertainment** 연극·영화·여흥 따위의 재미있고 흥겨운 오락 따위. **recreation** 일한 뒤에 하나의 즐거움으로 행하는 취미 활동. work에 상대되는 낱말. **pastime** 게임·독서 등 즐거운 마음으로 시간을 보내기 위해 행하는 취미 활동.

¶ ~으로(서) for pleasure; for *one's* amusement; by way of pastime; as a recreation 〔diversion〕 / 실내 ~ indoor amusements / 대중 ~ (a) popular 〔mass〕 entertainment / 하이킹은 건전한 ~이다 Hiking is a wholesome recreation. / 너는 ~으로 무엇을 하느냐 What do you do as a pastime? / 최근에는 미디어〔전달 매체〕의 발달로 눈으로 보는 ~이 늘고 있다 With the development of the media, there has been an increase in visual entertainment recently.

◉ ~가(街) an amusement quarter 〔district〕. ~물 a plaything; 《영화의》 a film for amusement. ~비 recreation expenditure. ~산업 amusement industry. ~설비〔시설, 기관〕 recreation(al) facilities; a means of public amusement; amusement facilities: ~시설을 마련하다 provide facilities for recreation / ~ 시설 완비 《게시》 Recreational facilities available. ~성 entertainingness: 고도의 ~성이 있는 영화 a very entertaining movie. ~실 an amusement hall; a recreation 〔game〕 room. ~잡지 a magazine for amusement 〔pleasure reading〕. ~장 a place for amusement 〔entertainment〕. ~프로 《라디오·텔레비전의》 an entertainment program.

**오락가락** coming and going; back and forth; to and fro; off and on. ~하다 come and go; go back and forth. ¶ 구름이 ~하다 the clouds come and go / 정신이 ~하다 *one's* mind wanders 〔strays〕 / 비가 ~한다 It rains 「off and on 〔by fits and starts〕.

**오랏줄** 《포승》 ⇨ 오라.

**오랑우탄** 〚동물〛 an orang(o)utan.

**오랑캐** 《여진》 uncivilized aborigines who lived north of the Tumen river; a barbarian; a savage.

**오랑캐꽃** a violet. ⇨ 제비꽃.

**오래** 《동안》 long; for a long time 〔while〕; a good while. ¶ ~ 전에 long ago; a long time ago / ~된 old; ancient; antique; old-fashioned; stale (음식물이) / 오랜 관습 an old custom / 오래지 않아 before long / ~ 계속되다 last long / ~ 걸리다 take long; take much time / ~ 살다 live long; outlive; enjoy longevity / ~ 끌다 drag on; be prolonged; 《병이》 linger / 그 일을 끝마치는 데 ~ 걸리겠습니까 Will it take you a long time to finish it? / ~ 걸려야 3일이겠지요 It will take three days at the longest. / ~ 기다리셨습니다 I'm sorry to have kept you waiting so long. / 그는 형제 중에서 제일 ~ 살았다 He outlived all his brothers. / 영어를 잘 하려면 ~ 걸린다 It takes a long time to master English. / ~ 기다리던 비가 어제 전국적으로 내렸다 The long-awaited rain fell throughout the nation yesterday.

**오래가다** last 〔keep〕 a long time; 《도구 등이》 stand long use; 《옷 따위가》 wear well; 《do not》 last 〔keep〕 long 〔well〕. ¶ 그 유행은 오래가지 않는다 That fashion will not prevail 〔last, continue〕 long. / 여름에는 생선이 오래가지 않는다 Fish do not keep long in summer. / 이런 가죽은 오래가지 못한다 This kind of leather does not wear well. / 좋은 날씨가 오래갈 것 같지 않다 I am afraid this fine weather will not hold. / 그의 금주(禁酒)는 오래가지 못할 거다 His abstinence will not continue long.

**오래간만** ¶ ~에 after a long time 〔interval, silence, absence, separation〕; for the first time in many days 〔years〕 / ~의 좋은 날씨 the first fine weather in quite a while; fine weather after a long spell of rain / 참 ~입니다 It has been a long time since I saw you last. *or* I haven't seen you for a long time. *or* We haven't met for ages. *or* It is an age 〔ages, a long time〕 since I saw you last. (★ It is… since…의 구문에서는 현재완료형은 사용되지 않는 것이 보통임: It is three years since the war ended. / Three years *have passed* since the war ended. 「전쟁이 끝난 지 3년이 되었다」. 또한 It 다음에 오는 명사가 복수더라도 be 동사는 단수형임) / 그한테서 ~에 편지를 받았다 I received a letter from him after a long silence. / 그는 ~에 영국에서 돌아왔다 He returned home after a long stay in England. / 그들은 ~에 만나 매우 기뻤다 They were very pleased to see each other after a long separation.

**오래다** be a long time; be of long standing; be long continued; (be) long. ¶ 오랜 습관 a custom of long standing; an old custom / 오랜 옛날 the (real) old days / 오랜 이야기 an old story / 오래지 않아 before long; not long after / 오랜 시일이 걸린다 It takes a long time 〔many years〕. / 그도 이젠 오래 살지 못할 것 같네 I am afraid his days are numbered. / 그를 본 지 ~ It is 〔has been〕 a long time since I saw him last. / 그가 미국에 간 지 ~ He has been in America long since. / 그가 죽은 지 ~ He has been long dead.

**오래도록** for long; for a long time; till late (늦게까지); forever. ¶ 밤에 ~ 앉아 있다 stay up till all hours / 아버지한테서 ~ 소식이 없다 do not hear from *one's* father for a long time / ~ 소식 전하지 못하여 미안합니다 I beg your pardon for my long silence.

**오래오래** for a long long time; very long; 《영원히》 forever. ¶ ~ 살다 live long; live to a ripe old age / ~ 해로(偕老)하다 live together in happy union till death parts them 〔us〕.

**오랫동안** for a long time 〔while〕. ¶ ~의 가뭄 a long spell of dry weather / ~의 분쟁〔교제〕 a dispute 〔an intercourse〕 of long standing / ~ 소식이 없다 hear nothing 《from *a person*》 for long / ~ 뵙지 못했군요 I haven't seen you for a long time. / ~ 소식을 못 드려 죄송합니다 I must apologize 〔Excuse me〕 for my long silence. / 서울에 얼마나 ~ 계실겁니까 How long are you going to stay in Seoul?

**오레오마이신** 〖약〗《상표》 aureomycin.

**오렌지** an orange. ¶ ~색의 orange; orange-colored. ◉ ~스쿼시 orange squash. ~주스 orange juice.

**오려내다** clip (out); cut out. ⇨ 오리다.

**오려붙이기** cut and paste.

**오로라** an aurora.

**오로지** alone; wholly; solely; exclusively; only; entirely. ¶ ~ 너 때문에 solely for your sake / ~ 사회 사업에 진력하다 give all *one's* energies 〔devote *oneself*〕 to social welfare work / ~ …의 연구에 몰두하다 devote 〔apply〕 *oneself* to the study of... / 그 책임은 ~ 너한테 있다 You are solely responsible for it. / 친구라곤 ~ 너뿐이다 You are the only friend I have. / 내 성공은 ~ 자네 덕분이네 I owe my success entirely to you.

**오롯하다** 《완전하다》 (be) perfect; complete; 《부족함이 없다》 (be) sufficient; 《원만하다》 (be) harmonious.

**오류**(誤謬) a mistake; an error; a fallacy. ¶ ~가 없는 free from mistakes 〔errors〕; correct; perfect; infallible / 계산상의 ~ an error in caculation / 문법상의 ~ a grammatical mistake 〔error〕 / ~를 깨닫다 see 〔realize〕 the error of *one's* ways / ~를 범하다 make a mistake 〔an error〕; commit an error / ~를 바로잡다 correct 〔rectify〕 an error / ~를 인정하다 admit 〔acknowledge〕 a mistake / 너의 작문에는 ~가 많다 Your composition has a lot of mistakes.

**오륜**(五倫) the moral rules to govern the Five Human Relations. ⇨ 삼강오륜.

**오륜**(五輪) ⇨ 올림픽. ◉ ~기(旗) the (five-ringed) Olympic flag; a flag bearing the five-ring Olympic emblem. ~마크 the five-ring Olympic emblem.

**오르가슴** (an) orgasm. ¶ ~에 도달하다 reach 〔have〕 orgasm.

**오르간** 〖악기〗 an organ; a harmonium. (★ 단순히 organ이라고 하면 보통 pipe organ을 가리킴. 우리가 말하는 풍금은 harmonium 또는 reed organ이라고 함). ◉ ~연주자 an organist.

**오르골** a music 〔musical 《영》〕 box.

**오르내리** ascent and descent; rise and fall; fluctuation (시세의).

**오르내리다** ① 《높은 곳을》 go up and down 《the steps》; ascend and descend. ¶ 층계를 ~ go up and down the stairs / 언덕을 ~ ascend and descend 〔go up and down〕 a hill. ② 《물가·온도 따위가》 rise and fall; go up and down; fluctuate. ¶ 물가가 ~ the price fluctuates / 온도가 20도에서 30도 사이를 오르내린다 The temperature varies 〔ranges〕 between 20 and 30 degrees. ③ 《먹은 것이》 do not settle. ¶ 먹은 것이 ~ suffer from indigestion. ④ 《남의 입에》 be talked about; be gossiped about; be in everybody's mouth. ¶ 그녀의 소행이 사람들 입에 오르내리고 있다 Her conduct is on every-body's lips.

**오르다** ① 《높이·높은 곳에》 go 〔come〕 up; rise; ascend; mount; climb (up). ¶ 나무에 ~ climb a tree / 단상〔연단〕에 ~ mount 〔step on〕 the platform / 산에 ~ climb a mountain / 지붕에 ~ get 〔go up〕 on the roof / 층계를 ~ go 〔walk〕 up the stairs / 하늘로 ~ soar 〔go up〕 in the air; soar skyward. ② 《탈것에》 take 《a bus, a plane》; ride 《a horse, a bicycle》; 《올라타다》 get on 〔into〕 《a train》; get into 《a car》; board 《a bus》; go 〔get〕 aboard 《a ship》. ⇨ 타다[2]. ③ 《물가 따위가》 rise; advance; go 〔come, look〕 up. ¶ 물가가 ~ prices go up / 시세가 ~ quotations 〔prices〕 advance 〔rise〕; rise 〔go up〕 in price / 부동산 가격이 급격히 올랐다 Property values went up 〔advanced〕 rapidly. /

내년부터 세금이 오른다 Taxes will be raised next year.
④ 《나아지다》 progress; make progress 〔headway〕; advance; improve. ¶ 성적이 ～ show a better school record / 능률이 ～ improve 〔increase〕 in efficiency.
⑤ 《승급·승진하다》 rise; be raised; be advanced 〔promoted〕; get promotion; 《왕위에》 ascend throne; accede 〔come〕 to the throne. ¶ 요직에 ～ be appointed to an important post 〔office〕 / 월급이 ～ get a salary raise / 지위가 ～ rise in rank; be promoted to a higher position / 그는 과장으로 올랐다 He was promoted to section chief.
⑥ 《밥상 등에》 be served; be brought; 《의제 등에》 come up; be placed before; be presented (무대에). ¶ 의제(議題)에 ～ come 〔be brought〕 up for discussion 〔debate〕; be placed on the agenda / 춘향전이 무대에 ～ the story of Ch'unhyang is put on the stage / 귀한 생선이 상에 올랐다 A rare fish was served on the table.
⑦ 《열·온도 등이》 rise; go up; get higher. ¶ 열이 ～ *one's* temperature rises 〔goes up〕; *one's* fever heightens / 온도가 ～ the temperature 〔mercury, thermometer〕 rises 〔goes up〕 / 기온이 30도로 올랐다 The temperature rose 〔went up〕 to 30°.
⑧ 《살이》 put on; gather; gain. ¶ 살이 ～ put on 〔gather, get〕 flesh; grow fleshy 〔in flesh〕; flesh up.
⑨ 《술·약기운 등이》 be effective; work. ¶ 술이 ～ be flushed 〔dazed〕 《by liquor》; become 〔get〕 tipsy 〔intoxicated〕 / 약기운이 ～ begin to feel the effect of a drug.
⑩ 《연기·김 따위가》 rise; go up. ¶ 김이 ～ steam; reek; emit 〔give off〕 steam / 굴뚝에서 연기가 ～ smoke rises from a chimney.
⑪ 《불길 등이》 blaze 〔light〕 up; burn 〔go〕 up (in a flame); burst into flames. ¶ 불기둥이 ～ a pillar of flames shoots up / 밤하늘에 불꽃이 솟아 올랐다 Fireworks were set off in the night sky.
⑫ 《실리다》 be recorded; be entered; be registered; be included. ¶ 이름이 전화 번호부에 ～ *one's* name is put in the telephone directory / 추문이 신문에 ～ a scandal is reported in a newspaper / 공적이 기록에 ～ *one's* achievement is placed 〔put〕 on record.
⑬ 《병독이》 be infected; be contracted. ¶ 옴이 ～ be infected with 〔get〕 the itch; suffer from the itch / 옻이 ～ be poisoned with lacquer; get poison ivy.
⑭ 《남의 입에》 become the talk of; be gossiped about; be on people's lips. ¶ 그녀의 행실이 동네 사람들의 입에 올랐다 Her conduct became the talk of the town.
⑮ 《물이》 rise. ¶ 나무에 물이 ～ the sap rises.
⑯ 《떠나다》 start; set out; leave. ¶ 귀로에 ～ leave for home; start on a homeward journey / 유럽 여행길에 ～ set out on a trip to Europe.
⑰ 《거슬러》 go upstream; go up 〔ascend〕 《a river》. ¶ 배를 저어 강을 거슬러 ～ scull 〔row〕 upstream.
⑱ 《약이》 be offended; feel vexed 〔annoyed〕 《with, at》; 《맛·향미 따위가》 ripen to full flavor. ¶ 노여움이 치밀어 ～ have a fit of anger / 그의 행동에 정말 약이 오른다 I am deeply offended by his conduct.
⑲ 《때가》 get dirty; become dirty 〔filthy〕.
⑳ 《성과·이익 등이》 produce; achieve; gain; be made. ¶ 좋은 성과가 ～ produce good 〔satisfactory〕 results / 이익이 ～ bring 〔give, fetch〕 《*a person*》 a profit / 집세로 월 50만 원의 수입을 올린다 I have a monthly income of 500,000 won from the house I rent.
㉑ 《기세 등이》 rise; become high-spirited 《by》. ¶ 기세가 ～ be in high spirits; be elated / 사기가 ～ become full of (fighting) spirit.
㉒ 《신·혼령 등이》 possess; be possessed. ¶ 무당에게 신이 올랐다 A god entered into the shaman.

**오르락내리락** rising and falling; going up and down; fluctuating. ～하다 = 오르내리다. ¶ 요새 물가가 ～하여 몹시 변동이 심하다 Prices are fluctuating and very unstable nowadays.

**오르막** an ascent; an uprise; an upward slope; uphill. ¶ 길은 줄곧 ～이다 The road runs 〔is〕 uphill all the way. / 거기서부터는 아주 가파른 ～이었다 From there we had a very steep climb. ◉ ～길 an uphill road; a rising hill.

**오른** (the) right. ◉ ～손 the right hand. ～팔 the right arm; 《심복》 a right-hand man; *one's* second self: 그는 나의 ～팔로 일하여 왔다 He has worked as my right-hand (man).

**오른쪽** the right (side). ¶ ～에 on *one's*

right; on the right of; to the right (★ 장소를 엄밀히 말할 때는 on보다는 at를 씀) / ～에 있는 사람 a person on *one's* right / ～에 앉다 sit at the right of / ～으로 꾸부러지다 turn to the right / ～으로 가다 keep to the right.

**오른편**(一便) the right (side). = 오른쪽.

**오름세**(一勢) 《물가의》 an upward tendency 《of the market》; a rising trend; 《증권의》 a bull (market). ¶ ～의 firm; bullish; strong / ～를 보이다 show rising trends / 꾸준히 ～를 보이다 rise steadily; be a firm trend.

**오리**[1] 《가는 조각》 a strip. ◉ 나무～ a strip of wood 〔board〕.

**오리**[2] 〚조류〛 a (wild) duck; a drake (수컷). ¶ ～ 사냥을 가다 go duck-shooting / ～가 울고 있다 A duck is quacking. ◉ 새끼～ a duckling.

**오리**(五里) five *ri.*

**오리**(汚吏) a corrupt official.

**오리건** 《미국의》 Oregon (생략 Oreg., Ore., Or.).

**오리나무** 〚식물〛 an alder; a black alder.

**오리너구리** 〚동물〛 a duckbill.

**오리다** cut 「off 〔away〕; cut 〔clip〕 (out). ¶ 가위로 종이를 ～ cut paper into strips with scissors / 신문에서 기사를 ～ clip 〔cut out〕 an article from a newspaper. 「board.

**오리목**(一木) 〚건축〛 a lath; a strip of

**오리무중**(五里霧中) ¶ ～이다 be in the dark 〔a fog〕 《about》; be all at sea 《in regard to》 / 그 살인사건은 여전히 ～에 빠져 있다 The murder case is as much in the dark as ever. / 무엇을 어찌해야 될지 ～이다 I don't have the foggist idea what to do.

**오리발** 《물갈퀴》 a webfoot; 《사람의》 a web-fingered hand. ¶ ～ 내밀다 [비유적] have the nerve to feign innocence; play innocent as if he knew nothing about 《it》.

**오리엔테이션** (an) orientation. ¶ 신입생에게 1주일 동안 ～을 한다 We shall give a week of orientation 〔an orientation session〕 to incoming freshmen. / 잊지 말고 그것을 ～에 갖고 오너라 Make sure you bring it to the orientation.

**오리엔트** 《동양》 the Orient.

**오리온자리** 〚천문〛 Orion; the Hunter.

**오리지널** an original. ¶ 사본과 ～을 구별하기 힘들다 It's difficult to tell the copy from the original.

**오막살이** (life in) a grass hut. ¶ ～를 하다 lead a hut life; be a hut-dweller.

**오만**(五萬) ①《수》 fifty thousand. ②《잡다함》 ever so much; innumerable; countless; thousands; millions. ¶ ～일 ever so many things 《to *do*》 / ～가지 물건을 팔다 sell things of every sort and kind / ～소리 다 한다 Cut the nonsense!

**오만**(傲慢) haughtiness; arrogance; overweening pride. ～하다 (be) haughty; arrogant; overbearing; 《구어》 stuck=up. ¶ ～불손한 insolent / ～한 태도를 취하다 act haughtily; assume a haughty attitude; hold *one's* head high / ～불손하게도 …하다 be so insolent as to 《*do*》; be insolent enough to 《*do*》.

**오만** 《나라 이름》 (the Sultanate of) Oman. ◉ ～사람 an Omani.

**오만상**(五萬相) a distorted 〔frowning, wry, puckered〕 face; a grimace; a scowl. ¶ ～을 짓다〔찌푸리다〕 distort *one's* face; make 〔pull〕 a wry face; make grimaces.

**오매불망**(寤寐不忘) remembering awake or asleep; unforgettableness. ～하다 remember when awake or asleep; bear in mind all the time. 「last.

**오메가** Omega; Ω, ω; 《사물의 맨끝》 the

**오면체**(五面體) 〚수학〛 a pentahedron.

**오명**(汚名) ①《더러워진 이름·불명예》 disgrace; dishonor; *one's* bad reputation; a stigma; a stain on *one's* honor; a bad name. ¶ ～을 남기다 leave a bad name behind 《*one*》. ② = 누명(陋名). ¶ 그는 가까스로 배신자라는 ～을 벗을 수 있었다 He managed to clear himself of the charge of being a traitor.

**오목** sunken-in; depressed; concave. ◉ ～거울 a concave mirror 〔reflector〕. ～누비 a kind of deep quilt-stitching. ～다리 quilt-stitched baby socks. ～렌즈 a concave lens.

**오목**(五目) 《play》 *omok,* a game of *paduk* with five checkers placed in a row.

**오목오목, 오목조목** sharply dented all over; sharply pressed 〔pushed〕 in; sunk here and there. ～하다 be sharply dented all over. ¶ 비에 땅이 오목오목 팼다 The ground is washed out in little hollows all over from the rain.

**오목하다** be sharply pressed 〔pushed〕 in; (be) sharply dented; sunk; depressed. ¶ 오목한 눈 deep-set 〔sunken〕 eyes.

**오묘**(奧妙) occultness; abstruseness;

reconditeness. ～하다 (be) abstruse; occult; recondite; esoteric. ¶ ～한 사상 profound ideas.

**오물**(汚物) 《분뇨》 night soil; 《더러운 것》 filth; dirt; muck; 《하수의》 sewage; 《부엌의》 garbage. ¶ ～ 처리 disposal of garbage. ◉ ～수거인 《분뇨의》 a nightman; 《쓰레기의》 a garbageman; an ashman 《미》. ～차(車) a night-soil cart; a garbage car. ～처리 공장 a sewage purification plant. ～처리 시설 filth-treating equipment; sanitation facilities.

**오물거리다** ① [장소가 주어] swarm 〔be crowded〕 《with》; crawl 〔be alive〕 《with》. ¶ 설탕 단지에 개미가 ～ A sugar bowl is alive with ants. ② 《입을》 chew with closed lips; mumble; chew on 《*one's* gum》; mouth; munch. ¶ 껌을 넣고 입을 ～ chew away at *one's* chewing gum. ③ 《말을》 mumble 《words》. ¶ 말을 ～ mumble *one's* words.

**오물오물** ① 《벌레 따위가》 in swarms. ② 《입 속에서》 mumbling; munching; mouthing; chewing on. ¶ 사과를 ～ 씹다 munch an apple. ③ 《말을》 mumblingly. ¶ ～ 말하다 mumble 〔mouth〕 *one's* words.

**오므라들다** get 〔become〕 narrower; contract; close; curl up; pucker up; wither. ¶ 나팔꽃은 정오가 되면 오므라든다 The flower of morning glory withers around noon. / 구멍이 오므라들었다 The opening has closed.

**오므라이스** an omelet with a filling of fried rice (containing minced beef and vegetables).

**오므리다** make 《*a thing*》 narrower; pucker; purse; close up; shut. ¶ 입을 ～ pucker up the mouth; purse (up) the lips / 날개를 ～ furl the wings / 그는 추워서 몸을 오므렸다 He huddled up with cold.

**오믈렛** an omelet(te).

**오미**(五味) the Five Tastes (*i.e.* sour, bitter, pungent, sweet, salty).

**오미자**(五味子) 〚한의〛 fruit of the *Maximowiczia chinensis.*

**오밀조밀**(奧密稠密) ～하다 ① 《면밀하다》 (be) very meticulous; scrupulous; circumspect. ¶ ～한 필치 a meticulous bit of writing. ② 《솜씨가》 (be) elaborate; exquisite; fine wrought. ¶ ～한 세공품 elaborate handiwork / ～하게 꾸민 정원 a garden of tasteful layout.

**오바댜서**(一書) 〚성서〛 The Book of Obadiah; 《약칭》 Obadiah (생략 Obad.).

**오발**(誤發) ① an accidental discharge 《of a gun》; accidental firing. ～하다 go off accidentally 〔by accident〕. ¶ 총의 ～을 방지하기 위해서는 안전 장치를 해 놓아야 한다 You should put the safety catch on your gun so that it doesn't go off accidentally. ② a slip of the tongue. ⇨ 실언(失言).

**오방**(午方) 〚민속〛 《남쪽》 the Direction of the Horse (=south).

**오배**(五倍) quintuple; five-times 《as many as》; fivefold. ～하다 multiply 《a number》 by five; quintuplicate.

**오백**(五百) five hundred. ¶ ～년째의 a quincentenary.

**오버** ① 《외투》 an overcoat. ¶ 털～ a fur overcoat. ② 《초과》 ～하다 go over; exceed. ¶ 비용은 예상액을 ～했다 The expenses exceeded the estimate. ③ 〚통신〛 《교신 끝》 Over (and out).

**오버네트** 《배구에서》 (a) reaching over the net.

**오버랩** 〚영화〛 (an) overlap; overlapping. ¶ 영상이 ～되다 Pictures are overlapping each other.

**오버런** (an) overrun. ～하다 overrun; overshoot (활주로에서). ¶ 활주로를 ～하다 overshoot 〔overrun〕 a runway.

**오버스로** 〚야구〛 an overhand 「throw 〔pitch, delivery〕.

**오버슈즈** 《덧신》 overshoes; galoshes.

**오버워크** overwork. ¶ ～로 병이 나다 become sick from overwork.

**오버코트** an overcoat. ¶ ～를 입다〔벗다〕 put on 〔take off〕 an overcoat.

**오버타임** overtime. ¶ 세시간 ～하다 work three hours overtime.

**오버핸드** ① 〚야구〛 ⇨ 오버스로. ② 〚테니스〛 overhand. ¶ ～ 스트로크 an overhand stroke.

**오버홀** 〚기계〛 an overhaul. ～하다 over-「haul 《an engine》.

**오버히트** overheat. ¶ ～된 엔진 an overheated engine.

**오벨리스크** 《뾰족한 기념탑》 an obelisk.

**오변형**(五邊形) a pentagon. ⇨ 오각형.

**오보**(誤報) an incorrect report; a false report; misinformation; wrong information. ～하다 misreport; misinform about 〔on〕; give a 「false report 〔wrong information〕. ¶ 그것은 ～였다 The report proved false 〔incorrect〕. / 그 신문은 가끔 ～를 낸다 That paper often gives wrong information.

**오보에** 〚악기〛 an oboe. ¶ ～ 연주자 an oboist.

**오복**(五福) the Five Blessings (*i.e.* longevity, wealth, health, love of virtue, peaceful death).

**오불관언**(吾不關焉) a detached 〔an unconcerned〕 air. ～하다 disregard; be indifferent 《to》; assume an unconcerned air. 「ly.

**오붓이** amply; abundantly; cozily; snug-

**오붓하다** (be) ample; substantial; sufficient; be a nice lot of. ¶ 오붓한 살림 a comfortable living / 오붓하게 살다 live in ease 〔plenty〕; be well off; live in a small way / 그들은 식구끼리 오붓하게 살고 있다 They live by themselves without any outsiders in the house.

**오븐** an oven; a quick oven. ¶ ～에 굽다 bake in an oven.

**오블라토** a wafer; an *oblaat* (D.).

**오비** 《졸업생》 a former student; 《미》 an alumnus (*pl.* -ni); 《영》 an old boy (생략 O.B.); 《골프에서》 out of bounds. ¶ 직장의 ～ an ex-colleague / 서클의 ～ an ex-member of a club / ～가 되다 《골프》 go out of bounds; put 〔drive〕 *one's* tee shot out of bounds; hit the ball out of bounds.

**오비이락**(烏飛梨落) A pear drops when a crow flies from the tree. → *or* It is just a coincidence that the two events have happened at the same time. → *or* the strangest coincidence that arouses other's suspicion.

**오빠** a girl's older brother.

**오사리**(五—) the early catch of fish at high tide. ◉ ～잡놈 a reprobate; a debauchee; scoundrel.

**오사바사하다** be likeable but capricious.

**오산**(誤算) 《계산 착오》 wrong estimate; miscalculation; 《잘못된 판단》 misjudgment. ～하다 make a wrong estimate; miscalculate; make an error in calculation; misjudge. ¶ ～에 의한 전쟁의 가능성 the possibility of war through miscalculation / 전략상의 ～ a strategic miscalculation / 그것은 나의 ～이었다 I misjudged it. / 그의 득표 예상은 큰 ～이었다 He made a huge error in estimating the number of possible votes he would get.

**오상**(五常) ① 《유교의》 the five constant virtues (*i.e.* benevolence, righteousness, propriety, knowledge, sincerity). ② ＝ 오륜(五倫).

**오색구름**(五色—) five-colored clouds; glowing 〔iridescent〕 clouds.

**오색딱따구리**(五色—) 〖조류〗 a great spotted woodpecker.

**오색영롱**(五色玲瓏) shining brilliantly in all the five colors. ～하다 shine brightly in various colors; (be) very colorful; resplendent.

**오색잡놈**(五色雜—) a reprobate; a rogue; a scamp. ⇨ 오사리잡놈.

**오서독스** orthodoxy; 《전통파》 the orthodox school; 《권위가 있는》 authoritative; 《근거가 있는》 authentic.

**오선**(五線) 〖음악〗 the staffs; the stave. ◉ ～보 staff notation. ～지 music paper; a music sheet.

**오성**(悟性) 〖심리〗 wisdom; 〖철학〗 understanding. ◉ ～론 〖철학〗 rationalism.

**오세아니아** 《대양주》 Oceania.

**오소리** 〖동물〗 a badger.

**오손**(汚損) stain 〔soilage〕 and damage. ～하다 stain; soil; damage; be stained 〔soiled〕.

**오솔길** a (narrow) path; a (lonely) lane; a trail. 「ta.

**오수**(午睡) midday sleep; a nap; a sies-

**오수**(汚水) dirty 〔filthy, foul〕 water; polluted water; 《하수》 sewage; 《부엌 구정물》 slops. ¶ 공장의 ～를 처리하다 treat waste water from the factory. ◉ ～관 a soil 〔waste〕 pipe. ～처리 sewage disposal 〔treatment〕: ～처리장 a sewage treatment plant.

**오순도순** in amity; on cordial terms; friendly; chummily; harmoniously. ～하다 (be) amiable; gentle; mild; kindly; conciliatory. ¶ 어린애들이 ～ 잘 논다 children play together well / 부부가 ～ 잘 지내다 man and wife live happily together.

**오스뮴** 〖화학〗 osmium (기호 Os).

**오스카상**(—賞) an Oscar. ◉ ～수상 배우〔여배우〕 an Oscar actor 〔actress〕.

**오스트레일리아** Australia. ¶ ～의 Australian. ◉ ～사람 an Australian.

**오스트리아** Austria. ¶ ～의 Austrian. ◉ ～사람 an Austrian.

**오슬오슬** shiveringly. ～하다 (be, feel) chilly; (be) shivery. ¶ ～ 춥다 feel a chill; be shivering with cold / ～ 떨다 shiver with cold / 열이 나서 ～하다 have chills 〔shakes〕 with the fever.

**오시**(午時) 〖민속〗 the Watch of the Horse (＝the period around between 11 a.m.-1 p.m.).

**오시아르** 〖컴퓨터〗 《광학 문자 판독(기)》 (an) OCR. [<*o*ptical *c*haracter *r*eader]

**오식**(誤植) 〖인쇄〗 a typographical 〔printer's〕 error; a literal error; a misprint; a slip of the press; an erratum. ～하다 misprint. ¶ ～이 없는 책 a book free from 〔of〕 misprints / (정오표에

서) "fail"은 "fall"의 ～ For "fail" read "fall." / ～이 많다 teem with 〔be full of〕 misprints / ～을 정정하다 correct errors in proof. ◉ ～정정표 a list of corrigenda; an errata.

**오실로그래프** 〖물리〗 an oscillograph.

**오실로스코프** 〖물리〗 an oscilloscope.

**오심**(誤審) ① 〖법〗 (a) miscarriage of justice; (a) misjudgment. ～하다 misjudge; judge wrongly. ② 〖스포츠〗 wrong (refereeing) decision. ～하다 give a wrong 〔bad, mistaken〕 decision.

**오십**(五十) fifty. ¶ 제～ the fiftieth / ～보 백보 (There is) little difference between the two; (There is) not much to choose between the two / 나이 ～을 바라보다 be close 〔hard〕 upon fifty; be on the short side of fifty. ◉ ～견(肩) a stiff and painful shoulder. ～년 축전 a semicentennial.

**오싹** 《shivering》 with a chill. ～하다 feel 〔have〕 a chill; shiver 《with fright, to think of》; shudder 《at, to think of》; thrill 《with horror》. ¶ 등골이 ～하다 [사물이 주어] send a chill 〔shiver〕 down *one's* spine / ～하게 하다 send a thrill 《of horror》 through 《*a person*》; freeze 〔chill〕 *one's* blood; make 《*a person*》 shudder; make 《*a person's*》 flesh creep / 생각만 해도 등골이 ～해졌다 The mere thought made me shudder. *or* I shuddered at the bare idea of it. / 일본의 두 도시를 무너뜨린 지진은 로스앤젤레스에 이런 지진이 일어났을 때 벌어질 오싹한 광경을 보여준다 The earthquake that flattened two Japanese cities provides a chilling picture of what the future could hold for Los Angeles.

**오싹오싹** shiveringly. ～하다 shiver with cold; be chilly; 《공포 따위로》 feel creepy.

**오아시스** an oasis (*pl.* -ses).

**오얏** a plum. = 자두.

**오언절구**(五言絶句) 〖문학〗 a quatrain with five syllables in each line.

**오엑스** true-false. ◉ ～문제 true-false questions. ～식 테스트 a true-false test.

**오엠아르** 〖컴퓨터〗 《광학 표시 판독(기)》 OMR. [＜*o*ptical *m*ark *r*eader]

**오역**(誤譯) (a) mistranslation; (a) wrong translation. ～하다 mistranslate; make 「a mistake 〔an error〕 in translation. ¶ ～을 지적하다 point out mistakes in a translation / 너의 번역에는 ～이 몇 군데 있다 You have made several slips in your translation. / 이 책은 ～투성이다 There are a lot of errors in this translation.

**오연**(傲然) (attitude of) haughtiness; arrogance. ～하다 show the attitude of haughtiness 〔arrogance〕; behave arrogantly 〔haughtily, overbearingly〕. ¶ ～히 haughtily; arrogantly; overbearingly / ～한 태도를 취하다 assume a haughty air; hold *one's* head high.

**오열**(五列) the Fifth Column; secret agents.

**오열**(嗚咽) a sob; sobbing; a fit of crying. ～하다 sob; cry out in sorrow; give a sob.

**오염**(汚染) contamination 《of water supplies》; 《air》 pollution. ～하다 pollute; contaminate 《the air》; taint. ¶ 대기～ air pollution / 환경～ environmental pollution / 공장 폐수에 의한 하천의 ～ industrial pollution of a river / ～되다 be contaminated; be polluted; be tainted / ～된 polluted 《air》; contaminated 《water》; tainted 《food》 / ～을 제거하다 remove pollutants; decontaminate / 공기를 ～시키다 pollute the air / 대기가 방사능〔자동차의 배기 가스〕에 의해 ～되어 있다 The atmosphere is contaminated by radioactivity 〔exhaust fumes from cars〕. *or* The air is polluted with radioactivity 〔exhaust fumes from cars〕. / 그것은 ～된 물에 의해 일어나는 특수한 질병이다 It is a specific illness caused by contaminated water.
◉ ～계(計) a contamination meter. ～대책 an antipollution measure; a measure (to be) taken against 《environmental, air》 pollution. ～도(度) a pollution level. ～물질 a pollutant; a contaminant. ～방지 prevention of 《air, water》 pollution: ～방지 조례 an antipollution ordinance / ～ 방지 장치〔설비〕 antipollution equipment. ～원(源) a pollution source. ～자 부담원칙 polluter pays principle.

**오욕**(汚辱) 《수치》 disgrace; dishonor; 《모욕》 insult; ignominy; opprobrium; obloquy. ¶ ～을 참다 endure obloquy; eat dirt.

**오용**(誤用) misuse; wrong use; misapplication (적용의); abuse (남용). ～하다 misuse; misapply; use 《*a thing*》 for a wrong purpose.

**오월**(五月) May. ¶ ～의 여왕 a May queen. ◉ ～단오(端午) the *Tano* festival on the fifth day of May of the lunar calendar.

**오월동주**(吳越同舟) bitter 〔implacable〕

enemies (placed by fate) in the same boat.

**오의**(奧義) profound meaning; recondite principles; the mysteries 《of an art》; secrets.

**오이** 〖식물〗 a cucumber. ¶ ~를 거꾸로 먹어도 제멋 《속담》 Every man to his taste. *or* Tastes differ. *or* There is no accounting for tastes.
◉ ~생채 cucumber salad. ~소박이 stuffed cucumber kimchi. ~지 cucumbers pickled in salt.

**오이시디** 《경제 협력 개발 기구》 OECD. [< the *O*rganization for *E*conomic *C*ooperation and *D*evelopment]

**오이엠** 〖경제〗《주문자 상표 부착 생산》 OEM. [< the *o*riginal *e*quipment *m*anufacturing] 「us.

**오인**(吾人) ① 《나》 I; me. ② 《우리》 we;

**오인**(誤認) a mistaken acknowledgment 〔recognition〕; (a) misconception. ~하다 take 〔mistake〕 A for B; misconceive; misrecognize; misidentify 《A as B》. ¶ 법정에서 사실에 대한 ~을 주장하다 claim in court that 《*his case*》 was based on an erroneous assumption of the facts.

**오일**(五日) five days; the fifth day of the month. ◉ ~장(葬) a five-day funeral. ~장(場) a five-day interval village market. 주(週)~근무제 a five-day workweek.

**오일** oil; 《휘발유》 gasoline; 《석유》 petroleum; 《원유》 crude oil. ¶ ~을 치다 oil / 네 차는 ~ 교환을 해야 한다 Your car needs an oil change. ◉ ~달러 petrodollars. ~버너 an oil burner. ~쇼크 the oil shock 〔crisis, squeeze〕. ~스토브 an oil stove. ~처리제 oil dispersing agents: 비행기가 좌초된 유조선으로부터 누출된 기름이 퍼지는 것을 막기 위해 ~처리제를 투하하고 있다 An airplane dumps oil dispersing agents to block the spreading the oil spill from the grounded tanker. ~탱크 an oil tank. ~펜스 an oil fence.

**오입**(誤入) debauchery; dissipation; extramarital sex. ~하다 dissipate; indulge in debauchery; lead a dissolute life; whore; frequent gay quarters; womanize 《구어》.
◉ ~쟁이 a libertine; a debauchee; a rake. ~판 the *demimonde* (F.).

**오자**(誤字) a wrong 〔miswritten〕 word; an erratum (*pl.* -ta); a misprint. ¶ 이 책은 ~투성이다 This book is full of wrong words.

**오장육부**(五臟六腑) the five vital organs and the six viscera; five viscera and six entrails; the internal organs in general. ¶ ~가 없는 사람 a white-livered person; a spiritless man / 그 이야기를 듣고 나는 ~가 뒤틀렸다 The story made my blood boil. *or* I was boiling with 「anger 〔rage〕 to hear the story.

**오쟁이** a small straw bag. ¶~진 사내 [비유적] a man whose wife is unfaithful; a cuckold.

**오전**(午前) the forenoon; the morning; a.m. 〔A.M.〕 (★ a.m.은 라틴어 *ante meridiem* (before noon)의 약자. 표제어나 시간표 이외에는 소문자로 쓰는 것이 보통이며, 반드시 시간을 나타내는 숫자 뒤로 옴). ¶ ~ 여덟 시, 8 a.m. / ~ 다섯 시 열차 the 5 a.m. train / ~(중)에 in the morning; on the morning 《of September 8, of the first of July》 / 일요일 ~에 on Sunday morning / 어느 추운 날 ~(중)에 on one cold morning (★ 단독으로 「오전중」이라고 할 때는 in을 쓰고, 날짜 또는 기상 상태를 나타내는 말과 함께 쓸 때는 on을 씀) / ~ 9시에 at nine in the morning; at 9 a.m. / ~중에는 집에 있다 be at home in the morning.

**오전**(誤傳) misinformation; an incorrect 〔a wrong, a false〕 report. ~하다 misreport; misinform; give a false report.

**오점**(汚點) a stain; a blot; a blotch; a (dirty) spot; a smear; 《결점》 a flaw; a blemish. ¶ ~이 없는 spotless / ~을 묻히다 put a blot 《on》 / 명성에 씻을 수 없는 ~을 남기다 leave an indelible stain on *one's* name 〔reputation〕.

**오젓** salted shrimps (made of the year's early catch).

**오정**(午正) noon; midday. =정오(正午).

**오제이티** 《현장 실습 교육》 OJT. [< *o*n-the-*j*ob *t*raining]

**오존** 〖화학〗 ozone. ¶ ~의 ozonic; ozonous / ~으로 처리하다 ozonize. ◉ ~경보 an ozone warning. ~계(計) an ozonometer. ~반응〔분해〕 ozonolysis. ~발생 장치 an ozone apparatus; an ozonizer. ~층(層) an ozone layer. ~홀 an ozone hole.

**오종경기**(五種競技) the pentathlon. ◉ ~선수 a pentathlete; a pentathlonist. 근대~ modern pentathlon.

**오종종하다** 《빽빽하다》 (be) dense; thick; compact; 《얼굴이》 (be) small and boring.

**오죽** very; indeed; how. ¶ 배가 ~ 고프겠느냐 You must be very hungry. *or*

I'll bet you are half starved. (★ I'll bet you…는 구어적 용법) / 그 애가 ~ 아프면 울겠느냐 The child must be in dreadful pain, otherwise he wouldn't cry. / 어머니가 너를 보면 ~ 기뻐하시겠니 How glad your mother will be to see you! / ~이나 낙담했겠나 I can well imagine your disappointment.

**오죽잖다** be not up to par.

**오줌** urine; water; 《비어》 piss; 《소아어》 pee. ¶ ~누다 urinate; pass 〔discharge〕 urine; pass 〔make〕 water; piss / ~이 마렵다 have a desire to urinate 〔pass water〕; feel nature's call; feel the urge to urinate; want to piss 《비어》 / ~이 잦다 have to urinate frequently / 자다가 ~을 싸다 wet the bed at night / ~을 참다 contain *one's* urine; retain 〔hold〕 *one's* water.
◉ ~똥 feces and urine; excreta. ~버캐 crust of urine stains. ~소태 frequency of urination; 〖의학〗 pollakiuria. ~싸개 a bedwetter. ~장군 a container for urine. ~통 《방광》 the bladder; 《통》 a urinal tub.

**오중**(五重) five fold; 《다섯 겹》 five layers. ¶ ~의 fivefold; quintuple.
◉ ~주〔창〕 a quintet(te). ~탑 a five-storied pagoda.

**오지**(五指) five fingers; four fingers and one thumb.

**오지**(奧地) the interior; the hinterland; the up(-)country; the back regions. ¶ ~의 up-country 《farms》 / ~로 《go》 up-country; 《head》 for 〔toward, into〕 the interior.

**오지그릇** pottery with a dark brown glaze.

**오지다** (be) solid; tight and strong. ⇨ 오달지다.

**오지랖** the lapels of an outer garment. ¶ ~ 넓다 《참견》 intrude; obtrude; intermeddle; thrust 〔poke〕 *one's* nose into.

**오직**(汚職) corruption; graft 《미구어》. 〔= 독직(瀆職).

**오직** only; merely; solely; but. ¶ ~ 울기만 하다 do nothing but cry / ~ 공부만 하다 be bent on *one's* work 〔studying〕 / 이것이 ~ 한 번의 기회다 This is my one and only chance. / ~ 그것뿐일세 That's all there is to it. / 친구라고는 ~ 너뿐이다 You are the only friend I have.

**오진**(誤診) 〖의학〗 a wrong 〔an erroneous〕 diagnosis. ~하다 make a wrong diagnosis; make an error in diagnosis; diagnose wrongly. ¶ 의사는 나의 증상을 맹장염으로 ~했다 The doctor wrongly diagnosed my case as appendicitis. ◉ ~율 the rate of wrong diagnosis.

**오짓물** glaze (in pottery).

**오징어** a squid; a calamary; a cuttle (-fish); an inkfish. ¶ ~는 먹물을 내뿜는다 A cuttlefish ejects ink.
◉ ~뼈 a cuttlebone; a pen. ~잡이 어선 a squid boat 〔jigger〕. ~포 dried cuttlefish.

**오차**(誤差) 〖수학〗 an (accidental) error. ¶ 허용 가능한 ~폭 a tolerance; an (acceptable) error range / 2 퍼센트 이내의 ~ errors of less than 2 percent / 우연 ~가 있다 There is an accidental error. ◉ 관측~ an observational error. 평균 ~ an average error.

**오찬**(午餐) a luncheon; a lunch; a midday repast (★ luncheon은 lunch보다 형식적인 표현이며, 공식 접대의 경우 등에 씀). ¶ ~을 들다 lunch; take lunch / ~에 초대하다 invite 《*a person*》 to a luncheon / 각계각층의 인사들과 ~을 나누다 (take) lunch with leading figures from various walks of life 《in》.
◉ ~회 《give》 a luncheon party.

**오채**(五彩) the five colors (*i.e.* blue, yellow, red, white, black).

**오체**(五體) the whole body 〔frame〕.

**오촌**(五寸) *one's* cousin's son 〔daughter〕; *one's* father's cousin. ◉ ~아저씨 a great-uncle's son; an uncle. ~조카 a cousin once removed.

**오카리나** 《악기》 an ocarina.

**오칭**(誤稱) a misnomer. ~하다 call by a wrong name; call wrongly 〔erroneously〕.

**오케스트라** an orchestra. ¶ 50인 편성의 ~ a 50-piece〔-member〕 orchestra / ~의 반주로 to an orchestral accompaniment.

**오케이** (an) O.K.; an okay; All right. ~하다 O.K. 〔okay〕 《a plan》; give an O.K. 《to》. ¶ 나는 ~다 It's OK with me. / 나의 요청에 그는 기꺼이 ~해 주었다 He willingly gave an OK to my request. / 그는 그 계획에 ~했다 He OK'd the plan. 《구어》 / 만사 ~다 Everything is OK 〔all right〕.

**오클라호마** 《미국의 주》 Oklahoma (생략 Okla.).

**오키나와** 《지명》 Okinawa. ¶ ~의 Okinawan. ◉ ~ 사람 an Okinawan.

**오탁**(汚濁) being filthy and turbid; muckiness. ~하다 be filthy and turbid; be mucky.

**오토레이스** an auto racing.

**오토리버스** 〖기계〗 autoreverse.

**오토메이션** automation. ¶ ~으로 제조하다 manufacture by an automation process / ～화하다 automate; automatize / 완전히 〔고도로〕 ～화된 공장 a fully 〔highly〕 automated factory. ◉ ～공장 an automated factory.

**오토매틱** automatic. ⇨ 자동(自動). ¶ ～도어 an automatic door.

**오토바이** a motorcycle; a motorbike (★ 《미》에서의 motorbike는 소형을 말함). ¶ ～ 뒷 좌석에 사람을 태우다 take a person on the pillion seat of *one's* motorcycle.

**오토자이로** 《회전익 비행기》 an autogiro.

**오톨도톨하다** ⇨ 우툴두툴하다.

**오트밀** oatmeal; 《죽으로 쑨》 porridge.

**오판**(誤判) misjudgement; miscalculation; a mistrial; miscarriage of justice 〔law〕.

**오팔** 〖광물〗 opal.

**오퍼** an offer. ～하다 make an offer. ¶ ～를 내다 offer; submit an offer; make an offer 《for goods》; put forward an offer / ～를 갱신〔수정, 연기〕하다 renew 〔modify, extend〕 an offer / ～를 받다 receive an offer. ◉ 구매～ a buying 〔buyer's〕 offer; a bid. 판매～ a selling offer; an offer.

**오퍼레이터** an operator.

**오페라** an opera. ¶ ～의 operatic. ◉ ～가수 an opera(tic) singer. ～하우스 an opera house. 국립 ～단 the National Opera Company.

**오페레타** an operetta.

**오펙** 《석유 수출국 기구》 OPEC. 〔<the *O*rganization of *P*etroleum *E*xporting *C*ountries〕

**오프 더 레코드** 《비공식》 off the record. ¶ ～발언 an off-the-record remark / 지금 내가 하고 있는 말은 ～입니다 I am now speaking off the record.

**오프리미츠** off limits; "no trespassing."

**오프사이드** 〖축구〗 offside. ¶ ～를 범하다 get a penalty for offside.

**오프셋** 〖인쇄〗 offset; setoff 《영》. ◉ ～인쇄 offset printing.

**오픈** open. ¶ 그 상점은 내월 초에 ～한다 The store will open at the beginning of next month. ◉ ～게임〔전〕 a preseason exhibition game. ～도어 an open door (policy). ～숍 〖노동〗 open shop. ～카 a convertible.

**오피스** an office. ◉ ～거리 a street lined with office buildings; a business district. ～걸 an office girl; a female office worker. ～ 오토메이션 《사무 자동화》 office automation (생략 OA). ～텔 a studio apartment; one room flat.

**오하이오** 《미국의 주》 Ohio (생략 OH.).

**오한**(惡寒) a chill; a cold fit; 〖의학〗 rigor; algor; ague. ¶ ～이 나다 feel 〔have〕 a chill; catch 〔take〕 a chill. ◉ ～증 = 오한.

**오합지졸**(烏合之卒) an undisciplined mob; a disorderly crowd; a rabble; the ruck.

**오해**(誤解) (a) misunderstanding; (a) misinterpretation; misapprehension; misconception. ～하다 misunderstand; have misunderstanding 《about》; get 《*a person*》 wrong; view 《*a matter*》 in a false light; 《잘못 생각하다》 deceive *oneself;* 《어구를》 put a wrong construction 《on》; misconstrue; 《나쁘게 생각하다》 take 《*something*》 amiss. ¶ ～하기 쉬운 misleading / ～를 사다 cause 〔invite〕 misunderstanding / ～를 받다 be misunderstood; be placed in a false position 〔light〕; leave the wrong impression 《on another》 / ～를 풀다 remove 〔clear away, correct〕 misunderstanding / ～를 일소하다 dispel misunderstanding / 그것은 너의 ～다 That's a misunderstanding on your part. *or* You've got it wrong. / ～하지 말게 Don't get me wrong. / 이 글은 명료해서 ～할 여지가 없다 This passage is clear and beyond misapprehension. / 너는 민주주의를 ～하고 있다 You have a wrong idea of democracy. / 자넨 그를 ～하고 있네 You are taking him wrong. / 너의 행동은 ～를 사기 쉽다 Your acts are misleading. / 나는 그를 부정직한 사람으로 ～했다 I was mistaken in thinking that he was dishonest.

**오행**(五行) 〖민속〗 the Five Elements; the five primary substance (*i.e.* metal, wood, water, fire, earth).

**오호**(嗚呼) Alas!; 《고어》 Alack!; Wo(e)! ¶ ～라 = 오호 / ～ 슬프다, 그는 가고 이젠 없도다 Alas! He is dead and gone!

**오호츠크해**(—海) 《러시아 동쪽의 바다》 the Sea of Okhotsk.

**오후**(午後) afternoon; p.m.. ¶ 오늘 〔어제, 내일, 그날〕 ～ this 〔yesterday, tomorrow, that〕 afternoon / ～수업 afternoon classes / ～에 in the afternoon / ～ 늦게 in the late afternoon / ～ 세 시(에) (at) three in the afternoon; (at) 3 p.m. / 월요일 ～에 on Monday afternoon / ～ 3시 10분 열차 the 3:10 〔three ten〕 p.m. train (★ 3:10 p.m. 처럼 콜론을 쓰는 것은 주로 미식이며 3.10 p.m.처럼 피리어드를 쓰는 것은 영식 용법. P.M. (대문자)보다 소문자 p.m.이 일반적임).

**오히려** ① 《차라리》 rather 《than》; sooner 《than》; preferably; 《그만큼 더》 all the more 〔better, worse〕. ¶ 거기 가느니보다 ~ 집에 있는 편이 낫겠다 I would rather stay (at) home than go there. / 이런 정신적 고통 속에 사느니 ~ 죽는 것이 낫다 I would rather die than live in this agony. / 이것이 저것보다 ~ 낫다 This is rather better than that. *or* I would rather have this than that. / 그는 시인이라기보다 ~ 소설가다 He is not so much a poet as a novelist. ② 《도리어》 on the contrary; instead. ¶ ~ 해가 되다 do more harm than good / 그것은 ~ 진보를 방해했다 It hindered rather than helped the progress. / 고마워하기는커녕 그는 ~ 나를 비난했다 Far from thanking me, he blamed me, instead.

**옥**(玉) ① 〖광물〗 jade; 《보석》 a gem; a jewel. ¶ ~을 닦다 polish a gemstone. ② [비유적] anything fine. ¶ 옥에 티 a flaw in a precious stone; a fly in the ointment / 그 사람 우유부단한 것이 옥에 티다 Irresolution is a defect in his otherwise perfect character. ◉ 옥가락지 a jade ring.

**옥**(獄) a prison; a jail. ¶ 옥에 갇히다 be imprisoned / 옥에 가두다 put 〔cast〕 《*a person*》 into prison; imprison 《*a person*》.

**옥고**(玉稿) 《원고》 《your, his》 esteemed manuscript.

**옥고**(獄苦) the hardships of prison life; a hard prison life. ¶ ~를 겪다 experience 〔suffer〕 a hard prison life / ~를 치르다 serve *one's* term of imprisonment.

**옥내**(屋內) the inside 〔interior〕 of a house. ¶ ~의 indoor; covered / ~에서 《exercise》 indoors; within doors / ~용의 관상 식물 a house plant. ◉ ~경기〔스포츠〕 an indoor game 〔sport〕. ~배선 interior 〔house〕 wiring; a service wire; 《안테나의》 a lead-in wire; a lead-in.

**옥니** 《옥은 이》 an inturned tooth. ◉ ~박이 a person with inturned teeth.

**옥다** ① 《안으로》 bend 〔get bent〕 in; turn in. ② 《밑지다》 lose 《at a business》; operate at a loss.

**옥답**(沃畓) fertile 〔rich〕 paddy fields.

**옥당목**(玉唐木) calico of inferior quality.

**옥도**(沃度) 〖화학〗 iodine (기호 I). ⇨ 요오드.

**옥돌**(玉―) a gemstone; (a) jade; a jadeite.

**옥돔**(玉―) 〖어류〗 a tile fish.

**옥동자**(玉童子) a (darling) baby boy; a precious son.

**옥문**(獄門) the gate of a jail; a prison gate.

**옥바라지**(獄―) ~하다 send in private supplies for a prisoner.

**옥사**(獄死) death in prison. ~하다 die in prison; end up in jail.

**옥사**(獄舍) a prison house; a jail. ◉ ~쟁이 a jailer; a guard; 《미》 a warder.

**옥사**(獄事) administration of the major criminal cases (such as murder and high treason).

**옥살산**(―酸) 〖화학〗 oxalic acid. ◉ ~암모늄 ammonium oxalate; oxalate of ammonium. ~염 an oxalate.

**옥살이**(獄―) prison life; life behind bars.

**옥상**(屋上) the rooftop 《미》; the roof. ¶ ~에서 on 〔from〕 the roof / ~ 가옥(架屋)하다 do something unnecessary; paint the lily. ◉ ~정원 a roof garden. ~주택 a penthouse.

**옥새**(玉璽) the Royal Seal; 《영국의》 the Privy Seal.

**옥색**(玉色) jade green.

**옥생각** misunderstanding; distortion; perversion; a biased interpretation; a distorted view. ~하다 misunderstand; distort; pervert.

**옥석**(玉石) ① 《옥돌》 a gemstone; (a) jade. ② 《좋은 것과 나쁜 것》 jade and stone; wheat and tares. ¶ ~을 가려내다 discriminate gems from pebbles 《in a most prudent way》. ◉ ~구분(俱焚) indiscriminate destruction of good and bad alike. ~혼효(混淆) 《be》 a mixture of wheat and tares 〔chaff and grain〕; a mixture 〔jumble〕 of good and bad.

**옥셈** miscalculation against *one's* own interest. ~하다 miscalculate 〔miscount〕 to *one's* own disadvantage.

**옥소**(沃素) 〖화학〗 iodine. ⇨ 요오드.

**옥쇄**(玉碎) an honorable death. ~하다 die (in battle) rather than surrender; die a hero's death. ◉ ~공격 a suicidal attack. ~전법(戰法) suicide tactics.

**옥수**(玉水) clear 〔crystal〕 water (as of a spring).

**옥수**(玉手) ① 《임금의》 the king's hand. ② 《미인의》 a (woman's) beautiful hand. ¶ 섬섬~ a slender 〔delicate〕 hand.

**옥수수** 〖식물〗 Indian corn; maize; 《미》 corn. ¶ ~를 재배하다 cultivate corn (plants). ◉ ~껍질 cornhusk. ~밭 a cornfield. ~수염 corn silk 〔floss〕. ~지대 《미국의》 the Corn Belt. 옥수숫대 a cornstalk.

**옥스퍼드** 《잉글랜드의 도시》 Oxford. ◉ ~대학 Oxford University.

**옥시풀** 『약』 Oxyful (상표명); hydrogen peroxide solution; 《줄여서》 peroxide.

**옥신각신** wrangling; altercating; arguing. ~하다 wrangle; altercate; squabble; argue; have a petty quarrel; skirmish. ¶ 서로 ~하다 wrangle with each other; exchange hot words with each other / 아무와 사소한 일을 가지고 ~하다 fight 〔argue〕 with *a person* over trifles.

**옥안**(玉顔) ① 《용안》 the king's face; the royal visage. ② 《미인의》 a (woman's) beautiful face.

**옥야**(沃野) fertile plains.

**옥양목**(玉洋木) muslin 《미》; calico 《영》; cambric.

**옥양사**(玉洋紗) fine calico.

**옥외**(屋外) outside the house; the outdoors; the open (air). ¶ ~의 outdoor; out-of-door; open-air / ~에서 in the open (air); out of doors; outdoors. ◉ ~경기 an outdoor game. ~광고판 《set up》 an outdoor billboard. ~노동자 an outdoor laborer. ~배관〔배선〕 outdoor piping 〔wiring〕. ~스포츠〔운동〕 outdoor 〔open-air〕 sports 〔exercise〕. ~작업 outdoor work. ~집회 an open-air meeting; an out-of-door gathering.

**옥음**(玉音) 《임금의》 the king's voice.

**옥이다** bend 〔turn〕 《*a thing*》 inward. ⇨ 욱이다.

**옥잠화**(玉簪花) 『식물』 a plantain lily.

**옥장이**(玉匠—) a jade cutter; a lapidary.

**옥졸**(獄卒) a jailer. ⇨ 옥사쟁이.

**옥좌**(玉座) the king's chair; the throne. ¶ ~에 앉다 sit on the throne; take the Royal seat.

**옥죄이다** feel cramped; be too tight for *one;* cut *one.* ¶ 옥죄이는 옷 a tight coat / 옷의 겨드랑이가 너무 옥죄인다 The coat cuts me under the arm. / 두 손을 묶은 포승이 몹시 옥죄여 들었다 The rope with which his hands were tied cut into the flesh.

**옥중**(獄中) ¶ ~에서 in prison 〔jail〕; behind bars. ◉ ~기(記) a diary written in prison.

**옥체**(玉體) ① 《임금의》 the king's 〔royal〕 person; the person of the king. ② 《편지에서》 your 〔his〕 health.

**옥타브** 『음악』 an octave. ¶ 한 ~ 올리다〔낮추다〕 raise 〔drop〕 《*one's* voice》 an octave higher 〔lower〕.

**옥탄가**(—價) 『화학』 the octane number 〔value, rating〕. ¶ ~가 높은 high-octane 《gasoline》; 《gasoline》 with a high-octane rating.

**옥토**(沃土) fertile land 〔earth〕; fertile 〔rich〕 soil. ¶ 메마른 땅을 ~로 만들다 make barren land fertile.

**옥토끼**(玉—) 《흰 토끼》 a white rabbit; 《달속의》 the rabbit (supposed to be) in the moon.

**옥편**(玉篇) a dictionary of Chinese characters; a Chinese-Korean dictionary.

**옥호**(屋號) the name 〔style〕 of a store 〔shop〕.

**옥화**(沃化) 『화학』 iodation. ⇨ 요오드화. ◉ ~물 an iodide; an iodid.

**옥황상제**(玉皇上帝) The Lord of Heaven (of Taoism); God of Providence.

**온** ① 《모든》 all; whole; entire; complete; perfect. ¶ 온 백성 the whole nation; all the people / 온 세상 all the world / 온 도시가 그를 환영했다 The whole town turned out to welcome him. ② = 온갖. ③ 《꼬박》 whole; full; just. ¶ 온종일 the whole day; all day long.

**온갖** [단수명사와 함께] every (possible, available); [복수명사와 함께] all (the); all sorts 〔kinds〕 of; of every shape; all manner of (★ 전체를 한 집단으로 볼 때에는 all the ~s, 전체의 하나하나를 의식할 때에는 all ~s를 씀: I told all the pupils (전교생에게). I told all pupils (학생 한 사람 한 사람에게). all보다는 every가 구어적임). ¶ ~ 수단 every possible means (★ means는 단수·복수 취급); every step; all the means in *one's* power / ~ (종류의) 책〔사람〕 all kinds 〔sorts〕 of books 〔people〕 (★ every kind of 라고는 안 함) / ~ 위험 dangers of every shape / ~ 방향으로 in every direction; in all directions / ~ 수단을 다 써보다 try every 「means available 〔possible means〕; leave no stone unturned / ~ 고생을 다하다 go through all kinds of hardship / ~ 죄를 다 저지르다 go through the catalog of crimes; have a long list of criminal acts / ~ 생각이 우리들 마음 속에 떠오른다 A crowd of ideas comes to our minds.

**온건**(穩健) moderateness; moderation. ~하다 (be) moderate; temperate; sensible; sound. ¶ ~하게 moderately / ~한 견해 moderate views 〔opinion〕 / ~한 인품 a temperate disposition. ◉ ~주의 moderatism: ~주의자 a moderatist; a moderate. ~파 the moderate party 〔wing〕; (the) moderates; middle-of-the-roaders; centrists.

**온고지신**(溫故知新) reviewing the old and learning the new; discover new things by studying the past.

**온기**(溫氣) warmth; warm air. ¶ ~가 있다〔없다〕 be 〔be not〕 warm / 이 방에는 아직도 ~가 남아 있다 There is still some warmth left in this room.

**온난**(溫暖) ~하다 (be) warm; mild; temperate; genial. ¶ ~한 기후 a mild 〔moderate, temperate〕 climate.
◉ ~전선(前線) 〖기상〗 a warm front.

**온당**(穩當) ~하다 (be) reasonable; right; just; fitting; proper; appropriate. ¶ ~하게 reasonably; justly; properly / ~한 언사 proper language / ~한 요구 a reasonable claim / ~한 조치 a just and proper measures / ~치 않다 be improper; be wrong / 그것이 그 문장의 ~한 해석이다 That is a sensible interpretation of the passage.

**온대**(溫帶) the Temperate 〔Variable〕 Zones. ◉ ~식물 a temperate (zone) plant; 《식물상》 the flora of the temperate zone. ~저기압 an extratropical cyclone. ~지방 the temperate regions 〔latitudes〕.

**온데간데없다** be completely 〔entirely〕 out of sight; vanish out of *one's* sight; vanish in(to) thin air; be nowhere to be seen.

**온도**(溫度) (a) temperature. ¶ 실내 ~ indoor 〔room〕 temperature / 체감 ~ sensible temperature / ~의 변화 (a) temperature change / 일정한〔높은, 낮은〕 ~에서 at a fixed 〔high, low〕 temperature / ~를 재다〔조절하다〕 take 〔adjust〕 the temperature / ~가 높다〔낮다〕 the temperature is high 〔low〕 / ~가 오르다〔내리다〕 the mercury 〔temperature〕 rises 〔falls〕; [사물이 주어] rise 〔fall〕 in temperature / ~가 영하로 내려가면 물이 언다 When thermometer is below zero water will freeze. / ~가 섭씨 40도 이상되는 곳에 두지 마시오 Do not store at temperatures above 40℃.
◉ ~조절 temperature control: ~조절장치 a thermoregulator; a thermostat.

**온도계**(溫度計) a thermometer; a pyrometer (고온계). ¶ ~가 오르다〔내리다〕 the mercury rises 〔falls, drops〕 / ~는 섭씨 25도를 나타내고 있다 The thermometer 「stands at 〔registers〕 「twenty-five degrees centigrade 〔25℃〕. / ~는 실내에서 섭씨 18도를 보이고 있다 The thermometer reads 〔stands at, registers〕 18℃ indoors.

**온돌**(溫突) *ondol;* the Korean under-floor heating system. ¶ ~방 an *ondol* room; a floor-heated room.

**온두라스** (the Republic of) Honduras. ◉ ~사람 a Honduran.

**온라인** on-line. ¶ 은행의 ~ 시스템 the on-line banking system / ~화(化)되다 go on-line / ~ 시스템이 있는 은행 a bank with on-line system / 은행의 ~이 한 시간이나 불통되었다 The on-line system in the bank was interrupted for an hour. ◉ ~ 기억장치 on-line storage. ~ 실시간(처리)방식 an on-line real time system. ~예금 an on-line deposit. ~처리 on-line processing: ~처리 시스템 an on-line processing system.

**온면**(溫麵) warm noodle soup.

**온몸** the whole body; [부사적] all over the body; from head to foot. ¶ ~이 멍투성이다 be black and blue all over the body / 그는 ~에 화상을 입었다 He got scalded all over his body. / 그녀는 ~을 떨면서 흐느꼈다 Sobs shook her frame. / 독이 ~에 퍼졌다 The poison pervaded 〔passed into〕 his whole system.

**온밤** all 〔the whole〕 night; all the night through. ¶ 간밤에 ~을 꼬박 뜬눈으로 새웠다 I couldn't sleep a wink throughout last night.

**온상**(溫床) a hotbed; a (warm) nursery; a forcing bed (속성 재배용). ¶ 혁명의 ~ a revolutionary forcing bed / 악의 ~ a hotbed of vice 〔social evils〕 / ~에서 모종을 기르다 raise seedlings in a hotbed / 빈민굴은 질병과 죄악의 ~이다 Slums are hotbeds of disease and vice.

**온색**(溫色) a warm color.

**온수**(溫水) warm 〔hot〕 water. ¶ 냉~가 나오는 설비 《an apartment with》 hot and cold (running) water / ~가 나오는 설비를 하다 install hot water / ~꼭지를 틀다 turn on a hot tap.
◉ ~공급 hot-water supply. ~기 a water heater: 순간 ~기 an instantaneous water heater. ~난방 hot-water heating. ~방열기 a hot-water radiator. ~보일러 a hot-water boiler. ~시설 a hot-water supply system. ~탱크 a hot-water tank. ~풀 a heated (swimming) pool.

**온순**(溫順) gentleness; docility; obedience. ~하다 (be) gentle; meek; docile; obedient; meek and mild. ¶ ~하게 gently; meekly; obediently / 양처럼 ~하다 be (as) meek as a lamb.

**온스** 《단위》 an ounce (생략 oz.).

**온실**(溫室) 《식물의》 a hothouse; a greenhouse; a glasshouse; 《속성 재배

용》 a forcing house; 《방》 a warm 〔hot〕 room. ¶ ～에서 자라다 《과보호로》 be brought up「like a tender plant 〔on a bed of roses〕/ ～에서 개화시키다 force 《a plant》 to bloom in a hothouse. ◉ ～식물 a hothouse plant. ～원예 greenhouse cultivation. ～재배 hothouse growth: ～ 재배하다 cultivate 《plant》 under glass. ～효과 〖기상〗 the greenhouse effect.

**온아**(溫雅) suavity; blandness; gracefulness. ～하다 (be) suave; bland; graceful. ¶ ～한 사람 a person of quiet grace.

**온욕**(溫浴) a warm 〔hot〕 bath. ◉ ～요법 a hot-water cure; treatment by warm water.

**온유**(溫柔) gentleness; mildness; clemency. ～하다 (be) gentle; mild.

**온음**(一音) 〖음악〗 a whole tone. ◉ ～계 the diatonic scale. ～음계 the whole-note〔-tone〕 scale. ～표 a whole note 《미》; a semibreve 《영》.

**온장**(一張) the entire sheet; a whole piece 《of paper, *etc.*》; uncut paper.

**온전**(穩全) ～하다 (be) sound; intact; unimpaired. ¶ ～하게 soundly; wholly; perfectly / ～한 접시가 하나도 없군 There is not a plate left whole 〔unbroken〕.

**온점**(溫點) 《피부의》 a hot point 〔spot〕.

**온정**(溫情) a warm heart; (a) kindly feeling; geniality; 《관대함》 leniency; tolerance. ¶ ～ 있는 kindly; warm-hearted; lenient; generous; tolerant / ～적인 판사 a lenient judge / 친구의 ～어린 말에 힘을 얻었다 I was encouraged by my friend's warm-hearted words.
◉ ～주의 paternalism.

**온종일**(一終日) all day (long); the whole day; all through the day; throughout the day. ⇨ 종일. ¶ ～ 야외에서 지내다 spend the whole day out in the open / ～ 책을 읽다 read books all day long / ～ 비가 온다 It rains all through the day. / 어제는 ～ 자네를 기다렸다 I waited for you all yesterday.

**온집안** 《가족》 the whole family; all (members of ) the family; 《집안》 all over the house. ¶ ～을 뒤지다 search all over the house / ～이 무사합니다 My family are all well.

**온채** the whole 〔entire〕 house. ¶ ～를 세내다 rent a house in whole.

**온천**(溫泉) a hot 〔thermal〕 spring; a spa. ¶ 온양 ～ the spa of Onyang; the Onyang hot spring(s) / ～에 가다 go to 〔visit〕 a spa 〔a hot-spring resort〕 / ～욕을 하다 take a hot spring bath. ◉ ～마을 a hot spring village. ～수 《마시는》 the thermal waters. ～여관〔호텔〕 a hot-spring inn 〔hotel〕: ～ 관광 호텔 a hot-spring tourist hotel. ～요법 hot-spring cure 〔therapy〕. ～장 a hot-spring resort; a spa; 《영》 a watering place. ～학 balneology.

**온축**(蘊蓄) *one's* stock of knowledge; erudition. ～하다 store *one's* mind with wide knowledge; acquire extensive knowledge.

**온탕**(溫湯) 《온천》 a hot spring; 《욕탕》 a (hot) bath; 《더운 물》 hot 〔warm〕 water.

**온통** all; wholly; entirely; altogether; everywhere; everything; all over. ¶ ～ 물바다가 되다 turn into a broad expanse of water; be entirely submerged 〔flooded, under water〕/ ～ 불바다가 되다 be entirely enveloped in flames / (어딜 가나) ～ 그 소문뿐이다 be the sole topic of conversation; be the talk of the town / 그것은 ～ 거짓말이다 It's a story made out of whole cloth. / 이익은 그가 ～다 차지했다 He took all the profits himself.

**온폭**(一幅) the whole 〔full〕 width 《of cloth 〔paper〕》.

**온혈동물**(溫血動物) a warm-blooded animal.

**온화**(溫和) 《기후의》 mildness; 《인품의》 gentleness; mildness; benignancy; geniality. ～하다 《기후 등이》 (be) mild; clement; genial; 《인품이》 (be) gentle; mild-tempered; benign. ¶ ～한 미소 a gentle smile / ～한 기후 a mild 〔genial〕 climate / ～한 인품 a gentle 〔genial〕 personality 〔nature〕.

**온후**(溫厚) gentleness; suavity. ～하다 (be) gentle; mild(-mannered); suave. ¶ ～한 사람 a mild-mannered person.

**올**[1] ⇨ 올해. ¶ 올 여름 휴가 《오는》 the coming summer vacation; 《지나간》 the last summer vacation / 올 안에 in (the) course of this year; before the end of this 〔the〕 year; before the year-end.

**올**[2] 《가닥》 a strand; a ply; 《피륙 따위의》 warp. ¶ 올이 성긴 coarse / 세 올 실 three-ply thread / 올이 고운 직물 close texture / 나일론 양말은 올이 가끔 풀어진다 Nylon stockings often run.

**올－** 《조생종》 early-ripening. ¶ 올벼 an early-ripening variety of rice / 올밤 an early chestnut.

**올가미** 《올무》 a noose; a snare; a las-so; a rope; 《함정》 a trick; a cheat; a trap; a snare. ¶ ~를 씌우다 put the rope on 《an animal》; trap 《*a person*》/ ~로 잡다 entrap; snare; ensnare; catch in a trap / 사슴을 ~로 잡다 catch 〔snare〕 a deer in a trap; trap a deer / ~를 놓다 lay a snare; set a trap / ~에 걸리다 be ensnared 〔trapped〕; be caught in a trap.

**올강거리다** be hard to chew; be tough. ¶ 고기가 올강거려 잘 씹히지 않는다 This beef chews hard.

**올곧다** ① 《마음이》 (be) honest; upright; straight; right-minded. ¶ 올곧은 사람 an upright person / 올곧게 살다 lead an honest life; live straight. ② 《줄이》 (be) direct; straight.

**올내년**(一來年) this and 〔or〕 next year.

**올되다** ① 《일되다》 mature young 〔early〕; be wise above *one's* age; be forward for *one's* age. ¶ 올된 아이 a precocious child. ② 《농작물이》 ripen early. ¶ 올되는 품종 an early-ripening variety 《of》. ③ 《피륙의 올이》 be tight.

**올드미스** an old maid; a spinster.

**올라가다** ① 《위로》 (***a***) 《높은 데로》 go 〔come〕 up; rise; ascend; mount; climb (up); soar. ¶ 비탈을 ~ go up 〔ascend〕 a slope; go uphill / 계단을 ~ go 〔walk〕 up the stairs / 산에 ~ climb 〔go up〕 a mountain; ascend 〔make an ascent of〕 a mountain / 연단에 ~ mount 〔step on〕 the platform / 지붕에 ~ get on the roof / 굴뚝에서 연기가 ~ smoke rises from a chimney / 승강기는 9층까지 올라갔다 The elevator went up to the ninth floor. (***b***) 《물가가》 rise; advance; go 〔come, look〕 up. ¶ 값이 ~ the price rises 〔goes up〕; [사물이 주어] rise 〔advance, go up〕 in price. (***c***) 《승진·승급(昇給)》 rise 《to》; be raised; be promoted 〔advance〕 《to》; be elevated 〔raised〕 《to》. ¶ 봉급이 ~ have *one's* salary raised; get a raise 〔rise 《영》〕 in *one's* salary / 지위가 ~ rise in rank; be promoted to a higher position. (***d***) 《이름이》 rise. ¶ 명성이 ~ rise in fame. (***e***) 《나아지다》 progress; make progress 〔headway〕; advance; improve. ¶ (학교) 성적이 ~ show a better school record. (***f***) 《열·기온·온도 등이》 rise. ¶ 기온이 ~ the temperature rises 〔goes up〕 / 신열이 ~ *one's* temperature mounts 〔rises, goes up〕; *one's* fever heightens. ② 《진출하다》 move into; advance to. ¶ 준결승에 ~ go to the semifinals; get 〔win *one's* way〕 into the semifinals. ③ 《상경하다》 go up to Seoul. ④ 《없어지다》 《property》 be lost. ¶ 화재로 살림살이가 몽땅 올라갔다 All our household goods were burned down by fire. ⑤ 《강을》 go 〔sail, steam〕 up. ¶ 강을 거슬러 ~ go up 〔sail up〕 a river / 이 강은 배로 몇 마일이나 올라갈 수 있는가 How many miles up is this river navigable? ⑥ 《건축되다》 be built; be put up; go up. ¶ 시내 곳곳에 고층 건물이 올라가고 있다 High buildings are going up in several parts of the city.

**올라서다** ① 《높은 곳으로》 mount 〔ascend〕 《a platform》; get up 《on a higher place》. ② 《지위가 높아지다》 rise to higher level 〔rank〕. ③ 《궤도에》 ¶ 사업이 드디어 궤도에 올라섰다 The undertaking finally got off the ground.

**올라오다** come up; rise. ¶ 위층에 ~ come upstairs / 서울에 ~ come up to Seoul / 무대로 올라오십시오 Please step up on the stage.

**올라타다** get on; get into; mount. ⇨ 타다[2]. ¶ 말에 ~ get on 〔mount〕 a horse / 열차에 ~ get on 〔into〕 a train / 다음 역에서 떠들썩한 고등 학생들이 차에 올라탔다 A bunch of noisy high school students came on board at the next station.

**올랑촐랑** 《담은 물이》 slopping from side to side; 《물결이》 lapping 《against》. ~하다 slop from side to side; lap 《against》. ¶ 물통의 물이 ~ 흔들리다 water slops back and forth in a bucket / 물결이 ~강가에 부딪치다 waves lap against the riverbank.

**올려놓다** put 《*something*》 on 《a place》. ¶ 책을 선반에 ~ put a book on a shelf / 손을 탁자에 ~ rest *one's* hands on a table / 불에 주전자를 ~ put a kettle on the fire.

**올려본각**(一角) 〚수학〛 (an angle of) elevation.

**올록볼록** rough; bumpy; uneven. ~하다 (be) rough; bumpy.

**올리다** ① 《위로》 raise; lift (up) (★ raise는 가장 일반적인 말. lift는 「지면에서 떼다」의 뜻이 강하며, 비교적 짧은 거리를 올릴 때 쓰임). ¶ 손을 ~ raise 〔hold up〕 *one's* hand / 연을 ~ raise 〔fly〕 a kite / 짐을 기차에 ~ lift baggage 〔luggage 《영》〕 up into a train / 기를 ~ lift 〔hoist, run up, fly〕 a flag / 책을 선반 위에 ~ put (up) a book on a shelf / 닻을 ~ pull up the anchor; weigh

anchor / 불꽃을 ~ set off fireworks.
② 《지위·비율을》 raise; promote; increase; boost. ¶ 월급을 ~ raise 《*a person's*》 salary 《to a million won》 / 월급을 올려받다 have *one's* salary raised / 지위를 ~ raise 《*a person's*》 rank; promote 《*a person*》 to a higher rank / 급수를 한 급 ~ promote 《*a person*》 to a higher class / 값을 ~ raise the price / 시가(市價)를 ~ raise the market price / 세율을 ~ raise the tariff / 온도를 ~ raise the temperature 《of a room》.
③ 《바치다》 offer; give; present. ¶ 기도를 ~ offer a prayer / 공양을 ~ make an offering / 재(齋)를 ~ have a mass read for the repose of a soul / 제가 써 올리지요 I will write it for you.
④ 《기록하다》 put on record; enter 《a name》. ¶ 전화 번호부에 이름을 ~ put 《*a person's*》 name in the telephone directory / 대장에 이름을 ~ enter a name in a book / 셈을 외상장부에 ~ charge the bill to *one's* account / 새 말을 사전에 ~ enter a new word in a dictionary.
⑤ 《내놓다》 bring up; place before; present. ¶ 음식을 밥상에 ~ serve food on the table / 회의에 의제를 ~ bring up a matter for discussion at a meeting / 무대에 ~ put 《a play》 on the stage; stage 《a play》.
⑥ 《병을 옮기다》 contract; be infected by. ¶ 옴을 ~ be infected with the itch; suffer from scabies / 옻을 ~ be poisoned with lacquer; get poison ivy.
⑦ 《점수·성과·효과를》 ¶ 훌륭한 성과를 ~ obtain 〔get, attain, gain, win, secure〕 excellent results / 생산성을 ~ increase 〔raise〕 the productivity 《of》 / 제품의 질을 ~ improve the quality of 「a product 〔manufactured goods〕 / 백만원의 순익을 ~ gain a net profit 《of one million won》 / (경기에서) 5점을 ~ score five points 〔runs〕.
⑧ 《칠을》 coat; apply; paint with. ¶ 나무에 칠을 ~ coat wood with paint / 사진틀에 금박을 ~ gild a picture frame / 반지에 얇게 금을 ~ plate a ring with gold.
⑨ 《소리를》 raise 《*one's* voice》; give 〔utter〕 《a cry》; scream (비명을). ¶ 환성을 ~ shout for joy; raise 〔give, let out, send up〕 a cheer.
⑩ 《식을》 hold 《a ceremony》; celebrate; observe. ¶ 결혼식을 ~ hold a wedding; celebrate a marriage.
⑪ 《기타》 ¶ 지붕에 기와를 ~ roof with tiles / 약을 ~ offend; exhaust *one's* patience; stir *one's* bile.

**올리브** 〖식물〗 an olive (tree). ◉ ~밭 an olive grove. ~유 olive oil.

**올림** ① 《증정》 presented by; with the compliments of. ¶ 남 선생님께 지은이 ~ To Mr. Nam with the compliments of the author. ② 《편지에서》 Yours very truly. ¶ 정순복 ~ Yours very truly, S.P. Chŏng.

**올림표**(一標) 〖음악〗 sharp (기호 ♯). ◉ 2중 ~ a double sharp.

**올림픽** 《경기》 the Olympics; the Olympic games. ¶ 국제 장애자 ~ the International Paraplegics Olympic Games; the paralympics / 근대 ~ the modern Olympics / 동계 ~ the Winter Olympics / 국제 ~ 위원회 the International Olympic Committee (생략 IOC) / 한국 ~위원회 the Korean Olympic Committee (생략 KOC) / 한국 대표로서 ~에 출장하다 represent Korea in the Olympic Games / ~에서 금메달을 따다 win a gold medal at the Olympics. ◉ ~기 the Olympic flag. ~기록 an Olympic record. ~선수 an Olympian; an Olympic sportsman; a member of the Olympic team. ~선수촌 the Olympic village. ~성화 the Olympic Flame 〔Torch〕. ~조직 위원회 the Olympic Organizing Committee (생략 O.O.C.): 서울 ~ 조직 위원회 the Seoul Olympic Organizing Committee. ~ 주경기장 the Olympic stadium. ~찬가 the Olympic anthem. ~헌장 the Olympic Charter. ~회의 the Olympic Congress.

**올망졸망** in lots of small units 〔pieces, lumps〕; all sorts of little things; various sized of small things; in clusters; in abundance. ~하다 be of various small sizes (★ 복수형으로 씀); come in lots of small units. ¶ ~한 초가집들 a cluster of small thatched cottages / ~한 아이들이 놀이터에서 놀고 있었다 Some little children were frolicking about in the playground.

**올무** a noose; a running knot. ¶ ~로 새를 잡다 noose a bird.

**올바로** uprightly; straightly; 《정직하게》 honestly; straightforwardly; frankly; 《정확하게》 correctly; properly; exactly; accurately. ¶ ~ 말하면 properly 〔strictly〕 speaking / ~ 말하다 speak straight out / ~살다 lead an honest life; pursue an honest career; live straight / ~ 행동하다 behave properly 〔correctly〕 / 마음을 ~ 먹어라 Be a good man.

**올바르다** (be) straight; upright; straightforward; honest. ¶ 올바른 사람 an upright person / 올바른 국가관과 역사 의식 the correct perception about *one's* nation and history / 그 말의 올바른 뜻으로는 in the proper sense of the word / 올바른 인식을 갖게 하다 make 《*a person*》 have correct understanding 《of》.

**올봄** this spring.

**올빼미** 〖조류〗 an owl. ¶ ～가 울다 an owl hoots. ◉ ～새끼 an owlet.

**올새** weave. ¶ ～가 성긴〔촘촘한〕 천 cloth with a loose 〔close〕 weave; cloth of open 〔close〕 texture / ～가 굵다〔가늘다〕 have rough 〔fine〕 weave.

**올차다** (be) energetic; peppy; be full of vigor; be small but solid; be of compact build. ¶ 올찬 사람 a person of compact build.

**올챙이** a tadpole; a polliwog 《미》. ◉ ～기자 a cub (reporter). ～배 potbelly; beer belly.

**올케** the wife of a girl's brother; a girl's sister-in-law.

**올콩** early-ripening beans.

**올통볼통하다** (be) bumpy; rough; uneven. ¶ 올통볼통한 길 a bumpy road.

**올팥** early-ripening red beans.

**올해** this year; the present 〔current〕 year. ¶ ～도 며칠 남지 않았다 We have only a few days left before the end of the year. / ～는 비가 많이 왔다 We have had much rain this year.

**옭다** ① 《잡아매다》 tie up; fasten; bind. ¶ 짐을 새끼로 ～ tie a bundle with a straw rope / 단단히 ～ tie fast; bind hard / 옭아서 단을 짓다 tie 《*a thing*》 into a bundle. ② 《올가미로》 put the noose on; collar. ¶ 개를 ～ put the noose on a dog. ③ 《죄를 씌우다》 entrap 《*a person*》; incriminate 《*a person*》; fasten the crime on 《*a person*》. ¶ 옭아 넣다 put 《*a person*》 under a false charge.

**옭매다** tie in a knot; tie fast; fasten; bind. ¶ 구두 끈을 ～ tie the shoe string in a knot.

**옭매듭** a flat 〔reef〕 knot; a square knot.

**옭아내다** ① 《올가미로》 put a rope around the neck and drag out; tie up and drag out. ¶ 아무를 ～ tie *a person* up and drag *him* out. ② ＝우려내다.

**옭아매다** ① 《잡아매다》 tie up; lash. ¶ 짐을 ～ tie up a package / 그는 인질을 밧줄로 기둥에 단단히 옭아매었다. He lashed the hostage securely to a post with rope. ② 《없는 죄를》 make a false charge against 《*a person*》.

**옭히다** ① 《올가미에》 get roped; have the rope on; be ensnared; be tied up. ¶ 사슴이 올가미에 ～ a deer is caught in a snare. ② 《얽히다》 be tied in a knot; be tangled. ¶ 실이 옭혀 풀리지 않는다 Thread is so tangled up that it is impossible to straighten it out. ③ 《걸려들다》 be dragged in; be hauled in; be roped in; be involved. ¶ 살인 사건에 옭혀 욕보다 be mixed up in a murder case and get a rough going-over.

**옮기다** ① 《이전》 move 〔remove〕 《to, into》; transfer. ¶ 가구를 ～ move the furniture / 집을 시골로 ～ move into the country / 새 집으로 ～ move into a new house / 학교를 ～ transfer to another school; transfer / 집을 아들의 명의로 ～ transfer the title of *one's* estate into *one's* son's name / 의자를 테이블 저쪽으로 옮겨라 Move your chair to the other side of the table.
② 《액체 따위를》 pour 〔empty〕 《into》; transfuse. ¶ 간장을 통에서 병으로 ～ pour soy sauce from the cask into bottles.
③ 《실행·이송》 carry; transfer. ¶ 결심을 실행에 ～ put *one's* decision into effect; carry out *one's* resolution / 사건을 대법원으로 ～ carry a case to the Supreme Court / 다음 문제로 옮기자 Let's get on to the next problem.
④ 《돌리다》 divert; turn; direct. ¶ 발길을 ～ turn *one's* steps / 집으로 발길을 ～ direct *one's* step toward home.
⑤ 《감염》 give; infect 《*a person* with a disease》; communicate; pass 《a disease on to *a person*》. ¶ 감기를 남에게 ～ pass 〔give〕 *one's* cold on to another.
⑥ 《말을》 pass 《it》 on. ¶ 말을 남에게 ～ pass words on to another; leak a secret.
⑦ 《번역》 translate 〔render, put, turn〕 《English》 into 《Korean》. ¶ 암호를 말로 ～ decipher 〔decode〕 a cryptograph into words / 이 말은 한국 말로 잘 옮길 수가 없다 This word does not bear well translated into Korean. / 이 글을 한국어로 옮기시오 Put 〔Translate〕 this sentence into Korean.

**옮다** ① 《이전》 move *one's* residence; move 〔remove〕 《to, into》. ¶ 부산서 서울로 ～ move from Pusan to Seoul.
② 《병이》 be infected; take; catch. ¶ 옮기 쉬운 병 an infectious 〔contagious〕

disease / 병이 ～ be infected with a disease / 남한테서 감기가 ～ catch a cold from another / 감기는 옮기 쉬운 병이다 We get easily infected with a cold. / 티푸스는 옮는다 Typhoid fever is infectious 〔contagious〕. / 하품은 옮는다 Yawning is catching.

**옮아가다** ① 《이사·전근》 move away 《to a place》. ¶ 종로로 ～ remove to the Chongno district. ② 《퍼져가다》 be diffused; spread. ¶ 홍역이 이웃 마을로 옮아갔다 Measles spread to a neighboring village. ③ 《넘어감》 pass 《to, into》; turn 《to》. ¶ 남의 수중으로 ～ pass into another's hands / 화제는 정치 문제로 옮아갔다 The conversation turned on political problems.

**옮아오다** ① 《다른 데서》 move in; move this way. ¶ 부산에서 서울로 ～ move up to Seoul from Pusan / 지점에서 본점으로 ～ be transferred from a branch office to the head office. ② 《퍼져오다》 be diffused; spread.

**옳다**[1] 《마음이》 (be) right(eous); upright; truthful; honest; 《행동·일·경우 따위》 (be) right; just; proper; correct; exact; rightful; 《합법적》 (be) lawful; legitimate; 《건전》 (be) sound. ¶ 옳지 않은 wrong; unjust; dishonest; improper; illegal; incorrect / 옳은 사람 a righteous man / 옳은 계산〔추론〕 a correct calculation 〔inference〕 / 문제의 옳은 해답 the right answer to a problem / 옳은 일을 하다 do a right thing; do right; do what is right / 네 말이 ～ You are right. / 너한테는 말하는 것이 ～고 생각한다 I think it only right to tell you. / 둘 중에 누가 옳은가 Which of the two men is in the right?

**옳다**[2] 《옳지·그래》 Right!; O.K.!; All right!; Right you are!; Right-oh! ¶ ～ 네 말이 맞았다 Yes indeed, you are right. / ～ 이제 알았다 Oh—now I get it! / ～ 됐다 Now I've got it. *or* That's fine.

**옳은길** the right road; the straight path; the road of righteousness. ⇨ 정도(正道). ¶ 아무를 ～로 이끌다 guide *a person* into the right path.

**옳은말** true words; an honest speech; the truth. ¶ ～을 하는 사람 a person who speaks truly 〔true〕.

**옴**[1] ① 〚의학〛 the itch; scabies; mange (말·개 등의). ¶ 옴딱지 scabies 〔mange〕 scabs / 옴쟁이 an itch sufferer / 옴이 오르다 catch 〔have〕 the itch; be infected with scabies. ② 《젖꼭지의》 the tiny bumps around the teats of a new mother.

**옴**[2] 〚물리〛 an ohm (기호 Ω). ¶ 옴의 법칙 Ohm's law. ◉ 옴미터 an ohmmeter. 옴수(數) ohmage. 옴저항 ohmic resistance.

**옴니버스** an omnibus.

**옴부즈맨** 《행정감찰관》 an ombudsman; an ombudsperson. ◉ ～제도 the ombudsman system.

**옴실거리다** swarm; squirm 〔wriggle〕.

**옴쏙** ～하다 (be) hollow; depressed; sunken. ¶ ～한 hollow; sunken / 눈이 ～들어간 사람 a person with sunken 〔deepset〕 eyes / ～해지다 become hollow 〔depressed〕; cave in; sink.

**옴질거리다** ① 《입을》 chew on 〔mumble〕 slowly. ¶ 옴질거리며 씹다 mumble 〔munch〕 《*something*》 / 껌을 넣고 입을 ～ chew on chewing gum slowly. ② 《주저》 be slow 《in *do*ing》; linger. ¶ 일을 ～ linger over *one's* work. ③ 《움직임》 move slowly 〔timidly〕; squirm. ¶ 벌레가 ～ a worm wriggles.

**옴질옴질** ① 《입을》 mumbling; slowly chewing. ¶ 사과를 ～ 씹다 slowly chew away on an apple. ② 《꾸물거림》 slowly; tardily; lingering. ③ 《움직임》 slowly; timidly. ¶ 벌레가 ～ 기어가다 a worm wriggles cautiously along.

**옴짝달싹** ¶ ～ 않다 be not at all daunted; do not turn a hair 〔move a muscle〕; do not budge 〔stir, move〕 an inch; stand as firm as a rock / ～ 못하다 cannot move 〔budge, stir〕 an inch; be helpless; be stuck / 빚은 늘어가고 장사는 안 되다 보니 지금 그는 ～ 못할 지경이다 With his debt increasing and his business diminishing, he doesn't know which way to turn.

**옴찔** ⇨ 움찔.

**옴츠러들다** huddle 〔curl〕 *oneself* up; shrink up; cower; flinch; quail 《at, before》; wince; recoil. ¶ 추워서 ～ be huddled up with the cold / 무서워서 ～ shrink with fear.

**옴츠러뜨리다** ① contract; huddle up; curl up; withdraw; draw 〔pull〕 in. ¶ 다리를 ～ draw in *one's* legs / 머리를 ～ duck *one's* head / 몸을 ～ huddle *oneself* up; 《용기를 잃고》 shrink up; flinch; cower; quail; wince / 꽃에서 벌을 보고 그는 손을 움츠러뜨렸다 Seeing a bee on the flower, he jerked his hand back. ② 《지질리게 하다》 make 《*a person*》 shrink up; scare. ¶ 고함으로 아무를 ～ scare *a person* with a loud shout.

**옴츠러지다** = 옴츠러들다.

**옴츠리다, 옴치다** = 옴츠러뜨리다.

**옴큼** a handful ⟪of rice⟫.

**옴파다** gouge 〔scoop〕 out; hollow out. ¶ 나무에다 자기 이니셜을 ~ gouge out *one's* initials on a tree.

**옴팡눈** deep-set 〔sunken〕 eyes; a person with deep-set eyes.

**옴패다** get pitted 〔dented, pushed-in, hollowed-out, sunken〕. ¶ 지면이 옴패여서 넘어질 뻔했다 I nearly tipped over because the road was pitted.

**옴폭** hollow; deep; sunken(-in); dented. ~하다 (be) hollow; deep; sunken (=in); dented. ¶ ~ 패인 곳 a depressed 〔hollowed〕 place; a cave-in / 눈이 ~하다 have deep-set 〔sunken〕 eyes.

**옵서버** an observer. ¶ ~로서 참석하다 attend ⟪a conference⟫ as an observer.

**옵션** ① ⟪선택할 수 있는 일〔것〕⟫ an option. ¶ 시내 관광은 ~입니다 The sightseeing tour around the city is optional. / ~ 상품은 다음과 같음(별도 요금) Optional parts are as follows (at extra cost). ② ⟪미식 축구의⟫ an option; an option play 〔pass〕.

**옷** clothes; clothing; garment; dress; wear; suit; apparel; an outfit; costume.

¶ 겉옷 outer garments / 비옷 a rain coat / 속옷 underwear / 잠옷 pajamas / 옷 한 벌 a suit of clothes / 옷을 입다 put on clothes; dress *oneself;* wear clothes / 옷을 개키다 fold *one's* clothes / 옷을 벗다 take off *one's* clothes; undress *oneself* / 옷을 걸치다 fling *one's* clothes on / 옷을 벗기다 strip ⟪*a person*⟫ of *his* clothes / 옷을 입혀 주다 put clothes on ⟪*a person*⟫; clothe ⟪a child⟫ / 아이의 옷을 벗겨 주다 help a child off with his clothes / 옷을 껴입다 wear one garment over the other / 옷을 빌어 입다 wear borrowed clothes; be in borrowed clothing 〔plumes〕; hire a garment ⟪for the day⟫ / 옷을 갈아 입다 change *one's* clothes / 검은 옷을 입고 있다 be (dressed) in black / 좋은〔나쁜〕 옷을 입고 있다 be well 〔poorly〕 dressed / 옷이 많다 have a large wardrobe / 그 옷은 너한테 잘 맞는다 The dress 〔suit〕 fits you perfectly. / 나는 입고 갈 옷이 없다 I have nothing to go in. / 아이가 자라서 옷이 맞지 않는다 The child has outgrown his garments. / 옷이 날개라 ⟪속담⟫ Clothes make the man. *or* The tailor makes the man. *or* Fine feathers make fine birds.

> (용법) **clothes** 실용적인 입장에서 본 의복을 말함. 가장 일반적으로 쓰이는 말로서 everyday clothes (일상복), work (-ing) clothes (작업복) 등. 항시 복수형. 셀 때는 a suit of clothes라고 말함. **clothing** 몸에 걸치는 것 모두를 집합적으로 볼 때의 총칭. 이 때의 의복 한 벌〔점〕은 an article 〔a piece〕 of clothing. **garment** 의복·옷을 격조 높게 일컫는 말. 의류 메이커들이 즐겨 씀. **dress** 장식적인 견지에서 본 의복. 이 말에는 보통 외투나 속옷이 포함돼 있지 않음. 여성복일 경우에는 원피스를 가리킴. 복합어로서 full dress (정장), evening dress (야회복), wedding dress (신부 의상), maternity dress (임신복)처럼 쓰임. **wear** 특별한 목적을 지닌 의복을 나타낼 때 쓰이며 대개의 경우 복합어로 나타냄. men's wear (신사복), children's wear (아동복), skiwear (스키복) 등. **suit** wear와 마찬가지로 목적을 나타내는 말과 함께 쓰임. bathing suit (수영복), business suit (양복), space suit (우주복) 등. **apparel** 속옷 등에 대한 겉옷을 나타내는 격식을 갖춘 말. 행사 등에서는 무게를 주기 위해 곧잘 쓰임. Fall Apparel Fashion Show (가을 패션쇼), Apparel Magazine (복식 잡지). **an outfit** 의복 한 벌. **costume** 시대〔국민〕 고유의 의복.

**옷가슴** the breast (of a garment). ¶ ~이 넓다〔좁다〕 be loose 〔tight〕 across the chest; be loose-〔close-〕breasted.

**옷가지** (several kinds of) garments.

**옷감** texture; stuff; (plain) cloth; drygoods; ⟪남자 양복감⟫ suit material; suiting; ⟪여자 양장감⟫ dress material. ¶ 얇은 ~ light stuff; thin cloth / ~을 마르다 cut cloth.

**옷걸이** a coat hanger; a clothes rack. ¶ 옷을 ~에 걸다 hang clothes on a hanger.

**옷고름** a breast-tie (of a Korean coat); a coat string. ¶ ~을 매다〔풀다〕 tie 〔untie〕 a coat string.

**옷기장** the length of *one's* clothes; *one's* dress length.

**옷깃** ⟪한복의⟫ the neckband; ⟪양복의⟫ a collar 〔lapel〕; ⟪셔츠 따위의⟫ a neck. ¶ ~차례(로) (in) order from left to right / ~을 세우다 turn up *one's* collar / ~을 여미다 adjust *oneself* 〔*one's*

dress]; straighten *oneself.*
**옷농**(—籠) a clothes chest.
**옷단** a tuck; a hem (좁게 감친); cuff; turn-up (접어 올린). ¶ ～을 감치다 hem.
**옷단장**(—丹粧) dressing [“dolling”] up. ～하다 dress [“doll”] up.
**옷맵시** ¶ ～가 좋다[없다] wear *one's* clothes stylishly [badly, poorly]; dress *oneself* in good [bad] shape; dress well [badly].
**옷보**(—褓) a cloth wrapper for clothes.
**옷상자**(—箱子) a chest [box] of clothes.
**옷셋집**(—貰—) a clothes-renting shop; a rental clothier [tailor].
**옷자락** the lower ends of clothes; 《여성의》 the skirt; the train; 《양복 바지의》 the bottom. ¶ ～을 끌다 trail [drag] *one's* skirt 《on the floor》 / ～을 걷어 올리다 tuck up *one's* skirt.
**옷장**(—欌) a clothes chest; a wardrobe.
**옷차림** *one's* attire; attiring *oneself;* personal appearance. ¶ ～이 얌전하다 be neat and tidy in *one's* dress / 그는 ～에 매우 까다롭다 He is rather particular about personal appearance.
**옷치레** dressing up; rich attire. ～하다 dress (*oneself*) up; wear fine clothes; be gaily [gaudily] dressed; be in *one's* (Sunday) best.
**-옹**(翁) an old [aged] man; old Mr. …. ¶ 김옹 the old Mr. Kim.
**옹고집**(壅固執) stubbornness; obstinacy; pigheadedness; perversity; mulishness; 《영구어》 bloody-mindedness. ¶ ～ 부리는 stubborn; obstinate; pigheaded; headstrong; perverse; mulish; uncompromising; stiff-necked / ～ 부리다 get [grow, become] obstinate / ～ 부리지 말게 Don't be so stubborn.
**옹골지다** 《실속있다》 substantial; solid; meaty; hard; full. ¶ 옹골진 과일 hard fruits / 더할 나위 없이 옹골진 생활을 하다 live life to the full(est).
**옹골차다** ⇨ 옹골지다. ¶ 옹골찬 사람 a person of sturdy build.
**옹그리다** ① ⇨ 옹송그리다. ¶ 옹그리고 자다 sleep curled up. ② 《팔·다리를》 contract; make *oneself* small (몸을). ¶ 다리를 ～ draw in *one's* legs / 팔을 ～ pull in *one's* arms / 입을 ～ purse *one's* lips.
**옹글다** (be) intact; whole; unbroken. ¶ 옹근 수 an unbroken number; a whole number.
**옹기**(甕器) pottery with a dark brown glaze. ◉ ～장수 a pottery dealer. ～장이 a potter. ～전(廛) a pottery shop.
**옹기옹기, 옹기종기** thickly; densely. ¶ TV앞에 옹기종기 모이다 form a little knot of togetherness around the TV.
**옹달-** small and hollow. ¶ 옹달샘 a small fountain [spring] / 옹달솥 a small deep iron pot / 옹달시루 a small deep earthenware steamer / 옹달우물 a small deep well.
**옹두리** a knot (on a tree); a knob; a node; a knurl; a knar; a gnarl. ◉ ～뼈 the leg bone 《of cattle》.
**옹립**(擁立) 《임금으로》 enthroning; 《떠받듦》 backing. ～하다 enthrone; give backing to; help 《*a person*》 to a position.
**옹벽**(擁壁) 『토목』 a breast [retaining] wall; a revetment.
**옹색하다**(壅塞—) ① 《생활·돈이》 be hard up; be in straitened [needy, narrow] circumstances. ¶ 돈에 ～ be pinched [pressed, hard up] for money / 옹색하게 살다 be badly off; live in poverty. ② 《비좁다》 (be) cramped; confined; narrow and close 《house》. ¶ 옹색한 방 a cramped room / 당분간 옹색한 대로 그냥 지내야겠다 We shall pig together for a time.
**옹생원**(—生員) a narrow-minded person.
**옹송그리다** curl [huddle] *oneself* up; squeez *oneself* 《in》; contract; draw [pull] in. ¶ 추워서 몸을 ～ huddle *oneself* up with cold / 방 한 구석에 몸을 옹송그리고 앉다 squat down in a corner of the room.
**옹송옹송하다** (be) hazy; confused.
**옹스트롬** 『물리』 《길이의 단위》 an angstrom (unit) (기호 Å).
**옹위**(擁衛) safeguard; escort. ～하다 guard; escort; 《군대·군함이》 convoy.
**옹이** a node; a knar; a gnarl; a knot. ¶ ～ 있는 gnarled; knotty.
**옹자배기** a tiny earthenware bowl.
**옹졸하다**(壅拙—) (be) narrow-minded; illiberal; hidebound; ungenerous; intolerant. ¶ 옹졸한 사람 a narrow-minded person / 생각이 ～ have a narrow(-minded) view 《of》.
**옹주**(翁主) a princess (by concubine).
**옹호**(擁護) 《보호》 protection; 《방호》 defense; 《변호》 (a) vindication; 《원조》 support. ～하다 support; back up; defend; protect 《A from B》; safeguard; vindicate. ¶ 자기의 권리를 ～하다 safeguard *one's* own rights / 자유를 ～하기 위해 싸우다 fight in the cause of freedom / 헌법을 ～하다 defend the constitution / 우리는 더 인권을 ～해야 한다 We should protect human rights more. ◉ ～자 a supporter; a defend-

er; a protector; a champion. 인권 ～가 a human rights advocate.

**옻** 《피부병》 lacquer poison.

**옻나무** 〖식물〗 a lacquer 〔varnish〕 tree.

**옻오르다, 옻올리다** be poisoned with lacquer; get poison ivy.

**옻칠**(—漆) varnishing with lacquer. ～하다 apply lacquer 《to》; lacquer. ¶ ～한 그릇 a lacquerware dish; lacquerware.

**옻타다** be sensitive 〔allergic〕 to lacquer 「poison.

**와**[1] 《일제히 움직이는 모양》 with a rush; all at once; in crowds; 《떠드는 모양》 with a great 「roar 〔noise〕; loudly; 《놀라는 소리》 Oh !; Wow ! ¶ 와 떠들다 make a great noise 〔roar〕 / 와 밀려가다 advance on with a rush / 와 웃다 roar with laughter; burst into laughter / 와 울다 burst out crying / 와, 신난다 Oh boy ! That's wonderful. / 사람들이 우리 집으로 와 몰려왔다 People rushed to my house in crowds.

**와**[2] 《마소를 멈출 때》 Whoa !; Wo !

**-와**[3] ① 《함께》 with; together with; in company with. ¶ 친구와 함께 together with my friend / 친구와 테니스를 하다 play tennis with a friend.
② 《열거》 and. ¶ 너와 나 You and I / 호랑이와 곰은 다 짐승이다 The tiger and the bear are both animals. / 그와 나는 같이 가겠다 He and I'll go together.
③ 《대항》 with; against. ¶ 친구와 싸우다 quarrel with a friend.
④ 《합치·협력》 with. ¶ 친구와 협력하다 cooperate with a friend.
⑤ 《접촉》 with. ¶ 친구와 만나다 meet with a friend / 사령부와 연락하다 get in touch with headquarters.
⑥ 《분리》 with; from. ¶ 친구와 작별하다〔관계를 끊다〕 part 〔break〕 with a friend.
⑦ 《관계》 with. ¶ 나는 너와 아무 관계가 없다 I have nothing to do with you.
⑧ 《비교》 with. ¶ …와 비교해서 as compared with / …와 대조해서 in contrast with.
⑨ 《유사》 (the same) as; like; (similar) to; (different) from. ¶ 바다와 비슷한 호수 a lake like 〔similar to〕 the sea.
⑩ 《혼합》 with. ¶ 달걀을 우유와 잘 섞어라 Mix up this egg with the milk.

**와가**(瓦家) a tile-roofed house.

**와각거리다** rattle; clatter. ¶ 수레 위에서 기와가 ～ roof tiles rattle on a cart.

**와각와각** rattlingly; clatteringly; with a rattling noise.

**와글거리다** ① 《북적이다》 《people》 swarm; crowd; throng. ¶ 광장에는 사람들이 와글거렸다 The square was crowded 〔jammed〕 with people. ② 《떠들다》 be clamorous 〔boisterous, tumultuous, noisy〕. ¶ 와글거리는 사람들 a clamorous crowd of people. ③ 《물이 끓다》 be hissing hot; be on the boil.

**와글와글** 《북적임》 in swarms 〔crowds, throngs〕; 《시끄럽게》 clamorously; in a boisterous manner; noisily. ～하다 make a lot of noise; make a boisterous noise. ¶ ～ 떠들어 대는 목소리 the confused murmuring of voices.

**와닥닥** 《갑자기》 suddenly; abruptly; 《급히》 hastily. ¶ ～ 일어서다 spring to *one's* feet / ～ 방에서 뛰쳐나가다 rush 〔bolt〕 out of the room.

**와당탕** clamorously; boisterously; noisily. ～하다 make a thumping sound; make a noise. ¶ 아이들이 마루 위에서 ～ 뛰어다니다 Children romp 〔jump〕 around boisterously on the floor.

**와드등와드등** with thuds 〔thumps〕; rumbling and clattering. ～하다 thump; (rumble and) clatter.

**와들와들** shiveringly; tremblingly. ¶ 손을 ～ 떨며 with trembling hands / ～ 떨다 tremble (all over); be all of a tremble; quiver; shiver 《with cold》 / 성이 나서〔무서워서〕 ～ 떨다 tremble with anger 〔fear〕.

**와락** with a start 〔rush, jerk〕; suddenly; abruptly; all at once. ¶ 줄을 ～ 잡아당기다 pull a rope with a jerk / 문을 ～ 열다 jerk a door open / 남의 목을 ～ 껴안다 fling *one's* arms round *a person's* neck / ～ 울음을 터뜨리다 burst out crying; burst into tears.

**와룡**(臥龍) a lying dragon; 《인물》 a great man in obscurity; a great man with no opportunity to display his talent.

**와르르** ① 《사람이》 with a rush. ¶ 군중들이 ～ 몰려 들어갔다 The crowd poured 〔surged〕 in. / 여학생들이 사인을 해달라고 그에게 ～ 몰려갔다 Girl students stormed him for his autographs. ② 《무너짐》 《fall》 in a confused heap; 《소리》 clattering down; crumbling all in a heap. ¶ ～ 무너지다 crumble all in a heap; fall down with a crash / ～ 떨어지다 clatter down / 마루에 높이 쌓아 올린 상자들이 ～ 무너졌다 Boxes stacked high on the floor 「fell down 〔collapsed〕 with a crash. ③ 《천둥 소리》 rolling; rumbling; thundering. ④ 《끓음》 seething; boiling.

**와륵**(瓦礫) pieces of broken tile.
**와병**(臥病) lying sick in bed. ~하다 be on *one's* sickbed; be ill in bed.
**와삭** rustlingly; with a rustle; with a rustling sound 〔noise〕. ~하다 give a rustle. ~거리다 rustle. ¶ 옷이 ~거리는 소리 the rustle of clothes / 나뭇잎이 바람에 ~거린다 The leaves rustle in the wind.
**와상**(渦狀) ¶ ~의 whirled; spiral. ◉ ~문 《지문의》 a whirl.
**와스스** 《떨어짐》 with a rustling sound; 《무너짐》 crumbling. ¶ 마른 잎이 ~ 떨어지다 dead leaves fall thick and fast / 낙엽이 바람에 ~ 소리를 냈다 The wind rustled the fallen leaves.
**와신상담**(臥薪嘗膽) struggling against difficulties for the sake of vengeance; sustained determination and perseverance. ~하다 go through unspeakable hardships and privations. ¶~하기를 10년 after ten years of hard struggles against fortune.
**와우**(蝸牛) 〖동물〗 a snail. ¶ ~ 각상(角上)의 싸움 a petty strife. ◉ ~각(殼) a snail shell; 〖해부〗 a cochlea (*pl.* -e, -s).
**와이** 《영어 자모》 Y. ◉ ~염색체 〖생물〗 a Y chromosome.
**와이더블유시에이** Y.W.C.A. 〔< *Y*oung *W*omen's *C*hristian *A*ssociation〕
**와이드스크린** 〖영화〗 a wide screen.
**와이셔츠** a shirt; a dress shirt (예복용). ¶ ~ 바람으로 in *one's* shirt(-sleeves).
**와이어** a wire. ¶ ~ 게이지 a wire gauge / ~ 로프 (a) wire rope. ◉ ~리스 마이크 a wireless microphone. ~메모리 〖컴퓨터〗 wire memory. ~브러시 a wire brush. ~커터 a wire cutter.
**와이엠시에이** Y.M.C.A. 〔< *Y*oung *M*en's *C*hristian *A*ssociation〕
**와이오밍** 《미국의 주》 Wyoming (생략 Wy(o).).
**와이투케이** 〖컴퓨터〗《2000년 연도 인식 오류》 Y2K 〔< *Y*ear *T*wo *K*ilo〕; the millennium bug (computer glitch). ¶원자력 발전소의 ~문제 the Y2K problem of the nuclear power plants / ~ 준비 상태에 대한 재평가 계획 a plan to reappraise 《the corporations'》 Y2K readiness.
**와이퍼** 《자동차의》 a (windshield) wiper; 《영》 a windscreen wiper.
**와이프** a wife (*pl.* wives); *one's* wife.
**와인** wine. ¶ 붉은 ~ red wine / ~ 글라스 a wineglass.
**와인드업** 〖야구〗 a wind-up. ~하다 wind up.
**와일드** 《야생의》 wild. ◉ ~라이프 《야생 동물》 wildlife. ~카드 《으뜸패·예측 불능한 일·리그전을 거치지 않고 출전할 수 있는 팀〔선수〕》 a wild card. ~캣스트라이크 《조합의 비승인 파업》 a wildcat strike. ~피치 〖야구〗 a wild pitch.
**와전**(瓦全) (living) a life of ease and inactivity; contenting *oneself* with safe mediocrity. ¶ ~을 부끄러이 여기다 be ashamed of having led a safe but mediocre life.
**와전**(訛傳) false telling; a false 〔distorted〕 report 〔story〕; a misrepresentation. ~하다 tell falsely 〔distortedly〕; misrepresent; hand down wrongfully. ¶ 그 보도는 ~된 것이었다 The report turned out 〔was〕 false.
**와중**(渦中) (in) a whirlpool; a vortex. ¶ …의 ~에 휩쓸려 들다 be drawn into the vortex 〔maelstrom〕 of 《war》; be involved 〔entangled〕 in 《a quarrel》.
**와지끈** smashing; crashing. ~하다 crash; go smash. ¶ ~뚝딱 with a smash-bang 〔crash-bang〕; crashing; smashing / 가구를 ~ 부수다 smash up furniture / 그릇들이 ~ 깨지다 dishes fall and smash to pieces / 부엌에서 ~거리는 소리가 들렸다 I heard a crash in the kitchen.
**와짝** ① 《힘껏》 forcefully; vigorously. ¶ 줄을 ~ 잡아당기다 give a rope a vigorous pull. ② 《갑자기》 all at once; all of a sudden; abruptly. ¶ 날이 ~ 추워지다 the weather gets cold suddenly. ③ 《부쩍》 in huge numbers. ¶ 요새 그의 환자가 ~ 늘었다 Recently his patients have increased a great deal.
**와트** 〖물리〗 a watt (of electricity). ¶ 100 ~의 전구 a 100-watt (electric) bulb. ◉ ~미터 a wattmeter. ~시(時) a watt-hour (생략 wh., whr.). ~시효율 watt-hour efficiency. ~조속기(調速機) a watt governor.
**와해**(瓦解) falling to pieces; crumbling; disintegration; breaking; collapse; a downfall; *débâcle* (F.). ~하다 fall to pieces; disintegrate; break up; collapse; be ruined. ¶ 정당의 ~ the collapse of a political party / 로마 제국의 ~ the fall of the Roman Empire / 내각은 머지않아 ~될 것이다 The Cabinet will soon be dissolved.
**왁다그르르** with a rattle. ~하다 rattle.
**왁스** wax. ¶ ~를 바르다 wax.
**왁시글** swarming; thronging; spreading out in crowds. ~거리다 swarm; throng; spread out in crowds.
**왁자그르르** boisterously; clamorously; uproariously; rowdily; with much

noise. ～하다 act boisterous [rowdy]; make a lot of noise.

**왁자하다** (be) noisy; boisterous; clamorous; uproarious; rowdy; 《왜자하다》 (be) widespread. ¶ 왁자지껄하다 ＝왁자하다 / 교실 안이 ～ the classroom is in an uproar / 그 사건으로 지난 석달 동안 세상이 왁자했다 The event kept the world astir for the last three months.

**왁친** 〖의학〗 vaccine. ⇨ 백신.

**완강**(頑强) obstinacy; stubbornness; doggedness. ～하다 (be) stubborn; obstinate; dogged; mulish; persistent; die-hard 《rightists》. ¶ ～하게 stubbornly; obstinately; doggedly; persistently / ～한 저항 a stubborn resistance / ～히 부정하다 deny persistently / 그들은 ～히 저항했다 They offered a stubborn resistance.

**완결**(完結) conclusion; completion; termination; finish; end. ～하다 conclude; complete; terminate; finish; end; bring 《a thing》 to an end [to completion]. ¶ ～되다 be completed; be concluded; be brought to an end / 사건을 ～짓다 bring the case to a conclusion / 그 책으로 이 시리즈는 ～된다 The book marks the close of the series. / 이 문학 전집은 30권으로 ～된다 This series of works of literature will be completed with the thirtieth volume. / 다음 호에서 ～《잡지 따위의 예고》 To be concluded (in next issue). ◉ ～편 the concluding volume [part] (of the novel).

**완고**(頑固) stubbornness; obstinacy; bigotry. ～하다 (be) stubborn; obstinate; bigoted; headstrong; 《끈질김》 persistent.

> 용법 **stubborn** 사람이나 동물의 성질이 나면서부터 완고하다는 뜻. **obstinate** 충고나 항의에 대해 이치에 맞지 않는 옹고집을 부리면서 목적·의견 등을 바꾸려 하지 않는 완고하고도 우매함을 말함. **headstrong** 하는 짓이 제멋대로이면서 고집스러움을 말함. 사람에게만 적용되는 용어. **persistent** 사람의 행동이나 일의 추진 등이 반대나 경고 또는 실패에도 불구하고 집요하게 추구됨을 말함.

¶ ～한 노인 an obstinate old man / ～한 사람 a hard-top; a holy terror / ～하게 의견을 고집하다 persist in *one's* own view.

**완곡**(婉曲) a roundabout way; circumlocution; euphemism. ～하다 (be) indirect; roundabout; periphrastic; euphemistic. ¶ ～하게 indirectly; in a roundabout way; by euphemism; gracefully / ～히 말하다 insinuate; say [tell *a thing*] in a roundabout way / 「발전도상국」이란 말은 「후진국」의 ～한 표현이다 The phrase 'developing countries' is a euphemism for 'underdeveloped countries'. / 때로는 ～한 표현을 쓰는 편이 좋다 It sometimes helps to say things in a roundabout way. ◉ ～법 〖수사학〗 euphemism; periphrasis.

**완공**(完工) completion. ⇨ 준공(竣工).

**완구**(玩具) a plaything; a toy. ¶ ～를 가지고 놀다 play with toys. ◉ ～상《사람》 a toy dealer. ～상자 a toy box. ～점 《미》 a toy store; 《영》 a toyshop. 한국～공업협동조합 Korea Toy Industry Cooperative.

**완급**(緩急) 《속도》 slowness and fastness; high and low speed; tempo. ◉ ～기호 〖음악〗 tempo notation.

**완납**(完納) full payment. ～하다 pay in full; pay the whole amount of 《*one's* tax》. ¶ 회비를 ～하다 pay up *one's* dues / 나는 세금을 ～했다 I have paid all my taxes [my taxes in full].

**완두**(豌豆) 〖식물〗 a pea; pease [총칭].

**완력**(腕力) physical [muscular, brute] strength; 《폭력》 brute force; violence. ¶ ～으로 by force / ～이 세다 have great physical strength; be strong-muscled / ～을 쓰다 use force / ～에 호소하다 resort [have recourse] to force [violence] / ～으로는 도저히 그를 당할 수가 없다 I am no match for him in mere physical strength. ◉ ～가 a strong(-armed) man; a man of muscle; a muscleman.

**완료**(完了) completion; finishing. ～하다 complete; finish; be over. ◉ ～시제 〖문법〗 the perfect tense.

**완만**(緩慢) slowness; inactivity; dullness; listlessness; slackness. ～하다 (be) slow(-moving); inactive; dull; listless; slack. ¶ ～한 흐름 a slow [gently flowing] stream / ～한 경사 a gentle [an easy] slope [grade] / ～한 내리막길 an easy descent / ～하게 gently; slowly; smoothly / ～한 플레이 a sloppy play / ～한 대응 slack measures / 동작이 ～하다 be slow-moving; be slow in *one's* movements.

**완미**(頑迷) asininity; bigotry; obstinacy; stubbornness; perversity. ～하다 (be) asinine; bigoted; stupidly obstinate;

stubborn. ¶ 너무 ～하여 여론의 동향을 모른다 He is so bigoted in his views that he is blind to the tide of public opinion.

**완벽**(完璧) perfection; completeness. ～하다 (be) perfect; flawless; impeccable; free from blemish. ¶ ～하게 perfectly; flawlessly / ～을 기하다 aim at 〔for〕 perfection / ～한 단계에 이르다 reach the stage of perfection / ～한 사람은 없다 Nobody is perfect.

**완본**(完本) an unabridged edition; 《전집》 a complete set of works.

**완봉**(完封) 〖야구〗 a shutout. ～하다 shut out. ¶ 투수가 ～하다 pitch a shutout.

**완비**(完備) perfection; completeness; complete provision 〔arrangement, preparation〕. ～하다 perfect; complete; make 《*a thing*》 perfect. ¶ 설비가 ～된 병원 a well-equipped hospital / ～되어 있다 be complete 〔perfect〕; 《설비가》 be fully equipped 〔furnished〕《with》/ 그 호텔은 설비가 ～되어 있다 The hotel is completely equipped./ 난방〔냉방〕～ 《게시》 Air-Conditioned. / 주차장이 ～되어있습니다 A parking lot is available.

**완상**(玩賞) enjoying; appreciation. ～하다 enjoy; appreciate. ¶ 국화를 ～하다 admire chrysanthemums.

**완성**(完成) completion; perfection. ～하다 complete; accomplish; finish; perfect; [사물이 주어] be finished 〔completed, perfected〕. ¶ 일을 ～하다 bring a work to completion; put the last hand to *one's* work / 그 건물은 가을에는 ～될 예정이다 The building is scheduled for completion in autumn. / 죽기 전까지 이 사업을 ～하고 싶다 I hope to see the work accomplished before I die. ◉ ～품 a finished product; finished goods.

**완수**(完遂) successful execution; accomplishment; completion. ～하다 bring 《*something*》 to a successful conclusion; accomplish; complete; carry through. ¶ 목적을 ～하다 attain *one's* object; accomplish *one's* purpose / 책임을 ～하다 discharge *one's* duty; fulfill *one's* responsibility / 큰 일을 ～하려면 인내심이 필요하다 It takes patience to accomplish a big project.

**완숙**(完熟) full ripeness 〔maturity〕. ～하다 come to 〔attain〕 full maturity; ripen into full maturity. ¶ ～한 fully ripe 〔ripened〕/ ～한 달걀 a hard-boiled egg.

**완승**(完勝) a complete 〔sweeping〕 victory. ～하다 win 〔score〕 a complete 〔sweeping〕 victory 《over》. ¶ ～을 거두다 have an out-and-out victory.

**완역**(完譯) a complete translation; a translation in full. ～하다 make a complete translation 《of》.

**완연하다**(宛然—) (be) clear; obvious; evident; patent. ¶ 봄빛이 ～ Spring has fairly set in.

**완월**(玩月) ～하다 enjoy the moon 〔moonlight〕; view the moon.

**완자** a meatball fried in egg batter; a kind of wonton.
◉ ～탕 a kind of wonton soup.

**완자**(卍字) ⇨ 만자(卍字). ◉ ～창 a window with a swastika-shaped frame.

**완장**(腕章) an armband; a brassard. ¶ ～을 두르다 wear an armband.

**완전**(完全) perfection; completeness; wholeness. ～하다 (be) perfect; complete; whole.

> 용법 **perfect** 모든 점에서 빠진 부분이나 결점이 없어 완전한. **complete** 필요한 것을 모두 갖춰 완전 무결한. **whole** 모든 구성 부분이나 구성원이 다 포함되어 제외된 것이 없는이란 뜻.

¶ ～히 to perfection; perfectly; completely; wholly; thoroughly; entirely; fully; quite / ～한 성공〔실패〕 a complete success 〔failure〕/ ～하게 하다 complete; perfect; make perfect; bring 《*a thing*》 to perfection / ～해지다 be made perfect; become complete; be brought 〔carried〕 to perfection / 결코 ～한 것이 못 되다 be far from perfect / ～에 가깝다 be nearly perfect / ～을 기하다 aim at perfection / ～의 경지에 달하다 attain 〔reach, touch〕 perfection / ～히 속다 be completely taken in / ～히 잊다 entirely forget / 그러나 그것은 예술품으로서는 ～했다 Yet as a work of art it was flawless. / 무슨 일이나 ～을 바랄 수는 없다 Perfection cannot be expected in anything. / 건축은 아직 ～히 끝나지 않았다 The building is not quite finished yet.
◉ ～가동〔조업〕 full operation; capacity operation. ～경기 〖야구〗 a perfect game. ～고용 full employment. ～무결 absolute perfection: ～무결한 absolutely perfect; perfect and faultless. ～범죄 a perfect crime. ～변태 〖동물〗 complete metamorphosis; perfect transformation. ～실업자 a wholly-unemployed person. ～연소 perfect combustion. ～

종지 〖음악〗 the perfect cadence. ~주의자 a perfectionist.

**완제**(完濟) full 〔complete〕 payment; liquidation. ~하다 pay in full; clear off 《*one's* debts》; complete payment of; liquidate. ¶ 채무를 ~하다 fully satisfy the obligations; pay up the liabilities.

**완제품**(完製品) a finished product; end products. ¶ ~보다 부품 수출에 좀더 중점을 두다 place more emphasis on the export of component parts rather than end products.

**완주**(完走) ~하다 run the whole distance 《of a marathon race》; complete 〔finish〕 the course 〔race〕.

**완충**(緩衝) shock-absorbing; concussion-deadening; buffing. ~하다 absorb shock; deaden concussion; buff. ◉ ~국 a buffer (state) 《against》. ~기(器) 《자동차의》 a bumper; 《철도 차량의》 a buffer. ~장치 a buffer; a shock absorber. ~지대 a buffer 〔neutral〕 zone; 《create》 a buffer 《against》.

**완치**(完治) a perfect 〔complete〕 cure. ~하다 cure 〔heal〕 completely. ¶ ~되다 be completely cured; heal completely / 그의 상처는 일주일만에 ~되었다 His wound completely healed in a week. / 그녀는 ~에 3개월이 걸리는 중상을 입었다 She has had a severe injury which will take three months to heal completely.

**완쾌**(完快) complete recovery 《from illness, of health》. ~하다 recover completely 《from》; be completely restored to health; get quite well / 그는 ~에 반년이 걸릴 것이라고 의사는 말한다 The doctor says it will be six months before he is completely well again.

**완투**(完投) ~하다 〖야구〗 pitch the whole game 〔the full nine innings〕; go the (whole) distance. ¶ 자이언트 투수로서 ~하다 go the distance for the Giants.

**완패**(完敗) a complete defeat. ~하다 suffer a complete defeat; be comprehensively defeated; 《구어》 be beaten hollow; be walloped. ¶ (테니스에서) 나는 그에게 6-0, 6-0으로 ~당했다 He walloped 〔whitewashed〕 me, 6-0, 6-0.

**완하제**(緩下劑) a laxative; an aperient.

**완행**(緩行) going 〔running〕 slow. ~하다 go slow; slow down. ◉ ~열차 a local 〔slow〕 train.

**완화**(緩和) 《고통의》 mitigation; alleviation; 《교통난의》 relief; 《제한 따위의》 relaxation; 《긴장의》 ease. ~하다 mitigate; alleviate; relieve; relax; ease; soften. ¶ 국제간의 긴장 ~ the *détente* (F.); an easing of strained political relations between nations / 교통난을 ~하다 ease traffic congestion / 규율을 ~하다 loosen discipline / 경계를 ~하다 lower *one's* guard 《against》 / 요구를 ~하다 moderate 〔tone down〕 *one's* demand 《for》 / 규제를 ~하다 deregulate / 정부는 수입의 제한을 ~했다 The government eased 〔relaxed〕 its restrictions on import. / 우회로의 개통에 따라 교통 정체가 좀 ~되었다 The traffic congestion was eased a little after the bypass was opened. ◉ ~정책 an appeasement policy. ~제 a mitigative; a palliative. ~책 an alleviating measure.

**왈가닥** a hussy; a minx; a tomboy; a hoyden; a flapper 《구어》. ¶ ~의〔인〕 tomboyish; hoydenish; flapperish / 그녀는 ~이다 She is a flapper. *or* She is past all sense of shyness.

**왈가닥거리다** rattle; clatter. ¶ 짐수레가 왈가닥거리며 가다 a cart clatters along.

**왈가닥달가닥, 왈각달각** rattling and clattering. ~하다 rattle and clatter.

**왈가왈부**(曰可曰否) argument pro and con. ~하다 argue pro and con. ¶ ~할 필요없다 It admits of no further discussion. *or* It is beyond further dispute. / 이제와서 ~해 보았자 소용없다 What's done cannot be undone. *or* What is done is done.

**왈딱** suddenly; abruptly; unceremoniously; brusquely; without warning. ¶ 먹은 것을 ~ 게우다 suddenly throw up all *one* has eaten / 자동차가 ~ 뒤집히다 a car overturns abruptly.

**왈왈하다** (be) quick-tempered; hot-tempered; rough; violent.

**왈츠** 《dance》 a waltz.

**왈칵** 《별안간》 all at once; all of a sudden; with a jerk. ¶ ~ 성내다 flare up; fly into a passion / 눈물을 ~ 쏟다 burst into tears; break into tears / ~ 잡아당기다 pull 《*a thing*》 with a jerk.

**왈칵하다** (be) quick-tempered; irascible.

**왔다갔다** coming and going. ~하다 come and go. ¶ 거리를 ~하다 stroll aimlessly through the streets / 그 두 사람 사이에 편지가 여러 번 ~했다 Many letters were exchanged between the two.

**왕**(王) 《임금》 a king; a queen (여왕); a monarch (군주); a prince (소국의);

a magnate (산업계의). ¶ 퇴위한 왕 an abdicated king / 왕 중 왕 the King of Kings / 백수의 왕 the king of beasts / 꽃중의 왕 the queen of flowers / 석유왕 an oil magnate / 타격왕 the batting champion / 왕을 세우다 enthrone a king / 왕을 폐하다 dethrone 〔depose〕 a king / 자본주의 사회에서는 소비자가 왕이다 In capitalist societies the consumer is King.

**왕** 《마소를 멈출 때》 Whoa!

**왕-**(王) 《큰》 large; big; king-size; giant. ¶ 왕밤 giant chestnuts.

**왕가**(王家) the royal family; a royal house.

**왕개미**(王—) 〖곤충〗 a (black) carpenter ant; a giant ant.

**왕거미**(王—) a garden spider.

**왕겨**(王—) chaff; rice husks 〔hulls〕.

**왕고모**(王姑母) a sister of *one's* grandfather; a grandaunt.

**왕골** 〖식물〗 a kind of sedge (plant). ◉ ~자리 a sedge mat.

**왕관**(王冠) a (royal) crown; a diadem. ¶ ~을 쓰다 wear a crown; 《즉위하다》 be crowned king.

**왕국**(王國) a kingdom; a monarchy.

**왕궁**(王宮) a king's 〔royal〕 palace.

**왕권**(王權) sovereign power 〔right〕; royal 〔regal〕 authority 〔rights, prerogatives〕. ◉ ~신수설(神授說) (the theory of) the divine right of kings.

**왕기**(王旗) a royal standard; the King's Color.

**왕녀**(王女) a royal princess.

**왕년**(往年) the years past 〔gone by〕; the past. ¶ ~의 former; one-time / ~의 씨름왕 a veteran *ssirŭm* player in (the) days gone by / ~의 명성 *one's* earlier fame / 그는 ~의 명투수였다 He was once a famous pitcher.

**왕눈이**(王—) a person with big eyes; a large-eyed person.

**왕당**(王黨) the Royalists; the Tories 「《영》.

**왕대비**(王大妃) the Queen Dowager; the Queen Mother.

**왕도**(王都) the capital of a kingdom; the royal capital.

**왕도**(王道) the royal road; the principles of royalty; kingship; the rule of right. ¶ ~로써 다스리다 rule *one's* people with justice / 학문에 ~ 없다 《속담》 There is no royal road to learning.

**왕따** "*wang-tta*", a malicious practice alienating fellow classmates 〔workers〕 in school 〔office〕. ¶ 요즘 학교에서 동급생들을 ~한다는 학생들의 이야기들은 온 나라에 충격을 주었다. In recent months, several stories of students maliciously alienating fellow classmates in school have shocked the nation.

**왕래**(往來) ① 《통행》 comings and goings; 《much》 traffic (교통). ~하다 come and go. ¶ 보행자의 ~ the pedestrian traffic / 차의 ~ the vehicular traffic / ~를 금하다 block traffic; be closed to traffic / ~가 많다〔적다〕 traffic is heavy 〔light〕 / 사람의 ~가 끊겼다 The street is deserted. / 이 거리는 차의 ~가 매우 심하다 This street has very heavy traffic. *or* This is a busy street.

② 《교제》 association; correspondence (서신 연락). ~하다 associate 《with》; be on visiting terms; be in correspondence. ¶ 그와는 ~가 없다 I have no contact with him. *or* He and I seldom see each other. / 그들은 아직도 ~가 잦다 They frequently see each other even now. / 요새 그와는 편지 ~가 없다 I have no correspondence with him these days.

**왕릉**(王陵) a royal tomb.

**왕림**(枉臨) your visit 〔coming, attendance〕. ~하다 (come to) visit; deign to visit; honor us with a visit. ¶ ~해 주시기 바랍니다 Kindly do us the favor of your company.

**왕립**(王立) ¶ ~의 royal. ◉ ~ 미술원 《영국의》 the Royal Academy of Arts (생략 R.A.): ~ 미술원 회원 a member of the Royal Academy of Arts. ~협회 《영국의》 the Royal Society (of London for the Advancement of Science) (생략 R. S.): ~ 협회 회원 a Fellow of the Royal Society.

**왕마디**(王—) a large knot; a large node 《of bamboo》.

**왕명**(王命) the king's order; a royal command. ¶ ~으로 by the royal orders / ~에 따라 in obedience to a royal command.

**왕모래**(王—) coarse sand; grit.

**왕밤**(王—) a large 〔giant〕 chestnut.

**왕방**(往訪) paying a visit. ⇨ 방문.

**왕방울**(王—) a large bell. ¶ 눈이 ~ 같다 have big eyes; have eyes like saucers.

**왕벌**(王—) 〖곤충〗 《큰 벌》 a large bee; a hornet (말벌); a carpenter bee (호박벌).

**왕복**(往復) a round trip; 《영》 a return trip; going and returning. ~하다 go and return; get there and back; run 《between》; make a round trip 《to,

between》; 《차·배가》 ply 《between》. ¶ AB 간을 ~하다 ply 〔be in service〕 between A and B (배가); shuttle between A and B (열차가) / 하루 두 번 ~하다 make two round trips a day 《between A and B》 / 서울 인천간을 ~하는 열차 a train running between Seoul and Inch'ŏn / 회사까지 ~ 3시간 걸린다 It takes me three hours to get to and fro between my home and office. / 걸어서 ~하는 데 얼마나 걸릴까요 How long does it take to walk there and back? / 부산까지의 ~ 요금은 얼맙니까 What is the fare to Pusan and back? / 급행 열차가 매시간 보스턴과 뉴욕 사이를 ~하고 있다 The express runs hourly between Boston and New York.
◉ ~비행 a round-trip flight. ~소요시간 turnaround (time). ~여비 expenses for a round trip. ~여행 a round trip; a trip with return. ~엽서 a reply=paid postcard; a double postal card. ~운동 《기계의》 a to-and-fro 〔back=and-forth〕 motion; a reciprocating motion. ~운임〔요금〕 a round-trip fare 《미》; a return fare 《영》: ~ 운임은 얼마입니까? How much is the round=trip fare? ~운행 shuttle service. ~차표 a round-trip ticket 《미》; a return (ticket) 《영》.

**왕비**(王妃) a queen; a queen consort.

**왕새우**(王—) 〖동물〗 a spiny lobster.

**왕생극락**(往生極樂) 〖불교〗 rebirth in paradise 〔Nirvana〕. ⇨극락(極樂).

**왕성**(旺盛) a prosperous 〔flourishing, thriving〕 condition. ~하다 (be) prosperous; flourishing; thriving. ¶ 원기가 ~하다 be in (good) spirits; be full of vigor 〔pep 《구어》〕 / 정력이 ~하다 be energetic / 식욕이 ~하다 have a strong appetite / 군의 사기는 매우 ~하다 The morale of the army is excellent. *or* The army is highly spirited.

**왕세손**(王世孫) the eldest son of the Crown Prince.

**왕세자**(王世子) the Crown Prince. ◉ ~비 the Crown Princess; the consort of the Crown Prince.

**왕손**(王孫) the grandchildren of a king; the royal grandchildren 〔descendants〕.

**왕수**(王水) 〖화학〗 nitrohydrochloric acid; aqua regia (L.).

**왕실**(王室) a royal household; a royal family.

**왕업**(王業) the rule 〔reign〕 of a king.

**왕왕**(往往) often; (every) now and then; every so often; from time to time; time and again. ¶ 이런 일이 ~ 일어난다 Such things are apt to happen. / 그런 학생이 ~ 눈에 띈다 Such a student is not unfrequently met with.

**왕위**(王位) the throne. ¶~에 오르다 accede to 〔mount〕 the throne / ~를 물려주다 resign *one's* throne to 《*one's* son》; pass the throne on to / ~를 버리다 abdicate (from) the throne; renounce the throne (스스로) / ~를 찬탈하다〔계승하다〕 usurp 〔succeed to, inherit〕 the throne / ~에서 쫓아내다 dethrone / ~에 있다 be on the throne / ~를 다투다 contend for the throne.
◉ ~계승 succession to the throne: ~계승권 the right of succession; the right to the throne.

**왕자**(王子) a royal prince; a prince of the blood (royal).

**왕자**(王者) 《임금》 a king; a monarch; 《통치자》 a sovereign; a ruler; 《경기의》 a champion. ¶ 축구의 ~, 한국 Korea, the winner of the football championships.

**왕정**(王政) the kingly rule; monarchy.
◉ ~ 복고 the restoration of Imperial rule; the re-establishment of Imperial regime.

**왕조**(王朝) a dynasty. ¶~의 dynastic.
◉ 조선~ the Chosŏn dynasty.

**왕족**(王族) the royal family; royalty [총칭]; 《한 사람》 a member of royalty; a royalty.

**왕좌**(王座) the throne; supremacy; first place. ¶~를 차지하다 occupy the premier position; be at the top 《of》; hold the 《heavyweight》 championship / ~를 겨루다 contend for the championship. ◉ ~결정전 a championship contest 〔tournament〕.

**왕지**(王旨) the king's order 〔directive〕.

**왕지네**(王—) 〖동물〗 a large centipede.

**왕진**(往診) a (doctor's) visit (to a patient); a house 〔home〕 call; 《밤의》 a night visit. ~하다 go and see a patient at *his* house; call on *one's* patient; make a house call. ¶ 야간 ~에 만 원을 받다 charge 10,000 won for a night call / 선생님은 ~ 나가셨습니다 The doctor is away on his round of visits. ◉ ~료 a doctor's fee for a visit; the house-call charge. ~시간 hours for visiting patients.

**왕청스럽다** (be) completely different; widely disparate; be poles apart.

**왕토**(王土) the royal domain.

**왕후**(王后) a queen; a queen consort.

**왕후**(王侯) the king and peers 〔feudal lords〕; princes and lords. ¶ ～의 영화 regal splendor / ～처럼 살다 live like a lord 〔prince〕.

**왜**(倭) Japan; Japanese. ¶ 왜놈 a Jap. / 왜말 Japanese language; Jap talk.

**왜** ① 《어째서》 why; how; what… for; 《구어》 how come…; for what reason 〔purpose〕; on what ground.

> **용법** **Why … ?** 는 까닭을 묻는 가장 일반적인 의문문. 대답에는 because를 쓰는 일이 많으나 반드시 일정한 것은 아님. **How … ?** 는 원래 '어떻게 해서'의 뜻인데, How is it that … ?의 표현으로서는 why와 같은 뜻임. **What … for ?** '무엇 때문에, 무슨 목적으로'의 뜻임. **How come … ?** 은 How did it come that … ? (…은 무슨 까닭이냐)의 단축형이며, why보다 다소 놀람을 나타내어 《구어》에 쓰임. **for what reason** 〔**purpose**〕는 좀 딱딱한 말임.

¶ 왜냐하면 because; for; the reason is… / 왜 그런지 without knowing why; somehow / 왜 늦었느냐 Why were you late? / 그가 왜 거절했을까 I wonder why he refused. / 왜 그렇게 웃느냐 What makes you laugh so? / 너 왜 그렇게 생각하지 Why do you 〔What makes you〕 think so? / 왜 그렇게 성적이 나쁘냐 How is it that you should do so poorly at school? / 왜 그런지 눈물이 자꾸 났다 I didn't know why, but the tears came to my eyes.
② [감탄사적] why. ¶ 왜, 무엇이 나쁘단 말인가 Why, what's the harm?

**왜가리** 〖조류〗 a heron.

**왜간장**(倭―醬) Japanese soysauce.

**왜건** 《자동차》 a (station) wagon; 《영》 an estate car.

**왜곡**(歪曲) distortion; perversion. ～하다 distort; pervert; make a false representation of.
¶ ～된 견해 a distorted view / ～된 해석 《편벽된》 a biased interpretation; 《억지의》 a strained 〔forced〕 interpretation / ～된 정의감 a perverted sense 〔idea〕 of justice / 감정적으로 ～된 판단 a judgment swayed 〔influenced〕 by passion / 한국에 관한 ～된 역사 기술 distorted historical accounts about Korea / 보도를 ～하다 slant 〔garble〕 the news / 이해할 수 없는 논리로써 진실을 ～하려 들다 attempt to distort the truth with a logic that can be hardly understood / 이것은 사실을 ～한 것이다 It is a distortion of (the) fact.

**왜골** a large indiscreet 〔impudent〕 person; a boor. 「ers.

**왜구**(倭寇) 〖역사〗 Japanese pirate raid-

**왜그르르** crumbly. ～하다 (be) crumbly. ¶ 밥이 ～하다 rice is too flaky 〔is not sticky enough〕.

**왜뚜리** a bulky 〔large〕 thing.

**왜뚤삐뚤** zigzag; wiggling; squiggly. ¶ ～ 걸어가다 go zigzag / 글을 ～ 쓰다 write up and down (all over) the line; write crooked letters; write letters in a crooked line / 산 언덕에 길이 ～ 나 있다 A road runs zigzag 〔wiggles〕 over the hillside.

**왜림**(矮林) a thicket of shrubs.

**왜바람** a changeable wind.

**왜색**(倭色) Japanese ways 〔manners, customs〕; things Japanese. ¶ ～을 일소하다 make a clean sweep of Japanese manners.

**왜성**(矮星) 〖천문〗 a dwarf star.

**왜소**(矮小) dwarfness. ～하다 (be) short and small; dwarf; dwarfish; undersized; diminutive; stunted. ¶ ～한 나무 a stunted 〔dwarf〕 tree. ◉ ～증 dwafism; nanism.

**왜식**(倭式) Japanese style.

**왜식**(倭食) Japanese food 〔cuisine〕. ◉ ～집 a Japanese restaurant.

**왜옥**(矮屋) a small flat house.

**왜인**(倭人) a Japanese; a Jap.

**왜인**(矮人) a midget; a pigmy; a dwarf.

**왜자하다** 《풍문이》 (be) widespread; rife.

**왜장**(倭將) a Japanese general.

**왜적**(倭敵) the enemy Japan; Japanese invaders.

**왜정**(倭政) the Japanese rule 〔regime〕. ◉ ～시대 the period of the Japanese rule of Korea (1910-45); the Japanese administration period.

**왜죽왜죽** with rapid strides. ¶ ～ 걷다 walk with rapid strides.

**왜퉁스럽다** (be) queer and silly.

**왜풍**(倭風) Japanese customs.

**왝왝** Urp urp!; Puke puke! ～하다 keck; retch. ¶ 먹은 것을 ～ 다 게우다 throw up all *one* has eaten.

**왱** with a whistle 〔whiz, buzz, drone〕. ～하다 whistle; whizz; buzz.

**왱그랑댕그랑** clink clank; with a clang; clattering. ¶ 종을 ～ 울리다 clang the bell.

**왱왱** ① 《바람이 부는 소리》 whistling. ～거리다 《the wind》 whistle. ¶ 바람이 돛줄 새로 ～ 스친다 The wind whistles through the rigging.

② 《길게 뽑는 소리》 《read》 aloud; noisily. ¶ 아이들이 ～ 글을 읽다 the boys read at the top of their voices.

③ 《벌레가》 droning; buzzing; booming. ～거리다 drone; buzz; boom. ¶ 벌이 ～ 날다 a bee buzzes about.

**외**(外) ① 《밖》 outside; outer; foreign. ¶ 외몽고 Outer Mongolia.

② 《그 밖》 except; but; with the exception of (…을 제하고는); beyond (이상은); besides; in addition to (그 위에). ¶ 한씨 외 5명 Mr. Han and five others / 이러한 원인 외에 above and beyond these causes / 일이 있을 때 외에는 except on business / … 외에는 아무도 no one else but… / 이 외에는 아무것도 가진 것이 없다 I have nothing but this. / 독서하거나 산책하는 것 외에는 아무것도 하는 것이 없다 There is nothing for me to do except to read or take a walk. / 자네 외에는 모두 준비가 되었다 Everyone is ready except you. / 월급 100만 원 외에는 아무 수입도 없다 I don't have any income beyond a million won of my salary. / 그 외에는 다른 도리가 없었다 We had 〔There was〕 no other way. / 그는 이 책 외에도 많은 그림을 주었다 Besides giving me this book, he also gave me many pictures.

③ [접두어] the mother's side of a family (외가쪽).

**외**(椳) 〖건축〗 a lath; a lattice-strip.

**외-** only; single; one; lone; sole; isolated. ¶ 외아들 an only son.

**외가**(外家) the home 〔family〕 of *one's* mother's side. ¶ ～ 친척 a relative on *one's* mother's 〔maternal, distaff〕 side.

**외가닥** a single strand.

**외각**(外角) 〖수학〗 an exterior 〔external〕 angle; 〖야구〗 the outcorner; the outside. ¶ ～을 찌르는 속구 an outside fastball. ◉ ～구(球) an outside ball 〔pitch〕; an outsider.

**외각**(外殼) a crust; a shell; an integument.

**외간**(外艱) mourning for *one's* father's death. ◉ ～상(喪) = 외간.

**외갈래** a (straight) line. ◉ ～길 a straight road; a road without a branch.

**외감**(外感) ① 〖한의〗 a cold. ② 《감각》 sense; sensation; feeling.

**외객**(外客) a guest; a visitor.

**외견**(外見) an (outward) appearance 〔show〕. ⇨ 외관(外觀). ¶ ～상(으로는) in appearance / ～을 중시하다 attach much importance to outward show / ～상 그는 얌전해 보인다 He is quiet in appearance.

**외겹** a single layer; one-ply.

**외경**(畏敬) reverence; awe. ～하다 stand in awe of 《*a person*》; hold 《*a person*》 in awe; revere. ◉ ～심 (a feeling of) awe: ～심이 일어나게 하는 awe-inspiring 《architecture》 / ～심에 사로잡히다 be struck with awe.

**외계**(外界) the external 〔outer〕 world; 《지구 밖》 the outer space. ¶ ～(로부터)의 external; from outside / ～의 사정 outward conditions / ～와의 교통이 두절되다 be shut off from the outer world. ◉ ～인 a space 〔an outer-space〕 man; an alien; an extraterrestrial (생략 E.T.).

**외고집**(一固執) single-minded stubbornness. ¶ ～의 obstinate; obdurate; headstrong; stubborn; perverse / ～을 부리다 be stiff-necked.

◉ ～쟁이 a pig-headed person: ～쟁이이다 be a stiff-necked person.

**외골목** a single alley.

**외곬** a single way; a single track; a single groove. ¶ ～으로 생각하다 see things from only one point of view / ～으로 생각하는 사람 a person with a one-track mind.

**외과**(外科) (the science of) surgery; 《병원의》 the surgical department. ¶ ～적(인) surgical / ～적 치료 surgical treatment. ◉ ～병동 a surgery ward. ～수술 a surgical operation; surgery: ～수술을 받다〔하다〕 undergo 〔perform〕 a surgical operation. ～의사 a surgeon.

**외과피**(外果皮) 〖식물〗 an exocarp; an epicarp.

**외곽**(外廓) ① 《성》 the outer wall (of a walled city). ② 《바깥 테두리》 an outer ring; the outer block; the outline.

◉ ～단체 an auxiliary organ; an outer 〔a fringe〕 organization; an extra-governmental 〔extra-departmental〕 organization 〔body〕 (관청의).

**외관**(外觀) the external 〔outside〕 appearance; an outward show 〔aspect〕; the exterior; externals; 《표면적인 인상》 appearances; the look. ⇨ 외양(外樣). ¶ ～상(으로) externally; seemingly; in appearance; to 〔by〕 all appearances / 건물의 ～ the exterior 〔external appearance〕 of a building / ～에 까다롭다 be particular about *one's* personal appearance / ～을 꾸미다 make outward show; put on a show; show off; be ostentatious / ～으로 사람을 판

단하다 judge a person by his appearance 〔looks〕 / ~이 나아지다 improve in appearance / 그의 집은 ~이 참 좋다 His house looks very fine.

**외교**(外交) ① 《외국과의》 diplomacy; a foreign policy (정책); diplomatic relations (국교). ¶ ~상 diplomatically / ~상의, ~적인 diplomatic / 강경〔약체〕 ~ a strong 〔weak(-kneed)〕 foreign policy / 한국의 대미 ~ Korea's policy toward the United States / ~적 수완 diplomatic talent 〔skill〕 / ~상의 비밀 a diplomatic secret / 필요한 모든 ~적 조치 all the necessary diplomatic steps / ~를 재개하다 revive 〔restore〕 diplomatic relations 《with》 / 분쟁을 ~로 해결하다 settle a dispute diplomatically 〔by diplomatic negotiations〕 / ~ 루트를 통해 확인하다 confirm through diplomatic channels / 무력〔평화〕 ~를 하다 practice gunboat 〔peaceful〕 diplomacy / 그렇게 하는 것은 ~적인 방식이 못된다 It is undiplomatic to do so. / 군인이 정치나 ~에 간섭하는 것은 바람직하지 않다 It is not desirable for military men to interfere in politics or diplomatic relations. / 현 정부는 ~보다 내정에 힘을 더 쏟고 있다 The present government is placing greater stress on domestic affairs than on foreign affairs.

② 《교섭·판매 등의》 canvassing; selling. ¶ ~를 잘하다 be a good 〔clever〕 salesman; be diplomatic; be a good diplomat / 그녀는 생명 보험 ~원 노릇을 한다 She sells life insurance (door-to-door).

◉ ~가 a diplomatist; a diplomatic person. ~감각 a sense of diplomacy; diplomatic sense. ~계 diplomatic circles. ~공세 a diplomatic offense. ~교섭〔협상〕 diplomatic negotiations; negotiations through diplomatic channels. ~기관〔경로〕 diplomatic machinery 〔channels〕. ~단 the diplomatic corps 〔body〕; 《파견된》 a diplomatic delegation. ~단절 a diplomatic break; diplomatic cessation; severance 〔a rupture〕 of diplomatic relations. ~무대 a diplomatic arena. ~문서 a diplomatic document 〔note, paper〕. ~문제 a diplomatic question 〔issue, problem〕. ~백서 a diplomatic white paper. ~부 the Ministry of Foreign Affairs: ~부 장관 the Minister of Foreign Affairs. ~사령(辭令) 《use》 diplomatic language. ~사절단 a diplomatic mission. ~수단 《take》 diplomatic measures: 그는 온갖 ~ 수단을 다 부렸다 He practiced all the wiles of diplomacy. ~수완 diplomacy; diplomatic talent 〔skill〕; 《세일즈맨의》 salesmanship: ~ 수완을 발휘하다 give full play to *one's* diplomatic skill; use diplomacy. ~안보 연구원 the Institute of Foreign Affairs and National Security (생략 IFANS). ~원 ⇨ 외판원. ~정책 (a) diplomatic 〔foreign〕 policy: 그들은 ~ 정책을 그르쳤다 They took a wrong diplomatic policy. ~특권 the diplomatic (privilege and) immunity.

**외교관**(外交官) a diplomatic official; a diplomat; the diplomatic service [총칭]. ¶ ~이 되다 enter the diplomatic service / ~이다 be a diplomat; be in the diplomatic service. ◉ ~시험 the Diplomatic Service Examination.

**외교관계**(外交關係) diplomatic relations. ¶ 양국 ~의 정상화 the normalization of diplomatic relations between the two nations / ~를 수립하다 establish diplomatic relations 〔ties〕 《with》 / ~를 단절하다 break off 〔sever〕 diplomatic relations 《with》 / 그 나라는 이웃 나라들과의 ~를 수립했다〔단절했다〕 The nation opened 〔broke off 〕 diplomatic relations with neighboring countries.

**외구**(外寇) a foreign enemy; a foreign invader.

**외구**(畏懼) awe; apprehension. ~하다 be awe-stricken; stand in awe of 《*a person*》. ¶ ~심을 갖다 be struck with awe.

**외국**(外國) a foreign country; 《정치·군사상의》 a foreign nation 〔power〕; 《낯선 땅》 a strange country 〔land〕. ¶ ~의 foreign; alien; oversea(s); 《외국풍의》 exotic / ~산(産)의 of foreign growth; foreign-produced / ~제의 of foreign make; foreign-made / ~식으로 on foreign lines; in foreign style / ~으로 나갈〔보낼〕 foreign-going 《cargos》; outbound 《ships》 / ~ 태생의 born abroad 〔overseas〕; foreign-born / ~에〔으로〕 가다 go abroad 〔overseas〕 / ~에서 돌아오다 return from abroad 〔from a foreign country〕 / ~에서 들어오다 come 〔be brought, be imported〕 from abroad / ~에 있다 be 〔stay〕 abroad 〔overseas〕 / ~에서 죽다 die abroad / ~ 땅을 밟다 set foot on foreign soil / ~의 침략을 받다 be invaded by a foreign country / ~의 영향을 받

지 않다 be untouched by alien influences / ～의 지배를 받고 있다 be under foreign rule / ～을 가는 사람은 해마다 늘고 있다 More people are 「going abroad 〔visiting foreign countries〕 every year. / 아버지는 자주 ～을 여행하신다 My father often travels abroad. / ～을 아는 가장 좋은 방법은 실제로 가보는 것이다 The best way to know a foreign country is to go there.
◉ ～무역 foreign trade. ～사신 a foreign envoy. ～상사 a foreign trading company. ～생활 living abroad; life overseas. ～시장 a foreign 〔an oversea(s)〕 market. ～영화 a foreign film. ～우편 mail from abroad; foreign mail. ～ 유명 상표 a famous foreign-brand label. ～자본 foreign capital. ～전보 an overseas 〔international〕 telegram. ～제품 foreign goods 〔products〕; 《수입품》 imported goods. ～채(債): 3푼 이자의 ～채 three percent foreign loan bonds. ～풍 foreign manners; foreignism; exoticism. ～항로 an overseas route: ～항로의 배 a ship on a foreign route; an ocean liner.

**외국어**(外國語) a foreign language. ¶ 제 2 ～ a second foreign language / ～를 읽고 쓰고 말할 수 있다 have a reading, speaking, and writing knowledge of a foreign language / 그는 ～에 능통하다 He is good at foreign languages. *or* He has a good command of foreign languages. ◉ 한국 ～ 대학교 Hankuk University of Foreign Studies.

**외국여행**(外國旅行) foreign travel; an overseas trip 〔tour〕; traveling abroad (★ trip은 대체로 짧은 여행, tour는 두루 돌아다니는 경우의 여행. overseas는 「바다를 건너」란 뜻이어서, 「육지로 이어진」 외국 여행에는 쓰지 않음). ¶ ～을 하다 make a trip abroad; travel abroad / ～을 떠나는 사람의 수가 최근 많이 늘었다 The number of people who travel abroad has increased lately.

**외국인**(外國人) a foreigner; 〖법〗 an alien. ¶ ～ 상대의 범죄 crimes against foreigners / 영국인은 미국에서 ～이다 An Englishman is an alien in the United States. / ～ 전용 《게시》 Foreigners only. ◉ ～관광객 a foreign tourist 〔visitor〕. ～노동자 an alien worker. ～등록 alien registration: ～등록법 Alien Registration Law. ～예능 경연 대회 《한국에 관한》 the Korean Folk Arts Contest for Foreigners. ～학생 a foreign student. ～ 한국어 웅변 대회 the Korean-Language Speech Contest for Foreign Nationals. ～혐오 xenophobia; 《사람》 a xenophobe.

**외국환**(外國換) foreign exchange. ◉ ～평형기금 exchange equalization fund(외화 매입 자금 조달책으로 발행되는 채권).

**외근**(外勤) outside duty 〔service〕; 《보험 따위의》 canvassing. ～하다 be on outside duty; work outside the office. ¶ 당신은 내근이오 ～이오 Do you work inside or outside? ◉ ～기자 a reporter; a legman 《미》. ～순경 a patrol(man). ～자 a person on outside duty; 《외무사원》 a canvasser. ～직원 an outdoor service employee.

**외기**(外氣) the (open) air; (the) fresh air; the air outside. ¶ ～에 쏘이다 air 《*a thing*》; expose 《*a thing*》 to the air / ～를 쐬다 expose *oneself* to the air; take the air; air *oneself*. ◉ ～권 〖기상〗 the exosphere.

**외길** the only road; a single path. ◉ ～목 the junction of roads.

**외김치** cucumber kimchi.

**외나무다리** a log bridge. ¶ ～를 건너다 cross 《a stream》 by a log bridge / ～에서 원수를 만나다 meet bad luck *one* cannot escape from / 원수는 ～에서 만난다 《속담》 Evildoing always catches up with you.

**외날** a single edge. ¶ ～ 면도날〔칼〕 a single-edged blade 〔razor〕.

**외다**[1] 《불편하다》 be inconvenient; be out of the way; be out of place; be off to one side. ¶ 손이 외 곳 a place located out of the way; a spot hard to reach / 손이 ～ be out of the way; be hard to reach; be unhandy.

**외다**[2] 《암기하다》 learn by heart; memorize; commit to memory. ¶ 외워 by heart 〔rote〕; from memory / 시를〔경을〕 ～ recite a poem 〔sutra〕 / 기도문을 ～ chant prayers / 내일까지 제1과를 외워야 한다 I have to memorize the first lesson by tomorrow. / 그는 셸리의 「종달새」를 외우고 있다 He knows Shelly's "Skylark" by heart.

**외대다**[1] 《반대로 일러주다》 tell 〔relate〕 untruthfully; tell contrary to the facts.

**외대다**[2] 《푸대접하다》 treat slightingly; slight; snub; 《배척하다》 reject.

**외대박이** ① 《배》 a single-masted boat. ② ⇨ 애꾸눈이.

**외도**(外道) 《오입》 debauchery; dissipation; dissoluteness; 《바르지 않은 길》 a wrong course; deviation from *one's* proper field 《of business》. ～하다 《오

입하다》 dissipate; lead a dissolute life; 《길을 어기다》 go astray; stray from *one's* proper field 《of business》.
**외돌다** keep aloof.
**외돌토리** a solitary 〔lonely〕 person. ¶ ~가 되다 be left alone; be left to *oneself.*
**외동딸** =외딸.
**외둥이** *one's* only son. ⇨ 외아들.
**외등**(外燈) an outdoor lamp.
**외따로** separated; isolated; solitarily; lonely; all alone. ¶ 도시에서 멀리 떨어져서 ~ 살다 live a lonely life far away from town.
**외딴** isolated; solitary; out-of-the-way. ¶ ~섬 a solitary island / ~집 an isolated house / ~곳에서 살다 live in a secluded place.
**외딴치다** 《혼자서 판치다》 play a one-man show.
**외딸** 《무남독녀》 an only daughter; 《남형제가 있는》 the only daughter.
**외딸다** (be) secluded; isolated; separated; out-of-the-way; lonely.
**외떡잎** 〖식물〗 a single seed leaf.
◉ ~식물 a monocotyledon; a monocotyledonous plant.
**외람**(猥濫) presumption; forwardness; impertinence. ~하다, ~되다 (be) presumptuous; forward; impertinent. ¶ ~된 짓을 하다 exceed *one's* authority; be presumptuous / ~된 말씀이오나 It is very presumptuous of me, but...; It is not for me to say, but ... / ~되오나 제가 그것을 설명하겠습니다 With your permission I will explain it.
**외래**(外來) ¶ ~의 foreign; (coming) from abroad; imported; outside 《help》 / ~문화 foreign culture(s).
◉ ~사상 foreign ideas 〔ideologies〕. ~식물 an exotic 〔a nonnative〕 plant. ~어 a word of foreign origin; a borrowed word; a loanword. ~자 a visitor; a stranger: ~자 출입 금지 《게시》 Outsiders are requested to keep out. ~종 an introduced species (식물 등의). ~진료소 an outpatient clinic. ~품 imports; imported goods; a foreign-made article: 특정 ~품 판매소 the Foreigner's Commissary. ~환자 an outpatient.
**외력**(外力) 〖물리〗 external force. ¶ ~이 가해지다 be pressed by external force.
**외로** to the left; to the left hand; 《비뚤게》 in the wrong direction; to the wrong path; to an evil course. ¶ 쇠줄을 ~ 감다 coil wire to the left / ~ 가다 go to the left; go astray; fall into evil ways.
**외로이** all alone; solitarily; lonely. ¶ ~ 지내다 lead a solitary life; live a lonely 〔lonesome〕 life / ~ 울다 cry all alone / 타향에서 ~ 죽다 die forlorn away from home.
**외롭다** be all alone; (be) solitary; lonely; lonesome. ¶ 외로움 loneliness / 외로운 마음 (a feeling of ) loneliness; lonesomeness / 외로운 사람 a lonely person / 외롭게 살다 lead a solitary life / 외로워하다 feel lonely 〔lonesome〕; miss 《*a person*》 / 그이가 없어서 무척 ~ I do miss him. *or* I miss him very much. / 부모를 여의기 전에는 외로움이란 것을 나는 미처 몰랐다 It was not until I lost my parents that I found myself lonely and forlorn.
**외륜산**(外輪山) 〖지질〗 the outer rim (of a volcanic crater); a somma.
**외륜선**(外輪船) a paddle steamer.
**외마디** 《동강》 a single piece; a section; 《소리》 a single cry 〔scream〕.
◉ ~설대 a pipe-stem made of a single section of bamboo. ~소리 an outcry of pain; a scream: 그는 칼에 맞아 ~ 소리를 지르며 쓰러졌다 When the sword hit him, he let out a scream and fell.
**외면**[1](外面) outward appearance; the exterior; the (outer) surface. ¶ ~의 outside; outward; exterior; external / ~으로는 outwardly.
◉ ~묘사 an external description.
**외면**[2](外面) ~하다 turn *one's* face away; look away; avert *one's* eyes; cut. ¶ 가난하고 고통받는 사람들을 ~하다 be indifferent to the poor and distressed / 그는 ~하고 지나갔다 He passed by with his face averted. *or* He cut me in the street. / 그는 ~하고 대답도 하지 않았다 He turned away 〔looked the other way〕 and gave no answer. / 그는 학급의 친구들로부터 ~당했다 The friends in the class turned the cold shoulder on him.
**외모**(外貌) an 〔*one's*〕 outward appearance; (*one's*) features; *one's* looks. ¶ 장사꾼 같은 ~ merchant-like appearance / ~를 꾸미다 keep up appearance; make outward show; save appearances / 사람을 ~로 판단하지 마라 Don't judge a man by his appearance. / 그녀의 ~는 그저 그렇다 She is ordinary 〔average〕 in appearance. *or* Her looks are just passable. / 그녀는 항상 ~에만 신경을 쓴다 She is always worrying about appearances.

worrying about appearances.

**외목** ① ⇨외길목. ② 《외목 장사》 monopoly (business).

**외몽고**(外蒙古) Outer Mongolia.

**외무**(外務) ① 《나라의》 foreign affairs. ② 《섭외》 = 외교(外交) ②. ◉ ~(분과) 위원회 the Foreign Affairs (Sub-)committee. ~원(員) = 외교원: 보험 ~원 an insurance salesman 〔canvasser〕.

**외미**(外米) rice from abroad; imported rice.

**외박**(外泊) staying out away from home; sleeping out. ~하다 stay out overnight; sleep out; sleep away from home. ¶ 말없이 ~하다 be absent all night without leave / 누이동생은 어제 ~했다 My sister stayed 〔sleep〕 out last night.

**외발제기** playing shuttlecock with one foot.

**외방**(外方) ① 《외국》 foreign lands; foreign parts. ② 《바깥》 outside. ③ 《서울 밖》 districts away from the capital 〔Seoul〕. ◉ ~살이 life as a government official out in the provinces.

**외배엽**(外胚葉) 〖생물〗 the ectoderm; the ectoblast.

**외벌** a single set. ◉ ~매듭 a single 〔simple〕 knot.

**외벽**(外壁) an outer wall.

**외부**(外部) the outside; the exterior; the outside world. ¶ ~의 external; outward; outside / 건물의 ~ the exterior of a building / ~(의) 간섭〔원조〕 outside interference 〔aid〕 / ~(의) 침략 external aggression / ~에 나타나다 appear on the outside / ~와 교통이 두절되다 be cut off from the outside world / 비밀이 ~에 샜다 The secret has leaked out. / 우리는 ~의 원조를 받았다 We got outside help.
◉ ~사람 an outsider; a man on the outside: 그것은 ~ 사람에 의한 범행이다 It is the offense of an outsider.

**외분**(外分) 〖수학〗 exterior division. ~하다 divide externally.

**외빈**(外賓) 《외국 손님》 a foreign visitor 〔guest〕; 《외부 손님》 a guest. ¶ ~용 침실 a guest room.

**외사**(外事) external 〔foreign〕 affairs. ◉ ~과 the foreign affairs section.

**외사촌**(外四寸) a maternal cousin.

**외삼촌**(外三寸) a maternal uncle. ◉ ~댁 the wife of a maternal uncle; an aunt; 《집》 the house of a maternal uncle.

**외상** credit; trust; tick 《영구어》. ¶ ~으로 on credit 〔tick, strap〕; on the cuff 《미구어》/ ~을 주다 give 《*a person*》 credit 〔tick〕/ ~값을 받다 collect a bill / ~으로 팔다 sell 《*a thing*》 on credit 〔tick, trust〕/ ~으로 사다 buy 《*a thing*》 on credit 〔tick, trust〕; buy on the cuff 《미구어》; have 《*a thing*》 charged to *one's* account / ~값을 받으러 가다 go to collect bills / ~값을 받으러 다니다 go round collecting bills / 깔린 ~값이 걷히지 않아 야단이다 be annoyed by a poor collection of bills / ~ 사절 《게시》 Sale on credit (absolutely) declined. *or* No credit (given). *or* Cash only. / 나는 이 물건을 ~으로 샀다 I bought this article on credit. / ~으로 해 주시오 Charge it to my account. *or* Put it on the cuff. / 그 가게에 ~이 십만원 있다 I owe the store a 100,000 won bill.
◉ ~값 an account; a bill. ~거래 credit transactions. ~매입 credit purchase. ~매출 credit sales: ~ 매출 계정 charge accounts; accounts of credit sales. ~손님 a charge 〔credit〕 customer. ~판매 a credit sale; sale 〔selling〕 on credit 〔tick〕.

**외상**(一床) a dining table for one; an individual table 《for dinner》. ¶ ~을 받다 be served meal on an individual table.

**외상**(外相) the Foreign Minister. ◉ ~회의 a Foreign Ministers' conference.

**외상**(外傷) an external wound 〔injury〕; 《정신적 상처를 주는 육체의》 a trauma (*pl.* ~s, -mata). ¶ 그는 교통사고로 심한 ~을 입었다 He suffered a heavy injury in the traffic accident.

**외서**(外書) a foreign book.

**외선**(外線) the outer line; outside wire; 《전화》 an outside line. ¶ ~ 부탁합니다 《전화 교환원에게》 Give me an outside line, please. / 9를 돌리면 ~과 연결됩니다 Dial 9, and you'll get an outside line. ◉ ~공사 outside wiring.

**외선작전**(外線作戰) 〖군사〗 an operation on exterior lines.

**외설**(猥褻) obscenity; indecency; scabrousness. ~하다 (be) obscene; filthy; indecent; pornographic; risqué; scabrous; 《미》 off-color. ¶ ~한 그림 an obscene 〔a pornographic〕 picture / ~한 이야기를 하다 talk smut; tell dirty 〔lowd〕 jokes. ◉ ~문서〔문학〕 obscene writings 〔literature〕; pornography. ~비디오 a pornographic video. ~서적 an indecent book; pornography. ~죄 public indecency: ~죄로 기소하다 indict 《*a person*》 on an obscenity charge. ~행위 《commit》 an act of obscenity; indecent behavior.

**외세**(外勢) ① 《형세》 external condition 〔situation〕. ② 《세력》 outside 〔alien, foreign〕 influence 〔power〕. ¶ ~에 의존하다 depend on the power of a foreign country / ~를 배격하다 denounce 〔drive out〕 foreign power.

**외손** one hand. ◉ ~뼉 a single palm: ~뼉이 울지 못한다 《속담》 It takes two to make a quarrel. ~잡이 a one-handed person.

**외손**(外孫) *one's* daughter's child; a grandchild; 《자손》 descendants in the daughter's line. ◉ ~녀 *one's* daughter's daughter; a granddaughter. ~자 *one's* daughter's son; a grandson.

**외손지다** get deprived of the use of one hand.

**외숙**(外叔) a maternal uncle. ◉ ~모 the wife of a maternal uncle; an aunt.

**외시골**(外—) outlying 〔remote〕 country districts.

**외식**(外食) eating 〔dining〕 out. ~하다 eat 〔dine〕 out. ¶ 점심은 보통 ~을 합니까 Do you usually eat lunch out? ◉ ~산업 the food-service industry; the restaurant industry. ~자 a diner=out.

**외식**(外飾) external ornament 〔embellishment〕; outward display; showiness; a show-off. ~하다 put on outside appearance; show off.

**외신**(外信) foreign news; a foreign message 〔telegram, cablegram〕. ◉ ~부 the foreign news department: ~부장 a foreign news editor. 서울 ~기자 클럽 the Seoul Foreign Correspondents' Club.

**외실**(外室) an outer room (for the menfolk).

**외심**(外心) 〖수학〗 a circumcenter; an outer center. ◉ ~각 an eccentric angle. ~점 the metacenter.

**외씨버선** small shapely socks.

**외아들** 《무매독자》 an only son; 《자매가 있는》 the only son.

**외야**(外野) 〖야구〗 the outfield. ◉ ~석 the outfield bleachers. ~수 an outfielder.

**외양**(外洋) the open sea; the ocean. ¶ ~항행의 ocean-going. ◉ ~어업 deep=sea fishing 〔fishery〕. ~항해선 a sea boat; an ocean liner (정기선).

**외양**(外樣) outward appearance; outward show. ¶ ~만의 false; feigned; make-believe / ~이 그럴듯하다 have a good appearance / ~을 꾸미다 put up a good front; keep up appearances / ~으로는 정직한 체하다 put on the appearance of honesty / 그는 ~이 반반하다 In person he is handsome.

**외양간**(喂養間) a stable; a cowshed. ¶ 소잃고 ~ 고치는 격이다 be (just like) locking the stable door after the horse is stolen.

**외어서다** step aside; get out of the way. ¶ 차가 오니 외어서라 A car is coming—get out of the way!

**외연**(外延) 〖논리〗 extension; denotation. ¶ ~적(인) extensive; denotative.

**외연기관**(外燃機關) an external combustion engine.

**외올** a single strand. ◉ ~뜨기 single=strand knitwork. ~베 hemp cloth woven of single strand. ~실 single=strand thread.

**외욕질** nausea; qualm; retch.

**외용**(外用) 《for》 external use 〔application〕. ~하다 use 〔apply〕 externally. ◉ ~약 a medicine for external use 〔application〕; an external remedy; 《약병에 쓰인 주의》 "For outward only."

**외우**(外憂) 《외환》 fears of foreign 〔outside〕 invasion; a foreign 〔an external〕 threat. ¶ ~ 내환에 시달리다 be beset with troubles both at home and abroad.

**외우**(畏友) *one's* respected friend.

**외우다** learn by heart. ⇨ 외다[2].

**외원**(外援) external help; foreign aid 〔assistance〕.

**외유**(外遊) a foreign tour 〔travel〕; a trip abroad; going abroad. ~하다 make a trip abroad; go 〔travel〕 abroad. ¶ ~ 길에 오르다 start on a tour abroad / ~에서 돌아오다 return from *one's* foreign tour.

**외유내강**(外柔內剛) being gentle in appearance, but sturdy in spirit. ¶ 그는 ~하다 He looks gentle but is tough inside.

**외음부**(外陰部) the vulva (*pl.* -vae, ~s). ¶ ~의 vulval; vulvar.

**외의**(外衣) an outer garment.

**외이**(外耳) 〖해부〗 the external ear. ◉ ~도 an (external) auditory canal 〔meatus〕. ~염 inflammation of the external ear; 〖의학〗 otitis externa.

**외인**(外人) 《외국인》 a foreigner; an alien; 《외부 사람》 an outsider; a stranger. ¶ 이 일은 ~이 알아서는 안 된다 This is between ourselves. ◉ ~부대 a foreign legion. ~사회 a foreign community. ~상사 a foreign (business) firm. ～주택 foreign residents' houses. ～촌 the foreign quarter of a city; a foreigners' residence area.

**외자**(外資) foreign capital [funds]. ¶ ～계의 foreign 《banks》; foreign-owned 《securities firms》/ ～계의 회사 a foreign firm; a foreign-owned[-affiliated] corporation.
◉ ～관리법 the foreign capital management law. ～도입 the induction [introduction] of foreign capital [funds]: ～ 도입법 the Foreign Capital Inducement Law / ～ 도입을 꾀하다 attract [invite] foreign investment. ～ 수용 태세 readiness for the induction of foreign capital; preparation for the receipt of foreign investments. ～유입 the inflow [influx] of foreign capital. ～유치 the inducement of foreign capital.

**외장**(外裝) 《포장》 wrapping(s); 《건물 등의》 (a) facing 《material》; the exterior (finish) 《of a building》; (a) cladding; 《자동차 따위의》 the paintwork; the finish. ¶ 자동차의 ～과 내장 the exterior and interior decor of a car.

**외장골**(外腸骨) 『해부』 the external iliac [flank] bone. ◉ ～동맥[정맥] the external iliac artery [vein].

**외적**(外的) external; outward. ◉ ～증거 external evidence.

**외적**(外敵) a foreign enemy [invader]. ¶ ～의 침입을 받다 suffer from a foreign invasion [attack, raid] / ～의 공격을 받다 be attacked by a foreign country; suffer an attack from a foreign enemy.

**외전**(外電) a foreign telegram [cable]; a dispatch 《from New York》. ¶ ～이 전하는 바에 의하면 foreign news says ...; according to foreign telegram....

**외접**(外接) 『수학』 circumscription. ～하다 circumscribe; be circumscribed.
◉ ～원 a circumcircle.

**외정**(外征) a foreign expedition [campaign]. ～하다 go on a foreign expedition; invade a foreign country.
◉ ～군 an expeditionary army.

**외정**(外政) foreign affairs [policies].

**외제**(外製) ¶ ～의 foreign(-made); 《goods》 made abroad; of foreign make.
◉ ～차 a foreign(-made) car; an imported car. ～품 foreign goods [products]; foreign-made goods: ～품 선호(경향) (a tendency toward) a preference of foreign products.

**외조모**(外祖母) a grandmother on *one's* mother's side; a maternal grandmother.

**외조부**(外祖父) a grandfather on *one's* mother's side; a maternal grandfather.

**외족**(外族) maternal relatives; a relative on the mother's side.

**외종사촌**(外從四寸) a maternal cousin. ⇨ 외사촌.

**외주**(外注) an outside order. ～하다 place an order outside the company. ¶ (자사 제품) 기계의 부품을 ～하다 place an order with an outside supplier for parts of a machine (produced in *one's* plant); contract 《*a thing*》 out / 우리는 이 부품을 ～로 낸다 We order these parts outside the company.

**외주**(外周) (a) circumference. ¶ 1마일의 ～a one-mile circumference.

**외줄** a single line [stripe].

**외줄기** a single stalk [stem].

**외지**(外地) 《외국》 an overseas land; a foreign country; 《내국의》 a strange [an outlying] region. ¶ ～용의 상품 goods for foreign markets / ～로 일하러 나가다 go to a foreign land to work. ◉ ～근무[생활] overseas service [life]. ～사람 a stranger. ～수당 an overseas allowance.

**외지**(外紙) a foreign newspaper; the foreign press [총칭].

**외지다** get [be] isolated [secluded, sequestered]; (be) remote. ¶ 외진 곳 an out-of-the-way place; a lonely place / 외진 산길 a remote mountain trail / 아주 외진 곳에 있는 오두막 a cottage in an out-of-the-way place.

**외직**(外職) a government post away from the capital; a local [provincial] government post.

**외진**(外診) an external examination. ～하다 see [examine externally] 《a patient》; make an external examination 《of》.

**외짝** (an odd) one of a pair; the pair [fellow] 《to》. ¶ ～ 양말[장갑] an odd sock [glove].

**외쪽** one side; a single direction; a single piece. ◉ ～생각 one-sided thinking; unilateral consideration.

**외채** a single building [structure].
◉ 외챗집 a detached house.

**외채**(外債) 『경제』 a foreign debt; a foreign loan [bond]. ¶ ～를 줄이다 reduce foreign liabilities / ～를 모집하다 raise [float] a foreign loan; place a loan on the foreign market / 무거운 ～ 부담을 줄이다 curtail 〔reduce〕 the heavy foreign debt burden / 증대하는 ～를 커버하는 유일한 방법은 수출을 증진하는 일이다 The only way of covering the escalating foreign debts is to promote exports. / 정부는 5,000만 달러의 ～를 모집하기로 결정했다 The Government decided to raise an fifty million dollar foreign loan. ◉ ～상환 기금 a redemption fund for foreign 〔external〕 bonds.

**외척**(外戚) relatives on the mother's side; a maternal relation 〔relative〕.

**외청도**(外聽道) = 외이도(外耳道).

**외출**(外出) going out. ～하다 go out. ¶ ～하기 좋아〔싫어〕하는 사람 a gadabout 〔stay-at-home, homeboy 《미》〕 / ～중에 while *one* is out; in *one's* absence / ～이 허가되다 be allowed out / ～하지 않다 stay at home; keep 〔stay〕 indoors / ～할 채비를 하다 get ready to go out; get dressed for going out / ～에서 돌아오다 return home from a visit / 그는 ～중이다 He is out 〔not at home〕. / 이런 폭풍우에는 ～할 수 없다 There is no going out in such a storm. / 그가 왔을 때 나는 마침 ～중이었다 I happened to be out when he called. / 비가 와서 ～하지 못했다 The rain prevented me from going out. *or* The rain confined me to my house.
◉ ～금지 《군인의》 confinement 《to the barracks》: ～ 금지령 a curfew (order). ～날 a leave day. ～복 a street wear 〔clothes, dress〕. ～시간 《군인의》 leave-time. ～허가증 a leave slip.

**외치**(外治) ① = 외교(外交). ② 『의학』 external 〔surgical〕 treatment. ～하다 treat externally; apply external 〔surgical〕 treatment.

**외치다** ① 《큰소리로》 shout; cry (out); let out a yell; utter 〔give〕 a cry; exclaim; 《비명을》 shriek; scream.
¶ 큰소리로 ～ cry 〔call〕 out; roar; howl / 「도둑이야」 하고 ～ cry "Thief !" / 「불이야, 불이야」 하고 ～ cry "Fire, fire !" / 사람살리라고 ～ cry 〔yell〕 for help / 찬성이라고 ～ give a cry of approval; shout approbation 〔*one's* approval〕 / 도와달라고 ～ cry for help / 찢어지는 소리로 ～ utter a piercing shriek / 목청껏 ～ cry at the top of *one's* voice / 목이 쉬도록 ～ shout *oneself* hoarse.
② 《강력히 주장하다》 cry 《for, against》; clamor 《for, against》; advocate 《birth control》. ¶ 개혁을 ～ cry (loudly) for reforms / 군축을 ～ cry for disarmament / 핵실험 금지를 ～ appeal for a ban on nuclear tests / 남북 통일을 ～ cry out for the unification of Korea.

**외침** a shout; a cry; an outcry; a yell; 《놀람·감탄의》 an exclamation; 《비명》 a shriek; a scream; 《항의의》 a clamor; 《노호》 a roar; a howl. ¶ 개혁의 ～ a cry for reforms / 한밤중에 여자의 ～소리를 들었다 I heard a woman scream at midnight.

**외탁하다**(外—) take after *one's* mother's side in appearance 〔character〕. ¶ 그 아이는 성질을 외탁했다 The boy gets his temperament from his mother's side.

**외톨** a single chestnut 〔garlic bulb〕. ◉ ～박이 《마늘》 a single-bulb garlic; 《밤》 a single-bur chestnut.

**외톨이** a single 〔lonely〕 person. ¶ (사람이) ～ 되다 be left alone; be left to *oneself;* be thrown on *one's* own resources.

**외통** 《장기의》 checkmate. ◉ ～수(手) a checkmate move: ～수로 몰리다 be checkmated.

**외투**(外套) an overcoat; a topcoat; a greatcoat 《영》. ¶ ～를 입고 있다 be in an overcoat; have on *one's* overcoat / ～를 벗다 take off *one's* overcoat / ～를 입다 put on 〔wear〕 *one's* overcoat (★ wear는 「입고 있다」라는 상태에 쓰이고, put on은 동작의 경우에 쓰임) / ～를 입혀〔벗겨〕주다 help 《*a person*》 on 〔off〕 with *his* overcoat / 그는 ～를 입은 채 방으로 들어왔다 He entered the room with his overcoat on 〔wearing his overcoat〕. / ～는 여기에다 맡기십시오 Please check your overcoat here.
◉ ～감 overcoating. ～걸이 an overcoat rack. ～막(膜) 《연체 동물의》 a mantle.

**외판**(外販) (a) traveling sale; canvassing. ¶ 가정용품을 ～하다 travel in domestic appliances. ◉ ～원 a salesman (남); a saleswoman (여); a canvasser: 서적 ～원 a (door-to-door) salesman in books.

**외팔** one arm. ◉ ～이 a one-armed person.

**외풍**(外風) ① 《바람》 a draft (of air); a draught 《영》. ¶ ～을 막다 cut off 〔prevent〕 drafts / 이 방엔 ～이 들어온다 There is a draft in this room. / 우리 집은 ～이 세다 My house gives free passage to draughts. ② 《외국풍》 foreign ways 〔fashion, manners, style〕; exotic fashion; a foreignism. ¶ ～에 물들다 take to foreign ways.

**외피**(外皮) = 겉껍질.

**외할머니**(外—) = 외조모.

**외할아버지**(外—) = 외조부.

**외항**(外港) an outer port; an outport.

**외항선**(外航船) an ocean-going ship; a ship for overseas service.

**외해**(外海) the open sea; the high seas. ¶ ～로 나가다 go out into the open sea.

**외향성**(外向性) 〖심리〗 extroversion. ¶ ～의 extrovert(ed); 《사교적인》 outgoing / ～의 사람 an extrovert.

**외형**(外形) an external 〔outward〕 form 〔shape〕; outward appearance. ¶ ～상(의) external; outward.

**외화**(外貨) 《외국 화폐》 foreign currency 〔money〕; 《외국환》 foreign exchange; 《외국 화물》 foreign goods. ¶ ～는 받지 않음 《게시》 Foreign money is refused / 한국이 보유하고 있는 ～ Korea's 「foreign-currency holding 〔foreign-exchange reserves〕.
◉ ～가득률 a foreign exchange earning rate. ～가득액 foreign exchange earnings. ～관리 management of foreign currency holdings. ～보유고 foreign currency holdings 〔reserve〕: 한국의 가용～ 보유고 Korea's usable 「foreign-exchange reserves 〔foreign-currency holdings〕. ～ 시장〔시세〕 =외환시장. ～ 어음 a foreign money bill. ～ 예금(預金) a foreign currency deposit. ～예산 a foreign exchange budget. ～ 유출 the diversion 〔outflow〕 of foreign currency. ～자금 foreign currency funds. ～절약 foreign currency saving. ～준비금 foreign currency reserve. ～ 채권 foreign currency bonds. ～획득 the acquisition of foreign currencies: 석유가 그 나라의 유일한 ～ 획득 수단이었다 Oil was the country's only source of foreign exchange. 특별〔일반〕 ～대출 제도 a special 〔general〕 foreign exchange lending system.

**외화**(外畫) a foreign film 〔movie〕.
◉ ～ 수입 쿼터 the foreign film import quotas.

**외환**(外患) fears of foreign 〔outside〕 invasion; foreign troubles. ◉ 내우～ domestic troubles and external threats: 내우 ～에 시달리다 be beset with troubles both at home and abroad.

**외환**(外換) foreign exchange.
◉ ～관리법 the Foreign Exchange Control Law: ～ 관리법 위반 혐의로 체포되다 be arrested on suspicion of violating the Foreign Exchange Control Law. ～관리부 the exchange control department. ～시장〔시세〕 foreign exchange market 〔rate〕. ～은행 a foreign exchange bank. ～준비금 foreign-exchange reserves.

**왼** left(-hand). ¶ 왼손 *one's* left hand / 왼발 the left foot / 왼쪽 the left (side).

**왼소리** news of *a person's* death.

**왼손** the left hand. ¶ 길의 ～ 쪽 the left-hand side of the street / ～으로 글을 쓰다 write with *one's* left hand.
◉ ～잡이 a left-handed person; a left-hander; a southpaw 《미구어》: ～잡이 투수 a southpaw (pitcher); a left-handed pitcher; a lefty 《미구어》.

**왼쪽** the left side; (the) left. ¶ ～의 left(-hand); left (★ left-hand는 「좌측의」, left-handed는 「왼손잡이」의 뜻) / 길 ～에 on the left(-hand side) of the street; to the left of the road / ～에서 오른쪽으로 from left to right / 자네 ～에 on your left / ～을 보다 look to the left / ～에 앉다 sit on the left side 《of》 / ～으로 돌다 turn to the left / ～에서 오른쪽으로 쓰다 write from left to right / ～은 바다입니다 We have the sea on our left. / ～에 보이는 것이 대궐입니다 On your left stands the Royal Palace.

**왼편**(—便) the left (side). ⇨ 왼쪽.

**요**(要) the main 〔essential, chief〕 point; the point. ¶ 요는, 요컨대 what is essential 〔important〕 is…; the point is…; in a word; in brief; in short / 요는 연습에 있다 The essential thing is practice.

**요**(褥) an underquilt; a (quilted) mattress; beddings. ¶ 요를 펴다 lay a mattress; put down 〔spread〕 an underquilt; make the bed / 요를 개다 put away the mattress 〔bed〕.

**요** ① 《얕잡을 때》 this little (one). ¶ 요까짓 … such a (little)… / 요놈 this fellow; this guy; You small thing! *or* You squirt! *or* You despicable 〔nasty, mean〕 fellow! *or* You villain! *or* You scoundrel! *or* Confound you! ② 《시간·거리》 this; these; right near at hand. ¶ 요새, 요즈막 these days; nowadays; lately; recently / 요 근처에 in this neighborhood; near here; around here / 요 너머에 정거장이 있다 There is a station right over the hill.

**요가** 《do》 yoga. ¶ ～의 수련자 a yogi.

**요강**(尿鋼) a chamber pot; a night stool 〔chair〕; a close-stool; a commode.

**요강**(要綱) the main principle(s); the general idea; the outline; the gist; 《취지서》 a prospectus. ◉ 입학～ a list of the entrance requirements 《for a college》.

**요건**(要件) 《중요 용건》 an important matter 〔business〕; 《필요 조건》 a necessary 〔required〕 condition 《of》; a requisite. ¶ ～을 구비하다 fulfill 〔satisfy〕 the necessary 〔required〕 conditions / 인생에서 건강은 성공의 제일 ～이다 Health is the first requisites for success in life.

**요격**(邀擊) (an) intercept(ion). ～하다 intercept 《enemy's bombers》; ambush; waylay. ¶ 우리 전투기가 적의 폭격기를 ～할 수 있을까 Can our fighter plane intercept the enemy's bombers? ◉ ～기 an interceptor (plane). ～용 미사일 an interceptor missile; 《미사일 대항의》 an antimissile missile (생략 AMM).

**요결**(要訣) a secret; a key; an essential meaning; a vital point 《of》; the cardinal principle. ¶ 성공의 ～ the secret of success; the key to success.

**요골**(腰骨) 〖해부〗 the hipbone; the hucklebone.

**요관**(尿管) 〖해부〗 a ureter.

**요괴**(妖怪) a ghost; an apparition; a specter; 《괴물》 a goblin; a hobgoblin. ～스럽다 (be) wicked and mysterious; eerie; weird; uncanny.
◉ ～담 a ghost 〔an uncanny〕 story.

**요구**(要求) 《청구》 a request; a requirement; 《보통 직권에 의한》 a demand; 《문서에 의한》 (a) requisition; 《권리에 의한》 a claim. ～하다 request; claim; call for; demand 《*a thing* of *a person*》; require 《*a person* to *do*, *a person* that...》; make a demand 《for *a thing* on *a person*》 (★ demand는 법률상의 요구에도 쓰임).

> 용법 **request** 격식차린 말로서 부탁하는 쪽이 역부족을 느끼거나, 상대방의 관심이 희박하여 승낙을 못 받아낼지도 모른다는 두려움으로 정중히 부탁한다는 뜻. **demand** 권리·권위를 갖고 있어서 강력하면서도 집요하게 요구하는 것. **require** demand와 같은 뜻으로도 쓰이지만, 법률·규칙·긴급 사태에 의하여 요구한다는 뜻이 있음. **claim** 상대방의 동의 여부와 관계없이 재산이나 지위 등을 자기 것이라고 주장하는 것.

¶ ～에 따라 on 〔upon〕 demand; in compliance with 《*a person's*》 request; at *one's* request / 임금 인상 ～ a demand for higher wages / 정당한 ～ a reasonable 〔fair〕 claim / 부당한 ～ an unreasonable demand / ～에 응하다 admit 《*a person's*》 claim; accede to 〔meet〕 《*a person's*》 demand; comply with 《*a person's*》 request / 과반수 회원의 ～로 총회를 열다 call a general meeting at the request of a majority of the members / 시대의 ～를 충족하다 fulfill the needs 〔requirement〕 of the times / 손해 배상을 ～하다 present 〔put in〕 a claim for damages; claim 《5,000,000 won》 for damages / 너의 ～에는 응할 수 없다 I cannot comply with your request. / 그들은 그 계약서에 서명을 ～했다 They have requested that I (should) sign the contract. / 회사측은 근로자의 임금 인상 ～에 응하기로 결정했다 The management has decided to meet the demand of the labor for the increased pay. / 이 법안은 시대적 ～에 맞는 것이다 This bill meets the needs of the times. / 그들은 총리에게 사임할 것을 ～했다 They called upon the Prime Minister to resign. / 주민들의 ～에 따라 새로운 공원이 만들어졌다 A new park was made at the inhabitants' request. / 그는 나에게 돈을 지급하라고 ～했다 He required me to pay the money. *or* He required that I should pay the money.
★ require, demand, suggest, insist 등 「요구, 제안, 의뢰, 명령」 등을 나타내는 동사에 연결되는 that절 안에서의 동사는 「should+동사원형」이 일반적이나, 《미》에서는 should를 생략하고 가정법 현재로 동사의 원형을 쓰는 경향이 많음: The contract *requires* that the rent (*should*) *be* paid by the first day of each month. (계약서에는 매월 1일까지 방값을 지불하도록 되어 있다) / I insisted that he (*should*) *resign* as chairman. (나는 그가 의장직을 그만 둘 것을 주장했다).
◉ ～불 《a bill》 payable on demand: ～불 어음 a note on demand; checking account deposits. ～조건 the terms desired.

**요구르트** yog(h)urt.

**요귀**(妖鬼) a ghost. ⇨ 요괴.

**요금**(料金) a charge; a fee; a rate; 《탈것의》 a fare; 《유료 도로 따위의》 a toll. ¶ ～을 청구하다 charge 〔make a charge of〕 《500 won for》 / ～을 안 받다 be free (of charge); make no charge / ～을 거두다 collect fees 〔a rate, a charge〕 / 비싼 ～을 물다 pay high rates 《to》 / 전기〔가스, 수도〕 ～을 징수〔지불〕

하다 collect 〔pay〕 the power 〔gas, water〕 rate(s) / ～ 선불 《게시》 Fare forward. / 주차 ～은 시간당 3,000원이었다 They charged 3,000 won for parking per hour. / 5월부터 공공 ～이 인상된다 Public utility charges will go up 〔be raised〕 next May. / 부산까지의 왕복 ～은 얼마입니까 What is the fare to Busan and back? / 1인용 객실의 ～은 얼마입니까 《호텔에서》 What 〔How much〕 is the charge for a single room? *or* How much do you charge for a single room?

> 용법 **charge** 주로 (공공) 서비스에 지급하는 요금. **rate** 수도, 전기, 우편, 주차 요금 따위처럼 일정한 기준에 의해 정해지는 요금. 단, charge와 rate는 구별없이 서로 바꿔 쓸 수 있는 경우가 많음. **fee** 전문직이나 학교, 클럽, (공공) 단체에 지불하는 요금. 입장료·면허료·허가료 따위가 이에 해당됨. **fare** 버스·택시·기차 따위 탈것에 지급되는 값. **toll** 도로 통행료나 도선료 따위.

◉ ～별납(別納) charges paid separately: ～별납으로 100통의 편지를 부쳤다 I mailed a hundred letters postpaid. ～별납우편 [표시] Postpaid 《미》; Post-free 《영》. ～인상〔인하〕 a raise 〔reduction〕 of the charge 〔rate〕; 《미》 a charge hike 〔cut〕. ～징수소 《유료 도로의》 a tollgate; a tollbooth. ～표 a tariff; a list of charges; a price list. ～함 《버스 따위의》 a fare box; 《공중전화 따위의》 a coin box.

부가～ a surcharge. 주차～ parking rate. 특별〔추가〕～ an extra charge: 나는 추가 ～ 지급을 요구받았다 I was asked to pay an extra charge.

**요기**(妖氣) a weird 〔ghostly〕 air. ¶ 이 집에는 ～가 서려 있다 There is something weird and ghostly about this house.

**요기**(療飢) appeasing 〔allaying, relieving〕 hunger. ～하다 take care of 〔relieve, allay, satisfy〕 *one's* hunger; fortify *oneself* with a meal. ¶ 햄버거로 ～하다 appease *one's* hunger with a hamburger.

**요긴**(要緊) essential importance. ⇨ 긴요. ～하다 be essentially important; be of vital importance. ¶ ～한 때에 at a critical moment; when badly needed / 그것은 우리 일상 생활에 ～한 것이 아니다 It is not essential to our daily life. ◉ ～목 《길목의》 a critical position.

**요까짓** ⇨ 이까짓.

**요나서**(一書) 〖성서〗 (The Book of) 「Jonah.

**요녀**(妖女) a temptress; an enchantress; a vamp; a witch; a siren. ⇨ 요부.

**요담**(要談) an important 〔a necessary〕 talk. ～하다 have a talk with 《*a person*》 on an important matter 〔business〕. ¶ ～중이다 be in the middle of an important consultation / ～이 있다 have an important matter to discuss / 사장님은 지금 ～중입니다 The president is now having an important business meeting.

**요도**(尿道) 〖해부〗 the urethra (*pl.* ～s, -thrae). ◉ ～검사 urethroscopy. ～경(鏡) a urethroscope. ～관 the urethral canal. ～구 the urethral meatus. ～염 inflammation of the urethra; urethritis. ～절개술 urethrotomy. ～ 협착 stricture of the urethra.

**요독증**(尿毒症) 〖의학〗 uremia; urine 〔uremic〕 poisoning.

**요동**(搖動) shaking; a shake; rocking; 《지진의》 a quake; 《배의》 pitching (세로의); rolling (가로의); 《자동차의》 jolting. ～하다 shake; quake; rock; pitch and roll; swing; sway; joggle; jolt. ¶ 배가 심하게 ～했다 The ship pitched and rolled badly. / 길이 험해서 차가 ～쳤다 The car jolted on the bad road.

**요들** a yodel. ◉ ～가수 a yodeler.

**요란**(擾亂) ① 《어수선함》 a commotion; a disturbance; disorders; confusion. ② 《시끄러움》 uproar; clamor; a tumult. ～하다, ～스럽다 (be) disorderly; noisy; loud; uproarious; clamorous; boisterous; tumultuous. ¶ ～하게 noisily; boisterously / ～하게 떠들다 clamor; shout to 〔at〕; make much noise / ～한 벨소리 the alarming sound of a bell / 열차가 ～한 소리를 내며 지나갔다 The train thundered past. / 경보 벨이 ～하게 울렸다 The warning bell rang furiously.

**요람**(要覽) a survey; a summary; an outline; 《안내서》 a handbook; a manual. ¶ 대학～ a college catalog / 회사～ a general survey of a company.

**요람**(搖籃) 《흔드는》 a cradle; a swinging cot; a nursery; 《요람지》 the cradleland 《of European civilization》; the birthplace. ¶ ～에서 무덤까지 from the cradle to the grave.

◉ ～기 the cradle; babyhood; infancy; the inchoate stage. ～지 the cradle; the place of origin; the cradleland: 문명의 ～지 the cradle of civilization.

**요략**(要略) a *résumé* (F.); a summary; an outline. ⇨ 요약.

**요량**(料量) 《헤아려 생각함》 a plan; an intention; an idea; a thought; 《판단》 discretion; judgment. ～하다 plan out; consider carefully. ¶ 어머니를 뵐 ～으로 with the intention of seeing *one's* mother / ～ 없다 have bad judgment; lack common sense; be absurd; be crazy / ～ 없는 말〔짓〕 an absurd remark 〔act〕 / 네 ～대로 해라 Act on your own discretion.

**요령**(要領) ① 《요점》 the (main) point; the gist; the sum and substance 《of *a matter*》; 《개요》 an outline; a summary. ¶ ～ 있는 pointed / ～ 없는 noncommittal; pointless; vague / ～ 있는 연설 a pointed speech / ～이 있다 be to the point 〔purpose〕 / ～이 없다 be not to the point; be pointless; be off the point / 그는 언제나 ～ 있게 말한다 He always speaks to the point. ② 《방법》 a knack; an art; the ropes 《구어》; the hang. ¶ ～ 있는〔없는〕 사람 a shrewd 〔tactless〕 man / 사람을 부리는 ～ the art of handling people / ～을 터득하다 get 〔learn〕 the knack 〔hang〕 of 《*doing*》 / ～을 알다 have a knack 《for》 / ～을 가르치다 teach 〔show〕 《*a person*》 the ropes 《of》 / ～을 배우다 learn how to 《drive a motorcar》 / 좀더 ～ 있게 해라 Do it more sensibly. / 일단 ～만 알면 그 일은 아주 쉽다 You will find the work very easy once you have the knack of it. / 그는 청중을 웃기는 ～을 터득하고 있다 He knows the trick of making his audience laugh.

**요령부득**(要領不得) pointlessness; irrelevancy; impertinency. ～하다 (be) pointless; irrelevant; be beside the point; be not to the point. ¶ ～한 이야기 a rambling 〔pointless〕 story / ～하게 말하다 speak beside the point; say nothing to the point / 너의 제안은 ～이다 Your suggestion is not to the point. / 자네 말은 도무지 ～이다 I can't catch 〔see〕 your point at all. *or* I can make neither head nor tail of what you say.

**요로**(要路) ① 《요직》 an important 〔influential〕 position 〔post〕; high office; authorities (당국). ¶ ～에 있는 사람들 those in (high) authority; the authorities / ～에 있다 be (high) in authority; occupy an important position. ② 《교통의》 a principal 〔an important〕 road; a main artery 《of traffic》. ¶ 교통의 ～에 있다 be in the main artery of traffic.

**요르단** 《나라 이름》 Jordan. ¶ ～의 Jordanian. ◉ ～강 the River Jordan. ～사람 a Jordanian. ～왕국 the Hashimite Kingdom of Jordan.

**요리**(料理) ① 《만들기》 cooking; cookery; cuisine (고급의); 《음식》 a dish; food. ～하다 cook 《food》; dress 《fish》; prepare 《a dish》; do 《meal》. ¶ 서양〔한국〕 ～ Western 〔Korean〕 food 〔dishes〕 / 중국식 ～ dishes prepared in Chinese style / 소고기와 야채 ～ a dish of beef and vegetables / 생선〔고기〕 ～ fishmeat 〔meat〕 dish / 일품 ～ one-course dinner / ～를 만들다 prepare a dish / ～를 내놓다 serve dishes; set dishes on the table / ～를 잘하다〔못하다〕 be a good 〔bad〕 cook; be a good 〔poor〕 hand at cookery / 이 ～는 맛이 있다 This is a delicious 〔palatable〕 dish. / 그녀는 ～솜씨가 좋다〔나쁘다〕 She is good 〔poor, bad〕 cook. *or* She is good 〔poor, bad〕 at cooking. / 이것은 내가 좋아하는 ～다 This is my favorite dish. / 저 호텔의 ～는 훌륭하다 The cuisine of that hotel is good. ② 《일 처리》 management; handling; administration. ～하다 manage; handle; administer. ¶ 나라 일을 ～하다 manage the affairs of a nation / 이 일은 나 혼자서 ～할 수 없다 I cannot manage the work alone. / 그는 상대를 간단히 ～했다 He defeated his opponent easily. ◉ ～교실 a cooking 〔cookery〕 class 〔course, school〕. ～기구 cooking utensils. ～대 a dressing table. ～법 a recipe: 이 수프는 맛이 아주 좋은데, ～법을 가르쳐 주세요 Your soup is quite delicious. Please 「give me the recipe 〔tell me how to cook it〕. ～사 a cook; a chef (F.) (주방장). ～점, 요릿집 a 《Korean》 restaurant; an eating house; a *kisaeng* house (고유의 한국요정): ～점 주인 the owner 〔proprietor〕 of a restaurant / 중국 요릿집 a Chinese restaurant. ～책 a cookbook 《미》; a cookery book 《영》. ～학 gastronomy. ～학원 a cooking school.

**요리** 《요렇게》 in this way; like this; so; 《요리로》 this way; this direction; here.

**요리조리** here and there; this way and that way; hither and thither. ⇨ 이리

저리. ¶ ～ 피하다 dodge about / 책임을 ～ 피하다 be cunning in dodging *one's* responsibility / ～ 핑계대다 make one excuse after another. 「(妖怪).

**요마**(妖魔) a goblin; a bogey. ⇨ 요괴

**요만것** this small 〔little〕 bit. ¶ ～도 모르느냐 Don't you even know this? / ～을 다 못 먹느냐 Can't you even eat this bit?

**요만큼** this (little) bit; to this small extent 〔degree〕. ¶ 그의 말에 거짓이라고는 ～도 없다 There is not even the slightest bit of falsehood in what he told me. / ～의 손해로 그쳤다는 것은 다행한 일이다 I must consider it fortunate to have got off with this much loss.

**요망**(妖妄) ～떨다, ～부리다 act frivolously 〔capriciously, flightily〕. ～스럽다, ～하다 (be) fickle; flighty; capricious; frivolous. ¶ 이 ～한 년 You wicked hussy!

**요망**(要望) a desire; a demand 《for》; a cry 《for》; 《희망》 *one's* wishes. ～하다 desire; demand; request; cry 《for》. ¶ ～에 응하다 meet the demand(s) 《of the age》 / …의 ～을 들어주다 comply with *a person's* wishes / 학생에게 자각이 ～된다 Conscientiousness is expected of a student. / ～하신 것을 충분히 고려하겠습니다 We will give due consideration to your request.

**요면**(凹面) a concave surface; concavity; concave. ◉ ～거울 a concave mirror.

**요모조모** ⇨ 이모저모.

**요목**(要目) important 〔principal〕 items; the (main) point; essential points; 《적요》 an epitome; 《강의 등의》 a syllabus (*pl.* ～es, -bi). ◉ 교수～ a syllabus of lectures.

**요물**(妖物) 《물건》 an uncanny thing; 《사람》 a wicked person; a crafty and malicious person.

**요번**(一番) this time. ⇨ 이번.

**요법**(療法) a method of treatment; a (medical) treatment; a remedy; a cure 《for dysentery》; 《약에 의하지 않는》 therapy. ¶ 식이 ～을 하다 be on a diet / 백신 ～을 받다 be treated with a vaccine / 그는 정신 ～을 받고 있다 He is undergoing mental treatment. ◉ 가정～ home treatment. 민간～ a folk remedy.

**요변**(妖變) ① 《사건》 a mysterious happening 〔event〕; a mystery. ② 《행동》 strange 〔suspicious, questionable, mysterious〕 behavior. ～스럽다 (be) strange; suspicious. ～떨다, ～부리다 act 〔behave〕 suspiciously 〔strangely〕. ◉ ～쟁이 a questionable 〔untrustworthy, treacherous〕 person.

**요부**(妖婦) an enchantress; a vamp(ire); a weird woman; a temptress; a siren. ¶ ～형의 여자 a woman of the vampire type / 그녀는 이 영화에서 ～역을 맡고 있다 In the film she plays the part of a seductive woman who ensnares men.

**요부**(要部) the essential 〔principal, main, important〕 parts. 「loins.

**요부**(腰部) the waist; the hips; the

**요분질** grinding (in sexual intercourse).

**요사**(夭死) an early death. = 요절.

**요사**(妖邪) ～하다, ～스럽다 (be) capricious; fickle; treacherous; wicked; vicious; weird; uncanny; crafty; cunning. ¶～피우다, ～떨다 behave in a capricious 〔vicious, weird, crafty〕 way.

**요사**(寮舍) ① 〖불교〗 a temple dormitory (for Buddhist monks). ② 《기숙사》 a hostel; a dormitory. 「urate.

**요산**(尿酸) 〖화학〗 uric acid. ◉ ～염 a

**요새**(要塞) 〖군사〗 a fortress; a stronghold; fortifications. ¶ ～화하다 fortify / ～를 구축하다 construct 〔build〕 a fortress. ◉ ～도시 a fortified city. ～지대 a strategic 〔fortified〕 zone.

**요새** 《근래》 recently; of late; lately; 《요즈음》 nowadays; these days; now; today; 《저번》 the other day; a few days ago; 《요전부터》 for some time past; these few days. ¶ ～의 recent; late; modern; present-day / ～ 사람 men of the present-day / ～ 청년 the present-day young people; the young people of today / ～ 일어난 일 a recent event / ～ 흔히 볼 수 없는 책이다 Such a book is rarely to be met with nowadays. / ～ 어떻게 지내십니까 How are you these days? / ～ 비가 많이 왔다 We have had much rain these days. 「calculus 〔stone〕.

**요석**(尿石) 〖의학〗 a urolith; a urinary

**요설**(饒舌) talkativeness; loquacity; garrulity.

**요셉** 〖성서〗 Joseph.

**요소**(尿素) 〖화학〗 urea. ◉ ～계 ureameter. ～수지 urea resins.

**요소**(要所) a key 〔an important, a strategic〕 point 〔place, position〕. ¶ ～요소에 at important points; at (every) strategic point / ～ 요소를 설명하다 explain the important points 《of 》/ ～에 군대를 배치하다 station troops at strategic points / 시내 ～에

는 경찰관이 배치되어 있었다 Policemen were posted at key places in the city.

**요소**(要素) an essential element; a 〔an important〕 factor; 《필수 조건》 a requisite; a constituent. ¶ 생산의 3대 ~ the three (great) requisites for production / 사회 생활의 한 ~ a factor in public life / …의 ~를 이루다 be essential 《to》; form an important factor 《of》; form 〔constitute〕 an essential part 《of》 / 건강은 행복의 ~다 Health is essential to happiness. / 희극에도 비극의 ~는 있다 Even a comic contains some tragic elements. / 공군력은 근대전의 결정적인 ~다 Air power is the decisive factor in modern warfare.

**요술**(妖術) ① 《마술》 (black) magic; black art; witchcraft; witchery; sorcery. ¶ ~을 부리다 use 〔practice〕 magic; practice sorcery; exercise witchcraft; work *one's* magic / ~로 속이다 delude 《*a person*》 by magical practices.
② 《눈속이는》 a juggler's trick; a conjuring 〔magic〕 trick; juggler's sleight of hand; legerdemain; a parlor trick (여흥적인). ¶ ~을 부리다 juggle; do 〔perform〕 conjuring tricks / ~의 속임수를 밝히다 explain the trick 〔catch〕; show the gimmick 《미》.
◉ ~방망이 a mallet of luck; the Aladdin's lamp. ~쟁이 a magician; a conjurer; a juggler; a wizard (남자); a witch (여자). ~지팡이 a magic wand 〔staff〕.

**요승**(妖僧) an evil-working 〔a wicked, a vicious〕 Buddhist priest.

**요시찰인**(要視察人) people on a surveillance list 〔blacklist〕. ◉ ~명부 a blacklist; a surveillance list: ~ 명부에 오르다 be on the blacklist; be blacklisted.

**요식**(要式) (the necessary) formalities; formal. ¶ ~의 formal. ◉ ~계약〔행위〕 a formal contract 〔act〕.

**요식업**(料食業) restaurant business. ◉ ~자 a restaurant owner.

**요신**(妖神) an evil spirit; a demon.

**요약**(要約) summation; condensation; summing up; 《요약한 것》 a summary; a condensed 〔an abridged〕 version; a digest; an epitome; a précis (★ 단·복수 같음. 발음은 단수 [preisíː], 복수 [preisíːz]); a ***résumé*** (F.). ~하다 summarize; epitomize; digest; condense; sum up; recapitulate; 《구어》 recap; 《줄이다》 abridge; brief 《미》. ¶ ~한 summarized; condensed; abridged; epitomized / ~하면〔해 말하면〕 to sum up; to make a long story short; in short 〔brief〕; in sum; in a word / ~해서 이야기하다 tell briefly; give the outline 《of》; sketch; outline; run over.

**요양**(療養) 《휴양》 recuperation; convalescence; 《치료》 (a) medical treatment 〔care〕. ~하다 《휴양하다》 recuperate; convalesce; 《치료받다》 receive 〔be under〕 medical treatment. ¶ 전지(轉地) ~하다 go 《a place》 for a change of air / 현재 ~중이다 be now under medical treatment; be recuperating 〔convalescing〕 《at *one's* home, at Haeundae》 / 그는 지금 해변에서 ~ 생활을 하고 있다 He lives at a seaside place nursing 〔recuperating〕 himself.
◉ ~소 a rest 〔nursing〕 home; a sanatorium (*pl.* ~s, -ria); a sanitarium 《미》. ~지 a health resort. 자택~ home 〔domiciliary〕 treatment; recuperation at home.

**요언**(要言) summarizing 〔setting forth〕 the essential points.

**요업**(窯業) 〖공업〗 the ceramic 〔pottery〕 industry; ceramics. ◉ ~가 a ceramist. ~소 a pottery. 「《약칭》 Joel.

**요엘서**(一書) 〖성서〗 The Book of Joel;

**요연하다**(瞭然一) (be) clear; evident; obvious; manifest; easy to see. ¶ 그것은 일목~ One can see it with half an eye.

**요염**(妖艶) voluptuous beauty; amorousness; sensual charm; the witchery of a woman's beauty. ~하다 (be) fascinating; bewitching; enchanting; voluptuous. ¶ ~한 눈매로 with coquettish eyes / ~한 모습 a charming 〔bewitching〕 figure / ~한 미인〔눈길〕 a voluptuous beauty 〔glance〕.

**요오드** 〖화학〗 iodin(e). ◉ ~팅크 tincture of iodine; iodine tincture.

**요오드포름** iodoform; tri-iodomethane.

**요오드화**(一化) 〖화학〗 iodation. ~하다 iodize. ◉ ~나트륨 sodium iodide. ~물 an iodide; an iodid. ~수소산 hydriodic acid. ~아연 zinc iodide; iodide of zinc. ~알루미늄 aluminum iodide. ~암모늄 ammonium iodide. ~에틸 ethyl iodide; iodide of ethyl. ~은 silver iodide; iodide of silver. ~철 iron iodide. ~칼륨 potassium iodide.

**요요** 《장난감》 a yoyo (*pl.* -s).

**요우**(僚友) a colleague; a comrade; a fellow official 〔worker〕.

**요원**(要員) the personnel necessary 〔required〕《for》; needed personnel. ¶ 몇 명의 보안 ~이 필요한가 How many personnel do you require for security? / ~의 부족이 반드시 능률의 저하를 가져오는 것은 아니다 A shortage of personnel does not always cause a drop in efficiency.

**요원**(遙遠·遼遠) ~하다 (be) very far away; far off; distant; remote. ¶ 전도 ~하다 [사람이 주어] have a long 〔far〕 way to go; have a long way before one; [사물이 주어] be far 〔a long way〕 off / 우리의 목표에 이르려면 아직 ~하다 We are still a long way from our object 〔goal〕.

**요원**(燎原) a prairie on fire. ¶ ~의 불길 a prairie fire; wildfire / ~의 불길처럼 퍼진다 It spreads like wildfire.

**요인**(要人) a leading 〔an important〕 person 《in political circles》; a pivot(-al) man; a key 〔leading〕 figure; a VIP 〔V.I.P.〕. [<*v*ery *i*mportant *p*erson] ¶ 재계의 ~ a VIP in the financial world. ◉ ~암살 assassination of key figures. 산업계~ those VIP's to various industries. 정부~ key figures in the government; high government officials.

**요인**(要因) a primary 〔an important〕 factor; a chief 〔main〕 cause; a prerequisite; a dominant cause. ¶ 능력은 성공의 한 ~이다 Ability is one factor of success. / 무엇보다도 운전자의 부주의가 그 사고의 ~이었다 The accident was caused, first of all, by the carelessness of the driver.

**요일**(曜日) a day of the week. ¶ 무슨 ~입니까 What day (of the week) is it? / ~에 관계 없이 방문해 주시오 Please come to see me any day of the week. / 금년 크리스마스는 무슨 ~이지 On which day of the week does Christmas (Day) fall this year?

**요전**(一前) 《요전날》 not long ago; the other day; just recently; just a short time back; 《전》 last; before; last time. ¶ 바로 ~ only the other day; quite recently / ~ 월요일 last Monday / ~ 음악회 the recent 〔last〕 concert / ~ 편지에 말한 대로 as I said in my previous letter / ~에 그를 만났을 때 the last time I saw him; when I saw him last / ~엔 실례(가) 많았습니다 I am sorry I caused you a lot of trouble last time.

**요절**(夭折) a premature 〔an early〕 death. ~하다 die young 〔prematurely〕; die at an early age.

**요절나다** ① 《못 쓰게 되다》 become unfit for use; become unserviceable; 《부서지다》 be spoilt 〔ruined〕; go to ruin; go to pieces; break; get broken; be damaged 〔destroyed〕; get out of order (기계 등). ¶ 내 구두가 요절났다 My shoes are worn out. / 수화기가 떨어져서 요절났다 The receiver dropped from my hand and got out of order. ② 《일이》 be spoiled; fall through; prove abortive. ¶ 지난 폭풍으로 모든 계획이 요절났다 The recent storm upset the whole plans.

**요절내다** spoil; ruin; mar; destroy.

**요절하다**(腰絶一) laugh *oneself* into convulsions; double up with laughter; be convulsed with laughter; hold 〔shake, burst, split〕 *one's* sides with laughter. ¶ 참 요절할 일이다 It is simply side-splitting. *or* How ridiculous it is!

**요점**(要點) the main 〔essential〕 point; the gist; the substance; the pith. ¶ 협정〔편지〕의 ~ the gist of an agreement 〔a letter〕 / 이야기의 ~ the pith of a speech / 전략상의 ~ a strategic point / ~을 벗어나다 be off the point / 문제의 ~을 파악하다 grasp 〔catch, get〕 the point of a subject; seize the essence of a matter / ~만 간단히 말하다 summarize; recapitulate / 바로 그것이 ~이다 That's the point 〔main thing〕. / ~을 말하면 다음과 같다 The main points may be summarized as follows. / 네 말은 ~을 모르겠다 I cannot see the point of your talk.

**요정**(了定) 《결정》 decision; 《끝마침》 completion; finish. ~나다 be decided; be settled 〔fixed〕; be finished; come to a close. ~짓다 decide; settle; fix (up); finish; conclude; bring 《*a matter*》 to an end; put an end to.

**요정**(妖精) a sprite; a fairy; 《꼬마 요정》 an elf (*pl.* elves). ¶ 숲〔나무〕의 ~ a dryad / 바다의 ~ a sea nymph / 물의 ~ a naiad; a nymph; a water sprite.

**요정**(料亭) a high-class Korean-style restaurant; a *kisaeng* house.

**요조**(窈窕) ~하다 (be) graceful; refined; elegant. ◉ ~숙녀 a lady of refined manners; an elegant 〔a graceful〕 lady; a chaste and modest woman.

**요즈음** now; at present; these days; nowadays; todays; 《최근》 recently; lately; of late (★ lately, of late는 현재완

료 시제에서만 쓰임).
¶ ~의 of today; today's; current; modern; recent; late / ~의 청년들 the young people of today / ~의 경향 the recent 〔modern〕 tendency / ~ 사건 a recent event / ~의 한국 present-day Korea; Korea (of) today / ~ 어떻습니까 How are you these days? / ~ 그 사람을 못 만난다 I haven't seen him lately. / ~ 그런 생각은 통하지 않는다 Your way of thinking won't do nowadays. / 아주 ~ 일입니다 It happened quite recently. / ~은 대부분의 가정에서 전기 기구를 사용하게 되었다 In these days electric instruments have come to be used at almost every house. (★ In those days라고 하면「그 당시에는」이란 뜻이 됨).

**요지**(要地) an important place; a strategic point 〔place〕. ¶ 상업상의 ~ a place of great commercial importance.

**요지**(要旨) 《요점》 the essentials; the gist; the point; the major points; 《취지》 the purport; the keynote; 《논지·서책 등의》 the argument; the substance; fundamental principles. ¶ …과 같은 ~의 《a lecture》 to the effect that… / ~를 말하다 set forth the essential points.

**요지경**(瑤池鏡) a magic glass; a toy peep show; a raree show. ¶ ~ 같은 인생 the kaleidoscope of life; shifts and changes of life.

**요지부동**(搖之不動) being unshakable; steadfastness. ~하다 stand as firm as rock; be unshakable 〔steadfast, adamantine, unyielding, invincible〕.

**요직**(要職) an important post 〔appointment〕; a key position 〔post〕; a responsible position 〔post〕. ¶ ~의 안배(按配) apportionment of key positions 〔posts〕 / 정부 ~에 있다 hold an important post in the Government / 부친께서는 L회사의 ~에 오르셨다 My father was appointed to an important post in L Company.

**요철**(凹凸) prominence and depression; unevenness; ruggedness; irregularity.

**요청**(要請) an important request; a claim; an urgent demand. ~하다 demand; request; call on 〔ask〕 《*a person*》 for 《aid》; make a bid for 《support》. ¶ 국가적 ~ a national demand / …의 ~에 의해서〔따라〕 at 〔by〕 the request of… / 시대의 ~에 따르다 meet the needs of the times / ~을 수락하다 comply with the request / ~에 응하다 accept 《*a person's*》 demand / 5백만 원을 ~하다 make a demand for five million won upon 《*a person*》 / 그는 연설을 해달라는 ~을 받았다 He was called upon to make a speech. / 그들은 사태를 수습하기 위해 군대의 출동을 ~했다 They requested 〔asked for〕 the mobilization of the army to save the situation. / 귀하의 ~대로 카탈로그 한 부를 무료로 즉시 보내드리겠습니다 A free copy of catalog will be promptly sent at your request.

**요체**(要諦) the secret 《of success》; the key 《to success》; the main 〔cardinal〕 point. ¶ 부지런함이야 말로 성공의 ~이다 It is diligence that is the secret of success.

**요추**(腰椎) 〖해부〗 the lumbar vertebra. ◉ ~마취 lumbar anesthesia; a spinal 〔lumbar〕 block.

**요충**(蟯蟲) a threadworm; a pinworm.

**요충**(要衝) 《군사상의》 a strategic point; a strategic position; 《중요 지점》 a key point; an important spot 〔position, place〕; an important center 〔focus〕. ¶ 지브롤터는 지중해의 ~이다 Gibraltar is the key (point) of the Mediterranean Sea.

**요컨대**(要—) in short; in a word; in fine; to cut a long story short; taking all in all; after all. ¶ ~ 그것은 이렇다 In brief it is like this. / ~ 그는 시민의 적이다 After all he is the citizens' enemy. / ~ 그는 거짓말쟁이다 In short he is a liar. / ~ 그들은 틀렸다 In a word, they are mistaken.

**요크셔** Yorkshire. ¶ ~종 돼지 a Yorkshire (pig).

**요탓조탓** with this excuse 〔complaint〕 and that.

**요통**(腰痛) 〖의학〗 lumbago; a pain in the lower back; (a) backache.

**요트** a yacht. ¶ ~를 타다 yacht; cruise in a yacht / ~를 달리다 sail a yacht. ◉ ~레이스 a yacht(ing) race. ~정박소 a yacht basin; a marina. ~조종자 a yachtsman.

**요판**(凹版) an intaglio. ◉ ~인쇄 intaglio printing.

**요포대기**(褥—) a baby quilt.

**요하다**(要—) need 《*do*ing, to *do*》; require; want; take (시간 따위를); demand; call for. ¶ 주의를 ~ require attention 〔care〕 / 휴식을 ~ need rest / 설명을 ~ call for an explanation / 수리를 ~ want mending / 이 작업은 숙련을 요하는 업무이다 The job demands skill and experience. / 거기까지 가는

데 2시간을 요했다 It took us two hours to get there. / 그 일은 비밀을 요한다 The matter requires secrecy.

**요한** 〖성서〗 John. ◉ ~계시록 the Revelation. ~복음 (The Gospel according to St.) John.

**요함**(僚艦) a consort ship; a comrade vessel.

**요항**(要項) the main 〔essential〕 points 〔items〕. ¶ 모집 ~ guidelines for applicants; an application guidebook. ◉ 지시~ the essential points for guidance.

**요항**(要港) a strategic 〔an important〕 port. ¶ 그 곳은 그 나라 북부의 유일한 ~이다 It is the only strategic port in the northern part of the country.

**요해**(要害) ① =요충(要衝). ②《몸의》 the vital parts of the body; a vital part.

**요행**(僥倖) luck (by chance); a piece 〔stroke〕 of good luck; a windfall. ¶ ~으로 by a stroke of good fortune 〔luck〕; luckily / ~을 바라다〔믿다〕 rely on chance / 그 학교에 입학하게 된 것은 ~이었다 It was sheer luck that got me into that school. / ~으로 그를 만났다 Luckily I met up with him. / 참 ~이로군 What a stroke of good luck! ◉ ~수 a fortunate move; a lucky chance.

**요혈**(尿血) 〖의학〗 bloody urine; bleeding in urination; hematuria.

**욕**(辱) ① 《욕설》 abusive 〔foul〕 language; abuse; 《중상》 (a) slander. ¶ 욕을 퍼붓다 heap abuses on 《*a person*》; curse (and swear) / (나한테) 욕하지 마시오 Don't call me names!

> **참고** 미국 사회에서 흔히 들을 수 있는 욕 중의 하나는 bitch이다. 여성에게는 그냥 bitch, 남성에게는 son of a bitch 라고 한다. 앞의 것은 「암캐」, 나중 것은 「암캐의 자식」이란 뜻이다. 나중 것은 머리글자만 모아 SOB (에스 오 비) 라고도 한다.

② 《치욕》 shame; humiliation; insult; disgrace. ⇨ 욕보다①, 욕보이다. ¶ 욕을 달게 받다 eat humble pie.
③ 《고생》 trouble(s); hardship(s); pains. ⇨ 욕보다②. ¶ 그의 집을 찾느라 욕을 봤다 I had a hell of a time looking for his house.

**욕**(慾) 《욕심》 a desire; a wish; a passion; an appetite; a thirst; a hunger. ¶ 권세욕 the will to power / 명예욕 a desire for fame / 금전욕 love of money; desire for wealth / 그는 지식욕에 불타고 있다 He is thirsty after 〔for, of〕 knowledge.

**욕가마리**(辱—) the person deserving of abuse.

**욕감태기**(辱—) a person who is called bad names by many people.

**욕객**(浴客) 《대중탕의》 a bathhouse customer; a bather; 《온천장의》 a visitor at a spa.

**욕계**(慾界) 〖불교〗 the world of desires; the greedy 〔avaricious, covetous〕 world.

**욕구**(欲求) want(s); (a) desire 〔wish〕 《for》; craving 《for》; an urge 《to *do*》. ~하다 want; desire; crave 《for》; aspire. ¶ 생의 ~ craving for life; the will to live / 성적 ~ sexual desire / ~를 채우다 satisfy 〔gratify〕 *one's* wants 〔desire〕 / 그녀는 지적 ~가 강하다 She has a strong desire to learn. / 「요즘 그는 왜 기분이 좋지 않니」—「아마, ~ 불만일 거야」 "Why is he in bad mood these days?"—"I guess he's frustrated." ◉ ~불만 〖심리〗 frustration.

**욕기부리다**(慾氣—) covet; be greedy for; be avaricious; be rapacious. ¶ 남의 것에 ~ covet another's property / 너무 욕기부리지 마라 You must not be so avaricious. / 왜 그렇게 욕기를 부리나 How covetous you are!

**욕념**(欲念) desire; craving; appetite; 《정욕》 (a) passion.

**욕되다**(辱—) be a disgrace; be shameful 〔disgraceful, dishonorable〕; bring disgrace upon *oneself*. ¶ 너 같은 자식은 가문에 욕(이)된다 A son like you is a disgrace to our family. / 그는 아랫사람한테 묻는 것을 욕되게 생각한다 He thinks it a disgrace to have to ask his subordinates questions.

**욕망**(欲望) a desire; a craving; an appetite; an ambition. ¶ ~을 억제하다 put a curb upon *one's* desire; suppress 〔control〕 *one's* desire / ~을 일으키다 arouse a desire 《in *a person* for *something*》 / ~을 채우다 gratify 〔satisfy〕 *one's* ambition 〔desire〕 / ~을 품다 harbor an ambition.

**욕먹다**(辱—) ① 《욕을》 be abused; suffer an insult; be slighted; be reviled; be fed insults. ② 《악평·비난을》 be spoken ill of; be disparaged; be spoken against; be slandered; be stigmatized; 《신문 등에서》 be criticized unfavorably; be attacked; be scolded; receive a rebuke.

**욕보다**(辱—) ① 《치욕》 be put to shame; be insulted 〔humiliated, abused, dishonored〕; disgrace *oneself.* ¶ 선불리 여자한테 말을 걸었다가 욕봤다 I approached the girl with so little tact I made a fool of myself. ② 《고생》 have a hard time; go through hardships; have a bitter experience; go through the mill; take pains. ¶ 돈 취하느라 ～ have a hell of a time getting a loan. ③ 《강간》 be raped; be assaulted; be violated.

**욕보이다**(辱—) ① 《치욕을》 humiliate; disgrace; bring disgrace on 《*a person*》; insult; put 《*a person*》 to shame. ② 《여자를》 rape; violate; assault.

**욕설**(辱說) 《악담》 curses; imprecations; swearwords; 《모욕적인 말》 insulting language. ～하다 utter curses; swear 《at》; throw insulting words. ¶ ～을 퍼붓다 curse (and swear); use abusive 〔bad, foul〕 language; call 《*a person*》 (bad) names.

**욕실**(浴室) a bath(room); a toilet 《미》.

**욕심**(慾心) 《탐욕》 greed; avarice; 《욕망》 desire; 《색욕》 lust; 《식욕·성욕》 (an) appetite; 《갈망》 (a) thirst; 《열망》 (a) hunger; 《야심》 ambition.

> 용법 **greed** 욕심을 뜻하는 가장 일반적인 말, 천박한 느낌을 나타냄. **avarice** greed보다 더 강조된 뜻의 격조 높은 말. **desire** 정신적 또는 육체적 욕망을 나타내는 말이지만, 성욕(sexual desire)의 뜻으로도 쓰임. **lust** 바람직스럽지 못한 것에 대한 강한 욕망. **appetite** 식욕·성욕 등 육체적인 욕망을 채우려는 마음을 말하며, 비유적으로 쓰임. **hunger, thirst**는 원래 각각 공복과 갈증을 뜻하지만, 절실히 바란다는 뜻으로도 쓰임. **ambition** 야심적인 욕망을 뜻함.

¶ ～에서 from a selfish motive; out of greed / ～을 부려 covetously; avariciously / ～ 없이 from 〔out of〕 a disinterested motive; with no ulterior motive (in mind) / ～꾸러기 a selfish 〔greedy〕 person; a hog 《구어》 / 돈에 대한 ～ desire for wealth; lust after money / ～을 누르다 put a curb upon *one's* desires; regulate *one's* desires / ～이 크다〔많다〕, ～이 사납다 be avaricious 〔covetous, rapacious, greedy, possessive〕 / ～이 없다 be unselfish; be disinterested; be simple / ～에 눈이 멀다 be blind with avarice; be blinded by love of gain; be ruled by avarice / 남의 것에 ～을 내지 마라 Do not covet things which belong to others. / 그는 매우 ～이 많다 He is very avaricious. *or* He has an itching palm. / 그는 ～ 덩어리이다 He is an incarnation of avarice. *or* He is avarice itself.

**욕의**(浴衣) a bathrobe; a bath gown.

**욕쟁이**(辱—) a foul-mouthed〔-tongued〕 person; a knocker; a slanderer.

**욕정**(欲情) feelings of passion; sexual desire; carnal desire 〔lusts〕. ⇨ 정욕(情欲). ¶ ～을 일으키다 [원인이 주어] inflame 〔excite, stir up〕 *one's* sexual desire.

**욕조**(浴槽) a bathtub; a bath.

**욕지거리**(辱—) abusive language; 《폭언》 a term of abuse; 《독설》 a biting tongue; bad names; insulting words. ～하다 say bitterly; call 《*a person*》 names; say bad things about 《*a person*》; abuse; use abusive language.

**욕지기** nausea; qualm; queasiness; a sickly 〔retching〕 feeling. ～하다 feel sick; feel nausea; *one's* stomach turns. ¶ ～ 나는 냄새 a nauseous 〔sickening〕 smell / ～가 날 정도로 to a sickening degree; revoltingly / ～(가) 나다 be nauseated; feel sick; feel queasy / 그를 보기만 해도 ～가 난다 The mere sight of him makes me sick 〔turns my stomach〕. / 그것을 보니 ～가 났다 At the sight of it nausea rose in me. / 그 냄새에 그녀는 ～가 났다 The smell made her sick.

**욕탕**(浴湯) a bathhouse. ⇨ 목욕탕.

**욕하다**(辱—) abuse; call 《*a person*》 names; speak ill of 《*a person*》; revile 《against, at》; scold; slander. ¶ 입이 걸게 ～ abuse 《*a person*》 in foul language / 아무를 뒤에서 ～ backbite *a person;* speak ill of *a person* behind *his* back / 그는 화가 나서 그들을 욕하기 시작했다 He was so angry that he began calling them names. / 그는 공개 석상에서 나를 욕했다 He railed at me in public.

**욕화**(浴化) the influence of virtue. ～하다 be influenced by virtuous examples.

**욕화**(慾火) ardent 〔burning〕 desire.

**욥기**(—記) 〖성서〗 the Book of Job; 《약칭》 Job.

**욧속**(褥—) cotton-wool used for lining a quilted mattress; cotton-wool stuffing; wadding 〔batting〕 for a mattress.

**욧잇**(褥—) a sheet-covering for a mattress.

**용**(茸) an antler. ⇨ 녹용.

**용**(龍) 《상상의 동물》 a dragon; 《큰 인물》

the great; 《왕에 관계되는 것》 pertaining to the king. ¶ 용이 되다 《크게 되다》 rise to greatness 〔eminence〕/ 개천에서 용나다 rise from humble family / 용이 구름을 얻은 듯하다 be in *one's* element / 미꾸라지가 용되었다 He has come a long way from ｢rags to riches 〔a small fly to a big shot〕.

**–용**(用) for (the use of). ¶ 남자용 《표시》 (For) Men. / 남자용 장갑 gloves for men; men's gloves / 여성용 우산 ladies' umbrellas / 이 수건은 손님용이다 These towels are for the guests.

**용감**(勇敢) bravery; courage (★ 전자는 행동에 중점을 두며, 후자는 정신적 면을 강조함); valor (주로 전쟁에서); heroism. ～하다 (be) brave; courageous; valiant; heroic. ¶ ～히 bravely; courageously; valiantly; heroically / ～한 시민 a valiant citizen / ～한 무사 a brave warrior / ～한 행위 a heroic deed; a deed of heroism / ～히 싸우다 fight bravely 〔heroically, gamely〕; fight a valiant battle 〔fight〕/ ～히 싸우다 죽다 die soldier's death.

**용건**(用件) (a matter of) business. ¶ 곧 ～에 들어가다 plunge at once into business / 빨리 ～을 말해라 Come to the point at once. / ～이 무엇입니까 What can I do for you? / 무슨 ～이냐 What is it?

**용골**(龍骨) 《배의》 the keel of a ship; a keel; 《화석》 mastodon bones.

**용공**(容共) pro-Communist. ¶ ～ 이적(利敵)하다 serve the interest of enemy, accommodating communism. ◉ ～단체 an organization accommodating communism. ～사상 pro-Communist thought: ～ 사상을 갖다 be sympathetic with Communism. ～정책 a pro-Communist policy.

**용광로**(鎔鑛爐) a blast 〔smelting〕 furnace. ¶ ～에 불을 때다 fire a blast furnace; blow a hot blast into the furnace.

**용구**(用具) a tool; an instrument; an implement. ◉ 교육～ teaching aids. 운동～ sporting goods. 필기～ writing instruments 〔implements〕.

**용궁**(龍宮) the Palace of the Dragon King; the Poseidon's Palace.

**용기**(用器) an instrument; a tool. ◉ ～화(畫) (an) instrumental 〔(a) mechanical〕 drawing.

**용기**(勇氣) courage; valor; bravery; nerve; pluck; grit. ¶ 무모한 ～ brute courage; foolhardiness / ～백배하여 with redoubled courage.

용기가: ～(가) 있는 courageous; valiant; brave; plucky; 《대담한》 bold; daring; intrepid / ～(가) 없는 cowardly; timid; fainthearted / ～가 나다 take heart. ⇨ ～를 얻다 / …할 ～가 있다 have the courage 〔heart, nerve〕 to 《*do*》; have the courage of 《*do*ing》/ ～가 꺾이다 be discouraged; lose courage / 옳다고 믿는 것을 실천〔말〕할 ～가 있다 have the courage of *one's* convictions.

용기를: ～를 내다 screw 〔pluck, summon, muster〕 up *one's* courage; call 〔gather〕 *one's* courage; summon up spirit 〔the blood〕; take 〔collect〕 courage 〔heart〕; get up *one's* 〔the〕 nerve 《to *do*》/ ～를 내어 in high spirits; gallantly / ～를 꺾다 discourage; dispirit; dishearten; unnerve / ～를 보이다 show *one's* nerve; display *one's* courage / ～를 얻다 be encouraged 《at, by》; take 〔derive〕 encouragement 《from》/ ～를 요하다 take nerve / ～를 잃다 lose courage 〔heart〕/ ～를 잃지 않다 keep a good 〔stout〕 heart; keep *one's* chin up.

¶ 말할 ～가 없었다 I didn't have the courage to speak. / 그의 말에 우리는 ～백배했다 His words inspired us with redoubled courage. / 그들은 그것을 보고 새로운 ～를 냈다 They drew fresh courage from the scene. / 낙심하지 말고 ～를 내라 Don't be dejected, take courage! / 그녀에게 구혼할 ～가 나지 않았다 I could not summon up the courage to propose to her. *or* I could never bring myself to ask for her hand.

**용기**(容器) a receptacle; a container; a case; a vessel.

**용기병**(龍騎兵) a dragoon.

**용꿈**(龍—) a dream about a dragon; a lucky dream. ¶ ～을 꾸다 dream 〔have〕 a lucky dream.

**용납**(容納) toleration; admission; approval; 《허용》 permission; allowance; 《용서》 pardon. ～하다 tolerate; admit; approve; permit; allow; pardon. ¶ ～할 수 없는 unpardonable / ～될 수 없다 cannot be tolerated / 지각을 ～치 않다 allow no excuse for being late / 이것은 어떠한 이유이든 결코 ～될 수 없는 극히 비인도적인 행위이다 This is an utterly inhuman act which can never be tolerated for any reason.

**용녀**(傭女) a hired girl; a maid servant.

**용녀**(龍女) the princess of the Dragon King.
**용뇌**(龍腦) ① 〖한의〗《용뇌향》 borneol. ② 〖식물〗《용뇌수》 the Borneo 〔Sumatra〕 camphor.
**용단**(勇斷) a courageous decision; a resolute 〔decisive〕 step 〔measure〕. ¶ ～을 내리다 make a brave 〔courageous〕 decision 《on *a matter*》; take a decisive 〔resolute〕 step / 당국의 ～을 촉구하다 demand a decisive measure on the part of the authorities / 학내 폭력 제거에 ～을 내리다 take more drastic measures against the school violence.
**용달**(用達) messenger 〔delivery〕 service. ～하다 deliver 《messages, goods, etc.》. ◉ ～사 a delivery agency. ～업 the delivery business. ～차 a delivery van 〔truck〕. 「bellflower.
**용담**(龍膽) 〖식물〗 a gentian; an autumn
**용도**(用度) supplies; expenditure. ◉ ～과(課) the supplies department.
**용도**(用途) a use; service. ¶ ～가 넓은 general purpose 《tables》 / ～가 많다 have various 〔many〕 uses; be used for various purposes 〔in various ways〕; be of wide use / 돈의 ～를 밝히다 account for how the money was spent; keep strict account of every cent / ～가 한정되어 있다 have (only) limited uses / ～ 불명 《출토품 따위에 붙이는 표시》 Use unknown.
**용돈**(用―) pocket 〔spending〕 money; 《미》 an allowance (주로 어린이의); pin money (여성의). ¶ 한 달에 오만 원을 ～으로 주다 allow 《*a person*》 fifty thousand won a month for pocket money / ～이 떨어지다 run out of *one's* pocket money / 이것이 이 달 네 ～이다 This is your allowance for the month. / 아버지는 한 달에 4만원씩 ～을 주신다 My father gives me an allowance of 40,000 won a month. / 그는 ～을 벌기 위해 아르바이트를 한다 He works part-time for spending money.
**용두**(龍頭) the winding knob 《of a watch》.
**용두레** 〖농업〗 a large water dipper (for irrigation); a scoop bucket.
**용두사미**(龍頭蛇尾) a bright beginning and a dull 〔tame〕 ending; an anticlimax. ¶ ～로 끝나다 end (up) in an anticlimax / 그 계획은 ～로 끝났다 The plan failed miserably after a good start. *or* The plan started well and ended in a fiasco. / 그녀의 연설은 ～같은 인상을 주었다 Our impression is that her speech started attractively but ended in an anticlimax.
**용두질** masturbation. ⇨ 수음(手淫).
**용략**(勇略) courage and strategy; bravery and artifice. 「분).
**용량**(用量) 《약의》 dosage; a dose (1회
**용량**(容量) (the measure of) capacity; 《용적》 cubic contents; volume. ¶ 기억～ 〖컴퓨터〗 storage capacity / 열～ thermal 〔heat〕 capacity / 물탱크의 ～ the (storage) capacity of a water tank / 이 통의 ～은 30갤런이다 This cask has a capacity of 30 gallons. ◉ ～분석 volumetric analysis. ～전류 a capacity current. 「courage.
**용력**(勇力) manly strength; physical
**용렬하다, 용렬스럽다**(庸劣―) (be) mediocre; inferior; stupid; awkward; clumsy; poor 《workmanship》. ¶ 용렬한 사람 an awkward 〔a stupid〕 fellow / 용렬한 짓을 하다 act foolishly; do a very foolish 〔stupid〕 thing.
**용례**(用例) an example; an illustration. ¶ ～를 들다 give 〔show〕 an example; cite 〔quote〕 an example; illustrate / 이 사전에는 동사 용법에 관한 많은 ～가 있다 This dictionary has many examples of how verbs are used.
**용립**(聳立) rising; soaring; towering. ～하다 rise high; tower.
**용마**(龍馬) a swift horse; a fleet steed.
**용마루** the ridge (of a roof). ¶ ～를 올리다 put up the ridge beam of a new house.
**용마름** the thatch covering 「on the ridge of the thatched roof 〔on a mud wall〕.
**용매**(溶媒) 〖화학〗 a (chemical) solvent; a dissolvent; a menstruum (*pl.* ～s, -strua).
**용맹**(勇猛) intrepidity; dauntlessness; valor; pluck; lionheartedness. ～하다, ～스럽다 (be) intrepid; dauntless; valiant; plucky; lionhearted. ◉ ～심 an intrepid spirit; indomitable courage: ～심을 불러일으키다 pluck up 〔take〕 courage; muster 〔summon up〕 *one's* courage.
**용명**(勇名) fame for *one's* bravery. ¶ ～을 떨치다〔날리다〕 be famous 〔renowned〕 for *one's* bravery; gain fame for *one's* bravery. 「in.
**용명**(溶明) 〖영화〗 a fade-in. ～하다 fade
**용모**(容貌) looks; (a cast of) features; the face. ¶ ～ 단정한 사람 a person of regular features 〔good looks〕 / ～가

변하다 get a new facial expression / 그녀의 ~가 맘에 안 든다 I don't like the looks of her. / 그녀는 ~가 아름답다 She has 「good looks 〔fine features〕. *or* She is good looking.

**용무**(用務) business; an engagement; work 〔things〕 to do. ¶ 급한 ~로 on urgent 〔pressing〕 business / ~를 마치다 finish 〔complete, carry out〕 *one's* business / 무슨 ~지요 May I ask your business? / 그는 급한 ~로 상경했다 Urgent business called him away to Seoul. / 나는 해야 할 중요한 ~가 있다 I have an important matter to attend to. / 달리 또 ~가 있어 실례하겠습니다 I must say good-bye, because I have another engagement.

**용법**(用法) (a) usage (관용); (a) use (용도); the way to use; how to use; the directions (for use) (사용법). ¶ 접속사의 ~ the uses of conjunctions / 그 약의 ~ the directions for the use of the medicine / 이 약은 ~을 잘 읽고 사용하시오 Apply the medicine after careful reading of the directions. / 그는 전치사의 올바른 ~을 가르쳐 주었다 He taught us how to use prepositions correctly.

**용변**(用便) ~하다 relieve *oneself;* go to stool; go to the bathroom 〔restroom〕.

**용병**(用兵) employment 〔manipulation〕 of troops; tactics; strategy. ~하다 employ 〔manipulate, maneuver〕 the troops. ¶ ~에 통달하다 be well versed in tactics; be a tactician.
◉ ~술 tactics; the science of war.

**용병**(傭兵) a mercenary (soldier); a hired soldier.

**용봉탕**(龍鳳湯) a mixture of chicken and carp soup.

**용불용설**(用不用說) 〖생물〗 the use and disuse theory; Lamarckism.

**용비**(冗費) unnecessary 〔wasteful〕 expenses 〔expenditure〕.

**용사**(勇士) a brave man 〔warrior〕; a hero; a man of courage; the brave [총칭]. ¶ ~ 중의 ~ the bravest of the brave / 대령은 역전의 ~로서 명성을 떨쳤다 The colonel won fame as a combat veteran.

**용상**(龍床) 《임금의 자리》 the King's seat; the royal throne.

**용상**(聳上) 〖역도〗 jerk.

**용색**(容色) features; (good) looks; 《미색》 beauty. ¶ ~이 곱다 be good-looking 〔beautiful〕 / 그녀는 노래도 잘하고 ~도 곱다 She is a good singer and has good looks as well.

**용서**(容恕) pardon; forgiveness. ~하다 forgive; pardon; excuse.

> 용법 **forgive**는 남의 죄나 잘못에 대하여 화를 내거나 처벌하는 대신에 용서하다. **pardon**은 원래 「죄인을 방면하다」란 뜻으로, 죄나 나쁜 짓에 대한 처벌을 면죄하다. **excuse**는 비교적 사소한 실수나 잘못을 용서하다.

¶ ~할 수 있는 pardonable; excusable; forgivable; justifiable / ~할 수 없는 unpardonable; inexcusable / ~를 빌다 beg 〔ask〕 *one's* pardon; apologize for / ~를 받다 be forgiven 《by》; obtain 《*a person's*》 pardon 〔forgiveness〕 / 과실을 ~하다 forgive 《*a person*》 for *his* fault / 무릎을 꿇고 ~를 빌다 beg a pardon on *one's* knees / 다시 이러한 짓을 하면 ~ 없다 If you do such a thing again, you will be sorry for. / 그들은 그의 죄를 ~해 주었다 They forgave him his crimes. / 이번은 저를 보아 그를 ~해 주십시오 Please forgive him this time for my sake.

**용석**(熔石) 〖광물〗 volcanic rock; lava.

**용선**(傭船) 《배》 a chartered ship 〔vessels〕; 《행위》 chartering; charterage; the hiring of a ship. ~하다 charter a ship; hire a ship. ◉ ~계약 charter; chartering. ~계약서 a charter (party). ~료 charterage; charter rates. ~업 chartering business. ~자 a charterer.

**용설란**(龍舌蘭) 〖식물〗 an agave; a pita.

**용소**(龍沼) the basin of a waterfall.

**용솟음**(湧—) 《끓음》 boiling; seething; bubbling up; 《분출》 gush; leaping up. ~치다 boil; seethe; bubble up; 《분출》 gush out; leap up; rise up. ¶ 샘이 ~쳐 나오다 a fountain gushes out / 피가 ~치게 하다 cause the blood to tingle; inflame the blood 《of》; stir *one's* blood.

**용수** a rice-wine strainer. ¶ ~(를) 지르다 use a strainer. ◉ ~뒤 the last of the wine; the bottom of the barrel.

**용수**(用水) water (available for use); 《관개용의》 water for irrigation. ¶ 농업〔공업〕~ water for agricultural 〔industrial〕 use. ◉ ~로 an irrigation channel 〔canal〕; a flume (발전소 등의). ~지(池) a reservoir. ~용 물통 a rainwater tank 〔barrel〕.

**용수철**(龍鬚鐵) a (coil 〔spiral〕) spring. ¶ 시계의 ~ the spring of a watch / ~ 장치의 장난감 spring-driven 〔clockwork, clockwork-driven, windup〕

toys / 이 쥐덫은 ～로 작동된다 This rat-trap works by a spring. *or* This rat-trap has a spring device. ◉ ～저울 a spring balance. ～침대 a spring bed; an inner-spring bed.

**용신**(容身) ① 《몸을 놀림》 moving (around); getting about to move. ～하다 move *one's* body; stir. ¶ ～ 못하다 cannot move about; cannot stir an inch; be unable to move / 방이 좁아서 ～할 수도 없다 The room is so narrow that I can't even move. ② 《겨우 살아감》 eking out (*one's* livelihood). ～하다 eke out a living.

**용신**(龍神) the Dragon God. ◉ ～제 the Dragon God festival.

**용심** 《심술》 malice; spite. ～ 부리다 wreak *one's* jealousy 〔spite〕; take *one's* grudge out 《on》. ◉ ～꾸러기〔쟁이〕 a malicious 〔spiteful〕 person.

**용심**(用心) 《마음 씀》 care; carefulness; prudence (신중). ～하다 take care of...; be careful 〔cautious〕 of...; take precautions against.

**용쓰다** ① 《기운을》 put forth all *one's* effort 〔strength〕; concentrate *one's* energy; strain (*oneself*). ② 《참다》 force *oneself* to bear up under stress.

**용안**(龍眼) 〖식물〗 a longan. ◉ ～육 longan.

**용안**(龍顔) the royal countenance.

**용암**(溶暗) 〖영화·TV〗 a fade-out. ～하다 fade out.

**용암**(熔岩) 〖지질〗 lava. ¶ 화산이 ～을 분출하다 a volcano spews out 〔vomits〕 lava. ◉ ～괴(塊) a lava boulder. ～대지(臺地) a plateau of lava. ～돔 a lava dome. ～류(流) a stream 〔flow〕 of lava; a lava flow. ～층 a lava bed.

**용액**(溶液) a solution. ¶ 묽은 ～ 《make》 a dilute 〔weak〕 solution 《of ammonia》 / 진한 ～ a concentrated 〔strong〕 solution.

**용약**(勇躍) [부사적] in high spirits; elatedly. ～하다 exult; be 〔get〕 spirited; take heart. ¶ 그들은 ～ 남극 탐험길에 올랐다 They went on their antarctic expedition in high spirits.

**용어**(用語) 《술어》 a term; (a) terminology [총칭]; 《말씨》 wording; diction; language; phraseology; 《어휘》 (a) vocabulary. ¶ 전문〔학술〕 ～ technical 〔scientific〕 terms 〔terminology〕 / 관청 ～ official 〔bureaucratic〕 language; officialese / ～의 선택 the choice of words / 의학〔군대〕 ～로 in「medical language 〔military parlance〕 / ～에 주의하다 be careful about wording / ～에 까다롭다 be particular as to the choice of words. ◉ ～집 a glossary.

**용언**(用言) 〖언어〗 a declinable word.

**용역**(用役) services. ¶ 재화와 ～ goods and services. ◉ ～단 service corps: 민간 ～단 civilian service corps. ～수출 service export.

**용왕**(龍王) the Dragon King.

**용왕매진**(勇往邁進) advance in a dashing spirit; a vigorous forward dash. ～하다 advance bravely; dash 〔push〕 on 〔forward〕; make a dash 〔push〕. ¶ ～의 기상 a dashing 〔daring〕 spirit.

**용융**(熔融) 〖야금〗 fusion; melting. ～하다 melt; dissolve. ◉ ～점 《녹는점》 a fusing 〔melting〕 point.

**용의**(用意) ① 《주의》 care; mindfulness; prudence; precaution. ¶ ～주도하다 be very careful; be cautious; be prudent; be circumspect / ～주도한 계획 a plan carefully arranged. ② 《준비》 preparedness; readiness.

**용의**(容疑) suspicion. ¶ 그는 절도 ～로 구류되고 있다 He is detained on suspicion of theft. *or* He is in detention, suspected of theft. ◉ ～자 〖법〗 a suspect; a suspected person; a person under suspicion: 유력한 ～자 a key suspect / 살인 ～자 a murder suspect.

**용이**(容易) ease; facility; simplicity. ～하다 (be) easy; simple; plain. ¶ ～하게 easily; simply; readily; with ease 〔facility〕; without difficulty 〔trouble〕 / 하기가 ～하다 be easy to do; be easily done / …을 ～하게 만들다 make 《*something*》 easy; facilitate / 외국어를 배운다는 것은 ～한 일이 아니다 It is「not easy 〔no easy matter〕 to learn a foreign language.

**용인**(容認) approval; admission. ～하다 《인정하다》 approve; admit; accept; 《허락하다》 allow; permit; tolerate. ¶ ～할 수 있는 tolerable; acceptable / 그녀의 부모는 그녀와 자네와의 결혼을 결코 ～하지 않을 것이다 Her parent will never approve of her marriage to you. / 이 이상 ～할 수 없다 This is the limit. *or* This is the last straw. / 일방적인 제도의 변경은 ～할 수 없다 We cannot accept the unilateral change of the system.

**용자**(勇者) a brave (man); a hero (*pl.* ～es); a person of courage 〔valor〕. ¶ ～만이 미녀를 얻을 자격이 있다 None but the brave deserve(s) the fair.

**용자**(容姿) the face and features; a

〔*one's*〕 figure; *one's* appearance 〔looks〕. ¶ ~ 단려하다 have a graceful 〔an elegant〕 figure.

**용장**(勇壯) bravery. ~하다 (be) brave; manly; stirring; heroic.

**용장**(勇將) a brave general. ¶ ~ 밑에 약졸 없다 A good general will make good men. *or* As is the master, so will his men be. *or* "Like master, like man."

**용재**(用材) materials (to make use of); 《목재》 timber; lumber.
◉ 건축~ building materials.

**용재**(庸才) a mediocre ability 〔talent〕; a loose head; inferior intelligence.

**용적**(容積) (cubic) capacity; volume (체적); bulk (크기). ¶ ~이 큰 capacious; bulky / 재화(載貨) ~ measurement capacity / 물체의 ~ the volume of a body / 이 상자의 ~은 약 4 리터이다 This box has a capacity 〔volume〕 of about four liters. ◉ ~량 the measure of capacity. ~률 〚건축〛 floor area ratio; floor space index. ~톤수 measurement tonnage.

**용전**(勇戰) brave fighting. ~하다 fight bravely 〔courageously〕; fight heroically 〔gallantly〕. ¶ ~ 감투하다 fight 《a battle》 courageously.

**용접**(鎔接) 〚공업〛 welding. ~하다 weld 《to, together》. ¶ 전기〔아크〕 ~ electric 〔arc〕 welding / ~용 마스크〔헬멧〕 a welder's helmet / 열 군데 ~하다 make ten welds / 철판을 ~하다 weld iron sheets. ◉ ~공 a welder. ~공장 a welding shop. ~기 a welding machine. ~봉 a welding rod. ~제 a welding agent 〔flux〕.

**용제**(溶劑) 〚화학〛 a solvent; a resolvent; a flux. ◉ ~접합 solvent sealing.

**용졸**(庸拙) ~하다 (be) mediocre; clumsy; shabby.

**용지**(用地) land (for the use of); 《부지》 a lot; a site. ¶ 건축 ~ a building lot; a site for a building / 목장 ~ pasture land; pasturage / ~를 선정하다 choose a site 《for a new school》 / ~를 매입하다 buy 〔purchase〕 a lot.

**용지**(用紙) paper (to use); a (blank) form; stationery; a blank; 《인쇄된》 a printed form. ¶ 답안 ~ a (blank) answer paper / 시험 ~ an examination paper / 신청 ~ an application form 〔blank〕 / 주문 ~ an order blank.

**용진**(勇進) a brave advance; dashing forward. ~하다 advance 〔march〕 bravely; push forward vigorously.

**용질**(溶質) 〚화학〛 a solute.

**용출**(湧出) gush; eruption. ~하다 gush out 〔forth〕; erupt; well (up); spring out.

**용출**(聳出) rising 〔towering〕 above. ~하다 rise 〔tower〕 above; soar.

**용춤** ¶ ~ 추다 yield 〔give in〕 to flattery / ~ 추이다 flatter 《*a person*》 till *he* gives in; wheedle 〔cajole〕 《*a person* into *doing*》.

**용퇴**(勇退) voluntary retirement; willing 〔graceful〕 retreat 〔withdrawal〕. ~하다 retire voluntarily; resign *one's* post of *one's* own accord. ¶ 정계에서 ~하다 retire from political life / ~하여 후진에게 길을 열어 주다 step down to make way for a junior.

**용트림** a big burp made on purpose. ~하다 let out a big burp.

**용틀임**(龍―) a dragon picture 〔engraving〕 in a building; dragon embellishments 〔decorations〕.

**용품**(用品) 《toilet》 articles; 《school》 things; supplies. ¶ 일~ daily necessities / 부엌 ~ kitchen utensils; utensils for kitchen use; kitchenware [총칭] / 여행 ~ a traveling outfit; traveling gear / 학〔사무〕~ school 〔office〕 supplies.

**용하다** ① 《재주가》 (be) skillful; deft; dexterous; brilliant; be good 《at》. ¶ 용한 점쟁이 a well divining fortuneteller / 무슨 일에나 재주가 ~ be a good hand at all things; be skillful in everything / (일을) 용하게 잘 처리하다 dispose of 《a case》 skillfully. ② 《장하다》 (be) admirable; wonderful; splendid; brave; great. ¶ 너 혼자 그 큰 일을 하였다니 정말 용한 걸 It is admirable that you did such a great work by yourself. / 그 큰 아이를 씨름에서 이기다니 너 ~ You have beaten the big boy in the wrestling—you are great.

**용해**(溶解) melting; dissolution; solution; liquefaction. ~하다 melt; dissolve; liquefy. ¶ ~한 dissolved; liquefied; solute / 물에 ~하다〔하지 않다〕 be soluble 〔insoluble〕 in water.
◉ ~도 solubility. ~량 meltage. ~력 solvency: ~력이 있는 solvent. ~성 solubility: ~성의 liquescent; soluble. ~액 a solution. ~열 the heat of dissolution. ~제 a solvent.

**용해**(鎔解) fusion; smelting. ~하다 smelt; fuse. ¶ ~성의 fusible / 불~성의 infusible / 불에 ~하다 smelt in the fire; be fused by fire. ◉ ～로 a smelting furnace. ～점 the smelting point.

**용호상박**(龍虎相搏) ～하다 be evenly-matched; be well contested; when Greek meets Greek, then comes the tug of war. ¶ ～의 싸움 a well-matched contest 〔fight〕; a Titanic struggle.

**용화**(熔化) melting; liquefaction. ～하다 melt; liquefy.

**용훼**(容喙) meddling; interference. ～하다 put in *one's* word; meddle 〔interfere〕 《in》. ¶ 남의 일에 ～하다 meddle in another's affair.

**용히** 《용하게》 skillfully; admirable; splendidly; remarkably; eminently. ¶ ～ 알아맞히다 make a good guess.

**우**(右) the right. ¶ 우와 여히 as above-mentioned / 우와 여히 상위(相違) 없음 the aforementioned is true to the best of my knowledge / 우로 봐 《구령》 Eyes right! / 우로 나란히 《구령》 Right dress! / 우향우 《구령》 Right turn 〔face〕! / 우회전 금지 《게시》 No right turn.

**우**(優) 《등급에서》 excellent; superior; 《성적에서》 good; fine; B.

**우** ① 《일시에 몰리는 모양》 all at once; with a rush; in a body. ¶ 사람들이 현장에 우 몰려 갔다 A crowd of people rushed to the scene. / 야구장에서 많은 사람들이 ～ 몰려 나왔다 A big crowd surged out of the baseball stadium. ② 《비·바람이》 all at once; suddenly. ¶ 소낙비가 우 쏟아졌다 A shower came on suddenly.

**우각**(牛角) a cow's 〔bull's〕 horn.

**우간다** 《나라 이름》 (the Republic of) Uganda. ¶ ～의 Ugandan. ◉ ～사람 an Ugandan.

**우거**(寓居) a temporary abode 〔residence〕. ～하다 reside 〔live〕 temporarily; take up *one's* (temporary) abode 〔quarters〕.

**우거지** ① 《푸성귀의》 the outer leaves (of cabbage, *etc*). ② 《절인 것의》 the dry and tasteless top layer of a crock of *kimchi* 〔salted shrimps〕.

**우거지다** [식물이 주어] grow thick 〔dense〕; grow rank (풀이); become luxuriant; luxuriate; flourish; [장소가 주어] be overgrown 〔covered〕 《with》. ¶ 우거진 thick(-growing); dense; luxuriant / 우거진 잡초 rank weeds / 우거진 잎 luxuriant foliage / 우거진 나무들 a dense 〔thick〕 growth of trees / 나무가 우거진 산 a thickly-wooded mountain / 나무가 우거져 있다 be overgrown 〔thickly covered〕 with trees; be thickly wooded / 뜰에는 잡초가 우거져 있다 The garden is overgrown with weeds. *or* The weeds are growing thick and rank in the garden.

**우거지상**(―相) a wry 〔sullen〕 face; a frowning face; distorted features; a grimace. ¶ ～의 sulky; morose / ～을 하다 make a wry face; (make a) grimace.

**우걱뿔** arched 〔inflexed〕 horns (of cattle). ◉ ～이 an ox with arched 〔inflexed〕 horns.

**우겨대다** cling stubbornly 《to *one's* notions》; hang on 《to》; force 《*one's* ideas on》; insist on *one's* own way; hold fast 《to》; persist. ¶ 제 생각만 ～ cling stubbornly to *one's* ideas / 그는 사실이 아닌 것을 사실이라고 우겨댔다 He insisted that what isn't, is. / 그만 우겨대고 내 말 좀 들어라 Don't be so hidebound—now, listen to me. / 그는 자기 말이 옳다고 우겨대고 있다 He asserts the statement to be true.

**우격다짐** high-handedness; forcible compulsion; coercion; pressure; browbeating. ～하다 resort to high-handed measures; put pressure 《on》; coerce; force. ¶ ～으로 high-handedly; by force; forcibly / ～으로 모든 일을 하다 take a high-handed policy in everything / ～으로 빚을 받다 force 《*a person*》 to pay *his* debt / ～으로 누르다 keep 《*a person*》 browbeaten / 돈을 내라고 ～하다 press 《*a person*》 for money / ～으로 합의케 하다 force 《*a person*》 to agree to 《the terms》.

**우격으로** against 《*a person's*》 will; forcibly; by force 〔compulsion〕. ¶ ～ 술을 먹이다 force 《*a person*》 to drink / ～ 그의 승낙을 얻으려는 것은 어리석은 일이다 It is quite silly of you to try to force him to consent.

**우견**(愚見) my humble opinion 〔view〕. ¶ ～으로는 from my point of view; in my humble opinion; to my thinking; to me; to express my opinion.

**우경**(右傾) veering 〔turning, tending〕 to the right side. ～하다 lean 〔swing〕 to the right; turn rightist. ◉ ～파 the Right Wing 〔Wingers〕; Rightist. ～학생 a rightist student.

**우계**(雨季) the rainy season. ＝우기(雨期).

**우골**(牛骨) cow bones; oxbone.

**우국**(憂國) patriotism. ◉ ～지사 a public-spirited man; a patriot. ～지심 a public spirit; a patriotic spirit. ～충정

*one's* intense patriotism: ～ 충정에서 우러나오다 be motivated by *one's* ardent patriotic sentiment.

**우군**(友軍) friendly forces 〔army〕; 《동맹군》 an allied troop 〔army〕; *one's* friends.

**우그러뜨리다** crush 〔bend〕 out of shape; make a dent 《in》; push in; dent. ¶ 밀짚 모자를 ～ crush a straw hat out of shape / 물통을 ～ dent a pail / 자동차의 옆을 ～ make a dent in the side of a car.

**우그러지다** be crushed out of shape; dent; get a dent in 《it》. ¶ 그 충격으로 내 차 옆이 우그러졌다 The impact dented the side of my car.

**우그르르** in swarms; 《물이》 simmering; 《벌레가》 swarming.

**우그리다** ⇨ 오그리다.

**우글거리다** swarm; be crowded; be alive 《with》; teem 《with》. ¶ 거리에는 거지가 우글거린다 The streets swarm with beggars. / 설탕에 개미가 우글거린다 The sugar is alive with ants.

**우글부글** bubbling; simmering. ～하다 bubble; simmer.

**우글우글** 《뒤끓는 모양》 in swarms; alive 《with》. ¶ 그 연못에는 물고기가 ～하다 The pond is alive with fish.

**우글쭈글** ～하다 (be) crumpled; rumpled; wrinkled; [서술적] be full of wrinkles. ¶ 옷이 ～해졌다 The clothes are all wrinkled.

**우금** a narrow (mountain) valley with a swift stream.

**우기**(右記) the above-mentioned〔-noted〕; the aforesaid.

**우기**(雨氣) signs of rain. ¶ ～를 띤 하늘 a watery sky.

**우기**(雨期) the rainy 〔wet〕 season; 《열대의》 the rains; 《인도 등지의》 the monsoon. ¶ ～에 접어들었다 The rainy season has set in.

**우기다** demand *one's* own way; force 《*one's* ideas on》; persist 《in *one's* opinion》; insist; impose 《*one's* views upon》; assert *oneself*. ¶ 사실이라고 ～ allege as a fact / 자기 의견이 옳다고 ～ stick to *one's* own opinion; hold fast to *one's* own views; carry *one's* point / 자기 생각을 ～ persist in *one's* ideas / 그는 자기만 옳다고 우겼다 He insisted he was the only one who was right. / 그는 아무 것도 모른다고 우겼다 He persisted in denying he knew anything about it.

**우김성**(一性) obstinacy; bullheadedness; headstrongness; stubbornness. ¶ ～이 많다 be pigheaded 〔headstrong, stubborn, self-asserting, obstinate, self-opinionated〕.

**우는살** an arrow with a turnip-shaped head that makes a sound as it flies.

**우는소리** a complaint; a whimper. ～하다 whimper; whine; complain.

**우단**(羽緞) velvet.

**우당**(友黨) a friendly 〔an allied〕 party.

**우당탕** with a thud 〔reverberating sound〕; thumping; bumping; banging. ～하다, 거리다 go thud. ¶ 무엇인지 마루에 ～ 떨어졌다 Something fell heavily on the floor. / ～ 소리 내며 층계를 내려갔다 He clattered down the stairway.

**우대**(優待) ① 《특별 취급》 preferential treatment. ～하다 give preferential treatment 《to》. ② 《융숭한 대접》 courteous 〔generous, warm〕 treatment; hospitality. ～하다 treat 《*a person*》 「courteously 〔with courtesy〕; give 《*a person*》 a warm 〔cordial〕 reception 〔welcome〕; receive 《*a person*》 warmly. ¶ 손님을 ～하다 be hospitable to *one's* guests; receive *one's* guest in a hospitable manner / 그들은 어디를 가나 ～받았다 They were 「treated 〔given warm reception〕 wherever they went. ◉ ～권(券) a complimentary ticket; a courtesy card; 《우대 할인권》 a discount coupon. ～금리(金利) prime rate. 경로～증 a Golden Age Passport 《미》.

**우도**(牛刀) a butcher knife. ◉ ～할계(割鷄) use an axe when a knife would be good enough; use sledgehammer to crack nuts; kill a fly with a long spear.

**우두**(牛痘) 〖의학〗 cowpox; vaccination; inoculation. ¶ ～를 놓다 vaccinate; inoculate 《*a person*》 for 〔against〕 smallpox; inoculate with vaccine / ～를 맞다 take vaccination; be vaccinated / ～가 잘 되었다 The vaccination took well. / ～가 잘 되지 않았다 The vaccination did not take. ◉ ～자국 a vaccination scar.

**우두둑** ① ⇨ 오도독. ② 《떨어지는 소리》 with a clatter 〔patter〕; pattering; clattering. ¶ 지붕에 ～ 떨어지는 비 the rain pattering on the roof / 우박이 ～ 떨어진다 The hail is clattering down.

**우두망찰하다** be flustered; be confused; be bewildered; be at a loss. ¶ 유일하게 밥벌이하는 사람이 죽어서 그 집안은 모두 우두망찰하고 있다 The death of their only breadwinner has bewildered the whole family.

**우두머리** ①《꼭대기》 the top. ¶ 나무의 ～를 자르다 cut off the top of a tree. ② 《사람》 the head; a leader; a chief; a boss. ¶ 인디언 부족의 ～ the chief of an Indian tribe / 남의 ～가 되다 become 〔be looked up to as〕 a leader; lead others.

**우두커니** blankly; absent-mindedly; listlessly; vacantly; idly; with an abstracted air; with *one's* head in the clouds; with *one's* mind a thousand miles away. ¶ ～ 서 있다 stand there with a vacant 〔idle〕 face / ～ 바라보다 look 〔gaze〕 blankly 《at》/ 또 아무 것도 안 하고 ～ 있구나 Woolgathering agains! / 그는 ～ 창 밖을 내다보고 서 있었다 He stood gazing vacantly out the window.

**우둔**(愚鈍) stupidity; dullness; imbecility; thick-headedness. ～하다 (be) stupid; dull; thick-headed; silly; obtuse.

**우둥퉁하다** ⇨ 오동통하다.

**우듬지** a treetop; the top branch of a tree.

**우등**(優等) excellence; 《학업 성적》 honors. ¶ 최～으로 with the highest distinction; 《미》 *summa cum laude* (L.) / ～으로 졸업하다 graduate 《from a college》 with honors 〔*cum laude*〕 / ～을 차지하다 take honors 《in English》; 《미》 make the honor roll.
◉ ～상 《win》 an honor prize. ～생 《미》 an honor(-roll) student; a prize pupil. ～졸업생 an honor graduate.

**우뚝** high; aloft. ～하다 《높이》 (be) high; upright; erect; tall; lofty; towering; soaring; 《뛰어나게》 (be) salient; prominent; conspicuous; outstanding. ¶ ～한 코 a high 〔shapely〕 nose / 키가 ～하다 be tall (in stature) / 산이 ～ 솟아 있다 A mountain rises 〔towers〕 high. / 그 애는 반에서 ～한 존재다 He stands head and shoulders above the other students in the class.

**우뚝우뚝** so that all are high 〔tall, towering〕. ～하다 be all high 〔tall, lofty, towering〕. ¶ 그 도시엔 굴뚝이 ～ 서 있다 The town bristles with chimneys.

**우라늄** 〖화학〗 uranium (기호 U, Ur).
◉ ～광 uranium ore. ～탄 〖군사〗 a uranium shell. 천연～ natural uranium.

**우락부락** rudely; roughly; wildly; harshly. ～하다 (be) rough; rude; harsh; wild. ¶ ～한 행동 impolite behavior / ～한 사람 a rough fellow / ～ 말하다 talk rudely / ～한 말을 하다 utter wild words / ～하게 굴다 behave rudely.

**우랄** 〖지리〗 Ural; Uralic. ◉ ～산맥 the Ural Mountains; the Urals. ～어족 the Uralic languages.

**우람하다, 우람스럽다** ¶ 우람스러운 모습 a dignified figure 〔pose〕.

**우량**(雨量) (a) rainfall; 〖기상〗 precipitation. ¶ 서울의 연간 평균 ～ the average annual rainfall in Seoul / ～이 많은〔적은〕 지역 a region of high 〔low〕 rainfall / 어제의 ～은 15밀리였다 Yesterday we had fifteen milimeters of rain. / ～이 적어서 저수지의 물이 줄었다 Lack of rain sank the reservoirs.
◉ ～계 a rain gauge; a hyetometer; a pluviometer. ～측정 pluviometry.

**우량**(優良) superiority; excellence. ～하다 (be) superior; excellent; fine. ¶ ～한 성적 an excellent result.
◉ ～기업 a blue chip company. ～도서 best 〔excellent〕 books 《of the year》. ～아 a superior child; a physically perfect child. ～종 a good breed: ～종의 highbred / ～종의 말 a horse of fine breed; a thoroughbred. ～주(株) blue chips; gilt-edged 〔superior〕 stocks; blue-chip stocks. ～품 articles of superior quality 〔grade〕; a choice lot: 최상의 ～품 superfine 〔extra-fine〕 goods.

**우러나다** soak out; come off. ¶ 짠맛이 우러나도록 생선을 물에 담그다 put a salted fish in water and leave it until the saltiness soaks out / 이 차는 잘 우러나지 않는다 This tea doesn't draw well.

**우러나오다** spring 〔well〕 up. ¶ 진정에서 우러나온 연설 a speech that came from *one's* heart / 진심에서 우러나오는 감사의 말 words of thanks from the bottom of *one's* heart.

**우러러보다** ① 《높은 데를》 look up 《at》; lift 〔raise〕 the eyes; look upward. ¶ 하늘을 ～ look up at the sky; raise *one's* eyes to heaven. ② 《사람을》 look up 《to》; respect. ¶ 스승으로 ～ look up to 《*a person*》 as *one's* teacher / 모두 그를 정치 지도자로 우러러보았다 He was looked up to as a political leader. / 사람들은 그를 국가의 기둥으로 우러러보았다 People looked up to him as a pillar of the state.

**우러르다** ① 《쳐들다》 lift *one's* head up. ② 《마음으로》 have (deep) respect 《for》; look up 《to》; revere 《God》.

**우럭우럭** flaring up; actively; furiously;

《술기운이》 flushingly. ¶ 술기운이 얼굴에 ~ 오르다 *one's* face flushes up with wine.

**우렁쉥이** 〖동물〗 an ascidian; a sea squirt.

**우렁우렁** thundering; rumbling; thumping. ~하다 thunder; rumble; thump. ¶ ~ 울리다 rumble; roll.

**우렁이** 〖조개류〗 a mud 〔pond〕 snail. ¶ 그의 마음은 우렁잇속 같다 He has an inscrutable mind.

**우렁차다** ① 《소리가》 (be) resounding; resonant; sonorous; rotund. ¶ 우렁찬 목소리 a rotund voice / 우렁차게 국가를 불렀다 We sang the national anthem with a sonorous voice. ② 《우람차다》 (be) imposing; impressive; grand; magnificent.

**우레** ① 《꿩을 부르는》 a birdcall 〔whistle〕 used to lure pheasants. ¶ ~(를) 켜다 imitate a pheasant call. ② 《천둥》 thunder. ¶ ~같은 thunderous / ~와 같은 박수 a thunder 〔storm〕 of applause / ~와 같은 환성(歡聲) thundering 〔vociferous〕 cheers. ◉ 우렛소리 a peal of thunder; the roll of thunder: 우렛소리가 나다 it thunders; the thunder rolls.

**우려**(憂慮) worry; anxiety; concern; apprehensions; solicitude 《about》. ~하다 fear; worry 《about, over》; be anxious 〔concerned〕 about; dread; be apprehensive 《of》; be troubled 《about》. ¶ ~해야 할 serious; worrying; alarming; grave / ~할 사태 a grievous 〔grave〕 situation 〔consequence〕 / 매우 ~할 만한 일 a matter of grave concern 〔great anxiety〕 / ~하는 태도로 with an air of concern / 사태에 대하여 ~하다 worry over the situation; view the situation with apprehension 〔concern〕 / 실업 문제는 매우 ~할 만한 사태에 이르렀다 The problem of unemployment has assumed very serious dimensions.

**우려내다, 우려먹다** ① 《억지로 얻어 내다》 extort; squeeze 《money》 out of 《*a person*》; screw. ¶ 돈을 ~ exact 〔wring, extort, squeeze〕 money 《from *a person*》 / 그는 그녀로부터 많은 돈을 우려냈다 He screwed 〔cheated〕 her out of a lot of money. ② exude; ooze (out); 《차를》 boil down 〔brew〕; make an infusion of; 《약을》 decoct; make a decoction of; 《떫은 맛을》 remove 《the astingency of persimmons》.

**우련하다** (be) obscure; dim; vague. ⇨ 아련하다. ¶ 우련하게 dimly; mistily; indistinctly; obscurely / 우련하게 나타나다 loom; appear indistinctly.

**우로**(雨露) the rain and the dew. ¶ ~를 막다 shelter *oneself* from the weather.

**우론**(愚論) a foolish opinion; an absurd view.

**우롱**(愚弄) mockery; derision; ridicule; scoff. ~하다 mock 《at》; ridicule; deride; fool; make a fool 〔fun〕 《of *a person*》; poke fun at; jeer 《at》; taunt. ¶ 나를 ~치 말라 Don't make fun of me. / 사람을 ~하는 짓은 그만해라 No more of your ridicule. / 그것은 전적으로 독자를 ~하는 짓이다 It is simply trifling with the readers.

**우루과이** 《나라 이름》 Uruguay. ¶ ~의 Uruguayan. ◉ ~ 라운드(무역협정) the Uruguay Round (trade pact). ~ 사람 an Uruguayan.

**우르르** ① 《물 끓는 소리》 simmering; boiling (up noisily). ¶ 물이 ~ 끓기 시작한다 The water begins to simmer. ② 《무너지는 소리》 clattering. ¶ 지붕이 ~허물어졌다 The roof came down with a clatter. ③ 《무더기로》 all in a heap; all over. ¶ ~ (겹쳐) 쓰러지다 fall down one upon another; fall 〔be knocked〕 over like ninepins / 담이 ~ 넘어지다 a wall falls over all in a heap / 사과가 자루에서 ~ 쏟아지다 apples tumble out of a sack all over. ④ 《여럿이》 all at once; rushingly; in a crowd; all in a group; stampeding. ¶ 병아리들이 ~ 달아나다 chicks run away all at once / 아이들이 학교에서 ~ 몰려 나왔다 Children poured out of the school all in one group. / 그들은 ~ 그 방으로 들어갔다 They poured noisily into the room. / 사람들이 여배우한테로 ~ 달려갔다 A crowd of people rushed the actress. ⑤ 《천둥소리》 rumbling; thundering; rolling; booming. ¶ ~ 울리다 roll; rumble; boom; thunder; grumble / 먼데서 천둥소리가 ~ 났다 The thunder boomed 〔rolled〕 in the distance.

**우리**[1] 《짐승의》 a cage (맹수의); 《가축의》 a pen; a corral; a fold (양의); a hutch (토끼 등 작은 동물의); a pigsty (돼지의). ¶ 호랑이를 ~에 가두다 cage a tiger.

**우리**[2] [인칭대명사] we; 《나》 I; 《우리의》 our; my; 《우리를·우리에게》 us; me; 《우리 것》 ours; mine; 《우리 자신》 ourselves; myself. ¶ ~ 한국인 we Koreans / ~들 일동 all of us / ~집〔아버지〕 my house 〔father〕 / ~ 집사람 my wife / ～끼리의 이야깁니다만 between ourselves〔you and me〕/ 한국의 첫번째 인공 위성 ～별 1호 Korea's first satellite, Uribyŏl〔Our Star〕No 1. ◉ ～말 our language; our mother tongue; the vernacular; Korean. ～사주 조합 the employee stock ownership association.

**우리 나라** our country〔land, nation〕. ¶ ～의 무역 our foreign trade / ～의 당면한 위기 a crisis facing this nation of ours.

**우리다** ① 《물에》 soak 《out》; steep; remove; take out. ¶ 도라지의 쓴맛을 ～ soak the bitterness out of broad bell=flower roots / 감을 ～ sweeten〔remove the astringency of〕persimmons. ② 《때리다》 slap hard. ¶ 빰을 ～ slap 《*a person*》 on the cheek.

**우마**(牛馬) cattle and horses. ¶ ～처럼 혹사하다 work 《*a person*》 like a beast of burden; work〔drive〕《*a person*》 hard.

**우매**(愚昧) stupidity and ignorance; asininity; imbecility; idiocy. ～하다 (be) stupid and ignorant; thick-headed; dumb 《미》; asinine; silly; imbecile; unenlightened; benighted; uncivilized. ¶ ～한 사람 a stupid and ignorant person / ～한 행동 a folly; a foolish move〔act〕; an act of folly / 그가 그런 거짓말을 하다니, 참 ～한 사람이군 It is very stupid of him to tell such a lie.

**우먼** a woman. ◉ ～리브 women's lib〔women's liberation〕《movement》. ～파워 woman power.

**우멍거지** a foreskin-covered adult penis; 〖의학〗 phimosis. ＝포경(包莖).

**우멍하다** be sunken in.

**우모**(羽毛) a feather; a plume; [총칭] feathering; plumage. ¶ ～ 있는 feathered.

**우무** gelidium jelly. ⇨ 한천.

**우묵-** ⇨ 오목-.

**우문**(愚問) a stupid〔silly〕question. ◉ ～우답 a silly dialog(ue). ～현답 a wise answer to a silly question.

**우물** a well. ¶ 깊게 판 ～ a deep-drilled well / ～ 안 개구리 a man of narrow outlook; "a big frog in a little pool" / ～가에서 at the well; by the side of the well / ～을 치다〔파다〕 clean〔dig, drill〕a well / 두레박으로 ～의 물을 긷다 draw water from a well with a bucket / ～을 파도 한 우물을 파라 《속담》 A rolling stone gathers no moss. *or* Success comes to him who can stick to his pursuit. / ～에서 숭늉 찾는다 《속담》 He seeks wool on an ass. ◉ ～가 공론 a house-wives' gossip (over the garden fence). ～귀신 the spirit of 《*a person*》 drowned in a well: ～귀신이 되다 drown *oneself* in a well. ～물 well water.

**우물거리다**[1] 《떼가》 squirm; swarm; be alive with 《fish》. ¶ 벌레가 ～ worms swarm.

**우물거리다**[2] 《말을》 mumble; mump.

**우물우물**[1] 《떼가》 in a swarm.

**우물우물**[2] 《입속에서》 mumblingly.

**우물지다** ① 《보조개가》 dimple. ¶ 그녀는 웃으면 볼에 우물이 진다 She has a dimple when she smiles. ② 《우묵해지다》 form a「dimple〔hollow〕《in》. ¶ 비가 와서 땅이 우물졌다 The rain formed small hollows in the ground.

**우물쭈물** vaguely; indistinctly; hesitantly; indecisively; half-heartedly. ～하다 be indecisive; be hesitant; be tardy〔slow〕(꾸물거리다); hesitate; 《구어》 dillydally; shilly-shally. ¶ ～ 말하다 speak ambiguously; equivocate; speak hesitantly; do not commit *oneself* / ～ 일하다 do a slow job; do a job half=heartedly; scamp *one's* work / ～하다가 기회를 놓치다 dally away *one's* opportunity / ～하지 마라 No hanging back! / ～하고 있을 때가 아니다 There is no time to lose. / 그는 ～ 농담으로 돌리려고 하였다 He tried to turn it off as a joke.

**우뭇가사리** 〖식물〗 an agar-agar.

**우미**(優美) prominent〔outstanding, superior〕beauty; grace; elegance. ～하다 (be) outstandingly beautiful; graceful; elegant.

**우민**(愚民) ignorant〔uninformed〕people; the unlettered masses. ¶ 국민을 ～ 취급하다 regard the people as ignorant. ◉ ～화 정책 an obscurantist policy.

**우민**(憂悶) worry; agony. ～하다 worry; be worried〔troubled〕; agonize; be agonized; be in agony.

**우박**(雨雹) hail; a hailstorm; 《한 알》 a hailstone. ¶ 별안간에 오는 ～ a sudden hailstorm / ～에 의한 농작물의 피해 the damage done to the farm crops by a hailstorm / ～이 오다 it hails / ～이 쏟아져 밭 채소가 피해를 입었다 Vegetables in the field suffered damage from a hailstorm.

**우발**(偶發) accidental〔incidental〕occurrence. ～하다 happen accidentally; occur〔come about〕by chance. ¶ ～

적 accidental; casual; 〚법〛 contingent / ～적으로 accidentally / ～적인 일이 없는 한 unless something unforeseen happens 〔occurs〕 / 그것은 ～적인 사건이었다 It was an accident.

◉ ～사건 an accident; a contingency; a chance occurrence; a happening. ～성(性) contingency. ～전쟁 an accidental warfare. ～증상 〚의학〛 an epiphenomenon (*pl.* -na). ～채무 contingent liabilities.

**우방**(友邦) a friendly nation 〔country〕.

**우범**(虞犯) liability to crime.

◉ ～자 a person liable to committing crime. ～지역 a crime-ridden area; a crime-prone area; the spots vulnerable to various crimes.

**우변**(右邊) (the edge on) the right side.

**우보전술**(牛步戰術) snail's-pace tactics; stalling 〔delaying, stonewalling, slow-motion〕 tactics. ¶ 그들은 논쟁 중인 PKO 법안의 통과를 지연시키기 위한 ～을 포기하기로 결정했다 They decided to drop stalling tactics to delay the passage of the controversial PKO bill.

**우부**(愚夫) a stupid fellow; a foolish man.

**우부**(愚婦) a stupid 〔foolish〕 woman.

**우부룩하다** (be) dense; thick. ¶ 뜰에는 잡초가 ～ The weeds are thick in the garden. *or* The garden is thick with weeds.

**우비**(雨備) rainwear; a raincoat (비옷); an umbrella (우산). ¶ 고무 입힌 ～ an Indian-rubber 〔a water-proof〕 raincoat / ～를 준비하다 prepare for rain / ～를 입다 put on a raincoat.

**우비다** poke; scrape 〔scoop, gouge〕 out; bore; pick. ¶ 콧구멍을 ～ pick *one's* nose / 귀를 ～ clean *one's* ears / 땅에 구멍을 우벼파다 scrape out hole in the ground / 담뱃대를 ～ poke a pipe.

**우비어넣다** twist 《*a thing*》 into 《a hole》; force in. ¶ 구멍에 막대기를～ twist a stick into a hole.

**우비어파다** scoop out; hollow out; scrape out; gouge; carve. ⇨ 우비다. ¶ 벽에 구멍을 ～ bore a hole in the wall.

**우비적거리다** keep poking 〔scraping out, boring, picking〕. ¶ 귀를 ～ pick *one's* ear incessantly.

**우빙**(雨氷) silver thaw; sleet; glaze 《미》; glazed frost 《영》.

**우사**(牛舍) a cowshed; a cowhouse.

**우산**(雨傘) an umbrella. ¶ ～을 받다〔쓰다〕 put up an umbrella; hold an umbrella / ～을 펴다 open 〔spread〕 an umbrella / ～을 접다 close 〔shut〕 an umbrella / ～을 같이 받고 가다 go 〔walk〕 under the same umbrella; share an umbrella 《with》 / 바람에 ～이 뒤집혔다 The wind turned 〔blew〕 my umbrella inside out.

◉ ～걸음 walking with a bounce. ～꽂이 an umbrella stand. ～대 the handle of an umbrella. ～살 umbrella ribs 〔frames〕. 핵～ the nuclear umbrella: 핵～ 밑에 under the shelter of 《the U.S.》 nuclear umbrella.

**우산이끼**(雨傘—) 〚식물〛 a (common) liverwort.

**우상**(羽狀) ¶ ～의 pinnate. ◉ ～엽 〚식물〛 a pinnate leaf.

**우상**(偶像) an idol; an icon; an image. ¶ ～화하다 idolize; idolatrize; make an idol 《of》 / ～을 파괴하다 break 〔smash, throw down〕 an idol / 젊은이의 ～이 되다 be an idol of the young people.

◉ ～숭배 idol worship; idolatry; iconolatry: ～숭배자 an idol worshipper; an idolater. ～파괴 iconoclasm: ～파괴자 an iconoclast.

**우색**(憂色) a worried 〔an anxious〕 look; a melancholy 〔gloomy〕 air. ¶ ～을 띠다 wear a worried look; look concerned 〔anxious, worried〕.

**우생**(優生) ¶ ～의 eugenic.

◉ ～결혼 a eugenic marriage. ～보호법 the eugenic protection law. ～학 eugenics: ～학상으로 eugenically / ～학자 a eugenist.

**우선**(優先) preference; priority; precedence. ～하다 be prior 《to》; have priority 《to, over》; take precedence 《over, of》. ¶ ～적(으로) preferential(-ly) / 공익은 사익에 ～한다 Public interest takes precedence of private interest. *or* Consideration is given to public interest before private interest. / 다른 법률의 규정과 모순될 경우는 이법률의 규정이 ～한다 When there is a contradictory stipulation in another law, the provisions of this law shall control. / 회원은 ～적으로 입장할 수있다 Members are given admission preference. / 이들 문제는 다른 것보다 ～되어야 한다 These questions should take precedence over the others. / 재해 발생시에는 인명 구조가 모든 일에 ～되어야 한다 Saving lives should be the first consideration when a disaster happens.

◉ ～감시대상국 〚경제〛 a priority watch

list (생략 PWL). ~배당 preference 〔preferred〕 dividends. ~사항 a priority item 〔matter〕: 최~사항 a matter of the highest priority; a top priority. ~순위 the priority order; the order of priority: ~순위처리 〖컴퓨터〗 priority processing. ~주(株) preferred stocks 《미》; preference share 《영》. ~협상대상국 priority foreign countries (생략 PFC).

**우선**(于先) 《첫째로》 first (of all); in the first place; before 〔above〕 everything; to begin with; for a start; 《좌우간》 anyway; anyhow. ¶ ~ …부터 하다 begin by …ing / ~이것을 해 치워야 한다 We must get this done first. / ~ 한숨 돌리고 보자 Let's take a rest first, at any rate. / 이쯤되면 ~은 안심이다 Well, we seem to be out of danger now. / ~ 물건이나 봅시다 Let me see the article anyway. / ~ 여러분께 진심으로 감사의 말씀을 드려야겠습니다 First of all, I must express my heartfelt thanks to you.

**우선권**(優先權) (the right of) priority 〔preference〕; a preferential 〔prior〕 right; precedence; the first claim. ¶ 통행의 ~ the right of way / ~이 있다, ~을 가지다 have priority (rights) 《to, over》; have preference 《to》; have the prior claim 《to》 / ~을 얻다 acquire a priority; take precedence 《over, of》; acquire the first claim to / ~을 주다 give priority 《to》; give 〔afford, offer〕 preference 《to》.

**우성**(優性) 〖생물〗 (genetic) dominance. ¶ ~의 법칙 the law of dominance. ◉ ~유전 prepotency. ~인자 a dominant gene. ~형질(形質) a dominant character.

**우세** ~하다 be put to shame; be humiliated; be sneered 《at》. ~스럽다 (be) humiliating.

**우세**(優勢) superiority; superior power; ascendancy; (pre)dominance; preponderance. ~하다 (be) superior; ascendant; predominant; leading. ¶ ~를 유지하다 maintain a superior position; hold the advantage 〔the edge〕 《over》; hold the upper hand 《of》 / 수에 있어 ~하다 be superior in numbers 《to the enemy》 / ~해지다 rise to predominance 《over》; become dominant; 《경기에서》 lead; 《토론 등에서》 gain ground / 지금 어느 팀이 ~하냐 Which team is leading now? / 그 후보자는 처음부터 ~했다 The candidate led from the first.

**우송**(郵送) mailing; sending by mail 〔post〕. ~하다 mail 《미》; post 《영》; send by mail 〔post〕. ¶ 책을 ~하다 send a book by mail 〔post〕 / 은행 카드는 별도로 ~해 드리겠습니다 We'll send your bank card by separate mail 〔post〕. ◉ ~료 postage 《on》. ~무료 postfree; postage free.

**우수**(雨水) ① 《빗물》 rain water. ② 《절기》 the second of the 24 seasonal divisions (=c. 18 Feb.).

**우수**(偶數) an even number. ⇨ 짝수. ¶ ~의 even(-numbered).

**우수**(憂愁) melancholy; gloom. ¶ ~의 melancholy; gloomy / ~의 빛 a melancholy air / ~에 잠기다 be oppressed with sorrow; be sunk in grief.

**우수**(優秀) excellence; superiority; predominance. ~하다 (be) predominant; superior; excellent. ¶ ~한 학생 a brilliant student / ~한 교사 a teacher of superior ability / ~한 성적을 올리다 achieve excellent results; gain 〔earn〕 high marks; make an excellent record / 그는 어느 방면의 학문에도 ~했다 There was no branch of learning in which he did not distinguish himself.
◉ ~성 excellency; prowess. ~팀 a crack team. 최~선수 the most valuable player (생략 MVP).

**우수리** ① 《거스름돈》 (money returned in) change. ¶ 백 원 ~를 주다〔받다〕 give 〔get〕 one hundred won change / ~는 네가 가져라 Keep 〔You can keep〕 the change. *or* Never mind the change. ② 《끝수》 a fraction; an odd sum (금액의). ¶ ~를 떨(어버리)다 omit 〔round off〕 fractions; round out 《the number》 / ~ 15원을 빼고 100원으로 하시오 Take off the odd fifteen won and make it a round hundred.

**우수수** 《fall, scatter》 in a multitude; in great masses; rustling down. ¶ 바람에 나뭇잎이 ~ 떨어졌다 A gust of wind shook a multitude of leaves off the trees.

**우스개** comicality; drollery; jocularity. ¶ ~로 삼다 make fun 〔sport〕 of; turn 《*a thing*》 into ridicule; laugh away 《*something*》. ◉ 우스갯소리 a joke; a jest: 우스갯소리를 하다 crack 〔make〕 a joke; joke; jest. 우스갯짓 clownery; drollery; waggery: 우스갯짓을 하다 play the fool; play droll trick.

**우스꽝스럽다** 《익살맞다》 (be) funny;

ludicrous; comic(al); laughable; 《바보스럽다》 (be) ridiculous; absurd. ¶ 우스꽝스러운 이야기 a funny story; a laughter-provoking story / 우스꽝스러운 짓을 하다 play the fool; play droll tricks; make a spectacle of *oneself*.

**우습게 보다** 《경멸》 look on with contempt; look down upon; disdain; slight; despise; belittle; 《경시》 make [think] little [light] of; do not think much of; hold 《*a person*》 cheap. ¶ 남의 학식을 ~ underrate another's scholarship / 아무를 ~ look down upon *a person* / 상관을 ~ be disrespectful to *one's* superior / 돈을 ~ make [think] light of money / 어린애라고 그를 우습게 보지 마시오 Don't underestimate him, just because he is a boy. / 그의 말을 우습게 볼 수 없다 What he says is not to be trifled with.

**우습다** ① 《재미있다》 (be) funny; amusing; 《가소롭다》 (be) laughing; laughable; ridiculous; absurd; ludicrous; droll; 《익살맞다》 (be) comic; 《기이하다》 (be) strange; unusual; singular; queer; funny; grotesque. ¶ 우스운 이야기 a funny story / 우스운 모습으로 in a funny style / 우스워 죽겠다 be tickled to death / 우습게 들리다 sound funny / 우스워하다 be amused [tickled] 《at》 / 우스운 것을 참다 refrain from laughter; keep a straight face / 뭣이 그리 우스우냐 What's so funny? / 참 우습기도 하다 How ridiculous! / 그런 이야기를 내가 믿을 줄 알고, 참 ~ It is ridiculous to expect me to believe such stories. / 이 거울로 보면 얼굴이 비뚤어져서 우습게 보인다 This mirror distorts *one's* features in a grotesque way.
② 《하찮다》 (be) trifling; trivial; small; 《쉽다》 (be) easy. ¶ 우스운 일 small [trifling] matters; (mere) trifles; a mere nothing / 우스운 일로 서로 다투다 argue with each other about a mere nothing / 우습게 여길 일이 아니다 It is not a small matter. *or* It is not an easy job.

**우승**(優勝) a victory; a championship. ~하다 win [capture] the victory [championship, 《미》 pennant, title]; come off [out] winner [victorious, the victor]. ¶ 연속 ~을 노리다 gun for *one's* second straight title / ~권 안[밖]에 있다 be in [out] of the winning / 그녀는 테니스에서 ~했다 She won [obtained] the tennis championship. / 그는 그 경주에서 ~했다 He came out victorious in the race. / 우리는 한 게임차로 ~을 놓쳤다 We lost the pennant by one game.
◉ ~결정전 a deciding match [contest] in a competition for a cup [pennant]. ~기 a pennant; a championship banner. ~다툼 a competition for victory; a pennant race; a flag chase. ~배[컵] a championship cup; a trophy; a cup. ~자 the (championship) winner. ~팀 the winning team. ~후보 the favorite [hopeful, top choice] for the championship; the best bet for the title. 개인[단체]~ the individual [team] championship. 준~ coming out second best.

**우승열패**(優勝劣敗) the survival of the fittest. ~하다 "the superior gains and the inferior loses"; the fittest survives; the weakest goes to the wall. ¶ ~는 세상사다 The survival of the fittest is the way of the world.

**우시장**(牛市場) a cattle market.

**우심하다**(尤甚—) (be) extreme; excessive; 《추위가》 (be) more severe; 《손해가》 (be) heavier.

**우썩** 《눈에 띄게》 markedly; considerably; very much; 《빠르게》 rapidly; 《힘있게》 vigorously; 《단번에》 all at once; 《갑자기》 all of a sudden. ¶ ~ 수가 늘다 increase markedly / 영어 회화 능력이 ~ 늘다 make rapid [much] progress in speaking English / ~ 추워지다 become [grow] 「very much [considerably] cold / ~우썩 자라다 《키가》 grow taller and taller / 요즘 형은 체중이 ~ 줄었다 My brother has lost a lot of weight lately. / 아버지는 백발이 ~ 늘고 있다 My father's hair is rapidly turning gray.

**우아**(優雅) elegance; grace(fulness); refinement. ~하다 (be) elegant; graceful; refined; polished.

> [용법] **elegant** 인위적인 우아함. **graceful** 자연 그대로의 우아함. **refined** 세련된 우아함. **polished** 스스로 단련시켜 익힌 우아함.

¶ ~하게 elegantly; gracefully / ~한 모습 a graceful figure [appearance] / ~한 문체 an elegant style / 태도가 ~하다 be elegant [graceful] in manners / ~하게 춤추다 dance gracefully [with grace].

**우아** ① 《기쁠 때》 Hurrah!; Oh joy!;

Goody-goody! ② ⇨ 와[1].

**우악스럽다**(愚惡—) (be) ferocious; cruel; atrocious; violent; wild; rough; rude. ¶ 우악스러운 사람 a rough fellow / 우악스럽게 생기다 have a ferocious look / 우악스럽게 다루다 handle 《*a thing*》 roughly / 그는 말버릇이 ～ He is rough-spoken.

**우안**(右岸) the right bank 《of a river》.

**우애**(友愛) 《형제의》 brotherliness; fraternity; 《친구의》 friendship; comradeship; fellowship. ¶ ～의 정 a friendly feeling / ～의 정신 the spirit of fraternity / ～롭다 be friendly; be brotherly. ◉ ～결혼 (a) companionate marriage.

**우어** 《마소를 멈출 때》 Whoa!

**우언**(寓言) an apologue; an allegory; a fable.

**우엉** 〖식물〗 a burdock; a cocklebur(r).

**우여**《새 쫓는 소리》 Shoo!

**우여곡절**(迂餘曲折) meandering; twists and turns; 《파란》 vicissitudes; 《착잡》 complications. ¶ 인생의 ～ the vicissitudes of life; the ups and downs of life / 많은 ～을 겪은뒤에 after much meandering; after many twists and turns / 교섭이 성립되기까지는 ～이 많았다 Agreement was reached after much complications.

**우역**(牛疫) cattle disease 〔epidemic〕.

**우연**(偶然) (a) chance; accident; fortuity. ～하다 (be) accidental; casual; incidental; fortuitous.
¶ ～히 accidentally; casually; incidentally; by accident; by chance; by haphazard / ～한 일치 a (strange) coincidence / ～한 만남 a chance meeting / ～히 알게 된 사람 a chance 〔casual〕 acquaintance / ～히 만나다 meet 《*a person*》 by chance; come 〔run〕 across / 그것은 단지 ～한 일〔사건〕이다 It is nothing but a mere accident. / 그의 성공은 결코 ～이 아니다 It is surely no accident that he succeeded (in life). / 그 말을 ～히 들었다 I happened to hear it. / 우리는 ～히 같은 차에 탔다 We just happened to take the same train. / 내가 거기서 그를 만난 것은 ～이었다 It was by mere chance that I met him there.

**우열**(優劣) superiority or inferiority; relative merits 〔superiority〕; comparative merits and demerits. ¶ ～의 법칙 〖유전〗 the law of dominance / ～이 없는 경주〔겨루기〕 a close contest; a level race / ～이 없는 level; even; equal; evenly matched / ～을 겨루다 contend 〔strive〕 for superiority; struggle for mastery / ～을 논하다 discuss the relative merits 《of A and B》 / ～을 매기다 put 〔place〕 《one thing》 above 《the other》; discriminate 《between A and B, in favor of A against B》 / 양자간에 ～은 거의 없다 There is little to choose between the two. / 이 신형차와 저 헌차와의 ～은 어떤가 How does this late-model car compare with that old one?

**우왕좌왕**(右往左往) ～하다 go this way and that; run about in confusion; rush about to no purpose. ¶ 출구가 어디인지 몰라서 우리는 ～했다 We moved around this way and that, not knowing where the exit was.

**우울**(憂鬱) gloom; depression; low spirit; melancholy; the blues 《미구어》; the dumps 《구어》. ～하다 (be) gloomy; melancholy; depressed; low spirited; sullen. ¶ ～한 날씨 gloomy weather / ～한 기분으로 with a heavy heart; in a depressed mood; in a melancholy frame of mind / ～해지다 be seized with melancholia; feel blue 〔gloomy, low〕; get in the dumps 《구어》 / ～하게 하다 give 《*a person*》 a melancholy feeling; make 《*a person*》 melancholy; cast a gloom on 《*a person*》 / ～한 얼굴을 짓다 look blue 〔depressed〕; pull 〔wear, put on〕 a long face / 그녀는 ～한 얼굴을 하고 있었다 She had a gloomy look on her face. / 오늘은 왠지 ～하다 I'm feeling rather blue today. *or* I'm rather depressed today. / 비오는 날이면 늘 ～해진다 Rainy weather always depresses me.
◉ ～증〔병〕 melancholy; mental depression; melancholia; hypochondria: ～증 환자 a hypochondriac; a melancholiac.

**우월**(優越) superiority; predominance; supremacy. ～하다 (be) superior 《to》; supreme; preponderant; surpassing. ¶ 그들이 우리보다 수적으로 ～하다 They are superior to us in numbers.
◉ ～감 a sense 〔feeling〕 of superiority; 〖심리〗 a superiority complex: ～감을 품다〔갖다〕 feel 〔have a sense of〕 *one's* own superiority 《to 〔over〕 *a person*》 / ～감을 꺾다 wound 《*a person's*》 pride.

**우위**(優位) superiority 《over》; predominance 《over》; a high 〔higher〕 position. ¶ 무관 ～ the superiority of military service 《to civil service》 / 군사적 ～를 확보하려는 정책 the policy aimed at gaining military superiority 《over》/ ~에 있다〔서다〕 have 〔gain〕 the superiority 《over》; have 〔win, gain〕 an advantage 《over》; 《지위가》 have a better position 《than》/ 힘의 ~를 유지하다 maintain the 「superiority in strength 〔the upper hand in power〕 《over》/ (힘의) ~를 확보하다 secure the superiority (in strength) 《over》/ 그 나라는 군사력에서 한국보다 ~에 서 있다 The country is superior to Korea in military power. / 토론에서는 그녀가 처음부터 ~에 섰다 She got the upper hand in the debate from the beginning. / 체력면에서는 그가 우리보다 단연 ~에 있다 His strength gives him a decided advantage over us.

**우유**(牛乳) (cow's) milk. ¶ ~를 살균하다 pasteurize milk / ~를 짜다 milk (a cow) / 아기를 ~로 기르다 raise a baby on cow's milk; bring up a baby on the bottle / ~를 배달하다 deliver milk. ◉ ~배달원 a milkman. ~배달차〔운반차〕 a milk wagon 〔cart〕. ~병 a milk bottle. 탈지~ skim milk.

**우유부단**(優柔不斷) irresolution; indecisiveness; indetermination; vacillation; hesitation. ~하다 (be) irresolute; indecisive; vacillating; wavering; shilly-shally; hesitant. ¶ 그는 ~한 사람이다 He is an irresolute man 〔a waverer〕. *or* He does not know his own mind.

**우음마식**(牛飮馬食) ~하다 drink like a fish and eat like a wolf; be immoderate in eating and drinking.

**우의**(友誼) friendship; friendly relations; amity. ¶ 따뜻한 ~ a good 〔warm〕 friendship / ~ 있는 amicable; friendly / ~로써 with friendship; in a friendly manner / ~로 봐서 being on friendly terms / ~를 맺다 form a friendship 《with》; make friends 《with》/ ~가 돈독하다 be a kind 〔warm〕 friend 《to》/ ~를 깨뜨리다 violate friendship / ~를 두터이 하다 promote friendly relations 《with》.

**우의**(雨衣) a raincoat. =비옷.

**우이**(牛耳) 《우두머리》 the leader; the head; 《쇠귀》 the ears of an ox; ox-ear. ◉ ~독경 《속담》 "preaching to deaf ears."

**우익**(右翼) 《정치상의》 the right wing 〔faction〕; 《사람》 right-wingers; rightists; 《대열》 the right flank 〔column〕; 《우측》 the right-hand side; 〖야구〗 the right field. ◉ ~단체 a right-wing organization. ~수 〖야구〗 a right fielder. ~운동 a Rightist movement; the movement of the Right. ~정당 the Right Wing; a Right group; the Rightists.

**우인**(友人) a friend; a companion; [총칭] company. =벗, 친구.

**우자**(愚者) a stupid person; a simpleton; a fool; a dunce; an idiot.

**우장**(雨裝) rain gear; rainwear; a rain outfit; a raincoat.

**우적우적** ① = 우썩. ② 《씹는 소리·모양》 munching; crunching. ¶ 오이 김치를 ~ 씹어 먹다 munch cucumber pickles. ③ 《무너지는 소리·모양》 creaking; squeaking. ¶ 울타리가 ~ 넘어간다 The fence is giving way with creaks.

**우정**(友情) = 우의(友誼).

**우정**(郵政) postal services 〔administration〕.

**우주**(宇宙) the universe; the cosmos; (outer) space.

> **용법** **the universe** 「존재하는 모든 것」을 의미하며 물질·현상 등의 총체로서의 우주. **the cosmos** chaos(혼돈)에 반대되는 질서와 조화의 체계로서의 우주. **space** 지구의 대기권 밖, 천체와 천체 사이의 무한한 공간으로서의 우주.

¶ ~의 universal; cosmic / ~의 신비 the mystery of space / ~ 중계로 via communication satellite / ~를 탐험하다 explore space / ~를 여행하다 go on a journey into space; travel into space / 인간을 ~에 보내다 launch a man in 〔into〕 space / 태양, 달, 별은 ~의 일부이다 The sun, moon, and stars are all part of the universe. ◉ ~개발경쟁 a space race. ~개발계획 a space development project 〔program〕. ~공간 (outer) space. ~공학 space engineering. ~공항 a spaceport. ~과학 space science. ~과학자 a space scientist. ~관 a 〔*one's*〕 vision of the universe. ~국제법 the international law of outer space. ~대폭발 생성론 the big-bang theory. ~로켓 a space 〔cosmic〕 rocket. ~무한 팽창설 the steady-state theory. ~물리(학) space physics. ~병 space sickness; space adaptation syndrome. ~병기 a space weapon. ~복 a space 〔pressure〕 suit. ~비행 a space flight. ~비행사 an astronaut 《미》; a spaceman 〔spacewoman〕; a cosmonaut 《러》. ~산업 the (aero-)space industry. ~생물학 exobiology; space biology. ~선(線) the cosmic ray; 〖수학〗 the world line.

~선(船) a space ship 〔craft, capsule〕: 유인〔무인〕 ~선 a manned 〔an unmanned〕 spacecraft. ~소설 a space fiction. ~속도 《궤도에 진입하기 위한》 orbital velocity; 《대기권을 벗어나기 위한》 escape velocity. ~시대 the space 〔cosmic〕 age. ~식 space food; food for astronauts. ~실험실 a space lab; a skylab. ~여행 space 〔interplanetary〕 travel; a journey into space. ~연구 space research. ~왕복선 a space shuttle. ~위성 a space satellite. ~유영〔산책〕 a spacewalk: ~유영을 하다 take 〔make〕 a spacewalk; walk in space. ~의학 space medicine. ~인 a spaceman; 《가상의 우주 생명체》 a visitor from (outer) space; an alien. ~인력 universal gravitation. ~자기 cosmic magnetism. ~정류장 a space 〔satellite〕 station; an interplanetary station. ~중계 a satellite relay. ~지리학 spatiography. ~진(입자) cosmic dust (particles). ~진화론 cosmogony. ~총 a space gun; a jet gun. ~탐색기 a space prove. ~탐험 space exploration. ~통신 space communications. ~학, ~론 cosmology: ~학자 a cosmologist. ~항공학 astronautics; cosmonautics. ~항법 astronautics; space navigation. ~협정 a space agreement. ~화학 cosmochemistry.

**우줄거리다** ⇨ 우쭐거리다.

**우중**(雨中) ¶ ~에 in the rain; while raining / ~에도 불구하고 in spite of the rain / ~에 나가다 go out in the rain.

**우중충하다** (be) gloomy; somber; dismal; dark and dull. ¶ 우중충한 날씨 dismal 〔gloomy〕 weather / 우중충한 방 a gloomy room / 우중충한 청색 sordid blue.

**우지**(牛脂) beef tallow 〔fat〕; suet.

**우지끈** with a snap 〔smash〕; crackling. ¶ 나뭇가지를 ~ 꺾다 break a twig with a snap / ~ 깨지다 smash to pieces.

**우지끈거리다** crackle; crack; keep popping. ¶ 기둥이 우지끈거리며 쓰러졌다 The pillar fell 〔collapsed〕 with a crack.

**우지직** ① 《타는 소리》 with a crackle; cracking; sputtering. ¶ 마른 짚이 ~ 불에 타다 dry straw crackles in the flames. ② 《부러지는 소리》 with a snap 〔crack〕. ¶ 나뭇가지를 ~ 꺾다 break twigs with a snap.

**우직하다**(愚直—) (be) stupid and tactless; simple 〔naive〕 and honest; be honest to a fault (★ to a fault는 「지나치게」의 뜻).

**우짖다** cry loud; shout; scream; yell; howl; 《작은 새가》 sing; chirp; twitter; warble.

**우쭐거리다** 《몸을》 keep dancing 〔swaying〕 rythmically. ⇨ 우쭐하다. ¶ 기쁨으로 몸을 좌우로 ~ dance 〔sway〕 *oneself* from side to side with joy.

**우쭐우쭐** 《몸체를》 dancing; swaying; 《걸음을》 strutting; swaggering. ¶ ~ 춤추다 dance up and down / ~ 걷다 strut along.

**우쭐하다** be proud 〔pompous〕; be puffed up 《with, by》; be elated 《with, by》; hold up *one's* head; have a swelled head. ¶ 우쭐해하다 be puffed up 《with *one's* success》 / 그렇게 너무 우쭐해 할 것 없어 Don't flatter yourself too much. *or* None of your cheeks. / 그의 우쭐해하는 태도에 기가 찼다 I'm amazed at his conceited attitude.

**우차**(牛車) an oxcart.

**우천**(雨天) a rainy 〔wet〕 day; rainy 〔wet〕 weather; 《예보에서》 "rain". ¶ 계속되는 ~ continued 〔a long spell of〕 rain / ~인 경우 in case of rain; if it rains 〔is rainy〕 / ~으로 인해 on account of 〔owing to〕 the rain / ~ 순연(順延) 《게시》 To be postponed till the first fine day in case of rain.

**우체국**(郵遞局) a post office. ◉ ~사무원 a mail clerk 《미》; a postal clerk 《영》. ~장 a postmaster (남자); a postmistress (여자). 군사 ~ an army post office (생략 APO).

**우체부**(郵遞夫) =우편 집배원.

**우체통**(郵遞筒) a mailbox; a postbox 《영》. ¶ 편지를 ~에 넣다 mail 〔post 《영》〕 a letter; drop a letter into a mailbox.

**우측**(右側) the right 〔right-hand〕 side. ¶ ~의 첫번째 방 the first room on the right / 길 ~에 on the right of a street / ~ 통행 《게시》 Keep to the right. / 미국에서는 차가 ~ 통행이다 Traffic moves on the right in America.

**우쿨렐레** 〚음악〛 a ukulele (악기).

**우크라이나** 《동유럽의 공화국》 Ukraine. ◉ ~사람 a Ukrainian.

**우툴두툴하다** (be) rugged; knotty; bumpy 《road》; granulated 《wood》; uneven; rough. ¶ 우툴두툴한 나무 a knotty timber / 우툴두툴한 길 a bumpy road / 우툴두툴한 가죽 granulated leather.

**우파**(右派) =우익(右翼) ①.

**우편**(右便) the right side 〔direction〕. 「= 우측.

**우편**(郵便) mail 《미》; post 《영》; 《우편제

도》 mail 〔postal〕 service. ¶ ～으로 by mail 〔post〕; in the mail / ～으로 보내다 send 《a parcel》 by mail 〔post〕; send 《a letter》 through the mail; mail 〔post〕 《a letter》 / ～으로 알리다 inform 〔notify〕 by mail 〔post〕 / ～으로 주문하다 order by mail 〔post〕 / 다음 ～으로 미루다 leave to the next mail / ～을 부치다 mail 〔post〕 《a letter》; put 〔drop〕 a letter in the post / ～이 와 있습니다 There is some mail for you. / ～을 이 주소로 전송해 주십시오 Please forward my mail to this address. / 내일 ～으로 보내드리겠습니다 We will send 〔forward〕 it to you by tomorrow's mail 〔post〕.

◉ ～규칙 the postal regulations. ～낭, ～가방 a mailbag 《미》; a postbag 《영》. ～료〔요금〕 postage; postal charges: ～요금 계기 a postal meter / 이 소포의 ～ 요금은 얼마입니까 What is the postage on this parcel? ～물 postal 〔mail〕 matter: 제1〔2, 3〕종 ～물 the first-〔second-, third-〕class mail matter. ～배달 mail 〔post〕 delivery: ～배달 구역 a postal delivery zone 〔district〕. ～번호 zip code 《미》; postcode 《영》; a postal code 〔number〕: ～번호제 postal number system; zip code system. ～보험 postal insurance. ～사서함 a post-office box (생략 P.O.B.). ～선 a mail boat. ～소인(消印) a postmark; a post-office stamp. ～업무 mail 〔postal〕 service. ～연금 a post-office annuity. ～엽서 a postal card 《미》; a postcard 《영》. ～저금〔예금〕 postal 〔post-office〕 savings 〔deposit〕: ～저금하다 deposit 《money》 in the post office. ～제도 the postal system. ～조약 a postal treaty. ～주문 a mail order. ～집배원 a mailman 《미》; a postman 《영》. ～차 《열차》 a mail train; 《자동차》 a mail 〔postal〕 van. ～폭탄 a mail bomb; a letter 〔parcel〕 bomb. ～투표 voting by mail. ～함 a mailbox 《미》; a letter box 《영》. ～환 a postal (money) order (생략 P.O.) 《미》; a post-office order (생략 P.O.O.) 《영》; 《소액환》 a postal (money) note: ～환으로 100,000원을 보내다 send 〔remit〕 100,000 won by money order / ～환을 현금으로 바꾸다 cash a money order.

국내〔국제〕～ domestic 〔international〕 mail 〔post〕: 국내〔외국〕 보통 ～ domestic 〔foreign〕 regular mail / 국제 특급 ～ international speedpost. 국제 ～ 요금 international postal tariff. 유치(留置)～ *poste restante* (F.); general delivery 《미》; a letter to be called for: 유치 ～으로 보내다 send 《*a person*》 a letter 「*poste restante* 〔to general delivery〕.

**우표**(郵票) a (postage) stamp. ¶ 100원짜리 ～ a one hundred won stamp / 50원짜리 ～ 열 장 ten fifty won stamps / ～를 붙이다 put a stamp on 《a letter》; affix 〔stick〕 a stamp to 《a letter》; stamp 《a letter》 / ～를 수집하다 collect stamps / 이 편지에는 얼마짜리 ～를 붙입니까 What is the postage for this letter?

◉ ～수집 stamp collecting; philately: ～ 수집가 a stamp collector; a philatelist / ～ 수집열 the stamp craze.

**우피**(牛皮) oxhide; cowhide.

**우행**(愚行) a folly; a foolish move 〔act〕.

**우향**(右向) ¶ ～ 앞으로 가 《구령》 Right wheel! / ～우 《구령》 Right turn 〔face〕!

**우현**(右舷) 〖항해〗 the starboard. ¶ ～으로 Starboard! / 키를 ～으로 잡다 starboard the helm / ～으로 기울다 list to the starboard.

**우호**(友好) friendship. ¶ ～적인 friendly; amicable / ～ 관계를 맺다 establish friendly 〔amicable〕 relations 《with, between》 / 양국의 ～를 촉진하다 promote friendship 〔amity〕 between the two nations / 세계 각국과 ～적인 관계를 유지하다 maintain friendly relations with all the nations of the world.

◉ ～관계 《establish》 friendly 〔cordial, amicable〕 relations: 이 역사적 회견은 양국간의 오랜 ～ 관계를 한층 더 강화할 것이다 This historic meeting will cement 〔promote〕 the friendship that has long existed between the two countries. ～국 a friendly nation. ～사절 a fraternal delegate. ～ 조약 a treaty of friendship 〔amity〕. ～협력조약 a friendship-cooperation treaty.

**우화**(雨靴) rain boots 〔shoes〕.

**우화**(寓話) an allegory; a fable; a parable. ◉ ～작가 a fable writer; a fabler; a fabulist. 이솝～집 Aesop's Fables.

**우환**(憂患) 《근심》 worry 〔troubles, cares, agony〕 「caused by 〔due to〕 illness; 《병》 illness; a disease. ¶ 오랜 ～ a long illness 〔trouble〕 / ～이 있다 have anxieties / 그의 병은 우리 집안의 큰 ～거리다 His illness is a great worry to our family. *or* His illness is a real thorn in the flesh to our family.

**우황**(牛黃) 〖한의〗 ox bezoar.

**우회**(迂回) a roundabout way; a circuit; a detour. ～하다 take a roundabout 〔circuitous〕 route; go round; make 〔take〕 a circuit 《round》; make a detour; detour; bypass 〔skirt around〕 《a town》. ¶ 산을 ～해서 가다 go around a mountain / 5마일 ～하다 make a detour of five miles / 1km 전방 임시 ～로 《게시》 Temporary detour 1km ahead. ◉ ～로 a bypass; 《게시》 Detour 《미》. ～무역 roundabout trade; commodity shunting. ～생산 circuitous 〔roundabout〕 production. ～선 a roundabout route; a loop (line). ～작전 an outflanking action.

**우회전**(右回轉) ～하다 turn to 〔toward〕 the right; make a right turn. ¶ ～금지 《게시》 No Right Turn.

**우후**(雨後) after the rain; after a rainfall. ¶ ～죽순처럼 나타나다 spring up like (so many) mushrooms after rain.

**욱기**(一氣) impetuosity; rashness; hot 〔hot-blooded〕 temper; hotheadedness. ¶ ～가 있다 be hot-tempered 〔hot-headed〕; have a wild disposition; be rough 〔wild〕.

**욱다** ① 《안으로》 get bent in; turn in; be dented. ② 《힘이》 get enfeebled 〔enervated〕; lose vigor. ¶ 기운이 ～ lose *one's* pep.

**욱시글거리다** swarm 〔teem〕 《with》; be crowded 〔thronged〕 《with》; [장소가 주어] crawl with 《worms》. ¶ 설탕에 개미떼가 욱시글거리다 Ants are swarming upon the sugar.

**욱신거리다** ① 《북적이다》 swarm; crowd; teem with; jostle one another; be 〔throng〕 together; be in a bustle. ¶ 장터에 사람이 ～ a market place swarms with people. ② 《쑤시다》 tingle; smart; [사람이 주어] feel a smarting pain 《in》; [환부가 주어] throb 〔smart〕 with pain. ¶ 찰과상이 아직도 ～ the scratch still smarts / 이가 욱신거린다 My tooth stings. / 어제 베인 손가락이 계속 욱신거린다 My finger keeps smarting from a cut I got yesterday.

**욱신욱신** 《북적임》 in swarms; 《쑤심》 pricking; throbbing 〔smarting〕 with pain.

**욱이다** bend 〔turn, batter〕 《*a thing*》 in; dent 《*a thing*》. ¶ 양철을 욱여넣다 a tin plate in.

**욱일**(旭日) the morning sun; the rising sun. ¶ 그는 ～ 승천지세(昇天之勢)다 His star is in the ascendant.

**욱적거리다** jostle all at one place. 「*one.*

**욱죄이다** feel cramped; be too tight for

**욱지르다** intimidate; browbeat. ¶ 욱질러 말을 못 하게 하다 shut 《*a person*》 down.

**욱하다** flare up impulsively; get impetuous; lose *one's* head; be distracted 《with, by》. ¶ 욱하고 성을 내다 burst into a sudden anger / 그는 걸핏하면 사소한 일에 욱한다 He gets like a madman on the slightest provocation.

**운**(運) fortune; luck; 《운명》 (a) fate; (a) destiny; (a) lot; 《기회》 chance.

> **용법** **luck** 인과 관계 없이 우연히 다가오는 운을 뜻하는, 가장 흔히 쓰이는 낱말. **fortune** luck 보다 좀더 중대한 것에 관한 운으로, 우연을 지배하는 힘에서 luck 보다 더 큰, 격식차린 느낌의 낱말. 위의 두 낱말 모두 행운과 악운에 두루 쓰인다: good 〔bad〕 *luck;* good 〔bad〕 *fortune.* 단, 형용사를 수반하지 않고 단독으로 쓰일 때는 「행운」이란 뜻이 된다. **chance** 행운·불운에 관계없이 우연성을 강조하는 낱말: Leave nothing to chance. (무슨 일이나 운에 맡기지 마라). ⇨ 운명.

¶ 운이 좋은 lucky; fortunate / 운이 나쁜 unlucky; unfortunate / 운(이) 좋게 fortunately; luckily; by good luck; as good luck would have it / 운(이) 나쁘게 unfortunately; unluckily; by ill luck; as ill luck would have it / 운이 기울다 be down on *one's* luck; be on the downgrade / 운이 좋다 be lucky; have a good luck / 운이 나쁘다 be unlucky; be out of luck / 운이 좋으면 if *one* is lucky (enough); if fortune smiles upon *one* / 운이 좋아 …하다 「be lucky enough 〔have the good fortune〕 to *do* / 운이 트이다 be in luck's way; *one's* fortune change(s) for the better; fortune 〔luck〕 turns in *one's* favor / 운이 안 트이다 have constant ill 〔bad〕 luck; have no luck / 운이 다하다 *one's* luck runs out; come to an end / 운을 하늘에 맡기다 trust to Providence 〔Heaven〕; resign *oneself* to fate; leave 《a matter》 to chance / 운을 잘 타고 나다 be born under a lucky star / 운에 맡기고 해보다 run the risk; try 〔take〕 *one's* chance / 사람의 운이란 모를 일이다 Fate is strange.

**운**(韻) a rime; a rhyme. ¶ 운을 맞추다 rhyme the lines / 운이 맞다 rhyme 《with, to》.

**운김** ① 《남은 기운》 a trace of warm air 〔vapor〕. ¶ 방에 ～이 아직 있다 There is still a little warmth lingering in the room. ② 《…하는 바람》 a sequel 《to》; (an) ardor 〔enthusiasm〕; (an) impetus; impulse. ¶ ～에 with an enthusiasm 〔ardor〕 《of》; on the impulse 〔spur〕 of circumstances.

**운니지차**(雲泥之差) a great 〔wide〕 difference; miles of difference 《between》.

**운동**(運動) ① 《신체의》 (physical) exercise; 《경기》 athletics; sports; games; 《체조》 gymnastics. ～하다 (take) exercise. ¶ 실내〔옥외〕～ indoor 〔outdoor, open-air〕 exercise / 가벼운〔격심한〕～ light 〔excessive〕 exercise / ～부족 lack of exercise / 적당히 ～하다 take moderate 〔proper〕 exercise / 하루에 2시간 ～하다 take two hours' exercise a day / ～ 삼아 걷다 walk for (the sake of) exercise / 「나 체중이 느는 것 같아」―「너 ～은 하니」―「응, 헬스 클럽에서 하고 있어」―"I'm afraid I'm getting overweight."―"Do you work out?"―"Yes, I do at the fitness center." / 적당한 ～은 건강에 좋다 Moderate exercise is good for the health. / 자네 ～을 좀 더 해야겠어 《운동 부족이란 뜻에서》 You don't get enough exercise.

② 〖물리〗 《물체의》 motion; movement. ～하다 move; be in motion. ¶ ～중의 물체 a body in motion / ～의 법칙 laws of motion / 지구는 중력 법칙에 따라 ～한다 The earth moves according to the laws of gravity.

③ 《목적을 위한 집단의》 a movement; a campaign; a drive; a crusade; 《선거》 electioneering 《영》; campaign(ing) 《미》; 《의원에의》 lobbying. ～하다 conduct a campaign 《for, against》; canvass 《for》; 《법안 통과의》 lobby. ¶ 금주～ a temperance movement / 노동～ a labor movement / 모금～ a fund=raising campaign / 가족 찾기 ～ family search campaign / 의안 통과 ～을 하다 lobby a bill / 사회 혁신 ～을 일으키다 inaugurate 〔initiate, start〕 a social reform movement / 결핵 박멸 ～에 참가하다 join the fight against tuberculosis.

④ 《노력·알선·진력》 an endeavor 《to seek *a person's* good office, *etc.*》; "pulling strings". ～하다 make an effort; pull (the) strings; use *one's* good offices. ¶ 김교수님의 ～으로 취직하다 obtain a position through the good offices of Prof. Kim / 친구의 ～으로 그는 석방되었다 Through the agency of his friend he was set free.

◉ ～가 《사회적인》 an activist 《in a political movement》; a crusader 《for women's rights》; 《체육의》 an athlete; a sportsman. ～감각 the sensation of movement. ～경기 athletic sports. ～구점 a sports store 〔shop〕. ～권 학생 activist students for the political struggle. ～기구 sporting goods; sport outfits. ～량 〖물리〗 momentum. ～마찰 〖물리〗 kinetic friction. ～모 a sports cap. ～복 sports clothes; sportswear; a gym suit. ～부 the department of athletics; 《학교》 an athletic club. ～부족 lack 〔shortage〕 of exercise: ～부족이다 be short of exercise. ～비(費) canvassing expenses. ～생리학 exercise physiology. ～선수 an athlete; a sportsman. ～시설 sports facilities. ～신경 the motor nerve: ～신경이 발달해 있다〔둔하다〕 be quick 〔slow〕 in *one's* movements; have quick 〔slow〕 control of *one's* muscles. ～에너지 〖물리〗 kinetic energy. ～열 a passion for sports; love of sports. ～원 《선거의》 a campaigner; a canvasser; an electioneering agent. ～자금 campaign funds. ～장 《학교의》 a playground; a play yard; 《경기장》 a playing field; sports grounds; a sports arena: 공설～장 a public stadium / 서울 ～장 the Seoul stadium / 서울 종합 ～장 the Seoul Sports Complex. ～장애 〖의학〗 motor disturbance. ～정신 sportsmanship. ～틀 gym equipment. ～팬츠 athletic 〔gym〕 pants 〔shorts〕. ～화 sports 〔gymnasium〕 shoes; 《고무 바닥의》 sneakers. ～회 a sports meeting; a field day (날); an athletic meet(ing) (육상 경기 대회): ～회는 비 때문에 연기되었다 Our field day was postponed because of rain.

**운두** ¶ ～가 높은〔낮은〕 신 a high-〔low=〕cut shoes.

**운명**(殞命) expiration of life; death. ～하다 breathe *one's* last; die; pass away. ⇨ 죽다.

**운명**(運命) (a) destiny; (a) fate; kismet; *one's* lot; fortune; luck; doom (불행한).

> [용법] **destiny, fate, doom** 모두 전생의 약속이라고 할 수 있는, 인력으로는 피할 수 없는 초자연적인 「숙명」을 뜻함. 특히 fate나 doom은 「죽음, 파멸」 따위의 비참한 결말을 뜻함. **fortune, luck** 선과 악에 관련된 두 가지 「운(運)」에 두루 쓰이나, 통상적으로 「호운(好運)」을 뜻함. ⇨ 운(運).

¶ ～의 총아 a fortune's favorite / ～의 장난 a quirk 〔an irony〕 of life; a trick of fortune / ～의 날 the fatal 〔fateful〕 day / ～에 맡기다 submit to (*one's*) fate; leave 〔abandon〕 《*a person, oneself, a thing*》 to fate / ～을 좌우하다 affect the fate 《of》; sway 〔influence〕 the destiny 《of》 / ～을 결정하다 decide 〔determine〕 the fate 《of》 / ～을 개척하다 carve (out) *one's* own future; mold *one's* destiny; seek *one's* fortune / (…와) ～을 같이 하다 cast 〔share〕 *one's* fortune with; throw in *one's* lot with… / ～과 싸우다 struggle against 〔with〕 fate / ～으로 받아들이다 accept 《*a matter*》 as fate / …할 ～에 있다 be destined 〔doomed, bound〕 to… / 그때 그들의 ～은 결정되었다 Their fate was sealed then. / ～의 여신은 우리 팀에게 미소를 지었다 Fortune smiled on our team. / ～의 날이 왔다 The fateful day arrived. / 그는 ～에 농락당하고 있었다 He was at the mercy of fortune. / 우리는 다시 만날 수 없는 ～이었다 We were destined never to meet again.

◉ ～론 fatalism: ～론자 a fatalist. ～선 《손금에서》 the line of Fate 〔Saturn〕. 공동 ～체 groups 〔nations〕 sharing a common destiny: 영국과 유럽 여러 나라는 공동 ～체이다 Britain and the countries of continental Europe form a natural community with a common destiny.

**운모**(雲母) 〖광물〗 mica. ◉ ～판 a mica plate. 백～ muscovite. 흑～ biotite.

**운무**(雲霧) cloud and mist 〔fog〕. ¶ ～에 싸이다 be shrouded by cloud and fog.

**운문**(韻文) verse; 《시》 a poem; poetry [총칭]. ¶ ～으로 쓰다 compose 〔write〕 in verse. ◉ ～극 a verse drama.

**운반**(運搬) conveyance; transport; transportation. ⇨ 운송. ～하다 carry; convey; transport.

> **용법** **carry** 손·수레·열차·배·항공기 따위로 「나르다, 운반하다」란 뜻의 가장 일반적인 낱말. **convey** carry보다 격식차린 말, 어떤 수단을 사용하여 「연속적으로」 운반하다의 뜻. **transport** 많은 사람이나 물품 따위를 매우 먼 거리까지 전문 수송 기관이 수송한다는 뜻.

¶ ～해 내다 carry 《*a thing*》 out of 《a room》 / ～해 들이다 carry 《*a thing*》 into 《a room》 / 철도〔배〕로 ～하다 convey 〔carry〕 by rail 〔ship〕.

◉ ～비 freight; carriage; cartage (차삯); haulage (철도 화물의). ～인 a carrier; 《인부》 a porter. ～차 a cart; a wagon; a (motor) lorry 《영》; a truck 《미》: 이삿짐 ～차 a removal van.

**운산**(運算) 〖수학〗 operation; calculation. ～하다 operate; calculate; figure out; do 〔work〕 at calculation (★ 한 문제를 계산할 때는 do 〔work〕 a sum이 됨).

**운석**(隕石) 〖광물〗 a meteorite; a meteoric 〔falling〕 stone.

**운성**(隕星) 〖천문〗 a shooting 〔falling〕 star; a meteor. ⇨ 별똥별.

**운세**(運勢) fortune; luck; *one's* star. ¶ ～가 좋다〔나쁘다〕 be fortunate 〔unfortunate〕; be born under a lucky 〔an unlucky〕 star; be lucky 〔unlucky〕 / ～를 봐 주다 tell *a person's* fortune / 나는 나의 ～를 보았다 I had my fortune told.

**운송**(運送) transport(ation); conveyance; carriage; forwarding; shipment 《미》. ～하다 transport; convey; ship; carry; forward. ¶ 육상 ～ overland transport / 해상 ～ marine transport; shipping / 여객 ～ passenger transport(ation) / ～ 중의 사고 an accident in transit / 철도〔배〕로 ～하다 transport 《goods》 by rail 〔ship〕.

◉ ～계약 a contract of carriage. ～료 forwarding 〔shipping〕 charge; freight charge; carriage. ～보험(保險) transport 〔freight, transit〕 insurance. ～비 cost of transport; freight; carriage 《of 〔on〕 goods》; shipping expenses. ～선 a transport (ship); 《화물선》 a cargo vessel. ～시설 transportation facilities. ～업 the transport 〔express, shipping, forwarding, freight〕 business 〔industry〕: ～업자 a shipping 〔freight, forwarding〕 agent; a carrier; 《미》 an expressman; 《이삿짐센터 따위》 a mover. ～점 a forwarding 〔a shipping, a freight〕 agency. ～품〔화물〕 freight; goods. ～회사 a transport 〔a shipping, a trucking, an express〕 company.

**운수**(運輸) traffic (service). ⇨ 운송.

◉ ～기관 means of conveyance 〔transportation〕. ～국 the transportation bureau. ～능력 carrying capacity. ～량 traffic. ～사업 the transportation business. ～협정 a traffic agreement. ～회사 a transport(ation) 〔a shipping, a forwarding, an express, a freight〕 company. 여객〔철도〕～ passenger 〔railway〕 traffic.

**운수**(運數) fortune; luck. ⇨ 운(運). ¶ ～가 좋다〔나쁘다〕 be lucky〔unlucky〕/ ～를 보아주다 tell〔read〕《*a person's*》 fortune; 《남이》 have *one's* fortune told 《by》/ ～ 좋게 피하다 have a lucky escape. ◉ ～소관 a matter pertaining to luck〔fortune〕: 실패를 ～ 소관으로 돌리다 attribute〔impute〕 *one's* failure to bad luck.

**운신**(運身) moving *one's* body. ～하다 move *one's* body; move around.

**운영**(運營) operation; (business) management; administration. ～하다 operate; run; manage; steer; administer. ¶ 사업을 ～하다 manage〔operate, run〕 a business / 학교를 ～하다 govern〔run〕 a school / 호텔을 ～하다 run a hotel / 조직을 ～하다 administer an organization / 이 클럽은 잘 ～되고 있다 This club is well run.
◉ ～규칙 managerial regulations. ～비 operational〔working〕 expenses. ～위원회《국회 등의》 a steering committee. ～자금 working〔operational〕 funds〔capital〕.

**운용**(運用) use; employment; working; application. ～하다 use; make use of (쓰다); employ; work; put in practice (실시하다); apply《to》(적용하다). ¶ 법률을 ～하다 apply a law / 자금을 ～하다 employ〔work〕 capital〔funds〕/ 시설을 잘 ～하고 있다 keep the facilities in good working order / 영어의 ～ 능력을 높이다 improve *one's* working knowledge of English.
◉ ～자본 working capital; operational funds. ～테스트《컴퓨터 등의》 an implementation test; an operation and control test.

**운운**(云云) so and so; such and such; and so forth〔on〕; *et cetera* (생략 etc., &c.). ～하다 say something or other 《of, about》; 《비판하다》 criticize; comment 《on》; 《언급하다》 mention; refer to. ¶ 지금은 그것을 ～할 때가 아니다 Now is not the time to criticize〔comment on〕 it. / 최근에 담배가 유해 ～하는 설이 있다 Of late, the opinion is heard that tobacco is harmful, etc.

**운율**(韻律) a rhythm; a beat; a cadence; a meter; a measure. ¶ ～의 rhythmical; metrical / ～이 없는 시 rhythmless verse. ◉ ～학 metrics; prosody.

**운임**(運賃) 《여객의》 a fare; rates; charge; 《화물의》 freight rates 《미》; goods rates 《영》; 《송료》 carriage (charges); 《해운비》 shipping expenses; 《운반비》 portage; cartage. ¶ 국내〔해양, 항공〕 ～ inland〔ocean, airway〕 freight / 편도〔왕복〕 ～ a one way〔round trip〕 fare / 여객 ～ a passenger fare / 특별 ～ extra rate / 버스의 ～이 다음달부터 인상된다 Bus fares will be raised next month. / ～이 비싸다〔싸다〕 The fare is high〔low〕.
◉ ～가산〔포함〕 가격 cost and freight price (생략 C. & F.). ～률 freight rates; a carriage rate. ～무료《게시》 Carriage Free. ～보험료 가산〔포함〕 가격(價格) C.I.F. price. [＜*C*ost, *I*nsurance and *F*reight]. ～선불 carriage〔freight〕 prepaid〔forward〕. ～수수료 가산〔포함〕 가격 cost, freight and commission (생략 C.F. & C.). ～완납 a carriage paid〔prepaid〕. ～청구서 a freight bill. ～표《여객의》 a fare table; 《화물의》 a freight list. ～협정 a tariff agreement. ～후불 freight to collect. 1〔2〕등칸 ～ the first〔second〕 class fare. 할인～ a reduced fare.

**운자**(韻字) a rhyming〔rhyme〕 character.

**운전**(運轉) working 《of a machine》; operation; running; driving; 《운용》 employment. ～하다 drive 《a car》; run 《a train》; operate〔put, set〕 《a machine》; work〔navigate〕 《a ship》. ¶ 기계의 ～을 멈추다 suspend the operation of a machine / 자동차 ～ 교습을 받다 take driving lessons; take a driving course / (자동차의) ～을 교대하다 take over the wheel / (차 흐름에 관계없이) 느리게 ～하는 사람 a Sunday driver / 졸면서 ～하다 doze off at the wheel (★ at the wheel은 「핸들을 잡고」의 뜻) / 그 기계는 ～ 중이다 The machine is「running〔in operation〕. / 안전벨트를 매고 조심해서 ～하시오 Drive carefully with your safety belt fastened. / 그는 음주 ～으로 체포되었다 He was arrested for drunken driving. / 그는 차 ～을 잘한다〔못한다〕 He is〔is not〕 a good driver. / 그녀는 ～이 난폭하다〔느리다〕 She drives (a car) recklessly〔slowly〕.
◉ ～교습소 a driving school. ～기술 driving skill; *one's* skill as a driver. ～대 a steering wheel. ～석《자동차의》 a driver's seat; 《열차의》 an engineer's seat: ～석 출입 금지《게시》 Keep out of driver's seat. ～자금〔자본〕 working funds〔capital〕. 시～ a road test; a test〔trial〕 run; 《기계의》 test working: 시～하다 make a trial run 《of》.

**운전기사**(運轉技士) 《자동차》 a driver; a chauffeur (자가용의); 《택시》 a taxi driver; a cabman; 《전차》 a motorman; 《기차》 an engineer; an engine driver: 《기계》 an operator. ◉ 교대～ a co-driver. 모범～ an exemplary driver.

**운전면허**(증)(運轉免許(證)) a driver's license 《미》; a driving license 《영》. ¶～를 따다 get 〔obtain〕 a driver's license / ～ 시험을 치다 take a driving test. ◉ 국제 자동차～ an international driving permit 〔license〕.

**운지법**(運指法) 『음악』 fingering.

**운집하다**(雲集—) swarm; gather in swarms 〔crowds〕; throng. ¶운집한 군중 a crowd 〔throng〕 people / 광장에는 군중이 운집해 있었다 A crowd had gathered at the square.

**운철**(隕鐵) 『광물』 meteoric iron.

**운치**(韻致) elegance; refinement; artistic effect; gracefulness. ¶～ 있는 tasteful; elegant / ～ 없는 tasteless; inelegant / ～ 없는 사람 a prosaic person / 그것은 ～라고는 조금도 없다 It is of sheer boorishness.

**운크라** UNKRA. [<*U*nited *N*ations *K*orean *R*econstruction *A*gency]

**운크타드** UNCTAD. [<the *U*nited *N*ations *C*onference on *T*rade *a*nd *D*evelopment]

**운필**(運筆) 《획》 strokes of the brush; 《운필법》 the way of 〔manner of handling〕 the brush 〔pen〕.

**운하**(運河) a canal; a waterway 《미》. ¶～를 파다 make 〔dig, build〕 a canal. ◉ ～지대 a canal zone. ～(통행)세 canal dues. 파나마〔수에즈〕～ the Panama 〔Suez〕 Canal.

**운항**(運航) 《탈것의》 navigation; (a) service; 《열차의》 a run; 《비행기의》 a flight; 《배의》 a sailing. ～하다 navigate; run; ply 《between》. ¶～ 중인 배 〔비행기〕 a ship 〔an airplane〕 in service / 항공기의 ～ an airline service / 인천·부산 간을 ～하는 배 a ship running 〔sailing〕 between Inch'ŏn and Pusan; a ship that runs 〔plies〕 between Inch'ŏn and Pusan / 시계(視界) 불량으로 그 비행〔선박〕편은 ～이 취소되었다 Owing to poor visibility, the flight 〔boat〕 has been canceled. ◉ ～등(燈) a navigation light. 안전～ 《항공기의》 the safe air passage.

**운해**(雲海) 《바다》 a clouded 〔overcast〕 sea; 《구름의》 a sea of clouds.

**운행**(運行) 《천체의》 revolution (자전·공전); movement; motion; 《차의》 running; moving; operation; service. ～하다 revolve 〔go, move, orbit〕 around 《the sun》; run; operate. ¶천체의 ～ movements of celestial bodies / 버스의 ～ 노선 a bus service route / 그 지역 일대를 ～하고 있는 버스 the buses that cover the area / 5분 간격으로 ～되다 《the buses》 be run at five-minute intervals on the course / 지하철은 러시 아워에 3분 간격으로 ～된다 The subways run every three minutes during the rush hour(s). / 행성은 그 궤도를 ～한다 The planets roll on in their courses. ◉ ～노선 a 《bus》 route: ～노선번호 a route number. ～정지 the suspension of operation 《for 5 days》. 임시 열차 ～ extra train service.

**운휴**(運休) suspension 〔stoppage〕 of (the) 《bus》 service. ¶다섯 개의 급행 열차가 ～되었다 The service of five express trains was suspended. / 폭설로 버스가 ～되었다 Bus service was canceled 〔suspended〕 because of the heavy snowfall.

**울**[1] 《겨레붙이》 relatives; family; kinsfolk; clan. ¶울을 믿고 행패(를)하다 play the bully, relying on his family to back him up.

**울**[2] ① 《울타리》 a fence; a hedge; an enclosure. ¶울 안에 inside the premises; in the compound / 울을 치다 fence round 《a house》; enclose 《a house》 with a fence. ② 《신발의》 the outer rim of shoes; 《그릇 등의》 the rim.

**울걱거리다** gargle. ¶양치질하느라고 ～ gargle (*one's* mouth).

**울근거리다** chew; mumble.

**울근불근하다** ① 《다투다》 be at odds 《with》; be in discord 《with》; be on bad terms 《with》. ¶그 부부는 늘 서로 울근불근한다 The couple are always 「at odds with each other 〔in each other's hair〕. ② 《앙상하다》 (be) bony; scraggy; rawboned; very lean. ¶뼈가 울근불근한 사람 a skinny man / 너무 말라서 갈빗대가 울근불근 보이다 be so emaciated *one's* ribs are showing.

**울근울근** 《씹는 모양》 chewing; mumbling. ¶질긴 고기를 ～ 씹다 chew on a tough piece of meat.

**울긋불긋** colorful; picturesque. ～하다 (be) colorful; picturesque. ¶들에 꽃이 ～ 피어 있다 The blooming field is ablaze with color.

**울기**(鬱氣) pent-up feelings; depression; melancholy; gloom.

**울컥** ¶ ~ 토하다 vomit; throw up / ~ 화가 치밀다 have a fit of anger; fly into a rage.

**울다** ① 《사람이》 cry (소리 치며); weep; shed tears (눈물을 흘리며); sob (흐느끼며); wail (통곡하며); blubber (엉엉); scream (날카로운 소리로); whimper (훌쩍이며); mewl (갓난애가 약한 소리로).

> 용법 **cry** 「큰소리로 울다」의 뜻으로 소리를 지르는 데 역점을 두고 있음. **weep** cry보다 격식차린 말로 「눈물 흘리며 울다」의 뜻. 눈물 흘리는 것을 강조하지만 종종 cry와 weep는 서로 바꿔 쓰임. **sob**는 「흐느껴 울다」「훌쩍훌쩍 울다」의 뜻으로 우는 것을 멈추려하거나, 울면서 말한다는 뜻이 내포되어 있음. **wail**은 슬픔이나 아픔으로 「울부짖다」. **blubber**는 아이들이 자기 뜻을 관철시키려고 「엉엉 울다」.

¶ 우는 얼굴 a tearful 〔tear-stained〕 face / 술취하면 우는 사람 a maudlin drinker; a sentimental 〔crying〕 drunkard / 울면서 with tears in *one's* eyes; crying; weeping / 아파서 ~ cry with pain / 기뻐서 ~ weep for 〔with〕 joy / 감동하여 ~ be moved to tears / 실컷 ~ weep *oneself* out; have a good cry / 엉엉 ~ cry bitterly / 마음 속으로 ~ weep at heart / 큰소리로 ~ cry loudly; howl; bawl; squall / 가슴이 미어지게 ~ cry *one's* heart out / 두 손에 얼굴을 파묻고 ~ cry into *one's* hands; cry with *one's* head (buried) in *one's* hands / 울며 세월을 보내다 spend *one's* days in tears; live in sorrow / 젖을 달라고 ~ cry for milk / 거짓 우는 체하다 pretend to be weeping; shed false tears / 목메어 ~ weep 〔cry〕 *oneself* out of breath / 울고 싶어지다 feel like crying / 베개에 얼굴을 묻고 ~ weep into *one's* pillow / 울며 매달리다 implore; entreat; supplicate 《*a person* for help, to *do*》.

② 《동물이》 cry; howl (짖다); 《고양이가》 mew; purr (그르렁대다); 《소가》 bellow; moo; low; 《말이》 neigh; whinny; 《당나귀가》 bray; 《원숭이가》 chatter; gibber; 《사슴이》 bell; 《양·염소가》 bleat; 《범·사자가》 roar; 《코끼리가》 trumpet; 《쥐가》 squeak; 《개구리가》 croak; 《벌레·새가》 chirp; sing; twitter; 《까마귀가》 caw; 《닭이》 crow (수탉); cluck (암탉); peep (병아리); 《오리가》 quack; 《부엉이가》 hoot; 《뻐꾹새가》 cuckoo; 《비둘기가》 coo; 《귀뚜라미가》 chirr; chirrup; 《칠면조가》 gobble; 《종달새가》 warble; 《벌이》 buzz; 《거위가》 goggle; 《학이》 whoop; 《매미가》 sing. ¶ 벌레가 울면 가을이 가까워진 징후이다 The chirping of insects is the sign that autumn is just around the corner.

③ 《종·천둥 등이》 = 울리다 ⑤.

④ 《세간·물체가》 creak; squeak; whistling; whizzing. ¶ 전깃줄이 바람에 윙윙 운다 The wind sets up a humming in the wires.

⑤ 《옷·벽지 따위가》 get wrinkled 〔crumpled〕; be shriveled.

⑥ 《귀가》 sing; ring; have a ringing 〔buzzing〕 in *one's* ears. ¶ 병후에 귀가 운다 I have a ringing in my ears after my illness.

⑦ 《우는 소리하다》 make complaints; grumble 《about, at》; whine 《about》. ¶ 하찮은 일에 우는 소리를 하다 whine about trifles.

**울대** 《새의》 the syrinx of a bird.

**울뚝불뚝** ① 《심술이 나서》 with repeated impetuosity 〔rashness〕. ¶ ~한 태도 a rude 〔rough〕 manner. ② 《불거진 모양》 rough; rugged; 《나무 따위가》 knotty; knaggy; gnarled; 《근육이》 muscular.

**울뚝울뚝** impetuously; rashly; roughly. ~하다 (be) impetuous; rash; rough.

**울렁거리다** ① 《가슴이》 palpitate; throb; thump; go pit-a-pat; pound; beat. ¶ 울렁거리는 가슴 a throbbing heart / 무서워서 가슴이 ~ palpitate with fear. ② 《물결이》 roll; surge. ③ 《메슥거리다》 feel sick (at the stomach); nauseate. ¶ 그 냄새를 맡자 속이 울렁거렸다 The smell made me sick.

**울렁울렁** ① 《가슴이》 pit-a-pat; palpitating; throbbing; thumping. ¶ 가슴이 ~하다 the heart palpitates 〔throbs, flutters〕. ② 《물결이》 tossing; rolling; surging. ③ 《속이》 heaving.

**울룩불룩하다** (be) rough; coarse; bumpy; uneven.

**울리다** ① 《사람을》 make 〔let〕 《*a person*》 cry; move 〔touch〕 《*a person*》 to tears (감동시켜). ¶ 사람을 울리는 이야기 a touching 〔pathetic, moving〕 story / 어린애를 울리지 마라 Don't let the child cry.

② 《소리를》 ring; sound; clang; blow (나팔); beat (북). ¶ 벨을 ~ ring a bell; jingle a bell (딸랑딸랑) / 경적을 ~《열차가》 sound an alarm whistle; 《자동차가》 sound a horn; honk / 누군가가

도어벨을 울리고 있다 Someone is ringing the doorbell.
③ 《명성이》 be widely known; be famous. ¶ 명성이 전국에 ~ win nationwide fame.
④ 《세력을》 be influential; wield (power); sway.
⑤ 《소리가》 ring; echo; resound; reverberate; 《천둥이》 thunder; rumble; roll. ¶ 종소리가 ~ a bell rings 〔tolls〕 / 고동이 ~ the siren blows 〔whistles〕 / 그의 목소리가 교실 안에 울렸다 The classroom rang with his voice. / 대포 소리가 산을 드르르 울렸다 The report of the gun reverberated through the hills. / 북소리가 둥둥 울린다 The drums beat loudly.

**울림** 《음향》 a sound; a noise; 《진동》 a vibration; 《반향》 an echo; 《굉음》 a roar; a boom (포성의); a report (총포의); a peal (종소리의). ¶ 대포의 ~ the roar 〔report〕 of a gun / 종의 ~ the peal of a bell / 북(소리)의 ~ the sound of a drum.

**울보** a crybaby; a blubberer.

**울부짖다** cry; howl; wail; scream. ¶ 울부짖는 부녀자와 아이들 screaming women and children / 멀리서 늑대가 슬프게 울부짖는 소리가 들린다 We can hear a wolf howling mournfully in the distance.

**울분**(鬱憤) pent-up feelings; resentment; grudge; animosity. ¶ ~을 참다 control *one's* anger / ~을 풀다〔터뜨리다〕 let out 〔relieve, vent, give vent to〕 *one's* pent-up feelings; let all *one's* frustrations out; let off steam 《구어》.

**울상**(―相) a crying face; a tearful 〔weeping〕 face; a face about to cry. ¶ ~을 하다 wear a tearful face; look sad; snivel; be ready to cry.

**울새** 〖조류〗 a robin; a redbreast.

**울쑥불쑥** jaggedly; bumpily. ~하다 (be) jagged; bumpy; stick up here and there. ¶ 산이 ~하다 the mountains are jagged.

**울안** a fenced-in place; an enclosure; a precinct.

**울울하다**(鬱鬱―) ① 《답답하다》 (be) dejected; melancholic; blue. ¶ 울울하게 gloomily; moodily; melancholily / 울울히 세월을 보내다 mope away *one's* time. ② 《울창하다》 (be) luxuriant.

**울음** crying; weeping. ¶ ~을 터뜨리다 burst 〔break〕 into tears; 「burst out 〔fall to〕 crying / ~을 참다 repress 〔gulp down〕 *one's* tears / ~을 그치다 stop weeping 〔crying〕; cry *oneself* out / ~으로 날을 보내다 spend *one's* days in tears; live in sorrow.

**울음소리** a tearful 〔weepy 《구어》〕 voice; a cry; 《맹수의》 a roar; 《새의》 a song; a note; a chirp; a twitter. ¶ ~로 말하다 sob out; say in sobs / 옆방에서 아기 ~가 들렸다 I heard a baby crying in the next room.

**울적**(鬱寂) melancholy; mental depression; low spirits; emptiness in the heart. ~하다 (be) depressed; gloomy; melancholy; in low spirits. ¶ ~한 기분으로 with a heavy heart; in a depressed mood / ~한 얼굴 a melancholy look / 궂은 날씨가 기분을 ~하게 한다 Bad weather depresses me.

**울증**(鬱症) melancholia; 〖의학〗 hypochondria.

**울창하다**(鬱蒼―) (be) luxuriant; thick; dense. ¶ 울창하게 thickly; densely; luxuriantly; in luxurious growth / 울창한 숲 a dense 〔thick〕 forest / (나무가) 울창하게 자라다 grow thickly 〔densely〕.

**울컥** ① 《토하는 모양》 《vomit》 suddenly; abruptly; with a puke. ¶ 먹은 것을 ~ 다 토하다 suddenly throw up all *one* has eaten. ② 《치미는 모양》 《get angry》 all of a sudden; with a burst 《of anger》.

**울타리** a fence; an enclosure; a hedge (산울타리); a hurdle (엮은); railing (목책). ¶ 대나무 ~ a bamboo fence / ~를 하다 make a fence / …주위에 ~를 두르다 put a fence around… / 뜰에 ~를 두르다 fence a garden; 「put up 〔build〕 a fence around a garden.

**울퉁불퉁하다** (be) bumpy; rough; rugged; uneven.

**울퉁불퉁하다** = 울툭불툭하다. ¶ 울퉁불퉁한 길 a bumpy 〔rough〕 road.

**울혈**(鬱血) 〖의학〗 congestion 〔engorgement〕 (of blood); hyper(a)emia.

**울화**(鬱火) pent-up anger; resentment. ¶ ~가 치밀다 feel the surge of anger 〔resentment〕 / (치미는) ~를 누르다 control 〔govern〕 *one's* temper / ~통이 터지다 burst into a fit of rage; explode with anger; blow *one's* top 《구어》 / ~통을 터뜨리다 loose *one's* temper; let loose *one's* anger; hit the ceiling 〔roof〕 《미구어》. ◉ ~병 hypochondria; a disease caused by frustration 〔pent-up feelings〕.

**움**[1] 《싹》 a bud; a tiller; a sprout; a shoot; an offshoot. ⇨ 움트다.

**움**[2] 《집》 a dugout; 《화채·채소의》 a pit;

《지하 저장고》 a cellar. ¶ 움을 파다 dig out a pit / 움에 채소를 저장하다 store 〔preserve〕 vegetables in a pit.

**움돋다** sprout. ⇨ 움트다.

**움막**(一幕) a rudely made underground hut; a dugout. ◉ ~살이 life in a mud hut.

**움실거리다** swarm; squirm in a swarm.

**움쑥하다** (be) hollow; sunken.

**움찔하다** flinch; draw back 《with fear 〔fright〕》; shrink; wince. ¶ 주사침을 보고 ~ flinch before a doctor's needle.

**움직거리다** stir; wriggle; move slowly 〔slightly〕. ¶ 지렁이가 ~ an earthworm wriggles along.

**움직이다**[1] [타동사] ① 《이동시키다》 move; remove; shift. ¶ 다리를 ~ move *one's* legs / 군대를 ~ move troops / 두 팔을 위아래로 움직여 보시오 Move your arms up and down. / 손발이 묶이어 몸을 움직일 수 없었다 Bound hand and foot, I was quite helpless.
② 《변경하다》 change; alter; 《흔들다》 shake. ¶ 움직일 수 없는 immovable; unchangeable 《fact》 / 움직일 수 없는 결심 an immovable 〔a firm〕 resolution.
③ 《기계를》 set 《a machine》 in motion; work 〔operate〕 《a machine》; drive. ¶ 이 기계를 움직일 수 있는 사람은 드물다 There are only a few people that can run this machine. / 이 기계를 움직이는 방법은 간단하다 This machine is easy to run 〔operate〕.
④ 《조종하다》 control; deal with 《*a person*》; 《경영하다》 manage; operate; carry on; run. ¶ 그는 회사에서 많은 사람을 움직인다 He directs a lot of people in the office. / 이 공장은 사실상 부사장이 움직인다 In fact, the factory here is run 〔managed〕 by the vice-president. / 그는 한국의 재계를 움직이는 사람이다 He is a man who moves Korean finance.
⑤ 《마음을》 move; touch; inspire; 《영향을 미치다》 affect; influence. ¶ 사람의 마음을 ~ move *a person;* sway the minds of men (인심을) / 그의 호소가 많은 사람들의 마음을 움직였다 His appeal touched the hearts of many people.
⑥ 《부인하다》 deny. ¶ 움직일 수 없는 사실 an undeniable 〔indisputable, established〕 fact / 움직일 수 없는 증거 a positive proof.

**움직이다**[2] [자동사] ① 《이동하다》 move; stir; budge; shift. ¶ 움직이고 있다 be in motion; be moving; be stirring; be on the go / 움직이지 않다 do not stir; stay; sit motionless (앉은 채) / 움직이지 않고 있다 be at rest; be at a standstill; remain still; stay put 《미구어》 / 움직이지 않게 되다 stop moving; come to a standstill; get stuck 《in the mud》 / 부러진 팔이 움직이지 않도록 부목(副木)을 대다 set a broken arm in splints to hold it in position / 사진 찍을테니 움직이지 마세요 Now I am about to shoot the picture, so please hold it. / 움직이면 죽는다 「Stir 〔Freeze or〕 you are a dead man.
② 《기계 등이》 work; operate; run; go. ¶ 전기로 ~ go by electricity / 전지로 움직이는 시계 a battery-operated clock / (차 따위가) 움직이지 않게 되다 break down; come 〔be brought〕 to a standstill / (기계 등을) 움직이지 않게 하다 put out of operation; jam (무언가를 끼워서) / 시계를 움직이게 하다 set 〔get〕 the watch going / 이 시계가 움직이지 않는다 This watch doesn't go.
③ 《흔들리다》 shake; swing; sway. ¶ 이빨이 ~ a tooth is loose / 시계추가 움직이고 있다 The pendulum is in motion.
④ 《마음이》 be moved 〔touched〕; be affected. ¶ (…하고 싶은) 마음이 ~ feel 〔be〕 inclined to 《*do*》; be itching 《to *do*》 / 마음이 움직이지 않다 be imperturbable; be immovable; remain firm; stand *one's* ground / 마음이 움직이기 쉽다 be easily affected 《by》.
⑤ 《좌우되다》 be influenced; be swayed; 《동요하다》 waver; fluctuate; be shaken. ¶ 감정으로 ~ be swayed by sentiment.

**움직임** ① 《운동》 motion; (a) movement (★ motion은 불규칙적인 동요나 이동, 또는 행성의 운행 등 과학적·기술적인 분야에서 쓰임. movement는 방향·목적·규칙성을 가진 사람이나 물체의 움직임, 사람의 구체적인 동작, 정치적·사회적 운동 등을 뜻함). ¶ 손의 우아한 ~ a graceful movement of the hand. ② 《활동》 action; activities; 《동향》 a trend; a drift; development. ¶ 세계의 ~ the trend of the world / 여론의 ~ the drift 〔trend〕 of public opinion / 피스톤의 ~ the play of the piston / 세계의 ~을 보아라 See how the world is moving. / 정계는 그것에 관해 아무런 ~도 보이지 않는다 There are no signs in the political circles of doing anything about it.

**움질거리다** ① 《움직이다》 move about; stir. ② 《주저하다》 hesitate; waver.

**움집** a dugout mud hut. ¶ ~살이하다

live in a cellar-hovel.

**움쭉거리다** ⇨ 움직거리다.

**움쭉달싹** ⇨ 옴짝달싹.

**움찔** with a flinch. ～하다 be startled 《at》; flinch; shrink back; wince.

**움츠러-** ⇨ 옴츠러-.

**움켜잡다** grab (at); grasp; seize (on, upon). ¶ 아무의 멱살을 ～ grab 〔seize〕 *a person* by the collar 〔lapels〕 / 그는 칼을 움켜잡고 내게로 다가왔다 Grabbing a knife, he closed in on me.

**움켜쥐다** grip; clutch; clench; hold tightly. ¶ 남의 손을 꼭 ～ squeeze *a person's* hand / 주먹을 ～ tighten 〔clench〕 *one's* fist.

**움큼** a handful 《of rice》; a fistful 《of sand》.

**움키다** ① 《꼭 쥐다》 clasp; clench; grasp; grip; clutch; hold; seize. ¶ 밤을 한 움큼 ～ grasp a handful of chestnuts in *one's* hand. ② 《짐승이》 seize 《with the claws》; claw hold of; grip; grasp; grab. ¶ 독수리가 병아리를 움켜챘다 An eagle grabbed a chick.

**움트다** bud; sprout; shoot. ¶ 초목이 움트는 시절에 when trees and grasses bud; when new buds begin to appear / 그 둘 사이엔 사랑이 움텄다 Love budded between the two. *or* The two began to have tender affection for each other.

**움파** scallions grown in a pit.

**움파리** 《물괸 곳》 a puddle.

**움펑눈** deep-set 〔sunken, hollow〕 eyes. ◉ ～이 a person with deep-set eyes.

**움푹** in hollow(s) 〔pit(s), depression(s)〕. ～하다 《지면 따위가》 be in hollows; (be) pitted; 《눈 따위가》 (be) hollow; deep; sunken; dented. ¶ ～한 눈 sunken 〔deep-set〕 eyes / 눈이 ～하다 have deep-set eyes / ～ 패다 become depressed 〔hollow〕; cave 〔fall〕 in; sink; subside / 비에 땅이 ～ 패였다 The ground was washed out in hollows by the rain.

**웁쌀** (a small quantity of) rice put on top of minor cereals to boil. ¶ ～ 얹다 put rice on top of cereals.

**웃-** the upper; the above; the outer.

**웃국** the upper, clear part of *sul* 〔soy sauce〕.

**웃기다** make 《*a person*》 laugh; provoke 〔excite〕 the laughter; raise a laugh; amuse. ¶ 청중을 ～ excite the laughter of *one's* audience; move the audience to laughter / 그는 농담으로 모두를 웃겼다 He made everyone laugh with his funny remarks. / 그는 익살로 청중을 왁자그르르 웃겼다 He brought down the house with his joke. / 네가 음악가가 돼, 웃기지 마라 You want to be a musician? Don't make me laugh! / 그가 프랑스어를 가르치다니 웃기는구나 He is teaching French? What a joke!

**웃날들다** 《날씨가》 clear (up); become fine. ¶ 웃날들었다 The sky 〔It〕 cleared up.

**웃다** ① 《소리내어》 laugh; 《미소짓다》 smile. ¶ 잘 웃는 사람 a good 〔an easy〕 laugher / 웃는 얼굴 a smiling face / 웃으면서 with a laugh 〔smile〕; laughingly; smilingly / (이를 드러내고) 싱긋이 ～ grin / 킥킥 ～ giggle / 낄낄 ～ chuckle / 싱겁게 ～ simper / 껄껄 ～ guffaw / 아이들의 장난을 보고 ～ smile to see the children's frolics / 농담에 ～ laugh over a joke / 눈물이 나도록 ～ laugh till the tears come out / 웃지 않을 수 없다 cannot help laughing / 웃어 넘기다 laugh off 〔away〕 《a request》 / 웃는 얼굴로 맞다 welcome with a smile / 웃으며 대답하다 answer with a smile; laugh a reply / 쓴웃음을 ～ smile a bitter smile / 경멸의 웃음을 ～ smile a smile of contempt / 큰소리로 ～ laugh out loud; give a loud laugh / 배를 움켜쥐고 ～ shake 〔hold〕 *one's* sides with laughter; laugh a hearty laugh / 자지러지게 ～ laugh *one's* head off; laugh fit to kill / 그는 그녀를 보고 싱긋 웃었다 He looked at her with a grin. / 그녀는 잘 웃는다 She laughs a lot. ② 《비웃다》 laugh 〔sneer〕 at; ridicule; jeer 〔scoff〕 《at》; deride. ¶ 웃을 만한 laughable; ridiculous / 아무의 무식을 ～ smile 〔laugh〕 at *a person's* ignorance / 네가 아무리 웃어도 나는 결심을 바꾸지 않는다 You cannot laugh me out of my decision.

**웃더껑이** a lid; a cover.

**웃도리** ⇨ 윗도리. ¶ ～를 벗다 strip to the waist; remove *one's* coat.

**웃돈** an extra; extra money (to a trade-in price); 《채권 등의》 a premium. ¶ ～을 치르다 pay (an) extra; add to a trade-in price; pay a premium / 더 좋은 방을 구하려면 ～을 주어야 한다 You must pay extra for a better room.

**웃돌다** top; be more than; exceed; be in excess of. ¶ 원가를 웃도는 이익 the gain over the cost 《of...》 / 총액은 10억 원을 훨씬 웃돌고 있다 The total is 「well over 〔way above〕 a billion won. / 수입이 수출을 10억 달러 웃돌았다 Imports exceeded exports by one billion dollars. / 올해 수확은 예상을 웃돌았다 This year's crop has exceeded the expected amount. / 집의 수리비는 100만 원을 웃돌았다 The repairs on my house cost more than one million won.

**웃비** a clearing rain. ¶ ~ 걷다 it stops raining; the rain lifts 〔clears〕.

**웃어른** *one's* elders; a senior.

**웃옷** ① 《겉옷》 an outer garment; a coat. ② 《상의》 an upper garment.

**웃을 일** a laughing matter. ¶ 이것은 ~이 아니다 This is no laughing matter, I tell you.

**웃음** a laugh; laughter; 《미소》 a smile; 《낄낄거리는》 a chuckle; a giggle; 《비웃음》 a derision; a sneer; a ridicule (★ laugh는 명랑하게 소리내어 웃는 웃음. 가장 일반적인 말. laughter는 laugh보다 오래 계속되는 웃음. 행위를 강조하는 말. chuckle은 재미있거나 내심으로 만족함을 나타내는 낮고 부드러운 웃음. giggle은 어린이나 여성이 빠르고 높은 소리를 내거나 반쯤 억눌러 참는 웃음. 당황·어리석음을 암시함.).
¶ 헛~ an empty laugh / 큰 ~ a loud laugh / ~이 터지다 burst out laughing; burst into (a roar of) laughter / ~을 띠다 wear a smile / ~을 참다 repress 〔suppress〕 a smile 〔laugh〕; swallow a laugh / ~을 터뜨리다 burst into a laugh / (남의) ~을 사다 incur derision; be laughed at; draw ridicule upon *oneself* / ~을 웃다 smile a smile; have a laugh / ~을 팔다 live as a prostitute; walk the streets / 그녀는 억지 ~을 지으며 근심의 빛을 감추었다 She hid her anxiety with a forced smile.
◉ ~거리 a laughingstock; a butt 〔an object〕 of ridicule: 남의 ~거리가 되다 become a laughingstock for others; become the butt of ridicule. ~소리 laughter; a laughing voice. ~판 a scene of boisterous laughter: 그의 이야기를 듣고 좌중이 ~판이 되었다 At his story the whole party burst into laughter.

**웃통** the upper part of the body. 《윗옷》 a coat; a jacket. ¶ ~을 벗다 strip *oneself* 〔be stripped〕 to *one's* waist / 그는 ~을 벗고 나에게 대들었다 He took his coat off and lit into me.

**웅거하다**(雄據—) hold and defend *one's* own territory; stand *one's* ground.

**웅그리다** ⇨ 옹그리다.

**웅긋쭝긋** sprouting up 〔standing out〕 here and there; bristling. ~하다 be bristly with points sprouting up here and there; bristle.

**웅기중기** ⇨ 옹기종기.

**웅담**(熊膽) 〖한의〗 bear's gall.

**웅대**(雄大) grandeur; magnificence; majesty. ~하다 (be) grand; magnificent; majestic; imposing. ¶ ~한 경치 a grand sight; a magnificent view / ~한 구상 a grand conception.

**웅덩이** a puddle; a pool; a plash. ¶ ~지다 form a puddle / ~에 빠지다 fall into a deep puddle.

**웅도**(雄途) a heroic 〔valiant〕 departure. ¶ ~에 오르다 make a heroic departure 《on an expedition》.

**웅도**(雄圖) a grand plan 〔scheme〕; an ambitious project. ¶ ~를 펴지 못하다 fail to realize *one's* great ambition / 예기치 못한 패배로 ~가 꺾이다 have *one's* ambition frustrated in an unexpected defeat.

**웅변**(雄辯) eloquence; oratory; fluency. ¶ ~을 토하다 speak fluently 〔eloquently, with eloquence〕; make an eloquent speech 《on》 / 결과가 이 사실을 ~으로 말해 주고 있다 The result eloquently speaks of this fact. / ~은 은이고 침묵은 금이다 《속담》 Speech is silver, silence is golden.
◉ ~가 an eloquent speaker; an orator: 그는 드물게 보는 ~가다 He has a rare gift of eloquence. ~대회 an oratorical 〔a speech〕 contest. ~술 oratory; elocution; the art of public speaking.

**웅비**(雄飛) a great leap 〔flight〕; an ambitious flight; launching out. ~하다 take a flying jump 〔a leap〕; soar up; launch (out) 《into》; embark on 《a career》. ¶ 해외로 ~하다 go abroad with a great ambition; embark on great ventures abroad / 정계에 ~하다 launch (out) into politics; soar up in politics / 디자이너로 세계에 ~하는 것이 그녀의 꿈이었다 It was her dream to take her place as a designer on the international stage.

**웅성**(雄性) 〖생물〗 maleness.
◉ ~ 배우자 a male gamete. ~식물 a male (plant).

**웅성거리다** be noisy; be in a commotion. ¶ 그가 연단에 오르자 장내는 웅성거렸다 When he appeared on the platform, there was a general stir in the audience.

**웅숭깊다** (be) deep; profound; inscrutable; subtle; broad(-minded); magnanimous. ¶ 웅숭깊은 사람 an unfathomable character; an inscrutable man; a deep fellow; a magnanimous man / 웅숭깊은 생각 a profound 〔far-reaching〕 idea.

**웅얼거리다** mutter; murmur; grunt; grumble; babble; jabber. ¶ 혼자 ~ mutter to *oneself* / 그는 언제나 입속에서 웅얼거릴 뿐 자기 의견을 분명히 말하지 않는다 He always mumbles rather than articulating his opinion clearly.

**웅얼웅얼** muttering; murmuring; grunting; grumbling; babbling. ¶ 그는 무어라고 ~ 혼자말을 하며 갔다 He went away muttering something to himself.

**웅예**(雄蕊) 〖식물〗 a stamen.

**웅자**(雄姿) a majestic figure; an imposing form; a gallant 〔brave〕 appearance. ¶ ~를 나타내다 cut 〔make〕 a brave 〔gallant〕 figure; make an imposing appearance / 안개가 걷히자 한라산의 ~가 우리 앞에 그 모습을 드러냈다 When the mist cleared, Mt. Halla appeared magnificently before us.

**웅장**(雄壯) grandeur; magnificence; majesty. ~하다 (be) grand; magnificent; majestic. ¶ ~한 경치 a magnificent view; a grand sight; spectacular scene / ~한 건물 a stately building / 나는 나이아가라 폭포의 ~함에 넋을 잃었다 I was fascinated with the grandeur of the Niagara Falls.

**웅지**(雄志) a noble aspiration; high ambitions.

**웅천** an unreliable person; a gascon; 「a gasbag.

**웅편**(雄篇) a great literary work; a masterpiece.

**웅혼**(雄渾) grandeur; sublimity. ~하다 (be) grand; sublime; virile; vigorous. ¶ ~한 필치 a grand 〔sublime〕 style; 《서체》 a bold 〔vigorous〕 hand.

**워낙** ① 《원래》 by nature 〔origin〕; constitutionally; 《처음부터》 from the first. ¶ 그는 ~ 몸이 약하다 He was born weak. / 그는 ~ 온순한 사람이라 난폭한 짓은 안 한다 He is born good-natured and will never behave rudely.
② 《몹시》 so; 《너무나》 too; too much; excessively; [부정] 《not》 very 〔quite, much〕. ¶ ~ 사람이 성실하기에 그를 채용했다 He was so sincere that I employed him. / 이 문제는 ~ 어려워서 나로서는 풀 수가 없다 This problem is too difficult for me to solve.

**워드프로세서** 《문서작성용 컴퓨터》 a word processor. ¶ 한국어 ~ a Korean language word processor / ~로 편지를 쓰다 write a letter on a word processor.

**워드프로세싱** 《컴퓨터에 의한 문서 처리》 word processing. ¶ ~ 시스템 a word processing system.

**워리** 《개 부르는 소리》 Here doggy !; Here 「boy !

**워밍업** a warm-up; warming up. ¶ ~을 하다 warm up; limber up.

**워싱턴** ① 《미국 초대 대통령》 George Washington (1732-99). ② 《미국의 수도》 Washington; Washington, D.C. (★ D.C.는 District of Columbia의 생략). ③ 《미국의 주》 Washington (State) (생략 Wash., WA).

**워즈워스** 《영국의 시인》 William Wordsworth (1770-1850).

**워치** a watch.

**워크로드** 《작업 부하》 work load.

**워크맨** 《상표명》 a Walkman.

**워크숍** 《연수회》 a workshop. ¶ 직업 보도 ~ a workshop in vocational guidance / 인사 관리에 관한 2일 간의 ~ a two-day workshop on personnel management.

**워크스테이션** 〖컴퓨터〗 a workstation.

**워크아웃** ① 《동맹 파업》 a walkout. ② 《기업 개선 작업》 workout.

**워키토키** a walkie-talkie.

**워터** water. ◉ ~마크 a watermark: ~마크를 넣다 watermark. ~슈트 a water chute. ~스포츠 water sports. ~컬러 a watercolor. ~ 탱크 a water tank.

**워터게이지** 《수면계》 a water gauge.

**워터펌프** a water pump.

**워터폴로** 《수구》 water polo.

**워터프루프** 《방수성》 waterproof.

**워더그르르** with a rattle. ~하다 rattle.

**워더글덕더글, 워더글워더글** rattling. ~하다 rattle.

**원** 《통화》 a won (기호 ₩, ₩). ¶ 천 원짜리 지폐 a 1,000 won note 〔bill〕.

**원**(員) 〖고제도〗 《수령》 a district magistrate.

**원**(圓) a circle; a circlet (작은). ¶ 원을 그리다 draw 〔describe〕 a circle / 원을 그리며 날다 fly in a circle / 삼각형 주위에 원을 그리다 describe a circle around a triangle / 서울을 중심으로 원을 그리다 draw a circle with Seoul as its center. ◉ 원 운동〔진동〕 a circular movement 〔oscillation〕.

**원**(願) 《소망》 a wish; (a) hope; a desire; (a) longing; 《요청》 a request; 《탄원》 an entreaty; a solicitation; 《기원》 a prayer. ¶ 원을 들어주다 grant 〔comply with〕 *a person's* wishes / 평생의 원을 이루다 realize *one's* dearest wishes; have *one's* cherished hope fulfilled / 원에 의해 면직되다 be relieved of *one's* post at *one's* own request / 아버지의 원으로 그는 의사가 되었다 At his father's wish he became a physician. / 모든 일이 원대로 되었다 Everything came out as I hoped it would.

**원** [감탄사] Gosh!; Gee!; Goodness!; gracious; Well, well; a Son of a gun! (더러운 놈); Jesus! ¶ 원, 그놈 뻔뻔도 하다 Gee, what a nerve he's got! / 이거 원, 자네에게 뭐라고 하지 Well, well. What shall I say to you?

**원-**(元·原) original; first; primary. ¶ 원계획 초안 the first draft of the plan / 원주소 original residence / 나의 원계획 my original plan.

**-원**(員) a member; a person engaged in; an employee. ¶ 사무원 a clerk.

**-원**(願) 《출원》 an application; 《청원》 a petition. ¶ 입학원 an application for admission / 사직원 a (written) resignation.

**원가**(原價) 〖경제〗 the cost (price); the prime cost. ¶ 생산 ～ the cost of production / ～ 이하로 with loss on cost; for less than 《it》 costs; below cost / ～로〔이하로〕 팔다 sell at 〔below〕 cost / ～를 계산하다 calculate 〔compute〕 the cost.
◉ ～계산 cost accounting; costing: ～계산 담당자 a cost accountant 〔clerk〕. ～견적 an estimate of the cost; a cost estimate: ～견적 초과 cost overrun. ～관리 cost control. ～구성 cost structure 〔formation, makeup〕. ～절감 cost reduction 〔retrenchment〕.

**원거리**(遠距離) a great 〔long〕 distance; a long range. ¶ ～의 long-distance; long-range / ～에 at a long 〔great〕 distance / ～에서 사격하다 shoot 《at the enemy》 at long range. ◉ ～통학 long-distance commuting (to school).

**원격**(遠隔) being far apart; being widely separated; remote(ness). ～하다 be far apart 《from》; be widely separated 《from》; (be) remote; faraway; far-off; distant.
◉ ～조작 remote operation: ～조작하다 operate 《a machine》 by remote control. ～조종〔제어〕 remote control: ～조종기(機) a radio-controlled 〔remote-controlled〕 plane. ～지 무역 long-distance trade.

**원경**(遠景) a distant view; 《in》 the background (그림 등의).

**원고**(原告) 〖법〗 《민사에서》 a plaintiff; a suitor; 《형사에서》 an accuser; a prosecutor. ¶ 그 증거는 ～에게 명백히 불리하다 The evidence is clearly 「against the accuser 〔not in the accusser's favor〕. ◉ ～대리인 the plaintiff's representative. ～측 변호사 an attorney 〔a lawyer〕 for the plaintiff.

**원고**(原稿) a manuscript (생략 MS. *pl.* MSS.); a copy; 《투고·기고》 a contribution; 《초안》 a draft; 《기사》 an article. ¶ 자필 ～ a manuscript written in *one's* own hand / 타이프로 친 ～ a typescript; a typewritten 〔typed〕 copy / ～를 쓰다 write *one's* manuscript; prepare *one's* copy / ～를 써서 생활하다 live by writing 〔*one's* pen〕 / ～를 모집하다 invite 〔solicit〕 contribution 《for 〔to〕 a magazine》 / ～를 채택하다 accept 《*a person's*》 contribution / ～ 없이 연설하다 speak without a note / 그에게 잡지의 ～를 청탁했다 We asked him to write for our magazine.
◉ ～료 copy money; contribution 〔manuscript〕 fees; remuneration 〔pay〕 for writing; a fee for an article 〔a manuscript〕: ～료는 1페이지당 얼마로 지급됩니다 You are paid for your manuscript at so much a page. ～정리원 《신문사의》 a copyreader; a copy editor. ～지 manuscript paper; 《한 묶음의》 a writing pad.

**원광**(圓光) 〖종교〗 a halo; a nimbus.

**원광**(遠光) a distant view; a light seen from afar.

**원교**(遠郊) outlying suburbs; the country around a city.

**원군**(援軍) rescue forces; reinforcements; relief. ¶ ～을 보내다 send reinforcements 《to》 / ～을 요청하다〔기다리다〕「ask for 〔wait for〕 reinforcements.

**원근**(遠近) far and near; distance. ¶ ～을 불문하고 irrespective 〔regardless〕 of distance / ～ 각처에서 from far and near. ◉ ～감 〖사진〗 perspective. ～법 perspective (representation): ～법에 맞다〔어긋나다〕 be in 〔out of〕 perspective. ～화〔도〕 a perspective; a picture in perspective.

**원금**(元金) 《이자에 대한》 the principal; 《자본》 capital. ¶ ～과 이자 principal and interest.

**원급**(原級) 〖문법〗 the positive degree; 《원래의 급》 the original 〔same〕 class.

**원기**(元氣) vigor; energy; vitality; 《구어》 pep. ¶ ～ 부족 lack of vigor / ～가 왕성하다 be full of vigor 〔pep〕; be in good 〔high〕 spirits / ～를 돋우다 cheer 《*a person*》 up; invigorate / ～를 회복하다 recover *one's* strength.

**원기둥**(圓―) 《기둥》 a column; a pillar; 〖수학〗 a cylinder. ¶ ～꼴〔모양〕의 columnar; cylindrical.

**원내**(院內) ¶ ～의 floor; parliamentary; inside the House 〔National Assembly〕/ ～ 발언의 자유 freedom from liability for speeches made in the House. ◉ ～교섭 단체 《be qualified as》 a parliamentary negotiating group. ～ 안정 세력 a stable force in the legislature. ～총무 the floor leader 《미》; the (party) whip 《영》: ～ 부총무 a deputy floor leader / ～ 총무 회담 a floor leaders' meeting.

**원년**(元年) the first year 《of an era or a king's reign, *etc.*》.

**원단**(元旦) (the) New Year's Day.

**원당**(原糖) raw sugar; crude sugar.

**원대**(原隊) *one's* (home, parent) unit. ¶ ～ 복귀하다 return to *one's* unit.

**원대**(遠大) ～하다 (be) far-reaching; ambitious; lofty. ¶ ～한 포부 a great ambition; a lofty aspiration / ～한 계획을 세우다 make 〔contrive〕 a grand 〔far-reaching〕 scheme / 일을 ～하게 꾀하다 formulate a far-reaching program; take a long view 《of》.

**원동기**(原動機) a motor.

**원동력**(原動力) motive power 〔force〕; the prime mover; generative power; a motive; a dynamic; 《추진력》 driving force. ¶ 사회의 ～ the driving force of society / 생산의 ～ the basic production factors / 활동의 ～ the mainspring of activity.

**원두막**(園頭幕) a lookout (shed) on a melon field.

**원래**(元來) 《본래》 originally; primarily; 《선천적으로》 naturally; by nature; 《본질적으로》 essentially; 《사실은》 really; properly speaking; 《처음부터》 from the first. ¶ ～대로 as ever 〔before〕; as 《it》 was before / ～부터 from the first 〔beginning, outset〕/ ～ 상태로 되다 return to normal; be restored (to the former state) / 책을 ～ 자리에 갖다놓다 put a book back (where it was) / 그는 ～ 정직한 사람이다 He is honest by nature. / 우리는 ～ 평화를 애호하는 국민이다 We are an essentially peace-loving people. / 그녀는 ～ 몸이 약하다 She is naturally delicate in health.

**원래**(遠來) coming from afar. ～하다 come 「from afar 〔from a distance〕. ¶ ～의 손님 a visitor (come) from afar.

**원려**(遠慮) long-sightedness; forethought. ¶ ～가 없다 be lacking in forethought; be imprudent.

**원령**(怨靈) a (re)vengeful 〔vindictive〕 spirit 〔ghost〕.

**원로**(元老) 《정계의》 an elder 〔a senior〕 statesman; 《고참》 a senior (member); an elder; a grand old man; an old-timer 《in newspaperdom》; a veteran. ¶ 실업계의 ～ an elder in business circles / 신문계의 ～ the dean of the newspaper world.
◉ ～원 〖역사〗 the senate; the senate house. ～정치 government by elder statesmen: ～ 정치가 a senior 〔an elder〕 statesman.

**원로**(遠路) a long way 〔distance〕; a long journey. ¶ ～의 여행 a long journey / ～를 무릅쓰고 오다 come a long way; come from far away / ～를 마다 않고 와 주셔서 감사합니다 Thank you for (your) coming such a long way.

**원론**(原論) a theory; the principles 《of》. ◉ 경제학～ the principles of economics.

**원료**(原料) raw material; materials; 《재료》 an ingredient. ¶ ～를 확보하다 secure 〔procure〕 raw materials / 초콜릿 ～ the ingredients of 〔for〕 chocolate / 이 나무는 종이의 ～가 된다 This tree is used for making paper. / 포도주는 포도를 ～로 한다 Wine is made from grapes. ◉ ～공업 the raw material industry; the primary product industry.

**원룸맨션** a one-room apartment; a studio 「apartment 〔flat 《영》〕.

**원리**(元利) principal and interest. ◉ ～합계액 an amount with interest added.

**원리**(原理) principles; 《원칙》 the fundamental truth. ¶ 경제학 ～ the principles of economics / 궁극적 ～ the ultimate principle / 생활의 지도 ～ the guiding principle of life / 민주주의의 기본 ～ the fundamental principles of democracy / ～를 규명하다 go into the principles 《of》; inquire into the ultimate truth / ～를 응용하다 apply the theory 《to》/ …와 같은 ～로 on the same principle as…; on a similar principle to….

**원만**(圓滿) 《완전》 perfection; integrity; soundness; 《조화》 harmony; concord; peace; 《만족》 satisfaction; contentment; 《원활》 smoothness. ～하다 (be) harmonious; amicable; peaceful; 《만족스럽다》 (be) satisfactory; 《성격이》 (be) well-rounded; smooth. ¶ ～한 가

정 a happy home / ～한 해결 a peaceful settlement / ～한 신사 《성질 따위가》 an amicable gentleman / ～한 인격 all-round character / ～히 harmoniously; satisfactorily; happily / ～히 지내다 live in harmony 《with》 / ～히 해결하다 settle 《a dispute》 amicably; bring 《*a matter*》 to an amicable settlement / ～치 못하다 be at odds 〔be inharmonious〕 with 《*a person*》; lack harmony / 그들의 가정 생활은 ～하다 They are in a harmonious condition of home life. / 파업은 ～히 해결되었다 The strike was settled amicably.

**원망**(怨望) 《원한》 ill will 〔feeling〕; a grudge; resentment; a rancor; spite; 《증오》 hatred; 《적개심》 enmity; 《불평》 a grievance; a complaint. ～하다 resent; reproach; bear 《*a person*》 a grudge; harbor rancor 〔enmity, spite〕 《toward》; make a grievance against. ¶ ～의 말을 하다 complain 《to *a person* about》 / 남의 ～을 사다 incur *a person's* grudge 〔ill will〕; make an enemy of 《*a person*》 / 제 자신을 ～하다 reproach *oneself* 《for》 / 하느님을 ～하다 curse Heaven; have rancor against Heaven / 나는 자네를 ～하지 않네 I have no resentment against you. / 나는 남의 ～을 받을 짓을 한 적이 없다 I have done nothing to incur anyone's enmity.

**원망스럽다**(怨望—) (be) reproachful; resentful; 《유감스러운》 regrettable. ¶ 원망스러운 얼굴 a reproachful face / 원망스러운 듯이 reproachfully; resentfully; with a reproachful look / 그녀는 그를 원망스러운 눈초리로 보았다 She gave him a reproachful glance.

**원맨쇼** a one-man show.

**원면**(原綿) raw cotton.

**원명**(原名) an original name; 《실제 이름》 a real name.

**원모**(原毛) raw wool.

**원모**(遠謀) a far-sighted scheme; a long-range plan.

**원목**(原木) raw 〔unprocessed〕 timber. ¶ 제지용 ～ pulpwood.

**원무**(圓舞) a circle dance; a 〔the〕 waltz; a round. ◉ ～곡 〖음악〗 a waltz.

**원문**(原文) 《본문》 the text; 《원서》 the original. ¶ ～대로 《의심스럽거나 틀린 원문을 그대로 인용할 때의 표시》 *sic* (L.) / ～으로 읽다 read 《a novel》 in the original / ～에 충실하게 번역하다 make a translation faithful to the original; translate literally.

**원반**(圓盤) a disk; 《영》 a disc; 《원반 던지기용》 a discus. ◉ ～던지기 the discus (throw): ～던지기 선수 a discus thrower.

**원방**(遠方) a remote area; a distant district; a faraway place; far-off parts.

**원배하다**(遠配—) exile to a remote place.

**원병**(援兵) reinforcements. ¶ ～을 보내다 send reinforcements 《to》 / ～이 포위된 수비대의 구원에 파견되었다 The reinforcements were sent to the relief of the besieged garrison.

**원본**(原本) the original (copy); the (original) text; 〖법〗 the script. ¶ 이것이 사본의 ～이다 This is the original of these copies.

**원부**(怨婦) a spiteful woman; a vindictive 〔malignant〕 woman.

**원부**(原簿) the original register; 〖부기〗 the original ledger; the original account book.

**원불교**(圓佛敎) *Won* Buddhism.

**원뿔**(圓—) 〖수학〗 a (circular) cone. ◉ ～곡선 a conic. ～대(臺) a truncated cone. ～면 a conical surface.

**원사**(元士) a sergeant major (육군); a master chief petty officer (해군); a master gunnery sergeant (해병대); a chief master sergeant (공군).

**원사**(寃死) 《원통한 죽음》 being put to death on a trumped-up charge. ～하다 be put to death on a trumped-up charge.

**원사이드게임** a one-sided game.

**원산**(原産) ¶ 동남아시아 ～의 뱀 a snake native to South-east Asia / 열대 ～의 식물 a tropical plant / … ～이다 originally come from 《Mexico》. ◉ ～물 a primary product.

**원산지**(原産地) the place 〔country〕 of origin; 《동식물의》 the (original) home; the habitat. ¶ ～ 불명의 of doubtful provenance / 설탕의 ～ the home of sugar / 그 사건은 한국의 일부 중요 수출품에 대한 ～ 문제를 제기시킬 것이다 The event will (actively) raise the country-of-origin issues for some of Korea's leading exports.
◉ ～증명 certification of origin: ～증명서 a certificate of origin (생략 C/O). ～표지〔레테르〕 country-of-origin marks 〔labels〕: 정부는 주요 수입품에 대해 ～표지 부착을 다음달부터 의무화하기로 하였다 The government will make it mandatory for major imported goods to carry country-of-origin labels

beginning next month.

**원상**(原狀) the original state; the former condition; 〚법〛 the *status quo ante* (L.). ¶ ～으로 회복〔복구〕하다 restore 《*a thing*》 to the original state 〔the former condition〕; 〚법〛 reestablish 〔restore matters to〕 the *status quo ante.*

**원색**(原色) 《기본색》 a primary color; 《원래의 색》 the original color(s). ¶ 삼～ the three primary colors. ◉ ～사진 a heliochrome (상표명); a color 〔colored〕 picture. ～판 《인쇄의》 (a) full-color reproduction; 《책》 a full-color edition.

**원생**(原生) ¶ ～의 primeval; primordial. ◉ ～대 the Proterozoic era. ～동물 a protozoan (*pl.* -zoa). ～림(林) a primeval 〔virgin〕 forest. ～생물 a protist. ～식물 a protophyte. ～토(土) residual 〔sedimentary〕 soil.

**원서**(原書) an original (language) edition; the original 《text, work》. ¶ 바이런을 ～로 읽다 read Byron in the original. ◉ ～강독 reading original texts in class.

**원서**(願書) an 〔a written〕 application; 《서식》 an application form 〔blank〕. ¶ ～를 제출하다 present 〔file, send in〕 an application 《for》 / ～를 접수하다 receive 〔accept〕 an application (form) / ～ 접수를 마감하다 stop receiving applications / ～를 작성하다 fill an application form.

**원성**(怨聲) murmur of grievances 〔complaints〕. ¶ ～을 사다 earn 《*a person's*》 grivance.

**원소**(元素) 〚화학〛 an (original) element; a chemical element. ¶ 몇 개의 ～로 분해하다 resolve into several elements. ◉ ～기호 the (chemical) symbol of an element. ～분석 elementary analysis. ～주기율 the periodic law of the elements. 불안정～ an unstable element.

**원손**(遠孫) distant 〔remote〕 descendants.

**원수**(元首) a sovereign; a ruler 〔head, chief〕 of state.

**원수**(元帥) 〚육군〛 a general of the army 《미》; a five-star general 《미구어》; a field marshal 《영》; 〚해군〛 a fleet admiral 《미》; an admiral of the fleet 《영》; 〚공군〛 a general of the air force 《미》; a marshal of the Royal Air Force 《영》.

**원수**(怨讐) 《사람》 an enemy; a foe; 《사물》 the object of *one's* grudge 〔grievances〕. ¶ ～지간 mutual enemies / 불구대천의 ～ a sworn 〔mortal〕 enemy 〔foe〕 / ～를 갚다 revenge *oneself* on 《*a person*》; get 〔take, have〕 *one's* revenge on 《*a person*》; 《구어》 get even with 《*a person*》; 《구어》 get *one's* own back on 《*a person*》 / ～ 지다 become an enemy 《of》 / 은혜를 ～로 갚다 do 〔return〕 evil for good / 그들은 서로 ～지간이다 They are enemies to each other.

**원수폭**(原水爆) atomic and hydrogen bombs; nuclear and thermonuclear bombs. ◉ ～금지 세계대회〔회의〕 a World Rally 〔Conference〕 Against Atomic and Hydrogen Bombs.

**원숙**(圓熟) maturity; mellowness; ripeness. ～하다 ripen; mature; mellow; grow accomplished; become perfect. ¶ ～한 mature; perfect; ripe; fully-developed / ～한 인격 mellowed character / ～한 사상 mature ideas / ～기에 접어들다 come to the ripening stage / ～의 경지에 달하다 attain 〔reach〕 maturity.

**원숭이** a monkey; an ape (유인원). ¶ ～상을 한 사람 a monkey-faced man / ～ 같은 apelike; monkeylike / ～를 놀리다 put a monkey through its paces; get the monkey to his tricks / ～도 나무에서 떨어진다 《속담》 "Even Homer sometimes nods."

**원시**(原始) 《처음》 the beginning; origin; genesis; 《본래의》 proto; 《자연 그대로》 the original 〔primitive〕 state of nature. ¶ ～적 primitive; primeval; original / ～적 생활 a primitive (form of) life; a primeval life / ～적 상태 a primitive state / ～적 본능 the primitive instinct. ◉ ～공동체 a primitive community. ～림 a virgin 〔primeval〕 forest. ～사회 primitive society. ～산업 the primitive industry. ～생물 a primitive organism. ～세포 a primordial cell. ～시대 the primitive age; primitive times. ～인 (a) primitive man; a primitive. ～종교 a primitive religion.

**원시**(遠視) ① 《바라봄》 looking far-off at. ② 〚의학〛 long sight; farsightedness; hypermetropia; 《영》 longsightedness. ¶ ～이다 《미》 be farsighted; 《영》 be longsighted. ◉ ～경(鏡) glasses for the farsighted. ～안(眼) a hypermetropic 〔far-sighted〕 eye.

**원심**(原審) ① 《원판결》 the original 〔initial〕 judgment 〔verdict, decision〕. ②

《하급 법원》 the court of original judgment; the lower court. ¶ ~대로 as originally decided / ~을 파기하다 reverse the original decision; overrule the original judgment.

**원심**(怨心) bitterness; ill will [feeling]; a grudge; resentment. ¶ ~을 품다 have [harbor, feel] a grudge《against》.

**원심**(圓心) 〖수학〗 the center (of a circle).

**원심력**(遠心力) 〖물리〗 centrifugal force.

**원심분리기**(遠心分離機) a centrifugal separator; a centrifuge.

**원심탈수기**(遠心脫水機) a centrifugal filter; a hydroextractor.

**원심펌프**(遠心—) a centrifugal pump.

**원아**(園兒) 《유치원의》 kindergarten children; 《유아원의》 nursery school children.

**원안**(原案) 《의안(議案)》 the original bill; 《계획》 the original plan; 《초안》 a draft. ¶ ~을 수정하다 amend the original bill / ~을 제출하다 produce a draft proposal [a rough draft] / ~을 지지하다 support the original bill [motion] / ~대로 가결하다 pass a bill in its original form.

**원앙**(鴛鴦) ① 〖조류〗 a mandarin duck. ② [비유적] a pair of lovebirds. ¶ 한 쌍의 ~ a couple of lovebirds; a happily married couple.
◉ ~금(衾) a coverlet [quilt] embroidered with mandarin ducks on it; the marriage bed: ~금을 나누다 share the marriage bed.

**원액**(元額·原額) the original sum [amount].

**원액**(原液) an undiluted solution.

**원야**(原野) 《벌판》 an uncultivated field; a plain; 《황야》 wasteland; a wilderness (★ 《미》에서 wilderness는 「황야」 「사막지대」뿐만 아니라 「삼림지대」도 포함해서, 태고 때의 자연 그대로의 모습을 간직하고 있는 모든 미개척지를 뜻함).

**원양**(遠洋) the open sea far from land; the deep sea; an ocean.
◉ ~어선 a deep-sea fishing vessel; a pelagic-fishing vessel. ~어업 deep-sea [pelagic] fishery [fishing]; ocean-going fisheries: ~어업 회사 a deep-sea fishery firm. ~항로 an ocean line: ~항로선 an ocean-going vessel; an ocean liner. ~항해 ocean navigation [voyage]; a long cruise: ~항해를 떠나다 set out on ocean navigation.

**원어**(原語) the original word [language]. ¶ ~로 읽다 read《a novel》in the original.

**원언**(怨言) grudging [spiteful] remarks; malignant [bitter] words.

**원영**(遠泳) a long-distance swim.

**원예**(園藝) gardening; 《원예학》 horticulture; 《화초 재배》 floriculture.
◉ ~가[사] a gardener; a horticulturist. ~술 the art [technique] of gardening. ~시험장 a horticultural experiment(al) station. ~식물 a garden plant. ~용구 gardening tools. ~작물 garden stuff [products]. ~장 a nursery. ~학교 a horticultural school.

**원외**(員外) nonmember(ship); supernumerary (status). ◉ ~교수 a professor extraordinary. ~자 a nonmember.

**원외**(院外) ¶ ~의 outside the House [National Assembly]; non-parliamentary. ◉ ~단 a nonparliamentary group of party members. ~운동 an outdoor agitation; 《미》 lobbying; lobbyism; lobby: ~운동을 벌이다 lobby. ~자 a lobbyist 《미》. ~투쟁 an out-of-the-National Assembly struggle.

**원용**(援用) ~하다 claim; 《인용》 quote; 《법률 등을》 invoke (조문을); cite 《a precedent》. ¶ 조항을 ~하다 invoke a clause.

**원유**(原油) crude oil [petroleum].

**원유회**(園遊會) a garden party. ¶ ~를 열다 give [hold] a garden party.

**원음**(原音) ① the original sound《of a character》; the original pronunciation (원음의 발음). ② 〖음악〗 the fundamental tone.

**원의**(原意) the original intention.

**원의**(原義) the primary [original] meaning《of a word》.

**원의**(院議) the decision of the House [National Assembly].

**원인**(原人) a primitive man; Dawn [Early] Man.

**원인**(原因) 《결과에 대한》 a cause; 《근원》 the origin; the source; the root; 《발단》 the origin; 《요인》 a factor. ¶ 문제를 일으키게 된 ~ the source of the trouble / 직접[간접] ~ an immediate [a mediate, an indirect] cause / 싸움의 ~ the origin of the quarrel / 분쟁의 ~ the root of trouble / ~ 불명의 《a fire》 of unknown origin; unaccountable / …이 ~이다 be caused by…; start [arise] from; be due to…; result from… / ~을 규명하다 try to find the cause 《of》; trace 《*something*》 to its origins / ~ 없는 결과란 없다 There are no results without causes. / 그녀의 병은 과로가 ~이다 Her sickness is the result of fatigue. / 그가 망한 것은 술이 ～이었다 Drink caused 〔was cause of〕 his downfall. / 병의 ～은 비타민 부족에 있었는지도 모른다 This disease may be caused by a lack of vitamins. ◉ ～결과 cause and effect. 궁극 ～ the ultimate cause.

**원인**(猿人) 〚인류〛 an ape-man. ◉ 자바 ～ the Java man.

**원인**(遠因) an underlying 〔a remote, distant〕 cause. ¶ …의 ～이다 form a remote cause 《of》.

**원인**(願人) an applicant; a petitioner.

**원일점**(遠日點) 〚천문〛 the aphelion (*pl.* ～s, -lia); the higher apsis.

**원자**(原子) 〚물리〛 an atom; a corpuscle. ¶ ～의 atomic; 《원자 병기의》 nuclear. ◉ ～가 atomic value; (a) valence 《미》; (a) valency. ～구조 atomic structure. ～기호 the symbol of an element. ～낙진 atomic 〔radioactive〕 fallout; death ash (죽음의 재). ～량(量) atomic weight. ～로(爐) an atomic reactor 〔furnace〕; an (atomic) pile: ～로 연료 reactor fuel / ～로 폐액(廢液) effluent waste from a nuclear reactor / ～로의 누출(漏出) 사고 a leakage accident at atomic reactor. ～론 the atomic theory; 《고대 그리스 철학의》 atomism: ～론자 an atomist. ～무기 〔병기〕 an atomic 〔a nuclear〕 weapon; atomic 〔nuclear〕 arms. ～물리학 atomic 〔nuclear〕 physics: ～ 물리학자 an atomic 〔a nuclear〕 physicist. ～번호 an atomic number. ～병(病) radiation sickness: ～병 환자 a sufferer from radiation sickness. ～ 부피 atomic volume (생략 at. vol.). ～분열 atomic fission. ～시(간) atomic time. ～시계 an atomic clock. ～식 an atomic formula. ～ 에너지 atomic 〔nuclear〕 energy. ～역학 atomic mechanics. ～열 atomic heat. ～운(雲) an atomic cloud; a nushroom cloud. ～질량 atomic mass: ～ 질량 단위 atomic mass unit. ～포(砲) an atomic gun 〔cannon〕. ～폭발 atomic explosion; a A-blast. ～(폭)탄 an atomic 〔atom〕 bomb; an A-bomb: ～탄두 an atomic warhead / ～탄 탑재기 an atomic bomber. ～핵 an atomic nucleus: ～핵 분열 〔반응·융합〕 nuclear fission 〔reaction, fusion〕 / ～핵 분열 물질 a fissionable materials / ～핵 파괴 장치 an atom smasher / ～핵 공학 nucleonics.

**원자력**(原子力) atomic 〔nuclear〕 energy 〔power〕. ¶ ～으로 움직이는 atom(ic)=〔nuclear-〕powered / ～의 평화적 이용 the peaceful uses of atomic 〔nuclear〕 energy; the use of atomic energy for peaceful purposes. ◉ ～ 공동 관리안 a plan for an atomic pool. ～관리 atomic energy control. ～국제 관리 the international control of atomic energy. ～로켓 a nuclear=powered rocket. ～발전 nuclear 〔atomic〕 power generation: ～ 발전기 a nuclear generator / ～ 발전소 a nuclear 〔an atomic〕 power station 〔plant〕. ～병원 the (Korea) Cancer Center Hospital. ～사고 an atomic energy accident. ～산업 nuclear power industry. ～(상)선 a nuclear(-powered) ship 〔vessel〕. ～시대 the atomic age. ～ 안전 센터 the Nuclear Safety Center. ～엔진 an atomic engine. ～연구소 the Institute of Atomic Energy Research: 한국 ～ 연구소 Korea Atomic Energy Research Institute. ～연료 nuclear 〔atomic〕 fuel. ～위원회 《유엔·미국의》 an Atomic Energy Commission (생략 AEC). ～잠수함 a nuclear(-powered) submarine. ～청 the Office of Atomic Energy (생략 OAE). ～추진 atomic 〔nuclear〕 propulsion: ～ 추진의 nuclear=propelled / ～ 추진 수중익선(水中翼船) a nuclear-powered〔-propelled〕 hydrofoil. ～ 평화 이용 계획 the atoms-for=peace program. ～ 항공 모함 a nuclear=〔an atomic-〕powered (aircraft) carrier. ～협정 an atomic energy agreement. 국제 ～ 기구 the International Atomic Energy Agency (생략 IAEA). 한국 ～ 문화 재단 the Organization for Korea Atomic Energy Awareness.

> 참고 「원자력」, 「핵분열」을 뜻하는 경우의 형용사로서, 최근에는 atomic보다 nuclear를 더 자주 사용한다. 예를 들면, 원자력 잠수함은 atomic(-powered) submarine보다 nuclear(-powered) submarine으로 부르는 경우가 더 많음.

**원자재**(原資材) raw material(s). ¶ 외국에서 ～를 수입하다 import raw materials from foreign countries.

**원작**(原作) an original (work) 《of art》. ◉ ～자 the (original) author 〔writer〕: ～자 불명의 책 a book of doubtful authorship.

**원장**(元帳) a ledger (생략 led.). ¶ ～에 기입하다 enter 《an item》 〔make an entry〕 in a ledger / ～과 대조하다 check 《the account》 with the ledger.

◉ ~잔액 a ledger balance. 총계정~〚부기〛 a general ledger.

**원장**(院長) the director ⦅of a hospital⦆; the president ⦅of an academy⦆.

**원장**(園長) the principal ⦅of a kindergarten 〔nursery school〕⦆; the curator ⦅of a zoo⦆.

**원저**(原著) the original work 〔book〕. ◉ ~자 the author.

**원적**(原籍) *one's* original domicile. ⇨ 본적(本籍).

**원전**(原典) the original text ⦅from which a translation or quotation is made⦆.

**원점**(原點) ⦅측량⦆ the datum 〔fiducial〕 point; ⦅좌표축의⦆ the origin (of the coordinate axes); ⦅출발점⦆ the starting point. ¶ ~으로 돌아가다 go back to the starting point / ~에서 다시 생각하다 consider ⦅*a thing*⦆ again from the beginning.

**원정**(遠征) ⦅군대·탐험대 등의⦆ an expedition; ⦅경기의⦆ a visit; a tour. ~하다 make 〔go on〕 an expedition ⦅into⦆; go on a tour ⦅to 〔of〕 the U.S.A.⦆; tour ⦅Britain⦆; visit.
◉ ~경기 an away match 〔game〕. ~군〔대〕 an expeditionary force; ⦅경기의⦆ a visiting 〔an away〕 team.

**원조**(元祖) ⦅창시자⦆ the originator; the founder; the father; ⦅발명자⦆ the inventor; ⦅제조원⦆ the original maker. ¶ 국제법의 ~ the father of international law / 당점은 마포 갈비의 ~입니다 Our restaurant is the originator of *Mapo Kalbi*.

**원조**(援助) ⦅조력⦆ assistance; aid; help; ⦅지원⦆ support. ~하다 assist; aid; support; help; back (up); stand by ⦅*a person*⦆; render assistance ⦅to⦆. ¶ 미국의 ~를 받는 나라 a U.S. aid-receiving nation / ~를 얻다 receive 〔secure, derive〕 assistance / ~를 주다 give 〔afford, lend〕 assistance 〔support〕 to; render help to; give 〔offer, render, extend〕 aid to...; lend 〔stretch〕 a helping hand ⦅to...⦆ / ~를 `(요)청하다 ask for 〔seek, invoke〕 ⦅*a person's*⦆ assistance; seek ⦅*a person's*⦆ help; call in ⦅*a person's*⦆ aid / 남에게 ~를 바라다 turn to *a person* for assistance.
◉ ~국 a donor country; an aid donor; an aid country: 피~국 an aid-receiving nation; aid-recipient country. ~금 an aid fund. ~물자 aid goods. ~사업 an aid project. ~자 a supporter. 경제〔군사, 식량〕~ economic 〔military, food〕 aid: 경제〔군사〕~를 제공하다 hand out ⦅$50 million⦆ in economic 〔military〕 aid. 재정(적)~ financial help 〔aid〕: 나는 그녀의 어머니로부터 재정적인 ~를 받았다 I was aided financially by her mother. 정신적〔물질적〕 ~ moral 〔material〕 support. 해외 ~ 계획 a foreign aid plan 〔program〕: 한국은 해외~ 계획을 재검토할 필요가 있다 Korea needs to reexamine its foreign aid policy.

**원족**(遠族) distant relatives of the same family origin.

**원죄**(原罪) 〚기독교〛 original sin.

**원죄**(冤罪) a false accusation. ¶ ~를 입다 be falsely charged with; be falsely accused of / ~를 씻다 clear *oneself* of a false charge.

**원주**(圓周) 〚수학〛 the circumference of a circle. ◉ ~율 the circular constant; the ratio of the circumference of a circle to its diameter; pi (기호 $\pi$).

**원주**(圓柱) a column. =원기둥.

**원주민**(原住民) a native; a aborigine; an aboriginal; [총칭] the native population. ◉ ~ 보호주의 nativism.

**원지**(原紙) stencil paper; a stencil; a master sheet.

**원진**(圓陣) a circle. ¶ ~을 치다 form a circle; stand 〔sit〕 in a circle.

**원질**(原質) an elementary substance; a protyle. ◉ 유전~ a gene.

**원채**(原—) 〚건축〛 the main building 〔house〕.

**원척**(遠戚) a distant connection; a remote relative.

**원천**(源泉) ⦅물의⦆ the fountainhead; the head-spring; the wellspring; ⦅근원⦆ a source; an origin. ¶ 힘의 ~ a source of strength / 지식의 ~ a fount of wisdom / ~을 거슬러 올라가다 go to the fountainhead / 수면이야말로 우리들의 활동의 ~이다 It is sleep that is the well-spring of our activity.
◉ ~과세 ⦅미⦆ (a) withholding tax; ⦅영⦆ pay-as-you-earn (생략 P.A.Y.E.): ~과세하다 tax 〔withhold taxes〕 at the source. ~징수 withholding 〔deducting〕 taxes at the (income) source: ~징수제도 a system of withholding taxes / ~징수표 a withholding slip; a W-2 form ⦅미⦆.

**원체**(元體) ① = 워낙. ② ⦅몸체⦆ the body.

**원촌**(原寸) actual 〔natural〕 size. ¶ ~ 크기의 full-scale〔-size(d)〕; of full size.

**원촌**(遠寸) distant kinship. ¶ ~의 distantly 〔remotely〕 related / ~이 되는 사람 a distant relative.

**원추**(圓錐) a cone. = 원뿔.
**원추꽃차례**(圓錐—) 〚식물〛 a panicle.
**원추리** 〚식물〛 a day lily.
**원칙**(原則) a fundamental rule; a (governing) principle; a general rule.
¶ ~(적)으로 as a (general) rule; in principle / ~에 반하다 go against 〔be contrary to〕 principle / ~에 의거〔입각〕하다 be based on a (basic) principle / ~을 세우다 formulate 〔establish〕 a principle / …하는 것을 ~으로 하다 make it a rule to 《*do*》 / ~적으로 동의하다 agree in principle / ~적으로 제안을 받아들이다 accept a proposition in principle / 돈을 빌리지도 꿔주지도 않는다는 것이 나의 ~이다 It's my principle neither to borrow nor to lend money. ◉ 기본~ a cardinal 〔basic〕 principle.
**원컨대**(願—) I wish…; I pray…; please; Would (to God) that …. ¶ 하느님, ~ 전쟁에 황폐된 이 나라에 복을 내리소서 O God, have mercy on this war-torn country. / ~ 그와 같은 사고는 두 번 다시 일어나지 않게 하소서 I pray to God an accident like that never happens again.
**원탁**(圓卓) a round table. ◉ ~토론〔회의〕 a roundtable discussion 〔conference〕.
**원통**(寃痛) ① 《분》 reproachfulness; resentment; 《유감》 ruefulness; regrettableness; 《억울》 mortification; chagrin; vexation. ~하다 (be) resentful; regrettable; vexing; mortifying. ¶ ~해서 이를 갈다 grind *one's* teeth with vexation / 뼈에 사무치도록 ~하다 taste the bitterest mortification.
② 《애통》 lamentation; grief; deep sorrow. ~하다 (be) grievous; lamentable. ¶ 그가 죽다니 참 ~한 일이다 I suffer deeply with grief at his death.
**원통**(圓筒) a cylinder. ¶ ~형의 cylindrical.
**원판** 《원래》 the original state of things.
**원판**(原板) 〚사진〛 a negative plate 〔film〕; a negative.
**원판결**(原判決) the original decision. = 원심(原審).
**원폭**(原爆) an atom(ic) bomb; an A-bomb. ¶ ~에 의한 보복 an atomic retaliation 〔reprisal〕.
◉ ~기지 an atomic base. ~실험 an atomic test; an A-test: ~실험 금지 an atomic test ban / ~실험을 하다 conduct an atomic test; test-explode an atomic bomb. ~운(雲) a mushroom cloud. ~증(症) radiation sickness; illnesses caused by atomic bomb radiation. ~투하 atomic bombing. ~희생자 A-bomb victims.
**원피**(原皮) raw hide; (a) green hide 〔skin〕.
**원피스** a one-piece dress.
**원하다**(願—) 《소망》 desire; wish; hope 〔long〕 for; 《요청》 want; ask for; request; 《간원》 wish; pray for; implore.

> 용법 **want** 필요하기 때문에 「…하고 싶다」는 뜻의 단도직입적인 표현. 보통 손윗사람에게는 안 씀. **wish** 「…이었으면 좋으련만」이라는 뜻으로서 실현성이 없을 경우에는 가정법과 함께 씀. 그 밖에 「기원하다」, 가벼운 명령조로서 「…해 주기 바라다」 등의 뜻이 있음. **desire** want, wish의 강한 표현. 격식을 갖춘 말. **hope** 실현 가능한 것을 「바라다」, 「기대하다」라는 뜻. **long** (**for**) 멀리 떨어져 있는 것, 또는 손쉽게 이루어질 수 없는 것을 「열망하다」「절실히 원하다」.

¶ 원한다면 if you please 〔wish, like, prefer〕 / 원하는 대로 as *one* pleases / 평화를 ~ wish for peace / 의사가 되기를 ~ wish to be a doctor / 훌륭한 사람이 되기를 ~ aspire to become a great man / 아들이 성공하기를 ~ wish success to *one's* son / 미국 가기를 ~ want to go to America / 돈과 명예 중 어느 쪽을 원하나 Which would you rather have, money or fame? / 그것이 바로 내가 원했던 것이다 That is just what I have wished for.
**원한**(怨恨) a grudge; spite; resentment; 《증오》 (a) hatred; rancor; 《악의》 ill will; malice; 《적의》 enmity; hostility. ¶ ~ 맺힌 원수〔적〕 *one's* mortal 〔deadly, sworn〕 enemy / ~에 의한 살인 murder from 〔for〕 grudge 〔revenge〕 / ~을 사다 incur 《*a person's*》 grudge 〔ill will, rancor〕; make an enemy of 《*a person*》 / ~을 품다 have 〔harbor, hold〕 a grudge 《against *a person*》; bear 《*a person*》 a grudge / ~을 풀다 pay off old scores; have 〔get〕 *one's* revenge 《on *a person*》 / ~을 잊다 forget *one's* grudge 《against》; forgive 《*a person*》 / ~이 뼈에 사무치다 have a deep-rooted rancor 〔grudge〕 《against》; bear 《*a person*》 a bitter grudge; be full of rancor 〔grudge〕 《against》 / 대체 내게 무슨 ~이 있느냐 What have you got against me?
**원항**(遠航) ocean navigation; a long cruise. ~하다 set out to navigate an ocean; be on a long cruise. ¶ ~중이다 be on a long(-distance) cruise.

**원해어**(遠海魚) a pelagic fish.

**원행**(遠行) a long 〔far〕 journey. ～하다 go on 〔make〕 a long journey; go a long way 《to》.

**원형**(原形) the original form. ¶ ～을 유지하다 retain *its* original form; remain intact / ～을 잃다 have no trace 〔vestige〕 of the original form; lose *its* original form / ～대로 복구되다 be restored to its original form / ～에서 달라지다 be out of shape; have no trace of the original form / 문화유산을 ～대로 보존하다 keep cultural heritage in the original form. ◉ ～부정사 『문법』 a bare infinitive. ～질 protoplasm: ～질체 a protoplast / ～질막 a cell membrane / ～질 분리 plasmolysis.

**원형**(原型) a model; a prototype (공학·발생학 등의); an archetype (문학·미술 등의); a mold (주물의); a cast (조각이나 주물의). ¶ A는 B를 ～으로 삼고 있다 B is a model for A. *or* A models after B.

**원형**(圓形) a round shape 〔form〕; a circle. ¶ ～으로 circularly; in a circle / ～으로 오려내다 cut out (in) a circle. ◉ ～극장 an amphitheater; a theater-in-the-round. ～탈모증 alopecia areata.

**원호**(援護) support; backing; protection; relief. ～하다 support; back (up); protect; give relief to; lend support to. ◉ ～기금 a relief fund. ～대상자 a relief recipient. ～병원 a relief hospital. ～회 a relief society.

**원호**(圓弧) 『수학』 a circular arc. ¶ ～를 그리다 describe 〔trace〕 circular arcs.

**원혼**(寃魂) the spirit of *one* put to death on a trumped-up charge.

**원화**(一貨) the won (currency). ◉ ～예치율 the won deposit rate.

**원화**(原畫) the original painting 〔picture〕.

**원활**(圓滑) smoothness; 《융화》 harmony. ～하다 (be) smooth; harmonious. ¶ ～하게 smoothly; harmoniously; amicably; without a hitch; in harmony / ～하게 작동하는 엔진 a smoothly running engine.

**원훈**(元勳) a man of the highest merit; 《원로》 a veteran statesman.

**원흉**(元兇) 《사람》 the ringleader 《of the riot》; 《사물의》 the source 〔cause〕 《of the evils》. ¶ 공해의 ～ the source of environmental pollution / 밀수단의 ～을 체포하다 arrest the ringleader of the smuggling ring.

**월** 《문장》 a sentence.

**월**(月) 《달》 the moon; 《한달》 a month. ¶ 월세계 the lunar world; the moon / 월 평균 on a monthly average / 월 1회의 once a month; monthly / 월 2회의 twice monthly; bimonthly; semimonthly.

**월가**(一街) 《뉴욕의》 Wall Street.

**월간**(月刊) monthly publication 〔issue〕. ¶ ～의 monthly. ◉ ～잡지 a monthly magazine.

**월갈** 『언어』 syntax.

**월경**(月經) menstruation; (menstrual) periods; the menses; 《구어》 the monthlies. ¶ ～중인 여성 a menstruating woman; a woman who is having her 〔a〕 period; 《완곡히》 a woman who is indisposed 〔unwell〕 / ～이 있다〔없다〕 have the 〔no〕 menses / ～을 하다 have the menses 〔monthlies〕 / ～중이다 be in *one's* menses; 《완곡히》 be in flowers; be unwell 《미》. ◉ ～과다 profuse menstruation. ～기 the menstrual 〔catamenial〕 period. ～대(帶) a sanitary belt 〔towel, napkin〕. ～불순 menstrual irregularity; irregular menstruation. ～순조 regular menstruation. ～연령 a menstrual age. ～통 menstrual pain 〔cramps 《미》〕; period pains. ～폐쇄기 the menopause; the change of life: ～폐쇄기의 여자 a woman at the menopause.

**월경**(越境) crossing the border; (a) border transgression; (a) violation of the border. ～하다 cross the border 〔frontier〕 《into》; transgress 〔violate〕 the border 《of a neighboring state》. ◉ ～비행 an overflight. ～사건 a border incident.

**월계**(月計) a monthly account. ～하다 cast accounts monthly. ◉ ～표 『상업』 monthly trial balance.

**월계관**(月桂冠) a laurel wreath 〔crown〕; [비유적] the highest honor: 승리의～을 쓰다 be crowned with the laurel of victory; carry off the honors.

**월계수**(月桂樹) 『식물』 a laurel (tree); a bay tree. ¶ ～잎 『요리』 a bay leaf.

**월계화**(月季花) 『식물』 a China rose.

**월광**(月光) moonlight; moonbeams; moonshine. ◉ ～곡 the Moonlight Sonata.

**월권**(越權) abuse of authority 〔confidence〕; arrogation. ～하다 exceed 〔overstep〕 *one's* authority; exceed the prerogatives of *one's* office; go beyond *one's* bounds 〔powers〕; arrogate power. ¶ 그런 일을 하는 것은 ～이다 It

is overstepping your bounds to do such a thing. *or* It is beyond your right to do so.
◉ ～행위 an act of arrogation; malfeasance: 그는 ～행위를 했다 He has exceeded〔overstepped〕his authority.

**월급**(月給) monthly pay; a (monthly) salary. ¶ 백만 원의 ～으로 《work》 at 〔for〕 a salary of one million won / 많은〔적은〕 ～을 받다 get〔receive, draw〕 a large〔small, low〕 salary〔pay〕 《from a firm》 / ～으로 살다 live on *one's* salary / ～이 오르다〔내리다〕 get a rise〔cut〕 in *one's* salary / 그 회사는 ～이 많다〔적다〕 The company pays good〔poor〕salaries.
◉ ～날 (a) payday. ～봉투 a pay envelope. ～쟁이 a salaried man〔worker〕; a white-collar worker (사무직의).

**월남**[1](越南) Vietnam. ＝베트남.

**월남**[2](越南) coming south (from North Korea). ～하다 《경계선을 넘어》 come south over the border; 《북한땅에서》 come from North Korea. ◉ ～동포《피난민》 North Korean refugees; 《귀순자》 North Korean defectors.

**월내**(月內) ¶ ～에 within the〔a〕month.

**월년생식물**(越年生植物) a biennial (plant).

**월당**(月當) monthly allocation〔distribution, allotment〕; monthly allowance.

**월동**(越冬) wintering; passing the winter. ～하다 winter 《at, in》; pass the winter. ¶ ～ 준비를 하다 prepare for coming winter months / 그 자동차는 ～장비가 갖춰져 있지 않다 The car is not winterized. / 많은 갈매기들이 호수에서 ～하는 것을 볼 수 있다 We can see a large number of wild ducks passing the winter at〔on〕the lake.
◉ ～계획 a winterization plan. ～대(隊) a wintering party〔team〕: 남극～대 the wintering party in the Antarctic. ～대책 measures for winterization. ～자금 winter relief fund; a winter allowance. ～준비 preparation for the winter; winterization.

**월드시리즈** 〚야구〛 the World Series.

**월드와이드웹** 〚컴퓨터〛 World Wide Web (생략 WWW; 인터넷에서 가장 많이 사용되는 이용 형태. 통칭 웹).

**월드컵** 〚스포츠〛 the World Cup. ¶ 한국은 2002년에 ～을 일본과 공동 개최하도록 지명되었다 Korea has been named co-host of the World Cup with Japan in 2002.

**월등**(越等) being superior by far. ～하다 (be) vastly different; extraordinary; singular; incomparable; [서술적] be superior by far; be by far the best. ¶ 반에서 ～한 학생 a student who is by far the best in class / ～히 by far / ～히 싼 값 an incredibly〔unbelievably〕low price / ～히 우수하다 be far superior / ～히 키가 크다 be outstandingly tall / ～히 낫다 be far better; be better by miles / 영어를 ～히 잘 하다 excel (others) in English / 그녀는 ～한 기억력의 소유자다 She has an extraordinary memory.

**월력**(月曆) a calendar. ⇨ 달력.

**월령**(月齡) the age of the moon.

**월례**(月例) ¶ ～의 monthly. ◉ ～경제 동향 보고 회의 a monthly economic briefing session. ～보고 a monthly report. ～회 a monthly meeting.

**월리**(月利) monthly interest.

**월말**(月末) 《at, toward》 the end of the month. ¶ ～에〔까지〕 at〔by〕 the end of the month / ～ 지급〔계산〕을 하다 pay the monthly bill / ～까지는 이 일을 끝내겠습니다 I'll finish this work by the end of this month. ◉ ～계산〔셈〕 month-end payment〔settlement〕.

**월면**(月面) the surface of the moon; the lunar surface. ◉ ～도 a selenographic chart. ～보행 a moon〔lunar〕walk. ～차 a lunar rover; a moon buggy. ～착륙 a 《manned》 lunar landing; a landing on the moon.

**월반**(越班) skipping a grade. ～하다 skip a grade. ¶ 그는 2학년에서 4학년으로 ～했다 He skipped the third grade and entered the fourth. / 재능 있는 학생은 ～할 수 있다 A talented student can skip grade(s). ◉ ～제도 grade skipping system.

**월변**(月邊) monthly interest.

**월보**(月報) a monthly report〔bulletin〕; monthly returns. ¶ 무역 ～ monthly trade returns.

**월부**(月賦) monthly payments; payment in〔by〕monthly installments. ¶ 매월 만 원씩 10개월 ～, 10 monthly payments of ten thousand won each / ～로 샀을 때 붙는 이자 a carrying charge / ～로 사다〔팔다〕 buy〔sell〕 《a TV set》 on the installment plan〔on hire purchase 《영》〕 / ～로 구두 한 켤레 맞추다 have a pair of shoes made on the monthly installment plan / 나는 2년 ～로 이 자동차를 샀다 I bought this car on the installment plan to be paid for over a period of two years. /

그녀는 TV의 ~금으로 매월 2만원씩 지불한다 She pays for the TV set in 〔by〕 monthly installments of twenty thousand won. *or* She pays an installment of twenty thousand won on the TV set every month.
◉ ~구입 installment buying. ~액 the amount allocated per month. ~지급 paying by monthly installments. ~판매 the (monthly) installment sale; installment selling; 《제도·방법》 the installment plan 《미》; (monthly) hire purchase (system) 《영》; 《구어》 the easy payment plan: ~ 판매를 하다 sell 《*a thing*》 on the installment plan.

**월북**(越北) crossing over 《the border》 into North Korea. ~하다 《경계를 넘어》 go north over the border; 《북한땅으로》 go to North Korea. ◉ ~작가 a writer who went to North Korea.

**월비**(月費) monthly expenses.

**월사금**(月謝金) monthly tuition 《미》; a (monthly) tuition 〔school〕 fee. ¶ ~을 내다 pay *one's* school fee / ~을 면제하다 exempt 《a student》 from tuition.

**월삭**(月朔) the first day of the month.

**월산**(月産) monthly production; (a) monthly output. ¶ 그 공장은 ~ 1,000톤의 비료를 생산한다 The plant produces 〔yields, manufactures〕 1,000 tons of fertilizer monthly 〔a month〕.

**월색**(月色) moonlight; moonbeam(s).

**월세**(月貰) monthly rent. ¶ 이 집은 ~ 30만 원이다 The house rents at three hundred thousand won a month.

**월세계**(月世界) the lunar world; the moon. ⇨ 달나라.

**월수**(月收) ① 《빚》 a loan at monthly interest. ② 《수입》 a monthly income. ¶ 그의 ~는 90만 원이다 His monthly income amounts to 900,000 won. *or* He makes 900,000 won a month.

**월수당**(月手當) a monthly allowance.

**월식**(月蝕) 〚천문〛 an eclipse of the moon; a lunar eclipse. ¶ 개기〔부분〕~ a total 〔partial〕 eclipse of the moon.

**월액**(月額) a monthly amount 〔sum〕.

**월야**(月夜) a moonlight 〔moonlit〕 night.

**월여**(月餘) more than a month. ¶ ~간이나 over 〔for more than〕 a month / ~ 전에 more than a month ago.

**월요병** blue Monday; Blue Monday.

**월요일**(月曜日) Monday (생략 Mon.).

**월일**(月日) the month and the day; 《날짜》 the date. ◉ 생년~ the date of *one's* birth.

**월장석**(月長石) 〚광물〛 moonstone.

**월전**(月前) a month ago.

**월정**(月定) contracting 〔arranging〕 by the month; a monthly contract. ¶ ~의 monthly; month-to-month / ~으로 by the month. ◉ ~고용 month-to-month engagement; hiring by the month. ~구독료 monthly subscription. ~구독자 a monthly subscriber.

**월차**(月次) ¶ ~의 monthly. ◉ ~계획 a monthly program. ~보고 a monthly report. ~(유급)휴가 a monthly paid holiday.

**월초**(月初) 《at》 the beginning of the month.

**월출**(月出) moonrise; the rise of the moon.

**월평**(月評) a monthly review 〔criticism, comment〕. ◉ 문단~ a monthly survey of the literary world.

**월표**(月表) a monthly list 〔table〕; monthly returns.

**웨딩** wedding. ◉ ~드레스〔마치〕 a wedding dress 〔march〕. ~벨 wedding bells. ~케이크 a wedding cake.

**웨버** 《자속(磁束)의 단위》 weber (기호 Wb).

**웨스턴** 《극》 a Western; 《음악》 country (=and-western) music.

**웨스트버지니아** 《미국의 주》 West Virginia (생략 W.Va.).

**웨이브** 《머리의》 a wave. ¶ ~진 머리 wavy hair / 머리에 ~를 하다 have *one's* hair waved.

**웨이스트** the waist. ¶ ~가 날씬하다 have a slim 〔slender〕 waist / 그녀의 ~는 58센티다 She measures 58 centimeters around the waist. / 이 스커트는 ~가 크다 This skirt is big around the waist. ◉ ~라인 the waistline.

**웨이스트볼** 〚야구〛 a waste ball 〔pitch〕.

**웨이터** a waiter. ¶ ~를 부르다 call for a waiter.

**웨이트리스** a waitress.

**웨이트 트레이닝** 〚운동〛 weight training.

**웨이팅 서클** 〚야구〛 the on-deck circle; the next batter's box.

**웨이퍼** 《과자》 a wafer.

**웨일스** 《영국의》 Wales. ¶ ~의 Welsh; Welch. ◉ ~말 Welsh. ~사람 a Welshman 〔Welshwoman〕; [총칭] the Welsh 〔Welch〕.

**웩웩** ¶ (게우려고) ~거리다 keck; retch.

**웬** what sort 〔kind〕 of. ¶ 웬 사람이냐 Who is the man? *or* What is he here for?

**웬걸** O my!; Why!; Why no!; Goodness no!; Gee!; Gosh! ¶ 산책 나가려고 했더니, ~ 소낙비가 쏟아졌다 I was going out for a walk, but by George, it started to shower. / ～ 그가 오늘 모임에 올까 Gee, I wonder if he isn't coming to the meeting after all. / ～ 이렇게 많은 사과를 가져 오셨습니까 My goodness gracious—what a lot of apples you have brought me! / 「인제 끝났니」—「웬걸, 막 시작한 참이야」 "Have you finished?"—"Why, I have only just begun."

**웬만큼** 《어느 정도》 to some extent; to a certain degree; 《어지간히》 fairly; passably; considerably; 《알맞게》 moderately; appropriately; properly.
¶ 영어를 ～하다 speak English fairly well / 술에 ～ 취하다 be rather tipsy / 고기가 ～ 익었다 The meat is done to a turn. / 농담도 ～ 해라 Don't go too far with your jokes. *or* Enough of your jokes. / ～ 마셔라〔먹어라〕 (Take it) easy on the liquor 〔food〕. / 그에게는 그 때 재산도 ～있었다 He was fairly rich then. / 우리의 계획은 ～ 성공했다 Our plan was successful to some extent.

**웬만하다** (be) fairly good; tolerable; passable; satisfactory; be pretty close to it; 《비꼬는 투로》 (be) terrific; tremendous; splendid. ¶ 수입이 ～ have a handsome income / 생김생김이 ～ be quite good-looking / 웬만하면 if you please; if you like; if you don't mind; how about (*do*ing…) / 그녀석 욕심도 웬만히 많군 What greed he has!

**웬일** what matter; what cause; what reason. ¶ ～인지 for some reason (or other) / ～이냐 What is all this? *or* What is the matter? *or* What's got into you? / ～로 왔는가 What has brought you here? / ～인지 그가 불쌍하게 여겨졌다 I felt sorry for him for reasons I couldn't understand.

**웰터급**(一級) the welterweight class. ¶ ～의 선수 a welterweight; a welter.

**웹** 〖컴퓨터〗 Web (World Wide Web의 생략). ◉ 웹브라우저 〖컴퓨터〗 a web browser (인터넷의 월드와이드 웹 정보를 검색하는 데 사용되는 프로그램). 웹사이트 Web site (웹 서비스를 제공하는 곳).

**위** ① 《위쪽》 the upside; the topside; the upper part; the above; a higher place. ¶ 위의 《…보다도》 upper / 위에 《위치》 on; above; over / 위로 《운동을 나타내어》 up; upward; onto; on to (★ above는 위치의 높음을 나타내지만 반드시 바로 위를 뜻하지는 않음. over는 수직적으로 「바로 위」에 있음을 보임. on은 「표면에 접하여」의 뜻: There is a fly *on* the ceiling. 「천장에 파리가 앉아 있다」/ I knocked *on* the door. 「나는 도어를 두드렸다」 upon도 거의 같은 뜻이지만 약간 문어적인 말. up, upward는 종종 운동을 나타내는 말과 함께 사용되어 「위를 향해서」의 뜻을 나타냄) / 위로 향한 upward; 《코 따위가》 turned-up / 테이블 위의 전등 the light over 〔above〕 the table / 위에서 말한 바와 같이 as we have said above / 언덕 위의 집 the house on the hill / 문 위의 간판 a sign above the door / 위에서 내려다 보다 look down at; look at 《*a thing*》 from above / 위를 쳐다보다 look upward / 이쪽을 위로 《게시》 This end up. *or* This side up. / 산봉우리는 구름 위로 솟아 있다 The peak rises above the clouds. / 비행기가 하늘 위를 높이 날고 있다 A plane is flying high up in the sky. / 우주에서는 위아래가 없으므로 몸의 방향은 문제가 안 된다 In space there is no up and down, so *one's* bodily position is immaterial.

② 《꼭대기》 the top; the summit. ¶ 맨 위의 topmost; uppermost / 위로부터 셋째 줄 the third line from the top / 위에서 아래까지 from top to bottom / 언덕 위로 올라가다 climb to the top of a hill / 나무 위에 새가 있다 A bird is up in a tree. / 위로 올라 오너라 Come up here.

③ 《표면》 the (upper) surface; the the surface (side); on. ¶ 책상 위의 책 the books on the desk / 해파리가 바다 위에 떠 있다 A jellyfish is floating on the surface of the sea. / 연못 위에 달이 비치고 있다 The moon is shining over the pond.

④ 《지위·나이·품질 등이 낫거나 높은 쪽》 ¶ 위의 《높은》 higher; 《…이상》 more than; above; over; beyond; 《나은》 superior; 《연상의》 older / 윗자리 a higher position 〔rank〕 / 위로부터의 명령 an order from above / 제일 위의 누나 my eldest sister / 윗 학교에 가다 attend a higher institution of education / 한 학년 위다 be a class ahead of 《*a person*》 / 기는 놈 위에 나는 놈 있다 《속담》 "There is no limit to those above us." / 그는 나보다 한 살 위이다 He is a year older than I. *or* He is older than I 〔senior to me〕 by one year. (★ elder는 *one's* elder brother처럼 한 가족내의 형제, 자매 관계를 나타내는 데 쓰이며, older는 그 이외의 경우에 사용됨. 다만 미국에서는 elder의 경우에도 older를 많이 씀. 그리고 구어에서는 than I 보다 than me가 많이 쓰임) / 너희들 중에서 누가 가

장 나이가 위냐 Who is the oldest among you? / 그는 지위가 나보다 위다 He is above me in rank. / 소령은 중위보다 두 계급 위다 A major is superior to a lieutenant by two ranks. / 위를 쳐다보면 한이 없다 [비유적] Don't compare yourself with those above you. ⑤《더욱·게다가》《in》addition; 《on》the top《of》. ¶ 그 위에 in addition to; moreover; besides; into the bargain; to boot; what's more / 그 위에 더 할 말이 없다 I don't have anything more to say.

**위**(位) ①《지위·등급》a place; a rank; a position. ¶ 제2위의 the second-ranking《Dodgers》/ 3위가 되다 take 〔gain, win〕 third place; be placed third / 소수 제2위까지 계산하다 calculate to the second decimal place / 그녀는 학급에서 10위로 떨어졌다 She has dropped to the tenth (place) in her class. / 한국은 연간 자동차 생산 대수가 세계 제3위다 Korea ranks third in the world in annual automobile production. ②《위패를 셀 때》¶ 영령 백위 one hundred heroic souls.

**위**(胃) 〖해부〗 the stomach. ¶ 위의 gastric / 위의 가스 gas 〔wind〕 on the stomach / 반추 동물의 제1〔2, 3, 4〕위 the paunch 〔honeycomb, manyplies, maw〕 of a ruminant / 위수술 an operation on the stomach / 위가 약한 사람 a person with a weak digestion 〔stomach〕 / 위가 아프다 have a stomachache; have a pain in *one's* stomach / 위가 튼튼하다〔약하다〕 have a strong 〔weak〕 stomach / 위를 상하다 get *one's* stomach out of order / 위가 거북하다 lie heavy on the stomach / 위를 튼튼히 하다 strengthen a weak stomach / 위의 내용물을 조사하다 examine the contents of《an animal's》stomach / 과음으로 위의 상태가 나빠졌다 Heavy drinking has upset my stomach.
◉ 위내시경 ⇨ 위경(胃鏡). 위신경증 gastric neurosis. 위절개(술) gastrotomy. 위점막 the gastric mucous membrane. 위카메라《구식의》a gastrocamera; 《내시경》a (gastro)fiberscope. 위카타르 〖의학〗 catarrh of the stomach; gastric catarrh. 위펌프 〖의학〗 a stomach pump.

**위**(緯)《위도》latitude; 《씨》the woof.

**위경**(危境) a critical situation; a crisis (*pl.* crises); danger; peril. ¶ ～을 당하다 face a crisis / ～을 벗어나다 tide over 〔pass through〕 a crisis.

**위경**(胃鏡) 〖의학〗 a gastroscope; a (gastro)fiberscope. ◉ ～검사법 gastroscopy.

**위경련**(胃痙攣) 〖의학〗 convulsions of the stomach; (stomach) cramps. ¶ ～을 일으키다 get 〔have〕 stomach cramps.

**위계**(位階) a grade of rank(s); a (court) rank. ◉ ～제 a hierarchy. ～질서 the order of ranks.

**위계**(僞計) a deceptive plan; a fraudulent stratagem. ¶ ～를 쓰다 use a deceptive scheme.

**위공**(偉功) a meritorious service; a great merit 〔deed〕. ¶ ～을 세우다 render great services; achieve a great deed.

**위관**(胃管) a stomach tube.

**위관**(偉觀) a grand sight 〔spectacle〕; a spectacular sight.

**위관**(尉官) 〖육군〗 a company officer; officers below the rank of major; a subaltern (소위·중위); 〖해군〗 officers below lieutenant commander.

**위광**(威光) authority; power; sway; influence. ¶ 대통령의 ～ presidential authority / 부모의 ～으로 through the influence of *one's* parents.

**위구**(危懼) fear; apprehensions; misgivings. ～하다 fear; be afraid 〔feel fear〕 of; be apprehensive over. ¶ ～심을 품다 entertain misgivings《about》; be apprehensive《of》.

**위국**(危局) a crisis; a critical situation. ¶ 경제적인 ～ an economic crisis / …을 ～으로 몰아넣다 bring ... to a crisis / ～을 넘기다 tide over a critical situation.

**위국하다**(爲國―) serve 〔benefit〕 *one's* country; be for (the benefit of) *one's* country; do *one's* country good.

**위궤양**(胃潰瘍) 〖의학〗 a stomach 〔gastric〕 ulcer; an ulcer of the stomach.

**위급**(危急) a crisis (*pl.* crises); an emergency. ～하다 (be) critical; exigent; urgent. ¶ ～시에 in case of emergency; in time of danger 〔need〕 / ～을 고하다 spread 〔give〕 the alarm; raise an alarm / ～에서 구하다 save《*a person*》from imminent danger; help《*a person*》at the most crucial time / ～할 때는 도와 주겠다 I will be by you in the hour of danger. / 우리는 국가 존망이 걸린 ～한 시기에 있었다 We were facing a national crisis.

**위기**(危機) a crisis (*pl.* crises); a critical situation; a critical moment 〔juncture〕; a crucial moment 〔hour〕.

¶ ～에 임하여 at the critical 〔crucial〕 moment; at a crisis / 정치적〔재정상의〕 ～ a political 〔financial〕 crisis / ～가 닥치다〔에 처하다〕 come to a crisis; be at a crisis / ～를 벗어나다 pass 〔get〕 through a serious crisis; tide over a crisis / ～에 빠지다〔빠져 있다〕 fall into 〔be in〕 crisis / 정부는 지금 중대한 ～에 직면해 있다 The Government is now facing a serious crisis. / 국제적 ～감은 완화되었다 There has been an easing of the atmosphere of international crisis. / 한국은 항상 에너지 ～의 가능성을 안고 있다고 생각한다 I think Korea always faces the possibility of an energy crisis. / IMF의 도움으로 우리는 금융 ～를 벗어났다 Help from the IMF tided us over the financial crisis. / 「그 백화점이 경영 ～란 소문이 들리고 있다」―「방만한 경영 때문이야」 "There is a rumor of a managerial crisis at the department store."―"Their management is very lax."
◉ ～감 a sense of crisis. ～관리 risk 〔crisis〕 management. ～일발: ～일발의 순간에 at the critical moment; in the nick of time / ～일발의 상황에서 벗어나다 escape 《death》 by a hair's breadth 〔by the skin of *one's* teeth〕; have a narrow 〔hairbreadth〕 escape.

**위난**(危難) a crisis and peril; (a) danger; jeopardy. ¶ ～을 당하다 encounter 〔meet with〕 a danger; be in peril 〔danger〕 / ～을 면하다 escape danger; get out of danger.

**위대**(偉大) greatness. ～하다 (be) great; grand (웅대한); 《강대한》 (be) mighty. ¶ ～한 국민 a great nation / ～한 업적 a great 〔stupendous〕 achievement / 그리스도의 ～함 the greatness of Jesus Christ / 그는 한국이 낳은 가장 ～한 정치가다 He is the greatest statesman that Korea has ever produced.

**위도**(緯度) 〖지리〗 latitude. ¶ ～의 latitudinal / ～상(으로) latitudinally / 고〔저〕～지방 high 〔low〕 latitudes / ～를 달리하다 be in different latitudes 《from》 / ～를 측정하다 determine the latitude / 그 지방의 ～는 북위 20도이다 The latitude of the region is twenty degrees north. ◉ ～선 a parallel. ～측정 determination of latitude.

**위독**(危篤) a critical 〔serious〕 condition of illness. ～하다 be critically 〔seriously, hopelessly〕 ill; be in a critical condition; 《입원 환자가》 be on the danger 〔critical〕 list. ¶ ～해 지다 [사람이 주어] fall into a critical 〔dangerous〕 condition; [병이 주어] take a critical 〔dangerous〕 turn.

**위락**(萎落) withering and falling. ～하다 wither and fall.

**위락시설**(慰樂施設) recreational 〔amusement〕 facilities.

**위란**(危亂) a (national) crisis; a critical situation. ～하다 (be) critical; tumultuous.

**위략**(偉略) an outstanding stratagem; a 「grand tactics.

**위력**(威力) 《힘·세력》 power 《of authority》; might; authority (권력); influence (세력). ¶ ～적인 powerful; mighty; formidable / ～적인 투구 a powerful pitch / 돈의 ～ the power of money 〔wealth〕 / 폭탄의 ～ the power of a bomb / 국가의 ～ the national authority / ～에 의한 업무 방해 〖법〗 forcible obstruction of business; obstructing business by force / ～을 떨치다 wield 〔exercise〕 *one's* power 《over people, in politics》; make *one's* influence felt; 《구어》 throw *one's* weight around / ～으로 굴복시키다 bring 《*a person*》 into submission by showing *one's* power / 그의 펀치는 굉장한 ～이 있다 His punch is very powerful. / 바람은 점점 그 ～을 더해갔다 The wind was gathering its force. / 그 폭탄의 어마어마한 ～이 그 전쟁에서 증명되었다 The terrible power of the bomb was proved in the war.

**위력**(偉力) great power 〔strength〕; mighty force. 「der〕; authority.

**위령**(威令) authoritative command 〔or-

**위령**(違令) violation 〔breach, infringement〕 of an order 〔a command, a decree〕. ～하다 violate 〔break, go against〕 an order.

**위령제**(慰靈祭) a memorial service. ◉ 전몰용사 ～ a memorial service for the war dead.

**위령탑**(慰靈塔) a memorial tower; a war memorial; a cenotaph 《built in memory of war victims》.

**위로**(慰勞) ① 《치사》 recognition 〔appreciation〕 of 《*a person's*》 services 〔efforts〕. ～하다 recognize; acknowledge 《*a person's*》 services. ¶ ～회를 열다 hold a party in acknowledgement of services.
② 《위안》 solace; consolation; comfort; entertainment. ～하다 console; solace; comfort; entertain (★ console은 낙담하거나 슬퍼하는 사람을 위로하다는 뜻이며, comfort에는 괴로움이나 슬픔을 달래어 희망을 준다는 적극적인 뜻이 포함되어 있음. sol-

ace는 낙담이나 슬픔뿐만 아니라 지루함이나 고독감을 달래주다의 뜻). ¶ ～의 말 words of comfort / 불행을 ～하다 console 〔solace〕 《*a person*》 in *his* misfortune / 병자를 ～하다 sympathize with a patient / 뭐라고 ～의 말을 해야 할지 몰랐다 I found myself at a loss for words of consolation.

◉ ～금 a bonus; a reward for *one's* services. ～연 a (dinner) party in appreciation of 《*a person's*》 services; a beanfeast; a 'thank-you' party. ～휴가 a special vacation 〔holiday 《영》〕 in appreciation of 《*a person's*》 services.

**위막**(胃膜) 〖해부〗 the coats of the stomach.

**위망**(威望) power and fame; authority 〔influence〕 and popularity.

**위명**(威名) renown; fame; prestige. ¶ ～이 혁혁한 장군 a general of high renown.

**위명**(僞名) a false 〔an assumed〕 name; 《특히, 범죄자의》 an alias. ¶ …라는 ～으로 under the false name of 《Big Jack》 / ～을 사용하다 use 〔assume〕 a false name / ～을 대다 give a false name.

**위무**(慰撫) pacification; soothing; consolation; comfort. ～하다 pacify; soothe; console; comfort. ¶ ～ 가다 go and comfort 《*a person*》; pay a sympathetic visit 《to》.

**위문**(慰問) 《환자의》 an inquiry (after *a person's* health); 《이재민 등에 대한》 (an) expression of *one's* sympathy 《for a sufferer》; 《방문》 a visit 〔call〕 of sympathy 〔consolation〕. ～하다 ask 〔inquire〕 after *a person's* health; pay a visit of inquiry to 《*a person*》; visit; show solicitude toward. ¶ ～ 가다 go and comfort 《*a person*》; pay a sympathetic visit 《to》; visit *a person* 《in hospital》.

◉ ～금 a solatium; a gift of money: 그녀는 이재민에게 줄 ～금을 모으고 있다 She is collecting money for the sufferers. ～대(袋) a comfort bag 〔kit〕 for 〔sent to〕 a soldier (at the front). ～방문 a call of inquiry. ～선(船) an amenity ship. ～편지 a consolatory letter; a letter of sympathy. ～품 a comfort; a present 〔gift〕 《to a sick person》.

**위반**(違反) 《법규의》 (a) violation; (an) infringement; an offense; 《명령 따위의》 disobedience; 《약속 따위의》 (a) breach. ～하다 violate 《a regulation》; break 《*one's* promise, a contract》; be 〔act〕 against 《a law》. ¶ 교통(법규) ～ traffic violation 〔offense〕 / 주차 ～ parking violation; illegal parking / 법률 ～ a violation of 〔an offense against〕 the law / 계약 ～ a breach of contract / …을 ～하여 in violation of / 선거법을 ～하다 infringe the election law / 조약을 ～하다 violate a treaty / 그는 예사로 약속을 ～한다 He does not hesitate to break his word. / 그는 속도 ～으로 적발되었다 He was caught for speeding. / 너의 행동은 규칙 ～이다 Your behavior is against the rule. / 그는 교통 ～으로 처벌 받았다〔벌금을 물었다〕 He was punished 〔fined〕 for a traffic offense. / 한 여자 경찰관이 주차 ～을 단속하고 있다 A policewoman is citing a parking violation.

◉ ～자 an offender; a violator: 이 법의 ～자는 1년 징역 또는 50만 원 이하의 벌금을 물게 된다 Violators of this law face up to a year in jail or a fine of up to 500,000 won. ～행위 an offense.

**위배**(違背) ＝위반. ¶ 올림픽 정신에 ～되다 《it》 run counter to the Olympic spirit.

**위법**(違法) violation of law; illegality; unlawfulness. ～하다 violate 《law》; break; infringe. ¶ ～의 unlawful; illegal / ～적으로 illegally; against the law / 폭발물의 차내 반입은 ～이다 It is ｢illegal 〔against the law〕 to bring explosives in 〔to〕 the coach.

◉ ～건축물 an illegally built house. ～성 illegality. ～자 a lawbreaker; an offender. ～처분 illegal disposition 〔measures〕. ～행위 an illegal act; 《공무원의》 malfeasance.

**위벽**(胃壁) 〖해부〗 the walls of the stomach; the stomach walls 〔lining〕.

**위병**(衛兵) a guard; a sentry; a sentinel. ¶ ～을 세우다 post a guard / ～을 서다 serve 〔act〕 as guard; mount 〔be on〕 guard 《at》.

◉ ～교대 the changing of the guard: ～교대식 the ceremony of changing the guard. ～근무 guard 〔sentry〕 duty: ～ 근무가 끝나다 come off guard / ～ 근무를 교대하다 relieve guard. ～소 a guardhouse; a guardbox. ～장교 an officer (in charge) of the guard.

**위병**(胃病) a stomach trouble; a stomach disorder; dyspepsia; indigestion. ◉ ～학 gastrology. ～환자 a dyspeptic.

**위복하다**(威服—) 《복종시키다》 awe 《*a person*》 into obedience; 《굴복하다》 submit to power.

**위본**(僞本) a fabricated book; a spurious copy; a forgery; 《해적판》 a pirated edition.

**위부**(委付) 〖법〗 abandonment. ～하다 abandon. ¶ ～조항 an abandonment clause.

**위부**(胃腑) the gastric region. ¶ ～의 gastric.

**위산**(胃散) 〖약〗 (medicinal) powder for the upset stomach.

**위산**(胃酸) stomach acids. ◉ ～결핍증 〖의학〗 anachlorhydria. ～과다 〖의학〗 excess(ive) acid in the stomach: ～과다의 hyperacid / ～ 과다증 hyperacidity.

**위상**(位相) 〖전기·물리〗 a phase. ◉ ～각(角) 〖물리〗 a phase angle. ～계(計) a phase meter 〔indicator〕. ～공간 〖수학〗 topological space; 〖물리〗 phase space. ～기하학 topology. ～변이 〖물리〗 phase shift. ～변조 〖전기〗 phase modulation (생략 PM). ～상수(常數) 〖물리〗 a phase constant; an initial phase. ～속도 〖물리〗 phase velocity. ～수학 topology; analysis situs. ～순서 〖컴퓨터〗 topological order. ～조정 phase adjustment: ～ 조정 변압기 a phase compensating transformer. ～차 a phase difference: ～차 현미경 a phase microscope; a phase(-contrast〔-difference〕) microscope.

**위생**(衛生) hygiene; sanitation (공중의); health (건강). ¶ 공중～ public health / 정신～ mental health 〔hygiene〕 / ～의, ～적인 hygienic; sanitary / ～에 좋은 good for (the) health; wholesome 《food》; healthy 《climate》 / ～에 나쁜 bad for (the) health; unwholesome; unhealthy / ～에 무관심하다 be careless about *one's* health / ～에 주의하다 be careful of *one's* health; attend to sanitation / ～에 해롭다 be insanitary; be unhealthful 〔unhealthy〕; be injurious 〔detrimental〕 to health; be bad for the health / 저 식당은 그다지 ～적인 것 같지 않다 That restaurant doesn't look very sanitary to me. / 식사 전에 손을 안 씻는 것은 비～적이다 It's unsanitary not to wash your hands before eating.
◉ ～감사 a sanitation check: 엄중한 ～ 감사를 받다 be subject to severe sanitation checks. ～공학 sanitary engineering. ～관념 sanitary thought; sense of hygiene 〔sanitation〕: 그들은 ～ 관념이 없다 They have no sense of hygiene. ～관리 health control 〔administration〕. ～대 《생리대》 a sanitary belt 〔napkin〕. ～법 hygiene; hygienics. ～병 〖군사〗 a hospital orderly; a medical corpsman; a medic 《구어》. ～복 disinfected overgarment. ～비 sanitation expenses. ～상태 sanitary conditions. ～시설〔설비〕 sanitary 〔health〕 facilities. ～시험소 a hygienic laboratory. ～실 a sanitary 〔medical〕 room. ～학 hygienics; sanitary science: ～학자 a hygienist; a sanitarian.

**위서다** accompany a bride 〔groom〕 to the wedding place; 《수행하다》 accompany 〔attend〕 an important person.

**위선**(僞善) hypocrisy. ¶ ～적(인) hypocritical; double-faced / ～을 행하다 behave hypocritically; play the hypocrite; do 〔practice〕 hypocrisy.
◉ ～자 a hypocrite; a pharisee.

**위선**(緯線) 〖지리〗 a parallel (of latitude); a latitude line.

**위성**(衛星) a satellite. ¶ 기상〔통신〕 ～ a weather 〔communications〕 satellite / 정지 ～ a stationary satellite / 정찰 ～ a reconnaissance satellite / 첩보〔공중사찰〕 ～ a spy 〔an eye-in-the-sky〕 satellite / 방송～ a telecommunication satellite / 달은 지구의 ～이다 The moon is a satellite of the earth. / 그 역사적인 행사는 ～으로 전세계에 중계되었다 The historic event was transmitted all over the world by satellite.
◉～ 관제 센터 a satellite control center. ～국(가) a satellite country 〔state〕; a satellite. ～궤도 the orbit 〔path〕 of a satellite. ～도시 a satellite town 〔city〕. ～발사 the launching of a satellite. ～방송 satellite broadcasting. ～사업〔비즈니스〕 satellite business. ～선(船) a satellite ship. ～송신 transmission via satellite. ～요격 무기〔미사일〕 〖군사〗 the antisatellite 〔ASAT〕 weapon 〔missile〕. ～중계 satellite relay: ～ 중계로 by 〔via〕 satellite relay / ～ 중계하다 transmit 《an event》 via satellite. 국제 상업 ～ 통신 기구 the International Telecommunications Satellite (생략 INTELSAT). 군사～ a military satellite. 미사일 탐지 ～ a missile warning satellite. 실용 ～ a practical satellite. 요격～ 〖군사〗 a killer satellite. 위성 공격용 ～ an anti=satellite interceptor (생략 ASAT). 지구 물리학 관측 ～ the Orbiting Geo-

physical Observatory.

**위세**(威勢) 《세력》 power; influence; authority; 《기운》 high 〔elated〕 spirits; dash. ¶ ~ 있는〔좋은〕 (high-)spirited; dashing; lively; energetic; vigorous / ~ 없는 listless; lifeless; spiritless / ~ 좋게 in high spirits; vigorously / ~를 부리다 exercise 〔wield〕 *one's* authority over 《*others*》 / ~를 보이다 make a display of *one's* influence; make *one's* influence felt / ~에 굴복하다 kneel 〔bow〕 to authority 〔power〕 / 그는 입으로는 ~를 떨지만 실제로는 소심한 사람이다 He certainly uses aggressive language but in reality he's something of a coward.

**위세척**(胃洗滌) 〖의학〗 gastrolavage. ~하다 wash out the stomach; carry out a gastric lavage. ¶ ~기 a stomach pump.

**위수**(衛戍) 〖군사〗 a garrison.
◉ ~근무 garrison duty. ~령 the Garrison Decree 〔Act〕: ~령을 발동하다 invoke the garrison act 《in》. ~병 garrison troops. ~병원 a garrison hospital. ~사령관 the commander of the garrison headquarters. ~지 a garrison town.

**위스콘신** 《미국의 주》 Wisconsin (생략 Wis., Wisc.).

**위스키** whisk(e)y. ¶ 물을 탄 ~ a whisky and water / ~를 스트레이트로 마시다 drink whisky straight 〔neat〕 / ~를 더블로 두 잔 주시오 Two double whiskies, please.
◉ ~소다 a whisky and soda; a highball 《미》. 버번~ Bourbon whisky. 스카치〔아이리시〕~ Scotch 〔Irish〕 whisky. 캐나디언 ~ Canadian whisky. 혼합~ blendid whisky.

> **참고** 미국에서는 보통, 국산 위스키를 whiskey, 수입한 것을 whisky로 철자하는 경우가 많다.

**위시하다**(爲始—) commence; begin; start. ¶ 김 박사를 위시해서 starting with 〔including〕 Dr. Kim / 그를 위시해서 다섯 명이 찾아왔다 Five men, including him, came to see me.

**위신**(威信) authority and confidence; prestige; dignity; honor. ¶ ~에 관계되다 affect 〔compromise, involve〕 *one's* dignity 〔prestige〕; be beneath *one's* dignity / ~을 잃다 lose authority 〔prestige〕; lose 〔lower〕 *one's* dignity; let *oneself* down / ~을 지키다 maintain 〔preserve〕 *one's* dignity 〔prestige〕 / ~을 손상하다 injure 〔dim〕 the prestige 《of》 / ~을 되찾다 recover *one's* lost prestige / 정부의 ~은 땅에 떨어졌다 The prestige of the Government is gone.

**위아래** 《위치》 up and down; top and bottom; 《신분의》 the upper and lower classes; high and low. ¶ ~로 up and down; above and below; high and low (높고 낮게) / ~ 구별없이 both high and low; irrespective of rank / 아무를 ~로 훑어 보다 look *a person* up and down; survey *a person* from head to foot.

**위아랫물지다** the different kind of two liquids seek separate levels; 《사람이》 people of different classes 〔age=groups〕 do not mix.

**위안**(慰安) 《위로》 (a) consolation; (a) solace; (a) comfort; 《오락》 (a) recreation; (an) amusement. ~하다 console; solace; comfort; amuse. ¶ 다소의 ~ some slight consolation / 다소의 ~이 되다 some comfort can be drawn 《from》 / ~을 주다 give comfort to 《*one's* employees》; afford solace / ~을 찾다 seek solace 〔comfort〕 《in religion》 / …에서 ~을 얻다 find *one's* comfort in…; take 〔derive, draw〕 comfort from… / 노인들을 ~하기 위해 병원을 방문하다 visit a hospital to comfort the aged / 이제는 독서가 그의 유일한 ~이다 Reading is the only pleasure left to him.
◉ ~물 a comfort; an article of comfort. ~부 a comfort woman 〔girl〕; a military prostitute: ~부 문제는 이제 다시 새로운 주목을 받게 되었다 The issue of comfort women has now gained renewed attention. ~시설 recreation facilities. ~회 a recreation meeting; an entertainment.

**위암**(胃癌) 〖의학〗 gastric 〔stomach〕 cancer; (a) cancer of the stomach.

**위압**(威壓) high-handedness; browbeating; coercion. ~하다 overawe; browbeat; treat with a high hand; coerce. ¶ ~적(으로) coercive(ly); high=handed(ly) / ~적인 태도 a coercive 〔domineering〕 attitude / ~당하다 be overawed 《by》; be cowed 《before》 / ~하여 사람을 침묵시키다 coerce *a person* into silence / 무력으로 적을 ~하다 overpower an enemy by using armed force.

**위액**(胃液) gastric 〔stomach〕 juices (★

juice는 복수형 juices로 쓰이는 일이 많음). ◉ ~분비(分泌) gastric secretions. ~선(腺) peptic 〔gastric〕 glands.

**위약**(胃弱) 〖의학〗 dyspepsia; indigestion; poor digestion. ~하다 (be) dyspeptic; suffer from indigestion; have a weak stomach.

**위약**(違約) a breach of promise 〔contract〕; a default (의무·채무 불이행). ~하다 infringe 〔violate〕 a contract; break a promise 〔contract, an agreement〕; default; renege. ¶ ~하지 않다 keep *one's* promise; act up to what *one* promises / A회사와의 계약을 ~하다 break the contract with A company / 그는 계약 조항을 ~한 업자를 상대로 소송을 제기했다 He brought a suit against the contractor reneged the terms of the contract. ◉ ~금 a penalty; an indemnity: ~금을 지급하다 pay the penalty 〔damages〕 for *one's* breach of contract. ~자 a person breaking a contract; a defaulter.

**위엄**(威嚴) dignity; majesty; stateliness. ¶ ~ 있는 dignified; majestic; stately; imposing / ~ 없는 undignified; cheap; unimpressive; unimposing / ~ 있는 사람 a man of dignified appearance / ~스럽다, ~ 차다 be dignified 〔stately〕 / ~을 보이다 show *one's* dignity / ~을 유지하다 keep 〔maintain〕 *one's* dignity / ~을 잃다 lose *one's* dignity / ~을 손상하다 impair *one's* dignity; be beneath *one's* dignity.

**위업**(偉業) a great undertaking 〔enterprise, venture〕; a great achievement. ¶ 획기적인 ~ a heaven-moving achievement / ~을 이루다 achieve a great work.

**위없다** (be) supreme; the best; unparalleled; unrivaled.

**위여** 《쫓는 소리》 shoo!

**위염**(胃炎) 〖의학〗 gastritis; inflammation of the stomach.

**위요**(圍繞) surrounding; encircling. ~하다 surround; encircle; center on. ⇨둘러싸다. ¶ …을 ~하고 centering 〔pivoting〕 around; in connection with …; concerning….

**위용**(偉容·威容) a dignified 〔imposing, commanding, grand〕 appearance 〔air〕; a majestic air. ¶ ~을 갖추고 in a dignified attitude / ~을 갖추다 assume a dignified attitude / ~을 보이다 present a grand 〔magnificent〕 appearance.

**위원**(委員) 《전체》 a committee; 《일원》 a member of a committee; a committeeman 《미》; 《정부의》 a commissioner 《미》. ¶ ~을 임명하다 appoint a committee / ~의 한 사람이다 be a member of the committee; be 〔sit〕 on the committee / 그녀는 학생회 ~으로 선출되었다 She was elected as a member of the student council. ◉ ~장 a chairperson; 《남성》 a chairman; 《여성》 a chairwoman: ~장 노릇을 하다 chair a committee. 부~장 the vice-chairperson 〔assistant chairperson〕 《of a committee》.

**위원회**(委員會) 《조직》 a committee; a commission; a board; 《집회》 a committee meeting.

> 용법 **committee** 일반적인 위원회의 통칭. **commission** 통상적으로 정부에서 조사·관리 등의 임무·권한을 위임받은 위원회. **board** 기업·법인·교육 기관 등의 관리·경영을 위임받은 위원회.

¶ 운영〔상임, 예산〕~ a steering 〔a standing, a budget〕 committee / 교육~ a board of education / 분과~ a subcommittee; 《회의》 a sectional committee meeting / 8인 ~ an eight-member committee / ~를 조직하다 form 〔organize〕 a commission / ~를 소집〔해산〕하다 call 〔discharge〕 a committee meeting / ~를 열다〔에 참석하다〕 hold 〔attend〕 a committee meeting / ~는 지금 그 문제를 심의하고 있다 The committee is in session on that question. ◉ ~ 결정사항 committee findings. 자격 심사~ a committee on qualifications. (적격)심사~ a screening committee.

**위의**(威儀) ① 《태도》 a dignified mien; a solemn manner. ¶ ~ 있는 dignified; solemn; stately / ~를 갖추고 in a dignified manner; with a solemnity of manner / ~를 갖추다 compose *one's* appearance; assume a dignified attitude / ~당당하다 be in a stately 〔dignified〕 manner. ② 《장례의》 a funeral procession.

**위인**(偉人) a great man; a master mind. ¶ 불세출의 ~ the greatest man that ever lived / 역사상의 ~들 the great names of history. ◉ ~전 the life 〔biography〕 of a great man.

**위인**(爲人) the man (that *one* is); 《사람 됨됨이》 *one's* nature 〔disposition, temperament, stamp〕; *one's* character 〔personality, make-up〕. ¶ 그는 출세할

～이 못된다 He is not「a 〔the sort of〕 man to succeed in life. / 새로 부임한 경찰서장은 어떤 ～이냐 What kind of (a) man is the new police chief?

**위인설관**(爲人設官) positions specially arranged to reward those figures for their meritorious contributions to the government in previous days.

**위임**(委任) trust; charge; commission; 《전권의》 delegation; authorization; commitment; 〖법〗 mandate. ～하다 entrust 〔leave〕 《*a matter*》 to 《*a person*》; entrust 〔charge〕 《*a person*》 with 《*a matter*》; commission 《*a person*》 to 《*do*》; give a commission to; authorize 〔empower〕 《*a person*》 to 《*do*》; commit 《*a matter*》 to 《*a person's*》 care 〔management〕. ¶ 권한의 ～ delegation of authority / ～ 받다 have 〔receive〕 a commission / 전권을 ～하다 entrust 《*a person*》 with full powers; give 《*a person*》 a carte blanche; give 《*a person*》 full power of attorney "on a blank sheet of paper" / 우리는 그 문제의 결정을 위원회에 ～했다 We left 〔entrusted〕 the problem to the decision of the committee.

◉ ～권 power of attorney. ～권한 competency of mandate. ～대리 〖법〗 representation of mandate: ～ 대리인 an authorized agent. ～명령 a delegated 〔an instructed〕 order. ～자 the mandator: 피～자 a trustee. ～장 a letter 〔warrant〕 of attorney; 《대리 투표의》 a proxy; credentials. ～제도 a mandate system. ～투표 proxy voting: ～투표하다 vote by proxy.

**위임통치**(委任統治) mandate; mandatory administration 〔rule〕. ◉ ～국 a mandatory (power). ～권 a mandate. ～령 a mandatory territory.

**위자료**(慰藉料) consolation money; a solatium; compensation (보상금); alimony (이혼·별거 수당). ¶ ～를 청구하다 demand compensation 《for》/ ～로 일백만원을 지급하다 pay one million won in compensation 《for the injury》/ 그녀는 그가 헤어지자고 하자 ～를 요구했다 She demanded that he pay「consolation money 〔alimony〕 when he wanted to leave her.

**위장**(胃腸) 〖해부〗 the stomach and intestines 〔bowels〕. ¶ ～의 gastrointestinal; gastroenteric / ～을 해치다 injure 〔disorder〕 the stomach / ～이 튼튼하다〔약하다〕 have a strong 〔poor〕 digestion. ◉ ～병 a gastroenteric disorder 〔trouble〕; a gastrointestinal upset. ～약 a medicine for the stomach and bowels; a digestive (소화제). ～염 gastroenteritis. ～장애 gastrointestinal trouble 〔disorder〕.

**위장**(僞裝) (a) camouflage; (a) disguise. ～하다 camouflage *a thing* 《as》; disguise *oneself* 〔*a thing*〕 《as》. ¶ 상선으로 ～한 군함 a warship disguised as a merchant ship / 거지로 ～하다 disguise *oneself* as a begger.

◉ ～공작 operation to disguise the fact. ～귀순 defection in disguise. ～망(網) a camouflage net. ～수출 fraud export. ～실업 disguised 〔hidden〕 unemployment. ～전입 a camouflaged move-in; a false resident registration 《to enter the so-called first-class high school》. ～취업자 students who entered firms as menial workers to incite labor unrest by concealing their high educational background. ～평화공세 《launch》 disguised peace offensive. ～폭탄 a booby trap.

**위적**(偉績) a great deed; glorious achievements.

**위정자**(爲政者) an administrator; a statesman. ¶ ～는 국민의 소리를 들어야 한다 Those who govern the people must listen to their voice.

**위조**(僞造) forgery; fabrication; falsification. ～하다 forge; counterfeit; fabricate; falsify. ¶ 화폐를 ～하다 counterfeit coins / 문서를 ～하다 fabricate 〔forge〕 a document / 수표를 ～하다 forge a check / 그는 ～죄로 기소되었다 He was prosecuted for forgery.

◉ ～단 a counterfeit ring. ～문서 a forged 〔spurious〕 document. ～수표 a forged check 〔cheque 《영》〕. ～자 a forger; 《화폐의》 a counterfeiter; coiner 《영》. ～지폐 a spurious 〔counterfeit, forged〕 bank note: 100달러 짜리 ～ 지폐 a counterfeit $100 bill / ～ 불가능 100달러 미국 지폐 a counterfeit-proof U.S. $100 bill / ～ 지폐를 사용하다 pass a counterfeit note. ～품 a forged article; a sham; a forgery; a fake; a counterfeit. 공문서～ the fabrication of the official documents.

**위주**(爲主) ¶ 자기 ～의 사고 방식 self-centered thinking / 남성 ～의 사회 male-oriented society / ～로 하다 put first (in importance); give the first consideration 〔primacy〕 to / 인격 함양을 ～로 하다 make character-building the prime object; aim at character-building / 장사는 이득 ~다 Profit making is the first consideration in business.

**위중하다**(危重—) be in a critical condition; (be) serious; grave. ¶ 위중해지다 get 〔become〕 worse 〔serious〕; take a turn for the worse / 병이 ~ be seriously 〔critically〕 ill.

**위증**(僞證) 〖법〗 false evidence; false testimony; perjury. ~하다 give false evidence; bear false witness; perjure *oneself*. ◉ ~자 a perjurer. ~죄 perjury: ~죄로 구속하다 put 《*a person*》 into custody on charges of perjury / ~죄로 기소되다 be accused of perjury.

**위지**(危地) 《장소》 a dangerous spot 〔place〕; 《처지》 a dangerous 〔perilous〕 position; a critical situation. ¶ ~에 빠지다 get 〔run, fall〕 into danger; get into a perilous position / ~에 빠뜨리다 put *a person* in peril / ~에 뛰어들다 get into danger; put *one's* head into a lion's mouth / ~에서 헤어나다 get out of danger.

**위쪽** the upper direction.

**위차**(位次) order of seats 〔ranks, positions〕.

**위채** 《집의》 the "upper" wing of a Korean house.

**위촉**(委囑) 《위임》 entrusting; commission; 《의뢰》 request; 《임명》 appointment; 《담당》 charge. ~하다 entrust 《*a person*》 with 《*a matter*》; commission 《*a person*》 to 《*do*》; give a commission 《to *a person*》; request 《*a person*》 to 《*do*》; ask. ¶ ~으로 by request; at the request 《of *a person*》 / 이 건을 그에게 ~하겠다 I will entrust him with this case. / 그녀는 그 연구를 ~받았다 She was placed in charge of the research. / 그는 운영 위원으로 ~되었다 He was appointed to the steering committee.

**위축**(萎縮) shrinking; shriveling; withering; contraction; 〖의학〗 atrophy (위축증). ~하다 《물체가》 wither; shrink; shrivel; dwindle. ¶ ~한 contracted; shrunken / ~되다 《사람이》 be daunted 〔dispirited〕 《by》 / 상사〔사장〕 앞에서 ~되어 그는 아무 말도 못했다 He quailed 〔cowered〕 before the boss and was unable to speak.
◉ ~병 〖식물〗 curl. ~신(腎) 〖의학〗 nephrosclerosis; atrophy of the kidney; the contracted kidney. ~위(胃) 〖의학〗 the leather-bottle stomach.

**위층**(—層) the upper floor 〔story, storey 《영》〕; upstairs. ¶ ~방 an upstair(s) room / ~에 올라가다 go upstairs.

**위치**(位置) a place; a position; a situation; a location; a site; 《신분·입장》 *one's* status 〔standing〕; a stand. ~하다 be situated 〔located〕; stand; lie.

> (용법) **place** 어떤 사람·사물이 점유하고 있는 특정한 위치. **position** 다른 것과 상대적인 관계에서의 어떤 사람·사물 등의 위치: I was in a good position to watch fireworks (불꽃놀이를 구경하기 좋은 장소에 있었다). **situation** 환경과 관련된 건물이나 주거지의 위치. **location**＝place; position. **site**＝position; location 건물·주거지·기념비 등이 과거에 존재했고, 현존하기도 하며, 장래 만들어지게 되어 있는 장소.

¶ 소설가로서의 ~ *one's* position among novelists / ~가 좋다〔나쁘다〕 be well 〔ill〕 situated / ~를 바꾸다 shift *one's* position / ~를 정하다 fix position; locate / 유리한 ~를 차지하다 hold an advantageous position / 학교는 좋은 ~에 있다 The school occupies an ideal site. / 일본은 한국의 동쪽에 ~하고 있다 Japan lies to the east of Korea. / 자네가 만일 나의 ~에 있다면 어떻게 하겠나 If you were in my place 〔position〕, what would you do?
◉ ~선정 location; positioning. ~에너지 〖물리〗 potential energy. ~천문학 〖천문〗 position astronomy.

**위친하다**(爲親—) honor 〔be devoted to〕 *one's* parents.

**위크** a week. ◉ ~데이 a weekday. ~엔드 a weekend.

**위클리** a weekly (magazine).

**위탁**(委託) trust; charge; commission; consignment (상품의). ~하다 entrust 《*a person* with *a matter*, *a matter* to *a person*》; place 〔put〕 《*a matter*》 in 《*a person's*》 charge; consign 《goods (for sale) to an agent》; 《일을》 commit 《*a matter*》 to 《*a person's*》 care; leave 〔give〕 《*a thing*》 in trust with 《*a person*》. ¶ ~을 받다 be entrusted; 《받고 있다》 have 《*something*》 to do on commission / ~으로 상품을 보내다 ship goods on consignment / 집의 매각을 부동산업자에게 ~하다 consign *one's* house (for sale) to a real estate agent / 이 상품의 판매는 대리점에 ~하고 있다 We have consigned these goods to our agent.
◉ ~가공 processing on commission:

～가공무역 processing trade. ～금 a trust fund; money in trust: ～보증금 consignment guarantee money. ～생산 production by commissioning. ～수수료 a consignment fee; a commission. ～연구 contract research. ～자 a truster; a consigner (위탁판매의); a client (의뢰인). ～주문〔구입〕 a purchase order; an official requisition (for supplies). ～판매 consignment 〔commission〕 sale; sale on commission: ～ 판매인 a commission agent; a consignee / ～ 판매하다 sell《goods》 on commission. ～품 goods on consignment; consigned goods. ～학생 a scholarship student.

**위태롭다, 위태하다**(危殆—) (be) dangerous; perilous; risky; 《병세가》 (be) critical; serious; grave; 《아슬아슬함》 (be) narrow; near; close. ¶ 위태롭게 하다 endanger; jeopardize; imperil / 위태로운 짓을 하다 run 〔take on〕 a risk; make a risky attempt / 그의 생명이 위태롭다 His life is in danger. / 그의 지위가 위태롭다 His position is very precarious.

**위턱** the upper jaw; the maxilla.

**위통**(胃痛) a stomachache; 『의학』 gastralgia.

**위트** wit. ¶ ～가 있는 witty.

**위패**(位牌) a mortuary 〔memorial〕 tablet. ¶ 조상의 ～ an ancestral tablet.

**위폐**(僞幣) ⇨ 위조 지폐. ◉ ～감식기 a counterfeit-bill detector. ～ 방지용 은행권 a forgery-free bank note; a counterfeit-resistant bill: 새로운 ～ 방지용 100 달러 지폐 the new, counterfeit=resistant $100 bill. ～범 a bank-note forger; a bogus note forger.

**위품**(位品) grade of official ranks.

**위풍**(威風) a stately 〔dignified〕 appearance; an imposing 〔a majestic〕 air; a commanding presence. ¶ ～당당한 majestic; imposing; commanding; awe-inspiring / ～당당한 인물 a man of commanding presence / ～당당히 majestically; in a stately 〔dignified〕 manner / ～에 압도되다 bend 〔bow〕 to 《*a person's*》 dignity; be overawed by 《*a person's*》 imposing air.

**위필**(僞筆) forged 〔feigned〕 (hand)writing; 《그림》 a forged 〔sham〕 picture. ～하다 forge; counterfeit.

**위하다**(爲—) 《공경·받듦》 serve; honor; respect; revere; look up to; venerate; adore; worship; 《존중》 make much of; value; esteem; have regard for; treat with care; take good care of; 《이롭게 함》 do for the good 〔sake, benefit〕 of; do in favor of 〔in behalf of〕. ⇨ 위하여. ¶ 예술을 위한 예술 art for art's sake / 논쟁을 위한 논쟁 argument for the sake of argument / 부모를 ～ honor *one's* parents; take good care of *one's* parents; be devoted to *one's* parents / 어린애들을 ～ be kind to children; love children / 조상을 ～ worship *one's* ancestors / 몸을 ～ take care of *oneself* / 회사를 ～ look to the interests of the firm / 명예보다 돈을 더 ～ be more interested in the money than the glory / 그는 학교를 위하는 마음에서 그렇게 했다 He did so out of concern for the school.

**위하수**(胃下垂) 『의학』 gastroptosis; gastric ptosis.

**위하여**(爲—) ① 《이익·편익》 for; for the sake 〔benefit〕 of; in the interests 〔favor, honor〕 of; in 〔on〕 behalf of (대신하여). ¶ 사회를 ～ in the interests of society / 조국을 ～ for the sake of the fatherland / 정의를 ～ in the cause of justice; for the sake of justice / 너를 ～ for your own sake / 나라를 ～ 몸을 바치다 lay down *one's* life for the nation / 공익을 ～ 일하다 work for the common good / 이것도 너를 ～ 하는 말이다 I say this on your behalf. / 너를 ～ 그것을 샀다 I bought it for you.
② 《목적》 in order to; to the end (that…); so as to 《*do*》; so that; for the purpose; with the intention of; with a view to. ¶ …하기 ～ (in order) that *one* may *do* / …하지 않기 ～ lest *one* should *do;* that *one* may not 《*do*》; so as not to *do* / 훈계하기 ～ by way of warning / 사업을 ～ for *one's* business / 영문학 연구를 ～ for the purpose of studying English literature; in order to study English literature / 자녀를 공부시키기 ～ 저축하다 save money toward the education of *one's* children / 사람은 살기 ～ 먹는 것이지 먹기 ～ 사는 것은 아니다 Man does not live to eat, but eats to live.

**위해**(危害) an injury; peril; harm; hazard. ¶ ～를 가하다 do 《*a person*》 harm 〔an injury〕; inflict an injury 《on *a person*》 / ～를 입다〔당하다〕 be harmed 〔injured〕 《by》; receive 〔sustain〕 an injury 《from》 / ～를 면하다 escape unhurt; escape with a whole skin 《구어》. ◉ ～물 a dangerous 〔hazardous〕 article.

**위헌**(違憲) (a) violation of the consti-

tution; unconstitutionality. ¶ ～적 unconstitutional; against the constitution / ～적 조치 an unconstitutional measure / ～이다 be unconstitutional; be against the constitution / 그것은 분명히 ～이다 It is decidedly against the constitution.
◉ ～입법 unconstitutional legislation.

**위험**(危險) 《위해》 (a) danger; (a) peril; 《모험》 (a) risk; (a) hazard; jeopardy. ～하다 (be) dangerous; risky; unsafe; perilous; hazardous; adventurous (모험적인).

> 용법 **danger** 「위험」을 의미하는 가장 일반적인 말. **peril** 상처를 입거나 생명과도 관계된 긴박한 위험. **risk** 위험의 가능성은 있지만 그것을 알고 스스로 무릅쓰는 위험. **hazard** peril만큼 긴박성은 없지만 직면하고 있는 사람이 제어할 수 없는 위험: the hazards of mountaineering (등산에 따르는 위험).

¶ 홍수의 ～ danger of a flood / ～한 작업 dangerous work; a hazardous job / ～을 면하다〔벗어나다〕 escape from 〔get out of〕 danger / ～을 무릅쓰고 at great (personal) risk; in face of danger; at the risk 《of》 / ～할 때는 in case 〔time〕 of danger / ～에 빠지다 get into 〔be in〕 danger; get in harm's way / ～에 빠뜨리다 put 《*a person*》 in danger; endanger; jeopardize / ～을 깨닫다 sense 〔suspect〕 danger / ～을 부담하다 〖보험〗 bear the risk / 생명의 ～을 무릅쓰다 risk *one's* life / 이제 ～한 고비는 넘겼다 The worst danger is now over. / 그는 ～이 닥쳐오는 것을 알지 못했다 He was not aware of the approaching danger. / 여기서부터 ～ 구간입니다 30km/h 《게시》 Danger zone begins. 30km/h / 폭발물, ～ 《게시》 Explosives! Danger!
◉ ～관리 〖경제〗 a risk management. ～사상 dangerous ideas 〔thoughts〕. ～상태 a dangerous 〔critical〕 condition. ～수당 danger money. ～요소 〔분자〕 dangerous elements. ～인물 a dangerous character 〔man, person〕; 《국가 안전상》 a security risk: ～ 인물로 보다 regard 《*a person*》 as a dangerous person. ～작업 dangerous work; a hazardous job. ～지대〔구역〕 a danger spot 〔zone, area〕; 〖컴퓨터〗 critical region. ～표지판 a warning (sign) post.

**위험물**(危險物) a dangerous article; a dangerous thing 〔object〕; 〖철도〗 explosives and combustibles; 《항해상의》 a danger; 《게시》 Hazardous commodities. ¶ ～ 반입 엄금 《게시》 Inflammables and explosives strictly prohibited to be brought in. / ～ 휴대 엄금 《게시》 Dangerous articles forbidden.

**위험부담**(危險負擔) 〖보험〗 risk-bearing. ¶ 소유주의 ～으로 at the owner's risk.
◉ ～자본 a venture 〔risk〕 capital.

**위험시**(危險視) ～하다 regard 《*a person, a thing*》 as dangerous; 《기도를》 regard 《an attempt》 as risky.

**위험신호**(危險信號) a danger signal; 《교통의》 a red light; a stop light; 〖철도〗 a red lamp (야간의). ¶ ～를 올리다 place 〔put up〕 a signal of danger.
◉ ～기 a red flag.

**위험천만**(危險千萬) ～하다 be extremely dangerous. ¶ ～한 짓을 하다 perform a hazardous feat; sleep on a volcano.

**위협**(威脅) (a) menace; intimidation; a threat. ～하다 menace; intimidate; threaten; scare; browbeat. ¶ ～적인 말 threatening language 〔words〕 / 평화에 대한 ～ a menace 〔threat〕 to peace / ～적 menacing; threatening; intimidatory / ～적으로 threateningly; menacingly / ～하여 by intimidation / ～을 느끼다 be menaced 《by, with》; be threatened 《with》 / ～이 되다 menace; threaten; be a menace to / 생활을 ～하다 threaten *one's* livelihood / ～적 태도를 취하다 take 〔assume〕 a threatening attitude / 그는 나를 죽이겠다고 ～했다 He threatened 「me with death 〔to kill me〕. ◉ ～사격 《fire》 a warning shot. ～자 an intimidator.

**위화감**(違和感) a sense of incongruity 〔incompatibility〕; a feeling that *one* does not belong 《in a place》. ¶ ～을 느끼다 feel a sense of incongruity / 사회적 ～을 심화시키다 deepen the social disharmony.

**위확장**(胃擴張) 〖의학〗 dilatation of the stomach; gastric dilatation.

**위훈**(偉勳) conspicuous merit; a brilliant exploit; a great achievement 〔deed〕. ¶ ～을 세우다 render distinguished services; accomplish a great achievement.

**윈도** 《진열장》 a (show) window. ◉ ～쇼핑 window-shopping: ～쇼핑을 하다 go window-shopping; do some window-shopping.

**윈도우** 〖컴퓨터〗 《운영체제》 Windows.

**윈드서핑** windsurfing.

**윈치** a winch; a hoist.

**윈터스포츠** winter sports.

**윗-** 《위의》 the upper; the above; the outer. ¶ 윗누이 an elder sister / 윗니 the upper teeth / 윗배 the upper part of the abdomen / 윗입술〔윗잇몸〕 the upper「lip 〔gum, teethridge〕/ 윗학교에 가다 attend a higher institution of education.

**윗길** ①《위쪽에 난 길》 the upper road. ②《우수한 품질의 것》 superior quality; better grade; top grade.

**윗도리** 《상체》 the upper part of the body; the upper body; 《상의》 a coat.

**윗목** the place on the floor away from the fireplace.

**윗물** ①《상류의》 the water in the upper part of a stream; upstream. ¶ ~이 맑아야 아랫물이 맑다 《속담》 A servant is only as honest as his master. ②《윗 국물》 water 〔liquid〕 floating on another without mixing with it.

**윗사람** *one's* seniors; *one's* elders; *one's* superiors 〔betters〕. ¶ ~에 대한 예의 manners towards a superior.

**윗수염**(一鬚髥) a mustache.

**윗자리** 《상좌》 the upper seat; the top 〔highest〕 seat; the seat of honor (주빈석); 《높은 지위》 a high 〔superior〕 rank; precedence. ¶ ~를 차지하다 take the top seat; rank high.

**윙** 《벌레 소리》 with a buzz 〔hum〕; 《기계 소리》 with a whir; 《바람 소리》 with a whistle 〔whiz(z)〕. ~하다 make a buzz 〔whir, whiz〕. ¶ 바람이 윙윙 불어 댔다 The wind hissed and raged.

**윙윙하다, 윙윙거리다** buzz and buzz; 《바람이》 whistle; 《탄알이》 ping; whiz.

**윙크** a wink. ~하다 wink 《at》; give a wink 《to》.

**유**(有) ①《존재》 existence; being. ¶ 무에서 유는 생기지 않는다 Out of nothing, nothing comes. ②《소유》 possession. ¶ 국유〔사유〕의 state-〔private-〕 owned.

**유**(酉) 〖민속〗 《십이지의》 the Sign of the Cock (=10th of the 12 Earth's Branches).

**유**(類) ①《종류》 a kind; a sort; a variety; a class; 〖논리〗 a genus. ¶ 이런 유의 사나이 a man of this type / 이런 유의 사기 this form 〔type〕 of swindling. ②《유례》 a similar; example 〔instance〕; 《동류》 a parallel; an equal; the like. ¶ 유가 없는 unparalleled; unique; unexampled; 《선례가 없는》 unprecedented; 《희귀한》 rare / 유유상종 Birds of a feather flock together. *or* Like attracts like. ③ 〖생물〗 ⇨ -류(類) ①, ②. ◉ 유개념 a genus.

**유가**(有價) having a fixed price; valuableness. ¶ ~의 valuable; negotiable. ◉ ~물 valuables.

**유가**(儒家) a Confucian (scholar); a student of Confucianism.

**유가족**(遺家族) a bereaved family; the family of the deceased. ¶ 군경 ~(의) 원호 relief for the bereaved families of the war dead / 슬픔에 싸인 ~들 the grief-stricken bereaved families. ◉ 전몰 ~ a war-bereaved family; the families of the war dead.

**유가증권**(有價證券) securities; stocks and bonds; a negotiable instrument 〔paper〕. ◉ ~시장 the stock 〔securities〕 market. ~투자 securities investment.

**유감**(遺憾) regrettableness; lamentableness; deplorableness; pity; 《불만족》 unsatisfactoriness. ~스럽다 be regrettable 〔sorry〕; 《한탄》 be deplorable; lamentable; 《불만》 be unsatisfactory. ¶ ~없는 《완전한》 perfect; (most) satisfactory; 《충분한》 thorough / ~없이 perfectly; fully; most satisfactorily; to *one's* heart's content / 재능을 ~없이 발휘하다 give full play to *one's* abilities / ~이다 regret; be sorry for; be regrettable / (…은) ~ 천만이다 it is really regrettable (that…); it is much to be regretted (that…); it is simply deplorable (that…) / ~의 뜻을 표하다 express *one's* regret 《at, for》/ ~ 천만이지만 거절하다 refuse「with much regret 〔with many regrets〕/ 일이 그렇게 되어 실로 ~이다 I regret that things should have come to such a pass.

**유감지진**(有感地震) 〖지질〗 a sensible 〔felt〕 earthquake.

**유개**(有蓋) having a lid 〔top, cover〕. ¶ ~의 lidded; covered; closed; roofed. ◉ ~마차 a covered carriage. ~자동차 a covered car. ~화차 a boxcar 《미》; a covered 〔roofed, box〕 waggon 《영》.

**유객**(幽客) a hermit; a recluse; an anchorite; an anchoret.

**유객**(遊客) ①《유람꾼》 a man on a pleasure trip; a tourist. ②《방탕꾼》 a playboy; a man leading an idle life; a loafer. ¶ ~ 한화(閑話) idle thoughts of an idle fellow.

**유거**(幽居) 《장소》 a hermitage; a sequestered retreat; a solitary 〔retired〕 residence; 《생활》 living seclusion; a secluded 〔retired〕 life. ～하다 live in seclusion; lead a retired life.

**유격**(遊擊) an attack by a mobile unit; a (commando) raid; a hit-and-run attack; a guer(r)illa attack. ～하다 divert; raid.

◉ ～대 a commando 〔ranger〕 group; a guerilla unit; a flying column 〔crops, party, army〕; mobile forces. ～병 partisans; guerillas; a ranger; a commando. ～수 〖야구〗 a short(stop). ～술 guerilla tactics; the hit-and-run tactics. ～전 guerilla 〔partisan, commando〕 warfare; hit-and-run raid 〔war〕. ～함대 a flying squadron.

**유경**(有莖) 〖식물〗 ¶ ～의 caulescent; stemmed; stalked. ◉ ～식물 a cormophyte.

**유계**(幽界) the other world; the world after death; Hades; the realm of the shades.

**유고**(有故) an accident; (a) trouble; a mishap; reason; cause; ground; an excuse. ～하다 have (some) trouble; have a reason 《for it》; be owing to some trouble; be justifiable.

◉ ～결석 absence owing to unavoidable circumstances. ～시 the time of an accident.

**유고**(遺稿) *one's* posthumous manuscripts; the writings left by the deceased. ¶ A씨의 ～를 정리하다 edit the unpublished writings left by the late Mr. A.

**유고**(諭告) advice; counsel; inculcation; instructions; admonition. ～하다 advise 〔counsel〕 《*a person* to *do*》; give instructions; issue an admonition.

**유곡**(幽谷) deep valley; a gorge; a ravine; a glen. ¶ 심산 ～ high mountains and deep valleys.

**유골**(遺骨) 《*a person's*》 remains; 《*a person's*》 (funeral) ashes. ¶ ～을 줍다 gather 《*a person's*》 ashes / ～을 담다 put 〔place〕 《*a person's*》 ashes 《in an urn》 / 아버님의 ～은 외국 땅에 묻혀 있다 My father's ashes rest in the soil of the foreign country.

◉ ～단지 a cinerary urn.

**유공**(有功) meritoriousness. ～하다 (be) meritorious. ◉ ～자 a man of merit. ～훈장 the order of merit.

**유공충**(有孔蟲) 〖동물〗 a foraminifer.

**유과**(油果) ⇨ 유밀과.

**유곽**(遊廓) licensed 〔gay, prostitute〕 quarters; a red-light district 《미》. ¶ ～에 드나들다 frequent gay quarters.

**유관**(有關) being related 〔concerned〕; having relation 〔concern〕. ¶ ～업체 a concern interested; its associated company / ～기관의 상호 협조 cooperation of the agencies 〔organs〕 concerned.

**유관**(油管) an oil pipe.

**유관속**(維管束) 〖식물〗 a vascular bundle ＝관다발. ◉ ～식물 a vascular plant.

**유관절류**(有關節類) 〖동물〗 an articulate.

**유광지**(有光紙) glazed paper.

**유괴**(誘拐) abduction; kidnap(p)ing. ～하다 kidnap; abduct 《*a person* from *his* home》; entice 《*a person*》 away 《from home》; shanghai; 《미구어》 snatch 《a child》. ¶ 어린아이를 ～하다 kidnap a child / 그녀는 ～되었음에 틀림없다 She must have been abducted. / 부호(富豪)의 아들을 ～한 범인은 5천만 원의 몸값을 요구했다 A rich man's son was kidnapped and the kidnap(p)er demanded a ransom of fifty million won. ◉ ～범 《범죄》 abduction; kidnap(p)ing; 《범인》 ＝유괴자. ～사건 an abduction 〔a kidnapping〕 case. ～자 an abductor; a kidnap(p)er.

**유교**(儒敎) Confucianism. ¶ ～의 Confucian. ◉ ～사상 Confucian ideas.

**유구무언**(有口無言) ¶ ～이다 have no word to say in excuse.

**유구하다**(悠久―) (be) eternal; everlasting; perpetual; permanent. ¶ 유구한 옛날부터 from time immemorial 〔out of mind〕.

**유권자**(有權者) the holder of a right; a qualified person; an eligible voter; the electorate [총칭]. ¶ ～ 총수는 5백만에 달한다 The electoral roll amounts to 5 million. ◉ ～명부(名簿) the electoral roll 〔register〕.

**유권해석**(有權解釋) an authoritative interpretation.

**유금류**(游禽類) natatorial birds; 〖조류〗 the swimmers; the web-footed birds.

**유급**(有給) ¶ ～의 paid; salaried. ◉ ～사원〔직원〕 staff members on the payroll. ～외판원 a salaried canvasser 〔salesman〕. ～휴가 a paid vacation 〔holiday 《영》〕; a vacation 〔holiday 《영》〕 with (full) pay: ～ 휴가 제도 a paid-leave system / 1주일간의 ～ 휴가 《take》 a week off with pay.

**유급**(留級) ～하다 stay back in the class; remain in the original class. ¶ ～되다 be left back to repeat 《the first year course》 / ～시키다 keep 《a student》 back (to repeat a grade). ◉ ～생 a repeater; a holdover.

**유기**(有期) ¶ ～의 terminable; limited; for a definite term. ◉ ～공채 a terminable [fixed-term] bond. ～연금 a limited annuity. ～징역 penal servitude for a definite term. ～형(刑) a sentence for imprisonment for a definite period: ～형을 선고받다 be sentenced to imprisonment for a definite term.

**유기**(有機) 〚화학〛 organic matter; an organism. ¶ ～적 organic; systematic; organized / ～적으로 organically / ～적 세계관 the organic view of the world. ◉ ～농업[농법] organic agriculture [farming]: ～ 농법으로 재배한 최고의 토마토 the finest, organically-grown tomatoes. ～물 organic matter; an organism. ～분자 an organic molecule. ～비료 an organic fertilizer. ～산(酸) (an) organic acid. ～수은 화합물 an organic mercury compound. ～재배 organic growth. ～질 an organic matter [substance]: ～질 비료 an organic fertilizer. ～체 an organism; an organic body. ～화학 organic chemistry. ～화합물 an organic compound.

**유기**(遺棄) abandonment; dereliction; desertion. ～하다 abandon; desert; leave 《*a thing*》 unattended. ¶ 직무～ neglect of duty / 시체를 ～하다 abandon a dead body; leave a dead body unattended. ◉ ～물 an abandoned thing; an article left; a left article; a derelict (해상의); refuse. ～시체 an abandoned corpse.

**유기**(鍮器) 《놋그릇》 brassware.

**유기음**(有氣音) 〚음성〛 an aspirate.

**유난** unusualness; fussiness; fastidiousness. ～하다[스럽다] (be) unusual; uncommon; exceptional; special; particular; fastidious; fussy. ¶ ～부리다[떨다] behave [talk] fastidiously / ～스럽게 굴다 be fastidious [particular, fussy] / 올 여름은 ～히 덥다 It is exceptionally warm this summer.

**유네스코** UNESCO. [<the *U*nited *N*ations *E*ducational *S*cientific and *C*ultural *O*rganization] ◉ ～헌장 the Constitution of UNESCO. 한국 ～ 협회 연맹 National Federation of UNESCO Association in Korea.

**유년**(幼年) infancy; childhood. ¶ 나의 ～시절은 행복했다 My childhood was happy. ◉ ～기[시대] infancy; childhood: ～ 시대에 in *one's* childhood / ～시대로부터 from *one's* infancy [childhood].

**유년**(酉年) 〚민속〛 the Year of the Rooster.

**유념**(留念) consideration; regard; attention. ～하다 consider; mind; regard; attend to.

**유뇨**(遺尿) bed wetting. ◉ ～증 〚의학〛 enuresis.

**유능**(有能) competence; ability. ～하다 (be) able; capable; competent; 《능률적인》 efficient.

> **용법** **able** 선천적 혹은 후천적으로 사람이 능력을 지니고 있다는 것을 나타내는 말. **capable** 어떤 종류의 일을 하거나 일정 목적을 달성하는 데 필요한 성질·자질을 갖추고 있음을, **competent** 특정 상태·직업·업무에서 필요로 하는 능력을 갖추고 있음을, **efficient** 업무 추진 능률이 좋음을 각각 말함.

¶ ～한 사람 a man of ability; an able [a competent] man / 그녀는 매우 ～한 변호사로 알려져 있다 She is known as a very able [competent] lawyer.

**유니버설** universal.

**유니버시아드** 《국제 학생 스포츠 대회》 the Universiade; the World University [Student] Games.

**유니버시티** 《종합대학》 a university.

**유니세프** 《국제 연합 아동 기금》 UNICEF. [<the *U*nited *N*ations *I*nternational *C*hildren's *E*mergency *F*und] (★ 지금은 the United Nations Children's Fund).

**유니섹스** 《남녀공통의》 unisex. ¶ ～의 옷 unisex clothes.

**유니언** union; a union. ◉ ～숍 a union shop. ～잭 《영국 국기》 the Union Jack.

**유니크하다** (be) original; unusual; out of the ordinary (run); unique (유일한) (★ 우리말에서는 「색다른」 「드문」 「독특한」 등을 나타내는 말로 쓰이고 있지만, 영어의 unique는 「비길 데 없는」 「유일한」 등의 뜻으로만 쓰임. 따라서 very [rather] unique 처럼 정도를 나타내는 부사와 함께 쓰는 것을 피해야 함). ¶ 그는 유니크한 존재이다 There is no one like him. / 그것은 유니크한 작품이다 It is a unique [an extremely original] work.

**유니폼** a uniform. ¶ ～을 입다 put on a uniform.

**유닛** 《한 단위》 a unit. ◉ ～가구 sectional [modular] furniture; unit furniture. ～시스템 the unit construction system.

**유다** 〚성서〛 Judas; Jude. ◉ ～서 the General Epistle of St. Jude (생략 Jude).

**유다르다**(類―) (be) conspicuous; uncommon; unusual. ¶ 유달리 conspicuously; unusually; uncommonly / 유달리 눈에 띄다 stand out conspicuously / 오늘은 유달리 바쁘다 This is an especially busy day.

**유단자**(有段者) 《유도·태권도 등의》 a blackbelt holder; a grade-holder 《in fencing, chess, *etc.*》.

**유당**(乳糖) 〖화학〗 lactose; milk sugar.

**유대** Judea. ¶ ～의 Jewish / ～계 학자 a scholar of Jewish origin. ◉ ～교 Judaism. ～교도 a Jew; a Judaist. ～교회당 a synagogue. ～민족 the Jewish race; the Jews: ～민족주의 Zionism. ～인 a Jew.

**유대**(紐帶) bonds; 《관계》 ties; relation; relationship. ¶ 사업상의 ～ a business tie / 우정의 ～ the ties of friendship / 정신적 ～ spiritual bonds / ～를 강화하다 strengthen the ties 《between》 / 긴밀한 ～를 맺다 come 〔be brought〕 into close relation 《with》 / 한미 ～를 공고히 하다 place Seoul-Washington ties on a firm footing / 상호 협력의 ～를 강화하다 step up mutual cooperative ties 《with》 / 정치적, 문화적으로 강한 ～를 가지다 retain strong political and cultural ties 《with》.

**유대류**(有袋類) 〖동물〗 the marsupial (animal).

**유덕**(有德) virtuousness. ～하다 (be) virtuous; good.

**유덕**(遺德) the「virtue 〔influence〕 of the departed.

**유도**(柔道) judo. ◉ ～가 a judo expert. ～복 a suit for judo practice. ～사범 an instructor of judo. ～유단자 a rank-holding judo man. 국제 ～ 연맹 the International Judo Federation (생략 IJF).

**유도**(誘導) ① 《유인》 guidance; inducement. ～하다 《안내하다》 conduct; lead; guide; 《꾀어서 …하게 하다》 lead 〔induce〕 《*a person*》 to do. ¶ 관제탑의 ～에 따라 착륙하다 make a landing following the instruction from the control tower; be talked down / 도선사가 배를 항구로 ～한다 A pilot guides the ship toward the port. / 소방훈련이 시작되면 학생들은 안전한 곳으로 ～된다 When the fire drill starts, students will be guided to a safe place.
② 《전기·자기의 작용》 induction.
◉ ～기(器) an induction machine; an inductor. ～기전력 induced electromotive force. ～단위 a derived unit. ～력〔성〕 inductivity. ～로 《비행장의》 a taxiway; taxiing way. ～물질 an inducing substance. ～반응 (an) induced reaction. ～발전기 an induction generator. ～법 〖의학〗 derivative; revulsion. ～병기 a guided weapon. ～용 계기 guidance instruments. ～자(者) an inducer; an encourager; an inductor; a conductor. ～자기장 an induction field. ～자화(磁化) induced magnetization. ～장치 a guidance system; guidance「equipment 〔controls〕; 《관제탑의》 a talking-down system. ～전기 induced electricity. ～전동기 an induction motor. ～전류 an induced current. ～제어 guidance control. ～질 〖화학〗 an inductor. ～체 a conductor. ～코일 an induction coil; an inductor. ～탄 a guided missile. ～회로 an inductive circuit. 원격～ remote control; teleguidance. 전자(電磁)～ electromagnetic induction. 지상 ～ 진압방식 the ground-controlled approach (생략 G.C.A.).

**유도**(儒道) Confucianism.

**유도신문**(誘導訊問) a leading question. ¶ ～을 하다 ask 〔put〕 a leading question; lead 《a criminal suspect》 to the point in question / ～에 걸려 불리한 진술을 하다 be led (against *one's* will) to make a disadvantageous statement by deliberate questions.

**유독**(有毒) noxiousness; venomousness. ～하다 (be) poisonous; noxious; venomous. ◉ ～가스 (a) poisonous gas. ～균류(菌類) venomous fungi. ～식물 a「poisonous 〔noxious〕 plant.

**유독**(惟獨·唯獨) only; singly; uniquely; alone. ¶ ～ 돈벌이만이 인생의 목적은 아니다 Moneymaking is not the sole end and aim of existence.

**유동**(流動) fluid. ～하다 flow (액체 등이); be fluid (정세·의견 등이). ¶ ～적인 fluid; mobile (이동하기 쉬운); not fixed (고정 안 된) / ～적인 사회 a mobile society / 그 문제에 관한 우리들의 생각은 ～적이다 Our ideas on the subject are not fixed. / 정세는 아직도 극히 ～적이다 The situation is still highly fluid. ◉ ～물 fluid substance. ～부채 current liabilities. ～성 liquidity; fluidity; (social) mobility: 국제 ～성 (금·외환 보유고 등) international liquidity / 노동의 ～성 mobility of labor / 고용의 ～성 mobility in employment. ～식(食) liquid food; a liquid diet. ～인구 a floating population. ～자본 circulating 〔floating, liquid〕 capital. ～자산 liquid 〔quick〕 assets. ～체 a fluid (기체도 포함); a liquid (액체만).

**유동**(遊動) ◉ ~원목(圓木) 《놀이기구》 a swinging pole. ~활차 a loose pulley.

**유두**(乳頭) 『해부』 a nipple; a teat. ◉ ~륜(輪) an areola; an halo. ~염 thelitis; acromastitis.

**유들유들** shamelessly; brazenfacedly. ~하다 (be) shameless; thick-skinned; unblushing; brazen-faced; cheeky. ¶ 자네 어지간히 ~하군 그래 You have plenty of cheek.

**유디티** 《수중 파괴반》 U.D.T. [< *u*nder-water *d*emolition *t*eam]

**유라시아** Eurasia; Europe and Asia. ¶ ~의 Eurasian; European and Asiatic. ◉ ~대륙 the Eurasian Continent. ~인 a Eurasian.

**유라톰** 《유럽 원자력 공동체》 Euratom. [< *Eur*opean *Atom*ic Energy Community]

**유락**(遊樂) amusement; enjoyment; pleasure; merrymaking; diversion. ~하다 enjoy 〔amuse〕 *oneself*.

**유람**(遊覽) sightseeing; a sightseeing tour; an excursion. ~하다 go sightseeing; do 〔see〕 the sights of 《a place》; sightsee 《around》. ◉ ~객 sightseers; tourists; excursionists; a vacationist. ~단체 a tourists' party; an excursion 〔a sightseeing〕 party. ~버스 a sightseeing bus. ~선 an excursion boat; a pleasure boat; a sightseeing boat. ~안내(서) a tourist guide book; an itinerary. ~여행 a pleasure trip 〔excursion〕. ~열차 an excursion train. ~지 a pleasure resort. ~지도 a tourists' map.

**유랑**(流浪) wandering; roaming; vagrancy. ~하다 wander 〔roam〕 「about 〔from place to place〕; rove. ¶ ~의 vagrant; wandering; roaming; nomadic. ◉ ~극단 a vagabond theatrical troupe. ~민 wanderers; a wandering 〔vagrant〕 tribe; 《유목민》 a nomadic people 〔tribe〕; nomads. ~벽 vagrant habits. ~생활 a wandering 〔vagrant〕 life; the life of an exile. ~여행 a roaming trip; wanderings. ~자〔인〕 a roamer; a vagabond; a tramp.

**유래**(由來) 《기원》 the origin; genesis; 《내력》 the history; 《출처》 the derivation; the source; 《원인》 the cause. ~하다 result 〔stem〕 《from》; originate 《in》; 《언어 등이》 be derived 《from》; 《…때부터》 date back 《to》. ¶ ~를 캐다 〔찾다, 더듬다〕 trace 《a custom》 to its source 〔origin〕; inquire into the origin of; study the history of / 나는 이 표현의 ~를 모른다 I don't know where this expression comes from.

**유량**(流量) 『물리』 flux; 《유수의 양》 the amount of flowing 〔inflowing〕 water. ◉ ~계 a flow meter.

**유러-** 《유럽의》 Euro-. ⇨유로.

**유럽** Europe. ¶ ~의 European / ~화하다 Europeanize / 이것이 ~의 관습이다 This is a European custom. ◉ ~개발은행 the European Bank for Reconstruction and Development (생략 EBRD). ~경제공동체 the European Economic Community (생략 EEC); 《속칭》 the Common Market. ~경제 협력기구 the Organization for European Economic Cooperation (생략 OEEC). ~공동체 the European Community (생략 EC). ~대륙 the (European) Continent. ~사람 a European. ~안보협력회의 the Conference on Security and Cooperation in Europe (생략 CSCE). ~연합 the European Union (생략 EU). ⇨이유 (EU). ~우주기구 the European Space Agency (생략 ESA). ~위원회 the European Commission. ~의회 the European Parliament. ~열강 the European Powers. ~ 자유무역연합 the European Free Trade Association (생략 EFTA). ~ 정치공동체 the European Political Community (생략 E.P.C.). ~ 통화단위 the European Currency Unit. ~회의 the Council of Europe (생략 CE).

**유려하다**(流麗―) (be) flowing 〔smooth, fluent〕 and elegant. ¶ 유려한 문체 a smooth and elegant style / 유려한 필치로 쓰인 편지 a letter written in an elegant hand.

**유력**(有力) ~하다 ① 《권세·영향력이 있는 상태》 (be) powerful; high-powered; influential; leading (일류의). ¶ ~한 신문 a leading newspaper / ~한 소식통 influential quarters / 협회의 ~한 회원 a leading 〔prominent〕 member of the society. ② 《가능성이 있는 상태》 《논쟁 등》 (be) weighty; cogent; 《증거 등》 (be) strong; convincing. ¶ ~한 찬성〔반대〕론 a strong 〔powerful〕 argument 「in favor of 〔against〕 《*a thing*》 / ~한 용의자 a key 〔prime〕 suspect / 가장 ~한 우승 후보 the likeliest winner; the top-rated contender for the title / 형사는 그 괴사건의 ~한 단서를 찾아냈다 The detective found 「a promising 〔an important〕 clue to the mystery. /

그는 다음 대통령감으로 가장 ～시되고 있다 He is regarded as the most likely presidential prospect.
◉ ～자 an influential person; a man of weight 〔influence〕; a dominant figure: 재계의 ～자 leading figures in the financial world; economic leaders.

**유력**(遊歷) a tour; an itinerancy; peregrination. ～하다 travel about; make a tour.

**유령**(幽靈) ① 《죽은이의》 a spirit of the dead. ② 《귀신》 a ghost; a bog(e)y; an apparition; a phantom; a specter 〔spectre 《영》〕; a supernatural visitor. ¶ ～ 같은 ghostlike / 저 집엔 ～이 나온다고 한다 They say that house is haunted. ◉ ～도시 a ghost town. ～선 a phantom ship. ～의 집 a haunted house. ～이야기 a ghost story. ～인구 a bogus 〔ghost〕 population. ～회사 a bogus 〔ghost, phantom〕 company; a paper company: ～ 회사를 차려놓고 많은 사람들로부터 1억원 이상이나 사취하다 swindle over 100 million won from a number of people running a bogus company.

**유례**(類例) a similar example 〔instance〕; a parallel case. ¶ ～없는 unique; unparalleled; without parallel; unexampled; unprecedented / 역사상 ～가 없다 be unparalleled in history.

**유로** 《유럽 사람》 a Euro; 《유럽의》 Euro-; 《EU의 통합 화폐 단위》 a Euro; a euro. ¶ 11개의 유럽 화폐들을 단일 통화인 ～로 통합한 것은 20세기 최대의 화폐 정책 성과 중의 하나이다 The merging of 11 European currencies into the single euro is truly one of the greatest monetary achievements of the 20th century. ◉ ～달러 Eurodollars. ～머니 Euromoney. ～뱅크 a Eurobank. ～본드〔채(債)〕 a Eurobond.

**유료**(有料) a charge. ¶ ～의 charged; feed; toll; paid / 무료 입장입니까 ～ 입장입니까 Is admission free or is there a charge? / 나는 그 공원이 ～ 입장인 줄을 몰랐다 I didn't know that admission to the park was charged.
◉ ～도로 a toll road 〔highway〕; a turnpike road. ～변소 a pay toilet. ～시사회 a 《film》 preview with an admission fee. ～전화 a pay telephone. ～주차장 a toll 〔paid〕 parking lot.

**유루**(遺漏) 《빠짐》 (an) omission; 《실수》 neglect; 《샘》 a leak. ～하다 omit; leave out; miss out; look over; make a careless mistake; 《새다》 leak. ¶ ～없이 《빠짐없이》 without omission; 《철저하게》 thoroughly; exhaustively / 만사 ～ 없도록 하시오 See that everything is done well.

**유류**(油類) oil [총칭]. ◉ ～ 절약 운동 an oil saving drive. ～파동 an oil crisis.

**유류**(遺留) leaving behind. ～하다 leave behind. ◉ ～분(分) 〖법〗 a legal portion of an heir; a reserve: ～분 권리자 a person entitled to a legal portion. ～품 an article left (behind); a thing left behind; a lost article; lost property: ～품 보관소 a lost property room.

**유리**(有理) ¶ ～의 rational. ◉ ～식〔수〕 a rational expression 〔number〕.

**유리**(流離) ⇨ 유리표박(流離漂泊).

**유리**(琉璃) glass; 《창유리》 a pane. ¶ ～ 같은 glassy; vitreous / 안전 ～ safety glass / 시계의 ～ a watch glass 〔crystal〕 / 젖빛 ～ frosted glass / 철사가 든 ～ wired glass / 창문에 ～를 끼우다 glaze a window; put a pane of glass in the window / 정치가의 생활은 ～를 낀 것처럼 투명해야 한다 Every aspect of a politician's life should be transparent for all to see.
◉ ～가게 a glass store. ～가루 glass dust; powdered glass. ～공(工) 《자르는》 a glass cutter; 《불어서 성형하는》 a glass blower. ～공장 a glassworks; a glass factory. ～관 a glass tube. ～구슬 a glass bead. ～그릇 glassware. ～문 a glass 〔glazed〕 door: ～문이 있는 책장 a glass-fronted bookcase. ～병 a glass bottle. ～섬유 glass fiber. ～세공 glasswork. ～잔 a glass. ～장수 a glazier; a glassman. ～조각 a piece of broken glass; a glass splinter (뾰족한). ～창 a glass window. ～칼 a glass cutter; a glazier's diamond.

**유리**(遊離) 《분리》 separation; 〖화학〗 isolation; extrication. ～하다 isolate; separate 《from》; come free; extricate. ¶ ～시키다 set free; let loose; 〖화학〗 extricate / 현실에서 ～되다 be removed 〔disengaged〕 from realities / 현실에서 ～된 정책 an unrealistic policy; a policy which is not based on the actual situation 《in the country》 / 염소는 이 방법으로 ～된다 Chlorine is released by this process.
◉ ～기(基) a free radical. ～산 free acid. ～산소 free oxygen. ～상태 a free state. ～에너지 〖물리〗 free ener-

gy. ～원자가 free valency. ～체 〖화학〗 an educt. ～핵 a free nucleus.

**유리**(瑠璃) lapis lazuli.

**유리표박**(流離漂泊) vagrancy; wandering. ～하다 vagabond; wander 〔roam〕 around; wander alone in a strange country.

**유리하다**(有利—) 《이로운》 (be) profitable; lucrative; remunerative; 《좋은》 (be) advantageous; favorable. ¶ 유리한 사업 a profitable enterprise / 유리한 장사 a lucrative business / 유리한 조건 remunerative terms / 피고에 유리한 증언 a witness favorable to the accused / 유리한 위치를 차지하다〔에 서다〕 have advantage over 《*a person*》; be in a better 〔stronger〕 position / 사태는 우리에게 유리하게 전개되었다 Things turned out (to be) favorable for us. / 젊은이들의 가치관에 순응하는 것이 우리에게 ～ It's our advantage to adapt to the values of young people. / 우리는 그를 이미 알고 있다는 점에서 유리했다 We had the advantage of already knowing him.

**유린**(蹂躪) 《침해》 infringement; 《겁탈》 violation; 《짓밟음》 trampling down; overrunning. ～하다 infringe (on); violate; trample upon 〔down〕; tread down; devastate; ravage. ¶ 인권 ～ an infringement of *one's* (human) rights / 개인의 자유를 ～하다 trample on the right of personal liberty / 남의 권리를 ～하다 ride roughshod over the rights of others / 정조를 ～하다 violate 〔dishonor〕 a woman / 국토를 ～하다 trample a country under foot / 국토를 ～당하다 have *one's* country trampled underfoot / 적군은 우리 조국을 ～했다 The enemy overrode 〔overran〕 our (mother) country. ◉ ～자 a devastator.

**유림**(儒林) (the class of) Confucian scholars.

**유막**(油膜) 〖기계〗 an oil film.

**유만부동**(類萬不同) ～하다 be different one from another; be of all different kinds.

**유망**(有望) a bright prospect 〔future, hope〕; great promise; rosy prospects. ～하다 (be) promising; hopeful; favorable; bright; full of promise. ¶ ～한 장래 a bright 〔rosy〕 future; a promising career / 전도 ～한 청년 a promising 〔up-and-coming〕 youth; a young man of (great) promise / ～하다고 보다 entertain a hopeful view of 《a plan》 / ～하지 않다 give little 〔no〕 hope / 우리 회사는 전도 ～하다 Our company has bright prospects for the future. ◉ ～주(株) 《주식》 a hopeful stock 〔share 《영》〕; 《사람》 an up-and-coming 《politician, player》.

**유망**(流網) a drift net. ◉ ～어업 drift-net fishing.

**유머** humor. ¶ ～가 풍부하다 be highly humorous; be full of 〔rich in〕 humor / ～가 있다 have a (fine) sense of humor / ～를 알다〔모르다〕 have a sense 〔have no sense〕 of humor. ◉ ～소설 a humorous novel 〔story〕. ～작가 a humorous 〔comic〕 writer; a humorist.

**유머러스** humorous.

**유머레스크** 〖음악〗 a humoresque.

**유머리스트** a humorist.

**유명**(幽明) ① 《어둠과 밝음》 darkness and light. ② 《이승과 저승》 this world and the other. ¶ ～을 달리하다 die; pass away; depart this life; return to dust 〔the earth〕.

**유명**(遺命) the dying injunctions 〔wishes〕 《of the king》; the last wishes 《of the king, of parents》. ¶ 아버지의 ～에 따라 according to *one's* dead father's will. 「자 a nominalist.

**유명론**(唯名論) 〖철학〗 nominalism. ◉ ～

**유명무실**(有名無實) ～하다 (be) nominal; titular; be in name only; be in nothing but the name. ¶ ～한 회장 a nominal 〔figurehead〕 president / 조약은 이젠 ～하다 The treaty has now become a mere scrap of paper. / 이 법은 ～하다 This law is a dead letter.

**유명세**(有名稅) a penalty of popularity 〔greatness〕; the price of fame. ¶ 너에게 그것은 일종의 ～이다 That's the price you have to pay for being famous. *or* Your name calls for that kind of sacrifice.

**유명인**(有名人) a celebrity; a public 〔well-known〕 figure; a big-name personage 《미》.

**유명하다**(有名—) (be) famous; noted; renowned; well-known; celebrated; 《악명으로》 (be) notorious. ¶ 유명한 사람 a celebrity / 유명한 사기꾼 a notorious swindler / 유명한 과자점 a well-known sweet shop / …로 ～ be famous for... / 치즈로 유명한 도시 a town noted for its cheeses / 유명해지다 become famous; rise into notice 〔fame〕; acquire fame; win a reputation; cut a figure; have *one's* name up; come to fame; 《악명으로》 gain notoriety / 정치가로 유명해지다 earn fame as a politician / 일약 유명하게 되다 leap 〔rocket〕 to fame / 그는 세계적으로 유명한 학자다 He is a scholar of worldwide fame 〔reputation〕. / 에디슨은 발명가로 유명하였다 Edison was renowned as an inventor.

> 용법 **famous** 좋은 뜻으로, 사람·사물이 「유명하다」란 뜻의 가장 일반적인 말. **noted** 전문 분야 등 특별한 자질에서 널리 알려져 「유명한」의 뜻. 나쁜 뜻으로도 씀. **renowned** 명성이 자자할 정도로 「유명하다」란 뜻. **well-known** 좋은 뜻으로나 나쁜 뜻으로나 「유명하게」 널리 알려진의 뜻. **celebrated** 사회적으로 높은 평가를 받아 「유명하다」란 뜻의 격식 차린 말. **notorious** 나쁜 뜻으로 「유명하게」 그 이름이 알려진의 뜻.

**유모**(乳母) a (wet) nurse; a nanny. ¶ 아기를 ~한테 맡기다 put a baby under a nurse's charge. ◉ ~차 a baby carriage 〔buggy〕; 《영》 a perambulator; a pram: ~차를 밀고 가다 wheel a baby carriage.

**유목**(流木) driftwood; drifting wood 〔logs〕.

**유목**(遊牧) nomadism. ~하다 nomadize; lead a nomadic life. ¶ ~의 nomad; nomadic. ◉ ~민 nomads; a nomadic people 〔tribe〕. ~생활 nomadism; a nomadic life. ~시대 the nomadic age.

**유무**(有無) existence and 〔or〕 nonexistence; existence; presence. ¶ 출석 의사의 ~를 묻다 ask 《*a person*》 whether *he* will be present or not / 관계 문헌의 ~를 조사하다 check for the existence of relevant literature / ~상통하다 minister to each other's wants; fill each other's needs; accommodate one another with.

**유묵**(遺墨) autographs of a departed person. ¶ 고(故) B씨의 ~ 전시회 an autographic exhibition of the late Mr. B.

**유문**(幽門) 〖해부〗 the pylorus (*pl.* -ri, -ruses). ◉ ~폐색 stoppage of the pylorus. ~협착 stricture of the pylorus; pyloric stenosis.

**유문**(遺文) posthumous writings; literary remains.

**유문암**(流紋岩) rhyolite.

**유물**(遺物) a relic; remains; vestiges; a hangover; a legacy (*pl.* -cies); a bequest. ¶ 과거의 ~ relics of the past / 봉건 시대의 ~ a holdover from the feudal times / 석기 시대의 ~ remains 〔vestiges〕 of the Stone Age.

**유물**(唯物) ¶ ~적인 materialistic / ~적으로 해석하다 interpret materialistically. ◉ ~론 〖철학〗 materialism: ~론자 a materialist. ~변증법 materialistic dialectic. ~사관 historical materialism; the materialistic conception of history.

**유미**(乳糜) 〖생리〗 chyle. ◉ ~관 a lacteal 〔chyle〕 duct; the lacteal vessels. ~즙 chyme.

**유미**(柳眉) beautiful eyebrows.

**유미**(唯美) ¶ ~적(인) (a)esthetic. ◉ ~주의 (a)estheticism: ~주의자 an (a)esthete / ~주의 운동 an (a)esthetic movement. ~파 the art-for-art's sake school.

**유민**(流民) drifting 〔wandering〕 people; the migrants.

**유민**(遊民) idle people; idlers; nonworkers.

**유밀과**(油蜜果) oil-and-honey pastry.

**유발**(乳鉢) a mortar.

**유발**(誘發) induction. ~하다 induce; cause 〔arouse〕 《*one's* anger》; lead to 〔bring about〕 《an event》; give rise to 〔set off, touch off〕 《a war》; trigger. ¶ 합병증을 ~하다 give rise to complications / 반일 데모를 ~하다 touch off anti-Japanese demonstration / 그 싸움이 폭동을 ~하였다 The fight triggered (off) the riot. / 비위생적인 환경이 병을 ~한다 Unhygienic conditions give rise to disease. / 운전기사의 과도한 스케줄이 그 버스 사고를 ~했다 The driver's overload schedule led to the bus accident.

**유방**(乳房) a breast; 〖의학〗 a mamma. ¶ ~이 큰〔작은〕 large-〔small-〕breasted 《girl》. ◉ ~암 a breast 〔mammary〕 cancer. ~염 mammitis; mastitis. ~절제(술) a mastectomy.

**유배**(流配) exile; banishment; deportation. ~하다 exile; banish. ¶ ~되다 be exiled 〔banished〕 《to a remote province》; be marooned; go into banishment. ◉ ~자 an exile; a deportee. ~지 a place of exile.

**유백**(乳白) ¶ ~색의 milk-white; milky white; opal. ◉ ~광 opalescence. ~제 an opalizer.

**유별**(有別) distinction; difference. ~나다 (be) distinctive; different. ¶ ~나게 distinctively; markedly; especially / ~난 사람 a peculiar person / 남녀 ~하다 There is a distinction between man and woman.

**유별**(類別) classification; categorization. ~하다 classify; grade; categorize.

¶ ～적인 classificatory.

**유보**(留保) reservation. ⇨ 보류. ～하다 reserve; hold over; keep back 《for》. ¶ 결정을 ～하다 reserve *one's* decision.

**유복**(有福) ～하다 (be) fortunate; lucky; blessed. ¶ ～한 가정 a blessed family.

**유복**(裕福) affluence; easy means; opulence. ～하다 (be) rich; affluent; opulent; well-to-do; well-off; wealthy. ¶ ～한 사람 a well-off 〔well-to-do〕 person; a person in easy circumstances / ～하게 지내다 live well; be well off; live in easy circumstances / ～해지다 grow rich; come to wealth / ～한 집안에 태어나다 be born rich; be born in a rich family / ～하게 자라나다 be bred up in luxury.

**유복자**(遺腹子) a posthumous child.

**유복지친**(有服之親) near relatives for whom mourning is due.

**유부**(油腐) 《a piece of》 fried bean curd. ◉ ～국수 noodles with fried bean curd. ～초밥 vinegared rice stuffed in fried bean curd.

**유부녀**(有夫女) a married woman.

**유비**(油肥) fertilizer made of animal fat; fatty fertilizer.

**유비무환**(有備無患) Be prepared, and you will have no cause for regrets. *or* Providing is preventing. *or* Provide for the worst, the best will save itself.

**유빙**(流氷) floating 〔drift〕 ice; an ice floe.

**유사**(有史) ¶ ～ 이래 since the dawn of history; in history / ～ 이전의 prehistoric; of prehistoric times / ～ 이래의 대전쟁 the greatest war in history / ～ 이래의 대홍수 the greatest flood on record / 그것은 ～ 이래 첫번째 실험이었다 It was the first experiment in history 〔since the dawn of history, on record〕.

**유사**(有事) emergency; crisis. ¶ ～시에 in time 〔case〕 of emergency; in an emergency / ～시에 대비한 입법 legislation to deal with emergencies / ～시에 대비하다 prepare for the worst; provide against emergencies.

**유사**(油砂) tar sand; oil sand.

**유사**(流砂) 《물속의》 silt; 《사막 등의》 shifting sand; quicksand.

**유사**(遊絲) 《시계의》 a hairspring.

**유사**(類似) (a) resemblance; (a) similarity; (a) likeness; an analogy; an affinity. ～하다 be similar 〔akin, analogous〕 《to》; (be) resemble; be like; bear resemblance 《to》. ¶ 심장은 펌프와 ～하다 The heart is analogous to a pump. / 지금의 네 상황은 나와 ～하다 Your present situation is similar to mine.

◉ ～뇌염 a suspected encephalitis case. ～사항 like matters. ～점 a (point of) similarity 〔resemblance〕: 이것과 그것과는 ～점이 없다 I see no likeness whatever between this and that. ～종교 a pseudo-religion. ～품 《모조품》 an imitation 《of the real thing》; 《비슷한 것》 a similar article; similar goods: ～품 주의 《표시》 "Beware of imitations". ～환자 a suspected case.

**유사분열**(有絲分裂) 〖생물〗 mitosis.

**유산**(乳酸) 〖화학〗 lactic acid. ◉ ～균 a lactobacillus (*pl.* -cilli).

**유산**(流産) (a) miscarriage; (an) abortion; 《실패》 failure. ～하다 have a miscarriage; miscarry; abort; 《고의로》 produce abortion; 《계획 따위가》 fail; fall through; prove abortive. ¶ 임신 3 개월째에 ～하다 have a miscarriage in the third month of pregnancy / 숙모는 또 ～했단다 Aunt has miscarried again, I hear. / 새 계획은 ～되었다 The new plan has miscarried 〔proved abortive〕.

**유산**(遊山) a picnic; an outing. ～하다 go on an outing. ◉ ～객 a picnicker.

**유산**(遺産) property left 《by》; an inheritance; a legacy; a bequest. ¶ 무형의 ～ incorporeal hereditament / ～을 남기다 bequeath 〔leave, hand down〕 a fortune 〔property, an estate〕 《to》; leave a bequest / ～을 가로채다 seize an inheritance / ～을 노리다 be after the inheritance / ～을 물려받다 inherit a fortune 〔property, an estate〕; succeed to an estate / ～을 분배하다 divide *one's* property 《among *one's* children》 / ～으로 주다 give and bequeath 〔devise, legate〕 / 1 억원의 ～으로 편히 살다 live comfortably on a legacy of ₩100,000,000 / 내게는 아버지의 ～이 좀 있다 My father has left me something. / 그는 군사 통치의 ～을 근절시키겠다는 공약을 다시 새롭게 하였다 He renewed his pledge to eradicate the legacy of military rule.

◉ ～관리 〖법〗 the administration of property (left by *a person*): ～ 관리인 an administrator 〔administratrix (여자)〕 of the property. ～다툼 a quarrel over an inheritance. ～분할 division of an estate. ～상속 inheritance: ～ 상속세 (an) inheritance 〔(a) succession〕

tax / ～ 상속인 an heir 〔heiress (여자)〕 to property; an inheritor; a legatee.
**유산계급** the propertied classes; the bourgeois class; the bourgeoisie.
**유산탄**(榴散彈) a shrapnel (shell).
**유상**(有償) ¶ ～의 〖법〗 onerous / ～으로 취득하다 obtain 《*something*》 for counter value. ◉ ～계약 an onerous contract. ～몰수 confiscation with compensation; confiscation for value. ～원조 credit assistance. ～취득 acquisition for value. ～행위 a juristic act done for a consideration.
**유상**(油狀) being oily. ¶ ～의 oily 《substances》; like oil.
**유상**(乳狀) ¶ ～의 milky; emulsified. ◉ ～액 (a) milky liquid; (an) emulsion; 《식물의》 latex: ～액을 분비하는 lactescent.
**유상무상**(有象無象) ① 《만상》 all things in nature; the universe; creation. ② 《어중이떠중이》 the rabble; the rank and file.
**유색**(有色) ¶ ～의 nonwhite; colored. ◉ ～야채 highly-pigmented vegetables. ～인종 colored races; non-white people.
**유생**(儒生) a Confucian (scholar); a student of Confucianism.
**유생물**(有生物) the animate; life; living things.
**유서**(由緖) a history. ¶ ～ 있는 historic; storied / ～ 있는 가문 a historic family; a family with history / ～ 깊은 땅 a place 〔spot〕 with its old associations; a place with a historic background / ～ 불명이다 The origin is unknown. / 이 소나무는 ～가 깊다 This pine tree has a history.
**유서**(遺書) a note left behind (by a dead person); a farewell note; 《자살의》 a suicide note; 《재산 분배의》 a testamentary letter; a will; (*one's* last will and) testament. ¶ ～를 쓰다 〔작성하다〕 make *one's* will 〔testament〕; draw (up) a will / ～를 남기다 leave a note 〔will〕 / ～를 남기고 죽다 die testate.
**유서**(類書) books of the same kind; similar 〔allied〕 books 〔works〕.
**유선**(有線) ¶ ～의 cabled; wired. ◉ ～방송 cable broadcasting. ～식 the wire system. ～전신 wire telegraphy. ～전화 wire telephone. ～중계 cable 〔wire〕 relaying. ～텔레비전 cable television 〔TV〕; cablevision; closed-circuit television (생략 CCTV); community antenna television (생략 CATV). ～ 텔레비전 방송 cable television broadcasting: 지방 ～TV 방송국 a local cable television station. ～통신 cable communications. 한국～ (텔레비전) 방송협회 the Korea Cable Television Association (생략 KCTA).
**유선**(乳腺) 〖해부〗 a mammary 〔lacteal〕 gland. ◉ ～염 〖의학〗 mastitis.
**유선형**(流線型) a streamline shape. ¶ ～의 streamline(d). ◉ ～자동차 a streamlined car.
**유성**(有性) ¶ ～의 gamic; sexual. ◉ ～생식 sexual reproduction; gamogenesis: ～생식을 하는 생물 a sexually reproducing organism. ～세대 a sexual generation.
**유성**(有聲) ¶ ～의 voiced; vocal. ◉ ～영화 a sound film 〔picture〕; a talkie. ～음 a voiced 〔vocal〕 sound: ～음화 vocalization; voicing. ～자음 a voiced consonant.
**유성**(油性) being oily 〔greasy〕. ¶ ～의 oil; oily; oleaginous; 《기름을 용제로 한》 oil-based. ◉ ～도료 an oil-based paint. ～페니실린 penicillin oil.
**유성**(流星) a shooting 〔falling〕 star; a meteor. ◉ ～군 a meteor stream. ～우(雨) a meteor shower; a shower of meteors.
**유성**(遊星) 〖천문〗 a planet. ⇨ 행성(行星).
**유세**(有稅) ¶ ～의 taxable; dutiable. ◉ ～지 dutiable land. ～품 dutiable goods.
**유세**(有勢) ～하다 ① 《유력하다》 (be) powerful; influential. ② =～떨다. ¶ ～떨다〔부리다〕 wield power 〔influence〕; be domineering; lord it over 《*one's* subordinates》; 《구어》 throw *one's* weight about 〔around〕 / 사람들은 좀 높은 자리에 앉으면 ～부리게 마련이다 People are likely to throw their weight around when they get a little authority.
**유세**(遊說) 《미》 stumping; a canvassing tour; an oratorical campaign; a campaign. ～하다 go canvassing; canvass; make an election tour; 《미》 stump 《*one's* electoral district》; 《지방을》 barnstorm 《through the Honam districts》.
¶ 단독 지방 ～ a solo whistle-stop trip 《미구어》 / 전국을 ～하다 go about the country electioneering; stump the whole country / 전국 ～의 길에 오르다 start on a speaking tour throughout the country / 대통령 자신이 ～에 나섰다

The President himself set out on a stumping tour.
◉ ~객〔인, 원〕 a campaign 〔stump〕 speaker; a stump orator; a canvasser. ~행각〔여행〕《go on》 a stumping 〔speaking〕 tour.

**유소**(幼少) infancy; childhood. ~하다 (be) infant; juvenile; young. ◉ ~년 children and toddlers; older and younger children.

**유속**(流速) the speed of a current. ◉ ~계 a current meter; a tachometer. ~측정 tachometry.

**유속**(遺俗) customs handed down to posterity; hereditary customs. ¶ 이것은 고대의 ~이다 This custom is of a very early origin.

**유수**(流水) running water; a flowing stream. ¶ 세월은 ~와 같다 Time flies (like an arrow).

**유수**(幽囚) confinement; imprisonment.

**유수**(有數) ~하다 (be) prominent; eminent; leading; distinguished; foremost. ¶ 한국 ~의 언어학자 one of the master philologists in Korea.

**유수정책**(誘水政策) 〖경제〗 a pump priming policy. ¶ ~을 쓰다 prime a pump.

**유숙**(留宿) lodging; boarding. ~하다 lodge 《at》; take up *one's* quarters 〔lodgings〕.

**유순**(柔順) submission; submissiveness; docility. ~하다 (be) submissive; docile; obedient; gentle; meek. ¶ ~히 obediently; gently; meekly; tamely / 아주 ~한 as gentle 〔meek〕 as a lamb / ~한 아이들 obedient 〔orderly〕 children.

**유스타키오관**(一管) the Eustachian tube; the syrinx (*pl.* syringes, ~es).

**유스호스텔** a youth hostel. ¶ ~을 이용하며 여행하다 go (youth-)hosteling.
◉ ~관리인 the warden 〔supervisor〕 of a youth hostel. ~이용자 a youth hosteler.

**유습**(遺習) a hereditary custom.

**유시**(幼時) childhood; infancy. ¶ ~의 체험 *one's* childhood experience.

**유시**(酉時) 〖민속〗 the Watch of the Cock; the 10th of the 12 double-hours (=the period between 5 and 7 p.m.).

**유시**(流矢) a stray arrow.

**유시**(諭示) admonition; instruction; inculcation. ~하다 admonish; instruct; inculcate. ¶ 대통령의 ~ a presidential instruction 〔message〕.

**유시계비행**(有視界飛行) visual flying; a visual flight. ⇨ 시계(視界).

**유시류**(有翅類) 〖곤충〗 *Pterygogenea* (학명).

**유시무종**(有始無終) having a beginning but no end; incompleteness. ~하다 (be) incomplete; endless.

**유시유종**(有始有終) completeness. ~하다 (be) complete.

**유식**(有識) scholarly attainment; scholarship; learning. ~하다 (be) learned; educated; cultured; cultivated. ¶ ~한 사람 learned men; knowledgeable people; the wise 〔learned, intelligent〕 / ~하게 말하다 speak in a refined way / ~한 체하다 pretend to know much; be pedantic / 그가 ~한 데 놀랐다 I am surprised at his erudition.

**유식**(遊食) an idle life. ~하다 live in idleness; live an idle life; loaf. ◉ ~지민(之民) idle people; the non-working 〔leisure〕 class.

**유신**(遺臣) a surviving retainer; a statesman 〔minister〕 of the previous dynasty.

**유신**(維新) renovation (혁신); the Revitalizing Reforms. ~하다 renovate; restore.

**유신론**(有神論) 〖철학〗 theism. ◉ ~자 a theist.

**유실**(流失) ~하다, ~되다 be washed 〔carried, swept〕 away 《by a flood》; be lost 《in a storm》/ 홍수로 약 천호의 가옥이 ~되었다 Some 1,000 houses were washed 〔swept〕 away by the flood. ◉ ~가옥 houses washed away by the flood.

**유실**(遺失) loss. ~하다 lose. ◉ ~자 a loser; the owner of a lost property.

**유실물**(遺失物) a lost article; lost property; things lost. ¶ 청구인이 없는 ~ an unclaimed lost article / ~을 청구하다 reclaim a lost article. ◉ ~광고 a lost advertisement. ~신고 a report on lost property. ~취급소〔보관소〕《미》 a lost and found (office); 《영》 a lost property office.

**유심**(唯心) ¶ ~적 spiritual; idealistic. ◉ ~론 〖철학〗 spiritualism; idealism; mentalism: ~론자 a spiritualist; an idealist; a mentalist.

**유심하다**(有心一) (be) attentive; careful; mindful; cautious. ¶ 유심히 attentively; carefully; with attention 〔care〕 / 유심히 듣다 hear attentively; listen to / 유심히 보다 look hard 《at》; have 〔take〕 a careful look 《at》.

**유아**(幼兒) an infant; a little child; a baby. ◉ ~교육 preschool education. ~기 babyhood; infancy. ~보험

infantile insurance. ～돌연사 증후군 sudden infant death syndrome (생략 SIDS). ～복 baby wear. ～사망률 the infant mortality (rate). ～살해 infanticide. ～식 baby 〔infant〕 food. ～어 baby talk. ～원 a (day) nursery.

**유아**(幼芽) a young sprout; a germ.

**유아**(乳兒) a suckling; a baby; an infant. ◉ ～식 baby food. ～원(院) a nursery.

**유아**(遺兒) a child of 《the late Mr. A.》; an orphan; an orphaned child.

**유아독존**(唯我獨尊) 《독선》 self-conceit; vainglory. ¶ 천상천하 ～ I am my own Lord 〔Holy am I alone〕 throughout heaven and earth. *or* I am not any man's man, but my own. 「lamp.

**유아등**(誘蛾燈) a light trap; a luring

**유아론**(唯我論) 『철학』 solipsism.

**유안**(留案) a pending question 〔problem〕. ～하다 leave 《*a matter*》 in abeyance; leave 《a question》 undecided (for future settlement); suspend 〔table〕 《a bill》 for further discussion.

**유안**(硫安) 『화학』 ammonium sulfate.

**유암**(乳癌) breast cancer. ⇨ 유방암.

**유압**(油壓) oil pressure. ¶ ～ 구동의 hydraulically-operated. ◉ ～계 an oil pressure gauge. ～브레이크 a hydraulic 〔an oil〕 brake. ～잭 a hydraulic jack.

**유액**(乳液) 『식물』 milky liquid; latex (*pl.* ～es, latices); 《화장품》 (a) milky lotion.

**유야무야**(有耶無耶) ～하다 (be) mystifying; vague; ambiguous; indecisive. ¶ ～가 되다 end in smoke; come to nothing; be dropped; become hazy / ～ 덮어 버리다 hush up 〔smother, suppress〕 《*a matter*》 / 결과를 ～로 만들다 obscure the matter / 그 문제는 ～가 되고 말았다 The issue simply faded from public awareness (without any clear-cut resolution).

**유약**(幼弱) ～하다 (be) young and fragile; juvenile and weak.

**유약**(柔弱) ～하다 (be) weak; unmanly; effeminate. ¶ 도시에서 자란 ～한 소년 a city-bred sissy boy / 그는 ～한 인물이다 He is a 「weak character 〔weak-kneed man〕.

**유약**(釉藥) 《도자기의》 glaze; overglaze; 《금속의》 enamel. ¶ ～을 칠하다 glaze 《pottery》; enamel 《a brooch》 / 도자기에 ～을 입히다 put glaze on pottery.

**유어**(類語) a similar word; 《동의어》 a synonym. ¶ …와 ～이다 be synonymous with…; be a synonym 《of a word》.

**유언**(流言) a groundless story 〔rumor〕; a wild rumor; a *canard* (F.); a false report. ¶ ～을 퍼뜨리다 set a false rumor afloat; spread 〔circulate〕 a wild story 〔rumor〕. ◉ ～비어 a wild rumor; a canard.

**유언**(遺言) *one's* will; *one's* last will and testament; *one's* dying wish; *one's* last words. ～하다 leave 〔make〕 a will 《that…》; say *one's* will 《that …》; express *one's* dying wish.

¶ ～에 의해 in accordance with 《*a person's*》 will 〔last wish〕 / ～을 실행하다 administer 〔carry out〕 《*a person's*》 will / ～을 남기고〔남기지 않고〕 죽다 die 「testate 〔intestate〕 / ～으로 남겨주다 leave 《two million won》 to 《*a person*》 in *one's* will; bequeath 《a person》 《two million won》 in *one's* will. ◉ ～자 a testator (남); a testatrix (여). ～장 *one's* last will and testament; a will; a testament: 자필 ～장 a holograph will / ～장을 만들다 make *one's* will 〔testament〕 / ～장을 만들게 하다 get 《a lawyer》 to write 〔make〕 *one's* will. ～집행자 an 〔a testamentary〕 executor. 「ness〕.

**유업**(乳業) the dairy industry 〔busi-

**유업**(遺業) work 〔business〕 left by 〔inherited from〕 《*a person*》; an unfinished work. ¶ ～을 계승하다 take over 《*a person's*》 unfinished work.

**유에스에이** U.S.A. [<the *U*nited *S*tates of *A*merica (미국); the *U*nited *S*tates *A*rmy (미국 육군)]

**유에프오** 《미확인 비행물체》 a UFO. [<an *u*nidentified *f*lying *o*bject]

**유엔** U.N. [<the *U*nited *N*ations] ¶ ～의 승인 a U.N. recognition / ～의 평화 유지 활동 the U.N. Peace-Keeping Operation (생략 PKO).

◉ ～ 경제 사회 이사회 the United Nations Economic and Social Council. ～경찰군 the U.N. Emergency Forces (생략 UNEF). ～교육 과학 문화 기구 the United Nations Educational, Scientific, and Cultural Organization (생략 UNESCO). ～군 the U.N. forces; the United Nations forces 〔troops〕: ～군 방송 the Voice of the United Nations Command (생략 VUNC) / ～군 사령부 the U.N. Forces Command. ～대학 the United Nations University. ～문장(紋章) the United

Nations Emblem. ～데이 United Nations 〔U.N.〕 Day. ～ 무역 개발회의 the United Nations Conference on Trade and Development (생략 UNCTAD). ～본부 the U.N. Headquarters. ～분담금 《Korea's》 financial contribution to the United Nations. ～사무국 the Secretariat of the United Nations. ～사무총장 the Secretary-General of the U.N. ～ 세계 식량 계획 the United Nations World Food Program (생략 WFP). ～ 안전 보장이사회 the United Nations Security Council (생략 UNSC). ～총회 the U.N. General Assembly. ～ 평화유지군 the U.N. Peace-Keeping Forces. ～ 한국대사 the Korean Ambassador to the U.N. ～헌장 the Charter of the United Nations; the U.N. Charter. ～회원국 a U.N. member (nation).

**유역**(流域) a (drainage) basin; 《큰 강의》 a (river) valley. ¶ 양쯔강 ～ the Yangtze valley / 아마존강 ～ the Amazon basin / 한강 ～ the basin of the Han River. ◉ ～면적 the size of a catchment area 〔basin〕.

**유연**(柔軟) ～하다 (be) soft; pliable; supple; flexible; pliant. ¶ 그녀는 몸이 ～하다 She has a pliant body. *or* She is lithe in build. / 사물을 좀더 ～하게 생각하라 You should take things more flexibly. ◉ ～성 softness; pliability; flexibility: ～성 있는 pliable; flexible; adaptable / 그의 법 해석에는 ～성이 없다 He「is too rigid 〔lacks flexibility〕 in his interpretation of the law. ～체조 light gymnastics; 《미용체조》 calisthenics: ～체조를 하다 limber *oneself* up.

**유연**(悠然) an air 〔attitude〕 of perfect composure. ～하다 (be) composed; calm; quiet; self-possessed. ¶ ～히 with an air of perfect composure; composedly; calmly; quietly; leisurely. ¶ 그는 언제나 ～하게 일에 대처한다 He aways deals with matters calmly.

**유연탄**(有煙炭) bituminous 〔soft〕 coal.

**유영**(游泳) 《헤엄침》 swimming; 《처세》 conduct of life; carrying *oneself*. ～하다 《헤엄치다》 (take a) swim; 《처세하다》 get on 〔make *one's* way〕 through the world. ¶ 우주를 ～하다 take 〔make〕 a space walk; walk in space. ◉ ～기관 〖동물〗 a natatorial organ; the flipper. ～류 〖동물〗 nekton; swimming insects. ～술 the art of swimming; 《처세술》 how to get along in the world.

**유예**(猶豫) ① 《망설임》 (a) delay; hesitation. ¶ 잠시도 ～할 때가 아니다 There is no time「to lose 〔to be lost〕. *or* The situation admits of no delay. ② 《예정 일시의 연기》 (a) postponement; (a) delay; grace (지급 기일의); 《형의》 〖법〗 suspension 《of a sentence》; a reprieve; a respite. ～하다 give *a person* 《a ten day's》 grace; grant *a person* a postponement 《of seven days》; 《형의 집행을》 grant 〔give〕 a reprieve 〔respite〕; reprieve. ¶ ～ 없이 without delay 〔hesitation〕 / 하루의 ～를 부탁하다 ask for a day's grace 《for the payment》 / 형의 집행을 ～하다 postpone 〔delay〕 execution; grant a stay of execution / 그녀는 형의 집행이 1년간 ～되었다 She was reprieved for a year.
◉ ～기간 an extension of time; 《보험료·어음 등 지급의》 《미》 a grace period; 《영》 days of grace; 〖노동〗 《냉각기간의》 a cooling-off period: 법정 ～기간 《채무 이행의》 a legal delay / 3개월의 ～기간 후 해고되다 be dismissed 〔fired〕 after three months' grace. ～미결 postponement and suspension. ～일수 days of indulgence 〔allowance〕; days of grace (어음 지급의).

**유용**(有用) usefulness; utility; use; serviceableness. ～하다 (be) useful; serviceable; good 《for》; of use 〔service〕. ¶ ～한 물건 a useful thing / 국가에 ～한 인물 a man useful 〔valuable〕 to the state / ～케 하다 turn 《*a thing*》 to account / 돈을 ～하게 쓰다 make the best use of *one's* money / 그녀는 회사에서 매우 ～한 인물이다 She is a valuable figure in the company. ◉ ～식물 a useful plant.

**유용**(流用) (a) diversion; (an) appropriation; 《착복》 (a) misappropriation. ～하다 apply 〔appropriate〕 《the money》 to 《some other purpose》; divert 《from one object to another》; misappropriate 《public money》. ¶ 그들은 가끔 공금을 ～했다 They often misappropriated 〔made use of〕 government funds. / 그 돈은 다른 목적에 ～되었다 The fund was diverted to some other purposes. ◉ 공금～ misappropriation of public money; peculation.

**유원지**(遊園地) an amusement park; amusement grounds; a (public) recreation 〔pleasure〕 ground. ¶ 아동 ～

an amusement park for children.
**유월**(六月) June (생략 Jun.).
**유월절**(逾越節) 〖유대교〗 Passover.
**유위**(有爲) capability; ability; efficiency; usefulness; serviceableness. ~하다 (be) capable; gifted; talented; useful; promising (유망한). ¶ ~한 인재 a man of parts 〔ability, promise〕/ ~한 청년 a promising young man.
**유유낙낙**(唯唯諾諾) ~하다 give ready 〔willing〕 consent 《to》; do willingly what *one* was told to do. ¶ ~ 그저 시키는 대로 일하다 work at 《*a person's*》 beck (and call).
**유유도일**(悠悠度日) ~하다 live idly 〔leisurely〕. 「slow; deliberate.
**유유범범**(悠悠泛泛) ~하다 (be) leisurely;
**유유상종**(類類相從) 《속담》 Birds of feather flock together. *or* Like attracts like.
**유유자적**(悠悠自適) ~하다 live in easy 〔comfortable〕 retirement; live free from worldly cares.
**유유하다**(悠悠—) ① 《아득하다》 (be) remote; be very far off. ② 《여유가 있다》 (be) leisurely; slow; unhurried; 《침착하다》 (be) calm: composed. ¶ 유유히 calmly; composedly; serenely; in leisurely fashion; slowly; quietly / 유유히 담배를 피우다 smoke serenely 〔at ease〕/ 거리를 유유히 걷다 walk leisurely along the street.
**유의**(留意) keeping in mind; mindfulness; attentiveness. ~하다 keep 〔bear〕 in mind; be mindful 《of》; be attentive 《to》; take care 〔notice〕 《of》; pay attention 《to》. ¶ ~해야 할 noteworthy; notable / …에 ~하면서 with an eye on 〔to〕… / ~해서 듣다 hear attentively 〔with attention, with care〕/ …에 ~하지 않다 give no heed to…; pay no attention 〔regard〕 to…; be inattentive to…; be unmindful of… / 건강에 ~하다 take care of *oneself* / 그는 위험 따위에는 ~하지도 않는다 He takes no heed of danger. 「식.
**유의유식**(遊衣遊食) an idle life. = 무위도
**유의의하다**(有意義—) (be) significant; meaningful.
**유익하다**(有益—) 《유리한》 (be) profitable; beneficial; advantageous; 《교육적인》 (be) instructive; edifying; salutary; 《유용한》 (be) useful; serviceable; helpful; good 《for》; 《가치있는》 (be) worthwhile; rewarding.
¶ 유익한 경험 a useful experience / 유익한 이야기〔교훈〕 an instructive talk 〔lesson〕/ 젊은이에게 유익한 책 books good for young people / 유익하게 쓰다 use 《*a thing*》 to good purpose; put 《*a thing*》 to a good use; use… profitably; turn… to advantage / 시간〔돈〕을 유익하게 쓰다 make good use of *one's* time 〔money〕; use *one's* time 〔money〕 to advantage / 그의 강연은 매우 유익했다 His lecture was very instructive. / 그는 우리에게 유익한 조언을 해 주었다 He gave us useful advice. / 해외 여행은 유익한 경험이다 Traveling abroad is 「an instructive 〔a profitable〕 experience.
**유인**(有人) ¶ ~의 manned; piloted. ◉ ~기(機) a manned 〔piloted〕 aircraft. ~우주 비행 manned space flight. ~우주선 a manned spaceship. ~우주센터 the Manned Spacecraft Center (생략 MSC). ~위성 a manned satellite. ~조종장치 〖우주〗 a manned maneuvering unit; a backpack.
**유인**(誘引) allurement; seduction; inducement; enticement. ~하다 allure 《*a person* with money》; seduce 《a girl》; entice 《*a person* into *doing*》; lead astray. ¶ ~해내다 lure 《*a person*》 out / 나쁜 짓을 하도록 ~하다 tempt 《*a person*》 into evil doing / 적을 위험한 곳으로 ~하다 lure the enemy into a dangerous position.
**유인**(誘因) a proximate 〔provoking, contributing〕 cause; an immediate occasion; an incentive; a motive. ¶ 전쟁의 ~ the cause of war / …의 ~이 되다 cause; induce; be the cause 〔occasion〕 of…; lead (up) to…; bring about….
**유인물**(油印物) printed matter. ◉ 불온 ~ subversive 〔anti-government〕 printed materials.
**유인성**(柔靭性) flexibility; elasticity. ¶ ~이 있다 be flexible 〔elastic〕.
**유인원**(類人猿) 〖동물〗 an anthropoid (ape).
**유일**(唯一) ~하다 (be) single; unique; solitary; sole; one (and only). ¶ ~한 the only; the sole; unique / ~한 상속인 the sole heir / ~한 예〔예외〕 a solitary instance 〔exception〕/ ~한 친구 *one's* only 〔sole〕 friend / 사고에서의 ~한 생존자 the sole 〔only〕 survivor of the accident / 이것이 그 주제에 관한 ~한 책이다 This is the only book on the subject. / 우리가 양보하는 것이 이 문제의 ~한 해결책이다 The only means of settling this problem is for us to

give in. ◉ ~신 the one and only God. ~신교 monotheism; Unitarianism.

**유일무이**(唯一無二) ~하다 (be) unique; peerless. ⇨ 유일. ¶ 독서가 그의 ~한 즐거움이다 Reading is his single pleasure.

**유임**(留任) remaining in office. ~하다 remain〔stay, continue〕in office. ¶ ~되다 be retained; stay on / ~을 권고하다 advise《*a person*》to stay in office / 각료 전원이 ~하는 것은 좋지 않다 It's bad that all the Cabinet ministers stay〔retain〕on their positions. ◉ ~운동 a movement to retain《*a person*》in *his* office.

**유입**(流入) (an) inflow; (an) influx; incoming. ~하다 flow〔stream, come〕in〔into〕. ¶ 외자 ~ an inflow〔influx〕of foreign capital / 인구 ~ the influx of the population / 정부는 미국 자본의 ~을 장려했다 The government encouraged American capital inflow. / 난민의 ~과 실업자의 증가와는 어떤 관계가 있느냐 Is there any relation between the influx of refugees and the rise in unemployment?

**유자**(柚子)〖식물〗a citron. ◉ ~나무 the citron (tree).

**유자**(遊資)〖경제〗《유휴자본》idle〔unemployed〕capital; floating money〔funds〕lying idle.

**유자격자**(有資格者) a qualified〔a competent, an eligible〕person《for a post》; an eligible《for》; a qualifier; the qualified [총칭]. ◉ 교원〔조종사〕~ a licensed teacher〔pilot〕.

**유자망**(有刺網) a drift net.

**유자생녀**(有子生女) ~하다 bring forth many sons and daughters.

**유자형**(U字型) ¶ ~의 U-shaped; U. ◉ ~ 볼트〔관〕a U bolt〔tube〕. ~ 커브 a hairpin curve〔bend〕.

**유작**(遺作) *one's* posthumous work(s).

**유장**(乳漿) whey; plasma; milk serum.

**유장하다**(悠長—)《길고 오래다》(be) long; lengthy;《지루하다》(be) tedious;《성미가 느릿하다》(be) leisurely; slow; deliberate.

**유저**(遺著) books that *one* has left behind; a posthumous work. ¶ 김 박사의 ~ writings of the late Dr. Kim.

**유적**(遺跡) remains; ruins; relics; vestiges. ¶ 고대 문명의 ~ the vestiges of ancient civilization / 선사 시대의 ~ a prehistoric site / 태고의 ~ the relics〔remains〕of an ancient age / 고대 로마의 ~을 찾다 visit the ruins of ancient Rome / 이 부근에는 역사적인 ~이 많다 This neighborhood abounds in historic sites.

**유전**(油田) an oil field; oil land. ¶ 해양 ~ an offshore oil field / ~을 발견하다 discover〔find〕an oil field; hit oil / ~을 개발하다 develop an oil field. ◉ ~지대 an oil (producing) region. ~탐사〔개발〕oil exploration.

**유전**(流轉)《유랑》wandering; vagrancy;《변전》continual change; vicissitudes《of life》;《윤회》transmigration. ~하다 wander《about》; rove; transmigrate. ¶ 만물은 ~한다 Nothing remains the same. *or* Everything changes. *or* All things are subject to vicissitude.

**유전**(誘電)〖전기〗induced electricity. ◉ ~체 a dielectric (substance).

**유전**(遺傳) heredity; (hereditary) transmission; (genetic) inheritance. ~하다 be hereditary; be transmitted《from *one's* parents》; run in the blood〔family〕; be handed down. ¶ ~성의, ~적인 hereditary; of hereditary nature; inherited; transmissible / ~적으로 hereditarily / ~적 장애《방사능에 의한》a genetic damage / 부모에게서 병이 ~되다 inherit a disease from *one's* parents / 어떤 버릇은 ~한다 Some habits are inherited. / 정신병은 그 집안의 ~이다 Insanity runs in that family. ◉ ~론 hereditism. ~병 a hereditary disease〔disorder〕; an inherited〔a genetic〕disease. ~성《of》hereditary nature; hereditary. ~인자 a genetic factor. ~학 genetics: ~학자 a geneticist. ~형질 a genetic trait〔character, endowment〕.

**유전기**(流電氣)〖전기〗galvanic〔voltaic〕electricity; voltaism; galvanism.

**유전스**〖상업〗usance. ◉ ~어음 a bill drawn at usance. ~제도 the usance bill system.

**유전자**(遺傳子) a gene. ¶ 면역 반응 억제 ~ an immune response inhibiting gene / 인공 ~ an artificial gene / 합성 ~ a synthesized gene / ~의 인위적 조작 genetic manipulation; manipulation of genes / ~ 변형 식품의 잠재적 위험 the potential dangers of genetically-modified food / ~를 합성하다 synthesize a gene. ◉ ~공학 the genetic engineering: ~ 공학자 a genetic engineer / ~ 공학 센터 the Genetic Engineering Research Center. ～은행 a gene bank. ～재결합 gene recombination. ～재조합 식품 genetically modified food. ～조작 gene manipulation. ～형 a genotype.

**유정**(有情) humaneness; warm-〔tender-〕heartedness; sympathetic 〔compassionate〕 feelings; sentience.

**유정**(油井) an oil(-producing) well; 《미》 an oiler. ¶ ～을 파다 sink an oil well; drill for oil. ◉ ～굴착기 an oil (drilling) rig. ～화재 oil well fire.

**유정**(遺精) involuntary emission of semen; nocturnal pollution; a wet dream; 〖의학〗 spermatorrhea.

**유제**(油劑) an oily medicine; a drug containing oil.

**유제**(乳劑) 〖약〗 an emulsion.

**유제**(類題) similar 〔like〕 questions.

**유제동물**(有蹄動物) 〖동물〗 a hoofed 〔an ungulate〕 animal.

**유제품**(乳製品) a milk product; dairy products.

**유조**(油槽) an oil tank. ◉ ～선 an oiler; a tanker; 《대형》 a supertanker; a mammoth tanker: 13만 5천 톤의 ～선 a 135,000-ton oil carrier / 노르웨이 선적의 ～선 the Norway-registered (oil) carrier. ～차 an oil tank truck 〔lorry〕.

**유족**(遺族) a bereaved 〔surviving〕 family; the family of the deceased. ¶ ～을 노두에 방황케 하다 leave the family without a means of livelihood / ～으로 부인과 두 아이가 있다 He is survived by his wife and two children. ◉ ～부조 aid to a surviving family: ～ 부조금 an allowance to the family of the dead; survivors' benefits. ～연금 《개인 보험의》 a survivor's annuity; 《사회 보험의》 a survivor's pension. 전사자 ～ the war bereaved (★ 복수 취급).

**유족하다**(裕足—) (be) abundant; sufficient; well-off. ¶ 유족하게 살다 be well 〔comfortably〕 off; live in affluence; live 〔be〕 in easy circumstances.

**유종**(有終) having an end; being completed 〔finished〕; perfection. ¶ ～의 미 a successful conclusion; crowning glory / ～의 미를 거두다 crown 《it》 with perfection; carry 《it》 to perfection; bring 《*a matter*》 to a successful conclusion; round off 《*one's* career》.

**유종**(乳腫) 〖의학〗 a breast tumor 〔abscess〕; mastitis.

**유죄**(有罪) guiltiness; guilt; culpability. ～하다 (be) guilty; culpable. ¶ ～를 선고하다 convict 《*a person*》 of 《a crime》; declare 〔sentence〕 《*a person*》 guilty / ～로 결정되다 be found 〔adjudged〕 guilty / ～로 결정하다 find 《the defendant》 guilty; 《배심원이》 return a verdict of guilty. ◉ ～인 a guilty person. ～판결 conviction; a guilty verdict; a judgment of guilty: ～ 판결을 하다 declare 〔sentence〕 《*a person*》 guilty.

**유주무량**(有酒無量) unbridled drinking.

**유주지물**(有主之物) objects that have an owner.

**유즙**(乳汁) milk.

**유증**(遺贈) testation; 《동산의》 bequest; bequeathal; 《부동산의》 devise. ～하다 leave 《*a thing*》 by will; bequeath 《50 million won to...》; devise 《*one's* real estate to...》. ◉ ～물 a bequeath; a legacy. ～자 the giver of a bequest; a legator; a devisor (부동산의): 피～자 a legatee; a devisee.

**유증**(類症) similar diseases 〔cases〕.

**유지**(有志) ① 《뜻이 있음》 having an interest; having sympathy 〔intention〕. ② 《사람》 an interested person; a supporter; a volunteer; a leading 〔an influential〕 figure (유력자). ¶ ～의 voluntary; interested / ～를 모으다 collect 〔raise〕 interested person / ～들의 참가를 환영합니다 Those interested are welcome to join us. / 이 병원은 ～들의 기부로 지탱되고 있다 This hospital is supported by voluntary contributions. ◉ ～일동 everyone 〔all the persons〕 concerned 〔interested〕 (in the matter). 지방～ those who work for the good of the locality; public-spirited men 〔leading figures〕 of the locality.

**유지**(油脂) oils and fats. ◉ ～공업 the oil and fat (manufacturing) industry.

**유지**(油紙) oiled paper; oil-paper.

**유지**(維持) maintenance; preservation; 《가옥·토지·자동차 따위의》 upkeep; 《후원》 support; 《생계의》 sustenance. ～하다 maintain; keep up; preserve; support; sustain; keep 《a club》 going. ¶ 건강을 ～하다 maintain *one's* health / 평화를 ～하다 maintain 〔keep〕 peace / 생명을 ～하다 maintain 〔preserve〕 life / 체면을 ～하다 keep up appearances / 지위를 ～하다 maintain *one's* position / 사회 질서를 ～하다 preserve public order / 젊음을 ～하다 keep *one's* youth / 미국과 친선 관계를 ～하다 maintain friendly relations with America / 이 협회는 어떻게 ～되는가 How is the society kept up?
◉ ～비 (the cost of) maintenance; upkeep 〔maintenance〕 expenses: 자

동차 1대의 ～비는 얼마나 드느냐 How much does it cost you to own a car? / 이 건물의 ～비가 1년에 100만원 든다 This building costs a million won a year in upkeep. ～책(策) a measure for maintenance.

**유지**(遺志) ⟪*one's* father's⟫ dying 〔last〕 wish (★ 이 표현은 「임종에서의 마지막 소원」이라는 뜻보다 넓은 의미로 쓰임); the wish 〔will, desire〕 of the deceased. ¶ 고인의 ～를 받들어 in obedience to the will of the deceased / ～를 따르다 〔실행하다〕 follow 〔carry out〕 the intention of the deceased.

**유직자**(有職者) the employed.

**유진무퇴**(有進無退) advance without retreat. ～하다 be over-advancing.

**유질**(流質) foreclosure (of the mortgage); a mortgage forfeit. ～하다 be foreclosed; forfeit a pawn.
◉ ～물 a forfeited article; an unredeemed pawn 〔pledge〕: ～물 공매처분 a foreclosure sale. ～처분 〖법〗 a foreclosure.

**유징**(油徵) oil indication; viable oil beds; signs of oil reserves. ¶ ～을 발견 못 하다 find no viable oil beds.

**유착**(癒着) ① 〖의학〗 adhesion; conglutination; healing up. ～하다 glue 〔knit〕 together; adhere ⟪to⟫; heal up; conglutinate. ¶ 늑막 ～ 〖의학〗 pleural adhesion / 수술 후 장의 ～ an intestinal adhesion after the operation. ② ⟪바람직하지 못한 맺어짐⟫ ¶ 정계와 재계의 ～ a back-scratching alliance of government and big business; a corrupt 〔cozy〕 relationship between political and business circles / 병기 제조업자와 정부 고관이 ～되어 있다고 비난받았다 The arms manufacturers and senior government officials were accused of being in each other's pockets. ◉ ～불능 ⟪골절의⟫ nonunion.

**유창하다**(流暢—) (be) fluent; flowing; smooth; facile. ¶ 유창하게 fluently; smoothly; with fluency / 유창한 문장 a flowing 〔an easy〕 style / 중국어를 유창하게 말하다 speak fluent Chinese / 그는 말이 ～ He is a fluent 〔ready〕 speaker. / 그의 영어가 유창한 데 놀랐다 I was surprised at the fluency with which he spoke English.

**유채**(油菜) 〖식물〗 a rape. ¶ ～꽃 rape flowers.

**유체**(有體) materiality. ¶ ～의 material; tangible; 〖법〗 corporeal. ◉ ～동산 corporeal movables. ～물 material things 〔objects〕; a materiality. ～자산 tangible assets 〔property〕; tangibles.

**유체**(流體) 〖물리〗 a fluid.
◉ ～공학 hydraulic engineering. ～동력학 hydrokinetics. ～압력 fluid pressure. ～역학 hydromechanics; hydrodynamics; fluid dynamics. ～정력학 hydrostatics.

**유촉**(遺囑) entrusting ⟪*a person*⟫ with everything after *one's* death; leaving last instructions 〔requests〕. ～하다 entrust with everything after *one's* death; leave a last request.

**유추**(類推) analogical inference; reasoning by analogy; (an) analogy; analogism. ～하다 analogize; infer; know by analogy. ¶ ～적 analogic(al) / …로 ～하여 on the analogy of... / 일부로 전체를 ～하다 analogize the whole out of a part. ◉ ～법 analogy. ～진단 〖의학〗 analogism. ～해석 analogical interpretation.

**유출**(流出) an outward flow; (an) outflow; spillage; (an) effluence; efflux; exodus; extrusion (용암의). ～하다 flow 〔run, drain〕 out; debouch; issue ⟪from⟫; spill. ¶ 두뇌의 ～ a brain drain / 원유의 ～ oil spillage / 금〔달러〕의 ～ an outflow of gold 〔dollars〕 / 대량의 원유가 좌초된 유조선에서 ～되었다 A large quantity of crude oil has spilled into the sea from the shipwrecked tanker. ◉ ～구 ⟪물의⟫ an outlet. ～량 the volume ⟪of water⟫ flowing from ⟪the dam⟫. ～물 effluence; an emanation. ～유(油) oil spill; spilled oil: ～유 제거 oil-spill cleanup / 해면에서 ～유를 떠내다 skim the oil spill off the sea surface.

**유충**(幼蟲) a larva (*pl.* -e). ＝애벌레. ◉ ～기 the larval stage.

**유취**(類聚) grouping in classes 〔species, *etc.*〕; collecting according to classes. ～하다 group in classes; classify.

**유취만년**(遺臭萬年) leaving an evil reputation forever 〔for all time〕.

**유층**(油層) an oil stratum; a pool of oil. ¶ ～을 찾아내다 strike oil / 동해의 해저 ～을 탐사하다 explore the bed of the East Sea for oil / 시굴에서 유망한 ～이 있을 가능성이 보였다 The appraisal drilling suggested the presence of promising reserves of oil. ◉ ～탐광(探鑛) oil exploration 〔prospecting〕.

**유치**(幼稚) infancy; babyhood; crudeness. ～하다 (be) childish; infantile; puerile; immature (미숙); primitive (원시적). ¶ ～한 생각 a childish notion

〔idea〕/ ~한 논문 an immature essay / ~한 연극 a sugary 〔slushy〕 play / 그 나라의 농업은 아직 ~하다 Agriculture in the country is still in its infancy. / 그 지방의 어업은 아주 ~하다 The methods of fishery there are in a very crude condition.

**유치**(乳齒) a milk 〔baby〕 tooth. ⇨ 젖니.

**유치**(留置) ① 〚법〛 (keeping in) custody; detention; lockup. ~하다 keep 〔hold〕 《*a person*》 in custody; detain; lock up. ¶ 경찰에 ~하다 take 《*a person*》 into custody of the police; detain 《*a person*》 at a police station / ~되다 be detained; be locked up. ② 《우편의》 being left till called for; general delivery 《미》. ~하다 leave till called for.

◉ ~권 〚법〛 《have》 a lien 《on》. ~료 a demurrage. ~우편 poste restante (F.); 《우편물 겉에 쓸 때》 "to be called for" poste restante; general delivery 《미》. ~장 a lockup; a police cell; a house of detention 〔custody〕: ~장에 갇히다 be detained in a police cell. ~전보 telegraphe restante (F.). 불법~ 〚법〛 detainer.

**유치**(誘致) attraction; a lure; invitation; enticement. ~하다 attract; lure; invite. ¶ 외국 관광객을 ~하다 attract foreign tourists 《to Korea》 / 외자를 ~하다 invite 〔induce〕 foreign capital / 공장을 ~하다 invite 《a manufacturing company》 to set up its plant 《in a place》 / 읍내에 병원을 ~하다 invite hospitals to the town.

**유치원**(幼稚園) a kindergarten; a nursery school; an infant school 《영》; a preschool 《미》. ¶ 아이를 ~에 보내다 send a child to a kindergarten. ◉ ~선생〔보모〕 a kindergarten teacher; a kindergartener.

**유칼리나무** a eucalyptus (*pl.* ~es, -ti).

**유쾌**(愉快) (a) pleasure; (an) amusement; (a) joy; (a) delight. ~하다 (be) cheerful; jolly; jovial; gay; pleasant; amusing; happy; delightful; nice; be (a lot of) fun.

¶ ~히 pleasantly; delightfully; merrily; cheerfully / ~한 이야기 an exhilarating story / ~한 대화 a pleasant conversation / ~한 사람 a jolly 〔cheerful〕 fellow / ~하게 웃다 laugh cheerfully / ~하게 하룻밤을 지새우다 《술 등을 마시며》 make a good night of it; spend a joyful night / ~하게 지내다 have a good 〔fine, nice, jolly〕 time (of it); enjoy *oneself.*

**유클리드** 《그리스의 수학자》 Euclid (B.C. 300년경). ◉ (비)~ 기하학 (non-)Euclidian geometry.

**유타** 《미국의 주》 Utah (생략 Ut.).

**유탄**(流彈) a stray bullet 〔shell〕; a random shot. ¶ ~에 맞다 be struck 〔hit〕 by a stray / ~에 맞아 죽다 be killed by a stray bullet.

**유탄**(榴彈) a howitzer shell; shrapnel.

**유탕**(遊蕩) dissipation; profligacy; riotous living. ⇨ 방탕(放蕩).

**유태**(猶太) Judea. ⇨ 유대.

**유택**(幽宅) a grave; a tomb; *one's* final resting place.

**유턴** 《차의》 a U-turn. ~하다 take 〔make, do〕 a U-turn. ¶ ~하지 마시오 《게시》 No U-turns. / 그 차는 갑자기 ~했다 The car suddenly made a U-turn.

**유토피아** (a) Utopia. ¶ ~의 Utopian.

**유통**(流通) ① 《화폐의》 circulation; currency; 《물자의》 distribution; 《어음의》 negotiation. ~하다 circulate; pass 〔go, run〕 current; 《어음 등이》 float. ¶ ~ 질서의 확립 establishment of order in the circulation 《of》 / ~시키다 circulate; publish; 《위폐 따위를》 give currency to; pass / ~하고 있다 be in circulation; 《어음이》 be afloat / 새 화폐를 ~시키다 put new coins in 〔into〕 circulation.

② 《공기의》 ventilation; circulation. ~하다 ventilate; circulate; flow. ¶ 공기 ~이 좋다〔나쁘다〕 be well 〔ill〕 ventilated / 공기 ~이 잘 되게 하다 facilitate ventilation; facilitate the circulation of air / 이 방은 공기 ~이 나쁘다 This room is poorly 〔ill〕 ventilated.

◉ ~경로(經路) a channel of distribution. ~구조 distribution structure: ~ 구조를 개선하다 improve 〔upgrade〕 the marketing structure 《for agricultural and fishery products》. ~기구(機構) the distribution network 〔system〕; distributive machinery. ~기한 the period of circulation 《of goods》; the shelf life 《of *one's* products》. ~량 《화폐의》 the amount of current money. ~산업 the distribution industry. ~성 《어음의》 negotiability. ~세 a circulation 〔transfer〕 tax. ~센터 a distribution center. ~시장 a circulation market. ~어음〔증권〕 a negotiable bill 〔bond〕. ~자본 a circulating 〔floating〕 capital. ~증권 a negotiable instrument 〔security, document〕. ~

질서 distribution order. ～혁명 a distribution revolution. ～화폐 current 〔circulating〕 money; currency in circulation.

**유틸리티 프로그램** 〖컴퓨터〗《기본 프로그램의 기능을 보강해주는》 utility program.

**유파**(流派) a school; a sect. ¶ 새로운 ～를 세우다 create 〔found〕 a new school 《of painting》.

**유폐**(幽閉) confinement; incarceration. ～하다 confine; shut 〔lock〕 up; hold 《*a person*》 incommunicado 〔in confinement〕; incarcerate. ¶ ～중이다 be in confinement; be confined 《in a house》 / ～당하다 be confined 《in *one's* own house》; be placed under confinement.

**유포**(油布) oiled cotton-cloth.

**유포**(流布) dissemination; diffusion; spread; propagation; circulation. ～하다 get abroad 〔afloat〕; take air 〔wind〕; be widespread; spread; disseminate; circulate. ¶ ～되고 있다 be in circulation; be current; be prevalent / 소문을 ～하다 set a rumor afloat / 거짓 풍설을 ～하다 circulate 〔disseminate〕 false reports.

**유품**(遺品) relics; an article left by the deceased. ¶ 칼라일에 관련된 ～ relics pertaining to Carlyle.

**유풍**(遺風) an old custom; a custom handed down from the preceding generations; usage inherited from *one's* forefathers; tradition; a remnant. ¶ 봉건 시대의 ～ customs 〔relics〕 of the feudal age / 중세(기)의 ～ survivals of medieval customs.

**유피**(鞣皮) (a) dressed skin; a tanned hide; leather; dressing skins. ◉ ～법 (the art of) tanning; tawing. ～업 tannery: ～업자 a tanner.

**유피아이** 《미국의 통신사》 UPI 〔<the *U*nited *P*ress *I*nternational〕; 《컴퓨터의 범용 단말 인터페이스》 UPI. 〔<*u*niversal *p*eripheral *i*nterface〕

**유하다**(柔―) ① 《부드럽다》 (be) soft; genial; amiable; kindly; benigh(ant). ¶ 유한 성질 a placid temper; a genial disposition / 사람이 ～ have a genial disposition. ② 《걱정이 없다》 (be) easygoing; happy-go-lucky; carefree.

**유하다**(留―) stay; lodge; stop; put up. ¶ 부산에서 하룻밤 ～ stay in Pusan overnight / 여관에 ～ put up 〔stop〕 at a hotel.

**유학**(留學) studying abroad. ～하다 study abroad; go abroad to study. ¶ 프랑스 ～중에 while studying in France / ～ 가다 go abroad for study / 국비로 ～하다 study abroad on a government scholarship / ～을 마치고 귀국하다 return from study abroad. ◉ ～생 a student studying abroad: 재미 한국 ～생 Korean students studying in the U.S. / 외국인 ～생 a foreign student.

**유학**(遊學) studying away from home. ～하다 study away from home.

**유학**(儒學) Confucianism. ◉ ～자 a Confucian(ist); a Confucian scholar.

**유한**(有限) limitedness; finiteness. ～하다 (be) limited; 〖수학〗 finite; terminable. ◉ ～급수 a finite series. ～꽃차례 〖식물〗 definite inflorescence. ～법화(法貨) limited legal tender. ～소수 a finite decimal. ～수 a finite number. ～직선 a finite straight line. ～집합 〖컴퓨터·수학〗 a finite set. ～책임 limited liability: ～ 책임 회사 a limited liability company / ～ 책임 사원 a limited partner. ～회사 a limited company.

**유한**(有閑) having leisure; being leisured. ¶ ～의 leisure. ◉ ～계급 the leisure(d) class(es); the idle rich. ～마담 a woman of leisure; a wealthy leisured lady. ～지 unused land.

**유한**(遺恨) a grudge; spite; rancor; (an) enmity. ¶ ～을 품다 bear 〔have〕 a grudge 《against *a person*》; have spite against 《*a person*》 / 오랜 ～을 풀다 pay off *one's* old scores; revenge *oneself* on 《*one's* father's murderer》.

**유합**(癒合) 〖의학〗 agglutination; conglutination; adhesion. ～하다 agglutinate; conglutinate; knit.

**유해**(有害) noxiousness; harmfulness; hurtfulness; injuriousness. ～하다 (be) noxious 〔bad, harmful〕; (be) detrimental 〔injurious〕 《to》; [서술적] do 《*a person*》 harm; have an injurious effect 《on》. ¶ ～무익하다 do more harm than good / 건강에 ～하다 be detrimental 〔injurious〕 to health; be bad for the health / 농작물에 ～하다 be harmful to the crops / 공중 도덕상 ～하다 be prejudicial 〔destructive〕 to public morals / 흡연은 건강에 ～하다 Smoking is 「bad for 〔harmful to〕 our health. / 과도한 운동은 ～하다 Too much exercise will do you harm. / 요즘은 청소년에게 ～한 TV 프로와 주간 잡지가 많다 These days there are

many TV programs and weekly magazines that are harmful to young people.
◉ ～가스 noxious gas. ～곤충 noxious insects. ～물 a hazardous article; a harmful object. ～물질 a toxic substance. ～식물 noxious plants. ～식품 poisonous food. ～폐기물 toxic waste(s).

**유해**(遺骸) the「dead body 〔mortal remains〕《of *a person*》; remains; 《유골》 ashes; bones. ¶ 한국전에서 전사한 미군의 ～를 찾아내기 위한 첫번째 작업 the first operations to recover remains of U.S. soldiers killed in the Korean War / ～를 인수하다 receive 《*a person's*》 body 〔mortal remains〕 / ～를 화장하다 cremate *a person's* remains / 그의 ～는 향리에 묻혔다 His remains 〔mortal body〕 was buried in his old home.

**유행**(流行) ① 《복장 따위의》 (a) fashion; vogue; style; a craze (대유행); a fad (일시적); 《인기》 popularity. ～하다 be in 〔come into〕 fashion 〔vogue〕; become 〔be〕 popular; be widely liked 〔favored〕.
¶ 짧은 치마의 ～ the vogue of short skirts / 일시적 ～ a passing fad / ～의 변천 change of fashion / 최신 ～의 of the latest fashion / ～이 되다 come into fashion 〔vogue〕 / 대～이다 be all the fashion; be the 〔in great〕 vogue; be very popular; be the craze / ～에 뒤지다 be behind the fashion / ～의 첨단을 걷다 lead 〔set〕 the fashion; be a trend-setter / ～을 만들어 내다 set 〔create〕 the fashion (of the hour) / ～을 좇다 follow 〔run after〕 the fashion / ～시키다 bring 《a style》 into vogue 〔fashion〕 / ～이 지나다 go 〔be〕 out of fashion 〔style〕; be outmoded / 비디오게임이 한때 아이들 사이에서 ～했다 Video games were popular among children at one time. / 이런 스타일의 드레스가 지금 ～이다 This style of dress is now in vogue 〔fashion〕. / 이것이 최신 ～의 수영복이다 This is the latest fashion in swim suits. / 한국 젊은이들 사이에는 스키가 대～이다 Skiing is all the rage with young people in Korea. / 프랑스는 ～의 본고장이다 France is the wellspring of fashion.
② 《병·폐단의》 prevalence. ～하다 be prevalent 〔prevailing, widespread〕; prevail; rage; be rampant. ¶ 성홍열의 ～ the prevalence of scarlet fever / 뇌물의 ～ the prevalence of bribery / 그해 콜레라가 전국에 ～했다 Cholera raged throughout the country that year. / 감기는 겨울에 ～된다 Colds are prevalent in winter.
◉ ～가 a popular song: ～가 가수 a pop singer; a singer of popular songs. ～병 an epidemic (disease); a pestilence; 《가축의》 an epizootic: ～병에 걸리다 be attacked with an epidemic / ～병이 돌다 an epidemic rages 〔spreads〕. ～어 a word 〔phrase〕 of the minute; a word 〔phrase〕 (that is) on everybody's lips; a vogue word; a cant. ～지(地) 《전염병의》 an infected district 〔locality〕: 콜레라의 ～지 a cholera-infected district. ～형 《형상》 a fashionable shape; 《양식》 an up-to-date style: (옷의) 최신 ～형 the latest style 〔fashion〕.

**유행성**(流行性) 〖의학〗 epidemicity. ¶ ～의 epidemic. ◉ ～간염 infectious hepatitis. ～뇌염 epidemic encephalitis. ～출혈열 epidemic hemorrhagic fever.

**유행성감기**(流行性感氣) influenza; (the) flu. ¶ ～에 걸리다 be attacked by influenza / 서울에는 지금 ～가 돌고 있다 Seoul is now in the grip of influenza.

**유향**(乳香) frankincense; olibanum.

**유혈**(流血) bloodshed. ¶ ～ 참사 a bloody 〔sanguinary〕 affair; an affair of bloodshed / ～로 끝나다 result in bloodshed / ～의 참극을 빚어내다 create a scene of bloodshed / ～ 사태로 번지다 develop into an affair of bloodshed.

**유형**(有形) materiality; concreteness. ¶ ～의 concrete; material; corporeal; tangible / ～화 하다 materialize; embody.
◉ ～ 고정 자산 tangible fixed assets. ～무역 visible trade. ～문화재 tangible cultural properties. ～물 a material being; a concrete object. ～자본 a corporeal capital. ～자산〔재산〕 tangible 〔material〕 assets; corporeal property. ～체 a material body.

**유형**(流刑) banishment; deportation; (an) exile. ¶ ～에 처(處)하다 condemn 《*a person*》 to exile; banish 〔exile〕 《to》; sentence to deportation 《to》 / 그는 먼 섬으로 ～되었다 He was exiled to a far-off island. ◉ ～수 an exile; a deportee. ～지 a penal colony; a place of exile.

**유형**(類型) a type; a pattern. ¶ ～적

typical; stereotype(d) / 그것들은 세가지 ～으로 분류된다 They can be divided into three types. ◉ ～학 〖심리〗 typology.

**유형무형**(有形無形) material(ity) and 〔or〕 immaterial(ity); visibility and 〔or〕 invisibility. ¶ ～의 material and immaterial; visible and invisible / ～으로 그 분의 도움을 받았다 I have received both material and moral support from him.

**유혹**(誘惑) (a) temptation; (an) allurement; (an) enticement; (a) seduction; a lure (악으로의). ～하다 tempt; lead 《*a person*》 into temptation; lure; entice; seduce 《a girl》; philander.
¶ 대도시의 ～ the allurements 〔temptations〕 of a large city / 바다의 ～ the lure 〔call〕 of the sea / 술의 ～ a temptation of drink / …하고 싶은 ～을 참다 resist 〔withstand〕 the temptation 《to *do*》 / ～을 이겨내다 overcome 〔get the better of 〕 temptation / ～과 싸우다 wrestle with temptation; fight 〔struggle〕 against temptation / ～에 지다 yield 〔give in〕 to temptation / ～에 빠지다 fall into temptation / ～에 빠지기 쉽다 be easily led into temptation / 돈으로 ～ 하다 allure 《*a person*》 with money / 그는 ～에 넘어가지 않는다 He is proof against temptation. / 대도시에는 젊은이들을 파멸로 이끄는 ～이 많다 There are in big cities various temptations which lead young people to ruin. ◉ ～물 a temptation; a lure; a decoy. ～자 a tempter; an enticer; a seducer.

**유화**(乳化) emulsification. ～하다 emulsify. ◉ ～유 emulsified oil. ～제(劑) an emulsifier; an emulsifying agent.

**유화**(油畫) 《그림》 an oil painting; 《화법》 oil painting. ¶ ～를 그리다 paint in oils. ◉ ～물감〔채료〕 oil colors. ～화가 an oil painter.

**유화**(宥和) appeasement. ～하다 appease; pacify. ◉ ～론자 an appeaser. ～정책 an appeasement policy.

**유화**(類化) assimilation. ～하다 assimilate; incorporate.

**유황**(硫黃) sulfur. ⇨ 황(黃) ②. ◉ ～연고 sulfur ointment. ～천(泉) a sulfur spring. ～화(華) sublimed sulfur; flowers of sulfur.

**유회**(流會) an adjournment of a meeting. ～하다 adjourn a meeting. ¶ ～되다 be adjourned; be called off / 회의는 성원 미달로 ～되었다 The meeting was「adjourned 〔called off, canceled〕 「for want 〔when it fell short〕 of a quorum.

**유효**(有效) 《법규 등의》 validity; affectiveness; 《표 따위의》 availability; 《약 등의》 efficiency; efficacy. ～하다 (be) valid; available; effective; efficacious; good; [서술적] hold 〔stand〕 good.
¶ ～하게 effectively; efficiently; effectually; validly / ～ 적절한 effective and well-directed / ～한 방법 an effective means; an effectual method / ～한 담보 a good security / ～한 계약 a valid contract / 시간〔돈〕을 ～하게 쓰다 make good use of *one's* time 〔money〕; put *one's* time 〔money〕 to a good use / ～하게 하다 confirm; validate; make valid 〔effective〕; give effect to 《a law》 / ～하게 되다 《법률이》 come into effect 〔force〕; become effective 〔operative〕; 〖법〗 enure; 《계약이》 become valid; take effect / 이 표는 발행 당일만 ～하다 This ticket is available 〔good, valid〕 on the day of issue only. / 이 계약은 1년 간 ～하다 This agreement 「holds good 〔remains in force〕 for a year. *or* This contract is valid for one year. / 그 판결은 아직도 ～하다 The decision still stands. / 인터페론은 암에 대해 ～하다고 한다 Interferon is said to be effective against cancer. / 내 운전면허는 앞으로 6개월 더 ～하다 My driver's license is good 〔valid〕 for another six months. / 이 법규는 교통 사고를 줄이는 데 ～할 것이다 These regulations will effectively cut down traffic accidents.
◉ ～거리 the effective distance 〔range〕. ～기간 the term of validity; the available period / ～ 기간의 만료(일) the expiration (date) of the validity time / ～ 기간이 지난 표 a ticket whose validity has expired; an expired ticket. ～사거리 the effective range of a gun. ～수요 〖경제〗 (an) effective demand. ～숫자 〖수학〗 a significant figure. ～열량 available heat. ～전류 an effective current. ～전압 effective voltage. ～증명 a certificate of validity; a testimonial. ～타 〖권투〗 a telling blow. ～투표 a valid ballot.

**유훈**(遺訓) *one's* last 〔dying〕 injunctions 〔instructions〕; the teachings 〔precepts〕 of the departed. ¶ 조상의 ～을 받들다 follow the teachings left by *one's* ancestors.

**유휴**(遊休) idleness; unemployment. ¶

～의 idle; unused; unemployed. ◉ ～공장 a nonoperating plant. ～물자 idle goods 〔commodities〕. ～생산력 idle production capacity. ～설비〔시설〕 idle facilities 〔equipment〕; spare plant capacity: ～설비를 활용하다 make use of the equipment that has so far remained unused. ～자금 idle 〔uninvested〕 money; floating money; idle funds. ～자본 idle 〔unemployed〕 capital. ～자산 idle properties. ～자재 idle materials; materials lying idle. ～지(地) idle land: ～지제 the idle land system.

**유흥**(遊興) merrymaking; amusement; pastime; pleasure seeking. ～하다 make merry; have fun; amuse 〔enjoy〕 *oneself.* ¶ ～에 빠지다 pursue 〔indulge in, give *oneself* up to〕 pleasure / 그는 ～에 돈을 아끼지 않았다 He didn't mind spending money to have fun. ◉ ～가(街) an entertainment 〔amusement〕 center; gay quarters. ～비 entertainment costs; the expenses of pleasures; amusement expenses. ～세 the entertainment 〔amusement〕 tax: ～세의 세율을 인상하다 raise the rate of the amusement tax. ～업소 a merrymaking 〔an entertainment〕 place; an amusement 〔entertainment〕 spot: 사치성 ～업소 a luxurious 〔an extravagant〕 entertainment establishment. ～음식세 the tax on amusements, food, and drink. ～장〔지〕 an amusement quarter.

**유희**(遊戱) 《오락》 amusements; a pastime; merrymaking; 《놀이》 a game; play; sports. ～하다 make merry; play; play (at) a game. ¶ ～를 즐기다 enjoy a game; amuse *oneself* at a game / 그것은 언어의 ～에 지나지 않는다 That's only playing with words. ◉ ～본능 play 〔sportive〕 instinct. ～실 a recreation hall; a playroom (어린이의). ～장 a playground; a place of amusement.

**육**(六) six. ¶ 제6, the sixth / 육연발총 a six-shooter / 6분의 1, one sixth.

**육**(肉) flesh; meat; beef (쇠고기); the flesh (육체). ¶ 영과 육 flesh and spirit; body and soul.

**육가**(六價) 〖화학〗 ¶ ～의 sexivalent. ◉ ～원소 a hexad.

**육각**(六角) ①〖악기〗 the Six Musical Instruments. ②《육모》 six angles; a sexangle; a hexagon. ¶ ～의 hexagonal; sexangular. ◉ ～형 a hexagon; a sexangle.

**육감**(六感) a sixth sense; (an) intuition; a hunch; extrasensory perception. ¶ ～으로 on the sixth sense; by a hunch / ～으로 알다 know 《*a thing*》 by intuition 〔the sixth sense〕 / ～이 맞았다 My hunch proved right 《구어》. / 나는 내가 미행당하고 있다는 것을 ～으로 알았다 My six sense told me that I was being followed.

**육감**(肉感) 《느낌》 the senses of the flesh; 《성적》 sexual feeling; sensual pleasure; carnal desire; voluptuousness. ¶ ～적인 suggestive; sensual; voluptuous / ～적인 미인 a voluptuous beauty / ～을 도발하다 excite 〔arouse〕 carnal desire 〔lust〕; be suggestive / 그 그림에는 ～을 자극하는 것이 있다 There is something suggestive about that painting. ◉ ～주의 sensualism.

**육갑**(六甲) the sexagenary cycle.

**육개장**(肉—) hot shredded beef soup (and rice).

**육계**(肉桂) 〖한약〗 cinnamon; cassia bark.

**육괴**(肉塊) a chunk 〔mass, lump〕 of flesh 〔meat〕.

**육교**(陸橋) an overhead bridge; 《고가도로·철도 등의》 《미》 an overpass; 《영》 a flyover; a footbridge (인도교); 〖지리〗 a land bridge. ¶ ～ 밑의 길 an underpass of a bridge / ～를 통해서 선로를 건너시기 바랍니다 《게시》 Passengers are requested to cross the line by the bridge.

**육군**(陸軍) 《군대》 the army; the land forces; the military service; 《군인》 a military man. ¶ ～의 army; military / ～에 입대하다 join 〔enter, enlist in〕 the army / ～에서 제대하다 leave the army. ◉ ～군악대 a military band. ～대장 a general; an army general. ～대학 the Military Staff College; the War College. ～무관 《대사관의》 a military *attaché* (F.). ～병원 a military 〔an army〕 hospital. ～비행대 an army flying corps. ～사관학교 the (Korea) Military Academy: ～ 사관 학교 생도 a military cadet / ～ 사관 학교 졸업식 the commencement ceremony for the (Korea) Military Academy. ～성 《미국의》 the Department of the Army; 《영국의》 the War Office. ～장관 《미국의》 the Secretary of the Army. ～장교 an army 〔a military〕 officer. ～참모 차장 the Vice Chief of Staff of the Army; the Vice Army Chief of Staff. ～참모총장 the Army Chief of Staff.

**육담**(肉談) vulgar talk; an 「improper 〔indecorous〕 story; a 「licentious 〔lewd〕 story.
**육대주**(六大洲) the Six Continents.
**육도**(陸稻) rice 〔a rice plant〕 grown in a dry field; the upland rice plant.
**육두문자**(肉頭文字) abusive 〔foul〕 language; the f-word.
**육로**(陸路) a land 〔an overland〕 route. ¶ ~로 by land; overland; by an overland route / ~로 가다 go by land; travel overland / ~로 부산을 향하다 leave for Pusan 「overland 〔by land〕. ◉ ~수송 overland transportation; transport by land. ~여행 a land 〔an overland〕 journey.
**육류**(肉類) meat; flesh; flesh meat. ¶ 1인당 ~ 소비량 per capita consumption of meat / ~를 피하다 abstain from flesh meat.
**육면체**(六面體) 〖수학〗 a hexahedron (*pl.* ~s, -hedra). ¶ ~의 hexahedral / 정~ a regular hexahedron; a cube.
**육모**(六—) a hexagon; a sexangle. ⇨ 육각. ¶ ~가 나다 be hexagonal.
◉ ~방망이 a 6-sided 「club 〔cudgel〕.
**육미**(六味) the Six Flavors (*i.e.* bitter, sour, sweet, pungent, salty and flat).
**육미**(肉味) flesh food; meat dishes.
◉ ~붙이 meat; meat dishes.
**육박**(肉薄) closing in upon; being close at hand. ~하다 close in upon 《the enemy》; press 《the enemy》 hard; come to close quarters 《with》; 《경쟁에서》 tread close on 《*a person's*》 heels; run 《a competitor》 hard 〔close〕. ¶ 적진에 ~하다 carry the fighting to the enemy's camp. ◉ ~전 《전투》 a hand-to-hand 「combat 〔fight〕; close 〔tight〕 battle; 《경기》 a close 「contest 〔game〕; a hard-fought game.
**육발이**(六—) a person with six toes on a foot.
**육배**(六倍) six times; sextuple. ~하다 sextuple; multiply by six.
**육법**(六法) the six codes of law.
◉ ~전서 a Compendium of Laws; the statute books.
**육봉**(肉峰) a hump.
**육부**(六腑) the six entrails (*i.e.* large intestine, small intestine, stomach, gall bladder, bladder and three foci). ⇨ 오장육부.
**육분의**(六分儀) a sextant. ◉ ~자리 〖천문〗 the Sextant; Sextans.
**육붕**(陸棚) a continental shelf. = 대륙붕.
**육붙이**(肉—) ⇨ 육미붙이.
**육사**(陸士) ⇨ 육군 사관 학교. ¶ ~ 17기 《한국의》 the Korea Military Academy in the 17th 「class 〔term〕.
**육삼삼제**(六三三制) 〖교육〗 the 6-3-3 「schooling 〔educational〕 system.
**육상**(陸上) 《on》 (the) land; 《on》 (the) ground; 《해상에 대하여》 (the) shore; ashore. ¶ ~에서〔으로〕 on land; on shore; ashore / ~으로 가다〔수송하다〕 go 〔transport〕 by land. ◉ ~경기 field and track events; athletic sports: ~ 경기 대회 an athletic meet; a field-and-track meet; a track and field competition / ~경기장 an athletics 「stadium 〔field〕. ~근무 《선박에 대하여》 shore 「duty 〔service〕; service ashore; 《항공에 대하여》 ground duty 〔service〕. ~부대 a land 「force 〔troop〕. ~생활 life on 「land 〔shore〕; land life. ~운송 overland 〔ground〕 transport; transport 〔carriage〕 by land: ~ 운송비 overland freight. 대한〔국제〕 ~ 경기 연맹 the 「Korean 〔International〕 Ama-teur Athletic Federation.
**육서**(陸棲) being terrestrial; living on land. ¶ ~의 〖동물〗 terrestrial; terraneous; living on land. ◉ ~동물 a land animal. ~생물 land life.
**육성**(肉聲) a live voice; a 「natural 〔human〕 voice; a lifelike tone. ¶ ~과 같은 음색을 내다 produce the correct sounds of the human voice / 마이크음과 ~은 다르다 Voices through a microphone differ from natural voices.
**육성**(育成) upbringing; rearing. ~하다 《기르다》 rear; nurture; bring up; 《조성하다》 foster; promote. ¶ 영재(英才)의 ~ the bringing up of gifted children / 그는 많은 신종 식물을 ~했다 He cultivated a large number of new species of plants. / 이런 기획들은 지방자치체에 의해 ~된다 These projects are promoted by the local authorities. ◉ ~재배 rearing and cultivating. ~회비 《학교의》 school supporting fees.
**육손이**(六—) a person with six fingers 「on a hand.
**육송**(陸送) land transportation; overland transport.
**육수**(肉水) beef-soup stock; thin meat 「juice 〔soup〕.
**육순**(六旬) sexagenarianism. ◉ ~노인 「a sexagenarian.
**육시처참**(戮屍處斬) posthumous decapitation. ~하다 behead 《the dead》 posthumously.
**육식**(肉食) 《사람의》 a meat diet; meat-eating; 《동물의》 flesh-eating; 《육미》

animal food; meat food; 《요리》 a meat dish. ～하다 eat meat; 《동물이》 eat flesh; live on flesh. ¶ ～의 carnivorous / ～을 끊다 abstain from eating meat / 나는 ～보다 채식을 좋아한다 I prefer a vegetable diet to animal food. / 사자는 ～ 동물이다 The lion is a beast of prey.
◉ ～가 a meat-eater. ～수〔류〕 a「carnivorous〔flesh-eating〕 animal; a carnivore. ～조 a predatory bird; a bird of prey. ～충 a predacious insect.

**육식처대**(肉食妻帶) 『불교』 a Buddhist priest eating meat and taking a wife. ～하다 《중이》 eat meat and take a wife.

**육신**(肉身) the flesh; the body; flesh and blood. ¶ 그의 ～은 흙으로 돌아갔다 His「body〔flesh〕 returned to dust.

**육십**(六十) sixty; threescore. ¶ 제 60, the sixtieth / 60분의 1, a sixtieth (part) / 60대의 사람 a sexagenarian; a person in his sixties.

**육십갑자**(六十甲子) ⇨ 육갑(六甲).

**육아**(肉芽) 『의학』 granulation; granulation tissue. ¶ ～가 생기다 granulate. ◉ ～종(腫) granuloma.

**육아**(育兒) childcare; upbringing〔nursing〕 of infants; child rearing. ～하다「bring up〔nurse〕 infants; rear children. ¶ 그녀는 ～에 전념했다 She devoted herself to the care of her child. ◉ ～법 the art of rearing infants; a method of child-rearing. ～비 childcare expenses. ～서 a book on childcare. ～수당 a nursery allowance. ～시간 nursing time. ～시설 childcare facilities. ～식(食) infant〔baby〕 food. ～실 a nursery (room). ～원 a baby farm; a nursery school 《미》; 《일반의》 a nursery home; 《기아의》 a foundling hospital; 《고아의》 an orphanage. ～휴가 a maternity leave.

**육안**(肉眼) the「naked〔unaided〕 eye. ¶ ～으로 보이는〔보이지 않는〕 곳에 within〔beyond〕 eyeshot / ～으로 볼 수 있는 별 stars visible to ordinary sight / ～으로 보다 see with the naked eye / ～에 보이다〔안 보이다〕 be「visible〔invisible〕 to the naked eye. ◉ ～검사 examination with the naked eye; macrography.

**육영**(育英) education. ～하다 educate. ◉ ～사업 educational work: ～사업에 평생을 바치다 devote *one's* life to education. ～자금 scholarship; the educational fund. ～회 an education association; a scholarship society.

**육욕**(肉慾) the appetites of the flesh; carnal〔sexual〕 desire〔lust〕; animal passions; sensual appetite. ¶ ～을 채우다 gratify〔satisfy〕 *one's* carnal「appetites〔lusts〕 / ～에 빠지다「indulge in〔be given to〕 sensual pleasures / ～을 억제하다 restrain〔control〕 *one's* passions. ◉ ～주의 sensualism; carnalism.

**육우**(肉牛) beef cattle.

**육운**(陸運) transportation by land; overland transportation. ◉ ～국(局) the Land Transportation Bureau. ～회사 a land transportation company.

**육이오**(六二五) 《한국전쟁》 the June 25th war of Korea; the Korean War (1950-53). ¶ ～의 충격을 겪지 못한 젊은 세대 the younger generation which did not go through the trauma of the 1950-53 Korean War.

**육자배기**(六字―) a brisk and lively folk tune (with six words to the line).

**육장**(六場) 《장날》 the market days being held six times in a month; [부사적] all the time.

**육적**(肉炙) beef shish kebab.

**육전**(陸戰) a land battle; ground combat; land warfare. ～하다 fight on land.

**육젓**(六―) salt-pickled shrimps caught in June.

**육종**(肉腫) 『의학』 a sarcoma (*pl.* ～s, -mata).

**육종**(育種) breeding 《of animals〔plants〕》.

**육중주**(六重奏) 『음악』 a sextet(te). ◉ ～단 a sextet(te).

**육중창**(六重唱) 『음악』 a sextet(te).

**육중하다**(肉重―) 《부피가》 (be) bulky and heavy; weighty; ponderous; massive (건물이); 《몸집이》 heavily-built; stout. ¶ 육중한 건물 a「massive〔ponderous〕 building / 육중한 걸음걸이로 with a heavy「step〔tread〕 / 몸이 ～ have a firm plump body.

**육즙**(肉汁) meat juice; beef soup; gravy; beef「broth〔bouillon〕.

**육지**(陸地) (the) land; 《바다에서 본》 (the) shore. ¶ ～에서 멀리 떨어져서 far away from land; far off the coast 《of》 / ～가 보이다 sight land; come in sight of land / ～를 밟다 set foot on land / ～로 둘러싸이다 be landlocked / 배는 ～를 떠났다 The boat left the shore. / 그들은 2개월 만에 ～에 올랐다 They went ashore for the first time in two months.

**육질**(肉質) fleshiness; fleshy substance; 《고기의 질》 the「quality〔grade〕 of meat; 《과육》 pulpy substance; pulp.

**육척**(六尺) six feet. ¶ ～의 사나이 a six-footer; a 6-foot man.

**육체**(肉滯) 〖의학〗 a dyspeptic ailment attributed to the eating of meat.

**육체**(肉體) the flesh; the body. ¶ ～의〔적〕 bodily; fleshly; physical; 《육욕의》 sensual; carnal / ～와 정신 body and spirit 〔soul〕; mind and body / ～적 쾌락 pleasure of the flesh; sensual pleasures / ～적 고통 physical suffering; bodily pain / ～적 결함 a physical defect / ～적 욕망 animal passions / ～적 요구 *one's* animal needs / ～를 바치다 give *oneself* up to 《*a person's*》 embrace / ～를 알다 have carnal knowledge of 《women》.

◉ ～관계 sexual relations; (sexual) intercourse: 그녀와 ～ 관계가 있다 have intercourse with her. ～노동 physical 〔muscular〕 labor; manual labor: ～노동자 a manual laborer / ～ 노동을 하다 do physical 〔manual〕 labor. ～문학 sensual literature. ～미 physical beauty; the beauty of the body. ～미인 a woman of great physical beauty; a curvaceous woman 〔beauty〕. ～파 a glamor (girl).

**육촌**(六寸) ① 《재종》 a 〔*one's*〕 second cousin. ② 《치수》 six inches.

**육축**(六畜) the six domestic animals (*i.e.* ox, horse, pig, goat, fowl, dog).

**육층**(六層) the sixth floor 〔story〕.

**육친**(六親) the six family relations (*i.e.* father, mother, older and younger siblings, wife, and children).

**육친**(肉親) a blood relative; *one's* flesh and blood; *one's* immediate relative. ¶ ～보다 더한 친절 a kindness exceeding even that of *one's* own family / ～에게 버림받다 be given up by *one's* own flesh and blood.

**육탄**(肉彈) a human bomb. ◉ ～공격 a suicide attack. ～전 a hand-to-hand battle 〔fight〕.

**육태질**(陸駄—) unloading a ship; landing; discharge; transport by land. ～하다 land 《cargo》; unload; discharge; transport overland.

**육포**(肉脯) jerked beef; a jerky.

**육풍**(陸風) a land breeze.

**육필**(肉筆) *one's* own handwriting; an autograph. ¶ ～의 autograph(ic); handwritten 《letter》.

**육해공**(陸海空) land, sea and air. ¶ ～군 the army, navy and air forces; the armed forces; the (fighting) services / ～군 장병 officers and men of the armed forces / ～군 합동 작전 a joint operations of the army, navy and air forces / ～의 입체 공격 coordinated attack of the army, navy and air forces.

**육해군**(陸海軍) the army and navy; the land and sea forces. ¶ ～의 확장 expansion of armaments on land and sea. ◉ ～인 soldiers and sailors.

**육혈포**(六穴砲) a six-chambered revolver; a six-shooter; a pistol.

**육회**(肉膾) a dish of minced raw beef.

**윤**(閏) ¶ ～의 intercalary.

**윤**(潤) luster; polish; gloss; shine; sheen. ¶ 윤을 내다 give a polish 《to》; put a polish 〔gloss〕 《on》; polish up; 《금속에》 burnish.

**윤간**(輪姦) gang 〔multiple〕 rape. ～하다 gang-rape; rape 〔violate〕 《a woman》 in turn 〔in succession〕.

**윤곽**(輪廓) ① 《겉모양》 contours 《of a human body》; outlines 《of a mountain》; skyline 《of a city》; 《역광시의》 a silhouette. ¶ 얼굴의 ～ the contour of *one's* face / 인체의 ～을 그리다 sketch 〔draw〕 the contour of the human body / 그녀의 얼굴은 ～이 뚜렷하다 She has 「very regular 〔well-chiseled, clear-cut〕 features. / 하늘이 어두워지자 집의 ～만이 보였다 I saw only the outline of the house against the darkening sky.

② 《대강》 an outline; a profile 《of the future of the town》; a general view 〔idea〕 《of》. ¶ 사건의 ～을 말하다 give an outline of the affair / ～을 파악하다 grasp a general idea 《of》; get a picture 《of》 / 마침내 그녀가 말하고 있는 내용의 ～을 알았다 I finally got a general idea of what she was talking about.

**윤기**(潤氣) luster; gloss; polish; sheen; shine. ¶ ～ 도는 머리 glossy 〔sleek〕 hair / ～가 없다 be lusterless 〔dry, dull, dim, dingy〕; have no gloss; 《얼굴에》 look sallow; be sallow-complexioned / 그의 얼굴에는 ～가 돈다 He has good color (on his face). / 흑단은 닦으면 ～가 난다 Ebony takes a polish when it is rubbed.

**윤나다**(潤—) be glossy 〔lustrous, bright, sheeny, shiny, polish〕; 《얼굴이》 be sleek 〔slick〕.

**윤납**(輪納) payment by rotation. ～하다 pay by turns.

**윤내다**(潤—) gloss; glaze; bring out the luster; brighten; put a polish

〔gloss〕 on; polish; make 《it》 glossy.
**윤년**(閏年) (a) leap year; an intercalary 〔a bissextile〕 year. ¶ ～은 4년마다 든다 Leap year comes around every four years. 「calary month.
**윤달**(閏—) a leap month; an inter-
**윤독**(輪讀) reading by rotation. ～하다 read by turns; take turns in reading.
**윤똑똑이** a smart alec 〔aleck〕; a shrewd one; a knowing chap 〔fellow〕.
**윤락**(淪落) ～하다 fall; ruin *oneself;* be ruined; be corrupted; go to ruin. ¶ 그녀는 방탕한 짓으로 인해 ～했다 She 「ruined herself 〔went to the dogs〕 by dissipation. ◉ ～가 a red-light district; the gay quarters. ～여성 a fallen 〔ruined〕 woman; a delinquent girl; a woman of the underworld. ～행위 방지법 the Anti-prostitution Law.
**윤리**(倫理) moral principles; ethics; morals. ¶～적 ethical; moral / ～적으로 ethically / ～적 행위 a moral act / 실천 ～ practical ethics / 의사의 ～ medical ethics / 그녀의 행동은 ～적 판단이 결여되어 있다 Her behavior lacks ethical judgment. / 수회 사건이 일어날 때마다 정치나 기업의 ～가 문제로 대두된다 Whenever a bribery scandal occurs, political and business ethics are called into question.
◉ ～학 ethics; moral philosophy 〔science〕: ～학자 an ethicist; a moral philosopher. 한국 신문 ～ 위원회 the Korea Press Ethics Committee.
**윤무**(輪舞) dancing in a circle; a round 〔circle〕 dance. ¶ ～를 추다 dance in a circle 〔ring〕.
**윤번**(輪番) turn; rotation. ～하다 take turns 《at…》 in rotation; rotate. ¶～으로 by turns; in turn; by rotation; on a rotation basis. ◉ ～제 a rotation system: 의장을 ～제로 하다 take the chair in rotation.
**윤삭**(閏朔) an intercalary month.
**윤색**(潤色) 《윤》 lustrous color; 《꾸밈》 (an) embellishment; ornamentation; coloring. ～하다 embellish 〔give color to〕 《*one's* story》; adorn; dress 《the facts》 up. ¶～한 문장 an ornate style of writing.
**윤생**(輪生) 〘식물〙 verticillation. ◉ ～엽 verticillate leaves. ～화 a cyclic flower.
**윤시하다**(輪示—) show around.
**윤음**(綸音) the king's words; a royal message. 「day.
**윤일**(閏日) an intercalary day; a leap
**윤작**(輪作) rotation of crops; crop rotation. ～하다 rotate crops 《in the fields》. ¶ 보리와 벼를 ～하는 농민이 있다 Some farmers rotate barley with rice. ◉ ～법 the crop rotation system.
**윤전**(輪轉) revolving; rotation. ～하다 turn round; rotate; revolve. ◉ ～기(機) a rotary press 〔printing machine〕: ～기를 돌리다 run a rotary press.
**윤창**(輪唱) 〘음악〙 a troll; a round. ～하다 troll; sing 《a song》 in a circular canon. ◉ ～곡 a troll.
**윤초**(閏秒) a leap second.
**윤택**(潤澤) ① 《광택》 gloss; luster; sheen; brilliance. ⇨ 윤기(潤氣). ② 《넉넉함》 abundance; plenty. ～하다 (be) abundant; ample; plentiful; copious; 《살림이》 (be) rich; wealthy; well-off. ¶ ～하게 abundantly; plentifully; in abundance; plenteously; 《살림이》 prosperously; richly / ～한 자원 abundant resources / ～해지다 become prosperous / 살림이 ～하다 be well-off; be 〔live〕 in comfortable circumstances / 자금이 ～하다 We have ample funds.
**윤허**(允許) royal 「permission 〔sanction, approval, grant〕. ～하다 grant (royal) sanction; be pleased to give sanction 《to》.
**윤형**(輪形) a wheel 〔round〕 shape; a ring; a circle. ¶ ～의 circular; round.
**윤화**(輪禍) a traffic accident. ¶ ～를 입다 have 〔meet with〕 a traffic accident / ～로 죽다 be killed in a traffic accident / 아이들을 ～로부터 지키다 protect children from traffic accidents.
**윤활**(潤滑) lubrication. ～하다 (be) smooth; lubricious; lubricatory.
◉ ～유 lubricating oil; lubricant: ～유 역할을 하다 [비유적] help (to) smooth 《the progress of negotiations》; reduce the friction 《between》.
**윤회**(輪廻) 《차례로 돌아감》 rotation; 〘불교〙 *Samsāra* (Sans.); the cycle of reincarnation; the transmigration (of the soul); metempsychosis. ～하다 rotate; transmigrate. ◉ ～설 transmigrationism.
**율**(律) ① 《기율》 a law; a rule; a statute; 《형률》 a criminal code; 《계율》 (Buddhist) commandments. ② 《음률》 a rhythm; 《시의》 a style of classical Chinese verse.
**율**(率) 《비율》 a rate; a ratio; a proportion; 《백분율》 a percentage; 〘물리〙 an index; 〘수학〙 a constant. ¶ 연율(年率) the annual rate / 평균율 the average rate / …의 율로 at the rate

of…; on a percentage of…; by a factor of… / 율을 높이다〔낮추다〕 raise 〔lower〕 the rate / 율을 정하다 fix the rate; designate the percentage / 율을 줄이다 decrease the rate.

**율격**(律格) 《규칙》 a rule; a statute; 《한시(漢詩)의》 rules of versification.

**율동**(律動) ① 《리듬》 (a) rhythm. ② 《주기적 운동》 (a) rhythmic movement. ¶ ∼적인 rhythmic(al) / 생의 ∼ the rhythm of life. ◉ ∼감(각) a rhythmic sense; a sense of rhythm. ∼미 rhythmical beauty. ∼체조 rhythm calisthenics.

**율령**(律令) a law; a statute; an ordinance.

**율모기** 〖동물〗 a ring(ed) 〔grass〕 snake.

**율무** 〖식물〗 adlay; adlai. ◉ ∼쌀 unshelled (grains of) adlay.

**율문**(律文) 《법조문》 articles of a criminal code; provisions; 〖문법〗 literature written in *yul* verse.

**율법**(律法) 《법률》 (a) law; a rule; 《계율》 commandments.

**율시**(律詩) a style of Chinese verse.

**융**(絨) cotton flannel.

**융기**(隆起) a protrusion; a bulge; 〖지질〗 a rise; an uplift; (an) elevation; upheaval. ∼하다 thrust itself up; upheave; bulge; rise; protrude. ◉ ∼산호초 an elevated coral reef. ∼해안 an uplifted coast.

**융단**(絨緞) a carpet; a rug (소형의). ¶ 페르시아〔터키〕 ∼ a Persian 〔Turkish〕 carpet 〔rug〕 / ∼을 깔다 spread 〔lay〕 a carpet; carpet 《a floor》 / 두꺼운 ∼을 깐 마루 a thick-carpeted floor. ◉ ∼청소기 a carpet sweeper. ∼폭격 carpet bombing.

**융모**(絨毛) wool; 〖해부〗 a villus (*pl.* -li).

**융비술**(隆鼻術) 〖의학〗 rhinoplasty; 《수술》 《make》 a rhinoplastic operation. ¶ ∼의 rhinoplastic.

**융성**(隆盛) prosperity. ∼하다 (be) prosperous; flourishing; thriving. ¶ 국운의 ∼ national prosperity / 한창 ∼하고 있다 be at the zenith of *one's* prosperity / ∼해지다 grow in prosperity; become prosperous; prosper; flourish / 그 당시 국운이 크게 ∼했다 The nation was in full flourish at that time.

**융숭하다**(隆崇―) highly respect 〔regard〕; think highly of; pay high 〔deep〕 esteem to. ¶ 융숭히 heartily; cordially; kindly; liberally / 융숭한 대접 warm 〔cordial, hospitable〕 treatment / 융숭한 대접을 받다 be received cordially; be treated hospitably; have a cordial 〔warm〕 reception.

**융자**(融資) 《대부》 financing; accommodation 〔advance〕 of funds; 《대출금》 a loan. ∼하다 finance 〔advance funds for〕 《an enterprise》; furnish 《a company》 with funds; accommodate 《*a person*》 with a loan. ¶ 구제 ∼ a relief loan / 조건부 ∼ conditional financing; a tied loan / 은행에 ∼를 요청하다 ask a bank for a loan / 그는 은행에서 1천만 원의 ∼를 받았다 He borrowed ten million won from the bank. *or* He got a loan of ten million won from the bank. / Y은행은 그 기업에 1억 원을 ∼했다 Y Bank provided one hundred million won to the enterprise. ◉ ∼금 a loan. ∼신청 a request for a loan. ∼알선 loan facilitation. ∼회사 a finance company.

**융점**(融點) 《녹는점》 the melting point; the fusing 〔fusion〕 point.

**융통**(融通) ① 《융자》 finance; accommodation; loan; 《유통》 circulation; negotiation (증권·어음 등의). ∼하다 accommodate; provide 〔advance〕 money; finance 《the project》; lend. ¶ 돈을 ∼해 주다 accommodate 《*a person*》 with a loan; finance; do financing / 그녀에게 100만 원을 ∼해 주다 lend her one million won / 은행에서 돈을 ∼하다 get financed through a bank. ② ＝융통성(融通性). ◉ ∼력 *one's* financing ability. ∼어음 an accommodation bill 〔draft, note〕. ∼자본 a circulating capital. ∼증권 a negotiable instrument.

**융통성**(融通性) adaptability; elasticity; flexibility; versatility. ¶ ∼이 있다 be adaptable 〔flexible, accommodating〕; be elastic (규칙 따위가) / ∼이 없다 be unadaptable 〔inflexible〕; be lacking in adaptability 〔flexibility〕; be strait-laced / ∼있게 굴다 adapt *oneself* to circumstances / 그는 ∼이 있는 사람이다 He is an adaptable 〔a flexible〕 person. / 그는 ∼이 없는 사람이다 He lacks flexibility.

**융합**(融合) ① 《녹아 합침》 fusion; merger. ∼하다 fuse; merge. ¶ 핵∼ nuclear fusion / 구리와 아연을 ∼하여 놋쇠를 만든다 make brass by fusing copper and zinc / 수소 원자가 ∼하면 막대한 에너지가 방출된다 Atoms of hydrogen fuse to give off an enormous amount of energy. ② 《인종 등의》 amalgamation; 《협조》 harmony. ∼하다 amalgamate; unite; harmonize; be in harmony 《with》. ¶ 헬레니즘은 그리스와 동양의 문화가 ～된 것이었다 Hellenism was a complex of Greek and Oriental cultures. ◉ ～유전 blended inheritance.

**융해**(融解) fusion; melting; dissolution; liquidation. ～하다 fuse; melt; dissolve; liquefy. ¶ 그 금속은 비교적 낮은 온도에서 ～했다 The metals fused at a relatively low temperature. ◉ ～열 (the) heat of fusion. ～온도[점] the melting temperature [point].

**융화**(融化) 〖화학〗 deliquescence. ～하다 deliquesce; soften.

**융화**(融和) reconciliation; harmony. ～하다 reconcile; harmonize [get along] 《with》; be reconciled 《with》; make peace 《with *a person*》. ¶ 양국간의 ～를 도모하다 attempt to establish the harmonious relationship between the two countries / 지역 사회와의 ～가 중요하다 It is important to get along with the (local) community.

**융흥**(隆興) (vigorous) prosperity; rise. ～하다 rise; prosper (vigorously); flourish.

**윷** ① 《놀이》 *yut;* the "Four-Stick Game". ② 《끗수》 the 4 points made by throwing the *yut* sticks so that all four faces come up. ③ ＝ 윷짝.

**윷놀이** playing *yut;* a game of *yut.* ～하다 play (a game of) *yut.*

**윷밭** a quarter of the *yut* board.

**윷짝** the sticks used in playing *yut.* ¶ ～ 가르듯 《distinguish》 sharply; clearly / ～ 가르듯 흑백을 가리다 discriminate clearly between good and bad [right and wrong]; separate clearly the sheep from the goats; know which end is up.

**윷판** 《윷노는 자리》 a scene of *yut* playing; 《말판》 a *yut* board.

**으깨다** ① 《부스러뜨리다》 crush (up); smash; squash; mash 《potatoes》. ¶ 호박을 으깨서 파이를 만들었다 We mashed pumpkins and made a pumpkin pie. ② 《억센 것을 부드럽게 하다》 rub into pulp; soften up; beat; knead.

**-으나** ① 《…하지만》 (be [do]…) but; though (it is [does]). ¶ 확실히는 모르나 …라고 한다 I don't know for sure, but I heard that… / 돈은 많으나 불행하다 Though he is rich, he is unhappy. / 가고 싶으나 시간이 없다 I'd like to come, but I haven't got the time. / 그는 열의는 있으나 재주가 없다 He has enthusiasm but no talent. / 애는 많이 썼으나 보람이 없었다 I tried very hard, but all in vain. / 그 곳에 가기는 갔었으나, 누님한테 들르지는 않았다 I was there to be sure, but I didn't stop by my sister's.
② 《어쨌든》 (whether…) or; or the like; or what not. ¶ 있으나 없으나 whether there is [was] or not / 크나 작으나 가리지 않고 regardless of whether it is big or small / 좋으나 싫으나 해야 한다 You must do it whether you like it or not.
③ 《퍽 …한》 that is very [quite]…; that is really [ever so]…. ¶ 넓으나 넓은 바다 a sea that is ever so wide / 높으나 높은 산 such a [a really] high mountain; ever so high a mountain / 깊으나 깊은 물 water ever so deep.

**-으나마** be… but anyway; however. ¶ 집은 작으나마 자리가 좋다 The house may be small, but it's nicely located.

**-으니** ① 《…하니까》 since (it is [does]); so; when (in the past) then; as. ¶ 너무 작으니 바꾸자 It's too small so let's exchange it. / 할 일이 없으니 산책이나 할까요 Since we have nothing to do, shall we take a walk? / 시간이 늦었으니 택시를 타고 갑시다 As it is late, let's go in a taxi.
② 《설명의 계속》 and also. ¶ 벼슬에 올랐으니 그때 그의 나이 스물이었다 He was appointed to a government post at the age of twenty.

**-으니까** 《…하므로》 since [as] it is [does]; so; and so; 《…한즉》 when (in the past) then; as; and [but] then. ¶ 한 서너 달 더 남았으니까 천천히 일해도 된다 As there are about three more months, we can take our time on the job. / 그 소식을 들으니까 마음이 놓인다 Now that I hear the news, I feel better. / 나이를 물으니까 그녀는 아직 30 아래라고 했다 When I asked her age, she said that she was still under 30. / 자세히 보니까 그것은 가짜 진주였다 When I looked it over closely, I found that it was an imitation pearl.

**으드득** with a crunch. ¶ 뼈를 ～ 깨물다 crunch on a bone / 이를 ～ 갈다 grind *one's* teeth.

**으드득거리다** ① 《…이》 crunch; be crunchy. ② 《…을》 grit; grate; grind 《*one's* teeth》. ¶ 이를 ～ grind *one's* teeth.

**으드득으드득** ①《깨무는 꼴》 crunching; with crunching sounds. ②《갈리는 꼴》 gritting; grating; grinding *one's* teeth.

**으드등거리다** bicker; spat; fuss; snarl; growl; feud 〔be at feud〕《with》; be at loggerheads《with》; be at outs 〔odds〕《with *one's* wife》. ¶ 서로 으드등거리며 지내다《부부 등이》 lead a cat-and-dog life / 그 둘은 앙숙처럼 늘 으드등거린다 Those two fight like cats and dogs.

**으드등으드등** bickering; fussing; at odds with each other.

**으뜸** ①《첫째》 the first; 《최고》 the top; the head; the best. ¶ 반에서 ~ 가는 아이 the top boy in a class / ~ 가다 be at the head《of》; occupy the first place; rank 〔stand〕 first; be (the) tops《구어》/ ~으로 졸업하다 graduate at the head of *one's* class / 반에서 영어는 그가 ~이다 He leads his class in English. / 돈 모으는 데에는 장사가 ~이다 The best (way) to make money is to go into business.
②《기본》 the basis; the foundation; the root; the core. ¶ 국어 교육은 모든 교육의 ~이 된다 The study of our national language forms the core of education as a whole.
◉ ~음 〖음악〗 a keynote; a tonic.

**-으라**《소원》¶ 한국에 통일이 있으라 Let there be unification in Korea! / 신의 은총이 있으라 May God bless you!

**-으라고**《명령》 telling 〔ordering〕 *someone* to *do*. ¶ 씻으라고 일러라 Tell him to get a wash.

**-으라는**《…하라는》¶ 그 물은 과일 잡수신 후에 손을 씻으라는 것입니다 The water is to wash your hands after you've eaten the fruit.

**-으락**《반복 상태·성질·동작·단속적》¶ …으락말락 be on the point 〔verge〕 of *do*ing; almost *do;* hesitate whether to *do* (or not) / 그의 얼굴이 붉으락푸르락 한다 His face gets red and blue《with anger》.

**-으러**《목적》《move》 for the purpose of; in order to. ⇨ -하러.

**으레** ①《관례·습관적으로》 customarily; habitually; usually; 《당연히》 (as a matter) of course; to be sure; naturally; no doubt; without question. ¶ 설날 아침에는 ~ 차례를 지내는 법이다 It is customary for Koreans to observe their ancestor-memorial rites on New Year's Morning. / 그것은 ~ 우리가 할 일이다 Needless to say it is our duty to do so. / ~ 이렇게 되는 법이다 This is quite in the nature of things.
②《어김없이》 usually; always; without fail; every time. ¶ 나는 조반 전에 ~ 산책한다 I make it a rule to take a walk before breakfast. / 그는 바깥에 나갈 때면 ~ 개를 데리고 간다 Whenever he goes out, he takes his dog with him. / 그들은 만나면 ~ 싸운다 They never meet without quarreling. *or* They quarrel whenever they meet.

**-으려고**《하고자 하여》 with the thought in mind《to *do*》; with the intention of《*do*ing》; with a view to《*do*ing》; with the desire《to *do*》; ready 〔prepared, willing〕《to *do*》. ~ 하다 intend《to *do*》; plan《to *do*》; want《to *do*》; be going《to *do*》; will《*do*》; be ready 〔prepared, willing〕《to *do*》; have《*a thing*》 in mind《to *do*》; be out《to *do*》; try《to *do*》; set out 〔about〕《to *do*》. ¶ 한 석달 더 있으려고 한다 I intend 〔am prepared〕 to stay another 3 months. ~ 들다 get 〔be〕 on the verge of《*do*ing》; be about《to *do*》; threaten《to *do*》; aim at《*do*ing》; try《to *do*》. ¶ 어린애가 가성소다를 사탕으로 알고 먹으려고 했다 The baby was about to eat the caustic soda, thinking it was candy.

**-으려도** ⇨ -려도. ¶ 죽으려도 죽을 수 없다 I cannot die in spite of myself.

**-으려면**《…으려 하면》¶ 냉면을 먹으려면 모두 그리 간다 Everybody goes there (who wants) to eat *naengmyŏn.*

**-으련만** ¶ 아버지가 빨리 오시면 좋으련만 I wish father would hurry back (but...).

**-으렴** ⇨ -려무나.

**으로** ①《수단》 by; by means of; through; with; in. ⇨ 로. ¶ 기차편~ by train / 배편~ by ship 〔sea〕(★ 교통기관 등을 나타낼 때에는 the를 안 붙임) / 망원경~ 보다 look through a telescope / 왼손~ 쓰다 write with the left hand / 돈~ 사다 buy《*a thing*》 with money / 붓~ 벌어 먹다 live by *one's* pen; depend upon the pen for bread / 서면~ 알리다 let《*a person*》 know by letter / 유화 물감~ 그리다 paint in oils / 청동~ 만들다 work in bronze.
②《원료》 from; of; out of. (★ from은 화학적 변화가 일어났을 때, of는 물리적인 변화가 일어났을 때 씀). ¶ 대리석~ 지은 집 a house made of marble / 헌 궤짝~ 테이블을 만들다 make a table out of an old box / 맥주는 대맥~ 만든다 Beer

is made from barley. / 와인은 무엇~ 만드느냐 What is wine made from?
③ 《원인·결과·이유》 for; as; with; from; through; because of; due to; as a consequence of; (in accordance) with. ¶ 그 까닭~ for that reason / 이것~ 말미암아 「as a consequence of 〔due to〕 this / 상용(商用)~ on business / 폭풍~ in a storm / 병~ 누워 있다 lie in bed with illness / 폐병~ 죽다 die of 〔from, with〕 consumption 〔T.B.〕 / 주로 자네의 도움~ 성공했네 I succeeded chiefly through your help. / 풍년~ 쌀값이 떨어졌다 With 〔Because of, As a result of〕 the good harvest (year), the price of rice has fallen.
④ 《지위·신분·자격》 ⇨ 으로서. ¶ 종~ 태어나다 be born a slave / 총각~ 살다 live as a bachelor / 양심 있는 선생~ 그런 말을 할 수 있나 As a teacher with a conscience, how can you say such a thing? / 여섯 살까지 소인(小人)~ 친다 Up to 6 you are counted 〔considered as〕 a child.
⑤ 《변화》 into; to; 《교환》 for. ¶ 산이 바다로 변하고 바다가 산~ 변하더라도 though mountains turn to seas, and seas to mountains / 헌 것을 새 것~ 바꾸다 change an old one for a new one / 번화하던 도시가 그만 쑥밭~ 변했다 The once-flourishing city had been reduced to a mere field of sage-brush.
⑥ 《방향》 to; toward(s); into (안으로); 《heading》 for. ¶ 이쪽~ this way / 부산~ 가는 기차 the train for Pusan / 연못 속~ 빠지다 fall into a pond / 방 안~ 들어오다 come into the room / 미국~ 떠나다 leave for America / 동쪽~ 가다 go toward(s) the east; go eastward / 왼편~ 가세요 Go to the left. / 산~ 가자 Let's go to the mountains. (★ to는 come, go, return 따위의 동사에 붙어 도착지를 나타내고, for는 leave, start 따위의 동사에 붙어 도달하기 위해 향하는 목적지를 나타냄. toward(s)는 단지 방향을 나타낼 뿐 "도달하기 위한"의 뜻은 없음).
⑦ 《액수》 for; in; at. ¶ 1,000원권~ in one thousand-won notes / 하루 8천 원~ 살다 live on eight thousand won a day / 2만원~ 사다〔팔다〕 buy 〔sell〕 《*a thing*》 for 20,000 won / 1킬로그램 천 원~ 사다 buy 《*a thing*》 at one thousand won a kilogram.
⑧ 《근거·기준》 by; from. ¶ 안색~ 미루어 judging from *a person's* look / 일급〔시간급〕~ 일하다 work by the day 〔hour〕 / 24를 3~ 나누다 divide 24 by 3 / 겉모양~ 판단하다 judge 《*a person*》 by appearances / 사람은 상종하는 벗~ 그 인품을 알 수 있다 A man can be judged by the company he keeps.
⑨ 《구성·성립》 of. ¶ …으로 되다 be composed of…; consist of…; be made of…; form / 의회는 상하 양원~ 되어 있다 The Parliament consists of the two Houses, upper and lower.
⑩ 《내용》 of; with. ¶ 설탕~ 가득 차다 be full of sugar.
⑪ 《정도》 as; in; with. ¶ 보통~ as a usual thing; usually; commonly.
⑫ 《시간 경과》 gradually more by (a unit of time). ¶ 아침 저녁~ 서늘해졌다 We have cooler mornings and evenings now.
⑬ 《목적의 선택》 ¶ 빵은 어떤 것~ 드릴까요 What shall I bring you in the way of bread? / 「우리 프랑스 빵~ 하세」—「그것을 주세요」 "Let's make it French bread."—"Bring us that." / 무엇~ 감사를 표해야 할는지요 What shall we give as a token of our appreciation?

**으로나** as 〔with, *etc.*〕 or the like; whether as 〔with, *etc.*〕. ¶ 양~ 질로나 해방된 우리 나라의 기백은 오로지 시단(詩壇)에서만 찾아볼 수 있다 Whether it be in quantity or quality, the spirit and will of liberated Korea can be seen only in the field of poetry.

**으로는** as for (its being) as 〔with, *etc.*〕. ¶ 양반~ 태어나지 않았지만 though he was not born of a noble family / 일본인~ 키가 퍽 크다 He's awfully tall for a Japanese. / 돈~ 내 결심을 바꾸지 못한다 Money cannot induce me to abandon my resolve. / 이것~ 안 된다 We can't do it with this. *or* This won't do.

**으로도** as 〔with, *etc.*〕 …also 〔either, even〕. ¶ 그이는 시인~ 이름이 있다 He is noted as a poet also. / 그는 선생~ 신문 기자로도 실패했다 He was a failure both as a teacher and as a news reporter. / 그 장관(壯觀)은 말로도 붓~ 형용할 수 없다 The grandeur of the scenery is beyond description by speech or pen.

**으로서** as; for; in the capacity of; 《…의 표시로》 in token of; as a token of (★ as 다음에 오는 명사에 관사가 붙지 않을 때에는 상태 그 자체를 가리키며 「…자격으로」의 뜻. 관사 a가 붙으면 「…자격을 갖는 개인」

의 뜻이 됨). ⇨로서. ¶ 사람~ 못할 짓이다 It is something that one can't do as a human being. / 그는 정치가로서보다도 시인~ 더 잘 알려져 있다 He is better known as a poet than as a statesman.

**으로써** ⇨로써. ¶ 그의 세력~ with all his influence.

**으르다** ① 《위협하다》 scare; threaten; menace; frighten; intimidate. ¶ 을러도 달래도 neither by threats nor by entreaties / 한편 을러대고 한편 달래고 하여 what with threats and coaxings / 죽이겠다고 ~ threaten with death / 을러대어 복종시키다 frighten 《*a person*》 into submission. ② 《으깨다》 mash 《wet rice》.

**으르렁** growling; snarling.

**으르렁거리다** ① 《짐승이》 growl; snarl. ¶ 개가 아무에게나 ~ a dog snarls at *a person*. ② 《사람끼리》 quarrel 〔dispute, wrangle〕 with; bicker with each other; 《불화》 feud with; be at outs with 《*one's* wife》.

**으름** 『식물』 an akebi fruit. ◉ ~덩굴 an akebi (shrub).

**으름장** a threat; intimidation; a menace. ¶ ~(을) 놓다 threaten; intimidate; browbeat; menace.

**-으리까** will it *do* 〔be〕? ¶ 누가 읽으리까 Who will read it?

**-으리니** as 〔since〕 it will happen. ¶ 내가 시를 읊으리니 너는 노래를 불러라 As I will be reciting a poem, you sing a song.

**-으리라** ¶ 그는 조만간 죽으리라 He will die sooner or later.

**으리으리하다** (be) awe-inspiring; magnificent; majestic; stately; grand; impressive. ¶ 으리으리한 저택 a stately 〔an imposing〕 mansion / 으리으리한 성당 a magnificent cathedral / 으리으리하게 살다 live like a lord.

**-으며** ① 《동시에》 do 〔be〕 and; while; as. ¶ 웃으며 말하다 say with a laugh / 그는 라디오를 들으며 편지를 쓰고 있다 Half listening to the radio, he is writing a letter. ② =-으면서.

**-으면** 《가설적 조건》 if; when; whenever. ¶ 시간이 있으면 if 〔when〕 you have time / 좀 더 있으면 after a little while / 그렇지 않으면 otherwise; (or) else / …으면 안 된다〔못 쓴다〕 it won't do to *do;* one must 〔ought, should〕 not *do* / …하지 않으면 안 된다 ought to 〔should〕 *do* / …했〔었〕으면 한다 I wish that; I hope that / …으면 좋겠다 (1) I hope it will; I wish it would; it would be nice if it did; it will be nice if it does. (2) it would be better to *do* / 집에 있지 않으면 안 된다 We ought to stay at home. / 가을이 가지 않으면 좋겠다 It would be nice if autumn would not leave. / 한국말을 잘했으면 좋겠다 I hope I speak Korean well. *or* I wish I spoke Korean well. / 자동차를 가졌으면 좋겠는데 I wish I had a car. / 날이 좋았으면 한다 I hope the weather's nice. / 그를 만났으면 좋겠는데 I wish I could see him. / 너무 많이 걸으면 피곤해진다 If you walk too much, you get tired.

**-으면서** 《동작·상태를 겸함》 while; at the same time. ¶ 음악을 들으면서 고향을 생각하다 think of home while listening to the music / 아침 밥을 먹으면서 신문을 읽다 read the newspaper over the breakfast table.

**-으면서도** while… yet; although… also; at the very same time that. ¶ 돈은 없으면서도 잘 쓴다 While 〔Though〕 you haven't (got) any money, you spend a lot.

**-으므로** as; so; so… that; since; because; because of 《illness》; owing to; due to; for; considering. ¶ 돈이 없으므로 since I have no money / 해가 짧으므로 일을 많이 할 수가 없다 Because the day is short I can't do much work. / 키가 작으므로 그를 꼬마라고 불렀다 We called him shorty because he is small.

**-으소서** please *do;* I beg you to *do.* ¶ 저의 간청을 들으소서 Pray listen to my plea.

**으스대다** 《우쭐거리다》 be proud 〔haughty〕; 《구어》 be stuck up; 《거드름 피우다》 stand on *one's* dignity; give *oneself* 〔put on〕 airs; 《호언하다》 talk big; brag; 《자랑하다》 pride *oneself* 《on》. ¶ 으스대는 arrogant; haughty; overbearing / 으스대며 걷다 swagger; strut 《about, along》.

**으스름달밤** a hazy 〔misty〕 moonlit night.

**으스름하다** 《moonlight》 (be) hazy; misty.

**으스스** shivering with cold; with *one's* blood running cold; with (cold) chills running up and down *one's* spine horrified. ¶ ~춥다 have a chill / 그를 보기만해도 ~ 몸서리가 쳐진다 The mere sight of the man gives me cold shivers.

**으슥하다** (be) secluded; retired; lonely; dim; dusky; deep. ¶ 으슥한 숲 속에서 in the gloom 〔depths〕 of a forest / 으

슥한 곳 a lonely place / 으슥한 방구석 a dim corner of a room.

**으슬-** ⇨ 오슬-.

**으슴푸레하다** (be) hazy; dim; misty. ¶ 달빛이 ~ the moon shines dimly.

**으쓱**[1] 《추위·무서움으로》 with a shudder of horror 〔chill〕. ~하다 (be) horrible; blood-curdling; hair-raising; chilling.

**으쓱**[2] 《어깨를》 with shoulders raised in pride. ~하다 《*one's* shoulders》 be raised; lift *one's* head up; be elated; be proud. ¶ 어깨가 ~하다 perk *oneself* up; be elated; be exultant; be proud / 그는 장관이 되어서 어깨가 ~했다 He was highly elated at becoming a member of the Cabinet.

**으쓱거리다** swagger; perk *oneself* up; give *oneself* airs.

**으악** 《놀래주는 소리》 Boo!; 《외마디 소리》 with a sudden shriek 〔outcry〕; 《울컥》 Puke!; with a puke. ¶ ~ 소리를 지르다 shriek; scream. 「smash.

**으크러뜨리다** crush; crumble; squash;

**으크러지다** get crushed 〔squashed〕.

**윽박다** bully; browbeat.

**윽박지르다** put 《*a person*》 to silence; talk 《*a person*》 down; shout 《*a person*》 down; browbeat 〔bully〕 *a person* 《into》. ¶ 그는 그녀를 윽박질러 제안을 받아 들이게 했다 He browbeat her into accepting the proposal.

**은**(銀) 〖광물〗 silver. ¶ 순은 pure 〔refined〕 silver; sterling / 은도금 silver plating; silver gilt / 은가루 silver dust; powdered silver / 은(제)의 silver / ~같은 silvery / 은을 입힌 silver-plated〔=gilt〕/ 은도금하다 plate 〔gild〕 with silver; silver / 구리 그릇에 은을 입히다 silver copperware. ◉ ~구슬〔방울〕 a silver bead 〔bell〕. ~그릇 silverware. ~중독 silver poisoning; argyria.

**-은** ① [형용사 어간에] …that 〔which〕 is; …who is. ¶ 작은 나무 a tree that is little; a little tree. ② [동사 어간에] …that 〔who〕 has done; …that 〔which〕 *one* has done; …that (*one*) did; …that (*one*) did to 〔from, with, for〕. ¶ 그 사람이 받은 편지 the letter that the man received; the letter that was received by the man / 그 사람이 밥을 먹은 집 the house that he ate his meal at.

**은거**(隱居) retirement 《from active life》. ~하다 live 〔dwell〕 in retirement; go into retirement.

**은고**(恩顧) a special favor; patronage. ¶ ~를 입다 receive favors 《from》.

**은공**(恩功) favor; merits.

**은광**(銀鑛) 〖광물〗 《광산》 a silver mine; 《광석》 silver ore.

**은괴**(銀塊) a silver ingot; silver bullion; 《막대 모양의》 bar silver.

**은근**(慇懃) ① 《정중》 politeness; courtesy; civility; 《간절》 earnestness; sincerity. ~하다 (be) polite; kind; attentive; courteous; civil. ¶ ~히 politely; courteously; with much courtesy. ② 《드러내지 않음》 (***a***) 《가만히 …함》 quietness; inwardness; secrecy; 《함축적임》 implicitness; indirectness. ~하다 (be) quiet; inward; implicit; indirect; secret. ¶ ~한 미소 a quiet smile / ~한 협박 a veiled threat / ~히 secretly; privately; inwardly; in *one's* heart / ~히 곯리다 cheat 《*a person*》 on the sly / ~히 걱정하다 feel anxious inwardly on 〔about〕 《*a person*》 / ~히 기뻐하다 laugh in *one's* sleeve 《at other's failure》 / ~히 비추다 hint 《at *something*》; drop a hint; suggest / …하기를 ~히 바라다 have a secret desire to 《*do*》; have a sneaky urge to 《*do*》. (***b***) 《남녀의 정·관계》 ¶ ~한 사이다 be on intimate terms 《with》; be intimate with 《a woman》; be thick 《with》.

**은근짜** 《매춘부》 an unlicensed prostitute; a streetwalker; 《의뭉스런 사람》 a sly 〔crafty, cunning, foxy〕 person.

**은기**(銀器) silverware; silver.

**은니**(銀泥) silver dust mixed in glue; silver paint.

**은닉**(隱匿) concealment; secretion. ~하다 conceal; hide; 《구어》 stash *something* (away); secrete; shelter; harbor 《a criminal》. ¶ 범죄자에게 ~처를 제공하다 provide shelters to criminals. ◉ ~물자〔재산〕 goods 〔assets〕 hidden 〔stashed〕 (away) 《in a secret place》. 장물 ~죄 secretion of stolen goods. 중범 ~죄 misprision of felony.

**은덕**(恩德) a beneficial influence 〔virtue〕; favor and indebtedness.

**은덕**(隱德) good done by stealth; a secret act of virtue 〔charity〕; a hidden virtue. ¶ ~을 베풀다 do good by stealth.

**은둔**(隱遁) retirement from the world; seclusion; sequestration; withdrawal from ordinary life. ~하다 retire from the world; sequester 〔seclude〕 *oneself* 「from the world 〔from society〕; renounce the world. ◉ ~생활 a life in seclusion; a retired 〔sequestered〕 life. ~자 a recluse; a hermit. ~처 a place of seclusion; a hermitage; a retreat.

**은막**(銀幕) the silver screen; 《영사막》 a screen; 《영화》 the films; the movies; the moviedom (은막계). ¶ ~의 여왕 the queen 〔heroine〕 of the silver screen; a movie 〔film〕 star.

**은메달**(銀—) a silver medal.

**은밀**(隱密) being secret 〔covert〕. ~하다 (be) secret; covert. ¶ ~히 confidentially; privately; in secret / ~히 조사하다 make confidential inquiries / ~히 처리하다 dispose of 《a matter》 「secretly 〔without its becoming public〕.

**은박**(銀箔) 《a piece of》 silver leaf (얇은 것); silver foil (두꺼운 것). ◉ ~지 silver paper; tin foil.

**은반**(銀盤) 《은쟁반》 a silver plate; 《달》 the moon; 《얼음판》 a skating rink; an ice rink. ¶ ~의 여왕 the queen on the ice.

**은발**(銀髮) silver(y) hair; silver(-white) hair (백발이 성성한); gray hair (반백의). ¶ ~의 silver-haired.

**은방**(銀房) a silver shop; a silversmith's; a jewelry (shop).

**은방울꽃**(銀—) 〖식물〗 a lily of the valley.

**은배**(銀杯) a silver cup.

**은백**(銀白) silver-white; silver-gray.

**은분**(銀粉) powdered silver; silver dust.

**은붙이**(銀—) [총칭] silverware.

**은빛**(銀—) silver color; silver; silveriness. ¶ ~의 silver(-colored); silvery; argentine.

**은사**(恩師) *one's* respected 〔beloved〕 teacher; *one's* (former) teacher.

**은사**(隱士) a hermit scholar (who refuses office); an anchorite; a recluse.

**은산**(銀山) a silver mine.

**은산덕해**(恩山德海) immeasurable favors 〔kindness〕.

**은세계**(銀世界) a silver world; the (whole) landscape covered with snow; a vast snowy scene. ¶ 아침에 일어나 보니 온통 ~였다 I awoke to find the whole place 「covered with 〔mantled in〕 snow.

**은세공**(銀細工) silverwork. ~하다 work silver. ◉ ~품 silverware.

**은수**(恩讐) love and hate. = 은원.

**은수저**(銀—) silver spoon and chopsticks; silver.

**은시계**(銀時計) a silver watch.

**은신**(隱身) rendering *oneself* invisible; hiding *oneself*. ~하다 hide *oneself*; 《가려서》 take cover. ◉ ~처 a hiding=place; a refuge; a hideaway; 《범죄자의》 a hideout 《구어》; a den.

**은실**(銀—) silver thread 〔strand〕.

**은애**(恩愛) favor and love; kindness and affection.

**은어**(銀魚) 〖어류〗 a "silver fish"; a 「sweetfish.

**은어**(隱語) secret language; (a) jargon 《of the trade》; 《thieves'》 cant; (a) 《criminals'》 argot. ¶ ~로 말하다 talk in secret language.

**은연중**(隱然中) in secret; without 《*a person's*》 knowledge; behind the scenes. ¶ 친구를 ~에 돕다 help a friend 「on the quiet 〔on the "Q.T."〕 / ~ 한 파벌을 이루다 form a party 「behind the scenes 〔in the back room〕.

**은연하다**(隱然—) (be) latent; hidden; secret; undercover; behind-the-scenes; backroom. ¶ 은연한 세력 a latent power; hidden 〔covert〕 influence.

**은옥색**(銀玉色) light green color.

**은우**(恩遇) beneficial 〔gracious〕 treatment. ~하다 treat 「beneficially 〔with kindness〕.

**은원**(恩怨) indebtedness and grudge; favor 〔benefaction〕 and spite.

**은유**(隱喩) a metaphor. ¶ ~적(으로) metaphorical(ly).

**은은하다**(殷殷—) (be) sonorous; booming; roaring; reverberating. ¶ 은은히 with roaring sounds; rumbling / 은은한 포성 the boom(ing) of guns / 은은히 울리다 boom; roar; reverberate.

**은은하다**(隱隱—) ① 《아련하다》 (be) dim; vague; indistinct (to the eyes). ¶ 은은하게 보이다 be seen dimly; be made out faintly (in the distance). ② 《소리가》 (be) dim; faint; distant (to the ears). ¶ 은은한 포성 the distant booming of cannons / 종 소리가 은은하게 들려 왔다 There came to my ears the distant peals of a bell. *or* The muffled sound of a distant bell came to my ears.

**은의**(恩義) indebtedness and obligation; favor and obligation. ¶ ~를 베풀다 put 《*a person*》 under an obligation.

**은익**(銀翼) 《은빛 날개》 silver wing; 《비행기》 an airplane.

**은인**(恩人) a benefactor 〔benefactress (여자)〕; a patron 〔patroness (여자)〕; a person to whom *one* is beholden; a person who has done *one* a great favor. ¶ 한국 음악계의 큰 ~ a great benefactor of music in Korea / 그는

내 ~이다 I owe him a debt of gratitude. / 그는 네 생명의 ~이다 You owe him your life.

**은인**(隱忍) bearing 〔suffering〕 in patience; patient endurance. ~하다 endure patiently 〔silently〕; bear up; put up with. ¶ ~자중하여 with patience and prudence / 그는 ~자중하며 기회가 무르익기를 기다렸다 He waited patiently for the opportunity to mature.

**은자**(隱者) ⇨ 은사(隱士).

**은잔**(銀盞) a silver cup 〔goblet〕.

**은장**(銀匠) a silversmith; a jeweler.

**은장도**(銀粧刀) an ornamental silver knife.

**은저울**(銀—) a precious-metal scale.

**은전**(恩典) special grace 〔favor〕; an act of grace; a special privilege. ¶ 특별 ~으로 by special grace / ~을 입다 receive 〔be granted〕 special favors.

**은전**(銀錢) a silver coin.

**은정**(恩情) benevolent 〔gracious〕 affection.

**은제**(銀製) 《은으로 된》 made of silver; 《제품》 silverware.

**은종이**(銀—) silver paper; tinfoil.

**은줄**[1](銀—) 《줄》 a silver cord.

**은줄**[2](銀—) 〖광물〗 a vein of silver.

**은총**(恩寵) favor; grace. ¶ 하느님의 ~ the grace of God / ~을 입다 be in 《*a person's*》 good graces / ~을 받다 gain grace; win 《*a person's*》 favor / ~을 잃다 fall into disfavor; lose favor 《with》 / 하느님의 ~을 빌다 pray for God's grace.

**은침**(銀鍼) a silver needle (used for acupuncture).

**은테안경**(銀—眼鏡) silver-rimmed spectacles.

**은퇴**(隱退) retirement from a post; withdrawal from public 〔active〕 life. ~하다 retire from *one's* post; withdraw from public 〔active〕 life; 《권투 선수가》 retire from ring; 《연예인 등이》 retire from the stage; 《영화 배우가》 retire from the screen; 《야구 선수가》 hang up the 〔*one's*〕 spikes 《미구어》. ¶ ~한 정치가 a retired politician / ~하여 시골에 가다 retire into the country / 정계에서 ~하다 retire from active politics / 그는 자진 ~한지 3년만에 정치 복귀를 선언했다 He declared his return to politics after three years of self-imposed retirement.
◉ ~경기 a farewell 《boxing》 match. ~생활 a retired life: 안락한 ~ 생활 an easy life in retirement / ~ 생활을 하다 live in retirement. ~연주회 a farewell concert.

**은파**(銀波) whitecaps; silvery moonlit waves.

**은폐**(隱蔽) concealment; hiding; covering up; coverture; suppression. ~하다 conceal; hide; cover up; suppress. ¶ 사실을 ~하다 cover up 〔suppress〕 a fact; slur a fact over / 죄상을 ~하다 cover up (the traces of) a crime.

**은하**(銀河) 〖천문〗 the Milky Way; the Galaxy. ◉ ~계 the galactic system: ~계 밖 성운(星雲) an external galaxy. ~면 the galactic plane. ~성단(星團) the galactic cluster. ~수 = 은하(銀河). ~ 좌표 the galactic coordinates.

**은행**(銀行) a bank. ¶ ~에 예금하다 deposit 〔put, place〕 money in a bank / ~에 백만 원을 예금하다 place a million won on deposit at a bank / ~에서 돈을 찾다 draw 〔withdraw〕 money from the bank / ~과 거래를 트다〔끊다〕 open an 〔close *one's*〕 account with a bank / ~에서 대부받다 make a loan at a bank; get 〔secure〕 a loan from a bank / ~과 거래하다 have 〔keep〕 an account with a bank / D ~에 30만원 예금이 있다 I have 〔keep〕 300,000 won in the D Bank. / H 은행에 그의 명의로 된 예금이 50만원 있다 There is ₩ 500,000 standing on deposit in his name at the H Bank.
◉ ~가 a banker. ~강도 《사람》 a bank robber; 《행위》 bank robbery: ~강도를 하다 rob a bank. ~계 banking circles. ~계정 a bank account; a checking 〔banking 《영》〕 account. ~공동관리단 the joint bank management body. ~권 a bank bill 〔note 《영》〕. ~금리 bank interest rates: ~금리 인하 bank interest cuts / ~ 금리의 상향 재조정 the upward realignment of bank interest rates. ~대리 an assistant manager 《of Kwanghwamun branch of the C Bank》. ~대출 bank credit. ~법 the Banking Law. ~부기 bank bookkeeping. ~비밀계좌 secret bank accounts. ~신용장 a bank credit. ~어음 a bank draft (생략 B/D); a bank note 《미》; a bank bill 《영》; bank paper [총칭]. ~업 banking; the banking business. ~업무 banking services. ~ 영업시간 banking hours. ~예금 a bank deposit. ~원 a bank clerk; the staff of a bank [총칭]. ~융자〔대출〕 a bank loan. ~이자 bank interest 〔rate〕. ~자동화 bank automation. ~잔고 bank balance. ~장〔총재〕 the president of a bank. ~

주 a bank stock. ～ 지급준비금 bank reserves. ～창구 bank windows: ～ 창구를 통한 사채 대출의 불법 거래를 막기 위한 조처 measures to prevent illegal transactions of curb loans through bank windows. ～통장 a bankbook; a passbook. ～할인 bank discount. ～환 a bank money order; a bank bill; exchange; a banker's draft.
국립～ a national bank. 국제결제～ the Bank for International Settlement (생략 B.I.S.). 국제 부흥 개발～ International Bank for Reconstruction and Development (생략 IBRD). 국책～ a national 〔state〕 policy bank. 기업～ Industrial Bank of Korea. 발권～ a bank of issue. 보통～ an ordinary commercial bank. 세계～ the World Bank. ⇨국제 부흥 개발 은행. 수출입～ an export-import bank. 시중～ a city bank; Seoul-based commercial banks. 안구～ an eye bank. 예금～ a deposit money bank. 외환～ a foreign exchange bank. 저축～ a savings bank. 중앙～ the central bank. 지방～ a local 〔provincial〕 bank. 학교～ a school bank. 한국산업～ the Korea Development Bank (생략 KDB). 한국수출입～ the Export-Import Bank of Korea. 한국외환～ the Korea Exchange Bank. 한국～ the Bank of Korea (생략 BOK). 한국주택～ the Korea Housing and Commercial Bank. 혈액～ a blood bank. 전국～협회 the Bankers' Association of Korea.

**은행**(銀杏) a gingko 〔ginkgo〕 nut. ◉ ～나무 a gingko (tree).

**은행거래**(銀行去來) bank account; banking account 〔transactions〕《영》. ¶ ～가 있다 be in 〔have an〕 account with a bank / ～를 트다〔끊다〕 open an 〔close *one's*〕 account with a bank.

**은혜**(恩惠) 《고마움》 a favor; a benefit; 《친절》 kindness; goodness; 《신세》 (moral) indebtedness; obligations; 《하느님의》 divine favor; grace; (a) blessing (⇨은총).
¶ 부모의 ～ *one's* debt to *one's* parents; parental love / 스승의 ～ the kind instructions 〔the goodness〕 of *one's* teacher; obligations *one* owes to *one's* teacher / ～를 알다 be grateful 〔appreciative〕 / ～를 모르다〔잊다〕 be thankless 〔ungrateful〕 / ～를 갚다 repay *one's* obligations; return a kindness 〔favor〕 / ～를 베풀다 do 《*a person*》 a favor; bestow favors 《on *a person*》 / ～를 입다 receive benefits; enjoy benevolent influence; be placed under an obligation / ～를 입고 있다 owe 《*a person*》 a debt of gratitude; be indebted to 《*a person*》; be under (an) obligation to 《*a person*》 / ～를 원수로 갚다 return evil for good; bite the hand that feeds *one* / 나는 그에게 많은 ～를 입고 있다 I am very much under (an) obligation 〔indebted〕 to him. / 당신의 ～는 결코 잊지 않겠습니다 I shall never forget what you have done for me. / 이 ～를 어찌 갚아야 할지 모르겠습니다 I don't see how I can ever repay your kindness. / 자식을 가져봐야 어버이의 ～를 안다 Without child, without true filial gratitude.

**은혼식**(銀婚式) a silver wedding. ¶ ～을 거행하다 celebrate silver wedding.

**은화**(銀貨) a silver coin. ◉ ～본위제 the silver standard.

**은화식물**(隱花植物) = 민꽃식물.

**은회색**(銀灰色) silver gray.

**을**(乙) ① 《십간의》 the second of the 10 Heaven's Stems. ② ⇨을방(乙方), 을시(乙時). ③ 《두번째》 the second; 《후자》 the latter. ④ 《성적》 the second; "B"; 《등급》 second grade.

**을** [조사] ① [타동사의 목적] ¶ 신문을 보다 read 〔look at〕 the newspaper / 사람을 찾다 visit 〔find, look for〕 a person / 말을 타다 mount 〔ride〕 a horse / 틈을 타다 seize 〔take advantage of〕 an opportunity / 돈을 빼앗다 rob 《*a person*》 of *his* money / 컵에 물을 채우다 fill a glass with water / 이 말을 그에게 전하시오 Give this message to him. / 그것을 보고 싶다 I'd like to see that.
② [수동태의 목적] ¶ 가슴을 채이다 get kicked in the chest / 약점을 잡히다 have *one's* weakness seized 〔played〕 upon / 목을 잘리다 get *one's* throat cut; "get fired" / 물건을 빼앗기다 be robbed of a thing.
③ 《목표·방향》 ⇨를.
④ 《움직임의 위치》 ¶ 하늘을 날다 fly (in) the sky / 강을 건너가다 cross a river / 산을 넘다 go over 〔cross〕 a mountain.
⑤ 《동안》 ¶ 사흘 동안을 기다리다 wait for three days / 두 시간을 자다 sleep (for) two hours.
⑥ 《목적》 ¶ 여행을 떠나다 set out on a trip / 영화 구경을 가다 go to see a movie.
⑦ 《차례》 ⇨를. ¶ 수석을 하다 go first;

rank first.
⑧ [동족 목적어] ¶ 잠을 자다 sleep (a sleep) / 춤을 추다 dance (a dance) / 숨을 쉬다 breathe (a breath) / 꿈을 꾸다 dream (a dream).
⑨ [구어적] ¶ 앞장을 서다 stand 〔lead〕 in the van; be in the lead / 마음을 먹다 have a mind 《to》.
⑩ 《관계》 ¶ 그것을 구실로 with 〔using〕 that for an excuse / 결혼을 조건으로 under the promise of marriage / 서울을 중심으로 with Seoul as the center.

**을러메다** threaten; menace; frighten; scare. ¶ 죽인다고 ~ threaten 《*a person*》 with death / 100 만원을 내지 않으면 그 일을 폭로하겠다고 ~ threaten to expose the affair unless given one million won.

**-을망정** ⇨ -ㄹ망정.

**을묘**(乙卯) 〖민속〗 the 52nd binary term of the sexagenary cycle.

**을미**(乙未) 〖민속〗 the 32nd binary term of the sexagenary cycle.

**을방**(乙方) 〖민속〗 east by southeast.

**을사**(乙巳) 〖민속〗 the 42nd binary term of the sexagenary cycle.

**을시**(乙時) 〖민속〗 the 8th of the 24 hour periods (＝6:30—7:30 a.m.).

**을씨년스럽다** ① 《보기에》 look miserable 〔shabby, wretched〕; 《날씨 따위가》 gloomy; dreary; dismal. ¶ 옷이 너절해서 ~ look wretched with shabby clothes / 을씨년스러운 날씨 gloomy weather. ② 《살림이》 (be) poor; miserable. ¶ 살림이 ~ live in poverty; live poor.

**을유**(乙酉) 〖민속〗 the 22nd binary term of the sexagenary cycle.

**을종**(乙種) class B; second grade.

**을축**(乙丑) 〖민속〗 the 2nd binary term of the sexagenary cycle.

**을해**(乙亥) 〖민속〗 the 12th binary term of the sexagenary cycle.

**읊다** 《낭송하다》 recite 〔sing〕 《a poem》; 《짓다》 compose 〔write〕 《a poem》. ¶ 시를 ~ recite a poem; compose a poem / 봄꽃을 시로 ~ write 〔sing〕 about spring flowers in a poem.

**읊조리다** recite 《a poem》; chant 《a hymn》.

**음**(音) ① 《소리》 a sound; a note; a tone. ¶ 높은〔낮은〕 음 a high 〔low〕 tone / 아름다운 음 a melodious 〔musical〕 sound / 음의 고저 pitch / 장〔단〕음 a long 〔short〕 sound. ② 《한문의》 the pronunciation 《of Chinese characters》. ¶ 한자를 음으로 읽다 read Chinese characters phonetically / 한자에 한글음을 달다 give the reading of Chinese characters in Hangul alphabet.

**음**(陰) 〖철학〗 "Yin"; the negative 〔female〕 principle in nature; 《어둠·그늘》 dark; shade; 《비밀》 secret; 〖수학〗 a negative 〔minus〕 sign. ⇨ 음으로(陰—).

**음가**(音價) 〖음성〗 phonetic 〔sound〕 value; 〖음악〗 a note value.

**음각**(陰刻) 〖미술〗 intaglio; depressed engraving. ~하다 intaglio; engrave in intaglio.

**음감**(音感) a sense of sound. ¶ ~이 좋다 have a good ear for music / 절대~ absolute 〔perfect〕 pitch. ◉ ~교육 auditory education; acoustic training.

**음경**(陰莖) 〖해부〗 the phallus; the penis (*pl.* ~es, -nes); the cock 《비어》. ◉ ~숭배 phallicism.

**음계**(音階) 〖음악〗 the (musical) scale. ¶ 단~ the minor scale / 반~ a chromatic scale / 장~ the major scale / 온〔전〕~ the gamut; a diatonic scale / 5음 ~ a pentatonic scale / 7음 ~ a seven-note scale / ~를 타다〔노래하다〕 play 〔sing〕 scales / ~연습을 하다 practice scales 《on the piano》.

**음곡**(音曲) music; musical performance. ◉ ~금지 the prohibition of musical entertainment.

**음극**(陰極) 〖전기〗 the negative pole; the cathode. ◉ ~강하 a cathode fall 〔drop〕. ~방식(防蝕) cathodic protection. ~선 the cathode rays: ~선관 a cathode-ray tube. ~액 catholyte. ~판 a negative 〔cathode〕 plate.

**음기**(陰氣) a chill; chilliness; gloominess; dreariness; melancholy. ¶ ~의 gloomy; melancholy / ~가 서린 방 a gloomy(-looking) room.

**음낭**(陰囊) 〖해부〗 the scrotum (*pl.* -ta); the balls 《미속어》. ◉ ~수종(水腫) hydrocele. ~염 scrotitis. ~헤르니아 scrotocele; scrotal hernia.

**음녀**(淫女) a lewd 〔an unchaste, a wanton〕 woman.

**음담**(淫談) a filthy 〔a foul, an obscene〕 talk 〔story〕; a bawdy talk; lewd 〔*risqué*〕 stories. ¶ ~을 하다 talk smut; tell lewd jokes. ◉ ~패설(悖說) ＝음담.

**음덕**(陰德) hidden virtue; kind acts done in secret; a secret act of charity (자선). ¶ ~을 베풀다 do 《*a person*》 private kindness; do good by stealth.

**음덕**(蔭德) the ancestor's virtue. ¶ (조상의) ～을 입다 be indebted to *one's* ancestors.

**음독**(音讀) 《한자의》 straight reading; 《소리내어》 reading aloud. ～하다 《소리내어》 read aloud / 시를 이해하려면 우선 ～을 해야 한다 To understand a poem, you should first read it aloud.

**음독**(飮毒) taking poison. ～하다 take poison. ¶ ～ 자살하다 commit suicide 〔kill *oneself*〕 by taking poison; poison *oneself* to death.

**음란**(淫亂) lewdness; lechery; lasciviousness; obscenity; incontinence. ～하다 (be) lewd; lascivious; lecherous; salacious. ¶ ～한 여자 a lewd 〔loose〕 woman. ◉ ～비디오 a lascivious sex video film. ～테이프 an obscene video tape.

**음량**(音量) the volume 《of voice, sound》. ¶ 라디오의 ～을 높이다〔줄이다〕 turn the volume up 〔down〕 on the radio / ～을 최대로 하여 스테레오를 켜다 play a stereo at top 〔full〕 volume. ◉ ～측정기 a sound-level meter.

**음력**(陰曆) the lunar calendar. ¶ ～ 정월 초닷새 January 5th of 〔according to〕 the lunar calendar / ～ 정월 보름날 "Full Moon" day, Jan. 15th of the lunar calendar / 이 지방에서는 아직도 ～을 쓰고 있다 In these parts they still use 〔go by〕 the lunar calendar. ◉ ～설 the Lunar New Year's Day.

**음료**(飮料) a beverage; a drink; something to drink; drinkables. ¶ ～로 알맞다 be fit for drink; be good to drink / ～로 쓰다 use for drinking purposes / 무슨 ～를 드릴까요 What kind of drink would you like? / 뜨거운〔찬〕 ～를 마시고 싶은데요 I'd like something hot 〔cold〕 to drink.
◉ ～수 drinking 〔potable〕 water; water to drink: 한해(旱害) 지역에 ～수 보내기 운동이 전국적으로 시작되었다 A nationwide campaign launched to send drinking water to drought-stricken areas. 혼합～ concoctions; cocktail; highball 《미》.

**음률**(音律) 《음조》 a tune; a note; a melody; 《음의 높낮이》 a pitch; (a) rhythm.

**음매** 《소울음》 a moo.

**음모**(陰毛) 〖해부〗 pubes; pubic hair.

**음모**(陰謀) a plot; a conspiracy; an intrigue; a dark design; a machination; a frame-up 《미구어》. ～하다 plot; conspire; form a conspiracy; intrigue. ¶ 암살을 ～하다 plot against 《*a person's*》 life / 정부의 전복을 ～하다 conspire 〔intrigue〕 against the government / 내란 ～죄로 기소되다 be indicted for plotting an insurrection.
음모에: ～에 가담하다 be implicated 〔initiated〕 in a plot / ～에 가담치 않다 not be a party to a plot / ～에 관계하다 be privy to a plot / ～에 말려들다 get entangled 〔entrapped〕 in a plot; be involved in an intrigue.
음모를: ～를 꾀하다 plot; lay 〔hatch, weave, concoct, brew, frame〕 a plot; form 〔lay〕 a conspiracy against 《*a person's* life》; intrigue against 《*a person*》 / ～를 눈치〔알아〕채다 scent treachery 〔a plot, an intrigue〕 / ～를 뒤엎다 thwart a conspiracy / ～를 파헤치다 expose 〔lay bare〕 a plot; unmask a conspiracy.
◉ ～단 a bank of conspirators; a cabal; a junta. ～자 a plotter; a conspirator; an intriguer; a schemer. 암살～ designs against 《*a person's*》 life; a conspiracy to kill 《*a person*》.

**음문**(陰門) 〖해부〗 the vulva; the vagina.

**음미**(吟味) 《맛봄》 tasting; sampling; 《감상》 appreciation; savoring 《of poems, songs》. ～하다 sample; taste; enjoy; appreciate; savor. ¶ 술맛을 ～하다 taste 〔take a taste of〕 liquor / 명작을 숙독하여 ～했다 I carefully read and appreciated the fine piece of literature.

**음반**(音盤) a (phonograph) record; a disk. ¶ ～을 틀다 play a record / ～으로 노래를 듣다 listen to a song on a record.

**음부**(淫婦) = 음녀(淫女).

**음부**(陰部) 〖해부〗 the pubic region; (the area of) the genital organs; the private 〔secret〕 parts; genitals. ¶ 외～ external genital organs.

**음산하다**(陰散―) (be) gloomy; depressing; dreary; dismal. ¶ 음산하게 gloomily; drearily; dismally / 음산한 하늘 an overcast 〔a leaden〕 sky / 음산한 날씨 gloomy 〔dismal〕 weather / 음산한 구름 heavy 〔sullen〕 clouds.

**음색**(音色) the quality of a tone 〔sound〕; a tone color; *timbre* (F.). ¶ ～이 좋다 sound beautiful; have a good *timbre* / 피아노와 바이올린은 ～이 다르다 Pianos and violins have different *timbre*. ◉ ～조절 (장치) (a) tone control.

**음서**(淫書) an erotic 〔a lascivious〕 book; [총칭] obscene literature; pornography.

**음성**(音聲) ① 〖언어〗 the phonetics 〔sounds〕 of a language. ② = 목소리[1]. ¶ 가짜 ~으로, ~을 속이어 in a feigned voice / 여자 ~을 내다 assume a woman's voice. ◉ ~기관 the vocal organs. ~기호 a phonetic sign 〔symbol〕; a phonetic notation. ~ 다중 방송 the sound multiplex broadcasting; the multichannel sound system. ~다중 TV a television set tunable to multiplex broadcasts: ~ 다중 TV 방송 a television broadcast using two audio frequencies; a sound multiplex television broadcast. ~언어 a spoken language. ~응답 시스템 an audio response system (생략 ARS). ~응답 유니트 an audio response unit (생략 ARU). ~인식 speech recognition: ~인식 다이얼 시스템 Voice Dial System (생략 VDS). ~체계 a phonetic system. ~테스트 audition. ~학 phonetics: ~학적 phonetic / ~학자 a phonetician. ~합성 voice synthesis.

**음성**(陰性) 《성격의》 passive character; passivity; passiveness; 《전기의》 negativity; 《병의》 dormancy. ¶ ~의〔적인〕 passive; 《원소·기(基)·전기가》 negative; electronegative; 《병이》 atonic; dormant; 《기질이》 gloomy / 그의 에이즈 검사 결과는 ~이었다 The result of his AIDS test was 〔proved〕 negative. ◉ ~거래 unlawful 〔illicit, under-the-table〕 deal 〔transaction〕. ~대전(帶電) negative electrification. ~반응 a negative reaction. ~수입 《관리의》 spoils; a perquisite: ~수입을 얻다 gain a perquisite; get extra benefits out of *one's* position. ~콜레라 dormant cholera.

**음소**(音素) 〖음성〗 a phoneme. ◉ ~기호 a phonemic symbol. ~론 phonemics. ~문자 alphabetic 〔phonemic〕 writing. ~체계 a phonemic system. ~학(學) phonemics. ~화(化) phonemicization: ~화하다 phonemicize.

**음속**(音速) 〖물리〗 the speed 〔velocity〕 of sound; acoustic velocity. ¶ ~의 sonic / ~ 이하의 subsonic / ~에 가까운 near-sonic 《speeds》 / ~의 3배의 속도 Mach 3 / ~(의 벽)을 돌파하다 break the sound 〔sonic〕 barrier / ~의 2배로 날다 fly at twice the speed of sound; fly at Mach 2. ◉ ~장벽 the sonic barrier. 극초(極超)~ hypersonic (speed). 아(亞)~ subsonic (speed). 초~ supersonic 〔ultrasonic〕 (speed): 초~학 supersonics.

**음수**(陰數) 〖수학〗 a negative (number); a minus 〔negative〕 quantity; a minus.

**음순**(陰脣) 〖해부〗 the labia (*sing.* -bium); 《구어》 the lips of the vulva. ◉ 대~ the labia majora. 소~ the labia minora; the nymphae.

**음습하다**(陰濕—) (be) dark 〔shady〕 and damp. ¶ 이 식물은 음습한 땅에서 자란다 The plant grows in damp, shady places.

**음식**(飮食) food; foodstuffs; a meal; food and drink; refreshments.
¶ ~을 먹다 eat and drink / ~에 조심하다 be careful about what *one* eats and drinks / ~에 까다롭다 be particular 〔finicky〕 about *one's* food / ~을 절제하다 be moderate in eating and drinking / ~ 대접을 받다 receive 《*a person's*》 hospitality; partake of hospitality; be feasted 〔entertained〕; be treated 《to macaroni》 / ~ 대접을 하다 entertain; give 《*a person*》 hospitality; give 《*a person*》 a dinner 〔feast〕; give a feast 〔dinner〕 / ~에 손도 대지 않다 leave the food 〔dish〕 untouched / 그것은 소화가 잘되는〔잘 안되는〕 ~이다 That is digestible 〔indigestible〕 food. / 그 식당은 ~이 좋다 That restaurant 「serves good meals and drinks 〔have a good bill of fare〕. ◉ ~물 food (and drink); foodstuffs (and beverages). ~점 an eating house; a restaurant; an eatery 《미구어》; 《간이 식당》 a chophouse: (대형) 호화 ~점 a (large-scale) deluxe restaurant 〔eatery〕.

**음신**(音信) 《소식》 news; correspondence; (a) communication; 《편지》 a letter.

**음심**(淫心) an inclination toward lewdness 〔licentiousness〕; a zest for lechery.

**음악**(音樂) music.

> 용법 **music** 하나 둘 셀 수 없는 불가산 명사로 복수형을 안 쓴다. 셀 때는 a piece of music (한 곡의 음악)으로 쓴다. 「곡, 선율, 노래」란 뜻을 나타내는 **tune** (곡, 선율), **melody** (곡, 선율), **song** (노래, 가곡) 따위는 가산 명사.

¶ ~적(인) musical; melodious / ~을 좋아하는 music-loving / ~의 밤 a musical evening 〔soiree〕 / ~의 대가 a great musician / ~을 배우다 take lessons in music / ~을 연주하다 play 〔perform〕 music / ~을 이해하다〔이해

못하다〕 can 〔cannot〕 appreciate music; understand 〔do not understand〕 music; have an 〔no〕 ear for music / ～에 취미가 있다 have a taste for music / ～에 맞추어 춤추다 dance to music.
◉ ～가 a musician. ～감독《영화 등의》a music 〔musical〕 director. ～감상실 a music hall. ～계 musical circles. ～교육 musical education; music training. ～당 a concert hall; 《야외의》 a bandstand. ～대 a (musical, brass) band: ～대 대장 a bandmaster. ～대학 the college 〔school〕 of music. ～사 the history of music. ～선생 a music teacher. ～애호가 a music lover; a lover of music. ～영화 a musical (film). ～이론 musical 〔music〕 theory. ～ 콩쿨 대회 a music contest. ～평론가 a music critic. ～학 musicology. ～학교 a music school 〔academy〕; a conservatory 《미》. ～회 a concert; 《독주·독창회》 a recital: 자선 ～회 an charity 〔benefit〕 concert / 야외 ～회 an outdoor concert / 열린 ～회 an open concert / ～회를 개최하다 give a concert 〔recital〕. ～효과 musical effects; the (background) music. 구체～ concrete music; *musique concrète* (F.). 극장～ scenic music. 색채～ color music. 피아노～ piano music. 한국～ Korean music.

**음양**(陰痒) 〖한의〗 a vaginal itch; pruritus.

**음양**(陰陽) ① 《상반되는 기운》 the cosmic dual forces; the interacting principles of 「the negative and positive 〔Yin and Yang〕; the male and female principles; 《해와 달》 the sun and the moon; 《그늘과 빛》 shade and light. ¶ ～의 화합 the harmony of the male and female principles. ② 《전기의》 negative and positive electricity; the cathode and anode.
◉ ～가(家) a necromancer; a diviner; a fortuneteller. ～각(刻) (raised) relief and bas-relief. ～오행설 the doctrine of the five natural elements of the positive and negative.

**음역**(音域) musical range; compass. ¶ 높은〔낮은〕 ～ the upper 〔lower〕 register 《of this instrument》 / ～이 넓은 목소리 a voice of great compass; a voice with a wide range / 그의 음성은 ～이 넓다 His voice has a wide range.

**음역**(音譯) (a) transliteration. ～하다 transliterate.

**음영**(吟詠) recitation of a poem. ～하다 recite 《a poem》.

**음영**(陰影) 《그림자》 shadow; 《그늘》 shade; 《그림의》 shade(s). ¶ ～이 지다 be shaded 《from the sun by a tree》 / (그림·사진에) ～을 넣다 put in the shadings.

**음욕**(淫慾) carnal desire 〔passion〕; sensual 〔sexual〕 appetite; lust. ¶ ～을 억누르다 control 〔restrain〕 *one's* passion; rule lust / ～에 탐닉하다 indulge in sexual pleasures; give rein to carnal passion.

**음용**(飮用) ¶ ～의 for drinking (purposes); potable / ～에 적합하다 be good 〔fit〕 to drink; be potable 〔drinkable〕 / ～에 부적합하다 be not good to drink; be unfit for drinking; be undrinkable. ◉ ～수(水) drinking water; water to drink; 《게시》 Fit to drink.

**음운**(音韻) 《음성》 a vocal sound; 《음소》 a phoneme; 《시의》 prosody; 《한문의》 the initial sound and final rhyme of a Chinese syllable. ◉ ～론〔학〕 phonemics; phonology: ～학자 a phonologist. ～변화 (a) phonetic change. ～조직 the sound system 《of a language》.

**음울**(陰鬱) gloominess; melancholy; dismalness. ～하다 (be) gloomy; dismal; dreary; cheerless; melancholy. ¶ ～한 이야기 a sad 〔melancholy〕 story / ～한 날씨 dark 〔gloomy〕 weather / ～한 하늘 a leaden 〔cloudy, overcast, gloomy〕 sky / ～한 표정을 하다 look melancholy 〔blue〕; wear a gloomy face.

**음위**(陰痿) 〖의학〗 impotence. ¶ ～의 impotent.

**음유시인**(吟遊詩人) a wandering 〔strolling〕 minstrel.

**음으로**(陰—) privately; implicitly; indirectly; secretly; in secret. ¶ ～ 양으로 publicly and privately; implicitly and explicitly / ～ 양으로 입은 은덕 favors received directly and indirectly.

**음이름**(音—) 〖음악〗 a pitch name.

**음이온**(陰—) 〖화학〗 a negative ion; an anion.

**음자리표**(音—標) 〖음악〗 a clef. ¶ 가온 ～ the C clef / 낮은～ the bass 〔F〕 clef / 높은～ the treble 〔G〕 clef.

**음전** dignified 〔proper〕 conduct 〔speech〕. ～하다 (be) proper; dignified; gentlemanly; ladylike. ¶ ～한 색시 a nice young lady.

**음전**(音栓) 《오르간의》 a stop (knob); 《관악기의》 a fipple.

**음전기**(陰電氣) 〖물리〗 negative 〔minus〕 electricity.

**음전자**(陰電子) 〖물리〗 a negative electron; a negatron.

**음전하**(陰電荷) 『전기』 (a) negative charge.

**음절**(音節) 『언어』 a syllable; 『음악』 a musical measure; a bar of music. ¶ ～로 나누다 syllabify; syllabicate; divide 《a word》 into syllables. ◉ ～문자 a syllabic (character); a syllabary. 단〔이, 삼, 다〕～어 a monosyllabic 〔dis(s)yllabic, trisyllabic, polysyllabic〕 word.

**음정**(音程) 『악기』 an 〔a musical〕 interval; a tone; a step. ¶ 4분 ～ a quarter tone. ◉ 단〔장〕～a minor 〔major〕 (interval). 반～ a semitone; a half step. 전～ a tone; a whole step.

**음조**(音調) 《가락》 a tune; 《선율》 melody; 《음색》 tone; 《음질》 (a) timbre; 《운율》 rhythm; 《발음의》 euphony; 《말의》 (an) intonation. ¶ 시의 ～ the timbre 〔prosodic quality〕 of a poem / ～의 변화 modulation; inflection of voice / ～가 좋은 pleasant (to the ear); melodious; sweet; euphonic / ～를 바꾸다 modulate.

**음주**(飮酒) drinking. ～하다 drink. ¶ ～의 폐단 the evil of drinking / ～에 빠지다 be given 〔addicted〕 to drinking / ～를 삼가다 be of sober habits / ～로 패가망신하다 drink *one's* fortune away / 그는 ～가 과하다 He is too fond of drink. / 과한 ～가 그의 건강을 해쳤다 Excessive drinking undermined his health. ◉ ～가 a drinker: 그는 대단한 ～가다 He is a heavy drinker. ～검사 a balloon 〔the breath〕 test. ～벽 drinking habit; a habit of drinking: ～벽을 고치다 get over 〔rid of〕 *one's* drinking habit. ～운전 drunken driving; driving while intoxicated: ～ 운전 강력 단속 캠페인 an intensive campaign against drunken drivers / ～ 운전자 a drunken driver. ～측정기 a breathalyzer; a drunkometer 《미》.

**음지**(陰地) a shady spot; a shaded lot 〔ground〕. ¶ ～와 양지 light and shade / ～가 양지되고 양지가 음지된다 《속담》 Every thing goes by turns. *or* The wheel of fortune turns.

**-음직하다** it is possible to; it is all right to; it is 〔seems〕 likely to; it is quite (+형용사); it is worth 《*do*ing》. ¶ 먹음직한 appetizing; tempting; delicious looking / 믿음직한 사람 a man you can trust / 수박이 먹음직하다 That watermelon looks good 〔delicious〕 eating.

**음질**(音質) the quality of sound; tone quality. ¶ 이 음반은 ～이 좋다〔나쁘다〕 This record has good 〔poor〕 sound quality.

**음충하다** (be) wily; guileful; crafty; tricky; insidious; snaky; sneaky; underhand(ed). ¶ 음충한 사람 a snake in the grass; a man to be wary of; a smiler with a knife.

**음치**(音癡) tone-deafness; lack of musical ability; lacking an ear for music. ¶ 나는 ～이다 I have no ear for music. *or* I'm tone-deaf.

**음침하다**(陰沈—) (be) gloomy; dismal; dreary; somber 〔sombre 《영》〕; cheerless; melancholy. ¶ 음침한 날씨 gloomy weather / 음침한 방 a dismal room / 음침한 집 a dismal 〔somber looking〕 house.

**음탐**(淫貪) a taste for lewdness; a yen for lust; a hunger for lechery. ～하다 (be) lecherous.

**음탕**(淫蕩) debauchery; dissoluteness; licentiousness; lechery and profligacy. ～하다 (be) debauched; dissipated; dissolute; profligate; licentious. ¶ ～한 눈으로 보다 give 《*a person*》 an amorous 〔a sultry〕 look / ～한 생활을 하다 lead a dissolute life; live a debauched life / 그는 그녀에게 ～한 짓을 했다 He did something 「dirty 〔indecent〕 to her.

**음파**(音波) a sound 〔sonic〕 wave. ¶ 초～ an ultrasonic wave / ～를 내다 put out sound waves. ◉ ～계(計) an audiometer; a sound wave meter. ～측정 phonometry: ～ 측정기 a phonometer; an audiometer. ～탐지기 a sonobuoy.

**음판**(陰板) 『전기·사진』 a negative 「(plate).

**음표**(音標) 『음악』 a musical note; a musical score; notation. ¶ 2분～ a half note; a minim 《영》 / 4분～ a quarter note; a crotchet 《영》 / 8분～ an eighth note; a quaver 《영》 / 16분～ a sixteenth note; a semiquaver 《영》 / 32분 ～ a thirty-second note; a demisemiquaver 《영》 / 64분～ a sixty-fourth note 《미》; a hemidemisemiquaver 《영》 / ～를 그리다 write notes 〔musical scores〕 / ～를 읽을 줄 알다 be able to read note. ◉ 겹점～ a double dotted note. 고～ the treble (score). 잇단～ a group of notes. 저～ the bass (score). 점～ a dotted note.

**음표문자**(音標文字) 『언어』 a phonetic alphabet 〔sign, symbol〕. ◉ 만국〔국

제] ~ the International Phonetic Alphabet (생략 IPA).

**음해**(陰害) damage done in secret. ~하다 damage 〔hurt, injure〕 secretly; stab 《*a person*》 in the back.

**음핵**(陰核) 〖해부〗 the clitoris; the phallus (*pl.* -li).

**음향**(音響) (a) sound; a noise (소음). ¶ ~을 막다 arrest sound / ~을 막는 벽 a sound-proof wall / ~을 흡수하다 absorb sound; be sound-〔noise-〕absorbent.

◉ ~설비 sound facilities. ~실 《악기의》 a sound box; a sound effects room. ~장치 《마이크 따위의 확성 장치》 a public-address system. ~전파 sound propagation. ~조절 sound conditioning. ~측심 echo sounding. ~측심기 an echo sounder; a sonic depth finder; 《상표명》 a Fathometer. ~측정기 a phonometer. ~탐지기 a sound detector; a sound detection gear. ~폭탄 a screamer bomb. ~학 acoustics: ~학자 an acoustician. ~효과 《극 등의》 sound effects; 《건물 내부의》 acoustics; 《음악의》 back-ground: 이 강당은 ~효과가 좋다〔나쁘다〕 The acoustics of this hall are good 〔bad〕.

**음험하다**(陰險—) (be) snaky; sneaky; treacherous; insidious; double-dealing; two-faced; untrustworthy; sly; tricky. ¶ 음험한 수단으로 by crafty means / 음험한 사람 an insidious man; a deep one; a snake / 음험한 수작을 부리다 use subtle tricks 〔treacherous measures〕.

**음화**(陰畫) 〖사진〗 a (photographic) negative.

**음훈**(音訓) 〖언어〗 the pronunciation and the meaning (of a Chinese character).

**음흉**(陰凶) wicked treacherousness. ~하다 (be) wicked and treacherous. ¶ ~한 사람 a tricky guy; a treacherous fellow. ◉ ~주머니 "a snake-in=the-grass".

**읍**(邑) *eup;* a town. ¶ 여주 읍 the town of Yŏju / 읍이 운영하는 town-managed 〔=run〕 / 읍에 가다 go up to town.

◉ 읍사무소 a town office. 읍소재지 the seat of a town office.

**읍**(揖) a polite 〔low〕 bow with *one's* hands in front. ~하다 make a low 〔polite〕 bow with *one's* hands in front.

**읍간**(泣諫) tearful remonstration. ~하다 remonstrate with tears.

**읍내**(邑內) 《in》 the town; the whole town (전체). ⇨ 읍(邑). ¶ 그녀는 ~에서 소문난 미인이다 She is famous in the town for her beauty.

**읍례**(揖禮) = 읍(揖).

**읍민**(邑民) the inhabitants of a town; townspeople; townsfolk. ¶ ~의 한 사람 a townsman; a townswoman.

**읍소**(泣訴) ~하다 implore 〔supplicate; appeal to〕 《*a person* for mercy》 with tears in *one's* eyes.

**-읍시다** let's. ⇨ -ㅂ시다. ¶ 소리내어 읽읍시다 Let's read aloud.

**읍장**(邑長) the mayor 《of a town》; a town manager; 《영》 a town mayor.

**읍청**(泣請) a sincere request (with tears). ~하다 implore; request sincerely (with tears).

**읍촌**(邑村) towns and villages.

**응** ① 《대답》 mmh; uh-huh; yeah; yes; all right; O.K.; 《부정》 no. ¶ 응, 꼭 갈께 Oh yes, I will come without fail. / 「너 안 가니」—「응, 안 간다」 "Don't you go ?"—"No, I don't." ② 《대답을 구할 때》 O.K?; huh? ¶ 극장에 가자, 응 Let's go to the theater, huh?

**응결**(凝結) 《피 따위의》 coagulation; 《우유 따위》 curdling; 《시멘트의》 setting; 《액체의》 congelation; solidification; freezing; 《기체의》 condensation. ~하다 coagulate; congeal; curdle; solidify; freeze; condense. ¶ 우유를 ~시키다 set 〔curdle〕 milk / 물은 ~하여 얼음이 된다 Water freezes into ice. / 수증기는 식으면 ~하여 물이 된다 Steam condenses into water when it cools. ◉ ~기(器) a freezer. ~물 a congelation 《of》. ~점 the freezing point. ~제 a coagulant; a coagulator.

**응고**(凝固) solidification; congelation (응결); coagulation (혈액의). ⇨ 응결. ~하다 solidify; congeal; coagulate; freeze; clot. ◉ ~점 the freezing 〔solidifying〕 point. ~제 a coagulating agent; a coagulant: 항~제 an anticoagulant.

**응급**(應急) emergency; makeshift. ¶ ~의 emergency 《supplies》; 《일시적인》 temporary; 《임시의》 stopgap 《measures》; makeshift.

◉ ~공사 an emergency work. ~물자 emergency supplies. ~병원 an emergency hospital. ~수단 = ~조치. ~수리 temporary 〔emergency〕 repairs: ~수리만을 하다 make temporary repairs only. ~실 a first-aid room; an emergency room. ～장치 emergency apparatus. ～조치 an emergency measure; a temporary expedient: ～ 조치를 취하다 take emergency measures; take a temporary expedient; employ 〔take〕 a stopgap. ～책(策) =～조치. ～환자 an emergency 〔urgent〕 case.

**응급치료**(應急治療) first aid; first-aid treatment. ¶ 화상의 ～(법) the first-aid treatment of burns / ～용 상자 a first-aid kit / ～를 하다 give 〔administer〕 first aid 《to *a person*》 / ～를 받는 환자 a first-aid patient / ～ 훈련을 하다 train 《*a person*》 in first aid.
◉ ～소 a first-aid room; a first-aid (dressing) station.

**응낙**(應諾) consent; assent; acceptance; acknowledgment; response. ～하다 consent 《to》; agree 《to》; respond 《to》; assent 《in》; accept 《a recommendation》. ¶ ～ 없이 without 《*a person's*》 consent.

**응달** the shade; (the place) where it is shady; the shady side. ¶ ～이 지다 be shaded 《by》 / ～에서 쉬다 take a rest in the shade / ～에 두다 keep 《*a thing*》 in the shade 〔out of the sun〕 / ～에서 말리다 dry 《*a thing*》 in the shade.

**응답**(應答) a response; a rejoinder; 《대답》 an answer; a reply. ～하다 respond; answer; reply to. ¶ 질의 ～ questions and answers; answers to questions. / 군중의 환호에 ～하다 respond to the cheers of the crowd / 그는 무슨 질문이든 ～에 막힘이 없다 He can give ready answers to any questions. / (두 사람이) 시편을 응답식으로 읽었다 The Psalms were read responsively. ◉ ～램프〔모드〕 『컴퓨터』 an answer lamp 〔mode〕. ～위치 『컴퓨터』 a response position. ～자 a respondent.

**응당**(應當) 《반드시》 for sure; without fail; 《당연히》 naturally; as a matter of course; necessarily. ¶ ～ 해야 할 일 a thing one 「ought to do 〔should do〕 / 그는 ～ 그 벌을 받아야 한다 He deserves the punishment.

**응대**(應對) ① 《남의 말에》 a response; an answer; a reply. ～하다 reply to; answer; rejoin.
② 《응접》 (a) reception. ～하다 receive 《guests》; wait on 《customers》; 《상대하다》 deal with 《*a person*》. ¶ ～를 잘하다〔서투르게 하다〕 be good 〔awkward〕 at dealing with people / 고객을 정중히 ～하다 wait on a customer politely / 어머니는 손님 ～에 바쁘시다 Mother is busy receiving visitors.

**응등그러지다** dry up; shrink up; shrivel.

**응등그리다** shrink *one's* body; shrug *one's* shoulders; huddle up.

**응력**(應力) 『기계』 stress.

**응모**(應募) 《기부 등의》 subscription; 《입학·취직 등의》 application; 《지원병의》 enlistment; 《회원 등의》 enrollment; 《참가》 entry; 《광고의》 response. ～하다 apply for; make an application for; subscribe for 〔to〕; enlist 《as a volunteer》 for; enter for 《a contest》. ¶ 경기에의 ～ an entry for a contest / 주식 모집에 ～하다 subscribe 「for shares 〔to stocks〕 / 그는 그 회사의 사원 모집에 ～했다 He applied for a position in the company. / ～ 자격에 제한이 없음 No special qualifications are needed to apply.
◉ ～신청 an application for subscription. ～액 the amount subscribed; *one's* subscription 《to a fund》. ～용지 an application form. ～원고 manuscripts entered 《for the prize》.

**응모자**(應募者) an applicant 《for a school》; a subscriber 《to》; an entrant; a volunteer. ¶ 현상 ～ a competitor 〔contester 《미》〕 for the prize / 현상 논문 ～ a prize essayist / ～가 굉장히 많았다 There were a great number of applicants 《for the prize》.

**응보**(應報) retribution; 《천벌》 nemesis. ¶ 인과～ a reward in accordance with a deed; As a man sows, so he shall reap.

**응분**(應分) ¶ ～의 《상당한》 appropriate; due; proportionate; reasonable; suitable; 《미치는 한의》 within *one's* power; 《분에 맞는》 according to *one's* circumstances 〔ability, means〕 / ～의 기부를 하다 contribute *one's* mite 〔due share〕 / ～의 대우를 받다 be given proper 〔due〕 treatment.

**응사**(應射) firing back; a return shot. ～하다 fire 〔shoot〕 back; respond to 《*a person's* firing》; return 《*a person's*》 fire. ¶ ～를 받다 bring 〔draw〕 return fire 《from the enemy》.

**응석** 《a child's》 playing on *one's* affections. ¶ ～ 받다 indulge; pamper; spoil; 《구어》 mollycoddle / ～ 부리듯 coaxingly / ～ 부리다 play on *one's* affections; behave like a spoilt child; play the baby / ～투로 말하다 speak in a coquettish tone. ◉ ～꾸러기〔둥이, 받이〕 a spoilt 〔pampered〕 child.

**응소**(應召) compulsory enrol(l)ment; levy; being drafted 〔conscripted〕. ～하다 be drafted 〔enlisted, enrol(l)ed〕. ◉ ～자〔병〕 a draftee; an enlisted man; a recruit (신병).

**응소**(應訴) 〖법〗 acceptance of a legal suit. ～하다 accept 〔answer〕 a legal suit.

**응수**(應手) 《바둑 등에서》 a countermove; a response. ～하다 make a countermove; respond 《to *one's* opponent's move》 with….

**응수**(應酬) 《대답》 a response; a reply; an answer; 《말대꾸》 a retort; 《답례》 a return; 《즉답》 a (verbal) riposte; 《주고받기》 an exchange 《of words》. ～하다 respond; reply; return; answer back; make a 《sharp》 retort. ¶ 지지 않고 ～하다 give tit for tat; make a repartee 〔riposte〕; retort 〔cast back〕 《an accusation》/ 그는 그 비난에 격하게 ～ 했다 He responded heatedly to the criticism.

**응시**(凝視) a steady gaze; a stare. ～하다 gaze at 〔on〕; stare at; watch intently; look hard at; fix 〔fasten〕 *one's* eyes on. ¶ 차가운 눈초리로 ～하다 give 《*a person*》 a cold stare.

**응시**(應試) applying 〔sitting 《영》〕 for an examination. ～하다 apply 〔sit〕 for an examination; take an exam. ◉ ～자 a participant in an examination; an examinee.

**응신**(應信) an answer 〔a response〕 to a signal; an answer signal. ～하다 answer 〔respond to〕 a signal.

**응애응애** mewling; whimpering. ¶ ～ 울다 cry; mewl; whimper.

**응어리** ① 《근육의》 a stiff muscle; a stiffness in a muscle. ¶ ～지다 go 〔get, become〕 stiff; harden / 어깨에 ～가 생기다 feel stiff in the shoulder; have a stiffness in the shoulder. ② 《감정의》 an unpleasant feeling. ¶ 사후(事後)에 ～를 남기다 leave an unpleasant feeling. ③ 《과일 등의》 the pith 《of fruit》; the core; the heart. ④ 《사물의》 the gist 〔nub, point, substance〕 of a matter; the heart 〔pith, core, crux〕 of the matter.

**응용**(應用) (practical) application. ～하다 apply; put 〔bring〕 into practice. ¶ ～적 applied; practical / ～할 수 있는 practicable; applicable / 널리 ～할 수 있는 of wide application / ～할 수 없는 inapplicable; impractical / 공식을 ～하다 apply a formula 《to a particular case》/ 과학을 산업에 ～하다 apply science to industry / 원리를 실지에 ～하다 make a practical application of the principle / 널리 ～하다 have wide application / 과학을 실지 ～하다 put science into practical use / 첨단 기술을 일상 생활에 ～하다 apply high technology to everyday life / 항해술은 천문학을 ～한 것이다 Navigation is an application of astronomy. / 그 발명은 ～의 범위가 넓다 The invention is of very wide application. *or* The invention has a wide range of application. ◉ ～경제학 applied economics. ～과학〔수학〕 applied science 〔mathematics〕. ～문제 an applied question; a question to test 《the students'》 ability to use 《their》 knowledge in practice; exercises(연습문제). ～물리학〔화학〕 applied physics 〔chemistry〕. ～미술 applied fine arts. ～식물학 practical botany. ～역학 applied dynamics. ～연구 applied research. ～프로그램〖컴퓨터〗 an application program.

**응원**(應援) ① 《도와줌》 aid; (an) assistance; help; reinforcement (증원); 《지지》 support; backing. ～하다 aid; assist; help; support; give support; reinforce; back (up). ¶ ～하러 오다〔가다〕 come 〔go〕 to aid 〔rescue〕/ ～을 청하다 call in *a person's* aid; ask 〔send〕 《*a person*》 for support 〔assistance〕/ 후보자를 ～하다 support a candidate. ② 《성원》 cheering; 《미구어》 rooting. ～하다 cheer; 《미구어》 root 《for》. ¶ 열렬히 ～하다 cheer 《*one's* team》 vigorously / K대학팀을 ～하다 cheer 〔root for〕 K university team / 그는 300명을 이끌고 ～하러 오겠다는 말을 전해 왔다 He has sent word that he will join up with three hundred men. ◉ ～가 a rooter's song. ～군〔병〕 reinforcements; troop support. ～기 a rooter's pennant. ～단 a cheer group; a cheering party; (a group of) cheerers; 《미구어》 rooters: ～단장 the leader of a cheer group; a head rooter; 《미식 축구·농구 등의》 a cheerleader 《미》. ～대 cheerers; rooters. ～석 a cheering section; fans' seats. ～연설 《make》 a campaign speech 《for a candidate》. ～자 a supporter; a backer; a cheering fan 〔enthusiast〕; a rooter; a booster.

**응전**(應戰) a response; taking up a challenge. ～하다 return the fire

〔shot〕; respond 〔reply〕 to the《enemy》fire; accept 〔take up〕 a challenge; accept battle; fight back. ¶아군 포화에 대한 적의 ~은 미약했다 The enemy's reply to our fire was weak.

**응접**(應接)《응대》(a) reception;《만나봄》interview. ~하다 receive《a visitor》; see; hold an interview with. ¶그녀는 방문객 ~으로 바쁘다 She is busy with visitors. ◉ ~시간 a call-hour; an at-home hour. ~실 a drawing room; a reception room; a parlor《미》: ~실로 안내하다 show《a visitor》into a parlor. ~원 a receptionist.

**응종**(應從) obedience; compliance. ~하다 obey; comply with.

**응집**(凝集) cohesion; condensation. ~하다 cohere; condense. ◉ ~력 cohesive power; cohesion: ~력이 있는 cohesive; condensable. ~반응 agglutination.

**응징**(膺懲) chastisement; punishment. ~하다 chastise; punish. ¶악을 ~하다 chastise vice; punish the wicked / ~과 보복을 받아 마땅하다 deserve *one's* punishment and retaliation.

**응천순인**(應天順人) obeying the will of heaven and following the voices of the people.

**응체**(凝滯)《막히거나 걸림》stoppage; impediment; delay. ~하다 get stopped; be impeded; be delayed.

**응축**(凝縮) condensation. ~하다 condense. ¶가스를 액체로 ~하다 condense a gas to a liquid. ◉ ~기 a condenser.

**응하다**(應—) ①《대답하다》answer; reply to; respond to; muster (소집에);《순종하다》obey. ¶질의에 ~ respond to 〔answer〕 questions / 왕명에 ~ obey the king's order / 적의 포화에 ~ reply to the enemy's fire / 명령에 응해서 오다 come in obedience to orders / 소집에 ~ answer the call 〔to the colors〕; be drafted.

②《승낙하다》comply with; accept; accede to. ¶요구〔제의〕에 ~accede to a demand 〔proposal〕/ 의뢰에 ~ accede to a request; comply with *a person's* request / 도전에 ~ accept a challenge / 당신의 지급 조건에 응할 수 없다 I cannot comply with your terms of payment. / 기꺼이 자네의 초대에 응하겠네 I shall be delighted to accept your invitation.

③《비례하다》scale; adjust; fit; make correspond; proportion. ¶ …에 응해서 in respond 〔reply, answer〕 to; in proportion to; according to / 능력에 응해서 according to *one's* ability / 필요에 응해서 as the need of the case demands; as occasion calls / 국력에 응하여 군비를 제한하다 limit the armament to the resources of the country.

④《응모하다》apply for; subscribe for; make application for. ¶학생 모집에 ~ apply for admission to a school / 회원 모집에 ~ apply for membership in a society / 국채 모집에 ~ subscribe for government bonds / 현상 논문 모집에 ~ enter a prize essay contest.

⑤《필요·수요에》meet; satisfy. ¶수요에 ~ meet a demand / 시대의 요구에 ~ meet the demand of the day 〔times〕/ 국가의 위급에 ~ rise to the national emergency.

**응혈**(凝血)《피》a clot of blood; coagulated 〔clotted, curdled〕 blood; gore;《작용》coagulation (of blood); blood clotting. ~하다 blood clots 〔coagulates, congeals〕; [원인이 주어] coagulate 〔clot, congeal〕 blood.

**의**(衣) garments; dress; clothing. ◉ 의생활 clothing habits.

**의**(義) ①《옳은 일》justice; righteousness; a just cause;《덕의》morality;《신의》faith;《의기》chivalry. ¶의를 위해서 죽다 die in the cause of justice 〔humanity〕/ 의를 위해 일어서다 stand for a good cause / 의를 중히 여기다 respect justice; value honor / 의를 보고 행하지 않음은 용기가 없음이니라 To see what is right and not to do it shows want of courage. *or* Knowing what is right without practicing it betrays *one's* cowardice.

②《맺혀진 관계》relationship; ties; bonds. ¶친구의 의 the ties of friendship / 군신(君臣)의 의 the relations of sovereign and subject / 의를 맺다 form the ties of friendship; pledge in a sworn relationship / 형제의 의를 맺다 pledge in a sworn brotherhood.

③《뜻》sense; meaning; signification.

**의**(誼)《정의》 relationship; relations. ¶의가 좋다〔나쁘다〕 be on good 〔bad〕 terms《with》/ 의좋게 on good terms; like good friends; in harmony / 의좋은 부부 a devoted 〔happy〕 couple / 의가 상하다 quarrel 〔fall out〕《with》; break《with》; be estranged《from》/ 그는 이웃 사람과 의가 좋다 He lives in harmony with his neighbors. / 그 부부는 의좋게 지낸다 The couple get along like a pair of lovebirds.

**의**(醫) 《의술》 medicine; 《의사》 a doctor; a physician. ¶ 의는 인술이다 Medicine is a benevolent art.

**의** ① 《소유·소속》 …'s; of; belonging to. ¶ 그의 책 his book / 너의 구두 your shoes / 한국의 경제 Korea's economy; the economy of Korea; Korean economy / 클럽의 회원 a member of a club / 돈의 가치 the value of money (★ 생물, 의인화된 물체 및 시간·거리·가격을 나타내는 관용구에는 —'s가 쓰임) / 나의 손을 잡다 take me by the hand.
② 《…에 관한》 in; at; on. ¶ 대수(代數)의 시험 an examination in algebra; an algebra exam / 교육계의 대가 a leading figure in the educational world / 생물학의 권위자 an authority on biology / 시(詩)의 천재 a genius in poetry.
③ 《…에 대한》 for; to. ¶ 지난달의 계산서 the bill for last month; last month's bill 〔account〕 / 뒷문의 열쇠 a key to the backdoor / 가문의 수치 a disgrace to the family.
④ 《작자》 by. ¶ 헤밍웨이의 소설 a novel (written) by Hemingway / 피카소의 그림 a painting by Picasso; a Picasso.
⑤ 《구성·재료》 (built, made) of; in. ¶ 4인의 가족 a family of four / 대리석의 상(像) a statue in marble.
⑥ 《분량》 ¶ 한 잔의 커피 a cup of coffee / 수십 대의 자동차 tens of cars / 찻숟가락 하나의 소금 a teaspoonful of salt / 10킬로의 쌀 ten kilograms of rice.
⑦ 《사람의 관계》 by; with; between; to. ¶ 사제(師弟)의 관계 the relations between teacher and pupil / 김씨의 조카 a nephew of Mr. Kim's; 《be》 nephew to Mr. Kim.
⑧ 《소재·장소》 at; in; on; over; from. ¶ 동래의 온천 the hot spring at Tongnae / 런던의 겨울 the winter in London / 이 선반의 책들 books on this shelf / 한강의 다리 a bridge over the Han River / 부산의 실업가 a businessman of 〔from〕 Pusan / 이 마을의 인구 the population of this village / 나주의 배 pears from Naju / 안성의 유기 brassware from Ansŏng.
⑨ 《시간·기간》 of; in; for. ¶ 오늘의 신문 today's newspaper / 한 시간의 휴식 an hour's intermission / 그 시대의 사람들 men of that time; people in those days / 지난달의 계산서 the bill for last month; last month's bill.
⑩ 《기타의 관계》 ¶ 문제의 사나이 the man in question / 열다섯 살의 소녀 a girl of fifteen / 음악의 도시 빈 Vienna, the city of music / 성공적인 삶의 비결 the key to success in life / 식욕의 계절인 가을 autumn, the season of vigorous 〔strong〕 appetite.
⑪ 《…와 같은》 like; of. ¶ 클레오파트라의 미 a beauty like Cleopatra's; the beauty of Cleopatra.

**의가**(衣架) 《옷걸이》 a clothes rack; a coat hanger.

**의가**(醫家) a medical man. ◉ ～서 a medical book.

**의거**(依據) 《증거에 따름》 《in》 conformity 〔accordance〕 《with》; according 《to》; 《기초·근거》 《on》 the basis 〔foundation, grounds〕. ～하다 conform 《to》; accord 《with》; be based on 〔due to, caused by〕. ¶ 헌법에 ～하여 in conformity 〔accordance〕 with the Constitution / …의 규정에 ～하여 under the provision of… / 자료에 ～하여 on the basis 〔authority〕 of the data.

**의거**(義擧) a worthy 〔laudable, noble〕 undertaking 〔uprising〕; a heroic 〔brave〕 deed; a movement in the public interest. ¶ 안중근 의사의 ～ the patriotic deed of Martyr Ahn Jung=Keun.

**의걸이(장)**(衣—(欌)) a wardrobe chest.

**의견**(意見) an opinion; a view; an idea; 《제안》 a suggestion.
¶ 내 ～으로는 in my opinion; according to my view / 다른 ～ different opinions / 반대 ～ an opposite view; an opposing opinion / 유력한 ～ an influential 〔a dominant〕 opinion / ～의 분열 a split in opinion / ～의 일치 a consensus; a unanimity of opinion; an agreement in views; an accord / ～의 불일치 a disagreement of opinion; a lack of consensus; failure to reach an agreement / ～의 충돌 a conflict 〔clash〕 of opinion / ～이 구구한 문제 a matter on which opinions are divided / ～을 말하다 give 〔express, state〕 *one's* opinion; set forth *one's* views / ～을 교환하다 exchange opinions 《with *a person* on a subject》 / ～을 같이하다 be of the same opinion; agree 《with *a person* about *a matter*》; share the view 《of》 / ～을 고수하다 stick to *one's* opinion 〔guns 《구어》〕 / ～을 발표하다 publish *one's* views / ～을 제안하다 put forth 〔voice〕

an opinion / ～을 품다 entertain 〔cherish, hold〕 an opinion / 아무의 ～을 받아들이다 accept *a person's* opinion / 아무의 ～을 묻다 ask *a person's* opinion; consult *a person* / 아무의 ～을 반박하다 refute *a person's* ideas / 아무의 ～에 찬성하다 favor *a person's* ideas / 아무의 ～을 존중하다 respect *a person's* opinion / ～이 맞지 않다 disagree with 《*a person*》; differ with 《*a person*》/ …라고 보는 ～이 지배적이다 a dominant opinion is 〔holds〕 that…; a majority of people believe that… / 그는 전연 반대 ～이었다 His opinion was quite to the contrary. / 이 문제에 있어 ～의 일치를 보지 못했다 On this matter no agreement was reached. / 그 문제에 대해서 우리는 ～이 일치하지 않는다 We don't see eye to eye on the subject. / 그것에 관해서 나는 별다른 ～이 없다 I have no opinion of my own about that. / 정부 부처간에 날카로운 ～ 대립이 있다 There are sharp differences (of opinion) within the Cabinet. / 그 점에 관해서는 너와 같은 ～이다 I agree with you on that point. / 그 일에 관하여 나는 ～을 말할 입장이 못 된다 I am not in a position to comment on that matter.

◉ ～광고 opinion 〔protest〕 advertising 《on an issue》: ～ 광고를 내다 take out an advertisement setting out *one's* opinion 《on a matter》. ～서 a written opinion; a statement of *one's* views.

**의결**(議決) a decision 《of a meeting》; a resolution. ～하다 decide (upon); resolve; 《투표로》 vote 《for, against, that》; pass a vote 《of》.

¶ 안(건)을 ～하다 vote for a scheme; vote on a bill; pass a resolution 《in favor of, against》/ …의 ～을 거쳐야 하다 be subject to the decision of… / 회원은 회장 불신임을 ～했다 The members passed a vote of no confidence in the president.

◉ ～권 a voting right; the right to vote: ～권을 행사하다 exercise *one's* vote. ～기관 a legislative 〔deliberative〕 organ. ～문 a letter of resolution. ～사항 matters for decision 〔resolution, deliberation〕.

**의고**(擬古) imitation of ancient literature. ～하다 write in (imitation of) ancient style. ¶ ～적 pseudo-archaic; pseudoclassic. ◉ ～문 a pseudoclassical style. ～주의 pseudo-archaism; archaism; pseudoclassicism. ～체 pseudoclassicism; archaism.

**의과**(醫科) the medical department (of a university); the medical school. ¶ ～를 나오다 graduate from a medical college. ◉ ～대학 a medical college; a college of medicine: ～대학생 a medical student.

**의관**(衣冠) gown 〔dress〕 and hat; 《옷차림》 attire. ¶ ～을 갖추다 be in full uniform; be in full dress. ◉ ～문물 civilization (of a nation). ～속대(束帶) 《wear》 a full court dress.

**의관**(醫官) a medical officer; a surgeon.

**의구**(依舊) being as formerly; being unchanged. ～하다 be as formerly; remain unchanged.

**의구**(疑懼) apprehension; misgiving(s); suspicion; fear; uneasiness. ～하다 doubt; suspect; apprehend; feel apprehensive; fear. ◉ ～심 misgivings; apprehensions; fear: ～심을 품다 entertain 〔feel〕 misgivings 《about》/ ～심에 사로잡히다 be swayed by misgivings.

**의기**(意氣) spirits; heart; mind; vigor; 《사기》 morale. ¶ ～ 왕성하다 be in high spirits; be elated 《at the victory》/ ～가 상통하다 be of a mind (★ 부정관사 a는 the same의 뜻임); be like-minded 《with *a person*》/ 그 소식에 우리들의 ～가 꺾였다 That news dampened our spirits. / 그와 ～ 상통했다 I found a congenial spirit in him.

**의기**(義氣) 《의협심》 chivalrous spirit; chivalry; heroism; 《공공심》 public spirit. ¶ ～ 있는 chivalrous; heroic; public-spirited / ～의 사나이 a man of chivalrous spirit; a public-spirited man.

**의기**(疑忌) ～하다 suspect and abhor; distrust and avoid.

**의기상투**(意氣相投) mutual understanding; affinity. ～하다 be of congenial temper; be of a mind; find a kindred 〔congenial〕 spirit in 《*a person*》. ¶ ～한 벗 congenial friends / 그들은 ～한다 They are like-minded. *or* There is a great affinity between them.

**의기소침**(意氣銷沈) depression 〔loss〕 of spirits; dejection; dispiritedness; the mopes. ～하다 droop; be dispirited 〔disheartened〕; be depressed in 〔in low〕 spirits 〔courage〕; be cast down; be in the dumps 〔blues, mopes〕; be crestfallen 〔downcast〕. ¶ ～한 모습으로 with a dejected air; pulling a long face; looking blue 〔gloomy〕.

**의기양양**(意氣揚揚) elation; a triumphant air. ～하다 (be) triumphant; exultant. ¶ ～한 표정 a triumphant 〔proud〕 look / ～하게 in high spirits; exultantly; triumphantly; proudly; in triumph.

**의기충천**(意氣衝天) ～하다 *one's* spirits rise to the skies; be in royal 〔high, towering, roaring〕 spirits.

**의기투합**(意氣投合) = 의기상투.

**의녀**(義女) a stepdaughter.

**의념**(疑念) (a feeling of) doubt; (a) suspicion; misgivings.

**의논**(議論) (a) consultation; (a) conference; a talk; 《구어》 a confab; 《구어》 a powwow; 《제의》 an offer; a proposal. ～하다 consult 《*a person,* with *a person* about *a matter*》; hold a consultation 《with》; have a talk 《with》; discuss 《*a matter* with *a person*》; talk with 《*a person* over *a matter*》; ask 《*a person's*》 advice. ¶ ～해서 after consultation; after consulting 《*a person*》; by mutual agreement 〔consent〕 / ～중이다 be in consultation / ～해서 합의보다 come to an agreement; come to terms 《with *a person*》 / ～할 이야기를 가져가다 approach 《*a person*》 with a proposal / 사장한테 ～해 보겠습니다 I'll have a conference with the president.

◉ ～상대 an adviser; 《믿는 사람》 a confident; a confidente (여성): ～ 상대가 없다 have no one「to consult with 〔to turn to for advice〕 / ～ 상대가 되어주다 give advice 〔counsel〕 《to》.

**의당**(宜當) as a matter of course; naturally; necessarily; justly; properly. ～하다 be a matter of course; be of necessity; (be) natural; right; proper. ¶ ～ …하여야 하다 ought to *do;* should *do;* it is (just and) proper that *a person* should *do* / ～ 받을 것을 받다 have 〔get〕 *one's* due / 정부는 ～ 실업 구제의 대책을 강구해야 한다 It is up to the Government to take some measure for relief of unemployment.

**의대**(衣帶) clothes and belt 〔girdle〕.

**의대**(醫大) ⇨ 의과 대학.

**의도**(意圖) an intention; an intent; an aim; an idea; a design; a plan; purpose. ～하다 intend; design; aim 《at》; drive 《at》.

¶ 죽일 ～로 with intent to murder 《*a person*》 / ～한 대로 just as *one* intended 〔designed〕; 《shape things》 to *one's* own design / ～적으로 on purpose; intentionally; by design / ～적으로 미리 계산된 폭력 행위 an act of deliberate and premeditated violence / ～를 숨기다 cover (up) *one's* tracks / 적의 ～를 좌절시키다 frustrate the enemy's design / 나는 그의 ～를 전연 모른다 I am in complete ignorance of his intention. / 질문하시는 ～는 무엇입니까 What is your intention in asking this question? / 나는 그가 ～적으로 그렇게 했다고 밖에 생각할 수 없다 I cannot help thinking that he did it on purpose.

**의례**(依例) following precedent. ～하다 follow precedent.

**의례**(儀禮) etiquette; courtesy; a ceremony (의식). ¶ ～적 ceremonial; formal / 외교적 ～ diplomatic etiquette / 가정 ～ 준칙 (the) family rite rules / ～적인 격식을 떠나서 without formality / ～적인 방문을 하다 pay a formal 〔courtesy, protocol〕 visit 〔call〕 《to》.

**의례건**(依例件) a matter of precedent; customary affairs; a customary task. ¶ ～으로 생각하다 task 《*things*》 for granted.

**의론**(議論) (an) argument; 《토의》 (a) discussion; 《토론》 (a) debate; 《논쟁》 (a) dispute; (a) controversy. ～하다 argue; dispute; controvert; debate.

> 용법 **argument** 사실이나 논리에 바탕을 두고 자기 의견을 주장하거나 상대방을 설득시키고자 하는 의론. **discussion** 문제의 해결을 위해 격식을 차리지 않고 서로의 의견을 제시·교환함을 말하며, 언제나 찬·반 양론으로 갈라짐을 뜻하는 것은 아님. **debate** 일정한 규칙에 따라서 진행되는 공개 석상에서의 토론. **dispute** 상대방의 주장을 뒤집기 위해 감정적으로 말이 오고감을 말함. **controversy** 중요한 문제에 관해 단체 사이에서 가지게 되는 장기간에 걸친 논쟁.

¶ ～을 좋아하는 argumentative / 격렬한 ～ a heated debate / 철저히 ～하여 해결하다 argue 《*something*》 out 〔thoroughly〕; thrash out 《a problem》 / ～할 여지가 없다 inarguable; indisputable / ～이 백출하여 결정을 내리지 못했다 There were so many disputes that we could not come to a decision.

**의롭다**(義―) (be) rightful; righteous. ¶ 의로운 사람〔행위〕 a righteous man 〔act〕.

**의롱**(衣籠) a wardrobe.

**의뢰**(依賴) ① 《부탁》 a request; solicitation. ~하다 request; make 《*a person*》 a request; ask 《*a person* to *do*》. ¶ ~에 따라 in answer [reply, response] to a request; by request; in compliance with 《*a person's*》 request / ~를 들어주다 grant [concede] a request / ~를 거절하다 decline [refuse] a request.

② 《맡김》 trust; commission. ~하다 entrust 《*a person* with *a matter*》; place 《*a matter*》 in 《*a person's*》 hands; leave 《*something*》 to 《*a person, a person's* charge》. ¶ (사건을) 변호사에게 ~하다 commit [leave] 《*a matter*》 to a lawyer [an attorney] / 재산의 관리를 ~하다 trust *a person* with *one's* property / 그 조사는 그에게 ~하겠다 I will trust [entrust] him with the investigation.

③ 《의지함》 dependence; reliance. ~하다 depend [rely] upon; lean on; turn [look] to 《*a person* for》; count [reckon] on. ¶ 남에게 ~하지 않다 rely on *oneself;* help *oneself.*

◉ ~비 《변호사 등의》 a retaining fee; a retainer. ~서 a letter of request; a written request. ~심 (a spirit of) dependence; reliance. ~인 《변호사 등의》 a client.

**의료**(衣料) clothing; clothes; garments. ◉ ~비 clothing expenses.

**의료**(醫療) medical treatment [care, attention]; medical service. ¶ 불법~행위 《conduct》 unauthorized medical treatment / 26명으로 구성된 한국군의 ~ 선발대는 어제 사우디아라비아로 떠났다 A 26-member advance unit of a Korean military medical team left yesterday for Saudi Arabia.

◉ ~기관 a medical institution. ~기구 medical appliances [instruments, equipment]; 《외과용》 surgical instruments: ~ 기구상 a dealer in medical appliances [supplies]. ~기사 a medical technician. ~기술 《an advance in》 medical technology. ~반 a medical team. ~법 the Medical Services Law. ~법인 a medical corporation; an [a legally] incorporated medical institution. ~보호법 the Medical Protection Law. ~봉사 volunteer medical services. ~비 a fee for medical treatment; medical expenses; a doctor's bill: ~비 공제 deduction for medical expenses. ~사고 medical malpractice: ~사고 소송 medical malpractice suit. ~산업 the medical industry. ~수가(酬價) medical (treatment) charges; medical fee; a fee for medical treatment; a doctor's bill: ~수가 규정 [기준] the rules [standards] for medical fees. ~시설 medical facilities. ~실 a clinic room. ~인 medical personnel. ~진 a medical team. ~품 medical supplies: ~품함(函) a medical kit. ~혜택 a medical benefit. 국립 ~원 the National Medical Center.

**의료보험**(醫療保險) medical (care) insurance. ¶ ~료 medical insurance premiums / ~ 제도 the medical insurance [security] system / ~ 혜택 《expand》 medical insurance benefits 《for》 / ~ 혜택자 [수혜자] the beneficiaries of medical insurance / ~ 조합 a medical insurance union. ◉ 한국 ~관리공단 the Korea Medical Insurance Management Corporation.

**의류**(衣類) clothing; clothes; garments; 《전 옷가지》 *one's* wardrobe. ¶ ~ 한 벌 a suit of clothes / ~ 한 점 an article of clothing: 작업용 ~ working clothes. ◉ ~봉제업 an apparel industry.

**의리**(義理) 《의무》 (social) duty; (an) obligation; 《바른 도리》 justice; 《신의》 fidelity; loyalty. (★ 「의리」에 해당되는 꼭 알맞은 영어는 없음).

¶ ~가 있다 be faithful [alive] to duty; be strong in the sense of justice; have a keen [strong] sense of honor [duty] / ~를 모르다[가 없다] have no sense of duty [justice]; be ungrateful; be unfaithful [disloyal] / ~를 지키다 be loyal to 《*a person*》 / ~를 위해 죽다 die in the cause of justice [humanity] / 그는 ~가 조금도 없는 사람이다 He is a brute devoid of all sense of duty and humanity. / ~상 그렇게 하지 않을 수 없다 I am duty=bound to do so. / 그 녀석은 ~와 인정이 없는 놈이다 He is a man lost to all sense of duty and humanity. / 그 돈은 ~상 받을 수 없다 I can't, in all conscience, accept this money.

**의모**(義母) 《의붓어미》 a stepmother; 《수양어미》 a foster mother; 《의로 맺은》 a sworn mother.

**의무**(義務) (a) duty; an obligation; liability 《for》; responsibility (책임).

¶ ~적인 obligatory; compulsory / ~적으로 from a mere sense of duty / ~로서 as a matter of duty / ~를 부과하다[지우다] impose duty 《upon *a person*》; place [put] 《*a person*》 under an obligation; obligate; assign a duty 《to *a person*》/ ～를 지다 owe a duty 《to》; have the obligation 《to》/ (…할) ～가 있다 ought to *do;* be under an obligation 《to *do*》; be bound 《to *do*》; be obligated to *do* / ～를 다하다 perform 〔discharge, do, fill, fulfill〕 *one's* duty; meet *one's* obligation / 납세의 ～를 지다 be liable to taxation; have the duty to pay taxes / …함을 ～로 삼다 make it *one's* duty to 《*do*》/ ～를 태만히 하다 neglect 〔fail in〕 *one's* duty / ～ 방어전을 치르다《권투에서》make an obligatory defense of *one's* title 《with》/ 빚은 갚을 ～가 있다 One ought 〔is bound, is obligated〕 to repay his 〔*one's*《영》〕 debts. / 너에게 그것을 공표할 ～는 없다 You are under no obligation to publish it. / 부모는 자식을 학교에 보낼 ～가 있다 Parents have an obligation to send their children to school. / 권리를 주장하려거든 먼저 ～를 다해야 한다 You must do 〔perform〕 your duties before you assert your rights.

> 용법 **duty** 양심·정의감·도덕심·직무 따위에 근거한 의무. 자기 또는 타인에 대해 마땅히 하여야 된다고 생각되는 것. **obligation** 특정한 약속·계약·관습·법률 등에 의해 행하여야 할 개인적인 의무. 자신이 아니라, 남에 대한 의무를 말함. 또 duty는 장기에 걸친 의무를, obligation은 1회에 한한 것을 뜻함. **liability**, **responsibility** 주로 법적·제도적 책임에 수반되는 의무.

◉ ～감 a sense of duty 〔obligation〕. ～교육 compulsory education: 중학 ～교육 the compulsory education for middle school / ～교육 제도 a compulsory education system. ～면제 excuse from duty. ～연한 an obligatory 〔a compulsory〕 term of service. ～이행 performance of a duty. ～자 an obligator; 〖법〗 an obligor (채무자); a responsible person; a person under special obligation.

**의무**(醫務) medical affairs. ◉ ～국 the medical bureau. ～기록 medical records. ～실《학교·공장 등의》a dispensary; a medical room 〔office〕.

**의문**(疑問)《의심》(a) doubt;《문제》a problem; a question. ¶ ～의 doubtful; questionable / ～의 인물《수상한》a questionable person;《수수께끼의》a riddle; a mystery man / ～의 죽음 a mysterious death / ～을 품다 have doubts 《about》; be skeptical 《about》; doubt / ～의 여지가 있다〔없다〕 be open to 〔be beyond〕 question / 사실인지 아닌지 ～이다 It is questionable whether it is true. / ～이 생기다 A question arises. / 그것에 관해선 ～이 없다 There is no doubt about that. / ～이 있으면 언제든 물어라 Ask me whenever (you are) in doubt.

◉ ～문〔대명사〕 an interrogative sentence 〔pronoun〕. ～부〔표〕 a question 〔an interrogation〕 mark. ～사 an interrogative. ～점 a point of 〔in〕 doubt; a question.

**의뭉스럽다, 의뭉하다** (be) subtle; be more subtle than *one* might think; be deeper than *one* thinks; look simpler 〔dumber〕 than *one* is; be deeper 〔smarter〕 than *one* looks.

**의미**(意味) (a) meaning; (a) sense; significance;《취지》(a) point; the effect; the purport; the import. ～하다 mean; signify; purport; imply.

> 용법 **meaning** 말이나 행위 등이 표현하는 내용을 말하며, 「의미」를 나타내는 가장 일반적인 말. **sense**는 낱말 또는 어구가 지니는 특정의 「의미」를 말하며, meaning보다 주관적인 뉘앙스를 풍기는 말. **significance** 공공연히 표명하지 않고 배후에 있는 뜻이라는 뉘앙스를 풍기면서, 우리말의 「의의(意義)」라는 뜻에도 부합되는 말.

¶ ～ 있는 significant; meaningful / ～없는 insignificant; meaningless; pointless; senseless; unimportant / 어떤 ～로는 in a sense; in a way / 넓은 ～로 in a broad 〔large〕 sense; in a wide meaning / 엄밀한〔좁은〕 ～로 in a strict 〔narrow〕 sense / 일반적인 ～로 in a general sense / ～심장하다 be profound in meaning; have a deep meaning; be of great significance / ～(가) 있다 have meaning; be significant / 좋은 ～로도 나쁜 ～로도 생각할 수 있다 can be taken in either a good or a bad sense / 그 여자는 ～ 있는 미소를 지었다 She gave a meaningful smile. / 그것은 무슨 ～입니까 What do you mean by that? ◉ ～론 〖언어〗 semantics.

**의법**(依法) 《in》 accordance with law. ◉ ～처단 punishment 〔penalty〕 according to law. ～처분 disposition 〔measures〕 according to law.

**의병**(義兵) an army in the cause of justice; a righteous army; loyal troops.

**의병**(疑兵) 〖군사〗 camouflaged 〔dummy〕 troops.

**의복**(衣服) clothes; 《한 벌의》 a suit; a dress; clothing [총칭]. ¶ ~을 입다 wear 〔put on〕 clothes / 좋은 ~을 입은 사람들 well-dressed persons. ◉ ~비 a clothing allowance.

**의부**(義父) 《의붓아비》 a stepfather; 《수양아비》 a foster father; 《의로 맺은》 a sworn father.

**의분**(義憤) righteous 〔just〕 indignation; public indignation 〔rage, resentment〕. ¶ ~을 느끼다 have righteous indignation 《about, against, with》 / ~을 참다〔누르다〕 repress *one's* righteous indignation.

**의불합**(意不合) incongruity of spirits; uncongeniality; disagreement. ~하다 (be) uncongenial.

**의붓** step. ◉ ~딸 a stepdaughter. ~아들 a stepson. ~아비 a stepfather. ~어미 a stepmother. ~자식 a stepchild.

**의사**(意思) 《생각》 idea; thought; 《의향》 a mind; an intention; a wish; a purpose. ¶ …할 ~는 없다 have no mind to *do* / ~를 표시하다 indicate *one's* intention; express *one's* will 《to *do*》; reveal 〔show〕 *one's* intention / ~를 밝히다 speak *one's* mind; make known *one's* intention; announce *one's* intention 《to *do*》 / ~가 서로 통하다 come to understand each other / 노사간에 ~의 소통이 된다〔안 된다〕 There is 〔is a lack of〕 understanding between management and labor. / 세대 간에 ~ 소통이 안 되게 되었다 Communication between the generations has broken down. ◉ ~결정 decision-making: 마지막 ~결정을 하다 make a final decision. ~능력 mental capacity: ~능력이 없다 be devoid of mental capacity.

**의사**(義士) a righteous 〔an upright〕 person; a martyr (신앙·주의 등의).

**의사**(擬似) false; suspected; para-. ◉ ~뇌염 false encephalitis. ~유전자 a pseudogene. ~증 a suspected case. ~콜레라 paracholera; a suspected case of cholera.

**의사**(醫師) a doctor; a medical man; a doc 《구어》; 《내과》 a physician; 《외과》 a surgeon; 《전문의》 a specialist; 《일반 개업의》 a general practitioner; 《여자의》 a woman 〔lady〕 doctor.

¶ 김~ Dr. Kim / ~가 되다 become 〔be〕 a doctor / ~를 부르다 call in a doctor; send for a doctor / ~의 치료를 받고 있다 be under medical treatment / ~의 진찰을 받다 consult a doctor / ~노릇을 하다 practice medicine / 곧 ~한테 보여라 Make him see the doctor without delay. / 저 ~는 환자가 많다 The doctor has a large practice.

> **용법** **doctor** 내·외과를 불문하고 의사를 가리키는 가장 일반적인 말. 《영》에서는 주로 physician을 가리키나 《미》에서는 surgeon이나 dentist까지 포함한 일상적인 용어로 쓰고 있음. **physician** 주로 내과의. **surgeon** 주로 외과의를 말하며, 군의·선의(船醫)에도 씀. **specialist** 전문의. **general practitioner** 내·외과를 다 보는 일반 개업의.

◉ ~ 국가 시험 the national examination for medical practitioners. ~면허 a medical license. ~법 the Medical Law. ~회 a medical association. 국경 없는 ~회 the Doctors without borders; *Médecins sans Frontières* (F). 단골~ *one's* (family) doctor.

**의사**(議事) 《토론》 deliberation; consultation; conference; 《심의 사항》 proceedings; business 《of the day》. ¶ ~를 진행하다 expedite the proceedings / 오늘은 ~가 없다 We have no session today.

◉ ~규칙 parliamentary rules. ~당 an assembly hall: 국회 ~당 the National Assembly Building; the Capitol 《미》; the Houses of Parliament 《영》. ~목록 an agenda. ~상정 introduction of business. ~정족수 a quorum (for commencing proceedings): ~ 정족수에 달하다 form 〔constitute〕 a quorum. ~진행 progress of proceedings: ~ 진행 방해 obstruction of proceedings; filibustering 《미》 / ~진행 방해자 an obstructionist; a filibuster(er) / ~ 진행을 방해하다 obstruct proceedings; filibuster 《미》.

**의사록**(議事錄) a minute book; the minutes 〔record〕 of the proceedings; proceedings; journals; 《국회의》 the (official) record of the proceedings of the Assembly; the Assembly Record. ¶ ~을 만들다 take minutes of 《the proceedings》 / ~에 올라 있다 be on the minutes. ◉ ~ 속기사 a stenographer to take an official note of the proceedings.

**의사봉**(議事棒) a gavel. ¶ ~을 두드리다 tap at 《the table》 with a gavel; bang the gavel.

**의사일정**(議事日程) the order of the day; an agenda; (the) floor schedules. ¶ 의제를 ~에서 제외하다 exclude an item from the agenda / ~에 오르다 be placed on the agenda; go on the calendar《미》/ 의제를 ~에 넣다 include an item in the agenda / ~을 변경하다 make a change in the agenda.

**의상**(衣裳) clothes; (a) dress (주로 여성의); garments; apparel; 《연극의》 costume; [집합적] clothing; wardrobe.

> 용법 **clothes** 상의·하의 등, 개개 의류의 집합체를 가리키는 말로 단수형으로는 쓰지 않음. **dress** ① 여성 원피스. ② 예복; 정장. **garment** 의상 한 벌을 가르키는 업자들의 점잔 뺀 말. **apparel** 의상을 격조 높게 부르는 말. **costume** 한 시대·국민을 상징하는 고유 의상 또는 무대 의상. **clothing** 의상을 집합적으로 말하는 총칭.

¶ 민속 ~ folk costume / ~을 입다「put on 〔wear〕 clothes; dress *oneself* in / 그녀는 ~이 많이 있다 She has a large wardrobe. *or* She has lots of dresses. ◉ ~담당자 《연극 따위의》 a costumer; a dresser. ~대여업자 a keeper of clothes for hire; a costumer. ~실 a dressmaker's (shop); 《고급의》 a couture house; a boutique; 〖연극〗 a wardrobe; a costume storeroom; a property room.

**의생**(醫生) a herb doctor; a herbalist.

**의서**(醫書) a medical book; a book on medicine.

**의석**(議席) a seat 《in an Assembly hall》; a Parliamentary seat; 《국회의》 the floor [총칭]. ¶ ~을 차지하다 《선거에서》 win seats / ~에 앉다〔~을 잃다〕 take 〔lose〕 *one's* seat / ~을 보유하다 hold a seat 《in the House》/ 그는 처음으로 국회의 ~을 차지했다 He won a seat in the National Assembly for the first time.

**의성**(擬聲) onomatopoeia; imitating sounds; (phono-)mimesis; sound=mimicry. ◉ ~법 onomatopoeia. ~어 an onomatopoeic 〔echoic〕 word; an onomatope.

**의수**(義手) an artificial 〔a false〕 arm 〔hand〕; an arm 〔a hand〕 prosthesis.

**의술**(醫術) medical 〔healing〕 arts; medical practice; the art of medicine. ¶ ~의 medical / ~은 인술이다 Medicine is a benevolent art.

**의식**(衣食) food and clothing 〔clothes〕; 《생계》 a livelihood; a living. ¶ ~지방(之方) means of livelihood 〔subsistence, living〕 / ~지우(之憂) worry over making a living; the problem of a livelihood / ~을 대주다 provide 《*a person*》 with food and clothes; feed and clothe 《*a person*》/ ~의 방도를 강구하다 find some means of living / ~이 족해야 예절을 안다 《속담》 Well-fed, well-bred. *or* Fine manners need a full stomach.
◉ ~주 food, clothing and shelter 〔abode〕; the necessities of life.

**의식**(意識) consciousness; awareness; *one's* senses. ~하다 be conscious 〔sensible〕 of; feel; be aware of.
¶ ~적(으로) conscious(ly) / ~의 흐름 the stream of consciousness / ~적인 범죄 a crime committed consciously / ~을 잃다 lose consciousness; lose *one's* senses; fall unconscious 〔senseless〕; (become) faint; swoon; pass out 《구어》/ ~을 회복하다 recover 〔regain〕 consciousness; come to *one's* senses 〔*oneself*〕/ ~이 몽롱하다 be in a semiconscious condition; have an indistinct consciousness / ~이 또렷하다 have a clear consciousness / ~을 회복시키다 bring 《a fainted person》 round / …을 ~하지 못하다 be unconscious 〔insensible〕 of... / 그는 남의 눈을 지나치게 ~한다 He is too conscious of the eye(s) of others. / 그는 죽을 때까지 ~이 뚜렷했다 He remained quite conscious to the last moment of his life. / 그는 언제 ~이 되돌아 왔느냐 When did he come to? / 점차로 그는 그녀의 존재를 ~하게 되었다 Gradually he became conscious of her presence. / 그는 죄 ~이 전혀 없었다 He had no sense of guilt. / 그녀는 ~불명인 채로 병원에 실려 왔다 She was taken to (the) hospital unconscious.
◉ ~개혁 the reform of consciousness. ~구조 *one's* way of thinking; a line of thinking. ~조사 《conduct》 an attitude survey. 권리~ sense of entitlement; awareness of *one's* rights: 각자의 권리 ~을 일깨우다 awaken everyone to his rights and entitlements. 귀속~ a sense of belonging.

**의식**(儀式) 《식전》 a ceremony; a ceremonial; 《예식》 formality; 《종교상의》 a rite; a ritual. ¶ ~을 거행하다 perform a ceremony. ◉ ~주의 formalism.

**의심**(疑心) ① 《의혹》 (a) doubt; 《의문》 question; 《불신》 mistrust; distrust.

～하다 doubt; distrust; mistrust. ¶ ～ 없다 be beyond doubt 〔question〕; be certain; there's no doubt about it / ～ 없는 undoubted; unquestionable / ～ 없이 undoubtedly; without 〔beyond〕 doubt / ～을 가지다〔품다〕 have 〔entertain, harbor〕 a doubt; have *one's* doubts / ～을 일으키다 raise 〔create〕 a doubt; make 《*a person*》 doubt / ～이 많다 be distrustful 〔incredulous, doubting〕 / ～이 생기다 begin to doubt / 보도의 사실여부를 ～하다 have doubt about the truth of the report / ～할 여지가 없다 leave no room for doubt; admit of no doubt; be past all doubt / ～할 여지가 있다 be open to doubt; leave room for doubt / 나는 내 눈을 ～했다 I could not believe my eyes.

② 《혐의》 suspicion. ～하다 suspect. ¶ ～을 받다〔사다〕 incur suspicion; fall under suspicion; be suspected 《of》 / ～을 일으키다 arouse 〔excite, breed〕 suspicion / ～을 풀다 clear *oneself* suspicion; dispel suspicion / 무식한 사람은 누구나 다 ～한다 The ignorant suspect everybody. / 나는 그를 사기꾼으로 ～했다 I suspected him to be a swindler. / ～ 받을 짓은 하지 마라 Avoid every cause of suspicion.

**의심스럽다**(疑心―) ① 《믿을 수 없다》 (be) doubtful; questionable; unreliable; uncertain; suspect. ¶ 올해 수출 목표액 달성을 의심스럽게 하다 place in doubt the attainment of the year's export goal 《of $50 billion》 / 그의 성공이 ～ I am doubtful of his success. / 그가 올 수 있을지 ～ I doubt he will be able to come. / 사실인지 ～ It is doubtful whether it is true. / 그를 믿기는 하나 역시 다소는 ～ I believe him with a grain of salt. / 그녀의 대답은 ～ Her answer is uncertain. / 그의 언동에는 의심스러운 데가 있다 There is something questionable in his speech and conduct.

② 《수상하다》 (be) suspicious; dubious; fishy 《구어》. ¶ 그의 동기가 의심스러웠다 I was suspicious of his motives. / 그는 의심스러운 눈초리로 나를 보았다 He cast a suspicious glance at me. / 서류는 다 제대로 갖춰져 있는데, 어딘지 좀 ～ All the papers are in order, but something smells fishy.

**의아**(疑訝) ～하다, ～스럽다 (be) dubious; suspicious; doubtful. ¶ ～스러운 듯이 dubiously; doubtingly; suspiciously; incredulously; wonderingly / ～스러운 얼굴을 하다 look dubious 〔suspicious〕; give a dubious look; wonder 《at》.

**의안**(義眼) an artificial 〔a false, a glass〕 eye. ¶ ～을 해 박고 있다 have a false eye.

**의안**(議案) a bill; a measure; an (item of) agenda. ¶ 정부 제출 ～ a Government bill 〔measure〕 / ～을 기초하다 draw up a bill / ～에 찬성하다 endorse 〔support〕 a bill / ～에 반대하다 oppose a bill / ～을 채택하다 adopt a bill / ～을 부결하다 reject 〔kill, vote down, vote against〕 a bill / ～을 수정하다 amend 〔revise〕 a bill / ～을 통과시키다 pass 〔approve, carry〕 a bill / ～을 철회하다 withdraw a bill / ～을 묵살하다 shelve 〔burke, quash〕 a bill / ～을 (의회에) 제출〔상정〕하다 present 〔introduce〕 a bill (to the Assembly); lay a bill (before the Congress).

**의약**(醫藥) 《약품》 (a) medicine; a medicinal drug; 《의술과 약품》 medical practice and pharmaceutical dispensing. ◉ ～분업 separation of dispensary from medical practice. ～품 pharmaceuticals; medicines; medical supplies.

**의업**(醫業) the medical profession. ¶ ～에 종사하다 practice medicine / 김씨 집안은 대대로 ～을 직업으로 삼아 왔다 The Kim's have been practicing medicine as a family profession.

**의역**(意譯) (a) free 〔liberal, broad〕 translation. ～하다 translate freely; give 〔make〕 a free translation. ¶ 그의 번역은 너무 ～에 치우쳤다는 비난이 있다 His translation is criticized of being too free.

**의연**(義捐) contribution; subscription; donation. ～하다 contribute 《money》 to 《a fund》; donate 《주로 미》; subscribe. ◉ ～금 a contribution; a subscription; a donation; alms: 수해 ～금 a relief fund for flood victims 〔sufferers〕 / ～금을 모집하다 invite subscriptions; raise a subscription for; pass round the hat (모자를 돌려서).

**의연**(毅然) ～하다 (be) dauntless; resolute; firm. ¶ ～한 태도 a dauntless 〔firm, resolute〕 attitude / ～히 resolutely; firmly; boldly; bravely; dauntlessly; with fortitude / ～한 자세를 보이다 display resolute attitude / ～히 역경을 견디다 heroically 〔stoically〕

endure adversity.

**의연**(依然) ～하다 be as it used to be; be as of old; be as ever; be as usual; be as remembered. ¶ 의연히 그대로 있다 remain unchanged; be just as it was / 섬유 산업은 의연히 침체 상태에 있다 The textile industry continues to stagnate.

**의열**(義烈) nobility of soul 〔spirit〕; heroism; gallantry. ～하다 (be) noble; heroic; gallant. ◉ ～지사(之士) a man of heroic and noble mind.

**의예과**(醫豫科) the premedical course; premed(ic) 《미구어》. ¶ ～ 학생 a premedical student; a premed(ic).

**의옥**(疑獄) a bribery case; a corruption scandal; 《미》 a graft case. ¶ 정치적 ～ 사건 a political scandal / ～(사건)에 연루되다 be involved in a bribery scandal.

**의외**(意外) ¶ ～의 《뜻밖의》 unexpected; unforeseen; unlooked-for; 《우연한》 accidental; 《놀라운》 surprising / ～로 unexpectedly; contrary to 〔beyond〕 *one's* expectation / ～의 일 a surprise / ～의 결과 an unexpected result / ～의 통지 a surprising report / ～로 생각하다 《놀라다》 be surprised 《at》; 《낙담하다》 be disappointed / ～로 어렵다 be more difficult than *one* may think / 그것은 ～의 일이다 That's a surprise to me. / 이 같은 뜨거운 환영을 받은 것은 ～이다 I am surprised that I should be accorded such a hearty welcome. / ～의 일로 실패했다 An unforeseen event checked my success. / 결과는 참으로 ～였다 The result turned out to be entirely beyond our expectation.

**의욕**(意慾) volition; (a) will; (a) desire; intention; motivation. ¶ ～적인 ambitious 《plan》 / ～이 강한 사람 a man with strong intention / …에 대한 ～이 대단하다 have a strong desire to *do;* be keen on *do*ing / 경영자측은 종업원들에게 일할 ～을 북돋아 주어야 한다 The management must 「motivate 〔provide motivation to〕 workers.

**의용**(義勇) loyalty and courage; heroism; bravery for a righteous cause. ◉ ～군 a volunteer army; a militia. ～병 a volunteer soldier; a militiaman.

**의용**(儀容) a mien; bearing; presence; manners. ¶ ～을 갖추다 tidy *oneself.*

**의원**(依願) 《in》 accordance with *one's* request. ◉ ～면직 dismissal 〔resignation〕 at *one's* request: ～ 면직되다 be relieved of *one's* post at *one's* own request.

**의원**(醫院) a doctor's 〔physician's〕 office; a (doctor's) surgery 《영》; a clinic (의사가 2인 이상의). ¶ 김 ～ Dr. Kim's office / 어머니는 안과 전문의로서 마포에서 ～을 하고 계시다 My mother, who is an eye specialist, is practicing in Mapo.

**의원**(醫員) a physician; a doctor (의사); a medical assistant (조수).

**의원**(議員) a member 《of an assembly》; an assemblyman; 《국회의원》 a member of the National Assembly; a House member; 《미》 a Member of Congress (생략 M.C.); 《하원의원》 《미》 a Congressman; a Representative; 《영》 a Member of Parliament (생략 M.P.); a Diet member; a Dietman (일본·덴마크); 《상원의원》 a Member of the Upper House; a Senator 《미》; a Lord 《영》; 《입법자》 a legislator; a lawmaker; a solon.
¶ 서울 출신 국회 ～ a member of the National Assembly for 〔from〕 Seoul; a Representative for Seoul / 서울시 ～ a member of the Seoul metropolitan assembly / 도〔시, 구〕～ a member of a provincial 〔municipal, ward〕 assembly / ～으로 당선되다 be elected a member 《of》 / ～이 되다 obtain a seat 《in Parliament》.
◉ ～석 the floor [총칭]. ～임기 the term of membership. ～입법 legislation at the instance of Assembly members. ～제출 법안 a (private) member's bill. ～총회 a general meeting of the Assembly members. ～회관 the Assembly Members' Office Building. 평(平)～ an ordinary 〔average〕 member; a backbencher.

**의원**(議院) the Assembly Chamber; the Parliament; the House. ◉ ～ 내각제 the parliamentary 〔cabinet〕 government system. ～제도 the parliamentary system.

**의의**(意義) (a) meaning; (a) sense; significance. ¶ ～ 깊은 말 a term of profound significance / ～(가) 있다 be significant 〔meaningful〕 / ～(가) 없다 be insignificant 〔meaningless, senseless〕 / ～ 있는 생활을 하다 live a meaningful life; lead a life worth living / ～없는 생활을 하다 live to no purpose / 1945년 8월 15일은 한국인에게 ～ 깊은 날이다 August 15, 1945 is a significant date for Koreans. / 그

의 한국 방문에는 하등의 정치적 ～가 없다 His visit to Korea has no political significance whatever.

**의인**(義人) 《의로운 사람》 a righteous man; 《의협적인 사람》 a public-spirited man; 《의에 죽는 사람》 a martyr.

**의인**(擬人) personification; impersonation. ～하다 personify; impersonate. ◉ ～법 personification; impersonation. ～화 personification: 동화에서는 동물들이 ～화되어 있다 Animals are personified in fairy tales.

**의자**(椅子) a chair. ¶ 긴～ a divan; a sofa; a couch; a settee; a bench / ～의 팔걸이〔등받이, 다리, 앉는 자리〕 the arm 〔back, leg, seat〕 of a chair / ～에 앉다 sit in 〔on〕 a chair; take a seat on a chair (★「의자에 앉다」의 전치사는 의자에 팔걸이가 있으면 보통 in이며, 팔걸이가 없으면 on을 씀). / ～를 늘어놓다 set chairs / ～를 앞으로 당기다 pull 〔draw〕 up a chair; drag *one's* chair forward / ～에서 일어서다 rise 〔get up〕 from a chair / ～에 앉기를 권하다 offer 《*a person*》 a chair. ◉ ～커버 a chair cover.

**의장**(衣欌) 《옷장》 a wardrobe.

**의장**(意匠) a (decorative) design. ¶ 공업～ an industrial design / 참신한 ～ a novel design / 공들여 ～을 한 elaborately designed / ～을 고안하다 think 〔work〕 out a design / ～을 만들다 draw 〔make〕 a design.
◉ ～가 a designer. ～권 a design right; the right(s) to a design. ～등록 registration of a design. ～료 a design fee. ～미술 the art of design.

**의장**(儀仗) ◉ ～대 the honor guards: ～대를 사열하다 inspect 〔review〕 the honor guards. ～병 an honor guard; a guard of honor.

**의장**(艤裝) rigging; fitting-out of a ship. ～하다 rig 《a ship》; fit 《a ship》 out 《for sea》. ◉ ～공 a rigger. ～공장 a fitting-out yard. ～품 fittings.

**의장**(議長) the president; the chairperson; the chair; the chairman; the chairwoman (★ chairman, chairwoman은 차별 용어로 기피되어 chairperson 또는 chair가 쓰임.); the Speaker (하원의); the President(상원의); 《호칭》 Chair! ¶ ～이 되다 be in 〔take〕 the chair / ～으로 뽑다 put 《*a person*》 in the chair / ～을 맡아보다 act 〔serve〕 as chairperson; preside over 〔at〕 《a meeting》; chair 《a meeting》 / ～에 취임하다 take over the presidency / …씨를 ～으로 하여 회의를 열다 open a meeting with Mr. ... in the chair.
◉ ～대리 a deputy chairperson. ～직권 the authority as chairperson.

**의장**(議場) an assembly hall; the chamber; 《의회》 《on》 the floor; the House. ¶ ～에서 소동을 일으키다 make a disturbance in the House / ～의 질서를 회복하다 《try to》 restore order in the House / ～은 대격론으로 수라장이 되었다 The floor was thrown into disorder with a great deal of discussion.

**의적**(義賊) a chivalrous robber; a benevolent picaroon; a Robin Hood.

**의전**(儀典) protocol. ＝의식(儀式).
◉ ～관 a master of ceremonies; a ceremonial officer. ～비서 a protocol secretary. ～실 the Office of Protocol.

**의절**(義絶) 《절연》 cutting off relationship; 《절교》 a breach (of friendship); 《자식과의》 disowning; disinheritance; 《부부간의》 legal separation of a married couple. ～하다 cut off relationship 《with》; break off 〔sever〕 friendly relations with; disown; renounce 《*one's* son》; separate legally from *one's* wife. ¶ ～당하다 《가족과》 be disowned; be cut off from *one's* family.

**의젓잖다** (be) undignified; flippant; unreliable; cheap; be lacking in dignity.

**의젓하다** (be) dignified; imposing; stately; commanding. ¶ 의젓이 with dignity; in a dignified manner; imposingly / 의젓하게 걷다 walk with slow and stately steps / 의젓하게 행동하다 behave with dignity; behave *oneself* respectably / 의젓한 어른이 되다 become a full-fledged adult.

**의정**(擬晶) 〖광물〗 mimetic crystals.

**의정**(議定) agreement by conference; decision by discussion. ～하다 confer and decide; confer and agree upon.
◉ ～서 a protocol.

**의정**(議政) parliamentarism; legislature; parliamentary politics 〔government〕. ¶ ～ 단상에 서게 되다 become 〔be elected〕 an Assemblyman.

**의제**(義弟) a sworn younger brother.

**의제**(擬制) 〖법〗 a (legal) fiction.
◉ ～자본 watered 〔fictitious〕 capital.

**의제**(議題) a subject 〔a topic, an item〕 for discussion; an agenda. ¶ ～로 삼다 place 〔put〕 《*a matter*》 on the agenda / ～로 오르다 come 〔be brought〕 up for discussion 〔debate〕; be placed on the agenda.

**의족**(義足) an artificial 〔a false, a wooden〕 leg; a prosthetic limb.

**의존**(依存) dependence; reliance. ～하다 depend 〔rely〕 《on》; be dependent 《on》. ¶ 상호～ interdependence / …에 ～하지 않고 independent of… / 아무에게 ～해서 살다 live in dependence on *a person* / 원모〔원면〕의 공급을 외국에 ～하지 않을 수 없다 We cannot help depending on foreign countries for the supply of raw wool 〔cotton〕. / 미국의 국방은 주로 미사일에 ～하고 있다 For its defense, the U.S. places its main reliance on missiles.
◉ ～도 dependence 《on》; reliance 《on》. ～명사 〖문법〗 an incomplete noun. ～증 《alcohol, drug》 dependence; morbid dependence 《on alcohol》.

**의중**(意中) *one's* inner thoughts 〔feelings, heart〕; *one's* mind 〔heart, intention〕. ¶ ～의 사람 the person *one* is thinking of; 《이성》 the man 〔girl〕 closest 〔nearest〕 to *one's* heart / ～을 떠보다 sound 《*a person's*》 views / ～을 밝히다 open *one's* heart 《to》; speak 〔lay bare, unfold〕 *one's* mind 《to》; unbosom *oneself* 《to》.

**의지**(依支) ① 《신뢰》 reliance; trust; 《의존》 dependence; 《도움》 help; support. ～하다 rely 〔depend, reckon, count〕 on; trust to; be dependent on; look 〔turn〕 to *a person* (for help). ¶ ～할 만한 친구 a dependable friend; a friend to turn to / ～할 곳 없는 helpless; forlorn / ～할 곳 없는 신세 *one's* helpless condition / ～할 곳 없는 사람들 the lonely and the helpless / ～가 되다 become a support; prove to be a support; be dependable 〔reliable〕; can be counted on (to help) / ～할 수 있다 be reliable; be dependable / 아들에게 ～하다 depend on *one's* son for support; lean on *one's* son / ～할 사람이 없다 have no one to turn 〔look〕 to (for help); have no one to depend on / 그는 친척을 ～하고 서울에 올라왔다 He came up to Seoul counting on his relative's help. / 형밖에 ～할 사람이 없다 I have no one to turn to but my older brother. / 곤란할 때 가장 ～할 수 있는 것은 친구다 Friends are the best resort in trouble. / 남에게 ～하지 마라 Self-reliance should be out first to principle.
② 《몸을 기댐》 leaning; reclining. ～하다 lean against 〔on, over〕; recline on 《a sofa》; rest against. ¶ 벽에 ～하여 앉다 sit with *one's* back against the wall / 지팡이에 ～하여 걷다 walk leaning on *one's* stick / 팔꿈치에 몸을 ～하다 lean on *one's* elbow / 그 소년은 내 어깨에 몸을 ～하고 잠들었다 The boy fell asleep on my shoulder.

**의지**(意志) (a) will; volition; 《의도》 an intention. ¶ 불굴의 ～ an indomitable 〔iron〕 will / ～가 강하다 be strong=willed; have a lot of will power; have a strong 〔an iron〕 will / ～가 약하다 have a weak will; be weak-willed / ～의 힘으로 그녀는 그 장애를 극복했다 She overcame the obstacle by the strength of will. / 그것은 그가 자기 ～로 결정한 것이다 He decided it 「of his own will 〔by himself〕. / 내 ～에 반하는 일 따위는 하고 싶지 않다 I don't like to do anything against my will. / 그는 자기 ～를 고수했다〔굽혔다〕 He stuck to 〔gave up〕 his will.
◉ ～력 will power; strength of will. ～박약 weakness of will: ～박약이다 have a weak will; be weak-willed.

**의지**(義肢) an artificial 〔a prosthetic〕 limb.

**의지가지없다** (be) helpless; forlorn; 《부모 없는》 (be) orphaned; [서술적] have no one to turn 〔look〕 to (for help); have no place to go. ¶ 의지가지없는 고아 a helpless orphan / 의지가지없는 사람들 the lonely and the helpless.

**의처증**(疑妻症) a morbid suspicion of *one's* wife's chastity; a groundless doubt of *one's* wife's faithfulness.

**의치**(義齒) an artificial 〔a false〕 tooth; 《틀니》 a set of false teeth; (full) dentures. ¶ ～를 해 박다 have a false tooth put in / ～를 끼우다〔빼다〕 put in 〔take out〕 *one's* false teeth / 그녀의 이는 모두 ～다 She wears 〔has〕 a full set of false teeth. ◉ ～술 dental prosthesis; prosthetics.

**의탁**(依託) 《의존·의뢰》 dependence; reliance; 《맡김》 trust; entrusting. ～하다 depend 〔rely〕 on; trust to; entrust *oneself* to 《*a person's* care》. ¶ 몹시 어려울 때 ～할 수 있는 사람 a person who is reliable 〔dependable〕 in a crisis / 딸에게 ～하다 depend on *one's* daughter for support / 자네 이외에는 ～할 사람이 아무도 없네 I have no one to 「look to 〔fall back on〕 but you. / 신에게 모든 것을 ～한다 God is my trust.

**의태**(擬態) 『생물』 (biological) mimicry; mimesis; simulation. ¶ ～를 하다 mimic. ◉ ～색 mimic coloring. ～어 a mimetic word.

**의표**(意表) ¶ ～를 찌르다 outwit 《*a person*》; frustrate 〔baffle〕 《*a person*》 in *his* design; baffle 《*a person's*》 expectations; take 《*a person*》 by surprise.

**의하다**(依—) ① 《…에 따르다》 depend 〔turn〕 on 《*something*》. ¶ 성공 여부는 앞으로의 자네 노력 여하에 의한다 Your success depends on 〔upon〕 how much effort you make from now on. / 결과는 그녀의 결정에 의해 정해진다 The outcome will ride on her decision.
② 《의거하다》 be based 〔founded, grounded〕 on 《*something*》. ⇨ 의하여. ¶ …에 의해 by 《the terms of Article 2 of the treaty》 / …에 의하면 according to 《rumors》; judging from 《reports》 / 그에 관해 아는 바에 의하면 from what I know of him / 미확인 런던발 보도에 의하면 according to an unconfirmed information originated in London / 이 추론은 잘못된 전제에 의한 것이다 This inference is based on false premises. / 신문에 의하면 국회는 8월에 휴회하리라고 한다 The newspapers have it that the National Assembly will recesses in August. / 미성년자에 대한 담배의 판매는 법률에 의해 금지되어 있다 The sales of cigarettes to minors is forbidden by law. / 한영(韓英) 양문장간에 상위(相違)가 있을 때에는 영문에 의한다 The English version will prevail if discrepancies exist between it and the Korean version.
③ 《수단으로 하다》 do 《anything》 by (means of); appeal to; have recourse to. ⇨ 의하여. ¶ …에 의하지 않고 without recourse to; disregarding…. / 정부는 힘에 의해 폭동을 진압하려 했다 The government resorted to force to suppress the riot.
④ 《원인이 되다》 be due to…; be caused by; be owing to 〔attributable to〕. ⇨ 의하여. ¶ 부주의에 ～ be due to carelessness / 나의 회복은 오직 그녀의 간호에 의한 것이다 My recovery is solely due to her care.

**의하여**(依—) 《…에 의거하여》 on the ground 〔strength〕 of; by 〔in〕 virtue of; in conformity to; 《…에 따라》 according to; in accordance 〔line〕 with; under; 《…에 응해서》 in compliance with; 《…의 이유로》 because of; by reason of; on account of; owing to; due to; 《…수단을 통해》 by; by dint 〔means〕 of; through; 《…의 결과로서》 in consequence of; as a result of.
¶ 귀명에 ～ by your order; in obedience 〔in accordance with, according to〕 your wishes 〔order, instructions〕 / 당국의 명에 ～ by order of the authorities / 법〔규칙〕에 ～ according 〔pursuant〕 to law 〔regulations〕 / 관례에 ～ in conformity with 〔according to〕 custom / 사정〔형편〕에 ～ according to circumstances / 이 조약에 ～ by 〔in〕 virtue of this treaty / 형법 제1조에 ～ under article 1 of the Criminal Code / 나라를 위해 진력한 공로에 ～ in appreciation 〔recognition〕 of *one's* services rendered for *one's* country / 충동에 ～ 움직이다 act on impulse / 포로는 각기 그 국적에 ～ 수용되었다 The prisoners of war were housed by nationality. / 사상은 언어에 ～ 표현된다 Thoughts are expressed 「by means of 〔through〕 words.

**의학**(醫學) medical science; medicine. ¶ ～적 medical / ～적으로 medically / 병원에서 ～ 실습을 하다 walk the hospital(s); intern 《at》 / ～을 연구하다 study medicine / 한국의 ～은 현저한 발전을 하였다 Korea has made remarkable progress in medical science. / 그는 ～ 연구차 도미했다 He went to the United States to study medicine there. / 이 병을 고친다는 것이 현재로서는 ～적으로 불가능하다 At present it is medically impossible to cure this disease.
◉ ～계 the medical world; medical circles: ～계의 업적 a great achievement in the field of medical science. ～박사 《사람》 a doctor of medicine; 《학위》 Doctor of Medicine (생략 M.D., D.M.). ～부 the medical department; a medical school 《미》. ～사 《사람》 a bachelor of medicine; 《학위》 Bachelor of Medicine (생략 B.M., M.B.). ～생〔도〕 a medical student. ～서 a medical book. ～실습생 an intern. ～자 a medical man 〔scientist〕. ～잡지 a medical journal.

**의향**(意向) an 〔*one's*〕 intention; an inclination; *one's* mind 〔idea〕.
¶ ～이 있다 be willing 《to *do*》; intend to 《*do*》; have an inclination to 《*do*》 / ～이 없다 have no intention of 《*doing*》 / ～을 비치다 disclose *one's* intention / ～을 묻다 ask 《*a person's*》

intention / ~을 타진하다 sound 《*a person*》 out on *his* intentions / ~을 확인하다 ascertain 《*a person's*》 intentions 〔mind〕 / …하고 싶은 ~을 보이다 signify 〔intimate〕 *one's* intention 《to *do*》 / 지금 결혼할 ~은 없다 I have no intention of getting married at this time.

**의협**(義俠) chivalry; heroism; gallantry. ¶ ~적인 heroic; chivalrous. ◉ ~심 a chivalrous spirit: ~심이 많다 be full of chivalry; be exceedingly chivalrous / ~심을 부리다 show chivalrous sentiments.

**의형**(義兄) a sworn elder brother.

**의형제**(義兄弟) *one's* sworn brothers. ¶ ~를 맺다 swear to be brothers 《with *a person*》.

**의혹**(疑惑) (a) suspicion; (a) doubt; (a) distrust. ¶ ~을 품다 entertain 〔have〕 doubts 《about》; harbor suspicion / 남의 ~을 일으키다〔사다〕 arouse 〔excite〕 another's suspicion / ~을 풀다 clear *one's* doubts 〔suspicions〕 / ~을 일소하다 dispel all doubts 〔suspicions〕 / ~의 눈으로 보다 look suspiciously 〔dubiously〕 《at》; look at 《*a person*》 with doubtful eyes; eye 《*a person*》 with (an eye of) suspicion / ~을 살 만한 것은 조금도 없었다 There was nothing in it to excite anyone's suspicions.

**의화학**(醫化學) medical chemistry.

**의회**(議會) an assembly; the National Assembly (한국의); the Diet (덴마크·스웨덴·일본의); Parliament (영국의); Congress (미국의) (★ Parliament, Congress에는 관사 불필요).

¶ 현~ the present session of Congress / 도〔시〕~ a provincial 〔municipal〕 assembly / 서울시 ~ the Seoul metropolitan assembly / 제84차 ~ the 84th session of Congress / ~를 해산하다 dissolve the Assembly / ~를 소집하다 convoke (a session of) the Assembly / 의안의 ~ 통과를 추진하다 push a bill through the House / ~는 내일 개회한다 Parliament meets tomorrow. / 시~가 개회 중이다 The municipal assembly is now in session.

◉ ~공작 lobbying. ~민주주의 parliamentary democracy. ~소집 convocation. ~ 운영 절차 parliamentary procedure. ~정치 parliamentary government; 《미》 Congressional government. ~제도 the parliamentary system. ~주의 parliamentarism.

**이**[1] ① 《치아》 a tooth (*pl.* teeth); 《속어》 grinders; choppers. ¶ 이가 좋다〔나쁘다〕 have good 〔bad〕 teeth; have a good 〔bad〕 set of teeth / 이가 나다 a tooth develops 〔comes through〕; [사람이 주어] cut a tooth; teethe / 이가 아프다 have (a) toothache / 이를 쑤시다 pick *one's* teeth / 이가 흔들리다 a tooth is loose / 이를 빼다 have 〔get〕 a tooth (pulled) out; pull out 〔take out, extract〕 a tooth / 이를 닦다 brush 〔clean〕 *one's* teeth / 이를 해 박다 have a false tooth put 〔set〕 in / 이를 악물다 clench 〔set〕 *one's* teeth / 이를 악물고 참다 bear 《*something*》 with clenched teeth / 이를 드러내고 싱긋 웃다 grin; smile a toothy smile / 분하여 이를 갈다 grind 〔gnash〕 *one's* teeth with vexation 〔chagrin, indignation〕 《at》 / 잇바디가 고르다〔고르지 않다〕 have a regular 〔an irregular〕 set of teeth / 너무 단 것을 먹으면 이가 썩는다 If you eat too many sweets, your teeth will decay. *or* Too much indulgence in sweets decays the teeth. / 아기의 이가 나오기 시작한다 The baby is cutting its teeth. / 이가 흔들려서 빼야겠다 I have a loose tooth, it will have to be pulled out. / 이 아이는 이를 갈기 시작했다 This child is just losing his baby teeth. / 이 없으면 잇몸으로 살지 《속담》 One can get along without something if necessary.

② 《톱의》 (a) tooth; 《톱니바퀴의》 a cog. ¶ 이 톱은 이가 많이 빠졌다 This saw has a lot of teeth missing.

③ 《그릇 등의》 ¶ 이가 빠지다 chip; be chipped / 이가 빠진 잔 a chipped cup / 그 접시는 이가 빠졌다 The plate has a chip in the edge.

**이**[2] 〖곤충〗 a louse (*pl.* lice). ¶ 이가 끓다 be infested with lice; be lousy / 이투성이 머리 a lousy head / (…의) 이를 없애다 delouse 《the bedding》; rid 《the bedding》 of lice / 이를 잡다 catch lice; hunt a louse / 이 잡듯이 뒤지다 comb 《*a place*》 for 《*a thing, a person*》; go through 《a suspect's apartment》 with a fine-tooth comb.

**이**[3] 《사람》 a person; a man; one. ¶ 읽는 이 the reader; the person reading / 지은이 the author; the writer; 《작곡가》 the composer / 다른 이 others; other people / 어떤 이 someone; some people / 김이라는 이 a man called Kim / 키 큰 이 a tall person / 잘생긴 이 a nice-looking one.

**이**[4] ① [관형사] this; these; present; current; the latter. ¶ 이 달 this month / 이 세상 this world; this life / 너의 이 책 this book of yours / 이 바보야 You, stupid! / 이 한 달 동안은 참 바빴다 I have been kept very busy during this month.

② [명사] this; it. ¶ 이 후 after this; in future / 이 외에 above this; besides / 이와는 반대로 contrary to this / 이는 곧 that is to say / 이에 불구하고 for all this / 이는 그의 무식을 드러낼 뿐이다 This only shows his ignorance. / 백만 원의 수표를 이에 동봉합니다 I enclose herewith a check for one million won. / 이로써 그의 진의를 짐작할 수 있다 His true intentions can be surmised from this.

**이**(二) two; 《제 2》 the second. ¶ 이삼일 two or three days; a couple of days / 이대 two generations; 《치세의》 two reigns / 이 삼은 육이다 Two times three makes six.

**이**(利) ① 《이문》 (a) profit; gain(s). ¶ 이가 많은 장사 a profitable 〔lucrative〕 business / 이가 적다〔박하다〕 give little profit; do not pay much; there is not much in it / 이가 남다 bring profits; yield a profit / 이를 보다 make a profit / 이를 탐하다 be covetous of gain / 이 장사는 이가 없다 This business does not pay. / 이는 적지만 많이 판다 The margin of profit is small, but they have a large turnover. / 그는 상당한 이를 보고 그것을 팔았다 He sold it at a considerable profit.

② 《유익》 benefit; an advantage; good. ¶ 자연〔지세〕의 이 a natural 〔geographical〕 advantage / 서로 이가 되다 be mutually advantageous / 이가 되다 benefit; do 《*a person*》 good / 지세의 이를 얻다 get the advantage of position / 그런 책을 읽어서 무슨 이가 있느냐 What is the good of reading such a book?

③ 《이자》 interest. ¶ 5푼 이의 공채, 5 percent bonds / 5푼 이가 붙다 bear 〔yield〕 5 percent interest / 6푼 이로 돈을 꾸다 borrow money at (the rate of) six percent interest.

**이**(里) ① 《거리의 단위》 a *ri* (0.4 km). ② 《행정 단위》 a *ri*; a village. ¶ 이장 a village headman.

**이**(浬) 《해리》 a nautical 〔sea〕 mile.

**이**(哩) 《마일》 a mile.

**이**(理) ① 《사리》 reason. ¶ 이에 닿지 않는 말을 하다 speak against all reason.

② 《원리》 a principle. ¶ 음양의 이 the principle of the negative and the positive.

**이가**(二價) 〖화학·생물〗 ¶ ~의 bivalent; divalent; diatomic. ◉ ~알코올 dihydric 〔diatomic〕 alcohol. ~원소 a dyad; a duad.

**이간**(離間) splitting up; alienation; estrangement. ¶ ~ 붙이다 alienate 《A from B》; estrange 《A and B》; part 《the lovers》; split up; separate 〔sever〕 《husband and wife》; set 《people》 at variance 〔odds〕; come between 《the two》 / ~당하다 get 〔be〕 alienated 《by *a person*》 / 그는 부부를 ~ 붙였다 He split the couple up. ◉ ~쟁이 a mischief-maker. ~질 = 이간. ~책 a plot to create dissension 《between》; mischief-making.

**이감하다**(移監—) transfer 《a convict》 to another prison.

**이 같은** such; of this kind 〔sort〕; like this; this sort 〔type〕 of; such... as this. ¶ ~ 일 a thing of this sort; such a thing (as this) / ~ 사정으로 under such circumstances as these / ~ 이유로 for such reasons (as mentioned).

**이같이** like this; in this way; so; thus; so much. ¶ ~ 많은 돈 such a big sum of money; so much money / ~ 추운 날은 처음이다 I have never seen such cold weather as this. / 그는 ~ 말했다 He spoke like this. / ~ 되리라고는 생각지 못했다 I didn't think things would come to this 〔to such a pass〕.

**이것** ① 《가까운 것》 this (*pl.* these); this one. ¶ ~으로 now; with this; here / ~뿐 no more; this much / ~으로써 보면 from what has been said; in view of these facts / ~은 싫다 I don't like this one. / ~은 안 된다 This will never do. / ~이 인생이다 Such is life. *or* This is the way life is. / ~ 참 Bless my soul! *or* Good gracious! ② 《부를 때》 ¶ ~ 좀 봐 I say. *or* Look here. / ~ 봐 어디 가나 Here 〔Say〕, where are you going?

**이것저것** this and 〔or〕 that; this one and the other; one thing or another. ¶ ~ 할 것 없이 with no further ado; without making a fuss; including everything; without discrimination / ~ 생각하면 after putting this and that together / ~ 생각하다 think of this and that; give consideration to various things / ~ 생각한 끝에 after thinking this way and that 《over *a* *matter*》/ ～ 해 보다 try one thing or another / ～ 생각하면 아무 결정도 지을 수 없다 If you keep worrying about this and that you will never make up your mind.

**이겨내다** 《어려움 등을》 tide 〔get〕 over 《difficulties》; weather 《a crisis》; overcome 〔surmount〕《obstacles》; resist 〔vanquish〕 《a temptation》. ¶ 병을 ～ get over *one's* disease / 자기를 ～ control 〔conquer〕 *oneself* / 유혹을 ～ overcome 〔get the better of 〕 a temptation; put the devil behind *one* / 여러 가지 국가적 시련과 모진 국제 환경을 ～ weather various national ordeals and hard international circumstances.

**이견**(異見) a different 〔dissenting, divergent〕 view 〔opinion〕; 《이의》 an objection; a protest. ¶ ～을 품은 사람 a dissident 〔dissentient〕 person / ～을 내세우다 hold a different 〔divergent〕 view; dissent 《from》; raise an objection 《to》; make a protest 《to》/ ～을 좁히다〔좁히지 못하다〕 narrow 〔fail to narrow〕 the differences 《between》.

**이겹실**(二—) a double-ply thread.

**이경**(二更) the 2nd watch of the night(= around 10 p.m.).

**이경**(耳鏡) 〖의학〗 an otoscope; an auriscope. ◉ ～검사 otoscopy.

**이경**(離京) departure from Seoul. ～하다 leave Seoul; leave the capital.

**이고** ① 《두 가지 이상의 사물》 and (also); or. ¶ 이것은 내 것～ 그것은 네 것이다 This is mine and that is yours. / 한 분은 의사～ 한 분은 변호사다 One is a doctor and the other is a lawyer. ② 《…이나, …이든》 any; …ever. ¶ 무엇～ whichever; anything / 정말～ 아니고 간에 whatever (it may be) true or not / 아무 연필～ 다 좋다 Any pencil will do. / 책～ 연필～ 가진 것을 다 가져오너라 Bring me whatever you have, book or pencil. / 무엇～ 하겠다 I'll do anything.

**이골나다** become used 〔accustomed〕 to; get inured to; grow experienced in; become skillful 〔good〕 at. ¶ 이골난 솜씨로 with a practiced hand; skillfully / 그는 교정에는 이골난 사람이다 He is an old hand at proofreading. *or* He is a veteran proofreader.

**이곳** this place; here. ¶ ～에(서) here; in this place / ～으로 here; hither; to this place / ～으로부터 from here; from this place / ～ 저곳에 here and there; in places; 《산재》 sporadically.

**이공**(理工) science and engineering 〔technology〕. ◉ ～과〔대학〕 a department 〔college〕 of science and technology: 나는 Y 대학교의 ～대학 1년생이다 I am a freshman in the college of science and technology at Y University.

**이과**(耳科) 〖의학〗 otology. ◉ ～의사 an otologist; an ear specialist.

**이과**(理科) 《학문》 science; 《학과》 the science course; 《학부》 the science department. ◉ ～대학 a college of science.

**이관**(移管) transfer of control 〔jurisdiction〕. ～하다 transfer the control 〔superintendence〕 of; place 《*a matter*》 under the authority 〔control〕 of another department. ¶ 국고에 ～하다 transfer to the national treasury.

**이교**(異敎) paganism; heathenism; heresy. ¶ ～의 heathen; pagan; heretical / ～를 전파하다 propagate heresy. ◉ ～도 a pagan; a heathen; a heretic.

**이구동성**(異口同聲) a unanimous voice; common consent. ¶ ～으로 with one voice; with one consent 〔accord〕; by common consent; unanimously; in unison / ～으로 찬성하다 agree unanimously.

**이국**(異國) an alien land; a strange land; a foreign country. ¶ ～적(인) exotic; alien; foreign / ～땅에서 죽다 die in a foreign land.
◉ ～사람 an alien; a foreigner. ～정서 an exotic atmosphere 〔mood〕; exoticism. ～취미 exoticism. ～풍 exoti(ci)sm; foreign customs.

**이군**(二軍) 〖야구〗 a farm 〔scrub〕 team. ◉ ～선수 a farmhand; 《미》 a scrub.

**이궁**(離宮) 《세자궁》 (the Palace of ) the Crown Prince; 《행궁》 a detached palace; a royal villa.

**이권**(利權) rights and interests; 《광산·철도 부설의》 concessions; 《기득권》 vested interests. ¶ ～에 급급한 사람 a concession hunter; a grafter 《미》/ ～을 얻다 acquire rights 〔concessions〕/ ～을 포기하다 renounce *one's* interests / ～을 좇다 hunt for concessions / 외국인에게 광산〔유전〕 개발의 ～을 부여하다 give foreigners mining 〔oil〕 concessions / 정치헌금은 큰 ～을 얻기 위한 목적으로 행해지는 경우가 많다 Political donations are often made in order to gain important concessions. ◉ ～양도〔획득〕 transfer 〔acquisition〕

of concessions. ～운동 graft(ing); hunting for a concession. ～추구 graft(ing); grabbing. ～회복 recovery of rights.

**이극**(二極) ¶ ～의 bipolar; double-pole / ～ 스위치 a double-pole switch.
◉ ～성(性) bipolarity. ～진공관 a diode. ～화(化) bipolarization.

**이글이글** 《불타는 모양》 (burning) lively 〔aglow〕; 《얼굴이》 deeply flushed. ～하다 (be) burning; glaring; glowing. ¶ 열정으로 ～ 불타는 눈 eyes burning with passion / 숯불이 ～ 피다 the charcoal burns lively / 그의 눈은 노여움으로 ～했다 His eyes glared with anger.

**이금**(泥金) gold dust; gold paint.

**이급**(二級) the second class. ¶ ～의 second-class〔-grade〕/ ～ 면허증 a second-class license.

**이기**(利己) selfishness; egoism; self=interest; self-centered. ¶ ～적(인) self=interested; selfish; egoistic / ～적이 아닌 unselfish; selfless; disinterested / ～적인 동기에서 from a selfish motive / ～적인 행동 a selfish action / ～적인 사고 방식 a selfish way of thinking. ◉ ～심 egoistic 〔selfish, egocentric, self-centered〕 mind. ～주의 egoism; selfishness: ～주의자 an egoist.

**이기**(利器) ① 《편리한 기구》 a convenience. ¶ 문명의 ～ a modern convenience; facilities of civilization. ② 《재능》 practical ability; useful talent. ③ 《연모·무기》 a sharp-edged tool; a sharp weapon.

**이기**(理氣) 〖철학〗 the "basic principles" and the "atmospheric force" of nature; the predisposition of nature (toward good or bad luck).

**이기다**[1] ① 《승리하다》 win; gain a victory 《over》; be 〔come off〕 victorious; get 〔have〕 the best of it; prevail; 《정복하다》 conquer; vanquish; triumph 《over》; 《쳐부수다》 beat; defeat.
¶ 싸움에 ～ win a war 〔battle〕; win victory in a war; win 〔gain〕 the day / 경주〔경기〕에 ～ win a race〔game〕/ 선거에 ～ win an election / 내리 ～ win 《three》 straight victories / 수월하게 ～ win an easy victory 《over》; walk over / 간신히 ～ barely win; win by a narrow margin / 이길 가망이 있다〔없다〕 have a 〔no〕 chance of victory / 투표에서 ～ beat 《*a person*》 at the poll / 적을 ～ defeat 〔beat〕 the enemy / 토론에 ～ beat 〔get the better of〕 《*a person*》 in argument / 재판〔소송〕에 ～ win a lawsuit / 결국 선은 악을 이긴다 Virtue will triumph over vice in the end. / 경기에서 Y대가 K대를 3대 1로 이겼다 In the game Y University beat 〔won〕 K University by three to one.

> 용법 **win** 경연·카드놀이·운동경기·전쟁 등에서 「이기다」「우승하다」「1위가 되다」란 뜻. 그 결과 「상을 타다」란 뜻도 포함. **beat** 「패배시키다」라는 뜻의 구어로 운동경기 등에서 상대방이나 그 팀을 최종적으로 패배시킨다는 뜻. **defeat** beat보다 딱딱한 말. 일시적으로 우위에 있다는 뜻이 포함되며 전쟁·운동경기·선거 등에서 적을 「패배시키다」란 뜻으로 쓰임. **prevail** defeat보다 격식차린 말로서 저항·토론 끝에 「우세하다」「이기다」란 뜻.

② 《극복하다》 overcome; surmount. ⇨ 이겨내다. ¶ 어려움을 ～ overcome 〔surmount〕 a difficulty / 유혹에 ～ overcome〔conquer, get the better of〕 temptation / 병에는 어느 누구도 이기지 못한다 No one can win against disease.

**이기다**[2] ① 《반죽하다》 knead 《dough》; work 《mortar》; mix up 〔together〕. ¶ 찰흙을 ～ work 〔knead〕 clay / 쌀가루를 이겨 경단을 만들다 knead rice-flour into dumplings. ② 《짓이기다》 beat 〔crush〕 to a pulp; mash; 《짓찧다》 mince; chop; pound into pieces. ¶ 감자를 ～ mash potatoes / 고기를 ～ mince meat.

**이기죽거리다** make invidious 〔insinuating, nagging〕 remarks.

**이까짓** this kind of; such a; so trifling 〔slight, little, small〕. ¶ ～ 것 such a trifle / ～ 돈 such a trifling sum of money / ～ 돈으로 무엇을 살 수 있나 What can I buy for only this much money? / ～ 일은 거저 먹기다 The job like this is nothing to me. / ～ 일로 놀랄 내가 아니다 I am not a man to be startled by such a trifle. / ～ 것하고 깔본 게 잘못이었다 I did wrong in making light of the matter.

**이깔나무** 〖식물〗 a kind of larch (tree).

**이끌다** 《인도하다》 guide; conduct; show 〔usher〕 in; 《지도하다》 guide; lead; 《인솔하다》 lead; head 《a party》; be at the head of; 《지휘하다》 command 《an army》. ¶ 군대를 이끌고 at the head of an army / 노구를 이끌고 in spite of *one's* old age / 아이의 손을 ～ lead a child by the hand / 나라를

번영의 길로 ~ steer *one's* country to prosperity / 사람을 바른 길로 ~ guide *a person's* steps in the path of righteousness / 후진을 ~ lead the younger generation / 그는 3만의 병력을 이끌고 전선으로 나아갔다 He went to the front with a force of 30,000 men under his command.

**이끌리다** 《인도되다》 be conducted to; be guided; be ushered into; 《지도받다》 be guided; be led; 《인솔되다》 be led; be commanded; 《감정 등에》 be driven by; be carried away by; succumb to 《curiosity》. ¶ 호기심에 이끌리어 under the impulse of curiosity; out of curiosity / 일시적 감정에 이끌리어 under the influence of a momentary passion / 이끌리어 가다 be led away; be taken along / 공명심에 ~ be driven by ambition / 호기심에 이끌리어 방안을 들여다 보다 peep into the room driven by curiosity.

**이끼**[1] 『식물』 moss; a lichen; a liverwort. ¶ ~가 끼다 moss grows 〔gathers〕; be moss-grown; be mossy / ~ 낀 나무 mossy trees / 구르는 돌에는 ~가 안 낀다 《속담》 A rolling stone gathers no moss.

**이끼**[2] Oh!; Oh my goodness!; Gracious me!; What a fright! ¶ ~나 = 이끼 / ~ 이건 또 뭐야 지진 아냐 There! What's that? An earthquake?

**이나** ① 《그러나》 but; (and) yet; however; 《한편》 while; 《…하기는 하나》 though; although. ¶ 분명히 그는 학자 ~ 상식이 없다 He is a learned scholar to be sure, but lacks common sense.

② 《정도》 as many 〔much, long, far〕 as; no less 〔fewer〕 than; nearly. ¶ 나이가 세 살~ 위다 be older 〔*a person's* senior〕 by three years / 이 책을 만 원~ 주고 샀다 I gave no less than 10,000 won for this book. / 그 일은 한 시간씩~ 걸리지는 않는다 It won't take so 〔as〕 much as an hour. / 그는 죽은 것~ 다름없었다 He was as good as dead.

③ 《선택》 or; any; either... or. ¶ 김군 ~ 내가 가야 한다 Either Mr. Kim or I must go. / 갓난아이는 조그만 것은 무엇 ~ 입에 넣는다 A baby puts any small object into its mouth. / 어느 것~ 좋다 I don't care which.

**이나마**[1] 《이것이나마》 although it is. ¶ ~ 없는 것보다 낫다 This is better than nothing.

**이나마**[2] 《우선 아쉬운 대로》 although; though 《it is》; even if; however. ¶ 헌 옷~ 입어야 하겠다 I'll just have to wear my old clothes. / 허름한 집~ 내 집을 하나 가졌으면 좋겠다 I wish I had a house of my own however humble it might be. / 한 달에 천 원~ 저축하고 싶다 I wish to save a minimum of a thousand won a month.

**이날** 《오늘》 this day; today; 《당일》 that day; the very 〔same〕 day; 《앞에 말한》 on the day in question; 《그때》 the occasion. ¶ 바로 ~ this very day / ~ 오후 this afternoon / ~ 이때 this time on this day / ~까지 till 〔until〕 today; up to 〔up until〕 this day / ~중으로 in the course of today; before the day is out; by the end of the day / 10년 전의 ~ ten years ago today; this day ten years ago / 내년〔작년〕~ this day coming 〔last〕 year / ~의 연사 the speaker of the day / ~에 이르기까지 그의 행방은 묘연하다 His whereabouts is unknown to this day. / ~ 날씨는 맑았다 The occasion was favored by fine weather.

**이날저날** this day and that day; from day to day; day after day. ~하다 put off from day to day. ¶ ~ 미루어 가다 keep putting 《*a matter*》 off day after day / ~ 살아가다 live from day to day.

**이남**(以南) south 《of》; South Korea. ¶ 38선 ~ south of the 38th parallel / 한강 ~ south of the Han River / 서울 ~ Seoul and southward; south of Seoul.

**이남박** a bowl with grooves running around the inside (used for washing rice); a rice-washing bowl.

**이내** ① 《바로》 at once; immediately; in an instant; soon 《after》; right away 《미》. ¶ 그는 나를 보자 ~ 달아났다 The moment he saw me he ran off. / 정거장에 닿거든 ~ 전화를 걸어라 Phone as soon as you get to the station. ② 《내처》 《not》 at all; ever since. ¶ 그가 집을 떠난 후 ~ 소식이 없다 I have had no news from him at all since he left home.

**이내**(以內) [형용사·부사적] inside of; inside the limit; within; less than; not more than; not exceeding (★ inside of는 within의 구어적 표현. 또 in이 within의 뜻으로 쓰일 때도 있음: The snow will be gone in 〔within〕 a week.). ¶ 1주일 ~ within a week; in less than a week / 10리 ~ not more than 10 *ri* away / 천 원 ~의 금액 a sum not exceeding 1,000 won / 자기 수입 ~에서 생활하다 live 〔keep〕 within *one's* income / 3일 ~에 책을 돌려 주겠다 You will have the book back within three days. / 당신 연설의 대강을 400 단어 ~로 쓰시오 You are required to write a synopsis 〔an outline〕 of your speech using less than 400 words.

**이냥** (in) this way; (in) the same way as this; as this is 〔was〕; still; with no change; with no let-up. ¶ ~ 두어두다 《현재대로》 leave 《*a thing*》 off (as it is); 《손 안 대고》 leave 《*a thing*》 intact / ~이라도 좋다 (1) 《복장·상태 따위》 I am all right as I am. (2) 《물건 따위》 You may leave them just as they are.

**이네(들)** these people.

**이년** You bitch !; You slut !

**이년**(二年) two years. ¶ ~생 a second-year〔-grade〕 pupil 〔student〕; 《대학의》 a sophomore 《미》 / ~생 식물 a biennial (plant).

**이념**(理念) an ideology; a doctrine; an idea. ¶ ~적 ideological / 국민에 대한 ~ 교육과 정신 교육 ideological and spiritual education of the people / ~이나 정치 체제의 차이를 초월하다 transcend differences in ideologies or political systems / 대학 교육의 ~ an idea of what university education ought to be / 간디는 죽을 때까지 비폭력 저항의 ~을 지켰다 Gandhi maintained the principle of nonviolent resistance until his death. ◉ ~형 a form 〔type〕 of reason 〔idea〕.

**이놈** this fellow 〔guy〕; this damn guy; this damn thing; it. ¶ ~아 You rascal ! *or* You villain 〔scoundrel〕! *or* You rat !

**이농**(離農) giving up farming. ~하다 give up 〔abandon〕 farming; leave the land. ◉ ~가 a farmer who has given up farming.

**이뇨**(利尿) urination; diuresis. ◉ ~곤란 difficulty in urination; difficult urination. ~작용 a diuretic effect: 수박은 ~ 작용을 한다고 한다 Watermelon is said to have a diuretic effect. ~제 a diuretic; a hydragog(ue).

**이니** or; and; and / or; what with... and. ¶ 공책~ 연필~ 잘 간수를 안 한다 do not take good care of notebooks and pencils and things like that / 과로니 영양 부족~ 하다 그는 병에 걸렸다 What with overwork and undernourishment, he was taken ill.

**이니(까)** as 〔since〕 it is; so; because (of). ¶ 환자가 자는 중~ 한 30분 기다릴 수 있겠습니까 As the patient is sleeping now, could you wait about 30 minutes ? / 저녁이 다 준비된 모양~ 식당으로 가십시다 As the dinner seems to be all prepared, let's go along to the dining room. / 토요일~ 오후엔 수업이 없을 게다 Today is Saturday so there probably won't be any classes in the afternoon.

**이니셔티브** initiative. ¶ ~를 잡다 take the initiative 《in》/ …에게서 ~를 빼앗다 take the initiative away from....

**이니셜** initials. ¶ ~로 서명하다 initial 《a document》.

**이닝** 〖야구〗 an inning; innings 《영》. ¶ 무득점 3~ three scoreless innings.

**이다**[1] 《머리 위로》 carry 〔put〕 on the head. ¶ 물동이를 머리에 ~ carry a water jar on *one's* head.

**이다**[2] 《지붕을》 cover; tile over (기와로); thatch (이엉으로); shingle (판자로); slate (슬레이트로). ¶ 짚으로 인 집 a straw-thatched cottage.

**이다**[3] ① 《지정하는 말》 be. ¶ A는 B~ A is B. / X~ It is X. / 악수는 오른 손으로 하는 것이 관례~ Using the right hand to shake hands is a convention. / 그는 보통의 인간~ He is the man in the street. ② 《…이 되다》 come; be. ¶ 이번 생일이 되면 스무 살~ I shall be twenty years old next birthday. ③ 《수량이》 number (수); weigh (무게); measure (도량); cover (면적). ¶ 키가 6 피트~ be six feet tall / 그것은 1미터~ It measures one meter.

**이다지** to this extent 〔degree〕; like this; thus; in this way; so (much). ¶ ~도 = 이다지 / ~ 부탁해도 for all my request / ~ 오래 so long / ~ 나쁠 줄은 몰랐다 I never figured it so bad. / 영어가 ~ 힘들어서야 어디 공부하겠나 With English as tough as all this, how can I ever learn it ! / 기차가 왜 ~ 늦담 Why is the train so damn late ?

**이단**(異端) ① 《유교에서》 all teaching that does not conform to Confucianism; 《기타 종교의》 heresy; heathenism; heterodoxy. ¶ ~을 배격하다 attack heresy / ~적 견해를 표명하다 express heretical views. ② 《사람》 a heretic; a heathen. ¶ ~시(視)하다 consider 《*a person*》 (to be) a heretic; regard 《a doctrine》 as heresy.

◉ ~사설(邪說) heresy and heterodoxy. ~자 = 이단 ②.

**이달** this month; instant (생략 inst.); the current 〔present〕 month. ¶ ~10일에 on the 10th instant 〔inst.〕; on the 10th of this month / ~ 그믐께 about the end of this month / ~중에 in the course of this month / ~ 월급 *one's* pay for this 〔the current〕 month / ~ 호 the current number 〔issue〕 / 그는 ~ 말까지는 돌아온다 He will be back by the end of this month.

**이대로** like this; as it is 〔stands〕; intact; as *one* is; as things now stand. ¶ ~ 가면 at this rate; as things are; judging from the present state of things / ~ 열흘만 비가 오면 if it keeps on raining at present rate for ten more days / 모임에 ~ 가도 좋으냐 May I go to the meeting as I am? / 가뭄이 ~ 오래 가면 큰 흉년이 들겠다 If the dry weather keeps on like this we will have a very bad year. / 책상 위에 책들을 ~ 두어라 Leave these books on the table just as they are. / ~ 가면 자넨 성공할 걸세 If things go at this rate, you will be successful.

**이데아** 〖철학〗 an idea; 《이상》 an ideal.

**이데올로기** ideology. ¶ ~의 ideological / ~의 분열〔대립〕 an ideological split 〔conflict〕 《between》.

**이도**(吏道) the duty of officials.
◉ ~쇄신 renovation of officialdom.

**이동**(以東) east 《of》. ¶ 서울 ~ east of Seoul; Seoul and eastward; from Seoul east.

**이동**(異同) (a) difference; (a) dissimilarity. ⇨ 차이(差異). ¶ 자본주의 경제와 사회주의 경제의 ~을 논하라 Explain the difference between capitalistic economy and socialistic economy.

**이동**(移動) (a) movement; locomotion; removal; (a) transfer; 《민족 따위의》 migration; drift. ~하다 move (from place to place); remove; travel; transfer; migrate. ¶ 보급품의 ~ the movement of supplies / 게르만 민족의 대~ the Germanic migration / 차를 ~시켜 주시오 Please move your car. / 유목민들은 목초를 찾아 끊임없이 ~했다 The nomads were constantly on the move looking for grass.
◉ ~경찰 the mobile 〔highway〕 police; railway police (열차내의); roving police. ~극단 an itinerant theatrical troupe. ~기중기 a traveling crane. ~노동자 a migratory laborer. ~도서관 a traveling 〔a mobile, an itinerant〕 library; a library on wheels; a bookmobile 《미》. ~무대 a movable 〔sliding〕 stage. ~병원 a hospital on wheels. ~성 고기압 〖기상〗 a migratory anticyclone. ~식 a movable 〔portable, mobile〕 type 〔style〕: ~식 ICBM a mobile ICBM. ~신고 a report of (*one's*) change of residence; a report of *one's* move. ~우체국 a mobile post office. ~율 turnover rate; 《조류·기류의》 drift. ~장치 a shifter. ~전람회 a mobile show 〔exhibition〕. ~전화 a mobile 〔cellular〕 phone 〔telephone〕. ~진료소 a traveling clinic. ~촬영 a moving shot.
인구~ the movement 〔drift〕 of population. 제2~ 통신 사업 the (nation's) second mobile phone project.

**이동**(異動) (a) change; shifting; reshuffle. ¶ ~을 단행하다 make changes 《in the staff》 / 이번 인사 ~에서 그는 부산 사무소로 전근되었다 In the recent personnel changes, he was transferred to the Pusan office. / 근간에 우리 회사에서는 사원의 대~이 있을 것으로 예상된다 A sweeping personnel change is expected 〔to be made〕 in our company one of these days.
◉ 내각~ the reshuffle of the Cabinet personnel. 인사~ changes of personnel; reshuffling of personnel; 《대이동》 a shake-up; a wholesale change 《of the membership》.

**이드거니** in rather large quantity 〔amount〕.

**이득**(利得) gains; profits; 《부동산 따위로부터의》 issue. ⇨ 이익. ¶ 부당 ~ 《행위》 profiteering; 《번 것》 an undue 〔excessive〕 profit / 부당 ~세 the excess profits tax / 부당 ~자 a profiteer / 부당 ~을 얻다 profiteer / ~에만 관심이 있는 interested only in gain / 서로 싸워봐야 누구의 ~도 되지 않는다 Nobody benefits from a quarrel.

**이든(지)** whether ... or; either ... or; or; 《무엇이나》 any; -ever. ¶ 그것이 사실~ 아니든지간에 no matter whether it is true or not / 연필~ 볼펜~ 너 좋을 대로 써라 You may write with either pencil or ball-point pen. / 어느 책~ 괜찮다 Any book will do.

**이듬-** 《다음》 next; the following; ensuing. ◉ 이듬해 the next 〔following〕 year; the year after.

**이듬** 《논밭의》 the second hoeing (of

the field); the second weeding; the second plowing. ～하다 give 《a field》 a second plowing.

**이등**(二等) 《2급》 the second class 〔grade, prize, place〕; 《2착》 the second. ¶ ～의 second; second-rate 〔=class〕 / ～으로 여행하다 travel second-class 〔cabin class 《배》〕 / ～으로 졸업하다 graduate second in *one's* class / 전람회에 ～으로 입선하다 take the second prize 〔place〕 at an exhibition; place second in the exhibition / 경주에서 ～이 되다 finish 〔come off〕 second in a race; get 〔win〕 second place in a race.

◉ ～국(國) a second-rate power; a nation of the second rank. ～병 〖육군·해병〗 a private; 〖해군〗 a seaman apprentice; an ordinary seaman; 〖공군〗 an airman. ～상 the second prize 〔award〕. ～선실 a second-class cabin. ～승객 a second-class passenger. ～차 a second-class car 〔carriage 《영》〕. ～차표 a second-class ticket. ～품 a second-grade〔-rate〕 article.

**이등변삼각형**(二等邊三角形) 〖수학〗 an isosceles 〔equilateral〕 triangle.

**이등분**(二等分) bisection. ～하다 divide 《*something*》 into two equal parts; cut 《*something*》 in half; 《선 따위를》 bisect. ◉ ～선 a bisector.

**이등친**(二等親) the second degree of kinship; a relative of the second degree 《to》.

**이디엄** (an) idiom.

**이따(가)** after a while; after a short time; a little later. ¶ 저녁을 좀 ～ 먹겠다 I will have dinner a little later. / ～ 전화를 하겠다 I'll call you later (on).

**이따금** from time to time; at times; sometimes; now and then; once in a while; at intervals; occasionally.

> (용법) **from time to time** 약간 문어적인 말로서 「어느 정도 정해진 간격을 두고」란 뜻. **sometimes** 「이따금」의 가장 일반적인 말. **now and then** 불규칙적으로 되풀이하여 일어나는 것으로, 강조하기 위해 every를 붙이는 경우도 있음. **once in a while** occasionally와 거의 같은 뜻으로 구어적인 표현. **at intervals** 「사이를 떼어서」란 뜻. **occasionally** 어쩌다가 일어나는 것을 나타내는 말.

¶ ～씩 every now and then; at intervals; from time to time / ～ 아들한테서 편지가 오다 receive occasional letters from *one's* son / 그는 ～ 찾아온다 He drops in sometimes 〔from time to time〕.

**이따위** a thing 〔person〕 of this sort; such a one; this kind 〔sort〕 《of》. ¶ ～ 책 this sort of book / ～ 일 a job of this kind / ～로 in this manner 〔way〕; like this / ～ 일은 다시는 안 하겠다 I shall do nothing of this sort again. / ～는 사서 무엇해 What do you buy such trash as this for?

**이때** 《at》 this time 〔juncture, moment, point〕. ¶ ～까지 until now; up to this day / 바로 ～(에) at this very moment / 이미 ～에는 by this time / 바로 ～ 한 남자가 방으로 들어왔다 At this point a man came into the room. / ～까지 이렇게 훌륭한 사람을 본 일이 없다 I have never seen such a great man. / ～에는 음악회가 이미 끝났었다 By this time the concert was already over.

**이똥** 《치아의》 impurities on the teeth; 《치석》 tartar.

**이라고** ¶ …이라고 자칭하다 give *oneself* out for…; represent *oneself* as…; pretend to be… / 이것을 무엇～ 하느냐 What do they call this? *or* What is this called? / 그까짓 것을 일～ 하고 있느냐 Why are you (wasting time) on that so called "job"? / 그 사람은 군인～했다 He said he was a serviceman.

**이라고는** 《…라고 하는 것은》 that (one) says it is; called; 《이렇다 할》 as for (the one that is called). ¶ 그 산에 꿩～ 한 마리도 없었다 There was not a single pheasant on that mountain. / 그를 악인～ 여기지 않는다 I don't think he is a rascal.

**이라니** ¶ 김군～ 어느 김군 말이냐 You said it was Mr. Kim but which Mr. Kim do you mean? / 네 소원～ 그럼 음악회에 가자 Since it's what you want to do, (then) let's go to the concert. / 악인～ 누구 말인가 Who(m) do you mean by a rascal?

**이라도** ¶ 어느 것～ 좋다 Either will do. / 내일～ 가볼까요 Let's go tomorrow, shall we? / 저는 어떤 명령～ 따르겠습니다 I shall obey whatever orders you give me.

**-이라면** ⇨ -라면.

**이라서** ¶ 오늘은 일요일～ 기차에 이렇게 사람이 많군요 The train is crowded because it is Sunday, I see.

**이라크** (the Republic of) Iraq; Irak. ¶ ～의 Iraqi. ◉ ～말 Iraqi. ～사람 an

Iraq**i**.

**이락**(利落) ¶ ～의 ex 「dividend 〔interest〕. ◉ ～채권 〖증권〗 an ex div. bond.

**이란** (the Islamic Republic of) Iran. ¶ ～의 Iranian. ◉ ～말 Iranian. ～사람 an Iranian.

**이란**《이라고 하는》 that is (called); 《이라고 하는 것은》 "as for (the one that is called)". ¶ 김～ 사람 a man called Kim / 인생～ 무엇인가 What is life? / 운명～ 참 야릇하다 Fate plays strange tricks. / 춘향～ 기생의 딸이 있었다 There was a *gisaeng's* daughter called Chunhyang.

**이란성**(二卵性) ¶ ～의 biovular. ◉ ～쌍생아 《one of》 fraternal 〔biovular〕 twins.

**이람** do you mean to say that it is?; really? ¶ 그런 놈도 사람～ Would you call the likes of him a human being?

**이랑**[1] 《밭두둑》 the ridge and the furrow of a field; 《고랑》 the furrow of a field. ¶ ～을 짓다 furrow 《a field》; make furrows; form ridges.

**이랑**[2] and; or; what with. ¶ 기쁨～ 부끄러움으로 with a mixture of joy and bashfulness / 이 일～ 저 일이랑 with one thing or another / 나는 슈퍼마켓에서 연필～ 공책 따위를 샀다 I bought pencils, notebooks, etc. at a supermarket.

**이래**(以來) (from) that time on; ever since; since.

> **용법** **since** 「과거의 어느 때부터 지금까지」란 뜻으로 보통 주절에는 현재완료형을 쓰고, since 절에는 과거형 또는 과거를 나타내는 어구를 씀. since는 다음 두 가지 구문을 취함. (a) Ten years have passed since I met him. (b) It is ten years since I met him. 단, 《미》에서는 종종 It has been ten years since...로 됨. 또 from a child, from olden times 등과 같이 (한 시점이 아니고) 어느 정도 폭을 가진 때를 나타내는 말로는 since 대신 from도 쓰임. 예: I have known him 「from 〔since〕 childhood. (나는 그를 어린 시절부터 알고 있다).

¶ 그때 ～ since then / 한국 해방 ～ since the liberation of Korea / 그가 미국에 간 ～ 소식을 들을 수 없다 I never hear from him any more since he went to America. / 그는 일 주일 전 자동차 사고를 당한 ～ 자리에 누워 있다 He was in an automobile accident a week ago and has been in bed since. / 이런 비는 10년 ～ 처음이다 It hasn't rained like this in ten years.

**이래** 《…이라 하다》 they say; I hear. ¶ 그녀의 이름은 제인～ 「I hear 〔They say〕 her name is Jane.

**이래도** ¶ ～ 나는 행복하다 「In my way 〔Such as I am〕, I'm a happy man.

**이래라저래라** ordering people about. ¶ 나한테 ～ 하지 마라 Stop bothering me about everything. / 그는 남의 일에 ～ 참견이 심하다 He is always poking his nose into other people's business and telling them what to do. / 나로서는 그녀에게 ～할 입장이 아니다 I am not in a position to tell her what to do.

**이래봬도** such as I am; humble as I am; whatever you may take me for; in spite of my appearance. ¶ ～ 나는 행복해요 Such as I am, I am happy. / ～ 나는 예술가야 I am an artist, humble as I am.

**이래서** This is why...; so. ¶ ～ 그는 신용할 수가 없다 This is why we can't trust him. / ～ 나는 가기 싫다고 했다 This is why I didn't want to go.

**이래저래** with this and that; for one thing or another. ¶ ～ 손해다 All these add to our loss. / ～ 바쁘다 I am busy with one thing or another.

**이랬다저랬다** this way and that way; changeable; fickle; unreliable. ～하다 be 「fickle 〔capricious, whimsical〕. ¶ ～하는 사람 a moody person; a 「capricious 〔whimsical〕 person / ～ 마음이 늘 변하다 be fickle as a cat's eye; be 「unstable 〔unpredictable, unreliable〕 / 그는 말을 ～한다 He says first one thing and then the opposite. / 너무 ～ 하지 말게 Don't be so fickle.

**이러** 《마소를 몰 때》 Get up!; Giddap!; Gee! (오른쪽으로); Haw! (왼쪽으로); 《빨리 몰 때》 Gee ho!; Gee-(h)up!

**이러구러** somehow or other; meanwhile; thus and thus. ¶ ～ 해가 저물었다 In the meantime the sun went down. / ～ 5년이 지났다 Five years have passed all too soon. *or* Meanwhile, five years went by.

**이러나저러나** at any rate; in any 「case 〔event〕; at all events; anyhow; anyway. ¶ ～ 해보는 게 좋다 At all events you had better try. / ～ 그건 어리석은 이야기다 Anyhow 〔At any rate〕, it is an idiotic story.

**이러니저러니** this and 〔or〕 that; one thing or another; for some reason or other. ¶ ～ 말할 것 없이 without saying this or that; without ado; without useless objections; with a good grace / ～ 말하다 say things; criticize; have a pert tongue; 《반대》 raise annoying objections 《to》; make complaints / 지금 와서 ～ 해야 소용없다 It is too late now to raise any objections. / 제발 내 일에 대해서 ～ 말 좀 말아주게 No meddling in my affairs, please! / 그는 ～ 핑계를 대고 일을 안 한다 He avoids the work on one excuse and another.

**이러다(가)** do 〔say, think〕 this way. ¶ 서둘러라, ～ 기차 놓칠라 Hurry up, or we will miss the train.

**이러루하다** 《it》 seem to be this way; be like this (one); be similar to this.

**이러저러하다, 이러이러하다** be so and so 〔such and such〕. ¶ 이러이러한 사람〔장소〕 such and such a person 〔place〕 / 이러저러한 이유로 for certain 〔such and such〕 reasons / 이러저러한 경우에는 이러이러하게 말하라고 가르쳐 주세요 Tell me to say so and so on such an occasion.

**이러쿵저러쿵** = 이러니저러니.

**이러하다** (be) such; be of this kind 〔of such a sort, like this〕. ¶ 이러한 일 a thing of this sort / 이러한 식으로 like this; in this way; thus / 사실인즉 ～ The fact is this.

**이럭저럭** somehow (or other); one way or another; 《어느덧》 before *one* knows; unnoticed; in no time. ¶ ～하는 동안에 in the meantime; meanwhile / ～ 해 나가다 get along somehow / ～ 살아가다 eke out a living; manage to keep the pot boiling / ～ 대학을 마치다 somehow or other manage to get through college / ～ 열 시가 되었다 It somehow got to be ten o'clock. / 그는 ～ 어떻게 해 냈다 He accomplished it in some way or another. / 지붕을 고치는 데 ～ 5십만 원 들었다 What with one thing and another it cost me five hundred thousand won to repair the roof. / 그가 미국에 간 지 ～10년이 되었다 Somehow ten years have passed since he went to America.

**이런[1]** 《이와 같은》 like this; such; this sort 〔kind〕 of. ¶ ～고로 for this reason / ～ 때에 at a time like this; at such a time / ～ 일 such a thing; a thing of this sort / ～즉 since it has come to this; such being the case / ～ 재미있는 책은 처음 읽었다 I have never read such an interesting book.

**이런[2]** [감탄사] Oh, dear!; Goodness!; Oh my!; What a surprise!; Indeed!; Well well!; My my! ¶ ～, 우산을 안 가지고 왔군 Oh dear, I forgot to bring my umbrella with me. / ～, 이게 뭐냐 Why! What is this?

**이렁저렁** = 이럭저럭.

**이렇게** in this way; like this; so; to that extent; that much. ¶ ～ 나쁜 so bad / ～ 비가 오는데도 for all this rain / ～ 부탁을 하는데도 for all my asking / ～ 말하고 with this; so saying / ～ 생각해 보면 considered 〔viewed〕 in this light / ～ 된 이상에는 since it has come to this; now that things have come to this pass / 일이 ～ 될 줄 누가 알았으랴 Who would expect things to come to this! / ～ 추운 날씨는 처음이다 I have never seen such cold weather as this. / ～ 재미있는 소설은 읽은 적이 없다 I have never read such an interesting story. / ～ 해라 Do it this way. / 나는 ～ 생각한다 This is 「what I think 〔how I feel〕 about it. / ～ 하면 문이 간단히 열린다 The door will open easily enough if you go about it like this. / ～ 말해서 뭣하지만, 그는 영어를 거의 모른다 I hesitate to speak out, but he has very little knowledge of English. / 그가 ～까지 어리석을 줄은 몰랐다 I didn't think him so stupid.

**이렇다** be this way; be like this; be as follows. ¶ ～ 할 (만한) to speak of; worth mentioning / ～ 할 이유도 없이 without any particular reason; for no good 〔special〕 reason; with nothing particular in mind / ～ 할 만한 영화 movies worth 「mentioning 〔to speak of〕; movies especially interesting / 그의 이야기는 대강 ～ His story runs somewhat like this. / 대통령이 발표한 성명은 ～ The statement issued by the President is as follows. / 여자란 ～ Women are like this. *or* That's the way women are. / 나는 ～ 할 취미도 없다 I have no particular hobby to speak of. / 어찌 사람이 이렇담 How can he do me this way! / 세상물정을 모르는 사람들은 늘 이렇단 말이야 It's always the way with those who know nothing of the world, you see.

**이렇다저렇다** 《say》 this or that. ¶ ∼ 말하다 say things; criticize; raise objections; make complaints / ∼ 말(이) 없이 without saying a word; with no further ado; without raising 〔voicing〕 any objections; uncritically / 그는 ∼ 남한테서 말을 들을 일이 없다 He is not open to criticism. / 지금 와서 ∼ 말한댓자 소용이 없다 It is too late now to make a fuss about it. / ∼ 말하지 말고 하라는 대로 해라 Stop fussing and do what you are told. / 이 일에 내가 ∼할 자격이 없다 I have no voice in this matter.

**이렇든저렇든** whether it is this or that; at any rate; in any case; in any event; anyhow; anyway.

**이렇듯** like this. ¶ ∼ 많은 so many 〔much〕 / ∼ 즐겁기는 난생 처음이다 I have never had such a pleasant time in life.

**이레** 《일곱 날》 seven days; 《초이레》 the seventh day (of the month); 《이레째》 the seventh day.

**이렛날** the seventh day; the seventh of the month.

**이력**(履歷) *one's* career; *one's* personal 〔life〕 history; *one's* past record; *one's* antecedents; 《학력·소양》 *one's* background. ¶ ∼이 좋다〔나쁘다〕 have an honorable 〔a poor〕 record of service / ∼에 오점을 남기다 leave a spot on *one's* record / ∼이 나다 become experienced; get used 〔accustomed〕 《to》 / 그는 이 방면에 많은 ∼을 쌓은 사람이다 He is rich in experience in this line. / 그는 어떤 ∼을 가진 사람이냐 What is his ｢background 〔past record〕? *or* What is his career?
◉ ∼서 a 〔*one's*〕 personal 〔life〕 history; a curriculum vitae [váiti:] (*pl.* curricula vitae) (생략 CV); 《미》 a résumé [rézuměi]: 그는 그 회사에 ∼서를 냈다 He sent his résumé to the company.

**이례**(異例) an exceptional 〔a singular〕 case; 《전례 없던》 an unprecedented case. ¶ ∼적인 rare; exceptional; singular; unprecedented; unusual / ∼적인 대우를 받다 enjoy exceptionally good treatment / 그의 승진은 ∼적이다 His promotion is exceptional.

**이로고** 《감탄·놀람의 뜻》 ¶ 못난 놈∼ How foolish you are! / 참 귀여운 아이∼ Oh, what a cute baby!

**이로다** ＝ 이다[3].

**이로되** it is ... but; though it is. ¶ 이 집은 남향이로되 약간 동으로 치우쳐 있다 This house faces south, but it is slightly tilted toward the east. / 회장은 회장이로되 실권은 없다 It is true that he is the chairman, but he has no power.

**이로부터** ① 《시간》 from now on; from this time forth; in (the) future; hereafter; henceforth. ¶ ∼ 더 조심해라 Be more careful from now on. ② 《이유·결과》 from this cause; hence; as a result of this. ¶ ∼ 여러 문제가 일어났다 Out of this many questions arose.

**이로써** now; here; with this. ¶ ∼ 판단하건대 judging from this / ∼ 내 자신이 어리석었다는 것을 깨달았다 Now I realized how foolish I was. / ∼ 내 인생은 끝장이다 This will be the end of me. *or* This will ruin me.

**이론**(異論) 《다른》 a divergent view; a different opinion; 《반대의》 an opposite view 〔opinion〕; an objection; a protest; a dissent. ¶ ∼ 없이 unanimously / ∼을 제기하다 object 《to》; interpose 〔raise〕 an objection; voice a protest / ∼이 있습니까 Have you any objection to it? / 이 일에는 ∼이 있을 리 없다 There can be no two opinions on this matter.

**이론**(理論) (a) theory. ¶ ∼적 연구 a theoretical study / ∼과 실천 theory and practice / ∼상 theoretically; in theory / ∼상의 theoretical / ∼을 세우다 theorize; advance a theory / ∼을 실천에 옮기다 put *one's* theory into practice; reduce a theory to practice / 되지도 않은 ∼을 늘어놓다 chop logic / 모두가 ∼으로서는 대단히 좋다 All is very well in theory. / ∼과 실제는 반드시 일치하지 않는다 Theory and practice do not always agree 〔go hand in hand〕. / 해군 장교들은 항해의 ∼과 실무를 이해해야 한다 Naval officers must understand both the theory and practice of navigation.
◉ ∼가 a theorist; a theoretician. ∼ 경제학〔물리학〕 theoretical economics 〔physics〕. ∼과학 theoretical science: ∼ 과학자 a theoretical scientist. ∼수학 abstract mathematics. ∼체계 a body of theory 《about energy》. ∼투쟁 《engage in》 a theoretical dispute; an ideological quarrel.

**이롭다**(利―) (be) profitable; lucrative; beneficial; salutary; 《유리하다》 (be) advantageous; favorable; 《좋다》 (be) good; 《교훈적이다》 (be) instructive; 《도움이 되다》 (be) helpful. ¶ 이로운 조건 advantageous terms / 이로운 사업 a profitable business / 소년들에게 이로운 책 a book good for youngsters / 이롭지 않다 be bad 《for》; do 《*a person*》 harm; be harmful 〔injurious〕 《to》; be against 《*a person's*》 interest; be disadvantageous 〔unfavorable〕 《to》 / 그의 충고를 좇는 것이 ~ It would be expedient to follow his advice. / 햇빛은 건강에 ~ Sunshine is beneficial to health. / 모든 일이 그에게 이로워졌다 Things turned out favorably for him.

**이루**(二壘) 〖야구〗 second base; second; the middle sack 〔cushion〕 《미》. ¶ ~를 지키다 act as second baseman.
◉ ~수 a second baseman 〔baser, sacker〕. ~심 the umpire at second base. ~타 a two-base hit; a two-bagger〔-baser, -sacker〕; a double (hit): 라이트 쪽에 ~타를 치다 hit a two-bagger 〔bang out a double〕 to right; double to right (field) / 우중간으로 빠지는 맹렬한 ~타를 날리다 send a mighty double between center and right.

**이루**(耳漏) discharge from the ear; 〖의학〗 otorrhea.

**이루** by any means; 《cannot》 possibly; utterly. ¶ ~ 말할 수 없는 indescribable; unspeakable; beyond description / ~ 헤아릴 수 없는 numberless; countless; innumerable / ~ 헤아릴 수 없다 be simply too many to count / ~ 형용할 수 없다 can hardly describe it / 그 참상은 ~ 말할 수 없었다 The disaster was beyond all description.

**이루다** ① 《성취하다》 accomplish; achieve; effect; attain; 《완성하다》 complete; 《실현하다》 realize; 《완료하다》 finish; conclude. ¶ 이루지 못할 unattainable; unrealizable / 이루지 못할 소망 an unattainable 〔impossible〕 desire / 이루지 못할 사랑 a hopeless love / 목적을 ~ achieve 〔gain〕 *one's* end; realize *one's* aim; accomplish 〔achieve〕 *one's* purpose / 뜻을 ~ effect *one's* purpose; have *one's* will; realize *one's* desire / 소원을 ~ have *one's* desire 〔wish〕 fulfilled; 《대망을》 attain *one's* ambition; realize *one's* wishes / 대사업을 ~ achieve a great work / 일가를 ~ make *oneself* master 《of an art》; make a name for *oneself;* establish *oneself* as an authority.
② 《형성하다》 constitute; form; make. ¶ 사회를〔촌락을〕 ~ form a society 〔community〕 / 한 가정을 ~ make 〔establish〕 a home; get married and settle down / 기암(奇岩)과 노송(老松)이 그곳에 절경을 이루었다 Curious rock formations and old pines have made the scenery there a grand sight.

**이루어지다** ① 《성취되다》 get 〔be〕 accomplished 〔achieved, realized, attained, effected〕. ¶ 뜻이 ~ *one's* purpose is realized / 나의 오랜 소망이 이제야 이루어졌다 My long-cherished desire is at last accomplished. ② 《형성되다》 be formed 〔made up, composed of, constituted〕. ¶ 이 대학교는 10개 단과 대학으로 이루어져 있다 This university is composed of ten colleges.

**이룩하다** ① 《이루어 내다》 accomplish; achieve; perform; carry 〔get〕 through; carry out; effect 《a reform》; make good; succeed in. ¶ 사업을 ~ go through with an undertaking / 큰일을 ~ achieve a great thing; perform a great deed / 나는 그가 그 큰 일을 이룩해 낼 것이라고 믿는다 I believe (that) he will carry the great work through. ② 《새로 세우다》 found; establish; make. ¶ 나라를 ~ found 〔establish〕 a new state / 가정을 ~ make 〔establish〕 a home; get married and settle down / 그는 젊어서 무일푼으로 큰 부를 이룩했다 He made 〔built up〕 a big fortune out of nothing while he was young.

**이류**(二流) ¶ ~의 second-class〔-rate〕; 《시시한》 minor; inferior. ◉ ~시인 a minor poet. ~인물 a second-rater. ~작가 a second-rate 〔minor〕 writer. ~호텔 a second-class〔-rate〕 hotel.

**이륙**(離陸) a takeoff; taking 〔flying〕 off; 《헬리콥터의》 whirl-off. ~하다 take 〔hop〕 off; take the air; leave the ground. ¶ ~ 때의 소음 takeoff noise. ◉ ~시간〔거리〕 takeoff time 〔distance〕. ~지점 a takeoff point. ~활주 a takeoff run 〔roll〕.

**이륜**(二輪) 《차바퀴》 two wheels; 《꽃송이》 two flowers. ◉ ~차 a two-wheeled vehicle; a two-wheeler; a bicycle.

**이르다**[1] 《때가》 (be) early; premature. ¶ 이른 아침〔봄〕 early morning 〔spring〕 / 이른 꽃 early flowers / 조금 이르게 떠나다 start a little earlier / 아직 시간이 ~ It is still early. / 이를수록

좋다 The earlier, the better. / 네가 결혼하기는 아직 ~ You are too young to get married. / 금년은 쌀수확이 ~ The rice crop is early this year. / 네가 독립하기엔 아직 ~ You are 「too young 〔not old enough〕 to stand alone.

**이르다**[2] ① 《알리다》 tell; inform; report. ¶ 내가 저녁 식사에 늦겠다고 어머니께 일러라 Tell mother that I will be late for dinner.
② 《타이르다》 tell; admonish; warn; explain; teach. ¶ 알아듣게 일러 주다 explain 《*a matter*》 to make it clear / 학생들에게 흡연하지 말도록 ~ admonish 〔tell, warn〕 the students against smoking / 사리 분별이 없는 아이에겐 아무리 일러줘도 헛수고다 It is useless to reason with children who are too young to judge anything.
③ 《고자질하다》 tell 〔carry〕 tales 《about, against, upon *a person*》; tell 〔squeal〕 on 《*a person*》; tattle; 《속어》 peach on 《*a person*》. ¶ 일러바치는 사람 a tale=teller; a tale-bearer / 아버지한테 이르겠다 I'm going to tell father on you.
④ 《말하다·부르다》 say; call. ¶ 이것이 소위 만유인력의 법칙이라고 이르는 것이다 This is what is called the law of gravitation. / 눈이 많이오는 해는 풍년이 든다고 옛날부터 일러지고 있다 It is proverbially said heavy snow foretells a bumper crop.

**이르다**[3] ① 《도달·도착하다》 arrive 《at, in》; reach; gain; get to. ¶ 이르는 곳마다 everywhere; wherever *one* goes; all over; throughout 《the country》; at every turn; anywhere you go / 처음부터 마지막에 이르기까지 from beginning to end; from start to finish / 행복에 이르는 길 a road to happiness / 결론에 ~ come to 〔reach, arrive at〕 a conclusion / (산)꼭대기에 ~ attain 〔reach, gain〕 the summit / 목적지에 ~ reach 〔arrive at〕 *one's* destination; get to *one's* journey's end / 성년에 ~ arrive at manhood.
② 《수량이》 reach; amount to; come (up) to; mount 〔run〕 up to. ¶ 길이 3피트에 ~ attain 〔reach〕 a length of three feet / 천문학적 숫자에 ~ run into astronomical figures / 나이 80에 ~ attain 〔reach〕 the age of 80.
③ 《통하다》 lead 《to》. ¶ 서울서 경주를 거쳐 부산에 이르는 철도 a railway leading from Seoul to Pusan by way of Kyŏngju / 이 길로 가면 강에 이른다 This road leads to the river.
④ 《결과》 end up; result 《in》; come to (the state of); get to (the point where); be brought to (the brink of). ¶ 믿기에 ~ come to believe / 자살하기에 ~ go so far as to commit suicide / 결국 그는 그녀와 결혼하기에 이르렀다 He finally ended up by marrying her. / 일이 여기에 이르리라고 누가 꿈엔들 생각했으랴 Who would have dreamed that things would come to this?
⑤ 《미치다》 come 《to》; get 《to》; extend 《to》; reach; cover. ¶ 오늘에 이르기까지 until now; to this day; up to the present time; even today / 1월에서 3월에 이르기까지 from January to March / 상세한 점에 이르기까지 설명하다 explain right down to the most minute details / 그 산맥은 국경에까지 이른다 The mountain range runs all the way to the frontier. / 위로는 사장에서 아래로는 사환에 이르기까지 전회사가 (한마음으로) 열심히 일한다 The whole company works hard from the president at the top to the office boy at the bottom.

**이르집다** 《껍질을》 pull off; peel; pick; 《말썽을》 make up; fabricate; cook up; fake up; frame up. ¶ 사건을 ~ frame up an affair; make up an incident.

**이른바** what is called; what you 〔they〕 call; as it is called; [경멸적] the so=called. ¶ ~ 멘델의 법칙 what is called the Mendel's law / 이러한 남자가 ~ 신사다 Such a man is what 「you 〔people〕 call a gentleman. / 이것이 ~ 10·26 사건이다 This is what was called the October 26 Incident.

**이를테면** ① 《말하자면》 as *one* might say; so to speak; as it were; in a way; in *one's* own way. ¶ 그는 ~ 산부처다 He is, so to speak, a living Buddha. / 그도 ~ 정치가다 He, too, is something of a politician (in his own way). ② 《예컨대》 for instance; for example; let us say; say; take (for instance). ¶ ~ 사자나 범 같은 맹수 beasts of prey, such as the lion and the tiger.

**이름** ① [일반적] a name; 《생략않은 정식의》 *one's* full name; 《성》 *one's* surname; *one's* family name; 《성에 대한》 *one's* personal 〔given, first〕 name; 《명칭》 a name; 《직함·표제》 a title.
¶ 그 ~대로, 그 ~과 같이 as the name implies; true to *one's* name / ~뿐인, ~만의 《a relative》 only in name;

nominal / ~이 A라는 목수 a carpenter by 〔of〕 the name of A; a carpenter called 〔named〕 A; a carpenter, A by name / ~을 짓다 give a name《to》; christen; name / ~을 대다 tell 〔give, mention〕 *one's* name / ~을 속이다 give a wrong name; falsify *one's* identity; assume a false name / 아무의 ~을 부르다 call *a person* by name / ~을 묻다 ask《*a person's*》 name / ~을 바꾸다〔고치다〕 change *one's* name / ~을 빼다 take *one's* name off《the list》/ 예수의 ~으로 기도하다 pray in Jesus' name / 아들의 ~으로 저금하다 deposit money in the name of *one's* son / 아버지의 ~으로 장사하다 do business under the name of *one's* father / 이 꽃의 ~이 무엇입니까 What is the name of this flower? *or* What do you call this flower? / 당신 ~은 무엇이오《사무적으로》 Your name, please. *or* What is your name? (★ My name is Kim.이라고 대답함. Who are you?란 물음에 대해서는 I am Kim. 따위로 대답) / 그런 ~의 사람은 모른다 I do not know anyone of that name. / 그 사람은 ~만 안다 I know him only by name. / 그는 ~만의 교수다 He is a professor in name only. / 그 별은 발견자의 ~을 따 지었다 The star is named after its discoverer. (★「그의 이름은 '창진'이라고 부른다」를 His name is called Ch'angjin.이라고 해서는 안 됨—His name is Ch'angjin. 또는 He is called Ch'angjin.이라고 해야 함. call과 name을 함께 쓰는 경우는 He called my name.「그는 나의 이름을 불렀다」나 They called him names.「그들은 그에게 욕을 했다」고 하는 경우뿐임).

> **용법** 미국이나 영국 사람의 이름은 John Fitzgerald Kennedy처럼 대개 세 부분으로 구성되어 있다. 첫째 이름은 first name, 또는 Christian name (세례명), given name (주어진 이름)이며, 가운데는 middle name이라 하며 initial로만 표기될 때가 많다. 마지막은 last name 또는 family name (가족 이름), surname (성)이라고 한다.

② 《명성》 a (famous) name; fame; (a) reputation; renown. ¶ ~ 있는 사람 (a) man with a name《in the world》; a famous 〔noted, renowned, reputed, well-known〕 person / ~ 없는 사람 a man of no name; a nameless 〔an unknown〕 person; an obscure man / ~이 알려지다 be well-known 〔noted, famous, popular〕 / ~을 후세에〔역사에〕 남기다 leave *one's* name「behind 〔in history〕 / ~을 내다〔날리다〕 hold *one's* name up (for the world to see); make 〔win〕 a name; distinguish *oneself;* make *oneself* famous / 부모의 ~을 더럽히다 stain *one's* family name; disgrace *one's* parents / ~을 팔다 trade on *one's* fame; take advantage of *one's* popularity; prostitute *one's* reputation / 그 작품으로 그는 ~이 났다 With that work his name was made. / 사람은 죽어도 ~은 남는다 A man lives but for one generation; his name for many.
③ 《명목》 cause; 《구실》 a pretext; a plea. ¶ 종교라는 ~ 아래 under the color 〔mask〕 of religion / 자선이라는 ~으로 in the cloak of charity / 국민의 ~으로 in the name of a nation / 대통령 ~으로 in the name of the President.

**이름나다** become famous 〔renowned〕《for》; win 〔gain〕 fame 〔renown〕《for》; win a reputation. ¶ 이름난 famous; noted; celebrated; well-known; renowned; 《나쁜 뜻으로》 notorious; infamous / 정계에서 이름난 사람 a celebrity in the political world / 이 고장은 피서지로 이름난 곳이다 This district「has a name 〔is famous〕 as a summer resort.

**이름씨** 〖문법〗 a noun.

**이리**[1] 《물고기의》 soft roe; milt《of fish》.

**이리**[2] 〖동물〗 a wolf (*pl.* wolves). ¶ ~떼 a pack of wolves / ~ 사냥개 a wolfhound / ~ 사냥꾼 a wolfer.

**이리**[3] ① 《이렇게》 in this way; like this. ② 《이곳으로》 this way; this direction; here; to this place. ¶ ~ 오십시오 This way, please. *or* Please come this way. / ~ 앉아라 Sit here.

**이리듐** 〖화학〗 iridium (기호 Ir).
◉ ~프로젝트 〖통신〗 Iridium Project.

**이리이리** so and so; such and such. ¶ ~ 하라고 말하다 tell《*a person*》 to do such and such.

**이리자리** 〖천문〗 the Wolf; Lupus.

**이리저리** 《이곳저곳》 this way and that; here and there; all about; 《이렇게 저렇게》 like this way and that; one thing or another. ¶ ~ 돌아다니다 wander 〔roam, ramble〕 about; loaf around / 책을 ~ 찾다 look high and low for a book / ~ 둘러보다 look this way and that; stare round; look curiously at / 배는 ~ 표류하고 있었다 The ship drifted hither and thither.

**이리하다** do like this.

**이마** ① 《사람의》 the forehead; the brow. ¶ 넓은〔좁은〕 ~ a broad 〔narrow〕 forehead; a high 〔low〕 brow / ~에 땀을 흘리며 by 〔in〕 the sweat of *one's* brow / ~를 맞대고 의논하다 put 《our, your, their》 heads together; 《구어》 go into 〔be in〕 a huddle / ~에 여덟팔자(八字)를 그리다 knit *one's* brows; frown. ② 《이맛돌》 the headstone of a fireplace.
◉ ~받이 striking with the head; butting; running into 《*a thing*》. ~빼기 =이마 ①. 이맛돌 = 이마 ②.

**이마적** lately; of late; recently; nowadays; these days.

**이만** to this extent; this much; this far. ¶ 오늘은 ~ 하자 So much 〔That will be all〕 for today. *or* Let's call it a day.

**이만것** such a small matter; a trifle like this. ¶ ~에 놀랄 그가 아니다 He is the last man to be disconcerted by such a trifling matter.

**이만저만** 《not》 to just this extent or that; 《more than》 so-so; 《hardly》 to any limited degree; 《not》 easy to dismiss; 《not》 in any offhanded way. ~하다 be 《not》 just so-so; be 《hardly》 describable. ¶ 더워도 ~ 덥지 않다 It is hot today, and there are no two ways about it. / 그는 영어를 해도 ~ 잘 하는 것이 아니다 He not only talks English, he talks it awfully well. / 미인도 ~한 미인이 아니다 She is a girl of unsurpassed beauty. *or* She is no everyday beauty. / 그 경치의 아름다움이란 ~한 것이 아니다 The scenery is lovely beyond all description. / 그는 노래 솜씨가 ~이 아니다 No one can match him in singing. / 자넨 실수도 ~한 실수를 한 것이 아니야 You just committed the blunder to end all the blunders.

**이만큼** 《양(量)이》 about this 〔so〕 much; 《수(數)가》 about this 〔so〕 many; 《크기가》 about so large 〔long〕; 《폭이》 about this width 〔wide〕; 《정도》 to this extent. ¶ ~이면 된다 This much will do. / 오늘은 ~ 해 두자 So much for today. / 2층에 책이 ~ 또 있다 I have just as many books upstairs as here. / ~만 있으면 당분간 용돈은 된다 This is enough for my pocket money for some time. / 어제 낚은 고기는 ~ 컸다 The fish I caught yesterday was this big.

**이만하다** be this much; be as much 〔big, many〕 as this; be to this extent. ¶ 이만한 손해는 아무 것도 아니다 Such a small loss is nothing to me. / 둑이 이만하면 튼튼하다 The dike is strong as can be now. / 내 책상은 ~ My desk is this large.

**이맘때** about 〔around〕 this time; (at) this time of day 〔night, year〕. ¶ 작년〔내년〕 ~ at this time last 〔next〕 year / 내일〔어제〕 ~ at this time tomorrow 〔yesterday〕/ ~면 by this time; by now / 작년 ~에는 쇠고기값이 한 근에 6,000 원이었다 Beef was selling at six thousand won a *Kun* a year ago at this time. / 작년 ~에는 큰 비가 왔었다 It was raining hard about this time last year. / 내일 저녁 ~ 또 와 뵙겠습니다 Tomorrow evening at this time I'll come and see you again.

**이맛살** wrinkles in 〔on〕 the forehead. ¶ ~을 찌푸리다 wrinkle (up) *one's* forehead; knit *one's* brows; frown.

**이맛전** ¶ ~이 넓다 have a broad forehead.

**이맞다** fit 《in》; come into gears; gear 《into, with》; mesh; engage.

**이매지네이션** 《상상(력)》 imagination.

**이메일** 〖컴퓨터〗 E-mail. [< *e*lectronic mail]

**이며** [조사] and; or; and/or. ¶ 책~ 돈~ 몽땅 잃었다 I have lost money, books, and everything. / 그는 군인~ 학자다 He is both a soldier and a scholar.

**이면**(二面) ① 《두 개의 면》 two faces 〔aspects〕; two sides; [형용사적] two=sided. ② 《둘째 면》 the second page 《of a newspaper》. ◉ ~각 〖수학〗 a dihedral angle. ~기사 items on the second page. ~성 two-facedness; two=sidedness.

**이면**(裏面·裡面) the back; the other 〔reverse〕 side; 《내면》 the inside; 《내막》 the inside story; the background; 《암흑면》 the dark 〔seamy〕 side 《of society》. ¶ 사회〔도시 생활〕의 ~ the dark 〔seamy〕 side of society 〔urban life〕 / 표지의 ~ the inside of the cover / 경화(硬貨)의 ~ the reverse side of a coin / ~의 뜻 the hidden meaning; the implication 《of *one's* words》 / ~에(서) behind 《*one's* back》; in secret; behind the scenes / ~에서

조종〔공작〕하다 maneuver behind the scenes; pull the strings 〔wires《구어》〕/ ~에서 활약하다 take 〔play〕 an active part in the background / ~에서 책동하다 act as a wirepuller behind the scenes / ~을 관찰하다 look at the other side《of》; look into the inside《of》/ 틀림없이 ~에 무언가 있다 I'm sure something lies behind it. *or* Something is going on behind the scenes. / ~을 보라 Please turn over (생략 P.T.O.).

◉ ~공작 behind 〔behind-the-scenes, backstage〕 maneuvering; underground activities; undercover work. ~부지(不知) a person displaying lack of judgment; behaving indiscreetly. ~사(史) an inside history; an account from within. ~사정〔사실〕 the inside affairs 〔facts〕. ~생활 *one's* intimate 〔private〕 life. ~술책 wirepulling.

**이면** [조사] if 〔when〕 it is; as for. ¶ 만일 내가 당신~ if I were you / 여기서 한 3분~ 간다 It's about three minutes (walk) from here.

**이명**(異名) an alias; a nickname.

**이명**(耳鳴) a ringing 〔buzzing, drumming〕 in the ears. ¶ ~이 있다 have a ringing 〔buzzing, drumming〕 in *one's* ears; *one's* ears ring 〔sing〕.

◉ ~증 『의학』 tinnitus.

**이명법**(二名法) 『생물』 binominal 〔binomial〕 nomenclature.

**이모**(姨母) *one's* mother's sister; a maternal aunt.

**이모부**(姨母夫) an uncle; the husband of a maternal aunt.

**이모작**(二毛作) double-cropping; two crops a year. ~하다 raise two crops a year.

**이모저모** this angle and that; every facet 〔side, view〕 of《*a matter*》. ¶ ~로 생각하다 view《*a matter*》 from every angle.

**이목**(耳目)《귀와 눈》the eye and ear; 《주의》public attention 〔notice〕. ¶ ~을 끌다 attract 〔arrest〕 public attention; catch the public eye / ~을 피하다 avoid public notice; shun publicity.

**이목구비**(耳目口鼻) ear, eye, mouth, and nose; features; looks. ¶ ~가 반듯하다 have well balanced features; have regular 〔fine〕 features.

**이무기** a python; a boa constrictor.

**이문**(利文) gain(s); profit; interests. ¶ ~이 있다 be profitable 〔lucrative, paying〕; pay / ~이 없다 be unprofitable; do not pay / ~이 적다 give 〔yield〕 little profit; do not pay much / 상당한 ~을 남기다 make a good profit.

**이문**(異聞) a strange report 〔episode, news, narrative, rumor〕; curious information; strange tales 〔accounts〕.

**이물** the prow of a boat; the stem. ¶ ~에서 고물까지 from stem to stern.

**이물**(異物) an alien 〔a foreign〕 substance.

**이미** ①《벌써》already; now; yet (의문문에); 《not》 any longer. ¶ ~ 때가 늦었다 It is now too late. / 그것은 ~ 끝났다 It's already finished. / 수업은 ~ 시작됐나요 Has school begun yet? / 내가 정거장에 닿았을 때 열차는 ~ 떠나고 없었다 When I arrived at the station, the train had already left. ②《앞서》before; previously; earlier. ¶ ~ 말한 바와 같이 as previously stated.

**이미지** an image. ¶ ~를 좋게 하다 improve the image《of a company, a new starlet》/ ~를 바꾸다 change *one's* (public) image; change the image《of *something* or *someone*》/ ~업〔다운〕하다 improve 〔damage〕 *one's* image / 세상 사람들은 유명인에 대하여 틀에 박힌 ~를 갖고 있다 People have a set picture in their minds about how famous people look.

◉ ~라이터 『컴퓨터』 image writer. ~빌더 image builder. ~통합《디자인의》 Corporate Identity (생략 CI).

**이미테이션** (an) imitation. ◉ ~보석 imitation jewelry. ~팔찌 an imitation bracelet.

**이민**(移民)《이주》emigration (외국으로); immigration (타국에서); 《이주자》 an emigrant (타국으로); an immigrant (타국에서); a settler (개척지의). ~하다 emigrate《from, into, to》; immigrate《from, into》; plant settlers 《on》; shift people 〔population〕. ¶ 우리 나라에서 많은 ~이 브라질로 갔다 A large number of people emigrated to Brazil from our country. / 해마다 많은 ~이 미국으로 온다 Many immigrants come to the United States each year.

◉ ~교섭 negotiations for immigration. ~귀화국(局)《미》the Immigration and Naturalization Service (생략 INS). ~노동자 an immigrant worker; imported labor. ~단 a group of emigrants《to Brazil》. ~문제 an emigration 〔immigration〕 problem. ~법 an emigration 〔immigration〕 law. ~알선

자〔회사〕 an emigration 〔emigrant〕 agent 〔company〕. ～정책 an emigration policy. ～제도 개혁위원회 《미》 the U.S. Commission on Immigration Reform. ～제한 restriction of immigration: ～제한법 the Immigration Restriction Law. ～협회 the Immigration Association. 가족～ emigration with *one's* family members.

**이바지하다** ① 《공급하다》 provide; furnish; supply. ② 《공헌하다》 contribute 《to》; render service 《to》; conduce 《to》; help; be helpful 《to, in》; make for 〔toward〕. ¶ 행복〔건강, 평화, 복지〕에 ～ conduce to happiness 〔health, peace, welfare〕 / 나라에 ～ serve *one's* country; do much for *one's* country / 한국의 경제 발전에 ～ contribute to the economical growth of Korea / 선교사들이 한국 교육계에 이바지한 바는 크다 Missionaries have done much to help Korean education.

**이박자**(二拍子) 〖음악〗 two-part time; double 〔binary, duple〕 time 〔measure〕.

**이반**(離反·離叛) (an) estrangement; alienation; defection 《from *a person*》; 《이탈》 (a) secession; a breakaway. ～하다 be estranged 〔alienated〕 《from》; be disaffected 《toward》; 《이탈하다》 secede 《from》; break 〔drift〕 away 《from》. ¶ 민심은 현정부에서 ～되어 있다 The public is alienated from the present government.

**이발**(理髮) a haircut; hairdressing. ～하다 get a haircut; have *one's* hair cut 〔trimmed〕. ◉ ～기 hair clippers. ～사 a barber; a haircutter; a hairdresser. ～소 《미》 a barbershop; 《영》 a barber's (shop): ～소 간판 a barber('s) pole. ～업 barbering; hairdressing. ～요금 the charge for 〔price of〕 a haircut. ～용구 hairdressing appliances.

**이밥** 《쌀밥》 plain boiled rice.

**이방**(異邦) an alien 〔a foreign〕 country. ◉ ～인 an alien; a stranger; a foreigner.

**이번**(一番) ① 《금번》 this time; the present; the current one; this one; 《최근》 the recent one. ¶ ～ 시험 the recent 〔last〕 examination / ～만 for this once; just this time; once for all / ～에 오신 선생님 the new teacher / ～만 용서해 주십시오 Please forgive me just this time. / ～ 전쟁에 사람이 얼마나 죽었습니까 How many people were killed in the recent 〔late〕 war? ② 《다음》 next time; the coming one; presently; shortly; now; next. ¶ ～ 일요일 next Sunday / ～ 여름 방학 the coming summer vacation / 그는 ～에 미국에 간다 He is going to America shortly. / ～에는 네 차례다 It's your turn (next). / ～ 가실 때에는 저도 함께 데리고 가 주세요 Take me there (the) next time you go.

**이번**(二番) number two; No.2; the second. ¶ ～ 타자 the second batter.

**이법**(理法) 《원리와 법칙》 principles and rules; a law; 《예법》 propriety and decorum. ¶ 자연의 ～ the law 〔order〕 of nature.

**이변**(異變) 《변고》 an extraordinary phenomenon; an unusual change; 《사고》 an accident; an untoward event; 《재해》 a disaster; a calamity. ¶ 날씨의 ～ an unusual change of weather / 태양의 ～ an extraordinary phenomenon in the sun / 금융계의 ～ a disturbance in financial circles / 그의 신상에 무슨 ～이라도 있는 것이 아닌가 I fear (that) something wrong has happened to him.

**이별**(離別) separation; parting; 《이혼》 (a) divorce. ～하다 separate 〔part〕 《from》; bid farewell 《to》; divorce 《*one's* wife》; get a divorce from 《*one's* husband》. ¶ 눈물의 ～ parting in tears; tearful parting / ～을 아쉬워〔섭섭해〕하다 be loath 〔reluctant〕 to part 《with》; express regret at parting / 친구들과의 ～이 그를 슬프게 했다 Separation from his friends made him sad. / 그는 어려서 양친과 ～했다 He was separated from his parents when he was a small child. ◉ ～가(歌) a song of farewell; a farewell song. ～주(酒) a farewell drink.

**이병**(罹病) contraction of a disease. ～하다 contract 〔catch, take, get〕 a disease; suffer from illness; 《감염되다》 be infected with 《cholera》. ◉ ～률 morbidity (rate); the incidence 《of influenza》. ～자 a sufferer 《from cholera》; a case 《of typhoid fever》.

**이보다** 《more, less, better, worse》 than this. ¶ ～ 앞서 prior to this; before this / ～ 나쁘다 be worse than this / 저것이 ～ 낫다 That is better than this. / ～ 더한 불행은 없다 There can be no greater misfortune than this.

**이복**(異腹) ¶ ～의 born of a different

mother. ◉ ~동생 *one's* younger sibling by a different mother; *one's* half brother 〔sister〕. ~형제 *one's* half brother 〔sister〕.

**이본**(異本) a variant《of the standard edition of》;《진본(珍本)》a rare book.

**이봐** Hi!; Hey!;《미》Say!; Look here! ¶ ~, 무엇하고 있나 Hey! What are you doing?

**이부**(二部)《두 부분》two parts;《제2부》the second part 〔section〕; Part Ⅱ (책차례의);《책의》two copies 〔volumes〕. ¶ ~로 되다 consist of two parts 〔divisions〕. ◉ ~수업 instruction in two shifts. ~작 a two-part work; a work consisting in two parts. ~제(制) the two-shift (school) system: ~제 수업의 학교 a school operated on the two-shift system. ~합창 a chorus in two parts: ~ 합창을 하다 sing《a piece of music》in two parts. ~형식 a two-part system.

**이부**(利附·利付) ¶ ~의 interest-bearing / 6푼 ~공채 a 6% interest-bearing bond.

**이부**(異父) a different father; a stepfather. ◉ ~형제 *one's* brother by a different father; *one's* half brother 〔sister〕.

**이부자리** bedding; bedclothes;《요》a mattress;《이불》a quilt. ¶ ~를 펴다 lay 〔make〕 a bed / ~를 개다 fold up bedclothes 〔bedding〕.

**이북**(以北)《북쪽》north《of》;《북한》North Korea. ¶ 서울의 ~ (to the) north of Seoul; (at) Seoul and northward / 삼팔선 ~ north of the 38th parallel / ~에서 온 사람 a man from North Korea.

**이분**(二分) division into two parts. ~하다 divide《*a thing*》in two 〔into two parts〕; halve; bisect《a line》. ¶ ~의 일 one 〔a〕 half / ~의 2박자 *alla breve* (It.); cut time.
◉ ~법 『논리』 dichotomy. ~쉼표 『음악』 a half rest. ~음표 『음악』 a half-note; a minim《영》. ~점〔경선〕『천문』 the equinoctial point 〔colure〕.

**이분자**(異分子) a heterogeneous element; an alien 〔a foreign〕 element; an outsider. ¶ (사람을) ~시(視)하다 regard《*a person*》as a foreign element; discriminate《against *a person*》as an outsider / ~를 축출하다 eliminate a foreign element; exclude an alien element《from a society》.

**이불** an overquilt; a quilt; a coverlet;《미》a comforter. ¶ ~ 속에서 활개 치는 사람 a blustering coward; (a man who is) a lion at home and a mouse abroad / ~을 덮다 put on a quilt / ~을 뒤집어쓰다 pull *one's* bed-clothes over *one's* head / ~을 덮고 자다 sleep under a coverlet. ◉ ~속 fillings. ~솜 batting. ~잇 a quilt cover.

**이브** ①《아담의 아내》Eve. ②《전야》an eve.

**이브닝** evening. ◉ ~드레스 an evening dress 〔gown〕. ~코트 an evening coat.

**이븐파** 『골프』 even par.

**이비**(耳鼻) the nose and ears. ◉ ~과 otorhinology. ~인후과 otorhinolaryngology; otolaryngology: ~인후과 병원 an ear, nose and throat hospital / ~인후과 의사 an otolaryngologist; an E.N.T. doctor.

**이사**(理事) a director;《공공 단체의》a trustee. ¶ 상무〔상임, 대표, 전무〕~ a managing 〔a standing, a representative, an executive〕 director / ~가 되다 obtain a seat on the board of directors《of an organization》.
◉ ~관 a grade-II-A official. ~국 a member country of the executive committee in an international organization: 유엔 안전보장 상임〔비상임〕~국 a permanent 〔nonpermanent〕 member of the UN Security Council. ~장 the chief director; the director general; the chairperson of the board of directors 〔trustees〕. ~회《기구》a board of directors; the governing body; a council;《회의》a directors' meeting.

**이사**(移徙) (house-)moving; (a) removal; a move. ~하다 change *one's* residence; move 〔remove〕《to, into》. ¶ ~가는 곳〔새 주소〕 *one's* new address / 새 집으로〔시골로〕 ~하다 move into a new house 〔the country〕 / 삼청동 1번지로 ~하다 move to No. 1 Samch'ŏngdong / ~가다〔오다〕 move out 〔in〕 / 아래 주소로 ~했습니다 We have moved to the following address. ◉ ~비용 (house-)moving 〔removal〕 expenses. 이삿짐 (the) furniture 〔property〕 to be moved《out of *one's* house》: 이삿짐 운반업자 a mover《미》; a remover《영》/ 이삿짐 운반차 a removal van.

**이사**(二死) 『야구』 two outs. ¶ ~ 만루 Two down, bases filled.

**이사분기**(二四分期)《during》the second quarter of the year.

**이사야서**(一書) 『성서』 (The Book of) Isaiah (생략 Isa.).

**이삭** an ear 《of grain》; a head; a spike. ¶ 벼~ an ear of rice / 떨어진 ~ gleanings; fallen ears / ~이 나오다〔패다〕 be in the ear; come into ears / (밭에서) ~을 줍다 glean (a field) / 보리 ~이 다 팼다 The ears of barley are all out. ◉ ~줍기 gleaning.

**이산**(離散) dispersion; scattering; breakup; separation (뿔뿔이). ~하다 scatter; disperse; be dispersed 〔scattered, broken up〕; separate. ¶ 그 가족은 일가 ~의 비운을 겪었다 The family had the misfortune to be broken up. / 그 전쟁으로 일가는 ~되었다 The war broke up the family.
◉ ~가족 the dispersed 〔separated〕 families: ~ 가족 찾기 운동 a campaign for reunion of dispersed family members; a "Search for Separated Family Members" campaign / ~가족의 재결합 reunion of *one's* dispersed family members / ~가족의 상봉을 바라는 피맺힌 절규 the painful outcries for the reunion of those divided families / 남북 ~ 가족의 교환 방문 the exchange visits of separated families in South and North Korea / ~ 가족 문제 the dispersed family members issue / ~ 가족의 재회를 실현시키다 realize the reunion of divided families / ~ 가족의 감동적인 재회를 텔레비전으로 지켜보다 watch on television the emotional reunion of separated families.

**이산화**(二酸化) 〖화학〗 dioxide. ◉ ~망간 manganese dioxide. ~물 (a) dioxide. ~탄소〔질소〕 carbon 〔nitrogen〕 dioxide. ~황 sulfur dioxide.

**이삼**(二三) ¶ ~의 two or three; a few; some / ~일 a few days; two or three days / ~회〔차〕 two or three times / ~명씩 in two or three.

**이상**(以上) ① 《수량》 not less than; or more; and over 〔up〕; above; over; more than; upward of.

> 용법 「6세 이상의 아동」이라고 할 때, more than, over, above 만으로는 6세를 포함하지 않는 것이 되므로, 엄밀하게는 children six years or 〔and〕 over 따위로 하여야 함. 「하나 이상」을 뜻하는 more than one은 의미상으로는 복수이나 문법적으로는 보통 단수 취급함. 또한 「1마일 이상」은 one mile over가 보다 정확한 표현임.

¶ 세 시간 ~ three hours or more; more than three hours / 10마일 ~ ten miles or more; more than ten miles / 50 ~ above fifty; fifty and over / 6세 ~의 아동 children over six years old; children of six and over; children from six years up.
② 《정도》 beyond; more than; further; past. ¶ 수입 ~의 생활을 하다 live beyond *one's* income; live above *one's* means / 상상 ~이다 be past 〔beyond〕 *one's* imagination; be more than *one* can imagine / 예상 ~이다 be beyond *one's* expectation; exceed *one's* expectation / 그 ~ 모른다 I know nothing beyond that. / 그 ~ 말할 것이 없다 I have nothing further 〔more〕 to say. / 그 ~ 말할 수 없다 I cannot say anything beyond that. / 그 ~ 더 잘 할 수는 없다 This is the best I can do.
③ 《…한 바엔》 since; now that; seeing that. ¶ 이렇게 된 ~은 now that things have come to such a pass / 약속을 한 ~ 지켜야 한다 Once you have made a promise, you should keep it. / 내가 온 ~ 이제 걱정은 말게 Now (that) I am here, don't worry any longer. / 그것을 본 ~ 우리에게 말해야 한다 Since you saw it, you must tell us about it. / 살아 있는 ~ 일해야 한다 So long as we live, we must work.
④ 《상기》 ¶ ~에 말한 the said; foregoing; above-mentioned〔-stated〕 / ~과 같이, ~ 말한 바와 같이 as mentioned 〔stated〕 above; as we have seen / ~은 그의 연설의 대요이다 The above is the gist of his speech.
⑤ 《이로써 끝》 that is all. ¶ ~ (끝) 《문서 등에서》 Concluded; 〖통신〗 Over.; 《아나운서 등의 말》 That's all 〔That's it〕 (for the moment).

**이상**(異狀) 《고장》 something wrong; trouble; 《nothing is》 the matter; disorder; (a) change (변화); 《신체의》 (a) disorder; (an) indisposition; 《마음의》 mental disorder; (mental) derangement; 《정상이 아닌 상태》 something unusual.
¶ ~이 있다 something is 「wrong 〔the matter〕 《with》; be abnormal; 《기계 등이》 be out of order; 《사람이》 be 「indisposed 〔sick, ill〕 / ~이 없다 be all right; be in good 「order 〔condition〕; be normal 〔sound〕 / ~을 보이다 show abnormal symptoms / 위의 ~을 호소하다 complain about *one's* stomach disorder / 정신 ~이 생기다 be 〔become〕 mentally disturbed; be

(mentally) deranged / 심장에는 별 ~이 없다 There is nothing wrong with the heart. / 전원 ~ 없음 《점호에서》 All present and accounted for. / 오른 팔에 ~이 있다 The right arm shows an abnormality. / 전선에 ~ 없다 All quiet on the front. / 엔진에 ~이 있다 Something is 「wrong 〔the matter〕 with the engine. / 실내에는 아무 ~이 없었다 We noticed nothing unusual in the room.

**이상**(異常) strangeness; abnormality. ~하다, ~스럽다 《보통이 아니다》 (be) unusaual; abnormal; extraordinary; uncommon; 《기이하다》 (be) strange; odd; queer; 《수상하다》 (be) dubious; suspicious.
¶ ~하게 strangely; queerly; abnormally / ~한 버릇 a peculiar habit / ~한 사람 a strange person; a queer fish / ~한 얼굴 a funny face / 머리가 ~하다 be out of *one's* mind; be off *one's* head / ~하게 들리다 sound strange / ~해 보이다 look strange 〔queer〕 / ~하게 느끼다 strike *one* as strange / ~히 여기다 wonder; be dubious of; feel 《*a thing*》 as strange / ~한 이야기지만 strange to say / ~하게 들릴지 모르지만 strange as it may sound / ~할 것이 없다 It is no wonder that... / ~하다, 내 시계가 어디 갔지 That's odd, where has my watch gone? / 자네가 그렇게 생각하다니 ~하다 It is strange that you should think so. (★ 감정을 나타내는 It is strange 〔It is a pity, *etc.*〕 that... 형태의 *that*-clause 에는 *should* 를 쓰는 일이 많음) / 그의 행동이 ~하다 His behavior is suspicious. / ~한 일도 다 있네 How can a thing like that happen, I wonder? / 저 사람은 어딘가 ~한 데가 있다 There is something strange about him. / 자네 오늘 좀 ~하군 그래 You are not yourself today. / 그는 ~한 사람이다 He is strange 〔eccentric〕. *or* He is a peculiar person. / 그녀는 ~한 성격의 소유자다 She is a woman of abnormal character. / 10월치고는 ~하게 덥다 It is unusually hot for October.
◉ ~건조 abnormal 〔unusual〕 aridity; abnormal dryness. ~기상 abnormal weather. ~난동(暖冬) an abnormally warm winter. ~아(兒) an abnormal child. ~접근 『항공』 a near miss; 《영》 an air miss. ~체질 《have》 an allergy 《to》; an idiosyncrasy; 『의학』 (a) diathesis.

**이상**(理想) an ideal. ¶ 높은 ~ a lofty ideal / ~적인 ideal / ~적인 남편〔교사〕 an ideal husband 〔teacher〕 / ~적인 남성상(像) *one's* idea of the perfect man / ~과 현실의 조화 the harmony of ideal 〔dream〕 and reality / 신혼 부부를 위한 ~적인 집 an ideal house for newlyweds / ~을 품다〔갖다〕 have 〔possess, entertain, conceive〕 an ideal / ~을 좇다 follow 〔pursue〕 an ideal / ~을 세우다 set 〔hold〕 up an ideal / ~을 달성하다 attain 〔reach〕 *one's* ideal / ~을 실현하다 realize *one's* ideal / ~에 맞다 meet 〔measure up to〕 *one's* ideal.
◉ ~가 an idealist. ~론 an idealistic thought 〔argument〕. ~주의 idealism: ~주의자 an idealist / ~주의적 idealistic. ~파 the idealistic school. ~향(鄕) an ideal land; a Utopia; an earthy paradise. ~형(型) an ideal type.

**이상야릇하다**(異常—) (be) odd; strange; queer; funny. ¶ 이상야릇한 냄새 unspeakably foul smell.

**이상화**(理想化) idealization. ~하다 idealize; sublimate. ¶ 그는 자기가 사랑하는 여성을 ~한다 He idealize the woman he loves.

**이색**(二色) two colors. ◉ ~인쇄 two-color printing. ~판 a two-color plate.

**이색**(異色) 《다른 색》 a different color; 《색다름》 novelty. ¶ ~적인 out of ordinary; unique; novel; unusual; singular / ~적인 작품 a 「novel 〔rare〕 work / 그는 문단에서 ~적인 존재이다 He is a unique personality in the literary world. ◉ ~인종 a race of a different color. ~작가〔화가〕 a unique novelist 〔artist〕.

**이생**(一生) this life 〔lifetime〕; this world. ¶ ~에서 이루지 못한 사랑 love unrealized in this life.

**이서**(以西) west 《of》; westward. ¶ 서울 ~ west of Seoul; Seoul and westward.

**이서**(裏書) 《수표 등의》 endorsement. ⇨ 배서(背書). ~하다 endorse. ¶ 여기에 ~해 주면 좋겠습니다 Would you please endorse it on the back? / 그는 자기 개인 어음에 ~해 주었다 He endorsed his personal check to me.

**이선**(離船) leaving the ship. ~하다 leave the ship; go ashore.

**이설**(異說) a different 〔conflicting〕 view 〔theory〕; a divergent opinion; 《이단》

a heterodoxy; a heresy. ¶ ～을 내세우다 dissent from 《the orthodox theory》/ 이 문제에 관해서 ～이 분분하다 Opinion differs 〔is divided〕 on this subject. *or* Many conflicting opinions have been expressed on this subject.

**이성**(異姓) a different surname.

**이성**(異性) 《성질》 different nature; 〖화학〗 isomerism; 《자웅》 the other 〔opposite〕 sex. ¶ ～간의 intersexual / ～과 사귈 기회 opportunities to meet people 〔members〕 of the opposite sex / ～을 알다 know a woman 〔man〕/ ～을 가까이하다 have connection with the other sex / 처음으로 ～을 알다 have *one's* first sexual experience; be sexually initiated / ～을 알 만한 나이가 되다 arrive at the age of puberty / ～ 교제가 넓다 have a large acquaintance with the other sex. ◉ ～관계 relationships with the opposite sex. ～애 heterosexual love. ～(질)체 〖화학〗 an isomer.

**이성**(理性) reason; rationality. ¶ ～적(인) rational; reasonable / ～적인 행동 rational conduct / ～적인 사람 a man of reason / ～이 없는 senseless; reasonless; irrational / 순수〔실천〕 ～ pure 〔practical〕 reason / ～과 경험에 비추어 in the light of reason and experience / ～에 호소하다 appeal to 《*a person's*》 reason 〔intellect〕/ ～을 따르다 follow the dictates of reason; listen to reason / ～에 따라 행동하다 act according to reason / ～을 잃다 behave irrationally; lose control (of *oneself*); 《구어》 lose *one's* cool / ～을 되찾다 regain *one's* reason / 인간은 ～적 동물이다 Man is a rational being. / 인간에게는 ～이 있다 Man has the power of reason. / 그녀는 ～을 잃고 소리질렀다 She lost her reason and screamed. / 그는 감정보다 ～쪽이 더 강하다 He is moved more by his head than (by) his heart. ◉ ～론 rationalism.

**이세**(二世) ① 《현세와 내세》 the present and the future world. ② 《제2세》 the Second; Junior (생략 Jr.); 《2대째》 a second generation. ¶ 존 에프 케네디 ～ John F. Kennedy, Jr. / 나폴레옹 ～ Napoleon Ⅱ (★ the Second라 읽음) / 미국에서 태어난 한국인 ～ an American-born Korean; a Korean American. ◉ ～교육 the education of children; juvenile education. ～국민 the children of the next 〔coming〕 generation.

**이속**(異俗) different 〔strange〕 customs.

**이솝** 《그리스의 우화 작가》 Aesop (619?-564 B.C.). ◉ ～이야기 Aesop's Fables.

**이송**(移送) transfer; removal; transportation (수송). ～하다 transfer; remove; transport; carry; convey. ¶ 화물의 ～ a freight transportation / 사건의 ～ removal 〔transfer〕 of a case.

**이수**(利水) irrigation; water-utilization. ～하다 utilize water 《for irrigation》. ◉ ～공사 irrigation works.

**이수**(里數) the number of *ri;* mileage; (a) distance.

**이수**(履修) completion. ～하다 study; complete 〔finish〕 《a college course》; take 《a course in psychology》. ¶ 본과를 ～하다 complete the regular course.

**이수**(離水) 《비행정의》 a takeoff from the water. ～하다 take 〔hop〕 off from the water; leave the water.

**이순**(耳順) sixty years old. ¶ ～이 되다 attain *one's* sixtieth year.

**이스라엘** (the State of) Israel. ¶ ～의 Israeli; 《고대의》 Israelite. ◉ ～사람 an Israeli (*pl.* -lis, [총칭] -li); 《고대의》 an Israelite.

**이스트** yeast. ◉ ～균 yeast; a yeast plant.

**이슥하다** (be) advanced; late. ¶ 이슥한 밤에 late at night; well into the night / 밤이 이슥하도록 till late at night / 밤이 이슥해 감에 따라 as the night wears 〔goes〕 on / 밤이 이슥해지다 the night is (getting) far advanced / 그는 밤이 이슥해서야 집에 돌아왔다 It was well into the night before he came home.

**이슬** ① 《맺힌 물》 dew; dewdrops (방울); 《눈물》 teardrops. ¶ 아침～ the morning dew / ～이 맺히다 dew forms; form dew; 《눈물》 become tearful / ～이 맺힌 꽃 dew-laden 〔dewy〕 flowers / ～이 내리다 it dews; dew falls 〔gathers〕/ ～에 젖다 be wet 〔moist, damp〕 with dew / 그녀 눈에는 ～이 맺혀 있었다 Her eyes were bedewed with tears. / 풀밭에 ～이 맺혀 있었다 There were dewdrops on the grass. ② 《덧없음》 ¶ ～ 같은 목숨 a life evanescent as the dew / 단두대의 ～로 사라지다 lose *one's* life on the guillotine. ③ 《모래집물》 amniotic fluid. ¶ ～이 비치다 the water breaks. ◉ ～떨이 (1) 《막대기》 a stick for clearing the dew from *one's* path. (2) = 이슬받이 ③. ～방울 a dewdrop;

drops of dew. ~아침 a dewy morning. ~점 〖물리〗 the dew point (temperature).

**이슬람** Islam. ¶ ~의 Islamic; Moslem / ~세계 the Islamic world. ◉ ~교 Islam; Mohammedanism. ~교국 a Mohammedan country. ~교도 《개인》 a Muslim (*pl.* ~(s)); [집합적] Islam. ~법 the Sharia. ~원리주의 Islamic Fundamentalism. ~화 Islamization.

**이슬받이** ① 《때》 the time when dew begins to form; dewfall. ② 《도롱이》 a grass kilt worn as protection from dew; a dew-kilt. ③ 《사람》 a person who clears the way of dewdrops for another; a dew-clearer. ④ 《길》 a dew-laden path.

**이슬비** a drizzle; a mizzle; a misty rain; a fog rain. ¶ ~가 내린다 It drizzles.

**이승** this world; this life. ¶ ~의 worldly; earthly; mundane / ~에(서) in this world; (on) this side of the grave / ~의 괴로움 the trials of this life / ~을 떠나다 go out of this earthly life; die; depart this life; pass away 〔on〕 / ~에 태어나다 be born into this world; come into existence; see the light (of day) / ~의 마지막을 고하다 bid 《*a person*》 the last farewell / 그것이 ~과의 작별이었다 It was our last meeting on this side of the grave.

**이식**(二食) 《take》 two meals a day.

**이식**(利息) interest. ⇨ 이자(利子). ◉ ~계산 calculation of interest. ~조견표 an interest ready reckoner.

**이식**(利殖) increase of wealth; moneymaking. ¶ ~의 재능이 있다 be clever at making money; have the Midas touch. ◉ ~법 the secret of moneymaking; how to make money.

**이식**(移植) transplanting; transplantation; 〖의학〗 a 《kidney》 transplant; 《피부 따위의》 grafting; a 《skin》 graft. ~하다 《식물의》 transplant; replant; 《장기·피부의》 transplant 《a kidney from a mother to her son》; graft 《skin》. ¶ 피부〔각막〕 ~ a skin 〔corneal〕 graft / 콩팥을 ~ 받다 receive a kidney transplant / 골수 ~을 받다 have 〔receive〕 a bone-marrow transplant / 나는 나무를 정원에 ~했다 I transplanted trees in the garden. ◉ ~수술 transplantation surgery: 심장~수술 《have》 a heart transplant operation.

**이신론**(理神論) 〖철학〗 deism. ¶ ~의 deistic(al). ◉ ~자 a deist.

**이실직고**(以實直告) ~하다 report 〔tell〕 the truth; speak out honestly; state the facts as they are.

**이심**(二心) 《두 마음》 duplicity; treachery; 《변덕》 fickleness. ¶ ~ 있는 double-faced〔-dealing〕; treacherous / ~을 품다 have two faces; play (a) double game.

**이심**(異心) a different intention 〔mind, idea, heart, design〕; a treasonous intention 〔thought〕. ¶ ~을 품다 have designs against; harbor treacherous intentions.

**이심**(離心) 〖수학〗 eccentricity. ¶ ~적 eccentric. ◉ ~각 an eccentric angle. ~궤도 〖천문〗 an eccentric orbit. ~률 eccentricity.

**이심전심**(以心傳心) telepathy (정신감응); tacit understanding; immediate communication 《of truth, *etc.*》 from one mind to another. ~하다 understand each other 「by telepathy 〔without speaking〕. ¶ ~으로 tacitly; by telepathy; telepathically / 그것을 ~으로 곧 알았다 I knew it right away by mental telepathy. / 우리는 ~으로 통하는 사이다 We are in tune with each other. *or* There is a sort of telepathy working between us.

**이십**(二十) twenty; a score. ¶ ~(번)째 the twentieth / ~분의 1 a twentieth / ~대의 여자 a young woman in her twenties. ◉ ~세기 the twentieth century.

**이십사금**(二十四金) pure gold; gold 24 karats 〔carats 《영》〕 fine.

**이십사시간**(二十四時間) twenty-four 〔24〕 hours. ¶ ~ 이내에 within twenty-four hours / ~ 영업하는 가게 a store open around the clock. ◉ ~방송 all-day 《TV》 broadcasting. ~제 the twenty-four-hour system; an around-the-clock system. ~조업 a round-the-clock operation.

**이십사절기**(二十四節氣) the 24 seasonal divisions of the year.

**이쑤시개** a toothpick. ¶ ~로 이를 쑤시다 use a toothpick; pick *one's* teeth.

**이아치다** ① 《손해입히다》 cause damage; lead to loss; spoil; ruin. ② 《방해되다》 be a hindrance; stand in *one's* way. ③ 《방해하다》 hinder; obstruct; interfere 《with》.

**이악하다** be keen for gain; be wide-awake to *one's* own interest; (be) shrewd; sharp; smart. ¶ 이악한 아이 a smart boy.

**이알** a grain of boiled rice. ¶ ~이 곤두선다 Don't be so cocky.

**이앓이** (a) toothache. ¶ ~를 하다 have 〔suffer from〕 a toothache / ~로 한쪽 뺨이 부었다 The toothache puffed out one side of my face.

**이앙**(移秧) transplanting rice seedlings; rice-planting. ~하다 transplant (rice seedlings); set 〔bed〕 out rice plants; plant rice. ◉ ~가(歌) a rice-planting song. ~기(期) the rice-planting season. ~기(機) a rice-planting machine.

**이야** 《강조·한정하는 뜻의 보조사》 ¶ 말~ 바른 말이지 to be frank 〔honest〕 (with you) / 앞일~ 누가 알 수 있으랴 When it comes to the future, who can tell? / 그 옷~ 어디 입을 수 있겠어 How on earth could I wear that dress? / 그 사람~ 그런 일 할 사람이 아니지 He would never do a thing like that! / 남~ 뭐라고 하든 조금도 상관 없다 I don't care a bit what other people say. / 그 쯤~ 나도 알고 있다 I know as much myself.

**이야기** ① 《담화》 (a) talk; (a) conversation; a discourse; 《한담》 a chat; a gossip; 《연설》 a speech; an address. ~하다 speak 《to *a person,* about 〔of〕 *something*》; talk 《to *a person,* about *something*》; have a talk 〔chat〕 《with》; make a conversation 《with》.

¶ ~할 때의 버릇 a peculiarity in talking / ~ 상대 someone to talk to; a companion (to talk with) / 장사 ~ a business talk / 우리끼리의 ~지만 between ourselves 〔you and me〕 / 그의 ~로는 according to his own story / 이상한 ~를 하는 것 같지만… it may sound strange, but… / ~를 걸다 address *oneself* to; speak to; accost / ~를 시작하다 begin to talk; enter into conversation / ~를 잘〔못〕 하다 be a good 〔poor〕 talker / ~를 꺼내다 draw out conversation / ~를 그치다 stop 〔wind up〕 talking / 혼자만 ~하다 do all the talking; monopolize conversation / 사냥 ~를 하다 talk about hunting / 영어로 ~하다 speak in English / ~로 밤을 새우다 talk all the night; talk the night away / 하고 싶은 ~가 좀 있습니다 I have something to talk about with 〔to〕 you. *or* I want a little talk with you. / 우리들은 식사를 하면서 ~했다 We talked over our dinner. / 그것 재미있는 ~로군 That sounds good 〔interesting〕. / 그렇게 되면 ~가 달라진다 That's another question 〔story〕. / 그는 현대 가족 제도에 대해서 ~를 했다 He gave a talk on the family system of the present day.

② 《설화》 a story; a tale; 《우화》 a fable; 《일화》 an episode; 《사실담》 a description; an account; a narrative; a romance; 《전설》 a legend. ~하다 tell a story 〔tale〕; relate; narrate; give an account 《of》; recount; make a description 《of》. (★ story는 실화나 가공적인 이야기. tale은 공상적·전설적인 가공담. account는 사실에 입각한 체험담 따위). ¶ 호랑이 ~ a story about a tiger / 신상(身上) ~ an account of *one's* life / 꾸민 ~ a made-up story; a fiction; a cock-and-bull story / 전쟁 ~를 하다 give an account of a battle / 어째 꾸며낸 ~ 같다 It sounds like (a) fiction. / 아이들은 ~ 듣기를 좋아한다 Children are very fond of listening to stories. / 그것은 정말 거짓말 같은 ~다 It is an incredible story. *or* That story sounds too good to be true.

③ 《화제》 a topic (of conversation); the subject. ¶ ~는 다르지만 by the way; to pass to another subject; to change the subject / ~는 바뀌어 in the meantime; meanwhile / ~를 돌리다 switch off the conversation; turn the conversation (to other matters) / ~를 바꾸다 change 〔turn〕 the subject; talk about something else / 이런 저런 ~를 하다 talk of one thing and another; chat about things generally; talk on various topics 〔subjects〕 / ~를 바꾸지 마라 Stick to the subject. / 너에게 할 ~가 많다 I have many things to tell you. / 이제 그 ~는 그만둡시다 Let's drop the subject. *or* Let's talk no more about it. / ~는 인공 위성에까지 미쳤다 The topic of conversation turned 〔drifted〕 to the artificial satellites.

④ 《소문·소식》 (a) rumor; (a) report; gossip; common talk; news. ~하다 speak 〔talk, gossip〕 about; talk of; rumor. ¶ 사실 무근의 ~ a groundless 〔an unfounded〕 gossip 〔rumor〕 / ~를 퍼뜨린 사람 the author of a rumor / 그렇다는 ~다 It is so rumored. *or* So I understand. *or* People say so. *or* So I am told. *or* That's what they say. / 자네에 관한 ~는 자주 들었다 I've often heard about 〔of〕 you. / 재미있는 ~가 있다 I have an interesting piece of news.

⑤《상담》a consultation; a negotiation (교섭); an agreement (합의); understanding (의사 소통). ～하다 talk with 《*a person*》 about 《*a matter*》; consult with 《*a person*》; discuss 《*a matter*》 with 《*a person*》. ¶ ～가 되다 arrive at 〔come to〕 an agreement with 《*a person*》; reach 〔come to〕 an understanding with 《*a person*》 / ～가 상통하다 have 〔keep〕 a good understanding with 《*a person*》 / ～가 다르지 않소 That's not 〔against〕 our understanding 〔agreement〕. / 난 결정할 수 없으니 사장과 ～하는 것이 나을 걸세 I cannot make the decision, so you had better consult (with) the president.

⑥《진술》a statement. ～하다 state; relate; tell. ¶ 의견〔입장〕을 ～하다 state *one's* view 〔case〕 / 그의 ～는 매우 듣기 힘들다 His statement is very hard to hear. / 그들의 ～가 일치하고 있다 They all talk the same story.

⑦《기타》¶ 그 제안을 받아들이는 것으로 ～가 매듭지어졌다 It has been decided that we will accept the offer. / 이제 ～를 매듭지었으면 합니다 I'd like to settle our talks now. / 그런 계획은 전혀 ～가 되지 않는다 A plan like that is out of the question.

◉ ～꾼 ＝～쟁이. ～상대 a companion; someone to talk to: ～ 상대가 없다 I have no one to talk to. ⇨말벗. ～쟁이 a storyteller; a teller of tales. ～책 a storybook. ～투 *one's* way 〔manner〕 of talking. 이야깃주머니 a person with lots of interesting things to tell.

**이야깃거리** a subject 〔topic〕 of conversation; something to talk about. ¶ ～가 되다 become a subject of conversation; be talked 〔gossiped〕 about / ～가 없어지다 run out of anything to talk about / 이것은 후세까지 ～가 될 것이다 This story will be handed down to posterity.

**이야말로**[1] 〔부사〕 this very one 〔thing, person〕; this indeed. ¶ ～ 정당한 비평이라 할 수 있다 This indeed can be called just criticism. / ～ 안성맞춤이다 This is the very thing for us 〔our purpose〕.

**이야말로**[2] 〔조사〕 indeed; precisely; exactly; just; none other than. ¶ 금강산～ 구경할 만한 산이다 Mount 〔Mt.〕 Kŭmgang is just the thing for you to see. / 이것～ 맹종(盲從)이라 하겠다 This indeed can be called servile submission.

**이양**(移讓) transfer; handing over; relinquishment. ～하다 transfer; hand over; relinquish. ¶ 정권을 ～하다 turn over the reins of government.

**이어링** 《귀고리》 earrings.

**이어받다** 《재산·성질을》 inherit; be heir to; 《지위를》 succeed to; take over. ¶ 뜻을 ～ follow in the footsteps of 《another》 / 아버지의 사업을 ～ succeed to *one's* father's business / 어머니의 성급한 성질을 ～ inherit a short temper from *one's* mother.

**이어(서)** 《다음에》 next; secondly; in the second place; 《그후에》 after; then; subsequently; soon after; 《계속해서》 continuously; without a break. ¶ 연～ one after another; in succession / 축사에 ～ 건배를 했다 Following 〔After〕 the congratulations, we drank a toast. / 그는 작년에 ～ 금년에도 우승했다 He has won the championship for the second straight year. / ～ 김군의 독창이 있겠습니다 As the next item on the program we have the vocal solo by Mr. Kim.

**이어지다** 《연결·계속되다》 be 〔get〕 connected; be joined 〔linked〕 together; get joined on; be continued; 《이끌다》 lead 《to》. ¶ 사건 해명으로 이어지는 물적 증거 physical evidence leading to the solution of the case / 전화가 이어졌다 The telephone connected 〔came through〕. / 부엌은 식당으로 이어져 있다 The kitchen connects with the dining room. / 태평양과 대서양은 파나마 운하로 이어져 있다 The Pacific and the Atlantic are linked together by the Panama Canal.

**이어폰** an earphone. ¶ ～으로 라디오를 듣다 listen to the radio through an earphone.

**이언**(二言) duplicity; double-dealing. ～하다 break 〔go back on〕 *one's* word 〔promise〕; be double-tongued.

**이언**(俚言) 《방언》 a dialect; 《속된 말》 a slang word 〔expression〕; vulgarism.

**이언**(俚諺) 《속담》 a proverb; a common 〔traditional, folk〕 saying.

**이엄이엄** continuously; uninterruptedly; without a break.

**이엉** straw thatching; thatch roofing. ¶ ～으로 지붕을 인 집 a thatch-roofed house; a (straw-)thatched house / 지붕을 ～으로 이다 thatch a roof with straw; thatch.

**이에** hereupon; thereupon; on this; at this point.

**이에서** than this. ⇨ 이보다.

**이에짬** a joint; a point of attachment; a juncture; a junction; a connection.

**이여** ¶ 미국～ 안녕 Adieu 〔Good-bye〕 to America.

**이여차** Yo-ho!; Yo-heave-ho! ¶ ～ 이여차 짐을 나르다 carry a load with the cry of yo-heave-ho.

**이역**(二役) a dual role 〔part〕. ¶ 1인 ～을 하다 take two parts; play a dual role; act two characters; play the parts of 《A and B》.

**이역**(異域) 《외국》 an alien land; a foreign country; 《타향》 a remote place; a different village. ¶ ～에서 죽다 die in an alien land.

**이역시**(─亦是) this too 〔also, again〕. ¶ ～ 고식적 정책에 지나지 않는다 This again is a mere temporizing policy.

**이연**(移延) postponement. ～하다 postpone; put off; defer.

**이연**(離緣) 《부부의》 the dissolution of marriage; a divorce; 《양자의》 the dissolution of adoption. ～하다 divorce 《*one's* wife》; cancel adoption.

**이연발총**(二連發銃) a double-barreled gun; a double-chambered rifle.

**이열**(二列) two rows; a double column 〔line〕. ¶ ～로 in two rows 〔ranks〕; two abreast / ～로 늘어서다 form two rows; be drawn up in two lines / ～을 지어 행진하다 march 〔walk〕 two abreast.

**이열치열**(以熱治熱) Like cures like. *or* Fight fire with fire.

**이염**(耳炎) 〖의학〗 otitis; inflammation of the ear. ¶ 내〔외〕～ otitis interna 〔externa〕 / 중～ otitis media.

**이염기산**(二塩基酸) 〖화학〗 dibasic acid.

**이염화**(二塩化) 〖화학〗 bichloride. ◉ ～물 a bichloride; a dichloride.

**이영차** ⇨ 이여차.

**이오니아** Ionia. ¶ ～의 Ionian; Ionic. ◉ ～식 the Ionic order.

**이온** 〖화학〗 an ion. ◉ ～교환수지(樹脂) ion exchange resin. ～층 ionosphere. ～화 ionization: ～화하다 ionize.

**이완**(弛緩) slackness; 《moral》 laxness; 〖의학〗 atony. ～하다 slacken; relax. ¶ ～된 slack; slackened; lax / 정신이～되다 *one's* mind 〔attention〕 relaxes / 병사들의 규율이 좀 ～되어 있다 There is some laxity in discipline among the soldiers.

**이왕**(已往) ① [명사] the past; bygones. ¶～지사 bygones / ～의 일은 묻지 마라 Let bygones be bygones. ② [부사] already; now that; as long as; since. ¶ ～ 늦었으니 천천히 가자 It is already late, so let's take our time. / ～ 그 일을 시작했으니 다 마치도록 해라 Now that you have started the job, try to finish it. ③ 《일단 …이라면》 if so; if that is the case. ¶ ～ …인 이상에는 since...; if... at all; once... / ～ 할 바에는 잘 해라 If you do it at all, do it well.

**이왕이면**(已往─) while 〔as long as〕 *one* is about 〔at〕 it; things being what they are; if you do at all. ¶ ～ 나하고 같이 가자 As long as you are going anyway, come along with me. / ～ 프랑스말을 배우겠다 As long as I am about it 〔While I'm at it〕, I might as well take French.

**이외**(以外) 《…을 제외하고》 except; but; except for; other than; save; 《…에 첨가하여》 besides; in addition to.

> 용법 **except** 제외하는 것을 강조하며, **but** 결과로서 제외된 상태를 나타냄. 이 의미로서의 but은 no, nothing, all, anything 따위나 who, what, where 따위 의문사 뒤에 쓰임. **except for** 「…은 별도로 하고 (apart from)」와 「…이 없으면 (but for)」의 뜻을 나타냄. **other than** 「…와는 별개의」란 개념으로 apart from, except와 같은 뜻으로 쓰임. **save** except (for)와 같은 뜻으로 쓰이는 격식차린 고어풍의 말.

¶ 일요일 ～에는 except on Sunday / 신문 기자 ～는 출입을 금함 《게시》 No admittance except reporters. / 그는 월급 ～에 다른 수입이 좀 있다 He has a little separate income besides his salary. / 학생 ～에는 할인하지 않습니다 Discount can be allowed only to students. / 나는 지켜보는 것 ～에는 아무것도 할 수 없었다 I could do nothing but watch. / 그는 사임하는 것 ～에 방법이 없었다 He has no choice but to resign. / 이곳에는 나 ～에 아무도 없다 There's no one here 「but 〔other than〕 me. / 이 도시에는 동물원 ～에는 볼만한 곳이 없다 There is nothing worth seeing in this town, except for the zoo. / 그는 독서 ～에 다른 취미가 없다 He has no hobbies other than reading. / 필수과목 ～에 최소한 다섯가지 선택 과목을 공부해야 한다 In addition to required subjects, we must take at least five electives. / 나는 그들이 무사히 도착하였다는 것 ～는 아무것도 모른

다 I have no news save that they arrived safely.

**이욕**(利慾) love of gain 〔money〕; greed; avarice; cupidity. ¶ ～에 눈이 멀다 be blinded by avarice; be tempted 〔allured〕 by gain / ～을 탐하다 be greedy for gain / ～을 떠나서 일하다 work disregarding 〔irrespective of〕 *one's* profit; work from disinterested motive(s).

**이용**(利用) ① 《이롭게 씀》 utilization; use. ～하다 use; utilize; make (good) use of; put 《*a thing*》 to (good) use; turn 《*a thing*》 to account 〔advantage〕; employ profitably; harness 《solar heat》; exploit.

> 용법 **use** 「이용하다」를 뜻하는 가장 일반적인 말. **utilize** 유용한 목적을 위해 이용하다. **make** (**good**) **use of**; **put... to** (**good**) **use** utilize와 거의 같은 뜻. **take advantage of** 사람이나 상황 따위를 자기에게 유리하도록 이용하다. **make the most** 〔**best**〕 **of** 최대한으로 이용하다. **harness**, **exploit** 자원 따위를 이용하는 경우. exploit는 남을 자기에게 유리하게 이용한다는 뜻도 있음.

¶ ～할 수 있는 utilizable; available / ～할 수 없는 unavailable; unusable / 충분히 ～되어 있지 않은 underutilized 《resources》 / 폐품 ～ the utilization of waste material / 시간을 잘 ～하다 make good use of *one's* time / 천연 자원을 ～하다 exploit 〔tap〕 natural resources / 원자력을 평화 목적을 위해 ～하다 make peaceful use of atomic energy; harness atomic energy for peaceful purpose / 너의 지식을 잘 ～해라 Turn your knowledge to good account. / 이 합성 물질은 자동차나 제트기 엔진에 더욱 많이 ～할 수 있게 되었다 This synthetic substance is finding increasing use in the engine of motorcars and jet planes.

② 《방편으로 씀》 ～하다 take advantage of; avail *oneself* of; make the most of; exploit; capitalize on; play on; 《사람을》 make a cat's-paw of. ¶ 기회를 ～하다 avail *oneself* of an opportunity; improve an occasion / 방학을 ～하다 take advantage of *one's* holidays / 약점〔허영심〕을 ～하다 trade on 《*a person's*》 weakness 〔vanity〕 / 남의 무지함을 ～하다 take advantage of 〔exploit〕 another's ignorance / 아무를 ～해 먹다 take advantage of *a person;* make a cat's-paw of *a person;* use *a person* as a tool.

◉ ～가치 usefulness; utility value: ～가치가 있다〔없다〕 be of 〔be of no〕 utility value. ～국 a user nation 《of the Suez Canal》. ～률 coefficient of utilization. ～법 a way to use; how to use: 이 기계의 ～법을 말해주세요 Tell me how to use 〔operate〕 this machine. ～자 a user; 《도서관 따위의》 a visitor.

**이용**(理容) = 이발(理髮). ◉ ～학원 a barbers' school.

**이우다** 《머리에》 help 《*a person*》 get 〔carry〕 《*a thing*》 on the head.

**이울다** ① 《시들다》 wither; wilt; droop; fade. ¶ 잎들이 이울었다 The leaves have withered. / 화병의 꽃이 이울었다 The flowers in the vase have wilted. ② 《달이》 wane. ¶ 달이 이울어 간다 The moon is on the wane. ③ 《쇠약해지다》 decline; fall off 〔away〕; wane; decay. ⇨기울다. ¶ 가운이 ～ *one's* family fortune declines.

**이웃** 《근처》 the neighborhood; vicinity; 《이웃집》 the (house) next door; the neighboring 〔adjoining〕 house; 《사람》 *one's* (nextdoor) neighbor.

¶ ～의 neighboring; next; adjoining / 오른 쪽에 사는 ～「*one's* neighbor 〔the next-door house〕 on the right / 한집 걸러 ～에 살다 live next door but one to *one's* house; live two doors away from *one's* house / ～의 웃음거리 the laughingstock of the neighborhood / ～과 잘 지내다 get along well with *one's* neighbors / 서로 ～해 있다 be next door to each other; neighbor 《on, with》/ ～으로 이사가다 move into the next house / ～ 사촌 《속담》 A good neighbor is better than a brother far off. / 그는 내 ～(집)에서 산다 He lives next door to me. / 너의 ～에는 누가 사느냐 Who lives next door to you? / 그녀는 ～과 별로 가깝게 지내지 않는다 She doesn't have much to do with the neighbors.

◉ ～나라 a neighboring 〔an adjacent〕 country. ～돕기운동 a help-your-neighbor campaign. ～방 the next 〔adjoining〕 room. ～사랑 love of *one's* neighbors.

**이원**(二元) duality. ¶ ～적(인) dual; dualistic. ◉ ～론 dualism: ～론자 a dualist. ～방송 simultaneous broadcast by two stations. ～방정식 an equation with two unknowns. ～성

dualism; duality.

**이원권**(以遠權) 〚항공〛 beyond rights; the right to fly beyond the《U.S.》 destination into third countries.

**이원제**(二院制) the bicameral system; the two-chamber〔-house〕 system.

**이월**(二月) February (생략 Feb.).

**이월**(移越) a transfer; a carry-over. ~하다 transfer《to, from》; bring forward 〔over, down〕《from》; carry forward 《to》; carry over《to, from》. ¶ 앞면〔전기〕에서 ~〚부기〛 brought forward (생략 BF) / 다음면으로〔차기로〕 ~〚부기〛 carried forward (생략 CF) / 다음 연도로 ~하다 carry《a sum》 forward to next year / 잔금을 다음달 분의 생활비로 ~하기로 했다 I've decided to transfer the balance to next month's living expenses.
◉ ~계정《다음으로의》 a carried forward account; 《앞에서의》 a brought forward account. ~금《앞에서의》 the balance〔amount of money〕 brought forward《from the previous account》; 《차기로의》 the balance〔amount of money〕 carried forward《to the next account》; a balance carried: 전기~금 a balance carried forward from the last account. ~손익〚상업〛 losses and profits brought forward. ~일 a contango day; a carrying over day.

**이위**(二位) 《석차》 the second place; 《사람》 a runner-up.

**이유**(理由) 《까닭》 (a) reason; cause; 《근거》 ground(s); 《동기》 a why; a motive; 《구실》 an excuse; a pretext (★「이 편지를 쓴 이유」는 my reason to write this letter라 않고 the reason why I wrote this letter 또는 my reason for writing this letter라고 함. reason 다음에 to+부정사가 오는 경우는「믿다, 바라다, 두려워하다」등 정신적 행위를 나타내는 동사일 때가 많음: He had no reason to fear it.「그는 그것을 두려워할 이유가 없었다」).

> **용법** **reason**「이유」를 나타내는 가장 일반적인 말로 아래의 낱말들 대신으로 쓸 수 있음. 어떤 행위나 의견을 조리있게 이성적으로 설명한다는 뜻을 내포함. **cause** 어떤 결과가 생기는 직접적인 원인을 나타냄. **ground(s)** 어떤 행위나 동기 따위의 근거를 나타내는 말. **motive** 사람이 어떤 행동을 취하게 하는 감정, 동기 따위를 나타냄.

¶ 결석한 ~ the reason for *one's* absence《from school》/ 자살의 ~ a motive for suicide / 정당한〔부당한, 그럴 듯한〕 ~ a justifiable〔unjustifiable, plausible〕 reason / 충분한〔빈약한, 표면상의〕 ~ a good〔slender, an ostensible〕 reason / ~있는 well=founded〔-grounded〕/ ~없는 groundless / ~가 있어서 with good reason / ~ 없이 without reason〔cause〕/ 이렇다 할 ~ 없이 for no particular reason / 무슨 ~로 for what reason; on what ground; why / …한 ~로 by reason of; on the ground of〔that〕; on account of; because of; for / ~를 들다 adduce reasons / ~를 말하다 give a reason《for》; state *one's* reasons / ~를 밝히다 clarify the reason; make 《it》 clear / 그는 정신착란이란 ~로 무죄가 되었다 He was acquitted on grounds of insanity. / 그렇게 말해서 안 될 ~가 어디 있느냐 Is there any good reason why I shouldn't say so? / 다만 가난하다는 ~로 남을 업신여겨서는 안 된다 You should not despise a man simply because he is poor. / 그녀의 말을 의심할 ~가 없다 There is no reason to doubt her word. ◉ ~서 a statement of reasons; an explanatory statement.

**이유**(離乳) weaning; ablactation. ~하다 wean《a baby from the breast》; be weaned. ◉ ~기(期) the weaning period: 그 아기는 지금 ~기에 있다 The baby is going through the weaning period. ~식(食) baby〔weaning〕 food.

**이유**《유럽연합》 the EU. [<the *E*uropean *U*nion]

**이윤**(利潤) (a) profit; returns. ¶ 초과〔정상〕 ~ excess〔normal〕 profits / ~분배 방식 the profit-sharing plan / ~이 높은 high-profit《business》/ ~이 많은 장사 a profitable business / 상당한 ~을 올리다 make a good profit.
◉ ~율 a profit rate; a rate of profit. ~추구 pursuit of profits; profit-seeking. ~통제 control of profits. ~폭 a profit margin.

**이율**(利率) the rate of interest. ¶ 은행 ~ the bank rate of interest / 협정 ~ the conventional rate of interest / ~을 인상하다 raise〔increase〕 the rate of interest / ~을 인하하다 lower 〔reduce, decrease〕 the rate of interest / 연 7푼 5리의 ~로 돈을 빌려주다 lend〔loan《미》〕 money at the rate of 7.5 percent per year.

**이율배반**(二律背反) 〚논리〛 antinomy. ¶ ~의 antinomic.

**이윽고** after a while; shortly; soon; in a short time; presently; before long. ¶ ~ 그는 병이 나았다 It was not long before he got well. / 해가 지고~ 달이 떴다 The sun set, and soon 〔in a short time〕 the moon appeared.

**이음**(異音) 〖음성〗 an allophone.

**이음매** a joint; a join; a juncture; a seam. ¶ ~가 없는 jointless; seamless / ~가 없는 레일 a welded rail / 관(管)의 ~에서 가스가 샜다 Gas leaked from where the pipes were connected 〔joined〕.

**이의**(異意) ① 《의견이》 a different view 〔opinion〕. ② = 이심(異心).

**이의**(異義) a different meaning; a different principle. ◉ 동음~어 a homonym.

**이의**(異議) 《반대》 an objection; a protest (항의); dissent (불찬성). ¶ ~ 없이 without any objection / ~를 제기하다 object 《to》; protest 《about, against》; raise an objection to; make 〔lodge〕 a protest 《against》 / …에 대해서 아무 ~도 없다 have no objection 〔complaint〕 to make about… / ~있습니까 Does anyone have an objection? / ~ 있습니다 Objection! / ~없습니다 No objection! ◉ ~신청 an exception; a formal objection: ~신청인 〖법〗 a demurrant; a demurrer.

**이익**(利益) ① 《이윤》 (a) profit; gain(s); returns. ¶~이 있다〔없다〕 be profitable 〔unprofitable, nonpaying〕 / ~이 나다 yield 〔make〕 a profit 《for *one*, to *one*》 / ~을 보다 profit 《by, at, from》; make a profit 《on》 / ~이 적다 give 〔yield〕 little profit; do not pay much / 많은 ~을 올리다 make a large profit / ~ 배분을 하다 give 《*a person*》 a profit participation / 사회에 ~을 환원하다 return *one's* profits to society / 나는 눈 앞의 ~만을 말하고 있는 것은 아니다 I am not talking about immediate economic gains. ② 《편익》 benefit; profit; advantage; good; *one's* interests. ¶ ~ 있는 advantageous; beneficial / …의 ~을 위하여 for the benefit of…; in the interests of… / 자기 ~을 꾀하다 look after 〔pursue〕 one's (own) interests / ~에 반(反)하다 be against *one's* interests / ~을 주다 benefit; do 《*a person*》 good / 공동의 ~을 증진하다 promote 《our 〔their〕》 common interests / 그런 책을 읽어서 무슨 ~이 있느냐 What is the good of reading such a book? ◉ ~금 gains; a profit: 총〔순〕 ~금 a gross 〔net〕 profit. ~대표 a person representing 〔voicing〕 the interests of a group. ~률 a profit rate; profitability. ~배당〔분배〕 profit sharing; distribution of profits; a dividend (주식·보험의): ~분배 제도 a profit-sharing system; industrial copartnership / ~분배를 받다 have a share in the profit. ~사회 a gesellschaft.

> (용법) **profit** 금전상의 「이익·이윤」이란 뜻으로 흔히 쓰임. **gain** loss의 반대어로 「이익·소득」의 뜻을 나타냄. 종종 도박 따위의 좋지 않은 수단으로 얻는 「수익」을 뜻하는 경우도 있음. **benefit** 「은혜·편익」이란 추상적 의미로 쓰임. **advantage** 다른 것보다 뛰어나거나 우수해서 생기는 「이익」을 뜻함.

**이인**(二人) two persons; two men; a couple. ◉ ~삼각(三脚) a three-legged race. ~승(乘) a two-seater. ~조 a pair 《of criminal》; 《구어》 a two-some; 《속어》 a duo (*pl.* ~s): ~조 강도가 그 집에 침입했다 A gang of two burglars broke into the house. ~칭 〖문법〗 the second person.

**이인**(異人) ① 《비범한 사람》 a genius; a prodigy. ② 《다른 사람》 a different person. ◉ 동명~ a different person with the same name.

**이인종**(異人種) a different 〔an alien〕 race.

**이임하다**(離任―) leave 〔quit〕 *one's* post 〔position〕.

**이입**(移入) import; shipping in. ~하다 import 《into》; bring in; introduce 《into》 (문물 등의); ship in. ◉ 감정~ 〖심리〗 empathy: 감정 ~설 empathy theory.

**이자**(利子) interest 《on a loan》. ¶ 정기 예금의 ~ interest on a fixed deposit / 1년 6%의 ~, 6% interest per annum / 비싼〔싼〕 ~로 at a high 〔low〕 interest / 무~로 without interest; free of interest / ~가 붙다 bear 〔yield〕 interest / ~가 비싸다〔싸다〕 the interest is high 〔low〕 / ~를 계산하다 compute 〔reckon〕 interest / ~를 받고 돈을 꾸어주다 put *one's* money out at interest / 5%의 ~로 돈을 빌리다 borrow money at 5 percent interest / ~를 붙여서 갚다 pay a debt with interest / ~를 물다 pay interest 《on a loan》 / ~물기가 벅차다 find it hard to pay *one's* interest.
◉ ~계산서 an interest note. ~부: ~

부 공채 an active 〔interest-bearing〕 bond / ~부 증권 an interest-bearing security. ~소득 the income from interest; interest income. ~지급 interest payment: ~ 지급 정지 suspension of interest payment. ~평형세 the interest equalization tax.

**이자택일**(二者擇一) selecting one alternative. ⇨양자택일. ~하다 make a choice; choose between the two.

**이장**(里長) the head of a village.

**이장**(移葬) exhuming and burying elsewhere. ~하다 exhume and bury in another place; change the burial site of.

**이재**(理財) management of financial affairs; moneymaking; economy; finance. ~하다 manage financial affairs. ¶ ~의 비결〔방법〕 the secret of moneymaking; how to make money 〔a fortune〕/ ~에 능하다〔밝다〕 be adept 〔efficient〕 at financial affairs; be clever at making money. ◉ ~가 an economist; a financier. ~국(局) the Financial (Management) Bureau.

**이재**(罹災) suffering from a calamity 〔disaster〕. ~하다 suffer from a calamity; fall a victim to a disaster. ◉ ~구호(기)금 a (disaster) relief fund. ~율 〖보험〗 the frequency of loss. ~지구 the afflicted 〔stricken〕 district 〔area〕: 홍수로 인한 ~지구를 방문하다 visit the area which suffered from the flooding.

**이재민**(罹災民) the victims of calamity; the sufferers from a disaster; the afflicted (people); the victims 《of》. ¶ 수해~ sufferers from a flood; flood sufferers 〔victims〕/ ~을 구호하다 carry out the relief of victims of a disaster. ◉ ~수용소 a refugee camp. 전쟁~ war victims.

**이적**(利敵) ~하다 benefit 〔profit〕 the enemy. ◉ ~행위 acts benefiting the enemy; an act advantageous to the enemy: 그는 ~ 행위라는 것을 알면서 그 일을 했다 He did it knowing that it would profit the enemy.

**이적**(異蹟) a miracle. ¶ ~을 행하다 work 〔perform〕 miracles; do wonders.

**이적**(移籍) the transfer of registration. ~하다 be transfer 《to》. ¶ (프로 선수가) 타이거스로 ~되다 be transferred to the Tigers. ◉ ~료 a waiver (프로야구의).

**이적**(離籍) 《호적에서》 removal of *one's* record 〔*one's* name〕 from the family register. ~하다 remove *one's* record from the family register. ¶ 결혼한 딸을 ~하다 remove *one's* married daughter's name from the family register.

**이전**(以前) 《현 시점에서》 ago; 《어떤 시점에서》 before; since; 《일찍이》 once; on an earlier occasion; 《옛날》 formerly; in former times.

> 용법 **ago** 현시점에서 「이전」이란 뜻이며, 항상 기간을 나타내는 어구를 앞에 두며, 대체로 과거형과 함께 쓰임. 간혹 과거 완료와 함께 쓰이기는 하나 현재완료 시제와는 함께 쓸 수 없음. **before** 현재·과거의 어떤 때로부터 「이전」이란 뜻. 흔히 과거형·현재〔과거〕 완료형과 함께 쓰임. **since** 본래 「그 이래, 그 후」의 뜻이나, ago의 뜻으로도 간혹 쓰임: He disappeared a month since. (그는 한 달 전에 실종됐다). **once** 「일찍이」, **formerly, in former days** 「옛날에」 모두 분명한 과거를 뜻하는 말이므로 과거시제와 함께 쓰임.

¶ ~의 previous; past; one-time; former / ~대로 as before / 50년 정도 ~에 about half a century ago / ~보다 더 열심히 공부하다 work harder than before 〔one used to〕/ ~에 그를 만난 적이 있다 I have seen him before. / 그는 ~에 대학교수였다 He was formerly a professor at a university. / 여기에 ~ 주소를 써 주시오 Please write your former address here. / ~에 비해서 지금은 훨씬 살기가 좋다 We are much better off than we used to be. / 나는 ~에 여기 살았었다 I used to live here. (★ used to [juːstə]+infinitive 에서의 used는 조동사와 같은 구실을 하는 말이다. 의문문에서는 *Did* he use [juːs] *to* live here?와 같이 did를 사용하는 것이 보통임) / ~부터 그를 알고 있다 I have known him for a long time. / 그 조각은 서기 300년 ~의 것으로 여겨지고 있다 The sculpture is thought to predate A.D. 300.

**이전**(移轉) 《집의》 (house) moving; a move; a removal; 《양도》 transfer (권리 따위의); demise (재산의); devolution (권리·의무·지위 등을 상속인에게). ~하다 《사람이》 move; remove; shift home; move *one's* residence 《from... to...》; 《양도》 transfer; change hands. ¶ ~할 수 있는 권리 transferable rights / 주식의 ~ the transfer of a stock / 재산의 ~ (a) transfer of property / 토지의 권리를 아내에게 ~하다 transfer a land deed to *one's* wife's name / 다른 집으로 ~하다 move into another house / ~한 곳을 비밀에 부치다 keep secret where *one* has removed to / 다음 주소로 ~했습니다 We have moved to the following address. ◉ ~공고〔통고〕 a removal notice; a notice of change of address. ~등기 registration of a transfer 《of *a person's* estate to *one*》: ~등기부 a transfer book. ~신고 a report of removal; a report of change of address. ~처 *a person's* new address. ~ 촉진 지역 relocation-promoted district. 권리~ a transfer of rights.

**이점**(利點) an 〔a point of〕 advantage; a merit. ¶ ~을 열거하다 point out the advantage 《of *a thing*》 / …라는 ~을 갖고 있다 possess the advantage of… / 다른 상점에 비해 그것이 이 상점의 ~이다 That is the advantage of this store over the others. / 이 기계는 운반과 조작이 편리하다는 ~이 있다 This machine has the advantage of being easy to carry and operate.

**이정**(里程) mileage; distance. ¶ 서울까지의 ~ the distance to Seoul. ◉ ~표(表) a table of distances. ~표(標) a milestone; a milepost.

**이제** now; this time 〔moment〕; the present (time).
¶ ~ 막 just; just now; a moment ago (★ just now는 현재완료와 함께 쓰이지 않음) / ~까지 until now; up to the present; so far / ~부터 from now on; from this time forth 〔forward〕; hence / ~껏 죽 all this while / ~껏 어디 있었는가 Where have you been all this while? / 그는 ~ 막 나갔습니다 He went out just a moment ago 〔just now.〕 / 그는 ~ 어린애가 아니다 He is no longer a boy. / 그것은 ~ 안 하겠다 I won't do that any more 〔again, any longer〕. / 자 ~ 가봐야겠습니다 Well, I think I must be going now. / 정말 더위는 ~부터다 The hottest season is yet to come. / ~ 더 할 말이 없다 I have nothing further to say. / ~부터 술을 삼가도록 해라 You must abstain from liquor from this day onward. / ~부터는 조심하도록 해라 Be careful after this. / ~야말로 우리가 궐기할 때다 Now is the time for us to rouse ourselves to action.

**이제와서** now; after so long a time; when it is too late. ¶ ~ 돌이킬 수 없는 일이지만 though it may be a case of crying over spilt milk / ~ 생각해 보니 when I「think of 〔look back to〕 it now / ~ 취소도 할 수 없다 It is too late to cancel it. / ~는 어쩔 수 없다 Nothing can be done now. *or* It can't be helped now. / ~ 그런 소릴 해보았자 소용없다 It is (of) no use to say such a thing now when it is too late. / ~ 그런 소릴 하면 곤란하다 You ought to have told me so before.

**이젤** 〖미술〗 an easel.

**이조**(吏曹) 〖고제도〗 the Civil Office Board.

**이조**(李朝) the Yi dynasty. ⇨ 조선.

**이족**(異族) 《다른 민족》 a different race; 《다른 씨족》 a different clan; a different surname.

**이종**(二種) two kinds; 《제2종》 the second class. ◉ 제~ 우편물 the second class mail (matter).

**이종**(異種) a different kind 〔species〕; a variety. ¶ ~의 of a different kind 〔species〕. ◉ ~교배 〖생물〗 hybridization; crossbreeding: ~ 교배하다 hybridize; crossbreed. ~번식 〖생물〗 crossbreeding; out-and-out breeding: ~ 번식하다 breed out and out.

**이종**(姨從) cousins by a maternal aunt.

**이종**(移種) transplantation of a seedling.

**이주**(移住) ① 《이사》 a move; a removal; shifting 〔changing〕 residence. ~하다 move 《to》; remove. ¶ 부산으로 ~하다 move to Pusan. ② 《이동》 migration; emigration (외국으로); immigration (외국으로부터). ~하다 migrate 《from, to》; emigrate 《to, into》; immigrate 《into》; settle 《in》.

> 용법 **migration** 사람이나 동물 따위가 어떤 지역에서 다른 지역으로 이동하는 것. **emigration** 모국을 떠나 외국으로 이주하는 것. **immigration** 외국으로부터 이주해 들어오는 것을 뜻함.

¶ 그녀는 프랑스에서 미국으로 ~했다 She emigrated from France to the United States. / 많은 한국인이 남아메리카로 ~해 왔다 A lot of Korean have immigrated to 〔into〕 South America. ◉ ~민〔자〕 《외국으로》 an emigrant; 《외국으로부터의》 an immigrant; 《미개척지의》 a settler: 그는 독일에서 온 ~자이다 He is an immigrant from Germany. ~지(地) 《행선지》 the place where *one* is going to live; 《이주한 곳》

the place in which *one* has settled. ～희망자 an intending emigrant.
**이주일**(二週日) two weeks; a fortnight.
**이죽거리다** = 이기죽거리다.
**이중**(二重) duplication; double(ness). ¶ ～의 double; duplex; dual; twofold; duplicate / ～으로 doubly; twice; over again / ～의 뜻 a double 〔twofold〕 meaning / ～턱의 double-chinned / ～연료의 bifuel 《rocket》 / ～바닥의 double-〔false-〕bottomed / ～으로 하다 double; duplicate; put on above the other / ～으로 싸다 wrap 《*a thing*》 double / ～으로 기입하다 make an entry 《of *a matter*》 twice 《over》 / ～으로 작성하다 make out 《an invoice》 in duplicate / ～의 목적을 이루다 fill a dual purpose / 그것은 ～의 수고가 든다 That would double the trouble.
◉ ～가격(제) a dual price (system). ～간첩 a double agent. ～결합 〖화학〗 a double bond. ～결혼 bigamy. ～고(苦) a double torture: 파산과 병마의 ～고에 시달리다 be under the double torture of bankruptcy and illness. ～곡가제 the dual grain price system; the two-tier pricing system for staple grains. ～과세(過歲) celebrating two New Years—one by the solar calendar and the other by the lunar calendar; the double celebration of the New Year. ～과세(課稅) double taxation: ～과세 방지 협정 double tax avoidance agreement. ～구조 〖경제〗 dual industrial structure. ～국적 dual nationality: ～국적자 a person with dual nationality. ～노출 double exposure. ～뚜껑 a double lid. ～모음 〖음성〗 a diphthong. ～문 double doors. ～방송 dual broadcasting. ～벽 a double(-framed) wall. ～부정 〖문법〗 a double negative. ～생활 a double life. ～성 dualism; duplicity. ～외교 dual diplomacy. ～인격 double 〔dual, split〕 personality: ～인격자 a double-faced person; a Jekyll and Hyde. ～인화 《사진의》 double printing; 《자막의》 superimposing. ～장부 《have》 dual bookkeeping for tax evasion. ～저당 a double mortgage. ～조종 dual control. ～주(奏)〔창(唱)〕 〖음악〗 a duet; a duetto. ～창(窓) a double-paned window. ～촬영 〖영화〗 an overlap. ～충돌 a double collision. ～판매 double sale. ～하이픈 a double hyphen.
**이즘** 《주의·설》 an ism.
**이지**(理智) intellect; intelligence. ¶ ～적(으로) intellectual(ly) / ～적인 사람〔용모〕 an intelligent 〔intellectual〕 person 〔countenance〕. ◉ ～주의 intellectualism.
**이지러지다** ① 《달이》 wane. ¶ 달이 이지러져 간다 The moon is on the wane. ② 《모서리가》 have a piece 《of china, glass, *etc.*》 break off; chip.
**이직**(移職) a change of occupation. = 전직(轉職).
**이직**(離職) leaving *one's* position; 《실직》 loss of employment. ～하다 leave 〔quit〕 *one's* job; lose employment. ¶ ～되어 있다 be unemployed; be out of work 〔employment〕. ◉ ～률 the jobless 〔unemployment〕 rate; the rate of people leaving their jobs; a turnover. ～자 an unemployed person; [총칭] the unemployed; the jobless.
**이진**(二陣) the second echelon 〔contingent〕. ◉ ～선수 the second-string players.
**이진법**(二進法) 〖수학〗 the binary 〔dyadic〕 system (of notation).
**이진숫자**(二進數字) 〖컴퓨터〗 a bit; a binary digit.
**이질**(姨姪) the children of *one's* wife's sister.
**이질**(異質) 《성질》 heterogeneity; 《재주》 a distinctive 〔an outstanding〕 quality or talent. ¶ ～의 different in kind; of a different nature; heterogeneous; 《외래의》 foreign 〔extraneous〕 《to》 / ～의 문화 culture of a different nature. ◉ ～동상〔동형〕 〖광물〗 allomerism; isodimorphism. ～배수성(倍數性) 〖유전〗 allopolyploidy. ～배수체(倍數體) 〖유전〗 an allopolyploid. ～용해 〖생화학〗 heterolysis. ～접합자 〖생물〗 a heterozygote. ～조직 〖의학〗 heterology.
**이질**(痢疾) 〖의학〗 dysentery; (bloody) flux.
**이질풀**(痢疾—) 〖식물〗 a kind of cranesbill.
**이집트** (the Arab Republic of) Egypt. ◉ ～말 Egyptian. ～문자 Egyptian script 〔hieroglyphs〕. ～사람 an Egyptian; [총칭] the Egyptian.
**이쪽** ① 《이편》 this side 〔direction〕; our side; this way. ¶ ～ 저쪽 this way and that / ～으로 가다 go this way / 은행은 길 ～에 있다 The bank is on this side of the street. / ～에 오시는 일이 있으면 꼭 들러 주십시오 If you come this way 〔When you are in this neighborhood〕, don't fail to drop in. ② 《우리 측》 our party; we; us. ¶ ～ 저쪽 we and they.

**이차**(二次) [형용사적] ① 《두번째의》 second; 《부차적인》 secondary. ¶ 제～세계 대전 the Second World War; World War Ⅱ / 그런 일은 ～적인 문제다 A question like that is of secondary importance. ② 〚수학〛 quadratic. ◉ ～감염 secondary infection. ～곡선 a curve of secondary degree. ～공해 secondary pollution. ～반응 〚화학〛 a second-order reaction. ～방정식 a quadratic equation. ～산업 the secondary industries. ～성징 a secondary sexual character. ～전지 a secondary battery. ～제품 secondary products.

**이차원**(二次元) two dimensions. ¶ ～의 two-dimensional.

**이차회**(二次會) a second meeting; 《술자리의》 a party after a party; an after-feast; an after-course of pleasure. ¶ ～를 가지다 《술자리》 have another spree 〔feast〕 at another place.

**이착**(二着) the second place; 《사람》 an runner-up (*pl.* runners-).

**이착륙**(離着陸) taking off and landing.

**이채**(異彩) brilliance. ¶ ～를 띠다 cut a conspicuous 〔brilliant〕 figure; be conspicuous 〔resplendent〕; figure 〔stand out〕 prominently (among others); stand out from others 〔in relief〕.

**이처럼** like this; in this way 〔manner〕; this much; so much. ¶ ～ 많이 so much 〔many〕/ ～ 와 주셔서 고맙습니다 Thank you for coming like this. / ～ 이른 아침에 어딜 가느냐 Where are you going at this hour of morning? / ～ 잘 될 줄은 몰랐다 I did not expect to succeed so well. / 그가 ～ 바보인 줄은 몰랐다 I thought he was much wiser.

**이첩**(移牒) notification to the authorities concerned; communication. ～하다 transmit 《an order, the information》 to the office 〔official〕 concerned; notify 《of, that》; refer 《to》; communicate 《to》.

**이첩기**(二疊紀) 〚지질〛 the Permian (period).

**이체**(異體) a variant. ◉ ～동심 being different in form but same in mind; being two in body, but one in mind. ～동형 〚생물〛 hormomorphy.

**이체**(移替) transfer. ～하다 transfer 《to, into》. ¶ 그 돈이 아직 ～되지 않은 것 같습니다 The money doesn't seem to have been transferred yet. / 가불금은 손익 계정으로 ～되어야 한다 You should transfer temporary payments to a profit and loss account.

**이초**(離礁) ～하다 get off the rock; refloat. ¶ ～시키다 refloat 《a ship》; get 《a ship》 off the rocks.

**이초점**(二焦點) ¶ ～의 bifocal 《lens》.

**이축**(移築) removing and reconstruction. ～하다 dismantle 《a historic building》 and reconstruct 《it》 in a different place.

**이취**(異臭) a nasty 〔foul〕 smell; a stink. ¶ ～를 발하다 give out a stench 〔foul smell〕; stink.

**이층**(二層) ① 《두 층》 2 stories 〔floors, levels〕. ② 《둘째 층》 the upper 〔second〕 story; the second floor 《미》; the first floor 《영》 (★ 영국에서는 1층을 ground floor, 3층을 the second floor라고 하는데 미국에서도 호텔 따위에서는 the second floor가 3층을 뜻할 때가 있음). ¶ ～방 an upstairs room; a room on the second floor / ～에(서), ～으로 upstairs / ～에 올라가다〔살다〕 go 〔live〕 upstairs / ～에서 내려오다〔떨어지다〕 come 〔fall〕 downstairs. ◉ ～버스 a double-deck bus. ～집 a two-story〔-storied〕 house.

**이치**(理致) 《도리》 (good) reason; 《원칙》 principle. ¶ 자연의 ～ a natural law / ～에 따라서 in accordance with what is reasonable; in line with reason / ～에 맞다 stand to reason; be reasonable / ～에 맞지 않다 be unreasonable; be contrary to reason / ～에 맞는 말 reasonable words / 네 말은 ～에 맞지 않는다 There is little reason in what you say. / 자식을 사랑하는 것은 자연의 ～다 It is in the nature of things that parents should love their children.

**이칭**(異稱) another name; another 〔a different〕 title.

**이카오** 《국제 민간 항공 기구》 ICAO. [<the *I*nternational *C*ivil *A*viation *O*rganization]

**이퀄** 《더하기에서》 be; make; equal; 《빼기》 leave; 《곱하기》 be; 《나누기》 equal; give; go. ¶ 5 곱하기 4 ～ 20, Five times four is 〔are〕 twenty. / 8 나누기 2 ～ 4, Two into eight goes four. / 2 더하기 3 ～ 5, Two and three make 〔makes, is, are〕 five. / 7 빼기 4 ～ 3, Four from seven leaves three.

**이큐** EQ; 《교육 지수》 educational quotient; 《감성 지수》 emotional quotient.

**이키**(나) Oh(, what a start)!; Oh, my goodness!

**이타**(利他) altruism. ¶ ～적 altruistic.

◉ ~주의 altruism: ~주의자 an altruist.

**이탄**(泥炭) peat; turf. ◉ ~지 a peat bog 〔moor〕; a turbary. ~층 peat deposits.

**이탈**(離脫) a secession; bolting; a breakaway. ~하다 secede《from a party》; bolt; break 〔drift〕 away《from》;《직장을》desert 〔quit〕《*one's* job》; walk off *one's* job. ¶ 국적을 ~하다 renounce 〔divest *oneself* of 〕 *one's* nationality / 그는 과격한 정책에 반대하여 당적을 ~했다 He left the party in protest at its radical policy. ◉ ~자 a seceder; a bolter.

**이탈리아** Italy. ¶ ~의 Italian. ◉ ~말 Italian. ~ 사람 an Italian.

**이탓저탓** with this excuse 〔complaint〕 and that; on one pretext or another; on some pretext or other.

**이태** two years. ¶ ~ 동안 for two years.

**이탤릭** 〖인쇄〗 italics; italic type. ¶ ~으로 하다 italicize; print in italic type.

**이토**(泥土) mud.

**이토록** so 〔this〕 much; like this. ¶ ~ 부탁을 하는데도 for all my asking / 영어를 가르치기가 ~ 힘든 줄은 몰랐다 I little dreamed that it was such hard work to teach English.

**이통**(耳痛) 〖의학〗 earache. ⇨ 귀앓이.

**이튿날** ①《다음날》the next 〔following〕 day; the day after. ¶ ~ 아침 the next morning / ~인 3월 10일에 on the following day, the tenth of March / 그가 떠난 ~에 on the day subsequent to his departure / 편지를 낸 ~ 그가 도착했다 He arrived the day after the letter was mailed. ②《초이틀》the second day (of the month).

**이틀**[1] ①《2일》two days. ¶ ~마다 every two days; every other day / ~ 후에 the next day but one; two days after 〔later〕 / ~ 걸러 every third day / 하루 ~에 in a day or two. ②《초이틀》the second day (of the month). ¶ 정월 초 ~ the second day of January; Jan. 2nd.

**이틀**[2] ①《턱뼈》the jawbone. ②《의치》a dental plate; a full denture. ¶ ~을 해 박다 insert a plate; fix a denture.

**이틀거리** 〖한의〗 a tertian fever; malaria. ¶ ~에 걸리다 be taken with tertian fever.

**이판암**(泥板岩) 〖광물〗 shale.

**이팔**(二八) sixteen. ◉ ~청춘 a sixteen-year-old; sweet sixteen; a man 〔girl〕 in the flower of youth.

**이팥** 〖식물〗 a kind of red bean.

**이페리트** 〖화학〗 yperite; mustard gas.

**이편**(一便) ①《이쪽》this side 〔way〕. ¶ 정거장은 길 ~에 있다 The station is on this 〔our〕 side of the street. ②《우리편》this 〔our〕 side; we; I. ¶ ~의 잘못 my 〔our〕 fault; a fault on my 〔our〕 part / ~으로선 for my 〔our〕 part.

**이피** an EP (record). 〔< *e*xtended *p*laying record〕

**이핑계저핑계** with this excuse and that excuse; on some pretext or other. ¶ ~ 대며 on one pretext or another / ~ 대며 일을 자꾸 미루다 keep putting the matter off with one excuse after another.

**이하**(以下) ①《수량》... or 〔and〕 below 〔less〕; no 〔not〕 more than; not exceeding; ... or under 〔fewer〕;《미만》less than; below; under. ¶ 4세 ~의 어린이 children of four and under; children less than five years old / 1,000원 ~로 for 1,000 won or less; for not more than 1,000 won / 신장이 160센티미터 ~인 사람 a man of one hundred (and) sixty centimeter tall or under / 6세 ~는 무료 입장《게시》Admission free for children of six years or under. / 밖의 기온은 섭씨 10도 ~이다 It is below ten degrees centigrade outside.

> **용법** 우리말에서는 「200이하」라고 할 경우 200도 포함되지만, 영어의 「less than 200」에서는 200이 포함되지 않는다. 따라서 「200개 이하의 주문에 대해서는 할인이 없습니다」라는 말을 엄밀히 영어로 표현하려면, There will be no discount on an order for 200 pieces or less.로 하여야 한다. 그러나 일상 구어에서는 그리 엄격히 구별하지 않고 두루 쓰이는 경우가 많다.

②《정도》under; below; beneath. ¶ 보통 ~ below the general level; below the average 〔mark, standard〕 / 중류 ~ below the middle class(es); middle class and below / 성적이 예상 ~이다 The result falls under what was expected. / 평년작 ~이다 The yield 〔crop〕 is below the average.

③《나머지》the following; the rest. ¶ ~ 같음 and so forth / ~ 여백 No more statement 〔detail〕 hereafter. / ~ 다음호에 To be continued. / ~ 생략 The rest (is) omitted. / ~ 이것에 따름 〔준함〕 The same rules apply correspondingly to the following. *or* The same shall apply hereinafter.

**이하부정관**(李下不整冠) Do nothing that may give rise to suspicion.

**이하선**(耳下腺) 〖해부〗 the parotid (gland). ◉ ～염(炎) parotitis; mumps.

**이학**(理學) natural sciences; 《물리학》 physical science. ◉ ～계 the scientific world. ～박사 《사람》 a doctor of science; 《학위》 Doctor of Science (생략 D. Sc.). ～부 the department of science; the science faculty. ～사 《사람》 a bachelor of science; 《학위》 Bachelor of Science (생략 B. Sc.). ～석사 Master of Science (생략 M. Sc.). ～자 a scientist; a physicist.

**이한하다**(離韓—) leave 〔depart, go away from〕 Korea.

**이함**(離艦) 〖군사〗 takeoff 《of an aircraft》 from a ship.

**이합사**(二合絲) double-ply thread.

**이합집산**(離合集散) meeting and parting; 《정당 따위의》 changes in 「political 〔party, factional〕 alignment. ¶ 해방 후 한국 정계는 ～의 연속이었다 There has been constant alignment and realignment in Korean politics since the 1945 Liberation (of Korea).

**이항**(二項) 〖수학〗 ¶ ～의 binomial. ◉ ～방정식 a binomial equation. ～분포 a binomial distribution. ～식 a binomial (expression). ～정리 the binomial theorem.

**이항**(移項) 〖수학〗 transposition (of a term); transposal. ～하다 transpose.

**이해** this year; the current 〔present〕 year. ¶ ～는 풍년이다 This is a bumper year.

**이해**(利害) gain and loss; advantages and disadvantages; interests.
¶ ～의 일치 identity of interests / ～의 상충 a clash 〔conflict〕 of interests / 유럽에 대한 미국의 ～ American interests in Europe / ～를 초월한 disinterested / ～에 관계되다 affect *one's* interests; be of 《great》 concern 《to *one*》 / ～를 같이 하다 have common interests 《in *a matter* with *a person*》 / ～에 영향을 미치다 affect *one's* interests / 그 건에 관해서 양자의 ～가 일치하고 있다 The two have common interests in that matter. / 이 협정에는 노사 쌍방의 ～가 얽혀 있다 This agreement is connected with the interests of both labor and management.
◉ ～상반 both gain and loss; both advantages and disadvantages; both benefit and harm: ～ 상반하다 be both profitable and unprofitable 〔favorable and unfavorable, advantageous and disadvantageous〕. ～타산 calculation 〔reckoning〕 of loss and gain 〔the profits and losses〕.

**이해**(理解) understanding; comprehension; apprehension; appreciation. ～하다 understand; comprehend; apprehend; grasp; appreciate; realize; see; get; make out.

> 용법 **understand** 이해한다는 뜻의 일반적인 말. **comprehend** 이해한다는 뜻이지만 understand보다 격식을 차린 말로서, 전후 관계·다른 사실과의 연관성까지도 포함해서 충분히 이해하고 있다는 뜻. **appreciate** 사람이나 사물의 진가를 이해한다는 뜻으로, 오해를 받고 있을 경우에 쓰임. **grasp** 사물을 이해〔파악〕한다는 뜻. **realize** 상상의 세계에만 있었던 사물을 구체적으로 명확히 이해함. **see** 《구어》 눈으로 보고 알아낸다는 뜻에서 머리로 사물을 이해하고, 생각해서 파악한다는 뜻. **get** 《구어》 손으로 받다〔잡다〕라는 뜻에서 의미를 파악〔이해〕한다는 뜻. **make out** 《구어》 가까스로 알게〔이해하게〕 된다는 뜻.

¶ ～ 있는 사람 a person of understanding; an intelligent person / ～곤란하다 be incomprehensible; be hard to understand; be beyond *one's* comprehension / ～가 부족하다 do not fully understand; want sympathy / ～가 없다 have no understanding; lack understanding / 올바르게 ～하다 have a right 〔proper〕 understanding 《of》 / ～가 빠르다 be quick of apprehension 〔understanding〕 / ～가 더디다 be slow to understand / …에 대해서 ～가 있다 be in sympathy with... / 상호간에 ～를 증진하다 promote 〔increase, deepen〕 mutual understanding; know each other better / 더 잘 ～하다 gain a better understanding 《of》 / ～할 수 있다 be understandable 〔comprehensible〕; make sense; can be appreciated / 문장의 뜻을 ～하다 pick out the meaning of a passage / 그는 남의 기분을 ～할 줄 모른다 He lacks consideration for the feelings of others. / 나는 자네 말을 ～할 수 없네 I can't catch your meaning. *or* I don't understand you. (★ understand what you say 라고는 안 함).

**이해관계**(利害關係) interests; a concern; stake. ¶ ～가 있다 have an interest 〔a concern〕 《in》 / 상충하는 ～의 조절

the adjustment of conflicting interests / 우리 나라는 이 문제에 중대한 ~를 가지고 있다 Our country has an important interest in this matter. *or* Korea is vitally interested in this matter. ◉ ~자 the persons interested [concerned]; the interested parties.

**이해득실**(利害得失) loss and gain; profit and loss; advantages and disadvantages; interests; 《장단》 merits and demerits. ¶ ~을 따지다 calculate [reckon] the loss and gain 《of》; balance the profits and losses 《of》; weigh losses against gains 《in *doing something*》 / 그는 ~에 밝다 He knows where his interests lie. / 모든 일에는 ~이 있다 Everything has its merits and demerits. / 이 방법의 ~을 설명해 주세요 Would you explain the 「advantages and disadvantages [pros and cons] of this method?

**이해력**(理解力) the comprehensive faculty; the power to understand; understanding. ¶ ~을 기르다 cultivate the power of understanding / ~이 없다[부족하다] lack understanding; have a poor understanding.

**이해심**(理解心) understanding; consideration; sympathy. ¶ ~이 있다 be considerate 《of other people's feelings》; be sympathetic 《about》 / ~이 없다 be unsympathetic; be inconsiderate / ~이 부족하다 want [lack] sympathy [understanding] / ~ 있는 아내 a sympathetic wife.

**이해타산**(利害打算) 《계산》 calculation [reckoning] of gains and losses; 《욕심》 self-interest; interestedness. ¶ ~에서 guided by self-interest / ~을 떠나서 apart from the consideration of gain / ~을 떠나서 …하다 do without a desire of gain.

**이행**(移行) a shift; a changeover (전환); a transition (추이). ~하다 change over 《from [to] *something*》; shift [switch] over 《to》; change over 《from, to》. ¶ 농업에서 공업으로 ~ the transition from agriculture to industry / 평화 산업으로 ~하다 switch over to peace industry.

◉ ~기간 a period of transition 《from the old to the new system》. ~조치 transitional [transition] measures: ~조치를 강구하다 work out [devise] special measures to be taken during a transition period.

**이행**(履行) performance 《of *one's* duty》; fulfillment 《of a promise》; discharge 《of an obligation》; execution 《of a contract》; implementation 《of a treaty》. ~하다 fulfill 《a promise》; carry out 《*one's* plan》; perform 《*one's* duties》; discharge 《an obligation》; execute 《a contract》; implement; put 《a principle》 into practice. ¶ 약속을 ~하다 fulfill *one's* promise; keep *one's* engagement; carry out a pledge / 채무를 ~하다 discharge *one's* liabilities / 계약을 ~하다 live up to [execute, fulfill, abide by] a contract / 채무 ~을 게을리하다 default on debt payments / 공무를 ~하기 위해 사생활을 희생하다 sacrifice *one's* private life to perform *one's* public duties / 그는 약속은 꼭 ~했다 He has never failed to keep *his* promise [word]. / 그는 충실하게 의무를 ~한다 He is faithful in the performance of his duties. / 그는 계약조차도 ~하려고 하지 않았다 He didn't even try to carry out the contract.

◉ ~자 a performer; an executor.

**이향**(離鄕) departure from *one's* native place. ~하다 leave *one's* native place; leave *one's* home.

**이형**(異形) 〖생물〗 heteromorphy; a heterogamete. ◉ ~배우자 heterogamate. ~분열 heterotype division. ~세포 an idioblast. ~염색체 a heterochromosome. ~질 alloplasm.

**이혼**(離婚) a divorce; the dissolution of marriage. ~하다 divorce 《*one's* wife [husband]》; get divorced from; have *one's* marriage annulled. ¶ 협의 ~(a) divorce by consent / …와 ~하다 get [obtain, secure] a divorce from… / 합의 ~하다 effect divorce by agreement [consent] / ~을 요구하다 seek [claim] a divorce / 그녀는 ~했다 She was divorced (from her husband).

◉ ~수당 an alimony. ~신고 a notice [report] of divorce; a divorce paper; divorce notice: ~ 신고를 하다 notify *one's* divorce; send in a divorce paper. ~율 a divorce rate. ~자 a divorcee; a divorced person. ~절차 divorce procedure [formalities]. 법정 ~ a judicial divorce.

**이혼소송**(離婚訴訟) a divorce suit; a suit for divorce; divorce proceedings. ¶ ~을 제기하다 file a suit [petition] for divorce 《against》; sue [petition] for divorce; start divorce proceedings.

**이화**(李花) 《꽃》 plum blossoms.

**이화**(梨花) pear blossoms.

**이화명충**(二化螟蟲) a rice(-stem) borer; a grass webworm.

**이화수분**(異花受粉) 〚식물〛 cross-pollination. ～하다 cross-pollinate. ¶ ～시키다 cross-pollinate.

**이화수정**(異花受精) 〚식물〛 cross-fertilization; allogamy; xenogamy. ～하다 cross-fertilize. ¶ ～시키다 cross-fertilize.

**이화작용**(異化作用) 〚생물〛 catabolism.

**이화학**(理化學) physics and chemistry; physicochemistry.
◉ ～교실 a science room 〔theater (계단식)〕. ～기계 physical and chemical appliances 〔apparatus〕. ～연구소 an institute of physical and chemical research.

**이환**(罹患) contracting a disease; suffering from illness. ◉ ～율 the attack rate; the rate of disease; morbidity. ～자 a patient; a sufferer 《from influenza》.

**이황화**(二黃化) 〚화학〛 ◉ ～망간 manganese disulfide. ～물 a disulfide; a bisulfide. ～수소 hydrogen disulfide. ～철 iron disulfide. ～탄소 carbon bisulfide.

**이회**(二回) two times; twice. ¶ 1일 ～ twice a day / 주 ～ twice a week; semiweekly / 월 ～ twice a month; semimonthly; 《영》 fortnightly / 연 ～ twice a year; semiannually / ～초〔말〕 〚야구〛 the first 〔last〕 half of the second inning(s).

**이후**(以後) 《금후》 after this; from now on; in future; hereafter; henceforth; 《장래는》 in (the) future; 《그 후》 after that time; thereafter; 《그후 죽》 since then; thenceforth. ¶ 5년 ～ five years hence / 그 ～에 생긴 일 subsequent events / 6월 8일 및 그 ～ on and after June the eighth / 그 ～ 오늘에 이르기까지 from that time down to this day / 신청은 8월 15일 ～ 접수한다 Applications will be accepted on and after August 15.

**익년**(翌年) the next year. ＝이듬해.

**익다** ① 《익숙하다》 get used to; be familiar 《with》; get accustomed 《to》; be experienced 〔skilled〕 《in》. ¶ 손에 익은 practiced; familiar / 익지 않은 new; unfamiliar; unexperienced / 익지 않은 일 an unfamiliar 〔unaccustomed〕 job / 귀에 익은 목소리 a familiar voice / 익은 솜씨로 with experienced hands; with clever hands; skillfully / 눈〔귀〕에 ～ be accustomed to see 〔hear〕; get used to seeing 〔hearing〕 / 고된 일에 ～ be inured to drudgery / 그는 가난한 농부의 아들이라 고생에는 익었다 The son of a poor farmer, he was inured to hardship. / 그는 이런 일에는 익은 사람이다 He is an old hand at such things.
② 《음식이》 get cooked; be done. ¶ 잘 익은 well-done〔-cooked〕 / 너무 ～ be overdone / 고기가 잘 익었다 The meat is well-done. / 감자가 잘 익지 않았다 The potatoes are underdone.
③ 《과실·기회가》 ripen; become ripe; mellow; mature. ¶ 익은 ripe; mature; mellow / 너무 익은 사과 an overripe apple / 익지 않은 과일 unripe 〔green〕 fruit / 기회가 익었다 The opportunity has developed. *or* The time is ripe. / 그는 기회가 익기를 기다렸다 He waited for an opportunity to ripen. / 벼는 익을수록 머리를 숙인다 《속담》 The boughs that bear most hang lowest.
④ 《장·술이》 become seasoned; be matured; ferment; mature; age.

**익더귀** 〚조류〛 the female Asiatic sparrow hawk; an accipiter.

**익명**(匿名) 《이름을 숨김》 anonymity; 《가명·필명》 a pseudonym. ¶ ～의 anonymous / ～으로 anonymously / ～을 희망한 미국의 한 고위 관리 a senior U.S. official who wish to remain anonymous / ～으로 기부하다 subscribe 《to the funds》 anonymously / ～으로 기고하다 contribute to 《a magazine》 anonymously / ～으로 해두다 keep 《*one's*》 anonymity.
◉ ～광고 a blind advertisement. ～기부 anonymous contributions. ～기증 an anonymous gift. ～비평 pseudonymous 〔unsigned〕 criticism. ～사원 a silent 〔《영》 sleeping〕 partner. ～자 an incognito (남자); an incognita (여자); an anonym. ～작가 an anonym; an anonymous author 〔writer〕. ～조합 an anonymous association. ～투고 an unsigned 〔anonymous〕 contribution. ～투서 an anonymous letter.

**익모초**(益母草) 〚식물〛 a motherwort.

**익사**(溺死) death by drowning. ～하다 be 〔get〕 drowned; drown. ¶ ～ 직전의 아이 a drowning child / ～할 뻔하다 be nearly drowned / ～ 직전의 사람을 구하다 save 〔rescue〕 *a person* from drowning.
◉ ～사고 a drowning accident. ～자 a drowned person; a case of drown-

ing. ～체 the body of a drowned person: ～체 하나가 바닷가로 밀려왔다 A drowned body was washed ashore.

**익살** drollery; waggishness; jocularity; comicality; 《농담》 a joke; a jest; (a) pleasantry; 《유머》 humor; 《기지》 a witticism; 《신소리》 a pun. ¶ ～ 떨다, ～피우다 = 익살부리다 / ～스럽다〔맞다〕 be funny 〔waggish, facetious, comical, clownish, antic, droll〕/ ～스럽게 이야기하다 speak humorously / 원숭이가 자전거 타는 것이 참 ～스러웠다 The monkey looked so funny on the bicycle. ◉ ～꾼 a jokester; a wag; a funnyman; a humorist; a buffoon; a clown; a harlequin; a comic; a comedian.

**익살부리다** play the fool; play antics; jest; joke; make joke; droll. ¶ 그는 언제나 익살을 부린다 He is always clowning 〔having his joke〕.

**익숙하다** 《친숙하다》 (be) familiar; long familiar; be well acquainted 《with》; be well versed 《in》; 《능숙하다》 be skilled 〔experienced, practiced〕 in; be good hand at; be at home in; be familiar with.

¶ 익숙한 일 a familiar job / 미국 사정에 익숙한 사람 a man familiar with things American / …에 익숙해지다 be accustomed 〔used〕 to *do*ing; get used to; be experienced in…; get familiar with / 무대에 ～ be at home on the stage / 교수법에 ～ be an experienced teacher / 그는 무슨 일이나 익숙하게 잘 한다 He does everything well and skillfully. / 그 사람은 연설이 ～ He is at home on the platform. / 이 길에 익숙합니까 Do you know this road well? / 나는 한국말에 점점 익숙해지는 것 같다 I think I am getting better and better in Korean. / 나는 이런 일에는 익숙하지 못합니다 I am unaccustomed 〔strange, new, raw〕 to this kind of business. / 지금은 이 동네에 익숙해졌다 I'm used to this town by now. (★ used [juːst]는 뒤의 to의 무성음 [t]의 영향을 받아, used to는 [juːstə]가 됨. 또 to의 뒤에는 명사 또는 동명사가 옴. 과거의 습관을 나타내는 used to와 혼동하지 말 것: I used to like him, but now I don't. 「옛날에는 그를 좋아했지만 지금은 그렇지 않다」).

**익숙히** with skill; skillfully; adroitly; expertly; with sure 〔practiced〕 hand; like 「an old-timer 〔a veteran〕.

**익스프레셔니즘** 《표현주의》 expressionism.

**익애**(溺愛) blind 〔doting〕 love. ～하다 dote upon; love 《*a person*》 to idolatry; lavish *one's* love upon 《a child》.

**익월**(翌月) the next 〔following〕 month.

**익일**(翌日) the next 〔following〕 day.

**익장**(翼長) 『항공』 the wingspan; the wingspread.

**익조**(益鳥) a beneficial 〔useful〕 bird.

**익충**(益蟲) a useful 〔beneficial〕 insect.

**익히** ¶ ～알다 know well 〔thoroughly, fully〕; be well informed of 《a fact》.

**익히다** ① 《익숙하게 하다》 make *oneself* familiar with; acquaint *oneself* with; accustom *oneself* to; habituate *oneself* to; inure *oneself* to; 《습득하다》 learn; 《훈련하다》 practice; get training in; 《숙련시키다》 gain 〔develop〕 skill in. ¶ 글씨를 ～ practice penmanship / 자동차 운전을 ～ learn how to drive a car / 영어 회화를 ～ practice English conversation / 추위에 몸을 ～ inure *oneself* to cold / 풍토에 ～ acclimate; acclimatize 《미》 / 노동을 익히게 하다 accustom 《*a person*》 to labor.
② 《익게 하다》 (***a***) 《음식을》 cook; boil; do 《meat》; give a boil. ¶ 감자를 ～ boil potatoes / 고기를 잘 ～ get the meat well-done. (***b***) 《과실을》 make ripe; ripen; mature; mellow. ¶ 풋과실을 ～ ripen green fruit. (***c***) 《발효 식품을》 brew; ferment; mature; age 《soysauce, wine, *etc.*》. ¶ 김치를 ～ get kimchi seasoned 〔flavored〕 / 술을 ～ brew rice wine.

**인**(仁) ① 《유교의》 perfect virtue; benevolence; humanity; humaneness; goodwill; charity. ② 《열매의》 a stone; a kernel; a core. ⇨ 핵(核).

**인**(印) a seal; a stamp. ⇨ 도장(圖章).

**인**(寅) 『민속』 ① 《십이지의》 the Sign of the Tiger (=the 3rd of the 12 Earth's Branches). ② ⇨ 인방(寅方). ③ ⇨ 인시(寅時).

**인**(燐) 『화학』 phosphorus (기호 P). ¶ 인의 phosphorous; phosphoric; phossy / 인중독 phosphorous poisoning; phosphorism / 인을 함유한 phosphorous / 인과 화합한 phosphuret(t)ed; phosphoret(t)ed / 인과 화합시키다, 인을 가하다 phosphorate.

**-인**(人) ¶ 문화인 a cultured man / 한국인 a Korean.

**인가**(人家) a house; (a) human dwelling 〔habitation〕. ¶ ～ 근처 an inhabited region; a built-up area / ～가 드문 sparsely 〔thinly〕 populated / ～와 동떨어진 far from human habitation / ～가 없는 deserted; desolate; uninhabited / ～가 많다 be crowded with houses; be thickly inhabited; be densely populated / 이 지역은 ～가 드물다 This area is sparsely populated.

**인가**(認可) approval; permission; 《행정 행위》 license; authorization; sanction. ～하다 approve; permit; give license 〔sanction〕 《to》; authorize. ¶ 교육부 ～의 authorized by the Ministry of Education / ～를 받다 obtain 〔secure, get〕 sanction 〔authorization〕 《from》; obtain a license 〔permit〕 《from》 / 당국의 ～를 얻어 하다 do with the approval of the authorities / ～를 신청하다 apply 《to the office》 for approval 《of the plan》 / 그 다리의 건설이 마침내 ～되었다 The construction of the bridge was approved 〔permitted〕 at last.

◉ ～영업 a licensed business. ～증 a certificate; a permit; a license; a written authority. ～학교 a school recognized 〔approved〕 by the authorities; an authorized 〔accredited〕 school.

**인가**(隣家) a neighboring 〔an adjoining〕 house; a neighbor's house; 《옆집》 the house next door.

**인각**(印刻) carving; engraving. ～하다 engrave 〔cut〕 a seal.

**인간**(人間) 《사람》 a human being; a human; a man; a mortal; flesh and blood; 《인물》 character; 《인류》 man; mankind; the human race.

> 용법 **human being** 다른 동물과 대비시켜 인간을 가리키는 말로 격식 차린 느낌의 말. **human** human being보다는 다소 구어적인 말로 남녀 구별 없이 씀. **man** 무관사 단수형일 때는 「인간·인류·사람」을 뜻하나, 관사 a가 붙으면 「(성인)남자」의 뜻이 됨. human being 보다 좀 문학적인 느낌을 주는 말: Man is mortal (인간은 죽게 마련이다). **mankind**는 인류 전체를 나타내는 좀 격식 차린 말. 성차별 폐지의 입장에서 최근에는 man이나 mankind 대신에 humankind, the human race 또는 human (being)을 쓰는 경향이 많음.

¶ ～의 human; mortal / ～다운 human / ～ 이상의 superhuman / ～ 이하의 subhuman / ～ 중심적인 man-centered; anthropocentric / ～다운 생활 《lead》 a life worthy of man / ～의 약점 human weakness / …하는 것은 ～ 이하〔초～적〕이다 it is less 〔more〕 than human to 《*do*》 / ～은 만물의 영장이다 Man is the lord of (all) creation. / 그들도 ～이다 They are human beings just like we are. / 그는 ～의 탈을 쓰고 있을 뿐이다 He is human only in appearance 〔shape〕. / ～의 손으로는 더 이상 잘 할 수 없다 No man living could do better. / 그것은 ～으로서는 할 수 없다 It is beyond human power. *or* It is humanly impossible. / 나는 그런 것을 할 수 없는 ～이다 I am just not born that way. / 성공을 하고 나서 ～이 변했다 The success has transformed his character. / 그는 절대로 우리를 배신할 ～이 아니다 He is the last person to betray us. / ～ 만사 새옹지마 《속담》 Inscrutable are the ways of Heaven.

◉ ～개조 reform in humanity. ～계 the world of mortals; the terrestrial world. ～고 human sufferings; bitterness of life. ～고락 the delights and sorrows of life. ～공학 human engineering; ergonomics. ～관계 human relations. ～국보 a living national treasure. ～독 a thorough medical checkup 〔examination〕: ～독에 들어가다 go into a hospital for a complete physical examination. ～문화재 human cultural assets 〔properties〕. ～미 humanity; a 〔the〕 human touch; humaneness: ～미가 있는 humane; warm-hearted. ～복제 cloning of human (embryos). ～사회 human society; the community of men. ～상(像) an image of man: 네가 간직하고 있는 그의 ～상은 실제와는 크게 다르다 The image of him you have is very different from what he really is. ～생태학 human ecology. ～성 human nature; humanity: ～성 말살 dehumanization / ～성이 풍부하다 be very human; be rich in human warmth. ～소외 dehumanization: 도시 생활자들은 ～소외에 빠지기 쉽다 Urbanites tend to lose human contact with the other members of the community. ～애 human love; 《인류애》 love of humanity. ～존중 respect for man's life and dignity. ～탐구 the study of man. ～폭탄 a human bomb. ～학 humanics. ～혐오 《성질》 misanthropy; misanthropism. ～형성 character building 〔formation〕. ～화 humanization: 비～화 dehumanization. ～환경선언 the Declaration of Human Environment.

**인감**(印鑑) 〖법〗 *one's* seal; *one's* signet;

《찍은》 a seal impression. ¶ ～ 등록을 하다 have *one's* seal impression registered. ◉ ～도장 *one's* legal 〔registered〕 seal. ～신고〔등록〕 the registration of a seal impression. ～증명 a certificate of a seal impression.

**인갑**(鱗甲) 《갑옷》 a scale armor; 《비늘과 껍데기》 scales and shells; 《동물의》 a scutum (*pl.* -ta); a scute.

**인건비**(人件費) personnel expenses 〔expenditures〕; labor costs. ¶ ～를 줄이다 cut down personnel expenses.

**인걸**(人傑) a distinguished person; an extraordinary man 〔character〕.

**인격**(人格) character; personality; individuality. ¶ ～적 감화 moral influence / ～을 갖추다 have a great personality / ～을 도야하다 build up *one's* character / ～을 존중〔무시〕하다 respect 〔ignore, disregard〕 《*a person's*》 personality / ～을 손상케 하다 injure *a person's* personality.

◉ ～교육 character building 〔training〕. ～권 personal rights. ～도야 the cultivation 〔formation〕 of character; character building. ～문제 a matter of personality. ～분열 dissociation 〔division, disintegration〕 of personality. ～상실 depersonalization. ～자 a man 〔person〕 of noble character; an upright man. ～주의 『철학』 personalism. ～형성 formation of character; character building 〔formation〕; personality development. ～화 impersonation; personification: ～화하다 impersonate; personify.

**인견**(人絹) artificial 〔synthetic〕 silk; rayon. ◉ ～사 rayon yarn.

**인견**(引見) an audience 〔a reception; an interview〕 《with the Queen》. ⇨접견. ～하다 receive 《*a person*》 in audience; give 〔grant〕 an audience to 《*a person*》.

**인경** 《옛날의》 a large curfew bell. ¶ ～을 치다 toll the curfew bell.

**인경**(隣境) an adjacent region; a neighboring land. 「bulbous plant.

**인경**(鱗莖) 『식물』 a bulb. ◉ ～식물 a

**인계**(引繼) 《사무의》 a transfer 《of duties》; 《이어받음》 taking over 《*another's* duties》; 《넘겨줌》 handing over 《*one's* duties》; transfer of business; transfer of control 〔administration〕. ～하다 hand over 〔transfer〕 《*one's* official duties, *one's* business》 to *one's* successor. ¶ ～받다 take over 《*a person's* duties》 / 전임자로부터 사무를 ～받다 take over business from *one's* predecessor / 후임자에게 사무를 ～하다 transfer 〔hand over〕 business to *one's* successor / 나는 내달 초하루에 사무를 ～받기로 되어 있다 I am to take over the business on the 1st of next month. / 사무 ～가 끝났다 Transfer of business has been completed.

**인공**(人工) human work 〔labor〕; 《기교》 human skill; art; artificiality. ¶ ～의, ～적 artificial; man-made〔-created〕; unnatural / ～적으로 artificially; by the art 〔hand〕 of man / ～을 가하다 apply work to; work upon; touch up by human skill / 천연과 ～이 잘 조화되어 있다 They combine nature and art in perfect harmony. / 자연계에는 ～으로 모방할 수 없는 것이 많다 There are many things in nature which defy human ingenuity to imitate.

◉ ～감미료 an artificial sweetener. ～강우 《행위》 rainmaking; 《비》 artificial rain. ～기흉(氣胸) artificial pneumothorax. ～두뇌 a mechanical brain. ～두뇌학 cybernetics: ～두뇌학자 a cybernetician; a cyberneticist. ～미 man-made beauty; the beauty of art. ～부화 artificial incubation. ～사육 artificial breeding. ～수분 artificial pollination. ～수정 artificial insemination (생략 A.I.); test-tube insemination: ～수정아 an artificially inseminated baby; a test-tube baby. ～수태 artificial conception. ～심장 a mechanical heart. ～심폐(心肺) a heart-lung machine. ～양식 artificial culture 《of oysters》. ～어(語) an artificial language. ～영양 《병자의》 feeding by artificial means; 《아기의》 bottle-feeding: ～영양아 a bottle-fed baby. ～유산 an (induced) abortion. ～유전자 an artificial gene. ～잔디 artificial turf. ～장기(臟器) an artificial internal organ. ～접종 artificial infection. ～중절 artificial abortion 〔interruption of pregnancy〕. ～지능 artificial intelligence (생략 AI). ～지진 a man-made earthquake. ～진주 an artificial 〔imitation〕 pearl. ～착색료(着色料) an artificial coloring agent 〔material〕. ～태양 광선 artificial daylight 〔sunlight〕. ～피임 artificial contraception. ～행성 a man-made planet. ～혈관 an artificial blood vessel. ～혈액 artificial blood. ～혜성 an artificial comet. ～호수 a man-made lake. ～호흡 artificial respiration; 《입으로의》 mouth-to-mouth respiration: ~ 호흡기 an artificial respiratory machine [apparatus]; a pulmotor / ~ 호흡을 시키다 practice [try] artificial respiration 《on *a person*》; try mouth-to-mouth respiration [resuscitation] 《on *a person*》.

**인공위성**(人工衛星) a satellite; an artificial [a man-made] satellite. ¶ ~을 발사하다 launch [blast off, shoot up] a satellite. ◉ ~시대 (the) satellite era.

**인과**(因果) 《원인과 결과》 cause and effect; 〖불교〗 karma; retribution (응보). ¶ 전세의 ~ the inevitable consequences of some fault committed in a previous existence / 피할 수 없는 ~ an inevitable retribution / ~로 여겨 단념하다 resign *oneself* to *one's* fate.
◉ ~관계 the relation of cause and effect; a causal relationship 《between two events》; causation; causality. ~법칙[율] the law of cause and effect; the law of causality. ~설 causationism. ~성 causality. ~응보 retributive justice (in the universe); retribution: ~ 응보라고는 하지만, 그의 말로(末路)는 참으로 비참했다 Though no one can escape retribution for evil-doing, he had a really tragic end.

**인광**(燐光) 〖물리·화학〗 phosphorescence. ¶ ~을 내다 shine with phosphorescence; phosphoresce.
◉ ~체 a phosphorescent body.

**인광**(燐鑛) 〖광물〗 mineral [rock] phosphate. ◉ ~석 phosphate rock. ~체 phosphor.

**인구**(人口) ① 《사람 수》 (a) population. ¶ ~가 많은 populous; thickly [densely] populated [inhabited] / ~가 적은 thinly [sparsely] populated [inhabited] / 낚시[골프] ~ the angling [golf-playing] population 《of Korea》/ ~가 조밀[희박]한 지역 a thickly-[sparsely-] populated district / ~ 5백만의 도시 a city with a population of five million inhabitants / 농촌 ~의 감소 rural depopulation / ~의 도시 유입 the drift of population to cities; an influx of people into cities / ~의 도시 집중화 the gravitation of population toward(s) cities / ~가 많다[적다] have a large [small] population / ~가 늘다[줄다] increase [decrease] in population / ~가 조밀[희박]하다 be densely [sparsely] populated; be thickly [thinly] peopled / 너희 나라의 ~는 얼마나 되느냐 What's the population of your country? / 농업[노동] ~가 증가했다 The farming [working] population has increased [grown].
② 《세간의 입·소문》 ¶ ~에 회자(膾炙)하다 be on everybody's lips; be well [widely] known / 이 속담은 ~에 회자되고 있다 This proverb is well known to everybody.
◉ ~감소 a decrease in population; population decrease. ~계획 population planning. ~과잉[과밀] overpopulation; overcrowding: ~ 과밀 지역 an overpopulated [overcrowded] district. ~구성 population composition [make-up 《구어》]. ~동태 demographics; population movements [trends]: ~동태 통계 dynamic statistics of population; vital statistics. ~문제 the 《world, Korean》 population problem. ~밀도 density of population; (a) population density. ~수 (a) population size. ~시계탑 a population clock tower. ~억제 population control: ~억제책 antipopulation measures. ~유발 시설 population increase facilities. ~유입 population influx [inflow]: ~유입을 억제하다 curb the population inflow 《into Seoul》; stem the inflow of population. ~정책 a population policy: ~분산 정책 a policy to disperse the population. ~조사 《국세조사》 a (national) census; a nose-count: ~조사를 하다 take a census (of the population). ~증가 an increase [a rise] in population; population growth: ~ 증가율 the rate of increase in population; a population growth rate / ~ 증가율 제로 zero population growth (생략 ZPG). ~집중 population concentration: 서울에 ~ 집중을 막다 prevent population concentration in Seoul. ~통계 population [vital] statistics: ~ 통계학 demography / ~ 통계학자 a demographer. ~폭발 (a) population explosion. ~학 demography.

**인국**(隣國) a neighboring country [nation]; an adjacent state.

**인권**(人權) human [personal] rights; the rights of man; civil liberties. ¶ ~을 박탈하다 deprive 《*a person's*》 civil rights; proscribe 《a man》/ ~을 지키다 defend human rights / ~을 유린하다 trample [infringe] upon personal [human] rights / ~을 침해당했다고 주장하다 allege encroachment upon personal rights / 너의 행위는 나의 ~을 침해 했다 Your act infringed upon

my personal rights.
◉ ～문제 a question of personal rights. ～상황 the human rights situation. ～선언 the Declaration ｢of the Rights of Man 〔of Human Rights〕. ～외교 human rights diplomacy. ～유린(蹂躪) an infringement of human rights. ～주간 Human Rights Week. ～침해〔유린〕 (a) violation of human rights; an infringement on personal rights. 기본적～ the fundamental human rights.

**인권옹호**(人權擁護) safeguarding 〔defending〕 human rights 〔civil liberties〕; the protection of human rights.
◉ ～위원 a Commissioner for the Protection of Fundamental Human Rights. ～한국 연맹 the Korean Civil Liberties Union. ～협회 the Civil Liberty Association. ～활동 civil liberty activities.

**인근**(隣近) neighborhood; vicinity. ¶ ～의 neighboring; nearby 《hospital》/ ～주민들 neighbors; [총칭] neighborhood / ～의 마을 a nearby village / ～의 나라들 neighboring countries / ～에 in the neighborhood 《of》; nearby; about 〔near, around〕 here 〔there〕.

**인금**(人―) *one's* personality; *one's* personal worth. ¶ ～이 잘나다 have an excellent personality; have capability / ～이 못나다 be worthless 〔good-for-nothing〕.

**인기**(人氣) popularity; popular 〔public〕 favor.
¶ 일시적〔덧없는〕 ～ a passing 〔an ephemeral〕 popularity / 폭발적 ～ tremendous popularity / ～를 얻으려는 정책 (a) vote-catching policy / ～위주의 언동 behavior aimed only at winning popularity / 세계적 ～ 가수 a singer of international appeal / 흘러간 ～ 가요 a once-popular song dear to the people's hearts / ～ 위주의 정책 a claptrap policy / ～ 있는 popular / ～가 있다 be popular 《with, among》; enjoy popularity; be in favor 《with》/ ～가 없다〔없어지다, 떨어지다〕 be 〔become〕 unpopular 《with》; lack 〔lose, fall in〕 popularity / ～가 오르다 become increasingly popular; rise in popularity / ～를 얻다〔끌다〕 win 〔gain〕 popularity; 《연극에서》 make a hit / ～를 유지하다 maintain *one's* popularity / ～를 잃다〔떨어뜨리다〕 fall 〔come〕 into *one's* popularity; become unpopular 《with, among》/ ～를 회복하다 recover 〔regain〕 *one's* popularity / ～에 영합하다 fawn on the public favor; curry favor with popular opinion / 대중의 ～를 누리다 command 〔win 《its》 way to〕 general popularity / ～를 얻으려고 애쓰다 make efforts to win public favor; seek popularity; play to the gallery 《구어》/ 그는 모든 학생에게 ～가 있다 He commands 〔wins〕 the popularity of all the students. / 그는 여성들한테 ～가 있다 He is popular among ladies.
◉ ～가수 a popular singer. ～경쟁 a popularity contest. ～배우 a popular actor 〔actress〕; a box-office star; a star at the height of his 〔her〕 popularity. ～선수 a star 〔popular〕 player. ～소설 a sensational 〔catching〕 novel. ～순위표 a popularity list. ～연기자 a show stopper. ～연예인 some popular entertainers and singers. ～인(人) a popular person. ～작가 a popular 〔star〕 writer. ～정책 a claptrap policy. ～주(株) an active 〔popular〕 stock. ～직업 an occupation dependent on public favor. ～투표 a popularity vote. ～품목 a popular item 〔article〕. ～프로 a hit 〔popular〕 program.

**인기척**(人―) 《show》 an indication 〔a sign〕 of a person being around. ¶ ～이 없다 show no indications of people being around / ～ 없는 거리 a deserted 〔an empty〕 street / 그 집에는 ～이 없었다 There was no signs of life in the house.

**인꼭지**(印―) the handle of a seal.

**인끈**(印―) the cord attached to the handle of a seal; a seal-chain.

**인날**(人―) 『민속』 the seventh of January (in the lunar calendar).

**인내**(人―) the smell of a human being.

**인내**(忍耐) perseverance; endurance; patience; fortitude. ～하다 be patient 《with》; endure; put up with; bear; persevere 《in》.

> 용법 **perseverance** 어려움·장애를 극복하여 어떤 목표를 달성하려는 적극적이고 부단한 노력. **endurance** 고통·어려움을 참고 견디는 능력, 즉 인내력·지구력의 뜻. **patience** 끈기와 참을성을 뜻하는 일반적인 말. 불쾌·고통·불행·늦어짐 등에 대해 불평하지 않고 냉정히 참고 견디는 덕을 뜻함. **fortitude** 고통·고뇌·어려움·역경 속에서도 이를 참으며 뚫고 나아가는 불굴의 정신을 뜻함.

¶ ~심이 강한 persevering; patient; stoical / ~심이 없다 lack in patience; be impatient / ~심을 시험하다 try 《*a person*》 patience / 나의 ~도 이제 한계에 이르렀다 My patience is worn out.
◉ ~력 (power of) endurance; perseverance; 《지구력》 staying power: ~력이 없는 《a man》 lacking in staying power 〔perseverance〕; impatient.

**인년**(寅年) 〖민속〗 the Year of the Tiger.

**인대**(靭帶) 〖해부〗 a ligament; a cord.

**인더스강**(—江) 《인도의 강》 the Indus River.

**인더스문명**(—文明) 〖역사〗 the Indus civ「ilization.

**인덕**(人德) *one's* natural virtue 〔qualities〕; *one's* personal magnetism. ¶ 그것은 그의 ~에 따른 것이다 That depends on his natural virtue.

**인덕**(仁德) benevolence; goodness; humanity.

**인데** ① [연결형] and; but; when. ¶ 이것은 내 책~ 보고 나서 돌려 주게 This is my book, return it to me when you are through with it. ② [종결형] ¶ 참 좋은 곳~ Why, it's a very nice place!

**인덱스** 《색인》 an index (*pl.* ~es, -dices). ¶ ~를 붙이다 index 《a book》; provide 《a book》 with an index; append an index to 《a book》 / ~를 만들다 compile an index. ◉ ~카드 an index card.

**인도**(人道) ① 《보도》 a footway; a footpath; a sidewalk 《미》; a pavement 《영》; a walk; a pedestrian way. ¶ ~와 차도의 구별이 없는 장소 a place without distinction of footpath and roadway / ~를 걷다 walk along a sidewalk. ② 《도덕》 humanity; morality. ¶ ~적 humanitarian; humane / 비~적 inhumane / ~적 원조 humanitarian aid / ~적 견지에서 from a humanitarian standpoint; on humanitarian grounds / ~를 위해 in the interest 〔cause〕 of humanity; for humanity's sake / ~를 무시하다 ignore humanity; disregard the laws of humanity / ~에 어긋나다 be contrary to humanity; be inhumane / ~적으로 다루다 treat 《*a person*》 humanely / ~적 견지에서 사형에 반대하는 사람도 있다 Some people are 「against 〔opposed to〕 capital punishment on humanitarian grounds.
◉ ~교 a footbridge; a pedestrian overpass. ~문제 a question touching humanity; a problem demanding a humanitarian solution. ~주의 humanitarianism: ~주의자 a humanitarian / ~주의의 이름으로 in the name of humanity.

**인도**(引渡) 《물건의》 delivery; 《재산 등의》 transfer; 《사람·물건의》 handing 〔turning〕 over; 《죄인의》 surrender; extradition (국제간의). ~하다 deliver; transfer; hand 〔turn, make〕 over; 《권리 등을》 give 〔deliver〕 up; transfer; 《포로·범인 등을》 surrender; extradite.
¶ 전쟁 범죄인의 ~ the extradition of a war criminal / 화물을 ~하다 deliver goods / ~받다 take delivery of 《*things*》 from 《*a person*》 / 재산을 ~하다 transfer 〔deliver up〕 property / 도둑을 경찰에 ~하다 hand 〔turn〕 over a thief to the police / 유해를 유족에게 ~하다 hand over 《*a person's*》 remains to *his* family / 점포를 채권자에게 ~하다 turn over *one's* business to a creditor / (국제간의) 범죄자의 ~를 요구하다 ask for the extradition of a criminal.
◉ ~가격 delivered cost. ~부족 short delivery. ~식 a handing-over ceremony. ~인 a deliverer. ~일〔시기〕 the date 〔time〕 of delivery; a settlement 〔delivery〕 day. ~장소 a place of delivery. ~조건 terms of delivery: 귀사의 ~조건을 알려 주십시오 Could you inform us of your terms of delivery? ~조약 《범죄인의》 an extradition treaty. ~필(畢) delivered; transferred.

**인도**(引導) 《지도》 guidance; 《선도》 lead. ~하다 guide; lead; show. ⇨ 안내. ¶ 신의 ~ divine guidance / 후진을 ~하다 give guidance to the younger generation / 아무를 바른 길로 ~하다 lead *a person* into the right path. ◉ ~자 a guide.

**인도**(印度) India. ¶ ~의 Indian.
◉ ~공화국 the Republic of India. ~말 Indian; 《공용어》 Hindi. ~사람〔인〕 an Indian. ~양 the Indian Ocean. ~철학 Hindu philosophy.

**인도네시아** (the Republic of) Indonesia. ¶ ~의 Indonesian. ◉ ~말 Indonesian. ~사람 an Indonesian.

**인도어** indoor. ◉ ~게임 indoor games. ~스포츠 indoor sports.

**인도유럽** ¶ ~어의 Indo-European.
◉ ~어(語) an Indo-European language. ~어족 the Indo-European family of languages.

**인도차이나** Indochina. ¶ ~의 Indochinese. ◉ ~사람 an Indochinese.

**인동**(忍冬) 《한약제》 dried honeysuckle

stems and leaves. ◉ ～덩굴 〖식물〗 a honeysuckle.

**인두** ① 《다림질의》 a small iron. ② 《납땜용》 a soldering iron. ◉ ～질 《다림질》 ironing; 《땜질》 soldering: ～질하다 iron; solder. ～판 an ironing board.

**인두**(咽頭) 〖해부〗 the pharynx (*pl.* ～es, -rynges). ◉ ～염 〖의학〗 pharyngitis.

**인두겁**(人—) a human mask; human shape; 《with》 the covering of a human. ¶ ～을 쓴 악마 a demon in human shape / 그는 ～만 썼지 사람이 아니다 He is a brute in human form.

**인두세**(人頭稅) a poll tax; a head 〔per capita〕 tax. ¶ ～를 매기다 levy a poll tax.

**인둘리다**(人—) get dizzy from overcrowding; feel sick 〔faint〕 from the jostling of a crowd.

**인들** granted that it be 〔is〕; even though it be 〔is〕. ¶ 세 살 먹은 아이～ even a little child / 아무리 무정한 사람～그 광경을 보고 눈물을 안 흘릴 수 없을 것이다 The most hard-hearted man would be moved to tears at the sight. / 낙화～ 꽃이 아니랴 쓸어 무삼하리요 Fallen blossoms are still blossoms—Do not sweep them away.

**인디고** indigo. 「paper; Bible paper.

**인디아** ＝ 인도(印度). ◉ ～페이퍼 India

**인디애나** 《미국의 주》 Indiana (생략 Ind.).

**인디언** an Indian; a Red Indian. ◉ 아메리카～ an American Indian; a Native American.

**인력**(人力) human strength 〔power〕; human agency (자연력에 대해); human efforts; man power (일률 단위). ¶ ～으로 움직이는 비행기 a man-powered aircraft / 기술 ～을 양성하다 nurture expert manpower / ～으로는 불가능하다 be beyond the power of man; be humanly impossible / 자연현상이란 ～으로 통제할 수 있는 것이 아니다 Natural phenomena are beyond human control. ◉ ～감사 manpower inspection. ～개발 development of human resources. ～난 manpower problems. ～동원 mobilization of manpower. ～배치표 a manpower loading chart. ～비행 (a) man-powered flight. ～수급계획 a manpower supply and demand plan. ～수출 manpower export; export of labor force.

**인력**(引力) 《지구의》 gravitation; (the force 〔pull〕 of ) gravity; (a) gravitational force 〔power, pull〕; 《자기의》 magnetism; 《물질간의》 attraction; (an) attractive power. ¶ ～있는 attractive / 태양〔지구〕의 ～ solar 〔terrestrial〕 gravitation / ～의 법칙 the law of gravitation / 조수의 간만은 달의 ～ 때문이다 The ebb and flow of the tide are due to the gravitation of the moon. ◉ ～권 the gravitational field; the sphere of gravitation.

**인력거**(人力車) a rickshaw; a ricksha. ¶ ～로 by rickshaw / ～에 타다 take 〔ride in〕 a rickshaw / ～로 가다 go by rickshaw / ～를 끌다 pull a rickshaw. ◉ ～꾼 a rickshaw man; a rickshaw puller.

**인류**(人類) man; mankind; humankind; humanity; the human species 〔race〕; human beings. ¶ ～의 human; man's 《future》; of mankind / ～의 복지 the welfare of man 〔mankind〕 / ～의 행복 human happiness / ～의 행복을 증진하다 further the happiness of the human race. ◉ ～사 the history of man; human history: ～사상에 in human history. ～사회 human society. ～애 love for humanity 〔mankind〕. ～학 anthropology: ～학자 an anthropologist / 문화〔형질〕 ～학 cultural 〔physical〕 anthropology.

**인륜**(人倫) ① 《인도(人道)》 humanity; humaneness; human duties. ② 《도덕》 morality; moral principles. ¶ ～에 어그러지는 행위 an act contrary to morality / ～에 어그러지다 go contrary to morality / ～을 짓밟다 transgress moral laws. ◉ ～도덕 ethics and morality. ～지 대사 the important 〔grave〕 matter of life.

**인마**(人馬) 《사람과 말》 (both) man and horse; 《마부와 말》 horseman 〔rider〕 and horse. ¶ ～의 왕래 the traffic of men and horses.

**인마르셋** 〖항해〗 《국제 해사 위성 기구》 INMARSAT. [<*In*ternational *Mar*itime *Sat*ellite Organization]

**인망**(人望) popularity; popular favor. ¶ ～이 있는 popular 《with》; of high reputation / ～이 없는 unpopular / ～이 있는 사람 a popular person 〔character〕; a person of wide 〔good〕 reputation / ～이 높다 enjoy a high reputation; be highly reputed; be very popular / ～을 얻다 win 〔acquire, attain, gain〕 popularity; become popular / ～을 잃다 lose *one's* popularity; forfeit people's esteem; lose public support / 그는 이웃에서 ~이 있다 He is popular with his neighbors. ◉ ~가 a popular person; a person of wide reputation.

**인맥**(人脈) personal relationships [connections]; a line of personal contact. ¶ ~을 형성하다 form a line of personal contact / 그것은 그의 ~ 덕택이다 His personal connections did it.

**인면**(人面) a human face. ◉ ~수심(獸心) a beast with a human face; man in face but brute in mind.

**인멸**(湮滅) extinction; destruction. ~하다 destroy 《evidence》; make away with. ¶ …이 ~되다 be extinct; get lost [destroyed] / 증거를 ~하다 destroy [make away with] the proofs 《of》; destroy [stifle] evidence 《of *one's* crime》.

**인명**(人名) a person's name. ◉ ~록 a directory; a Who's Who. ~부 a roll; a list of names; a directory: ~부를 찾아보다 look up 《*a person's* name and address》 in a directory. ~사전 a biographical dictionary; 《신사록》 a Who's Who.

**인명**(人命) (human) life. ¶ 많은 ~을 희생하여 at a great sacrifice of life / ~에 관계되다 affect 《*a person's*》 life; endanger life / ~을 구조하다 save a life / ~을 존중하다 respect (human) life; hold life sacred / ~을 경시하다 make light of (human) life / 그 화재는 많은 ~을 앗아갔다 The fire 「took a heavy toll of lives [caused a great loss of life]. / ~은 재천이다 《속담》 Every bullet has its billet.
◉ ~구조 saving a life; lifesaving. ~손실 a loss [the toll] of lives.

**인문**(人文) human knowledge [inquiry]; civilization; culture; humanity. ¶ ~의 발달 the advance of civilization.
◉ ~ 고등학교 an academic high school. ~과목 humanities. ~과학 the humanities. ~주의 humanism: ~주의의 humanistic / ~주의자 a humanist. ~지리 human geography. ~학 humanities; humane studies.

**인물**(人物) 《사람》 a person; a man; a character (별난); a figure (거물); a personage (명사 등); 《인품》 character; personality; 《인재》 an able man; a talented man; 《작품 중의》 a character; a personage.
¶ 위대한 ~ a great man [mind] / 세계적 ~ a world figure; a person of worldwide fame / 위험 ~ a dangerous person / 주의 ~ a person on the black list / 중요 ~ an important person; a VIP / 변변치 않은 ~ a worthless character; a good-for-nothing fellow / ~이 못 생긴 사람 an ill-favored person / 장래가 기대되는 ~ a promising young man / ~이 좋다 be of good character; be personable / ~을 양성하다 train personal ability / ~을 시험하다 put 《*a person's*》 character [ability] to the test; take 《*a person's*》 measure / ~을 보증하다 answer for 《*a person's*》 character / ~을 그리다 《그림에서》 paint a human figure; 《소설에서》 draw [delineate] a character; characterize 《*a person*》 / ~ 그림에 서툴다 be poor at figure painting / ~본위로 생각하다 judge 《*a person*》 primarily in the light of *his* personal character / 그는 어떠한 ~인가 What sort of person is he? / 그는 재주는 있지만 ~이 작다 He has talent all right, but lacks greatness. / 지금 정계에는 ~이 적다 There are few men of caliber [ability] on the political scene at present. / 이 소설에는 ~이 잘 묘사되어 있다 The characters are all well delineated in this novel.
◉ ~ 가난 a dearth [shortage] of talented men. ~묘사 a character sketch; a profile. ~시험 a character [personality] test. ~양성 character building; training of men of ability. ~점묘 a personal sketch; a personality profile; a profile 《of a scholar》. ~평 personal criticism; a character sketch. ~평가 character grading. ~화 a figure painting [picture, piece]; a portrait.
작중~ the characters in the story.

**인민**(人民) the people [citizens]; the populace; the public; the subjects. ¶ ~의, ~에 의한, ~을 위한 정부 a government of the people, by the people, for the people / ~의 권리 the civil rights / ~을 보호하다 protect the people / 북한의 ~군 North Korean People's Army (생략 KPA).
◉ ~공사 《중국의》 a people's commune. ~공화국 a people's republic. ~당 the people's party. ~위원 《옛 소련의》 a (People's) Commissar: ~ 위원회 the Council of People's Commission. ~재판 a people's [kangaroo] court: ~재판을 받다 be tried in a kangaroo court / ~재판을 하다 subject 《*a person*》 to a kangaroo court.

～전선 the people's 〔popular〕 front. ～정부 the people's government. ～주권 popular sovereignty. ～해방군 the People's Liberation Army.

**인박이다** fall 〔get〕 into the habit of 《*do*ing》; get 〔become〕 addicted to; 《속어》 get hooked 《on heroin》. ¶ 인박인 사람 a habitual user 《of》.

**인방**(引枋) 〖건축〗 the lintel (of a door or window); a molding; a cornice; a baseboard.

**인방**(寅方) 〖민속〗 the Direction of the Tiger (=northeast-by-east).

**인방**(隣邦) a neighboring 〔an adjacent〕 country.

**인벤토리** 《재고 목록》 (an) inventory. ¶ 회사 비품의 완전한 ～를 만들다 make a complete inventory of the company equipment.

**인보이스** 〖상업〗 an invoice. ¶ 이들 품목에 대한 개별적인 ～를 보내겠습니다 We will be invoicing you separately for these items.

**인복**(人福) the good fortune to have kind friends.

**인본**(印本) a printed book.

**인본주의**(人本主義) 〖철학〗 humanism. ◉ ～자 a humanist.

**인부**(人夫) 《일꾼》 a workman; a sundry laborer; 《영》 a navvy; a coolie; 《운반부》 a porter; a carrier.
◉ ～십장 a foreman; a coolie-master. 선로～ a lineman; a railway worker. 토목～ a construction laborer; a navvy.

**인분**(人糞) (human) feces; excrement(s); ordure; night soil. ◉ ～비료 human manure; night soil for manure.

**인비**(人秘) secrecy of personnel affairs.

**인비**(燐肥) 《인산 비료》 phosphatic manure 〔fertilizer〕; superphosphate.

**인비늘**(人―) scaly skin (on a human); skin peelings; dandruff (비듬).

**인사**(人士) men of society; people; persons. ¶ 거물급 ～ an important figure; a VIP. ◉ 반정부～ an anti-government personage. 재야～ an opposition personage.

**인사**(人事) ① 《사교상의》 greeting; salutation; respects; the time of day (아침 저녁의); compliments (말); an address (식사). ～하다 greet; salute; say hello; pay *one's* respects; meet; pass the time of day; give an address; pay a visit of courtesy 《to》. ¶ 작별 ～ a farewell address; parting words / 아침〔작별〕 ～를 하다 say good morning 〔goodby(e)〕 / ～를 주고받다 exchange greeting 《with *a person*》 / ～시키다 《소개》 introduce / 모자를 들어 ～하다 raise 〔lift〕 *one's* hat to 《*a person*》 / 모자를 흔들어 ～하다 wave *one's* hat in greeting / 신임 ～를 하다 《연설》 make an inaugural address; 《답례》 make *one's* inaugural calls / ～말도 없이 가 버리다 leave without even saying good-bye / 아직 ～를 나누지 못했는데 제 이름은 한일수올시다 I don't think we've met yet. My name is Ilsu Han. / 두 분이 ～를 하셨습니까 Have you met each other? / 김 박사와는 이미 ～를 나눈 사이일세 I have already met Dr. Kim. / ～를 하고 수업을 받는다 After passing the time of day we take lessons.
② 《절》 a bow; a kowtow; a salutation. ～하다 bow 《low, politely》; make a 《polite》 bow 《to》; kowtow. ¶ 어른한테 ～를 하다 make a bow to *one's* elder / ～를 받다 receive the bows of 《*one's* students》.
③ 《감사의 답례》 thanks; gratitude; acknowledgment; a present (in acknowledgment). ～하다 thank; acknowledge; make a present (in acknowledgment). ¶ 그에게 선물을 받았는데 무엇으로 ～를 할까 What shall I give him in return for his present?
④ 《예의》 manners; decorum; etiquette; civility; courtesy. ¶ ～를 알다〔모르다〕 have good 〔no〕 manners / ～차 방문하다 pay a courtesy call / 그렇게 하는 것은 ～가 아니다 It is bad manners to do so.
⑤ 《사람의 일》 human 〔personnel〕 affairs; what men (can) do. ¶ ～를 다하고 천명을 기다리다 do *one's* best and leave the rest to Providence.
⑥ 《의식》 consciousness; senses. ⇨ 인사불성(人事不省).
⑦ 《인사행정》 personnel affairs; personnel management 〔administration〕. ¶ 공무원의 ～는 지연, 학연, 혈연을 따지지 않고 공정히 이루어져야 한다 Personnel management in officialdom should be fairly conducted without adherence to regionalism, school relations, and kinship.
◉ ～고과 performance rating; merit rating; (the) assessment of an employee's performance. ～과 the personnel section 〔office〕: ～ 과장 the head of a personnel section. ～관리〔행정〕 personnel management 〔administration〕. ～권 the right of personnel management: ～권을 행사하다

exercise the right to enforce personnel administration. ～기록 a personnel record. ～담당관 an officer [a director] in charge of personnel administration. ～란 a personal column; personal notes. ～말 greetings; compliments; an address (연설). ～부 a personnel division. ～부장 a personnel manager. ～비밀 secrecy of personnel affairs. ～소송 a personal suit. ～위원회 the personnel committee. ～이동 personnel changes; a shake-up; a turnover; a reshuffle: ～이동의 발령 an official announcement of personnel changes. ～장 a greeting card; 《전임·이전 따위의》 a notice.

**인사교류**(人事交流) an interchange of personnel 《between》. ¶ 부처간의 ～ interministerial personnel reshuffle.

**인사불성**(人事不省) ① 《기절》 unconsciousness; loss of consciousness; stupor; suspended animation. ¶ ～의 unconscious; insensible; senseless / ～이 되다 lose consciousness; fall [become] unconscious [insensible, senseless]; fall into a swoon; pass into a state of coma / ～이 되도록 마시다니, 어리석다 It's stupid of you to drink yourself into senselessness [unconsciousness]. ② 《무례》 having no sense of propriety.

**인사성**(人事性) courteousness; sociability. ¶ ～이 밝다[없다] have good [no] manners; be well-[ill-]mannered.

**인산**(燐酸) 〖화학〗 phosphoric acid. ◉ ～ 마그네슘 magnesium phosphate. ～비료 phosphatic fertilizer [manure]; phosphate. ～석회 phosphate of lime. ～암모늄 phosphate of ammonium. ～칼륨 potassium phosphate. ～칼슘 calcium phosphate.

**인산인해**(人山人海) hordes of people. ¶ 교회 앞은 ～를 이루었다 A crowd gathered before the church.

**인삼**(人蔘) a ginseng. ¶ 한국은 고품질의 ～으로 전세계에 평판이 나 있다 Korea is well reputed worldwide for its top-quality ginseng. / 한국 ～은 정력을 북돋우는 데 가장 효과적이라고 널리 알려져 있다 Korean ginseng is widely known to be the most effective in building-up stamina. ◉ ～정과 ginseng preserved in honey. ～주[차] ginseng liquor [tea]. 한국 ～ 연초 연구소 the Korea Ginseng and Tobacco Research Institute.

**인상**(人相) 《얼굴 생김새》 looks; facial features; 《관상학상의》 physiognomy. ¶ ～이 좋지 않은 evil-[ill-]looking / ～이 천한[고귀한] vulgar-[noble-]looking / 천한 ～ a low cast of countenance / ～이 좋지 못한 사내 a man of evil physiognomy; an evil-looking man; a hard-featured man / ～을 보다 read [judge] 《*a person's*》 character by the face; tell 《*a person's*》 fortunes by physiognomy / 그 녀석 ～이 마음에 안 든단 말야 I don't like his looks. / 범인의 ～을 기억하고 있습니까 Do you remember the looks [features] of the criminal? ◉ ～서(書) a personal description: ～서와 부합하다 answer [fit, meet] the description of 《*a person*》. ～학 physiognomy; metoposcopy: ～학자 a physiognomist.

**인상**(引上) ① 《끌어올림》 pulling [drawing] up; 〖역도〗 the snatch (lift). ～하다 pull [draw] up.
② 《가격 따위의》 raising; a raise; (an) increase. ～하다 raise; hike; increase; up 《구어》. ¶ 운임을 ～하다 raise fare / 기본 임금의 ～을 요구하다 demand a raise of the wage base / 가격이 5백 원으로 ～되었다 The price was raised to 500 won.

**인상**(印象) an impression. ⇨ 느낌. ¶ ～적 impressive / 첫～ the first impression / 좋은 ～ a good [favorable] impression / 나쁜 ～ a bad [an unfavorable] impression / 사라지지 않는 ～ an indelible [ineffaceable, ineradicable] impression / 잊을 수 없는 ～ an unforgettable impression / 유쾌한 ～ a pleasant [an agreeable] impression / 불쾌한 ～ a disagreeable [an unpleasant] impression / ～을 남기다 leave an impression behind / ～을 받다 receive [get, gain] an impression / 깊은 ～을 받다 be deeply impressed / ～을 주다 impress 《*a person*》; give an impression; make an impression 《on *a person*, on *a person's* mind》 / 좋은[나쁜] ～을 주다 leave [exercise, have] a favorable [an unfavorable] impression 《upon *a person*, upon *a person's* mind》; give 《*a person*》 a favorable [an unfavorable] impression / 첫～을 말하다 tell the first impressions 《of》 / 서울의 ～이 어떻습니까 How did Seoul impress [strike] you? / 이것이 미국에서 받은 ～이다 These are the impressions I brought away from America. / 그의 ～이 마음 속 깊이 남아 있다 His image is deeply impressed

on my mind. / 그의 연설은 청중에게 깊은 ~을 주었다 His speech produced a deep impression on the audience.
◉ ~비판 impressionistic criticism. ~주의 impressionism: ~주의자 an impressionist. ~파 the impressionist school; the impressionists: ~파 화가 an impressionist painter.

**인상**(鱗狀) scale-like(ness); scaliness. ¶ ~의 scale-like; scaly; squamous.

**인색**(吝嗇) stinginess; 《영》 meanness; niggardliness; tightfistedness; parsimoniousness. ~하다 (be) stingy; niggardly; miserly; tightfisted; close-fisted; parsimonious; 《미》 cheap; 《영》 mean. ¶ ~한 사람 a miser; a stingy [close-fisted] fellow; a niggard; 《미》 a penny pincher; a skin; a screw / 그는 돈에 정말 ~하다 He is very mean about money. / ~하게 굴지 마라 Don't be so stingy. / 그의 공을 찬양하는 데 ~하지 않다 I don't grudge [stint] due praise for his meritorious deed. / 나는 잘못을 인정하는 데 ~하지 않다 I feel no reluctance in acknowledging my errors.

**인생**(人生) man's [human] life; (*one's*) life; human existence.
¶ ~의 human; life / ~의 부침(浮沈) the ups and downs of fortune / ~의 목적[의미] the aim [meaning] of life / ~의 종말 *one's* journey's end / ~의 쾌락 the pleasures of life / ~에 지치다 find life a bore / ~을 낙관하다 take an optimistic [a cheerful] view of life; look on the bright side of life / ~을 비관하다 take a pessimistic [gloomy] view of life; look on the dark side of life / ~을 꿈결처럼 보내다 dream away *one's* life / ~ 불과 50년 Man's span of life is but [only] fifty years. / 그것이 ~이야 Such is life. *or* This is how the world wags on. / 제목이 「하숙생」이란 한국 노래의 가사는 「~은 나그네길, 어디서 왔다가 어디로 가느냐」로 시작된다 A Korean song, titled "Hasuksaeng," whose lyric lines starts as "Life is a vagabond's path. Where do we come from? and Where are we heading for?"
◉ ~관 *one's* view of life; *one's* 「outlook on [attitude toward] life: 진지한 ~관을 가진 사람 a man of a serious outlook on life. ~기록 a human document. ~문제 the problem of life. ~예찬 a psalm of life. ~철학 a philosophy of life. ~ 칠십고래희(七十古來稀) Men seldom [Few people] live to be seventy. ~파 the humanists. ~항로[행로] the tenor [path] of *one's* life; *one's* course of life.

**인석**(人石) the two stone statues before a king's grave.

**인선**(人選) the choice of the personnel; the selection of a suitable person. ~하다 select [choose] a (suitable) person 《for》. ¶ 각료의 ~ the selection of Cabinet members / ~난이다 find difficulty in choosing the right person / ~을 잘못하다 choose the wrong man / 그는 ~에서 빠졌다 He was left out of the choice. / 그의 후임자를 지금 ~중이다 They are now looking for his successor.

**인성**(人性) human nature; humanity; humanism; 《본능》 human instinct. ¶ ~은 본래 선(善)한 것이다 All men are born good. *or* Man is intrinsically good. ◉ ~론 Treatise of Human Nature. ~주의자 a humanist. ~학 ethology.

**인세**(印稅) 《인지세》 the stamp duty; 《저작물의》 royalties 《on a book》. ¶ 책의 정가에 대하여 1할의 ~를 지급하다 pay a royalty of [to] 10% upon the published price of the book / 나는 책의 정가의 5%를 ~로 받게 되어 있다 I'm to receive a royalty of five percent on sales of the book. (★ 이 경우의 sales는 「매상고」를 뜻함).

**인솔**(引率) leading; guiding. ~하다 lead; head; guide; be in charge of 《a party》. ¶ 선생님의 ~ 아래 headed [led] by a teacher / 그는 학생들을 ~하여 소풍을 떠났다 Leading his pupils, he set out on an excursion. ◉ ~자 a leader; a guide.

**인쇄**(印刷) printing; presswork. ~하다 print; put into print; print [work, strike, run] off 《800 copies》. ¶ 색도 ~ color(ed) printing / ~의 잘못 a misprint / ~에 부치다 send [put] 《a book》 to press / ~중이다 be printing; be in (the) press; be in the printer's hand / 작은 글자로 ~하다 print in small types / 3도쇄로 ~하다 print in three colors / ~가 선명하다 be clearly printed / ~가 선명치 않다 the 《words, pictures》 do not come out well; be poorly printed / 이 책은 1만 부 ~되었다 This book had a printing of ten thousand copies.
◉ ~공 a printer; a pressman; a machine man. ~공장 a printing house

〔office, shop〕. ～국 the Printing Bureau. ～기(계) a printing machine 〔press〕; a press. ～물 printed matter; 《영》 printed papers. ～부수 《서적 등 1회의》 a print 〔press〕 run; a run. ～소 a printing house 〔office, shop〕. ～술 (the art of) printing; a printing technique. ～업 the printing industry 〔business〕. ～용 《for》 printing purposes. ～(용)지 printing paper. ～인 a printer. ～잉크 printing 〔printer's〕 ink. ～체 문자 a print letter. ～판 a printing plate; a press plate.

**인수**(人數) the number of people 〔persons〕; numerical strength. ¶ ～가 늘다〔줄다〕 increase 〔decrease〕 in number / ～를 세다 count the heads / ～를 제한하다 limit the number.

**인수**(引受) 《맡음》 undertaking; charge; 《어음 따위의》 acceptance; 《주식·사채·공채의》 underwriting; 《보증》 guaranty; security. ～하다 《일 따위를》 undertake; 《책임지다》 take charge of; answer for; hold *oneself* responsible for; go 〔stand〕 security for; 《어음을》 accept; guarantee; 《인계받다》 take over 《*a person's* business》.
¶ ～필의 accepted; underwritten / 부채를 ～하다 hold *oneself* liable for a debt; shoulder another's debt (남의 부채를) / 사건을 ～하다 take (up) an affair in hand / 책임을 ～하다 assume the responsibility / 어려운 문제를 ～받다 undertake a difficult problem / 미안하지만 이 일은 ～할 수 없다 I'm sorry, but I can't take on 〔up〕 this work.
◉ ～거절 nonacceptance; dishonor. ～어음 an accepted 〔acceptable〕 bill. ～은행 an accepting 〔undertaking〕 bank. ～채권 assumed bonds. 조건부〔단순〕 ～ qualified 〔absolute, clean〕 acceptance.

**인수**(因數) 〖수학〗 a factor. ¶ 2와 3은 6의 ～다 2 and 3 are factors of 6.
◉ ～분해 resolution into factors; factorization: ～분해하다 resolve 〔solve, break up〕 《a quantity》 into factors; factorize.

**인수인**(引受人) 《보증인》 a surety; a guarantor; 《수락자》 an acceptor (환어음의); an underwriter (공채·사채 모집의); 《시체·분실물 따위의》 a claimer; a claimant. ¶ ～ 없는 시체 an unclaimed body.

**인수합병**(引受合併) merger and acquisition (생략 M & A).

**인술**(仁術) 《의술》 the healing art; the science of medicine.

**인슈트** 〖야구〗 an inshoot.

**인슐린** 〖약〗 insulin. ◉ ～쇼크 an insulin shock.

**인스턴트** instant. ◉ ～식품 instant food; precooked food; fast 〔convenience, service〕 food. ～커피 instant coffee.

**인스피레이션** (an) inspiration. ⇨ 영감(靈感).

**인습**(因習·因襲) a long-established custom 〔usage〕; convention; conventionality. ¶ ～적(으로) conventional(ly) / ～을 좇다 follow the convention / ～을 타파하다 break usage; do away with 〔break through〕 conventionalities / ～에서 벗어나다 depart from convention; leave the beaten track / ～에 사로잡히다〔얽매이다〕 be a slave to 〔of〕 convention; be 「fettered by 〔enslaved by, tied down to〕 tradition. ◉ ～도덕 conventional morality 〔morals〕. ～주의 conventionalism. ～타파 iconoclasm.

**인시**(寅時) 〖민속〗 the Watch of the Tiger. ① the 3rd of the 12 double-hours (=the period between 3 and 5 a.m.). ② 5th of the 24 hours (= 3:30–4:30 a.m.).

**인시류**(鱗翅類) 〖곤충〗 Lepidoptera.

**인식**(認識) awareness; cognition; recognition; perception; understanding; knowledge. ～하다 recognize; perceive; have cognizance of; be cognizant of; understand; realize; see; know; become aware 《of, that ...》. ¶ 바르게 ～하다 have a correct understanding 《of》; duly recognize 《the fact that ...》; look at 《*a matter*》 in the right light; show a true perception 《of》 / ～을 새로이하다 see 《it》 in a new light; find a new meaning 《in》; be awakened to 《its》 new significance / 그 문제의 중요성을 잘 ～하고 있다고 생각한다 I think I'm fully aware of the importance of the matter. / 그 문제에 대한 일반 시민의 ～은 아직 깊지 않다 The public has only a superficial understanding of the matter. ◉ ～력 cognitive faculty. ～론 〖철학〗 epistemology; the theory of knowledge: ～론자 an epistemologist. ～비판 〖철학〗 critique of cognition. ～작용 〖철학·심리〗 cognition. ～표 〖군사〗 an identification tag 〔disk〕; 《속어》 a dog tag.

**인식부족**(認識不足) lack of (adequate) understanding 〔knowledge〕; ignorance. ¶ ～이다 have little understanding 《of》; be ignorant 《of》; be ill-informed 《about》/ 심한 ～을 나타내다 [사물이 주어] exhibit 〔show〕 *one's* gross ignorance 《of》.

**인신**(人身) 《몸》 the human body; 《신상》 *one's* person. ◉ ～공격 a personal attack 〔abuse〕: ～공격하다 make a personal attack on 《*a person*》. ～매매 flesh 〔human〕 traffic; the slave trade; trade in human life: ～ 매매자 a slave dealer 〔trader〕 / ～매매하다 traffic in human beings. ～보호법 the Protection of Personal Liberty Act; the Habeas Corpus Act (영국의).

**인심**(人心) ① 《사람의 마음·인정》 a man's mind 〔heart〕. ¶ ～이 좋다 be good-hearted; be genial; be generous. ¶ ～ 쓰다 be generous; grant 《*a person* a favor》; act generously; display *one's* liberality / 남의 것으로 ～ 쓰다 rob Peter to pay Paul; be generous at another's expense.
② 《민심》 people's mind; the hearts of the people; the public mind; the popular sentiments; the feelings of the general public. ¶ ～의 동요 public unrest / ～을 얻다〔잃다〕 win 〔lose〕 the hearts of the people / ～을 살피다 perceive the drift of public sentiments / ～을 안정시키다 stabilize the feelings of the people / ～을 통일시키다 unify public sentiment / ～이 동요하다 the people are agitated / 그 소문으로 ～이 불안해졌다 The rumor made public feelings uneasy. / ～을 일신해야 한다 We should try to change the sentiment of people.
◉ ～소관 dependence on *one's* mind; a matter of consideration.

**인심**(仁心) a benevolent heart; charitable feeling; kind-heartedness; benevolence; humanity; humaneness; goodness.

**인애**(仁愛) kind love; humane affection. ¶ ～심이 있는 benevolent; humane.

**인양**(引揚) pulling; 《배의》 salvage; refloatation; 《시체의》 recovery. ～하다 pull up; salvage; refloat; recover. ¶ ～되다 be refloated / 침몰된 배를 ～하다 salvage a sunken ship.
◉ ～작업 《배의》 salvage work; refloatation 〔salvage〕 operations. ～장치 lifting gear.

**인어**(人魚) ① 《상상의》 a merman (남자); a mermaid (여). ② 〖동물〗 a dugong; a sea-pig.

**인연**(因緣) 《인과》 cause and occasion; 〖불교〗 karma; fatality; fate; destiny; 《연분》 affinity (bond); a relation; ties. ¶ ～을 맺다 form ties 《with》/ ～을 끊다 break off relations; cut connection / ～이 깊다 be closely related 〔associated〕/ ～이 멀다 have little relation / 부부의 ～을 끊다〔맺다〕 break up 〔consummate〕 a marriage / 이것도 ～이다 There is an act of Providence. / 돈과는 ～이 없다 Money and I are strangers. / 당신과 결혼하게 된 것도 ～인가 보오 It must be an act of Providence that I should come to marry you.

**인욕**(忍辱) fortitude; endurance; forbearance.

**인용**(引用) quotation; citation. ～하다 quote 《from a book》; take 《a line》 from 《an author, a book》; adduce 《a quotation from》; cite; borrow from. ¶ ～할 만한 quotable / 밀턴의 한 귀절을 ～하다 quote a passage from Milton / 내 말은 앞뒤가 무시된 채 ～되었다 I was quoted out of context. / 그녀는 자주 이야기 중에 성서로부터 ～한 귀절을 사용한다 She frequently uses quotations from the Bible in her speech.
◉ ～구〔문〕 a quotation; 《구어》 a quote: ～구의 출처를 밝히다 identify a quotation; trace a quotation to its original source. ～부(호) quotation marks; 《구어》 quotes. ～서(적) reference books; books referred to.

**인원**(人員) 《인원수》 the number of persons; the complement (정원); 《직원》 the staff; the personnel; hands (작업의). ¶ 가용～ available hands / ～이 남다 be over-staffed / ～ 부족이다 be short-staffed; be short of hands / ～을 제한하다 limit the number of persons / ～을 줄이다 cut the number of employees; curtail the personnel 《of the office》; decrease the working force. ◉ ～구성 personnel setup. ～배치표 a personnel allotment table. ～점호 a roll call: ～ 점호를 하다 call the roll. ～정리 a personnel slash 〔reduction〕; a personnel cut 〔retrenchment〕: ～정리를 하다 curtail 〔reduce〕 the personnel 《of》; cut the number of employees.

**인위**(人爲) human work; human power 〔agency〕; 《인공》 artificiality. ¶ ～적인 artificial; man-made; factitious / ～적 artificially / ～적(인) 시세 artificial 〔manipulated〕 market price / ～적으로 가격을 올리다 raise the price artificially. ◉ ～도태〔선택〕〖생물〗 artificial selection. ～법 an artificial law.

**인육**(人肉) human flesh. ◉ ～시장 a white slave market; a house of prostitution.

**인의**(仁義) benevolence and righteousness; humanity and justice. ◉ ～충효 humanity, justice, loyalty, and filial piety.

**인일**(寅日) 〖민속〗 the Day of the Tiger.

**인입선**(引入線) 〖전자〗 a service wire 〔line〕; 《전화의》 a telephone drop; 《TV》 a lead-in (wire); a (down-)lead.

**인자**(人子) 《그리스도》 the Son of Man.

**인자**(仁者) a benevolent person; a man of goodwill.

**인자**(仁慈) (love and) benevolence; benignancy; clemency. ～하다 (be) benevolent; benign; clement; merciful.

**인자**(因子) a factor. ◉ ～분석 〖심리〗 factor analysis. 가속도～ 〖경제〗 an accelerator.

**인장**(印章) 《도장》 a seal; 《인발》 the imprint of a seal. ¶ ～을 새기다 engrave 〔cut〕 a seal / ～을 위조하다 counterfeit a seal. ◉ ～위조 forgery of a seal: ～위조자 the counterfeiter of a seal. 위조～ a forged seal.

**인재**(人材) 《총칭》 talent; a talented 〔capable〕 person; a person of talent. ¶ 천하의 ～ all the talents of the world / ～를 등용하다 open positions to persons of talent; promote people 「on the basis of their talent 〔on their merits〕 / ～를 구하다 look out for talent / ～를 발탁하다 pick out good men and assist them to get on / ～가 부족하다 be short of talented people / 우리는 널리 ～를 구해 등용하는 과감한 조치를 취해야 한다 We must take a bold step to call in the best brains and open the offices to them.
◉ ～등용 selection of fit persons for higher position. ～발굴 talent hunt. ～스카우트 a headhunter 《구어》. ～은행 a talent bank; a job bank 《미》; an employment agency for people with special talent or skills.

**인재**(人災) a man-made calamity 〔disaster〕. ¶ 그 사고는 ～로 인한 것이었다 Human error caused the accident. / 지난 2년여 동안 ～로 인한 대형 사고들이 온 나라를 뒤흔들어 놓았다. Man-made catastrophes rocked whole nation over the last two years.

**인적**(人的) (being) human. ¶ 불은 크게 났었지만 ～ 피해는 없었다 Though it was a big fire, no one was hurt.
◉ ～손해 the loss of manpower. ～자원 human 〔manpower〕 resources; manpower: ～ 자원의 부족 lack of human resources / ～ 자원이 풍부하다 be rich in human resources / ～ 자원을 최고도로 활용하다 make the best use of manpower. ～지원 physical support.

**인적**(人跡) human traces 〔tracks, footsteps〕. ¶ ～ 미답(未踏)의 unexplored; untrodden 《regions》; virgin 《peaks》 / ～ 미답의 땅 a region untrodden by men; a region where no human being has ever set foot / ～이 드문 unfrequented; out-of-the-way; 《a place》 away from the haunts of men / ～이 끊어지다 be completely deserted.

**인절미** cake made from glutinous rice.

**인접**(隣接) contiguity; adjacency. ～하다 adjoin; be adjacent 〔contiguous〕 《to》; be 〔lie〕 next 《to》; be 〔lie, stand〕 close by; border on (국가·영토 등이). ¶ ～한 나라들 neighbor nations; countries having a common boundary / ～한 마을 neighboring towns and villages / 우리집은 교회에 ～해 있다 My house adjoins the church. / 화재는 ～한 공장으로 번져나갔다 The fire spread to the adjacent 〔neighboring〕 factory.

**인정**(人情) 《욕망》 human desire 〔passions〕; 《인간 본성》 human nature; 《마음》 the heart of a people; 《물정》 the condition of the world and humanity; 《동정심》 humaneness; sympathy; 《자애심》 the heart; kindness; tenderness; 《동정하는 마음씨》 a spirit of empathetic generosity; 《인간성》 humanity. ～스럽다 (be) warmhearted; kindhearted; tenderhearted; sympathetic; considerate; thoughtful.
¶ ～의 따뜻함 the milk of human kindness / ～이 있다 〔두텁다〕 be humane 〔kind〕 / ～이 없다 be coldhearted 〔heartless, inhumane, unfeeling〕 / ～ 있는 사람 a warm 〔tenderhearted〕 person / ～에 약하다 be easily moved; be tenderhearted / ～에 반(反)하다 be against humane nature / ～에 끌리다 be prompted by pity; be touched with pity; be moved with compassion / ～상 그런 일은 할 수 없다 I can't find it in my heart to do so. *or* How can I do such a thing as a man? / 그렇게 생각하는 것

이 당연한 ~이다 It is quite natural that one should think so. / 어디를 가나 ~에는 변함이 없다 Human nature is the same everywhere 〔all over〕. / 세상 ~은 얼음장같이 차다 The public are as cold as ice to me. / 그를 ~상 해고시킬 수 없었다 I didn't have the heart to dismiss him. / 요즘 사람들~은 예전 같지 않다 These days people are not as warm-hearted as before.
◉ ~미(味) a human touch; human warmth; warm-heartedness: ~미 넘치는 warm-hearted 《person》; heart-warming 《story》 / 그녀는 ~미 넘치는 사람이다 She is full of human warmth. *or* She has a lot of heart 〔human touch〕. ~풍속 customs and manners.

**인정**(仁政) benevolent government 〔administration, rule〕. ¶ ~을 베풀다 govern 〔rule〕 《people》 with benevolence.

**인정**(認定) recognition; acknowledgment; 《동일하다는 것의》 identification; 《승인》 approval; 《인가》 authorization; sanction; 《허가》 permission. ~하다 admit 《a fact》; recognize; acknowledge 《*one's* fault》; concede 《that...》; accept; approve 《of》 《a plan》; sanction 《a usage》.

> **용법** **admit** 사물의 옳고 그름, 사실 여부 등을 인정하다. **recognize** 권위·자격 있는 자가 어떤 지위나 존재를 사실로서 인정하다. **acknowledge** 밝히지 않았거나 비밀로 하던 일을 인정하다. **concede** 진실·타당하다고 인정하다. 또는 패배 등을 내키지 않는 마음으로 인정하다. **accept** 사실로서 또는 만족스러운 것으로서 용인하다. 마지못해 인정하는 경우도 있음. **approve** 제의된 것을 좋다고 생각하여 인정하다.

¶ 일반에게 ~을 받다 win public recognition / 크게 ~ 받다 receive 〔gain, win〕 much recognition / 시인으로서 ~을 받다 be acknowledged as a poet / 무죄로 ~하다 resume 《*a person's*》 innocence; presume 《*a person*》 to be innocent / 정치적인 실체의 존재를 ~치 않을 수 없다 be compelled to recognize the existence of a political entity / 네가 옳다고 ~한다 I own 〔admit〕 that you are right. / 나는 그 요구를 옳다고 ~한다 I admit the claim. / 미국 정부는 모든 신앙의 자유를 ~한다 The United States government is tolerant toward all the religious beliefs. / 그가 나보다 뛰어난 것을 ~한다 I acknowledge him as my superior. / 그는 유망한 작가로서 ~되고 있다 He is recognized as a promising writer. / 사실의 ~은 증거에 의한다 Facts shall be found on the basis of evidence.
◉ ~과세 taxation with the standard of assessment fixed by the authorities. ~서 a written recognition 《of championship》. ~시험 a certification examination.

**인정신문**(人定訊問) 〖법〗 identity questioning; an identity interrogation. ~하다 question 〔interrogate〕 the identity 《of an accused》.

**인제** 《지금》 now; 《앞으로》 from now on. ¶ ~도리가 없다 Nothing can be done now. / ~ 그렇게 안하겠습니다 I will never do so in the future. / ~야 그이가 왔다 He has just come at long last. / ~야 생각이 난다 Now I remember.

**인조**(人造) artificiality. ¶ ~의 artificial; man-made; 《모조》 imitation; 《합성》 synthetic.
◉ ~가죽 synthetic 〔imitation〕 leather; leatherette. ~견사 artificial 〔synthetic〕 silk; rayon. ~다이아몬드 an artificial diamond. ~대리석 artificial 〔imitation〕 marble. ~고무 synthetic rubber. ~금 imitation gold. ~버터 margarine. ~비료 an artificial fertilizer 〔manure〕. ~빙 artificial ice. ~석〔상아〕 artificial 〔imitation〕 stone 〔ivory〕. ~석유 synthetic oil 〔petroleum〕. ~섬유 synthetic 〔chemical〕 textiles; man-made fibers. ~육(肉) synthetic meat. ~인간 a mechanical man; a robot. ~진주 an artificial 〔an imitation, a false〕 pearl. ~호(湖) an artificial 〔a man-made〕 lake.

**인종**(人種) the human race; a race; an ethnic group. ¶ ~의〔적인〕 racial; ethnic / ~간의 racial 《tension》; interracial 《understanding》 / 황〔백〕색 ~ the yellow 〔white〕 race(s) / 유색 ~ the color race(s) / ~의 평등 racial equality / ~적 차별 대우 racist 〔racialist〕 practices / ~적 특성 racial characteristics / ~적 반감 racial 〔race〕 antipathy / ~적 편견 racial prejudice; racism; racialism / ~간의 반목〔대립〕 race antagonism / 같은 ~이다 be of the same race / 미국은 다양한 ~으로 구성된 다민족 국가이다 The United States of America is a multiracial

nation composed of various races. / ～이나 종교를 이유로 사람을 차별해서는 안 된다 We must not discriminate against a person on the basis of race or religion.
◉ ～개량 the production of fine (human) offspring; racial eugenics: ～개량론자 a eugenist / ～개량학 eugenics. ～격리 정책《남아공화국의》 apartheid. ～문제 the race 〔racial〕 problem 〔issue〕. ～분규 a racial conflict. ～의식 racial 〔color〕 consciousness. ～투쟁 racial strife; a racial quarrel. ～폭동 an ethnic 〔a race, a color〕 riot. ～학 ethnology: ～학적 ethnological / ～학자 an ethnologist.

**인종**(忍從) submission; self-surrender. ～하다 submit 〔resign *oneself*〕 《to》; suffer; lie down 《under》.

**인종차별**(人種差別) racial discrimination; a color bar; 《미》 segregation (흑·백인간의); 《남아공화국의》 apartheid. ～하다 discriminate against colored 〔nonwhite〕 people; draw the color line; segregate 《the blacks》. ¶ ～의 철폐 abolition of racial discrimination; desegregation; integration / ～을 없애다 desegregate; abolish 〔do away with〕 racial discrimination; remove racial inequalities.
◉ ～주의 racism: ～주의자 a racist. ～철폐론자 an integrationist.

**인주**(印朱) a red inkpad 〔stamp pad〕.

**인줄**(人—) 『민속』 a rope hung across the gate 〔entrance〕 to guard against evil spirits.

**인중**(人中) the philtrum; the groove of the upper lip.

**인즉** [조사] to speak of; speaking of; as for. ¶ 사실～ in fact; to tell the truth / 기회～ 좋은 기회다 As for the opportunity, it is a good one. / 말～ 옳소 What he says is true.

**인증**(引證) quotation; citation; illustration (예증). ～하다 quote 《a fact》; cite 《an instance》; adduce 《evidence》.

**인증**(認證) 『법』 authentication; certification; attestation. ～하다 authenticate; attest; confirm; certify. ¶ ～이 있는 등본 a certified 〔an authenticated〕 copy; an attestation copy / 아무의 진술을 ～하다 authenticate *a person's* statement.
◉ ～서 a certificate of attestation; a note of authentication. ～시험 《산업인력의 등급평가》 Information Technology and Qualification (생략 ITQ).

**인지**(人指) a forefinger. ＝집게손가락.

**인지**(人智) human wisdom 〔intellect, knowledge〕. ¶ ～의 발달 the advancement of human knowledge / ～가 미치지 못하는 beyond 〔above〕 human knowledge 〔understanding〕; beyond the wit of man.

**인지**(印紙) a (revenue) stamp. ¶ 100원짜리 ～ one hundred won revenue stamp / ～를 붙이다 affix a revenue stamp 《to》; put 〔stick〕 a revenue stamp 《on》; stamp 《a paper》 / ～로 납부하다 pay in revenue stamps.
◉ ～세 (revenue-)stamp duty: ～세법 the Stamp Act. ～판매소 a stamp=office; 《게시》 Stamps on sale.

**인지**(認知) legal recognition; acknowledgment; cognition (인식). ～하다 recognize 〔acknowledge〕 《a child as *one's* own》. ¶ 심령 연구는 정당한 과학으로 ～되지 않고 있다 Psychical research is not acknowledged as legitimate science. ◉ ～과학 cognitive science. ～소송 a legal action for recognition. ～심리학 cognitive psychology.

**인지** 《막연한 의문》 I wonder 《if, whether, how, what, when, who, where》. ¶ 정말～ Can it be true? *or* I wonder whether it can be true. / 오늘이 무슨 요일～ 모르겠다 What day of the week is it today, I wonder?

**인지라** as it is; since it is. ¶ 학교에 가는 길～ 지금 들르지 못하겠소 I'm on my way to school, so I can't stop in now.

**인지상정**(人之常情) humaneness; humanity; human nature. ¶ 그렇게 생각하는 것이 ～이다 It is 「quite natural 〔only human〕 that one should think 「so 〔that way〕.

**인질**(人質) a hostage. ¶ ～로 잡다 take 〔hold〕 《*a person*》 (as a) hostage / ～로 잡히다, ～이 되다 be held 〔taken〕 as hostage / 총을 가진 사내가 한 여자를 ～로 잡았다 A man with a gun took 〔held〕 a woman hostage. / 어서 ～을 석방하고 밖으로 나와라 Release all the hostages and give yourself up right away. ◉ ～석방금〔몸값〕 (a) ransom.

**인책**(引責) taking the responsibility on *oneself;* assuming the responsibility 《of 》. ～하다 take the responsibility on *oneself;* assume the responsibility 《for》; hold *oneself* responsible 《for》.
◉ ～사직 assuming the responsibility

and resigning *one's* post 〔office〕: ～ 사직하다 take the responsibility 《for *something*》 on *oneself* and resign / 시장은 오직사건으로 ～사직하여야 했다 The Mayor had to resign from the office holding himself responsible for the「corruption 〔bribery〕 case.

**인척**(姻戚) a relative 〔relation〕 by marriage; *one's* in-law 《구어》. ¶ ～ 관계이다 be related by marriage 《to》.

**인체**(人體) the human body 〔organism〕; flesh (육체). ¶ ～에 영향을 주다 affect the human body / ～에 위해를 가하다 inflict a bodily injury upon 《*a person*》.

◉ ～구조 the structure of the human body. ～기생충 a human parasite. ～모형 an anatomical model of the human body; 《인형》 a manikin. ～실험 a living-body test; an experiment on a human body; human experimentation. ～학 somatology. ～해부 dissection of a human body: ～해부도 an anatomical chart / ～해부학 human anatomy.

**인축**(人畜) men and 〔or〕 livestock 〔animals, beasts〕; living creatures. ¶ ～의 피해는 없었다 No harm was done to men or cattle. / ～에 무해 《살포제 등의 표시》 Harmless to humans and animals.

**인출**(引出) 《예금 등의》 (a) withdrawal; drawing out. ～하다 draw out 〔from〕; withdraw. ¶ 초과 ～ overdraft / 특별 ～권 special drawing rights (생략 SDR) / 은행에서 예금을 ～하다 draw *one's* money from the bank; check out *one's* deposit (수표로) / 5만원을 ～하셨죠, 맞습니까 《은행 창구 등에서》 The amount withdrawal is fifty thousand won, isn't it?

**인치** an inch (생략 in.). ¶ 6～ 반 six and a half inches; six inches and a half / 그는 키가 6피트 1～이다 He is six feet one inch tall. *or* He is 〔stands〕 six-foot-one.

**인칭**(人稱) 〖문법〗 person. ¶ 제1〔제2, 제3〕～ the first 〔second, third〕 person. ◉ ～대명사 a personal pronoun.

**인커브** 〖야구〗 an incurve.

**인큐베이터** an incubator.

**인터내셔널** international. ◉ 인터내셔널리즘 internationalism.

**인터넷** 〖컴퓨터〗 internet; 《통신망》 INTERNET; the Internet. 〔<network of networks〕 ¶ ～서비스 제공자 an Internet service provider (생략 ISP).

> 참고 인터넷(Internet)— 전세계적으로 구성되어 있는 컴퓨터 통신망으로, 세계 도처에 산재해 있는 국지적인 네트워크의 집합체로 구성되어 있다. 수천만의 사람들이 거미줄처럼 연결된 이 통신망을 통해 원하는 자료의 검색을 하거나 상대에게 전자 우편을 보낼 수 있다. 200만의 가입자를 가지고 있는 미국의 PC통신 'CompuServe'도 인터넷에서는 하나의 네트워크에 불과하다.

**인터벌** an interval. ¶ ～트레이닝 training 〔practicing〕 with regular intervals rest.

**인터뷰** an interview. ～하다 interview 《*a person*》; have an interview 《with》. ¶ 전화〔단독〕 ～ a telephone 〔an exclusive〕 interview / 기자와의 ～ a press interview / ～하는 사람〔받는 사람〕 an interviewer 〔interviewee〕 / …와의 ～에서 in an interview with… / 신문 기자와 ～하다 give an interview to newsmen.

**인터체인지** an interchange. ¶ 클로버형 ～ a cloverleaf (interchange) / 어느 ～에서 호남고속도로로 들어가면 좋겠습니까 What 〔Which〕 interchange should we enter the Honam Expressway at?

**인터페론** 〖약〗 interferon. ¶ 유전 공학 기술을 응용함으로써 항암제인 새로운 형태의 ～을 개발하다 develop a new type of interferon, the anticancer drug, by applying genetic engineering technology.

**인터페이스** 〖컴퓨터〗 interface. ¶ 그래픽 사용자 ～ graphic user interface (생략 GUI).

**인터폰** an interphone; an intercom; 《장치》 an intercommunication system.

**인터폴** 《국제경찰》 the Interpol. 〔<the *Inter*national Criminal *Pol*ice Organization (생략 ICPO)〕

**인턴** 《수련의》 an intern. ¶ ～으로 근무하다 intern 《at》; serve *one's* internship 《at》; 《영》 walk a hospital.

◉ ～제도 the internship system.

**인테리어** 《내부》 the interior. ¶ 현대적인 ～ a modern interior. ◉ ～디자이너 a interior designer 〔decorator〕. ～디자인 interior design 〔decoration〕.

**인텔리(겐치아)** an educated person; an intellectual; a highbrow 《미구어》; an egghead 《미구어》; 〔총칭〕 the intelligentsia; the intellectuals. ¶ 창백한 ～ pale-faced intellectuals / 그는 ～다 He is an intellectual. ◉ ～계급 the intellectual class.

**인텔샛**《국제 상업 통신 위성》Intelsat. [< the *In*ternational *Tele*communication *Sat*ellite]

**인토네이션**〖음성〗(an) intonation. ◉ ~곡선 an intonation contour.

**인파**(人波) a (surging) crowd; a flood of people; waves 〔a tide, a surge〕 of humanity. ¶ ~에 밀리다 be jostled by the crowd; be buffeted by the waves of humanity / ~를 헤치고 나아가다 jostle through a crowd / 나는 ~를 헤치고 나가 거기에 닿았다 I reached there pushing my way through the crowd.

**인파이터**〖권투〗an infighter.

**인파이트**〖권투〗infighting.

**인편**(人便) ¶ ~에 by means of someone; through the agency of a person; by 〔through〕 a person / ~으로 들은 이야기 a piece of hearsay; a piece of information acquired at second hand / ~으로 듣다 hear from someone / ~이 닿는 대로 보내다 send at the first opportunity.

**인편**(鱗片)〖동물·어류〗a scale;〖동·식물〗a squama (*pl.* -mae);〖식물〗a ramentum (*pl.* -ta). ¶ ~상(狀)의 scaly.

**인품**(人品) *one's* personal dignity 〔appearance〕; character; personality. ¶ ~이 좋다 have a fine personality 〔looking〕; a good-natured person / ~이 좋은 사람 a man of respectable appearance / ~이 야비하다 have a coarse personality.

**인프라**《산업기반 시설》an infrastructure.

**인플레이션**〖경제〗inflation. ¶ 천정부지의 ~ runaway inflation; hyperinflation / 잠재적 ~ latent inflation / 악성 ~ vicious inflation / 두 자리 숫자의 ~ double-digit inflation; inflation greater than 10 percent / ~이 없는 경제 성장 non-inflationary economic growth / ~을 초래하다 cause inflation / ~을 막다 combat 〔check〕 inflation / ~을 저지하다〔잡다〕 stop 〔halt〕 inflation / ~을 피하다 avoid inflation / ~으로 물가가 폭등하고 있다 Prices are soaring owing to inflation. / ~이 계속되고 있다 Inflation is still going on. ◉ ~경기 an inflation boom. ~경향 an inflationary trend 〔tendency〕. ~대책 counter-inflation measures. ~심리 the inflationary psychology; inflation mentality 〔psychology〕. ~악화 aggravation of inflation. ~정책 an inflationary policy. 갤러핑〔급성〕~ galloping inflation. 크리핑〔완만한〕~ creeping inflation.

**인플루엔자**〖의학〗influenza; (the) flu(e)《구어》. ¶ 악성 ~ malignant influenza / ~에 걸리다 contract 〔suffer from〕 influenza; catch flu / ~가 크게 유행하고 있다 There's a lot of flu about. ◉ ~바이러스 an influenza 〔a flu〕 virus.

**인피**(靭皮)〖식물〗bast. ◉ ~부(部) phloem. ~섬유 liber; phloem 〔bast〕 fiber.

**인하**(引下) lowering; (a) reduction; a cut《in wages》. ~하다 lower; bring down;《물가를》reduce; cut down; roll back (통제하여). ¶ 가격 ~ 경쟁 a price war / 가격 ~ 판매 a mark-down sale / 임금 ~ (a) reduction in wages; a wage cut / 값을 2할 ~하여 at a reduction of 20 percent / 가격을 ~하다 cut a price down; reduce 〔lower〕 the price《to》/ 금리는 내달에 ~된다 Interest rates will be reduced 〔lowered〕 next month.

**인하다**(因—)《말미암다》be due 〔owing〕 to; be caused by; be attributable《to》; come《from》; be a consequence《of》. ¶ 부주의로 인한 due to carelessness / 병으로 인해서 결석하다 be absent because of illness / 사고로 인하여 죽다 die from 〔on account of〕 an accident / 그 사고는 부주의한 운전으로 인해 일어났다 The accident was due to careless driving.

**인해전술**(人海戰術)《adopt》human=wave tactics《in attacking the enemy's fortress》.

**인허**(認許) recognition; approval; authorization. ~하다 recognize; approve; authorize.

**인형**(人形) a doll;《꼭두각시》a puppet; a marionette. ¶ ~ 같은 doll-like / ~을 가지고 놀다 play (with) dolls / ~을 부리다 manipulate a puppet 〔marionette〕. ◉ ~극 a doll play; a puppet show; a marionette performance.

**인형**(仁兄) you;《편지에서》Dear Friend.

**인화**(人和) harmony among men; peace and amity within the nation; national concord. ¶ ~를 도모하다 promote 〔advance〕 the harmony among men.

**인화**(引火) catching fire; ignition. ~하다 catch 〔take〕 fire; ignite. ¶ ~하기 쉬운, ~성의 inflammable; flammable / 발화 또는 ~ 염려가 있다 be liable to cause combustion or ignition / 담뱃불이 가스에 ~했다 The cigarette ignited the gas. / 휘발유는 ~하기 쉽다 Gasoline catches fire easily. / 불꽃이

휘발유에 ~되어 불이 났다 The gasoline caught fire from the spark, causing the fire. ◉ ~물질 the inflammables. ~성 (in)flammability; ignitability: ~성 물질—20 미터 이내 금연《게시》Flammable: No smoking within 20m. ~점 the flash point; the ignition point. ◉

**인화**(印畫)《작업》printing; 《인화한 것》 a print. ~하다 print; make a print of. ◉ ~지 printing 〔sensitized〕 paper.

**인화**(燐火)《인광석의》phosphorous light; phosphorescence; 《도깨비불》an elf fire; a jack-o'-lantern; a will-o'-the-wisp.

**인환**(引換) exchange; change. ~하다 exchange; change. ◉ ~권《경품 등의》a coupon; 《화물 등의》a claim ticket.

**인회석**(燐灰石)〖광물〗apatite.

**인후**(咽喉) the throat. ◉ ~병〖의학〗a swelling 〔swollen〕 sore throat. ~염 a sore throat: 만성 ~염 a clergyman's sore throat. ~카타르 catarrh of the throat.

**일** ①《사항》a matter; a thing; an affair; 《우발적 사건》an incident; an event; an occurrence; a happening; 《사정》circumstances; 《사태》things; a matter; 《사고》an accident; a mishap; 《말썽》(a) trouble.

¶ 좋은 일 a good thing; a happy event / 기분 나쁜 일 an unpleasant matter; something unpleasant; a nasty business / 빤한 일 an obvious fact / 중대한 일 a matter of grave concern / 귀찮은 일 an awkward proposition / 돈에 관한 일 a matter of money; a money matter / 무슨 일이 있더라도 under any circumstances; whatever happens / 급한 일이 있을 때는 in case of emergency / 아무 일 없이 without incident (emergency); uneventfully; without accident 〔a hitch〕; peacefully; smoothly / 그 일이라면 for that matter / 그 일에 관해서는 as to 〔concerning〕 the matter / 일을 저지르다 cause 〔make〕 trouble / 학교 일에 관해서 이야기하다 speak about the school affairs / 아주 사소한 일에 화를 내다 get angry on the slightest provocation 〔for nothing〕 / 무슨 일이 있기를 바라다 hope for something to happen / 일의 진부를 확인하지 않으면 안 되겠다 I must ascertain 〔make sure of〕 the fact. / 이 일은 전적으로 당신의 재량에 맡기겠습니다 I leave the matter entirely to your arrangement. / 내가 관여할 일이 아니다 That's no business of mine. / 내 일은 염려 마라 Don't trouble yourself about me. / 일이 복잡해지지나 않을까 I am afraid that will complicate the matter. / 일이 이렇게 되었으니 하는 수 없다 Now that things have come to such a pass, we can't help it. / 무슨 일이냐, 어디 아프냐 What's the matter with you? Are you sick or something? / 참 이상한 일이다 It is a curious thing indeed.

②《작업》work; labor; business; a job; 《직업》employment; *one's* trade; an occupation; (a) vocation (천직); 《사업》an undertaking; 《임무》*one's* duties; a mission (임무). ⇨ 일하다, 일삼다.

> **용법** **work** 일정한 목적을 갖고 하는 육체적·정신적 일. 가장 일반적인 말. play (놀기)의 반대말. **labor** 고된 육체적인 일. **business** 영리를 목적으로 하는 일, 또는 직업상의 일. **job** 작업 내용이 정해진 구체적인 일로서, 수입이 따르는 일. **employment** 남에게 고용되어 하는 일. **trade** 수공업적인 훈련을 쌓아야 할 직업의 일. **occupation** 규칙적으로 종사하고 있거나 그러기 위해 훈련을 받은 전문적인 일.

¶ 쉬운 일 an easy job / 힘든 일 a hard job; a difficult task; hard work; toil / 하룻일 a day's work / 한창 일할 나이 the prime 〔noon〕 of life / 일하는 시간 working hours / 나날의 일 *one's* daily routine / 일이 빠른〔느린〕 사람 a quick 〔slow〕 worker / 일하는 동안에 at *one's* work; while working / 아무의 밑에서 일하다 work under *a person* / 일을 찾다 look for work 〔employment, job〕; seek a job / 일에 착수하다 set 〔begin〕 to work / 일에 몰리다 be pressed with business; be very busy / 일을 얻다 get a job; find work / 일을 쉬다 absent *oneself* 〔stay away〕 from work / 일을 끝내다 finish 〔get over〕 *one's* work / 일을 시키다 put 《*a person*》 to work / 일을 너무 시키다 overwork 《a servant》 / 일을 맡다 accept 〔take〕 a job / 일을 급히 하다 rush *one's* work / 일이 없다 have nothing to do / 일이 없어 놀다 be out of work 〔employment, job〕 / 일을 배우다 learn a trade / 일을 가르치다 train 《*a person*》 to some trade / 일을 해주고도 칭찬을 못 받다 do thankless task / 일이 손에 잡히지 않다 be unable to bring *oneself* to work; cannot concentrate on *one's* work / 오늘은 일이 없었다 I had a blank day. / 나는 오늘

할 일이 많다 I have lots of things to do today. / 그는 요새 술 마시는 것이 일이다 He does nothing but drink these days. / 아드님은 무슨 일을 합니까 What line of business is your son in?

> **참고** **workaholic** —「일 밖에 모르는 사람, 일에 중독된 사람」work(일)와 alcoholic (알코올 중독)의 holic을 합성해서 만든 말. 경제적으로 어려워서가 아니라 일하는 것이 즐겁다고나 할까, 일을 하지 않으면 좀이 쑤셔서 못견디는 사람을 말한다. 한국인에도 이 workaholic에 속하는 사람이 많지만, 미국인들 사이에도 이런 사람들이 의외로 많다고 한다. 다음의 대화를 읽으면서, 마치 우리집 이야기를 하는 것 같다고 느끼실 분도 많을 것이다.
> Jane: 요즘 네 남편 전혀 볼 수 없구나. I never see your husband lately.
> Lucy: 너만 못 보는게 아냐, 나 역시 그래. You're not the only one. I hardly see him myself.
> Jane: 일을 무척 좋아하시는 모양이지? He must really love his job.
> Lucy: 응, 그이야말로 일에 중독된 사람 같다니까.
> Yes, he's a real **workaholic**.

③《용무》business; an errand. ¶ 회사 일로 on the business of the firm / 무슨 일인가 묻다 inquire *one's* business / 무슨 일인지요 What do you want with me? / 무슨 일이든지 분부만 하십시오 I'm always at your service. / 서울엔 무슨 일로 왔소 What has brought you to Seoul? *or* On what business have you come to Seoul? / 일 없는 사람은 들어오지 마시오《게시》No admission except on business. *or* No trespassing.
④《계획》a plan; a program(me); a project; a scheme; an idea;《음모》a plot; a trick. ¶ 일을 꾀하다 make a plan; form a scheme;《음모를》conspire 〔intrigue〕《against》/ 일을 진행시키다 carry a program forward / 일이 순조롭게 잘 되어 간다 The plan is on a fair way to success.
⑤《경험》(an) experience. ¶ …한 일이 있다 have ever *done;* once *did;*《과거완료》had ever 〔once〕 *done* / …한 일이 없다 have never *done;* never *did;*《과거완료》had never *done* / …하는 일이 있다 sometimes *do* / …하는 일이 없다 never *do* / 비행기를 타 본 일이 없다 I've never traveled by plane. / 한국으로부터 편지를 받으신 일이 한번도 없습니까 Have you never received a letter from Korea? / 중국에 가 본 일이 있느냐 Have you ever been to China? / 그에게서 한 번 편지를 받은 일이 있다 I once got a letter from him.
⑥《공적》an achievement; merits; services. ¶ 훌륭한 일을 하다 render distinguished services《to》; distinguish *oneself*《in》.

**일**(一)《하나》one;《첫째》the first; an ace (카드·주사위의). ¶ 1인 1표 one man one vote / 1원 one won / 1등 first; number one; first class / 하트의 1 the ace of hearts.

**일**(日) a day. ¶ 3일 three days / 5월 2일《on》the 2nd of May;《on》May 2.

**일가**(一家) ①《가정》a family; a household; a home. ¶ ~의 family; domestic / ~의 가장 the master of a house / 김씨 ~ the (whole) Kim family; (all) the Kims / ~를 이루다 create a new family; establish a house of *one's* own / ~를 거느리다 keep house; look after the family.
②《친척》*one's* family and relatives; *one's* kinsfolk. ¶ 먼 ~ a distant relation / 먼 ~ 되는 사람 a distant relative / 그는 나의 먼 ~가 된다 He is a remote relative 〔distant kinsman〕 of mine.
③《유파》a school. ¶ ~를 이루다 develop 〔find〕 a style of *one's* own; establish《as a novelist》; establish *oneself* as a master; be an authority《on》/ 그는 식물학자로서 ~를 이루고 있다 He is a botanist of established reputation.
◉ ~단란 a happy family 〔home〕 circle; the pleasures of a happy 〔sweet〕 home: ~ 단란하다 sit in a happy family circle; enjoy the pleasures of a happy home. ~동반 자살 a collective family suicide; suicides by all family members. ~몰살 annihilation of an entire family. ~문중 *one's* close and distant kinsfolk. ~붙이 family relations; relatives; *one's* kinsfolk. ~친척 *one's* relatives「by blood and marriage 〔in blood and law〕; *one's* kith and kin. ~화합 harmony in a family: ~ 화합하다《a family》be harmonious.

**일가**(一價)〖화학〗univalence; monovalence. ¶ ~의 univalent; monovalent; monatomic. ◉ ~원소 a monad.

**일가견**(一家見) *one's* own opinion; an (independent) opinion of *one's* own;

a personal view. ¶ 그 문제에 관해 그는 ~이 있다 He has well-informed opinions on the problem.

**일가족**(一家族) one family; 《전 가족》 the whole family; all the family.

**일각**(一刻) a minute; a moment; an instant. ¶ ~을 다투는 문제 a problem that needs a speedy solution; a burning question / ~도 지체 없이 without a moment's delay; in no time; immediately / ~을 아끼다 grudge even a minute / ~의 여유도 없다 There isn't a moment to lose. *or* We don't have a moment to spare. / ~이 천금 Every moment is precious. *or* Time is money. / ~이 여삼추(如三秋) A minute is like three years 〔seems like a lifetime〕.

**일각**(一角) a corner; a section. ¶ 정계의 ~ a section of political circles / 빙산의 ~ the tip of an iceberg.
◉ ~대문 〖건축〗 a front gate with two posts and a roof. ~수(獸) a unicorn.

**일간**(日刊) daily publication 〔issue〕. ¶ ~의 daily. ◉ ~신문〔지〕 a daily newspaper; a daily; the daily press [총칭].

**일간**(日間) [부사적] soon; before long; in a few days; at an early date; in the near future. ¶ ~ 다시 찾아 뵙겠습니다 I will call again one of these days.

**일간두옥**(一間斗屋) a small one-room house; a hut; a humble house.

**일갈**(一喝) a thundering cry; a roar. ~하다 thunder (out) 《at》; cry in a thunder of voice; yell 《at *a person*》; roar. ¶ 그는 버릇없는 아이들에게 ~했다 He barked 〔snapped〕 at the naughty children.

**일개**(一介) mere; only. ¶ 나는 ~ 가난한 학생이다 I am but a poor student.

**일개**(一箇) one; a piece. ¶ ~년 one year / ~월 one month / 만 ~년 a full year / ~년의 수입 an annual income.

**일개미** a worker (ant); an ergate.

**일개인**(一個人) an individual; a private person. ⇨ 개인(個人). ¶ 나 ~의 생각 my personal view / ~의 자격으로 in *one's* private 〔individual〕 capacity; in the character 〔capacity〕 of an individual 〔a private citizen〕.

**일거**(一擧) one action; one effort. ¶ ~에 by one effort; at a (single) stroke 〔blow〕; at one swoop / 문제를 ~에 해결하다 solve a problem at a stroke / 적을 ~에 분쇄하다 beat 〔crush〕 the enemy at a blow. ◉ ~양득 killing two birds with one stone; attaining two advantages at one move: 그렇게 하면 ~양득이다 It serves two ends.

**일거리** a piece of work; a job. ¶ ~가 있다 have work to do; have a business to attend to / ~가 없다 be out of job; have nothing to do / ~를 주다 assign a task 《to *a person*》 / 오늘은 ~가 많다 We have plenty of work to do for today.

**일거무소식**(一去無消息) no tidings since departure.

**일거수일투족**(一擧手一投足) *one's* every move 〔action〕. ⇨ 일거일동.

**일거일동**(一擧一動) *one's* every action 〔move, movement〕; everything *one* does. ¶ ~에 주의하다 be careful about every little thing *one* does / 남의 ~을 살피다 watch every movement of others / 경찰은 용의자의 ~을 지켜보았다 The police watched every move the suspect made. / 세상 사람들은 그의 ~을 지켜보고 있다 His movements are being carefully watched by the public.

**일건**(一件) an affair; a matter; a case. ¶ 그 ~은 아직 종결되어 있지 않다 The matter has not been settled yet.
◉ ~서류 all the papers 〔documents〕 relating to an affair; a dossier 《on a criminal case》.

**일격**(一擊) a single blow; a stroke. ¶ ~에 at a 〔one〕 blow; with one stroke; by a (single) blow / 맹렬한 ~ a smashing blow / ~을 가하다 strike 〔give〕 《*a person*》 a blow; strike 〔deal, launch〕 a blow 《at, on, against》.

**일견**(一見) a look; a sight; a glance; a glimpse. ~하다 have 〔take〕 a look 《at》; (cast a) glance 《at》; get a glimpse 《of》. ¶ ~할 가치가 있다 be worth seeing 〔taking a look at 《구어》〕 / ~ 그는 장사꾼 같았다 He was apparently a merchant. / ~하여 가짜라는 것을 알았다 I saw at a glance that it was a fake. / 백문이 불여~ 《속담》 Seeing is believing. *or* An eye finds more truth than two ears.

**일계**(一計) a plan. ¶ ~를 생각해내다 think 〔work〕 out a plan.

**일계**(日計) daily account(s); daily expenses. ◉ ~표 daily trial balance.

**일고**(一考) consideration; a thought. ~하다 take 《*a matter*》 into consideration; give a thought 《to》; bestow some consideration 《on》. ¶ ~의 여지가 있다 leave room for consideration / 이것은 ~를 요하는 문제다 This is a matter for consideration. / 그 일에 대해 부디 ~해 주십시오 Please give some consideration to the matter.

**일고**(一顧) a notice; heed. ¶ ~의 여지〔가치〕도 없다 be beneath *one's* notice; do not deserve even a passing notice; be quite worthless / ~도 하지 않다 take no notice〔account〕《of》; give no heed《to》.

**일곱** seven. ¶ ~째 the seventh / ~살 먹은 아이 a child of seven (years old); a seven-year-old (child) / ~시 반 half past seven. ◉ ~이레 the 49th day after a baby's birth.

**일공**(日工)《날품일》daily employment; a day-to-day engagement; day labor; 《날품삯》daily pay; a day's wage.
◉ ~쟁이 a day laborer.

**일과**(一過) ~하다 pass away. ¶ ~성의 temporary; transitory; fugitive / ~성 치통 phantom odontalgia.

**일과**(日課) daily work; a daily task; (daily) routine (판에 박힌);《학과》a daily lesson. ¶ ~를 주다 impose a daily task on《*a person*》; give《*a person*》daily lessons / ~를 게을리하다 neglect *one's* daily work / ~를 마치다 do *one's* daily stint〔task〕/ 나는 저녁 식사 후에 산책하는 것을 ~로 삼고 있다 I make it a rule to take a walk after supper. ◉ ~표 a daily schedule (일상적인); *one's* schedule for the day (예정된); a school timetable (학과의).

**일곽**(一郭) a block; a quarter.

**일관**(一貫)《시종여일》consistency; coherence; unswerving. ~하다 be consistent〔coherent〕; be unswerving〔faithful〕. ¶ ~하여 consistently; from first to last / ~된 정책 a consistent〔coherent〕policy / ~성이 없다〔결여되다〕be wanting in consistency; be inconsistent〔incoherent〕/ 초지 ~하다 go through with〔carry out〕*one's* original idea / 시종 ~ 충성을 다하다 remain faithful《to the King》to the last; be unswerving in *one's* allegiance〔devotion〕《to》/ 그는 시종 ~ 과학의 발전을 위하여 진력했다 He devoted himself to the development of science throughout his life.
◉ ~성 consistency; coherence: 그의 발언에는 ~성이 없다 His statement lacks consistency. ~작업 integrated work; one continuous operation; a thorough process: 현대의 과학 기술은 ~ 작업으로 대량 생산을 가능케 했다 Modern technology has made mass production possible through integrated production process.

**일괄**(一括) a bundle; a lump. ~하다 make〔tie up〕into a bundle; lump together; 《개괄하다》sum up; summarize. ¶ ~하여 in a lump; collectively; *en bloc;* in bulk / 세 의안이 ~ 상정되었다 The three bills were brought up en bloc〔together〕for discussion. / 그 문제들은 ~ 처리할 수 있다 Those problems can be dealt with collectively. / 그들은 교재를 ~하여 주문했다 They ordered teaching materials in bulk.
◉ ~계약 a contract in bulk; a blanket contract; 《make》a package deal. ~구입《make》a blanket purchase 《of necessities》. ~배급 collective rationing. ~사표 *en masse* resignations. ~소송 a wholesale suit; a package suit. ~안〔제안〕a package plan〔proposal〕. ~지급 a lump-sum payment: 차의 대금을 ~지급하다 pay for a car in a lump sum. ~처리〖컴퓨터〗batch processing. ~타결 a package〔an overall〕settlement; a package solution. ~판매 (a) sale in bulk; buying and selling in bulk.

**일광**(日光) sunshine; sunlight; sunbeams; the rays of the sun. ¶ ~의 작용 the action of the sunlight.
◉ ~반사기〖물리〗a heliotrope. ~소독 disinfection by sunlight; sterilization by sunning. ~시 the daylight hours; 《길이》the span of daylight. ~요법 heliotheraphy; suncure. ~욕 a sunbath: ~욕하다 bathe〔bask〕in the sun; sunbathe; take a sunbath. ~절약 daylight saving: ~ 절약 시간 daylight saving time (생략 D.S.T.); summer time《영》.

**일교차**(日較差)〖기상〗daily (temperature) range.

**일구난설**(一口難說) being difficult to explain「in a word〔briefly〕.

**일구다**《개간하다》reclaim《waste land》; clear《woodland》(for cultivation); bring《land》under cultivation; 《밭을》cultivated《the fields》; plow《미》; turn over《the soil》; 《두더지가》raise a mound; burrow in.

**일구월심**(日久月深)《시간》《with》the lapse of time; [부사적] earnestly〔intently〕as time passes by; with all *one's* heart. ¶ 그녀는 ~ 남편만을 기다렸다 She waited only for her husband with all her heart.

**일구이언**(一口二言) being double=

tongued; double-dealing. ～하다 contradict *oneself;* be double-dealing 〔double-tongued〕; 《약속을 어기다》 break *one's* word 〔promise〕. ¶ 나는 절대로 ～하지 않는다 I never go back on 〔fail to keep〕 my word.

**일국**(一國) a nation; a country; one state; 《온 나라》 the whole country. ¶ ～의 수상 a prime minister of a country / ～을 뒤흔든 사건 an event that shakes the whole country.

**일군**(一軍) 《전군》 the whole army; 《제1군》 the First Army. ¶ ～의 지휘관 a commander-in-chief / ～사령관 the Commander of the First Army.

**일그러지다** be distorted; be contorted; be twisted. ¶ 고통으로 일그러진 얼굴 a face drawn 〔contorted, twisted〕 with pain / 그는 화가 나서 얼굴이 일그러졌다 His face was distorted by rage.

**일금**(一金) (the sum of ) money. ¶ ～ 1만원 (the sum of) ten thousand won.

**일급**(一級) 《최상》 the first class; 《한 등급》 one class; one grade. ¶ ～의 first-class; first-rate; of the highest 〔best〕 quality / ～호텔 a first-class 〔first-rate〕 hotel / 그는 나보다 ～ 위〔아래〕이다 He is one class 〔grade〕 above 〔below〕 me. ◉ ～품 first-class goods: 이 포도주는 ～품이다 This wine is (of) the best quality.

**일급**(日給) daily wage 〔pay〕; a day's wage. ¶ ～ 30,000원 a day's wage of 30,000 won / ～으로 일하다 work by the day / ～으로 지급〔고용〕하다 pay 〔hire〕 《*a person*》 by the day.
◉ ～노동자 a day laborer. ～제 the day-rate plan (system).

**일긋거리다** be shaky 〔unsteady〕; be rickety. ¶ 책상 다리가 좀 일긋거린다 The legs of the table are a bit shaky.

**일기**(一期) ① 《일생》 *one's* span of life; *one's* whole life. ¶ 60세를 ～로 죽다 die at the age of sixty. ② 《기간》 a term; a period; 《병의》 a stage. ¶ 제～생 the first term students / 제～의 결핵 tuberculosis in its first stage / ～에 3만 원의 소득세를 내다 pay an income tax of 30,000 won for a term. ◉ ～배당금 a regular 〔quarterly〕 dividend.

**일기**(一騎) a (single) horseman. ¶ ～당천의 용사 a match for a thousand; a matchless 〔mighty〕 warrior.

**일기**(日記) a diary; a journal. ¶ ～를 쓰다 keep 〔write〕 a 〔*one's*〕 diary; diarize / ～에 적다 write down 〔record〕 《*a matter*》 in *one's* diary. ◉ ～문학 diaries (as a branch of literature). ～장 a diary; 『부기』 a daybook. 여행～ *one's* diary of a travel; a travel diary. 영문～ an English diary. 학생～ a student diary.

**일기**(日氣) the weather. ⇨ 날씨.
◉ ～개황 a general weather condition. ～불순 unseasonableness 〔changeableness〕 of weather.

**일기예보**(日氣豫報) a weather (fore)cast 〔report〕. ¶ 내일의 ～ the weather forecast for tomorrow / ～에 의하면 according to the weather forecast; the weatherman says... / ～를 하다 make a weather forecast; forecast the weather / ～에 내일은 맑을 거라고 한다 The weather forecast says it will be fine tomorrow. ◉ ～담당자 《TV 등의》 a weatherman; a weather forecaster.

**일깨우다** ① 《자는 사람을》 wake 〔awake, arouse〕 《*a person*》 up early in the morning. ② 《가르쳐서》 make 《*a person*》 aware of; make 《*a person*》 realize 《*something*》; open 《*a person's*》 eye to 《*something*》; enlighten 《the natives》. ¶ 민중을 ～ enlighten the public / 그의 잘못을 일깨워 주었다 I brought to his attention what he had done wrong.

**일껏** with (much) trouble; at great pains. ¶ ～ 번 돈을 쓰지 않으면 안 되었다 I had to spend my hard-earned money. / ～ 애쓴 일이 허사가 되고 말았다 All my pains went for nothing.

**일꾼** ① 《노동자》 a laborer; a workman; a worker; a farm hand 〔worker〕(농가의); 《품팔이》 a wage earner; a wage-worker; 《막일의》 a coolie; a navvy. ¶ ～이 많이 모자란다 We are terribly short of workers. ② 《역량 있는 사람》 an able man 〔hand〕; a man of ability. ¶ 그는 사회의 큰 ～이 될 것이다 He will become a pillar of society.

**일끝** the end 〔finish〕 《of a matter》. ¶ ～을 맺다 finish the matter up; complete *one's* work.

**일년**(一年) a 〔one〕 year. ¶ ～에 한 번씩 once a year; annually / ～에 두 번씩 twice a year; semiannually / ～내내 all the year round 〔through〕; throughout the year / ～ 걸러 every other 〔second〕 year; biennially / ～반 one year and a half; one and a half year. ◉ ～감 a tomato. ～생 a first-year〔-grade〕 boy 〔girl〕; a first grader; 《대학 등의》 a freshman 《미》. ～생식물〔풀〕 an annual 〔a yearly〕 plant.

**일념**(一念) 《한결같은 마음》 a single

〔whole〕 heart; a concentrated mind; a determined soul; 《소원》 an ardent wish. ¶ 만나보고 싶은 ~으로 out of sheer desire to see 《*a person*》.

**일다**[1] ① 《연기·바람 따위가》 rise; go up; 《파도가》 run high. ¶ 연기가 ~ Smoke rises. / 바람이 일 것 같다 The wind seems to be rising. / 파도가 일고 있다 The sea is running high. / 먼지가 구름처럼 일고 있다 The dust is rising in clouds. ② 《성해지다》 become active; gain force; increase in power; 《번창하다》 prosper; flourish. ¶ 불길이 일고 있다 The fire is burning briskly 《in the fireplace》. / 세력이 ~ gain in influence / 그 회사는 호경기로 사운이 크게 일었다 The company has prospered because of a business boom. ③ 《보풀 따위가》 be nappy 〔fluffy〕. ¶ 보풀을 일게 하다 nap; fluff; raise nap 《on cloth》.

**일다**[2] 《쌀 따위를》 wash out useless elements. ¶ 사금을 ~ wash for gold; pan gold / 쌀을 ~ wash 〔rinse〕 rice (to remove grits and stones, *etc.*).

**일단**(一旦) 《한번》 once; 《우선》 first; in advance; 《일시》 present 〔moment, time being〕; 《만약의 경우》 in case of. ¶ ~ 승락한 이상은 Once you have agreed 〔consented〕, … / ~ 유사시에는 in case of emergency / ~ 약속을 하면 지켜야 한다 Once you have made a promise, you should keep it. / ~ 결정하면 변경할 수 없다 Once agreed upon, it cannot be changed. / 그 사건은 ~ 끝났다 The case was closed for the moment. / ~ 그의 의견을 들어보자 We will first hear his opinion. / ~ 이것으로 끝마칩시다 Let's stop here for the present.

**일단**(一段) ① 《단계》 one stage; the first stage. ¶ 자동차의 ~기어를 넣다 put a car into first 〔bottom〕 gear / 로켓의 ~을 분리하다 detach the first stage of a rocket. ② 《층계》 a step 《of a staircase》. ③ 《등급》 a grade; the first grade (초단). ¶ (바둑 등에서) 초단인 사람 a first grader. ④ 《문장의》 a passage; a paragraph; 《신문의》 a column. ¶ ~광고 a one-column ad.

**일단**(一端) 《한쪽 끝》 one end; 《일부》 (a) part; 《대강》 an outline. ¶ 문제의 ~을 논하다 touch on the fringe of the question / 감상의 ~을 피력하다 express a fragment of *one's* impression / 이것으로 그의 성격의 ~을 엿볼 수 있다 This enables us to get a glimpse of his character.

**일단**(一團) a body; a group; a party; a band; a company; 《악당 등의》 a gang; 《배우 등의》 a troupe.

> **용법** **body** 공동으로 무엇인가를 하는 단체. **group** 비교적 소수의 집단. **party** 공통의 목적을 위한 일시적인 집단. **company** 함께 있거나 함께 무엇인가를 하는 집단을 가리키는 일이 많음.

¶ ~이 되어〔을 이루어〕 in a body 〔group, party, flock〕 / ~의 관광객 a party of tourists / 순회 배우의 ~ a company 〔troupe〕 of traveling actors / 악당의 ~ a pack 〔gang〕 of scoundrels 〔rascals〕.

**일단락**(一段落) a pause (for the present). ¶ ~을 짓다 settle 《*a matter*》 for the time being; complete the first stage 《of the work》; come to the end of the first stage / 지금 진행 중인 일을 ~ 지으면 when I am finished with what I am doing, … / 그들은 교섭을 ~지었다 They have finished the first phase of the negotiations.

**일당**(一堂) ¶ ~에 모이다 gather 〔meet together〕 in a hall 〔room〕.

**일당**(一黨) a party; partisans; a clique (파벌); a ring; a gang (폭력단의). ¶ ~ 일파에 치우치지 않다 be free from partisan spirit / ~은 모두 검거되었다 All the fellow conspirators were nabbed. *or* The whole gang was arrested. ◉ ~국회 an one-party legislature. ~독재 one-party rule 〔dictatorship〕.

**일당**(日當) a daily allowance; daily pay 〔wages〕; earnings of the day. ¶ 여비(의) ~ daily traveling allowance / ~ 3만원을 지급하다 pay 〔grant〕 30,000 won a day / ~으로 일하다 work by the day. ◉ ~계산 payment by the day; daily payment. ~근로자 a day laborer. ~제 a day-rate system.

**일당백**(一當百) one (person) that is worth a hundred (persons). ¶ ~의 용사 a match for a hundred; a matchless 〔mighty〕 warrior.

**일대**(一大) [형용사적] great; grand; remarkable; very important; of great importance. ¶ ~ 발견 a discovery of great importance / ~ 성황을 이루다 (모임이) be a great success / ~ 용단을 내리다 take a decisive step; make a brave decision.

**일대**(一代) ① 《일세대》 one 〔a〕 generation; the age (당대). ¶ ～의 영웅 the greatest hero of the age. ② 《일생》 *one's* lifetime. ¶ 일생～의 실책 the gravest fault committed in *one's* whole career / ～에 쌓아올린 재산 a fortune built up in *one's* lifetime / 이 소설은 그의 ～의 걸작이다 This is the best novel that has ever come out of his pen. ◉ ～기 a life history; a biography. ～잡종 an $F_1$ hybrid.

**일대**(一隊) a body; a group; a company; a party; a band; a squad. ¶ 병사의 ～ a company of soldiers / 탐험가의 ～ a party of explorers.

**일대**(一帶) the area 〔district〕; the neighborhood 《of》; a tract 《of land》; a stretch 《of open country》. ¶ 그 주변 ～ the whole neighborhood 〔district〕 / 어젯밤 호남 지방 ～에 눈이 내렸다 Snow fell all over Honam region last night. / 경찰은 주변 ～를 수색했다 The police searched the whole neighborhood.

**일대사**(一大事) a matter of great importance 〔of grave concern〕; a serious 〔grave〕 affair; an emergency. ¶ 국가의 ～ an affair of vital importance to the State; a national crisis.

**일대일**(一對一) one to one. ¶ ～의 승부 〔대결〕 a single-handed combat 〔fight〕; a man-to-man fight.

**일더위** the early summer heat; the heat of early summer.

**일도양단**(一刀兩斷) ～하다 cut 《*a person, a thing*》 in two with a slash 〔a single stroke〕 of the sword; cut the Gordian knot. ¶ ～의 조치를 취하다 take a drastic 〔decisive〕 measure; solve a problem once for all.

**일독**(一讀) reading through once; a perusal. ～하다 read 《a book》 through 〔once〕; look 《a report》 over; run *one's* eyes over 《a paper》. ¶ ～할 만하다 be worth reading; be worthy of a perusal.

**일동**(一同) all the persons present 〔concerned〕; all (of us 〔them〕). ¶ 가족 ～ all *one's* family / 회원 ～ all the member / 사원 ～ the whole company / 저희들 ～ we all; all of us / ～모두 in a body; all together / ～을 대표하여 on behalf of all / ～을 대신하여 감사의 말씀을 올리고자 합니다 Let me speak a few words of thanks on behalf of all of us.

**일동일정**(一動一靜) every bit of conduct 〔movement, motion〕.

**일되다** mature early; grow early; ripen early. ¶ 올해는 벼가 일되었다 The rice crops are early this year.

**일득일실**(一得一失) one merit and one demerit; an advantage set off by a disadvantage.

**일등**(一等) the first class; the first rank 〔grade〕; 《제1위》 the first place. ¶ ～석으로 여행하다 travel first class; 《선박의》 travel in a first class cabin / 죄～을 감하다 reduce the penalty 〔commute the sentence〕 by one degree. / 그녀는 ～을 했다 《경주에서》 She came in first; 《경연 등에서》 She won the first prize; 《시험에서》 She took first place in the examination.
◉ ～국 a first-class 〔first-rate〕 power: ～국이 되다 rank among the greatest powers of the world. ～급 first degree. ～기관사 a first engineer. ～병 ⇨ 일병. ～상 《win》 (the) first prize. ～성 〖천문〗 a star of the first magnitude. ～(승)객 a first-class passenger. ～지(地) the best 《residential》 district 《of the town》: 그의 가게는 이 시내의 ～지에 있다 His store is located in the best commercial district in town. ～차〔차표〕 a first-class carriage 〔ticket〕. ～친(親) 〖법〗 a relation of the first degree. ～품 a first-class article; the finest 〔first〕 stuff. ～항해사 the chief 〔first〕 officer 〔mate〕.

**일락서산**(日落西山) ～하다 the sun sets 〔goes down〕 behind the western hills 〔in the west〕.

**일란성**(一卵性) 〖의학〗 ¶ ～의 monozygous; monovular. ◉ ～쌍생아 one-egg 〔monovular〕 twins; identical twins.

**일람**(一覽) ① 《일견》 a look; a glance; a view(ing); a perusal; 《일독》 a reading; 《검토》 an inspection. ～하다 take 〔have〕 a look at; look 〔read〕 through; run through; run *one's* eyes over. ¶ ～후 30일불(拂)의 payable at thirty days after sight / ～하신 후에 되돌려 주십시오 Please return it to me after looking through it. / 그 계획서는 중역 회의 ～용으로 제출되었다 The program was presented at the board meeting for inspection.
② 《개요》 a summary; an epitome; a synopsis; 《안내》 a prospectus; a catalog(ue). ¶ 서울 명소 ～ (A List of) Places to See in Seoul / 대학 ～ a university catalog(ue) 〔prospectus〕.
◉ ～불(拂) payable at sight; sight payment: ～불 어음 a bill payable at

sight 〔on demand〕; a sight bill 〔draft〕/ ～불의 payable at sight. ～표 a table (체계적인); a chart; a list (항목별); a schedule (열차표 등의): 졸업생 ～표 a list of graduates / 출판물 ～표〔목록〕 a catalog of publications.

**일러두기** explanatory notes; introductory remarks; a legend (지도 등의).

**일러두다** 《지시하다》 tell 〔direct, instruct, order〕 《*a person* to *do*》; bid 《*a person do*》; 《부탁하다》 ask; request. ¶ 집을 잘 보라고 그에게 일러두고 왔다 I left him (with instructions) to take care of the house.

**일러바치다** inform (a superior) 《against, on》; tell 〔squeal〕 on 《*a person*》; tell 〔carry〕 tales 《about, against, upon》; 《학생이》 sneak 《영속어》. ¶ 일러바치는 사람 a telltale; a talebearer / 엄마한테 일러바치지 마라 You don't tell mother on me.

**일러주다** ① 《알려주다》 let 《*a person*》 know; inform 《*a person* of, that...》; tell 《*a person*》; announce; notify 《*a person* that...》; tip off about. ¶ 형은 어머님 병환을 나한테 일러주지 않았다 My brother kept mother's sickness from me. ② 《가르치다》 tell; advise; admonish; teach; inculcate; instruct. ¶ 글을 ～ teach reading / 다음부터 더 조심하라고 그에게 일러주어라 Tell him to be more careful from now on.

**일렁거리다** bob up and down; toss; rock (on the waves).

**일렉트론** 〖물리〗 an electron.

**일력**(日曆) a daily pad calendar.

**일련**(一連) ① 《연속》 a series 《of》; a chain 《of》; a succession 《of》. ¶ ～의 successive; connected; a chain 〔train〕 of; a series of / ～의 사건 a chain of events / ～의 거래 a series of transactions. ② 《종이 따위》 a ream 《of paper》. ◉ ～번호 serial 〔consecutive, running〕 numbers: ～번호를 붙이다 number 《the cards》 consecutively.

**일렬**(一列) 《가로의》 a row; a line; a rank; 《세로의》 a file. ¶ ～로 in a line 〔queue, row〕; in a (single) file / ～로 서다 stand in a line 〔row〕; stand in (single) rank 〔file〕; stand in a queue (무엇을 사려고) / ～을 짓다 form a line 〔row〕/ ～로 행진하다 march in a single file 〔line〕. ◉ ～종대: ～종대로 나아가다 march (in) single 〔Indian〕 file.

**일례**(一例) an example; an instance; a case; an illustration. ¶ ～를 들면 for example; for instance; to cite 〔give〕 an instance 〔example〕/ ～로서 for example 〔instance〕; by way of example; as an example / ～를 들다 cite an instance 〔example〕; give 〔mention〕 an instance; take it for one thing / …의 ～가 되다 afford an example of...; serve as an example of... / 이것은 ～를 든 데 불과하다 We merely cited this as an instance of numerous cases. *or* This is only an instance out of many.

**일로**(一路) a straight road; a way; a course; 《곧바로》 straight. ¶ ～매진하다 go 〔advance〕 straightly; 《노력하다》 strive only for 《a matter》/ ～ 샌프란시스코로 향하다 head 〔go〕 straight 〔direct〕 for San Francisco / 환자는 쇠약 ～에 있다 The patient is growing weaker and weaker. / 인구는 증가 ～에 있다 The population shows a steady growth.

**일루**(一縷) a single thread; a thin wreath 《of smoke》; a ray 〔gleam, flush, shred〕 《of hope》. ¶ ～의 희망을 품다 cling to *one's* last hope / ～의 희망마저 잃다 lose the last hope / 그의 병세에는 아직 ～의 희망이 있다 There is still a ray of hope of his recovery.

**일루**(一壘) 〖야구〗 first base. ¶ 4구를 얻어 ～에 나가다 walk to the first base on four balls.

◉ ～선 the first base line. ～수 the first baseman: ～수를 맡다 play first base. ～심 the umpire at first base. ～측 스탠드 the right stand. ～타 a 〔one〕 timer; a base hit; one bagger.

**일류**(一流) ① 《제일위》 the first class 〔rank〕. ¶ ～의 first-class〔-rank, -rate〕; top-ranking 《미》; of the first class 〔order〕; (one of) the best; leading; foremost; top-notch 《구어》; first=string; bang-up 《구어》; 《증권 따위》 blue-chip / 당대 ～의 음악가 one of the best 〔foremost〕 musicians of the day / ～메이커 one of the leading manufacturers / 그는 ～ 외교관이다 He is a diplomat of the first rank. / 그는 산업계에서 ～에 속하는 인물이다 He is one of the foremost men in industrial circles. ② 《유파》 a school. ¶ ～를 이루다 found a school.

◉ ～가수 a top class singer. ～국가 a first-rate nation 《in the coming century》. ～극장 a first-class theater. ～기술자 a top-notch 〔an A-1〕 engineer. ～병 a first-class kick; a fad (passion) for top class: 학부모들은 ～병에

걸려 있다 Parents of pupils are on the first-class school kick. ～선수 a ranking player. ～신문 leading newspapers. ～음악〔영화〕 first-rate music 〔cinema〕. ～작가 a first-rate writer; a name writer; one of the best 〔leading〕 writer 《of Korea》. ～정치가 a politician of the first rank. ～증권 gilt-edged securities. ～학교 a prestige school; (one of ) the best-known schools. ～학자 a scholar of the first order 〔highest standing〕. ～호텔 the first-class〔-rate〕 hotel. ～회사 (one of ) the top-ranking companies; a leading company 〔firm〕.

**일류미네이션** 《조명》 illumination. ¶ ～장치를 한 illuminated.

**일륜차**(一輪車) a monocycle; 《손수레》 a wheelbarrow.

**일률**(一律) ① 《한결같음》 uniformity; evenness; equality; indiscrimination (무차별). ¶ ～적으로 uniformly; equally; evenly; indiscriminately (차별없이); without variation / 7퍼센트의 ～적인 승급(昇給) an across-the-board wage increase of 7 percent / 그 두 개는 ～적으로 논할 수 없다 The two cannot be mentioned in the same breath. / 이 규칙은 ～적으로 적용될 수 없다 This rule cannot be applied in all cases. ② 《죄》 an offense 〔a crime〕 that deserves the death penalty.

**일리**(一理) ① 《어떤 이치》 some reason; some truth. ¶ 네 말에도 ～가 있다 There's some truth in what you say. *or* Your view is true in a way. / 그것도 ～는 있다 There is something 〔some reason〕 in that. ② 《같은 이치》 (one and) the same reason.

**일리노이** 《미국의 주》 Illinois (생략 Ill.); 《속칭》 Prairie State. ¶ ～의 Illinoisan / ～사람 an Illinoisan.

**일막**(一幕) one act; 《제1막》 the first act. ◉ ～극 a one-act play.

**일말**(一抹) ¶ ～의 애수를 느끼다 feel a touch of sadness 《about her》 / ～의 불안을 느끼다 feel slightly uneasy 《about》; feel some 〔a certain〕 anxiety 《about》 / 그녀에게는 ～의 외로움이 감돌고 있다 There is a touch of loneliness about her.

**일망**(一望) a sweep of the eye. ¶ ～천리의 바다 an unlimited 〔a boundless〕 expanse of waters; a boundless ocean / ～천리의 옥야(沃野) a vast sea 〔stretch〕 of fertile plain.

**일망무제**(一望無際) 《끝없이 펼쳐짐》 endlessness; boundlessness. ～하다 (be) endless; boundless. ¶ ～의 바다 an unlimited 〔a boundless〕 expanse of waters; a boundless ocean.

**일망타진**(一網打盡) having a big haul at a single cast of the net; a wholesale arrest. ～하다 catch 《the whole herd》 with one throw; make a wholesale 〔summary〕 arrest 《of smugglers》; round up 《a gang of criminals》.

**일매지다** (be) even; uniform; be all alike. ¶ 잔디밭을 일매지게 깎다 trim the lawn evenly / 이 김 다발은 일매지지 않다 These packs of (dry) laver are (of ) all different sizes.

**일맥**(一脈) a vein. ¶ ～ 상통하다 have a thread of connection 《with》; have something 「to do with 〔in common with〕.

**일면**(一面) ① 《물체의》 a surface; 《사물의》 a 〔one〕 side; 《양상》 an aspect; a phase 《of American life》. ¶ 시대상의 ～ a sign of the times / ～만을 본 견해 a one-sided view / 어두운〔약한〕 ～이 있다 have *one's* dark 〔weak〕 side / 이 문제에는 또 다른 ～이 있다 There is another side to the question. / 나는 그의 성격의 또 다른 ～을 알고 있다 I know another phase of his character. / 그 이야기의 ～에는 슬픈 사연이 있다 The story has a sad side to it. / 그에게는 완고한 ～이 있다 He has a streak of obstinacy in him. / 그가 저지른 일은 비난받을 만하나 ～ 동정할 점도 있다 Of course he should be blamed for what he did, but, on the other hand, he also deserves our sympathy. ② 《신문 따위의》 the first 〔front〕 page. ¶ ～ 기사 first page news; a front-page item / 그 사건은 모든 미국 신문의 ～ 기사가 되었다 The affair hit 〔made〕 the front pages of newspapers throughout the U.S. / 그것에 관한 기사가 신문의 ～ 톱에 나왔다 An article about it appeared at the top of the front page. ③ 《한번 만남》 a single meeting. ～하다 meet 〔confront〕 for the first time. ④ 《행정 구역》 the whole *myŏn*.

**일면식**(一面識) a sight acquaintance. ¶ …와 ～이 있다 be slightly acquainted with…; be on bowing terms with …; know 《*a person*》 by sight / 그와는 ～도 없다 He is a complete stranger to me. *or* I have never met him. / ～

도 없는 사람을 추천할 수는 없다 I cannot recommand a person whom I have never met.

**일면여구**(一面如舊) being very friendly (like old pals) at the first meeting.

**일명**(一名) ① 《한 사람》 one person. ¶ 타이피스트 ~ 채용 《광고》 A typist wanted. ② 《딴 이름》 another 〔a second〕 name; an alias. ¶ 송명철 ~「꼬마」 Song Myŏngch'ŏl, alias *kkoma* / 김군은 ~ 갑돌이다 Kaptol is another name of Mr. Kim. *or* Mr. Kim goes by the name of Kaptol.

**일명**(一命) a life. ¶ 나라를 위해 ~을 바치다 offer 〔lay down〕 *one's* life for *one's* country.

**일모**(日暮) 《일몰》 sunset; sundown 《미》; 《황혼》 dusk; twilight; 《저녁때》 evening.

**일모작**(一毛作) raising a single crop a year; single-crop farming. ◉ ~전답 a single-crop field.

**일목요연**(一目瞭然) ~하다 (be) quite obvious; plain; [서술적] be as clear 〔plain〕 as day 〔daylight〕; be clear at glance. ¶ 그의 보고서는 ~했다 His report was clear at a glance. *or* His report was「quite obvious 〔as clear as day〕.

**일몰**(日沒) sunset; sundown 《미》. ¶ ~ 후〔전〕 after 〔before〕 sunset / 일출부터 ~까지 from sunrise to sundown / ~ 후에 그들은 행동을 개시했다 They went into action after the sunset.

**일무**(一無) nothing; not even one. ◉ ~가관(可觀) nothing worth seeing. ~가취(可取) nothing worth taking. ~소득 no profit 〔gain〕 at all. ~소식 no tidings 〔news〕 at all; not a single word.

**일문**(一門) ① 《한집안》 a family; a clan; *one's* kinsfolk. ¶ 고인의 제사에 ~이 모두 모였다 All of the clan gathered to have a memorial service for the dead. ② 《대포의》 《a piece of》 gun.

**일문일답**(一問一答) (a series of) questions and answers; question-and-answer; detailed questioning and answering. ~하다 give an answer to each question; give an interview; answer questions.

**일물**(逸物) a superb article; an excellent thing; 《걸작》 a masterpiece.

**일미**(一味) a good flavor; relish; deliciousness. ¶ 이 요리는 천하 ~다 This cuisine 〔dish〕 is out of this world. *or* There is nothing like this delicious dish in the whole world.

**일박**(一泊) a night's lodging; an overnight stay. ~하다 stay overnight; stop for the night; put up 《at a hotel》 for the night; pass 〔spend〕 a night 《at, in》. ◉ ~여행 《make》 an overnight trip 《to》: 부산으로 ~여행을 가다 make an overnight trip to Pusan.

**일반**(一般) ① 《전반》 the whole; the all; general. ¶ ~의〔적〕 《전반의》 general; over all; whole; all; 《보편적인》 universal; 《보통의》 common; usual; ordinary; 《대중의》 popular / ~적으로 generally; in general; universally; commonly; ordinarily; as a rule; on the whole; by and large; on an 〔the〕 average / ~적으로 말하면 generally speaking / ~ 사람 the general public; people 〔the public〕 at large; the common run of people; an ordinary person; a man in 〔on〕 the street / ~에게 공개하다 open 《a garden》 to the public / 그는 ~론부터 개개의 문제까지 논급했다 He reasoned from the generalities to the particulars. / 성적은 ~적으로 우수하다 The results are on the whole excellent. / 아이들은 ~적으로 사탕을 좋아한다 Children in general are fond of candy. / 그것이 ~의 의견이다 That is the common opinion of all. ② 《매일반》 the same 《as》. ◉ ~감각 general sensation. ~개념 a general concept 〔idea, notion〕. ~경향 a general tendency. ~교서 《미》 the President's State of the Union Message (to Congress). ~교양 general 〔liberal〕 education: ~ 교양 과목 liberal arts; general subjects / ~ 교양과정 liberal education course. ~규정 a general rule; general provisions. ~독자 readers in general; common readers. ~론 (a) generalization. ~명사(名辭) a general term. ~미(米) traditional rice; rice of traditional breed. ~법 a general law 〔statute〕. ~사면(赦免) a general pardon. ~석 《극장 등의》 a general admission seat. ~성 generality. ~식 〖수학〗 a general expression. ~원칙 broad 〔general〕 principles. ~의(醫) a general practitioner. ~입찰 an open public tender 〔bid〕. ~직(職) 《공무원의》 《be in》 administrative grade 《of the Civil Service》; 《민간 기업의》 《be in》 the general=duties grade; 《have》 a secretarial 〔general-duties〕 post 〔position, job〕. ~투표 a referendum; a popular vote.

~표준 the average. ~화 generalization; 《보급》 popularization: ~화하다 generalize; popularize. ~회계 the general account: ~ 회계 예산 the general account budget.

**일발**(一發) 《총 따위의》 a 〔one〕 (single) shot 〔pop〕; 《탄알의》 one 〔a〕 round. ¶ ~의 총성 the report of a gun 〔shot〕 / ~로 at a shot.

**일방**(一方) 《한 쪽》 one side 〔hand〕; 《다른 한 쪽》 the other side 〔hand〕; a party; 《당사자의 한 쪽》 the other party. ¶ ~적(으로) one-sidedly; unilateral(ly); lopsided(ly) / ~적(인) 경기 a one-sided game / ~적인 승리 《win》 a lopsided victory; an overwhelming victory; a runaway victory / ~적인 견해 a one-sided view / ~적인 주장 one=sided allegations / 조약을 ~적으로 파기하다 abrogate a treaty one-sidedly. ◉ ~무역 a one-way trade. ~통행 one=way traffic; 《게시》 One way (only): ~통행로 one-way street / 그 길은 ~통행이다 That is a one-way street.

**일배**(一杯) 《한 잔》 a cup; a glass; a cupful; a glassful.

**일번**(一番) Number One; the first. ¶ ~의 first; foremost; top / ~으로 합격하다 pass an examination first on a list / ~ 문제에 답하시오 Answer question No. 1. *or* Answer the first question. ◉ ~열차 the first train. ~타자 〖야구〗 the first 〔lead-off〕 batter.

**일벌** 〖곤충〗 a worker bee; a worker.

**일변**(一邊) 《한쪽》 one side; 《한편》 one hand; the other side.

**일변**(一變) 《아주 바뀜》 a (complete) change. ~하다 change completely; undergo a complete change; turn round; be transformed. ¶ 형세의 ~ a drastic 〔sweeping〕 change of the situation / 사람이 ~하다 become quite another man; turn over a new leaf / 태도를 ~하다 change *one's* attitude altogether 〔entirely〕; reverse *one's* attitude / 국면이 ~하다 the situation ｢takes on 〔assumes〕 a new aspect / 병세가 ~하다 a disease takes a new turn / 원자 무기의 발명으로 전술이 ~했다 The invention of atomic weapons brought about a change in warfare.

**일변**(日邊) daily interest 〔rate〕. ¶ ~ 500원의 이자 interest of five hundred won per day.

**일변도**(一邊倒) wholehearted 〔complete〕 devotion to one side; being single=hearted. ¶ 미국 ~다 be completely pro-American; be an out-and-out 〔unqualified, unquestioning〕 supporter of America; be totally committed to America 〔the American cause〕. ◉ ~정책 a lean-to-one-side policy.

**일별**(一別) parting; separation. ~하다 part 《from》; separate 《from》. ¶ ~ 이래 since we parted; since our last meeting; since we last met; since I saw you last.

**일별**(一瞥) a glance; a glimpse; a look. ~하다 glance 《at, on》; cast 〔throw, take〕 a glance 《at》; have 〔catch, get〕 a glimpse 《of》; take a quick look 《at》. ¶ ~할 가치도 없다 be beneath notice / 그는 ~했을 뿐이다 He only gave it a glance.

**일병**(一兵) 〖육군·해병〗 a private first class (생략 Pfc.) 《미》; 〖해군〗 a seaman 《미》; a leading seaman 《영》; 〖공군〗 an airman second class 《미》; a senior aircraftman 《영》.

**일보**(一步) a 〔one〕 step. ¶ ~ 일보 step by step / 개선의 제 ~ the first step toward improvement / ~전진〔후퇴〕하다 take a step forward 〔backward〕 / ~도 양보하지 않다 do not budge 〔yield〕 an inch / …의 ~ 직전에 있다 be on the brink 〔verge〕 of 《ruin》.

**일보**(日報) 《보도·보고》 a daily report; 《신문》 a daily newspaper. ¶ 동아 ~ the Dong-A Daily News.

**일보다** take care of a business; handle a job; work. ¶ 교장 부재중에는 그가 대리로서 일본다 In 〔During〕 the absence of the principal, he is in charge of the school.

**일복**(一福) 《할 일이 많음》 ¶ ~이 많다 have plenty 〔a lot〕 of work to do / ~을 타고 나다 be destined to do a lot of work through life.

**일본**(日本) Japan. ¶ ~의 Japanese / ~식의 Japanesque / ~식으로 in Japanese style / ~화하다 Japanize. ◉ ~뇌염 Japanese encephalitis. ~말 Japanese; the Japanese language. ~사람 a Japanese (*pl.* Japanese); the Japanese (people) [총칭]. ~열도 the Japanese Islands 〔Isles, Archipelago〕. ~요리 Japanese dishes 〔cooking, cuisine〕. ~정부 the Japanese Government. ~차(茶) Japanese 〔green〕 tea.

**일봉**(一封) an envelope enclosing money (as a gift). ¶ 금~ an enclosure 〔a gift〕 of money / 그는 금~을 받았다 He got a gift of money.

**일부**(一夫) one man; one husband.

◉ ～다처 polygyny; polygamy. ～양처 bigamy; having two wives. ～일처(一妻) monogamy: ～일처의 monogamous; monogamic / ～일처주의자 a monogamist. ～제(制) monandry; the monandrous system. ～종사 serving but a single husband: ～종사하다 serve but a single husband. ～종신 having but a single husband during life.

**일부**(一部) ① 《일부분》 a part; a portion; a section.

> 용법 **part** 「일부분」을 뜻하는 가장 일반적인 낱말. 「…의 일부」라고 단수를 나타내는 경우는 관사 a를 생략하는 일이 많음. **portion** 할당된 part, 즉 「몫」을 나타냄. **section** 구획된 또는 떼어낸 한 부분으로서의 part를 뜻함.

¶ ～의 some; partial; sectional / ～의 사람들 some people; a certain circle / ～의 과격파 a small group 〔section〕 of extremists / 필요 기재의 ～ part of the needed machinery / 재산의 ～ a portion of the property / ～를 수정하다 amend partially 〔in part〕; make a partial amendment 《of》 / ～를 이루다 form (a) part of... / 그것의 ～는 나무로, ～는 금속으로 되어 있다 It is made partly of wood, and partly of metal. / 그건 ～ 내 잘못이다 It is partly my fault. / 그의 이야기는 ～만이 사실이다 Only part of his story is true. / ～ 학생은 게으르다 Part of the students are idle (★ part가 사람이나 동물처럼 셀 수 있는 것에 쓰일 때는 복수동사를 취함). / 이것은 그녀의 수집품의 극히 ～에 지나지 않는다 This is only (a) part of her collection.

② 《책》 a (single) copy. ¶ 근저(近著) ～를 증정하겠습니다 I will make you a present of a copy of my new book.

◉ ～결정 partial decision. ～수정 partial amendment. ～용선(傭船) a part=cargo charter. ～인사 certain circles; some people. ～주권국 a state having partial sovereignty; a semi-independent country.

**일부**(日附) a date; dating. =날짜. ¶ ～가 없는 편지 an undated letter / 그 편지는 3월 10일의 ～가 있었다 The letter was dated March 10. ◉ ～변경선 the (international) date line. ～인(印) a date stamp.

**일부**(日賦) daily installments. ¶ ～로 갚다 pay by daily installment.

◉ ～금 daily installment payment. ～판매 sale on daily-installment terms.

**일부러** 《고의로》 on purpose; purposely; intentionally; deliberately; by design; 《짐짓》 knowingly; wittingly; 《특히》 specially; expressly; 《멀리서 이렇게》 all the way. ¶ ～…하다 take the trouble 《to *do*》; trouble 〔bother〕 《to *do*》; go to all the trouble 《of *do*ing》 / ～울다 force a weeping / ～ 한 것이 아니니 용서해 주십시오 Pardon me, please, for it was quite accidental. / 너 ～ 그랬지 You did it on purpose, didn't you? / 그것은 내가 ～ 한 말이다 I said that on purpose (to fool you). / ～ 거기 갈 것은 없다 You don't have to take the trouble to go there. *or* Don't bother to go there. / 방금 어머니가 그것을 사러 ～ 나가셨다 Mother has just gone out for the express purpose of buying it. / 너를 보려고 ～ 서울에 왔다 I've come all the way to Seoul to see you. / 먼 길을 ～ 와 주셔서 고맙습니다 It is very kind of you to come all the way to see us. *or* How good of you to come all the way to see us!

**일부분**(一部分) one part 〔portion, section, division〕. ⇨ 일부(一部) ①.

**일분**(一分) ① 《100분의 1》 one hundredth; one percent. ② 《시간·각도》 a minute. ¶ ～ 1초도 어김없이 as accurate as chronometer; on the minute. ③ 《온도》 point one. ¶ 36도 ～ thirty=six degrees point one.

**일비**(日費) daily expenses 〔expenditure〕.

**일사**(一事) one thing; a single item.

◉ ～ 부재리(不再理) 〖법〗 a prohibition against double jeopardy: ～ 부재리의 원칙 the principle of not reopening a settled case; the principle of not deliberating the same measure twice; *ne bis in idem*(L.). ～부재의(不再議) 〖법〗 (the principle of) not deliberating the same measure twice during the same session (of the National Assembly).

**일사**(一死) 〖야구〗 one out. ¶ ～ 만루가 됐다 The bases were loaded with one out.

**일사병**(日射病) 〖의학〗 sunstroke; heliosis. ¶ ～에 걸리다 be sunstruck; have 〔be affected by, suffer from〕 sunstroke.

**일사분기**(一四分期) 《during》 the first quarter of the year. ¶ 한국 경제는 올해 ～중 작년 동기에 비해 9.7퍼센트나 성장했다 The Korean economy grew by 9.7% during this year's first quarter over the same period of last year.

**일사불란**(一絲不亂) perfect order; thorough consistency. ~하다 be in perfect 〔strict〕 order; (be) shipshape; thoroughly consistent. ¶ ~한 논지(論旨) a thoroughly consistent argument / ~하게〔으로〕 in perfect 〔strict〕 order; shipshape; in a shipshape manner / 그의 논법은 ~했다 His argument was perfectly airtight.

**일사천리**(一瀉千里) rapid advance; torrential eloquence. ¶ ~로 at top speed; in a hurry; with (great) rapidity; 《단숨에》 at full stretch 〔heat〕 / ~로 사무를 처리하다 dispatch business at full gallop; make short work of it / 의안을 ~로 통과시키다 rush a bill through / ~로 써내려가다 dash off 《a letter》 at a stretch.

**일삯** wages; pay.

**일산**(一酸) 〚화학〛 ¶ ~의 monoacidic. ◉ ~화물 monoxide. ~화 질소〔탄소〕 nitrogen 〔carbon〕 monoxide.

**일산**(日産) ① 《생산고》 a daily output. ② 《일본제》 Japan-made; 《of 》 Japanese make.

**일삼다** 《일로 삼다》 make it *one's* business to 《*do*》; 《전념》 devote *oneself* to; 《탐닉》 give *oneself* up to; do nothing but.... ¶ 술 마시기를 ~ do nothing but drink; be given to drink / 낚시질을 일삼고 집안을 돌보지 않다 indulge in fishing and neglect *one's* family.

**일상**(日常) 《매일》 every day; daily; 《평소》 usually. ¶ ~의 daily; everyday; usual; ordinary / ~의 행실 *one's* everyday conduct / ~하는 일 (*one's*) daily work 〔business〕; routine work; (daily) routine / ~ 쓰는 물건 things of daily necessity / 그것은 ~ 다반사다 It's a daily occurrence 〔happening〕. *or* It's an everyday affair. / 나는 ~의 일들을 일기에 적는다 I write down 「daily events 〔everyday affairs〕 in my diary.

◉ ~복 an everyday dress 〔suit〕; everyday 〔ordinary〕 clothes; a housedress. ~사 an everyday experience 〔occurrence, affair, happening〕. ~생활 everyday 〔daily〕 life. ~어 everyday language. ~업무 daily business; routine work. ~용어 everyday words. ~회화 daily conversation.

**일색**(一色) ① 《한 빛》 one color. ¶ 파랑 ~으로 all in blue color. ② 《미인》 a distinguished beauty. ③ 〔비유적〕 ¶ 천하~ a peerless beauty (in the world) / 위원회는 민주당 ~이다 The committee seats are exclusively occupied by Democrats. / 서울은 야당 ~이었다 Seoul was swept by the Opposition.

**일생**(一生) a lifetime; *one's* (whole) life. ¶ ~의 사업 *one's* lifework / ~의 소원 *one's* lifelong desire; a desire cherished for life / ~에 한 번 once in a lifetime / ~ 한 번의 좋은 기회 the chance of a lifetime; a once-in-a-lifetime chance / ~을 통하여 throughout (*one's*) life; all *one's* life; as long as *one* lives / ~을 걸다 stake *one's* life 《for》 / ~을 보내다 pass through life / ~을 바치다 devote 〔dedicate, consecrate, give〕 *one's* life 《to》 / 구사(九死) ~을 얻다 have a narrow escape from death; be snatched from the jaws of death / ~을 그르치다 make a failure of *one's* life; wreck *one's* chances in life; ruin *one's* career / ~을 마치다 end 〔close〕 *one's* life 〔career, days〕; finish *one's* life / ~을 독신으로 지내다 stay 〔remain〕 single 〔unmarried〕 all *one's* life; live and die a bachelor (남자가); live and die a spinster (여자가) / ~을 편히 지내다 spend *one's* life in easy circumstances; live comfortably to the end of *one's* life / ~동안 불구가 되다 become a cripple for life. ◉ ~일사(一死) living and dying; life and death.

**일생일대**(一生一代) *one's* lifetime. ¶ ~의 once in a lifetime; of *one's* lifetime / ~의 걸작 *one's* life's masterpiece; *one's* magnum opus.

**일석**(日夕) ⇨저녁. ◉ ~점호 the evening roll call.

**일석이조**(一石二鳥) (killing) two birds with one stone; *One stone, two birds.* (★ Two favorable results come from a single effort.의 뜻). ¶ 그것은 ~이다 It serves a double purpose.

**일선**(一線) 《줄》 a line; 《전쟁·실무의》 the front (line); the first 〔fighting〕 line. ¶ ~ 외교관들 the first-line diplomats / ~에 서다 stand 〔be〕 in the fire front 《of 》 / ~에서 활약하다 be active in the first line 《of the business world》 / ~을 긋다 draw a line 《between》 / …와(의 사이에) 명확한 ~을 긋다 set up 〔make〕 a clear distinction 《between》; draw a clear 〔sharp, neat, firm〕 line of demarcation 《against》 / 그는 제 ~에서 물러났다 He has retired from active work

〔participation〕. ◉ ～근무 field 〔active〕 service.

**일설**(一說) 《하나의 설》 one report 〔opinion, view, version〕; 《다른 설》 another report; another opinion 〔view〕 (의견); another version (해석). ¶ ～에 의하면 according to one theory 〔authority, account〕; one theory holds that...; someone says...; 《다른 설에 의하면》 according to another view; to quote another authority.

**일세**(一世) 《일대》 a generation; an age; 《일생》 a lifetime; 《그 시대》 the time; the age; the day; 《왕조의》 the first; 《이민의》 a first-generation immigrant. ¶ ～의 of the age; of *one's* life / ～의 영웅 the greatest hero of the day / 나폴레옹 ～ Napoleon I 〔the First〕 / ～를 풍미하다 dominate the (literary) world / ～를 경악케 하다 startle the whole world.

**일세기**(一世紀) one 〔a〕 century; 100 years.

**일세대**(一世代) a 〔one〕 generation.

**일소**(一笑) a laugh. ¶ ～에 부치다 laugh 《*a matter*》 away 〔off〕; dismiss 〔carry off〕 《*a matter*》 with a laugh / 그녀는 나의 구혼을 농담으로 여기고 ～에 부쳤다 She laughed off my proposal of marriage as a joke.

**일소**(一掃) a (clean) sweep. ～하다 sweep away 〔off〕; drive off; clear (away, off); stamp 〔root〕 out; 《구어》 get rid of; eradicate; uproot. ¶ 악습을 ～하다 sweep away abuses; eradicate evil customs / 오리(汚吏)를 ～하다 make a clean sweep of the corrupt elements / 세상의 오해를 ～하다 dispel current misapprehensions / 의혹을 ～하다 clear away *one's* suspicion / 적을 ～하다 clear 〔sweep〕 《the place》 of the enemy; drive the enemy off 《the place》 / 주자(走者)를 ～하다 〖야구〗 clean the bases.

**일손** ① 《일》 work in hand. ¶ ～을 놓다 stop working / ～을 붙들다 〔잡다〕 start working / ～을 쉬다 take a work break. ② 《솜씨》 a skillful hand; skill at a job. ¶ ～이 오르다 improve in *one's* skill / ～이 떨어지다 fall off in *one's* skill. ③ 《사람》 a (hired) hand; a worker; a help; 《도움》 help. ¶ 농촌의 ～돕기 운동 a (nationwide) drive to help farmers 《in their busiest harvest season》 / ～을 돕다 provide a helping hand / ～이 모자라다 be short-handed; be short of hands; be undermanned; suffer from a lack of hands / ～을 빌다 ask for another's help; get 〔procure〕 assistance from another / ～이 필요하다 We need helping hands. / 그는 ～을 빌리지 않고 그 일을 했다 He did the work by himself. / 많은 중소 기업들은 ～부족으로 고통받고 있다 Many small-to-medium sized enterprises are suffering from a shortage of workers.

**일수**(日收) a loan collected by daily installment. ¶ ～로 돈을 꾸다 〔꾸어주다〕 borrow 〔lend〕 money at daily interest. ◉ ～놀이 moneylending by 〔in〕 daily installments. ～쟁이 a moneylender who collects by daily installments. 일숫돈 money payable by daily installments.

**일수**(日數) ① 《날 수》 the number of days. ¶ 입원 치료의 ～ days of hospital treatment / 많은 ～가 걸리다 take a great number of days 〔a long time〕. ② 《날의 운수》 a day's luck. ¶ ～가 사납다 have a bad day('s luck) / ～가 좋다 the day is lucky.

**일수판매**(一手販賣) = 총판(總販).

**일숙박**(一宿泊) a night's lodging. ⇨ 일박. ～하다 stay overnight.

**일순**(一巡) a round; a patrol (경찰의). ～하다 make a round 〔tour〕 《of》; take a round; patrol.

**일순간**(一瞬間) an instant; a moment; a flash. ¶ ～의 momentary / ～에 in an instant 〔a flash, a wink〕 / ～도 소홀히 해서는 안 된다 We cannot waste even a moment.

**일습**(一襲) 《옷의》 a suit; 《가구의》 a suite 《of furniture》; 《용구의》 a (complete) set 《of》. ¶ 동복～ a suit of winter clothes / 다기(茶器) ～ a set of tea things / 등산 장비 ～ a complete set of equipment for mountain climbing.

**일승일패**(一勝一敗) one win against 〔and〕 one defeat. ¶ ～의 경기 a ding-dong contest; an even match.

**일시**(一時) ① 《한때》 《at》 a time; 《at》 one time; once. ¶ 그는 ～ 서울에서 살았다 He lived in Seoul at one time. / ～ 그의 생명이 절망적이었다 At one time his life was despaired of. ② 《동시》 ¶ ～에 at the same time; simultaneously 《with》; concurrently. ¶ ～에 두가지 일을 할 수는 없다 You cannot do two things at the same time. / 모든 청중이 ～에 일어섰다 Simultaneously the whole audience stood up.

③《잠시》 for a time 〔while〕; momentarily; temporarily. ¶ ～적(인) momentary; temporary; passing; impermanent / ～적 분노 the anger of the moment / ～적 인기 a mere mushroom 〔transient〕 popularity / ～적 현상 a passing phenomenon / ～적 방편 a temporary expedient; a stopgap 〔temporary〕 measure / ～적 충동에 이끌리다 be carried away by the impulse of the moment / 그의 명성도 ～에 지나지 않았다 His fame was only momentary. / 이 불경기가 ～적 현상이기를 바란다 I hope this business depression is a passing phenomenon.
④《갑자기》 ¶ ～에 suddenly; all at once / 그는 ～에 갑부가 되었다 He became a millionaire overnight. / 그는 이 소설로 ～에 유명해졌다 He made a name all at once by this novel. / 학생들이 ～에 떠들기 시작했다 The students got noisy all at once.
◉ ～귀휴(歸休) 제도 the layoff system. ～금〔급(給)〕 a lump-sum allowance. ～미봉책 a stopgap remedy; a makeshift; a temporary expedient. ～보관 temporary custody《of baggage》: ～ 보관소 a cloakroom; a checkroom《미》; a baggage checking office / ～보관증 a claim check. ～불(拂) payment in a lump sum; a lump-sum payment. ～정지《make, come to》 a halt. ～차입금 a floating debt; a temporary loan.

**일시**(日時) the date (and time); the time. ¶ 우편으로 ～를 알려 드리겠습니다 We will let you know the date and time by mail.

**일시동인**(一視同仁)《공평》 impartiality; impartial treatment; 《동포애》 universal brotherhood 〔benevolence〕; fraternal spirit. ¶ ～의 impartial; cosmopolitan.

**일식**(日蝕) 〖천문〗 an eclipse of the sun; a solar eclipse. ¶ 개기〔부분〕～ a total 〔partial〕 eclipse of the sun.

**일신**(一身) *one's* self 〔body〕. ¶ ～상의 문제 *one's* personal affairs / ～상의 중대사 a matter of great personal importance / ～의 이해를 돌보지 않고 regardless of *one's* own interests / ～의 이익을 꾀하다 consult 〔pursue〕 *one's* own interests / 중망을 ～에 모으다 have public hopes centered upon *one* / ～을 바치다 devote 〔offer〕 *oneself* 《to》 / ～상의 사정으로 사직하다 resign for personal reasons.

**일신**(一新) renovation; a complete change; renewal. ～하다 renovate; change completely; renew; revolutionize. ¶ 면목을 ～하다 undergo a complete change / 민심을 ～하다 renew popular sentiments / 생활을 ～하다 turn over a new leaf / 주거가 바뀌면 기분이 ～된다 A change of abode brings about a change of mind. / 기분을 ～하기 위해 며칠간 시골에 가야겠다 I need a few days in the country 「to restore my spirits 〔to put me back in top form〕. / 그는 개각을 단행해서 민심을 ～해보려 했다 He tried to rekindle public 「enthusiasm 〔support〕 by carrying out a Cabinet reshuffle.

**일신**(日新) daily renovation 〔improvement〕. ～하다 be daily renovated; undergo a daily improvement.

**일신교**(一神教) 〖종교〗 monotheism; a monotheistic religion. ¶ ～의 monotheistic. ◉ ～도 a monotheist.

**일심**(一心) ①《한마음》 one mind; 《일념》 a single heart; wholeheartedness; undivided attention. ¶ 온 국민이 ～이 되다 the whole nation unites as one. ②《전념》 concentration 〔absorption〕 of mind on one thing. ¶ ～으로 with all *one's* mind; heart and soul / ～으로 …하다 set *one's* heart on; devote *oneself* to; be absorbed in 《*something*》. ◉ ～동체 being one in flesh and spirit: 부부는 ～동체이다 Man and wife are one flesh. / ～동체가 되다 become one flesh. ～만능 Nothing is impossible to a determined mind. ～전력 *one's* whole heart and all *one's* might 〔energies〕.

**일심**(一審) the first trial 〔instance, court〕. ¶ ～에서 패소하다 lose a case at the first trial / ～에서 무죄가 되다 be aquitted 〔be free of charge〕 at the first trial. ◉ 제 ～법정 a court of the first instance.

**일심불란**(一心不亂) *one's* whole heart; wholeheartedness; single-hearted devotion. ～하다 give *one's* whole mind 〔heart〕 《to》; put *one's* heart and soul 《into》; devote *oneself* 《to》; throw *oneself* 《into》. ¶ ～하게 공부하다 concentrate single-mindedly on *one's* work.

**일심시차**(日心視差) 〖천문〗 the heliocentric parallax.

**일쑤** a habitual 〔usual〕 practice. ¶ …하기가 ～이다 be always *do*ing (something unpleasant) / 그는 남을 비웃기

~다 He's always sneering at others. / 그는 거짓말하기 ~다 He tells a lie every time he turns around. / 그녀는 울기 ~야 She's a constant crybaby.

**일약**(一躍) one bound 〔leap, jump〕; [부사적] at a (single) bound 〔jump〕. ¶ ~ 최고 지위에 오르다 rise to the highest position at a jump / ~ 유명해지다 spring 〔leap〕 into fame / 그는 그 소설로 ~문단에 알려졌다 He leaped into literary eminence by writing that novel. / 그는 무일푼에서 ~ 백만 장자가 되었다 From a penniless man he became a millionaire at a bound.

**일양일**(一兩日) a day or two (★ a day or two가 가장 일반적임. one or two days 라고도 할 수 있지만 one day or two라고는 관용상 안함. 단, 「시간」의 경우는 one hour or two라고도 할 수 있음). ¶ ~간 for a couple of days.

**일어**(日語) Japanese; the Japanese language. ¶ ~ 교과서 a Japanese text (-book); a textbook of the Japanese language.

**일어나다** ① 《기상하다》 get up; get out of bed; rise; 《잠을 깨다》 wake up; awake. ¶ 아침 일찍 ~ get up early in the morning / 병석에서 ~ get up from a sickbed; leave *one's* sickbed / 일어날 시간이다 It's time for me to get up. / 환자는 일어나 다닐 수 있게 되었다 The patient is now so well he can be up and about. / 밤늦게까지 자지 않고 일어나 있으면 안 된다 You should not sit up too late at night. / 자, 일어나거라 Hey! Wake up!

② 《일어서다》 get up; stand up; rise (to *one's* feet); pick *oneself* up (넘어졌다가). ¶ 의자에서 ~ rise 〔get up〕 from the chair / 벌떡 ~ spring 〔leap, start〕 to *one's* feet / 힘겹게 가까스로 ~ scramble to *one's* feet / 그는 넘어졌으나 일어나서 다시 달렸다 He stumbled, picked himself up and ran again.

③ 《사건 따위가》 happen; occur; take place; break out; arise.
¶ 어떤 일이 일어나더라도 whatever may happen / 민중 사이에서 자연 발생적으로 일어난 운동 a movement rising spontaneously from among the people / 매일 일어나는 일 the events of the day; daily happenings; everyday occurrence / 전쟁이 ~ a war breaks out / 신문은 세계에서 일어나는 일을 알려 준다 The newspaper tells us what is going on in the world. / 학교에서 소동이 일어났다 Trouble broke out in the school.

> 용법 **happen** 원인이나 계획·의도 유무에 관계없이 일·사건 따위가 「일어나다」란 뜻으로 가장 폭넓게 쓰이는 일반적인 말. **occur** happen보다 격식차린 말로, 어떤 특정한 일이 특정한 때에 일어남을 뜻함. 그러나 happen과 같은 뜻으로 쓰이는 경우도 많음. **take place** 예정되었던 일이 일어남을 뜻함. **break out** 화재·전쟁·소동 따위가 예고없이 갑자기 「일어나다」란 뜻. **arise** 원인이 있어서 그 결과로서 「일어나다」란 뜻.

④ 《생겨나다》 spring up; come into existence 〔being〕. ¶ 최근 각종 새로운 공업이 일어났다 Various new industries have sprung up lately. / 또 다른 불온한 사건이 일어나려 하고 있다 Another disturbing incident is in the making.

⑤ 《번성하다》 rise; flourish; prosper; be prosperous; revive. ¶ 나라가 크게 ~ a nation rides the wave of a great prosperity / 그의 대에 이르러 그의 집안은 크게 일어났다 In his days, the family prospered.

⑥ 《불이》 burn; be kindled; get lively; 《a flame》 rise. ¶ 불이 잘 일어난다 The fire is burning lively.

⑦ 《바람이》 rise; blow; come up. ¶ 별안간 큰 바람이 일어났다 All of a sudden, a great wind came up.

⑧ 《열·전기가》 be produced 〔generated〕. ¶ 물체를 마찰하면 열과 전기가 일어난다 Friction generates heat and electricity.

⑨ 《기인하다》 arise 〔spring, result〕 《from》; come of; originate 《in》; have its origin 《in》. ¶ 병은 종종 과식에서 일어난다 Sickness often results from eating too much. / 싸움은 오해에서 일어났다 The quarrel originated in 〔from〕 a misunderstanding.

**일어서다** ① 《기립하다》 ⇨ 일어나다 ②. ¶ 내가 들어오자 그는 일어섰다 He got to his feet as I entered. ② 《분기하다》 rise up; brace *oneself* up; bestir *oneself*. ¶ 압제에 반항해서 ~ rise against oppression / 이제야 말로 무기를 들고 일어설 때다 It is the time for us to rise up in arms.

**일어탁수**(一魚濁水) One man's 「mistake 〔error, misconduct〕 does damage 〔injury, mischief〕 to many.

**일억**(一億) a 〔one〕 hundred million.

**일언**(一言) a (single) word; one word. ~하다 speak 〔say〕 a word. ¶ ~지하

에 거절하다 reject 《*a person's* request》 pointblank 〔flatly〕 / ～지하에 거절당했다 I was met by a flat refusal. / 남아 ～ 중천금 A man's word of honor is as good as a bond. ◉ ～일행 every word and deed 〔act〕.

**일언반구**(一言半句) a 〔one〕 word. ¶ ～의 사과도 없이 without a single word of apology / ～도 없다 do not utter a word / ～도 함부로 말하지 않다 weigh *one's* words carefully; be very careful in *one's* choice of words / 그는 ～의 변명도 없이 자리를 떴다 He left us without a single word of excuse.

**일언이폐지**(一言以蔽之) One sentence can cover the whole. ～하다 express in a single word.

**일없다** (be) needless; useless; unwanted; there is no need for; have no use for. ¶ 의사는 나한테 ～ I have no use for a doctor. / 옷은 일 없으니 돈이나 주시오 I don't want clothes, give me money. / 이렇게 많이는 ～ I don't need so many.

**일여덟** seven or eight.

**일엽편주**(一葉片舟) a light skiff; a small boat.

**일요**(日曜) ⇨일요일. ◉ ～예배 Sunday service(s). ～특집 a Sunday supplement. ～판(版) a Sunday edition. ～학교 a Sunday school. ～화가 a Sunday 〔weekend〕 painter.

**일요일**(日曜日) Sunday (생략 Sun.). ¶ ～이외의 날 the weekday(s) / ～에(는) on Sunday / ～에는 언제나 on Sundays; Sundays 《미》 / 지난〔다음〕 ～에 last 〔next〕 Sunday; on Sunday last 〔next〕 / ～ 아침에 on Sunday morning / ～에는 학교에 가지 않는다 We have no school on Sundays. / 오늘은 ～이다 It is Sunday today. *or* Today is Sunday. / 우리는 ～도 없이 일한다 We work even on Sundays. ◉ ～ 특별프로 Sunday features. ～특집 《신문의》 a Sunday supplement. ～판 《신문의》 a Sunday edition.

**일용**(日用) daily 〔everyday〕 use. ¶ ～의 daily; for daily 〔everyday〕 use; of daily necessity.
◉ ～기구 ordinary utensils; utensils of daily use. ～범백(凡百) 〔백화(百貨)〕 all the articles of daily use; daily necessaries; living necessities ～사전 an everyday 〔all-purpose〕 dictionary. ～영어 everyday English. ～품 daily necessities; articles of daily use.

**일원**(一元) ¶ ～적인 unified; unitary.
◉ ～론 〖철학〗 monism. ～설 monogenesis. ～화 unification: ～화하다 unify.

**일원**(一員) a member 《of society》.

**일원**(一圓) ＝일대(一帶). ¶ 호남 ～에 throughout 〔all over〕 the Honam district.

**일원제**(一院制) the single-chamber system; the unicameral system.
◉ ～의회 a unicameral legislature.

**일월**(一月) January (생략 Jan.).

**일월**(日月) 《해와 달》 the sun and the moon; 《시간》 time and tide; days and months. ◉ ～성신(星辰) the sun, the moon and the stars. ～식 solar and lunar eclipse(s).

**일위**(一位) ① 〖수학〗 《1의 자리》 the unit's place. ② 《첫 자리》 the first 〔foremost〕 place; the premier position; No. 1; the first rank. ¶ ～를 차지하다 《경기 등에서》 come in first; win 〔get〕 first place; 《성적 등에서》 stand 〔rank〕 first; head the list 《of》; be at the top of 《a class》; hold the foremost place 《among》.

**일으키다** ① 《세우다》 pick 《*a person*》 up; raise; set up. ¶ 일으켜 세우다 make 《*a person*》 stand / 넘어진 사람을 ～ help a person to his feet / 쓰러진 기둥을 ～ put a fallen post back up / 아이가 넘어졌는데도 아무도 일으켜 주지 않았다 The boy fell down, but nobody set him on his feet. / 넘어진 손수레를 일으키려 하였지만, 내겐 너무 무거웠다 I tried to set the fallen cart up 〔upright〕 but it was too heavy for me.
② 《야기하다》 raise 《a commotion, *etc.*》; create; cause; make; give rise to; stir up 《a trouble》; 《촉발하다》 provoke; invite. ¶ 의심을 ～ raise a doubt / 호기심을 ～ excite 《*a person's*》 curiosity / 흥미를 ～ arouse *one's* interest / 소동을 ～ raise a disturbance; stir up troubles; start a riot; raise Cain / 전쟁을 ～ bring about war / 말썽을 ～ ferment a trouble / 그의 연설이 물의를 일으켰다 His address elicited much criticism.
③ 《개시하다》 start 《a movement》; begin; launch 〔undertake〕 《a new enterprise》; get 《*a matter*》 under way; 《발기하다》 promote; organize; 《설립하다》 set up; establish 〔found〕 《a school》. ¶ 새로운 사업을 ～ launch 〔father〕 a new enterprise / 반부패 운동을 ～ start 〔set up〕 an anti-corruption movement.
④ 《흥하게 하다》 bring to prosperity;

revive; make prosperous. ¶ 나라를 크게 ~ bring a nation to great prosperity / 쓰러진 집안을 ~ resuscitate a ruined family.
⑤ 《불을》 make; kindle. ¶ 불을 불어 ~ blow up the fire / 난로에 불을 ~ make a fire in the stove.
⑥ 《각성시키다》 wake up; awake; arouse. ¶ 그 광경은 내게 연민의 정을 일으켰다 The sight woke pity in my breast.
⑦ 《전기·열을》 generate; produce 《heat》; raise; excite. ¶ 전기를 ~ generate electricity / 마찰로 열을 ~ produce heat by friction.
⑧ 《제기하다》 ¶ 소송을 ~ institute 〔bring〕 an action 〔a suit〕 against; start 〔raise〕 a lawsuit 《against》.
⑨ 《발병하다》 fall 〔get, be taken〕 ill; be attacked with 〔by〕. ¶ 뇌빈혈을 ~ have an attack of cerebral anemia / 기관지염을 ~ set up 〔cause〕 bronchitis / 두통을 일으키기 쉽다 be subject to headaches.

**일의대수**(一衣帶水) ¶ 한국과 일본은 ~를 끼고 있다 Only a narrow channel lies between Korea and Japan.

**일이**(一二) one or two. ¶ ~년 a year or two; one or two years / ~회 once or twice / 그는 학교에서 늘 ~위를 다툰다 He is always one of the two top boys at school.

**일익**(一翼) a part 〔role〕 (to play). ¶ ~을 담당하다 act 〔perform〕 a part 〔role〕 《of》; bear a part 《in》 / 그는 그 사업의 ~을 담당하고 있다 He is equally responsible for carrying out the project.

**일익**(日益) every day; day by day; as (the) days go on. ¶ ~ 차도가 있다 get better every day 〔day by day〕 / 사태가 ~ 악화하다 the situation is getting worse day by day.

**일인**(一人) one person; one man.
◉ ~당 for every 〔each〕 person; per head; per capita: ~당 연간 소득 annual income for each person / 인구 ~당 per head of population. ~독재 one-man dictatorship. ~분 a portion for one person: 《식사의》 one helping 〔serving〕: ~분 식사 a plate / 빵 ~분 one portion of bread. ~승 비행기〔자동차〕 a single-seater. ~이역 《play》 a double role. ~일기(一技) a man, a trade: ~일기 실기 교육에 중점을 두다 give special emphasis to the "a man, a trade" vocational training. ~일표 one man, one vote. ~자 the number-one man; the leading figure 〔light〕; the outstanding authority. ~지도 체제 a unitary leadership. ~천하: ~ 천하이다 be the sole master 《of》; stand unchallenged 〔without a rival〕. ~칭 〖문법〗 the first person: ~칭 단수〔복수〕 the first person singular 〔plural〕 / ~칭 소설 a first-person novel.

**일일**(一日) 《하루》 a 〔one〕 day; 《초하루》 the first day (of a month). ¶ 제~ the first day / ~이 천추 같다 feel as if one day were years / ~지장(之長)이 있다 be a little ahead of 《*a person*》; be *one's* superior 《in》.
◉ ~생활권 a one-day life zone: 전국을 ~생활권에 들게 하다 shrink the entire nation into a one-day life zone.

**일일이** 《일마다》 everything; all things; in every thing 〔case〕; all; without omission. ¶ ~ 간섭하다 meddle in everything / 하는 일에 ~ 잔소리를 하다 find fault with everything *one* does.

**일일이**(一一—) ① 《하나씩》 one by one; singly; individually. ¶ ~ 조사하다 examine 《*things*》 one by one / 은숟가락을 ~ 닦다 polish the silver spoons one by one / 모든 사람과 ~ 악수하다 shake hands all around. ② 《상세히》 in detail; in full; (in) all particulars. ¶ ~ 설명하다 explain in detail 〔point by point〕 / ~ 보고하다 report in full.

**일임**(一任) entrusting; committing 《*a matter*》. ~하다 leave 《*a matter*》 entirely to 《*a person*》; commit 《*a matter*》 to 《*a person's*》 care; leave 〔place〕 《*a matter*》 in 《*a person's*》 hands; entrust 《*a person*》 with 《*a matter*》. ¶ 모든 것을 당신에게 ~하겠습니다 I shall leave everything to you 〔your discretion〕. / 그건 제게 ~해 주십시오 Leave it to me. / 그 건은 너에게 ~할 수 없다 I can't let you handle the matter. / 나는 학교의 운영을 ~받고 있다 I have been put in sole charge of the affairs of the school. *or* The management of the affairs of the school has been entrusted on me.

**일자리** a job; a position; a place; employment; an opening.
¶ 청년에게 좋은 ~ a good opening for a young man / ~를 찾다 seek a job 〔an employment〕; look for a position; scout for work; look 〔hunt〕 for work 〔a job, a position〕 / ~를 잃다 lose *one's* job; be discharged / ~를 얻어주다 procure a position for 《*a person*》;

find 《*a person*》 a job / ～를 얻다 find 〔get〕 a job; find a position; obtain employment / ～를 찾았다 I've found a job.

**일자무식**(一字無識) illiteracy; (utter) ignorance. ¶ ～의 unlettered; illiterate; ignorant. ◉ ～꾼 an (utterly) unlettered 〔illiterate〕 person; an illiterate person; an ignoramus.

**일장**(一場) ① 《연극의》 a scene; the first scene (제1장). ② 《한바탕》 a time; a round; a spell (of action). ◉ ～연설 a speech; an address: ～연설을 하다 make 〔deliver〕 a speech; address 《an audience》. ～춘몽 a spring dream; an empty dream; a crushed hope: ～ 춘몽으로 끝나다 vanish like「a spring dream 〔visions〕/ 인생은 ～ 춘몽이다 Life is but an empty dream. ～풍파 a tumult; an uproar; a turmoil; a commotion: ～ 풍파가 일어날 것 같다 Trouble is brewing.

**일장일단**(一長一短) merits and demerits; strength and weakness. ¶ 사람은 누구나 ～이 있다 Every man has his merits and demerits.

**일전**(一戰) 《전투》 a battle; a fight; 《승부》 a game; a contest; a bout. ¶ ～을 겨루다 fight 〔engage in〕 a battle 《with》; (make a) fight 《with》; have a passage of arms 《with》; 《승부하다》 have a game 〔bout〕; cross bats (야구에서) / ～을 불사하다 be ready to fight; be prepared to fight.

**일전**(一轉) a complete change; a turn. ～하다 《돌다》 turn round; 《바뀌다》 undergo a complete 〔sudden〕 change. ¶ 심기 ～하다 turn over a new leaf / 그 사건 이후 상황이 ～하였다 The situation has completely changed since that happened.

**일전**(日前) the other day; a few days ago; last time; previously. ¶ ～ 편지에 in *one's* last letter / ～부터 for some days (past) / ～ 그를 만났을 때엔 아주 건강해 보였다 The last time I saw him, he looked quite well.

**일절**(一切) altogether; wholly; entirely; positively. ¶ ～ …하지 않다 never *do;* not *do* at all / 사례는 ～ 사절합니다 We positively decline any form of reward. *or* No gratuities accepted. *or* No tipping please. / 외상 ～ 사절 Positively no credit. / 본건에 관해서는 ～ 관계없다 I have nothing to do with this affair.

**일절**(一節) 《단위》 a section; 《문장》 a passage; a paragraph; 《시의》 a stanza; 《노래의》 a verse. ¶ 제3장 제1절 Chapter III, Section I / 영국 국가의 첫 ～ the first verse of 'God Save the Queen'.

**일점**(一點) 《한 점》 a point; a dot; 〖야구〗 a run; 《한 개》 an article; a piece 《of furniture》. ¶ 《경기에서》 ～을 따다 score a point 〔run〕.

**일정**(一定) fixation; regularity; 《획일》 uniformity; 《표준》 standard. ～하다 (be) fixed; set; settled; regular; established; uniform; 《표준의》 standard. ¶ ～하게 uniformly / ～ 불변의 fixed (and unchangeable); constant; invariable / ～하지 않은 irregular; unsettled / ～한 표준 a fixed standard / ～한 서식 a prescribed 〔set〕 form / ～한 규칙 an established rule; a standing rule / ～한 직업 a regular occupation; a steady job / ～한 장소 a fixed 〔an appointed, a designated〕 place / ～한 목적 a definite object / ～한 기한 for a given period of time; a specified period; a limited time / ～한 수입 a regular 〔fixed〕 income / ～한 비율 an invariable ratio / ～하게 하다 standardize; unify / ～한 속도로 달리다 run at a fixed speed / ～한 기간 내에 within a fixed period / ～한 간격을 두고 at regular intervals / ～한 비율로 at a fixed rate / 가격은 ～하지 않습니다. 종류에 따라 다소 차이가 있습니다 The price is not uniform; there are small differences according to the type.

**일정**(日程) the day's program 〔schedule〕; 《경기의》 a fixture; 《의사 진행의》 the order of the day; the day's agenda. ¶ 빡빡한 ～ a tight schedule / 세부 ～ 《여행 따위의》 detailed itinerary / ～을 변경하다 alter the day's program / ～을 마치다 complete 〔go through〕 a day's program / 시험 ～을 발표하다 announce the examination schedule / 여행 ～을 정하다 make out the schedule for *one's* trip / ～에 올리다 place 〔put〕 《a bill》 on the order of the day; place on the day's agenda / ～에 올라 있는 사항 the items on the day's agenda /「금주의 일정은 어떻습니까」―「빡빡합니다」 "What about your schedule for this week?"—"It's very tight." ◉ ～표 a schedule; 《여행의》 an itinerary.

**일제**(一齊) ¶ ～히 all together; in unison; in a body; with one accord; 《동시에》 all at once; simultaneously; 《이

구동성으로》 in chorus; unanimously; with one voice / 전국에서 ～히 simultaneously throughout the country / ～히 반대하다 be against 《to *a matter* 〔*a person*〕》 / ～히 사직하다 resign in a body 〔*en bloc*〕 / 그들은 ～히 소리쳤다 They set up a roar all at once. / 그들을 향해서 ～히 공격을 가했다 We made a concerted attack upon them. / 지금 시내에서 속도 위반 ～ 단속이 실시되고 있다 A citywide crackdown on speeding offenses is now going on. ◉ ～검거 a blanket 〔wholesale〕 arrest; a roundup: ～검거하다 make a wholesale arrest; round up.

**일제**(日帝) Japanese imperialism; imperialist Japan. ¶ ～ 때 under the rule of Japanese imperialism.

**일제**(日製) Japanese make 〔manufacture〕. ¶ ～의 Japanese-made; of Japanese make; made in japan. ◉ ～상품 Japanese(-made) goods; products made in Japan.

**일제사격**(一齊射擊) a volley (of fire); a fusillade; a salvo (*pl.* ～(e)s) (포의); a broadside (fire) (군함 현측의). ¶ ～을 (가)하다 volley; fire a volley 〔volleys〕; fire by volleys 〔in salvo〕; discharge in a volley; fusillade; deliver a broadside (fire) (현측에서).

**일조**(一兆) 《미》 a trillion; 《영》 a billion.

**일조**(一助) ¶ ～가 되다 be helpful 《to *a person*, in *do*ing》; be of some help 《toward》 / 이 책이 영어 학습자에게 ～가 된다면 그것으로 충분합니다 I would feel amply rewarded for my efforts if this book proved helpful to students of English.

**일조**(日照) sunshine. ◉ ～계 a heliograph. ～권 a right to (enjoy) sunshine; the right to light (in *one's* home): 계획중인 빌딩은 이웃사람들의 ～권을 위협한다 The planned building threatens the neighboring people's right to sunshine. ～시간 hours of sunlight; daylight hours. ～율 the percentage of sunshine.

**일조일석**(一朝一夕) a brief space 〔span〕 of time. ¶ ～에 in a (single) day; in a short time; in a short 〔brief〕 space of time / 그 일은 ～에 되는 것이 아니다 It is not to be done in a day. / 큰 사업이란 ～에 이루어지는 것이 아니다 Rome was not built in a day.

**일족**(一族) all *one's* family and relatives; *one's* kinsmen; 《가족》 *one's* whole family; 《친족》 relatives; 《씨족》 the 《*Namgung*》 clan. ¶ ～의 웃어른 the head of a clan.

**일종**(一種) a kind; a sort; a species; a description. ¶ 제～ 우편물 first-class mail matter / 벼는 풀의 ～이다 The rice plant is a kind 〔variety〕 of grass. / 그는 ～의 천재이다 He is a genius in a sense. / 그의 문장에는 ～의 독특한 묘미가 있다 His style is marked by a charm all his own. / 그가 하고 있는 짓은 ～의 배신 행위이다 What he is doing is a sort of betrayal.

**일주**(一周) a 〔one〕 round; 《주항(周航)》 a circumnavigation; 《경기장의》 a lap; 《회전》 a revolution. ～하다 go 〔travel, sail, revolve〕 round; make a round 《of》. ¶ ～ 200미터의 트랙 a running track two hundred meters around / 뛰어서 트랙을 ～하다 run once around the race track / 세계를 ～하다 go 〔travel, sail, fly〕 around the world; make an around the world trip / 비행기는 도시 상공을 ～했다 The plane circled over the city. / 지구는 1년 걸려 태양을 ～한다 The earth goes 〔revolves〕 round the sun once in a year. ◉ ～기(期) 『천문』 a period. ～기(忌) the first anniversary of *a person's* death. ～여행 a round trip: 세계 ～여행을 하다 make a round-the-world trip.

**일주**(一週) 《for》 a week. ⇨ 일주일.

**일주권**(日周圈) 『천문』 the diurnal circle.

**일주년**(一周年) a full year. ◉ ～기념 the first anniversary: 창립 ～ 기념식을 거행하다 observe the first anniversary of the opening 《of the school》.

**일주시차**(日周視差) 『천문』 the diurnal parallax.

**일주야**(一晝夜) a whole day and night; 《for》 twenty-four hours.

**일주운동**(日周運動) 『천문』 diurnal motion.

**일주일**(一週日) a week. ¶ ～에 한번(의) once a week; weekly / ～의 휴가 a week's holiday / ～간 내내 비가 왔다 It has been raining for a week. / ～에 한 번 영화 구경을 간다 I go to the movies once a week.

**일지**(日誌) a diary; a journal. ＝일기(日記).

**일직**(日直) day duty. ～하다 be on day duty; do day duty. ¶ 나는 오늘 ～이다 I'm on day duty today. ◉ ～장교 an orderly officer; an officer of the day.

**일직선**(一直線) a straight line. ¶ ～으로 straight; in a straight line; in a beeline; as the crow flies / ～으로 나아가다 go 〔keep〕 straight on; make straight for; make a beeline for.

**일진**(一陣) ①《군사의》 a military camp. ②《선봉》 the vanguard. ③《바람》 a gust 〔blast, puff〕《of wind》. ◉ ～광풍 a strong gust 〔puff〕 of wind. ～청풍 a puff of breeze.

**일진**(日辰) 〖민속〗《간지》 the binary designation of the day according to the sexagenary cycle; 《운수》 the day's luck. ¶ 오늘은 ～이 나쁘다 This is not a lucky day for me.

**일진월보**(日進月步) rapid progress 〔advance〕. ～하다 make rapid progress. ¶ ～하는 rapidly-advancing; ever-progressing / 전자 공업은 ～한다 Electronics is advancing by leaps and bounds.

**일진일퇴**(一進一退) advance and retreat; ebb and flow. ～하다 advance and retreat; ebb and flow; fluctuate. ¶ ～의 경기 a seesaw 〔dingdong〕 game 〔match〕 / 싸움은 ～였다 The struggle seesawed to and fro. / 환자의 병상이 ～하고 있다 Sometimes the patient gets a little better but then he gets worse again. *or* The patient is better one day and worse the next.

**일찌감치** a little early 〔earlier〕; ahead of time; in good time. ¶ ～ 떠나다 leave home a bit earlier than usual / ～ 오면 더 좋다 If you come a bit earlier, all the better.

**일찍** 《이르게》 early. ¶ 아침 ～ early in the morning; at an early hour / ～일어나다 get up early / ～ 자고 ～ 일어나다 keep early 〔good〕 hour / ～ 죽다 die young / 열차가 10분 ～ 닿았다 The train arrived ten minutes ahead of time. / 그는 ～ 부모를 여의었다 He lost his parents at an early age. / 좀 더 ～ 왔더라면 좋았을 것을 You should have come earlier.

**일찍이** ① ＝일찍. ②《전에》 earlier; once; one time; formerly (★ once는 「일찍이」의 뜻의 경우는 동사(be 동사 제외)의 앞 또는 글머리에 쓰이며, 「한 번」의 뜻일 때에는 원칙적으로 동사 뒤에 옴: I once went there. 「일찍이 거기 가본 일이 있다」, I went once. 「한 번 그 곳에 간 일이 있다」). ¶ 이런 일은 ～ 들어 본 일이 없다 I have never heard of such a thing. / 그는 ～ 벼슬한 일이 있다 He was in government service at one time. / ～ 그것을 본 일이 있다 I have (once) seen it. (★ 완료시제에서 「일찍이」의 뜻이 이미 나타나 있을 때는 once를 생략하는 것이 보통).

**일차**(一次) 《한번》 one time; once; 《첫번》 the first; 〖수학〗 linear. ¶ ～의 first; primary / 제～ 처칠 내각 the first Churchill Cabinet / 거기에 ～ 가본 적이 있다 I have been there once. ◉ ～냉각수 a primary 〔first-stage〕 coolant. ～냉각장치 a primary cooling system. ～반복법 〖수학〗 linear iteration. ～방정식 a linear 〔first-degree, simple〕 equation. ～산업 primary industries. ～산품 primary products. ～시험 a primary examination. ～전지〔코일〕 a primary battery 〔coil〕.

**일차원**(一次元) ¶ ～의 one-dimensional; unidimensional. ◉ ～배열 〖컴퓨터〗 one-dimensional array. ～분산분석 〖컴퓨터〗 on-way variance analysis.

**일착**(一着) 《경주의》 the first (arrival); the first (person 〔runner〕) to arrive 〔come in〕. ～하다 come in first; finish first; be the first to come in; win the first place.

**일책**(一策) an idea; a plan. ¶ ～을 생각해내다 think out a plan.

**일처다부**(一妻多夫) polyandry. ¶ ～의 polyandrous.

**일천**(日淺) ～하다 be a few days old; be not long since…. ¶ 회사를 창립한 지 아직 ～하다 It is only a short time since the company was founded. *or* The company is but of yesterday's birth.

**일체**(一切) 《모든 것》 all; (any and) every thing; the whole; 〔관형사〕 all; every; entire; whole. ⇨ 일절(一切). ¶ ～ 비용 the total cost 〔expense〕 / ～의 편의 every facility / ～의 관계를 끊다 cut off all relations 《with》; wash *one's* hands of 《*a matter*》 / 나는 이 일과는 ～ 관계가 없다 I have nothing whatever to do with this affair. ◉ ～중생 all living beings 〔things〕; all creature; all life 〔flesh〕. ～형 all in one: ～형 오디오 all-in-one audio system / ～형 마이크로 컴퓨터 〖컴퓨터〗 an all-in-one microcomputer.

**일체**(一體) ①《한몸》 one body; a single body. ¶ ～가 되다 become one (body); unite; be united / ～가 되어 in a body; as one / ～가 되어 일하다 work as one body / 부부는 ～다 Man and wife are one flesh. ② ＝전부(全部). ◉ ～감 a sense of unity. ～화 unification; integration.

**일촉즉발**(一觸卽發) a delicate 〔touch-and-go〕 situation. ¶ ～의 상태 a touch-and-go 〔an extremely delicate〕 situation / 양국의 관계는 ～의 위기에 처해 있다 Relations between the two countries have been strained to the breaking point. / 대만 해협의 전역(全域)은 ～의 위험을 안고 있었다 The whole region of the Taiwan Straits was a tinderbox.

**일축**(一蹴) 《참》 a kick; 《거절》 a flat rejection; a refusal; 《이김》 beating easily. ～하다 kick; reject; refuse flatly; turn down; spurn. ¶ 가볍게 ～하다 《거절》 reject flatly; turn down 《*a person's*》 proposal; 《경기에서》 beat easily.

**일출**(日出) sunrise; sunup 《미》. ⇨ 해돋이. ¶ ～에서 일몰까지 from sunup to sundown. ◉ ～시각 (the time of) sunrise; sunup.

**일취월장**(日就月將) daily progress and monthly advance. ～하다 make progress day after day and month after month; make steady progress.

**일층**(一層) ① 《단층》 one story; floor level; 《밑층》 the 「first 〔ground 《영》〕 floor (★ 영국에서는 the first floor가 「2층」을 가리킴). ¶ ～집 a one-storied〔=story〕 house / 그의 사무실은 ～에 있다 His office is on the first floor. ② 《한결》 more; still 「more 〔further〕; all the more. ¶ ～의 진보 further progress / ～ 더 재미있는 more interesting / ～ 더 낫게 보이다 look to advantage.

**일치**(一致) ① 《합치》 agreement; consistency; accord; 《부합》 coincidence (우연의); correspondence (대응); 《조화》 a harmony; 《의견의》 consensus. ～하다 agree 《with》; accord 《with》; coincide 《with》; correspond 《with》; harmonize 《with》; 《되어 있다》 be in 「agreement 〔accord, harmony, line〕 《with》.

> **용법** **agree** 의견이나 사물의 형편 따위가 딱 들어맞게 일치한다는 뜻의 가장 일반적인 말. **accord** 특히 본질·정신 따위가 조화·일치된다는 뜻의 말. **coincide** 생각·성격·취미·판단 따위가 완전히 일치하는 것. 때로는 사건 따위가 우연히 일치한다는 뜻도 됨. **correspond** 양자의 주된 특징 따위가 유사 또는 좀 달라도 서로 잘 대응해서 조화를 이루어 일치한다는 뜻. **harmonize** 두 개, 두 가지 사항이 뚜렷한 차이가 있지만, 잘 조화되어 어울려 있음을 뜻함.

¶ 증언의 ～ consensus of testimony / 의견의 ～를 보다 come to an agreement / 의견의 ～를 보지 못하다 fail to reach an accord 《on》 / 전원의 의견이 ～하다 reach (a) consensus 《on *a matter*》 / 나의 견해와 그의 견해가 ～한다 My views are in accord with his. / 그는 언행이 ～하지 않는다 His words are not in 「keeping 〔accord〕 with his deeds. / 양쪽 이야기는 서로 ～한다 The two stories agree with each other. / 그의 행동은 공무원의 본분과 ～하지 않는다 His conduct is not consistent with his duty as a public servant. /이상과 실제는 결코 ～하지 않는다 The ideal and the real never coincide. /외관과 실제가 ～하는 일은 극히 드물다 Appearance and reality seldom correspond.
② 《단합》 union; unity; concert. ～하다 unite; act in concert 《with》. ¶ ～하여 unitedly; in concert 《with》; in union / 동의를 만장 ～로 가결하다 carry a motion without dissent / 전국민이 ～하여 대적했다 The people were united in patriotism against the enemy. / 만장 ～로 그는 대장으로 선발됐다 He was elected captain by a unanimous vote. *or* They unanimously elected him captain.
◉ ～단결 union; solidarity: ～단결하다 unite 《with》; act in union 《with》; be united; be solid 《for, with》 / 관민이 ～단결하여 with unanimity between the government and people / ～단결하여 일하다 work in concert. ～점 a meeting point; a point of 「agreement 〔concurrence〕. ～협력 united 〔combined〕 efforts; cooperation: ～협력하다 make combined efforts; act in concert; cooperate 《with》.

**일컫다** ① 《칭하다》 call; name; designate. ¶ 명삼이라고 일컫는 사람 a man 「called 〔by the name of〕 Myeongsam / 하와이는 흔히 태평양의 낙원이라 일컬어진다 Hawaii is often referred to as the Paradise of the Pacific. ② 《칭찬하다》 praise; laud; extol; admire. ¶ 모든 사람이 그의 덕을 일컬었다 Everybody extolled his supreme virtue.

**일탈**(逸脫) (a) departure 《from》; (a) deviation 《from》. ～하다 deviate 〔depart, stray〕 《from the path of good conduct》. ¶ (규범을) ～한 행동 deviant behavior / 권한을 ～하다 overstep *one's* authority / 이 계획은 원래의 목적에서 ～한 것이다 This plan is a departure from our original aim.

**일터** the place where *one* works; *one's* job site; a workshop; 《사무소》 *one's* office; 《공사장》 a construction site.

**일파**(一派) 《파벌》 a faction; a party; 《유파》 a school; 《종파》 a sect. ¶ 이씨

～ Lee faction; Lee and his followers / ～를 창설하다 create a school; 《종교의》 found a sect.

**일패**(一敗) ¶ 3승 ～ three wins and one defeat. ◉ ～도지(塗地) a complete 〔crushing〕 defeat: ～도지하다 meet with complete defeat; suffer a crushing defeat.

**일편**(一片) a piece; a bit; a fragment; a scrap. ¶ ～의 양심 a bit 〔modicum〕 of conscience. ◉ ～단심 a sincere 〔devoted〕 heart; fidelity: ～단심으로 섬기다 serve faithfully; devote *oneself* to; do 《*something*》 in all sincerity.

**일편**(一篇) a piece 《of poetry, *etc.*》.

**일평생**(一平生) a lifetime; *one's* whole life. ¶ ～ 잊지 못할 never-to-be-forgotten / ～의 소원 *one's* lifelong desire; a desire cherished for life / ～을 마치다 end *one's* life / ～을 바치다 dedicate 〔devote〕 *one's* life / ～ 독신으로 지내다 remain a bachelor 〔spinster (여자가)〕 all *one's* life.

**일폭**(一幅) a scroll; a piece. ¶ 동양화 ～ a scroll of Oriental painting.

**일품**(一品) ① 《벼슬의》 the first rank of office. ② 《상품》 an article of top quality; a superior article. ¶ 천하～ an article of peerless quality. ③ 《요리》 one dish of food. ◉ ～요리 one=course service; a one-dish meal 〔dinner〕; an *a la carte* dish.

**일품**(逸品) an unusual 〔a rare〕 article; an excellent piece; 《걸작》 a masterpiece. ¶ 이 책은 수집품 중의 ～이다 This volume is the gem of the whole collection.

**일필휘지**(一筆揮之) dashing off with one stroke of a brush. ～하다 write with one stroke 〔dash〕 of a brush.

**일하다** 《노동하다》 work; labor; 《근무하다》 serve 《at》; be in the service 〔employ〕 《of》. ⇨ 일. ¶ 열심히 ～ work hard; be hard at work / 바쁘게 ～ busy *oneself* 《(in) *do*ing》 / 부지런히 ～ work diligently 〔assiduously〕; work away; toil and moil / 생계를 위해 ～ work for *one's* living / 농장에서 ～ work on a farm / 일하러 가다 go to work / 우리 가정부는 일을 잘 한다 Our maid serves us well. / 그녀는 사장 비서로 일한다 She works as secretary to the president.

**일할**(一割) 10 percent. ¶ 1다스 사시면 ～ 할인해 드립니다 If you buy a dozen of it, I will allow you ten percent discount.

**일행**(一行) ① 《동아리》 a party; *one's* suite; a company; a troupe (배우 등의). ¶ 관광단 ～ a tourist group; a party of sightseers / 남씨 ～ Mr. Nam and his party 〔suite〕 / ～에 끼다 join a party / ～은 8명이었다 The party consisted of eight (members). ② 《한 줄》 a line; a row; 《시의》 a line of verse. ¶ 이 원고는 ～에 20자 박이다 This copy is written at the rate of twenty characters a line. 「혈.

**일혈**(溢血) 〖의학〗 extravasation. ⇨ 뇌일

**일호**(一號) number one; No. 1. ◉ ～홈런 〖야구〗 the virgin homer.

**일화**(日貨) 《돈》 Japanese money; 《상품》 Japanese goods. ¶ ～ 배척 a boycott of Japanese goods.

**일화**(逸話) an anecdote; an episode. ¶ 그에게는 많은 ～가 있다 Many anecdotes are told of him. ◉ ～집 a collection of anecdotes.

**일확천금**(一攫千金) making a big fortune 「on a single occasion 〔with one swoop〕. ～하다 make a fortune at a stroke. ¶ ～을 노리는 사람 a person who 「chases to 〔plans to make〕 quick money / ～을 꿈꾸다 dream of making a fortune at a 「stroke 〔single bound〕 / ～의 꿈은 깨지게 되어 있다 The get-rich-quick scheme is bound to fail.

**일환**(一環) a link (in a chain). ¶ …의 ～으로서 as a part of… / …의 ～을 이루다 form a part of… / 정책의 ～을 이루다 form 〔mark〕 a line in the chain of policy.

**일회**(一回) 《횟수》 one time; once; 《승부의》 a round; an event; a game; 〖야구〗 an inning; 〖권투〗 a bout. ¶ 주 ～ once a week / 연 ～씩 annual(ly). ◉ ～분 《약의》 a dose. ～전 the first game; the first round 〔inning〕.

**일흔** seventy; threescore and ten.

**일희일비**(一喜一悲) ～하다 have joy and sorrow in quick alternation; be now glad, now sad 《at》; be glad and sad by turns; cannot put *one's* mind at ease / ～하면서 restlessly; in suspense / 그런 하찮은 일에 ～하는 것은 어리석다 It's silly to let yourself be affected by such a trifle.

**읽다** ① 《책 따위를》 read; peruse (정독하다); recite (암송하다); chant (경문을). ¶ 읽기 reading; 《학과》 reading lessons / 읽고 쓰기 reading and writing / 읽기 쉬운 easy to read; 《필적이》 readable; legible / 읽기 어려운 hard to read; 《필적이》 illegible / 책〔신문〕을 ~ read a book 〔newspaper〕 / 신문에서 ~ read about 《*a matter*》 in a newspaper / 읽어 주다 read 《a letter》 for 《*a person*》 / 읽어달래다 have 《a book》 read 《by *a person*》 / 잘못 ~ misread; read 《*a thing*》 wrong; 《발음을》 mispronounce / 소리내(어) ~ read aloud / 대충대충 ~ glance over 〔through〕; run *one's* eye over 《the list》 / 급히 ~ take a quick read 《at a book》 / 띄엄띄엄 ~ skim over; read skipping here and there / 정신(을) 들여 ~ peruse; read carefully / 산만하게 ~ browse 《in a book》 / 다 ~ read 〔get〕 through / 책을 ~가 잠이 들다 read *oneself* to sleep / 소설을 읽으면서 울다 cry over a novel; be moved to tears by a novel / 이 잡지는 읽을 것이 없다 This magazine has little reading matter in it. ② 《파악·이해하다》 read; see; understand. ¶ 행간의 숨은 뜻을 ~ read between the lines / 상대의 수를 ~ read the next move of the opponent / 그의 의도를 읽었다 I saw 〔understand〕 his intention. / 그는 사람의 마음을 잘 읽는다 He is good at reading other people's heart.

**읽을거리** reading; reading matter; literature. ¶ 좋은〔재미없는〕 ~ good 〔dull〕 reading / 어린이의 ~ books for children; children's books.

**읽히다** 《읽게 하다》 get 《*a person*》 to read; set 《*a person*》 to reading; have 《a book》 read 《by *a person*》; 《읽혀지다》 be widely-read. ¶ 많이 읽히는 책 a widely-read book / 어린 아이들에게 동화를 ~ get children to read fairy tales / 성서는 어떤 책보다도 많이 읽히는 책이다 The Bible is the most widely read of all books.

**잃다** lose; miss; 《빼기다》 be bereft 〔deprived〕 of. ¶ 이성을 잃은 사람 a man bereft of reason / 기회를 ~ miss 〔lose〕 an opportunity 〔a chance〕 / 어머니를 ~ lose 〔be bereaved of 〕 *one's* mother / 희망을 ~ lose *one's* hope / 신용을 ~ lose *one's* credit; lose the confidence 《of》 / 시력〔청력〕을 ~ lose sight 〔hearing〕 / 도박으로 전재산을 ~ gamble away *one's* entire fortune / 직업을 ~ lose *one's* position; get out of job / 면목〔체면〕을 ~ lose *one's* face; bring disgrace upon *oneself* / 목숨을 ~ lose *one's* life / 길을 ~ lose *one's* way; lose *oneself;* get lost / 선수권을 ~ lost the championship.

**임** 《연인》 a sweetheart; a lover (남); a love (여). ¶ 임 그리운 마음 a heart pining for an absent love / 임을 그리다 miss *one's* love.

**임간**(林間) the interior of a forest 〔wood〕. ¶ ~에(서) in a wood 〔forest〕. ◉ ~학교 「an open-air 〔an outdoor, a camp〕 school.

**임검**(臨檢) 《검사》 an (official) inspection; a visit of inspection; 《수색》 a raid; a search; 《배의》 boarding. ~하다 《검사하다》 (visit and) inspect; make an inspection 《of》; 《수색하다》 (raid and) search 〔make a raid on〕 《a house》; swoop down on; 《선박을》 (board and) search 《a ship》. ¶ 현장을 ~하다 make an official inspection of the spot; 《범죄 현장을》 view the place of a crime / 선박을 ~하다 institute a search on vessels. ◉ ~반 a raiding party; 《배의》 a boarding party. ~증 an inspection certificate.

**임계**(臨界) 〚물리·수학〛 ¶ ~의 critical. ◉ ~각〔고도〕 the critical angle 〔altitude〕. ~량 critical mass. ~상태〔점〕 the critical state 〔point〕. ~실험 a critical experiment: ~ 실험 장치 〚원자물리〛 a critical assembly. ~온도〔압력〕 the critical temperature 〔pressure〕.

**임관**(任官) (an) appointment (to an office); (an) installation (in an office); a commission (장교의). ~하다 get appointed (to an office); be installed (in an office); 《장교로》 be commissioned. ¶ 소위로 ~하다 be commissioned second lieutenant. ◉ ~식 《hold》 an inaugural ceremony. ~장교 a commissioned officer.

**임균**(淋菌) 〚의학〛 a gonococcus (*pl.* -cocci). ◉ ~성 요도염 gonorrheal urethritis.

**임금**(賃金) wages; pay. ¶ 기준 ~ the standard 〔basic〕 wages / 명목〔실질〕~ nominal 〔real〕 wages / 최고〔최저〕~ maximum 〔minimum〕 wages / 능률〔할증〕~ efficiency 〔extra〕 wages / 시간제〔작업량제〕~ time 〔piece〕 wages / 현물~ wages in kind / 최저 ~제 a (uniform) minimum wage system / ~이 낮은 근로자 an ill-paid wage earner / 노동 조합이 규정한 ~ union wages / 이틀치 ~ two days' wages 〔pay〕 / 좋은 ~으로 at good wages / 반액의 ~으로 for half wages / 1일 3만원의 ~으로 일하다 work at a wage 〔for wages〕 of 30,000 won a day / 싼 ~으로 일하다 work at low wages; work at 〔for〕

poor pay / ～을 올리다〔내리다〕 increase 〔lower, cut down〕 wages / ～을 지급하다 pay wages / ～을 받다 receive wages / 하루 5만원의 ～을 받다 be paid fifty thousand won a day / 괜찮은 ～을 받고 있다 have good wages / 적당한 ～을 지급하다 pay reasonable wages / ～에 영향을 미치다 affect wages / ～에서 빼다 《지각 따위의 경우》 dock *one's* wages / ～이 싸다〔비싸다〕 Labor is cheap 〔dear〕.

◉ ～가이드라인 a wage guideline. ～격차 wage disparity; a wage differential. ～노동 wage labor; wageworking: ～노동자 a wage earner; a wageworker 《미》. ～대장 a wage ledger; a payroll (book). ～동결 freezing of wages; wage freeze. ～률 a wage 〔pay〕 rate. ～물가체계 the wage-price structure. ～베이스 an average wage; level up the wage base. ～삭감 a cut in wages; a wage cut. ～생활자 a wage earner; a wageworker. ～수준 a wage level. ～ 슬라이드제〔연동제(連動制)〕 the sliding scale system of wages; the elevator system; a sliding pay scale. ～안정 wage stabilization. ～ ～외 급부 fringe benefits. ～인상 a wage increase 〔raise〕: ～ 인상 요구 a wage-hike demand / ～인상을 요구하다 demand 〔ask for〕 higher wages 〔pay〕; demand a raise in *one's* wages / ～ 인상을 외치다 cry for a boost in pay. ～인하 a wage decrease 〔cut〕. ～정책 a wage policy. ～제도 a wage system. ～지급일 a payday. ～지수 a wage index. ～체계 a wage structure. ～통제 wage control(s). ～(인상) 투쟁 a wage struggle; a struggle 〔strike〕 for higher wages; a wage-boost strike. ～협정 a wage agreement.

**임금** a king; a monarch; a sovereign.

**임기**(任期) *one's* term of office 〔service〕; *one's* tenure; 《의원의》 a term of membership; 《지사의》 governorship. ¶ 남은 ～ the remainder 〔unexpired portion〕 of *one's* term of office / ～중 during *one's* term 〔tenure〕 of office / ～가 차다 the time is up; *one's* term of office expires / ～를 연장하다 extend *one's* term / ～를 마치다, ～를 채우다 wind up *one's* service; finish up *one's* tenure of office / 대통령의 ～는 5년이다 The President holds office for five years. *or* (The length of ) Presidential tenure is five years.

◉ ～만료 completion 〔expiration〕 of *one's* term of office: ～만료와 함께 at the expiration 〔completion〕 of *one's* term of office 〔membership tenure〕 / ～만료 전에 해임되다 be dismissed before *one's* term expires.

**임기응변**(臨機應變) adaptation to circumstances. ～하다 act according to the circumstances; adapt *oneself* to circumstances 〔the moment〕; take such steps as the occasion demands. ¶ ～의 expedient; emergency / ～으로 as occasion may demand 〔require〕; according to circumstances / ～의 조치를 취하다 resort to a temporary expedient; take measures suited to the occasion; take proper steps to meet the situation.

**임대**(賃貸) 《토지·가옥 따위의》 lease; letting out (on hire); 《물품의》 hiring out; 《배의》 charter. ～하다 lease; locate (토지·가옥 등); hire out 《a boat》; rent 《a house》; charter 《a ship》. ¶ ～로 on lease / 자동차를 시간제로 ～하다 hire out a car by the hour / 집을 ～하다 put out a house to lease; rent a house 《to》.

◉ ～가격 a rental value; a value of lease. ～계약(서) a lease (contract). ～료 (a) rent; hire (자동차 등의); charterage (배의). ～물 an article for lease 〔rent 《미》, hire 《영》〕. ～방식 the rental system. ～아파트 a rental 〔leased〕 apartment. ～업 leasing service. ～인(人) a lessor. ～주택 a rental house. ～지(地) leased land.

**임대차**(賃貸借) lease; letting and hiring; 《선박의》 charter. ¶ ～계약 a lease contract.

**임독**(淋毒·痳毒) a gonorrheal infection; gonorrhea; clap 《속어》. ◉ ～균 a gonococcus (*pl.* -cocci).

**임률**(賃率) rate; 《화물의》 freight rates; 《노임의》 a wage scale.

**임립**(林立) standing close together. ～하다 stand close together; bristle 《with chimneys》. ¶ ～한 굴뚝 a forest of chimneys.

**임면**(任免) appointment and dismissal 〔removal〕. ～하다 appoint and dismiss 〔remove〕. ◉ ～권 the power to appoint and (to) dismiss.

**임명**(任命) appointment; nomination; designation. ～하다 appoint 《*a person* to the post of mayor》; nominate 〔name〕 《*a person* for a position》; ordain; designate; commission. ¶ ～제로 하다 make 《an office》 appointive /

후임자로 ～하다 appoint 《*a person*》 as *one's* successor / 그는 주미 대사로 ～되었다 He was appointed (to the post of) Ambassador to the United States. ◉ ～권 appointive power. ～식 the ceremony of appointment; an investiture. ～자 an appointer: 피～자 an appointee. ～장 a letter of appointment; an appointment letter.

**임무**(任務) (a) duty; (a) task; official duties; service; a function; 《사명》 a mission. ¶ 중대 ～ an important duty; a great task 〔mission〕 / ～를 수행하다 discharge 〔do, carry out〕 *one's* duties; perform duties; do *one's* part; accomplish *one's* task; fulfill *one's* mission / ～를 주다 assign 《*a person* to a task, to do *something*》 / ～에 충실하다 be faithful *one's* duties / ～를 태만히 하다 neglect *one's* duties / 특별 ～를 띠고 가다 go on a special service 〔on an extraordinary mission〕.

**임박**(臨迫) approaching; impending. ～하다 draw near; approach; impend; be close 〔near〕 at hand; be imminent. ¶ 죽음이 ～하다 *one's* time is drawing near; [사람이 주어] be on the verge 〔brink〕 of death / 시험이 ～해 있다 The examination is (near) at hand. *or* The examination is hanging over us.

**임부**(妊婦) a pregnant woman; 《초산부》 an expectant mother. ◉ ～복 a maternity dress 〔robe, gown〕.

**임산물**(林産物) forest products.

**임상**(臨床) ¶ ～의 clinical / ～적으로 clinically / ～적 연구 a clinical study 《of》 / ～의 권위자 a clinical authority / ～ 신문 a clinical examination. ◉ ～강의 a clinical lecture; a clinic. ～경험 《have a wealth of》 clinical experience. ～데이터 clinical data. ～병리과 the clinical laboratory. ～병리학 clinical pathology. ～실험〔실습〕 clinical tests 〔trials〕: 그 약은 ～실험 중이다 The medicine is undergoing clinical testing (on patients). ～심리학 clinical psychology. ～의(醫) a clinician; a therapist. ～의학 clinical medicine; clinics. ～일지 a physician's diary. ～진단 (a) clinical diagnosis. ～진찰 a clinical examination.

**임석**(臨席) attendance; presence. ～하다 attend; be present 《at》; present *oneself* 《at》. ¶ 아무의 ～하에 with *a person* in attendance; in the presence of *a person* / 귀하의 ～을 부탁드립니다 We request the honor of your presence at the party. ◉ ～경관 a policeman in attendance; a policeman assigned 《to a theater》. ～자 a person present; [총칭] those present; the attendance.

**임술**(壬戌) 〖민속〗 the 59th binary term of the sexagenary cycle.

**임시**(壬時) 〖민속〗 the last of the 24 hour periods (＝10:30—11:30 p.m.).

**임시**(臨時) 《일시·잠정적》 being temporary 〔provisional〕; 《특별한》 being extra 〔extraordinary〕; 《시험적인》 being tentative; 《시기에 임함》 presence of an occasion 〔opportunity〕. ¶ ～의 temporary; provisional; special; extra; extraordinary; expedient; makeshift; improvised / ～로 specially; extraordinary; temporarily; provisionally / ～로 만들다 extemporize; improvise; rig 《a building》 / ～로 고용하다 engage 《*a person*》 temporarily / ～로 그렇게 해 두자 Let it be so for the present. ◉ ～결의 a provisional resolution. ～결정 a tentative decision. ～고용인 a temporary employee; an extra hand; a part-time worker; a part-timer. ～공(工) a casual laborer. ～공사 provisional construction work. ～구호 본부 a temporary rescue headquarters. ～국회 《convene》 an extraordinary session of the National Assembly. ～규정 provisional 〔tentative〕 rules. ～뉴스 news special; a special newscast. ～면허 a temporary 〔provisional〕 license. ～비 《지출》 extraordinary 〔incidental〕 expenses; 《예산》 a reserve fund for contingencies. ～사무소 a temporary office. ～소집 an emergency call-up. ～수당 a special allowance. ～수입〔지출〕 extra 〔occasional〕 income 〔expenditure〕. ～숙소 a temporary dwelling 〔house〕; a provisional residence. ～승급 a special pay rise. ～시험 a special examination. ～열차 a special 〔extra〕 train 《for》. ～영업 temporary business: ～영업하다 carry on business temporarily / ～영업소 a temporary office 〔place of business〕; temporary (office) quarters. ～예산 a provisional budget. ～의장 an acting chairperson. ～접수 interim 〔provisional〕 acceptance. ～정류장 a temporary car 〔bus〕 stop. ～정부 a provisional government: 상해 ～ 정부 the Korean Provisional Government in Shanghai. ～조

교 a teaching assistant (생략 T.A.). ～증간(增刊) an extra edition; a special issue《of a magazine》. ～직 a temporary post〔position, office〕. ～직원 a temporary employee. ～총회 an extraordinary general meeting. ～특례 a provisional exception. ～협정 a provisional agreement. ～휴교 a temporary school closing; cancellation of classes. ～휴업 a special〔an extra〕holiday; temporary closure《of a shop》;《게시》No business today. *or* Closed temporarily.

**임시변통**(臨時變通) a makeshift; a temporary expedient; a stopgap. ～하다 conduct〔manage〕through a makeshift; make shift with《*a thing*》; manage《with》; make《*a thing*》do. ¶ ～의 temporary; makeshift; stopgap; make-do / ～으로 for a shift; as a stopgap; by way of makeshift / ～의 대책 a makeshift〔stopgap〕measure〔action〕/ ～으로 만든 의자 an impromptu chair / 이것으로 ～할까 한다 I am thinking of using this as a makeshift. / 이만한 돈이면 ～이 된다 I can make shift with this money. / ～으로 이것을 쓰십시오 Use this as a makeshift.

**임시채용**(臨時採用) probation; appointment on trial. ～하다 take〔admit〕《*a person*》on probation; employ《*a person*》on trial. ¶ ～의 probational; probationary. ◉ ～자 a candidate on probation; a probationer.

**임신**(妊娠) pregnancy; conception; gravidity. ～하다 conceive《a child》; get〔become〕pregnant. ¶ 상상 ～ pseudopregnancy; false pregnancy / 원치 않는 ～ an unwanted pregnancy / ～중에 during the period of maternity / ～중이다 be in the family way; be (big) with child; be expecting a baby / ～ 6개월이다 be six months「pregnant〔gone with child〕/ ～시키다 get《a girl》with child; cause pregnancy. ◉ ～ 가능기간 the child-bearing period (of a woman). ～기간 a pregnancy period. ～부 a pregnant woman. ～조절 birth control. ～중독(증) toxemia of pregnancy;〖의학〗gestosis. ～중절 (an) artificial abortion. 자궁외～ extrauterine〔ectopic〕pregnancy.

**임야**(林野) a forest land; forests and「fields.

**임업**(林業) forestry. ◉ ～시험장 an experimental forestry station.

**임용**(任用) appointment; employment. ～하다 appoint《*a person* to a post》. ◉ 공무원 ～령 the Official Appointment Regulations.

**임원**(任員) an officer; an official; a person in charge;《전체》the board; the staff;《회사의》a director; an executive《미》. ◉ ～석 seats for the officials; officers' seats. ～회 an officers'〔executives'〕meeting; the staff meeting;《중역회》a directors'〔board〕meeting.

**임의**(任意) option; discretion; voluntariness. ¶ ～의 free; any; optional (선택 자유의); voluntary (자발적인); arbitrary (제멋대로의) / ～의 삼각형 any triangle / ～의 장소 any place《*a person* likes》/ ～로 at *one's* option; at *one's* pleasure; as *one* pleases〔chooses〕; at *one's* discretion; of *one's* own accord〔free will〕; voluntarily / ～롭다 (be) voluntary / ～로 행동하다 act at *one's* discretion / ～에 맡기다 leave《*a matter*》to *a person's* discretion〔option〕/ 그것은 네 ～로 처리해도 좋다 You may do with it as you please. *or* It is in your discretion as to how you dispose of it. ◉ ～단체 a private organization (neither controlled nor protected by law). ～ 동행: 경찰관은 그에게 경찰서까지 ～동행을 요구했다 The policeman asked him to go voluntarily to the police station with him. ～법 voluntary law. ～선택 option; free choice. ～성(性) voluntariness. ～수색《가택 수색의》house search with consent. ～자백 a voluntary confession. ～추출법〖통계〗random sampling (method). ～출석 voluntary appearance〔attendance〕: ～출석을 요구하다 ask《*a person's*》voluntary appearance《at the police》. ～퇴직 voluntary retirement.

**임인**(壬寅)〖민속〗the 39th binary term of the sexagenary cycle.

**임자** ①《소유자》the owner; the proprietor (경영자). ¶ ～ 없는 ownerless; belonging to nobody / ～가 바뀌다 [사물이 주어] change hands; pass into someone else's possession / ～불명의 토지 land of uncertain ownership / 이 책 ～는 누구냐 To whom does this book belong? / 이 자동차의 ～가 누구요 Who owns this car? ②《자네》you;《부부간》(my) dear; darling; honey.

**임자**(壬子)〖민속〗the 49th binary term of the sexagenary cycle.

**임전**(臨戰) going into battle. ～하다 go into battle 〔action〕. ◉ ～무퇴 knowing no retreat at the battlefield. ～태세 preparations for action: ～태세를 갖추다 be prepared for war; be ready for a fight.

**임정**(林政) forestry administration.

**임정**(臨政) a provisional government. ◉ ～요인 leading figures of the provisional government.

**임종**(臨終) ① 《죽음에 임함》 facing death; 《죽는 때》 *one's* dying hour; *one's* last moment of life; *one's* deathbed. ¶ ～의 말 *one's* last 〔dying〕 words / ～의 고백 a deathbed confession / ～에 at *one's* death; on *one's* deathbed / ～시에 부르다 call 《the family》 to *one's* deathbed / ～이 다가오다 *one's* end is near; be at death's door 〔near death〕 / 그는 ～을 눈 앞에 두고 있었다 He was nearing his end. / ～이십니다 He 〔She〕 is now in his 〔her〕 last moments.
② 《임종의 배석》 attendance 〔presence〕 at 《*one's* parent's》 deathbed. ～하다 be with 〔wait upon〕 《*one's* parent's》 deathbed; be present at the moment of 《the parent's》 death. ¶ 유감스럽게도 아버지가 돌아가실 때 ～을 못 했다 I regret I could not be present at my father's deathbed. / 어머님 ～에 늦지 않게 되기를 간절히 바랐다 I ardently wished to be in time for the death of my mother.

**임지**(任地) the place of *one's* appointment; *one's* post. ¶ ～로 떠나다 leave for 〔proceed to〕 *one's* new post / 그는 어제 저녁 새 ～인 런던으로 떠났다 Last night he left for his new post in London.

**임직**(任職) appointment to an office.

**임진**(壬辰) 〖민속〗 the 29th binary term of the sexagenary cycle. ◉ ～왜란(倭亂) Japanese Invasion of Korea in 1592.

**임질**(淋疾) 〖의학〗 gonorrhea; the clap 《속어》. ¶ ～에 걸리다 suffer from gonorrhea. ◉ ～균 a gonococcus (*pl.* -cocci). ～환자 a gonorrheal patient; a case of gonorrhea.

**임차**(賃借) 《부동산의》 lease; renting; 《물건·차·선박의》 hire. ～하다 lease 《land》; rent 《a house》; hire; pay hire for; hold a lease 《on land》; take a lease 《of a building》. ◉ ～가격 a rental value; the value of lease. ～권 a 〔the〕 right of lease. ～료 (a) rent; (the charge for) hire. ～부동산 leasehold estate. ～용 가옥 a house 「for rent 〔to let 《영》〕. ～인 a hirer; a tenant; a lessee; a leaseholder. ～지 leased land.

**임파**(淋巴) 〖생리〗 lymph.

**임포텐스** impotence (남성의 발기 불능).

**임피던스** 〖전기〗 impedance.

**임하다**(臨―) ① 《면하다》 look out on 〔onto〕; face (onto, on); front (onto, on). ¶ 큰 거리에 임한 집 the house facing 〔fronting〕 (onto) the street / 바다에 임해 있다 face the sea.
② 《방문》 deign to pay a visit; 《도착》 arrive; approach; impend. ¶ 전쟁터에 임하여 on a battlefield / 개회식에 ～ attend 〔be present at〕 the opening ceremony.
③ 《군림·대함》 deal with. ¶ 부하에게 관대하게 ～ deal with *one's* subordinates with generosity; be generous 〔lenient〕 to *one's* subordinates.
④ 《직면》 stand 〔be〕 in the presence 《of》; meet; face 《a danger》; be confronted with 〔by〕 《difficulties》. ¶ 그 때에 임하여 at that juncture 〔very moment〕 / 죽음에 임하여 in the presence 〔at the moment〕 of death; on 〔at〕 *one's* deathbed / 그는 조용히 죽음에 임했다 He met his death calmly.

**임학**(林學) forestry; dendrology (수목학). ◉ ～자 a dendrologist; a forestry expert.

**임항**(臨港) ◉ ～선 《철도》 a harbor railroad.

**임해**(臨海) the seashore; the seaside. ¶ ～의 coastal; seaside. ◉ ～공업 단지 〔지대〕 a coastal industrial complex 〔region〕. ～도시 a coastal city. ～실습 marine practice. ～실험소 a marine (biological) laboratory. ～지역 littoral districts. ～학교 a seaside 《summer》 school. ～행락지 a seaside resort.

**입** ① 《사람·동물의》 the 〔*one's*〕 mouth (★ mouth의 복수형 mouths의 발음은 [mauðz]. 일반적으로 -th로 끝나는 명사의 복수형은 앞이 장모음이나 이중모음인 때에는 [θs]가 아니고 [ðz]. months [mʌnθs], paths [pɑːðz]); 《입술》 lips; *os* (*pl. ora*) (L.).
¶ 입의 oral / 예쁜 입 a pretty mouth / 입 속 (the interior of) the mouth / 꽉 다문 입 a firm-set mouth 〔lips〕 / 입이 큰 bigmouthed / 한 입에 at a bite / 입가에 미소를 띄우고 with a smile about *one's* mouth / 입을 벌리다 open *one's* mouth / 입을 다물다 shut *one's* mouth / 입을 오므리다 purse *one's* lips / 입을 축이다 moisten *one's* lips / 입에서 냄새가 나다 have foul 〔bad〕 breath; [입을 주

어로] smell / 입에 풀칠하다 earn *one's* living / 입에 거미줄 치다 starve; go hungry / 입에서 신물이 나다 be sick (and tired) 《of》; be bored 《with, by》; be fed up 《with》 / 손등으로 입을 씻다 wipe *one's* mouth with the back of *one's* hand / 벌어진 입을 다물지 못하다 《기가 막혀서》 be dum(b)founded; be speechless 《with surprise》; be agape 《in wonder》; be struck dumb / 그 소문은 그의 입에서 나왔다 He spread the rumor. / 그는 한 입에 삼키려 했다 He attempted to swallow it at a gulp. / 술은 입에 댄 일도 없다 Liquor has never touched my lips. / 저 녀석은 입만 앞세운다 He is all talk and no action. / 그는 그 건에 대해 자기도 모르게 입을 잘못 놀렸다 He made a slip of the tongue about the matter. ② 《말》 tongue; speech; words. ¶ 입이 뜨다 〔무겁다〕 be slow to speak; be taciturn 〔reticent〕 / 입이 가볍다 be talkative 〔glib-tongued, voluble〕 / 입을 열다 break the silence; confess; disclose / 입이 걸다 be foul-mouthed; be slanderous; be sharp-tongued; use violent language / 입 밖에 내다 talk 〔speak〕 of; mention; let out; let slip; spill 《a secret》 / 입 밖에 내지 않다 keep 《*a matter*》 secret; keep *one's* mouth shut / 입을 다물다 clamp *one's* lips together; hold *one's* tongue; fall silent; 《도중에》 cut *oneself* short / 남의 입에 오르다 be gossiped about; be in everyone's mouth / 너는 입만 살았다 You are bold in word only. / 결코 입 밖에 내서는 안 돼 Say nothing to anyone. *or* Keep it strictly to yourself. / 그 소문이 모든 사람 입에 올랐다 The rumor is on everybody's lips.

③ 《식구》 a mouth to feed; a dependent. ¶ 입이 많다 have a large family.

④ 《부리》 a bill (넓적한); a beak (갈고리 모양의).

⑤ 《구미》 *one's* taste; *one's* palate. ¶ 입에 맞다 be to *one's* taste; suit *one's* palate; be palatable / 입에 맞는 떡 just the right thing; just what *one* wants 〔needs〕 / 입이 까다롭다 have a delicate taste; be particular about food / 술은 내 입에 안 맞는다 Wine is not to my taste. / 입에 꼭 맞는다 It tastes just right to me.

**입가** ¶ ～에 about the mouth; at *one's* lips / ～에 미소를 띠고 with a smile on *one's* lips; with a smile playing about *one's* lips 〔mouth〕.

**입가심** 《입을 가심》 rinsing (out) *one's* mouth; 《뒷맛을 가심》 taking away the aftertaste from *one's* mouth; chasing (a strong taste). ～하다 rinse 〔wash〕 (out) *one's* mouth; take away 〔kill〕 the aftertaste; chase. ¶ 약을 먹고 사과로 ～하다 eat an apple to chase the medicine taste.

**입각**(入閣) entry into 〔joining〕 the Cabinet. ～하다 enter 〔join〕 the Cabinet; become a Cabinet member.

**입각**(立脚) ～하다 be based 〔grounded〕 《on》; take *one's* ground 《on》; rest on the basis of. ¶ …에 ～하여 on the ground of... 〔that...〕 / 사실에 ～하다 be based on facts / 그의 의견은 사실에 ～하고 있다 His views are well grounded on the fact. ◉ ～점 a standpoint; a viewpoint; a point of view; an angle; 《입장》 a footing.

**입간판**(立看板) a billboard; a standing signboard.

**입감**(入監) imprisonment. ～하다 imprison. ¶ ～중이다 be serving a term in prison.

**입거**(入渠) ～하다 go into (a) dock; enter a dock. ◉ ～료 dockage. ～시설 docking accommodation.

**입건**(立件) ～하다 book 《*a person*》 on charge 《of》. ¶ 형사 ～되다 be criminally booked 《on charge of..., in connection with...》 / 경찰은 과실 치사 혐의로 그를 ～했다 Police booked him on charge of the accidental homicide.

**입경**(入京) entering the capital; arrival in the capital; coming up to Seoul. ～하다 enter 〔arrive in〕 the capital; come up to Seoul.

**입고**(入庫) warehousing; storage in warehouse; 《자동차 따위의》 entering a car shed. ～하다 deposit 《*a thing*》 in a warehouse; put into a warehouse; store; be stocked; enter a (car) shed. ¶ 감자가 다량 ～되었다 Great quantities of potatoes have been stocked.

**입고병**(立枯病) 《농작물의》 damping-off.

**입관**(入棺) placing the corpse in the coffin. ～하다 place (a corpse) in the coffin. ◉ ～식 the rites of placing the body in the coffin; the coffin rites.

**입교**(入校) entrance 〔admission〕 into a school. ⇨ 입학(入學).

**입교**(入敎) entering a faith 〔a sect, a religious order, the church〕; baptism. ～하다 enter the church; be converted.

**입구**(入口) an entrance 《to》; a way in; a door 《to》; a gate 《to》. ¶ 터널의 ～ the approach to a tunnel / 항구의 ～

the「mouth of [entrance to] a harbor / 고속도로 ~ the「access [entrance] road to an expressway / ~를 막다 stop up the entrance / ~로 들어가다 go [come] in by [at] the entrance (door) / ~에서 기다리다 wait at the entrance (door) / 이 ~로 들어오지 못함《게시》 No entrance by this door.

**입국**(入國) entry [entrance] into a country; 《이민의》 immigration. ~하다 enter [be admitted to] a country; 《이민이》 immigrate into a country. ¶ 불법~ unlawful [illegal] entry / ~을 허가하다 admit 《*a person*》 to a country / ~을 거절하다 refuse [deny] 《*a person*》 entry into a country / 그는 그 나라에 불법 ~했다 He entered the country illegally.
◉ ~관리국 the Immigration Bureau. ~관리 사무소 the Immigration Office. ~기록 카드 a disembarkation card; a landing card. ~날짜 the date of entry 《to Korea》. ~사증(査證) entry visa: ~사증 면제 협정 a visa waiver accord. ~세(稅) a landing [entry] tax. ~수속 entry formalities. ~신고서 a disembarkation card. ~자 명단《공항의》 an inbound passenger list. ~ 절차 formalities for entry: ~절차를 간소화하다 simplify the entry formalities of foreigners into the nation. ~허가(장) an entry permit.
무비자~ no-visa entry: 그 두 나라는 무비자 ~협정을 맺었다 The two countries signed a pact on no-visa entry.

**입국**(立國) ①《건국》 the founding [establishment] of a state. ②《나라의 존립·발전》 ¶ 공업[산업]~ an industrial nation.

**입궐**(入闕) attendance at the Royal Court. ~하다 proceed [go] to the Royal Court.

**입금**(入金)《받음》 receipt of money; 《받은 돈》 receipts; money received [paid in]; 《받을 돈》 money due; money coming in; 《일부금》 part payment; payment on account. ~하다 receive 《some money》; pay (on account). ¶ 어제 그 회사로부터 10만 원의 ~이 있었다 I received hundred thousand won from the company yesterday. / 그 돈은 6월 1일까지 ~해야 한다 The payment is due on June 1. ◉ ~전표 a deposit slip; a receiving [paying-in] slip. ~통지서 a credit advice.

**입길** gossip. ¶ ~에 오르내리다 be talked about by people [others]; be the talk of town.

**입김** ①《내쉬는 숨의》 the steam of breath; puffs of *one's* breath. ¶ ~이 거세다 breathe hard [heavily, rapidly] / 유리창이 사람 ~에 흐려졌다 The windowpanes were steamed up with people's breath. / 그는 언 손에 후후 ~을 불었다 He blew on his frozen hands. ②《영향력》 (an) influence. ¶ ~이 세다 be influential [powerful]; have great influence 《over, with on, upon》 / ~이 미치다 influence...; have [exert] an influence on... / 그는 사장의 ~을 (등에) 업고 있다 He is backed up by the president. *or* He has the backing of the president.

**입납**(入納) Please deliver to 《Mr. A》; To.... ¶ 송씨댁 ~ To Mr. Song.

**입내**[1] 《흉내》 mimicry; imitation. ¶ 남의 ~를 내다 mimic another; imitate another's way of speaking. ◉ ~쟁이 a mimic(ker); an impersonator.

**입내**[2] 《구취》 bad [foul] breath; 〖의학〗 halitosis. ¶ ~가 나다 have bad [foul] breath.

**입노릇** eating; munching; having a bite. ¶ ~을 하다 have a bite; eat; munch.

**입다** ①《착용하다》 put on (★ 다만, 목적어가 대명사일 때는 put it on이 됨); slip into 《a dressing gown》 (걸치다); 《입고 있다》 wear; have on; be dressed [clad] 《in white》. ¶ 제복을 입은 대학생 a college student in uniform / 양복을 ~ wear [dress in] European clothes / 옷을 잘 ~ be well dressed; dress well / 입고 있다 be wearing; wear / 외투를 입어 보다 try on an overcoat / 외투 입은 채로 계십시오 Keep your overcoat on, please. / 무엇을 입고 갈까 What shall I go in? / 이런 옷을 입고는 나갈 수 없다 I can't go out in these (clothes).
②《받다》 get 《a favor》; receive; 《손해를》 suffer 《a loss》; sustain. ¶ 은혜를 ~ receive [enjoy] favors; be favored with patronage; share in the benefit / 피해를 ~ suffer damage; be damaged; be injured / 적은 큰 손해를 입고 퇴각했다 The enemy retreated with great loss. / 홍수로 경인선이 곳곳에서 큰 피해를 입었다 The Seoul-Inch'ŏn line was seriously damaged in places by the flood.
③《거상을》 ¶ 상을 ~ be in [go into] mourning 《for *a person*》.

**입단**(入團) joining an organization. ~하다 join [enter] an organization;

enroll in 《the Boy Scouts》.

**입담** word power; skill at talking; volubility; speaking; the impact of *one's* words. ¶ ～이 좋다 be glib 〔voluble, loquacious〕; *one's* words "pack a wallop" / ～ 사납다 be foul-tongued.

**입당**(入黨) joining a political party. ～하다 join 〔become a member of, accede to〕 《the Democratic Party》. ¶ 개별 ～하다 join a party on an individual basis.

**입대**(入隊) enlistment; recruitment; enrollment. ～하다 join 〔enlist in〕 the army; 《징병되어》 be conscripted 〔drafted〕 into the army; get recruited (★ 해군·공군 등에 입대하는 경우는 the army 대신에 the navy, the air force를 쓴다). ◉ ～식 the parade 〔ceremony〕 of new recruits. ～자 a recruit.

**입덧** morning sickness. ～나다 feel sick in the morning; have morning sickness. ¶ ～이 심하다 have bad morning sickness / ～은 대개 임신 3개월이 지나면 가라앉는다 Morning sickness usually disappears after the third month of pregnancy.

**입도선매**(立稻先賣) pre-harvest sale of rice crop. ～하다 sell rice before the harvest.

**입동**(立冬) *Iptong;* onset of winter, the first day 〔beginning〕 of winter (= one of the 24 seasonal divisions).

**입뜨다** (be) reticent; taciturn; be slow of speak; hold *one's* tongue. ¶ 입뜬 사람 a man of few words.

**입력**(入力) 《전기의》 power input; 《컴퓨터의》 input (★ 1회의 입력은 an input라고 하며 one input라고 하지 않음. 또 복수형은 쓰지 않음). ¶ 컴퓨터에 정보〔데이터〕를 ～하다 input information 〔data〕. ◉ ～신호 an input 〔incoming〕 signal. ～장치 an input unit. ～전류 an input; an incoming current. ～정보 input.

**입론**(立論) argument; argumentation; setting up a theory. ～하다 argue; make 〔put forward〕 an argument; set up a theory.

**입막음하다** seal 〔close〕 《*a person's*》 lips; forbid 《*a person*》 to say anything (to anybody) about 《*a thing*》; impose silence on 《*a person*》; muzzle 《*a person*》. ¶ 입막음하는 돈 hush money; a bribe.

**입맛** appetite; *one's* taste; *one's* palate. ¶ ～에 맞다 suit *one's* palate 〔taste〕; be palatable; be to *one's* taste / ～을 잃다 lose *one's* appetite / ～이 없다 have no appetite / ～을 돋우다 stimulate 〔excite, provoke, arouse〕 *one's* appetite / 나는 요새 ～이 좋다 I have good appetite these days. / 운동을 좀 하면 ～이 난다 A little exercise will give you an appetite.

**입맛다시다** ① 《먹고 싶어》 smack *one's* lips; smack appreciative lips 《over a dish》; enjoy 《*one's* favorite dish》. ¶ 입맛다시며 먹다 eat smacking *one's* lips; eat with much gusto 〔relish〕 / 사과를 보고 ～ lick *one's* chops at the sight of an apple; *one's* mouth waters at seeing an apple. ② 《못마땅해서》 click *one's* tongue; tut-tut. ¶ 아무가 하는 짓에 ～ click *one's* tongue 〔tut-tut〕 at a person's behavior.

**입맛쓰다** taste bitter; feel wretched 〔bad, sick〕; be chagrined. ¶ 입맛 쓴 듯이 with a perplexed air; in a puzzled way / 낙제해서 ～ I feel miserable for failing the examination.

**입맞추다** ① 《키스하다》 kiss 《*a person, a person* on the cheek》; give 《*a person*》 a kiss; 《소리를 내며》 give a smacking kiss. ¶ 손에 ～ kiss *a person's* hand / 느닷없이 ～ snatch kiss. ② 《말을 맞추다》 make sure 《their》 stories agree; arrange not to contradict each other; arrange beforehand to tell the same story 〔say the same thing〕 《to the police》.

**입멸**(入滅) 〖불교〗 entering Nirvana; death (of a Buddhist saint). ～하다 enter Nirvana; pass away; die.

**입모습** shape of the mouth. ¶ ～이 예쁘다 have a lovely mouth / ～이 예쁜 소녀 a sweet-mouthed girl.

**입목**(立木) a living 〔standing, growing〕 tree; standing timber (목재로서의).

**입문**(入門) ① 《첫걸음》 an introduction 《to》; a guide; a primer. ¶ 경제학 ～ an introduction to economics / 라틴어 ～ a Latin primer. ② 《제자가 됨》 entrance into 〔admission to〕 a private school. ～하다 enter a school; become a pupil 〔disciple〕 《of *a person*》. ◉ ～서 a guide; a manual; a primer.

**입바르다** (be) plain-spoken; straightforward. ¶ 입바른 소리 plain speaking; a straight talk / 입바른 소리를 잘 하는 사람 a plain-spoken person; an outspoken person / 입바른 소리를 하다 speak plainly; call a spade a spade.

**입방**(立方) 〖수학〗 cube. ⇨ 세제곱.

**입방아찧다** nag 《at》; cavil 《at, about》;

carp ⦅at, about⦆; prattle ⦅on, about⦆. ¶ 그녀는 입방아를 찧어 남편을 혼나게 했다 She nagged her husband half to death.

**입방체**(立方體) ⇨ 정육면체.

**입버릇** *one's* manner of speech; *one's* way of talking; ⦅판박이말⦆ *one's* favorite 〔stock〕 phrase; *one's* favorite 〔pet〕 saying. ¶ ～이 사납다 be foul-tongued; be evil-mouthed; be nasty / ～처럼 말하다 always say; be in the habit of saying; never fail to say.

**입법**(立法) 〖법〗 legislation; law-making. ～하다 legislate; make 〔enact〕 laws; pass a new law. ¶ ～의 legislative / ～정신에 위배되다 be contrary to the spirit of the legislation.
◉ ～권 ⦅exercise⦆ legislative 〔law-making〕 power. ～기관〔부〕 a legislative organ 〔body〕; the legislature. ～자 a legislator; a lawgiver; a law-maker. ～화 legalization: ～화하다 legalize. ～회의 a legislative council.

**입병**(一病) a sore mouth; a mouth disease.

**입비뚤이** a person with a crooked 〔twisted〕 mouth.

**입사**(入社) entering 〔joining〕 a company. ～하다 enter 〔join〕 a company; become a member of a firm; obtain a position in a concern. ¶ 그는 일류 상사에 ～가 내정되어 있다 He has been informally promised employment at a top-rate trading company. /「조지, 스티브와 인사하게. 오늘부터 우리와 일할 사람이야」―「스티브씨, ～를 환영합니다」 "George, meet Steve. He'll be working with us beginning today."―"Hi, Steve. Nice to have you with us." *or* "Hello, Steve. Welcome aboard!"
◉ ～시험 an entrance 〔employment〕 examination ⦅of, for⦆; a test for employment ⦅in a firm⦆; ⦅면접⦆ a personal interview: ～시험을 통해 채용하다 employ ⦅*a person*⦆ through an entrance examination.

**입사**(入射) 〖물리〗 incidence. ◉ ～각 an incidence angle; an angle of incidence. ～광선 incident rays: 거울의 ～광선 a ray of light incident upon a mirror.

**입사**(立嗣) designating heir. ～하다 designate ⦅*a person*⦆ as heir.

**입산**(入山) ① ⦅산에 들어감⦆ entering a mountain area. ～하다 go into 〔enter〕 a mountain area; ⦅함부로⦆ step in a reserved forest; ⦅은거하다⦆ retire (from society) into the mountains. ¶ ～금지 ⦅게시⦆ Keep out of the mountain. *or* A reserved forest. ② 〖불교〗 retiring to a mountain to enter the priesthood. ～하다 enter 〔join〕 priesthood; renounce the world.
◉ ～수도 mountaineering asceticism: ～수도사 a mountaineering ascetic.

**입상**(入賞) winning a prize. ～하다 win 〔get, receive, carry off〕 a prize. ¶ 일등으로 ～하다 win 〔take〕 the first prize / 그녀는 ～한 사진을 미술관에 기부했다 She donated her prize-winning photograph to the art museum.
◉ ～자 a prize winner; a winning contestant. ～화(畫) a prize picture.

**입상**(立像) a (standing) statue; ⦅작은⦆ a statuette.

**입상**(粒狀) ¶ ～의 granular ⦅starch⦆; granulated ⦅sugar⦆. ◉ ～전분 granular starch. ～조직 granular texture.

**입석**(立席) ⦅극장 따위의⦆ the gallery; standing room ⦅미⦆. ¶ ～뿐임 ⦅게시⦆ Standing Room Only. (생략 S.R.O.) / ～도 만원(滿員)이다 There's no room even for standing.
◉ ～손님 a standee.

**입선**(入選) being selected 〔accepted〕 for a competition. ～하다 get selected; be accepted. ¶ 그의 조각이 국전에 ～됐다 His piece of sculpture was accepted 〔selected〕 for the National Art Exhibition. ◉ ～논문 a winning essay. ～자 a winner; a winning 〔successful〕 competitor 〔contestant〕; the winners [총칭]. ～작(作) a winning (piece of) work.

**입성**(入城) an 〔a triumphal〕 entry into a fortress 〔city〕. ～하다 make a triumphal 〔formal〕 entry into a fortress 〔city〕; enter a city triumphantly 〔in triumph〕. ◉ ～식 formal 〔triumphal〕 entry.

**입소**(入所) ① ⦅연구소 등으로의⦆ entrance ⦅into⦆; admission ⦅to⦆. ～하다 enter 〔be admitted to〕 ⦅an institution⦆. ¶ ～훈련 initiatory training.
② ⦅교도소로의⦆ imprisonment; incarceration; ⦅수용소로의⦆ internment; confinement. ～하다 ⦅교도소에⦆ be put in 〔into〕 prison; be sent to 〔cast into〕 prison; be imprisoned; ⦅수용소로⦆ be put into 〔sent to〕 a (concentration) camp; be interned. ¶ 교도소에 ～되어 있다 be in prison 〔jail〕.

**입속말** a murmur; a mutter. ～하다 mutter to *oneself;* grumble ⦅at, over, about⦆; murmur ⦅at, against⦆.

**입수**(入手) acquisition; receipt; obtainment. ~하다 receive; obtain; procure; get; come by; [사물이 주어로] come to hand. ¶ 그 악보를 ~하기는 어렵다 The musical note is hard to obtain. / 마침내 그 물품을 ~했다 At last the article came to 〔fell into〕 my hands. ◉ ~경로 means of acquisition. ~난 difficulty of obtaining: ~난이다 be difficult to obtain.

**입술** the lips. ¶ 얇은 ~ thin lips / 두툼한 ~ full 〔thick〕 lips / 윗〔아랫〕~ the upper 〔lower〕 lip / 터진 ~ chapped lip(s) / ~을 깨물다 《분해서》 bite *one's* lip in frustration 〔chagrin〕; 《초조해서》 nervously chew 〔gnaw〕 *one's* lip / ~을 훔치다 steal a kiss 《from *a person*》 / ~을 비죽거리다 make a lip; pout *one's* lips / ~을 오므리다 purse *one's* lips. ◉ ~소리 『언어』 labial sounds. ~연지 (a) lipstick; rouge: ~연지 묻은 담배 꽁초 a cigarette butt with lipstick on it.

**입시**(入試) an entrance examination. ¶ ~를 치르다 take 〔sit for, face, undergo〕 an entrance examination 《for》 / ~에 합격하다 〔실패하다〕 pass 〔fail〕 an 〔*one's*〕 entrance examination 《for a university》 / ~ 준비를 하다 prepare for an entrance examination. ◉ ~문제 entrance examination papers 〔questions〕. ~지옥 exam hell; the narrow gate to an upper school: ~지옥을 완화하다 ease off the exam hells. ~합격자 a successful candidate for the entrance examination.

**입식**(立食) a stand-up meal; 《뷔페 형식의》 buffet. ~하다 have a stand-up meal. ¶ ~파티 a buffet-style dinner party.

**입신**(立身) establishment of *oneself* in life; success in life; a rise in the world. ⇨출세. ~하다 establish *oneself* in life; succeed 〔advance〕 in life; rise in the world. ¶ ~을 꾀하다 seek *one's* fortune. ◉ ~양명 rising in the world and gaining fame. ~출세 success in life; a successful career: ~출세주의 the cult of success; careerism / ~출세주의자 a (social) climber; a status seeker; a (single-minded) careerist / ~ 출세담 an up-from-the-bottom story / ~출세하다 succeed in life.

**입심** boldness 〔brazenness〕 in words; volubleness; eloquence. ¶ ~이 좋다 be bold 〔brazen〕 in words; talk big; be glib 〔voluble, loquacious, eloquent, talkative〕 / ~사납다 have a spiteful 〔bitter〕 tongue.

**입싸다** (be) talkative; have a loose tongue; be a blabbermouth.

**입쌀** unglutinous rice.

**입씨름** 《말다툼》 bickering; (exchange of) high words; a brawl; an altercation; a wrangle; a dispute; an argument. ~하다 bicker; have high words 《with》; wrangle; altercate; argue 〔dispute〕 《with》.

**입씻기다** buy 《*a person's*》 silence; pay hush-money. ¶ 입씻기기 위해 만 원을 내놓다 offer 10,000 won to keep dumb about 《it》. / 1만 원을 주어 그의 입을 씻겼다 I gave him 10,000 won to keep his mouth shut.

**입씻이** ① 《입씻기는》 hush money; bribe money. ② =입가심.

**입아귀** the corner(s) of the mouth.

**입안**(立案) ① 《안을 세움》 drafting; drawing 〔setting〕 up (a draft); planning. ~하다 make 〔form, draw up, map out〕 a plan; design; devise; draft. ¶ 이 안은 그가 ~한 것이다 This idea originated with him. / 총리는 새로운 외교 정책을 ~했다 The prime minister designed a new foreign policy. ② 『역사』 an official certificate. ◉ ~자 a drafter; a deviser; a planner: 정책 ~자 a policy maker / 도시계획의 ~자 a city planner.

**입양**(入養) adoption. ~하다 adopt 《a child as *one's* son》; receive into *one's* family 《as a daughter》; affiliate. ¶ ~되다 be adopted 《into a family》. ◉ ~신고 a report of adoption of an heir. ~아 an adopted child 〔son, daughter〕.

**입어**(入漁) ~하다 fish in the restricted waters. ◉ ~권 an entrance right to a fishing lot; a right of entry into a fishing ground; the common of piscary 〔fishery〕. ~료 charges for fishing in another's piscary; fishing fee.

**입영**(入營) entering barracks; enrol(l)ment; enlistment. ~하다 enter barracks; enlist in 〔join〕 the army; 《징집되어》 be drafted into the army. ¶ ~중이다 be in the army; be serving with the colors.

**입욕**(入浴) bathing; a bath. ~하다 take 〔have〕 a bath; bathe; 《영》 bath. ¶ ~시키다 give 《a baby》 a bath; bathe 《a baby》.

**입원**(入院) hospitalization; admission into a hospital. ~하다 go into 〔enter, be admitted to] hospital; be hospitalized; check into a hospital《미》. ¶ ~중(中)이다 be in the hospital; 《영》 be in hospital / ~시키다 get 〔have〕《*a person*》 admitted to hospital; hospitalize; 《의사가 환자를》 admit 《*a person*》 to hospital / ~ 가료를 요하다 require treatment in (a) hospital. ◉ ~료〔비〕 hospital charges. ~절차 hospital admission procedures 〔formalities, red tape〕; formalities connected with inpatient treatment. ~실 a (sick) ward. ~치료〔가료〕 hospital treatment. ~환자 an inpatient: ~환자 명부 a list of inpatients / 장기 ~환자 a long-stay patient.

**입자**(粒子) 〖물리〗 a particle. ¶ 반(反)~ an antiparticle. ◉ ~량(量) particle weight. 경(輕)~ a lepton.

**입장**(入場) entrance; 《관객의》 admission; admittance. ~하다 enter; get in; 《관객이》 be admitted 《to, into》; gain entrance. ¶ (선수가) 경기장에 ~하다 enter the stadium / ~을 허락하다 admit 《*a person*》 to 〔into〕 《a place》; give 〔grant〕 《*a person*》 admission 《to, into》 / ~을 거절하다 refuse admission / 일반의 ~을 허락하다 be open to the public / ~금지 《게시》 Keep out. *or* No admittance. *or* No entrance. / ~환영 《게시》 Welcome to all visitors. / 7세 미만의 어린이는 ~할 수 없습니다 《게시》 Children under 7 are not admitted. / ~무료 《게시》 Admission 〔Entrance〕 free. *or* Free to all. / 연소자 ~ 불허 《게시》 Adults only. ◉ ~권(權) ingrees; *entrée* (F.); right of admission. ~권(券) an entrance 〔admission〕 ticket; 《역의》 a platform ticket: ~권 매표소 a ticket 《미》 〔booking 《영》〕 office / 특별~권 a complimentary ticket. ~료 an entrance 〔admission〕 fee: ~료를 받다 charge admission / ~료를 안 받다 charge no admission / ~료는 얼마입니까 What is the admission? *or* How much do you charge for admission? / ~료 2000원 Admission ₩2,000. ~세 an admission tax. ~식 an opening ceremony. ~자 visitors 《to a theater》; spectators; an attendance [총칭]: 유료 ~자 (a) paid attendance. ~행진 an entrance march 〔procession〕.

**입장**(立場) 《경우》 a position; a situation; 《당연한 처지》 a footing; *one's* ground; a standpoint; a ground; 《관점·시점》 a point of view; an angle 《구어》. ¶ 정치적 ~에서 from a political standpoint / 대등한 ~에서 on an equal footing 《with》 / 외교적인 ~에서 from a diplomatic 「point of view 〔standpoint〕 / 곤란한 ~에 있다 be in a difficult situation; be in a tight place / 묘한 ~에 있다 be placed in a delicate position / 불리한 ~에 있다 be behind the eight ball 《미속어》 / 괴로운 ~에 있다 find *oneself* in a painful position / 자기의 ~을 밝히다 define *one's* position; clarify *one's* attitude / ~을 달리하다 be on a different footing / ~을 고수(固守)하다 hold fast to *one's* 《earlier》 stance / 남의 ~이 되어보다 put *oneself* in another's place 〔shoes〕 / 나는 그것을 할 수 있는 ~에 있지 않다 I am not in a position to do it. / 네가 내 ~에 있다면 어떻게 하겠느냐 What would you do if you were in my place? / 내 ~ 좀 되어 봐주게 Look at my side of it. / 너는 자신의 ~을 분명히 해야 한다 You should make your standpoint 〔position〕 clear. / 하인의 ~으로서 주인을 따를 수 밖에 없었다 Being a (mere) servant (as I was), I could do nothing but obey my master. ◉ 기본~ *one's* basic stance.

**입장단**(―長短) humming along to dance rhythm. ¶ ~을 치다 hum along to dance rhythm.

**입적**(入寂) death of a saint. =입멸(入滅).

**입적**(入籍) official registration as a family member. ~하다 have *one's* name entered in the family register; enter 《*a person's* name》 in *one's* family register.

**입전**(入電) a telegram received. ¶ 홍콩으로부터 ~된 바에 의하면 according to a cablegram from Hong Kong / …내용의 ~이 있었다 We have received a telegram to the effect that….

**입정**(入廷) entrance into the courtroom. ~하다 enter 〔appear in〕 the courtroom.

**입정놀리다** keep *one's* mouth busy to eat; eat incessantly between meals.

**입정사납다** ① 《입이 걸다》 (be) nasty; foul-tongued; foul-mouthed. ② 《탐식하다》 (be) greedy; voracious; ravenous.

**입조**(入朝) attendance at 〔a visit to〕 the Royal Court. ~하다 attend the Royal Court; be present at the Royal Court.

**입주**(入住) ~하다 move in(to) 《an

apartment house》; 《가정에》 live in; live with 《a family》; become an inmate 《of》. ¶ 새 집에 ~하다 move into a new house / ~ 가능한 일자리를 찾다 get a living-in position; obtain a resident post / 이 시영 아파트에는 모자 가정이 20세대 ~해 있다 Twenty fatherless families occupy this apartment building managed by the city. / 「이 아파트에는 언제 ~하셨습니까」—「지난 달입니다」 "When did you move into this apartment?" — "Last month."

◉ ~ 가정교사〔가정부〕 a resident 〔living-in〕 tutor 〔maid〕. ~자 a tenant; an occupant; a resident; a dweller. ~제 a living-in system.

**입증**(立證) proof; demonstration; establishment 《of a fact》; substantiation 《of *one's* statement》. ~하다 give proof; prove 《*one's* theory》; establish 《a fact》; substantiate 《the testimony of a witness》; [사물이 주어] testify 《a fact》; attest to 《a fact》; corroborate; bear out; bear *one's* testimony. ¶ …을 ~하는 사실 facts corroborative of 《a crime》; facts in support of 《*one's* statements》/ …을 ~하기 위하여 in support 〔proof〕 of … / 유죄를 ~하다 prove 《*a person*》 guilty / 무죄를 ~하다 prove 《*a person*》 not guilty; establish *one's* innocence / …의 우수성을 ~하다 demonstrate the superiority of… / 이 약은 암에 효과가 있다고 ~되었다 This drug has been proved effective against cancer.

◉ ~자료 supporting evidence.

**입지**(立志) fixing *one's* aim in life. ~하다 make a strong resolution; fix *one's* aim in life. ◉ ~전 the biography of a self-made man; *one's* success story: ~전적인 인물 a (successful) self-made man.

**입지**(立地) (a) location. ~하다 be located. ◉ ~조건 conditions of location: ~조건이 좋다〔나쁘다〕 be conveniently 〔inconveniently〕 located; be located favorably 〔unfavorably〕; be in a favorable 〔an unfavorable〕 situation / 공장 건립에는 ~ 조건을 충분히 검토할 필요가 있다 You must thoroughly investigate conditions at the location where you are planning to set up a factory.

**입직**(入直) taking *one's* turn in office 〔at night duty〕.

**입질** 《낚시에서》 a bite; a strike. ~하다 bite; take 〔have〕 a bait. ¶ ~이 없다 have 〔feel〕 no bite / ~이 있었다 I had 〔felt〕 a strike 〔bite〕.

**입짓** making a mouth; moving *one's* lips. ~하다 make a mouth.

**입짧다** have a small appetite; 《구어》 eat like a bird. ¶ 입짧은 사람 a light 〔poor, small〕 eater.

**입찬말**, **입찬소리** bragging; hot air 《속어》.

**입찰**(入札) a bid; a tender; bidding. ~하다 tender 〔bid〕 《for》; offer 〔put on〕 *one's* bid 〔tender〕 《for》; make a bid 《for》.

¶ 공개〔일반〕 ~ an open tender / 경쟁 ~ a public tender; competitive bidding / ~에 부치다 《경매 입찰》 sell 《articles》 by (public) tender; put 《*a thing*》 out to tender; 《공모하다》 invite tenders 《for》; call for bids / 남보다 싸게〔비싸게〕 ~하다 underbid 〔outbid〕 others / 신교사 건축 ~공고 《게시》 Bids are invited for the new school-building. / 도로 공사의 ~이 행해졌다 Bids were invited for the construction of the road. / 회사는 그 교량 공사의 ~에서 낙찰되었다 Our tender for the bridge construction was accepted. / 상기 ~ 희망자는 1주일 이내에 신청할 것 Any person who wishes to bid for the above shall apply within a week.

◉ ~가격 the price tendered; a bidding price. ~공고 a notice of tender 《for engineering work》; a bid announcement. ~기일 time appointed for handing in tenders. ~보증 a bid bond. ~보증금 security for a tender 〔bid〕; bid bond. ~일 the day of tender 〔bidding〕. ~자 a tenderer; a bidder: 최고 ~자 the highest bidder.

**입천장**(—天障) the roof 〔vault〕 of the mouth; the palate. = 구개(口蓋). ¶ ~의 palatal; palatine.

**입체**(立體) a solid (body). ¶ ~의 solid; cubic / ~적(인) three-dimensional; 〖미술〗 plastic / ~적인 그림 a three-dimensional picture. / ~적으로 고찰하다 consider 《*a matter*》 from many angles.

◉ ~각 a solid angle. ~감 solidity; 〖미술〗 plasticity; a three-dimensional 〔stereoscopic〕 effect (사진·영화 등의): ~감이 있다 look solid. ~교차 《도로의》 a two-〔multi-〕level crossing; a grade separation; a crossing with an overpass 〔underpass〕; an overhead crossing: ~교차로 a flyover roadway / ~교차로의 윗길〔아랫길〕 an overpass 〔underpass〕. ~교차점 an overpass 《미》; a flyover 《영》. ~기하학 solid geometry. ～묘사 cubic 〔solid〕 delineation. ～미 solid beauty. ～방송 a stereo (phonic) 〔binaural〕 broadcast. ～사진 a stereoscopic photograph. ～영화 a three-dimensional 〔3-D〕 film 〔movie〕. ～음향〔음악〕 a stereophonic sound 〔music〕: ～음향 장치 a stereophonic sound system. ～작전 《영》 combined operations. ～전 three-dimensional warfare. ～파 〖미술〗《화풍》 cubism; 《유파》 the cubists: ～파의 그림 a cubist picture 〔painting〕. ～화법 stereography.

**입체**(立替) temporal payment on *a person's* behalf. ～하다 pay temporarily 《for *a person,* on *a person's* behalf》. ¶ 우선 내가 ～해 놓을게 I'll pay for you and we'll settle up later.

**입초**(立哨) standing watch; sentry duty. ¶ ～서다 stand watch / ～세우다 place 〔mount〕 a guard. ◉ ～병 a sentry; a sentinel.

**입초**(入超) 〖경제〗 an excess of imports (over exports); an unfavorable 〔adverse〕 balance of trade; a foreign trade deficit. ¶ 지난 달에는 50만 달러의 ～를 냈다 Imports exceeded exports by $500,000 last month. / 작년도의 무역 수지는 100억 달러의 ～였다 The balance of foreign trade for the last year showed an excess of imports of ten billion dollars.

**입추**(立秋) *Ipch'u;* the day which signals the arrival of autumn by the traditional Korean 〔seasonal〕 calendar; the 「first day 〔beginning〕 of autumn (around 8 or 9 Aug.).

**입추**(立錐) ¶ ～의 여지도 없다 be closely packed; be densely crowded; be filled to capacity / 극장은 관중으로 ～의 여지도 없었다 The theater was packed full with audiences.

**입춘**(立春) *Ipch'un;* the day which signals the arrival of spring by the traditional Korean 〔seasonal〕 calendar; the 「first day 〔beginning〕 of spring (around 3 or 4 Feb.).

**입태자**(立太子) the official investiture of a Prince as Heir Apparent to the Throne.

**입하**(入荷) a fresh supply of goods; arrival 〔receipt〕 of goods. ～하다 arrive; be received. ¶ 오렌지 20톤이 ～됐다 Twenty tons of oranges were received. / 예약 주문한 새로운 기종의 컴퓨터의 ～를 기다리고 있다 We have placed an advance order and been waiting for the new model of the computer to arrive. ◉ ～통지 an arrival notice.

**입하**(立夏) *Iph'a;* the first day of summer; onset of summer, one of the 24 seasonal divisions (around 5 or 6 May).

**입학**(入學) entrance into 〔admission to〕 a school; 《대학의》 matriculation. ～하다 enter 〔be admitted, gain admission to〕 a school 〔university〕; matriculate 〔be matriculated〕 《in a university》. ¶ ～준비를 하다 prepare for a school 〔college〕 / ～을 지원하다 apply for admission 《to a university》 / ～을 허가하다 grant admission 《to》 / 톰은 하버드 대학에 ～했다 Tom got into Harvard.
◉ ～규칙 admission regulations. ～금 an entrance 〔enrollment〕 fee. ～난 the difficulty in entering a school. ～생 a new student; an incoming student; the entering class. ～시험 an entrance examination: ～시험을 치르다 take 〔sit for〕 an entrance examination. ～식 an entrance ceremony. ～원서 《용지》 an application form: ～원서를 내다 send in an application for admission 《to》. ～자 a new student; a newly registered 〔enrolled〕 student. ～자격 qualifications 〔requirements〕 for admission. ～절차 entrance formalities: ～절차를 밟다 register 〔complete registration〕 for 《a university》. ～정원 a 《college》 admission quota; 《a college's》 quota of students. ～지원자 a candidate 〔an applicant〕 for admission 《to》. ～허가 admission (to a school); 《대학의》 matriculation: ～허가서 《미국 유학의》 I-20 form.

**입항**(入港) entry into port; arrival 《of a ship》 in port. ～하다 enter 〔make, put into〕 port; arrive in 〔come into〕 port. ¶ ～해 있다 be in port 〔harbor〕 / 인천항에 ～하다 put into Inch'ŏn / 그 배는 어제 ～할 예정이었다 The boat was scheduled to make port yesterday. ◉ ～선 an incoming 〔inbound〕 vessel. ～세 port 〔harbor〕 dues; keelage. ～수수료 an entrance fee. ～신고 an entrance notice. ～예정일 the expected time of arrival (생략 ETA). ～절차 clearance inwards.

**입향순속**(入鄕循俗) When you are in Rome, do as the Romans do. *or* Do in Rome as the Romans do.

**입헌**(立憲) establishment of a constitution; constitutionalization. ¶ ～적(인) constitutional / ～적으로 constitutionally; on constitutional lines.

◉ ～군주국 a constitutional monarchy. ～군주〔민주〕정체 constitutional monarchy 〔democracy〕. ～정치 constitutional government; constitutionalism. ～주의 constitutionalism.

**입회**(入會) entrance 《into》; admission. ～하다 enter 〔join〕 a society; be admitted to 〔into〕 an association; become a member of a society. ¶ ～를 신청하다 apply 〔make application〕 for admission / ～를 허락하다 admit 《*a person*》 to membership 〔to a society〕 / 누구든지 ～할 수 있다 Membership is open to everybody. ◉ ～권 〖법〗 ((the) right of) common. ～금 an entrance 〔admission, enrollment〕 fee. ～식 an initiation (ceremony). ～자 an entrant; a new member.

**입회**(立會) ① 《출석》 presence; attendance; 《증인으로의》 witnessing. ～하다 attend; be present 《at an interview》; be (a) witness 《to, of》. ¶ 증인 ～하에 in the presence of a witness / 증인으로서 ～하다 be present as a witness / ～를 요청하다 request 〔ask for〕 《*a person's*》 presence 《at the meeting》 / 나도 선거 개표에 ～했다 I was among the witness 〔the election judges〕 at the opening of the ballot. ② 《증권거래소의》 a session.

◉ ～경관 a policeman in attendance. ～인〔자〕 an observer; a witness (증인); a teller (개표의).

**입후보**(立候補) candidacy 《미》; candidature 《영》. ～하다 run 〔stand〕 in an election; be 〔become〕 a candidate; stand 〔come forward〕 as a candidate 《for an election》; run for 《an election, an office》.

¶ ～를 선언하다 announce 〔declare〕 *one's* candidacy 《for》 / 국회 의원에 ～하다 run for election to the National Assembly / 서울에서 ～하다 run as a candidate in Seoul / ～를 사퇴하다 decline the nomination for candidacy (공천 과정에서) / ～를 단념하다 give up *one's* candidacy / 그가 ～하자 모두 놀랐다 His candidacy surprised everybody. / 그는 대통령 선거에 ～할 것이다 He will run for the presidency. / 그는 다음 선거에서 무소속으로 ～할 것이다 He's going to be an independent candidate in the next election. ◉ ～공탁금 a deposit for filing candidacy. ～등록 registration of *one's* candidacy. ～자 a candidate: ～자 지명 nomination of a candidate.

**입히다** ① 《옷을》 dress; clothe; put on. ¶ 어린 아이에게 옷을 ～ dress a child / 외투를 입혀주다 help 《*a person*》 (on) with *his* overcoat / 외투를 입혀 보다 try an overcoat on 《*a person*》. ② 《거죽에》 coat; plate; gild; veneer; paint; cover. ¶ 고무를 입힌 coated with Indian rubber / 금을 입힌 plated with gold / 은을 입힌 술잔 a silver-plated winecup / 무덤에 떼를 ～ cover a grave with sod. ③ 《손해를》 inflict 《injury》 on 《*a person*》; cause 《damage, loss》; subject 《*a person*》 to; do 《harm》. ¶ 아무에게 손해를 ～ inflict losses on *a person* / 화를 ～ do 《*a person*》 an evil.

**잇**[1] 《이불 따위의》 a (mattress 〔pillow〕) cover. ¶ 베갯잇 a pillow cover; a pillowcase.

**잇**[2] 〖식물〗 a safflower.

**잇다** ① 《연결하다》 join 〔link〕 《*a thing* to another》; piece 〔put〕 together; connect 《*a thing* with another》; piece 《*a thing* to another》. ¶ 줄을 ～ link strings together / 끈을 ～ link up string / 두 가닥의 새끼를 ～ tie together two pieces of rope / 실을 ～ piece threads together / 조각을 ～ join fragments together / 책상을 이어 붙이다 place the tables end to end.

② 《계승하다》 succeed 《to *one's* father's trade》; inherit; follow (in the footsteps of). ¶ 가산을 ～ inherit an estate / 왕위를 ～ succeed 〔come〕 to the throne / 대를 ～ carry on a family line / 그는 자기의 뒤를 이을 자손이 없다 He has no heir. *or* There is no one to carry on his family or inherit his property. / 그는 홍씨의 뒤를 이어 장관이 되었다 He succeeded Mr. Hong as Minister 《of Foreign Affairs & Trade》. ③ 《생명을》 maintain; sustain; preserve 《life》. ¶ 생명을 겨우 이어가다 eke out a bare existence; keep body and soul together / 빵과 물로 목숨을 이어가다 sustain *oneself* on bread and water.

**잇달다** ① 《이어 달다》 join; put together; link; connect; attach. ¶ 두 헝겊을 ～ piece 〔sew〕 two bits of cloth together. ② 《연달다》 come 〔occur〕 in succession. ⇨ 잇따르다. ¶ 잇단 행운〔불운〕 a run of good 〔bad〕 luck.

**잇달아** consecutively; successively; one after another. ¶ 세 번 ～ three times in succession 〔in a row〕 / 닷새나 ～

for five days running 〔on end〕; for five consecutive 〔straight〕 days / 홍수에 ~ 질병이 발생했다 Disease followed on the heels of the flood.

**잇닿다** continue (in contact); go on; be adjacent to.

**잇대다** ① 《연결하다》 put together; join; link; connect; couple. ¶ 두 책상을 ~ put two tables together / 기관차에 객차를 ~ couple a locomotive with passenger cars. ② 《계속하다》 continue 《*a thing*》; go on; keep 《*a thing*》 up. ¶ 잇대서 continuously; without a break; uninterruptedly.

**잇따르다** 《잇달다》 occur in succession; follow one after another; ensue. ¶ 잇따른 불행 a run of ill luck / 잇따른 가뭄 a long spell of dry weather / 잇따라 in succession; one after another 〔the other (둘의 경우)〕 / 잇따라 손해를 보다 suffer loss upon loss / 잇따라 다섯 번 이기다 win five consecutive victories / 잇따라 총회가 있었다 Then a plenary meeting followed. / 기근이 전쟁에 잇따랐다 Famine followed in the wake of the war. / 사람들이 사회당을 잇따라 탈당했다 People left the Socialist Party one after another. / 불행이 잇따랐다 Misfortunes came one after another.

**잇몸** the gums; the teethridge. ¶ ~을 드러내고 웃다 (show *one's* teeth and) grin. ◉ ~출혈 gingival bleeding.

**잇바디** a row of teeth. ⇨ 치열(齒列).

**잇새** the crevice between 〔*one's*〕 teeth. ¶ ~를 쑤시다 pick *one's* teeth / 그는 ~가 떴다 His teeth are set far apart. / ~에 고기가 끼었다 I got a shred of meat stuck between my teeth.

**잇소리** 〖음성〗 a dental (sound). ⇨ 치음.

**잇속** the shape of a tooth 〔of *one's* teeth〕. ¶ ~이 좋다〔나쁘다〕 have a regular 〔an irregular〕 set of teeth.

**잇속**(利—) source of profit 〔gains〕. ¶ ~이 있다 be profitable 〔lucrative〕 / ~이 없다 be unprofitable; be lean / ~에 밝다 be alive 〔wide-awake〕 to *one's* interests; have a quick eye for a profit / ~ 있는 장사 a profitable business.

**잇자국** a tooth mark; a bite. ¶ ~이 나다 have 〔show〕 a tooth mark.

**잇줄**(利—) a lucrative connection; a road to gains.

**잇집** the socket of a tooth.

**있다** ① 《존재하다》 there is 〔are〕; be; exist; be in existence; 《책임·죄 따위가》 rest with; depend on. ¶ 그건 지금도 ~ It still exists. / 여기 열쇠가 ~ Here is a key. / 「내 책이 어디 있느냐」—「책상 위에 ~」 "Where's my book?" — "It's on the desk." / 책상 위에는 무엇이 있느냐 What is on the desk? / 책상 위에는 책이 있다 There is a book on the desk. / 세상에는 불가사의한 일들이 많이 있다 There are a lot of 「mysterious 〔strange〕 things in the world. / 옛날에 어진 임금이 있었다 Once there lived a wise king. / 너 어디 있었느냐 Where have you been? / 성패는 너의 수완 여하에 ~ The success depends on your ability. / 그 책임은 너에게 ~ The fault rests with you. / 네 뒤엔 내가 있으니 안심해라 Don't be anxious because I will always be behind you.
② 《머무르다》 stay; stop. ¶ 집에 ~ stay in; 《영》 stop in 〔indoors〕 / 너는 여기 있거라 You stay here.
③ 《시간의 경과》 time elapses. ¶ 좀 더 있으면 a little bit later on / (지금부터) 며칠 ~가 in a few days; a few days from now.
④ 《위치하다》 be; be located 〔situated〕; stand (건물이); lie (도시·호수 등이); run (도로·강 등이). ¶ 강가에 있는 절 a temple standing by the river / 일본은 한국 동쪽에 ~ Japan lies to the east of Korea. / 교회는 마을 한복판에 ~ The church stands 〔is located〕 in the center of the town. / 산 뒤에 시내가 ~ Behind the hill there runs a brook. / 학교 뒤에는 야산이 ~ A hill rises behind the school. / 서점은 여기서 걸어 10분 걸리는 곳에 ~ The bookstore is a ten-minute walk from here.
⑤ 《내재하다》 consist in; lie in. ¶ 행복은 만족에 ~ Happiness consists in contentment. / 그 작품의 매력은 이 점에 ~ The charm of this book lies 〔exists〕 in this point. / 결정권은 이사회에 ~ The power of decision resides in the board of directors.
⑥ 《소유하다》 have; possess; own; keep; contain; 《타고나다》 be endowed 〔blessed (좋은 것이)〕 with; be cursed with (나쁜 것이). ¶ 아들이 둘 ~ have two sons / 명성이 ~ bear a reputation / 그의 딸은 음악에 재주가 ~ His daughter 「is endowed with 〔posesses〕 musical talents. / 있는 돈을 다 썼다 I spent all the money I had. / 그녀에게는 막대한 재산이 ~ She has 〔owns〕 a vast fortune / 여가와 돈이 있으면 무엇을 하겠느냐 What would you do if

you had time and money to spare?/ 그 집에는 넓은 정원이 있다 The house has a large garden (to it).
⑦ 《휴대·판매하다》 carry; keep; sell; have; 《발견·입수하다》 find; get; [물건이 주어] be got; [사람이 주어] can get. ¶ 미제 담배 있나 Do you carry American cigarettes?/이것은 백화점에만 ~ This can be had only at a department store./비누 있습니까 Do you sell 〔keep〕 soaps?/그것은 어느 가게에나 ~ You can get it at any store./있던 데 갖다 둬라 Put it back where it was 〔you found it〕.
⑧ 《개최·거행되다》 be held; take place; open; come off. ¶ 다음 모임은 언제 있느냐 When is the next meeting to be held?/축하연은 언제 있소 When will the celebration come off?/어제 수학 시험이 있었다 We had an examination in mathematics yesterday./3시부터 교수 회의가 ~ The faculty meeting begins at three o'clock.
⑨ 《실재하다》 be. ¶ 있을 수 없는 impossible/있을 법한 probable; likely/그런 일이 있을 수 있을까 How can that be?/그런 이야기가 어디 있어 That is an impossible story./그런 일이 있을지도 모른다 That may be the case. *or* That may well be./그것은 있을 법하지도 않다 That, I think, is hardly likely.
⑩ 《발생하다》 break out; occur; happen; take place; there is 〔are〕. ¶ 무슨 일이 있든지 no matter what happens; come what may/신청이 있으면 in case 〔when〕 a request has been made/사고가 있었던 장소 the scene of a disaster/자주 있는 일 an everyday affair/있을 수 있는 잘못 a common mistake/간밤에 화재가 있었다 A fire broke out last night. *or* There was a fire last night./그 부부 사이에 무슨 일이 있었는지 나는 모릅니다 I don't know what has passed between that couple./그 한 해 동안에 많은 일이 있었다 Many things happened in that one year./이런 일은 두 번 다시 있어서는 안 된다 Such a thing must never happen again.
⑪ 《경험하다》 ¶ 이번 여행 중에는 여러 가지 일이 있었다 I have experienced various things during this trip./그에게 좋은 때가 있었다 He has seen better days./경주에 가본 일이 있습니까 Have you ever been to Kyŏngju?/이렇게 아름다운 경치를 본 일이 있습니까 Have you ever seen such a beautiful sight? (★ Did you ever see ...?는 「설마 없을 테지」의 뜻이 강해짐)/그 사람과는 한 번 만난 일이 ~ I remember seeing him once. *or* I have met him only once.
⑫ 《포함하다》 be contained 《in》; be included 《in》. ¶ 그 책에는 참고 문헌 목록이 ~ The book contains a bibliography./이 책에는 재미있는 이야기가 많이 ~ This book contains many interesting stories.
⑬ 《부속하다》 have 《*a thing*》 attached to 《it》; 《설비가》 be equipped; be fitted; be provided 《with》. ¶ 학교에는 기숙사가〔부속 병원이〕 ~ Our school has a dormitory 〔hospital〕 attached to it./집에는 목욕탕이 ~ The house is provided with a bathroom.
⑭ 《유복하다》 be rich 〔wealthy〕. ¶ 있는 사람 a well-off person/있는 집에 태어나다 be born rich; be born in a rich family; be born of rich parents.
⑮ 《동작의 계속》 be *do*ing; 《상태의 존속》 be; remain; keep *do*ing. ¶ 서 ~ keep standing/먹지 않고 ~ go without food/독신으로 ~ remain single/그는 책을 읽고 ~ He is reading./형은 장사를 하고 ~ My brother is engaged in business./담이 무너져 ~ The wall is broken.

**잉걸불** a lively burning charcoal fire.

**잉글랜드** England. ⇨ 영국(英國).

**잉꼬** 〖조류〗 a parakeet; a macaw; a cockatoo. ◉ ~부부 a devoted couple.

**잉아** 《직기의》 threads used to hold up the warp while weaving; warp ties.

**잉앗대** a warp-tie stick (on a loom).

**잉어**(一魚) 〖어류〗 a carp.

**잉여**(剩餘) surplus; the remainder; the residue; what is left over.
◉ ~가치 〖경제〗 surplus value. ~금 a surplus (fund). ~노동력 surplus labor. ~농산물 surplus agricultural 〔farm〕 products: 한미 ~ 농산물 협정 the Korea-U.S. Agreement for Surplus Agricultural Commodities/~농산물 도입 import of 《U.S.》 surplus farm products. ~물자〔식량, 재료〕 surplus articles 〔food, materials〕: ~ 물자 매각 surplus sales.

**잉잉** ¶ ~ 울다 whimper.

**잉카** Inca. ◉ ~문명 the Incan civilization. ~사람 an Inca(n). ~제국 the Inca empire. ~족 the Incas.

**잉크** ink. ¶ ~ 얼룩 an ink stain; an inkblot/등사〔제도〕 ~ copying 〔drafting] ink / ～ 냄새가 물씬 풍기는 새 신문 a newspaper fresh from the press / 펜과 ～로 쓰다 write with pen and ink / 펜촉에 ～를 찍다 dip a pen in ink / ～가 번지다 ink runs 〔spreads〕/ 빨간 ～로 쓰다 write in red ink. ◉ ～병 an ink bottle. ～스탠드 an inkstand. ～지우개 an ink eraser. 만년필(용) ～ ink for the fountain pen. 불변색～ indelible ink.

**잉태**(孕胎) = 임신(妊娠).

**잊다** ① 《물건을》 forget 《*a thing*》; forget to take 〔bring〕 《*a thing*》; leave 《*a thing*》 behind. ¶ 시계를 잊고 안 가져왔다 I forgot to bring my watch. / 자동차 키 갖고 오는 것을 잊었다 I forgot my car key. / 버스 안에 책을 놔둔채 잊고 왔다 I left my book (behind) in the bus. (★ 잊은 장소를 나타내는 부사구가 있는 문장에서는 left 대신 forget을 쓸 수 없음) / 뭐 잊어버리고 온 것은 없니 Are you sure you have not left anything behind?

② 《망각하다》 forget; be forgetful 〔oblivious〕 《of, about》; [사물이 주어] slip *one's* mind; escape *one's* memory. ¶ 잊을 수 없는 날 a never-to-be-forgotten day / 잊지 않고 without forgetting / 침식을 ～ forget *one's* sleep and food; be devoted to 《*a thing*》 (몰두하다) / 은혜를 ～ forget 《*a person's*》 kindness; be ungrateful / 본분을 ～ be unmindful of *one's* duty / 잊기 잘 하다 be forgetful 〔oblivious〕 / 사람의 이름을 잘 ～ have a bad memory for people's names / 근심 걱정을 잊고 독서하다 read unmindful of cares and worries / 한시도 잊지 않고 있다 keep 《*a matter*》 in mind all the time / 잊지 말고 손을 씻어라 Don't forget to wash your hands. / 일 년 동안에 영어를 다 잊었다 Here, it is only a year and I have forgotten all my English. / 그의 이름을 깜박 잊었다 His name has quite escaped me. / 아무래도 오늘 아침 무언가 잊어버린 게 있는 것 같은데 I can't help feeling there's something I forgot this morning. / 나이를 먹으면 잊기를 잘 한다 One's memory fails (one) with age. / 평화가 오래 계속되면 평화의 귀중함을 잊기 쉽다 We tend to forget the value of peace after a long spell of peace.

③ 《의식적으로》 get 《*a matter*》 off *one's* mind; put 《*a matter*》 out of *one's* mind; think no more of; dismiss 《*a matter*》 from *one's* mind. ¶ 그는 그녀를 잊을 수 없었다 He couldn't put her out of his thoughts. *or* He couldn't get her out of his mind. / 그것은 잊을래야 잊을 수 없다 It haunts my memory. / 그 일은 다 잊어라 Don't think about it any more. *or* Forget all about it. / 그는 술로 슬픔을 잊으려고 애를 썼다 He tried hard to drown his sorrows.

**잊히다** be forgotten; escape *one's* memory; slip 〔pass from〕 *one's* mind; be buried in oblivion. ¶ 잊히지 않는 일 an unforgettable event / 세상에서 잊혀지다 be sunk 〔buried〕 in oblivion; die from the memory of the world / 그녀가 잊혀지지 않았다 She was always on my mind.

**잎** a leaf (*pl.* leaves); 《작은》 a leaflet; 《풀잎》 a blade; 《침엽》 a needle; 《양치류의》 a frond; [총칭] foliage; leafage. ¶ 나뭇잎 leaves of the tree / 풀잎 blades of grass / 우거진 잎 thick foliage / 잎이 우거진 leafy / 잎이 없는 leafless; bare / 잎이 무성한 버드나무 a willow with thick leafage / 잎이 나오다 the leaves are 〔come〕 out; [나무가 주어] come into 〔be in〕 leaf / 잎이 떨어지다 become leafless / 잎이 다 떨어졌다 The leaves are all gone off the trees.

**잎나무** brushwood.

**잎눈** 『식물』 a leaf bud.

**잎담배** leaf tobacco.

**잎맥**(一脈) 『식물』 a vein (of a leaf); a nerve; a nervure.

**잎벌레** a (green-)leaf insect.

**잎사귀** a leaf; a leaflet.

**잎샘** a cold spell in early spring (when trees start leafing); lingering cold in the leafing season. ¶ ～을 하다 get cold in leafing time.

**잎자루** 『식물』 a petiole; a leafstalk.

**잎차례**(一次例) 『식물』 a phyllotaxy.

**잎채소**(一菜蔬) green vegetables; edible herbs.

**잎파랑이** 『식물』 《엽록소》 chlorophyl(l). ⇨ 엽록소(葉綠素).

ㅈ

**자**[1] ① 《길이를 재는》 a ruler; a (measuring) rule; a straightedge (직선의); a measure; a (T) square (직각의). ¶ 자로 재다 measure with a rule / 자로 잰 것처럼 as precisely as a square; like clockwork; to a T 〔tee〕 / 자를 대고 줄을 긋다 rule lines 《on paper》; draw lines with a ruler. ② 《길이 단위》 *cha;* the Korean foot(=30.3 cm). ¶ 옷감을 자로 팔다 sell cloth by the measure / 자가 모자라다 be short of measure; be wanting in length / 이 옷감은 꼭 다섯 자다 This cloth measures five *cha* exactly. 「자작(子爵).

**자**[1](子) ① 《자식》 a son; a child. ② ⇨

**자**[2](子) 『민속』 ① 《십이지의》 the Sign of the Rat 〔Mouse〕 (=the first of the 12 Earth's Branches). ② ⇨ 자방(子方). ③ ⇨ 자시(子時).

**자**(字) ① 《글자》 a letter; a character; 《낱말》 a word; an ideograph (한자 등). ¶ 큰 자 a big letter / 작은 자로 쓴 written in tiny lettering / 낫 놓고 기역자도 모르다 be utterly illiterate / 영어라고는 한 자도 모른다 I do not know a word of English. ② 《이름》 a name 〔style〕 taken at the age of twenty; *one's* "courtesy name"; a pseudonym.

**자**(者) 《사람》 a person; a fellow; one. ¶ 그 자 he; that fellow / 김이란 자 one 〔a〕 Kim; a man named Kim / 죽은 자와 다친 자 the dead and (the) injured / 그는 홍길동이란 자이다 His name is Hong Kildong. / 그 자리에서 죽은 자도 있다 Some were killed on the spot. / 가난한 자는 복이 있나니 Those who are poor shall be blessed.

**자**[2] 《주의 환기》 Come on!; Come now!; Here!; Here you are! ¶ 자, 그것 봐라 I told you! / 자, 오너라 Come on! / 자, 가자 Come, let us go! / 자, 한잔 마시자 Come on, let's have a drink. / 자, 택시가 왔다—빨리 타라 Here comes your cab—get in quick. / 자, 출발합시다 Let's start now, shall we? / 자, 그럼 잘 있거라 So-long. / 자, 네게 선물이다 Here's a present for you. / 자, 쏠 테면 쏘아라 Go ahead and shoot, if you are going to. / 자, 어때요, 내가 말한 대로죠 There, I told you so.

**자**-(自) 《부터》 from…. ¶ 자오전 10시 지(至)오후 3시 from 10 a.m. to 3 p.m.

**자**-(雌) 《암컷》 she-; female.

-**자** ① 《어미》 let's. ¶ 가자 Let's go. / 먹자 Let's eat. / 앉자 Let's sit down. / 어디 보자 Let's see now. ② 《…하자 곧》 as soon as; no sooner than; when; on; at. ¶ 집에 들어가자… on entering the house / 소식을 듣자… at the news 《of》 / 나를 보자 도망쳤다 He ran off the moment he saw me. / 그는 아침에 일어나자 곧 의사에게 갔다 The first thing in the morning he went to the doctor. / 그녀는 나를 보자 울음보를 터뜨렸다 On seeing me, she burst into cry. *or* No sooner had she seen me, she burst into cry.

**자가**(自家) *one's* own house 〔family〕. ¶ ~제의 homemade; 《a boat》 of *one's* own making; 《a chair》 *one* made *oneself* / 이것은 ~제의 포도주다 This is homemade wine.
◉ ~당착 self-contradiction: ~당착하다 contradict *oneself* / ~당착의 의론 a self-contradictory argument. ~발전장치 an independent (electric) power plant. ~수분(受粉) 『식물』 self-pollination. ~수정 『생물』 self-fertilization. ~시설 *one's* own facilities: ~ 시설을 갖춘 출판사 a publishing firm with its own printing plant. ~전염 autoinfection. ~중독 autotoxemia; autointoxication: ~ 중독을 일으키다 cause autotoxemia 〔autointoxication〕. ~치료 self-treatment; home treatment: ~ 치료를 하다 doctor 〔treat〕 *oneself;* try home treatment.

**자가용**(自家用) ① 《개인용》 private 〔domestic〕 use; personal use; family use (가정용). ¶ ~의 for private 〔domestic, family〕 use; for home consumption; private; personal. ② 《자가용차》 a private car 〔automobile〕; an automobile for *one's* personal use; an owner-driven car. ¶ 너를 내 ~으로 부산까지 데려다 주겠다 I'll drive you down to Pusan in my car. ◉ ~운전사 a chauffeur in *one's* employ. ~족

those who have their own cars; 《자신이 운전하는》 an owner driver.

**자각**(自覺) consciousness; self-consciousness; self-knowledge; (self-) awakening; awareness. ～하다 become conscious 〔aware〕 of; realize; awaken to. ¶ 아무에게 그의 직책의 중대함을 ～시키다 awaken *a person* to the importance of *his* position / 자기의 결점을 ～하다 realize 〔become conscious of〕 *one's* deficiencies / 국민의 ～을 기다리다 wait for the self-awakening of the nation / 그에게는 사회인이라는 ～이 없다 He isn't conscious that he is an adult member of society. / 공해를 막는 일에는 시민의 ～이 필요하다 Citizens have to be aware (of) what they should do to control pollution. ◉ ～증상 a subjective symptom: 이 병은 종종 환자에게 전혀 ～ 증상이 없는 경우가 있다 Patients with this disease very often have no subjective symptoms (of it).

**자간**(子癎) 〖의학〗 eclampsia.

**자갈** gravel; (small) pebbles; shingle (강변의); ballast (철길에 까는). ¶ 길〔철길〕에 ～을 깔다 「gravel a road 〔ballast a railroad〕 / 도로에 ～이 깔려 있다 The road is graveled 〔covered with gravel〕. ◉ ～길 a gravel(ed) road 〔walk〕. ～밭 a gravelly field. ～채취 gravel-digging: ～채취장 a gravel pit. ～하치장 a gravel yard.

**자갈색**(紫褐色) purplish brown.

**자강**(自强) strenuous efforts. ～하다 make strenuous efforts. ◉ ～불식(不息) ceaseless endeavors. ～술 the art of 「health building 〔physical fitness〕; (ways of) keeping *oneself* fit.

**자개** mother-of-pearl; nacre. ¶ ～를 박다 inlay with mother-of-pearl. ◉ ～그릇 a wooden 〔vessel〕 inlaid with mother-of-pearl. ～단추 a mother-of-pearl button. ～세공 《a piece of》 mother-of-pearl work. ～장〔상〕 a cabinet 〔table〕 inlaid with mother-of-pearl.

**자개미** the armpit; the crook 〔hollow〕 of the knee 〔arm〕.

**자객**(刺客) an assassin; an assassinator; a killer. ¶ ～의 손에 죽다〔쓰러지다〕 die at the hands of an assassin; be assassinated; fall a victim to an assassin's dagger.

**자격**(資格) 《신분》 capacity; 《지위·직업 등의》 qualification(s); a requirement (필요 요건); eligibility (입회 자격); 《능력》 competence; 《권리》 a right. ¶ …의 ～이 있는 qualified; competent; certified; capable; eligible / …의 ～으로 in *one's* capacity as 《a stockholder》 / 개인 ～으로 in *one's* individual capacity / …할〔의〕 ～이 있다 be qualified 〔competent〕 「to *do* 〔for…〕 / …할〔의〕 ～이 없다 be unqualified 〔incompetent〕 「to *do* 〔for *do*ing〕; have no right 「to *do* 〔for *do*ing〕 / ～을 잃다 be disqualified 《for, as》 / ～을 주다 qualify 《*a person* for a teacher》; entitle 《*a person* to admission》 / ～을 얻다 obtain qualifications 《for》 / ～을 빼앗다 disqualify 《*a person* from 〔for〕 a teacher》 / 그녀는 간호사 ～이 있다 She is qualified as a nurse. / 그에겐 그것을 비평할 ～이 있다 He is competent to criticize it. *or* He has a right to criticize it. / 회원 ～에 남녀의 제한은 없다 Membership is not limited by sex. / 정회원이 될 ～이 있다 You are eligible to full membership. / 그는 대표자 ～으로 파견되었다 He was sent in a representative capacity. / 그는 교사로서의 ～을 충분히 갖추고 있다 He is quite a competent teacher. / 그녀는 시간 강사 ～으로 고용되었다 She was employed as a part-time teacher. / 나는 개인〔공인〕 ～으로 이것을 말씀드립니다 I am expressing this to you in a private 〔public〕 capacity. / 이익 분배에 참여할 ～은 나에게도 있다 I am entitled to a share in the profit. ◉ ～검정시험 a qualifying examination. ～기준 qualification criteria. ～상실 disqualification. ～심사 an examination of the applicants' 〔the candidates'〕 qualifications; a (preliminary) qualification exam; screening. ～정지 suspension of qualification. ～증명서 a certificate of qualification.

**자격지심**(自激之心) 《자책》 a guilty conscience; a feeling of self-accusation 〔self-reproach〕. ¶ ～을 가지다 have a guilty conscience / 그것은 그의 ～에서 나온 말이다 He said that out of self-accusation.

**자결**(自決) ① 《스스로 결정》 self-determination. ～하다 determine by *oneself*. ¶ 민족 ～ racial self-determination. ② 《자살》 suicide. ～하다 kill *oneself*; commit suicide. ¶ 군중 앞에서 ～하다 commit suicide in the presence of the crowd.

**자경단**(自警團) a vigilante group 〔corps〕. ¶ ～원 a vigilante.

**자계**(自戒) self-discipline. ~하다 admonish *oneself;* caution *oneself* 《against》; take care 《not to repeat the same error》.

**자계**(磁界) a magnetic field. = 자기장(磁氣場).

**자고**(鷓鴣) 〖조류〗 a partridge; a francolin.

**자고깨면** whenever *one* awakes from sleep; all the time; every (waking) minute; always; from morning till night. ¶ 그는 ~ 그것만 생각한다 The matter is ever present in his mind. / 그들은 ~ 정치 이야기다 Politics is constantly on their lips.

**자고로**(自古―) from ancient 〔old(en)〕 times; since early times; traditionally. ¶ ~ 성공한 사람은 반드시 시간을 중히 여겼다 There never was a man who won success without husbanding his time. / ~ 이런 사건은 없었다 There is no parallel to this incident in all history. / 몽고 민족은 ~ 유목민이었다 Mongolians have been nomads from time immemorial.

**자고새면** when the day breaks; if only another day breaks; one more night and….

**자괴지심**(自愧之心) a sense of shame. ¶ ~이 있다 have 〔feel〕 a sense of shame; be sensible to shame / ~이 전혀 없다 be lost 〔dead〕 to all sense of shame.

**자구**(字句) terms; words and phrases; wording; 《법률의》 the letter 《of the law》. ¶ ~의 verbal / ~에 구애되다 be letter-bound; adhere too closely to the wording; keep 〔stick, adhere〕 to the letter 《of the law》 / ~를 수정하다 make some changes in the wording / ~ 그대로 해석하다 interpret literally / 번역을 할 때는 원문 ~에 지나치게 구애되어서는 안된다 In translation you must not adhere blindly to the original wording.

**자구행위**(自救行爲) 〖법〗 self-help. ¶ ~를 하다 take action for self-defense; take self-defense measures.

**자국** 《흔적》 a mark; traces (★ 보통 복수형); 《눌러진》 a print; an impression; a stain (얼룩); a track (한줄기의); a trail (지나간); a spoor (짐승의); a scar (상처의). ¶ 이빨 ~ (a) toothmark (*pl.* teethmarks) / 신발 ~ a shoe mark; a footprint / 눈물 ~ trace of tears / 물린 ~ a mark made by biting; a bite / 긁힌 ~ a scratch / 수레가〔차량이〕 지나간 ~ the track of a wagon 〔a car〕; ruts (바퀴의) / 지운 연필 ~ traces of erased pencil marks / 마마 ~이 있는 얼굴 a pockmarked face / ~(이) 나다 get marked / ~을 남기다〔남기지 않다〕 leave 「*one's* traces 〔no trace〕 behind *one* / 발~을 쫓다 follow up a trace 〔track〕; follow the trail 《of a criminal》; trail; trace; track / 시체에는 칼~이 있었다 The body bore marks of a knife. / 카펫에 커피를 흘리면 ~이 남는다 If you spill coffee on the carpet, it will leave a mark (on it). ◉ ~눈 light snow. ~물 water gathered in footmarks; a small puddle.

**자국**(自國) *one's* (own) country; *one's* native land; *one's* fatherland; *one's* home 〔mother〕 country. ¶ ~의 native; home; 《언어의》 vernacular / ~ 제품의 homemade. ◉ ~민 *one's* fellow countrymen. ~어 *one's* mother 〔native〕 tongue; the vernacular: ~어 신문 vernacular dailies / 그녀는 영어를 ~어처럼 말한다 She speaks English as if she were born to it. *or* She speaks English like a native (speaker).

**자궁**(子宮) the womb; 〖해부〗 the uterus (*pl.* -ri). ¶ ~의 uterine. ◉ ~경암(頸癌) cervical cancer; cancer of the cervix. ~근종(筋腫) a myoma of the uterus. ~내막염 endometritis. ~병 a uterine disease. ~암 uterine cancer; cancer of the womb. ~염 metritis. ~외 임신 extrauterine 〔ectopic〕 pregnancy. ~전굴 anteflexion. ~절개 hysterotomy. ~절제(술) hysterectomy. ~출혈 metrorrhagia. ~후굴 retroflexion 〔retroversion〕 of the uterus.

**자귀**[1] 《연장》 an adze; an adz. ¶ ~질하다 adz(e); dress roughly with an adze. ◉ 자귓밥 chips from an adze.

**자귀**[2] 〖수의〗 a dog 〔pig〕 ailment caused by overeating.

**자그마치** a little; a few; some; [반어적으로] as much 〔many, long〕 as. ¶ 술을 ~ 마셔라 Don't drink too much. / 그 열차 사고에 ~ 20명이나 사상자가 났다 As many as twenty passengers were killed or wounded in that train wreck. / ~ 10만 원이나 손해가 났다 The loss is as much as 100,000 won.

**자그마하다** (be) smallish; small; small=sized; be of a somewhat small size; be rather on the small side. ¶ 자그마한 rather small; small statured; undersized / 키가 자그마한 사람 a person of smallish stature / 그는 몸집이 자그마한 편이었다 He was rather of small build.

**자극**(刺戟) 《자극물》 an incentive; a spur; a stimulus (*pl.* -li); an impetus; an impulse; 《자극하는 일》 stimulation; impulsion; incitement; 《격려》 encouragement. ～하다 stimulate; excite; incite; give an impetus 《to》; irritate 《the skin》. ¶ ～이 강한 exciting; thrilling; sensational / ～이 없는 dull; boring; monotonous / ～성의 stimulative; irritant; incentive; excitant; pungent (향기·냄새 따위가) / …에 ～ 받아 under the stimulus of…; spurred by… / ～이 되다 be a stimulus 《to》; serve as a stimulus 《to》 / ～을 받다 receive stimulation / ～을 찾다 look for some excitement / ～에 반응하다 react to a stimulus / 새로운 ～을 받다 receive a fresh impetus 《from》 / 신경을 ～하다 stimulate the nerves; 《the sounds》 get 〔jar〕 on *one's* nerves / 호기심을 ～하다 excite *one's* curiosity / 식욕을 ～하다 stimulate *one's* appetite / 흥미는 공부하는 데 ～이 된다 Interest is an incitement to study. ◉ ～성 음식 pungent food and drink; spicy food. ～제〔물〕 a stimulant; an excitant; an irritant.

**자극**(磁極) 〖물리〗 a magnetic pole. ◉ ～성 magnetic polarity.

**자금**(資金) funds; (a) capital (자본); 《기금》 a fund. ¶ 운전〔운동, 회전, 건축, 구제, 준비, 기밀〕 ～ a working 〔campaign, revolving, building, relief, reserve, discretionary〕 fund / ～ 고갈 fund starvation / ～ 공급 funding; financing; bankrolling / ～ 회전 turn of capital / 풍부한 ～ ample funds / ～이 있다 〔떨어지다〕 be in 〔out of〕 funds / ～이 부족하다 be short of funds; be poorly 〔insufficiently〕 funded / ～을 대다 furnish 〔provide〕 funds; finance 〔fund〕 《an enterprise》 / ～을 조달하다〔모으다〕 raise capital 〔funds〕 《for》 / ～을 융통해주다 accommodate 《*a person*》 with money / ～ 사정의 어려움을 겪다 suffer from financial difficulties / 적은 ～으로 장사를 시작하다 start business with a small amount of capital / ～ 출처를 조사하다 probe into the sources of funds 〔money〕 / 그 회사는 ～ 공급이 원활하다 The company is well-financed. / 새 공장을 짓는 데 ～이 모자란다 We are short of funds for building a new factory. ◉ ～공여협정 agreement on loan provision. ～동결 freezing of funds. ～부족 shortage of funds: ～ 부족으로 for lack of funds. ～수급계획 a fund supply and demand program. ～수요 demand for credit 〔finance〕; capital requirements. ～순환 money flow: ～ 순환 분석 money-flow analysis. ～압박 the financial strains. ～조달 financing: ～ 조달 운동 a fund-raising campaign. ～원(源) a source of funds. ～출처 《probe 〔dig〕 into》 the sources of (operation) funds 〔money〕. ～화 capitalization: ～화하다 capitalize; convert 《goods》 into money.

**자금난**(資金難) financial difficulty; lack of funds; difficulty in cash flow. ¶ ～으로 for lack 〔want〕 of funds / ～을 완화하다 ease *one's* 〔its〕 financial difficulties / 우리 회사는 ～에 빠져 있다 Our company is in financial difficulty. / 사업은 ～으로 궁지에 처해 있다 The business came to a standstill for lacks of capital.

**자급**(自給) self-support; self-sustenance. ～하다 support *oneself;* provide for *oneself;* be self-sustaining. ¶ ～하는 self-supporting; self-sustaining / 우리는 식량 ～을 위해 노력해야 한다 We should try to become self-sufficient in food production. ◉ ～경제 self-sufficient economy; autarky: ～경제주의 autarky. ～률 (the degree of) self-sufficiency 《in oil》.

**자급자족**(自給自足) self-sufficiency. ～하다 be self-sufficient 《in》. ¶ ～의 self-sufficient; self-sustaining; self-sufficing; self-contained / ～을 위한 정책 a self-sufficient policy / ～ 상태 the condition of self-sufficiency / 경제적 ～ economic independence; autarky / 경제적 ～을 이루다 achieve 〔attain〕 economic self-sufficiency / 그는 ～ 생활을 하고 있다 He provides for himself. *or* His life is self-sufficient. / 북한은 아직 식량을 ～하지 못하고 있다 With regard to food, North Korea has not yet attained self-sufficiency.

**자긍**(自矜) 《자만》 self-conceit; 《긍지》 pride; self-esteem. ～하다 pride *oneself* 《on》; feel proud 《that…》. ◉ ～심 pride.

**자기**(自己) *one's* self; oneself. ¶ ～의 *one's* own; personal; private / ～ 스스로 *oneself;* personally; for 〔by〕 *oneself;* single-handed / ～ 생각만 하다

think of *oneself* only / ～ 마음대로 하다 do as *one* pleases / ～를 반성하다 reflect on *oneself* / ～를 대단한 존재로 생각하다 think much of *oneself;* be self-conceited / ～ 자신을 알다 know *oneself* / ～ 과시욕이 강하다 be「self-assertive 〔pushy, obtrusive〕; be excessively self-confident / ～의 이익을 꾀하다 look to *one's* own interests / 그녀는 ～ 옷은 자기가 만든다 She makes her own dress. / ～ 일은 자기가 해라 Look after yourself. / 그는 ～가 옳다고 생각한다 He believes himself in the right. / 그는 기자라고 ～ 신분을 밝혔다 He identified himself as a reporter. / 그는 ～ 중심적이기 때문에 나는 그와 교제를 계속할 수는 없다 I can't keep up with him, because he's self-centered. ◉ ～감응 〖전기〗 self-induction. ～개혁 self-reformation. ～경멸 self-contempt. ～과시 self-display. ～관찰 self-observation. ～기만 self-deception. ～도취 narcissism; self-absorption: ～ 도취증 narcissism; narcism. ～류: ～류의 《(a painting》 after *one's* own style; self-taught / ～류로 in *one's* own way; after 〔in〕 *one's* own style. ～만족 self-satisfaction〔-contentment〕; (self-)complacence. ～모순 self-contradiction: ～모순의 self-contradictory; inconsistent. ～방위 self-protection. ～변호 self-justification; an excuse: ～ 변호하다 defend 〔justify〕 *oneself.* ～보존 self-preservation. ～본위 egotism; egoism; egocentricity; self-centeredness; selfishness: ～ 본위의 사람 a self-centered person; an egotist; an egoist. ～부담: ～ 부담하다 pay *one's* own expenses / 교통비는 ～부담이다 Everyone must pay his own carfare. ～부정 self-denial. ～분석 self-analysis. ～비판 self-criticism: ～비판하다 criticize *oneself* 〔*one's* own faults, *one's* past deeds〕. ～선전 self-advertisement; self-display: ～ 선전을 하다 advertise *oneself;* seek publicity. ～소개 self-introduction; ～ 소개를 하다 introduce *oneself.* ～소외 〖철학〗 self-alienation. ～수양(修養) self-culture; self-discipline. ～숭배(崇拜) self-worship. ～실현 self-realization. ～암시 autosuggestion: ～암시에 걸리다 be subjected to autosuggestion. ～앞수표 a cashier's check; a bank 〔banker's〕 check. ～억제 self-restriction〔-restraint〕; self-control. ～의식 a sense of self; self-identification. ～일 *one's* own 〔personal〕 affair: *one's* personal concern: ～ 일처럼 슬퍼하다 sorrow 《over a friend's misfortune》 as if it were *one's*「personal concern 〔own affair〕. ～자금 *one's* own money. ～자본 equity 〔owned〕 capital. ～조정 self-adjustment〔-regulation〕. ～주장 self-assertion: ～ 주장을 하다 assert *oneself* / 그는 ～ 주장이 강하다 He is very self-assertive. *or* He insists on having his own way. ～중심= ～본위. ～중심주의 egocentrism. ～증식 〖생물〗 self-reproduction; self-replication. ～최면 autohypnosis; self-hypnosis: ～ 최면에 걸린 self-hypnotized. ～충족 self-fulfillment: 물질적 성공보다 ～ 충족을 중시하다 stress self-fulfillment over material success. ～포기 self-renunciation. ～현시욕: ～현시욕이 강한 self-assertive; pushy; aggressively self-confident; obtrusive. ～혐오 self-abhorrence; self-hatred; self-hate: ～ 혐오에 빠지다 yield to self-hatred. ～희생 self-sacrifice.

**자기**(自記) 《자신의》 writing by *oneself;* 《자동 장치의》 self-registration. ¶ ～의 self-recording〔-registering〕. ◉ ～온도계〔우량계〕 a self-registering thermometer 〔rain gauge〕.

**자기**(瓷器) china(ware); porcelain.

**자기**(磁氣) 〖물리〗 magnetism. ¶ ～를 띤 magnetic / ～를 띠게 하다 magnetize; make a magnet of / ～를 없애다 demagnetize. ◉ ～감응〔저항〕 〖물리〗 magnetic induction 〔reluctance〕. ～검출기 a magnetoscope. ～공명 〖물리〗 magnetic resonance. ～권 the magnetosphere. ～기뢰 a magnetic mine. ～나침의 a magnetic compass. ～녹음 magnetic recording. ～디스크 〖컴퓨터〗 a magnetic disc. ～부상 열차 a magnetically-levitated 〔maglev〕 train. ～유도 〖물리〗 magnetic induction. ～잉크 magnetic ink. ～자오선 the magnetic meridian. ～측정 magnetometry. ～테이프 magnetic tape; mag tape. ～폭풍 a magnetic storm. ～학 magnetics: ～학자 a magnetist.

**자기력**(磁氣力) 〖물리〗 magnetic force 〔power, attraction〕; magnetism. ¶ ～의 magnetic / ～(작용)으로 magnetically. ◉ ～계(計) a magnetometer. ～선 a line of magnetic force.

**자기장**(磁氣場) 〖물리〗 a magnetic field. ¶ ～의 세기〔방향〕 the intensity 〔direction〕 of the magnetic field.

**자기화**(磁氣化) 〖물리〗 magnetization. ～

하다 magnetize; become 〔be〕 magnetized. ◉ ～율 susceptibility. ～전류 a magnetizing current.

**자깝스럽다** 《조숙하다》 pretend to be older than *one* be; pose as a grown=up man; put on an oldish air; assume a dignified air.

**자꾸** ① 《되풀이하여》 repeatedly; again and again; over and over; 《자주》 often; frequently. ¶ 문을 ～ 두드리다 knock repeatedly on the door / 같은 실험을 ～ 하다 repeat the same experiment over and over / 시청자로부터 문의 전화가 ～ 걸려 왔다 We had repeated telephone calls from TV viewers inquiring about it. ② 《잇달아·늘》 constantly; incessantly; always; continuously; 《열심히》 hard; eagerly; intently. ¶ ～ 얼굴을 보다 look hard at 《*a person*》 / ～ 권하다 urge 《*a person*》 strongly 《to *do*》 / 비가 ～ 온다 It keeps on raining. / 그 아이는 사과를 ～ 달란다 The child keeps asking for an apple. / 그는 ～ 나에게 구혼해 왔다 He eagerly proposed me to marry him.

**자나깨나** (whether) awake or asleep; waking or sleeping. ¶ ～ 그 여자를 잊을 수가 없었다 I could not get her out of my mind awake or asleep. / 그는 ～ 그 일만 생각하고 있다 The thought is ever present in his mind. / ～ 그 일이 마음에 걸려 있다 Waking or sleeping, it's on my mind. 「Pole.

**자남극**(磁南極) the South Magnetic

**자낭**(子囊) 〖식물〗 spore case; an ascus (*pl.* asci); a sporangium. ◉ ～균 an ascomycete; a sac fungus. ～포자 an ascospore.

**자네** you. ¶ ～의 your / ～것 yours / ～자신 yourself / ～들 자신 yourselves / ～ 집 your house / ～ 여기 앉게나 You sit here. / 어, 자넨가 Oh, it's you.

**자녀**(子女) sons and daughters; children; offspring. ¶ ～의 교육〔교육비〕 「the education 〔the educational expenditure〕 of *one's* children / "한 ～ 낳기" 운동 the "one child per family" campaign / "두 ～ 이하 낳기" 운동 the "two-or-less-children-a-family" campaign / 그들은 양가집 ～이다 They come of a good family.

**자늑자늑하다** (be) soft-moving; gentle; swaying; supple; graceful. ¶ 그녀는 몸가짐이 ～ She has a graceful deportment.

**자다** ① 《잠을》 sleep; go 〔get〕 to sleep (★ get to sleep는 부정문에서 쓰임); slumber; fall asleep; 《자리에 들다》 go 〔get〕 to bed; retire (to bed); 《구어》 turn in. ¶ 잘 시간 bedtime / 잠을 잘〔못〕 ～ sleep 「well 〔badly〕 / 푹 ～ sleep soundly; lie sound asleep / 곤드라지게 ～ sleep like a log / 낮잠 ～ take a (midday) nap / 밤새껏 한잠 못 ～ lie awake all night / 잠 안 자고 간호하다 watch 〔sit up〕 with 《an invalid》 / 잠 안 자고 있다 sit up (all night); 《못 자고》 lie 〔be kept〕 awake / 일찍 ～ go to bed early / 일찍 자고 일찍 일어나다 keep early hours / 늦잠 ～ sleep late / 너무 ～ oversleep *oneself* / 잠 안 자고 기다리다 wait up 《for》 / 잠 안 자고 생각하다 「consult with 〔take counsel of〕 *one's* pillow / 두서너 시간 ～ get two or three hours' sleep; sleep (for) two or three hours / 옷 입은 채 ～ sleep without changing dress / 잘 시간이다 It is bedtime. *or* It is time for you to go to bed. *or* It is time you went to bed. (★ 「이미 자고 있었을 시간」이란 뜻으로 과거형인 went를 취함). ② 《물결·바람이》 calm down; die down; abate; get lulled; go down; abate; subside. ¶ 바람이 ～ a wind 「dies 〔goes, sinks〕 down / 파도가 ～ a sea goes down. ③ 《결이》 get 「pressed 〔smoothed〕 down; take a set. ¶ 머리가 ～ *one's* hair sets. ④ 《기계가》 stop; run down. ¶ 시계가 ～ a clock 「stops 〔runs down〕.

**자단**(紫檀) 〖식물〗 a red sandalwood; a rosewood; 《재목》 rosewood.

**자담하다**(自擔—) pay *one's* own way; bear *one's* own expense; take care of *one's* own share.

**자당**(慈堂) your 〔his, her〕 (esteemed) mother. 「saccharose.

**자당**(蔗糖) cane sugar; 〖화학〗 sucrose;

**자동**(自動) automatic 「movement 〔motion, action, operation〕; automatism. ～하다 move automatically. ¶ ～식의 automatic / 반～식의 semiautomatic / ～적으로 automatically; 《기계적》 mechanically / ～적으로 태엽이 감기는 self-winding 《watch》 / 이 기계는 ～적으로 움직인다 The machine works by itself. / 이 문은 ～적으로 개폐된다 This door opens and closes automatically. ◉ ～감지기 an automatic sensing device. ～개찰기 an automatic 「turnstile 〔ticket gate〕. ～권총 an automatic (pistol). ～금전 출납기 an automatic paying machine. ～기계 an automatic machine; an automaton. ～노출 automatic exposure. ～문 an automatic door; a self-operating door. ~방향 탐지기《항공기의》 automatic direction finder(생략 ADF). ~번역기 an automatic translation machine. ~변속 장치 an automatic transmission〔drive〕. ~성(性) automatism. ~소총 an automatic rifle. ~소화장치《건물 내부의》 sprinkler system. ~식자〔주식〕기 a monotype; a linotype. ~안정 장치 〖항공〗 a stabilizer; a gyrostabilizer. ~엘리베이터 an automatic elevator. ~연결 장치 an automatic coupler. ~예금기《은행의》 an automatic depositor. ~유도 장치 a homing device. ~인형 an automaton (*pl.* -ta, ~s). ~작용 an automatic action. ~장치 an automaton (*pl.* -ta, ~s). ~점화기 an automatic lighter. ~제어 〖기계〗 automatic control: ~제어(장치) an automatic controller / ~ 열차 제어(장치) automatic train control (생략 ATC). ~조작 automatic operation; 〖기계〗 automation. ~조정 self-adjustment: ~ 조정기 an automatic regulator. ~조종 장치《비행기·배 등의》 an automatic pilot; an autopilot; a gyropilot. ~추적: ~ 추적하다 automatically follow and find《a target》; 《레이더·미사일 등의》 lock onto *something*. ~판매기 a vending〔slot《영》〕machine; 《식품의》 an automat: 담배〔캔음료〕 ~ 판매기 a cigarette〔soft-drink〕vending machine; vending machine for cigarettes〔soft-drink〕. ~피아노 a Pianola; a player piano. ~현금 지급기 an automated cash dispenser; a cash machine. ~화기 automatic weapons〔firearms〕. ~화재 경보기 an automatic fire alarm. ~휴회 an automatic〔a spontaneous〕recess.

**자동사**(自動詞) an intransitive verb; a verb intransitive (생략 vi.). ¶ 불완전 ~ an incomplete intransitive verb.

**자동승인**(自動承認) automatic approval. ◉ ~제 the automatic approval system. ~품목 immediate import liberal items.

**자동차**(自動車) a (motor) car; an automobile; 《미구어》 an auto (*pl.* ~s); a motor vehicle [총칭]. ¶ 화물 ~《미》 a truck; 《영》 a lorry / 소형〔중형, 대형〕 ~ a compact〔medium-sized, large〕car / 지붕 개폐형 ~ a convertible car / 자가용〔경주용, 대절용〕 ~ a private〔racing, rental〕car / 배달용 ~ a delivery truck / 자갈을 만재한 화물 ~ a fully loaded gravel truck / ~의 행렬 a motorcade《미》 / ~의 안전성 car safety / ~로 by car / ~ 한 대분의 짐 a truck-load《of *something*》 / ~를 몰다〔운전하다〕 motor; drive a car; have a motor ride / ~를 타다 ride in〔get in, get on〕a car; take〔have〕a motor ride / ~에 태우다 give《*a person*》 a ride〔lift〕in a car / ~로 가다 go by car〔in a car〕; drive〔motor〕《to Pusan》 / ~로 드라이브 가다 go out for a drive《to》 / ~로 역까지 가다 drive〔taxi〕to the railroad station / ~에서 내리다 get off〔alight from〕a car / ~를 세워두다 park a car / 집에까지 ~로 데려다주다 drive《*a person*》 home in *one's* car / 여기에 ~를 주차시켜서는 안 된다 You must not park your car here.

◉ ~경주 an auto race; motor racing: ~ 경주 선수 a racing driver / ~경주장 an auto〔a motor〕race track. ~공업〔산업〕《미》 the automobile〔car〕industry; 《영》 the motor〔car〕industry. ~공해 automobile pollution. ~도둑《사람》 a car〔an auto〕thief〔lifter〕; 《행위》 car〔auto〕theft. ~매매업자 a car〔motor〕dealer. ~메이커〔회사〕 an automaker; an automobile company. ~번호판 a number plate. ~보험 automobile insurance. ~부대 〖군사〗 a motorized unit. ~부품 an autocomponent. ~사고 a motor(-ing)〔an auto〕accident; 《구어》 a car crash〔smash〕: 총 ~ 사고의 93.4 퍼센트는 운전자들의 부주의에 의한 것으로 밝혀졌다 It was found that 93.4 percent of the total auto accidents were attributed to the carelessness of the drivers. ~상용자《자가용의》 a motorist. ~세 the automobile tax. ~속도계 an autometer; a speedometer. ~손해배상 책임보험 (mandatory) automobile third party liability insurance. ~쇼 a motor show. ~수리공 a car〔garage〕mechanic. ~ 수리 공장 an auto-repair shop. ~여행《make》 a motor〔car〕trip: ~여행자 a motorist / ~여행을 하다 take〔make〕a trip by car. ~ 운수 사업법 the Auto Transportation Business Law. ~운전면허증 a driver's license《미》; a driving license《영》. ~운전기사 an automobile〔a motor〕driver; 《자가용의》 a chauffeur. ~이용 인구 the motoring population. ~ 전용 도로 an expressway; a superhighway《미》; a motorway《영》. ~전화 a car phone

〔telephone〕. ～정비공 an auto(mobile) mechanic. ～제조업자 a car manufacturer. ～주차장 a parking place; a parking lot 《미》; a car park 《영》; a motor pool; an autopark; 《차고》 a garage. ～판매업자 an automobile dealer. ～퍼레이드 a motorcade; an autocade. ～학원 a driver's school; a driver training school. ～회사 an automobile company.

한국산～ Korean-made automobiles. 한국 ～ 보험 회사 the Korea Automobile Insurance Company.

**자두** 〖식물〗 a plum (tree); a prune (말린 것).

**자득**(自得) ① 《터득》 apprehension; self-acquirement. ～하다 apprehend; understand; acquire by *oneself*. ② 《만족》 self-satisfaction. ～하다 feel self-satisfied; be self-complacent.

**자디잘다** (be) very small; tiny; fine; 《사람이》 (be) meticulous; overscrupulous. ¶ 자디잔 사람 a petty-minded person; a meticulous 〔an overscrupulous〕 person / 글씨를 자디잘게 쓰다 write microscopically / 파를 자디잘게 썰다 cut a scallion up fine; mince a scallion.

**자라** 〖동물〗 a snapping 〔soft-shelled, mud〕 turtle; a terrapin. ¶ ～ 보고 놀란 가슴 소댕 보고 놀란다 《속담》 "Once bitten 〔burned〕, twice shy." *or* The burnt child dreads the fire.

◉ ～목 《스웨터》 a turtleneck (sweater); a pullover(-sweater); a poloneck (sweater) 《영》. ～자지 a shrivelled-up penis; a deceptively small penis.

**자라다**[1] ① 《충분하다》 (be) sufficient; enough. ¶ 이 연료가 겨우내 자랄까 Will this fuel last out the winter? ② 《미치다》 reach; get at (손이); come up 《to》. ¶ 손이 자라는 곳에 within *one's* reach / 힘이 ～ be within *one's* power 〔ability, reach〕 / 내 손은 천장까지 자란다 I can reach 〔touch〕 the ceiling. / 제 힘이 자라는 데까지 하겠습니다 I'll do it to the best of my ability.

**자라다**[2] 《성장하다》 grow (up); be bred; be brought up. ¶ 한창 자라는 아이 a growing child / 모유〔우유〕로 자란 아이 a breast-fed 〔bottle-fed〕 child / 빨리 자라는 나무 a fast-growing tree / 도회지〔시골〕에서 자란 아이 a city-bred 〔country-bred〕 child / 자람에 따라 with *one's* age; as *one* 「grows up 〔becomes older〕 / 너무 ～ overgrow *oneself* / 지혜가 ～ grow in wisdom / 키가 ～ grow taller / 가난하게 ～ be bred in poverty; be cradled in the lap of penury / 호사스럽게 ～ be bred 〔reared〕 in luxury / 무럭무럭 ～ grow up fast 〔rapidly〕 / 네 손톱이 너무 자랐다 You have let your nails grow too long. / 너 요전보다 더 자랐구나 You have grown since I saw you last. / 이 땅에는 장미가 잘 자라지 않는다 Roses won't grow well in this soil. / 이 개는 자랄 대로 다 자랐다 This dog has reached his full growth. / 한국의 무역은 더 자랄 수 있다 Korea's trade is capable of further growth 〔expansion〕.

**자라풀** 〖식물〗 a frogbit; a frog's-bit.

**자락** 《옷의》 the skirt 《of a gown》; the lower edges 〔the ends〕 of garments; the train (여성복의); the hem 《of a cloth》. ⇨옷자락. ¶ 바지 ～을 걷어 올리다 tuck up *one's* trousers.

**자락자락** 《버릇없이 구는》 impertinently; impudently; saucily. ¶ 보자 하니 ～ 더 한다 I have been overlooking it, but now his impudence is getting worse.

**자란자란** 《넘칠 듯한》 overflowing; to the brim; brimfully. ～하다 (be) brimful; overflowing. ¶ 잔에 술을 ～ 붓다 fill the glass to the brim with wine; fill up the glass.

**자랑** pride; a boast; bragging; 《얼굴·옷 따위》 vanity; 《자찬》 self-respect; self-praise. ～하다 brag 〔boast〕 《of, that》; be boastful; be proud 〔boastful〕 of; pride *oneself* 《on》; talk big 《구어》.

> 용법 **be proud of** 「자랑하다」의 가장 일반적인 표현. 좋은 뜻, 나쁜 뜻으로 두루 쓰임. **boast**와 **brag**는 나쁜 뜻으로 쓰이는 것이 일반적임. 「자랑스레 떠벌리다」란 뜻이 boast, 「호들갑스럽게 으스대다」, 「허풍떨다」가 brag임.

¶ 나라 ～ patriotic pride / ～삼아, ～스러운 듯이 proudly; boastfully; braggingly / …을 ～으로 삼다 make a boast of…; take pride in… / …을 ～해 보이다 make a display 〔show〕 of *something*; show off 《*one's* new car》 / 힘 ～을 하다 boast about 〔of〕 *one's* strength / 제 ～을 하다 sing *one's* praises; blow *one's* own trumpet / ～은 아니지만 Though I say it myself, …; I rather flatter myself that…; Do not take what I am saying as boastful, but…; Without boasting I may say… / ～할 만한 것은 아니다 It's

nothing to boast of. *or* That's nothing to be proud of. / 불국사는 한국의 ~이다 Pulguk Temple is the pride of Korea. / 그렇게 제 ~하는 사람은 처음 본다 I've never seen anyone who praised himself so much! / 그녀가 아들 ~하는 것도 무리가 아니다 She may well be proud of her son.
◉ ~거리 a source of pride; the pride and joy《of》; pride; boast; a feather in *one's* cap; something to brag about: 새 모자가 그 여자의 ~거리다 The new hat is her pride and joy. / 그는 양친의 ~거리였다 He was the pride of his parents. *or* He was the apple of his parents' eye. / 그 여배우는 미모가 ~거리였다 The actress was vain about her beauty. ~이야기 a boastful talk; a brag; bragging.

**자랑스럽다** (be) boastful; proud; braggish; triumphant; be「full of〔glowing with〕pride. ¶ 자랑스럽게 boastfully; proudly / 자랑스러운 얼굴 a boastful〔triumphant〕look / 자랑스럽게 여기다 be proud of; boast of / 자랑스럽게 이야기하다 speak boastingly《of》; brag《of》/ 그는 아들이 공부를 잘하는 것이 자랑스러웠다 He took great delight in his son's progress at school.

**자력**(自力) *one's* own strength; self-effort; *one's* own exertion. ¶ ~으로 by *one's* own efforts〔ability〕; by〔for〕*oneself;* single-handed / ~으로 하다 do by *oneself;* do without help; do on *his* own. ◉ ~갱생 regeneration by *one's* own efforts; pulling *oneself* up by *one's* own bootstraps; self-reliance: ~ 갱생하다 work out *one's* salvation by *one's* own effort.

**자력**(資力) means; funds; (financial) resources; the wherewithal. ¶ ~에 따라 according to *one's* means / ~의 부족으로 from lack of funds / ~이 있는〔없는〕사람 a man of〔without〕means / ~이 충분하다 have plenty of funds《for》/ 그에게는 그것을 완성시킬 만한 ~이 없었다 He lacked the wherewithal to complete it. / 그 계획은 ~ 부족으로 좌절되었다 The plan was frustrated for lack of money.

**자력**(磁力)〖물리〗magnetism. =자기력. ◉ ~선 lines of magnetic force.

**자료**(資料) material; data(★ material은 「자료」의 뜻으로는 단수형이 보통. data는 datum의 복수형이지만,《미》에서는 종종 this data처럼 단수로도 씀). ¶ ~를 수집하다 collect material〔data〕《for》/ ~를 제공하다 furnish〔afford〕data《to》/ 이것으로는 ~가 모자란다 These data are not enough. / 이 ~는 내용적으로 의문점이 너무 많다 There are too many questions about the content of this material / 나는 UFO에 관한 ~를 모으고 있다 I'm collecting data on UFO (★ UFO는 *u*nidentified *f*lying *o*bject (미확인 비행 물체)의 생략형).
◉ ~실 a reference room; a morgue (신문사 등의). 연구~ research material〔data〕. 통계~ statistic(al) data; material for statistics.

**자루**[1]《부대》a sack; a bag.

> **용법** **sack** 즈크나 질긴 재료로 만들어 곡물·석탄·야채 등의 저장·운송에 주로 쓰이는 것. **bag** 직물·가죽·종이 따위로 만든 것.

¶ 한 ~ 가득 a bagful; a sackful / 한 ~의 감자 a sack of potatoes / ~에서 꺼내다 take《*something*》out of bag / 쌀을 ~에 담다 put rice into a sack.
◉ 쌀〔콩〕~ a rice〔bean〕bag.

**자루**[2]《도구의》a handle; a grip (기계 따위의);《칼 따위의》a haft; a hilt; a shaft (창 따위의). ¶ 해머 ~ the handle of a hammer / 빗~ a broomstick / ~가 긴 숟가락 a long-handled spoon / ~를 끼우다 fit〔put〕a handle《to》/ 식칼 ~가 빠졌다 The handle has come off the kitchen knife.

**자루**[3]《세는 단위》a unit; a stick; a pair (가위 따위의); a stand (총 따위). ¶ 분필 한 ~ a piece of chalk / 연필 두 ~ two pencils / 소총 세 ~ three stands of rifles / 가위 한 ~ a pair of scissors.

**자류**(磁流)〖물리〗magnetic flux.

**자르다** ①《절단하다》cut (off); carve《roast beef》; hash (다지다); chop (토막내다); saw (톱으로); slice《off a piece of meat》(얇게); shear《a sheep》(가위로). ¶ 사과를 반으로 ~ cut an apple into halves / 도끼로 나무를 ~「chop firewood〔cut up a log〕with an ax / 아무의 목을 ~ cut *a person's* head off; behead *a person* / 판자를 톱질해서 둘로 ~ saw the board into two / 손톱을 ~ trim *one's* fingernails / 양파를 잘게 ~ chop the onions.
②《해고하다》dismiss; discharge; fire《구어》. ¶ 사장은 당장에 그의 목을 잘랐다 Boss fired him out in no time.
③《단호하게 거절하다》refuse flatly; give a flat〔square〕refusal. ¶ 그녀는 그의 제의를 딱 잘라 거절했다 She flatly

refused his offer.
④《단언하다》¶ 잘라 말하다 state positively; declare; assert / 이것이 진실임을 나는 잘라 말할 수 있다 I have no hesitation in saying that this is the truth.

**자리** ①《좌석》a seat; a place. ¶ ~에 앉다 take *one's* seat; sit in *one's* seat; seat *oneself;* sit down / ~에 앉아 있다 be seated / ~에 앉히다 seat《*a person*》; place《*a person*》in a seat / ~에서 일어서다 get up 〔rise, arise〕 from *one's* seat / ~를 떠나다 leave *one's* seat / ~를 비우다 clear 〔vacate〕 the seat / ~에 돌아오다 return to *one's* seat / ~를 같이하다 sit side by side together / ~를 양보하다 offer *one's* seat《to *a person*》; make room for《*a person*》/ ~를 빼앗기다 lose *one's* place / ~를 다투다 (make a) rush for seats / ~를 맡아 놓다 keep 〔hold, save〕 a seat for《*a person*》/「이 ~ 비었습니까」―「예, 비어 있습니다」《극장 따위에서》"Is this seat taken ?" *or* "Has anybody taken this seat ?"— "No, it's not 「taken 〔occupied〕." / 그는 지금 ~에 없습니다《사무실 따위에서》He is not at his desk now. *or* He is away from his desk now. / 나는 그 비행기에 ~를 예약했다 I reserved a seat on the plane.
②《공간》space; (a) place; (a) room. ¶ ~를 너무 차지하다 take (up) too much space / 관람석에는 발 디딜 ~도 없었다 Every available space in the stand was filled. / 한 사람 더 들어갈 ~가 있다 There is room left for one more.
③《특정한 장소·때》a scene; a spot; an occasion (경우). ¶ 화재가〔살인 사건이, 사고가〕 났던 ~ the scene of a fire 〔a murder, an accident〕/ 그 ~에 있던 사람들 the people on the spot / 그 ~에서 체포하다 arrest《a thief》「on the spot 〔there and then〕/ 그 ~에 맞는 옷차림을 하다 be properly dressed for the occasion.
④ a site (집터); a seat (소재지); a location; a place. ¶ 도서관이 설 ~ the site where the library will stand / 절이 있었던 ~ the place where a temple used to be / 이 ~에 새 공장이 들어선다 A new factory will go up on this site.
⑤《위치》a position; a situation; a location. ¶ ~잡다 take *one's* position 〔place〕; place *oneself;* occupy a position / ~가 좋다〔나쁘다〕 be well 〔badly〕 situated; be conveniently 〔inconveniently〕 located / ~가 좋아서 장사가 잘 된다 The good location of the store brings a great deal of business / 경찰서는 마을 중앙에 ~하고 있다 The police station is located 〔situated〕 in the center of the town.
⑥《직책·일자리》a position; a status; a post; a place; a job;《빈자리》an opening; a vacancy. ¶ 중요한 ~ an important position 〔post〕/ ~가 있다 find a place 〔position〕/ ~를 채우다 fill (up) a vacancy / 마땅한 ~가 없을까요 「Is there 〔Could you suggest〕 a suitable position for me ? / 그는 그 보험 회사의 좋은 ~에 있다 He holds a good position with that insurance company. / ~가 나면 자네 문제를 고려해 보겠네 You will be considered when there is a vacancy. / 그 학교에 선생 ~가 났다 There is an opening for a teacher at that school. / 자네가 만일 내 ~에 있다면 어떻게 하겠는가 If you were in my position 〔place〕, what would you do ?
⑦《정착》settling down《in life》; establishment; stability. ¶ ~가 잡히다 get on the (right) track; settle down; establish *oneself;* get in the saddle / 서울에 ~잡다 settle down in Seoul / 정부도 이젠 ~가 잡혔다 The government is in the saddle now. / 일이 ~가 잡혔다 My work is on the right track. / 그는 늘 떠돌더니, 이젠 ~가 잡힌 모양이다 He was a regular "rolling stone", but now he seems to have settled down and found his place in life.
⑧《흉터》a mark; a scar; an impression. ¶ 총에 맞은 ~ (the mark of) a bullet wound / 개한테 물린 ~ a scar from a dog bite / 이것은 우두 맞은 ~다 This is a vaccination scar.
⑨《깔개》a mat; a cushion;《침구》bedding; a bed. ¶ ~를 보다 make 〔prepare〕 a bed; lay a bed / ~를 펴다 make a bed; spread a mat《on the floor》.
⑩《병석》a sickbed. ¶ ~에 눕다 lie in *one's* sickbed / 병이 나서 하루 종일 ~에서 꼼짝 못했다 I was confined to my bed all day long. *or* I was laid up with illness all day long.
⑪《숫자의》a figure; a unit; a place. ¶ 네 ~의 수 a number of four figures / 한 ~내리다 take a figure down

one place / 소수점 이하 네 ~까지 구하라 Calculate down to four places of decimals.

◉ ~끼 bedtime drinking-water. ~보전 lying in *one's* sickbed: ~보전하다 lie in *one's* sickbed; be sick in bed. ~옷 ⇨ 잠옷. 자릿수 〖수학〗 the order (of decimals). 자릿조반 a light breakfast in bed.

**-자리** 〖천문〗 constellation. ¶ 오리온자리 the Orion / 큰곰자리 the Great Bear; Ursa Major.

**자리다** be numbed. ⇨ 저리다.

**자리다툼** a scramble for seats 〔position〕. ~하다 scramble for seats (좌석을); compete with 《*a person*》 for a post 〔position〕.

**자리바꿈** 《좌석의》 changing *one's* seat; 〖음악〗 (a) inversion; 〖언어〗 《격변화》 declension.

**자리자리하다** 《저리다》 be numbed; go 〔become〕 numb; 《구어》 have pins and needles. ¶ 발이 ~ I have pins and needles in my feet.

**자린고비**(玼吝考妣) a notorious miser; a niggard; a skinflint; a tightwad 《구어》; a close file; cheapskate 《구어》.

**자립**(自立) 《독립》 independence; 《자활》 self-support〔-reliance〕. ~하다 become independent; stand on *one's* own feet; establish *oneself;* support *oneself.* ¶ ~하여 independently; on *one's* own account / ~해서 장사하다 do business on *one's* own account / 정신적으로 ~하다 achieve emotional autonomy / 직업 훈련을 확충함으로써 신체 장애자들이 ~하도록 돕다 help handicapped people stand on their own feet by expanding vocational training / ~ 생활을 할 수 있다 I can get along on my own income. / 그 나라는 아직 ~할 수 없다 That country is still unable to stand on her own legs. / 그는 아직 ~할 수 없다 He can't support himself yet.

◉ ~경제 self-supporting economy; economic independence; autarky. ~성장 self-sustained growth. ~심 self-reliance: 부모가 과보호하는 아이들은 ~심이 결여되는 경향이 있다 Children whose parents are over-protective are prone to lack in self-reliance.

**자릿자릿** ~하다 《저리다》 be benumbed; 《마음이》 (be) thrilling; suspenseful; be thrilled; be on tenterhooks. ¶ ~해하다 be thrilled at; be on tenterhooks over / 줄타기 곡예사를 ~해서 볼 수가 없다 The tightrope walker keeps me in such suspense, I can't watch.

**-자마자** as soon as; no sooner... than ...; hardly 〔scarcely〕... when 〔before〕; directly; immediately 《on》; the moment. ¶ 그는 나를 보자마자 나가 버렸다 He had no sooner seen me than he went out. *or* The moment he saw me he went out. / 그는 대학을 나오자마자 실업계에 투신했다 Immediately on graduating from the university, he went into business.

**자막**(字幕) 〖영화〗 a (film) title; 《제목명 등의》 a (cinema) caption; 《번역 자막》 subtitles; superimposition. ¶ ~을 넣다 superimpose subtitles 《on the film》 / 한글 ~을 넣은 미국 영화 an American film with Korean subtitles.

**자막대기** a measuring stick; a yardstick; a foot rule.

**자만**(自慢) 《자찬》 self-admiration; self-praise; self-applause; self-conceit (과대 평가); vanity (용모 따위의); pride (자랑); 《큰소리》 brag; boast. ~하다 《입으로》 boast 《of, that...》; be boastful; 《마음으로》 be proud 《of》; pride *oneself* 《on》; take pride 《in》. ¶ ~하는 사람 a boaster; a braggart / ~하는 것은 아니나… Don't take what I am saying as boastful, but...; Without boasting I may say... / 너무 ~하지 마라 Don't be too conceited. / 그녀는 자기 용모에 ~하고 있다 She prides herself on her good looks. ◉ ~심 (self-)conceit; self-opinion; vanity: 그는 ~심이 강하다 He is full of conceit.

**자매**(姉妹) sisters. ¶ 친~ a full sister; sister-german / 이복 ~ a half sister / 박씨~ the Park sisters / ~와 같은 sisterly. ◉ ~결연 establishment 〔setting up〕 of sisterhood relationship 〔ties〕: ~ 결연을 맺다 set up sisterhood relationship 《with》. ~기관 sister agencies. ~도시〔학교〕 a sister city 〔school〕 《to》. ~편 《책의》 a companion 〔sister〕 volume 《to》. ~회사 a sister 〔an affiliated〕 company.

**자맥질** diving; ducking. ⇨ 무자맥질.

**자멸**(自滅) self-destruction; self-ruin; a suicide (자살). ~하다 ruin 〔destroy〕 *oneself;* cut *one's* own throat. ¶ ~적인 self-destructive; suicidal / ~을 초래하다 lead to self-destruction / 정치적 ~을 하다 commit political suicide / 그들은 머지않아 ~할 것이다 They will come to ruin sooner or later.

◉ ~책 a suicidal policy.

**자명종**(自鳴鐘) an alarm clock. ¶ ~을 6시에 맞추어 두다 set an alarm clock for six.

**자명하다**(自明—) (be) self-evident; self-explaining; axiomatic. ¶ 자명한 이치 a self-evident truth; a truism; an axiom / 그것은 ~ It tells its own tale.

**자모**(字母) ① 〖언어〗 an alphabet; a letter; a syllabic. ② 〖인쇄〗《모형(母型)》 a matrix (*pl.* ~es, -trices). ◉ ~순(順) alphabetical order. ~표 an alphabetical table.

**자모**(慈母) an affectionate mother; a loving 〔tender〕 mother.

**자모음**(子母音) 〖언어〗 consonants and vowels.

**자못** very (much); exceedingly; greatly; remarkably. ¶ ~ 기뻐 보이다 look highly 〔quite〕 pleased / 그 일은 ~ 어렵다 It's an exceedingly hard job. / 나는 그에게 신세진 바가 ~ 크다 I owe him a great deal.

**자몽** 〖식물〗 a grapefruit; a pomelo.

**자문**(諮問) an inquiry; a consultation. ~하다 consult; inquire《with *a person* about *a matter*》; 《문의하다》 submit 〔refer〕《*a matter* to *a person*》. ¶ ~에 응하다 provide advice and suggestions as requested / 그들은 정부 ~에 응했다 They responded to the government's request for advice. ◉ ~기관 an advisory organs 〔body〕. ~안 a draft submitted for deliberation. ~위원회 an advisory 〔a consultative〕 committee; a trial board.

**자문자답**(自問自答) (a) soliloquy; a monologue. ~하다 《혼자말로》 talk to *oneself;* soliloquize; 《소리를 내어》 answer *one's* own questions; 《마음속으로》 wonder to *oneself.*

**자문하다**(自問—) question 〔ask〕 *oneself.*

**자물쇠** a lock; a padlock (맹꽁이자물쇠); a snap lock 〔bolt〕 (자동식의). ¶ ~를 잠그다 lock《a door》; fasten a lock / ~를 달다 put a lock on / ~를 열다 unlock / ~를 비틀어 열다 wrench away 〔break open〕 a lock / ~가 잘 안 잠긴다 The lock won't catch 〔lock〕/ 이 문에는 ~가 달려 있지 않다 There is no lock on the door / 이 문은 ~가 잠겨〔열려〕있다 The door is locked 〔unlocked〕. *or* The door is on 〔off〕 the lock.

**자바** 《인도네시아의 섬》 Java. ◉ ~어〔인〕 Javanese. ~커피 Java coffee.

**자바라**(啫哱囉) 〖악기〗 small cymbals.

**자박** 〖광물〗 a gold nugget.

**자반**(佐飯) salted 〔salt-cured〕 fish. ¶ 고등어 ~ a salted mackerel. ◉ ~뒤집기 jactitation; writhing in agony: ~뒤집기하다 toss restlessly about《in》; writhe in agony.

**자반**(紫斑) 〖의학〗 a purple spot. ◉ ~병 purpura. 출혈성~ purpura hemorrhagica.

**자발** ¶ ~(머리)없다 be quick-tempered 〔impatient, restless〕.

**자발성**(自發性) spontaneity.

**자발적**(自發的) voluntary; spontaneous. ¶ ~으로 voluntarily; on *one's* own initiative; spontaneously; of *one's* own accord / ~으로 행동하다 act spontaneously / ~으로 사직하다 resign voluntarily / 나는 ~으로 그 일을 맡았다 I undertook the work of my own accord. / 학생들은 ~으로 교실을 청소했다 The pupils cleaned the classroom on their own initiative. ◉ ~실업 voluntary unemployment. ~활동 self-activity.

**자방**(子方) 〖민속〗 the Direction of the Rat(-north).

**자방**(子房) 《씨방》 〖식물〗 the ovary of a plant.

**자배기** a deep round pottery bowl.

**자백**(自白) confession; 《시인》 admission; 《자인》 acknowledgment. ~하다 confess《to》; make a confession; own up《to》; admit. ¶ 강요된 ~ confession made under duress / 강요되지 않은 상태에서 한~ confession made in a state free of any coercion / ~의 신빙성 결여 the lack of credibility of the confession / 증거의 뒷받침 없는 ~ confession which is not supported by evidence / 범행을 ~하다 confess *one's* guilt; confess to a crime / 깨끗이 모두 ~하다 make a clean breast《of》; make a full confession of《*one's* crime》/ …에게 ~을 강요하다 force a confession from《*a person*》; force《*a person*》into confession / 고문으로 ~시키다 extort a confession by torture / 을러대어 ~시키다 threaten《*a person*》into confession / 그를 ~시킬 수가 없었다 We failed to produce confession from him.

**자벌레** 〖곤충〗 a measuring worm; an inchworm.

**자본**(資本) (a) capital; a fund. ¶ ~의 회전 circulation of capital / ~의 부족 lack of funds 〔capital〕 / ~의 집적(集積)과 집중(集中) concentration and centralization of capital / ~ 집약형 산업 capital-intensive industry / ~과 경영의 분리 separation between capital and administration / ~의 축적 the accumulation of capital / ~의 유입(流入) the influx 〔inflow〕 of capital / ~의 유출 (a) capital outflow / …의 ~으로 with a capital of... / ~을 투자〔투입〕하다 invest 〔lay out〕 capital 《in an enterprise》; sink capital 《in, into》 / ~을 조달하다 raise capital 《for》 / ~을 변통하다 employ 〔rotate〕 capital / ~을 공급하다〔대다〕 provide capital for 《an enterprise》; finance; furnish 〔supply〕 《*a person*》 with capital 〔funds〕 / ~을 놀려 두다 let capital lie idle / 천만 원의 ~으로 장사를 시작하다 start business with a capital of ten million won / 건강이 나의 유일한 ~이다 [비유적] Health is the only asset I have.

◉ ~가 a capitalist; a financier: ~가와 노동자 capitalist and laborer / ~가 계급 the capitalist class. ~거래 capital transaction. ~계수(係數) a capital coefficient. ~계정 capital account. ~과세(課稅) capital levy. ~구성 capital composition; the capital structure 《of a firm》. ~금 capital; a fund; 《주식 자본》 a share capital; capital stock 《미》: 그 회사의 ~금은 2백만 달러이다 The company is capitalized at $2,000,000. *or* The company has a capital of $2,000,000. ~도피 capital flight. ~력 the capital strength 《of an enterprise》. ~론 《책 이름》 *Das Kapital;* the Capital. ~생산성 capital productivity. ~소득 capital income. ~시장 the capital market. ~잉여금 capital surplus. ~재(財) capital goods. ~주(主) a financier; a financial supporter. ~준비금 a capital reserve. ~집약적 산업 capital-intensive industries. ~초과 overcapitalization. ~투자 capital investment. ~화 capitalization: ~화하다 capitalize. ~회전율 capital turnover.

**자본주의**(資本主義) capitalism. ¶ ~의 capitalistic; capitalist / 독점〔수정〕 ~ monopoly 〔modified, revised〕 capitalism. ◉ ~경제 capitalistic economy: ~ 경제조직 the capitalistic economic system. ~국가 a capitalistic country 〔state〕. ~자 a capitalist. ~제도 the capitalistic system. ~진영 the capitalist camp.

**자볼기** a whipping 〔verbal lashing〕 from *one's* wife. ¶ ~ 맞다 take a beating 〔verbal lashing〕 from *one's* wife; be henpecked.

**자봉틀**(自縫―) ⇨ 재봉틀.

**자부**(子婦) a daughter-in-law; 「*one's* son's wife.

**자부**(自負) self-conceit; self-confidence; pride. ~하다 be (self-)conceited; be self-confident; think highly of *oneself;* be proud of; flatter *oneself* 《that...》. ¶ 그는 획기적인 제품을 개발했다고 ~하고 있다 He takes pride in having developed an epoch-making product.

◉ ~심 self-conceit〔-confidence, -importance〕; pride 《in *one's* achievements》: ~심이 강한 사람 a very self-conceited person; a person with a high opinion of himself / 그는 ~심이 강하다 He has a high opinion of himself. *or* He is self-confident.

**자부**(慈父) a loving 〔an affectionate〕 father.

**자북**(磁北) magnetic north. ◉ ~극 the North Magnetic Pole.

**자비**(自費) *one's* own expense 〔charge〕. ¶ ~로 at *one's* own expense / ~로 출판하다 publish 《a book》 「on *one's* own account 〔at *one's* own expense〕.

◉ ~생 a private 〔self-paying〕 student. ~유학생 a student studying abroad *one's* own expense.

**자비**(慈悲) 《동정》 compassion; pity; mercy; 《자선》 charity; benevolence; 《관용》 clemency. ¶ ~를 베푸시는 셈치고 for mercy's sake; in mercy's name / ~를 베풀다 do 《*a person*》 an act of charity; have mercy 〔compassion〕 on 《*a person*》; show mercy 〔clemency〕 to(ward) 《*a person*》 / ~롭다 be compassionate 〔merciful, charitable〕 / ~를 빌다 beg 〔appeal, ask〕 for mercy; beseech charity.

◉ ~심 a merciful 〔benevolent〕 heart; mercy: ~심 깊은 kind-hearted; tender-hearted / 저 친구에게 ~심 따위는 없다 He has a heart of stone.

**자빠뜨리다** 《뒤로 넘어지게 하다》 make 《*a person*》 fall on *his* back; knock 〔push, pull, throw〕 《*a person*》 down on *his* back; trip up (걸어서); 《물건을》 knock 〔push, pull, throw〕 《*a thing*》 down; level; 《바람이》 blow down.

**자빠지다** ① 《뒤로 넘어지다》 fall on *one's* back; tumble over backward; go 〔fall〕 over; tumble down. ¶ 빙판 위에 ~ fall down on the ice / 큰대자로 ~ fall full length 《on the floor》 / 바람에 많은 나무들이 자빠졌다 The wind knocked down many trees.

② 《눕다》 lie down; lay *oneself* down; stretch *oneself* out; 《빈둥거리다》

lounge; loll; lollygag. ¶ 늘 자빠져 있지 말고 일 좀 해라 Stop lollygagging around and do some work.

**자빡** definite refusal 〔rejection〕. ¶ ～대다 flatly refuse; turn down / ～맞다 be refused point-blank; be given a brush-off.

**자산**(資産) property; a fortune; means; 《회사 따위의》 assets. ¶ 은닉 ～ hidden assets / 현금〔자본, 명목〕 ～ cash 〔capital, nominal〕 assets / ～과 부채 assets and liabilities / ～의 동결 freezing of (foreign) assets 〔funds〕 / ～을 만들다 make 〔amass〕 a fortune / ～을 남기다 leave a fortune / ～을 공개하다 make *one's* property 〔assets〕 public / 당신만큼 ～이 있다면 무슨 일이든 할 수 있다 A man of your means can do anything. / 그의 ～은 헤아릴 수 없을 정도로 많다 He has a large fortune beyond measure.
◉ ～가 a man of property 〔means〕; a wealthy 〔rich〕 person: ～가 계급 the propertied classes. ～가치 the value of *one's* property 〔assets〕; property 〔asset〕 value. ～계정 assets account. ～목록 assets; a statement 〔an inventory〕 of assets. ～상태 *one's* financial standing. ～소득 income from property. ～재평가 revaluation of property. ～주(株) income stocks 〔shares〕. ～평가 valuation of assets.

**자살**(自殺) suicide; self-murder. ～하다 kill *oneself;* commit suicide; take *one's* own life; put an end to *one's* own life. ¶ ～적 suicidal / ～할 목적으로 with suicidal intent / ～을 기도하다 attempt suicide / 권총 ～을 하다 shoot *oneself* to death / 음독 ～을 하다 commit suicide by taking poison / 절망한 끝에 ～하다 kill *oneself* in despair / 철로에 뛰어들어 ～하다 kill *oneself* by jumping in front of a (running) train / ～에 실패하다 fail in an attempted suicide / ～ 직전에까지 몰리다 be driven to the very verge of suicide / 타살이 아니라 ～로 판명되다 be found to be a case of suicide, not of murder / 그는 목을 매어 ～했다 He hanged himself. / 그녀는 가스를 마시고 ～했다 She killed herself by inhaling gas. / 그는 분신 ～했다 He burned himself to death. / 그녀는 강에 투신 ～했다 She jumped in the river to kill herself. ◉ ～골 《축구의》 《score》 an own goal; an accidental scoring against *one's* own team. ～미수 an attempted suicide. ～방조 aiding and abetting suicide: ～방조죄 the crime of aiding self-destruction. ～자 a suicide. ～특공대 a suicide commando. ～행위 a suicidal act.

**자상**(仔詳) minuteness; carefulness. ～스럽다, ～하다 (be) cautious and careful; thoughtful; kind; considerate; 《자세하다》 (be) minute; meticulous; be in detail. ¶ ～하게 in detail; minutely; in full / ～한 배려 attentive consideration.

**자상**(刺傷) a stab; a pierced wound.

**자상행위**(自傷行爲) 〖법〗 self-inflicted injury; injuring 〔crippling〕 *oneself* 《to avoid military service》.

**자새** a (small) reel. ◉ ～질 reeling.

**자색**(姿色) a fair face; good looks; personal beauty 《in a woman》; comeliness. ¶ ～이 아름답다〔곱다〕 be beautiful; have a graceful figure / ～이 뛰어나다 surpass 《others》 in beauty.

**자색**(紫色) purple; violet. ¶ 연한 ～ light purple.

**자생**(自生) natural 〔spontaneous〕 growth; self-generation; autogeny; abiogenesis. ～하다 grow wild 〔spontaneously, naturally〕; be autogenous. ¶ ～의 native; autogenous. ◉ ～식물 self-sown plants; native plants.

**자서**(自序) the author's preface. ～하다 write *one's* own preface 《to *one's* work》.

**자서**(自書) ～하다 write in *one's* own hand; autograph. ⇨ 자필(自筆).

**자서**(自署) an autograph; a signature. ～하다 affix *one's* signature; sign *one's* name; autograph. ¶ ～한 사진 a signed 〔an autographed〕 photograph / 책에 ～하다 autograph a book.

**자서전**(自敍傳) an autobiography; *one's* life story. ¶ ～체의 autobiographic / ～을 쓰다 write the story of *one's* own life; write *one's* life story. ◉ ～소설 an autobiographical novel; a fictionalized autobiography.

**자석**(磁石) a magnet; a loadstone; 《나침반》 a compass. ¶ ～의 magnetic / ～의 인력 magnetic attraction / ～은 철을 당긴다 A magnet attracts iron. ◉ ～식 전화기 a magnetotelephone set. ～이불〔요〕 magnetic bedclothes 〔matresses〕. 막대～ a bar magnet. 천연～ a natural magnet; a loadstone.

**자석영**(紫石英) ＝ 자수정(紫水晶).

**자선**(慈善) charity; benevolence; beneficence; 《구호》 almsgiving. ¶ ～의 char-

itable; benevolent / ～하는 마음으로 for charity's sake / 가난한 사람에게 ～하다 render aid to the poor in charity; give alms to the poor / 그는 전재산을 ～ 사업에 바쳤다 He left 〔gave〕 his entire fortune to charities.
◉ ～가 a charitable 〔benevolent〕 person; a philanthropist. ～공연 a benefit (performance). ～기금 a charity fund. ～냄비 a charity pot (for collecting public contributions). ～단체 a charitable institution 〔organization〕. ～바자 a charity 〔benefit〕 bazaar. ～병원 a charity hospital. ～사업 charitable 〔philanthropic〕 work; charities: 수익을 ～ 사업에 기부하다 give 〔make over〕 the proceeds to charitable work. ～쇼〔흥행〕 a charity show 〔performance〕. ～시설 a charitable institution. ～심 a benevolent spirit; (a sense of) charity. ～음악회〔무도회〕 a charity concert 〔ball〕. ～행위 an act of charity.

**자선**(自選) ～하다 select 《some》 out of *one's* own works. ◉ ～시집 a collection of poems selected by the poet himself. ～집 the author's (own) selection (of stories 〔writings〕).

**자설**(自說) *one's* own opinion 〔view, theory, doctrine〕. ¶ ～을 고집하다 persist in 〔maintain〕 *one's* view; stick to *one's* opinion / ～을 굽히다 change 〔switch, revise, revamp〕 *one's* thinking; 《변절하다》 turn *one's* coat.

**자성**(自省) 《자기 관찰》 self-examination; reflection; reflexion; 《내성》 introspection. ～하다 examine 《*oneself*》; reflect 《on *oneself*》; introspect. ¶ ～적 introspective; reflective / ～을 촉구하다 ask 《*a person*》 to reflect on *himself*.

**자성**(雌性) 〘생물〙 femininity; feminity; femaleness.

**자성**(磁性) 〘물리〙 magnetism; magnetic properties. ¶ ～의 magnetic / ～을 띠게 하다 magnetize. ◉ ～산화철 magnetic oxide of iron. ～인력 polarity. ～체 a magnetic substance. 반～체 a diamagnet.

**자세**(姿勢) (a) posture; a pose; a position; 《몸가짐》 a carriage; 《태도》 an attitude. ¶ 좋은〔나쁜〕 ～ a good 〔poor〕 posture / 앉은 ～로 in a sitting posture / ～가 좋다〔나쁘다〕 have a fine 〔poor〕 figure / ～를 취하다 posture; pose / ～를 바르게 가지다 keep a straight posture / ～를 바로잡다 straighten *oneself;* 《고치다》 correct *one's* carriage / 차려 ～를 취하다 stand at 〔come to〕 attention / 편한 ～로 앉다 sit in a comfortable position / 방어〔대결〕 ～를 취하다 get ready for a defensive 〔an aggressive〕 attitude / 매우 비타협적인 ～를 취하다 adopt 〔assume〕 a very uncompromising position 《on the issue》 / 그는 언제나 긍정적인 ～로 사물에 대처한다 He always copes with matters in a positive 〔forward-looking〕 attitude. ◉ ～검사 a posture examination. ～반응 postural reflex.

**자세하다**(仔細—) (be) minute; detailed; circumstantial; full; in-depth.
¶ 자세한 이야기〔지도〕 a detailed account 〔map〕 / 자세한 일〔것〕 details; particulars; further information / 자세히 minutely; in detail; in full; at length / 자세히 이야기하다 go 〔enter〕 into details / 자세히 설명하다 give a full explanation; explain in full 〔in detail, in full detail〕 / 자세하게 심문하다 question minutely / 자세하게 점검하다 make a close inspection 《of》 / 자세한 것은 제3장을 보라 For particulars 〔details〕, turn to Chapter Ⅲ. / 시간이 없어 자세한 이야기는 못 한다 I have no time to tell you the full of it. / 이 사전이 다른 사전보다 설명이 ～ This dictionary gives fuller explanation than others. / 참 자세히도 알고 있네 그려 You certainly are well informed about the matter. *or* You talk like a book. / 그로부터 자세한 전말을 들었다 I got a full account from him. / 우리는 사건의 자세한 내용을 상사에게 보고하였다 All the details 〔particulars〕 of the event were reported to our superiors.

**자속**(磁束) 〘물리〙 (a) magnetic flux.

**자손**(子孫) a descendant; an offspring; [총칭] posterity; offspring; progeny. ¶～에게 전하다 hand down 《*a thing*》 to *one's* posterity / …의 ～이다 be descended from…; be a descendant of…; trace *one's* descent to… / ～을 남기다 leave offspring.

**자수**(自首) 〘법〙 self-surrender; voluntary confession. ～하다 give *oneself* up 《to the authorities》; surrender 〔deliver〕 *oneself* 《to the police》.
◉ ～기간 《set》 a surrender period.

**자수**(刺繡) embroidery; needlework; 《무늬》 an embroidered design 〔pattern〕. ～하다 embroider 《a pattern on a dress》; do embroidery 《on》.

◉ ～본, ～무늬 embroidery designs. ～사(師) an embroiderer. ～실 embroidery thread. ～틀 an embroidery-frame; a taboret.

**자수**(自手) ¶ ～로 with *one's* own hands; in person; without help.
◉ ～성가 making a home by *one's* own hand; making *one's* own fortune: ～ 성가하다 make *one's* fortune by *one's* own effort. 「quartz.

**자수정**(紫水晶) 〖광물〗 amethyst; violet

**자숙**(自肅) self-discipline; self-control 〔=restraint〕. ～하다 discipline 〔control〕 *oneself;* exercise 〔practice〕 self-discipline〔-control〕; voluntarily refrain 《from》.

**자습**(自習) self-teaching〔-study〕. ～하다 teach *oneself;* study by *oneself;* study without a teacher; be *one's* own teacher. ◉ ～문제 homework; 《숙제 따위》 hometask. ～서 a self-teaching 〔teaching yourself〕 manual; a book for self-study; a key; a pony 《미속어》; a horse 《미속어》; a crib 《구어》: 영어 ～서 《표제》 English Self-Taught / ～서의 사용은 금한다 The use of cribs is prohibited. ～시간 study hour(s). ～실 a study hall; a (private) study room.

**자승자박하다**(自繩自縛―) be caught in *one's* own trap; fall in a trap set by *oneself;* lose *one's* freedom of action as a result of *one's* own actions.

**자시**(子時) 〖민속〗 the Watch of the Rat. ① the first of the 12 double-hours (=the period between 11 p.m. and 1 a.m.). ② the first of the 24 hours (=11:30 p.m.—12:30 a.m.).

**자시하**(慈侍下) having only *one's* mother alive to serve.

**자식**(子息) ① 《아들딸》 *one's* children; *one's* sons and daughters; offspring; issue. ¶ 사람의 ～ a human being / ～이 많다 have a brood of children / ～이 없다 be childless; have no children; be without issue / ～복이 있다 be blessed with children / 귀여운 ～에게 매를 주어라 《속담》 Spare the rod and spoil the child. / 자식을 키워 보고 비로소 부모의 은혜를 안다 Only after a person is himself a parent does he know how indebted he is to his own parents. ② 《욕이나 친근한 뜻으로》 a guy; a chap; a fellow; a bloke; a so-and-so; a bastard. ¶ 개～ son of a bitch 〔gun〕 / 이 후레～ You wretch. / 저 ～은 사기꾼이다 That guy is a damn swindler.

**자신**(自身) *one's* self; *oneself;* itself; (the) self. ¶ 나 ～ myself / 너 ～ yourself / 그 ～ himself / 그녀 ～ herself / 자기 ～ *one's* own self / ～이 by *oneself;* 《자기 힘으로》 for *oneself;* 《몸소》 personally; in person / ～의 생명을 내걸다 risk *one's* life / ～의 나갈 길을 개척하다 make *one's* way in the world / 그 ～이 (직접) 그것을 만들었다 He made it for himself. / 너 ～을 알라 Know yourself 〔thyself〕.

**자신**(自信) self-confidence; self-assurance. ～하다 be confident 《of, that ...》.

> 용법 **confidence** 자기 자신, 자신의 힘에 대한 자신감. **assurance** confidence 보다 더 뜻이 강하며, 때로는 교만한 태도로 나타날 수 있는 자신을 말함. confidence가 이성적인 면을 뜻하는 반면, assurance는 결과의 옳고 그름을 문제시 않는 감정적인 면이 있음.

¶ ～이 있는 confident; self-confident / 확고한 ～을 가지고 with firm 〔unwavering〕 confidence / ～ 있는 사람〔태도〕 a (self-)confident person 〔manner〕 / ～만만한 청년 a young man of unbounded assurance / ～이 있다 be confident 《of》 / ～이 없다 be diffident 《of》 / 큰 ～을 갖고 있다 have great confidence in *oneself* / (성공)할 ～이 있다 be confident 〔sure〕 of (*one's* success) / ～을 얻다〔잃다〕 gain 〔lose〕 confidence in *oneself* / ～만만하다 be full of confidence / 이번 시험에는 ～이 있다 《앞으로 있을》 I'm sure I can do well in the coming examination. *or* 《이미 끝난》 I'm sure, I have done well in the examination. / 항상 ～을 가지시오 Always be sure of your success. / 나는 이 일을 잘 해낼 ～이 있다 I am confident of success in this work. 「망연 자실.

**자실**(自失) stupefaction; abstraction. ⇨

**자심**(滋甚) getting worse; aggravation. ～하다 be getting 〔growing〕 worse. ¶ 어려움이 ～하다 be in an extreme difficulty.

**자아**(自我) 〖철학〗 the 〔*one's*〕 self; 〖심리〗 (the) ego; the "I". ¶ ～가 강한 egotistic; egoistic; self-centered; self-willed / ～의 발전 self-development / ～의 완성 self-perfection / ～의 주장 self-assertion. ◉ ～망각 self-effacement. ～보존 self-preservation. ～비판 self-criticism〔-accusation〕. ～억제 self-repression. ～의식 self-consciousness〔-awareness〕. ～이상 the ego ideal. ～해방 emancipation of ego.

**자아내다** ① 《실을》 draw out (thread); reel off; spin. ¶ 고치에서 실을 ～ reel silk off cocoons / 솜에서 실을 ～ spin thread out of cotton. ② 《액체·기체를》 extract 《liquid, steam, gas》 by machine; draw; suck; pump. ③ 《느낌을》 evoke 《feeling》; arouse. ¶ 슬픔을 ～ make 《*a person*》 feel sad / 동정심을 ～ evoke 《*a person's*》 sympathy / 의심을 ～ arouse suspicion.

**자아올리다** suck up (water); draw up; pump up. ¶ 펌프로 우물에서 물을 ～ pump up water from a well.

**자애**(慈愛) affection; love; kindness; benevolence. ¶ ～로운 affectionate; loving; benevolent; kind / 부모의 ～ parental affection / ～가 넘치다 be full of affection / ～로운 눈으로 보다 look with affection / 그녀는 어릴 때부터 어머니의 ～를 모르고 자랐다 From her childhood she has been a stranger to mother's affection 〔love〕.

**자애**(自愛) self-love. ～하다 take care of *oneself;* look after *oneself* 〔*one's* health〕. ¶ ～적 self-regarding / 자중 ～하시기를 빕니다 Please take good care of yourself. ◉ ～주의 selfishness; egoism.

**자약하다**(自若—) (be) self-possessed; calm; composed; cool. ¶ 자약하게 calmly; coolly; with composure; with self-possession / 태연～ keep *one's* calm; have presence of mind; be firm as a rock.

**자양**(滋養) nutrition; nourishment; alimentation. ¶ ～(분)이 있는 nutritive; nourishing / ～(분)이 많다 be full of nutrients; be nutritious.

◉ ～물 nutritious food; nourishment; a nutrient. ～분 a nutritious element; nutritious matter; nutritive material; nutrients: ～분이 적은 음식 food of poor nutritive value / ～분을 섭취하다 take nutritious food.

**자업자득**(自業自得) the natural consequences of *one's* own deed 〔misdeed〕. ¶ 그것은 그의 ～이다 He asked for it. *or* That serves him right. *or* He has brought it on himself. / ～이니까 내버려 두어라 It's his own fault. Let him stew in his own juice. / 그의 가난은 ～이다 His poverty is of his own making.

**자연**(自然) nature. ¶ ～의, ～적인 natural; 《천성이》 instinctive; 《타고난》 native; inborn; inherent; 《자연 발생적인》 spontaneous; 《꾸미지 않은》 unstudied; unaffected; 《야생의》 wild / ～히 naturally; spontaneously; of *one's* own accord; 《자동적으로》 automatically; 《저절로》 by *itself* 〔*oneself*〕; 《나도 모르게》 in spite of *oneself* / ～의 힘 the force of nature (바람·물의 힘 따위); the natural agencies (자연계의 작용) / ～의 묘(妙) the mystery of nature / ～의 법칙 the law of nature / ～의 섭리에 따라 in the course of nature / ～을 벗삼다 live with nature / ～히 생겨나다 come of *itself* / ～(의 섭리)에 어긋나다, ～스럽지 않다 be against nature / ～의 섭리에 따르다 let *a matter* take *its* own course / 상처가 ～히 아물었다 The wound healed all by 〔of〕 itself. / ～ 경관을 보호합시다《게시》 Keep nature beautiful. *or* Conserve nature. / 과도한 개발로 ～이 파괴되어 가고 있다 Nature is being ruined by excessive development. / 한국의 ～은 나날이 파괴되어가고 있다 Nature is being destroyed in Korea day by day.

◉ ～개조 the remodeling 〔reshaping〕 of nature. ～계 the natural world; (the world of) nature. ～공원 a natural park. ～과학 natural science. ～관 *one's* view of nature. ～대수(對數) 〚수학〛 natural logarithm. ～도태〔선택〕 natural selection. ～묘사 description of nature. ～미 natural beauty; the beauties of nature. ～발생 spontaneous genesis 〔generation〕; 《생물》 autogeny; abiogenesis: ～ 발생적으로 spontaneously. ～발화 spontaneous combustion. ～보전 구역 nature-preservation district. ～분리 avulsion. ～분만(법) (a) natural childbirth. ～사 (a) natural death. ～생태 보호 지역 a natural ecology protection area. ～수 a natural number. ～숭배 nature 〔elemental〕 worship; nature cult: ～숭배자 a nature worship(p)er. ～시인 a nature poet. ～식품 natural foods. ～신교(神教) deism. ～신학 natural theology. ～애호가 a nature lover. ～요법 naturopathy; physical therapy. ～유량 a rate of flow. ～인 《미개인》 a natural man; 《법인이 아닌 개인》 a natural person. ～자원 natural resources. ～재해 a natural disaster. ～종교 natural religion. ～주의 naturalism: ～주의자 a naturalist. ～증가 a natural increase 《in population》: ~증가율 the rate of natural increase. ~증수(增收) a natural increase in revenue. ~지리학 physical geography. ~철학 natural philosophy. ~치유 self-healing; spontaneous recovery. ~파괴 the destruction of nature. ~현상 a natural phenomenon. ~환경 the [a] natural environment: ~ 환경 보호 지구 《designate as》 natural environment preservation district.

**자연**(紫煙) tobacco smoke.

**자연보호**(自然保護) conservation [preservation] of nature; protection of the natural environment; wildlife conservation. ¶ 우리는 ~에 더 박차를 가해야 한다 We must speed up our efforts at the conservation of nature.
◉ ~단체 a conservation group. ~운동 a (nature-)conservation movement; a nature-protection campaign: ~ 운동가 a nature conservationist. ~지역 a wildlife sanctuary; a nature reserve.

**자연스럽다**(自然—) (be) natural; unartificial; unaffected. ¶ …은 극히 자연스러운 이치다 be quite in the nature of things / 파티에서는 자연스럽게 행동해라 Be yourself at the party.

**자엽**(子葉) 〖식물〗 a seed leaf. =떡잎.

**자영**(自營) self-management; self-sustenance; self-support. ~하다 do 《business》 independently [on *one's* own account]. ¶ ~의 self-supporting [=sustaining]; independent; self=employed / ~으로 장사하다 do business on *one's* own; run *one's* own business. ◉ ~사업 an independent enterprise.

**자오선**(子午線) 〖천문〗 the meridian (line). ◉ ~고도 the meridian altitute. ~관측 meridian observation. ~통과 《천체의》 transit.

**자외선**(紫外線) 〖물리〗 ultraviolet rays. ◉ ~방사 ultraviolet radiation. ~요법 (an) ultraviolet treatment; ultraviolet light therapy. ~전구 an ultraviolet lamp. ~현미경 an ultraviolet microscope.

**자우**(慈雨) a welcome [beneficial, good] rain; a seasonable rain. ¶ 가뭄 끝에 기다리던 ~ long-awaited [blessed] rain after a long spell of dry weather.

**자욱하다, 자우룩하다** (be) dense; thick; heavy. ¶ 자욱하게 in thick clouds; thickly; densely; obscurely / 자욱한 안개 a dense fog / 연기가 ~ The smoke is thick. / 방안은 담배 연기로 자욱하였다 The room was dim [filled, heavy, clouded] with tobacco smoke.

**자웅**(雌雄) ① 《암수》 male and [or] female; the two sexes. ¶ ~ 양성의 bisexual / ~을 감별하다 determine the sex 《of》; sex 《a chicken》.
② 《승부·우열·강약》 victory and defeat; (relative) supremacy. ¶ ~을 결하다 fight a decisive battle 《with *a person*》 for hegemony; try conclusion 《with》; fight it out 《with》; determine the stronger or the weaker / ~을 겨루다 vie [contest] 《with *a person*》 for supremacy; strive 《with an opponent》 for mastery; contend 《with *a person*》 for hegemony.
◉ ~눈 a pair of eyes that are not the same size: ~눈이 a person whose eyes do not match. ~도태[선택] sexual selection. ~동주(同株) monoecism. ~동체(同體) hermaphrodite. ~이주(異株) dioecism. ~이체(異體) gonochorism. ~이화(異花) diclinism.

**자원**(自願) volunteering. ~하다 volunteer 《for》. ¶ ~해서 voluntarily / ~ 입대하다 volunteer for military service.
◉ ~(봉사)자 a volunteer (worker): 한국 해외 ~ 봉사자 a Korea Overseas Volunteer (생략 KOV).

**자원**(資源) 〖경제〗 (natural) resources. ¶ 국가의 ~ national resources / 유한한 ~ finite resource / 미개발 ~ undeveloped [unexploited, untapped] resources / ~이 풍부하다 be full of resources; be rich [abundant] in resources / ~이 빈약하다 be poor in resources / ~을 개발하다 develop [exploit] natural resources / 전쟁은 국가의 ~을 고갈시킨다 A war is a great drain upon the country's resources.
◉ ~개발 exploitation of resources. ~공급국 resource-supplying countries [nations]. ~관리법 the Resources Management Law. ~문제 the [a] resource(s) problem. ~배분 allocation of resources. ~보호 conservation of resources. ~부국 a resource-rich nation [country]. ~빈국 a resource=poor nation [country]. ~산출국 resource-producing countries [nations]. ~애호 conservation of resources. ~유한시대 an era of limited natural resources. ~탐사 위성 a remote-sensing [an earth resources] satellite.

**자위**[1] 《붙박인 것·태아의》 the area 〔point〕 of contact between an object and the base it rests on 〔is set in〕; the fixed position in which an object is lodged; a fixed position 〔state〕. ~뜨다 budge; stir; leave 〔make, show〕 a slight opening. ¶ 태아의 ~가 돌았다〔떴다〕 The fetus has started to move 〔quicken〕. / 바위가 마침내 ~ 뜨기 시작했다 The rock began to 「give 〔yield, budge〕 a little at last.

**자위**[2] 《달걀·눈의》 the white 〔yolk〕 of an egg; the white 〔colored〕 part of the eye. ¶ 달걀의 흰〔노른〕 ~ the white 〔yolk〕 of an egg / 눈의 흰〔검은〕 ~ the white 〔pupil〕 of the eye.

**자위**(自慰) ① 《자기 위안》 self-consolation. ~하다 console *oneself.* ¶ …이라 생각하고 ~하다 comfort *oneself* with the thought that…. ② 《수음》 masturbation; self-abuse; onanism.

**자위**(自衛) self-defense; self-protection〔-preservation〕. ~하다 protect 〔defend〕 *oneself* 〔*one's* country, *etc.*〕 《from, against》. ¶ ~의 in 〔by way of〕 self-defense / ~책을 강구하다 take a step to protect 〔defend〕 *oneself;* think out means of self-preservation / ~ 행동을 취하다 take action for self-defense.

◉ ~권 the right of self-defense〔-protection〕: ~권의 발동 invocation of self-defense power / ~권을 주장하다 claim the right of defense 《of the nation》. ~대 《일본의》 the Self-Defense Forces: 육상〔해상〕 ~대 the Ground 〔Maritime〕 Self-Defense Force. ~력 self-defense capabilities. ~본능 the protective instinct. ~수단 a measure of self-defense. ~전력 war potential for self-defense; self-defense war potential. ~책 《adopt》 a self-protecting policy.

**자유**(自由) freedom; liberty. ~롭다, ~스럽다 (be) free; unrestricted; liberal.

> **용법** **freedom** 속박·억압 등이 없는 절대적인 의미의 자유. **liberty** 과거의 속박·제한·압력 등에서 해방된 상태를 뜻하는 말. 노예가 석방되어 자유를 얻게 되는 것 등이 이에 해당됨.

¶ 개인의 ~ personal liberty; freedom of the individual / 언론〔신앙, 출판〕의 ~ freedom of speech 〔worship, the press〕 / (판문점의) ~의 집〔다리〕 the Freedom House 〔Bridge〕 / ~로(이) 《마음대로》 freely; unrestrictedly; at will 〔liberty〕; at *one's* pleasures; as *one* wishes 〔likes, pleases〕; 《거침없이》 without reserve 〔restraint〕; 《편히》 with ease / ~로운 몸이〔~롭게〕 되다 become 〔get〕 free; be set free; be liberated / ~로이 활동하다 have free play / ~스럽게 의견을 말하다 state *one's* own views freely / ~로 사용하다 make free use 《of *a thing*》 / 아무에게 ~를 주다 give *a person* liberty; give *a person* his head / 신체의 ~를 구속하다 restrain *one's* liberty / ~를 외치다 cry for liberty / ~를 옹호〔획득〕하다 defend 〔obtain〕 *one's* liberty / 언론의 ~를 억제하다 curb free speech / 생명보다 ~를 존중하다 prize freedom more than life; prize liberty above life / ~롭게 하여 주다〔해방하다〕 set 《*a person*》 free 〔at liberty〕; liberate / (아무의) ~에 내맡기다 give 〔leave〕 《*a person*》 a free hand; let 《*a person*》 have his 〔her〕 own way / 행동의 ~를 잃다 be tied hand and foot / ~를 박탈하다 deprive 《*a person*》 of his 〔her〕 liberty / ~로운 행동을 취하다 take 〔go〕 *one's* own way / ~ 아니면 죽음을 달라 Give (me) liberty or (give me) death. / 손발이 묶여서 몸이 ~롭지 못했다 Bound hand and foot, I was quite helpless. / ~는 자칫 방종으로 흐르기 쉽다 Liberty often degenerates into lawlessness. / 「김 양은 프랑스 말을 ~롭게 말하지, 안 그래」—「그럼요, 그녀는 프랑스 사람처럼 말해요」 "Miss Kim is fluent in French, isn't she?" —"Yes, she speaks it as well as a native speaker."

◉ ~가격 the free 〔open〕 price. ~결사 a voluntary association. ~결혼 free marriage 〔union〕; 《내연관계》 common-law marriage. ~경쟁 free 〔open〕 competition. ~경제 a free economy. ~계약 a free contract: ~계약 선수 『야구』 a free agent / ~계약자 a free-lancer. ~권 civil liberties. ~근무 시간제 the flextime. 〔<*flex*ible *time*〕. ~금리 unregulated interest rates. ~기업 a free enterprise: ~기업 경제 free-enterprise economy. ~노동 조합 a free trade union; the Solidarity Trade Union (폴란드의): 국제 ~ 노동 조합 연합회 the International Confederation of Free Trade Union (약칭 ICFTU). ~노무자 a free 〔casual〕 laborer. ~당 《영국의》 the Liberal Party; the Liberals. ~도시 『역

사》 a free city. ～로 the Freedom Road. ～무역 free trade: ～ 무역주의자 a free trader / ～ 무역항 a free port / ～ 무역 지대 a free trade zone. ～민 a free citizen; a freeman; 《노예 신분에서 해방된》 a freedman; a freed slave. ～민권론 democratic rights. ～민권 운동 the Movement for Civic Rights and Freedom (in the 1880 s). ～방임 noninterference; 〖경제〗 laissez-〔laisser-〕faire: ～방임주의 the principle of laissez-faire; a let-alone policy. ～사상 liberal ideas; 《종교상의》 free thought. ～선택 free choice: ～선택 과목 an elective 〔optional 《영》〕 subject. ～세계 《공산권에 대해서》 the free world. ～시간 《단체 여행 따위에서의》 free time; time at leisure. ～시장 a free market. ～업 a liberal profession. ～연구 independent research. ～연기 (演技) optional exercise. ～의사 free will 〔volition〕; spontaneity: ～ 의사로 하다 do 《*something*》 of *one's* 「own free will 〔own accord〕. ～인 a freeman. ～작문 an essay; free composition. ～종목 《체조 경기의》 free exercises. ～주의 liberalism: ～주의의 liberal / ～주의 세계 the free world / 철저한 ～주의자 a liberalist to the backbone. ～진영 the Free World; the Western Camp. ～토의 (a) free discussion; (특히 미국 의회의) (a) colloquy. ～통항권(通航權) the right of free passage. ～학습 open classroom: ～ 학습의 날 a no textbook day; a textbook-free day. ～항 a free port. ～행동 free 〔independent〕 action: ～ 행동을 취하다 act at *one's* own discretion; act for *oneself* / ～ 행동을 허락하다 give 〔allow〕 《*a person*》 a free hand / ～ 행동을 할 수 있다 have 〔get〕 a free hand. ～형 《수영》 a freestyle swim(ming); 《레슬링》 catch-as-catch-can.

**자유왕래**(自由往來) 《국경 따위의》 free cross-border travel.

**자유자재**(自由自在) ～하다 (be) free; unrestricted; free and easy. ¶ ～로 freely; at *one's* pleasure; at will; with perfect freedom; as *one* pleases / ～한 필치 a free and bold hand / 왼손으로 ～로이 글씨를 쓰다 write freely with *one's* left hand / 영어를 ～로 구사하다 have good command of English.

**자유재량**(自由裁量) latitude; discretion; a free hand. ¶ ～에 맡기다 give 《*a person*》 a free hand; leave to the discretion 《of *a person*》 / 약간의 ～을 허용하다 allow a little latitude. ◉ ～권 《have no》 discretionary power.

**자유화**(自由化) liberalization 〔freeing〕 《of trade》; removal of restrictions 《on trade》. ～하다 liberalize; free. ¶ 고교생의 두발과 복장의 ～ the liberalization of hair styles and the abolition of school uniforms for secondary school / 한국의 무역을 95퍼센트까지 ～하다 liberalize 〔remove restrictions〕 95 percent of Korea's trade. ◉ ～상품 liberalized goods. ～율 extent of trade liberalization. ～조처 liberalization measures. ～품목 리스트 a liberalization list.

**자율**(自律) self-regulation; self-control; 〖철학〗 autonomy. ¶ ～적 self-regulating; autonomous / 학원의 ～ the campus autonomy. ◉ ～신경 an autonomic nerve: ～ 신경계 the autonomic nervous system / ～ 신경 실조증 autonomic ataxia 〔imbalance〕.

**자율규제**(自律規制) self-imposed control 《on》; voluntary 〔self-imposed〕 restraint(s) 《on》; self-regulation. ¶ 수출용 면제품의 ～는 제대로 잘 이행되었다 Self-imposed control on cotton textile exports worked out right. / 그들은 한국이 내년도에도 미국에 대한 자동차 수출 대수의 ～를 계속하도록 요구했다 They demanded that Korea should continue its voluntary restraints on the number of motorcars exported to the U.S. in the coming year.

**자음**(子音) 〖음성〗 a consonant. ¶ ～의 consonantal. ◉ ～자 a consonant (letter). ～중복 gemination.

**자음**(字音) the pronunciation of a Chinese character; the sound of a word.

**자의**(自意) *one's* own will 〔volition〕. ¶ ～(대)로 voluntarily; of *one's* own accord.

**자의**(字義) the meaning of a word. ¶ ～대로 literally; to the letter / ～를 밝히다 ascertain the meaning of a word / 글자를 ～대로 해석하다 interpret a word literally.

**자의**(恣意) arbitrariness; wantonness. ¶ ～적인 arbitrary; willful / ～로 arbitrarily; willfully.

**자의식**(自意識) 〖심리〗 self-consciousness. ¶ ～이 강하다 be highly 〔keenly, very〕 self-conscious.

**자이로스코프** a gyroscope.

**자이로컴퍼스** a gyrocompass.

**자이르** 《아프리카 국가》 (the Republic of ) Zaire.

**자인**(自認) self-acknowledgment; admission; a confession. ～하다 acknowledge 〔own〕 *oneself* 《to be in the wrong》; admit 《*one's* fault》; confess. ¶ 실패를 ～하다 admit *one's* failure / 그는 패배를 ～했다 He owned his defeat. / 피고는 자기에게 죄가 있음을 ～했다 The accused made acknowledgment of his guilt.

**자일**(子日) 〖민속〗 the Day of the Rat.

**자일** 《등산용》 a (climbing) rope; a *Seil* (G.).

**자임하다**(自任—) fancy 〔think, flatter〕 *oneself* 《to be a pioneer》; consider 〔regard〕 *oneself* 《as》. ⇨ 자처하다. ¶ 큰 학자로 ～ fancy *oneself* a great scholar / 호걸로 ～ play the hero; assume the airs of a great man.

**자자손손**(子子孫孫) *one's* descendants; *one's* offspring; posterity; *one's* children's children. ¶ ～에 이르기까지 (even) to *one's* remotest descendants / ～에 전하다 hand 《*a thing*》 down to posterity / ～에 전해지다 go 〔hand〕 down to posterity.

**자자하다**(藉藉—) be widely spread; be spread abroad. ¶ 칭찬이 ～ win wide admiration / 명성이 ～ be highly reputed 〔renowned〕; enjoy a high reputation / 그 계획에 대해서는 세간의 비난이 ～ The people are loud against the plan. / 그 도시에서는 그가 명의라는 평판이 ～ He has the reputation of an excellent physician in the town.

**자작**(子爵) a viscount. ◉ ～부인 a viscountess.

**자작**(自作) *one's* own making 〔work, production, composition〕. ～하다 make 《*a thing*》 *oneself;* 《농작물을》 cultivate *one's* own farm. ¶ ～의 of *one's* own making 〔writing, composing, growing〕 / ～한 감자 potatoes of *one's* own growing / ～ 소설 a novel of *one's* own pen 〔writing〕. ◉ ～농 an independent 〔an owner, a landed〕 farmer. ～시 *one's* own poem. ～자급 self-sustenance. ～자연: ～자연하다 play 〔perform, read〕 *one's* own work.

**자작**(自酌) pouring wine for *oneself;* selfservice. ～하다 pour 《wine》 for *oneself;* serve 《wine》 *oneself;* help *oneself* to wine. 「적거리다.

**자작거리다** drag 《*oneself*》 along. ⇨ 저

**자작나무** 〖식물〗 a white birch.

**자잘하다** (be) all fine 〔small, tiny, minute〕. ¶ 자잘한 글씨 a small letter 〔character〕. 「자기장.

**자장**(磁場) 〖물리〗 a magnetic field. ⇨

**자장가**(—歌) a lullaby; a cradle song; a nursery song. ¶ ～를 불러서 아이를 재우다 sing 〔lull, croon〕 a baby to sleep / ～를 들으며 자다 fall asleep to a lullaby. 「bean sauce.

**자장면**(酢醬麪) noodles with blackish

**자장자장** rockabye; hushaby. ¶ ～ 잘도 잔다 Rockabye 〔Hushaby〕, baby—go to sleep now.

**자재**(自在) ⇨ 자유자재. ¶ 신축 ～이다 be capable of expansion and contraction; be elastic 〔flexible〕.

**자재**(資材) resources; materials. ¶ 건축 ～ building 〔construction〕 materials. ◉ ～과 supply section.

**자저**(自著) *one's* own work.

**자적**(自適) self-satisfaction; complacency; self-contentment. ～하다 be self-satisfied; be complacent. ¶ 유유 ～한 생활을 하다 lead a life of ease and contentment; live free from worldly cares.

**자전**(字典) a dictionary; a lexicon. ◉ 한한(漢韓)～ a dictionary of classical Chinese explained in Korean.

**자전**(自轉) rotation; the turn 〔spin〕 《of the earth》 on its (own) axis. ～하다 turn on its axis; rotate. ¶ 지구는 ～한다 The earth rotates 〔turns round〕 on its axis. / 지구의 ～으로 밤과 낮이 생긴다 The rotation of the earth causes day and night. ◉ ～주기 a rotation period.

**자전거**(自轉車) a bicycle; a cycle; 《구어》 a bike; 《영구어》 a pushbike. ¶ 어린이 〔어른〕용 ～ a children's 〔full-size〕 bicycle / 경주용 ～ a racing bicycle / ～ 타는 사람 a bicycle rider; a cyclist / ～를 타다 ride (on) 〔get on〕 a bicycle / ～로 가다 go by bicycle; go on a bicycle / ～를 탈 줄 아느냐 Can you cycle? *or* Can you ride a wheel? 《미》 / ～ 주행 금지 《게시》 No bicycles. ◉ ～경주 a bicycle 〔bike〕 race: ～경주선수 a cycle racer / ～ 경주장 a bicycle bowl 〔track〕; a cyclodrome; a velodrome. ～여행 a bicycle trip; a cycling tour. ～전용도로 a cycle track; a cycling path 〔lane〕; 《미》 a bikeway. ～점 a bicycle shop. 「tricity.

**자전기**(磁電氣) 〖물리〗 magnetic elec-

**자전지계**(自全之計) a measure of self-protection.

**자정**(子正) 《at》 midnight.

**자정**(自淨) self-cleansing; self-purification. ◉ ~력: 원래 하천에는 상당한 ~력이 있다 Under natural conditions, rivers have very considerable powers of self-cleansing. ~작용: 자연의 ~작용 the self-cleansing action of nature; 『생물』 biological purification.

**자정향**(紫丁香) 『식물』 a lilac.

**자제**(子弟) sons; children; young people. ¶ 남씨의 ~ Mr. Nam's children / 명문의 ~ sons of an illustrious family [a noble stock].

**자제**(自制) self-restraint; self-control; self-repression; continence. ~하다 control *oneself;* exercise self-restraint; check *oneself* 《from *do*ing》. ¶ 그는 술을 마시게 되면 ~를 잃고 만다 He lets himself go when he drinks. ◉ ~력[심] (the power of) self-control; command over *one's* temper: ~력을 잃다 lose control 《over *oneself*》; lose *one's* self-control; let *oneself* go / ~력이 없다 be incontinent; lack self-restraint [=control].

**자제**(自製) *one's* own making [manufacture]. ¶ ~의 of *one's* own making; 《자가제의》 homemade. ◉ ~품 an article of *one's* own making.

**자조**(自助) self-help. ¶ ~의 정신 the spirit of self-help / ~는 최선의 도움 Self-help is the best help. ◉ ~정신 the spirit of self-help.

**자조**(自嘲) self-ridicule; self-scorn; self-mockery. ~하다 scorn *oneself.* ¶ ~적인 self-mocking / ~적으로 《say》 as if in self-mockery; as if to mock *oneself.*

**자족**(自足) self-sufficiency. ~하다 be self-sufficient. ⇨ 자급(自給).

**자존**(自存) self-existence. ~하다 exist of [by] itself.

**자존**(自尊) self-respect; self-esteem; self-importance; (self-)conceit; pride. ~하다 respect [esteem] *oneself;* have self-respect; be self-conceited; be proud. ¶ 민족의 ~과 안녕 national self-esteem and public well-being.

**자존심**(自尊心) (a sense of) self-respect; pride; self-esteem. ¶ ~이 있는 self-respecting; proud / ~이 강한 사람 a man of great self-respect / ~을 누르다 swallow *one's* pride; put *one's* pride in *one's* pocket / ~을 잃다 lose *one's* self-respect / ~을 상하게 하다 hurt 《*a person's*》 pride / 너는 ~도 없느냐 Why do you hold yourself so cheap ? / 나도 ~은 있다 I have my pride, too.

**자주**(自主) independence; autonomy. ¶ ~적인 independent; autonomous; 《주동적》 active / ~적으로 voluntarily; of *one's* own accord [free will] / ~(독립)의 정신 the spirit of independence / ~적 외교 an independent foreign policy; an autonomous diplomacy / ~적 관리 self-management / ~적으로 방침을 정하다 decide upon a course of action on *one's* own will / 좀더 ~적인 생각을 가져라 Have a more independent idea.
◉ ~관리 self-management. ~국 an independent state. ~국방 태세 a self-reliant defense position. ~권 autonomy; sovereign rights: ~권의 상실 frustration of autonomy. ~독립 independence; autonomy. ~성 autonomy; (*one's*) independence: ~성이 없다 lack independence (in *one's* behavior).

**자주** frequently; often; repeatedly; many times; again and again. ¶ ~ 있는 일 a common [an every day] affair / 청년들에게 ~ 있는 과오 a blunder (that) young men are apt to make / 젊은이들에게 ~ 있는 일인데 as is usual with young men / 그와는 ~ 만난다 I see much [a great deal] of him. / 비가 ~ 온다 It rains quite often. / 이 시기에는 불이 ~ 일어난다 Fires are frequent at this time of (the) year.

**자주포**(自走砲) a mobile gun.

**자줏빛** purple; amethyst; claret. ¶ 짙은 ~ deep [dark] purple / ~을 띤 purplish / ~으로 물들이다 dye 《*a thing*》 purple. ◉ ~물감 claret [purple red] dye.

**자중**(自重) 《자애》 self-love; taking care of *oneself;* 《조심》 prudence; caution; circumspection. ~하다 take care of *oneself;* 《조심》 use prudence; be cautious [circumspect]. ¶ 앞으로 더욱 ~하겠습니다 I will be more prudent [cautious] from now on.

**자중지난**(自中之亂) a fight among themselves; (an) internal strife.

**자지** the penis (*pl.* ~es, penes); the cock 《비어》.

**자지러뜨리다** shrink; double up; frighten 《*a person*》 to death; give 《*a person*》 shudders [the creeps, the willies 《미구어》]. ¶ 놀라서 몸을 ~ shrink [freeze] with fear; be scared out *one's* senses; be terrified / 배가 아파서 몸을 ~ double up with stomach pain.

**자지러지다**[1] shrink; cower; crouch. ¶ 자지러지게 놀라다 shrink with fright;

be petrified 〔frightened〕/ 자지러지게 웃다 hold *one's* sides laughing; laugh fit to kill 《미구어》/ 자지러지게 울다 cry as if *one's* heart would break; cry *one's* heart out.

**자지러지다**[2] 《그림·조각·음악 등이》 (be) exquisite; superb; charming; fascinating.

**자진**(自進) volunteering (*oneself*). ~하다 volunteer (*oneself*). ¶ ~하여 of *one's* own accord 〔volition, will〕; voluntarily / 일을 ~해서 하다 do a job of *one's* own accord / ~ 입대하다 volunteer for military service / ~해서 책임을 맡다 take the responsibility of *one's* own will / 그는 ~해서 사임했다 He resigned 「of his own accord 〔voluntarily〕. ◉ ~신고 a voluntary report: ~ 신고 기간 the voluntary reporting period.

**자질** measuring with a rule. ~하다 measure with a rule.

**자질**(資質) natural disposition; temperament; 《재능》 a talent. ¶ 그는 의사로서의 ~이 없다 He's not the stuff that doctors are made of. ◉ ~향상 upgrading the quality: 은행원들의 ~ 향상 방안을 마련하다 work out ways of upgrading the quality of bank clerks.

**자질구레하다** be all of a small size; be evenly small; (be) petty; trifling; slight. ¶ 자질구레한 밤 small-sized chestnuts / 자질구레한 일 a trifling matter; a trifle.

**자찬**(自讚) self-admiration. = 자화자찬.

**자채**(벼)(紫彩(—)) a variety of early-ripening rice plant. ◉ 자채볏논 a field of *chach'ae*.

**자책**(自責) self-accusation〔-reproach, -reproof, -condemnation〕. ~하다 accuse *oneself;* blame *oneself.* ◉ ~감〔심〕 a guilty conscience; 《가책》 pangs 〔prick〕 of conscience; 《후회》 remorse: ~감〔심〕에 사로잡히다 have 〔suffer from〕 a guilty conscience; be conscience-stricken; be seized with remorse; feel remorse 《for what *one* has done》. ~점(點) 『야구』 an earned run (생략 e.r., er).

**자처**(自處) ① 《자결》 suicide. ~하다 commit suicide. ② 《자임》 pretension. ~하다 flatter *oneself* 《that...》; fancy 〔think〕 *oneself* (as, to be); regard 〔look upon〕 *oneself* 《as》. ¶ 스스로 예술가임을 ~하다 profess 〔claim〕 to be an artist; fancy *oneself* as an artist / 시인으로 ~하다 have pretensions as a poet; think of *oneself* as a poet / 사회적 지도자로서 ~하다 look upon *oneself* as a social leader.

**자천**(自薦) self-recommendation. ~하다 recommend *oneself.*

**자철**(磁鐵) 『광물』 magnetic iron. ◉ ~광 magnetite; loadstone.

**자청**(自請) volunteering. ~하다 volunteer.

**자체**(自體) itself; 《제 몸》 *one's* own body. ¶ 물(物) 그 ~ 《칸트 철학의》 the thing-in-itself / 그 ~의 무게로 쓰러지다 fall of its own weight / 그 생각 ~가 어리석다 The idea itself is absurd. / 그 문제 ~는 매우 명료하다 The matter itself is very clear. ◉ ~감사 self-inspection. ~조사 an inhouse investigation 〔probe〕 《on》.

**자체**(字體) the shape 〔form〕 of a letter 〔character〕; 《활자의》 type; print. ¶ 정~로 명확하게 쓰다 write clearly in the square style.

**자초**(自招) ~하다 bring 《trouble》 on *oneself;* incur 《blame》; court 《danger》. ¶ 화를 ~하다 bring misfortune on *oneself* / ~한 실책이니 누구를 탓하랴 He has none to blame but himself, for the blunder was of his own making.

**자초지종**(自初至終) from the beginning to the end; from start to finish; the whole story; all the details; full particulars. ¶ ~을 다 듣다 hear the whole story / ~을 알다 be acquainted with every detail; know everything about 《it》 / ~을 이야기하다 give full particulars 《of》; give a complete account 《of》.

**자축**(自祝) celebrating by *oneself.* ~하다 celebrate 《an event》 by *oneself.*

**자축거리다** hobble; limp. ¶ 자축거리며 걷다 hobble 〔limp〕 along.

**자춤발이** a lame person; a cripple.

**자취** a trace; a track; a trail; *one's* whereabouts; marks; indications; signs; evidences; vestiges. ¶ 옛 영화의 ~ traces of former glory / ~를 감추다 cover up *one's* tracks; conceal *one's* whereabout; disappear / ~를 남기지 않다 leave no trace behind / ~도 없다 there is nothing left of 《the castle》 / 그의 ~를 찾을 수 없다 I can find no trace of him. / 이 탑만이 옛 문명의 ~를 남기고 있다 This tower is all that is left to give evidence of that ancient civilization.

**자취**(自炊) cooking food for *oneself.* ～하다 cook for *oneself;* cook *one's* own food; do *one's* own cooking. ¶ 그는 ～하고 있다 He cooks his own meals. ◉ ～생 a self-boarding student. ～설비 《a room with》 cooking facilities.

**자치**(自治) self-government 〔rule〕; self-administration; autonomy; home rule. ～하다 govern *oneself.* ¶ ～의 self-governing; autonomous / 읍면의 ～ the self-government of towns and villages / 학생들에게 ～를 허용하다 allow students to govern themselves / ～를 요구하는 집회를 갖다 hold meetings to demand their autonomy. ◉ ～권 the right of self-government; autonomous rights; autonomy. ～능력 power of 〔capacity for〕 self-government; autonomous ability. ～단체 a self-governing body. ～령 a dominion. ～제(도) a self-governing system. ～행정 self-governing administration. ～회 《학생의》 a student council; a students' self-government association.

**자치기** tipcat. ～치다 play tipcat. ¶ ～의 치는 막대기 a bat; a stick / ～의 맞히는 나무토막 a tipcat; pussy.

**자치체**(自治體) a self-governing body; an autonomy.

**자친**(慈親) a loving mother; *one's* (own) mother.

**자침**(磁針) a magnetic needle. ◉ ～방위 magnetic bearing. ～편차도 a magnetic variation chart.

**자침하다**(自沈―) scuttle 《*one's* boat》.

**자칫** 《까딱하면》 (very) nearly; barely; almost; at the slightest slip 〔provocation〕. ¶ ～하면 …하기 쉽다 be apt 〔liable, inclined, prone〕 to *do* / ～ 목숨을 잃을 뻔하다 come near losing *one's* life / ～ 잘못하면 큰일이 난다 One little mistake and you're in trouble. / ～ 기차를 놓칠 뻔했다 I was very near missing the train. / 그는 ～ 모든 것을 털어 놓으려는 참이었다 He was on the verge of telling all.

**자칭**(自稱) [형용사적] self-styled; self-appointed; self-professed; would-be. ～하다 style 〔profess, call, describe〕 *oneself;* represent *oneself.* ¶ 시인을 ～하다 profess *oneself* to be a poet / 그는 백만장자라고 ～한다 He calls 〔styles〕 himself a millionaire. / 그는 ～ 변호사다 He is a self-styled lawyer. ◉ ～시인 a would-be poet. ～신사 a self-styled gentleman.

**자타**(自他) *oneself* and others; 〖철학〗 subject and object. ¶ ～의 관계 *one's* relations with others; relations between *oneself* and others / ～가 모두 다 both *oneself* and others / 그는 ～가 인정하는 시인이다 He is generally acknowledged to be a poet. / 그가 뛰어난 역사가임은 ～가 공인하는 바이다 It is commonly acknowledged that he is a prominent historian.

**자탄**(自歎) ～하다 complain 〔grieve〕 to *oneself;* feel grief for *oneself.* ¶ 실패를 ～하다 grieve for *one's* failure.

**자태**(姿態) personal appearance; a pose; a figure; a person. ¶ 아름다운 ～ a beautiful figure / 요염한 ～ a bewitching 〔lovely〕 figure; 《포즈》 an alluring pose / 한라산의 웅장한 ～ the grand figure of Mt. Halla.

**자택**(自宅) *one's* (own) house; *one's* home. ¶ ～에서 at *one's* home / ～의 주소 *one's* home address / ～의 전화번호 *one's* home telephone number / ～에 있다〔없다〕 be 〔be not〕 at home; stay in 〔out〕 / ～ 대기령을 받다 be told to stand by at home (until instructed to return to work). ◉ ～연금 house arrest; domiciliary confinement: ～연금 시키다 place 《*a person*》 under house arrest. ～요법 a home treatment 〔remedy〕.

**자퇴**(自退) leaving 《*one's* post, *etc.*》 voluntarily; resigning of *one's* own accord. ～하다 leave 《*one's* post, *etc.*》 of *one's* own accord; resign voluntarily; back out of 《the enterprise》. ¶ 입후보를 ～하다 withdraw *one's* candidacy of *one's* own free will.

**자투리** odd ends of yardage 〔yard goods〕; remnants of dress goods. ◉ ～땅 a small piece of land (in downtown areas).

**자파**(自派) *one's* (own) party 〔faction〕.

**자판**(自判) ① 《판명》 becoming clear of itself; becoming evident 〔known〕 of its own accord; self-evident. ～하다 become self-evident. ② 《상급 법원의》 a superior court's judgment on a case reversing the original decision. ～하다 reverse (the decision).

**자판**(自辦) ① 《스스로 처리함》 doing things 〔handling matters〕 in person; disposing of matters *oneself.* ～하다 do 〔handle〕 in person. ② 《자변》 payment of the expenses *oneself.* ～하다 pay *one's* own expenses.

**자판기**(自販機) a vending machine; an automat(음식의). ⇨ 자동판매기.

**자폐선**(自閉線) 〖수학〗 a folium (*pl.* -lia);

a looped curve.
**자폐증**(自閉症) 〖심리〗 autism. ¶ ～의 아이 an autistic child.
**자포자기**(自暴自棄) self-abandonment; desperation; despair. ～하다 abandon *oneself* to despair; give *oneself* up to despair; get 〔grow, become〕 desperate. ¶ ～의 desperate; abandoned / ～로 in despair / ～가 되어 in (*one's*) desperation; 「out of 〔in〕 despair / ～가 되다 get 〔grow, become〕 desperate 《at *one's* failure》 / ～의 술을 마시다 drown *one's* cares in liquor / ～하지 마라 Don't abandon yourself to despair. / 실연으로 ～하는 젊은이들도 있다 There are some young men who are thrown into despair by disappointment in love.
**자폭**(自爆) blowing *oneself* up; suicidal 〔self-blasting, suicide〕 explosion; self-destruction; suicidal attack. ～하다 destroy *oneself;* make a suicidal attack; 《비행기가》 crash *one's* plane into the target; 《함선이》 blow up *one's* own ship. ¶ 수류탄으로 ～을 기도하다 try to blow *oneself* up with a grenade / 그는 적함에 그의 비행기를 부딪쳐 ～하였다 He crashed his plane into an enemy ship.
**자필**(自筆) *one's* own handwriting; 《법》 a holograph; an autograph. ¶ ～로 in *one's* own handwriting; autographically / ～의 autograph(ic); of 〔written in〕 *one's* own handwriting; written by *oneself;* holograph; holographic(al) (유서 등의) / ～의 원고 an autograph manuscript. ◉ ～이력서 *one's* personal history in *one's* own handwriting. ～증서 a holograph deed.
**자학**(自虐) self-torture; self-torment; masochism. ～하다 torture *oneself.* ¶ ～적인 masochistic; self-tormenting / 그녀는 ～성이 있다 She is masochistic. ◉ ～증 masochism. ～행위 a cruelty to *oneself.*
**자해**(字解) a glossary.
**자해**(自害) self-injury; 《자살》 suicide. ～하다 injure 〔hurt〕 *oneself;* kill *oneself;* commit suicide. ¶ ～적인 self-injurous; self-harming.
**자행**(恣行) ～하다 do 〔practice, commit〕 as *one* pleases; be self-indulgent; have *one's* own way. ¶ 폭력행위를 ～하다 commit 〔resort to〕 violence / 나쁜 짓을 ～하다 commit a crime; do wrong 〔evil〕.
**자형**(字形) the shape of a character; the form of a letter; type; print.
**자형**(姉兄) *one's* elder sister's husband; *one's* brother-in-law.
**자혜**(慈惠) charity; philanthrophy; benevolence. ◉ ～병원 a charity hospital. 「기화.
**자화**(磁化) 〖물리〗 magnetization. ⇨자
**자화상**(自畫像) 〖미술〗 a self-portrait. ¶ ～을 그리다 paint 〔draw〕 *one's* own portrait. 「tion.
**자화수정**(自花受精) 〖식물〗 self-fertiliza-
**자화자찬**(自畫自讚) self-admiration; self-praise. ～하다 praise 〔admire〕 *oneself;* blow *one's* own trumpet; sing *one's* own praises. ¶ 그녀는 자기 작품에 대해 ～하고 있다 She praises herself about her own work.
**자활**(自活) self-support. ～하다 support 〔sustain〕 *oneself;* earn *one's* (own) living. ¶ ～하는 여자 a woman who fights her own way in the world / ～의 길을 찾다 seek a living for *oneself* / ～의 길을 열어 주다 put 《*a person*》 in the way of getting *his* living.
**자회사**(子會社) a subsidiary 〔an affiliated〕 company; a daughter firm.
**자획**(字畫) the number of strokes in a Chinese character.
**작**(作) ① 《작품》 a work; a production. ¶ 이광수 작의 소설 a novel by Yi Kwangsu. ② 《농작》 a crop; a harvest; a yield. ¶ 평년작 an average crop / 풍〔흉〕작 a good 〔poor〕 harvest.
**작**(爵) a degree of nobility; peerage. ¶ 작의 5등급 the five degrees of peerage / 세습작 hereditary nobility / 작을 주다 bestow a title (of the peerage).
**작**(勺) 《a unit of measure》 a *chak* (= 0.018 liters, 1/10 *hop*).
**작가**(作家) a writer; an author; 《소설가》 a novelist. ¶ 신진 여류～ a rising woman writer / 인기～ a popular 〔favorite〕 writer.
**작가**(作歌) songwriting; versification. ～하다 write 〔compose〕 a song.
**작고**(作故) decease; death. ～하다 decease; die; pass away. ¶ ～한 the late / ～한 사람 the deceased [총칭].
**작곡**(作曲) (musical) composition. ～하다 compose; write music. ¶ A씨 ～ composed by Mr. A; music by Mr. A / 노래를 ～하다 《가사에 곡을 붙이다》 set a song to music; write the music to a song / 그는 이 노래의 작사 ～을 했다 He wrote both words and music for this song. / A씨 작사, B씨 ～ Words by A, music by B. ◉ ～가 a

composer. ～기술 compositional technique.

**작금**(昨今) 《현재》 these days; nowadays; 《최근》 recently; lately; of late. ¶ ～의 추위 the recent 〔present〕 cold / ～에 시작된 일은 아니다 It is of no recent date. ◉ ～양년(兩年) both last and this year. ～양일(兩日) both yesterday and today.

**작년**(昨年) last year. ¶ ～의 오늘 today last year / ～ 여름 last summer / ～ 5월에 last May; in May (of) last year; a year ago last May (★ last May는 지나간 금년 5월을 지칭할 수도 있음).

**작다** 《크기가》 (be) small; little; tiny; be of a small size; 《어리다》 (be) young; little; 《마음이》 (be) narrow-minded; small-minded; 《사소하다》 (be) petty; trifling; trivial; insignificant; 《얼마 안 되는》 (be) slight; minor; small. ¶ 제일 작은 아이 *one's* youngest child / 그릇이 작은 사람 a small mind; a small-minded person; a person of small caliber / 키가 작은 사람 a short 〔small-statured〕 person / 작은 집 a small house / 작은 아이들 little ones; little kids / 작은 목소리 a low voice / 작아지다 become smaller; dwindle; diminish / 이 구두는 나한테 너무 ～ This pair of shoes are too small for me. / 옷이 작아졌다 I have outgrown my clothes. / 작은 고추가 맵다 《속담》 The smaller, the shrewder.

**작다리** a person of short stature; a little fellow; a short person; a shorty.

**작달막하다** be sort of small; be rather short (of stature). ¶ 작달막한 체격 short build.

**작달비** 《장대비》 rain pouring down in pitchforks; a driving 〔pouring, pelting〕 rain; a drenching shower; a (torrential) downpour.

**작당**(作黨) ～하다 form a gang; band together. ¶ ～하여 in a group; in a league.

**작대기** ① 《버팀대》 a pole; a rod; a stick with a forked head; a propping stick. ② 《작대기표》 the mark of failure 《in a test》; the mark of elimination; a cross; a crossing off or out; an "X" marking a mistake. ¶ 작문에 ～를 긋다 put a failing mark on a (composition) theme. ◉ ～바늘 a darning 〔big〕 needle.

**작도**(作圖) 〖기하〗 construction; 《도면》 drawing; designing. ～하다 construct 《a triangle》; draw a figure 〔chart, diagram〕. ◉ ～문제 〖기하〗 a problem for construction.

**작동**(作動) ～하다 《기계 등이》 operate; move; come into action; work. ¶ 이 장치는 전기로 ～된다 This device is worked by electricity. / 이 기계의 ～법을 압니까 Do you know how to work this machine?

**작두**(斫一) a straw cutter; a fodder-chopper; 《사진용》 a print trimmer. ◉ ～질 chopping fodder.

**작두콩**(斫一) 〖식물〗 a sword bean.

**작량**(酌量) consideration; allowance; extenuation. ⇨참작. ～하다 consider; take into consideration 〔account〕.

**작렬**(炸裂) explosion; 《펀치의》 landing. ～하다 explode; burst. ¶ 공중에서 ～하다 explode in the air / 안면에 레프트를 ～시키다 sock a left into 《*one's* opponent's》 face.

**작명**(作名) naming; christening. ～하다 name; christen (세례명을).

**작문**(作文) (literary) composition; writing; a theme; an exercise in composition. ¶ ～을 짓다 make a composition; write a theme / ～을 연습하다 practice the art of composition; get practice in writing / ～의 제목을 내다 set a subject for composition / 자유라는 제목으로 ～을 쓰다 write a composition on 'Liberty'. ◉ ～제목 a subject for composition; a theme. 영～ English composition. 자유～ free composition.

**작물**(作物) crops; farm products 〔produce〕. ⇨농작물. ¶ ～이 되지 않았다 The harvest failed. / 이런 날씨는 ～에 좋다〔나쁘다〕 This weather is good 〔bad〕 for the crops. / 금년은 ～이 나오는 것이 이르다〔늦다〕 The crops are early 〔backward〕 this year.

**작반**(作伴) accompanying each other (on a way); keeping company; going together. ～하다 keep company 《with》; accompany; go together 〔with〕.

**작법**(作法) ① 《글 등의》 composition method; how to write 〔compose, make, *etc.*〕. ② 《법칙 제정》 making a rule 〔regulation, law〕; legislation. ◉ 소설～ how to write novels.

**작벼리** the pebbly sands 《at shore》.

**작별**(作別) leave-taking; good-by(e); a farewell. ～하다 part; take leave; say good-by. ¶ ～ 인사 a farewell 〔parting〕 word; a parting 〔farewell〕 call / ～할 때에 at 〔on〕 parting; in parting from 《*a person*》 / ～을 고하다 say good-by(e) 《to》; bid 《*a person*》 farewell / 친구와 ~하다 take leave of *one's* friends / ~ 인사를 하러 가다 go to say good-by 《to》; make a farewell call 《on》/ 이제 ~해야겠다 I must say good-by now. *or* I think I must be going now / 나는 그녀에게 ~의 키스를 했다 I kissed her good-by. / 나는 그와 ~의 악수를 했다 I shook his hand good-by.

**작부**(作付) 《농작물의》 planting; sowing. ~하다 plant 《rice》; put in a crop. ◉ ~면적 the acreage under cultivation: 보리의 ~ 면적을 줄이다 cut back on barley acreage.

**작부**(酌婦) a barmaid; a waitress.

**작사**(作詞) lyric making; writing songs. ~하다 write lyrics 〔the words〕. ¶ 김동진 ~작곡 words and music by Kim Dong-jin / 이 노래는 그가 ~ 작곡했다 He wrote both the words and music for this song. ◉ ~자 a lyric writer; a songwriter; a lyricist.

**작사리** cross-sticks (used as props).

**작살** ① 《물고기 잡는》 a (pronged) fish spear; a harpoon. ¶ ~을 쏘다 harpoon 《a whale》; fire a harpoon / ~로 고기를 잡다 spear 〔harpoon〕 fish. ② ⇨ 작사리.

**작성**(作成) drawing up; framing; preparation. ~하다 draw up; frame; make out; write out 《a contract, *etc.*》; prepare 《a deed, *etc.*》. ¶ 계약서를 2통 ~하다 make out a contract in duplicate / 증서를 ~하다 draw up a deed / 유언장을 비밀리에 ~하다 make 〔draw up〕 *one's* will secretly / 내가 그 서류를 ~하고 그가 서명하였다 I draw up the papers and he signed.

**작시**(作詩) versification; verse writing. ~하다 compose a poem; write a verse; versify. ◉ ~법 the art of verse making; 《운율법》 versification; prosody.

**작신거리다** tease 〔pester, importune〕 《*a person*》 for 《*something*》; put the squeeze 〔bite〕 on 《*a person*》.

**작심**(作心) resolve; resolution; determination. ~하다 resolve; be determined; make up *one's* mind. ◉ ~삼일(三日) a resolution good for only three days; a short-lived resolve.

**작약**(芍藥) 『식물』 a peony.

**작약하다**(雀躍—) jump for joy; exult over 《*one's* success》; leap with joy.

**작업**(作業) work; operations (조업); fatigue duty (군대의). ~하다 conduct operation; work. ¶ ~중에 while at work; while working / ~을 개시〔중지〕하다 commence 〔suspend〕 operations; start 〔stop〕 working / 강에 다리를 놓는 ~ 계획 a work project to build a bridge across the river / ~ 구간 끝 《게시》 End work / ~중 《게시》 In operation / ~중 출입 금지 《게시》 No Admittance During Working Hours / 그는 ~중에 다쳤다 He got hurt 「while working 〔at work〕. / 이제 슬슬 ~을 시작하자 Let's start working, shall we? ◉ ~강도 intensity of work. ~계획 a work project. ~공정 a working process. ~교대 work shift(s). ~능률 operation efficiency. ~대 a workbench; a worktable. ~량 amount of work done; a man-day (하루의); a man-hour (시간당). ~명령 a job order. ~모 a fatigue cap. ~반 a work 〔working〕 party; a fatigue party (군대의): ~반장 a foreman. ~복 working clothes 〔dress, uniform〕; 《직공의》 overalls; 《군대의》 fatigues. ~비 working 〔operating〕 expenses. ~시간 working hours: ~ 시간표 a time card. ~실 a workroom. ~요법 『의학』 occupational therapy. ~원 a worker. ~일 a workday; a working day. ~장 《공작소》 a workshop; 《공사장》 a job site. ~전표 a job slip. ~조건 《환경》 working conditions; 《필요조건》 job requirements. ~중지 suspension of operation; a work stoppage: ~중지 기간 a 「down 〔work stoppage〕 period. ~진척도 the rate of progress. ~허가 a work permit. ~화 work shoes. ~환경 working environment; 《improve》 the working conditions (for workers). ~훈련 on-the-job training.

**작열**(灼熱) red 〔white〕 heat; broiling 〔scorching〕 heat; incandescence. ¶ ~하는 scorching; burning; red-hot; incandescent / ~하는 태양 the scorching 〔burning〕 sun / ~하는 사막 sun-baked desert.

**작용**(作用) (an) action; working; operation; process; 《기능》 a function; 《효과》 an effect. ~하다 act 《on》; work 〔operate〕 《on》; function 《as》; affect. ¶ 동화~ the process of assimilation / 부~ a side (ill) effect / 상호~ (an) interaction / 심리~ a psychological 〔mental〕 process / 정신~ operation of the mind; mental function / 화학~ a chemical action / ~과 반작용 action and reaction / 식물에 대한 빛의 ~ the effects of light on plants / 자연의 ~ the working of nature / 산(酸)이 금속에 끼치는 ~ the action of an acid on a metal / 소금의 ~으로 by the action of salt / 지구 인력의 ~으로 under the influence of gravity / …에 ~하다 act 〔operate, work〕 upon; affect / 서로 ~하다 interact / 그건 전기의 ~으로 움직인다 That's electrically worked. / 어떤 초자연적인 힘이 ~하고 있는지도 모르겠다 Some supernatural power might be at work. / 브레이크의 ~으로 차는 멈춘다 The car stops by the working of the brake. ◉ ~범위 the working realm. ~점 《지렛대의》 the point of action 《of a lever》. ~중심 『물리』 the center of action.

**작위**(作爲) artificiality; 『법』 commission; feasance. ¶ 부(不)~ nonfeasance; omission / ~의 intentional; deliberate / ~의 죄 a sin of commission. ◉ ~동사 『문법』 a factitive 〔causative〕 verb (★ cause him to fall의 cause 같은 것). ~범 『법』 a crime of commission.

**작위**(爵位) a (noble) title; peerage. ¶ ~를 수여하다 grace 《*a person*》 with a title.

**작은곰자리** 『천문』 the Little Bear; the Ursa Minor; the Little Dipper.

**작은북** a small 〔snare〕 drum; a side drum (군악대의).

**작은아버지** *one's* father's younger brother; *one's* uncle.

**작은어머니** wife of *one's* father's younger brother; *one's* aunt.

**작은집** ① 《아우·아들의 집》 *one's* son's 〔younger brother's〕 house; a branch 〔collateral〕 family. ② 《첩의 집》 *one's* concubine's house; 《첩》 *one's* concubine 〔mistress〕. ¶ ~을 두다 keep a mistress.

**작인**(作人) a tenant farmer; a sharecropper; [총칭] tenantry. ⇨ 소작인.

**작자**(作者) ① 《소작인》 a sharecropper; a tenant farmer. ② 《만든 사람》 a maker; 《저작자》 the author; the writer. ¶ ~ 불명의 of unknown authorship; anonymous / 이 소설의 ~는 헤밍웨이다 This novel was written by Hemingway. ③ 《위인》 《구어》 a fellow; a guy. ¶ 미친 ~ a crazy guy; a screwball / 그 ~는 어디 갔지 Where has the fellow gone away? ④ 《살 사람》 a buyer; a purchaser. ¶ ~가 나서다 find a buyer / ~가 없다 find no buyers.

**작작** 《적당하게》 moderately; properly; not too much. ¶ 술 좀 ~해라 Don't drink too much. / 농담 좀 ~해라 Don't go too far with your jokes.

**작작**(綽綽) freedom and ease 《of the mind》; leisureliness. ~하다 (be) free and easy; leisurely. ¶ 여유가 ~하다 be free and easy; have energy to spare; have more than enough.

**작전**(作戰) 『군사』 (military) operations (행동); strategy (전략); tactics (전술). ~하다 plan a campaign. ¶ ~상 operationally; strategically; tactically / ~상 중요한 《a spot》 of strategic importance / ~을 짜다〔세우다〕 elaborate 〔consider, map out〕 a plan of operations / ~을 잘못하다 commit a tactical error / ~을 변경하다 change *one's* tactics / 그렇게 하는 것은 ~상 좋지 않다 It is strategically unwise to do so. / 우리의 ~이 기막히게 적중했다 Our plan worked remarkably well. ◉ ~개념 an operational concept: 한반도의 특수 상황에 맞는 ~ 개념을 개발하다 develop an operational concept tailored to specific conditions of the Korean Peninsula. ~개시일 the D-day. ~계획 《map out》 a plan of operations. ~과 the operation division. ~구역 an operating area. ~기지 a base of operations. ~명령 an operation order. ~목표 the objective of operations. ~본부실 an operations room. ~부대 a task force (육·해·공군의). ~지 a field of operations. ~지도 an operational map. ~책임 전술 지역 『군사』 the tactical area of operational responsibility (생략 TAOR). ~타임 《스포츠의》 (a) timeout. ~통제 the operational control: 한국군의 평화시 ~ 통제권이 44년만에 미국으로부터 한국으로 이관되었다 The peacetime operational control of the South Korean Armed forces has been transfered from the U.S. to Korea after 44 years. ~회의 a council of war; a tactical planning conference.

공중~ airborne operations. 방어~ defensive operations. 수세〔공세〕~ passive 〔active〕 operations; defensive 〔offensive〕 operations.

**작정**(作定) 《결정·결심》 a decision; a determination; 《의향》 an intention; a plan; an idea; a thought; a notion; 《목적》 a purpose; a project; a goal. ~하다 decide; determine; plan; propose; intend to 《*do*》; make up *one's* mind to 《*do*》; fix *one's* mind on 《*do*-

ing》. ¶ …할 ～으로 with the intention of *do*ing; with a 〔the〕 view to 〔of〕 *do*ing; in expectation 〔anticipation〕 of…; in the hope of *do*ing; for the purpose of *do*ing / …할 ～이다 be decided 〔resolved, determined〕 to *do;* have the intention of *do*ing; plan to *do;* be going to *do;* intend to *do;* mean to *do;* be thinking of *do*ing / 나는 그것을 할 ～이다 I am going to do it. / 너는 무엇을 할 ～인가 What do you mean to do? / 나는 그것을 팔 ～으로 샀다 I bought it with the intention of selling. / 하숙을 옮길 ～이다 I am thinking of changing lodgings. / 나는 여기를 떠날 ～이다 I plan to leave here. / 자동차는 팔기로 ～했다 I decided to sell my automobile.

**작중인물**(作中人物) a character who appears in the work.

**작차다** 《꽉차다》 get full up; get quite full.

**작태**(作態) a conduct; a practice. ～하다 put on airs; assume an attitude. ¶ 과거의 못된 ～ the evil practices of the past / 구시대의 못된 정치 ～ evil political practices of the bygone days / 지난날의 바람직하지 못한 정치 ～와 불신 풍조가 다시 없도록 막다 prevent the revival of the undesirable political evils and a trend of mutual distrust.

**작파**(作破) ～하다 give up 《trying》; leave off; abandon. ¶ 계획을 ～하다 lay aside 〔drop〕 a scheme.

**작폐**(作弊) making trouble; making a nuisance. ～하다 make trouble; make a nuisance; exert an evil influence.

**작품**(作品) a (piece of) work; a product; a production; 《특히 음악의》 an *opus* (L.). ¶ 문학～ a literary work / 예술～ a work of art / 현대 조각가 ～전 an exhibition of works 〔pieces〕 by contemporary sculptors / 「이것은 누구의 ～입니까」—「헤밍웨이의 유명한 ～중의 하나다」 "Whose work is it?" — "It's one of Hemingway's famous works." / 셰익스피어의 ～을 읽어 보았느냐 Did you ever read a Shakespeare? ◉ ～집 the works 《of Thomas Hardy》.

**작풍**(作風) a style 《of writing》; a literary style; 《음악·미술의》 idiom. ¶ 바흐의 ～ the idiom of Bach / 남의 ～을 모방하다 model *one's* style on another's.

**작황**(作況) a harvest; a crop; a yield. ¶ ～이 좋다〔나쁘다〕 have a good 〔bad〕 crop 《of rice》; the crops are in good 〔bad〕 condition; the crops are doing well 〔ill〕. ◉ ～보고 a crop report 〔return〕. ～예보 crop 〔harvest〕 prospects; 《예상 수확고》 the estimated crop 〔yield〕 《of rice》. ～지수(指數) a crop-situation index.

**잔**(盞) ① 《술잔》 a wine cup 〔glass〕. ¶ 잔에 술을 따르다 fill a cup with wine / 잔을 받다 accept a cup / 잔을 돌리다 pass the cup round / 잔을 주고받다 exchange cups. ② 《컵》 a cup; a glass. ¶ 찻잔 a teacup / 물을 두 잔 마시다 drink two glasses of water.

**잔가시** fine bones 《of fish》.

**잔가지** a twig; 《꽃·잎이 달린》 a sprig; a spray. ¶ ～를 치다 lop off twigs.

**잔걸음** 《걸음걸이》 walking with short steps; 《움직임》 walking within a short distance. ～치다 walk back and forth within a short distance.

**잔고**(殘高) ＝잔액(殘額). ¶ 이월 ～《차기로의》 the balance carried forward; 《전기로부터의》 the balance brought forward / ～를 전부 인출하다 draw the balance to nothing. ◉ ～증명 a certificate of balance. ～표 a balance sheet. 은행 예금 ～ the balance at the bank.

**잔고기** (a) small fish; 《치어》 fry.

**잔광**(殘光) 《해질 무렵의》 an afterglow. ¶ 석양의 ～ the afterglow of a sunset.

**잔교**(棧橋) ① 《부두의》 a (landing) pier; a landing stage. ⇨선창(船艙). ¶ 배를 ～에 대다 bring a boat alongside the pier. ② 《계곡의》 a bridge laid across ravines; a suspension bridge.

**잔글씨** small characters; fine letters. ¶ ～를 쓰다 write small characters / ～로 편지를 쓰다 write a letter in fine 〔small〕 letters.

**잔금** fine 〔thin〕 wrinkles; fine 〔small〕 lines.

**잔금**(殘金) 《잔고》 the balance; 《남은》 the surplus 〔rest〕 (of the money); the remainder; the money left over. ¶ ～을 치르다 pay the balance 〔remainder〕 / 부채의 ～을 갚다 pay the remainder of *one's* debt / ～은 이것뿐이다 This is all the money left.

**잔기**(殘期) the remaining time; the remainder of a period 〔term〕.

**잔기침** a hack; a slight 〔hacking〕 cough. ～하다 hack; have a hacking cough.

**잔꾀** little selfish wiles; petty guile 〔tricks〕. ¶ ～를 부리다 indulge in petty wiles / ～ 부리지 마라 None of your cheap tricks!

**잔당**(殘黨) the remnants (of a defeated

party or gang); the survivors《of the rebellion》. ¶ 과격파의 ～몇 명이 체포되었다 A few of the remaining radicals were arrested.

**잔돈** (small) change; small money; loose money 〔cash〕; 《속어》 peanuts; beans; 《거지에게 주는》 handout. ¶ ～으로 100원 a hundred won in change / 천원짜리를 ～으로 바꾸다 change 〔break〕 a thousand-won bill into small money / ～으로 치르다 pay in small change 〔with small money〕 / ～이 없습니다 I have no change. / ～바꾸는 곳 《게시》 Small change and coins. / ～ 준비하시오 《게시》 Have change ready. *or* (Please have) correct change. / ～이 준비돼 있지 않습니다. 토큰이나 정액을 넣어 주십시오 《게시》 We do not make change. Token or exact coin only. ◉ ～지갑 a coin purse; a small change purse.

**잔돈푼** 《소액의 돈》 a small sum of money; petty cash; odd money. ¶ ～을 벌기 위해서 일하다 do an odd job to earn some for *one's* own petty expenses / ～깨나 모으다 save a pretty sum of money.

**잔돌** a pebble(stone); a small stone 〔rock 《미》〕; [총칭] gravel (자갈).

**잔등이** ＝등.

**잔디** 〖식물〗 turf; sod; (a patch of) grass. ¶ ～ 깎는 기계 a lawn mower / ～를 깎다 cut the grass / ～를 깔다 lay 〔turf〕 a lawn; lay turf / 뜰에 ～를 심다 plant grass 〔a lawn〕; put a yard in turf. ◉ ～구장 a lawn soccer field; a lawn ground. ～밭 a lawn; a grassplot; a patch of grass: ～밭을 깎다 mow the lawn / ～밭에 물을 뿌리다 sprinkle the lawn / ～밭에 들어가지 마시오 《게시》 Keep off the grass !

**잔뜩** ① 《꽉 차게》 (to the) full; fully; to capacity; 《많이》 in plenty; abundantly; heavily. ¶ ～ 마시다〔먹다〕 drink 〔eat〕 *one's* fill / ～ 취하다 be loaded 《with liquor》; be dead-drunk / 술을 잔에 ～ 붓다 fill a cup with wine to the brim / 옷을 ～ 껴입다 be heavily clothed / 할 일이 ～ 있다 have *one's* hand full / 빚을 ～ 지고 있다 be under a heavy debt / 돈을 ～ 모으다 save a lot of money / 책장에 책이 ～ 있다 The shelves are loaded with books. ② 《몹시》 intensely; heavily; extremely; firmly. ¶ ～ 찌푸린 날씨 a heavily leaden 〔sullen, overcast〕 sky / 아무의 얼굴을 ～ 노려보다 stare *a person* in the face; look straight at *a person* / ～ 골이 나다 start fuming; begin to boil (with anger) / …을 ～ 믿다 firmly believe that… / ～ 버티고 움직이지 않다 will not stir an inch.

**잔루**(殘壘) 〖야구〗 runners left 〔stranded〕 on base. ～하다 be left on base. ¶ 주자는 3루에서 ～로 끝났다 The runner was left on third base. / ～ 없음 Nobody left on base.

**잔류**(殘留) remaining; staying behind. ～하다 remain 〔stay〕 behind. ¶ 공습경보가 발령되었는데도 그 건물에 2, 3명의 남녀가 ～해 있었다 A few men and women stayed behind in the building after the air-raid warning was given. ◉ ～감각 〖심리〗 aftersensation. ～농약 residual agricultural chemicals. ～물 a residual substance; a residue. ～부대 remaining forces. ～선 residual rays. ～자기(磁氣) residual magnetism. ～조(組) a group ordered to remain.

**잔말** small talk; prattle; chatter; small complaints; nagging; scolding. ＝잔소리. ～하다 say useless things; twaddle; chatter; nag; scold; rebuke. ¶ ～ 말고 어서 일이나 해라 Cut the chatter and get down to work.

**잔명**(殘命) the remainder of *one's* doomed life. ¶ 그는 ～이 얼마 안 남았다 His days 〔years〕 are numbered. *or* He has one foot in the grave.

**잔무**(殘務) remaining business; unsettled affairs. ¶ ～를 정리하다 clear up the remaining business; settle the remaining 〔pending〕 affairs; wind up the affairs 《of》 / ～를 끝내려고 잔업하다 work overtime to finish *one's* unsettled affairs.

**잔물결** ripples; wavelets. ¶ ～이 일다〔을 일으키다〕 ripple; ruffle / 바람이 호수면에 ～을 일으켰다 The wind rippled the surface of the lake.

**잔병**(一病) constant slight sickness; a slight indisposition; sickliness. ¶ ～이 많다 be constantly 〔frequently〕 sick; be sickly. ◉ ～꾸러기 a sickly person. ～치레 always getting sick.

**잔부**(殘部) the remaining part; the remainder; the rest; what is 〔are〕 left.

**잔상**(殘像) 〖심리〗 an afterimage.

**잔서**(殘暑) the lingering (late) summer heat; the heat of late summer.

**잔설**(殘雪) lingering snow; the remaining 〔unmelted〕 snow on the ground.

**잔셈** a small account. ¶ ～은 나중에 하자 Let's settle small accounts later on.

**잔소리** ① 《잔말》 useless 〔small〕 talk; empty 〔idle〕 talk; empty prattle. ～하다 talk idle; say useless things; 《쫑알거리다》 nag 《at》; find fault 《with》; 《불평하다》 complain 《of》; grumble 《at, over》. ¶ ～가 심한 여자 a nagging 〔faultfinding〕 woman / 그녀는 늘 아이들에게 ～를 늘어놓는다 She keeps grumbling at her children. / 그녀는 늘 남편의 귀가 시간이 늦다고 ～했다 She kept nagging her husband for coming home late. ② 《꾸지람》 (a) scolding; a rebuke; preaching. ～하다 scold; give 《*a person*》 a scolding; rebuke; reprimand. ¶ ～를 듣다 be scolded; catch it / ～를 퍼붓다 give 《*a person*》 a good scolding / ～ 그만해 Enough of your preaching. ◉ ～꾼 a chatterbox; a nagger.

**잔손** fine 〔elaborate, detailed〕 hand work; a little touch; minute attention 〔care, trouble〕. ¶ ～이 드는 일 laborious 〔troublesome〕 work; a piece of work requiring elaborate care / ～이 많이 들다〔가다〕 demand a lot of fine touches; take a lot of trouble. ◉ ～질 a small touch; a final touch: ～질하다 give 《*a thing*》 small touches; give a final touch to; put the final touch(es) on.

**잔솔** a young pine (tree). ◉ ～밭 a grove 〔wood〕 of young pines: ～밭에서 바늘찾기 "trying to find a needle in a haystack".

**잔술**(盞―) liquor by the cup 〔glass〕; a glassful of liquor. ◉ ～집 a pub that sells draft liquor.

**잔심부름** sundry errands 〔jobs〕; miscellaneous services; odd jobs.

**잔악**(殘惡) cruelty; atrocity; inhumanity. ～하다 (be) cruel; atrocious; inhumane. ¶ 온갖 ～한 짓을 다하다 employ every means of atrocity that *one* can think of.

**잔액**(殘額) the balance (in an account); the remainder. ⇨ 잔고·잔금. ¶ 은행의 예금 ～ the balance at the bank / 미불금 ～ arrears 《of rent》 / 차입금 ～ the balance of the loan / ～을 지불하다 《차액을》 pay the balance of 《*a person's*》 account; 《잔금을》 pay the remainder of the money due to 《*a person*》.

**잔업**(殘業) overtime 〔extra hours〕 work; working overtime. ～하다 work overtime 〔extra hours〕. ¶ 어제는 2시간 ～했다 I worked two hours overtime yesterday. ◉ ～수당 pay for overtime; an overtime-work allowance; overtime pay: ～수당을 받다〔지급하다〕 get paid 〔paid〕 for overtime (work).

**잔여**(殘餘) the remainder; the remnants; the rest; the balance; the surplus; 《화학 처리·유산 등의》 the residue. ¶ ～의 remaining; residual / 이것은 석유를 정제할 때의 ～ 생산물이다 This is a residual product of oil refining. ◉ ～액 the balance; the remainder. ～재산 remaining assets; a residuary estate.

**잔인**(殘忍) cruelty; atrocity; inhumanity. ～하다 (be) cruel; atrocious; brutal; inhuman; cold-blooded; cruel=hearted. ¶ ～한 살인 a cold-blooded murder / ～한 짓 a cruel act; a cold=blooded act / ～한 사람 a cruel 〔brutal〕 person / ～한 짓을 하다 do a cruel thing; commit cruelties / ～하게 대하다 treat 《*a person*》 cruelly; be cruel to 《*a person*》; be hard on 《*a person*》 / 그런 짓을 하는 것은 ～하다 It is cruel to do such a thing. ◉ ～무도 abominable cruelty; inhumanity. ～성 *one's* brutal nature.

**잔일** 《자질구레한》 a trifling 〔minor〕 matter; 《잔손이 가는》 troublesome work; sundry jobs; 《가사의》 (household) chores.

**잔입** the limited appetite *one* has on getting out of bed. ¶ ～이 되어서 입맛이 없다 I don't feel like eating because I just got up.

**잔잔하다** 《바람·물결·사태 따위가》 (be) quiet; still; calm; tranquil; placid; peaceful; serene; smooth. ¶ 잔잔히 quietly; placidly / 잔잔한 물결 gentle waves / 잔잔한 바다 a calm 〔smooth〕 sea / 잔잔한 미소 a serene smile / 잔잔한 목소리로 in a quiet 〔gentle〕 voice / 바람이 점차로 잔잔해졌다 The wind has gone down 〔died away〕. / 잔잔한 물이 깊다 《속담》 Still waters run deep.

**잔잔하다**(潺潺―) (be) murmuring. ¶ 잔잔히 murmuring(ly) / 잔잔한 시냇물 a murmuring stream / 잔잔히 흐르다 flow murmuringly; murmur along.

**잔재**(殘滓) remnants; leftovers; 《앙금》 dregs; 《찌끼》 waste matter; 《흔적》 a vestige. ¶ 봉건주의〔군국주의〕의 ～ remaining vestiges of feudalism 〔militarism〕 / 일제(日帝)의 ～ vestiges of

Japanese imperialism.

**잔재미** an amusement 〔a pleasure〕 in a small way; a subtle pleasure. ¶ ~가 있는 사람 a nice person to have around / ~를 보다 have a nice little time of it; make a hit in a small way (성공); turn a tidy profit (이익); fish up a nice bit of catch (낚시).

**잔재주**(—才—) a petty artifice; a trick; a device. ¶ ~를 부리다 play 〔resort to〕 petty tricks; employ petty shifts / ~로는 이 위기를 넘길 수 없다 cheap tricks won't get us through this crisis.

**잔적**(殘敵) the remnants of a defeated enemy; stragglers. ¶ ~을 소탕하다 mop up 〔clean up〕 the remnants of (shattered) enemy troops. ◉ ~소탕전 a mopping-up operation; a mopper-up.

**잔존**(殘存) survival. ~하다 survive; remain; be left; be still alive 〔in existence〕. ¶ ~하고 있는 surviving; extant. ◉ ~기관(器官) a vestigial 〔residual, rudimentary〕 organ. ~동물〔식물〕 relic fauna 〔flora〕. ~물 (a thing that is) a hangover; a survival. ~생물 a relict. ~자 a survivor. ~종(種) 〚동·식물〛 a relict species.

**잔주름** fine wrinkles 〔lines〕; crow's-feet (눈가의). ¶ ~이 지다 finely wrinkled 《skin》. ◉ ~살 skin with fine wrinkles in it.

**잔줄** a fine line.

**잔지바르** 《아프리카 동해안의 섬》 Zanzibar (Island). ◉ ~사람 a Zanzibari.

**잔챙이** the smallest one; a small one; small fry. ¶ ~ 물고기 small fry 〔fish〕 / ~를 골라 내다 pick 〔sort〕 out a small 〔inferior〕 one.

**잔치** a (ceremonial) feast (축연); a banquet (공식적인); a party. ¶ 생일~ a birthday party / 돌~ a birthday party for one-year old baby / 혼인 ~ a wedding feast / 환갑 ~ a banquet given on *one's* sixtieth birthday / ~를 열다〔벌이다〕 give a banquet 〔feast〕 / ~에 손님을 초대하다 invite guests to a feast / ~가 한창이다 The feast is at its height. ◉ 잔칫집 a banqueting house: 소문난 잔칫집에 먹을 것 없다 《속담》 Much noise and no substance.

**잔칼질** mincing; chopping. ~하다 mince; chop. ¶ 고기를 ~하다 mince meat.

**잔털** fine hairs; down (솜털).

**잔품**(殘品) leftover stock; unsold goods; the remaining stock. ¶ ~이 얼마 없다 The stock is running short 〔low〕. ◉ ~정리〔매출〕 a clearance 〔rummage〕 sale.

**잔학**(殘虐) outrage; (a) cruelty; (an) atrocity; brutality; inhumanity. ~하다 (be) cruel; outrageous; inhuman; ruthless. ¶ ~한 행위 a brutal act; brutalities; an atrocity / ~하게 대하다 treat 《*a person*》 cruelly 〔brutally〕; subject 《*a person*》 to inhuman treatment / ~한 짓을 하다 do something cruel; commit atrocities (★ atrocity는 복수형으로 쓰는 일이 많음).

**잔해**(殘骸) 《배·건물 등의》 the wreck; 《잔류물》 ruins; the remains 《of》; 《시체의》 a corpse; a carcass; 《무너진 것》 debris; [총칭] the wreckage 《of》. ¶ 비행기의 ~ the wreck(age) of an airplane; the remains of a wrecked plane / 옛 성이 ~로 남아 있었다 The old castle was 〔lay〕 in ruins.

**잔향**(殘響) (a) reverberation. ¶ 절의 종소리의 ~ the reverberation(s) of a temple bell. ◉ ~계(計) 〚물리〛 a reverberation meter. ~시간 reverberation time.

**잔허리** the small of the back.

**잔혹**(殘酷) (a) cruelty; (a) brutality; (an) atrocity; ruthlessness; mercilessness. ~하다 (be) cruel; atrocious; brutal; ruthless; merciless. ⇨ 참혹.

**잘** ① 《만족스럽게, 훌륭〔유리〕하게》 well; nicely; satisfactorily; favorably; fortunately. ¶ 잘 생기다 be good-looking / 잘 먹다〔자다, 살다〕 eat 〔sleep, live〕 well / 아무에 대해 잘 말하다 speak well 〔favorably〕 of *a person* / 아무에게 잘 보이다 win the good opinion of *a person;* find favor in the eyes of *a person* / 잘 있었니 How have you been? / 이 고기는 잘 익었다 This meat is well done. / 만사가 생각했던 것보다 잘 되었다 Everything went better than I had expected. / 이 문은 잘 닫힌다〔닫히지 않는다〕 This door 「shuts well 〔does not work well〕. / 그녀에 관하여는 어머니로부터 잘 들었다 I've heard much of her from my mother.
② 《상세히》 well; closely; thoroughly; intimately. ¶ 잘 알다 know well / 잘 생각하다 consider well; give much thought to; think over / 잘 모르겠다 I don't know for certain. *or* I am not sure about it. / 이 말 뜻을 잘 모른다 I don't know exactly what this word means. / 잘 생각해보니, 3시에 약속이 있는 걸, 이 얘기는 다음에 하세 Come to think of it, I have an appointment

at 3 o'clock, so we'll have to table our discussion.
③ 《익숙·능란하게》 well; excellently; expertly. ¶ 잘 지껄이는 사내 an inveterate punster; a voluble talker; a talkative man / 말〔음식〕을 잘 하다 talk 〔cook〕 well / 피아노를 잘 치다 play the piano well / 잘 빠져나가다 make *one's* escape good; explain away.
④ 《주의하여·탈없이》 well; carefully. ¶ 잘 보다 look at 《*a thing*》 carefully 〔closely〕; have a good look at / 잘 듣다 listen (to) carefully / 잘 가거라〔있거라〕 Good-bye!
⑤ 《많이》 lots; a lot; in large numbers; in nice quantity; sufficiently; 《자주》 lots; a lot; often; in nice frequency. ¶ 잘 …하곤 하였다 used to 《*do*》; would 《*do*》 (★ used to는 would 보다 규칙적인 경우임) / 영화관에 잘 가다 go to the movies a lot / 비가 잘 온다 It rains a lot. / 그는 학교를 잘 쉰다 He often「stays away from school 〔skips school〕. / 그 상점엔 손님이 잘 온다 The store has lots of customers.
⑥ 《걸핏하면》 readily; easily; on the slightest provocation. ¶ 잘 웃다 laugh readily; be fond of laughing / 잘 성내다 be apt to get angry; get angry readily / 그는 남하고 잘 싸운다 He is apt to pick quarrels with others.
⑦ 《알맞게》 well; suitably; properly. ¶ 옷이 잘 맞다 a dress fits nicely.
⑧ 《마침》 well; timely; at a good time. ¶ 너 참 잘 왔다 You've come at just the right moment. Welcome, welcome! / 이번 비는 잘 왔다 This was a good rain.

**잘가닥** with a snap 〔click, crack〕. ~하다 give a snap 〔click〕; slap; slurp. ~거리다 snap 〔click〕 away; slap and slap; slurp and slurp. ¶ 문의 자물쇠를 ~ 걸다 click the door shut / 사진을 ~ 찍다 snap a picture.

**잘가당** with a snap 〔click〕. ~하다 give a snap; click.

**잘각-** ⇨ 잘가닥-.

**잘그랑-** ⇨ 절그렁-.

**잘금-** ⇨ 짤끔-.

**잘나다** ① 《잘생기다》 (be) handsome; good-looking; comely. ¶ 얼굴이 잘난 소년 a handsome boy / 잘난 청년 a fine-looking young man / 그 사람 잘났군 He is quite handsome. ② 《뛰어나다》 (be) distinguished; great; excellent. ¶ 잘난 사람 a distinguished 〔great〕 person; a person of great caliber. ③ [반어적] (be) worthless; useless. ¶ 이 잘난 책을 무엇하러 읽느냐 I don't see why you are reading such a "great work"(=such a stupid book) as this.

**잘난 체하다** assume 〔put on〕 airs 〔an air of importance〕; give *oneself* airs; look big; think *oneself* somebody; think highly of *oneself*. ¶ 잘난 체하는 사람 a self-important fellow; a snob; a braggart / 잘난 체하며 말하다 speak with an air (of importance) / 녀석은 잘난 체한다 He acts big.

**잘다** 《크기가》 (be) fine; small; tiny; minute; 《인품이》 (be) small; stingy; fussy; be of small caliber 〔calibre 《영》〕. ¶ 잔 모래〔자갈〕 fine sand 〔gravel〕 / 잔 사람 a man of small caliber / 잔 글씨를 쓰다 write small characters 〔letters〕 / 잘게 베다 cut 《*a thing*》 fine 〔small〕 / 고기를 잘게 썰다 chop meat into small pieces; mince meat / 그는 사람이 ~ He is a small-minded 〔fussy〕 man.

**잘되다** ① 《일·성과가》 go well; come off fine; come out well 〔successfully〕; make good progress; 《농사·장사 따위》 prosper; thrive. ¶ 잘되지 않다 go wrong 〔amiss〕; be unsuccessful / 지금까진 잘돼가고 있어 "so far so good" / 잘되면 제 탓 못 되면 조상 탓 take personal credit when things go well, and blame *one's* ancestors when they do not / 올해는 벼가 잘된다 The rice plants are doing nicely this year. / 장사가 전처럼 잘되지 않는다 Business never goes quite so smoothly as before. / 잘됐군 그래 How lucky you are! *or* Good for you. / 모든 일이 잘되었다 Everything has gone well with me. ② 《출세하다》 succeed in life; rise in the world; be promoted (승진). ¶ 가장 잘된 사람 the most successful man. ③ 《완전하다》 be complete; be thoroughgoing. ¶ 이 식당은 위생 설비가 잘되어 있다 The restaurant has complete sanitary facilities. / 이 집은 손질이 잘돼 있다 This house is in good repair.

**잘똑거리다** limp. ⇨ 절다[2].

**잘라내다** cut off 〔out, away〕; cut 〔hew〕 down 《lumber》; nip; snip; clip; 《손발을》 amputate; 『외과』 《일부를》 resect. ¶ 가위로 ~ cut 《*a thing*》 with scissors 〔shears〕; shear; 《정원수를》 trim 〔prune〕 《a tree》 / 나무의 새순을 ~ nip shoots off a tree / 신문

기사를 ～ cut 〔clip〕 an article from a newspaper.

**잘라 말하다** say 〔assert, state〕 positively; say definitely; declare; affirm; swear; vouch; give 〔pledge〕 *one's* words. ¶ 잘라 말하기를 꺼리다 hesitate to say positively / 승낙 못 하겠다고 잘라 말하는 것이 좋겠다 You had better tell him once for all that you cannot comply with his request.

**잘라먹다** ① 《동강내어》 eat by cutting 〔breaking〕 into pieces. ¶ 떡을 ～ break a cake and eat it. ② 《안 갚다》 deliberately forget to return 《*a thing*》; make 《a borrowed thing》 *one's* own. ¶ 빚을 ～ welsh on *one's* debt / 외상을 ～ bilk 〔ignore〕 *one's* bill / 술값을 ～ do not pay for *one's* drink; leave *one's* bar bill unpaid / 빚을 잘라먹고 도망가다 bolt without paying *one's* debts / 빚을 잘라먹을 셈이냐 Do you mean to disown your debt?

**잘랑거리다** jingle; clink; tinkle. ¶ 주머니의 돈을 ～ jingle the coins in *one's* pocket.

**잘랑잘랑** jingling; clinking; tinkling. ¶ 말방울이 ～ 울린다 The horse bells are jingling.

**잘래잘래** shaking *one's* head.

**잘록잘록** ～하다 (be) pinched 〔sloped〕 in (in many places).

**잘록하다** be constricted (in the middle); be pinched 〔sloped〕 in; (be) slender; narrow. ¶ 잘록한 허리 a pinched-in 〔slender〕 waist / 허리가 잘록한 여자 a woman with a wasp waist / 조롱박은 허리가 ～ A gourd 「has a neck 〔narrows in the middle〕.

**잘리다** ① 《끊어지다》 be snapped; cut 《off》; 《해고》 get fired; get the ax(e). ¶ 목이 ～ be decapitated 〔beheaded〕 / 이 통나무는 잘 잘리지 않는다 This log won't chop. / 그는 자동차에 치어서 팔이 잘렸다 He was run over by a car and lost one arm. ② 《떼어먹힘》 lose (*a thing* by lending or entrusting it to *a person*). ¶ 그에게 돈을 잘렸다 He swindled me out of money. / 저 녀석에게 100만원 잘렸다 He has bilked 〔swindled〕 me out of one million won. ③ 《졸라매이다》 be tied up tight.

**잘못** ① 《과실·틀림》 a mistake; an error; a blunder; a slip; a fault; a failure; a wrong; a blame (죄과); bobble. ～하다 《…이》 do wrong; be in the wrong; make 「a mistake 〔an error〕; blunder.

> **용법** **mistake** 큰 잘못, 작은 잘못 할 것 없이 잘못에 대한 일반적인 말로, 견해나 행위, 판단 등의 그릇됨을 가리킴. 비난의 뜻은 error나 blunder보다 약함. **error** mistake와 같은 뜻으로 쓰이지만, 부주의로 정확성이나 행위가 기준을 벗어났음을 뜻함. **blunder** 부주의로 저지르게 되는 어처구니없는 실수. **slip** 서두르거나 방심해서 생기는 작은 잘못. **fault** 사람이 지니고 있는 결점(shortcomings)의 뜻으로, 언제나 비난의 뜻이 담겨 있는 것은 아님. **blame** 실수나 잘못에 대한 비난의 뜻이 강한 말.

¶ 문법의 ～ a grammatical mistake / 인쇄의 ～ a misprint / ～해서 by mistake / ～을 봐 주다 overlook 《*another's*》 faults; shut 〔close〕 *one's* eyes 《to》; connive at 《*another's*》 fault; pass over 《*a matter*》 in silence / ～을 범하다 commit a fault; make 〔commit〕 an error; bobble / ～을 깨닫다 see 〔perceive, realize〕 *one's* faults; see the error of *one's* ways; be convinced of *one's* error / ～을 사과하다 apologize 《to *a person*》 for *one's* fault / 아무한테 ～하다 do *a person* wrong; wrong *a person* / ～했다고 하다 own *oneself* in the wrong / ～을 고치다 《과오를》 mend *one's* ways; correct the errors of *one's* past; 《틀린 데를》 correct an error / 어서 ～했다고 해라 Come on, now, and say you're sorry. / ～이 있으면 고치시오 《틀린 데를》 Correct errors, if any. / 정부가 이런 정책을 쓰는 것은 ～이다 It is a big mistake for the Government to adopt such a policy. / 그는 ～해서 다른 기차를 탔다 He got on the wrong train by mistake. / 그것은 내 ～이다 That is my mistake 〔fault〕. *or* I was wrong. *or* I am to blame. / 계산에 ～이 있다 There is something wrong in the accounts. / 그 사람을 믿은 것이 네 ～이다 It is your mistake that you trusted him. / 누구에게나 ～은 있게 마련이다 Anyone can make a mistake. *or* Nobody's perfect. *or* To err is human.

② 〔부사적〕 by mistake; wrongly; erroneously; mistakenly. ～하다 《…을》 do wrongly 〔improperly, amiss〕; misdo. ～되다 go wrong 〔amiss, awry〕. ¶ ～된 생각 the wrong idea; a misjudgment / ～된 정책 the wrong policy; a mistaken (political) course / 정치를 ~하다 misrun the government; misconduct the affairs of state / ~ 발음하다 mispronounce / ~ 생각하다 misunderstand; misjudge; mistake / ~ 생각하고 있다 be in error; be under a wrong 〔false〕 impression; be misled 《about *a matter*》 / ~ 계산하다 miscalculate / ~ 듣다 mishear / ~ 두다 misplace / ~ 보도〔인용〕하다 misreport 〔misquote〕 / ~ 보다 《오인》 mistake 〔take〕 《A》 for 《B》; misidentify 《A》 as 《B》; 《평가》 make a mistake 《about》; misjudge; 《빠뜨림》 miss; fail to see 《a mistake, a misprint》 / 사람을 ~ 보다 misjudge *a person* / 나의 생각이 ~된 것이 아니라면 if I am not mistaken; 《기억이》 if I remember right; if my memory is correct / 네가 ~ 생각했다 You have the wrong idea. / 그는 겸손에 대해서 ~ 생각하고 있다 He has a mistaken idea of modesty. / 사람을 ~ 보지 말라고 What do you take me for? / 그를 ~ 보았다 I am disappointed in him. / 그녀를 남자로 ~ 보았다 I mistook her for a man. / 실례했습니다, 제가 사람을 ~ 봤군요 Excuse me. I thought I knew you. / 모든 일이 ~되었다 Everything went wrong.

**잘못짚다** guess wrong; make a wrong guess; misjudge 《the result》; make a miscalculation 《about》; shoot at the wrong mark.

**잘박거리다** splash 《about》. ¶ 잘박거리며 걷다 splash along / 아이들이 잘박거리며 시내를 건너고 있다 The children are splashing across the stream.

**잘박잘박** splashing along; with splash after splash. ¶ ~ 걷다 splash along.

**잘살다** be well 〔comfortably〕 off; live in affluence.

**잘생기다** (be) good-looking; handsome; beautiful; pretty; fair. ¶ 잘 생긴 남자 a handsome 〔good-looking〕 man / 잘 생긴 여자 a beautiful 〔good-looking〕 woman / 얼굴이 ~ have a handsome face.

**잘잘** ① 《끓음》 bubbling; simmering; seething; boiling. ¶ 물이 ~ 끓는다 The water is simmering. / 그는 열이 있어 몸이 ~ 끓는다 His body is burning with fever. ② 《끌림》 dragging 《on the ground》. ¶ 치맛자락을 ~ 끌다 drag the ends of *one's* skirt. ③ 《쏘다님》 darting about; going around hurriedly. ¶ 어디를 그렇게 ~ 돌아다니느냐 What are you doing, darting about so much! ④ 《흔듦》 shaking; jingling 《in *one's* hand》. ⑤ 《기름·윤기》 being oily; greasy; glistening; sleek. ⑥ ⇨잘래잘래.

**잘잘못** right and 〔or〕 wrong. ¶ ~간에 (regardless of whether) right or wrong / ~을 가리다 know 〔tell〕 the right from the wrong / ~간에 싸울 것 없다 No matter who is right or wrong, you shouldn't quarrel. / 어린 애는 ~을 가리지 못한다 A baby is not a moral being.

**잘카닥-, 잘칵-** ⇨ 잘가닥-.

**잘하다** ① 《익숙·능란·훌륭》 do well 〔skillfully, expertly, cleverly〕; 《올바르게》 do a right thing; do right. ¶ 말 잘하는 사람 a smooth talker / 음식 ~ cook well / 계산을 ~ be good at figures / 영어를 ~ speak English well; have a good command of English / 말을 ~ be a good speaker / 아무에게 ~ be good to *a person* / 잘해내다 manage 《*a matter*》 successfully; make a good job of it; hit *one's* stride / 그가 그르고 네가 잘했다 He is wrong and you are right. / 정말 잘했다 Well done! *or* Good for you! There you go. / 잘하면 성공할 지도 모른다 With good luck, I might succeed. / 당신은 사람 다루기를 잘하시는군요 You are dexterous in 〔at〕 handling men, aren't you? ② 《걸핏하면》 do a lot; do often. ¶ 웃기를 ~ laugh a lot.

**잠** ① 《수면》 sleep; slumber. ¶ 깊은〔얕은〕 잠 a deep 〔light〕 sleep / 잠을 자다 sleep; go to sleep / 잠이 들다 fall asleep / 잠이 부족하다 have not had enough sleep / 잠이 엄습하다 be overpowered with drowsiness / 잠에서 깨다 awake 〔start〕 from *one's* sleep / 잠을 못 이루다 fail to go sleep; be sleepless; lie awake / 잠을 험하게 자다 have a disorderly sleeping manner; toss about in sleep / 간밤엔 잠을 못 잤다 I could not get to sleep last night. / 잠을 못 자서 머리가 아프다 I spent a restless night and now I have a headache. / 잠을 자야 꿈을 꾸지 《속담》 There are no results without causes. / 그 일을 생각하느라 밤새 한 잠도 못 잤다 I never slept a wink all night for thinking of the matter. ② 《누에의》 the dormant period of the silkworm. ③ 《푸한 것의》 compression; pressing 〔smoothing〕 down; setting; tamping.

**잠결** while asleep. ¶ ~에 in *one's* sleep;

while asleep / ～에 듣다 hear half asleep / ～에 '불이야' 하는 소리를 들었다 Half sleep and half awake, I heard the cry "Fire!" / ～에 총소리를 들었다 In my sleep I heard the sound of a rifle shot.

**잠귀** *one's* hearing while asleep; *one's* wakeability. ¶ ～가 밝다 awake from *one's* sleep at the slightest noise; sleep lightly; be a light sleeper / ～가 어둡다 sleep heavily; be a heavy sleeper / ～가 질기다 be a hard person to rouse / 노인은 대개 ～가 밝다 Old men are mostly light sleepers. / 그는 ～가 밝다 He sleeps in one eye open.

**잠그다**[1] 《여닫는 것을》 lock; fasten (the lock of). ¶ 문〔서랍, 집, 방〕을 ～ lock a door 〔drawer, house, room〕/ 수도를 ～ turn off the water 〔faucet〕/ 문에 자물쇠를 분명히 잠갔니 Are you sure you locked the door? / 열쇠를 차 안에 놔둔채 문을 잠그고 나왔다 I'm locked out of my car.

**잠그다**[2] ①《물에》 immerse; soak; steep; dip; submerge; sink. ¶ 머리를 물 속에 ～ immerse 〔plunge〕 *one's* head in the water / 빨기 전에 옷을 물에 ～ let clothes soak before washing them / 스펀지를 더운 물에 ～ soak a sponge in hot water / 손가락을 물에 잠갔다 I dipped my fingers in water. ②《투자》 invest 《capital》 in 《a permanent holding》; sink 《funds》.

**잠기다**[1] 《여닫는 것이》 lock; be locked. ¶ 이 문은 자동적으로 잠긴다 This door locks automatically. *or* This is a self-locking door. / 문이 잠기지 않는다 The door won't lock. / 책상 서랍이 잠겨 있다 The desk drawer is locked.

**잠기다**[2] ① 《물 속에》 sink 《in the water》; submerge; 《홍수로》 be flooded 〔submerged〕. ¶ 배가 강 밑에 잠겼다 The boat sank to the bottom of the river. / 이 바위는 밀물 때 물 속에 잠긴다 This rock submerges at high tide. / 홍수로 아래층이 물에 잠겼다 The downstairs (rooms) were under water owing to the flood. ② 《목이》 become hoarse; hoarsen; get a frog in *one's* throat. ¶ 목소리가 ～ become hoarse; hoarsen / 목이 잠겨서 말을 못하겠다 I lost my voice and I can't talk. ③ 《돈이》 《capital》 be tied down; be sunk. ¶ 돈이 광산업에 ～ *one's* money is sunk in the mining industry. ④ 《생각·습관 따위에》 be absorbed in; be sunk 〔lost〕 in; indulge in; give *oneself* up to; be given (over) to. ¶ 악습에 ～ indulge *oneself* in a bad habit / 비탄에 ～ be overwhelmed by sorrow; 《구어》 eat *one's* heart out / 생각에 ～ contemplate / 그는 명상에 잠겼다 He was sunk 〔lost〕 in contemplation.

**잠깐** (for) a moment 〔while〕; (for) a (little) while; (just) a minute; a short time. ¶ ～ 사이〔동안〕에 in a minute 〔moment〕; in no time / ～ 생각하고 나서 after a moment's thought / ～ 있으면 in a little while 〔short time〕/ ～ 있다가 after a little while 〔short time〕/ 그 문제는 ～ 별도에 부치기로 하고 apart from 〔setting aside〕 the question of... / ～ 기다리십시오 Wait a few moments, please. / ～ 뵐 수 있습니까 May I see you for a minute? *or* I should like to see you for a few minutes. / ～ 다녀오겠다 《나갈 때》 I won't be gone long. / ～ 실례합니다 Could you spare me a few minutes? / ～ 보여 주시오 Let me have a look.

**잠깨다** awake from *one's* sleep. ¶ 자명종 소리를 듣고～ wake to an alarm clock.

**잠꼬대** talking in *one's* sleep; somniloquy; 《엉뚱한 말》 silly talk; nonsense; bosh. ～하다 talk in *one's* sleep; say silly things; talk nonsense; talk bosh. ¶～하는 버릇이 있는 사람 a sleep talker; a somniloquist.

**잠꾸러기** a sleepyhead; a great 〔heavy〕 sleeper; "a slugabed".

**잠동무** a bedfellow.

**잠두**(蠶豆) 『식물』 a broad bean; a horse bean.

**잠들다** fall asleep; drop off to sleep; 《죽다》 die; pass away. ¶ 깊이 ～ fall fast asleep; sleep like a log / 술을 마시고 ～ drink *oneself* to sleep / 영원히 ～ go to *one's* long sleep; sleep the final 〔eternal〕 sleep / 아기가 울다가 잠들었다 The baby cried himself to sleep. / 영혼이여 고이 잠드소서 May he rest in peace. *or* May his soul rest in peace.

**잠란**(蠶卵) a silkworm egg 〔seed〕. ◉ ～지(紙) a silkworm-egg card.

**잠망경**(潛望鏡) a periscope.

**잠바** a jacket; a zip-up jacket; a jumper. ⇨ 점퍼.

**잠방이** unlined shorts; farmer's knee-breeches. ¶ 얻은 ～ something got from someone else that is no great marvel.

**잠버릇** *one's* sleep habit. ¶ ～이 나쁘다 be an untidy sleeper.

**잠복**(潛伏) ① 《숨음》 hiding; concealment; ambush; latency. ～하다 conceal *oneself;* hide; lurk; be hidden. ¶ 그 살인범은 서울 시내에 ～중이다 The murderer is now in hiding in Seoul. ② 《병의》 incubation; latency. ～하다 be dorment; be latent. ◉ ～감염 a latent infection. ～근무(하다) (be on the) ambush (sentry) duty; 《미구어》 stakeout (경찰의). ～기 the latent 〔incubation〕 period: 그 병은 ～기가 길다 The disease has a long incubation period. ～성 latency: ～성 보균자 an incubatory carrier / ～성 질환 latent disease. ～장소 《범인의》 a shelter; a hide out; 《동물의》 a shelter; a cover; 《사냥꾼의》 a blind. ～초소 an ambush sentry box.

**잠비아** 《아프리카의 공화국》 Zambia.

**잠사**(蠶絲) silk yarn 〔thread〕. ◉ ～업 silk-reeling 〔sericultural〕 industry.

**잠수**(潛水) diving; submerging; submergence. ～하다 dive; go under water; submerge.
◉ ～공작원 〖군사〗 a frogman. ～구 an aqualung (호흡기); a diving apparatus. ～모 a diving helmet. ～모함 a submarine tender. ～병(病) caisson disease; (the) bends. ～복 a diving suit 〔dress, gear〕. ～부〔사〕 a diver. ～업자 a diving contractor. ～영법(泳法) subaqueous 〔underwater〕 swimming. ～정 a minisub. ～함 a submarine; 《구어》 a sub: ～함 승무원 a submariner / 원자력 ～함 a nuclear submarine / ～함 탐지기 a sonar; an asdic / ～함대 a submarine 〔an undersea〕 fleet / ～함 발사 미사일 a submarine-launched missile / ～함 방어망 an antisubmarine net / ～함 탑재 미사일 a submarine-borne missile / 난파된 ～함에서 상륙한 26명의 북한 공비들 중 22명이 살해 또는 시체로 발견되었다 Twenty-two of 26 North Korean infiltrators who came ashore from the wrecked submarine have been killed or found dead. 심해 ～정 a deepsea vehicle: 무인 심해 ～정 an unmanned deepsea vehicle; the autonomous underwater vehicle(생략 AUV).

**잠시**(暫時) a short time; for some time; (for) a (little) while; a minute; a moment. ¶ ～ (동안) for a short time; for a little while / ～ 후에 after a while; a little later on / ～ 머무르다 stay for a short time / ～ 기다려 주세요 Wait a little while, please. *or* 《전화 따위에서》 Will you hold on a moment, please?

**잠식**(蠶食) encroachment; an inroad; invasion. ～하다 encroach 《upon》; make inroads upon 〔into〕; eat into; gain on. ¶ …의 영토를〔영역을〕 ～하다 encroach on the territory 〔province〕 of... / 해외 시장을 ～하다 make inroads into foreign markets; [상품이 주어] erode 《*other's*》 market share in overseas markets.

**잠실**(蠶室) a silkworm-raising room.

**잠아**(潛芽) 〖식물〗 a latent bud.

**잠약**(—藥) a sleeping pill 〔draft, potion〕.

**잠언**(箴言) an aphorism; an adage; a maxim; a proverb. ¶ 솔로몬의 ～ the Proverbs of Solomon.

**잠업**(蠶業) sericulture; the sericultural industry. ◉ ～시험장 the Sericulture Experiment Station.

**잠열**(潛熱) 〖물리〗 potential 〔latent〕 heat; 《인체의》 dormant temperature.

**잠옷** nightwear; night clothes; pajama 《미》; 《여성·어린이용》 a nightdress; a nightgown. ¶ ～을 입고 자다 sleep in *one's* night clothes.

**잠입**(潛入) infiltration. ～하다 smuggle 〔sneak〕 *oneself* 《into》; steal 《into》; infiltrate 《into》; get 〔slip〕 in. ¶ 무장간첩이 서울에 ～해 있다 The armed agents have infiltrated into Seoul. / 그 폭력조직들은 지하로 ～해 버렸다 The organized groups of gangsters went underground. ◉ ～자 an infiltrator.

**잠자다** ① 《수면하다》 sleep; go to bed 〔sleep〕. ¶ 잠자는 아기 a sleeping child (★ 이 경우는 child에 강세가 주어지나, a sleeping car 「침대차」에서는 sleeping에 강세가 옴. 전자의 sleeping은 분사, 후자는 동명사임) / 늦도록 ～ sleep late / 한데서 ～ sleep in the open air / 잠잘 시간이다 It is time to sleep. ② 《푸한 것이》 be 「smoothed down 〔pressed down, compressed〕. ¶ 이불 솜이 ～ the cotton of the quilt is well set / 머리가 ～ *one's* hair gets nicely set.

**잠자리**[1] 〖곤충〗 a dragonfly.

**잠자리**[2] ① 《자는 곳》 a sleeping place; a bed; bedding. ¶ ～를 펴다 make a bed / ～를 걷다 put away beddings / ～에 들다 go to bed / ～에서 일어나다 get out of bed / ～에서 책을 읽다 read in bed / ～가 편합니까 Is the bed comfortable enough for you? / ～에

들자마자 그는 곯아떨어졌다 No sooner had he gone to bed than he fell asleep. ②《동침》 sexual intercourse; sleeping together. ¶ ~를 같이하다 sleep together; share the same bed《with》.

**잠자코**《말 없이》 without a word; 《조용히》 silently; 《공손히》 without question; obediently; 《무단히》 without leave 〔permission〕. ¶ ~ 있다 keep silence; keep mum / ~ 바라보다 《방관》 stand by / ~ 서 있다 be standing in silence / ~ 가버리다 go away without a word 〔saying anything〕 / ~ 하라는 대로 해라 Do as I tell you without question. / 왜 그 일을 ~ 있었니 Why did you keep the thing to yourself? / 이런 일은 ~ 있을 수 없다 I can't let such a thing go without objection. / 그는 멸시를 당하고 ~ 있을 사람은 아니다 He is not the sort of man to stand any nonsense. / 뭐라 대답할지 몰라, ~ 있었다 Not knowing what to answer, I remained silent.

**잠잠하다**(潛潛—) (be, keep) silent; quiet. ¶ 잠잠하게 quietly / 잠잠해지다 quiet 〔calm〕 down; become calm / 거리는 ~ All is quiet in the street. *or* The street looks deserted. / 자정이라 사방이 ~ It is midnight and there is a hush on all sides. / 그의 말에 모두 잠잠해졌다 They were all struck dumb at his remark.

**잠재**(潛在) latency; dormancy; potentiality. ~하다 lie dormant; (be) latent; potential. ¶ ~적 latent; dormant; subconscious; potential / ~적인 위협 a potential threat / 그들의 사고 방식에는 군국주의가 ~하고 있다 Militarism is latent in their way of thinking. / 두 나라 사이에는 ~적인 적의가 존재한다 There are latent hostilities between the two countries. / 현대 사회에는 갖가지 위험이 ~해 있다 Various dangers are lurking in the present society.
◉ ~구매력 latent purchasing power. ~능력 potential; latent faculties: potential capacities. ~력 potential (energy); latent force: ~력을 발달시키다 develop the powers latent within *one.* ~병원균 latent disease germs. ~수요 potential 〔latent〕 demands. ~실업 latent 〔invisible〕 unemployment: ~실업자 the hidden jobless. ~의식 subconsciousness; the subconscious: ~의식의 subconscious; subliminal / ~의식의 영역 the realm of the subconscious. ~주권 residual sovereignty. ~통화 latent currency. 「재우다.

**잠재우다** let 《*a person*》 go to sleep. =

**잠적하다**(潛跡—) conceal 〔hide〕 *oneself;* get in 〔into〕 hide; decamp; abscond; cover *one's* tracks 〔traces〕; disappear; go into hiding. ¶ 그는 갑자기 잠적했다 He suddenly disappeared.

**잠정**(暫定) being tentative 〔provisional〕. ¶ ~적인 provisional; tentative; temporary / ~적인 합의 a provisional agreement / ~적으로 provisionally; tentatively; temporarily; for the time being / ~적인 조치를 취하다 take tentative 〔temporary〕 measures 〔steps〕. ◉ ~안 a tentative plan. ~예산 a provisional budget. ~조약 a provisional treaty. ~조치 a temporary step; a stopgap measure. ~협정 a provisional 〔an interim〕 agreement; a *modus vivendi;* ~협정을 맺다 set up a *modus vivendi.*

**잠종**(蠶種) silkworm eggs. ◉ ~개량 silkworm species improvement.

**잠지** a baby's penis.

**잠투정** a baby's peevishness before 〔after〕 sleep. ~하다 get peevish 〔be fretful〕 before 〔after〕 sleep. ¶ 이 아이는 잘 때마다 ~한다 This baby always starts fretting when he is sleepy.

**잠함**(潛函) a caisson; a pontoon. ◉ ~공법 the caisson method. ~병 caisson disease; the bends; 〖의학〗 decompression sickness.

**잠항**(潛航) an underwater cruise; submarine navigation; a submarine voyage. ~하다 cruise 〔move, navigate〕 underwater; submerge (수중에 잠기다). ¶ ~의 신기록을 세우다 make 〔create〕 a new immersion record of 《60 days》. ◉ ~시간 underwater time. ~정 《소형 잠수함》 a submarine boat.

**잠행**(潛行) traveling in disguise. ~하다 travel incognito 〔in disguise〕; go underground (지하로). ◉ ~분자 undercover agents. ~성 질병 an insidious disease. ~활동 underground activities.

**잡가**(雜歌) a vulgar song; a folk song.

**잡감**(雜感) miscellaneous impressions 〔thoughts〕 《of》.

**잡거**(雜居) mixed residence; mixed living. ~하다 live 〔dwell, reside〕 together; live cheek by jowl 《with》. ¶ 이 집에는 3개 세대가 ~하고 있다 Three families live together in this house.
◉ ~지(地) a mixed-residence quarter.

**잡건**(雜件) miscellaneous items 〔matters〕; sundries.

**잡것**(雜―) ①《물건》 odds and ends; miscellaneous junk; impurities (불순물). ②《사람》 miscellaneous rough 〔uncouth〕 people; trash; ragtag-and=bobtail; every Tom, Dick and Harry.

**잡계정**(雜計定) 〖부기〗 sundry 〔miscellaneous〕 accounts.

**잡곡**(雜穀) miscellaneous 〔minor〕 cereals 〔grain〕. ◉ ~밥 boiled rice and cereals. ~상 a dealer in cereals; a corn merchant 〔dealer〕. ⌈spirits.

**잡귀**(雜鬼) minor demons; sundry evil

**잡균**(雜菌) various 〔sundry〕 germs 〔bacteria〕; unwanted bacteria.

**잡급**(雜給) sundry payment.

**잡기**(雜技) miscellaneous games; gambling. ◉ ~꾼 a gambler. ~판 a gambling place; a gaming house.

**잡기**(雜記) miscellaneous notes; miscellanea. ◉ ~장 a notebook; an exercise book.

**잡년**(雜―) a bad 〔loose〕 woman; a slut. ¶ 이 ~아 You slut!

**잡념**(雜念) distracting thoughts; worldly 〔evil, idle〕 thoughts. ¶ ~을 버리다 get rid of distracting thoughts; banish worldly thoughts from *one's* mind; put all other thoughts out of *one's* mind / 이제는 모든 ~을 버리고 공부에 몰두해야 한다 Now you must put all other thoughts out of your mind and devote yourself to studying.

**잡놈**(雜―) a loose fellow; a dissolute fellow; a no-good.

**잡다** ①《손으로》 hold; take 〔catch〕 hold of; seize; take; catch; grasp; grip. ¶ 아무의 멱살을 ~ seize *a person* by the neck / 공을 ~ catch a ball / 아무의 손을 ~ take *a person* by the hand; grasp 〔clasp〕 *a person's* hand; 《악수》 shake hands with *a person* / 꽉 ~ grasp firmly; hold tight 《to the railing》 / 잡은 손을 늦추다 loosen *one's* grasp of…; relinquish *one's* grip on 《the rope》 / 이 밧줄을 잡고 놓지 마세요 Take hold of this rope, and don't let go of it. / 물에 빠진 사람은 지푸라기라도 잡는다 《속담》 A drowning man will catch at a straw.

②《범인·적군 등을》 capture; catch; arrest; 《짐승·물고기 등을》 catch; get; seize; take. ¶ 도둑을 ~ catch a thief / 적병을 ~ capture an enemy soldier / 새를 ~ catch a bird / 고기를 잡으러 가다 go fishing.

③《권한·기회·세력·증거 따위를》 take 《power》; assume; wield; seize. ¶ 정권을 ~ come into political power / 기회를 ~ seize 〔catch〕 an opportunity / 권력을 잡고 있다 be in 〔have〕 power / 증거를 ~ get hold of evidence 〔a proof〕 / 패권을 ~ hold the supremacy 《in》; 《스포츠에서》 win the championship / 그 정당은 장기간 정권을 잡고 있다 The party has been in power for a long time. / 회사의 실권은 그녀가 잡고 있었다 The real power over the company was in her hands.

④《담보로》 hold 《in mortgage, pawn》; take 《as security》. ¶ 저당잡고 on mortgage / 자동차를 잡고 돈을 빌려주다 lend money on a car / 집을 저당 ~ hold a mortgage on a house.

⑤《예약하다》 get 《a room》; (pre-) engage; book; reserve; 《결정하다》 fix; decide; settle; 《선정하다》 choose; select. ¶ 골라 ~ choose 〔pick out, select〕 《*a thing*》 / 날짜를 ~ fix the date 《for》 / 일자리를 ~ get a job; find a position; obtain employment / 호텔에 방을 ~ get a room at hotel / 하숙을 ~ pick a boardinghouse to live in / 극장에 자리를 잡아 놓았다 I've reserved a seat at the theater.

⑥《차지하다》 take up; occupy. ¶ 자리를 너무 많이 ~ take up too much space.

⑦《약점·탈을》 find 《fault with》; point to 《a shortcoming》. ¶ 흠을 ~ find fault with 《*a person*》 / 물건의 흠을 ~ pick flaws 〔holes〕 in an article / 남의 약점을 잡아 이용하다 take advantage of *a person's* weakness 〔weak points〕 / 말에 트집을 ~ find fault with 《*a person's*》 remark.

⑧《이해·파악하다》 grasp; comprehend. ¶ 의론의 요점을 ~ grasp 〔catch, get〕 the point of argument / 뜻을 잡기 힘들다 The meaning is beyond my understanding. *or* I can hardly grasp the meaning.

⑨《요량·어림하다》 estimate 〔put〕 《at》; compute; rate. ¶ 대충 잡아서 at a rough estimate / 최대한으로 잡아서 at the highest estimate; at most / 최소한으로 잡아서 at the lowest estimate; at least / 지나치게 많이 ~ overestimate / 지나치게 적게 ~ underestimate / 비용을 5만 원으로 ~ put the expense at 50,000 won.

⑩《마음을》 steady *one's* mind; get a grip on *oneself;* collect 〔calm〕 *oneself;* hold 〔put〕 《*one's* passion》 under

control. ¶ 들뜬 마음을 ~ hold rein over *one's* erratic mind; keep a firm hand on *oneself* / 마음을 잡고 공부하다 study in a settled frame of mind.
⑪ 《도살하다》 butcher; kill 《animals》; slaughter. ¶ 돼지를 ~ butcher a hog.
⑫ 《모해하다》 plot against; lay a trap 《for》; slander. ¶ 사람 잡을 소리 그만해 Stop slandering me!
⑬ 《불을》 put out; extinguish; hold 〔get〕 《a fire》 under control. ¶ 물〔모래〕로 불을 ~ quench the fire with 「water 〔sand〕 / 그들의 필사적인 진화 작업으로 불길을 잡았다 With their desperate efforts, the firemen put the fire under control.
⑭ 《택시 따위를》 find 〔pick up〕 《a taxi》; take 〔get, catch〕 《a cab》. ¶ 서울 번화가에서는 택시 잡기가 매우 힘들다 It is very hard to 「catch 〔pick up〕 a taxi on the streets in downtown Seoul.
⑮ 《균형을》 balance; keep 《*one's* balance》. ¶ 균형이 잘 잡힌 체격 balanced physique / 그녀는 몸의 균형을 잡지 못해서 넘어졌다 She lost her balance and fell.
⑯ 《바로잡다》 unbend; straighten out. ¶ (굽은) 화살을 ~ straighten arrows out / 굽은 못을 바로 ~ make a bent nail straight.
⑰ 《주름을》 gather into folds; make a crease. ¶ 주름을 ~ pleat; pucker; crease; shirr / 치마에 주름을 ~ pleat a skirt / 바지 주름을 ~ crease trousers.
⑱ 《만류하다》 (try to) prevent 《*a person*》 from leaving (손님 따위를); detain; 《저지하다》 keep 《*a thing*》 back; check. ¶ 오래 머물도록 잡지 않겠습니다 I won't keep 〔detain〕 you long.

**잡다하다**(雜多—) 《갖가지의》 (be) miscellaneous; 《뒤죽박죽의》 (be) unarranged; unsorted. ¶ 잡다한 정보 miscellaneous information / 잡다한 사람들 people of all sorts and conditions; a mixed crowd of people.

**잡담**(雜談) idle 〔small〕 talk; light conversation; a chat; a gossip; chit=chat. ~하다 have an idle talk 《with》; gossip; chat 《with》; have a chat 《with》; engage in 「chit-chat 〔small talk〕 《with》. ¶ ~을 즐기다 enjoy chatting / ~으로 시간을 보내다 pass time gossiping / 우리 차를 마시며 ~이나 하자 Let's chat over tea.

**잡답**(雜沓) 《사람의》 a crowd; a throng; 《상태》 a (traffic) jam; congestion; hustle and bustle. ~하다 (be) crowded; thronged; bustling. ¶ 대도시의 ~에서 벗어나다 get out of the hustle and bustle of a big city.

**잡도리** supervision. ~하다 supervise; superintend; oversee; take care of.

**잡동사니** useless 〔worn-out〕 articles; sundries; odds and ends; rubbish; junk.

**잡되다**(雜—) be 「loose 〔lax〕 in morals; (be) wanton; lewd; 《천한》 (be) indecent. ¶ 잡된 사람 「a dissolute 〔an indecent〕 person / 잡된 생각 the wanton thoughts.

**잡록**(雜錄) miscellaneous notes 〔records〕; miscellanies; miscellanea.

**잡맛**(雜—) an impure taste; a taste other than the original one.

**잡목**(雜木) miscellaneous small trees; scrubs; scrub trees. ◉ ~숲 scrub; a thicket; a copse; a coppice.

**잡무**(雜務) sundry duties; routine 「business 〔duties〕; odds and ends to do; 《가정의》 domestic chores. ¶ ~로 바쁘다 be 「busy 〔pressed〕 with routine business / ~를 처리하다 dispose of routine business.

**잡문**(雜文) miscellaneous writings. ◉ ~가 a miscellanist.

**잡물**(雜物) ① 《잡것》 miscellaneous 「things 〔articles〕; sundries. ② 《불순물》 foreign ingredients; impurities.

**잡배**(雜輩) low type of persons; vulgar people; trash; riffraff; small fry.

**잡병**(雜病) various diseases.

**잡보**(雜報) sundry reports; miscellaneous items of news; general news. ◉ ~란 the general-news column(s).

**잡부**(雜夫) an odd-job man; a handyman.

**잡부금**(雜賦金) miscellaneous fees. ¶ 특별 활동을 빙자한 ~ 징수 collection of miscellaneous fees under the pretext of the special activities / ~을 일소하다 prohibit the collection of miscellaneous fees.

**잡비**(雜費) sundry 〔petty〕 expenses; incidental expenses; incidentals. ¶ ~를 덜다 exclude the incidental expenses / ~가 꽤 많이 든다 Sundries come up to a considerable amount. ◉ ~ 계정 a petty expenses account.

**잡상스럽다**(雜常—) 《난잡하다》 (be) disorderly; messy; confused; pell-mell; 《상스럽다》 (be) vulgar; vile; low; mean; gross; 《음탕하다》 (be) wanton; lewd; licentious. ¶ 성품이 잡상스러운 사람 a man of vile character / 잡상스

럽지 않은 respectable; decent.

**잡상인**(雜商人) miscellaneous traders; small tradesman; peddlers. ¶ ~ 출입 금지 《게시》 No hawkers. *or* No peddlers. *or* No soliciting. *or* No solicitors allowed.

**잡색**(雜色) 《빛깔》 various colors; variegation; 《사람》 all kinds of people; a motley crew. ¶ ~의 parti-colored; variegated; varicolored; motley.

**잡서**(雜書) ① 《각종의 책》 miscellaneous books. ② 《여러 내용의》 a book on miscellaneous subjects.

**잡석**(雜石) rough broken stones; rubble.

**잡설**(雜說) an unorthodox theory; a tale 《of gossip》; idle talk; smutty talk; a dirty story.

**잡성화**(雜性花) 〖식물〗 polygamous flowers.

**잡세**(雜稅) miscellaneous 〔sundry〕 taxes; various taxes.

**잡소리**(雜—) 《잡된 말》 obscene 〔dirty〕 talk; smut; 《잡담》 useless 〔idle〕 talk; prattle; nonsense.

**잡손질**(雜—) idle fingering; useless touching; playing 〔idling〕 with *one's* fingers. ~하다 play with *one's* fingers.

**잡수다** ① 《먹다》 eat; drink; have; partake 《of》. ¶ 술을 ~ drink / 많이 잡수시오 Help yourself, please. ② 《제사를》 perform an ancestor-memorial service.

**잡수입**(雜收入) 《개인의》 miscellaneous income; 《공공 단체의》 miscellaneous revenues 〔receipts〕.

**잡스럽다**(雜—) = 잡되다.

**잡식**(雜食) 〖동물〗 polyphagia. ~하다 feed on both animal and vegetable substances; be omnivorous. ¶ ~의 omnivorous; polyphagous. ◉ ~동물 an omnivorous animal 〔feeder〕. ~류 〖동물〗 the Omnivora. ~성 〖동물〗 polyphagia.

**잡신**(雜神) (sundry) evil spirits.

**잡아가다** take 〔walk〕 《a suspect to a police station》; haul 〔bring〕 《*a person*》 before 《the police authorities》.

**잡아내다** 《결점 등을》 pick at 《flaws》; criticize 《shortcomings》; 《밖으로》 throw 《*a person*》 out 《of the door》. ¶ 흠을 ~ point out mistakes / 잡아내라 Kick him out!

**잡아당기다** pull; draw; 《배로》 tug; 《밧줄로》 tow; 《힘을 주어》 haul; 《갑자기》 jerk. ¶ 아무의 소맷자락을〔귀를〕 ~ pull *a person* by the sleeve 〔ear〕 / 밧줄을 홱 ~ give the rope a jerk / 문을 ~ pull the door open 〔shut〕 / 그는 밧줄을 세게 잡아당겼다 He gave a strong pull at the rope. / 너무 잡아당기면 끊어진다 It'll break if you pull too hard.

**잡아들이다** seize and bring in; drag 〔draw〕 in 〔into〕; bring 〔take〕 in; arrest. ¶ 주모자를 잡아들여라 Arrest the ringleader and bring him in.

**잡아떼다** ① 《떼내다》 pull 《jointed or attached things》 apart; take 〔tear〕 off. ¶ 코트의 단추를 ~ tear a button off the coat. ② 《부인하다》 deny with an innocent face; give a barefaced denial; refuse flatly; feign 〔pretend〕 ignorance; play the innocent. ¶ 그는 그런 일은 전혀 모른다고 잡아뗐다 He put on an innocent air and denied any knowledge of the affair. / 끝끝내 모른다고 잡아뗄 셈이냐 How dare you feign ignorance all this time? / 아무리 물어도 그는 모른다고 잡아뗐다 However much I asked, he persisted in feigning ignorance.

**잡아매다** tie up; bind; fasten. ¶ 책을 한데 ~ tie books up in a bundle; bundle up books / 아무를 나무에 ~ tie 〔bind〕 *a person* to a tree / 선창에 배를 ~ moor a boat to the pier.

**잡아먹다** ① 《잡아서 먹다》 slaughter and eat; devour. ¶ 잡아먹느냐 먹히느냐의 싸움 a struggle for life and death; a war of survival / 돼지를 ~ slaughter a hog and eat it / 서로 ~ feed on each other; devour one another / 뱀은 개구리나 쥐를 잡아먹고 산다 The snake lives on frogs, mice, and rats. ② 《괴롭히다》 torment; torture; harass; be hard on; treat 《*a person*》 harshly. ¶ 그는 늘 나를 잡아먹지 못해 안달이다 He is needling me all the time. *or* He treats me very harshly all the time. ③ 《요하다》 take; need; require; occupy (차지하다). ¶ 장소를 ~ occupy 〔take up〕 much room 〔space〕 / 이 사업은 많은 돈을 잡아 먹는다 This job eats lots of money. / 이 차는 많은 연료를 잡아먹는다 This car consumes a lot of gas. / 이 일에 꽤 많은 시간을 잡아 먹었다 We devoted much time to complete this work.

**잡아뽑다** pluck (up, off, out); pull out. ¶ 닭의 털을 ~ pluck a chicken / 무를 ~ pull out a radish.

**잡아찢다** tear up 〔off〕; tear 〔pull〕 to pieces; rip up; rend. ¶ 편지를 ~ tear up a letter; tear a letter to 〔in, into〕

pieces.

**잡아채다** snatch 《*a thing*》 (away) 《from》; take 《*a thing*》 by force; tear 《*a thing*》 from 《*a person*》. ¶ 핸드백을 잡아채이다 have *one's* handbag snatched away.

**잡어**(雜魚) small fish 〔fry〕 (of various kinds).

**잡역**(雜役) miscellaneous services; odd jobs; 《특히 군대의》 fatigue duty; chores 《미》. ◉ ～부(婦) a maid-of-all-work; 《날품팔이》 a charwoman. ～부(夫) an odd-job man; a handyman.

**잡용**(雜用) ① ＝잡비. ② 《씀씀이》 sundry uses 〔expenses〕.

**잡음**(雜音) ① 《소음》 noise(s); 《라디오의》 radio noise; jarring and grating; 《레코드의》 the surface noise; 〚의학〛 《기관의》 souffle; murmur. ¶ 도시의 ～ city 〔town〕 noises / 심장의 ～ a heart murmur / ～이 없어졌다 The noise abated. / 라디오에 ～이 들린다 The radio program is hampered 〔disturbed〕 by noises. *or* The radio is affected static. ② 《이의·반대》 dissenting voices; objections; complaints; censure; 《참견》 interference; (an) irresponsible criticism (of an outsider). ¶ 남의 이야기에 쓸데없는 ～을 넣지 마라 Stop putting in irrelevancies from aside. *or* Don't interfere in our talk. ◉ ～지수 a noise figure 〔factor〕.

**잡인**(雜人) an outsider.

**잡일**(雜―) miscellaneous affairs. ¶ 신변 ～ *one's* personal 〔private〕 affairs / 가사의 ～ the household chores.

**잡종**(雜種) a hybrid; a cross 《between》; a crossbre(e)d; a mixed breed; a mongrel. ¶ ～의 crossbred; half-bred; hybrid; mongrel; 《잡다한》 miscellaneous / ～을 만들다 cross one breed with another; cross two breeds; interbreed; hybridize.
◉ ～강세 〚생물〛 heterosis; hybrid vigor. ～개 a mongrel (dog); a dog of mixed breed. ～불임성 hybrid sterility. ～제1대 〚생물〛 the first filial generation (생략 $F_1$).

**잡지**(雜誌) a magazine; 《전문의》 a journal; 《정기 간행물》 a periodical.
¶ 주간〔월간, 계간〕～ a weekly 〔monthly, quarterly〕 magazine / 종합〔문예〕～ a general 〔literary〕 magazine / 연 4회 발행의 ～ a quarterly / 월 2회 (간행)의 ～ a semimonthly magazine / 수험용의 ～ a guide-magazine for examinees / ～에 기고하다 write for a magazine; contribute to a magazine / ～를 구독하다 subscribe for a magazine; take a magazine / ～를 편집하다 edit a magazine / 이것은 과학 ～이다 This is a science magazine.
◉ ～광고 magazine advertising. ～기사 a magazine article. ～기자 a magazine writer 〔reporter〕; a magazinist. ～꽂이 a magazine rack. ～사 a magazine house. ～편집자 a magazine editor.

**잡채**(雜菜) 〚요리〛 a mixed dish of vegetables and sliced meat; chopsuey 《미》.

**잡초**(雜草) weeds. ¶ ～가 우거진 weedy; 《a garden》 overgrown with weeds / ～처럼 생명력이 강하다 have a strong hold on life like weeds / ～를 뽑다 weed 《a garden》 / 뒤뜰에는 ～가 우거져 있다 Weeds have overrun the back yard.

**잡치다** botch; mangle; mar; spoil; ruin; butcher; make a mess 〔bungle〕 of; fall through. ¶ 아무의 기분을 ～ hurt *a person's* 〔*one's*〕 feeling; offend 《*a person*》 / 입맛을 ～ spoil 《*a person's*》 appetite 〔taste〕 / 일을 ～ make bungling work of; make a mess of it / 초를 너무 쳐서 맛을 ～ spoil food by putting too much vinegar in / 너 때문에 계획을 완전히 잡쳤다 You have upset my whole plan. / 비밀이 새어 계획을 잡쳤다 When the secret leaked out, our plan was spoiled. / 단 한 번 실수가 그의 일생을 잡쳤다 Just a single failure ruined his life.

**잡칙**(雜則) miscellaneous rules 〔regulations〕.

**잡탕**(雜湯) 〚요리〛 pot-au-feu; a mixed soup; an olio; 《뒤범벅》 a hodgepodge 《미》; a hotchpotch; a medley; a jumble; a hash; a mishmash. ¶ ～이 되다 be mixed up; be jumbled together; be an admixture / ～을 만들다 jumble together; mix up / 그 음식은 중국과 인도 음식의 ～ 같았다 The food was like a mixture of Chinese and Indian (food).

**잡품**(雜品) sundries; miscellaneous articles.

**잡혼**(雜婚) (sexual) promiscuity; promiscuous sexual relations. ～하다 have promiscuous sexual relations 《with》.

**잡화**(雜貨) miscellaneous 〔sundry〕 goods; sundries; general goods 〔merchandise〕; notions 《미》. ¶ ～를 적재하고 with a cargo of general merchandise; with a general cargo / 그들은 온갖 ～를 취급하며 폭넓게 장사를 하고 있

다 They trade widely in all kinds of sundry goods. ◉ ~매장 《백화점의》 a household goods 〔sundries〕 department. ~상 a dealer in miscellaneous goods; 《식료품의》 a grocer 《미》: ~상을 경영하다 be in the grocery line. ~점 a general store 《미》; miscellaneous store 〔shop〕; 《식품 취급의》 a grocer's.

**잡히다**[1] ① 《손에》 be held 〔grasped, seized〕. ¶ 손에 잡히는 곳에 within grasping distance; within *one's* reach 〔grasp〕. ② 《붙잡히다》 be caught 〔seized, taken, captured, arrested〕; be detained; be beset 《by》; fall in hands of. ¶ 경찰관한테 ~ be arrested by the police / 청어가 많이 ~ get a good catch of herrings / 포로로 ~ be taken prisoner by the enemy / 다람쥐가 한 마리 잡혔다 One squirrel was caught. / 그는 아직 잡히지 않고 있다 He is still at large. (★ at large는 「잡히지 않고」의 뜻). ③ 《도조(賭租)가》 get estimated at; be rated. ¶ 도조가 30섬 잡혔다 The farm rent is rated at thirty bushels in kind. ④ 《모해를 입다》 fall into 《*a person's* scheme, plot》; get trapped; be maneuvered into; get taken in. ⑤ 《불이》 be got 〔brought, held〕 under control. ¶ 그 불은 새벽녘이 되어서야 겨우 잡혔다 The fire was finally brought under control toward daybreak. ⑥ 《마음이》 turn steady; settle 〔calm〕 down; be under control; concentrate. ¶ 마음이 잡히지 않다 feel uneasy 〔restless〕; be ill at ease / 일이 손에 잡히지 않다 cannot settle down to (*one's*) work; be in no mood for work. ⑦ 《곧게》 get 〔be〕 straightened out. ⑧ 《주름이》 get 〔be〕 pleated 〔puckered, creased〕; get 〔be〕 wrinkled. ¶ 주름이 잘 잡힌 바지 well creased trousers / 이마에 주름이 ~ become wrinkled on *one's* forehead. ⑨ 《기타》 ¶ 모양이 ~ take a form / 균형이 ~ be well balanced / 시내는 다시 질서가 잡혔다 Order was restored to the city. / 그의 행방에 대해서는 아직 이렇다 할 단서가 잡히지 않았다 No clue has yet been found to his whereabouts.

**잡히다**[2] ① 《잡게 하다》 cause 《*a person*》 to take 〔catch〕. ② 《담보로》 put in pawn 〔mortgage〕; have 《*something*》 taken as security. ¶ 외투를 2만 원에 ~ pawn an overcoat for 20,000 won / 집을 ~ mortgage *one's* house / 집을 잡혀서 돈을 꾸다 borrow money on the (security of *one's*) house. ③ 《약점·탈을》 have 《a weakness》 discovered 〔taken advantage of〕; have to listen to complaints about 《*one's* shortcomings》. ¶ 트집을 ~ be found fault with / 아무한테 흠을 ~ be found out *one's* weakness by *a person;* have *a person* take advantage of *one's* shortcomings / 남한테 흉을 ~ be spoken ill of; be caviled at; have 《*something*》 harped on. ④ 《풍류를》 have 《music》 play.

**잡힐손** handiness; serviceableness. ¶ ~있는 사람 a serviceable person; a handyman; a Jack of all trade.

**잣** pine nuts 〔seeds〕. ¶ 잣가루 ground 〔chopped〕 pine nuts / 잣기름 pine-nut oil / 잣나무 a nut pine; a Korean white pine / 잣송진 pine resin; turpentine / 잣죽 a gruel made of rice and pine nuts; pine nuts gruel 〔porridge〕 / 잣집게 a pine-nut cracker.

**잣눈**[1] 《눈금》 the gradation markings on a measuring rule; ruler notches.

**잣눈**[2] 《눈》 snow a foot deep; one foot of snow.

**잣다** 《물을》 draw up; suck up; pump up; 《실을》 spin out. ¶ 물을 ~ suck 〔draw〕 up water; 《펌프로》 pump up water / 목화에서 실을 자아내다 spin thread out of cotton; spin cotton into yarn.

**잣대** a yardstick.

**잣박산**(—薄—) a honey cake of glutinous rice flavored with pine nuts.

**잣새** 〚조류〛 a crossbill; a crossbeak.

**잣송이** a pine-nut cone.

**잣징** 《작은 징》 a tiny hobnail.

**장**(丈) ① 《길이 단위》 a *jang;* a measure of length (=10 *ja*). ② 《어른》 an (esteemed) elder. ¶ 노인장 an elderly person / 춘부장 your (venerable) father.

**장**(長) ① 《길이》 length; long. ② 《우두머리》 the head; the chief; the chairman; the boss 《미》; the director; 《사령관》 the commander. ¶ 만물의 장 the lord of all creation / 한 집안의 장 the head of a family. ③ 《장점》 a merit; a strong 〔good〕 point; *one's* forte; an advantage. ¶ 일장 일단이 있다 Each merit has its demerit. *or* Each advantage has its disadvantage.

**장**(章) 《책의》 a chapter; a section; 《기장》 a sign; a mark; a badge; an emblem; 《인장》 a seal. ¶ 제2장 the second chapter; Chapter 〔Chap.〕 Ⅱ / 새로운 장 a new chapter 〔era〕/ 새로운 장을 열다 open a new chapter 《in》/ 한국에 관한 장 the chapter on Korea / 이 책의 문학 비평의 장은 특히 재미있다 The chapter of literary criticism in this book is particularly interesting.

**장**(張) 《종이 등의》 a sheet; a leaf. ¶ 종이 두 장 two sheets of paper / 접시 열두 장 a dozen plates / 10원짜리 우표 두 장 two ten-won stamps / 첫 장에서 끝 장까지 from cover to cover; from title page to colophon / 책을 한 장씩 넘기다 turn over the leaves of a book.

**장**(將) ① 《군대의》 a general; a commander. ② 《장기의》 the king. ⇨장군(將軍) ②. ¶ 장이야 Check! *or* Mate!

**장**(場) ① 《시장》 a market; a mart; 《정기적인》 a fair. ¶ 5일장 a five day interval (village) market / 장보러 가다 go shopping / 장에 물건을 내다 bring commodities to the market / 장이 서다〔열리다〕 a fair is held 〔opened〕/ 다음 장은 8일에 선다 The next fair is on the 8th. / 장마다 망둥이 나랴 《속담》 Good luck does not always repeat itself. ② 《…하는 장소》 a ground; a track; a place; a spot. ¶ 골프장 a golf course; golf links / 사격장 a rifle range / 장내〔외〕에 in 〔out of〕 the ground / 정치의 장에서 국정을 논의하다 discuss national affairs on the political stage. ③ 〚물리〛 a field. ¶ 자(기)장 the magnetic field. ④ 《연극의 장면》 a scene. ¶ 2막 4장의 극 a play in two acts and four scenes / 제3막 제1장 Act Ⅲ, Scene Ⅰ (★ act three, scene one 으로 읽음).

**장**(腸) 〚해부〛 the intestines; the entrails; the entera; the bowels; the guts 《구어》. ¶ 장의 intestinal; enteric / 장의 병 a bowel disease; an intestinal trouble 〔disorder〕/ 장이 나쁘다 have a bowel trouble; have weak intestines; have a trouble in the intestines; suffer from a bowel complaint.

**장**(醬) soy sauce; soybean sauce; 《간장과 된장》 soy and bean paste.

**장**(欌) a wardrobe; a cabinet; a closet. ¶ 단층〔이층〕장 a single 〔double〕 chest of drawers / 새장 a bird cage / 옷장 a wardrobe; a chest of drawers.

**장**(臟) the five vital organs of the body (*i.e.* heart, liver, lungs, kidney, spleen); the vitals; the viscera; the internal organs.

**장가** 《결혼》 a marriage; a wedding; taking 〔get〕 a wife. ~들다〔가다〕 take 〔get〕 a wife; take 《a girl》 to wife; marry. ¶ ~들이다 marry 《a son》 to 《a woman》; get 《a son》 married / ~들었나 Are you married?

**장가**(長歌) a long poem 〔song〕.

**장가스**(腸—) gas (on the stomach).

**장가처**(—妻) *one's* legal 〔first〕 wife.

**장갑**(掌匣) gloves; 《벙어리 장갑》 mittens; 《권투용》 a muffle; 《승마·크리켓용》 a gauntlet. ¶ 고무~ rubber gloves / ~ 한 켤레 a pair of gloves 〔mittens〕/ ~ 낀 손 a gloved hand / ~을 끼다〔벗다〕 put on 〔pull off〕 gloves / ~을 낀 채 악수하는 것은 실례가 된다 It is impolite to shake hands with gloves on.

**장갑**(裝甲) armoring. ~하다 armor. ¶ ~한 armored; ironclad; armor-plated. ◉ ~부대 an armored 〔a panzer〕 corps 〔unit〕. ~차 an armored car 〔truck〕; a panzer. ~판 an armor plate. ~포대 an armored battery.

**장거**(壯擧) a splendid 〔heroic〕 undertaking 〔scheme〕; a daring attempt 〔enterprise〕. ¶ 세계 일주 비행의 ~ the grand project of a round-the-world flight.

**장거리**(長距離) a long 〔great〕 distance; 《사격 등의》 a long range. ◉ ~경주 a (long-)distance race. ~비행 a long(-distance) 〔long-range〕 flight. ~선수〔주자〕 a (long-)distance runner. ~수송 long-distance transportation 〔transport, haulage〕. ~열차 a long-distance train. ~전화 a long-distance telephone 〔call〕; a trunk call 《영》: ~ 직통 전화 방식 the direct distance dialing system; the DDD system / ~ 전화를 걸다 telephone 《*a person*》 by long-distance / 부산으로 ~ 전화를 부탁합니다 I want a long-distance call to Pusan. ~탄도탄 a long-range ballistic missile. ~트럭 《장거리 화물 수송용》 a long-haul 〔long-distance〕 truck. ~포 a long-range gun. ~폭격기 a long-range bomber.

**장거리**(場—) a market place.

**장검**(長劍) a sword. ¶ ~을 차다 wear a sword 《at *one's* side》.

**장결핵**(腸結核) 〚의학〛 intestinal tuberculosis.

**장경**(長徑) the major axis. ⇨ 긴지름.

**장고**(長考) ~하다 think for a long time 《about what move to make》.

**장골**(壯骨) a strongly-built man; a Hercules; stout-built physique.

**장과**(漿果) 〖식물〗 a berry; a bacca (*pl.* -ae).

**장관**(壯觀) a grand 〔thrilling〕 sight; a magnificent view 〔sight, spectacle〕. ¶ 알프스의 ~ the grand panorama 〔the amazing grandeur〕 of the Alps / ~을 이루다 offer a grand spectacle; present a magnificent sight / 천하의 ~이다 be one of the grandest sights imaginable / 그 ~은 필설로 표현키 어렵다 The grandeur of the scenery beggars (all) description.

**장관**(長官) a Cabinet minister; a minister (of state); a director; 《미국 각 부(部)의》 a Secretary; 《지방의》 a governor. ⇨ 내각.

> 용법 영국에는 secretary와 minister로 불리우는 두 종류의 장관이 있음. 미국의 장관은 모두 secretary라고 하지만, 법무장관(Attorney General)처럼 secretary라고 부르지 않는 장관도 있음. 「청」(Agency)은 「부」(Ministry)와 기능면에서는 비슷하지만, 「부」처럼 규모가 크지 않은 것을 말함. 「청」의 장은 보통 the director general이라고 함. 우리 나라의 장관은 영국식을 따라서 minister라고 함.

¶ 무임소 ~ a minister without portfolio / 지방 ~ a provincial governor / ~직 a portfolio; ministership / 국무~ 《미》 the Secretary of State / 그녀는 ~이 되었다 She became a Cabinet minister. *or* She was named to a Cabinet post. / 그는 ~직을 사임했다 He resigned from the Cabinet.

**장관**(將官) 《육군의》 a general (officer); 《해군의》 a flag officer; an admiral. ¶ ~급 장교 a general-grade officer.

**장광설**(長廣舌) a long talk; a long-winded talk 〔speech〕. ¶ ~을 늘어놓다 make a 「long-winded speech 〔long harangue〕; give a long talk / 그의 ~은 관중들을 지루하게 했다 He made a long speech and tired the audience with it.

**장교**(將校) an officer; a commissioned officer. ¶ ~와 사병 officers and soldiers 〔privates〕 / 육군〔해군, 공군〕 ~ a military 〔a naval, an air force〕 officer / 고급〔하급〕~ a high-ranking 〔low-ranking〕 officer.

**장구** a *chang-gu;* a double-headed drum pinched in at the middle; an hour-glass-shaped drum. ¶ ~를 쳐야 춤을 추지 《속담》 Help is needed. ◉ ~채 a *chang-gu* drumstick.

**장구**(長久) a long period of time; permanence. ~하다 be of long standing; be lasting; be long-range. ¶ ~지계(之計) a long-range plan / 무운 ~를 빌다 wish 《*a person*》 good luck in war / ~한 시일을 요하다 require a long period of time.

**장구**(長軀) tall stature; towering height.

**장구**(葬具) a funeral outfit; funeral necessities 〔goods〕.

**장구**(裝具) an outfit; equipments; gear; 《실내의》 fittings; 《말의》 harness; trappings. ¶ ~를 갖추다 fit 《*a thing*》 out; equip; harness 《a horse》.

**장구머리** a bulging head; 《사람》 a person with a bulging head.

**장구면**(長球面) 〖기하학〗 a prolate spheroid.

**장구벌레** 〖곤충〗 the larva of a mosquito; a w(r)iggler.

**장국**(醬—) soup flavored with soy sauce. ◉ ~밥 beef soup with rice in it.

**장군** an earthenware jar 〔barrel, cask〕. ¶ 오줌 ~ a urine cask 〔barrel〕.

**장군**(將軍) ① 〖군사〗 a general; a commander in chief. ② 《장기·체스 등의》 "check" in chess. ¶ ~받다 make a defensive move against a checkmate; get out of check.

**장궤양**(腸潰瘍) 〖의학〗 an intestinal ulcer.

**장기**(長技) special skill 〔ability〕; *one's* specialty; *one's* favorite performance; *one's* forte. ¶ …을 ~로 하다 be good 〔skillful〕 at; have a forte for; be at home in / 그의 ~는 무엇이냐 What is his specialty?

**장기**(長期) a long time 〔period, term〕. ¶ ~의 long(-dated); long-term; protracted / ~에 걸친 long-pending; protracted; prolonged / ~적으로는 in the long run / ~에 걸치다 be prolonged; extend over a long (period of) time / 인체에 미치는 ~적인 영향 the long-term health effects / 교섭은 ~에 걸쳤다 The negotiations took a long time. / 그는 서울에 ~간 체류했다 He stayed in Seoul for a long time. ◉ ~거래 long-term transaction. ~결석 a long 〔prolonged〕 absence. ~계획 a long-range 〔long-term〕 plan. ~공채(公債) a long-term (public) bond. ~근속 long service; years of labor: ~근속 수당 longevity allowance / ~ 근속자 a long-service man. ~대출 a long-term loan: ~대출금 long-term loans receivable. ~신용 long-term credit. ~

어음 a long-dated bill. ～예금자 a long-term depositor. ～예보 a long-range《weather》forecast. ～전 a long 〔prolonged, drawn-out〕 war: 이 문제는 서둘러 해결하려 하지 않고 ～전으로 나가는 것이 좋겠다 We had better not try a hasty solution but should find a long-term strategy to tackle the problem. ～전략 long-term strategies: 일본 시장에 파고들기 위한 ～ 전략을 세우다 map out long-term strategies to penetrate into the Japanese markets. ～정책 a long-range 〔long-term〕 policy. ～집권 a prolonged one-man rule. ～차입금 long-term loans payable. ～채권 noncurrent receivables. ～체류 a prolonged stay. ～회사채 a long-term bond. ～흥행 a long-run《of a play》.

**장기**(將棋) *changgi,* Korean chess. ¶～를 두다 play *changgi*《with》; have a game of *changgi.* ◉ ～짝 a piece; a chessman. ～판 a chessboard.

**장기**(臟器) 〖해부〗 the viscera; the intestines; the internal organs; the bowels. ¶～의 불법 거래 (the) illegal trafficking of human organs.
◉ ～이식 〖의학〗 an (internal) organ transplant: 요즘 ～이식을 필요로 하는 환자가 급격히 늘고 있다 The number of the patients who need organ transplants has been rapidly increasing in recent years. 한국 ～기증자 프로그램 the Korea Organ and Tissue Donor Programs (생략 KOTDP).

**장김치**(醬—) Kimchi pickled in soy sauce.

**장꾼**(場—) marketeers and marketers; market crowds.

**장끼**《수꿩》 a cock-pheasant.

**장난**《놀이》 a game; play; (children's) sport; 《못된 짓》 mischief; prank; a practical joke; 《심심풀이》 fun; amusement; pastime; hobby. ～하다〔치다〕 play; 《만지작댐》 toy《with》; trifle; tamper; fumble; monkey; 《짓궂게》 do mischief; do a naughty thing; play a trick; play a practical joke; 《심심풀이》 amuse *oneself*《with》; kill time.
¶～기 있는 mischievous; naughty / 공～ a game of ball / 어린아이의 ～ children's games / 어린아이 같은 ～ childish mischief / 운명의 ～ a tribute of fortune; the irony of fate / ～으로 for 〔out of〕 fun; in joke; as a pastime 〔hobby〕 / ～으로 말하다 speak in fun; joke; jest / 반～으로 하다 do half in fun; do《*a thing*》in play (★ in play 의 반대는 in earnest) / 어린이들한테 ～을 못 하게 하다 keep children out of mischief / 공을 가지고 혼자 ～하다 amuse *oneself* with a ball / 아무한테 ～하다 play a trick on *a person* / 불을 가지고 ～하다 play with fire / 장전된 총을 가지고 ～하다 fool with a loaded gun / 그저 ～을 한 것에 불과하다 I did it just for fun.

**장난감** a toy; a plaything; 《노리개》 a sport; a baby rattle. ¶～ 같은 집 a toy 〔match box〕 of a house / ～으로 삼다 make sport of; make a toy 〔plaything〕 of; make fun 〔sport〕 of; sport 〔trifle〕 with / 아무를 ～으로 삼다 play 〔flirt〕 with *a person;* make a plaything of *a person* / (여자가) 남자를 ～으로 삼다 turn 〔twist〕 a man round her little finger; fool 〔make a fool of〕 a man / ～이 되다 be made a plaything《by》; become a toy《of》/ 너는 ～을 가지고 놀 나이가 아니다 You have outgrown your playthings.
◉ ～가게 a toyshop. ～기차〔말〕 a toy train 〔horse〕. 국제～박람회 the 《Seoul》 International Toy Fair《'99》.

**장난기** playfulness; mischievousness; mischief. ¶～ 어린 눈으로 with mischievous 〔impish〕 eyes / ～가 있는 playful; sportive; full of play 〔fun〕; mischievous; impish.

**장난꾸러기, 장난꾼** 《아이》 a mischievous child; a naughty boy; an urchin; a little monkey; 《어른》 a naughty fellow; a mischief-maker; a rogue.

**장날**(場—) a market 〔fair〕 day.

**장남**(長男) the first-born son; the 〔*one's*〕 eldest son; 《아들이 둘일 경우》 *one's* elder son.

**장내**(場內) the inside of the hall 〔grounds, premises〕. ¶～에서 in the hall 〔grounds〕; on the premises / ～가 꽉 차다 The hall is overcrowded. / 이 곳은 ～ 금연이다 You are not allowed to smoke here in the hall. / ～ 방송으로 공고가 있었다 An announcement was made over the public address system in the stadium.
◉ ～정리 crowd control in the hall. ～정치 intra-Assembly politics. ～조명《극장의》 the houselights.

**장내박테리아**(腸內—) intestinal bacteria.

**장녀**(長女) the first-born daughter; the 〔*one's*〕 eldest daughter; 《딸이 둘일 경우》 *one's* elder daughter.

**장년**(壯年) 《in *one's*》 manhood; 《in》 the prime of life. ¶～의 사내 a man

in the prime of life / ~이 되다 reach (the prime of *one's*) manhood.
◉ ~기=장년.

**장뇌**(樟腦) 〖화학〗 camphor. ¶ ~를 넣다 camphorate. ◉ ~유(油) camphor oil. ~정(精) the spirit of camphor.

**장님** 《맹인》 a blind person; [총칭] the blind; 《문맹인》 an illiterate. ¶ 눈뜬~ an unlettered 〔illiterate〕 person (문맹인) / ~이 되다 go 〔become〕 blind; lose *one's* sight / 그 아이는 나면서부터 ~이다 The child was born blind.

**장다리** a flowering stalk 《of radishes, cabbages, *etc.*》. ¶ ~가 나다 go 〔run〕 to seed. ◉ ~무 a seed radish.

**장단**(長短) ① 《길이》 (comparative) length. ¶ 물건의 ~을 재다 measure the length of a thing.
② 《장점과 단점》 merits and demerits; strong and weak points; 《득실》 relative merits 〔importance〕. ¶ …의 ~을 생각하다 consider the relative merits of... / ~이 상쇄되다 the merits and demerits offset each other / 사물에는 모두 ~이 있다 Things have both merits and demerits.
③ 《박자》 time; (a) rhythm; the beat (of a tune). ¶ ~을 맞추다 keep time with 〔to〕 《the music》 / ~ 치다 beat out a tune / 발로 ~을 맞추다 beat 〔keep〕 time 〔lead the tune〕 with *one's* foot / 남의 ~에 춤추다 play into another's hands / 그는 손으로~을 맞추며 노래를 불렀다 He sang keeping 〔beating〕 time with his hands.

**장담**(壯談) assurance; vouching; guarantee; assertion; affirmation. ~하다 assure; guarantee; vouch 《for》; affirm. ¶ 그것이 사실임을 나는 ~한다 I affirm it to be a fact 〔true〕. / 그 점은 좀 ~할 수 없다 I am not positive about it. / 나는 어떻다고도 ~ 못 하겠다 I can not commit myself either way.

**장대**(長—) a 《bamboo》 pole; a rod. ¶ ~로 하늘 재기 attempting the impossible. ◉ ~높이뛰기 pole jump; pole vault 《미》: ~높이뛰기 선수 a pole= jumper〔-vaulter〕 / ~높이뛰기를 하다 pole-jump〔-vault〕.

**장대하다**(壯大—) (be) big and strong; husky; sturdy; mighty. ¶ 허우대가 장대한 사나이 a man with big and strong physique.

**장도**(壯途) an important mission; an ambitious 「undertaking 〔course of action, enterprise〕. ¶ ~에 오르다 start on the ambitious course / 북극 탐험의 ~에 오르다 embark on the enterprise of an arctic expedition.

**장도**(粧刀) an encased ornamental knife (hung at the belt).

**장도리** 《망치》 a hammer; 《노루발》 a claw hammer. ¶ ~ 대가리 a hammer-head / ~ 자루 the handle of a hammer / ~로 치다 hammer / ~로 못을 빼다〔박다〕 extract 〔drive in〕 a nail with a claw hammer.

**장독**(醬—) a crock 〔jar〕 of soy sauce. ◉ ~간 a place to keep jars of soy sauce. ~대 a terrace where soy sauce crocks are placed. ~소래기 the lid of a soy sauce crock.

**장돌림, 장돌뱅이**(場—) an itinerant 〔a roving〕 market trader 〔dealer〕.

**장두**(長頭) a longhead; dolichocephaly.

**장두**(檣頭) a masthead; the head of a mast. ¶ 국기를 ~에 올리다 hoist the national flag at the masthead.
◉ ~등(燈) a top light; a top lantern.

**장딴지** the calf (of the leg).

**장땡** 《노름에서》 a pair of tens; 《제일·최고》 the happiest 〔luckiest〕 lot. ¶ ~ 잡다 come across the happiest lot / 시치미만 떼면 ~이냐 To pretend to know nothing will give no help to settle the problem.

**장떡**(醬—) rice-cake seasoned with soy sauce.

**장래**(將來) the future; the time to come; 《전망》 the (future) prospects; [부사적] in (the) future (★ the가 없는 경우는 막연한 장래를 나타냄). ¶ ~의 future 《events》; prospective 《candidates》 / 밝은 ~ a bright 〔brilliant〕 future; bright prospects / 어두운 ~ a dark future; gloomy prospects / ~가 유망한 청년 a young man with bright prospects; a promising young man / ~를 내다 본 행동 a farsighted action / 먼 ~에 in the remote 〔distant, far-off〕 future / 가까운 ~에 in the near 〔foreseeable〕 future / 머지 않은 ~에 in the not-too-distant future; before too long / ~를 생각하다 look to the future; think of the future / ~의 계획을 세우다 form a plan for *one's* future; sketch out *one's* future / 이 사업은 ~가 유망하다 This business has great prospect. / 그는 ~에 엔지니어가 되려고 한다 He plans to become an engineer. / 나는 ~에 학자가 될 작정이다 I should like to establish myself as a scholar. / 이것들은 ~ 너희들이 세상에 나갈 때 크게 도움이 될 것이다 These things will prove useful some day

when you go out into the world. / ~에 무슨 일이 있을 지 모른다 There is no knowing what will happen in the future. / 너는 ~가 유망한 청년이다 You are a「promising 〔hopeful〕 young man.
◉ ~성 a prospect; future possibilities: 한국 산업의 ~성 Korean industrial possibilities / 그는 ~성이 있다 He has a bright future before him. / 이 사업은 ~성이 없다 There is no future (possibilities) in this business.

**장려**(壯麗) grandeur; splendor; magnificence. ~하다 (be) grand; magnificent; imposing. ¶ 그 옛 궁전의 ~함에 저절로 입이 딱 벌어졌다 The magnificient sight of the old palace made us catch our breath.

**장려**(奬勵) encouragement; stimulation; promotion (촉진). ~하다 encourage; promote; put 〔place〕 a premium《on》. ¶ 사회 봉사의 ~ the encouragement of social service / 산업〔학문, 저축〕을 ~하다 encourage「industry 〔learning, saving〕 / 운동을 ~하다 encourage athletic sports / 그것은 사기를 ~하는 것과도 같다 That would be offering a premium to fraud.
◉ ~금 a subsidy; a bounty: 생산 ~금 a subsidy for manufacturing. ~임금 incentive wages. ~자 a promoter; a supporter. 연구~보조금 grants for the encouragement of research.

**장력**(張力) 〖물리〗 tension; tensile strength. ¶ 표면~ surface tension.
◉ ~계(計) a tensiometer. ~시험 a「tension 〔tensile〕 test. ~시험기 tension testing machine.

**장렬**(壯烈) heroism; intrepidity; bravery. ~하다 (be) heroic; brave; glorious; sublime. ¶ ~한 죽음 a heroic death / ~한 행동 heroic 〔brave〕 deeds / ~한 죽음을 맞이 하다 die gloriously; meet a heroic death《in action》.

**장례**(葬禮) funeral「ceremonies 〔rites〕; a「funeral 〔burial〕 service. ¶ ~를 지내다 conduct 〔hold〕 a funeral; perform a funeral service《for》/ ~에 참례하다 attend 〔be present at〕 a funeral《for Mr. Kim》/ 그의 부친 ~는 교회에서 행해졌다 His father's funeral was held in church.
◉ ~비 funeral expenses. ~식 a funeral (service); burial 〔funeral〕 rites: ~식에 모인 사람들 the funeral「party 〔group, attendants〕. ~위원 a person in charge of funeral arrangements; a funeral commissioner: ~위원장 the chief funeral commissioner. ~집행 위원회《chairman of》the executive committee of the funeral service. ~차 a funeral car; a hearse. ~행렬 a funeral procession. 합동 ~식 the joint funeral (ceremony).

**장로**(長老) ① 《원로》 an elder; a senior; a superior. ¶ 정계의 ~ an elder statesman. ② 《교회의》 a presbyter; an elder. ◉ ~교〔교회〕 the Presbyterian「denomination 〔church〕.

**장롱**(欌籠) a wardrobe; a chest (of drawers); a bureau《미》.

**장루**(檣樓) a crow's nest; a top.

**장르** a *genre* (F.); a category; a kind. ¶ 이 책장은 ~ 별로 구분되어 있다 This bookshelf is classified according to genre.

**장리**(掌理) management; direction; control; superintendence. ~하다 manage; direct; control; administer.

**장마** the「rainy 〔wet〕 season; the long spell of rainy weather in (early) summer. ¶ 계속되는 ~ a continuous rain; a long spell of「wet 〔rainy〕 weather / ~(가) 지다, ~철로 접어들다 the rainy season sets in / ~가 걷히다 the rainy season is over. ◉ ~전선 a seasonal rain front. ~철 the「rainy 〔wet〕 season.

**장마루**(長—) 〖건축〗 a floor made of long planks instead of inlaid blocks.

**장막**(帳幕) a tent; a canopy; a hanging; a curtain. ¶ 철의 ~ the iron curtain / 밤의 ~ the veil of「night 〔darkness〕 / ~을 치다 pitch a tent; hang curtains / ~을 늘어뜨리다 hang《a window》with a curtain / 신비의 ~에 싸이다 be「wrapped 〔shrouded〕 in mystery / 모든 것이 밤의 ~에 싸이고 말았다 All were covered in the veil of darkness.

**장만** making; getting; getting ready; procurement; preparation. ~하다 make; get; get ready; buy; provide *oneself* with. ¶ ~한 돈이 없다 have no money prepared / ~한 옷이 많다 have a lot of clothes「prepared 〔made ready〕 / 돈을 ~하다 get 〔raise, make〕 money / 점심을 ~하다 prepare luncheon / 옷을 새로 ~하다 have a new suit made; buy a new suit / 집을 ~하다 get a house / 재산을 ~하다 amass a fortune / 땅을 잡혀 돈을 ~하다 raise money on *one's* land / 모든 것이 다 ~

되었느냐 Is everything ready? / 그녀는 시집가려고 옷을 많이 ～해 두었다 She has prepared many dresses for her marriage.

**장면**(場面) 《소설·영화 따위의》 a scene; 《장소》 a place; 《무대 따위의》 a setting; 《연극의》 a situation; 《광경》 spectacle; a sight. ¶ 연애 ～ a love scene / (극중의) ～ 전환 a 《quick》 set change / ～이 바뀌다 the scene shifts / ～을 활기띠게 하다 enliven the scene / ～은 전시 중의 런던이다 The scene is laid in London during the war. / 어제 귀가길에 감동적인 ～을 목격했다 Yesterday I 「came upon 〔witnessed〕 a moving scene on my way home.

**장명등**(長明燈) ① 《무덤 앞의》 a stone lantern that guards a grave. ② 《추녀·대문의》 a hanging lantern on the gate 〔at the end of the eaves〕.

**장모**(丈母) *one's* wife's mother; *one's* 〔a man's〕 mother-in-law.

**장모음**(長母音) a long vowel.

**장문**(―門) a wide-open door 〔gate〕.

**장문**(長文) a long article; a lengthy piece of writing; 《편지》 a long letter. ¶ ～의 전보 a long telegram.

**장물**(贓物) stolen 〔pilfered〕 property; stolen 〔hot 《미》〕 goods. ¶ ～을 은닉하다 secrete stolen goods. ◉ ～매매 dealing in stolen goods; fencing. ～아비 a dealer in stolen goods; a fence. ～취득 receiving stolen goods; fencing: ～취득하다 receive 〔purchase〕 stolen goods.

**장미**(薔薇) 〖식물〗 a rose; a rosebush. ¶ 들～ a wild rose; a brier / 장밋빛의 rosy; rose-colored; rose-pink / 장밋빛 같은 입술〔뺨〕 rosy lips 〔cheeks〕 / 가시 없는 ～는 없다 No rose without thorns. ◉ ～꽃 a rose. ～나무 a rose tree; a rosebush.

**장미계**(長尾鷄) 〖조류〗 a long-tailed 「rooster.

**장바구니**(場―) a shopping basket.

**장바닥**(場―) the market area; a marketplace.

**장발**(長髮) long hair; 《사람》 a long-haired person; a long hair. ¶ ～의 long-haired / ～을 하고 있다 wear *one's* hair long. ◉ ～족(族) a "hippie" style long-haired youth; long-hair wearers; long-haired mimickers; longhairs.

**장방형**(長方形) a rectangle. = 직사각형.

**장벽**(障壁) 《벽》 a fence; a wall; a barrier; 《장애》 an obstacle; a barrier. ¶ 언어 ～ a language barrier / ～을 쌓다 build 〔erect, set up, raise〕 a barrier 《between》 / ～을 없애다 remove 〔break down〕 a barrier 《between》 / ～이 되다〔을 이루다〕 constitute a barrier 《to》; be an obstacle 《to》; be in the way 《of》 / 관세의 ～을 쌓다 raise a 「tariff wall 〔customs barrier〕.

**장벽**(腸壁) the intestinal wall.

**장변**(場邊) interest on a loan for a period of five days (from one market to the next); a loan at high interest. ¶ ～리 =장변(場邊) / ～ 놀이하다 lend money at high interest; practice usury; be a loan shark.

**장병**(長病) a long 〔protracted〕 illness. ¶ ～을 앓다 suffer from a long illness; be ill 〔sick〕 for a long time.

**장병**(將兵) officers and men; military men.

**장보**(長―) 〖건축〗 a long beam which runs all the way without the support of templets.

**장보다**(場―) ① 《저자를 열다》 open a booth at a market. ② 《장에 가다》 go to market; go shopping.

**장복**(長服) habitual use 《of a medicine》; constant use. ～하다 use 《a medicine》 constantly; use habitually.

**장본**(張本) a (fatal) cause; the origin; the root. ¶ 그 정당에 든 것이 그가 망한 ～이 되었다 His joining that party was what led to his downfall.

**장본**(藏本) *one's* books 〔library〕.

**장본인**(張本人) the very man (who did *something*); the author 《of a plot》; the ringleader. ¶ 그가 그 음모의 ～이다 He is the very man who is behind the plot. *or* He is the very ringleader of the plot.

**장부** 〖건축〗 a tenon; a dovetail. ◉ ～촉 이음 mortise and tenon joint. 장붓구멍 a mortise.

**장부**(丈夫) 《장성한》 a full-grown man; 《사내다운》 a reliable man 〔gentleman〕. ¶ ～ 일언 중천금 A man's word is as good as a bond. ◉ 대～ a manly man.

**장부**(帳簿) a book; an account book; a ledger (원장); a register (대장). ¶ 상업 ～ trade books / 외상 ～ a charge account / 허위 ～ 기재 phony bookkeeping / ～에 기입하다 book; make an entry in a book; enter account in a book; enter 《an item》 in the book / ～를 매기다 keep books 〔accounts〕 / ～를 마감하다 close the books / ～를 검사하다 examine 〔inspect〕 the books; audit the accounts; check records

(조사) / ~를 속이다 falsify 〔juggle〕 accounts; 《영구어》 cook the books / ~를 정리하다 adjust the accounts. ◉ ~가격 book value. ~감사 auditing. ~기록계(係) a bookkeeper; an accountant: ~기록계의 일을 보다 be in charge of bookkeeping. ~정리 adjustment of accounts.

**장부끝**(帳簿—) the balance of accounts. ¶ ~을 맞추다 make the accounts balance; make (both) ends meet / ~을 속이다 doctor 〔falsify, manipulate, cook〕 accounts / ~이 맞지 않다 the accounts does not balance.

**장비**(裝備) equipment; outfit; rigging (선박의); 〖군사〗 armament. ~하다 equip 《a ship, *a person* with *a thing*》; mount 《a gun》; outfit 《with》; fit out; rig 《a ship》. ¶ ~가 좋은〔나쁜〕 well-〔ill-, poorly-〕equipped / 완전~의 fully equipped; 《200 men》 with full equipment / 우수한 ~를 갖춘 군함 a well-equipped warship / 그 군함은 20인치 포 9문을 ~하고 있다 The warship carries nine 20-inch guns. / 그 배에는 무전기가 ~되어 있다 The ship is equipped with radio. *or* The ship has radio equipment. / 그런 가벼운 ~로 겨울 산에 오르는 것은 매우 위험하다 It's very dangerous to climb a mountain in the winter wearing such a light outfit. ◉ ~과 the equipment division.

**장사** trade; business; commerce; 《거래》 transaction; a deal. ~하다 engage in trade; run a business. ¶ 장삿속 a commercial spirit; a mercantile mind; a profit-making 〔mercenary〕 motive / 음식〔술〕 ~ the restaurant 〔liquor〕 business / 수지 맞는〔맞지않는〕 ~ a paying 〔nonpaying〕 business / ~가 잘 되다 *one's* business thrives; do a brisk business / ~에 소질이 있다〔없다〕 have a good 〔poor〕 business 「head 〔sense〕 / ~가 번창하다 *one's* business prospers; drive a roaring trade / … ~를 하다 deal in 《rice》; be 《a tailor》 by trade; 《경영》 carry on business 《in coffee》 / ~를 바꾸다 change *one's* trade / 무슨 ~를 하세요 What kind of business are you in? / 요새 ~가 시원치 않다 Business is slack 〔slow〕 these days. ◉ ~꾼 a trader; a merchant; a dealer: ~꾼 기질〔근성〕 a mercenary spirit. ~판 trade; commercial 〔business〕 pursuits.

**장사**(壯士) a muscular 〔strong〕 man; a Hercules. ¶ 힘이 ~다 be as strong as Hercules.

**장사**(葬事) a funeral; a burial. ¶ ~지내다 hold a funeral; bury. ◉ 장삿날 a funeral day.

**장사진**(長蛇陣) a long 「line 〔queue, file, row〕. ¶ ~을 치다 make 〔stand in〕 a long line 〔queue《영》〕 / 극장 입구까지 사람들이 ~을 치고 있었다 A long queue was winding 〔snaking〕 its way to the entrance of the theater.

**장살**(杖殺) clubbing to death. ~하다 club to death.

**장삼**(長衫) a Buddhist monk's robe.

**장삼이사**(張三李四) (every) "Tom, Dick, and Harry"; everybody.

**장색**(匠色) a (handi)craftsman; an artisan; a worker.

**장생**(長生) long life; longevity. ~하다 live long; enjoy a long life. ¶ 불로 ~의 비결 the secret of perpetual youth.

**장생불사**(長生不死) eternal life; immortality. ~하다 enjoy eternal life; share immortality. ¶ ~의 영약 the elixir of life.

**장서**(藏書) a collection of books; *one's* (private) library. ~하다 build a library; collect books. ¶ 천 권의 ~가 있다 have a collection 〔library〕 of 1,000 volumes. ◉ ~가 the owner of a fine library; a book collector; a bibliophile. ~목록 a library catalog. ~벽(癖) bibliomania. ~인(印) the owner's signet 《affixed on a book》. ~표(票) a bookplate; an ex libris (생략 ex lib.).

**장석**(長石) 〖광물〗 feldspar; felspar.

**장선**(長線) 〖건축〗 an underfloor support beam; underflooring.

**장선**(腸線) a catgut; a gut.

**장성**(長成) growth; maturity. ~하다 grow up; grow to maturity. ¶ ~한 아이 a child all grown up / ~해서 어른이 되다 grow into an adult.

**장성**(將星) generals. ¶ 육해군 ~ army and navy celebrities.

**장성**(長城) a long wall. ¶ 만리~ the Great Wall of China.

**장소**(場所) 《지점》 a place; a spot; a point; 《좌석》 a seat; 《여지》 room; space; 《위치》 a location; a situation; a district; 《부지》 a site; 《현장》 a scene. ¶ 약속한 ~ the appointed place / 화재〔살인, 사고〕가 있었던 ~ the scene of a fire 〔a murder, an accident〕 / ~가 없어서 for want of space / ~를 너무 차지하다 occupy 〔take up〕

much「room 〔space〕/ ～를 가리지 않다 do not take due notice of the occasion / ～가 좋다〔나쁘다〕 be「well 〔badly〕 situated; be「conveniently 〔inconveniently〕 located / ～가 장소인지라 잠자코 있었다 Considering where I was, I refrained from referring to it. / ～가 좋아서 장사가 잘 된다 The locality brings a great deal of business.

**장손**(長孫) the eldest grandson by the first-born son.

**장송**(長松) a tall pine tree; 《널》 a long「pine board.

**장송**(葬送) escorting 〔attending〕 a funeral. ～하다 escort a funeral; attend at a funeral. ◉ ～곡 a funeral march.

**장수** 《상인》 a trader; a dealer; a seller; 《소매점 주인》 storekeeper; shopkeeper; 《행상》 a peddler; a hawker; a vendor. ◉ 생선～ a fishmonger. 술～ a wine dealer. 책～ a bookseller.

**장수**(長壽) (a) long life; longevity. ～하다 live long; enjoy longevity; live to a great age. ¶ 그는 ～하는 집안 출신이다 He comes of a long-lived family. / 그는 90세까지 ～를 누렸다 He lived to be ninety. / 그는 형제 중에서 가장 ～했다 He outlived all his brothers.
◉ ～법〔비결〕 the secret of longevity. ～식(食) 연구 macrobiotics. ～자 a macrobian. ～프로그램 a long-lived program (방송의). ～학 gerontology. 불로～약 the elixir of life (전설상의).

**장수**(將帥) a general; a commander; a commander-in-chief.

**장수**(張數) the number of「leaves 〔sheets〕.

**장수벌**(將帥―) 《여왕벌》 a queen bee.

**장승** 《마을 어귀의》 a totem pole 《at the village entrance》; a guardian idol; 《키다리》 a tall person; a gangling fellow. ¶ ～같이 크다 be as tall as a lamppost.

**장시간**(長時間) many (long) hours; long time. ¶ ～에 걸쳐 for (many) hours / ～ 회담하다 have a long talk 《with》.

**장시세**(場時勢) the market price 〔rate〕. ¶ ～의 변동 market fluctuations (주가 등의) / ～가 올랐다〔내렸다〕 The market (price)「advanced 〔declined〕.

**장시일**(長時日) a long (period of ) time; (for) years. ¶ ～에 걸치다 extend over a long period of time.

**장식**(裝飾) (an) ornament; ornamentation; (a) decoration; (an) adornment; (an) embellishment; 《점포의》 dressing. ～하다 ornament; adorn; decorate; deck out. ¶ ～용 for decoration; for「ornamental 〔decorative〕 purposes / ～적 decorative; ornamental / ～이 없는 plain; unadorned; unornamented; with no decoration / ～에 사용하다 use for decoration / 진열장을 ～하다 decorate 〔dress〕 a shop window / 방을 꽃으로 ～하다 decorate a room with flowers / 이 사진틀은 조개로 ～되어 있다 This picture frame is decorated with seashells. / 이 도자기는 단순히 ～용이다 This china is only for show (and not for use).
◉ ～단추 an ornamental button; a fancy button. ～물〔품〕 an ornament; decorations: 건축용 ～물 architectural ornaments. ～미술 decorative「art 〔painting〕. ～비 decoration expenses. ～사 《실내의》 an interior decorator; 《점포의》 a window dresser. ～술 decorative art. ～유리 ornamental glass. ～음 〖음악〗 a grace note; [총칭] grace. ～조각 ornamental carving; carved decorations. ～조명 decorative illumination. 머리～ an ornament for the head 〔hair〕; headdress. 무대～ stage decoration.

**장신**(長身) a tall「figure 〔stature〕. ¶ ～의 tall; 《미》 rangy / ～의 농구선수 a tall basketball player.

**장신구**(裝身具) personal ornaments; personal outfittings; trinketry; 《여성용》 accessories; 《남성용》 furnishings.

**장아찌** a dish of dried slices of radish or cucumber seasoned with soy sauce, *etc.*

**장악**(掌握) hold; grasp; seizure; command. ～하다 have a hold on; completely grasp 《the situation》; have at *one's* command. ¶ 정권을 ～하다 come into power; take (over) the reins of government / 실권을 ～하다 hold real power / 제공권을 ～하다 get 〔have〕 the command of the air / 그는 부하들을 잘 ～하고 있다 He has a good hold on his staff members.

**장안**(長安) the capital (city).

**장애**(障礙·障碍) 《방해되는 것》 an obstacle; an obstruction; an impediment; a hindrance; a barrier; a hurdle; a stumbling block; a difficulty; a hitch; a snag; 《신체상의》 trouble; a disorder; 〖의학〗 a lesion.
¶ 무역 ～ a trade barrier / 언어～ a speech「impediment 〔defect〕; an impediment in *one's* speech / 위장～ gastrointestinal disorder / 진보의 ～

an obstacle 〔a barrier, a stumbling block〕 to progress; a drag on the progress 《of》/ 예기치 않은 ~ an unexpected 〔unforeseen〕 obstacle 《to》/ 중대한 ~ a serious obstacle / ~가 되다 be an obstacle 《to》; be deterrent 《to》; hinder; impede; be 〔come, get〕 in the way 《of》/ ~에 부딪치다 encounter 〔meet with〕 an obstacle; hit 〔strike, run against〕 a snag / ~를 극복하다 overcome 〔surmount〕 an obstacle 〔a difficulty〕; get over a barrier; tide over 〔overcome〕 a difficulty / ~를 돌파하다 break through an obstacle; demolish 〔break down〕 a barrier / ~를 일소하다 clear away every obstacle; sweep all obstacles away / ~가 생긴다 A hitch arises. / 여하한 ~라도 뚫고 목적을 관철할 결심이다 Nothing shall prevent me from accomplishing my purpose.
◉ ~물 an obstacle; an obstruction; a hurdle (육상 경기의); a (jumping) bar (경마의); a bunker (골프의): ~물 경주 an obstacle race; a hurdle race (육상 경기의); a slalom (스키의); a steeplechase (경마의) / ~물 코스 an obstacle course / ~물을 뛰어넘다 jump 〔clear〕 an obstacle 〔a hurdle〕/ ~물을 제거하다 get obstacles out of the way. ~요소 an obstacle. ~인 a handicapped person; the handicapped [집합적]: ~인 학교 a school for the handicapped / ~인의 해 the Year of the Disabled / (전국) ~인 기능경기 대회 the Vocational Training Competition for Handicapped People / 한국 ~인 재활(再活)협회 the Korean Society for Rehabilitation of the Disabled / 정신 ~인 a mentally handicapped person / 시각 ~인 a blind person; a visually handicapped person. ~(인) 공제 《세금의》 a tax deduction for handicapped persons. ~인 교육 education of physically and mentally handicapped people. 방사선~ radiation sickness. 정서~ an emotional disorder.

**장액**(腸液) intestinal juice 〔secretion〕.

**장액**(漿液) 〖생리〗 serum.

**장어**(長魚) 〖어류〗 an eel; a common eel. ◉ 민물~ a freshwater eel.

**장엄**(莊嚴) majesty; solemnity; sublimity; grandeur; magnificence. ~하다 (be) majestic; solemn; sublime; impressive; grand. ¶ ~한 음악 solemn music / ~한 경관 sublime 〔majestic〕 scenery / 의식은 ~하게 거행되었다 The ceremony was conducted in a solemn atmosphere. ◉ ~미사 〖가톨릭〗 a High 〔Solemn〕 Mass.

**장염**(腸炎) 〖의학〗 enteritis; inflammation of the (small) intestine; intestinal catarrh.

**장염전증**(腸捻轉症) 〖의학〗 a twist in the intestines.

**장옷**(長―) 〖역사〗 a kind of long hood formerly worn by women.

**장외**(場外) ¶ ~의〔에〕 outside the room 〔hall, grounds, parliament〕/ 관중이 ~에까지 넘쳤다 The spectators overflowed the grounds.
◉ ~거래 〖증권〗 over-the-counter trading; off-board transactions; transactions on the third market. ~마권 an off-track betting ticket: ~ 마권 판매소 an off-track betting office. ~정치 the out-of-parliament politics; politics outside the stage 〔parliament〕. ~호머〔홈런〕 an out-of-the-park homer; a homer hit out of the ball park: ~ 호머를 날리다 hit a home run out of the (ball) park.

**장원**(壯元) 〖역사〗 ① 《수석 합격》 the highest passing mark in the state examination. ~하다 win the first place in the state examination. ¶ ~ 급제하다 =~하다. ② 《사람》 a candidate who won the first place in the state examination.

**장원**(莊園) 〖역사〗 a manor. ◉ ~제도 the manorial system.

**장유**(長幼) old and young. ¶ ~유서(有序)하다 The younger should give precedence to the elder. *or* The elder shall preside.

**장유**(醬油) soy sauce and sesame oil.

**장음**(長音) a long sound; 〖음성〗 a long vowel. ◉ ~부호 〖언어〗 a macron; a length mark; a long vowel mark.

**장음계**(長音階) 〖음악〗 the major (scale); the gamut.

**장의**(葬儀) a funeral. ⇨ 장례(葬禮). ¶ 성대한 ~ a pompous funeral / ~를 치르다 hold a funeral 《for》; perform 〔conduct〕 a funeral service 《for》.
◉ ~사(社) an undertaker's shop; a funeral parlor 《미》; a funeral home; a mortuary. ~ 준비 위원회 a (organizing) funeral committee.

**장의자**(長椅子) a sofa; a couch; a lounge; a bench.

**-장이**(匠―) a professional doer of …; -er.

**장인**(丈人) the wife's father; a man's 〔*one's*〕 father-in-law.

**장인**(匠人) an artisan; a craftsman. ◉ ~기질 the artisan spirit; (pride in *one's*) craftsmanship: 그렇게 하는 일은 그의 ~기질이 허락치 않는다 His artisan spirit will not allow him to do such a thing.

**장일**(葬日) the day of the funeral.

**장자**(長子) the eldest 〔oldest〕 son. ◉ ~상속권 the right of primogeniture. ~상속법 primogeniture.

**장자**(長者) 《어른》 an elder; *one's* senior; *one's* superior; 《덕망가》 an elder of virtue; a man of moral influence; 《부자》 a rich 〔wealthy〕 man. ¶ 백만~ a millionaire / ~를 공경하다 respect *one's* superiors / ~에게는 자리를 양보함이 당연하다 It is natural that one should give place to his superiors.

**장자**(莊子) 《중국의 사상가》 Chuangtzu (365-290 B.C.).

**장자석**(場磁石) 〖물리〗 a field magnet. ◉ ~ 가속 계전기 a field accelerating relay. ~극(極) a field pole. ~저항기 a field rheostat. ~전류 a field current. ~조정기 a field regulator. ~코일 field coil. 회전~ a revolving field.

**장작**(長斫) firewood. ¶ ~을 패다 split 〔chop〕 firewood / ~을 지피다 feed a fire with firewood. ◉ ~간 a woodshed; a woodhouse. ~개비 a piece of firewood. ~단 a fagot. ~불 wood fire. ~스토브 a wood(-burning) stove. ~패기 wood chopping.

**장장**(長長) very long; at great length; lengthily. ¶ 회의는 ~ 6시간이나 계속되었다 The meeting went on and on for six long hours. ◉ ~추야(秋夜) the long nights of autumn. ~하일(夏日) the long days of summer.

**장전**(裝塡) a charge 《of a gun》; loading. ~하다 charge 《a gun》; load. ¶ 총에 탄환을 ~하다 load *one's* gun with bullets.

**장절**(章節) chapters and verses. ¶ ~로 나누다 divide into chapters and verses.

**장점**(長點) a strong 〔good〕 point; an advantage; a merit; *one's* forte; a virtue; the saving grace. ¶ ~과 단점 strength and weakness; merits and demerits; (*one's*) forte and foible / 남의 ~을 인정하다 see the good in others / …라는 ~이 있다 have the advantage of… / 정직함이 그의 ~이다 Honesty is termed his saving grace. / 그것이 그의 ~의 하나다 It is one of his good 〔strong〕 points. / 그는 신제품의 많은 ~을 늘어놓았다 He claimed many advantages for the new product.

**장정**(壯丁) a strong young man; a sturdy youth; a strapping fellow; 《징병 적령자》 a young man of conscription age. ◉ ~명부 a list of conscripts.

**장정**(長征) a long march; 《중국군의》 the 「Long March.

**장정**(長程) a long way; a great distance. ¶ ~ 5만 마일 a distance of 50,000 miles.

**장정**(裝幀) binding; book cover design; getup 《구어》. ~하다 bind (a book); design 《a book cover》. ¶ 견고한 ~ durable binding / 그 책은 아담한 가죽 ~이다 The book is neatly bound in leather.

**장조**(長調) 〖음악〗 a major key.

**장조림**(醬―) beef boiled in soy sauce.

**장조카**(長―) the oldest 〔eldest〕 son of *one's* oldest 〔eldest〕 brother.

**장족**(長足) a great stride; a strong pace. ¶ ~의 진보 rapid progress / ~의 진보를 하다 make great 〔long〕 strides 《toward》; make rapid 〔remarkable〕 progress 《in》.

**장죽**(長竹) a long (smoking) pipe; a bamboo pipe.

**장중**(壯重) solemnity; gravity; impressiveness. ~하다 (be) solemn; grave; impressive. ¶ ~하게 solemnly; with solemnity / ~한 광경 an impressive scene / ~한 음악 solemn music / ~한 어조로 in a solemn tone.

**장중**(掌中) 《in》 *one's* hand; 《within》 *one's* power 〔grip〕. ⇨ 수중(手中). ◉ ~물 a thing in *one's* hand; *one's* possessions. ~보옥 a jewel in *one's* hand; the apple of *one's* eye: ~보옥처럼 사랑하다 love 《*one's* child》 like a precious jewel; treat as the apple of *one's* eye / ~보옥을 잃다 lose a prize within *one's* grasp.

**장지**(障―) a *changji* (screen); a paper sliding door; a sliding screen. ¶ 유리를 낀 ~ a glass-fitted sliding door / ~를 열다〔닫다〕 open 〔shut〕 a paper sliding door / ~를 바르다 paper 〔repaper〕 a sliding screen. ◉ ~문 = 장지. ~종이 sliding-screen paper. ~틀 sliding-door frame.

**장지**(長指) the middle finger.

**장지**(葬地) a burial ground 〔place〕.

**장질**(長姪) ⇨ 장조카.

**장차**(將次) in (the) future; some day. ¶ ~ 어떤 일이 일어날지 아무도 모른다

Nobody can tell what will happen in the future.

**장착**(裝着) installation; furnishing; fitting; mounting. ¶ 체인을 ～한 차 a car with tire chains on.

**장창**(長槍) a long spear 〔lance〕.

**장천**(長天) the boundless sky.

**장총**(長銃) a (long-barreled) rifle.

**장축**(長軸) 〖수학〗 the major axis; 〖천문〗 the apse line.

**장출혈**(腸出血) 〖의학〗 enterohemorrhage.

**장치**(裝置) equipment; installation; (an) apparatus; a (mechanical) contrivance; a device; 《무대의》 a setting. ～하다 equip 《with》; fit up 《with》; install. ¶ 급수～ a feeding apparatus / 기폭～ a trigger device; a fuse / 발화 ～ an ignition device / 안전 ～ a safety device / 조명〔난방〕～ a lighting 〔heating〕 system / …을 ～하다 fit 〔equip〕 《*a thing*》 with…; install; arrange / (…의) ～가 되어 있다 be equipped 《with》; be fitted 《with》 / 그 어선에는 레이더 ～가 없었다 The fishing boat had no radar equipment. *or* The fishing boat was not equipped with radar. / 그것에는 자동 발화 ～가 되어 있다 It is contrived so as to ignite automatically. / 이 승강기에는 안전 ～가 달려 있다 This elevator has a safety catch 〔device〕.

**장침**(長枕) a long pillow (that serves as an armrest).

**장침**(長針) a long needle; 《시계의》 the long hand; the minute hand.

**장카타르**(腸—) 〖의학〗 intestinal catarrh.

**장쾌**(壯快) being exciting and delightful; splendidness; thrillingness. ～하다 (be) exciting and delightful; splendid; thrilling. ¶ ～한 거사 a stirring 〔an exciting〕 attempt.

**장타**(長打) 〖야구〗 《hit》 a long hit. ◉ ～자 a long-ball hitter.

**장탄식**(長歎息) a heavy 〔deep〕 sigh. ～하다 draw 〔heave〕 a heavy sigh.

**장터**(場—) a market place 〔site〕.

**장티푸스**(腸—) 〖의학〗 typhoid fever. ◉ ～균 a typhoid bacillus. ～ 예방주사 anti-typhoid inoculation; a typhoid shot. ～환자 a (case of) typhoid.

**장파**(長波) 〖물리〗 a long wave. ◉ ～라디오 (수신기) a long-wave radio set. ～방송 a long-wave broadcast.

**장판**(壯版) a floor covered with laminated paper. ◉ ～방 a room with paper-covered floor. ～지(紙) (a sheet of) oiled floor paper.

**장편**(長篇) a long work 〔piece〕. ◉ ～소설 a long novel; a full-length novel. ～영화 a long film; a full-length film; a feature (film).

**장편**(掌篇) a very short piece of writing. ◉ ～소설 a short story; a *conte*.

**장폐색(증)**(腸閉塞(症)) 〖의학〗 obstruction 〔constriction〕 of the intestines; an intestinal blockage; ileus.

**장하다**(壯—) 《훌륭하다》 (be) great; grand; splendid; magnificent; wonderful; 《갸륵하다》 (be) praiseworthy; admirable; brave; 《놀랍다》 (be) remarkable; striking. ¶ 장한 행실 an admirable 〔a praiseworthy〕 conduct 〔deed〕 / 장한 어머니상 the "Great Mother" award / 장한 구경 거리 a grand spectacle / 장한 일을 하다 achieve a great thing / 그녀의 용기를 장하게 여기다 admire her courage / 참 장한 일을 했다 Well done! / 일등상을 탔다니 참 ～ It is splendid of you taking first prize.

**장하다**(長—) be proficient 《in》; be adept 《in》; be a good hand at 〔in〕; excel 《in》; be skilled 《in》. ¶ 그림에 ～ be excel in painting.

**장학**(奬學) encouragement 〔promotion〕 of learning. ～하다 encourage learning. ◉ ～관〔사〕 a government school inspector; 《도·시의》 a provincial 〔municipal〕 school inspector. ～금 a scholarship; a (student) grant 《영》: ～금을 주다〔받다〕 award 〔obtain, win〕 a scholarship / ～금을 받고 있다 be supported by a scholarship; hold 〔have〕 a scholarship / ～금 제도를 마련하다 found 〔establish, create〕 a scholarship / 그는 미국에서 ～금을 받아 공부하였다 He studied in America on a scholarship. ～기금 a scholarship fund. ～생 a scholarship student; a student on scholarship; a scholarship holder. ～(위원)회 a scholarship committee.

**장해**(障害) ＝장애(障礙·障碍).

**장형**(杖刑) flogging. ～하다 flog 《a criminal》.

**장형**(長兄) the eldest brother.

**장화**(長靴) high 〔long〕 boots; Wellington boots. ¶ 고무～ rubber boots.

**장황하다**(張皇—) (be) lengthy; tedious; long-winded; long and boring. ¶ 장황한 연설 a lengthy 〔long-winded〕 speech / 장황하게 설명하다 make a long-winded explanation / 얘기를 장황하게 늘어놓다 speak tediously 〔in a roundabout way].

**잦다**[1] 《뒤로》 lean back; get sway-back(ed). ¶ 뒤로 잦은 의자 a sway-back chair.

**잦다**[2] 《바람 등이》 go down; sink; fall; subside; 《물 등이》 dry (up); boil down.

**잦다**[3] 《빈번하다》 (be) frequent; be very often; repeated; 《빠르다》 (be) quick; rapid. ¶ 잦은 걸음 short [quick] steps / 잦은 걸음으로 걷다 walk at a quick pace [rapid steps, a brisk pace] / 최근 철도 사고가 잦았다 We have had frequent railroad accident lately. / 겨울에는 화재가 ~ Fires are frequent in wintertime. / 공항을 왕래하는 버스편이 ~ The buses for the airport run at frequent intervals.

**잦뜨리다** throw [bend] 《*one's* head》 back. ¶ 고개를 잦뜨리고 의자에 앉다 sit in a chair with *one's* head thrown back.

**잦아들다** keep going down [sinking, falling]; run dry; 《끓어서》 boil down. ¶ 물이 끓어 ~ water boils down / 가뭄으로 연못 물이 잦아들었다 The pond water sank with the drought.

**잦아지다** sink; go down; fall; dry up.

**잦추다** 《재촉하다》 press; hurry (up); urge on; rush. ¶ 아무한테 일을 ~ hurry *a person* with *his* work / 빚을 갚으라고 ~ press 《*a person*》 for the payment of a debt.

**잦혀놓다** ① 《뒤집어 놓다》 turn 《*a thing*》 over [down] and leave it; lay 《*a thing*》 face down [upside down]. ¶ 접시를 ~ turn over a plate. ② 《열어 놓다》 leave 《a swing door, *etc.*》 flung open. ¶ 문을 ~ keep a door flung open. ③ =제쳐놓다.

**잦히다**[1] ① 《뒤집다》 turn over; turn 《*a thing*》 upside down; lay 《*a thing*》 face down. ¶ 책장을 ~ turn over leaves of a book; open a book / 접시를 ~ turn a plate over. ② 《뒤로》 pull [bend] back; lean backwards. ¶ 몸을 ~ straighten *oneself* up; stick out *one's* chest / 어깨를 ~ pull back *one's* shoulders. ③ 《열다》 fling open; open wide. ¶ 문을 ~ fling a door open. ④ 《일 따위를》 put aside (*one's* work); set apart; lay aside. ¶ 하던 일을 잦히고 친구를 만나다 meet a friend laying aside what *one* was doing.

**잦히다**[2] 《밥을》 let the rice stand on a low flame; stew; simmer down.

**재**[1] 《타고 남은》 ash(es). ¶ 재가 되다 be reduced to ashes; convert into ash / 재 같은 ashy; ashen / 재투성이의 full of ashes / 죽어서 재가 되다 be cremated / 담뱃재를 떨다 knock [tap] the ash off *one's* cigarette 《into an ashtray》 / 많은 집들이 불에 타 재가 되었다 Many houses were burned to ashes.

**재**[2] 《고개》 a (mountain) pass; a (mountain) peak; a hill. ¶ 무악재 the Muak Pass / 재를 넘다 cross over a pass; go over a hill.

**재**(齋) 〖불교〗 the Buddhist service of praying for the souls of the dead; Buddhist mass for the dead. ¶ 재를 올리다 pray for the happiness of the dead; have a mass read for the repose of a soul.

**재-**(再) re-. ¶ 재군비 rearmament / 재정리 rearrangement; readjustment / 재검표(再檢票) ballot recounting.

**재가**(在家) staying [being] at home; 〖불교〗 studying Buddhism at *one's* home. ~하다 be (at) home; stay [keep] at home; lead a Buddhist life staying at *one's* home. ◉ ~승(僧) a married Buddhist priest.

**재가**(再嫁) remarriage 《of a woman》. ~하다 (a woman) remarry. ⇨ 개가(改嫁).

**재가**(裁可) approval; sanction. ~하다 approve; give sanction to. ¶ ~를 바라다 submit 《*a matter*》 to 《*a person's*》 sanction / ~를 얻다 obtain 《*a person's*》 sanction.

**재간**(才幹) 《능력》 ability; talent; capability; 《재주》 skill. ¶ ~이 있다 be able [capable]; be talented / ~ 많은 사람 a man of many gifts / ~ 있는 able; talented; gifted; resourceful / ~을 발휘하다 show *one's* ability [skill] 《in》 / 학식과 ~이 남보다 뛰어나다 excel others both in talent and learning.

**재간**(再刊) republication; reissue; reprint(ing); second edition. ~하다 republish; reissue; reprint.

**재갈** a bit; 《사람에게 물리는》 a gag. ¶ ~을 물리다 gag 《*a person*》; put a gag in 《*a person's*》 mouth / 말에 ~을 물리다 bit a horse; put a bit in the mouth of a horse / (말이) ~을 물다 《a horse》 takes the bit.

**재감**(在監) 〖법〗 imprisonment; being [staying] in prison. ¶ ~중이다 be in prison. ◉ ~자 a prison inmate; a prisoner.

**재감염**(再感染) reinfection.

**재강** 《술찌끼》 the sediment of fermented liquor; lee. ◉ ~장 soy sauce steeped in liquor lees. ～죽 gruel made with liquor lees and sticky rice.

**재개**(再開) reopening; resumption. ～하다 reopen; resume; hold ⟪a meeting⟫ again. ¶ 교섭〔무역〕을 ～하다 reopen 〔resume〕 negotiations 〔foreign trade〕/ 경기를 ～하다 resume play / 국회가 ～되었다 The National Assembly has resumed work. *or* The National Assembly session 「has been 〔was〕 resumed. / 회의는 오후 1시에 ～된다 The meeting will be resumed 〔reopened〕 at 1 p.m. / 한미 교섭이 ～되었다 The negotiations between Korea and America were reopened 〔resumed〕.

**재개발**(再開發) redevelopment. ～하다 redevelop. ¶～ 공사 현장 a redevelopment construction site. ◉ ～지역 a redevelopment area 〔zone〕.

**재건**(再建) reconstruction; rebuilding; rehabilitation; re-erection. ～하다 reconstruct; rebuild; re-erect. ¶ 전후의 ～ postwar reconstruction / ～에 착수하다 embark on the reconstruction ⟪of⟫ / 도시를 ～하다 rebuild a town from ruin / 조국을 ～하다 restore 〔rehabilitate〕 *one's* country (to its former prosperity) / 그들은 피해 입은 가옥을 ～했다 They rebuilt a damaged house. ◉ ～비 rebuilding expenses. 산업〔경제〕 ～ industrial 〔economic〕 reconstruction.

**재검사**(再檢査) (a) reexamination; (a) reinspection. ～하다 reexamine; recheck; check over again; reinspect. ¶ 너의 위는 ～가 필요하다 Your stomach must be examined again.

**재검토**(再檢討) (a) reappraisal; (a) reexamination; (a) review; rethinking. ～하다 reappraise; reexamine; rethink; review. ¶ 대통령은 국방 계획의 ～를 명했다 The President ordered a review of the nation's defense plans. / 그 문제는 ～하도록 하자 Let us reexamine 〔review〕 the matter. / ～한 뒤 그 제안은 기각되었다 After reexamination, the proposal was rejected. / 이 정책은 충분히 ～할 필요가 있다 A good deal of rethinking is needed on this policy.

**재결**(裁決) (a) decision; (a) judgment; ruling; arbitration. ～하다 pass decision 〔judgment〕 ⟪on⟫; decide; arbitrate. ¶～에 따르다 abide by a decision / ～을 내리다 pass judgment ⟪on⟫ / ～을 바라다 ask ⟪*a person*⟫ for decision; ask for ⟪*a person's*⟫ decision / 그 문제의 ～은 당국에 맡기는 것이 좋겠다 You had better leave the problem to the authorities' judgement. ◉ ～권 a casting vote. ～서 a written verdict 〔decision〕.

**재결합**(再結合) recombination; reunion. ～하다 reunite ⟪with⟫; recombine; rejoin together. ¶ 이산 가족의 ～ reunion of *one's* dispersed family members / 전부인과 ～하다 be reconciled 〔reunited〕 with his former wife.

**재경**(在京) staying in the capital; staying in Seoul. ～하다 stay in Seoul; be 〔reside〕 in Seoul. ¶～의 벗 a friend in Seoul / ～중(에) during *one's* stay in Seoul; while in the capital 〔in Seoul〕. ◉ ～동창생 alumni in Seoul. ～외국인 foreign residents in Seoul.

**재경**(財經) finance 〔financial administration〕 and economy.

**재경하다**(再耕—) till ⟪a field⟫ a second time; plow again; replow.

**재계**(財界) the financial world 〔circles〕; the money market; ⟪경제계⟫ the economic world; economic circles; ⟪실업계⟫ the business world; (big=) business circles. ¶～의 거두 a leading financier; a tycoon ⟪미⟫; a financial magnate; a financial leader / ～의 안정〔동요〕 financial stability 〔unrest〕/ ～의 위기 a financial crisis / ～의 불황 a business 〔an economic〕 depression / ～가 활기를 띠다 The financial world shows signs of activity. / 그는 ～의 위기를 건전한 상태로 되돌려 놓았다 He rehabilitated the financial crisis. ◉ ～사정 financial affairs. ～인 ⟪금융가⟫ a financier; ⟪실업가⟫ a businessman; ⟪자본가⟫ a capitalist.

**재계**(齋戒) (religious) purification; ablution. ～하다 perform purification; purify *oneself.* ¶ 목욕 ～하고 기도드리다 offer prayers performing purification (of mind and body).

**재고**(再考) reconsideration; rethinking. ～하다 reconsider; think ⟪it⟫ twice 〔over〕; think better of; think over again; rethink. ¶～한 후에 on reflection; on second thoughts / ～를 요함 *ad referendum* (L.) / ～를 촉구하다 urge ⟪*a person*⟫ to reconsider / ～를 요청하다 ask ⟪*a person*⟫ to reconsider ⟪the matter⟫ / ～의 여지가 없다 There is no room for reconsideration. / 한번 더 ～해 주시지 않겠습니까 Would you think it over once more?

**재고**(在庫) stock; the stockpile. ¶～의 in store; in stock / ～가 있다〔없다〕 be in 〔out of〕 stock / ～가 부족하다 do not have sufficient quantities in stock; the stock has run short / 그 책의 ～는 많다 We have a large stock of the book.

◉ ～과잉 excess stock; over-stocking; a glut 《of eggs》 (on the market). ～관리 control of goods in stock; inventory control 《미》. ～대장 a stock book. ～량 the total stock. ～부족 a shortage of goods in stock. ～순환 inventory cycle. ～율 inventory-sales ratio. ～율 지수 an index of inventory=sales ratio. ～ 정리 대매출 a clearance sale; 《게시》 Clearance sale. ～조사 stocktaking; (an) inventory: ～ 조사하다 take stock 〔an inventory〕 of *one's* goods on hand; check the stock. ～조정 inventory 〔stock 《영》〕 adjustment: 아직 ～ 조정 국면은 끝나지 않았다 The phase of inventory adjustment is not over yet. ～투자 inventory investment.

**재고품**(在庫品) goods in store; warehouse goods. ¶ ～ 목록 a stock list; an inventory / ～이 있다 [사람이 주어] have 《goods》 in stock; [물건이 주어] be in stock.

**재교**(再校) the second proof 《from the printer》; (the second) revision. ¶ ～를 보다 read the second proof. ◉ 요(要)～ a second proof required.

**재교부**(再交付) a reissue; a regrant. ～하다 reissue 《a passport》; regrant. ¶ 패스포트의 ～를 신청하다 apply for a new passport.

**재교육**(再教育) reeducation; retraining; reorientation; in-service training (재직자의). ～하다 reeducate; retrain; reorient. ¶ ～을 받다 be reeducated; be retrained. ◉ 직업～ vocational reeducation; job retraining.

**재구성**(再構成) reconstruction; recomposition. ～하다 reconstruct; recompose.

**재구속**(再拘束) 〖법〗 (a) remand. ～하다 remand 《*a person*》 (in custody).

**재군비**(再軍備) rearmament. ～하다 rearm; remilitarize. ⇨ 재무장.

**재귀**(再歸) reflection; reflexive(ness); recursive(ness); recurring; relapsing; recurrent. ◉ ～대명사〔동사〕 a reflexive pronoun 〔verb〕. ～열(熱) 〖의학〗 a relapsing fever: ～열 스피로헤타 a spiroch(a)eta (*pl.* -tae) recurrentis.

**재규어** 〖동물〗 a jaguar.

**재근**(在勤) ～하다 hold office; serve; work. ¶ ～중에 while in office; during *one's* term of office / 해외 ～ 수당 a foreign service allowance / 5년 이상 ～한 사람들 those in service for more than five years.

**재기**(才氣) talent; a flash of wit. ¶ ～있는 학생 an apt pupil / ～ 발랄하다 be very witty.

**재기**(再起) a return to popularity 〔power, *one's* former position〕; 《구어》 a comeback; 《회복》 (a) recovery. ～하다 come back; make 〔stage〕 a comeback; 《회복하다》 recover; be 〔get〕 on *one's* feet again. ¶ ～불능이다 be disabled for active service; be past 〔beyond all〕 hope of recovery / 그는 가수로서 ～ 불능이다 His singing career is over. / 그는 ～ 불능이라고 선고되었다 His recovery has been pronounced as hopeless 〔impossible〕. / 그는 무대 배우로 ～했다 He made a comeback as a stage actor.

**재깍** ① 《소리》 with a click 〔clack, snap〕. ～하다 give a click 〔snap, thud〕. ¶ ～거리다 keep clicking 〔snapping〕 / ～ 부러지다 snap 《off》. ② 《일을》 with dispatch; speedily; quickly. ¶ 일을 ～하다 do *one's* work with dispatch.

**재깍재깍** 《소리가》 with repeated clicks 〔snaps〕; 《일처리를》 with dispatch; speedily; quickly.

**재난**(災難) a calamity; a disaster; 《불운》 a misfortune; a mishap; 《사고》 an accident.

> 용법 **misfortune** 불행, 재난을 나타내는 일반적인 말. 대체로 중대한 사항에 쓰임. **disaster** 커다란 손해를 가져오거나 갑자기 닥치는 불행·재난. **calamity** 재해·재난 따위로 초래된 손해나 고통 따위가 대단히 큰 것을 뜻하는 말.

¶ 불의의 ～ an unexpected calamity / ～의 연속 a series of accidents 〔misfortunes〕; a run of ill luck / ～을 당하다 meet with a misfortune; have 「an accident 〔a mishap〕 / ～을 면하다 escape a disaster / ～을 가져오다 invite a disaster; bring a disaster 《upon *oneself*》 / 언제 어떤 ～이 닥쳐도 당황하지 않도록 대비하여라 Be prepared not to get upset, no matter what misfortune befalls you at any time.

**재넘이** a mountain wind 〔blast〕; a wind blowing down a mountain.

**재년**(災年) an unfortunate year.

**재능**(才能) ability; capability; capacity; gift; talent; genius.

> 용법 **ability** 선천적·후천적인 능력. **capability** 일을 추진할 때 발휘되는 실제적인 능력. **capacity** 사물을 이해하고 받아들이는 역량. **talent** 예술·예능 등 어떤 특수한 것에 대한 타고난 재능. 훈련에 의해서 나타남. **gift** 타고난 재질로서 아무런 노력 없이 발휘되는 재능. **genius** 창조적인 일에서 발휘되는 범상치 않은 재능.

¶ ～이 있다 have talent; be talented / ～이 없다 lack ability 〔talent〕; be talentless 〔untalented, incapable〕 / ～이 있는 talented; gifted; able; capable / ～이 없는 talentless; incapable / ～이 있는 사람 a talented person; a man of talent / 어학적 ～ linguistic talent / 숨은 ～ a hidden talent / 타고난 ～ *one's* natural gift / ～을 발휘하다 show 〔demonstrate〕 *one's* talent 〔ability〕 / ～을 닦다 cultivate *one's* talents; improve *one's* ability / 그는 뛰어난 ～을 타고났다 He is richly gifted by nature. / 그녀에게는 음악적 ～이 있다 She has a talent 〔genius〕 for music. / 나는 어학에 ～이 없다 I have no gift for languages. *or* I have no linguistic talent 〔ability〕. / 그 일이라면, 나도 ～을 충분히 발휘할 수 있을 것이다 In that work, I will be able to show my ability.

**재다**[1] ① 《넓이·길이를》 take measure of; 《도량을》 measure; gauge; weigh (무게를); survey (측량); 《수심·인심 등을》 fathom; sound; guess. ¶ 자로 ～ take measurements with a ruler / 키를 ～ take 〔measure〕 *one's* height / 강의 깊이를 ～ sound 〔fathom〕 the depth of a river / 풍력을 ～ gauge the strength of the wind / 양복의 치수를 재게 하다 have *one's* measurements taken / 거리를 ～ measure the distance / 체온을 ～ take *one's* temperature / 체중을 ～ weigh *oneself* on the scale / 산의 높이를 ～ measure the height of a mountain / 아무의 마음을 ～ sound (out) *a person;* enter into *a person's* feelings / 시간은 시·분·초로 잰다 Time is measured by the hour, minute and second. / 강수량을 재는 방법을 아느냐 Do you know how to gauge 〔measure〕 the amount of rainfall ? / 야드는 길이를 재는 단위다 A yard is a unit in measuring length. ② 《평가하다》 estimate; measure; judge; 《계산하다》 calculate; compute; 《헤아리다》 guess; presume; take 《*something*》 into consideration. ¶ 자기 척도로 남의 역량을 ～ measure 〔judge〕 others by *one's* own standard / 앞뒤를 ～ take every possible consequence 〔situation〕 into consideration; look before and after / 일을 재서 하다 carry out *one's* plan with discretion / 여러모로 재보다 view 《*a matter*》 from various angles / 그 가치는 돈으로 잴 수 없다 Its value cannot be measured by money. / 재산으로 사람의 가치를 잴 수는 없다 We cannot measure a person's worth by his wealth. / 행복을 돈으로는 잴 수 없다 Happiness can't be measured in terms of money.

**재다**[2] ① 《탄약을》 load 《a gun》 《with》; charge 〔tamp〕 《with》. ¶ 총에 탄환을 ～ load a gun. ② 《김·솜 따위를》 have 《*a thing*》 pressed; smooth 《down》; let set 〔settle〕. ¶ 김을 ～《쟁이다》 let the seaweed get pressed / 솜을 ～《재우다》 have the (ginned) cotton pressed.

**재다**[3] ① 《동작이》 (be) quick; fast; alert; nimble; agile. ¶ 몸이 잰 사람 a nimble person / 걸음이 ～ be nimble on *one's* feet; have quick steps / 입이 ～ be talkative; be loose-tongued / 손이 ～ have nimble fingers. ② 《으스대다》 be proud of; make a boast of; be high-browed; give *oneself* 〔put on〕 airs; assume an air of importance. ¶ 그것은 잴 만한 일이 못 된다 That is not much to be proud of.

**재단**(財團) 〖법〗 a foundation. ¶ ～ 설립의 학교 a foundation 〔an endowed〕 school / ～이 후원하는 foundation-sponsored 《research》 / 우수한 학생을 해외로 보내기 위해 ～이 설립되었다 A foundation was established to send excellent students abroad. ◉ ～법인 a foundation; an 〔a legally〕 incorporated foundation; a juridical person.

**재단**(裁斷) ① 《마름질》 (garment) cutting. ～하다 cut out 《a dress》. ② ＝재결. ◉ ～기 a cutter; a cutting machine. ～법 cutting; a cut. ～사 a (tailor's) cutter; a cloth-cutter.

**재담**(才談) a witty talk 〔remark〕; witticism. ～하다 talk wittily. ◉ ～꾼 a witty talker.

**재당숙**(再堂叔) a male second cousin of *one's* father.

**재당질**(再堂姪) a son of *one's* male second cousin.

**재덕**(才德) talents and virtues. ¶ ~을 겸비한 부인 a virtuous and talented lady / ~을 겸비하다 be both talented and virtuous.

**재독**(再讀) a second reading. ~하다 read 〔peruse〕 again; reread. ¶ 그 기사는 ~할 만한 가치가 있다 The article is worth a second reading.

**재돌입**(再突入) 《우주선 등의》 re-entry. ¶ 대기권에 ~하다 re-enter the atmosphere; make a (successful) re-entry into the atmosphere.

**재동**(才童) a talented child; a child 「prodigy.

**재두루미** 〖조류〗 a white-naped crane.

**재떨이** an ashtray; 《스탠드식》 a smoking stand. ¶ ~와 부자(富者)는 모일수록 더럽다 《속담》 Greed grows with possessions.

**재래**(在來) former times; the past; conventional. ¶ ~의 traditional; usual; common; customary; conventional; ordinary / ~의 습관 traditional 〔old〕 customs / ~의 물품과는 전혀 다르다 be quite different from 「an ordinary article 〔the existing kind〕. ◉ ~기술 traditional 〔old〕 technology. ~무기 conventional weapons. ~식 conventional type. ~종 a native kind; the natural and not improved species: ~종 딸기 native strawberries.

**재래**(再來) a second 「coming 〔advent〕; reincarnation. ~하다 come again. ¶ 나폴레옹은 카이사르의 ~라고 일컬어져 왔다 Napoleon has been called a second Caeser. ◉ ~환자 a person on the sick list.

**재략**(才略) resourcefulness; a clever scheme; tacts; resource(s). ¶ ~이 있다 be 「resourceful 〔tactful, adroit〕.

**재량**(裁量) discretion; judgment. ¶ 자유 ~으로 at *one's* discretion / ~껏 하다 use *one's* discretion / ~에 맡기다 leave 《*a matter*》 to 《*a person's*》 discretion; give 《*a person*》 a free 「hand 〔rein〕 《for *a matter*》 / 자네 ~껏 하게 You can do with it as you think best. / 재판장의 ~으로 그를 가석방 할 수 있다 It is within the discretion of the presiding judge to release him on parole. ◉ ~처분 discretional 〔discretionary〕 disposition.

**재력**(財力) financial 〔money〕 power 〔ability〕; 《재산》 wealth; means. ¶ ~이 있는 사람 a man of 「means 〔wealth〕 / ~을 과시하다 let *one's* money talk.

**재련**(再鍊) 《쇠 따위의》 resmelting; reforging. ~하다 reforge; resmelt.

**재론**(再論) reargument; rediscussion. ~하다 reargue; rediscuss.

**재롱**(才弄) 《아기의》 cute tricks. ¶ ~스럽다 《아기 동작이》 《be》 cute; sweet / ~(을) 부리다 act cute; do cute things. ◉ ~둥이 a cute baby; a sweet baby doing cute things.

**재료**(材料) [일반적] material(s); matter; stuff; 《원료》 raw material(s); 《요소》 a factor; an element; 《성분》 ingredients; 《제재(題材)》 subject matter; 《자료》 data. ¶ 풍부한〔빈약한〕 ~ abundant 〔scanty〕 materials / ~를 입수하다 procure 〔get〕 materials / ~를 수집하다 collect (necessary) materials 《for》 / ~를 제공하다 afford 〔furnish〕 materials 〔data〕 《for》 / ~를 모으다 assemble materials 《to *do*》 / 이 집은 좋은 ~로 세워졌다 This house is built of good materials. / 이 케이크의 주된 ~는 무엇이냐 What are the main ingredients of this cake? ◉ ~고갈 exhaustion of materials. ~비 the cost of materials; material costs. ~시험 material testing. 건축~ building 〔construction〕 materials. 실험~ materials for experiments.

**재류**(在留) residence. ~하다 reside; stay; dwell. ¶ ~의 resident; living 《in, at》. ◉ ~민 Korean residents abroad. ~외국인 foreign residents 《in Korea》: 서울 ~ 외국인 foreign residents in Seoul.

**재림**(再臨) 〖기독교〗 reincarnation; a second 「coming 〔advent〕. ~하다 be reincarnated; come again. ¶ 예수의 ~ the Second Advent of Christ. ◉ ~파 Adventist. 예수~설 Adventism.

**재명**(才名) talent and fame; fame for *one's* talent.

**재목**(材木) wood; lumber 《미》; timber 《영》; 《통나무》 a log (★ lumber는 미국·캐나다에서는 제재된 목재·판자를 가리키며 영국에서는 미가공된 목재를 가리킨다. timber는 미·영에서 건축용 재목의 뜻으로 쓰이나 특히 영국에서는 판자를 가리키는 경우가 있음). ¶ ~감을 벌채하다 cut down trees for lumber; lumber 《in, at》 / ~을 건조시키다 season the wood. ◉ ~상 《사업》 the lumber business; 《사람》 a 「lumber 〔timber〕 dealer 〔merchant〕. ~운반선〔트럭〕 a lumber 「carrier 〔truck〕. ~적재장 a lumberyard; a timber yard.

**재무**(財務) financial affairs. ¶ 그는 ~ 담당이다 He is in charge of financial affairs.

◉ ~감독관 a comptroller (of the treasury). ～감사 financial audit. ～고문 a financial advisor. ～관 a financial agent 〔commissioner〕. ～관리 financial management. ～구조 the financial structure 《of enterprises》. ～보고서 financial reports. ～부〔성〕 the Department of the Treasury 《미》: ～부 장관 the Secretary of the Treasury 《미》. ～위원회 the Finance Committee. ～제표(諸表) financial statements. ～행정 financial administration.

**재무장**(再武裝) rearmament. ～하다 rearm 《itself》; remilitarize 《a country》. ¶ 나는 ～에 절대 반대이다 I am absolutely against rearmament.
◉ ～계획 rearmament program. 도덕～운동 Moral Rearmament Movement (생략 MRA).

**재물**(財物) property; effects; goods; means; treasures; a fortune. ¶ ～에 눈이 어두워지다 be dazzled by riches / 남의 ～을 빼앗다 rob *a person* of *his* property / 많은 ～을 모으다 amass a vast fortune.

**재미** ① 《즐거움·흥미》 interest; amusement; enjoyment; fun. ¶ ～있다〔나다〕 be interesting 〔amusing, entertaining, enjoyable; full of fun〕 / ～ 없다 be uninteresting 〔unamusing, dull, flat, insipid〕 / ～있는 사람 a man of humor / ～있는 이야기〔책〕 an interesting 〔amusing〕 story 〔book〕 (★ 현재 분사형과 과거 분사형의 뜻의 차이에 주의. 보기: interested spectators 「재미있어〔흥겨워〕하는 구경꾼」이란 뜻) / ～ 없는 소문 unpleasant 〔unsavory〕 rumors / ～를 보다 have a good 〔profitable〕 time; have fun; enjoy *oneself* / ～를 붙이다 take interest 《in》; take pleasure 《in》; be interested 《in》 / ～ (많이) 보십시오 《놀러 가는 이에게》 Have fun, good-by! / ～ (많이) 보셨습니까 Did you have a good time? *or* Was it fun? / 그는 낚시질의 ～를 모른다 He can not see the fun of fishing. / 이 책을 아주 ～있게 읽었다 I have read this book with great interest. / 이것은 ～가 있을 거야 This should be fun.
② 《만족》 satisfaction. ¶ 결과는 ～ 없었다 The result was unsatisfactory. / 이거 ～가 적은데 The prospects are not encouraging. *or* Things are getting worse. / 이거 ～있게 되는군 There is a good time coming. *or* Things are warming up.
③ 《장사의》 favorableness; satisfactoriness; good. ¶ 요새 장사 ～가 어떻습니까 How is your business getting along? / ～ (많이) 보십시오 《가게를 떠나면서》 Good business to you, good-by!
④ 《취미》 a pastime; a hobby; recreation; fun; comfort. ¶ ～로 기르다 grow 《flowers, *etc.*》 for a hobby / 낚시질이 그의 유일한 ～다 Fishing is his sole comfort.

**재미**(在美) residing in America. ¶ ～의 in America / ～중에 while in America / ～중이다 be in America. ◉ ～교포 a Korean resident 〔living〕 in the United States. ～유학생 Korean students studying in America.

**재민**(災民) ＝이재민(罹災民). ¶ 한해(旱害)～ sufferers from the drought.

**재발**(再發) ① 《병·사고 등의》 reappearance; relapse 〔return〕 《of a disease》; recurrence; recrudescence. ～하다 [병이 주어] recur; return; recrudesce; redevelop (암이); [사람이 주어] relapse 《into》; have 〔suffer〕 a relapse 〔return〕 《of》; have a second attack 《of》. ¶ 전쟁의 ～ the recurrence of war / 유사한 사건의 ～을 방지하기 위한 보장 guarantees to prevent a recurrence of a similar incident / 한반도에서의 전쟁의 ～을 막다 prevent the recurrence of war on the Korean Peninsula / ～ 방지에 노력하다 make efforts to prevent the recurrence 《of》 / 병의 ～을 막다 prevent a disease (from) returning / 그는 병이 ～했다 He has had a return 〔second attack, relapse〕 of the disease. / 통증이 ～했다 The pain has returned. / 그는 늑막염이 ～했다 He has relapsed into pleurisy. / 이것은 아마 비슷한 사고의～을 막는 가장 알맞은 대책이 될 것이다 This is probably the best possible measure to keep similar accidents from happening again.
② 《재발송》 a second dispatch 〔sending〕 《of a letter》. ～하다 《다시 보내다》 send out 〔dispatch〕 again.

**재발견**(再發見) rediscovery; recovery. ～하다 rediscover; recover. ¶ 잊혀진 기술을 ～하다 recover a lost art.

**재발급**(再發給) reissuance; (a) reissue. ～하다 reissue.

**재발족**(再發足) a restart; a fresh start. ～하다 make a restart; make a fresh start; begin anew 〔afresh〕.

**재발행**(再發行) (a) reissue. ～하다 reissue.

**재방송**(再放送) a rebroadcast; a repeat (performance); rebroadcasting. ～하다 rebroadcast.

**재배**(再拜) ①《절》bowing twice; a second bowing 〔obeisance〕. ~하다 bow twice. ②《편지의 맺음말》"Sincerely yours"; "As ever".

**재배**(栽培) cultivation; culture; growing; raising. ~하다《과수·초목 등을》cultivate; grow;《야채를》raise. ¶ 비닐하우스〔온실〕에서 야채를 ~하다 grow vegetables 「in a plastic greenhouse 〔in a hothouse〕/ 그는 과실을 ~하고 있다 He is growing fruit. / 이 지방은 차 ~에 적합하다 This part of the country is suited for tea culture. ◉ ~기술 cultivation techniques. ~법 a method of cultivation. ~식물 a cultivated 〔domesticated〕 plant. ~어업 aquaculture. ~자 a grower; a cultivator. 담배~ tobacco farming 〔raising〕.

**재배치**(再配置) reassignment; relocation; realignment. ~하다 reassign; relocate; realign. ¶ 군의 전국적인 ~ the relocation of army units throughout the country / 공격을 위한 병력의 ~를 끝내다 complete the redeployment of its《key》military forces for aggression.

**재벌**(財閥) a financial combine 〔clique, group〕; a great financial conglomerate; a large conglomerate;《가족》a giant family concern; a *chaebol;*《부유계급》the plutocracy; the plutocrats;《개인》a big businessman; a plutocrat;《미국에서》the plutes; "Wall Street". ¶ ~의 횡포 plutocratic despotism / S~ the S financial combine 〔group〕; the S interests; the S *chaebol.* ◉ ~기업 a (business) conglomerate; a business group: ~기업군 giant business groups. ~해체 the dissolution of the *chaebol.*

**재범**(再犯) a second offense; a second conviction; the repetition of an offense. ~하다 commit a second offense. ◉ ~자 a second offender.

**재벽**(再壁)〘건축〙second plastering; overplastering.

**재변**(災變) a (natural) calamity; disaster.

**재보**(財寶) treasure(s); valuable(s); riches; wealth; precious things.

**재보험**(再保險)〘경제〙reinsurance. ~하다 reinsure. ◉ ~금 reinsurance claims 〔money〕. ~자 reinsurer. ~조항 a reinsurance clause. ~중개인 a reinsurance broker. 의무~ obligatory reinsurance. 임의~ facultative reinsurance. 피~자 the reinsured.

**재복무**(再服務) reenlistment; extension of *one's* military service. ~하다 reenlist; extend *one's* military service.

**재봉**(裁縫) sewing; needlework; tailoring; dressmaking. ~하다 sew; do needlework. ¶ ~을 배우다 take lessons in sewing / ~을 잘 하다〔못 하다〕 be clever 〔awkward〕 in sewing; be good 〔poor〕 at needlework. ◉ ~공임〔삯〕 sewing charges. ~대 a sewing table. ~도구 sewing requisites 〔things〕; a sewing set. ~사 a tailor; a tailoress (여자); a dressmaker. ~상자 a sewing box. ~실 a sewing room. ~함 a sewing box.

**재봉틀**(裁縫—) a sewing machine. ¶ ~로 박다 sew《*a thing*》by machine; run up a seam on the machine / 이건 손으로 꿰맨 것입니까 ~로 박은 것입니까 Was the sewing done by hand or by machine? *or* Is this hand-sewed or machine-sewed? ◉ ~기름 sewing-machine oil. ~바늘 a sewing-machine needle. 손~ a hand sewing machine.

**재분배**(再分配) redistribution; reallotment. ~하다 redistribute; reallot. ¶ 부(富)의 ~ redistribution of wealth.

**재빠르다** (be) quick; nimble; agile; alert. ¶ 재빠른 사람 a shrewd person / 재빠르게 quickly; swiftly; quick as a flash / 원숭이처럼 재빠르게 with the agility of a monkey / 재빠르게 행동하다 act smartly / 손이 ~ have nimble fingers / 재빠르게 모습을 감추다 disappear in a flash.

**재사**(才士) =재자(才子). ¶ ~ 다병(多病) Men of talent are often of delicate health.

**재산**(財産) property; (material) possessions; a fortune (큰 재산);〘법〙an estate; assets (자산).

> **용법** **fortune** 많은 액수의 돈, 막대한 소유물. **property** 합법적인 소유권이 있는 유형·무형의 모든 재산. **estate** 법률상 상속의 대상이 되는 동산 및 부동산. **assets** 개인회사의 처분가능한 자산이란 뜻.

¶ 수백만 달러 상당의 ~ many million dollars worth of property / 전~ *one's* whole fortune / 먹고 살 만한 ~ a competence / ~이 손에 들어오다 come into a fortune / ~을 날리다 ruin *one's* fortune; lose *one's* property / ~을 남기다 leave an estate 〔a fortune〕《of ten million won》/ ~을 물려받다 inherit 〔succeed to, come into〕 a fortune / ~을 만들다 make a fortune; amass *one's* wealth / ~을 축내다 reduce 〔damage〕 *one's* fortune / ~을 탕진하다 run through 〔fritter away〕 *one's* fortune 《in》; dissipate *one's* fortune; muddle 〔sweep〕 away *one's* fortune / ~을 탐내어 다투다 claim 〔lay claim to〕 a fortune / ~을 압류하다 seize 〔attach〕 the property / 천만 원의 ~이 있다 have ten million won (to *one's* name) / 먹고살 만한 ~이 있다 have enough means to live on / ~을 노리고 결혼하다 marry for money / 생명과 ~을 보호하다 protect the life and property 《of the people》/ 막대한 ~이 굴러 들어오다 a big fortune comes into *one's* hand / ~을 관리하다 administer 〔manage〕 *one's* property / 내겐 ~이라고 할 만한 것이 없다 I have no property to speak of. / 그는 그 사업으로 한 ~을 이뤘다 He made a large fortune from the business.

◉ ~가 a man of property 〔wealth, fortunes, means〕; a wealthy 〔rich〕 person. ~계정 〖부기〗 a property 〔an assets and liabilities〕 account. ~관리 property management. ~관리인 an administrator 〔a custodian〕 of property. ~권 〖법〗 the right to own property; property rights. ~목록 a list of property; an inventory. ~ 반환청구 a claim for recapture of property. ~법 〖법〗 the law of property. ~분배 distribution of property. ~상속 inheritance of property; succession to an estate. ~상태 *one's* financial status 〔conditions〕. ~세 property tax. ~압류 attachment 〔seizure〕 of property. ~양도 conveyance 〔transfer〕 of an estate: ~ 양도세 a tax on transfer of properties. ~처분 disposition of property. ~ 청구권 기금 the Property Claims Fund. ~취득세 tax on purchasing property. ~평가 property valuation. ~ 해외도피 property 〔capital〕 flight to overseas.

**재산공개**(財産公開) the public disclosure of personal assets; asset disclosure; the disclosure of assets. ~하다 make public *one's* assets; disclose *one's* assets; 《가족의》 disclose the assets of *one's* family members.

**재삼**(再三) again and again; over and over (again); time and time again; repeatedly; more than once. ¶ ~ 시도하다 try again and again; make several attempts; try and try again / ~ 경고하다 give repeated warnings / 그는 ~ 말해도 듣지 않는다 He turns a deaf ear to my repeated warnings. / ~ 시도해 보았으나 허사였다 I tried over again only to fail. ◉ ~재사(再四) over and over again; repeatedly.

**재상**(宰相) the prime minister; the premier (under the king); the chancellor (독일의).

**재상영**(再上映) a rerun. ~하다 rerun 《a movie》; show 《a film》 again.

**재색**(才色) wits and beauty. ¶ ~을 겸비하다 be beautiful and talented; have 〔be endowed with〕 both intelligence and beauty / ~을 겸비한 여인 a lady equipped with brains and beauty.

**재생**(再生) ① 《소생》 revival; resuscitation; a return to life; 《갱생》 revival; (a) rebirth; regeneration; 《원기회복》 rejuvenation. ~하다 《소생하다》 return to life; revive; resuscitate; 《갱생하다》 be born again; make a fresh start in life; 《다시 만들다》 remake; regenerate. ¶ ~의 은혜를 입다 owe 《*a person*》 *one's* life / 그는 이제 ~했다 He is now regenerated. / 이 물고기는 몸의 잃은 부분을 ~할 수 있다 This fish can regenerate lost parts of its body.
② 《녹음·녹화의》 (a) playback. ~하다 play back; reproduce; replay. ¶ 녹음을 ~하다 play back the recording / 그녀의 목소리를 생생하게 ~하다 reproduce her voice vividly / 나는 야구 방송을 비디오로 ~했다 I played back (the broadcast of ) a baseball game on a VTR.
③ 《폐품 따위의》 reclamation; recycling. ~하다 recycle 《newspaper》; reclaim 《glass from old bottles》. ¶ 우리는 폐품의 ~과 이용을 고려해야 한다 We must think about recycling our waste materials.
◉ ~가능 에너지 a renewable 〔recyclable〕 energy. ~고무 reclaimed rubber. ~능력 《생물·자연 등의》 regeneration power(s). ~법 reproduction method. ~불량성 빈혈 〖병리〗 aplastic anemia. ~산업 the reproductive industry. ~섬유 regenerated fiber. ~양모 mungo; shoddy. ~유(油) reclaimed oil. ~이용 recycling; reclamation. ~장치 《녹음·녹화의》 playback equipment; 《보일러 등의》 a regenerative apparatus. ~지(紙) recycled paper.

~타이어 a recapped tire. ~품 reclaimed 〔made-over〕 articles; recycled products.

**재생산**(再生産) reproduction. ~하다 reproduce. ◉ ~론 the theory of reproduction. 축소〔확대〕~ reproduction on a regressive 〔a progressive, an enlarged〕 scale.

**재선**(再選) reelection; a second 〔repeated〕 selection. ⇨ 재선거. ~하다 reelect 《*a person* as chairperson》; select a second time. ¶ ~되다 be reelected / 그는 이 시의 시장으로 ~되었다 He was reelected mayor of this city.

**재선거**(再選擧) the renewal of election; (a) reelection; a recall election. ¶ ~를 실시하다 hold an election again; hold a recall election.

**재선적**(再船積) reshipment. ~하다 reship; ship back. ◉ ~표 a reshipping slip. ~품 reshipments; returned goods.

**재세**(在世) ¶ ~의 living; in life / ~시 during (the time of) *one's* life; while *one* lives / ~중의 그를 알고 있던 사람들 people who knew him in life.

**재소자**(在所者) a prisoner; a prison inmate; [총칭] the criminal population; the inmates.

**재송**(再送) ~하다 send again; (re)forward.

**재수**(再修) ~하다 cram to repeat a college entrance exam; prepare for the entrance examinations after *one* left high school; take 《a year》 out. ¶ 나는 2년 ~했다 I have spent two years preparing for the entrance examinations after I left high school. / 그는 1년 ~하고 희망하는 대학에 입학했다 He spent one year preparing for the entrance examination after he left high school and entered a university that he wanted.
◉ ~생 a high-school graduate who has failed to enter a college and 「is waiting for another chance 〔is studying to try again〕; 《낙제생》 a holdover 《from》; a repeater.

**재수**(財數) luck; fortune. ¶ ~가 있다〔좋다〕 be lucky; be in luck; be fortunate; have 〔be blessed with〕 a good luck / ~가 없다 be unlucky; be unfortunate; be out of 〔off *one's*〕 luck; have no luck / ~ 좋게도 luckily; fortunately; as luck would have it / ~ 없게 unluckily; by ill luck; unfortunately / ~ 좋은 사람 a lucky 〔fortunate〕 person / 뜻하지 않은 ~ a stroke of luck / ~가 트이다 luck turns in *one's* favor; be in luck's way / 저런, ~ 없는 소리 말게 Good God! Don't croak! / 너는 ~가 좋다 You're in luck. / 이건 ~ 좋으라고 갖고 다닌다 I carry this around for luck. / 신발을 잃으면 ~가 없다고 한다 Losing *one's* shoes is said to be an omen of misfortune.

**재수입**(再輸入) reimport; reimportation. ~하다 reimport. ◉ ~면장 a reimport permit (세관의). ~신고서 a reimport declaration. ~품 reimported goods; reimports.

**재수출**(再輸出) reexport; reexportation. ~하다 reexport. ◉ ~품 reexports; goods reexported 〔for reexport〕.

**재스민** 〖식물〗 a jasmin(e); a jessamin(e); 《향수》 jasmin(e).

**재승덕박**(才勝德薄) superior talents and inferior virtue. ~하다 be more talented than virtuous.

**재시합**(再試合) rematch 《of a game》; a return game 〔match〕.

**재시험**(再試驗) a retest; a reexamination: 《미구어》 a make-up; 《영》 resit. ~하다 test 〔examine〕 again; reexamine; give 〔have〕 a make-up test. ¶ ~을 치르다 take a reexamination; make up an examination (불합격 과목의).

**재실**(在室) ~하다 be in *one's* room; stay 〔remain〕 in the 〔*one's*〕 room.

**재심**(再審) reexamination; 〖법〗 a retrial; a second hearing; a new trial. ~하다 reexamine; retry; hear again; review; have a new trial; try a second time. ¶ ~을 청구하다 move for a rehearing; apply for a new trial / 하급 법원의 판결을 ~하다 review decisions of a lower court.
◉ ~법원 a court of review. ~소송 an action for renewal of procedure.

**재심사**(再審査) reexamination; reinspection; rejudging. ~하다 reexamine; reinspect; rejudge.

**재앙**(災殃) 《재난》 a calamity; a disaster; woes; 《불행》 misfortune; evils. ¶ ~을 내리다 《하늘이》 ruin; do harm / ~을 당하다 meet with a misfortune 〔calamity〕 / ~을 자초하다 bring a calamity upon *oneself* / ~을 피하다 keep off a misfortune / 그녀의 부주의가 ~을 가져왔다 Her carelessness caused 〔brought on〕 the disaster.

**재액**(災厄) a calamity; a disaster; a misfortune; a mishap.

**재야**(在野) ¶ ~의 《a party》 out of office 〔power〕; 《parties》 in opposition;

non-Government 《parties》 / ～ 시절에 when 〔while〕 out of office 〔power〕 / 재조 ～를 막론하고 whether in office or out of office / ～의 명사 distinguished men out of office.

**재언**(再言) repetition; reiteration. ～하다 say over again; repeat; reiterate. ¶ 여기서 ～할 필요가 없다 It needs no repetition here.

**재연**(再演) 《영화·연극 등》 rerunning 《of a movie》; a second presentation; another showing 〔performance〕. ～하다 stage 〔present〕 《a play》 again; show 《a movie》 again; perform again; repeat 《a movie, a play, *etc.*》. ¶ 범행을 ～하다 reconstruct *one's* crime / 그 연극은 ～되었다 The play was presented again.

**재연**(再燃) a fresh outbreak; recurrence; recrudescence; revival. ～하다 flare up again; rekindle; revive; come to the fore again. ¶ 인플레이션의 ～ (a) recurrence of inflation / ～시키다 rekindle 《the old debate》; revive 《old quarrels》; reignite 《a border dispute》; reheat 《the international crisis》 / 문제가 ～됐다 The problem has come to the fore again.

**재예**(才藝) talent and accomplishment. ¶ ～가 출중하다 be highly accomplished.

**재외**(在外) ¶ ～의 abroad; overseas 《offices》; 《staff》 resident abroad. ◉ ～공관 embassies and legations abroad; diplomatic establishments abroad; overseas agencies of the Ministry of Foreign Affairs & Trade: ～ 공관장 the chief of the overseas diplomatic mission 〔establishment〕. ～교포 Korean residents abroad; overseas Korean residents. ～예금 foreign deposit. ～자산 overseas 〔external〕 assets.

**재욕**(財慾) greediness for wealth. ¶ ～이 많다 be greedy for wealth.

**재우** fast; quickly; nimbly; agilely. ¶ 요술쟁이의 ～ 놀리는 손재주 a magician's nimble handling of his tricks.

**재우다** 《잠을》 put 《*a person*》 to sleep; send to sleep; afford 《*a person*》 lodging; put 《*a person*》 up. ¶ 나그네를 하룻밤 ～ take a traveler in for the night; give a traveler a night's lodging / 아이를 잠 ～ get *one's* baby off to sleep / 노래를 불러 ～ sing 《a baby》 to sleep / 아이를 열시에 ～ put *one's* child to bed at ten o'clock.

**재우치다** finish up quickly; dispatch 《work》. ¶ 일을 ～ finish a job up quickly; make short work of it.

**재원**(才媛) a gifted 〔talented〕 young lady.

**재원**(財源) financial 〔economic〕 resources; a revenue source; a source of revenue; funds; finances; means. ¶ ～이 풍부〔빈약〕하다 be rich 〔poor〕 in financial resources; be resourceful 〔resourceless〕 / ～을 고갈시키다 drain 〔exhaust〕 the resources / 그들은 새로운 ～을 찾고 있다 They are looking for a new source of revenue 〔income〕. / 급여 인상을 위한 ～이 없다 We have no means of financing a raise in the wages.

**재위**(在位) (*one's*) reign. ～하다 be on the throne; reign. ¶ 장기간 ～하고 있는 국왕 a long-reigning king / ～ 중에 in *one's* reign; during the reign of 《Queen Victoria》 / ～ 30년 후에 after a reign of 30 years. ◉ ～기간 the period of 《Queen Victoria's》 reign.

**재음미하다**(再吟味―) reexamine; review.

**재의**(再議) reconsideration; rediscussion. ～하다 consult afresh; discuss again; reconsider. ¶ ～에 부치다 submit 《*a matter*》 for reconsideration / ～는 불필요하다 The matter needs no reconsideration.

**재인**(才人) 《광대》 an acrobat; an acrobatic tumbler; 《재사》 a man of talent.

**재인식**(再認識) recognizing 〔appreciating〕 anew 《the merit of a thing》; a new understanding; reappraisal. ～하다 see 《*a matter*》 in a new light; take another look at; look into further; have a new understanding 《of》; recognize again. ¶ 정세를 ～하다 have a new understanding of the situation / 이 문제의 중요성을 ～했다 I again realized the importance of the matter.

**재일**(在日) residing 〔living〕 in Japan. ◉ ～교포〔동포〕 Korean residents in Japan; Koreans living in Japan: ～ 교포 모국 방문단 a home-visiting group of Korean residents in Japan / ～동포의 법적 지위 향상 the improvement of the legal status of Korean residents in Japan. ～본 대한민국 민단 the Korean Residents Union in Japan.

**재임**(在任) being in office. ～하다 hold office; be in office. ¶ ～중 while in

office; during *one's* term of office.
◉ ～자 an incumbent.

**재임**(再任) reappointment. ～하다 get reappointed; reappoint 《*a person* to a post》.

**재입국**(再入國) reentry 《into a country》. ～하다 reenter. ◉ ～허가 a reentry permit.

**재입학**(再入學) readmission 《to a school》; reentrance. ¶ ～을 허가하다 readmit 《*a person* to a school》.

**재자**(才子) a young man of talent; a clever youth. ¶ ～ 가인(佳人) a young man of talent and a girl of beauty / ～ 다병 Whom the gods love die young.

**재작년**(再昨年) the year before last.

**재작일**(再昨日) the day before yesterday.

**재잘거리다** chatter; prattle; gibber; wag *one's* tongue 〔jaw〕. ¶ 한 시간 동안이나 ～ rattle 〔prattle〕 on for an hour.

**재적**(在籍) 《호적》 being on *one's* family register; 《학적》 enrol(l)ment; register. ～하다 be on the register 〔roll〕. ¶ 이 대학에는 총 3,000명의 학생이 ～하고 있다 This college has a total enrollment of 3,000 students. / 그는 S 대학에 ～하고 있다 He is on the roll 〔register〕 of S University.
◉ ～자 《학생》 students on the register: ～자 수 the number of students on the register; the enrollment figure; the number enrolled / 그 학교는 ～자 수가 2천 명이다 The school has 2,000 students on the register. ～증명서 《학교의》 a certificate of enrollment; 《단체의》 a membership certificate.

**재적**(材積) the volume the lumber 〔stone〕.

**재정**(財政) finance(s); 《상태》 financial affairs. ¶ 국가〔지방〕 ～ national 〔local〕 finance / 건전 ～ sound 〔balanced〕 finance / 적자 ～ red-ink 〔unbalanced〕 finance / ～상의 financial; fiscal / ～의 위기 financial crisis / ～상 이유로 on financial grounds; for financial reasons / 국가 ～의 재건 reestablishment of national economy; reconstruction of the government finances / ～적 부채 financial obligation / ～적 원조 financial support 〔help〕 / ～이 풍부하다 《개인이》 be well off; 《국가 등이》 be in good financial circumstances / ～이 곤란하다 《개인이》 be badly off; 《국가 등이》 be in financial difficulties / ～적으로는 걱정이 없다 have no financial worries / ～을 확립하다 put the finances 《of a company》 on a firm basis / ～을 긴축하다 tighten the belt / 국가〔가정〕의 ～을 손에 쥐다 hold the strings of the government 〔family〕 purse / 우리 회사의 ～은 건전하다 Our company's finances are sound. / ～ 기반이 약한 많은 회사는 금년 안에 파산할 것이다 Many financially weak firms will go bankrupt within this year.
◉ ～가 a financier. ～경제부 the Ministry of Finance and Economy: ～경제부 장관 the Minister of Finance and Economy. ～계획 a financial program. ～고문 a financial adviser. ～규모 a fiscal 〔budget〕 scale. ～난 《get into》 financial difficulties 〔trouble〕. ～면 financial aspects. ～문제 a financial question 〔problem〕. ～법안 a financial bill. ～보증 financial guarantee: ～보증인 a financial guarantor. ～상태 the financial standing; financial conditions. ～원조자 a financial supporter 〔backer〕. ～위기 a financial crisis. ～자금 the fund for public finance. ～적자〔흑자〕 red 〔black〕 figures in finance. ～전문가 a financial expert. ～정리 (re)adjustment of the finances. ～정책 a financial 〔fiscal〕 policy: 긴축 ～정책 a tight money policy; a tight-financing policy. ～증권 a treasury bill. ～통 a financial expert. ～통계 finance statistics. ～투융자 treasury loans and investments: 《국가의》 ～투융자 계획 a national investment and loan program. ～투자 financial investments. ～핍박 financial straits; financial stringency. ～학 (public) finance. ～혼란 financial derangement.

**재정**(裁定) (a) decision; an award; arbitration; ruling. ～하다 decide; rule 《on》; adjudge; arbitrate; hand down a decision 《on》. ¶ 의장의 ～으로 본안은 폐기되었다 The Speaker, asked to arbitrate, decided that the bill should be scrapped.
◉ ～거래 arbitrage. ～서(書) an award. ～시세 arbitrated rate (of exchange). ～안 an arbitration proposal. ～자 an adjudicator. ～조항 《노사간의》 an arbitration clause. ～환율 arbitrated rate of exchange.

**재제**(再製) remanufacture; reproduction; reprocessing. ～하다 remake; reproduce; rebuild; reprocess; reclaim. ⇨ 재생(再生). ◉ ～염(塩) refined salt. ～원모(原毛) shoddy. ～품 reprocessed 〔made-over〕 articles.

**재조**(在朝) ¶ ～의 now in power 〔office〕; governmental / ～ 재야의 명사 noted people in and out of official life.

**재조사**(再調査) reexamination; reinvestigation. ～하다 reexamine; reinvestigate.

**재조정**(再調整) readjustment; reregulation. ～하다 readjust; reregulate. ¶ 구조 ～ restructuring / 금리를 ～하다 readjust interest rates. 「reorganize.

**재조직**(再組織) reorganization. ～하다

**재종**(再從) a second cousin. ◉ ～간 second-cousinship. ～고모 a female second cousin of *one's* father. ～매(妹) a female (younger) second cousin. ～손(孫) the grandson of a cousin. ～숙(叔) a male second cousin of *one's* father. ～제(弟) a male (younger) second cousin. ～조(祖) a cousin of *one's* grandfather. ～질(姪)〔질녀〕 a son 〔daughter〕 of *one's* second cousin. ～형 a male (older) second cousin.

**재주**(才—) 《재능》 talent; gifts; ability; 《솜씨》 skill; dexterity; 《재치》 wit; intelligence. ¶ 손～ hand skill; dexterity 〔deftness〕 of hand / 음악의 ～ a talent for music / ～껏 to the best of *one's* ability; as much as *one* can do / ～가 있다 be talented 〔gifted〕 / ～있는 able; talented; gifted; witty / ～있는 사람 a talented man; a man of talent 〔ability, parts〕 / ～없는 talentless; dull-witted; witless; stupid / ～를 보이다〔나타내다〕 show 〔display〕 *one's* talent / ～를 충분히 발휘하다 give full to *one's* ability / ～를 부리다 exercise *one's* talent; 《잔꾀를》 use tricks; intrigue; figure out a scheme; 《재주넘기를》 do acrobatic feats / 너는 ～가 메주다 You are all thumbs.

**재주**(在住) residence. ～하다 live; reside; dwell. ◉ ～자 a resident.

**재주**(齋主) 〖불교〗 the person who requests a Buddhist priest to read a mass for the soul of the dead.

**재주꾼**(才—) a person of talent; a talented person. ¶ 그는 대단한 ～이다 He is clever to the fingernails. 「set.

**재주넘기**(才—) a somersault; a somer-

**재주넘다**(才—) make a somersault. ¶ 비행기가 재주를 넘다 An airplane loops the loop. *or* An airplane performs a looping feat.

**재중**(在中) ¶ ～의 containing / 견본 ～ 《우편》 "Samples (only)" / 사진 ～ 《우편》 "Photos (only)" / 인쇄물 ～ 《우편》 Printed matter (only).

**재즈** 〖음악〗 jazz; jazz music. ¶ 모던 ～ modern jazz / 핫～ hot jazz / ～(음악)에 맞추어 춤추다 dance to jazz / ～를 연주하다 play jazz; jazz / ～화하여 연주하다 jazz up. ◉ ～댄스 jazz dancing: ～댄스를 추다 jazz dance; do jazz-dancing. ～밴드 a jazz band. ～싱어 a jazz singer. ～음악 jazz music. ～팬 a jazz fan.

**재지**(才智) talent and wisdom; wit; intelligence. ¶ ～ 있는 talented; witty; intelligent / ～에 찬 full of wisdom 〔wit〕; tactful; resourceful.

**재직**(在職) ～하다 hold office; be in office. ¶ ～ 5년 이상의 사람들 those in service for more than five years / ～중에 while in office; during *one's* term of office / 그 회사에 3년간 ～중에 during *one's* three years in that company / 그는 본교에 ～한 지 20년이 된다 He has served 〔taught at〕 this school for twenty years. / 그 사건은 그의 ～ 중에 일어났다 The trouble happened during his tenure of office. / ～중에 많은 신세를 졌습니다 I am very grateful to you for your kind care of me while I was in office. ◉ ～기간 *one's* tenure of office; *one's* period of service in a position. ～연한 the length of *one's* service. ～자 the holder of a position; an incumbent.

**재질**(才質) natural gifts; natural endowment; talent. ¶ ～을 살리다 make the best use of *one's* talent.

**재질**(材質) the quality of the material.

**재차**(再次) (for) the second time; twice; again; 《한번 더》 once more 〔again〕. ¶ ～ 방문하다 pay a second visit / ～ 시도하다 try again; make another 〔a second〕 attempt.

**재채기** a sneeze; sneezing. ～하다 sneeze; kerchoo. ¶ 연달아 ～하다 have a fit of sneezing.

**재천**(在天) ¶ ～의 in heaven; heavenly / 인명은 ～이다 Life and death are providential.

**재청**(再請) 《두번째》 a second request; an encore; 《찬성》 seconding 《a motion》. ～하다 request a second time; encore; 《찬성》 second 《a motion》.

**재촉** pressing; urging. ～하다 press

〔importune〕《*a person* for》; urge《*a person* to *do*》. ¶ 아무한테 빚을 갚으라고 ~하다 dun *a person* for payment of a debt; urge *a person* to pay a debt / 술을 더 가져오라고 ~하다 call 〔yell〕 for more wine / 일을 ~하다 hasten 〔hurry up〕 the work / 열차를 놓칠 것 같아 운전 기사를 ~했다 I hurried up the driver for fear I should miss the train. / 그는 어서 옷을 입으라고 아이를 ~했다 He tried to hurry his son up in getting dressed. / 그는 ~ 하지 않으면 일을 안 한다 He will not do anything unless he is pressed. / 그는 빚을 조금도 ~하지 않았다 He was very easy with me over the debt.

**재출발**(再出發) a new start 〔departure〕; a restart. ~하다 make a new departure; restart; make a fresh start 〔beginning〕. ¶ 그는 직장을 옮겨서 ~하기를 바랐다 He wished to start afresh in a new post.

**재취**(再娶) 《재혼》 (a man's) remarriage; a second marriage; 《후처》 a second wife. ~하다 remarry (after the death of *one's* first wife); marry again.

**재치**(才致) wit; quick 〔ready〕 wit; tact; resource. ¶ ~가 있다 be witty; be quick-witted / ~ 있는 사람 a man of tact; a tactful 〔witty, quick-witted〕 person / ~있는 말을 하다 make a witty remark / 그는 ~있게 그 문제를 수습했다 He had the tact to settle the matter.

**재침(략)**(再侵(略)) a reinvasion. ~하다 reinvade.

**재킷** ① 《상의》 a jacket. ② 《레코드의》 a jacket; 《영》 a sleeve.

**재탕**(再湯) the second brew 〔decoction〕 《of the same stuff》; [비유적] a rehash. ~하다 make the second brew 《of》; make a rehash 《of》. ¶ ~ 커피 a second brew of coffee / 김 박사 논문의 ~ a rehash of Dr. Kim's article.

**재택**(在宅) ~하다 be (at) home.
◉ ~간호 in-home care 《for》. ~근무 working at (*one's*) home for *one's* company; 《데이터 통신을 이용한》 telecommuting. ~근무자 a homeworker for *one's* company; a telecommuter.

**재투자**(再投資) reinvestment. ~하다 reinvest; plow back 《the profits of a business》.

**재투표**(再投票) revoting. ~하다 take a vote again.

**재티** cinders; (dust of) ashes. ¶ ~가 튀다 cinders fly / ~가 눈에 들어가다 get cinders in *one's* eye.

**재판**(再版) (a) reprint; 《제2쇄》 a second impression; 《개정판》 a second edition; 《반복》 a repetition 《of past event》. ~하다 reprint; put out of a second edition 《of》. ¶ ~ 3천부 a second impression of 3,000 copies / ~이 되다 run into a second edition / 우리는 1950년의 ~을 두려워한다 We are anxious that it may be 1950 over again.

**재판**(裁判) justice; 《판결》 judgment; decision; 《공판》 a trial; a hearing. ~하다 judge 《*a person*, a case, *etc.*》; try 《a lawsuit》; decide 〔pass judgment〕 on 《a case》. ¶ 공정한 ~ fair justice; impartial judgment / ~의 공시 publication of a judgment / ~의 방청인 a spectator at a trial / ~을 받다 face (a) trial; be tried; stand trial 《for murder》; be on trial / ~에 부치다 put 《a case》 on trial; bring 《*a matter*》 to trial 〔judgment〕; try 《*a person*》 (in court) / ~이 되다 be laid before the court; be tried; be put on trial / ~에 지다〔이기다〕 lose 〔win〕 a case 〔suit〕 / ~을 열다 hold a court / ~ 날짜를 결정하다 assign a day for trial / 그 사건은 지금 ~중이다 The matter is pending in court. *or* The case is now on trial. / ~은 피고〔원고〕의 승소로 끝났다 The case was decided in favor of the defendant 〔accused〕. / 그는 살인 혐의로 ~을 받았다 He stood trial for murder.
◉ ~관 = 법관. ~권 《have》 jurisdiction 《over》. ~비용 judicial costs. ~사건 a court case. ~일 a court day. ~장 the chief 〔presiding〕 judge; 《미》 the chief justice. ~절차 court procedure 〔proceedings〕. ~청구권 the right of access to courts.

**재편(성)**(再編(成)) reorganization; a reshuffle; reshuffling; 《구조 개혁》 restructuring. ~하다 reorganize; regroup; reshuffle; reform; restructure. ¶ 학급을 ~하다 rearrange classes / 위원회를 ~하다 reorganize a committee.

**재평가**(再評價) (a) revaluation; (a) reappraisal; reassessment. ~하다 revalue; reassess; reappraise. ¶ 자산 ~ revaluation of property. ◉ ~액 revaluation amount. ~적립금 revaluation reserves.

**재포장**(再包裝) repacking. ~하다 repack.

**재학**(在學) being in school. ~하다 be in 〔at〕 school 〔college〕. ¶ ~ 중에

while at 〔in〕 school 〔college〕; while (*one* is 〔was〕) a student 〔an undergraduate〕/ 그는 ~ 중에 운전 면허를 땄다 He got a driver's license while in 〔at〕 school. ◉ ~기간 the period of attendance at school; *one's* school days: 그의 ~ 기간은 짧다 He has not had much schooling. ~생 a student: ~생은 약 3천명이다 There are about 3,000 students (enrolled) in the school. *or* The school has 3,000 students. ~증명서 verification 〔a proof〕 of enrollment; a certificate of student status; a student ID card (학생증).

**재할인**(再割引) 〖경제〗 a rediscount. ~하다 rediscount. ◉ ~어음 a rediscount bill. ~율 rediscount rate.

**재합성**(再合成) resynthesis. ~하다 resynthesize; synthesize again.

**재해**(災害) a calamity; a disaster. ¶ 특별~지구 a special disaster zone / ~를 입다 suffer from a disaster; be struck by disaster; meet with an accident / ~의 연속 a series of accidents; a spell of ill luck / 지난 해는 ~가 많은 해였다 Last year was indeed remarkable for frequent disasters. ◉ ~관리법 a disaster control law. ~구호법 the Disaster Relief Act. ~대책 measurers against disasters; countermeasures to deal with (natural) calamities: ~ 대책 위원회 the (national) anticalamity measures committee / 중앙 ~ 대책 본부 the Central Anti=Calamity Headquarters (생략 CACH). ~방지 prevention of disasters. ~보험 disaster 〔accident〕 insurance. ~복구비 (natural) disaster relief expenditure 〔fund〕. ~수당〔보상〕 accident 〔disaster〕 allowance 〔compensation〕. ~지 a (disaster-)stricken 〔devastated〕 district 〔area〕; an afflicted area.

**재행**(再行) a husband's first visit to *his* wife's home after the marriage. ~하다 pay a first visit 《to *one's* bride's home》.

**재향군인**(在鄕軍人) an ex-soldier 〔ex=serviceman〕; a reservist; a veteran (soldier) 《미》. ◉ ~회 the association of reservists; the American Legion 《미》: 대한 민국 ~회 the Korean Veterans Association.

**재현**(再現) reappearance; reemergence; readvent; revival; emersion; 《재현하기》 (a) reproduction. ~하다 reappear; reemerge; revive; reproduce. ¶ 그 그림은 당시의 생활을 ~하고 있다 The picture reproduces the life of those days.

**재형저축**(財形貯蓄) the property-formation savings (system) for workers; worker's tax-free〔-exempt〕 assets=making deposit; 'nest-egg' savings.

**재혼**(再婚) remarriage; a second marriage; deuterogamy; digamy. ~하다 remarry; marry again; be married again. ¶ ~을 권하다 advise 《*a person*》 to remarry / 그녀는 돈때문에 부자인 상인과 ~했다 She remarried 〔got married again to〕 a rich merchant for money. ◉ ~자 a remarried person; a deuterogamist; a digamist.

**재화**(災禍) 《재난》 a calamity; a disaster; 《불행》 a misfortune; an evil. ⇨ 재난(災難). ¶ ~를 당한 지역 the (disaster-)stricken area.

**재화**(財貨) 《상품》 goods; commodities; 《재산》 money and property; wealth.

**재확인**(再確認) reaffirmation; reconfirmation. ~하다 reaffirm; reconfirm. ¶ 예약을 ~하고 싶은데요 I would like to reconfirm my reservation. / 아시아에서 한반도의 전략적 중요성을 ~하다 reaffirm the strategical importance of the Korean Peninsula in Asia.

**재활**(再活) rehabilitation; reform. ~하다 be rehabilitated. ◉ ~시설 rehabilitation facilities.

**재활용**(再活用) the recycling 〔reuse, reutilization〕 (of waste materials). ~하다 recycle 〔reuse〕 《of discarded articles》; reutilize; reclaim. ¶ ~ 휴지 recycled tissue paper / ~ 비누 recycled soap / 수집된 ~품의 양은 지난해의 239,000톤에서 340,000톤으로 42퍼센트가 증가했다고, 조사 기관은 말했다 Amount of recyclable goods collected increased 42 percent to 340,000 tons over 239,000 tons from last year, the survey said.

**재회**(再會) meeting again; reunion. ~하다 meet again. ¶ 이산 가족의 ~ the reunion of the separated families / ~를 기약하다 promise to meet again / ~를 기약하고 헤어지다 part in the hopes of meeting again; say *au revoir* / 그는 5년만에 아버지와 ~했다 He met his father for the first time in five years.

**재흥**(再興) revival; restoration; reestablishment; resuscitation; rehabilitation. ~하다 revive; restore; reestablish; rehabilitate. ¶ 민족 문화의 ~

rehabilitation of national culture.
◉ ～자 a reviver; a restorer.

**잭** 《기중기》 a jack; 《트럼프》 the knave; the jack.

**잭나이프** a jackknife.

**잼** 《apple, strawberry》 jam. ¶ 잼 바른 빵 bread and jam.

**잼버리** a jamboree.

**잽** 〖권투〗 a jab. ¶ 잽을 먹이다 jab 《*one's* opponent》. ◉ 라이트〔레프트〕～ a right (=hand) 〔left(-hand)〕 jab.

**잽싸다** (be) nimble; agile; quick. ¶ 잽싸게 quickly; swiftly; nimbly / 잽싸게 달아나다 escape 〔run away〕 quickly / 그는 잽싸게 그것을 알아차렸다 He was quick to notice it.

**잿더미** a heap of ash. ¶ ～로 변하다 be reduced 〔burnt down〕 to ashes / ～에서 일어나다 rise from the ashes.

**잿물** ① 《세탁용》 lye; caustic soda (가성소다). ¶ ～을 받다〔내리다〕 render lye from ashes. ② ⇨ 양잿물. ③ 《유약》 glaze; enamel. ¶ 도자기에 ～을 올리다 put glaze on pottery.

**잿밥**(齋—) rice offered to Buddha. ¶ 부처님께 ～을 올리다 offer rice to Buddha.

**잿빛** ash(en) color; gray 《미》; grey 《영》. ⇨ 회색. ¶ ～이 도는 grayish; ashy / 그의 얼굴이 ～으로 변했다 His face went 〔turned〕 ash-pale.

**쟁**(箏) 《악기》 a kind of 13-stringed musical instrument.

**쟁**(錚) 《꽹과리》 a gong.

**쟁강** 《금속 소리》 with a clank; with a clink. ～하다 give a clank 〔clink〕.

**쟁강거리다** clank; clink.

**쟁강쟁강** clanking; clinking; jingling.

**쟁권**(爭權) contention of power; a struggle for supremacy 〔power〕. ～하다 contend for supremacy 〔power〕.

**쟁그랑-** =쟁강-.

**쟁기** 〖농업〗 a Korean plow 〔plough 《영》〕. ◉ ～꾼 a plowman. ～질 plowing. 쟁깃술 the blade-guard of a plow.

**쟁단**(爭端) a cause 〔source〕 of strife 〔dispute, discord〕.

**쟁론**(爭論) a dispute; a contention; a controversy; an altercation; polemic. ～하다 dispute; argue; altercate; quarrel. ⇨ 논쟁(論爭).

**쟁반**(錚盤) a shallow round plate; a tray; a salver; a server.

**쟁의**(爭議) 《분쟁》 (a) trouble; a dispute; a strife; 《노동자의》 a labor 〔an industrial〕 dispute; industrial action 《영》; 《파업》 a strike; a walkout. ¶ ～를 일으키다 start a dispute; initiate a dispute; beget 〔cause〕 a dispute 〔strife〕 / ～를 중지하다 stop a dispute; halt 〔call off〕 a strike / ～를 조정하다 mediate 〔adjust〕 a dispute / ～중이다 be on (a) strike / ～를 해결하다 settle a dispute 〔strike〕 / ～ 조정의 수고를 맡다 take upon *oneself* the trouble of mediating the strike 《between》 / ～는 원만히 수습되었다 The dispute was settled amicably. / 이번의 노사간의 ～는 오래 끌 것 같다 This dispute between the employer and the employees seems to drag on.
◉ ～권 the right to 〔of〕 strike. ～수단 dispute tactics. ～위원회 a dispute committee. ～점 the point at issue. ～지령 a strike order. ～해결 settlement of a dispute. ～행위 a strike; a labor dispute: ～행위 금지 명령 a labor injunction.

**-쟁이** a constant doer of; -monger; a man who does…. ¶ 관상쟁이 a physiognomist; a fortuneteller.

**쟁이다** lay one on top of another; make a neat pile 《of》; accumulate; pile 〔heap〕 up. ¶ 김을 ～ lay pressed laver sheets one on top of another (so that seasonings may soak through) / 고기를 ～ leave sliced meat in piles 〔stacks〕 / 쌀가마가 쟁여져 있다 Bags of rice are piled up.

**쟁쟁하다**(琤琤—) ① 《구슬 소리가》 (be) clear; have a nice ring to it; (be) sonorous; resonant. ¶ 쟁쟁한 목소리 a clear (ringing) voice. ② 《귀에》 ring 《in *one's* ears》. ¶ 그의 말이 아직도 귀에 ～ His words are still ringing in my ears.

**쟁쟁하다**(錚錚—) ① 《금속 소리가》 (be) clear; have a nice ring to it; (be) sonorous; resonant. ② 《출중하다》 (be) resounding; prominent; outstanding; distinguished. ¶ 쟁쟁한 명성 resounding fame / 쟁쟁한 인물 an outstanding man; a prominent figure / 쟁쟁한 음악가 a prominent musician / 당내의 쟁쟁한 인물중 한 사람 one of the shining lights of the party / 쟁쟁한 명선수 a crack player.

**쟁점**(爭點) the point at issue; the point of 〔in〕 dispute; a disputed point. ¶ 법률상〔사실상〕의 ～ an issue of law 〔fact〕 / ～을 벗어난 발언 remarks off the point.

**쟁취**(爭取) ～하다 win; gain; obtain; secure; score. ¶ 승리를 ～하다 win (out) 《over》; gain 〔secure, clinch〕 a victory 《over》 / 권리를 ～하다 secure *one's* rights / 그는 마침내 세계 헤비급 선수권을 ～했다 He finally won the heavyweight championship of the world.

**쟁탈**(爭奪) a scramble; a struggle; a contest; a competition. ～하다 scramble 〔struggle, contend, fight〕 《for》. ¶ 정권의 ～ a struggle for political power / 우승배를 ～하다 compete for a trophy.

**쟁탈전**(爭奪戰) a scramble; a contest; a struggle; a competition. ¶ 우승배 ～ a contest for the championship trophy / 선수권 ～ a championship series / 선수권 ～을 하다 play for the title / 지금 그 도시의 ～이 벌어지고 있다 A battle for the possession of the city is now in progress.

**쟁패전**(爭霸戰) a struggle 〔fight, contest〕 for supremacy; 《경기의》 a championship game; a pennant race.

**저**[1] 《피리》 a kind of flute; a fife.

**저**(著) *one's* writing(s); [형용사적] written by.... ¶ 이광수 저(의 소설) (a novel) written by Yi Kwangsu.

**저**(箸) (a pair of) chopsticks. ⇨ 젓가락.

**저**[2] 《나》 I; me; 《자기》 oneself; self. ¶ 저 생각만 하다 be thinking only of *oneself* / 저는 잘 모르겠습니다 I don't know very well, sir.

**저**[3] ① 《저기에 있는》 that (over there); the. ¶ 저 사람〔집〕 that person 〔house〕. ② 《저것》 that (one); that thing; the more remote one; it. ③ 《저이》 that person; he; she; that one. ¶ 저 같은 사람 a man like him; the like of him; such a man as he.

**저**[4] [감탄사] well; by the way; say; if you please; 《말이 나오지 않을 때》 er-r-r...; uh.... ¶ 저, 내일 돌아오시지요 By the way, you're coming back tomorrow, aren't you? / 저, 아까 뭐라고 말했죠 Well, what was it you said a while ago?

**저간**(這間) that time; then; that occasion; 《요즈음》 recent 〔these〕 days. ¶ ～의 사정 the circumstances of the occasion 〔days〕.

**저감**(低減) a fall 《in profits》; a drop 《in turnover》; a decrease 《in output》. ～하다 fall; drop (off); decline; decrease. ¶ 생산의 ～ decrease in production / 경비 ～을 위해 노력하다 make efforts to reduce costs 〔expenses〕.

**저같이** like that; (in) that way; so. ¶ ～ 해라 Do like that. / 저 소녀를 ～ 호되게 나무라지 않아도 좋을 텐데 He shouldn't have scolded the little girl so severely.

**저개발**(低開發) underdevelopment. ¶ ～의 underdeveloped / ～지역 an underdeveloped area. ◉ ～국 an underdeveloped country; a developing country (★ 요즘은 developing country (개발 도상국)이란 말로 저개발국을 지칭함).

**저것** that thing (over there); that one; that person. ¶ 이것 ～ this and that / 이것 ～ 생각 끝에 after a great deal of thinking / 이것 ～ 생각해 보면 taking everything into consideration; putting this and that together / ～봐 Look there!

**저격**(狙擊) shooting; sniping; sharpshooting. ～하다 shoot 〔fire, snipe〕 at. ¶ ～을 당하다 be shot 《by》. ◉ ～대 a sharp shooting squad. ～수 a sniper; a marksman. a shooter.

**저고리** *chŏgori;* a Korean jacket; a coat. ¶ ～를 입다〔벗다〕 put on 〔take off〕 *one's* coat.

**저공**(低空) a low sky 〔altitude〕. ¶ ～을 비행중인 항공기 a low-flying aircraft / ～으로 비행하다 fly at a low altitude; fly low. ◉ ～비행 a low-altitude flight; low-level flying; flying low. ～폭격 low-altitude bombing.

**저금**(貯金) 《돈》 savings; a deposit; saving money; 《행위》 saving. ～하다 save money; lay 〔put〕 money by; deposit money 《in a bank》. ¶ 은행 ～ a bank deposit / 적립〔우편〕 ～ installment 〔postal〕 savings / ～을 찾다 draw 〔withdraw〕 *one's* savings out; take *one's* savings out 《of 〔from〕 the bank》 / ～을 다 써 버리다 exhaust *one's* savings; spend all *one's* savings / 은행에 ～이 200만원 있다 have 2,000,000 won deposited in a bank / 나는 매월 8만원씩 ～하고 있다 I save eighty thousand won a month. ◉ ～통 a saving box; a piggy bank (돼지 모양의). ～통장 a (savings) bankbook; a deposit book.

**저금리**(低金利) low interest (rate); cheap money. ¶ ～로 인해 은행에서 빠져 나간 유휴 자금 the idle funds withdrawn from banks due to low interest (rates) / ～로 돈을 빌려달라고 부탁하다 ask for the loan with low interest. ◉ ～정책 (the) low interest policy; a cheap 〔an easy〕 money policy. ～체제 the low interest rate system.

**저급**(低級) low class 〔grade〕; inferiority. ~하다 be of an inferior sort; (be) low(-grade); vulgar; cheap. ¶ ~한 노래 a vulgar song; a cheap tune / ~한 취미 (a) low 〔poor, bad, vulgar〕 taste / ~한 잡지 a cheap magazine / ~한 TV 프로를 보지 마라 Don't watch vulgar TV programs. ◉ ~품 low-grade articles.

**저기** that place; over there; yonder. ¶ 여기 ~ here and there / ~에 there; over 〔up, down〕 there / ~까지 there; as far as there / ~ 있는 저 건물이 도서관이다 The building over there is the library.

**저기압**(低氣壓) ① 〖기상〗 low (atmospheric) pressure; an atmospheric depression. ¶ ~의 중심 the center of a low pressure area / 우세한 ~ the dominant low / ~의 내습 the approach of a depression / ~이 발생하다 a low pressure develops / 제주도 부근에서 발생한 ~ the low atmospheric pressure which originated near the Cheju / ~이 남동으로 진행하고 있다 The low pressure area is moving southeast. ② 《기분》 a bad temper; sullenness. ¶ 그는 오늘 ~이다 He is in a bad temper 〔out of sorts〕 today.
◉ ~지대〔권〕 a low-pressure area.

**저까짓** that kind of; such a; so trifling 〔trivial, slight, small, worthless, poor〕. ¶ ~ 것 such a worthless thing as that; such trifles / ~놈이 무엇을 할 줄 알겠나 What did you expect from a person like that?

**저나마** although it is (nothing more than) that. ¶ ~ 그런 대로 《poor, worthless, trivial》 as that is 〔may be〕 / 구두가 헐었지만 ~ 신을 수밖에 없다 I have to put on that pair of shoes, worn out though they are.

**저냐** 〖요리〗 fried meat or fish rolled in flour and egg; saute.

**저냥** (in) that way; (in) the same way as that; as that is 〔was〕; still; with no change; with no letup; as it is. ¶ ~ 내버려 두다 leave 《*a thing, a person*》 as it 〔*he*〕 is; leave 《*a thing*》 alone.

**저널리스트** a journalist. ¶ ~의 문장 《좋은 뜻》 journalitic style (간결한); 《나쁜 뜻》 journalese.

**저널리즘** journalism.

**저네(들)** those people (over there); 「they; them.

**저녁** ① 《때》 evening; dewfall; dusk; eventide; sunset. ¶ ~ 나절 late afternoon; early evening / 오늘〔내일, 어제〕 ~ this 〔tomorrow, yesterday〕 evening / 다음 날 ~에 the next 〔following〕 evening / ~마다 evening by evening / ~이 될 무렵에 toward evening.
② 《식사》 the evening meal; supper (가벼운); dinner (정찬). ¶ ~거리 groceries for supper; supper makings / ~ 후 after supper / ~에 초대하다 invite to dinner / ~을 짓다 prepare supper; get dinner ready / ~을 먹다 take 〔have〕 supper; sup / ~을 못먹다 miss out *one's* supper / ~ 준비는 되었느냐 Is supper ready? / 그녀는 ~을 들고 있다 She is at supper. / 그는 ~을 먹지 않고 잠자리에 들었다 He went to bed supperless.
◉ ~놀 an evening glow; a red sunset. ~볕〔햇살〕 the westering 〔afternoon, declining〕 sun.

**저녁때** = 저녁 ①. ¶ ~까지는 by evening / ~에 귀가하다 return home toward evening.

**저녁밥** (a) supper; (a) dinner. = 저녁 ②.

**저놈** 《사람》 that fellow 〔guy〕; that damn guy (over there); he; him; 《물건》 that damn thing; that one.

**저능**(低能) low intelligence; feeble-mindedness; mental deficiency; imbecility; idiocy; moronism. ~하다 (be) feeble-minded; backward; retarded; moronic; imbecile. ¶ ~한 사람 a mentally deficient person.

**저능아**(低能兒) a weak-minded 〔feeble-minded〕 child; a backward 〔retarded〕 child. ◉ ~교육 the education of the feeble-minded (children).

**저다지** to that degree 〔extent〕; like that; so (much); in that way. ¶ ~ 서두를 것이 무어람 What's the hurry?! / ~ 돈을 모아서 무엇하나 Why is he so eager to pile up money? / ~ 완고한 녀석은 본 일이 없다 He is the most obstinate fellow I have ever seen.

**저당**(抵當) (a) mortgage; (a) security. ~하다 mortgage; give 《*a thing*》 as security. ¶ 동산 ~ chattel mortgage / 이중 ~ a double mortgage / 1번〔2번〕 ~ a first 〔second〕 mortgage / 집을 ~ 잡히다 mortgage a house / 토지를 ~잡다 take land as security / ~을 잡고 대부하다 lend money on security / …을 ~에 넣다 place a mortgage on… / 나는 집을 ~으로 은행에서 800만원을 빌렸다 I mortgaged my house to the bank for eight million won. / 이 땅은 4천만원에 ~잡혀 있다 There is a mortgage of forty million won on this estate. ◉ ～권 mortgage; hypothec: ～권 설정 settlement of mortgage / ～권 설정자 a mortgagor / ～권자 a mortgagee. ～대부금 a loan on security: 무 ～대부금 an unsecured loan; a loan without security. ～물 a security; a pledge; a hostage; a thing mortgaged; a collateral 《미》: ～물의 유질(流質) foreclosure / …의 ～물에 담보권을 행사하다 foreclose on *a person.* ～증서 a mortgaged bond.

**저대로** like that; as it is 〔stands〕; in that condition. ¶ ～ 두다 leave 《*a thing, a person*》 just as it 〔*he*〕 is; let 〔leave〕 《*a thing*》 alone.

**저도모르게** unintentionally; unconsciously; undesignedly; in spite of *oneself.* ¶ ～ 죄를 범하다 commit a crime in spite of *oneself* / ～ 눈물을 흘리다 shed tears involuntarily 〔in spite of *oneself*〕.

**저돌**(猪突) recklessness; foolhardiness; rashness. ～하다 rush recklessly; make a headlong 〔reckless〕 rush 《at》. ¶ ～적인 rash; foolhardy; reckless; headlong / ～적으로 recklessly; foolhardily; precipitately / ～적으로 돌진하다 rush recklessly; make a rush 《at》.

**저들** those people (over there); they; 「them.

**저따위** a thing 〔person〕 of that sort; such a …; that kind 〔sort〕 《of》. ¶ ～ 사람 a man like him; the like of him; his like / ～는 처음 본다 I have never seen such a person in all my life. / ～ 집은 사서 무엇 하나 What are you buying that sort of shabby house for? 「세의). ⇨ 하락(下落).

**저락**(低落) fall; depreciation; decline (시

**저래** like that; so; that way. ¶ ～서는 변변한 위인이 될 수 없을 게다 If he goes that way he will never amount to much. / ～도 영리한 데가 있다 He is clever after a fashion. / ～도 몸은 튼튼하다 He is sturdier than he looks.

**저런**[1] 《저 같은》 like that; that sort of; such (★ 뒤에 종종 as를 수반함). ¶ ～ 사람 such a man 《as he》 (★ 부정관사의 위치에 주의); a man like him / ～ 책 a book of that sort / ～ 일 봤나 What a 《sorry》 sight! / 이런 일 ～일로 매우 바쁘다 I am very busy what with one thing and another.

**저런**[2] [감탄사] Oh dear!; Goodness!; Oh my!; What a surprise!; Indeed!; Well well!; My my! ¶ ～, 참 고생하셨겠습니다 Goodness—you must have had a hard time of it.

**저렇게** like that. ¶ 그가 ～까지 유명한 줄은 몰랐다 I did not know he was so 〔that〕 famous. / ～도 못난 사람은 처음 본다 I've never seen anyone so stupid.

**저렇다** be like that; be that way. ¶ 이렇다～ 말이 많다 say this and that; say things; criticize; be critical 《about》; make objections; raise a fuss / 그는 언제나 ～ That's always the way with him.

**저력**(底力) potential 〔latent〕 power 〔energy〕. ¶ 경제적인 ～ economic staying power / ～ 있는 of preserving strength; energetic; powerful; strong / ～이 있다 have sufficient bottom / ～을 보이다 show 〔display〕 *one's* reserved strength / 그의 목소리에는 ～이 있다 He has a deep voice. / 그는 아직 ～이 있음을 보여 주었다 He showed himself still strong enough. / 이제야말로 그에게 너의 ～을 보여 줘라 Now's the time you show him your 「real ability 〔full potential〕.

**저렴**(低廉) cheapness; inexpensiveness; a low price; moderateness. ～하다 (be) cheap; low in price; inexpensive; moderate.

> 용법 **cheap** 값이 싼 정도로 품질도 그만큼 나쁜 것을 암시하는 낱말. cheap necklace라고 하면 「싸구려 목걸이」라는 뜻으로 흔히 해석됨. **inexpensive** 「물건에 비해 값이 비싸지 않다」는 점에 역점이 주어지며 품질이 나쁘다는 뜻은 없음. **low** 값이나 급료 따위 액수에 관하여 쓰임. **moderate** 기본적인 뜻은 「알맞은 정도의, 중간 정도의」란 뜻이지만, 흔히 완곡한 표현으로 「중간 이하의」란 뜻으로 쓰임.

¶ ～한 가격 a moderate price / ～한 가격의 물품 low-priced articles 〔goods〕.

**저류**(底流) an undercurrent; an underflow. ¶ 의식의 ～ the subconscious current / …의 ～를 이루고 있다 underlie 《a country's foreign policy》; lie 〔exist, flow〕 beneath 《*a person's* conduct》 / 그는 혁명의 ～를 이루는 정치사상에 관하여 말했다 He talked about the political ideas underlying the revolution.

**저리**(低利) low interest; a low rate of interest. ¶ ～로 돈을 빌려주다〔빌리다〕 lend 〔borrow〕 money at low interest. ◉ ～금융 cheap credit. ～대출금 a low interest loan; a loan at cheap interest. ~자금 low interest funds; easy 〔cheap〕 money.

**저리** ①《저렇게·저다지》 in that way; like that; so; to that extent. ②《저리로》 there; that way; that direction; over there. ¶ 이리 ~ here and there / ~ 가라 Over there! *or* Go away! / ~ 가면 어디입니까 Where does that road over there lead to? / ~ 좀 비키시오 Step aside please!

**저리다** ①《쑤시다》 be sore; have a dull pain; feel sore 《in *one's* joints》. ¶ 온 뼈마디가 ~ feel pain in *one's* every joint / 발이 저려 따끔따끔하다 I have pins and needles in my legs. ②《마비되다》 become 〔go〕 numb; be numbed; be benumbed; be asleep; be paralysed. ¶ 한쪽 발이 ~ My foot is asleep. / 추위로 손발이 저렸다 My hands and legs were numb with cold.

**저마다** each (one); everyone. ¶ ~ 제가 옳다고 한다 Every man claims that he himself is right. / 사람은 ~ 장점과 단점을 갖고 있다 Each person has his merits and demerits.

**저만큼** so (much); that much; like that; to that extent. ¶ ~ 공부하는 이도 드물다 Few men study as hard as that. / ~ 만 영어를 하면 좋겠는데 I wish I could speak English that much.

**저만하다** be that much 〔so much〕; be to that extent; be as much as that. ¶ 저만한 인물 a man of that caliber / 저만한 미인 so beautiful a woman; a woman of such great beauty / 저만한 돈이 있는데도 with all that money; for all *one's* riches / 저만하면 충분하다 That much is good enough for me.

**저맘때** about 〔around〕 that time; (at) that time of day 〔night, year〕. ¶ 나도 ~에는 심한 장난꾸러기였다 I was quite a naughty boy when I was his age.

**저면**(底面) the bottom. ⇨ 밑면.

**저명**(著名) eminence; prominence; distinction. ~하다 (be) eminent; prominent; distinguished; celebrated; well=known; illustrious. ¶ ~한 실업가 a prominent businessman / ~한 학자 a celebrated scholar. ⇨ 유명하다.
◉ ~인사 a person of fame; a man of distinction; a celebrity.

**저물가**(低物價) low prices. ◉ ~시대 times of low prices. ~정책 a low=price policy.

**저물다** 《날이》 grow 〔get〕 dark; 《해·계절 등이》 end; close; come to an end 〔a close〕. ¶ 저물도록 till late; till dark / 날이 저물기 전에 before it gets dark; before sundown / 날이 저문 후에 after dark / 길 저문 나그네 a belated traveler / 날이 ~ it grows dark; the day draws to a close; night 「falls 〔gathers in〕 / 요새는 일곱 시에 날이 저문다 It grows dark at seven these days. / 날이 저물자마자 비가 내리기 시작했다 It started raining as soon as it got dark. / 가을이 저물었다 Autumn is over. / 이 해도 저물어가고 있다 This year is drawing to a close.

**저미다** slice 《meat》; cut thin. ¶ 고기를 얇게 ~ cut meat into thin slices / 저며 내다 slice off 〔away〕.

**저버리다** ①《약속 따위를》 break 〔go back on〕 《*one's* promise》; 《기대 따위를》 be contrary to 《*one's* expectation》; 《신뢰·충고 따위를》 betray; disobey 《*one's* father》. ¶ 은혜를 ~ go back on *one's* obligation / 그는 나와의 약속을 저버렸다 He went back on his promise with me. / 그는 나의 신뢰를 저버렸다 He betrayed my trust in him. / 남의 호의를 저버리지 마라 You should know better than to refuse another's kind offer.
②《돌보지 않다》 desert; forsake; abandon. ¶ 그녀는 남편을 저버렸다 She deserted her husband. / 그는 가족을 저버렸다 He forsook 〔deserted〕 his family. / 나를 저버리지 마세요 Don't abandon me.

**저벅** with a heavy footstep. ~거리다 walk with a thud; tramp; trample. ¶ 군인들이 ~거리며 지나가는 소리가 들렸다 Soldiers were heard tramping by.

**저벅저벅** with heavy footsteps; tramping. ~하다 make a crunching sound; crunch.

**저번**(這番) the last time; the other day; lately; previously. ¶ ~의 last; recent; previous; of the other day / ~ 일요일 last Sunday / ~ 편지 the previous letter / ~에 만났을 때 when I saw him last; the last time I saw him / ~에 말씀드린 바와 같이 as I let you know last time; as previously announced.

**저변**(底邊) = 밑변. ¶ 사회의 ~ the lowest stratum of society.

**저부**(底部) the bottom; the base.

**저상**(沮喪) dispiritedness; demoralization; dejection. ~하다 be depressed;

lose heart 《at》; be in low spirit; *one's* heart sinks (within *one*). ¶ 의기 ~하여 with a dejected air; pulling a long face; looking blue 〔gloomy〕 / 의기를 ~시키다 damp 〔depress〕 《*a person's*》 spirits; dishearten 《*a person*》 / 의기 ~하여 있다 be in low spirits; droop; be despondent / 적군은 의기가 ~되어 있다 The enemy troops are demoralized.

**저서**(著書) a (literary) work; a book; *one's* writings; a production. ¶ 예술에 관한 ~ a book on art / 그는 ~가 많다 He has written many books.

**저성**(低聲) a low voice 〔tone〕; a subdued voice. ¶ ~으로 in a low voice; *sotto voce* (It.).

**저세상**(一世上) the other 〔next〕 world; the afterlife. ¶ ~에서 in the other world; in the beyond / ~으로 가다 die; go to Heaven.

**저소득**(低所得) a low 〔small〕 income. ◉ ~층 the low-income brackets 〔classes〕: ~층의 실질 소득을 보장하다 ensure substantial income to people in the low-income brackets.

**저속**(低俗) vulgarity; baseness. ~하다 (be) vulgar; base; low. ¶ ~한 취미 low taste / ~한 영화 a film for lowbrows / ~한 소설〔노래〕 a vulgar novel 〔song〕 / 보는 이로 하여금 눈살을 찌푸리게 하는 원색적이고 ~한 내용의 광고 the advertisements, whose contents are raw or vulgar enough to cause readers to frown / ~한 잡지를 단속하다 crack down on pulp magazine / 이 프로는 ~하다는 평이지만 시청률은 매우 높다 Although this program is said to be vulgar, it has a high rating.

**저속(도)**(低速(度)) (a) low speed. ¶ 저속으로 하다 slow down / 저속으로 slowly; at a low speed; in low gear / 당신은 여기서 저속으로 운전해야 한다 You are requested to drive slowly here.

**저수**(貯水) storage of water; reservoir water; 《물》 stored(-up) water. ~하다 keep (water) in store; build up a reservoir. ◉ ~량 pondage; the volume of water kept in store. ~탱크 a (water) tank.

**저수지**(貯水池) a (storing) reservoir; 《관개용의》 an irrigation reservoir. ◉ ~댐 a storage dam.

**저술**(著述) 《글쓰는 일》 writing; 《쓴 것》 a 《literary》 work; *one's* writings. ~하다 write 《a book》; compose 《a work》. ¶ 원예에 관한 ~ books on gardening / 이것은 누구의 ~인지 모른다 This is of unknown authorship. / 그는 많은 ~을 했다 He has written a number of books. ◉ ~가 a writer; an author; 《여자》 an authoress. ~업 the literary profession; writing (as a career): ~업에 종사하다 be engaged in literary work.

**저습**(低濕) ¶ ~한 low and moist 《land》. ◉ ~지 a low, swampy place.

**저승** 《황천》 the world beyond; the other 〔next〕 world; the world of the dead; the afterlife. ¶ ~으로 가다, ~사람이 되다 pass away; die; go to Heaven; leave this world; pass to the other shore. ◉ ~길 the road to Hades. ~말 the Pale Horse. ~사자 ⇨ 사자(使者) ②.

**저압**(低壓) low pressure; 〖전기〗 low tension 〔voltage〕. ◉ ~부(部) 《공기 따위의》 a low-pressure area; a locality of low pressure. ~선 a low tension 〔voltage〕 cable. ~전류 a low-voltage current. ~ 증기기관 a low pressure steam engine. ~측 the low-tension side. ~터빈 low pressure turbine. ~회로〔케이블, 코일〕 a low-tension circuit 〔cable, coil〕.

**저액**(低額) small amount. ◉ ~소득자 a small-income earner; a person with a small income; [집합적] people in the low(er)-income brackets; under-paid people: ~소득자층 the low-income classes.

**저어새** 〖조류〗 a blackfaced spoonbill.

**저어하다** be afraid; fear. ¶ 일이 또 잘 안 될까 저어합니다 I am afraid that the thing would fail again.

**저열**(低熱) low heat; 《신열》 a low (body) temperature; a slight fever.

**저열하다**(低劣—) (be) low; despicable; contemptible; mean; base. ¶ 저열한 사람 a mean 〔base〕 fellow.

**저온**(低溫) low temperature. ¶ 일기 예보에 의하면 금년 겨울은 ~일 것이라고 한다 According to the (long-range) weather forecast, the temperature will be low this winter. ◉ ~건류(乾溜) low temperature carbonization. ~공업 the low temperature manufacturing industry. ~냉동 low temperature refrigeration. ~도 a low (degree of) temperature. ~물리학 cryophysics. ~소독〔살균〕 pasteurization at (a) low temperature. ~수송 refrigerated transport. ~유통체계 cold chain (생략 CC). ~ 처리〔포장〕법 《통조

림의》 cold pack. ～학 cryogenics.

**저울** a balance; 《대저울》 a steelyard; 《천칭》 a pair of scales; 《대형 계량기》 a weighing machine; 《자동 저울》 a dial scale. ¶ 부정한 ～ an unlawful balance / ～에 달다 weigh 《*a thing*》 on the balance / ～을 속이다 give short weight / ～을 후하게 달아주다 give good weight. ◉ ～대 the beam (of a balance or steelyard); the scale beam. ～추 the weight (of a balance). ～판 the pan of a balance; a scale.

**저울눈** notches on a balance beam; scale markings; measure of weight. ¶ ～을 속이다 cheat weight; give short weight.

**저울질** weighing; scaling; putting on the scales. ～하다 weigh; scale; put on the scales.

**저위**(低位) a low position 〔rank〕; a 「low degree.

**저위도**(低緯度) low latitudes.

**저유**(貯油) storage of oil. ◉ ～소 an oil reservoir. ～탱크 a storage tank.

**저육**(豬肉) pork. ⇨ 제육.

**저율**(低率) a low rate. ¶ ～의 low-rate; low / ～의 이자(로) (at) low interest 〔rate〕.

**저음**(低音) a low tone; a low-pitched sound; a low voice; 『음악』 bass. ¶ ～의 매력 the spell of *one's* deep voice / ～으로 on the lower keys; in bass. ◉ ～가수 a low-voiced singer; a *basso;* 《여성의》 a *contralto* (It.). ～부(部) the bass register: ～부 기호 a bass clef; an F clef.

**저의**(底意) *one's* original purpose; *one's* real intension; *one's* will 〔motive〕; *one's* inmost thought; an ulterior 〔underlying〕 motive. ¶ ～ 없이 without reserve; frankly / ～를 간파하다 pierce into 《*a person's*》 meaning / 너의 ～를 알 수 없다 I can't understand what you really mean to do. *or* I don't know what you are really getting at.

**저이** that person; he 〔him〕; she 〔her〕. ¶ ～들 those people; they 〔them〕.

**저인망**(底引網) a dragnet; trawling. ◉ ～어선 a trawler. ～어업 dragnet fisheries.

**저임금**(低賃金) low wages. ¶ ～의 일 a low-paying work 〔job〕. ◉ ～근로자 a low-wage earner. ～노동 cheap labor. ～정책 a low-wage policy.

**저자** ① 《시장》 a market; a fair. ¶ ～ 보다 go to market 《to buy, sell》. ② 《가게》 a market 〔grocery〕 stand.

**저자**(著者) a writer; an author; 《여류의》 an authoress; a lady writer. ¶ ～ 목록 〔색인〕 an author catalog 〔index〕 / ～ 불명의 anonymous / ～ 불명의 책 a book of unknown authorship / ～임을 주장하다 claim the authorship 《of》.

**저자세**(低姿勢) a modest 〔humble〕 attitude; low profile. ¶ ～를 취하다 assume a low posture; take 〔adopt〕 a low 〔low-profiled, modest〕 attitude 《toward》; behave *oneself* humbly / 그녀는 내 앞에서는 언제나 ～다 She's always humble in 「front of me 〔my presence〕. / 우리 정부는 이 문제에 관해서는 이웃 나라의 반감을 사지 않으려고 ～를 취해 왔다 Our government has maintained a low profile on this issue, so as not to antagonize its neighbor. ◉ ～외교 low-profile diplomacy.

**저작**(咀嚼) chewing; mastication. ～하다 chew; masticate. ⇨ 씹다. ◉ ～구(口) 『곤충』 a mandible. ～근(筋) 『해부』 a muscle of mastication. ～력 *one's* chewing power.

**저작**(著作) writing; authorship; 《저서》 a (literary) work; a book. ～하다 write a book. ¶ ～에 종사하고 있다 be engaged in writing / ～으로 생활하다 live by the (*one's*) pen. ◉ ～가, ～자 a writer; an author; 《여자》 a woman writer; an authoress. ～물 a (literary) work; a book: 그에게는 건축에 관한 ～물이 많이 있다 He has written widely on the subject of architecture.

**저작권**(著作權) copyright (기호 ©). ¶ ～이 있는 책 a copyrighted book / ～을 소유하다〔획득하다〕 hold 〔acquire, obtain〕 the copyright 《of》 / ～을 침해하다 infringe the copyright 《of》; pirate 《*a person's* work》. ◉ ～등록 copyright registered; copyright registration. ～법 a copyright law. ～사용료 a royalty. ～소유 ownership of copyright; 《표시》 Copyright reserved. *or* Copyrighted: ～ 소유자 a copyright holder. ～침해 an infringement of copyright; piracy: ～ 침해자 a (literary) pirate. 국제～조약 Universal Copyright Convention (생략 UCC).

**저장**(貯藏) storing; storage; keeping; preservation (보존); 『컴퓨터』 save. ～하다 store (up); lay 〔put〕 《*something*》 up 〔by〕; preserve. ¶ ～해 둔 in store / ～하고 있다 have 《*things*》 in store; have a store 〔stock〕 of

《*things*》/ ～되어 있다 be held in storage / ～할 수 있는 storable《products》/ 소금에 절여서 ～하다 preserve《*a thing*》in 〔with〕 salt / 겨울에 대비하여 연료를 ～하다 store up fuel for the winter / 오래 ～하기 어렵다 be of limited storage life.
◉ ～고 a storehouse; a storage house. ～량 the amount of stock. ～물〔품〕 stored goods; stores; stocks; supplies; a provisions《of food》. ～미〔야채〕 stored rice 〔vegetables〕. ～비 storage expenses. ～소 a storing place. ～실 a storeroom. ～파일 〖컴퓨터〗 an archived file.
냉동～ cold storage; refrigeration: 냉동 ～하다 keep《food》in cold storage.

**저적거리다** drag《*oneself*》along; shuffle 〔drag〕 *one's* weary feet.

**저절로** of 〔by〕 itself; of its own accord; spontaneously; by a natural process; automatically. ¶ 촛불이 ～ 꺼졌다 The candle light went out all by itself. / 이 문은 ～ 열린다 This door opens automatically. / 그분 앞에선 고개가 ～ 수그러진다 I can't help bowing in respect for him.

**저조**(低調)《가락의》a low tone; an undertone;《침체》dullness; weakness (시장 경기가);《운동 선수의》a slump;《활동의》lack of enthusiasm 〔activity〕. ¶ ～한 low-toned; inactive; inanimate; dull; sluggish; in a slump / ～한 타선 poor batting / ～한 성적 poor results 〔achievements〕 / 시장 경기가 ～하다 The market is sluggish.

**저조**(低潮) 〖지리〗 low tide; low water. ◉ ～선 a low-water mark.

**저주**(咀呪) imprecation; a curse; malediction; execration. ～하다 curse; call down a curse《upon》; imprecate evil《upon》; wish ill《toward》. ¶ ～받을 cursed; execrable / ～받은 cursed; doomed / ～받고 있다 be under a curse; carry a curse / 세상을 ～하다 curse the world / 그 놈을 ～한다 My curse shall be on his head.

**저주파**(低周波) low frequency (생략 LF).

**저지**(低地) low(-lying) land 〔ground〕; a lowland area;《강가의》《미》bottomland(s). ¶ 폭우로 그 지역내의 ～가 침수되었다 As a result of the heavy rain, the low-lying districts of the area were flooded.

**저지**(沮止) impediment; obstruction; hindrance; interception. ～하다 stop; resist; oppose; stand in the way; hinder; hamper; impede; obstruct; check; hold back; block. ¶ 진보를 ～하다 impede 〔block〕 progress; halt the advance / 아무의 행동을 ～하다 deter *a person* from acting 〔an action〕 / 초목의 성장을 ～하다 hinder 〔stop, check, deter〕 the growth of the plants / 발달을 ～하다 check the growth; arrest the development / 적의 진격을 ～하다 check the enemy's advance; hold the enemy in check / 통화 팽창의 경향이 현저히 ～되었다 The inflational trend has been considerably checked.

**저지**《심판원》a judge. ◉ ～페이퍼 a judge paper.

**저지레** spoiling; ruining; marring. ～하다 spoil; ruin; mar.

**저지르다** commit 〔perpetrate〕《a crime》; make《a terrible blunder》; make a real mess《of *things*》; spoil《a plan》. ¶ 일을 ～ cause trouble / 잘못을 ～ commit an error; make a mistake / 그는 어마어마한 일을 저질렀다 He has set the Thames 〔world, river〕 on fire, indeed. / 그가 또 무슨 일을 저지를지 알 수 없다 There is no knowing what he will be up to next.

**저질**(低質) low quality. ◉ ～탄 coal of low quality; poor-grade coal.

**저쪽** ①《방위》that side 〔direction〕; over there; the other side 〔direction〕. ¶ ～에 there; over there; on other 〔far〕 side; yonder; that way / ～에 있는 집 the house over there / ～에 보이는 산 the mountain you see over there / ～으로 가라 Go there. *or* Go away. / 이쪽 ～에서 반대하는 소리가 나왔다 Objections were heard on all sides. ②《파·사람》the other party; they; them; he; him. ¶ ～의 제의 the proposal of the other party / 이쪽 ～을 다 봐 줄 수 없어 입장이 난처하다 I'm in a fix 〔dilemma〕, being unable to satisfy both sides. / (전화에서) ～에서 무어라고 하는지 들리지가 않는다 I cannot hear what the man on the other end is saying.

**저처럼** like that; so; to that extent.

**저촉**(抵觸)《충돌》(a) conflict; (a) collision;《모순》(a) contradiction;《위반》(an) infringement; (a) contravention. ～하다《충돌하다》conflict 〔clash, collide〕 with; run counter to;《모순되다》be contrary to; be incompatible with;《위배되다》infringe on. ¶ 법에 ～되다 be 「in contravention of

〔contrary to, in conflict with〕 the law / 법에 ~되는 짓은 하지 않았다 I have done nothing contrary to the law. / 실험 결과는 그들의 이론과 ~되는 것이었다 The results of the experiment conflicted with their theory.

**저축**(貯蓄) saving; storing; 《저금》 savings. ~하다 save (up); lay by 〔aside〕; store up; put 〔set〕 by; hoard. ¶ ~의 날 the Savings Day / 소액 ~ 비과세(非課稅) 제도 a tax-free small deposits system / ~이 있다〔없다〕 have some 〔no〕 savings / ~을 장려하다 encourage savings / 수입에서 얼마를 ~하다 save something from 〔out of〕 *one's* income / 만일의 경우에 대비해서 ~하다 save against a rainy day / 그는 매월 급료의 2할을 ~한다 He saves 20 percent of his pay every month.
◉ ~금 savings; reserve funds. ~기관 a thrift institution. ~률 a rate of savings. ~성 예금 time and savings deposits. ~성향 a propensity to save. ~심 the spirit of saving; thriftiness: ~심이 있는 saving; thrifty / ~심이 있는〔없는〕 사람 a provident 〔an improvident〕 man. ~예금 a savings deposit. ~운동 a savings campaign. ~은행 a savings bank. ~채권 a savings bond 〔debenture〕.

**저탄**(貯炭) a stock of coal. ◉ ~소, ~장 a coal yard; a coal depot; a coaling station; 《배의》 a bunker.

**저택**(邸宅) a residence; a mansion. ¶ 훌륭한 ~ a lordly 〔stately〕 mansion; a fine house 〔mansion〕 / 훌륭한 ~을 짓다 build a fine mansion.

**저편** =저쪽.

**저하**(低下) a decline; a fall; a drop; 《품질의》 deterioration; 《가치의》 depreciation. ~하다 fall; drop; depreciate; deteriorate. ¶ 수준의 ~ a lowering of standards / 품질의 ~ a falling-off in quality (of goods); deterioration in the quality / 생활 수준의 ~ a decline in the standard of living / 능률이 ~하다 show a drop in efficiency; drop off in efficiency / ~시키다 let fall; lower; reduce; deteriorate / 생산을 ~시키다 curtail production / 학생들의 학력이 현저히 ~되어 있다 There is a marked decline in the students' scholastic performance. / 요즘 나는 시력이 ~되어 안경이 필요하다 I need glasses because my eyesight has been getting weaker. 「〔grades〕.

**저학년**(低學年) the lower classes

**저항**(抵抗) 《반항》 resistance; defiance; 《반대》 opposition; 〖물리〗 resistance. ~하다 make 〔offer〕 resistance 《to》; stand 〔struggle, hold out〕 against; withstand; resist; defy; oppose. ¶ ~하기 어려운 irresistible / 최후의 ~ the last-ditch stand / 공격에 ~하다 resist an attack; withstand an attack / 권위에 ~하다 revolt against authority / 완강한 ~을 시도하다 offer a stubborn 〔stout〕 resistance / ~을 받다 meet with resistance / 운명에 ~하다 strive against fate / 공기의 ~을 감소시키다 dwindle the air resistance / …하는 데 ~을 느끼다 《심리적으로》 be reluctant to *do;* do not feel like *do*ing / 사람은 일반적으로 가장 ~이 적은 방식을 택한다 People generally choose the line of least resistance.
◉ ~계 〖전기〗 an ohmmeter. ~권 the right of resistance. ~기 a resistor. ~력 resisting power 〔force〕; (power of) resistance: ~력을 줄이다〔늘리다〕 lower 〔increase〕 the power of resistance 《to》 / ~력을 얻다 acquire resistance 《to》 / 질병에 대한 ~력이 적다〔있다〕 have little 〔good〕 resistance to disease / 수면부족으로 감기에 대한 ~력이 약해졌다 Lack of sleep lowered my resistance to the flu. ~상자 〖전기〗 a resistance-box. ~운동 the Resistance. ~자 a resistant. ~코일 a resistance coil. 내〔외〕~ 〖물리〗 internal 〔external〕 resistance. 마찰~ frictional resistance.

**저해**(沮害) a hindrance; an impediment; an obstruction; blocking; a check; 〖심리〗 a blockage. ~하다 check; hinder; impede; hamper; obstruct; block; 《지연시키다》 delay; retard. ¶ 활동을 ~하다 hinder *one's* activity / 발전〔발달〕을 ~하다 check 〔arrest〕 the development 〔growth〕 《of》 / 진보를 ~하다 impede 〔hinder〕 the progress 《of》 / 사회의 안정과 발전을 ~하는 온갖 비리를 뿌리뽑다 root out all sorts of illegal acts detrimental to social stability and development.

**저혈압**(低血壓) low blood pressure; 《저혈압증》 hypotension. ¶ ~이다 have low blood pressure; be hypotensive.

**저희** 《우리》 we; us; 《저 사람들》 they; those people. ¶ ~(들) we; they / ~(들)의 희망 our 〔their〕 hope.

**적**(敵) ① 《원수》 an enemy; a foe; the enemy. ¶ 평화〔사회〕의 적 an enemy to peace 〔society〕/ 적군 the enemy forces; the enemy / 적기 an enemy plane / 적과 싸우다 fight against the enemy / 많은 적을 만들다 make many enemies / 적에게 붙다 go over to the enemy / 적의 수중에 떨어지다 fall into the enemy's hands / 적을 소탕하다 clear 《the land》 of the enemy / 아무를 적으로 삼다 have *a person* for an enemy / 적은 마침내 격퇴되었다 The enemy was beaten off at last. / 그들은 앞 뒤에서 적의 공격을 받았다 They were attacked in the front and rear. ② 《싸움의 상대》 an opponent; an antagonist; 《필적자》 an adversary; 《경쟁자》 a rival; a competitor; a match; *one's* equal. ¶ 너는 그의 적이 될 수 없다 You are no match for him. *or* You have got no chance against him. / 그가 가는 곳에 적이 없다 He carries everything before him.

**적**(籍) a register; 《본적》 the census register; domicile; 《단체의》 membership. ¶ 적을 두다 《*a person*》 register; enrol 《in school》; be enrolled 《at a university》; become a member 《of a party》/ 적에 올리다〔적에서 빼다〕 have *one's* name entered in 〔struck out from〕 the register / 그 학교는 천 명의 학생이 적을 두고 있다 The school has 1,000 students on the register.

**적** ① 《때》 the time (when); (on) the occasion. ¶ 옛적에 once upon a time; in the old days / 그가 왔을 적에 난 없었다 When he came to see me I was away. ② 《경험》 an experience. ¶ 그런 말을 들은 적이 있다 I've heard such talk too. / 비행기 여행을 한 적이 없다 I've never traveled by plane. / 그에게서 편지를 한번 받은 적이 있다 I once received a letter from him.

**-적**(的) ¶ 가급적 so far as possible / 경제적 economic(al) / 동양적 Oriental / 세계적 worldwide; all over the world / 직업적 professional / 역사적 historic(al) / 일반적으로 in general / 일시적 momentary / 역사적으로나 지리적으로나 both historically and geographically; in terms of history and geography / 그의 집은 매우 가정적인 분위기였다 His house had a very homely 〔honey〕 atmosphere to it. / 그는 독일인이지만 한국적인 사고방식의 소유자다 Although he is a German, he has a Korean way of thinking.

**적갈색**(赤褐色) a reddish brown (color).

**적개심**(敵愾心) a hostile feeling; hostility; animosity; enmity. ¶ ～에 불타서 influenced by a hostile feeling / ～을 일으키다 arouse hostility / …에 대해서 ～을 품다 harbor enmity toward… / ～을 자극하다〔부추기다〕 excite 〔provoke, arouse〕 《*a person's*》 hostility toward 《*his* adversary》; inflame 〔stir up〕 《*a person's*》 animosity 《against》/ 그들은 ～이 솟구쳤다 Their animosity ran very high.

**적격**(適格) conformity to the standard 〔qualification〕. ¶ ～의 qualified; competent; eligible; adequate / 그녀는 이 일에 ～이다 She is qualified 〔eligible〕 for this job. / 그녀는 친절해서 간호사로서 ～이다 She is cut out to be nurse because she is so kind. ◉ ～심사 위원회 a screening committee. ～자 a qualified 〔a competent, an eligible〕 person; a person qualified 《for》. ～품 standard 〔acceptable〕 goods.

**적공**(積功) long-standing labor 〔efforts, services〕; building up merit. ～하다 put a long-standing effort 《into》; render lasting service; build up merit.

**적교**(吊橋) a suspension bridge. ¶ ～를 놓다 suspend a bridge 《over a river》; construct a suspension bridge 《over》.

**적구**(赤狗) 《공산당 앞잡이》 the Reds; a communist; a commie.

**적국**(敵國) a hostile 〔an enemy〕 country 〔nation〕.

**적군**(敵軍) the enemy force; enemy troops; the hostile army.

**적권운**(積卷雲) a cumulocirrus (cloud).

**적극**(積極) ¶ ～적인 positive; active; aggressive; 《열심인》 keen 《on》; enthusiastic 《about, over》/ ～적으로 positively; actively / ～적인 사람 a very energetic person; a go-ahead / ～적 태도를 취하다 adopt a positive attitude / ～적으로 원조하다 give positive aid 《to *a person*》/ ～적으로 활동하다 work on positive lines / ～적인 태도로 나오다 take up a positive attitude / …의 방침을 수행하는 데 매우 ～적이다 be very aggressive in pursuing the policy of… / 내각은 ～적인 재정 정책을 취하기로 결정하였다 The Ministry has decided upon a positive financial policy. ◉ ～론자 an activist; a positivist. ～성 positiveness; aggressiveness; enterprising spirit; 《구어》 push: ～성이 있다 be positive / ～성이 없다 lack something positive / 그는 ～성이 없다 He has not enough enterprising spirit. ～외교 positive 〔active〕 diplomacy. ～정책 a positive policy. ～주의 positivism.

**적금**(積金) installment savings; an installment deposit. ¶ ～을 하다 save up 〔deposit〕 by installments; lay down a sum of money.

**적기**(赤旗) a red flag; 《공산당·노조의》 the Red Flag.

**적기**(摘記) a summary; an epitome. ～하다 summarize; sum up; epitomize. ¶ 회답의 개요를 ～하면 다음과 같다 The gist of the reply may be summarized as follows.

**적기**(適期) the proper 〔appropriate, adequate, suitable〕 time; a season (for). ¶ ～의 timely; opportune / 지금이 ～이다 the present is most opportune 《for *do*ing *something*》.

**적기**(敵機) an enemy plane.

**적꼬치**(炙—) a spit; a skewer for barbecue; *shish kebab* (Turk.).

**적나라**(赤裸裸) ① 《발가벗음》 nakedness; nudity. ～하다 (be) naked; bare. ② 《숨김없음》 straightforwardness; frankness; openness. ～하다 (be) frank; plain. ¶ ～하게 plainly; frankly; without reserve / ～한 사실 a naked 〔bald〕 fact / ～한 생의 모습을 보다 see life in the raw / 자신의 기분을 ～하게 이야기하다 speak plainly about *one's* real feelings / 그녀는 잘못한 과거의 일들을 ～하게 고백했다 She made a clear breast of her past evil deeds.

**적남**(嫡男) sons by the legal wife.

**적녀**(嫡女) daughters by the legal wife.

**적년**(積年) many years; an accumulation of years. ¶ ～의 공 efforts of many years / ～의 원한 a long-standing feud.

**적다**[1] 《수가》 (be) few; small; not many; be a small number of; do not have many; 《양이》 (be) little; not much; be a small quantity of; do not have much; 《부족하다》 (be) scarce; scanty; insufficient 《in》. ¶ 적은 수입 a small income / 적지 않은 손해 a considerable loss / 적지 않게 in no small number 〔quantity〕; not a little 〔few〕 / 적게 잡아도 at the lowest estimate / 그것보다 적게 less than that / 적어지다 get fewer 〔less〕; decrease; diminish; lessen / 파티 참석자는 적었다 Attendance at the party was poor 〔small〕. / 이 식품은 칼로리가 ～ This food is low in calories. / 그는 말이 ～ He is a man of few words. / 그는 성공할 가망이 ～ He has slim chance of success. / 교회 가는 사람이 극장 가는 사람보다 ～ Fewer 〔Less〕 people go to church than to theaters. (★ 수를 나타낼 때는 보통 fewer를 씀) / 그 소식에 적지 않게 놀랐다 I was not a little surprised at the news.

**적다**[2] 《기록하다》 write 〔put, take〕 down; make 〔take〕 a note of; put 《*a thing*》 on record; record; enter 《an account》 in 《a ledger》. ¶ 연필로 ～ write with a pencil; write in pencil / 잉크로 ～ write in ink / 영어로 ～ write in English / 친구의 주소를 수첩에 ～ write down a friend's address in a pocketbook / 하루 일을 일기에 ～ write 〔record〕 the day's events in *one's* diary / 아무의 공적을 글로 ～ record *a person's* achievements in writing / 나는 그의 강의의 요점을 적었다 I wrote 〔put〕 down the important points of his lecture.

**적당**(適當) appropriateness; suitability; fitness. ～하다 (be) suitable; proper; befitting; appropriate; adequate; apposite; apt; be fit 《for》. ¶ ～히 fittingly; suitably; properly; adequately; reasonably; as you think fit 〔proper, right〕; timely / ～한 집〔직업〕 a suitable house 〔job〕 / ～한 운동 moderate exercise / 아이들에게 ～한 책 a proper book for children / ～한 분량 an adequate amount / ～한 값으로 at a reasonable price / ～한 조건으로 on fair 〔reasonable〕 terms / ～한 때에 at a 〔the〕 proper time 〔season〕 / ～한 속도로 at a moderate speed / ～한 시기를 택하다 choose the proper time / ～히 조처하다 manage 《*a matter*》 「at *one's* discretion 〔as *one* thinks fit〕 / ～하다고 인정하다 think 《it》 fit 〔proper〕 / ～히 해라 Do as you see fit. / ～히 갈라 주시오 Please divide 《it》 as you think fit. / ～한 운동은 건강에 좋다 Proper exercise will do your health good. / ～하다고 생각되는 사람을 뽑아 주시오 Please choose a person you think competent. / 이 옷은 오늘 저녁 파티에는 ～치 않다 This dress won't be appropriate for the party this evening. / 대강대강 ～히 해라 Take it easy; you don't have to be perfect.

**적대**(敵對) hostility; antagonism. ～하다 show hostility 《toward》; be hostile 《to》; oppose; defy; revolt 〔fight〕 《against》. ¶ 두 나라는 ～ 관계에 있다 Both countries are hostile to each other. ◉ ～국 a hostile country. ～시 (regarding with) hostility; enmity: ～시하는 태도 a hostile attitude / ～시하다 look on 《*a person*》 as an enemy; regard with hostility; show enmity 《toward》; be hostile 《to》. ～행위 a hostile act; hostilities; hostile actions 〔operations〕: 공공연한 ～ 행위 open hostilities / ～ 행위를 취하다 open 〔commence〕 hostilities.

**적도**(赤道) the equator; the line. ¶ 자기 ～ the magnetic equator / ～(직하)의 equatorial / ～ 직하에서 directly under the equator / ～ 직하에 있다 be on the equator / ～를 가로지르다 cross the line. ◉ ～면 an equatorial plane. ～무풍대 the doldrums; the zone of equatorial calms. ～선 the equator line. ～역류(逆流) the Equatorial Countercurrent. ～의(儀) an equatorial telescope. ～제(祭) the ceremony of crossing the equator 〔line〕. ～지대 the equatorial region.

**적도기니**(赤道一) 《아프리카의 공화국》 (the Republic of ) Equatorial Guinea.

**적동**(赤銅) 〖광물〗 an alloy of copper and gold. ◉ ～광(鑛) cuprite; red copper (ore). ～색 bronze: ～색의 bronze; copper-colored.

**적란운**(積亂雲) 〖기상〗 a cumulonimbus.

**적량**(適量) a proper quantity; 《약의》 a proper dose. ¶ ～의 물 a suitable amount of water / ～이 넘게 과식〔과음〕하다 take 《*a thing*》 too much; 《술을》 drink to excess / ～의 소금을 치다 add a suitable amount of salt / ～의 술은 몸에 좋다고 한다 Liquor taken in proper quantity is said to be good for the health.

**적량**(積量) carrying capacity; tonnage. ¶ 배의 ～ the carrying capacity of a vessel; a ship's tonnage.

**적령**(適齡) the right age 《for》. ¶ ～에 이르다 attain the right age 《for》; be old enough 《to》 / 결혼 ～기에 이르다 reach 〔attain〕 the marriageable age; be old enough to marry / 그녀는 결혼 ～기가 지났다 She is past marriageable age.

**적례**(適例) a good example; an apt instance; a case in point. ¶ ～를 들다 cite an apt instance / 다음은 그 한 ～이다 The following is an example in point.

**적록색맹**(赤綠色盲) red-green (color) blindness; Daltonism.

**적리**(赤痢) 〖의학〗 dysentery. ⇨ 이질. ◉ ～균 a dysentery bacillus. ～환자 a dysentery patient; a case of dysentery.

**적린**(赤燐) red 〔amorphous〕 phosphorus.

**적립**(積立) reserving; laying by; saving. ～하다 save up (money); lay by; reserve; accumulate; amass. ¶ 한 달에 2만 원씩 ～하다 lay aside 20,000 won every month / 봉급의 일부를 매달 ～하고 있다 I save up part of my salary every month. ◉ ～금 a reserve (fund); a deposit: 법정 ～금 a legal reserve / 별도 ～금 a special reserve / ～금으로 붓다〔넣다〕 transfer 〔put〕 《a sum of money》 to reserve. ～배당금 accumulated dividends. ～저금 installment 〔regular〕 savings.

**적막**(寂寞) loneliness; solitude. ～하다 (be) lonely; solitary; lonesome; desolate; forlorn. ¶ ～한 광경〔광야〕 a dreary 〔desolate〕 sight 〔wasteland〕. ◉ ～감 a lonely feeling.

**적멸**(寂滅) 〖불교〗 annihilation; death; Nirvana. ～하다 be annihilated; pass away; go to Nirvana.

**적목질**(赤木質) 〖식물〗 heartwood.

**적바림** 《글로 적어 둠》 making a note of 《*a thing*》. ～하다 write 〔note, put, take〕 《*a thing*》 down; put 《*a thing*》 on record.

**적반하장**(賊反荷杖) (being an instance of ) evil-doer's audacity. ¶ ～이란 바로 이런 것이다 This is what they mean by 'the audacity of the thief'.

**적발**(摘發) exposure; disclosure. ～하다 expose; unmask; lay bare 〔open〕; uncover; disclose. ¶ 부정 사건을 ～하다 expose 〔lay bare〕 a scandal / 금제물을 ～하다 uncover contrabands / 마약 밀수단이 경찰에 ～되었다 A narcotic smuggling gang was unearthed by the police. / 그 회사의 탈세가 ～되었다 The company's tax evasion was exposed. ◉ ～자 a denunciator.

**적법**(適法) legality; lawfulness. ～하다 (be) lawful; legal; legitimate. ¶ ～이 아니다 be unlawful; be illegal / ～이다 be lawful 〔legal〕. ◉ ～성 legality; lawfulness. ～수단 lawful means. ～조치 a lawful measure. ～행위 a legal 〔lawful〕 act.

**적병**(敵兵) an enemy soldier; the enemy (전체). ¶ ～을 포로로 잡다 take an enemy prisoner.

**적부**(適否) 《일의》 propriety; 《사람·사물의》 suitability; fitness; 《적성》 aptitude. ¶ 인물의 ～ the fitness of a person /

장소의 ~ the suitability of a place / 직업의 ~ employment aptitude / ~를 판단하다 judge whether 《*a thing*》 is proper or not; determine the suitability. ◉ ~심사 review of the legality 《of detention》.

**적부적**(適不適) ⇨ 적부(適否). ¶ 그 일에는 사람에 따라 ~이 있다 Some are fitted for the work, but others are not. / 직업 선정시에는 그 ~을 생각해야 한다 In selecting your occupation, you must consider whether it suits you or not.

**적분**(積分) 〖수학〗 integral calculus. ~하다 integrate. ¶ ~의 integral / 면〔선〕~ a 「surface 〔curvilinear〕 integral. ◉ ~방정식 an integral equation. ~법 integration: 부분 ~법 integration by parts. ~상수 a constant of integration. ~인수 an integrating factor. ~학 integral calculus. ~함수 integral function.

**적빈**(赤貧) dire 〔extreme〕 poverty; destitution. ~하다 be in dire poverty; suffer from utter destitution.

**적산**(敵産) enemy property. ¶ ~을 몰수하다 confiscate enemy property. ◉ ~관리법 Enemy Property Administration Law.

**적삼** *chŏksam,* an unlined Korean summer jacket. ¶ ~ 벗고 은가락지 낀다 behave improperly; do beyond *one's* means.

**적색**(赤色) ① 《빛깔》 red color; red; crimson (진홍); scarlet (주홍). ¶ ~의 red(-colored). ② 《공산주의》 communism; communist; Red. ◉ ~분자 a Red; a red element. ~리트머스 시험지 red litmus paper. ~안료 red pigment. ~테러 Red terrorism. ~혁명 (a) Red revolution.

**적서**(嫡庶) children born of the legal wife and those born of the concubine.

**적선**(敵船) an enemy ship.

**적선**(積善) accumulation of virtuous deeds; practice of charities. ~하다 accumulate good deeds; practice charities. ¶ ~합쇼 Alms for the poor!

**적선지대**(赤線地帶) a red-light district; prostitute quarters.

**적설**(積雪) (fallen) snow; deep snow. ¶ ~로 열차가 불통이다 All the trains are snowbound. *or* The train is snowed up. / ~이 30센티미터에 달했다 The snow lay 〔piled up〕 thirty centimeters deep. ◉ ~계 a snow gauge. ~량 (a) snowfall: 많은 ~량 a heavy snowfall. ~조사 a snow survey.

**적설초**(積雪草) 〖식물〗 a ground ivy.

**적성**(適性) aptitude; fitness. ¶ ~과 능력에 맞는 일 a job appropriate to *one's* aptitude and capability / ~을 계발시키다 develop *one's* aptitude / 그에겐 교사로서의 ~이 있다 He is suitable 〔fit〕 for a teacher. *or* He has an aptitude for teaching. / 성급한 사람은 버스 운전기사로서는 ~이 맞지 않는다 A short-tempered person is not fit to be a bus driver. ◉ ~검사 an aptitude test: ~ 검사를 받다 undergo a quality 〔an aptitude〕 test.

**적성**(敵性) animosity; hostility. ◉ ~국가 a hostile country.

**적세**(敵勢) the strength of the enemy; the morale of the foe. ¶ ~를 크게 꺾다 shatter 〔break〕 the enemy's morale.

**적소**(適所) the right 〔proper〕 place; a proper 〔suitable〕 position. ¶ 적재~ the right man in the right place / ~를 구하다 gain a proper place 〔position〕; find a niche for *oneself.*

**적손**(嫡孫) grandchildren by the legal wife; posterity.

**적송**(赤松) 〖식물〗 a Korean red pine.

**적송**(積送) shipment; 《위탁판매를 위한》 consignment. ~하다 ship; forward; consign. ¶ 철도~ shipment 〔forwarding〕 by rail. ◉ ~인 a shipper; a forwarder. ~품 a shipment; a consignment.

**적쇠**(炙—) a gridiron; a grill. ◉ 적쇳가락 (a pair of ) large grill sticks.

**적수**(赤手) = 빈손. ◉ ~공권 empty hands and naked fists; being without any financial support.

**적수**(敵手) a rival; a competitor; an adversary; an opponent. ¶ 호~ a good rival 〔match〕 / 나는 그의 ~가 못 된다 I am no match for him. / 아무리 해 봐도 도저히 자네의 ~는 못 되겠네 Try what I will, I don't think I am quite a match for you.

**적습**(敵襲) an enemy attack 〔raid〕. ¶ ~을 받다 be attacked 〔raided〕 by the enemy.

**적시**(適時) ¶ ~의 timely; opportune. ◉ ~타(打) 〖야구〗 a timely hit.

**적시다** wet; moisten; dampen; 《담그다》 soak; drench; dip. ¶ 옷을 ~ get *one's* clothes wet / 손을 물에 ~ get *one's* hands wet; 《담그다》 dip *one's* hands in water / 눈물로 소매를 ~ wet *one's* sleeves with tears / 적시지 않다 keep 《*a thing*》 dry.

**적신호**(赤信號) 《교통 신호》 a red (traffic) light; stoplight; 《위험 신호》 a 「red 〔danger〕 signal. ¶ ～를 보고 차를 멈추다 stop 〔brake〕 the car for a red light / ～를 무시하고 달리다 run through a red light / ～를 무시하고 길을 건너다 cross a street against the red light / 그 할머니는 ～를 무시했다 The old lady ignored the stoplight.

**적실**(嫡室) *one's* legal 〔lawful〕 wife.

**적십자**(赤十字) 《단체》 the Red Cross; 《기장》 a Red Cross. ◉ ～구호반 the Relief Corps of the Red Cross Society; a Red Cross relief squad. ～병원 a Red Cross Hospital. ～사 the Red Cross (Society): 국제 ～사 the International Committee of the Red Cross (생략 ICRC) / 대한 ～사 the Korea National Red Cross(생략 KNRC). ～사업 Red Cross work. ～조약 the Red Cross Convention. 남북 ～ 회담 Talks between the South and North Korean Red Cross Societies.

**적어도** at (the) least; at a minimum; to say the least (of it). ¶ ～ 30분은 걸릴 것이다 It will take at least 30 minutes. / ～ 2만 원은 들 것이다 It will cost you at least 20,000 won. / 하루에 ～ 새 단어를 다섯 개는 외워라 Learn at least five new words every day.

**적업**(適業) the right vocation; a good line of work (to be in).

**적역**(適役) a suitable 「post 〔position, office〕; 《연극의》 a well-cast 「role 〔part〕. ¶ 그 일엔 그가 가장 ～이다 He 「is cut out 〔is the right man〕 for the work. / 그는 그 역에 ～이었다 He was well cast in the role.

**적역**(適譯) a 「good 〔proper, nice〕 translation; an exact rendering. ～하다 render exactly 《into Korean, English, *etc.*》; give a good translation 《of》; translate properly. ¶ 그 낱말에 대한 영어의 ～이 없다 There is no exact English equivalent for the word.

**적외선**(赤外線) infrared 〔ultrared〕 light 〔rays〕. ◉ ～램프 an infrared lamp. ～분광기 an infrared spectrometer. ～사진 infrared photography: ～사진기 an infrared camera. ～암시(暗視)장치 noctovision. ～요법 infrared therapy. ～필름 infrared film.

**적요**(摘要) a synopsis; a compendium; an epitome; a summary; 《개요》 an outline; 《발췌》 an abstract. ～하다 summarize; sum up; epitomize. ¶ 연설의 ～ an abstract of *one's* speech. ◉ ～란 the remarks column.

**적요하다**(寂寥—) (be) desolate; lonely; lonesome.

**적용**(適用) application. ～하다 apply 《a rule to》. ¶ 법의 ～ the application of a law / ～할 수 있는〔없는〕 applicable 〔inapplicable〕 《to》 / 모든 경우에 ～할 수 있는 법칙 a rule applicable to all cases / 규칙에 ～시켜 in conformity with the rule / ～되다 be applicable 《to a rule》 / ～ 범위가 넓다 be of wide application / 규칙을 잘못 ～하다 misapply a rule; make a wrong application of the rule / 이 규칙이 ～되지 않는 경우는 거의 없다 There are few exception to this rule. / 이것은 그와 같은 사람에게는 ～ 안 된다 This is not true of such a man as he. / 이 규칙은 어린이에게는 ～되지 않는다 This regulation does not apply to children. / 그는 실험에 그 이론을 ～했다 He applied the theory in actual practice.

**적운**(積雲) a cumulus. ＝뭉게구름.

**적위**(赤緯) 〖천문〗 declination.

**적응**(適應) adaptation; accommodation. adjustment; fitness. ～하다 adapt 〔adjust, accomodate〕 *oneself* 《to》; be 「fit 〔adapted〕 for 〔to〕; be suited to 〔for〕; get acclimated 《to》 (풍토에).

> 용법 **adapt** 유연성을 갖고 또는 스스로 새로운 상황에 적응하다. **adjust** 비교적 작은 차이를 계산이나 판단으로 조절하여 기계 부품처럼 들어맞게 하다. **accommodate** 변화 등에 그럭저럭 적응해 나가다란 느낌을 주는 말.

¶ ～시키다 adapt 《*a thing*》 《to》; adjust; accommodate; fit 〔suit〕 《*a thing*》 《to》 / 환경에 ～ 못 하는 사람 a maladjusted person / 새 환경에 ～하다 adapt *oneself* to new circumstances / 현재의 일자리에 그는 잘 ～하고 있다 He is well adapted for his present position. / 이 동물은 추위에 ～하는 능력을 가지고 있다 This animal has an ability to adapt itself to the cold. ◉ ～방산(放散) 〖생물〗 adaptive radiation. ～설 〖생물〗 an adaptation theory. ～성 adaptability; flexibility: ～성이 있는 adaptable; adaptive; flexible / ～성이 없다 be inadaptable; lack adaptability. ～증 a disease which is susceptible to treatment 《by a particular medicine》. ～형질 an adaptative character.

**적의**(適宜) appropriateness; suitableness; suitability. ～하다 (be) suitable; fit; befitting; appropriate; apposite. ¶ ～하게 suitably; properly; fittingly; at *one's* own discretion (자기 재량으로) / ～ 조치하다 do as *one* thinks fit; take proper steps; take (what *one* regards as) appropriate measures.

**적의**(敵意) hostile feelings; hostility; enmity; animosity; 《악의》 malice; ill will; spite; 《원한》 (a) grudge. ¶ ～가 있는 hostile; inimicle; antagonistic / ～를 품다 harbor animosity 《toward》; be hostile 《to》; bear a grudge 《against》; entertain hostile feelings 《against *a person*》 / ～를 보이다 show animosity 《toward》 / ～를 일으키다 arouse 〔rouse〕 the animosity.

**적이** some; somewhat; to some extent; in some measure; slightly; quite a bit; rather; quite. ¶ 그 소식에 ～ 안심되오 I am slightly relieved at the news.

**적이나** at the very least; ever so little; a little at least; if at all possible. ¶ 그가 ～ 후회하니 다행이다 I'm glad he was sorry a little at least.

**적임**(適任) fitness to the post; suitability; competence. ¶ ～이다 be fit 〔suitable〕 《for the office》; be suited 《to the job》; be competent 《for》; be well qualified 《for》 / ～이 아닌 unfitted; unsuited; incompetent / 그 자리에는 그가 ～이다 He is the right 〔best〕 man for the position.
◉ ～자 a person fit for the post; a well-qualified person; a suitable person; the right man 《for the position》: 최～자이다 be the very man 〔just the man〕 《for the post》.

**적자**(赤字) 《재정상의》 a deficit; a loss; the red. ¶ 상당한 ～ a sizable deficit / 수지의 ～ an adverse balance of payments / 예산의 ～ a budget deficit / ～가 나다 have a deficit / ～를 내다 go 〔get, run〕 into the red 《미》; show 〔suffer〕 a loss 〔deficit 《영》〕; go into red ink / 10억 원에 달하는 ～를 내다 go into the red to the extent of a billion won; show a loss of a billion won / ～를 메우다 cover 〔make up〕 the deficit / ～를 내고 있다 be in the red / ～를 벗어나다 get 〔come〕 out of the red / ～를 내지 않도록 하다 keep out of the red / 우리집 가계는 매월 ～다 Our household budget runs into the red every month.
◉ ～경영＝～운영. ～공채 a deficit-covering (public) bond. ～노선 《버스 등의》 a deficit-ridden 《bus》 line 〔route〕; a loss-making 《railroad》 line. ～보전(補塡) deficit covering. ～생활 red-ink living. ～예산 an unbalanced budget; a deficit budget. ～요인 deficit-causing factors. ～운영 deficit operation: ～운영을 하다 operate at a loss 〔in the red〕. ～인생 a financially hard-pressed life. ～재정 deficit financing 〔finances〕. ～지출 deficit spending.

**적자**(嫡子) sons by *one's* legal wife.

**적자**(適者) those fit; the fit; a fit person. ◉ ～생존 the survival of the fittest: ～생존의 법칙 the law of the survival of the fittest.

**적장**(敵將) the enemy's general; the enemy commander.

**적재**(適材) a man fit for the post; the right man for the job. ◉ ～적소 the right man in the right place: ～적소에 배치하다 assign 〔put〕 the right man in the right post / ～적소가 아니다 be a case of a square peg in a round hole.

**적재**(積載) carrying; loading. ～하다 load; carry; 《배에》 have 《cargo》 on board; take on 〔in〕. ¶ 밀을 ～한 with a cargo of wheat / 배에 화물을 ～하다 load a ship with goods / 우편물 및 화물을 ～하다 take on mail and cargoes.
◉ ～능력 carrying 〔loading〕 capacity 〔power〕. ～량 loadage; a load (of). ～배수량 《a ship of 5,000 tons》 load displacement. ～지점 a loading point. ～톤수 capacity 〔freight〕 tonnage. ～하중 live load. ～화물 cargo on board.

**적적하다**(寂寂―) (be) lonely; lonesome; solitary; desolate; deserted. ¶ 적적한 느낌 a lonely feeling; loneliness; lonesomeness / 적적한 곳 a lonely place / 적적하게 지내다 lead 〔live〕 a lonely life / 나는 말벗이 없어서 ～ I feel lonely having no one to talk to. / 당신이 없어서 무척 ～ I feel lonely because you are not here. *or* I miss you very much. (★ miss는 「…이 없어 적적하다」는 뜻) / 아이들이 없어서 집안이 ～ The house is lonely without children.

**적전**(敵前) ¶ ～의〔에〕 before 〔in the face of, in front of〕 the enemy / ～에 상륙하다 land in the face of the enemy / ～에서 도망치다 turn *one's* back to the enemy; fly before the enemy.
◉ ～도하 a forced crossing of a river against an enemy. ～상륙 a landing

in the face of the enemy.

**적절**(適切) appropriateness; fitness; pertinence. ～하다 (be) suitable; fit; appropriate; proper; adequate.

> (용법) **suitable, fit** 어떤 조건·상황·목적·용도 따위에 「어울리는, 알맞은」이란 뜻의 가장 일반적인 낱말. **appropriate** 어떤 목적·조건에 「딱 들어맞는」이란 뜻. **proper** 사회의 도덕·관습·의례 따위의 견지에서 볼 때 기준에 맞기 때문에 「적절하다」는 뜻. **adequate** 어떤 목적을 이루기에 「충분한」, 필요한 자질을 「갖춘」이란 의미에서 「적절하다」는 뜻.

¶ ～치 않은 impertinent; unfit / ～한 말 an apt 〔a happy〕 remark; an opportune remark; a well-placed remark / ～한 보기〔예〕 an apt example; a good example / ～한 비유 a fitting simile / ～한 비평 an apt 〔a pertinent〕 criticism / 귀하의 제안은 이 시점에서 참으로 ～합니다 Your proposal at this time is certainly in order. / 그것을 설명할 ～한 말이 떠오르지 않았다 I couldn't think of a fitting 〔suitable〕 explanation for it. *or* I couldn't find suitable words to express it. / 이런 때에 웃는 것은 ～치 않다 Laughing is improper in such a case. / 서울은 국제 회의를 개최하는 데 ～한 장소다 Seoul is a logical place for holding an international conference. / 그 경우에 정부가 취한 행동은 ～하지 못했다 The action of the government was not appropriate to the occasion.

**적정**(敵情) the enemy's movements. ¶ ～을 살피다 feel the enemy out; reconnoiter the enemy's movements.

**적정**(適正) propriety; appropriateness; reasonableness. ～하다 (be) proper; appropriate; reasonable; just; right. ¶ ～한 분배 a fair 〔judicious〕 distribution / ～한 수단 (an) appropriate means / ～한 평가 a fair 〔correct〕 evaluation / ～ 가격을 유지하다 maintain prices at a reasonable level.
◉ ～가격 a reasonable price. ～고용 optimum employment. ～수준 optimum level. ～이윤 (a) reasonable profit. ～인구 optimum population. ～통화량 optimum money supply.

**적조**(赤潮) a red 〔reddish brown〕 tide; red water. ◉ ～현상 조기 경보제 an early red tide warning system.

**적조**(積阻) being remiss in writing. ～하다 be remiss in writing; be a poor correspondent. ¶ 오랫동안 ～했습니다 Pardon me for my long silence.

**적중**(的中) a (good) hit. ～하다 hit the mark; make a good hit; 《짐작 등이》 guess right; 《급소 등에》 go 〔strike〕 home; 《예언 등이》 come 〔turn out, prove〕 true. ¶ ～하지 않다 miss 〔be wide of〕 the mark; guess wrong / 그의 예언이 ～했다 His prediction has come true. / 탄환은 모두 ～했다 Every shot told. / 내 추측이 ～했다 I was right in my guess 〔conjecture〕.
◉ ～률 a hitting ratio.

**적지**(敵地) the enemy's territory 〔land, country〕. ¶ ～에 침입하다 advance into the enemy's country / ～에 깊숙이 들어가다 penetrate deep into the enemy's territory.

**적지않은** not a few 〔little〕; no small; considerable; great. ¶ ～ 돈 no small amount of money; a considerable sum of money / ～ 책들이 분실되고 없었다 Not a few books were missing. / 나는 그의 어머님께 ～ 신세를 졌다 I owe a great deal to his mother.

**적지않이** in no small way; to no small extent; not a little; considerably; greatly. ¶ ～ 애쓰다 take no little pains / ～ 놀라다 be not a little surprised / 이 책에는 오식이 ～ 있다 There are more than a few misprints in this book.

**적진**(敵陣) the enemy's camp; the enemy's position; the enemy line. ¶ ～을 돌파하다 break through the enemy line / ～을 공격하다〔빼앗다〕 attack 〔carry〕 the enemy's position.

**적철광**(赤鐵鑛) 〖광물〗 hematite.

**적체**(積滯) the pileup (of goods to be handled); accumulation 《of undelivered goods》; backlog; 《교통 등의》 congestion; a jam. ～하다 accumulate; pile up; form a backlog. ¶ 그 사고로 교통이 ～되었다 The accident jammed traffic. / 파업으로 인해 우편물이 ～되어 있다 Owing to the strike, undelivered mails are piling up.

**적출**(嫡出) legitimacy. ¶ ～이다 be born in lawful wedlock. ◉ ～자 a legitimate child 〔son〕.

**적출**(摘出) removal; extraction. ～하다 remove; extract 《from》; pick 〔take〕 out. ¶ 상처에서 총알을 ～하다 remove 〔extract〕 the bullet from a wound.

**적출**(積出) shipment; forwarding.
◉ ～인 a shipper. ～항 a port of shipment: 석탄 ～항 a coal-shipping

port; a coal loading port.

**적치**(積置) piling-up; heaping; amassing. ～하다 pile up; heap; amass.

**적탄**(敵彈) 《소총의》 the enemy's bullets; 《대포의》 the enemy's shells. ¶～을 무릅쓰고 in the face 〔teeth〕 of enemy's fire / ～에 쓰러지다 fall under the enemy's fire; be shot dead by the enemy; be killed by a bullet from the enemy.

**적토**(赤土) red clay 〔earth〕.

**적통**(嫡統) ① 《적출의》 legitimate lineage. ¶～의 자손 a person of legitimate lineage. ② 《정통파》 the main line of descent; the orthodox school.

**적평**(適評) a just criticism; an appropriate comment. ¶～을 내리다 hit the mark; make a pertinent remark 《on *a matter*》.

**적폐**(積弊) deep-rooted evils; vices of long standing; accumulated evils. ¶～를 일소하다 clear 〔sweep〕 away deep-rooted evils.

**적포도주**(赤葡萄酒) red wine.

**적함**(敵艦) an enemy warship 〔ship〕.

**적합**(適合) suitability; fitness; appropriateness. ～하다 (be) suitable 《to》; fit; suit; be fit 〔fitted〕 《for》. ¶…에 ～하게 하다 adapt 《*a thing, a person*》 to… / 초심자에 ～한 책 a book suitable for beginners / 식용〔건강〕에 ～하다 be good to eat 〔for the health〕 / 기질에 ～하다 be congenial to *one's* disposition / 목적에 ～하다 suit *one's* purpose / 이 벼는 추운 지방에서 재배하기에 ～하다 This rice is suitable for planting in cold climates. / 채용 조건에 ～한 응모자가 없었다 There were no applicants who fitted the requirement of the job.

**적혈**(赤血) red blood. ◉ ～구 〖해부〗 a red (blood) corpuscle; a red (blood) cell; an erythrocyte: ～구 수 검사 《do》 a red cell count / ～구 침강 속도 검사 a blood sedimentation 〔precipitation〕 test.

**적화**(赤化) communization; Bolshevization; Sovietization. ～하다 communize; Bolshevize; Sovietize; turn 〔go〕 red; go communist. ¶ 한반도 ～ 통일의 망상 a fanatic dream of communizing the entire Korean Peninsula / ～를 방지하다 check the spread of communism. ◉ ～선전 Red 〔Bolshevization〕 propaganda. ～운동 a Red movement.

**적화**(赤禍) the red peril.

**적화**(積貨) 《적재》 shipping; loading; lading; 《짐》 a cargo; a freight; a load. ～하다 load 《a truck with goods》; put 《goods》 on board. ¶～를 부리다 discharge 〔unload〕 goods 《from a truck》; unload 《a ship》. ◉ ～량 《중량》 intake weight; 《용적》 intake measurement. ～명세서 a freight list. ～목록 a shipping invoice; the (cargo) manifest. ～보험 cargo insurance; insurance on cargo. ～비용 loading 〔cargo〕 costs. ～수령증 a shipping receipt. ～안내 an advice of shipment. ～중량 manifest weight. ～항 the port of shipment.

**적확**(的確) precision; accuracy; exactness; infallibility. ～하다 (be) precise; accurate; exact. ¶～한 숫자 exact figures / ～한 증거 a positive proof / 말의 ～한 뜻 the exact meaning of a word / ～한 보고 a precise report / ～한 묘사 an accurate description.

**적환**(積換) transshipment; reshipment. ～하다 transship; reship. ◉ ～비(費) a transshipment charge. ～항 a transshipment port. ～화물 transshipment goods.

**적흑색**(赤黑色) reddish black. ¶～의 dark-red.

**적히다** be recorded; be put on record; be written down; be inscribed. ¶이름을 ～ have *one's* name noted down / 의사록에 적혀 있다 be recorded in the minutes / 편지에는 이렇게 적혀 있다 The letter goes like this.

**전** 《가장자리》 a brim; a rim; an edge. ¶～이 넓은 꽃병 a vase with a broad brim.

**전**(田) a dry field; a farm.

**전**(典) 《법전》 a code; 《의전》 a ceremony.

**전**(前) ① 《시간의 미달》 《six minutes》 to 《ten》; 《a little》 before 《nine》; earlier than 《usual》; 《연령 등의》 《be》 under 《twenty》; 《지정된 날짜 이전》 《a week》 in advance. ¶열시 십오분 전 a quarter before 〔to〕 ten / 서력 기원전 before Christ (생략 BC) / 표는 1주일 전부터 판다 sell tickets a week in advance / 그녀는 아직 30 전이다 She is yet under thirty. ② 《앞서의》 former; last; previous; ex-; onetime; retired (퇴직한). ¶전 총리 the ex-Prime Minister / 전 남편 *one's* former husband / 전 주소 *one's* former address / 이 도시의 전 시장 the ex-mayor of this city / 나는 전의 계획이 나중의 것보다 좋다 I prefer the former plan to the latter. ③ 《이전·과거의》 before; ago; since

(…이래); previous. ¶ 오래 전 long ago / 이틀 전 신문 a newspaper a couple of days old / 전날 밤 the night before; the previous night / 전에 말한 바와 같이 as previously stated / 전부터 from way back 〔long ago〕; for some time now / 전에 그것을 들은 일이 있다 I have heard it before. / 그는 전과 다름이 없었다 He hasn't changed since. / 그건 얼마 전의 일입니까 How long since is it ? / 이 절은 천년 전에 세워졌다 This temple is a thousand years old. / 그것은 오래 전 일이다 It happened a long time ago. / 전에도 이런 일이 있었나 Did anything like this ever happen before ? (★ ago는 현재의 시점에서 앞인 때, before는 모든 경우에 쓰임).
④ 《…하기 전》 prior to; before; earlier than. ¶ 그가 도착하기 전 before his arrival / 수업 시간이 되기 전에 before (it gets to be time for) class / 외출 전에 식사하다 eat before going out / 아버지는 내가 태어나기 전에 돌아가셨다 My father died before I was born.
⑤ 《앞면》 the front; the fore part. ¶ 역전 the station front / 사고는 내 면전에서 일어났다 The accident happened right in front of me.
⑥ 《편지에서》 Dear; Sir. ¶ 어머님전 상서 Dear Mother.

**전**(煎) fried food. ¶ 전을 부치다 fry; prepare a fried dish / 생선전을 부치다 fry filleted fish.

**전**(廛) a shop; a store; 《노점》 a booth; a stall. ¶ 싸전 a rice shop / 어물전 a fish shop.

**전**(錢) ① 《화폐 단위》 a Korean cent; a *chŏn* (=1/100 won). ② 《돈》 money; a coin (주화).

**전-**(全) whole; all; entire; total; full; pan-. ¶ 전국 the whole nation / 전패 a total defeat / 전세계 the whole world.

**-전**(殿) 《궁궐·불각》 a palace; a Buddhist temple. ¶ 복마전 an abode of demons; pandemonium / 대웅전 the main building of a temple.

**-전**(戰) 《전투》 a battle; a fight; combat; 《경기》 a match; a game. ¶ 시가전 street fighting / 육박전 a hand-to-hand fight; a close combat / 공중전 an air battle 〔war〕 / 1회전 the first game 〔round〕.

**전가**(全家) the whole family; all the family.

**전가**(傳家) ¶ ~의 ancestral; hereditary; successive / ~지보(之寶) an heirloom / ~의 보도(寶刀) a sword treasured in the family; [비유적] 《비장의 수단》 《resort to》 *one's* last measure; 《play》 *one's* trump card.

**전가**(轉嫁) 《넘겨 씌움》 imputation; ascription. ~하다 impute; ascribe; lay 〔throw〕 《the blame on *a person*》; shift 〔shuffle off〕 《a responsibility on another's shoulder》; pass on 《to》; 《구어》 pass the buck 《to》. ¶ 죄를 남에게 ~하다 impute a crime to *a person* / 허물을 남에게 ~하다 lay the blame on a *person* / 남에게 책임을 ~하지 마라 Don't shift the responsibility on to others. / 임금 코스트의 증가는 소비자에게 ~되었다 Increased wage costs have been passed on to the consumers. / 그는 실패의 책임을 타인에게 ~하려고 했다 He tried to shift the blame for his failure onto someone else.

**전각**(全角) 〖인쇄〗 an em.

**전각**(殿閣) a royal palace.

**전갈**(全蠍) 〖동물〗 a scorpion. ◉ ~자리 〖천문〗 Scorpio; the Scorpion.

**전갈**(傳喝) a verbal message. ~하다 give a (verbal) message; send word 〔a message〕. ¶ ~을 전하다 deliver a (verbal) message / ~을 받다 receive a message; get word / 저의 ~을 받았습니까 Did you get my message ?

**전개**(展開) unfolding; development; 《군대의》 deployment; 〖수학〗 expansion; development. ~하다 《진전되다》 unfold; develop; evolve; roll out; 《확대하다》 spread 〔open〕 out; 《군대가》 deploy; 〖수학〗 expand. ¶ 이론을 ~하다 develop 〔expand〕 *one's* theory / 새로운 국면을 ~하다 take a new turn / 이 사건은 앞으로 어떻게 ~될까 What will be the future developments of this affair ? / 사태가 어떻게 ~될지 기다려 보자 Let's wait and see how things shape up. / 이야기는 뜻밖의 결말로 ~되어 갔다 The story developed into an unexpected ending. / 웅대한 경관이 서서히 눈 아래 ~되기 시작했다 A magnificent landscape began to spread out below. ◉ ~도(圖) 〖수학〗 a development figure. ~부(部) 〖음악〗 a development section. ~식 〖수학〗 an expansion.

**전거**(典據) authority; authenticity; documentation; a source. ¶ ~ 있는 학설 an authoritative 〔an authenticated, a well-documented〕 theory / ~가 확실한 of good authority / ~ 없는 without authority / ~를 보이다 give chapter and verse / ~를 들다 name 〔cite〕 the authority / ~를 밝히다 verify *one's* references / 그 이야기에는 확실한 ~가 없다 There are no definite sources for that story.

**전거**(轉居) removal of residence; change of address. ~하다 change *one's* residence 〔abode〕; move 《to》. ⇨ 이전, 전출. ¶ ~를 통지하다 give a notice of *one's* change of address.

**전격**(電擊) 《전기에 의한 충격》 an electric shock; 《급습》 a lightning attack. ¶ ~적(인) lightning; sudden; immediate / ~적으로 공격을 받다 be blitzed; be attacked with a blitz / 국회는 그 법안을 ~적으로 통과시켰다 The National Assembly has passed the bill with lightning speed. ◉ ~결혼 a sudden marriage. ~요법 《전기 치료》 electroshock therapy 〔treatment〕. ~작전 lightning 〔blitz〕 tactics. ~전 a lightning war; blitz warfare.

**전경**(全景) a complete view; a panoramic view; a bird's-eye view (위에서 본); a panorama. ¶ 경기장의 ~ a general view of the stadium / 시가지의 ~을 내려다보다 command a view of the whole city / 서울의 ~을 보다 see the whole view 〔a panorama〕 of Seoul / 창에서 해안과 바다의 ~을 볼 수 있다 From the window we can enjoy a panorama of beach and sea.
◉ ~사진 a panoramic photograph: ~사진기 a pantoscope; a pantoscopic camera.

**전경**(前景) the front view; the foreground.

**전고**(典故) an authentic precedent.

**전곡**(田穀) dry-field grain 〔crop〕.

**전곡**(全曲) ¶ ~녹음 (a) full-length recording / ~연주 a full-length performance 《of Carmen》.

**전곡**(錢穀) money and grain.

**전골** a *chŏngol;* a beef casserole; beef with vegetables cooked in casserole. ◉ ~틀 a casserole (pan).

**전공**(前功) past services; former merit.

**전공**(專攻) a special study; *one's* major 《미》; *one's* (main) subject; *one's* (academic) specialty. ~하다 study 《a subject》 specially; make a specialty of; specialize in; major in 《미》. ¶ 정치학을 ~하다 major in political science / 대학에서 무엇을 ~하셨습니까 What did you major in 〔What was your major〕 at the university? / 비서학을 ~할 수 있습니까 Can I take a major in Secretarial Science?
◉ ~과목 a subject of special study; a major 《미》; a speciality 《영》. ~분야 a major field of study; a field of specialization. 부~ a minor: 부~ 과목 a minor subject / 부~으로 배우다 minor 《in》.

**전공**(電工) an electrician.

**전공**(戰功) military merit 〔distinction〕; meritorious 〔distinguished〕 services in war. ¶ ~ 있는 장교 an officer with a fine war record / ~을 세우다 distinguish *oneself* on the field of battle; render distinguished military services / 그는 ~으로 훈장을 받았다 He was awarded a medal for his distinguished military service.

**전과**(全科) the whole 〔full〕 curriculum; the full course (offered by a school); the complete course. ¶ ~를 이수하다 complete the whole required course.

**전과**(前科) 〖법〗 a previous conviction 〔offense〕; a criminal record. ¶ 절도 ~가 있는 남자 a man with a past conviction for theft / ~ 3범의 남자 a man with three previous convictions / ~가 있다 be an ex-convict; have a criminal 〔police〕 record. ◉ ~기록 a rap sheet 《속어》. ~자 an ex-convict; an old offender; a man with a criminal record; an ex-con 《속어》; an old lag 《영》; a jailbird 《구어》.

**전과**(戰果) war results; military achievements 〔results, gains〕. ¶ 혁혁한 ~를 올리다 make marked military achievements; achieve brilliant 「war results 〔results in war〕.

**전과**(轉科) change of *one's* major study 〔course, field〕. ~하다 change *one's* major; be 〔get〕 enrolled in another 〔a different〕 course.

**전관**(前官) 《전임자》 the predecessor 《in a post》; 《자신의》 *one's* former post. ¶ ~ 예우를 받다 be granted the privileges of *one's* former post.

**전관**(專管) exclusive jurisdiction 〔management〕. ~하다 have the exclusive jurisdiction 《over》; have power 《over》. ◉ ~구역 an exclusive jurisdiction. ~어업〔어로〕수역 an exclusive fishing zone 〔waters〕.

**전광**(電光) 《번개》 a flash of lightning; a bolt; 《전깃불》 electric light. ¶ ~석화같이 like a bolt of lightning; in a flash; (as) quick as lightning / ~을 내다 emit electric sparks. ◉ ~간판 an electric sign 《of a store》. ~(게시)판 an electric bulletin board; 《경기장의》 an electric(al) scoreboard. ~뉴스

an illuminated sign spelling out news items; an electric news tape; 《광고용의》 a sky sign.

**전교**(全校) 《학교 전체》 the whole school; 《모든 학교》 all the schools. ¶ ～생 all the students of a school; the entire student body / ～생에게 연설하다 speak to the whole school.

**전교**(傳教) ① 《왕의 명령》 ＝하교(下教) ①. ② 《종교》 ⇨ 포교.

**전교**(轉交) sending 《a letter》 in care of *a person;* delivery [transfer] through *a person;* care of (생략 c/o). ～하다 send in care of *a person.* ¶ A씨 ～ B씨 귀하 《편지 겉봉에》 Mr. B, care of [c/o] Mr. A / …전교로 편지를 내다 address a letter in care of….

**전구**(電球) the bulb of an electric lamp; an electric [a light] bulb. ¶ 백 와트짜리 ～ a 100 watt bulb / 끊어진 ～ a burnt-out light bulb / 소켓에 ～를 끼우다[빼다] screw a bulb into [out of] a socket / ～가 끊어졌다 The light bulb has burned out. ◉ 가스～ a gas-filled bulb. 반투명[젖빛]～ a frosted bulb. 백열[색]～ an incandescent [a colored] bulb. 섬광～ a flash bulb. 소형[꼬마]～ a miniature bulb. 탄소선 ～ a carbon-filament bulb.

**전국**(全國) the whole country [nation]. ¶ ～의[적인] national; nationwide; countrywide / ～적으로 all over [across] the country; all the country over; throughout the land; in all parts of the country; on a national scale / ～을 통해[에 걸쳐] throughout [all over] the country [land]; across the nation / ～적으로 유명한 사람 a man with national reputation / ～평균 the national average / ～적인 운동 a campaign on a nationwide [national] scale / ～적인 운동을 일으키다 start a nationwide movement / ～적으로 퍼지다 spread all over the country / ～에서 모이다 gather from all over the country / 그 방송은 ～에 중계되었다 The broadcast was carried on a national network. / 그 회사는 ～에 지점이 있다 The company has branches in all parts of the country. / 그들은 ～적인 규모로 환경보호 운동을 벌였다 They started a nationwide campaign for the protection of the environment. ◉ ～경제인 연합회 the Federation of the Korean Industries (생략 FKI). ～대회 《정당의》 a national convention; 《스포츠의》 a national athletic meet: ～체육대회 the National Sports [Athletic] Meet / ～ 대회를 열다 hold a national meeting [conference]. ～방송 a broadcast on a national network [hookup]; a national network broadcast; 《방송 프로》 a nationwide program. ～소년체전 the National Children's Sport's Meet. ～중계 (방송) a nationwide hookup. ～지(紙) a newspaper with nationwide circulation. ～체전 the National Games: 제80차 ～체전 the 80th National Games.

**전국**(戰局) the war situation; the state [aspect] of the war; the progress of the war; the tide of war. ¶ ～이 바뀌다 the war situation changes / ～은 일진일퇴이다 The war situations hang in the balance. / 그것으로 ～은 일변했다 That turned the tide of the war.

**전국구**(全國區) the national constituency; the Nation-wide Proportional Seats. ¶ 당의 ～ 지명자 순위 14번 the 14th slot on the list of the party's national constituency nominees. ◉ ～의원 a National Assembly Member on a Nation-wide Proportional Seat; a member of the National Assembly elected from the national constituency. ～제 the national constituency system. ～후보자 명단 the national constituency list.

**전국민**(全國民) the whole [entire] nation. ¶ ～의 national; nationwide / 그 사건은 ～의 주목을 끌었다 The incident attracted national [nationwide] attention.

**전국시대**(戰國時代) the Age of Wars; the turbulent age [period]; 《중국사》 the Age of the Warring States.

**전군**(全軍) 《군대의》 the whole army [force]. ¶ ～을 지휘하다 command the whole army.

**전권**(全卷) 《전집류의》 a complete set 《of the encyclopedia》; 《한 권 전체》 the entire [whole] volume; 《영화의》 the whole reel. ¶ 이광수 전집～ a set of complete works of Lee Kwang=su / ～을 통독하다 read the book from cover to cover; read through the book.

**전권**(全權) plenary [full] power; plenipotentiary power; absolute authority [power]; 《백지 위임》 *carte blanche* (F.). ¶ ～을 위임하다 invest [entrust] 《*a person*》 with full power 《to *do*》 / ～을 장악하다 hold full power 《over》 / 회사의 ～을 잡다 hold absolute power over the company / 그는 조약 개정에

관한 ~을 갖고 미국에 갔다 He went to America with full power to revise the treaty. ◉ ~공사 a minister plenipotentiary. ~대사 an ambassador plenipotentiary: 특명~대사 an ambassador extraordinary and plenipotentiary. ~위원 a plenipotentiary. ~위임장 a commission of full power.

**전권**(前卷) the preceding volume.

**전권**(專權) an exclusive right; arbitrary power. ~하다 exercise arbitrary power.

**전극**(電極) 〖전기〗 an electrode; a pole.

**전근**(轉勤) transference 《to another office》. ~하다 get 〔be〕 transferred 《to another office》. ¶ 부산 지점으로 ~되다 be transferred to the Pusan branch.

**전근**(轉筋) a cramp 《in the leg》; a charley-horse 《미구어》.

**전근대적**(前近代的) premodern. ¶ ~사고 방식 a premodern way of thinking.

**전기**(前記) ¶ ~의 above-mentioned; aforementioned; referred to above; 《the》 said 《*person*》; foregoing / ~의 금액 the said sum / ~의 사람들 the persons above-named / ~와 같이 as above-mentioned; as said 〔stated〕 above / ~와 같은 사정이오니 such being the case / ~ 장소로 이전하다 move to the above address / ~한 것은 몇 가지 보기에 불과하다 The foregoing are only a few of the instances.

**전기**(前期) ① 《첫번째의》 the first term; the first half year (상반기); the first semester (학기의); 〖생물〗 the prophase. ② 《앞서의》 the earlier term; the recent 〔last, latest〕 term.
◉ ~결산 settlement for the first half year. ~국회 the last session of the National Assembly. ~대학 the first-group universities 〔colleges〕; universities 〔colleges〕 in the first (screening) group. ~시험 the first semester exams. ~이월금 the balance brought over from the last account. ~총회 the last session of the general meeting.

**전기**(傳奇) ① 《소설·희곡》 a novel; a romance. ② 《세상에 전하기》 disclosing to the world 〔writing up〕 a strange 〔a curious〕 matter.

**전기**(傳記) a biography; a life (story). ¶ ~의 biographical / 슈바이처 ~ a life (story) of Albert Schweitzer. ◉ ~물 〔문학〕 biographical writings 〔literature〕. ~소설 a fictionalized 〔fictional〕 biography. ~작가 a biographer.

**전기**(電氣) 〖전기〗 electricity; an electric light (전등); an electric current (전류). ¶ ~의 electric; electrical; [연결형] electro- (★ electric은 「전기성(性)의」, electrical은 「전기에 관한」이란 뜻임. 그러나 electrical은 electric과 같은 뜻으로 쓰이기도 함. 전기에 관한 학문·기계 등의 용어에는 electro-라는 연결형을 쓰는 경우가 많음) / ~를 켜다 put 〔switch, turn〕 on the (electric) light / ~를 끄다 switch off 〔put out, turn out〕 the (electric) light (★ 최근에는 「전등」의 뜻인 경우에도 electric을 생략하고 그냥 the light라 하는 것이 보통임. 「전차」의 경우도 마찬가지로 the train이라고 하는 경우가 많음) / ~를 일으키다 generate electricity / 취사는 모두 ~로 한다 We do all our cooking by electricity. / 이 전선에는 ~가 통해 있다 This wire is 「live 〔charged with electricity〕. / 이 기계는 가정용~로 작동된다 This machine operates on domestic current 〔voltage〕.
◉ ~감응 electric induction. ~검사〔검침〕원 an electricity checker 〔inspector〕. ~경보기 an electric alarm. ~계기(計器) an electric meter. ~계량기 a voltameter. ~계통 an electrical system. ~공(工) an electrician. ~공사 electric work. ~공업 the electric industry. ~공학 electrical engineering; electrotechnology. ~광학 electro-optics. ~기계 an electric machine. ~기관차 an electric locomotive. ~기구 an electric appliance; electrical apparatus (공업·실험용의): 가정용 ~기구 household electric appliance / ~(기구)상점 an electric appliance store 〔shop〕. ~기사 an electrical engineer. ~기타 〖악기〗 an electric guitar. ~난로 an electric heater 〔stove〕. ~난방 electric heating. ~냉장고 an electric refrigerator 〔freezer〕. ~다리미〔담요, 시계〕 an electric iron 〔blanket, clock〕. ~도금 electrogilding (금의); electroplating (은의): ~ 도금을 하다 electroplate; galvanize. ~도체 an electric conductor. ~도화선(導火線) an electric fuse. ~동(銅) electrolytic copper. ~동력계 an electrodynamometer. ~드릴 an electric drill. ~량 the quantity of electricity. ~레인지 an electric range. ~로(爐) an electric furnace. ~마사지 electromassage. ~마취 electronarcosis. ~메스 a radio knife (외과용). ~면도기 an electric

shaver 〔razor〕. ~발동기 an electromotor. ~밥솥 an electric rice-cooker. ~방사〔방사기〕 electric radiation 〔radiator〕. ~방석 a heating pad. ~뱀장어 〖어류〗 an electric eel. ~분석 electroanalysis. ~분해 electrolysis: ~ 분해물 an electrolyte. ~사업 the electrical industry; electric enterprises. ~사형 electrocution. ~삼투 electroosmosis. ~석 〖광물〗 tourmalin. ~설비 electric installation 〔equipment〕. ~세탁기 an electric washing machine 〔washer〕. ~스탠드 a desk lamp. ~야금(학) electrometallurgy. ~역학 electrodynamics. ~요금 electric charges 〔rates〕; power rates. ~요법 electrotherapy; electropathy; electrical treatment. ~용광〔용접〕 electric smelting 〔welding〕. ~의자 an electric chair; a hot seat 《속어》: ~ 의자에 앉다 be electrocuted; get the chair 《미구어》/ ~ 의자에 앉히다 electrocute; send 《a prisoner》 to the chair. ~이발기 an electric hair clipper. ~자동차 a battery 〔an electric〕 car; an electromobile. ~자석 an electromagnet. ~장치 an electric device: ~ 장치의 operated 〔worked〕 by electricity; electric. ~재봉틀 an electrical sewing machine. ~저항 electric resistance: ~저항계 an ohmmeter. ~전도 electric(al) conduction. ~절연〔절연체〕 electric insulation 〔insulator〕. ~제어 electric control. ~제품 an electric appliance 〔apparatus〕. ~조각 electroengraving. ~조명 electric illumination. ~(진공)청소기 an electric vacuum cleaner. ~집진기 (集塵機) an electric 〔electrostatic〕 precipitator. ~철도 an electric railroad. ~충격 an electric shock. ~침 an electric needle (외과용). ~타이머 《수영 경기 등의》 an automatic (touch) timer 〔timing machine〕. ~토스터 an electric toaster. ~톱 a power saw. ~통신 electro communication: 한국(~)통신 (공사) the Korea Telecom(munication Authority) (생략 Korea Telecom) / 한국 ~ 통신 연구소 the Korea Electrotechnology and Telecommunication Research Institute. ~판〔판술〕 〖인쇄〗 an electrotype 〔electrotypy〕. ~표백(법) electric 〔electrolytic〕 bleaching. ~풍로 an electric cooking stove. ~학 electrology; the science of electricity. ~합성 〖화학〗 electrosynthesis. ~해리(解離) ionization. ~화학 electrochemistry. ~회로 an electric circuit. ~회사 an electric(al) company. 공중~ atmospheric electricity. 화력~ steam power electricity.

**전기**(電機) electrical machinery and appliances; electrical equipment 〔supplies〕. ◉ ~공업 electrical equipment 〔machinery〕 industry.

**전기**(戰記) a record of war; an account of war; a military history. ¶ 태평양~ a history of the Pacific War.

**전기**(戰機) the time for fighting 〔battle〕. ¶ ~가 무르익다 The time for fighting is now ripe.

**전기**(轉記) 〖부기〗 posting. ~하다 post 《an item》. ¶ 대장(臺帳)에 ~하다 post in the ledger.

**전기**(轉機) a turning point; a point of change. ¶ 생애의 ~ the turning point in *one's* life / …을 ~로 하여 with... as a turning point / ~에 서다〔처하다〕 be on 〔at〕 a turning point / 정국(政局)의 ~를 만들다 make a turning point in the political situation / 이것은 나에게 일생의 큰 ~가 될 것이다 This is going to be a major turning point in my life. / 석유 파동은 우리나라 산업계에 하나의 큰 ~였다 The oil crises were an important turning point for the industrial world of our country.

**전기료**(電氣料) electric(al) charges 〔rates〕.

**전깃불**(電氣—) = 전등(電燈).

**전나무** 〖식물〗 a fir (tree).

**전날**(前—) the previous 〔preceding〕 day; the day before; 《과거의 어느 날》 the other day; some 〔a few〕 days ago. ¶ 크리스마스 ~ the day before Christmas / 불이 난 ~ 밤에 on the evening before the fire broke out / ~의 약속을 잊지 마라 Don't forget what you promised the other day.

**전남편**(前男便) *one's* ex-husband; *one's* former 〔divorced, late〕 husband.

**전납**(全納) payment in full; full payment. ⇨ 완납. ~하다 pay in full.

**전납**(前納) payment in advance. = 예납(豫納).

**전내기**(全—) 《물 타지 않은》 pure 〔undiluted〕 liquor.

**전내기**(廛—) ready-made goods; goods for the market.

**전년**(前年) 《작년》 last year; 《지나간 해》 past years; former years; the other year; a few years ago. ¶ 그 ~ the year before / ~ 여름 in the previous summer / 전쟁이 일어나기 ~ the last prewar year. ◉ ~도 the previous 《fiscal》 year.

**전념**(專念) undivided attention; concentration of mind. ～하다 concentrate (*one's* mind 〔thoughts〕) 《on》; devote *oneself* 《to》; be absorbed 《in》; be intent 《on》; apply *oneself* closely 《to》. ¶ 공부에 ～하다 put *one's* heart and soul into *one's* studies; give *oneself* to study / 생업에 ～하다 work hard to get a living / 그는 연구에 ～했다 He was absorbed 〔lost〕 in his research. *or* He gave himself up to his research.

**전뇌**(前腦) 〖해부〗 the forebrain; the prosencephalon.

**전능**(全能) omnipotence. ～하다 (be) almighty; all-powerful; omnipotent. ¶ 전지～한 omniscient and omnipotent / ～한 신 the Almighty; Almighty God.

**전능력**(全能力) *one's* full ability 〔capacity〕; all *one's* ability. ¶ ～을 기울여 with the utmost effort; to the best of *one's* ability; at full capacity / 일에 ～을 기울이다 train 〔bend, channel〕 all *one's* ability into a task.

**전단**(全段) 《신문의》 a whole page; the whole space. ◉ ～표제 a banner (headline); a bannerline.

**전단**(專斷) arbitrary decision; arbitrariness. ～하다 act high-handedly; do 〔manage〕 arbitrarily. ¶ ～으로 arbitrarily; at *one's* own discretion; on *one's* own authority 〔responsibility〕 / ～적 조치 an arbitrary measure 〔act〕 / ～적 조치를 취하다 act arbitrarily 〔on *one's* own authority〕.

**전단**(傳單) a bill; a leaflet; a handbill. ¶ ～을 뿌리다 distribute handbills 〔leaflets〕; drop leaflets 《from a plane》; broadcast leaflets / ～을 붙이다 put up a poster; stick 〔paste up〕 a bill.

**전단**(戰端) the cause of war; the opening of hostilities; hostile operations; hostilities. ¶ ～을 열다 open hostilities; go to war 《with》; make war 《on》; take up arms against.

**전달**(前—) 《지난달》 last month; 《전의 달》 the preceding 〔previous〕 month.

**전달**(傳達) delivery; transmission; communication; notification. ～하다 deliver; pass on; transmit; convey; communicate; notify. ¶ 음향의 ～ traveling of sound / 명령을 ～하다 serve 《*a person*》 with an order / 취지를 정부에 ～하다 communicate the purport to the government / 소리의 ～은 빛보다 느리다 Sound travels slower than light. / 그에게 곧 오도록 ～하여 주시오 Tell him to come at once.
◉ ～경로 an avenue of communication. ～사항 a message; information to be conveyed 《to》. ～속도 《전파·음향의》 velocity of propagation; propagation velocity. ～수단 a means of communication. ～자 a messenger.

**전담**(全擔) the whole responsibility; complete charge. ～하다 take 〔assume, bear〕 complete 〔full〕 charge of; be wholly responsible for. ¶ 비용을 ～하다 be charged with the whole expenses.

**전담**(專擔) exclusive responsibility 〔charge〕. ～하다 take 〔bear, assume〕 exclusive charge 〔responsibility〕 《of》; be wholly 〔exclusively〕 responsible 《for》. ¶ 소매치기 ～반(班) a pickpocket squad.

**전답**(田畓) dry fields and paddy fields.

**전당**(典當) pawning; pledge. ¶ ～을 잡히다 give 〔put〕 《*a thing*》 in pawn; pawn, pledge / ～을 잡다 take 《*a thing*》 in pawn 〔pledge〕; hold 《*a thing*》 in pledge / ～에 잡혀 있다 be in 〔at〕 pawn; be in hock 《미속어》 / 그는 외투를 만 원에 ～잡혔다 He pledged his overcoat for ten thousand won.
◉ ～물〔품〕 a pawned article; an article placed in pawn: ～물을 찾다 redeem a thing in pledge / ～물이 유질(流質)되다 be forfeited. ～포 a pawnshop; a pawnbroker's (shop); 《미구어》 a hock shop: 공설 ～포 a public pawnshop / ～포업 pawnbroking / ～포 업자 a pawnbroker / ～포에 드나들다 frequent a pawnshop. ～표 a pawn ticket.

**전당**(殿堂) 《궁전》 a palace; 《신전》 a sanctuary; 《사원》 a temple; a shrine. ¶ 학문의 ～ a sanctuary of learning / 예술의 ～ a sanctuary of the fine arts.

**전당대회**(全黨大會) the national convention 《of a party》. ¶ 1999년도 민주당 ～ the 1999 Democratic Party Convention.

**전대**(前代) 《이전의 세대》 the previous generation; 《이전의 시대》 the last period.

**전대**(戰隊) a battle corps; a 《naval》 squadron. ¶ 수뢰～ a torpedo boat flotilla.

**전대**(轉貸) sublease; underlease. ～하

다《토지를》sublease; underlease;《가옥을》sublet; subrent. ¶ 가옥을 ～하다 sublet a house. ◉ ～인 a sublessor. ～차(借) subletting and subleasing.

**전대**(纏帶)《허리에 차는》a money belt.

**전대미문**(前代未聞) ¶ ～의 unheard-of 〔unparalleled〕 in history; unprecedented / ～의 대재난 an unprecedented calamity / 역사상 ～의 사건 an event unparalleled 〔an unheard-of〕 event in history.

**전대야** a brimmed washbasin.

**전도**(全島) the entire 〔whole〕 island. ¶ ～에 all over 〔throughout〕 the island.

**전도**(全道) the whole province. ¶ ～에 all over 〔throughout〕 the province.

**전도**(全圖) a complete diagram 〔drawing〕; a whole 〔complete〕 map. ◉ 서울〔대한민국〕～ a complete map of Seoul 〔Korea〕. 세계～ a world map.

**전도**(前途)《여정》the distance to be covered《on a journey》; the road before *one;*《장래》*one's* future;《전망》prospects; an outlook. ¶ ～ 유망한 청년 a promising 〔hopeful〕 youth; a young hopeful / ～가 유망하다 have a bright future 〔prospects〕《before *one*》/ ～가 요원하다 have a long way to go; be far off / ～가 암담하다 have a gloomy prospects / ～를 그르치다 spoil 〔ruin〕 *one's* career 〔future〕 / ～를 근심하다 be anxious about *one's* future / ～를 축복하다 wish《*a person*》success 〔a happy future〕 / ～를 내다보다 see *one's* future / 너에게는 ～가 있다 Life lies in front of you. / 우리의 ～는 다난하다 Our future is full of difficulties.

**전도**(前渡)《돈의》payment in advance;《물품의》delivery in advance. ◉ ～금 an advance; an advancement.

**전도**(前導) leading the way; guidance. ～하다 lead; guide. ◉ ～자 a guide; a leader.

**전도**(傳道) gospel preaching; evangelical work; missions; mission work; evangelism. ～하다 engage in mission work; evangelize; preach the gospel; propagate *one's* religion. ¶ 기독교를 ～하다 engage in Christian mission work. ◉ ～부인 a bible woman; a lady evangelist. ～사 a preacher; a missionary; an evangelist. ～사업 missionary work. ～서 『성서』(The Book of ) Ecclesiastes. ～여행 an evangelical tour.

**전도**(傳導) 『물리』 conduction《of heat, electricity》; transmission《of sound, light, momentum》; drive《of automotive power》. ～하다 conduct; transmit. ¶ 열을 ～하다 conduct heat / 전선은 전기를 ～한다 Wires transmit electricity. ◉ ～기 an intermedium. ～력〔율, -성〕 conductivity. ～체 a conductor; a transmitter: 부～체 a nonconductor / 초～체 a superconductor.

**전도**(顚倒)《엎드러짐》falling down; a fall; an upset;《거꾸로》turning upside-down; overturning; upsetting. ～하다《…이》fall (down); overturn; tumble;《…을》turn upside down; reverse; invert. ¶ 본말을 ～하다 put the cart before the horse; mistake the means for the end; invert the order; get *one's* priority wrong.

**전동**(電動) electric motion; electromotion. ¶ ～식의 electrically-powered 〔-driven, -run〕《machines》; electric《typewriters》. ◉ ～개폐기 a motor-operated switch. ～공구 an electric tool. ～기 an electric motor; a motor; an electromotor: ～기 부하〔회로〕 a motor-load〔-circuit〕/ 교류〔직류〕 ～기 an alternating 〔a direct〕 current motor; an AC 〔a DC〕 motor. ～력 electromotive force. ～발전기 a motor dynamo 〔generator〕. ～자(子) an amature. ～차 an electric railcar.

**전동**(傳動)《장치》gearing; transmission; drive. ～하다 gear; drive. ◉ ～나사 a drive screw.

**전동**(箭筒) a quiver (for arrows).

**전두**(前頭) the forehead; 『해부』 the sinciput. ◉ ～골 the frontal bone. ～엽 the frontal lobe.

**전두리** the circumference of a rim; the edge of a rim《of jar 〔lid〕》.

**전등**(電燈) an electric lamp 〔light〕. (★ 자명한 경우는 단순히 a light, 또는 a lamp로 하는 것이 보통임). ¶ 밝은 ～빛 bright lamplight / ～을 달다 install electric lights; have electric lights installed / ～을 켜다〔끄다〕 turn on 〔turn off 〕 the light / ～이 밝다〔어둡다〕 The light is bright 〔dim〕. / 갑자기 ～이 꺼졌다 Suddenly the light went out. / 그는 ～을 켜 놓은 채 잠들었다 He went asleep with the light on. / ～이 켜져 있을 때는 이 문은 열리지 않습니다《게시》When light on, this door closed. ◉ ～갓 a lampshade.

**전라**(全裸) total nudity; stark nakedness. ¶ ～의 stark-naked; absolutely nude / ～의 몸으로 stark-naked; with nothing on; in the altogether / ～가 되다 strip *oneself* of everything; be stripped stark naked / ～로 수영하다 swim in the nude; swim with nothing on; skinny-dip《구어》.

**전락**(轉落)《나쁜 처지에 빠짐》a downfall; a fall; degradation (타락). ～하다 fall; degrade; be「degraded〔reduced〕; degenerate《into》. ¶ 3위로 ～하다 slide down to third place / 그는 거지로 ～했다 He degenerated into a beggar. / 그 정부는 이미 하나의 지방 정권으로 ～했다 The Government has already been reduced to a local government.
◉ ～자 a「fallen〔dissolute〕person.

**전란**(戰亂) strife; the disturbances of war. ¶ ～통 times of strife / ～의 위협 the threat of war / ～의 아시아 war-torn〔war-shattered〕Asia / ～의 도가니 the「scene〔seat〕of「war〔hostilities〕; a scene of deadly strife and carnage / ～이 일어나다 a war breaks out. ◉ 대～ a great war.

**전람**(展覽) exhibition; show(ing); display. ～하다 exhibit; show; display; put〔place〕《*a thing*》on display.
◉ ～물 exhibits. ～실 a showroom; a salon《미》. ～회 an〔a public〕exhibition; a show: ～회에 출품하다 exhibit an article in an exhibition / ～회를 열다 hold an exhibition / ～회장 an exhibition gallery.

**전래**(傳來) transmission (조상으로부터); introduction (외국으로부터). ～하다 get transmitted; be handed down; be introduced; be imported; be brought in. ¶ 조상 ～의 가보 an heirloom; patrimonial goods / 한국 ～의 의술 traditional Korean「medicine〔medical practices〕/ 신유행의 ～ the introduction of a new fashion / 불교는 중국에서 한국에 ～됐다 Buddhism was introduced into Korea from China. / 이것은 조상 ～의 가보이다 This is our family treasure handed down from generations.

**전략**(前略) heading omitted; omission of what precedes. ～하다 omit the preface. ¶ ～하옵고《편지에서》「I hasten〔Just a line〕to inform you that... (★ 영미인의 편지에는 우리처럼 편지 서두에 으레 들어가는 계절·안부에 관한 인사 치레의 말없이, 바로 용건으로 들어가는 것이 일반적이다. 인사말을 생략한다는 뜻의「전략하옵고…」란 표현은 영어에는 없다).

**전략**(戰略) (a) strategy; a stratagem. ¶ ～상(으로 보아) from the strategical point of view; strategically / ～적(인) strategic / ～적 후퇴〔지점〕a strategic「retreat〔point〕/ ～을 써서 by stratagem / ～상의 목적으로 for strategic purposes / ～으로 이기다 outgeneral〔outmaneuver〕《a *person*》/ ～을 꾸미다 elaborate〔plan〕a strategy / ～을 세우다 map〔work, think〕out *one's* strategy; devise a stratagem.
◉ ～가 a strategist. ～공군 a strategic air force: ～ 공군 사령부《미》the Strategic Air Command (생략 SAC). ～목표 a strategic target. ～무기 strategic arms: ～ 무기 감축 회담 the Strategic Arms Reduction Talks (생략 START) / ～무기 제한회담 Strategic Arms Limitation Talks (생략 SALT). ～무역정책 a strategic trade policy. ～물자 strategic goods. ～방위구상 the Strategic Defense Initiative (생략 SDI). ～산업 a strategic industry: ～산업으로서 집중적으로 육성되다 be intensively fostered as strategic industries. ～수립자 a strategy-maker. ～수출품목 a strategic export item. ～이론 strategic theory. ～폭격 strategic bombing: ～ 폭격기 a strategic bomber. ～핵무기 a strategic nuclear weapon. ～회의 a strategy meeting.
국제～연구소 International Institute for Strategic Studies (생략 IISS).

**전량**(全量) the whole quantity.

**전량**(錢糧) money and provisions.

**전량계**(電量計) a coulometer; a voltameter.

**전력**(全力) all *one's*「strength〔might, power〕; all *one's* energies; *one's*「best〔utmost〕. ¶ ～을 다하다 do *one's*「best〔utmost〕; do all *one* can; do everything in *one's* power; exert *oneself* to the utmost;《구어》go all out / ～을 다하여 with all *one's* might; with might and main; to the best of *one's* ability / …에 ～을 기울이다 devote all *one's* energies to...; give body and soul to...; concentrate *one's* energies on... / 학생은 공부에 ～을 기울여야만 한다 Students should devote their best efforts to their studies. / 그는 ～ 투구로 시험 준비를 하고 있다 He is devoting all his energy to preparing for the exam.

**전력**(前歷) *one's*「past〔previous〕record; *one's* personal history; *one's* antecedents. ¶ ～을 조사하다 inquire into《*a person's*》past record / 그의 ～은 공무원이었다 He once served in a government office. / 그녀는 매우 다채로운 ～의 소유자다 She has had a very 「varied 〔checkered〕 career. / 그녀가 어떤 ～을 가진 사람인지 알고 싶다 I would like to know something about her (past) 「career 〔background〕.

**전력**(電力) electric 「power 〔energy〕; electricity; power. ¶ ～(의) 낭비〔절약〕 waste 〔economy〕 of electric power / 10만 마력의 ～ 100,000 electrical horsepower / ～을 공급하다 supply (electric) power / 그 기계는 대단히 많은 ～을 소비한다 That machine consumes an enormous amount of power.
◉ ～개발 electrical power development. ～계 a wattmeter. ～공급 (the) supply of electric power; (the) power supply. ～공사 power supply works. ～공업 an electric power industry. ～기근 power famine. ～부족 an electric power shortage; a short supply of electricity: ～부족의 power-short 《areas》 / 5년 이내에 심각한 ～ 부족이 있을 것이다 There will be a serious power shortage within five years. ～사정〔요금〕 the (electric) power condition 〔rates〕. ～생산 electric power production: 수력 발전에 의한 ～ 생산량 hydroelectric power output. ～선 a power line. ～소비 power consumption: ～ 소비는 여름철에 절정에 이른다 Power consumption peaks in summer. ～수요 (the) demand for (electric) power 〔for electricity〕. ～자원 (electric) power resources. ～제한 power restrictions. ～채 electric power (company) bonds. ～통제 power control. ～학 electrodynamics. ～회사 a 〔an electric〕 power company. 한국～공사 the Korea Electric Power Corporation (생략 KEPOC).

**전력**(戰力) military strength; fighting power; war 「potential 〔capacity, power, capability〕. ¶ ～의 증강 the 「strengthening 〔build-up〕 of war potential / ～ 없는 군대 troops 〔an army〕 without war potential / ～은 조금씩 증강되고 있다 「Military strength 〔War potential〕 is being built up little by little. ◉ ～유지〔상실〕 the 「maintenance 〔loss〕 of war potential. 미사일～ missile capability.

**전력**(戰歷) a battle record; a war record 〔career〕; *one's* 「war experience 〔combat career〕. ¶ 많은 ～을 가진 군인 a soldier of many campaigns.

**전령**(傳令) a written official order; an official message; 《사람》 a messenger; an orderly. ～하다 convey 〔deliver〕 an official message. ¶ ～을 보내다 send a message; send an orderly.
◉ ～근무 an orderly duty. 기마～ a cavalry orderly.

**전령**(電鈴) an electric bell. ¶ ～을 울리다 ring an electric bell.

**전례**(典禮) a ceremony; a ritual. ◉ ～주의 ritualism.

**전례**(前例) a precedent; a previous 「example 〔instance〕. ¶ ～없는 unprecedented 《matter》 / ～에 의해서 according to precedent / ～에 반해서 against precedent / ～가 되다 give precedent 《for》; become a precedent / ～를 깨뜨리다 violate 〔depart from〕 precedents / ～로 삼다 take 《*a thing*》 as a precedent / ～를 따르다 follow a precedent / 이것에 관해서는 ～가 전혀 없다 There is no precedent for this.

**전로**(轉爐) 〖야금〗 a revolving furnace; a converter. ◉ ～강 converter steel.

**전류**(電流) an electric current; a current of electricity. ¶ ～가 통한 철망 live wire; wire charged with electricity / ～의 역류 reversal of current / ～를 통하다 send an electric current 《to》; charge 《*a thing*》 with electricity / ～를 끊다 cut 〔shut〕 off the current; switch off / 이 선에는 ～가 흐르고 있다 This wire is live (with electricity).
◉ ～계 a galvanometer; an amperemeter; an ammeter. ～단위 a current unit. ～밀도 current density. ～전환기 a commutator. ～제한기〔차단기〕 a current 「limiter 〔breaker〕. ～증폭기 an electric current amplifier. ～측정 current measuring; galvanometry. ～표시기 an electric current indicator. ～학 galvanism. ●고압 ～ a high voltage current. 교류〔대류, 전도, 직류〕～ 「an alternating 〔a convection, a conduction, a direct〕 current.

**전륜**(前輪) a front wheel. ◉ ～구동 front-wheel drive (생략 FWD): ～구동차 a front-wheel-drive car.

**전리**(電離) 〖물리〗 ionization; electrolytic dissociation. ～하다 ionize. ◉ ～압력계 an ionization gauge. ～장치 an ionizer. ～층 the ionosphere.

**전리품**(戰利品) a war trophy; 《약탈품》 booty; spoils of war.

**전립선**(前立腺) 〖해부〗 the prostate (gland). ◉ ～비대 enlargement of the prostate gland. ～염 prostatitis.

**전마선**(傳馬船) a lighter.

**전말**(顚末) 《사정》 the circumstances; 《상세》 the particulars; the details; 《사실》 the facts; 《경위》 the course of events. ¶ 사건의 ～을 말하다 give an account of the accident / 사직하게 된 ～을 설명하다 explain the circumstance which led to *one's* resignation / ～을 자세히 보고하다 report all the circumstances in detail.
◉ ～서 a report; an account.

**전망**(展望) a view; a prospect; an outlook. ～하다 have a view 《of》; view; look out 《upon, over》.
¶ 정치계의 ～ a view of the political world / 앞으로의 ～ the future prospect / 산정에서의 ～ a view from the mountain top / ～이 좋다 have a good prospect; have 〔command〕 a fine view 《of the sea》 / 서울 전시가지를 ～하다 have a panoramic view of the whole city of Seoul / ～을 방해하다 obstruct the view 《of》 / ～이 밝다 The prospects are bright. / ～이 흐리다 The prospects are discouraging. *or* The future is gloomy. *or* It presents a gloomy outlook. / 이 사업은 ～이 좋지 않다 This enterprise has no future.
◉ ～대 an observatory; an observation platform. ～차 an observation car; a parlor car. ～탑 an observation tower; 《잠수함의》 a conning tower.

**전맞춤**(廛—) special-order goods; goods that have to be ordered from the factory.

**전매**(專賣) a monopoly; monopolization. ～하다 monopolize; make a monopoly 《of》; hold a monopoly 《for tobacco》. ¶ 술을 정부의 ～로 하다 make the sale of liquor a government monopoly. ◉ ～권 monopoly; exclusive right(s): 정부는 소금의 ～권을 갖고 있었다 The Government held the monopoly in salt. ～사업 the monopoly enterprise. ～제도 the monopoly system. ～주의 monopolism. ～청 《administrator of》 the Office of Monopoly. ～품 monopoly goods; monopolies.

**전매**(轉賣) (a) resale. ～하다 resell. ¶ ～할 수 있는 resalable / 불법 주택 ～ illegal housing sales.

**전매특허**(專賣特許) a patent. ⇨ 특허(特許)③.

**전면**(全面) 《전체의 면》 the whole 〔entire〕 surface 〔page〕. ¶ ～적 all-out; overall; general; full-scale / ～적인 개정 a sweeping 〔an overall〕 change 〔revision〕 / ～적 통제 full control / ～적으로 generally; extensively; in a wholesale way / ～에 걸쳐 all over the surface / ～적으로 지지하다 give solid 〔wholehearted〕 support to 《*a person*》; 《지면 전부》 the whole 〔entire〕 page / 전쟁 발발의 뉴스가 신문 제1면의 ～을 가득 채웠다 The news of the outbreak of the war filled the whole front page of the newspaper.
◉ ～강화 an all-out 〔overall〕 peace. ～공격 《launch》 an all-out attack. ～광고 a full-page advertisement. ～전쟁 《develop into》 an all-out war; a general 〔full-scale, total〕 war; the global war. ～파업 an overall strike. ～핵전쟁 an all-out nuclear war.

**전면**(前面) the front (side 〔part〕); the frontage; 《건물의》 the facade. ¶ ～에 in front 《of》; in the foreground / ～의 적 the enemy in front / ～을 돌로 장식하다 be fronted with stone.
◉ ～공격 a frontal attack.

**전멸**(全滅) (suffering) total destruction; 《절멸》 annihilation; extermination; extirpation. ～하다 get annihilated; be totally destroyed; be wiped out; be exterminated. ¶ ～시키다 annihilate; totally destroy; wipe out / ～할 각오로 싸우다 fight to the last (man) / 마을은 해일로 ～하였다 The village was wiped out by tsunami. / 연대는 ～했다 The whole regiment was annihilated. / 우리 부대는 적의 공격을 받고 ～했다 Our unit has suffered a crushing defeat under the attack of the enemy.

**전모**(全貌) the whole aspect; the full picture 《of》. ¶ ～를 밝히다 give the entire picture; bare the whole picture 《of》; get the full story 《of》; reveal in its entirety / 그것으로 사건의 ～가 밝혀졌다 It throws light upon the whole affair. / 나는 그 사건의 ～를 알고 싶다 I want to know all about the affair. / 사건의 ～를 밝히는 것은 결국 불가능하였다 It was impossible, in the end, to bring the whole affair to light.

**전몰**(戰歿) death in battle. ～하다 die 〔be killed〕 in battle. ◉ ～용사 fallen heroes. ～자〔장병〕 《개인》 a fallen soldier; the war dead [총칭]: ～자 기념비 a war memorial.

**전무**(全無) total nonexistence; total

lack; total absence. ~하다 be wholly lacking 〔wanting〕; do not exist 〔cannot be found〕 at all. ¶ 나는 법률 지식이라고는 ~합니다 I have not the least knowledge of law. / 구인 광고를 냈으나 응모자가 ~했다 Nobody applied for the job we advertised. / 이 계획은 성공할 가망이 ~하다 This plan doesn't have any chance of success.

**전무**(專務) ① 《사무》 exclusive 〔special〕 duty; principal business. ② 《사람》 an executive 〔a managing〕 director. ◉ ~이사 ⇨ 전무(專務) ②.

**전무후무**(前無後無) the unprecedented 〔unparalleled〕 in history; the unheard-of; record-breaking; the unique; the epoch-making. ~하다 be never heard 〔seen〕 before or since; (be) unprecedented; unparalleled; unheard-of; unique. ¶ ~한 대발견 an epoch-making discovery / ~한 대전쟁 the greatest war on record / (…은) ~한 일이다 It is the first and probably the last (that…).

**전문**(全文) the full text 《of an address》; a whole statement 〔sentence〕. ¶ 조약의 ~ the full text of a treaty / ~을 인용하다 quote 《a letter》 in full 〔in its entirety〕.

**전문**(前文) the above (passage); the foregoing remark; 《조약 따위의》 a preamble 《to, of》.

**전문**(前門) a front gate.

**전문**(專門) a specialty 《미》; a speciality 《영》; a special subject of study. ¶ ~적〔의〕 special; 《기술상》 technical; 《직업상》 professional; expert / ~으로 specially; professionally; technically / ~적인 지식 expert 〔technical〕 knowledge / 심장 ~의 a heart specialist / ~으로 하다 make a specialty of 《importing liquors》 / ~으로 연구하다 make a special study 《of》; specialize 《in》 / 경제학은 나의 ~이다 Economics is my particular line. / 그것은 나의 ~이 아니다 It is out of my field. *or* It is not in my line. / 그의 ~은 화학이다 His specialty is chemistry. *or* He majors in chemistry. / 이 회사는 농기구를 ~으로 만들고 있다 This company specializes in making agricultural machines.
◉ ~가 a specialist; an expert; 《아마추어에 대하여》 a 《golf》 professional. ~과목 a specialized subject. ~교육 (a) technical 〔professional〕 education; professional 〔specialized〕 instruction. ~기술 expert skill. ~대학 a (junior) college: 공업 ~대학 a junior college of technology; a technical junior college. ~분야 a 〔*one's*〕 (special) field (of study); *one's* line 〔field〕: 너의 ~ 분야는 무엇이지 What do you specialize in? *or* What is your (special) field? ~서적 a technical book. ~어 a technical term; [총칭] (technical) terminology. ~위원 an expert advisor; a technical expert. ~의 a medical specialist: 안과 ~의 an eye specialist; an oculist. ~점 a specialty store; a store specializing in 《computers》. ~지 a technical journal 〔magazine〕. ~지식 expert 〔technical〕 knowledge; expertise: 이것을 충분히 이해하려면 원자물리학에 관한 ~ 지식이 필요하다 To understand it fully requires a special knowledge of nuclear physics. ~학교 a special 〔vocational〕 school; a college. ~화 specialization: ~화하다 specialize.

**전문**(電文) 《문구》 the message 〔text〕 of a telegram; 《전보》 a telegram; a telegraphic message.

**전문**(傳聞) hearsay; a report; a rumor. ~하다 hear from others; hear as a rumor; learn by hearsay; know by report; be told. ¶ ~한 바에 의하면 from what I hear; according to a rumor 〔report〕; I hear that….
◉ ~증거 hearsay evidence. ~증인 a hearsay witness.

**전물**(奠物) offerings 《to gods, to Buddha》.

**전미**(全美) the entire United States; all America; the whole of America. ¶ ~선수권 an all-American championship.

**전박**(前膊) a forearm.

**전반**(全般) the whole. ¶ ~의 whole; general; overall / ~에 걸쳐 generally; by and large; across the board / 국민〔사회〕 ~ the people 〔world〕 at large / 과학 ~에 걸치다 cover the whole field 〔range〕 of science / … ~에 걸쳐 연구하다 make a general study 《of》; study 《a subject》 in all its bearings 〔aspects〕 / 심리학 ~에 걸쳐 연구하다 make a comprehensive study of psychology / 일을 ~에 걸쳐 환히 알다 have the whole gamut of business at *one's* fingers' ends.

**전반**(前半) the first half; 《축구 따위의》 the first period. ¶ 1980년대 ~ the early 1980's / 20세기 ~ the first half of the twentieth century / 20대 ~

《in》 *one's* early twenties. ◉ ~기 the first half year. ~전 the first half of a game.

**전반사**(全反射) 〖물리〗 total reflection.

**전반적**(全般的) general; overall; across-the-board. ¶ ~으로 generally; overall; across the board; on an across-the-board basis / ~인 감세 a wholesale 〔an across-the-board〕 tax reduction / ~으로 논하다 make a general comment 《on》 / ~으로 고찰하다 consider 《*a matter*》 by and large; study 《*a matter*》 in all its aspects / 대회는 ~으로 보아 성공이었다 On the whole, the convention was successful. *or* The convention was by and large a success.

**전방**(前方) the front (line); forward area; 《일선 지역》 front-line areas. ¶ ~의 front; forward / ~에 ahead 《of》; in front 《of》; forward / 100미터 ~에 one hundred meters ahead / 군대를 ~ 지역 가까이 이동시키다 move troops close to front-line areas / ~약 2킬로 되는 곳에 농가가 있다 A farm house stands some two kilometers ahead. / 사고의 원인은 운전기사의 ~주시 태만이었다 The accident was due to inattention on the part of the driver. ◉ ~기지 〖군사〗 an advanced base; an outpost. ~부대 a forward unit; a unit on the front line. ~위문 공연 《미》 a foxhole circuit. ~지휘소 a forward command post.

**전방**(廛房) a store; 《영》 a shop. ⇨ 가게.

**전방위**(全方位) ¶ ~(성)의 omnidirectional. ◉ ~외교 omnidirectional diplomacy.

**전방향**(全方向) ¶ ~안테나 an omnidirectional antenna.

**전배**(前杯) drinks taken prior to attending 《a party》. = 전작(前酌).

**전번**(前番) the other day; a former occasion. ¶ ~의 last; previous; former / ~에 last (time); before this; previously; some times ago; lately; recently / ~에 그를 만났을 때 when I saw him last / ~에 상경했을 때엔 1주일밖에 머물지 않았다 The last time I came to Seoul, I stayed only a week.

**전범**(戰犯) 《죄》 war crimes; 《사람》 a war criminal. ¶ B급 ~ a class B war criminal. ◉ ~법정 a war crimes court. ~용의자 a suspected war criminal; a war criminal suspect.

**전법**(戰法) tactics; strategy; a plan of campaign.

**전벽**(全壁) 〖건축〗 a blind 〔blank〕 wall.

**전별**(餞別) giving a farewell party; sending off; farewell. ⇨ 전송(餞送). ◉ ~금 a parting 〔farewell〕 gift.

**전병**(煎餠) pancakes. ◉ ~코 ⇨ 납작코.

**전병사**(戰病死) death caused by a disease 〔illness〕 while at war. ~하다 die of an illness while at war. ◉ ~자 the death from a disease contracted at the front.

**전보**(電報) a telegram; a telegraph; a telegraphic message; a wire; 《해외의》 a cable. ~ 치다 send a telegram; wire; cable. ¶ ~로 by wire 〔telegraph, cable〕 / ~ 접수 《게시》 Telegrams (Accepted). / …라는 보고의 ~ a telegram reporting that… / ~를 배달하다 deliver a telegram / 고향에서 부친 위독의 ~가 왔다 I received a telegram from home announcing that my father was seriously ill. / ~를 치시려면 115로 전화해 주십시오 Dial 115 to send telegrams from your home, office or hotel. / 낸시 결혼식에 축하 ~를 쳤다 I sent a congratulatory telegram to Nancy for her wedding. ◉ ~료 a telegram fee 〔charge〕. ~배달원 a telegram deliverer. ~사무 telegram service. ~약호 a cable code address. ~용지 a telegram form 〔blank〕. ~주문 a cable order. ~환 a telegraphic transfer 〔remittance〕. 국내〔국제〕~ a domestic 〔an international〕 telegram. 발신〔수신〕~ an outgoing 〔incoming〕 telegram. 신문~ a newspaper dispatch. 암호〔친전〕~ a code 〔confidential〕 telegram. 편지~ a lettergram.

**전보**(塡補) ~하다 《채우다》 fill (up); 《보상하다》 make up 《for》; compensate; 《보충하다》 supply; replenish. ¶ 결손〔손실〕을 ~하다 make up the deficit 〔loss〕.

**전보**(戰報) war intelligence 〔news〕; a war report.

**전보**(轉補) transfer(ence); shuffling. ~하다 transfer. ¶ ~되다 be transferred to another position.

**전복**(全鰒) 〖조개류〗 an ear shell; a sea-ear; an abalone 《미》. ◉ ~쌈 a dish of sliced abalone wrapped with pinenuts. ~죽 abalone porridge. ~초(炒) a dish of chopped abalone boiled in oil and soysauce. ~탕 abalone soup.

**전복**(顚覆) overthrow; overturn; subversion; upset; a capsize (선박의). ~하다 overthrow; overturn; subvert; upset; capsize. ¶ 정부의 ~을 꾀하다

plot against [to overthrow] the government; scheme for the overthrow [subversion] of the government / 열차를 ~시키다 overturn a train / 내각을 ~시키다 overthrow the Cabinet / 배가 ~했다 The ship turned turtle [was capsized]. / 열차가 태백역 구내에서 탈선 ~했다 The train (was) derailed and overturned in the T'aebaek Station yard. ◉ ~사고 a rollover accident.

**전봇대**(電報—) = 전주(電柱).

**전부**(全部) all parts; the whole; all; the entire; the full; [부사적] wholly; entirely; completely; in full; in *its* entirety. ¶ 이 책들 ~ all of these books / ~ (합)해서 in all; in full; altogether; all put together; all told / 이야기를 ~ 듣다 hear 《*a person*》 out (to the end) / 책을 ~ 읽다 read through a book; read a book from cover to cover / 대금을 ~ 치르다 pay purchase money in all / 이것이 ~나 Is this all? / 돈이 ~는 아니다 Money is not everything. / ~가 틀렸다 Everything went wrong. *or* All is lost. / 신문에 그 사건이 ~ 발표되었다 A full account of the incident appeared in the newspaper. / ~해서 얼마입니까 How much is it altogether? / ~해서 10,000원입니다 It sums up to [amounts to, comes up to, totals] ten thousand won. / 이것이 내가 가진 돈의 ~다 This is all the money I have. / 나는 스필버그 감독의 영화는 ~ 보았다 I've seen all the films directed by Spielberg.

**전부**(前夫) *one's* former [divorced, late] husband. ¶ ~의 자식 a child by *one's* former husband.

**전부**(前部) the front part; the forepart; the front. ¶ 배의 ~ the forepart of a ship / 최~ the foremost part 《of》; the very front.

**전분**(澱粉) starch. ¶ ~질의 starchy; farinaceous / ~이 많은 식품 starchy foods. ◉ ~ 당화 효소 amylase.

**전비**(前非) *one's* past error [sin, misdeeds]. ¶ ~를 깨닫다 see the error of *one's* ways / ~를 뉘우치다 repent of *one's* previous misdeeds [error, sin].

**전비**(戰費) war expenditure(s); war funds; the cost of war.

**전비**(戰備) war(like) preparations; armaments. ¶ ~를 갖추다 prepare [make preparations] for war.

**전사**(全史) a complete history.

**전사**(戰士) a soldier; a warrior; a fighter. ¶ 자유의 ~ a champion of liberty / 산업~ an industrial worker.

**전사**(戰史) a military [war] history; the history of a war. ¶ 제2차 세계 대전 ~ a history of World War Ⅱ / ~에 남다 be mentioned [recorded] in a war history.

**전사**(戰死) death in battle [action]. ~하다 die [fall] in battle; be killed 「in action [in the war]; die on the battlefield. ¶ 명예롭게 ~하다 die [meet] a glorious death on the battlefield. ◉ ~상자 the war dead and wounded; war casualties. ~자 a fallen soldier; the war dead [총칭]: ~자 명부 a roll of honor / ~자 유족 a war bereaved family.

**전사**(轉寫) transcription; copying. ~하다 transcribe; copy. ◉ ~기 a transcriber. ~법 a transfer(ring) process. ~잉크 [지] transfer ink [paper]. ~효소 transcriptase. ~화(畵) a transfer.

**전산**(電算) computation [calculation] by computer. ◉ ~기 a computer: 소형 ~기 a minicomputer. ⇨ 컴퓨터. ~사식 조판시스템 a computer type-setting system (생략 CTS). ~화 computerization.

**전상**(戰傷) a war wound. ~하다 be wounded in action [a battle]. ◉ ~병 a wounded soldier. ~자 the war wounded [총칭]; a wounded veteran [soldier, airman, sailor].

**전색맹**(全色盲) total color-blindness; 〖의학〗 achromatopsia.

**전생**(前生) 〖불교〗 *one's* previous [former] life; *one's* previous existence. ¶ ~의 인연 destinies arranged in a previous existence; a predestined relation; a karmic relation / ~의 죄 sins committed in a previous existence / ~에서부터의 숙명 predestination; *one's* fate / 옷깃만 스쳐도 ~의 인연이다 Even a chance acquaintance is due to the karma in a previous life.

**전생애**(全生涯) *one's* entire [whole] life. ¶ ~를 통하여 throughout [in all] *one's* (whole) life; from (the) cradle to (the) grave / ~를 바치다 devote [dedicate] *one's* whole life 《to》.

**전서**(全書) a complete book [collection]; 《개설서》 a compendium (*pl.* ~s, -dia).

**전서**(前書) *one's* previous letter; the first letter. ◉ 고린도~ 〖성서〗 the First Epistle of St. Paul to the Corinthians.

**전서**(傳書) transmittance of a letter. ◉ ~구〔비둘기〕 a carrier pigeon.

**전서**(篆書) a seal character; writing in seal characters.

**전선**(全線) the whole line (of a railroad); 《전장의》 the entire battle line. ¶ ~에 걸쳐 all up and down 〔all along〕 the line / 중앙선은 ~에 걸쳐 불통이다 Service has been cut all along the Chung-ang Line.

**전선**(前線) ① 〖군사〗 the front; the front 〔battle〕 line; the battle 〔war〕 front; the forward edge (of battle area) (생략 FEBA). ¶ ~의 장병 officers and men at the front / ~에서 싸우다 fight in 〔on〕 the front line / 병력을 ~으로 보내다 send troops up to the front line / ~으로 떠나다〔에 있다〕 go up to 〔be in〕 the front line. ② 〖기상〗 a (weather) front. ¶ ~의 발생 frontogenesis / 한랭〔온난〕 ~이 남하했다 The cold 〔warm〕 front pushed southward. / 동서로 뻗어 있는 ~이 전국에 머물고 있다 A front extending east and west is stationary over the country. / 장마 ~이 북상하고 있다 A seasonal rainfront is advancing north. ◉ ~기지 an advanced base. ~돌파 a breakthrough. ~부대 frontline troops.

**전선**(電線) 《전기의》 (an) electric(al) wire 〔line〕; an electric cord; 《해저의》 a cable; 《전화의》 a telephone 〔telegraph〕 wire. ¶ ~을 가설하다 lay electric wires / 강풍으로 ~이 끊어졌다 The electric wire was broken because of the strong wind.

**전선**(傳線) 《양말의》 a run 《미》; a ladder 《영》 [<デンセン(日)]. ¶ ~이 생기지 않는 양말 runproof 〔ladderproof〕 stockings / 스타킹에 ~이 갔다 There is a run in this stocking.

**전선**(戰線) the battle 〔fighting〕 line; the (battle) front. ¶ 통일~ a united front / 적의 ~ 후방에 behind the enemy lines / 서부 ~에 on the western front / ~에 나가다 go to the front; be at the front; take part in the front / ~을 축소하다 shorten the line / 적의 ~을 돌파하다 break through the enemy line / …에 대한 공동 ~을 펴다 form a united front against…. ◉ ~이탈자 a deserter.

**전설**(前說) *one's* previous view 〔doctrine〕; theories 〔views, doctrines〕 of predecessors; earlier theories 〔views〕. ¶ ~을 번복하다 change 〔renounce, withdraw〕 *one's* former views.

**전설**(傳說) a legend; a tradition; 《민간전승》 folklore; a folk tale 〔story〕. ¶ ~적인 legendary; traditional; fabulous / ~적 인물 a legendary person / 그 집에 관해 전하는 ~ the legend that has grown up around the house / ~에 의하면 according to tradition 〔legend〕 / 로빈후드는 영국의 ~상의 영웅이다 Robin Hood is a legendary English hero. ◉ ~시대 the legendary age 〔period〕.

**전성**(全盛) the height of prosperity. ~하다 be at the height of *its* 〔*one's*〕 prosperity; be in the heyday of *its* 〔*one's*〕 power; be in (all) *its* glory. ¶ 그의 ~기에 in his best days. ◉ ~시대〔기〕 the golden age; the heyday 《of》; *one's* best days; the days of *one's* glory: 그의 ~시대는 지났다 He has seen his best days.

**전성**(展性) 〖금속〗 malleability. ¶ ~이 풍부하다 be malleable.

**전성관**(傳聲管) a voice pipe 〔tube〕; 《미》 a speaking tube.

**전세**(前世) ① 《전대》 former time 〔generations〕; past 〔prehistoric〕 ages. ② =전생(前生).

**전세**(專貰) charter; reserving; reservation; 《영》 booking; engaging; 《게시》 Reserved. ¶ ~의 《대절의》 chartered; 《예약한》 reserved; 《영》 booked / ~내다 charter; engage; book; 《미》 reserve; make reservation. ◉ ~버스〔비행기〕 a chartered bus 〔plane〕. ~요금 charterage. ~자동차 a rental car 《미》; a hire car 〔auto〕.

**전세**(傳貰) the lease of a house 〔room〕 on a deposit basis; a contract to rent a house 〔room〕 with deposit 〔key〕 money. ¶ ~놓다 lease 《a house 〔room〕》 on a deposit basis. ◉ ~금 deposit 〔key〕 money for the lease of a house 〔room〕: ~금 융자 a loan to pay for the lease of a house 〔room〕. ~방〔전셋집〕 a room 〔house〕 for rent on a deposit money basis.

**전세**(戰勢) the war situation; the progress of a battle; the tide of the war. ¶ ~를 결정적으로 뒤집다 turn the tide of the war decisively 《against》 / ~가 불리하다 The war is not going in our favor. / ~가 역전되어 유리해졌다 The (war) situation turned in our favor.

**전세계**(全世界) the whole world; all the world. ¶ ~에〔의〕 all over 〔throughout〕 the world; the world over; across 〔around〕 the globe / ～의 사람들 people throughout the world; people the world over / ～에서 모이다 come from all parts 〔corners〕 of the world / ～에 알려지다 be known all over the world; be well known to the whole world / ～에서 선발되다 be selected from all the nations of the world / ～를 여행하다 travel all over the world 〔round the world, world wide〕 / ～를 놀라게 하다 astonish the whole world / ～가 그의 죽음에 충격을 받았다 The whole world 〔All the world〕 was shocked by his death. (★「all+the+명사(복수 또는 단수형)와, 「the+whole+명사(단수 또는 복수형)」에서는 the의 위치에 주의).

**전세기**(前世紀) the last century; 《어떤 시점에서 보아》 the previous 〔preceeding〕 century. ¶ ～의 유물 a relic from an earlier 〔a former〕 age; a museum piece; an antediluvian.

**전소**(全燒) total destruction by fire. ～하다 be entirely 〔totally, completely〕 destroyed by fire; be burned down 〔to the ground〕. ¶ ～된 가옥 a house totally destroyed by fire / 그 건물은 ～하였다 The building was burned down 〔to the ground〕.

**전속**(專屬) ～하다 belong exclusively 《to》; be under the exclusive control 《of》. ¶ ～의 exclusive; attached to / 저 코미디언은 그 나이트 클럽에 ～되어 있다 That comedian belongs exclusively to the nightclub.
◉ ～가수 a singer attached to 〔under exclusive contract with〕 《the MBC》. ～관할 〖법〗 exclusive jurisdiction. ～극작가 a playwright belonging to 〔who write specially for〕 《a company》. ～배우 an actor 〔actress〕 attached to 《a M company》; an actor 〔actress〕 under exclusive contract 《with》. ～부관 an aide-de=camp. ～악단 an orchestra attached to 《the KBS》; the 《KBS》 studio orchestra.

**전속**(轉屬) (a) transfer 《to another unit》. ～하다 be transferred 《to another section》; transfer 《to another corps》. ¶ 그는 A중대에서 사단본부로 ～되었다 He was transferred from A company to the division headquarters.

**전속력**(全速力) full 〔top〕 speed. ¶ ～으로 at full 〔top〕 speed; 《비행기·배가》 at full power; 《말이》 at full gallop; 《배가》 at 〔under〕 full steam / ～을 내다 put forth full speed / ～으로 뛰다 run at full speed; 《단거리 경기》 sprint / 자동차는 ～을 냈다 The car pulled out at full speed.

**전손**(全損) 〖보험〗 total loss. ¶ ～을 보다 suffer a total loss. ◉ ～담보 security for total loss only (생략 T.L.O.).

**전송**(電送) electrical 〔wireless〕 transmission. ～하다 telegraph; wire; transmit; send 《*something*》 by wireless. ¶ 사진을 ～하다 transmit 〔send〕 a picture by telephotography. ◉ ～사진 a telephotograph; a telephoto; a photo facsimile. 사진～ telephoto service; radiophoto transmission: 사진 ～ 장치 telephoto apparatus.

**전송**(傳送) transmission; conveyance; delivery. ～하다 transmit; convey; deliver.

**전송**(餞送) seeing 《*a person*》 off; (a) send-off. ～하다 see 〔send〕 《*a person*》 off; give a send-off. ¶ 공항까지 ～하다 go to an airport to see 《*a person*》 off / 그를 ～하기 위해 많은 사람들이 정거장에 모였다 A large crowd gathered at the station to see him off. ◉ ～객 persons 〔people〕 present for a send-off. ～회 a farewell party.

**전송**(轉送) forwarding; transmission. ～하다 forward; transmit; send on. ¶ 내게 오는 편지는 이 주소로 ～하여 주십시오 Please forward all letters for me to this address.
◉ ～처 a forwarding address.

**전수**(全數) the whole; the total number 〔figure〕; [부사적] all; totally.

**전수**(專修) exclusive study; specialization. ～하다 make a special study 《of》; specialize 〔major〕 《in》. ◉ ～과 a special course: 영어 ～과 a course specializing in English. ～과목 a specialized subject; a major 《미》. ～학교 a vocational school.

**전수**(傳受) inheriting; receiving. ～하다 get handed down 《*a thing*》; receive 《instruction》; be instructed; be taught.
◉ ～자 an initiate.

**전수**(傳授) handing down; handing over 《to》; transmission; initiation; instruction. ～하다 hand over 《to》; deliver 《to》; transmit; instruct; initiate. ¶ ～받다 receive instruction; be instructed / 비법을 ～하다 initiate 《*a person*》 into the secrets (of arts).
◉ ～자 an initiator.

**전수금**(前受金) money received in

advance; 〖법〗 an advancement.

**전술**(前述) the above-mentioned; the foregoing. ¶ ～의 above-mentioned; foregoing; preceding / ～한 바와 같이 as aforesaid; as stated 〔mentioned〕 above.

**전술**(戰術) tactics; the art of war; a plan of campaign. ¶ ～상의 tactical / ～상의 요지 a tactical point / ～상의 잘못 a tactical error / 교묘한 ～ a brilliant 〔clever〕 piece of tactics; sharp tactics / ～적으로 tactically / ～로 이기다 outgeneral; outmaneuver / 우리들의 요구를 충족시키기 위해서는 다른 ～을 시도할 필요가 있다 We need to try different tactics to fulfill our demands.
◉ ～가 a tactician. ～공군 tactical air forces: ～공군 사령부 〖미군〗 the Tactical Air Command (생략 TAC). ～전환 a change of tactics. ～정보 처리시스템 the Action Automation System. ～폭격기 a tactical bomber. ～핵무기 tactical nuclear weapons. 고등～ grand tactics. 국지～ minor tactics.

**전습**(傳襲) inheritance. ～하다 inherit.

**전승**(全勝) a complete victory. ～하다 win 〔gain〕 a complete victory 《over》; sweep the field; 《경기에서》 sweep 〔win〕 all games 〔matches, bouts〕; make a clean record.

**전승**(傳承) 《일》 handing down; 《전설》 (an) oral tradition; (a) word-of-mouth tradition; 《민화》 folklore. ～하다 hand down 《orally》; pass 《a story》 down (from generation to generation). ◉ ～문학 oral 〔traditional〕 literature. ～서사시 an oral epic.

**전승**(戰勝) a victory; a triumph. ¶ ～을 기원〔축하〕하다 pray for 〔celebrate *one's*〕 victory. ◉ ～국 a victorious country 〔power〕. ～기념일 an anniversary of a victory; a victory day.

**전시**(全市) the whole city. ¶ ～에 걸쳐 citywide / ～를 눈 아래 내려다보다 see 〔view〕 the whole city below *one's* eyes.

**전시**(展示) exhibition; display. ～하다 exhibit; put 〔place〕 《*things*》 on display. ¶ ～용 견본 a sample for display / ～되다 go 〔be placed〕 on display / ～되어 있다 be on display 〔show〕 / 여러 가지 상품이 ～되어 있다 A variety of things are displayed for sale. / 그 화랑에는 인상파의 그림이 ～되어 있다 Impressionist paintings are exhibited in the art gallery.
◉ ～관 a pavilion. ～물〔품〕 an exhibit; exhibition [총칭]. ～실 a gallery; an exhibit hall 〔room〕; an exhibition hall: 본관 ～실 the main exhibition hall. ～장 an exhibition hall 〔room, area〕. ～판매 an exhibition and sale 《of paintings》; a display with the exhibits on sale. ～회 a show; an exhibition: 도서 ～회 a book exhibition 〔fair, show〕 / 사진 ～회 a photo exhibition. ～효과 a demonstration effect. 한국종합～장 the Korea Exhibition Center (생략 KOEX).

**전시**(戰時) wartime; time of war. ¶ ～중 during the war; in time of war / ～나 평시를 막론하고 whether in peace or in war. ◉ ～경기 a war boom. ～경제 wartime economy. ～국채〔공채〕 war bonds; a war loan. ～금제품 contraband of war. ～내각 a war cabinet. ～모리배 a wartime profiteer. ～배상위원회 《UN의》 the War Reparations Committee. ～보상 war indemnity 〔compensation〕. ～보험 war risk insurance. ～산업 industry in wartime. ～상태 a state of war; belligerency; wartime conditions: ～상태 종결 선언 a declaration of the termination of the state of war / 준 ～상태 《be in》 a semi-war state; a quasi-state of war. ～수당 war bonus. ～재정 wartime finance. ～체제 《establish, build up》 a war regime; 《on》 a war footing; the wartime structure: ～체제하에 있다 be on the wartime structure 〔footing〕. ～편성 a war footing 〔organization〕: ～편성 사단 a division at war 〔fighting〕 strength.

**전시대**(前時代) former ages 〔times〕; past generations.

**전신**(全身) the whole body; 《사진·그림의》 the full length. ¶ ～의 힘을 다하여 with *one's* whole strength / ～을 떨다 shake all over; shake from head to foot / ～이 땀투성이가 되다 get all in a sweat / ～에 화상을 입다 burn *oneself* all over / 그는 ～에 상처를 입고 있었다 He was covered with wounds.
◉ ～마취 general anesthesia: ～마취를 시키다 subject 《*a person*》 to general anesthesia. ～불수 total paralysis. ～사진〔상(像), 화〕 a full-length photograph 〔figure, picture〕. ～운동 exercise for the whole body: 수영은 ～운동이 된다 Swimming gives exercise to every parts of your body.

**전신**(前身) *one's* former self; the predecessor; *one's* past life [history]. ¶ 고려 대학교의 ~인 보성 전문 학교 Posŏng College, the predecessor of the present Korea University / ~을 조사하다 look up ⟪*a person's*⟫ antecedents; investigate ⟪*a person's*⟫ past life.

**전신**(電信) telegraphic communication; telegraph; telegram; (a) wire; ⟪해외 전신⟫ a cable. ¶ ~의 telegraphic / ~으로 by telegraph [wire] / ~을 보내다 telegraph; wire; cable / ~으로 송금하다 remit money ⟪to *a person*⟫ by telegraphic transfer / 폭풍우로 ~이 두절되었다 Telegraphic communications were interrupted by the storm. / 부산과의 ~이 재개되었다 Telegraphic service with Pusan was resumed. ◉ ~국 a telegraph station [office]. ~기 a telegraphic instrument; a telegraph. ~기사 a telegraph operator; a telegrapher. ~사무 telegraphic service. ~송금 telegraphic transfer (생략 T/T). ~암호 a telegram code: ~암호장 a code book. ~약호 a telegraphic [cable] address. ~전화국 a telecommunication office: 국제 ~ 전화국 the Korea International Telecommunication Office(생략 KIT). ~주 a telegraph pole. ~환 a telegraphic transfer [remittance]: ~환으로 부치다 wire [remit] ⟪money⟫ ⟪to *a person*⟫ by telegraphic transfer.

**전실**(前室) *one's* former wife. ◉ ~자식 the children by *one's* former wife.

**전심**(全心) *one's* whole heart [soul]. ¶ ~을 기울여 with *one's* whole heart [soul] / ~전력을 다하다 put *one's* heart and soul into ⟪*one's* work⟫; devote all *one's* energies to ⟪*one's* work⟫.

**전심**(專心) concentration of mind; undivided attention; the whole heart. ~하다 devote *oneself* [all *one's* energies] ⟪to⟫; put heart and soul ⟪into⟫; contract [concentrate] *one's* mind ⟪upon, on⟫. ¶ ~으로 wholeheartedly; single-mindedly; with all *one's* heart and soul; intently / 그는 연구에 ~하고 있다 He applies himself in his researches.

**전아**(典雅) elegance; refinement. ~하다 (be) refined; elegant; graceful. ¶ ~한 궁정 음악 elegant court music.

**전압**(電壓) (a) voltage. ¶ 100볼트의 ~ ⟪have⟫ a voltage of 100 / 높은[낮은] ~ (a) high [low] voltage / ~을 높이다[낮추다] increase [drop] voltage / ~이 높다[낮다] The voltage is high [low]. ◉ ~계 a voltmeter. ~전류계 a voltameter. ~조절기 a [an automatic] voltage regulator.

**전액**(全額) the total [full] amount; the (sum) total. ¶ ~ 부담하다 cover all the expenses / 다음 주에 ~ 지불하겠다 I will pay in full next week. ◉ ~납입: ~납입의 fully paid-up ⟪stocks⟫. ~담보 full coverage. ~보험 full insurance. ~지급 full payment; payment in full: ~ 지급의 fully paid [covered] ⟪by⟫.

**전야**(前夜) the previous night; the night before; the eve (축제일 등의). ¶ 성탄절 ~에 on Christmas Eve / 혁명 ~에 on the eve of the revolution / 결혼 ~에 on the night before the wedding. ◉ ~제 an eve: ~제를 지내다 celebrate the eve ⟪of a festival⟫.

**전약**(煎藥) a medicinal decoction.

**전어**(錢魚) 〖어류〗 a gizzard shad.

**전언**(前言) ⟪앞서의 말⟫ *one's* previous remarks [words, statement]. ¶ ~을 취소하다 withdraw [retract, take back] *one's* words; eat [swallow] *one's* words (부득이) / ~을 어기다 go back on *one's* word; back down from what *one* said.

**전언**(傳言) a (verbal) message. ~하다 give ⟪*a person*⟫ a message; leave a message for ⟪*a person*⟫; send [bring] ⟪*a person*⟫ word. ¶ ~을 남기다 leave word [a message] ⟪with *a person*⟫ / ~을 부탁받다 be asked to give a message. ◉ ~판 a message board.

**전업**(專業) a special [principal] occupation; a full-time job. ¶ …을 ~으로 하다 make a specialty of…; devote *oneself* (full-time) to ⟪writing⟫ / 그는 꽃 재배를 ~으로 하고 있다 He specializes in growing flowers. *or* He is a floriculturist by profession. ◉ ~농부 a full-time farmer. ~주부 a full-time housewife; a homemaker.

**전업**(電業) the electrical industry.

**전업**(轉業) a job change; a change of occupation. ~하다 change *one's* occupation [job]. ◉ ~자 a person who changed his occupation. ~자금 funds for occupational change.

**전역**(全域) ⟪through⟫ all the area; ⟪in⟫ all parts ⟪of⟫; the whole area [region]. ¶ 호남 지방 ~에 걸쳐 throughout [all over] the Honam districts / …의 ~에 영향을 미치다 affect every field of ⟪natural science⟫.

**전역**(全譯) a complete 〔whole〕 translation; an unabridged translation. ~하다 translate 《*Macbeth*》 completely 《into Korean》; translate the whole of 《Shakespeare》. ◉ ~성서 a complete translation of the Bible.

**전역**(戰役) a war; a campaign. ⇨ 전쟁.

**전역**(戰域) a war 〔battle〕 area; a theater of war. ¶ ~을 확대〔축소〕하다 extend 〔reduce〕 the area of operations. ◉ ~핵무기〔미사일〕 theater nuclear weapons 〔missiles〕. ~핵전력 theater nuclear forces (생략 TNF).

**전역**(轉役) ~하다 discharge from service; transfer 《to the first reserve》. ¶ 현역에서 예비역으로 ~시키다 transfer 《*a person*》 from the active list to the reserve list.

**전연**(全然) wholly; utterly. ⇨ 전혀.

**전열**(前列) the front rank 〔row〕. ¶ ~ 왼쪽에서 세 번째 the third from the left in the front row.

**전열**(電熱) electric heat. ◉ ~기(器) 《난방용》 an electric heater; 《취사용》 an electric range 〔stove, cooker〕; a hot plate.

**전열**(戰列) a battle line; a line (of battle). ¶ ~에 참가하다 join 〔go into〕 the line(s) / ~을 이탈하다 leave 〔desert〕 the line of battle / ~을 가다듬다 straighten up the line of battle.

**전염**(傳染) 《접촉의》 contagion; 《간접의》 infection. ~하다 [병이 주어] be contagious 〔infectious, catching 《구어》〕; [사람이 주어] be infected with; catch. ¶ ~예방을 위하여 격리되다 be isolated to prevent infection / 디프테리아는 ~됩니까 Is diphtheria contagious 〔catching〕? / 하품은 ~된다 Yawning is catching 〔infectious〕.
◉ ~경로 a route of infection. ~력 virulence. ~매체 a germ carrier: 말라리아는 모기가 ~매체이다 Malaria is carried by mosquitoes. *or* Mosquitoes are malaria carriers. ~병 ⇨ 전염병. ~성 contagiousness: ~성의 contagious; infectious / 그 병은 ~성이 매우 강하다 The disease is very contagious. ~원 a source of infection. 공기~ aerial 〔airborne〕 infection: 공기 ~병 an air-carried disease. 자가~ autoinfection. 접촉~ contact infection: 접촉성 ~병 a disease which spreads through contact. 직접〔간접〕 ~ direct 〔indirect〕 infection.

**전염병**(傳染病) 《접촉에 의한》 a contagious 〔communicable〕 disease; 《공기에 의한》 an infection; an infectious disease; 《유행병》 an epidemic. ¶ 제1종 ~ the 1st class communicable disease / 그 지방에는 ~이 유행하고 있다 An epidemic is prevalent in the area. ◉ ~병동 a contagious 〔an isolation〕 ward. ~병원 a hospital for contagious disease; a quarantine; an isolation hospital. ~연구소 the Infectious Diseases Research 「Laboratory 〔Institute〕. ~예방법 the Infectious 〔Contagious〕 Diseases Prevention Act. ~유행지 an infected area; an area hit by an epidemic. ~환자 a case of infectious disease; a contagious 〔infectious〕 case.

**전옥**(典獄) the warden 《미》. ⇨ 교도소장.

**전와**(戰渦) a turmoil 〔the maelstrom〕 of war. ¶ ~에 휘말리다 be involved in the maelstrom of war.

**전와**(轉訛) corruption (of a word). ~하다 be 〔get〕 corrupted 《from, into》. ◉ ~어 a corrupt word; a corruption; a corrupted form.

**전용**(專用) exclusive 〔private〕 use. ~하다 use exclusively; be private. ¶ ~의 exclusive; 《개인의》 private / 외국인 ~의 나이트클럽 a night club reserved only for foreign customers / 야간 ~ 전화 a 〔the〕 telephone for night use only / 이 승강기는 직원 ~이다 This elevator is only for the employees. / 여성 ~《게시》 Ladies Only.
◉ ~권 《독점 사용권》 the sole right of use; the right of exclusive use. ~기 a plane for *one's* personal use: 대통령 ~기 a presidential plane; 《미》 Air Force One. ~실 *one's* private room. ~전화선 an exclusive line: 시장 ~의 전화선 the Mayor's private telephone line. ~차 a 〔*one's*〕 private car; a car for *one's* personal use: 사장 ~차 the president's private car. ~회선(回線) a leased 〔private〕 line.

**전용**(轉用) diversion; appropriation. ~하다 divert 〔use〕 《*a thing*》 to other purposes; convert; misappropriate. ¶ 공금을 ~하다 misappropriate public money / 자금을 다른 데에 ~하다 divert funds to other purposes.

**전우**(戰友) a fellow soldier; a comrade (in arms); a war brother.

**전운**(戰雲) war clouds. ¶ 중동에 ~이 감돌고 있다 War clouds hang (low) over the Middle East.

**전원**(田園) 《시골》 the country; rural districts; 《교외》 the suburbs. ¶ ~의

rural; pastoral / ~ 생활을 즐기다 taste the pleasure of rural life. ◉ ~곡 〚음악〛 pastorale (*pl.* -li). ~도시 a garden city. ~문학 pastoral literature. ~생활 (a) rural 〔country〕 life; life 〔living〕 in the country: ~생활을 하다 lead a rural life; live in the country. ~시 a pastoral poem; an idyllic poem; an eclogue: ~시인 a pastoral poet; an idyllist. ~주택 a house for rural 〔country〕 life: ~주택지 a garden suburb. ~풍경 a rural landscape 〔scene〕. ~화 ruralization.

**전원**(全員) all the members; the entire staff; 《배 등의》 the whole crew; all hands. ¶ ~일치로 unanimously; 《consent》 with one voice / ~의 승낙 unanimous consent / ~ 출동하다 be present in full force / 학급의 ~이 게임에 참가했다 All the class participated 〔took part〕 in the game. / 제안은 ~ 일치의 찬성으로 승인되었다 The proposal was accepted with unanimous approval.

**전원**(電源) 《전력원》 the source of electric power; a power source; 《콘센트》 an outlet. ¶ ~을 차단하다〔끊다〕 cut the power supply; shut off the power / 코드를 ~에 꽂다 put a plug in an outlet 〔a socket〕 / 이 면도기의 ~은 건전지이다 This shaver runs 〔operates〕 on batteries. *or* This shaver is powered by batteries. ◉ ~개발 development of power resources.

**전월**(前月) last month; 《어떤 달의 전달》 the previous month. ◉ ~호 《잡지 따위의》 the last month's issue.

**전위**(前衛) 《선구》 an advance(d) guard; the van(guard); 〚구기〛 a forward; 〚럭비〛 a rusher; 〚미식축구〛 a lineman. ¶ ~적 《사상·행동이》 radical; forward; *avant garde*(F.) / ~를 보다 play forward (구기에서); play at the net (테니스에서). ◉ ~음악〔미술, 문학, 영화〕 *avant-garde* music 〔art, literature, picture〕. ~파 an avant-gardist.

**전위**(電位) 〚전기〛 (an) electric potential (★ 복수로 쓸 수 없음. 또 an 대신 one을 써서도 안됨). ¶ 양〔음〕~ positive 〔negative〕 potential. ◉ ~강하 a drop in potential. ~계 an electrometer. ~차 a potential difference (생략 p.d.); a difference of (electric) potential.

**전위**(轉位) (a) transposition; 《원자의》 (a) dislocation; 《염색체의》 translocation.

**전유**(全乳) whole milk (지방질을 제거하지 않은).

**전유**(專有) exclusive possession; monopoly (독점). ~하다 have 〔take, enjoy〕 sole possession 《of》; monopolize 《a right》; have 《*a thing*》 to *oneself*. ◉ ~권 exclusive rights; (a) monopoly. ~자 a sole 〔private〕 owner.

**전율**(戰慄) a shiver; a shudder; trembling. ~하다 shudder; shiver; tremble 《with fear》. ¶ ~할 (만한) terrible; horrible / ~할 광경 a horrible 〔bloodcurdling〕 sight / ~케 하다 make 《*a person*》 shudder; make *one's* blood run cold / 그 광경을 보기만 하고도 그들은 ~했다 The very sight was enough to make their flesh creep.

**전음**(全音) 〚음악〛 a whole tone. ⇨ 온음.

**전음**(顫音) 〚음악〛 a trill. = 떤꾸밈음.

**전의**(戰意) a fighting spirit (투지); the will to fight; aggressive 〔hostile〕 intentions. ¶ ~가 없다 have no will to fight; have no intention of fighting / ~를 잃다 lose *one's* fighting spirit; lose the will to fight / ~를 북돋우다 whip up war sentiment.

**전의**(轉義) a transferred 〔figurative〕 meaning; a derivative meaning 《of a word》. ¶ ~의 figurative.

**전이**(轉移) 《변화》 (a) change; 《환부의》 spread 《of a disease》 from its original site to another part of the body; 〚의학〛 metastasis; 〚정신분석〛 transference. ~하다 change; spread (by metastasis); metastasize; transfer. ¶ 폐암이 위로 ~한 것 같다 It seems that the lung cancer has spread to the stomach. / 복부 수술을 해보니 암은 이미 환자의 위에서 간장으로 ~되어 있었다 An abdominal operation showed that cancer cells had already transferred from the patient's stomach to his liver.

**전인**(全人) ◉ ~교육 education for the whole man.

**전인**(前人) a predecessor; a forerunner. ¶ ~ 미답의 unexplored; unprecedented; untrodden; virgin 《forest》.

**전인격**(全人格) *one's* whole personality.

**전일**(前日) 《일전》 the other day; a few days ago; formerly; previously; before; some time ago; 《전날》 the previous day; the day before.

**전일제**(全日制) a full-time system. ¶ ~ 고등학교 a full-time high school.

**전임**(前任) ① 《사람》 *one's* predecessor; a former official. ② 《벼슬》 the post previously occupied; a previous appointment. ¶ ~의 preceeding; former / ~ 대사 the preceeding ambassador. ◉ ～자 a predecessor in office: 당신의 ～자는 누구였던가요 Who preceded you in the post? *or* Who held the post before you? ～지 *one's* former [last] post.

**전임**(專任) exclusive duty; full service; sole charge. ～하다 do exclusive duty; be in full service; be in sole charge 《of》. ¶ ～의 full-time / 회사의 ～ 법률고문 a full-time legal adviser to a company. ◉ ～강사 an instructor (대학의); a full-time lecturer. ～교사 a full-time teacher: 그는 그 학교 ～교사로 있다 He is a full-time teacher at that school.

**전임**(轉任) change of post; transference. ～하다 be transferred to another post [service]; change *one's* post. ◉ ～자 a person transferred. ～지 *one's* new post.

**전입**(轉入) transference; moving in [into] 《a place》. ～하다 move in [into]; be transferred 《to》. ◉ ～생 a transfer student; a student [pupil] transferred from another school. ～신고 a moving-in notification.

**전입학**(轉入學) ～하다 enter a school from another school; be transferred to a school from another.

**전자**(前者) ① 《전번》 some time ago; the other day. ¶ ～에 some time ago; formerly. ② 《the latter에 대하여》 the former; 《this에 대하여》 that; 《the other에 대하여》 the one. ¶ ～와 후자 the former and the latter / 그들은 말과 소를 기른다. ～는 승마용이고 후자는 우유를 얻기 위한 것이다 They keep horses and cattle; the former for riding, the latter for milking.

**전자**(電子) 〖물리〗 an electron. ¶ ～의 electronic.

◉ ～계산기 a [an electronic] computer. ～공업[산업] electronics industry: ～산업을 2000년대의 유망 산업으로 육성하다 foster the electronics industry into promising industry during 2000s. ～공학 electronics: ～ 공학과 the department of electronics engineering / ～공학 제품 electronic products [goods]. ～관(管) an electron tube. ～광학 electron optics. ～교환기 《전화의》 an electronic exchanger. ～구름 〖물리〗 an electron cloud. ～구조 electronic structure. ～기기 electronic equipment [총칭]. ～기체 〖물리〗 electron gas. ～냉동 electronic refrigeration; thermoelectric cooling. ～냉방 electrocooling. ～대책(對策) an electronic countermeasure (생략 ECM). ～두뇌 an electronic brain. ～레인지 a microwave oven. ～렌즈 an electron lens. ～망원경 an electron telescope. ～문서 교환방식 Electronic Data Interchange (생략 EDI). ～미술 electronic art. ～밀도 electron density. ～방출 〖물리〗 electron emission. ～번역기 an elec-tronic translating machine. ～볼트 〖원자물리〗 an electron volt (생략 EV, e.v.). ～빔 an electron beam. ～사진 an electrophotograph. ～상거래 e-commerce (transactions). ～설 the electron theory. ～수첩 an electronic notebook. ～스위치 an electronic switch. ～시계 an electronic clock [watch]. ～식 음주측정기 an electronic alcohol detector. ～신문[잡지] an electronic newspaper [magazine]. ～악기 an electronic musical instrument. ～오락실 an electronic game [amusement] room; a video game room: 법정 시설 기준 미달의 무허가 ～ 오락실 unlicensed video game rooms without appropriate facilities compatible with legal standards. ～오락업 electronic amusement business. ～오르간 an electronic organ. ～우편 〖컴퓨터〗 electronic mail; E-mail (컴퓨터를 이용한 메시지 교환). ～음(音) an electronic sound. ～음악 electronic [electrophonic] music. ～장치 an electronic device [gadget]. ～전(戰) electronic warfare. ～전기제품 상가 an electronic and electric products (sales) center. ～정보수집[정찰] electronic intelligence (생략 ELINT). ～정보 처리시스템 an electronic data processing system (생략 EDPS). ～조명 electroluminescence. ～조종 장치 《비행기의》 electronic controls. ～총 《컬러 TV의》 an electron gun. ～출판 electronic publishing. ～친화력 electron affinity. ～카메라 an electron camera. ～파일 an electronic file. ～핵공학(核工學) nucleonics. ～현미경 an electron microscope. ～회사 an electronics company: 한국의 ～회사들은 올해에 국내외로부터의 점증하는 도전에 직면하게 될 것 같다 Korea's electronics companies are likely to face a growing challenge from home and abroad this year. ～ 회절(回折) 〖물리〗 electron diffraction.

극소～공학 molectronics. 한국～기술연구소 the Korea Institute of Electronic Technology. 한국～전시회 the

《'99》 Korea Electronic Show.
**전자**(電磁) electromagnetic.
◉ ~단위 an electromagnetic unit (생략 EMU, emu). ~석 an electromagnet. ~유도 electromagnetic induction. ~자물쇠 an electronic door lock. ~장 an electromagnetic field. ~조리기 an electromagnetic cooker. ~파 electromagnetic waves; a radio wave: ~파포(砲) a railgun.
**전자**(篆字) a "seal" character.
**전자기**(電磁氣) electromagnetism. ¶ ~의 electromagnetic. ◉ ~학 electromagnetics.
**전작**(田作) 《밭농사》 dry-field farming; 《농작물》 farm crops; dry-field crops.
**전작**(前酌) cups *one* has taken previously; the drinks *one* has had; earlier 〔beforehand〕 drinking. ¶ ~이 있습니다 I had a few (drinks) before I came here. 「in *one's* possession.
**전장**(田庄·田莊) *one's* farmstead; fields
**전장**(全長) the full 〔total〕 length; the overall length. ¶ ~이 백 피트다 have an overall length of 100 feet.
**전장**(前章) the preceding 〔foregoing〕 chapter; the last 〔prior〕 chapter.
**전장**(前場) 〖경제〗 《증권시장의》 the morning stock market session; the morning market.
**전장**(電場) 〖물리〗 an electric field.
**전장**(戰場) a battlefield; a battleground; the theater 〔seat〕 of war; the front. ¶ ~에서 on the battlefield; in battle / ~에 가다 go to the front / ~의 이슬로 사라지다 end *one's* life on the battlefield.
**전재**(戰災) war damage 〔disaster〕. ¶~를 입다〔면하다〕 suffer 〔escape〕 war damage. ◉ ~고아 a war orphan. ~도시 a war-ravaged city. ~민 war refugees 〔victims〕. ~지구 a war=damaged〔-devastated〕 area.
**전재**(轉載) reproduction; reprinting. ~하다 reproduce; reprint. ¶ 「라이프」지에서 ~하다 reprint 《the article》 from *the Life* / ~불허 《표시》 Reproduction forbidden. *or* All rights 〔Copyright〕 reserved. / B씨의 승낙을 받고 ~ Reprinted by courtesy of Mr. B.
**전쟁**(戰爭) (a) war; warfare; hostilities. ~하다 make 〔levy, go to〕 war 《with》; wage war 《against》; 《전투》 fight 《a battle》; 《개전》 open hostilities. ¶ 국내 ~ a civil war / 6.25 ~ the June 25th war of Korea / 전면~ a total 〔an all=out〕 war / 제한~ a limited war / 침략~ a war of aggression / ~의 상처 the scars of war / ~의 참화 the calamity 〔horrors, ravages〕 of war / 오래〔질질〕 끄는 ~ a protracted 〔long=drawn〕 war / ~을 좋아하는 warlike; bellicose / ~중의 《교전중의》 belligerent; warring / ~중이다 be at war 《with》 / ~을 시작하다 open hostilities; go to war 《with》 / ~을 수행하다 wage war / ~을 확대하다 expand 〔escalate〕 a war / ~이 발발하다 a war breaks out / ~에 이기다〔지다〕 win 〔lose〕 a war / ~에 대비하다 be prepared for war / ~에 휩쓸리다 be involved in a war / ~에 참가하다 enter a war / ~에 돌입하다 rush into war / ~에 개입하다 intervene in a war / ~을 일으키다 provoke 〔bring on〕 war / ~에 반대〔찬성〕하다 be against 〔for〕 war / ~을 끝내다 put an end to war / ~을 회피하다 avoid war / ~은 곧 끝날 것이다 The war will be over soon. / 그들에게는 ~ 체험이 없다 They have no war experience. / 중동에서 ~이 일어났다 A war broke out in the Middle East. / 양국간의 국경 분쟁은 ~으로 발전할 것이다 The border dispute between the two countries will develop into a war. ◉ ~경기(景氣) a war 〔wartime〕 boom. ~고아 a war orphan. ~공포증 war-phobia. ~기념관 the War Memorial 《in Yongsan》. ~놀이 playing soldiers. ~도발 warmongering: ~도발자 a war-monger; a warmaker. ~문학 war literature. ~미망인 a war widow: ~ 미망인이 되었다 She was widowed by the war. ~반대 운동 an antiwar movement. ~범죄 war crimes: ~ 범죄자 a war criminal / ~범죄자 재판소 a war=criminals court. ~사생아 a war baby. ~소설〔영화〕 a war novel 〔film〕. ~수행능력 war potential. ~신경증 psychoneurosis of war. ~추방 the outlawry of war. ~포기 the renunciation of war. ~행위 an act of war; warfare. ~협력자 war collaborators. ~화 a battle picture. ~확대 expansion 〔widening〕 of war. ~희생자 a war victim.
**전쟁상태**(戰爭狀態) a state of war; belligerency. ¶ ~종결 선언 a proclamation 〔declaration〕 of the termination of the state of war / 준~ a quasi-war state / ~에 있다〔들어가다〕 「be in 〔enter into〕 a state of war.
**전적**(全的) (being) overall; complete; whole; the full. ¶ ~인 협력 whole=

hearted co(-)operation / ～으로 동의하다 give blanket consent / ～으로 실패하다 meet with utter failure.

**전적**(典籍) classical books. ⇨서적(書籍).

**전적**(戰跡) an old battlefield; 《visit》 the trace of battle.

**전적**(戰績) 《전쟁의》 a war record; military achievements; 《경기의》 results; a record; a score. ¶ 빛나는 ～ brilliant achievements; a splendid record.

**전적**(轉籍) ～하다 transfer *one's* domicile 〔family register〕; enter 《another's》 family register.

**전전**(戰前) prewar days; 〖국제법〗 *jus postliminii* (L.). ¶ ～의 prewar; before the war; antebellum; *avant-guerre* (F.) / 그녀는 ～에 미국에서 살았다 She lived in America before the war. ◉ ～세대 the prewar generation.

**전전**(前前) former times; the one before last. ¶ ～번 time before last. ◉ ～날 the day before yesterday (그저께); two days ago 〔earlier〕. ～달 month before last.

**전전긍긍**(戰戰兢兢) trembling from fear; trepidation; timidness; nervousness. ～하다 be trembling with fear; be filled with trepidation; be in great fear. ¶ ～하여 with fear and trembling; with trepidation; in great fear gingerly; timidly / 그는 추문이 탄로나지 않을까 ～하고 있었다 He was in constant fear that the scandal would come to light.

**전전하다**(轉轉—) 《임자를 바꾸다》 pass from hand to hand; change hands many times; 《헤매다》 wander from place to place; roam about. ¶ 직업을 바꾸어 ～ work at a variety of occupation; change from job to job / 그 사람은 각지를 전전했다 The man wandered from one place to another. / 그 시계는 여러 사람의 손을 전전했다 The watch passed from hand to hand.

**전절**(前節) the preceding 〔foregoing〕 paragraph; the last 〔prior〕 paragraph.

**전정**(前庭) ① 《앞뜰》 the front yard 〔garden〕. ② 〖해부〗 the vestibule. ◉ ～기관 a vestibular organ.

**전정**(剪定) 〖원예〗 pruning; trimming. ～하다 prune; trim. ◉ ～가위 pruning shears.

**전제**(前提) (a) presupposition; 〖논리〗 a premise; prerequisite. ～하다 set 《*something*》 forth as a premise. ¶ …을 ～로 하고 on the assumption 〔premise〕 that; assuming; supposing; presupposing / 우리는 결혼을 ～로 교제하고 있다 We are dating with marriage in mind. ◉ ～조건 《교섭의》 a precondition; 《필요한》 a prerequisite.

**전제**(專制) absolutism; despotism; autocracy; dictatorship. ¶ ～적인 autocratic; despotic; absolute. ◉ ～국 an absolute monarchy. ～군주 a despot; an autocrat; a tyrant; an absolute monarch: ～군주 정체 an absolute monarchy. ～정치 absolute 〔despotic〕 government; autocracy. ～주의 absolutism; despotism.

**전조**(前兆) 《길흉의》 an omen; 《조짐》 a presage; a sign; 《불길한》 a foreboding; a portent; 《병의 징후》 a (premonitory) symptom. ¶ 눈이 올 ～ a sign of snow / 좋은〔나쁜〕～ a good 〔a bad, an evil〕 omen / …의 ～이다 (fore)bode 《rain》; presage; be a sign of; be ominous of; portend; augur 《ill, well》 / 이 검은 구름은 폭풍우의 ～이다 This black cloud is a sign of a storm. / 그의 불면(不眠)은 노이로제의 ～인지도 모른다 His insomnia may be a premonitory symptom of neurosis.

**전조**(前條) the preceding item 〔clause〕; the foregoing article.

**전조**(轉調) 〖음악〗 transition; modulation.

**전조등**(前照燈) 《자동차의》 a headlight.

**전족**(纏足) foot-binding. ～하다 bind *one's* feet.

**전주**(前奏) 〖음악〗 a prelude; an introduction. ¶ 세계 대전의 ～ [비유적] a prelude to a world war. ◉ ～곡 an overture; a prelude.

**전주**(前週) 《그 전주》 the preceding week; the week before; 《지난 주》 last week. ¶ ～의 오늘 this day last week.

**전주**(電柱) an electric pole; a telegraph 〔telephone〕 pole. ◉ ～광고 a poster on a telegraph pole.

**전주**(錢主) a financier (자본주); a creditor (대여자); a money owner (소유자). ¶ ～가 되다 finance 《an enterprise》 / 이 사업의 ～는 김씨다 This enterprise is financed 〔financially backed up〕 by Mr. Kim.

**전중**(典重) courteousness; civility. ～하다 (be) courteous; civil.

**전지**(田地) cultivated land; farmland; fields.

**전지**(全知) omniscience. ～하다 (be) omniscient; all-knowing. ◉ ～전능 omniscience and omnipotence: ～전능의 omniscient and omnipotent / ～전능의 신 Almighty God.

**전지**(全紙) 《자르지 않은》 the whole sheet of paper; 《전지면》 the whole surface of a sheet of paper; the whole space of paper.

**전지**(剪枝) 『원예』 lopping; trimming; pruning. ～하다 lop; trim; prune. ◉ ～가위 pruning shears.

**전지**(電池) an electric cell; a battery (★ cell이 모인 것이 battery임). ¶ ～를 충전하다 charge a battery / ～를 교환하다 replace a battery with a new one / ～가 닳았다 The battery 「ran down 〔died, was dead〕.
◉ ～개폐기 a battery switch. ～시계 a battery watch. ～용량 battery capacity. ～충전 battery charging. ～회로 a battery circuit.

**전지**(戰地) the battlefield; the front. ¶ ～에 나가다 go to the front / ～로 출발하다 start for the front.
◉ ～근무 field service.

**전지**(轉地) a change of air 〔climate〕. ～하다 go 《to *a place*》 for a change of air; take 〔get〕 a change of air 《for *one's* health》. ◉ ～요법 treatment by change of air. ～요양 《taking》 a change of air for *one's* health.

**전직**(前職) the office 〔post〕 held previously; *one's* former office. ¶ ～교사 a former teacher / ～장관 an ex-minister.

**전직**(轉職) a job-change; a change of job 〔occupation〕. ～하다 change *one's* occupation 〔job〕; switch jobs 《to》. ¶ 그는 은행원에서 교사로 ～했다 He resigned his post as bank clerk and became a teacher.

**전진**(前進) moving forward; an advance; progress; 《구령》 Forward! ～하다 advance; move forward; go ahead; make headway (배 등의). ¶ 일보 ～하다 take a step forward / 군대는 ～을 계속했다 The troops kept advancing.
◉ ～각(角) 『항공』 a sweepforward angle. ～기지 an advance 〔a forward〕 base 〔post〕; an outpost. ～력 driving power. ～명령 《give》 orders for advance: ～명령을 내리다 give orders to advance / 그들은 ～명령을 기다리고 있었다 They were waiting for the go-ahead. ～배치 forward deployment: ～배치된 군대의 수를 증가시키다 increase the numbers of 'forward deployed' troops 《along its border》. ～부대 the foremost troops 《of an army》. ～운동 a forward movement; forward motion.

**전진**(戰陣) 《대형》 battle array 〔formation〕; 《진영》 a military camp; 《전장》 a battlefield; the front.

**전진**(戰塵) the dust of combat 〔of the battlefield〕. ¶ ～을 씻다 wash off the dust of combat.

**전질**(全帙) a complete set 《of books》.

**전집**(全集) *one's* complete works; a complete collection. ¶ 셰익스피어 ～ the complete works of Shakespeare.
◉ ～물 a complete works series. ～붐 a boom (in publication) of collected works. 개인～ complete works of an individual (writer).

**전차**(前借) borrowing in advance. ～하다 borrow 〔draw〕 《money》 in advance.
◉～금 money borrowed in advance.

**전차**(電車) an electric car; 《시내 전차》 a streetcar 《미》; a trolley car 《영》; a tram(car); an electric train (★ a train은 2량(輛)이상 연결한 것). ¶ 교외～ a suburban train / ～로 by streetcar 〔train, car〕 (★ 교통기관을 나타낼 때엔 흔히 무관사) / ～를 타다〔내리다〕 get on 〔get off〕 a streetcar 〔tram〕; 《교통 수단으로서》 take a 〔the〕 tram 《to Inch'ŏn》; go 《to Inch'ŏn》 by tram / ～편이 좋다〔나쁘다〕 be convenient 〔inconvenient〕 for getting on a streetcar / ～를 운전하다 run 〔operate〕 a tram(car) / 오는 ～마다 만원이었다 Car after car was full 〔overcrowded〕.
◉ ～삯 a car 〔tram〕 fare. ～선로 a streetcar line 〔track〕; a tramway 《영》. ～운전사 a motorman. ～정류장 a streetcar stop. ～차고 a tram shed; a car barn 《미》. ～차장 a streetcar conductor 〔conductress〕.

**전차**(戰車) 『군사』 a tank. ¶ 경〔중〕～ a light 〔heavy〕 tank / 대지뢰～ 《지뢰 폭발 장치를 갖춘 전차》 a flail tank.
◉ ～병 a tankman. ～부대 tank forces; a tank unit 〔outfit, corps〕. ～장애물 a tank barrier 〔obstacle〕. ～전(戰) tank warfare 〔battle〕. ～포 a tank gun: 대～포 an antitank gun; a bazooka (대전차 로켓포). ～호 a tank trap; an antitank trench.

**전차**(轉借) 《부동산의》 a sublease; (a) subtenancy; borrowing at second hand (임차인에게 다시 빌림). ～하다 borrow at second hand; borrow 《*something*》 indirectly; 《부동산을》 sublease. ¶ 그는 8년간 그 집을 ～하고 있다 He has been subleasing the house for 8 years. ◉ ～인 a sublessee; a subtenant.

**전차후옹**(前遮後擁) ～하다 guard the

van and protect rear.

**전채**(前菜) 〖요리〗 an *hors d'oeuvre* (F).

**전채**(戰債) 〖경제〗 war debt(s); war bonds.

**전책임**(全責任) full responsibility 《for》. ¶ ~을 지다 take 〔assume〕 full responsibility 《for》.

**전처**(前妻) *one's* former wife; an ex-wife. ¶ ~ 소생의 자식 a child by *one's* former wife.

**전천후**(全天候) all-weather. ◉ ~기(機) 〔요격기, 카메라〕 an all-weather 「plane 〔fighter, camera〕. ~농업〔영농〕 all-weather agriculture; farming free of drought. ~도로 all-weather highway. ~비행 all-weather flying.

**전철**(前轍) the track of a preceding wheel; a precedent. ¶ ~을 밟다 tread in 《*a person's*》 steps; follow 《*a person's*》 example; make the same 「mistake 〔error〕 as *one's* predecessors; repeat the same failure 《as...》.

**전철**(電鐵) an 「electric 〔electrified〕 railroad 〔railway〕. ◉ ~화(化) electrification of railroad: 서울과 위성 도시간의 ~화가 시급하다 Electrification of railroad is urgent between Seoul and its satellite cities. ~회사 an electric railroad company. 수도권 ~노선도 a metropolitan subway line map.

**전철**(轉轍) 〖철도〗 (railroad) switching. ◉ ~기 a switch 《미》; the points 《영》. ~수 a switchman; a pointsman.

**전첩**(戰捷) a victory; a triumph. ¶ ~을 올리다 win a victory.

**전체**(全體) the whole; the totality. ¶ ~의 whole; entire; general / ~적으로 generally; entirely; on the whole; in general / ~에 걸쳐서 all over; throughout / ~로서 as a whole; collectively; in the aggregate / ~ 합해서 in all; all told / 이 학급의 학생들은 ~적으로 머리가 좋다 The students of this class are generally (very) clever. ◉ ~주의 totalitarianism: ~주의의 totalitarian / ~주의 국가 a totalitarian state. ~회의 a plenary 「session 〔meeting〕; a general 「meeting 〔assembly〕.

**전초**(前哨) an outpost; an advanced post. ◉ ~기지 an advanced base. ~부대〔근무〕 outpost 「troops 〔duty〕. ~선 the outpost line. ~전(戰) a combat in outpost; a (preliminary) skirmish: 총선거의 ~전 a skirmish of the general election.

**전축**(電蓄) an electric gramophone; 《라디오 겸용》 a radiophonograph; 《영》 a radiogram; 《영》 a radio gramophone. ◉ 하이파이 ~ a high-fidelity gramophone.

**전출**(轉出) 《이주》 removal of residence; change of address; moving out; 《전임》 transfer (of post). ~하다 change *one's* 「residence 〔address〕; move out 《to》; transfer 《to another post》. ¶ 방계 회사로 ~되다 be transferred to a subsidiary company. ◉ ~신고 a moving-out notification; a removal notice; a report of a change of address. ~증명 certification of moving-out. ~지 the place of moving out. ~처 *one's* new address.

**전충**(塡充) filling; tamping; plugging. ~하다 fill (up); tamp; plug.

**전취**(前娶) *one's* former wife. ⇨ 전처.

**전취하다**(戰取—) fight to win; gain by fighting.

**전치**(全治) a complete cure; full recovery. ⇨ 완치. ~하다 completely 「cured 〔healed〕 《of》; completely cure; recover completely 《from》.

> **용법** 우리말에서는 「전치(全治)」라고 해도 영어에서는 단순히 「낫다」로 생각하고 표현해도 좋은 경우가 있음. **cure** 일반적으로 질병에 관해 쓰임. **heal** 상처에 관해 쓰임. **recover** 원래의 건강 상태로 돌아오다, 즉 「회복하다」란 뜻.

¶ ~ 2주의 부상 an injury which will take two weeks to heal completely / 그의 상처는 1주일만에 ~되었다 His wound healed in a week. / 그는 자동차 사고로 ~ 2주간의 부상을 입었다 In the car accident, he suffered an injury which would take two weeks to heal completely.

**전치사**(前置詞) 〖문법〗 a preposition. ¶ ~적 용법 a prepositional use / 이 동사에는 어떤 ~가 붙는가 What preposition is 「required 〔called for〕 after this verb? *or* What preposition follows this verb? ◉ ~구 a prepositional phrase.

**전칙**(典則) a law; a rule.

**전칭**(全稱) 〖논리〗 the generic; the universal. ◉ ~긍정〔부정〕 a universal 「affirmative 〔negative〕. ~명사(名辭) a general term. ~명제 a universal proposition. ~판단 a universal judgment.

**전토**(田土) cultivated lands; fields.

**전토**(全土) the entire 「country 〔land, territory〕; the whole land. ¶ 한국 ~에 걸쳐 all over Korea.

**전통**(傳統) (a) tradition; 《관습》 (a) convention. ¶ ~적(으로) tradition-al(ly) / 오랜 ~ a time-honored tradition / ~적인 문학 conventional literature / 80년의 ~이 있는 대학 a university with eighty years' tradition / ~적인 남아(男兒) 선호 사상 the conventional notion of preferring sons to daughters 《in our society》 / 오랜 ~의 감화를 받아서 influenced by hoary tradition / ~적인 한국의 축제 a traditional Korean festival / ~을 어기다 violate 〔break with〕 tradition / ~을 무시하다 ignore tradition / ~을 따르다 follow (a) tradition / ~을 존중하다 make much of tradition; value 〔cherish〕 tradition / 그들은 오랜 ~을 굳게 지키고 있다 They stick 〔adhere〕 to time-honored traditions. ◉ ~문화 a cultural heritage. ~주의 traditionalism: ~주의자 a traditionalist.

**전투**(戰鬪) a battle; a combat; an action; a fight; an engagement.

> 용법 **battle**은 일련의 교전 행위에서 이루어지는 전투: the battle of Waterloo / a naval battle. **combat**는 좁은 뜻에서의 전투 (보급·수송 따위를 포함하지 않는), 결전, 대결, 1대 1의 싸움 따위의 뜻을 내포. **fight**는 가장 일반적인 말이나, 종종 군사 행동 이외의 뜻으로도 씀: a fight for freedom (자유를 향한 투쟁). **action** 한번에 달성된 「행위」란 뜻에서, 지속적이 아닌 일과성의 격렬한 「전투·교전」의 뜻으로 쓰이는 말. **engagement** 「혼약·약속·계약·고용」 등의 여러 뜻이 있지만, 「교전·전투」를 뜻하는 격식차린 표현으로도 쓰임.

¶ ~적(인) militant; combatant / ~를 개시하다 go into action 〔battle〕; open hostilities; begin a combat 《미》 / ~를 중지하다 break off a battle; cease hostilities / ~중인 병사 a soldier in combat / ~에 참가하다 take part in 〔come into〕 action; join battle. ◉ ~경찰대 the combatant 〔riot〕 police unit. ~교련 combat drill; field training. ~기 a fighter. ~대형 battle formation: ~ 대형으로 in battle array / ~ 대형을 이루다 form in fighting order. ~력(力) 《augmentation of》 combat strength 〔capabilities〕; fighting power 〔strength, efficiency〕: ~력을 상실하다 be disabled; be put out of action. ~모(帽) a field(-service) cap. ~병과 장교 an arm branch 〔a combat arm〕 officer. ~복 combat uniform 〔fatigues〕. ~부대 a combat unit 〔troop〕: ~부대의 전방 배치 the forward deployment of combat units. ~비행 combat flying. ~상태 a state of hostilities 〔war〕: ~ 상태로 들어가다 enter a state of war; go to war (with each other) / 두 나라는 오랜 기간 ~ 상태에 있다 The two countries have been in a state of war 〔at war〕 for a long time. ~요격기 a fighter-interceptor. ~원 a combatant; a combat crew. ~준비 preparation for action; clearing for action; 《구령》 To arms!; Clear the deck! (해군의). ~중지 suspension of hostilities. ~지대 a battle 〔combat〕 zone. ~지휘관 a combat commander 〔leader〕. ~태세 combat readiness. ~폭격기 ⇨ 전폭기. ~함 a battleship. ~행위 an act of hostility. ~화(靴) combat shoes. ~훈련 battle practice; field training. 야간~ night fighting.

**전파**(全破) complete destruction. ~하다 destroy completely; demolish. ¶~되다 be completely destroyed; be razed to the ground. ◉ ~가옥 a razed 〔completely destroyed〕 house.

**전파**(電波) 〖물리〗 an electric wave; a radio wave. ¶ ~를 통하여 over the air / ~에 싣다 put 《a program》 on the air / ~에 실리다 be broadcast (by radio); go on the air. ◉ ~감시 monitoring of radio waves. ~강도 radio field intensity 〔strength〕. ~계 a 〔an electric〕 wavemeter; a cymoscope. ~관리 radio regulation. ~망원경 a radio telescope. ~매체 broadcast media. ~발신음 electronic beeps. ~방해 jamming: ~방해로 라디오 청취나 TV프로 시청을 거의 할 수가 없다 I can hardly hear radio programs or see television because of jamming. ~스모그 electronic smog. ~영상경(映像鏡) 《레이더의》 a radarscope. ~전(戰) radio warfare. ~조종 radio control. ~천문학 radio astronomy: ~천문학자 a radio astronomer. ~탐지기 a radar; a radiolocator. ~탐지법 radiolocation. ~파장 wave length. ~항법 radio navigation.

**전파**(傳播) propagation; spreading; circulation; diffusion; dissemination. ~하다 propagate; transmit; spread abroad; disseminate; circulate. ¶ 열의 ~ transmission of heat / 음향의 ~ propagation of sound / 병균의 ~ dissemination 〔spread〕 of disease germs / 문명의 ～ the spread of civilization. ◉ ～속도 propagation velocity. ～오류 〖컴퓨터〗 an propagated error. ～지연 〖컴퓨터〗 propagation delay: ～지연 시간 propagation delay time.

**전파수신기**(全波受信機) an all-wave receiver 〔radio set〕.

**전판**(全一) all; the whole; the entire lot. ¶ 나는 그녀를 ～ 모른다 I don't know her at all. / 그는 가진 것을 ～ 잃었다 He lost his all.

**전패**(全敗) a complete 〔crushing〕 defeat; a rout. ～하다 be 〔get〕 completely 〔totally〕 defeated; lose all *one's* games 〔matches, bouts〕.

**전편**(全篇) the whole book; the whole volume. ¶ ～을 통해서 from cover to cover; from title page to colophon.

**전편**(前篇) the first volume 〔part〕; part I.

**전폐**(全廢) total abolition. ～하다 do away with; abolish (completely). ¶ 노예 제도의 ～ the abolition of slavery. ◉ ～론 abolitionism: ～론자 an abolitionist.

**전포**(廛鋪) a store 《미》; a shop 《영》.

**전폭**(全幅) the full width 《of cloth》; the whole piece 《of cloth》. ¶ 비행기 날개의 ～ the wing span of an airplane / ～적으로 to the full; fully / ～적으로 지지하다 give 《*a person*》 full support / ～적인 all; every; full; utmost / ～적인 동정을 보이다 extend 〔show〕 wholehearted sympathy 《to *a person*》 / ～적으로 신뢰하다 put 〔place〕 full confidence in 《*a person*》; trust 《*a person*》 fully 〔wholeheartedly〕 / 그녀의 제안에 ～적인 동의를 했다 We agreed with her suggestions a hundred percent.

**전폭기**(戰爆機) a fighter-bomber. ¶ 전천후 ～ an all-weather fighter-bomber.

**전표**(傳票) a voucher; a slip; a chit; a check 《미》; a bill. ¶ ～를 떼다 sign 〔give〕 a chit; issue a voucher / ～와 교환으로 지급하다 pay 《money》 in exchange for a slip. ◉ 매출～ a sales check. 수납〔지불〕～ a receiving 〔paying-out〕 slip.

**전하**(殿下) 《2인칭》 Your (Royal) Highness; 《3인칭》 His 〔Her〕 Highness; Their Highness (★ 2인칭, 3인칭에 따르는 동사는 모두 3인칭). ¶ 동궁 ～ His Royal Highness; the Crown Prince.

**전하**(電荷) 〖전기〗 (an) electrical charge. ◉ 양〔음〕～ (a) positive 〔negative〕 charge.

**전하다**(傳一) ① 《말·소식을》 inform; notify; communicate; convey; tell; report.

> 용법 **inform** 「알리다」라는 뜻으로서, 어떤 상황을 파악하는데 필요한 사실이나 소식을 전달한다는 뜻. **notify** (정식으로) 「통지하다」, 「알리다」라는 뜻. 문서 따위로 「통지〔연락〕하다」 라는 뜻도 됨. **communicate** 지식·정보·의견·기대·감정 등을 「알리다」, 「전달하다」라는 뜻. 특히 전달 여부의 결과를 강조함. **convey** 생각·의견·감정 등을 「전달하다」, 「알리다」라는 뜻. 「매개체가 되어서」라는 뜻도 지니고 있음. **report** 보거나 조사한 것을 「보고하다」라는 뜻.

¶ 전하는 바에 의하면 according to reports; it is reported 〔said〕 that... / 허보를 ～ give 〔spread, circulate〕 a false report / 비보를 ～ break the sad news 《to the family》 / 말을 ～ convey a message / 정보를 ～ give 〔pass on〕 information 《to *a person*》 / 말을 전하라고 부탁받다 be asked to give a message 《to *a person*》 / 출석할 뜻을 ～ signify 〔notify of〕 *one's* intention to be present / 그에게 곧 오라고 전해 주시오 Tell him to come at once. / 이 말을 그에게 전하시오 Please convey this message to him. / 그한테 전화 좀 해 달라고 전해 주십시오 Will you tell him to give me a ring ? / 뉴욕타임스가 그 사건을 자세히 전하고 있다 The New York Times reports the affair in full. / 부인께 인사 말씀 전해 주십시오 Please remember me to your wife. / 전하실 말씀 있으세요 《전화에서》 May I take your message ? *or* Would you care to leave a message ?

② 《물려주다》 hand down; pass on; bequeath; leave; transmit. ¶ 가보로 전해진 검 a sword handed down as an heirloom / 후세에 ～ hand down to posterity / 가보를 대대로 ～ hand down *one's* heirloom from generation to generation.

③ 《전수하다》 impart; initiate; teach; introduce; bring. ¶ 제자에게 지식을 ～ impart knowledge to *one's* disciple / 아무에게 비법을 ～ initiate *a person* into the mysteries.

④ 《전달하다》 bring; take. ¶ 편지를 아무한테 ～ take 〔bring〕 a letter to *a person* / 이 꾸러미를 전하라는 말씀이었습니다 He asked me to hand this bundle to you.

⑤ 《열·전기·빛 따위를》 conduct; transmit; propagate. ¶ 구리는 전기를 잘 전한다 Copper conducts electricity well. ⑥ 《문물을》 introduce 《an invention into a country》. ¶ 기독교를 한국에 ~ introduce Christianity into Korea.

**전학**(轉學) change of schools. ~하다 change *one's* school; change 〔transfer〕 (to another school). ◉ ~생 a transfer student.

**전학급**(全學級) the whole class.

**전함**(戰艦) 『군사』 a warship; a battleship.

**전항**(前項) the preceding clause; the foregoing paragraph; 『수학·논리』 the antecedent.

**전해**(前—) the previous 〔preceding〕 year.

**전해**(電解) 『물리』 electrolysis; electrolyzation. ~하다 electrolyze. ◉ ~분리 electrolytic dissociation 〔analysis〕. ~소다 electrolytic soda. ~조(槽) an electrolytic cell; an electrolyzer. ~질〔액〕 an electrolyte.

**전해듣다**(傳—) hear 《from others》; hear at second hand; learn by hearsay. ¶ 전해 들은 말 hearsay; secondhand 〔hearsay〕 information / 그것은 전해 들어서 알았네 I have got it by hearsay.

**전향**(轉向) changing directions; switching courses; conversion. ~하다 shift; switch over 《to》; turn 《to》; be converted 《to》; turn *one's* coat. ¶ 우익으로 ~하다 swing to the right / 180도 ~을 하다 do a complete about=face; make a complete volte-face / 그는 급진파에서 보수파로 ~하였다 He turned from Radical to Conservative. / 그녀는 회사를 그만두고 화가로 ~했다 She left her company and became a painter. ◉ ~자 a convert 《from》. ~점 a turning point.

**전혀**(全—) 《not》 at all; entirely; wholly; quite; completely; utterly; totally; altogether; in any shape or form.
¶ ~ 모르는 사람 a total stranger / ~ 다르다 be quite different; 《사실이 아니다》 be not true 〔so〕 at all / ~ 관계가 없다 be not connected in any shape or form 《with the matter》 / ~ 들은 바 없다 hear nothing 《of》 / ~ 생각해 보려고도 안 하다 do not even try to think 《a question》 / 동정심이라곤 ~ 없다 He doesn't have a particle of sympathy. / 그를 ~ 모릅니다 I don't know him at all. / 「그것을 아느냐」—「아니오 ~ 모릅니다」 "Do you know of it?"—"No, not a bit (of it)." / 기계에 관해선 ~ 모른다 I know nothing (whatever) about machine. / 그것은 ~ 믿을 수 없는 일이다 It's quite unbelievable. / 난 ~ 상관없다 I have nothing to do with it. *or* I don't mind what so ever.

**전형**(典型) a model; a type; a specimen; a pattern. ¶ ~적인 model; typical; representative / ~적인 보기 a typical example / 남성의 ~ a model of manhood / 그는 ~적인 학자다 He is a typical scholar. / 그녀는 ~적인 미인이다 She is a paragon of beauty.

**전형**(銓衡) screening; selection; choice. ~하다 screen; select; choose. ¶ ~에서 누락되다 fail to be selected; be not chosen / 제1차 ~에 합격하다 get through the first selection. ◉ ~기준 a criterion for selection. ~시험 a screening test. ~위원 a member of screening 〔a selection〕 committee: ~위원회 a selection committee.

**전호**(前號) the preceding 〔last〕 number 〔issue〕. ¶ ~에서 계속 《표시》 Continued (from the last issue).

**전화**(電化) electrification. ~하다 electrify. ¶ 철도를 ~하다 electrify the railroad / 철도가 ~되기까지는 아직 여러 해 있어야 할 것이다 It may be years before the railroad system is electrified. ◉ ~구간 an electrified section. ~사업〔계획〕 an electrification work 〔program〕. ~주택 an electrified home. 농촌~ rural electrification 《program》.

**전화**(電話) a telephone; a phone. ~하다 telephone; phone; call; call up; ring up 《영》; make 〔place〕 a telephone call 《to》.
¶ ~로 by (tele)phone; through the telephone / ~로 이야기하다 talk 〔speak〕 《to *a person*》 over the telephone / ~를 받고 있다 be on the phone / ~가 통하지 않다 cannot reach 《*a person*》 on the phone / ~를 걸다 make a phone call / ~를 끊다 ring off; hang up / ~를 가설하다 install a phone; have a phone installed / ~가 오다 the phone rings; have a phone call / ~로 불러내다 get 《*a person*》 on the phone / ~ 공사중 《게시》 Telephone repair ahead. / ~를 좀 써도 되겠습니까 May I use your telephone? / ~를 끊지 마시오 Hold the line, please. / ~왔습니다 You're wanted on the phone. *or* A phone for you. *or* There is a call for you. *or* You have a call. / 그에게는 언제 ~ 걸어도 통화중이다 Every time I try to call him up, the line is busy. / 「전화를 몇 번에 거

셨습니까」—「735국에 1984입니다」 "What number did you dial?"—"I dialed 735-1984." (★ 보통 seven three five one nine eight four라고 읽음) / ～ 잘못 거셨습니다 You have the wrong number. *or* The wrong number. / 나중에 다시 ～하겠습니다 I'll call you back later. / ～가 멀군요. 좀 더 크게 말씀하세요 I can't hear you. Speak a little louder, please. / 댁에 ～가 있습니까 Is there a telephone installed in your house? / 「《교환원》 UCLA 입니다. 하신 ～를 어디로 연결해 드릴까요」—「김달선 교수 연구실로 연결해 주십시오」—「기다려 주세요」 "UCLA. How may I direct your call?"—"Connect me with the office of Professor Dal-sun Kim, please."—"Please hold the line while I transfer your call." / 미스터 강으로부터 ～가 왔었습니다. ～를 걸어달라고 하시던데요 You had a call from Mr. Kang. He wanted you to call him back. / 그는 지금 다른 ～를 받고 있습니다 He is on another line at the moment. / 누구와 ～통화하시길 원하십니까 Who are you calling?

◉ ～가설료 charge for telephone fixture. ～가입자 a telephone subscriber. ～교환국 a telephone exchange. ～교환대 a (telephone) switchboard. ～교환원 a telephone operator 〔girl〕; a hello girl 《미구어》. ～국 a telephone office. ～기〔통〕 a telephone (apparatus). ～네트워크 『컴퓨터』 a (tele)phone network. ～도수제(度數制) the call system. ～리퀘스트쇼 《라디오·TV》 a call-in 〔phone-in〕 show. ～박스 a telephone booth; a call box 《영》. ～번호 a telephone number (★ 명함 따위에 전화 번호를 넣을 때에는 tel: 보다 phone: 이 보통임). ～번호부 a telephone directory 〔book〕: ～번호부에 실려 있다 be (listed) in the phone book. ～선 a telephone wire 〔line〕. ～세 a telephone service tax. ～수화기 a (telephone) receiver. ～연락: 계속해서 ～ 연락을 취하다 keep in constant telephone communication 《with》. ～요금 telephone 〔call〕 charges: ～요금 청구서 a telephone bill. ～전보 a telephone telegram. ～주문 an order by telephone. ～카드 (telephone) calling card.

괴롭힘～ a harassing call. 교환～ an extension (tele)phone. 국제～ an international telephone service: 국제 수동 ～ international operator-assisted calls / 국제 자동 ～ international subscriber dialing (생략 I.S.D.). 긴급～ emergency calls. 누름단추식～ a push-button (tele)phone. 대표～ the main number 《for》; the general information number. 도청방지～ a scrambler telephone. 장거리～ a long-distance telephone 〔call〕 《미》; a trunk=call 《영》: 장거리 자동～ direct distance dialing (생략 DDD) / 장거리 자동 공중～ DDD public phone. 화상～ a videophone.

> 참고 전화의 종류: 공동 전화 a party line. 다이얼식 전화 a rotary dial phone. 벽걸이 전화 a wall phone. 비디오〔TV〕 전화 a videophone (상표명). 《부재중의》 자동응답 전화 an answering machine; a message phone. 자동차 전화 a car 〔cellular〕 phone. 직통 전화 a direct line. 휴대용 전화 a portable 〔cellular〕 phone.

**전화**(戰火) 《전쟁에 의한 화재》 the fires of war; 《전쟁》 a war. ¶ 아시아를 ～로부터 구하다 save Asia from war.

**전화**(戰禍) the disasters 〔devastation, ravages, afflictions, horrors〕 of war; war damage. ¶ ～를 입은 war-torn; war-shattered / ～를 입다 suffer the damages of war / ～를 입은 유럽 war=torn Europe.

**전화**(轉化) transformation; change. ～하다 transform 《from, into》; change 《from, to, into》; be transformed.

**전화면**(全畫面) full screen. ◉ ～표시장치 『컴퓨터』 (a) full-page display.

**전화위복**(轉禍爲福) good coming out of evil. ～하다 a misfortune turns into a blessing. ¶ 이런 경우를 ～이라고 한다 This is a case of good coming out of evil.

**전환**(轉換) conversion; changeover; diversion; reconversion; switchover; turnover; commutation; switching (of electric current); transposition. ～하다 convert 《*a thing* to》; divert 《*one's* mind from》; reconvert; switch over; commutate; switch. ¶ 기분 ～으로 for a change; 《take a walk》 for a diversion / 방향을 ～하다 change *one's* direction / 180도(의) ～ 《태도·의견 따위를》 《make》 a complete about-face / 기분 ～을 위해 사냥을 가다 go for sports for a change / 군수 산업을 평화 산업으로 ～하다 convert the munition industries to a peacetime basis.

◉ ∼가치 〖경제〗 a conversion factor 〔value〕. ∼기(期) a turning point; a transitional period 〔stage〕: 역사적인 ∼기 a turning point in history / ∼기의 문학 literature at the turning point / ∼기의 한국 Korea in transition. ∼기(器) a commutator; a switch. ∼로(爐) 〖원자물리〗 a converter reactor. ∼사채(社債) a convertible (corporate) bond 〔debenture〕 (생략 CB). ∼스위치 a changeover switch. ∼점 a turning point. ∼주(株) a convertible stock.

**전황**(戰況) the progress of a battle; the war situation. ¶ ∼을 보고하다 report on the war situation / ∼은 아군에 유리하게 전개되고 있다 The war is going in our favor. ◉ ∼뉴스 war news 〔reports〕.

**전회**(前回) the last 〔preceding, prior〕 time; an earlier occasion. ¶ ∼의 last; previous; preceding / ∼의 강의 the last 〔previous〕 lecture / ∼까지의 줄거리 the outline of the story up to the last installment.

**전회**(轉回) rotation; revolution; alternation; evolution. ∼하다 rotate; revolve.

**전횡**(專橫) despotism; absolutism; autocracy; tyranny; arbitrariness; high-handedness. ∼하다 be despotic; tyrannize; act arbitrarily. ¶ ∼적인 행동을 하다 have *one's* own way; tyrannize 〔domineer〕 《over》; carry matters with a high hand.

**전후**(前後) ① 《위치의》 before and behind; the front and the rear; 《때의》 before and after. ⇨ 앞뒤. ¶ ∼곡절〔사연〕 all the circumstances; all the details 《of an affair》 / ∼좌우로 "before and behind, right and left"; in every direction; on all sides / ∼하여 《시간적으로》 at about the same time / 한국 전쟁을 ∼해서 우리 사회에 큰 변동이 있었다 There was a general upheaval in Korea about the time of the Korean War.
② 《처음과 끝·순서·사리》 the preceding and the following; sequence; order. ¶ 참사의 ∼ 사정 details of a disaster / ∼ 생각도 없이 reckless of the consequences; without reflecting on the consequences; thoughtlessly / ∼를 통하여 from the first to the last; throughout / ∼가 모순되다 be (self=) contradictory.
③ 《약》 about; thereabout; approximately. ¶ 40 ∼의 남자 a man of about forty / 그녀는 20세 ∼다 She is around twenty.
◉ ∼관계 《문장의》 the context: 이들 문장은 ∼ 관계를 무시하고 인용되고 있다 These passages have been taken out of context. ∼좌우 all directions: 나는 ∼ 좌우를 주의깊게 둘러 보았다 I looked about 〔around〕 me carefully.

**전후**(戰後) postwar days; [형용사적] postwar. ¶ ∼의 한국 postwar Korea / ∼ 문제 postbellum questions / ∼의 사회 상태 afterwar social conditions; postbellum social state / ∼ 수년간 for several years after the war / ∼ 최대의 위기 the worst crisis since the war / ∼ 49년을 경과했다 forty-nine years have passed since the close of the war. ◉ ∼세대 the *après-guerre* generation 〔school〕; the postwar generation: ∼세대의 청년들 young men of the postwar type.

**전훈**(電訓) telegraphic instructions 「〔order〕.

**절**[1] 《사찰》 a Buddhist temple. ¶ 절간 a Buddhist temple; temple buildings / 절에 불공 드리러 가다 go to a temple 「to worship 〔to offer a Buddhist service〕; visit a temple for worship.

**절**[2] 《인사》 a bow (on *one's* knees); a deep bow; an obeisance. ∼하다 bow; make 「a bow 〔an obeisance〕 《to》. ¶ 큰절 a bow on ceremonial occasion; a ceremonial bow / 공손히 절하다 bow politely; make a low bow / 그들은 서로 절을 하였다 They exchanged bows.

**절**(節) ① 《글》 a paragraph; a passage; a section; a stanza; a verse. ¶ 제1장 제2절 chapter I, section II. ② 〖문법〗 a clause. ③ 《절개》 loyalty; chastity.

**-절**(折) folding. ¶ 12절 duodecimo; 12 mo / 2절로 하다 fold in two 〔half〕.

**-절**(節) 《절기》 a season; 《명절》 a festival. ¶ 성탄절 Christmas / 삼일절 the anniversary of the *Samil* Independence Movement.

**절감**(節減) curtailment; retrenchment; economy. ∼하다 reduce; curtail; retrench; cut (down on). ¶ 비용을 ∼하다 cut expenses; cut down on expenses / 우리는 에너지의 소비를 ∼하여야 한다 We have to cut down on our consumption of energy.

**절감하다**(切感―) feel keenly 〔acutely〕. ¶ 어학의 필요성을 ∼ feel keenly the necessity of linguistic knowledge.

**절개**(切開) 《외과》 (an) incision; an operation; (a) section. ∼하다 incise; cut 〔lay〕 open; operate 《upon》. ¶ 제

왕 ∼(수술) a Caesarean operation / 환부를 ∼하다 cut out the affected parts / 종기를 ∼하다 incise a tumor. ◉ ∼수술 a surgical operation; incision; surgery. 십자∼ crucial incision. 위∼술 gastrotomy.

**절개**(節槪) 《충절》 integrity; honor; 《순결·정조》 chastity; 《신의》 faith. ¶ ∼가 있는 사람 a man of integrity / ∼를 지키다 remain faithful to *one's* cause; 《여자가》 keep *one's* chastity.

**절검**(節儉) economy; thrift; frugality. ∼하다 economize; save. ⇨절약.

**절경**(絶景) a magnificent view; fine scenery; a scenic masterpiece; a fine sight. ¶ 천하∼ the grandest view under the sun.

**절교**(絶交) breaking off friendship; a breach of friendship; a rupture in relation; breaking relations. ∼하다 break 《with》; break off *one's* relationship 〔friendship〕 with; cut *one's* connection 《with》; be done 〔through〕 with. ¶ 나는 그녀와 ∼했다 I broke off my relationship with her. *or* I'm through with her. *or* I have nothing to do with her any more. ◉ ∼장(狀) a letter of breaking off *one's* relationship with 《*a person*》; 《미구어》 a Dear John (letter) (여자가 남자에게 보내는).

**절구** a 《stone, wood》 mortar. ¶ ∼에 쌀을 찧다 pound rice in a mortar. ◉ ∼질 pounding grain in a mortar: ∼질하다 pound grain in a mortar. ∼통 the body of a mortar: 그 여자는 ∼통이다 She has no waist. *or* She is built like a washtub 〔silo〕. 절굿공이 a (wooden) pestle.

**절구**(絶句) 『문학』 a four-line stanza of Chinese poetry; a Chinese quatrain.

**절규**(絶叫) (an) exclamation; (an) ejaculation. ∼하다 exclaim 〔shout〕 at the top of *one's* voice; ejaculate; cry out; scream. ¶ 피맺힌 ∼ the painful outcries.

**절그렁** with a clink; jingling; rattling. ∼하다, ∼거리다 clink; jingle; rattle. ¶ 열쇠를 ∼거리다 rattle *one's* keys.

**절기**(絶忌) abhorrence; abomination.

**절기**(絶技) wonderful arts and crafts.

**절기**(絶奇) exquisiteness; excellence. ∼하다 strange; wonderful; 《절묘하다》 exquisite; excellent.

**절기**(節氣) the subdivisions of the seasons; the 24 solar terms 〔seasonal divisions〕.

**절꺼덕** with a snap 〔click〕. ∼하다 make a snap; click; slap; slurp. ∼거리다 snap 〔click〕 away; slap and slap. ¶ 자물쇠를 ∼ 잠그다 click 《the door》 shut; fasten a lock with a snap.

**절다**[1] 《소금에》 get (well) salted; get salted through and through. ¶ 이 청어는 잘 절었다 These herrings are well salted.

**절다**[2] 《다리를》 limp; hobble. ¶ 다리를 ∼ limp (in the legs); hobble; be lame / 다리를 몹시〔약간〕 ∼ limp heavily 〔slightly〕 / 한 쪽 다리를 ∼ be lame of one leg / 오른편 다리를 ∼ limp in the right leg / 다리를 절며 걷다 limp 〔hobble〕 along / 부상자는 다리를 절며 가버렸다 The wounded man hobbled away.

**절단**(切斷·截斷) cutting; severance; abscission; 《손발의》 amputation. ∼하다 cut 《off》; sever; amputate; 『컴퓨터』 《계산에서 수치 조정》 truncate; 《연결을 끊음》 disconnect. ¶ 둘로 ∼하다 cut 《*a thing*》 in two / 다리를 ∼하다 amputate a leg. ◉ ∼기 a cutting machine; a cutter. ∼도 a drawing in section. ∼면 a section; a cutting plane (제도에서). ∼오차 『컴퓨터』 a truncation error. ∼환자 an amputee.

**절대**(絶對) absoluteness. ¶ ∼의 absolute; unconditional; unconditioned / ∼로 absolutely; unconditionally; positively / ∼의 진리 (an) absolute truth / ∼불변의 immutable; permanent / ∼로 금하다 prohibit positively / ∼로 필요하다 be absolutely necessary / 명령에 ∼로 복종하다 obey orders without question / 그것은 ∼로 불가능하다 It is absolutely impossible. / 그런 일은 ∼로 하지 않겠습니다 I swear I will never do such a thing. / ∼로 허용치 않겠다 I won't allow it on any account. / ∼로 그녀를 떠나지 않겠다 I will never leave her. / 신은 ∼적 존재이다 God is the absolute being. / ∼로 그렇지 않습니다 Cross my heart, I'm not telling a lie. / 나는 ∼로 가지 않겠다 I positively decline to go. *or* Blame my hide if I go. / 과학을 ∼시하는 것은 위험하다 It's dangerous to place absolute trust in science.

◉ ∼가격 absolute price. ∼값 『수학』 the absolute value; the modulus (*pl.* -li). ∼개념 absolute concept. ∼고도 absolute altitude. ∼공간 absolute space. ∼군주 an absolute monarch: ∼군주제 (an) absolute monarchy. ∼권 absolute right: ∼ 권력 absolute authority 〔power〕. ～금주(禁酒) total abstinence: ～금주주의 teetotalism. ～농지 exclusive farmland. ～다수(를 차지하다〔얻다〕) (enjoy 〔win〕) an absolute majority. ～단위 〖물리〗 an absolute unit. ～대표권 exclusive representation. ～등급 〖천문〗 absolute magnitude. ～론자 an absolutist. ～명령 〖철학〗 categorical imperative; 〖컴퓨터〗 absolute instruction. ～명사 〖논리〗 an absolute term. ～무기 an ultimate weapon. ～반대 positive opposition: ～ 반대이다 be positively 〔dead〕 against 《a proposal》/ ～ 반대의 입장을 취하다 stand positively against 《it》. ～번지 지정 〖컴퓨터〗 absolute addressing. ～복종 absolute 〔unconditional〕 obedience: ～ 복종을 요구하다 demand 《*a person's*》 absolute obedience. ～선(善) the absolute good. ～속도 〖물리〗 absolute velocity (speed). ～습도 〖물리〗 absolute humidity. ～아(我) 〖철학〗 absolute ego. ～안정 (a) complete 〔(an) absolute〕 rest: ～ 안정을 취하고 있다 take a complete rest / 환자는 ～ 안정을 요한다 The patient must be kept absolutely at rest. ～압(력) 〖물리〗 absolute pressure. ～액(額) 《숫자상의》 an absolute figure. ～언어 〖컴퓨터〗 an absolute language. ～오차 〖컴퓨터〗 an absolute error. ～온도〔영도〕 〖물리〗 absolute temperature 〔zero〕. ～우위 an absolute advantage 《over》: ～ 우위에 서다 gain an absolute advantage over 《another》. ～운동 〖물리〗 absolute motion. ～원리 an absolute principle. ～음감(音感) (the sense of ) absolute 〔perfect〕 pitch. ～음악 absolute music. ～자 〖철학〗 the Absolute; the absolute being. ～주의 absolutism. ～평가 absolute evaluation. ～항 〖수학〗 an absolute term.

**절대량**(絶對量) an absolute quantity. ¶ ～이 많다〔적다〕 be large 〔small〕 in absolute quantity / 식량의 ～을 확보하다 secure the absolutely needed quantity 〔supply〕 of food / ～이 부족하다 We are short of absolute quantity.

**절대빈곤**(絶對貧困) absolute poverty. ¶ 정부후원으로 실시된 한 통계에 의하면, 300만 명 이상의 국민이 ～에서 생활하고 있는 것으로 나타났다 A government-sponsored survey shows that more than 3 million people live in "absolute poverty".

**절대적**(絶對的) absolute; unconditional; positive; imperative. ¶ ～ 실업 absolute unemployment / ～ 요소 an absolute / ～ 존재 the absolute being.

**절도**(節度) moderation. ¶ ～를 지키다 be moderate 《in drinking》; exercise moderation.

**절도**(竊盜) 《행위》 (a) theft; pilferage (작은 것을 조금씩); 〖법〗 larceny; 《사람》 a thief (*pl.* thieves). ¶ 시계 ～의 혐의로 (charged) with the larceny of a watch / ～질하다 steal; commit a theft; pilfer; filch / ～혐의로 잡히다 be arrested on the suspicion of theft. ◉ ～범 《죄》 larceny; theft; 《사람》 a thief; a larcenist. ～죄 larceny; theft.

**절뚝거리다** limp; hobble. ⇨ 절다[2].

**절뚝절뚝** limping; hobbling.

**절량농가**(絶糧農家) a food-short farm household; food-short farmers. ¶ ～의 구호 대책을 세우다 map 〔work〕 out relief measures for food-short farmers.

**절레절레** shaking *one's* head.

**절륜**(絶倫) being peerless 〔matchless〕. ～하다 (be) peerless; matchless; unparalleled; unique. ¶ 정력(精力)이 ～한 사람 a man of unequaled energy.

**절름발이** a lame person. ¶ 그는 심한 ～다 He is badly lame. *or* He is seriously crippled.

**절망**(切望) an earnest desire; an eager wish; an entreaty. ～하다 sincerely hope; eagerly wish; earnestly desire. ¶ 그는 귀국을 ～하였다 He was anxious to return to his country.

**절망**(絶望) despair; hopelessness. ～하다 despair of; be driven to despair; give up 〔surrender〕 all hope. ¶ ～적인 hopeless (가망 없는); desperate (절망 상태의); despairing (낙담해 있는) / ～하여 in despair; despairingly / ～한 나머지 out of despair; driven 〔overcome〕 by despair / ～적인 상태 a desperate state of affairs / ～케 하다〔시키다〕 make 《*a person*》 despair; drive 《*a person*》 to despair; throw 《*a person*》 into despair / ～에 빠지다 abandon *oneself* to despair / ～의 구렁텅이에 빠져 있다 be (sunk) in the depths of despair / ～한 나머지 자살하다 take *one's* life out of despair / 그의 생존은 이제 ～적인 것 같다 There is no hope that he is alive. *or* His possible survival is hopeless. / 환자는 ～적이다 The patient is past hope. / 반드시 ～적인 것은 아니다 There is still some hope. / 앞일은 완전히 ～적이다 There is not a slim chance before us.

**절멸**(絶滅) annihilation; extermination; extinction; eradication. ~하다 《없애다》 annihilate; exterminate; eradicate; wipe out (of existence); 《없어지다》 go out of existence; become extinct; die out. ¶ ~의 위기에 처하다 be on the verge [brink] of extinction; face extinction; be in danger of extinction / 핵전쟁은 인류를 ~시킬 것이다 Nuclear war would 「wipe out [exterminate] the human race.

**절명**(絶命) death. ~하다 die; expire; pass away; breathe *one's* last. ¶ 두 시간 후에 ~했다 He passed away two hours later.

**절묘**(絶妙) exquisiteness; superbness; excellence. ~하다 (be) exquisite; superb; superexcellent. ¶ ~한 예술품 exquisite works of art / ~한 재주 a miraculous feat / ~한 필치 an exquisite touch.

**절무**(絶無) none [nothing] (at all); nought; nil; total absence. ~하다 be none at all; be nil; be totally absent.

**절미**(節米) economy in rice consumption; rice saving. ~하다 economize on [in] rice. ◉ ~계획 a rice-saving program. ~운동 a movement for saving rice; a save-the-rice campaign.

**절박**(切迫) ① 《급박함》 urgency; pressure; imminence; impendence. ~하다 (be) imminent; urgent; pressing; impending. ¶ ~한 위기 an impending crises / 마감 기일이 ~하다 the deadline is drawing [getting] near / 시간이 ~하다 Time presses [is pressing]. / 우리는 ~한 상황하에 있다 We are in an urgent condition. ② 《긴장·심각》 acuteness; tension. ~하다 (be) acute; tense; serious. ¶ 사태가 ~하다 The situation is serious [tense]. / 방 안에는 ~한 분위기가 감돌고 있었다 There was a tense atmosphere in the room. ◉ ~감 a sense of urgency.

**절반**(折半) a half. ~하다 cut in halves; divide 《*a thing*》 into halves; halve. ¶ ~의 크기[값] half the size [price] / ~의 확률 a fifty-fifty chance 《of survival》 / ~씩 나누다 go halves [shares] 《with *a person* in *a thing*》 / 이제 ~은 왔다 We have covered half the distance. / 그 값의 ~이라도 비싼 셈이다 It would be expensive at half that price.

**절버덕** with a splash. ~거리다 splash 《about》; dabble. ¶ ~거리며 걷다 splash along / 물을 손으로 ~거리다 splash [dabble] *one's* hands in the water / 흙탕물을 ~거리다 splatter muddy water.

**절벅절벅** splashing along; with splash after splash. ¶ ~ 걷다 splash along.

**절벽**(絶壁) 《낭떠러지》 an inaccessible precipice; 《해안 따위의》 a cliff; a bluff. ¶ ~을 기어오르다 scale [clamber up] a cliff / ~에서 추락하다 fall over a precipice.

**절삭**(切削) cutting. ~하다 cut. ◉ ~공구 a cutting tool.

**절상**(折傷) a fracture. ~하다 suffer a fracture; fracture.

**절색**(絶色) an unsurpassed [a rare] beauty; a woman of peerless [matchless] beauty; the loveliest of all.

**절세**(絶世) ① 《뛰어남》 the unequaled in the world; the peerless; the matchless. ¶ ~ 미인 a rare beauty; a woman of matchless [peerless] beauty. ② 《은둔함》 retirement from the world. ~하다 retire from the world.

**절손**(絶孫) the extinction of *one's* family line. ~하다 *one's* family line die out; have [leave] no posterity. ¶ 그 집안은 ~했다 The family (line) has died out.

**절수**(節水) water saving [economy]. ~하다 save water; economize in water consumption. ¶ 우리는 ~해야 한다 We have to go easy on water.

**절식**(絶食) ① 《단식》 fasting; a fast; abstinence from food. ⇨단식(斷食). ~하다 fast; go on a fast 《of a week》; abstain from food. ¶ 2일간의 ~ a two-day fast / 나는 건강 진단을 위해 ~하고 있다 I haven't eaten anything for a medical. ② 《절량》 running out of provisions. ~하다 lack food; run out of provisions.

**절식**(節食) moderation [temperance] in eating; a diet. ~하다 be moderate [temperate] in eating; eat moderately [sparingly]; eat less; be on a diet. ¶ 그는 건강을 위해 ~하고 있다 He's on a diet for his health.

**절실**(切實) ~하다 (be) earnest; fervent; 《긴급한》 urgent; pressing; 《중대한》 serious. ¶ ~히 《통절히》 acutely; keenly; 《충심으로》 sincerely; heartily / ~한 소원 an earnest wish / 그 필요를 ~히 느끼다 feel keenly [strongly] the necessity of it / 물의 부족은 지금 ~한 문제이다 Lack of water is an urgent problem. / 그것은 나에게 있어서

～한 문제이다 That is an important problem for me. / 평상시의 노력이 중요하다는 것을 ～히 느꼈다 I 「keenly 〔acutely〕 felt that everyday efforts are important.

**절약**(節約) economy; saving; 《검약》 frugality; husbandry; thrift. ～하다 economize 《on》; spare; save; be 「thrifty 〔frugal, economical〕; 《절감하다》 cut down 《on》; curtail.

> 용법 **economy** 돈·시간·노력 따위의 낭비를 하지 않는 것. **saving** 장래를 위해 돈 등을 모으는 일. **frugality** 특히 음식물이나 비용 등의 절약을 위해 소비·소모를 절감하는 것. **thrift** 돈이나 물품을 마구 쓰지 않고 삼가 사용하는 것.

¶ 전기를 ～하다 「economize on 〔save〕 electricity / 비용을 ～하다 cut down expenses / 가스를〔석탄을〕 ～하다 spare 「gas 〔coal〕 / 모든 ～을 다하다 practice every retrenchment / 가능한 한 ～을 하시오 Save in every way you can. / 그것은 시간과 노력의 ～이 된다 It saves time and trouble. / 우리는 에너지를 ～하여야 한다 We must conserve energy. / 연료비 ～이 판매면에서 우리 상품의 강점이다 Our selling point is the saving in fuel bills. ◉ ～가 a 「thrifty 〔frugal〕 person. 시간〔비용〕～ economy 「of time 〔in expenditure〕.

**절연**(絶緣) ① 《인연·관계를》 severing relations; breaking off *one's* connection. ～하다 break off relations 《with》; sever 〔cut〕 *one's* connections 《with》. ¶ 과거와 ～하다 break 〔part〕 with *one's* past / 종교와 ～된 과학 science divorced from religion / 그와 ～했다 I have done with him. *or* I am through with him. ② 〖물리〗 insulation; isolation. ～하다 insulate; isolate. ◉ ～기(器) an insulator; a switch. ～기(機) an insulating machine. ～내력(耐力) dielectric strength. ～선 an insulated wire. ～성 nonconductivity. ～시험 an insulation test. ～유 insulating oil. ～장 a letter breaking off *one's* relationship 《with *a person*》. ～재 an insulating material. ～저항 insulation resistance. ～지 insulating paper. ～체 〖전기〗 an insulator; an isolator; a nonconductor. ～테이프 《전깃줄에 감는》 (a) friction 〔(an) insulating 《영》〕 tape.

**절연**(節煙) temperance in smoking. ～하다 smoke less; be 「moderate 〔temperate〕 in smoking. ¶ 나는 지금 ～중이다 I'm trying to smoke less. *or* I cut down on my smoking.

**절의**(節義) fidelity to *one's* principle; integrity; honor. ¶ ～를 지키다 adhere to *one's* principles.

**절이다** preserve 〔pickle〕 with salt; salt (down); souse; corn (쇠고기 따위). ¶ 절인 배추 salted cabbage / 생선을 소금에 ～ preserve fish with salt; salt fish.

**절전**(節電) power saving; economy in power consumption. ～하다 economize (in) power; save 「electricity 〔electric power〕. ¶ ～ 효과가 나타나기 시작했다 The effects of conserving electricity are beginning to be seen. ◉ ～운동 a power-saving campaign.

**절절이**(節節 —) word by word; each word; phrase by phrase. ¶ ～ 가슴에 와닿는다 Every phrase is touching.

**절정**(絶頂) 《산의》 the top; the summit; 《정점》 the peak; the zenith; the acme; the height; a climax. ¶ 호경기의 ～ the peak of the boom / 번영의 ～ the zenith of *one's* prosperity / ～에 달하다 climb 〔mount〕 to the summit; reach 〔attain〕 the 「peak 〔climax〕 《of》 / 인기 ～에 있다 be at the height of *one's* popularity / 행복의 ～에서 불행의 나락으로 떨어지다 be knocked down from the 「height 〔apex〕 of happiness into the depth of misery.

**절제**(切除) 〖의학〗 resection; excision; (a) surgical removal. ～하다 excise; cut off; resect; remove 《the diseased part》. ¶ 신경～(술) neurotomy / 폐～(술) pneumonectomy / 종양을 ～하다 excise a tumor.

**절제**(節制) moderation; 《음식의》 abstinence; temperance. ～하다 practice temperance; be moderate 〔temperate〕 《in》; abstain from 《drinking》. ¶ ～하여 moderately; temperately / 음식〔언행〕의 ～ temperance in 「eating and drinking 〔speech and conduct〕 / 술을 ～하다 be 「temperate 〔moderate〕 in drinking / 욕망을 ～하다 control *one's* passions. ◉ ～가 a temperate person; a person of temperate habits. ～생활 temperate living.

**절조**(節操) integrity; constancy; fidelity; chastity (정조). ¶ ～가 없는 unprincipled; inconstant / ～가 있는 사람 a principled person; a man of 「principle 〔integrity〕 / ～를 지키다 be 〔remain〕 faithful to *one's* principles;

keep 〔hold, live up〕 to *one's* principles / ～를 팔다 sell *one's* honor; prostitute *oneself.*

**절종**(絶種) 《일》 extinction of species; 《종》 an extinct species. ～하다 become extinct; go out of existence; a species die out.

**절주**(節酒) moderation in drinking; temperance (★ temperance는 「금주」의 뜻으로도 쓰임). ～하다 be moderate in drinking; drink moderately; practice temperance.

**절지동물**(節肢動物) an arthropod.

**절차**(節次) formalities; procedures; steps; 《소송의》 proceedings. ¶ ～상 for the sake of formalities / ～상의 procedural / ～에 따라서 according to the procedures / 수출 ～ export procedures / 재판의 정식 ～ the formalities of judicial process / 법률상의 번거로운 ～ the cumbersome processes of the law / 관료적인 번거로운 ～《cut through the》 red tape / ～를 밟다 follow the necessary procedures 《for》; go through the formalities; take (the necessary) steps 《in a matter》/ 정식 ～를 마치다 complete the regular formalities / 퇴학 ～는 어떻게 밟아야 합니까 What procedure is necessary for leaving the school? / 재산 상속에는 갖가지 번거로운 ～가 필요하다 You have to go through 「complicated formalities 〔annoying red tape〕 when you inherit property. ◉ ～법 procedural law; an adjective law. ～위반 deviation from the procedures.

**절차탁마**(切磋琢磨) "cutting and polishing" (as precious stones); indefatigable assiduity. ～하다 apply *oneself* closely 《to *one's* study》.

**절찬**(絶讚) extolment; the highest praise. ～하다 extol; praise highly; admire greatly; speak very highly of 《*a person, a thing*》; speak of 《*a person, a thing*》 in the highest terms. ¶ ～을 받다 win great admiration 《from the public》; win the highest praise; be praised sky-high 《by》/ ～을 받을 만하다 deserve the highest terms of praise / 그의 발명에는 ～을 아끼지 않는다 My highest praise goes to his invention. / ～리 상영 중 《광고문》 Now showing amid enormous popular acclaim!

**절창**(絶唱) an excellent piece of poetry; a superb song; 《사람》 a superb singer.

**절처봉생**(絶處逢生) 「finding life in 〔escaping〕 the jaws of death; finding a way out of a fatal situation.

**절충**(折衷) (a) compromise; compromising. ～하다 make 〔arrange, work out〕 a compromise 《between》; compromise 《with》. ¶ 한양(韓洋)식 ～ 《be》 a compromise between Korean and Western styles; a blending of Korean and Western styles / 한양식 ～의 집 a semiforeign house / 정치적 ～을 모색하다 seek political compromise / 노사 쌍방의 ～으로 쟁의는 해결되었다 The strike came to a settlement through a compromise between labor and management. ◉ ～가격 a compromise price. ～설(說) eclecticism; a compromise on conflicting views. ～안(案) a compromise plan 〔suggestion, proposal〕. ～주의 『철학』 eclecticism.

**절충**(折衝) 《담판》 negotiation(s); a parley. ～하다 negotiate 〔parley〕 with 《*a person*》 about 《a matter》. ¶ ～을 거듭한 후에 after repeated negotiations / 외부와의 ～을 맡다 engage in negotiations with the public / 그 일은 지금 ～중이다 The matter is now under negotiations. / 협정이 성립되려면 아직 상당한 ～이 필요하다 Considerable negotiating lies ahead before an agreement can be reached.

**절취**(竊取) stealing; pilfering; embezzling. ～하다 steal; pilfer; embezzle.

**절취선**(切取線) the line along which to cut 《a section》 off; 《점선》 a dotted line; 《바늘 구멍》 a perforated line.

**절치**(切齒) ～하다 gnash *one's* teeth. ¶ ～부심(腐心)하다 gnash *one's* teeth with rage and hatred.

**절친**(切親) a close friendship; intimacy. ～하다 be on intimate 〔friendly〕 terms 《with》 (★ intimate는 「이성간에 성교섭을 가질 정도로 친밀하다」란 뜻이 있어 주의를 요함); be on the warmest 〔best〕 terms 《with》; be very good friends 《with》. ¶ 두 사람은 ～한 사이다 They are very friendly with each other.

**절터** a temple site.

**절토**(切土) 『토목』 cutting (off); cutting the ground. ¶ ～와 성토를 하다 cut and fill.

**절통하다**(切痛—) (be) extremely regrettable; bitterly mortifying.

**절판**(絶版) going out of print. ～하다 discontinue the publication 《of a book》. ¶ ～된 책 an out-of-print book / ～되다 go 〔be〕 out of print.

**절편** 《떡의 일종》 a rice cake with flower pattern imprinted.

**절품**(絶品) a superb 〔an exquisite〕 piece of work; a unique article; a rarity.

**절필**(絶筆) ① 《마지막 글》 *a person's* last (hand) writing 〔work〕. ② 《붓을 꺾음》 ～하다 give up writing; make an end of *one's* literary career.

**절핍**(絶乏) exhaustion; drain. ～하다 get exhausted; be drained; give out.

**절하**(切下) 《값·비용 등의》 (a) cut; (a) reduction; 《평가의》 devaluation (of currency). ～하다 cut; reduce; 《평가의》 devaluate; devalue. ¶ 달러를 10% ～하다 devalue the dollar by 10 percent. / 또 한 차례 달러의 ～가 행해졌다 There's been a further devaluation of the dollar.

**절해**(絶海) the farthest seas. ¶ ～의 고도 a lonely island in the far-off sea; an isolated island.

**절호**(絶好) ¶ ～의 (the) best; capital; splendid; excellent; 《완벽한》 perfect / ～의 기회 a golden opportunity; a rare chance; the best chance 《to study abroad》 / 이것은 ～의 기회다 This is the chance of lifetime. *or* This is the best chance that offers.

**절후**(節候) ＝절기(節氣).

**젊다** (be) young; youthful. ¶ 젊었을 때 in *one's* youth; when (*one* was) young / 젊은 동안 while young / 젊었을 때부터 from *one's* youth / 젊은 여자 a young woman 〔girl〕 / 젊은 혈기 youthful passion 〔enthusiasm〕; ardor of youth / 젊은 혈기로 저지른 과오 a youthful indiscretion; youthful follies / 한창 젊은 때이다 be in the prime of youth; be in *one's* hot youth; be in the flower of life / 나이보다 ～ look young for *one's* age / 두 세살 젊게 보이다 [사람이 주어] look two or three years younger 《than *one* really is, than *a person*》; [사물이 주어] take two or three years off *one's* age / 마음이 ～ be young at heart; have young ideas / 젊은 시절은 다시 오지 않는다 Young days will never come again./ 그는 언제 보아도 ～ He always looks young. / 자네는 아직 젊으니 괜찮아 You have still a number of hopeful years to live. / 그녀는 젊었을 때 미인이었다 She was a beauty in her day. / 그는 나보다 다섯 살이나 ～ He is five years younger than I. *or* He is five years my junior. / 그는 젊어서 결혼했다〔죽었다〕 He married 〔died〕 young. (★ 위의 문장에서 왜 young이라는 형용사가 씌어졌는가 하면 이 young은 결혼〔사망〕했을 때의 「상태」를 나타냄. 즉 married 〔died〕는 「결혼〔사망〕했다」는 뜻을 나타냄과 동시에 He와 young을 결합시키는 구실을 함).

**젊은이** a young person; a lad; a youth; a youngster; [총칭] the young; the youth. ¶ ～의 피를 끓게 하다 stir the blood of youth.

**젊음** youthfulness; youth. ¶ ～을 유지하다 keep *one's* youth; remain young / ～은 두 번 다시 없다 You are only young once.

**점**(占) divination; fortunetelling. ⇨ 점치다. ¶ 점쟁이에게 점을 보다 consult a fortuneteller 《about》; have *one's* fortune told by a fortuneteller / 길흉화복을 점치다 tell fortunes.

**점**(點) ① 《표》 a point; a dot. ¶ 점을 찍다 mark with a dot; put a dot; dot / i자에 점을 찍어라 Dot your 〔the〕 i's. / A점과 B점 간의 거리는 얼마냐 How long is it between point A and B?
② 《성적의》 《미》 a grade; a mark; point (in grading). ⇨ 점수. ¶ 60점으로 합격하다 pass an examination with 60 marks / 100점 만점에서 90점을 따다 get 〔obtain〕 90 out of 100 (marks) / 영어에서 70점을 받다 get a grade of 70 in English.
③ 《경기의》 a point; a score; 〖야구〗 a run. ¶ 2점을 올리다 score two points / 야구에서 5점이 나다 score 5 runs at baseball / 원정 팀의 실책으로 첫번째 점수를 얻다 earn the first score on the misplay of the visitors / 1회에 두 점을 따다 〖야구〗 score two runs in the first inning.
④ 《문제되는 점》 a point; a respect; a way; 《관점》 a standpoint; a point of view. ¶ 좋은〔나쁜〕 점 a strong 〔weak〕 point / 문제점 a point in dispute / 의문점 a point in question / 요점 an important point / 그 점에 있어서 on that point; in that respect 〔regard〕; for that matter / 어떤 점에서는 in some respects 〔ways〕 / 그 밖의 점에서는 in other respects; otherwise / 이 점에서 보면 in view of this; from this viewpoint 〔standpoint〕 / 어느 점으로나, 모든 점에서 in every respect; in all respects; on all counts / 남의 좋은 점을 보라 See the good in others. / 이 점이 중요하다 This is the main point. *or* It is this point that counts

〔matters〕. / 그것이 곤란한 점이다 That is where the difficulty lies.
⑤ 《물품의 수》 an item; a piece. ¶ 가구 몇 점 several articles of furniture / 의류 8점 eight pieces of clothing.
⑥ 《기준이 되는 점》 a point. ¶ 출발점 the starting point / 소수점 a decimal point.
⑦ 《반점》 a spot; a speck; a drop; 《피부의》 a birthmark; a nevus (모반). ¶ 태양의 흑점 a sunspot / 흰 점 박힌 검정 개 a black dog with white spots / 구름 한 점도 없는 하늘 a sky without a speck of cloud in it.
⑧ 〖바둑〗 a piece (돌); a cross (판의).
⑨ 《고깃조각》 a piece 《of meat》; a cut; a slice (얇은).

**점가**(漸加) a gradual increase. ～하다 increase gradually; accelerate. ◉ ～속도 acceleration of velocity.

**점감**(漸減) a gradual decrease. ～하다 decrease 〔diminish〕 gradually.

**점거**(占據) occupation; possession. ～하다 occupy; hold; capture. ¶ 폭도들이 그 건물을 ～했다 The mobs occupied the building. ◉ ～자 an occupant. ～지 an occupied territory. 불법 ～ illegal 〔unlawful〕 occupation 《of》: 그들은 그 건물을 불법 ～했다 They occupied the building illegally.

**점검**(點檢) a check; (an) inspection; (an) examination. ～하다 inspect; make an inspection of; check; examine. ¶ 불시 ～ a spot check 〔test〕 / 엔진 ～ an engine checkup / 인원을 ～하다 call the roll; take a roll call / 정기적인 ～을 하다 make a routine check 《on》 / ～을 받다 undergo 〔have〕 an inspection / 가스 기구를 ～하다 inspect 〔check〕 gas fittings / 자동차 ～을 받았다 I had my car examined 〔checked〕. / 출발 전에 차량 ～ 《게시》 Check vehicles before departure.

**점고**(漸高) a gradual rise 〔elevation〕. ～하다 rise gradually.

**점괘**(占卦) a divination sign. ¶ ～가 좋다 〔나쁘다〕 have a good 〔an ill〕 divination sign.

**점근**(漸近) a gradual approach; drawing near; getting near. ～하다 approach gradually; draw near; get near. ◉ ～곡선 an asymptotic curve. ～급수 〖수학〗 asymptotic series. ～선 〖수학〗 an asymptote; an asymptotic curve. ～원 〖수학〗 an asymptotic circle.

**점대**(占一) the lots 〔sticks〕 cast for divination. ¶ ～로 점을 치다 divine by casting lots.

**점도표**(點圖表) 〖통계〗 a scatter 〔dot〕 diagram; a scattergram.

**점두**(店頭) a storefront 《미》; a shop front 《영》; a store 〔shop〕. ¶ ～에서 《be sold》 over the counter; at the store 《미》; in the shop 《영》 / 물건을 ～에 진열하다 display articles in the show window / 물건을 ～에 내놓다 put goods on sale. ◉ ～거래 〖증권〗 an over-the-counter transaction 〔trading〕. ～견본 《기구·가구 등의》 a display 〔floor 《미》〕 model. ～광고 a show-window advertisement. ～매매〔판매〕 〖증권〗 over-the-counter dealings. ～장식 window dressing. ～주(株) an over-the-counter stock; a counter share.

**점둥이**(點一) ① 《개》 a brindled dog. ② 《개이름》 "Spot(ty)." ③ 《사람》 a person with 「a birthmark 〔a spot〕.

**점등**(點燈) lighting. ～하다 light up; turn 〔switch〕 on a light; light a candle 〔lamp〕. ◉ ～시간 lighting-up time; the lighting hour. ～장치 lighting system.

**점등**(漸騰) a gradual rise 《of price, *etc.*》. ～하다 rise gradually.

**점락**(漸落) a gradual fall 《of price, *etc.*》. ～하다 fall gradually.

**점령**(占領) occupation; capture; possession. ～하다 occupy; seize; take; capture. ¶ 도시의 ～ the capture of a city / ～하에 있다 be under occupation. ◉ ～국 an occupying nation. ～군 the occupation forces. ～정책 an occupation policy. ～지 an occupied territory 〔area〕. ～지대 a zone of military occupation.

**점막**(粘膜) 〖생물〗 a mucous membrane; a mucosa. ◉ ～분비물 rheum; a mucous discharge. ～선 a mucous gland.

**점멸**(點滅) blinking; glimmering. ～하다 go 〔flash〕 on and off; turn 〔blink, switch〕 《lights》 on and off. ¶ 경고〔주의〕 신호가 ～하고 있다 A warning signal goes on and off. / 목적지에 도착하게 되면 등불을 ～시켜 신호해 주십시오 Please signal by switching the light on and off when you get to the destination. ◉ ～기 a switch. ～신호 a blinking signal.

**점멸등**(點滅燈) a blinker (light); 《자동차의》 a front 〔rear〕 turn signal; a front 〔rear〕 blinker.

**점묘**(點描) 〖미술〗 a sketch; a profile

《of》; 《그림》 painting with dots; pointillism(e). ¶인물～ a personal sketch; the profile of a person. ◉ ～주의, ～파 pointillism. ～화가 a pointillist. ～화법 pointillism; stippling.

**점박이**(點—) ① 《동물》 a dapple 〔brindled〕 animal. ② 《사람》 a person with a birthmark 〔spot〕. ③ 《손가락질 받는》 (a person who is) a laughingstock.

**점보제트기**(—機) a jumbo jet(liner).

**점서**(占書) a book on divination; a fortune(telling) book.

**점선**(點線) a dotted line; a perforated line (절취선). ¶～으로 표시된 부분 the part shown in dotted line / ～을 긋다 draw a dotted line / ～부분을 떼어 내시오 《지시》 Tear on the perforated line.

**점성**(占星) a horoscope. ¶(점성가에게서) ～을 보다 have *one's* 「fortune told by the stars 〔horoscope read〕. ◉ ～가 an astrologer. ～술 astrology.

**점성**(粘性) viscosity; viscidity. ◉ ～률 a coefficient of viscosity.

**점수**(點數) ① 《성적의》 (grade) marks; a grade 《미》. ¶～가 박하다 severe in marking / ～가 깎이다 lose a mark / ～를 매기다 give 《students》 marks / 좋은 ～를 따다 get good marks 《in》/ 저 선생님은 ～가 후하다 That teacher is generous with his marks. ② 《경기의》 a point; a score; 〖야구〗 a run. ¶많은 ～를 따다 make a good score. ③ 《물품의 수》 items; pieces; (the number of) articles.

**점술**(占術) the art of divination; prognostication; fortunetelling.

**점신세**(漸新世) 〖지질〗 the Oligocene age.

**점심**(點心) lunch; luncheon 《영》 (★ lunch는 dinner를 저녁으로 할 경우의 점심을 말하며 가벼운 식사를 가리킴. luncheon은 점심때 접객용으로 나오는 가벼운 식사를 말하기도 하며, 노동자 등이 오전 열시쯤 드는 가벼운 새참의 뜻으로도 쓰임).
¶～을 먹다 have lunch / ～ 준비가 되었습니다 Lunch is ready. / ～ 먹을 시간도 없다 We haven't time enough to have lunch. / ～ 식사는 어디로 하러 가겠느냐 Where do you want to go for lunch? / 우리는 ～을 함께 하며 그것에 관해 이야기했다 We talked about it over lunch. ◉ ～나절 the forenoon: ～나절에 toward noon. ～때 lunchtime; noontime; noon. ～시간 lunchtime: ～시간에 at lunchtime; in the lunch hour. ～약속 a lunch engagement.

**점안**(點眼) ～하다 apply eyewash 〔eye lotion〕; administer eye drops. ◉ ～기 an eyedropper. ～수〔약〕 eyewash; eye drops 〔lotion〕.

**점액**(粘液) mucus; mucilage; viscous liquid. ¶～성의 mucous; viscous; sticky / ～을 분비하는 muciferous; mucific. ◉ ～변 mucous feces 〔stool〕. ～분비 secretion of mucus. ～선 a mucous gland. ～소 mucin. ～질 phlegmatic temperament: ～질의 사람 a person of phlegmatic temperament.

**점원**(店員) a (store) clerk 《미》; a salesclerk 《미》; a salesperson; a salesman; 《여자》 a saleswoman; 《영》 a shop assistant; 《영》 a shopgirl.

**점유**(占有) possession; occupation; 〖법〗 occupancy. ～하다 take possession of; possess; occupy; 〖법〗 be seized of. ◉ ～권 the right of possession; a possessory right: ～권을 취득하다 acquire the right of possession. ～물 a thing possessed; a possession; property. ～율 《시장의》 a (market) share: 세계 무역에 있어서의 한국의 ～율 Korea's share in world trade / 컴퓨터 시장에서의 우리 회사 ～율 our company's share of the computer market. ～자 an occupant; a possessor; a seizer; an occupier. 불법～ 〖법〗 detention; deforcement. 토지 ～권 a possessory title to land.

**점음표**(點音標) 〖음악〗 a dotted note.
◉ 겹～ a double dotted note.

**점입가경**(漸入佳境) ～하다 enter the region of delights; approach the climax; get to the best part. ¶이야기가 ～하다 The story reaches the most interesting part. *or* The plot thickens.

**점자**(點字) Braille; braille. ¶～를 읽다 read Braille / ～로 옮기다 put 〔transcribe〕 into braille / ～로 발행하다 publish 《a book》 in braille.
◉ ～기 a braillewriter. ～번역자 a braille transcriber. ～법 (the) braille. ～블록 a studded paving block (to aid the blind). ～서〔책〕 a book in braille (type). ～악보 Braille music. ～인쇄물 《우편 겉봉의 표기》 literature for the blind. ～읽기 finger reading.

**점잔** a dignified air. ～빼다, ～부리다 assume a dignified air; play the gentleman; behave in a genteel way; give *oneself* 〔put on〕 airs; be affected 〔precious〕/ ~빼며 말하다 speak with an air of dignity.

**점잖다** (be) dignified; well-bred; well=behaved; respectable; genteel; decent; grave; be a gentleman. ¶ 점잖은 사람 a fine gentleman / 점잖게 굴다 behave like a gentleman; behave *oneself* / 점잖지 못하다 be disrespectable 〔ill-bred, ill-mannered, misbehaved, vulgar〕/ 점잖은 말을 하다 use refined 〔graceful〕 language / 점잖은 개가 부뚜막에 오른다 People who look like gentleman are the first to grab something for themselves.

**점재**(點在) scattering. ~하다 [장소가 주어] be dotted 〔scattered, studded, interspersed〕 with 《cottages》; [물건이 주어] be scattered 〔dotted〕 about 《the countryside》. ¶ ~한 dotted; dotty; sporadic / 섬들이 ~한 바다 the island-studded sea.

**점쟁이**(占—) a fortuneteller; a diviner; a prognosticator.

**점적**(點滴) 《물의》 falling drops of water; 《비의》 raindrops; 《약액의》 an intravenous drip (정맥 내); a drip. ¶ 약액을 ~하다 give 〔administer〕 an intravenous drip injection to 《*a person*》; put 《*a person*》 on a 《glucose》 drip. ◉ ~기 《혈관에의》 an instillator; 《안약 등》 a (medicine) dropper; an eyedropper. ~반응 〖화학〗 a spot reaction. ~배양 drop culture. ~병 a dropping bottle; a dropper (안약 등). ~분석 a spot analysis. ~수혈 drip transfusion. ~약 medicinal drops.

**점점**(漸漸) by degrees; little by little; gradually. ¶ 일이 ~ 익숙해지다 become more and more accustomed to the work / ~ 더 더워지다 be getting 〔growing〕 hotter and hotter / ~ 나빠지다 go from bad to worse / ~ 더 적어지다 grow less and less / 해가 ~ 길어진다 The day is getting longer (and longer). / 길은 ~ 험해졌다 The road becomes steeper. / 나는 영어가 ~ 재미있어진다 I have got more and more interested in English.

**점점이**(點點—) ① 《여기저기》 here and there; sporadically; scattered. ¶ ~ 흩어져 있다 [물건이 주어] lie scattered (about); [장소가 주어] be dotted 〔interspersed〕 《with》 / ~ 흩어지다 be all scattered about / 하늘에는 반짝이는 별이 ~ 수놓아져 있다 The sky is studded 〔strewn〕 with twinkling stars. / 공원에 진달래가 ~ 피어 있다 The park is dotted 〔interspersed〕 with blooming azaleas. ② 《하나씩》 item by item; article by article; one by one.

**점주**(店主) a store-owner; a storekeeper 《미》; a shopkeeper 《영》; the proprietor 〔proprietress (여자)〕 《of a store》.

**점증**(漸增) a steady 〔gradual〕 increase. ~하다 increase steadily 〔gradually〕. ¶ ~하는 실업자 the ever-increasing unemployed.

**점지** ~하다 《신불이》 bless 《*a person*》 with a baby. ¶ 자식을 ~하여 주기를 빌다 pray for offspring.

**점진**(漸進) gradual progress; a steady advance. ~하다 make gradual progress. ¶ ~적인 gradual; moderate (의견·정책 등이) / ~적으로 gradually; progressively; step by step; by ｢gradual degrees 〔progressive stages〕. ◉ ~주의 gradualism; moderatism: ~주의자 a gradualist; a moderatist.

**점찍다** mark out 《*a person, a thing* for some purpose》; 《골라서》 single 〔pick〕 out 《a house for rent》; spot 《a man》; fix *one's* choice on 《*a person*》; select 《*a thing*》 as desirable. ¶ (마음속에) 점찍어 놓은 사람 a man 〔girl〕 of *one's* heart.

**점차**(漸次) gradually; by degrees; little by little; step by step. ¶ 환자는 ~ 나아져 가고 있다 The patient is getting better every day. / 시황(市況)이 ~로 바뀌기 시작했다 A gradual change began in the market.

**점착**(粘着) adhesion; viscosity. ~하다 stick 〔adhere, be glued〕 《to》. ◉ ~력 adhesive power; adhesiveness; viscosity. ~성 adhesiveness; viscosity; stickiness: ~성의 cohesive; sticky; gluey / ~성이 없는 inadhesive. ~제 an adhesive; gluing agent. ~테이프 an adhesive tape.

**점철**(點綴) interspersion. ~하다 intersperse; dot; stud.

**점치다**(占—) tell 《*a person's*》 fortune; divine 《the future》; forecast 《from》; prognosticate; augur 《*a person's* failure》. ¶ 카드로 아무의 운을 ~ read 〔tell〕 *a person's* fortune with cards.

**점토**(粘土) clay; 《상표》 Plasticine (조소용). ¶ ~질(의) clayey; clayish / ~질 철광석 clay ironstone. ◉ ~세공 claywork. ~암 clay stone. 내화~ fireclay.

**점판암**(粘板岩) 〖광물〗 argillite; (clay) slate.

**점퍼** a jacket; a jumper; a windbreaker; a wind-cheater (두건이 달린). ¶ 가죽～ a leather jacket.

**점포**(店舗) a store《미》; a shop《영》. ¶ ～를 내다 set up *one's* store / ～를 열다[닫다] open 〔close〕 a store;《폐업하다》shut 〔close〕 up store; wind up business. ◉ ～정리 판매 a winding-up 〔clearance〕 sale.

**점프** a jump. ～하다 jump. ◉ ～볼 『농구』 a jump ball. ～슛 a jump shot.

**점하다**(占—) occupy; hold. ⇨ 차지하다.

**점호**(點呼) (a) roll call; (a) call-over; a muster. ～하다 call the roll; take the roll call. ¶ 예비역으로 있는 중에 두 번 ～를 받다 be called out twice while on the reserve list / ～는 오전 6시 Roll call will be at 6 A.M.
◉ 일조[일석]～ 『군사』 the morning 〔evening〕 roll call. 임시[불시]～ a check 〔surprise〕 roll call.

**점화**(點火) lighting; ignition. ～하다 light; fire; ignite; kindle; 《폭발물에》 set off. ¶ ～하기 쉬운 easy to ignite; easily ignited / 다이너마이트에 ～하다 detonate 〔set off〕 a charge of dynamite. ◉ ～관(管) an ignition tube. ～기 a lighter. ～약 priming powder; a priming 〔an ignition〕 charge; a detonator. ～장치 an ignition system; a firing mechanism; 《엔진의》 the ignition. ～플러그 《내연 기관의》 a plug; a spark plug; 《영》 a sparking plug.

**접** a 〔one〕 hundred 《fruit, bulbs, tubers》. ¶ 감 한 접 a hundred persimmons.

**접**(椄) 『식물』 grafting. ¶ 접(을) 붙이다 graft; engraft / 자두나무에 배를 접붙이다 graft the pear upon the plum.

**접각**(接角) 『수학』 an adjacent angle.

**접객**(接客) reception of a guest; entertaining a guest. ～하다 receive a guest; entertain a guest; wait on customers. ¶ ～용의 for customers / 저 식당은 ～하는 태도가 좋다고 평판이 자자하다 That restaurant has a reputation for offering good service.
◉ ～업 an entertainment business; a service trade: ～업자 hotel and restaurant traders 〔keepers〕. ～원 a receptionist.

**접견**(接見) an interview; a reception; an audience. ～하다 give 《*a person*》 an interview 《to》; receive 《*a person*》 in audience; grant an audience 《to》. ¶ 대통령께서는 청와대에서 내외 기자들을 ～하셨다 President received home and foreign journalists in *Chŏngwadae.* ◉ ～실 a reception room 〔hall〕; an audience chamber 〔room〕. ～일 a reception day.

**접경**(接境) a border line; a border land 〔area〕. ～하다 be contiguous 《to》; border 《on》; share borders 《with》; abut 《on》.

**접골**(接骨) bonesetting. ～하다 set (a fractured 〔broken bone〕); coapt. ¶ 나는 부러진 오른 쪽 다리를 ～했다 I had my broken right leg set. ◉ ～술 (the art of) bonesetting. ～원 a bonesetter's (office). ～의(醫) a bonesetter.

**접근**(接近) access; (an) approach; proximity (인접). ～하다 approach; make an approach 《to》; draw 〔come, get〕 near; come 〔get〕 close 《to》; 《배가》 close 《another boat, the land》; 《교제》 (try to) associate with. ¶ ～하기 쉬운 사람 an easily accessible 〔approachable〕 person / ～하기 쉽다[어렵다] 《물리적으로》 be easy 〔difficult〕 to approach; be easy 〔difficult〕 of access; 《심적으로》 be approachable 〔unapproachable〕 / …와의 ～을 꾀하다 bring about better relationships between 〔with〕... / 폭발물에 ～하지 마시오 Keep away from an explosive! / 태풍이 호남 지방으로 ～하고 있다 A typhoon is approaching the Honam district. / 그는 재계의 거물에게 ～했다 He approached a man of financial influence. / 최근 미국과 러시아의 ～은 국제 관계에서 새로운 시대의 도래를 의미하는 것인지도 모른다 The recent approachment between the U.S. and Russia may symbolize the coming of a new era in international relations.
◉ ～경로 an access route. ～전(戰) a close combat; 『권투』 infighting.

**접다** ① [일반적] fold; furl; collapse. ¶ 접을 수 있는 책상 a collapsible desk / 종이를 네 겹으로 ～ fold a paper into four / 우산을 ～ close 〔furl〕 an umbrella / 부채를 ～ fold 〔close〕 a fan. ② 《접어주다》 (***a***) 《너그럽게 대해주다》 treat an inferior a little generously. (***b***) 《핸디캡》 give (a handicap). ¶ 한 수(를) ～ give a handicap; make due allowance.

**접대**(接待) (a) reception; a 《warm》 welcome. ～하다 receive 《a guest》; entertain 《*one's* guests with refreshments》; attend to 《a guest》; welcome. ¶ 손님을 ～하다 receive 〔entertain〕 guest(s) / 손님 ～를 잘하다 be hospitable; be of good service / 손님

을 ~하는 데 조금도 소홀한 점이 없었다 The best possible care was taken in receiving the guests. / 우리는 다과를 ~ 받았다 We were entertained with refreshments. ◉ ~계〔원〕 a receptionist; the person in charge of receiving guests. ~부 a maid; a waitress; a barmaid. ~비 entertainment expenses; an entertainment allowance.

**접두사(어)**(接頭辭(語)) 〖문법〗 a prefix.

**접등**(摺燈) a folding 〔collapsible〕 lantern.

**접때** not long ago 〔before〕; a short time back; a few days ago. ¶ ~부터 for some past / ~ 편지에 in *one's* late letter / ~ 그를 만났을 때 the last time I saw him.

**접목**(椄木·接木) 〖농업〗 grafting; 《나무》 a grafted tree. ~하다 graft (trees) together; graft 《one tree》 on another. ◉ ~법 (en)grafting.

**접미사(어)**(接尾辭(語)) 〖문법〗 a suffix.

**접변**(接變) 〖언어〗 progressive assimilation (of sounds). ~하다 undergo 〔show〕 progressive assimilation.

**접본**(椄本) a tree to which a graft is put; a grafted tree.

**접붙이다**(椄 —) graft. ⇨ 접목.

**접사**(接辭) 〖언어〗 an affix.

**접선**(接線) ① 〖수학〗 a tangent (line). ② 《접촉》 a contact. ~하다 make contact 《with》; contact; come in(to) contact 《with》.

**접속**(接續) connection; joining; junction; 《전기의》 (electric) contact; 〖컴퓨터〗 interface. ~하다 connect 《with》; join 《on》; link; adjoin. ¶ 이 전선을 저 전선에 ~해 주시오 Connect this wire (up) with 〔to〕 that. / 이 열차는 부산행 열차와 ~된다 The train「connects 〔make a connection〕 with one for Pusan. ◉ ~곡 〖음악〗 a medley; a *potpourri* (F.). ~기 〖컴퓨터〗 an adapter; an interface adapter. ~선 a connecting line. ~역 a junction (station). ~연관(鉛管) 〖전기〗 a lead sleeve. ~플러그 〖전기〗 a connecting plug. ~함 〖전기〗 a joint 〔junction, connection, splice〕 box. ~항(港) a port of connection.

**접속사**(接續詞) 〖문법〗 a conjunction; a connective (word). ¶ 등위〔종속〕~ a coordinate 〔subordinate〕 conjunction.

**접수**(接收) requisition(ing); seizure. ~하다 take over; requisition 《a building》; commandeer. ¶ 토지의 ~ the requisitioning of land / 철도를 ~하다 take over a railroad / ~를 해제하다 derequisition / ~되어 있다 be under requisition; be taken over 《by》/ 그 건물은 점령군에게 ~되었다 The building was taken over by the Occupation (Forces). ◉ ~가옥 a requisitioned house.

**접수**(接受) receipt. ~하다 receive; be in receipt of; accept 《application》. ¶ 원서 ~ 기한 the time for application / 무전을 ~하다 pick up a wireless message / 원서는 3월 1일부터 ~한다 Applications will be accepted on and after March 1. ◉ ~계원 an information man; a receptionist; an usher. ~구 an information window 〔desk〕; a reception counter. ~번호 the receipt number. ~처 an information office.

**접시** a plate; a dish (★ 음식을 담아 놓는 접시가 a dish, dish의 요리를 덜어서 직접 먹는 접시가 a plate); a saucer (받침 접시); [총칭] plates; flatware; 《저울의》 a scalepan; a pan. ¶ 고기 한 ~ a dish of meat / ~를 씻다 wash dishes / 음식을 ~에 담아 내놓다 serve food「in a dish 〔on a plate〕/ 음식을 ~에 덜어 놓다 dish out 《potatoes》/ 음식을 ~에 덜어서 먹다 eat off 〔out of〕 a plate / 오믈렛을 두 ~ 먹다 eat two helpings of omelet. ◉ ~닦기 《행위》 dish-washing; 《영》 washing-up; 《사람》 a dishwasher. ~돌리기 a dish-turning〔-spinning〕 trick. ~세척기 a dishwasher. ~안테나 a dish 〔parabolic〕 antenna. ~저울 a balance.

**접시꽃** 〖식물〗 a hollyhock; a rose mel「low.

**접신**(接神) being possessed of a spirit. ~하다 be possessed of a spirit. ◉ ~론 theosophy.

**접안**(接岸) ~하다 come alongside the pier 〔quay, berth〕. ¶ 동시 ~ 능력 the simultaneous berthing capacity.

**접안렌즈**(接眼—) 〖물리〗 the eyepiece 《of a telescope》; an ocular (piece); an eye lens.

**접어넣다** fold in; turn 〔tuck〕 in; make「a tuck in.

**접어들다** ① 《방향·목표로》 take; pick up 《a road》. ¶ 길을 북으로 ~ pick up the road to the north. ② (*a*) 《계절·때·나이 등에》 approach; set in; begin. ¶ 선거전이 종반에 ~ the election campaign enters its last days / 가을철로 접어든다 The autumn season draws near. / 장마철에 접어들었다 The rainy season has set in. / 이 달에 접어들더

니 몹시 추워졌다 The weather has been extremely cold since the beginning of this month. (***b***) 《어느 지점에》 come to near; approach; near. ¶ 배가 해협에 접어들고 있다 The ship is entering the straits.

**접어주다** ① 《봐주다》 give a head start of; give a handicap 〔odds〕 of; give an edge 〔advantage〕 of. ¶ 다섯 점～ give a 5-point handicap 《in playing *paduk*》/ 그한테 몇 점을 접어 주느냐 What odds do you give him in playing the game ? ② [비유적] give 《*a person*》 vantage ground; make due allowances 《for *a person*》.

**접영**(蝶泳) the butterfly stroke.

**접자**(摺 —) a carpenter's rule; a jointed measuring stick; a folding ruler.

**접전**(接戰) a close combat 〔battle〕; a hand-to-hand fight; a close contest 〔game〕. ～하다 fight hand to hand; fight a close fight; have a close game 〔contest〕. ¶ (경기에서) 일대 ～을 벌이다 stage neck-to-neck battle; be in keen competition 《with》; have a close contest 〔game〕 《with》.

**접점**(接點) 〖수학〗 a point of contact.

**접종**(接種) 〖의학〗 inoculation; vaccination. ～하다 inoculate; vaccinate. ¶ 병균을 ～하다 inoculate 《*a person*》 with (a) virus / 천연두 ～을 실시하다 vaccinate 〔inoculate〕 《children》 against small pox. ◉ ～요법 a vaccine cure. 비시지～ inoculation of BCG.

**접종**(接踵) following on the heels 《of》. ～하다 follow in the wake 《of》; occur one after another; arise in quick succession. ¶ 전후에는 여러 불행이 ～했다 Miseries followed in the wake of a war. / 크고 작은 사건들이 ～했다 Events, great and small, occurred in rapid succession.

**접지**(接地) 〖전기〗 ground 〔earth〕 connection; grounding; earthing; an earth. ～하다 ground; earth. ¶ 전자 레인지를 ～시켰다 I grounded the microwave oven. ◉ ～선 a ground 〔an earth〕 wire; an earthing 〔a grounding〕 conductor. ～회로 an earthed 〔a grounded〕 circuit.

**접지**(椄枝) 〖식물〗 a branch graft(ing); a slip 《from a plant》. ～하다 graft.

**접지**(摺紙) folding paper; paper folding. ～하다 fold paper 《to bind a book》.

**접질리다** get sprained; be wricked. ¶ 발목을 ～ *one's* ankle is sprained.

**접착**(接着) 〖화학〗 adhesion; glueing; 〖생물〗 synapsis. ～하다 glue; bond; stick to; adhere to. ¶ 깨진 화병의 조각들을 ～하다 glue the broken pieces of the vase together. ◉ ～력 adhesive strength. ～재(材) 〖전기〗 a binder; a binding material. ～제(劑) adhesives; a bonding 〔an adhesive〕 agent. ～테이프 adhesive tape.

**접촉**(接觸) contact; touch; 〖전기〗 (electrical) contact. ～하다 touch; make 〔come into〕 contact 《with》; 《처음으로》 get 「in touch 〔into contact〕 《with》; establish contact 《with》. ¶ 아무와 ～함으로써 through contact with *a person* / 아무와 ～을 지속하다 keep in contact 〔touch〕 with *a person* / 예비 ～을 갖다 make preliminary contacts 《with》/ 남북 ～에 큰 진전을 보다 make good progress in the South-North contact / ～이 끊기다 lose touch 《with》; get out of touch 《with》/ 개인적인 ～이 있다 have a personal contact 《with *a person*》/ A를 B와 ～시키다 bring A into contact with B / 여러 사람과 ～하다 come into contact with all sorts of people / 세상과의 ～을 끊다 be out of contact with the world / 그는 사업상 여러 사람들과 ～한다 The nature of his business throws him into contact with all sorts of men. / 그는 외국인과 ～할 기회가 많다 He has a lot of chances to come into contact with foreigners.

◉ ～각 a contact angle. ～감염 《spread by》 contagion. ～곡선 an osculating curve. ～기 〖전기〗 a contactor. ～면 a contact surface. ～반응 〖화학〗 a catalysis. ～법 the contact process. ～부 《기계 등》 a contacting part. ～비행 〖항공〗 contact flying. ～사고 《가벼운》 a minor collision; 《have》 a scrape 《with another vehicle》; a fender-bender 《미구어》: ～사고를 일으키다 have a minor collision 《with》/ 나는 출근길에 가벼운 ～사고를 당했다 I had a fender-bender on my way to work. ～식 화면 〖컴퓨터〗 a touch screen; a touch-sensitive screen. ～원 an osculating circle. ～음 a touch tone: ～음 다이얼링 touch tone dialing / ～음 전화 a touch tone telephone. ～작용 contact action; 〖화학〗 catalytic action; catalysis. ～전기 contact electricity. ～점 a point of contact; a point of tangency.

**접치다** ① ⇨접다. ② ⇨접치이다.
**접치이다** get folded; be furled.
**접칼**(摺—) a pocketknife; a folding 〔clasp〕 knife.
**접칼**(椄—) a grafting knife.
**접피술**(接皮術) 『의학』 skin grafting; transplantation of skin.
**접하다**(接—) ① 《접촉·대면하다》 touch; come 〔be〕 in contact 《with》. ¶ 많은 사람과 ~ come into contact with many people / 방문객을 ~ receive visitors. ② 《인접하다》 border 《on》; adjoin; be adjacent 《to》; be contiguous 《to》. ¶ 두 집이 서로 ~ two houses adjoin each other / 북쪽은 시베리아와 접해 있다 be bordered on the north by Siberia. ③ 《경험하다》 meet with; 《받다》 receive; get. ¶ 희보에 ~ receive happy news / 급보에 ~ receive urgent news / 이런 기묘한 사건에 접해 본 일이 없다 I have never met with such a strange case as this. / 아직 상세한 보고에 접하지 못하였다 Particulars are not yet to hand. ④ 《결합하다》 piece together; connect.
**접합**(接合) union; joining; junction; 『생물』 zygosis; conjugation; 『의학』 inosculation (혈관의). ~하다 unite 《with》; connect; put together; join; splice (로프·필름 등의); 『의학』 inosculate (혈관 등을); 『생물』 conjugate. ◉ ~자, ~체 『생물』 a zygote; a zygospore. ~재(材) a binder. ~제(劑) glue; cement.
**접히다** ① 《종이 등이》 get folded; be furled. ¶ 세 겹으로 ~ be folded in three. ② 《바둑 등에서》 a handicap is given; receive odds; take a handicap. ¶ 두 점이 ~ take odds of two points.
**젓** salted fish guts; matured 〔pickled〕 fish foods with salt. ¶ 새우〔조개〕젓 salted shrimps 〔clams〕 / 오징어젓 soused cuttlefish / 새우젓을 담다 preserve shrimps with salt for maturing 〔seasoning〕.
**젓가락** chopsticks. ¶ ~ 한 쌍 a pair of chopsticks / 나무~ 《일회용》 half-split chopsticks / ~으로 김칫국을 집어 먹을 놈 a stupid person / ~으로 집어 들다 pick up 《*a thing*》 with chopsticks / 대부분의 외국인들은 ~을 잘 쓰지 못한다 Most foreigners are clumsy with chopsticks. ◉ ~통 a chopstick stand.
**젓갈** salted sea foods. ⇨젓.
**젓국** salted-fish juice; juice of matured sea foods with salt.
**젓다** ① 《섞다》 stir; churn; beat; whip. ¶ 달걀을 ~ beat eggs / 국을 숟가락으로 ~ stir soup with a spoon. ② 《노를》 paddle; row; scull; pull an oar; work at oars. ¶ 배를 ~ row 〔paddle〕 a boat / 노를 ~ work a scull / 한 번 (크게) ~ row a (long) stroke. ③ 《손을》 wave; sign; gesticulate; 《머리를》 shake 《*one's* head》. ¶ 그는 우리에게 잔디밭으로 들어가지 말라고 손을 저었다 He waved us to keep off the grass.
**정**[1] 《연장》 a chisel (for shaping stone); a burin (조각용).
**정**(丁) ① 《십간의》 the 4th of the 10 Heaven's Stems. ② ⇨정방(丁方). ③ ⇨정시(丁時). ④ 《성적》 the fourth grade; "D".
**정**(正) 《옳음》 justice; righteousness; 《정식의》 regular; ordinary.
**정**(疔) 『의학』 a carbuncle.
**정**(町) 《거리》 *chŏng;* a unit of distance (= c. 109 m); 《면적》 *chŏng;* a unit of area (= c. 99 acres).
**정**(情) ① 《애정》 (an) affection; love; heart. ¶ 부부의 정 conjugal affection / 부모 자식간의 정 affection between parents and child(ren) / 어머니에 대한 정 affection for *one's* mother / 정에 얽매이다 be overcome by *one's* affection; be tied of 《*a person*》 by affection / 여자한테 정이 들다 「become attached to 〔grow fond of〕 a girl / 정을 통하다 《간통하다》 「become intimate 〔have an amour〕 with 《*a woman*》; 《내통하다》 have an intrigue with. ② 《인정》 compassion; sympathy; tender feelings. ¶ 연민의 정 a sentiment of pity; pity / 정이 많다 〔두텁다〕 be warm-hearted 〔kind-hearted〕 / 정에 약하다 be emotional 〔tender-hearted, susceptible〕. ③ 《감정》 feeling(s); (a) sentiment. ¶ 그리운 정 longing; yearning / 애국의 정 the sentiment of patriotism. ④ 《정상》 circumstances; conditions. ⇨정상(情狀).
**정**[2] 《정말로》 really; quite; indeed; very.
**-정**(整) 《금액》 net 〔neat〕 amount. ¶ 5만 원정 a clear 50,000 won.
**-정**(錠) a tabloid; a tablet 《of medicine》.
**정가** 『식물』 a pigweed; a goosefoot.
**정가**(正價) a normal 〔true, fair〕 price.
**정가**(定價) the fixed 〔labeled, regular, list, marked〕 price. ¶ ~로 팔다 sell at a fixed price / ~를 3할 할인하다 make a discount of 30% on the list price / ~를 정하다 set a price 《on *a thing*》 / ~를 올리다〔내리다〕 raise

〔lower〕 the price / 이건 ~가 얼마요 What is the price of this article? ◉ ~표(票) a price tag: 물건에 ~표를 붙이다 fix a price tag to an article. ~표(表) a price list.

**정가극**(正歌劇) 〖음악〗 a grand opera.

**정각**(正刻) the exact time. ¶ 열 시 ~에 at exactly ten o'clock; at ten sharp / ~ 한 시에 오너라 Come at one o'clock sharp.

**정각**(定刻) the appointed hour; the fixed time. ¶ 기차는 ~에 도착하였다 The train came on time. / 오늘 그는 ~에 30분 늦었다 He is half an hour behind time today. 「꼭지각.

**정각**(頂角) 〖수학〗 a vertical angle. ⇨

**정간**(停刊) suspension 《of publication》. ~하다 suspend publication of. ¶ 신문의 ~을 해제하다 release the suspension of a newspaper.

**정갈스럽다**, **정갈하다** (be) clean; neat; be neat and proper 《in appearance 〔garb〕》. ¶ 정갈한 요리 솜씨 neat culinary art.

**정감**(情感) feeling; sentiment. ¶ ~있게 말하다 speak with feeling 〔emotion〕 / 피아노를 ~있게 치다 play the piano with great feeling.

**정강**(政綱) a political principle 〔creed〕; 《정당의》 a party platform 《미》; a plank 《미》. ¶ 신당의 ~ the platform of a new party.

**정강마루** 〖해부〗 the ridge of the shin.

**정강말** "shanks' mare 〔pony〕"; *one's* own legs. ¶ ~을 타다 ride "shanks' mare".

**정강이** the shin; the shank. ¶ 아무의 ~를 차다 kick *a person* in the shin / ~를 까다 bark 〔scrape〕 *one's* shin / 의자에 ~를 부딪치다 hit *one's* shin against a chair. ◉ ~받이 leggings; 《경기용의》 leg 〔shin〕 guards. ~뼈 the shinbone.

**정객**(政客) a politician; a statesman.

**정거**(停車) stopping; a stop; halt. ~하다 make a stop; stop; halt; come to a halt. ¶ 급〔비상〕~ a sudden 〔an emergency〕 stop / 10분간의 ~ a ten minutes' stop / ~시키다 stop 《a vehicle》 / 기차는 역마다 ~한다 The train stops at all stations. / 요다음 ~하는 데가 어디냐 What is the next station we stop at? / 자동차가 갑자기 ~했다 The car came to a sudden stop.

**정거장**(停車場) a railroad station (기차의); a bus stop (버스의). ¶ ~구내 the station yard / ~ 대합실 a station waiting room / ~을 떠나다〔지나다〕 leave 〔pass〕 a station / 다음 ~이 어디냐 What is the next station 〔stop〕?

**정격**(正格) a proper form 〔formality〕; regularity. ¶ ~의 regular; correct; orthodox. ◉ ~활용 〖언어〗 a regular conjugation.

**정견**(定見) a definite view 〔opinion〕; a settled conviction; set 〔fixed〕 ideas. ¶ ~이 없다 have no definite opinion of *one's* own / ~이 없는 사람 a man without settled convictions.

**정견**(政見) *one's* political view 〔opinion〕. ¶ ~의 차이 differences in political opinion; political differences / ~을 발표하다 state 〔give out〕 *one's* political views / ~을 달리하다 differ 《from *a person*》 in political opinions. ◉ ~발표회 a campaign meeting; the hustings. ~방송 a 《TV, radio》 broadcast of political opinions by election candidates.

**정결**(貞潔) chastity; faithfulness. ~하다 (be) chaste and pure; faithful. ¶ ~한 부인 a chaste 〔faithful〕 wife.

**정결**(淨潔) neatness and cleanliness. ~하다 (be) clean and neat; undefiled. ¶ 방을 ~하게 하다 keep *one's* room neat as a new pin / 몸을 ~히 하여라 Keep your body clean.

**정경**(政經) politico-economic(s); politics and economics. ◉ ~유착 politics-business collusion; political=business nexus. ~학부 the political and economic 〔politico-economic〕 faculty.

**정경**(情景) a pathetic 〔touching〕 scene; a sight; a view. ¶ 참담한 ~이다 present a frightful sight.

**정경분리**(政經分離) the separation of economy and politics. ~하다 separate economy from politics. ◉ ~론 divisibility of politics and economy. ~정책 a policy separating economy from politics. 「eage.

**정계**(正系) a legitimate line; direct lin-

**정계**(定界) 《경계》 a fixed 〔an established〕 boundary; 《경계의 확정》 delimitation; demarcation. ~하다 fix the boundaries; delimitate; demarcate the frontier line.

**정계**(政界) the world of politics; the political world 〔arena〕; political circles. ¶ ~ 소식통 informed political circles / ~의 거물 a great political figure 〔leader〕; a prominent figure in politics / ~의 불안 a political unrest; unrest in the political world / ～의 움직임 a political trend / ～의 정화 the purification 〔a cleanup〕 of political circles / ～에 들어가다〔나서다〕 enter the political world; enter upon a political career; go into politics; take up politics as a career; go in for politics / ～에서 물러나다〔떠나다〕 retire from political life; quit (the stage of) politics / ～의 사정에 훤하다 be familiar 〔conversant〕 with political affairs / ～는 매우 활기를 띠고 있다 Political circles are in a animated state.

**정계**(淨界) the holy confines; an undefiled place; 《정토》 the Pure Land; Paradise.

**정곡**(正鵠) the bull's-eye; the mark; the main point. ¶ ～을 찌르는 appropriate; proper / ～을 찌르다 hit the mark; hit the nail on the head; be to the point / ～을 찔리다 be spotted right / ～을 벗어나다 miss the mark; be wide of the mark.

**정골**(整骨) bonesetting. ⇨ 접골.

**정공**(正攻) a frontal attack. ～하다 make a frontal attack; fight openly and squarely; play fair. ◉ ～법 a frontal attack; the regular tactics for attack.

**정과**(正果) fruit 〔ginger, lotus root, ginseng〕 preserved in honey.

**정관**(定款) 〖법〗 the articles of association 〔incorporation〕; a statute. ¶ ～ 제1조 Art. 1 of the articles of association / ～으로 규정되다 be fixed by the articles of association.

**정관**(精管) 〖해부〗 a spermatic duct; a seminal duct; a *vas deferens* (*pl. vasa deferentia*). ◉ ～결찰(結紮)수술 (a) vasoligation. ～절제(수)술(을 받다) 《undergo》 (a) vasectomy.

**정관**(靜觀) serene contemplation. ～하다 watch 〔look on〕 calmly; quietly contemplate; wait and see. ¶ 사태를 ～하다 calmly watch the development of the situation / ～적인 태도를 취하다 assume a wait-and-see attitude 《toward》 / 좀더 ～해 보기로 하자 Let's wait a little longer and see. ◉ ～주의 a wait-and-see policy.

**정관사**(定冠詞) 〖문법〗 the definite article.

**정교**(正教) ① 《사교(邪教)에 대하여》 orthodoxy. ② 〖기독교〗 ＝ 정교회(正教會).

**정교**(政教) 《정치와 종교》 politics and religion; Church and State; 《정치와 교육》 politics and education; State and School. ◉ ～분리 《the principle of》 separation of 「Church and State 〔government and religion〕; politico-religious separation; separation of religion from politics. ～일치 the unity 〔union〕 of 「Church and State 〔religion and politics〕.

**정교**(情交) ① 《우정》 close friendship. ～하다 form friendship; have close relations 《with》. ② 《남녀의》 illicit (sexual) intercourse; a sexual liaison. ～하다 have illicit intercourse 《with》; establish a sexual liaison 《with》; have sexual intercourse 《with》. ¶ ～를 강요하다 force *one's* (sexual) attentions upon 《a girl》; press 《a woman》 to have sex with *one*.

**정교**(精巧) exquisiteness; elaborateness. ～하다 (be) elaborate; exquisite; delicate; fine. ¶ ～한 기계 an elaborate 〔a delicate〕 machine; a machine of mechanical excellence / ～한 세공품 an article of exquisite workmanship / 세공은 아주 ～하다 The workmanship is exquisite.

**정교사**(正教師) a regular 〔full〕 teacher.

**정교수**(正教授) a full professor.

**정교회**(正教會) the (Greek 〔Eastern〕) Orthodox Church.

**정구**(庭球) tennis.

**정국**(政局) the political situation. ¶ ～의 추이〔진전〕 a political development / ～의 불안정 political instability / ～의 위기 a political crisis; a tense 〔serious, grave〕 political situation / ～의 타개책 a measure to break a political deadlock / ～을 안정시키다〔수습하다〕 bring stability to the political situation / ～에 전기(轉機)를 가져오다 mark 〔make〕 a turning point in the political situation / ～이 불안해진다 The political situation becomes uneasy. / ～은 혼미상태에 빠져 있다 The political situation is in confusion. / ～은 예상 밖의 변화를 맞이했다 The political situation has taken an unexpected turn. / 그는 ～을 안정시키고자 하였으나 실패했다 He vainly tried to stabilize the political situation. / 내각의 총사퇴로 ～은 일변했다 The general resignation of the Cabinet brought about a complete change in the political situation. ◉ ～경색 a political deadlock: ～경색의 타개를 도모하다 try to break the political deadlock.

**정권**(政權) 《정치권력》 political 〔administrative] power; 《정부》 an administration 《미》; a government. ¶ 클린턴 ~ the Clinton Administration / ~을 쥐다 come to power; take office; take the helm of state / ~을 잃다 lose [drop] the reins of government; get [go] out of power / ~을 유지하다 stay in power / ~을 이양하다 turn over the reins of government / ~을 다투다 scramble for political power / ~에 복귀하다 return to power / 선거에 이겨 ~을 잡다 be elected to office / 민주당이 ~을 잡고 있다 The Democratic Party is in power. ◉ ~교체 a change of 「regime [government]: 평화적인 ~교체 a peaceful 「turn-over [transfer] of political power / 비평화적 ~ 교체 non-peaceful transfer of power. ~다툼 a 「struggle [scramble] for political power. ~수립 the establishment of a government. ~욕 ambition [desire] for political power. ~이양 a 「transition [transfer] of power 《to》. ~쟁탈전 a scramble for political power. ~타도 the overthrow of a government. ~획득 accession to power.

**정규**(正規) formality; regularity. ¶ ~의 regular; formal; proper; 《합법적》 legitimate; legal / ~ 교육을 받다 have regular school education / ~ 과정을 [절차를] 밟다 go through the regular 「course [formalities] / 그녀는 ~ 경로를 거쳐 취직했다 She got her job through normal channels. / 그녀는 ~ 간호사이다 She is a qualified nurse. ◉ ~군 a regular army. ~병 regulars. ~전 regular warfare.

**정규**(定規) ① 《규칙》 (fixed) rules; regulations. ② = 자[1].

**정극**(正劇) 「a traditional [a legitimate, a conventional, an orthodox] drama.

**정근**(精勤) hard work; diligence; industry; 《근무자의》 good [regular] attendance. ~하다 work hard; apply *oneself* 《to》; (be) diligent; industrious; attend 《the office》 regularly. ¶ 10개년의 ~ *one's* 10-year service with a clean record. ◉ ~상 a prize for 「good [regular] attendance. ~자 a worker with a good attendance; a regular attender.

**정글** the jungle. ◉ ~전 jungle fighting. ~지대 a jungle region. ~짐 《운동 시설》 a jungle gym; 《영》 a climbing frame.

**정금**(正金) ① 『경제』 《지폐에 대한 정화》 specie. ¶ ~으로 지급하다 pay in specie. ② 《순금》 pure gold; solid gold; bullion. ◉ ~결핍 shortage of specie. ~은행 a specie bank.

**정기**(正氣) ① 《바른 기풍》 a fair and equitable spirit; uprighteousness. ② 《천지의》 the spirit which animates and controls the universe.

**정기**(定期) a 「fixed [stated] period. ¶ ~의 fixed; regular; scheduled; periodic(al) / ~적으로 periodically; at 「regular [stated] intervals; at a fixed time; regularly / 모임은 ~적으로 개최하도록 되어 있다 The meeting is to be held 「periodically [at regular intervals]. / 관광 버스는 ~적으로 운행되고 있다 The sightseeing bus runs at a fixed time. ◉ ~간행물 a periodical (publication). ~개선 a periodical reelection. ~검사 a periodic(al) inspection. ~검진 a periodic medical 「check-up [examination]. ~국회 a regular session of the National Assembly. ~대부 a time loan; time money. ~매매 time transactions. ~선 a (regular) liner; a ferry (ship): 유럽 항로 ~선 a European liner. ~승급 a regular (annual) pay raise. ~승차권 a 「commutation [commuter('s)] ticket; 《영》 a season ticket; 《영구어》 a season: ~승차권으로 다니는 승객 a commuter; a commutation passenger 《미》; a season=ticket holder / ~승차권 케이스 a commutation ticket holder / ~승차권으로 다니다 commute. ~시험 a 「periodic [regular] examination. ~여객기 an airliner. ~연금 a terminable annuity. ~예금 a 「time [fixed] deposit: ~예금자 a time depositor. ~전 a regularly=scheduled 「game [match]. ~총회 a regular general meeting. ~편 a regular 「service [run, flight]; a scheduled flight. ~항공 a scheduled flight; a regular airplane service: ~ 항공기 an airliner / ~ 항공로 an airway. ~항로[운행] a regular 「line [run]. ~항해 a regular steamer service. ~휴일 a regular holiday.

**정기**(精氣) ① 《정신과 기력》 spirit and energy; 《만물의 기》 the spirit of all creation. ② 《정력》 energy; vigor; vitality. ¶ ~가 넘치다 be full of energy [life].

**정나미**(情—) attachment; fondness; liking. ¶ ~(가) 떨어지다 be disgusted 《with, at, by》; be disgusting; fall out of love 《with》; be out of patience 《with》; be disaffected 《toward》/ 그가 하는 짓을 보니 ～가 떨어진다 I am disgusted at his behavior. / 네겐 이제 ～가 떨어진다 I'm quite out of patience with you!

**정남방**(正南方) due south.

**정낭**(精囊) 〖해부〗 a seminal vesicle; a spermatic sac.

**정녀**(貞女) 《동정녀》 a virgin; a maiden; 《정절녀》 a chaste woman.

**정년**(丁年) full age; (*one's*) majority. ¶ ～에 이르다 come of age; reach 〔attain〕 *one's* majority / ～ 미달이다 be under age. ◉ ～자 a man of full age; an adult.

**정년**(停年) retiring age; the age limit; the compulsory 〔mandatory〕 retirement age.
¶ ～에 달하다 reach the age limit; reach retiring age / ～으로 퇴직하다 retire (at the age limit); leave *one's* job on reaching retiring age / 공무원의 ～을 60세로 하다 set the retirement age of government officials at 60 / 교사의 ～은 62세다 The teachers retire at 62. / 나는 금년으로 ～입니다 I am due to retire this year. / ～ 후에도 일하고 싶어하는 사람이 많지만, 취업 상황은 신통치 않다 Many people want to work after the retirement age, but their job situation is not very good.
◉ ～법〔제〕 the age-limit law 〔system〕. ～전역 discharge from military service due to age limit in grade. ～퇴직 retirement under the age limit: ～퇴직 연령을 높이다 upgrade the retirement age / ～퇴직자 a retired person 〔worker〕.

**정념**(情念) emotion(s); passion(s). ¶ 증오나 복수심 같은 어두운 ～ dark emotions like hatred and the desire for revenge.

**정녕**(丁寧) without fail; by all means; certainly; surely; for sure. ¶ ～코＝정녕 / ～ 그러냐 Are you sure? / ～ 그렇습니다 I assure you it is so.

**정다각형**(正多角形) 〖수학〗 a regular 〔an equilateral〕 polygon.

**정다면체**(正多面體) 〖수학〗 a regular polyhedron.

**정담**(政談) a political talk 〔chat〕; a discussion of politics.

**정담**(情談) a friendly talk; 《남녀의》 a lover's talk; a tête-à-tête (F.).

**정답다**(情—) (be) affectionate; loving; kind; tender; friendly. ¶ 정다운 친구 a good 〔close〕 friend / 정다운 태도 an endearing manner / 정다운 여자 a warm-hearted woman; an affectionate woman / 정다운 인사 warm greetings / 정답게 affectionately; tenderly; warmly; 《화목하게》 happily; harmoniously / 손님을 정답게 맞다 receive a visitor warmly / 아이들을 정답게 바라보다 look fondly 〔affectionately〕 at *one's* children / 그 부부는 정답게 지낸다 They are an affectionate couple.

**정당**(正當) justness; rightfulness; legitimacy. ～하다 (be) just; right; rightful; proper; legitimate; lawful; legal.
¶ ～한 사유 a good reason; a just cause / ～한 변명 a good excuse / ～한 수단으로 by fair means / ～한 이유 없이 without good 〔sufficient〕 reason / ～한 법률상의 절차를 밟지 않고 without due process of law / ～히 rightly; rightfully; properly; legitimately; duly; reasonably; lawfully / ～히〔하게〕 평가하다 do 《*a person*》 justice; do justice to 《a subject》; set due value on 《*a matter*》; duly appreciate 《*a thing*》 / 그가 ～하다 He is right 〔justified〕. / 그는 ～히 행동했다 He played fair. / 사실로 보아 그의 주장은 ～하다 The fact warrants his statement. / 비록 자네가 ～하다 하더라도 그렇게 말하는 게 아니다 Though you may be right, you must not say such a thing to him.
◉ ～방위 〖법〗 (legitimate) self-defense; legal defense: ～ 방위로 《kill a man》 in self-defense / ～ 방위를 주장하다 plead self-defense.

**정당**(政黨) a political party.
¶ ～출신의 각료〔수상〕 a party minister 〔premier〕 / ～간의 interparty 《cooperation》 / 2대(大) ～ two major political parties / 2대 ～제 a two-party system / 진보〔급진〕～ a progressive 〔radical〕 party / ～에 적을 두다 belong to 〔be a member of〕 a political party / ～에 관계하고 있지 않다 be not connected with any political party / 새 ～을 만들다 form a new political party / ～을 초월하다 be supraparty.
◉ ～강령 a party platform 〔programme 《영》〕. ～관계 party affiliations. ～내각 a party cabinet. ～법 the Political Party Law. ～원 a member of a political party; a party man. ～정치 party politics; party government. ～정파 political parties and groups: ～정파에 관계가 없는 nonpartisan. ～조직 party organization.

참고 우리 나라의 주요 정당
열린 우리당 the Uri Party / 한나라당 the Grand National Party (GNP) / 민주 노동당 the Democratic Labor Party (DLP) / 새천년 민주당 the Millennium Democratic Party (MDP) / 자유 민주 연합(자민련) the United Liberal Democrats (ULD)

**정당**(精糖) 《정제》 sugar refining; 《정제당》 refined sugar.

**정당화**(正當化) justification. ～하다 justify 《the means》; warrant 《a measure》. ¶ 목적은 수단을 ～한다 The end justifies the means. / 그 같은 폭력은 어떤 이유로도 또는 어떤 명분으로도 ～될 수 없다 Such violence cannot be justified by any excuse or under any pretext.

**정도**(正道) the right path 〔track〕; the path of righteousness; justice. ¶ ～에 어긋나는 행위 an unrighteous act / ～를 밟다 tread on the path of righteousness; 《구어》 keep on the straight and narrow / ～로 들어서게 하다 set 《*a person*》 on the right track / ～에서 벗어나다 stray 「from the straight and narrow 〔from the right path〕 / 아무를 ～로 이끌다 guide *a person* into the right path / 일단 ～에서 벗어나면 되돌아가기가 어렵다 Once you stray from the right path, you will find it difficult to get back on to it.

**정도**(征途) a military expedition; a journey. ¶ ～에 오르다 go on an expedition; start 〔set out〕 on a journey.

**정도**(程度) 《분량》 (a) degree; extent (범위); 《표준》 a grade; a standard; a level; 《한도》 a limit; 《대략》 about. ¶ 손해의 ～ the extent of damage 〔loss〕 / 고등 학교 ～ the high-school level / 입학 시험의 ～ the standard of an entrance examination / 고교 졸업 ～ the senior high-school graduate standard / 중학 ～의 학교 a school of the middle-school standard / 대학 ～의 학교 an institution of the university grade / 어느 ～까지 to 「a certain 〔what〕 extent / 문명 ～가 높다 〔낮다〕 be in a high 〔low〕 state of civilization / ～를 넘다 exceed 〔go beyond〕 the limits; get out of bounds 〔out of hand〕 / ～를 지키다 keep within bounds; use moderation / ～를 높이다 〔낮추다〕 raise 〔lower〕 the standard / 그것은 ～문제다 It is a matter 〔question〕 of degree. / 어느 ～까지 그녀의 말을 믿어야 하나 To what extent can I believe her? / 이 책은 ～가 높다 This book is of higher standard. / 가격은 〔수는, 양은, 거리는, 나이는〕 어느 ～냐 How much 〔many, much, far, old〕 ...? / 더운 ～가 아니다 "Hot" is not the word. / 네 말엔 어느 ～ 진리가 있다 There is a certain degree of truth in what you say. / 불가능이라 해도 좋을 ～다 It is almost 〔practically, next to〕 impossible. / 술을 마시는 것도 좋지만 ～ 문제다 You may drink, but you must use moderation. / 그녀는 2천만 원 ～의 연수입이 있다 Her income is on the order of 20 million won a year. / 「10달러 ～의 멋진 선물이 있습니까」—「이 하모니카는 어떻습니까」 "Do you have a nice gift for about $10?" —"How about this harmonica?"
◉ 생활～ the standard of living: 그의 생활～는 꽤 높다 〔낮다〕 His standard of living is rather high 〔low〕.

**정독**(精讀) a careful 〔close〕 reading; intensive reading. ～하다 read carefully 〔intensively〕; peruse.

**정돈**(停頓) a deadlock; a stalemate; a standstill. ～하다 come to a standstill; reach a deadlock. ¶ ～상태에 빠지다 reach a stalemate; come to a standstill / ～상태에 있다 be stagnant; be at a standstill / ～된 국면을 타개하다 bring a deadlock to an end / 교섭이 ～ 상태에 빠졌다 The negotiations came to a deadlock. / ～상태를 타개하기 위하여 여러 가지 일이 시도되었다 There were many attempts to break the deadlock.

**정돈**(整頓) putting in (good) order; proper arrangement; tidying (up). ～하다 arrange 〔put〕 in order; put 〔set〕 to rights; arrange properly; tidy up; 《대열을》 dress. ¶ ～된 (neat and) tidy 《rooms》; in (good) order; orderly; well-organized / 방을 ～하다 tidy up a room; straighten *one's* room up / ～해 두다 have 〔keep〕 《everything》 in good order / 잘 ～돼 있다 be in trim 〔apple-pie〕 order / ～이 되어 있지 않다 be in disorder; be out of order / 대열을 ～시키다 dress the ranks; dress 《the men》 in line / 서류를 ～해 두어라 Put your papers in order. / 그는 항상 방을 ～해 둔다 He always keeps his room tidy.

**정동**(精銅) refined copper.

**정동방**(正東方) due east.

**정들다**(情—) grow fond 《of》; become

attached 《to》; acquire affection 《for》; fall in love 《with》; become intimate 《with》. ¶ 정든 님 *one's* beloved 〔love, lover〕 / 정들인 여자 a girl that *one* has come to love / 정든 학생들 *one's* beloved students / 여자한테 ~「become fond of 〔fall in love with〕 a girl / 정든 부모의 슬하를 떠나 그는 외국 유학을 떠났다 He left his tender parents and went abroad to study.

**정떨어지다**(情—) get disaffected 《with》; be disgusted 《with》; be sick 《of》. ¶ 여자한테 ~ fall out of love with a girl; *one's* affection is turned from a girl / 정떨어지는 이야기 a disgusting story / 하는 짓에 정이 떨어지다 be disgusted with the way *a person* behaves / 그의 어리석음에는 정말이지 정떨어졌다 I am quite disgusted at 〔with〕 his stupidity.

**정략**(政略) ①《정치적 책동》 political tactics; a political maneuver 〔move〕; a policy. ¶ ~적(인) political / 그것은 일시적인 ~에서 나온 조치이다 It is a measure dictated by political expediency. / 그것은 ~으로서 극히 졸렬한 조치이다 It is a very impolitical step. ②《책략》 an artifice; 《방편》 an expedient. ¶ ~으로 by artifice / ~을 쓰다 use artifice 〔tricks〕; resort to an expedient. ◉ ~가 a clever political tactician. ~결혼 (a) marriage of convenience 〔expediency〕; a marriage for political reasons.

**정량**(定量) a fixed 〔determinate〕 quantity; a standard capacity; 《내복약의》 a dose. ¶ ~의 quantitative. ◉ ~분석 〖화학〗 quantitative analysis.

**정려**(精勵) hard work; industry; diligence; assiduity. ~하다 work hard; apply *oneself* 《to *one's* studies》; be industrious 〔diligent, assiduous〕.

**정력**(精力) energy; vigor; vitality; 《구어》 go; 《성적인》 *one's* sexual capacity 〔powers〕; virility; potency. ¶ ~적인 energetic; vigorous; 《구어》 full of go; dynamic / ~의 소모 loss of energy / ~이 왕성한 사람 a man of unbounded 〔immense〕 virility 〔potency〕 / ~이 다하다 have *one's* energy exhausted / ~을 기울이다 put all *one's* energies 《into》 / ~을 회복하다 regain *one's* vigor; show renewed vitality / 그는 물리학 연구에 ~을 기울였다 He applied his energies to the study of physics. / 젊은 까닭에 ~이 왕성하다 Being young, he has lots of energy. / 그는 ~이 쇠퇴하고 있다 His powers are falling. *or* His energy is declining. / 그의 성공은 ~적인 성격 때문이다 His success is due to his dynamic personality. / 그는 ~이 매우 왕성해서, 1주일만에 그 책을 다 써냈다 He was so energetic that he completed the book in a week. ◉ ~가 an energetic man; 《구어》 a bundle of energy; 《구어》 a ball of fire: 그는 ~가 이다 He is a (real) bundle of energy. ~제 a stimulant for the sex drive.

**정련**(精練) ①《연습》 good training 〔drill〕. ~하다 drill 〔train〕 well. ②《섬유의》 scouring; degumming (견사의). ~하다 scour; degum. ◉ ~제 a scouring agent.

**정련**(精鍊) refining; smelting. ~하다 refine 《metals》; smelt 《copper》; reduce 《ores》. ◉ ~소 a refinery; a smelting works. ~업 the refining industry.

**정렬**(貞烈) chastity; virtue. ◉ ~부인 a lady of virtue.

**정렬**(整列) standing in a row; an array; a lineup. ~하다 stand in a row; form a line; line 〔be lined〕 up. ¶ ~하여 기다리다 wait in line / 3열로 ~하다 line up in three files / 길의 양쪽에 ~하다 line both sides of the street / ~시키다 dress 《the men》.

**정령**(政令) a government order 〔ordinance〕.

**정령**(精靈) 《혼백》 the soul (of the deceased); the spirit; the ghost; 《혼령》 a spirit; a sprite; a genius (*pl.* genii). ◉ ~설 animism; spiritualism.

**정례**(定例) usage; a custom. ¶ ~의 regular; ordinary; usual / ~에 의하여 according to usage. ◉ ~국무회의 a regular 〔an ordinary〕 Cabinet meeting. ~기자회견 a regular press conference 〔interview〕. ~회의 a regular meeting: ~회의가 내일 열린다 There will be a regular meeting tomorrow.

**정로**(正路) ①《대로》 the main road. ②《올바른》 the right path 〔track〕; the path of righteousness.

**정론**(正論) a sound 〔fair〕 argument. ¶ ~을 펴다 「come out with 〔put forth〕 a sound argument.

**정론**(定論) an established theory; an established 〔a settled〕 view 〔opinion〕; the orthodox theory.

**정론**(政論) political arguments 〔discussions〕; politics. ¶ ~을 벌이다 discuss (current) political affairs 〔matters〕; talk politics.

**정류**(停留) stoppage; a stop. ~하다

stop 〔halt〕《at》; come to a halt; make a stop. ◉ ～장 a 《bus》 stop: 다음 ～장은 어디입니까 What is our next stop? *or* Where does the bus stop next? / 여기서 역까지 ～장이 몇 군데나 있습니까 How many stops are there from here to the station?

**정류**(精溜) 〖화학〗 rectification (of a chemical substance); purification; refinement. ～하다 rectify; purify; refine. ◉ ～기 a rectifier. ～주정(酒精) rectified spirit.

**정류**(整流) 〖물리〗 rectification; commutation; 〖전자〗 detection. ～하다 rectify; adjust; commutate; commute; detect. ◉ ～관 a rectifying tube. ～기 a rectifier. ～자(子) a commutator.

**정률**(定律) 〖물리·화학〗 a fixed law; 〖음악〗 a fixed rhythm.

**정률**(定率) a fixed rate. ◉ ～세 proportional taxation.

**정리**(正理) truth; reason; logic.

**정리**(廷吏) a court clerk.

**정리**(定理) 〖수학〗 a theorem. ◉ 다항〔2항〕～ polynomial 〔binomial〕 theorem.

**정리**(情理) humaneness; humanity. ¶ ～를 다하여 타이르다 expostulate; persuade earnestly; reason with 《*a person* about *a matter*》.

**정리**(整理) ① 《정돈》 arrangement; (re)adjustment; order; regulation. ～하다 (re)arrange; put 《*a thing*》 in order; put 〔set〕 《*something*》 to rights; (re)adjust; straighten (out); keep *a thing* tidy. ¶ 경지 ～ readjustment of arable land / 가사(家事)를 ～하다 adjust *one's* household affairs / 교통을 ～하다 regulate 〔control〕 the traffic / 서랍을 ～하다 put the drawer in order / 소지품을 ～하다 arrange *one's* personal belongings properly / 유고(遺稿)를 ～하다 arrange 〔edit〕 《*a person's*》 posthumous works / 회의장을 ～하다 restore order in the chamber / 장부를 ～하다 《은행원이》 adjust accounts / 자료를 ～분류하다 pigeonhole data / 재정을 ～하다 readjust finances; 《집안의》 readjust *one's* financial affairs / 회의 전에 서류를 ～하다 arrange *one's* papers before the meeting / 말하기 전에 생각을 ～하는 것이 필요하다 It is necessary to put our thoughts in order before we speak.
② 《해소·해체》 liquidation; disorganization; reorganization; 《지불 관계의》 full payment; settlement. ～하다 liquidate; disorganize; reorganize; consolidate; 《지불 관계를》 clear 〔pay〕 off; pay in full; settle 《*one's* debts》. ¶ ～회사 《정리가 필요한》 a company in need of reorganization; 《정리중의》 a company in liquidation; 《정리된》 a liquidated company; 《합병된》 an absorbed company / 채무를 ～하다 pay off 〔clear away〕 *one's* debt; settle *one's* debts.
③ 《감원》 retrenchment; curtailment; a shake-up (대규모의); 《매각·처분》 disposition; clearance. ～하다 retrench; curtail; cut down 《on》; reduce; 《처분》 dispose of; sell. ¶ 가재(家財)를 ～하다 dispose of *one's* household goods and furniture / 잔품을 ～하다 clear off the unsold goods / 사장은 인원을 ～할 계획이다 The boss is planning to cut down on the staff.
◉ ～공채 a consolidated public loan; funded loans. ～기금 consolidated funds. ～번호 a reference number. ～부 《신문사의》 the copydesk; the make-up department. ～안 a readjustment plan. ～위원 an adjustment committee. ～자 an adjuster; a regulator. ～자금 consolidated capital. ～장(欌) a commode. ～함 《서류의》 a filing cabinet: 서랍식 ～함 《책상 위에 놓는》 pigeonholes.

**정립**(定立) 〖논리〗 a thesis (*pl.* theses).

**정립**(鼎立) a triangular position. ～하다 take 〔be in〕 a triangular position; be in a three-cornered contest; stand in a trio. ¶ 3국이 ～하다 the three countries are opposed to one another.

**정말**(正―) ① 《참말》 (the) truth; reality; a fact. ¶ ～ 같은 likely; probable; plausible / ～은 really; in fact; as a matter of fact; in reality / ～로 여기다 accept 《a story》 as true; take 《a word》 seriously; believe / ～같은 이야기 a likely-sounding story; a story having the ring of truth about it / ～같은 거짓말 a plausible lie / ～인가 Is it true? / ～입니다 Believe me. *or* Take my word for it. / 그 소문은 ～이었다 The rumor proved (to be) true. / 듣기는 했어도 ～ 같지 않았다 I could not believe my ears. / 그게 ～일까 Can it be true? *or* I wonder if it is true. / 그 이야기는 ～ 같지 않다 I can't accept the news as true. / 그의 말은 ～ 같이 들린다 His words ring 〔sound〕 true.
② [부사적] truly; really; quite; indeed;

very; so help me. ¶ 나는 ~ 슬펐다 I was really 〔right 《구어》〕 sad. / ~ 감사합니다 I thank you very much. / 그는 ~ 총명한 사람이다 He is really a very clever man. / ~ 위험천만이구나 It is, so help me, one of the most dangerous things. /「이것 ~ 큰일이군」—「~그래」 "This is really a serious matter." — "You said it."
③ [감탄사] 《놀라서》 Really ?; 《설마》 Not really ?; You don't say (so)!

**정맥**(精麥) 《보리》 cleaned 〔polished〕 barley; 《일》 barley cleaning. ◉ ~기(機) a barley cleaning machine.

**정맥**(靜脈) a vein. ¶ ~의 venous; venose / 굵은 ~이 불거진 손 a heavily veined hand. ◉ ~경화증 phlebosclerosis. ~류(瘤) a varix (*pl.* varices): ~류가 생겨났다 have varicose veins. ~염 phlebitis. ~주사 《give》 (an) intravenous injection 《to》. ~혈(血) venous blood. 소~ a veinlet. 안면~ a facial vein.

**정면**(正面) the front; the front side 〔part〕; the facade (건물의).
¶ ~의 front; frontal / ~에 in front 《of》 / ~으로 directly; sheer / 바로 ~에 full in the face; right in front 《of》; just opposite / ~에서 보다 take a front view 《of》 / ~에서 본 얼굴 a full face / ~의 입구 the front 〔main〕 entrance 《of a hotel》 / ~에 앉다 sit in front / ~으로 공격하다 make a frontal attack on 《the enemy》; attack 《*a person*》 openly / ~으로 반대하다 be (dead) against 《*a matter*》; publicly oppose / 바람을 ~으로 받다 face the wind / 우체국은 정거장의 ~에 있다 The post office is right in front of the station.
◉ ~공격 a frontal attack 《against》. ~도(圖) a front view. ~돌파 a frontal breakthrough. ~석 《의회의》 the front bench; 《극장의》 the dress circle. ~충돌 a head-on collision 《with》; 《의론·교섭 등에서》 a frontal clash: ~ 충돌하다 collide 〔clash〕 head-on 《with, against》 (★ clash는 자동차에 관하여는 쓰지 못함); run head-on into *something* / 트럭과 버스가 ~ 충돌했다 The truck collided head-on with a bus. / 회기의 연장을 둘러싸고 여당과 야당의 ~ 충돌이 예상된다 A frontal clash between the Government Party and the Opposition is expected over the extension of the Assembly session.

**정모**(正帽) a full-dress hat; a formal hat.

**정묘**(丁卯) 〖민속〗 the 4th binary term of the sexagenary cycle.

**정묘**(精妙) exquisiteness; fineness. ~하다 (be) exquisite; fine; subtle. ¶ ~히, ~하게 exquisitely; finely.

**정무**(政務) state 〔political〕 affairs; government business. ¶ ~를 보다 attend to government affairs; administer the affairs of state. ◉ ~위원 a political committeeman; a political committee [총칭]. ~장관 the Minister of State for Political Affairs: 제1 ~장관 the first state minister for political affairs. ~차관 a parliamentary vice-minister 〔undersecretary〕. ~회의 《정당의》 an executive policy council.

**정문**(正文) the (official) text. ¶ 협약의 ~ the text of an agreement.

**정문**(正門) the front 〔main〕 gate; the main entrance. ¶ ~으로 들어가다 go in at the front gate; enter by the main gate.

**정문**(頂門) the crown of the head; the pate. ◉ ~일침(一鍼) an incisive remonstrance; a vital warning; a home-thrust: ~일침을 놓다 give an admonition to the point.

**정물**(靜物) stationary things; inanimate objects; [총칭] still life. ◉ ~사진 a still photo. ~화 a (picture of) still life; a still-life painting 〔picture〕: ~화가 a still-life painter.

**정미**(丁未) 〖민속〗 the 44th binary term of the sexagenary cycle.

**정미**(正味) ¶ ~의 net; clear / ~1파운드 one pound net.

**정미**(精米) rice polishing 〔cleaning〕; 《정백미》 polished 〔cleaned〕 rice. ~하다 polish 〔clean〕 rice. ◉ ~기(機) a rice-cleaning machine. ~소 a rice (=cleaning) mill.

**정미**(精微) fineness; delicacy; minuteness; subtlety. ~하다 (be) fine; delicate; minute; subtle.

**정밀**(精密) 《상세함》 minuteness; 《정확함》 precision; accuracy. ~하다 (be) minute; precise; detailed; exact; accurate; close.

> 용법 **minute** 세밀한 부분까지 주의를 기울인. **precise** 세밀한 부분까지 정확한. **detailed** 자세하고 세밀하게 기술한. **exact** 엄밀하게 정확한. **accurate** 모델이나 정해진 수준에 충실히 따른. **close** 철저하게 면밀한.

¶ ～하게 minutely; closely; in detail; precisely; accurately / ～한 지도 a detail(ed) map / ～한 조사 a close investigation / ～한 계획 a blueprint; a detailed plan / ～한 기술 precision techniques / 이 기계는 ～하게 검사되었다 A thoroughgoing investigation has been made with this machine. / 그는 그 약품에 대하여 ～한 검사를 했다 He did a detailed analysis of that medicine.
◉ ～검사 a close [thorough] examination ⟪of⟫. ～계기 a precision gauge. ～공업 the precision (machinery) industry; the precision manufacturing. ～공학 precision engineering. ～과학 an exact science. ～기계[기구] a precision machinery [apparatus, instrument]: ～기계 공장 a precision machine plant. ～도 a detailed drawing. ～작업: 그녀들은 손끝이 야무져서, ～작업에는 안성맞춤이다 Their nimble fingers make the girls ideal for precision work. ～폭격 pinpoint [precision] bombing.

**정박**(碇泊) anchoring; anchorage; mooring. ～하다 (lie at) anchor; take up moorings ⟪at⟫; berth; ⟪기항⟫ stop [call, put in] ⟪at⟫; ⟪투묘⟫ drop anchor. ¶ ～중인 배 a ship at anchor; a ship on the berth / ～해 있다 be [lie] at anchor; be [stay] in port; be moored ⟪at the pier⟫. ◉ ～기간 lay days. ～등(燈) an anchor light. ～료[세] anchorage fees [dues]. ～선(船) a ship at anchor [on the berth]. ～시설 harbor accommodation(s). ～지[소] an anchorage (area); a moorage; a roadstead. ～항 an anchorage harbor.

**정박아**(精薄兒) ⇨ 정신박약아.

**정반대**(正反對) the direct opposition; the exact reverse [opposite]. ¶ ～의 directly opposite / ～로 in direct opposition ⟪to⟫; diametrically; on the contrary / ～이다 be just the opposite ⟪of⟫; be diametrically opposed [opposite] ⟪to⟫; be the exact reverse ⟪of⟫; be quite contrary ⟪to⟫ / ～ 방향으로 나가다 go just in the opposite direction / 사실은 ～입니다 The fact is just the opposite. / 나는 ～로 생각했다 I thought quite the opposite. / 그는 총명하기는 커녕 그 ～입니다 He is the reverse of [far from being] intelligent.

**정반합**(正反合) 〚철학〛 thesis-antithesis=synthesis.

**정방**(精紡) (fine) spinning. ◉ ～기 a (fine) spinning machine.

**정방형**(正方形) = 정사각형.

**정배**(定配) exile. ⇨ 유배. ¶ ～ 보내다 condemn ⟪*a person*⟫ to exile; exile ⟪*a person*⟫.

**정백**(精白) pure white. ◉ ～당(糖) refined sugar. ～미 polished rice.

**정벌**(征伐) ⟪토벌⟫ subjugation; conquest; ⟪진압⟫ suppression; ⟪원정⟫ an [a punitive] expedition. ～하다 conquer; subjugate; suppress ⟪a revolt⟫. ¶ ～하러 가다 go on an expedition ⟪against⟫ / 적을 ～하다 conquer the enemy.

**정범**(正犯) 〚법〛 the principal offender.

**정변**(政變) a political change; a change of government; ⟪무력에 의한⟫ a *coup d'état* (F.). ¶ 페루에서 ～이 일어났다 A *coup d'état* took place in Peru.
◉ 갑신～ the *Kapshin* coup (in December 1884).

**정병**(精兵) a crack [an elite] troop [corps]; the flower of the army. ¶ ～ 2천 a picked army [crack troop] of 2,000.

**정보**(情報) ⟪a piece of⟫ information; intelligence; a report; news.

> **용법** **information** 「정보」란 뜻에서는 「셀 수 없는 명사」, 따라서 수를 나타내려면 그 앞에 piece, item 등을 써야 함. That's a useful piece [item] of information. (유용한 정보.) **intelligence** 주로 적측에 관한 정보를 뜻함: military intelligence (군사 정보).

¶ (…에 관한) 한 유익한 ～ a useful piece of information ⟪about, on⟫ / 믿을 만한 소식통으로 부터의 ～ information from a reliable source / 엉터리 ～ ⟪미구어⟫ phony information / …라는 ～에 접하고 having received information that… / …라는 ～가 있다 it is reported that… / ～를 모으다 [수집하다] gather [collect] information ⟪on⟫ / 넌지시 ～를 얻어내다 fish for information / …에서 ～를 끄집어 내다 derive information from ⟪a chat⟫ / ～에 어둡다 be not well informed ⟪about⟫ / ～를 제공하다 give information / 적의 ～를 얻다[입수하다] obtain [get] intelligence [information] of the enemy / ～를 누설하다 tip off [leak] information / 그녀는 그 건에 관한 ～를 나에게 주었다 She gave me some information about [on] the matter. / 그것은 매우 흥미 있는 ～다

That's a very interesting piece of information. / 경찰에 그 ~를 흘린 자가 누구냐 Who tipped off the police about it? / 우리는 적의 계획에 관한 비밀 ~를 가지고 있다 We have secret intelligence of our enemy's plans.
◉ ~검색 information retrieval (생략 IR). ~계 an intelligence branch. ~고속 도로 an information superhighway. ~공개법 a public information act; 《미국의》 a sunshine law, the Freedom of Information Act. ~공학 information engineering. ~과(課) the intelligence division. ~과잉 a surfeit 〔glut〕 of information. ~과학 information science. ~국 an intelligence section 〔bureau〕: 중앙~국 《미국의》 the Central Intelligence Agency (생략 CIA). ~기관 a secret 〔an intelligence〕 service; a counter-intelligence corps (방첩 부대). ~기술 Information Technology (생략 IT). ~누설 a leakage of information; an intelligence leak. ~루트 a pipeline; a 《secret》 channel of information. ~망 an intelligence network; networks of intelligence 〔information〕: ~망을 깔아 놓다 set up an intelligence network. ~부대 an intelligence unit 〔organization〕. ~부 요원 an intelligence agent 〔officer〕; a secret agent. ~산업 the information industry 〔business〕; the business of communications. ~수집 information gathering: ~수집함 an intelligence vessel 〔ship〕. ~시대 an information age; the age of information. ~원 《경찰에의》 an informer; an agent. ~원(源) a news source; information sources: 문제가 되는 것은 그것의 ~원이다 What matters is where 〔what source〕 they got 〔obtained〕 the information from. ~이론 the information theory. ~장교 an intelligence officer. ~정치 tip-off politics; politics sustained by intelligence activities. ~제공자 an informant; an informer. ~처리 data 〔information〕 processing: ~처리 산업 the data processing industry / ~처리 제품 a information product. ~통 a person in the know 《about》; a well-informed person. ~통신부 the Ministry of Information and Communication. ~혁명 the information revolution. ~화사회 an information-oriented society. ~활동 intelligence activities. 허위~ a false 〔wrong〕 tip. 국가~원 《한국의》 the National Intelligence Service.

**정복**(正服) a formal dress; a full uniform. ◉ ~경찰관 a policeman in full uniform.

**정복**(征服) conquest; subjugation; mastery; defeat. ~하다 conquer; subjugate; overcome; subdue; master 《English》; defeat.

> (용법) **conquer** 힘을 사용하여 사람 또는 사물을 정복하다. **overcome** 어려움을 극복하여 물질 이외의 힘과 싸워 이겨내다. **subdue** 저항심을 잃게 하여 영속적으로 복종시키다. **master** 어떤 상황을 극복하여 그 처리 방법을 터득하다. **defeat** 「…을 패배시키다」란 뜻에서 「정복하다」로 개념이 발전된 것.

¶ ~할 수 없는 unconquerable / 산정을 ~하다 conquer the summit / 자연을 ~하다 subdue nature / 노르만인은 11세기에 영국을 ~했다 The Normans conquered England in the eleventh century. / 그는 돌파하기 어려워 보이는 난관을 기어이 ~했다 He finally overcome what looked an insurmountable obstacles. ◉ ~욕 lust 〔desire〕 for conquest. ~자 a conqueror; a vanquisher; a subjugator.

**정본**(正本) 《원본》 the original text 〔copy〕; 《공문서의 등본》 an officially certified copy; 《법률 용어》 an exemplification. ¶ ~과 사본 the original and copy.

**정부**(正否) right or wrong. ¶ 일의 ~를 판별하다 tell 〔distinguish〕 right from wrong; judge whether *something* is right or wrong.

**정부**(正副) 《직위》 principal and vice; 《서류의》 original and duplicate 〔copy〕. ¶ ~2통을 작성하다 prepare 〔make out〕 《a document》 in duplicate / ~2통의 원서를 내야 한다 The application shall be presented in duplicate. / 일건 서류 ~2통을 송부할 것 Send both the original and a copy of all the documents bearing on the affair.
◉ ~의장 the speaker and vicespeaker; the chairperson and vicechairperson. ~통령 the president and VicePresident.

**정부**(政府) a government; 《어떤 나라의》 the Government; 《미국의》 the Administration; 《내각》 the cabinet; the ministry 《영》. ¶ ~(측)의 government(-al) / 현~ the present Government

〔Cabinet〕/ 한국 ~ the Korean Government / 클린턴 ~ the Clinton Administration / ~를 수립하다 establish 〔set up〕 a government / ~를 지지하다〔공격하다〕 support 〔attack〕 the Government / ~를 타도〔전복〕하다 overthrow 〔subvert, overturn〕 the Government / ~관련 기관 a government-related organization / ~의 예산안이 국회를 통과했다 The government=drafted budget passed the National Assembly. / 나는 현~의 외교 정책에 반대한다 I am against the foreign policy of the present government.
◉ ~간행물 government 〔official〕 publications. ~고시 가격 the government-set official 〔fixed〕 price: ~ 고시 표준 건축비 the government-set standard building cost 《of apartment》. ~고위층 high-ranking government officials. ~기관 a government body 〔agency〕. ~당국 the government authorities. ~대표 a government representative. ~(보유)미 state-held 〔government-controlled〕 rice: 정부는 물가 안정을 위해 ~보유미를 무제한 방출할 것이다 To stabilize the price, the government will release 〔supply〕 unlimited amounts of state-held rice. ~보조금 government subsidies. ~보증 government guarantee. ~소식통 government sources 〔circles〕. ~소재지 the seat of government; the capital. ~수반 the head of government. ~(제출법)안 a government 〔an administration〕 bill 〔measure〕. ~조직법 『법』 the National Government Organization Act. ~종합청사 《한국의》 the Unified 〔Integrated〕 Government Building. ~특혜 government's favors. 세계~ a world government. 중앙〔지방〕~ the central 〔local〕 government.

**정부**(情夫) a (male) lover; a paramour. ¶ ~를 두다 carry on with a lover.

**정부**(情婦) a mistress; a (lady)love; a paramour. ¶ 그의 ~ his girl; his woman / ~를 두다 get a mistress.

**정북(방)**(正北(方)) due north.

**정분**(情分) a cordial friendship; affection; intimacy. ¶ ~이 두텁다 be on terms of intimacy.

**정비**(正比) 『수학』 direct ratio.

**정비**(整備) 《기계·도구 등의 수리·점검·조정》 maintenance; service; tuning up; 《구어》 a tune-up; repair (수리); 《배의》 fitting-out; 《정돈하여 갖춤》 preparation; putting in good order. ~하다 《수리·점검·조정하다》 repair 《a tool》; fix 《a car》; service 《an airplane》; fit out 《a ship》; 《정돈·갖추다》 put 《*a thing*》 in good order; equip 《a factory》 fully with 《machinery》; provide 《a laboratory》 with 《many equipment》; 《개선하다》 improve. ¶ ~가 잘 되어 있는 차 a car kept in good repair / 도로를 ~하다 repair a road / 경기장을 ~하다 put the ground(s) in good condition / 잘 ~해 두다 keep 《a machine》 in good repair 〔condition〕/ 인원을 ~하다 reshuffle the personnel / 기업을 ~하다 consolidate an enterprise / 각종 법령을 시민 생활의 현실적인 필요에 맞게 ~하다 improve various laws and regulations in such a way to meet the realistic needs of civil lives / 엔진은 잘 ~되어 있다 The engine is finely tuned.
◉ ~공장 a repair 〔maintenance〕 shop; 《자동차의》 an auto repair shop. ~불량 poor maintenance. ~사〔공〕 《비행기의》 a ground man; a ground-crew; 《기계의》 a repairman; 《자동차의》 a car 〔garage〕 mechanic.

**정비례**(正比例) 『수학』 direct proportion 〔ratio〕. ~하다 be in direct proportion 《to》. ¶ …에 ~해서 in direct proportion to.

**정비례**(定比例) definite 〔constant〕 proportion.

**정사**(正史) 《야사에 대하여》 authentic 〔true〕 history; 《정부 편찬의》 an official 〔authorized〕 history.

**정사**(正邪) right and 〔or〕 wrong; good and 〔or〕 evil. ¶ ~를 구별하다 discriminate between right and 〔from〕 wrong; know right from wrong; have a clear sense of right and wrong.

**정사**(正使) the chief envoy.

**정사**(政事) political affairs; administrative business; administration. ¶ ~를 돌보다 manage the administrative business 〔affairs of state〕.

**정사**(情死) a lovers' suicide; a double suicide; a joint suicide 《with a woman》. ~하다 die together for love; commit 〔attempt〕 a double suicide. ¶ 젊은 한 쌍이 호텔 방에서 ~했다 A young couple committed a double suicide in a hotel room. ◉ ~미수 an attempted double suicide. 억지~ a forced double suicide.

**정사**(情事) a love affair; an affair of the heart; a romance; an amour; 《밀통》 a liaison. ¶ 혼외~ extramarital intercourse 〔love affairs〕.

**정사**(精査) (a) minute investigation; a careful examination; a close inspection. ~하다 look closely into 《a matter》; examine carefully; investigate minutely; scrutinize.

**정사각형**(正四角形) 〖수학〗 a (regular) square; a perfect 〔an exact〕 square.

**정사면체**(正四面體) 〖수학〗 a regular tetrahedron.

**정사영**(正射影) 〖수학〗 an orthogonal projection. ◉ ~법 orthography.

**정사원**(正社員) a regular member; a full member of the staff; a member on the regular payroll.

**정산**(精算) exact calculation; an accurate account; adjustment; 《결산》 settlement of accounts. ~하다 keep an accurate account; adjust; settle accounts; settle up. ¶ 운임을 ~하다 adjust the traffic fares / 계산은 지금 내가 할 것이니, 나중에 ~하자 I'll pay the bill now; we can settle up later. ◉ ~서 a settlement of accounts. ~소 a fare adjustment office. ~액 the adjusted amount. ~인 an average adjuster.

**정삼각형**(正三角形) 〖수학〗 a regular triangle; an equilateral triangle.

**정상**(正常) normalcy; normality. ¶~의 〔적인〕 normal / ~이 아닌 abnormal; irregular / ~적인 정신 상태 normal mental state / ~적인 행동 normal behavior / ~으로 작동하다 work normally / ~으로 돌아가다 return 〔get back〕 to normal; be restored to normality 〔normalcy〕 / 열차 운행은 ~으로 돌아갔다 The train schedule has been restored to normal. / 그녀가 ~임은 의심할 여지가 없다 Her sanity is beyond doubt. / 사춘기의 젊은이가 부모의 권위에 도전하는 일은 ~이다 It is normal for the adolescent to challenge parental authority.
◉ ~가격 a normal price. ~궤도 the right track: 국민 경제를 ~ 궤도에 올려놓다 place the national economy on the right track. ~능률 normal efficiency. ~상태 the normal condition 〔state〕. ~속도 a normal speed. ~위치 a normal position 〔posture〕. ~아 a normal child. ~조업 regular operation.

**정상**(定常) regularity. ◉ ~상태 〖물리〗 a stationary state. ~파 〖물리〗 a stationary 〔standing〕 wave.

**정상**(政商) a businessman with political background 〔connections〕. ◉ ~배 businessmen with political affiliations 〔influence〕.

**정상**(頂上) ① 《산의》 the peak; the top; the summit (★ top은 산 이외에 수목, 기둥, 머리 꼭대기 등에도 쓰임). ¶ 산의 ~에 on 〔at〕 the top of a mountain; atop a hill / ~에 오르다 gain 〔get to〕 the summit; top the mountain peak / 산 ~에는 1년 내내 눈이 덮여 있다 The mountain is covered 〔capped〕 with snow all the year round / 우리는 그 산의 ~을 정복했다 We attained the summit of the mountain.
② 《절정》 the peak; the highest point; the zenith; 《수뇌》 the summit; the head. ¶ 그녀의 인기는 지금 ~에 있다 Her popularity is now at its peak. *or* She is now at the peak of her popularity. / 물가가 ~에 달했다 Prices have hit the ceiling.
◉ ~급 회담 a summit-level conference. ~외교 summit diplomacy. ~회담 summit talks; a summit conference: 남북한~ 회담 South-North Korean summit talks; an inter-Korean summit meeting / 여러 문제의 해결을 위한 길을 트기 위하여 태평양 ~ 회담 개최를 제안하다 suggest holding a Pacific summit talks to pave the way for solution of problems 《about》.

**정상**(情狀) circumstances; conditions. ¶~을 참작해서 in consideration 〔view〕 of the (extenuating) circumstances / ~을 참작하다 take the circumstances into consideration 〔account〕 / 그의 죄상은 ~을 참작할 여지가 없다 Nothing can extenuate his guilt.

**정상화**(正常化) normalization. ~하다 normalize. ¶ 국교 ~ the normalization of diplomatic relations 《with》 / ~되다 return to normalcy 〔normal conditions〕 / 몹시 혼잡한 철도 (수송) 사정을 ~하다 straighten out the badly congested railroad traffic conditions / 두 나라의 국교는 1980년에 ~되었다 Diplomatic relations between the two countries were normalized in 1980.

**정색**(正色) 《빛깔》 the primary colors; 《안색》 a serious countenance 〔look〕; a solemn air; 《진지함》 seriousness; earnestness; gravity. ~하다 show *one's* seriousness 〔earnestness, sincerity〕; assume a solemn air 〔countenance〕; wear a sober look; put on a grave 〔serious〕 look. ¶~하고 말하다 speak in a stiff manner / ~하고

남을 나무라다 reprove *a person* with a solemn air. 「color reaction.

**정색**(呈色) 〖화학〗 coloration. ◉ ~반응

**정서**(正書) 《또박또박 쓰기》 square-hand 〔printed-style〕 characters. ~하다 write in the square style.

**정서**(淨書) neat writing 〔copying〕. ~하다 make a fair 〔clean〕 copy 《of》.

**정서**(情緖) 《감정》 emotion(s); feeling(s); sentiment; 《분위기》 a mood; an atmosphere. ¶ ~가 풍부한 full of artistic effect; charming / 이국~ an exotic atmosphere / ~가 넘치는 거리 a street with a lot of atmosphere / ~가 넘쳐 흐르다 be overcome with emotions / ~가 불안정하다 be emotionally unstable. ◉ ~교육 culture of (aesthetic) sentiments. ~불안정 emotional instability. ~장애 an emotional disturbance: ~장애아 an emotionally disturbed child.

**정서(방)**(正西(方)) due west.

**정석**(定石) 《바둑·장기의》 a set move (in *paduk*); established tactics; 《공식》 a formula; 《원칙》 the cardinal principle. ¶ ~대로 《play》 by the book / 그것이 정치의 ~이다 That is an accepted formula in politics.

**정선**(停船) stoppage of a ship; detention of a boat (전시중의); 《검역을 위한》 quarantine. ~하다 《a vessel》 stop; heave 〔lie〕 to; bring 《a ship》 to. ¶ ~을 명하다 stop 《a vessel》; order a ship to stop / 안개로 인하여 ~하다 be held up in the fog.

**정선**(精選) careful selection. ~하다 select 〔sort out〕 carefully; pick out with care. ¶ ~된 well-selected; choice; hand-picked / 이 도서실에는 ~된 양서가 있다 In this library there are carefully selected good books. ◉ ~품 choice goods: 여름 상품의 ~품 a fine selection of summer goods.

**정설**(定說) 《학계의》 an established theory; 《개인의》 a settled 〔definite〕 opinion 〔view〕; 《일반의》 an widely accepted opinion. ¶ ~을 뒤집다 overthrow an established theory / 비만이 심장병의 원인이 된다는 것이 ~로 되어 있다 It is the accepted view that being overweight contributes to heart disease.

**정성**(精誠) a true heart; sincerity; earnestness; devotion. ~스럽다 (be) sincere; earnest; devoted. ¶ ~껏 with *one's* utmost sincerity; wholeheartedly; devotedly / ~어린 선물 a gift with *one's* best wishes / ~을 들이다 devote *oneself* 《to》; give *one's* whole mind to; spare no pains / ~을 다하다 do *one's* best; make every effort 《to do》; exert *one's* utmost strength / ~껏 키우다 bring up with great 〔the utmost〕 care / 그는 ~껏 우리를 대접했다 He did his utmost to entertain us. 「analysis.

**정성분석**(定性分析) 〖화학〗 qualitative

**정세**(情勢) the state of things 〔affairs〕; the situation; conditions; circumstances; the appearance. ¶ 현재의 ~ the present status of affairs; the *status* (*in*) *quo* / 세계 〔유럽〕의 ~ the world 〔European〕 situation / 일반 ~ the general drift of affairs 《in Asia》 / 수습할 수 없는 ~ an unmanageable 〔uncontrollable〕 situation / ~의 변화 a change in the situation / ~의 악화 comedown 〔deterioration, worsening〕 of the situation / 현(現) ~에 비추어 in view of the situation; as the situation now stands / 지금의 ~로는 as matters 〔things〕 stand now; under the present circumstances; judging by the situation / (만일) ~가 호전된다면 should the situation improve / ~를 관망하다 watch the development of the situation / ~를 파악하다 grasp 〔take in〕 the situation / ~를 판단하다 judge 〔size up, assess〕 the situation / 새로운 ~에 대처하다 meet a new phase of the situation / 국제~ 변화에 능동적으로 대처하다 cope actively with the changing international circumstances / 지금의 ~는 어떠한가 How do things stand now ? *or* What is the present situation ? / ~가 어떤지 확실히 말해 주시오 Tell me exactly how matters stand. / ~는 점점 심각해지고 있다 The situation is becoming serious. ◉ ~판단 (a correct) analysis (and judgment) of the situation. 국내~ the domestic situation.

**정수**(正手) 《바둑·장기의》 the proper move.

**정수**(正數) 〖수학〗 a positive number.

**정수**(定數) 《일정수》 a fixed number; 《정족수》 a quorum. ¶ 출석자가 ~에 미달시에는 unless a quorum is present / ~에 차다 make a quorum; make up the full number / ~를 채우다 fill the necessary quorum / ~를 넘다 exceed the fixed number.

**정수**(淨水) clean water. ◉ ~기 a water purifier. ~장 a cleaning bed; a 「filtration 〔purification〕 plant. ～장치 a water-purifying device; a water purification system; a 「cleaning 〔filter〕 bed. ～지(池) a 「clean 〔pure〕 water reservoir.

**정수**(精水) semen; spermatic fluid.

**정수**(精髓) ① 《뼛속의》 marrow. ② 《사물의》 the essence; the quintessence; the 「spirit 〔soul〕; the pith. ¶ 기독교의 ～ the essentials of Christianity / ～를 골라내다 take essence of / 그의 작품은 한국 민속 예술의 ～를 나타내고 있다 His work embodies the quintessence of Korean folk art. / 부처님의 가르침에서 그 ～는 모든 사람을 사랑하라는 것이라고 나는 생각한다 I think the essence of Buddha's teaching is love for all men.

**정수**(靜水) still water. ◉ ～(역)학 hydro「statics.

**정수**(整數) 〖수학〗 an integral number; an integer; a whole number. ◉ ～론(論) the number theory.

**정수리**(頂—) the crown of the head; the pate. ＝정문(頂門).

**정숙**(貞淑) chastity; female virtue; feminine modesty. ～하다 (be) chaste; virtuous. ¶ ～하다는 평판이 있다 have a reputation for womanly virtue / 그녀는 ～한 아내이다 She is faithful to her husband.

**정숙**(靜肅) stillness; silence. ～하다 (be) still; silent; quiet. ¶ ～하게 silently; quietly; in an orderly manner / ～ 《게시》 Silence (please). / ～히 《의장의 발언》 Order ! order !; 《재판관의 발언》 Order in (the) court ! / ～히 하여라 Keep quiet. *or* Don't make a noise.

**정승**(政丞) 〖고제도〗 a minister of States; a prime minister (in the Kingdoms of Korea).

**정시**(正視) looking straight. ～하다 look 《*a person*》 in the face; look 「squarely 〔straight〕 《at》. ¶ 사실을 ～하다 look at a fact squarely. ◉ ～렌즈 an orthoscopic lens. ～안(眼) 〖안과〗 emmetropia.

**정시**(定時) fixed 〔regular〕 time; a 「stated 〔fixed〕 period. ¶ ～의 periodical; ordinary / ～에 regularly; periodically / ～운행하다 《a train, *etc.*》 move on schedule; operate regularly / ～에 발차하다 leave 「at the scheduled time 〔on schedule〕 / ～에 회의를 열다 meet at stated intervals / ～퇴근 《게시》 No overtime. ◉ ～제(制) 〖교육〗 the part-time (schooling) system.

**정식**(正式) proper 〔regular〕 form; formality. ¶ ～의 formal 《procedure》; regular 《education》; official 《name》; due 《formality》; full-dress 《debate》 / ～으로 formally; in due form; duly; officially / ～으로 신청하다 make a formal application for / ～절차를 밟다 go through due formalities / ～으로 방문하다 make a formal call 《at, on》; pay a formal visit 《to》 / ～ 재판을 신청하다 apply to the court for a formal trial / 두 사람은 아직 ～으로 결혼하지 않았다 The two are not 「legally 〔formally〕 married yet. / 나는 ～으로 피아노를 배우지 않았습니다 I have not taken regular piano lessons. / 연습 시합은 그만두고 우리 ～으로 해보세 Let us stop the practice game and do the thing in style. / 나는 아직 ～ 절차는 밟지 않고 있다 I haven't gone through the regular formalities yet. ◉ ～결혼 legal marriage. ～계약 a formal agreement. ～교섭 formal negotiations. ～교육 regular school education. ～멤버 a regular 〔card-carrying〕 member. ～방문 a formal visit. ～소개 a regular introduction. ～승인 (a) *de jure* recognition. ～식사 a 「regular 〔full-course〕 dinner. ～재판 a formal trial.

**정식**(定式) 「an established 〔a prescribed〕 form; a formula.

**정식**(定食) ① 《식당의》 a 「regular 〔set〕 meal. ② 《요리점의》 *table d'hôte* (F.); a dinner; *à prix fixe* (F.); the menu of the day. ¶ 만원 짜리 ～ a ten-thousand-won *table d'hôte* / 저녁으로 ～을 먹다 have a set supper / 오늘의 정식 《게시》 Today's Special.

**정식**(程式) 〖수학〗 a formula; forms.

**정식**(整式) 〖수학〗 an integral expression. ⇨ 다항식.

**정신**(艇身) a boat's length. ¶ 1～의 차로 지다 lose the race by a boat's length.

**정신**(精神) mind; soul; spirit; 《의지》 will; 《근본이념》 the spirit 《of the law》; 《민족·사회 등의》 ethos.

> 용법 **mind** 물질(matter)에 상대적인 말. 감정적이 아니라 판단·사고 등을 행하는 지적·이성적인 마음 즉 지력(知力)을 뜻함. **soul** 육체(body)를 떠나도 존재한다고 생각되는 「영혼」을 뜻하는 말. **spirit** 육체(flesh)에 상대되는 말. soul보다 더 육체로부터의 독립을 강조하는 말. **will** 「의지」를 뜻하는 말.

¶ ～적(인) spiritual; mental; moral; emotional (감정적인) / ～(적)으로 spiritually; mentally / ～적인 과로 mental fatigue / ～적인 원조〔압력〕 moral support 〔pressure〕 / ～적인 공백 a spiritual vacuum / ～적인 타격 a mental blow; a shock / ～적인 동요 emotional upset(s) / ～적인 유산 a mental heritage / 한국인의 귀중한 ～ 유산 the valuable spiritual asset of the Korean people / ～적인 사랑 platonic love / 법의 ～ the spirit of the law / 비열한 ～ a base mind; a mean spirit / 숭고한 ～ a noble spirit / ～적 지지〔압박〕 moral support 〔pressure〕 / ～이 훌륭한 noble〔high〕-minded; high-souled / ～이 썩은 corrupt; depraved / ～적으로 자립하다 achieve emotional autonomy / ～을 쏟아넣다 《일에》 do 《a job》 with heart and soul; devote *oneself* entirely to 《a job》; put *one's* (heart and) soul into 《*one's* work》 / ～을 잃다 lose *one's* senses 〔consciousness〕 / ～을 집중하다 concentrate *one's* attention on 《*something*》 / ～을 차리다 collect *one's* mind; pay attention / ～이 나가다 grow absent-minded; become foolish / ～이 없다 have a poor memory; have no spirit; be distracted 〔absent-minded, blank〕 / ～은 똑똑하다 be in *one's* right mind / 기본 ～에 어긋나다 run counter to the fundamental spirit 《of》 / ～에 이상을 가져오다, ～에 이상이 있다 be 〔get〕 mentally deranged; have a mental breakdown; 《미치다》 become insane; go mad 〔out of *one's* mind〕 / ～을 수양하다 cultivate 〔train〕 the mind; discipline *oneself* / …에 ～이 팔리다 be absorbed in; be intent on / ～을 바짝 차리다 strain every nerve; be all attention / ～적으로 지쳐 있다 be mentally exhausted 〔tired out〕 / 헌법 ～에 위배되다 be contrary to the spirit of the constitution / ～을 차려서 하여라 Put your heart into it. / ～차려 Look sharp! *or* Be on the alert! *or* Keep up your nerve! / 제발 ～ 차리시오 For goodness' sake, pull yourself together. / ～ 일도 하사 불성 (精神一到何事不成) Where there is a will, there is a way. *or* Nothing is impossible to a willing mind. / 건전한 ～은 건전한 육체에 깃든다 A sound mind in a sound body. / 우리는 법률의 조문 뿐만 아니라, 그 ～에 따라야 한다 We should obey the spirit as well as the letter of the law.

◉ ～감응 psychomancy. ～감정 a psychiatric test: ～감정을 하다 test 《*a person's*》 sanity. ～계 the mental world. ～과 psychiatry; psychopathy: ～과 의사 a psychiatrist. ～과학 mental science. ～교육 moral 〔spiritual〕 education: ～교육을 강화하다 intensify the spiritual education. ～구조 *one's* mental make-up 〔structure〕. ～노동 mental 〔brain〕 work: ～노동자 a mental 〔brain〕 worker. ～력 mental power; spiritual strength: (환자가) ～력으로 버티고 있다 stay 〔keep〕 alive by the sheer strength of 《*his*》 will to live. ～론 idealism. ～무장 mental 〔spiritual〕 armament. ～문명 moral 〔spiritual〕 civilization. ～문화 연구원 the Academy of Korean Studies (생략 AKS). ～물리학 psychophysics. ～발생학 psychogenesis. ～병리학 psychopathology: ～ 병리학자 a psychopathologist. ～분열증 split personality; schizophrenia: ～ 분열증 환자 a schizophrenic. ～상태 a mental condition; a state of mind; mentality / ～ 상태가 불안정하다 be emotionally unstable. ～생활 *one's* spiritual 〔mental〕 life. ～수양 mental training; moral cultivation: ～수양을 하다 discipline *one's* mind. ～신경증 psychoneurosis (*pl.* -ses): ～ 신경증의 psychoneurotic / ～ 신경증 환자 a psychoneurotic. ～신체의학 psychosomatic medicine; psychosomatics. ～안정제 a tranquilizer. ～연령 mental age: 그는 ～연령이 어리다 Mentally he is still a child. ～외과 psychosurgery. ～요법 a mind cure; psychotherapy; psychotherapeutics. ～위생 mental hygiene. ～의학 psychiatry: ～의학자 a psychiatrist. ～이상 mental disorder 〔derangement〕; psychosis: ～ 이상자 an insane 〔a mentally deranged〕 person; a lunatic; a psychopath. ～자세 《renew》 *one's* spiritual attitude. ～작용 mental function; mentation. ～장애 a mental disability 〔disorder〕. ～주의 idealism; spiritualism: ～주의자 an idealist; a spiritualist. ～지체 〖심리〗 mental retardation: ～지체아 a mentally retarded child. ～진단(학) psychognosis. ～질환 a mental disease: ～ 질환자 a mental patient; a mentally deranged person; mentally-disordered people. ～착란 mental derangement; insanity. ～측정 psychometry. ～통일 concentration of mind; mental concentration. ～현상 a mental phenomenon.

**정신대**(挺身隊) a group of comfort women (for Japanese soldiers during the World War II).

**정신박약**(精神薄弱) mental weakness; mental deficiency; feeble-mindedness. ◉ ～아(兒) a mentally-handicapped〔=retarded〕child; a「weak-minded〔feeble-minded〕child: ～아 수용시설 a home for retarded children. ～자 a「feeble-minded〔weak-minded〕person; a mentally deficient person; [집합적] the mentally handicapped; mentally「retarded〔backward〕people.

**정신병**(精神病) (a) mental illness; a mental disease; a disease of the mind; a psychosis (*pl.* -ses). ◉ ～동 a「psychiatric〔psychotic〕ward. ～자 a mentally deranged person; an insane person; a lunatic; a psychopath. ～전문의 a psychiatrist; a mental specialist. ～학 psychiatry: ～학자 a psychiatrist. ～환자 a「mental〔psychiatric〕patient; 《구어》 a mental case.

**정신병원**(精神病院) a mental hospital; a sanatorium for the insane; a lunatic asylum; 《구어》 a madhouse. ¶ ～에 들어가다 be「confined to〔put into〕a mental hospital.

**정신분석**(精神分析) psychoanalysis. ¶ ～학적인 psychoanalytical / ～학적으로 psychoanalytically / ～을 하다 psychoanalyze. ◉ ～학자 a psychoanalyst.

**정실**(正室) *one's*「lawful〔legal〕wife.

**정실**(情實) personal〔private〕considerations〔motives〕; favoritism (편중). ¶ ～에 좌우되다〔흐르다〕be「influenced〔swayed〕by personal considerations; take personal circumstances into consideration / ～을 배제하다 thrust personal considerations aside 《in public affairs》/ 실력보다 ～에 의하여 지위를 얻다 win a position more by favor than by merit / ～로 승진하다 be promoted through favoritism / 공적인 일에 ～은 금물이다 Private considerations must not enter into public affairs. ◉ ～인사 the appointment 《of *a person* to a position》 through favoritism.

**정악**(正樂) 〖음악〗 classical music; court music. ◉ 국립～연주단 the National Classical Music Orchestra.

**정압**(定壓) 〖물리〗 constant pressure.

**정압**(靜壓) 〖물리〗 static pressure.

**정애**(情愛) affection; love.

**정액**(定額) a fixed「sum〔amount〕; the required amount; a flat sum. ¶ ～에 달하다 come up to the required amount. ◉ ～등 a fixed-rate lamp. ～소득 a fixed income. ～예금 fixed amount savings; a fixed deposit: 그녀는 매월 5만원의 ～예금을 하고 있다 She puts 50 thousand won in a fixed deposit (account) every month. ～임금 a fixed wage. ～제 a flat sum system: ～제 요금 a flat rate.

**정액**(精液) ① 〖생리〗 semen; sperm. ¶ ～의 seminal; spermatic. ② 《순수액체》 an extract; an essence. ◉ ～사출 ejaculation; an ejection of semen. ～은행 a sperm bank.

**정양**(靜養) (a) rest; 《병후의》 convalescence; recuperation. ～하다 rest quietly; convalesce; recuperate; take a rest. ¶ ～차 for (the sake of) *one's* health; for recuperation / 의사는 병 치료를 위해 ～하라고 처방하였다 The doctor prescribed a rest cure for my illness. / 그녀는 두 달 정도 집에서 ～하면 완전히 기운을 되찾을 것이다 She will be completely restored to health by convalescing at home for two months or so.

**정어리** 〖어류〗 a sardine. ◉ ～통조림 canned〔tinned 《영》〕sardines.

**정언적**(定言的) 〖논리〗 categorical. ◉ ～명령〔판단〕 categorical「imperative〔judgment〕. ～명제 a categorical proposition.

**정업**(定業) a regular occupation; (a) fixed「employment〔job〕.

**정역학**(靜力學) 〖물리〗 statics.

**정연**(整然) orderliness. ～하다 (be) orderly; regular; systematic; well-regulated. ¶ ～하게 in (good) order; in an orderly manner; systematically / 그의 이론은 논리 ～하다 His argument is perfectly logical. / 모든 것이 질서 ～하다 All are arranged in good order.

**정열**(情熱) passion; enthusiasm; zeal. ¶ ～적 passionate; ardent; fervent / ～적인 사랑 passionate love / ～에 불타다 burn with passion / ～을 기울이다 put *one's* heart (and soul) into 《*one's* work》/ 그는 평화의 중요성에 관해 ～적으로 이야기하였다 He spoke passionately about the importance of peace.

**정염**(正塩) normal salt.

**정염**(情炎) the fires of passion; the flame of *one's* passion. ¶ ～에 불타다 burn with passion / ～을 불태우다 kindle the passions; have a burning passion 《for *a person*》.

**정예**(精鋭) the pick 〔best〕 《of the airmen》; the flower 《of an army》; elite 〔choice, picked〕 troops. ¶ ～의 picked; crack / 소수 ～ a small number of elite members / 5,000의 ～군대 a troop 5,000 strong / 팀의 ～ the best players of the team / 우리 부대는 ～로 편성되어 있다 Our unit is made up of the best soldiers. ◉ ～부대 a crack 〔an elite〕 unit; picked troops.

**정오**(正午) noon; high noon; midday. ¶～에 at (high) noon; at midday / ～전〔후〕에 before 〔after〕 noon.

**정오**(正誤) correction (of typographical errors). ◉ ～문제 a true-false question. ～표 a list of errata 〔corrigenda〕; an errata (slip): 완전한 ～표를 싣다 give a full list of errata.

**정온**(定溫) a fixed temperature. ◉ ～기 a thermostat. ～동물 a homoiothermic animal.

**정욕**(情慾) carnal 〔sexual〕 desire; lust; passions. ¶ ～의 노예 a slave of passions / ～을 억제하다 restrain *one's* carnal desire / ～에 빠지다 indulge in *one's* carnal pleasures / ～에 불타게 하다 inflame 《*a person*》 with sexual desire / ～을 채우다 gratify *one's* lust / 남자의 ～을 자극하다 stimulate 〔arouse〕 men's sexual desire.

**정원**(定員) 《정해진 수》 the fixed number 《of regular personnel, students, *etc.*》; the number limit; the full 「number 〔strength〕 (of staff); the quota; a quorum (정족수); 《수용인원》 the (seating) capacity. ¶ 버스의 ～ the seating capacity of a bus / ～이 500명인 영화관 a movie-house capable of seating 500; a movie-house with a seating capacity of 500 / ～ 외의 supernumerary / ～을 줄이다 reduce an establishment / ～에 달하다 reach the regular number / 이 버스는 ～이상의 손님을 태우고 있다 This bus is overloaded. / 회의는 ～ 미달로 연기되었다 The meeting was adjourned for want of a quorum. / ～엄수 《게시》 The seating capacity observed. / 이 차의 ～은 60명이다 This car is capable of carrying 〔has the capacity of〕 sixty passengers. / 금년은 지원자 미달로 ～을 못 채우는 대학이 생길지도 모른다 It is quite possible that some universities will not make 〔meet〕 their quota because of the shortage of applicants this year. ◉ ～초과 exceeding capacity; overcrowdedness.

**정원**(庭園) a garden; a park (큰). ¶ 옥상～ a roof garden / ～을 만들다 make 〔lay out〕 a garden / ～을 손질하다 tidy (up) a garden. ◉ ～가꾸기 gardening. ～사 a gardener. ～석〔수〕 a garden rock 〔tree, plant〕. ～술 landscape gardening.

**정월**(正月) January (생략 Jan.). ¶～ 초하루 New Year's Day / ～ 보름 the First Full Moon Day.

**정위치**(定位置) *one's* regular position.

**정유**(丁酉) 〖민속〗 the 34th binary term of the sexagenary cycle.

**정유**(精油) 《기름》 refined oil; essential oil (식물성의); 《정제》 oil refining. ◉ ～공장 an oil refinery. ～회사 an oil refining company.

**정육**(精肉) lean meat; dressed meat (적당한 크기로 포장한). ◉ ～상〔업자〕 a butcher; a meatman. ～업 the meat industry. ～점 a meat 〔butcher 《미》〕 shop; a butcher's (shop) 《영》.

**정육면체**(正六面體) a regular hexahedron; a cube.

**정은**(正銀) solid 〔pure〕 silver.

**정의**(正義) justice; right; righteousness. ¶ ～의 righteous; just / ～를 위한 싸움 a righteous war; fighting for a rightful cause / ～의 투사 a champion of right / ～를 옹호하다 defend the right / ～를 위해 싸우다 fight 「in the cause 〔for the sake〕 of justice / 힘은 ～이다 Might is right. / ～는 결국 승리한다 Right will prevail in the end. / ～는 우리 편이다 Right and justice are on our side. / 그는 자유와 ～를 위한 싸움에서 전사했다 He was killed in the war for freedom and justice. ◉ ～감 a sense of justice: ～감이 강하다 have a strong sense of justice. ～사회 a just society: ～ 사회 구현 the realization of a just society / ～사회를 구현하다 realize a society of justice.

**정의**(定義) a definition. ～하다 define. ¶ 사전의 ～ a dictionary definition / 「전쟁」이라는 낱말의 ～ a definition of the word "war" / ～를 내리다 give 〔lay down〕 a definition; define 《as》 / ～를 내리기 어렵다 be hard to define; be indefinable; defy a definition.

**정의**(情意) emotion and will; feelings.

◉ ～상통 mutual understanding〔feeling, affection〕: ～상통하다 enjoy mutual understanding〔affection〕.

**정의**(情誼) friendly feelings; affections. ¶ 깊은 ～ deep friendship / ～가 두텁다 be warm-hearted〔friendly〕/ 옛 ～를 생각해서 for old acquaintance('s) sake.

**정의**(精義) the exact meaning; a detailed exposition. ¶ 영문법 ～《책이름》 *A Commentary on English Grammar.*

**정일**(定日) the fixed date〔day〕; the appointed day.

**정자**(正字) the correct form of a character. ¶ ～로 기재하시오 Please write〔type〕clearly. ◉ ～법 orthography.

**정자**(亭子) a bower; an arbor; a summerhouse. ◉ ～나무 a big tree serving as a shady resting place in a village.

**정자**(精子) a sperm; 《동물의》 a spermatozoon (*pl.* -zoa); 《식물의》 a spermatozoid. ◉ ～낭 a spermogonium (*pl.* -nia); a spermagonium (*pl.* -nia). ～선 a sperm gland; a spermary. ～세포 a spermatid. ～은행 a sperm bank. ～형성 spermatogenesis.

**정자각**(丁字閣) a T-shaped shrine for ceremonial rites before a royal tomb.

**정자형**(丁字形) a T-shape; the figure T.

**정작** reality; actuality; practice; [부사적] really; actually; practically. ¶ ～ …하려면 if *one* has to; when occasion demands; when it comes to a showdown / ～사려고 하면 살 수 없다 When you actually try to buy one, they are not to be had. / ～해보면 어렵다 When one comes to doing it, one finds it considerably difficult.

**정장**(正裝) formal dress; full dress; full uniform. ～하다 dress up; be formally attired; dress formally; be in full 「dress〔uniform〕. ¶ ～을 갖추어야 할 모임 a dress affair; a dress-up party / ～으로 연회에 나가다 attend the banquet in full dress / ～하실 필요 없음《초대장에서》No formal dress.

**정장석**(正長石) 〖광물〗 orthoclase.

**정장제**(整腸劑) medicine for intestinal disorders.

**정재**(淨財) estate〔property, money〕 for votive offerings; a subscription. ¶ ～를 모으다 collect voluntary subscription《for》/ ～를 희사하다 make a votive offering of money《to a temple》.

**정쟁**(政爭) political strife〔controversy, dispute, issue〕. ¶ ～의 소용돌이 속에 몰아넣다 drive into the whirlpool of a political strife / ～의 도구로 삼다 make a political issue of / 정치가들은 밤낮 ～을 일삼고 있다 Politicians are spending all their time on political infighting.

**정적**(政敵) a political rival〔foe, opponent〕.

**정적**(靜的) passive; quiet; calm; static. ¶ ～으로 statically.

**정적**(靜寂) stillness; quiet; silence. ¶ ～을 깨뜨리다 break the silence / 무거운 ～이 방 안에 감돌았다 A gloomy silence hung over the room.

**정전**(正殿) the palace where the king used to hold morning audience; the royal audience chamber.

**정전**(停電) 《전등의》 a blackout; 《전기 공급의》 a power failure〔stoppage〕; a power cut; an interruption of the power supply; power suspension. ～하다 cut off the electricity〔power〕. ¶ ～이 되다 the electricity fails; the power supply is cut off / ～이다 the power is off / 어젯밤은 폭풍으로 ～이 되었다 Our electric light was cut off by storm last night. / 아, ～이다 Oh, the lights went out. (It must be a power failure.) / 어젯밤 ～이 있었다 We had a blackout last night.

**정전**(停戰) a cease-fire; a truce; an armistice; cessation of hostilities. ～하다 cease fire; make a truce; suspend hostilities. ¶ ～을 명하다 order to suspend hostilities.
◉ ～명령〔회담〕 a cease-fire order〔conference〕. ～조약《conclude》 a treaty of armistice《with》. ～협상 cease-fire negotiations. ～협정 an armistice〔a cease-fire〕agreement: ～협정을 체결하다 conclude a cease-fire agreement.

**정전기**(靜電氣) 〖물리〗 static electricity. ◉ ～학 electrostatics.

**정전압**(定電壓) constant voltage.

**정절**(貞節) faithfulness; fidelity; chastity. ¶ ～을 지키다 lead a chaste life / ～을 지키는 faithful; chaste; constant; true / ～이 없는 unchaste; frail / ～을 지키는 아내 a faithful〔virtuous〕wife.

**정점**(定點) a definite〔fixed〕point. ◉ ～관측〖기상〗fixed point observation: ～관측선 a ship weather station.

**정점**(頂點) 《산의》 the top; the summit;

《절정》 the summit; the peak; the climax; the zenith; 《삼각형 등의》 an apex; a vertex. ¶ 삼각형의 ~ the apex of a triangle / 영화(榮華)의 ~에 있다 be at the height 〔zenith〕 of *one's* prosperity / 이로써 그의 인기는 ~에 달했다 This marked the climax of his popularity.

**정정**(亭亭) 《우뚝 섬》 standing alone 《as a mountain peak》; standing high; lofty; towering; 《몸이》 being hale and hearty. ~하다 stand alone; (be) hale and hearty; old but vigorous. ¶ ~한 노인 a man in his green old age; a hale old man / 그는 90이 넘었으나 아직 ~하다 He is turned (of) ninety and still going strong.

**정정**(訂正) correction; rectification; revision. ~하다 correct; rectify; revise. ¶ ~을 부탁하다 submit 《a composition to *a person*》 for correction / 이 책은 ~할 필요가 있다 This book needs correction. / 그는 발언을 ~해야만 했다 He had to amend his statement. ◉ ~판 a revised edition.

**정정**(政情) a state of political affairs; a political situation 〔condition〕. ¶ ~의 안정 the stability of a political situation; political stability / ~의 불안정 political instability 〔unrest〕 / ~에 밝다 be familiar 〔conversant〕 with political conditions 《in 〔of〕 Japan》.

**정정당당**(正正堂堂) ~하다 (be) fair and square; open and aboveboard. ¶ ~히 open and aboveboard; on the square; fairly / ~한 승부 a fairly contested match / ~하게 싸우다 play 「fair 〔on the square〕; fight openly and squarely; play the game / 그녀의 태도는 ~하였다 Her attitude was open and aboveboard.

**정정법**(政淨法) the Political Purification Law.

**정제**(精製) refining; refinement. ~하다 refine. ¶ ~한 refined; purified. ◉ ~공장 a refinery. ~당〔식염〕 refined sugar 〔salt〕. ~법 a refining process. ~유 refined oil. ~품 a refined article 〔product〕.

**정제**(整除) 『수학』 divisibility. ¶ ~되는 (exactly) divisible / ~되지 않는 indivisible. ◉ ~수 aliquot part; an exact divisor.

**정제**(整齊) regularity; symmetry. ~하다 arrange in regular order; make symmetrical 〔regular, even, uniform〕.

**정제**(錠劑) a tablet; a pill.

**정조**(貞操) chastity; (feminine) virtue; (female) honor; constancy; faithfulness; 《처녀성》 virginity; maidenhood. ¶ ~가 굳은 chaste; virtuous; faithful; constant / ~가 굳은 여자 a chaste woman / ~가 굳지 않은 unchaste; profligate; inconstant / ~ 관념이 희박하다 have a weak sense of virtue; be a woman of easy virtue / ~를 잃다 lose *one's* chastity 〔virtue〕; fall from chastity; stray from the path of virtue / ~를 농락하다 〔짓밟다, 더럽히다〕 defile 〔violate, trifle with〕 《a girl's》 chastity; seduce 〔dishonor, ruin, deflower〕 《a girl》 / ~를 바치다 surrender *one's* chastity to 《a man》; give *oneself* to 《a man》 / ~를 (소)중히 여기다 prize chastity / ~를 지키다 remain faithful 〔chaste, true〕 to 《*one's* husband》 / ~를 팔다 sell *one's* chastity; prostitute *oneself* / 그녀는 ~관념이 없다 She is a lady of easy virtue. ◉ ~관념 a sense of virtue. ~대(帶) a chastity belt. ~유린 a violation of chastity.

**정조**(情調) a mood; a tone; an atmosphere.

**정조**(情操) 『심리』 a sentiment. ¶ 고상한 ~ a noble sentiment. ◉ ~교육 culture of (aesthetic) sentiments.

**정족**(鼎足) the legs of a tripod. ¶ ~지세(之勢) a triangular position.

**정족수**(定足數) 『법』 a quorum. ¶ ~에 달하다 form 〔be enough for〕 a quorum / 오늘 국회 본회의는 의원 ~ 미달로 유회되었다 Today's National Assembly plenary session was adjourned because of lack of a quorum.

**정종**(正宗) refined rice wine.

**정좌**(正坐) sitting up straight. ~하다 sit upright 〔straight〕 (on *one's* seat); sit square.

**정좌**(靜坐) sitting quietly; sitting in meditation. ~하다 sit quietly; sit in meditation.

**정주**(定住) settlement; domiciliation; settling down. ~하다 reside permanently 《at, in》; establish a domicile; settle down; domiciliate. ¶ 서울에 ~하다 settle down 〔make *one's* home〕 in Seoul / 그들은 영국에 ~했다 They have settled in England. ◉ ~자 a permanent resident. ~지 *one's* fixed 〔permanent〕 place of residence.

**정중**(正中) the very middle. ◉ ~동맥〔신경〕 a median artery 〔nerve〕.

**정중**(鄭重) earnestness; gravity; courtesy; civility. ~하다 (be) polite; courteous; respectful. ¶ ~히 politely;

courteously; with courtesy; civily / ～한 서한 a courteous letter / ～한 말로 in courteous words 〔terms〕 / ～히 다루다 treat 《*a person*》 courteously 〔with consideration〕 / ～한 대우를 받다 receive courteous treatment / 돕겠다는 제의를 ～히 거절하다 politely decline 《*a person's*》 offer to help.

**정지**(停止) ① 《멈춤》 a stop; a standstill. ～하다 stop; come to a standstill 〔a stop〕; cease. ¶ ～시키다 stop; put an end to; make an end of; suspend; interrupt. ② 《금지》 a ban. ～하다 ban; place 〔put〕 《a paper》 under a ban; place 〔put〕 a ban on. ¶ K일보가 당국에 의해 발행 ～를 당했다 The K Daily News was banned by the authorities. ③ 《중지》 suspension; 《정체》 (a) deadlock. ～하다 suspend. ¶ 영업〔지급〕을 ～하다 suspend business 〔payment〕 / ～해 있다 be suspended / 그는 1개월간의 운전 면허 ～를 당했다 His driver's license was suspended for a month. / 거래는 지금 ～상태에 있다 Business is currently at a standstill.
◉ ～가격 a stopped price. ～선 a stop line. ～신호 a stop signal. ～조건 〖법〗 a condition precedent.

**정지**(静止) stillness; (a) standstill; rest; quiescence. ～하다 rest; stand still; come to a standstill; become stationary. ¶ ～한 자세 the posture of repose / ～상태에 있다 be at a standstill; be 〔remain〕 stationary.
◉ ～궤도 a geostationary 〔geosynchronous〕 orbit. ～위성 a geostationary satellite.

**정지**(整地) 《건축을 위한》 leveling of ground; site preparation; 《경작지의》 land readjustment; soil preparation. ～하다 level the land 《for construction》; readjust the land 《for construction》; prepare the soil 《for planting》.

**정직**(正直) honesty; uprightness; integrity; veracity; truthfulness. ～하다 (be) honest; upright; straightforward; truthful.

> 용법 **honest** 진실되고 바르고 솔직한, 남에게 대해서 거짓이 없다는 뜻. **upright** 도덕적인 행동 규범에 맞게 바르다. **straightforward** 숨기거나 꾸밈없이 솔직하다는 뜻. **truthful** honest와 같은 뜻이나, 좀 딱딱한 말.

¶ ～히〔하게〕 honestly; frankly; straightforwardly; truthfully / 저렇게 ～한 사람 such an honest man as he (is) / ～하게 번 이익 honest profits / ～한 자가 손해를 보는 세상 the world where honesty does not pay / ～해 보이는 honest-looking / ～하게 말하면 to tell the truth; speaking truthfully; to be frank 〔honest〕 with you / 사실 그대로 ～히 말하다 call a spade a spade / 너에게는 아주 ～히 말하마 I shall be quite honest with you. / ～히 말하면 용서해 주마 I will let you go unpunished, if you speak the truth.

**정직**(定職) a regular 〔fixed〕 occupation; a fixed employment; (a) steady job. ¶ ～을 얻다 find 〔get〕 a regular job / ～에 있다 be in regular work; have a steady job / 그는 ～이 없다 He has no regular work 〔job〕.

**정직**(停職) suspension from office. ¶ ～을 명하다 suspend 《*a person*》 from *his* office / ～되다 be suspended from *one's* office.

**정진**(精進) ① 《열심히 노력함》 devotion; close application; assiduity. ～하다 devote *oneself* 《to》; apply *oneself* 《to》; work hard; be industrious. ¶ 학업에 ～하다 devote *oneself* to the study / 직무에 ～하다 attend diligently 〔apply *oneself* closely〕 to *one's* duties; be assiduous in performing *one's* duties. ② 〖불교〗 《수행》 devotion to the pursuit of *one's* faith. ～하다 devote *one's* life to the pursuit of *one's* faith. ③ 《채식》 abstinence from (eating) fish and meat. ～하다 abstain from eating fish and meat.

**정차**(停車) = 정거(停車). ◉ ～선 stop line. ～시간 stoppage time.

**정착**(定着) ① 《정주》 settlement: domiciliation. ～하다 settle down; domiciliate. ¶ 부산에 ～하다 settle down in Pusan / 그는 미국에 ～ 하였다 He fixed himself in America. ② 《달라 붙음》 fixing; fixation. ～하다 fix; fixate; become established; 《사상·생각 등이》 take 〔strike〕 root. ¶ 한국에 민주주의가 ～한지는 얼마 되지 않았다 It hasn't been long since democracy took root in Korea. ◉ ～금 resettlement funds. ～물 a fixture. ～수당 resettlement allowance. ～액 〖사진〗 a fixative; a fixing solution; a fixing agent.

**정찬**(正餐) a (formal) dinner.

**정찰**(正札) a price tag 〔mark, label〕. ¶ ～을 붙이다 set 〔put, mark〕 a price 《on an article》; price《all the goods in the store》/ 만 원의 ～이 붙은 상품 an article marked〔labeled〕10,000 won / ～제 ―에누리 없음《게시》Fixed price, no haggling. *or* Prices clearly marked, and no overcharge. *or* No price reduction. *or* No reduction allowed / ～제이오니 가격을 깎지 마십시오 We are practicing a price marking system and no discount is allowed. ◉ ～가격 a marked〔fixed〕price. ～제 a price tag〔marking〕system; a fixed price system: ～제 판매 sale at a fixed〔set, labeled〕price.

**정찰**(偵察)〖군사〗reconnaissance; scouting. ～하다 reconnoiter; scout; patrol. ¶ ～하러 가다 go scouting / 적정을 ～하다 reconnoiter〔spy upon〕the enemy / 적진을 ～하다 scout the enemy's camp. ◉ ～기 a reconnaissance plane. ～대 a reconnaissance party; a patrol; scouts. ～병 a scout. ～비행 a reconnaissance flight: ～비행을 하다 make〔go on〕a scouting〔reconnaissance〕flight. ～위성 a reconnaissance〔spy〕satellite. ～장치 reconnaissance equipment.

**정찰하다**(精察―) closely examine.

**정채**(精彩)《광채》brilliance; brightness;《활기》liveliness; vitality; vividness. ¶ ～가 있는 colorful; vivid / ～가 없다 lack vividness; be lifeless.

**정책**(政策) (a) policy. ¶ ～상의 문제 a matter of policy; a policy issue / 한국의 대일(對日) ～ Korea's policy toward Japan / 선린～ a good-neighbor policy / 외교〔대외〕～ a diplomatic〔foreign〕policy / ～을 결정하다 fix〔decide on〕a policy / ～을 쓰다 employ〔adopt〕a policy / ～을 바꾸다〔전환하다〕change *one's* policy / ～을 바꾸지 않다 make no departure from *one's* policy / ～을 세우다 frame〔formulate, shape〕a policy / ～을 실행하다 carry out a policy / ～을 심의하다 deliberate on a policy / ～을 지지하다 support a policy / 전임 장관의 ～을 답습하다「take over〔succeed to〕the policy of the preceding minister / 새 ～을 발표하다 announce〔publish〕a new policy / 당의 ～에 따르다 follow the party line; be a faithful party liner. ◉ ～강령 a platform. ～결정 a policy decision. ～노선 a line of policy; party line《미》. ～논쟁 an argument〔a controversy〕over policy. ～수립〔입안〕policy making: ～입안자 a policy maker. ～위원회 a policy planning〔policy-making〕committee. ～자문기구 a (presidential) consultative body. ～전환 a policy switch. ～질의 an interpellation.

**정처**(正妻) the〔*one's*〕lawful wife.

**정처**(定處) a fixed place; a definite destination; some one place. ¶ ～없이 떠돌다 wander from place to place; wander aimlessly.

**정철**(精鐵) refined iron.

**정청**(政廳) a government office〔house〕.

**정체**(正體) the real form; *one's* true character〔colors〕;《신분》(an) identity. ¶ ～ 모를 strange; mysterious; funny / ～ 불명의 unidentified; 《a man》with dubious backgrounds / ～ 모를 사람 a stranger; a mystery man / ～를 드러내다 reveal *one's* real shape; show *one's* true colors; throw off *one's* mask / ～를 밝히다 disclose 《*a person's*》identity / ～를 숨기다 wear a mask; disguise *oneself* / ～를 파악하다 grasp the true character 《of》; get to the root《of an affair》/ 그것이 그녀의 ～다 That's what she really is.

**정체**(政體) a form〔system〕of government; a government system. ¶ ～를 바꾸다 change the form of government.

**정체**(停滯) stagnation;《연체》delay. ～하다 be stagnant; stagnate; congest; accumulate; be delayed〔retarded〕. ¶ ～된 stagnant / 자금의 ～ a tie-up of funds / 화물의 ～ an accumulation〔a congestion〕of goods / 장마 전선의 ～로 인한 큰 비 a heavy rain due to a lingering seasonal rain front / 우편물이 ～되어 있다 The mail has piled up. / 경기는 당분간 이대로 ～ 될 것이라고 예상된다 The economy is expected to remain stagnant for a while. ◉ ～전선〖기상〗a stationary front.

**정초**(正初) the first ten days of January. ¶ ～에 early in January.

**정초식**(定礎式) the laying of the「cornerstone〔foundation stone〕. ¶ ～을 올리다 lay the cornerstone.

**정축**(丁丑)〖민속〗the 14th binary term of the sexagenary cycle.

**정취**(情趣)《느낌》sentiment; mood; touch; flavor;《분위기》atmosphere;《아취》an artistic effect《in a painting》. ¶ ～가 있는 정원 a tasteful garden / ～를 맛보다 taste〔experience〕a mood〔an atmosphere〕/ 고전적 ～가 있다

have a classical touch to it / 아무 ~도 없다 be dull; be flat / 그의 그림에는 독특한 ~가 있다 In his paintings there is something peculiar which appeals to our artistic sentiment.

◉ 이국~ an exotic mood; exoticism.

**정치**(定置) fixation; setting. ~하다 station. ¶ ~의 fixed; stationary.

◉ ~망 a fixed shore net; a stationary net: ~망 어업 fixed shore net fishing; stationary net fishery.

**정치**(政治) politics; 《행정》 government; administration; political affairs (정무). ¶ ~상 politically; from the political point of view / ~적 political / 비~적인 unpolitical / 깨끗한 ~ clean politics / ~의 빈곤 lack of proper government 〔political ingenuity〕/ ~적 무관심 political apathy / ~적 수완 political ability 〔ingenuity〕; statecraft; statesmanship; 《외교》 diplomacy / ~적 해결 settlement 《of a problem》 through the political channel / ~의식이 강한 사람들 politically conscious people / ~적 상황〔전망〕 the political landscape / ~적 열의 political fever / ~를 하다 govern the country; administer 〔conduct〕 the affairs of state / ~에 참여하다 be engaged in politics / ~적으로 이용하다 politicize / …에 대한 주민들의 반대를 ~적으로 이용하려 들다 try politicize local citizens' objections to... / ~ 도구로 이용되다 be capitalized on as a political tool / ~에 관계하다 take up politics; dabble 〔meddle〕 in politics / ~에 관계하지 않다 let 〔leave〕 politics alone / ~를 논하다 talk 〔discuss〕 politics; politicize / 그들은 ~적인 자유를 요구하고 있다 They are demanding political freedom 〔liberties〕.

◉ ~가 a statesman; a politico (*pl.* ~(e)s); a politician (★ statesman에 비해 낮은 호칭): 선동 ~가 a demagog(ue) / 직업 ~가 a career politician. ~감각 *one's* political sense. ~결사 a political organization 〔association〕. ~계 political circles. ~공작 political maneuvering; 《구어》 politicking. ~광(狂) 《병》 politicomania; 《사람》 a politicomaniac. ~권력 political authority. ~기관 the organ of government; the political machinery. ~기구 (a) political structure 〔machinary〕. ~기자 a writer on political affairs; a political writer 〔correspondent〕. ~깡패 political hoodlums; a political henchman. ~꾼 a politician. ~단체 a political body 〔organization〕. ~도덕 political morality. ~력 *one's* political power 〔influence〕: ~력의 빈곤 lack of political power 〔influence〕; poor statesmanship. ~범 《범죄》 political offense; 《사람》 a political offender; a prisoner of conscience. ~보복 political retaliation. ~부 《신문사의》 the politics department. ~브로커 a political broker. ~사 (a) political history. ~사상 a political idea 〔thought〕. ~사찰 political surveillance. ~생명 a political life. ~생활 *one's* political life 〔career〕. ~안정 《maintain》 political stability. ~연수원 a political training institute. ~열 political fever. ~외교학과 the department of political science and diplomacy. ~운동 a political movement 〔campaign〕. ~윤리 political ethics. ~이념 political belief. ~자금 political funds; money for political activities: ~자금법 the Political Fund Law / ~자금 규제법 the Act for the Regulation of Political Funds. ~재판 a political trial. ~적 책임 (*one's*) administrative responsibilities. ~정화 the political clean-up; the purification of politics. ~조작극 a premeditated political conspiracy. ~조직 a political system; (a) political organization. ~지망생 a political aspirant. ~철학 political philosophy. ~체제 a political structure. ~테러 political terrorism. ~투쟁 a political struggle; politics strife. ~판도 political spectrum. ~평론가 a political commentator 〔journalist, columnist〕. ~학 political science: ~학과 the department of political science / ~학자 a political scientist. ~해금(解禁) the lifting of the political ban or old-time politicians: ~해금자 a reinstated politician. ~헌금 political donation. ~ 현안 문제 the pending political issues. ~협상 political negotiations. ~형태 a form of political organization; (a) polity.

권력~ power politics. 무단~ military government 〔rule〕; government by the bayonet: 무단 ~를 하다 govern by the bayonet; rule *one's* people with the rod of iron. 유엔 총회 특별~위원회 the Special Political Committee, UN General Assembly. 혁신~ reformist politics.

**정치**(精緻) exquisite fineness; delicacy;

minuteness; subtlety. ～하다 (be) minute; fine; delicate; nice; subtle.

**정치문제**(政治問題) a political problem 〔issue〕. ¶ ～로 삼다 make a political issue《of a matter》/ ～로 삼지 않다 keep《a question》out of politics / ～로 발전하다 develop into a political issue.

**정치의식**(政治意識) political awareness. ¶ 그들은 ～이 발달되어 있다 They are very politically minded.

**정치(적)망명**(政治(的)亡命) political asylum; political exile (추방에 의한). ¶ ～을 하다 flee from *one's* own country for political reason / 한국으로 ～을 원하다 seek political asylum 〔refuge〕 in the Republic of Korea. ◉ ～자 a political exile 〔refugee〕; a defector (★ defector는「국가 기밀을 가지고 망명하는 사람」이란 뜻이 함축되어 있음).

**정치풍토**(政治風土) the political climate. ◉ ～쇄신 the renovation of the political climate: ～ 쇄신 특별 조치법 the Special Measures Law for Renovating the Political Climate.

**정치활동**(政治活動) political activities. ¶ ～ 정화법 the Political Purification Law / ～ 피규제자 the former politicians whose political activities are banned (under the Political Renovation Law) / ～을 하다 engage in politics 〔political activity〕.

**정칙**(正則) a regular system; regularity; normality.

**정칙**(定則) an established rule; a law.

**정크**《평저 범선》a (Chinese) junk.

**정크본드**〖경제〗《미》a junk bond (신용도가 낮아 위험 부담이 많은 채권).

**정탐**(偵探) scouting; spying. ～하다 spy; spy on. ◉ ～꾼 a scout; a spy.

**정태**(靜態) stationariness. ¶ ～의 static(al); stationary. ◉ ～경제학 static economics. ～사회학 static sociology. ～통계학 static statistics.

**정토**(淨土)〖불교〗Sukkāvatī; pure land; 「Paradise.

**정통**(正統) ①《바른 계통》orthodoxy; legitimacy. ¶ ～의 legitimate; orthodox / ～적인 견해 an orthodox point of view / ～적인 정부 a legitimate government. ②《국왕》lineal descent of royalty. ◉ ～극 a legitimate drama. ～주의 legitimism. ～파《당파》an orthodox party 〔faction〕;《종파》an orthodox sect. ～학파 an orthodox school.

**정통**(精通) complete knowledge; being at home; being well versed. ～하다 be well versed《of》; be well informed 《of, on》; be at home《in》; have a thorough knowledge《of》; be familiar 〔acquainted〕 with; have《*something*》at *one's* fingertips. ¶ 그 일에 ～하다 be well acquainted with the matter / 핵무기에 ～하다 be an authority on nuclear weapons / 그는 중국 사정에 ～하다 He is well acquainted with Chinese affairs. / 그녀는 영어는 물론 프랑스어에도 ～하다 She is well versed in French as well as English. / 그는 고전에 ～하다 He has classic literature at his fingertips.

**정파**(政派) a faction (in a political 「party).

**정판**(整版)〖인쇄〗recomposition; justification. ～하다 recompose; justify. ◉ ～공 a maker-up; a justifier.

**정평**(正評) right 〔fair〕 criticism.

**정평**(定評) an established reputation; a settled opinion; public acknowledgment. ¶ ～ 있는 acknowledged; recognized; (well-)established / ～ 있는 물건 a popular article / ～있는 인물 a man of established reputation; a recognized figure / ～이 있다 it is generally agreed 〔acknowledged〕 / 좋다는 ～을 얻다 secure a verdict in *one's* favor / …하다는 일반의 ～이다 It is generally agreed that… / 그의 작품의 우수성은 이미 ～이 나 있다 The world acknowledges the superiority of his work. / 우리 회사 제품의 품질에 대해서는 우수하다는 ～이 있다 We enjoy a high reputation for the quality of our goods.

**정표**(情表) a love token; a keepsake; a memento. ¶ 애정의 ～ a《small》token of *one's* love and affection / 감사의 ～로서「in token 〔as a token〕 of *one's* gratitude.

**정풍운동**(整風運動) purification drive; the rectification campaign.

**정하다**(定—)《결정하다》decide; fix; arrange; settle《*a matter*》;《결심하다》be resolved 〔determined〕《to *do*》; make up *one's* mind《to *do*》;《선택하다》choose;《태도를》define《*one's* attitude》;《시일·장소를》set; fix; appoint;《규정하다》lay down; establish. ¶ 정한 시간에 at an appointed hour / 법이 정하는 바에 따라 as provided by law / 정해지다 be decided; be determined; become settled;《뽑히다》be chosen / 날짜를 ～ fix a date / 법을 ～ lay down a law / 결혼하기로 ～ decide to get married / 값을 ～ fix the price / 분량을 정하여 마시다 drink 〔take〕 a fixed quantity《of》/ 정해 놓고 …하

다 make it a rule to *do;* be in the habit of *do*ing / 우리는 그녀를 우리들의 지도자로 정했다 We decided on her 「to be 〔as〕 our leader. / 나는 미국으로 유학가기로 마음을 정했다 I resolved to go to the United States to study. / 우리는 내일 출발하기로 정했다 We fixed tomorrow as our departure date. / 나는 모든 것을 팔기로 정했다 I settled on selling everything.

**정하다**(淨—) (be) clean; pure; clear.

**정하중**(靜荷重) 〖물리〗 dead 〔static〕 load.

**정학**(停學) suspension (from school). ¶ 1주일의 ～ one week's suspension from school / ～에 처하다 suspend 《*a student*》 from school / ～을 맞다〔당하다〕 get suspended from school. ◉ 무기～ indefinite suspension from school.

**정한**(定限) a fixed period 〔limit, degree, extent〕; limits.

**정한**(精悍) intrepidity; fierceness. ～하다 (be) dauntless; intrepid; fierce.

**정해**(丁亥) 〖민속〗 the 24th binary term of the sexagenary cycle.

**정해**(正解) a correct interpretation; a correct answer; a correct solution. ～하다 interpret correctly; give a correct answer 〔solution〕. ◉ ～자 one who gives a correct answer.

**정해**(精解) precise 〔accurate〕 explaining. ～하다 explain 〔clarify〕 precisely.

**정해지다**(定—) ① 《결정되다》 be decided; be settled; be determined; be fixed; 《합의되다》 be arranged; be agreed upon. ¶ …에 의해 ～ depend on…; be determined by… / 정해진 regular; fixed; definite / 그것은 미리 다 정해져 있었다 It was all arranged beforehand. / 조건은 아직 정해지지 않았다 The terms have not yet been agreed on. / 결혼식 날짜는 5월 25일로 정해졌다 The wedding has been set for May 25. ② 《규정되다》 be laid down; be prescribed; be provided; be established; be stipulated. ¶ 근로 시간은 법률로 정해져 있다 Working hours are prescribed by low.

**정핵**(精核) 〖생물〗 a sperm nucleus.

**정향**(丁香) 〖한의〗 dried clove buds. ◉ ～나무 a clove (tree). ～유 clove oil. 「사인 ③.

**정현**(正弦) 〖수학〗 a sine (생략 sin). ⇨

**정형**(定形) a set 〔fixed〕 form 〔shape〕. ◉ ～동사 〖문법〗 a finite verb.

**정형**(定型) a set pattern; a fixed 〔regular〕 type 〔form〕; a standard. ¶ ～의 fixed; regular. ◉ ～시(詩) set-form 〔=rhymed〕 verse; a fixed form of verse. ～화(化) standardization: ～화하다 standardize.

**정형**(整形) 〖의학〗 [형용사적] orthopedic. ◉ ～수술 orthopedic surgery; an orthopedic operation: ～수술을 받다 have 〔undergo〕 an orthopedic operation. ～외과 orthopedics: ～외과의(醫) an orthopedist.

**정혼**(定婚) arranging a marriage; betrothal; affiance. ～하다 arrange a marriage; betroth.

**정화**(正貨) specie. ¶ ～로 in specie / ～의 유출〔유입〕 the outflow 〔inflow〕 of specie. ◉ ～결핍 shortage 〔lack〕 of specie. ～보유고 the specie holdings. ～수송점 a gold 〔specie〕 point. ～은행 a specie bank. ～준비 specie reserve. ～지급 a specie payment.

**정화**(淨化) ① 《맑게 하기》 purification; purgation; elutriation. ～하다 purify; cleanse; deterge; elutriate; 〖정신분석〗 abreact. ¶ 정교한 공기 ～ 시스템 an elaborate air purification system / 오수는 하수 처리장에서 ～된다 Sewage is purified in the sewage treatment plant. / 이것은 물을 ～하는 장치이다 This is a device to purify water. ② 《부정 따위의》 a cleanup; purgation (숙정). ～하다 clean up; purge 〔purify〕 *one's* soul 《of sin, evil thoughts》; purge 《the party of corrupt members》. ¶ 정계의 ～ the cleanup of political circles / 총리는 정부내의 부패 ～에 노력하여야 한다 The Prime Minister should clean up corruption in the Government. ◉ ～설비〔시설〕 《하수의》 sewage disposal facilities; sanitation facilities. ～운동 a cleanup movement 〔campaign, drive〕: 선거 ～ 운동 a "clean election" campaign 〔movement〕. ～장치 a purifier; an apparatus for purifying. ～조 《하수·화장실 등의》 a septic tank 《for sewage》. 사회～ social purification: 사회 ～ 위원회 the Social Purification Committee.

**정화**(精華) the essence; the flower; the cream; the quintessence. ¶ 기사도의 ～ the flower of chivalry.

**정화수**(井華水) 〖민속〗 water drawn from the well at daybreak.

**정확**(正確) correctness; exactness; accuracy; exactitude; precision. (★ correctness가 가장 뜻이 약하며, precision이

가장 강함. 또 precision은 사람에게 쓰이는 경우가 많음). ∼하다 (be) correct; exact; accurate; precise; right.

> 용법 **correct** 「잘못·틀림이 없는」이란 뜻의 가장 일반적인 낱말. **accurate** 계산·통계 지식 따위가 사실·표준 등에 완전히 일치한다는 강한 뜻의 낱말. **precise** 극히 「세부적인 부분에 이르기까지 정확한」이란 뜻. **exact** 치수를 바르게 잰 것처럼 「정밀하게 들어맞는」이란 뜻. **right** correct와 거의 같은 뜻으로 쓰이나, 보다 넓은 의미를 지니면서, 답이나 시간 따위가 「올바른, 정확한」이란 뜻으로 흔히 쓰임.

¶ ∼히 correctly; exactly; accurately / ∼한 발음 correct pronunciation / ∼한 시간 correct 〔exact〕 time / ∼한 조준 폭격 a pinpoint bombing / ∼히 말하면 to be exact; correctly speaking / 과학적으로 ∼히 with scientific exactitude / ∼한 지도 an accurate map / 시계처럼 ∼히 with clockwork precision / 시간을 ∼히 지키다 be punctual / ∼한 관찰을 하다 make accurate observations / ∼을 기하기 위해 고심하다 take much trouble to ensure correctness / ∼히는 모른다 I don't know for certain. *or* I cannot say for certain. / 이 시계는 ∼하다 This watch keeps good time. ◉ ∼도 accuracy.

**정황**(政況) the political outlook.

**정황**(情況) conditions; circumstances; a situation; the state of things 〔affairs〕. ¶ 지금 ∼으로는 under 〔in〕 the present circumstances; as matters stand now; under the existing conditions. ⇨ 상황. ◉ ∼증거 circumstantial 〔presumptive〕 evidence.

**정회**(停會) the suspension of a meeting; 《휴회》 adjournment; 《의회의》 prorogation. ∼하다 suspend 《a meeting》; adjourn.

**정회**(情懷) affectionate remembrances; fond recollection; dear memories.

**정회원**(正會員) a regular member. ¶ ∼의 자격 full membership.

**정훈**(政訓) troop information and education (생략 TI & E). ◉ ∼요원 TI & E personnel.

**정휴일**(定休日) a regular 〔set〕 holiday.

**정히**(正—) exactly; precisely; surely; certainly; no doubt; truly; really.

**젖** ① 《유즙》 milk. ¶ 소젖 cow's milk / 어머니 젖 mother's milk / 젖빛 milk-white 〔milky〕 color / 소의 젖을 짜다 milk a cow / 젖 짜는 사람 a milkman (남자); a milkmaid (여자) / 아기한테 젖을 빨리다 〔먹이다〕 suckle a baby (on *one's* breast); give the breast to a baby / 젖이 마르다 《*one's* breasts》 run dry; 《*one's* breasts》 go off milk / 젖을 떼다 wean 《a baby from its mother》 / 젖을 달라고 울다 cry for milk / 젖으로 기르다 nourish 《a baby》 on mother's milk / 이 소는 젖이 많다 This cow milks well. / 울지 않는 애 젖 주랴 《속담》 Let your wants be known.
② 《식물의 진》 latex; milk 《of a plant》; any sticky white fluid.
③ 《유방》 the breast(s); the udder (소·염소의). ¶ 젖이 붓다 the breast is swollen; the breasts fill / 아기가 젖을 빨다 a baby suckles at its mother's breast / 아기에게 젖을 물리다 give the breasts to a baby.

**젖가슴** the breast; the bosom.

**젖꼭지** the teat(s); the nipple(s).

**젖내** the smell of milk. ¶ ∼ 나다 smell of milk; 《유치함》 be (still) a suckling; be (still) in swaddling clothes; be babyish 〔childish, puerile, immature, green〕; "be still wet behind the ears".

**젖니** a milk tooth; the first set of teeth.

**젖다** ① 《물 따위에》 get wet 〔soaked, drenched〕; be damp 〔moistened〕. ¶ 젖은 옷 〔땅〕 wet clothes 〔ground〕 / 비에 ∼ get wet in the rain / 땀에 ∼ be wet with perspiration / 물에 ∼ get 〔be〕 wet; get 〔be〕 soaked / 함빡 ∼ be wet to the skin; be soaking wet.
② 《귀에》 ring (in *one's* ears); be accustomed to hear; be familiar with. ¶ 귀에 ∼ ring in *one's* ears; be familiar to *one's* ear; be impressed on *one's* mind; soak 〔be soaked〕 in thoroughly / 네 말은 귀에 젖도록 들었다 That's enough of you.
③ 《빠지다》 be given over to; indulge in. ¶ 술에 ∼ be given over to drinking.

**젖당**(—糖) 〖화학〗 milk sugar; lactose.

**젖동생**(—同生) a foster brother 〔sister〕.

**젖떨어지다** be 〔get〕 weaned. ¶ 젖 떨어진 아이 a weaned child; a weanling.

**젖떼다** wean; cease to suckle. ¶ 어린 아이를 ∼ wean a baby.

**젖먹이** a sucking child; a suckling; a baby.

**젖멍울** 《젖샘》 a mammary gland; 《유선염》 mastitis. ¶ ∼이 서다 《a woman》 suffer 〔fill out〕 from mastitis.

**젖몸살** mastitis. ¶ ～을 앓다 suffer from mastitis; have inflamed mammary glands.

**젖병**(一甁) a nursing bottle; a nurser.

**젖산**(一酸) 〖화학〗 lactic acid. ◉ ～균 a lactic acid bacterium (*pl.* -ria); a lactobacillus. ～음료 a lactic acid drink.

**젖소** a milk 〔milking〕 cow; [총칭] dairy cattle.

**젖어머니** a wet nurse. ⇨ 유모.

**젖퉁이** the breast(s).

**제**[1] ① 《나·저》 ¶ 제가 이 학교 교장입니다 I am the principal of this school. ② 《나의》 my; my own. ¶ 제 모자 〔집〕 my hat 〔house〕 / 제 생각으로는 for my part; as for me / 모두 제 잘못인데 누굴 원망하랴 I have no one but myself to blame. ③ 《자기의》 *one's* 〔his, her〕; *one's* own; personal; private. ¶ 제가 좋아서 하는 일 a self-imposed work / 제 일로 on (*one's*) private business; on *one's* own business / 제 멋대로 as *one* pleases; at will / 제 생각만 하다 be thinking only of *oneself;* be full of *oneself;* be self-centered / 제 판단으로 행동하다 act at *one's* own discreation / 제 이익만 생각하다 look to *one's* own interest / 제 일은 제가 해야 한다 One should look after *one's* own business.

**제**[2] 《저기》 that place; there. ¶ 그가 제 있다 He is there.

**제-**(第) No.; number...; -th. ¶ 제일 the first / 제1과 the first lesson / 제2 number two (생략 No. 2); the second / 제4조 제3항 the third Clause of Article IV.

**제-**(諸) several; many; all. ¶ 제비용〔경비〕 sundry expenses; costs / 제형(兄) dear friends.

**-제**(制) a system; an institution. ¶ 8시간제 the eight-hour system / 4년제 대학 a four-year college.

**-제**(祭) 《제사》 an ancestor memorial service; 《축제》 a festival; a fête. ¶ 기념제 a commemoration / 50년제 a jubilee / 백년제 a centennial / 200년제 a bicentenary.

**-제**(製) manufacture; make. ¶ 목제의 wooden; made of wood / 강철제의 made of steel / 한국제의 made in Korea; Korean-made / 외국제의 foreign-made / 가죽제의 책 《표지》 a book bound in leather / Y사제의 만년필 a fountain pen made 〔manufactured〕 by Y Company / 외국제의 물건 articles of foreign 「make 〔manufacture〕 / 미국제의 미사일 an American-built missile / 이것은 이탈리아제 가방이다 This is an Italian-made bag. *or* This bag is of Italian make.

**-제**(劑) a medicine; a drug; a dose. ¶ 소화제 an aid to digestion; a digestive.

**제가**(諸家) ① 《여러 대가》 various 〔many〕 masters; all the schools 《of art, *etc.*》. ② 《여러 집안》 the whole family; all the relatives.

**제가하다**(齊家一) govern 《a family》; manage 《a household》.

**제각기**(一各其) each; respectively; individually; separately. ¶ 그 회의에 모인 학생들은 ～ 의견을 말했다 Each one of the students present at the meeting expressed his ideas. / 아이들이 ～ 기를 들고 있다 The children each have a flag. (★ 복수대명사 뒤의 each는 앞말과 동격) / 사람에게는 ～ 장점과 단점이 있다 Each man has his merits and faults.

**제감**(除減) deduction; subtraction. ～하다 deduct; take away; subtract.

**제강**(製鋼) steelmaking; steel manufacture. ◉ ～법 the steelmaking process. ～소 a steel mill; a steelworks; a steelmaking plant. ～업 the steel industry: ～업자 a steelman; a steelmaker.

**제거**(除去) exclusion; removal; elimination. ～하다 exclude; remove; get rid of; eliminate; weed out (가려서). ¶ 불안을 ～하다 remove misgivings / 장애물을 ～하다 clear 〔remove〕 obstacles / 원인을 ～하다 remove a cause / 바람직하지 않은 회원은 ～되었다 Undesirable members were 「weeded out 〔eliminated〕.

**제것** *one's* possession 〔belongings〕. ¶ ～으로 만들다 make 《*a thing*》 *one's* own; take 《*a thing*》 to *oneself;* have 《*a thing*》 for *one's* own; appropriate for *oneself* / ～이 되다 fall into *one's* possession 〔hands〕.

**제격**(一格) becoming 〔being suitable, proper, *etc.*〕 to *one's* status; befitting *one's* station. ¶ 그 자리는 그에게 ～이다 He is the very man for the post. / 그는 그 일엔 ～이다 He is 「cut out 〔the right man〕 for the work.

**제고**(提高) ～하다 raise; lift; promote; improve; heighten. ¶ 생산성 ～ the heightening of productivity / 새로운 기계 설치로 우리회사 제품의 품질이 크게 ～되었다 The installation of the new machine has greatly improved the quality of our products.

**제고장** (*one's*) native place; the (original) home.

**제곱** 〖수학〗 a square; squaring. ∼하다 square 〔multiply〕《a number》. ◉ ∼근 a square root: ∼근을 구하다 extract the square root《of》; find the square《of》/ 3은 9의 ∼근이다 Three is the square root of 9. ∼근 풀이 evolution; extraction of a square root: ∼근 풀이하다 extract the square root《of》. ∼비 (a) subduplicate ratio. ∼수 a square number. 거듭∼ involution.

**제공**(提供) an offer; 〖법〗 a tender. ∼하다 (make an) offer; present; furnish; tender; put《*a thing*》at《another's》service; provide; 《방송》 sponsor《a TV program》. ¶ (상품의) 특별 ∼ a special offer / ∼을 받다〔거절하다〕 accept 〔decline〕 an offer《of support》/ 장기를 ∼하다《이식을 위해》 donate 〔provide〕 an organ / 그에게 32만 원을 ∼하다 offer him 320,000 won / 나는 그녀에게 신뢰할 만한 시장 정보를 ∼해 주었다 I provided 〔furnished〕 her with reliable market tips. / 이 프로는 C회사 ∼이었습니다 This program has been sponsored by C corporation. ◉ ∼가격 the price offered. ∼물 an offer; a present 〔gift〕. ∼자 an offerer; a sponsor (프로 등의); a《kidney》 donor / 정보 ∼자 an informant; an informer (경찰의) / 대한 적십자사는 혈액 ∼자를 찾고 있습니다 The Korea National Red Cross is looking for blood donors.

**제공권**(制空權) 〖군사〗 air supremacy; (the) mastery 〔command〕 of the air. ¶ ∼을 잡다〔잃다〕 secure 〔lose〕 the mastery of the air / ∼을 잡고 있다 have 〔hold〕 the command of the air; command the air / 미국 공군이 태평양 상의 ∼을 잡고 있다 The U.S. Air Force has command of the air over the Pacific Ocean.

**제과**(製菓) confectionery. ◉ ∼업 the confectionery 〔candy〕 industry: ∼업자 a confectioner; a candy-maker. ∼점 a confectioner's shop; a confectionery. ∼회사 a confectionery company.

**제관**(祭官) ①《제사 맡은 자》 one who superintends ceremonial rites; an officiating priest. ②《제사 참례자》 those who participate in ceremonial rites.

**제관**(製罐) can manufacturing; canning 《미》; tinning《영》. ◉ ∼공장〔업〕 a can-manufacturing plant 〔industry〕. ∼업자 a canner.

**제구**(祭具) ritual utensils.

**제구력**(制球力) 〖야구〗 *one's* (pitching) control. ¶ ∼이 없다〔있다〕 have poor 〔good〕 ball control / 투수에게는 구속(球速)과 함께 ∼이 필요하다 A pitcher needs control as well as speed.

**제구실** ①《해야 할 일》 *one's* function; *one's* duty; *one's* obligation; what is expected of *one*; *one's* share 〔bit〕. ¶ ∼을 하다 perform *one's* function 〔duty〕 worthily; do「what is expected of *one* 〔what has to be done〕; discharge *one's* obligation; do *one's* bit; keep up *one's* end; prove adequate; be worth *one's* salt / ∼을 못 하다 fail to do as *one* should; behave improperly; be not worth *one's* salt; be good-for-nothing; "be not worth a damn"; be useless. ②《홍역 따위》 the usual childhood epidemic diseases that everyone has to go through. ¶ ∼을 하다 have *one's* measles 〔smallpox, *etc.*〕.

**제국**(帝國) an empire. ¶ ∼의 imperial. ◉ ∼주의 imperialism: ∼주의적 imperialistic / ∼주의자 an imperialist / 반∼주의 감정 anti-imperialist sentiment. 로마∼ the Roman Empire.

**제국**(諸國) all 〔various, many〕 countries.

**제군**(諸君) you; 《호칭》 Gentlemen !; My「friends.

**제금** 〖악기〗 small cymbals.

**제금**(提琴) 〖악기〗 a violin. ◉ ∼가 a「violinist.

**제기**[1] 《유희》 a kind of shuttlecock game played with the feet. ¶ ∼를 차다 play shuttlecock with the feet.

**제기**(祭器) ritual dishes or utensils.

**제기**(提起) presentation; introduction; institution (소송의). ∼하다 bring up 〔forward〕《a proposal》; raise《a question》; pose《a problem》; propose. ¶ 이론(異論)을 ∼하다 raise a question in argument / 소송을 ∼하다 institute 〔lodge〕 a lawsuit / 그녀는 중요한 문제를 ∼했다 She brought up a very important question. / 새로운 정책의 ∼가 물의를 일으켰다 The presentation of the new policy has given rise to criticism.

**제기**[2] 《제기랄》 Damn (it)!; Confound it !; Shucks !; Darn it ! ¶ ∼ 비싸기도 하다 It's damn expensive.

**제기다**[1] ①《빠지다》 slip out; sneak away. ②《알제기다》 get 〔have〕 a white spot in the pupil of an eye.

**제기다**[2] ① 《지르다》 kick with the heel; nudge with the elbow; heel; elbow. ② 《깎다》 whittle at 《a piece of wood》. ③ 《붓다》 pour 《water, soup》 a little at a time. ④ 《맞히다》 hit *one's* target (in a money-tossing game).

**제깐에** in *one's* own estimation 〔opinion〕; to *one's* own thinking. ¶ 그는 ～ 잘 한 줄 안다 He believes 〔fancies〕 himself to have done well. / 그는 ～는 시인이라고 생각한다 He thinks he is a poet.

**제너레이션** a generation. ¶ ～갭 《세대간의 단절》 the generation gap.

**제네바** 《스위스의 도시》 Geneva; Genève. ◉ ～협정 the Geneva Conventions.

**제단**(祭壇) an altar (for sacrifice). ◉ ～자리 〖천문〗 the Altar; Ara.

**제당**(製糖) sugar manufacture; sugar refining 〔milling〕. ◉ ～공장 a sugar mill 〔refinery〕. ～업 the sugar-manufacturing industry. ～회사 a sugar=manufacturing company.

**제대**(除隊) 〖군사〗 discharge from military service. ～하다 be discharged from service; discharge. ¶ ～되다 get discharged from service; be mustered out 《미》; 《병으로》 be invalided out 《of the army》. ◉ ～군인 a discharged soldier; an ex-G.I. 《미》. ～명령 discharge orders from military service. 명예〔만기〕～ (an) honorable discharge. 불명예～ (a) dishonorable discharge. 의가사〔의병〕～ discharge from service 「by family hardships 〔of illness〕; a hardship 〔compassionate〕 discharge.

**제대**(梯隊) 〖군사〗 an echelon.

**제대**(臍帶) 〖해부〗 an umbilical cord.

**제대로** ① 《있는 대로》 as it is; intact; untouched. ¶ ～두다 leave it just as it is; let it alone. ② 《잘·순조로이》 《do, go, progress》 as it should; smoothly; well; all right; without a hitch; in (good, proper) order; in orderly fashion. ¶ 일이 ～ 되다 *one's* work goes well / 일이 ～ 잘 되면 내달에는 끝나겠다 If all goes well, this job will be finished next month. ③ 《변변히》 properly; fully; well; enough. ¶ ～ 읽지도 않고 without reading 《a book》 properly / 그는 편지 하나 ～ 못 쓴다 He can't even write a letter properly. / 나는 ～ 교육도 못 받았다 I have had no regular education.

**제도**(制度) a system (방식); an institution (관례); an organization (기구); a regime (체제). ¶ 현행～ the existing system / 새로운 ～ a new system 〔regime〕 / 교육〔사회〕 ～ an education 〔a social〕 system / 문물～ culture and institutions / 새 ～하의 교육 education under the new system / 신〔구〕 ～하에 under the new 〔old〕 system / 서양에서 도입된 여러 ～ institutions imported from the West 《in the Chosŏn period》 / 미국의 ～를 본떠서 after the American system; on the American plan / ～를 개선하다 improve 〔reform〕 the system / ～를 고치다 renovate the system; remodel an institution / ～를 시행하다 enforce a system; put a system in operation / ～를 확립〔폐지〕하다 establish 〔abolish〕 a system / ～적 장치를 마련하다 make institutional devices 《to》 / 이 지방에는 독특한 가족 ～가 남아 있다 An unusual family system remains in this area. / 그 ～는 미국의 현행 ～를 본따서 만들어졌다 The system is 〔was〕 modeled on that in use in America.

**제도**(製陶) pottery manufacture; porcelain making. ◉ ～술(術) the ceramic art.

**제도**(製圖) drafting; drawing; cartography. ～하다 draft; draw 《a plan》. ◉ ～가 a draftsman; a cartographer. ～기구 drawing instruments. ～실 a drafting room; a drawing room. ～용구 a draftsman's outfit. ～용지 drafting 〔drawing〕 paper. ～판 a drawing board.

**제도**(諸島) (a group of) islands; an archipelago. ¶ 하와이 ～ the Hawaiian Islands.

**제도**(濟度) 〖불교〗 salvation; redemption. ～하다 save; redeem. ¶ ～할 수 없다 be past 〔beyond〕 redemption; be incorrigible / ～할 수 없는 사람 a lost soul; an incorrigible person.

**제도화**(制度化) institutionalization; 《체계화》 systematization. ～하다 institutionalize; systematize.

**제독**(除毒) ＝해독(解毒).

**제독**(提督) an admiral; a commodore. ¶ 넬슨 ～ (Fleet) Admiral Nelson.

**제독주다**(制毒—) humble 《*a person*》; take 《*a person*》 down a notch or two; take the wind out of 《*a person's*》 sails.

**제동**(制動) braking; damping (of electricity); 《스키의》 stemming. ¶ ～을 걸

다 apply 〔put on〕 the brake. ⇨ 브레이크. ◉ ~거리 《자동차 등의》 braking distance. ~기(機) a brake: 진공〔자동〕~기 a vacuum 〔an automatic〕 brake. ~레버 a safety lever. ~수 〖철도〗 a brakeman 《미》; a brakesman 《영》. ~자(子) a damper; a brake shoe. ~장치 a braking system; a damping device; 〖항공〗 an arresting gear: 2중 ~장치 a dual braking system. ~활강 〖등산〗 a glissade; 〖스키〗 a stemming; a stem. ~회전 〖스키〗 a stem turn.

**제등**(提燈) a (paper) lantern. ◉ ~행렬 a lantern parade.

**제등수**(諸等數) 〖수학〗 a compound number.

**제딴은** = 제깐에.

**제때** an appointed 〔a scheduled, a proper〕 time. ¶ 김장은 ~에 해야 한다 You have to make your kimchi at the right season. / 그는 ~가 지났는데 아직도 안 돌아 온다 It's past his usual time, but he's still not home.

**제라늄** 〖식물〗 a geranium.

**제련**(製鍊) 〖공업〗 smelting; refining. ~하다 refine 《metals》; smelt 《copper》; reduce 《ores》. ◉ ~소 a refinery; a smeltery. ~업 the refining industry: ~업자 a refiner; a smelter.

**제령**(制令) regulations; laws.

**제례**(祭禮) sacrificial 〔religious〕 rituals; ancestor-memorial ceremonies.

**제로** zero. ¶ 그는 인간으로서 ~다 He is nothing of a man. / 그는 교사로서는 ~였다 He was a complete failure as a teacher. ◉ ~게임 〖테니스〗 a love game; 〖야구〗 a scoreless game; a shut-out (제로패). ~디펙츠 〖경영〗 《무결점 운동》 zero defects. ~섬 게임 a zero-sum game. ~섬 사회 the zero-sum society. ~성장 〖경제〗 a zero economic growth.

**제록스** 《상표명》 Xerox. ¶ ~로 복사하다 xerox (a copy).

**제마**(製麻) manufacture of hemp (goods). ~하다 manufacture hemp (goods). ◉ ~회사 a hemp-dressing company.

**제막**(除幕) unveiling 《a statue, *etc.*》. ~하다 unveil. ◉ ~식 an unveiling ceremony 〔exercise 《미》〕: 내달 2일에 고(故) H박사의 동상 ~식이 거행된다 The bronze statue of the late Dr. H will be unveiled on the 2nd next month.

**제멋** *one's* own taste 〔fancy, style〕.

**제멋대로** at *one's* convenience; as *one* pleases; arbitrarily. ¶ ~ 굴다 have *one's* own way; do what *one* likes; behave as *one* pleases / ~ 하게 내버려 두어라 Let him have his way.

**제면**(製綿) ginning cotton. ~하다 gin cotton.

**제면**(製麪·製麵) noodle making. ~하다 make noodles. ◉ ~기〔업, 소〕 a noodle-making machine 〔business, plant〕.

**제명**(除名) striking off a name; dismissal from membership; (an) expulsion. ~하다 strike 〔take〕 《*a person's*》 name off the list; expel 〔oust〕 《*a person*》 from 《the club》; dismiss 《*a person* from membership》. ¶ ~ 처분을 받다 be expelled from 《the party》 / 자유당은 그의 ~을 결의했다 The Liberals have decided to strike his name off the roll.

**제명**(題名) a title 《of a book, *etc.*》. ¶ …의 ~으로 출판되다 be published under the title of… / 어제 「언어」라는 ~의 책을 샀다 I bought a book entitled *Language* yesterday. (★ 작품명은 보통 이탤릭체로 씀).

**제모**(制帽) a regulation 〔uniform〕 cap. ¶ 제복 ~의 경찰관 a policeman in uniform.

**제모**(製帽) manufacture of headgear; hat-making.

**제목**(題目) 《주제》 a subject; a theme; 《표제》 a title; 《화제》 a topic.

> 용법 **subject** 주제라는 뜻의 가장 일반적인 말. **theme** 논문·문학 작품 등에서 전개되고 상세히 기술되는 제목. **title** 책 등의 제목·표제라는 뜻. **topic** 구어적인 낱말로, 토론이나 수필 등에서 다루어지는 공통의 화제라는 뜻. 격식을 차리지 않을 경우에는 subject나 theme 대신으로도 쓰임.

¶ 「자유」라는 ~의 논문 an essay entitled "Liberty" / ~을 붙이다 give a title 《to》; entitle 《a book》 / 「봄」이라는 ~으로 쓰다 〔이야기하다〕 write 〔speak〕 on the subject of "Spring".

**제문**(祭文) a funeral oration 〔ode〕.

**제물** ① 《물·국물》 the original water in which food was cooked; liquid left after food is cooked. ② 《순수한 것》 genuine 〔pure〕 stuff. ◉ ~묵 pure green-pea jelly.

**제물**(祭物) things offered in sacrifice; an ancestor-memorial offering. ¶ 신에게 ~을 바치다 offer a sacrifice to a deity.

**제물낚시** a fly; an artificial fly; a fishing fly; a fly hook. ¶ ～질하다 do fly-fishing / ～로 낚다 flyfish; fish with a fly; angle with an artificial fly; get 《a fish》 on a fly.

**제물에** of its 〔*one's*〕 own accord; of *itself;* by *itself.* ¶ 상처가 ～ 나았다 The wound healed of itself. / 불이 ～ 꺼졌다 The fire went out of itself.

**제바람** its own power 〔influence, steam〕. ¶ ～에 under its own steam; of *itself;* by *oneself.*

**제반**(諸般) all sorts. ¶ ～의 various; several; all sorts 〔kinds〕 of; every / ～정세 all circumstances; the general state of things / ～의 준비를 갖추다 make every preparation 《for》; complete preparations 《for》. ◉ ～사(事) various matters 〔affairs〕; all things.

**제반미**(祭飯米) rice (to be cooked and) offered in memorial service.

**제발** for heaven's 〔God's, goodness'〕 sake; for the love of Mike; I beg of you; please; pray. ¶ ～ 떠들지 마라 For heaven's sake, be quiet. / ～ 문 좀 닫아 주오 Kindly oblige me by closing the door. / ～ 와 주시오 Do come, please. / ～ 용서하시오 Excuse me, please. *or* I humbly beg your pardon. / ～ 농담 좀 그만두게 Don't go too far with your jokes, please. / ～ 살려 줍쇼 Spare me for mercy's 〔Peter's〕 sake.

**제발 덕분에**(―德分―) for mercy's sake; (please) for my sake; I pray you. ¶～ 그를 관대히 봐 주십시오 Please, show him your leniency.

**제방**(堤防) a bank; an embankment; a dike; a levee 《미》. ¶ ～을 쌓다 construct 〔build〕 an embankment 〔a dike〕 / ～이 무너지다 the levee 〔dike〕 breaks down 〔collapses〕 《in several places》. ◉ ～공사 bank revetment; banking; shore-protection works.

**제백사**(除百事) laying aside everything; neglecting everything else. ～하다 lay everything aside. ¶ ～하고 before everything else; above all things / ～하고 찾아 뵙겠습니다 I'll let everything else go and visit you.

**제번**(除煩) saving trouble; being without ceremony. ～하다 save trouble; be without ceremony; get right to the subject. ¶ ～하옵고 I hasten to inform you that.... ｢cutting.

**제벌**(除伐) 〖임업〗 improvement 〔salvage〕

**제법** the way things ought to be; nicely; quite (good); fairly; pretty; beyond expectation. ¶ ～ 덥다 it is quite 〔nice and〕 warm / 독어를 ～ 잘 하다 speak German pretty well / ～이다 be quite good 〔up to the mark, up to snuff〕 / 그는 그림을 ～ 잘 그린다 He draws fairly well.

**제법**(除法) 〖수학〗 division.

**제법**(製法) a method 〔process〕 of manufacture; a process; how to make; 《과자·요리의》 a recipe 《for making a cake》. ¶ 케이크의 ～을 가르치다 teach 《*a person*》 how to make a cake; give 《*a person*》 a recipe for (making) a cake / ～을 보고 만들다 make 《*something*》 from a formula 〔recipe〕 / 이 검은 모자는 전통적인 ～으로 만들어진다 This black hat is made by a traditional process 〔method〕.

**제복**(制服) a uniform; regulation dress. ¶ 학교의 ～ school uniform / ～을 입은 uniformed; 《a girl》 in uniform / ～ 제모로 in 《school》 cap and uniform / ～을 입은 경관 a uniformed policeman; a police officer in uniform.

**제복**(除服) going out of mourning; expiration of mourning period. ～하다 go out of 〔leave off〕 mourning.

**제복**(祭服) liturgical robes.

**제본**(製本) bookbinding. ～하다 bind 《a book》. ¶ ～중이다 be at the binder's / ～이 잘 되어 있다 be well bound / 나는 논문을 ～하게 했다 I had my thesis bound. ◉ ～소 a book bindery; a bookbinder's. ～업 the bookbinding industry: ～업자 a bookbinder. 고급 양장～ high quality hardcover bookbinding.

**제분**(製粉) (flour) milling; pulverizing; grinding. ～하다 mill; pulverize; grind (grains) to flour. ◉ ～기, ～소 a (flour) mill. ～업 the milling industry: ～업자 a miller. ～회사 a flour mill company.

**제붙이** ＝제살붙이.

**제비**[1] 《추첨》 a lot; a lottery; a draw; a raffle. ¶ ～(를) 뽑다 draw 〔cast〕 lots / ～에 꽝을 뽑다 draw a blank / ～ 뽑아 결정하다 decide by lot / ～를 뽑아 당첨되었다 The lot fell to me. / ～로 첫 순번을 결정짓자 Let's cast lots for the first move. *or* Let's toss up to decide who's first. / ～ 뽑기에서 연필을 탔다 I won some pencils in a lottery.

**제비**[2] 〖조류〗 a swallow.

**제비꽃** 〖식물〗 a violet.

**제비족**(―族) a gigolo (extortionist). ¶

~인 김(金)은 남편에게 그들의 관계를 폭로하겠다고 위협하여 여인에게 많은 돈을 요구했다 Kim, a gigolo extortionist, requested a large sum of money from the woman, threatening her that he would reveal their relations to her husband.

**제비추리** beef from the inside ribs.

**제비턱** (a person with) a chubby chin.

**제빙**(除氷) deicing; defrosting. ~하다 deice; defrost. ◉ ~장치 a deicing device; a deicer; a defroster.

**제빙**(製氷) ice manufacture. ~하다 make 〔manufacture〕 ice. ¶ ~용 접시 《냉장고의》 an ice (cube) tray / 자동~장치 an automatic ice-maker. ◉ ~공장 an ice plant 〔manufactory〕. ~기 an ice machine; an ice=maker. ~회사 an ice(-manufacturing) company.

**제사**(第四) the fourth; number four (생략 No. 4). ◉ ~계급 《무산자》 the proletariat; 《언론인》 the fourth estate; journalists. ~세대 항생제 the 4th=generation antibiotic. ~차원 the fourth dimension.

**제사**(祭司) a 〔an officiating〕 priest; an officiant.

**제사**(祭祀) 《종교상의》 a religious service; sacrificial rites; 《조상의》 a memorial service 《for *one's* ancestor(s)》; an ancestor-worship ceremony 〔rite〕. ¶ 조상에게 ~지내다 hold 〔perform〕 a memorial service for the repose of *one's* ancestors / 아버님의 3주기(★ 3주기(週忌)는 사후 만 2년임) ~를 지냈다 We held a memorial service on the second anniversary of my father's death. ◉ 제삿날 a memorial service day; the anniversary of 《*a person's*》 death.

**제사**(製絲) spinning; 《생사의》 silk reeling; filature; drawing silk; making thread. ~하다 reel; draw silk; make thread. ◉ ~공 a silk-reel worker. ~공장 a spinning mill; a filature; a silk mill. ~기계 a reeling machine. ~업 the spinning 〔silk-reeling〕 industry: ~업자 a silk manufacturer.

**제사기**(第四紀) 〖지질〗 the Quaternary period.

**제사날로** as *one* wants; according to *one's* own desires; of *its* own accord.

**제산제**(制酸劑) an antacid (agent).

**제살붙이** a blood relative 〔relation〕; *one's* kin; a relative (by blood).

**제삼**(第三) the third; number three (생략 No. 3); the tertiary. ¶ ~의 third; tertiary / ~으로 thirdly; in the third place / ~의 물결 《책이름》 *the Third Wave* (앨빈 토플러 저).
◉ ~계급 the bourgeoisie; 《평민》 the third estate. ~공화국 the Third Republic. ~국 a third country 〔power〕: ~국으로의 망명을 요청하다 ask for political asylum to a third country. ~기(紀) 〖지질〗 the Tertiary period. ~기(期) the third term 〔period〕: ~기 매독 tertiary syphilis. ~세계 the Third World. ~세력 a third force; the third partisan group (정당). ~자 a third person 〔party〕; an outsider (국외자): ~자 보험 third-party insurance / ~자의 위치에 서다 stand outside; take *one's* position as a third party. ~제국 《나치의》 the Third Reich. ~차 산업 (the) tertiary industries.

**제상**(除霜) ~하다 defrost; deice. ◉ ~장치 a defroster; a deicer.

**제상**(祭床) a sacrificial table; a table used in a religious 〔memorial〕 service.

**제석**(帝釋) ① 〖민속〗 the Harvest God (= a shamanistic deity). ② ⇨ 제석천. ◉ ~풀이 〖민속〗 the shamanistic rite celebrating the Harvest God: ~풀이하다 celebrate the Harvest God.

**제석**(祭席) a mat used in religious 〔memorial〕 services.

**제석천**(帝釋天) 〖불교〗 *Sakra devānām Indra* (Sans.).

**제설**(除雪) snow removal. ~하다 remove 〔clear (away)〕 the snow 《from the street》. ◉ ~기 a snowplow. ~작업 snow-removing 〔snow-clearing〕 work: 거리 ~작업에 종사하다 engage in clearing snow (away) from the city streets. ~차 a snowplow car 〔locomotive〕.

**제설**(諸說) various views 〔opinions, theories, accounts〕. ¶ 이 문제에 대해서는 ~이 분분하다 Various views are expressed on this problem.

**제세**(濟世) salvation of the world. ~하다 save the world. ◉ ~안민(安民) saving the world and relieving the people.

**제소**(提訴) 〖법〗 instituting a lawsuit. ~하다 bring a lawsuit 《against》; sue. ◉ ~자 a suitor; a complainant.

**제수**(弟嫂) *one's* younger brother's wife; *one's* sister-in-law.

**제수**(除數) 〖수학〗 the divisor; the number to be divided by. ◉ 피~ a dividend.

**제수**(祭需) things needed in the sacrificial 〔ancestor-memorial〕 service; expenses of the service.

**제스처** a gesture. ¶ 단순한 ～에 불과하다 It's simply a gesture.

**제습**(除濕) dehumidification. ～하다 dehumidify. ◉ ～기(器) a dehumidifier. ～제 a dehumidifying agent.

**제시**(提示) presentation 《of ideas, *etc.*》. ～하다 present; indicate; bring up; come up with 《an idea》; cite; 《보여주다》 show. ¶ ～하는 대로 at 〔on〕 presentation / 검문소에서 운전 면허증 ～를 요구받았다 I was asked to show 〔present〕 my driver's license at a checkpoint. / 건물 안에 들어가려면 신분증을 ～하여야 한다 You must show your ID card to get into the building. ◉ ～부 〖음악·연극〗 exposition.

**제시간**(一時間) the appropriate 〔proper, scheduled〕 time. ¶ ～에 on time / ～에 못 대다 be too late 《for》 / 회의장까지 간신히 ～에 대어 갔다 I got to the place of meeting just in time.

**제식**(制式) ⇨ 규정(規定). ◉ ～교련〔훈련〕 〖군사〗 close-order drill.

**제씨**(弟氏) your esteemed younger brother.

**제씨**(諸氏) gentlemen; Messrs. ¶ 애독자 「～ my reader(s).

**제안**(提案) a proposal; a proposition; a suggestion; a motion; an offer. ～하다 propose; suggest; make 「a proposal 〔a proposition, an offer〕; put forward a suggestion; offer 〔advance〕 a suggestion; move 《for》.

> 용법 **propose** 고려·토의·채택해 주도록 제안함. 「propose＋목적어＋to 부정사」의 형식으로는 쓰지 못함: propose terms of peace 「휴전 조건을 제안하다」 / propose a friend for a club 「친구를 클럽에 추천하다」. **suggest** 「시사하다」에서, 「…은 아닌가, …하면 어떤가」하고 제언하는 정중하고 사교적 표현. to부정사 또는 「사람」을 목적어로 취하지 않음: suggest a stroll after lunch 「식사 후 산책을 제안하다」.

¶ 아무 조건도 붙지 않은 ～ a proposal with no strings attached / ～에 동의하다 agree to a proposal / 반대 ～을 하다 make a counterproposal / ～ 이유를 설명하다 describe the proposition 《that...》 / …라는 ～이 있다 It is proposed that... / 평화를 위한 일련의 건설적인 ～들을 제시하다 offer a steady stream of constructive proposals for peace / 그는 모임에서 새 계획을 ～할 것이다 He will propose a new plan at the meeting. / 시의회는 그 ～을 가결〔부결〕했다 The municipal assembly 〔council〕 adopted 〔rejected〕 the proposal. / 그녀는 시청에서 만나자고 ～했다 She suggested meeting at the City Hall.
◉ ～설명 enunciation of a proposal. ～자 a proponent; a proposer: 의장은 ～자에게 ～이유를 설명하라고 요청하였다 The chairperson requested the proposer to explain the proposal.

**제압**(制壓) control; supremacy; mastery. ～하다 bring under *one's* control; gain supremacy 〔mastery〕 over 《the enemy, the sea, *etc.*》.

**제야**(除夜) the New Year's Eve; the watch night. ¶ ～의 종 the watch-night bell; the bell speeding 〔ringing out〕 the old year / ～의 종을 울려서 새해를 맞이하다 ring in the new year.

**제약**(制約) a restriction; a limitation; 《조건》 a condition; a constraint. ～하다 restrict; control; dominate. ¶ 시간의 ～을 받다 be restricted by time / 유형무형의 ～을 받다 be curbed physically and spiritually 《from》 / 사회 생활에는 갖가지 ～이 있다 Our social life is hampered by a lot of obstacles. / 비용면에서 ～이 있다 We must do it with a limited sum (of money). ◉ ～적 판단 〖철학〗 conditional judgment.

**제약**(製藥) 《약의 제조》 medicine 〔drug〕 manufacture; pharmacy; 《만든 약》 a manufactured drug. ～하다 manufacture drugs 〔medicines〕.
◉ ～공장 a pharmaceutical factory. ～사(師) a pharmacist; an apothecary. ～업 the pharmaceutical industry. ～업자 a drug manufacturer; a pharmacist. ～화학 pharmaceutical chemistry. ～회사 a pharmaceutical 〔drug〕 company.

**제어**(制御) control; governing; check(-ing); restraint. ～하다 control; govern; check; restrain; rein. ¶ ～하기 쉬운 easy to control; controllable; manageable; tractable / ～하기 어려운 hard to control; uncontrollable; unruly; unmanageable; refractory.
◉ ～공학 control engineering. ～기 a controller; a regulator. ～력 (power to) control. ～반(盤) a control console 〔board〕. ～봉 《원자로의》 a control rod. ～장치 a control device; controls: 자동 ～ 장치 an automatic control system 〔device〕. ～프로그램 a control program. (중앙)～실 the central control room.

**제언**(提言) a suggestion; a proposal. ⇨제안.

**제역**(除役) ① 《면역》 release from office. ∼하다 release from office. ② 《병역 면제》 exemption from military service; immunity from conscription. ∼하다 exempt from military service.

**제염**(製塩) salt manufacture. ∼하다 manufacture salt. ◉ ∼소 a saltern; a saltworks. ∼업 the salt industry.

**제오**(第五) the fifth; number 〔No.〕 5. ¶ ∼차 경제 사회 개발 5개년 계획 the fifth five-year economic and social 〔socio-economic〕 development plan. ◉ ∼공화국 the Fifth Republic. ∼성병 the fifth venereal disease. ∼세대 컴퓨터 the 5th generation computer. ∼열 《간첩》 a fifth column.

**제왕**(帝王) an emperor; a king; a sovereign. ¶ ∼의 imperial. ◉ ∼신권설 the theory of the divine right of kings. ∼절개(수술) 〖의학〗 a Caesarean operation 〔section〕: ∼ 절개 분만 (a) Caesarean birth.

**제외**(除外) exception; exclusion. ∼하다 except 《from》; exclude. ¶ …을 ∼하고(는) except; save; but; excepting; exclusive of; with the exception of; except for / 하나를 ∼하고 모두 all but one / 몇몇 예외를 ∼하고 with a few exceptions / 이자를 ∼한 만원 10,000 won, exclusive of interest / 전항의 규정에 의한 경우를 ∼하고 apart from cases governed by the provision of the preceding paragraph / 다른 특별한 규정이 있는 경우를 ∼하고는 unless otherwise provided / 여기 오신 분은∼하고 except those present / 몇 군데 잘못된 곳을 ∼하고는 잘된 번역이다 The translation is good except for a few mistakes. ◉ ∼조항 an escape clause.

> 용법 「…을 제외하고」에 가장 적합한 영어는 **except**임. but는 no, all, anything, everywhere 등의 뒤에서만 쓰임. **except for**는 not… except…의 뜻으로 이 어구는 보통 긍정문의 뒤에 쓰임. (그들을 제외하고는 교실에 아무도 없었다) There was no one in the classroom except 〔but〕 them. *or* The classroom was empty except for them.

**제요**(提要) a summary; a compendium; an epitome. ◉ ∼서 a manual.

**제욕**(制慾) the control of passion; self=control. ∼하다 control *one's* passion; control *oneself.* ◉ ∼주의 asceticism.

**제웅** 〖민속〗 a straw effigy for exorcism.

**제위**(帝位) the imperial throne; the Crown. ¶ ∼에 오르다 ascend the throne / ∼를 계승하다 succeed to the throne / ∼를 선양(禪讓)하다 abdicate the throne 《in favor of another》/ ∼를 빼앗다 usurp the throne / ∼를 다투다 contend 〔rival〕 for the throne.

**제위**(祭位) the spirit to whom a sacrificial rite is offered. ◉ ∼답(畓) paddy 〔ordinary〕 fields set apart so that their produce will maintain the annual ancestor-memorial services.

**제위**(諸位) gentlemen.

**제유**(製油) oil manufacture. ◉ ∼소 an oil factory 〔refinery〕.

**제육** pork. ◉ ∼구이 roast pork. ∼전 a pork butcher 〔shop〕.

**제육감**(第六感) a sixth sense. ⇨ 육감(六感).

**제융**(製絨) wool-weaving. ◉ ∼소 a woolen factory; a wool mill.

**제의**(提議) an offer; a proposal. ⇨ 제안. ¶ (…의) ∼로 at the motion 〔instance〕 《of》/ 강화를 ∼하다 make peace overtures; make overtures for peace / 계획을 ∼하다 put forward a plan; move for a plan 《of》/ ∼에 응하다 accept an offer / ∼를 거절하다 decline an offer / 이 ∼는 Y씨가 한 것이다 This offer emanates from Mr. Y. / 그 문제에 관해 ∼하고 싶은 것이 있다 I have a proposal to make about that matter. ◉ ∼자 a proposer; a proponent.

**제이**(第二) the second; number 〔No.〕 2. ¶ ∼의 the 〔a〕 second; secondary (★ a second는 another의 뜻을 나타내는 일이 있음: a second time 「또 한번」; a second coat 「다른 옷」) / ∼의 고향 *one's* second home / ∼의 천성 second nature / ∼의 나폴레옹 a second Napoleon / ∼의 문제 a matter of secondary importance; a secondary consideration. ◉ ∼당 the second largest party. ∼보충역 retired replacement status. ∼인칭 〖문법〗 the second person. ∼종우편(물) the second-class mail (matter). ∼주제 〖음악〗 the subsidiary (theme). ∼차 세계 대전 the Second World War; World War II. ∼차 집단 〖사회〗 a secondary group. ∼후보 the second string. 산화∼동(銅) cupric oxide.

**제일** *one's* own (personal) affair. ¶ ∼처럼 as if 《it》 were *one's* own affair /

친구가 성공했다는 소식을 듣고 그는 ～처럼 자랑스럽게 느꼈다 He heard of the success of his friend and felt a sort of personal pride.

**제일**(除日) the last day of the year.

**제일**(祭日) a sacrificial day; 《제삿날》 an ancestor-worship day; a memorial service day.

**제일**(第一) the first; number one (생략 No. 1); the most important (thing). ¶ ～의 first; primary; foremost; initial (★ first는 형용사·명사로서 흔히 the를 수반함: the first train; He was the first to come. 그러나 다음과 같은 관용구에서는 관사가 안 붙음: at first sight; at first hand) / ～ 좋은〔나쁜〕 best 〔worst〕 / ～ 아름다운 most beautiful / ～ 앞의〔뒤의〕 foremost 〔hindmost〕 / ～ 먼저 first(ly); in the first place; first of all; before everything else / ～류의 first-class〔-rank, -rate〕; topnotch 《미》; leading; A—1 / ～의 목적 the primary object / 세계 ～의 부자 the richest man in the world / 세계에서 ～ 높은 산 the highest mountain in the world / ～ 중요하다 be of the first importance; be most important 《to》 / 건강이 ～이다 Health is above everything else. / 여기는 한국 ～의 명승지이다 This is the most picturesque place in Korea. / 그녀는 글씨 쓰기가 학급에서 ～이다 She leads the class in handwriting. / 건강을 위해서는 시골로 가는 것이 ～이다 In order to improve your health, you had best go into the country. / 그를 만나기가 ～ 싫다 He is the last man that I want to see. / 성공에는 인내가 ～이다 Perseverance is the first essential to success. / 미국은 공업과 상업에 있어 세계 ～의 나라이다 America holds the first rank in the world for industry and commerce. ◉ ～과 the first lesson; lesson one. ～국민역 eligible conscription status. ～기 the first term 〔period〕; 《병 따위의》 the first 〔initial, primary〕 stage: ～기 납입 payment of the first installment / ～기생 one of the first-time graduates. ～단계 the primary stage. ～당(黨) the leading party. ～방송 network 〔channel〕 No. 1; the first (transmission) program. ～보충역 standby replacement status. ～서기 the First Secretary (of the Communist Party). ～심(審) the first trial 《in court》: 그는 ～심에서 이겼으나 제이심에서 패소했다 At the first hearing he won the case, but was defeated at the second. ～야당 the major opposition party. ～위 the first (rank): ～위를 차지하다 stand 〔rank〕 first. ～종 우편(물) first-class mail (matter). ～주자 the lead-off man. ～차산업 primary industries. ～차 세계 대전 the First World War; World War I. ～차 제품 primary products 〔produce〕. ～착(着) the first「to arrive 〔to reach the goal〕; the first in the race.

**제일보**(第一步) the first step 《to, toward》; an initial step; 《발족》 a start. ⇨첫발. ¶ ～를 내딛다 take the first step; make 〔get〕 a start / ～를 그르치다 make a false start; start in the wrong way.

**제일선**(第一線) 《최전선》 the first 〔foremost〕 line; vanguard; 《군사》 the fighting line; the front. ⇨일선. ¶ 방위의 ～ the first 〔an advance〕 line of defense / ～에 서다 stand 〔be〕 in the forefront 《of》.

**제일성**(第一聲) the first speech. ¶ 귀국 ～ *one's* first public speech after *one's* return from abroad.

**제일인자**(第一人者) the number-one man; the leading expert 〔man〕; the first among *one's* peers. ¶ 그는 이 분야에서는 ～이다 He is a leading expert in this field. / 그는 현존 작가 중 ～이다 He stands foremost among the living writers. / 그는 실업계의 ～이다 He is a topflight 〔topnotch〕 businessman.

**제자**(弟子) a disciple; a follower; a pupil; an apprentice. ¶ 소크라테스의 ～ followers of Socrates / ～가 되다 become 《*a person's*》 disciple / ～로 삼다 take 《*a person*》 as *one's* pupil.

**제자**(諸子) ① 《제군》 you; gentlemen. ② 《아들들》 *one's* sons. ③ 《중국의》 masters; sages. ◉ ～백가 all philosophers and literary scholars.

**제자**(題字) a title; a heading; an inscription (at the head of a book).

**제자리** 《마땅한 자리》 the proper place; 《본래 자리》 the original 〔former〕 place. ¶ 책을 ～에 갖다 놓다 put a book back (where it was). ◉ ～멀리〔높이〕 뛰기 a standing long 〔high〕 jump. ～물가 시대 a zero-price increase era.

**제자리걸음** 《제자리에서 걷는 동작》 marking time; 《정체 상태》 a stalemate; a standstill. ¶ ～하다 mark time; 《정체하다》 be at a standstill; make no progress 〔headway〕 / 음악에 맞춰 ～

하다 mark time to the music / 그 교섭은 ～을 하고 있다 The negotiations are at a standstill.

**제작**(製作) manufacture; production. ～하다 manufacture; produce; make; turn out. ¶ 공동～(a) co-production / ～중이다 be in the making; be manufacturing / 그 영화는 ～에 3년이 걸렸다고 한다 I hear it took three years to make that movie.

◉ ～물〔품〕a manufactured article; products; manufactured goods. ～비 production cost(s). ～소 a factory; a works (★ 흔히 단수 취급); a plant. ～자 a manufacturer; a maker; 《영화의》a film producer: 공동～자 a co-producer. 국립 영화 ～소 the National Film Production Center. 한국 영화 ～가 협회 the Association of Korean Movie Producers.

**제잡담하다**(除雜談 —) leave off idle talk; "cut (out) the chit-chat". ¶ 제잡담하고 "without palaver"; without useless words.

**제재**(制裁) sanctions; punishment; discipline. ～하다 take〔apply〕sanctions〔disciplinary action〕《against》; inflict punishment《upon》; punish. ¶ 경제적〔사회적, 군사적〕인 ～《apply》economic〔social, military〕sanctions / ～를 풀다〔완화하다〕lift〔ease〕sanctions / 폭력으로 ～를 가하다 take the law into *one's* own hands / 법의 ～를 받다 be brought under the law; be brought to justice / 미국은 이라크에 경제 ～를 가했다 The U.S. applied economic sanctions against Iraq. / 그는 사회적인 ～를 받고 있다 He is suffering social punishment.

**제재**(製材) sawing; lumbering. ～하다 lumber; do lumbering; saw (up) 《logs into boards》. ◉ ～목 sawn wood; lumber《미》; timber《영》. ～소 a sawmill; a lumbermill. ～업 the lumbering〔sawing〕industry: ～업자 a lumberer; a sawmiller.

**제재**(題材) subject matter; a theme; material《for a novel》.

**제적**(除籍) removal from a register. ～하다 remove《*a person's*》name from the register〔roll〕; strike《*a person's*》name off the list; 《학적에서》expel〔turn out〕《*a person*》(from school). ¶ 학교에서 ～을 당하다 get removed from a school register; be expelled〔dismissed〕from school / ～ 학생을 복귀시키다 reinstate the students expelled from school / 호적에서 ～하다 remove《*one's* name》from the family register / 그는 당규 위반으로 당에서 ～당했다 He was struck off from our party register for infringement of party discipline.

**제전**(祭典) religious celebration; a festival (rite); a fête. ¶ ～을 베풀다 hold〔celebrate〕a festival.

**제절**(諸節) ① 《댁내 여러분》all the family; all of you. ¶ 댁내 ～이 무고하신지요 How are your people? *or* How is your family? ②《여러 가지 일》various affairs; everything.

**제정**(制定) establishment by law; enactment; institution. ～하다 establish《a law》; enact《provisions》; formulate〔lay down〕《a rule》; institute《an order》. ¶ 국기를 ～하다 decide on the national flag《of Korea》/ 법률을 ～하다 enact〔make〕laws; legislate 《against, for》. ◉ ～법 an act of Congress〔Parliament《영》〕; a statute law. ～자 a legislator.

**제정**(帝政) imperial government〔rule〕; imperialism. ◉ ～러시아 Tsarist〔Czarist〕Russia. ～시대 the monarchical period; 《러시아의》the Czarist era〔period〕.

**제정**(祭政) church and state. ◉ ～일치 unity of church and state; theocracy.

**제정**(提呈) presentation. ～하다 present; offer《to a high personage》; submit. ¶ 신임장을 ～하다 present *one's* credentials《to》.

**제정신**(—精神)《기절에 대해》consciousness; sense;《미친 것에 대해》sanity; reason; right mind;《술기운에서 깬》soberness. ¶ ～의《미치지 않은》sane; 《안 취한》sober / ～으로 in *one's* right mind〔senses〕; in earnest; in soberness / ～을 잃다 lose *one's* senses; lose consciousness; become unconscious;《미치다》go〔get〕mad; lose *one's* sanity〔reason〕/ ～이다 be sound in mind; be in *one's* right mind / ～이 아니다 be out of *one's* senses; be not in *one's* right mind / ～이 들다 return to consciousness; recover〔regain〕consciousness; recover〔come to〕*oneself;* come round / 취하여 ～을 잃다 drink out of *one's* senses / ～으로 돌아오게 하다 bring《*a person*》to *himself*〔*his* senses〕; bring《*a person*》round.

**제제다사**(濟濟多士) a group〔galaxy〕of talented people.

**제조**(製造) making; manufacture; production. ～하다 manufacture (★ 주로 기계를 사용한 대량 생산을 뜻함); produce; make; turn out. ¶ 자동차〔무기〕의 ～ the production of automobiles 〔arms〕 / 미국에서 ～한 American-made; of American make / 펄프에서 종이를 ～하다 make paper from pulp / 넝마로 벽지를 ～하다 manufacture rags into wallpaper / 그는 신발의 ～ 판매를 하고 있다 He makes and sells shoes. / 질적 양적으로 외국에 뒤지지 않는 물품을 ～하고 있다 They turn out goods comparable to those of foreign nations in both quality and quantity. ◉ ～공정 a manufacturing process. ～능력 manufacturing capacity. ～번호 the (manufacturer's) serial number 《on a TV》. ～법 a manufacturing process 〔technique〕. ～소 a works; a plant; a factory; a mill. ～업 the manufacturing industry: ～업자 the manufacturer; the maker / ～업 경쟁력 manufacturing competitiveness. ～연월일〔일자〕 the date of manufacture. ～원가 manufacturing 〔production〕 cost; cost to manufacture. ～인〔원(元)〕 a manufacturer; a producer; a maker. ～지 the place of production. ～품 manufactured goods; a product.

**제주**(祭主) 《만상제》 the chief mourner; 《주재자》 the master of religious rites.

**제주**(祭酒) rice wine for use in a sacrificial rite. ¶ ～를 올리다 offer wine before the alter.

**제중**(濟衆) salvation of the people; saving the (distressed) masses.

**제지**(制止) (a) restraint; a check; control. ～하다 keep 《*a person*》 from 《*do*ing》; hold 〔keep〕 《crowd》 back; check; control; restrain. ¶ 나의 ～를 뿌리치고 in defiance of my remonstrance / ～할 수 없게 되다 [대상이 주어] get beyond 〔out of〕 *one's* control; go out of hand; [사람이 주어] lose control 《of》 / ～를 받다 be under 〔subject to〕 restraint; be restrained / ～를 받지 않다 be free from restraint / 경찰은 폭도들을 ～할 수 없었다 The police lost control of the mob. / 그들은 수위의 ～를 무릅쓰고 건물 안으로 들어가려고 하였다 They tried to force their way into the building, defying the porter.

**제지**(製紙) paper manufacture; papermaking. ～하다 manufacture paper. ◉ ～공장 a paper mill 〔factory〕. ～기계 a paper-making machine. ～업 the paper(-manufacturing) industry: ～업자 a paper manufacturer; a paper-maker. ～용 펄프 paper pulp. ～원료 paper stock; pulp. ～회사 a paper=manufacturing company.

**제창**(提唱) 《제안》 (a) proposal; 《창도》 advocacy. ～하다 advance 《a new doctrine, *etc.*》; put forward; propose; advocate. ¶ 화평의 ～ a peace proposal / 인류의 평등을 ～하다 proclaim 〔advocate〕 the equality of men / 자유주의를 ～하다 advocate liberalism. ◉ ～자 an advocate; a proponent.

**제창**(齊唱) singing in unison. ～하다 sing 《the national anthem》 in unison.

**제철** the (right) season; the best time 《for》. ¶ ～의 사과 apples of the season / ～에 맞는 물건 장수 a dealer in seasonable articles / ～이다 be in season / ～이 지나다 be out of season.

**제철**(製鐵) iron making 〔manufacture〕; 《제강》 steel manufacture; steelmaking. ～하다 manufacture iron. ◉ ～소 a steelworks; an ironworks (★ 단·복수 취급); a steel mill. ～업 iron industry: ～업자 a steel producer. ～회사 an iron-manufacturing company; a steel(-manufacturing) company. 종합～공장 an integrated (iron and) steel mill: 세계에서 가장 최신의 효율적인 종합 ～ 공장 the world's most up-to=date and efficient integrated steel mill.

**제철**(蹄鐵) a horseshoe. ⇨ 편자.

**제청**(祭廳) a place in front of a grave, where a sacrificial rite is held as part of the funeral.

**제쳐놓다** ① ＝제치다. ② lay 〔set〕 aside; put aside; leave out; set apart. ¶ 내일을 위해 ～ save 《*a thing*》 for tomorrow. ③ 《무시하다》 ignore; disregard; slight. ¶ 그것은 제쳐놓고 aside from that / 비용 문제는 제쳐놓고 apart from the question of expense / 하던 일을 제쳐놓고 친구를 맞으려 일어서다 get up to meet a friend, laying aside what *one* was doing / 담임 교사를 제쳐놓고 교장과 담판하다 negotiate directly with the headmaster over the head of the teacher in charge of the class / 급하지 않은 일은 제쳐놓고 급한 일을 먼저 해라 Put aside what can be done later and take care of the urgent things first.

**제초**(除草) weeding. ～하다 weed《a garden》; do weeding. ◉ ～기 a weeder; a grass cutter. ～제 a weed-killer; a herbicide.

**제출**(提出) presentation; proposition. ～하다 present; submit; bring forward《evidence》;《원서·답안을》send 〔hand〕 in;《의견을》advance;《의안을》introduce;《항의를》lodge;《사표를》tender. ¶ 증거를 ～하다 bring forward evidence; produce proof / 원서를 ～하다 hand 〔send〕 in *one's* application / 의견을 ～하다 advance an opinion; set forth *one's* views / 예산안을 ～하다 introduce the budget / 답안을 ～하다 send 〔give〕 in an examination paper / 정부는 새 법안을 ～할 것이다 The government will introduce a new bill. ◉ ～기한 a deadline: 리포트의 ～ 기한은 7월 10일이다 The deadline of this paper is July 10. ～물《서류의》the documents for submission; 〖법〗 an exhibit. ～자《서류의》a presenter;《안 등의》a proposer.

**제충**(除蟲) extermination of insects. ～하다 get rid of insects 〔worms〕; exterminate 〔repel〕 insects. ◉ ～분 insect powder. ～제 an insect repellent; an insectifuge;《살충제》an insecticide.

**제충국**(除蟲菊) 〖식물〗 a (Dalmatian) pyrethrum;《구충제》powdered pyrethrum flowers.

**제취**(除臭) deodorization. ～하다 deodorize. ◉ ～제 a deodorant; a deodorizer.

**제치다** clear away; put out of the way; omit; leave out.

**제칠**(第七) the seventh; number seven (생략 No. 7). ◉ ～천국 the seventh heaven. ～함대 the Seventh Fleet.

**제키다** get abraded; get rubbed raw.

**제트** jet. ¶ ～4기 장치의 비행기 an four=jet 〔four-engined jet〕 plane. ◉ ～기 a jet (plane): ～기로《go》by jet / ～기 조종사 a jet pilot / ～기의 굉음 the high whine of a jet plane. ～기류 the jet stream. ～수송기 a jet transport (plane). ～엔진 a jet engine 〔motor〕. ～여객기 a jet (air)liner. ～전투기〔폭격기〕 a jet fighter 〔bomber〕. ～항공로 a jet airline.

**제판**(製版) 〖인쇄〗 plate making; engraving. ～하다 plate; make a (stereotype 〔an electrotype〕) plate. ¶ 사진～ photoengraving / 전기 ～ electrotype process. ◉ ～소 a plate-maker's shop; an engraver's shop.

**제팔**(第八) the eighth; number eight (생략 No. 8).

**제패**(制覇) conquest; domination; supremacy. ～하다 conquer; dominate 〔mastery〕《over》;《경기에서》win 〔gain〕 the championship《of》; gain supremacy. ¶ 세계 ～ domination of the world; world hegemony / ～를 다투다 contend 〔compete〕 for supremacy / 그녀는 세계 ～를 꿈꾸고 있다 She dreams of winning the《tennis》championship in the world.

**제퍼슨**《미국의 정치가》 Thomas Jefferson (1743-1826).

**제풀로, 제풀에** ＝제물에.

**제품**(製品) manufactured goods 〔articles〕; a product. ¶ 실크 ～ silk goods 〔products〕 / 은～ silverware / 국내～ home products / 한국 ～ Korean(-made) goods; products made in Korea / ～을 시장에 팔다 market the products / 이 냉장고는 당사의 ～입니다 These refrigerators are the products of our company.
◉ ～원가 the cost (of products).

**제하다**(除—) ①《나누다》divide. ¶ 30을 6으로 ～ divide 30 by 6. ②《빼다》leave out; except; exclude. ⇨ 제외(除外). ③《공제하다》take out; subtract; deduct; subduct. ¶ 세금을 제하고 50만원의 수입 an income of 500,000 won after tax reduction / 이자를 제하고 10만원, 100,000 won, exclusive of interest / 봉급에서 ～ deduct《a sum》from *one's* salary / 비용을 다 제하면 남는 것이 없다 After I take out the expenses I won't have anything left.

**제한**(制限) (a) restriction; a limit; (a) limitation; (a) restraint;《자격의》qualifications. ～하다 restrict; limit; restrain; put 〔impose, place〕 restrictions《on》. (★ restrict는 제한·조건을 붙여 「금〔구속〕하다」란 뉘앙스를 가진 반면, limit는 정도·분량 등에 「한계를 설정하다」란 뜻). ¶ 수량～ quantitative restrictions / 전력 소비 ～ restrictions on power consumption / 시간 〔연령〕의 ～ time 〔age〕 limit / ～ 내에서 within the limits / ～없이 without limit 〔restriction〕 / 스페이스에 ～이 있어서 because of space limitations / ～부로 under certain restrictions / ～을 받다 be subject to restriction / 음식을 ～하다 put《*a person*》on a diet / 행동을 ～받다 be restricted in *one's* movements / 수에 ～이 있다 be limited 〔restricted〕 in number / ～을 완화〔해제〕하다 relax

〔lift〕 restrictions《for》/ 연설은 10분으로 ～되어 있다 Speeches are limited to ten minutes. / 회원은 100명으로 ～돼 있다 The membership is limited to a hundred. / 회원 자격에 남녀의 ～은 없습니다 Membership is not limited by sex. / 이 고속도로에서는 시속 90km로 속력이 ～되어 있다 Speed is limited to ninety kilometers per hour on this expressway.
◉ ～구역 a limited area. ～속도 a speed limit; the regulation speed: ～속도 준수가 교통사고를 방지하는 길이다 Keeping within the speed limit is a way to prevent traffic accidents. ～송전 power limit: ～송전하다 limit the supply of electricity. ～시간 the time limit; the restricted hours. ～전쟁 a limited 〔restricted〕 war; limited warfare.

**제한적**(制限的) restrictive. ¶ ～〔비～〕 용법 『문법』 the restrictive 〔nonrestrictive〕 use《of relative pronouns》.

**제해권**(制海權) the command of the sea; naval supremacy. ¶ ～을 장악하다〔잃다〕 secure 〔lose〕 the command of the sea / ～을 되찾다 regain the lost command of the sea / ～을 잡고 있다 hold 〔have〕 the mastery of the sea; command the sea.

**제행**(諸行) 『불교』 ①《만물》 all things in the universe; all worldly things. ②《수행》 (various) ascetic practices.
◉ ～무상 All things are in flux and nothing is permanent.

**제헌**(制憲) establishment of the constitution. ◉ ～국회 the Constitutional Assembly: ～국회의원 a member of the Constituent Assembly. ～절 Constitution Day.

**제혁**(製革) tanning; leather manufacturing. ◉ ～소 a tannery. ～업 the tanning industry: ～업자 a tanner.

**제현**(諸賢) gentlemen.

**제형**(梯形) a trapezoid; an echelon formation.

**제형**(諸兄) (dear) my friends.

**제형**(蹄形) hoof shape; U-shape. ¶ ～의 hoof-shaped; U-shaped. ◉ ～자석 a horseshoe magnet. ～체 an ungula.

**제호**(題號) the title《of a book》.

**제화**(製靴) shoemaking. ◉ ～공 a shoemaker. ～공장 a shoe(making) factory. ～기 a shoemaking machine. ～업 the shoe(making) industry: ～업자 a shoemaker.

**제후**(諸侯) feudal princes 〔lords〕.

**제휴**(提携) cooperation; a tie-up; coalition (정치적); a hookup. ～하다 cooperate with; act in concert 〔unison〕 with; fall 〔act〕 in line with; move in harmony; go hand in hand with; join 〔clasp〕 hands with; join together; tie up with; form an affiliation with; be aligned with.
¶ 기술～ a technical tie-up 〔cooperation〕《between》; (an agreement for) technical cooperation / …와 ～하여 in concert 〔cooperation〕 with / ～를 하고 있다 be aligned《with》; be bound in the same camp / ～를 계속하다 continue in partnership / ～하여 공동의 적에 맞서다 be leagued together against the common enemy / 그는 미국 회사와의 더 밀접한 ～를 주창하고 있다 He advocates a closer alignment with an American firm. / 그는 노동당과 ～하였다 He identified himself with the Labor Party. / 우리는 B사와 ～하여 새 사업을 시작하기로 결정했다 We decided to start the new business in cooperation with B company. / 이 약은 당사와 A사와의 기술 ～로 개발되었다 This medicine has been developed under a technical tie-up between ourselves and A company. ◉ ～회사 an affiliated concern.

**젠장** Hang 〔Damn〕 it !; Gosh !; Hell !; How vexatious !; Confound it 〔you〕! ¶ ～ 비가 오네 Confound the rain !

**젠체하다** put on (superior) airs; assume an air of importance; puff *oneself* up. ¶ 젠체하는 affected; conceited; self-important / 젠체하고 affectedly; conceitedly / 젠체하는 사람 an affected person / 그는 언제나 젠체한다 He always puts on airs. / 그는 너무 젠체하지만 않으면 좋은 사람인데 He'd be quite a nice fellow, if he didn't put on so much airs. / 그렇게 젠체할 것 없어 Don't put on airs like that.

**젠틀맨** a gentleman.

**젤라틴** 『화학』 gelatin(e). ¶ ～ 모양의 gelatinous.

**젤리** jelly; 《과자》 a jelly. ¶ ～ 모양으로 되다〔만들다〕 jellify; jelly.

**젯날**(祭―) = 제일(祭日).

**젯메**(祭―) sacrificial boiled rice.
◉ ～쌀 raw rice to be boiled for a sacrifice offering.

**젯밥**(祭―) boiled rice that has been offered in sacrifice.

**조**[1] 『식물』 (foxtail 〔Italian〕) millet.

**조**[2] that little《thing over there》. ¶ 조 놈 that little man 〔guy, so-and-so〕.

**조**(兆) a trillion 《미》; a million million; a billion 《영》 (★ billion은 《미》에서 「10억」, trillion은 《영》에서 「백만조」의 뜻).

**조**(組) a company; a party; a team; a crew; a gang. ¶ 2인조 a pair 《of robbers》; a couple; a duet / 3인조 a trio; a triad / 4인조 a group of four / 조를 짜다 make up a party; team up 《with》.

**조**(條) an article; a clause; an item. ¶ 제5조 Article 〔Section〕 V / 제5조 제4항과 같다 be the same as Article V Clause 4 / 그것은 제7조 제1항에 규정되어 있다 It is stipulated in Article 7, Paragraph 1.

**조**(朝) a dynasty; 《치세》 a reign. ¶ 고려조 the Koryŏ Dynasty.

**조**(調) ① 《음조》 a pitch; a tone; 《박자》 time; a tempo (*pl.* ~s, -pi); 《시의》 a meter; 〖음악〗 a key. ¶ 장〔단〕조 major 〔minor〕 key. ② 《행동·말투》 an air 〔a manner, an attitude〕 《of》; 《…조로》 -ly. ¶ 장난조로 jokingly / 시비조로 defiantly; with a truculent attitude / 비난조로 critically; with an air of censure.

**-조**(造) built; made. ¶ 목조의 (built 〔made〕) of wood; wooden / 연와조의 집 a brick(-built) house.

**조가**(弔歌) an elegy; a dirge.

**조가비** a shell. ¶ ~를 줍다 gather 〔collect〕 shells. ◉ ~세공 shellwork.

**조각** a piece; a bit; a fragment (단편); a splinter (뾰족뾰족한); a slice (얇은); a strip; a slip; a flake. ¶ 유리~ a piece of broken glass; splinters of glass / 깨진 접시 ~ a fragment of a broken dish / 헝겊 ~ (a piece of) cloth / 종이 ~ bits 〔scraps〕 of paper / 빵 한 ~ a slice of bread.
◉ ~달 a crescent (moon); a waxing moon (상현달); a waning moon (하현달). ~보(褓) a patchwork wrapping-cloth.

**조각**(組閣) formation of a Cabinet 〔Ministry〕. ~하다 form a Cabinet; organize a Ministry. ◉ ~본부 the Cabinet organization headquarters.

**조각**(彫刻) sculpture; engraving; carving. ~하다 sculpture; engrave; carve. ¶ ~적인 sculptural / ~ 같은 얼굴 chiseled features / 나무에 상(像)을 ~하다 carve an image in wood.
◉ ~가 a sculptor; an engraver. ~도 a chisel; an engraving knife; a graver (동판용). ~물〔품〕 a (piece of) sculpture; an engraving; a carving; a statue (조각상). ~술 sculptural art; sculpture; the plastic art; engraving.

**조각나다** ① 《갈라지다》 be broken to pieces; split in pieces; break into splinters; splinter; break; cleave. ¶ 산산이 ~ go 〔be smashed〕 to pieces 〔into fragments〕 / 두 ~ break 〔be broken〕 in two. ② 《의견이》 have a split in opinion; differ.

**조각조각** in 〔to〕 pieces 〔bits, fragments, shreds〕. ¶ ~ 부서지다 break to pieces / ~ 찢다 tear to pieces / 헝겊을 ~ 이어서 이불을 만들다 make 〔piece together〕 a patchwork quilt.

**조간**(朝刊) a morning edition 〔issue〕. ¶ 오늘 ~의 일면 기사는 무엇이지 What is the front-page article of today's morning paper?
◉ ~신문 a morning paper.

**조갈**(燥渴) thirst. ¶ ~이 나다 feel 〔get〕 thirsty; be easily parched. ◉ ~증 a disease attended by great thirst.

**조감도**(鳥瞰圖) a bird's-eye view; an airscape; 《항공 사진》 an air view.

**조감독**(助監督) 〖영화〗 an assistant director.

**조갑**(爪甲) nails; fingernails (손톱); toenails (발톱).

**조강**(粗鋼) crude steel.

**조강지처**(糟糠之妻) a wife who has shared *one's* difficulties; *one's* wife married in poverty; *one's* old life partner. ¶ ~는 불하당(不下堂) One should respect his wife who has shared his adversity.

**조개** a clam; (a) shellfish; a bivalve. ¶ ~를 캐다 dig (for) shellfish 〔clams〕.
◉ ~관자 the adductor muscle (of shellfish). ~구름 a cirrocumulus. ~껍질 a shell; a clamshell. ~무지 a shell heap 〔mound〕. ~볼 《볼》 protruding 〔plump〕 cheeks. ~탄 oval briquettes. ~탕 shellfish soup. 조갯살 the flesh of a shellfish; clam meat.

**조객**(弔客) a caller for condolence; a person calling to express his sympathy. ◉ ~록 a guest book for condolers.

**조건**(條件) a condition; 《지급 등의》 a term; a proviso (단서); a qualification (제한); a requirement (필요 조건). ¶ 첫째 ~ the first prerequisite / 계약의 ~ the terms of a contract / 열악한 노동~ poor working conditions / 부대~ a collateral condition / 필수~ an indispensable condition; a precondition / 지급~ terms of payment / 매매 〔거래〕의 ~ the terms of sale 〔trade〕/ 회원이 될 수 있는 ～ a membership requirement / 무리가 없는 ～ reasonable terms / …을 고르는 세 가지 ～ the three terms for choosing 《a spouse, a job》/ 필요하고도 충분한 ～ the necessary and sufficient condition / 아무 ～도 없이 with no strings attached.

조건으로: 무～으로 unconditionally / 유리한 ～으로 on favorable terms / 불리한 ～으로 on unfavorable condition / 동등한 ～으로 on equal terms; on even board 《with》/ 상당한 ～으로 on fair terms / 몹시 까다로운 ～으로 under the toughest conditions / …한다는 ～으로 on condition of 《our surrender》; on condition 〔under the condition〕 that 《we should surrender immediately》; provided 〔on the understanding〕 that 《he should resign》/ 분배에 참여한다는 ～으로 on condition of sharing 《in》/ 적어도 60일 전에 통고한다는 ～으로 subject to at least sixty day's previous notice / …라는 ～으로 허락하다 give permission on condition that 《he shall return it in a week》/ …을 ～으로 하다 make it a condition that … / …을 ～으로 하고 있다 be subject to 《your consent》; be contingent on 《your agreement》/ …을 ～으로 하는 약속 a promise conditional on 《*one's* resignation》.

조건을: ～을 붙이다 make 〔set〕 conditions; attach a condition 《to *one's* proposal》; impose conditions 《on》/ 까다로운 ～을 붙이다 set 〔lay down〕 iron-bound conditions / ～을 받아들이다 accept a condition / ～을 어기다 violate conditions / ～을 지키게 하다 hold 《*a person*》 to terms / 그 기부에 아무런 ～을 붙이지 않다 tie no strings to *one's* gift / 일정한 ～을 설정하다 stipulate for certain terms / ～을 변경하다 modify the terms / ～을 채우다〔만족시키다〕 meet the qualifications / 제기한 ～을 철회하다 waive conditions mentioned / ～을 가급적 완화하다 make the condition as easy as possible / ～을 정하고 약속하다 promise on fixed condition.

¶ 회사측은 그 ～을 받아들였다 The management side accepted the terms. / 보수를 준다는 ～이라면 하겠다 I will do it, if I get paid. / 더 좋은 ～을 다른 바이어가 제의하였다 Better terms were offered by other buyers. / 건강은 행복의 필요 ～이다 Health is a necessary condition of happiness. / 이 계약은 몇 가지 ～이 붙어 있다 This contract imposes several conditions. / 그것을 승낙하는 데 있어 한가지 ～이 있다 I agree to it on one condition. / ～에 따라서는 자네 제의를 받아들일 수도 있다 According to the terms, I may accept your proposal.

◉ ～문 〖문법〗 a conditional (sentence). ～반사 〖생리〗 a conditioned reflex: ～반사를 일으키다 cause a conditioned reflex; condition. ～반응 〖심리〗 a conditioned response. ～법 〖문법〗 the conditional mood. ～절 〖문법〗 a conditional (clause).

**조건부**(條件附) ¶ ～의 conditional; conditioned; qualified / ～로 conditionally; with conditions attached; with (a) proviso / …라는〔한다는〕 ～로 on condition that 《you stay at least for three years》/ ～로 승낙하다 give a qualified consent / 몇가지 ～로 동의한다 I will agree with some reservations. ◉ ～계약〔협정〕 a conditional contract 〔agreement〕. ～권리 a conditional right. ～매매 conditional sales. ～법률행위 a juristic act subject to conditions. ～선적지시서 a conditional shipping order. ～승낙 a qualified consent. ～승인 conditional approval. ～유산 a conditional legacy; an estate upon condition. ～의무 an obligation subject to conditions. ～인수〔배서〕 conditional acceptance 〔endorsement〕. ～채용 《임용》 a conditional appointment; 《고용》 a conditional employment.

**조견표**(早見表) a chart; a table. ◉ 계산 ～ a ready reckoner. 전화번호～ telephone numbers at a glance.

**조경**(造景) landscape architecture. ◉ ～가 a landscape architect 〔gardener〕. ～술 landscape architecture 〔gardening〕.

**조계**(早計) rashness; prematurity. ¶ ～의 premature; rash; hasty.

**조계**(租界) a settlement; a concession. ◉ 영국～ a British concession.

**조계종**(曹溪宗) 〖불교〗 the *Chogye* Order. ◉ 대한불교 ～ 총무원장 the executive chief of the Korean Buddhist *Chogye* Order.

**조고**(祖考) *one's* deceased grandfather.

**조곡**(弔哭) wailing in mourning; keening. ～하다 wail in mourning; keen.

**조곡**(組曲) 〖음악〗 a (musical) suite.

**조공**(朝貢) 〖고제도〗 tribute (to a country from a vassal state). ～하다 pay tribute《to a country》. ◉ ～국 a tributary state.

**조관**(條款) an article; a clause; a provision; a stipulation. ◉ 최혜국～ a most-favored nation provision.

**조관**(朝官) a court official; a courtier; [총칭] the court.

**조광**(躁狂) a mad excitement; a frenzy; 「a mania.

**조광권**(租鑛權) a mineral right; a mining concession.

**조교**(助敎) an assistant teacher 〔instructor〕; an assistant (조수).

**조교**(照校) collation. ～하다 collate. ◉～전보 a collated telegram.

**조교**(調敎) training; breaking. ～하다 break (in) 《a wild horse》; train《a horse》; tame《a tiger》. ◉ ～사 a 《horse》 trainer 〔breaker, tamer〕.

**조교수**(助敎授) an assistant professor.

**조국**(祖國) *one's* fatherland 〔motherland, homeland〕; *one's* native 〔mother〕 country. ¶ ～을 방위하다 defend *one's* fatherland / ～을 위하여 싸우다 fight for *one's* fatherland / ～을 버리다 leave *one's* country; expatriate *oneself*. ◉ ～근대화 the modernization of *one's* fatherland. ～순례 대행진 the Grand March through the Fatherland. ～애 love for *one's* country; patriotism: ～애에 불타다 burn with love for *one's* country.

**조규**(條規) articles《of a law, of a regulation》; provisions; a stipulation.

**조그마하다, 조그맣다** ⇨ 자그마하다.

**조그만큼** just a little 〔few〕.

**조금** ①《양》 a little (★ a few, a little은 각각 수·양에 있어서 긍정을 나타내며, few, little은 부정에 중점을 둠); a small quantity《of》; some. ¶ 아주 ～ only a very little; just a little 〔bit〕 / ～ 더 a little more《water》/ ～씩 little by little; a little at a time; bit by bit / 물을 ～ 탄 위스키 whisky with a splash 〔dash〕 of water / 양념으로 후춧가루를 ～ 넣다 season with a dash of pepper / ～ 밖에 돈이 없다 I have only a little money. / 돈이 ～ 필요하다 I need some money. / 차를 ～ 더 주시오 Give me some more 〔a little〕 tea, please.
②《수》 a few; a small number《of》; some. ¶ 그는 친구가 ～은 있다 He has a few friends. / 그는 친구가 ～밖에 없다 He has few friends. / 이 작문에는 오류가 ～ 있다 There are some mistakes in this composition. / 책을 ～ 더 보여 주십시오 Please show a few more 〔some more〕 books.
③《정도》 slightly; a little; a bit; a trifle; somewhat; a shade. ¶ ～씩 by degrees; gradually / ～이라도 친절한 마음이 있다면 if you have a spark of kindness in you / ～은 알고 있다 have some knowledge《of》/ 오늘은 기분이 ～ 좋다 I feel a little 〔shade〕 better today. / 그는 머리가 ～ 이상하다 He is a little out of his mind. / ～ 숙달되었습니까 Have you made any progress? / ～ 놀랐을 뿐이오 It just surprised me a little, that's all. / ～만 주의하면 그런 일은 방지할 수 있었을 것이다 A little care would have prevented it. / ～ 조용히 해 주게 Less noise, please. / 그는 귀가 ～ 안 들린다 He is slightly 〔a little〕 deaf. /「너 프랑스 말을 할 줄 아니」—「～ 하지」 "Do you speak French?"—"Yes, I do, but just a little." / 그는 일하는 것이 ～씩 나아진다 His work is improving little by little. / 그의 병세가 ～ 나아졌다 He is slightly 〔a little〕 better.
④《시간》 (for) a moment; just; a (little) while. ¶ ～지나면 in a little while; in a short time; a little later; shortly; soon / ～ 전에 a little while ago; not long ago / ～ 있다 오너라 Call again a little later. / ～만 기다려 주시오 Wait a moment 〔bit〕, please. *or* Just a moment.
⑤《거리》 a little way; a short distance. ¶ ～ 떨어져서 a little way off / ～씩 앞으로 나아가다 advance inch by inch / ～ 가니까 강이 나왔다 A little way on, we came to a river. / 경찰서는 ～ 더 가면 있다 The police station is a little way off.

**조금**(潮一) the neap tide.

**조금도** 《not》 in the least; 《not》 at all; 《not》 in the slightest degree. ¶ 나는 ～ 놀라지 않았다 I was not a bit surprised. / 그것을 ～ 예기치 않았다 That is the last thing I expected. *or* I did not expect it at all. / 나는 그것에 대해서 ～ 모른다 I know nothing about it. / 그것에 비하여 ～ 뒤지지 않는다 This is just as good as that. / 공사는 ～ 진척되지 않았다 The works did not show 〔make〕 any progress.

**조급**(早急) ¶ ～히 immediately; at once; without delay; as quickly as possible / ～한 회답 요망 A prompt answer is required. / 이 문제는 ～히 해결할 필요가 있다 This matter needs an

immediate 〔a prompt〕 solution.
**조급**(躁急) ∼하다 (be) quick-tempered; hasty; impatient. ¶ ∼한 사람 a person of impetuous disposition; a hothead / ∼히 impetuously; hastily; impatiently / 마음이 ∼하다 be driven by impetuosity / 그렇게 ∼히 굴지 마라 Don't be so impatient. *or* There is no hurry.
◉ ∼증 a quick 〔hot, short〕 temper; impatience; hastiness.
**조기** 〖어류〗 a croaker. ◉ ∼젓 salted 〔pickled〕 croakers.
**조기**(弔旗) a mourning flag; 《반기》 a flag at half-mast. ¶ ∼를 달다 hang 〔hoist〕 a flag at half-mast; display 〔put out〕 a flag draped in black.
**조기**(早起) getting up early; early rising. ∼하다 get up early in the morning; rise early.
**조기**(早期) an early stage 〔period〕. ¶ ∼에 발견하다 detect 〔find, spot〕 《a disease》 in early stages; find 〔spot〕 《a disease》 early (enough) / 이런 종류의 암은 ∼에 발견하면 고칠 수 있다 This sort of cancer can be cured if it is discovered early enough.
◉ ∼경보 체제 the early warning system. ∼교육 early education; 《학령전의》 preschool education. ∼발견 early detection 《of cancer》. ∼사용 an early use; advance use. ∼상환 advanced redemption. ∼졸업 the early graduation of superior 〔excellent〕 students. ∼진단 early diagnosis; an early checkup: ∼진단을 받다 be diagnosed in good time. ∼치료 early treatment: ∼치료로 목숨을 건졌다 An early treatment has saved his life. ∼타결 early rapprochement; an early settlement of issues (pending between...). ∼탐지 early detection 《of the enemy infiltration》. ∼퇴직 early retirement.
**조깅** jogging. ¶ ∼을 하다 practice jogging / ∼은 살을 빼고 건강을 증진시키는 좋은 방법이다 Jogging is a good way to lose weight and improve *one's* health.
**조끼**[1] 《옷》 a vest 《미》; a waistcoat 《영》. ◉ ∼적삼 a sleeved vest.
**조끼**[2] 《맥주 따위의》 a beer mug; a tankard; a jug. ¶ 한 ∼ 가득한 맥주 a jugful of beer.
**조난**(遭難) a disaster; an accident; 《배의》 (a) shipwreck. ∼하다 meet with a disaster 〔an accident〕; be in distress; be wrecked. ¶ 그들은 산에서 ∼당했다 They met with a disaster in the mountains. / 태풍으로 많은 선박이 ∼당했다 A lot of ships were wrecked by the typhoon.
◉ ∼구조대 a rescue party 〔team〕. ∼구조선 a rescue boat; 《항공기 사고의》 a crash boat. ∼선 a ship in distress (조난 중의); a wrecked ship (난파한). ∼신호 《pick up》 a distress signal 〔call〕; 《무선의》 《send》 an SOS (call): ∼신호를 내다〔받다〕 send out 〔pick up〕 an SOS. ∼자 a victim; a sufferer; 《생존자》 a survivor: 철도 사고의 ∼자 victims of a railroad accident / ∼자의 이야기를 듣다 hear the account of a survivor. ∼지 the place of a disaster; a disaster area. ∼현장 the scene of a disaster 〔an accident〕.
**조달**(調達) supply (공급); procurement (일용품 등); purveyance (식료품의); raising (돈의); preparation (조제); fulfillment (주문의). ∼하다 supply; provide; furnish 《*a person* with *a thing*》; raise 《money for...》; purvey. ¶ 자금을 ∼하다 raise funds / 여행비를 ∼하다 raise the money for the trip / 정부는 이재민을 위해 식량을 ∼했다 The government furnished the sufferers with food. ◉ ∼과 the purchasing 〔supplies〕 section. ∼기관 a procurement agency. ∼청 the Supply Administration. 해외∼ offshore procurement. 현지∼률 《부품 따위의》 domestic content.
**조당**(粗糖) raw 〔unrefined〕 sugar.
**조대** a clay 〔bamboo〕 pipe.
**조도**(照度) 〖물리〗 intensity of illumination. ◉ ∼계 an illuminometer.
**조동사**(助動詞) 〖문법〗 an auxiliary verb.
**조라떨다** 《경망스럽게 망치다》 bungle by a rash 〔flighty〕 act; mess up; upset the apple cart.
**조락**(凋落) 《식물의》 withering; 《영락》 decline; decay. ∼하다 wither; decline; wane; decay. ¶ ∼의 길을 걷다 head for ruin 〔downfall〕 / 자연주의 문학의 ∼ the decay of the naturalist school in literature.
**조력**(助力) aid; help; assistance. ∼하다 aid; help; assist; lend 《*a person*》 a helping hand; give 〔render〕 《*a person*》 assistance 《in, at》 (★ assist *a person* to do this라고는 하지 않음). ¶ …의 ∼으로 with 〔by〕 *a person's* kind assistance; by 〔with〕 the help of... / 남의 ∼을 빌지 않고 without another's

help; by *oneself;* single-handed / ～을 청하다 ask for《*a person's*》help; look to《*a person*》for assistance / 그의 ～으로 궁지를 벗어났다 He helped me out of the difficulty.
◉ ～자 a helper; an assistant.

**조력**(潮力) tidal energy〔power〕.
◉ ～발전 tidal power generation. ～발전소 a tidal-powered electric plant.

**조련**(操鍊) ①《훈련》training exercises; military drill; maneuvers. ～하다 drill; train. ②《괴롭힘》afflict; torment; harass; distress; torture. ～하다 torment; harass. ◉ ～질 afflicting; tormenting; harassing.

**조령모개**(朝令暮改) inconsistent〔changeable〕behavior; lack of principle; an unsettled course of action. ¶ ～의 정책 a fickle〔an inconsistent〕policy; an on-again-off-again policy.

**조례**(弔禮) the forms observed for condolence; condolence etiquette.

**조례**(條例) regulations; rules; laws; an ordinance; acts.

> 용법 **ordinance** 법률 요건으로서 국회의 심의를 필요로 하지 않는 지방공공단체 따위가 정하는 법규. **law** 국회의 심의가 필요한 것. **regulation** law나 ordinance에 규정된 범위 안에서 내려지는 공적인 명령에 의한 「규칙, 규정」.

¶ 시 ～ a municipal ordinance / ～를 반포하다〔취소하다〕issue〔revoke〕regulations〔an ordinance〕.

**조례**(朝禮) a morning assembly.

**조로**(早老) premature old age; premature senility〔decrepitude〕;〖의학〗progeria. ¶ ～의 prematurely old〔aged〕/ 그는 ～해 보인다 He looks older than his age. ◉ ～현상 symptoms of premature old age.

**조로**(朝露) morning dew. ¶ ～같은 인생 transient life.

**조로아스터** 〖종교〗Zoroaster. ◉ ～교 Zoroastrianism: ～교도 a Zoroastrian.

**조롱**(吊籠) a hanging cage〔basket〕.

**조롱**(鳥籠) a (bird)cage.

**조롱**(嘲弄) ridicule; derision; mockery; scorn; a scoff; raillery; jeering. ～하다 laugh at; ridicule; deride; scoff《at》; rail〔jeer〕《at》; make a fool of. ¶ ～하여 in ridicule《of》/ ～당하다 be ridiculed; be held in derision; be treated with scoff / 비겁하다고 ～하다 taunt《*a person*》with cowardice / 그는 나를 ～했다 He made game〔a mock〕of me. ◉ ～자 a scoffer.

> 용법 **ridicule** 남을 조롱하는 것으로서 때로는 악의를 품고 놀리는 것. **mockery** 흉내를 내면서 비웃는 것. **scorn** 말이나 태도로 멸시하는 것. **scoff** 오만·불신 등의 생각을 품고 비웃는 것으로서 보통 복수형으로 쓰임.

**조롱박** ①《호리병박》a bottle gourd. ②《쪽박》a water dipper made of that gourd.

**조롱이** 〖조류〗a sparrow hawk.

**조루**(早漏) 〖의학〗(a) premature ejaculation. ◉ ～증〔환자〕a case〔patient〕of premature ejaculation.

**조류**(鳥類) birds; fowls; the feathered tribe. ◉ ～보호 bird protection. ～학 ornithology: ～학자 an ornithologist.

**조류**(潮流) ①《조수》a (tidal) current; a tide. ¶ ～가 세다 The tide runs strong. / ～는 저쪽에서 방향을 바꿔 흐른다 The tide runs in a different direction over there. ②《풍조》a current; a trend; a tendency. ¶ 시대의 ～를 따르다 swim〔go〕with the current (of the times) / 시대 ～에 역행하다 go against the current of the times.

**조류**(藻類) 〖식물〗an alga (*pl.* algae [ǽldʒiː]); seaweed (해조); a waterweed (수초). ¶ ～의 algoid.
◉ ～학 algology: ～학자 an algologist.

**조르개**《줄》a tightening string〔cord〕.

**조르기** 〖유도〗choking techniques; a strangle hold.

**조르다** ①《팽팽하게》tighten;《매다》tie (up); bind;《끈 등을》put on《a tie》; buckle;《목을》strangle; wring (비틀듯이). ¶ 허리띠를 ～ tighten〔draw up〕*one's* belt / 가야금의 줄을 ～ tighten〔screw up〕the strings of a Korean harp / 닭의 목을 ～ wring the neck of a chicken / 목을 졸라 죽이다 strangle《*a person*》(to death).
②《졸라대다》ask〔pester〕for; keep after《*a person*》for; beg〔importune, press〕for. ¶ 어머니한테 돈을 달라고 ～ beg〔pester〕mother for money / 새 옷을 사 달라고 남편을 ～ keep after *one's* husband to buy a new dress / 엄마를 졸라서 과자를 사다 coax *one's* mother into buying sweets for *one.*

**조르르** ①《물줄기가》trickling; dribbling; running in a thin stream. ¶ 수돗물이 ～ 흐르다 water dribbles from the faucet / 눈물이 ～ 그녀의 뺨을 흘러

내렸다 Tears streamed down her cheeks. ② 《잽싼 걸음걸이》 at a dash; with one rush. ¶ ~ 달려가다 make a dash 《for》; go off at a dash.

**조리**(笊籬) a (bamboo) mesh dipper; a (bamboo) strainer. ¶ ~로 쌀을 일다 rinse rice using a (bamboo) strainer. ◉ ~자지 over-frequent urination; polyuria.

**조리**(條理) logic; reason. ¶ ~가 닿다 be logical; be reasonable; stand to reason / ~가 닿는 reasonable; logical; consistent; coherent / ~에 닿지 않는 unreasonable; illogical; inconsistent; lacking consistence 〔coherence〕 / ~가 닿지 않는 소리를 하다 talk incoherently; utter an incoherent remark.

**조리**(調理) ① 《조섭》 care of health. ~하다 take care of *one's* health. ② 《요리》 cooking; cookery. ~하다 prepare (food); cook. ③ 《처리》 appropriate disposal 〔handling〕 of a matter. ~하다 deal with 《*a matter*》 properly. ◉ ~대 a dresser; a kitchen table. ~법 the art of cooking; cookery; cuisine. ~사 a licensed cook. ~실 a cuisine; a kitchen.

**조리개** 《사진기의》 an iris (*pl.* ~es, irides); a diaphragm.

**조리다** boil 《fish》 down. ¶ 고기를 간장에 ~ boil beef down in soy sauce / 생선을 은근한 불에 ~ let fish simmer gently / 과일을 조리어 잼을 만들다 boil fruit down into jam.

**조리돌리다** drag 〔march〕 《a criminal》 through the streets.

**조리차하다** spend 〔use〕 sparingly; stint; be sparing of.

**조림** boiled food. ¶ 통~ canned food. ◉ 쇠고기~ beef boiled with soy sauce.

**조림**(造林) afforestation; forestation. ~하다 afforest 《a mountain》; plant trees. ◉ ~계획 a tree-planting 〔an afforestation〕 project. ~면적 an afforestation area. ~장려 encouragement of afforestation. ~정책 an afforestation 〔a reforestation〕 policy. ~지 an afforested land; a plantation (삼림). ~학 forestry.

**조립**(組立) construction; structure; fabrication; constitution (구성); 《기계의》 assembly; assembling. ~하다 assemble; construct; put 〔fit, piece〕 together; frame; set 〔fix〕 up. ¶ 기계를 ~하다 build 〔frame, construct〕 a machine; assemble 〔put together〕 a machine / 라디오〔자동차〕를 ~하다 assemble a radio 〔an auto〕 / 그의 취미는 모형 비행기 ~이다 His hobby is building model airplanes. / 우리나라에서 처음으로 ~된 F-16 전투기가 사천 공장에서 출고되어 나왔다 The nation's first assembled F-16 fighter plane rolled out from the Sach'on plant. ◉ ~공 an assembler; a fitter. ~공장 an assembly plant 〔shop〕. ~(식) 주택 a prefabricated house; a prefab. ~(식) 책장 a sectional 〔collapsible〕 book-case.

**조릿조릿하다** be held in suspense; be nervous 〔uneasy, anxious〕 about; be on the edge.

**조마**(調馬) horse training 〔breaking〕. ~하다 train 〔break in〕 a horse. ◉ ~사 a horse trainer. ~장 a riding ground; a paddock.

**조마조마하다** (be) fidgety; agitated; edgy; feel anxious 〔uneasy, nervous〕; be held in suspense; be on pins and needles. ¶ 조마조마하게 하다 put 《*a person*》 into a flutter; keep 《*a person*》 in suspense; make 《*a person*》 nervous / 그의 아버지가 화내실까 ~ I am nervous at the thought that his father might get angry. / 그가 무심결에 그 일을 입 밖에 내지 않을까 몹시 조마조마했다 I was in great fear lest he should blurt it out.

**조막** a size smaller than fist. ¶ ~만하다 be smaller than the size of a fist.

**조막손** a clubhand; a claw hand. ◉ ~이 a claw-handed person.

**조만간**(早晩間) sooner or later; in (the course of) time; by and by. ¶ 이런 종류의 일은 ~ 폭로된다 This sort of thing is bound to come out sooner or later. / 내각은 ~ 총사직할 것이다 The general resignation of the Cabinet is only a question of time.

**조망**(眺望) a view; a prospect; a lookout (전망). ~하다 have a distant view of; command a view of; look out upon 〔over〕. ¶ ~이 좋다 [장소가 주어] afford 〔command〕 a fine view / 이 언덕은 ~이 좋다 This hill commands a fine view. *or* We (can) get a magnificent view from this hill. / 나무숲이 ~을 가로막고 있다 The cluster of trees obstructs the view. ◉ ~권 the right to a view.

**조망**(鳥網) a fowling 〔bird, fowler's〕 net.

**조매**(嘲罵) abuse; a jeer; revilement; insulting remarks. ~하다 revile;

taunt; rail 《at, against》; flout 《at》; ridicule.

**조면**(繰綿) cotton ginning. ◉ ~공장 a ginnery. ~기 a cotton gin.

**조명**(照明) lighting; illumination. ~하다 illuminate; light (up). ¶ ~이 불충분하다 be poorly illuminated / 이 교실은 ~이 좋다〔나쁘다〕 This classroom is well 〔badly〕 lighted.
◉ ~공학 illumination engineering. ~기구 lighting fixtures 〔equipment〕. ~기사 an illuminator; a lighting technician; a spotlightman. ~등 《street, tunnel》 lighting. ~실 a lighting room. ~차 a floodlight car. ~탄 a flare (bomb); a star shell. ~효과 lighting effects.

**조명**(助命) = 구명(救命).

**조명나다**(嘲名—) have a bad reputation; have an ill name; be notorious.

**조모**(祖母) a grandmother.

**조목**(條目) articles; clauses; items. ¶ ~조목 item by item / ~별로 쓰다 itemize / 그것은 이 ~에 해당한다 It comes under this clause.

**조무래기** ① 《물건》 small articles; sundries; odds and ends. ② 《아이》 small children; little kids; kiddies; small fry.

**조문**(弔文) a (written) funeral address; a letter of condolence; a memorial address.

**조문**(弔問) a call of condolence. ~하다 make a call of condolence; call 《on *a person*》 to express *one's* condolence 〔sympathy〕. ¶ ~을 받다 receive callers for condolence. ◉ ~객 a condoler; a condolence caller. ~사절 condolence delegations; a 《U.S.》 delegation to memorial service.

**조문**(條文) 《본문》 the text 《of regulations, *etc.*》; 《조항》 provisions. ¶ ~에 있는 바와 같이 as stipulated in the text / 조약의 ~ the text of a treaty / 헌법의 ~ the provisions of the Constitution / ~에 명기되어 있다 be specified 〔expressly stated〕 in the text 《of the law》.

**조물주**(造物主) the Creator; the Maker (of the universe); Supreme Being; God.

**조미**(調味) seasoning; flavoring. ~하다 season; flavor; give flavor 《to》.
◉ ~료 a seasoning; a condiment; a flavor enhancer: 인공 ~료 a synthetic flavoring matter; artificial flavors.

**조밀**(稠密) density. ~하다 (be) dense; thick; close; crowded. ¶ 인구가 ~하다 [장소가 주어] be densely 〔thickly〕 populated; have a high population density / 그 근처에는 인가가 ~하다 Houses are closely crowded in that neighborhood.

**조바심하다**[1] 《조의 타작》 thresh millet.

**조바심하다**[2] be cautious 《about》; be nervous 〔anxious〕 《about》; worry *oneself;* feel impatient 〔restless〕. ¶ 일이 잘 안될까 ~ be nervous that things might go wrong / (아무가) 돌아오기를 조바심하며 기다리다 wait in anxious suspense for 《*a person's*》 arrival.

**조박**(糟粕) 《재강》 brewers' grains; draff; lees; 《학문의》 lees; dregs; leavings. ¶ 고인의 ~을 핥다 imitate the styles of old masters; follow the beaten tracks.

**조반**(朝飯) breakfast. ¶ ~을 들다 take breakfast; eat 〔have〕 *one's* breakfast.

**조발**(調髮) a haircut; hairdressing.

**조발성**(早發性) 〖의학〗 (being) precocious. ◉ ~치매(癡呆) schizophrenia.

**조밥** boiled millet (and rice).

**조방**(助幇) pandering; pimping; procuring. ¶ ~을 보다 pimp; pander.
◉ ~꾼, ~꾸니 《오입판의》 a pander; a pimp; a procurer; 《놀이동무》 a children's attendant 〔nurse, companion〕.

**조방**(粗放) ~하다 (be) reckless; careless. ◉ ~농법 extensive farming. ~농업 extensive agriculture.

**조백**(早白) having gray 〔white〕 hair in youth; premature growth of gray hair. ~하다 《*one's hair*》 turn gray early in *one's* life; have gray hair while (*one* is still) young.

**조뱅이** 〖식물〗 a kind of thistle.

**조변석개**(朝變夕改) changeableness; inconsistency; capriciousness; fickleness. ~하다 change constantly; take an unsettled course of action; keep changing 〔revising〕. ¶ ~의 정책 a fickle 〔an inconsistent〕 policy.

**조병창**(造兵廠) an armament works 〔factory〕; an arsenal; an armory.

**조복**(朝服) 〖고제도〗 a court 〔an official〕 dress 〔suit〕; court attire.

**조부**(祖父) a grandfather. ◉ ~모 grandparents.

**조분**(鳥糞) bird droppings; guano (바다새의). ◉ ~석 guano (deposit).

**조붓하다** be a bit narrow; be on the narrow side.

**조비**(祖妣) *one's* deceased grandmother.

**조사**(弔詞) words 〔a letter〕 of condolence; a memorial address. ¶ ~를 하다 express *one's* condolence.

**조사**(早死) a premature 〔an untimely, an early〕 death. ~하다 die young; die an early death; die at an early age; die before *one's* time.

**조사**(助詞) 〖문법〗 a postpositional word; a postposition. 「sect 〔school〕.

**조사**(祖師) the founder of a (religious)

**조사**(照射) irradiation. ~하다 irradiate. ¶ 뢴트겐을 ~하다 apply X-rays 《to》; X-ray 《*a person's* chest》.

**조사**(調査) (an) investigation; (an) examination; an inquiry; a survey; 《인구의》 (a) census. ~하다 investigate; check; inspect; probe; examine 《into》; inquire 〔look〕 into; make inquiries 《about》; make an investigation; take a census 《of the population》.

> **용법** **investigate** 「조사하다」, 「수사하다」의 뜻으로 조직적으로 추적하여 사실 관계를 밝힌다는 뜻. **check** 「조사하다」, 「확인하다」의 뜻으로 대조하여 바른지 어떤지를 조사하는 것. **inspect** 「검사하다」의 뜻으로 기준에 비추어 결점이나 잘못, 흠의 유무를 상세히 조사하는 것. **examine** 사실·본질·특징·상태 등을 면밀히 조사 또는 검사하는 것.

¶ 당국의 ~에 의하면 according to the investigation made by the authorities / ~해 보니 upon investigation / ~중이다 [사물이 주어] be under investigation / 원인을 ~하다 investigate the cause; inquire into the cause / …을 철저히 ~하다 make a thorough 〔an intensive〕 investigation 《into》; investigate *something* thoroughly / 고대 유적을 ~하다 survey the remains of ancient times / ~한 결과 그것은 단순한 소문으로 판명되었다 On 〔Upon〕 investigation it was found to be a mere rumor. / 위원회는 분쟁을 ~했다 The commission made an inquiry into the dispute. / 당국은 사고의 원인을 ~하기 시작했다 The authorities have started to investigate the cause of the accident.

◉ ~결과 findings. ~과 the investigation division. ~관 an examiner; an investigator. ~단 an inquiry commission; a research group; a study team 《to》. ~보고 a report of investigation; a surveyor's report; finding. ~부 an inquiry section. ~용지 《여론 따위의》 a questionnaire. ~원 an investigator; an examiner. ~위원 a committee of inquiry: ~위원회 an investigation committee. ~자료 data for investigation.

**조산**(早産) premature birth 〔delivery〕. ~하다 [산모가 주어] give birth to a baby prematurely; have *one's* baby prematurely; be prematurely delivered of a child; [아이가 주어] be born prematurely. ◉ ~아 a prematurely born infant: ~아실 a premature babies room.

**조산**(助産) midwifery. ◉ ~사(師) a maternity nurse; a midwife (*pl.* -wives).

**조산**(造山) an artificial mound (in a garden); a miniature hill; a rockery. ◉ ~운동 〖지질〗 orogenic 〔mountain-making〕 movements; orogeny.

**조삼모사**(朝三暮四) swindling by a clever trick. 「《with a mourner》.

**조상**(弔喪) condolence. ~하다 condole

**조상**(早霜) an early frost. ~하다 have an early frost.

**조상**(祖上) an ancestor; a forefather; a progenitor. ¶ ~의 ancestral / ~ 전래의 ancestral; hereditary / ~을 숭배하다 worship ancestors / ~의 이름을 더럽히다 bring disgrace upon the good name of *one's* fathers / 이것은 ~ 전래의 보물이다 This is a family heirloom. ◉ ~숭배 ancestor worship.

**조상**(彫像) a (carved) statue; sculptured figure. ¶ 대리석 ~ a statue of marble. 「rite for *one's* ancestors.

**조상굿**(祖上—) 〖민속〗 a shamanistic

**조색**(調色) mixing colors. ◉ ~판 a painter's palette. 「species.

**조생종**(早生種) 〖농업〗 a precocious

**조서**(詔書) a royal edict 〔rescript〕.

**조서**(調書) a record; a written evidence. ¶ ~를 받다 put 《a deposition》 on record / 경찰은 용의자의 진술을 ~에 기록했다 The police put the suspect's confession on record.

**조석**(朝夕) 《때》 morning and evening; 《밥》 morning meal and evening meal. ¶ 목숨이 ~에 있다 be on the brink 〔verge〕 of death. ◉ ~반(飯) breakfast and supper.

**조석**(潮汐) 《간만》 ebb and flow; 《조수》 a tide. ◉ ~운동 a tidal movement.

**조선**(造船) shipbuilding; ship construction. ~하다 build a ship.

◉ ~계획 a shipbuilding program. ~공 a shipbuilding worker; 《목선의》 a shipwright. ～공학 marine engineering. ～기사 a marine 〔naval〕 engineer 〔architect〕; a shipbuilder. ～능력 shipbuilding capacity. ～대 a shipway; 《경사진》 a slipway; a slip. ～량 shipbuilding tonnage. ～소 a shipbuilding yard; a shipyard; a dockyard. ～술(術) shipbuilding. ～업 the shipbuilding industry; the shipyard business: ～업계 the shipbuilding circles. ～학 naval architecture.

**조선**(朝鮮) 『역사』 *Chosŏn;* Korea. ¶ ～왕조 실록 *the True record of the Chosŏn dynasty.* 「(調理) ①.

**조섭**(調攝) the care of health. ＝조리

**조성**(助成) furtherance; aid; assistance. ～하다 《보조하다》 assist; aid; 《촉진하다》 further; promote. ¶ 농업～ 계획 a farm subsidy program. ◉ ～금 a subsidy; a bounty; a grant: 주택～금 housing subsidies / ～금을 지급하다 subsidize; grant a bounty.

**조성**(造成) 《토지의》 development; creation; preparation 《of a housing site》; 《매립》 reclamation. ～하다 make up; build up; create 《land》; prepare 《the ground for housing》; reclaim 《land from the sea》. ¶ 택지～ development of residential sites / 택지를 ～하다 develop land for housing lots; prepare a housing site / 산림을 ～하다 make a woodland; afforest a mountain / 사회 불안을 ～하다 create social unrest / 공포 분위기를 ～하다 produce 〔create〕 a terror atmosphere.

**조성**(組成) 《구성 내용》 composition; 《물건의 구조》 constitution; formation; 《조립》 make-up. ～하다 compose; constitute; form; make up. ◉ ～물 a composite; a composition. ～체 an organism.

**조세**(租稅) taxes; taxation. ¶ ～를 과하다 lay 〔impose, levy〕 a tax 《upon》 / ～를 납입하다 pay taxes / ～를 부담하다 be burdened with a tax / ～를 면제하다 exempt from taxes / 과중한 ～에 신음하다 groan under the heavy burden of taxation.

◉ ～감면 규제법 the Regulation Law on Tax Reduction and Exemption. ～감면 혜택 《various》 tax privileges. ～범 처벌법 the Law on Punishment of Tax Evaders. ～법정주의 no taxation without representation. ～부담 a tax burden. ～부담률 ratio of taxation against national income. ～수입 internal 〔inland〕 revenues. ～징수 tax collection. ～체납 tax delinquency 〔arrears〕.

**조소**(彫塑) 『미술』 carving and sculpture (조각과 소상); a carved clay model (소상); the plastic arts (조형미술). ◉ ～가 a plastic artist.

**조소**(嘲笑) a sardonic smile; a scornful laugh; a ridicule; derision; a sneer. ～하다 laugh derisively; laugh with scorn; deride; ridicule; mock; scoff 《at》; jeer 《at》. ¶ ～적(으로) scornful(ly); mocking(ly); derisive (-ly) / ～받다 be mocked and derided; be jeered 〔laughed〕 at / 세인의 ～를 사다 excite the public derision; bring ridicule upon *oneself* / ～거리가 되다 be a laughing-stock 《of》; find *oneself* amid the jeers and laughter of everyone.

**조속기**(調速機) a speed regulator.

**조속히**(早速―) as soon as possible; at the earliest possible moment; at your earliest convenience.

**조수**(助手) an assistant; a helper. ¶ ～로 일하다 serve as an assistant; assist. ◉ ～석 《자동차의》 the passenger seat; the assistant driver's seat. 여자～ a coadjutress. 연구～ a research assistant. 외과～ a surgeon's mate; a surgical assistant. 운전～ an assistant driver.

**조수**(鳥獸) birds and beasts; fur and feather; 《야생 동물》 wildlife. ¶ ～보호 및 수렵에 관한 법률 《violate》 the Law on the Protection of Birds and Beasts and Hunting / 부근에는 ～와 어류가 많다 Fur, fin and feather abound in the neighborhood. ◉ 야생～보호 wildlife conservation: 야생～ 보호구 a wildlife sanctuary. 「a tide table.

**조수**(潮水) the tide; tidewater. ◉ ～표

**조숙**(早熟) early maturity; premature growth 〔ripeness〕; precocity. ～하다 mature 〔ripen〕 early; grow early. ¶ ～한 premature; precocious; prematurely developed / 대체로 서양인은 한국인보다 ～하다 Broadly speaking, Westerners mature earlier than Koreans. ◉ ～아 a precocious child.

**조식**(粗食) a plain 〔poor〕 diet; simple 〔plain〕 food; coarse 〔plain〕 fare; a frugal meal. ～하다 take a simple meal; live on poor food 〔a frugal diet〕. ¶ ～에 익숙해지다 become accustomed to plain fare.

**조식**(朝食) breakfast. ⇨ 조반(朝飯).

**조신**(朝臣) court officials; courtiers.

**조신**(操身) carefulness of conduct 〔behavior〕; circumspection. ～하다 be careful of *oneself;* exercise circumspection.

**조실부모**(早失父母) losing *one's* parents early in life. ～하다 lose parents early in life. ¶ 그는 ～했다 He lost his parents at an early age.

**조심**(操心) 《주의》 carefulness; care; heed; 《신중》 prudence; circumspection; 《경계》 precaution; vigilance; guard. ～하다 take care 《with》; be careful 〔cautious〕 《about》; take precautions 《against》; watch out 《for》; guard 《against》; use prudence 《in》; be circumspect 《in》; beware 《of》. ¶ ～하여 carefully; cautiously; with care / 말을 ～하다 be careful in *one's* speech / 몸을 ～하다 be careful of *one's* health; take care of *oneself* / 속지 않게 ～하다 be careful not to get cheated / ～해서 걷다 walk with care / 어두워서 안됐지만, ～해 가십시오 I'm sorry it's so dark, be careful on your way home. / 그는 위험 인물이니 ～해라 He is a dangerous character, watch your step around him. / 앞으로는 ～하겠습니다 I will be more cautious in the future. / 개～《게시》 Beware of the dog. / 길 건널 때는 자동차를 ～해라 Watch out for cars when you cross the road. ◉ ～성 cautiousness; carefulness; discretion; prudence; circumspectness. 불～ precaution against fire; 《게시》 Watch out for fires ! *or* Beware of fire ! *or* Fire danger ! *or* Inflammable ! *or* Flammable !

**조아리다** knock (*one's* forehead) on the floor 〔ground〕; kowtow; give a deep bow (in reverence).

**조아팔다** sell in small lots 《of》; break 《it》 up into small lots to sell.

**조악**(粗惡) coarseness; crudeness. ～하다 (be) coarse; crude; inferior. ¶ 품질이 ～하다 be coarse in 〔be of coarse〕 quality. ◉ ～품 coarse 〔crude〕 articles; goods of poor 〔inferior〕 quality.

**조암광물**(造岩鑛物) rock-forming minerals.

**조야**(粗野) rusticity; rudeness; boorishness; coarseness; vulgarity; grossness. ～하다 (be) coarse; rude; rustic; rough; vulgar; unrefined; gross.

**조야**(朝野) the government and the people 〔public〕; the (whole) nation. ¶ ～의 명사 men of distinction both in and out of the government.

**조약**(條約) a treaty; a convention; an agreement; a pact. ¶ ～상의 권리〔의무〕 treaty rights 〔obligations〕 / ～에 조인하다 sign a treaty / ～을 맺다 conclude 〔make, enter into〕 a treaty 《with》 / ～을 지키다〔어기다, 깨뜨리다〕 observe 〔violate, break〕 a treaty / ～을 폐기하다 abrogate 〔denounce〕 a treaty / 강화 ～이 두 나라 사이에서 조인되었다 A peace treaty was concluded between the two countries. ◉ ～가맹국 signatory countries; the members of a treaty. ～개정 the revision 〔renewal〕 of a treaty; a treaty revision. ～국 treaty 〔signatory〕 powers. ～규정 treaty provisions 〔stipulations〕. ～비준 the ratification of a treaty. ～체결권 treaty-making powers. 보호～ a protectorate treaty. 상호 원조～ a mutual assistance pact 〔treaty〕. 평화〔통상〕～ a peace 〔commercial〕 treaty: 한국은 중국과 통상～을 맺고 있다 Korea has a commercial treaty with China.

**조약돌** gravel stone(s); bits 〔pieces〕 of gravel; pebbles.

**조어**(造語) 《말》 a coined word; a coinage; 《만들기》 coinage. ¶ 한자가 지니고 있는 고도의 ～력 the high word-forming ability of Chinese characters. ◉ ～법 word formation.

**조언**(助言) counsel; advice (★ 셀 때는 a piece 〔some bits〕 of advice로 함); a hint; a suggestion. ～하다 advise; counsel; give 《*a person*》 advice 〔counsel〕; suggest. ¶ 전문가의 ～ professional advice / ～을 구하다 ask advice 《of *a person*》 / ～을 받아들이다 take 〔listen to〕 《*a person's*》 advice / 자네 ～이 없었으면 실패했을 거네 I should have failed but for your advice. ◉ ～자 an adviser; a counselor.

**조업**(操業) work; operation. ～하다 run 《a factory》; operate 《a mine》; work 《a mill》. ¶ ～을 단축하다 reduce 〔cut down〕 operation / ～을 개시〔중지〕하다 start 〔stop〕 operation / ～을 재개하다 get back in operation; resume operation / 최근의 불경기로 우리는 ～을 단축해야 한다 We have to curtail 〔cut down, reduce〕 operations because of the recent economic recession. ◉ ～단축 short-time operation; reduction 〔curtailment〕 of operation 〔working hours〕. ～비 operating expenses. ～시간 operating hours. ～일

수 days operated. ~제한 output restriction. ~중지 a shutdown. 8시간 ~ an eight hour run 《of a factory》. 완전~ full operation: 그 공장은 완전~을 하고 있다 The factory is in full operation.

**조역**(助役) 《거드는 사람》 a helper; an assistant; 《역의》 an assistant stationmaster. ◉ ~꾼 an assistant of rough work.

**조연**(助演) support; supporting performance. ~하다 assist 〔support〕 《the leading actor》; play a supporting 〔minor〕 role 《in》. ¶ 주연 K, ~Y, starred by K, supported by Y / 최우수 ~배우(상) (an award for) the best supporting actor. ◉ ~자 a supporting player 〔actor, actress〕; a byplayer; a costar.

**조영**(造營) building; (a) construction; (an) erection. ~하다 build; erect; construct. ◉ ~물 a building; a structure. ~비 building expenses.

**조예**(造詣) knowledge; attainments. ¶ ~가 깊다 have a profound 〔deep〕 knowledge 《of》; be deeply versed 〔learned〕 《in》; be at home 《in》; possess high attainments 《in》 / 학문에 ~가 깊은 사람 a man of great erudition.

**조용하다** 《잠잠하다》 (be) quiet; still; silent; tranquil; calm; placid; 《온건하다》 (be) peaceful; serene; gentle; soft; 《점잖다》 (be) graceful; 《한적하다》 (be) deserted.

> 용법 **quiet** 시끄럽거나 떠들썩하지 않고 조용하다는 뜻. **still** 소리뿐만 아니라 움직이는 기색조차 없는 조용함을 말함. **silent** 소리가 전혀 없고 고요할 때, 또는 사람이 입을 다물고 조용히 있을 때처럼 목소리나 다른 소리가 들리지 않는다는 뜻. **calm** 바다나 마음 등이 평온하고 잔잔히 가라앉은 상태. **soft** 음악 등이 부드럽고 조용한 느낌을 주는 것을 말함. **tranquil** 마음의 동요나 들뜸이 없으면서 차분하고 조용한 상태.

¶ 조용한 목소리로 in a quiet voice / 조용한 곳 a quiet spot; a secluded place / 조용한 거리 a deserted street / 조용한 사람 a quiet(-mannered) person / 조용해지다 become 〔get, grow〕 still 〔calm, quiet〕; calm 〔quiet〕 down; 《가라앉다》 subside; become tranquil; quiet 〔die〕 down / 쥐 죽은 듯이 ~ be still with a deathly hush; be as silent as the grave / 정치 파동 후 나라가 다시 조용해졌다 The country calmed down again after the political upheaval.

**조용히** quietly; silently; calmly; gently; peacefully. ¶ ~ 하다 keep quiet 〔still〕; be silent / ~ 자고 있다 sleep quietly 〔in peace〕 / ~ 이야기하다 speak in a calm tone / ~ 하고 있다 keep quiet 〔still〕 / ~ 살다 live in quiet; lead a quiet life / ~ 들어오다 come in softly / 나중에 ~ 좀 만나지 I'll see you alone later! / ~ 다시 이야기합시다 Let's talk it over again privately. / 떠들지 말고 ~ 이야기하자 Now, let's not get excited but talk it over calmly. / 좀 ~ 해 주십시오 I wish you wouldn't make so much noise. / ~ 하시오 《게시》 Quiet, please. *or* Keep quiet. *or* No noise. / 말을 ~ 합시다 《게시》 Only quiet talk permitted here. *or* Please converse quietly.

**조우**(遭遇) ① 《신임》 winning royal confidence. ~하다 win royal confidence. ② 《만남》 an encounter; a casual meeting. ~하다 meet with 《an accident》; come across; encounter. ¶ 근접~ a close encounter / 적과 ~하다 encounter the enemy. ◉ ~전 an encounter 《action, battle》; an incidental operation.

**조운**(漕運) marine transportation. ⇨ 해운.

**조울병**(躁鬱病) 〖의학〗 a manic-depressive insanity. ◉ ~환자 a manic-depressive.

**조원**(造園) landscape gardening. ~하다 make 〔lay out〕 a garden; do the landscaping; landscape. ◉ ~가 a landscape gardener.

**조위**(弔慰) (the expression of) condolence. ~하다 condole 《with *a person* upon the death of *his* father》; offer *one's* condolences 《to》. ¶ ~의 전보를 치다 telegraph *one's* condolence 《to *a person*》. ◉ ~금 condolence money; a solatium: 유족에게 ~금을 보냈다 We sent some money as a token of condolence to the bereaved.

**조율**(調律) tuning. ~하다 tune; put 《a piano》 in tune. ¶ ~이 잘못된 피아노 a badly tuned piano / 이 피아노는 ~하지 않으면 안 된다 This piano needs tuning. ◉ ~기 a key; a regulator. ~료 a charge for tuning 《a piano》. ~사 a tuner.

**조음**(調音) 《목소리의》 articulation; modulation; 《악기의》 tuning. ~하다 articulate; tune.

**조음**(噪音) (a) noise.

**조의**(弔意) mourning; condolence; sympathy. ¶ ～를 표하다 express *one's* deep sorrow 《to》; show *one's* mourning 《for》; offer 〔express〕 *one's* condolences 《to》 / 유가족에게 우리들은 삼가 ～를 표합니다 We respectfully tender the bereaved family our condolence and sympathy. / 아버님이 돌아가셨다니 참으로 안됐습니다. 삼가 ～를 표합니다 I'm sorry your father has passed away. My condolences!

**조이스** 《아일랜드의 소설가·시인》 James Joyce (1882-1941).

**조인**(鳥人) an airman; a birdman; an aviator.

**조인**(調印) signing; signature. ～하다 sign; affix 〔set〕 *one's* seal 《to a document》; affix 〔put〕 *one's* signature 《to》; sign and seal 《a note》. ¶ 조약의 ～ a signature to the treaty / 가(假) ～하다 initial (an agreement) / 조약은 ～됐다 The treaty has been signed and sealed. ◉ ～국 a signatory (power). ～식 a signing ceremony. ～자 a signer; a signatory. ～장소 the place of signature.

**조인트** a joint. ◉ ～광고 a joint advertisement. ～리사이틀 a joint recital. ～벤처 a joint venture. ～콘서트 a joint concert.

**조작**(造作) 《제조》 manufacturing; 《날조》 invention; concoction; fabrication; falsification. ～하다 manufacture; fabricate; forge; invent; cook up; make up; concoct. ¶ ～된 이야기 「a made-up 〔an invented〕 story; a fiction / ～된 재판 a frame-up trial / ～된 민의 falsified will of the people / ～기사 a fabrication; a fabricated report / 그것은 순전히 ～이었다 It was 「a pure fabrication 〔a mere fake〕. ◉ ～극 a put-up job; a frame-up; a got-up affair; a build-up; a fabrication.

**조작**(操作) (an) operation; (a) handling; (a) manipulation. ～하다 operate 〔work〕 《a machine》; manipulate 《the market》. ¶ 금융〔시장〕～ monetary 〔market〕 manipulation / 원격～ remote control / 인위적 ～ artificial manipulation 《of prices》 / 자동～ automatic operation / 기계의 ～을 잘못하다 mishandle a machine / 이 새 컴퓨터는 ～하기 쉽다 This new computer is easy to operate. / 나는 이 기계의 ～에는 익숙지 않다 I'm not used to handling this machine.

**조잡**(粗雜) crudeness; coarseness; rudeness; roughness. ～하다 (be) rough; rude; coarse; crude; gross; shoddy. ¶ ～한 건물 a crude building / ～한 제본 loose 〔careless〕 binding / ～한 시공 shoddy construction.

**조장**(助長) furtherance; promotion. ～하다 encourage; promote; further; foster; bolster 《up》. ¶ …의 발달을 ～하다 foster 〔promote〕 the development of… / 악폐를 ～하다 aggravate 〔promote〕 evils / 폐해를 ～하다 bolster up an abuse / 국제간의 친선을 ～하다 promote international friendship / 부모의 과보호는 아이들의 의타심을 ～한다 Overprotective parents encourage their children to grow more dependent. / 그 계획은 개발도상국의 경제 성장을 ～할 것이다 The plan will promote the economic growth of developing countries.

**조장**(組長) a head; a foreman.

**조장**(鳥葬) sky burial.

**조전**(弔電) a telegram of condolence; a telegraphic condolence. ¶ ～을 치다 telegraph *one's* condolence 《to *a person*》; send a telegram of condolence 《to *a person*》.

**조절**(調節) regulation; adjustment; control; 《음성의》 modulation; 《라디오의》 tuning in. ～하다 regulate; adjust; control; modulate; tune in 《the radio》. ¶ 물가의 ～ the 「regulation 〔control〕 of prices / 음성의 ～ modulation of *one's* voices / 방의 온도를 자동적으로 ～하다 automatically regulate the temperature of a room. ◉ ～기(器) a regulator. ～미(米) 《release》 (government=held) rice to cushion rice price hike. ～판 a 「regulator 〔control〕 valve. 남북～위원회 the South-North Coordinating Committee.

**조정**(朝廷) the (Imperial) Court.

**조정**(漕艇) rowing; boating. ～하다 row a boat. ◉ ～경기 a boat race.

**조정**(調定) settlement. ～하다 settle. ◉ ～세액 the tax amount settled. ～액 the settled amount. ～인원 the number of persons to be settled.

**조정**(調停) mediation; arbitration; intervention; 『법』 conciliation. ～하다 mediate 《between two persons》; arbitrate 《in a case》; reconcile 《a quarrel》; intervene 《in an affair》; settle 《a dispute》.

¶ …의 ～으로 through the mediation

of… / ～에 부치다 submit 〔refer〕《a dispute》 to arbitration / ～의 수고를 하다 take the trouble of mediating 《a labor dispute》; take upon *oneself* the trouble of mediating 《between the two parties》 / 교전국 사이를 ～하다 mediate between two warring nations / 파업을 ～하다 intervene in a strike / 관계 당국의 ～으로 분쟁은 무사히 해결됐다 Through the mediation of authorities concerned, the strife came to a settlement. / 저작권에 관한 분쟁 ～이 위임되었다 The dispute over the copyright was「referred 〔submitted〕 to arbitration. / 유엔은 두 나라 사이의 국경 분쟁에 관한 ～에 나섰다 The United Nation set「about 〔to〕 the mediation of the dispute between the two countries over the border dispute.

◉ ～서(書) 《법원에서 작성하는》 a consent decree. ～신청서 a written application for mediation. ～안 an arbitration proposal; a mediation plan; a compromise plan. ～역할 a mediation role. ～위원 a member of mediation committee: ～위원회 a mediation committee; a conciliation commission. ～자 a mediator; an arbitrator; 《중재자》 a peacemaker; 《중개자》 an intermediary; a go-between. ～재판 court arbitration: ～재판소 a court of arbitration. (가정)분쟁～ grievance mediation.

**조정**(調整) regulation; adjustment; coordination; modulation (음조의). ～하다 regulate; adjust; put 《*a thing*》 in order; coordinate; control; modulate; 《상이한 의견 등을》 iron out. ¶ 가격을〔속도를〕 ～하다 adjust 〔control〕 the「prices 〔speed〕 / 서로 충돌하는 의견을 ～하다 iron out conflicting views / 나는 그들의 상치되는 의견 ～을 시도했다 I tried to coordinate their different views. / 정부는 수입 억제로 국제 수지를 ～하려고 하였다 The government attempted to regulate the balance of payments by controlling imports.

◉ ～기 a regulator; 《가스의》 a governor. ～위원회 a coordinating committee. ～자 a coordinator. 연말～ 《세금의》 the year-end tax adjustment.

**조제**(粗製) slipshod manufacture; coarse 〔crude, careless〕 manufacturing. ～하다 manufacture crudely; produce crude articles. ¶ ～의 coarse; crude. ◉ ～남조(濫造) mass production of inferior goods: ～남조하다 produce 〔manufacture〕 inferior articles in large quantities. ～설탕 raw 〔unrefined〕 sugar. ～염 crude salt. ～품「a crude 〔an inferior〕 article; coarse manufactures.

**조제**(調製) making; manufacture; preparation; 《주문품의》 execution. ～하다 make; prepare; execute; make 《*a thing*》 to order. ◉ ～법 a recipe. ～품 a preparation.

**조제**(調劑) 《약의》 preparation 〔compounding〕 of medicines. ～하다 prepare 〔compound〕 a medicine; 《처방에 따라》 fill 〔make up〕 a prescription. ¶ ～시키다 have the prescription filled / 처방대로 ～하다「make up 〔fill〕 a prescription; dispense a prescription / 약을 잘못 ～하다 compound a medicine in a wrong way / 약국에서 두통약을 ～해 달라고 했다 I got my headache prescription filled in the drugstore. ◉ ～법 pharmacy. ～실 a dispensary. ～약 a mixture; a preparation. ～학 pharmaceutics.

**조조**(早朝) early morning. ¶ ～할인 영화 《see》 a movie shown at reduced admission fees for (early) morning.

**조종**(弔鐘) a funeral bell; a knell.

**조종**(祖宗) ancestors 〔forefathers〕 of a king.

**조종**(操縱) 《기계·비행기 따위의》 steering; piloting; control; operation; handling; 《사람의》 management; maneuvering. ～하다 manage 《*one's* wife, a boat, *etc.*》; handle; control; operate; maneuver; manipulate (기계를); pilot (비행기를); steer (배를); drive (차를); pull the wires (뒤에서).

¶ ～하기 쉽다〔힘들다〕 be「easy 〔hard〕 to manage 〔control, *etc.*〕 / 기계를 ～하다 work 〔operate 《미》〕 a machine / ～의 자유를 잃다 lose control of 《an airplane》 / 남편을 마음대로 ～하다 twist 〔turn〕 her husband round her little finger; make her husband do whatever she wants / 교묘히 ～하여 …시키다 maneuver 《*a person*》 into *do*ing / 파업자들은 전적으로 그에게 ～당하고 있다 The strikers are perfectly under his thumb. / 그는 경비행기를 ～할 수 있다 He can fly a lightplane.

◉ ～간(桿) a control「stick 〔lever〕; a joystick 《구어》. ～법 operation; control: 비행기의 ～법을 배우다 learn how to fly an airplane. ～사 a pilot; an aviator; 《여류》 an「aviatrix 〔aviatress〕: 부～사 a copilot. ～석 a pilot's seat; a cockpit. ～실 a cockpit: ～실 음성기록 장치 a cockpit voice recorder (생략 CVR). ～자 a manager; a manipulator; 《배후의》 a wire puller. ～장치 controls; a steering gear: 공동 ～ 장치 《연습 비행기의》 dual controls.

**조주**(助奏) 〖음악〗 *ob(b)ligato* (It.).

**조준**(照準) aim; aiming; laying; sight. ～하다 aim 《at》; take aim 《at》; sight 《a rifle》; lay 《a gun》; collimate (망원경 따위를). ¶ 대포의 ～각 the elevation of a gun / ～연습 사격 a sighting shot / ～을 맞추다 set 〔get〕 *one's* sight 《on》; take a careful sight; adjust the sight; lay 《a gun》 / ～이 틀리다 be faulty at aim / 신중하게 ～을 하고 쐈다 I took a careful sight and fired.
◉ ～기(器) sights; a sighting device. ～망원경 a sighting telescope. ～선 a line of sight. ～수 《대포의》 a gun layer; a pointer. ～폭격 precision bombing. 상하～ laying for elevation. 전시(全視)～ panoramic sight. 직접〔간접〕～ direct 〔indirect〕 laying.

**조지다** ① 《단단히 맞춤》 fix tightly; tighten up; screw up. ¶ 사개를 ～ screw 〔make, fix〕 a joint tight. ② 《단속》 exercise strict control 《over》; make double-sure; hold 《*a person*》 to.

**조지아** 《미국의 주》 Georgia (생략 Ga.).

**조직**(組織) 《구성》 formation; construction; 《사회·단체 등의 통일체》 (an) organization; (a) structure; (a) constitution; 《계통·제도》 (a) system; 《생물의》 tissue. ～하다 form; organize; constitute; compose; set up; incorporate (회사 따위를).
¶ ～적(으로) systematic(ally); methodical(ly); organic(ally) / 사회의 ～ the social structure; social system / 인체의 ～ the organization of the human body; human anatomy / ～의 손상 《생물의》 tissue damage / ～적 운동 an organized movement / 강팀을 ～하다 get together a strong team / 내각을 ～하다 organize 〔form〕 a Cabinet / 클럽을 ～하다 form a club / 남극 탐험대를 ～하다 organize an expedition to the South Pole / ～적으로 연구하다 make a systematic study 《of》 / …으로 ～되다 「consist 〔be composed, be made up〕 of... / 영어를 ～적으로 연구하다 make a systematic study of English / 근로자들은 노동조합을 ～했다 The workers organized a labor union. / 위원회는 6명의 위원으로 ～되어 있다 The committee is 「made up 〔composed〕 of six members. *or* The committee consists of six members.
◉ ～력 organizing ability; systematizing talent. ～망 a network of system. ～배양 《make》 (a) tissue culture. ～범죄 an organized crime. ～위원회 an organizing committee. ～자 an organizer. ～책 a chief organizer. ～체 an organism. ～폭력 organized violence. ～표(票) 《선거의》 block votes 《of a labor union》. ～학 〖생물〗 histology.

**조직화**(組織化) organization; systematization. ～하다 organize; systematize; structure. ¶ 고도로 ～된 사회 a highly structured society.

**조짐**(兆朕) 《징조》 symptoms; signs; indications; 《전조》 an omen; a foreboding. ¶～을 보이다 show signs 〔symptoms〕 《of》; betoken; forebode / 폐렴의 ～이 나타나다 develop symptoms of pneumonia / 모든 ～으로 보아 by all indications / ～이 좋다 have 〔make〕 a good omen; be propitious; be of good omen / 그건 불길한 ～이다 It carries an ominous foreboding of evil. / 당분간 비가 올 ～은 안 보인다 There is no sign of immediate rain.

**조차**(租借) lease 《of a house, land, territory》. ～하다 lease; hold 《land》 by 〔on〕 lease. ¶～ 기한을 연장하다 extend the lease. ◉ ～권 lease; leasehold: 99개년의 ～권을 얻다 obtain a 99 years' lease. ～지 a leased territory; a leasehold.

**조차**(潮差) the range of tide; tidal range.

**조차**(操車) 〖철도〗 marshaling. ◉ ～원 a train dispatcher. ～장 a switchyard 《미》; a marshaling yard 《영》.

**조차** 《…도》 even; 《게다가》 besides; in addition; into the bargain. ¶ 그것은 들은 일～ 없다 I have never even heard of it. / 너～ 그럴 줄은 몰랐다 I didn't know that (even) you would do that. / 그는 제 이름～ 못 쓴다 He cannot even 〔as much as〕 write his own name. / 자네뿐 아니라 그 사람～ 그런 말을 하데 As if it weren't enough for you to say it, he said it too. / 그 사람은 만나기～ 힘들다 It's difficult even to get to see him. / 점심도 못 먹고 저녁～ 굶었다 I didn't eat any lunch and then skipped dinner as well. / 몹시 추운데 눈～ 내리기 시작했다 It was very cold, and then it began to snow into the bargain.

**조찬**(朝餐) breakfast. ⇨ 조반(朝飯).

◉ ～회 a breakfast meeting; a meeting-over-breakfast: ～ 기도회 a breakfast prayer meeting.

**조처**(措處) a measure; a step; a move; action; disposal. ～하다 take measures 〔steps〕; take action; dispose of; manage 《an affair, a matter》. ¶ 신속한 ～ a speedy disposal / 적절한 ～ a measure suited to the occasion; an appropriate measure / 잘못 ～하다 take a wrong step 〔measure〕; make an error in dealing with 《an affair》/ 강경한〔과감한〕 ～를 취하다 take strong 〔drastic〕 action 《against》/ 즉각적인 ～를 취하다 take an immediate step / 현명한 ～를 취하다 adopt a wise policy; act wisely / 필요한 (모든) ～를 취하다 take (all) necessary measures 〔steps〕; take necessary action / 그것은 내가 알아서 ～하겠습니다 I'll see to it. / 다음 ～를 취해 두지 않으면 안전하지 못하다 You don't stand on a safe ground, if you have not done the next step.

**조청**(造清) glutinous starch syrup.

**조촉**(弔燭) a funeral candle.

**조촐하다** (be) neat; nice; tidy; dapper (옷차림이); spruce; trim; clean-cut. ¶ 조촐히 neatly; nicely / 조촐한 집 a trim house / 옷 입은 것이 ～ be dapper in dress / 조촐하게 생기다 have a neat appearance.

**조총**(弔銃) a (rifle) volley for the dead. ¶ ～을 쏘다 fire a volley for the dead.

**조총**(鳥銃) 《새총》 a fowling piece.

**조총련**(朝總聯) *Jochongnyeon;* the pro-North Korean residents' league in Japan.

**조치**(措置) ＝조처(措處). ¶ 보완～ 《take》 complementary measures / 후속～ 《take》 follow-up measures.

**조칙**(詔勅) a Royal edict. ＝ 조서(詔書).

**조카** a nephew. ¶ …의 ～ a nephew of 〔to〕…. ◉ ～딸 a niece. ～며느리 a nephew's wife. ～뻘 the relation of nephew: 그는 내 ～뻘이다 He stands to me in the relation of nephew. ～사위 a niece's husband.

**조커** 〖카드놀이〗 a joker.

**조타**(操舵) 〖항해〗 steering; steerage. ～하다 steer. ◉ ～기〔장치〕 steering gear. ～수 a steersman; a helmsman. ～실 a steering 〔wheel〕 house; a pilot-house; a control room.

**조탁**(彫琢) 《보석 따위의》 carving and polishing 《gems》; 《문장 따위의》 polishing 《writings, *etc.*》; elaboration. ～하다 carve and polish; elaborate.

**조탄**(粗炭) coarse 〔low-grade〕 coal.

**조퇴**(早退) leaving 《school, the office》 earlier than usual. ～하다 leave 《school》 early; leave 《the office》 earlier than usual. ¶ 두 시간 일찍 ～하다 leave 《work》 two hours early.

**조판**(組版) 〖인쇄〗 typesetting; composition; a form. ～하다 set (up) in type; put 《a manuscript》 in type; compose (type); do typesetting. ¶ 원고는 지금 ～ 중에 있다 The manuscript is now in type.

**조팝나무** 〖식물〗 a bridal wreath.

**조팝나물** 〖식물〗 a hawkweed.

**조폐**(造幣) mintage; coinage. ～하다 mint coins. ◉ ～국 the Mint (Bureau): ～국장 the Director 〔Treasurer 《미》〕 of the Mint (Bureau). 한국～공사 the Korea Minting, Security Printing & ID Card Operating Corp.

**조포**(弔砲) a salute of minute guns; a funeral salute. ¶ 대통령의 장례식 ～가 울렸다 The funeral salute was fired in honor of the late President.

**조품**(粗品) ① ＝조제품(粗製品). ② 《선물할 때》 a small gift; a trifle present. ¶ ～이지만 받아 주십시오 This is a small present for you but I hope you'll like it.

**조하다**(躁—) (be) hasty; quick-tempered; impatient; impetuous.

**조함**(造艦) naval shipbuilding. ◉ ～계획 a naval construction program. ～능력 naval shipbuilding capacity.

**조합**(組合) ① 《단체》 an association; a guild (동업자의); a union (근로자의). ¶ 협동～ a cooperative society; a coop / 어용 ～ a company-dominated union / ～을 만들다 organize an association; form a union 〔guild〕/ ～에 가입하다 join the association; become a union member / ～에 넣어 주다 admit 《*a person*》 into the association. ② 〖수학〗 combination. ◉ ～간부 a union leader 〔official〕. ～규약 the articles of association; a union constitution 〔charter〕. ～근로자 [총칭] organized 〔union〕 labor. ～비 union dues. ～운동 a union movement. ～원 a member of an association; 《노조의》 a unionist; a union member: 비～원 a nonunionist / ～원증 a union card. ～장 a union president 〔boss〕. ～전임자(專任者) a full-time union officer; a paid union officer. ～조직 union organization. ～활동 union activities.

**조합**(調合) ① 《섞음》 mixing 《medicines, dyes》; compounding; preparation. ~하다 compound; mix; prepare; make up. ¶ 처방대로 ~하다 fill 〔make up, dispense〕 a prescription / 두 가지의 가루약을 ~하다 mix two powders together. ② 《조미》 seasoning 《food》; flavoring; dressing. ~하다 season; add flavor(ing); dress.
◉ ~물 a mixture; a preparation.

**조항**(條項) an article; a clause; a provision; a stipulation. ¶ ~을 규정하다 enact a provision / 계약 ~을 이행하다 carry out contract stipulations / 계약서에 …취지의 ~을 첨가하다 add to the contract a clause to the effect that 《the principal shall be repaid in two years》/ 그 계약에는 많은 ~이 있다 The contract contains many stipulations.

**조현병**(調絃病) 〖의학〗 schizophrenia. ~환자 a schizophrenic.

**조혈**(造血) blood formation; hematogenesis; hematosis. ¶ ~의 hematogenous; hematogenic. ◉ ~기관 a blood-forming organ. ~기능〔조직〕 blood-forming functions 〔tissues〕; hematogenous functions 〔tissues〕. ~제 a blood-forming medicine; a hematic 〔hematinic〕 (drug).

**조형**(造形) molding; modeling. ~하다 mold; model; shape. ◉ ~미술 formative 〔the plastic〕 arts.

**조혼**(早婚) early marriage. ~하다 marry early 〔young〕. ¶ ~을 장려하다 encourage early marriage / 그녀는 ~했다 She married young. / 이 나라에는 오래 지속된 ~의 관습이 있었다 There was a long-standing custom of early marriage in this country.

**조혼전**(助婚錢) a gift of money that is made to a poor bride by the groom in order to cover the wedding expenses.

**조홍**(潮紅) flush (in the face); blushing. ⇨홍조.

**조화**(弔花) funeral flowers; a funeral wreath (화환); floral tributes. ¶ ~사절 《부고의 말》 No flowers.

**조화**(造化) 《창조》 creation; nature; 《신통함》 the mysterious; the marvelous; the wonderful. ¶ ~의 신 the Creator; the Maker / ~의 묘 the wonder(s) of nature / ~의 변덕〔장난〕 a freak of nature.

**조화**(造花) an imitation 〔artificial〕 flower.

**조화**(調和) 《일치》 harmony; accord; agreement. ~하다 harmonize; be in harmony 〔keeping〕 《with》; match; accord 〔go, agree〕 with. ¶ ~된 harmonious; well-matched / ~ 안 되는 inharmonious; out of keeping 《with》/ 색의 ~ harmony of colors / ~를 이룬 배색 a harmonious arrangement of colors / 성장과 안정의 ~ the harmony of growth and stability / ~시키다 harmonize; match; adjust / ~되지 않다 lack harmony; be out of keeping with; be out of place with / 양탄자와 커튼이 ~가 안 된다 The carpet and the curtain do not match. *or* The carpet does not 「match 〔go well〕 with the curtain. / 그것은 그 장소의 분위기와 ~되지 않았다 It was out of tune with the atmosphere of the place. ◉ ~비례〔함수〕 〖수학〗 a harmonic proportion 〔function〕. ~운동 〖물리〗 harmonic motion.

**조회**(朝會) a morning assembly.

**조회**(照會) (an) inquiry 〔enquiry〕; a query; (a) reference. ~하다 inquire 《of *a person* about *a thing*》; refer 〔apply, write〕 《to *a person* for information》; make reference 《to》; make inquiries 《as to, about》. ¶ ~중이다 be under inquiry / 신원을 ~하다 inquire 〔check〕 into 《*a person's*》 background 〔history〕 / B씨의 성품에 관해서 전(前)회사에 ~하다 refer to Mr. B's former company for his character / 상세한 것은 사무실로 ~해 주십시오 For particulars apply to the office. / 본사에 직접 ~해주십시오 Please refer 〔write〕 directly to our main office. / ~한 결과 그것이 사실임을 알았다 On inquiry I found it was true. / 나는 그 건에 관하여 본사에 ~했다 I referred to the main office for information about the matter. / 당신에 관한 것을 누구에게 ~하면 되겠습니까 Who are your references? / 나의 신원은 김 교수님께 ~해 주십시오 Please refer me to Professor Kim. ◉ ~장〔서〕 a letter of inquiry. ~처 《신용·신원 따위의》 a reference.

**족**(足) ① a foot 《of a cow》; trotters (양·돼지 등의). ② 《켤레》 a pair 《of socks》.

**족**(族) 《종족》 a tribe; a race; 《일족》 kin(s)folk; 《가족》 a family; 《족속》 a gang. ¶ 고양이족 the cat family / 몽골족 a Mongol tribe / 사양족 a declining upper-class family / 마이카족 an owner driver / 폭주족 a motorcycle gang.

**족대기다** force; constrain; compel; make; press; urge. ¶ 아무를 족대기어 일을 시키다 force *a person* to work /

아무를 족대기어 세금을 받다 force taxes out of *a person* / 기부금을 내라고 ～ press 《*a person*》 to contribute.

**족두리** *chokturi,* a black crown-like headpiece worn by women on formal occasions. ◉ ～하님 a servant taken along by the bride to her new home.

**족발**(足—) 《돼지의》 pettitoes; pig's trotters.

**족벌**(族閥) a clan; a clique. ◉ ～정치 clan government. ～주의 nepotism.

**족보**(族譜) a genealogical table 〔record〕; a clan register; genealogy; pedigree. ¶ ～를 캐다 look into 〔trace〕 *one's* genealogy 〔pedigree〕 / ～를 만들다〔편찬하다〕 draw up 〔compile〕 a genealogy 《of》.

**족생**(簇生) gregarious growth. ～하다 grow gregariously 〔in clusters〕. ◉ ～식물 a social plant.

**족속**(族屬) a clan; a clansman; a kinsman; 《패거리》 a party; a band; a gang. ¶ 깡패 ～ a gang of thugs.

**족쇄**(足鎖) fetters; shackles (for the feet); leg irons. ¶ ～를 채우다 fetter; shackle; put 《*a person*》 in fetters; place leg irons 《on prisoners》.

**족인**(族人) clansmen; relatives.

**족자**(簇子) a hanging scroll 〔picture〕. ◉ ～걸이 a pole with hooks for hanging a scroll. ～축 a roller (for a scroll).

**족자리** ears (on both sides of a pot).

**족장**(族長) a patriarch; the head of a family 〔clan〕; the chief of a tribe. ◉ ～시대 the patriarchal age.

**족적**(足迹·足跡) a footprint; a footmark; traces; tracks. ¶ ～을 남기다 leave *one's* footprints 〔footmarks〕 / ～을 따라가다 track 《an animal》; follow 《*a person's*》 footsteps; follow 《a lion's》 tracks.

**족제비** 〖동물〗 a weasel. ◉ ～얼레 a kind of long thin bobbin 〔spindle〕.

**족족** 《마다》 every occasion (that); whatever time (that); whenever; every time; as often as. ¶ 오는 ～ whenever 〔every time〕 *one* comes; each 〔every〕 time *one* calls / 여러번 해 보았으나 하는 ～ 실패했다 I made several attempts and failed as many times.

**족집게** ① 《털 뽑는》 《a pair of》 tweezers. ¶ ～로 가시를 뽑다 pluck 〔pull〕 a thorn out 《of *one's* finger》 with tweezers. ② ⇨ 족집게 장님. ◉ ～장님 a blind fortuneteller who is very good at perceiving what has happened in 《*a person's*》 past.

**족척**(族戚) relatives; kindred.

**족치다** ① 《줄이다》 reduce; diminish (in size); shorten. ② 《결딴내다》 break 《up》; destroy; ruin; mangle. ¶ 살림을 ～ break up 〔ruin〕 a home / 산의 나무를 ～ fell 〔destroy〕 the trees on a mountain. ③ ＝ 족대기다.

**족편**(足—) cow's foot jelly 〔gelatin〕; gelatined cow's foot.

**족하다**(足—) 《충분하다》 (be) enough; sufficient; suffice; 《만족하다》 be satisfied 《with》; be content(ed) 《with》. ¶ 마음에 ～ be satisfactory / …을 마음에 족해 하다 be satisfied 〔content〕 with … / 열 사람이 먹기에 족한 음식 sufficient food for ten / 생활하기에 족한 급료 enough salary to live on / 한 마디로 ～ One word will suffice. / 한 달에 100만원이면 족하겠다 One million won will do for a month.

**족히**(足—) enough; sufficiently; in plenty; fully; well (worth). ¶ ～ 만 명은 수용할 수 있다 be large enough to accommodate ten thousand people / ～볼 만하다 be well worth seeing / ～ 칭찬할 만하다 be worthy of praise / ～ 다섯 시간은 걸린다 It takes you a full five hours. / 그와는 ～ 정치를 논할 만하다 He is well worth talking politics with.

**존** a zone. ¶ 스트라이크 존 〖야구〗 the strike zone / 존디펜스 zone defense.

**존경**(尊敬) respect; veneration; esteem; reverence; deference; (a) high regard. ～하다 respect; esteem; venerate; hold 《*a person*》 in respect 〔esteem〕; think highly 〔much〕 of; look up to; have respect 〔a high regard〕 for. ¶ 나의 ～하는 선생님 my revered teacher / …을 ～하여 in deference to…; out of respect for… / ～을 받다 win the respect 《of all》; command respect 〔esteem〕; enjoy the esteem 《of 》; be held in (a great, high) esteem 〔respect〕 / ～을 표시하다 show *one's* respect 《for》 / ～을 못 받다 lose 《*a person's*》 respect; forfeit 《*a person's*》 esteem / ～할 만하다 deserve 〔be worthy of〕 respect; be honorable 〔estimable〕 / 우리는 그를 스승으로서 ～하고 있다 We look up to him as our master. / 그는 ～할 만한 인물이 못 된다 He doesn't deserve to be respected. / 내가 가장 ～하는 사람은 우리 아버지이다 The person I have the highest regard for is my father.

**존공**(尊公) your esteemed father.

**존귀**(尊貴) nobility. ～하다 (be) high and noble.

**존당**(尊堂) your esteemed mother.

**존대**(尊待) treatment with respect. ～하다 treat with great respect; hold 《*a person*》 in esteem. ¶～ 받다 be esteemed; be held in esteem; be thought highly of.
◉ ～어 honorific language; a term of respect; honorifics.

**존립**(存立) existence; subsistence. ～하다 exist; subsist. ¶ ～을 위태롭게 하다 endanger 〔threaten〕 the existence 《of》.

**존망**(存亡) life or death; existence; destiny; fate. ¶ 국가 ～에 관한 문제 a life-or-death question for the nation / 국가의 ～을 걸다 stake the existence of a nation 《upon》/ 우리는 지금 국가 ～의 위기에 처해 있다 We are now facing a national crisis.

**존비**(尊卑) the high and the low; aristocrat and plebeian. ¶～귀천 할 것 없이 irrespective of rank; without distinction of rank; high and low alike.

**존속**(存續) continued existence; continuance; continuation; duration. ～하다 continue to exist; continue; last; keep up. ¶～시키다 continue; maintain; keep up; retain.

**존속**(尊屬) 〖법〗 an ascendant. ¶ 직계〔방계〕～ a lineal 〔collateral〕 ascendant. ◉ ～살해 parricide; 《부친》 patricide; 《모친》 matricide. ～친 〖법〗 lineal consanguinity.

**존안**(尊顔) your (esteemed) countenance; you (sir). ¶～을 뵙다 have the honor of seeing you.

**존엄**(尊嚴) dignity; prestige; majesty. ～하다 (be) dignified; solemn; sacred. ¶ 인간의 ～성 the dignity of man / ～을 손상하다 impair the dignity 《of》/ 법의 ～을 지키다 uphold the majesty 〔dignity〕 of law. ◉ ～사 death with dignity.

**존영**(尊影) your 〔his〕 (esteemed) portrait 〔picture〕.

**존의**(尊意) your (esteemed) opinion 〔view〕.

**존장**(尊長) a (venerable) elder.

**존재**(存在) existence; being. ～하다 exist; be in existence 〔being〕; 《잔존하다》 be extant; remain. ¶～하지 않는 nonexistent / 신의 ～ the existence of God / 이 세상에서 가장 비참한 ～ the most miserable being in existence / ～를 인정하다 recognize the existence 《of》/ ～를 인정받다 be recognized 《as a critic》; win recognition / …의 ～를 무시하다 take no notice of 《*a person*》; ignore / 신의 ～를 믿다 believe in god / 자기의 ～를 (남에게) 의식하게 하다 make *one's* presence felt / 그는 이 분야에서는 귀중한 ～이다 He is a most valuable person in this field. / 신은 ～한다 God is 〔exists〕. / 그는 기회 있을 때마다 자신의 ～를 내세웠다 He asserted himself at every opportunity. / 그녀는 역사적으로는 ～하지 않는 가공 인물이다 She is a fictitious character that has no existence in history.
◉ ～론 〖철학〗 ontology. ～이유 a reason for being; *its* 〔*one's*〕 justification for existence; *raison d'être* (F.): 은행은 신용 즉 공신력을 어기면 바로 그 ～이유를 잃게 된다 Banks lose their very *raison d'être* if they violate credibility or trustworthiness.

**존절**《절약》 frugality; economy; saving; thrift. ～하다 economize 《on》; be economical 〔sparing〕 《of》. ¶ ～히 frugally / 돈을 ～히 쓰다 be economical of money; make economical use of money.

**존존하다** be finely woven; be of fine weave.

**존중**(尊重) respect; esteem; deference. ～하다 respect; esteem; value; hold dear; think much 〔highly〕 of; hold 《*a thing*》 in esteem 〔respect〕; set store by; have a high regard for.
¶ ～할 만한 respectable; estimable / …을 ～하여 in deference to 《the wishes of *one's* parents》/ 여론을 ～하다 pay regard to public opinion / 금전 이상으로 명예를 ～하다 prize 〔value〕 honor above money / 학문을 ～하다 hold learning in esteem / 그는 생명보다도 명예를 ～한다 He holds honor dearer than his life. / 민주 정치란 정치가가 여론을 ～하는 데 있다 Democracy means that politicians are to set store by public opinion.

**존체**(尊體) your (esteemed) self 〔health〕.

**존칭**(尊稱) a title of honor 〔respect, esteem〕; an honorific title. ～하다 address honorifically.

**존폐**(存廢) maintenance or abolition; existence. ¶ 조만간 우리 기구의 ～에 관해 토의해야 한다 Sooner or later we'll have to discuss whether we should maintain our organization or not.
◉ ～문제 the question of maintenance (or abolition); the problem of keeping or discarding: 학교의 ～ 문제

the question of continuing or closing the school.

**존함**(尊銜) your (esteemed) name. ¶ ～이 어떻게 되십니까 May I have your name, please? *or* What's the name, please? *or* 《전할 경우》 What name shall I say?

**졸**(卒) 《장기의》 a Korean-chess pawn. ¶ 졸을 잡다 take a pawn.

**졸** 〖화학〗 sol; colloidal solution. ◉ 졸화 solation.

**졸가리** ① 《가지》 dry bits of twig. ② 《줄기》 a stripped stalk 〔stem〕. ③ 《골자》 an outline; a summary.

**졸경치(르)다**(卒更—) have bitter experiences; have a hard 〔bad〕 time of it 《with *a person*》; pay dearly 《for》.

**졸년**(卒年) the year of 《*a person's*》 death.

**졸다**[1] 《잠이 와서》 doze (off); drowse; snooze; fall into a doze. ¶ 졸면서 운전하다 doze (off) 「at the wheel 〔while driving〕; drive 《a car》 asleep / 깜박 ～ drop off to sleep; doze off; fall 〔drop off〕 into a doze / 자리에서 ～ drowse in *one's* seat / 책을 읽다가〔일하다〕 ～ doze over *one's* book 〔work〕 / 청중은 대부분 졸고 있었다 Most of the audience were asleep. / 졸면서 운전하는 것은 매우 위험하다 It's very dangerous to drive (a car) when sleepy.

**졸다**[2] ① 《액체가》 get boiled down; be boiled dry. ② ＝줄다.

**졸도**(卒倒) fainting; a faint; a swoon; swooning; 〖의학〗 syncope. ～하다 fall down in a faint; faint (away); (fall in a) swoon; fall unconscious. ¶ 더위로 ～하다 faint from the heat / 그녀는 무서워서 ～했다 The fright made her sink down in a swoon. / 그는 오늘 아침 뇌일혈로 ～했다 He had a stroke of apoplexy this morning.

**졸들다** be 〔get〕 hampered in development; be stunted; be shriveled; be withered; be wilted. ¶ 졸든 아이 a stunted child / 보리가 ～ barley gets blighted.

**졸때기** ① 《일》 a small-scale affair; a petty job. ¶ ～ 장사 small trade. ② 《사람》 a petty 〔an unimportant〕 person; a petty underling; small fry [총칭]. ¶ ～ 공무원 a petty official.

**졸라대다** pester for; badger 《*a person* to *do*》; tease; beg 〔cry, clamor, importune, press〕 for. ¶ 과자를 달라고 ～ clamor for candies / 아버지에게 카메라를 사 달라고 ～ badger *one's* father to buy *one* a camera / 그는 돈을 더 달라고 어머니에게 졸라댔다 He pestered his mother for more money.

**졸라매다** fasten tightly; tie up; tighten; constrict; strangle. ¶ 허리띠를 ～ tighten up *one's* belt; wear a belt tight / 목을 졸라매어 죽이다 strangle 〔throttle〕 《*a person*》 to death.

**졸래졸래** flippant(ly); frivolous(ly). ¶ ～ 돌아다니다 gad about.

**졸렬**(拙劣) clumsiness; inexpertness; maladroitness; awkwardness. ～하다 (be) clumsy; awkward; poor; bungling; blundering; unskillful. ¶ ～한 수단 a bungling step; a clumsy measure / ～한 변명 an awkward excuse / ～한 문장 a crude style of writing.

**졸론**(拙論) ① 《자기의》 my (unworthy) opinion 〔view〕; my argument. ② 《보잘것 없는》 a poor opinion 〔view〕.

**졸리다**[1] 《잠이 오다》 get 〔become〕 sleepy; feel sleepy 〔drowsy〕. ¶ 졸려 뵈는 sleepy; drowsy; sleepy-looking / 졸린 듯이 sleepily; drowsily / 졸려 견딜 수 없다 I suffer from sleepiness.

**졸리다**[2] ① 《매어짐》 get 〔be〕 tightened. ② 《남에게》 get pestered 〔annoyed〕; be kept after; be pressed 〔begged, coaxed〕.

**졸막졸막** in various small sizes or quantities. ～하다 be of 〔come in〕 various small sizes or quantities.

**졸망졸망** 《옹기종기》 small things in a group; 《올통볼통》 all bumpy. ～하다 be small-sized; be all bumpy. ¶ ～한 아이들 a bunch of little children.

**졸문**(拙文) ① 《졸렬한 글》 poor writing; poor composition. ② 《자기의 글》 my (poor) writing 〔composition〕.

**졸병**(卒兵) a (common) soldier. ＝병졸.

**졸부**(猝富) an overnight millionaire; [집합적] the newly rich. ¶ ～가 되다 suddenly become a rich.

**졸사**(猝死) sudden death. ～하다 die suddenly; drop 〔fall〕 dead.

**졸속**(拙速) ¶ ～의 rough-and-ready; hasty / ～공사의 관행 the-faster-the=better construction practices. ◉ ～주의 a rough-and-ready method 〔rule〕: 그가 하는 일은 언제나 ～주의다 His work is always rough-and-ready.

**졸아들다** shrink; contract; 《수분이》 be boiled down; boil down. ¶ 시럽은 곧 졸아들었다 The syrup boiled down in a very short time.

**졸아붙다** 《액체가》 get boiled dry; boil down to nothing.

**졸아지다** be boiled away 〔down〕; be contracted; be reduced; shrink.

**졸업**(卒業) graduation; completion of a course 《of study》. ~하다 graduate 〔be graduated〕 《from Yale》《미》; graduate 《at》《영》; complete a course 《of study》; finish school. (★ graduate 를 《영》에서는 「학위를 받고 졸업하다」의 뜻으로만 쓰인다. 따라서 초등 학교 등의 졸업에는 finish를 씀. 《미》에서는 이런 구별이 없다. 또 graduate는 수동태 형식으로 쓰면 격식차린 표현이 된다).
¶ ~ 후 after graduation; after leaving the school / 대학을 갓 ~한 젊은이 a young man fresh from college / 중학교를 ~하다 complete the junior high school course / 대학을 ~하다 graduate 〔be graduated〕 from 〔at〕 a university / 수석으로 ~하다 graduate first on the list / 우등으로 ~하다 graduate with honors / 요즘에는 고학하며 대학을 ~하는 학생이 많다 In these days many students work their way through college. / 나는 S대학의 법학부를 ~했다 I graduated in law from S University. / 너는 대학 ~ 후 무엇을 할 생각이냐 What do you intend to do after graduation from college?
◉ ~논문 a graduation thesis. ~반 《students of》 the graduating class. ~시험 a graduation examination. ~장 a diploma; a certificate (of the completion of a school course); a sheepskin 《미구어》. ~정원(제) the graduation quota (system).

**졸업생**(卒業生) a graduate; an ex-student; a school leaver (초·중학교의); 《미》《남자》 an alumnus (*pl.* -ni); an old boy 《영》; 《여자》 an alumna (*pl.* -nae); an old girl. ¶ 고교 ~ a senior high school graduate / 대학 남자〔여자〕 ~ a male 〔female〕 university graduate / 4년제 대학 ~의 초임금 the starting salary for a four-year university graduate / 300명의 ~을 내다 turn out 300 boys 〔girls〕 / 그는 1992년도 ~이다 He graduated with the class of 1992.
◉ ~명부 a list of graduates.

**졸업식**(卒業式) a graduation ceremony; graduation exercises 《미》; the commencement (exercises) 《미》. ¶ ~날 the graduation day; 《미》 the commencement day; a speech day 《영》 / ~에서 최고 영예인 대통령상을 타다 be awarded the top honor with the presidential citation at the commencement ceremonies.

**졸연하다**(猝然—) (be) sudden; abrupt; unexpected. ¶ 졸연히 suddenly; abruptly; unexpectedly.

**졸음** sleepiness; drowsiness; a sleepy spell. ¶ ~이 오다 get 〔feel, become〕 sleepy 〔drowsy〕 / ~을 물리치다 shake off sleepiness / ~ 운전을 하다 doze (off) 「at the wheel 〔while driving〕 / ~을 물리치기 위해 차를 한 잔 마셨다 I had a cup of tea to keep me awake. / 나는 몹시 ~이 왔다 A great drowsiness grew 〔fall〕 upon me. / 이 알약을 먹으면 ~이 올지도 모릅니다 These tablets may 「cause drowsiness 〔make you drowsy〕.

**졸이다** ① ⇨줄이다. ② 《속을》 feel anxious 〔uneasy, nervous〕. ¶ 마음을 ~ be fidgety 〔agitated, edgy〕; be on edge; be held in suspense; be excited; be nervous 〔uneasy, anxious〕 《about》; worry / 낙제할까봐 마음을 ~ be nervous at the possibility that *one* might fail / 마음을 졸이며 공중 곡예를 보다 watch aerial acrobatics 「on the edge of *one's* seat 〔with excitement〕 / 돌아오기를 마음 졸이며 기다리다 wait in anxious suspense for 《*a person's*》 return. ③ 《끓여서》 boil down 〔hard〕. ¶ 고기를 간장에 ~ boil beef down in soy sause.

**졸작**(拙作) ① 《졸렬한》 a poor work; trash; rubbish. ¶ 이 시는 ~이다 This poem is rubbish. ② 《자기의》 my (poor) work.

**졸장부**(拙丈夫) a small-minded man; a petty little fellow; an unmanly man; a sissy.

**졸저**(拙著) my (poor) work.

**졸졸** ① 《흐름》 trickling; bubbling; murmuring; babbling. ¶ 시냇물이 ~ 흐르다 a brook murmurs along / 수돗물이 ~ 나오다 water trickles down 《from the faucet》. ② 《따라다님》 《follow *a person*》 persistently; hanging on; sticking close; tagging along. ¶ 그 아이는 항상 엄마를 ~ 따라다닌다 The child is always tagging at his mother's heels.

**졸중풍**(卒中風) 〖의학〗 apoplexy. ¶ ~에 걸리다 have a fit 〔stroke〕 of apoplexy.

**졸지에**(猝地—) suddenly; unexpectedly; all of a sudden; abruptly; out of the blue. ¶ ~ 사고를 당하다 have an accident all of a sudden.

**졸참나무** 〖식물〗 a bristletooth oak.

**졸책**(拙策) ① 《졸계》 a poor 〔an inadequate〕 plan 〔policy〕; an awkward plan; an imprudent 〔injudicious〕 measure. ②《자기 계책》 my humble plan.

**졸필**(拙筆) ①《악필》 poor writing; a poor hand. ¶ 그는 ～이다 He has bad handwriting. ②《악필가》 a person with poor handwriting; a poor writer; a scribbler. ③《자기 필적》 my clumsy writing; my handwriting.

**졸하다**(卒—) die; pass away; decease.

**졸하다**(拙—) ①《용렬》 (be) clumsy; awkward; poor. ¶ 졸한 정책 a poor policy / 글씨가 ～ write a poor hand. ②《사람됨이》 (be) narrow-minded. ¶ 졸한 사람 a narrow-minded person.

**좀**[1] 〖곤충〗 a clothes moth; a bookworm; a silverfish; [비유적] a person 〔a thing〕 that slowly destroys from within; a "termite". ⇨ 좀먹다. ¶ …하고 싶어 좀이 쑤시다 be itching 「to *do* 〔for action〕; be impatient to *do* / 책이 온통 좀이 먹었다 The books are all worm-eaten.

**좀**[2] ①《조금》 a bit; a little; a few; [긍정·평서문에서]《얼마큼·어딘가》 some; to some extent 〔degree〕; rather; [의문·부정문에서] anything; somewhat. ¶ 좀 있다가 after a while; a little 〔while〕 later; soon; shortly / 좀 피곤하다 be somewhat weary / 달걀이 냉장고에 좀 있다 There are a few 〔some〕 eggs in the refrigerator. / 나는 영어를 좀 말할 수 있다 I can speak English a little. / 기분이 좀 나아졌습니까 Do you feel any better now? / 오늘은 기분이 좀 좋다 I feel a little 〔bit〕 better today. / 오늘은 좀 선선하다 It is rather cool today. / 그 사람은 좀 이상한 데가 있다 There is something strange about him. / 할 얘기가 좀 있는데 I want (to have) a word with you. / 좀 놀랐을 뿐이에요 It just surprised me a little, that's all.

> 참고 **some**의 용법 : 조건·의문문에서 권유·의뢰·희망 따위의 뜻을 포함할 때 some을 쓸 경우가 있는데, 이 경우 조건문에서는 가정적 뜻이 약해지고, 의문문에서는 긍정적 대답을 예측하는 경우가 됨: Would you lend me *some* money? 「돈 좀 빌려 주시겠소?」/ Won't you have *some* beer? 「맥주 좀 드시지 않으렵니까?」. 또한 회화에서는 의문문에서도 some을 any와 같이 사용할 때가 있음: Do you have *some* 〔any〕 pencils?

②《제발》 please; just. ¶ 내일 좀 오십시오 Please come tomorrow. / 확답을 좀 주십시오 Please give us a definite answer. / 말씀 좀 여쭈어도 되겠습니까 Excuse me, but may I ask you a question?

**좀**[3] 《그 얼마나》 how; what; how much 〔many〕. ¶ 그녀가 그것을 들으면 좀 기뻐할까 How glad she will be to hear it! / 그 소식에 좀 놀라셨겠습니까 What a surprise it must have been for you to hear the news! / 아드님이 멀리 가서 좀 쓸쓸하시겠습니까 How lonely it must be for you now that your son is away!

**좀-** petty; small. ¶ 좀생원 a narrow-minded person / 좀것《사람》 a petty person; 《물건》 small things; trifles.

**좀꾀**《잔꾀》 petty wiles; little 〔cheap〕 tricks. ⇨ 잔꾀. ¶ ～를 쓰다〔부리다〕 indulge in petty wiles.

**좀노릇** petty jobs; trifling work; small-time business.

**좀더**《양》「a little 〔some〕 more; 《수》 a few 〔some〕 more; 《시간》 a little longer; 《거리》 farther; 《정도》 further (★ farther는 거리에, further는 정도에 사용하나 이 구별은 엄밀치 않음). ¶ ～ 드시겠습니까 Won't you have some more? / ～ 주십시오 Please give me some more. / ～ 가자 Let's go farther 〔further〕.

**좀도둑** a pilferer; a sneak (thief); a petty thief; a snatcher. ¶ 집을 비운 동안에 ～이 들었다 The house was broken into while we were away.
◉ ～질 petty theft; pilfering: ～질을 하다 pilfer 《a handbag》; filch; commit petty theft; sneak; snatch.

**좀먹다**《벌레먹다》 be 〔get〕 moth-eaten; 《서서히 나쁘게 하다》 undermine; spoil; affect. ¶ 좀먹은 책 a moth-eaten book / 동심을 ～ spoil the child's mind / 수면 부족은 건강을 좀먹는다 Lack of sleep affects 〔ruins〕 your health. / 부패(행위)가 나라의 심장부를 좀먹고 있다 Corruption is eating at the heart of the country.

**좀생이** ① 〖천문〗 the Pleiades. ～보다 〖민속〗 check the Pleiades and their position from the moon on the first of (lunar) February to foretell the year's crop. ②《잔 물건》 small things.

**좀스럽다** ①《마음이》 (be) small-minded; petty. ¶ 좀스런 사람 a petty person / 좀스럽게 굴다 be too meticulous / 좀스럽게 별것 다 알려고 한다 Why are you so curious to know about such petty matters? ②《규모가》 (be) small; petty; trifling. ¶ 좀스런 일 a small-time business; petty jobs.

**좀약**(一藥) a mothball.

**좀처럼** 《여간해서는》 rarely; seldom; hardly; scarcely; 《쉽사리》 easily; readily; lightly.
¶ 그는 ~ 오지〔외출〕 않는다 He seldom comes here 〔goes out〕. / 이런 기회는 ~ 없다 It is a chance in a thousand. / 이 책은 ~ 찾아 볼 수 없다 This book is rarely found. / 보통 실력으로는 그 학교에 ~ 입학 못한다 You will hardly get into that school without much studying. / 문이 ~ 안 열린다 The door will not open easily. / ~ 해서는 그의 승낙을 얻기 힘들걸 I am afraid he will not give a ready consent. / 그는 ~ 성내지 않는다 He is slow to take offense.

**좀쳇것** a so-so thing; a common 〔an ordinary〕 thing; an unimpressive 〔unspecial〕 thing.

**좀팽이** a petty little person; a small-minded person.

**좁다** ① 《폭이》 (be) narrow; 《공간 범위가》 (be) small; limited; 《집 따위가》 (be) small; cramped; 《숨 막히도록》 (be) poky; stuffy; close; 《옷의 품 따위가》 (be) tight. ¶ 좁은 길 a narrow road 〔path〕 / 좁은 방 a poky 〔stuffy〕 little room; a small room (★ a narrow room은 폭이 좁은 방) / 좁은 시야 a narrow horizon / 좁은 문 the strait gate (마태복음 VII) / 좁은 활동 범위 a limited sphere of activity / 교제 범위가 ~ have a small circle of friends / 땅이 ~ be small in area / 가구가 많아서 방이 ~ The room is crowded with furniture and we are cramped for room. / 이 옷은 품이 ~ This coat is tight under the arm. / 세상이란 참 ~ How small the world is !
② 《도량·소견이》 (be) narrow (-minded); illiberal. ¶ 좁은 마음 a narrow mind / 좁은 뜻으로 in a narrow sense / 견해가 ~ be narrow in *one's* opinion; have a narrow view; be short-sighted.

**좁다랗다** (be) narrow and close; rather narrow; narrowish.

**좁쌀** ① 《조》 hulled millet. ¶ ~ 한 섬 두고 흉년 들기를 기다리다 be unrealistic (in *one's* preparations). ② [비유적] a petty 〔tiny〕 thing. ◉ ~과녁 a person with a broad flat face. ~뱅이 a petty person. ~영감 a petty old man.

**좁아지다** (get) narrow; become narrower. ¶ 골짜기는 갈수록 좁아졌다 The valley narrowed more and more. / 그 길은 여기서 좁아진다 The road gets narrow here. / 유명 대학 입학의 문은 더욱 좁아졌다 It has become more and more difficult to enter prestigious universities.

**좁히다** 《폭·범위를》 make narrow; straiten; restrict; 《간격을》 close; compact. ¶ 소매를 ~ take in the seam of the sleeves / 문제의 범위를 ~ limit the field of a problem / 좁혀 앉다 sit close 〔closely〕 / 선두의 두 주자 사이가 좁혀지고 있다 The gap between the front runners is narrowing.

**종**[1] 《마늘 따위의》 (the end of) a stalk 《of garlic》.

**종**[2] 《노비》 a servant; a slave; a bond(s)-man. ¶ 종의 근성 a servile temper / 계집〔여〕종 a slave girl; a female slave / 종으로 삼다 make a slave 《to, of》 / 종으로 팔리다 be sold for a slave / 종같이 부리다 put 《*a person*》 to a practical slave labor; use 《*a person*》 at *one's* beck and call / 종같이 일하다 work like a slave; drudge. ◉ 종노릇 slavery; serfdom: 종노릇하다 serve as a slave; be a slave 《to》.

**종**(終) the end; the finish.

**종**(種) ① 〖생물〗 a species. ¶ 종의 기원 《책명》 *the Origin of Species* / 여러 종의 나비 every species of butterflies. ② 《종류》 a sort; a kind; a class; a variety; a type. ¶ 3종 우편 third-class mail / 일종의 귀금속 a kind of precious metals / 여러 종의 우표 수집 a collection of a large variety of stamps. ③ 《품종》 a breed; a stock. ¶ 외국종의 말 a horse of foreign breed / 잡종 hybrid; crossbred. ④ 《종자》 a seed; a grain; a breed; a stock. ¶ 종마 a breeding 〔stud〕 horse; a stallion / 종우 a breeding cow; a stud bull.

**종**(縱) (a) length. = 세로.

**종**(鐘) a bell; a handbell (손종); a gong (징); a doorbell (초인종). ¶ 종소리 a sound of a bell / 저녁종 vesper bells / 종치는 방망이 a wood bell-hammer / 종을 달다 put a bell 《on》 / 종을 치다 strike 〔toll〕 a bell / 학교종을 울리다 ring 〔toll〕 a school bell / 종을 울려서 묵은해를 보내고 새해를 맞다 ring out the Old Year and ring in the New. ◉ 종지기 a bell ringer.

**종-**(從) a second-degree relative. ¶ 종자매 female cousins.

**-종**(宗) 《종파》 a religious sect; a denomination. ¶ 조계종(曹溪宗) the *Chogye* Sect.

**종가**(宗家) the main 〔head〕 family 〔house〕.

**종가래** a small spade 〔plow, shovel〕.

**종가세**(從價稅) an *ad valorem* duty.

**종각**(鐘閣) a bell house 〔pavilion〕.
**종간**(終刊) = 폐간(廢刊). ◉ ~호 the final number.
**종개념**(種槪念) 〖철학〗 specific concept.
**종견**(種犬) a breeding dog.
**종결**(終結) termination; (a) conclusion; an end; a close. ~하다 end; terminate; come 〔be brought〕 to an end 〔a close〕; be concluded; be settled. ¶ 전쟁의 ~ the end of the war / 토론의 ~ the conclusion of a discussion / ~시키다 bring 《*a matter*》 to an end 〔a conclusion〕; terminate 《state of war》 / 전쟁 ~의 교섭을 시작하다 begin negotiations for an end to the state of war.
**종고모**(從姑母) a female cousin of *one's* father.
**종곡**(終曲) 〖음악〗 the finale.
**종관**(縱貫) running 〔penetrating〕 lengthwise.
**종교**(宗敎) (a) religion; (a) (religious) faith. ¶ 계시〔자연〕~ (a) revealed 〔natural〕 religion / 기존의 ~ the established religions / 신흥~ a newly-born religion / ~상의, ~적 religious / 비~적 nonreligious / ~를 믿다 believe in a religion; embrace 〔profess〕 a religion / ~를 버리다 abjure *one's* religion / ~를 금하다 proscribe 〔ban〕 a religion / ~를 전도하다 propagate a religion; spread a faith / ~를 박해하다 persecute a religion / ~에서 위안을 찾다 seek solace 〔consolation〕 in religion / 그들은 각각 ~가 다르다 They are followers 〔adherents〕 of different faiths. /「당신의 ~는 무엇입니까」—「기독교입니다」 "What is your religion ?" — "I'm a Christian." / 나는 ~가 없다 I don't have any particular religion.
◉ ~가 a man of religion; a religious man; a believer. ~개혁 religious reformation; the Reformation. ~계 religious circles; the religious world. ~광 a religious crank 〔maniac〕; a fanatic. ~교육 religious education. ~극 a religious drama; a miracle play (기적극). ~단체 a religious body 〔organization〕. ~문제 a religious question 〔problem〕. ~문학 religious literature. ~미술 religious art. ~박해 religious persecution. ~법인 a religious corporation. ~사 (a) history of religions. ~서적 religious books; a book on religion (단권). ~심 a religious sentiment: ~심이 있는〔없는〕 religious 〔irreligious〕; pious 〔impious〕. ~열 religious enthusiasm. ~음악 sacred music. ~의식 a religious ceremony. ~재판 the Inquisition. ~조각 religious sculpture. ~철학 philosophy of religion. ~학 the science of religion: 비교 ~학 comparative religion / ~학 교수 a professor of religion. ~화(畵) a holy 〔sacred, religious〕 picture. ~회의 a religious conference; an ecclesiastical meeting.
**종국**(終局) an end; a close; a termination; a finale; a conclusion; a denouement. ¶ ~의 final; ultimate; eventual / ~에 가서는 after all; ultimately; in the long run / 인생 ~의 목적 the ultimate purpose of life / ~의 승리 ultimate victory / ~에 가까워지다 draw to an end / ~을 고하다 come 〔be brought〕 to an end 〔a close〕; be settled / 전쟁은 드디어 ~을 고했다 The war came to an end at last.
**종군**(從軍) joining the army; service in a war; going to the front. ~하다 follow 〔join〕 the army; go to the front; serve in the war. ¶ ~하고 있다 be at the front; be on active service (in the war) / ~을 자원하다 apply for attachment to the army / ~ 허가를 얻다 obtain permission to join the army. ◉ ~간호사 a (Red Cross) nurse attached to the army. ~기자 a war correspondent. ~기장(記章) a war medal. ~위안부 "comfort girls" (attached to the army); women being forced to work in Japanese military-run brothels during World War II.
**종극**(終極) finality; extremity; the ultimate. ¶ ~의 final; extreme; ultimate.
**종기**(終期) the end (of a term); the close; the termination.
**종기**(腫氣) a swelling; a boil; an abscess; a tumor. ¶ 악성~ a malignant tumor / 등에 ~가 나다 get 〔have〕 a boil on *one's* back.
**종내**(終乃) at (long) last; finally. ⇨ 마침내.
**종내기**(種—) a breed; a stock; a species. ¶ ~가 같다〔다르다〕 be of the same 〔a different〕 breed.
**종년** a servant 〔slave〕 girl.
**종놈** a servant; a slave.
**종다래끼** a small bamboo basket; 《잡은 고기 담는》 a small fishing basket; a creel.
**종다수**(從多數) following the views of the majority. ~하다 follow 〔agree〕 the views of the majority. ¶ ~ 결정하다 pass a resolution 〔decide 《*a matter*》〕 by majority vote.

**종단**(宗團) a religious order.

**종단**(縱斷) vertical; cutting from north to south; 《분할》 a division; a split. ～하다 《절단하다》 cut 〔divide〕 《*something*》 vertically; 《장소를》 traverse; run through 《a field》; travel down through 《the Americas》; travel the length of 《Africa》. ¶ 그 철도는 대평원을 ～하고 있다 The railroad runs through the prairie. / 그녀는 한국 ～여행을 계획하고 있다 She is planning to travel through Korea from North to South. ◉ ～면 a longitudinal 〔vertical〕 section. ～철도 a railroad running through 《the mainland》.

**종달새** 『조류』 a skylark; a lark.

**종답**(宗畓) paddy fields set apart as provision for sacrificial purposes; clan fields.

**종당**(從當) as a matter of course; after all; in the end.

**종대**(縱隊) a column (of troops); a file. ¶ 4열 ～로 in column of fours / ～를 짓다 form a file / 2열 ～로 행진하다 march in double file.

**종돈**(種豚) a breeding pig; 《수컷》 a boar; 《암컷》 a breed sow.

**종두**(種痘) (a) vaccination. ⇨ 우두(牛痘).

**종람**(縱覽) 《마음대로 봄》 (general) inspection; reading (열람). ～하다 inspect; go over; visit; read. ¶ ～케 하다 make 《the list of electors》 available for public inspection / ～을 환영〔사절〕하다 invite 〔decline〕 inspection / ～수의(隨意)〔사절〕 《게시》 Available 〔Not available〕 to the public. / 회의 의사록은 누구나 ～할 수 있음 The minutes of official meetings are open to public inspection. ◉ ～실 an exhibition 〔a reading〕 room. ～자 a visitor; a reader; 《참관자》 a spectator.

**종래**(從來) hitherto; heretofore; up to now; so far. ¶ ～의 old; former; usual / ～와 같이 as before; as usual 〔ever〕; as of old; as in the past / ～의 사업 the former business / ～의 악폐를 일소하다 make away with the existing evils.

**종량세**(從量稅) a specific duty.

**종려**(棕櫚) 『식물』 a hemp palm. ◉ ～나무 a palm tree. ～유 palm oil.

**종렬**(縱列) a file; a column. ¶ 소대〔중대, 분대〕 ～로 in a column of platoons 〔companies, squads〕 / ～을 이루다 form a file / ～로 행진하다 defile.

**종료**(終了) an end; (a) conclusion; a close; completion (완료); expiration (기한의). ～하다 《마치다》 end; close; conclude; complete; 《끝나다》 come to an end; 《완료하다》 be completed; be finished. ¶ 전쟁을 ～시키다 bring the war to an end / 점검이 ～된 것은 오전 5시가 지나서였다 Our checkup was not finished until after 5 in the morning.

**종루**(鐘樓) a belfry; a bell tower; a bell pavilion.

**종류**(種類) a kind; a sort; a variety; a class; a description; a species (동식물의); a type (형); a nature (성질).

> (용법) **kind** 동일한 성질을 가지고 있어서 자연적으로 하나의 무리로 분류 또는 구분할 수 있는 종류. **sort** kind처럼 엄밀하지는 않지만, 어느 정도의 유사점을 가지고 있는 종류. 종종 kind와 같은 뜻으로도 쓰임. **variety** 같은 부류 속에 있으면서도 세부적인 면에서 질적으로 다른 점이 있음을 강조하는 뜻을 가진 종류. **class** 동일한 성질을 가지고 있는 부류의 집단으로, 등급·우열·품위 따위의 가치 판단을 암시하는 뜻의 종류. **type** 다른 것과 뚜렷하게 구별할 수 있는 특징을 가진 종류.

¶ 온갖 ～의 all kinds 〔sorts〕 of; of every kind 〔description〕 / ～가 다른 of a different kind / 여러 ～의 물건 things of various kinds / 이런 ～의 사건 events of this nature / 여러 가지 ～의 우표 수집 a collection of a large variety of stamps / 세 가지 ～의 글 three kinds of sentence(s) (★ 「수사+kinds of+가산명사」의 경우 그 명사는 복수형을 쓰는 것이 보통) / 이 ～의 나무들 these 〔this〕 kind of trees (★ these는 kind of trees를 형용하며 「몇 종류인가의 나무들」의 뜻이 됨. 다만, 「이 종류의 사람들」과 같은 경우는 these kind(s) 〔this kind〕 of people의 세 가지 표현이 가능. 또 kind를 쓸 경우, 동사는 복수·단수 양쪽을 다 씀. sort의 경우도 같음) / 이런 ～의 사기 this type 〔form〕 of swindling / ～별로 나누다 classify; assort / 세 ～로 나누다 divide 《*things*》 into three classes / 온갖 ～의 사람들이 모였다 All manner of people gathered together. / 어떤 ～의 케이크를 제일 좋아합니까 What kind of cake do you like best?

**종마**(種馬) a breeding horse; a stud; a stallion (at stud).

**종막**(終幕) ① 《연극 따위의》 the last 〔final〕 act 《of a play》; a curtain fall. ② 《사건의》 an end; a close; 《대단원》

a denouement. ¶ ~을 고하다 come 〔be brought〕 to an end.

**종말**(終末) a close; a conclusion; an end. ¶ ~을 고하다 come 〔be brought〕 to「an end 〔a conclusion, a close〕; be concluded / 전쟁도 ~이 가까워지고 있다 The war is drawing to a close. ◉ ~론 『종교』 eschatology.

**종매**(從妹) a female younger cousin.

**종목**(種目) an item; a line; 《경기의》 an event. ¶ 영업~ items of business / 알파인 ~ the Alpine events / 제품을 ~별로 리스트하다 list products by item.

**종묘**(宗廟) the royal ancestors' shrine; the ancestral temple of the royal family.

**종묘**(種苗) 《씨·묘목》 seeds and saplings; seedlings; 《씨·모종을 심음》 planting a seedling 〔sapling〕. ◉ ~장 a field for seedling; a nursery (garden). ~회사 a nursery company.

**종무**(宗務) religious affairs. ◉ ~소 a temple office.

**종무**(終務) the closing of offices for the year. ◉ ~일 the last business day of the year at the offices.

**종반전**(終盤戰) 《바둑·장기의》 an end game; 《선거 등의》 《get into》 the last 〔final〕 stage(s) 〔phase〕 《of an election campaign》. ¶ 선거 운동도 사실상 ~에 들어갔다 The election campaign is effectively in its final stages. / 프로야구 시즌은 마침내 ~에 들어갔다 The professional baseball season has entered its final phase at last.

**종발**(鍾鉢) a small bowl.

**종범**(從犯) 『법』 《죄》 participation in a crime; 《사람》 an accessory 《to a crime》; an accomplice. ¶ 살인 ~ an accessory to murder. ◉ 사전〔사후〕~ an accessory before 〔after〕 the fact.

**종별**(種別) (a) classification; (an) assortment. ~하다 classify 《into》; divide into classes; assort.

**종복**(從僕) a servant; an attendant.

**종사**(宗嗣) a descendant 〔heir〕 of the main 〔head〕 family of a clan.

**종사**(從死) killing *oneself* to follow 《*a person*》 in death. ~하다 die in attendance on 《*a person*》; follow to the grave.

**종사**(從事) 《일에》 attending to 《*one's* work》; 《직업·사업에》 following a profession; pursuing 《a calling》. ~하다 《일에》 attend to 《*one's* work》; engage in 《business》; 《직업에》 pursue 《a calling》; follow 《a profession》. ¶ …에 ~하고 있다 be engaged in; be occupied with 〔in〕; be at work / 공무〔무역〕에 ~하고 있다 be engaged in official duties 〔trade〕 / 건설업에 ~하다 work on the building trades / 교육에 ~하다 employ *oneself* on education / 주민의 대부분은 농업에 ~하고 있다 Most of the inhabitants are farmers. / 그는 무슨 직업에 ~하고 있습니까 What business is he engaged in? *or* What is he by occupation 〔profession〕? / 나는 인쇄업에 ~하고 있다 I am in the printing line.

**종사**(縱射) 『군사』 a raking fire; an enfilade. ~하다 rake (with fire); enfilade; sweep. ◉ ~포 a raker.

**종산**(宗山) a clan 〔an ancestral〕 graveyard.

**종서**(縱書) vertical 〔up-and-down〕 writing. ~하다 write vertically 〔in vertical lines〕.

**종선**(縱線) a vertical 〔longitudinal〕 line; 『음악』 a bar (마딧줄).

**종성**(終聲) 『언어』 a final consonant.

**종속**(從屬) subordination; dependence. ~하다 be subordinate 《to》; be subject 《to》; be dependent 《on》. ¶ ~적인 subordinate; dependent; secondary / ~시키다 subordinate 《*a thing*》 to 《*a person*》 / 홍보과를 판매부에 ~시키다 subordinate the advertisement section to the sales department. ◉ ~관계 subordinate relationship. ~국가 a dependent state; a dependency. ~이론 the theory of dependence. ~절〔구〕 『문법』 a subordinate clause 〔phrase〕. ~접속사 『문법』 a subordinate conjunction.

**종손**(宗孫) the eldest grandson of the main family.

**종손**(從孫) the grandson of *one's* brother; a grandnephew.

**종손녀**(從孫女) the granddaughter of *one's* brother; a grandniece.

**종숙**(從叔) a male cousin of *one's* father.

**종숙모**(從叔母) the wife of *one's* father's cousin.

**종시**(終始) = 시종(始終).

**종시**(終是) = 끝끝내.

**종시속**(從時俗) conforming to the times; following the customs of the day. ~하다 conform to the times; follow the customs of the day.

**종식**(終熄) cessation; an end; eradication (근절). ~하다 cease; come 〔be brought〕 to an end; 《근절》 be eradicated 〔extirpated〕; be stamped out

(전염병의). ¶ ~시키다 put an end 〔a stop〕 to 《a war》/ 제2차 세계대전은 1945년에 ~되었다 World War II came to an end in 1945.

**종신**(宗臣) ① 《원훈》 a distinguished minister of state. ② 《왕족》 a minister from the royal family.

**종신**(終身) 《한평생》 a whole life; all *one's* life; 《죽음》 the end of life; *one's* death; 《임종》 being at *one's* parent's deathbed. ~하다 live out *one's* life; end *one's* days; be at 〔on〕 *one's* parent's deathbed. ¶ ~의 life; lifelong; lifetime / ~ 사업 *one's* life work / ~지계 a plan to live by through *one's* life.
◉ ~고용제 a lifetime 〔lifelong〕 employment system. ~보험 straight 〔whole〕 life insurance. ~연금 a life annuity 〔pension〕. ~직 a life office; an office for life; a life tenure 《of office》. ~형 life imprisonment; penal servitude for life; a life sentence: ~형을 선고받다 be sentenced to life imprisonment / ~형을 살다 serve a life sentence. ~회원 a life member.

**종실**(宗室) the royal family; royal clansmen.

**종심**(終審) 〖법〗 the final judicial examination; the final trial. ◉ ~법원 the court of last instance.

**종씨**(宗氏) a clansman (of the same surname).

**종씨**(從氏) ① 《자기의》 a paternal cousin older than *oneself*. ② 《남의》 a paternal cousin of 《*a person*》.

**종아리** the calf. ¶ ~를 맞다 get whipped on the calf / ~를 때리다 lash 〔whip〕 《*a person*》 on the calf /「나는, 우리 교수들이 그들을 제대로 교육시키지 못한 것을 안타깝게 생각하며, 스스로 내 ~를 때리고 싶은 심정이다」라고 그는 말했다 "I regret that we professors did not educate them properly and I feel like whipping my own legs with a rod," he said. ◉ ~뼈 〖해부〗 a fibula; a splint bone. ~채 a switch; a cane 《미》.

**종알거리다** mutter; murmur 《in complaint》; spatter; babble; prattle. ¶ 혼자 ~ mutter to *oneself*.

**종야**(終夜) all night; the whole night; all the night through; through the night.

**종양**(腫瘍) 〖의학〗 a tumor; a neoplasm. ¶ 뇌 ~ a cerebral tumor / 악성〔양성〕 ~ a malignant 〔benign〕 tumor.
◉ ~학 oncology; phymatology.

**종언**(終焉) 《죽음》 last moments; the end of life; death; 《종말》 an end; a close; expiration; completion; finish. ~하다 die; end; finish; complete. ¶ ~을 고하다 end; come to an end.

**종업**(從業) work in service; attending to *one's* work. ~하다 be employed; be in the service; be in employment.

**종업**(終業) 《기업체의》 finishing 〔the end of〕 work; 《학교의》 the close of school. ~하다 end 〔complete〕 *one's* work. ◉ ~시간 finishing time; 《구어》 knocking-off time (공장 등의); closing time (상점의). ~식 the closing ceremony 〔exercises〕: ~식은 24일이다 School will break up on the 24th. ~일 《학년말, 학기말의》 the breaking-up day; the last day of school.

**종업원**(從業員) 《1인》 an employee; a worker; [총칭] men; the work force. ¶ 이 공장에는 약 200명의 ~이 있다 There are about two hundred workers in this factory.
◉ ~교육 the training of employees; employee education 〔training〕. ~대표 a spokesman of the working men. ~명부 a name-list of employees. ~전용: ~전용 승강기 a service elevator 〔lift 《영》〕/ ~전용 입구 a staff 〔an employees'〕 entrance. ~조합 an employees' union. ~지주제(持株制) employee stock ownership plan. ~출입구 a private doorway for employee. ~퇴직 수당 적립금 a reserve for employees' retirement allowance.

**종연**(終演) the end of a show; the close 《of a run of performances》. ~하다 end; finish; close 《a theater, the performance》. ¶ 오후 10시 ~ The curtain falls at 10 p.m.

**종용**(慫慂) 《유도》 inducement; 《설득》 coaxing; persuasion; suggestion; advice. ~하다 coax; persuade; suggest; advise. ¶ 아무의 ~으로 at *a person's* suggestion 〔instance〕/ 나는 그에게 경찰에 자수하기를 ~했다 I advised him to surrender himself to police officers.

**종우**(種牛) a breeding cow 〔bull〕; a seed bull.

**종유**(種油) 《씨의》 seed oil; 《평지의》 rape(-seed) oil; colza oil.

**종유동**(鍾乳洞) a stalactite cavern 〔cave, grotto〕.

**종유석**(鍾乳石) stalactite.

**종이** paper. ¶ ~한 장 a sheet of paper / ~ 1첩〔1련〕 a quire 〔ream〕 of paper / ~로 만든 made of paper;

papermade / ~를 뜨다〔만들다〕 make paper / ~에 적다 write 〔put down〕 on paper / ~로 싸다 wrap 〔do up〕 《*a thing*》 in paper / ~를 접어 학을 만들다 fold a piece of paper into the figure of a crane / ~를 바르다 paper 《a wall》 / ~ 한 장의 차이다 There is but slight difference between them. ◉ ~꾸러미 a paper parcel 〔package〕. ~냅킨 a paper napkin 〔serviette〕. ~돈 paper money. ~접기 the art of folding paper into various forms. ~쪽 a piece 〔scrap, strip, slip〕 of paper. ~컵〔잔〕 a paper cup; a Dixie (cup). ~테이프 a paper tape; 《환영·환송용의》 paper streamers. ~표지 a paperback; a paper cover. ~호랑이 a paper tiger.

**종일**(終日) all day (long); all the day; the whole day; from morning till 〔to〕 night; throughout the day. ¶ ~ 공부하다 study all day long / 어제는 ~ 비가 왔다 It rained yesterday from morning till night. / 나는 ~ 기다렸다 I was kept waiting all through the day. / 비 때문에 하루 ~ 집에 있었다 I have been at home all day long because of rain. / 아버님은 ~서재에서 책을 읽으셔도 지루하지 않으신 것 같다 My father does not seem to be tired of reading books in his study all day.

**종자**(從者) a follower; an attendant; a valet; a (body) servant; 《수행원들》 a retinue; a suite.

**종자**(種子) ① = 씨[1]. ② 《사람》 an offspring. ◉ ~돈 seed money. ~식물 a seed plant.

**종자매**(從姉妹) female cousins.

**종작없다** (be) pointless; desultory; senseless; nonsensical; absurd. ¶ 종작없는 말 senseless remarks; nonsense.

**종잡다** get the gist; get a rough idea; get at the main idea; get the point; roughly understand. ¶ 나는 그의 말을 종잡을 수 없다 I can't see what he's driving at. *or* There is no logic in his remark.

**종장**(終章) the last of the 3 verses of a (*shijo*) poem; the last part of a song.

**종장**(終場) 〖증권〗 closing. ◉ ~가격〔시세〕 the closing price 〔quotations〕.

**종적**(蹤迹) *one's* traces; *one's* tracks; *one's* whereabouts. ¶ ~을 감추다 cover *one's* tracks; leave no trace behind; disappear / 소년이 ~을 감춘지 며칠 된다 The boy has been missing from his home for some days.

**종적**(縱的) longitudinal; lengthwise; vertical (수직의). ¶ ~ 연락 vertical contact.

**종전**(從前) ¶ ~의 previous; past; former; old; usual / ~에 hitherto; heretofore; formerly; before / ~의 관계 *one's* past connections 《with *a person*》 / ~과 같이 as in the past; as usual; as before; as hitherto / ~과 같다 be same as before / 그는 모든 것이 ~ 그대로이기를 원했다 He wanted everything to be the way it had been. / ~에는 이런 문제들을 어떻게 처리해 왔느냐 How have you dealt with problems like this in the past?

**종전**(終戰) the end of a war; the termination 〔cessation〕 of hostilities. ¶ 제2차 세계대전 ~ 기념일 the anniversary of the end of the 2nd World War / ~후의 postwar / ~ 당시에 at the time of the war's end / ~이 되다 the war comes to an end.

**종점**(終點) the terminal (station); 《영》 the terminus; the last stop; 《미》 the end of the line; 《버스의》 a bus terminal. ¶ 자 ~에 다 왔다 Now we are at the last stop.

**종정**(宗正) 〖불교〗 the (Order's) supreme patriarch.

**종제**(從弟) younger male paternal cousins.

**종조모**(從祖母) a grandaunt; the wife of *one's* granduncle 〔great-uncle〕.

**종조부**(從祖父) a granduncle; a great-uncle.

**종족**(種族) a race; a tribe; 《동식물의》 phylum (*pl.* -la); a family; a genus; a species. ¶ ~을 늘리다 spread 〔produce more of〕 《their》 kind / ~간의 intertribal; interracial (민족간의) / ~ 보존의 본능 the instinct of preservation of the species.

**종종**(種種) ① 《가지가지》 several 〔various, diverse, different〕 kinds. ② 《가끔》 often; frequently; every now and then. ¶ ~ 친구를 찾다 visit a friend every now and then / ~ 놀러 오십시오 Come and see us often. / ~ 폐를 끼쳐 미안합니다 I am sorry to trouble you so often. / 이 곳에는 늦은 여름에 태풍이 ~ 온다 Typhoons are frequent here during late summer.

**종종** with short quick paces; with hurried steps. ~거리다 walk with hurried steps.

**종종걸음** short and quick steps; a

quick pace; hurried 〔mincing〕 steps; tripping. ¶ ～ 치다 walk with hurried steps; walk with short and quick steps; go pit-a-pat.

**종주**(宗主) a suzerain. ◉ ～국 a suzerain state. ～권 suzerainty: ～권하에 있다 be under the suzerainty of….

**종중**(宗中) the families of the same clan.

**종지** a small dish 〔bowl, cup〕.

**종지**(宗旨) the fundamental meaning; the main purport; a tenet; principles.

**종지**(終止) termination; cessation; an end; a stop. ～하다 terminate; cease; stop; come to an end.

◉ ～부 a full stop; a period: ～부를 찍다 put a period 〔an end〕 《to》. ～사(詞) the sentence-final form.

**종지뼈** the kneecap; the patella. ⇨무릎뼈, 슬개골.

**종진**(縱陣) a column; a line ahead. ¶ ～으로 in a line ahead; in single file / ～을 펴다 form a column.

**종질**(從姪) a male cousin's son.

◉ ～녀 a male cousin's daughter. ～부 the wife of a male cousin's son.

**종착역**(終着驛) a terminal (station); a terminus (*pl.* -ni, ～es). ¶ 인생의 ～ the terminus of *one's* life / 부산은 경부선의 ～이다 The Kyŏngbu line terminates in Pusan.

**종창**(腫脹) 〖의학〗 tumefaction.

**종축**(種畜) breeding stock. ◉ ～장 a livestock breeding farm.

**종축**(縱軸) a vertical axis; 〖수학〗 the axis of ordinates. ＝세로축.

**종친**(宗親) 《임금 친척》 kindred of the king; royal clansmen. ¶ ～회 《친족의》 a family 〔clan〕 council 〔meeting〕.

**종콩** a kind of small white bean.

**종탑**(鐘塔) a bell tower; a belfry.

**종파**(宗派) ① 《지파에 대한》 the main branch of a family 〔clan〕. ② 《파벌》 a sect; a denomination. ¶ ～적(인) sectarian; denominational. ◉ ～심 sectarianism. ～싸움 a sectarian strife.

**종파**(縱波) a longitudinal wave.

**종피**(種皮) 〖식물〗 a testa (*pl.* -tae).

**종합**(綜合) (a) synthesis (*pl.* -ses); generalization; 〖논리〗 colligation. ～하다 synthesize; generalize; unite; put 〔piece〕 together. ¶ ～적 synthetic; composite; overall; comprehensive; 《미》 all-around / ～운영 integrated 〔well-coordinated〕 management / ～적으로 synthetically / 이들 각종 보고를 ～해보니 putting these various reports together / ～해서 생각하다 think of collectively / 이것을 ～하면 아마 이렇게 될 것이다 Summing up, this will come to the following result.

◉ ～개발 overall 〔comprehensive〕 development. ～경기 all-around games 〔events〕; 《체조의》 combined exercises: 개인 〔단체〕 ～경기 individual 〔team〕 combined (exercises) / 잠실 ～경기장 the Seoul Sports Complex. ～계획 an all-out plan; a comprehensive program 〔plan〕. ～과세 consolidated 〔aggregate〕 taxation. ～과학 a synthetic science. ～대학교 a university. ～무역 상사 a general trading company. ～병원 a general hospital; a polyclinic (hospital). ～보험 comprehensive 〔umbrella〕 insurance. ～비타민 〖약〗 vitamin complex; multiple vitamin: ～비타민제 a vitamin complex preparation 〔pill〕; a multivitamin pill. ～사진 a composite photograph. ～선수권 the all-around championships. ～소득세 a composite income tax. ～예술 a composite art. ～잡지 an all-around magazine; a (general) magazine. ～재산세제 the integrated properties tax system. ～지수 all-items index. ～철학 synthetic philosophy. ～청사 the Integrated Government Building. ～토지세제 an integrated land tax system. ～판단 (a) synthetic judgment.

**종형**(從兄) an older (male) cousin.

**종형제**(從兄弟) (male) cousins.

**종회**(宗會) a clan 〔family〕 meeting. ¶ ～를 열다 hold a family meeting.

**종횡**(縱橫) perpendicular and 〔or〕 horizontal; length and breadth. ¶ ～으로 《세로 가로로》 lengthwise and crosswise; vertically and horizontally; 《사방 팔방으로》 in all directions; in every direction; throughout the length and breadth 《of》 / ～무진으로 freely; at will; most actively / ～으로 뻗은 철도망 a network of railroads covering the country / ～무진한 재치 a wealth of wit / 문제를 ～무진으로 논하다 discuss 〔deal with〕 a problem from all angles.

**좆** the penis.

**좇다** ① 《뒤를》 follow; go 〔run〕 after; trail; track; pursue. ¶ 명리(名利)를 ～ follow 〔run after〕 wealth and fame / 아무의 뒤를 ～ follow *a person;* dog *a person's* footsteps. / 그녀는 허황된 꿈만을 좇고 있다 She is always running after dreams.

② 《그대로 함》 follow; conform *oneself*

to; act on 〔upon〕. ¶ 관습을 좇아서 in conformity with custom; according to custom / 선례를 ～ follow a precedent / 유행을 ～ follow the fashion / 대세에 ～ conform to the times / 충고를 ～ take 〔follow〕《*a person's*》 advice / 남이 하는 대로 좇아 하다 follow 《another's》 example; follow in 《another's》 steps / 공자의 가르침을 ～ follow Confucius teachings / 원칙에 좇아 행하다 act on a principle.

③《복종하다》 obey; abide by; submit 〔give in〕 to. ¶ 아무의 지시를 ～ follow 〔take〕 *a person's* direction / 명령을 ～ obey 《*a person's*》 orders 〔commands〕 / 법을 ～ obey 〔be obedient to〕 the law / 아무의 뜻에 ～ submit to *a person's* will.

**좋다**[1] ①《모양·상태·성질 등이》 (be) good; fine; nice. ¶ 좋은 집〔그림, 길, 책〕 a good house 〔picture, road, book〕 / 좋은 냄새 a nice 〔sweet〕 smell / 좋든 나쁘든 for better or for worse; if things are good or bad / 마음씨가 ～ be good-natured〔-humored〕 / 집안이 ～ be of 〔come from〕 a good family / 그는 머리가 ～ He is bright 〔smart, clever〕. / 그게 그의 좋은 점이다 That's one good thing about him. / 좋은 물건을 주지 Here is something nice for you. / 그거 좋은 생각이다 That's a good idea. / 그는 기억력이 ～He has a good 〔retentive〕 memory. / 날씨가〔날이〕 ～ It's a lovely day.

②《유익하다》 (be) beneficial; favorable; good. ¶ 두통에 좋은 약 a medicine good for headache / 몸〔위〕에 ～ be good for the health 〔stomach〕 / 먹기에 ～ be good to eat / 우유는 어린이에게 ～ Milk is good for children. / 그렇게 하는 것이 ～고 생각했다 I thought it good to do so.

③《적당하다》 (be) right; proper; suitable; good. ¶ 좋은 실례 a good example / 좋은 기회 a good opportunity 〔chance〕 / 좋을 대로 하다 do as *one* pleases; suit *oneself* / 어찌 해야 좋을지 모르다 don't know what to do / 마침 좋은 때에 왔네 You have come just at the right time. *or* You have come just in time.

④《재능이》 (be) able; skilled; good. ¶ 손재주가 ～ be dexterous; be good 〔clever〕 with *one's* hands / 재간이 ～ be talented / 입심이 ～ have a glib tongue / 필적이 ～ write a good hand / 영어 실력이 ～ have a good command of English.

⑤《좋아하다》 like; 《비교·선택하다》 (be) better; preferable; superior 《to》. ¶ 훨씬 ～ be far 〔much〕 better / 나는 이것이 ～ I like this. / 나는 그것보다 이것이 좋다 I like this better than that. *or* I prefer this to that. (★ I love her more than Mary.라고는 쓸 수 있지만 I like this more than that.으로는 할 수 없음. like를 쓸 경우 better than이 보통) / 나는 귤보다 사과가 ～ I like apples better than tangerines. / 「홍차와 커피 중 어느 쪽이 좋습니까」—「커피가 좋습니다」 "Which would you prefer, tea or coffee ?"—"I prefer coffee." / 빨리하면 할수록 더욱 ～ The sooner done the better.

⑥《바라다》 wish; hope; desire. ¶ 자동차가 있으면 좋겠다 I wish I had a car. / 그래 내가 죽으면 좋겠니 So, do you wish me dead ? / 내가 새라면 좋겠는데 I wish I were a bird. / 내일 날이 맑으면 좋겠다 I hope it will be fine tomorrow. / 오디션에 통과만 하면 좋겠는데 If only I could pass the audition.

⑦《…이 낫다》 (had) better (*do*). ¶ 그 책을 읽는 것이 ～ You had better read the book. *or* You should read the book. (★ had better는 should보다 더욱 강한 충고를 나타냄. ought와 should는 대체로 같은 뜻으로 마땅히 해야 할 것을 뜻함. 또 You had better do it.의 과거형은 You had better have done it.) / 그런 짓은 하지 않는 것이 ～ You had better not do such a thing. (★ had better는 조동사적으로 취급되며, not은 뒤에 옴) / 너는 곧 가는 것이〔가지 않는 것이〕 ～ You had better go 〔not go〕 at once. (★말하는 이에게 「체념적 기분」과 같은 소극적 태도가 있을 때에는 You may as well go at once.) / 하지 않는 편이 ～ You (had) better not try.

⑧《귀하다》 (be) precious; valuable; noble (고귀). ¶ 좋은 자료 valuable 〔precious〕 material / 저 사람은 좋은 집안의 태생이다 He comes of a noble family.

⑨《괜찮다》 may; can; do not mind 《*doing*》; do not care (if) (★ may의 부정은 must not, cannot이 보통 쓰임: You may go... You must not 〔cannot〕 go.) ¶ 가도 ～ You may go. / 「담배 피워도 좋습니까」—「네, 좋습니다」 "May I smoke ?"—"Yes, you may." / 이 과자 먹어도 좋습니까 Can I have this cake ? (★ Can I...?보다 May I...?가 더 정중한 표

현. 대답은 Yes, you may 〔can〕. 보다 certainly, sure 따위를 쓰는 것이 보통) / 하다 못해 잘못했다는 말은 해도 좋지 않겠어 You might at least apologize. / 얼마라도 좋으니 돈 좀 빌려줘 Lend me whatever sum you can spare. / 사람들이 무어라고 해도 ～ I don't care what people say about me.

⑩《무방하다》 do not have to; need not; can get along without. ¶ 좋은 것이 아니라도 ～ It doesn't have to be good. / 내일 오지 않아도 ～ You don't need to come tomorrow. / 일부러 설명 안 해도 ～ You need not trouble yourself to explain. / 그가 없어도 ～ We can do very well without him. / 「내일 낸시와 드라이브 가지 않겠니」—「그거 좋지」 "How about going for a drive with Nancy tomorrow ?"—"I wouldn't say no."

⑪《길하다》 (be) good; lucky; happy; auspicious; favorable. ¶ 좋은 조짐 a good omen / 좋은 번호 a lucky number / 좋은 날 a lucky day.

**좋다**[2] 《느낌》 Good !; Well !; All right !; O.K.; 《환성》 Whoopee !; Goody !; Oh boy !; Whee ! ¶ ～ 내가 떠맡겠다 All right, I will undertake the work. *or* O.K., I'll take it on. / ～ 그렇게 하지 Very well 〔All right〕, I'll do so.

**좋아지내다** be on intimate terms 《with》; be good friends 《with》. ¶ 그 둘은 서로 좋아 지낸다 The two of them are hand and 〔in〕 glove with each other.

**좋아지다** ①《상태가》 improve; become 〔get〕 better; 《병세가》 get better; take a turn for the better; 《날씨가》 clear up; 《아름다워지다》 become finer 〔more beautiful〕. ¶ 날씨가 ～ the weather clears up; the weather becomes better 〔improves〕 / 경기가 ～ business is improving 〔picking up, looking up〕 / 그는 병세가 점점 좋아지고 있다 He is getting better. *or* He is on the road to recovery.

②《좋아하게 되다》 get 〔come, learn〕 to like 《*a thing*》; become 〔grow〕 fond of; take a fancy 〔liking〕 to. ¶ …이 점점 ～ develop a liking for… / 나는 이 집이 좋아졌어요 I've become fond of this house.

**좋아하다** ①《기호》 like; 《사랑》 love; be fond 《of》; have a liking 〔fancy, taste〕 for; 《특별히》 be partial to; 《주로 음식을》 have a weakness for 《apples》; 《선택》 prefer 《*a thing*》 to 《another》; 《주로 부정문, 의문문에》 care 《for *something*, to *do*》.
¶ 좋아하든 싫어하든 whether *one* likes or not / 좋아하는 이 *one's* lover; a sweetheart / 좋아하는 책 *one's* favorite book / 좋아하는 일을 하다 do what *one* likes; follow *one's* own bent / 그리 좋아하지 않다 do not care much for 〔to *do*〕 it / 음악을 ～ be fond of music / 장미보다 백합을 ～ prefer lilies to roses / 자네가 좋아하는 가수는 누군가 Who is your favorite singer ? / 그들은 서로 좋아하는 사이다 They are in love with each other. / 그는 스포츠를 매우 좋아한다 He is partial to sports. / 그는 술을 좋아한다 He has a weakness for wine 〔liquor〕. / 그는 한국을 몹시 좋아하는 미국인이다 He is a great pro=Korean American. / 나는 그(를 좋아하기)보다는 그녀를 더 좋아한다 I love her more than him. (★ more than he면 「그와 나 두 사람 중 내가 그녀를 더 좋아한다」의 뜻이 됨).

②《기뻐하다》 be glad 《of, to *do*, that …》; be pleased 〔delighted〕 《with, at, to *do*》; (take) delight 《in》; rejoice 《at, over》. ¶ 장난치며 좋아하는 아이들 boys taking delight in doing mischiefs / 껑충껑충 뛰면서 ～ dance with joy / 그는 그 말을 듣고 무척 좋아했다 He was much pleased to hear that. / 그 소식에 모두들 좋아했다 All were delighted at the news. / 그는 무언가 읽으며 혼자 좋아하고 있었다 He was chuckling to himself over what he was reading.

**좋이** well; full; good; fully. ¶ ～ 10마일 a good ten miles / ～ 세 시간 a full 〔good〕 three hours / ～ 60은 넘다 be well over sixty / ～ 두 되는 된다 It makes a full measure of 2 *toe*. / 키가 6피트는 ～ 된다 He stands full six feet tall. / 거기까진 ～ 다섯 시간 걸린다 It takes a good five hours to get there.

**좋지않다** ①《도덕상》 (be) bad; evil; wrong; immoral; sinful. ¶ 좋지 않은 일 a wrong; an evil deed; a misdeed / 좋지 않은 짓을 하다 do wrong; commit a sin 〔crime〕.

②《악하다》 (be) bad; evil; wicked; ill-natured; malicious; villainous; roguish. ¶ 좋지 않은 사람 a wicked man; a rascal.

③《해롭다》 (be) bad; harmful; injurious; detrimental; 《불리하다》 (be) disadvantageous; impolitic; unadvis-

able. ¶ 눈에 ~ be bad for [be injurious to] the eyes / 이런 책을 아이들이 읽는 것은 ~ Such books should not be placed in boy's hands.
④《품질이》(be) bad; inferior; be of low grade; be of inferior quality.
⑤《머리가》(be) poor; weak. ¶ 머리가 ~ be weak-[muddle-]headed.
⑥《날씨가》(be) bad; foul; inclement (사나운); nasty. ¶ 좋지 않은 날씨 foul [bad, nasty] weather.
⑦《불길하다》(be) ill; unlucky; bad; ominous. ¶ 좋지 않은 징조 a bad [an ill] omen.
⑧《평판이》(be) bad; ill; unsavory. ¶ 좋지 않은 소문 an unsavory rumor.
⑨《건강이》(be) ill; sick; be [feel] unwell. ¶ 위가 ~ have a weak stomach / 안색이 ~ look pale; have a bad complexion.
⑩《기분이》feel unwell [poorly, ill, indisposed]; be [feel] out of sorts. ¶ 기분이 좋지 않아서 in an unhappy frame of mind; in bad humor / 오늘 아침은 기분이 ~ I feel rather out of sorts this morning.

**좌**(左) 《방향》 (the) left; 《사상》 a leftist; the left [총칭]. ¶ 좌측의 left; left-hand (★ left-handed는 「왼손잡이의」란 뜻임에 주의) / 첫 모퉁이에서 좌로 방향을 바꾸시오 Turn left at the first corner. *or* Turn the first corner to the left. / 그는 (사상이) 좌에 속해 있다 He belongs to the left (wing). / 좌로 나란히《구령》Left 「turn [face]! / 좌로 봐《구령》Eyes left!

**좌**(座) ① a seat. ⇨ 좌석. ②《지위》a position. ¶ 권좌에 있는 사람들 men in power.

**좌경**(左傾) inclination to the left; radicalization; Bolshevization; leftism; leftist. ~하다 incline to the left; become [turn] leftist; turn red [pink, communist]. ¶ ~적 leftist(-leaning); radical; Red; Bolshevized / ~ 색채가 농후한 잡지 a journal of pronouncedly leftist color. ◉ ~문학 leftist literature. ~분자 radical [leftist] elements. ~사상 leftist thinking. ~운동 a left movement. ~파 Left Wing: ~파 지도자 a left wing leader. ~학생 a radical [Red] student.

**좌고**(坐高)《앉은키》*one's* sitting height.

**좌고우면**(左顧右眄) a look to left and right; looking around; irresolution; vacillation. ~하다《망설이다》vacillate; be unable to make up *one's* mind (wondering how others' opinions will be). ¶ ~(하며) 어찌 할 바를 모르다 look this and that way; waver in *one's* attitude.

**좌골**(坐骨) 〖해부〗 the hip [huckle] bone; the ischium (*pl.* -chia). ◉ ~신경 the sciatic nerve: ~ 신경통 hip gout; 〖의학〗 sciatica.

**좌기**(左記) the undermentioned (statement); the following. ¶ ~와 같이 as follows [undermentioned, underwritten] / ~서류 the following documents.

**좌담**(座談) a table talk; (a) conversation; a colloquy. ¶ ~이 능하다 be a good talker [conversationalist].
◉ ~회 a round-table talk; a discussion meeting; a symposium (*pl.* ~s, -sia): ~회를 열다 hold a symposium 《on》; have a discussion meeting.

**좌대**(座臺) a pedestal.

**좌르르** with a great rush; with a splash. ¶ 물이 ~ 쏟아지다 water comes rushing out.

**좌변**(左邊) the left side.

**좌변기**(坐便器) 《양변기》 a stool-type flush toilet.

**좌불안석**(坐不安席) being unable to sit comfortably 《from anxiety, *etc.*》. ~하다 be unable to rest; fidget; squirm anxiously. ¶ 걱정으로 ~했다 Fear kept me restless.

**좌상**(坐像) a sedentary [seated] figure [(statue)].

**좌상**(座上) ①《좌중》《in》the company; the party; all those present. ②《연장》the elder in a 「company [party].

**좌서**(左書) 《왼쪽에서부터》writing from left to right; 《왼손글씨》left-handed writing. ~하다 write from left to right; write left-handed.

**좌석**(坐席) 《자리》 a seat; a cockpit (조종사의); a pew (교회의); (sitting) room (여지). ¶ 앞[뒷] ~ a front [back, rear] seat 《of a car》/ 창쪽[통로쪽] ~ a window [an aisle] seat / ~에 앉다 take *one's* seat; seat *oneself* 《at a table, in a chair》; have *one's* seat 《미》/ ~을 잡다 get [take, secure] a seat 《in a bus》/ ~을 잡아 두다 save a seat 《for *a person*》/ ~을 예약하다 reserve a seat 《in a theater [train]》/ ~을 양보하다 offer [give up] *one's* seat 《to *a person*》; make room 《for》/ 혼자 3명분의 ~을 차지하다 occupy [take up] room for three people / ~을 지정 받으신 후 입장하십시오 Please get seat assignment before entering. / 이 강당에는 500명이 앉을 수 있는 ~이 있다 This auditorium [hall] has

a seating capacity of 500 people. / ~ 만원 《게시》 Standing Room Only (생략 S.R.O.).
◉ ~권 a ticket. ~배치도 the (theater) seat-plan. ~버스 a seat bus. ~번호 the seat number. ~정원(수) seating capacity 〔accommodation〕. ~조절용 레버 a seat adjustment lever. ~지정권 a reserved-seat ticket. ~표 a seating list. 지정~ a reserved seat.

**좌선**(左旋) rotation to the left; 『물리·화학』 levorotation; levorotary. ~하다 turn 〔rotate〕 to the left.

**좌선**(坐禪) 『불교』 sitting in Sŏn 〔Zen〕 meditation; *Dhyāna Pāramitā* (Sans.). ~하다 sit in meditation.

**좌시**(坐市) a marketplace. ◉ ~터 a marketplace.

**좌시**(坐視) watching idly 〔with indifference〕. ~하다 look on idly 〔with indifference〕; remain a mere spectator 〔looker-on〕. ¶ 너의 곤경을 ~할 수 없다 I cannot bear to be an idle spectator of your difficulties.

**좌안**(左岸) the left bank (of a river).

**좌안**(左眼) the left eye.

**좌약**(坐藥) 『의학』 a suppository.

**좌완투수**(左腕投手) a left-handed pitcher; a southpaw (pitcher); a lefty 《미구어》.

**좌욕**(坐浴) a sitz 〔hip〕 bath.

**좌우**(左右) 《좌우측》 right and left; 《측근》 *one's* attendants; people in attendance; 《지배·영향》 sway; influence; control. ~하다 《지배하다》 dominate; command; control; sway; gain control of; have *a person* under *one's* thumb; 《영향을 미치다》 affect; influence; have 〔exert〕 an influence 《upon》.
¶ ~에 (on) right and left; on both sides; on either side (★ either side는 「한쪽」의 뜻도 되므로 뜻이 애매해질 우려가 있을 때는 쓰지 않는 것이 좋음) / ~로 흔들리다 roll from side to side / ~를 둘러보다 look all around; glance about / ~로 갈리다 part right and left / 시장을 ~하다 control 〔gain control of〕 the market / 운명을 ~하다 hold sway over *one's* destiny; decide 〔control〕 *one's* destiny. ¶ 감정에 ~되다 be carried away by sentiment; be swayed by emotion / 인간은 환경에 ~되기 쉽다 Man is easily influenced by his surroundings. / 신문은 여론을 ~한다 Newspapers influence the current of thought.

**좌우**(座右) the right side of where *one* is sitting. ¶ ~에 비치하다 keep 《*a thing*》 at 「hand 〔*one's* elbow〕. ◉ ~명 a favorite proverb 〔motto, maxim〕.

**좌우간**(左右間) at any rate; in any event; anyhow; anyway 《주로 미》; in any case; at all events. ¶ ~ 그렇게 해 보겠다 I will do so anyway. / ~ 정오까지는 그를 기다리고 있겠다 Well, at any rate, I will wait for him till noon. / ~ 무슨 대책을 강구해야지 After all, a measure should be taken to it. / ~ 거기에 대한 준비는 할 것이다 In any case 〔At all events〕, I will make preparations for it. / 실패할지 모르지만 ~ 해보겠다 My plan may prove a failure, but anyway I'll try it.

**좌우균제**(左右均齊) symmetry.

**좌우익**(左右翼) ① 『군사』 left and right wings of the army; the left and right flank. ② 《사상》 left-wing and 〔or〕 right-wing (ideas).

**좌익**(左翼) ① 《대형의》 the left wing 〔flank〕. ② 『야구』 the left field. ③ 《주의》 the left (wing); 《사람》 the leftist; the left-winger. ¶ ~적(인) leftist; left-wing / ~적 경향 《exhibit》 leftist leanings. ◉ ~단체 a leftist organization; a group of radicalists. ~분자 a left-wing element. ~사상 leftism: ~사상에 물들다 be tinctured with radicalism. ~수 『야구』 a left fielder. ~운동 a leftist movements; a left 〔radical〕 movement. ~정당 a leftist political party.

**좌장**(座長) the senior person present (in a seated group).

**좌절**(挫折) ① 《계획의》 a breakdown; ruin; collapse; a reverse; a setback; frustration. ~하다 miscarry; be baffled; get ruined; be upset; break down; collapse; fall through; fall to the ground; suffer a setback; get frustrated; be thwarted. ¶ ~시키다 frustrate 《*a person's* plan》; balk 《*a person* in *his* plan》; disappoint 《*a person's* plans, hopes》 / 공격이 ~되다 an attack is frustrated; an attack suffers a setback / 인간은 수많은 ~을 이겨내면서 커간다 One 〔A man〕 can grow in stature by overcoming a series of frustrations 〔failures〕. / 그의 계획은 ~되었다 His plan miscarried 〔fell through〕. *or* He was frustrated 〔foiled〕 in his scheme.
② 《마음·기운의》 discouragement. ~하다 get discouraged 〔disheartened, daunted〕. ¶ ~시키다 discourage.
◉ ~감 (a sense of) frustration; a sense of failure: 여러 번 ~감을 맛보다

experience frustrations 《before completing a project》/ 입학 시험에 떨어졌을 때 그는 ~감을 맛보았다 He felt frustrated when he failed (in) the entrance examination. ⌈seat.

**좌정하다**(坐定―) sit; be seated; take a

**좌중**(座中) ¶ ~의 한 사람 one of those present; one of the company / ~을 둘러보다 look over the whole assembly 《of people》.

**좌지우지**(左之右之) having 《*a person*》 at *one's* beck and call; having a free hand. ~하다 have 《*a person*》 at *one's* beck (and call); have 《an organization》 under *one's* thumb; 《구어》 lead 《*a person*》 by the nose. ¶ 사장은 은퇴했지만 아직도 회사를 ~하고 있다 The president is retired but he still controls the company.

**좌천**(左遷) degradation; relegation; downgrading; demotion 《미》. ~하다 relegate; transfer 《*a person*》 to a lower position; demote 《미》; be downgraded 〔demoted〕; 《좌천되다》 be relegated. ¶ 지점으로 ~당하다 be relegated to a branch office / 그의 이번 전임은 사실 ~이다 His new appointment is a virtual demotion.

**좌초**(坐礁) running aground; stranding. ~하다 strike 〔run on〕 a rock; strand; be stranded 〔aground〕; run aground 〔ashore〕. ¶ ~한 배 a stranded ship / 폭풍우로 배는 ~되었다 The tempest drove the ship on the rocks.

**좌충우돌**(左衝右突) ~하다 dash this way and rush that; plunge forward on this side and dash in on that.

**좌측**(左側) the left side; the left. ¶ ~의 left(-hand) / 길의 ~에 on 〔to〕 the left (side) of the street / ~통행 《게시》 Keep (to the) left.

**좌파**(左派) the left wing; the left faction (of a party); 《사람》 the left wingers; the leftists. ¶ ~의 leftist; left-wing. ◉ 사회당~ the Left-Wingers of the Socialists.

**좌표**(座標) 〚수학〛 coordinates. ◉ ~계 the coordinate system. ~기하학 coordinate geometry. ~축 the axis of coordinates. 가로~ an abscissa (*pl.* ~s, -sae). 구면~ spherical coordinates. 극~ polar coordinates. 세로~ an ordinate. 직각〔사각(斜角)〕~ rectangular 〔oblique〕 coordinates.

**좌향**(左向) ¶ ~ 좌 《구령》 Left turn 〔face〕! / ~ 앞으로 가 《구령》 Left wheel!

**좌향**(坐向) 〚민속〛 geomantic aspect; the lay of a site 《of a house, a grave》.

**좌현**(左舷) 《배의》 port. ¶ ~에〔으로〕 on the port side / ~ 이물〔고물〕에 on the port bow 〔quarter〕/ ~으로 기울다 list to port.

**좌회전**(左回轉) a left-hand turn; a turn to the left. ~하다 turn (to the) left; make 〔take〕 a turn to the left. ¶ ~금지 《게시》 No Left Turn.

**좍** 《퍼지는 모양》 widely; far and wide; broadly; extensively. ¶ 좍 알려져 있다 be widely known / 소문이 순식간에 좍 퍼졌다 The rumor ⌈spread 〔got about〕 far and wide in a flash. / 화재가 사방으로 좍 퍼졌다 The fire spread quickly in all directions.

**좍좍** ① 《쏟아짐》 《it rains》 in torrents 〔in sheets, in buckets〕. ¶ 비가 ~ 퍼붓는다 It's raining cats and dogs. *or* The rain is pouring down in buckets. ② 《거침없이》 with ease; fluently; smoothly. ¶ 시를 ~ 외다 recite a poem fluently / 모든 문제를 ~풀다 solve all the problems with such beautiful ease.

**좔좔** with a gush 〔rush〕; gushing; flowing freely. ~거리다 gush; pour down. ¶ 물이 ~ 흐르다 water runs freely; water gushes along.

**좨기** a cake of cooked vegetables

**좽이** a casting 〔cast〕 net. ⌊〔flour〕.

**죄**(罪) 《법률상의》 a crime; an offense (비교적 가벼운); guilt; 《종교·도덕상의》 (a) sin; a vice; 《허물》 fault; blame; 《책임》 responsibility; 《벌》 a punishment; 《과외》 a fault. ¶ 죄 있는 guilty; sinful; blamable / 죄 없는 not guilty; blameless / 죄의식 a sense of guilt 〔sin〕; an awareness of *one's* sinfulness / 간음죄 the sin of adultery / 죄받을 짓 a sinful act / 신체 및 재산에 대한 죄 crimes against persons and property / 죄책감에 괴로워하는 사람 guilt-ridden people / 죽을 죄 a grave sin 〔crime〕/ 죄를 짓다 commit a crime; be guilty of 《murder》; 《도덕적인》 commit a sin 《against God》/ 죄를 묻다 accuse 《*a person*》 of a crime; bring 〔level〕 a charge against 《*a person*》/ 죄를 규명하다 make inquiries into 《*a person's*》 crime / 죄를 용서하다 pardon a sin / 죄를 남에게 씌우다 fasten the crime on 〔upon〕 *a person;* put the blame on *a person* / 죄를 면하다 escape punishment; be acquitted of a charge / 죄를 거듭하다 commit one crime after another / 죄를 짊어지다 hold *oneself* blamable 〔responsible〕 《for》; take the guilt 〔blame〕 upon *oneself* / 죄를 받다 meet with 〔suffer〕 punishment / 죄를 감하다 mitigate 〔reduce〕 《*a person's*》 punishment / 경찰에 죄를 자백하다 confess *one's* crime to the police / 죄에 빠뜨리다 incriminate 《*a person*》 / 죄는 미워하되 사람은 미워하지 마라 Condemn the offense but not the offender. / 이 실패는 누구의 죄냐 Who is 「responsible 〔to blame〕 for the failure ? / 그녀가 오지 않는다 해도 내 죄는 아니다 I cannot help it if she doesn't come. / 내게 무슨 죄가 있습니까 I haven't done anything wrong. *or* I am not to blame. / 그는 무슨 죄로 잡혀갔나 On what charge was he arrested ? / 그녀는 무고하게 죄를 뒤집어 쓰고 투옥되었다 She was sent to prison for a crime she did not commit. / 뇌물 수수는 가벼운 죄가 아니다 Taking a bribe is not a minor offense. / 그는 죄가 없음이 판명되었다 He turned out to be not guilty. / 나는 그 실패에 대해 죄의식을 느꼈다 I felt a sense of guilt about the failure.

**죄과**(罪科) an offense 〔offence 《영》〕; a sin; a crime; guilt. ¶ ～를 묻다 make inquiry into a crime.

**죄과**(罪過) a crime; a sin; a wrong; a fault (과오).

**죄다**[1] ① 《바싹》 tighten (up); stiffen; strain; stretch; 《줄을》 string. ¶ 느슨한 밧줄을 ～ tighten a loose rope; stretch a rope tight; tighten up a rope / 가야금의 줄을 ～ tighten a *kayakŭm* 〔Korean harp〕 string / 나사를 ～ tighten up a bolt. ② 《마음을》 feel anxious 〔uneasy, nervous, tense〕; tense up. ¶ 마음을 ～ be fidgety 〔edgy〕; be held in suspense; be worry 〔nervous, uneasy, anxious〕 / 결과가 어찌 될까 마음을 ～ be worried over the result; be worried over how it will turn out; be anxious about the outcome.

**죄다**[2] 《모두》 all; everything; everyone; each and every one; in all; all together; wholly; entirely. ¶ ～ 자백하다 confess everything / ～ 가져오너라 Bring here all of them. / 학교 도서실의 책을 ～ 읽었다 I have read every book in the school library.

**죄명**(罪名) the name of a crime 〔an offense〕; a charge. ¶ 절도〔사기〕의 ～으로 on a charge of theft 〔fraud〕; charged with theft 〔fraud〕.

**죄목**(罪目) a charge; crimes; offenses.

**죄밑**(罪—) 《죄의식》 a guilty conscience; 《죄의 진상》 the fact of wrongdoing. ¶ 그는 ～이 있어 나를 늘 피한다 He always avoids me because of the fact of wrongdoing he has done me.

**죄받다**(罪—) suffer 〔incur〕 punishment; be punished. ¶ 죄받을 짓 a sinful act / 죄받을 짓을 하다 do a 「cruel 〔wicked〕 thing / 그 가엾은 노인에게 사기를 치다니 죄받을 짓이었어 It was wicked of him to cheat that poor old man. / 그런 짓을 하면 죄받는다 You will suffer punishment for it if you do that.

**죄벌**(罪罰) (a) punishment for a crime.

**죄상**(罪狀) the nature of a crime; the circumstances of a crime; criminality; guilt; charges. ¶ ～을 불다 confess *one's* crime / ～을 조사하다 inquire into 《*a person's*》 guilt / ～이 명백해지다 be proved guilty 《of》 / ～을 시인하다〔부인하다〕 plead guilty 〔not guilty〕 to a criminal charge / ～의 정도에 따라 according to the degree of culpability / ～이 밝혀짐에 따라, 그녀는 3년 징역에 처해졌다 Her guilt becoming clear, she was sentenced to three years at hard labor.

**죄송**(罪悚) regret; feeling sorry. ～하다 be sorry 《for》; regret. ～스럽다 (be) regretable; troubled. ¶ ～하지만 I am sorry to trouble you, but...; Excuse me, but... / 기다리게 해서 ～합니다 I am very sorry to have kept you waiting. / 공부에 방해를 해서 정말 ～합니다 I am very sorry to trouble your studies. / ～하지만 담뱃불 좀 빌려 주십시오 May I trouble you for a light ? / ～합니다만 당신 책을 잃어버렸어요 I'm sorry, but I'm afraid I've lost your book. / 불편을 끼쳐 드렸다면 ～합니다 I'm sorry to have caused you any inconvenience.

**죄수**(罪囚) a prisoner; a convict; 《구어》 a jailbird; 《속어》 a con. ◉ ～복 (a) prison uniform. ～호송차 《미》 a patrol wagon; 《영》 a police 〔prison〕 van; 《영구어》 a Black Maria.

**죄악**(罪惡) 《법률상의》 a crime; 《종교·도덕적》 (a) sin; a vice. ¶ 인도(人道)에 대한 ～ a crime against humanity / ～을 범하다 commit a sin 〔crime〕 / ～시하다 consider *something* a sin / 시간의 낭비는 일종의 ～이다 Waste of

time is a sort of sin.
◉ ~감 a sense of sin 〔guilt〕.

**죄어들다** become tighter 〔narrower〕; get tightened 〔drawn up〕; cut into. ¶ 수사망이 ~ the dragnet moves in / 자일이 내 손에 죄어 들었다 The climbing rope cut into my hands.

**죄어치다** 《바싹》 tighten; 《재촉》 press; urge; rush; dun. ¶ 일을 빨리 하라고 ~ urge 《*a person*》 to do a quick job / 방세를 내라고 ~ dun 《*a person*》 for the rent / 수사망을 ~ tighten the dragnet.

**죄업**(罪業) 〖불교〗 a sin; a sinful act. ¶ ~을 쌓다 commit many sins; live a sinful life; live in sin. ◉ ~망상 〖의학〗 delusion of culpability.

**죄이다** ① 《죔을 당하다》 get tightened; be constricted; stiffen. ¶ 가슴이 죄이는 느낌 a constriction in the chest. ② 《마음이》 be braced up; become tense; feel 〔be〕 anxious 〔uneasy, nervous〕; be fidgety 〔edgy〕; be held in suspense / 그 소식에 마음이 죄였다 I became tense at the news. *or* I was braced up by the news.

**죄인**(罪人) ① 《법률상의》 a criminal; an offender; a culprit (미결수); a convict (기결수); a wrongdoer; 《종교·도덕상의》 a sinner; a transgressor. ② 《상중의》 I; me.

**죄임성**(一性) eager expectation; a hankering; being on pins and needles.

**죄장**(罪障) 〖불교〗 sins. ¶ ~을 소멸하다 expiate *one's* sins. ◉ ~소멸 expiation (of sins).

**죄적**(罪迹) proofs 〔traces〕 of guilt; evidence of a crime. ¶ ~을 감추다 cover (up) the traces of *one's* guilt / ~을 들추다 trace out a crime.

**죄주다**(罪一) punish; penalize; disciple. ¶ 죄과에 따라 ~ punish 《*a person*》 for *his* crime.

**죄증**(罪證) proofs 〔evidence〕 of a crime; proofs 〔evidence〕 of guilt. ¶ ~을 인멸하다 destroy all the proofs 〔evidence〕 of *one's* guilt.

**죄질**(罪質) the nature of a crime 〔an offense〕.

**죄짓다**(罪一) commit a crime 〔an offense〕; 《종교상》 commit a sin; sin.

**죄책**(罪責) the liability for a crime 〔an offense〕. ¶ ~을 묻다 charge with a crime 〔an offense〕. ◉ ~감 a guilty conscience; an awareness of *one's* sinfulness: ~감을 느끼다 feel guilty; have a guilty conscience.

**죄형법정주의**(罪刑法定主義) the principle of *"nulla poena* 〔*nullum crimen*〕 *sine lege"*; the principle of legality.

**죔쇠** a tool used to insert and tighten a wooden piece; a vise; a buckle; a clasp; a clamp.

**죔틀** a vise.

**주**(主) ① 《주장·근본》 the main 〔chief〕 part; the principal part. ¶ 주된 principal; chief; main; important / 주로 mainly; chiefly; principally; primarily / 주목적 *one's* main object / 주된 임무 *one's* main duty / 주가 되어 …하다 take the lead in *do*ing / 인격 양성을 주목적으로 하다 make character=building the prime object / 청중은 주로 여성들이었다 The audience consisted mainly of women. ② 《주인·임자》 *one's* master; an owner; a chief; *one's* employer. ③ 《천주》 the Lord; the Savior. ¶ 주여, 우리를 가엾이 여기소서 Lord, have mercy upon us.

**주**(朱) vermilion; Chinese red; 〖광물〗 cinnabar.

**주**(州) 《미국의》 a state; 《캐나다의》 a province; 《영국의》 a county. ¶ 캘리포니아주 the State of California / 주립대학 a state university / 주로 승격하다 《미》 attain statehood.

**주**(洲) ① 《퇴적》 a sandbank. ¶ 삼각주 a (river) delta. ② 《대륙》 a continent. ¶ 아시아주 the Continent of Asia / 오대주 the Five Continents.

**주**(株) ① 《주식》 a stock 《미》; a share 《영》; 《투자 대상으로의》 an interest 《in a business》 (★ 개인의 출자 총액이 stock 이고, 그것을 일정한 단위로 분할한 단위주가 share. 미국에서는 양 뜻으로 stock을 쓰지만, 「30주」와 같이 일정한 주수를 말할 때는 미국에서도 share를 씀).

¶ 보통주 an ordinary 〔a common〕 share / 신〔구〕주 new 〔old〕 shares / 우량주 superior stocks; gilt-edged stocks; blue chip / 성장주 growth stocks / 전력주 electric power shares / 전액 불입주 a full-paid stock / 주를 모집하다 invite subscriptions for shares; offer stocks for subscription / 주를 사다 buy 〔invest in〕 stocks; take stock 《in》; buy an interest 《in a business》 / 그 회사주를 1,000주 사다 buy 1,000 shares of the company / 주를 갖다〔처분하다〕 hold 〔liquidate〕 shares / 주로 재미〔손해〕 보다 make 〔lose〕 money on the stock market / 주에 손을 대다 speculate 〔dabble〕 in stocks; play the market 《미》 / 한 주에 대해 …의 특별 배당을 받다 receive an extra dividend of… a share / 주의 시

세가 변동하다 shares fluctuate in price. ② 《그루》 a tree. ¶ 나무 세 주 three trees.

**주**(週) a week. ¶ 금〔전, 내〕주 this 〔last, next〕 week / 그 회사는 주 5일 근무제가 됐다 The firm has established a five-day work week.

**주**(註) explanatory notes; annotations; footnotes; commentary. ¶ …에 주를 달다 annotate; make 〔write〕 notes on.

**주-**(駐) resident 〔stationed, staying〕 《in》. ¶ 주미의 resident 〔stationed〕 in America / 주미 한국 대사 the Korean Ambassador to the United States.

**주가**(株價) stock prices; the price of a stock. ¶ ～의 상승〔하락〕 a rise 〔fall〕 in stocks / ～를 조작하다 manipulate stock prices / ～가 오르다 stocks rise 〔go up〕; 《사람의》 *one's* reputation rises; rise in public estimation; gain in 《*a person's*》 estimation. ◉ ～지수 the price index of stocks: 종합 ～지수 the composite price index of stocks. 평균～ stock price average.

**주간**(主幹) 《회사의》 an executive in charge of 《an affair》; the chief manager; 《편집의》 the chief editor; the editor in chief; 《논설의》 the editorial writer in chief. ～하다 manage 《affairs》; edit 《a magazine, *etc.*》.

**주간**(晝間) the daytime; day. ¶ ～에 in the daytime; during the day; by day / ～에 일하고 야간에 학교에 나간다 He works by day and attends school by night. ◉ ～근무 day-duty. ～인구 the daytime population 《of Chongno》.

**주간**(週刊) weekly publication. ¶ ～의 (published) weekly. ◉ ～(잡)지 a weekly (magazine 〔journal〕): 시사 ～지 a weekly newsmagazine; a newsweekly / 여성 ～지 a women's weekly / 너는 무슨 ～지를 읽고 있느냐 What weeklies do you read?

**주간**(週間) a week. ¶ 2～ two weeks; a fortnight / 몇 ～동안 for weeks / 불조심 강조 ～ Fire Prevention Week. ◉ ～논평 a weekly review.

**주객**(主客) ① 《주인과 손》 host and guest. ② 《사물의》 principal and auxiliary 〔subsidiary〕. ¶ ～간에〔의〕 between host and guest / 이내 ～이 전도됐다 Very soon the tables were turned. / 그것은 ～전도다 That is putting the cart before the horse. *or* You are giving priority to something less important.

**주객**(酒客) a drinker; a tippler; a thirsty soul.

**주거**(住居) a (dwelling) house; a residence; an abode. ¶ ～를 정하다 take up *one's* abode 《in》; settle (down) 《in》; fix *one's* residence 《in the city》 / ～를 서울로 옮기다 remove *one's* residence to Seoul. ◉ ～면적 living space: 1인당 ～ 면적 living space per person; per capita living space. ～비 housing expenses. ～생활 housing life. ～인 an occupant (of a house); a resident; an inhabitant. ～지(址) 〚고고학〛 a dwelling 〔habitation〕 site; the site of a 《prehistoric》 settlement. ～지역 a residential area 〔district, quarter〕. ～침입 homebreaking; violation of domicile.

**주거니 받거니** exchanging 《wine cups》. ¶ ～하며 마시다 drink together exchanging cups of wine.

**주걱** 《밥주걱》 a rice scoop; 《구둣주걱》 a shoehorn; a long shoehorn (긴 것). ◉ ～상(相) a pushed-in face. ～턱 a turned-up chin; a spoon-like chin; a jutting chin.

**주검** a (dead) body; a corpse. ⇨ 시체(屍體).

**주격**(主格) 〚문법〛 the nominative 〔subjective〕 case. ◉ ～보어 〚문법〛 a subjective complement.

**주견**(主見) *one's* own opinion 〔view〕; an independent opinion 〔idea〕; a principle; a fixed view. ¶ ～이 없다 be lacking a principle; have no fixed views of *one's* own.

**주경야독**(晝耕夜讀) spending the days in the field and the nights at *one's* books.

**주고받다** give and take; exchange; reciprocate. ¶ 술잔을〔인사를〕 ～ exchange 「cups of wine 〔greetings〕 / 편지를 ～ exchange letters 《with》; correspond 《with》.

**주곡**(主穀) staple grains. ◉ ～자급 self-sufficiency in staple grains.

**주공**(住公) ⇨ (대한) 주택(공사). ◉ ～아파트 the KNHC-built apartment.

**주공**(鑄工) a caster; a cast-iron worker.

**주관**(主管) management; superintendence; supervision. ～하다 manage; be in charge 《of》; superintend; supervise. ◉ ～사항 matters in *one's* charge. ～자 a superintendent; a supervisor; a manager.

**주관**(主觀) 〚철학〛 subjectivity.

¶ ~적(으로) subjective(ly) / ~적 비평 subjective criticism / ~적으로 말하면 subjectively speaking / ~적으로 보다 take a 「subjective 〔personal〕 view 《of》 / ~에 치우치다 be too subjective / ~을 섞지 말고 설명해 주시오 Explain it without being subjective. / 그의 판단은 전적으로 ~적인 것이어서 공평하다고 할 수 없다 His judgment is entirely subjective and therefore quite unfair. / 면접에는 시험관의 ~이 개입된다 The subjective views of the examiners enter into interviews.
◉ ~론〔주의〕 subjectivism: ~주의자〔론자〕 a subjectivist. ~성 subjectivity. ~식 문제 a subjective question.

**주광성**(走光性) 〖생물〗 phototaxis. ¶ ~의 phototactic.

**주광전구**(晝光電球) a daylight lamp.

**주교**(主教) ① 《성직자》 a bishop. ② 《주된 종교》 a 「dominant 〔major〕 religion. ◉ ~구 a diocese. ~미사 a pontifical mass. ~제도 episcopacy. ~직 bishopric; episcopate.

**주교**(舟橋) a 「pontoon 〔floating〕 bridge.

**주구**(走狗) ① 《개》 a hunting dog; a hound. ② 《앞잡이》 a tool; a cat's paw. ¶ 공산당의 ~ a mere tool of communists / 남의 ~가 되다 be made a cat's paw of *a person*.

**주구**(誅求) exaction; extortion. ~하다 exact; extort; squeeze; lay under tribute.

**주군**(主君) *one's* (liege) lord; *one's* master.

**주권**(主權) sovereignty; sovereign authority; supreme power. ¶ ~을 잡다 assume 〔take over〕 the sovereignty / ~을 침해하다 violate 〔infringe on〕 the sovereignty 《of》 / ~을 회복하다 regain 〔restore〕 sovereignty / ~을 존중하다 respect the sovereignty.
◉ ~국 a sovereignty; a sovereign state. ~자 a sovereign; a supreme ruler. ~재민 the principle that sovereignty rests with the people. ~침해 infringement of sovereignty.

**주권**(株券) 《미》 a stock (certificate); 《영》 a share (certificate). ¶ 무기명 ~ a stock certificate to bearer / 기명 ~ a registered share / ~으로 1백만 원 가지고 있다 have 1,000,000 won in share certificates / ~을 현금으로 바꾸다 cash shares.

**주근깨** freckles; flecks; 〖의학〗 lentigo (*pl.* -tigines). ¶ ~ 낀 freckled 《face》; sprinkled 〔peppered〕 with freckles / ~가 끼다〔나다〕 freckle; get freckled.

**주금**(株金) capital; a stock. ¶ ~ 납입의 청구 a call on shareholders / ~을 납입하다 pay up *one's* shares. ◉ ~계정 capital account (생략 a/c).

**주금류**(走禽類) 〖조류〗 the runners; cursorial birds.

**주급**(週給) weekly 「wage(s) 〔pay〕. ¶ 그는 ~ 25만 원이다 He gets wages of 250,000 won a week.
◉ ~제 the weekly payment system: 이 공장에서는 임금이 ~제이다 In this factory the wages are paid on a weekly basis.

**주기**(酒氣) the 「odor 〔smell〕 of liquor; an alcoholic smell; 《술기운》 the influence of liquor; 《취기》 intoxication. ¶ ~를 띠고 있다 be under the influence of liquor; breath smell of liquor; be 「intoxicated 〔drunk〕.

**주기**(周忌·週忌) an anniversary of 《*a person's*》 death. ¶ 아버지의 3 ~ the second anniversary of *one's* father's death (★ 사후 만 2년).

**주기**(週期) a period; a cycle. ¶ ~적 periodic(al); cyclical / ~적으로 periodically / ~적 운동 a periodic motion / 행성의 ~ the period of a planet / 경기(景氣)의 ~ a business cycle / ~적으로 증감을 되풀이하다 have cyclic ups and downs / 이 현상은 ~적인 것이다 This phenomenon occurs periodically. ◉ ~성 periodicity. ~율 〖화학〗 the periodic law: ~율표 〖화학〗 a periodic table (of the elements). ~전류 a periodic current. ~혜성 〖천문〗 a periodic comet.

**주기도문**(主祈禱文) the Lord's Prayer.

**주낙** a (fishing) reel and line with multiple hooks. ¶ ~으로 고기를 잡다 fish with reel and multiple hooks.

**주년**(週年·周年) an anniversary. ¶ 10 ~ the tenth anniversary 《of》.

**주눅** timidity; shyness; diffidence. ¶ ~(이) 들다 feel timid; lose *one's* nerve / ~(이) 좋다 be brazen-faced; be impudent; be shameless; be unabashed.

**주니어** a junior. ◉ ~스타일 〖양재〗 junior 〔teenage〕 style. ~웨어 junior wear. ~칼리지 《2년제 단기 대학》 《미》 a junior college.

**주다** ① [일반적] give; present; bestow; furnish; provide; supply; feed; let 《*a person*》 have 《*a thing*》.
¶ 주어진 시간 the time allowed / 일을 ~ provide work 《for *a person*》 / 지식을 ~ impart knowledge 《to *a per-*

*son*》/ 편의를 ～ afford 《*a person*》 facilities 《for》/ 힌트를 ～ drop a hint 《to *a person*》/ 환자에게 약을 ～ give medicine to a patient / 아무에게 먹을 것을 ～ give *a person* something to eat / 꽃에 물을 ～ water flowers / 닭에게 모이를 ～ feed the chickens / 아기한테 젖을 ～ give a baby the breast; feed a baby / 주고 받다 give and take; exchange / 한 번 더 기회를 주시오 Give me another chance. / 그는 아들에게 매달 20,000 원의 용돈을 준다 He allows his son twenty thousand won a month. / 태양은 우리들에게 빛과 열을 준다 The sun gives us light and heat. / 그것을 나에게 주십시오 Give it to me. 《미》/ 그는 가난한 사람들에게 활수하게 돈을 주었다 He gave his money generously to the poor. / 동물에게 먹이를 주지 마시오 《게시》 Please refrain from feeding the animals. / 연구를 위해 온갖 편의가 그에게 주어졌다 He was supplied with all sorts of facilities for his research. / 정부는 신체 장애자에게 직업을 주려고 노력하고 있다 The government is trying to provide employment for the handicapped.

② 《치르다》 pay 《for》; pay out. ¶ 4천 원에 고기 한 파운드를 사다 pay 4,000 won for a pound of meat / 얼마 주었느냐 How much did you pay for it?

③ 《수여하다》 give; award; confer; grant. ¶ 박사 학위를 ～ confer the doctorate; give the doctor's degree 〔the Ph. D.〕/ 상을 ～ award a prize / 정부는 그에게 장학금을 주었다 The government granted a scholarship to him.

④ 《할당·부과하다》 assign; allot; give. ¶ 숙제를 ～ assign homework 《to students》/ 몫을 ～ allot a share 《to *a person*》.

⑤ 《끼치다》 cause; inflict; bring about; bring to bear. ¶ 손해를 ～ do damage 《to》; inflict a loss 《on》/ 고통을 ～ cause pain 《to》/ 영향을 ～ exert 〔have〕 influence on 《*a person*》/ 타격을 ～ give a blow 《to *a person's* business》/ 폭풍우는 벼농사에 피해를 주었다 The storm inflicted damage on the rice crops.

⑥ 《줄 등을》 let 《a line》 out; feed 《a line》 out; give 《line》. ¶ 연실〔낚싯줄〕을 ～ give kite 〔fish〕 line.

⑦ 《힘을》 put 《strength, force》 in; put forth 《*one's* strength》. ¶ 줄을 힘주어 당기다 pull a rope with all *one's* strength / 힘주어 말하다 emphasize *one's* words; accentuate; speak with emphasis / 더 힘주어 노래해라 Sing with more life.

⑧ [조동사] do as a favor for 《*a person*》; favor 《*a person*》 with. ¶ 책〔장난감〕을 사 ～ buy 《*a person*》 a book 〔toy〕/ 어린아이의 옷을 입혀 ～ help a child on with clothes; dress a child / 아무를 때려 ～ beat 〔hit〕 *a person*; give *a person* a taste of *one's* fist / 이런 일 다시 하면 혼내 준다 Don't do this again, or I'll let you have it! / 그는 내 말을 들어 주지 않았다 He wouldn't listen to me. / 영어 편지 한 장 써 주십시오 Please write me a letter in English.

**주단**(紬緞) silks and satins; silk goods.

**주당**(酒黨) a drinker.

**주도**(主導) leading; the initiative. ～하다 lead; assume leadership 《of》; take the lead 〔initiative〕 《in》; spearhead 《a movement》. ¶ 민간 ～의 경제 private initiated economy / ～적 역할을 하다 play a leading role 《for》; play a leading part 《in》/ 자동차 산업이 불황 탈피의 ～적 역할을 했다 The auto industry played the trigger role in getting the economy out of recession.
◉ ～산업 a leading 〔trigger〕 industry. ～자 a leader 《of a movement》; a prime mover.

**주도**(周到) ～하다 (be) scrupulous; cautious; careful; circumspect; thorough(going). ¶ ～하게 carefully; thoroughly; scrupulously / ～한 계획 a carefully worked-out plan; a well-laid plan / 그는 일을 도모함에 있어 ～면밀했다 In working out his plans he was as cautious and circumspect as could be. / 그녀는 무슨 일에나 ～면밀하다 She is scrupulously careful about everything.

**주도**(酒道) a drinking manner; a drinker's etiquette.

**주도권**(主導權) the leadership; the initiative. ¶ ～ 싸움 a struggle for leadership; a leadership struggle / ～을 잡다〔쥐다〕 take the leadership 〔initiative〕 《in》/ ～을 빼앗다 wrest 〔take〕 away the initiative 《from》/ ～을 잃다 lose the initiative 《to the enemy》/ 우리는 교섭의 ～을 잡고 있다 We have the leadership 〔initiative〕 in the negotiations. / ～은 우리 손에 다시 돌아왔다 The initiative has passed to us again.

**주독**(酒毒) alcohol poisoning. ¶ ～이 오

르다 get a red spot on *one's* face.
◉ ～코 a red nose (from drinking); a coppernose.

**주동**(主動) motive power; leadership. ¶ ～이 되다 take the lead / 불순 조직에 의하여 ～되다 be masterminded by an impure organization.

**주동자**(主動者) the prime mover; the moving spirit; the mastermind; the leader. ¶ ～가 되다 take the lead 《in》; lead 《a movement》/ 데모 ～를 구속하다 arrest the leader of the demonstration.

**주되다**(主―) (be) chief; principal; main; major; leading; important.

> (용법) **chief** 권력·계급·중요성 등이 최고이며, 특히 사람에 있어서는 「으뜸가는」. **principal** 크기·지위·중요성이 다른 모든 것 위에 있다는, 다소 격식차린 말. **main** 사물의 크기·중요성이 「뛰어난」. **major** 특히 다른 것과 비교하여 뛰어나다는 뜻을 강조하는 말. **leading** 선도적인 역할을 하는 뜻을 강조하는 말.

¶ 주된 특징 the main features 《of》/ 주된 목적 the main 〔chief〕 purpose / 주된 회원 leading members / 한국의 주된 도시 the principal cities of Korea / 이 부품이 사고의 주된 원인이다 This part is the major cause of the accident. / 운동회는 학교의 주된 연중 행사의 하나이다 The athletic meet is one of the main annual events in school. / 호남 지방의 주된 산물은 무엇이냐 What are the principal products of Honam district?

**주두**(柱頭) ① 〖건축〗《대접받침》 a capital; a headpiece on a column. ② 〖식물〗《암술머리》 a stigma.

**주둔**(駐屯) stationing. ～하다 be stationed 《at, in》; station; stay. ¶ 한국에 ～하고 있는 미군 U.S. troops stationed in Korea / 군대를 ～ 시키다 station troops.
◉ ～군 stationary troops; 《점령지의》 an occupation army; occupation forces; 《수비의》 a garrison: ～군 지위 협정 the Status of Occupation Forces Agreement. ～지 a post; an army post; a garrison.

**주둥아리, 주둥이** ① 《새의 부리》 a bill; a beak (★ bill은 물새·오리 따위의 납작하거나 가느다란 주둥이, beak은 솔개·매 따위 육식조의 부리). ¶ 갈고리처럼 구부러진 ～ a hooked beak / ～로 쪼다 peck 《at》/ ～로 쪼아 구멍을 뚫다 《birds》 peck at a hole 《in the sack》. ② 《사람·동물의 입》 the mouth; the muzzle (개 등의); 《물건의 개구부》 a mouth(piece); an opening; a nozzle (호스 등의). ¶ ～를 까다 have a glib tongue; be a chatterbox / ～가 싸다 be glib(-tongued); be talkative; be quick to talk back / ～를 놀리다 wag *one's* tongue / 어디서 건방지게 그따위 ～를 함부로 놀리느냐 How impudent you are to talk to me like that!

**주라**(朱喇·朱螺) 〖악기〗 a red conch born.

**주란사**(―紗) cloth woven from gassed cotton thread. ◉ ～실 gassed cotton thread.

**주람**(周覽) a round trip of observation.

**주랑**(柱廊) a pillard corridor; a colonnade (그리스식).

**주량**(酒量) *one's* drinking 〔alcoholic〕 capacity. ¶ ～이 크다 be a heavy drinker; drink much / ～이 늘다〔줄다〕 gain 〔lose〕 drinking capacity; come to drink more 〔less〕 than *one* used to / 그의 ～은 대단하다 His drinking capacity is astonishing. / 너는 요새 ～이 상당히 늘었다 You have become a pretty good drinker.

**주렁주렁** in clusters; in full bearing. ¶ 열매가 ～ 열린 나무 a tree in full bearing / ～ 달리다 [열매가 주어] hang 〔grow〕 in clusters; [나무가 주어] be heavy-laden 《with fruit》/ 사과나무에 사과가 ～ 달렸다 The tree is loaded 〔laden〕 with apples.

**주력**(主力) the main force 〔strength, body〕. ¶ ～을 집결하다 concentrate the main force / 적의 ～은 아군의 좌측을 압박했다 The enemy's main force pressed on our left flank.
◉ ～부대 main-force units; hard-core units. ～산업 (the) key 〔major〕 industries. ～상품 key commodities. ～업종 a central 〔core〕 business. ～주 〖증권〗 leading 〔key〕 stocks 〔shares〕. ～함 a capital ship. ～함대 the main fleet 〔squadron〕.

**주력**(注力) ～하다 concentrate 〔focus〕 *one's* efforts 《on》; exert *oneself* 《for》; devote 〔apply〕 *oneself* 《to》.

**주렴**(珠簾) a blind woven with strings of beads.

**주례**(主禮) 《예식의 주장》 officiating at a ceremony; 《사람》 an officiator; the one in charge of a ceremony. ¶ 결혼식은 김 교수의 ～로 행해졌다 Professor Kim officiated at the wedding. ◉ ～목사 an officiating pastor 〔minister〕.

**주로**(走路) 《경기장의》 a track; 《마라톤 등의》 a course.

**주로**(主―) mainly; chiefly; principally; primarily; in the main; 《대개》 mostly; for the most part; generally. ¶ 여름은 ~ 바닷가에서 보낸다 I spend the summer mostly at the seaside. / 그것은 ~ 기후의 변화에 의한다 It is mainly due to climatic changes. / 학생들은 ~ 지방 출신이다 The students are, for the most part, from the provinces. / 청중은 ~ 여자들이었다 The audience consisted mainly of women.

**주루**(走壘) 〚야구〛 base running. ¶ ~를 잘 하다 be good at base running.

**주룩주룩** ① 《주름이》 with wrinkles 〔rumples, folds〕. ¶ ~ 주름이 가다 be all wrinkled; have winkles in it. ② 《비가》 pouring down off and on; in sudden downpours. ¶ ~ 오는 비 pouring 〔pelting〕 rain.

**주류**(主流) the main current(s) 《of Korean literature》; the mainstream. ¶ 사회 불안의 ~ the main current of social unrest. ◉ ~파 the leading 〔main-current〕 faction 《of a political party》; the main-stream faction 〔group〕; the faction in power: 비~파 anti-mainstream group; the factions out of power.

**주류**(酒類) alcoholic drinks 〔beverages〕; liquors. ¶ 비~음료 a soft drink / ~의 판매 liquor selling.
◉ ~소매점 《미》 a package store. ~판매점 a liquor store 〔shop〕. ~판매 허가증 a liquor license. 「rheotactic.

**주류성**(走流性) 〚생물〛 rheotaxis. ¶ ~의

**주륙**(誅戮) death punishment. ~하다 punish 《*a person*》 with death; execute.

**주르르** trickling; dribbling; running. ¶ 눈물이 ~ 흐르다 shed big drops of tears / 상처에서 피가 ~ 흘렀다 Blood was oozing from the wound.

**주르륵** gurgling. ¶ ~ 소리가 나다 gurgle.

**주름** wrinkles; 《피부의》 lines; furrows (깊은); 《눈가의》 crow's-feet; 《물건의》 creases; folds; a pleat (접은 줄). ¶ ~진 《피부가》 wrinkled; lined; furrowed; 《천·종이가》 crinkled; crumpled / ~ 지지 않는 《천 따위가》 crease-resistant; wrinkle-proof 《fabrics》; wrinkle-free 《polyester clothing》 / 스커트의 ~ the folds on a skirt / 옷에 ~이 가다〔잡히다〕 *one's* clothes are wrinkled / 얼굴에 ~이 지다〔잡히다〕 *one's* face is wrinkled 〔furrowed〕 / 이마에 ~을 짓다 knit *one's* brows; frown; gather *one's* brows in a frown / 치마에 ~을 잡다 pleat a skirt / 바지에 ~을 잡다 crease 〔put a crease in〕 *one's* trousers / ~을 펴다 smooth (out) the creases; press out the wrinkles 《of a dress》; iron out / 이 천은 ~이 지지 않는다 This fabric won't wrinkle. *or* This fabric is wrinkle-free. / 스커트의 ~이 펴졌다 The pleats on the skirt had come out.
◉ ~상자 bellows (on a camera). ~치마 a pleated skirt. 잔~ fine wrinkles 〔lines〕; crow's-feet.

**주름잡다** ① 《옷 따위를》 pleat; crease; fold; make a pleat 《in a skirt》; gather 《a skirt》. ② 《지배하다》 have command of; dominate; gain control of; sway. ¶ 오늘날 세계를 주름잡는 사람들 the men who have the sway of 〔over〕 the world today / 시장을 ~ gain control of the market / 금융계를 ~ have a firm grip on the banking business / 그녀는 그 위원회를 주름잡고 있다 She takes the leadership in the committee. *or* She controls the committee.

**주리** "the leg screw" torture. ¶ ~(를) 틀다 impose leg-screw torture.

**주리다** 《배를》 starve; go hungry; be famished; 《갈망하다》 be hungry for 〔after〕; hanker for; hunger 〔thirst〕 for 〔after〕. ¶ 주린 hungry; starving; famished / 애정〔돈〕에 ~ be hungry for affection 〔money〕 / 지식에 ~ be thirsty for 〔after〕 knowledge.

**주립**(州立) [형용사적] state-established; state-founded; province-established; provincial. ◉ ~대학〔병원, 공원〕 a state 〔provincial〕 university 〔hospital, park〕.

**주릿대** 《형구》 the wooden sticks used for leg-screw torture; 《사람》 a bad man; a wicked 〔an evil〕 person. ¶ ~ 안기다 inflict a cruel punishment on.

**주마**(走馬) a running horse; running a horse. ~하다 gallop 〔drive〕 a horse.
◉ ~가편(加鞭) whipping an already galloping horse; urging 〔inspiring〕 《*a person*》 to further efforts. ~간산(看山) seeing the hills while passing on horseback; giving a hurried 〔cursory〕 glance: ~간산식 관광 여행 《make》 a Cook's tour 《of 》. ~창(瘡) 〚한의〛 boils that spread all over the body.

**주마등**(走馬燈) 《등》 a revolving lantern; [비유적] a moving 〔shifting〕 panorama; rapid change; a kaleidoscope. ¶ ~(과) 같은 kaleidoscopic; ever-changing〔-shifting〕; protean / ～같이 변하다 change kaleidoscopically / 여러 가지 생각이 ～처럼 나의 뇌리를 스쳤다 Many images came and went in my mind's eye.

**주막**(酒幕) a tavern; an inn. ¶ ～에 들다 put up at an inn. ◉ ～거리 a road lined with「taverns〔inns〕. ～쟁이 a tavern keeper; an innkeeper.

**주말**(週末) a weekend. ¶～을 진해에서 지내다 weekend at Chinhae; stay at Chinhae over the weekend / ～을 지내러 시골 친구 집을 찾다 visit a friend in the country for a weekend / 우리와 함께 ～을 지내러 오시지요 Please come and stay with us over the weekend. ◉ ～농장 a weekend farm. ～여행 a weekend trip: ～여행을 떠나다 go「away〔on a trip〕for the weekend / ～ 여행자 a weekender.

**주맥**(主脈) 《산의》 the main range 《of mountains》; 《광맥의》 the main mineral vein.

**주머니** ① 《돈주머니》 a purse; a bag. ¶ ～가 가볍다 have a light purse / ～를 털다 spend *one's* last penny; spend all the money *one* has / ～를 차다 wear a purse 《at *one's* waist》; carry a purse / ～가 비다 *one's* purse becomes empty.
② 《호주머니》 a pocket; 《물건을 담는》 a bag; 《부대》 a sack; 《행낭》 a pouch. ¶ 뒷〔안〕～「a hip〔an inside〕pocket / 저고리〔바지〕 ～ coat 〔trouser〕 pocket / ～에 넣다 put 《*a thing*》 into *one's* pocket / ～에서 시계를 꺼내다 take a watch out of *one's* pocket / 손을 ～에 넣고 있다 keep *one's* hands in *one's* pockets.
◉ ～끈 purse strings. ～돈 pocket money (reserved for an emergency). ～떨이 everybody emptying his pockets and pooling the money to pay for joint refreshments. ～사정 financial 〔pecuniary〕 circumstances; *one's*「finances〔funds〕. ～칼 a pocketknife.

**주먹** a fist. ¶ ～만한 돌 fist-sized stone / ～을 부르쥐고 with a clenched fist / ～으로 위협하다 threaten 《*a person*》 with *one's* fist / ～을 쥐다 double 〔clench〕 *one's* fist / ～으로 아무를 치다 strike *a person* with *one's* fist / 빈 ～으로 장사를 시작하다 start in business empty-handed / 맨～으로 싸우다 fight with naked fists / ～으로 테이블을 치다 strike *one's* fist on the table; bang on the table with *one's* fist.
◉ ～밥 《뭉친》 a rice ball. ～심 the power of *one's* fist 《to hit》; 《완력》 physical strength. ～싸움 a fist fight. ～장 〖건축〗 a pole plate with a fist-shaped head. ～코 a snub nose.

**주먹구구**(一九九) ① 《손가락셈》 finger-counting. ¶～로 셈하다 count on the fingers. ② 《어림》 rule of thumb. ¶～로 어림치다 estimate by rule of thumb; make a rule-of-thumb estimate.

**주먹다짐** ① 《때림》 striking 《*a person*》 with *one's* fist. ～하다 strike 《*a person*》 with *one's* fist; give 〔deal〕 《*a person*》「a blow〔blows〕. ② 《윽박지름》 threats of violence; intimidation. ～하다 threaten; intimidate. ¶ ～에 못 이겨 돈을 빌려 주다 be coerced into lending money.

**주먹질** shaking *one's* fist 《at *a person*》; 《때리기》 a fistic fight; (a bout of) fisticuffs; an exchange of blows. ～하다 shake *one's* fist 《at *a person*》; fight (with fists); exchange blows 《with》; come to「blows〔fisticuffs〕 《with》. ¶ 하늘에다 대고 ～하다 beat the air / 마침내 그들은 ～까지 하게 됐다 They finally came to blows.

**주명곡**(奏鳴曲) 〖음악〗 a sonata.

**주모**(主謀) heading a「conspiracy〔plot, scheme〕. ～하다 lead a「conspiracy〔scheme, plot〕; stir up; organize; mastermind.
◉ ～자 a prime mover; a ringleader; a leader; a mastermind: 반란의 ～자는 누구냐 Who「led〔masterminded〕the mutiny? / 그가 ～자임에 틀림없다 He must be at the bottom of the affair. / 그가 개혁안의 ～자다 He is the chief mover in the scheme of reform.

**주모**(酒母) ① 《술밑》 distiller's grains; yeast; ferment. ② 《작부》 a barmaid.

**주목**(朱木) 〖식물〗 a yew (tree).

**주목**(注目) attention; observation; notice; note; watch. ～하다 give〔pay〕attention to; take notice of; observe; watch; keep an eye on; turn *one's* attention to; take note of.
¶ ～의 대상 the center〔object〕of (public) attention / ～할 만한 noticeable; noteworthy; remarkable; significant; striking / ～할 만하다 be worthy of notice; be worth noticing / ～을 받지 않다 be unnoticed / 세인의 ～을 끌다 attract public attention; hold the public eye / 위험 인물로서 경찰의 ～을 받다 be watched by the police as a dangerous man / 그 일의 귀추가 대단

히 ~되고 있다 The development of the matter is being watched with keen interest. / 여기를 ~해 주십시오 May I have your attention, please?

**주무**(主務) chief control 《of an affair》; an official who has chief control. ~하다 have chief control; be in charge. ◉ ~관청〔부, 장관〕 the competent authorities 〔Ministry, Minister〕. ~자 a person in charge; the chief official (in charge of affairs); a supervisor.

**주무르다** ① 《만지다》 finger; fumble 《with, at》; play 《with》. ¶ 흙을 ~ finger 〔play〕 with clay / 그녀는 장갑을 주무르며 앉아 있었다 She sat playing 〔toying〕 with her gloves. ② 《안마하다》 massage. ¶ 어깨를 ~ massage *one's* shoulders / 등을 주물러 드리죠 Let me massage your back for you. ③ 《농락하다》 inveigle; cajole; coax; humor; have 《*a person*》 under *one's* thumb. ¶ 마음대로 ~ have 《*a person*》 completely under *one's* control; make a puppet of 《*a person*》.

**주문**(主文) 《판결의》 the text; 『문법』 the principal clause.

**주문**(注文) ① 《맞춤》 an order; ordering. ~하다 order 《*a thing*》 from 《a firm》; 《사람에게》 order 《*a thing*》 from 〔of〕 《*a person*》 (★ order to a person 이라고는 결코 안 함); give 〔put in〕 an order 《for an article to a firm》; give an order to 《*a person*》 for 《*a thing*》; place an order 《with *a person* for》. ¶ 구두(口頭) ~ a verbal order / 재〔추가〕 ~ a reorder / 매도〔매입〕 ~ 《주식의》 a sell 〔buy〕 order / 급한 ~ an urgent 〔a rush〕 order / ~하시는 대로 곧 upon receipt of your order / ~에 따라 in compliance with 〔obedience to〕 your order / ~이 쇄도하다 have a rush of orders / ~을 이행하다 fill 〔complete〕 an order / ~에 응하다 accept 〔take up〕 an order / ~을 받다 receive an order; get an order 《from abroad》; take 《*his*》 order / ~에 따라 만들다〔쓰다〕 make 〔write〕 《*a thing*》 to order / ~을 취소하다 cancel 〔withdraw〕 an order / 대량〔소량〕의 ~이 들어오다 have a 「large 〔small〕 order 《for goods from…》 / 그녀는 그 상점에 새 커튼을 ~했다 She ordered new curtains from the store. / ~이 점점 줄어들고 있다 Orders are falling off. / 그 책은 이미 영국에 ~되어 있다 The book is already on order from England. / 이것은 내가 ~한 것과 다르다 This is not what I ordered. / 이 책의 ~이 각지에서 쇄도했다 Orders for this book poured in from all over the country. / 이 드레스는 ~해서 만든 것이다 This dress is 「made-to-order 〔custom-made〕. / 웨이터가 와서 ~을 받아 갔다 《식당에서》 A waiter came up and took our orders. / 「그 뻐꾸기 시계는 어디서 샀느냐」―「우편을 통해서 구입했다」―「어디다 ~하였느냐」 "Where did you buy the cuckoo clock?" ― "I bought it through the mail." ― "Where did you order it from?"
② 《요구》 a request; a demand; a desire; a wish (희망). ~하다 request; demand; ask; desire; make a request. ¶ 어려운 ~ a delicate request / 무리한 ~ an unreasonable request; a tall order / 그건 무리한 ~이다 That is too much to ask. *or* It's an absurd desire. / 네게 ~이 하나 있다 《부탁》 I want to ask a favor of you. / 자네 ~대로 된다면 참 좋겠는데 If things turn out as you wish, all well and good.
◉ ~변경 modification of orders. ~복 a suit made to order; a custom-made suit; a tailor-made suit. ~생산 order production. ~서 a written order; an order form 〔sheet〕. ~식단제 *à la carte* system: 전국 모든 음식점에서 ~ 식단제가 실시된다 *À la carte* system will be in force in all restaurants across the nation. ~자 an orderer. ~장(帳) an order book. ~주택 a custom-built house; a house built to order. ~처 《주문자》 the orderer; 《인수자》 the receiver of an order. ~취소 an order cancellation. ~품 goods ordered; an article on order; an article made to order. ~형 반도체 computer chips on demand.

**주문**(呪文) a magic formula; an incantation; magic words; a spell; a charm. ¶ ~을 외다 make an incantation; chant a spell; say the magic words.

**주문자 상표부착 생산(자)**(注文者商標附着生產(者)) (an) original equipment manufacturing 〔manufacturer〕(OEM).

**주물**(鑄物) a casting; cast-iron ware; a cast-iron product. ◉ ~공장 a foundry.

**주물럭거리다** finger; fumble with; knead; massage.

**주물럭주물럭** fingering; fumbling.

**주미**(駐美) ¶ ~의 resident 〔stationed〕 in America. ◉ ~한국대사 the Korean ambassador to the United States.

**주민**(住民) residents; inhabitants; dwellers; 《전주민》 the population. ¶ 그는 뉴욕의 ～이다 He is a resident of New York. / 이 마을의 ～은 모두 200명이다 The population of this village is 200 at most.
◉ ～등록 resident registration: ～등록증 a certificate of residence; a (personal) resident registration card; a resident card / ～등록 번호 a resident registration number / ～ 등록표 a copy of family residential registration papers. ～세 an inhabitant tax; a resident tax. ～운동 a citizens' movement. ～자치 citizen autonomy. ～투표 the inhabitants' vote; a local referendum; a poll of residents: ～투표로 결정하다 decide by the inhabitants' vote.

**주밀**(周密) 《일에》 thoroughness; cautiousness; prudence; carefulness; completeness. ～하다 (be) thorough(-going); scrupulous; meticulous; careful; cautious; prudent; exhaustive. ¶ ～하게 circumspectly; scrupulously; carefully; cautiously; meticulously / ～한 설계 thoroughgoing design.

**주발**(周鉢) a brass rice-bowl. ◉ ～뚜껑 the lid of a brass rice-bowl. 통～ a cheap brass rice-bowl.

**주방**(廚房) a kitchen; a cookery; a cookroom; a cuisine (호텔 따위의); a galley (배 안의) (★ kitchen은 보통 부엌을 말하지만 cuisine은 「요리법, 요리」의 뜻으로도 쓰임: Chinese cuisine은 「중국 요리」). ¶ 음식점의 ～을 손님들에게 보이게 하다 have restaurants' cooking places open to the customers.
◉ ～용품 kitchen utensils. ～장 a head cook; a *chef* (F.).

**주번**(週番) 《be on》 weekly duty. ¶ ～이다 be on duty for the week. ◉ ～사관 the duty officer of the week.

**주벌**(誅伐) a punitive expedition. ～하다 send a punitive expedition.

**주벌**(誅罰) punishment; chastisement. ～하다 punish; chastise.

**주범**(主犯) 《사람》 the principal offender; the chief criminal; the main culprit; 《죄》 a principal offense.

**주법**(主法) the principal 〔major〕 laws.

**주법**(走法) (a) form of running. ¶ ～이 틀리다 run in a wrong form.

**주법**(奏法) 〖음악〗 (a style of ) rendition; execution; how to play 《the violin》. ¶ ～이 좋다〔나쁘다〕 be well 〔badly〕 executed.

**주벽**(酒癖) *one's* behavior under the influence of alcohol; a drinking habit. ¶ ～이 심하다〔나쁘다〕 be quarrelsome in *one's* cups; be a quarrelsome drinker; turn nasty when drunk.

**주변** resourcefulness; tactfulness; flexibility; adaptability; 《융통성》 versatility; ability to shift about 〔to make shift with〕; shiftiness; shiftability. ¶ ～이 있는〔좋은〕 사람 a man of ability / ～머리 없는 shiftless; resourceless; incapable; incompetent; good-for-nothing / ～이 있다〔좋다〕 be resourceful; be quick on *one's* feet; "be on the ball" / 그는 말 ～이 좋다 He has a way with words. *or* He has the gift of gab. / 돈도 없고 ～머리도 없다 He is neither rich nor versatile.
◉ ～머리 = 주변.

**주변**(周邊) ① 《주위》 the circumference; 《도시 따위의》 the outskirts; the environs. ¶ …의 ～에 around…; on the outskirts of 《Seoul》 / 서울 및 그 ～에 in and around Seoul; in Seoul and its outskirts 〔suburbs〕. ② = 부근. ¶ 이 ～에 somewhere about here; in this neighborhood / ～을 둘러보다 look about 〔around〕 / ～의 경치를 보고 즐겼다 I enjoyed the surrounding scenery. / 이 도시 ～에는 공장이 많다 There are lots of factories around 〔in the neighborhood of 〕 this city.
◉ ～기기 〖컴퓨터〗 peripherals. ～단말장치 〖컴퓨터〗 peripheral and terminal equipment.

**주병**(酒餠) wine 〔liquor〕 and rice cake.

**주병하다**(駐兵―) station troops.

**주보**(酒保) a canteen; a camp shop; 《미》 a post exchange (생략 PX).

**주보**(週報) a weekly (paper)(신문); a weekly bulletin (공보); a weekly report (보고).

**주봉**(主峰) the main 〔highest〕 peak 《of a mountain range》.

**주부**(主部) the main 〔principal〕 part; 〖문법〗 the subject.

**주부**(主婦) a housewife (*pl.* -wives); the mistress 〔lady〕 of a house. ¶ ～가 되다 manage 〔run, mother〕 *one's* household / 그녀는 ～이며 두 아이의 어머니이기도 하다 She is a housewife and mother of two.

**주부코** a red bulbous nose; a whisky nose.

**주비** 〖식물〗 a variety of millet.

**주빈**(主賓) the guest of honor; a principal guest. ¶ …를 ～으로 하여 만찬회

를 열다 give a dinner in honor of 《*a person*》. ◉ ～석 《take》 the seat of honor.

**주뼛주뼛** shy and hesitant. ～하다 (be) shy and hesitant.

**주사**(主事) a junior official; the clerical staff [총칭].

**주사**(走査) 〖TV〗 scanning. ～하다 scan. ◉ ～기 a scanner. ～면(面) a scanning area. ～밀도 scanning density. ～변환 〖컴퓨터〗 a scan conversion. ～선〔점〕 a scanning line 〔spot〕. ～장치 a scanning apparatus. ～진폭 scanning frequency.

**주사**(注射) an injection; 《구어》 a shot; 《구어》 a jab; 《예방 접종》 inoculation. ～하다 inject; give 《*a person*》 an injection 〔a shot〕; inoculate. ¶ 포도당을 ～하다 administer an injection of glucose / 캠퍼 ～를 놓다 inject camphor 《into the leg》 / 티푸스의 예방 ～를 맞다 be inoculated with an antityphoid vaccine; be inoculated 〔injected〕 against typhus / 팔에 ～를 맞다 have an injection 〔a shot〕 《of antibiotic》 in the arm / 그 환자는 ～의 힘으로 간신히 버틴다 The patient barely lives under the influence of injections. / ～의 효과가 있어 열이 내렸다 The injection worked on me and my fever went down. / 의사는 내 팔에 진통제를 ～했다 The doctor injected a painkilling drug into my arm. *or* The doctor injected my arm with a painkilling drug. ◉ ～기 an injector; a syringe. ～액〔약〕 an injection. ～침〔바늘〕 an injection syringe; a needle.

**주사**(酒邪) disorderly acts under the influence of alcohol; delirium tremens. ¶ ～가 있는 사람 a vicious drinker; a person who loses his temper over his cups / ～가 있다 be a vicious 〔bad〕 drinker; be quarrelsome in *one's* cups.

**주사위** a dice (★ 단·복수 동형); a die (★ "The die is cast"의 경우에만 쓰임). ¶ ～의 눈 the spots 〔pips〕 on 〔of〕 a dice / ～를 던지다 throw 〔shoot, cast〕 the dice 《for a drink》/ ～는 던져졌다 The die is cast. ◉ ～놀이 diceplay; 《도박》 gambling with dice; dicing (for money).

**주산**(主山) a guardian mountain (located to the north of a town or a grave).

**주산**(珠算) abacus calculation; calculation on the abacus. ～하다 count 〔figure〕 on an abacus. ◉ ～경시대회 an abacus calculation contest.

**주산물**(主産物) main 〔chief, prime, principal〕 products.

**주산지**(主産地) the chief producing place 〔center, district〕.

**주상**(主上) the Sovereign; His 〔Your〕 Majesty 〔Highness〕; the King.

**주상**(主喪) the chief mourner.

**주상**(酒傷) illness from drinking alcohol.

**주색**(朱色) vermilion (color).

**주색**(酒色) wine and women; sensual pleasures; dissipation and debauchery. ¶ ～에 빠지다 give *oneself* up to liquor and sex 〔women〕; be addicted to sensual pleasures / 그는 ～으로 몸을 망쳤다 His dissipation was his ruin. ◉ ～잡기 wine, women and (gambling) games.

**주서**(朱書) writing in red; rubrication. ～하다 rubricate; write in red.

**주석**(主席) 《자리》 the top 〔head〕 seat; 《사람》 the head; the chief; 《중국의》 the head of a state; (the) state president; the Chairman.

**주석**(朱錫) tin. ¶ ～으로 만든 tin; (made) of tin / ～을 입히다 tin. ◉ ～도금 tinning. ～박(箔) tin foil. ～제품 tinware.

**주석**(柱石) pillars and cornerstones; a mainstay; a main prop; a pillar. ¶ ～지신(之臣) a pillar of a state / 국가의 ～(으로 추앙되다) (be looked up to as) the pillar of a state.

**주석**(酒石) 〖화학〗 crude tartar. ◉ ～산 tartaric acid. ～영(英) cream of tartar.

**주석**(酒席) a drinking party; a banquet; a feast. ¶ ～에서 시중들다 wait 〔serve〕 at a banquet / ～을 베풀다 give a banquet.

**주석**(註釋) (explanatory) notes; annotation; a commentary. ～하다 annotate; write notes 《on a book》. ¶ ～이 달린 책 an annotated book / 이 책에는 권말에 많은 ～이 있다 This book has plenty of notes at the end. ◉ ～자 an annotator; a commentator.

**주선**(周旋) 《알선》 good 〔kind〕 offices; 《중개》 mediation; agency. ～하다 use *one's* influence; exercise *one's* good offices; act as an agent 〔intermediary〕. ¶ 친구의 ～으로 through the good offices of a friend / 취직을 ～해 주다 find 《*a person*》 a job / 숙부의 ～으로 현재의 직업을 얻었다 I have got this job through the good offices of my uncle. ◉ ～료 brokerage; commission. ～업 brokerage; 《고용인의》 employment agency. ～인 an agent;

an intermediary.

**주선**(酒仙) a hard 〔heavy〕 drinker.

**주섬주섬** 《picking them up》 one by one. ¶ ~ 줍다 pick up「piece by piece 〔one by one〕; gather / 옷을 ~ 싸다 pack *one's* clothes one by one.

**주성**(走性) 『생물』 (a) taxis (*pl.* taxes); (a) tropism. ¶ ~의 taxic; tactic. ◉ ~운동 taxic 〔tactic〕 movement.

**주성분**(主成分) the principal ingredient(s); chief element(s); main component(s). ¶ 이 약은 요오드가 ~이다 The chief ingredient of this medicine is iodine. 「Liquor Tax Law.

**주세**(酒稅) the liquor tax. ◉ ~법 the

**주소**(住所) *one's* dwelling (place); *one's* residence; *one's* address 〔domicile〕. ¶ 현~ the present address / ~를 정하다 take up *one's* residence; fix *one's* abode / ~를 변경하다 change *one's* address / ~를 속이다 give a false address / ~가 일정치 않다 have no fixed abode; be a floater 《미》 / 봉투에 수신인 ~ 성명을 쓰다 address the envelope / 그의 ~를 알 수가 없다 I cannot obtain his address. / ~가 어디시죠 What is your address, please? *or* May I have your address? / 김 선생님 ~를 아십니까 Do you have Mr. Kim's address? / 다음 ~로 이사했습니다 I have moved to the following address. ◉ ~록 an address book; a directory. ~불명 the address unknown. ~성명 *one's* name and address: ~성명을 말하시오 Give me your name and address.

**주술**(呪術) incantation; sorcery; an occult art. ¶ ~로 병을 고치다 charm 〔conjure〕 away an illness; cure an illness by a charm.

**주스** juice; fruit juice; fruit-flavor soft drink. ¶ 오렌지 ~ orange juice.

**주시**(注視) a steady gaze; close observation; scrutiny. ~하다 stare 〔gaze〕 at; fix *one's* eye on; observe 〔look at〕 《*a thing*》 closely; watch carefully. ¶ 아무의 얼굴을 ~하다 look 〔gaze〕 *a person* in the face / ~의 대상이 되다 become the center of attention; have every eye fixed on *one*.

**주시다** give; bestow 《on》; confer 《a title on *a person*》. ⇨ 주다.

**주식**(主食) the staple 〔principal〕 food; a (diet) staple; the chief article of food. ¶ 쌀을 ~으로 하다 live on rice / 쌀은 동양 여러 나라의 ~이다 Rice is the staple food of Oriental nations.

**주식**(株式) stocks 《미》; shares 《영》. ¶ ~을 모집하다 offer stocks for subscription / ~을 양도하다 transfer stocks / ~을 매매하다 deal in stocks 〔shares〕 / ~의 명의 변경을 정지하다 suspend transfers of stocks. ◉ ~거래 stock trading: ~거래소 = 증권거래소. ~공개 offering of stock to the public; going public. ~매매 dealing in stocks 〔shares〕; stock-jobbing (부정한). ~발행 a stock issue: ~발행가격 the issue prices of stocks / ~발행액 issued stocks. ~배당 a stock dividend. ~시세 stock prices. ~시세표 a stock 〔share〕 list. ~시장 a stock 〔share〕 market; stock exchange. ~시황(市況) stock quotations. ~액면가 the face value of a stock. ~응모 a stock subscription. ~자본 capital stock. ~중매(업) stockbroking; stockbrokerage. ~중매인 a stockbroker. ~청약금 application money for stocks. ~청약서 an application for stocks. ~청약인 a subscriber for shares. ~투자 investment in stocks.

**주식**(酒食) wine and food.

**주식**(晝食) a midday meal; lunch.

**주식회사**(株式會社) a joint-stock company; 《미》 a stock company 〔corporation〕 (★ 회사명과 함께 쓸 경우에는, 《미》..., Inc.; 《영》... Co., Ltd라고 생략함).

**주심**(主審) 《스포츠의》 the chief umpire 〔judge〕; the umpire-in-chief; 《축구·권투 따위》 a chief referee.

**주악**(奏樂) playing music; a musical performance. ~하다 play 〔perform〕 music. ¶ 악대의 ~ band music / 국가의 ~리에 amid the music of the national anthem.

**주안**(主眼) the prime 〔principal〕 object; the chief aim 〔end〕; the object in view; the principal point. ¶ 인격 양성을 ~으로 하여 with an eye to character-building / …에 ~을 두다 aim at …; have an eye to... / 우리가 ~으로 삼는 것은 …이다 Our principal object is …. ◉ ~점 the essential 〔main〕 point; the keynote.

**주안상**(酒案床) 《술상》 a table of「side dishes 〔tidbits〕 taken with alcoholic drinks.

**주야**(晝夜) day and night. ¶ ~ 교대로 in day and night shifts / 2 ~ two days and nights / ~겸행하다 work day and night; work without rest / ~로 바쁘다 be busy day and night. ◉ ~장천 day and night ever passing; unceasingly.

**주어**(主語) 〖문법〗 the subject (of a sentence).

**주역**(主役) 《역할》 the「leading〔principal〕part〔role〕; 《배우》 the leading「actor〔actress (여자)〕; a star; 《중심인물》 a kingpin. ¶ ～을 맡다 take〔play〕the leading「part〔role〕《in a play》; head the cast / ～은 누구지 Who is the leading「actor〔actress〕? / 신인이 그 영화의 ～으로 뽑혔다 A new face was singled out for the star of the movie. / 내가 ～을 맡고 그녀가 조역이 되었다 I played (the) lead and she played「second〔a supporting role〕.

**주역**(周易) the Book of *Changes* (= a Chinese classic on divination).

**주연**(主演) playing the leading part; starring. ～하다 play the leading「part〔role〕《in》; star《in》. ¶ K ～의 영화 a picture starring K / 이 영화의 ～은 누구지 Who is starring in the film? / 그녀는 많은 영화에서 ～을 맡아 왔다 She has starred in many pictures. ◉ ～배우 a leading「actor〔actress〕; a star; a leading「man〔lady〕《미》.

**주연**(酒宴) a banquet; a feast; a drinking「bout〔party〕. ¶ ～을 베풀다 give a feast; hold a banquet / 밤새도록 ～을 벌이다 feast〔drink〕the night away / ～이 한창이다 The banquet is at its height.

**주영**(駐英) ¶ ～의 resident〔stationed〕in「Great Britain〔England〕/ ～ 한국 대사관 the Embassy of the Republic of Korea in London. ◉ ～한국 대사 the Korean Ambassador to「Great Britain〔the Court of St. James's〕.

**주옥**(珠玉) a gem; a jewel; [총칭] jewelry. ¶ ～ 같은 글 a literary gem; a writing of rare beauty / ～의 명작 a masterpiece; a jewel of a literary work.

**주요**(主要) the principal; the important; the main; the essential. ～하다 (be) principal; main; leading; staple; important; essential; chief. ¶ ～한 작가 a「leading〔prominent〕writer / ～한 점 the main points《of an argument》/ ～한 역할을 맡아 하다 play a prominent part.

◉ ～경기종목 the main events《of today》. ～도시 major〔chief〕cities. ～목적 the main object. ～부 the principal part; the head and front. ～사실 〖법〗 a fact in issue; an ultimate fact. ～산물 staple products. ～산업 key industries: ～ 산업 및 공공 시설 major industrial and public facilities. ～성분 the「main〔principal〕ingredients: 설탕은 사탕의 ～ 성분이다 Sugar is the main constitution of candy. ～ 수입품 the staple for import. ～수출국 the principal exporting nations. ～수출품 the「chief〔principal〕exports. ～ 시장 a primary market. ～역 main〔principal〕stations. ～원인 main「cause〔reason〕. ～인물 the leading characters (극의); the key figures (사건의).

**주워내다** pick out; take out; sort out.

**주워담다** pick up and「put〔stuff〕in. ¶ 흩어진 사과를 바구니에 ～ pick up scattered apples and put them back in a basket.

**주워대다** enumerate glibly; mention all sorts of things; pick out of the air. ¶ 이유를 ～ pick excuses out of the air / 거짓말을 ～ make up lies.

**주워듣다** learn by hearsay; hear incidentally; pick up《a bit of information》. ¶ 주워들은 지식 knowledge picked up from others / 남한테서 이야기를 ～ pick a story up from others.

**주워먹다** pick up and eat; take and eat; grab a bite to eat. ¶ 이것저것 ～ grab a bite of this and that.

**주워모으다** collect; gather. ¶ 주워 모은 것 (a collection of) odds and ends.

**주워섬기다** chatter; rattle on; say all sorts of things *one* heard of and saw. ¶ 윗사람들의 결점을 ～ run〔go〕through a list of *one's* superiors' faults.

**주위**(周圍) 《둘레》 the girth (나무 등의); 〖기하〗 the circumference (원의); the perimeter (다각형의); 《주변부》 the periphery《of the city》; 《환경》 the surroundings; the environment; 《부근》 the「environs〔neighborhood〕《of》. ¶ ～의 surrounding《hills》; encompassing《mountain ranges》; neighboring《villages》/ ～의 사정 circumstances; all the surrounding things and conditions / ～의 사람들 those「around〔close to〕*a person;* 《가족》 *a person's* family; *a person's* friends and acquaintances / 도시의 ～ the environs of a city / ～의 영향을 받다 be influenced by the surroundings / ～에 울타리를 두르다 fence around《a house》/ (이상한 듯) ～를 둘러보다 look around (in wonder) / ～에는 아무도 없다 There is nobody about. / 호수는 ～가 10마일 된다 The lake is ten miles around

〔in circumference〕. / 공원 ~에는 나무가 둘러있다 The park is bordered by trees. / 아마 그의 ~ 사람들이 가만히 있지 않을 테죠 Probably those around him will not remain 「silent 〔impassive〕.

**주유**(舟遊) boating; a cruise. ⇨ 뱃놀이.

**주유**(周遊) a (circular) tour; an excursion; a pleasure trip. ~하다 make a tour; make 〔take〕 an excursion; take a cruise (바다를). ¶ 제주도를 ~하다 make a tour around 〔through〕 Cheju island / 세계를 ~하다 make around-the-world tour.

**주유**(注油) 《윤활유 등의》 oiling; lubrication; 《급유》 refueling. ~하다 oil 《an engine》; lubricate; refill 《a car》 with gas; refuel 《an airplane》. ¶ ~를 받다 be lubricated; receive lubrication / 기계에 ~하다 oil 〔lubricate〕 a machine. ◉ ~기 a lubricator. ~소 a gas(oline) station; a filling 〔refueling〕 station; a service station.

**주육**(酒肉) wine and meat.

**주의**(主義) a principle; a doctrine; a cause; an ism; 《방침》 a line; a basis.

> 용법 **principle** 자기의 행동·선택·결정 등에 대하여 개인이 세우는 기준. **doctrine** 종교·정치 등의 교의·주의·신조. **cause** 개인 또는 집단이 거기에 헌신하고, 목표·이상으로 삼는 대의명분. **ism** 「주의·학설」을 뜻하는 말. 추상 명사를 만드는 어미로도 사용됨.

¶ ~로써 on 〔by〕 principle; as a matter of principle / ~가 있는〔없는〕 사람 a man of 「principle 〔no principle〕 / …을 ~로 삼다 make it a principle 〔point〕 to *do* / ~를 위해서 죽다 die for 〔be a martyr to〕 *one's* cause 〔principles〕 / ~에 따라 행동하다 act on principle; live up to *one's* principles / 현금 ~로 장사를 하다 do business on a cash basis / ~를 실행하다 carry out *one's* principles / ~를 지키다 stick to *one's* principles; live up to *one's* principles / ~를 버리다 abandon *one's* principles / ~를 굽히다 sacrifice 〔make a compromise with〕 *one's* principles / ~를 옹호하다〔배반하다〕 defend 〔betray〕 a cause / ~에 반하다 be against *one's* principles / 그런 비열한 짓은 내 ~에 어긋난다 It's against my principle to play dirty trick like that. / 저 병원은 돈벌자는 ~이다 That hospital is run for profit. ◉ ~주장 *one's* ideas and principles. 공화~ republicanism. 비관~ pessimism. 안전제일 ~ the motto of "Safety First."

**주의**(注意) ① 《주목·유의·관심》 attention; notice; heed; note; care. ~하다 pay 〔give〕 attention 〔heed〕 《to》; take notice of; attend to; 《관찰》 observe; 《특히 명령문에서》 mind (명심하다). ¶ ~해야 할 《주목할 만한》 remarkable; striking; noteworthy; significant (중요한) / ~하지 않다 take no notice 〔heed〕 of; 《경시하다》 neglect / ~가 모자라다〔산만하다〕 be careless 〔inattentive〕 / ~를 끌다 attract 〔draw, catch〕 《*a person's*》 attention / ~를 불러일으키다 arouse 〔provoke, stimulate〕 《*a person's*》 attention / ~를 게을리하다 relax *one's* attention; be negligent 《of》 / ~를 돌리다 turn 〔direct〕 *one's* attention 《to》; distract 〔divert〕 《*a person's*》 attention 《from》 / ~를 촉구하다 call 〔draw〕 《*a person's*》 attention 《to》 / ~를 집중하다 concentrate attention / 내 말을 ~해서 들어라 Attend to what I say. *or* Listen to me carefully 〔attentively〕. / 그 사실에 상당히 ~해야 한다 Careful attention must be paid to the fact. / 그녀는 늘 복장에 ~하고 있다 She is always attentive to her dress.

② 《조심》 care; 《경계》 watchfulness; caution; 《예방》 precaution. ~하다 「take care 〔be careful〕 《of》; be cautious 《about》; be watchful 《of, against》; guard 《against》. ¶ ~ 깊은 careful; cautious; watchful / ~가 모자라는 careless; negligent / ~해서 with care 〔caution〕; carefully; cautiously / 건강에 ~하다 take care of *oneself* 〔*one's* health〕 / 당연히 취해야 할 ~를 게을리하다 fail to take necessary precautions 《against》 / 음식에 ~해라 Be careful about what you eat. / 화재 방지에 특별한 ~를 해라 Take special precautions to prevent fire. / 나무에서 떨어지지 않도록 ~해라 Be careful lest you fall from the tree. / 유혹에 빠지지 않도록 항상 ~하시오 Be always watchful against temptations. / 맹견 ~ 《게시》 Beware of the dog! / 취급 ~ 《게시》 Handle with care.

③ 《충고》 advice; suggestion; counsel; 《경고》 (a) warning; admonishment. ~하다 advice; give advice 《to》; counsel; 《경고하다》 warn; caution 《*a person* against》; admonish. ¶ ~시키

다 warn; caution; advise / ～를 주다 give 《*a person*》 warning 〔advice〕; offer cautions / ～를 무시하다 disregard a caution / 내가 ～한대로 하시오 Follow my advice.

◉ ～력 (the power of) attention; attentiveness. ～보 〖기상〗 a warning: 폭풍～보 a storm warning / 파랑(波浪) ～보 a heavy seas warning. ～사항 matters that demand special attention; N.B. 《*nota bene* (L.)》. ～서(書) 《주석》 notes; 《지시》 instructions; 《약 등의》 directions: ～서를 잘 읽고 나서 사용해 주십시오 Please read the instructions before use. ～신호 a warning signal. 요(要)～인물 a suspicious 〔dangerous〕 character; a person under observation 〔the eyes of the police〕.

**주익**(主翼) 〖항공〗 the main wings (of an aircraft).

**주인**(主人) ① 《가장》 the master 《of a house》; the head 《of a family》; 《남편》 *one's* husband. ¶ ～과 하인 master and servant / ～을 섬기다 serve *one's* master / ～ 계십니까 Is the master at home? / ～은 외출 중입니다 The master is out. / 댁의 ～ 직업이 뭡니까 What is the occupation of your husband? ② 《임자》 the owner; the proprietor; 《고용주》 the employer; the master; 《여관·하숙집 등의》 the landlord; the landlady. ¶ ～과 고용인 the employer and employee(s) / 가게 ～ a storekeeper / ～ 없는 개 an ownerless dog; a stray (dog) / ～이 바뀌다 be now under new ownership / ～ 행세를 하다 act as if *one* owned the place; assume a proprietary air. ③ 《손님에 대한》 the host; the hostess. ¶ ～과 손님 host and guest / ～ 노릇을 하다 act as host 〔hostess〕; play host 〔hostess〕.

**주인**(主因) the primary 〔principal, chief〕 cause; the prime 〔main〕 factor. ¶ ～은 …이다 be chiefly due to… / 무역 부진의 ～은 생산 부족에 있다 The trade inactivity is mainly due to low production.

**주인공**(主人公) ① = 주인(主人). ② 《소설·극 등의》 a protagonist: a hero (*pl.* ～es); a heroine (여자). ¶그 소설은 귀환 병사가 ～이다 The novel has a returned soldier as its hero.

**주일**(主日) the Lord's day; Sunday; the Sabbath. ◉ ～날 = 주일(主日). ～학교 a Sunday school.

**주일**(週日) a week(day). ¶ 이번〔지난, 오는〕 ～ this 〔last, next〕 week / 한～ 동안의 여행 a week's journey (★ 소유격 어미 's는 사람·동물 이외에 시간·거리·금액 등을 나타낼 경우에도 쓰임: ten minutes' walk 「10분간의 산책」 / at arm's length 「팔을 뻗으면 닿을 곳에」 / a dollar's worth 「1달러의 가치」) / 한서너 ～ 걸리겠다 It will take a few weeks. / 크리스마스까지는 아직 2～ 남았다 We have still two weeks left until Christmas.

**주일**(駐日) ¶ ～의 resident 〔stationed〕 in Japan. ◉ ～한국 대사관 the Embassy of the Republic of Korea (accredited) 「to Japan 〔in Tokyo〕.

**주임**(主任) the person in charge 《of》; a head; a chief; a manager. ¶ ～을 명하다 put 《*a person*》 in full charge 《of》.

◉ ～교사 the teacher in charge: 그는 3학년 ～교사다 He is in charge of a third-year class. ～교수 a head professor: 영어과 ～교수 the chief instructor of English; the head of the English department. ～기사 a chief engineer. ～수당 《학교의》 an allowance for a senior teacher with administrative responsibilities. ～제 《학교의》 the system of assigning teachers to certain designated administrative responsibilities. 영업부～ the head 〔manager〕 of the sales 〔business〕 department. 회계～ a chief treasurer.

**주입**(注入) 《액체 따위의》 pouring into; injection (약액 등의); 《사상 등의》 infusion; instillation; 《교육의》 cramming. ～하다 《부어넣다》 pour 〔put, pump〕 《*something*》 into; 《고취하다》 infuse 《a spirit》 into 《*a person's* mind》; instill 《an idea》 into 《*a person's* mind》; 《약액을》 inject 〔infuse〕 into; 《공부 따위를》 cram. ¶ 지식을 머리에 ～하다 cram 〔stuff up〕 *one's* head with knowledge / 그는 새로운 사상을 학생들에게 ～시켰다 He inculcated the students with new ideas. / 그는 침체하고 있는 경제계에 활기를 ～했다 He pumped new life into the economic stagnation. ◉ ～식 cramming method: ～식 교육 the cramming (system of) education / ～식 수업 grinding. ～액(液) 〖의학〗 an infusion (식염수 따위).

**주자**(走者) 《달리기의》 a runner; 《야구》 a (base) runner. ¶ 제1～ 《릴레이의》 the starting runner / 2루에 ～를 두고 with a runner on the second (base) / ～를 내보내다 send a runner 《to》 / ～를 일소하다 〖야구〗 clear the bases (of the runners).

**주자**(奏者) a player. ⇨ 연주자.

**주자**(鑄字) a metal printing type.
◉ ～기 a type-caster. ～소 a type foundry.

**주장**(主張) 《고집》 insistence; persistence; 《창도》 advocacy; 《견해·주의》 *one's* opinion 〔doctrine〕; 《논점》 *one's* contention 〔point, argument〕; 《권리의》 a claim; 《요구·주장 따위의》 (an) assertion; 《지론》 *one's* opinion. ～하다 《자기 주장 따위를》 insist 《on, that》; assert; argue; maintain; claim; allege (근거 없이); plead (법정에서); 《강조하다》 emphasize; lay stress 《on》; 《창도하다》 support 《trade liberalization》; advocate 《women's rights》.
¶ 권리를 ～하다 assert *one's* rights; stand on *one's* rights; claim the right 《to *do*》; lay claim 《to *a thing*》/ 판권을 ～하다 lay claim to the copyright / 자유의 중요성을 ～하다 emphasize 〔laid stress on〕 the importance of freedom / 정당 방위를 ～하다 plead self-defense / 개혁을 ～하다 advocate reform / 무죄를 ～하다 assert *one's* innocence; 《법정에서》 plead innocence 〔not guilty〕 / ～을 관철하다 carry 〔gain〕 *one's* point / ～을 굽히다 concede a point; compromise / 자기 ～을 굽히지 않다 stick 〔hold firm〕 to *one's* convictions 〔opinions〕; stick to *one's* positions 〔guns〕 / 그녀는 자기의 말이 사실이라고 ～한다 She asserts that her statement is true. / 그의 ～은 옳다〔그르다〕 His opinion is 「right 〔wrong〕. / …하다는 것이 그의 ～이다 His opinion is that…. / 우리의 ～은 수락되지 않았다 Our contention was not accepted. / 그는 자기 ～이 강하다 He is extremely self-assertive. / 그는 자기가 그 토지의 소유자라고 ～했다 He claimed to be the owner of the land.
◉ ～자 《권리의》 a claimant; 《주의의》 an advocate.

**주장**(主將) 《팀의》 the captain 《of a baseball team》; 《군대의》 the commander in chief; a chief general.

**주재**(主宰) supervision; presiding; superintendence. ～하다 preside over 《a society》; supervise; superintend; run. ¶ …의 ～하에 under the superintendence 〔supervision〕 of… / A씨가 ～하는 잡지 a magazine run 〔edited〕 by Mr. A / …이 ～하는 위원회 a committee under the presidency of… / 회의를 ～하다 preside over the meeting.
◉ ～자 the president; the chairperson; the leader.

**주재**(駐在) stay; residence. ～하다 reside 《at, in》; be stationed 《at, in》. ¶ ～의 residing 〔resident〕 《in a country》/ 파리 ～ 외교관 a diplomat residing in Paris / 내 형은 신문 기자로 L.A.에 ～하고 있다 My elder brother is stationed in L.A. as a newspaper reporter.
◉ ～관 a resident officer 〔official〕; an officer 〔official〕 resident in a country. ～국 the country of residence. ～원 《신문사의》 a resident reporter. 미국 ～ 한국 대사 the Korean Ambassador in America.

**주저**(躊躇) hesitation; indecision; vacillation; scruples. ～하다 hesitate 《to *do*》; be irresolute; have scruples 《about》; waver; vacillate.
¶ ～하면서 hesitatingly; with hesitation; reluctantly; irresolutely / ～없이 without hesitation; readily / …함을 ～하지 않다 have no hesitation in *doing*; make no scruple to *do* 〔of *doing*〕 / 그는 ～하고 있었다 He was in a state of indecision. / 그는 돈벌이라면 무슨 일이든지 ～하지 않고 한다 He does not hesitate to do anything for money-making. / 그는 제 생각을 ～없이 말했다 He did not hesitate to tell me what he thought. / 그는 입당할까 말까 아직도 ～하고 있다 He is still hesitant about joining the party.

**주저앉다** ① 《맥없이》 drop 《on *one's* knees》; fall 〔sink〕 down; collapse 《on》 (쓰러지듯); 《털썩》 sit down plump. ¶ 의자에 털썩 ～ sink 〔drop, plop down〕 into a chair / 그는 너무 피곤해서 길가에 주저앉았다 He was so tired that he collapsed on the roadside. ② 《가라앉다》 sink; cave in; 《내려앉다》 collapse; subside. ¶ 지붕이 ～ a roof caves 〔falls〕 in. ③ 《그대로 머물다》 stay on; sit on; settle down. ¶ 그는 사직하려다 그대로 주저앉았다 He stayed on in his office and gave up the idea of resigning.

**주저앉히다** 《의자 따위에》 force 《*a person*》 to sit 〔squat〕 down; 《못 떠나게》 make 《*a person*》 stay on.

**주전**(主戰) ¶ ～투수 《야구》 the chief pitcher; an ace hurler 〔pitcher〕.
◉ ～론 a pro-war argument; advocacy of 〔support for〕 war; militant patriotism: ～론자 a war advocate; [집합적] the pro-war party / ～론을 펴다 advocate war.

**주전**(鑄錢) coinage; minting; mintage. 「～하다 mint; coin.

**주전부리** snacking between meals. ~하다 take snacks between meals.

**주전자**(酒煎子) a (copper, brass) kettle; a teakettle. ¶ ~에 물을 끓이다 boil water in a kettle / ~를 불에 얹어 놓다 put a kettle 「over the fire 〔on the stove〕. ◉ ~뚜껑〔주둥이, 손잡이〕 the lid 〔spout, bail〕 of a kettle.

**주절**(主節) 〖문법〗 the main 〔principal〕 clause.

**주점**(酒店) a (Korean-style) bar; a tavern; a saloon; 《영》 a pub; a public house. = 술집.

**주접들다** be stunted 〔blighted〕; be in poor shape. ¶ 주접든 나무 stunted trees / 보리가 ~ barley gets blighted / 잘 먹지 못해 ~ be in bad shape from poor eating.

**주접스럽다** (be) greedy; avaricious; gluttonous.

**주정**(舟艇) a boat; a craft. ¶ 상륙용 ~ a landing craft.

**주정**(酒酊) misconduct affected by liquor; drunken frenzy. ~하다 be a bad drunk. ¶ 그는 술을 마시면 ~부린다 He is a 「bad drunk 〔vicious drinker〕. *or* He loses his reason when he is drunk. ◉ ~꾼〔뱅이〕 a drunken brawler; a bad drunk.

**주정**(酒精) alcohol; spirits; 〖화학〗 ethanol. ¶ ~의 alcoholic; spirituous / 공업용 ~ industrial alcohol / ~화 하다 alcoholize; turn into alcohol. ◉ ~계 an alcoholometer. ~분 alcoholic content. ~음료 alcoholic beverages 〔drinks〕.

**주정설**(主情說) 〖철학〗 emotionalism; emotivism.

**주제** ① 《몰골》 seedy 〔wretched〕 appearance; shabby 〔humble〕 looks. ¶ ~사납다 have a shabby appearance; be shabbily 〔poorly〕 dressed / 차마 이런 ~로 그녀 앞에 나갈 수가 없다 I simply cannot appear before her with this shabby appearance. / 그런 ~를 하고 가면 멸시당할 거야 You will be slighted, if you go so poorly dressed. ② 《형편·처지》 ¶ 신출내기 ~에 though being only a 「beginner 〔greenhorn〕 / 돈도 없는 ~에 though in need of money / 지금의 내 ~로는 그런 것을 할 수가 없다 In my present circumstances I cannot possibly afford to do it.

**주제**(主題) 《주 제목》 the (principal, main) subject; 《작품의》 the theme; the motif. ¶ ~의 thematic / ~의 발전 thematic development / 영국 시골 생활을 ~로 희곡을 쓰다 write a play based on the rural life of England. ◉ ~가 a theme song 《of a motion picture》.

**주제넘다** (be) presumptuous; impudent; impertinent; forward; cheeky; conceited; saucy; sassy.
¶ 주제넘게 impertinently; impudently; presumptuously; obtrusively / 주제넘은 녀석 an impertinent 〔insolent〕 fellow; a smart aleck / 지나치게 ~ be too forward / 주제넘은 말을 하다 talk fresh / 주제넘게 남의 말을 가로채다 have the cheek to cut in; interrupt impertinently / (남의 일에) 주제넘게 나서다 put 〔thrust〕 in *one's* oar; meddle in 〔poke *one's* nose into〕 (the affairs of others) / 주제넘게 굴지 마라 Don't be so forward. *or* I want none of your cheek. / 주제넘습니다만 … Excuse me for interfering, but…. / 그는 아무데나 주제넘게 나선다 He thrusts himself in everywhere. / 그는 주제넘게도 나에게 그런 말을 하였다 He had the impudence to tell me so.

**주조**(主調) 〖음악〗 the keynote; the dominant 〔fundamental〕 note.

**주조**(主潮) the main tide 〔current〕. ¶ 유럽 문예의 ~ the main current of European literature.

**주조**(酒造) 《양조》 《beer》 brewing; 《증류》 《whisky》 distilling. ~하다 brew; distill. ◉ ~가 a brewer; a 《whisky》 distiller. ~업 the brewing 〔distilling〕 industry. ~장 a brewery; a distillery.

**주조**(鑄造) casting; founding; 《화폐의》 coinage; minting; mintage. ~하다 cast; found 《a bell》; 《화폐를》 coin; mint. ¶ 활자를 ~하다 cast metal types. ◉ ~비 coinage charges. ~소 a foundry; 《화폐의》 a mint. ~업 foundry. ~인 a founder; a caster. ~화폐 a metallic coin.

**주종**(主從) 《주인과 종자》 master and servant; lord and retainer 〔vassal〕; 《주체와 종속》 the principal and the accessory 〔subordinate〕. ¶ ~의 맹세를 하다 plight to be lord and vassal. ◉ ~관계 the relation between master and servant: ~관계에 있다 stand in the relation of master and servant.

**주주**(株主) a stockholder 《미》; a shareholder 《영》. ¶ 회사의 ~ stockholders in company. ◉ ~권 a stockholder's right. ~명부 a stockholders' list. ~배당금 a dividend to stockholder. ~의 결권 the voting right of stockholders. ~총회 a general meeting of stockholders; a stockholders' 〔sharehold-ers'〕 meeting. 대〔소〕～a large 〔small〕 stockholder.

**주지**(主旨) the general purport; the main meaning; the tenor; the drift; the gist.

**주지**(住持) 《절의》 the head 〔chief〕 priest of a Buddhist temple.

**주지**(周知) ¶ ～의 known to every-body; universally 〔widely〕 known; well-known / ～의 사실 a matter of common knowledge; a well-known fact / ～하는 바와 같이 as is generally 〔commonly, universally〕 known; as everybody knows / …은 ～의 사실이다 It is (a matter of) common knowl-edge that… / 흡연이 건강에 해롭다는 것은 ～의 사실이다 It is well known that smoking is bad for the health.

**주지사**(州知事) 《미》 the governor of a state. ◉ ～선거 a gubernatorial elec-tion. 「〔banquet〕.

**주지육림**(酒池肉林) a sumptuous feast

**주지주의**(主知主義) 〖철학〗 intellectual-ism. ◉ ～자 an intellectualist.

**주차**(駐車) parking. ～하다 park 《a car》. ¶ ～중인 차 a parked car / 다른 차 곁에 나란히 ～하다 double-park / 그 가로에는 ～할 곳이 없었다 There was no parking place 〔space〕 along the street. / ～금지 《게시》 No parking. / 주요 도로상의 ～는 금지되어 있다 Park-ing on main streets is prohibited. ◉ ～ 금지 구역 《미》 a no-parking 〔=stopping 《영》〕 zone. ～난 parking difficulties 《in downtown areas》. ～료 a parking charge 〔fee〕. ～단속원 《미》 a meter maid 《여》. ～미터 a parking meter. ～빌딩 a parking build-ing. ～위반 (a) parking violation; illegal parking: ～위반 딱지 a parking ticket / ～ 위반을 하다 violate the parking regulations; get 〔pick up〕 a parking ticket / ～위반의 과태료를 물다 pay a parking ticket; be fined for a parking violation. ～장 a parking lot 〔zone, place〕 《미》; a car park 《영》: ～장법 the Parking Lot Act / ～장 시설 a parking lot installation.

**주창**(主唱) advocacy; promotion. ～하다 advocate 《peace》; promote; suggest. ¶ …의 ～으로 at the instance of…; on the suggestion of… / 그들은 인종차별의 폐지를 ～했다 They advocated abol-ishing racial distinctions. ◉ ～자 an advocate; a promoter; the high priest 《of modern education》.

**주책** a definite view; a fixed opinion. ¶ ～이 없다 have no definite opinion of *one's* own; be wishy-washy; be spineless; be indecisive / ～없이 말하다 talk senselessly 〔pointlessly〕; talk nonsense / ～없는 짓을 하다 behave disgracefully 〔indecently〕. ◉ ～망나니〔바가지〕 a wishy-washy 〔spineless, indecisive〕 person.

**주철**(鑄鐵) cast iron. ◉ ～소 an iron=foundry〔-works〕. 「〔Emperor〕 《for》.

**주청**(奏請) ～하다 petition the king

**주체** ～하다 cope with 〔take care of〕 *one's* troubles. ⇨ 주체 못 하다.

**주체**(主體) the main body; 〖철학〗 the subject; 《중핵》 the nucleus; the core. ¶ ～적인 independent; subjec-tive / ～적인 행동 independent action / 권리의～ the subject of rights / …이 ～가 되어 …을 하다 take the initiative in *do*ing 《for》 / 북한의 ～ 사상 the North Korea's "*juche*" 〔self-reliance〕 ideology / 대학생을 ～로 하는 단체 a group 〔an organization〕 mainly com-posed of college students. ◉ ～성 independence; autonomy; identity: ～성을 확립하다 establish *one's* independence. ～세력 the main group 〔body〕 《of》. ～의식 a sense of sovereignty (and independence): 전국민에게 ～의식의 강화를 호소하다 make a nation-wide plea for strengthening of a sense of sovereignty and inde-pendence. 「ing.

**주체**(酒滯) indigestion caused by drink-

**주체못하다** do not know what to do 《with》; find 《*a person*》 unmanage-able; be too much 〔many〕 《for》; be beyond 〔out of〕 *one's* control; be unmanageable 〔uncontrollable〕. ¶ 일이 많아서 ～ have more work than *one* can manage / 나는 시간을 주체 못한다 Time hangs heavy on my hands. / 그는 주체 못 할 만큼 돈이 많다 He has more money than he knows what to do with. / 그는 뚱뚱해서 제 몸을 주체 못 한다 He is so fat he can hardly get along with himself.

**주체스럽다** (be) unmanageable; un-wieldy; burdensome; be hard to han-dle 〔manage〕.

**주첼덩어리** a nuisance 《to the family》; a bother; an encumbrance; a white elephant; a black sheep. ¶ 그는 가족내의 ～이다 He is the 「black sheep 〔nuisance〕 in his family.

**주최**(主催) sponsorship; auspices. ～하

다 host 《a speech contest》; sponsor. ¶ …의 공동 ~로 under the joint auspices of… / 교육부 ~로 under the auspices 〔direction〕 of the Ministry of Education / 그 전람회는 한 신문사 ~로 열렸다 The exhibition was 「held under the sponsorship of 〔sponsored by〕 a newspaper company. ◉ ~국 《초대 행사의》 the host country. ~단체 the host organization; the organization that hosts the contest 〔athletic meet, *etc.*〕. ~자 the pro-moter; the sponsor.

**주추**(柱—) 〖건축〗 the stone on which a pillar rests; a cornerstone.

**주축**(主軸) 〖공학〗 the main 〔principal〕 axis; 《중심 인물》 the central 〔leading〕 figure. ¶ 그는 신인이면서도 팀의 ~이 되었다 Rookie though he was, he was given a key role in the team.

**주춤거리다** hesitate; waver; hold back; balk at. ¶ 주춤거리면서 hesitatingly; hesitantly; waveringly / 주춤거리며 말하다 stammer out; falter / 결단을 내리지 못하고 ~ be hesitant to make a decision / 그는 잠시 주춤거린 후에 그것을 사기로 했다 He decided to buy it after a short period of hesitation. / 그는 뱀을 보자 잠시 주춤거렸다 On seeing the snake, he held back for a while.

**주춤주춤** hesitatingly; hesitantly; falteringly; waveringly.

**주춧돌**(柱—) a foundation stone. =주추.

**주치**(主治) ~하다 take charge of 《a case》. ◉ ~의 the physician in charge 《of》; 《가정의》 *one's* (family) doctor; general practitioner (생략 GP): 나의 ~의는 전문의에게 가보라고 권유했다 My GP advised me to go and see a specialist. ~효능 the chief virtues 《of a medicine》.

**주택**(住宅) a house; a residence; a dwelling; a residential building; [총칭] housing. ¶ 조립식 간이 ~ 《미》 a prefab / 모델 ~ a model dwelling / 근로자용 ~ houses for the working class / M씨의 ~ Mr. M's house / 가구가 딸린 ~ a house partly 〔fully〕 furnished / 그 건물은 ~으로 마땅치 않다 The building is not fit to live in. / 급속도로 증가하는 인구에 ~을 공급한다는 것은 어려운 일이다 It is difficult to provide housing for the rapidly increasing population.
◉ ~가 a residential street. ~건설 산업 home-building industry. ~건설 촉진법 the Housing Construction Expediting Law. ~계획 a housing project. ~구역〔지역〕 the residence section 《of the city》; a residential district 〔quarter〕. ~단지 a housing complex. ~문제 the housing problem. ~부족 (a) shortage of housing accommodation; housing accommodation; housing shortage. ~비 housing expenses. ~사정 the housing situation. ~수당 a housing allowance. ~용지 a housing lot: ~용지를 확보하다 secure a housing lot. ~융자 (a) housing loan. ~조합(제도) a housing cooperative (system). ~지 a residential quarter 〔district, area, section〕: 이름있는 ~지 a noted dwelling-ground. ~지구 《도시계획의》 a residence zone. ~채권 housing bonds: ~채권 입찰제 the bond bidding system. ~청약 예금 an apartment-application deposit 《bank note》. ~행정〔정책〕 the housing administration 〔policy〕. 대한 ~공사 the Korea National Housing Corporation (생략 KNHC).

**주택난**(住宅難) (a) shortage of house; housing shortage 〔trouble〕; a house famine. ¶ ~으로 고생을 하다 suffer from scarcity of house / ~을 완화하다 ease the housing shortage / ~은 큰 사회 문제로 되어 있다 The house famine poses 〔forms〕 a big social problem.

**주파**(周波) a cycle. ¶ 고〔저〕~ a high 〔low〕 frequency.

**주파수**(周波數) frequency. ¶ ~ 750 킬로헤르츠로 방송하다 broadcast in the band 〔frequency〕 of 750 kilohertz.
◉ ~계 a frequency meter. ~대 a frequency band. ~변조 〖방송〗 frequency modulation (생략 FM). ~조정 amplitude modulation. ~증폭기 a frequency amplifier.

**주파하다**(走破—) run 〔cover〕 the whole distance 《between》. ¶ 1 마일을 4 분대에 ~ cover 〔run〕 one mile in four minutes.

**주판**(籌板·珠板) an abacus (*pl.* -cuses, abaci); a counting board. ¶ ~을 놓다 work 〔use〕 an abacus; count 〔reckon〕 on an abacus / ~을 잘 놓다 be clever with *one's* abacus. ◉ ~알 a counter; a bead (on an abacus).

**주포**(主砲) 〖군사〗 the main armament; the principal battery 〔guns〕 《of a warship》.

**주피터** 〖로神〗 Jupiter.

**주필**(主筆) the chief editor; the editor-in-chief. ¶ 부~ an assistant editor; a subeditor 《주로 영》.

**주필**(朱筆) a brush for red ink; a red brush. ¶ ~을 가하다 correct; 《구어》 red-pencil 《a book》; 《개정하다》 revise.
**주한**(駐韓) ¶ ~ 미군 U.S. Armed Forces in Korea / ~ 미군 방송 the American Forces Korea Network (생략 AFKN) / ~ 외교 사절단 the diplomatic corps in Korea / ~ 일본 대사 the Japanese Ambassador to Korea 〔in Seoul〕.
**주항**(周航) circumnavigation; cruising. ~하다 circumnavigate; cruise; sail around. ◉ 세계~ sailing around the world; a round-the-world cruise.
**주해**(註解) (an) annotation; (explanatory) notes; a commentary; a comment. ~하다 annotate; comment 〔make notes〕 upon; give notes. ¶ ~가 붙은 annotated; with notes / ~를 단 책 an annotated book; a book with notes. ◉ ~서 an annotated edition 《of *Hamlet*》; 《미구어》 a trot. ~자 an annotator; a commentator.
**주행**(舟行) going by boat; sailing; navigation. ~하다 go by boat; sail along; navigate.
**주행**(走行) traveling; covering. ~하다 travel 《from A to B》; cover 《100 miles in an hour》. ¶ 차의 ~ 마일수를 살펴보다 check the mileage of a car / ~중에 운전 기사에게 잡담하지 마시오 《게시》 Don't speak to the driver without good reason while the bus is in motion. ◉ ~거리 (a) distance covered 《in a given time》; 《마일로 표시된》 mil(e)age: ~거리계(計) an odometer; a mileage indicator / 이 차의 ~거리는 약 만 킬로이다 The mileage on this car is about ten thousand kilometers. ~선 a driving lane. ~시간 time taken in「traveling 《from A to B》〔covering the distance 《between A and B》〕; 《열차의》 rail time.
**주행성**(晝行性) ¶ ~동물 a diurnal animal; an animal of diurnal habit(s).
**주향**(酒香) the flavor of liquor.
**주혈흡충**(住血吸蟲) a blood fluke; a schistosome. ◉ ~병 schistosomiasis.
**주형**(主刑) the principal penalty.
**주형**(鑄型) a mold; a matrix; a cast. ¶ ~을 뜨다 cast a mold / ~에 붓다 pour 《metal》 into a mold. ◉ ~공 a molder. 「속어》 a boozer.
**주호**(酒豪) a hard 〔heavy〕 drinker; 《영
**주홍**(朱紅) scarlet (red); vermilion.
**주화**(鑄貨) coinage; mintage; 《화폐》 a coin. ¶ 기념~ 《issue》 commemorative coins / 불량 유사 ~는 넣지 마시오 《게시》 Do not use odd coins.
**주화론**(主和論) advocacy of peace. ◉ ~자 an advocate of peace; a pacifist.
**주황**(朱黃) orange color.
**주효**(奏效) efficacy; (an) effect. ~하다 be effectual; be effective; take effect; work well; be fruitful; pay off 《미》. ¶ 그의 시도는 ~하지 않았다 His attempt yielded no results. *or* His attempt proved ineffectual. / 우리의 정치 운동은 ~했다 Our political campaigning paid off.
**주효**(酒肴) wine and tasty dishes.
**주휴**(週休) a weekly holiday 〔day off〕. ◉ ~2일제 《institute, go over to》 a five-day workweek 〔working week 《영》〕.
**주흥**(酒興) 《홍취》 elation from drinking; feeling high; merrymaking. ¶ ~에 겨워 under the influence of wine; in *one's* drunken exhilaration / ~을 돕다〔깨뜨리다〕 heighten 〔dampen〕 「the merriment 〔the life to the party〕 / 그 일 때문에 모처럼의 ~이 깨지고 말았다 That brought a chill over the merrymaking party.
**죽**(粥) (rice-)gruel (묽은); porridge (되직한); hot cereal; pap (유아용). ¶ 죽을 쑤다 boil rice into 《thick, thin》 gruel / 겨우 죽이나 먹고 살다 live on a crust / 죽거리도 없다 have no grain to make porridge; live in poverty.
**죽**[1] 《열 벌》 ten pieces; ten 《plates, garments》. ¶ 접시 한 죽 ten plates.
**죽**[2] ① 《한 줄로》 in a row 〔line〕. ¶ 죽 서다 stand in a row / 죽 늘어놓다 make an array 《of》; display / 자동차가 죽 늘어서 있었다 There was an array of motorcars. / 그 거리의 한편에는 책방이 죽 늘어서 있다 On one side of the street is an unbroken succession of bookshops. / 길가에 군인들이 죽 늘어서 있었다 The streets were lined with troops.
② 《찢는 소리》 tearing; ripping; with a rip. ¶ 봉투를 죽 찢다 tear open an envelope / 손수건을 죽 찢다 rip a handkerchief.
③ 《물·기운 등이》 《recede》 utterly; completely; all the way; all down the line; easily. ¶ 큰 물이 죽 빠졌다 The flood receded completely. / 기운이 죽 빠졌다 I am utterly exhausted.
④ 《줄곧》 all during; throughout; all the time; straight (through). ¶ 아침부터 죽 all through the morning / 일년 동안 죽 all the year round / 지금까지

죽 기다렸습니다 I have been waiting for you all this while. / 역에서 집까지 죽 걸어왔다 I have walked home all the way from the station. / 그때부터 죽 여기서 살고 있습니다 I have lived here ever since. / 전쟁 중에는 죽 부산에 있었다 I stayed in Pusan all through the war.

⑤《대강》roughly; quickly; briefly. ¶ 죽 훑어보다 look 〔glance, run〕 through; look over / 신문을 죽 훑어보다 run through the paper / 편지를 죽 훑어보다 pass *one's* eyes over a letter.

**죽기**(竹器) a bamboo ware 〔utensil〕.

**죽는 소리** ①《엄살》talking 〔making a〕 poor mouth. ⇨ 엄살. ～하다 talk poor mouth. ¶ ～ 좀 그만 해라 Stop talking poor mouth. ②《비명》a shriek; a scream; a screech. ¶ ～를 지르다 utter a shriek; screech / 아파서 ～를 지르다 give a cry of pain; shriek with pain.

**죽다** ①《숨이 끊어지다》die (★ 병으로 죽을 때는 die of, 다른 원인으로 죽을 때는 일정치 않음. 보기: die by the sword, die from wounds, die by violence, die through neglect, die of thirst 〔hunger, sorrow, disappointed love〕); 《완곡어》pass away; be gone; breathe *one's* last; 《목숨을 잃다》meet *one's* end 〔death〕; lose *one's* life; be killed; perish (★ perish는 문어적인 말); 《일생을 마치다》close *one's* day 〔life〕; end *one's* career; 《저승 가다》leave this world; go to the better world; 《자살하다》kill *oneself;* commit suicide.

¶ 죽은 dead; the late 《Mr. A》; departed; deceased / 죽을 각오로 at the risk of *one's* life / 죽느냐 사느냐의 문제 a matter of life and 〔or〕 death / 죽은 숙부 *one's* dead 〔deceased〕 uncle / 죽은 사람들 the dead / 죽어라 하고 〔죽자 사자〕 싸우다 fight to death / 죽어라 하고 도망하다 run for *one's* life / 죽어도 말 못하겠다 cannot tell for *one's* life / 죽을 지경에 빠지다 get to 〔be at〕 death's door; get (in) on the brink of death / 죽을 지경이다 be in a tight situation; be in a corner / 타〔얼어, 굶어〕 ～ be burnt 〔frozen, starved〕 to death / 병〔암〕으로 ～ die of「a disease 〔cancer〕 / 교통 사고로 ～ be killed in a traffic accident / 보고 싶어 죽겠다 be dying to see / 피곤해〔심심해〕 죽겠다 be tired 〔bored〕 to death / 인간은 죽기 마련이다 Man is mortal. / 그가 죽은지 5년이 된다 It is five years since he died. / 죽은 자식 나이 세기 《속담》It is no use crying over spilt milk. / 우스워서 죽을 뻔했다 I nearly died of laughing. / 그 둘은 죽자 사자 좋아한다 Those two are mad about each other. / 돈이 없어 죽을 지경이다 I am very hard up for money. / 그때는 정말 죽는가 보다 생각했다 Then I really felt my last hour had come. / 욕을 보는 것보다 죽는 게 낫다 I would rather die than live and be humiliated. / 이 나이에 영어를 배우자니 죽을 노릇이다 This business of learning English at my age is killing me. / 아이고 죽겠다 Brother, it's murder! / 그저 죽지 못해 산다 For all I get out of life I might as well be dead. / 너 같은 것은 죽어라 Drop dead! / 은혜는 죽어도 잊지 않겠습니다 I shall never forget your kindness.

②《기가》get crestfallen 〔downcast, out of spirits〕; feel small 〔depressed, dispirited〕. ¶ 그녀의 말에 그는 풀이 죽었다 When she said that it really took the starch out of him.

③《초목이》wither; die; perish; be dead; be blasted (서리 따위로). ¶ 이 나무는 물이 부족해서 죽어가고 있다 This tree is dying from lack of water.

④《생기가》lack life; be lifeless. ¶ 이 그림은 생동감이 죽어 있다 This painting is lifeless 〔lacks life〕.

⑤《불이》die out; go out. ¶ 죽어 가는 불 a dying fire / 불이 죽지 않게 하다 keep the fire alive.

⑥《동작이 멎다》run down; stop. ¶ 시계가 죽었다 The clock has stopped.

⑦《장기·바둑에서》be captured 〔lost〕; 〖야구〗 be (put) out.

**죽담** 《돌담》a stone wall. ¶ 마당 둘레에 ～을 쌓다 put up a stone wall around the garden.

**죽데기** side-splits from whole logs (used as firewood); long side-splits.

**죽도**(竹刀) 《대칼》a bamboo knife; 《검도의》a bamboo sword.

**죽림**(竹林) a bamboo grove.

**죽마**(竹馬) a bamboo horse (외대의); stilts (두 대의). ¶ ～를 타다 walk on stilts. ◉ ～지우(之友) a bosom friend from childhood; a childhood friend; an old chum 〔playmate〕.

**죽물**(粥—) thin 〔watery〕 rice gruel.

**죽방울** 《장난감》a diabolo; a cup and ball. ¶ ～ 받다 play with a diabolo; [비유적] make fun of 《*a person*》 with mixed praise and mockery.

**죽살이** (a matter of) life and 〔or〕

death. ~치다 make desperate 〔frantic〕 efforts. 「bamboo ware.
**죽세공**(竹細工) bamboo work. ◉ ~품
**죽순**(竹筍) a bamboo shoot 〔sprout〕. ¶ 우후~처럼 나오다 shoot 〔spring〕 up like mushrooms after rain.
**죽술**(粥—) a few spoonfuls of (rice) porridge. ¶ ~이나 먹고 살아가다 lead a meager life.
**죽어라하고** desperately; frantically; like hell; for life; as hard as *one* can; with utmost effort; tooth and nail. ¶ ~ 달리다 run as fast as *one's* legs can carry *one* / ~ 도망치다 run for *one's* life / ~ 일하다 work away like *one* possessed.
**죽어지내다** live under oppression; live a life of subjugation. ¶ 그는 아버지〔아내〕 앞에 죽어지낸다 He lives under his father's 〔wife's〕 thumb.
**죽은목숨** a life 〔person〕 as good as dead; a person beyond the realm of hope 〔help〕 (such as a sick person); a hopeless case; a person who might as well be dead. ¶ 너는 이제 ~이다 You are a dead 〔marked〕 man now.
**죽을둥살둥** desperately; frantically; life and death; tooth and nail. ¶ ~ 덤비다 go it as if *one's* life depends on it; go after at it tooth and nail.
**죽을병**(—病) a fatal 〔mortal〕 disease. ¶~에 걸리다 catch 〔suffer from, contract〕 a fatal disease.
**죽을뻔살뻔** by the skin of *one's* teeth; at the peril of *one's* life; within an inch of *one's* life; having a close shave (with death). ¶ ~ 삼팔선을 넘었다 I came across the 38th parallel by the skin of my teeth.
**죽을상**(—相) an agonized look; a frantic 〔desperate〕 look.
**죽을힘** the last effort; a frantic 〔desperate〕 effort. ¶ ~을 다해서 frantically; desperately; for *one's* life / ~을 다해서 헤엄치다〔도망치다〕 swim 〔run〕 for *one's* life / ~을 다해서 싸우다 fight a desperate fight; fight to the death.
**죽음** (a) death; decease; demise. ¶ ~에 임하여 on *one's* deathbed / ~을 무릅쓰고 at the risk of *one's* death / ~ 같은 고요 a deathlike silence / ~의 재 radioactive fallout; deadly radioactive ash; "death ash" / ~의 공포 the fear of death / ~이 멀지 않은 비슬거리는 노인 a decrepit old man with one foot 〔leg〕 in the grave / ~에 이르게 하다 cause 《*a person's*》 death; cause 《*a person*》 to die / ~에 직면하다 face death; look death in the face / ~에서 다시 살아나다 rise from the dead; resurrect / ~으로 속죄하다 atone for 《*one's* crime》 with death / ~이 다가오다 be near 〔approach〕 *one's* final hour / ~이 다가옴을 알다 feel *one's* life ebbing away / ~을 재촉하다 hasten 〔quicken〕 *one's* death / ~을 당하다 meet *one's* death; suffer death; lose *one's* life; be killed / 간신히 ~을 모면하다 have 〔make〕 a narrow escape; escape death by a hair's breadth; be snatched from the jaws of death / ~을 각오하다 prepare for death; be ready to die / 영광스러운 ~을 하다 die a glorious death / 수치스러운 ~을 하다 die a shameful death / ~은 평등하다 Death is a leveler. *or* All are equal in the grave. 「tain.
**죽의장막**(竹—帳幕) the Bamboo Cur-
**죽이다** ① 《살해하다》 kill; slay (고의로); put 《*a person*》 to death; take 《*a person's*》 life; put an end to 《*a person's*》 life; 《모살하다》 murder; 《학살하다》 slaughter; massacre (대량으로); 《도살하다》 butcher.

> 용법 **kill** 사람·동식물을 「죽이다, (말라) 죽게 하다」란 뜻의 일반적인 말. **slay** 사람에 대해서, kill보다 뜻이 강하고 문어적인 말. **murder** 사람을 계획적·불법적으로 죽이다. **slaughter** 짐승이나 사람을 잔인한 방법으로 죽이다. 대량 학살도 포함됨. **massacre** 무고한 사람들을 무자비하게 대량으로 학살하다. 한 사람에 대해서는 쓰지 않음.

¶ 목을 졸라 ~ strangle 《*a person*》 (to death) / 때려 ~ beat 《*a person*》 to death / 독약을 먹여 ~ dose 《*a person*》 to death / 사람을 죽이고 사형이 되다 be executed 〔hanged〕 for murder 〔homicide〕 / 죽여 버린다고 위협하다 threaten 《*a person*》 with death / 그는 나를 죽이려 했다 He made an attempt on my life. / 살리든 죽이든 마음대로 해라 I am at your mercy. / 한 걸음이라도 움직이면 죽여 버린다 Stir a step, and you shall die. *or* Stick 〔Stay〕 right where you are, or you're a dead man. / 이 죽일 놈아 Damn you! *or* Be damned to you. / 그놈 죽일 놈이군 He is a rascal, indeed.
② 《잃다》 suffer the death 〔loss〕 of; lose 《a son, a chessman》. ¶ 졸 하나

를 ~ lose a pawn / 전쟁에 아들을 ~ lose a son in the war.
③ 《억제하다》 hold back; restrain; deaden; muffle. ¶ 말소리를 죽이어 in a whisper 〔low tone〕 / 숨을 ~ hold *one's* breath / 발소리를 ~ muffle *one's* footsteps.
④ 《기·재능을》 ¶ 기를 ~ break 《*a person's*》 spirits; damp 〔dampen〕 *one's* spirits; depress; dispirit; dishearten / 재능을 ~ destroy 〔suppress〕 *one's* talent.
⑤ 《동작을》 stop 《a timepiece, a top, a motor》; allow 《it》 to stop.
⑥ 《불을》 put out 《a fire, a light》; let 《it》 go out.

**죽자꾸나하고** with great fortitude (불굴의 정신으로); resolutely (단호히); 《필사적으로》 desperately; frantically. ¶ ~ 일하다 work like a devil.

**죽장**(竹杖) a bamboo cane 〔stick〕.
◉ ~망혜 a bamboo stick and straw sandals.

**죽장기**(—將棋) (being) a poor chess player; a poor hand at chess. ¶ ~를 두다 play a poor hand of chess.

**죽젓개질**(粥—) ~하다 stir gruel; 《훼방하다》 interfere; stir up.

**죽죽** ① 《줄을》 in rows 〔lines〕; row after row; in streaks. ¶ 줄을 ~ 긋다 draw line after line. ② 《비가》 in sheets; in showers. ¶ 비가 ~ 내린다 The rain comes down in sheets. ③ 《찢다》 into shreds; in 〔to〕 pieces. ¶ ~ 찢다 tear to pieces. ④ 《기운차게》 briskly; 《꾸준히》 steadily; increasingly. ¶ 나뭇가지의 잎을 ~ 훑다 strip leaves off a twig briskly / 키가 ~ 자라다 grow taller and taller / 사업이 ~ 번창하다 a business expands steadily.

**죽지** 《어깨의》 a shoulder blade; a scapula; the shoulder joint; 《날개의》 the wing joint.

**죽창**(竹槍) a bamboo spear.

**죽치** goods sold by the tens 〔dozens〕; wholesale coarse 〔cheap〕 goods.

**죽치기** wholesale (trade). ¶ ~로 사다 buy wholesale.

**죽치다** confine *oneself* to 〔be confined in〕 《*one's* house》; stay put at home; shut 〔lock〕 *oneself* up 〔in〕; stay 〔remain〕 indoors. ¶ 종일토록 방안에 죽치고 있다 keep to *one's* room all day long.

**죽침**(竹針) = 대바늘.

**죽통**(粥筩) 《구유》 a feeding trough.

**죽피**(竹皮) a bamboo sheath. ◉ ~방석 a cushion made of bamboo sheaths.

**준-**(準) quasi-; semi-; associate. ¶ 준급행 a semi-express; a local express 《미》 / 준사법권 quasi-judicial power / 준여당 a quasi-government party; 《친여 정당》 a pro-government party / 준현행범 a quasi-flagrant offense / 준회원 an associate member.

**준거**(準據) authority cited; standard referred to; going to a standard 〔reference〕; referring to a precedent 〔rule〕. ~하다 base 《a decision》 on; conform to; follow; go by. ¶ …에 ~해서 on the authority of; in accordance with; in conformity to / …의 ~하는 바를 밝히다 give the authority of... / 법률〔선례〕에 ~하다 comply with the law 〔precedent〕 / ~할 규정이 없다 We have no rule to go by.

**준걸**(俊傑) a man of eminent 〔great〕 ability; a great man; a hero.

**준결승(전)**(準決勝(戰)) a semifinal (game). ¶ ~에 진출하다 go on to the semifinals / ~에 나가다 play 〔run〕 in the semifinals / 고교 야구 선수권 대회 ~에서 K 고교 팀은 Y 고교 팀을 물리쳤다 The K High School team defeated the Y High School nine at a semifinal of the High School Baseball Championship.
◉ ~출전자 a semifinalist.

**준골**(俊骨) an eminent physique; a man of eminent physique 〔ability〕.

**준공**(竣工) completion. ~하다 be completed; be finished. ¶ ~이 가깝다 be nearing completion 《of a house》 / 새 교사가 ~되었다 The new schoolhouse has been completed.
◉ ~검사 《건물의》 a permit for building completion; the permit on the completion 《of a building》. ~기 the time of completion. ~도(圖) 《건물의》 a drawing showing how a building will look when completed. ~식 a ceremony to celebrate the completion 《of a bridge》.

**준교사**(準敎師) an assistant teacher; a teaching assistant.

**준금치산**(準禁治産) = 한정치산(限定治産).

**준동**(蠢動) wriggling (like worms); squirming; activities. ~하다 《벌레가》 crawl; wriggle; 《무리가》 be active; stir; plan mischief. ¶ 불평분자의 ~ the (behind-the-scenes) maneuvering of discontented elements.

**준령**(峻嶺) a steep mountain pass; a dangerous high range.

**준마**(駿馬) a fine horse; a swift horse; a fleet steed.

**준말** a shortened word; an abbreviation; an abbreviated word. ¶ phone은 telephone의 ～이다 'Phone' is short for 'telephone'.

**준법**(遵法) law-abiding; obeying the law. ～하다 observe 〔obey, abide by〕 the law. ◉ ～정신 a law-abiding spirit; respect for law: ～ 정신을 앙양하다 promote law-abiding spirit. ～투쟁 a law-abiding labor struggle; work-to-rules strikes: ～ 투쟁의 전술 work-to-rules tactics / ～ 투쟁을 하다 follow work-to-rules tactics to disrupt efficient operation 《of the subway》.

**준봉**(峻峰) a steep peak; a lofty peak.

**준비**(準備) preparation(s); (preliminary) arrangements; preparedness; readiness; 《예비》 a reserve 《of money》. ～하다 prepare 《for》; ready; arrange 《for》; make preparations 《for》; get ready 《for》; provide for 《against》. ¶ ～ 없는 연설 an extempore 〔off-the-cuff 《미구어》〕 speech / ～부족의 ill-prepared 《attempt》 / ～중이다 [사람이 주어] be getting ready 《for》; [사물이 주어] be in (course of) preparation / ～를 갖추다 be ready 《for》 / ～에 바쁘다 be busy getting ready for 《*one's* trip》; be busy preparing for 《an examination》; be in active preparation 《for departure》 / 식사 ～를 하다 prepare 〔set〕 the table; provide 《for》 a dinner; get a dinner ready / 출발 ～를 하다 get 〔make〕 ready to start / 시험 ～를 하다 prepare (*oneself*) 〔study up〕 for an examination / 여행 ～를 하다 get (*oneself*) ready for a journey / 전투 ～를 하다 get readied for battle; 《해군이》 clear the decks / 환대 ～를 하다 make arrangements for the reception / …에 대비한 ～를 하다 prepare for 〔against〕 《an emergency》; stoke the fires against 《a visitor》 / 필요한 ～를 하다 make (all) necessary preparations 〔arrangements〕 《for》 / 만일의 경우를 위해 ～해 두다 provide against a rainy day / 손님을 위해 방을 ～하다 make a room ready for guests / 그는 노후에 걱정이 없도록 ～를 해 두었다 He has provided well for his old age. / 그 방을 회의에 쓰도록 ～해 두시오 Make the room ready for the meeting. / 필요한 돈은 ～되어 있다 I have the necessary sum ready to hand.
◉ ～공사 preparatory works. ～금 a reserve (fund); money (kept) 〔held〕 in reserve: 비상 ～금 an emergency fund / 손실에 대비한 ～금 a reserve against loss. ～기간 preparatory 〔breaking-in〕 period. ～실 a preparation room. ～운동 warming 〔limbering〕 up; warming-up exercises; 《경주말의》 sweating; a sweat: ～운동을 하다 warm up; limber (*oneself*) up. ～위원회 a preparatory committee 《for founding a college》. ～은행 《미국의》 a reserve bank. ～절차 『법』 preparatory proceedings; preliminaries. ～통화 a reserve currency.

**준사관**(准士官) a warrant officer.

**준사원**(準社員) a junior employee.

**준설**(浚渫) dredging. ～하다 dredge 《a harbor》. ¶ 강바닥을 ～하다 dredge up mud at the bottom of a river; dredge the river bottom. ◉ ～기 a dredging machine. ～선 a dredger; a dredging vessel. ～작업 dredging operations 〔work〕. 대한 ～ 공사 the Korean Dredging Corporation.

**준수**(俊秀) superiority in talent and elegance. ～하다 excel in talent and elegance; (be) superior and refined. ¶ ～한 젊은이 a young man of outstanding talent; 《외모가》 a well-set, handsome youth.

**준수**(遵守) observance; compliance; conformity. ～하다 observe 《rules, the law》; obey; abide by; follow; comply 《with》; conform to. ¶ ～하는 사람 an observer / 법률의 ～ law-observance / 법률을 잘 ～하는 국민 a law-abiding people / 법률〔규칙〕을 ～하다 observe the law 〔rules〕.

**준엄**(峻嚴) stringency; sternness; severity; rigor; strictness. ～하다 (be) stringent; severe; rigorous; stern; strict. ¶ ～한 검사 a relentless prosecutor / ～한 태도 a stern attitude / ～한 얼굴을 하다 look stern / 그 나라에서 영화는 ～한 검열을 받도록 되어 있다 The movie films are subjected to the strictest censorship in the country.

**준열**(峻烈) ～하다 (be) severe; sharp; stern; relentless; rigorous. ¶ ～한 비판 a sharp criticism.

**준우승**(準優勝) coming out a second best. ～하다 finish second 《in a tournament》. ◉ ～자 a winner of the second prize; a runner-up.

**준위**(准尉) a sub-officer; a warrant officer (생략 WO).

**준장**(准將) a brigadier general 《미육·공군》; a brigadier 《영육군》; a commodore

《해군》; an air commodore 《영공군》.
**준재**(俊才) 《재주》 eminent ability 〔talent〕; 《사람》 a brilliant 〔talented〕 man; a man of talent.
**준족**(駿足) 《말》 a swift 〔fast〕 horse; a fleet steed; 《사람》 a swift runner. ¶ ~의 fleet-〔swift-〕footed / ~이다 be fleet 〔swift〕 of foot; be a fast runner.
**준준결승(전)**(準準決勝(戰)) a quarterfinal (game); the quarterfinals.
**준치** 〖어류〗 a kind of herring.
**준칙**(準則) a standing rule; working rules; 《기준》 a standard; a criterion (*pl.* ~s, -ria). ¶ 법률은 행위의 ~이다 Law is the rule to action.
**준평원**(準平原) a peneplain.
**준하다**(準—) 《따르다》 act on 《a rule, precedent, *etc.*》; follow; go by; be based on; conform to; apply correspondingly 《to》; 《모방하다》 model after; 《비례하다》 be proportionate 《to》; be in proportion 《to》. ¶ …에 준하여 in accordance with…; in proportion to 《*one's* exertion》; in proportion as 《*one* exerts *oneself*》 / 회원에 ~ be treated the same as a regular member / 이하 이에 준함 This applies correspondingly to the following cases. / 작업량에 준하여 보수를 지급하겠다 We'll pay you in proportion to the amount of work you do.
**준행**(準行) ~하다 follow 〔put into effect〕 in accordance with the rule.
**준험**(峻險) steepness; precipitousness. ~하다 (be) steep; precipitous.
**준회원**(準會員) an associate member.
**줄**[1] ① 《끈》 a string; a cord; a rope; a line. ¶ 줄을 매다〔풀다〕 tie 〔untie〕 the strings. ② 《악기의》 a string. ¶ 바이올린에 줄을 달다〔갈다〕 string 〔restring〕 a violin / 줄을 죄다 tighten the string / 줄이 끊어지다 The string snaps. ③ 《선》 a line. ¶ 종이에 줄을 치다 rule 〔line on〕 paper / 줄을 긋다 draw a line. ④ 《행렬》 a line; a row; a rank; a file; a queue. ¶ 한 줄로 늘어선 나무 a line of trees / 줄을 짓고 차례를 기다리는 사람들 people standing in queues awaiting their turn / 한줄로 서다 stand in a line; line up in one file / 줄에 끼어 들다 break into a line 《of waiting people》 / 줄을 섭시다 Please wait 〔stand〕 in line. *or* Please wait your turn. *or* Form a line and wait your turn. ⑤ 《무늬》 a stripe; a band; a strip. ¶ 줄진 바지 striped trousers / 흰 줄이 둘 있는 모자 a cap banded with two white stripes / 그 옷감은 노랑 바탕에 흰 줄이 있다 The material is yellow with white stripes. ⑥ 《나이의》 a level 《of years of age》. ¶ 30줄의 남자 a man in his thirties / 50줄에 접어들다 enter the fifties. ⑦ 《거미줄》 a spider's thread; threads of spider silk. ⑧ 《광맥》 a vein (of ore). ⑨ 《엮어 묶은》 a tied bunch; a sheaf 《of tobacco leaves》.
**줄**[2] 《연장》 a file; a rasp. ¶ 줄로 쓸다 file; rasp 《away, off》 / 줄로 쓸어 매끈하게 하다 file 《*a thing*》 smooth.
**줄**[3] ① 《방법》 the how; the way (how to). ¶ 헤엄칠 줄(을) 알다 know how to swim / 글 쓸 줄(을) 모르다 do not know how to write / 영어를 할 줄 아세요 Do you know (how to speak) English? *or* Can you speak English? ② 《셈속》 the assumed fact; likelihood; probability. ¶ 그 애가 지금 자고 있는 줄 알아 Do you think that the boy is in bed now? / 그가 집에 있는 줄 알았다 I supposed that he was at home. / 네가 그런 줄 알았다 I thought you would do that. / 너를 여기서 만날 줄이야 꿈에도 생각지 않았다 I never dreamed I'd run into you here. / 그가 그런 줄(을) 몰랐다 I had no idea he would be that way. / 제 똥 구린 줄을 모른다 People are blind to their own defects. / 그가 간첩인 줄 누가 알았으랴 Who ever suspected that he was a spy? / 그가 나한테 편지를 쓸 줄은 몰랐다 I didn't know that he was going to write a letter to me. / 버스를 타고 거기 갈 줄은 모르지만 걸어서 갈 줄은 안다 I don't know to get there by bus, but I can get there on foot.
**줄거리** ① 《줄기》 a stalk; a stem; a caulis; a leafstalk; a petiole. ② 《골자》 an outline; a plot; a summary; a synopsis 《of a play》. ¶ 연극의 ~ the plot of a play / 이야기의 ~를 말하다 outline a plot.
**줄걷다** 《광대가》 walk (on) a tightrope.
**줄곧** all the time 〔way〕; at all hours; all along; through(out); constantly; continually. ¶ ~ 지절거리다 keep chattering all the time / 그녀는 ~ 잠자코 있었다 She remained silent throughout. / ~ 비가 온다 It rains day in and day out. / 그 집안에는 ~ 나쁜 일이 일어난다 That family is in constant trouble. / 그에게는 ~ 의사가 붙어 있다 The doctor is in constant attendance upon him. / 기차가 혼잡하여 ~ 서 있었

다 The train was so crowded that I had to keep standing all the way.

**줄긋다** draw a line; line 〔rule〕 paper; underline; run a line through.

**줄기** ① 《나무의》 a trunk; a stem; a stalk; a cane; a haulm. ② 《물 따위의》 a watercourse. ¶ 물～ the course of a stream 〔river〕. ③ 《산 따위의》 a mountain range. ¶ 산～ a range of mountains. ④ 《소나기의》 a shower; a downpour. ¶ 소나기가 한～ 올 것 같다 It looks like we're in for a bit of a downpour. ⑤ 《빛 따위의》 a line; a strip; a streak; a column 《of smoke》. ¶ 한～의 빛 a streak 〔ray〕 of light.

**줄기세포**(―細胞) stem cells. ¶ 배아 ～연구 embryonic stem-cell research.

**줄기줄기** ① 《시냇물이》 in streams 〔streamlets〕. ¶ 물이 ～ 흐르다 water flows in streamlets. ② 《산이》 in ranges 〔chains〕. ¶ 산이 ～ 뻗어 나가다 a mountain spreads out into ranges.

**줄기차다** (be) vigorous; exuberant; be bursting 〔streaming〕 with vitality. ¶ 줄기차게 strongly; vigorously / 줄기찬 비 a driving 〔pouring〕 rain / 4일 동안 줄기차게 내린 비 the downpour of rain which persisted for four days / 줄기차게 비가 내리다 rain hard 〔incessantly〕; pour down / 줄기차게 항거하다 offer a stout resistance / 시냇물이 줄기차게 흘러간다 The stream rushes along exuberantly.

**줄나다** be produced in less than estimated quantity; fall short of the production goal.

**줄넘기** 《줄을 돌리면서》 skipping (race); ropeskipping; 《줄을 팽팽히 하고》 rope jumping. ～하다 skip 〔jump〕 rope; turn a skipping rope.

**줄다** get smaller 〔less〕; lose size 〔quantity〕; decrease; dwindle; diminish; shrink; run low; abate; subside; go down. ¶ 양이〔수가〕 ～ decrease in quantity 〔number〕 / 체중이 ～ lose weight / 강물이 ～ the river sinks / 병력이 줄었다 The forces were thinned. / 최근 매상이 줄었다 There has been a decrease in sales recently. / 올해는 티푸스 환자가 작년에 비해 줄었다 This year has seen fewer cases of typhoid than last year. / 저수지의 물이 줄었다 The water in the reservoir went down. / 수출이 2퍼센트 줄었다 Our exports 「showed a decrease of 〔decreased by〕 two percent. *or* The exports have fallen off by 2 percent. / 이 옷감은 빨면 준다 This material shrinks when washed.

**줄다리기** a tug-of-war. ～하다 「play at 〔have〕 a tug-of-war.

**줄달다** follow one after another (in an unbroken succession or line). ¶ 줄달아 continuously; without interruption; successively; in line 〔row〕 / 손님이 줄달아 찾아 오다 have a continuous flow of visitors / 자동차의 왕래가 줄달아 끊이지 않는다 There is a line of traffic a mile long!

**줄달음질** running; dashing; darting. ～하다〔치다〕 run hard; rush; dart. ¶ 집 밖으로 ～쳐 나가다 dash out into the street.

**줄대다** keep 《*a thing*》 running 〔flowing〕 without interruption; go on; keep on. ¶ 줄대어 continuously; uninterruptedly; in succession; in a row / 줄대어 서다 stand in a line; queue up.

**줄드리다** ① 《늘어뜨리다》 hang a rope. ② 《꼬다》 make 〔twist, strand〕 a rope.

**줄띄우다** stretch out a rope 《to measure a distance.

**줄모** 『농업』 young rice plants bedded out in lines 〔rows〕. ¶ ～를 심다 bed out young rice plants in lines.

**줄목** the keypoints 《of *a matter*》; the outstanding 〔salient〕 points; a crucial 〔critical〕 moment. ¶ ～을 쥐다 grasp the key-points.

**줄무늬** stripes. ¶ ～의 striped.

**줄무더기** ① 《잡동사니》 a medley; a motley (of colors); a patchwork. ② 《연줄》 a kite string pieced together. ◉ ～형제 half-siblings with all different mothers.

**줄밑걷다** track 〔pin〕 down; trace; find out.

**줄바둑** a poor (game of) *paduk*. ¶ ～두는 사람 a poor *paduk* player.

**줄밥**[1] 《매의》 the feed attached to an end of the string given a falcon during its training period. ¶ ～에 매로구나 serve 《another's》 interest through *one's* own greed.

**줄밥**[2] 《줄질할 때의》 (metal) filings.

**줄방귀** a succession of breaking wind; breaking wind time after time.

**줄방석**(―方席) a rush seat-mat.

**줄버들** a row of willow trees.

**줄불** a string of firecrackers.

**줄사(닥)다리** a rope ladder.

**줄어들다** dwindle away; grow smaller; shrink; diminish; decrease. ¶ 점점 줄어들어 없어지다 dwindle away into nothing / 인구가 5만으로 ~ the population falls to 50,000 / 이 스웨터는 세탁해도 줄어들지 않는다 This sweater won't shrink in the wash.

**줄이다** 《감소하다》 reduce; diminish; lessen; decrease; 《단축·삭감하다》 cut down; pare down; shorten; curtail; condense; boil down; 《생략하다》 abbreviate; abridge. ¶ 비용을〔경비를〕 ~ reduce 〔pare down〕 (*one's*) expenses / 생산〔속력〕을 ~ reduce production 〔speed〕 / 예산을 바짝 ~ make the utmost retrenchment in the budget / 문장을 ~ condense a sentence / 두서너 줄로 ~ boil down 《an article》 into a few lines / 수명을 ~ shorten *one's* life / 옷의 길이를 ~ take a dress up; have *one's* dress shortened / 웨이스트를 줄여 주십시오 Please take the waist in.

**줄자** a tape measure; a tapeline. ¶ ~로 재다 tape-measure / 이 ~로 자네의 키를 재어주지 I will measure your height with this tapeline.

**줄잡다** make a moderate 〔conservative〕 estimate of; estimate low; underestimate. ¶ 줄잡아서 at a moderate estimate; at the inside / 최하로 줄잡아서 at the lowest estimate / 비용을 ~ make a rock-bottom estimate of the expenses / 줄잡아 어림하다 make a conservative estimate 《of》 / 비용이 줄잡아도 10만 원은 들겠다 It will cost at least 100,000 won. / 이것은 줄잡아 들어야 한다 It must be taken with a grain of salt. / 손해는 줄잡아서 천만 원이다 Ten million won is a conservative estimate of the damage.

**줄줄**[1] ⇨ 졸졸. ¶ 땀을 ~ 흘리다 swelter; sweat / 상처에서 피가 ~ 흐르고 있었다 The wound was bleeding profusely.

**줄줄**[2] 《막힘없이》 smoothly; without stopping 〔a hitch〕; fluently. ¶ 시를 ~ 외다 recite a poem fluently.

**줄줄이** in row after row; all in rows; all rows.

**줄짓다** stand in (a) line 〔row〕; form in (a) line 〔queue 《영》〕; line up; rank. ¶ 일렬로 ~ 《세로로》 stand in a line; stand behind one another; 《가로로》 stand in a row; stand side by side / 두 줄로 ~ form 〔stand in〕 two lines / (차례를 기다려) 줄지어 서다 line 〔queue〕 up / 헌 책방이 줄지어 선 거리 a street lined with the secondhand bookstores.

**줄치다** ① draw a line. ⇨ 줄긋다. ② 《거미가》 weave a web. ③ 《밧줄 등》 stretch a rope.

**줄타기** tightrope walking 〔dancing〕; a high-wire act. ~하다 walk a tightrope; walk the wire. ¶ 위태위태한 ~를 하다 run a risk; make a risky attempt; go out on a limb 《속어》. ◉ ~광대〔곡예사〕 a tightrope walker 〔dancer〕; a high-wire acrobat 〔artist, performer〕.

**줄타다** walk a tightrope.

**줄팔매(질)** (stone-)slinging; a sling (of a stone).

**줄행랑**(―行廊) ① 《행랑채》 the front wing of a house; the outhouses. ② 《도망》 running away; flight; abscondence. ¶ ~을 치다 run away; take flight; dart off.

**줌** ① 《움큼》 a handful; a fistful; a grip; a grasp. ¶ 소금 한 줌 a handful of salt. ② 《주먹》 the fist. ③ ⇨ 줌통.

**줌** 《확대·축소하는》 zoom. ◉ ~렌즈 a zoom lens.

**줌밖에 나다** get out 《*a person's*》 hands 〔clutches, grasp, control〕; be uncontrollable 〔unmanageable, ungovernable〕. ¶ 아무의 ~ 「be freed from 〔slip out of〕 *a person's* grasp.

**줌벌다** be too big to get *one's* fingers around; be too many 〔much〕 to get hold of. ¶ 줌이 벌어 잡지 못하겠다 [물건이 주어] be too thick to get fingers around.

**줌안에 들다** fall into 《*a person's*》 hands 〔clutches, grasp, control〕; slip under 《*a person's*》 control; be controllable 〔manageable, governable〕. ¶ 아무가 ~ have *a person* 「under *one's* control 〔in *one's* clutches〕.

**줌통** 《활의》 the handle of a bow.

**줍다** pick up; 《채집》 gather (up); 《발견》 find; 《이삭을》 glean; gather; 《다투어》 scramble for. ¶ 주운 물건 a found article; anything picked up 〔found〕/ 이삭을 ~ glean 〔gather〕 ears of corn / 밤을 ~ gather chestnuts / 마루에 흩어져 있는 종잇조각을 ~ pick up the scraps of paper lying about on the floor / 길에서 이 시계를 주웠다 I found this watch on the road. / 아이들은 다투어 땅콩을 주웠다 The children scrambled for peanuts.

**줏대** the metal rim of a wheel.

**줏대**(主―) fixed principles; strength of character; moral fiber〔fibre〕; backbone. ¶ ~ 있는 사람 a man of principle / ~가 없다 lack backbone 〔moral fiber〕.

**중** a Buddhist priest; a monk. ¶ 중이 되다 become a monk; enter the priesthood / 중이 제 머리 못 깎는다《속담》 You cannot scratch your own back.

**중**(中) ①《정도》 the middle; medium. ¶ 중키의 사람 a man of medium height / 그의 성적은 중 이상이다 His (school) records are above average.
②《…중에서》 of; among; in; amid(st); out of; between (★ 「…중에서」는 최상급 다음에 명사가 있으면 보통 among, 또는 in을 쓰며, of를 쓰지 않음: He is the cleverest boy among them 〔in his class〕. / He is the cleverest of all the boys.). ¶ 십 중 팔구 nine out of ten / 왕 중의 왕 the king of kings / 이 둘 중에서 어느 것이 좋으냐 Which of these two is better? / 현대 미국 작곡가 중에서 나는 코플랜드가 제일 좋다 Of contemporary American composers I like Copland (the) best. / 그는 형제 중 키가 제일 크다 He is the tallest among his brothers.
③《동안》 the time during which…; (the) while. ¶ …중에 during; while; in; within / 휴가중(에) during the vacation / 금주 중에 in the course of the week; within the week; before the week is out / 내달 중에 sometime during next month / 건축 중의 집 a house under construction / 식사 중이다 be at table / 일은 현재 진행중이다 The work is now in progress 〔under way〕. / 홍 선생은 수업중이십니다 Mr. Hong is (now) teaching (his class). / 통화중입니다《전화》 The line is busy 〔engaged《영》〕. / 바쁘신 중에 이처럼 일을 도와 주셔서 대단히 감사합니다 I'm very grateful to you for helping me in my work when you are busy. / 그는 편지를 쓰는 중이다 He is writing a letter. / 그 사건은 지금 조사 중이다 The matter is under investigation. / 우리가 자고 있는 중에 도둑이 들었다 A burglar broke into the house while we were sleeping.
④《내내》 all over; throughout. ¶ 오전 중 내내 all through the morning.
⑤《등급》 the second class 〔quality〕.

**-중**(重)《겹》 fold. ¶ 2중의 twofold; double / 3중의 threefold; triple.

**중간**(中間) the middle; the midway. ¶ ~의 middle; midway; intermediate; 《기간의》 interim / …의 ~에 (halfway, midway) between…; in the middle of … / …의 ~에 서다 mediate between…; act as a go-between for《two parties》/ 두 지점 ~에 있다 lie halfway between two places.
◉ ~결과《조사의》 interim findings. ~결산 interim closing. ~관리직 a middle manager; [집합적] the middle management. ~낭설 a groundless rumor. ~노선 neutrality; middle-of-the-road: ~노선을 취하다〔걷다〕 take 〔steer〕 a neutral course. ~무역 intermediate trade. ~배당 an interim dividend. ~보고 an interim report. ~상인 a broker; a middle man. ~색 a neutral tint 〔color〕. ~생산물 intermediate product. ~선거《미국의》 an off-year election. ~숙주 an intermediary host. ~시험〔고사〕 a midterm examinations. ~역 a way station 《미》; an intermediate station《영》. ~음〖음악〗 an intertone; an intermediate tone. ~이득 intermediary profiteering. ~정책 the middle-of-the-way policy. ~착취(搾取) intermediary exploitation. ~층 the middle class(es); middle-brows (취미 등의). ~파 the neutrals; the middle-of-the-roaders. ~휴식 a rest; a recess; a break; 《경기의》 half time.

**중간**(重刊) republication; reprint; reissue. ~하다 reprint; reissue; republish.

**중간자**(中間子)〖물리〗 a mes(otr)on.
◉ 뮤~ a mu-mesotron; a muon. 중(重)~ a heavy meson.

**중간치**(中間—) in-between things 〔sizes, prices, quality, *etc.*〕; a thing of medium size 〔price, quality, *etc.*〕.

**중갈이**(中—)〖농업〗 vegetables in all seasons.

**중갑판**(中甲板) the middle deck.

**중값**(重—) a great 〔high, dear〕 price.

**중개**(仲介) (inter)mediation. ~하다 (inter)mediate. ¶ …의 ~로 through the mediation of / ~역을 하다 act as a go-between 〔an intermediary〕/ 그의 ~로 그들은 이 조건들에 화해했다 They compromised on these terms by 〔through〕 his agency. ◉ ~국 a mediating power. ~무역 merchant 〔commission, intermediary〕 trade. ~물 a medium; a channel. ~수수료 brokerage (commission). ~업 brokerage; the brokerage business. ~인〔자〕 an intermediary; a middleman; a go-between; a mediator. ~판매 sale on commission.

**중거리**(中距離) a medium 〔an intermediate] range distance. ◉ ~경주 a middle-distance race. ~선수 a middle-distance runner. ~탄도탄 an intermediate range ballistic missile (생략 IRBM); a medium-range ballistic missile (생략 MRBM). ~핵무기 intermediate-range nuclear forces (생략 INF).

**중견**(中堅) ① 《중군》 the main body; 《사회의》 the mainstay; the nucleus; the backbone; the hard core. ¶ 회사의 ~이 되다 form [prove *oneself*] the backbone of a company / 중산 계급은 국가의 ~이다 The middle class forms the backbone of the nation. ② 《야구장의》 the center [centre 《영》] field. ◉ ~수 『야구』 a centerfielder. ~인물 a leader; leading figures. ~작가 a writer of medium [middle] standing.

**중경상**(重輕傷) serious and [or] slight injuries. ¶ ~을 입다 be seriously or slightly injured [wounded]; suffer a major or minor injury / 승객 50명이 ~을 입었다 Fifty passengers were injured either slightly or seriously. ◉ ~자 major and minor casualties.

**중계**(中繼) 『방송』 relay; 《방송국간의》 hookup 《미》; rebroadcasting; 『전신』 translation; 《무역 따위의》 intermediation. ~하다 relay; broadcast; translate. ¶ 신임 대통령의 취임 연설이 TV로 전세계에 ~되었다 The new President's inaugural speech was broadcasted all over the world. / 올림픽 개회식이 위성으로 ~되었다 The opening ceremony of the Olympic Games was relayed by satellite. /「재즈 축제가 생~된다고 하는군」—「놓칠 수 없지」 "I hear the jazz festival is live from the spot."—"I can't miss it."
◉ ~국(局) a relay station. ~무역 intermediate [transit] trade. ~방송 outside [relay] broadcasting; 《프로그램》 an outside broadcast; a hookup 《미》: 전국에 ~ 방송을 하다 broadcast over a nation-wide network [hookup]. ~선 a junction line. ~점 a relay point. ~차 an outside broadcast van. ~항 a transit port. ~회로 a junction circuit.

**중고**(中古) ① 『역사』 the Middle Ages; medieval times. ¶ ~의 medieval. ② 《헌》 the somewhat used; the slightly old; the second-hand 《article》. ¶ ~를 사다 buy 《*a thing*》 (at) second=hand. ◉ ~사[문학] medieval history [literature]. ~차 a used car: ~차 시장 a used car market. ~품 a (slightly) used article; second-hand goods: 신품과 다름없는 ~품 an article slightly used but almost 「brand-new [as good as new].

**중고층**(中高層) ¶ ~아파트 high and medium-height apartment houses.

**중공**(中空) 《중천》 midair; 《비어있음》 hollowness. ¶ ~에 in midair; in the air / ~의 hollow.

**중공업**(重工業) heavy industry [industries]. ◉ ~도시 a city with heavy industry. ~회사 a heavy industry company.

**중과**(衆寡) disparity in numbers; odds. ¶ ~부적이다 We are outnumbered [overcome by numbers]. *or* There is no contending against odds.

**중괄호**(中括弧) a brace (기호 { }).

**중구**(中歐) Central Europe.

**중구**(衆口) public rumor; popular criticism. ¶ ~난방이다 It is difficult to stop the voice of the people.

**중국**(中國) China. ¶ ~의 Chinese / ~대륙 the continent of China. ◉ ~공산당 the Chinese Communists. ~말 Chinese; the Chinese language. ~사람 a Chinese (*pl.* Chinese); the Chinese [총칭]. ~옷 a China dress; a Chinese suit [robe]. ~요리 Chinese food [dishes]; Chinese cuisine [cooking] (요리법): ~요리점 a Chinese restaurant. ~인거리 a Chinatown; the Chinese quarter. ~통(通) a person versed in things Chinese. ~학(學) sinology; study of things Chinese [Chinese culture]: ~학자 a sinologist; a China scholar.

**중궁(전)**(中宮(殿)) 《왕후》 the Queen.

**중권**(中卷) the middle [second] volume of a set of three.

**중근동**(中近東) the Middle and Near East.

**중금속**(重金屬) 『화학』 a heavy metal.

**중금주의**(重金主義) 『경제』 the mercantile system. ⇨ 중상주의.

**중급**(中級) an intermediate grade. ¶ ~의 medium; of the middle class. ◉ ~영어 intermediate English. ~품 fair average quality.

**중기**(中期) the middle (years) 《of an era》; 《세포 분열의》 the metaphase. ¶ 조선 ~의 in the middle of the *Chosŏn* dynasty. ◉ ~계획 a medium-range plan.

**중기**(重機) heavy machinery.

**중기관총**(重機關銃) a heavy machine 「gun.

**중길**(中—) 《물건》 an article of medium quality; average-grade goods; middlings.

**중남미**(中南美) Central and South America. ¶ ～사람들 Latin Americans.

**중년**(中年) middle age; *one's* middle years. ¶ ～의 middle-aged / ～을 넘은 여인 an elderly woman / ～ 남자 a middle-aged man; a man in his middle life 〔years〕 / ～에 죽다 die in middle age. ◉ ～기 the middle years of *one's* life. ～신사 a middle-aged gentleman. ～여자 a woman in middle age. ～층 the middle-aged; the middle generation.

**중노동**(重勞動) heavy 〔hard〕 labor. ¶ ～을 하다 engage 〔be engaged〕 in heavy labor / ～ 3년의 형을 받다 be sentenced to three years at hard labor. ◉ ～자 a heavy worker.

**중노인**(中老人) ＝중늙은이.

**중농**(中農) a middle-class farmer.

**중농정책**(重農政策) an agriculture-first policy.

**중농주의**(重農主義) physiocracy; physiocratism. ◉ ～자 a physiocrat.

**중뇌**(中腦) the midbrain; mesencephalon.

**중늙은이**(中—) a person in well advanced middle age; an elderly man.

**중단**(中段) ① 《층계의》 the middle part of a staircase. ② 《글의》 the middle part of a book. ③ 《검도의》 ¶ ～자세를 취하다 be at middle guard.

**중단**(中斷) discontinuance; interruption; suspension. ～하다 discontinue; interrupt; suspend; break off; give up. ¶ ～되다 be 「interrupted 〔discontinued, suspended〕 / 그 소동으로 연주가 ～되었다 The concert was interrupted by the uproar. / 그는 하던 일을 ～하고 전화를 받았다 He interrupted his work to answer the phone.

**중대**(中隊) 《보병·공병 따위의》 a company; 《포병의》 a battery; 《비행》 a squadron. ◉ ～장 a company commander.

**중대**(重大) importance; gravity; seriousness. ～하다 (be) important; serious; weighty; momentous.
¶ ～한 문제 an important question; a serious problem / ～한 과실 a gross mistake 〔negligence〕 / ～한 책임 grave responsibility / …에게 ～한 영향이 있다 have an important influence upon ... / ～해지다 get 〔grow, become〕 serious; assume serious proportions / 그것은 나에게는 ～한 문제이다 The matter is 「of great importance 〔very important〕 to me. / 총선거의 결과는 우리들의 생활에 ～한 영향을 끼친다 The result of the general election has an important influence upon our lives.
◉ ～관심사 a matter of the utmost 〔gravest〕 concern. ～문제 a serious 〔vital〕 question; a grave issue; a matter of grave concern: 그것은 우리에게 있어서 아주 ～문제이다 It is a matter of vital importance to us. ～사건 a matter of great importance; a serious affair; a momentous event. ～성 importance; gravity; seriousness: 시국의 ～성 the gravity of the situation. ～성명 《announce》 a serious statement.

**중대가리** 《머리》 a shaven head; 《사람》 a shaven-headed person.

**중대문**(中大門) the inner gate.

**중대시**(重大視) taking 《*a matter*》 seriously. ～하다 attach great importance to 《*an affair*》; take a serious view of 《*a matter*》; regard 《*a thing*》 as serious; take 《*a matter*》 seriously. ¶ 그들은 우리의 행동을 ～하고 있다 They are taking a grave view of our conduct.

**중대화**(重大化) becoming critical 〔serious〕; aggravation (악화). ～하다 become 「serious 〔critical〕; assume serious proportions; aggravate.

**중덜거리다** grumble 《at, about》; complain 《of》; mutter 《at, against》; murmur 《at, about》.

**중도**(中途) ¶ ～에서 halfway; midway; in the middle / 일을 ～에서 그만두다 stop halfway through; give up halfway; leave 《*a thing*》 half done / ～에서 돌아서다 turn back halfway 〔midway〕 / ～에서 퇴학하다 leave school without finishing the course / 일의 ～에서 쓰러지다 break down in the middle of *one's* work.
◉ ～퇴학 leaving school in mid course: ～퇴학자 a school dropout.

**중도**(中道) the middle road 〔path〕; the mean. ¶ ～를 걷다〔지키다〕 take 〔choose〕 a moderate course; take 〔follow〕 the golden 〔happy〕 mean.
◉ ～정당 a centrist party. ～정책 《미》 the middle-of-the-road policy. ～파 (the) middle-of-the-roaders.

**중독**(中毒) poisoning; toxication; 〖병리〗 toxicosis (중독증); 《마약의》 addic-

tion. ¶ 식~ poisoning from eating / ~되다 be 〔get〕 poisoned《by fish》; 《마약에》 get 〔become〕 addicted《to narcotics》; 《속어》 get hooked《on heroin》/ 그는 마약〔알코올〕 ~이다 He is「a drug addict 〔an alcoholic〕.
◉ ~사 death from poisoning. ~성 toxicity: ~성의 toxic; poisonous / ~성 빈혈 toxic anaemia. ~증상《show》 toxic symptoms; 《present 〔develop〕》 symptoms of poisoning.

**중동**(中—) the middle 〔center〕 part; the waist. ¶ 생선의 ~ the center cut of fish / ~이 길다〔짧다〕 be long=waisted 〔short-waisted〕.
◉ ~끈 the belt to a skirt; a sash.

**중동**(中東) the Middle East; the Mideast. ◉ ~사태 the Middle East situation. ~전쟁 the Middle East war. ~조약 기구 the Middle East Treaty Organization (생략 M.E.T.O.).

**중동**(仲冬) midwinter; the 11th lunar month.

**중동무이**(中—) leaving《*a thing*》 half-done 〔unfinished〕; stopping halfway. ~하다 leave《*a thing*》 half-done 〔unfinished〕; go 〔give up〕 halfway; do《*a thing*》 by halves.

**중등**(中等) 《질》 medium quality; 《등급》 the secondary level; the middle 〔second〕 class. ¶ ~의 middle; medium; middling; average / 그의 학교 성적은 ~ 이상이다 His school record is above average.
◉ ~교원 a secondary school teacher. ~교육 secondary education: ~ 교육과 the secondary education section. ~품 an article of medium quality; medium-quality〔-grade〕 goods. ~학교 a secondary school.

**중략**(中略) an omission of a middle part《of sentence》. ~하다 omit; skip. ¶ ~ 표시로 점점을 찍다 put suspension periods 〔points〕《between the two words》(★ 이 점점은 three spaced periods (…)가 원칙임).

**중량**(重量) weight. ¶ 항공 우편물의 ~ air mail poundage / ~ 한도를 초과한 화물 an overweight baggage 〔luggage《영》〕/ 짐의 ~을 달다〔재다〕 weigh the baggage / ~감이 있다 be massive; look heavy and bulky; look solid / ~을 속이다 cheat on weight; give short weight / ~이 5파운드 나가다 It weighs five pounds. / 이 기계의 ~은 얼마입니까 How much does this machine weigh? ◉ ~급 the heavy weight class: ~급 권투 선수 a heavy-weight boxer. ~부족 short weight. ~분석 〖화학〗 gravimetric analysis. ~제한 weight 〔《미》 load〕 limits. ~초과 overweight: 화물의 ~ 초과 요금을 지불하다 pay for excess baggage. ~톤 a deadweight ton: ~톤수 deadweight tonnage 〔capacity〕. ~화물 weight cargo; heavy 〔hard〕 goods.

**중량급**(中量級) the middle weight class.

**중러**(中—) ¶ ~의 Sino-Russian; Russo=Chinese. ◉ ~관계 Chinese-Russian relations.

**중력**(重力) gravity; gravitation; gravitational pull; G-force. ¶ (우주 정거장 안의) 인공 ~ artificial gravity / ~의 법칙 the law of gravity / ~의 중심 the center of gravity / 그는 우주의 무~ 상태에서 거꾸로 떠있다 He is suspended upside down in the weightlessness of space. ◉ ~ 가속도 acceleration of gravity. ~계 a gravimeter. ~단위 a gravitational unit. ~장 the gravity field. ~전지 a gravity cell. ~파 a gravity 〔gravitational〕 wave.

**중령**(中領) 〖육군·해병〗 a lieutenant colonel; 〖해군〗 a commander; 〖공군〗 a lieutenant colonel《미》; a wing commander《영》.

**중론**(衆論) public opinion. ⇨ 중의(衆議).

**중류**(中流) ①《강의》 the middle reaches (상류·하류에 대하여); 《강폭의 중앙》 midstream. ¶ ~는 수심이 깊다 The river is deep in midstream. ②《정도·계급》 the middle classes. ¶ 대부분의 한국 사람은 자기가 ~계급에 속한다고 생각한다 Most Koreans think (that) they belong to the middle class.
◉ ~가정 a middle-class family: 그는 ~가정 출신이다 He is from a middle=class family. ~계급 the middle class(-es): ~ 계급의 사람들 middle-class people; the middle classes.

**중립**(中立) neutrality. ¶ ~의 neutral; 《불개입의》 indifferent / 스위스의 영세 ~ the permanent neutrality of Switzerland / ~적인 태도를 취하다 take a neutral attitude / ~을 지키다 maintain 〔keep, observe〕 neutrality; remain 〔stand〕 neutral / ~을 선언하다 declare 〔proclaim〕 neutrality / ~ 노선을 따르다 follow a neutralist policy / ~을 침해〔존중〕하다 violate 〔respect〕《a country's》 neutrality.
◉ ~내각 a neutral cabinet: 다가오는 대통령 선거의 공정한 관리를 위하여 ~내각을 세우다 set up a neutral cab-

inet for fair management of the coming presidential election. ～보장 security of neutrality. ～선언 a declaration of neutrality. ～성 neutrality; impartiality. ～위반 a violation 〔breach〕 of neutrality. ～의원 a neutral member. ～정책 a neutrality 〔neutralist〕 policy. ～조약 a neutrality pact. ～주의 neutralism: 적극적〔비무장〕 ～주의 positive 〔unarmed〕 neutralism. ～지대 a neutral zone. ～파 a neutral party 〔faction〕; the neutrals; the neutralists; the neutralist wing. ～화 neutralization: ～화하다 neutralize.

**중립국**(中立國) a neutral state 〔power〕. ◉ ～감시 위원회 the Neutral Nations Supervisory Commission (생략 NNSC). ～선박 neutral ships. ～인 a neutral (citizen).

**중망**(衆望) public confidence 〔expectation〕; popularity. ¶ ～에 어긋나지 않다 meet public expectation / ～을 받고 있다 be the center of popular hopes; enjoy public confidence / ～을 한 몸에 모으다 become a popular hero; win great popularity / ～을 얻어 입후보하다 stand 《for the National Assembly》 with popular support.

**중매**(仲媒) matchmaking. ～하다 arrange a (marriage) match 《between》; act as (a) go-between. ～들다 serve as a matchmaker 〔go-between〕. ¶ …의 ～로 through 《*a person's*》 good offices / 친구의 ～로 결혼하다 get married through a friend's matchmaking. ◉ ～결혼 (an) arranged marriage; a marriage arranged by a go-between. ～쟁이 a matchmaker; a go-between.

**중매**(仲買) brokerage. ～하다 act as broker. ◉ ～구전〔수수료〕 a broker's commission; brokerage. ～인 a broker; a middleman; a commission 「merchant 〔agent〕. ～점 a brokerage house 〔firm〕.

**중목**(衆目) public attention; every eye; all eyes. ◉ ～소시(所視) what every eye saw; the cynosure of all eyes: ～소시가 되다 become the focus of public attention; be the cynosure of all eyes.

**중문**(中門) an inner gate.

**중문**(重文) 〖문법〗 a compound sen「tence.

**중미**(中米) rice of medium quality.

**중미**(中美) Central America; Middle America. ¶ ～의 나라 a Central American country.

**중반전**(中盤戰) 《바둑 등의》 the middle game; 《선거 등의》 the middle phase. ¶ ～에 들어 가다 《바둑 등이》 get into the thick of a game; 《선거 등이》 reach the peak 《of the election campaign》 / 선거는 이제 ～에 접어들었다 The election campaign is now in full swing.

**중방**(中枋) ⇨ 중인방.

**중배**(中—) ① 《물건의》 a bulged-out middle; "a pot belly". ¶ ～ 부르다 be bulged out in the middle; be pot-bellied. ② 《새끼》 an animal born after the first litter.

**중배엽**(中胚葉) 〖생물〗 the mesoderm; the mesoblast.

**중벌**(重罰) severe punishment; heavy penalty. ¶ ～에 처하다 punish 《*a person*》 severely; inflict a severe punishment on 《*a person*》.

**중범**(重犯) ① 《중대범》 felony; 《중범인》 a felon. ② 《거듭 저지름》 repetition of crimes; 《사람》 a perpetrator of several crimes; an old 〔a repeated〕 offender. ¶ ～의 경우에는 in the case of a repeated offense.

**중병**(重病) a serious illness 〔disease〕. ¶ ～에 걸리다 be attacked by a serious illness; fall 〔get, be taken〕 seriously ill / ～으로 누워 있다 be seriously ill in bed. ◉ ～환자 a serious case.

**중보**(重寶) treasure of great value; priceless treasure. ¶ 가전(家傳)의 ～ a treasured heirloom.

**중복**(中伏) the 「middle period 〔second 10-day period〕 of the dogdays.

**중복**(中腹) 《중턱》 the mountain's breast; the mid-slope of a mountain; halfway up 〔down〕 a hill.

**중복**(重複) repetition (되풀이); (an) overlap (부분적); duplication (이중); redundancy (여분). ～하다 overlap; duplicate; be repeated; be redundant. ¶ ～된 duplicate; overlapping; repeated; redundant; 《어구 등의》 tautological; pleonastic / ～을 피하다 avoid overlapping 〔duplication〕 / ～ 신청의 경우는 무효가 된다 If you make a double application, it will be declared invalid.

**중복부**(中腹部) 〖해부〗 the mesogastrium (*pl.* -ria); the middle abdomen.

**중부**(中部) the middle 〔central〕 part; the midsection 《of a country》; the center. ◉ ～갑판 the middle deck. ～고속도로 the *Chungbu* 〔Central〕 Highway. ～전선 the central front; the central front-line areas. ～지방 the central districts 〔area, region〕. ～태평양 mid-Pacific.

**중부하**(重負荷) 〖기계〗 heavy loading.

**중뿔나다**(中—) be nosy 〔meddlesome, impertinent, presumptuous, intrusive〕. ¶ 중뿔난 사람 a nosy person / 중뿔나게 말하다 make uncalled-for 〔impertinent〕 remarks.

**중사**(中士) 〖육군〗 a sergeant first class.

**중산계급**(中産階級) the middle class (-es); people in the middle-income brackets (of society); the bourgeoisie; a bourgeois (한 사람). ¶ ～의 bourgeois.

**중산모(자)**(中山帽(子)) a derby (hat) 《미》; a bowler (hat) 《영》.

**중상**(中傷) (a) slander; a slur; defamation; 《정계의》 mudslinging. ～하다 slander; defame; injure 《*a person's*》 reputation; cast a slur on 《*a person's*》 good name; sling 〔fling, throw〕 mud at 《*a person's*》 reputation. ¶ ～적(인) slanderous; defamatory; libelous / ～적 보도 a slanderous 〔libelous〕 report / 그는 ～ 잘 하는 사람이다 He is given to slander. *or* He is a scandalmonger. / 그는 동료로부터 심한 ～을 당했다 He was bitterly slandered by his fellow workers. / 그 기사는 나를 ～하고 있다 The article defames me. ◉ ～자 a slanderer; a scandalmonger; a mudslinger; a libelist.

**중상**(重喪) double mourning (=losing *one's* parents one after another within three years).

**중상**(重傷) a severe 〔serious〕 wound 〔injury〕. ¶ ～을 입다 receive 〔sustain〕 a serious wound; be badly 〔seriously〕 injured / ～을 입히다 injure 《*a person*》 seriously; inflict a severe injury upon 《*a person*》 / 그는 머리에 ～을 입었다 He was wounded seriously in the head. / 부상자 5명 중 1명은 ～이다 Five persons were injured, one seriously. ◉ ～자 a seriously wounded 〔injured〕 person: 그 사고로 인한 사망자는 3명, ～자는 7명이었다 Three were killed and seven were severely injured in the accident.

**중상주의**(重商主義) mercantilism; the mercantile system. ◉ ～자 a mercantilist.

**중생**(衆生) mankind; all living beings; all creatures. ¶ ～을 제도(濟度)하다 save mankind.

**중생대**(中生代) 〖지질〗 the Mesozoic (era). ¶ ～의 Mesozoic 《life》. ◉ ～층 a Mesozoic formation.

**중서부**(中西部) 《미국의》 the Middle West; the Midwest. ¶ ～의 Middle Western; Midwestern.

**중석**(重石) 〖광물〗 tungsten; scheelite.

**중석기시대**(中石器時代) 〖고고학〗 the Mesolithic Age. ¶ ～의 Mesolithic.

**중선거구**(中選擧區) a medium constituency 〔electoral district〕. ◉ ～제 the medium constituency (electorate) system; a medium-sized electoral system.

**중설**(衆說) public opinion.

**중성**(中性) 〖문법〗 the neuter gender; 〖화학〗 neutrality; 〖생물〗 sexlessness; 〖식물〗 sterility. ¶ ～의 《문법의》 neuter; 《화학의》 neutral; 《생물의》 sexless; 《식물의》 sterile / ～의 남자〔여자〕 a sexless man 〔woman〕. ◉ ～반응 a neutral reaction. ～세제 a neutral detergent. ～염 neutral salt. ～지(紙) neutral paper. ～화(花) a neutral flower.

**중성**(中聲) 〖언어〗 the medial of a Korean orthographic syllable; the vowels (and semivowels) of a Korean syllable.

**중성미자**(中性微子) 〖물리〗 a neutrino (*pl.* ～s). ¶ 반(反)～ an antineutrino.

**중성자**(中性子) 〖물리〗 a neutron. ¶ 반(反) ～ an antineutron. ◉ ～로 a neutron reactor. ～탄 a neutron bomb.

**중세**(中世) the Middle Ages; the medieval times. ¶ ～의 medieval. ◉ ～기 the Middle Ages. ～사〔건축〕 the medieval history 〔architecture〕. ～암흑 시대 the Dark Ages. ～영어 Middle English. ～취미 medievalism.

**중세**(重稅) a heavy tax; heavy taxation. ¶ ～를 과하다 impose 〔levy〕 a heavy tax 《on》; impose heavy duties on 《imports》 / ～에 시달리다 groan 〔labor〕 under 「heavy taxation 〔the heavy burden of taxation〕 / ～를 부담하다 bear a heavy duty.

**중소**(中小) 〔형용사적〕 medium and small. ◉ ～상공업자 merchants and industrialists of small and medium-sized enterprises.

**중소기업**(中小企業) a small and medium(-sized) enterprise; smaller 〔minor〕 enterprises 〔business〕. ¶ 부친은 ～을 경영하신다 My father runs a small 〔medium-sized〕 business. / 정부는 ～ 육성책 강화를 다짐했다 The government pledged to step up measures

to help development of medium and small enterprises.
◉ ~경영자 minor enterprisers. ~공제기금 a mutual-aid fund for small business. ~자금 bank loans for small=medium industries. ~주(株) the small-to-mid sized companies' stocks. ~진흥공단 the Small and Medium Industry Promotion Corporation. ~청 the Small & Medium Business Administration (생략 SMBA). ~특별위원회 the Presidential Commission on Small and Medium Business. ~협동조합중앙회 the Korean Federation of Small Businesses (생략 KFSB).

**중속환이**(—俗還—) an ex-bonze〔-Buddhist monk〕.

**중송아지**(中—) a full-grown calf.

**중수**(重水) 〖화학〗 heavy water; deuterium oxide.

**중수**(重修) repairing 《a building》; remodeling; restoration. ~하다 repair; remodel; restore. ｢deuterium.

**중수소**(重水素) 〖화학〗 heavy hydrogen;

**중순**(中旬) the middle ten days of a month. ¶ 오월 ~에 in mid-May; in the middle of May / 이달 ~경에 about the middle of this month.

**중시**(重視) (taking) a serious view 《of》. ~하다 attach importance 《to》; lay stress 《on》; make 〔think〕 much of; regard 《*a thing*》 as important; take 《*a matter*》 seriously. ¶ ~되다 be accounted / 그리 ~되지 않다 be accounted little / 국제무역을 ~하다 regard international trade as important / 그녀는 발음 연습을 너무 ~한다 She attaches too much importance to pronunciation practice. / 우리는 그녀의 의견을 더 ~해야 한다 We should take much more of her opinion.

**중신**(重臣) a chief minister 《of state》; a senior statesman. ◉ ~회의 a conference of senior statesmen.

**중심**(中心) ① [일반적] the center; 《중앙》 the middle 《of the road》; 《중심부》 the heart; 《중핵》 the nucleus; the core 《of an apple, of *a matter*》; 《초점》 the focus; 《중추》 the pivot.

> **용법** **center** 둘레의 여러 점에서 같은 거리의 중심점. **middle** 양끝에서 같은 거리의 점·선 및 부분. **heart** 중심에 국한되는 것이 아니라 가장 중요한 지점.

¶ ~의 central; middle / 원〔중력〕의 ~ the center ｢of a circle 〔of gravity〕/ 금융의 ~ the pivot of financial operation / ~을 벗어난 out of center 〔focus〕; eccentric / …을 ~으로 하여 centering around 《*a thing*》; with 《*a person*》 as leader 〔the central figure〕/ ~이 되어서 일하다 take the lead in some work / 김 박사를 ~으로 회를 조직하다 form an organization ｢around Dr. Kim 〔with Dr. Kim as the central figure〕/ 지구는 태양을 ~으로 돌고 있다 The earth revolves round the sun as a center.
② 《균형》 balance. ¶ ~을 잡다〔잃다〕 keep 〔lose〕 *one's* balance / ~을 잃고 넘어지다 lose *one's* balance and stumble / 한 발로 서서 몸의 ~을 잡다 balance *oneself* on one leg.
◉ ~가 the main street. ~과제 the key subject. ~기압 〖기상〗 the central (air) pressure. ~도시 a kingpin town. ~력 a centripetal force. ~문제 the central problem 〔question〕. ~부 the central part; the heart 《of a city》: 태풍 ~부의 바람 the center wind of a typhoon. ~사상 the central idea. ~선 a center line. ~세력 a central force; the main strength 《of the party》. ~시도(示度) 〖기상〗 the central pressure: ~ 시도 1,000 밀리바, 1,000 mb. at the central pressure. ~점 the center; the central 〔center〕 point. ~지 a center; a central place: 미술의 ~지 an art center / 교통의 ~지 a transport center / 공업의 ~지 an industrial center / 상업의 ~지 a commercial center. ~축 the central axis. ~타선 〖야구〗 the leading 〔central〕 batters 《of a team》.

**중심**(重心) 〖물리〗 the center of gravity.

**중심인물**(中心人物) the central 〔leading〕 figure; the major 〔focal〕 character. ¶ 혁명의 ~ the central figure of a revolution / 그는 일행의 ~이다 He is the leader of the party.

**중압**(重壓) (heavy) pressure; 《부담의》 heavy burden. ¶ ~을 가하다 bring pressure on 《*a person* to *do*》; put pressure on 《*a person*》. ◉ ~감 an oppressive feeling.

**중앙**(中央) 《중심점》 the center; 《중앙부》 the middle; 《중심부》 the heart; 《서울》 a metropolis. ¶ ~의 central; middle / 도시 ~에 in the center 〔heart〕 of a city / ~으로 모이다〔모으다〕 centralize; concentrate / 도시 ~에 있다 be (situated) in the center of the town / 그 가수는 ~에서는 인기가 없다

The singer is not popular in the metropolitan area.
◉ ～공무원교육원 《행정자치부의》 the Central Officials Training Institute. ～관청 the central government agencies. ～교육 연수원 the National Institute for Educational Research & Training. ～난방〔냉난방〕 central heating 〔airconditioning〕. ～노동위원회 the Central Labor Relations Committee. ～돌파 《경기 등에서》 a frontal breakthrough. ～문단 literary circles in the metropolis. ～방송국 a central 〔key〕 broadcasting station. ～부 the central part; the midsection. ～분리대 a median strip 《미》; a central reservation 《영》; 《게시》 "divider." ～선 《violate》 the central line 《of a highway》; 《철도의》 the Central Line. ～선거관리위원회 the Central Election Management Committee. ～시장 the central market. ～아시아〔아메리카〕 Central Asia 〔America〕. ～우체국 the Central Post Office (생략 CPO). ～은행 a central bank. ～인사위원회 the Civil Service Commission. ～전화국 the central telephone office. ～정보부 《미국의》 the Central Intelligence Agency (생략 CIA). ～정부 the central government; 《미국의》 the federal government. ～ 집행 위원 a member of the central executive committee: ～집행위원회 a central executive committee. ～처리 장치 《컴퓨터의》 Central Processing Unit (생략 CPU). ～행정 state administration.

**중앙아프리카공화국**(中央―共和國) the Central African Republic.

**중앙집권**(中央集權) centralization of 「government 〔administrative power〕.
◉ ～제 centralism: ～제로 하다 centralize. ～화 centralization of power: ～화하다 centralize; get centralized / 중앙 정부의 비～화 노력 the central government's decentralization efforts.

**중양(절)**(重陽(節)) the ninth day of the ninth lunar month.

**중언(부언)**(重言(復言)) repetition; reiteration. ～하다 repeat; reiterate; say over again.

**중얼거리다** mutter; murmur; 《불평을》 grumble. ¶ 혼자 ～ mutter to *oneself* / 그는 무어라고 중얼거리며 가버렸다 He went away muttering to himself.

**중얼중얼** muttering; murmuring; grumbling; in a mutter. ¶ ～ 혼자 말하다 mutter to *oneself*.

**중역**(重役) a director; [집합적] the board of directors. ¶ ～이 되다 become a director; obtain a seat on the board of directors. ◉ ～회의 a directors' 〔board〕 conference.

**중역**(重譯) (a) secondhand translation; (a) translation from a translation; a retranslation. ～하다 retranslate; translate a translation. ¶ 이것은 톨스토이 작품의 영역본을 한국어로 ～한 것이다 This is the Korean translation from the English version of Tolstoi.

**중엽**(中葉) the middle part (of a period). ¶ 19세기 ～ the mid-nineteenth century / 조선조 ～에 about the middle of the time of the Choson dynasty.

**중외**(中外) ① 《내외》 the inside and the outside; home and abroad. ¶ ～의 internal and external; home 〔domestic〕 and foreign; home and abroad / ～에 at home and abroad / ～에 선언하다 declare 〔announce〕 to the world / 명성을 ～에 떨치다 win a worldwide reputation. ② 《조정과 민간》 the government and the people. ③ 《서울과 시골》 the capital and the provinces.

**중요**(重要) importance; significance; consequence. ～하다 (be) important; momentous; weighty; essential; consequential; be of importance.
¶ 군사상의 ～ 지점 places of military importance / 역사상의 ～ 사건 some highlights 〔salient events〕 of history / ～한 사람 a person of importance 〔consequence〕 / ～한 역할을 하다 play an important part 〔role〕 / 그는 회사에서 ～한 지위를 차지하고 있다 He has an important position with his company. *or* He occupies a prominent position in the firm. / 그녀의 의견은 나에게 조금도 ～치 않다 Her opinion carries no weight with me at all. / 심장과 폐는 ～한 기관이다 The heart and lungs are vital organs. / 그는 우리 팀의 ～한 멤버이다 He is a valuable member of our team. / 이 일은 내게 매우 ～하다 This work means a lot to me. *or* This is a matter of great importance to me.
◉ ～기사 news of value; front page news; the highlights 《in today's paper》. ～문제 an important 〔a serious〕 question. ～문화재 an important cultural property 〔asset〕: ～ 무형 문화재 an important intangible cultural

asset. ～물자 key commodities. ～법안 important 〔must《속어》〕 bills. ～사항 an important matter; a matter of consequence 〔moment〕. ～산물 staple products. ～산업 key 〔major〕 industries. ～상품 staple commodities. ～서류 important documents 〔papers〕. ～인물 a (very) important person; a VIP《구어》;《핵심 인물》a key figure 〔man〕; a prominent person. ～증거(물) an important 〔a crucial〕 piece of evidence. ～지위 an important position. ～참고인《증인》a key witness.

**중요성**(重要性) importance; gravity. ¶～이 있다〔없다〕 be「of 〔of no〕 importance / ～을 띠다「take on 〔acquire, assume〕 importance / 그것은 문제로서 ～이 없다 It carries no weight 〔It figures small〕 in the matter.

**중요시**(重要視) ⇨중시(重視).

**중용**(中庸) ①《중정》the (golden) mean; the 〔a〕 middle course 〔way〕; moderation. ¶～을 취한 mean; moderate; reasonable / ～을 취하다 use 〔exercise〕 moderation; take the golden mean; strike the happy mean / ～을 지키다 be moderate; observe moderation《in everything》/ ～을 잃다 be immoderate / 그 일에는 ～을 취하는 것이 중요하다 It is a question of finding the happy medium. ②《책이름》The Doctrine of the Mean.
◉ ～지도(之道) the middle course 〔way〕; the golden mean.

**중용**(重用) ～하다 give《*a person*》an important position; appoint《*a person*》to a position of trust. ¶～되고 있다 hold an important position《in a company》.

**중우**(衆愚) the ignorant 〔vulgar〕 crowd; the mob; the blind populace. ◉ ～정치 mobocracy; ochlocracy; mob rule.

**중원**(中元) the 15th day of the 7th lunar month.

**중원**(中原)《경쟁장》the field of contest;《나라의》the central districts《of a country》. ¶～의 패권을 다투다 compete for supremacy in a country.

**중위**(中位)《정도》medium; average (평균);《등급》second rate. ¶～의 medium; middle; moderate;《평균의》average;《원만한》passable / ～이상〔이하〕의 above 〔below〕 average.

**중위**(中尉)〖육군〗a first lieutenant《미》; a lieutenant《영》;〖해군〗a lieutenant junior grade《미》; a sublieutenant《영》;〖공군〗a first lieutenant《미》; a flying officer《영》(★ lieutenant의 발음은 영국에서는 [(육군) lefténənt, (해군) ləténənt], 미국에서는 육·해군 아울러 [luːténənt]).

**중위**(中衛)〖축구〗the halfback;〖배구〗the middle guard.

**중유**(重油) heavy 〔crude〕 oil; crude 「〔raw〕 petroleum.

**중음**(中音)〖음악〗《여성의》contralto;《남성의》baritone;《음역》the middle register 〔range (악기의)〕. ◉ ～부 기호 the alto clef.

**중음**(重音) a double sound.

**중의**(衆意) public 〔popular, general〕 opinion. ¶그가 적임자라는 것에 ～가 일치했다 It is universally admitted that he is fit for the post.

**중의**(衆議) public discussion; general consultation; public opinion. ¶～로 결정하다 let public opinion decide / 이것은 ～에 의하여 결정함이 타당하다 It is proper that this should be decided by majority of votes.

**중이**(中耳)〖해부학〗the middle ear; the tympanum (*pl.* ～s, -na). ◉ ～염 tympanitis; otitis media; inflammation of the middle ear.

**중이층**(中二層) a mezzanine (floor).

**중인**(中印) China and India. ¶～의 Sino-Indian《border dispute》.

**중인**(衆人) the multitude; the crowd; the public; the people. ¶～ 앞에서 in public; before all the people; in the presence of the whole company / ～이 보는 앞에서 모욕하다 insult《*a person*》in public.

**중인방**(中引枋)〖건물〗a horizontal wall 「strut.

**중임**(重任) ①《중대 임무》a heavy responsibility; an important duty 〔task, mission〕. ¶～을 띠고 on an important mission / ～을 맡다〔떠맡다〕 take a heavy trust on *oneself;* take upon *oneself* an important task; shoulder a heavy responsibility / ～을 맡고 있다 have a heavy responsibility on *one's* shoulders; be entrusted 〔charged〕 with an important mission / ～을 견뎌내다〔감당하다〕 be equal to an important duty. ②《재임용》reappointment;《개선》reelection. ～하다 be reappointed 〔reelected〕. ¶～을 반대하지 않다 have no objection to《*a person's*》reappointment.

**중장**(中章) the middle verses of a *shijo* 「poem.

**중장**(中將)〖육군·해병〗a lieutenant general;〖해군〗a vice admiral《미》; a vice-admiral《영》;〖공군〗a lieutenant general《미》; an air marshal《영》.

**중장비**(重裝備) heavy (construction) equipment. ¶ ~의 heavily equipped 《division》. ◉ ~공장 a heavy (construction) machinery shop.

**중재**(仲裁) mediation; arbitration; peacemaking. ~하다 mediate 《between》; arbitrate 《between》; make up; act as peacemaker. ¶ 싸움의 ~를 하다 mend 〔mediate〕 a quarrel / ~를 요청하다 solicit 《*another's*》 mediation; ask for arbitration / ~로 쟁의를 해결하다 settle a dispute by arbitration / ~를 제의하다 offer mediation / ~에 맡기다 go to arbitration / ~ 역할을 하다 play go-between role / 쟁의는 그의 ~로 해결되었다 The dispute was settled through his mediation.
◉ ~결정 an arbitration award. ~위원회 an arbitration committee; 《정당 따위의》 a trouble-shooting committee. ~인〔자〕 an arbitrator; a peacemaker; a mediator. ~재정(裁定) an arbitration ruling 〔decision, award〕. ~재판 arbitration (tribunal): ~ 재판소 a court of arbitration. ~조약 an arbitration treaty.

**중전**(中殿) the Queen. ◉ ~마마 Her Majesty the Queen.

**중전기**(重電機) heavy electrical equipment.

**중전차**(重戰車) a heavy tank.

**중절**(中絶) discontinuance; interruption; 《임신의》 an abortion. ~하다 discontinue; interrupt. ¶ 임신을 ~하다 have an abortion; interrupt pregnancy (by abortion).

**중절모**(中折帽) a felt 〔soft〕 hat; a trilby 《영》; a wide-awake (hat).

**중점**(中點) 〖수학〗 the middle point; the median; the central point.

**중점**(重點) 《강조》 emphasis; stress; 《중요》 importance; 《우위》 priority. ¶ ~적으로 in priority; 《apply policies》 selectively / ~을 두다 lay 〔put, place〕 stress 〔emphasis〕 《on》; attach importance 《to》; give priority 《to》 / 영어를 ~적으로 공부하다 concentrate more on the study of English than any other subject / 그는 그 방을 ~적으로 조사했다 He made a priority investigation of the room. ◉ ~배급 priority rationing; rationing on priority basis. ~생산 priority production. ~정책 a policy with overriding priority. ~주의 the principle of establishing clear priorities; a policy of concentrating (only) on (the) essentials.

**중정**(中正) impartiality; fairness. ~하다 (be) impartial; fair; unbias(s)ed.

**중정**(中庭) a courtyard; a 〔an inner〕 court.

**중정**(重訂) a second revision; a re-revision.

**중정석**(重晶石) 〖광물〗 barite.

**중조**(重曹) 〖화학〗 bicarbonate of soda.

**중죄**(重罪) (a) felony; a grave 〔capital〕 offense 〔crime〕. ¶ ~를 범하다 commit a grave crime. ◉ ~인〔범〕 a felon.

**중주**(重奏) 〖음악〗 a duet(t). ¶ 현악 4~ a string quartet.

**중증**(重症) a serious 〔dangerous〕 illness; a severe case. ¶ 그는 ~으로 생명이 위독하다 He is seriously ill and has no hope of recovery. ◉ ~환자 a serious case.

**중지**(中止) discontinuance; suspension; cancellation; interruption; stoppage; 《연기》 postponement. ~하다 stop; discontinue; cancel 《a meeting》; call off 《a strike》; leave off 《work》; give up 《doing》. ¶ ~되다 be discontinued 〔suspended, interrupted, stopped〕; fall into abeyance; be called off / 공사를 ~하다 discontinue the work / 연설을 ~시키다 stop the speaker / 경기는 ~되었다 The match was called off. / 모임은 ~되었다 The meeting was canceled. / 그 모임은 명령에 의해 ~되었다 The meeting was suppressed by order. / 우리는 그 일을 ~하지 않으면 안된다 We must put a stop to the work. / 모임은 우천으로 ~되었다 The party was called off on account of rain. *or* The party was rained out.

**중지**(中指) the middle 〔long〕 finger.

**중지**(衆智) wisdom of many people. ¶ ~를 모으다 gather the wisdom of many people; put 《our》 heads together; ask a large number of people for their advice 〔opinion〕.

**중지상**(中之上) the higher class of the medium grade; "B plus".

**중지중**(中之中) the middle class of the medium grade; "B".

**중지하**(中之下) the lower class of the medium grade; "B minus".

**중직**(重職) an important office; a responsible post; a position of trust. ¶ ~을 차지하다 occupy 〔hold〕 a responsible 〔an important〕 post.

**중진**(重鎭) ① 《중요한 인재》 a holder of a strategic post; a man of influence; a prominent 〔leading, influential〕 figure; a leader; a pillar; 《국가·사회의》 a mainstay; 《학계의》 an authority. ¶

우리 나라 영문학계의 ~ a leading scholar of English 〔an authority on English〕 in this country / 언론계〔교육계〕의 ~ leading journalists 〔educators〕 / 양당간의 ~ 회담 the high-powered bipartisan talks. ② 《문진》 a heavy paperweight.

**중진국**(中進國) a semideveloped country〔nation〕.

**중질**(中秩) an article of medium quality.

**중창**(中―) 《구두의》 an insole.

**중창**(重唱) 〖음악〗 a vocal ensemble; a part song. ¶ 4~ a vocal quartet / 3~ a trio.

**중책**(重責) 《책임》 a heavy responsibility; an important mission 〔duty〕. ¶ ~을 맡다 assume 〔shoulder〕 a heavy responsibility / ~을 맡고 있다 be entrusted with an important mission.

**중천**(中天) midair; the midheaven; the zenith. ¶ 해가 ~에 걸려 있다 The sun shines in the zenith.

**중첩**(重疊) 《반복》 reiteration; 《겹침》 being piled one on another. ~하다 be repeated 〔reiterated, duplicated〕; be piled one upon another; be heaped up; be amassed. ¶ 산악이 ~하여 하늘을 찌를 듯이 솟아 있다 Mountain upon mountain soars into the blue.

**중추**(中樞) 《중심》 the center; the pivot; the hub; the backbone; a mainstay. ¶ ~의 central; leading; pivotal / 사회의 ~ the backbone 〔mainstay〕 of society / ~ 역할을 하다 play a pivotal role 《for, in》.

◉ ~산업 a pivotal 〔key〕 industry. ~신경 a central nerve: ~신경 계통 the central nervous system / ~신경 조직 a central nervous tissue. ~인물 a leading figure; a key man; a mainstay. 신경~ 〖해부학〗 a nerve center.

**중추**(仲秋) the 8th lunar month; midautumn. ◉ ~명월 the harvest moon.

**중축**(中軸) the pivot; the axis; 《중심 인물》 the leading figure.

**중층**(中層) the middle stratum 〔layer, class, story, floor〕.

**중치**(中―) a thing of medium size 〔price〕. ⇨ 중간치.

**중침**(中針) a needle of medium size.

**중크롬산**(重―酸) 〖화학〗 dichromic acid. ◉ ~소다〔나트륨〕 sodium bichromate. ~염 dichromate; bichromate. ~전지 a bichromate cell. ~칼륨 potassium bichromate.

**중키**(中―) 《키의》 medium 「height 〔stature, size〕. ¶ ~의 남자 a medium-sized man.

**중탄산**(重炭酸) 〖화학〗 bicarbonate. ◉ ~소다, ~나트륨 bicarbonate of soda. ⇨ 탄산수소 나트륨. ~염 bicarbonate. ~칼륨 bicarbonate of potassium.

**중탕하다**(重湯―) cook 〔warm up〕 the vessel containing 《*something*》 in hot water.

**중태**(重態) a serious 〔grave〕 condition; a critical state 〔stage〕; the seriousness of *one's* illness. ¶ ~이다 be critical; be seriously 〔dangerously〕 ill 《with encephalitis》; be in a serious condition / ~에 빠지다 《병자가》 fall into a critical condition; 《병이》 take a serious turn; assume a grave character / 그는 암으로 ~이다 He is seriously ill with cancer. / 그는 부상을 입어 ~였다 He was wounded and in a serious condition.

**중턱**(中―) 《산의》 the breast of a hill; the mid-slope of a mountain; 《입체물의》 the middle part. ¶ ~에(서) halfway up 〔down〕 《a mountain》 / 산 ~에서 한숨 쉬다 take a short rest halfway up 〔down〕 the mountain / 산 ~에 절 하나가 있다 Halfway up the mountain there is a temple.

**중토**(重土) 〖화학〗 baryta. ◉ ~수 baryta water.

**중퇴**(中退) leaving school without completing the course; dropping out of school. ~하다 leave school halfway; drop out (of school). ¶ ~자 a (school) dropout / 대학을 ~한 청년 a young man 「who got only halfway through college 〔who gave up a university course halfway〕.

**중파**(中波) 〖전파〗 a medium wave. ◉ ~방송 medium-wave broadcasting. ~수신기 a medium-wave receiver. ~장 a medium wavelength.

**중판**(重版) 《거듭 인쇄》 a second 〔another〕 impression 〔printing〕; a reprint; 《개정판》 a second 〔revised〕 edition. ¶ 여러 번 ~되었다 The book went into many impressions 〔editions〕.

**중편**(中篇) 《제2권》 the second part; the middle 〔2nd〕 volume; 《중편의 글》 a medium-length story. ◉ ~소설 a medium-length story; a short novel; a novelette.

**중평**(衆評) public opinion 〔criticism〕. ¶ 이 문제에 관한 ~은 각색이다 Public opinion is divided as to this question.

**중포**(重砲) a heavy gun; [총칭] heavy artillery. ¶ ~에 의한 포격 (a) heavy artillery bombardment. ◉ ~병〔대〕 heavy artillery; 《한 사람》 a heavy artilleryman.

**중포격**(重砲擊) heavy bombardment. ~하다 bombard heavily.

**중폭격**(重爆擊) heavy bombing. ~하다 bomb heavily. ◉ ~기 a heavy bomber.

**중품**(中品) medium quality (goods).

**중풍**(中風) 〚한의〛 palsy; paralysis. ¶ ~에 걸리다 have a stroke of paralysis; be stricken 〔taken〕 with paralysis / 그는 ~으로 오른쪽 반신을 못 쓴다 He is paralyzed on his right side.
◉ ~ 환자 a paralytic.

**중하**(仲夏) midsummer; the fifth lunar month.

**중하**(重荷) 《짐》 a heavy burden; an encumbrance; 《책임》 heavy responsibility.

**중하다**(重—) 《중대하다》 (be) important; serious; momentous; grave; grievous; critical; 《귀중하다》 (be) precious; invaluable. ¶ 중한 죄 a grave sin / 중한 책임 a heavy responsibility / 중한 병 a serious illness / 중한 자리 a key post; an important job.

**중학교**(中學校) a middle school; 《미》 a junior high school. ¶ ~에 다니다 go to a junior high school / ~를 졸업하다 graduate from junior high school.
◉ ~과정 a junior high school course. ~학생 a middle school boy 〔girl〕; a junior high school pupil.

**중합**(重合) 〚화학〛 polymerization. ~하다 polymerize. ◉ ~유 polymerized oil. ~체 a polymer.

**중핵**(中核) the kernel; the core; the nucleus (*pl.* -clei, -uses).

**중형**(中型) a medium 〔middle〕 size. ¶ ~의 medium-〔middle-〕sized. ◉ ~차 a medium vehicles; a medium=sized passenger car.

**중형**(重刑) a severe punishment; a heavy penalty. ¶ ~에 처하다 sentence 《*a person*》 to a severe punishment; impose 〔inflict〕 a heavy penalty 《upon *a person*》.

**중혼**(重婚) bigamy; a bigamous marriage. ~하다 commit bigamy. ¶ ~의 bigamous / ~죄를 범하고 있다 be guilty of bigamy.
◉ ~자 a bigamist. ~죄 bigamy.

**중화**(中和) 〚화학〛 neutralization; 《독 따위》 counteraction. ~하다 neutralize; counteract. ¶ 독성을 ~하다 neutralize the effects of poison / 알칼리는 산을 ~한다 Alkalis neutralize acids.
◉ ~력〔제〕 a counteractive; a counteragent. ~열 heat of neutralization. ~점 the neutral point.

**중화**(中華) China. ◉ ~민국 the Republic of China (대만). ~사상 Sinocentrism. ~요리 Chinese dishes 〔food, cuisine〕: ~ 요리점 a Chinese restaurant. ~ 인민공화국 the People's Republic of China.

**중화기**(重火器) heavy weapons 〔firearms〕.

**중화학공업**(重化學工業) the heavy and chemical industry.

**중환**(重患) a serious illness. ◉ ~자 (a patient who is) a serious case; a patient on the danger list. ~자실 an intensive care unit (생략 I.C.U.).

**중후**(重厚) gravity and generosity. ~하다 (be) grave and generous; profound; imposing; deep. ¶ ~한 인물 a man of substance / ~한 태도 a grave and serious attitude / 그는 ~한 느낌을 주는 사람이다 He impresses one as being a man of depth.

**중흥**(中興) restoration; revival; rehabilitation. ~하다 revive; be restored; be rehabilitated. ¶ 민족~의 아버지 the father of the national restoration / 민중과 동떨어져 있는 연극의 ~을 위해서 궐기하다 rise for the restoration of dramatic performance that has been separated from the populace.
◉ ~지주(之主) the restorer 《of a kingdom, a dynasty》; a revivalist.

**중히**(重—) with care 〔caution, respect〕. ¶ 아무를 ~ 쓰다 appoint *a person* to a post of trust; give *a person* an important position / ~ 간수하다 take good care of 《*a thing*》 / ~ 여기다 《중시하다》 attach importance to; regard as of great consequence; take a serious view of; 《소중히 하다》 hold it in esteem; value; prize; respect; honor / 문제를 ~ 여기다 take a serious view of the matter / 책임을 ~ 여기다 respect 〔have a deep sense of〕 responsibilty / 명예를 ~여기다 respect 〔think much of〕 *one's* honor / 생명보다 명예를 ~ 여기다 put honor above life; hold *one's* name dearer than *one's* life / 무엇보다 건강을 ~여기다 set health before everything else / ~ 여기지 않는다 have no regard for; make light of; slight; attach little importance to / 그들은 그의 의견을 ~ 여기지 않았다 They didn't set much store by his opinion.

**쥐**[1] 《생쥐》 a mouse (*pl.* mice); 《시궁쥐》 a rat. ¶ 쥐가 시끄럽게 찍찍거리다 Rats are squeaking noisily. / 그는 이제 독 안에 든 쥐와 같다 Now he is like a rat in a trap. / 쥐가 많은 빌딩 a rat=infested building / 물에 빠진 쥐 같다 be wet as drowned rat / 쥐가 날뛰다 The rats run about. / 쥐도 궁지에 몰리면 고양이를 문다 A stag at bay is a dangerous foe. ◉ 집〔들〕쥐 the house 〔field〕 mouse. 쥐잡기 운동 an anti-rat drive.

**쥐**[2] 〖한의〗 a cramp; a charley horse. ¶ 다리에 쥐가 오르다〔나다〕「have a cramp 〔get cramped〕 in the leg; get a charley horse in the leg.

**쥐구멍** a mousehole; a rathole. ¶ ~으로 소 몰려고 한다 attempt to force the impossible / 부끄러워서 ~이라도 찾고 싶었다 I could have sunk through the floor. *or* I was so overwhelmed with 〔by〕 shame that I wished the floor would open and engulf me. / ~에도 볕들 날이 있다 《속담》 Fortune knocks at our door by turns. *or* Every dog has his day.

**쥐꼬리** a rattail. ¶ ~만한 월급 a small 〔low〕 salary; a poor 〔small〕 pay / ~만하다 be very small. ◉ ~톱 a kind of long thin saw.

**쥐눈이콩** 〖식물〗 a kind of small bean; *Rhynchosia volubilis* (학명).

**쥐다** grip; clench; clasp; take 〔get, have〕 hold of; hold. ¶ 주먹을 ~ clench *one's* fist / 멱살을 ~ seize 《*a person*》 by the collar 〔lapels〕 / 권력을 ~ take 〔assume〕 power / 정권을 ~ take over state affairs; come into power / 남의 비밀을 ~ get 〔have〕 hold of *a person's* secret / 사람을 쥐었다 폈다 하다 twist *a person* round *one's* little finger.

**쥐덫** a mousetrap; rattrap. ¶ ~을 놓다 set a trap for rats / ~으로 쥐를 잡다 catch a mouse with a mousetrap.

**쥐똥나무** 〖식물〗 a wax tree; privet. ◉ ~벌레 〖곤충〗 a wax insect.

**쥐라기**(一紀) 〖지질〗 the Jurassic period. ◉ ~공원 the Jurassic Park (영화명).

**쥐락펴락** controlling 《*a person*》 perfectly; having 《*a person*》 under *one's* thumb. ~하다 control 《*a person*》 perfectly; have 《*a person*》 under *one's* thumb; twist 《*a person*》 (a)round *one's* little finger. ¶ 남편을 마음대로 ~하다 have *one's* husband under *one's* thumb.

**쥐며느리** 〖동물〗 a sow 〔pill〕 bug; a wood louse.

**쥐방울** 〖식물〗 a Dutchman's-pipe.

**쥐뿔** a worthless thing. ¶ ~ 같다 be worthless 〔useless〕.

**쥐살** foreshank of beef.

**쥐색**(一色) (dark) gray.

**쥐손이풀** 〖식물〗 a herb Robert.

**쥐숨듯(이)** without leaving any trace.

**쥐악상추** young lettuce.

**쥐알봉수** a petty and crafty person; a fox.

**쥐약**(一藥) rat poison.

**쥐어뜯다** pluck (off); pick; tear 〔rip〕 off; scratch off. ¶ 창자를 쥐어 뜯는 것 같은 heartrending / 머리털을 ~ tear *one's* hair / 닭털을 ~ pluck (feather from) a chicken.

**쥐어박다** deal a blow; hit; punch; sock. ¶ 가슴을 ~ punch 《*a person*》 on the chest.

**쥐어주다** 《돈을》 put 《*a thing*》 in *a person's* hand; let 《*a person*》 have; hand over; slip (money) into 《*a person's*》 hand; 《뇌물을》 grease 《*a person's*》 palm; bribe 《*a person*》; 《팁을》 tip. ¶ 입막음으로 돈을 ~ bribe 《*a person*》 into secrecy 〔silence〕.

**쥐어짜다** ① 《수분 따위를》 wring; squeeze; 《주스 따위를》 squeeze 《a lemon》; press; extract (기계 따위로). ¶ 젖은 수건을 ~ wring 〔twist〕 the wet towel / 옷을 쥐어짜서 물기를 빼다 squeeze water from the clothes; wring a damp clothes dry / 오렌지에서 주스를 ~ squeeze the juice from an orange; press the juice out of an orange. ② 《생각·목소리 따위를》 ¶ 머리〔지혜〕를 ~ rack *one's* brains; strain *one's* wits / 목소리를 ~ strain *one's* voice; be at the top of *one's* voice. ③ 《돈 따위를》 squeeze 〔extort, wring〕 《money from 〔out of〕 *a person*》; exploit (착취하다). ¶ 마지막 1원까지 ~ bleed 《*a person*》 white 〔dry〕.

**쥐어흔들다** grab and shake. ¶ 어깨를 ~ shake 《*a person*》 by the shoulders.

**쥐엄나무** 〖식물〗 a honey locust.

**쥐엄발이** a shriveled foot; a person with a shriveled foot.

**쥐엄쥐엄** "grab it! grab it!"

**쥐엄질** 《재롱》 the way a baby opens and closes its hands; playing "grab it!".

**쥐여지내다** be placed under 《*a per-*

son's》 control; live in the grips 《of》; live under 《*a person's*》 thumb; be dominated 《by》. ¶ 마누라한테 ~ be tied to *one's* wife's apron strings; be henpecked; be under the petticoat government.

**쥐오줌풀** 『식물』 a valerian.

**쥐잡듯** ① 《샅샅이》 one by one; thoroughly. ¶ ~ 뒤지다〔살피다〕 comb 《the files for a missing letter》; go through 〔over〕 《a suspect's apartment》 with a fine-tooth(ed) comb. ② 《거칠게》 violently; rudely; roughly. ¶ (남을) ~하다 treat 《*a person*》 roughly; manhandle 〔maltreat〕 《*a person*》.

**쥐정신**(―精神) forgetfulness; a short memory. ¶ ~이다 be forgetful; have a poor 〔bad〕 memory.

**쥐젖** a small wart.

**쥐죽은듯** as still as can be; all hushed and still; as quiet as a mouse; deathly quiet. ~하다 (be) deathly quiet; be silent as the grave. ¶ 주변은 ~ 고요했다 All was silent around there. *or* I could have heard a pin fall. / 거리가 ~이 고요하다 There is a deathly hush in the streets.

**쥐참외** 『식물』 a snake gourd 〔cucumber〕.

**쥐치** 『어류』 a filefish; a leatherfish.

**쥐코밥상**(―床) a poor 〔humble〕 table.

**쥐코조리** a small-minded 〔petty〕 man.

**쥘부채** a folding fan.

**쥘손** a handle; a grip; a knob; a pull (서랍의); 《주전자의》 a catch; an ear.

**즈런즈런** 《살림이》 in affluence; in abundance; plentifully; richly; abundantly. ~하다 (be) affluent; opulent; abundant; plentiful. ¶ 살림이 ~하다 be well off; lead an abundant life; live in clover.

**즈봉** (a pair of) trousers; breeches (주로 반즈봉); 《미》 pantaloons; pants. ◉ 반~ (a pair of) breeches; shorts.

**즈음** the time (when). ¶ 이 ~에 these days; lately / 그 ~에 in those days; at that time / ~하여 when; at the time 《of》; in case 《of》; on the occasion 《of》 / 출발에 ~하여 at the time of *one's* departure / 창립 50주년에 ~하여 on the occasion of the fiftieth anniversary of the foundation / 떠남에 ~하여 인사의 말 몇 마디 드리고자 합니다 At the moment of my departure I should like to speak a few parting words.

**즈크** [< *doek* (D.)] duck; canvas. ◉ ~신 canvas shoes; tennis shoes.

**즉**(卽) ① 《곧》 that is (to say); namely; or; i.e.; in other words; viz.

> 용법 **that is** 흔히 문장 전체를 바꿔 말할 때 쓰이고, **namely**, **or**는 어구를 바꿔 말하려고 할 때 쓰임. 특히 or를 「즉」이란 뜻으로 쓰는 경우는 처음 듣거나 어려운 말을 바꿔 말하려 할 때 쓰임: 「에스컬레이터 즉 움직이는 계단」 "an escalator *or* a moving staircase". **i.e.**는 라틴어 *id est*의 약어로 [ðǽtíz] 또는 [ái íː]로 읽으며 문서나 전문 서적 등에서 쓰임. **viz** 라틴어 *vedelicet*의 약어로 흔히 namely로 읽음.

¶ 그녀는 2주 전, 즉 6월 10일에 미국으로 떠났다 She left for the U.S. two weeks ago, that is, on June 10. / 그 일을 할 수 있는 사람은 단 하나, 즉 너다 Only one person can do the job, namely you. ② 《바로》 precisely; exactly; just; indeed; 《다름아닌》 nothing but; neither more nor less. ¶ 그것이 즉 그의 위대한 점이다 That's what is great about him. / 그것이 즉 내가 바라는 바다 That's just the thing I want.

**즉각**(卽刻) [부사적] 《즉시》 instantly; at once; on the instant; on the spot; immediately; at once; right away; in a moment. ¶ ~ 효험을 나타내다 《약 따위가》 work at once; take 〔give an〕 immediate effect / ~ 실행하겠습니다 It shall be done without delay. / ~ 물러날 것을 명령받았다 I was ordered to quit without delay.

**즉결**(卽決) a prompt 〔immediate〕 decision; 《구어》 a snap decision 〔judgment〕; 《재판의》 a summary decision. ~하다 decide promptly 〔on the spot〕; try 〔deal with〕 summarily. ¶ ~로 without debate (회의 따위에서). ◉ ~재판 summary justice 〔conviction〕; a summary trial 〔decision〕: ~재판을 하다 deal with 《*a person*》 summarily; try 《*a person*》 by a summary action. ~재판권 summary jurisdiction. ~재판소 a summary court. ~처분 summary punishment.

**즉낙**(卽諾) a ready consent 〔assent, agreement〕. ~하다 readily consent 〔agree〕 《to》.

**즉납**(卽納) immediate 〔prompt〕 payment. ~하다 pay immediately.

**즉단**(卽斷) a prompt 〔an immediate〕 decision. ~하다 decide promptly 〔on the spot〕.

**즉답**(卽答) a prompt 〔ready〕 answer; an immediate reply. ～하다 give an immediate 〔a ready〕 answer; reply promptly 〔on the spot, at once〕. ¶ ～을 요구하다 ask for a prompt reply / ～을 피하다 choose to answer later.

**즉매**(卽賣) a spot sale; a sale on the spot. ～하다 sell on the spot.

**즉사**(卽死) instantaneous 〔instant〕 death. ～하다 die on the spot; be killed instantly. ¶ 총탄에 맞아 그는 ～했다 A bullet killed him on the spot. ◉ ～자 a person killed instantly.

**즉석**(卽席) ¶ ～의 impromptu; offhand; extempore; improvised / ～에서 on the spot; offhandedly; extemporarily; impromptu; off-the-cuff 《구어》; instantly / ～에서 …하다 do offhand 〔on the spot〕; extemporize 《a speech》; improvise 《a poem》; ad-lib 《a song》 / ～에서 시를 짓다 improvise a poem / ～에서 대답하다 give an answer on the spot / 수상은 ～ 기자 회견을 가졌다 The premier gave an impromptu press conference. / 나는 ～에서 그의 제의를 거절했다 I declined his offer then and there. / ～에서는 응해드릴 수가 없습니다 We cannot have it ready at a moment's notice.
◉ ～복권 an instant lottery ticket. ～식품 instant food. ～연설 an impromptu 〔offhand〕 speech: ～ 연설을 하다 speak extempore; make an impromptu speech. ～요리 instant meal; a pickup dish. ～커피 an instant coffee.

**즉시**(卽時) instant. ¶ ～로 instantly; immediately; on the spot; in no time; at once; promptly; without delay / ～ 의사를 부르다 call a doctor at once / ～ 정전(停戰)을 요구하다 call for an immediate ceasefire / 이 문제는 ～ 해결해야 한다 This problem calls for immediate solution. / 부르거든 ～ 오너라 Come right away if I call you. / 그는 나에게 ～ 찬성했다 He gave me a ready assent. ◉ ～불 spot 〔down〕 payment. ～인도 spot delivery. ～지급 어음 a sight bill. ～통화 direct distance 〔《영》 trunk〕 dialing.

**즉위**(卽位) accession to the throne; enthronement. ～하다 accede 〔come〕 to the throne; ascend the throne.
◉ ～식 an enthronement ceremony; 《대관식》 a coronation: ～식을 행하다 perform the ceremony of accession to the throne; hold a coronation ceremony.

**즉응**(卽應) prompt conformity; immediate adaptation. ～하다 conform immediately 《to》; adapt 〔accommodate〕 *oneself* 《to》; meet promptly. ¶ …에 ～하여 in conformity with…; in response to… / 시대적 요구에 ～한 교육 education adapted to the times / 시대 요구에 ～하다 (promptly) meet the needs of the times.

**즉일**(卽日) the same day. ¶ ～로 on the (very) same day / ～로 돌아오다 return on the same day; make a one day trip / 투표는 ～로 개표할 예정이다 The ballot is expected to be opened on the very day.

**즉행**(卽行) 《떠남》 prompt departure; 《행함》 prompt execution 〔action〕. ～하다 depart at once; go promptly; execute 〔carry out〕 promptly; act at once. ¶ 옳다고 생각하는 일은 ～하라 Do at once what you think is right.

**즉효**(卽效) an immediate effect 《of medicine》. ¶ ～가 있다 produce 〔have〕 an immediate effect 《on》; 《고통에 대하여》 give quick relief. ◉ ～약 an instant(aneous) 〔a quick〕 remedy 《for》; a quick cure.

**즉흥**(卽興) impromptu amusement. ¶ ～적인 improvised; impromptu; offhand; ad-lib; extempore; extemporaneous / ～적으로 짓다 compose 《a poem》 extempore / 나는 ～적으로 말했는데, 모두 못마땅하게 여겼다 I ad=libbed and they didn't like it. ◉ ～곡 〖음악〗 an impromptu. ～시 an improvised poem. ～시인 an improviser.

**즐거움** joy; delight; gladness; pleasure; happiness (행복). ¶ 전원 생활의 ～ delights of rural life / ～에 겨워하다 be overcome with joy / 인생의 ～과 슬픔을 다 맛보다 taste both the joys and sorrows of life / …하는 것을 ～으로 여기다 take pleasure 〔delight〕 in *do*ing / 독서가 나의 유일한 ～이다 Reading is my only pleasure.

**즐거이** delightfully; with delight; joyfully; pleasantly; merrily. ¶ 친구를 ～ 맞다 receive a friend with pleasure; be delighted to receive a friend / 시간을 ～ 보내다 pass happy hours.

**즐겁다** (be) delightful; pleasant; joyful; merry; glad; happy. ¶ 즐겁게 joyfully; happily; merrily; cheerfully / 즐거운 우리 집 our sweet home / 즐거운 옛 생각 happy memories / 즐겁게 놀다 play merrily / 즐겁게 지내다 live happily;

have a good time of it / 즐겁게 하다 please; delight; amuse; give pleasure 《to》; 《환대하여》 entertain / 즐거운 한 때를 보내다 have a good 〔happy〕 time / 눈을 즐겁게 하다 delight the eye; [사람이 주어] feast *one's* eyes 《on *a thing*》 / 즐거운 하루를 보내세요 Have a nice day!

**즐겨** ① 《소망하여》 by 〔from〕 choice; willingly; by preference; 《자진하여》 of *one's* own accord 〔free will〕; by (*one's* own) choice; willing to 《do》. ¶ ~ 독서를 하다 take pleasure in reading / 그는 지금까지 ~ 나쁜 짓을 해왔던 것은 아니다 Vice has never been his choice. ② 《종종》 often; frequently. ¶ ~ 그림을 그리다 care to paint a picture frequently; draw a picture very often.

**즐기다** enjoy 《a meal, a film》; get 〔obtain〕 pleasure 《from》; find pleasure 〔delight〕 《in music》; 《즐겁게 보내다》 enjoy *oneself*; have fun 〔a good time〕; amuse *oneself* 《*doing*》. ¶ 독서를 〔인생을〕 ~ enjoy reading 〔life〕 / 음악을 ~ delight in music / 보고 ~ take pleasure in looking at / 술을 ~ be fond of liquor / 나는 가끔 만화를 즐긴다 I sometimes amuse myself by reading comics.

**즐비하다**(櫛比—) stand closely together; stand in a continuous row. ¶ 길가에 상점이 ~ Shops and stores closely line the streets.

**즙**(汁) 《과일의》 juice; 《초목의》 sap; 《고무나무 따위의》 latex. ¶ 고기즙 meat juice / 과일〔사과〕즙 fruit 〔apple〕 juice / 레몬즙을 짜다 squeeze 〔extract〕 juice from a lemon / 즙이 많다 be juicy 〔succulent〕 / 사과를 즙내다 juice an apple; press the juice out of an apple. 「〔juiceless〕.

**즙액**(汁液) juice. ¶ ~이 많은〔없는〕 juicy

**증**(症) 《증세》 symptoms. ¶ 중독증 toxic symptoms / 현기증이 나다 feel dizzy.

**증**(證) ① 《증거》 (a) proof; evidence; testimony. ② 《증서》 a certificate; a warrant. ¶ 학생증 a student's (identification) card / 졸업증 a diploma / 영수증 a receipt.

**증가**(增加) (an) increase; (an) augmentation; (an) increment; a gain; (an) addition; 《인구 등》 growth. ~하다 increase; be on the increase; grow; rise; step up 《production》. ¶ 체중의 ~ a gain in weight / 청소년 비행의 ~ the increase 〔rise〕 in juvenile delinquency / 인구〔수〕가 ~하다 increase in population 〔number〕 / ~ 일로에 있다 be on the increase / (작년에 비해) 2할의 ~를 보이다 show a 20% 〔twenty percent〕 increase (over last year) / 교통 사고가 놀랄만큼 ~하고 있다 Traffic accidents are increasing alarmingly. / 한국의 무역은 해마다 ~한다 Korea's trade grows larger every year. / 이 도시를 방문하는 관광객의 수가 요즘 크게 ~했다 The number of tourists who visit this town has increased greatly in recent years.
◉ ~액 the amount of increase; an increment. ~율 a rate of increase; an increasing rate; percentage increase. 자연~ a natural increase.

**증간**(**호**)(增刊(號)) a special 〔an extra〕 number 〔issue〕 《of a magazine》.

**증감**(增減) increase and 〔or〕 decrease; rise and 〔or〕 fall; fluctuation; variation. ~하다 increase and 〔or〕 decrease; 《하천의 물이》 rise and 〔or〕 fall; fluctuate; vary 《*in quantity*》. ¶ …에 정비례하여 ~하다 vary in direct proportion to… / 소득이 달에 따라 ~하다 *one's* income varies from month to month / 이 잡지는 구독자의 ~이 아주 심하다 There are sharp fluctuations in this magazine's circulation.

**증강**(增強) (a) reinforcement; (an) increase; augmentation; a 《military》 build-up. ~하다 reinforce; increase; augment; build up. ¶ 병력을 ~하다 reinforce troops 〔an army〕 / 군사력을 ~하다 build up the military strength / 수송력을 ~하다 increase the carrying 〔transport〕 capacity / 영업력을 ~하다 strengthen sales capability.

**증거**(證據) evidence; (a) proof; 『법』 《증언》 (a) testimony; witness.
¶ 충분한〔불충분한〕 ~ sufficient 〔insufficient〕 evidence / 확실한〔결정적인, 명백한〕 ~ certain 〔decisive, clear〕 evidence / 물적(物的) ~ (physical) evidence / …에게 불리한 ~ evidence against 《*a person*》 / …의 ~로서 in evidence…; as (a) proof of… / ~ 불충분으로 for lack 〔want〕 of (good) evidence; on the ground of insufficient evidence / 확실한 ~에 입각하여 on trustworthy evidence / …의 ~가 되다 be evidence 〔proof〕 of…; prove; testify / ~를 잡다〔쥐다〕 hold 〔obtain〕 proofs 《of》; secure evidence 《of》 / ~를 들다 give 〔produce, bring forward〕 evidence 《to show that…》;

cite *something* as proof 《of》/ ～로서 채택되다 be adopted as evidence / ～를 제출하다 produce testimony 〔evidence〕《of》; produce 《*a thing*》 in evidence 〔as a proof〕/ ～를 수집하다 gather 〔collect〕 evidence / 사실을 뒷받침하는 ～를 확보하다 secure evidence supporting the fact / 결정적 ～를 못 잡다 cannot obtain a conclusive point of evidence 《on a culprit》/ 이 사실은 그의 증언이 허위라는 ～다 This fact bears testimony to his falsehood. / 그가 유죄라는 ～는 없다 There is no evidence of his guilt. / 그것은 그가 너를 사랑한다는 ～다 It shows that he loves you. / 그는 ～ 불충분으로 석방되었다 He was released for want of material evidence.

◉ ～금 a deposit; deposit money. ～능력 admissibility of evidence. ～물〔품〕 (a piece of) evidence; an exhibit (of evidence). ～보전 preservation of evidence. ～서류 documentary evidence. ～수집 the gathering 〔collecting〕 of proofs 〔evidence〕. ～인멸 destruction of evidence: ～ 인멸하다 destroy evidence 《of, as to》/ ～ 인멸을 꾀하다 try to hide traces of the crime. ～자료 corroborative facts. ～조사 the taking of evidence. 내적 ～ internal evidence.

**증권**(證券) 《공사채》 a bond; 《주식증권》 a certificate (of stock 〔share〕); 《환어음 등》 a bill; 《공채·주권 등의 유가증권》 securities (★ 보통 복수형); 《보험증권》 an insurance policy. ¶ (은행의) 예탁 ～ a deposit certificate / ～화하다 convert 《funds, deposits》 into securities / ～에 손을 대다 speculate 〔dabble〕 in stocks; play the market 《미》.

◉ ～거래법 the Securities and Exchange Act. ～거래소 the stock 〔securities〕 exchange: 한국 ～ 거래소 the Korea Stock Exchange. ～거래원 a bill broker; a (licensed) stock broker: ～ 거래원 수수료 brokerage; commission. ～거래 위원회 《미국의》 the Securities and Exchange Commission (생략 S.E.C.). ～매매 dealing in bonds and securities. ～분석가 a securities analyst. ～소유자 a security holder. ～시세 stock quotations 〔prices〕. ～시장 a stock(-exchange) market; a securities market. ～업 securities business; stockbroking: ～업자 a stockbroker; a bill broker. ～투자 investment in securities; securities investment. ～회사 a securities 〔stock〕 company; a stockbrokerage firm. 국고～ a treasury bond 《미》; an exchequer bond 《영》. 대용～ collateral securities. 선화(船貨)～ a bill of lading (생략 B/L). 유통～ a negotiable instrument. 정부(발행)～ government securities.

**증급**(增給) a pay 〔wage, salary〕 increase; a pay raise. ～하다 increase 〔raise〕 《*a person's*》 pay 〔wages, salary〕. ¶ 200,000원의 ～ a two hundred thousand won increase in *one's* salary / 1할 ～하다 give 《*a person*》 a 10% increase of salary.

**증기**(蒸氣) 《김》 steam; 《수증기》 vapor. ¶ ～를 발생하다 generate steam / ～를 뿜다 (give off) steam / ～로 움직이다 be driven 〔powered〕 by steam.

◉ ～관 a steam pipe. ～공(孔) 《화산 등의》 a fumarole. ～기관 a steam engine. ～기관차 a steam locomotive. ～난방 steam heating: ～ 난방 장치 a steam-heating system 〔apparatus〕; a steam heater. ～다리미 a steam iron. ～력 steam power. ～선 a steamship. ～소독 steam disinfection; autoclaving (의료 기구의). ～압 steam pressure. ～욕 a steam bath. ～탕 Turkish bath. ～터빈 a steam turbine. ～펌프 a steam pump.

**증답**(贈答) an exchange of gifts 〔presents〕. ～하다 exchange gifts 〔presents〕. ◉ ～품 a gift; a present.

**증대**(增大) enlargement; augmentation; (an) accretion; (an) increase; (an) increment; a step-up. ～하다 《커지다》 become 〔grow, get〕 larger 〔bigger, greater〕; 《크게 하다》 make *something* bigger 〔larger, greater〕; enlarge; increase; augment; swell 《the total》; enhance; gather 〔gain〕 《speed》; step up 《the amount》. ¶ 불안의 ～ the buildup of suspense / 생산의 ～ a step-up in production / 인구의 ～ a swell 〔an increase〕 in population / ～하는 세계 위기 a mounting world crisis / 권력을〔부를〕 ～하다 increase *one's* power 〔wealth〕/ 수요가 ～하다 the demands rise 《for it》; be more in demand / 국내 산업의 국제 경쟁력을 ～시키다 increase domestic industries' international competitive edge.

◉ ～판 《issue》 an enlarged edition. ～호 an enlarged number: 신년 ～호 the enlarged January number 《of》.

**증량**(增量) (an) increase in quantity.

~하다 increase the quantity《of》.

**증류**(蒸溜) distillation. ~하다 distill.
◉ ~관 a distiller tube. ~기 a distiller; a still. ~수 distilled water. ~액 distillate. ~장치 distillation apparatus〔equipment〕. ~주 spirits;《미》(distilled〔hard〕) liquors.

**증명**(證明)《증거》(a) proof; evidence;《확증》authentication; corroboration;《검정》certification;《논증》demonstration;《입증》verification;《증언》testimony; attestation. ~하다《실증하다》prove; show; bear out;《증언하다》testify《to》; bear witness《to》;《입증하다》verify;《문서로》certify; demonstrate; authenticate;《신원을》identify.

> (용법) **proof** 주장의 정당성·타당성을 확증하는 증거. **evidence** proof보다 품위 있는 말로서 어떤 일이 사실임을 밝혀내는 것. **testimony** 진위를 증명하는 공적인 증언을 의미함.

¶ 무죄를 ~하다 prove《*a person's*》innocence / 학설을 ~하다 verify〔confirm〕a theory / 오류임을 ~하다 prove that *something* is wrong; disprove *something* / ~할 수 없다 be unprovable; be unverifiable / 실험에 의해서 이론을 ~하다 prove a theory by experiment / 이 사람은 본교 교원임을 ~함 This is to certify that this person is a teacher at our school. / 이 약은 효능이 있음이 ~되었다 This drug has been proved (to be) effective. / 너는 그 날 어디에 있었는지 ~할 수 있느냐 Can you prove where you were (on) that day? / 그 시간에 네가 집에 있었다는 것을 ~할 수 있느냐 Can you prove that you stayed home (at) that time? / 그 사실로 그녀의 말이 진실임이 ~되었다 The fact proved the truth of her remark. / 그 이론은 아직 과학적으로 ~되어 있지 않다 The theory is not yet scientifically established.
◉ ~서 a certificate; a testimonial (인물·자격 등의); a warrant (허가증): 건강 ~서 a health certificate / 신분 ~서 an identification card / 원산지 ~서 a certificate of origin / 결혼 ~서 a marriage certificate / 출생〔사망〕~서 a birth〔death〕certificate / ~서를 내주다〔받다〕give〔get〕a certificate.

**증모**(增募) raising extra《troops, laborers, subscriptions》; an increased〔intensified〕enrolling〔recruiting, collecting〕. ~하다 raise〔enroll, recruit〕extra.

**증발**(蒸發)《액체의》evaporation; vaporization;《사람의》(a) mysterious disappearance. ~하다 evaporate; vaporize;《물이》steam;《사람이》disappear〔vanish〕into thin air. ¶ ~하기 쉬운 volatile / 물은 ~한다 The water turns into vapor. / 그는 큰 돈을 가지고 ~했다 He disappeared without a trace「carrying〔taking〕a lot of money. ◉ ~계 vaporimeter. ~기 an evaporator. ~력 evaporative power. ~성 evaporativity: ~성의 volatile (휘발성); evaporative (기화되는). ~열 evaporation heat. ~접시 an evaporating dish.

**증발**(增發)《통화의》an increased issue;《열차의》operation of an extra train. ~하다 issue additional paper money; operate〔run〕a special〔an extra〕train. ¶ 적자 공채의 ~ a further issue of "red-ink" bonds / 임시 열차를 ~하다 operate〔run〕a special train.

**증배**(增配)《배당의》an increased dividend; a bonus;《배급의》an increase of rations. ~하다《주식의 배당을》pay an increased dividend;《배급을》increase the ration《of rice》.

**증병**(增兵) reinforcement(s). ~하다 reinforce the troops; dispatch reinforcements.

**증보**(增補) enlargement; supplementation. ~하다 enlarge; supplement. ¶ ~와 개정을 가하여 발행하다 be published with additions and up-to-date corrections.

**증빙**(證憑) (a) proof; evidence; (a) testimony.
◉ ~서류 documentary evidence.

**증산**(增産) increased output〔production〕; a production increase; an increase〔a step-up〕in production;《농산물의》an increased yield《of rice》. ~하다 increase〔step up〕production《of》; increase the yield. ¶ 쌀의 ~ a higher〔an increased〕yield of rice / 식료품 ~이 급선무다 It is of burning necessity to turn out foodstuffs in increasing amount.
◉ ~계획 a program for the increased production《of》: 철강의 장기 ~ 계획 a long-range program for increasing the output of steel. ~운동 a production increase campaign; a drive for production increase. ~의욕《farmers'》willingness to produce more: ~의욕을 북돋우다 encourage《*a person's*》will to produce more.

**증상**(症狀) symptoms (징후); the conditions of illness (병세). ¶ 독감의 ～을 보이다 develop 〔show〕 symptoms of influenza / 감기와 비슷한 ～으로 앓다 suffer from symptoms similar to those of a cold / 「어떤 ～입니까」—「재채기가 나고 콧물이 나오며, 눈이 가렵습니다」 "What symptoms do you have?"—"Sneezing, a runny nose, and my eyes itch." ◉ 자각～ subjective symptoms. 중독～ toxic symptoms.

**증서**(證書) 《채무의》 a bond; 《양도 따위의》 a deed; 《증거 서류》 a document; a paper; 《영수증 따위》 a voucher; 《증명서》 a certificate; 《졸업의》 a diploma. ¶ 차용～ an IOU (=I owe you); a bond of debt / ～와 교환으로 in exchange for a bond / ～를 작성하다 prepare 〔write out, draw out〕 a deed; execute a deed (법규정대로) / 그는 ～에 조인했다 He signed a deed. ◉ 국채～ government bonds. 졸업～ a diploma.

**증설**(增設) (an) increase (of buildings); enlargement; extension. ～하다 increase; establish 《five》 more 《shools》; install more 《telephones》. ¶ 학교를 ～하다 build more schools / 지점을 2개소 더 ～하다 establish 〔set up〕 two more branches.

**증세**(症勢) symptoms; the condition of illness. ⇨증상. ¶ 너는 학질 ～가 있다 You have 〔show〕 the symptoms of malaria. / 환자의 ～가 좀 어떻습니까 How is the patient progressing?

**증세**(增稅) a tax increase; increased taxation. ～하다 increase 〔raise〕 taxes 《on *a thing,* on *a person*》. ¶ 10%의 ～ a ten percent increase in taxation. ◉ ～계획 an increased taxation plan. ～안 a tax increase bill.

**증손**(曾孫) a great-grandchild (*pl.* -children). ◉ ～녀 a great-granddaughter. ～부 the wife of *one's* great=grandson. ～서(婿) the husband of *one's* great-granddaughter. ～자 a great-grandson.

**증쇄**(增刷) an additional printing. ～하다 print in addition. ¶ 1,000부를 ～하다 print additional 1,000 〔1,000 more〕 copies.

**증수**(增水) the rise 〔rising〕 of a river; flooding. ～하다 rise; swell. ⇨붇다②. ¶ 호우로 인해 한강이 2m ～됐다 As a result of the heavy rainfall, the Han river has risen (by) two meters. ◉ ～기 a flooded season; the annual flooding period. ～표 a floodmark.

**증수**(增收) 《수입》 an increase of receipts 〔income, revenue〕; 《수확》 an increased yield; an increase of crop. ～하다 《*one's* income, the revenue, the crop》 increase 《by 5%》. ¶ 세금의 자연 ～ automatic increases in tax revenues / 쌀의 ～를 꾀하다 increase the yield of rice / 우리의 대차대조표는 작년 같은 달보다 약 5퍼센트의 ～를 보인다 Our balance sheet shows an increased revenue of about five percent over the same month of last year.

**증수회**(贈收賄) (official) corruption; bribery. ◉ ～사건 a bribery case.

**증식**(增殖) propagation; multiplication; (an) increase; 〖생물〗 proliferation. ～하다 increase; propagate; multiply; proliferate. ◉ ～로 《원자로의》 a breeder reactor: 고속 ～로 a fast breeder reactor (생략 FBR). ～속도 a multiplication rate. 병적 ～ 《피부 조직의》 vegetation. 세포이상～ hyperplasia of cells. 자기～ self-reproduction.

**증압**(增壓) ～하다 raise 〔get up〕 the pressure 《of》. ◉ ～반사 〖생리〗 a pressor reflex.

**증액**(增額) the increased amount 《of money》; (an) increment; (an) increase. ～하다 increase (the amount); raise; augment. ¶ 국방비의 ～ an increase in the national defense budget / 예산의 ～을 요구하다 demand an increase in *one's* budget allocation / 월급을 130만 원으로 ～하다 increase 《*a person's*》 salary to one point three million won. ◉ ～분 the increased amount.

**증언**(證言) 〖법〗 (verbal) evidence; testimony; witness; attestation. ～하다 testify 《to a fact》; bear witness 《to》; depose 〔swear〕 《to》; give evidence. ¶ 목격자의 ～ eyewitness evidence; the testimony of an eyewitness / ～의 일치 consensus of testimony / …한 것을 ～하다 testify 〔bear testimony〕 to the fact that… / 법정에서 ～하다 give *one's* evidence in court / 무죄를 ～하다 testify to *a person's* innocence / 피고에게 유리〔불리〕한 ～을 하다 testify 「in favor of 〔against〕 the accused / 목격자의 ～에 의하면 용의자는 빨간 재킷을 입고 있었다 According to an eye witness' testimony, the suspect wore a red jacket.

◉ ～대《take》the witness stand《미》; the witness box《영》. ～서 a written testimony. ～자 a witness.

**증여**(贈與) donation; presentation; gift. ～하다 give; make a present of《a thing》; present; donate《money》.
◉ ～물 a gift; a present. ～세 a donation〔gift〕tax. ～자 a giver; a donator; a donor: 피～자〖법〗a donee; a donatory. ～재산 a donated property.

**증오**(憎惡) hatred; detestation; abhorrence. ～하다 hate; detest; abhor. ¶ ～할 hateful; detestable; abhorrent / ～를 사다 incur《*a person's*》hatred / 그녀는 그에 대한 ～심을 떨쳐 버릴 수 없었다 She couldn't get rid of her hatred for him.

**증원**(增員) an increase of personnel〔the staff〕. ～하다 increase the number of staff; augment the personnel《of》. ¶ 50명을 ～하다 increase the staff by 50 / 직원을 50명에서 80명으로 ～하다 increase the staff of fifty to eighty.

**증원**(增援) reinforcement. ～하다 reinforce《an army》. ◉ ～부대《dispatch》reinforcements.

**증음기**(增音器) a sound amplifier; 《오르간의》 a knee swell.

**증인**(證人) a witness; an eyewitness (목격자); an attestor (증서 작성의); a testifier (증언자); a deponent (선서 증인); a surety (보증인). ¶ ～이 되다 bear witness《to》; 《사건의》 testify《to》; 《법정에서》 give evidence; 《신원의》 stand surety for《*a person*》/ ～을 소환하다 call a witness; summon a witness《to appear in court》/ ～으로 세우다 call《*a person*》to〔as〕witness / ～으로 나서다 present *oneself* as a witness.
◉ ～대 the witness stand《미》; the witness box《영》: ～대에 서다 be in the (witness) box《영》; go on〔take〕the (witness) stand《미》. ～심문 the examination of a witness. 검사〔피고〕측 ～ a prosecution〔defense〕witness.

**증인**(證印) a seal affixed to a document; a notary seal.

**증자**(增資) (an) increase of capital; (a) capital increase. ～하다 increase the capital; 《주식회사가》 increase its〔their〕stock. ◉ ～(신)주 additional stocks《미》; additional shares《영》; newly issued stocks.

**증정**(增訂) supplementing〔enlarging〕and correcting〔revising〕. ～하다 supplement and correct; enlarge and revise. ◉ ～판 an enlarged and revised edition.

**증정**(贈呈) presentation; proffering; 《저서에》 "With the author's compliments"; 《선물 따위에》 To〔Presented to〕《Mr. A》 (with best wishes from...). ～하다 present《*a person* with *a thing*, *a thing* to *a person*》; make a present〔gift〕of《*a thing* to *a person*》; proffer; give. ¶ 목록 무료 ～《게시》 Catalog offered free. / 은퇴하는 시장에게 푸짐한 선물이 ～되었다 A handsome presentation was made to the retiring mayor.
◉ ～본 a presentation〔complimentary〕copy; a keepsake; a gift book; an author's copy. ～식 the ceremony of the presentation《of》. ～자 a giver; a donor; a presenter. ～품 a present; a gift.

**증조고**(曾祖考)《돌아가신》 the deceased great-grandfather.

**증조모**(曾祖母) a (paternal) great-grandmother.

**증조부**(曾祖父) a (paternal) great-grandfather.

**증조비**(曾祖妣)《돌아가신》 the deceased great-grandmother.

**증좌**(證左)《증거》 corroborative evidence; proof.

**증지**(證紙) a certificate stamp.

**증진**(增進) promotion; furtherance; (an) increase. ～하다 promote; increase; further. ¶ 사회 복지의 ～ promotion of social welfare / 문화 교류의 ～ the promotion of cultural exchanges / 건강을 ～하다 improve〔build up〕*one's* health / 능률을 ～하다 increase〔improve〕efficiency / 식욕을 ～하다 promote〔sharpen〕*one's* appetite.

**증차**(增車) raise the number of cars〔vehicles〕. ¶ 철도청은 설날 연휴동안 열차를 ～할 예정이다 The Office of Railroads schedules more trains during the New Year season.

**증축**(增築) enlargement〔extension〕of a building. ～하다 extend〔enlarge, add to〕a building; build an annex〔extension〕to《the main building》. ¶ 새로 ～한 건물 a new extension building / 현재 ～중이다 An extension is now under construction. / 우리집 2층에 방 하나를 ～하고 있다 We are adding a room on the second floor of our house. ◉ ～공사 extension work. ～비 the cost of extending a building.

**증파**(增派) reinforcement; additional dispatch. ～하다 reinforce《an army》;

send 〔dispatch〕 more 《troops, warships》. ¶ 함선을 ~하다 send 〔dispatch〕 more warships 《to》 / 정부는 재해지에 구조대를 ~하기로 결정했다 The government decided to send more rescue parties to the stricken area.

**증편**(蒸—) steamed rice-cake.

**증폭**(增幅) amplification. ~하다 amplify. ¶ 확성기를 통해서 소리가 ~되었다 The sound was amplified through a loudspeaker. ◉ ~기 an amplifier.

**증표**(證標) a voucher; a certificate. ¶ 검사필의 ~ a certificate of inspection.

**증회**(贈賄) giving a bribe; bribery. ~하다 give 《*a person*》 a bribe; grease 〔oil, tickle〕 《*a person's*》 palm 〔hand〕. ◉ ~사건 a bribery case. ~자 a briber. ~죄 bribery: ~죄를 범하다 commit bribery / ~죄로 고소되다 be charged with bribery. 「drome.

**증후**(症候) = 증세(症勢). ◉ ~군 a syn-

**지** (the time) since; from the time when. ¶ 고향을 떠난 지 벌써 10년이나 된다 It is already ten years since I left home. *or* Ten years have passed since I left home. (★ Ten years is a long time.의 경우 ten years는 단일체이고, ...have passed의 경우는 일년 일년의 모임인 ten years임에 주의) / 햇빛을 본 지가 오래다 It's been a long time since we saw any sunshine. / 여기 오신 지가 얼마나 됩니까 How long have you been here? / 그 분과 작별한 지 얼마나 되죠 How long is it since you saw him last? / 편지 받은 지 두 달 된다 It's been two months since I got a letter.

**지**(知) 《지성》 intelligence; intellect.

**지**(智) wisdom.

**지-**(至) 《까지》 to...; till...; until. ¶ 자(自) 오전 열시 지 오후 세시 from 10 a.m. to 3 p.m.

**-지**(地) ① 《땅〔곳〕》 ¶ 목적지 *one's* destination. ② 《옷감》 ¶ 양장지 dress material.

**-지** ① 《의문》 ¶ 어떻게 하는 것인지 가르쳐 주시오 Tell me how to do it. / 목욕물이 준비됐는지 물어 봐다오 Please ask if the bath is ready. / 그가 올지 안 올지 모르겠다 I don't know whether he will come or not. ② 《말끝》 ¶ 오늘은 누가 오겠지 Someone may come to see me today. / 부(否)가 3표에 가(可)가 10표였지 There were ten ayes against three noes. ③ 《부정》 저 배에는 사람이 타고 있지 않다 That ship has no passengers on board. / 사람이 많은데도 능률이 오르지 않는다 Sufficient efficiency is not obtained in spite of the large numbers of workers.

**지가**(地價) the price 〔value〕 of land; a land prices 〔value〕. ¶ 법정 ~ the assessed value of land / ~가 오른다 Land rises in value 〔price〕. ◉ ~수정 revaluation 〔reassessment〕 of land.

**지가**(紙價) the price of paper.

**지각**(地殼) 〚지질〛 the earth's crust; the lithosphere. ◉ ~변동 diastrophism. ~운동 tectonic 〔crustal〕 movements. ~평형 isostasy.

**지각**(知覺) ① 〚심리〛 perception; 《의식》 consciousness. ~하다 perceive; be conscious of; feel. ¶ ~할 수 없는 imperceptible / ~을 잃다 lose consciousness; fall insensible.
② 《철》 sense; judgment; wisdom; discretion. ¶ ~없이 against all sense; senselessly; thoughtlessly; imprudently; indiscreetly / ~날 나이 an age of discretion / ~이 있다〔없다〕 have 〔have no〕 sense; have 〔lack〕 prudence 〔discretion〕 / ~(이) 나다, ~(이) 들다 attain discretion; get *one's* senses; become sensible; cut 〔*one's*〕 wisdom teeth / 나이가 그만하면 ~날 때도 되었다 You are old enough to have more sense than that. / 그는 아직도 ~이 없다 He doesn't have sense enough to know better. / ~없는 말을 한다 You are saying foolish 〔absurd〕 things.
◉ ~기관 the organs of perception. ~동사 〚문법〛 a verb of perception. ~력 perception; perceptivity; the ability to perceive. ~마비 stupor. ~상실 a stupefaction; an(a)esthesia. ~신경 a sensory nerve. ~연령 〚법〛 age of discretion. ~착란 mental derangement.

**지각**(遲刻) a tardy; being late; lateness. ~하다 be late 《for》; be behind time; come late. ¶ 학교에 ~하다 be late for school / 직장에 ~하다 reach *one's* office late / ~하지 않고 회사에 가다 get to work on time / 그는 늘 ~한다 He is always behind time. *or* He always comes late. / 그는 내가 ~한 것을 나무랐다 He censured me for being late. ◉ ~생〔자〕 a tardy student; a latecomer. ~일수 the number of days late.

**지갑**(紙匣) 《동전용》 a purse; 《지폐용》 a pocketbook; a wallet; 《미》 a billfold. ¶ 가죽 ~ a leather pocketbook / 두툼한 ~ a well-lined purse; a plump purse / ~이 가볍다 have a light purse; be short of money; 《구어》 be feeling the draft / ～을 톡톡털다 spend *one's* last penny; spend all the money ⌊*one* has.

**지검**(地檢) ⇨지방 검찰청.

**지게** 《짐지는》 a coolie rack (for carrying things); an A-frame (carrier); a carrying rack; a back rack. ¶ ～를 지다 carry the A-frame on *one's* back / 물건을 ～에 얹다 put 〔load〕 《*things*》 on the A-frame carrier.

◉ ～꾼 an A-frame coolie; a burden carrier; a bearer. ～질: ～질하다 carry things on an A-frame. ～차 a forklift (truck). 지겟다리 the legs of an A-frame carrier.

**지게미** ① 《술의》 residue left after rice wine is drained; lees. ② 《눈곱》 eye mucus; gum (in the corner of the eye); 《구어》 sleep. ③ ＝비듬.

**지겹다** 《진저리나다》 (be) tedious; wearisome; tiresome; 《넌더리나다》 (be) loathsome; detestable; disgusting; repulsive. ⇨지긋지긋하다. ¶ 지겨워하다 be bored (with); feel disgusted 《at》; be fed up 《with》; be 〔get〕 sick of / 지겨운 듯이 disgustedly / 지겨운 녀석 a damnable 〔an accursed〕 fellow / 아이구 지겨워 Confound it! *or* Damn it! / 지겨운 비다 Damn this rain! / 생각만 하여도 ～ The bare idea makes 〔turns〕 me sick. / 이 지저분한 것을 치워야 한다니, 정말 ～ It's a pain in the neck when I have to clean this mess.

**지경**(地境) ① 《경계》 a boundary; a border. ¶ 인접지와의 ～ the boundary with the neighboring land / ～을 정하다 fix the boundary. ② 《형편》 a situation; a condition; circumstances. ¶ (…할) ～에 있다 be on the point 〔verge, brink〕 of; be about to; 《직면하다》 face / 죽을 ～이다 be in a bad fix / 파멸할 ～이다 stand on the brink of ruin / 그 회사는 파산 ～에 있다 The company stands face to face with bankruptcy. ⌈(창고).

**지계**(地階) 〖건축〗 a basement; a cellar

**지고**(至高) sublimity; supremacy. ～하다 (be) highest; most sublime; supreme. ◉ ～선(善) the supreme good.

**지골**(肢骨) bones of the extremities.

**지골**(指骨) a phalanx (*pl.* ～es, -langes); a phalange. ◉ ～관절 a knuckle joint.

**지공무사**(至公無私) supreme fairness and impartiality. ～하다 (be) absolutely fair 〔just〕.

**지공지평**(至公至平) supreme fairness; absolute justice. ～하다 (be) absolutely fair.

**지관**(地官) a geomancer.

**지구**(地球) the earth; the globe. ¶ ～ 표면 the surface of the earth / ～ 인력 terrestrial gravitation / ～의 공전〔자전〕 the revolution 〔rotation〕 of the earth / ～상에 있는 모든 생명 all life on 〔of〕 the earth / ～ 이외의 장소에 생물이 존재할 수 있는 가능성 the possibility of extraterrestrial life / ～의 반대쪽에서 half the globe 〔world〕 away / ～는 지축을 중심으로 자전한다 The earth revolves on its axis. / ～는 태양의 주위를 돈다 The earth goes 〔moves〕 around the sun.

◉ ～과학 earth science. ～ 관측위성 an earth observation satellite. ～궤도 the earth's orbit. ～물리학 geophysics. ～본〔의(儀)〕 a (terrestrial) globe. ～역학 geodynamics. ～온난화 global warming. ～인 an earthling; an earthman. ～중심설 the geocentric theory. ～촌 a global village. ～화학 geochemistry. ～환경금융 Global Environment Facility (생략 GEF).

**지구**(地區) a district; a zone; a region; an area; a section 《미》. ¶ 경인～ the Seoul-Inch'ŏn area 〔district〕.

◉ ～당 a (electoral) district party chapter; a (party's) constituency chapter: ～당 위원장 the chairperson of a district party chapter; a district leader 《미》 / ～당을 개편하다 reorganize a district party chapter; reorganize a provincial branch.

**지구**(地溝) 〖지질〗 a rift (valley); a trough. ◉ ～대(帶) a rift valley; a graben.

**지구**(持久) endurance; sustenance; durability; persistence. ～하다 hold out; endure; sustain; stay; persist.

◉ ～력 staying power; endurance; perseverance; tenacity; 《육체적》 stamina. ～책 a plan for holding out; dilatory tactics 〔measures〕; a Fabian policy: ～책을 강구하다 form a plan for holding out.

**지구전**(持久戰) ① 《전투》 a protracted 〔long-drawn-out〕 struggle 〔war〕. ¶ ～으로 돌입하다 get into the stage of position warfare. ② 《스포츠》 a contest 〔game〕 of endurance; an endurance contest 〔game〕.

**지국**(支局) a branch (office). ¶ 신문사 ～ a branch office of a newspaper.

◉ ～장 the head 〔manager〕 of a

branch; the branch manager.

**지그르르** simmering.

**지그시** ①《참는 모양》 patiently; perseveringly; with patience [perseverance]. ¶ 고생을 ~ 견디다 endure *one's* hardship stoically / 모욕을 ~ 참다 patiently put up with the insult. ②《누르거나 당기는 모양》 gently; softly; quietly. ¶ 소녀의 손을 ~ 잡다 hold a girl's hand tenderly / 소매를 ~ 잡아당기다 tug gently at 《*a person's*》 sleeve / 눈을 ~ 감다 close *one's* eyes gently.

**지그재그** zigzag. ¶ ~로 《walk》 in zigzags / ~로 나아가다 (go) zigzag; follow [trace] a zigzag course. ◉ ~ 행진 《데모대 등의》 《stage》 a snake dance; snake dancing.

**지극하다**(至極—) (be) extreme; utmost; exceeding. ¶ 그는 어머니에 대한 효성이 ~ He is extremely devoted to his mother.

**지극히**(至極—) extremely; exceedingly; very. ¶ ~ 아름다운 경치 a scene of exceeding beauty / ~ 중요한 문제 a very important matter; a problem of the greatest importance / ~ 겸손하다 be extremely modest; be modest 「to a high degree [in the extreme] / 그는 ~ 만족스러워 보였다 He looked highly pleased.

**지근**(支根) 『식물』 a rootlet; a radicle.

**지근**(至近) ¶ ~거리 the shortest range; point-blank range / ~탄 a near hit.

**지근거리다** ①《집적거리다》 annoy; bother; tease; make a nuisance 《of》; needle. ¶ 아무를 ~ needle *a person* / 지근거리며 돈을 달라다 pester 《*a person*》 for money / 지근거리지 말고 나를 가만 내버려 둬라 Don't bother me. Just leave me alone. ② 《머리가》 have a shooting pain 《in *one's* head》. ③ 《씹다》 chew softly.

**지글거리다** sizzle; simmer; bubble [foam] up; seethe.

**지글지글** sizzling; simmering; bubbling [foaming] up; seething. ¶ ~ 끓다 sizzle / 미움으로 속이 ~ 타다 *one's* mind seethes with hatred.

**지금**(只今) ① 《현재》 the present (time); this time [moment]; now; 《오늘날》 the present day. ¶ ~의 present (=day) / ~의 대통령 the present President 《of France》 / ~의 학생 students of today; present-day students; students nowadays / ~의 상태 the existing state of things / ~까지, ~껏 till [untill] now (★ until과 till은 대체로 같은 뜻이지만 until이 약간 강조적이며 clause, phrase가 주문(主文)에 선행하는 경우에 많이 씀); up to the present; by this time; up [down] to date; hither to / ~부터 from now (on); after this; hence / ~부터 10년 전 ten years ago / ~부터 50년 후 fifty years hence / ~이나 옛날이나 for all ages; now as in ages past / ~와서 돌이켜 볼 때 when I 「think of [look back to] it now / ~은 여름이다 It is summer now. / 그는 ~쯤 뭣하고 있을까 What can he be doing now? / 그가 ~쯤은 거기에 닿았겠다 I suppose he's there by this time. / ~에 와서 무엇을 근심하는 거냐 You needn't make yourself so uneasy now. / 때는 바로 ~이다 Now (is the time) or never. / ~부터라도 늦지 않다 It is not too late even yet. / ~까지 뭣하고 있었느냐 What have you been doing all this time [while]? / ~으로서는 자네의 도움이 필요 없네 For the time being, your help isn't necessary.
②《지금 막》 just; only [but] just; but [even] now; just now; a moment ago. ¶ ~ 다섯 시를 쳤다 It struck five just now. / 아버지는 ~ 막 떠나셨습니다 Father went out just a moment ago.
③《지금 곧》 soon; at once; (just) in a moment; immediately. ¶ ~ 지불해 주시오 Pay me this very instant. *or* Pay right away [off, now] / ~ 갑니다 I will come at once. *or* I am coming. / ~ 곧 오너라 Come here this very minute. / ~ 당장은 더 필요 없다 I don't need any at the moment.

**지금**(地金) ingot gold; 《토대가 되는》 ground metal; 《화폐의》 bullion.

**지금거리다** chew gritty; be gritty to the teeth. ¶ 밥이 ~ the rice is gritty.

**지금지금** gritty. ¶ ~ 씹히다 chew gritty.

**지급**(支給) 《공급》 provision; supply; furnishment; 《지불》 payment; defrayment. ⇨ 지불(支拂). ~하다 supply [provide] 《*a person*》 with 《*a thing*》; furnish; give; pay; grant; allow. ¶ 현금 ~ cash payment / 전액 ~의 《the expenses》 fully 「paid [covered] 《by》 / 의식(衣食)을 ~하다 supply 《*a person*》 with food and clothing / 여비를 ~하다 grant 《*a person*》 traveling allowance / 월급 100만 원을 ~하다 pay a salary of one million won / 재해자에게 식량을 ~하다 provide food to the victims.
◉ ~거절 refusal of payment. ~계정 an account payable. ~고 the amount

of payment. ～기일 the date for payment. ～기한 the time for payment; the date due: ～ 기한이 되다 《어음의》 fall 〔become〕 due; mature / ～ 기한을 넘다 be overdue. ～능력 solvency; ability to pay (세금의): ～ 능력이 있다 be solvent. ～명령 an order for payment. ～보증 《bank's》 payment guarantees; certification of payment: ～보증수표 a certified check. ～불능 inability to pay; insolvency: ～ 불능 기업 an insolvent enterprise. ～승낙 a guarantee for payment. ～액 the amount payable 〔paid〕. ～어음 a bill payable. ～유예 a moratorium; (a) postponement of payment; 《20 days》 grace: 오늘이 ～ 기한이지만, 1주간의 ～ 유예를 인정해 주었다 Payment is due today, but I gave him a week's grace. ～인 a payer; 《어음의》 a drawee. ～일 《급료의》 a pay-day; a pay-off. ～전표 a debit 〔payment〕 slip. ～정지 suspension of payment: ～ 정지 은행 a bank in suspension / ～ 정지를 하다 stop 〔suspend〕 payment. ～조건 terms of payment. ～준비금 a reserve fund for payment; payment reserves. ～준비제도 《은행의》 a reserve requirement system. ～지 the place of payment. ～창구(窓口) the paying teller's window. ～청구 a demand for payment: ～청구서 a written application for payment / ～청구를 하다 ask for 〔demand〕 payment.

**지급**(至急) utmost urgency; exigency. ～하다 (be) urgent; pressing; immediate. ¶ ～히 urgently; promptly; immediately; at once; without delay; with dispatch; with all haste 〔speed〕; as soon as possible / "～ 친전"이라고 써 있는 편지 a letter marked "private and urgent" / ～편으로 보내다 send 《a mail》 by express / 그 일은 ～을 요한다 The matter is pressing. ◉ ～전보〔전화, 편지〕 an urgent telegram 〔call, letter〕.

**지긋지긋하다** ① 《넌더리나다》 (be) tedious; wearisome; tiresome. ¶ 지긋지긋한 일 a tedious 〔boring, wearisome〕 task / 비도 지긋지긋하게 온다 We have had enough of rain. / 이젠 정치 싸움에는 지긋지긋해졌다 I am fed up with political bickering.
② 《지겹다》 (be) loathsome; detestable; tedious; repulsive; horrible. ¶ 지긋지긋한 광경 a horrible sight / 지긋지긋한 날씨 abominable weather / 생각만 해도 ～ It makes me sick even to think of it.

**지긋하다** be advanced in years; be well up in years. ¶ 나이(가) 지긋한 사람 an elderly person; a man well advanced in years.

**지기**(知己) 《아는 사람》 an acquaintance; 《친한 친구》 a close friend.

**지기**(志氣) will and spirit; spirit. ¶ 애국의 ～ spirit of patriotism / ～상합(相合)하다 be of a spirit; fall in with another's spirit.

**지기**(紙器) paper ware; a paper container.

**-지기**[1] 《논밭의》 an area 〔a measure〕 of land. ¶ 닷마지기 a plot of land that will take 5 *mal* of seed / 두 섬지기 a stretch of land requiring 2 *sŏm* of seed / 닷되지기 a field that takes 5 *toe* of seed.

**-지기**[2] 《사람》 a keeper; a guard. ¶ 등대지기 a lighthouse keeper / 산지기 a forest ranger / 능지기 a grave caretaker 〔keeper〕 / 문지기 a gatekeeper.

**지기지우**(知己之友) a close friend.

**지꺼분하다** ① 《눈이》 (be) dirty; gummy; mattery; be gummed-up; be full of gum. ¶ 지꺼분한 눈 gummy eyes. ② 《물건이》 (be) shabby; squalid. ¶ 물건을 지꺼분하게 늘어놓다 litter things up; leave litter around.

**지껄이다** talk garrulously; jabber; gibber; gabble; chatter. ¶ 잘 지껄이는 사람 a chatter-box; a great talker / 알 수 없는 말을 ～ talk jargon 〔nonsense〕; jabber / 함부로 ～ talk too freely; shoot off *one's* mouth 《구어》 / 그는 지껄이게 내버려두면 한이 없다 He would go on talking forever. / 이 일은 함부로 지껄이면 곤란해 Be sure and keep your mouth shut about this. *or* Mind you don't blab out this. / 너무 빨리 지껄이지 말고 천천히 말해 Speak more slowly, don't gabble.

**지끈** with a snap 〔crack, crash〕. ～하다 snap; give a snap; crack; crash. ¶ ～하고 부러지다 snap off; snap short / 돛대 부러지는 소리가 ～했다 There was the sound of the mast snapping.

**지끈지끈** ① 《부러지는 소리》 with a snap; snappingly. ② 《아픈 모양》 ¶ 골치가 ～ 아프다 I have a splitting 〔racking〕 headache.

**지나가다** ① 《통과하다》 go past; pass by. ¶ 지나가는 사람 a passerby / 문 앞을 ～ pass by the gate / 숲을 ～ go through a forest / 우연히 ～ happen

〔chance〕 to pass (by); pass by casually; happen along / 태풍은 지나갔다 The typhoon has passed. / 지나가는 길에 한번 들르시오 Please drop in sometime when you are passing by. ② ⇨ 지나다 ②, ③.

**지나다** ① 《통과하다》 pass (by); go past; pass through. ¶ 대구를 지났습니까 Have we passed Taegu yet? ② 《경과하다》 pass; elapse; go by. ¶ 지난 last; previous; former / 지난밤 last night / 지난 일 the past; bygones; a thing of the past / 지난달〔해〕 last month 〔year〕 / 6개월이 지나서 after six months; a half year later / 지난 일요일에 last Sunday; on Sunday last / 때가 지남에 따라 with the lapse of time; as days 〔years〕 go by / 지난 5년간 for the last 〔past〕 five years / 오랜 시일이 지났다 A long time has passed. / 그는 1주일이 지나면 돌아온다 He will come back in a week. (★ within a week는 「1주일 이내에」의 뜻) / 지난 일은 잊어버리자 Let's forget what's happened. *or* Let bygones be bygones. / 나는 지난 주의 오늘 대구에 있었다 I was in Taegu this day week. ③ 《한도·기한이》 exceed (the limits); go beyond. ¶ (…에) 지나지 않다 be nothing but; be more than; be only 〔mere, merely〕 / 기한이 ～ the term 〔time limit, date〕 expires; pass a fixed term; be overdue / 그것은 단지 추측에 지나지 않는다 It is no more than a guess. / 벌써 열 시가 지났다 It's already past ten o'clock. / 이 차표는 기한이 지났다 This ticket has expired. / 그는 일개 학생에 지나지 않는다 He is nothing but a student. / 그것은 구실에 지나지 않는다 That's a mere excuse.

**지나새나** night and day; day in day out; all the time. ¶ ～ 철학을 논하다 talk philosophy morning and night.

**지나오다** ① 《통과해 오다》 come by 〔along, through〕; pass by. ¶ 숲을 ～ come through a forest / 벌써 그 집을 지나온 것 같다 We must have passed that house. / 지금 지나온 정거장 이름은 무엇입니까 What is the name of the station we have just passed? ② 《겪다》 go through; undergo. ¶ 많은 간난을 ～ go through hardships and privations / 지나온 일을 생각하다 remember things gone by.

**지나치다** ① 《과도하다》 exceed; go beyond; go too far; overdo 《*it*》; go to excess; do 《*a matter*》 too much. ¶ 지나치게 먹다 overeat *oneself;* eat too much / 지나치게 일하다 work too hard; overwork *oneself* / 지나치게 술을 마시다 drink too much; drink to excess / 지나치게 똑똑하다 be too clever / 그에게 잔소리를 좀 지나치게 한것 같다 I am afraid I have given him too much of a scolding. / 그건 지나친 생각〔걱정〕일세 You take it too seriously. / …라고 해도 지나친 말은 아니다 It is not too much to say that… / 농담이 좀 ～ You carry your joke a little too far. / 운동이 지나쳐서 병이 났다 He made himself ill by his indulgence in sports. / 지나침은 모자람과 같다 Too much is as bad as too little. ② 《통과하다》 pass by; go past; pass through. ¶ 조는 사이에 두 정거장이나 지나쳤다 I dozed off and missed my station by two stops.

**지난**(至難) extreme difficulty. ～하다 (be) extremely 〔most〕 difficult. ¶ 이 기록을 깨뜨리는 것은 ～한 일이다 It is next to impossible 〔a task of extreme difficulty〕 to break this record.

**지난날** old days 〔times〕; days gone by; bygone days. ¶ ～의 추억 the memory of old days; old memories / ～을 그리워하다 think of the good old days / ～을 말하다 talk over old times / ～을 회고하다 look back on the past / ～의 아무를 회상하다 recall the memories of *a person*.

**지난번**(—番) the other day; some time ago; the last time; the most recent (time); the latest. ¶ ～ 받은 편지 the last letter received / ～ 그를 만났을 때에 when I saw him last; the last time I met him / ～ 말씀 드린 바와 같이 as I told you last time / ～에는 실례했습니다 I must beg your pardon for being rude to you the other day. / ～ 오셨을 때에는 별로 대접도 못 해드려 죄송합니다 I am awfully sorry there was but little to entertain you with when you came to see us the other day.

**지날결** in passing; when going by. ¶ ～에 잠깐 들렀습니다 I just dropped in to see you while passing by.

**지남석, 지남철**(指南石(鐵)) ① 《자석》 a magnet. ② ＝자침.

**지내다** ① 《살아가다》 pass; spend (time); live; get along. ¶ 하루를〔밤을〕 ～ pass a day 〔night〕 / 독서로 ～ spend *one's* time in reading / 외투 없이 겨울을 ～

go through the winter without an overcoat / 하루하루를 어렵게 ~ scrap a living from day to day; live from hand to mouth / 행복하게〔편히〕 ~ live happily 〔comfortably〕/ 휴가를 해변에서 ~ spend *one's* holidays by the seaside / 과부로 ~ live in widowhood / 어떻게 지내십니까 How are you getting along? / 그는 적은 봉급으로 겨우 지낸다 He ekes out life on a tiny salary. / 지난 여름을 어떻게 지냈느냐 How was your summer?

② 《겪다》 pursue 〔follow〕 a career; serve; go through; experience. ¶ 형사를 지낸 사람 a former detective / 관리를 ~ pursue an official career; be in the government service / 도지사를 지냈다 He has been a Governor.

③ 《치르다》 hold; celebrate. ¶ 장례를 ~ hold a funeral; perform a funeral service / 제사를 ~ perform ancestral rites / 생일을 ~ celebrate *one's* birthday.

**지내듣다** take no notice 《of》; pay little attention 《to》; give no heed 《to》. ¶ 남의 말을 ~ pay little attention to what others say.

**지내보다** go through; experience; get acquainted with. ¶ 사람은 지내봐야 안다 It takes time to really get to know a person. / 그는 지내볼수록 좋은 사람이다 He is the sort of man who improves on acquaintance. / 지내보니 좋은 친구였다 On further acquaintance I found him a jolly fellow.

**지네** 〖동물〗 a centipede; a scolopendrid. ¶ 침먹은 ~ [비유적] a person who is tongue-tied; a scaredy-cat; a coward.

**지네고사리** 〖식물〗 a wood fern.

**지노**(紙—) (a) paper string. ¶ ~를 꼬다 twist 〔twine〕 paper into a string.

**지느러미** a fin. ¶ 등〔가슴, 배, 꼬리, 뒷〕 ~ a dorsal 〔a pectoral, a ventral, a caudal, an anal〕 fin / ~가 있는 finned / ~가 없는 finless. ◉ ~발 a flipper; a pinna (*pl.* ~s, -nae).

**지능**(知能) intellectual 〔mental〕 faculties; intelligence; intellect. ¶ 보통 ~의 사람 a person with average intelligence / ~이 우수한 사람들 men of high intellectual power / ~이 높은〔낮은〕 사람 a person of high 〔little〕 intelligence / ~이 낮은 아이 a mentally retarded child / ~이 낮다 be feeble-minded; show little intelligence (★ strong-mined는 「의지가 강하다」는 뜻.) / ~을 계발하다 develop *one's* intellectual powers; improve *one's* mind. ◉ ~검사 an intelligence test: ~ 검사를 하다 give an intelligence test. ~로봇 an intelligent robot. ~발달 intellectual growth. ~범 《범죄》 an intellectual offense 〔crime〕; 《범인》 a thinking 〔smart 《구어》〕 criminal. ~연령 the mental age. ~정도 an intellectual standard. ~지수 intelligence quotient (생략 I.Q.): ~ 지수가 130이다 have an IQ of 130.

**지니다** 《보전하다》 keep; preserve; retain; maintain; 《가지다》 carry; have; 《품다》 hold; entertain; cherish; 《기억하다》 keep in mind; commit to memory; remember. ¶ 장서를 많이 ~ have a large library / 몸에 ~ take with; carry; bring; 《무기를》 be armed / 비밀을 ~ cherish a secret / 몸에 권총을 ~ carry a pistol with *one* / 늘 지니고 다니다 carry 《*a thing*》 always about 〔on〕 *one* / 병독을 ~ carry a poisonous virus / 기념으로 시계를 ~ keep a watch as a memento / 그는 모든 학생의 인기를 한 몸에 지니고 있다 He commands the popularity of all students.

**지닐성**(—性) the quality of carrying 〔preserving, remembering〕.

**지다**[1] ① 《짐을》 carry on the back; bear. ¶ 짐을〔지게를〕 ~ carry a pack 〔an A-frame〕 on the back / 무거운 짐을 ~ bear a heavy burden.

② 《빚을》 owe (money); get into debt. ¶ 빚을 ~ get into debt; owe money / 그에게 빚을 얼마 졌나 How much (money) do you owe him?

③ 《신세를》 owe; be indebted 〔due〕 《to》; be under an obligation 《to》. ¶ 신세를 ~ be indebted 《to *a person*》; owe 《*a person*》 a debt of gratitude; be under indebtedness to 《*a person*》; be a burden to; be under the care of / 신세를 많이 졌습니다 I am indebted to you for kindness.

④ 《책임을》 assume 《a responsibility》; bear; take. ¶ 그가 모든 책임을 지고 그 것을 했다 He did it on his own responsibility. / 이 이상 책임을 질 수 없다 I can't be saddle with any more responsibilities. / 그는 분실물에 대해서 책임을 지지 않는다고 말했다 He refused to be liable for lost articles. / 자네가 전력을 다한다면 결과에 대한 책임은 내가 지지 If you do your best, I will answer for the consequences.

**지다**[2] ① 《꽃·잎이》 (fade and) fall; be shed; be gone; be strewn 《to the ground》. ¶ 지기 시작하다 begin to fall / 곧 꽃이 지겠다 The flowers will soon be gone. / 벚꽃이 다 졌다 The cherry blossoms are all gone.
② 《해·달이》 set; sink; go down; decline; grow 〔get〕 dark (저물다). ¶ 지는 달 the sinking 〔setting〕 moon / 해가 ~ the sun sets 〔sinks〕 / 해질 무렵 at dusk 〔nightfall〕; toward evening / 해가 지고 나서 after dark 〔sunset〕 / 해가 지기 전에 before (it is) dark; before sundown 〔sunset〕 / 해는 동쪽에서 떠서 서쪽으로 진다 The sun rises in the east and sets in the west.
③ 《목숨이》 breathe *one's* last breath; give up *one's* breath; expire; die.
④ 《때 등이》 come off 〔out〕; be removed; be taken out; wash off 〔out〕; fade away. ¶ 아무리 빨아도 얼룩이 지지 않는다 The stains will not come out, however hard I may try to wash them off.

**지다**[3] 《패배하다》 get 〔be〕 defeated; be beaten 〔outdone〕; lose; be bested; 《굴하다》 give in 《to》; yield 《to》; succumb 〔give way〕 《to》; 《못하다》 be inferior 《to》; be second 《to》; fall behind; be behind.
¶ 지기 싫어하는 unyielding; unbending / 전쟁〔소송, 경기〕에 ~ lose a war 〔lawsuit, game〕 / 유혹에 ~ give way to temptation / 일부러 져주다 《승부에서》 concede 〔yield〕 《*a person*》 the palm of victory; lose a game just to please the opponent; throw a game / 매수되어 져주다 be paid to throw the game / 일시적 감정에 ~ be carried away by the feeling of the moment / 경쟁에 ~ lose in a contest 〔competition〕 / 큰 득점차로 ~ be beaten by a large score / 유혹에 지지 않다 withstand temptation / 그는 아직 누구에게도 져본 일이 없다 He remains unbeaten. *or* He has never met his match yet. / 그에게 지지 않으려고 더한층 노력했다 Not to be outdone by him, I worked harder. / 그의 재주는 누구에도 지지 않는다 As far as talent is concerned, he is second to none. / 그런 사람에겐 지기 싫다 I don't want to give in to somebody like him. / 우리는 2대 1로 시합에서 졌다 We were defeated in the 《baseball》 game by two to one. *or* We lost the 《baseball》 game by two to one. / 당신에 대한 사랑은 누구에게도 지지 않아요 I yield to none in my love for you. *or* I love you more than anyone else does. (★ does를 빼면 anyone else가 주격인지 목적격인지 불분명해짐). / 그녀는 지기 싫어하는 성격이다 She hates losing 〔to lose〕.

**지다**[4] ① 《그늘이》 cast a shadow; shade; get shady 〔shaded〕; form shade; be shaded. ¶ 그늘진 길 a shady path / 나무 때문에 집에 그늘이 너무 진다 The trees 「shade the house too much 〔overshadow the house〕.
② 《얼룩이》 be stained; get spotted. ¶ 얼룩이 ~ get stained; be smudged.

**지다**[5] 《장마가》 set in. ¶ 홍수가 ~ 《집·논밭이》 be flooded; be under water; be inundated / 장마가 졌다 The rainy season has set in.

**지다**[6] 《되어 가다》 get to be; become; grow. ¶ 좋아〔나빠, 추워, 더워, 피곤해〕 ~ get better 〔worse, colder, warmer, tired〕 / 공부가 싫어 ~ get tired of studying / 기울어 ~ 《it》 tilt / 날이 차차 길어진다 The days are getting longer and longer. / 이제는 음악이 좋아졌다 Now I've come to like music. / 폭풍우는 점점 더 심해졌다 The storm grew more and more severe.

**지다위** ① 《기댐》 leaning 〔relying〕 on 《*a person*》; 《괴롭힘》 pestering. ~하다 look 〔turn〕 to 《*a person*》 for help; importune 〔pester, tease〕 《*a person*》 for 《money》. ② 《전가함》 laying *one's* responsibility on 《another》. ~하다 lay *one's* responsibility on 《another》; lay the blame at 《another's》 door.

**지당하다**(至當—) (be) quite right 〔true, natural, reasonable〕; proper; fair; just. ¶ 지당하신 말씀이오 You are right. / 그 말도 지당하기는 하다 There is some truth in what you say.

**지대**(支隊) a detachment; detached troops.

**지대**(地代) land 〔ground〕 rent. ¶ ~가 비싼〔싼〕 high-〔low-〕rented / ~의 인상 the raising of ground rents / ~를 받다 collect ground rents / ~로 생활하다 live on the revenue from lands.

**지대**(地帶) a zone; an area; a belt; a region. ¶ 구릉 ~ hilly districts / 공장〔주택〕 ~ an industrial 〔a residential〕 area 〔zone〕 / 녹 ~ a green belt / 면화 ~ 《미국 남부의》 the Cotton Belt / 사막〔산림〕 ~ a desert 〔forest〕 region.

**지대공**(地對空) ¶ ~의 ground-to-air.
◉ ~미사일 a ground-to-air missile.

**지대지**(地對地) ¶ ～의 ground-to-ground. ◉ ～미사일 a ground-to-ground missile.

**지대하다**(至大—) (be) immense; vast; enormous; very great. ¶ 지대한 관심사 a matter of great interest / 그는 한국 부흥에 지대한 공헌을 하였다 He has greatly contributed to the rehabilitation of Korea.

**지더리다** (be) mean; vile; low; gross; vulgar; dirty. ¶ 천성이 ～ be low-minded; be a man of vile character.

**지덕**(地德) the auspicious effect of a site.

**지덕**(知德) knowledge and virtue. ¶ 그는 ～을 겸비한 사람이다 He combines 〔is gifted with〕 knowledge and virtue.

**지도**(地圖) a map; 《지도책》 an atlas; 《해도》 a chart.

> 용법 **map** 지구의 표면 또는 그 일부, 또는 그 위에 있는 건조물 등을 나타낸 지도. **atlas** 몇 개의 map나 chart를 철해서 한 권의 책으로 만든 지도. **chart** 항공 또는 항해용 지도.

¶ 간단한 ～ a rough map / 상세한 ～ a detailed map / 정확한 ～ an accurate map / 한국〔세계〕 ～ a map of Korea 〔the world〕 / 도로 ～ a road map / 백분의 일 ～ a map on a one-hundredth scale / 20만분의 1 ～ a map on a scale of 1 to 200,000 (★ one to two hundred thousand라고 읽음. scale은 「축척」의 뜻.) / ～로 찾다 search a map for 《a place》; look up 《a place》 on a map / ～에 있다〔없다〕 be 〔be not〕 on maps 〔the map〕 / ～를 그리다 draw a map 〔plan〕 / ～ 보는 법을 배우다 take lessons in map-reading / ～ 보는 법을 잘 알고 있다 be good at reading maps / ～를 보다 consult 〔read〕 a map / 그 나라는 ～에서 사라졌다 The country was wiped off the map. ◉ ～제작 cartography: ～제작자 a cartographer; a map-maker; a mapper. ～책 an atlas. 괘～ a wall map. 구면(球面)～ a globular map. 역사～ a historical map. 접～ a folding map.

**지도**(指導) guidance; leadership; leading; direction; coaching (경기 등의). ～하다 guide; lead; instruct; coach; direct; run. ¶ ～층 인사(人士)들 people in the leadership class / …의 ～ 밑에 under 《*a person's*》 guidance; under the leadership 〔guidance, direction〕 of… / 홍 교수 ～ 밑에서 연구하다 study under the guidance of Prof. Hong / 잘못 ～하다 misdirect; misguide; lead 〔direct, guide〕 *a person* wrongly 〔amiss〕 / ～에 따르다 follow the lead / ～적 역할을 하다 play the part of the leader; take the lead; play a leading part 《in》 / ～를 바라다 look to 《*a person*》 for guidance / ～의 임무를 맡다 assume the leadership 《of》; undertake the task of teaching 〔coaching〕 / ～적인 입장에 있다 be in a position of leadership.
◉ ～교사 a guidance teacher. ～교수 a tutor; an (academic) adviser. ～권 leadership; hegemony; ascendency 《over》: ～권을 쥐다 assume 〔grasp〕 the leadership. ～료 a consultancy fee: 기술 ～료 a technical guidance fee. ～반 a guiding group. ～방침〔원리〕 guiding principle(s); guidelines. ～법 a method of guidance; how to guide 《*one's* pupil》. ～부 a guidance 〔fostering〕 division. ～서 a guide (= book); a manual. ～안 a guidance plan; 《학과의》 a teaching plan. ～요령 〖교육〗 guidelines. ～원(員) an instructor; a supervisor; an advisor: …를 위해 ～원을 파견하다 dispatch an advisor to give proper guidance about…. ～위원(회) a direction 〔steering〕 committee; a guidance committee (정당의). ～정신 a guiding spirit 〔idea〕; a governing principle. ～층 the leadership. 단일〔집단〕～체제 a one-man 〔a collective〕 leadership system.

**지도력**(指導力) *one's* leadership; qualities of 〔the capacity for〕 leadership. ¶ 대단한 ～이 있다 have great leadership / ～을 발휘하다 exercise *one's* leadership.

**지도리** hook-and-eye hinges; hinges.

**지도자**(指導者) a leader; a guide; a director; the mentor (of a group); a coach; a rudder. ¶ ～의 교체 a change of 〔in〕 leadership; 《make》 a leadership change 《in the Socialist Party》 / ～가 되다 become a leader; assume leadership 《of, in》.

**지독하다**(至毒—) ① 《독하다》 (be) vicious; venomous; vitriolic; atrocious; spiteful; ferocious. ¶ 지독한 말 vicious 〔vitriolic〕 remarks / 지독한 여자 a spiteful woman / 지독한 짓 an atrocious act / 지독한 모욕 a gross insult.
② 《모질다》 (be) hard; severe; terri-

ble; extreme; dreadful; awful; exorbitant; outrageous; terrific. ¶ 지독한 구두쇠 an awful miser / 지독한 추위 severe 〔bitter〕 cold / 지독한 눈〔비〕 a heavy snow 〔rain〕 / 지독하게 공부하다 study awfully hard / 지독한 감기에 걸리다 catch a nasty cold / 그는 지독한 근시다 He is dreadfully nearsighted. / 정말이지 지독한 날씨다 What terrible 〔nasty〕 weather we're having! / 지독한 더위다 It is terribly 〔awfully, exceedingly〕 hot.
③《완강하다》(be) tough; unflinching; dogged; die-hard; stubborn; stiff; hard-boiled; bigoted. ¶ 지독한 사람 a very determined person; a die-hard.

**지동**(地動) ①《지진》 an earthquake. ②《공전·자전》 the terrestrial movement; the revolution and the rotation of the earth. ◉ ～설 the heliocentric theory; the Copernican theory 〔system〕.

**지둔**(至鈍) extreme stupidity. ～하다 (be) extremely stupid 〔dull〕.

**지둔**(遲鈍) dullness; slowness; stupidity. ～하다 (be) slow; dull; stupid.

**지디피** 《국내 총생산》 GDP. 〔< *G*ross *D*omestic *P*roduct〕

**지딱** hurriedly and at random; recklessly. ～지딱하다, ～거리다 do 《it》 hurriedly.

**지라** 〚해부〛 the spleen; the milt.

**지란지교**(芝蘭之交) sweet and noble friendship.

**지랄** an epileptic fit; (an attack of) epilepsy (간질); a fit (of hysteria, unreasonableness). ～하다 act unreasonably; behave rampageously; get out of line; make a fuss; make a scene; go crazy; have a fit; get hysterical. ◉ ～버릇 fitfulness; freakishness; whim; capriciousness; fickleness; irregularity; unreliability; unpredictability. ～병 epilepsy: ～병 환자 an epileptic. ～쟁이 《변덕쟁이》 a capricious 〔an unreliable, an irresponsible〕 person.

**지략**(智略) 《슬기》 cleverness; strategy; resourcefulness. ¶ ～이 풍부한 사람 a man of resources; a resourceful mind / ～이 풍부하다 be resourceful; be full of resources.

**지러지다** wither; shrivel; get stunted. ¶ 그늘이 너무 지면 꽃이 자라지 못하고 지러진다 The flowers won't have a chance to grow if the place is too shady—they'll get stunted.

**지런지런** ①《넘칠 듯》 to the brim; brimfully. ②《닿을락 말락》 scraping close; almost touching.

**지렁이** 〚동물〛 the earthworm; 《낚시 미끼》 an angleworm; fishworm. ¶ ～도 밟으면 꿈틀한다 《속담》 Even a worm will turn. *or* Even the meekest will lose his temper finally.

**지레**[1] 《지렛대》 a lever; a handspike. ¶ ～질하다 lever / ～로 들어올리다 raise 《*a thing*》 with a lever.
◉ ～작용 leverage; purchase.

**지레**[2] 《미리》 in advance; beforehand. ¶ ～알리다 let 《*a person*》 know beforehand 〔in advance〕; give prior 〔advance〕 notice / 돈을 ～ 찾아 쓰다 get an advance of money.

**지레짐작**(—斟酌) guesswork; a hasty conclusion 〔deduction〕. ～하다 guess; jump to conclusions; form 〔come to〕 a hasty conclusion. ¶ …이라고 ～하다 run away with the idea that… / 쌀값이 오를 것을 ～하고 쌀을 사 두다 buy up rice in hasty anticipation of a rise in price.

**지레채다** know beforehand; foresee; perceive in advance; anticipate. ¶ 눈치를 ～ foresee 〔anticipate〕 《*a person's*》 intention 〔motive〕 / 남의 이야기를 ～ guess the point of another's story in advance.

**지력**(地力) fertility of soil. ◉ ～체감(遞減) diminishing fertility.

**지력**(智力) intellectual power; mental capacity; intellect; mentality. ¶ ～이 발달한 intellectual; intelligent / 그는 12세 아이의 ～정도이다 He has a mentality of a 12-year old. *or* His I.Q. 〔mental〕 age is not above 12.

**지력선**(指力線) 〚물리〛 lines of force.

**지령**(指令) an order; a directive; an instruction; 〚컴퓨터〛 a command. ¶ ～을 내리다 issue an order; give directions; instruct / 조합원에게 파업 ～을 내리다 order the union members out on strike / 무전으로 ～을 받다 receive radio instructions 《from》.
◉ ～서 written instructions 〔orders〕. 비밀～ a secret order.

**지령**(紙齡) the issue number of a periodical.

**지론**(持論) *one's* cherished opinion 〔view〕; *one's* pet theory; a stock argument. ¶ ～을 굽히지 않다 stick 〔hold fast〕 to *one's* opinion; persist in *one's* views / ～대로 실행하다 act up to *one's* opinion / 나의 ～은 이렇다 I am of (the) opinion that….

**지뢰**(地雷) a (land) mine. ¶ ～를 묻다 lay 〔charge〕 a mine / 적의 ～를 폭파하다 spring a mine laid by the enemy / ～를 제거〔회수〕하다 remove 〔retrieve〕 mines / ～를 매설하는 군인 a miner. ◉ ～밭〔원, 지대〕 a mine field. ～탐지기 a mine detector. 핵～ Atomic Demolition Munitions (생략 ADMs); nuclear land mines.

**지루하다** (be) tedious; tiresome; wearisome; boring. ¶ 지루한 여행〔강연〕 a tedious journey 〔lecture〕 / 지루하고 긴 장마 a long and tiresome rainy season / 이야기가 지루해서 넌더리나다 get bored with a tedious talk / 지루해 죽겠다 Time hangs heavy on my hands. / 이 책은 ～ This book bores me. / 그것은 지루했다 It turned out to be boring.

**지류**(支流) a tributary; a branch stream; an affluent. ¶ 한강과 그 ～ the Han River and its tributaries.

**지르다** ① 《소리를》 holler; yell; scream; cry aloud. ¶ 고함을 ～ yell; shout; holler / 비명을 ～ let out a shriek; scream / 오라고 소리를 ～ shout for 《*a person*》 to come.
② 《차다》 give a hard kick 《at》; kick hard; 《치다》 strike; hit; beat. ¶ 발로 정강이를 ～ kick 《*a person's*》 shin / 공을 ～ kick a ball / 얼굴을 ～ strike 《*a person*》 across 〔in〕 the face.
③ 《꽂아 넣다》 insert; thrust 〔stick, put〕 in. ¶ 빗장을 ～ bolt 〔bar〕 a door / 머리에 비녀를 ～ stick a hairpin in *one's* hair; wear a hairpin.
④ 《불을》 set fire to. ¶ 집에 불을 ～ set a house on fire.
⑤ 《자르다》 cut off; snip; nip. ¶ 순을 ～ cut 〔nip〕 off the buds.
⑥ 《기운을 꺾다》 crush; damper; cast a damp over 《*a person's* spirits》. ¶ 적의 예기를 ～ break the brunt of the enemy.
⑦ 《질러 가다》 shorten 《the way》; take a shorter way. ¶ 길을 질러 가다 take a short cut.
⑧ 《걸다》 stake; wager. ¶ 판에 돈을 ～ lay (down) a bet 《on the gambling table》; put money down.

**지르되다** grow slowly; be of slow growth.

**지르르** ① 《윤기·기름기가》 dribbling; dripping; glossy with grease. ¶ 개기름이 ～ 도는 얼굴 *one's* face glossy with grease. ② 《저린 느낌》 with a dull pain 《in the joints》.

**지르박** 《춤의 하나》 the jitterbug.

**지르신다** slip 《shoes》 halfway on; wear shoes half-on; wear socks slipped down over the heels.

**지르잡다** hold the soiled part of a garment and wash it off. ¶ 지르잡아 빨다 wash off a spot / 얼룩을 ～ wash the stain out; wash out the stain.

**지르코늄** 〖화학〗 zirconium (기호 Zr).

**지르콘** 〖광물〗 zircon. ◉ ～산 zirconic acid.

**지르퉁** sulky; sullen; pouting. ～하다 (be) sulky; sullen; pouting. ¶ 무엇 때문에 ～해있나 What makes you so sulky? / 그는 ～하여 말이 없었다 He was in a sulky mood and wouldn't say a word.

**-지를** ¶ 도리어 결과가 좋지를 못했다 On the contrary the results were no good at all.

**지름** 《직경》 a diameter. ¶ ～이 10미터다 It is 〔measures〕 ten meters in diameter. ◉ 반～ a radius.

**지름길** a shorter road; a short cut. ¶ 성공으로 가는 ～ a short cut to success / 신당동으로 빠지는 ～ a short cut to Shindang-dong / ～을 잡아들다 take a shorter way / 정거장으로 가는 ～을 가르쳐 주십시오 Show me a short cut to the station. / 저축의 증대는 외채를 줄이는 ～이다 Increasing savings is the shortcut to reducing the foreign debts. / 우리는 ～로 왔다 We came by a short cut.

**지릅뜨기** (a person with) upturned eyes.

**지릅뜨다** cast an upturned glance. ¶ 성이 나서 눈을 ～ cast an upturned glance at 《*a person*》 with anger.

**지리**(地理) 《지형》 geographical features; topography; the lay of the land; 《지리학》 geography. ¶ ～상의 geographical; topographical / ～적 위치〔조건, 분포〕 geographical position 〔conditions, distribution〕 / 그 곳 ～에 밝다 be quite familiar with that place; know the geography of the place / 나는 이 곳 ～에 어둡다 I am a stranger here. ◉ ～정보 geographic information. ～책 a geography (book). ～학자 a geographer. 인문〔정치〕～(학) human 〔political〕 geography.

**지리**(地利) ① 《편리·이점》 advantages of a locality 〔situation〕; geographical advantages. ② 《생산》 profits from land; production; produce.

**지리다**[1] 《냄새가》 (be) smell of urine.

**지리다**[2] 《조금 싸다》 wet 〔soil〕 *one's* pants.

**지리멸렬**(支離滅裂) 《부조리》 incoherence; inconsistency; 《사분오열》 disruption; breaking up in pieces; separation; split. ～하다 be incoherent 〔irrelevant〕; 《사분오열하다》 be disrupted; be torn asunder; break up; come to pieces; split 《into fractions》. ¶ ～한 대열 a disordered line / ～이 되다 lose *its* coherence; fall into a chaotic condition. 「《of laundry》.

**지린내** the smell of urine; a stale smell

**-지마는, -지만** but; however; yet; though; although; notwithstanding the fact that. (★ "「나이는 젊지만 직무에 밝다」의 Though young, yet he is well up in his profession.에서 yet을 but로 써도 되는가"—이 yet은 앞의 though와 상관적으로 쓰여 though를 강조하는 뜻이므로 생략은 해도 되나 but로 대체할 수는 없음. but을 쓰면 He is young, but…로 됨). ¶ 영웅이었지만 hero as he was, … (★ 이 경우 명사는 무관사.) / 나이는 먹었지마는 though he is old; old as he is / 그는 훌륭한 학자지만 Fine scholar as he is … (★ 이 구문에서는 단수형 보통명사라도 a가 붙지 않음: Young teacher as he is… ) / 역설같이 들릴지는 모르지만 Paradoxical as it may sound, … / 그에게 결점은 있지만 그래도 나는 그가 좋다 I like him none the less for his faults. / 몇 번이고 해 보았지만 번번히 실패였다 I tried over and over again, only to fail each time. / 그는 나이는 어리지만 충분히 그 일을 해 낼 힘이 있다 Young as he is, he is equal to the task. / 비가 오지마는 나는 간다 Although it is raining, I will go. / 가난하지마는 그는 남을 잘 도와준다 Though he is poor, he is willing to help others. / 그렇지만 나는 네 계획에 찬성할 수 없다 I cannot approve of your plan, however. / 그가 오기야 오겠지마는 너무 늦지 않았으면 좋겠다 He's sure to come, all right, but I hope he won't be too late. / 가고는 싶었지만 시간이 없었다 I wanted to come, but I had no time.

**지망**(志望) a wish; a desire; an aspiration; an ambition; 《선택》 choice. ～하다 desire; aspire to; wish; apply for; choose; 《좋아하다》 prefer. ¶ ～대로 as *one* wishes / 외교관을 ～하다 wish to be a diplomat; aspire to a diplomatic career / 나는 신문 기자를 ～한다 I wish to be a journalist. *or* I aspire to be a pressman. / ～하는 직업을 기입해라 State the profession preferred. ◉ ～학과 the desired course of study. ～학교 the school of *one's* choice; the school preferred. 제1〔제2〕～ *one's* first 〔second〕 preference 〔choice〕.

**지망자**(志望者) an applicant; an aspirant; a candidate. ¶ 문학 ～ a literary aspirant / 취직 ～ an applicant for employment / 입학 ～ an applicant for admission to a school / 여배우 ～ prospective 〔would-be〕 actress / 많은 ～가 있었다 There were many applicants 《for a post》.

**지망지망** carelessly; heedlessly; thoughtlessly; indifferently. ¶ 일을 ～ 하다 do a slipshod 〔slapdash〕 job.

**지맥**(支脈) 《식물의》 a spur; an offset; 《수맥의》 feeder; 《산맥의》 a branch of a mountain range.

**지맥**(地脈) a stratum (*pl.* -ta, ～s); a layer; a vein 《of rock》.

**지면**(地面) 《지표》 the surface of land; the ground (땅바닥); 《지상》 the earth. ¶ ～에서 5미터 위에 five meter above the ground / ～에 털썩 주저앉다 sit flat 〔directly〕 on the ground / ～에는 눈이 3미터나 쌓여 있다 The snow lies three meters deep on the ground. / 비행기가 ～에 추락했다 The airplane crashed to the ground. / 나는 ～이 흔들리고 있는 것을 느꼈다 I felt the earth shake.

**지면**(知面) acquaintance.

**지면**(紙面) 《신문의》 paper; a sheet; 《여백》 space. ¶ ～관계로 on account of limited space; for want of space / ～이 허락하면 if space permits 〔allows〕 / …에 많은 ～을 할애하다 devote a good deal of space to… / ～을 확장하다 increase the printed columns of a paper / 그녀의 결혼 기사가 신문 ～을 장식했다 An article about her marriage appeared in the newspaper.

**지면**(誌面) the space 〔pages〕 of a magazine 〔journal, periodical〕. ¶ ～에 in a magazine / ～을 통해 through a magazine.

**지멸있다** (be) steady; faithful. ¶ 지멸있게 steadily; constantly; faithfully; persistently.

**지명**(地名) the name of a place; a place name; a geographical designation. ◉ ～사전 a geographical dictionary; a gazetteer.

**지명**(知名) a wide reputation. ¶ ～의 well-known; noted; distinguished; eminent; celebrated. ◉ ～인사 a man of fame 〔note, distinction〕; a well=

known person; a celebrity. ～작가 an eminent author 〔writer〕.

**지명**(知命) ① 《천명을 앎》 knowing the decrees of Heaven. ② 《50세》 the age of fifty years.

**지명**(指名) naming; nomination; designation; appointment. ～하다 nominate; designate; name; mention; call on 《*a person*》 to *do;* pick (on) 《a student to answer the question》. ¶ ～순으로 in the order of the persons called 〔mentioned〕 / 의장으로～하다 nominate for chairperson / 그는 대통령 후보로 ～되었다 He was nominated for a presidential candidate. / 그는 아들을 후계자로 ～했다 He designated his son as his successor. / 미국의 대통령 후보 ～은 선거가 있는 해의 여름에 행해진다 Nominations for President of the United States take place in the summer before the election. ◉ ～수락 연설 an acceptance speech. ～수배 a search for the named suspect (under an arrest warrant): ～수배자 a most wanted criminal / 전국 ～수배 all-points bulletin (생략 APB) / ～수배하다 put 《*a person*》 on the wanted list. ～스트라이크 a strike 〔walkout〕 by union-designated workers. ～입찰 a tender by designated companies. ～자 a nominator; a designator: 피～자 a nominee. ～타자 《야구의》 a designated hitter (생략 DH). ～통화 《전화에서》 a person-to=person call; a personal call 《영》. ～투표 a roll-call vote. ～해고 the dismissal of named 〔designated〕 workers.

**지명도**(知名度) name value; how well one is known; 《악명의》 notoriety. ¶ ～가 높은 well-known; noted / ～에 따라 사람을 평가하다 judge *a person* by how widely *he* is known / 우리 회사는 아직 이 지방에서 ～가 낮다 Our company is 「not well-known 〔of little note〕 in this district.

**지모**(智謀) ingenuity; resourcefulness. ¶ ～가 풍부한 사람 a man of resources / ～가 뛰어나다 be resourceful.

**지목**(地目) the classification of land category; land classification. ◉ ～변경 reclassification of land; a change in the category of land: ～ 변경 신고 declaration of change of land category.

**지목**(指目) pointing out; indication. ～하다 point out; spot; indicate; designate; put the finger on. ¶ 그를 범인으로 ～하다 spot him as a criminal / 나는 그를 주모자로 ～하고 있다 I think he must be at the bottom of the affair.

**지문**(地文) the physical features and changes of the earth. ◉ ～학 physical geography; physiography: ～학자 a physiographer.

**지문**(指紋) a fingerprint; a finger mark; a dactylogram; a thumb print (엄지 손가락의). ¶ ～을 채취하다 take 《*a person's*》 fingerprints; fingerprint 《*a person*》 / ～을 남기다 leave *one's* fingerprints 《on *a thing*》 / ～을 남기지 않도록 장갑을 끼다 wear gloves to avoid leaving fingerprints / ～을 찾아내다 detect fingerprints. ◉ ～감식 fingerprint identification. ～날인 fingerprinting: ～날인 문제 the fingerprinting issue / ～날인을 거부하다 refuse to be fingerprinted. ～채취 fingerprinting: 재일 외국인의 ～ 채취 제도 the system of fingerprinting for foreigners residing in Japan / ～ 채취 등록 제도에 항의하다 protest against the fingerprinting registration system. ～학 dactylography.

**지물**(紙物) paper goods. ◉ ～포 a paper goods store.

**지미**(地味) the quality 〔nature〕 of soil. ¶ 비옥한 ～ fertile 〔rich〕 soil.

**지미**(至美) supreme beauty. ～하다 (be) supremely beautiful.

**지반**(地盤) ① 《토대》 the base; the foundation; 《지면》 the ground. ¶ 단단한 ～ firm 〔solid〕 ground / ～을 굳히다 solidify 〔harden〕 the foundation. ② 《발판》 footing; foothold; position. ¶ 확고한 ～ a firm foothold / ～을 닦다 establish *one's* footing. ③ 《세력 범위》 a sphere of influence; 《선거구》 a constituency. ¶ 선거의 ～을 쌓다 nurse *one's* constituency; mend *one's* (political) fences 《미》 / 서울을 ～으로 출마하다 run for election with Seoul as *one's* constituency / 그의 ～은 굳은 편이다 His constituency is pretty solid. / 그는 Y씨의 ～을 파고 들어갔다 He has encroached upon Mr. Y's sphere of influence. ◉ ～침하(沈下) 《토지의》 ground 〔land〕 subsidence; 《정당 따위의》 a decline in support.

**지반자**(紙—) 〖건축〗 a papered ceiling.

**지방**(地方) 《지구》 a locality; a district; a region; an area; a section (of the

country); 《시골》 the country; the provinces; 《부근》 the neighborhood; the vicinity.
¶ ～의, ～적인 local; sectional; regional; provincial / 서울 ～ Seoul and its neighboring districts / 서북 ～ northwestern districts / 이 ～ this part [section] of the country; these parts / ～ 사람 country people / ～적 편견 localism; sectionalism / ～에 가다 go to [into] the country / ～에서 상경하다 come up from the country.
◉ ～거래처 a local client. ～검사 a district attorney. ～검찰청 the district public prosecutor's office. ～경찰 the local police. ～계획 regional planning. ～(공공)단체 a local [regional] public body. ～공무원 a local government employee [worker]; a provincial government official. ～공연 a provincial tour: ～공연을 하다 make a provincial tour; go on [take] the road 《미》. ～관청 a local government. ～교부세 (the portion of national) tax revenue allocated to local government. ～기사 local news. ～노선(路線) 《철도의》 a local line. ～도시 a provincial city [town]. ～법원 a district court: ～ 법원 판사 a district judge. ～분권(分權) (the) decentralization of power [authority]. ～사투리 a local accent [dialect (방언)]; a brogue: ～ 사투리가 심하다 speak with a brogue [broad provincial accent]. ～색 local color; localism: 이 민요는 ～색이 잘 나타나 있다 This folksong is full of local color. ～선거 a local election: ～의회 선거 a local assembly election. ～선거구 a prefectural constituency. ～선거법 local (autonomy) election laws. ～세 local taxes 《미》; the council taxes 《영》: ～세법 the local tax law. ～시 local time. ～신문 a local news paper. ～은행 a local bank. ～의회 a local assembly: ～ 의회 의원 a local assembly man. ～자치 local autonomy: ～ 자치단체 a local government; the State [County, City, etc.] government 《미》; a local authority 《영》 / ～ 자치법 the Local Autonomy Law / ～ 자치제의 조기실시 the early implementation of local autonomy system. ～장관 a prefectural [local] governor; the governor of a prefecture: ～ 장관 회의 a gubernatorial [governors'] conference. ～재정 local [provincial] finance: ～ 재정법 the local financial law. ～정책 a local policy. ～정치 local politics. ～판(版) a local-news section [page]; an out-of-town [a provincial, a local] edition. ～행정 local administration. ～화 localization: ～화하다 localize.
광역～의회선거 a large-unit local election.

**지방**(脂肪) grease; fat; 《돼지의》 lard; 《소·양 등의》 suet; 《고래의》 blubber.
¶ 식물성[동물성] ～ vegetable [animal] fat / ～이 많은 음식물 fatty food / ～이 많은[없는] 고기 fat [lean] meat / ～을 빼다 remove (surplus) fat; slim; 《운동으로》 exercise fat off / 먹기만 하고 운동을 안하면 배에 ～이 붙는다 You'll put on fat around the stomach, if you eat too much and get no exercise. ◉ ～간 a fatty liver. ～과다 excess of fat; obesity. ～분해 효소 lipolytic enzyme; lypase. ～산 a fatty acid. ～선(腺) the sebaceous glands. ～세포 a fat cell. ～유 fatty oil. ～조직 adipose tissue. ～질 greasy [oily] matter: ～질의 fatty. ～층 a layer of fat.

**지방**(紙榜) an ancestral paper tablet.

**지방순회**(地方巡廻) a provincial tour 《of a theatrical troupe》. ¶ ～판매원 a traveling salesman / ～를 하다 make a country tour 《미》; be on the road.

**지배**(支配) 《운영》 management; 《관리》 control; superintendence; 《지휘》 direction; 《통치》 rule; governing; domination; sway. ～하다 manage; control; direct; superintend; 《통치하다》 rule; govern; dominate.
¶ 법의 ～ the reign of law / 백인이 ～하는 사회 a white-dominated society / 강국에 의한 약소국의 ～ the domination of a weak country by a strong one / ～를 받다 be (put) under the control [rule] of; be subject to / 여론을 ～하다 sway public opinion / 환경을 ～하다 be master of *one's* circumstances / 환경에 ～되다 be at the mercy of *one's* circumstances / 감정에 ～되다 be influenced [swayed] by *one's* feelings / 세계를 ～하다 dominate the world / ～하에 두다 keep [bring, place] 《*a person, a thing*》 under *one's* control [rule] / 바다를 ～하는 자는 곧 세계를 지배하는 자다 Those who have command of the seas have control of the world. / 만물은 자연의 법칙에 ～된다 Everything is subject to the laws of nature. / 이상한 고요가[침묵이]

온 시내를 ～하고 있다 A strange quiet rests over the entire city.
◉ ～계급 the ruling 〔governing〕 class(es). ～권 control; supremacy; management. ～능력 physical intelligence. ～력 governing power; leadership. ～민족 a master 〔ruling〕 race. ～자 a ruler; a master; a dominator. ～회사 a controlling company.

**지배**(遲配) 《우편물의》 delay in mail delivery.

**지배인**(支配人) a manager; an executive; an superintendent; a director; a cashier (미국 은행의). ¶ 호텔 ～ the manager of a hotel; a hotel manager. ◉ ～ 대리 an acting manager.

**지배적**(支配的) dominant; predominant; overriding. ¶ 그 생각이 ～이다 The idea is dominant over all the others. / 프랑스에서는 가톨릭이 ～이다 Catholicism is the predominant religion in France.

**지벅거리다** stumble 《along》; walk with difficulty.

**지벅지벅** stumblingly. ¶ ～ 걷다 stumble along.

**지번**(地番) a (land) lot number.

**지벌**(一罰) 『민속』 ¶ ～입다 incur the divine wrath; be cursed 《with》.

**지벌**(地閥) social standing and (noble) lineage.

**지범거리다** pick up one by one 〔piece by piece〕.

**지범지범** picking 《them》 up one by one 〔piece by piece〕.

**지변**(地變) 《지질 변동》 an extraordinary geographical phenomenon; a terrestrial upheaval; 《자연재해》 a natural calamity; the convulsion of nature.

**지병**(持病) a chronic 〔an inveterate〕 disease; an old complaint. ¶ ～이 도지다 have an attack of *one's* chronic disease / ～으로 자리에 눕다 be confined to bed by an attack of *one's* chronic disease / 두통이 나의 ～이다 Headaches are chronic with me.

**지보**(至寶) most valuable treasure; the greatest 〔a cherished〕 treasure. ¶ 나라의 ～ a great national asset; 《사람》 the pride of a nation / 한국 문단의 ～적 존재 the most prominent figure in Korean literary circles.

**지복**(至福) the supreme bliss; beatitude. ◉ ～천년 『기독교』 the millennium.

**지부**(支部) a branch (office) 《of a society, an association》; a chapter; 《미》 a local 《of a union》. ◉ ～장 the manager of a branch office; the president of a chapter.

**지부럭거리다** annoy; pester; tease; needle; razz; make fun of.

**지분**(脂粉) rouge and powder; cosmetics. ◉ ～내 a (seductive) fragrance of cosmetics.

**지분거리다** annoy; pester; harass. ¶ 전화로 ～ pester 《*a person*》 by telephone.

**지분지분** annoying; pestering.

**지불**(支拂) payment; defrayment. ⇨ 지급(支給). ～하다 pay; pay out; defray 《expenses》; clear 《*one's* debts》; settle 《*one's* accounts》. ¶ ～을 연기하다 postpone 〔put off, delay〕 payment / 전액을 ～하다 pay in full / 벌써 그것은 ～했다 I have already paid for it. / 식사 대금은 신용 카드로 ～했다 I paid for our meal by credit card. / 「대금 ～은 어떤 방법으로 하면 좋을까요」—「은행 불입으로 하여 주십시오」 "What form of payment would you like?"—"Please pay into our bank account." / ～필 (You are) all paid up (★ 스탬프 따위로는 PAID로 함).

**지붕** a roof. ¶ 둥근 ～ a dome / 초가 ～ a thatched roof / 자동차의 ～ the roof of a car / ～ 이는 사람 a roofer; 《초가의》 a thatcher / 기와로〔슬레이트로, 이엉으로〕 ～을 이다 roof a house with tiles 〔slate, thatch〕 / ～이 새다 the roof leaks.

**지브롤터** 《스페인의 항구》 Gibraltar. ◉ ～ 해협 the Strait of Gibraltar.

**지빠귀** 『조류』 a thrush.

**지사**(支社) a branch (office). ¶ 해외 ～ an overseas branch.

**지사**(志士) a (zealous) supporter of a noble cause 〔ideal〕. ¶ 근왕의 ～ a king's loyalist / 우국～ a patriot.

**지사**(知事) a (provincial) governor. ¶ 경기도 ～ K씨 Mr. K, Governor of Kyŏnggi Province. ◉ ～관사 gubernatorial mansion 〔residence〕. ～선거 a gubernatorial election. ～직 governorship. ～후보 a gubernatorial candidate.

**지상**(至上) the supreme; the highest. ¶ 인생의 ～ 목적 the supreme end of life. ◉ ～권 supreme power; supremacy; sovereignty. ～명령 a supreme order; 『철학』 a categorical imperative.

**지상**(地上) 《on, above, over》 the ground. ¶ ～의 ground; earthly; terrestrial; surface / ～에(서) on 〔above, over〕 the ground; on (the) earth / ～ 130층의 세계 최고의 건물 the highest

building in the world with 130 stories above the ground / ~ 15층 지하 2층의 빌딩 a building with fifteen stories above and two under the ground / ~ 2백 미터에 at 200 meter above the ground / ~에서 모습이 사라지다 disappear off the face of the earth / ~에는 아직 눈이 남아 있다 The ground is still covered with snow. / 그는 ~ 7미터 되는 곳에서 뛰어내렸다 He jumped down from a point of seven meters above the ground.
◉ ~경(莖) 〖식물〗 an aerial stem. ~관제센터 a ground control center. ~관제소 〖항공〗 a ground control station. ~군 a ground 〔land〕 army; ground forces. ~권(權) surface rights; superficies: ~권 설정 creation of superficies / ~권 설정자 the creator 〔grantor〕 of superficies / ~권을 가지다 hold 〔enjoy〕 superficies. ~근무 ground service: ~근무원 a ground crew member; ground personnel. ~낙원 a heaven 〔paradise〕 on earth; the Earthly Paradise. ~병력 ground forces 〔strength〕; land forces. ~부대 a ground unit; ground forces 〔troops〕. ~시설 ground facilities. ~유도 착륙방식 〖항공〗 ground-controlled approach 〔GCA〕 method. ~작전 a ground operation. ~전 ground warfare; land war. ~전투 ground fighting 〔action〕. ~정비원 《항공기 등의》 a groundman; a mechanic; a ground crew [총칭]. ~(통신)국 《항공 연락 무선국》 an aeronautic(al) station. ~편향 〖항공〗 a ground loop. ~포화 ground fire. ~핵실험 above-ground nuclear testing.

**지상**(地相) 《지형》 configuration of the ground; the lay of the land.
◉ ~학 physiography.

**지상**(地象) terrestrial phenomena.

**지상**(紙上) ¶ ~에(서) on paper; in print; in the newspaper / 본 ~에서 in our columns / ~의 논전 paper warfare / ~에 실리다 appear in a newspaper.
◉ ~계획 a paper plan. ~공문(空文) mere paper talk; a "mere scrap of paper". ~상담란 a personal advice column.

**지상**(誌上) ¶ ~에 in a magazine 〔journal〕 / 다음 호 ~에 발표함 To be made public in the next number. ◉ ~대담 a conversation 〔tête-à-tête talk〕 in the magazine 〔journal〕.

**지새다** the day breaks (and the moon sets); it dawns. ¶ 지새는 달 a wan morning moon.

**지새우다** 《밤을》 see the night out; stay up 〔awake〕 all night. ¶ 뜬눈으로 ~ do not sleep a wink; be wakeful all night / 술로 밤을 ~ drink the night away; drink all night long; make a night of it / 하룻밤을 이야기로 ~ talk together throughout the night; talk the night away together.

**지서**(支署) a branch office 〔station〕; a substation; a local branch; 《경찰의》 a police substation 〔box〕.

**지석**(誌石) a memorial stone; a slate inscribed with the deceased's date of birth and death together with his works and deeds.

**지석묘**(支石墓) 《고인돌》 a dolmen.

**지선**(支線) 《철도 등의》 a branch line; a feeder (line); 《지방 철도》 a local line.

**지선**(至善) the highest 〔supreme〕 good. ~하다 (be) supremely good.

**지성**(至誠) perfect 〔absolute〕 sincerity; devotion; wholeheartedness; *one's* true heart. ⇨ 정성(精誠). ¶ ~으로 heart and soul; with all *one's* heart; wholeheartedly; in all sincerity / ~이면 감천이라 Sincerity moves heaven.

**지성**(知性) intellect; intelligence; mentality. ¶ ~적(인) intellectual; intelligent / ~이 보통인〔높은, 낮은〕사람 a man of average 〔high, low〕 intelligence / 그의 학설은 ~에 호소하고 있다 His theory appeals to our intelligence. ◉ ~인 an intellectual; a highbrow.

**지성소**(至聖所) 〖성서〗 the sanctuary; 「the holy of holies.

**지세**(地貰) land rent; ground rent.

**지세**(地稅) a land tax.

**지세**(地勢) physical features of a place; geographical 〔natural〕 features; topography (지세도); the lay 〔lie〕 of the land. ¶ ~로 보아 topographically.

**지세븐** 《선진 7개국 재무 장관 회의》 the G-7; the Group of Seven Major Industrial Nations. 「tion.

**지소**(支所) a branch office; a substa-

**지소사**(指小辭) 〖문법〗 a diminutive.

**지속**(持續) continuance; continuation; duration. ~하다 《계속시키다》 continue; carry on; 《계속하다》 last; hold out 〔up〕; endure; 《버티다》 maintain; keep up. ¶ ~적인 lasting; continuous / 생명을 ~하는 데에는 공기가 필요하다 Air is necessary to support life. / 그 협회는 오래 ~되지 않았다 The society did not continue long in existence. ◉ ~기간 a duration period. ~력 sustaining 〔staying〕 power; tenacity; persistency. ~성 durability: ~성이 있는 durable. ~음 a continuant sound.

**지수**(指數) an index (number); 〚수학〛 an exponent. ◉ ~급수〔함수〕 an exponential 「series 〔function〕.

**지스러기** waste; odds and ends; trash 《미》. ¶ 실 ~ waste threads.

**지시**(指示) indication; denotation; pointing out; instructions; directions; guidance. ~하다 《나타내다》 show; indicate; 《지적하다》 point to; 《지령하다》 instruct; direct; give 「directions 〔instructions〕 《to》. ¶ ~에 따라 as instructed 《by *a person*》/ ~에 따르다 follow 《*a person's*》 instructions / ~를 기다리다 wait for instructions 《from *a person*》/ ~된 대로 사용하시오 《게시》 Use only as directed. / 남의 ~ 따위는 안 받겠다 I will take no orders from anyone. *or* I won't be ordered about. ◉ ~대명사 〚문법〛 a demonstrative pronoun. ~서 directions; an order. ~약 〚화학〛 an indicator. ~인 a director; 《지정된 사람》 a designated person. ~판 a notice board; a finger post. ~형용사 〚문법〛 a demonstrative adjective.

**지식**(知識) knowledge; 《견문》 information; 《학문》 (book) learning; theory; 《전문 지식》 know-how.
¶ ~이 있는 well-informed; educated / ~이 없는 ignorant; uninformed / 최신 ~ up-to-date 「knowledge 〔information〕 / 단편적인〔빈약한, 전문적인, 피상적인〕 ~ 「a fragmentary 〔a poor, an expert, a superficial〕 knowledge / 불완전한 ~ an imperfect knowledge; incomplete information / 심원한 ~ a 「profound 〔deep〕 knowledge / 산 ~ a 「working 〔serviceable, practical〕 knowledge / 어학의 ~ linguistic 「knowledge 〔attainments〕 / 읽을〔말할〕 정도의 영어 ~ a 「reading 〔speaking〕 knowledge of English / 경제학의 초보 ~ 「an elementary knowledge 〔the ABC〕 of economics / 독어의 ~이 다소 있다 have some knowledge of German / ~이 늘다 advance in knowledge / ~을 쌓다 accumulate 〔store up〕 knowledge; stock *one's* mind with knowledge / ~을 보급시키다 popularize knowledge; spread 〔propagate, disseminate, diffuse, publicize〕 knowledge 《of》/ ~을 얻다 get 〔acquire, gain, obtain〕 knowledge 〔information〕; derive *one's* knowledge 《from》/ ~을 향상시키다 improve *one's* 「mind 〔knowledge〕 / ~이 없다 lack 「knowledge 〔information〕 / ~을 흡수하다〔넓히다〕 assimilate 〔widen〕 *one's* knowledge / 나는 그 문제에 대해서 전혀 예비 ~이 없다 I have no previous knowledge of the subject. / 그는 문법 ~이 부족하다 He is lacking in grammatical knowledge. ◉ ~계급 the educated class(es); the intellectuals; the intelligentsia; the highbrows. ~산업 the knowledge industry. ~인 an intellectual; a highbrow. ~집약 산업 the knowledge-intensive industry. ~체계 a body of knowledge.

**지식욕**(知識慾) a thirst for knowledge; intellectual appetite; a desire to learn. ¶ ~에 불타다 have a voracious appetite for knowledge; have a thirst for knowledge; have a strong desire to learn / ~을 만족시키다 gratify *one's* thirst for knowledge.

**지신**(地神) the god of the earth.

**지실** evil 〔calamity〕 caused by ill luck.

**지심**(地心) the 「center 〔core〕 of the 「earth.

**지싯거리다** hang on to *one's* demand; insist upon; ask for persistently; keep begging; importune.

**지싯지싯** 《ask for》 persistently; insistently; importunately.

**지아비** 《남편》 a 〔*one's*〕 husband.

**지아이** 《미국 군인》 a GI (*pl.* GI's). 〔< *G*overnment *I*ssue〕

**지악**(至惡) ① 《극악》 ~하다 (be) heinous; atrocious; most wicked; devilish; 《악랄》 (be) knavish; villainous; wily. ¶ ~한 놈 an accomplished villain; a devil; a fiend / ~한 수단 knavish tricks; villainous measures.
② 《악착》 ~스럽다 (be) fussy; hard; sedulous. ¶ ~스럽게 fussily; busily; hard; sedulously / ~스럽게 일하다 toil and moil; plod away; work hard.

**지압**(指壓) finger-pressure therapy; acupressure. ¶ ~을 하다 practice 〔perform〕 finger-pressure therapy. ◉ ~사 an acupressurist. ~요법 = 지압.

**지양**(止揚) 〚철학〛 sublation; *Aufheben* (G.) ~하다 sublate; *aufheben*.

**지어내다** make up; turn out; produce; invent; devise. ¶ 지어낸 말 a 「cooked-up 〔made-up, fabricated〕 story; a fabrication; an invention / 하루에 옷을 열벌씩 ~ produce ten suits of clothes a day / 새 말을 ~ coin 〔make up〕 a new word.

**지어먹다** gather 《*one's* wits》; apply 〔gather〕 《*one's* mind》. ¶ 마음을 ~ gather *one's* wits; give 〔apply〕 *one's* mind 《to》; keep *one's* mind 《on》.

**지어미** 《아내》 a 〔*one's*〕 wife.

**지언**(至言) most reasonable remarks; a wise saying. ¶ ~이다 It is well 〔wisely〕 said that….

**지엄**(至嚴) extreme strictness 〔sternness〕. ~하다 (be) extremely strict 〔stern, rigid〕.

**지업상**(紙業商) 《상점》 a paper store; 《상인》 a dealer in paper.

**지에(밥)** 《고두밥》 steamed rice used for brewing rice wine.

**지에스피** 《일반 특혜 관세 제도》 GSP. [< *G*eneralized *S*ystem of *P*reference]

**지엔피** 《국민총생산》 GNP. [< *G*ross *N*ational *P*roduct] ¶ ~의 6퍼센트를 국방비에 쓰다 spend 6 percent of the GNP as defense expenses.

**지역**(地域) an area; a region; a zone; a district (지구).

> **용법** **area** 넓이와는 관계 없이 한 지역을 나타내는 가장 일반적인 말. **region** 상당히 넓은 지역으로 문화·사회·지리적인 특징을 갖고 있어서 다른 지방과 구별되는 곳. **zone** 특색에 따라 나누어진 지대이며, 지도상에 획을 그어서 나타낼 수 있는 범위. **district** 행정·교육·선거 등의 목적으로 나눈 지구.

¶ ~적(인) local; regional / ~별로 by regional groups / 방화~ a fire zone / 자연 보존 ~ nature-preservation district / 산업의 ~분포 geographical distribution of industries / ~ 실정에 맞는 계획 projects suitable to regional conditions / 광대한 ~ a vast area / ~에 따라 다르다 differ from place to place; vary 「according to the locality 〔in different localities〕 / ~ 감정을 촉발시키다 touch off the regional emotion 《of》 / ~차를 없애다 iron out regional differences.

◉ ~간 격차 regional disparity. ~개발 community development. ~구 《선거의》 local constituencies; electoral district. ~단체 a local 〔regional〕 society. ~방언 a regional dialect. ~ 수당 an area allowance. ~ 안보 체제 a system of regional security. ~연구 area studies. ~재개발 계획 an area redevelopment program. ~정보 통신망〔네트워크〕 local area network (생략 LAN). ~주민 a local resident; [총칭] local citizenry 〔populace〕. ~특성 the (province's) regional characteristics.

**지역권**(地役權) 〖법〗 easement; servitude. ◉ ~자 a servitude holder.

**지역대표**(地域代表) the delegation 〔delegates〕 of a district 〔region〕; 《조합의》 local union delegates. ◉ ~제 regional representation (system).

**지역사회**(地域社會) a (local) community; a local society. ¶ ~를 위해 일하다 work for the good of the (local) community. ◉ ~개발 community development. ~학교 a community school.

**지연**(地緣) regional relation; regionalism; old provincial connections. ¶ ~, 혈연을 따지다 stick to regionalism and kinship / ~, 학연(學緣) 및 혈연을 배격하다 reject regionalism, school relations, and kinship / 혈연, ~에 따른 정실(情實)은 공직자 사회에서 완전히 뿌리뽑아야 한다 Any favoritism out of blood relations, regionalism should be totally eradicated in the bureaucratic society. ◉ ~사회 a territorial society.

**지연**(遲延) delay; procrastination; retardation; postponement (연기). ~되다 delay; be delayed; be retarded; 《연착》 be overdue. ¶ 오래 ~된 long-deferred / 예정보다 2시간이나 ~하여 two hours behind the schedule / 출발이 ~되다 be delayed in *one's* departure / ~시키다 delay; retard; put off; postpone. ◉ ~작전 stalling 〔delaying〕 tactics: ~작전을 쓰다 stall for time. ~책 a delaying move; a dilatory policy 〔motion〕.

**지열**(止熱) the abatement of temperature 《in sickness》; dropping of temperature. ~하다 the temperature falls; *one's* fever breaks.

**지열**(地熱) terrestrial 〔geothermal〕 heat. ¶ ~의 geothermal. ◉ ~발전 geothermal power generation: ~발전소 a geothermal (generating) plant.

**지엽**(枝葉) 《가지와 잎》 branches and leaves; 《중요하지 않은 일》 minor details; nonessentials. ¶ ~적인 minor; unessential; unimportant / ~적인 문제 a side issue; a mere detail 〔trifle〕 / ~으로 흐르다 go into unimportant details; deviate from the main issue; digress from the subject.

**지옥**(地獄) a hell; an inferno; the pit (of hell); Hades. ¶ ~ 같은 hellish;

infernal; a hell of a... / 생～ a hell on earth / ～과 극락 heaven and hell; Hades and Paradise / ～에 떨어지다 go to hell; land in hell / ～에 떨어뜨리다 condemn 《*a person*》 to hell; let 《*a person*》 fall into hell / ～의 고통을 받다 suffer hell / 그는 ～에서 부처님을 만난 기분이었다 [비유적] He was greatly relieved to find such a good friend in his distress.

**지온**(地溫) soil 〔ground〕 temperature.

**지용**(智勇) wisdom and courage; sagacity and valor. ¶ ～을 겸비하다 unite wisdom and valor / 그는 ～을 겸비한 명장이다 He is a great general remarkable for both wisdom and valor.

**지우**(知友) a close friend.

**지우개** an eraser; a cleaner. ¶ 고무 ～ 《주로 미》 an eraser; 《영》 a rubber (★ 《미》에서 a rubber는 콘돔의 뜻으로 쓰임) / ～로 지우다 rub out 《a pencil mark》 with an eraser.

**지우다**[1] ① 《짐을》 put 《*a thing*》 on 《*a person's*》 back; make 《*a person*》 carry on *his* back; burden; load. ¶ 말에 짐을 ～ load a horse up / 지게꾼에게 짐을 ～ hire a coolie to carry *one's* pack. ② 《의무를》 charge 《*a person* with duty》; lay 《on》; impose 《on *a person*》 / 빚을 아무에게 ～ let *a person* bear *one's* debt / 큰 임무를 ～ entrust 《*a person*》 with a grave task.

**지우다**[2] ① 《떨어지게 하다》 scatter 《flowers》; 《숨을》 die; expire; 《아이를》 have a miscarriage. ② 《없애다》 rub out; wipe out; erase; efface; strike out. ¶ 칠판의 글자를 ～ erase the words on the blackboard / 글씨를 고무로 ～ erase words (with an eraser) / 옷에 묻은 얼룩을 ～ wipe a stain off clothes / 이름을 명부에서 ～ strike a name off the list / 두 낱말을 ～ delete 〔strike out, cross out〕 two words.

**지우다**[3] 《눈물·그늘을》 form; make. ¶ 눈물을 ～ shed tears / 그늘(을) ～ form shade.

**지우다**[4] 《이기다》 beat; defeat; get the better of; put 《*a person*》 to the worse; worst; down; 《구어》 lick. ¶ 논쟁에서 ～ beat 〔get the better of〕 《*a person*》 in argument / 언제건 그를 지우고 말겠다 I'll get the better of him someday. / 그는 상대를 지울 것이다 He will down his opponent.

**지우산**(紙雨傘) a bamboo-and-oilpaper umbrella.

**지원**(支援) support; backup; aid. ～하다 support; back (up); aid. ¶ 정신적인 ～ moral support / 적극적인 ～ active 〔positive〕 support / ～을 청하다 ask 《*a person's*》 support; seek support from... / 그는 우리 운동을 ～하고 있다 He supports 〔backs〕 our movement. ◉ ～부대 backup 〔support〕 forces. ～연설 《선거의》 a campaign speech 《for a candidate》. ～자 a supporter; a patron; a backer.

**지원**(志願) 《지망》 wish; desire; aspiration; 《신청》 application; 《자원》 volunteering. ～하다 aspire to; wish; desire; volunteer 《for》; apply 《for》. ¶ 입학을 ～하다 apply for admission to a school / ～을 받아들이다 grant 《*a person's*》 application / 간호사를 ～하다 volunteer *one's* service as a nurse / 군복무를 ～하다 volunteer for military service. ◉ ～병 a volunteer (soldier): ～병제도 the volunteer system. ～서 a written application. ～자 an applicant; a volunteer; an aspirant; 《후보자》 a candidate. ～제도 the volunteer system.

**지위**(地位) 《신분》 (*one's*) status; (social) standing; *one's* station (in life); 《직위》 a position; a post; 《계급》 a rank. ¶ ～ 있는 사람 a man of (high) position 〔rank〕 / 사회적 ～ a social position 〔status〕 / 책임 있는 ～ a post of trust 〔responsibility〕 / 교수의 ～ a post as professor / ～의 상징 a status symbol; a symbol 〔sign〕 of status / ～가 높다〔낮다〕 be high 〔low〕 in position; be of high 〔low〕 social standing; stand high 〔low〕 socially / ～가 오르다 rise in (social) standing; improve *one's* position 〔station〕; reach a higher rank / ～를 차지하다 occupy 〔fill, take, hold〕 a position / ～에 오르다 take a position 《as》; assume the position 《of》 / ～를 얻다 gain 〔get, acquire, secure〕 a position; be given a place 《in the government》 / ～를 높이다 raise 〔elevate〕 《*a person's*》 position 〔status〕 / ～를 향상시키다 improve *one's* position / 높은 ～에 있다 hold a high rank 《among》; stand high 《among》 / ～를 잃다 lose *one's* position 〔station, place〕 / ～를 회복하다 recover 〔regain〕 *one's* lost position; come back to *one's* former office / ～를 다투다 try 〔compete〕 for a position / ～를 남용하다 abuse *one's* position 〔authority〕 / ～를 굳히다 consolidate *one's* position / 남의 ～를 차지하다 supplant *a* *person;* step into《*a person's*》shoes / ～가 높은 사람부터 낮은 사람의 순으로 in descending order of status / 회사에서 그는 어떤 ～에 있는가 How is he placed in the firm? / 전후 여성의 사회적 ～가 향상되었다 Woman's status in society has been raised 〔elevated〕 since the war. ◉ 주한 미군 ～ 협정 the Korea-U.S. Status of Forces Agreement (생략 SOFA).

**지위지다**《몸이》get 〔be〕 worn out; be exhausted;《살림이》get 〔become〕 poor; be reduced.

**지육**(枝肉) beef 〔pork〕 carcass. ¶ ～값이 6백 그램 한 근당 2백원 떨어졌다 The price of beef 〔pork〕 carcass dropped by 200 won per 600 grams.

**지육**(智育) intellectual 〔mental〕 training; mental culture 〔education〕. ¶ ～에 치우치다 over-emphasize mental training.

**지은이** a writer; an author.

**지의**(地衣) 〖식물〗 lichen.

**지인**(知人) an acquaintance; a friend (★ acquaintance는 friend보다 교제가 얕은 사람). ¶ 부친의 ～ an acquaintance of my father's / ～이 많다 have a wide 〔large〕 circle of acquaintances; have many contacts《특히 미》.

**지인용**(智仁勇) wisdom, benevolence and valor.

**지일**(至日) 〖천문〗 the solstices.

**지자**(知者) a man of intelligence; a man of knowledge and experience; [총칭] the intellect.

**지자**(智者) a man of wisdom; a wise man; a sage; [총칭] the wise. ¶ ～는 불혹이다 A wise man knows his own mind. *or* A wise man never wavers. / ～도 천려(千慮)에 일실(一失)은 있다 Even the wise are not free from perplexity. *or* No one is wise at all times.

**지자기**(地磁氣) terrestrial magnetism; geomagnetism.

**지장**(支障)《장애》a hindrance; an obstacle; an impediment; interference;《곤란》a trouble; a difficulty;《불편》an inconvenience;《해》harm. ¶ ～이 없으면 if nothing happens 〔interferes〕; if all goes well; if it suits *one;* if it is convenient to you / ～이 있다 have trouble 〔difficulty〕; have something happen / ～을 주다 [사물이 주어] cause *one* inconvenience; hinder *one*《in *one's* work, from *do*ing》; impede / ～이 없다《불편을 느끼지 않다》experience 〔suffer〕 no inconvenience;《곤란하지 않다》have no difficulty 〔trouble〕《in *do*ing》;《선약이 없다》have no previous engagement; be disengaged; be free;《이의가 없다》have no objection《to》;《해나갈 수 있다》be able to get along;《없어도 되다》can do without;《해가 안 되다》do《*one*》no harm; be harmless / 공부에 ～이 있다 interfere with *one's* study / ～이 있으시다면 나중에 또 뵙죠 If I have come at an inconvenient time, I will call again later. / 네가 참가하면 만사가 ～ 없이 잘 될 것이다 If you join us, everything will go smoothly. / …하는 데 ～ 없다 I see no harm in *do*ing. / 책 읽는 데 ～이 없다 I have no difficulty in reading.

**지장**(指章) a thumbprint; a thumb impression. ¶ ～을 찍다 seal《a document》with the thumb.

**지장**(智將) a resourceful general.

**지저귀다** sing; twitter; chirp; warble (휘파람새 등이); chatter (재잘거리다). ¶ 참새가 지저귀는 소리 a sparrow's chirpings / 참새처럼 ～ chatter like a sparrow.

**지저깨비**《나무 조각》a chip of wood.

**지저분하다**《어수선하다》(be) messy; untidy; disordered; messed up;《더럽다》(be) dirty; unclean; filthy. ¶ 지저분한 방 a room in a mess; a messed-up room / 지저분한 거리 a dirty street / 지저분하게 먹다 eat in a messy way.

**지적**(地積)《면적》acreage.

**지적**(地籍) a land register. ◉ ～도(圖) a cadastral map; a land registration map. ～측량 a cadastral survey.

**지적**(知的) intellectual; intelligent; mental.

> **용법** **intellectual** 충분한 교양과 지성을 갖추고 있는 것. **intelligent** 선천적으로 이해력이 있으며 총명한 것을 뜻함. 따라서 어린 아이를 말할 때는 intellectual이란 표현은 쓰지 않음. **mental** 「마음의, 정신의, 지적인」의 뜻에서 발전된 말, 한정적인 뜻으로만 쓰임: mental exercise (지적 훈련).

¶ ～ 감정 intellectual feeling / ～ 작용 intellection / ～수준 an intellectual level / ～생활 (an) intellectual life / ～노동(자) brain work(er) / ～교류 intellectual interchange / ～활동 mental activities / ～직업 an intellectual occupation / 그는 아무리 봐도 ～이지 않다 He is not intellectual in any respect. / 그녀는 매우 ～인 얼굴을 하고 있다 She looks very intelligent. ◉ ～능력 *one's* intellectual powers; *one's* mental faculties. ~재산권 intellectual property (rights). ~ 재산권보호 protection of intellectual property.

**지적**(指摘) pointing out; indication. ~하다 point 《out》; indicate; lay *one's* finger on. ¶ 위에 ~한 바와 같이 as pointed out above / 잘못을 ~하다 point out mistakes.

**지전**(紙錢) 《지폐》 paper money; currency 〔bank〕 notes.

**지전류**(地電流) 〖물리〗 an earth current.

**지점**(支店) a branch; a branch office 〔store〕. ¶ 해외~ overseas branches 〔offices〕 / 한국 은행 부산 ~ Pusan Branch of the Bank of Korea. ~을 내다〔설치하다〕 open 〔establish〕 a branch office 《in, at》 / ~으로 전근되다 be transferred 〔assigned〕 to a branch office. ◉ ~망 a branch network. ~장 a branch manager.

**지점**(支點) 〖물리〗 a fulcrum (*pl.* ~s, -cra); 〖건축〗 a bearing.

**지점**(地點) a spot; a point; a place; a position. ¶ 유리한 ~ a vantage point / 예정한 ~ the intended spot / 두 개의 도로는 이 ~에서 만난다 Two roads meet at this point.

**지정**(至情) ① 《정분》 close intimacy 〔friendship〕. ② 《친척》 close relative. ③ 《충정》 *one's* sincere heart; sincerity; deep feelings. ¶ ~에 감동되다 be moved 〔touched〕 by 《*a person's*》 sincerity.

**지정**(指定) designation; specification; appointment; assignment; authorization. ~하다 designate; name; specify; mark; appoint; assign; authorize. ¶ (교육부) ~의 designated by (the Ministry of Education) / ~한 대로 as specified / 별도 ~이 없는 한 unless otherwise designated 〔specified〕 / 날짜〔장소〕를 ~하다 appoint a day 〔place〕 / 특별히 장소 ~은 하지 않았다 No place in particular was designated. / 회의의 일시를 ~해 주십시오 Please set 〔decide〕 the time and date of the meeting.
◉ ~가(격) the limits. ~공장 a designated factory. ~권(券) a ticket for reserved seat. ~대리인 an authorized agent. ~사(詞) 〖문법〗 a copula (word). ~상품〔품목〕 specified stocks. ~석 a reserved seat. ~시간〔장소〕 the designated hour 〔place〕; the appointed time 〔place〕. ~은행 a designated bank. ~인 〖법〗 an appointor. ~일 a designated day; a specified date. ~ 좌석권 a reserved-seat ticket. ~품목 〖금융〗 specified stocks. ~통화 a designated 〔specified〕 currency. ~호텔 a hotel designated 《by》. ~후견인 a designated guardian.

**지정거리다** loiter on the 〔*one's*〕 way; waste *one's* time on the way 〔road〕; dawdle along the road; linger; delay.

**지정학**(地政學) geopolitics. ¶ ~의 geopolitic(al). ◉ ~자 a geopolitician.

**지조**(地租) the land tax; the tax on land. ◉ ~미 rice paid as land tax.

**지조**(志操) purpose; principle; 《절조》 constancy; fidelity; integrity. ¶ 정치가의 ~ political fidelity / ~가 고결한 사람 a man of high principles / ~가 없는 inconstant; unprincipled / ~를 굳게 지키다 be true 〔devoted〕 to *one's* principles / ~가 굳다〔약하다〕 be firm 〔weak〕 of purpose; have a firm 〔weak〕 purpose.

**지존**(至尊) His Majesty; the King.

**지주**(支柱) a prop; a stay; a support; a strut. ¶ ~를 대다 prop 《a house》 up; provide 《a structure》 with supports / 한 집안의 ~ [비유적] the prop and stay of a family; the mainstay of a family.

**지주**(地主) a landowner; a landholder; a landlord; a landed proprietor. ¶ 대~ a large 〔great〕 landowner / 부재(不在)~ an absentee landlord. ◉ ~계급 the landed class.

**지주**(持株) *one's* (stock) holdings; *one's* shares. ◉ ~회사 a holding company. 종업원 ~ 제도 a stock-sharing plan for the employees.

**지중**(地中) ¶ ~의 underground; subterranean; subterraneous / ~에 in the earth; under the ground / ~에 묻다 bury in the earth / ~에서 파내다 dig 《*a thing*》 out of the ground; unearth. ◉ ~송전선 an underground transmission line. ~온도계 an earth thermometer.

**지중해**(地中海) the Mediterranean (Sea). ¶ ~(연안)의 Mediterranean.

**지지** 《소아어》 Dirty! ¶ 에이 ~, 아가 만지지 마 Oh, it's dirty—Baby mustn't touch.

**지지**(支持) support; upholding; backing. ~하다 support 《*a person*》; stand by 〔behind〕 《*a person*》; be for 〔in favor of〕 《a proposition》; uphold 《a policy》; back 《*a person*》 (up); prop up; sustain. ¶ 여론의 ~ 《have》 the

backing of public opinion / 정신적 ~ 《give *a person*》 moral support / 국민의 ~를 얻다 be supported by the people; have 〔get〕 the support of the people / 아무의 주장을 ~하다 support *a person's* claim / 여성들로부터 상당한 ~를 얻다 gain considerable support from women / 나는 그의 발언을 ~한다 I will show my support to what he says. / 나는 이 계획을 ~하는 연설을 했다 I made a speech in support of this plan.
◉ ~물 a support. ~율 the approval rate: 최근의 여론 조사에 의하면, 현 내각의 ~율은 아직 25퍼센트 이하를 맴돌고 있다 According to a recent public-opinion poll, support for the present cabinet is still lingering below 25 percent. ~자 a supporter; an upholder; a backer. ~층 the base of *one's* support: 그의 ~층은 두텁다 He has a broad base of support.

**지지**(地誌) a (local) topography.
◉ ~학 (the science of) topography.

**지지**(遲遲) slowness; lagging; tardiness. ~하다 (be) slow; lagging; tardy. ¶ ~하게 slowly; tardily; languidly / ~부진하다 make slow 〔little〕 progress / 건설 공사는 ~부진이다 The work of construction is making progress at a snail's pace.

**지지난달** the month before last.

**지지난밤** the night before last.

**지지난번**(一番) the time before last.

**지지난해** the year before last.

**지지다** ① 《끓이다》 stew. ¶ 생선을 ~ stew fish. ② 《지짐질하다》 pan-fry; *sauté* (F.); grill. ¶ 고기를 기름에 ~ pan-fry meat / 저냐를 ~ make fish *sauté* / 빈대떡을 ~ make green-pea griddle cake. ③ 《인두 따위로》 cauterize; sear; scorch; brand. ¶ 인두로 상처를 ~ sear a wound with a hot iron. ④ 《머리 따위를》 friz(z); frizzle; singe; crimp; crinkle; wave. ¶ 지진 머리 frizzled hair; friz(z); curls / 머리를 ~ friz(z) 〔curl, singe〕 *one's* hair; put a wave 〔curl〕 into hair.

**지지랑물** 《낙숫물》 musty drippings from the thatched roof.

**지지르다** ① 《무거운 것으로》 press down; weigh on. ¶ 돌로 ~ press 《*a thing*》 under a stone. ② 《기운을》 overawe; overbear; overpower. ¶ 그는 내가 제기하는 이견(異見)은 무엇이든지 모두 지질렀다 He overbore whatever objections were raised by me.

**지지리** awfully; frightfully; shockingly; terribly; unbearably; horribly; exceedingly. ¶ ~도 못나다 《얼굴이》 be awfully ugly-looking; 《태도가》 be downright stupid / ~ 고생하다 go through terrible 〔unbearable〕 hardships.

**지지하다** 《시시하다》 (be) trifling; trivial; poor; worthless. ¶ 지지한 책 a worthless book; a dull book / 지지한 소리하다 say silly things; talk rot / 지지한 일로 걱정하다 worry about trifles; bother *one's* mind over a trivial matter.

**지진**(地震) an earthquake; a quake; a shock (of earthquake); 《미진》 a 〔an earth〕 tremor. ¶ ~의 seismic; seismal / 대~ a strong 〔severe〕 earthquake / ~의 중심 the center of an earthquake; a seismic center / ~이 잦다 be subject to frequent earthquakes / ~이 나다 an earthquake occurs; have an earthquake / 어젯밤 강한 ~이 있었다 A strong earthquake 〔shock〕 was felt last night. *or* There was a strong earthquake last night.
◉ ~계 a seismograph; a seismometer. ~관측 seismological observation; seismometry; seismography: ~관측소 a seismological observatory; a seismographic station. ~대 an earthquake zone 〔belt〕; a seismic area. ~대책 anti-earthquake procedures 〔measures〕. ~도 a seismogram. ~설계기준 《Japanese》 earthquake-design standards. ~연구소 an earthquake research institute. ~예보 earthquake prediction. ~파 a seismic 〔an earthquake〕 wave. ~학 seismology: ~학자 a seismologist. ~현상 seismism; earthquake phenomena. ~활동 seismic activity.

**지진아**(遲進兒) a (mentally) retarded child.

**지질**(地質) geological features; the nature of the soil (토질).
◉ ~공학 geotechnology. ~도(圖) a geological map. ~분석 a soil analysis. ~시대 the geological age; geologic time (지질학적 기록밖에 없는 고시대); a geologic era 〔age〕 (지질학상의 한 시대). ~연구소 the Geological Survey Office. ~조사 a geological survey. ~학 geology: ~학상의 geological / ~학자 a geologist / 고대 ~학 paleogeology / 구조 ~학 structural 〔tectonic〕 geology / 동력〔경제〕 ~학 dynamical 〔economic〕 geology / 해저 ~학 submarine 〔ocean bottom〕 geology.

**지질**(紙質) the quality of paper.

**지질리다** ①《무게로》get pressed down; be weighed on. ②《기가》get overawed; be overpowered; cower; quail.

**지질지질** watery; soft. ～하다 (be) watery; soft. ¶ 밥이 ～하게 되다 rice gets done on the soft side.

**지질펀펀하다** ①《평평하다》(be) level; even; smooth; flat. ¶ 지질펀펀한 길 a smooth road. ②《질고 펀펀하다》(be) wet and open. ¶ 지질펀펀한 들 a broad expanse of wet field.

**지질하다** ①《싫증나다》(be) tedious; wearisome; boresome; tiresome. ¶ 지질한 일생 a dull life / 지질한 사람 a bore; a drip《속어》/ 그의 연설은 지질했다 His speech was long and boring. ②《변변치 못하다》(be) worthless; good-for-nothing; poor; wretched; trashy. ¶ 지질한 놈 a good-for-nothing / 지질한 시(詩) a wretched poem / 지질한 소리 하다 talk nonsense; say silly things.

**지짐거리다**《비가》it rains off and on.

**지짐이** (a) stew. ¶ 고기 ～ meat stew.

**지짐질** making griddlecakes; panfrying. ～하다 pan-fry.

**지참**(持參) bringing; bearing. ～하다《가져오다》bring《*a thing*》with *one;*《가져가다》take 〔carry〕《*a thing*》with *one.* ◉ ～금 a dowry; a marriage portion; a dot: 딸에게 ～금을 주다 dower 〔endow〕 a daughter at marriage. ～인 a bearer: ～인불(拂) payable to bearer / ～인불 어음 a bill 〔note〕 (payable) to bearer / 이 편지 ～인에게 그 책을 건네어 주십시오 Please hand the book over to the bearer of this letter.

**지참**(遲參) late attendance. ～하다 arrive 〔come〕 late; be behind time. ◉ ～자 a latecomer.

**지척**(咫尺) a very short distance. ¶ ～을 분간할 수 없을 만큼 어두운 밤 a pitch-dark night / ～지간이다 be very close; be within a foot / ～을 분간할 수 없을 만큼 안개가 짙었다 The fog was so dense that nothing was to be seen an inch ahead. / ～이 천리이다《속담》Though it is close-by, the lack of news makes one feel as if it were a thousand miles away.

**지척거리다**《걸음을》drag along; scuff(le); trudge.

**지천**(至賤) ①《천함》the most base. ～하다 (be) most base 〔vulgar, mean, low, humble〕. ¶ 그는 ～한 집안에서 태어난 사람이었다 He was a man of very humble birth. ②《풍부》abundance. ～하다 (be) abundant. ¶ ～으로 in great abundance; ever so much 〔many〕.

**지청**(支廳) a branch (government) 「office.

**지청구** grumbling (without good reason); murmuring; mumbling; complaining; bitching《구어》. ～하다 grumble (without good reason); murmur; mumble; complain; bitch《구어》.

**지체** lineage; birth; pedigree; family stock. ¶ ～가 높다〔낮다〕 be of noble 〔humble〕 birth.

**지체**(肢體) the limbs and the body. ¶ ～가 부자유한 lame; crippled. ◉ ～부자유자 a physically handicapped person; a disabled person.

**지체**(遲滯) (a) delay; deferment; retardation; procrastination. ～하다 delay; hold off;《지불 등이》be in arrears; be overdue; be delinquent (납세 등이). ¶ ～ 없이 without delay; promptly; immediately / 업무가 ～되어 있다 The work is behind schedule. / 마을 사람들은 세금을 ～ 없이 납부했다 The villagers paid their taxes without delay. / 본건은 어떤 ～도 허용 안된다 The matter 「will not bear any delay 〔admits of no delay〕. ◉ ～일수 (number of) days overdue.

**지촉**(紙燭) paper and candle.

**지축**(地軸) the axis of the earth. ¶ ～을 뒤흔드는 듯한 요란한 소리 deep, earthshaking rumble.

**지출**(支出) disbursement; (an) outlay; expenses; expenditure; (an) outgoings; payment. ～하다 disburse; make an outlay; defray; expend; pay. ¶ 수입과 ～ revenue and expenditure; incomings and outgoing / 부당～ an unjust disbursement / 예산외～ defrayment unprovided for in a budget; extra-budgetary expenditures / ～이 많다〔적다〕 have many (few) expenses / ～을 억제하다 hold down expenditure 〔expenses〕/ 많은 ～을 하다 make a great outlay《to》/ ～을 삭감하다 cut down 〔curtail〕 *one's* expenses / ～이 수입을 초과했다 Expenditure 〔Outlays〕 exceeded revenues. / 금주에는 ～이 많았다 We had to pay heavy expenses this week. *or* Our expenses ran up this week. / 물가가 올라 ～이 자꾸 늘어 간다 Owing to rising prices, our expenses keep growing. ◉ ～액 the expenditure; the amount expended 〔disbursed〕. 정부〔재정〕～

government expenditure. 총〔경상, 임시〕~ total 〔ordinary, extraordinary〕 expenditure.

**지층**(地層) 〖지질〗 a (geological) stratum (*pl.* ~s, -ta); a layer. ¶ ~(상)의 stratigraphic. ◉ ~학 stratigraphy: ~학상의 stratigraphical.

**지치** 〖식물〗 a gromwell.

**지치다**[1] 《피로하다》 get 〔be〕 exhausted 〔fatigued〕; get 〔be〕 tired (out); be worn out (★ 「지쳐있다」고 하는 상태에는 be, 「지치다」라는 상태의 변화에는 get 을 씀). ¶ 지칠 줄 모르는 tireless; unwearied / 기다리다 ~ be tired of waiting 《for *a person*》/ 지칠 대로 ~ be utterly worn out; be fagged out / 일에 ~ be tired from *one's* work / 너무 지쳐서 아무것도 먹을 수 없다 be too tired to eat / 나는 먼 길을 걸어서 지쳤다 I have walked such a long way that I am worn out. / 그는 더위에 지친 모양이다 It seems he's exhausted from the heat.

**지치다**[2] 《얼음 따위를》 slide 《on, over》; skate 《on》. ¶ 얼음지치기 skating; sliding / 얼음을 지치는 사람 a 〔an ice〕 skater / 얼음을 ~ skate 〔slide〕 on the ice / 연못으로 얼음을 지치러 가다 go skating on a pond.

**지치다**[3] 《문을》 close 《a door》 without locking it; leave 《a door》 unlocked but closed; close 《a door》 softly 〔lightly〕.

**지친**(至親) close relatives; members of *one's* immediate family.

**지침**(指針) ① 《계기의》 an index; an indicator; a pointer; a needle; 《자석의》 a compass needle. ② 《길잡이》 a guide 《to》; 《지도 방침》 a guiding principle 《in *one's* life》; a guideline 《for governmental action》. ¶ 행동의 ~을 제시하다 indicate 〔set forth〕 guidelines for *a person's* conduct / 그는 나에게 인생의 ~을 가르쳐 주었다 He has given me the principle that guides my life. ◉ ~서 a guide (book): 수험 ~서 a guide to examinations; a guide book for examinees.

**지칭**(指稱) ~하다 call; name; designate. ¶ 그들은 그를 "A교수"라고 ~했다 They pointedly called him "Professor A".

**지켜보다** watch (intently); stare 〔gaze〕 《at》; watch 〔keep watch〕 《over》; (wait and) see (관망). ¶ 사태의 진전을 ~ watch the development of events; follow the evolution of events / 형세를 ~ watch the turn of an event; see which way the cat jumps.

**지키다** ① 《살피다》 watch; keep a watch; 《호위》 stand guard; guard; 《보호》 protect; 《방어》 defend.

> 용법 **guard** 경계하거나 망을 보아 「지키다」라는 뜻. **protect** 사전에 어떤 방어 수단을 써서 「보호하다」의 뜻. **defend** 실제의 위험이나 공격에 저항해서 「지키다」라는 뜻의 일반적인 말.

¶ 양떼를 ~ watch a flock of sheep / 나라를 ~ defend the country / 집을 ~ look after 〔take care of〕 a house / 몸을 ~ defend *oneself* 《against attack》/ 자기의 이익을 ~ protect 〔look after〕 *one's* interests 《from》/ 무기고를 잘 지키라는 명령을 받았다 He was ordered to keep the arsenal under close guard. / 내 자리 좀 지켜 다오 Please keep 〔save〕 this seat for me.
② 《준수하다》 keep; fulfill; observe; obey; abide by; follow; stick 〔adhere〕 《to》 (주의 따위를). ¶ 중립을 ~ observe neutrality / 약속을 ~ keep *one's* engagements; keep 〔be true to〕 *one's* word / 규칙을 ~ keep 〔stick〕 to the regulations / 내야〔외야〕를 ~ 〖야구〗 play infield 〔outfield〕 / 법을 ~ abide by the law / 비밀을 ~ keep a secret / 신의를 ~ keep faith / 본분을 ~ fulfill *one's* duty; stick 〔keep〕 to *one's* lot in life / 절개를 ~ remain faithful to *one's* allegiance 〔loyalty〕; keep *one's* integrity; follow 〔observe〕 *one's* principles; stick to *one's* colors 〔guns〕; maintain chastity / 예의를 ~ observe good manners / 침묵을 ~ keep silence / 시간을 ~ observe the time / 시골에서는 옛 관습을 아직도 지키고 있다 The old customs are still kept up in the country districts. / 교통 신호를 지켜라 Observe traffic signals. / 우리는 법을 지키지 않으면 안 된다 We must observe the laws.

**지탄**(指彈) ~하다 《손가락을 튀기다》 fillip; flick; flip; 《비난하다》 censure 〔condemn, blame〕 《*a person* for *his* fault》; accuse 《*a person* of telling a lie》; denounce 《*a person* as a hypocrite》; criticize; reproach 《*a person* for ingratitude》; lay the blame 《on *a person*》. ¶ ~ 받다 be blamed 〔censured〕 《for》; lay *oneself* open to censure; incur blame / 그는 여러 가지로 ~ 받았다 Much was said in blame of him.

**지탱하다**(支撐—) keep (up); prop up; preserve; support; maintain; sustain. ¶ 집안을 ~ maintain *one's* family / 건강을 지탱해 나가다 preserve *one's* health / 그는 자본이 모자라 가게를 더 지탱할 수 없었다 He couldn't keep his store going any longer because he was running short of capital. / 적 병력에 압도되어 지휘관은 진지를 더 이상 지탱할 수 없었다 Outnumbered by the enemy, the officer in command found the position no longer tenable.

**지통**(止痛) allaying 〔relieving, killing〕 pain. ~하다 allay 〔relieve, kill〕 pain. ◉ ~제 an anodyne; a painkiller.

**지파**(支派) 《혈족·부족의》 a branch of a family 〔tribe〕; 《종파》 a sect; 《분파》 a subbranch; an offshoot; 《정당의》 a faction.

**지판**(地板) 《관의》 the bottom piece of 「a coffin.

**지팡이** a (walking) stick; a cane; a staff. ¶ ~를 짚다 use a stick / ~를 짚고 걷다 walk with a stick / ~를 들고 다니다 carry a cane 〔stick〕 / ~에 의지하다 hang on 〔lean upon〕 *one's* stick. ◉ 대(나무)~ a bamboo cane. 등산용 ~ an alpenstock.

**지퍼** a zipper; a (slide) fastener. ¶ ~ 달린 《a bag》 with a zipper; zippered 《bag》 / ~를 채우다 zip (up) 《a coat》 / ~를 끄르다 unzip 《a coat》 / 가방의 ~를 채우다 zip a brief case shut / (등의) ~를 좀 채워 주시겠어요 Zip me up, will you?

**지평**(地平) 《대지의 평면》 the surface of the earth; 《지평선》 the horizon.
◉ ~각 a horizontal angle. ~면 the horizontal plane. ~부각(俯角) the dip of the horizon. ~시차 the horizontal parallax.

**지평선**(地平線) the horizon; a horizontal line; the skyline. ¶ ~상에 above 〔on〕 the horizon / ~상에 오르다 rise above the horizon / ~ 밑으로 가라앉다 sink below the horizon / 해가 ~ 쪽으로 기울었다 The sun sank toward the horizon.

**지폐**(紙幣) paper money; a (bank) note 《영》; a bill 《미》. ¶ ~의 남발 excessive issue of paper currency / ~(의) 뭉치 a roll 〔wad, bundle〕 of bills / 1,000원짜리 ~ a thousand-won note 〔bill 《미》〕 / ~를 발행하다 issue paper money / ~를 위조하다 forge paper money; counterfeit 《10,000-won》 bills / ~를 회수하다 recall bank notes.
◉ ~발행 issue of paper money: ~발행고 a note issue / ~ 발행권 the note-issuing right; the right of issue / ~ 발행 은행 a note-issuing bank; a bank of issue. ~본위(제) the paper standard.

**지폭**(紙幅) the width of paper.

**지표**(地表) the surface of the earth.
◉ ~수 surface water. ~온도 ground temperature; temperature at ground level.

**지표**(指標) ① 《표지》 an index (*pl.* ~es, indices); an indicator; a pointer; a directing 〔guide〕 post. ② 『수학』 a characteristic.

**지푸라기** bits of straw. ¶ 물에 빠지면 ~라도 잡는다 《속담》 A drowning man will catch at a straw.

**지프** 《산악·전투용 자동차》 a jeep.

**지피다** 《불을》 kindle; burn; build 〔feed, make〕 a fire. ¶ 아궁이에 불을 ~ get a fire going in the fireplace / 석탄〔장작〕을 ~ burn coal 〔wood〕 / 스토브에 불을 ~ make a fire in the stove; light a stove 〔heater〕.

**지피에스** 《위성 위치 확인 시스템》 G.P.S. 〔< *G*lobal *P*osition *S*ystem〕 ¶ ~버그 a GPS bug.

**지필**(紙筆) paper and pens 〔writing brushes〕. ◉ ~묵 paper, brushes 〔pens〕 and ink.

**지하**(地下) ① 《땅속》 underground; subterranean. ¶ ~에서 일하다 work underground / ~에 파묻다 bury 〔lay〕 《*a thing*》 underground / ~ 20미터까지 파다 dig 20 meters under 〔below〕 (the) ground / ~에 잠입하다 go underground; go into hiding. ② 《무덤·저승》 the grave; Hades; the underworld. ¶ ~의 벗 *one's* friend in the grave / ~에 잠들다 sleep in the grave; rest in peace.
◉ ~갱도 an underground tunnel. ~경(莖) 『식물』 a subterranean stem; a rootstock; a rhizome. ~경제 the underground economy. ~공작 underground operations 〔maneuvering〕. ~근(根) a subterranean root. ~(보)도 an underground passage; an underground pedestrian walk; a subway 《영》; an underpass 《미》; 《성곽의》 a gallery. ~상가 an underground shopping area 〔complex〕. ~선 an underground cable. ~수 underground water. ~수위 an underground water level; 《지하 수면》 the water table. ~식물 a geophyte. ~실 a basement; a

cellar. ～요새 an underground fortress. ～운동 an underground movement. ～2층 the 2nd basement; basement 2. ～자원 underground resources: ～자원이 풍부하다 be rich in underground resources. ～정부 an underground 〔an invisible, a hidden〕 government. ～조직 an underground organization: ～(조직)망 《establish》 underground networks. ～주차장 an underground parking lot. ～차도 underground motorways. ～핵실험 an underground nuclear test (blast).

**지하철**(地下鐵) an underground railway; 《미》 a subway; 《영》 the underground 〔Underground〕; the Tube (런던의); 《파리 등의》 the Metro. ¶ ～을 타다 take a subway train 〔the Underground〕/ ～로 가다 go by subway 〔underground〕/ 나는 ～을 타고 집으로 돌아오는 길이었다 I was going home on the subway. / ～로 종로역까지 세 정거장을 갔다 I took the subway three stops to the Chongno station. ◉ ～건설 본부 《director general of》 the subway construction headquarters. ～역 a subway station. ～이용자 an undergrounder. ～2호선 the No.2 〔second〕 subway line. 서울～공사(公社) Seoul Metropolitan Subway Corporation.

**지학**(地學) physical geography; earth 「science.

**지한**(知韓) pro-Koreanism. ◉ ～파 the pro-Korean (group): ～파이다 be pro-Korean.

**지함**(紙函) a bandbox; a cardboard 「box; a carton.

**지해제**(止咳劑) a cough medicine 〔lozenge (정제)〕.

**지핵**(地核) 〖지질〗 the centrosphere; the nucleus 〔core〕 of the earth.

**지행**(知行) knowledge and conduct.

**지향**(志向) (an) intention; (an) aim; (an) inclination; (an) orientation. ¶ 미래 ～형의 future-oriented.

**지향**(指向) ～하다 point 《to》; head 《for, toward》. ◉ ～성 〖무선〗 directivity: ～성 안테나 a directional antenna. ～송신〔수신〕 directional transmission 〔reception〕.

**지혈**(止血) stopping 〔arrest〕 of bleeding; 〖의학〗 hemostasis. ～하다 stop 〔check, arrest〕 bleeding. ◉ ～대 a tourniquet. ～법 styptic treatment; a hemostatic method; the stanching. ～제 a styptic; a hemostatic.

**지협**(地峽) an isthmus (*pl.* ～es, -mi); a land bridge; a neck of land. ¶ ～의 isthmian. ◉ 수에즈～ the Isthmus of Suez.

**지형**(地形) configuration of the ground; the lay 〔lie〕 of the land; the topography. ¶ ～(학)상의 topographical. ◉ ～답사 〖지질〗 reconnaissance; survey. ～도 a topographical 〔terrain〕 map; a contour map (등고선 표시); a relief map (등고선·음영·색채 등의 방법을 이용). ～측량 a topographical survey. ～판단 〖군사〗 estimation of ground. ～학 geomorphology; topography.

**지형**(紙型) 〖인쇄〗 a *papier-mâché* mold; a paper mold. ¶ ～을 뜨다 make a paper mold; take a *papier-mâché* mold.

**지혜**(智慧) wisdom; sense; wits; brains; intelligence; sagacity; resourcefulness.

> (용법) **wisdom** 현명하게 적절한 선택과 결정을 내릴 수 있는 지혜. **sense** 사려·분별·양식이라는 뜻에서의 지혜, common 〔good〕 sense라고도 함. **wit** 머리의 회전이 빠른 것을 말함. **brain(s)** 이해력이나 사고력이라는 뜻에서의 지혜. **intelligence** 지능이 높고 이해가 빠르다는 뜻에서의 지혜.

¶ 생활의 ～ wisdom for living 〔of life〕/ ～ 있는 wise; sagacious; resourceful; intelligent / ～ 없는 unintelligent; unwise; stupid; silly; brainless / ～를 짜내다 cudgel 〔rack〕 *one's* brains / ～롭다 be wise 〔sagacious〕/ ～를 빌리다 pick 《*a person's*》 brains; take advice 《from *a person*》.

**지호**(指呼) beckoning. ～하다 beckon 《to *a person*》. ¶ ～지간에 있다 be within hail 〔call〕; be near at hand.

**지화**(指話) 《use》 finger 〔hand〕 language. ◉ ～법〔술〕 dactylology.

**지화자** a shout to mark time in accompanying singing or dancing.

**지환**(指環) a ring. ⇨ 가락지, 반지.

**지효**(至孝) the utmost filial piety.

**지휘**(指揮) command; 《지시》 directions; instructions; 《감독》 superintendence; supervision. ～하다 command; take command of 《troops》; lead; direct; instruct; superintend; 《악단을》 conduct; lead; direct; baton. ¶ B씨의 ～로 「conducted by 〔under the baton of 〕 Mr. B. / …의 ～하에 《be》 under (the) command of…; 《be》 under *a person's* direction; 《연주》 《be》 under

the baton of... / ~를 맡다 take 〔assume, hold〕 command 《of an army》; take 〔assume〕 the leadership 《of》; assume direction 《of》 / ~를 요청하다 ask orders 《from》 / ~를 받다 be under 《*a person's*》 command; be presided over 《by *a person*》; be under 《*a person's*》 supervision / 만사를 그의 ~에 의지했다 I looked to his guidance 〔directions〕 in everything.
◉ ~계통 a chain of command. ~관 a commander; an officer in command; a commanding officer 〔generals〕: 군 주요 ~관들 key military leaders; the commanding military generals / ~관의 교체 a change of command / 최고 ~관 the supreme commander; a captain general (*pl.* captains general). ~권 the (right of) command. ~능력 《군인의》 command ability. ~대 《연주의》 a podium (*pl.* -dia); a platform. ~도 a saber; a parade sword. ~봉 a baton. ~자 a commander; a director; a leader; 《음악의》 a conductor; a (musical) director: ~자로서 출연하다 make a podium appearance. ~차 a commander's car.

**직** 《발작》 an attack. ¶ 학질을 한 직 앓다 suffer from an attack of malaria.

**직**(職) 《일자리》 employment; work; a job; a situation; a position; 《직무》 *one's* duties; 《관공직》 an office; 《직업》 an occupation; a calling; a trade. ¶ 직을 구하다 seek employment; look for a position 〔job〕 / 직을 얻다 get 〔obtain〕 a job 〔position, situation〕 / 직을 잃다 lose *one's* job 〔employment〕; 《실직중》 be out of work / 직에 머물다 stay 〔remain〕 in office / 직에 앉다 take a position 《as a clerk》; 《취임하다》 take office / 직에서 밀려나다 be relieved of *one's* office; be dismissed; be fired 《미구어》 / 직을 그만두다 quit *one's* job.

**직**(直) 《당번》 duty; watch; guard; lookout. ¶ 일직 day duty.

**직-**(直) 《곧은》 straight; upright; perpendicular; direct. ¶ 직선 a straight line / 직수입 direct import.

**직각**(直角) 〖수학〗 a right angle. ¶ ~의 right-angled; rectangular / …와 ~으로 at a right angle to...; perpendicular to... / (…와) ~을 이루다 make a right angle 《with》; be 〔meet, cross〕 at right angles 《with》.
◉ ~삼각형 《미》 a right triangle; 《영》 a right-angled triangle. ~선 a perpendicular line. ~원기둥 〖수학〗 a right cylinder. ~원뿔 〖수학〗 a right circular cone. ~자 a square.

**직각**(直覺) intuition; direct perception. ~하다 intuit; know intuitively. ¶ ~적 intuitive; intuitional / ~적으로 알다 know by intuition. ◉ ~력 intuitive power. ~설 intuitionism. ~판단 intuitive judgment.

**직간**(直諫) direct 〔personal〕 admonition 〔remonstrance〕. ~하다 admonish directly 〔openly〕; reprove 《*a person*》 face to face.

**직감**(直感) intuition; 《구어》 a hunch; 《구어》 a gut feeling. ~하다 know by intuition 〔intuitively〕; perceive intuitively; feel 《*a thing*》 in *one's* bones. ¶ ~적으로 intuitively; by intuition / ~에 의존하다 rely on *one's* intuition / ~으로 알다 learn 「intuitively 〔by intuition〕 / 내 ~으로는 그가 살인범이 아니다 「My intuition tells 〔I have a gut feeling〕 that he is not the murderer.

**직거래**(直去來) direct 〔spot〕 transaction. ~하다 transact direct(ly) 《with》; make a direct deal 《with》. ¶ 외국인과 ~하다 deal directly with foreigners.

**직격**(直擊) direct hit. ◉ ~탄 a direct hit 〔shot〕: ~탄에 맞다 be hit directly by a bomb.

**직결**(直結) direct connection 〔coupling〕. ~하다 connect 〔link, couple〕 《*a thing*》 directly 《with》. ¶ ~되다 be connected 〔linked〕 directly 《with》; be directly linked 《to》 / 실험의 성패는 인류 번영과 ~되어 있다 The success (or failure) of the experiment is directly linked to the prosperity of mankind. / 그 문제는 국민 생활에 ~되어 있다 The problem is directly connected with national life. / 한국의 안전은 미국의 안전과 ~되어 있다 The security of Korea is vital to 〔for〕 the security of the United States.

**직경**(直徑) 〖수학〗 the diameter. ⇨ 지름.

**직계**(直系) a direct line (of descent). ¶ ~의 lineal / ~(의) 자손 a direct 〔lineal〕 descendant / 그는 드골 ~의 정치가이다 He is a direct descendant in the political line of de Gaulle.
◉ ~가족 family members in a direct line. ~존속[비속] a lineal ascendant 〔descendant〕. ~혈족 a lineal relation. ~회사 a directly affiliated firm 〔concern〕.

**직계**(職階) a job classification. ◉ ~제 a job-ranking 〔job classification〕

system; 《관청의》 a classified civil service system.

**직고**(直告) informing 〔reporting〕 truthfully. ～하다 inform 〔tell, report〕 truthfully.

**직공**(職工) a workman; a worker; an operative; a (factory) hand; a mechanic (기계공). ◉ ～기질 an artisan 〔a craftsman〕 spirit. ～장 a foreman.

**직관**(直觀) intuition. ⇨ 직각(直覺), 직감(直感). ◉ ～력 intuition; intuitive power. ～주의 intuition(al)ism.

**직교**(直交) ～하다 cross 〔meet〕 at right angles. ◉ ～좌표 『수학』 rectangular coordinates.

**직교역**(直交易) direct barter trade.

**직구**(直球) 『야구』 a straight ball 〔pitch〕. ¶ ～를 던지다 throw 〔pitch〕 a straight ball.

**직권**(職權) *one's* (official) authority 〔power〕. ¶ ～ 외의 outside *one's* authority; extraofficial / ～에 의하여 in virtue of *one's* office; *ex officio* (L.) / ～ 외의 일을 하다 overstep *one's* authority / ～을 행사〔남용〕하다 exercise 〔abuse〕 *one's* authority / 남의 ～을 침해하다 encroach on another's functions / ～을 위임하다 authorize 《*a person* to *do*》; invest 《*a person*》 with the authority / 의장의 ～으로써 귀하의 퇴장을 명한다 On my authority as chairman I order you to leave the room. / ～으로 사장은 최종 결정을 내렸다 By virtue of his position, the president made the final decision. ◉ ～남용 abuse of *one's* authority; wrongful exercise of authority. ～조정 mediation by virtue of *one's* authority 《as chairman》.

**직급**(職級) = 직계(職階).

**직기**(織機) a (weaver's-)loom; a weaving machine.

**직납**(直納) ～하다 deliver directly to 《a retailer》.

**직녀**(織女) a woman weaver; 《직녀성》 Vega; the Weaver.

**직능**(職能) a function. ¶ 판사의 ～ the function of a judge. ◉ ～검사 a performance test. ～급 wages based on job evaluation: 우리 급료는 ～급으로 되어 있다 Our wages are paid according to function. ～대표(제) vocational 〔functional〕 representation (system). ～별 조합 a craft union.

**직답**(直答) 《즉답》 a prompt 〔ready〕 answer 〔reply〕; 《직접 답변》 *one's* personal reply. ～하다 give a ready answer; answer personally. ¶ 나는 너의 ～을 들어야겠다 I would have your ready answer.

**직력**(職歷) *one's* business 〔professional〕 experience 〔career〕; *one's* work experience.

**직렬**(直列) 『물리』 a series; an electrical series. ◉ ～변압기 a series transformer. ～회로 a series circuit.

**직로**(直路) a straight road; a direct route.

**직류**(直流) 『물리』 direct current (생략 DC); continuous current; series flow. ◉ ～발전기 a DC generator 〔dynamo〕. ～변류기 a DC converter. ～회로 a direct current circuit.

**직립**(直立) standing erect. ～하다 stand erect 〔straight, upright〕. ¶ ～해서 upright; erect; in an upright position / ～보행하다 walk erect 〔upright〕 / 그는 사령관 앞에서 ～ 부동 자세를 취했다 He stood at attention before the commander in Chief. ◉ ～면〔선〕 『수학』 a perpendicular plane 〔line〕. ～원인(猿人) the Java man; *Pithecanthropus erectus* (학명).

**직매**(直賣) direct 〔spot, hand-to-hand〕 sale. ～하다 sell directly 〔on the spot〕; carry out direct sales. ¶ 산지 ～의 사과 apples sold directly by the producers / 이 야채는 생산자가 ～하고 있다 These vegetables are sold directly from the producers. ◉ ～소〔점〕 a direct-sales store 〔stall〕. ～품 articles sold directly.

**직면**(直面) ～하다 face; confront; meet face to face 《with》; be faced 《with》; be confronted 《by》; come up against 《a trouble》; be on the point 〔verge〕 of. ¶ ～한 문제 the problems that *one* faces / 불경기에 ～하여 in the face of business depression / 위험〔어려운 문제〕에 ～하다 be faced with danger 〔difficult problems〕 / 파멸에 ～하다 stand on the brink of ruin / 파산에 ～하다 be on the verge of bankruptcy / 회사는 경영 위기에 ～해 있다 The firm is in a financial crisis. / 그는 죽음에 ～했다 Death stared him in the face.

**직명**(職名) 《직업명》 a job name; (the name of) *one's* occupation; 《직책명》 *one's* official title; the title of *one's* office 〔position〕.

**직무**(職務) *one's* duty; an office; a function; a job. ¶ ～상의 official; ex officio / ～를 수행하다〔다하다〕 discharge 〔perform, do〕 *one's* duties; perform 〔fulfill〕 *one's* function(s) / ~를 게을리하다 neglect 〔be negligent of〕 *one's* duties; be derelict 〔remiss〕 in *one's* duties 〔work〕 / ~를 분담하다 divide duties 《among》 / ~에 반(反)하다 be inconsistent with *one's* duty 〔function〕 / ~에 충실하다 be faithful to *one's* duties 〔job〕 / ~에 힘쓰다 attend diligently to *one's* duties / 그렇게 하는 것은 당신 ~ 밖의 일이다 You overstep your authority to do so. / ~상 하는 일이니 나쁘게 생각하지 말았으면 싶네 I am doing this as a matter of duty. I hope you will not take it amiss.

◉ ~규정 office regulations. ~급 ⇨ 직능급. ~내용 job specifications. ~방해 interference with *one's* work 〔*a person's* duty〕. ~분담 distribution 〔allotment〕 of (office) duties. ~분석(표) a job analysis (sheet). ~수당 a service allowance; wages attached to a post. ~수행 performance of *one's* duty. ~유기 dereliction 〔delinquency〕 of *one's* duty: ~ 유기로 고소당하다 be charged with dereliction of *one's* duty. ~정지 suspension of performing *one's* duties. ~집행 performance of *one's* duties: ~ 집행을 방해하다 interfere with 《an official》 in the performance of his duty. ~평가 a job evaluation.

**직무태만**(職務怠慢) neglect 〔dereliction〕 of duty; delinquency. ¶ ~으로 면직이 되다 be dismissed 〔discharged〕 for 〔on a charge of〕 neglect of duty; lose *one's* job through neglect of duty / ~이다 be neglectful of *one's* duties. ◉ ~자 a defaulter; a delinquent.

**직물**(織物) textile fabrics; textiles; 《천》 cloth; 《제품》 woven goods.
◉ ~공업 the textile industry. ~공장 a textile factory. ~류 woven goods; fabrics; drapery. ~상 a textile 〔dry goods 《미》, drapery 《영》〕 dealer. ~시장 the cloth market. ~업 《제조》 textile manufacture; 《판매》 the textile 〔dry goods 《미》, drapery 《영》〕 business.

**직배**(直配) direct delivery 〔distribution〕. ~하다 deliver 〔distribute〕 directly. ¶ 산지 ~의 사과 apples distributed directly by the producers / 이 야채는 생산자가 ~하고 있다 These vegetables are delivered directly from the producers.

**직분**(職分) *one's* duty; *one's* job. ¶ ~을 다하다 do 〔discharge〕 *one's* duty (to the full); fulfill *one's* duty / ~을 지키다 perform *one's* job responsibly 〔faithfully〕; be faithful to *one's* duty / 그는 자기의 ~을 알고 있다 He knows his place.

**직불카드** a debit card. ¶ ~로 결제하다 pay for 《the radio》 with *one's* debit card.

**직사**(直射) ① 《광선의》 direct rays (of the sun). ~하다 《the sun》 shine 〔beat〕 directly 《upon》. ¶ 일광의 ~를 받다 be exposed to the direct rays of the sun. ② 《포화의》 direct 〔frontal〕 fire. ~하다 fire direct 《upon》; fire point-blank 《at》. ¶ 포화의 ~를 받으며 under direct fire. ◉ ~광선 a direct ray of light. ~일광 《avoid》 direct sunlight: ~일광을 피할 것 《게시》 Keep out of the sun. ~포 a direct-firing gun; a gun (firing point-blank).

**직사각형**(直四角形) 〖수학〗 a right-angled tetragon; a rectangle. 「shape.

**직삼**(直蔘) ginseng dried in its original

**직삼각형**(直三角形) 〖수학〗 a right-angled triangle.

**직선**(直線) a straight line; a beeline. ¶ ~으로 in a straight line; straight / ~을 긋다 draw a straight line / ~으로 늘어서다 line up in a straight line / 두 점을 ~으로 연결하시오 Draw a straight line between those two points. ◉ ~기선 a straight baseline. ~미 linear beauty. ~운동 rectilinear movement; a rectilinear 〔straight=line〕 motion. ~코스 a straight course.

**직선거리**(直線距離) one-line distance. ¶ ~로 in a beeline 〔a crow line, an air line 《미》〕 / 집에서 서울까지는 ~로 40킬로 된다 It is forty kilometers from my house to Seoul 「in a beeline 〔as the crow flies〕.

**직설**(直說) "straight talk"; plain speaking; frankness. ~하다 talk frankly 〔straight from the shoulder〕; speak out; speak up; speak without reserve. ◉ ~법 〖문법〗 the indicative mood.

**직성풀리다**(直星—) be satisfied 〔gratified〕; be appeased; feel relieved; [사물이 주어] appease 〔satisfy〕 *one's* conscience. ¶ 직성이 풀리지 않다 be not satisfied; feel regret 《for》 / 그는 무엇이건 자신이 직접 하지 않고선 직성이 안 풀린다 He is not satisfied with anything unless he does it by him-

self. 「direct tax section.
**직세**(直稅) a direct tax. ◉ ～과 the
**직소**(直訴) a direct appeal 〔petition〕. ～하다 appeal directly; make a direct appeal 《to the President》. ¶ ～를 기도하다 attempt a direct appeal 《to the Emperor》.
**직속**(直屬) directly belonging 《to》; being directly attached. ～하다 belong directly 《to》; be directly owned 《by》; be under direct control 《of》.
¶ ～의 under direct control 《of》/ ～부하 a subordinate under direct control / 그는 나의 ～ 상관이다 He is the senior officer I directly belong to. *or* I am directly responsible to him.
**직손**(直孫) direct 〔lineal〕 descendants; descendants in the direct line.
**직송**(直送) direct delivery 〔shipment〕. ～하다 send direct(ly) 《to》. ¶ 산지 ～의 야채 vegetables sent directly from the growing district; vegetables direct 〔fresh〕 from the farm.
**직수굿하다** (be) docile; obedient; quiet; reserved. ¶ 직수굿한 아이 a docile child.
**직수입**(直輸入) direct import(ation). ～하다 import 《goods》 direct(ly) 《from》/ 저 상점은 런던에서 ～한 구두를 팔고 있다 That store sells shoes imported direct from London. ◉ ～무역 direct import trade. ～상 a direct importer. ～품 direct imports; articles 〔goods〕 imported direct from abroad.
**직수출**(直輸出) direct export(ation). ～하다 export 《goods》 direct(ly) 《to》. ◉ ～상 a direct exporter. ～품 direct exports.
**직시**(直視) looking in the face. ～하다 look 《*a person*》 in the face; look straight 〔squarely〕 at; face. ¶ 사실을 ～하다 face facts as they are; confront facts boldly / 현실을 ～하다 face up to the reality.
**직시류**(直翅類) 〖곤충〗 *Orthoptera* (학명).
**직심**(直心) an honest heart; honesty; straightforwardness. ¶ ～스럽다 (be) honest; straight; straightforward.
**직언**(直言) plain speaking; direct 〔frank, open〕 speech; speaking without reserve; outspoken advice. ～하다 speak plainly 〔frankly, without reserve〕; speak out; tell 《*a matter*》 to 《*a person's*》 face. ¶ ～ 직행하다 speak plainly and act immediately; don't beat about the bush / 충신은 임금에게 ～하기를 꺼리지 않는다 A loyal subject does not mince his words to his lord. ◉ ～가 a plain-spoken 〔a free-spoken, an outspoken〕 person.
**직업**(職業) a job; *one's* occupation; a vocation; a career; *one's* business; a line of work; a calling; 《전문적》 a profession; 《장사·수공 따위》 a trade.

> 용법 **job** 직업을 나타내는 구어적 표현, 「직장·업무·직업」 등의 뜻으로 널리 쓰이는 말. **occupation** 우리말의 「직업」이라는 딱딱하고 격식을 차린 표현에 딱 들어맞는 말. 신상 명세서나 그 밖의 서류의 「직업」란에는 이 말을 씀. **vocation** 원래는 천직이라는 뜻의 말이었으나, 지금은 오랜 기간의 훈련을 필요로 하는 기술적인 일을 가리키는 말. **career** 특별한 훈련이나 기술을 필요로 하며, 평생의 업으로 삼으려는 직업을 가리키는 말. **business** 영리를 목적으로 하는 장사라는 뜻으로 넓은 범위의 일을〔업무를〕 가리키는 말. **work** 어떤 종류의 일에 대해서도 쓸 수 있는 말로, occupation 또는 vocation과 바꿔 쓸 수 있는 평이한 말. **profession** 상당히 높은 학력 등을 필요로 하는 전문적인 직업. **trade** 특히 상업 혹은 손으로 하는 일.

¶ ～별의 classified by occupations / ～별로 according to occupations; 《classify》 by occupation / ～이 없는 jobless; unemployed / ～을 구하다 seek employment; look for a position 〔job〕 / ～을 고르다 choose an occupation / ～을 얻다 get 〔obtain〕 a job 〔position, situation〕; be employed / ～을 바꾸다 change *one's* line of work; change *one's* occupation; switch jobs / ～을 바꾸지 않다 stick to *one's* occupation / ～에 종사하다 follow 〔engage in〕 an occupation / ～은 인쇄공이다 be a printer by trade / 의사를 ～으로 하다 make a business 〔profession〕 of a doctor; be a physician by profession / ～을 익히다 learn a trade / ～이 무엇입니까 What line of business are you in? *or* What is your occupation? *or* What do you do (for a living)? / ～에 귀천이 없다 All legitimate trades are equally honorable. / 나는 ～상 자주 여행을 하여야 한다 My business 〔job〕 requires a good deal of traveling. / 자기에게 맞는 ～을 찾는다는 것은 매우 중요하다 It is very important to find the right job. ◉ ～경력 *one's* occupational career. ～교육 vocational education. ～군인 a professional 〔career 《미》〕 soldier

〔military officer〕. ～대표제 the professional representative system. ～댄서 a taxi dancer. ～별 전화번호부 a classified telephone directory. ～별 조합 a craft union. ～병 an occupational disease. ～보도 vocational guidance 〔training〕: ～ 보도소 the Public Vocational Training Agency. ～분야 fields of work. ～선수 a professional (player); a pro (*pl.* ～s) 《구어》. ～소개소 an employment agency 〔office〕; a placement bureau 《미》. ～안내란 a "Help Wanted" column (★「구직란」은 a 'Situation Wanted' column). ～안정법 the Employment Security Law. ～안정소 《공공 직업 안정소》 the employment office 《미》; a job centre 《영》; the Public Employment Security Office. ～여성 a working 〔career〕 woman. ～외교관 a career diplomat. ～윤리 《the establishment of》 professional 〔vocational〕 ethics. ～의식 occupational consciousness; professional sense; pride in *one's* job; awareness of the responsibilities of *one's* profession. ～적 professional: 반～적 semi-professional. ～적성 vocational aptitude: ～적성 검사 a vocational aptitude test. ～전선 the struggle for jobs. ～전환 (a) change of *one's* occupation. ～정치가 a professional politician. ～학교 a vocational 〔trade〕 school. ～화 professionalization: ～화하다 professionalize. ～훈련 vocational training: ～훈련원〔소〕 a vocational training center.

**직역**(直譯) a literal 〔strict, close, direct, verbatim, word-for-word〕 translation. ～하다 translate 「literally 〔word for word〕. ¶ ～적인 metaphrastic / 전체 문장을 ～하다 translate the whole sentence literally 〔word for word〕.
◉ ～주의 literalism.

**직영**(直營) direct management; direct control. ～하다 manage 〔operate〕 《a store, *etc.*》 directly. ¶ 호텔 ～의 레스토랑 a restaurant managed by the hotel (in which it is housed) / 정부의 ～ 사업 an enterprise under government management / 정부의 ～이다 be under the direct management of the government.

**직원**(職員) an employee; a member of the staff; 《대학 등의》 the faculty; [총칭] the staff; the personnel. ¶ 철도청 ～ the staff of the (Korean) National Railroad Administration / ～의 이동 a change in the staff; a reshuffle of personnel / 회사 ～으로 있다 be on the staff of a company / 그는 그 중학교 ～이다 He is on the staff of the middle school.
◉ ～공제 조합 a mutual aid association of personnel. ～단체 an employees' organization. ～명부〔록〕 a staff list 〔register〕; 《공무원의》 a list of government officials. ～실 《학교의》 a teachers' 〔faculty〕 room. ～일동 all the members of the staff; all the staff. ～회(의) a 「staff 〔teachers'〕 meeting. ～훈련 staff training.

**직유**(直喩) 〖수사법〗 a simile.

**직인**(職印) an official seal; 《정부의》 a government seal.

**직임**(職任) *one's* office 〔official〕 duties.

**직장**(直腸) 〖해부〗 the rectum (*pl.* -ta). ¶ ～의 rectal. ◉ ～경 〖의학〗 a rectoscope. ～암 rectal cancer; cancer of the rectum. ～염 procititis. ～탈〔탈출〕 prolapse of the rectum.

**직장**(職長) a foreman.

**직장**(職場) *one's* place of work 〔employment〕; *one's* workplace; 《공장》 a workshop; the office (where *one* works). ¶ ～의 꽃 a beauty in the office / ～에 충실하다 stick to *one's* post 〔office〕 faithfully / ～을 지키다 stick to *one's* post / ～을 버리다〔이탈하다〕 desert 〔walk off 〕 *one's* post 〔job〕; walk out (on *one's* job) / ～에서 쫓겨나다 be forced 〔compelled〕 to leave *one's* position / ～에 돌아가다 return to work / ～을 그만두다 quit 〔throw up〕 *one's* job / ～을 자주 바꾸다〔옮기다〕 change *one's* employment with (great) frequency / ～을 찾다 seek employment; look for a position 〔job〕 / ～을 얻다 get 〔obtain〕 a job 〔position, situation〕; be employed 〔hired〕.
◉ ～경력 *one's* employment history. ～내결혼 marriage between people working in the same place. ～대표 《노동 쟁의의》 a shop deputy. ～대항 노래 자랑 a singing contest of companies 〔workshops〕. ～대회 a workshop 〔shop-floor〕 rally 〔meeting〕. ～보도(輔導) training within industry (생략 T.W.I.); 《직장 연수》 on-the-job training. ～복귀(운동) back-to-work (movement): ～ 복귀령 a "return-to-work" order; a "halt-strike" order. ～이탈 job desertion; a walkout 《미》. ～투쟁 a workshop struggle. ～폐쇄 the

lockout. ～환경 *one's* work environment. 「functions.

**직장**(職掌) the division of official duties;

**직재**(直裁) ① 《즉시 재결》 a prompt decision. ～하다 make a prompt decision; decide promptly 〔on the spot〕. ② 《몸소 재결》 a direct 〔personal〕 decision. ～하다 make direct decision; decide personally.

**직전**(直前) ¶ ～에 right 〔just, immediately〕 before; just prior to / 완성 ～의 그림 a painting just before completion / 전쟁 ～에 on the eve of the war; just before the war / 출발 ～에 그를 방문했다 I called on him just prior to my departure.

**직접**(直接) ¶ ～의 direct; immediate; personal (★ 대리가 아닌 본인의) / ～으로 directly; immediately; at firsthand; 《몸소》 personally; in person / ～ 간접으로 directly and 〔or〕 indirectly; one way or another / 사고의 ～원인 the immediate cause of the accident / ～얻은 정보 a firsthand information / ～행동하다 take a direct action / ～ 보다 have a firsthand look 《at》; witness 《*a thing*》 with *one's* own eyes / ～ 전달하다 deliver 〔hand over〕 《*a thing*》 personally; transmit directly / …에 ～적인 영향을 주다 have a direct influence on… / (…와) ～ 관계가 있다 have an immediate connection 《with》; be directly concerned 《in》 / 사람을 ～ 만나 보다 see a person personally / 그 일을 내가 ～ 보았다 I witnessed it with my own eyes. / 네가 그에게 ～ 말해라 You tell him personally. / ～ 간접으로 수고가 많았습니다 I owe you many obligations, directly and indirectly. / 그녀를 ～ 만나보는 것이 좋겠다 You had better see her 「in person 〔personally〕. / 내가 ～ 그에게 편지를 쓰겠습니다 I will write direct to him. (★ I will write directly to him.이면 「나는 곧 그에게 편지를 쓰겠다」는 뜻이 됨) / 본인 ～ 내담(來談)할 것 《게시》 Apply in person. / 나는 그와는 ～ 관계가 없다 I have no direct connection with him. / 나는 본인에게서 ～ 들었다 I have got the news at firsthand.

◉ ～거래 direct dealings. ～매매 spot sales. ～목적어 〖문법〗 a direct object. ～비 direct cost. ～선거 a direct election. ～세 a direct tax. ～영향 a direct influence. ～원인 a direct cause; an immediate cause 〔occasion〕. ～조명 direct illumination. ～청구 a direct claim to 《a local government》. ～투자 direct investment. ～행동 《take》 direct action. ～협상 direct negotiation. ～홍보활동 direct public relation. ～화법 〖문법〗 direct discourse 〔speech 《영》〕.

**직접담판**(直接談判) direct negotiation; a personal consultation. ～하다 have direct negotiation 《with》; negotiate 〔talk〕 directly 《with *a person*》.

**직제**(職制) 《기구》 the organization 〔setup〕 of an office. ¶ ～를 개편하다 reorganize an office.

◉ ～개편안 a reorganization plan.

**직조**(織造) weaving. ～하다 weave.

◉ ～공 a weaver. ～공장 a weaving shop; a textile mill. ～기 a loom; a weaving machine.

**직종**(職種) the kind 〔type, sort〕 of occupation; an occupational category. ¶ ～별로 by 〔according to〕 occupation / ～의 난이도와 책임도에 따른 호봉제 a (different) payment grade system in accordance with the difficulty and responsibility of their duties. ◉ ～분류 occupational classification.

**직직** ① 《긋는 소리》 with repeated written strokes; 《찢는 소리》 tearing; rending. ¶ ～ 찢다 tear 〔rend〕 《paper》 to pieces. ② 《지면을 끄는 모양》 dragging. ¶ 신발을 ～끌다 drag *one's* shoes noisily. ③ 《대소변 소리》 with repeated sounds of bird-droppings.

**직직거리다** keep dragging 〔scuffing〕 *one's* shoes.

**직진**(直進) ～하다 go straight on 〔ahead〕; make straight for; make a straight 「drive 〔advance〕 on. ¶ 빛은 ～한다 Light travels straight. / 그 차는 점멸등을 켠 채로 교차점을 ～했다 The car went straight through the intersection with its blinkers on.

**직책**(職責) the responsibilities of *one's* work 〔job〕; *one's* duty; (official) responsibility. ¶ ～상 as a matter of duty; in view of *one's* position (직책에 비추어) / ～을 다하다 discharge 〔perform〕 *one's* duties / ～을 중시하다 have a strong 〔keen〕 sense of duty 〔responsibility〕 / 그것은 과장인 자네 ～상의 일이다 As the chief of your section, you are responsible for it.

◉ ～수당 allowance for the post attached.

**직통**(直通) ① 《교통·통신의》 through traffic; direct communication. ～하다 communicate directly 《with》; 《도로가》

lead directly 《to》. ¶ 이것이 나의 ～전화 번호이다 If you dial this number, you can make direct contact with me. ② [비유적] 《즉효》 an immediate effect 《on》. ¶ 이 약은 통증에 ～이다 This medicine has 〔produces〕 a quick effect on pain. ◉ ～전화(선) a direct telephone line 〔service〕; 《정부 수뇌간의》 a hot line.

**직품**(職品) the grades of official ranks.

**직필**(直筆) unbiased writing; uncolored writing; straight reporting.

**직하**(直下) ① 《바로 밑》 ¶ ～에〔의〕 directly 〔just, right〕 under / 적도 ～의 섬 an island right 「on 〔under, below〕 the equator (line). ② 《내려감》 a perpendicular fall; falling plumb down. ～하다 fall perpendicularly 〔plumb down〕. ¶ 급전～하다 make a rapid 〔swift〕 movement; take a rapid turn. ◉ ～형 지진 a (strong) local earthquake.

**-직하다** it is possible 《to》; it is all right 《to》; it is 〔seems〕 likely; it is quite; 《…만하다》 it is worth. ¶ 있음직한 이야기 a likely story / 바람～ be desirable; it is to be desired 《that …》 / 믿음～ be reliable 〔trustworthy〕 / 있음직한 곳은 모두 찾다 look for 《*a thing*》 in every likely place.

**직할**(直轄) direct control; direct jurisdiction. ～하다 control directly; hold under direct jurisdiction. ¶ 교육부～의 학교 a school under the direct control of the Ministry of Education / …의 ～로 만들다 transfer 《it》 to the direct control of… / ～이 되다 come under the direct control 《of》.
◉ ～시(市) a special city under the direct control of the central government. ⇨ 광역시. ～식민지 《영국의》 the crown colony. ～파출소 a police box under the direct control (of the police station).

**직함**(職銜) the title of a position; *one's* official title. ¶ 어마어마한 ～ a high-sounding title / ～이 있는 with a title to *one's* name; titled / ～이 없는 without any title; untitled.

**직항**(直航) 《기선의》 sailing directly; a direct voyage; 《비행기의》 a nonstop flight 《to》. ～하다 sail direct(ly) 《to, for》; make a nonstop flight 《to》. ¶ 이 배는 홍콩 ～이다 This ship is bound direct for Hong Kong. / 그는 비행기로 런던에 ～했다 He flew straight to London. ◉ ～로 a direct line; 《항공의》 a direct air route. ～선(船) a direct steamer 《for》.

**직행**(直行) going direct 〔nonstop〕. ～하다 go straight 〔direct〕 《to》; run through 《to》. ¶ 사고 현장에 ～하다 rush right 〔straight〕 to the scene of the accident / 갈아타지 않고 ～하다 《기차 등이》 go 〔run〕 through without making a change / 열차는 정거하지 않고 ～합니다 The train goes through without a stop. / 그녀는 파리에서 ～으로 왔다 She came straight 〔direct〕 from Paris. ◉ ～버스 a through 〔nonstop〕 bus; a direct bus; a semi-express bus. ～열차 a through train. ～운행 through operation. ～편 《비행기의》 a nonstop 〔direct〕 flight 《to》.

**직후**(直後) ¶ ～의〔에〕 《때》 immediately 〔directly, right〕 after 《the war》; 《장소》 just behind; at the back 《of》 / 나는 사건 ～에 그녀를 보았다 I saw her immediately after the incident. / 6·25 전쟁 ～의 한국은 혼란스러웠다 Right after the Korean War, Korea was in a chaotic condition.

**진**(辰) 『민속』 《십이지의》 the Sign of the Dragon (= the 5th of the 12 Earth's Branches).

**진**(津) 《나무의》 resin; gum; sap; 《생리의》 secretion; 《담배의》 nicotine; tar. ¶ 송진 pine resin / 담뱃진 (tobacco) tar / 진을 내다 sap / 진이 나다 secrete gum 〔resin〕 / 담뱃대가 진으로 막혔다 The pipe is clogged up with tar.

**진**(陣) 《진영》 a military camp; 《진형》 a (battle) formation; a battle array; 《진지》 a position; 《대열》 lines; ranks. ¶ 장사진 a long line / 진을 치다 encamp; pitch a camp; take up (a) position / 진을 거두다 strike a camp; withdraw from a position.

**진** 《술》 gin. ¶ 드라이진 dry gin / 진피즈 gin fizz / 진토닉 gin and tonic.

**진** 《a pair of 》 jeans. ¶ 블루진 blue jeans / 진을 입은 젊은이 a young person in (blue) jeans / 진을 입다〔입고 있다〕 put on 〔have on, wear〕 jeans.

**진-**(眞) true; real; genuine. ¶ 진면목 *one's* true character.

**진가**(眞價) true 〔real, intrinsic〕 value; true worth 〔merit〕. ¶ 교육의 ～ the true value of education / ～를 발휘하다 prove *one's* merits 〔worth〕; give full play to *one's* ability / ～를 인정하다 appreciate 〔recognize〕 the value 《of》 / ～가 있다 have intrinsic value.

**진간장**(—醬) nicely aged soysauce.
**진갈이** 〖농업〗 ～하다 plow wet fields after rain.
**진갑**(進甲) *one's* 61st birthday. ◉ ～잔치 the celebration of *one's* 61st birthday.
**진개**(塵芥) dust; dirt; rubbish; refuse.
**진객**(珍客) a rare guest; a least-expected visitor 〔guest〕.
**진걸레** a wet scrub cloth or mop.
**진격**(進擊) 《진군》 a march onward; an advance; 《공격》 an attack; an assault; a drive; a charge(돌격). ～하다 march 〔advance〕 《against, on》; make an attack 《upon》; assault; charge 《at, on》. ◉ ～군 an attacking force. ～명령 the order to advance. ～부대 a storming party; an attack force.
**진경**(鎭痙) 〖의학〗 ¶ ～성의 spasmolytic. ◉ ～제 〖약〗 a spasmolytic; an antispasmodic.
**진계**(塵界) this dirty 〔filthy〕 world.
**진공**(眞空) 〖물리〗 a vacuum. ¶ ～의 evacuated 《vessels》 / ～으로 만들다 evacuate 《a flask》; make a (perfect) vacuum / ～이 되다 be evacuated; a vacuum forms 〔is created〕 / 병 속은 ～이다 The inside of the bottle has no air. ◉ ～건조기 a vacuum drier. ～계(計) a vacuum gauge. ～관 《미》 a vacuum tube; 《영》 a vacuum valve. ～도 the degree of a vacuum. ～방전 〖전기〗 vacuum discharge. ～브레이크 a vacuum brake. ～청소기 a vacuum cleaner 〔sweeper〕. ～펌프 a vacuum pump. ～포장 vacuum packing: ～포장하다 vacuum-seal 《frankfurters in a plastic package》 / ～포장의〔된〕 vacuum-packed 《smoked salmon》 / ～포장에 의한 저장 vacuum storage / ～포장된 냉장육 vacuum-packed chilled meat.
**진공**(進攻) an attack. ⇨ 진격.
**진과**(珍果) rare 〔uncommon〕 fruit.
**진과**(珍菓) rare dainties 〔delicacies〕.
**진구렁** a mud hole; a slough; a bog; 《곤경》 a quagmire; a morass. ¶ ～에 빠지다 fall in a mud hole; bog (down); sink in a bog; be 〔get〕 bogged / ～에 빠져들다 [비유적] bog down; be bogged 〔mired〕 down; get stuck in a bog; be driven into a quagmire / ～에서 빠져 나오다 find a way out of the swamp / ～에 점점 깊이 빠져들다 get bogged deeper in the mud.
**진국**(眞—) ① 《전국》 undiluted 〔unrefined〕「liquor 〔soysauce, *etc.*〕. ② 《사람》 a simple-hearted person; an honest person; "the salt of the earth".
**진군**(進軍) a march; (an) advance. ～하다 march; advance 《on, against》. ¶ ～나팔을 불다 sound (the bugle for) the march / ～중이다 be on the march / ～을 명하다 order the advance. ◉ ～가 a marching song.
**진귀**(珍貴) preciousness; valuableness. ～하다 (be) rare and precious; valuable; priceless.
**진급**(進級) (a) promotion. ～하다 be promoted 《to》; 《학년 등의》 move up 《to a higher class》. ¶ ～시키다 promote 〔advance〕 《*a person* to》 / ～이 빠르다〔늦다〕 be rapid 〔slow〕 in promotion / 대령으로 ～하다 be promoted to (be) a colonel / 3학년에 ～하다 be moved up to the third grade. ◉ ～상신(上申) a recommendation for promotion. ～시험 an examination for promotion.
**진기**(珍奇) rarity; novelty; curiosity; queerness. ～하다 (be) rare; curious; singular; queer; strange; fantastic. ¶ ～한 현상 a strange phenomenon / ～한 것 a rarity; a curiosity / ～한 듯이 《look at *a thing*》 curiously; with curiosity / ～해하다 regard 《*a thing*》 as unusual.
**진기**(津氣) stickiness; viscousness; persistency. ¶ ～ 있는 viscous.
**진기**(珍器) a rare article; a curio.
**진나다**(津—) ① 《진이 나다》 ⇨ 진(津). ② 《시달려》 get pestered 《by *a person*》.
**진날** a rainy 〔wet〕 day. ¶ ～ 개 사귀기 meeting with an unpleasant and troublesome affair / ～ 나막신 찾듯 asking for a long-neglected friend in time of need.
**진노**(震怒) wrath; rage; fury. ～하다 burst with anger; be enraged. ¶ 신의 ～를 달래다 appease the wrath of God.
**진눈깨비** sleet. ¶ ～가 오다 it sleets; it rains with a mingling of snow.
**진단**(診斷) 《질병·사물의》 diagnosis. ～하다 diagnose; make a diagnosis 《of》; give *one's* diagnosis 《of》. ¶ ～적 평가 〖교육〗 diagnostic evaluation / 조기 ～ an early check up / ～을 잘하는 의사 a doctor who is skilled in diagnosis / 의사의 ～을 받다 consult 〔see〕 a doctor / 정확하게 ～하다 make a correct diagnosis / ～을 잘못하다 err in diagnosis; make a wrong diagnosis / 병을 말라리아로 ～하다 diagnose 《*a*

*person's*》 sickness as malaria / 장티푸스로 죽은 것이라고 ～하다 pronounce 《*a person*》 dead of typhoid fever / 회사의 현황을 ～하다 make *one's* diagnosis of the firm's present situation. ◉ ～기술 diagnostic skill; a diagnostic technique. ～서 a diagnosis; a medical certificate: 사망 ～서 a death certificate. ～학 diagnostics. 종합～ a comprehensive medical testing.

**진달래** 〖식물〗 an azalea.

**진담**(珍談) a strange 〔funny〕 story; an amusing 〔intriguing〕 story. ¶ 저 사람에 대해서 많은 ～이 있다 There are many anecdotes told of him.

**진담**(眞談) a serious talk. ¶ 농담을 ～으로 듣다 take a joke seriously / 이번에는 ～이다 I mean business this time.

**진도**(進度) (the rate of ) progress. ¶ 학과의 ～ the progress of classwork / 반에 따라 ～가 다르다 Progress is different from class to class. / 이 학급은 영어 ～가 앞서〔뒤져〕 있다 This class is forward 〔backward〕 in English. ◉ ～표 a teaching schedule 《for the year》; a progress chart.

**진도**(震度) seismic intensity. ¶ 리히터 ～계 the Richter scale / ～ 5의 강진 a very strong earthquake of five degrees intensity; a tremor of the 5th degree on the seismic scale / ～ 7.8을 기록하다 register 7.8 on the Richter scale.

**진동**(振動) 〖물리〗 oscillation; vibration; a swing (시계추의). ～하다 oscillate; vibrate; swing. ¶ 공기의 ～ air vibrations / ～을 일으키다 set up vibrations 〔swing motion〕 / ～을 멈추다 stop the vibration. ◉ ～계 a vibrometer; a vibroscope. ～기 a vibrator; an oscillator. ～수 the number of vibrations; the frequency of vibration. ～시간 the oscillation time. ～전류 〖전기〗 an oscillating current. ～주기 period of vibration. ～파 an oscillating wave. ～판 a diaphragm; 《초인종 등의》 a trembler. ～회로 oscillation circuit. ～회수 frequency.

**진동**(震動) a shock; vibration; a tremor; a quake; concussion; 《엔진 등의》 throbbing 〔throbs〕 《of the engine》. ～하다 shake; quake; tremble; vibrate; throb. ¶ ～을 느끼다 feel a shock / ～시키다 shake; vibrate / 약간의 ～을 깨닫다 notice a slight tremor / 이 차는 ～이 심하다〔적다〕 This car shakes horribly 〔runs smoothly〕. / 집이 심하게 ～하였다 The house rocked violently. ◉ ～시간 the duration of the shock 〔vibration〕.

**진동항아리**(—缸—) 〖민속〗 ① 《무당의》 a spirit tablet in a shaman's home. ② 《항아리》 a jar where some money and rice are kept as a token to insure peace and prosperity.

**진두**(陣頭) 《at》 the head 《of an army》; the front. ¶ ～에 서다 take the lead 《in the sales promotion campaign》; be at the head 《of 》; lead the van 《of 》/ ～ 지휘하다 act as the leader 《of an army》; lead 《the search party》.

**진드근하다** (be) staid. ⇨ 진득하다.

**진드기** 〖동물〗 a tick; a mite; an acarid; an acarus (*pl.* -ri). ¶ ～ 같은 사람 a barnacle; a hanger-on / ～에 물리다 be bitten by a tick / ～같이 달라붙다 fasten on 《*a person*》 like a tick; cling 〔stick〕 to 《*a person*》 like a leech.

**진득거리다** ① 《들러붙다》 keep sticking 〔holding on, adhering〕. ② 《검질기다》 resist cutting; (be) stubborn; tough; steadfast; unyielding. ¶ 페인트가 아직 진득거린다 The paint is still sticky 〔wet and smeary〕.

**진득이** gravely; sedately; with dignity; in earnest; soberly; quietly; patiently. ¶ ～ 공부하다 settle down to *one's* studies.

**진득진득** 《끈적끈적》 stickily; adhesively; 《검질긴 모양》 stubborn(ly); unyielding(ly). ～하다 (be) sticky; gluey; stubborn; tough; tenacious.

**진득하다** (be) staid; sedate; sober; dignified; grave; earnest; quiet; patient. ¶ 진득한 성격 a staid character.

**진디** 〖곤충〗 ① an aphid; an ant cow; a plant louse. ② ⇨ 진드기. ◉ ～등에 a gnat; a sandfly. 진딧물: 진딧물 내리다 《a plant》 be infested with plant lice.

**진땀**(津—) sticky 〔greasy〕 sweat. ¶ ～나다 sweat hard / ～ 빼다 have a hard time; have an awful 〔a hell of a〕 time / 시험 치르느라 ～ 빼다 sweat out an exam.

**진력**(盡力) 《애씀》 endeavor(s); effort(s); exertion(s); 《돌봄》 service(s); good offices. ～하다 try hard to *do;* endeavor; make efforts; exert *oneself;* render services. ¶ 그의 ～에 의하여 through his good offices / ～에 보답하

다 reward *a person's* service / 교육 사업에 ~하다 render services to the educational work / 사회 복지 증진에 다소 ~하다 do something toward social welfare / 인류를 위하여 크게 ~하다 do 〔render〕 great services to mankind.

**진력나다**(盡力—) get sick (and tired) 《of》; tire 〔get tired〕 《of》; become disgusted 《with》. ¶ 차츰 이 일에 진력이 나기 시작했다 I'm getting tired of this job.

**진로**(進路) a course (to advance); a way; a route; *one's* path in life. ¶ ~에 in the course 《of》 / 졸업 후의 ~를 정하다 decide on the course 〔the career to pursue〕 after graduation / ~가 막히다 be blocked the way / ~를 가로막다 block 〔stand in〕 《*one's*》 way / ~를 개척하다 cut 〔cleave〕 *one's* way / 인생의 ~를 그르치다 take a wrong turning in life / 후진을 위해 ~를 열어 주다 make way for *one's* juniors / 태풍의 ~에 놓여 있다 be in the path of the typhoon / 태풍은 ~를 동쪽으로 바꿨다 The typhoon shifted toward the east 〔turned its course eastward〕. ◉ ~지도 〖교육〗 academic and career counseling.

**진료**(診療) medical examination and treatment. ~하다 give medical treatment; treat. ¶ ~받다 receive (medical) treatment; be treated / ~신청서 작성하는 곳 《게시》 Fill out medical treatment application form here. ◉ ~소 a clinic; a medical office. ~순위표 a treatment order chart. ~시간 consultation 〔office 《미》〕 hours. ~실 an examination 〔a consultation〕 room; a medical office.

**진루하다**(進壘—) 〖야구〗 advance. ¶ 2루에 ~ advance 〔move on〕 to second base.

**진리**(眞理) truth. ¶ ~의 추구 the pursuit of truth; a search for truth / 만고 불변의 ~ an eternal 〔a permanent〕 truth / 움직일 수 없는 ~ an uncontrovertible 〔unquestionable〕 truth / ~의 탐구자 a seeker after truth / 보편적 ~ a universal truth / 과학적 ~ the truths of science; the scientific truths / ~를 탐구하다 seek (after) truth / 그의 말에도 일면의 ~가 있다 There is some truth in what he says.

**진맥**(診脈) feeling 〔taking〕 the pulse (for diagnosis). ~하다 feel 〔take〕 《*a person's*》 pulse.

**진면목**(眞面目) *one's* true self 〔character〕. ¶ ~을 발휘하다 show 〔exhibit〕 *one's* true character 〔ability, gifts〕.

**진멸**(殄滅) annihilation; extermination. ~하다 annihilate; exterminate. ¶ 이단을 ~하다 exterminate the heresy.

**진목**(珍木) a rare tree.

**진무**(鎭撫) pacification; placating. ~하다 pacify; placate; calm; quell; quiet; mollify. ¶ 폭도를 ~하다 placate 〔quell〕 the mob / 정부 정책은 민중의 분노를 ~하지는 못하였다 The government policy failed to quiet 〔quell〕 the anger of the people down.

**진무르다** be blistered 〔sore, inflamed〕; fester; be bleared 〔bleary〕 (눈이). ¶ 진무른 sore; inflamed; festered / 빨갛게 진무른 살 an inflamed raw skin / 진무른 눈 blear 〔sore〕 eyes.

**진문**(珍問) a strange 〔an extraordinary〕 question.

**진문**(珍聞) rare news; a curious story.

**진물** ooze 〔watery discharge〕 from a sore. ¶ ~이 흐르는 부스럼 a running sore / ~이 나다 a sore oozes discharge; run with discharge.

**진물진물** ~하다 (be) all inflamed 〔blistered〕.

**진미**(珍味) 《맛》 a delicate flavor 〔taste〕; 《음식》 a dainty; a delicacy; a delicate tidbit; "goodies". ⇨ 산해진미(山海珍味). ¶ 계절의 ~ delicacies of the season / 갖은 ~를 먹다 have all sorts of delicacies / 이건 ~로구나 What a delicacy this is!

**진미**(眞味) true taste; genuine appreciation. ¶ 동양화의 ~를 알다 appreciate what Oriental painting is all about.

**진박새** 〖조류〗 a coal tit; a titmouse.

**진발** muddy feet 〔shoes〕. ¶ ~로 마루를 더럽히다 soil the floor with muddy feet 〔shoes〕.

**진방**(辰方) 〖민속〗 the Direction of the Dragon (=southeast-by-east).

**진배없다** be equal 《to》; be as good as; be on a level 《with》; be on a par 《with》; be no worse 《than》. ¶ 죽은 거나 ~ be virtually 〔as good as〕 dead / 새거나 ~ be as good as new / 그런 말은 모욕이나 ~ Such a speech practically amounts to an insult.

**진버짐** 〖한의〗 eczema; a watery ringworm. ¶ ~이 난 얼굴 an eczematous face.

**진범**(인)(眞犯(人)) the true culprit; the real offender 〔criminal〕.

**진법**(陣法) 〖군사〗 disposition of troops; plan of campaign; battle array. ¶ 방

어〔공격〕 ～ defensive 〔offensive〕 disposition.

**진보**(進步) progress; (an) advance; advancement; (an) improvement. ～하다 (make) progress; advance; improve.

> (용법) **progress** 눈에 띄는 비교적 현저한 발달. **advance** 목표를 향한 전진을 뜻하며, 진보의 정도에 관해서는 뜻하는 바 없음. **improvement** 불만스러운 점이나 미비한 점을 개선해 나아가는 진보.

¶ ～적인 progressive ⇨진보적 / 위대한 ～ great progress / 놀라운 ～ marvelous 〔wonderful〕 progress / 급속한〔현저한〕 ～ rapid 〔remarkable〕 progress / 과학의 ～ the progress of science / ～한 국민 an advanced nation / ～가 빠르다〔더디다〕 make rapid 〔slow〕 progress / ～를 그치다 make no further progress / ～를 조장하다 further 〔facilitate〕 the progress / 별로 ～하지 않다 make little progress / ～를 저해하다 hinder 〔retard, impede〕 progress / 착실히 ～하다 make steady progress / 그의 영어는 매우 ～하였다 He has made great progress in his English. ◉ ～주의 progressivism: ～주의자 a progressive. ～파 the progressives; a progressive group 〔faction〕.

**진보적**(進步的) progressive; advanced. ¶ ～인 사람 a man of progressive ideas 〔advanced views〕; a forward-looking〔-thinking〕 man / ～인 사상 a progressive idea.

**진본**(珍本) a rare (old) book.

**진본**(眞本) an authentic 〔unforged〕 piece of writing 〔painting〕. ¶ 루벤스의 ～ a genuine Rubens.

**진부**(眞否) truth or falsehood; truth (or otherwise). ¶ ～를 확인하다 ascertain 〔find out〕 whether it is true or not; check the truth 《of a statement》.

**진부**(陳腐) staleness; triteness; commonplaceness; banality. ～하다 (be) stale; hackneyed; old-fashioned; antiquated; commonplace; worn-out. ¶ ～한 말 a trite remark / ～한 학설 a worn-out theory / ～한 격언 a copybook maxim / ～한 문구 a hackneyed phrase; a *cliché* (F.) / ～한 표현 a trite expression / ～한 생각 a commonplace idea / ～한 익살 a stale joke / 그의 이론은 모두 ～하고 평범하다 His arguments are all cut and dried.

**진사**(陳謝) an apology. ～하다 apologize 《to *a person*》 《for》; express *one's* regret. ¶ ～의 편지 a letter of apology / ～할 것을 요구하다 demand an apology 《from》.

**진사**(進士) 〖고제도〗 a person who passed the primary state examination only.

**진상**(眞相) the truth; the actual 〔real〕 facts. ¶ ～을 밝히다 disclose 〔reveal〕 the truth; give a true account 《of》 / ～을 추궁〔규명〕하다 inquire into the real state of affairs / 일의 ～을 알다 know the truth about an affair; see a matter in its true light / ～을 말하다 lay bare the truth of 《*a matter*》 / ～을 파악하다 get at the truth 〔real state of affairs〕 / ～을 흐리다 put a false color on 《*a matter*》 / 불원간 ～이 드러나겠지 The truth will be out some day. / ～이 밝혀졌다 The truth has come out. / 조금씩 ～을 알게 되었다 Bit by bit the real situation dawned on me. ◉ ～조사단〔위원회〕 a fact-finding mission 〔committee〕.

**진상**(進上) the offering 〔presentation〕 《of local product》 to the king. ～하다 offer 〔present〕 《a local product》 to the king. ◉ ～물 a present to the king.

**진서**(珍書) a rare 〔treasured〕 book.

**진선미**(眞善美) truth, good(ness) and beauty. 「〔view〕.

**진설**(珍說) a novel 〔strange〕 opinion

**진성**(眞性) ① 《천성》 *one's* inborn nature. ② 〖의학〗 genuineness. ¶ ～의 genuine; true. ◉ ～뇌염 genuine encephalitis: ～뇌염 환자 a genuine encephalitis case; a genuine case of encephalitis. ～콜레라 (a case of) genuine 〔true〕 cholera.

**진세**(陣勢) the position of troops; the disposition of forces; 《군세》 military strength.

**진세**(塵世) this dirty 〔filthy〕 world; this mortal life. ¶ ～의 번거로움 worldly cares; this mortal coil / ～를 벗어나다 seclude *oneself* from the world; keep aloof from the world / ～를 버리다 renounce the world.

**진솔** ① 《새 옷》 brand-new clothes. ② ⇨진솔옷. ◉ ～옷 ramie-cloth garments made in spring or fall. ～저고리 a brand-new coat.

**진수**(珍羞) rare dainties; delicacies. ◉ ～성찬 a sumptuous meal 〔feast〕: ～성찬을 대접받다 be entertained with all kind of delicacies.

**진수**(眞髓) 《본질》 the essence; 《정수》 the quintessence; the spirit; the soul; 《핵심》 the pith; the core. ¶ 민주주의의 ~ the essence of democracy / 화랑도의 ~ the spirit of *Hwarangdo* / 불교의 ~ the soul of Buddhism.

**진수**(進水) launching 《a vessel》. ~하다 《배를》 launch; 《배가》 be launched; take the water. ◉ ~대 the launching platform 〔ways〕. ~식 a launching ceremony.

**진술**(陳述) a statement; a deposition (증인의). ~하다 state; set forth; give 〔make〕 a statement; expound 〔explain〕 《*one's* views on a subject》. ¶ 거짓 없는〔허위의〕 ~을 하다 make a true 〔false〕 statement / ~을 취소하다 withdraw 〔retract〕 *one's* statement / 자기 입장을 ~하다 state *one's* case 〔situation〕 / 의견을 ~하다 state 〔set forth〕 *one's* views / 증인은 피고에게 유리〔불리〕한 ~을 하였다 The witness made a statement for 〔against〕 the defendant. ◉ ~서 a (written) statement 〔declaration〕: ~서를 제출하다 send 〔hand〕 in a statement.

**진시**(辰時) 〚민속〛 the Watch of the Dragon; the 5th of the 12 double-hours (=7−9 a.m.); the 9th of the 24 hours (=7 : 30−8 : 30 a.m).

**진실**(眞實) truth; fact; reality; 《성실》 sincerity. ~하다 (be) true; real; sincere; genuine. ¶ 역사적인 ~ historical truth / ~하게〔로〕 truly; really; in reality; sincerely / ~하지 않은 insincere; unfaithful; false / ~을 말하자면 to tell the truth; the fact is… / ~하게 대하다 act sincerely 《toward *a person*》 / ~을 왜곡하다 bend 〔twist〕 the truth / ~을 밝히다 reveal the truth / ~을 말하다 tell 〔speak〕 the truth / ~을 증명하다 prove the truth 《of》 / 안됐지만 그것은 ~이다 That is only too true. / ~은 밝혀지기 마련이다 The truth is bound to come to light anyway. / 경찰은 그의 말이 ~인지 의심했다 The police doubted the truth of his statement.

**진실성**(眞實性) the truth 〔veracity, authenticity〕 《of a report》; fidelity (충실성). ¶ 보고의 ~을 의심하다 doubt the truth of a report / ~이 없다 there is no truth 《in his statement》/ 그 이야기는 ~이 없다 The story lacks reality. / 그녀의 이야기에는 ~이 있는 것 같았다 There was a ring of truth in what she said.

**진심**(眞心) a true heart; sincerity (성심); earnest. ¶ ~어린 sincere; hearty; heartfelt; wholehearted; cordial; warm / ~으로 sincerely; heartily; from (the bottom of) *one's* heart / ~에서 우러나오는 감사 thanks from the bottom of *one's* heart / ~으로 성공을 바라다 sincerely hope for success / ~을 토로하다 speak out of *one's* heart; lay *one's* heart open 《to》 / ~으로 이야기하다 speak from *one's* heart / ~을 밝히다 unbosom *oneself* 《to》; open *one's* heart 《to》 / ~으로 감사하다 thank 《*a person*》 from the bottom of *one's* heart; express *one's* hearty thanks 《to》; thank a million / ~으로 성공을 축하합니다 My sincere and hearty congratulation for your success. / 그가 과연 ~으로 그런 소리를 했을까 I wonder if he really meant what he said.

**진압**(鎭壓) suppression; repression; subjugation. ~하다 suppress; repress; subdue; quell; subjugate; put down. ¶ 폭동을 ~하다 quell 〔put down〕 a riot / 반란은 그날 안으로 ~되었다 The riot was suppressed within the day. / 경찰은 시위를 ~했다 The police put down the demonstration. ◉ ~경찰 《데모·난동 등의》 the riot police. ~책 a repressive measure.

**진애**(塵埃) dust; dirt. ¶ ~ 속에 버려두다 expose 《*a thing*》 to dust.

**진액**(津液) resin; gum; sap; extract. ¶ ~이 많은 resinous / 포도나무를 베면 ~이 나온다 A grape vine bleeds when cut.

**진언**(進言) 《a piece 〔word〕 of》 advice; counsel; a suggestion. ~하다 advise; counsel; suggest; propose. ¶ 그는 총리에게 양국간의 무역 증진에 대해 ~했다 He made a proposal to the Prime Minister about increasing trade between the two countries.

**진열**(陳列) (an) exhibition; (a) show; (a) display. ~하다 exhibit; display; put 《*something*》 on show 〔exhibition〕. ¶ ~중인 상품 wares on show 〔display〕 / 화랑에 ~되어 있는 그림 the paintings on exhibition at the art gallery / ~되어 있다 be placed on show; be on show 〔display〕; be exhibited / 팔려고 ~하다 lay 《articles》 out for sale. ◉ ~관 a 《commercial》 museum; a gallery (미술품의). ~대 a display stand 〔counter〕. ~실 a showroom. ～장(欌) a showcase; a display 〔an exhibit〕 case. ～창 a show 〔display〕 window. ～품 an exhibit; articles on display 〔show〕.

**진영**(陣營) a (military) encampment; a camp; quarters. ¶ 전체주의 ～ the totalitarian camp / 동서 양～ 간의 긴장 the tension between the two camps of the East and the West / ～을 치다 encamp; pitch a camp / ～을 철거하다 break camp; decamp / 양～으로부터 중립을 지키다 stand aloof from both camps. ◉ 공화〔민주〕당～《미국의》 the Republican 〔Democratic〕 camp. 민주～ the democratic camp. 반공～ the anticommunist camp. 혁신～ the progressive camp.

**진영**(眞影) a true image; a portrait. ¶ 세종 대왕의 ～ a portrait of King Sejong.

**진용**(陣容)《군대의》 a battle array 〔formation〕; a disposition; 《스포츠 팀·내각의》 a line-up. ¶ 신내각의 ～ the line-up of the new Cabinet / ～을 갖추다 《군대의》 array 《troops》 for battle; put 《troops》 in battle formation; 《팀의》 rearrange 〔reorganize〕 the 《team》 line-up; 《내각의》 carry out a cabinet reshuffle / ～을 재정비하다 reorganize the battle front / 다음 경기를 위해 ～을 바꾸다 change *one's* line-up for the next match.

**진원(지)**(震源(地)) 〖지학〗 the seismic center; the center of an earthquake; the epicenter; [비유적] the source. ¶ 그 ～은 삼척 부근이었다 The epicenter lay near Samchŏk.

**진위**(眞僞) truth (or falsehood); authenticity; genuineness. ¶ ～를 확인하다 ascertain the truth 《of》 / ～를 조사하다 examine 〔look into〕 the genuineness 《of an article》 / ～를 분별하다 discriminate truth from error / 그 ～를 보증할 수 없다 I cannot vouch for the truth 《of the report》. / ～가 불명하다 It is not known whether it is true or not. *or* It remains to be confirmed.

**진의**(眞意) 《의도》 *one's* real intention; 《동기》 *one's* real motive; *one's* ultimate purpose; 《의미》 the true meaning. ¶ 그의 ～가 무엇인지 알 수 없다 I cannot see what he really means. *or* I can't make out what he's driving at. / 이 논문 필자의 ～는 무엇입니까 What does the author of this essay really mean?

**진의**(眞義) the true meaning 〔signification〕.

**진인**(眞因) the true 〔real〕 reason 〔motive, cause〕. ¶ 죽음의 ～ the real cause of 《*a person's*》 death.

**진일** wet housework; chores in which *one's* hands get wet. ¶ ～로 손이 거칠어졌다 My hands (have) got chappy owing to the washing and scullery work.

**진입**(進入) entry 《into *a place*》; penetration. ～하다 enter; go 〔penetrate〕 into; make 〔find〕 *one's* way 《into》. ¶ 궤도에 ～하다 achieve 〔go into, enter into〕 orbit / 제차(諸車) ～금지 《게시》 Don't enter. *or* No entry. *or* No thoroughfare. / 시위대가 광장으로 ～했다 The demonstrators made their way into the square. / 열차가 2번선에 ～하고 있었다 The train was approaching on Track Two. ◉ ～구 an admission part. ～등(燈) 〖철도·항공〗 an approach light. ～로 an access road; 《고속 도로의》 an approach ramp; a ramp; a slip road 《영》; 〖항공〗 an approach way. ～밸브 an admission valve. ～선회 〖항공〗 an approach turn. ～지시기 〖철도〗 an approach indicator. 지상 관제 ～ 방식 〖항공〗 the ground controlled approach system (생략 G.C.A.).

**진자**(振子) 〖물리〗 a pendulum.

**진자리** ①《출산·임종의》 the spot where 「a child was just born 〔a person just died〕. ② 《똥오줌 싼》 a spot soiled by a child's urine 〔feces〕. ③ 《그 자리》 the very place 〔spot〕. ¶ ～에서 on the spot; on the occasion.

**진작**(振作) stimulation 《to action》; promotion; rousing. ～시키다〔하다〕 stir 〔shake, brace〕 up; stimulate to action; rouse. ¶ 사기를 ～시키다 stir up the morale 《of troops》.

**진작** 《좀더 일찍·그때에》 then and there; on that occasion; 《벌써》 earlier. ¶ 왜 ～ 말하지 않았느냐 You might have said so then and there. / ～ 말씀을 못 드려 죄송합니다 I apologize for not having said this before. / ～ 갔어야 했다 You should have gone earlier.

**진재**(震災) an earthquake disaster.

**진저리** ①《몸을 떠는》 a shiver; a quiver; a shudder. ¶ ～치다 shudder 《at》; shiver 《with cold》; tremble 《for fear》. ② 〔= 진절머리.

**진저에일** 《음료》 ginger ale.

**진전**(進展) development; progress; advance. ～하다 develop; advance; (make) progress. ¶ 사건의 ～과 함께

with the development of affairs / ~이 빠르다 make rapid progress / 연구에 ~을 보다 advance in *one's* studies / 원활하게 ~되다 go on smoothly; make good progress / 올해는 과학이 큰 ~을 이루었다 Science made great progress this year. / 교섭은 예상 밖의 방향으로 ~되었다 The negotiation has progressed in an unexpected direction.

**진절머리** disgust; repugnance; aversion. ¶ ~(가) 나다 be sick (and tired) 《of》; be 〔feel〕 disgusted 《with, at》; [사물이 주어] bore 〔weary〕 *one* to death / 이런 음식은 보기만 해도 ~가 난다 The mere sight of such food revolts me. / 그 생각만 해도 ~가 난다 It makes me sick even to think of it. / 전쟁이란 소리를 듣기만 해도 ~가 난다 The mere mention of a war makes me shudder.

**진정**(眞正) genuineness; authenticity. ~하다 (be) genuine; authentic; real; true; pure. ¶ ~한 의미에서 in the true sense of the word / ~한 사랑 a true love / ~한 학자 a scholar in the true sense of the word.

**진정**(眞情) ① 《진심》 *one's* real feelings; *one's* true 〔genuine〕 sentiments; sincerity. ¶ ~의 true; sincere; earnest / ~으로 sincerely; truly; seriously / ~을 토로하다 express *one's* true sentiments; speak from *one's* 〔the〕 heart / ~을 보이다 reveal *one's* true intention / ~을 다해 돌봐주다 look after 《*a person*》 with great kindness / 그 말씀은 ~이십니까 Do you mean what you say 〔to say so〕? / 그의 말이 ~인지 모르겠어 I wonder if his words are meant seriously. ② 《사정》 the true facts of a case; the true state.

**진정**(陳情) a petition; an appeal. ~하다 《청원하다》 make a petition 《to》; petition 《the authorities》; appeal 《to the mayor》; 《고충을 말하다》 complain 《about, of》. ¶ ~을 받아들이다〔받아들이지 않다〕 accept 〔reject〕 a petition / 쌀값의 인하를 관계 당국에 ~하다 appeal to the authorities concerned for lowering the price of rice.
◉ ~단 《국회에의》 a group of lobbyists; a lobby 《미》. ~서 a (written) representation; a petition; a memorial: ~서를 제출하다 send in a petition; file a petition 《with the government》. ~자 a petitioner; a lobbyist 《미》.

**진정**(進呈) ⇨ 증정(贈呈). ~하다 present 《*a person* with *a thing*》; offer.

**진정**(鎭定) suppression; repression; subdual. ~하다 suppress; repress; subdue; pacify; quell; tranquil(l)ize.

**진정**(鎭靜) pacification; appeasement; tranquil(l)ity; calm. ~하다〔시키다〕 become calm 〔quiet〕; 《고통 등을》 soothe; appease; allay; 《소란 등을》 pacify; tranquil(l)ize. ¶ 마음을 ~하다 calm *oneself* down / 노여움을 ~하다 《자신의》 appease *one's* anger; 《남의》 calm 〔appease〕 《*a person's*》 anger / 약을 먹여 환자를 ~시키다 put a patient under sedation / 소동이 ~되었다 The commotion subsided 〔died down〕. / ~하게 Don't get excited. *or* Calm yourself. *or* Take it easy.
◉ ~작용 sedation. ~제 a sedative (drug); a tranquil(l)izer.

**진종일**(盡終日) the whole day; all day long; from morning till night; throughout the day. ¶ 어제는 ~ 비가 왔다 It rained yesterday from morning till night. / ~ 기다렸다 I was kept waiting all the day.

**진주**(眞珠) a pearl. ¶ ~와 같은 pearly / ~를 박은 반지 a ring set with a pearl / ~와 같은 광택 a pearly luster / ~와 같다 be like pearls / 돼지 앞에 진주를 던지다 cast 〔throw〕 pearls before swine. ◉ ~목걸이 a pearl necklace. ~세공 pearl work. ~양식 pearl culture: ~ 양식장 a pearl farm 〔bed〕. ~잡이 《채취》 pearl fishery; pearling; 《채취자》 a pearl diver 〔fisher〕; a pearler. ~조개 a pearl oyster 〔shell〕. 진줏빛 pearl gray. 흑〔핑크색〕~ a black 〔pink〕 pearl.

**진주**(進駐) 《군대의》 occupying 《*a place*》 and staying; advancing and staying. ~하다 advance 《into》; make an (armed) entry 《into》; occupy (점령하다); be stationed 《at》. ¶ 미군은 일본에 ~했다 The United States Army occupied Japan. ◉ ~군 stationary troops; 《점령지의》 occupation forces.

**진주만**(眞珠灣) Pearl Harbor.

**진중**(陣中) [부사적] in camp; in the field; at the front; in the ranks. ¶ 적 ~에 난입하다 rush into the ranks of the enemy. ◉ ~근무 duties in the field; field duty. ~생활 a camp life. ~위문 visiting men 〔soldiers〕 at the front. ~일기 a staff diary.

**진중하다**(珍重―) ① 《보중(保重)하다》 treasure 《*a thing*》; value highly;

think much of. ¶ 좋은 선물 오래도록 진중하겠습니다 I shall long treasure your nice present. ②《귀중하다》(be) precious; valuable.

**진중하다**(鎭重—) (be) reserved; dignified; grave; sedate. ¶ 그는 행동이~ He is prudent in his behavior.

**진지** a meal; dinner. ¶ ~ 잡수셨습니까 Have you had your meal〔dinner〕?

**진지**(陣地) 〖군사〗 a military camp site; a position; an encampment. ¶ ~를 점령하다 occupy a position / ~를 탈환하다 recover a position / ~를 지키다〔차지하다〕 hold〔take up〕 a position / ~를 철수하다 evacuate〔withdraw from〕 a position; decamp; break camp / ~를 구축하다 build up a strong point〔position〕/ 적을 ~에서 몰아내다 dislodge the enemy from their position. ◉ ~전 position warfare; stationary warfare.

**진지**(眞摯) sincerity; earnestness; seriousness. ~하다 (be) sincere; earnest; sober; serious. ¶ ~하게 in《real, good》earnest; seriously; sincerely / ~한 사람 a serious-minded person; a man of sober habits / ~한 노력 an earnest effort / ~한 태도 a serious〔sincere〕 attitude / ~하게 생각하다 take《*a matter*》seriously〔soberly, gravely, earnestly〕/ 그런 농담은 그만하고 좀 ~한 얘기를 하자 I have had enough of such jokes. Let's talk sense.

**진진하다**(津津—) ¶ 흥미~ (be) very〔intensely〕 interesting; fascinating; of immense interest / 이 이야기가 어떻게 전개될지 흥미~ It'll be very interesting to see how this story develops.

**진짜**(眞—) a genuine article; the real stuff〔thing〕. ¶ ~ 고려 자기 an authentic piece of Koryŏ pottery / ~ 커피 honest coffee / 아주 ~같이 만들다 imitate to the life / ~와 가짜를 가리다 tell the real〔originals〕 from the false〔imitations〕/ 이 조화는 꼭 ~ 같다 These artificial flowers are so lifelike. / 그는 그것을 ~라고 속여 팔았다 He played it off as genuine.

**진찰**(診察) (a) medical examination; diagnosis (진단). ~하다 examine〔see〕《a patient》. ¶ 의사의 ~을 받다 see〔consult〕 a doctor; take medical advice from a doctor / ~ 무료《게시》 Consultation free. / 그는 정밀한 ~을 받았다 He was put to a very thorough examination. / 너는 ~받는 게 좋겠다 You had better consult a doctor. ◉ ~권 a consultation card〔ticket〕. ~료 a doctor's fee〔bill〕; a fee for medical advice. ~시간 consultation hours. ~실 a consultation〔consulting〕 room; a surgery《영》. ~일 a consultation day.

**진창** mud; a muddy place〔spot〕《in a road》; mire. ¶ ~에 발이 빠지다 fall in the mire / ~에 발이 박히다 get stuck in the mud / ~ 속을 걷다 trudge in the mud / ~에서 빠져 나오다 pull *oneself* out of the mire / 우리는 발목까지 빠지는 ~을 헤치고 나아갔다 We proceeded in the ankle-deep quagmire. ◉ ~길 a muddy road《caused by the melting of snow》; a slushy road.

**진척**(進陟) progress; (an) advance. ~하다 make (good) progress; make headway; proceed; advance. ¶ ~중이다 be (well) under way; be in progress / ~시키다 hasten; speed up; accelerate / ~이 없다 make no〔little〕 progress / 공사의 ~을 꾀하다 hasten the construction / 현저한 ~을 보이다 show marked progress / 계획을 ~시키다 forward a plan / 이 일은 많이 ~되었다 I have gone far with this work.

**진천동지**(震天動地) shaking heaven and earth; rending the air (음향이). ~하다 shake the whole universe; make the whole world wonder; rend the air.

**진출**(進出) advance; 〖군사〗 debouchment;《진입》entry; penetration. ~하다 advance〔enter〕《into》; gain ground; go〔launch〕《into》; find *one's* way《into》; forge ahead;《군대가》debouch. ¶ 정계〔영화계〕에 ~하다 go into politics〔the movies〕/ 세계 시장으로 ~하다 make inroads into the world market / 결승전에 ~하다 advance to〔go into〕 the finals / 한국의 상품이 해외로 대거 ~하였다 Korean products found a large market abroad. / 최근 여성의 직장 ~이 현저하게 증가했다 In recent years women who follow occupations have remarkably increased. / 한국의 자동차 산업은 해외 각지로 ~해 있다 The car industry of Korea is「branching out〔making its way〕 into various foreign countries.

**진취**(進取) ¶ ~적인 progressive; pushing; go-ahead《미》; enterprising / ~

적인 기상 an enterprising〔a go-ahead〕spirit / ~적인 기상이 있는 사람 a man of great enterprise / ~적인 기상이 왕성하다 be「endowed with〔full of〕a progressive〔an enterprising〕spirit / 여러분들은 구습에 얽매이지 말고, ~적인 기상으로 맡겨진 일에 임해 주기를 바란다 I expect you all to attend to your jobs with an enterprising spirit, unshackled by old ways and customs. ◉ ~성 a progressive〔an enterprising〕spirit.

**진치다**(陣—) pitch a camp; encamp;《위치를 점유하다》place〔install〕*oneself*《at, in》; take *one's* stand《at, in》; occupy《a corner of the room》. ¶그는 출입구에 진치고 서서 들어오는 사람들을 검문했다 He took up his stand at the door and checked the people coming in.

**진탕**(—宕) to *one's* heart's content; as much as *one* likes; heartily. ¶~ 먹다〔마시다〕eat〔drink〕*one's* fill.

**진탕**(震盪) concussion; shock. ◉ 뇌~〖의학〗cerebral concussion.

**진토**(塵土) dust and dirt.

**진통**(陣痛) labor pains; the pains of childbirth. ¶~의 시작 an outset labor pains / ~을 느끼다 have labor pains; feel pains / 그녀의 ~이 잦아졌다〔심해졌다〕Her labor pains have quickened. / 그녀의 ~이 시작되었다 She felt the beginnings of labor. / 그 나라는 지금 혁명의 ~기에 있다 The country is now in the throes of revolution.

**진통**(鎭痛) alleviation of pain. ◉ ~제 an anodyne; a lenitive; an analgesic; a pain-killer: 모르핀과 코데인은 지금도 ~제로 처방된다 Morphine and codein are still prescribed for pain.

**진퇴**(進退) advance or retreat; movement;《처신》*one's* course of action;《사임 혹은 유임》resigning or remaining in office. ¶~를 결정하다 decide on *one's* course of action / ~를 정하지 못하다 be at a loss (as to) which way to take / ~를 적절히〔잘못〕하다 take the right course〔a wrong course〕of action; act properly〔unwisely〕/ ~의 자유를 잃다 be lose freedom of movement; be〔get〕stalled《in the mud》/ ~를 함께 하다 share *one's* lot with《*another*》; throw〔cast〕in *one's* lot with / ~양난(兩難)이다, ~유곡(維谷)에 빠지다 be in a dilemma〔fix〕; be at the end of *one's* rope; be driven〔pushed〕to the wall.

**진폭**(振幅)〖물리〗amplitude (of a swing). ◉ ~변조〖전기〗amplitude modulation (생략 AM).

**진폭**(震幅) the amplitude of an earthquake.

**진품**(珍品) a rare article; a rarity; a curio. ¶그건 ~이다 It is something out of〔above〕the common thing.

**진품**(眞品) a genuine article; a real

**진피** stubbornness; willfulness. ¶~부리다 act stubbornly〔willfully〕. ◉ ~아들 an extremely ugly-looking person; a mere idiot.

**진피**(眞皮)〖해부·동물〗the thick skin; the true〔inner〕skin; the corium (*pl.* -ria); the derma.

**진필**(眞筆) *one's* own handwriting; an autograph; a genuine writing. ¶이것은 위필이냐 ~이냐 Is this writing forged or genuine〔his own〕?

**진하다**(盡—) be exhausted; be used up; be spent; come to an end; run out《of luck》. ¶기운이 ~ feel exhausted / 운이 ~ run out of luck.

**진하다**(津—) ①《빛깔·화장이》(be) deep; dark; saturated. ¶진한 감색 deep blue; dark navy blue / 진한 색 dark color / 진한 눈썹 thick eyebrows / 진하게 하다 deepen (the color) / 화장을 진하게 하다 wear heavy make-up. ②《액체가》(be) thick; rich; strong. ¶진한 국물 thick soup / 진한 차 strong tea / 차를 진하게 하다 make tea strong.

**진학**(進學) ~하다 go on to〔enter, proceed to〕the next stage of education〔a school of higher grade〕; go on to《high school, university》. ◉ ~률 the ratio of students who go on to the next stage of education. ~적성검사 a scholastic〔an academic〕aptitude test. ~지도《고교의》counselling on choice of college: 담당 선생님으로부터 ~지도를 받는 것이 좋겠다 You had better consult the teacher in charge about which school to choose. ~희망자 students who wish to go (on) to the next stage of education. 대학~코스 a college-preparatory course.

**진합태산**(塵合泰山) Many a little〔pickle〕makes a muckle〔mickle〕. *or* Many drops make a shower.

**진항**(進航) sailing out. ~하다 sail《out, toward》; steam ahead. ¶16노트의 속력으로 ~하다 steam at 16 knots.

**진해제**(鎭咳劑) a cough remedy.

**진행**(進行) (an) advance; progress; progression. ~하다 advance; make progress 〔headway〕; move onward 〔forward〕; go on; proceed. ¶ ~중인 열차 a moving train; a train in motion / ~중이다 be in progress; be going on; be underway / ~이 빠르다〔더디다〕 make rapid 〔slow〕 progress / 착착 ~하다 make steady progress / 의사를 ~시키다 expedite the proceedings / 순조롭게 ~하다 progress favorably / 교섭을 ~시키다 go on 〔ahead〕 with negotiations / 폐결핵의 ~을 막다 arrest tuberculosis / 계획대로 ~시키다 proceed with the program as arranged / 하역 작업이 ~중이었다 Unloading was in process. / 선거 운동은 이미 ~중이다 The election campaign has already been under way. / 「일의 ~은 어떻게 되고있느냐」—「잘 ~되고 있다」 "What sort of progress are you making with your job?"—"It's coming along fine."

◉ ~계(係) a person charged with expediting the proceedings 《of a conference》; a program director; 《사회자》 the master of ceremony. ~신호 〖철도〗 a clear 〔proceed〕 signal. ~파 〖전기·공업〗 a traveling 〔progressive〕 wave. ~형 〖문법〗 the progressive form: 현재 〔과거, 미래〕 ~형 the present 〔past, future〕 progressive form.

**진행성**(進行性) 〖의학〗 ¶ ~의 progressive / ~ 근위축증(筋萎縮症) progressive muscular dystrophy.

**진형**(陣形) a (battle) formation 〔array〕. ◉ 공격〔수비〕~ an offensive 〔a defensive〕 disposition.

**진혼**(鎭魂) repose of souls. ◉ ~곡 a requiem. ~제 a service for the repose of the deceased 〔departed soul〕.

**진홍**(眞紅) crimson; scarlet. ¶ ~색 옷을 입다 be dressed in crimson 〔scarlet〕.

**진화**(進化) 〖생물〗 evolution; development. ~하다 evolve 〔develop〕 《from... into...》. ¶ ~적(인) evolutional; evolutionary / ~ 과정을 거쳐서 through an evolutional process; evolutionally / ~하여 …이 되다 evolve into... / 인간은 원숭이로부터 ~하였다 Man has evolved from the ape.

◉ ~론 the theory of evolution; 《modern》 evolutionary theory: ~론자 an evolutionist.

**진화**(鎭火) putting out a fire; extinguishing of a fire. ~하다 extinguish; put out; bring under control. ¶ ~되다 be extinguished; be put out / 불이 저절로 ~되었다 The fire burnt itself out. / 불은 3시에야 겨우 ~되었다 The fire was at last 「brought under control 〔put out〕 at three.

**진흙** ① 《차진》 (potter's) clay. ② 《질척질척한》 mud. ¶ ~의 muddy; dirty / ~투성이의 muddy; covered with mud; miry / ~ 속의 연꽃 a lotus flower in the mud / 그의 옷은 ~투성이였다 His clothes were covered with dirt.

**진흥**(振興) promotion; furtherance; rousing; encouragement. ~하다 《…을》 promote; forward; encourage; stir up; arouse; 《…이》 be encouraged; be stirred up; be aroused. ¶ 과학 지식의 ~ the advancement of scientific knowledge / 경제 ~계획 a program for the stimulation of the economy / 무역을 ~하다 promote 〔stimulate〕 foreign trade / 산업의 ~을 꾀하다 promote the development of industry. ◉ ~책 a measure for the promotion 《of》. 대한 무역 투자 ~공사 the Korea Trade=Investment Promotion Agency (생략 KOTRA).

**질**(帙) ① 《책갑》 a folding case for books; a bookwrapper. ② 《한 벌》 a set of books. ¶ 이 책은 여섯 권이 한 질이다 This book is complete in six volumes.

**질**(膣) 〖해부〗 the vagina; the vaginal canal. ¶ 질벽〔구, 부〕 the vaginal wall 〔opening, region〕 / 질경(鏡) a vaginal speculum; a colposcope / 질경(痙) vaginismus; vaginodynia / 질막(膜) the vaginal tunic.

**질**(質) 《품질》 quality; 《바탕》 matter; substance; 《성질》 nature; character. ¶ 동물〔식물, 광물〕질 animal 〔vegetable, mineral〕 matter / 질이 좋은〔나쁜〕 비누 soap of good 〔bad〕 quality / 질이 좋다〔나쁘다〕 be of good 〔bad〕 quality / 질이 떨어지다 be inferior in quality / 질을 올리다〔떨구다〕 improve 〔debase〕 the quality / 양보다 질을 목표로 하다 aim at quality rather than quantity / 손님의 질이 좋다〔나쁘다〕 have refined 〔low〕 customers / 대학 교육의 질을 높이다 raise 〔upgrade〕 the quality of education at the colleges / 담배 질이 떨어져 간다 The quality of tobacco is declining. / 이 제품은 질이 좋다〔나쁘다〕 This product is of good 〔bad〕 quality. / 이쪽 것이 질이 좀 떨어지는 것 같다 This seems to be little inferior in quality. / 양보다 질이 중요하다 Quality matters more than quantity. / 우리 회사는 좋은 질의 제품을 만든다 Our company makes good quality products.

**-질** (the act of) doing. ¶ 양치질 rinsing the mouth / 톱질 sawing / 서방질 adultery.

**질겁하다** get appalled 〔dismayed, taken aback〕; be transfixed 〔startled〕; be absolutely astonished 〔staggered, 《구어》 flabbergasted〕 《at》. ¶ 질겁해서 말을 못하다 be struck dumb with consternation / 총소리에 ~ start at the sound of a rifle shot / 질겁해서 소리지르다 cry out in consternation / 개 짖는 소리에 도둑은 질겁해서 달아났다 The burglar was frightened away by the barking of the dog.

**질겅질겅** chewing; gnawing. ¶ ~ 씹다 chew away at 《it》.

**질경이** 〖식물〗 a (broad-leaved) plantain; a whiteman's foot.

**질곡**(桎梏) fetters; bonds; a yoke. ¶ ~에서 벗어나다 break 〔shake off〕 the fetters 〔bonds〕 《of》; throw off 〔break away from〕 the yoke 《of》 / 우리는 인습의 ~에서 탈피하지 않으면 안 된다 We must break through the shackles of convention.

**질권**(質權) the right of pledge. ◉ ~설정자 a pledger; a mortgager. ~자 pledgee; a mortgagee.

**질그릇** unglazed earthenware; biscuit (ware); clayware.

**질근질근** 《새끼 꼬는 모양》 《make 〔twist〕 a rope》 slowly 〔leisurely, idly〕; 《씹는 모양》 chew repeatedly.

**질금거리다** trickle; dribble; fall 〔run down〕 off and on. ¶ 비가 ~ 《it》 rains off and on.

**질기다** ① 《물건이》 (be) tough; durable; lasting. ¶ 질긴 고기〔종이〕 tough meat 〔paper〕 / 질긴 옷감 durable cloth. ② 《성질이》 (be) tenacious; persisting; pertinacious; persevering; tough. ¶ 성질이 ~ be tenacious by nature.

**질기와** an unglazed tile.

**질깃질깃** ~하다 (be) tough; stiff; rigid; stark; stubborn.

**질깃하다** rather 〔somewhat〕 tough.

**질끈** 《tying》 tight(ly); firmly; fast. ¶ 머리에 ~ 동여맨 수건 a twisted towel worn around *one's* head / 짐을 ~ 동이다 tie a bundle up tight / 허리끈을 ~ 동여매다 tie *one's* sash tight.

**질녀**(姪女) a niece.

**질다** ① 《반죽이·밥이》 (be) soft; slushy; watery. ¶ 밥이 너무 질게 되었다 The rice has come out too soft 〔slushy〕. ② 《땅이》 (be) muddy; slushy; messy; wet. ¶ 진 길 a muddy road.

**질동이** a clay jar to carry water in.

**질뚝배기** a large clay bowl.

**질량**(質量) 〖물리〗 mass; quantity of matter. ¶ ~ 불변의 법칙 the law of conservation of mass / 이들 두 물체의 ~은 같다 These two bodies have equal mass.

◉ ~단위 《원자의》 a mass unit; an atomic mass unit. ~분석계〔기〕 a mass spectrometer 〔spectrograph〕. ~수(數) mass number. ~스펙트럼 a mass spectrum. ~차(差) mass defect.

**질러가다** take a shortcut. ¶ 질러가는 길 a shorter road / 길을 ~ go by a shorter way.

**질러오다** come by a shortcut.

**질력나다** be sick 〔sick and tired〕 《of》; be bored 《with, by》; be fed up 《with》 《구어》. ¶ 진력나게 하다 bore; weary; sicken / 진력나는 강의 a boring 〔tedious, tiresome〕 lecture.

**질리다** ① 《채다》 receive a kick; get kicked 《in the...》; be struck; get hit. ¶ 정강이를 ~ be kicked in the shin / 되게 내~ be struck hard; be pommeled; get a sound thrashing.

② 《빛깔이》 (take) dye unevenly. ¶ 옷감에 물이 ~ a cloth gets 〔is〕 dyed unevenly.

③ 《진저리나다》 become 《thoroughly, quite》 disgusted with; get sick of; have enough of; become tired (to death); become fed up with. ¶ 이 일에는 질렸다 I am tired of this work. / 그의 불평은 질릴 정도로 들었다 His grumbling tires me.

④ 《기가》 be amazed 〔stunned, aghast, dumbfounded〕; 《겁내다》 cower; be cowed; be overawed. ¶ 질려서 말도 못하다 be (struck) dumb with amazement; be dumbfounded / 두려움으로 파랗게 ~ turn 〔become〕 deadly pale with horror; be scared stiff / 그는 아버지 앞에서는 기가 질려서 말 한마디 못한다 When his father is present, he loses his nerve and can't say a thing.

⑤ 《값이》 cost *one;* set *one* back.

**질문**(質問) a question; 《문의》 an inquiry; 《의문·반대》 a query; 《심문》 an interrogation; 《국회에서의》 an interpellation; 《영》 parliamentary question. ~하다 ask 《*a person*》 a question; put a question 《to》; ask a question of 《*a person*》; make inquiries

《about》; 《국회에서》 interpellate. ¶ 엉뚱한 ～ a question beside the mark / 긴급〔일괄, 일반〕～《국회에서의》 an emergency 〔an overall, a general〕 interpellation / 급소를 찌르는 ～ a pointed 〔home〕 question / ～의 연발 a barrage 〔volley〕 of questions / ～에 대답하다 answer a question / ～을 받다 be questioned / ～을 슬쩍 넘기다 parry a question / ～을 퍼붓다 rain questions 《on》; fire questions 《at》/ 귀찮게 ～하다 trouble 〔bother〕 《*a person*》 with questions / ～을 종결짓다 bring interpellation to a close / ～이 있습니까 Have you any questions to ask? / ～이 있습니다 I have a question to ask you. / ～을 하여도 좋습니까 May I ask you a question? / 이 ～에 대답을 해 주십시오 Please answer me this question. / 그들은 그에게 ～ 공세를 폈다 They plied him with questions.
◉ ～권(券) a question coupon. ～서 a written inquire; 《앙케트의》 a questionnaire. ～자 a questioner; an interrogator.

**질물**(質物) a pawn; a pledge.

**질박**(質樸·質朴) simplicity. ⇨소박. ～하다 (be) simple (and unadorned); plain; simple-minded.

**질벅-** = 질척-.

**질병**(疾病) a disease; sickness. ¶ ～의 예방 prevention of a disease / ～과 싸우다 combat 〔fight〕 a disease / ～관리 센터 the Center for Disease Control (생략 CDC).

**질부**(姪婦) the wife of a nephew.

**질빵** a shoulder-pack strap; a backstrap. ¶ ～을 지다 have a back-pack strapped across *one's* chest.

**질산**(窒酸) 〖화학〗 nitric acid. ¶ 묽은 ～ dilute nitric acid. ◉ ～균 〖식물〗 nitrate-forming bacteria. ～동〔암모늄, 카드뮴〕 copper 〔ammonium, cadmium〕 nitrate. ～셀룰로오스 cellulose nitrate. ～염 a nitrate. ～은 silver nitrate; nitrate of silver; lunar 〔common〕 caustic: ～은 용액 a nitrate of silver solution. ～제거 denitration: ～을 제거하다 denitrate.

**질색**(窒塞) shock; horror; dismay; abhorrence. ～하다 be appalled; be shocked; be dismayed; abhor; abominate. ¶ ～할 노릇은 to *one's* disgust / 그런 녀석은 딱 ～이다 I cannot endure him. / 나는 그런 일은 아주 ～이다 I hate it so much. *or* I wouldn't do it for anything. / 터무니 없는 값을 불러 ～했다 I was shocked 〔dismayed〕 at the exorbitant price. *or* When I heard the price, it took my breath away.

**질서**(姪壻) the husband of a niece.

**질서**(秩序) order; system; method; regularity; discipline. ¶ ～ 있는 orderly; systematic; methodical / ～ 없이 disorderly; unsystematically; irregularly; confused / 새 ～ a new order / 국민의 공공 ～ 의식 people's sense of public orderliness / 사회의 ～ social 〔public〕 order / ～가 정연하다 be in good order; be systematical / ～를 지키다 keep 〔maintain〕 order / ～를 확립하다 establish order / 사회의 ～를 문란케 하다 disturb public order / ～ 있게 일을 하다 do 《*a thing*》 systematically 〔in orderly fashion〕 / 그의 일엔 ～가 없다 There is no system 〔method〕 in his work. / 시내의 ～는 회복되었다 Order was restored to the city.

**질소**(窒素) 〖화학〗 nitrogen (기호 N). ¶ 공중에 있는 ～ atmospheric nitrogen / ～를 함유한 nitrogenous / ～와 화합시키다 nitrify. ◉ ～가스 nitrogen gas. ～고정(법) nitrogen fixation. ～공업 nitrogen industry. ～비료 (a) nitrogenous manure 〔fertilizer〕. ～산화물 nitrogen oxide (생략 NOx). ～순환 the nitrogen cycle. ～포화(飽和) nitrification. ～폭탄 a nitrogen bomb.

**질소화물**(窒素化物) 〖화학〗 a nitride.

**질시**(嫉視) regarding with jealousy 〔dislike〕; jealous looks. ～하다 be jealous of 《*a person*》; regard with jealousy; keep a jealous eye 《on》. ¶ ～를 받다 be regarded with jealousy.

**질식**(窒息) suffocation; a choke. ～하다 suffocate; smother; choke; be 「suffocated 〔smothered; choked〕.

> 용법 **suffocate** 산소가 없어 숨을 쉴 수 없게 하다. **smother** 덮개·뚜껑 따위로 덮어두었기 때문에 산소 부족으로 숨을 쉴 수 없게 하다. **choke** 목을 조르거나 호흡 기관을 막히게 하든가 해서 숨쉬기 어렵게 하다.

¶ ～성의 suffocative / ～시키다 suffocate; choke; stifle; smother / ～하여 죽다 suffocate; be suffocated; choke 〔be choked, be smothered〕 to death; die from suffocation / 연기로 ～할 것만 같았다 The smoke almost choked me. ◉ ～사 death from [by] suffocation.

**질염**(膣炎) 〖의학〗 vaginitis; colpitis.

**질의**(質疑) a question; an inquiry; 《국회에서의》 an interpellation; 《영》 a parliamentary question. ～하다 question; inquire; interpellate. ¶ ～에 답하다 answer a question.
◉ ～응답 question and answer: ～ 응답란 a question-and-answer column / ～ 응답 시간 a question [discussion] period / ～ 응답이 있은 후 의안이 표결되었다 After questions and answers the bill was put to the vote. ～자 a questioner; an interrogator. 대정부～ 《국회에서의》 an interpellation.

**질적**(質的) qualitative. ¶ ～으로 qualitatively; in quality / ～으로 우수하다 be superior in quality / ～으로나 양적으로나 quantitatively as well as qualitatively; both in quality and in quantity / ～으로 보면 후자가 낫다 So far as the quality is concerned, the latter is better.

**질정**(叱正) (a) correction.

**질주**(疾走) running rapidly; a scamper; a scud; speeding. ～하다 run at full speed; scamper; scurry; scuttle; dash. ¶ ～하는 차 a speeding car / 차가 ～해 왔다 An automobile came tearing along.

**질질** ① 《끄는 모양》 draggingly; trailingly. ¶ ～ 끌다 drag 《a heavy thing》 / 신을 ～ 끌다 drag [shuffle] *one's* shoes / 치마를 ～ 끌며 걷다 walk with a trailing skirt / ～ 끄는 병 a languishing illness / 전쟁이 ～오래 끌었다 The war dragged on. ② 《흐르는 모양》 dribbling; oozing. ¶ 눈물을 ～ 흘리다 let tears trickle / 오줌을 ～ 싸다 dribble urine / 얼굴에 기름기가 ～ 흐른다 His face almost oozes oil.

**질책**(叱責) a scolding; 《구어》 a telling-off; (a) reproof; a reproach; reprimand. ～하다 scold; 《구어》 tell 《*a person*》 off; reprove; reproach; berate; castigate; reprimand. ¶ ～을 받다 be reproved [reprimanded]; be called to task / 나는 그를 몹시 ～했다 I pitched into him. / 그러한 부주의에 대해 그는 톡톡히 ～당할 만하다 He ought to be well told for such carelessness as that.

**질척거리다** be wet and soft; be muddy; be gooey. ¶ 길이 질척거려서 가까스로 목적지에 도착하였다 The roads were so muddy that we could reach our destination only with great difficulty. / 눈이 녹아서 질척거렸다 The snow has melted into slush.

**질컥거리다, 질컥하다** (be) gooey; sticky.

**질타**(叱咤) scolding. ～하다 give a scolding; scold; berate; spur 《*a person* to *do*》.

**질탕**(佚宕) ～하다 (be) riotous; racketing. ¶ ～하게 놀다 go on a racket [the spree]; revel it.

**질투**(嫉妬) jealousy; envy. ～하다 be jealous of 《*a person's* success》; be envious of; envy 《*a person*》. ¶ ～가 나서 from jealousy; out of (sheer) envy / ～에 눈이 멀어 in a fit of jealous rage / ～가 많다 be jealous; be envious / ～로 속을 태우다 be consumed with jealousy / ～한 나머지 그녀는 남편을 죽이려 했다 Driven by jealousy, she attempted to murder her husband. ◉ ～심 (feelings of) jealousy; envy: ～심이 일어나다 get [feel, become] jealous 《of, over》.

**질퍼덕거리다, 질퍽거리다** squish and squash; slosh away.

**질퍽질퍽** sloppily; sloshily; slushily. ～하다 sloppy; sloshy; slushy.

**질편하다** ① 《땅이》 (be) broad and level. ¶ 질편한 들 a broad expanse of fields. ② 《게으르다》 (be) sluggish; slovenly; idle. ¶ 질편하게[히] sprawlingly; sluggishly; slothfully / 방에 질편하게 누워 있다 sprawl around the room / 질편하게 세월을 보내다 lead an idle life; idle *one's* time away / 질편히 의자에 앉아 노닥거리다 talk while lolling in a chair.

**질풍**(疾風) a strong wind; a gale; 〖기상〗 a fresh breeze. ¶ ～과 같이 like a gust of wind / ～신뢰(迅雷)와 같이 as quick as lightning; like a whirlwind.
◉ ～경초(勁草) [비유적] a man who never yields his integrity even in adversity.

**질항아리** an earthenware [clay] jar.

**질화**(窒化) 〖화학〗 nitrification; nitration. ～하다 nitrify; nitrate. ◉ ～물 a nitride. ～작용 nitrification; nitration.

**질환**(疾患) a disease; an ailment (가벼운); a 《heart》 complaint; 《chest》 trouble; a disorder.

**질흙** (potter's) clay. ⇨ 진흙.

**짊어지다** ① 《짐을》 pack on the back; saddle [burden] *oneself* with; bear; shoulder. ¶ 짐을 ～ shoulder a pack / 그녀는 보따리를 짊어지고 있었다 She had a bundle on her back. ② 《빚을》

get 〔run〕 into (debt); incur (debt). ¶ 빚을 많이 ~ be heavily in debt. ③《의무 따위를》 bear; assume; be charged with 《duty》; take upon *oneself;* shoulder. ¶ 책임을 ~ shoulder responsibilities / 우리는 앞날의 한국을 짊어지고 나갈 사람들이다 We are the support and driving force of future Korea.

**짐** a load; a burden; 《수화물》 packages; packs; parcels; baggage; 《영》 luggage; 《배의》 cargo; 《기차의》 freight; 《영》 goods; 《소지품》 *one's* things 〔belongings〕.
¶ 짐스러운, 짐이 되는 burdensome; bothering / 짐을 만재한 배 a heavily laden ship / 짐을 싸다〔꾸리다〕 pack up; pack goods / 짐이 무겁다 be too heavy 《for *a person*》; 《부담이》 be too hard 〔much〕 《for *a person*》 / 짐을 덜다 relieve 《*a person*》 of *his* burdens / 짐이 되다 be a burden 《to *a person*》; be burdensome / 짐을 짊어지다 《부담》 assume 〔saddle *oneself* with〕 a burden / 마차에 짐을 싣다 load a cart / 말의 짐을 풀다 unpack a horse / 이 짐을 부치는 데 얼마입니까 How much is it to send this package? / 그런 것들은 가지고 가지 마라, 가지고 가면 짐만 된다 Don't take such things with you, they will only encumber you. / 무거운 짐에서 벗어난 기분이다 I feel as if the load were off my shoulders. / 짐은 어디에 놓을까요 Where should I put my belongings?

**짐**(朕) I; Me; We. ¶ ~의 My.

**짐꾼** a carrier; a porter; a coolie.

**짐마차**(一馬車) a (freight) wagon; a cart; a dray.

**짐바리** a load (on a pack animal); a pack.

**짐받이** the bed 《of a truck》; a roof rack 《for a car》; the carrier 《of a motorcycle》.

**짐배** 《화물선》 a cargo boat; a freighter; 《거룻배》 a lighter; a barge.

**짐수레** a wagon; a cart; a dray. ◉ ~꾼 a carter; a drayman; a wagoner.

**짐스럽다** (be) burdensome; cumbersome; troublesome. ¶ 짐스럽게 여기다 find 《it》 burdensome; regard 《*a person*》 as a nuisance.

**짐승** a beast; a brute; an animal. ¶ ~ 같은 놈 You brute! / 그 녀석은 ~만도 못한 놈이다 He is worse than a brute.

**짐자동차**(一自動車) 《미》 a truck; 《영》 a lorry.

**짐작**(斟酌) 《요량》 discretion; judgment; 《어림》 guess; conjecture; estimation. ~하다 use *one's* own discretion 〔judgment〕; guess; conjecture; estimate. ¶ 내 ~에는 in my estimation / 손~ measuring roughly with *one's* hands / 눈~ eye measure; measure by eye / ~이 맞다 guess right; be right in *one's* conjecture / ~이 가다 can guess 〔imagine〕; have (an idea) in mind; come to form an idea of / 네 ~에 얼마나 먼 것 같으냐 How far do you think it is? / 그게 어떤건지 ~이 안 간다 I have no idea of what it is like. / 겉으로 보아 그의 나이가 스물은 될 것으로 ~했다 From his appearance I guessed his age at 20.

**짐짐하다** ① 《맛이》 be just salty without much flavor to 《it》. ② 《마음에》 《it》 weigh on *one's* mind; feel uncomfortable 《about a situation》. ¶ 모든 일이 다 ~ I don't feel very good about the whole affair.

**짐짓** deliberately; on purpose; intentionally. ¶ ~ 냉정한 태도를 취하다 deliberately assume an indifferent attitude / 그는 ~ 모르는 체했다 He affected ignorance.

**짐짝** a package; a pack; a parcel; an item of freight 〔baggage〕. ¶ ~ 세 개가 있다 have three pieces of baggage.

**짐차**(一車) 《미》 a freight car; 《영》 a goods van 〔wagon〕.

**집** ①《사는 곳》 a house; a home; a dwelling (거처); a residence.

> 용법 **house** 일반적으로 독채로 된 가옥. **home** 가족과 함께 살고 있는 가정이라는 뜻의 집. 따라서 home은 반드시 독채집이어야 할 필요는 없고, 아파트나 셋방살이라도 무방함. 《미》에서는 home을 house와 같은 뜻으로 쓰는 경우가 많음. **dwelling** 「주거」하는 곳이란 뜻. 사무실·상점 따위와 구별하는 격식 차린 투의 말로 법률 용어. **residence** 「살고 있는 장소」라는 뜻으로, 객관적인 느낌을 주는 격식차린 투의 말.

¶ 집 안〔밖〕에서 inside 〔outside〕 the house; indoors 〔outdoors〕 / 초가〔기와〕집 a thatch-〔tile-〕roofed house / 좋은〔초라한〕 집 a fine 〔shabby〕 house / 쓰러져 가는 집 a house ready to tumble down / 자기 집 a house of *one's* own / 집에 있다 stay at home / 집 없는 신세가 되다 lose *one's* home; be rendered homeless / 집에 없다 be out; be away from home / 집으로 돌아 가다 go

〔return〕 home / 같은 집에 살다 live under the same roof / 집을 비우다 vacate a house (퇴거하다); stay out (외박) / 집을 세내다 rent a house 《from *a person*》 / 집을 세주다 rent 〔let〕 a house 《to *a person*》 / 집을 헐다 tear down a house / 집을 짓다 build 〔put up〕 a house / 김 선생은 집에 계십니까 Is Mr. Kim 「at home 〔in〕? / 나는 아저씨 집에 살고 있다 I am staying at my uncle's (house). / 옆집에는 누가 살고 있습니까 Who lives next door (to you)? / 집 모양을 봐서 병원임에 틀림없다 Judging from the style of the house, that must be a doctor's office.
② 《동물의》 ¶ 개집 a doghouse; a kennel / 새집 a nest; a bird's-nest; a birdhouse / 벌집 a beehive; a comb.
③ 《가정》 a home; a household; a family. (★ household는 집합적으로 고용인을 포함한 한 가족 전부를 뜻하며, 또 「살림살이」란 뜻도 있음. family는 집합명사인데 하나의 단체로 보는 경우는 단수동사로, 개개 가족에 대해 서술하는 경우는 복수동사로 받음: His family *is* rather small. / His family *are* all well.) ¶ 큰집 the main branch of a family; the main line of descent; the oldest brother's home / 작은집 a branch family; a younger brother's home / 가난한〔잘 사는〕 집에 태어나다 be born poor 〔rich〕 / 집 생각이 나다 think of home; get homesick.
④ 《끼거나 담아 두는》 a box; a case; an incasement; a protector; a sheath. ¶ 칼집 a sheath; a scabbard / 두꺼비집 a fuse box / 아기집 a womb.
⑤ 《집사람》 *one's* spouse 〔wife〕; 《첩》 a concubine; a kept mistress. ¶ 전주집 *one's* concubine from *Chŏnju* / 우리 집사람 my wife.
⑥ 《바둑의》 a point; 《한 칸》 a square (on a *paduk* board). ¶ 네 집 이기다 〔지다〕 win 〔lose〕 by four points.

**집**(集) a collection. ¶ 수필집 a collection of essays / 단편집 a collection of short stories / 걸작집 a collection of masterpieces.

**집**(輯) a series. ¶ 제2집 the second series.

**집가시다** 〖민속〗 purify a house of evil spirits (after a funeral).

**집게** tongs; tweezers; forceps; pincers; nippers; pliers. ¶ 부～ fire tongs / ～로 집다 pick up with tweezers / ～로 못을 뽑다 pull a nail out with pliers. ◉ ～발 claws; pincers: ～발로 집다 nip with its claws. ～벌레 an earwig. ～뼘 the length between extended thumb and index finger. ～손가락 a forefinger; an index finger.

**집결**(集結) assembly; concentration 《of troops, *etc.*》. ～하다 《모으다》 assemble; concentrate; gather; mass 《its troops》; 《모이다》 be concentrated; gather; assemble. ¶ 국경에 적군이 ～하다 the enemy concentrates along the border / 대군을 ～시키다 concentrate a large army / 많은 폭도가 시내 각처에 ～했다 Large numbers of rioters were concentrated at various quarters in the city. ◉ ～지 《군대의》 an assembly place 〔area〕; 《출동을 위한》 a staging area.

**집계**(集計) totaling; a total (집계량). ～하다 add 〔sum〕 up; total. ¶ ～를 내다 find the total 《of》; total / 비용을 ～하니까 300달러가 되었다 The costs totaled 〔added up to〕 $300. / 각 지점은 매달 매상을 ～하여 본점에 보고한다 Every month each branch office of the company adds up the sales figures for the past month and reports them to the head-office. ◉ ～표 a tabulation; a summary sheet.

**집광**(集光) 〖광학〗 ～하다 concentrate light. ◉ ～기(器) a light-concentrating instrument; a condenser. ～렌즈 a condensing 〔collecting〕 lens; a condenser.

**집괴**(集塊) a mass; a cluster.

**집구석** ¶ ～에 within 〔inside〕 the house; indoors / ～에 박혀 있다 stay 〔keep〕 indoors; keep to the house; stick indoors.

**집권**(執權) grasping 〔coming into〕 political power. ～하다 come to 〔into〕 power; hold the reins of power; take the helm of state affairs. ¶ 평화적 ～연장 peaceful extension of power; peaceful prolonged seizure of political power / 재 ～하다 return to power / 한 사람에 의한 장기 ～을 막다 prevent long-term seizure of power by one man. ◉ ～당 the party in power; the ruling party.

**집권**(集權) centralization of power 〔authority〕. ～하다 centralize power. ¶ 중앙～ centralization of power / 중앙～제도〔주의〕 centralism; the centralizing system; centralized administration.

**집기**(什器) ＝집물. ¶ 사무용 ～ 《a piece of》 office fixtures.

**집나다** ① a house is put up for sale. ②《바둑》a nest is formed; a square is made.

**집내다** ① empty 〔vacate〕 a house; offer 〔put up〕 *one's* house for sale. ②《바둑》form a nest; make a square.

**집념**(執念) a deep attachment《to》; tenacity of purpose. ～하다 be deeply attached《to》; have a constant passion 〔ardor〕《for》. ¶ ～이 강한 tenacious of *one's* purpose / 그는 그 계획 수행에 ～을 불태웠다 He devoted himself intensely to the pursuit of that project. / 이 사업이 완성될 수 있었던 것은 무엇보다도 그의 ～덕분이다 It is his tenacity of purpose more than anything else that contributed to the completion of this project.

**집다** pick up; take up. ¶ 집게로〔젓가락으로〕 ～ pick up with tongs 〔chopsticks〕/ 길에 떨어진 돈을 ～ pick up a coin on the street / 소금을 한 줌 ～ pick up a handful of salt.

**집단**(集團) a group; a mass; a body. ¶ ～으로《act》in a group; en masse / ～적으로 as a group; collectively / ～ 지향의 group-oriented《society》/ ～을 이루다 form a group / ～ 탈주하다 run away 〔break out〕 en masse《from a reformatory》/ 그들은 ～으로 진정(陳情)했다 They made their appeal as a group.
◉ ～감염 (a) mass infection. ～강도 an organized 〔a gang of〕 burglars. ～검거 mass arrest; wholesale arrest; a rounding up. ～검진 a mass examination 〔checkup〕《for》. ～결근 mass absenteeism. ～결혼 (a) group marriage: ～결혼식 a group wedding. ～경기 a group game. ～노동 group work. ～농장 a collective farm; a *kolkhoz* (Russ.). ～반응 (a) mass reaction. ～발생 a mass outbreak《of》. ～보험 group insurance. ～살인 multiple murder. ～생활 living in a group; communal living 〔life〕: 새들은 다양한 이유로 ～생활을 한다 Birds form colonies for a variety of reasons. ～소개(疎開) group evacuation. ～소송 a class action 〔suit〕: ～ 소송을 일으키다 take 〔bring, file〕 a class action《against》. ～식중독 mass food poisoning. ～심리(학) group psychology. ～안전 보장《a system of》collective security. ～요법 a group therapy. ～의식 group consciousness: 일본인은 ～ 의식이 강하다 The Japanese are group-minded〔-oriented〕. ～이민 collective 〔mass〕 emigration. ～자살 mass suicide: 일가족 ～ 자살 a family suicide. ～자위 collective self-defense. ～주택 group housing. ～지도 collective guidance 〔leadership〕: ～ 지도제《be under》a collective leadership system. ～체조 massed calisthenics 〔gymnastics〕. ～탈당 collective defection《to the other party》. ～토론 group discussion. ～폭행 mob violence;《윤간》gang rape. ～표본 추출 〖컴퓨터〗 cluster sampling. ～학살《인종에 대한》genocide. ～행동 group 〔collective〕 action; collective behavior. ～화 collectivization. ～히스테리 group hysteria.

**집대성**(集大成) (a) compilation. ～하다 compile《all the available data》into one book; make 〔give〕 a comprehensive survey of《past studies on a subject》. ¶ 한국 민화를 ～하다 compile all the folktales in Korea into a book / 이 책은 그의 연구를 ～한 것이다 The book contains 〔brings together〕 the result of all his studies.

**집도**(執刀) the performance of an operation. ～하다 operate 〔perform an operation〕《on *a person* for cancer》. ¶ 그 수술은 김 박사의 ～로 행해졌다 The operation was performed by Dr. Kim. ◉ ～자 an operating surgeon.

**집돼지** a barnyard pig.

**집들이**《파티》a housewarming (party). ～하다 give a housewarming (party); do the honors of *one's* new establishment. ◉ ～선물 a housewarming present.

**집무**(執務) conducting *one's* official duties. ～하다 attend to *one's* duties; work《from 9 a.m. to 5 p.m.》. ¶ ～중이다 be on duty; be at *one's* desk 〔work〕/ ～중 면회 사절《게시》Visitors declined during office hours. ◉ ～시간 office 〔business, working〕 hours. ～실 an office;《미국 대통령의》the Oval Office. ～지침〔편람〕 a guide to office routine.

**집문서**(—文書) a house deed; the title of a house; the deed to a house. ¶ ～를 잡히고 돈을 빌다 「get a loan 〔borrow money〕 on security of *one's* house / ～는 은행으로 넘어갔다 The title of the house passed to a bank.

**집물**(什物) household furniture and utensils; miscellaneous household goods.

**집배**(集配) collection and delivery. ～하

다 collect and deliver. ◉ ～원 《우편의》 《미》 a mail carrier; a mailman; 《영》 a postman.
**집비둘기** a dove; a house pigeon.
**집사**(執事) 《집일을 맡는》 a steward; a butler; 《교회의》 a deacon; a deaconess (여자).
**집산**(集散) gathering and distribution. ～하다 《사람이》 meet and part; 《산물이》 gather 〔collect〕 and distribute. ◉ ～지 a distributing 〔trading〕 center; an entrepôt: 이 도시는 과일의 ～지이다 This town is a trading center for fruit.
**집산주의**(集産主義) collectivism. ◉ ～자 a collectivist.
**집성**(集成) (a) compilation 《of historical materials》. ～하다 collect; compile; gather 《the facts》 together (into a whole); codify 《traffic rules》.
**집세**(一貰) (a) (house) rent. ¶ ～를 내다 pay *one's* rent; pay 《a sum》 for the house / ～를 올리다〔내리다〕 raise 〔lower〕 the rent / ～가 밀려 있다 be behind with *one's* rent / ～는 얼마인가 What is the rent 《for the house》? / 그 집의 ～는 한 달에 5만 원이다 The house rents at fifty thousand won a month. / 이 집은 ～가 비싸다 This house has a high rent.
**집시** a gypsy 〔Gypsy〕; a gipsy 〔Gipsy〕. ¶ ～의 gypsy 《music》. ◉ ～족 the Gypsies.
**집안** ① 《가족》 a family; a household (세대); 《가문》 the (social) standing 〔status〕 of a family; 《가정》 a 〔*one's*〕 home; 《일가》 *one's* kin; *one's* clan; *one's* relatives. ¶ ～의 domestic; family / ～끼리의 private; informal; inside / 온 ～ the whole family; all the family / ～ 식구 the family (members); *one's* inmates of a house / 김씨 ～ the Kim's clan 〔family〕; the Kims / 다른 ～ another family / 식구가 많은〔적은〕 ～ a large 〔small〕 family / ～의 큰일 a matter of great concern to the family / ～에서 쉬쉬하는 비밀 a family secret / 좋은 ～에 태어나다 come of good stock 〔family〕 / ～도 좋고 교양도 있다 be well-born and well-bred / ～이 모두 안녕하시냐 How's the family? / 그는 알려진 ～출신이다 He is from a well-known family. / 의식은 ～끼리만 모여 행하였다 The ceremony was performed within the family circle. / ～ 수치를 밖으로 드러내지 마라 Wash your dirty linen at home. / 그의 ～은 급속히 몰락해 가고 있다 His family is going fast down hill. ② 《집 속》 the inside of the house. ¶ ～ 공기 the indoor atmosphere / ～에서 기르는 housebroken 《cats》 / ～에 들어박히다 remain 〔stay〕 indoors / ～을 치우다 clean the house up. ◉ ～사정 *one's* family reasons 〔circumstances〕; *one's* family affairs. ～심부름 errands around the house: ～심부름을 하다 do errands around the house. ～싸움 a domestic quarrel; a family trouble 〔squabble〕: ～싸움을 하다 have a family quarrel 〔trouble〕. ～일 housework; household affairs; chore: ～일을 처리하다 manage *one's* family affairs.
**집알이** a courtesy call to a newly-moved family. ～하다 pay a courtesy call to a newly-moved family; visit 《*a person's*》 new house for the first time.
**집약**(集約) ～하다 《모으다》 put 《all *one's* ideas》 together; 《요약하다》 summarize 《the results》; abridge 《the novel》; condense 《the report》. ¶ ～적인 intensive / 자본〔노동〕 ～적 capital-〔labor-〕intensive 《industries》 / ～적인 방법 the intensive method / 나는 그 모임에서 우리가 토의한 내용을 ～했다 I summarized what we discussed in the meeting. ◉ ～농업 intensive agriculture 〔farming〕. ～투자 intensive investment.
**집어넣다** ① ＝넣다. ¶ 가방에 서류를 ～ stuff the documents into a briefcase / 휴지통에 ～ throw 《*a thing*》 into the wastebasket. ② 《투옥하다》 throw 《*a person*》 into prison; imprison. ¶ 도둑을 교도소에 ～ throw a thief into prison.
**집어등**(集魚燈) a fish-luring〔-gathering〕 light.
**집어먹다** ① 《음식을》 pick up and eat. ¶ 손으로 음식을 ～ pick up food with *one's* fingers and eat it. ② 《착복하다》 embezzle; pocket 《구어》; make off with. ¶ 큰 돈을 ～ pocket 〔peculate〕 a large sum / 공금을 ～ embezzle public money 〔funds〕; divert public money into *one's* own pocket / 친구(의) 돈을 ～ make off with a friend's money.
**집어삼키다** ① 《음식을》 pick up and swallow. ② ＝집어먹다 ②. ¶ 아무의 재산을 ～ dispossess *a person* of *his* property.
**집어주다** ① 《건네주다》 pick up 《*a thing*》 and hand it over; pass; reach

《*a thing*》 for 《*a person*》; help 《*a person*》 to 《some potatoes》. ¶ 소금을 ~ pass the salt / 그 책을 좀 집어 주십시오 Please reach me the book. / 어머니는 아이에게 푸딩을 한 조각 집어 주었다 The mother helped the child to a piece of pudding. ② 《뇌물을》 offer 〔give〕 a bribe to 《*a person*》; grease 《*a person's*》 palm; bribe 《*a person*》 to *do*; 《팁을》 tip 《the waitress a dollar》. ¶ 얼마 집어 주고 입을 막다 bribe 《*a person*》 into secrecy 〔silence〕.

**집어치우다** put 〔stow〕 away; leave off; set aside; lay aside; give up; do away with; clear away. ¶ 일을 ~ lay aside *one's* work; leave off work / 장사를 ~ quit *one's* business / 학교를 ~ leave 〔give up〕 school / 의사 노릇을 ~ relinquish medical practice.

**집요**(執拗) tenacity; persistence; obstinacy. ~하다 (be) obstinate; stubborn; tenacious; persistent. ¶ ~하게 stubbornly; obstinately; tenaciously; persistently / ~한 반항 stubborn resistance / ~하게 묻다 pester 〔harass〕 《*a person*》 with persistant questions.

**집적**(集積) (an) accumulation; 〖물리〗 integration. ~하다 accumulate; pile (up); heap up 〔together〕; amass; 〖물리〗 integrate. ◉ ~회로 〖전자〗 an integrated circuit (생략 I.C.): 고밀도 ~회로 a large-scale integrated circuit (생략 LSI) / 초고밀도 ~회로 《반도체의》 a very large-scale integrated circuit (생략 VLSI). 탄약~소 an ammunition dump.

**집적거리다** ① 《건드리다》 tease; needle; razz. ¶ 개를 ~ tease a dog / 아무를 ~ needle *a person*. ② 《참견하다·손대다》 meddle 《with》; dabble 《in》; have a finger 《in》; poke *one's* nose 《into》. ¶ 남의 일에 ~ meddle with *a person's* business; poke *one's* nose into another's affairs / 정치에 ~ dabble in politics.

**집적집적** ① 《건드림》 teasing; needling; razzing. ② 《참견》 meddling; dabbling.

**집정**(執政) governing; administration; 《사람》 an administrator. ~하다 hold the power of state; govern; administrate. ◉ ~관 〖역사〗 a consul.

**집주인**(一主人) ① 《가장》 the master of a house; the head of a family. ② 《집임자》 the owner of a house; a landlord; a landlady (여자).

**집중**(集中) concentration; centralization. ~하다 《모으다》 concentrate; 《upon》; centralize; mass 《troops》; 《모이다》 concentrate; converge 《into, on》; focus 《on》; center 《on, around》. ¶ 인구의 ~ the gravitation of the population 《toward》 / 에너지의 ~ concentration of energy / 주의를 ~하다 concentrate *one's* attention 〔mind〕 on 《*one's* work》 / 목적에 전력을 ~하다 bend all *one's* energies on *one's* aim; bring all *one's* energies to bear on *one's* object / 질문은 그 점에 ~되었다 Questions centered on that point. / 권력은 모두 이들 몇 사람에게 ~ 되어 있다 All of the power is centralized among these few people. / 나는 공부에 전력을 ~한다 I focus 〔concentrate〕 all my energies on the study. / 나는 그 문제를 ~적으로 연구했다 I made an intensive study of the subject. / 국회에서 질문이 총리에게 ~되었다 Questions in the National Assembly were concentrated on the Prime Minister.
◉ ~강의 an intensive course 《in Korean literature》; a closely-packed series of lectures. ~공격 《make, launch》 a concentrated attack 《on, against》. ~력 *one's* ability to concentrate; (powers of) concentration: 이 일은 ~력을 요구한다 This job requires concentration. / 그의 ~력은 칭찬할 만하다 His ability to concentrate upon anything he does is quite admirable. ~배제 decentralization. ~사격〔포화〕 converging 〔concentrated〕 fire. ~안타 〖야구〗 an avalanche 〔a rally, a volley〕 of hits. ~자료처리(시스템) a centralized data processing (system). ~치료 《be under》 intensive care: ~ 치료실 an intensive care unit (생략 ICU). ~폭격 saturation bombing 《미》. ~호우 a localized torrential downpour 〔rainfall〕; a concentrated heavy rain. ~훈련 intensive 〔centralized〕 training: ~ 훈련을 받다 undergo centralized training.

**집진기**(集塵器) a dust collector.

**집집** each and every house; house after house. ¶ ~마다, ~이 at 〔in〕 every house 〔door〕; from house 〔door〕 to house 〔door〕 / ~마다 국기가 휘날리고 있었다 The national flag was fluttering at every house.

**집착**(執着) 《애착》 attachment; adhesion; 《끈기》 tenacity; persistence. ~하다 be attached 《to》; stick 〔adhere〕 《to》; cling 《to》; hold fast 《to》. ¶ 생에 대한 ~ tenacity for life; attachment to life / 낡은 관습에 ～하다 cling to an old custom / 그는 일을 끝낼 때까지 ～하는 성격이다 He will stick to his task until it is finished. / 승부에 너무 ～하지 마라 Don't get too hung up on the outcome of the game.

◉ ～력 tenacity; pertinacity; adhesive power. ～심 attachment 《to, for》; tenacity of purpose: 그녀는 금전에 대한 ～심이 너무 강하다 She is too attached to money.

**집찰**(集札) collection of tickets. ～하다 〖철도〗 collect tickets. ◉ ～원 a ticket collector.

**집채** (the bulk of) a house. ¶ 큰 ～ a house of huge size; a great bulk of a house / ～ 같다 be of great size 〔bulk〕; be as big as a barn / ～만한 황소 a great hulking bull; an enormous bull / ～같은 파도 mountainous waves.

**집치장**(一治粧) the (interior) decoration of a house. ～하다 decorate (the interior of) a house; do the interior decorating. ¶ ～이 잘 되어 있다 be nicely decorated.

**집터** a (housing) site; a (housing) lot. ¶ ～를 닦다 level a site for a house / ～를 사다 buy a lot for a building.

**집필**(執筆) writing. ～하다 write; do writing. ¶ ～을 의뢰받다 be asked to contribute 《an article》 / 잡지에 ～하다 write for a magazine. ◉ ～료 payment for writing. ～자 the writer; the author; 《기고자》 the contributor.

**집하**(集荷) gathering of goods; 《화물》 goods gathered. ～하다 gather goods; collect 〔pick up〕 cargos. ◉ ～장 a (cargo-)pickup point; 《부두의》 a container freight station.

**집합**(集合) (a) gathering; collection; (a) meeting; an assembly; 〖수학〗 a set. ～하다 《모이다》 get together; gather; collect; assemble; meet; swarm; flock; congregate; throng; 《모으다》 gather (together); call 〔get, put〕 together; collect; assemble; summon; muster. ¶ 집합 《구령》 Gather around! / 학생들은 강당에 ～하였다 The pupils assembled 〔were assembled〕 in the (school) hall.

◉ ～나팔 a muster call. ～론 〖수학〗 the theory of sets; set theory. ～명령 a gathering cry. ～명사 〖문법〗 a collective noun. ～시간 the hour of meeting; the time appointed for meeting. ～장소 the meeting place; the rendezvous (point); the roll-call 〔assembly〕 point. ～점 〖기하〗 a concurrence. ～체 an aggregate. ～표상(表象) 〖사회〗 a collective representation.

**집행**(執行) execution; enforcement; 《의식 등의》 performance. ～하다 execute; enforce; carry out; perform. ¶ 형을 ～하다 execute a sentence / 직무를 ～하다 perform 〔discharge〕 *one's* duties / 압류를 ～하다 serve an attachment 《on》 / 형의 ～을 유예하다 place *a person* on probation.

◉ ～관 [일반적] an executor; a sheriff; 《법원의》 a bailiff. ～기간 the term for execution. ～기관 an executive organ. ～기일 the date of 〔fixed for〕 execution. ～부 the executive(s). ～영장〔명령〕 a writ 〔an order〕 of execution. ～위원 an executive committeeman; a member of the executive committee: ～위원회 an executive committee. ～자 an executor (★ 여성형은 executrix (*pl.* ～es, -trices)); an executant; 《사형의》 an executioner. ～절차 execution proceedings. ～정지 suspension of executant. ～처분 an executive measure.

**집행유예**(執行猶豫) 〖법〗 a stay of execution; probation; 《판결》 a suspended sentence. ～하다 place 《*a person*》 on probation; allow 《*a person*》 to go on probation; grant 《*a person*》 a stay of execution. ¶ ～ 판결을 내리다 give a suspended sentence / ～가 되다 be granted a stay of execution; be given a suspended sentence 《of two years》 / 징역 6월 ～ 2년을 선고받다 be sentenced to six months in prison with a stay of execution for two years / 그는 지금 ～ 중이다 He is on probation 《for two years》.

**집현전**(集賢殿) 〖역사〗 *Chiphyŏnjŏn*, the Hall of Worthies. ¶ 세종 임금께서는 한글의 중요함과 그 필요성을 절감하시고 한글을 창안하도록 ～에 학자들을 모아 연구하게 하셨다 King Sejong firmly believed in the necessity and the importance of *Hangŭl* and enlist the services of scholars in the Hall of Worthies to originate *Hangŭl*.

**집형**(執刑) execution of a sentence. ～하다 execute a sentence.

**집화**(集貨) collection of cargos. ⇨ 집하.

**집회**(集會) a meeting; a gathering; an assembly; a congregation; a rally. ～

하다 assemble; gather; meet together; hold a meeting.

> 용법 **meeting** 토론·결정 등을 목적으로 하는 「모임·집회」. **assembly** 정치·사회·종교 따위의 명확한 목적을 가진 모임. **gathering** 어떤 일정한 목적·주장·규칙 따위에 얽매이지 않은 허물없는 모임. **congregation** 주로 종교적인 목적을 가진 집회. **rally** 정치적 시위 따위를 목적으로 하는 군중 집회.

¶ ~의 자유 freedom 〔liberty〕 of assembly (★ 일반적으로 freedom을 쓰지만 억압이나 제한이 있었던 것을 암시해서 liberty를 쓰는 일도 있음) / ~를 방해하다 thwart 〔disturb, interrupt〕 an assembly / ~에 참석하다 attend a meeting / 3시부터 ~를 갖겠습니다 We will have 〔hold〕 a meeting at three.
◉ ~신고 a notice of an assembly; gathering permits. ~ 및 시위에 관한 법률 《violate》 the Law on Assembly and Demonstration. ~장(소) a meeting place; an assembly hall.

**집히다** get picked up; 《it》 pick up. ¶ 손에 집히는 대로 먹다 eat anything *one* can put *his* hands on / 바늘은 잘 집히지 않는다 The needle is hard to pick up.

**짓** an act; a deed; behavior; conduct; a motion; a gesture; a movement. ¶ 손짓 a motion of the hand; a wave; a hand signal / 몸짓 a gesture; gesticulation / 눈짓 a sign with the eyes; an eye-signal; eyeing; giving the eye 《to》 / 나쁜 짓 bad conduct / 이게 무슨 짓이냐 Where are your manners? / 또 그 짓이야 The same old game! / 미친 짓이다 That is act of madness. / 너 하는 짓은 밤낮 그 모양이다 Nothing you do ever amounts to anything. / 무슨 생각으로 그런 바보같은 짓을 했느냐 What's the idea of making such an ass of yourself?

**짓거리** ① a gesture 〔an act〕 out of merriment; a bit of fun; a thing done just for fun. ② = 짓.

**짓고땡** ① a game in which each player gets 5 cards 〔dominoes〕 at a time, with three of them used to make a *mudae* (= 10, 20 score) and the remaining two used for matching other players. ② 《뜻대로 됨》 a smooth going of a job.

**짓궂다** (be) annoying; bothersome; harassing; troublesome; insistent; persistent; nagging. ¶ 짓궂은 비 a plaguing rain / 짓궂은 장난꾼 a practical joker / 짓궂게 조르다 pester for; insist on 《having》; importune.

**짓누르다** weigh down; press down; press upon 《*a thing*》; 《억누르다》 put down; 《마음을》 weigh heavily on 《*one's* mind》. ¶ 그 빚이 그의 마음을 짓눌렀다 The debt lay like a heavy weight on his mind.

**짓눌리다** be weighed 〔pressed, put〕 down; be crushed 〔squashed〕. ¶ 슬픔에 ~ be crushed with grief 《over》.

**짓다**[1] ① 《만들다》 make; manufacture; fashion. ¶ 잘 지은 옷 well-tailored 〔=cut〕 clothes / 구두를 ~ make shoes / 어머니가 새 옷을 지어 주셨다 Mother made a new dress for me.
② 《집을》 build; construct; erect. ¶ 돌〔나무〕로 지은 집 a house built of stone 〔wood〕 / 집을 ~ build a house / 새가 집을 지었다 The bird built a nest. / 이 집은 반 년 걸려 지었다 The building 〔construction〕 of the house took six months.
③ 《글을》 make; compose; write. ¶ 시를 ~ compose 〔write〕 a poem / 작문을 ~ write a composition / 그는 여덟 살 때 시를 짓기 시작했다 He began to compose a poem when he was eight years old.
④ 《밥을》 cook; prepare. ¶ 밥을 ~ cook 〔boil〕 rice / 저녁을 ~ prepare 〔fix 《미》〕 supper / 어머니는 늘 밥을 지어놓고 나를 기다리셨다 Mother always waited for me with a meal ready.
⑤ 《줄을》 form; make. ¶ 열을 ~ form a line 〔queue〕; line up / 줄을 지어 나아가다 advance in ranks 〔files〕 / 많은 사람들이 극장 앞에 줄을 지어 있었다 A large number of people queued up before the theater.
⑥ 《농사를》 cultivate; farm; crop; grow; raise. ¶ 농사를 ~ do farm work; till the soil / 논농사를 ~ till a rice-field / 보리 농사를 ~ raise 〔grow〕 barley / 여기는 밀농사를 많이 짓는다 Here much wheat is grown.
⑦ 《죄를》 commit; perpetrate. ¶ 죄를 ~ commit a sin 〔crime〕 / 내가 무슨 죄를 지었습니까 In what have I offended?
⑧ 《표정을》 show; express; put forth 《a look》. ¶ 지은 웃음 a forced smile; a smirk / 웃음을 ~ put forth 〔wear〕 a smile / 슬픈 표정을 ~ give 〔take on〕 a sad look / 눈물 ~ be moved to tears;

*one's* eyes swim 〔dim〕 with tears. ⑨《끝장을》 settle. ¶ 일의 결말을 ～ settle 〔wind up〕 a matter; bring an affair to a conclusion / 그들끼리 그 사건을 해결지었다 They have settled the matter among 〔between〕 themselves. ⑩《약을》 prepare; compound 《medicine》; fill a prescription (처방에 의하여). ¶ 약을 ～ prepare medicine; make up 〔fill〕 a prescription. ⑪《허구》 make up; invent; fabricate. ¶ 지어낸 이야기 a made-up 〔an invented〕 story; an invention.

**짓다**[2] 《아이를》 miscarry; abort. ¶ 아이를 ～ have a miscarriage.

**짓무르다** be sore 〔inflamed〕; become blistered. ¶ 빨갛게 짓무른 피부 an inflamed raw skin / 상처가 짓물렀다 The cut is inflamed.

**짓무찌르다** smash; crush; beat; rout; slaughter. ¶ 적을 ～ crush 〔smash〕 the enemy.

**짓밟다** ①《발로》 stamp 〔trample〕 down; tread on. ¶ 꽃을 ～ tread flowers down / 불을 짓밟아 끄다 stamp 〔tread〕 out a fire. ②《유린하다》 trample 《*something*》 underfoot; crush under *one's* feet; infringe (on); override. ¶ 남의 감정을 ～ trample on *a person's* feelings / 남의 권리를 ～ infringe *a person's* rights / 국민의 자유를 ～ ride over the liberties of the people / 그는 도와 주겠다는 내 호의를 짓밟았다 He was ungrateful enough to reject my kind offer to help him.

**짓밟히다** get 《*something*》 trampled under foot; be trampled down 〔upon〕; get overridden; get overrun. ¶ 짓밟혀 죽다 be trampled to death; be crushed to death under foot.

**짓씹다** chew thoroughly 〔well〕; masticate.

**짓이기다** beat to a pulp; knead to a mash; mash. ¶ 감자를 ～ mash potatoes / 아무를 ～ beat a person to a jelly; thrash a person / 진흙을 ～ knead mud.

**짓찧다** ①《빻다》 pound hard; pulverize. ¶ 절구에 고추를 ～ pulverize red pepper in a mortar. ②《부딪치다》 strike 〔hit, bump〕 hard. ¶ 벽에 이마를 ～ bump *one's* head against the wall.

**징**[1] 〖악기〗 a gong. ¶ 징을 치다 〔울리다〕 strike a gong.

**징**[2] 《구두의》 a hobnail. ¶ 징을 박은 부츠 hobnailed boots / 구두창에 징을 박다 put hobnails on shoe soles.

**징거두다** ①《바느질》 ⇨징그다. ②《준비》 make advance preparation. ¶ 내일 할 일을 ～ do preparation for tomorrow's work.

**징건하다** (be) heavy 〔stodgy, stuffy〕 (on the stomach); remain undigested in the stomach.

**징검다리** stepping stones (across a stream). ¶ ～를 건너다 cross a stream by the stepping stones; step from stone to stone.

**징검징검** ①《꿰매다》 sewing loosely; saddle-stitching. ¶ ～ 꿰매다 sew loosely. ②《걸음을》 stepping; skipping. ¶ ～ 걷다 walk with long steps.

**징계**(懲戒) an official reprimand; a disciplinary punishment; discipline. ～하다 discipline; reprimand.
◉ ～위원회 a disciplinary committee: ～위원회에 회부하다 refer 《a case》 to the Disciplinary Committee. ～조치〔처분〕 a disciplinary measure 〔punishment, action〕: ～조치를〔처분을〕 받다 be subjected to disciplinary punishment 〔action〕. ～파면〔면직〕 a disciplinary dismissal 〔disposition〕: ～파면이 되다 be dismissed in disgrace.

**징그다** 《듬성듬성 꿰매다》 sew loosely 〔with long stitches〕 for reinforcement; give reinforcing stitches 《to》; 《접어서 호다》 make a tuck 《in a dress》.

**징그럽다** (be) crawly; creepy; repulsive; feel creepy; make *one's* flesh creep. ¶ 징그러운 벌레 creepy insects / 징그러운 느낌 a creepy sensation / 보기만 해도 ～ The sight made me crawly. / 뱀은 보기에 ～ Snakes are uncanny-looking. / 이런 징그러운 것을 어떻게 먹나 I wouldn't eat odious stuff like this.

**징글징글하다** (be) crawly; creepy; repulsive.

**징모**(徵募) levy; enlistment; recruiting. ～하다 recruit; enlist; levy; raise.

**징발**(徵發) requisition; commandeering; levy; forage. ～하다 commandeer; levy; requisition; forage. ¶ ～된 토지 commandeered land / 식량의 ～ requisition for provisions / ～을 면하다 be exempted from requisition / ～되다 be placed under requisition / 말을 군용으로 ～하다 requisition horses for troops / 마을에서 트럭을 ～하다 requisition a town for motor trucks.
◉ ～권 the right of requisition. ～대 a foraging party. ～령 a requisition order. ～법 the Requisition Law. ～병

a forager. ～보상 compensation for commandeered properties. ～선(船) a requisitioned ship.

**징벌**(懲罰) disciplinary punishment; discipline; chastisement. ～하다 punish; discipline; castigate; chastise. ¶ ～을 받다 be subject to punitive action. ◉ ～규정 a disciplinary provision. ～동의 a motion for disciplinary measures 《against *a person*》.

**징병**(徵兵) conscription; enlistment; 《미》 the (military) draft; compulsory draft; 《영》 the call-up. ～하다 draft; conscript. ¶ ～되다 be enlisted; be enrolled; 《미》 be drafted; 《미》 be inducted 《into the U.S. Army》; 《영》 be called up / ～을 면제받다 be exempted from military service / ～을 기피하다 evade 〔shirk〕 conscription; evade the draft 《미》.
◉ ～검사 a physical examination 〔medical checkup〕 for conscription: ～ 검사를 받다 be examined for conscription. ～관 a conscription officer; a recruiter. ～구 a conscription district. ～기피 evasion of conscription 〔military service〕; evasion of the draft 《미》: ～기피자 a draft dodger; a slacker. ～사무소 an enlistment station. ～적령(適齡) draft 〔conscription〕 age: ～ 적령자 a young man of conscription 〔draft〕 age. ～제도 the conscription 〔draft〕 system.

**징세**(徵稅) tax collection; collection of taxes. ～하다 collect 〔levy〕 taxes 《from》. ◉ ～목표 a tax collection goal.

**징수**(徵收) levy; assessment; collection. ～하다 levy; tax; collect; assess; charge. ¶ 세금을 ～하다 collect 〔levy〕 taxes / 부가 ～하다 levy additional (taxes); collect additional dues 〔fees〕 / 1인당 3,000원의 회비를 ～했다 I collected a fee of three thousand won per person. ◉ ～료 a collection fee. ～액 the collected amount.

**징역**(懲役) penal servitude; imprisonment with hard labor. ～ 살다 serve (time) in prison; be in jail. ¶ ～ 가다 be sent to prison; go to jail / ～을 받다 be given a jail sentence / ～ 2년에 처해지다 be sentenced 〔condemned〕 to two years' imprisonment / 10년 ～을 복역하다 serve a sentence of ten years' penal servitude; serve ten years' sentence / 2년의 ～을 마치다 finish *one's* two years' prison term.
◉ ～꾼 a convict; a prisoner. ～살이 a prison life; a life behind bars; imprisonment.

**징용**(徵用) the (work) draft; drafting; commandeering; requisition. ～하다 draft; commandeer; requisition. ¶ ～가다 be drafted / 중년의 남자들도 군에 ～되었다 Even middle-aged men were drafted into the army. ◉ ～자 draftees. ～해제 derequisition.

**징잡이** a gong player.

**징장구** 〖악기〗 gongs and drums.

**징조**(徵兆) a sign; an indication; an omen; a presage; a symptom. ¶ 좋은 〔나쁜〕 ～ a good 〔an evil〕 omen / …의 ～가 있다 show signs 〔give indications, be a sign, be ominous〕 of…; betoken; forebode / 열이 있는 것은 병의 ～이다 Fever indicates illness. / 무지개는 날이 갤 ～이다 The rainbow promises fair weather.

**징집**(徵集) ① 《징병》 conscription; enlistment; enrollment; recruitment; draft. ～하다 draft; conscript; enlist; press 《*men*》 into service; levy 《troops》. ¶ 학생의 ～ 연기 특전 the privilege of student conscription deferment / ～되다 be drafted / 고교생의 ～을 졸업 때까지 연기하다 allow high school students to have their draft deferred until graduation. ② ＝징수(徵收).
◉ ～기피 evasion of conscription; draft dodging: ～ 기피자 a slacker; a draft dodger. ～면제 exemption from conscription 〔enlistment, the draft 《미》; military service〕: ～ 면제의 특전 the privilege of exemption from conscription / ～ 면제가 되다 escape conscription; be exempted from conscription 〔the draft〕. ～연기 postponement of enlistment 〔recruitment〕; temporary exemption from conscription 〔military service〕: ～연기자 persons deferred from recruitment / ～ 연기가 되다 be temporarily exempted from military service. ～연도 conscription year. ～영장 《미》 a draft card; 《영》 *one's* call-up papers. ～유예 temporary draft exemption.

**징크스** a jinx; a saying; a popular belief. ¶ …라는 ～가 있다 There is a saying 〔a popular belief〕 that… (★ There is a jinx that…라고는 아니함. 영어에서는 There seems to be a jinx on this house 「이 집은 재수가 없다」라는 식의 사용법 이외는 없음) / ～를 깨다〔믿다〕 break 〔believe in〕 the jinx.

**징후**(徵候) a symptom (of disease); [일반적] a sign; an omen; an indication; a foretoken. ¶ 폭풍이 닥쳐올 ～ an indication of an approaching storm / ～를 나타내다 give indications 〔show signs〕 《of》 / 구름은 비가 올 ～이다 Clouds are signs of rain. / 그는 말라리아의 ～가 여실하다 He has all the symptoms of malaria. / 사태가 좋아질 ～가 충분하다〔없다〕 There is every 〔no〕 indication that things will soon improve.

**짖다** ① 《개·여우가》 bark; 《늑대·개가》 howl; 《맹수가》 roar; 《사냥개 따위가》 bay. ¶ 멀리서 개 짖는 소리 the howling of a dog / 달을 보고 ～ howl at the moon / 그 개는 낯선 사람만 보면 짖는다 He barks at a stranger. / 짖는 개는 물지 않는다 《속담》 Barking dogs seldom bite. ② 《까막까치가》 caw; croak.

**짙다** ① 《색이》 (be) deep; rich; dark. ¶ 짙은 푸른 빛〔그림자〕 deep blue 〔shadows〕 / 짙은 갈색 dark 〔deep〕 brown (color) / 짙은 화장 heavy toilet; a thick make-up / 짙은 눈썹 thick eyebrows. ② 《농후》 (be) thick; dense. ¶ 짙은 안개 a thick fog / 커피를 짙게 타서 마시다 drink coffee strong. ③ 《숲·나무 등이》 (be) thick; heavy; gross. ¶ 짙은 숲 a thick forest.

**짙푸르다** (be) deep blue.

**짚** straw [총칭]. ¶ 볏짚 rice straw / 밀짚 wheat straw / 밀짚 모자 a straw hat / 짚을 다발로 묶다 tie up straw in sheaves / 짚을 깔다 spread straw; 《외양간에》 litter down 《a horse》.

**짚가리** a stack of rice straw; a rick. ¶ ～를 쌓다 heap up in rick; stack.

**짚다** ① 《대다》 touch; feel; pat. ¶ 맥을 ～ take 〔feel, examine〕 the pulse / 열이 있나 이마를 ～ feel *one's* forehead to see if *one* has fever / …에 팔꿈치를 ～ rest *one's* elbow(s) upon… / 땅 짚고 헤엄치기다 That's quite an easy job. *or* That's a cinch 《미구어》. ② 《지팡이 따위를》 put *one's* hand 《on a cane》 for support. ¶ 지팡이를 ～ use a cane / 지팡이를 짚고 걷다 walk with a stick 〔cane〕. ③ 《헤어보다》 count on the fingers. ¶ 달수를 ～ count the months on *one's* fingers. ④ 《짐작하다》 guess; make a shot 〔random guess〕. ¶ 그 추측은 제대로 짚었다 That was a good 〔lucky〕 guess. ⑤ 《지목하다》 point out; indicate; put a 〔*one's*〕 finger 《on》. ¶ 낱말을 ～ point out a word.

**짚단** a sheaf of straw. ¶ ～을 만들다 tie up straw in sheaves.

**짚둥우리** a straw basket.

**짚북데기** a heap of straw.

**짚불** a straw fire. ¶ ～을 피우다 make fire with straw.

**짚수세미** a scrub brush made of straw; a straw scrubber.

**짚신** straw sandals 〔shoes〕. ¶ ～을 삼다 make straw sandals / ～감발하다 put on 〔wear〕 straw sandals and foot-wraps; equip *oneself* for walking trip / ～감발하고 길을 떠나다 set out for a journey lightly outfitted.

**짚이다** 《마음 속에》 (happen to) know of; have in mind; suspect; have a glimmering 〔inkling〕 of. ¶ 전혀 짚이는 데가 없다 have not faintest 〔slightest〕 idea 《of》 / 당신 시계를 누가 훔쳤는지 짚이는 데가 있습니까 Have you any idea who stole your watch?

**짚자리** straw matting.

**짚재** straw ashes.

**짜개** a piece of bean (or the like) split in two. ¶ 콩～ split beans. ◉ ～황밤 split chestnuts.

**짜깁기** invisible mending. ～하다 mend 《the trousers》 invisibly.

**짜다**[1] ① 《제작》 piece together; assemble; construct; make. ¶ 궤를〔책상을〕 ～ make a chest 〔table〕 / 나무로 찬장을 ～ make a cupboard of wood. ② 《편성》 form; organize; compose. ¶ 영어반을 ～ form an English class / 도당을 ～ band together; form a faction / 편을 ～ form a faction; make sides / 편을 짜서 놀자 Let's play sides. / 어떻게 팀을 짜야 할지 모르겠다 I don't know how I can manage to make up the team. ③ 《실 따위로》 weave. ¶ 무명〔비단〕을 ～ weave cotton 〔silk〕 cloth / 털실로 트위드를 ～ weave wool into tweeds / 그녀는 융단을 짜고 있다 She is weaving a rug. ④ 《뜨개질》 knit; crochet. ¶ 털실로 양말을 ～ knit stockings out of wool. ⑤ 《공모》 act in league 〔concert〕 《with》; plot together; collude 《with》; conspire with 〔together〕. ¶ 아무와 짜고 in collusion 〔league, conspiracy〕 with *a person* / 서로 짜고 공금을 횡령했다 They got together and embezzled public funds in cahoots. ⑥ 《계획을》 work over; make 《*one's*

plan》 carefully. ¶ 생각을 짜내다 ponder over *one's* ideas; rack *one's* brains / 장래의 계획을 ~ plan (of) *one's* future.
⑦ 《활자를》 set up (in type); set type; compose.

**짜다²** ① 《즙·기름을》 squeeze; press; extract. ¶ 오렌지의 즙을 ~ squeeze juice from an orange / 눈물을 ~ squeeze out a tear / 소젖을 ~ milk a cow / 참기름을 ~ press oil from sesame seeds. ② 《빨래 따위를》 wring; squeeze. ¶ 젖은 수건을 ~ wring out a wet towel / 빨래를 한 번만 짜라 Give that wash just a wring. ③ 《착취》 exploit; squeeze; extort 《from》. ¶ 농민의 고혈을 ~ squeeze (sweat and blood from) the farmers / 돈을 짜내다 extort 〔squeeze〕 money from 《*a person*》.

**짜다³** ① 《맛이》 (be) salty; briny. ¶ 짠맛 a salty taste / 짠 음식 salted foods. ② 《달갑지 않다》 (be) unpleasant; displeased; sour. ¶ 마음에 ~ feel unpleasant. ③ 《점수가》 be severe 〔strict〕 in marking.

**짜드락나다** be found out; get out; be exposed 〔disclosed〕; come to light.

**짜디짜다** (be) very salty.

**-짜리** ① 《가치》 worth; value. ¶ 백 원짜리 동전 a 100-won coin / 천 원짜리 모자 a thousand-won hat. ② 《양》 amount. ¶ 이십 킬로짜리 가마니 a twenty-kilogram bag of rice.

**짜릿짜릿** ~하다 (be) thrilling; tingly; [서술적] be suspenseful. ¶ 이 이야기에는 ~한 장면이 많다 This is a suspense-laden story.

**짜릿하다** 《맛이》 (be) pungent; spicy; 《마음이》 (be) tingly; smart.

**짜이다** ① 《규모·규격 등이》 get put 〔pieced〕 together; get assembled 〔constructed, made〕. ② 《조직·이론 등이》 get formed 〔organized, framed, structured〕. ¶ 잘 짜인 팀 a close-knit team / 꽉 짜인 일정 a crowded schedule / 잘 짜인 소설 줄거리 the well constructed plot of a novel / 조직이 잘 ~ be well organized / 이론이 잘 ~ a theory is well framed 〔nicely structured〕. ③ 《피륙이》 get woven. ④ 《편물이》 get knitted 〔crocheted〕.

**짜임** ① 《구성》 being put 〔pieced〕 together; being made 〔formed, assembled〕. ② 《언어의》 getting compounded; compounding. ③ 《조직의》 being systematized 〔organized, put in order〕. ◉ ~새 the make; makeup; structure; the way something is put together: ~새가 거칠다 be open 〔loose〕 in weave.

**짜장면** ＝ 자장면

**짜증** fret; annoyance; irritation; a temper; (a fit of) anger; a tantrum (어린이의). ¶ ~을 내다, ~이 나다 lose *one's* temper; be vexed; get irritated; be peevish; fly into a passion 〔tantrum〕 / ~이 나게 하다 annoy; irritate; make anger; put out of temper / ~을 참아내다 control 〔keep〕 *one's* temper / 내 대답에 그는 ~을 냈다 He lost his temper at my reply. / 그녀는 나를 ~나게 한다 She gets in my hair.

**짜하다** (be) widespread abroad; well aired 〔circulated〕. ¶ 그 소문이 짜하게 퍼졌다 The rumor spread like a wildfire.

**짝¹** ① 《쌍을 이루는》 one of a pair 〔couple〕; the mate 《to》; the fellow 《of》; the partner 《to》; the other one. ¶ 양말〔장갑〕 한 짝 an odd sock 〔glove〕 / 짝을 짓다〔채우다〕 pair; match; couple / 이 구두 한 짝이 어디갔나 Where is the other shoe (to this one)? / 새가 짝을 부르고 있다 The bird is calling his mate. / 결혼하려 해도 알맞은 짝이 없다 I wish to marry but cannot find a fit mate. / 윷놀이에서 나는 그녀의 짝이 되었다 I was her partner at *yut*. ② 《상대》 a match; a peer. ③ 《짐 따위의》 an item.

**짝²** ① 《편》 a side; one side. ② 《갈비》 a 〔one〕 side 《of beef 〔pork〕 ribs》. ③ 《아무짝》 ¶ 아무짝에도 못 쓴다 It's no good anywhere. / 그게 무슨 짝이냐 A shame it is!

**짝³** ① 《찢는 소리》 ripping; tearing. ¶ 종이를 짝 찢다 rip paper. ② 《활짝》 wide-open. ¶ 입을 짝 벌리다 open *one's* mouth wide; gape.

**짝귀** ears which are not the same size; mismated ears; a person who has one ear bigger than the other.

**짝눈** eyes which are not the same size; mismated eyes; a person who has one eye bigger than the other.

**짝맞다** match with another one.

**짝맞추다** match (two things); make match.

**짝사랑** one-sided love; a crush. ~하다 love 《*a girl*》 secretly; worship 《*a girl*》 at a distance. ¶ 그의 사랑은 ~이었다 His love was not reciprocated 〔returned〕. / 낸시는 잘 생긴 선생님을

~하고 있다 Nancy has a crush on her handsome teacher.

**짝수**(—數) an even number. ¶ ~의 even; even-numbered / ~의 해 even years / ~ 날은 휴무다 We are off duty on days bearing even numbers.

**짝신** an unmatched 〔a mismated〕 pair of shoes; wrongly paired shoes.

**짝없다** ①《비길 데 없다》(be) matchless; incomparable; be without a peer. ¶ 기쁘기 ~ be happy beyond measure / 미안하기 짝이 없어요 I'm ever so sorry for what I did. ②《대중없다》(be) preposterous; incongruous; be unmatched《in absurdity or irrelevance》. ¶ 짝없는 말 preposterous remarks.

**짝자래나무** 〖식물〗 a kind of buckthorn.

**짝짓다** pair; make a match; mate. ¶ 새를 ~ mate a bird / 둘씩 셋씩 짝지어 오다 come by twos and threes.

**짝짜꿍** a baby's hand-clapping game; "pat-a-cake". ¶ "~ 짝짜꿍, 곤지곤지, 죔죔, 도리도리" "Clap it, clap it, mark it, mark it, grab it, grab it, roll it, roll it!"

**짝짜꿍이** ①《다툼》a clash; a fight; a commotion; a scene. ~하다 clash 〔fight〕 with each other. ¶ ~ 일다 raise a commotion; make a scene. ②《밀계》a secret scheme. ~하다 secretly scheme.

**짝짝** ①《끈끈한 것이》clinging fast 〔close, tight〕. ¶ 껌을 ~ 씹다 chew a stick of gum audibly / 젖은 셔츠가 몸에 ~ 달라붙다 a wet shirt clings to *one's* body. ②《입맛을》smacking. ¶ 입맛을 ~ 다시다 smack *one's* lips; lick *one's* chops. ③《신발을》dragging; slap-slap; slop-slop; slupping 〔slopping〕 along. ¶ 신을 ~ 끌다 drag *one's* shoes. ④《찢는 소리》ripping; tearing up. ¶ 옷을 ~ 찢다 rip up a dress.

**짝짝거리다** ① ⇨ 짝짝거리다. ②《신발을》drag. ③《찢다》rip; tear up.

**짝짝이** an unmatched pair; a wrongly matched pair. ¶ ~ 양말을 신다 wear unmatched socks / 이 구두는 ~다 These shoes are wrongly paired. / 그는 눈이 ~다 One of his eyes is bigger than the other.

**짝채우다** match; make a set. ¶ 찻잔 하나를 사서 ~ buy a teacup to match the set.

**짝하다** become a partner; partake.

**짠물** salt water; brine; seawater.
◉ ~고기 saltwater fish; a sea fish.

**짠지** radish kimchi preserved with salt.

**짠하다** feel depressed 〔sad, "blue"〕.

**짤까닥, 짤깍** ① ⇨ 잘가닥. ②《들러붙음》clinging fast 〔close, tight〕.

**짤끔거리다** ①《물 따위가》trickle; dribble. ② = 찔름거리다[2].

**짤따랗다** (be) shortish; rather short.

**짤라뱅이** a short object; an undersized thing; a dwarf; a runt; a midget; a miniature.

**짤래짤래** shaking *one's* head.

**짤막짤막** all short(ly); all briefly. ~하다 (be) all shortish 〔short〕; all brief. ¶ 오이를 ~하게 썰다 cut cucumbers in small pieces / 글을 ~하게 쓰다 write choppy sentences.

**짤막하다** (be) shortish; choppy; rather 〔somewhat〕 short. ¶ 짤막한 인사말 a brief address.

**짤짤거리다**《돌아다니다》go around hurriedly; dart about.

**짤짤이** a person who dashes about unceremoniously; a bustling fellow.

**짧다** ①《시간·길이》(be) short;《간결한》(be) brief; concise. ¶ 짧게 briefly / 짧게 말하면 in short; to be brief; to make a long story short / 짧은 여행 〔이야기, 생각〕 a brief trip 〔talk, thought〕/ 짧은 일생 a short span of life; a brief life / 짧은 바지 knee 〔short〕 breeches; knee trousers 〔pants〕/ 다섯 자 ~ be short by five feet / 짧아지다 shorten; grow shorter / 짧게 하다 shorten; cut short / 그의 머리는 ~ He has short hair. / 그 코트의 소매는 좀 ~ The coat is a little short in the sleeves. / 날이 점점 짧아져 간다 The days are getting shorter. / 사람의 일생은 ~ Our life is but a span. / 그는 굵고 짧게 사는 것이 좋다고 생각한다 He believes in a short life and a merry one. / 그의 짧은 말 속에는 만감이 교차하는 심경이 담겨 있다 All of his complex feelings are encapsulated in those few words. ②《까다롭다》(be) particular 〔fussy, fastidious, overnice〕《about》; be choos(e)y《about》. ¶ 그녀는 입이 ~ She is fussy 〔particular, finicky〕 about her food. *or* She picks and chooses what she eats. ③ = 모자라다 ①.

**짬** spare time; leisure (hours). ⇨ 틈.

**짬뽕**《뒤범벅》a mixture; a medley;《중국 음식》a Chinese-style hotchpotch noodle of vegetables and seafood.

**짬짜미** a secret promise 〔agreement, contract, pact〕; undercover negotiations 〔bargaining〕. ~하다 promise secretly; indulge in undercover negotiations.

**짭질찮다** ① 《안 좋다》 (be) poor; no good; mediocre; so-so. ¶ 솜씨가 ~ be rather poor at it. ② 《천하다》 (be) vulgar; mean; low; base.

**짭짤하다** ① 《맛이》 (be) nice and salty; have a good salty taste 《to》; (be) tasty. ¶ 짭짤한 고기 반찬 a nicely salted meat dish. ② 《짜임새 따위가》 (be) acceptable; respectable; be quite a…. ③ 《쑬쑬함》 be fairly good at. ¶ 짭짤한 부자 a quite well-to-do person / 솜씨가 ~ be quite good at / 그들의 살림살이는 하나같이 ~ The household effects they have are all substantial.

**짱짱하다** (be) sturdy; stout; strong.

**-째** 《보통, 기본수를 나타내는 명사 뒤에 붙어 차례·등급을 나타내는 말》 ¶ 첫〔둘, 셋〕째 first 〔second, third〕 / 첫〔둘, 셋〕째로 firstly 〔secondly, thirdly〕 / 두번째의 결혼 a second marriage / 둘째 형 the second oldest brother / 세계에서 다섯째로 큰 산 the fifth highest mountain in the world / 둘째를 차지하다 take the second place; rank second / 셋째로 떨어지다 drop to third place / 첫째로 졸업하다 graduate at the head of *one's* class / 그는 두번째로 왔다 He was the second to come. / 내가 여기 온 것은 이번이 세 번째이다 This is the third time I have been here. / 그녀는 우리 집에서 넷째 번 집에 살고 있다 She lives in the fourth house beyond us. *or* She lives three doors off from us. (★ four doors off는 「네 집 걸러」의 뜻이므로 결국 다섯째 집이 됨에 주의).

**째** 《통째로·그대로》 and all; together with; inclusive of; as it is. ¶ 사과를 껍질 째 먹다 eat an apple, peel and all / 생선을 가시 째 삼켜 버리다 devour a fish, bones and all / 나무를 뿌리 째 뽑다 pull up a tree by the roots.

**째깍-** ⇨ 재깍-.

**째다**[1] 《찢다》 cut open 《a boil, *etc.*》; open; lance; incise. ¶ 종기를 ~ lance a boil / 소매치기가 주머니를 칼로 째고 돈을 가져 갔다 A pickpocket cut my pocket open with a knife and took my money.

**째다**[2] ① 《부족하다》 be insufficient; be short of. ¶ 살림이 ~ be in want; be needy / 일손이 짼다 We are short of hands. ② 《작다》 be too small (to wear comfortably); be too tight 《for》. ¶ 이 옷은 너무 짼다 The suit is too tight for me.

**째마리** 《물건》 trash; rubbish; junk; waste; 《사람》 a good-for-nothing; a scum; a human waste 〔debris〕.

**째보** ① 《언청이》 a harelipped person. ② 《잔망한 사람》 a weak and frivolous person.

**째(어)지다** split; rend; tear; rip; cleave. ¶ 길게 째진 눈 long slanted eyes / 깃발이 바람에 갈가리 째졌다 The flag was torn to ribbons by the wind. / 이런 종이는 쉽게 째어진다 Paper of this quality tears easily.

**짹짹거리다** tweet; twitter; chirp. ¶ 새들이 짹짹거리고 있다 Birds are chirping.

**쨍그랑** ⇨ 쟁강. ¶ 접시가 ~ 마룻바닥에 떨어졌다 The dishes fell on the floor with a crash.

**쨍쨍** 《the sun shines》 blazing(ly); bright(ly); glaring(ly). ~하다 (be) bright; blazing. ¶ 해가 모래 위에 ~ 내리쬐었다 The sun glared down upon the sand.

**쨍쨍거리다** snap 〔nag, snarl〕 《at》; speak snappishly 〔snarlingly〕 《to》; be snappish 《with》; give the rough side of *one's* tongue.

**쩌렁쩌렁하다** (be) resonant; sonorous. ¶ 쩌렁쩌렁한 목소리 a resonant voice.

**쩌쩌** ① 《혀차는 소리》 Tsk tsk tsk! ② 《소 몰 때》 Haw!

**-쩍다** feel (like); give 〔have〕 a feeling 《of》. ¶ 겸연쩍다 be abashed 〔shamefaced, embarrassed〕 / 괴이쩍다 be queer 〔strange〕 / 미심쩍다 be doubtful 〔suspicious〕 / 미안쩍다 be 〔feel〕 sorry 《for》.

**쩍말없다** leave nothing to be said; have nothing to complain 《of》; (be) perfect; have nothing better.

**쩍쩍거리다** smack *one's* lips; lick *one's* chops. ¶ (입을) 쩍쩍거리며 먹다 smack *one's* lips while eating.

**쩍하면** on the slightest movement; easily; with the slightest provocation.

**쩔레쩔레** shaking *one's* head.

**쩔쩔매다** fluster *oneself;* be all in a hurry; be flurried 〔confused, flustered〕; lose *one's* head; be solely perplexed; be at a loss what to do. ¶ 바빠서 ~ be so busy that *one* doesn't know the left from the right / 시험장에서 ~ be snowed under by 〔with〕 the examinations / 상관한테 ~ be shaken up by *one's* superior / 쩔쩔매며 어찌할 바를 모르다 be at a loss to know what to do / 그는 돈이 없어 쩔쩔맨다 He is hard up for money.

**쩝쩝** licking *one's* chops; smacking *one's* lips. ～하다〔거리다〕 lick *one's* chops; smack *one's* lips. ¶ 입맛을 ～ 다시다 lick *one's* chops; smack *one's* lips / ～거리며 먹다 smack *one's* lips while eating.

**쨍쨍** ①《권세가》 resounding; powerful; mighty. ¶ 세력이 ～ 울리다 enjoy resounding influence. ②《갈라지는 소리》 cracking. ¶ 얼음이 ～ 갈라지다 the ice cracks.

**쩨쩨하다** 《인색》 (be) niggardly; miserly; stingy; close-fisted; tight-fisted; illiberal; 《다랍다》 (be) mean; humble; shabby; poor; 《시시하다》 (be) worthless. ¶ 쩨쩨한 사람 a miser; a stingy person / 쩨쩨한 생각 a narrow-minded idea / 쩨쩨하게 stingily; niggardly / 쩨쩨한 소리 하지 마라 Don't be stingy. *or* Be liberal.

**쪼개다** split; cleave; chop 《wood》; divide; cut. ¶ 둘로 ～ divide 《it》 in two / 도끼로 통나무를 ～ split the log with an ax.

**쪼개지다** split; be split; 《균열》 crack; be cracked; break; be broken; be smashed.

**쪼그랑박** a withered gourd.

**쪼그랑할멈** a withered old woman.

**쪼그리다** ① ＝쭈그러뜨리다. ②《몸을》 crouch; squat; bend low. ¶ 쪼그리고 앉다 crouch 〔squat〕 down.

**쪼글쪼글** ⇨쭈글쭈글.

**쪼다** ①《부리 따위로》 peck at; pick up. ¶ 새가 콩을 ～ a bird pecks at beans. ②《정 따위로》 chisel. ¶ 정으로 돌을 ～ cut a stone with a chisel.

**쪼들리다** be hard pressed; be oppressed; be in straitened circumstances. ¶ 돈에 ～ be pressed 〔strapped〕 for money / 가난에 ～ be pinched with poverty / 빚에 ～ be harassed with debts / 생활에 ～ be in straitened circumstances; be hard up for living / 돈에 쪼들리고 있는 미국방부는 낡은 군사 장비를 할인 가격으로 판매하여 수십억 달러를 마련한다는 계획을 고려하고 있다 The cash-strapped Pentagon is weighing a plan to raise billions of dollars through the cut-price sale of used military equipment.

**쪼르르, 쪼르륵** ⇨주르르, 주르륵. ¶ 수도에서 물이 쪼르륵 흐르다 water dribbles from the faucet.

**쪼아먹다** peck (at and eat).

**쪽**[1] 〖식물〗 the indigo plant.

**쪽**[2] 《부인의》 a chignon. ¶ 쪽을 찌다 do *one's* hair up in a chignon.

**쪽**[3] 《조각》 a piece; a slice; a cut. ¶ 마늘 한 쪽 a clove of garlic / 참외 한 쪽 a slice of melon.

**쪽**[4] 《방향》 a direction; a side; a way. ¶ 오른〔왼〕쪽 the right 〔left〕 side / 동〔서〕쪽 the east 〔west〕 / 이〔저〕쪽 this 〔that〕 way / 우리 쪽 our side / 양쪽 both sides; both parties / 길 건너기 전에 양쪽을 잘 살펴라 Look carefully both ways before crossing the street. / 죄는 그 쪽에도 있다 The other party has its share of the blame too. / 범인은 서울역 쪽으로 달아났다 The criminal escaped in the direction of Seoul Station.

**쪽다리** a one-plank bridge.

**쪽마루** a veranda of one or two floor-boards 〔planks〕.

**쪽매** parquetry-work; parquet; a marquetry. ¶ ～붙임하다 inlay parquet strips on (a base board) / ～질하다 make 〔decorate〕 (a wooden vessel) with parquet strips; make (a parquet vessel).

**쪽문**(―門) a wicket (gate); a side door 〔gate〕.

**쪽박** a small gourd; a gourd dipper.

**쪽발이** ①《외발》 a thing which has only one leg left; a one-legged thing. ②《두 갈래진》 a cloven foot 〔hoof〕. ③《왜놈》 a Jap 《속어》.

**쪽빛** indigo (blue); indigotin.

**쪽소매(책상)** a desk with drawers on one side.

**쪽자**(―字) 〖인쇄〗 a single piece of printing type made by combining parts taken from other pieces.

**쪽잘거리다** chew by bits; eat half-heartedly.

**쪽지**(―紙) a slip of paper; a tag; a note (left behind). ¶ ～에 몇 자 적다 jot 〔put〕 a few words down on a slip.

**쪽찌다** do up (*one's* hair) in a chignon. ¶ 쪽찐 머리 a (round) chignon.

**쫀득거리다** keep sticking.

**쫀득쫀득** sticky; glutinous; adhesive; elastic.

**쫀쫀하다** 《천이》 (be) finely woven; be of fine weave.

**쫄깃쫄깃하다** (be) chewy; sticky.

**쫄딱** completely; wholly; altogether; utterly. ¶ ～ 망하다 be completely ruined; go completely to the dogs.

**쫑긋거리다** ①《입술을》 work (the mouth); move the lips; mumble. ¶ 입을 ～ move the lips; curl *one's* lips; make a lip. ②《귀를》 move the ears; cock 〔prick up, strain〕 *one's* ears. ¶

그 말은 양귀를 쫑긋거렸다 The horse cocked up the ears.

**쫑알거리다** ⇨ 종알거리다.

**쫓겨나다** 《내쫓기다》 be expelled; be turned 〔sent, driven〕 out; be kicked out 《of》; 《직위에서》 be ousted 〔expelled〕 《from a position》; 《해고당하다》 be dismissed 〔fired〕; lose *one's* place. ¶ 집에서 ~ be thrown out of house / 클럽〔학교〕에서 ~ be expelled from the club 〔school〕 / 고향에서 ~ be driven out of *one's* hometown / 직장에서 ~ be dismissed 〔fired〕 from *one's* post; be forced to leave *one's* position.

**쫓기다** ① 《뒤쫓기다》 be pursued 〔chased〕 (after); be run 〔taken〕 after; be trailed. ¶ 쫓는 자와 쫓기는 자 the pursuer and the pursued / 그는 경찰에 쫓기고 있다 He is hunted 〔chased〕 by the police. ② 《일 따위에》 be kept busy; be pressed with 《*one's* business》; be up to *one's* neck 《in work》. ¶ 가사에 ~ be kept busy with domestic cares / 시간에 ~ be pressed for time / 나는 언제나 일에 쫓기고 있다 I'm always tied down by my business. / 무엇인가에 쫓기는 듯한 기분이다 I feel as if I were being hastened on by something.

**쫓다** ① 《물리치다》 drive out 〔away〕; shoo away (동물을); expel. ¶ 새를 ~ shoo birds away / 파리를 손으로 ~ fan the flies away with *one's* hand / 아무를 나라에서 ~ expel *a person* from the country. ② 《뒤쫓다》 pursue; chase; run after. ¶ 사냥감을 ~ chase game / 도망하는 도둑의 뒤를 ~ run after a fleeing thief / 유행을 ~ follow the fashion / 명리를 ~ pursue wealth and fame / …의 발자국을 쫓고 있다 be on the track 〔trail〕 of 《a bear, a criminal》. ③ 《겨루다》 compete with; rival; equal; keep up with. ¶ 아무도 그의 학식을 쫓을 수 없다 No one can match him in scholarship.

**쫓아가다** ① 《뒤쫓아서》 go in pursuit; pursue; follow; run after. ¶ 패주하는 적을 ~ give chase to the retreating enemy / 애들이 나비를 쫓아간다 Children run after butterflies. ② 《추종하다》 follow suit; follow in 《*a person's*》 foot-steps; take after; copy after. ¶ 남이 하는 대로 ~ do the same as others do; follow suit; copy after others / 지도자를 ~ follow the leader. ③ 《따라잡다》 catch up with; keep up with. ¶ 앞서가는 사람을 ~ catch up with a person ahead. ④ 《겨루다》 compete with; rival; equal. ¶ 그 여자의 요리 솜씨는 아무도 쫓아갈 수 없다 No one can match her cooking. ⑤ 《함께 가다》 follow; accompany; go with. ¶ 아무를 ~ go with 〔accompany〕 *a person* / 사절단을 ~ accompany a delegation; join the retinue of a mission.

**쫓아내다** turn 〔drive, send〕 《*a person*》 out 《from》; throw 〔kick〕 《*a person*》 out; expel; 《지위에서》 oust 《*a person*》 《from a position》; 《해고하다》 fire; dismiss; 《셋집 등에서》 evict; eject. ¶ 학생을 학교에서 ~ expel a student from school / 하녀를 ~ give a maid the sack / 선동자를 모임에서 쫓아냈다 We ejected an agitator from the meeting.

**쫓아다니다** 《뛰어다니다》 run about 〔round〕; 《붙어다니다》 follow about 〔around〕; dangle about 〔after〕. ¶ 여자 꽁무니를 ~ dangle after girls.

**쫓아버리다** drive 〔run〕 《*a person*》 away; turn 〔send〕 away 〔off, out〕; disperse 〔scatter〕 《the crowd》. ¶ 경관이 군중을 쫓아버렸다 The police scattered the crowd.

**쫓아보내다** 《돌려보내다》 drive back 〔out〕; 《방문자 등을》 send away; show 《*a person*》 the door.

**쫓아오다** ① 《추적해 오다》 come in pursuit; follow at 《*a person's*》 heels. ¶ 나를 쫓아오너라 Follow me. ② 《바싹 따라오다》 keep up with; catch up with. ¶ 너무 빨리 걸어서 그는 쫓아오지 못했다 I walked too fast for him to catch up with me. ③ 《겨루다》 compete; rival; equal. ¶ 바둑에서 나를 쫓아오려면 아직 멀었다 It will be a long time before you can take me on in *paduk*.

**쬐다**[1] 《비치다》 shine on 〔over〕; beat 〔strike〕 (down) on. ¶ 볕이 내리 ~ burn; beat down on / 쨍쨍 내리쬐는 햇볕 아래 in the fierce heat of the sun.

**쬐다**[2] ① 《불에》 warm *oneself* 《at the fire》; put 《*a thing*》 over the fire; hold up to the heat; take warmth. ¶ 손을 불에 ~ warm *one's* hands over the fire / 젖은 옷을 불에 ~ put wet clothes up to the fire. ② 《볕에》 expose 《*a thing*》 to the sun; bathe 〔bask〕 in the sun (일광욕); dry 《*a thing*》 in the sun (말리다). ¶ 햇볕을 ~ bask 〔bathe〕 in the sun; sun *oneself;* take the sun / 이불을 햇볕에 ~ expose bedding to the sun; air bedding.

**쭈그러뜨리다** press 〔squeeze〕 out of shape; crush. ¶ 모자를 납작하게 ~ crush a hat flat.

**쭈그러지다** ① 《우그러지다》 get pressed 〔squeezed〕 out of shape; be crushed. ¶ 쭈그러진 모자 a battered hat. ② 《쪼글쪼글해지다》 wither; shrivel. ¶ 쭈그러진 얼굴 a worn face.

**쭈그렁이** ① 《물건》 a thing crushed out of shape. ② 《늙은이》 a withered old person.

**쭈그리다** ① = 쭈그러뜨리다. ② 《구부리다》 crouch; bend forward 〔low〕; stoop; 《쭈그리고 앉다》 sit down on *one's* heels; squat down. ¶ 쭈그린 자세로 in a squatting position / 몸을 ~ bend *oneself* low; stoop 《over a desk》 / 그는 쭈그리고 꽃을 땄다 He stooped to pick the flowers.

**쭈글쭈글** withered; wrinkled. ~하다 (be) withered; wrinkled. ¶ ~ 구겨진 옷 crumpled clothes / ~한 노파 a withered(-up) old woman / ~한 얼굴 a wrinkled face / ~ 늙다 be withered with age.

**쭈르르, 쭈르륵** ⇨ 주르-.

**쭈뼛하다** ① 《솟아있다》 be bulged out; rise. ② 《머리끝이 서는 듯하다》 (be) hair-raising; bloodcurdling; spine-chilling; horrible; [서술적] be filled with horror 《at》; shudder 《with horror》. ¶ 머리끝이 쭈뼛해지다 [사람이 주어] feel a shudder; [사물이 주어] make *one's* hair stand on end; make *one's* blood curdling / 머리끝이 쭈뼛했다 I felt a cold chill pass through me. *or* A shiver ran through my limb. / 어두운 뜰에서 사람 그림자를 보고 쭈뼛했다 My blood ran cold as I saw a figure in the dark garden.

**쭉** ⇨ 죽[2].

**쭉정이** empty heads of grain; blasted ears.

**쭝얼거리다** ⇨ 중얼거리다.

**-쯤** ① 《정도》 about (so much); approximately; around; nearly; ...or so; some (★ some은 주로 수사에 붙음: some 20 boys). ¶ 네 시간쯤 about 4 hours / 그는 내 나이쯤 된다 He is about my age. / 그쯤 해 두자 Let's leave it (about) there. / 얼마쯤 주었느냐 About how much did you pay? / 90프로쯤 완성됐다 The work is nearly completed. / 500명쯤의 군중이 모였다 A crowd of around 500 (people) gathered 〔assembled〕.
② 《무렵》 at about (a certain time). ¶ 네 시쯤 about 4 o'clock / 몇 시쯤 해서 about what time / 내주쯤 또 오겠습니다 I will come again some time next week. / 열흘쯤 전의 일이다 It was 〔happened〕 around 10 days ago.
③ 《까지》 by (a certain time). ¶ 내일쯤 by tomorrow / 지금쯤 by now; by this time.
④ 《적어도》 at least. ¶ 잡지 하나쯤은 네게 거져줄 수 있다 I can give you at least a copy of a magazine for nothing. / 사과의 말쯤은 해야 할 게 아닌가 At any rate, you have to apologize for what you have done.

**쯧쯧** 《혀차는 소리》 tut, tut! ¶ ~하고 그는 혀를 찼다 "Tut, tut!" He clicked his tongue.

**찌** 《낚시의》 ⇨ 낚시찌.

**찌개** a pot stew. ¶ 된장 ~ a pot stew with *toenjang* (= bean paste) as its main ingredient / 생선 ~ a fish pot stew / ~그릇 a stew bowl.

**찌그러뜨리다** crush; smash; squash; distort; contort.

**찌그러지다** be crushed 〔smashed, squashed〕; be contorted, be battered. ¶ 찌그러진 얼굴 a wry 〔distorted〕 face / 구두가 찌그러졌다 My shoes have lost their shape.

**찌긋거리다** ① 《눈을》 wink (an eye) at 《*a person*》. ¶ 아무한테 눈을 ~ wink at *a person;* give *a person* an eye-signal. ② 《옷을》 pull 《*a person*》 by the sleeve (to call *his* attention).

**찌꺼기** 《앙금》 dregs; lees (주류의); grounds (커피 등의); sediment; residue; 《위로 뜬 것》 scum; 《불용물》 refuse; leavings; remains; remnants; leftovers; waste. ¶ 밥 ~ residue of rice / 차 ~ tea grounds / 콩 ~ bean refuse / ~사과 the worst of the apples 《in a basket》 / 먹다 남긴 ~ leftovers of food / ~가 남다 the dregs settle; it leaves sediment / 이런 사람들은 말하자면 인간의 ~다 These kind of people are, so to speak, the dregs of mankind.

**찌끼** = 찌꺼기.

**찌다**[1] 《살이》 grow fat; gain weight; put on flesh. ¶ 살찐 암탉 a fat hen / 돼지를 살찌게 하다 fatten a pig / 그는 너무 살이 쪘다 He is overweight.

**찌다**[2] 《날씨가》 get steaming hot; be sultry; be humid. ¶ 찌는 듯한 더위 the sweltering heat / 날이 찌는 듯이 덥다 It is steaming hot.

**찌다**[3] 《뜨거운 김에》 steam. ¶ 찐 고구마 steamed sweet-potatoes / 감자를 ~ steam potatoes / 찬밥을 ~ heat up cold rice with steam.

**찌득찌득하다** (be) tough; be stiff to cut.

**찌들다** ① 《더러워지다》 get 〔become〕 dirty 〔grimy〕; be stained with dirt. ¶ 찌든 grimy; dirty; grubby. ② 《여위다》 be careworn; be hardened 《by bitter experiences》. ¶ 살림에 ~ be 〔look〕 worn with domestic 〔family〕 cares.

**찌르다** ① 《뾰족한 것으로》 pierce; prick; stab; thrust. ¶ 바늘로 손가락을 ~ prick a finger with a needle / 단도로 등을 ~ stab 《*a person*》 in the back with a dagger.
② 《밀고하다》 inform 《on, against》; tip 《off》; squeal 〔squeak〕 《on》; report 〔tell〕 《on》; betray 《*one's* accomplices》. ¶ 경찰에 ~ tip the police off / 공범자가 ~ an accomplice squeals.
③ 《밑천을 들이다》 put in 《money》; lay out; invest 《in》. ¶ 장사에 밑천을 ~ invest *one's* money in a business.
④ 《자극하다》 strike; touch. ¶ 그의 말이 가슴을 찔렀다 His remark hit home. *or* What he said was brought home to me. / 그는 나의 아픈 데를 찔렀다 He touched me on a sore spot. *or* His words stung me to the quick.
⑤ 《냄새가》 be pungent; stink. ¶ 불쾌한 냄새가 코를 찔렀다 An offensive smell assailed my nostrils.
⑥ 《공격하다》 attack. ¶ 적의 배후를 ~ attack the enemy in the rear.
⑦ 《충천하다》 rise 〔soar〕 high up. ¶ 하늘을 찌르듯이 soaring to the sky; sky-high.

**찌르레기** 〚조류〛 a (gray) starling.

**찌르륵** with a slurp (as through a straw). ~하다 give 〔make〕 a slurp.

**찌무룩하다** (be) sullen; sulky; be in a bad temper. ¶ 찌무룩한 얼굴을 하다 look cross 〔sullen, displeased〕.

**찌부러뜨리다** crush; squash; smash; batter. ¶ 모자를 ~ crush a hat.

**찌부러지다** be crushed (out of shape); be squashed; be smashed 〔battered〕. ¶ 찌부러진 공 a crushed ball.

**찌뿌드드하다** 《몸이》 feel unwell 〔out of sorts〕; be indisposed 《with a slight fever》; 《날씨가》 (be) heavy; overcast.

**찌푸리다** ① 《날씨가》 be gloomy 〔overcast〕; cloud over. ¶ 찌푸린 날씨 cloudy weather. ② 《얼굴을》 grimace 《at》; frown 〔scowl〕 《at, on》; knit the brows; wrinkle up. ¶ 눈살을 ~ knit *one's* brow / 얼굴을 ~ make a wry face / 어머니는 얼굴을 찌푸리고 나를 보고 계셨다 Mother was frowning at me. / 그는 고통으로 얼굴을 찌푸렸다 His face was distorted with pain. *or* He grimaced because of a sharp pain.

**찍** ① 《미끄러지는 모양》 ¶ 찍 미끄러지다 get a slip; slip. ② 《긋는 모양》 ¶ 선을 찍 긋다 draw a line with a (vigorous) stroke. ③ 《찢는 소리》 ¶ 찍 찢다 rip up 《*one's* clothes》; tear up 《paper》. ④ 《쥐 따위의 울음 소리》 ¶ 찍하고 울다 squeak.

**찍다** ① 《인쇄물·도장 따위를》 imprint; impress; stamp; seal; set 〔affix〕 a seal 《to》; print. ¶ 편지에 소인을 ~ imprint a postmark on a letter / 서류에 도장을 ~ affix *one's* seal to a document / 1,000부를 ~ print off one thousand copies.
② 《묻히다》 dip 《into》. ¶ 펜에 잉크를 ~ dip the pen into the ink / 설탕을 찍어 먹다 eat 《*a thing*》 with sugar.
③ 《점 따위를》 place 《a dot, *etc.*》; mark with a point; dot; point off; earmark; designate. ¶ 소수점을 ~ place a decimal point.
④ 《눈여겨 두다》 pick out; have an eye 《on》; spot (범인 따위를). ¶ 범인을 점찍어 놓았다 The culprit is spotted. / 저 세 사람을 수상하다고 점찍고 있다 I have an eye to those three, whom I suspect to be the offenders.
⑤ 《도끼 따위로》 chop 《with an ax》; hew; hack; cut. ¶ 도끼로 나무를 찍어 넘기다 chop a tree down with an ax.
⑥ 《차표 따위에 구멍을》 punch.
⑦ 《사진을》 take 《a photograph》; shoot; snap. ¶ 사진을 ~ take a picture 〔snapshot〕; have *one's* picture taken / 영화를 ~ take a motion picture; shoot pictures; film / 이 사진은 잘 찍혔다 This photograph has been taken 〔come out〕 well.
⑧ 《작살 따위로》 catch with a hook; pierce; thrust. ¶ 갈고리로 나무를 ~ hook a log / 작살로 고기를 ~ spear a fish.

**찍소리** a chirp; a tweet; a word; a syllable. ~하다 give a chirp 〔tweet〕; open *one's* mouth. ¶ ~ 없다 (be) silent / ~ 없이 in silence; without a word; without complaining / ~ 없이 순종하다 obey without a whimper / ~도 못 하게 하다 be silenced; be beaten hollow; put 〔reduce〕 《*a person*》 to silence / 그는 요새 ~ 없다 He isn't around these days. / 그는 ~도 못 했다 He couldn't utter a syllable in reply.

**찍어매다** sew (up); stitch 《two pieces of cloth》 together lightly; stitch 《*a* *thing*》 onto; tack 《a ribbon to a hat》. ¶ 터진 데를 ~ stitch up a tear 〔rip〕. 「《쥐가》 squeak.

**찍찍거리다** 《새가》 tweet; twitter; chirp;

**찍히다** get imprinted 〔impressed, stamped〕; get dipped 《into》; get pointed off 〔earmarked, designated〕; get chopped 〔hacked, cut〕; get punched; get taken (사진이); get hooked.

**찐빵** a steamed bun stuffed with sweet bean paste; a bean-jam bun.

**찐쌀** rice processed by steaming unripe grains.

**찔끔하다** get struck with fear; be intimidated. ¶ 아버지가 묻는 말에 찔끔했다 My heart stood still at father's question. / 나는 그의 말에 찔끔했다 His word came home to me.

**찔레**(**나무**) 〚식물〛 a wild 〔multiflora〕 rose; a brier. 「over the brim.

**찔름거리다**[1] 《넘치다》 brim over; flow

**찔름거리다**[2] 《조금씩 주다》 give in small amounts 〔in driblets〕; give a little at a time; give off and on.

**찔름찔름** piecemeal; in dribs and drabs. ¶ 돈을 ~ 주다 give money out piecemeal / 돈을 ~ 쓰다 use *one's* money in dribs and drabs.

**찔리다** 《뾰족한 것에》 get 《*something*》 pierced 〔stabbed, pricked, thrust into〕; 《가슴에》 go home to *one's* heart. ¶ 가시에 손을 ~ get a hand pricked by a thorn / 등을 찔려 죽다 be stabbed in the back to death / 그의 말에 가슴이 찔렸다 I had 〔felt〕 a prick of conscience at what he said.

**찜** 《요리》 a steamed 〔smothered〕 dish. ¶ 닭찜 steamed chicken.

**찜질** fomentation; applying a poultice 〔a compress〕. ~하다 apply a poultice 《to》; put a poultice 〔compress〕 《on》. ¶ 모래~ 《take》 a (hot) sand bath; treatment by the sand bath / 얼음 ~ applying an ice pack / 더운〔냉〕 ~ a hot 〔cold〕 compress / 더운 물수건으로 무릎을 ~하다 apply a hot towel to the knee.

**찜찜하다** feel awkward 〔embarrassed〕; feel ill at ease. ¶ 돈 문제는 말하기가 ~ It is awkward to speak about money 「matters.

**찝찔하다** ⇨ 짭짤하다.

**찡그리다** 《얼굴을》 frown; scowl; grimace; pull a long face; make a wry face; 《눈썹을》 knit 〔gather, contract〕 *one's* brows. ¶ 눈썹을 찡그리고 with a frown; with knitted brows / 얼굴을 ~ make a grimace 〔wry face〕 / 어머니가 얼굴을 찡그리고 나를 보셨다 Mother was frowning at me. / 그는 고통으로 얼굴을 찡그렸다 His face was distorted with pain. *or* He grimaced 〔twisted〕 his face with pain.

**찡긋거리다** 《눈을》 wink at; signal 〔make a sign〕 with *one's* eyes; 《얼굴을》 twist 〔wrinkle up〕 *one's* face at 《*a person*》; make a mouth at.

**찡얼거리다** ① 《투덜거리다》 grumble; murmur. ② 《애가》 whimper; fuss; whine. ¶ 애가 왜 이렇게 찡얼거릴까, 어디가 아픈가 The baby is quite fretful today, I wonder he 〔she〕 is sick.

**찡찡거리다** ＝찡얼거리다.

**찡찡하다** ① ＝찜찜하다. ② 《코가》 be stuffed 〔stopped〕 up. ¶ 코가 ~ My nose is stuffed up. / 추우면 코가 자주 찡찡해진다 The cold often makes my nose stuffy.

**찢기다** get torn 〔rent, ripped〕. ¶ 갈기갈기 ~ be torn to ribbons / 그의 옷이 가시 철망에 찢겼다 His clothes were rent on barbed wire. / 기는 갈갈이 찢겨 있다 The banner is rent to pieces. / 못에 소매가 걸려 찢겼다 I tore my sleeve on a nail.

**찢다** tear; rend; rip. ¶ 입장권을 둘로 ~ tear an admission ticket in two / 편지를 갈기갈기 ~ tear a letter to pieces / 공책을 한 장 찢어 내다 tear off a sheet from a notebook / 자루를 찢어서 열다 rip a bag open / 찢어 죽이다 tear 《*a person*》 limb from limb / 그는 손수건을 찢어 상처를 감았다 He tore off his handkerchief and bandaged the bruise.

**찢어발기다** tear to threads; rip to ribbons. ¶ 찢어발겨도 시원찮은 놈이다 Nothing can allay my anger toward 〔against〕 him.

**찢어지다** be 〔get〕 torn; be rent; tear; rip. ¶ 가슴이 찢어지는 듯한 heart-rending / 찢어지기 쉽다 tear easily / 그 헝겊을 너무 잡아당기면 찢어진다 If you pull on the cloth too hard, it will split. / 이 천은 좀처럼 찢어지지 않는다 This cloth will not tear / 그는 찢어지게 가난하다 [비유적] He is as poor as a church mouse. / 입이 찢어져도 그것은 말할 수 없다 For the life of me I cannot tell you about it.

**찧다** pound; hull; ram (부딪다). ¶ 절구에 쌀을 ~ pound rice in a mortar / 코방아 ~ fall flat on *one's* face / 벽에 이마를 ~ ram *one's* head against a wall / 엉덩방아를 ~ plop down with a thud.

**차**(此) 《이(것)》 this; these; present; current. ¶ 차제에 now; on this occasion; at this juncture〔time〕/ 차로써 보면 in view of these facts.

**차**(車) ① 《탈것》 a vehicle; a conveyance; 《자동차》 a car; 《영》 a motorcar; 《주로 미》 an automobile; 《구어》 an auto; 《버스》 a bus; 《택시》 a taxi; a cab; 《화물차》 a truck; a van. ¶ 차를 타다 「get in(to)〔take〕 a car; take a taxi; get on a bus / 차를 타고 가다 ride in〔on〕 a car / 차에서 내리다 get out of a car; get off a bus / 차로 가다 go by car〔taxi〕; take a bus 《to》/ 차를 운전하다 drive a car / 차로 운반하다 carry〔transport〕《goods》 in a car〔truck〕/ 차에 태우다 give 《*a person*》 a ride; pick 《*a person*》 up; give 《*a person*》 a lift / 차를 멈추다 《주행 중인》 stop a car / 차를 세우다 《손을 들어》 stop〔hold up, flag (down)〕《미》」 a cab / 자기 차를 몰다 drive *one's* own car / 대문 앞에 차가 대기하고 있습니다 The car is waiting (for you) at the gate. / 여기서 공항까지는 차로 20분 걸린다 The airport is a twenty minutes' ride from here. / 차를 부를까요 Shall I call a taxi? / 차를 불러 주시겠어요 Will you get me a taxi, please? / 차가 급정거했다 The car stopped short. / 이 차에는 8명이 탈 수 있다 This car 「holds〔seats〕 eight people. / 그는 차로 직장에 다닌다 He goes to the office by〔in〕 a car. / 나는 그녀를 차로 집까지 데려다 주었다 I drove her home. *or* I took her home by car. / 차로 마중 나와라 Please come to pick me up. / 역까지 차에 좀 태워 줄 수 있겠습니까 Could you 「give me a lift〔drive me〕 to the station? / 「죄송합니다. 차가 막혀서 늦었어요」—「괜찮습니다. 서울의 교통 체증은 꽤 심하니까요」 "I'm sorry. I'm late. I was tied up in traffic." — "That's all right. Traffic jam in Seoul is so terrible." / 차를 좀 앞으로〔뒤로〕 빼주시겠습니까? 제 차가 두 차 사이에 끼어서 나갈 수가 없군요 Would you mind 「moving〔backing〕 up a little, please? I'm sandwiched between two cars and can't get out. (★일상 대화에서는 Would you를 생략하고 간단히 "Mind moving〔backing〕 up a little, please?"가 더 잘 쓰임).

② 《장기의》 a "chariot"; 《체스의》 a castle; a rook.

◉ 차사고 a car〔vehicular〕 accident.

**차**(茶) tea (★ tea는 보통 「홍차」를 뜻함); green tea (녹차); black tea (홍차); 《잎》 tea leaves; 《나무》 a tea plant〔bush〕. ¶ 차 한 잔 a cup of tea / 진한〔묽은〕 차 strong〔weak〕 tea / 차를 끓이다 make tea; prepare the tea / 차를 따르다 pour out tea / 차를 찻종에 따르다 pour tea into a cup / 차를 마시다 drink〔take〕 tea / 차를 홀짝이다 sip tea / 차가 우러나다 tea brews〔draws, steeps〕/ 손님에게 차를 대접하다 offer a guest tea; serve a guest with tea / 차를 마시며 이야기하다 talk over (a cup of ) tea.

◉ 차거르개 a tea strainer. 차도구 tea things. 차산지〔고장〕 a tea-growing district; a tea-producing area. 차찌꺼기 tea grounds; used tea leaves. 차통 a tea canister〔caddy〕.

**차**(差) 《차이》 (a) difference; 《격차》 a gap (의견 따위의); (a) disparity (불균형); (a) discrepancy (상위); 《득표·가격 등의》 a margin; (a) balance (차감의); 《임금의》 a (wage) differential; 《우열의》 odds; 〚수학〛《잉여》 the remainder.

¶ AB의 차 the difference between A and B / 견해의 차 a difference in view / 신분의 차 disparity in social standing / 역량의 차 discrepancy in ability / 연령의 차 an age difference 《of two years between A and B》; (a) disparity in age / AB간의 품질의 차 the difference in quality between A an B / 차가 있다 there is a difference 《between》; differ 《from》/ (그다지) 차가 없다 there is no difference 《between A and B》; make little difference; differ little 《from》/ (차가) 크게 벌어지다 differ greatly〔a great deal〕《from》.

차로: 근소한 차로 이기다 win by a narrow margin 〔small majority〕/ 백표의 차로 당선하다 win an election by a majority 〔plurality〕 of 100 (votes) / 1점차로 지다〔이기다〕 lose 〔win〕 the game by one point / 근소한 차로 2위가 되다 make a close second《in a race》.

차를: 차를 구하다 find the remainder / 차를 두다 discriminate《between, against》; make a discrimination;《차등을》grade; graduate / 소득세에 차를 두다 graduate the income tax / 차를 두지 않고 indiscriminately; without discrimination; equally; evenly; uniformly / 차를 내다〔벌이다〕《경기에서》establish 〔build up, open〕 a lead《on *one's* opponent》/ 차를 좁히다 narrow the lead《of another》.

¶ 5분 차로 기차를 놓쳤다 I missed the train by (just) five minutes. / 빈부 차가 심하다 There is a big gap 〔gulf〕 between the rich and the poor. / 기온차가 심하다 There are great changes in temperature. / 그들은 세대 차를 느끼고 있다 They feel a generation gap between them. / 정치 체제상 북한과 남한은 큰 ~가 있다 In regard to their political systems, there is a 「lot of 〔great〕 difference between North and South Korea.

**차**(次)《…하려던》moment; just as; (on) the point 〔verge〕 of《*doing*》;《…하는 김에》while; when; by the way 〔by(e)〕; on the occasion; in passing. ¶ 부산에 가는 차에 on the way to Pusan / 만나려던 차에 마침 그가 왔다 He came at the very moment when I was going to see him.

**-차**(次) ①《목적》to; for the purpose《of》; with the intention《of》; by way《of》. ¶ 연구차 for the purpose of studying / 구경차 서울에 오다 come to Seoul for sightseeing / 인사차 방문하다 call on《*a person*》to pay *one's* respect. ②《숫자 뒤에서》order; sequence; time (횟수);〖수학〗degree. ¶ 1차 방정식 a simple equation; an equation of the first degree / 1차〔2차〕 코일 a primary 〔secondary〕 coil / (제)2차 발표 the second announcement / 제2차 세계 대전 World War II; the Second World War.

**차가**(借家)《집》a rented 〔hired〕 house;《세듦》renting a house; taking a house for rent. ~하다 rent 〔hire〕 a house. ◉ ~료 a house rent. ~인 a tenant.

**차가다** snatch (off, away)《from》; swoop off; carry off. ⇨채다[2]. ¶ 병아리를 ~《an eagle》snatch away a chick; pounce away with a chick.

**차간거리**(車間距離) the distance 〔space〕 between (two) cars (going in same direction). ¶ ~를 지키다 observe the proper distance between cars / ~를 충분히 유지하시오 Maintain a safe distance between your car and the one in front of you. / 그는 추돌을 피하기 위해 충분한 ~를 유지했다 He left enough room between the two cars in order to avoid running into the car ahead. / 그는 ~를 너무 좁게 잡아서 추돌했다 He ran into the car in front because he was driving too close to it.

**차감**(差減)《뺌》(a) deduction; (a) subtraction;〖법〗(a) recoupment;《계정의》(striking) a balance; margin. ~하다 take away 〔off〕; deduct; subtract;〖법〗recoup; balance《an account》. ¶ 대차(貸借)를 ~하다 strike a balance / 손익을 ~하다 balance the profit and loss. ◉ ~공제액〖법〗an amount deducted《from》; a recoupment 〔deduction〕. ~잔액 the balance.

**차갑다**《온도·날씨가》(be, feel) cold; chill(y); icy; freezing;《매몰차다》(be) cold; frigid; cold-hearted; unfriendly; inhospitable; unsympathetic. ¶ 차가운 날씨 cold 〔chilly〕 weather / 차가운 물 cold water / 차가운 사람 a cold-hearted 〔an icy〕 person / 차가운 태도 a cold 〔unfriendly〕 attitude / 얼음처럼 ~ be as cold as ice; be ice-cold / 차가운 눈으로 보다 look at《*a person*》coldly; cast a cold eye 〔steely glance〕 on《*a person*》; give《*a person*》a stony 〔chilling〕 stare / 차가워지다 get 〔become〕 cold 〔chilled〕/ 마시기 전에 냉장고에 넣어 차갑게 하다 chill《the white wine》in the refrigerator before serving / 그녀의 태도는 요즘 퍽 차가워졌다 Her attitude toward me has become chilly lately.

**차고**(車庫) a car shed; a carbarn;《기차·전차의》a train 〔tram〕 depot 〔shed〕;《자동차의》a garage; a carport (지붕만의). ¶ ~에 넣다 put《a streetcar》into a barn; put《a car》into a garage / ~에 넣어 두다 keep《a bus》in a barn; garage《a car》.

**차곡차곡** in orderly fashion; neatly; in a neat pile; one by one; one after another. ¶ 옷을 ~ 개다 fold (up) clothes neatly / 책을 ~ 쌓아 놓다 stack the books up neatly 〔in good order〕.

**차골광**(車骨鑛) 〖광물〗 bournonite; cogwheel ore.

**차관**(次官) a vice-minister; an undersecretary; a deputy secretary 《미》. ¶ 교육부 ~ the Vice-Minister of Education / ~급의 《*a person*》 of the vice-minister class / 사무〔정무〕 ~ a permanent 〔parliamentary〕 vice-minister / 남북한간의 ~(급) 회의 inter-Korean vice-minister level talks; the South-North vice-ministers' talks.
◉ ~보 an assistant secretary 《미》.

**차관**(借款) a loan. ¶ 단기〔장기〕 ~ a short-time 〔long-term〕 credit / 민간〔상업, 재정〕 ~ a private 〔commercial, financial〕 loan / 현금 ~ a cash loan; loans in cash / ~을 신청하다 ask 〔apply〕 for a loan / ~을 얻다 obtain a loan 〔credit〕 / ~을 제공하다 grant 〔extend, give〕 a credit 《to》 / ~을 체결하다 contract a loan 《of one billion dollars》 / 그들은 우리나라에 30억 달러의 ~을 요청했다 They asked our country for a loan of three billion dollars. ◉ ~계약 a loan contract. (국제적) ~단 a consortium (*pl.* ~s, -tia). ~업체 a foreign loan-financed firm; a loan-backed firm 〔company〕. ~융자 credit financing. ~협정 a loan agreement.

**차관**(茶罐) a teakettle; a teapot.

**차광**(遮光) shading the light; covering over the light. ~하다 shade 〔shield〕 the light; darken the light. ◉ ~막 a blackout curtain (창문의); a shade (등화 주변의); 《TV 카메라의》 a flag. ~장치 shading; 《카메라의》 an iris shutter.

**차근차근** methodically; systematically; carefully; scrupulously; step by step; steadily. ~하다 (be) methodical; slow and careful; scrupulous. ¶ 일을 ~ 처리하다 dispose of a matter 「step by step 〔carefully〕 / 난문제를 ~ 해결하다 solve a difficult problem by going at it systematically.

**차금**(借金) a debt; a loan. ⇨ 빚.

**차기**(次期) the next term 〔period〕. ¶ ~ 대통령 the President for the next term / ~ 정권을 노리다 aspire 〔aim〕 to take over the reins of government / ~ 대통령에 입후보하다 run for the next presidency. ◉ ~국회 the next session of the National Assembly. ~이월 〖부기〗 carried forward (생략 c/f): ~이월 손실금 loss to be carried forward / ~이월 이익금 balance to be carried forward. ~정권 the next administration.

**차기**(此期) this 〔the present〕 term 〔period〕.

**차꼬** 《옛 형구》 a foot-cangue; fetters; shackles. ¶ ~를 채우다 fetter; shackle; put 《*a person*》 in the stocks.

**차꼬막이** 〖건축〗 《용마루의》 crescent-shaped tiles placed at both sides of the ridge of a tiled house; 《박공머리의》 a square rafter and tile fitted to the edges of a gable.

**차끈하다** (be) very cold; feel chilled 〔very cold〕; feel freezing cold.

**차나무**(茶—) 〖식물〗 a tea plant 〔bush〕. ◉ ~밭 a tea plantation 〔garden〕.

**차남**(次男) *one's* 〔the, a〕 second son.

**차내**(車內) the inside of a car 〔train〕. ¶ ~에서 in the car / ~에서는 금연입니다 《게시》 Passengers are requested to refrain from smoking in the car. *or* Please don't smoke in the car. / 이 자동차의 특징은 넓은 ~ 공간입니다 The roominess of the interior is the outstanding features of this car.
◉ ~검표 the inspection of tickets in the car. ~광고 publicity 〔advertising〕 posters (displayed) in the train. ~등 an interior light. ~회견 an interview in the train.

**차녀**(次女) *one's* 〔the, a〕 second daughter.

**차다**[1] 《온도·날씨가》 (be) cold; icy; chill(y); frosty; 《냉담하다》 (be) cold; cold-hearted. ¶ 찬물 cold water / 찬 날씨 cold 〔chilly〕 weather / 찬 바람 a chilly 〔cold〕 wind / 마음이 찬 사람 a cold-hearted 〔an icy〕 person / 차게 하다 cool; 《얼음으로》 ice; cool 《drinks》 with ice; 《냉장 장치로》 refrigerate / 차게 한 cooled 《water》; iced 《drinks》 / 차게 해 두다 keep 《*a thing*》 cool on ice / 차지다 get 〔become〕 cold 〔chilled〕 / 얼음장같이 ~ be ice-cold; be as cold as ice / 바깥 날씨가 몹시 ~ It is freezing cold outside. / 날씨가 매섭게 ~ There is a nip in the air. / 뜨거운 여름 날에는 찬 맥주 한 잔이 제일이다 There's nothing like a glass of cold beer on a hot summer day.

**차다**[2] ① 《가득 차다》 (***a***) 《사물이》 fill; become full 《of》; be filled 〔replete〕 《with》; brim 《with》; 《시간·일·자리 등이》 be engaged; be occupied. ¶ 독에 물이 ~ water fills a jar; a jar is filled (up) with water / 배가 ~ *one's* stomach is full / 방에 사람이 그득 ~ a room is jammed 〔crowded〕 with people / 기백에 차 있다 be full of spirit / 해학에 차 있다 be「full of 〔replete with〕 wit 〔humor〕/ 앞날이 희망에 차 있다 *one's* future is full of hope / 스케줄이 꽉 차 있다 have a heavy 〔close-packed, tight〕 schedule. (***b***) 《달이》 wax. ¶ 달이 ~ the moon waxes / 달도 차면 기운다 《속담》 Every flow 〔tide〕 has its ebb.

② 《흡족하다》 be satisfied 〔pleased〕 《with》; be content(ed) 《with》; content *oneself* 《with》; [사물이 주어] be satisfactory. ¶ 마음에 ~ meet with satisfaction; prove 〔be〕 satisfactory; be contented with / 며느리가 마음에 ~ be satisfied with *one's* daughter-in-law / 밥이 양에 ~ have enough rice (to satisfy *one's* appetite) / 마음에 차지 않다 《사물이》 be unsatisfactory 〔unsatisfying〕; be not good enough; leave something 〔much〕 to be desired; 《사람이》 be dissatisfied 〔not satisfied〕 《with》.

③ 《한도에》 measure up 《to》; come (up) to; amount to; be as much as; be all of. ¶ 말이 ~ it is one *mal* full; it is one whole *mal* / 쌀이 서 말이 ~ the rice measures a good three *mal* / 인원수가 ~ the number is complete 〔filled up〕/ 정원에 ~ reach 〔obtain, come up to〕 the regular number; have 〔form〕 a quorum (정족수) / 정원이 차지 않다 lack 〔want〕 a quorum (정족수) / 돈이 액수에 차지 못하다 The money is short of a certain amount.

④ 《기한이》 expire (임기가); 《어음 등이》 mature; reach maturity; fall 〔come〕 due. ¶ (임신부의) 달이 ~ *one's* time (of delivery) comes / 어음 기한이 ~ a bill matures 〔is due for payment〕/ 그의 임기는 내달에 찬다 His term of office expires next month.

**차다**[3] ① 《발로》 kick 《at》; give 《*a person*》 a kick. ¶ 공을 ~ kick a ball / 정강이를 ~ give 《*a person*》 a kick on the shin / 발길로 차서 쓰러뜨리다 kick 《*a person*》 down; kick 《*a thing*》 over / 차 넣다 kick in / 발길로 차서 열다 break open 《a door》 by kicking; kick 《a door》 open / 차올리다 kick up; give an upward kick / 자리를 차고 방을 나가다 leave 〔storm out of〕 the room indignantly; fling 〔stamp〕 out of the room.

② 《거절하다》 refuse; reject; repulse; turn down. ¶ 요구를 차 버리다 repel 〔turn down〕 a request / 제의를 차 버리다 reject 〔spurn〕 an offer.

③ 《혀를》 click; clack. ¶ 혀를 ~ click *one's* tongue; tsk; go tsk; tut / 혀차는 소리 a click of the tongue; Tut, tut.

④ 《채뜨리다》 take (by force); snatch (away) 《from, off》; wrest 《from》. ⇨ 차가다.

**차다**[4] ① 《몸에》 attach; fasten on; carry; put on; wear; bear. ¶ 시계를 ~ put 〔strap〕 on a watch; wear a watch / 칼을 ~ wear a sword at 〔by, on〕 *one's* side; gird on a sword / 허리에 ~ carry 《*a thing*》 by *one's* side / 훈장을 ~ wear 〔pin on〕 a decoration / 패물을 ~ wear trinkets.

② 《쇠고랑 등을》 be handcuffed 〔manacled〕. ¶ 쇠고랑을 ~ have *one's* hands handcuffed / 쇠고랑을 찬 죄수 a handcuffed prisoner.

**차단**(遮斷) interception; isolation; 《방역을 위한》 quarantine. ~하다 intercept; isolate; cut 〔shut, wall〕 off; block (up) 《a street》; quarantine; 『전기』 break. ¶ 광선을 ~하다 intercept 〔shut out〕 the light / 교통을 ~하다 hold up 〔cut off, suspend〕 traffic / 길을 ~하다 block 〔bar〕 the way; bar the passage / 보급로를 ~하다 block the supply route / 외부의 음향을 ~하다 exclude (the) outside sounds / 퇴로를 ~하다 intercept 〔cut off〕 the 《enemy's》 retreat; block the way of retreat / 이 높은 벽이 광선을 ~하고 있다 This high wall shuts out the light. / 그 거리는 3시간 동안 교통이 ~되었다 Traffic on the street was stopped 〔held up〕 for three hours. / 폭설로 인해 교통이 ~되었다 The traffic was interrupted by the heavy snow.

◉ ~기 『전기』 a (circuit 〔contact〕) breaker; 《건널목의》 a crossing gate; a lifting gate (오르내리는). ~장치 a cutoff; 《배의》 a cutout gear.

**차대**(車臺) a chassis.

**차도**(車道) a roadway; a carriageway 《영》; a traffic lane; 《미》 a driveway (도로에서 현관으로 들어오는). ¶ ~를 횡단할 때는 잘 살피도록 해라 Take good care in crossing the roadway. / 어린 아이가 ~로 뛰어들어 차에 부딪쳤다 A child ran into the roadway and was hit by a car.

**차도**(差度) improvement 《of illness》. ¶ 병이 ~가 있다 《an illness》 take「a favorable turn 〔a turn for the better〕; 《an illness》 progresses favorably; [사람이 주어] improve; get better / 환자는 점차 ～가 보인다 The patient is well on the road to recovery.

**차돌** 《석영》 quartz. ¶ ～ 같은 사람 a tough 〔steadfast〕 guy; a regular little ball of fire. ◉ ～모래 quartz 〔silica〕 sand; glass silica.

**차동**(差動) 〖물리〗 differential motion. ¶ ～의 differential. ◉ ～도르래 a differential pulley. ～장치 a differential (gear). ～전동기〔전류계〕 a differential motor 〔galvanometer〕. ～전위계 a differential electrometer. ～톱니바퀴 a differential gear.

**차드** 《아프리카 중부의 나라》 (the Republic of ) Chad.

**차등**(差等) gradation; graduation; (a) difference. ¶ ～이 있다 be different in grade(s) / ～을 두다 grade; graduate; discriminate. ◉ ～세율 a graded〔differential〕 tariff.

**차디차다** (be) very cold; frigid; icy; be ever so cold; be cold as can be; be as cold as ice.

**차라리** rather 〔sooner〕 (than); better (than); first; preferably; in preferance; if anything. ¶ ～ 가는 것이 좋겠다 You had better go. *or* I would rather go. / 나는 ～이 편을 택하겠다 I'd rather take this one. *or* I prefer this one. / 그렇게 하느니 ～ 하지 않는 것이 낫겠다 It would be better not to do it at all than to do it that way. / 그들은 굴복하느니 ～ 죽음을 택한다 They would die before yielding. / 굴욕을 당하느니 ～ 죽는 것이 낫다 I would rather 〔sooner〕 die than suffer disgrace. *or* I had rather die than live in dishonor. (★ 이처럼 had와 would는 어느 쪽도 좋지만 1인칭에서는 had, 2·3인칭에서는 would를 흔히 씀).

**차랑거리다** ① ⇨ 치렁거리다. ② 《소리가》 clink; rattle; tinkle; jingle; ting. ¶ 열쇠 뭉치를 차랑거리며 걷다 walk along clinking a bunch of key.

**차랑차랑** ① ⇨ 치렁치렁. ② 《소리》 clinking; rattling; ting-a-ling; ting-ting.

**차량**(車輛) vehicles; cars; 《객차》 a (railroad) coach; 《미》 a car; 《영》 a carriage; 《철도·운송 회사의》 the rolling stock [총칭]. ¶ 한 ～분의 화물 a carload 《of goods》 / ～에 의한 수송 wheeled transport / ～의 정비 불량 poor maintenance of the vehicles / 오늘 오전 6시부터 오후 1시까지 남산 및 그 주변 일대의 ～ 통행이 제한된다 Vehicle traffic will be limited in and around Namsan, Seoul from 6 a.m. until 1 p.m. / ～ 통행 금지 《게시》 No thoroughfare for vehicles. ◉ ～검사 vehicle (maintenance) inspection; vehicle safety inspection. ～격일제 운행제도 the alternative-day-no-driving system. ～고장 a car trouble; a breakdown: 다음 열차는 ～고장으로 10분 정도 지연되겠습니다 Owing to a breakdown, the next train will be ten minutes late. ～등록 vehicle registration. ～번호판 《자동차의》 a (license) plate: ～번호판의 마지막 숫자 the final figure of the car registration number. ～부족 car shortage. ～십부제 운행제도〔규칙〕 the '10th-day-no-driving' system 〔rule〕. ～정비 vehicle maintenance. ～중량 the dead-weight 《of a freight car》. ～회사 a rolling stock (manufacturing) company.

**차려** 《구령》 Attention!; 'Shun! ¶ ～자세를 취하다 come to attention; stand at 〔to〕 attention; place *oneself* in an attitude of attention.

**차력**(借力) ～하다 enhance 〔boost〕 *one's* physical strength by 「taking a tonic 〔spiritual concentration〕.

**차례** ① 《순서》 (an) order; (a) sequence; 《순번》 (*one's*) turn. ¶ 내〔네〕 ～ my 〔your〕 turn / ～로 in good 〔regular〕 order; by turns; in turn; one by one / 크기의 ～로 according to size / ～를 따라 according to the order 〔program〕; in due order 〔course, succession〕; in regular sequence / ～없이 in random order; disorderly / ～가 뒤바뀌다 be out of order; be in wrong order / ～가 오다〔되다〕 *one's* turn comes round / ～로 서다 stand in 「order 〔a queue〕 / 키 ～로 서다 stand in order of height / ～대로 늘어놓다 put 《*things*》 in order / ～로 일하다〔망보다〕 work 〔watch〕 by turns / ～를 기다리다 wait for *one's* turn (to come around); be on the waiting list / 줄지어 ～를 기다리는 사람들 people standing in queues awaiting their turn / ～를 (앞)당기다 move up the order 《of》 / ～를 바꾸다 change the order / 연주회는 오후 9시부터 프로그램에 따라 ～대로 진행되었다 The concert 「proceeded 〔went on〕 from 9 p.m. in the order shown in the program. / 내가 읽을 ～다 It is my turn to read. / 누구 ～지 Whose turn 〔move〕 is it? *or* Who is next?

② 《횟수》 time; round. ¶ 한 ~ once / 두 ~ twice / 세 ~ thrice; three times / 여러 ~ several times / 책을 세 ~ 읽다 read a book three times / 한 ~ 이기다 win one round of a game / 술잔을 세 ~째 돌리다 pass the winecup for the third round of drinks.
③ 《목차》 a table of contents (★ 책의 차례 면에는 보통 Contents로 씀). ¶ ~를 달다 attach a table of contents 《to a book》. ◉ ~표 a program.

**차례**(茶禮) 《추석 등의》 ancestor-memorial services 〔rites〕. ¶ ~를 지내다 observe a worship service for family ancestors on 《*Ch'usŏk* morning》.

**차례차례** in due 〔regular〕 order; in order; in regular sequence; one by one; one after another; in succession. ¶ 사람을 ~ 불러들이다 call in men one after another / 일을 ~ 처리하다 dispose of matters in due order; settle things one by one 〔one after another〕 / 키대로 ~ 서다 stand one after another in order of height.

**차롓걸음** proceeding in due order 〔course, succession〕; proceeding step by step; orderly management.

**차로**(叉路) a forked road; a branch=road; a crossroad (십자로).

**차로**(遮路) the blockage of the road 〔street〕; interception of the passage. ~하다 blockade 〔block off〕 the road 〔street〕; bar 〔obstruct〕 the passage.

**차륜**(車輪) a wheel. ⇨ 차바퀴. ¶ 착륙용 ~ a landing wheel. ◉ ~제동기 a wheel brake.

**차르랑** 《쇳소리》 with a clink 〔rattle〕. ~하다, ~거리다 give a clink 〔rattle〕.

**차리다** ① 《마련하다》 (***a***) 《장만·채비를 하다》 prepare; make 〔get〕 《it》 ready; make; give; arrange. ¶ 밥상을 ~ spread 〔set〕 the table (for dinner) / 저녁상을 ~ get supper ready; prepare 〔fix 《미》〕 supper / 잔치를 ~ hold 〔give〕 a feast 〔banquet〕 / 제단을 ~ prepare 〔set up〕 an altar / 길 떠날 채비를 ~ prepare 〔make preparations〕 for a journey; equip 〔outfit〕 *oneself* for a trip. (***b***) 《새로》 open; start; found; establish; set up. ¶ 살림을 ~ make 〔set up〕 a new home; make *one's* home / 점포를 ~ open 〔set up〕 a shop 〔store〕.
② 《외관을》 equip *oneself* 《for》; be equipped 《in》; dress (*oneself*) up; deck out; adorn *oneself*. ¶ 옷을 차려 입다 dress up; deck out / 외관을 잘 ~ show up; make a show 《of》 / 잘 차려 입다 be richly dressed; be in *one's* best clothes; be in *one's* gala attire 〔dress〕 / 화려하게 차려 입다 be gaily 〔gaudily〕 dressed / 분주하게 차려 입고 나서다 go out after having dressed in a hurry.
③ 《정신을》 (***a***) 《의식을》 keep; collect; come to (*one's* senses); come round (to *oneself*). ¶ 의식을 ~ recover 〔regain〕 consciousness / 정신을 바싹 ~ preserve *one's* consciousness; keep *one's* senses; harden *one's* heart / 정신(을) 차리게 하다 bring 《*a person*》 to *himself* 〔*his* senses〕; bring 《*a person*》 round / 정신을 차리고 보니 내가 땅에 누워 있었다 When I came to my senses, I found myself lying on the ground.
(***b***) 《주의하다》 take care 《of》; be careful 《of》; be mindful 《of》; 《집중하다》 attend to; give 〔pay〕 attention 《to》; be attentive 《to duty》; 《경계하다》 look out 〔sharp〕 《for》; watch (out). ¶ 속지 않게 정신을 ~ keep *one's* eyes open so as not to be cheated / 정신을 차려 일하다 do the job carefully; be intent upon *one's* work; devote *one's* attention to the task at hand / 정신을 바짝 차리고 있다 be attentive; be wide-awake; have *one's* wits about *one*.
④ 《예의를》 keep; maintain; save; preserve; observe; pay attention 《to》. ¶ 인사를 ~ observe decorum; keep up the common civilities of life / 체면을 ~ keep up appearances; save (*one's*) face.
⑤ 《실속 등을》 seek; intend 《to *do*》; aim at. ¶ 제 이익을 ~ seek 〔look to〕 *one's* own interests.

**차림** 《행색·옷차림》 (personal) appearance; guise; dress; attire; an outfit. ¶ 행상인 ~의 사내 a man looking like a peddler / 단정한 ~으로 decently dressed / ~이 초라하다 be shabbily 〔poorly〕 dressed; look shabby / 선원 ~이다 be rigged out as a sailor / 옷 ~이 얌전하다 〔야하다〕 be neatly 〔loudly〕 dressed / 이런 ~으로는 남 앞에 못 나간다 I am not fit to be seen. *or* I am not presentable.

**차림새** ① 《살림의》 the setup; arrangements; furnishings; installation; decoration. ¶ 살림 ~가 훌륭하다 a home is nicely furnished; be a nice setup for living. ② 《옷의》 *one's* manner of dressing; *one's* garb 〔getup, clothes, attire〕. ⇨차림. ¶ ～만 봐도 그녀의 성격을 알 수 있었다 Her appearance betrayed her character. *or* You could judge her character through her outfit.

**차림표** 《식단》 a menu; a (menu) card; a bill of fare. ¶ ～에 올라 있다 be (listed) on the menu / ～를 보다 consult 〔look at〕 a menu / 오늘 ～에는 무슨 요리가 올라 있지 What's on the menu today?

**차마**(車馬) horses and vehicles. ¶ ～의 통행 vehicular traffic / ～ 통행 금지 《게시》 No thoroughfare for horses and vehicles.

**차마** for (all) the world; for *one's* life. ¶ ～ 그대로 볼 수 없어서 (being) unable to stand (idly) by (any longer) / ～ …을 못 하다 do not have the heart 《to punish him》; be reluctant 〔averse〕 《to *do*》; cannot allow 〔bring〕 *oneself* 《to leave》 / ～ 눈뜨고 볼 수가 없다 cannot bear 〔endure〕 to see; be unable to bear 〔stand〕 the sight of / ～ 그대로 보아 넘길 수 없다 be unable to let 《it》 pass unnoticed; cannot remain indifferent / ～ 그런 짓은 못 하겠다 I cannot find it in my heart to do so. / 그를 ～ 해고시킬 수 없었다 I didn't have the heart to dismiss him. / 그의 간절한 부탁을 ～ 거절 못했다 I found it impossible to refuse his earnest entreaties.

**차멀미**(車—) carsickness; motion sickness. ～하다 get 〔feel〕 carsick. ¶ 그녀는 버스만 타면 ～를 한다 She gets sick every time she rides on a bus. *or* Bus rides always make her sick.

**차면**(遮面) ～하다 《얼굴을》 hide 〔veil〕 *one's* face; 《사람을》 put a wall 〔screen〕 between people.

**차명**(借名) ～하다 use 〔assume, borrow, take〕 《*a person's*》 name. ¶ ～으로 under the assumed name of….
◉ ～계좌 a 「borrowed-name 〔false=name〕 bank account.

**차밍** charming. ～하다 (be) charming; attractive. ¶ ～한 처녀 a charming 〔an attractive〕 girl; a charmer.

**차바퀴**(車—) a wheel. ¶ ～ 자국 a (wheel) track; a rut; the print of a wheel / ～ 밑에 깔리다 be run over by 《a car》 / ～에 기름을 치다 put oil on the wheels / ～가 빠졌다 The wheel has come off.

**차반**(茶盤) a tea tray 〔board, server〕.

**차버리다** kick off 〔away〕; 《거절하다》 refuse; turn down; jilt. ⇨차다[3] ②. ¶ 애인을 ～ jilt *one's* lover.

**차변**(借邊) the debit 〔debtor〕 (생략 dr.); the debit 〔debtor〕 side. ¶ ～과 대변 debtor and creditor / ～에 기입하다 debit 《a sum》 against 《*a person*》; debit 《*a person's*》 account with 《a sum》; enter 《an item》「on the debit side 〔to *a person's* debt〕. ◉ ～계정 a debtor account. ～기입 a debtor entry. ～잔고 a debtor balance. ～표 a debit note. ～항목 a debit item.

**차별**(差別) discrimination; distinction; differentiation. ～하다 discriminate 《against》; draw 〔set up〕 a distinction 《between》; differentiate 《one from another》. ¶ 인종～ racial discrimination; racism; racialism / ～ 없이 without discrimination; indiscriminately / 남녀의 ～ 없이 irrespective of sex; men and women alike / 신분의～ 없이 irrespective(ly) of social standing / ～을 두다 discriminate 《against A, in favor of B》; make a discrimination / ～적인 대책 a discriminatory 〔discriminating〕 measure / 고용에 있어서 남녀의 ～을 폐지하다 abolish 〔do away with〕 sex discrimination in employment / 이 여행에는 남녀노소의 ～ 없이 누구나 참가할 수 있다 You can join in this tour without any distinction of age and sex. / 그 회사는 사람을 고용할 때 외국인을 ～한다 That company discriminates against foreigners in its hiring.
◉ ～관세 discriminatory tariffs; differential duties. ～세율 the rate of discriminatory 〔differential〕 tariff 〔texation〕. ～용어 discriminatory terms. ～임금 differential wages. ～조항 a discriminatory regulation. ～철폐 《인종의》 abolition of racial discrimination.

**차별대우**(差別待遇) discriminatory treatment; discrimination. ¶ ～를 하다 treat 《*a person*》 with discrimination; discriminate against / ～를 하지 않다 treat every person just and fair; treat all alike / ～를 받다 be treated discriminately.

**차부**(車夫) a driver; a carter (짐수레「의).

**차부제**(次副祭) 〚가톨릭〛 a subdeacon.

**차분하다** (be) calm; quiet; serene; self=composed; collected; sedate; self=possessed. ¶ 차분한 태도 a composed manner / 차분한 무늬〔색깔〕 a quiet pattern 〔color〕 / 차분한 기분으로 in a calm 〔collected〕 frame of mind / 차분히 calmly; quietly; with composure / 차분히 공부하다 settle down to *one's* studies / 차분히 생각하다 think 《it》 over; ponder 《on, over》.

**차비**(車費) a 《taxi, railroad》 fare; a carfare; 《교통비》 traffic expenses; 《약간의 사례금》 a small consideration. ¶ ~를 내다 pay the fare / ~를 할인하다 discount 〔reduce〕 railroad fares 《for parties》 / 서울까지의 왕복 ~는 얼마입니까 What is the fare to Seoul and back? / ~정도 사례해도 그녀는 도우러 올 것이다 For a small consideration she'll come and help you.

**차사**(差使) 〖고제도〗 a policeman sent to arrest a criminal; a messenger 〔an emissary〕 (sent by a governor).

**차석**(次席) the next position 〔seat〕. ¶ ~의 next (in rank); ranking next 《to》 / ~이다 rank next 《to》.
◉ ~자 《관리 등의》 an official next in rank; an associate; 《수상자 등》 the second winner; the runner-up.

**차선**(次善) the second 〔next〕 best.
◉ ~책 the second 〔next〕 best policy; the best alternative plan: ~책이 있다 have two strings to *one's* bow.

**차선**(車線) a (traffic) lane. ¶ 4~ 도로 a four-lane road / ~을 지키다 keep *one's* lane; stay in one lane / ~을 바꾸다 change *one's* lanes / 서울—대전간의 고속 도로를 8~으로 확장하다 expand the Seoul-Taejŏn Expressway into an eight-lane road. ◉ ~분리대 a divisional strip 〔island〕. ~분리선 a (painted) lane marking. 다인승 전용 ~ the carpool lane. 4~ 고속도로 a four-lane highway 〔expressway〕.

**차세대전투기**(次世代戰鬪機) the next generation fighter (plane). ¶ 차세대 지원 전투기 the next generation support fighter (plane).

**차손**(差損) a loss from the fluctuations in the market (price); 《환차손》 a foreign-exchange loss.

**차수**(差數) difference (in number); balance.

「=압류(押留).

**차압**(差押) (an) attachment; (a) seizure.

**차압계**(差壓計) a differential pressure gauge; a differential manometer.

**차액**(差額) the difference; the balance; a margin. ¶ 큰〔작은〕 ~ a wide 〔narrow〕 margin / 무역의 ~ the balance of trade / 양쪽 값의 ~ the difference between the two prices / ~을 메우다 make up the difference / ~을 지불하다 pay the balance 〔difference〕.

**차양**(遮陽) ① 《차일》 a sunshade; a sunscreen (발); 《창문의》 a blind; 《가게 앞 등의》 an awning; 《창이나 문 위의》 a pent roof. ② 《모자의》 a peak; the visor of a 「cap 〔hat〕; 《운동모 등의》 an eyeshade; an eye shield. ¶ ~이 달린 모자 a peaked 〔visored〕 cap.

**차용**(借用) borrowing; use on loan. ~하다 borrow; have 〔get〕 a loan 《of》. ¶ 돈의 ~을 부탁하다 ask 《*a person*》 for a loan of money / 일금 10만 원을 ~함 I owe you 100,000 won. / 위 금액을 틀림없이 ~함 I acknowledge the loan of the amount above inscribed.
◉ ~금 borrowed money; a loan. ~인 a borrower. ~증(서) an I.O.U. (*pl.* ~s, ~'s); a written acknowledgement of a debt 〔loan〕: 50만 원에 대한 ~증을 쓰다 write an I.O.U. for 500,000 won.

**차용어**(借用語) 〖언어〗 a loan-word. ¶ 우리말에는 중국어나 영어에서 온 ~가 많다 Korean has borrowed heavily from Chinese and English.

**차원**(次元) a dimension. ¶ 다~의 multi-dimensional / ~이 낮은 low-grade; vulgar; unworthy / 4~의 세계 the four-dimensional world / ~이 다르다 be on 〔belong to〕 a different level 〔order〕 / 나의 견해와 그의 견해는 ~이 다르다 My view belongs to a different level from his. / 그는 늘 ~이 낮은〔높은〕 이야기만 한다 He always talks about vulgar 〔lofty〕 topics.

**차월**(借越) a debt balance; 《당좌 예금의》 overdrawing; an overdraft. ~하다 overdraw. ¶ ~로 하다 let a debt stand over; leave a debt outstanding / 그 은행에는 백만 원의 ~이 되어 있다 I have overdrawn my account by a million won from the bank.

**차위**(次位) the second rank 〔place, position〕.

**차이**(差異) (a) difference; a divergence (의견 등의); 《불균형》 (a) disparity; 《불일치》 (a) discrepancy; 《격차》 a gap; a gulf; a margin. ¶ 의견의 ~ a difference 〔divergence〕 of opinion 〔view〕 / 취미의 ~ disparity of tastes / 연령 〔신분〕의 ~ (a) discrepancy 〔disparity〕 in age 〔social standing〕 / 상당한〔근소한〕 ~로 by a considerable 〔narrow〕 margin / 2점 ~로 이기다〔지다〕 win 〔lose〕 by two points. 차이가: 큰 ~가 있다 there is a great difference 《between》; differ greatly 《from》 / ~가 없다 there is no difference《between》.

차이를: ～를 두다《차별을》 discriminate《between, against》; make a discrimination;《차등을》 grade; graduate / ～를 밝히다 clarify the distinction《between》; make clear the difference《between》/ ～를 넓히다《경기에서》 increase〔stretch〕*one's* lead. ¶ 양자 사이에는 아무런 ～도 없다 There is no difference between the two. / 양자간에는 큰 ～가 있다 They differ greatly. *or* There is a great difference between the two. / 듣는 바와 실제는 큰 ～가 있다 There is miles' difference between hearsay and the fact. / 그녀는 나와 다섯 살 ～다 She is five years senior〔junior〕by five years. / 빈부의 ～가 크다 There is a big gap〔gulf〕between the rich and the poor.

◉ ～법〚논리〛the method of difference. ～점 a point of difference: A와 B의 ～점을 밝히다 make it clear where A is different from B; clarify the distinction between A and B.

**차익**(差益) a (profit) margin. ¶ 환～ exchange gain〔profit〕/ 매매～ trading profit.

**차일**(遮日) an awning; a marquee; a tent. ¶ ～을 치다 fix a marquee; pitch a tent; shade《*a thing*》from the sun.

**차일피일**(此日彼日) delaying from day to day; putting off day by day. ～하다 put off from day to day; delay day by day; procrastinate. ¶ 일을 ～ 미루다 keep putting the job off day after day / ～하고 빚을 갚지 않다 defer payment on the debt time and again.

**차임**(借賃)《부동산·물건의》(a) rent;《물건·탈것의》hire; a hire charge.

**차임** a chime. ◉ ～벨 a chime bell.

**차입**(差入) sending in to a prisoner. ～하다 send in《*a thing*》to a prisoner. ◉ ～물 things sent in to a prisoner. ～식사 a meal sent in to a prisoner. ～자 a prison caterer.

**차입**(借入) borrowing. ～하다 borrow; have〔get〕the loan《of》. ◉ ～금 a loan (of money); borrowed money; a debt: ～금 계정 a loan account / 일시 ～금 a temporary loan; a floating debt / 장기〔단기〕～금 a long-term〔short-term〕debt. ～주(株) borrowed stock.

**차자**(次子) *one's*〔the〕second son.

**차작**(借作)《대작》vicarious writing〔making〕; ghostwriting;《작품》a vicarious work. ～하다 make〔write, compose〕for《*a person*》; ghostwrite. ◉ ～자 a ghostwriter.

**차장**(次長) an assistant director; a vice-chief; a deputy-chief; a deputy manager〔head〕(은행의). ¶ 편집～ a senior editor; an associate editor. ◉ ～검사 the assistant prosecutor general.

**차장**(車掌) a conductor;《여자》a woman conductor; a conductress;《영》a guard (열차의). ◉ ～실 the conductor's compartment;《화물차의》a caboose; a guard's〔brake〕van《영》.

**차점**(次點) the second highest mark〔number of points〕;《표수》the second largest number《of votes》; the largest number of votes obtained by the runner-up. ¶ ～이 되다 stand second (on the list of successful candidates) / 그는 (선거에서) ～이었다 He came next to the successful candidates. *or* He was the runner-up in the election. ◉ ～자 the second winner; the person who gets the second highest mark〔score〕;《선거·경기의》the runner-up《in a contest》.

**차제**(此際) ¶ ～에 now; on this occasion; at this juncture〔time〕;《지금의 형편》under〔in〕these circumstances / ～에 여러분께 감사의 말씀을 드립니다 Let me take this opportunity of thanking you.

**차조**〚식물〛glutinous millet.

**차조기**〚식물〛a beefsteak plant.

**차좁쌀** hulled glutinous millet.

**차주**(車主) a car owner; the owner of a car〔vehicle〕.

**차주**(借主) a borrower; a debtor; a renter (가옥의); a tenant (부동산의); a hirer (임차인); a lessee (토지의).

**차중**(車中) ①《차 안》¶ ～에서 in〔on〕a train; in a car. ②《차 탄 동안》while aboard《the train》; while in the car.

**차중음**(次中音)〚음악〛tenor.

**차지**[1] occupancy; possession. ～하다 occupy; hold; have; take (up);《손에 넣다》make《*a thing*》*one's* own; secure; take〔get, gain〕possession of;《비율을》account for. ¶ 높은 지위를 ～하다 secure〔occupy〕a high position / 제1위를 ～하다 rank first; hold〔win〕the first place; head the list《of》/ (세간 등이) 자리를 너무 ～하다 occupy〔take up〕much room

〔space〕/ 절대 다수를 ～하다 command an overwhelming majority《in the National Assembly》/ 천하를 ～하다 conquer〔reign over〕the whole land / 철도 사고의 2할을 ～하다 account for 20 percent of all railway accidents / 그녀는 언제나 학급에서 수석을 ～한다 She is always at the top of her class. / 외국인 학생이 이 대학에서는 3분의 1을 ～하고 있다 Foreigners account for a third of the students in this university. / 이 나라는 철의 생산량에 있어서 세계 제2위를 ～하고 있다 This country stands second in the world as regards the output of iron.

**차지**(借地) leased land; rented ground; a leasehold;《행위》lease of land.
◉ ～권 a lease; a leasehold. ～료 (a) (land) rent; (a) ground rent《영》. ～법 the Land Lease Law. ～인 a tenant; a leaseholder; a renter;〖법〗a lessee: 공동 ～인 a joint tenant; a cotenant. ～증서 a lease of land.

**차지**〖축구〗charge. ～하다 charge.

**차지다** (be) sticky; glutinous; viscid. ¶ 차진 밥 sticky rice.

**차질**(蹉跌·蹉躓)《헛디딤》stumbling;《잘못됨》something wrong〔amiss〕;《실패》a failure; a miscarriage; a fiasco; a setback; a deadlock; a snag. ¶ ～이 생기다 fail《in *one's* attempt》; miscarry; hit a snag; go wrong〔amiss〕/ 계획에 ～을 가져오다 [원인이 주어] upset〔frustrate〕*one's* plan; [사람이 주어] be frustrated〔baffled〕in *one's* scheme / 사업에 ～이 생겼다 The business struck a snag. / 그 계획은 사소한 잘못으로 ～이 생겼다 The project「received a setback〔ended in a fiasco〕because of a slight error.

**차질다** (be) stickily wet; viscous; tenacious; persistent.

**차차**(次次) ①《점차》gradually; by degrees〔inches〕; bit by bit; step by step; little by little; more and more (더하여); less and less (덜하여). ¶ ～ 어려워지다 become increasingly difficult / ～ 추워지다〔따뜻해지다〕be getting colder〔warmer〕/ ～ 일에 익숙해지다 become more and more accustomed to the work / ～ 좋아지다〔나아지다〕show gradual improvement / ～ 높은 지위로 승진하다 advance to a higher position step by step / 해가 ～ 길어진다 The days grow longer and longer. / 권투의 인기가 ～ 높아가고 있다 There has been a gradual increase in the popularity of boxing game. / 소음은 ～ 심해졌다 The noise became louder and louder.
②《조만간》by and by; in due course (of time); in due time; later; eventually. ¶ ～ 갚을 테니 너무 돈 재촉을 마시오 Stop dunning me, I'll get the money paid back eventually. / ～ 알게 될 겁니다 You will come to understand it by and by. / 돈은 ～ 갚아도 됩니다 You may return the money later on at your convenience.

**차창**(車窓) a car〔bus, train〕window. ¶ ～ 밖에 비치는 경치 the scenery seen from a car〔train〕window / ～ 밖을 내다보다 look out (of) the car〔train〕window.

**차체**(車體) a car body; the body《of a car》; the chassis《of a carriage》; the frame《of a bicycle》. ¶ ～가 낮은 자동차 a low-slung car.

**차축**(車軸) an axle.

**차츰차츰** little by little; gradually; by degrees; step by step; inch by inch; more and more. ⇨ 차차.

**차치하다**(且置—) set〔put〕aside〔apart〕; let alone. ¶ 농담은 차치하고 joking aside〔apart〕/ 만사 차치하고 before everything〔anything〕else; first of all / 이 문제는 차치하고 apart from this question; setting〔leaving〕aside this question / 그들은 사치품은 차치하고 일상의 필수품도 없다 They lack the necessities of life, to say nothing of luxuries. / 비용은 차치하고 거기에는 많은 시간이 필요할 것이다 Aside from the expenses, it will take a lot of time.

**차탄**(嗟歎)《개탄함》a sigh; lamentation; deploration;《감탄》admiration. ～하다 sigh; lament; deplore;《감탄하다》admire.

**차탈피탈**(此頉彼頉) one excuse or another; some excuse or other; all sorts of excuses. ～하다 make〔give〕one excuse or another; make all sorts of excuses.

**차편**(車便) a (public) conveyance;《by way of》a vehicle. ¶ ～으로 여행하다 travel by (a) vehicle / 지하철 ～이 좋다 be convenient to the subway / 그곳까지는 버스 ～을 이용할 수 있다 A bus service is available as far as there. *or* You can get there on the bus〔by bus〕.

**차폐**(遮蔽) cover; shelter;〖전기〗screening; shielding. ～하다 cover; shelter;

screen《*a thing* from observation》; shade《a light》; blackout《a window》. ◉ ～막 a blackout curtain. ～물 a cover; a shelter: 온갖 ～물을 이용하여 making use of everything available for shelter. ～진지 a covered position. ～포대 a masked battery.

**차표**(車票) a ticket. ¶ ～를 사는 줄 a ticket line〔queue〕/ ～를 사다 get〔buy〕a ticket《for Pusan》/ 대구까지 직행 ～를 사다 book through to Taegu; buy a through ticket to Taegu / ～를 검사하다 examine tickets / ～를 찍다《개찰하다》punch〔clip〕a ticket / ～를 보여 주세요 Ticket please. / 이 ～는 3일간 유효함 This ticket is valid for three days. /이 ～는 판매 당일만 유효함 This ticket is available on the day of issue only. ◉ ～자동판매기 a ticket (vending) machine. ～판매소 a ticket office《미》; a booking office《영》;《창구》a ticket〔booking〕window. ～판매원 a ticket agent《미》; a booking clerk《영》. 「for *one*.

**차필**(借筆) ～하다 have《*a person*》write

**차하지다**(差下—) be inferior to《another》by comparison; fall behind《another》when compared; do not stand (up to) comparison.

**차항**(次項) the next clause〔item〕; the following clause〔item〕. ¶ ～ 참조 Confer the next item〔clause〕.

**차호**(次號) the next number〔issue〕.

**차회**(次回) next time; the following sequence; the next round (경기의).

**차회**(此回) this time;《on》this occasion.

**차후**(此後) after this; hence(forth); hereafter; in (the) future (★ in future는「지금과는 달리 앞으로는」이라는 뜻인데 비해서, in the future는 단순히「미래에는」이란 뜻); from this time on; from now on. ¶ ～의 future; coming / …은 ～의 문제다 it remains to be proved that… / ～로는 더욱 조심해라 Be more careful in future.

**착** ①《붙는 모양》close(ly); tight(ly). ¶ (끈끈한 것이) 착 붙다 stick fast《to》; stick together / (남에게) 몸을 착 붙이다 nestle close《to *a person*》/ 몸을 벽에 착 붙이다 stand〔hold *one's* body〕close to the wall; hug the wall / 땅에 착 엎드리다 lie flat on the ground. ②《늘어진 모양》flaccidly; limply. ¶ 착 가라앉은 목소리(로) (in) a subdued voice / (몸이) 착 까부라지다 be dead tired; feel languid〔dull〕/ 착 늘어지다 dangle; hang limply.

**-착**(着) ①《도착》arrival; reaching; getting to. ¶ 최근착의 타임지 the latest issue of *Time* / 5시 부산착의 열차 the train due at Pusan at 5. ②《레이스 등의》¶ 1〔2〕착 the first〔second〕to finish〔arrive, come in〕/ 2착이 되다 come in〔finish〕second.

**착각**(錯覺)《감각기관의》an (optical) illusion;《잘못 생각》(a) misapprehension; (a) misunderstanding; misjudgment; a mistaken idea. ～하다 have an illusion; be under an illusion; misapprehend; guess wrong. ¶ 도둑으로 ～하다 mistake《*a person*》for a robber / ～하고 있다 be mistaken; be under a misapprehension; be under an illusion《about, as to, that》/ …라는 ～에 빠져 있다 be possessed with the illusion that… / 자네가 갈 것으로 ～하고 있었네 I was under the false impression that it was you who were to go there. / 당신은 나를 어떤 딴 사람으로 ～하고 있군요 You've got me mixed up with somebody else. / 나는 마치 내 방에 있는 듯한 ～에 빠져 있었다 I was under the false impression that I was in my own room. / 나는 마치 몸이 공중에 떠 있는 것 같은 ～을 일으켰다 I felt as if I were floating in「the air〔midair〕.

**착검**(着劍) ¶ ～하고 with a fixed bayonet; with bayonets fixed / ～《구령》Fix bayonets!

**착공**(着工) starting work. ～하다 start〔begin〕(construction) work. ¶ 그 공사는 다음주에 ～된다 The construction work will be started next week. ◉ ～식 a ground-breaking ceremony.

**착념**(着念) ～하다 keep in mind; be mindful of; pay attention to.

**착란**(錯亂) distraction; derangement. ～하다 be distracted〔deranged〕; go mad; be〔go〕off *one's* head. ¶ 정신～ dementia;《a state of》mental derangement; insanity / 정신 ～이 일어나다 go〔run〕mad〔distracted〕; be mentally deranged;《구어》go〔be〕off *one's* head / 정신을 ～시키다 drive《*one*》distracted; derange *one's* mind. ◉ ～상태 a state of dementia.

**착륙**(着陸) (a) landing; touchdown (활주로에 바퀴가 닿음). ～하다 land《at, on》; make a landing; touch〔set《미》〕down. ¶ 도중에 ～하다 make a stop on the way / ～하기 위해 진입하다 come in for a landing / 공항에 ～하

다 land on an airport / 훌륭히 ～하다 make a good landing / 강제 ～시키다 force 《an aircraft》 down / ～ 실패로 대파하다 crash on landing / 야간 ～을 하다 make a night landing / 비행기는 비행장에 무사히 ～했다 The airplane landed safely at the airfield.
◉ ～선 《우주 탐사용》 a landing module. ～장 a landing field 〔ground, strip〕. ～장치 landing gear; 《raise, lower》 the undercarriage: 자동 ～장치 automatic landing gear. ～지 a landing zone; 《공정대의》 a jump area. ～지시기 a landing indicator. ～지점 a touchdown point 〔spot〕.

**착모**(着帽) ～하다 put on 〔wear〕 a hat. ¶ 갱내에서는 헬멧의 ～가 필수적이다 Those who enter the pit are required to wear a hard helmet.

**착발**(着發) ① 《발착》 arrival and departure. ～하다 come and go; arrive and depart. ② 《격발》 (firearm) percussion; detonation by impact. ～하다 percuss; detonate by impact.
◉ ～신관 a percussion fuse. ～탄 a percussion shell.

**착복**(着服) ① 《착의》 dressing. ～하다 dress 〔clothe〕 *oneself* 《in》; put on clothes. ② 《횡령》 embezzlement. ～하다 embezzle; pocket 《구어》; misappropriate; help *oneself* to 《two million won》; divert 《public money》 into *one's* own pocket. ¶ 거액의 공금을 ～하다 embezzle 〔misappropriate〕 a large sum of public fund / 그는 수금한 돈을 ～했다 He pocketed the money that he had collected. ◉ ～자 《돈의》 an embezzler.

**착살맞다** (be) mean; indecent; nasty; petty; fussy. ¶ 착살맞은 사람 a niggardly person.

**착살하다** (be) mean; nasty. ⇨ 착살맞다.

**착상**(着床) 〖생물〗 《수정란의》 implantation. ～하다 be implanted 《in the uterine wall》.

**착상**(着想) an idea; a conception; a notion. ～하다 conceive; 「hit on 〔be struck with〕 《a plan》. ¶ 좋은 〔독창적〕 ～ a clever 〔an original〕 idea / 기발한 ～ a novel idea / ～이 좋다 be cleverly conceived; be a clever conception 〔idea〕 / ～이 떠오르다 an idea occurs to *one;* hit on an idea.

**착색**(着色) coloring; coloration. ～하다 color; paint; stain. ¶ 스케치에 ～하다 put in colors to an outline picture / 이 식품은 인공 ～되어 있다 This food is artificially colored. ◉ ～법 coloring. ～사진 a colored photograph. ～유리 stained 〔colored〕 glass. ～제 a coloring agent; a colorant: 인공～제 함유 《식품의 표시》 Contains artificial colorants. ～화 a colored picture 〔print〕.

**착생**(着生) 〖생물〗 insertion. ◉ ～식물 an epiphyte; an epiphytic plant; an aerial 〔air〕 plant.

**착석**(着席) ～하다 take *one's* seat 〔place〕; take a chair; sit (down). ¶ ～순으로 in the order of seats / ～해 있다 be seated; be in *one's* seat 〔place〕 / ～시키다 seat 《*a person*》 / 여러분 ～해 주십시오 Please be seated, ladies and gentlemen. ◉ ～자 one who is seated.

**착수**(着水) 〖항공〗 alighting 〔landing〕 on the water; 《우주선의》 (a) splashdown. ～하다 alight 〔land〕 on the water; splash down (우주선이). ¶ 우주선은 태평양에 무사히 ～했다 The spaceship made a safe splash down in the Pacific. ◉ ～장치 《비행기의》 the landing gear. ～판(板) a hydrovane.

**착수**(着手) a start; commencement. ～하다 start (on); 《미》 start in on; commence; begin (on); set about 《business》; get to 《work》; undertake; take up; set *one's* hand to; enter upon 《*one's* work》; 《새 사업에》 embark on; launch (upon). ¶ 일에 ～하다 set 〔get〕 to work; set about *one's* business / ～하고 있다 have 《the work》 in hand / 계획에 ～하다 set a plan on foot / 그는 새로운 사업에 ～했다 He embarked on a new enterprise. / 곧 일을 ～하겠다 I'll launch out on my work at once. / 공사는 아직 ～되지 않고 있다 No start has yet been made with the work. / 무엇부터 ～할까 What shall we 「do first 〔start〕? *or* What shall we begin with? / 우리는 곧 조사에 ～했다 We immediately set about making inquiries.

**착수금**(着手金) money paid to initiate a work; a deposit; a retainer; earnest money; a retaining fee (변호사의). ¶ ～으로 30만 원이 필요하다 We want ₩300,000 to start the work with.

**착시**(錯視) 〖심리〗 an optical illusion.

**착신**(着信) arrival of the post 〔mail〕; 《전신》 a message received. ◉ ～국(局) a receiving 〔the destination〕 post office.

**착실**(着實) ～하다 ① 《진실·견실하다》

(be) steady (and honest); stable; sound; sincere; sober; reliable; trustworthy. ¶ ～한 사람 a steady person; a trustworthy person / ～한 사업 a good solid business; a business on a sound basis / ～한 상인 a trustworthy merchant / ～한 생각 a solid 〔sober〕 view / ～한 성격 a stable 〔steady〕 character / ～한 회사〔영업 방식〕 a sound business firm 〔method〕 / 일을 ～히 하다 do *one's* work faithfully / 일에 ～한 진전을 보이다 make steady progress in *one's* work / 그 회사는 ～히 운영되고 있다 That firm is run on a sound business method. ② 《알차다》 (be) full; substantial; meaty; solid; well-off; moneyed. ¶ 자력이 ～한 부자 quite a rich person; a well-heeled person / 내용이 ～한 저술 a substantial work / 돈냥깨나 ～히 모으다 amass quite a lot of money.

**착안**(着眼) an aim; observation; the point; 《견지》 a viewpoint; a standpoint. ～하다 aim 《at》; pay attention to; fix *one's* eyes upon; take notice of (주목하다); turn *one's* attention to (유의하다). ¶ ～이 좋다 be right in 「*one's* way of looking at 〔*one's* view of〕 the matter / 자네 ～을 참 잘 했네 Your aim is right. *or* You are well advised in your approach to the subject. (논문 따위에 관해) / 자네의 기발한 ～에는 경탄하겠네 I admire the originality of your observation.

**착안점**(着眼點) the point aimed at; the point of *one's* observation; 《견지》 a point of view; *one's* viewpoint. ¶ 이것이 우리가 고려해야 할 문제의 ～이다 This is the aspect 〔point〕 of the question which we must consider. / 우리는 ～이 다른 것 같다 We seem to be directing our attention to different points.

**착암기**(鑿岩機) 〖광산〗 a rock drill.

**착어증**(錯語症) 〖의학〗 paraphasia. ¶ ～의 paraphasic.

**착오**(錯誤) a mistake; an error; a slip. ～하다 err 《in》; slip. ¶ 시행 ～ trial and error / ～ 없는 free from mistakes 〔errors〕 / ～에 빠지다 fall 〔drift〕 into an error; make 〔commit〕 a mistake. ◉ ～검색 〖컴퓨터〗 false retrieval. 시대～ anachronism: 그의 착상은 시대～에 지나지 않는다 His ideas are nothing but an anachronism.

**착용**(着用) 《동작》 putting on; 《상태》 wearing. ～하다 put on; wear; have 《a coat》 on. ¶ 제복을 ～하고 있다 be in uniform / 행사에는 예복을 ～할 것 A dress suit is to be worn on the occasion. *or* 《안내장 따위에서》 Dress: Formal. *or* Evening dress. ◉ ～품 (wearing) apparel; habiliments.

**착유**(搾油) oil expression. ～하다 press oil 《from》. ◉ ～공장 an oil mill. ～기 an oil press.

**착유**(搾乳) milking. ～하다 milk 《a cow》. ¶ ～하는 여자 a milkmaid; a dairymaid / 1회의 ～량 a milking. ◉ ～기 a milker; a milking machine; 《임산부의》 a breast pump. ～장 a dairy (farm).

**착의**(着衣) getting dressed; dressing; *one's* clothes 〔clothing〕. ～하다 get dressed; dress (*oneself*); get 〔put〕 on clothes.

**착임**(着任) arrival at *one's* post. ～하다 arrive at *one's* post. ¶ 그는 주미 대사로 ～했다 He arrived at his post as the ambassador to U.S.

**착잡**(錯雜) complication; intricacy; involution. ～하다 (be) complicated; intricate; knotty; entangled; be mixed up. ¶ ～한 표정 an expression of mixed feelings.

**착전**(着電) the arrival of a telegram; a telegram received.

**착정**(鑿井) well drilling 〔sinking〕. ～하다 bore 〔drill, dig, sink〕 a well.

**착지**(着地) ① 《비행기 따위의》 (a) landing; touchdown. ⇨ 착륙. ② 《체조 따위의》 landing. ～하다 land 《on a mat》. ¶ 잘 ～하다〔～에 실패하다〕 make a good 〔poor〕 landing.

**착착** steadily; in orderly fashion; step by step. ¶ ～ 진행되다 make steady 〔good〕 progress 〔headway〕; progress steadily / 공사는 ～ 진척되고 있다 The work is well under way.

**착출기**(搾出機) 《플라스틱 등의》 an extruding machine.

**착취**(搾取) ① 《짜냄》 squeezing out; extracting; expression; extraction. ～하다 squeeze out; press; extract. ② 《고혈의》 exploitation; squeezing; "sweating". ～하다 extort; exploit; sweat 《*a person*》; squeeze 《money》 out of 《*a person*》; "bleed"; "soak". ¶ 자본가의 ～ capitalist exploitation / 식민지를 ～하다 exploit a colony / 백성의 고혈을 ～하다 exploit 〔bleed〕 the people; grind the people down / 고용주가 고용인을 ～한다 The employer sweats his workers. / 조합측은 경영진이 ～를

하고 공장의 설비 개선에 충분한 투자를 하지 않았다고 비난했다 The union has accused management of milking and not investing enough in plant improvement.
◉ ~〔피~〕계급 the exploiting 〔exploited〕 class. ~노동 sweated labor; sweatshop labor. ~산업 a sweated industry. ~제도 the sweating system. 중간~ intermediary exploitation.

**착탄**(着彈) 《미사일 등의》 impact.
◉ ~거리 the range 《of a gun》: ~거리 내에 들어오다 come within range / ~거리 내에〔밖에〕 있다 be in 〔out of〕 range / ~거리를 측정하다 find the range. ~지점 an impact area.

**착하**(着荷) the arrivals 〔receipts〕 of goods. ~하다 arrive. ◉ ~인도〔불(拂)〕 delivery 〔payment〕 on arrival.

**착하다** 《아이·마음씨가》 (be) good; nice; good-natured; tenderhearted; kindhearted. ¶ 착한 사람 a good man; a good-natured person / 착한 아이 a good child; a good 〔nice〕 (little) boy 〔girl〕 / 착한 일 a good work 〔deed〕; a virtuous act / 마음이 ~ be kindhearted; have *one's* heart in the right place / 착한 일을 하다 do something good; do (what is) good; practice virtue / 착하게 굴다 act in a virtuous 〔kindly〕 manner; be good 〔nice〕 to 《*a person*》 / 착하지, 울지 마라 Don't cry, there's a good boy 〔girl〕. / 착하기도 해라 What a good boy 〔girl〕!

**착함**(着艦) 《비행기의》 deck-landing; 《귀함》 returning to *one's* warship. ~하다 《비행기가》 land 《on a carrier》.

**착항**(着港) arrival (in port). ~하다 make port 〔harbor〕; arrive in port 〔harbor〕. ◉ ~가격 landed terms.

**찬**(贊·讚) praise; eulogy; a legend; a panegyric. ¶ 그림에 찬을 쓰다 write a legend on 〔over〕 a painting.

**찬**(饌) subsidiary articles of diet; a (side) dish. ⇨ 반찬. ¶ 찬이 많다 have many side dishes / 찬이라곤 야채절임 뿐이다 We have nothing but pickles to eat along with rice.

**찬가**(讚歌) a song 〔poem〕 in praise 《of》; a paean. ¶ 올림픽 ~ a song in praise of the Olympics.

**찬간자** a bluish-gray horse with white face.

**찬국** a cold summer soup (made from water, soysause, and vinegar).

**찬기**(―氣) 《찬 공기》 cold air; cold draft(스며드는); 《냉기》 a chill. ¶ ~가 돌다 be chill with cold air; have a cold fit / ~를 느끼다 feel chilly; feel a chill / ~를 쐬다 be exposed to cold air.

**찬동**(贊同) approval; approbation; support; endorsement. ~하다 approve of 《a plan》; give *one's* approval 〔support〕 to 《a proposal》. ¶ ~을 구하다 ask 《*a person's*》 approval 《for a plan》 / ~을 얻다 [사람이 주어] obtain 《*a person's*》 consent 〔approval〕; [사물이 주어] meet with 《*a person's*》 approval / ~을 얻어서 with 《*a person's*》 approval 〔consent, support〕.

**찬란하다**(燦爛―) (be) brilliant; shining; bright; glittering; lustrous; radiant; dazzling. ¶ 찬란한 별 bright 〔glittering〕 stars / 찬란한 보석 a brilliant 〔radiant〕 jewel / 찬란하게 brightly; brilliantly; radiantly; lustrously / 광채가 ~ have bright colors; be lustrous / 찬란하게 빛나다 shine bright(ly) 〔brilliantly〕.

**찬립**(簒立) usurpation of the throne. ~하다 usurp 〔seize〕 the throne.

**찬모**(饌母) a woman cook in charge of making side dishes.

**찬무대** a cold current. ⇨ 한류(寒流).

**찬물** cold water. ¶ ~을 끼얹다 pour 〔put〕 cold water over *oneself;* get shower with cold water; [비유적] discourage 《*a person* from》; throw cold water on 《a scheme》; throw a wet blanket over 〔on〕; put a damper on / ~을 한 잔 들이켜다 drink a cup of cold water.

**찬미**(讚美) praise; admiration; adoration; glorification (신을). ~하다 praise; admire; glorify; extol; chant hymns of praise 《to》. ¶ 신을 ~하다 praise God; sing the praises of God / 신을 ~하는 노래 a hymn of praise to God / 인생을 ~하다 sing 〔chant〕 the praises of life. ◉ ~자(者) an admirer; an adorer.

**찬미가**(讚美歌) = 찬송가.

**찬바람** a cold 〔chilly, bleak〕 wind; cold air (공기). ¶ 살을 에는 듯한 ~ a cutting 〔biting, nipping〕 wind / ~을 쐬다 expose *oneself* to a cold wind.
◉ ~머리 the (time of) setting in of the chill winds of autumn.

**찬반**(贊反) for and against; ayes or noes. ¶ 여야(與野)의 ~ 토론 pros and cons among the rival parties. ◉ ~양론(兩論) ⇨ 찬부양론: ~양론에 귀를 기울

이다 listen to the pros and cons 《of *a matter*》.

**찬밥** cold (cooked) rice.

**찬방**(饌房) a storeroom for food supplies; a pantry.

**찬부**(贊否) approval and 〔or〕 disapproval; yes and 〔or〕 no; ayes and 〔or〕 noes. = 찬반. ¶ ~를 묻다 take the ayes and noes; put 《a question》 to the vote (투표로) / ~를 결정짓다 《투표에서》 vote on 《*a matter*》 / ~ 반반이다 The ayes and nays split evenly. ◉ ~양론 pros and cons; arguments for and against: 그 의안에 대해서는 ~양론이 있다 There are arguments both for and against the bill.

**찬사**(讚辭) a eulogy; praise(s); a compliment; laudatory remarks; a panegyric. ¶ 아낌없는 ~ 《give》 unstinted praise / ~를 드리다〔보내다〕 eulogize; pay *one's* tribute of praise 《to》; compliment 《*a person* on *his* performance》 / ~를 아끼지 않다 be unsparing of 〔in〕 *one's* praise / 그의 공적은 어떠한 ~로써도 다 표현할 수 없다 One cannot speak too highly of his achievements 〔merits〕.

**찬성**(贊成) approval; agreement; support; 《동의에 대한》 seconding. ~하다 approve of 《a plan》; give *one's* approval 《to》; agree 《to *a person's* proposal, with *a person*, with *a person's* opinion》; fall in with 《*a person's* view》; second 《a motion》; support 《a bill》; vote for 《a proposal》. ¶ ~하는 쪽 the consenting party; the affirmative side / 계획에 ~하다 「give *one's* approval to 〔endorse〕 a plan / 의안에 ~하다 「come out 〔be〕 in favor of a bill; vote for a bill / 만장 일치로 ~하다 reach unanimous agreement; consent unanimously / (토론에서) ~하는 측에 서다 take the affirmative / 자기 의견에 ~케 하다 win 《*a person*》 round to *one's* own view / 남의 의견에 진심으로 ~하다 heartily endorse another's opinion; be in earnest agreement with another's view / 의안은 ~ 180표, 반대 120표로 통과되었다 The bill was passed with 180 in favor to 120 against.
찬성의: ~의 의견을 말하다 speak in favor 《of》 / 손을 들어 ~의 뜻을 표하다 show *one's* hand in favor 《of a plan》.
찬성을: ~을 얻다 gain 〔win〕 the approval 《of》; meet with the approbation 《of》 / …의 ~을 얻어 supported by… / ~을 구하다 ask (for) 《their》 approval 〔support〕 / 위원회의 과반수 ~을 얻다 win 〔meet with〕 the approval of the majority of the committee / ~을 표명하다 express *one's* approval.
¶ 그것에 ~이다 I am for it. / 나는 전적으로 네 의견에 ~이다 I completely 「agree to 〔concur in〕 your opinion. *or* I'm all for you. / 나는 전적으로 ~할 수 없다 I can't quite agree. / 자네 계획에는 ~할 수가 없네 I don't much care for your plan. / ~이 오십 반대가 백이다 There are 50 ayes 〔votes for〕 and 100 nays 〔votes against〕. *or* Fifty are for and a hundred are against. / ~하는 분은 손을 들어 주시오 Those in favor 〔The ayes〕 are requested to raise their hands. *or* All those in favor, signify by raising your hands. ◉ ~론 a supporting argument. ~연설 a speech in support of 《a measure》. ~의원 a member in favor of 《a bill》. ~자 an approver; a supporter; a seconder (동의의): ~자가 많다 The ayes have it. ~투표 a vote in favor of 《a bill》; an approval ballot: ~투표를 하다 vote for 〔in favor of〕 《a bill》; cast a favorable 〔an aye〕 vote for 《a measure》.

**찬송**(讚頌) glorification. ⇨ 찬미.

**찬송가**(讚頌歌) a hymn; a psalm. ¶ ~를 부르다 sing a hymn; chant a psalm. ◉ ~작가 a hymnist; a hymnodist; a psalmist. ~집〔책〕 a hymnbook; a hymnal.

**찬술**(撰述) writing; composing. ~하다 write (a book); compose.

**찬술**(纂述) editing; compilation. ~하다 edit; compile.

**찬스** a chance; an opportunity. = 기회. ¶ 절호의 ~ a golden 〔perfect〕 opportunity; a chance not to be missed / ~를 잡다〔만들다, 얻다〕 seize 〔make, get〕 a chance / ~를 놓치다 lose 〔pass up〕 a chance / 유일한 ~를 놓치다 miss *one's* only chance / ~를 엿보다 wait for an 〔*one's*〕 opportunity / 이것은 일생에 한 번 오는 ~다 This is the chance 〔opportunity〕 of a lifetime. / 지금이 ~다 Now is your chance. ◉ ~메이커 a heads-up player.

**찬양**(讚揚) praise; commendation; admiration; laudation. ~하다 praise; commend; admire; laud. ¶ 공(功)을 ~하여 in appreciation 〔recognition〕 of 《*a person's*》 services / ~할 만하다 be worthy of praise / 용기를 ~하다

praise 《*a person*》 for his courage / …을 ～하는 연설을 하다 give an address of homage to 《Goethe》 / 극구 ～하다 praise 〔extoll, laud〕 《*a person*》 「to the skies 〔sky-high〕; speak in the highest praise of / 그녀는 모든 사람으로부터 ～을 받았다 She was the admiration of all beholders.

**찬역**(簒逆) usurpation; seizure. ～하다 usurp; seize.

**찬연**(燦然) brilliancy; resplendence; radiance. ～하다 (be) brilliant; radiant; resplendent. ¶ ～한 광휘 brilliancy; radiant brightness / ～히 빛나다 shine brilliantly.

**찬위**(簒位) = 찬탈(簒奪).

**찬의**(贊意) approval. ¶ ～를 표하다 express 〔show, give, nod, voice〕 *one's* approval 《to》; give *one's* assent 《to》.

**찬이슬** cold dew; the night dew. ¶ ～ 맞는 놈 a night thief.

**찬장**(饌欌) a pantry chest; a cupboard; a sideboard.

**찬조**(贊助) support; backing; patronage; sponsorship; auspices; 《지지·승인》 endorsement; approval; 《장려》 encouragement. ～하다 support; back (up); patronize; sponsor; endorse; render assistance. ¶ 김씨의 ～하에 「supported by 〔under the support of〕 Mr. Kim / ～를 얻다 have 〔obtain〕 《*a person's*》 patronage 〔approval, support〕 / ～를 청하다 solicit 《*a person's*》 support. ◉ ～금 a contribution; donation: ～금을 내다 make a donation 〔contribution〕. ～연설 a supporting speech; a campaign speech 《for a candidate》: ～연설을 하다 speak for a candidate. ～자 a supporter; a patron. ～출연 appearance as a guest (artist): ～출연하다 appear as a guest star 〔artist〕. ～회원 a supporting 〔patron〕 member.

**찬찬하다** ① 《꼼꼼하다》 (be) meticulous; attentive; very careful; scrupulous; thorough; considerate; punctilious; cautious. ¶ 그의 일은 ～ His work is thorough. ② 《침착하다》 (be) composed; staid; self-possessed; collected; calm; cool; quiet; placid; leisurely; deliberate. ¶ 그는 성격이 아주 ～ He is very placid and attentive.

**찬찬히** ① 《꼼꼼히》 meticulously; attentively; very carefully; scrupulously; painstakingly; thoroughly. ¶ ～ 만들다 make with patient care / 교정을 ～ 보다 read the proof with religious care / 남의 얼굴을 ～ 뜯어보다 get a good look into *a person's* face; take a close look at *a person.* ② 《침착히》 composedly; calmly; staidly; unperturbedly; coolly; with great self-possession; in a leisurely way 〔manner〕; deliberately. ¶ ～ 겨냥을 하다 take deliberate aim / ～ 걷다 walk along unperturbed.

**찬칼**(饌—) a kitchen knife; a carver.

**찬탄**(贊嘆·讚嘆) admiration; praise. ～하다 admire; praise; extoll; speak highly 《of》; be filled with admiration 《at》. ¶ ～할 만하다 deserve praise; be worthy of the highest admiration; merit the highest praise / ～하여 마지않다 be lost in admiration 《for》.

**찬탈**(簒奪) usurpation. ～하다 usurp; seize. ¶ 왕위를 ～하다 usurp the throne / 왕위 ～을 꾀하다 plot to supplant the king. ◉ ～자 a usurper.

**찬평**(讚評·贊評) praising and criticizing; a favorable criticism 〔comment〕. ～하다 comment 〔criticize〕 favorably.

**찬표**(贊票) a favorable 〔an aye〕 vote. ¶ ～를 던지다 vote 「for 〔in favor of〕 《a bill》; cast a favorable vote for 《*a matter*》.

**찬합**(饌盒) a nest 〔tier〕 of boxes; a picnic box. ¶ ～에 담다 pack 《food》 in a nest of boxes; fill a nest of boxes with 《rice》 / ～에 담은 음식 food packed in a nest of boxes.

**찰-** 《차진》 sticky; glutinous; 《지독한》 extreme; deadly; dire.

**찰가난** penury; dire 〔extreme〕 poverty. ◉ ～뱅이 a pauper; a very poor person.

**찰거머리** ① 《거머리》 a sticky leech. ② 《사람》 a leech; a persistently sticky person. ¶ ～ 같다 fasten on 《*a person*》 like a tick; cling 〔stick〕 to 《*a person*》 like a leech.

**찰과상**(擦過傷) an abrasion; a scratch; a brush burn; an excoriation. ¶ ～을 입다 sustain 〔get〕 a scratch 《on the shoulder》; suffer an abrasion / 아주 가벼운 ～이다 It's only a scratch. / 그는 나무에서 떨어졌지만 ～도 입지 않았다 He fell down from a tree, but did not even get the slightest scratch.

**찰그랑-** ⇨ 절그렁-.

**찰기**(—氣) stickiness. ¶ ～가 있다 be sticky 〔glutinous, viscid〕.

**찰깍** ① 《붙는 모양》 sticking tight 〔close, fast〕. ¶ ～ 붙다 stick fast 《to》.

② 《소리》 with a slap 〔snap, click〕. ¶ ~거리다 keep slapping 〔snapping〕 / 셔터를 ~ 누르다 click the shutter.

**찰깍쟁이** a "sticky" 〔nasty, mean〕 miser.

**찰깍찰깍** ① 《붙는 모양》 all sticking tight 〔close, fast〕. ② 《소리》 with slap after slap; snapping and snapping.

**찰나**(刹那) a moment; an instant. ¶ ~적인 momentary; transient 《pleasures》 / 그 ~에 (just) at that very moment 〔instant〕 / 그가 뚜껑을 여는 ~에 the instant 〔moment〕 he opened the lid / 자동차를 피하는 ~에 in (the act of) dodging a motorcar / ~적인 충동에 이끌리다 be driven by an impulse of the moment / ~적(인) 환락에 빠지다 「indulge in 〔be addicted to〕 momentary pleasures. ◉ ~주의 the principle of living only for (the pleasure of) the moment; impulsiveness.

**찰딱거리다** cling 《to》; stick 《to》.

**찰떡** rice cake made of glutinous rice.

**찰락거리다** trickle.

**찰랑거리다** lap; splash; slop; slosh. ¶ 찰랑거리는 잔물결 laughing wavelets / 물결이 해안에 ~ waves lap (at) the shore / 독 안의 물이 찰랑거린다 The water in a jar is slopping from side to side.

**찰랑찰랑** 《그득 차서》 to the brim 〔full〕; overflowingly; sloppily; 《물결이》 splashily. ¶ 잔에 ~하도록 술을 따르다 fill a glass (up) to the brim with wine; brim a cup with wine / 독에 ~하도록 물을 붓다 fill a jar with water to the brim.

**찰밥** cooked glutinous rice; cooked dish of glutinous rice.

**찰벼** 『식물』 glutinous rice.

**찰부꾸미** a glutinous rice pancake.

**찰상**(擦傷) an abrasion. ⇨ 찰과상.

**찰쇠** a metal ring around a pivot.

**찰싹-** ⇨ 철썩-.

**찰쌈지** a tobacco pouch carried by 「*one's* side.

**찰짜** a meticulous 〔over-scrupulous, pertinacious〕 person.

**찰찰** ⇨ 철철.

**찰찰하다**(察察—) (be) exact; punctil-「ious; meticulous.

**찰카닥, 찰칵, 찰카당** ⇨ 잘가닥, 잘가당.

**찰흙** clay; 《상표명》 Plastacine (소상용(塑像用)). ¶ ~의 clay / ~질의 clayey 《soil》; argillaceous 《rocks》 / ~으로 만들다 make 《a model》 of clay; model 《an image》 in clay.

**참**[1] 《진실·사실》 the truth; the reality; the actuality; the fact; 《성실》 sincerity; faithfulness; a true heart. ¶ 참의 《진실의》 true; real; 《실제의》 actual; 《정직한》 honest; sincere; 《진짜의》 genuine / …이 참임을 증명하다 certify the truth of ….

**참**[2] ① 《참으로》 really; truly; in truth; indeed; in fact; very; much; quite; exceedingly; extremely; actually; surely. ¶ 참 좋다 be quite good / 참 난처하군 I am in a nice fix. / 참 놀랐다 I was surprised indeed. / 오늘은 참 더운데 It's awfully 〔very〕 hot today. / 자네 시계는 참 좋은데 Your watch is really good. / 참 재미있었다 I have had 「such a good time 〔lots of fun〕. / 그것 참 안됐군요 I am very sorry to hear that. / 그는 참 훌륭한 인격자다 He is a man of virtue, indeed. / 영어는 참 어렵구나 English is really very difficult to learn.

② [감탄사적] What!; How!; Oh!; Well!; Uh…!; Well now…!; Really now…!; Really! ¶ 그것 참 그렇구나 How true that is! / 참 훌륭한 솜씨로군 How (very) skillful he is! / 참 바보로구나 How foolish (he is)! / 참 오늘이 수요일이지 Oh, it's Wednesday, isn't it? / 참 별 사람 다 보겠다 Really now, I have never seen such a dreadful person! / 참 별소리 다 듣겠다 Just what do you mean talking to me that way?

③ [접두어] real; true; genuine. ¶ 참말 the truth; a true remark / 참마음 sincerity; a true heart / 참용기 true 〔genuine〕 courage / 참이야기 a true story.

**참**(站) ① 《역참》 a post; a stage; a station. ② 《쉬는 곳》 a stop; a resting place. ¶ 층계참 a (mean) landing; a halfpace. ③ 《휴식》 a (short) rest; a break; a recess. ④ 《…하려는 때》 time; moment. ¶ 막 …하려는 참이다 be 「going 〔just about〕 to 《*do*》; be on the point 〔verge〕 of 《*doing*》.

**참가**(參加) participation; joining; entry. ~하다 participate in 《a project》; take part in 《a discussion》; join (in) 《a party》; enter 《a war》; be a party 《to》; sit in 《on a conference》.

¶ ~를 신청하다 enter for 《a contest》 / 경기에 ~하다 take part 〔participate〕 in a game / 전쟁〔회의〕에 ~하다 participate in a battle 〔conference〕 / 여름 강습회에 ~하다 be enrolled in a class at the summer school / 정치 운동에 ~하다 join (in) the political movement / 조약에 ~하다 become a party to a treaty / 웅변 대회에 ~를 신청하다 send in *one's* name for a speech contest / 클럽 활동에 적극적으로 ~하다 take an active part to the club activities / 40개국이 그 조약에 ~하고 있다 Forty countries are parties to the treaty. / 그들은 그녀에게 그 집회에 ~할 것을 촉구했다 They urged her to participate in the meeting.

◉ ~교(校) an entrant school. ~국〔팀〕 a participating「nation〔team〕. ~료 an entry fee. ~상 a prize for participation《in an event》. ~의식 a sense of participation. ~자 a participator; a participant《in a rally》;《경기 등의》 an entrant: ~자 명부 an entry; a list of participants. ~증서 a participation certificate. 불~ nonparticipation.

**참게** 〖동물〗 a「king〔horse-shoe〕 crab.

**참견**(參見) ①《관여》 participation. ~하다 participate〔take part〕《in》; have a「share〔hand〕《in》. ¶ 계획에 ~하다 participate in a plan; be involved in a scheme / 회사일에 ~하다「take part〔have a finger〕 in company business. ②《간섭》 interference; meddling. ~하다 interfere「in〔with〕; meddle「with〔in〕; poke〔put, thrust〕 *one's* nose into《another's affair》. ¶ ~쟁이 a meddler; a meddlesome person / 말 ~하다 put in a word; break〔cut, butt〕 in / 일일이 ~하다 meddle in everything / ~ 못하도록 하다 keep《*a person*》 in *his* place / 남의 일에 웬 ~이야 Don't poke your nose into other's business. / 네가 ~할 바가 아니다 It is none of your business. *or* You have no right to「interfere in〔butt in on〕 the matter. / 쓸데없는 ~ 좀 말게 None of your lips! *or* Mind your own business.

**참경**(慘景) a terrible sight; a pitiful〔pitiable〕 spectacle. ⇨ 참상.

**참고**(參考) reference; consultation. ~하다 refer to《the notes》; consult《a book》. ¶ ~로 for reference; for *one's*「information〔guidance〕/ ~가 되다 [책 따위가 주어] furnish〔provide〕《*a person*》 with useful information;《도움이 되다》be「of help〔helpful〕 to《*a person* in *doing*》/ …에게 ~로 말하다 tell《*a person something*》 for *his* information; inform《*a person* of *a thing*》 by way of suggestion / 주석을 ~하며 본문을 읽다 read the text, consulting the annotations / 서류를 후일의 ~로 보존하다 keep a document for later reference / 계획을 세우기 전에 여러 사람의 의견을 ~하다 consult (the views of) several people before setting the plan up / ~로 말씀드립니다만… May I suggest that…? / ~되는 말씀을 해 주셔서 고맙습니다 Thank you for your suggestion. / 이 책은 영문학 연구에 큰 ~가 된다 This book is a good guide to the study of English literature. / 그것에 관해서는 ~할 만한 문헌이 거의 없다 There is very little literature to refer to about it.

◉ ~도서 a reference book. ~문헌 a bibliography; literature cited. ~물 a specimen for reference. ~서류 reference documents. ~서목(書目) a bibliography (권말의). ~인《증인》a witness: 중요 ~인으로 경찰서에 임의 출두하다 respond to a request to appear voluntarily at the police station as an important witness. ~자료 reference「data〔materials〕.

**참고서**(參考書)《참고 도서》 a reference book;《학습용의》 a study-aid book; a guide book. ¶ ~류 books for reference / 수학 ~ a reference book for the study of mathematics.

**참관**(參觀) a visit; inspection;《입회》 witnessing. ~하다 visit; inspect; pay a visit of inspection; make an inspection《of》;《증인으로서》witness. ¶ 공장을 ~하다 pay a visit of inspection to a factory / 수업을 ~하다 visit〔inspect〕 a class (at work) / 개표〔투표〕를 ~하다 witness「the ballot counting〔the voting〕/ 학교를 ~하다 inspect〔look into〕 a school / ~할 수 있다〔없다〕 [사물이 주어] be「open〔closed〕 to visitors.

◉ ~인 a visitor;《선거의》 a witness: ~인 명부 a visitors' book / 투표 ~인 a voting witness. ~일 a visiting day.

**참괴**(慙愧) shame; humiliation;《회한》 compunction. ~하다 feel shame《at》; be ashamed《of, to》. ¶ ~케 하다 put《*a person*》 to shame; overwhelm《*a person*》 with shame / ~하여 마지않다 be「overwhelmed〔overcome〕 with shame; feel heartily ashamed《of *oneself*》.

**참극**(慘劇) a tragedy; a tragic event; an atrocity. ¶ 순찰차가 ~의 현장으로 달려 갔다 A (police) patrol car ran to the scene of the tragedy.

**참기름** sesame oil; gingili.

**참깨** 〖식물〗 sesame; sesame seeds (씨). ¶ ～를 빻다 pound sesame seeds / ～가 기니 짧으니 한다 《속담》 There is little to choose between them.

**참나리** 〖식물〗 a tiger lily.

**참나무** 〖식물〗 an oak (tree). ◉ ～산누에나방 〖곤충〗 an emperor moth; a tussah.

**참녜**(參—) ⇨참여. ¶ 잔치에 ～하다 attend a party; be present at a banquet.

**참다** ① 《견뎌내다》 put up with; endure; bear; stand; forbear; suffer 《insolence》; tolerate; 《인내하다》 persevere 《in》; be patient 《with》. ¶ 잘 ～ bear and forbear / 굴욕을 ～ suffer humiliation; eat dirt 〔humble pie〕; put up with an insult / 더운 것을 ～ stand 〔bear up under〕 the heat / 불행을 꾹 ～ bear *one's* misfortune with stoical fortitude / 졸음을 ～ withstand sleepiness / 이가 쑤시는 것을 지그시 ～ bear 〔stand〕 a toothache stoically / 참을 수 있다 be bearable; can be endured; be tolerable / 참을 수 있는 데까지 ～ bear to the best of *one's* capacity / 참을 수(가) 없다 [사물이 주어] be unbearable 〔intolerable, insufferable〕; be past 〔beyond〕 endurance; [사람이 주어] cannot bear 《*a person,* the noise》 / 참을 수 없는 unbearable; intolerable; unendurable; insufferable / 참을 수 없게 되다 become unendurable 〔intolerable〕; lose patience 《with》; exhaust *one's* patience; *one's* patience becomes exhausted / 참을 수 없는 고통이다 My suffering is more than I can bear. / 그는 아파서 참을 수가 없었다 He could no longer stand the pain. / 이 조건으로 당분간 참아 주십시오 Please put up with these terms for the time being. / 참는 것도 한도가 있다 There is a limit to my patience. / 이건 도저히 못 참겠다 This is not to be endured. *or* This is too much for me. / 뭐 그렇게 잠자코 참고만 있어야 할 이유가 없네 There's no reason why you should endure it in silence.
② 《자제하다》 control 〔restrain〕 *oneself;* check *oneself* 《from *doing*》; repress; suppress; contain; hold 〔keep, choke〕 back; gulp down 《*one's* sobs》. ¶ 노여움을 ～ control *one's* temper; repress 〔suppress, keep down, swallow〕 *one's* anger; choke down *one's* rage; restrain *one's* wrath / 눈물을 ～ keep 〔fight, hold〕 back *one's* tears; keep tears from *one's* eyes / 똥 마려운 것을 ～ repress the movement of the bowels; resist the call of nature / 오줌(마려운 것)을 ～ contain *one's* urine; hold *one's* water / 선하품을 ～ stifle 〔suppress〕 a yawn / 웃음을 ～ suppress *one's* laughter; swallow a laugh / 한 잔 하고 싶은 것을 ～ repress *one's* thirst for drink / ～ 못 해서 웃음을 터뜨리다 be unable to control *oneself* from bursting into laughter / ～ 못 해서 화를 내다 get impatient and blow *one's* top / 나는 ～ 못 해서 울음을 터뜨렸다 I could not help bursting out crying. / 그는 울고 싶은 것을 꾹 참았다 He resisted an impulse to cry out.

**참담**(慘憺) ～하다 《비참하다》 (be) miserable; wretched; grim; dire; terrible; horrible; 《가련하다》 (be) pitiful; pitiable; miserable. ¶ ～한 광경 a frightful 〔gruesome〕 spectacle; a horrible sight / ～한 상태 《be in》 a wretched 〔sore〕 plight / ～한 패배 《suffer》 a crushing defeat / ～한 생활 a wretched 〔miserable〕 life; a life of misery / ～한 지경에 처하다 be in 「extreme distress 〔dire want〕; be in depth of misery / 불탄 거리의 광경은 실로 ～했다 The fire-destroyed street presented a horrible sight.

**참답다** (be) true; real; honest; genuine; faithful; truthful; sincere. ⇨참되다. ¶ 참다운 친구 a true friend / 참다운 영웅 a hero worthy of the name / 참다운 의미에 있어서 in the true 〔proper〕 sense of the word 〔term〕 / (마음을 잡아) 참다운 사람이 되다 become a new man; turn over a new leaf.

**참대** 〖식물〗 a common bamboo.

**참돔** 〖어류〗 a red sea bream; a porgy.

**참되다** (be) true; honest; truthful; faithful; sincere; genuine; right-minded. ¶ 참되게 honestly; faithfully / 참된 이야기 a true story / 참된 사람 a genuine 〔an honest, a sincere〕 person / 참된 용기 true 〔genuine〕 courage / 그이야 말로 참된 학자다 He is (what I call) a real scholar. *or* He is a scholar worthy of the name.

**참따랗게** truly; faithfully; truthfully; sincerely; really; genuinely.

**참뜻** the true meaning 〔sense, signification〕; *one's* real intention. ¶ ～을 오해하다 misjudge *one's* real motives / ～과는 크게 다르게 far from *one's* true intention / 나는 그의 ～을 모르겠다 I can't see what he really means.

**참렬**(參列) attendance; presence. ⇨참석.

**참례**(參禮) 《식에》 attending a ceremony; 《참석》 attendance; presence. ～하다 attend 《a ceremony》; be present 《at》; present *oneself* 《at》. ¶ 장례식에 ～하다 attend a funeral / ～자가 많았다 There was a large attendance 《at the funeral》. *or* Lots of people were present 《at the ceremony》.

**참말** a true remark 〔story〕; a (real) fact; an authentic story 〔account〕; the truth. ¶ ～(로) 《실로》 truly; really; in truth; actually; indeed; 《확실히》 surely; to be sure; 《매우》 very; much; (ever) so; such 《a pleasant time》; exceedingly; tremendously; awfully; 《충심으로》 heartily / ～ 같은 이야기 a likely-sounding story; a story having the ring of truth about it / ～ 같은 거짓말 a plausible lie / ～(로) 좋다 be very good / ～(로) 놀라다 be really surprised / ～로 믿다〔받아들이다〕 believe 《a statement》 (to be true); take 《*a thing*》 for truth; accept 《a remark》 (as true) / 아무의 말을 ～로 믿다 take *a person* at *his* word / ～을 하다 tell the truth; speak true / ～입니까 《놀라서》 Indeed? *or* Really? *or* You don't say so! (설마) / 그게 ～인가 Is that true? *or* Do you mean what you say? / ～일까 Can it be true? *or* I wonder if it is true. / ～입니다 Believe me. / 그 소문은 ～인가 Is there any truth in the rumor? / ～로 글씨를 잘 쓰는구나 You write a very good hand. / 그 이야기는 어쩐지 ～인 것 같다 The story 「has some color 〔bears the stamp〕 of truth. / 그것을 누가 ～로 믿는담 Who would believe it? *or* Tell it to the marines. / 너 ～ 잘 왔다 How nice of you to come. / 그는 ～로 교양이 있다 He is, in a very true sense of the word, cultured. / ～이지 어떻게 사과를 드려야 할지 모르겠군요 I really don't know how to apologize to you. / 베풀어 주신 도움 ～로 고맙습니다 I thank you from the bottom of my heart for your kind help. / ～이지 유감입니다 It is really a matter for regret. / ～이지 잘 된 작품이다 This is certainly a bit of good work.

**참매** 〖조류〗 a goshawk.

**참매미** 〖곤충〗 a robust cicada.

**참먹** an ink-stick of good quality.

**참모**(參謀) 《군대의》 a staff officer; [총칭] the staff; 《상담역》 an adviser; a counselor; a brain truster 《to *a person*》; a brain (trust) 《구어》; [집합적] the brains. ¶ 김씨의 ～역 Mr. Kim's brain trust; an adviser 〔a brain truster〕 to Mr. Kim / …의 ～로서 활동하다 act as adviser to… / 저 사람은 사장의 ～다 The man is a member of the president's brain trust.
◉ ～본부 the General Staff Office. ～장 the chief of staff. ～장교 a staff officer. ～총장〔차장〕 the Chief 〔Deputy Chief〕 of the General Staff. ～회의 a staff conference; a council of war. 일반～ the general staff. 합동～본부 the Joint Chiefs of Staff.

**참밀** 〖식물〗 (common) wheat.

**참바** a heavy rope; a hawser.

**참배**(參拜) worship; visiting a place of worship. ～하다 (go and) worship at 《a shrine》; visit 《a shrine》; enter 《a temple》 and pray before the altar.
◉ ～자 a worshiper; a visitor 《to a shrine》.

**참벌** a honeybee. ⇨ 꿀벌.

**참변**(慘變) a disastrous accident; a tragic incident; a (terrible) disaster. ¶ ～을 당하다 suffer a disastrous accident.

**참빗** a fine-tooth(ed) bamboo comb.

**참빗살나무** 〖식물〗 a spindle tree.

**참사**(參事) a counselor; a secretary.
◉ ～관 an adviser; a councilor of an embassy.

**참사**(慘死) a tragic 〔miserable〕 death. ～하다 「meet with 〔come by〕 a tragic death; be cruelly murdered. ¶ 교통사고로 ～하다 be killed in a traffic accident. ◉ ～자 a person killed 《in a plane crash》. ～체 a mangled body.

**참사**(慘事) a tragedy; a disaster; a disastrous 〔terrible〕 accident; a catastrophe. ¶ 탄광의 ～ a terrible accident in a coal mine / 철도 ～ a terrible railway accident / ～를 일으키다 cause a terrible accident / 여객기 추락은 대～였다 The (air)plane crash was a tragic accident.

**참사람** a true 〔an honest〕 man; a good citizen. ¶ ～이 되다 become a new man; turn over a new leaf; reform *oneself*.

**참사랑** true love.

**참살**(斬殺) beheading; decapitation. ～하다 behead; decapitate. ¶ ～당하다 have *one's* head cut off; be beheaded 〔decapitated〕.

**참살**(慘殺) murder; slaughter; massacre (다수의). ～하다 slaughter; massacre; butcher; murder cruelly; kill without mercy. ¶ 일가족 7명이 ～되었다 All seven members of the family were brutally murdered. / 마을 사람들은 한 명도 남김없이 ～당했다 All the villagers were massacred in cold blood. ◉ ～사건 an atrocious murder case. ～시체 a mangled body 〔corpse〕. ～자 a brutal murderer.

**참상**(慘狀) a horrible 〔dreadful, terrible〕 scene; a miserable condition 〔state〕; a misery. ¶ 기근의 ～ the misery of a famine / 전쟁의 ～ the horrible scenes of war / ～을 보이다 〔드러내다〕 present a terrible sight 〔spectacle〕; be in a miserable 〔wretched〕 condition / ～을 목격하다 witness the terrible scene of a disaster / 사고 현장의 ～은 차마 눈뜨고 못 볼 지경이었다 The scene of the accident was too dreadful to behold. *or* The scene of the accident 「presented a horrible sight 〔was absolutely shocking〕.

**참새** 〖조류〗 a sparrow. ¶ ～떼 a flock of sparrows / ～처럼 재잘거리다 chat like a sparrow / ～가 죽어도 짹한다 《속담》 Tread on a worm, it will turn.

**참새우** 〖동물〗 a prawn.

**참서**(讖書) a book of prediction; a prophetic book.

**참석**(參席) attendance; presence; participation. ～하다 attend 《a meeting》; be present 《at a meeting》; present *oneself* 《at》; participate in; take part in. ¶ …～하에 with... in attendance; in the presence of... / 회의에 ～하다 sit as a member at a meeting / 많은 친구들이 그의 결혼식에 ～했다 A lot of friends 「attended 〔were presented at〕 his wedding. / 내일 밤의 축하 파티에 ～해 주시겠습니까 Won't you attend the celebration party tomorrow night? ◉ ～자 an attendant 《at》; 〔총칭〕 attendance; those present; 《참가자》 a participator.

**참선**(參禪) 〖불교〗 meditation in *Zen* Buddhism; 《수행》 practices of 〔in〕 *Zen* meditation. ～하다 practice *Zen* meditation 《in a temple》. ◉ ～자 a *Zen* practicer; a votary 〔votaress(여)〕.

**참섭**(參涉) 《참견》 meddling; meddlesomeness; interference; officiousness. ～하다 meddle in 〔with〕; interfere in; pry into; poke *one's* nose into. ¶ 남의 일에 ～하다 meddle in another's affairs / 사사로운 일에 ～하다 pry into 《*a person's*》 intimate affairs.

**참소**(讒訴) a false charge; (a) slander; calumny. ～하다 make a false charge 《against》; slander; calumniate. ◉ ～자 a slanderer; a calumniator.

**참수**(斬首) beheading; decapitation. ～하다 behead; decapitate. ¶ ～를 당하다 be beheaded; have *one's* head cut off.

**참숯** hardwood charcoal.

**참스쿨** 《신부 학교》 a charm school.

**참신**(斬新) originality; novelty. ～하다 (be) novel; original; up-to-date; innovative. ¶ ～한 디자인 a novel design / ～한 교수법 an up-to-date method of teaching / ～한 느낌이 들다 find something fresh 《in》/ ～한 맛을 내다 strike a fresh note; show originality 《in》.

**참언**(讒言) a false charge; (a) slander; calumny; defamation. ～하다 slander; calumniate; defame; make a false charge 《against》. ¶ ～에 빠지다 fall a victim to 《another's》 slanderous tongue. ◉ ～자 a slanderer; a calumniator.

**참언**(讖言) a prediction; a prophecy.

**참여**(參與) participation 《in public affairs》. ～하다 take part 〔participate〕 in. ¶ 국정에 ～하다 take part in the conduct of state affairs / 경영에 ～하다 have a voice in the management 《of》/ 이익 배당에 ～하다 share in the profits / 총선거는 국민이 국정에 직접 ～하는 유일한 기회다 The general election is the nation's sole chance directly to participate in government. ◉ ～정부 the participatory government.

**참예**(參詣) a visit 《to a temple 〔shrine〕》; worship; a pilgrimage. ～하다 visit 〔pay a visit to〕 《a temple 〔shrine〕》; worship at 《a shrine》; make a pilgrimage 《to》. ◉ ～자 a visitor 《to a shrine》; a worshiper; a pilgrim (순례자).

**참외** 〖식물〗 a (musk) melon. ◉ ～밭 a melon field 〔patch〕.

**참월**(僭越) presumptuousness; presumption; forwardness. ～하다 (be) presumptuous; arrogant; insolent; forward; audacious.

**참으로** 《정말》 truly; really; indeed; 《매우》 very; (very) much; quite; 《감탄》 how; what. ¶ ～ 고맙다 Thank you very much. / …은 ～ 유감스런 일이다 It is much to be regretted that.... *or* It is pity that.... / 그 소년은 ～ 영리하다 The boy is very clever indeed. / ～ 아름다운 장미다 What a beautiful rose it is! *or* How beautiful the rose is! / ~ 뻔뻔한 놈이군 What a nerve he's got! / 그는 ~ 위대한 정치가였다 He was a truly great politician.

**참으아리** 〖식물〗 a traveler's-joy.

**참을성**(—性) patience; endurance; forbearance; perseverance. ¶ ~이 있다 be patient; have patience; be forbearing; be persevering / ~이 없다 be impatient; lack patience 〔perseverance〕 / ~ 있게 patiently; with patience 〔perseverance, forbearance〕; perseveringly / 그는 ~ 있게 기다렸다 He waited patiently. / 그는 ~이 없다 He can stick to nothing.

**참의원**(參議院) the House of Councilors; the Upper House; the Senate (미국의). ◉ ~의원〔의장〕 a member 〔the President〕 of the House of Councilors.

**참작**(參酌) consideration; reference; allowance(s). ~하다 consider; take 《*a thing*》 into consideration 〔account〕; allow 〔make allowance(s)〕 for; refer to. ¶ ~할 만한 사정 extenuating circumstances / 정상을 ~하여 in consideration of extenuating circumstances; allowing for circumstances / …을 ~하지 않고 without any consideration of …; relentlessly / 사정을 ~하다 take circumstances into consideration; 「take account of 〔make allowances for〕 the circumstances / 정상을 ~하여 사형에서 한 등급 감형하다 commute the penalty of death by one degree on account of extenuating circumstances / 우리들은 그가 아직 어리다는 점을 ~해 주어야 한다 We have to make allowances for his youth.

**참작약**(—芍藥) 〖식물〗 a Chinese peony.

**참전**(參戰) participation in a war; entry into a war. ~하다 participate 〔take part〕 in the war; enter 〔join in〕 the war; go to war. ¶ ~하지 않다 stay 〔stand〕 out of a war / 유엔 측으로 ~하다 enter the war on the part of the United Nations.

**참정**(參政) participation in government. ~하다 participate in government.

**참정권**(參政權) suffrage; franchise; the right to vote. ¶ ~을 주다 enfranchise; grant 〔give, extend〕 the suffrage 〔franchise〕 《to》 / ~을 획득하다 acquire the franchise / ~을 잃다 forfeit the franchise. ◉ 여성~ woman 〔female〕 suffrage: 여성 ~ 운동 a movement for female suffrage / 여성 ~운동자 a suffragette; a woman suffragist.

**참조**(參照) reference; comparison; consultation. ~하다 refer to; consult; see; compare 《with》. ¶ 사전을 ~하다 consult 〔refer to〕 a dictionary / 앞 장(章)을 ~하다 refer to a preceding chapter / ~하라 see; *confer* (생략 cf.) (L.); *vide* (생략 v., vid.) (L.) / 제2장 ~ See 〔Cf.〕 chapter 2. / 30페이지 ~ See 〔Cf.〕 page 30. / (괄호 안에서) 그 항(項) ~ *quod vide* (생략 q.v.) (L.); which see / 각주(脚註)를 ~하라 Refer to the footnotes. *or* "See footnotes." / 자세한 것은 별지를 ~하여 주십시오 Please refer to the attached sheet for details. ◉ 전후~ 《같은 책 안에서의》 cross reference.

**참조기** 〖어류〗 a yellow corbina 〔croaker〕.

**참주**(僭主) a usurper (of the throne); a tyrant; a despot.

**참죽(나무)** 〖식물〗 a kind of redoak.

**참참**(站站) repeated stops 〔recesses, breaks〕; every stage. ¶ ~이 at intervals; once in a while; after a short interval / ~이 아프다 ache by fits and starts.

**참척하다** 《전념하다》 devote *oneself* 《to》; give *oneself* up wholly 《to *one's* work》; lose *oneself* 《in *one's* work》. ¶ 그는 무서운 열의로 일에 참척했다 He plunged into the work with a dreadful zest.

**참치** ① ⇨참치방어. ② 《통칭》 a tuna. ◉ ~방어 〖어류〗 a kind of yellowtail; *Elagatis bipinnulatus*(학명).

**참칭**(僭稱) assumption of a title; an unjustified title. ~하다 pretend to 《a throne》; assume the title 《of》; arrogate 《a title》 to *oneself*.

**참패**(慘敗) a crushing 〔a disastrous, a heavy〕 defeat; 《영패》 a shutout. ~하다 suffer 〔sustain〕 a crushing 〔disastrous〕 defeat; be beaten hollow; be crushed; be utterly 〔completely〕 defeated; 《영패하다》 be shut out (야구에서). ¶ 지난 번 선거에서 나는 상대 후보에게 ~당했다 In the last election, I was swamped by the other candidate.

**참하다** ① 《얌전하다》 (be) nice; pretty; fair; good; 《상당히 좋다》 (be) decent; respectable; 《성품이》 (be) gentle; mild; quiet; meek; modest. ¶ 참해 보이는 mild-looking〔-appearing〕; quiet=looking / 참한 아가씨 a pretty 〔nice=looking〕 girl; a modest girl / 참한 얼굴 a fair countenance 〔face〕 / 옷차림이 ~ be decently dressed. ② 《말쑥하다》

(be) trim; tidy; neat; smart; fair. ¶ 참한 방 a neat little room / 참한 집 a neat 〔snug〕 house; a house to *one's* taste 〔after *one's* fancy〕.

**참하다**(斬—) behead; decapitate; slay; put《*a person*》to the sword. 「date.

**참한하다**(—限—) wait till the due

**참해**(慘害) heavy 〔ruinous〕 damage. ¶ 전쟁의 ～ the horrors 〔ravages〕 of war / 폭격의 ～ bomb devastation / ～를 입다 suffer heavy 〔severe〕 damage《from a typhoon》; be hard hit / ～를 입히다 work havoc with《the crops》; wreak havoc on《the city》; cause severe damage.

**참형**(斬刑) decapitation; beheading. ¶ ～에 처하다 behead; cut the head off《a criminal》/ ～을 당하다 have *one's* head cut off; be beheaded.

**참형**(慘刑) a cruel 〔terrible〕 punishment; a merciless penalty.

**참호**(僭號) a self-assumed title.

**참호**(塹壕) a trench; a dugout; a sap. ¶ ～를 파다 dig 〔open〕 trenches; get entrenched; dig in. ◉ ～공사 trench work. ～생활 trench life. ～선 a trench line; entrenchments. ～열 〖병리〗 trench fever. ～전 trench warfare 〔fight〕.

**참혹**(慘酷) ①《잔인》(a) cruelty; (a) brutality; (an) atrocity. ～하다 (be) cruel; brutal; inhuman; atrocious; merciless. ¶ ～한 살인 a cruel 〔cold=blooded〕 murder / ～하게도 …하다 be cruel enough to《*do*》; have the cruelty to《*do*》/ ～한 짓을 하다 do a cruel thing; commit cruelties 〔atrocities〕/ 정말 ～하다 What a cruelty (it is). ②《비참》pitiableness; miserableness; wretchedness; distress. ～하다 (be) pitiable; piteous; miserable; wretched; terrible. ¶ ～한 생활《lead》a wretched life / 그지없이 ～하다 be in the depths of misery / ～한 죽음을 당하다 meet with a tragic death; die in misery 〔like a dog〕; die a miserable death / ～해서 눈뜨고 볼 수 없는 광경이었다 The sight was shocking 〔too miserable〕 to look at.

**참화**(慘禍) a terrible disaster; a crushing calamity; a tremendous catastrophe. ¶ 원폭의 ～ the great damage 〔ravage〕 by the atomic bomb / 전쟁의 ～를 입다 suffer the ravages 〔horrors〕 of war.

**참회**(參會) attendance. ⇨참석. ～하다 attend 〔be present at〕《a meeting》.

**참회**(懺悔)《뉘우침》penitence; repentance;《고백》(a) confession《of *one's* sins》. ～하다 repent《of *one's* sins》; be penitent; confess; make a confession《of》. ¶ ～의 눈물 penitential tears / ～의 생활 a penitential 〔penitent's〕 life / ～를 듣다 listen to《*a person's*》confessions《of》/ ～시키다 draw a confession from《*a person*》/ ～하여 죄를 용서받다 be confessed of a crime / ～하면 죄를 씻는다 Repentance wipes out sin. / 그녀는 자신의 죄를 신부에게 ～했다 She confessed her sins to the priest. ◉ ～록《책이름》*Confessions.* ～실 a confessional. ～자《개심한 사람》a repentant sinner; a penitent;《참회하는 사람》a confessant.

**참획**(參劃) participation in planning. ～하다 participate 〔have a hand〕《in》; take part《in》.

**찹쌀** glutinous rice; sticky rice. ¶ ～경단 rice-flour dumplings.

**찹찹하다** ①《물건이》be neatly piled 〔heaped〕 up; be stacked in good order. ②《마음이》(be) calm and serene; self-possessed; composed.

**찻간**(車間) the inside of a train 〔car〕; a railway carriage; a compartment. ¶ ～에 들여오다 take 〔bring〕《*a thing*》into the carriage.

**찻감**(茶—) stuff to make tea out of.

**찻길**(車—) ①《궤도》a (train) track; a railroad. ②《차도》a roadway; a driveway《미》.

**찻물**(茶—) tea (to drink). ¶ ～이 잘 우러나다 tea draws 〔brews〕 well.

**찻삯**(車—) (a) (car)fare; traffic expenses;《운반료》carriage; cartage.

**찻숟가락**(茶—) a teaspoon. ¶ ～으로 하나 a teaspoonful《of sugar》.

**찻잎**(茶—) tea leaves.

**찻잔**(茶盞) a teacup. 「for tea-things.

**찻장**(茶欌) a tea cabinet; a cupboard

**찻종**(茶鍾) a teacup; a teabowl. ¶ 차를 ～에 따르다 pour tea into a cup.

**찻집**(茶—) a teahouse; a tearoom; a coffeehouse. ⇨다방(茶房).

**창**[1]《구두의》sole leather; the sole of a shoe. ¶ 밑창 an outer sole / 속창 an inner sole / 안창 a liner / 창이 나가다 shoe soles get 〔are〕 worn out / 창을 갈(아대)다 put a new sole《on》; resole;《시켜서》have *one's* shoes resoled《by》.

**창**[2]《구멍》a hole made in paper 〔cloth〕; a tear; a rent. ¶ 저고리에 난 창 a tear in the coat / 창(이) 나다 a hole is made 《in cloth》; get a hole in 《*a thing*》 / 창이 난 곳을 깁다 《옷의》 cover a hole.

**창**(窓) a window; a sash window (내리닫이); a casement (window) (여닫이); 《배의》 a port(hole); 《채광창》 a skylight.
¶ 창틀 a window frame; a window sash / 창가에 서다 stand at a window / 창을 열다 open a window; raise 〔pull up〕 a window / 창을 열어 두다 leave a window open 〔up〕 / 창을 닫다 shut 〔close, let down〕 a window / 창을 닫아 두다 keep a window shut 〔closed, down〕 / 창 밖을 내다보다 look out (of) a window / 창으로 안을 들여다보다 look into 〔in at〕 a window / 창 밖으로 몸을 내밀다 lean out of a window / 창 밖으로 머리를 내밀다 stick *one's* head out of a window / 창으로 들어가다 get in by a window / 창에서 뛰어내리다 jump (down) from a window / 창 밖의 경치가 좋다 The window commands a very fine view. / 창 너머는 잔디밭이다 The window looks out upon a lawn. / 도둑은 창으로 침입했다 The thief entered by the window. / 눈은 마음의 창이다 The eyes are the windows of the mind.

**창**(槍) a spear; a javelin (투창 경기의); a lance (기병 등의). ¶ 창대 a spear handle / 창끝 a spearhead / 창으로 찌르다 spear 《*a person*》; thrust 〔plunge〕 a spear 《into an enemy's breast》 / 창을 쓰다 wield 〔brandish〕 a spear / 창을 꼬나잡다 couch *one's* spear.

**창가**(娼家) a brothel; a house of ill fame; a bawdy house.

**창가**(唱歌) 《노래함》 singing; 《노래》 a song; vocal music. ～하다 sing.
◉ ～집 a collection of songs.

**창간**(創刊) the first publication 〔edition〕; foundation 《of a periodical》. ～하다 launch 《a newspaper》; found 〔start〕 《a periodical》. ¶ 그 잡지는 ～된 지 10년이 되었다 The magazine has been in existence for ten years. / 1920년 ～《표시》 Founded 〔First published〕 in 1920. ◉ ～기념호 a special number in commemoration of the foundation. ～호 the first 〔initial, inaugural〕 number 〔issue〕: ～호를 내다 issue 《*its*》 initial number.

**창갈이** 《구두의》 resoling; sole-repairing. ～하다 resole (shoes); put a new sole 《on》; 《시켜서》 have *one's* shoes resoled 《by》.

**창건**(創建) foundation; establishment; organization; inauguration. ⇨ 창업(創業). ～하다 found; establish; organize; start; inaugurate; create. ¶ 그 회사는 ～된 지 오래지 않다 It is not very long since the company was established.

**창견**(創見) an original view 〔idea〕; 「originality; invention.

**창고**(倉庫) a warehouse; a storehouse; a depot (building). ¶ ～에 보관하다〔넣다〕 warehouse; store 《goods》; put 〔deposit〕 《goods》 in storage 〔a warehouse〕. ◉ ～계원〔관리인〕 a warehouseman; a storekeeper. ～과 a warehouse section. ～료 warehouse charges. ～업 warehousing; the warehousing industry: ～업자 a warehouseman. ～인도 『상업』 ex store 〔warehouse〕. ～증권 a warehouse bond. ～회사 a warehouse 〔storage〕 company.

**창공**(蒼空) a blue 〔an azure〕 sky; the blue heavens; the vault of heaven.

**창구**(窓口) a window; a wicket; 《은행 따위의》 a counter. ¶ ～에서 사무를 보다 attend at the window / ～의 서비스가 나쁘다〔를 개선하다〕 give poor 〔better〕 service at the window / 등기 우편은 6번 ～입니다 Registered mail is handled at window No. 6. / 5번 ～로 가십시오 《은행 따위에서》 Please go to window No. 5. /공공요금은 이 ～에서 내실 수 있습니다 You can pay your public utility bills at this counter.
◉ ～계원 a clerk at the window. 매표～ a ticket window. 출납～ a cashier's 〔teller's (은행의)〕 window 〔cage〕.

**창구**(創口) a cut; a gash; a slit.

**창구**(艙口) 『해양』 a hatch; a hatchway.

**창궐**(猖獗) rage; fury; rampancy; rifeness; virulence. ～하다 rage; be rife 〔virulent, rampant〕. ¶ 유행성 감기가 ～하고 있다 Influenza is raging (just now).

**창극**(唱劇) a Korean classical opera.
◉ ～조(調) an aria.

**창기**(娼妓) a prostitute. ⇨ 창녀(娼女).

**창나무** 《키의》 a tiller; a helm.

**창난젓** salted pollack guts.

**창녀**(娼女) a prostitute; a street-girl; a trollop; a streetwalker; a woman of the street; a harlot; a whore. ¶ ～출신 an ex-prostitute / ～가 되다 enter into 〔practice〕 prostitution / ～로 팔리다 be sold for prostitution / ～와 놀다 consort with a whore; go to bed with a prostitute / 몸값을 물고 ～를 빼내다 ransom 〔buy the freedom of〕 a prostitute / ～생활을 하다 live on the street.

**창달**(暢達) development; growth; promotion; progress. ¶ 언론 ～에 공헌하다 contribute to the promotion of the freedom of speech.

**창당**(創黨) the formation 〔organization〕 of a political party. ～하다 form 〔organize〕 a political party. ¶ ～식을 거행하다 inaugurate a political party / 그는 2년에 걸친 은퇴를 거두고 정치 복귀와 그의 ～계획을 발표했다 He announced his political comeback after two years' retirement and his plan to create a new party.
◉ ～당원 a charter member of a party. ～이념 founding ideology (of a party). ～정신 the founding spirit of a party; the spirit underlying the formation of the party.

**창던지기**(槍—) the javelin (throw). ～하다 throw a javelin. ◉ ～선수 a javelin thrower.

**창도**(唱道) advocacy. ～하다 advocate; propose; preach; advance 〔introduce〕 《a new doctrine》. ¶ 자유를 ～하다 espouse the cause of liberty; preach 〔uphold〕 liberty / 신학설을 ～하다 advance 〔introduce〕 a new theory. ◉ ～자 an advocate; a proponent.

**창독**(瘡毒) 〖한의학〗 the infection in a boil; the virus of a boil.

**창립**(創立) founding; foundation; establishment; organization. ～하다 establish; found; organize; build; set up; start. ¶ ～ 50주년을 축하하다 celebrate the 50th anniversary of the foundation 《of a school》 / 이 학교는 ～된 지 30년이 된다 This school has reached the 30th year of its existence. / 하버드 대학은 1636년에 ～되었다 Harvard University saw the light of day in 1636. / 그 회사는 ～된 지 얼마 안 된다 It is not very long since the company was established. ◉ ～기념식 a ceremony marking the 《school's 50th》 founding anniversary. ～기념일 the anniversary of the founding 〔establishment〕 《of a school》. ～위원회 〔사무실〕 an organizing committee 〔office〕. ～자 the founder 〔foundress (여자)〕; the organizer. ～총회 the inaugural 〔first general〕 meeting. ～취지서 a prospectus. 대학 ～이사장 the chairperson of a university foundation.

**창만**(脹滿) 〖의학〗 abdominal dropsy.

**창망**(蒼茫) a boundless 〔vast〕 expanse 《of water》. ～하다 (be) vast; boundless.

**창문**(窓門) a window. ⇨ 창(窓). ¶ ～ 밖으로 손이나 얼굴을 내밀지 마라 Don't put your head or hands out of the window.

**창받다** 《신바닥에》 put a sole on (a shoe); 《버선에》 put a patch on (a sock).

**창백**(蒼白) pallor; pallidness. ～하다 (be) pale; deathly white 〔pale〕; pallid; white (as a sheet). ¶ 얼굴이 ～해지다 turn pale 〔white〕 《with fear》 / 친구의 갑작스런 부음(訃音)에 그의 얼굴은 ～해졌다 When he heard the unexpected news of his friend's death, he turned pale.

**창법**(槍法) spearmanship.

**창병**(槍兵) a spearman; a lanceman.

**창병**(瘡病) 《매독》 syphilis; a secret disease 《미구어》.

**창부**(倡夫) an actor.

**창부**(娼婦) a prostitute. ⇨ 창녀(娼女).

**창살**(窓—) 《문의》 a lattice; a latticework; a lattice strip; a frame; a grille; iron bars (감옥의). ¶ ～ 없는 감옥 a prison without bars. ◉ ～문 a latticed door.

**창상**(創傷) a gash; a wound 〔injury〕 (by an edged weapon); a cut.

**창생**(蒼生) the people; the populace; the masses.

**창설**(創設) establishment; founding; organization. ⇨ 창립(創立).

**창성**(昌盛) prosperity; flourishing; thriving. ～하다 prosper; thrive; flourish; be prosperous; do well.

**창세**(創世) the creation of the world. ◉ ～기 〖성서〗 The Book of Genesis; 《약칭》 Genesis (생략 Gen.).

**창술**(槍術) spearmanship; the art of spearfighting. ◉ ～가 a spearman; an expert with the spear.

**창시**(創始) origination; creation; establishment; foundation. ～하다 originate; create; found; establish; initiate. ¶ 그건 K씨가 ～한 것이다 It originated with 〔It was invented by〕 Mr. K. ◉ ～자 the originator; the founder; the initiator.

**창안**(創案) an original plan 〔idea〕. ¶ 이 것은 그의 ～이다 The idea 〔plan〕 originated with him. / 이 기계는 A박사가 ～한 것이다 This machine has originated from 〔is originally designed by〕 Dr. A. ◉ ～자 the originator; the inventor.

**창애** a trap; a gin. ¶ ～에 걸리다 get caught in a trap.

**창업**(創業) ①《국가의》 the foundation 〔establishment〕 of a country. ～하다 found 〔establish〕 a country. ②《사업의》 inauguration of an enterprise. ～하다 inaugurate 〔start〕 an enterprise. ¶ ～한 이래 since the foundation / ～30주년을 축하하다 celebrate the 30th anniversary of foundation / ～은 쉬우나 이를 지키기는 어렵다 The difficulty is not to start an enterprise, but to carry it to final success. / 폐사는 ～된 지 100년이 되었습니다 It is one hundred years since this company was established. ◉ ～비 initial expenses 〔expenditure〕; the costs of starting up a business 〔an enterprise〕. ～자 the founder.

**창연**(蒼鉛) 〖화학〗 bismuth. ¶ ～의 bismuthal; bismuthic. ◉ ～산 bismuthic acid. ～중독 bismuth poisoning; bismuthism. 차질산(次窒酸)～ bismuth subnitrate.

**창연하다**(愴然—) (be) sad; sorrowful. ¶ 창연히 sadly; sorrowfully; mournfully.

**창연하다**(蒼然—) 《푸릇푸릇하다》 (be) dark blue; bluish; 《어둑어둑하다》 (be) dim; gloomy; gray; shady; somber; 《고색이》 (be) antiquated; patinated; timeworn. ¶ 고색 창연한 antique-looking / 고색 창연한 옛절 an old temple with the patina of age.

**창유리**(窓琉璃) 《끼워져 있는》 a (window-) pane; 《창문용 유리》《a pane of》 window glass. ¶ ～를 깨(뜨리)다 break a windowpane / ～를 끼우다 glaze a window. ◉ ～닦개《자동차의》 a windshield washer 〔cleaner〕.

**창의**(創意) an original idea; 《독창성》 originality; 《연구·발명의 재능》 ingenuity. ¶ ～적인 original; inventive; ingenious / ～력이 부족하다 lack originality 〔creative power〕; be lacking in invention / ～력을 발휘하다 use *one's* originality; exercise 〔exert〕 *one's* ingenuity / ～적인 기술 개발로 값싼 고급 상품을 개발하기 위해 노력하다 make efforts to develop cheap but quality commodities through creative development of technologies / 그녀는 ～력이 풍부하다 She is a woman of ideas. *or* She has a creative talent. / 그것은 전적으로 그의 ～에 의한 것이다 It is entirely original with him. *or* That comes entirely from his originality.

**창이**(創痍) a wound. ¶ 만신 ～가 되다 be covered all over with wounds; be thoroughly hurt 〔injured〕; have cuts all over *one's* body.

**창일**(漲溢) overflow; inundation. ～하다 overflow; inundate; flood.

**창자** 《대장·소장》 the intestines; the bowels; 《내장》 the entrails; the guts (동물의). ¶ ～의 intestinal; enteric / 생선의 ～를 빼내다 remove the guts from a fish; gut a fish / ～가 끊어지듯이 배가 아프다 have a splitting stomachache.

**창작**(創作) 《만들어 냄》 creation; 《제작》 production; 《소설을 씀》 story 〔fiction〕 writing; 《창작품》 a creative 〔an original〕 work; a creation 《of a great artist》; 《소설》 a novel; fiction [총칭]. ～하다 create; invent; 《소설을 쓰다》 write a novel 〔story〕. ¶ ～적인 creative; original / ～에 종사하다 engage in writing a creative 〔an original〕 work; engage in the profession of letters / ～을 그만두다 quit writing 〔penning〕 novels. ◉ ～가 a creator; an originator; a creative 〔story, fiction〕 writer; a novelist. ～력 creative power 〔talent〕. ～연습 practices in creative writing. ～욕 a creative urge. ～활동 creative activity; writing.

**창제**(創製) (an) invention; creation; origination. ～하다 [사람이 주어] create; invent; [사물이 주어] originate with 《*a person*》.

**창조**(創造) creation. ～하다 create; make; call into being. ¶ ～적(인) creative; 《독창적》 original / ～적 예술〔예술가〕 a creative art 〔artist〕 / ～적 진화 creative evolution / ～의 재능 creative genius / 천지 ～의 신화 a creative myth / 천지～ 이래 since the creation of the world / 하느님은 만물을 ～하셨다 God created all things. ◉ ～력 creative power 〔faculty〕; creativity; originality (독창성). ～물 a creature; creation [총칭]. ～성 creativity. ～자 a creator; 《신》 the Creator. 천지～ the Creation.

**창졸**(倉卒) suddenness; abruptness; unexpectedness; precipitation; hurry. ～하다 (be) sudden; unexpected; hurried. ¶ ～간에 suddenly; abruptly; in the midst of great hurry / ～히 떠나게 되어 그에게 작별 인사도 못했다 I was in such a rush that I didn't even get to say good-by to him. / ～간이라서 그 사람 이름을 묻는 것도 잊었

다 In the hurry of the moment I forgot to ask his name. 「tympanites.

**창증**(脹症) 〖한의〗 abdominal dropsy;

**창창하다**(蒼蒼—) ① 《푸르다》 (be) deep blue 〔green〕; azure. ¶ 창창한 바다 the blue sea; the deep / 창창한 하늘 a deep blue sky. ② 《멀다》 be far off 〔away〕; 《아득하다》 (be) remote; dim; uncertain; long; 《끝없다》 (be) vast; boundless. ¶ 갈 길이 아직도 ~ still have a long way to go 〔before *one*〕 / 앞길이 ~ be still young; have a long future before *one*.

**창천**(蒼天) a blue 〔an azure〕 sky.

**창칼** ① 《작은 칼》 a small knife; a pointed knife (공작용). ② 《찬칼》 a kitchen knife.

**창틀**(窓—) a window frame.

**창파**(滄波) sea waves; billows; big rollers. ¶ 만경~ ⇨ 만경창파.

**창포**(菖蒲) 〖식물〗 an iris (*pl.* ~es, irides); a (sweet) flag; a sweet rush.

**창피**(猖披) shame; disgrace; dishonor; (a) humiliation; an insult (모욕). ~하다, ~스럽다 be a shame; (be) shameful; scandalous; disgraceful; ignominious; 《초라하다》 (be) unsightly; shabby; miserable; unpresentable.

¶ 큰 ~ an open 〔a public〕 disgrace; a burning 〔crying〕 shame / ~한 일 a shame; a disgrace / ~를 〔~한 꼴을〕 당하다 be put to shame; disgrace 〔humiliate〕 *oneself;* bring disgrace upon *oneself;* be put out of countenance; be disgraced 〔insulted〕 in public / ~를 주다 shame; put 〔bring〕 《*a person*》 to shame; make 《*a person*》 blush 〔ashamed〕; put 《*a person*》 out of countenance; humiliate 《*a person*》; insult; 《크게》 shame 〔disgrace〕 《*a person*》 publicly / ~를 알다 have a sense of honor / ~해서 머리를 숙이다 hang *one's* head for shame / ~해서 얼굴을 붉히다 blush with shame / ~를 무릅쓰고 돈을 꿔달라하다 swallow *one's* pride to ask 《*a person*》 to lend *one* money / …하는 것을 ~하게 여기다 think 〔feel〕 shame to 《*do*》 / ~하게 여기지 않다 be lost 〔dead〕 to (all sense of) shame / ~하다 어서 가자 What a disgrace, let leave here at once. / 그게 무슨 ~니 What a disgrace! *or* Shame on you! / ~하게 이런 초라한 옷으로야 어디 나다닐 수 있나 I can't possibly go out in such miserable clothes.

**창해**(滄海) a blue expanse of water; the (vast blue) sea; the ocean.
◉ ~일속(一粟) a drop in the ocean.

**창호**(窓戶) windows and doors. ~하다 paper a window frame 〔a doorframe〕.
◉ ~지 window paper; paper for doors: ~지를 바르다 paste the paper on the window frame 〔doorframe〕.

**창화**(倉貨) warehouse goods.

**창황**(蒼黃·倉皇) hurry; haste; precipitation; flurry. ~하다 be in haste; be in a great hurry; be in a rush 〔flurry〕. ¶ ~히 with precipitation; hastily; hurriedly; in great haste 〔great hurry〕 / ~히 달아나다 run away helter-skelter; beat a hasty retreat.
◉ ~망조(罔措) a flurry: ~망조하다 be panic-stricken; be upset; lose *one's* head.

**찾다** ① 《행방·소재를》 search 《for》; be on the search 《for》; look for 〔up〕; seek for 〔after〕 (★ seek for는 사람·물건을 찾을 때, seek after 「탐구·추구하다」는 추상적인 뜻에 쓰임: seek for 《a person, a place, an object》; seek after 《happiness, truth》); 《수색하다》 hunt (up); track down; locate (소재를); make inquiry 〔a search〕 for. ¶ …을 찾아(서) 《start》 in search of 《the lost child》 / 집안을 ~ search a house 《for *something*》 / 실종된 사람을 ~ track down a missing person / 지도에서 부산을 ~ look up 〔out〕 Pusan on 〔in〕 a map / 집주소를 ~ look for the location of a house; try to locate a house / 찾고 있다 be in search for 〔of〕; be looking for; be on the look out for / 찾아 헤매다 search 〔look〕 about for 《*a thing*》; scout 〔scrounge〕 around 《for》 / 여기저기를 찾아 헤매다 hunt 「up and down 〔everywhere〕 / 책을 찾느라고 온 집안을 뒤지다 look all over the house for a book / 찾을 것이 있다 have something to look for / …을 찾으러 가다 go looking for...; go in search 〔quest〕 of... / 잔디밭에서 바늘 찾기 looking for a needle in a haystack.

② 《찾아내다》 find (out); discover; detect; locate; run down; hunt 〔seek〕 out; rummage 《the barn for a shovel》; ferret 〔pry〕 out; scent 〔smell, sniff〕 out; trace. ¶ 범인을 ~ trace a criminal / 아무의 거처를 ~ locate 〔find out〕 *a person's* whereabouts / 잃어버린 반지를 ~ find *one's* lost ring / 우연히 보물을 ~ find a treasure by accident.

③ 《구하다·요구하다》 seek 《for》; look

out for; look for; hunt for; be out after. ¶ 행복을 찾아 in search 〔pursuit, quest〕 of happiness / 셋집을 ~ look for a house to let / 연줄을 ~ hunt up connections / 일자리를 ~ hunt for 〔look out for〕 a job.

④ 《방문하다》 call on 《*a person*》; call at 《a house》; visit; pay 〔make〕 a visit to; come 〔go round〕 to see; pay 《*a person*》 a call. ¶ 찾아온 사람 a caller; a visitor / 친구를 ~ call on a friend / 갑자기 찾아가다 pay a surprise visit to 《*a person*》 / 찾는 사람도 없이 외롭게 살고 있다 live in unvisited loneliness / 단풍을 보러 설악산을 ~ visit Mt. Sŏrak to see the autumn leaves / 떠나기 전에 찾아볼 사람이 몇 있다 I have a few calls to make before I leave. / 어제 시골서 친구가 찾아 왔었다 I had a visit yesterday from a friend from the country. / 언제쯤 찾아뵐까요 When shall I call at your house 〔on you〕? / 내주 찾아 뵙겠습니다 I'll come and see you next week. (★ 상대방의 집을 방문할 때는 go가 아니고 come).

⑤ 《원리·근원 따위를》 trace. ¶ 근원을 ~ trace 《*something*》 to *its* origin 〔source〕; get at the root of 《*something*》 / 어원을 ~ trace the etymology of a word.

⑥ 《사전 따위를》 look up 《a word in a dictionary》; refer to 〔consult, go to〕 《a dictionary》. ¶ 낱말의 뜻을 알기 위해 사전을 ~ consult a dictionary for the meaning of a word / 사전 찾는 법을 모른다 I do not know how to 「go to 〔consult〕 a dictionary. / 그 단어의 철자를 모르거든 사전을 찾아보아라 Refer to a dictionary if you cannot spell the word.

⑦ 《되찾다》 take 〔get〕 back; have 《it》 back; retake; regain; retrieve; restore; 《잡힌 것을》 redeem 《a mortgage, pawned goods》; 《미》 lift 〔pay off〕 《a mortgage》. ¶ 빌려준 돈을 다시 ~ get back the money which had been lent / 잃었던 영토를 ~ regain *its* lost territory / 이전 지위를 다시 ~ retrieve *one's* former position / 전당포에서 시계를 ~ redeem 〔reclaim〕 a watch from the pawnshop; get a watch out of hock.

⑧ 《예금을》 draw out 〔from〕. ¶ 은행에서 예금을 ~ draw *one's* money 《deposit》 from *one's* bank; check out *one's* deposit (수표로) / 은행에서 수표로 50만원을 ~ draw a check on the bank for 500,000 won.

**찾을모** 《장점》 a merit; a good 〔strong〕 point; 《가치》 value; worth. ¶ ~ 없는 worthless; good-for-nothing / 이 책에는 ~가 하나도 없다 This book has nothing to recommend it.

**채**[1] 《길이》 the length (of a long and slender object).

**채**[2] 《수레·가마의》 (bearing) poles; shafts. ¶ 가마 채 a palanquin pole / 상여 채 pallbearers' poles on a funeral bier.

**채**[3] ① 《채찍》 a whip; a rod; a cane; a switch. ⇨ 채찍. ¶ 종아리 채 a cane to use on the legs / 파리 채 a fly swatter 〔flap〕. ② 『악기』 a drum-stick; a stick; a pick.

**채**[4] 《고루 안 먹은 물》 uneven dye; spotty 〔streaky〕 coloring. ¶ 채가 지다 be uneven 〔streaky〕 in dyeing; be dyed unevenly.

**채**[5] ① 《건물》 a section of a building; a building; a wing. ¶ 본 채 the main house 〔building, wing〕 / 딴 채 a separate building / 사랑 채 a detached building 〔the detached wing of a house〕 used for a reception room. ② 《집을 셀 때》 ¶ 집 두 채 two houses / 이 마을에는 20채 안쪽의 농가가 있다 This hamlet consists of less than twenty farmhouses.

**채**[6] 《잘게 썰기》 shredding vegetables, cutting in thin strips; 《썬 것》 thin strips (of a vegetable); shredded vegetables; vegetable shreds. ¶ 무를 채치다 cut a radish into fine strips.

**채**[7] ① 《아직》 《not》 yet; as yet; so far; before; 《겨우》 only. ¶ 날이 채 밝기도 전에 before light / 3분도 채 못되어 in less than three minutes / 열 달이 채 되지 못하다 it is not yet ten months / 사과가 채 익지 않다 an apple isn't ripe yet / 그의 말이 채 끝나기도 전에 before he could finish his sentence / 채 자리가 잡히지 않다 《일이》 be not yet on the right track / 1마일도 채 못가서 소나기를 만났다 I had not gone a mile before I was caught in a shower.

② 《정도에 덜 참》 completely; up to. ¶ 쌀이 열 말이 채 되지 못하다 rice doesn't amount to ten *mal;* rice falls short of ten *mal.*

**채**[8] 《그대로》 just as it is 〔stands〕; intact; with no change; (in) the original state of. ¶ 불을 켠 채로 자다 sleep with the electric light on / 미해

결인 채로 남아 있다 remain unsolved 〔unsettled〕/ 산 채로 묻다 bury 《*a person*》 alive / 나무는 넘어진 채로 있다 The tree lies as it fell. / 아기가 입을 벌린 채 잠자고 있다 The baby is sleeping with its mouth open. / 책은 펼쳐진 채였다 The book was lying open. / 그는 모자를 쓴 채 나에게 인사했다 He greeted me with his hat on. / 신을 신은 채로 들어와도 좋다 You can come right in with your shoes on. / 의자에 앉은 채 그는 우리를 맞았다 He greeted us from his chair (without getting up). / 누가 수돗물을 틀어 놓은 채로 두었는가 Who has left the water running?

**채**(菜) 《반찬의》 vegetable salad; a cold dish of sliced vegetables dressed with seasonings and vinegar. ¶ 오이채 a cold dish of sliced cucumbers.

**채결**(採決) ballot taking; a vote; 《미》 a roll call; 《영》 a division (의회 등에서). ~하다 vote 〔take a vote〕 《on》. ¶ ~에 부치다 put 《*a matter*》 to a vote / ~에 들어가다 come to a vote / 가부(可否)를 ~하다 take the ayes and noes / ~을 요구하다 call for a division 〔vote〕 《on *a matter*》.

**채고추** long fine slices of (red) pepper.

**채광**(採光) lighting. ~하다 light; let in light; admit light. ¶ ~이 좋은〔나쁜〕 방 a well-〔poorly-〕lit room / ~이 나쁘다 be ill lighted. ◉ ~창 《천창》 a skylight; 《문 위의》 a fanlight; 《미》 a transom (window).

**채광**(採鑛) mining. ~하다 mine; work 《a mine》; dig for 《minerals》. ◉ ~공학 mine engineering. ~권 mining rights. ~기계 mining machinery.

**채굴**(採掘) mining; digging; exploitation; working. ~하다 dig out; mine 《gold, coal》; work 〔exploit〕 《a mine》. ¶ 금광을 ~하다 work 〔exploit〕 a gold mine / 석탄을 ~하다 mine 〔extract, dig〕 coal. ◉ ~권 mining rights; a mining concession. ~량 outturn; output. ~료 mining rent. ~업자 a mine operator. ~장 a stope (계단식의). ~지 diggings. ~출원인 a digging applicant.

**채권**(債券) 〖경제〗 a (loan) bond; a debenture. ¶ ~의 소유자 a bondholder / 5푼 이자의 ~ five percent (loan) bonds / ~을 발행〔상환〕하다 issue 〔redeem〕 bonds / ~을 사다 buy a bond. ◉ ~액면(가격) the face value of a bond. ~입찰제 the bond bidding system; 《아파트의》 the bond-accompanied apartment bidding system. 개발~ a development bond. 기명~ a registered bond: 무기명 ~ a bond to bearer. 무담보~ a plain bond. 유기한〔무기한〕~ a redeemable 〔perpetual〕 bond.

**채권**(債權) credit; a claim. ¶ ~ 확정의 소송 an action for settling claims / 그에 대한 ~이 있다 I'm his creditor. *or* I have a claim on 〔against〕 him. ◉ ~국 a creditor power 〔nation〕. ~담보 security for an obligation. ~법 the law of obligations. ~순위 the order of credit. ~신고 기간 the period for reporting obligation. ~압류인 a garnisher. ~압류통고 garnishment. ~양도 cession 〔assignment〕 of an obligation. ~자 a creditor; an obligee: ~자들이 몰려들다 have *one's* door thronged 〔besieged〕 by creditors. ~표 a list of claims.

**채귀**(債鬼) a dun; a creditor. ¶ ~에 시달리다 be dunned; be harassed 〔tormented〕 by creditors; have many duns at *one's* heels.

**채그릇** a wicker vessel; wickerware.

**채근**(採根) ~하다 《뿌리를》 dig roots out; 《근원을》 trace 《*a thing*》 to its origin; 《독촉하다》 press 《*a person* for *a thing*》; urge 《*a person* to *do*》; demand; call upon 《*a person* to *do*》.

**채금**(採金) mining gold; gold mining. ~하다 mine 〔dig〕 gold.

**채꾼** a boy cowhand.

**채널** 〖TV〗 a channel. ¶ ~7에 on Channel 7 / ~을 맞추다 pick up 〔select〕 a channel / ~을 딴 데로 돌리다 change the channel / 제4 ~로 돌리다 turn to Channel 4 / (집에서) ~권을 쥐고 있다 have 〔hold〕 a monopoly of the TV channels 《in *one's* family》 / ~3번에서는 무엇을 하나 What is on Channel 3? / 우리 TV는 ~6의 화면이 선명치 않다 Channel 6 is poorly received on our TV set. ◉ ~간 접속기 〖컴퓨터〗 a channel to channel adapter. ~다툼 a dispute over which television program 《they》 should watch.

**채다**[1] 《값이》 the price rises 〔goes up〕 a little.

**채다**[2] ① snatch 《*a thing*》 away 《out of, off》; take 《*a thing*》 by force; tear 《*a thing*》 from 《*a person*》; 《가로채다》 steal 〔snatch, take〕 《*a thing*》 out of 《*a person's*》 possession 〔hands〕; 《덮치어》 swoop off. ¶ 병아리를 채가다 《솔개

등이》 pounce on a chicken and fly off with it / 한 젊은 사내가 그녀의 손에서 핸드백을 채갔다 A young man snatched the handbag from her hand and rushed away.
② 《확 당기다》 jerk; pull with a jerk. ¶ 낚싯대를 ~ jerk *one's* fishing rod out / 소매를 잡아 ~ jerk 《*a person*》 by the sleeve.

**채다**[3] 《눈치·낌새를》 sense; suspect; spot; smell out 《the secret》; get wind 〔scent〕 of; become aware 《of, that》. ¶ 좋아하지 않음을 눈치 ~ sense that people don't like *one* / 알아채게 하다 make 《*a person*》 aware 《of》 / (남에게) 눈치(를) 채지 못하도록 하다 avoid 《*another's*》 suspicion.

**채다**[4] ① 《걷어채다》 get kicked; get a kick; 《돌부리에》 stumble 《over, upon, against》. ¶ 당나귀에 ~ get kicked by a donkey / 돌부리에 ~ trip on 〔against〕 a stone / 옆구리를 ~ get a kick 〔get kicked〕 on the side. ② 《빼앗기다》 get 《*something*》 snatched 〔seized, taken, stolen〕. ¶ 돈지갑을 ~ have *one's* purse snatched. ③ 《딱지맞다》 be rejected 〔rebuffed〕; be refused; 《특히 애인에게》 be jilted.

**채단**(綵緞) silk stuffs; silks.

**채도**(彩度) 〖미술·사진〗 chroma; saturation.

**채독**(菜毒) a vegetable-borne disease. ¶ ~에 걸리다 get 〔suffer from〕 a vegetable-borne disease.

**채동지**(蔡同知) a 〔an empty〕 boaster; a braggart; a gasbag.

**채둥우리** a large wicker basket.

**채록**(採錄) recording in a book. ~하다 select 〔extract〕 《a passage》 and put 《it》 on record; record. ¶ ~되어 있다 [책이 주어] contain 《a word》; [낱말 등이 주어] be given 〔found〕 《in a dictionary》.

**채롱**(一籠) a box-shaped wicker basket; a hamper.

**채료**(彩料) coloring materials; (an artist's) colors; pigment; paints. ¶ 수채화〔유화〕 ~ water 〔oil〕 colors / ~로 그리다 paint; color 《a picture》. ◉ ~그릇 a palette.

**채마**(菜麻) garden vegetables. ⇨ 채소(菜蔬).

**채무**(債務) a debt; a financial obligation; liabilities. ¶ ~가 있다 have debts 《of 3 million won》; be liable for debts; owe 《*a person* 600,000 won》; be 〔stand〕 in 《*a person's*》 debt / ~를 상환하다 refund 〔repay〕 *one's* debt / ~를 이행하다 meet 〔discharge〕 *one's* liabilities 〔obligations〕; settle 〔pay〕 *one's* debt / ~를 청산하다 liquidate *one's* liabilities; clear up *one's* debts / 그 사람한테 ~가 있다 I stand in his debt. *or* I am indebted to him. / 그 나라는 우리 나라에 대해 5년 상환의 ~를 지고 있다 That country holds liabilities repayable over five years to our country.
◉ ~국 a debtor country 〔nation〕. ~면제 waiver of an obligation. ~불이행 default on 〔nonfulfillment of〕 financial obligations. ~상환 redemption of a debt: ~상환 비율 debt service ratio (생략 DSR). ~소멸 expiration of an obligation. ~승계 succession to liabilities. ~승인 acknowledgment of an obligation. ~이행 fulfillment of an obligation: 그는 나에게 ~이행을 독촉했다 He urged me to pay my debt to him. ~자 a debtor; a loanee; 〖법〗 an obligor. ~증서 a bond; an obligation. 고정~ fixed liabilities 〔indebtedness〕.

**채문**(彩紋·彩文) a design; 《지폐의》 a watermark.

**채반**(一盤) ① 《그릇》 a wicker tray. ¶ ~이 용수가 되게 우긴다 be stubbornly unreasonable. ② 《신부의》 (a bride's) delicacies taking home 《to her parents》.

**채반상**(一盤相) 《얼굴》 a moon 〔big round flat〕 face; 《사람》 a person who has a flat face.

**채받이** beef rump.

**채발** a long and slender foot.

**채벌**(採伐) (tree) felling; deforestation. ⇨ 벌채. ~하다 fell; cut down.

**채변** polite hesitancy (to accept *something*). ¶ ~ 말고 많이 드십시오 Don't feel you have to be polite, take lots. *or* Please help yourself without ceremony.

**채비**(一備) 《준비》 preparations; (preliminary) arrangements; 《치장》 a getup; (an) outfit; equipment. ~하다 prepare 《for》; make arrangements 〔preparations〕 《for》; get ready 《for, to *do*》; 《치장하다》 equip *oneself*; get *oneself* up; fit 〔fix 《미》〕 *oneself* out. ¶ 아무 ~도 없이 without any preparation / 길 떠날 ~를 하다 make preparations for a journey; equip *oneself* 〔fit *oneself* out〕 for a trip / 외출할 ~를 하다 fix *oneself* for going out / 파티를 치를 ~는 다 되었다 Everything is all set 〔ready〕 for the party.

**채산**(採算) (commercial) profit. ¶ ~을 무시하고 with no thought of profit /

～이 맞다〔안 맞다〕 pay 〔do not pay〕; be「profitable 〔unprofitable〕; be「paying 〔not paying〕; can 〔cannot〕 make「both 〔two〕 ends meet / ～이 맞는 사업이다 This is a paying business. / 이 일은 ～이 맞지 않는다 I cannot make two ends meet on this job. / 하려면 할 수는 있지만 ～이 맞지 않는다 Though possible, it is not commercially practicable. / 자네는 지나치게 ～만 따진다 You are too「calculating 〔profit-conscious〕.
◉ ～가격 a remunerative price. ～성 payability: 이 제품의 ～성에는 문제가 없습니다 This product should have no trouble in turning a profit.

**채색**(彩色) coloring; painting. ～하다 color; paint; add colors《to a picture》. ¶ ～한 colored; painted / 지도에 ～하다 color a map. ◉ ～도판 a colored plate. ～인쇄 color printing. ～판 chromatic printing; a colored print. ～화 a colored picture.

**채색**(菜色)《빛깔》a green color;《굶주린 얼굴빛》a starved look; a sallow complexion.

**채석**(採石) quarrying. ～하다 quarry《marble》; cut《stone》. ◉ ～공 a quarryman; a quarrier; a stonecutter. ～권 stone-quarrying rights. ～기 a quarrying machine. ～장 a quarry; a stone pit.

**채소**(菜蔬) vegetables; greens; greenstuff; garden products; garden「stuff 〔truck〕《미》. ¶ 푸른 ～ a green vegetable / 생～ raw vegetables / ～가꾸기 kitchen 〔truck〕 gardening / ～를 가꾸다 raise 〔grow〕 vegetables;《시장에 내려고》grow garden「truck 〔stuff〕《미》/ 될 수 있는대로 많은 ～를 먹도록 하여라 Try to have as many vegetables as possible.
◉ ～가게 a greengrocery; a vegetable store《미》. ～밭《가정의》a「vegetable 〔kitchen〕 garden;《농가의》a vegetable field; a truck「garden 〔farm〕《미》; a market garden《영》. ～샐러드 vegetable salad. ～수프 vegetable soup. ～요리 a vegetable dish. ～장수 a greengrocer;《미》a vegetableman.

**채송화**(菜松花)〖식물〗a sun plant; the rose moss; a garden portulaca.

**채식**(菜食) a vegetable diet; a vegetarian meal. ～하다 live on vegetables; lead a vegetarian existence. ◉ ～동물 a「herbivorous 〔grass-eating〕 animal. ～주의 vegetarianism; vegetarian principles: ～주의자 a vegetarian.

**채약**(採藥) gathering medicinal「plants 〔herbs〕. ～하다 dig 〔gather, pick〕 medicinal「plants 〔herbs〕.

**채용**(採用) ①《고용》employment;《임용》appointment. ～하다 employ; appoint; take《*a person*》into service. ¶ 그를 비서로 ～하다 employ him as a secretary / 서기로 ～하다 engage 〔employ〕《*a person*》as a clerk / 졸업생 5명을 ～하다 employ five graduates / 임시로 ～하다 take《*a person*》on trial / ～해 줄 것을 부탁하다 offer *one's* service(s); apply for a position / 그의 ～여부는 2, 3일내로 결정될 것이다 In a few days his employment will be decided upon. ②《채택》adoption. ⇨ 채택(採擇).
◉ ～시험 an examination for service. ～신청 an application for employment. ～조건 hiring「specifications 〔qualifications, requirements〕. ～통지 a notification of employment. ～후보자 a prospective employee. 무서류～시스템《인터넷을 이용한》a Paperless Recruiting System.

**채우다**[1]《잠그다》fasten; lock. ¶ 단추를 ～ fasten buttons; button (up)《*one's* coat》/ 훅을 ～ hook (up)《a dress》/ 자물쇠를 ～ fasten a lock; turn the key in the lock; lock《the door》; lock up《a box》/ 자물쇠를 채워두다 keep《*a thing*》locked; keep 〔have, place〕《*a thing*》under lock and key.

**채우다**[2]《몸에》make 〔let, have〕《*a person*》wear《*something* pinned, *etc.*》; put 〔fasten〕 on《*something* for another》. ¶ 수갑〔쇠고랑〕을 ～ handcuff; manacle; slip 〔place, put〕 handcuffs 〔manacles〕 on《*a person*》.

**채우다**[3]《찬물·얼음에》put 〔keep〕《*a thing*》「in cold water 〔on ice〕; keep《*a thing*》cool; soak《in cold water》. ¶ 맥주를 찬물에 ～ keep beer cool in cold water / 생선을 얼음에 ～ keep fish on ice / 수박을 찬물에 ～ put 〔keep〕 a watermelon in cold water.

**채우다**[4] ①《수량을》complete《a number》; make up for; make good; fill up. ¶ 백을 ～ make《it》100; make a round hundred / 수를 ～ make up the number / 부족액을 ～ replenish a shortage; make up a deficit.
②《가득하게》fill (up);《꽉》pack (in); cram; charge. ¶ 배를 ～ fill up (*one's* stomach); eat *one's* fill; satisfy *one's* appetite / 병에 물을 ～ fill a

bottle with water; bottle water / 술잔을 ～ fill a glass with wine; fill a wine glass / 가방에 옷을 ～ pack (in) a suitcase with clothes / 컵에 물을 3분의 2가량 ～ fill a glass about two-thirds full with water.
③ 《충족시키다》 satisfy; gratify; appease 《*one's* appetite》; answer; meet; fulfill. ¶ 채워지지 않는 욕구 an unfilled desire / 사복(私腹)을 ～ stuff 〔fill, line〕 *one's* own pocket(s) 〔purse〕; enrich *oneself* / 수요를 ～ supply 〔meet〕 the demand / 욕망을 ～ satisfy 〔gratify〕 *one's* desire / 정욕을 ～ gratify *one's* lust / 조건을 ～ meet the conditions.
④ 《기한을》 complete 《a period, term》; see 《it》 through. ¶ 계약 기한을 ～ see *one's* contract through; fulfill the period 〔term〕 of a contract / 임기를 ～ complete 〔finish up〕 *one's* tenure of office; serve out *one's* term.

**채유**(菜油) rape(-seed) oil; colza oil.

**채유**(採油) 《식물 등에서》 extracting oil; 《석유의》 drilling for oil. ～하다 extract oil 《from》; drill for oil. ◉ ～권 an oil concession; drilling rights.

**채이다**[1] 《빼앗기다》 get 〔have〕 《*something*》 snatched 〔taken, stolen〕 away; 《발길에》 get kicked; 《딱지 맞다》 get refused 〔rebuffed〕; be turned down; be kicked out; 《특히 애인에게》 《구어》 be jilted. ¶ 나는 그녀에게 채였다 I was rejected by her. *or* She turned me down. / 그는 여자에게 채이고 자살했다 He was jilted by a girl, and committed suicide.

**채이다**[2] 《눈치를》 get 《*something*》 sensed 〔suspected, spotted, found out, detected〕. ¶ 눈치 채이지 않도록 하다 avoid 《*a person's*》 suspicion / 둘의 사랑을 부모들이 눈치챘다 The love between the two was sensed by their parents.

**채자**(採字) 〖인쇄〗 type-picking. ～하다 pick type.

**채잡다** take charge of; take the lead 《in》; preside over 〔at〕; play first violin. ¶ 일을 채잡아 하다 take charge of matters; take things in hand.

**채전**(菜田) a vegetable garden.

**채전에** 《…하기 전에》 beforehand; in advance; ahead of time; 《오래 전에》 a long time 〔while〕 ago. ¶ ～ 통보하겠습니다 I'll inform you beforehand. / 그녀의 결심을 ～ 알고 있었다 I had advance knowledge of her decision. / 왜 ～ 그런 말을 하지 않았소 Why didn't you tell me so before?

**채점**(採點) marking; grading; rating 《미》; scoring (경기의). ～하다 give 〔award〕 marks; mark 《test papers》; grade 《students》; score 《a skater 5》. ¶ 답안 ～으로 바쁘다 be busy looking over the test papers / 100점 만점으로 ～하다 mark 《a paper》 out of 100 / ～이 후〔박〕하다 be a good 〔bad〕 marker; be generous 〔severe〕「in (*one's*) marking 〔in giving marks〕 / ～에 출석을 반영하다 consider a student's attendance record when giving marks.
◉ ～부 a mark 〔grade〕 book; 《경기의》 a score book. ～자 a marker; a grader; scorekeeper (경기의). ～표 a list of marks; a grade list 〔sheet〕.

**채종**(採種) seed gathering. ～하다 gather seeds 《of》.

**채주**(債主) a creditor; an obligee.

**채지다** 《물들인 것이》 get 〔be〕 dyed unevenly; be streaky 〔spotty〕 in coloring. ¶ 채지지 않게 칠하다 paint evenly.

**채질** whipping; flogging. ⇨ 채찍질.

**채집**(採集) gathering; collection. ～하다 gather; collect; make a collection 《of》. ¶ 식물～상자 a vasculum / 나비를 ～하다 catch butterflies for specimens / 식물을 ～하다 collect plants; gather herbs 〔grass〕 / 식물을 ～하러 가다 go botanizing / 바닷속의 플랑크톤을 ～하다 gather marine planktons.
◉ ～가 a collector.

**채찍** a whip; a rod; a cane; a lash (끈 달린); a horsewhip (말채찍). ¶ ～소리 the crack 〔whistle〕 of a whip / ～자국 a wale; a wheal; a welt / ～끈 a whipcord; a (whip)lash / ～과 당근 정책 a carrot-and-stick policy / 말을 ～으로 때리다 whip 〔lash〕 a horse; trail *one's* whip across the horse (가볍게) / ～을 휘두르다 wield 〔flip〕 a whip; flick a whiplash 《at》 / ～을 울리다 crack 〔swish〕 a whip / ～을 가하여 말을 몰다 touch 〔whip〕 up *one's* horse; whip a horse on.

**채찍질** whipping; lashing; flogging; 《격려》 urging on; spurring on. ～하다 whip; lash; take a whip to; 《격려하다》 lash; spur 〔urge〕 《*a person*》 into 《action》; cheer 《*a person*》 on; encourage. ¶ 말을 ～하다 whip *one's* horse (on); flick a horse with *one's* whip / 달리는 말에 ～을 가하다 [비유적] urge on a willing person; make 《*a* *person*》 redouble *his* efforts.

**채취**(採取) picking; gathering; 《추출》 extraction. ～하다 pick; collect; gather; get; fish 《pearls》; glean; harvest; extract; mine 《coal》. ¶ 해초를 ～하다 gather seaweeds / 지문을 ～하다 take 〔get〕 《*a person's*》 fingerprints; fingerprint 《*a person*》; register 〔record〕 《*a person's*》 fingerprints / 올리브 열매에서 기름을 ～하다 extract oil from olives. ◉ ～경제 a gathering 〔collecting〕 economy. ～자 a picker; a gatherer; a collector.

**채치다**[1] ① 《빼앗다》 snatch 《from, off》; seize. ¶ 남의 손에서 책을～ snatch a book out of another's hand. ② 《당기다》 jerk; pull with a jerk. ¶ 팔을～ jerk at 《*a person's*》 arm. ③ 《독촉하다》 press; urge; rush; dun.

**채치다**[2] 《채를 썰다》 shred; slice; cut 《a radish》 into a fine strips; cut into small pieces. ¶ 오이를 ～ shred a cucumber 《for salad》.

**채칼** a chef's knife; a knife for shredding 〔chopping〕 vegetables.

**채탄**(採炭) coal mining. ～하다 mine coal. ◉ ～량 the output of coal. ～부 a coal miner; coalface worker; a collier. ～장 a coal mine; a colliery.

**채택**(採擇) 《선택》 choice; option; selection; 《채용》 adoption; taking. ～하다 select; adopt; choose; carry 《a resolution》. ¶ 교과서의 ～ the choice of textbooks / 결의안을〔메시지를〕 ～하다 adopt a resolution 〔message〕 / 새 방법을 ～하다 adopt a new method / ～여부를 일임하다 leave 《*a matter*》 to 《*a person's*》 option / 그 동의는 투표 결과, 찬성 30, 반대 10으로 ～되었다 The motion was carried by 30 votes to 10. ◉ ～원고 manuscripts accepted.

**채편**(―便) the side of a drum to be struck; the beating side.

**채필**(彩筆) a paintbrush; a brush.

**채혈**(採血) blood-gathering〔-collecting〕; 《검사용》 drawing blood; blood taking. ～하다 gather 〔collect〕 blood 《from a doner》; draw blood 《from a vein》; take a blood sample. ¶ 나는 어제 병원에서 ～했다 Yesterday I had my blood taken at a hospital.
◉ ～기관 a blood-gathering agency. ～기구 blood-collecting equipment. ～차 a bloodmobile.

**채화**(彩畫) 〖미술〗 a colored picture; a painting. ¶ 수～ a watercolor (painting); a painting in watercolors.

**채화**(菜花) flowers on vegetables.

**책**(册) a book; a volume (한 권); a work (작품); reading (읽을 거리). ¶ 역사책 a book on history / 의학책 a medical book; a book on medicine / 지리책 a geography book / 책 갈피에 끼어 놓다 put 〔keep〕 《a letter》 between the leaves of a book / 책으로 만들어 내다 publish 《essays》 in book form / 한 권의 책으로 엮다 collect 《essays》 into a single volume (모아서); compile 《data》 into a book (편집해서) / 책을 내다〔쓰다〕 publish 〔write〕 a book / 많은 책을 읽다 read much 〔many books〕 / 책을 읽다가 잠들다 read *oneself* to sleep / 책을 읽어(들려)주다 read to 《*a person*》 / 책장을 하나하나 넘기다 turn over the leaves of a book / 자네는 정말 책벌레〔독서광〕일세 그려 You are quite a bookworm. *or* You spend all your time in reading. / 그 책은 대출 중이다 The book is out. / 그 책은 품절이다 The book is out of stock now.

**책**(柵) ① 《울》 a picket fence; a railing; a palisade; a corral (가축용); a stockade (방어용). ¶ 책을 두르다 make 〔set up, put up〕 a fence 〔stockade〕 《round》; enclose 《a place》 with a palisade; fence round 〔in, up〕; rail in. ② 《둑의》 a log dike.

**-책**(責) a responsible person; a person in charge 《of》. ¶ 조직책 an organizer.

**-책**(策) 《계획》 a plan; a scheme; 《정책》 a policy; 《수단》 a step; a measure; a means; an expedient (방편). ¶ 궁여지책 a shift; the last expedient / 대응책 countermeasures / 해결책 a means of settling a problem.

**책가위**(册―) a book cover; a (dust) jacket. ～하다 jacket; put cover on 《a book》.

**책갑**(册匣) a bookcase. 「price.

**책값**(册―) the price of a book; a book

**책권**(册卷) a volume; a book. ¶ 그 사람 ～깨나 갖고 있다 He has quite a lot of books. *or* He has a large library.

**책궤**(册櫃) a book box.

**책글씨**(册―) penmanship used for hand-written books; a hand-writing style used for books.

**책꽂이**(册―) a bookstand; a bookrack; a bookshelf.

**책동**(策動) maneuvers; machinations; scheming. ～하다 maneuver 〔intrigue〕 《behind the scenes》; machinate 《a plot》; scheme 《for power》; pull strings 〔wires〕《to get a post》. ¶ 정치가들의 비열한 ~ the contemptible maneuvers of politicians. ◉ ~가 a maneuverer; a machinator; a schemer; a wirepuller.

**책뚜껑**(冊—) a (book) cover.

**책략**(策略) a stratagem; a ruse; an artifice; a trick; tactics; strategy; a scheme; wiles; a frame-up 《미속어》. ¶ ~을 꾸미다 contrive 〔devise〕 a stratagem / 온갖 ~을 다 쓰다 use every artifice 〔trick〕; resort to every possible stratagem; play every mean trick on 《*a person*》/ ~을 써서 《escape》 by 〔with〕 a trick 〔stratagem〕/ ~에 능하다 《사람이》 be a shrewd tactician 〔schemer〕/ ~으로 적을 진지내로 유인해 들이다 maneuver the enemy into position / 그것은 인심을 얻기 위한 ~이다 It is a policy to win the hearts of people. / 그것은 당을 분열시키려는 ~이다 It is a trick to split the party. ◉ ~가 a tactician; a schemer.

**책력**(冊曆) a book calendar; an almanac.

**책망**(責望) 《질책》 reproach; rebuke; (a) reproof; scolding; 《비난》 blame; censure; a charge. ~하다 rebuke 《*a person* for *something*》; reprove; reprimand; scold; 《비난하다》 blame; censure; 《문책하다》 call 〔bring〕《*a person*》 to task 〔account〕. ¶~을 듣다 get reproached; be reproved 〔rebuked〕; be scolded; receive a reproof 〔reprimand〕《from》; draw a reproof 《from》/ 부주의를 ~하다 reproach 〔reprove〕《*a person*》 for *his* carelessness / 잘못을 ~하다 blame 《*a person*》 for *his* fault / 돈을 많이 쓴다고 ~하다 blame 《*a person*》 for spending too much money / 자기를 ~할지언정 남을 ~하지 마라 Be severe with yourself but lenient with others.

**책무**(責務) (a) duty; (an) obligation; (a) responsibility (책임). ⇨ 의무, 책임. ¶ 국가에 대한 ~ *one's* duty to *one's* country / ~를 다하다 discharge 〔fulfill〕 *one's* obligations; do 〔perform〕 *one's* duty 〔duties〕.

**책받침**(冊—) a cardboard 〔celluloid board〕 (used under writing paper).

**책방**(冊房) a bookseller's; a bookstore 《미》; a bookshop 《영》. ⇨ 서점. ¶ ~을 경영하다 keep a bookstore. ◉ ~주인 a bookseller; a bookdealer; the proprietor of a bookshop.

**책벌**(責罰) (reprimand and) punishment; 《법률상의》 penalty. ~하다 punish; inflict penalty on 《a culprit》. ¶ ~받다 be punished; receive 〔bear, suffer〕 punishment.

**책벌레**(冊—) 《벌레》 a bookworm; 《사람》 a bookworm; a literary glutton.

**책보**(冊褓) a cloth wrapper for books. ¶ ~에 싸다 wrap 《books》 in a kerchief.

**책사**(策士) a man of resources; a tactician; 《나쁜 뜻의》 a machinator; a schemer.

**책상**(冊床) a (writing) table; a desk. ¶ ~에 앉다 sit 〔be〕 at *one's* desk / ~위의 서류를 치우다 clear the papers from 〔off〕 the top of *one's* desk / ~을 사이에 두고 앉다 sit across a table. ◉ ~보 a table cloth.

**책상다리**(冊床—) ① 《책상의》「a leg 〔legs〕 of a table 〔desk〕. ② 《가부좌》 sitting on crossed legs; sitting with *one's* legs crossed. ~하다 sit 〔squat (down)〕 cross-legged; sit with *one's* legs crossed.

**책상물림**(冊床—) a novice from the ivory tower; a naive academic; a person inexperienced in the ways of the world. ¶ ~이다 know nothing of the world / 그는 ~이라 세상일은 아무것도 모른다 He is a novice from the ivory tower and knows nothing of the world.

**책송곳**(冊—) a bookbinding 〔book-binder's〕 awl.

**책실**(冊—) bookbinding thread.

**책싸개**(冊—) book wrappers; a dust jacket.

**책씻이**(冊—) 《책례》 treating *one's* teacher and friends to celebrate the completion of a course. ~하다 treat teacher and friends upon finishing a course.

**책임**(責任) 《결과에 대한》 responsibility; 《법률상의》 (a) liability (지불의); 《의무》 an obligation; *one's* duty. ¶ 무거운 ~ heavy 〔high〕 responsibility / 법률에 대한 ~ responsibility to the law / 사고에 대한 ~ liability for an accident / 의무 이행의 ~ responsibility for the fulfillment of obligation / 가족 부양의 ~ a family responsibility / 전쟁의 ~ war guilt; responsibility 〔accountability〕 for war / ~있는 지위 a responsible post; a position of trust / ~ 있는 회답 a responsible answer / ~이 있다 be responsible 〔answerable, accountable〕《to *a person* for *something*》; be to blame 《for》/ ～은 …에 있다 the responsibility rests 〔lies〕 with…; the fault lies with… / ～의 소재를 밝히다 clarify where the responsibility lies; find out who is responsible 《for》.

책임으로: 자기 혼자 ～으로 on *one's* own sole responsibility / …의 ～으로 돌리다 lay 〔place, throw, cast〕 the responsibility on…; charge 《*a thing*》 to 《*a person's*》 account; lay the blame at the door of 《*a person*》/ 자기 ～으로 하다 act 〔do〕 on *one's* own responsibility.

책임을: ～을 느끼다 be sensible of *one's* responsibility 《for》/ ～을 느끼고 사퇴하다 resign from a sense of responsibility / ～을 다하다〔이행하다〕 fulfill *one's* responsibility; discharge *one's* obligation(s); do *one's* duty / ～을 묻다 call 〔bring〕 《*a person*》 to account; take 〔call〕 《*a person*》 to task 《for》/ ～을 전가하다 shift 〔shuffle〕 the responsibility for 《*something*》 on to 《*a person*》; pass the buck to 《*a person*》/ ～을 지다 bear 〔assume, take, shoulder〕 the responsibility 《for, of》; hold *oneself* responsible 〔accountable〕 《for》; answer 《for》; be liable 〔answerable〕 《for》; take the blame 《for》; 《보증하다》 assure; guarantee; pledge *oneself* to; go 〔stand〕 security for (신원 따위) / 일체의 ～을 지지 않다 disclaim all the responsibility 《for》; hold no liability 《for》/ ～을 지우다 place 〔put, thrust〕 the responsibility 《for *something*》 on 《*a person*》; saddle 《*a person*》 with the responsibility 《for》; lay the blame on 〔at the door of〕 《*a person*》/ ～을 함께 나누다〔지다〕 share the responsibility 《for *something*》 with 《*a person*》/ ～을 해제하다 absolve 〔release〕 《*a person*》 from *his* responsibility 〔liability〕/ ～을 회피하다 avoid 〔abdicate, evade, shirk〕 *one's* responsibility 《for》.

¶ 내 ～은 아니다 I'm not responsible 〔to blame〕 for it. / 결정하는 것은 자네의 ～이다 It lies with you to decide. / 우리는 그의 행위에 ～을 지지 않는다 We cannot answer for his actions. / 부모를 봉양하는 것은 당신의 ～이다 It lies upon you to provide for your parents. / 학생에게 공부시키는 것은 교사의 ～이다 It is a teacher's business to make boys learn. / 너는 이 실패의 ～을 져야 한다 You have to account for this failure. / 책임의 태반은 은행측에 있다 Much of the blame belongs with the bank. / 이 대화재의 발생은 누구의 ～이냐 Who is to blame for starting this big fire? / 그것은 내게 맡겨라. 내가 ～지고 하겠다 Leave it to me. I'll take care of it.

◉ ～교료(校了) 〖인쇄〗 《표시》 O.K. with corrections. ～내각 《내각책임제에서》 a Cabinet responsible to the Parliament 〔Diet〕. ～보험 liability insurance. ～분담 the division of responsibility. ～자 a responsible person; a person in charge 《of》: 우리 학교의 식당 ～자는 누군가 Who is in charge of our school cafeteria? ～전가 buck-passing 《미속어》. ～정치 responsible politics. ～해제 release from responsibility; acquittal from liability. ～회피 evasion 〔shirking〕 of responsibility; buck=passing 《미속어》: ～회피를 하는 사람 a buck passer 《미속어》.

**책임감**(責任感) a sense of responsibility 〔duty〕. ¶ ～을 느끼다 feel a sense of responsibility / ～이 강하다 have a strong sense of responsibility / ～이 없다 lack all sense of responsibility.

**책임능력**(責任能力) the ability to fulfill *one's* responsibilities 《as》. ¶ ～이 있다〔없다〕 be 〔be not〕 《criminally》 responsible (for *one's* actions) / 교장으로서의 그의 ～을 의문시하는 사람들도 있다 Some people question his ability to fulfill his responsibilities as principal. (★ as에 이어지는 명사가 「관직·역할·자격」따위를 나타낼 경우는 무관사임).

**책자**(冊子) a booklet; a leaflet; a pamphlet. ¶ 소～ a pamphlet; a leaflet. ◉ 선전～ a propaganda pamphlet.

**책잡다**(責—) find fault with 《*a person*》; call 《*a person*》 to account 《for》; take 《*a person*》 to task 《for》; blame 〔reproach〕 《for》. ¶ 아무의 실언을 ～ take *a person* to task for *his* slip of tongue / 과실을 책잡아 면직시키다 dismiss 《*a person*》 for his error.

**책잡히다**(責—) get blamed 〔reproached〕 for; be found fault with; be called to account; be taken to task. ¶ 직무 태만으로 ～ be accused of having neglected *one's* work; be taken to task for neglecting *one's* duty / 회사 돈을 썼다고 ～ be blamed for appropriating company money.

**책장**(冊張) a leaf of a book; the pages. (★ a page는 책장의 한 면만을, leaf는 그 양면을 말함. 즉 a leaf는 two pages임).

¶ ～을 넘기다 turn (over) the leaves 〔pages〕 of a book; thumb 〔leaf〕 through the pages / ～을 뜯다 tear off 〔rip out〕 a page.

**책장**(冊欌) a bookshelf; a book chest; a bookcase.

**책정**(策定) 《예산 등의》 appropriation; 《가격 등의》 fixing 《prices》. ～하다 appropriate 〔apply, assign〕 《to》; allot; earmark 《sums of money》 for; fix (up). ¶ 가격을 ～하다 fix a price / 시간을 ～하다 map 〔plot〕 out *one's* time / 학교 보조금으로 천만 원을 ～하다 appropriate ten million won for school aid / 해마다 G.N.P.의 10퍼센트를 군비로 ～하다 earmark 10% of 《its》 G.N.P. each year for military preparedness. ◉ 봉급～ arrangement of a salary scale.

**책치레**(冊—) a (decorative) design of book.

**책하다**(責—) reproach; reprove; take 《*a person*》 to task; call 《*a person*》 to account. ⇨ 책망하다.

**책형**(磔刑) crucification. ¶ ～에 처하다 crucify 《*a person*》 / ～을 받다 be crucified; die on the cross.

**챔피언** a champion; a champ 《구어》. ¶ 수영의 세계 ～ the swimming champion of the world / 헤비급 세계 ～ the heavy-weight 《boxing》 champion of the world / ～이 되다 win 〔gain〕 a championship / ～의 자격이 있다 be entitled to become a champion.
◉ ～십 (a) championship.

**챗국** a cold soup with shredded radish in it.

**챙** a sunshade. ⇨ 차양(遮陽).

**챙기다** ① 《한데 모으다》 gather all together; collect; 《짐을》 pack. ¶ 소지품을 ～ get *one's* things together; gather up *one's* belongings / 짐을 챙겨 상경하다 come up to Seoul with *one's* things packed. ② 《정리하다》 tidy up; put 《*things*》 in order; 《처리하다》 manage; take care of; 《치우다》 put 〔lay〕 《*a thing*》 away 〔up, by〕; stow (away); keep. ¶ 서류를 ～ get papers in order / 소중하게 챙겨두다 treasure (up); lock away / 안전한 곳에 ～ take 《*a thing*》 into safe keeping / 일한 뒤에 연장을 ～ put the tools in order after *one* has finished *his* work / 그애는 너무 어려서 제 몸 하나 챙길 줄 모른다 The child is too young to take care of himself.

**처**(妻) a wife (*pl.* wives); *one's* better half 《속어》. ⇨ 아내. ¶ 내연의 처 the unwedded wife; 〖법〗 a common-law wife / 처를 얻다 take 〔get〕 a wife; marry 《a girl》 / 처로 삼다 make 《a woman》 *one's* wife; take 《a woman》 to wife; have 〔get〕 《a woman》 for *one's* wife / 처에게 쥐어 지내다 be henpecked; be tied to *one's* wife's apron string / 처에게 쥐어 지내는 남편 a henpecked husband / 악처(惡妻)를 만나다 be cursed with a bad wife.

**-처**(處) 《곳》 a place; 《정부 기구》 an office. ¶ 근무처 *one's* place of employment; *one's* office / 법제처 the Office of Legislation.

**처가**(妻家) the home 〔house〕 of *one's* wife's parents; *one's* wife's home.
◉ ～살이 living in *one's* wife's home: ～살이하다 live in *one's* wife's home.

**처결**(處決) decision; settlement; disposal; disposition. ～하다 decide; settle; dispose of.

**처깔하다** fasten the doors securely.

**처남**(妻男) *one's* wife's brother; *one's* brother-in-law.

**처넣다** 《밀어넣다》 press in(to); thrust 〔shove, tuck〕 in(to); throw 〔cast〕 in; 《잔뜩》 stuff 〔cram, pack〕 into. ¶ 모든 옷을 여행가방에 ～ cram 〔jam〕 all *one's* clothes into the suitcase / 교도소에 ～ cast 〔throw, clap, fling〕 《a culprit》 into prison 〔jail〕 / 가방에 책을 ～ pack 〔stuff〕 a bag with books / 머릿속에 ～ cram 《knowledge》 into *one's* head / 바닷속에 ～ 《배에서》 throw 《*a thing*》 overboard / 쓰레기통에 ～ throw 《*things*》 into a wastebasket / 헛간에 ～ put 《*things*》 into a barn / 있는 돈을 모조리 주식에 ～ put all *one's* money into stocks.

**처녀**(處女) a maiden; a virgin. ¶ ～의 virgin; maiden / ～다운 maidenly; maidenlike; virginal / ～답게 like a maiden; in a maidenlike manner / ～다움 maidenliness / 숫～ an immaculate virgin / 시골〔도시〕 ～ a country 〔city〕 girl / 한창 때의 ～ a girl in the flower of maidenhood; a girl in the bloom of youth / ～가 애를 낳아도 할 말이 있다 《속담》 Every evildoer has his reason.
◉ ～궁 〖천문〗 Virgo. ～림 a virgin forest. ～막 the hymen; the maidenhead. ～봉 a virgin 〔an untrodden〕 peak. ～비행〔항해〕 a maiden flight 〔voyage〕: ～ 항해를 떠나다 set out on her maiden voyage. ～시절 《in》 *one's* girlhood; maidenhood; virginhood. ～자리 〖천문〗 the Virgin; Virgo. ～작〔출판〕 *one's* maiden work 〔publication〕.

**처녀성**(處女性) virginity; virginhood;

maidenhood. ¶ ～을 잃다〔빼앗기다〕 lose〔be deprived of〕*one's* virginity; be deflowered / ～을 지키다 abide virgin; remain a virgin; retain *one's* virginity.

**처녀지**(處女地) virgin soil; (a) virgin territory. ¶ ～를 개척하다 turn up the virgin soil; break the fresh〔new〕ground.

**처녑** 《소 따위의》 the manyplies; an omasum (*pl.* -sa).

**처단**(處斷) 《결단》 decision; judg(e)ment; 《처벌》 disposition; punishment. ～하다 decide; dispose 《of》; punish; deal〔do〕with. ¶ 엄중 ～하다 punish〔deal with〕《an offender》 severely.

**처대다** ① 《대주다》 keep supplying〔providing〕. ② 《불에》 put on the flames; burn on a fire.

**처덕**(妻德) ① 《덕행》 the virtue of a wife. ② 《은덕》 *one's* wife's favor〔help〕; obligations *one* owes to *one's* wife. ¶ ～으로 성공했다 Thanks to his wife's help, he could succeed.

**처덕거리다** ① 《방망이로》 keep beating with paddles; paddle; slap; beat. ¶ 빨래를 ～ paddle the laundry. ② 《바르다》 slap 《papers》 together; paste〔assemble〕haphazardly; 《분·칠 따위를》 paint thick(ly); dab; daub 《paint on》. ¶ 벽에 종이를 ～ paste papers all over a wall in a haphazard way / 얼굴에 분을 ～ paint *one's* face thick; powder *one's* face too thickly.

**처덕처덕** 《빨래를》 paddling; slapping; beating; 《바르다》 pasting up haphazardly; thick(ly); all over (온통). ¶ 분을 ～ 바르다 paint〔plaster〕《*one's* face》 thickly.

**처든지르다** eat greedily; shove〔shovel〕down 《food》. ⇨ 처먹다.

**처때다** burn (a fire) high; feed a fire with heaped 《wood》.

**처뜨리다** 《아래로》 hang down; droop. ¶ 어깨를 ～ droop *one's* shoulders / 개가 귀를 ～ a dog droops his ears / 띠를 뒤로 매어 ～ have *one's* sash tied behind with the ends hanging.

**처량하다**(凄凉—) ① 《쓸쓸하다》 (***a***) 《황량해서》 (be) desolate; dreary; bleak; deserted. ¶ 처량한 광경 a desolate scene; a bleak view; a pathetic sight; a ghastly view / 처량한 벌판 a wind swept〔desolate〕plain; a wilderness. (***b***) 《적적해서》 (be) lonely; lonesome. ¶ 처량하게 살다 lead a lonely life. ② 《마음이》 (***a***) 《구슬퍼서》 (be) plaintive; doleful; mournful; sad; melancholy; pensive. ¶ 처량한 노래 a plaintive song / 처량한 심사 melancholy〔pensive〕mood. (***b***) 《비참해서》 (be) helpless; cheerless; dreary; wretched; forlorn; inconsolable. ¶ 처량한 생각이 들다 feel miserable; find no solace in anything / 처량한 생활을 하다 lead a wretched〔miserable〕life / 처량해지다 feel miserable〔wretched〕/ 처량한 얼굴을 하지 마라 None of you wretched face! / 처량한 소리 말고 기운 좀 내라 Cheer up! Don't be faint-hearted. / 남편과 사별하니 그녀는 처량한 마음이 들었다 She felt forlorn and helpless on the death of her husband.

**처럼** 《…와 같이》 like; (the same) as; as...as; so...as; as if〔though〕. ¶ 여느 때 ～ as usual; in *one's* usual way; as is usually the case with 《*one*》/ 한 집안 식구 ～ like members of one family / 아무 일도 없었던 것～ as if nothing had happened / …～ 보이다 it seems〔appears〕that…; look like … / 자기 자식～ 귀여워하다 love 《a child》 like *one's* own / 미치광이～ 달리다 run like〔as if *one* were〕mad / 한 식구～ 대하다 treat 《*a person*》 as one of the family / 남～ 굴다 behave like a stranger; have a distant manner〔air〕/ 대낮～ 밝았다 It was light as day. / 네가 미치지 않은 것～ 그도 미치지 않았다 He is no more mad than you are. / 음식이 육체에 영양을 주는 것～ 독서는 정신을 함양한다 As food nourishes the body, so does reading the mind.

**처리**(處理) 《취급》 management; dealing 《with》; 《처분》 disposal; 〖법〗 disposition; 《화학상의》 treatment; 《원료 등의》 processing; 《컴퓨터에서의》 data processing; 《사무 등의》 conduct〔transact〕《business》. ～하다 handle; manage 《*a matter*》; conduct 《business》; dispose of 《*a matter*》; deal with 《an affair》; transact; settle 《*a matter*》; 《원료 등을》 process; 《화학적으로》 treat; 《컴퓨터에서》 process. ¶ 쓰레기〔하수〕～ garbage〔sewage〕disposal / 폐기물을 ～하다 dispose of waste materials / 문제를 ～하다 treat〔deal with〕a problem / 열～를 하다 treat 《metals》 by heating; heat-treat 《metals》/ 황산으로 ～하다 treat 《a substance》 with sulfuric acid / 집안 일을 ～해 나가다 manage household affairs; run a household / 제 일을 스스로 ～하다 manage *one's* own affairs /

~되다 be settled; be disposed of / 적절히 ~해 주게 I leave (the transaction of) the matter to your discretion. / 사건을 어떻게든지 빨리 ~해 주시오 I want you to settle the matter one way or another as soon as possible. / 나는 그 사건의 ~를 위임받았다 I was entrusted with bringing the affair to conclusion. / 쓰레기 ~는 어느 시에서나 심각한 문제이다 Refuse disposal is a serious problem in any city. / 그 공장에서 나오는 폐기물은 모두가 미~된 상태로 바다에 버려지고 있다 All the waste from the factory was passing untreated into the sea. ◉ ~장 a processing plant; 《하수 따위의》 a treatment plant. 사무~ the transaction of business 〔affairs〕.

**처마** 〖건축〗 the eaves. ¶ ~의 홈통 a gutter; an eave trough / ~에서 떨어지는 빗물 raindrops falling from the eaves / ~ 밑에서 잠시 비를 피하다 take short shelter from rain under the eaves. ◉ ~끝 the edge of the eaves.

**처매다** tie tightly 〔fast〕; fasten tight; 《붕대를》 bandage 《a wound》 up thoroughly.

**처먹다** eat greedily; dig 〔tuck〕 in; shove 〔shovel〕 down; devour. ¶ 떡을 ~ shovel down rice cake / 처먹어라 Dig 〔Tuck〕 in!

**처먹이다** feed immoderately; stuff 《*a person*》 with food.

**처박다** ① 《때려서 박다》 drive 〔strike〕 in(to); ram down 《a stake》; wedge in (쐐기 등을). ¶ 못을 ~ drive 〔hammer〕 a nail into 《a wall》. ② 《처넣다》 thrust 〔shove, tuck〕 in(to); stuff 〔cram, pack〕 into; ram in(to); 《물 속에》 dive; dip. ¶ 서랍 속에 ~ shove 〔cram〕 《*a thing*》 in a drawer / 트렁크에 옷을 ~ ram clothes into a trunk / 헛간에 ~ put 《*things*》 into a barn. ③ 《가두다》 shut in 〔up〕; lock in 〔up〕; confine. ¶ 처박아 두다 keep 《*a person*》 penned (up) 《in a place》 / 처박혀 있다 confine *oneself* to 〔in〕 《a room》; shut *oneself* up; be confined 〔closeted〕 in 《*one's* room》; remain 〔keep〕 indoors / 하루 종일 방에 처박히다 keep (in) *one's* room all day long.

**처방**(處方) 〖의학〗 (a) prescription; a recipe. ~하다 prescribe 《a medicine for stomach》. ¶ 의사의 ~대로 as prescribed by a physician / ~을 잘못하다 make out a wrong prescription 《for》 / ~대로 약을 짓다 prepare a medicine as prescribed; make up 〔dispense, fill〕 a prescription / 이 ~으로 약을 조제해 주세요 Please prepare some medicine according to this prescription. / ~ 조제 《표시》 Prescription filled. ◉ ~전(箋) a (medical) prescription (slip): ~전을 쓰다 write 〔make out〕 a prescription 《for a disease》.

**처벌**(處罰) punishment; (a) penalty. ~하다 punish 《*a person* for a crime》; inflict 〔impose〕 a penalty on 《*a person* for an offense》. ¶ 범죄(행위)에 대한 ~ punishment for a crime / 가벼운〔무거운〕 ~ 《impose》 a light 〔heavy〕 penalty / 엄중하게 ~하다 punish severely; inflict severe 〔heavy〕 punishment on 《*a person*》; deal strictly with / ~받다 be 〔get〕 punished; incur a penalty / ~을 받지 않고 무사히 넘기다 go unpunished; get off scot-free / 교통 위반으로 ~받다 be punished for violation of the traffic regulations / ~받을 만하다 deserve 〔merit〕 the punishment 《of》 / 그는 증거 불충분으로 ~을 면했다 He was 「set free 〔unpunished〕 because of lack of evidence.

**처부모**(妻父母) the parents of *ones* wife; 「a man's parents-in-law.

**처분**(處分) 《처치》 disposal; disposition; dealing 《with a problem》; 《조치》 a measure; 《처벌》 punishment; penalty. ~하다 dispose of; deal 〔do〕 with; make a clearance of 《unsold goods》; 《처벌하다》 punish. ¶ 재산을〔토지를〕 ~하다 dispose of *one's* property 〔land〕 / 관대히 ~하다 deal leniently with 《*a person*》 / 행정 ~을 하다 take an administrative measure / 그는 징계 ~을 받았다 He was subjected to disciplinary punishment. / 「차는 어떻게 했느냐」—「~해 버렸다」 "What did you do with the car?"—"I got rid of it." ◉ 부당 ~ an unwarrantable proceeding 〔measure〕; wrongful dealing: 압류품의 부당 ~ breach of the arrestment.

**처사**(處士) a retired gentleman (who holds no office); scholar in retirement.

**처사**(處事) management (of an affair); dealing 〔handling〕 with (a matter); 《행위》 behavior; an act; action; conduct; 《조치》 a measure; a step. ¶ 매정한 ~ cold treatment / ~를 잘하다 take a proper step; deal with 《*a matter*》 properly / 처에 대한 그의 ~는 전혀 이해할 수 없다 I simply can't understand the way he treats his wife.

**처삼촌**(妻三寸) *one's* wife's uncle.

**처상**(妻喪) *one's* wife's death; mourning for *one's* wife.

**처서**(處暑) one of the 24 seasonal divisions (=about August 23rd).

**처세**(處世) conduct of life. ～하다 go 〔walk〕 through the world; get on in the world; conduct *oneself;* carry *oneself.* ¶ ～의 길 the rules of conduct in the life / 그는 ～에 능하다〔능하지 못하다〕 He knows 〔doesn't know〕 how to get on in the world. *or* He knows 〔doesn't know〕 the secret of success in life. / 정직함이 그의 ～방법이다 Honesty is the guiding principle of his life. ◉ ～법 ⇨처세술. ～훈(訓) the (guiding) motto 〔principle〕 for *one's* life; rules of conduct in life.

**처세술**(處世術) a rule of life; the secret of success in life; the art 「of living 〔of managing in society〕; how to get on in the world; social politics. ¶ ～에 능하다 know how to get on in life 〔how to swim with the current〕 / ～이 서투르다 be lacking in worldly wisdom.

**처소**(處所) 《장소》 a place; 《거처》 a living place; *one's* residence; a place of abode (숙소); *one's* address (주소). ¶ ～를 잡다 make 〔take up〕 *one's* abode / ～를 알아 내다 locate 《*a person*》; find out 《*a person's*》 address; follow up 《*a person's*》 residence.
◉ 임시～ *one's* temporary residence 〔abode〕.

**처숙**(妻叔) *one's* wife's uncle.

**처시하**(妻侍下) being henpecked; a henpecked husband; a man tied to his wife's apron string. ¶ ～이다 be a henpecked husband; be wife-ridden; be tied to *one's* wife's apron strings.

**처신**(處身) behavior; deportment; demeanor; conduct. ～하다 behave 〔conduct〕 *oneself* 《like a gentleman》. ¶ 겸허하게 ～하다 bear *oneself* in modesty and moderation / 점잖게 ～하다 behave *oneself* well; bear *oneself* gracefully / ～이 좋다〔나쁘다〕 be well=behaved 〔ill-behaved〕 / 모든 경우에 ～을 잘 하기란 쉬운 일이 아니다 It is not easy to act properly on every occasion.

**처우**(處遇) treatment. ～하다 treat; deal 〔do〕 with. ¶ 그녀는 우리를 공평하게 ～했다 She treated us fairly.
◉ ～개선 better treatment: ～개선하다 better 〔improve〕 treatment; give better treatment to 《workers》.

**처음** ① 《시작》 the beginning; the opening; the commencement; 《발단》 the start; the outset; 《최초》 (the) first; 《기원》 the origin. ¶ ～의 first; initial; early (초기의); the former (전자의); 《본디의》 original / 맨～ the very beginning / ～이 잘되다 make a successful beginning; make a good start / ～이 그릇〔잘못〕되다 begin at the wrong end; make a false 〔wrong〕 start / ～꺼내다 break the ice; speak first.
처음에: ～에 in the beginning; at the beginning 〔start〕; at the (very) outset; first(ly) / 장(章) ～에 at the beginning of the chapter.
처음에는〔은〕: ～에는 at first; at the start 〔outset〕; 《본디는》 originally; primarily / ～에는 …하게, 마지막에는 … at first... and at last....
처음부터: ～부터 끝까지 from (the) beginning to (the) end; from start 〔first〕 to finish 〔last〕; from A to Z / ～부터 끝까지 다 읽다 read 《a book》 from cover to cover / ～부터 다시 하다 do all over again; begin afresh; make a new start / ～부터 그 제안에 반대하다 be against the proposal from the beginning.
¶ 모든 일은 ～이 어렵다 Everything is hard at the beginning. / 그건 ～부터 알고 있었네 I have known it all along. / ～이 중요하다 A good beginning is half the battle. *or* Well begun is half done. / 이것이 ～이자 마지막이다 This is the first and the last. / ～치고는 그의 작품이 그리 나쁘지 않다 As a beginner, his work is not so bad. / ～에는 회원이 단 3명이었다 We had only three members to start with. / 이 회사도 ～에는 조그마했다 This company started in a small way. / ～엔 어렵다고 생각했다 I found it difficult at first.
② 《첫번》 first (of all); prior; the first time. ¶ ～(으로) for the first time (in *one's* life) / 그 사람 만난 것은 이번이 ～이다 This was the first time I had met him. / ～ 뵙겠습니다 How do you do? (★ 이에 대한 답도 How do you do?라고 함) *or* Pleased 〔Glad〕 to meet you. / 이곳에 온 것은 ～이다 I have never been here. *or* I am quite a stranger here. / 서울은 이번이 ～입니까 Is this your first visit to Seoul? / 그 분을 ～ 만난 것은 3년 전이다 I first

met him three years ago. *or* It is three years since I first met him. / 그런 사람은 생전 ~ 보았다 I saw such a person for the first time in my life. / 며칠 후 ~으로 사실을 알았다 It was not until a few days later that I learned the truth. / 연단에 선 것은 이번이 ~이다 This is the first time that I have ever stood on the platform.

**처자**(妻子) *one's* wife and children; *one's* dear(est) ones; 《가족》 *one's* family. ¶ ~를 돌보지 않다 have no regard for *one's* wife and children / ~를 부양하다 support 〔provide for〕 *one's* family / ~를 버리다 discard 〔desert〕 *one's* wife and children.

**처재**(妻財) *one's* wife's property 〔dowry〕.

**처쟁이다** pile 〔heap〕 up 《*things*》 by pressing down.

**처절**(悽絶) extreme sadness 〔melancholy, sorrow〕; ghastliness; gruesomeness. ~하다 (be) extremely sad 〔melancholy, wretched, miserable〕; extremely weird 〔gruesome, lurid, ghastly〕. ¶ ~한 광경 a gruesome scene 〔picture〕.

**처제**(妻弟) *one's* wife's younger sister; 「*one's* sister-in-law.

**처조모**(妻祖母) *one's* wife's grandmother.

**처조부**(妻祖父) *one's* wife's grandfather.

**처조카**(妻―) *one's* wife's niece 〔nephew〕.

**처족**(妻族) *one's* wife's relatives.

**처지**(處地) ① 《형편》 a situation; a state; a condition; circumstances; *one's* lot; 《입장》 a position; a stand; a footing; a standpoint; 《신분》 a station 〔condition〕 in life. ¶ ~의 변화 a change in *one's* circumstances / 곤란한 ~ a difficult situation / 어떤 ~에 있건 under 〔in〕 any circumstances; however circumstanced *one* may be; in any condition in life / 지금 ~로는 in the present circumstances / 대등한 ~에서 on an equal footing 《with》 / 같은 ~에 있다 be in the same circumstances / 괴로운〔곤란한〕 ~에 있다 「find *oneself* 〔be placed〕 in 「a dilemma 〔an awkward situation, a delicate position〕 / 괴로운 ~에 빠지다 be placed in a sad plight; be put in a (nice) fix / 어려운 ~에 있다 《살기가》 be in needy circumstances; be badly off / 남의 ~가 되어보다 put 〔place〕 *oneself* in another's place 〔shoes〕 / 남의 ~를 부러워하다 envy *a person's* lot / 자기 ~에 만족하다 be contented with *one's* lot / 자신의 ~를 모르다 do not know where *one* is 〔stands〕 / 지금의 내 ~로는 그것에 관해 분명한 것을 말할 수 없다 I am not in a position to tell you anything definite about it now. / 지금 ~로는 그런 것은 살 수 없다 In my present circumstances I cannot afford (to buy) such a thing. / 그런 큰 집은 네 ~에 과하다 A big house like that is beyond your means. / 우리는 각기 ~가 다르다 We are all differently circumstanced. / 가지 않을 수 없는 ~가 되었다 I was compelled 〔forced〕 to go away.

② 《사이》 relationship; terms; friendship. ¶ 우리 ~에 고만 일을 가지고 싸울 수야 있겠나 In view of the friendship between you and me, surely we can't quarrel over such a petty thing.

**처지다** ① 《끝이 늘어지다》 hang (down); droop; 《한가운데가》 sag. ¶ 처진 어깨 drooping shoulders / 귀가 처진 개 a dog with drooped ears 〔with a button ear〕; a flap-eared dog / 옷의 뒤가 ~ *one's* dress sags in the back / 천장이 처져 있다 The ceiling is sagging. / 열매가 많이 열려서 나뭇가지가 축 처져 있다 The branches are drooping under the weight of the fruit.

② 《내려앉다》 go down; droop; sink. ¶ 위(胃)가 ~ *one's* stomach suffers a prolapse 〔gastroptosis〕.

③ 《뒤처지다》 (***a***) 《뒤지다》 fall 〔remain, stay〕 behind; 《낙오되다》 draggle; straggle; drop behind 〔to the rear〕; 《학문·일 등에》 get 〔hang〕 behind; lag behind; allow 《another》 to get the start of; be backward; 《달리기에서》 trail 《미구어》. ¶ 혼자만 뒤에 ~ remain behind all alone / 행군하다 ~ fall out while on the march / 처지지 않고 따라가다 keep up 〔pace〕 with 《*a person*》 / 나는 다른 사람보다도 일이 처지고 있다 I am behind the others in 〔with〕 my work. (***b***) 《…만 못하다》 compare unfavorably 《with》; be inferior 《to》.

**처지르다** put 〔throw〕 《logs》 on 〔in〕 the fire; shovel 《coal into a stove》; cram 《*a thing*》 into.

**처질**(妻姪) 《처조카》 *one's* wife's niece 「〔nephew〕.

**처참**(處斬) decapitation; beheading. ~하다 cut 《*a person's*》 head off; decapitate; behead.

**처참**(悽慘) ~하다 (be) gruesome; grim; appalling; ghastly; lurid; miserable; wretched. ¶ ~한 광경 a gruesome scene 〔picture〕; an appalling 〔a heart-rending] sight / ～한 싸움이었다 It was a bloody battle. / 현장은 몹시 ～했다 The scene presented a ghastly sight.

**처처**(處處) everywhere; 《in》 every quarter; at every turn. ⇨ 곳곳.

**처첩**(妻妾) *one's* wife and concubine.

**처치**(處置) ① 《처리》 disposal; management; dealing with 《*a thing*》; 《조치》 a measure; a step; 《치료》 《give》 medical treatment 《to》. ⇨ 조처. ～하다 dispose of; deal 〔do〕 with; handle; manage; take measures 〔steps〕 against; 《치료하다》 treat; give medical treatment 《to》. ¶ 적절한 ～를 취하다 use *one's* discretion in dealing with 《*something*》; deal with 《*a thing*》 as *one* thinks fit / 잘못 ～하다 take the wrong measures / 부상자에게 응급 ～를 취하다 give first aid to the wounded / …이 ～곤란이다 do not know what to do with …; be at a loss what to do 〔how to deal〕 with… / 그것은 내가 ～하겠다 I'll see to it. / 그들은 무법자에 대하여 단호한 ～를 취했다 They took strong 〔decisive〕 measures against outlaws.
② 《제거》 removal; doing away with it; disposing of it; getting rid of it. ～하다 remove; take 〔clear, move〕 away; get rid of; do away with. ¶ 책상을 어디로 ～해야겠다 We have to move the table away somewhere. / 그 놈을 ～해 버리기로 하자 Let's make up our minds to get rid of him.

**처하다**(處—) ① 《놓이다》 be placed 《in》; get 〔be〕 faced 《with》. ¶ 나쁜 환경에 ～ be placed in bad surroundings; have an unfavorable environment / 역경에 ～ be in adversity; be down (up)on *one's* luck; be under unfavorable circumstances / 곤란한 처지에 ～ be in a fix; be in a quandary; find *oneself* "behind the eight ball" / 위기에 ～ be at 〔come to〕 a crisis; be in a ciritical condition; face a crisis.
② 《처벌하다》 sentence; condemn. ¶ 구류에 ～ order detention for 《*a person*》 / 사형에 ～ sentence 〔condemn〕 《a criminal》 to death / 5일간의 구류에 처해지다 be sentenced to five days' detention.
③ 《대처하다》 manage; deal with; cope with; dispose of; treat. ¶ 난국에 ～ cope with a difficulty; deal with a knotty problem. 「sister-in-law.

**처형**(妻兄) *one's* wife's elder sister; *one's*

**처형**(處刑) punishment; (an) execution (사형 집행). ～하다 inflict punishment 《on》; punish; 《사형에》 execute; send 《a criminal》 to the scaffold 〔gallows〕. ¶ 범인의 공개 ～ (an) open execution of criminals / ～되다 be punished; be executed / 살인범은 오늘 아침 교도소에서 ～되었다 A murderer was hanged at the jail this morning. ◉ ～대 a scaffold; a gallows (★ 단·복수 같음). ～장 an execution ground.

**척**[1] ① 〖기계〗 a chuck; a vise. ¶ 척 선반 a chuck lathe. ② 《지퍼》 a zip 〔slide〕 fastener; a zipper.

**척**[2] pretense; pretending. ＝체[3].

**척**(尺) a Korean foot (=about one foot). ¶ 척수가 길다 〔짧다〕 be long 〔short〕 length / 척수가 모자라다 be wanting in length; be short of measure / 척으로 팔다 sell by the measure.

**척**(隻) vessels; ships. ¶ 배 한 척 a vessel; a ship / 한 척분의 뱃짐 a shipload / 한 척의 배에 싣다 load in one ship.

**척**[3] ① 《단단히》 sticking fast; close; tight. ¶ 손에 척 들러붙다 stick fast to *one's* hand / 젖은 옷이 몸에 척 들러붙다 wet clothes cling tight to *one's* body.
② 《처짐》 drooping low; loosely. ⇨ 축[2]. ¶ 척 늘어지다 hang loose.
③ 《선뜻》 without delay 〔hesitation〕; readily; 《즉각》 instantly; right off 〔away〕; offhand; quickly; speedily. ⇨ 척척. ¶ 척 대답하다 answer (questions) readily; give a ready answer / 돈을 척 내걸다 bet *one's* money without hesitation; be a ready bettor / 한 번 척 보고 그가 사기꾼임을 알아보았다 One glance was enough to see through his fraud.
④ 《의젓하게》 imposingly; in a dignified manner; 《멋지게》 smartly; becomingly; dashingly. ¶ 안경을 척 쓰다 look good in spectacles; put on *one's* glasses imposingly / 칼을 척 차다 wear a sword dashingly.

**척결**(剔抉) ～하다 《긁어 발라내다》 gouge 〔hollow〕 out; scrape out; 《들춰내다》 expose 《a crime, fraud》; lay bare 《an evil design》. ¶ 부정 사건을 ～하다 expose a scandal.

**척골**(尺骨) 〖해부〗 the ulna (*pl.* ～s, -nae). ◉ ～동맥 〔신경〕 the ulna artery 〔nerve〕.

**척골**(脊骨) 〖해부〗 the backbone; the spine; the spinal column. 「(bone).

**척골**(蹠骨) 〖해부〗 the metatarsal

**척도**(尺度) 《계측의 도구·단위》 a (linear)

measure; a scale; a gauge; 《지표》 an index; 《평가의 기준》 a standard; a yardstick; a criterion (*pl.* ~s, -ria). ¶ 문명의 ~ an index 〔barometer〕 of civilization / 선악의 ~ standards of morality / …을 재는 ~가 되다 be a measure 〔a barometer, an index〕 of…; be a yardstick for… / 센티미터는 길이의 ~이다 Centimeters measure length. / 시력이 떨어지는 것은 노화의 한 ~이다 Failing eyesight is a sign of 「growing old 〔aging〕.

**척량**(脊梁) ① 〖해부〗 the spinal 〔vertebral〕 column; the spine; the line of the backbone. ② 《산줄기의》 a mountain ridge.

**척박**(瘠薄) barrenness; sterility; infertility 《of soil》; meagerness. ~하다 (be) barren; sterile; infertile. ¶ ~한 땅 barren 〔sterile, unproductive〕 soil 〔land〕/ 땅을 ~하게 하다 impoverish the soil.

**척분**(戚分) kinship; (ties of) relationship.

**척살**(刺殺) 《죽임》 stabbing to death; 〖야구〗 touching out. ~하다 stab 《*a person*》 dead 〔to death〕; 〖야구〗 put 〔throw, touch〕 《a runner》 out.

**척색**(脊索) 〖동물〗 a notochord. ◉ ~동물 a chordate (animal).

**척수**(脊髓) 〖해부〗 the spinal cord 〔marrow〕; the spine.

◉ ~마비 spinal paralysis. ~마취 spinal anesthesia. ~병 a spinal disease. ~신경 the spinal nerves: ~신경절(節) a spinal ganglion. ~액 the spinal fluid. ~염(炎) myelitis. ~주사 a spinal injection. 뇌~ the brain and spinal cord: 뇌~액 cerebrospinal fluid / 뇌~염 encephalomyelitis.

**척식**(拓殖) 《개척》 reclamation; 《식민》 colonization. ~하다 reclaim; colonize; establish a colony. ◉ ~은행 a colonial bank. ~자 a colonist. ~회사 a colonization company.

**척신**(隻身) single life; 《독신》 celibacy.

**척주**(脊柱) 〖해부〗 the spinal column. ⇨ 척추. ◉ ~교정판 a backboard. ~지압요법 chiropractic.

**척지**(尺地) 《작은 땅》 a single square foot of land; a small strip of land; 《가까움》 a foot away; a stone's throw.

**척지**(瘠地) barren land; arid soil.

**척지다**(隻—) come to hate each other.

**척짓다**(隻—) earn 《*a person's*》 grudge; incur grudge 〔an enmity〕; create a situation leading to mutual hatred.

**척척** ① 《차곡차곡》 fold by fold (개킴); heap by heap (쌓음); in orderly fashion. ¶ 옷을 ~ 개키다 fold up *one's* clothes / 쌀 가마니를 ~ 쌓다 stack up rice bags.
② 《감기다》 coil by coil; twining; clinging. ¶ ~ 감기다 twine 〔coil〕 itself round; twist about / 칡넝쿨이 몸에 ~ 감기다 arrowroot vines entangle *one's* body.
③ 《달라붙다》 all sticking fast; close; tight; adhesively. ¶ ~ 붙다 be sticky on; stick to 〔on〕; adhere to / 젖은 옷이 몸에 ~ 달라붙다 wet clothes cling fast to *one's* body.
④ 《지체없이》 all without delay 〔hesitation〕; readily; right off; 《시원시원하게》 promptly; quickly; speedily; easily; in a businesslike way; with dispatch 〔promptitude〕. ¶ 일을 ~ 처리하다 dispose of the matters snappily 〔handily〕; be prompt in *one's* work / 묻는 말에 ~ 대답하다 answer questions readily / 어려운 문제를 ~ 풀다 solve a hard question easily / 그는 일을 ~ 처리하는 사람이다 He has a brisk way of disposing of things.

**척척하다** (be) wet; moist; damp(ish); clammy; [서술적] feel wet. ⇨ 축축하다. ¶ 척척한 손 moist 〔clammy〕 hands / 척척한 옷 wet clothes / 마룻바닥이 ~ the floor is damp / 밤이슬을 맞아 ~ be wet 〔damp〕 with night dew / 오줌을 싸서 옷이 ~ clothes have been wet with urine.

**척추**(脊椎) 〖해부〗 the backbone; the spine; the spinal 〔vertebral〕 column. ¶ ~가 있는 vertebrated.
◉ ~골 the vertebra. ~관절 돌기 a zygapophysis (*pl.* -physes). ~동물 a vertebrate (animal): 무~동물 an invertebrate (animal). ~마취 spinal an(a)esthesia. ~만곡 spinal curvature; scoliosis. ~염 〖의학〗 spondylitis. ~카리에스 〖의학〗 spinal caries.

**척축**(斥逐) expulsion; driving 〔turning〕 out; ouster. ~하다 expel; drive 〔turn, send〕 out; oust.

**척출**(斥黜) ousting; dismissal 〔removal〕 from office. ~하다 oust; dismiss 〔remove〕 from office.

**척출**(剔出) extraction; removal; excision. ~하다 extract; excise; remove; cut 〔gouge〕 out. ¶ 눈알〔탄알〕을 ~하다 remove 「an eyeball 〔a bullet〕.
◉ ~기 an extractor.

**척탄**(擲彈) a (hand) grenade. ◉ ~통(筒) a grenade (bomb) thrower; a grenade discharger.

**척토**(尺土) a foot 〔patch〕 of land 〔territory〕; a small bit of land.

**척토**(瘠土) arid soil. ⇨ 척지(瘠地).

**척하다** =체하다.

**척후**(斥候) 《업무》 scouting; patrolling; 《사람》 a scout; a patrol; a feeler. ~하다 scout; reconnoiter 《the area》. ¶ ~를 내보내다 send out scouts / ~로 나가다 go out scouting. ◉ ~대 a scouting 〔reconnoitering〕 party: ~ 대장 a patrol leader. ~병 a scouting 〔reconnoitering〕 soldier. ~전 skirmishes of scouts; a partol encounter 〔action, clash〕. 전투〔정찰〕 ~ a combat 〔reconnaissance〕 patrol 〔scout〕.

**천** 《피륙》 woven stuff; cloth; fabric. ¶ 천 조각 a piece of cloth / 고급천 quality cloth / 양복 천 suiting; suit 〔dress (여자의)〕 materials / 두꺼운 〔얇은〕 천 a piece of thick 〔thin〕 cloth / 좋은 〔나쁜〕 천 good 〔bad〕 stuff / 천이 고운 〔거친〕 of fine 〔coarse〕 texture / 천을 끊다 buy a piece of cloth / 천을 짜다 weave cloth / 이 천은 질깁니다 This stuff wears well.

**천**(千) a thousand. ¶ 수천의 thousands of 《people》 / 천배(倍)의 thousandfold; of a thousand times / 5천 five thousand (★ 수사가 복수라도 s를 붙이지 않음) / 천만 ten million / 천만 장자 a multimillionaire / 천분의 1, a 〔one-〕 thousandth / 천에 하나 one in a thousand / 천 명이나 되는 사상자 casualties that could be counted by the thousand; thousands of casualties / 천 배로 하다 increase thousandfold / 천 단위로 표시되다 be shown 〔expressed〕 in thousands / 그의 말은 천근(斤)의 무게가 있다 His word has the weight of authority.

**천**(薦) recommendation. ⇨ 추천(推薦).

**천간**(天干) 〖민속〗 the ten celestial stems; the ten calendar signs.

**천개**(天蓋) a coffin lid.

**천거**(薦擧) recommendation; support. ~하다 recommend 《*a person*》; say 〔put in〕 a good word for. ⇨ 추천.

**천격**(賤格) 《품격》 mean character; mean style; 《사람》 a person of low birth; a mean countenance. ~스럽다 (be) mean; low; humble; vulgar; base.

**천견**(淺見) a superficial idea; a shallow view. ◉ ~박식(薄識) little experience and small learning; superficial learning and a shallow view.

**천계**(天界) 《하늘》 the skies; the heavens; 《천상 세계》 the celestial sphere.

**천계**(天啓) (divine) revelation; revelation 〔a sign〕 from Heaven.

**천고**(千古) 《태고》 remote antiquity; 《영원》 eternity; all ages. ¶ ~불멸의 everlasting; eternal; immortal / ~의 명언 an eternal truth; an unchangeable maxim / ~의 영웅 the greatest hero that ever lived.

**천고마비**(天高馬肥) ¶ ~의 계절 autumn with the sky clear and blue, and horses growing stout.

**천골**(賤骨) 《사람》 a person of low birth; 《용모》 a mean countenance 〔look, physiognomy〕.

**천공**(天功) Nature's work; wonders 〔work〕 of Nature. ¶ ~의 미(美) natural 〔scenic〕 beauty.

**천공**(天空) the sky; the air; the firmament; the heaven. ¶ ~으로 skyward(s); heavenward; into the air / ~으로 높이 오르다 shoot up skywards / ~을 날다 fly high in the air.

**천공**(穿孔) perforation; boring; punching. ~하다 drill; perforate; bore; punch. ◉ ~기 a boring 〔drilling〕 machine; a drill; a borer; a perforator; a key 〔card〕 punch (카드 따위의). ~선반 a boring lathe. ~성 복막염 perforative peritonitis. ~카드 〖컴퓨터〗 a punch(ed) card. ~테이프 〖컴퓨터〗 a punched 〔perforated〕 tape.

**천공해활**(天空海濶) ~하다 be serene as the sky and open as the sea. ¶ ~의 기질 a spacious 〔an oceanic〕 mind.

**천구**(天球) 〖천문〗 the celestial sphere. ◉ ~도(圖) a celestial map. ~의(儀) a celestial globe. ~적도(赤道) the celestial equator.

**천국**(天國) Heaven; Paradise; the Kingdom of Heaven 〔God〕; the Celestial City. ¶ ~의 heavenly; celestial / 지상 ~ an earthly 〔a terrestrial〕 paradise; a heaven on earth / 보행자 ~ a pedestrian's paradise; a (car-free) mall / ~에 가다 go to Heaven; die.

**천군만마**(千軍萬馬) thousands of troops and horses. ¶ ~지간의 맹장 a veteran of many battles.

**천궁도**(天宮圖) a horoscope. ¶ ~를 펼쳐 별점을 치다 cast a horoscope.

**천극**(天極) 〖천문〗 the celestial poles.

**천금**(千金) a lot of money; a thousand pieces of gold; fortune. ¶ 일확 ~을 꿈꾸다 dream of making a fortune at a stroke; plan to get rich at a single bound / 그것은 ~을 주고서도 못 산다 It is a priceless treasure 〔above price〕. / ～을 준다 해도 그건 못 하겠다 I wouldn't do that for anything 〔for all the world〕.

**천기**(天氣) =일기(日氣), 날씨. ◉ ～도(圖) a weather map 〔chart〕.

**천기**(天機) ① 《자연의 기밀》 the profound secrets of nature; the hidden plans of Providence. ② 《큰 기밀》 a deep 〔profound〕 secret; a state secret (국가의). ¶ ～를 누설 마라 The secret must not be divulged. *or* It must be kept (a) secret.

**천기**(喘氣) a light case of asthma.

**천녀**(天女) a heavenly maid; a celestial nymph.

**천녀**(賤女) a woman of humble 〔low〕 birth; a lowly 〔humble〕 woman.

**천년**(千年) a thousand years; a millennium. ¶ ～의 millenary / ～만년 【부사적】 (for) long; for ever; everlastingly.

**천당**(天堂) Heaven; the palace of Heaven; Paradise. ⇨ 천국.

**천대**(賤待) (a) contemptuous 〔scornful, disdainful〕 treatment. ～하다 treat with contempt 〔inhospitably〕; slight; 《등한히 하다》 neglect; be negligent 《of》. ¶ ～받다 be treated contemptuously; get disdainful treatment / 그 소년은 의붓자식이라고 몹시 ～를 받았다 Being a stepchild, the boy suffered a real ill-treatment.

**천더기**(賤—) a despised person; a poor wretch; a child of scorn. ¶ 사회의 ～ a pariah; an outcast / ～ 노릇을 하다 be treated as a child of scorn.

**천덩거리다** 《끈기 있는 액체가》 keep dripping in drops. 「다 =천덩거리다.

**천덩천덩** dripping in sticky drops. ～하

**천도**(天桃) ① 《전설의》 a heavenly peach. ② 《품종》 a variety of peach with its reddish yellow flesh.

**천도**(天道) ① 《천지의 도리》 the way of Heaven; Providence; the way of Providence; Heaven. ¶ ～도 무심하다 God is indifferent. ② 【천문】 the orbits of heavenly bodies.

**천도**(遷都) the transfer of the capital 《to》; the removal of the seat of government. ～하다 transfer the capital 《to》; move 〔remove〕 the seat of government 《to》.

**천도교**(天道敎) 【종교】 "*Ch'ŏndoism*" 《*Ch'ŏndo* religion, founded in southern Korea by Ch'oe Che-wu in 1859》. ◉ ～도 a *Ch'ŏndoist.*

**천동설**(天動說) the Ptolemaic 〔geocentric〕 theory 〔system〕; geocentricism.

**천둥** thunder; a peal 〔roar, roll〕 of thunder; cracks of thunder. ～하다 thunder; thunder rolls 〔rumbles, cracks〕. ¶ ～에 개 뛰어 들듯 become frightened 〔startled〕; be petrified with terror 〔fright〕 / 멀리서 ～ 소리가 울려왔다 Rolls of thunder were heard in the distance.

**천둥벌거숭이** a rough-and-tumble amateur; a man of reckless valor; a reckless simpleton; a daredevil. ¶ ～라 아무 것도 모르며 덤비기만 한다 He is a rank amateur but has to get mixed up in everything.

**천둥지기** rice paddies that depend on rainfall for water; rain-dependent farmland. 「Star.

**천랑성**(天狼星) 【천문】 Sirius; the Dog

**천래**(天來) ¶ ～의 heavenly; heaven=sent; divine; 《천부의》 innate.

**천량** money and food; wealth; possessions. ¶ ～이 다 떨어지다 have run out of food and money both.

**천려**(淺慮) indiscretion; imprudence; a shallow 〔foolish〕 idea; thoughtlessness; lack of prudence 〔foresight〕.

**천려일실**(千慮一失) an oversight 〔a slip〕 of a wise man; a mere slip.

**천렵**(川獵) river fishing; fishing in a river. ～하다 fish in a river.

**천륜**(天倫) the natural relationships of man; moral laws. ¶ ～을 어기다 violate 〔transgress〕 moral laws.

**천리**(千里) a thousand *ri;* 【비유적】 a long distance. ¶ ～만리 떨어져 있는 곳 a place far far away / 천릿길도 한 걸음부터 A journey of a thousand miles starts with but a single step. *or* Step by step one goes a long way. ◉ ～마 a swift horse; a fleet 〔gallant〕 steed.

**천리**(天理) natural laws; the laws of nature. ¶ ～에 어긋나다 violate 〔be contrary to〕 the laws of nature; go against nature.

**천리안**(千里眼) 《투시》 clairvoyance; second sight; 《통찰력》 insight; penetration. ¶ ～을 가진 사람 a person gifted with second sight; a clairvoyant (남자); a clairvoyante (여자) / ～이다 be gifted with second sight / ～을 가지고 있다 have 〔possess〕 clairvoyant powers.

**천마**(天馬) 《나는 말》 a flying horse; 【그神】 Pegasus; 《명마》 a fine steed.

**천막**(天幕) a tent; 《큰》 a pavilion; a

marquee《영》; 《작은》 a shelter tent (피난용 따위의); 《배의》 an awning; [총칭] tentage. ¶ 원뿔형 ~ a bell tent / ~용 기둥 a tent pole / ~의 로프를 매는 말뚝 a tent peg / ~을 치다 pitch 〔set up, put up〕 a tent / ~을 걷다 strike 〔pull down, fold up〕 a tent. ◉ ~생활 camping (out); camp life; 《방랑의》 a nomadic life: ~ 생활을 하다 camp out. ~촌 a tent 〔camp〕 village.

**천만**(千萬) 《1천만》 ten million; 《무수》 a countless number; a myriad; 《매우》 exceedingly; extremely; very much. ¶ 수~의 tens of millions of / ~의 말씀 《당찮은》 an inappropriate remark; a remark wide of the mark; 《과분한》 an undeserved compliment 〔courtesy〕 / ~의 말씀입니다 Don't mention it. *or* Not at all. *or* You're welcome. 《미》 / 유감 ~이다 That's too bad. *or* It is 「really regrettable 〔quite deplorable〕 (that ...). *or* It is much to be regretted (that ...). / 찾아 뵙지 못해 유감 ~입니다 I am very sorry that I was unable to call on you. / 「수고해 주셔서 고맙습니다」—「원 ~에요」 "Thank you for your trouble."—"Oh, no, not at all."

◉ ~고(古) remote antiquity; most ancient days. ~금 millions of money. ⇨천금. ~년 ten million years; myriad years; a long long time. ~사 all things 〔affairs〕; everything; all matter; all. ⇨ 만사. ~세(世) countless generations; all ages: ~세에 걸쳐 for all ages to come; through all ages; forever. ~세(歲) hundreds of millions of years. ~인 ten million people; millions of people; so many people. ~장자 a billionaire; a multimillionaire. ~층 countless classes 〔strata, varieties〕; innumerable 〔various〕 ranks 〔classes, grades〕; all levels: 물건도 ~층이다 There is an endless variety of articles in the world.

**천만다행**(千萬多幸) being extremely fortunate; a stroke of good luck 〔fortune〕; a godsend. ~하다 (be) extremely fortunate; very lucky. ¶ ~으로 luckily; fortunately; by good luck / 다친 것이 그만하기 ~입니다 You were lucky not to have been hurt seriously 《in the auto accident》. / 병이 그만하시다니 ~입니다 It is wonderful to hear that you are getting along so well. / 그곳에서 그를 만난 것은 ~이었다 It was by a stroke of good luck that I met him there. *or* I found him there by pure luck.

**천만뜻밖**(千萬 —) being quite unexpected 〔unforeseen, unanticipated〕; a great surprise. ¶ ~의 quite unexpected; unlooked-for; unforeseen; unanticipated; never dreamed of / ~의 일 the last thing *one* can think of; a (great) surprise; a bolt from the blue / ~에 quite unexpectedly; contrary to *one's* expectation; surprisingly enough; all of a sudden / ~에 그를 노상에서 만났다 I met 〔ran into, bumped into〕 him quite unexpectedly on the street. / 그가 성공한 것은 ~이다 His success is really surprising.

**천만번**(千萬番) ten million times; [부사적] ever so many times; over and over again; repeatedly. ¶ 너 같은 놈은 ~ 죽어 마땅하다 Thousands of death are too good for the likes of you. *or* The likes of you cannot die too often.

**천만부당**(千萬不當) being utterly 〔entirely, absolutely〕 unjust; being unright 〔unlawful, unreasonable, inappropriate〕. ~하다 (be) utterly 〔entirely, absolutely〕 unjust; be entirely 〔quite〕 unreasonable 〔unright, inappropriate〕. ¶ ~한 말 an absolutely unreasonable remark; an utterly inappropriate remark / ~한 요구 an extravagant demand / 당국의 조처는 ~하다 The measure taken by the authorities is absolutely injudicious.

**천명**(天命) ① 《수명》 *one's* (preordained span of) life. ¶ ~이 다하다 come to the end of *one's* journey / 그가 일찍 죽은 것도 ~이다 He was meant to die young. ② 《하늘의 뜻》 God's will; Providence; a mandate from Heaven; 《운명》 fate; destiny; Karma. ¶ ~으로 알다 submit to Heaven's will; resign *oneself* to *one's* fate / 할 일을 다하고 ~을 기다리다 do *one's* best and leave the rest to Heaven / 이렇게 된 것도 ~이다 This has been ordained by Providence. / 총알에 맞고 안 맞는 것은 ~이다 Every bullet has its billet.

**천명**(闡明) clarification; elucidation. ~하다 make clear; clarify; explain; give an explanation; elucidate; explicate. ¶ 중외(中外)에 ~하다 affirm before 〔declare to〕 the world.

**천묘**(遷墓) relocating a grave. ⇨ 이장(移葬).

**천무이일**(天無二日) Heaven cannot support two suns, nor the earth two masters.

**천문**(天文) 《현상》 astronomical phenomena; 《천문학》 astronomy; 《점성술》 astrology. ¶ ～을 보다 make astronomical observations; 《점성》 cast a horoscope. ◉ ～년〔일, 시, 조수〕 astronomical year 〔day, time, tide〕. ～단위 an astronomical unit. ～대 an (astronomical) observatory. ～도 an astronomical chart. ～연표 an astronomical chronology. ～항법 〖항공·해양〗 celestial navigation.

**천문동**(天門冬) 〖한의〗 the root of a kind of asparagus.

**천문학**(天文學) astronomy; uranology. ¶ ～적〔상의〕 astronomical / ～적 숫자에 달하다 run into astronomical figures 〔numbers〕. ◉ ～자 an astronomer.

**천민**(賤民) a person of low 〔humble〕 birth; [총칭] lowly 〔humble〕 people; the lowly; the humble.

**천박**(淺薄) shallowness; superficiality. ～하다 (be) shallow; superficial; half-baked. ¶ ～한 사람 a shallow-minded person / ～한 생각 a superficial way of thinking; a half-baked 〔shallow〕 idea; a superficial view 《of life》/ ～한 짓을 하다 do a silly thing / 온갖 일에 ～한 지식을 내세우다 show off *one's* superficial knowledge in everything.

**천방지축**(天方地軸) ① 《덤벙댐》 a stupid flurry; rashness; recklessness; [부사적] rashly; recklessly; headlong. ¶ ～ 덤비다 rush recklessly; make a headlong rush. ② [부사적] 《허둥허둥》 precipitately; utterly discomfited; hurry-scurry; helter-skelter. ¶ ～ 도망치다 beat a hasty retreat; run away with the tail between the legs.

**천백번**(千百番) ever so many times.

**천벌**(天罰) Heaven's vengeance; divine punishment 〔retribution〕; the wrath of God; nemesis. ¶ ～을 받다 be punished by Heaven; incur the wrath of God; provoke nemesis / ～이 내리도록 빌다 imprecate 〔call down〕 the vengeance of Heaven upon 《*a person*》/ 그런 짓을 하면 ～을 받는다 Heaven will punish you for it. / 드디어 그에게 ～이 내렸다 Retribution at last overtook him. / 그것은 네가 거짓말을 한 ～이다 It is a judgment on you for having lied.

**천변**(川邊) a riverside; a streamside; a riverbank; an edge of a river. ¶ ～에 by 〔on〕 a river; on the banks 〔shores〕 of a river / ～에서 at the side of a river; at the riverside.

**천변**(千變) a thousand changes; countless variations; kaleidoscopic changes. ～하다 change endlessly; make kaleidoscopic changes.

**천변**(天變) extraordinary phenomena in the heavens; a convulsion of nature. ⇨ 천변지이(地異).

**천변만화**(千變萬化) innumerable 〔kaleidoscopic〕 changes; an endless series of changes; immense 〔infinite〕 variety. ～하다 change 〔vary〕 endlessly; undergo kaleidoscopic changes. ¶ ～의, ～하는 ever-changing; kaleidoscopic / ～하는 광경 shifting scenes / ～하는 세상 the ever-changing 〔kaleidoscopic〕 world.

**천변지이**(天變地異) an extraordinary natural phenomenon; a convulsion of nature; a cataclysm.

**천병만마**(千兵萬馬) vast numbers of infantry and cavalry; a big army.

**천복**(天福) a heavenly blessing; benediction. ¶ ～을 받다 be blessed by Heaven.

**천부**(天賦) ¶ ～의 natural; native; inborn; innate; gifted; inherent; endowed / ～의 재능 a natural gift 〔endowment〕; an innate talent / ～의 인권 the natural 〔inherent, absolute〕 rights of man / ～의 음악 소질〔재능〕이 있다 be endowed (by nature) with musical talent; have a natural talent for music; be a born musician. ◉ ～론 nativism.

**천부당만부당**(千不當萬不當) ⇨ 천만부당.

**천분**(天分) 《천성》 *one's* nature; 《천부의 재주》 *one's* natural talent(s) 〔gifts〕. ¶ ～이 있다〔～을 타고나다〕 be endowed with talents 《for》; have an aptitude 《for》; be born with great talents / ～이 있는 사람 a talented 〔gifted〕 man / ～이 없다 be untalented 〔ungifted〕; be endowed with no genius / ～을 발휘하다 give full play to *one's* natural talent / ～을 키우다 develop *one's* natural talent.

**천비**(賤婢) a lowly maidservant.

**천사**(天使) an angel; 《아기 천사》 a cherub (*pl.* ～s, -ubim); [총칭] hierarchy. ¶ ～의〔같은〕 angelic 《smiles》; seraphic; cherubic; an angel of 《a woman》/ 대～ an archangel / 수호～

a guardian angel / ～ 같은 데가 있다 《모습이》 have something angelic in the expression of *one's* features.

**천사만고**(千思萬考) deep meditation; mature consideration; careful deliberation. ～하다 meditate deeply; deliberate carefully; consider well.

**천사슬**(天—) doing things nature's way; letting nature take its course.

**천산**(天産) = ～물. ◉ ～물 natural products; [총칭] natural produce: (여러 가지) ～물이 풍부하다 be rich in natural products (of all kinds).

**천산갑**(穿山甲) 〖동물〗 a pangolin; a scaly anteater.

**천산지산** with all sorts of excuses; profuse excuses. ¶ 핑계를 ～ 늘어놓다 「come out with 〔make, produce〕 all sorts of excuses.

**천상**(天上) the heavens. ¶ ～의 heavenly; celestial; ethereal / ～에서 from heaven; from above; from on high / ～천하에 그런 나쁜 놈은 없다 There is no worse rascal in the whole world. / ～천하 유아독존 I am my own Lord 〔I am holy alone〕 throughout heaven and earth.

**천상바라기**(天上—) a person with a habitual upturned face.

**천생**(天生) ① [명사적] what is produced by Heaven; what is destined 〔preordained〕 by Heaven; what is natural. ¶ ～의 natural; born; designed by nature; destined by Heaven / ～의 음악가 a born musician.
② [부사적] by nature; naturally; for ever; as ever. ¶ 그는 ～ 학자다 He is a scholar by nature. *or* He was meant to be a scholar. / 너는 ～ 사기꾼밖에 못해 먹겠다 A swindler 「is all 〔is the most〕 that you will ever be.
◉ ～배필 a match made in Heaven; a predestined marriage; a well=matched couple. ～연분 matrimonial ties preordained by Providence.

**천석꾼**(千石—) a person who has a crop of 1,000 bag of rice; a wealthy farmer; a large 〔great〕 landowner.

**천성**(天性) (*one's*) nature; *one's* natural 〔innate〕 disposition 〔character〕; 《기질》 temperament. ¶ ～의〔적인〕 natural; born; inborn; innate (★ natural 재능·성질 따위를 「태어날 때부터 가지고 있는」의 뜻. born 「타고난」이란 뜻의 가장 일반적인 말. inborn 좀 딱딱한 표현의 문어적인 말로 born과 같은 뜻. innate 성질 따위가 「천부의, 선천적인」이란 뜻의 말.) / ～이 정직하다 be honest by nature / ～이 온순하다 have a gentle disposition; be tenderhearted by nature / 습관은 제2의 ～이다 Habit is second nature. / 사랑과 미움은 사람의 ～이라 마음대로 할 수가 없다 Love and hatred are instinctive and can't be controlled at will. / 최소 노력으로 최대 이익을 얻으려는 것은 인간의 ～이다 It is human nature to want to gain the greatest profit by the smallest effort.

**천세**(千歲) a thousand years; a millennium; eternity; a long time. ¶ 이름을 ～에 남기다 immortalize *one's* name; win immortal 〔undying, everlasting〕 name; hand *one's* name down to posterity / ～ 만세 무강하십시오 Long live! ◉ ～력 a thousand year almanac; a perpetual calendar.

**천세나다** be much in demand; hard to get; become scarce 〔rare〕; run short.

**천수**(天水) rainwater. ◉ ～답 paddies dependent rainwater.

**천수**(天壽) *one's* natural term of existence; *one's* natural span of life. ¶ ～를 다하다〔누리다〕 live out *one's* allotted span of life; die a natural death; complete the natural span of *one's* life / ～를 누리지 못하고 죽다 die early; die before *one's* time.

**천수**(天數) ① 《천명》 *one's* natural span of life. ⇨ 천명(天命) ①, 천수(天壽). ② 《천운》 destiny; fate.

**천시**(天時) ① 《기회》 a good 〔favorable, heaven-sent〕 opportunity; help from Heaven; the psychological moment. ¶ ～를 기다리다 wait *one's* time; watch for a chance 〔good opportunity〕 / ～를 포착하다 seize 〔take〕 the good opportunity; take the tide as it offers. ② 《자연 현상》 spells of natural phenomena.

**천시**(賤視) contempt. = 멸시(蔑視).

**천식**(喘息) 〖의학〗 asthma; 《수의(獸醫)》 whistling. ¶ ～(성)의 asthmatic / ～의 발작 an asthma attack. ◉ ～환자 an asthmatic (patient).

**천신**(天神) the heavenly gods. ◉ ～지기(地祇) the gods of heaven and earth.

**천신**(薦新) 《신에게 올림》 offering 〔presenting〕 a new product to the gods; 《굿》 a shamanist rite in spring 〔autumn〕. ～하다 offer 〔present〕 a new product 〔fruits〕 to the gods; have a spring 〔autumn〕 exorcism.

**천신만고**(千辛萬苦) all sorts of hardships and privations; arduous labor;

(severe) trials. ～하다 undergo 〔go through〕 all sorts of hardships and privations; take great pains. ¶ 그는 ～로 겨우 살림을 꾸려 간다 He goes through all sorts of hardships to earn a bare living. / 그는 ～ 끝에 그 기계를 발명하였다 He had gone through all sorts of hard works before he got the machine invented.

**천심**(天心) ①《하늘의 뜻》 the will of Heaven; the divine will; Providence. ¶ ～은 헤아릴 수 없다 Inscrutable are the ways of Heaven. / 민심은 ～이다 The voice of people (is) the voice of God. ②《하늘 한복판》 the zenith. ¶ 달이 ～에 걸렸다 The moon has reached 〔is at〕 its zenith. *or* The moon is hanging at the zenith.

**천안**(天顔) the King's countenance. ¶ ～을 배알하다 be received in audience by His Majesty.

**천안문**(天安門) 《중국 북경의》 *Tienanmen* Gate; Gate of Heavenly Peace. ◉ ～광장 the *Tienanmen* Square.

**천앙**(天殃) Heaven's punishment; divine retribution.

**천애**(天涯) ①《하늘 끝》 the horizon. ②《먼 곳》 a distant land; a far-off country; a remote region. ¶ ～의 고아 a lonely orphan. ◉ ～지각(地角) the four corners of the earth.

**천야만야**(千耶萬耶) ～하다 《높다》 (be) lofty; sky-high; 《깎아지르다》 (be) sheer; precipitous; [서술적] tower up steeply; 《깊다》 (be) unfathomable. ¶ ～한 계곡 an unfathomable ravine; an abyss.

**천양**(天壤) heaven and earth. ¶ ～지간 the whole universe; the space between heaven and earth.

**천양지차**(天壤之差) a world of difference; all the difference in the world; a great 〔wide〕 difference 《between》. ¶ ～다, ～가 있다 be poles 〔worlds〕 apart; be as different as light from darkness 〔as day from night〕; there is a world of difference 《between》 / 그와 나의 사회적 지위는 ～다 He and I are wide 〔poles〕 asunder 〔apart〕 in social standing. / 그 두 작품에는 ～가 있다 There is all the difference between the two works.

**천양지판**(天壤之判) a wide difference 《between》. = 천양지차.

**천언만어**(千言萬語) countless 〔innumerable〕 words; endless arguments.

**천업**(賤業) a mean 〔discreditable〕 occupation; a dishonorable 〔shameful〕 calling 〔trade〕; a dirty job.

**천여**(天與) a godsend; a Heaven's gift. ¶ ～의 Heaven-sent; God-given; god=sent; natural / ～의 재능 a God-given talent; (a) natural gift / ～의 자원이 풍부하다 be rich in natural resources.

**천역**(賤役) a mean 〔humble〕 job 〔service〕; dishonorable work.

**천연**(天然) nature. ¶ ～의 natural; unartificial; native (금속 등의); spontaneous (자생의); wild (야생의) / ～의 미 natural beauty; the beauty of nature / ～으로 naturally; unartificially; spontaneously; in nature / ～으로 나는 금 native gold / ～ 그대로의 암석 a living 〔natural〕 rock / 바위가 ～으로 그렇게 생겼다 A rock is so shaped by nature.

◉ ～가스 natural gas: ～ 가스 매장지 a natural gas field / 액화 ～ 가스 liquefied natural gas (생략 LNG). ～기념물 a natural monument 〔treasure〕: ～ 기념물로 지정하다 designate 《*a thing*》 as a precious natural treasure. ～물 a natural substance 〔object〕. ～색 (a) natural color: ～색 사진 a color photograph 〔picture〕 / ～색 영화 a color film 〔movie〕. ～석 native rock. ～수 natural water. ～자원 natural resources: ～자원의 공동 개발 joint development of natural resources 《between》.

**천연**(遷延) delay; procrastination; postponement. ～하다 delay; procrastinate; put off; postpone. ¶ 일을 ～하다 delay *one's* work / ～이 허용되지 않다 [사물이 주어] admit of no delay.

◉ ～책 a delay move; a dilatory policy 〔measure〕; a time-gaining measure.

**천연덕스럽다**(天然—) = 천연스럽다.

**천연두**(天然痘) 〖의학〗 smallpox. ¶ ～에 걸리다 have 〔suffer from〕 smallpox.

◉ ～균 a smallpox germ 〔virus〕. ～자국 a pockmark. ～환자 a case of smallpox.

**천연스럽다**(天然—) ①《자연스럽다》 (be) natural; unartificial; 《꾸밈없다》 (be) unstudied; unaffected; 《그럴 듯하다》 (be) plausible; specious; looking like the truth. ¶ 천연스러운 자세 a natural posture / 천연스러운 안색 a natural expression of face / 천연스러운 태도 an unaffected attitude / 천연스럽게 거짓말을 하다 tell a lie that sounds like truth; tell a clever lie / 천연스럽게 눈

물을 흘리다 shed crocodile tears / 천연스럽게 말하다 talk with much show of truth.
② 《태연하다》 (be) unmoved; unperturbed; cool; 《무관심하다》 (be) unconcerned; indifferent. ¶ 천연스럽게 calmly; coolly; with an innocent look; as if nothing had happened; 《무관심하게》 unconcernedly; with utter indifference / 부끄러워하는 빛도 없이 ~ be barefaced; show no sign of humiliation / 술을 한 되나 마시고도 ~ remain quite sober after drinking a *doe* of *sul* / 그는 아무 일도 없었던 것처럼 천연스런 얼굴이었다 He looked indifferent 〔unconcerned〕 as if nothing had happened to him.

**천왕성**(天王星) 『천문』 Uranus.

**천우신조**(天佑神助) God's 〔providential〕 help; the grace of Heaven; divine grace. ~하다 Heaven helps and God assists. ¶ ~의 providential / ~로 by the grace of God 〔Heaven〕 / ~를 믿다 trust in divine favor / ~를 빌다 invoke the help of Heaven 《for》 / ~로 목숨을 건졌다 I escaped death by the grace of Heaven.

**천운**(天運) 《운명》 destiny; fate; the will of Heaven; 《운》 fortune. ¶ ~에 맡기다 leave 《*a matter*》 to chance; trust to Providence / ~으로 여기고 단념하다 resign *oneself* to fate; submit to fate / ~을 감사하다 thank 〔bless〕 *one's* stars 《for》.

**천은**(天恩) 《하늘의》 the grace 〔goodness〕 of Heaven; heavenly blessings; 《임금의》 Royal favor; the king's grace.

**천의**(天意) the divine will; God's will; Providence. ¶ ~에 따르다 follow 〔bow to〕 the will of Heaven / ~에 어긋나다 be against the will of Heaven.

**천의무봉**(天衣無縫) perfect beauty with no trace of artifice. ¶ ~의 flawless; perfect; artless and endearing.

**천인**(天人) 《하늘과 사람》 God 〔Heaven〕 and man; 《사람》 a heavenly being. ¶ ~공노할 만행〔죄악〕 a heinous atrocity 〔offence〕 / 그들은 ~공노할 죄를 저질렀다 They have sinned against God and man.

**천인**(賤人) a person of low 〔humble〕 origin; a lowly man.

**천일**(天日) ① 《해》 the sun; sunshine; sunlight. ② 《하늘과 해》 the sky and the sun. ③ 《천도교의》 Heaven Day (in the *Ch'ŏndo* religion) (=April 5). ◉ ~염 bay salt; sun-dried salt.

**천일야화**(千一夜話) 《책이름》 *The Arabian Nights; The Thousand and One Nights; The Arabian Nights' Entertainments.*

**천일초**(千日草) 『식물』 a globe amaranth.

**천자**(千字) 1,000 characters. ◉ ~문 the Thousand-Character Text; a primer of Chinese characters.

**천자**(天子) 《황제》 an emperor; a son of Heaven.

**천자**(天資) natural endowments; (a) nature. ¶ ~ 총명한 endowed with high intelligence.

**천자만태**(千姿萬態) an endless variety of forms; multifariousness. ¶ ~의 multifarious.

**천자만홍**(千紫萬紅) a colorful display (of flowers); a resplendent 〔dazzling〕 variety of beautiful flowers. ¶ 뜰에는 ~의 꽃들이 한창 어우러져 피어 있다 The garden is a riot of colors with a variety of flowers in full glory.

**천잠**(天蠶) 『곤충』 a wild silkworm; a tussah. ◉ ~나비 『곤충』 an emperor moth. ~사(絲) silk from the wild silkworm; tussah.

**천장**(天障) the ceiling; the roof 《of a cave》. ¶ 둥근 ~ a dome; a vault / ~이 낮은〔높은〕 방 a low-〔high-〕ceilinged room / ~이 높다〔낮다〕 have a high 〔low〕 ceiling; be high-〔low-〕ceil(ing)ed / ~에 매달려 있다 be hanging from the ceiling / ~을 기어다니다 creep over 〔on〕 the ceiling / ~에 반자를 하다 ceil 《a room》 with boards; board a ceiling / ~에 파리가 많이 붙어 있다 There are a lot of flies on the ceiling. ◉ ~널 a ceiling board. ~등(燈) an overhead 〔a ceiling〕 light. ~반자 a boarded ceiling. ~선풍기 a ceiling fan. ~화 a painting on the ceiling.

**천장**(遷葬) reburial; reinterment. ⇨ 이장(移葬). ~하다 bury again; rebury.

**천재**(天才) 《사람》 a (man of) genius; a prodigy; 《재능》 genius 《for》; a natural gift 〔talent 《for》〕. ¶ ~적(인) 《사람이》 gifted; talented; 《능력이》 outstanding 《ability》; prodigious 《intelligence》 / 수학의 ~ a genius in mathematics / 뛰어난 ~ a great 〔transcendent〕 genius / 세상의 인정을 못받는 ~ an unappreciated genius 《for》 / 어학에 ~다 be endowed with linguistic talent; be a born linguist / ~적인 데가 있다 have a touch of genius; have something of the genius in *one* / ~를 발휘하다 give full

play to *one's* genius; bring *one's* talent into full play / 어려서 이미 ～성이 드러나다 *one's* genius asserts itself early / 그는 ～적인 시인이다 He is a 「born 〔highly gifted〕 poet. / 에디슨은 ～란 「1%의 영감과 99%의 노력」이라고 말했다 Edison defined genius as '1% inspiration and 99% perspiration.'
◉ ～교육 (the) education of gifted children. ～아 an infant prodigy; a gifted child; a boy 〔girl〕 wonder 《미》. ～화가 a highly-gifted artist; a born artist; an artistic genius.

**천재**(天災) a natural calamity 〔disaster〕; an act of God (불가항력). ¶ ～를 입다〔당하다〕 be 「visited 〔struck〕 by a calamity / ～로 돌려 단념하다 accept 《it》 as *one's* destiny / 해일, 가뭄 같은 ～에 기인하는 손해를 최소화하기 위한 예방책을 강구하다 work out preventive measures to minimize damages caused by such natural disasters as tidal waves and drought / ～라 어쩔 수 없다 It is an act of God and beyond human control. *or* There is no help to it, for it is an act of God. / 그것은 ～가 아니라 인재(人災)였다 It was not a natural disaster but a man-made one. / ～는 거의 예상치 않을 때 찾아온다 A natural calamity will happen when we least expect it. ◉ ～지변(地變) a natural disaster 〔calamity〕; the disturbances of the elements.

**천재**(千載) a thousand years; a long time. ◉ ～일우(一遇) what happens once in a thousand years; the chance of a lifetime; a very rare opportunity: ～일우의 좋은 기회 a golden opportunity / ～일우의 기회를 놓치다 throw away 〔miss〕 a golden opportunity 〔chance〕; lose the chance of a lifetime.

**천적**(天敵) 〚생물〛 a natural enemy; a natural check 《on rats》. ¶ 들쥐의 ～은 뱀이다 The snake is a natural enemy of the field mice.

**천정**(天井) ⇨ 천장.

**천정**(天定) ⇨ 천생(天生).

**천정**(天頂) 〚천문〛 the zenith; the vertex. ◉ ～거리 the zenith distance. ～의(儀) a zenith telescope. ～점(點) the zenith.

**천정부지**(天井不知) skyrocketing. ¶ ～의 물가 skyrocketing 〔soaring〕 prices / ～다 be soaring high; be skyrocketing; no ceilings are foreseen / 요즘 물가가 ～로 오르고 있다 Prices are 「skyrocketing 〔going sky-high〕 these days.

**천제**(天帝) the Lord of Heaven; God of Providence; the Creator.

**천조**(天助) Heaven's 〔Providential〕 help; heavenly assistance.

**천주**(天主) 〚가톨릭〛 the Lord of Heaven; God; *Deus* (L.). ◉ ～경(經) the Lord's Prayer; 《say》 a pater 〔paternoster〕. ～삼위(三位) the Trinity. ～십계(十誡) the Ten Commandments; the Decalog(ue).

**천주**(天誅) 《하늘의 벌》 Heaven's punishment; punishment from Heaven; 《하늘을 대신하는》 well-deserved punishment. ¶ ～를 가하다 inflict (just) punishment 《on *a person*》; kill 《*a person*》 as divine punishment for *his* wrong doing / ～를 받다 be punished by Heaven.

**천주교**(天主教) Roman Catholicism. ＝「가톨릭.

**천지**(天地) ① 《하늘과 땅》 heaven and earth; 《우주》 the universe; 《세상》 the world; 《자연》 nature. ¶ ～의 of heaven and earth; universal; mundane / ～의 진동 a convulsion of nature / ～를 진동시키다 《위엄 따위로》 make the whole world wonder; shake the sphere 〔earth and sky〕; 《음향 따위가》 rend the air / 둘 사이에는 ～의 차가 있다 There is 「a world of difference 〔all the difference in the world〕 between them. / (세상) ～에 그렇게 착한 사람은 없다 He is the best man in the world. / (세상) ～에 그런 일은 없다 It is simply impossible! *or* It is incredible! / ～간에 가장 귀한 것은 사람이다 Man is the noblest of all creatures in the world. / 포성이 ～를 뒤흔들었다 The guns rent heaven and earth.
② 《세계·곳》 a world; a land; 《경지》 a realm; a sphere. ¶ 별～ a different world; a world by 〔in〕 itself; a world of its own / 신～ a new world / 자유～ a free land; the land of freedom / 신～가 열리다 a new world opens (up) / 신～를 개척하다 exploit a new sphere of activities / 별～에 온 것 같은 기분이다 feel as if *one* were in a different world.
③ 《매우 많음》 being full 《of》; (an) abundance; (a) plenty; richness. ¶ 거지 ～다 [장소가 주어] swarm 〔be crowded〕 with beggars / 사람 ～다 be crowded 〔thronged〕 with people / 그 책은 온통 오자(誤字) ～다 That book

is full of misprints.
◉ ～만물 all creatures; the creation; the universe; universal 〔all〕 nature. ～창조 the Creation: ～ 창조의 신 the Creator of the universe / ～ 창조 이래 since the beginning of Creation; since the Creation.

**천지**(天池) the crater lake 《on Mt. Paektu》.

**천지개벽**(天地開闢) ① 《창조》 the Creation (of Heaven and Earth); the beginning of the world. ～하다 create Heaven and Earth. ⇨천지 창조. ② 《큰 변혁》 a cataclysmic change; an upheaval; a revolution. ～하다 undergo a cataclysmic change; revolutionize.

**천지신명**(天地神明) the gods of heaven and earth; deity; divinity. ¶ ～의 가호(加護) the protection of God; the grace of Heaven / ～께 맹세하건데 나는 그것을 하지 않았다 I swear by heaven and earth I did not do it.

**천직**(天職) a calling; a (real) vocation; a mission (in life); *one's* divinely appointed work (in life). ¶ 단순한 생활 수단이 아닌 ～ a divine calling, not a mere means for making a living / 목사를 ～으로 알다 feel a call to the ministry / ～을 다하다〔찾아내다〕 fulfill 〔find out〕 *one's* mission / 가르치는 것이 내 ～이다 Teaching is my duty in life. / 이것이 내 ～이다 Heaven has called me to this work. / 여성(들)의 ～은 가정에 있다 Women's natural place is in the home.

**천직**(賤職) a mean 〔a humble, an ignoble〕 occupation; a shameful calling.

**천진난만**(天眞爛漫) innocence; *naïveté* (F.); naivety; simplicity; lack of sophistication; artlessness. ～하다 (be) simple (and innocent); innocent; naive; artless; unaffected; simple-hearted〔-minded〕; unsophisticated; ingenuous. ¶ ～한 생각 a simple 〔an unsophisticated〕 idea / ～한 아이 a simple and innocent child / ～한 태도 an innocent 〔unsophisticated, unaffected〕 air / ～하게 웃다 laugh an innocent laugh / ～한 소리를 하다 talk like a child; say childish things / 그의 행동에는 ～한 데가 있다 He has a sort of *naïveté* 〔naivety〕 and openness of demeanor.

**천질**(天質) *one's* innate nature; natural endowments 〔disposition〕; a temperament.

**천차만별**(千差萬別) infinite variety 〔gradation〕. ～하다 (be) varied; [서술적] have infinite variety 〔gradation〕; come in all sorts and kinds. ¶ ～의 multifarious; of various kinds; an infinite variety of 《opinions》; in a thousand different ways / ～의 사람들 all sorts of people; various kinds of people / 사람의 마음은 ～이다 So many men, so many minds.

**천착**(穿鑿) 《구멍의》 boring; excavation; 《학문 따위의》 search; inquiry; scrutiny. ～하다 bore; excavate; scrutinize; rake; search; see 〔look〕 for; inquire into; poke and pry; dig 〔pry, delve〕 into. ¶ ～을 좋아하는 inquisitive; prying; curious; nos(e)y / 속속들이 ～하다 prove 《*a matter*》 to the bottom.

**천착하다**(舛錯—) 《심정이》 (be) perverse and disorderly; untoward; ill-natured; meanspirited; 《생김새·행동이》 (be) vulgar; low; mean; untoward. ¶ 천착한 얼굴 an ugly face; vulgar features / 천착한 말씨 a vulgar (way of) expression.

**천창**(天窓) a skylight; 《갑판의》 a companion; a scuttle.

**천천하다** (be) slow; tardy; unhurried.

**천천히** slowly; unhurriedly; at a slow speed; by (slow) degree; patiently; without haste 〔hurry〕; leisurely.
¶ ～ 걷다 walk leisurely; walk at a leisurely pace; walk slow 〔slowly〕 (★ walk slow는 walk slowly보다 구어적 표현으로 「걷다」라는 동작보다는 「느리게」라는 상태에 중점이 있음. 단 어느 쪽을 쓰느냐는 문맥의 어조에 따라 정해짐. 「천천히 가다」는 go slow가 더 관용적 표현임. slow, slowly는 How로 시작되는 감탄문에서가 아니고는 언제나 동사 뒤에 옴) / ～ 나아가다 advance slowly 〔at a slow pace〕; make *one's* slow way 《toward》; make slow time 《toward》 / ～ 생각하다 ponder over 《*a matter*》; take time to think / 시기를 ～ 기다리다 wait patiently for an opportunity / 식사를 ～ 하다 eat leisurely; take *one's* time with the meal / (일을) ～ 하다 take *one's* time 《in *do*ing》 / ～ 하시오 Take your time. / 좀더 ～ 운전하시오 Drive more slowly. *or* Don't drive so fast. / 길이 미끄러우니 ～ 가는 것이 좋겠다 The road is slippery, you had better slow down. / 그 일은 뒤에 ～ 생각하겠다 I'll think it over at my leisure. / (전화에서 상대에게) 좀 ～ 똑똑하게 말씀해 주시지 않겠습니까 Would you please speak slowly and clearly?

**천첩**(賤妾) ① 《첩》 a concubine of low

birth. ②《여자의 자칭》I.

**천체**(天體)「a heavenly 〔a celestial, an astronomical〕 body; 「a celestial 〔an astronomical〕 object. ¶ ～를 관측하다 observe (the) heavenly bodies; make an astronomical observation; survey the starry heavens.
◉ ～관측 an astronomical observation: ～관측학 astrometry. ～기상학 astrometeorology. ～도(圖) a celestial map. ～망원경 an astronomical telescope. ～물리학 astronomical physics; astrophysics: ～ 물리학 관측소 an astrophysical observatory / ～ 물리학자 an astrophysicist. ～분광술 astronomical spectroscopy. ～사진 the photograph of a「star 〔heavenly body〕: ～사진술 astrophotography; stellar photography. ～역학 celestial mechanics. ～운동 the movement of heavenly bodies. ～좌표 celestial coordinates. ～측량 uranometry. ～학 uranography; uranology.

**천추**(千秋)《천년》 thousand years;《긴 세월》many 〔long〕 years; [부사적] for ever. ¶ ～의 한(恨) a matter of「eternal 〔great〕 regret / 하루가 ～같이 기다려지다 wait impatiently for《*a person*》; look eagerly forward to《*a thing*》; be impatient for《the news》; await《*a person's* arrival》with「a craned neck 〔on tiptoe〕/ 훌륭한 이름을 ～에 남기다 win (an) immortal fame.
◉ ～만세(萬世) ＝천만년.

**천축**(天竺)《인도》India.

**천출**(賤出) a child born of a mean concubine; an illegitimate child.

**천층만층**(千層萬層) ⇨ 천만층.

**천치**(天癡·天痴) idiocy;《사람》an idiot. ⇨ 백치. ¶ ～의〔같은〕 idiotic / 이런 ～ 같은 놈 Oh, you (big) fool!

**천칭**(天秤) a balance. ⇨ 천평칭.

**천칭**(賤稱)《call by》a depreciatory「term 〔name〕; a derogatory term.

**천태만상**(千態萬象) all kinds of forms and figures; multifariousness.

**천트다**(薦―) ①《추천받다》get recommended《for》. ②《손대다》try for the first time; turn *one's* hand to; embark on《an unexperienced work》.

**천편일률**(千篇一律) monotony; humdrumness; lack of variety. ¶ ～의 monotonous; humdrum; stereotyped; dull / ～적인 문장 stereotyped 〔monotonous, dull〕 writing / ～적으로 되다 get 〔fall〕 into a groove / 그의 말은 ～적이다 He always harps on the same string.

**천평칭**(天平秤) a balance; a pair of scales. ¶ ～에 달다 weigh《*a thing*》「in the balance 〔on the scale〕.

**천품**(天稟)《성품》nature; character;《재질》a natural endowment; natural talents. ¶ 영특한 ～ a wonderful natural gift / 훌륭한 ～을 타고 나다 be born with an admirable disposition.

**천하**(天下) ①《한 나라》the whole country; the (whole) land; the State;《세상》the public; the earth;《세계》the world;《지배권》ruling power; the reins of government. ¶ ～없어도 whatever happens; under any circumstances / ～없이 without parallel; unrivaled / ～ 무비의 unequaled; unparalleled; unique; matchless; incomparable.
천하의: ～의 공론 public opinion / ～의 대사 a matter of grave concern to the state / ～의 영웅 the greatest hero ever known / ～의 대세 the general world「situation 〔trend〕/ ～의 형세를 살피다 observe the「situation 〔trend〕 of「public affairs 〔the political world〕.
천하에: ～에 under the sun; under heaven; in the world; on the world / ～에 둘도〔다시〕 없는《유일한》only; unique;《비길 데 없는》peerless; matchless; unequaled; unparalleled; unrivaled / ～에 무적이다「have no rival 〔be unrivaled〕 in the world / ～에 이름을 떨치다 make a「noise 〔name〕 in the world; spread *one's* name around the world; become worldfamous.
천하를: ～를 다스리다 reign 〔rule〕 over the whole country / ～를 잡다〔차지하다〕《정권을》「come to 〔get into〕 power; gain political power; become the ruler of the country; conquer the whole country;《통일하다》unify a country; bring the whole country under *one's*「rule 〔sway〕/ ～를 호령하다 dictate to the world.
¶ ～가 태평하다 All is right with the world. *or* Peace reigns in the land. / 지금은 민주당 ～다 The Democratic Party is now in power. / 이런 훌륭한 경치는 ～에 둘도 없을 게다 The place「unequaled 〔has no equal〕 in its scenic beauty. / ～는 그의 손 안에 들어왔다 The whole country came under his rule.
②《마음대로 함》having *one's* own way. ¶ 지금은 그의 ～다 Now he has his own way in everything. / 이곳은 오직 나 한 사람의 ～다 Here I am

absolutely my own boss 〔master〕. / 그가 없어졌으니 우리들 ~다 Now that he is gone, we are our own masters. / 한때 한국은 군벌의 ~였다 The militarists once ruled over Korea.
◉ ~명창 a great 〔an excellent〕 singer in the world; a world-famous singer. ~일색 a woman of matchless beauty; the fairest of the fair; a peerless beauty. ~장사 a matchless warrior; the strongest man in the world; a Hercules; an Atlas.

**천하다**(賤―) ①《사회적 신분 등이》(be) humble; low(ly); ignoble; obscure; low-born. ¶ 천한 몸 a person of low 〔ignoble〕 birth / 천한 신분 a humble station in life; *one's* lowly status / 천한 지위 a low position / 천한 직업 a mean 〔humble〕 occupation / 천한 집안에서 태어난 사람이다 be a man of humble birth.
②《천격스럽다》(***a***)《상스럽다》(be) vulgar; mean; low; base; gross; rude; immodest. ¶ 천한 계집 a low woman / 천한 티 a vulgar streak / 인품이 천하지 않은 사람 a decent-looking person / 말씨가 ~ be vulgar in *one's* speech / 천한 말을 쓰다 use vulgar language. (***b***)《야비·비열하다》(be) base; mean; despicable; dastard(ly); dirty; ignoble; vile. ¶ 천한 근성 a base spirit; a mean mind / 천한 짓 a mean 〔an ignoble〕 action; a dastardly act / 나는 그따위 천한 짓은 않는다 I am above such meanness.
③《흔하다》(be) plenty; superabundant; superfluous;《값싸다》(be) cheap. ¶ 요즘은 천한 것이 사과다 Apples are very cheap these days.

**천하일품**(天下一品) a unique article; a nonesuch; the best specimen in existence; the first on earth. ¶ ~이다 be unique 〔peerless〕; be beyond comparison; defy all comparison; there is nothing like it in the whole world. *or* It is unsurpassed by anything. / 이 작품은 ~이다 This work is supreme 〔without peer〕. / 그 아름다움이란 정말이지 ~이다 A fairer one was never seen. / 자네 부인의 요리 솜씨는 ~이다 Your wife's cooking is out of this world.

**천학**(淺學) shallow learning; superficial knowledge. ¶ ~비재(菲才)를 무릅쓰고 in spite of my want of knowledge and ability; though I have no pretentions either to learning or ability(★ 이러한 표현은 겸손을 나타내는 매우 한국적인 발상으로, 영미에서는 이런 표현은 쓰지 않는다).

**천행**(天幸) the blessing 〔help〕 of Heaven; a piece of good luck 〔fortune〕; a godsend. ¶ ~으로 luckily; fortunately; by (a stroke of) good luck; as good luck would have it / ~으로 살아나다 have a narrow escape by good luck / 전쟁 중 무사했으니 ~이다 You are fortunate to have been safe during the war.

**천험**(天險) a natural fastness 〔stronghold, defense〕. ¶ ~에 의지하다 take to a natural fastness.

**천혜**(天惠) Heaven's blessing; a gift of nature; natural advantage. ¶ ~의 요새 a fortress blessed with natural barriers for defense / ~가 풍부한 나라 a country blessed with natural resources / ~가 많다〔적다〕 be favored 〔ill-favored〕 by nature.

**천후**(天候) the weather. ⇨ 날씨. ¶ ~의 급변 an abrupt 〔a sudden〕 change in (the) weather.

**철**[1] ①《계절》a season; the time of the year. ¶ 제철이 아닌 out of season; unseasonable; off-season / 사철 four seasons; all the year round / 철따라 피는 꽃 flowers of the season / 철 늦은 behind the season / 철에 상관없이 in all seasons; all the year (round); in and out of season / 철이 바뀌다 a season changes; the seasons change / 봄철이 들다 spring begins 〔sets in〕; spring comes / 철이 이르다〔늦다〕 a season is early 〔late〕 in coming / 철따라 옷을 갈아 입다 change *one's* clothes according to the season / 경치는 철따라 바뀐다 The scenery varies from season to season. / 나는 철이 바뀔 때 자주 병에 걸린다 I am often taken ill when the season changes.
②《한창 …인 때》the season; the best time《for》. ¶ 복숭아철 the peach season / 사냥철 the season for shooting 〔hunting〕 / 철 이른〔늦은〕 사과 early 〔late〕 apples / 제철을 만나다 《사람이》 be in *one's* heyday 〔*one's* prime〕; be in *one's* palmy days; have *one's* best days / 송이버섯이 지금 제철이다 Mushrooms are now in season. / 꽁치철이다〔철이 지났다〕 The mackerel pike season is on 〔off〕.

**철**[2]《분별》good sense; discretion; prudence; judgment; reasonableness; wisdom. ¶ 철(이) 들 나이 an age of discretion / 철이 들다〔나다〕 attain the age of discretion; reach the age of reason; begin to understand things / 철이 들고 나서부터 since *one* was old enough to understand things; ever since *one* could remember / 철이 있다 have sense 〔discretion〕; be sensible; have a head on *one's* shoulders / 철이 없다 have no sense 〔discretion〕; be indiscreet 〔thoughtless, injudicious, foolish〕 / 철없는 짓을 하다 act 〔behave〕 thoughtlessly / 철도 들기 전에 아버지를 여의다 lose *one's* father 「before *one* can remember 〔while still a little child〕 / 그는 이제 철들 나이가 되었다 He is now old enough to have some sense about him. / 이젠 좀 철이 나야지 You ought to know better now.

**철**(鐵) 《쇠》 iron; steel (강철). ⇨쇠. ¶ 철의 ferrous; iron / 철제의 iron; (made) of iron / 철문 an iron gate / 철을 함유한 containing iron; ferrous; ferriferous / 철의 장막 the Iron Curtain / 철의 장막에서 망명해 오다 defect from behind the Iron Curtain.

**-철**(綴) filing; binding; a file. ⇨철하다. ¶ 서류철 a file of documents 〔papers〕 / 신문철 a newspaper file; a file of newspaper.

**철각**(鐵脚) iron legs. ¶ ~을 자랑하는 선수 a runner of iron legs.

**철갑**(鐵甲) 《장갑》 an iron covering; ironclad; 《갑옷》 iron armor; 《칠갑》 a coating; a crust. ~하다 form a coating. ◉ ~상어 『어류』 a sturgeon: ~상어의 알젓 caviar(e). ~선 an ironclad (ship).

**철강**(鐵鋼) (iron and) steel. ¶ ~제의 (made) of steel; steel / ~으로 되다〔만들어지다〕 be made 〔built〕 of steel. ◉ ~업 the steel industry. ~제품 steel manufactures.

**철거**(撤去) 《제거》 removal; demolition (파괴); clearing away (치워 없애기) pulling down (부수기); 《군대의》 withdrawal; 『컴퓨터』 demount. ~하다 《제거하다》 remove; take 〔clear〕 away; dismantle (장비 등을); 《부수어서》 demolish; pull 〔take〕 down. ¶ 무허가 판자집의 ~ removal of illegally built shacks / 빈민가의 ~ the clearing of slums / 장애물을 ~하다 remove the obstacles; clear 《the passage》 of obstacles / 군사 시설을 ~하다 dismantle 〔take away〕 military facilities / ~되다 be removed; be dismantled; be taken away; 《건물이》 be demolished; be pulled 〔taken〕 down.

**철겹다** be behind the season; be out of season; be unseasonable. ¶ 철겨운 꽃 a flower 「late for the 〔out of〕 season / 철겨운 옷 clothes worn beyond the season.

**철골** a bony 〔skeletal, emaciated〕 appearance. ¶ ~이 되다 become thin 〔emaciated〕; look haggard.

**철골**(鐵骨) 《튼튼한 몸》 (a) strongly=built physique; 《철근》 an iron 〔a steel〕 frame; a steel skeleton. ¶ ~로 건조하다 build with iron frames / 저 공장은 ~ 슬레이트 지붕이다 The factory has a slate roof on iron frames. ◉ ~건물 a steel-frame〔-skeleton〕 building. ~건축 《a building of》 steel=frame construction. ~공사 steel-frame work. ~구조 a cage; steel-frame structure; skeleton construction.

**철공**(鐵工) an ironworker; an ironsmith. ◉ ~소 an ironworks; an iron foundry: ~소 주인 an ironmaster. ~장(場) = ~소.

**철관**(鐵管) an iron pipe 〔tube〕. ¶ ~을 묻다 lay iron pipes / ~이 파열하다 an iron pipe bursts.

**철광**(鐵鑛) an iron mine; 《광석》 iron ore. ◉ ~천(泉) chalybeate springs 〔waters〕; a ferruginous spring.

**철교**(鐵橋) an iron bridge; a railroad 〔railway〕 bridge (철도의). ¶ ~를 놓다 build 〔construct〕 an iron bridge 〔a railway bridge〕 《over》 / ~를 지나가다 pass an iron bridge.

**철군**(撤軍) withdrawal 〔evacuation〕 of troops; military withdrawal. ~하다 withdraw troops 《from》; evacuate 《a place》. ¶ ~의 규모와 일정 the size and timetable of the pull-out (of the troops) / ~을 요구하다 demand troop withdrawal(s); demand evacuation / ~을 거부하다 refuse to withdraw the army; refuse evacuation.

**철권**(鐵拳) a strong fist; a clenched fist. ¶ ~을 먹이다 give 《*a person*》 a taste of *one's* fist; use *one's* fists 《on》; strike 《*a person*》 with *one's* fist / ~을 퍼붓다 rain blows upon 《*a person*》 / ~을 휘두르다 shake *one's* fist 《at *a person*, in *another's* face》. ◉ ~통치 iron-fisted rule.

**철권제재**(鐵拳制裁) a fist law. ¶ ~를 가하다 administer fist law to 《*a person*》; hit 《*a person*》 with *one's* fist as punishment / ~를 당하다 be subject to fist law.

**철궤**(鐵軌) a 〔an iron〕 rail.
**철궤**(鐵櫃) a steel safe; an iron 〔a money〕 box 〔chest〕; a strong box.
**철그렁-** ⇨ 절그렁-.
**철근**(鐵筋) 〖건축〗《콘크리트 속의》 a 〔an iron〕 reinforcing rod 〔bar〕.
◉ ~절단기 a bar cutter.
**철근콘크리트**(鐵筋 —) ferroconcrete; reinforced concrete. ¶ ~(의) 건물 a ferroconcrete 〔reinforced concrete〕 building / ~로 되어 있다 be (built) of reinforced concrete.
**철기**(鐵器) ironware; hardware 《미》; ironmongery 《영》. ⇨ 철물(鐵物).
◉ ~시대 〖고고학〗 the Iron Age.
**철길**(鐵 —) a railroad 〔railway 《영》〕 track; a rail line. ¶ ~ 보행의 위험 the danger of walking on a railroad track.
**철꺽** with a snap 〔click〕.
**철끈**(綴 —) a binding string 〔strip〕.
**철도**(鐵道) a railroad; a railway 《영》; a rail line. ¶ ~의 운행 railroading; operation of railroad / ~로 운반되는 화물 rail-borne goods / ~로 연결되어 있다 be linked by rail 《with》 / ~로 여행하다 travel by rail 〔train〕 / ~편으로 부치다 send 《*a thing*》 by rail / ~를 놓다 lay 〔build, make, construct〕 a railroad / ~를 이용하다 take the train 《to Seoul, to get there》; go 《to a place》 by train; use the train service / 여기서 안동까지 ~가 통해 있다 A railroad runs from here to Andong. / 폭설로 ~가 일부 불통되었다 The railroad service was interrupted by the heavy snow. / 도시에서는 많은 사람들이 ~를 이용해서 출근한다 There are many people in the cities who go to work by train.
◉ ~경비대 the railroad guard corps. ~공안원 a railroad security officer; a railroad policeman. ~공학 railroad engineering. ~기관사 a locomotive engineer 《미》; an engine driver on the railway 《영》. ~망 a railroad system 〔network〕. ~병원 a hospital for railroad employees. ~부설 railroading 《미》; the construction 〔building〕 of railroad: ~ 부설권 a railroad charter; railroad building concession. ~부속지 a railroad zone. ~사고〔참사〕 a railroad accident 〔disaster〕: 어젯밤 ~사고가 있었다 There was a railroad accident last night. ~선로 a railroad track; a rail line; [총칭] trackage: ~(선로) 보선공 a trackman; a linesman. ~수송 transportation by rail; railroad transport(ation). ~승차권 a railroad ticket: ~ 승차권 자동 발매기 an automatic ticket vending machine. ~안내소 a railroad information bureau 《미》; a railway enquiry office 《영》. ~여객 a railroad passenger: ~여객 운임표 a fare table; a railroad tariff. ~여행 railroad traveling 〔journey〕: ~여행자 a rail traveler. ~연락 railroad connection. ~요금〔운임〕《여객의》 a railroad fare; 《화물의》 freight 〔goods〕 rates; freightage. ~용지 《미》 a right-of-way (*pl.* rights-of-way, right-of-ways). ~우편 the railroad postal service 《미》; the railway post service 《영》. ~원 ⇨ 철도 종업원. ~자살: ~자살하다 throw *oneself* under a train; commit suicide by throwing *oneself* under a train. ~종업원 《미》 a railroad worker 〔man, employee〕; 《영》 a railwayman. ~차량 a railway vehicle 〔carriage〕; 《객차》 a (railroad) coach 〔car〕; 《화차》 a (railroad) freight car; a railroad car. ~청(廳) the National Railroad Administration. ~침목 crossties; ties; sleepers. ~편(便) railroad transportation; transportation by rail: 그 짐을 ~편으로 보내주시오 Please send the parcel by rail. ~행정 railroad administration. ~회사 a railroad corporation 《미》; a railway company 《영》.
고가~ an elevated 〔overhead〕 railroad. 고속~ a high-speed railroad. 관광~ a scenic railroad. 교외~ a suburban railroad. 복선~ a double-track railroad; a two-track line.

> **참고** 영·미의 철도
> 영국의 철도는 런던 주변의 일부 지하철(tube)를 제외하고는 모두 국유(國有)이며, British Rail이라고 한다. 미국에는 사설 철도가 많으나, 철도의 만성적인 적자를 해소시키기 위해 정부가 앞장서서 전미(全美) 철도 수송공사(National Railroad Passenger Corporation, 통칭으로 앰트랙 Amtrak 즉, American travel by track의 약칭)을 설립하여 여객 수송을 담당케 하고 있다. 또 동부·중서부의 화물·통근 수송에는 콘레일공사(公社)(Conrail, 즉 Consolidated Rail Corporation의 약칭)을 설립하여 반관 반민의 형태로 경영을 하고 있다.

**철두철미**(徹頭徹尾) [부사적] from beginning to end; from first to last; through and through; out and out;

thoroughly. ～하다 (be) thorough; thoroughgoing; exhaustive; complete; out-and-out; be an utter…; be an all-out…. ¶ ～한 연구 「a thorough 〔an exhaustive〕 study / ～한 조사 a thoroughgoing investigation / ～한 학자 a scholar to the 「core 〔bone〕; a scholar 「through and through 〔to the last inch〕 / ～ 반대하다 oppose in every particular; be dead set against 《it》; oppose 《it》 tooth and nail / ～ 애국자다 be a patriot to the core / 그 후보자는 ～한 개혁주의자였다 The candidate was an out-and-out reformist. / 나는 ～ 그를 지지해 왔다 I have supported him 「throughout 〔from beginning to end〕.

**철떡거리다** cling 《to》; stick 《to, on》; adhere 《to》. ¶ 옷이 젖어서 철떡거린다 My clothes are wet and cling to my body.

**철렁거리다** lap; slop; slosh. ¶ 물결이 해변에 ～ waves lap the shore.

**철로**(鐵路) a railroad. ＝철도(鐵道).

**철리**(哲理) the philosophical principles 《of》; the 「philosophy 〔metaphysics〕 《of》. ¶ ～를 실천하다 carry *one's* philosophy into action / ～를 탐구하다 study the philosophy 《of *a matter*》.

**철마**(鐵馬) a (railroad) train; an iron horse 《미구어》.

**철망**(鐵網) ① 《철사로 엮은》 wire net; wire gauze (눈이 촘촘한); wire netting 〔cloth〕. ¶ 창(窓)의 ～ a window screen / ～ 친 창 a wire-mesh window / ～을 치다 cover 《*a thing*》 with wire netting. ② ⇨ 철조망.

**철매** soot. ¶ ～투성이의 sooty; sooted; soot-covered / ～를 떨어내다 sweep away 〔off〕 soot.

**철면**(凸面) a convex surface. ⇨ 볼록면. ◉ ～경〔렌즈〕 a convex 「mirror 〔lens〕.

**철면피**(鐵面皮) a brazen face; shamelessness; impudence; 《구어》 cheek. ～하다 (be) brazen-faced; thick-skinned; shameless; unblushing; impudent; cheeky; show (a lot of) brass or nerve. ¶ ～하게도 …하다 have the 「impudence 〔cheek, gall, face〕 to 《*do*》 / 끝까지 ～하게 굴다 brazen 〔cheek〕 it out; steel *one's* forehead against all shame / 그는 ～다 Nothing can abash him. / 정말이지 ～한 녀석이다 What nerve he has got! / ～하게도 그가 돈을 또 빌려 달란다 He has the 「nerve 〔brass, gall〕 to ask for a loan again. *or* He has the 「impudence 〔cheek〕 to ask for some money again.

**철모**(鐵帽) a 「steel 〔battle〕 helmet; a 「trench 〔shrapnel〕 helmet. ¶ ～를 쓴 군인 a helmeted soldier.

**철모르다** have no 「sense 〔discretion〕; lack judgment; be 「indiscreet 〔injudicious, thoughtless〕; be 「simple-minded 〔innocent, unversed, untutored〕. ¶ 철모르는 애 an innocent child; a thoughtless child / 철모르는 소리 a thoughtless remark.

**철문**(鐵門) an iron gate 〔door〕.

**철물**(鐵物) iron 〔metal〕 goods; ironware; hardware; ironmongery 《영》; metal fittings. ◉ ～상(商) 《사람》 a hardwareman 《미》; a hardware 「dealer 〔merchant〕; an ironmonger 《영》. ～세공 metal work. ～전 a hardware 「store 〔shop〕 《미》; an ironmongery 《영》; an ironmonger's (shop) 《영》.

**철바람** a seasonal wind; a monsoon (인도양·남아시아의).

**철버덕** with a splash.

**철버덩** with a 「plop 〔dull splash〕. ¶ 물속에 ～ 뛰어들다 jump into the water with a splash; make a splash dive / (물에) ～ 떨어지다 drop into 《the water》 with a 「plop 〔dull splash〕; fall plop into 《the water》.

**철벅** with a splash; dabbling. ～거리다 《물 따위를》 splatter; dabble; 《물 속에서》 splash 《about》. ¶ ～거리며 물 속을 걷다 splash (*one's* way) 〔slosh〕 through the water; splash along / ～거리며 내를 건너다 splash across the stream; wade a stream / 발을 물 속에 담그고 ～거리다 dabble *one's* feet in the water.

**철벽**(鐵壁) an iron wall; 《견고한》 an impregnable fortress. ¶ ～같은 방어진을 치다 build up impregnable defenses. ◉ 금성～ an impregnable fortress 〔castle〕.

**철병**(撤兵) military withdrawal. ⇨ 철군(撤軍).

**철봉**(鐵棒) ① 《쇠막대》 an iron rod 〔bar〕; an iron club (곤봉). ② 《체조용의》 a horizontal bar; 《종목》 the horizontal bar. ¶ ～을 하다 exercise on the horizontal bar.

**철부지**(一不知) ① 《어린애》 a mere child; just a child. ¶ 아직 아무 것도 모르는 ～다 be just a child who does not know his mind as yet / 철부지가 한 짓이니 용서하십시오 Please forgive his behavior, he is only a child. ② 《지각없는》 a person who lacks good sense; a person who doesn't have a lick of sense; a stupid 〔foolish〕 person. ¶ ～ 노릇을 하다 behave like a mere child; play a fool / 나이 삼십인데도 아직 ～다 Although he is already thirty he doesn't have a lick of sense. / 나는 ～가 아닐세 I was not born yesterday.

**철분**(鐵分) iron (content). ¶ ～이 있는 〔함유된〕 containing iron; ferric; ferrous; chalybeate《water, springs》/ ～이 많다〔적다〕 be rich 〔poor〕 in iron; be high 〔low〕 in iron / 이 물은 ～이 많다 The water is strongly impregnated with iron.

**철분**(鐵粉) iron powder 〔filings〕. ¶ 미세한 ～ finely ground iron.

**철빈**(鐵貧) destitution; extreme 〔dire, abject〕 poverty; indigence.

**철사**(鐵絲) (a) wire; [총칭] wiring. ¶ ～ 같은 wiry / ～로 묶다 wire together / ～를 뽑다 draw a wire; wiredraw; draw《a metal》into wire.

◉ ～게이지 a wire gauge. ～그물 a wire net. ～세공 wirework.

**철상**(撤床) clearing the offertory table. ～하다 clear the (offertory) table; remove the cloth.

**철새** a migratory 〔passage〕 bird; a bird of passage; [총칭] migrants.

**철색**(鐵色) steel 〔iron〕 blue; dark blue.

**철석**(鐵石) ①《쇠와 돌》iron and stone. ②《몹시 굳음》¶ ～ 같은 adamant; firm; steadfast; strong; impregnable / ～ 같은 마음 an iron will; a steadfast resolution / ～ 같은 마음을 가진 사람 a man of iron will / ～ 같은 언약 a solemn promise.

**철석간장**(鐵石肝腸) a hard heart; a firm mind 〔purpose〕; an adamant resolution. ¶ ～이 녹다 *one's* firm purpose gives way; *one's* steadfast resolution is shaken; *one's* hardheartedness softens / ～을 녹이다 disarm *one's* hardheartedness; make *one's* firm purpose waver; shake *one's* resolution.

**철석영**(鐵石英) 〖광물〗 ferruginous quartz.

**철선**(鐵線) an iron wire. ⇨ 철사.

**철설**(鐵屑) scrap metal 〔iron〕; ferrous 〔steel〕 scrap; filings (줄밥).

**철수**(撤收) withdrawal; evacuation; removal. ～하다 withdraw; evacuate; remove. ¶ 군대를 ～시키다 pull the troops out of; call《the armed forces》home (본토로) / 캠프를 ～하다 strike camp / 군대의 ～를 거부하다 refuse to withdraw the army; refuse evacuation. ◉ ～명령 an evacuation order. ～자 an evacuee.

**철시**(撤市)《시장·저자를》closing up stores; suspension of business. ～하다 close the market; close up stores; suspend business. ¶ ～한 상가(商街) a closed shopping street; a shopping street in suspension.

**철심**(鐵心) ①《마음》a firm mind; an iron 〔adamantine〕 will. ②《심》an iron core; a metal supporting frame. ¶ ～을 넣은 안경테 a spectacle frame with a metal support inside.

**철썩** ①《파도가》with splashes 〔plashes〕; with spattering noise. ～하다 splash; plash. ②《때리는 소리》with a spank 〔slap, bang〕. ～하다 make a spanking sound; slap; bang; clash; slam. ¶ 따귀를 ～ 갈기다 slap《*a person*》in the face / 볼기를 ～ 때리다 spank《*a person*》on the bottom / 채찍으로 ～ 때리다 switch《*a person*》with a whip; whip with a crack.

**철썩거리다** keep lapping; keep splashing; keep spanking 〔slapping〕. ¶ 철썩거리며 해안에 부딪치는 파도 the waves lapping 〔beating〕 on the beach / 해안에 파도가 ～ the waves lap 〔wash〕 the shore; the waves slap against the beach.

**철썩철썩**《파도 소리》splashing; plashing; with splashes 〔plashes〕;《때리는 소리》spanking 〔slapping〕 away; with slaps 〔spanks〕.

**철야**(徹夜) an all-night vigil 〔sitting〕. ～하다 sit 〔stay, be〕 up all night; keep an all-night vigil. ¶ 시험 공부하느라 ～하다 sit up all night preparing for the examination; cram for an examination throughout the night / ～로 회의를 하다 have an all-night conference / 섣달 그믐날에 ～하다 sit out New Year's Eve; see the new year in / ～로 간호하다 sit up all night with《an invalid》; keep an all=night vigil over《a sick child》/ 나는 숙제를 하기 위해 간밤에 ～를 했다 I stayed up all night to finish my assignment. ◉ ～운행《버스 따위의》all-night service: ～운행하다《the buses》run all night long. ～작업 all=night work: ～작업하다 work all night.

**철없다** (be) indiscreet; thoughtless; foolish; [서술적] be like a mere child; have no sense 〔discretion〕. ¶ 철없는

짓을 하다 act thoughtlessly 〔foolishly〕; behave like a mere child.

**철옷** clothes of 〔for〕 the season; seasonal attire. ¶ ~으로 갈아입다 change the clothes of the season.

**철옹성**(鐵甕城) a strong 〔an impregnable〕 fortification; an iron-clad bastion. ¶ ~ 같다 be very 〔ever so〕 strong.

**철완**(鐵腕) an iron arm. ◉ ~투수 a pitcher with an iron arm.

**철음**(綴音) the sound of a syllable.

**철의장막**(鐵—帳幕) the Iron Curtain. ¶ ~에서 망명해 오다 defect 〔flee〕 from behind the Iron Curtain.

**철인**(哲人) a philosopher; a man of wisdom 〔intelligence〕. ¶ ~처럼 행세하다 pose as a philosopher. ◉ ~정치가 a philosopher-statesman.

**철인**(鐵人) an iron man.

**철자**(綴字) spelling; orthography (정자법). ~하다 spell. ¶ 정확한 ~ the exact spelling / ~가 틀리다 misspell; be misspelled / ~가 틀린 단어 a misspelt word / ~를 생략지 않고 정식으로 쓰다 spell out; spell 《*one's* name》 in full / 그 사람의 이름 ~가 틀립니다 That is not the way to spell his name. / 그 단어의 ~를 가르쳐 주세요 Tell me how to spell the word.

**철자법**(綴字法) the rules 〔system〕 of spelling. ⇨ 맞춤법.

**철재**(鐵材) iron 〔steel〕 material; an iron frame. ¶ ~로 집을 짓다 build a house with iron frames.

**철저**(徹底) thoroughness. ~하다 (be) thorough; thoroughgoing; complete; exhaustive; consistent (일관); out-and-out; radical; drastic; [서술적] be an utter...; be an all-out.... ¶ ~한 대책 a radical 〔drastic〕 measure / ~한 변혁 a sweeping 〔drastic〕 change / ~한 연구 a thorough 〔an exhaustive〕 study / ~한 태도 a thoroughgoing 〔consistent〕 attitude / ~한 해결 a final solution 〔settlement〕 / ~한 이기주의자 an out-and-out egoist; an egoist down to *one's* marrow / ~하지 못한 조사 an inexhaustive investigation / 그의 검약은 ~하다 His thrift is thoroughgoing. / 그는 병원에서 ~한 검사를 받았다 He had a thorough medical examination at the hospital. / 그는 ~한 애국자다 He is a patriot to the core.

**철저히**(徹底—) thoroughly; thoroughgoingly; completely; exhaustively; all-out; through and through; all the way; down the line; (up) to the hilt. ¶ ~하다 do 《*something*》 thoroughly; go the whole hog; go all length; carry 《it》 out 〔through〕 to 《its》 logical conclusion / ~ 심어 넣다 《사상 등을》 dye in (the) grain 〔in the wool〕 / ~ 연구하다 make a thorough study 《of》 / ~ 이해하다 understand thoroughly / ~ 이해시키다 bring 《a fact》 home to 《*a person's*》 mind / ~ 조사하다 probe 〔search, sift〕 《*a matter*》 to the bottom; make 「a thorough(going) 〔an exhaustive〕 investigation 《of *a matter*》 / ~ 증명하다 prove to the hilt / 취지를 ~하다 press a point home / 자기의 뜻을 ~ 이해시키다 have *oneself* fully understood 《by》 / 싸우려면 ~ 싸워라 Fight it out to the end if you are going to fight at all. / 공부를 하려면 ~ 해라 If you study at all, be sure to master your subject. / 우리들은 이 문제를 ~ 조사할 것이다 We will prove the matter to the utmost limit. *or* We will make a thoroughgoing investigation of the matter.

**철제**(鐵製) ¶ ~의 (made of) iron; steel. ◉ ~기구 an iron tool; ironwork; ironware.

**철제**(鐵蹄) ① 《편자》 a horseshoe. ② 《말》 a strong 〔swift〕 horse; a sturdy and gallant steed 〔horse〕.

**철제**(鐵劑) 〖의학〗 iron; a ferric medicine; ferrous medicaments.

**철조망**(鐵條網) (barbed) wire entanglements; 〖군사〗 a hedgehog. ¶ ~을 둘러 친 건물 building with barbed-wire entanglements / ~을 치다 stretch 〔set〕 barbed-wire around 《a place》 / ~에 걸리다 get entangled in barbed wire / ~을 뚫다 break through wire entanglements.

**철주**(掣肘) (a) restraint; restriction; control; (a) check; interference. ~하다 restrain. ¶ ~를 가하다 restrain; restrict; put 〔place〕 restrictions 《on》; check; control; curb / ~를 받다 be restricted; be under restraint.

**철주**(鐵柱) an iron pole; a steel prop.

**철주자**(鐵鑄字) 〖인쇄〗 an iron 〔metal〕 type; [총칭] iron type.

**철쭉** 〖식물〗 a royal azalea; a rhododendron. ◉ ~꽃 a royal azalea blossom.

**철창**(鐵窓) 《창》 an iron-barred〔steel-barred〕 window; 《감옥》 prison bars;

the bars; a jail; a prison. ¶ ～에 갇히다 be placed behind prison bars; be cast 〔put〕 into prison; be imprisoned / ～에서 신음하다 pine behind (the) bars. ◉ ～생활 life behind (the) bars: ～ 생활 10년 《pass》 ten years in prison.

**철찾다** suit the season; be seasonable; fit the season.

**철책**(鐵柵) an iron railing 〔paling, fence〕. ¶ ～으로 보호하다 protect 《the lawn》 by iron railings / ～을 두르다 stretch an iron fence 《around》; enclose 《a garden》 with an iron railing / ～을 쳐서 사람을 못 들어오게 하다 keep people away with a wire fence.

**철천지원수**(徹天之怨讎) a sworn 〔mortal〕 「enemy 〔foe〕.

**철천지한**(徹天之恨) deep-rooted enmity; a lasting regret; an inveterate grudge. ¶ ～을 품다 have 〔cherish, nurse〕 《*a person*》 a deep-rooted rancor 〔grudge〕 《against》; bear 《*a person*》 a deep 〔bitter〕 grudge; bear 〔have〕 a blood feud 《against》; cherish an implacable hostility 《toward》/ ～을 풀다 vent *one's* inveterate grudge; satisfy 〔wreak, work off〕 *one's* deep-rooted grudge / 우리는 그들에게 ～이 있다 We have deep-rooted rancor against them.

**철철** 《넘침》 brimming over; overflowing; running over. ¶ ～ 넘치도록 to the brim; to the full / ～ 넘치도록 술을 따르다 fill a glass to the brim with wine / 물이 ～ 넘치다 be brimming over with water.

**철철이** each and every season; from season to season.

**철총이**(—驄—) a horse with a dark blue marking on its body.

**철추**(鐵椎) = 철퇴(鐵槌).

**철칙**(鐵則) an iron 〔ironbound〕 law; a hard-and-fast rule; an invariable principle. ¶ ～을 만들다 make 〔lay down〕 ironbound laws.

**철커덕-**, **철컥-** ⇨ 잘가닥-.

**철탑**(鐵塔) a steel tower; 《고압선용의》 a 「pylon.

**철통**(鐵桶) an iron 〔a steel〕 tub. ¶ ～ 같다 be strong; be impregnable 〔impenetrable〕; be airtight 〔watertight〕; 《경비가》 be closely 〔rigorously〕 guarded; be on strict watch 〔guard〕 / ～ 같은 방비 impregnable fortification / ～같은 방어진 an impenetrable defense cordon 〔position〕 / ～같은 경계망 a strict police cordon / ～같은 경계망을 펴다 throw 〔lay〕 a tight cordon 《around》 / ～같은 방위 태세를 유지하다 maintain an iron-tight defense posture / ～같이 경계하다 be on strict watch; guard rigorously / ～같이 에워싸다 surround 《a place》 like a ring of iron / 수도 방위 태세는 ～같다 The defense system of the capital is just perfect.

**철퇴**(撤退) (a) withdrawal; (an) evacuation; a pullout; a retreat (퇴각). ～하다 withdraw 〔draw off〕 《troops》; evacuate 《a place》; fall back 《from》; pull out 《of a place》. ¶ 병력을 (진지에서) ～시키다 withdraw troops (from a position). ◉ ～명령 an evacuation order: 그 도시로부터의 ～ 명령을 받다 be ordered out of the city. 부분～ a partial pullout; a thinout. 전면～ a general pullout.

**철퇴**(鐵槌) an iron hammer. ¶ ～를 가하다〔내리다〕 deal 〔give〕 a hard 〔heavy〕 blow 《to》/ 거리의 불량배에게 ～를 가하다 crack down on street roughs.

**철판**(凸版) letterpress; relief 〔anastatic, surface〕 printing. ◉ ～인쇄 letterpress; relief 〔anastatic〕 printing. ～잉크 letterpress 〔typographic〕 ink. 사진～술 phototypography: 사진 아연～술 photozincography.

**철판**(鐵板) an iron 〔a steel〕 plate; a sheet of steel 〔iron〕; 《번철》 a griddle; a hot plate. ¶ 총알이 ～을 뚫다 the bullet penetrates 〔goes through〕 iron plate. ◉ ～구이 《요리》 meat 〔seafood〕 and vegetables roasted on a hot plate; 《요리법》 cooking on an iron griddle.

**철편**(鐵片) a piece 〔scrap〕 of iron. ¶ 앏「은 ～ taggers.

**철편**(鐵鞭) an iron rod 〔whip〕.

**철폐**(撤廢) abolition; removal. ～하다 cancel; withdraw 《a measure》; abolish 《a provision》; remove; do away with; repeal 《a law》; lift 《a ban》. ¶ 물품세를 ～하다 repeal the excise tax / 법률을 ～하다 rescind a law / 야간 통금을 ～하다 lift the curfew / 제한을 ～하다 remove 〔take away〕 the restriction / 차별 대우를 ～하다 「do away with 〔abolish〕 the discrimination / 통제를 ～하다 take off controls; decontrol.

**철폐**(鐵肺) an iron lung; a Drinker res「pirator.

**철필**(鐵筆) 《펜》 a pen; 《등사판용》 a steel pen; a stylus. ¶ ～로 쓰다 write with a pen / ～로 원지를 긁다 cut a stencil with a stylus. ◉ ～대 a pen holder. ～촉 a pen point.

**철하다**(綴—) file; bind. ¶ 서류를 ~ file papers / 신문을 철해 놓다 keep newspapers on 〔in a〕 file.

**철학**(哲學) ① 《학문》 philosophy. ¶ ~적(으로) philosophical(ly) / ~적 사색 philosophical speculation / 그나름의 독특한 ~ a philosophy of all his own / ~적으로 생각하다 consider philosophically; philosophize 《about》 / ~을 논하다 talk philosophy / ~에 뜻을 두다 take up the study of philosophy / ~을 연구하다 study philosophy.
② 《경험에 바탕을 둔 사고 방식》 ¶ 나에게는 나대로의 ~이 있다 I have a philosophy of my own. / 그는 낙천적인 인생 ~을 가지고 있다 He has an optimistic philosophy of life.
◉ ~개론 an introduction to 〔an outline of〕 philosophy. ~과 《대학의》 the philosophy department: 대학 ~과 출신 a university graduate in philosophy. ~박사 《학위》 Doctor of Philosophy (생략 Ph. D.); 《사람》 a doctor of philosophy. ~사 the history of philosophy. ~서(書) a philosophy book. ~자 a philosopher; a man of philosophy: ~자 같은 데가 있다 be something of a philosopher. ~체계 a body of philosophy; a philosophical system.
귀납〔연역, 비판, 경험, 자연〕~ inductive 〔deductive, critical, empirical, natural〕 philosophy. 도덕~ moral philosophy. 동양〔서양〕~ Oriental 〔Occidental〕 philosophy. 법~ philosophy of law. 분석~ analytical philosophy. 사회~ social philosophy. 선험적~ 《칸트의》 a *priori* philosophy (of Kant). 실존~ existential philosophy; existentialism. 실증~ positive philosophy; positivism. 실험~ experimental philosophy. 역사~ philosophy of history. 인생~ the philosophy of life. 종교~ philosophy of religion. 처세~ a philosophy of living.

**철혈**(鐵血) blood and iron; man and arms. ◉ ~재상 the Iron Chancellor. ~정책 a blood-and-iron policy.

**철형**(凸形) convexity. ¶ ~의 convex.

**철회**(撤回) ① 《취소》 withdrawal; revocation; repeal; retraction. ~하다 withdraw; take back; revoke 《a permission》; retract 《a statement》. ¶ 사표를〔의안을〕 ~하다 withdraw *one's* resignation 〔a bill〕 / 소송을 ~하다 withdraw 〔call off, drop, discontinue〕 a case / 약속을 ~하다 retract *one's* promise / 요구를 ~하다 withdraw 〔retract〕 *one's* claims 〔demands〕 / 전언(前言)을 ~하다 withdraw 〔take back〕 *one's* words; back down on what *one* said / 제안을 ~하다 get the proposal abandoned / …의 ~를 요구하다 demand a retraction of ... / 당신이 한 말을 ~하면 나도 하겠습니다 If you will take back what you said, I will do the same.
② 《철거》 removal; demolition; pulling down. ⇨ 철거(撤去).

**첨가**(添加) annexing; addition. ~하다 add 《to》; annex 《to》; append 《to》; affix 《to》; attach 《to》. ¶ 방부제를 ~하다 add preservatives 《to food》 / ~기입하다 add 《*something*》 in writing / 추신(追伸)을 ~하다 add a postscript 《to》 / ~해서 말하다 make an additional remark / 원금에 이자를 ~하다 add the interest to the principal / 이 소시지에는 방부제가 ~되어 있다 This sausage contains preservatives.
◉ ~물 an additive; an annex(e); an appendix: 식품 ~물 a food additive / 인공 ~물 an artificial additive / ~물이 없는 additive-free / 이 제품에는 인공 ~물이 전혀 포함되어 있지 않습니다 This product contains no artificial additives. ~어 ⇨ 교착어.

**첨단**(尖端) ① 《뾰족한 끝》 a pointed end 〔head〕; an extreme point; the point; the tip. ¶ 송곳의 ~ an awl point; a drill point / 곶의 ~ the tip of the cape.
② 《맨 앞장》 the spearhead; the vanguard. ¶ ~적인 ultramodern; up-to-date; up-to-the-minute; up-to-the-second; 《유행의》 ultrafashionable / 유행의 ~ the ultrafashionable mode 〔style〕; an up-to-date fashion / 농업용 ~ 기계 high-tech machinery for farm use / 시대〔유행〕의 ~을 걷는 사람 a trendsetter / 유행의 ~을 걷다 lead 〔set〕 the fashion / 시대의 ~을 가다 lead 〔be in〕 the van of the new era / 신사조(新思潮)의 ~을 걷다 spearhead the latest ideas.
◉ ~기술 high 〔frontier, up-to-date, high-advanced〕 technology; high-tech: ~기술 도입 the introduction of high technology / ~기술의 개발 the development of high technology. ~방전 『물리』 point discharge. ~산업 a high-tech 〔high-technology〕 industry.

**첨대**(籤—) ① 《댓조각》 a piece of bamboo used as a marker. ② ⇨ 점대.

**첨벙** with a splash 〔plop, plunge〕. ¶ ～ 뛰어들다 jump 〔plunge〕 with a splash 《into the water》/ 물속으로 ～ 떨어지다 drop into the water with a plop.
「vance guard point.
**첨병**(尖兵) a point (생략 pt.); an ad-
**첨부**(添附) attachment; appending; annexing. ～하다 attach 《*a thing* to another》; append; annex; add 〔tack〕 on; be accompanied 《by》. ¶ 책에 색인을 ～하다 add 〔append〕 an index to a book / 원서에 사진을 ～하여 제출하다 submit an application along with *one's* photograph / 가격표를 ～합니다 《팩스 따위에서》 We 「attach 〔are attaching, have attached〕 a price list. *or* A price list is 「attached 〔to follow〕. *or* You will find a price list 「attached 〔to follow〕.
◉ ～물 a supplement. ～사진 the accompanying photograph. ～서류 attached 〔appended〕 papers; an annex(e); 《증거 서류》 exhibits.
**첨삭**(添削) correction. ～하다 correct; look over; touch up. ¶ 작문의 ～을 받다 have *one's* composition corrected 《by》/ ～을 요청하다 submit 《*one's* composition to *a person*》 for correction; ask 《*a person*》 to look over 《*one's* composition》. ◉ ～료 a correction fee.
**첨서**(添書) an addition 《of a note, *etc.*》; a postscript (생략 P.S.); an added note. ～하다 add 《*something*》 in writing; append; 《편지에》 write a postscript to 《a letter》.
**첨예**(尖銳) ～하다 (be) sharp; acute; radical. ¶ 이 점에 대해서는 의견이 ～하게 대립하고 있다 There is a sharp conflict of opinion on this point.
◉ ～분자 radicals; (the) radical 〔extreme〕 elements.
**첨예화**(尖銳化) ～하다 《분쟁 등이》 become 〔get〕 acute 〔intense〕; be aggravated; 《사상 등이》 be radicalized; become more radical 《in *one's* ideas》; get 〔become〕 militant. ¶ ～하는 분쟁 a sharpening conflict / 노동쟁의는 점점 ～되어 가고 있다 The labor dispute is becoming increasingly radical 〔militant〕.
**첨작**(添酌) pouring additional wine into an offertory cup. ～하다 pour an additional amount of wine. ¶ 술을 두 번 ～하다 add more wine to the cup twice.
**첨지**(籤紙) a piece of paper used as a marker; a tab; a tag; a card.
**첨첨** layer on layer; pile after pile; heap upon heap. ¶ 벽돌을 ～ 쌓다 lay one brick upon another.
**첨탑**(尖塔) a steeple; a spire; a pinnacle (작은 것); a minaret (회교사원의).
**첨하**(檐下) under the eaves. ¶ ～에서 비를 피하다 take shelter from (the) rain under the eaves 《of a house》.
**첩**(妾) a concubine; a (kept) mistress. ¶ 첩의 집 a mistress's house / 첩살림 living with a concubine / 첩살림을 하다 keep a second 〔separated〕 establishment 《완곡어》/ 첩을 두다 keep 〔set up〕 a mistress 〔concubine〕/ 남의 첩노릇을 하다 be 〔become〕 *a person's* concubine / 첩이 정실로 들어앉다 a mistress becomes 《*a person's*》 legal wife / 첩의 소생이다 be born of a concubine; be a child by a concubine.
**첩**(貼) a package (of prepared herbs); a pack (of herb medicine). ¶ 약 두 첩 two packages of prepared herbs.
**-첩**(帖) an album; a (note) book. ¶ 견본첩 a sample book / 발췌첩 a scrap=book / 사진첩 a photo(graph) album.
**첩경**(捷徑) ① 《쉬운 방법》 a short 〔quick, easy〕 way; 《지름길》 a shortcut; a nearer 〔shorter〕 way. ¶ 성공에의 ～ a shortcut to success / 영어를 배우는 ～ a quick way to learn English / 경제적 안정을 이루는 ～ a shortcut to economic stability / 학문에는 ～이 없다 《속담》 There is no royal road to learning.
② [부사적] most likely; in all probability; apt to; liable to; easily; readily. ¶ 돈을 빌려주면 ～ 잃기 쉽다 If you lend money, you are liable to lose it. / 정신차리지 않으면 장사꾼한테 ～ 속기가 일쑤다 If you are not wide-awake, you will easily be cheated by merchants.
**첩며느리**(妾—) *one's* son's concubine; the concubine of *one's* son.
**첩모**(睫毛) eyelashes. ⇨ 속눈썹. ◉ ～난생(亂生) 〖의학〗 introverted eyelashes: ～난생증 〖의학〗 trichiasis.
**첩박다** board up 《a door》; fasten the gate with nails. ¶ 문을 ～ board a door up.
**첩보**(捷報) news of a victory. ¶ 얼마 안 있어 ～가 날아들었다 It was not long before word came that they won the battle.
**첩보**(牒報) a written report to a superior official. ～하다 report to a supe-

rior official.

**첩보**(諜報) intelligence; secret information. ◉ ～기 a spy plane: 대한 항공 보잉 747 점보기를 미군 ～기로 오인하다 mistake the Korean Air Lines Boeing 747 jumbo jet for a U.S. spy plane. ～기관 an intelligence organization 〔agency〕; a secret service. ～망〔조직〕 an espionage 〔intelligence〕 network; a spy ring. ～부 an intelligence department 〔bureau〕; 《방첩》 a counterintelligence office. ～수집활동 an intelligence-gathering activity. ～원 an intelligence man 〔operative〕; a secret agent; a spy. ～위성 an intelligence satellite. ～활동 espionage.

**첩부**(貼付) pasting 〔sticking, putting, affixing, applying〕 on 〔up〕. ～하다 paste 〔stick, put, affix, apply〕 on 〔up〕. ¶ 편지에 우표를 ～하다 put 〔stick〕 a stamp on a letter; stamp a letter / 벽에 광고를 ～하다 paste a poster 〔an advertising bill〕 on a wall.

**첩실**(妾室) a concubine. ⇨ 첩(妾).

**첩약**(貼藥) medicinal herbs in packages; a pack of prepared herb medicine.

**첩자**(諜者) a spy; an (espionage) agent; a secret agent; an informer (밀고자); 《속어》 a rat (배신자). ¶ 이중～ a double agent / ～ 노릇을 하다 act as spy; engage in espionage / ～를 보내다 send out a spy; send a spy 《into》/ ～를 침투시키다 plant 〔infiltrate〕 spies. 「(with due ceremony).

**첩장가**(妾—) ～들다 take a concubine

**첩지** an ornamental hairpin (worn on ceremonial occasions).

**첩지머리** ① 《첩지를 쓴》 *one's* head with a *ch'ŏpchi* hairpin on it. ② 《머리 모양》 a girl's hairdo (with the side hairs plaited so that the ends cover her ears).

**첩첩산중**(疊疊山中) ¶ ～에 in the heart of mountains rising one above another; deep in the mountains; far up (in) the mountain / ～에 살다 live in the heart of the mountains.

**첩첩수심**(疊疊愁心) anxiety on anxiety; worry on top of worry. ¶ ～에 싸이다 have a lot of anxiety; have worries upon worries.

**첩첩이**(疊疊—) fold upon fold; layer upon layer; pile upon pile; piled high; heap (up)on heap. ¶ ～산처럼 쌓여 있다 be piled up mountain-high; lie in a huge pile / 그의 책상 위에는 자주 쓰이는 사전들이 ～ 쌓여 있다 On his desk is a pile of dictionaries which he often consults.

**첩출**(妾出) being born of a concubine; a child by a concubine.

**첩출**(疊出) arising 〔happening〕 in succession 〔one after another〕; repeated 〔frequent〕 occurrence. ～하다 arise 〔happen〕 in succession 〔one after another〕; occur frequently 〔at short intervals〕. ¶ 곤란한 문제가 ～하다 difficult problems arise one after another / 불행한 일이 ～하다 have one misfortune after another; have a series of misfortunes.

**첩치가**(妾置家) ～하다 set up a separate home with a concubine.

**첫** the first; new; maiden; starting; the beginning. ¶ 첫째 the first / 첫경험 *one's* first experience / 첫글자 the first letter 《of a word》; 《이름의》 an initial (letter) / 첫등장 *one's* debut; *one's* first appearance on the stage / 첫아이 *one's* firstborn child / 첫차 the first bus 〔train〕 / 첫출전 《make》 *one's* first campaign; a maiden battle / 첫항해 a maiden voyage.

**첫가을** early autumn 〔fall 《미》〕; the beginning of autumn.

**첫걸음** the first step 《to》; an initial step; a start; 《초보·기본》 the rudiments 《of 》; the ABC 《of 》; a beginners' course 《in English》. ¶ 영어～ elementary 〔beginner's〕 English; "First Steps in English" / 성공에의 ～ the first step to success / ～을 그르치다 make a false start; start in the wrong way / ～을 내딛다 take the first step; make a start. 「winter.

**첫겨울** early winter; the beginning of

**첫고등** the start; the outset; the beginning. ¶ ～에 실패하다 fail at the outset; make an unsuccessful start; 《좌절되다》 be baffled at the start.

**첫공개**(—公開) the first opening 〔unveiling, exhibition〕 to the public.

**첫공연**(—公演) the first public performance 〔presentation〕; the *première* performance.

**첫국밥** the first seaweed soup and rice taken after childbirth. ¶ ～을 먹다 take soup and rice for the first time after the delivery of a child.

**첫기제**(—忌祭) the first anniversary of 《*one's* parent's》 death after the two=year mourning period.

**첫길** ① 《초행길》 an unaccustomed

course 〔route〕; *one's* first trip 《to》; a road *one* is on for the first time. ¶ ～이 되어 생소하다 I am not familiar with the road. *or* It is new to me. ② 《신행길》 《being on》 the way to *one's* wedding.

**첫나들이** 《갓난아이의》 going out for the first time after *one's* birth; 《신부의》 the first outing of a bride after marriage. ～하다 go out for the first time after *one's* birth; 《신부가》 make her first post-marriage outing.

**첫날** the first day 〔night〕; the opening day; 《연극의》 the *première*. ¶ 학년의 ～ the first day of school 〔of the school year〕 / 연극의 ～ the opening day 〔the *première*〕 of a play / 회의의 ～ the opening session.

**첫날밤** the bridal 〔wedding〕 night; the first night of a married couple.

**첫낯** an unfamiliar face; a stranger; a first meeting.

**첫눈**[1] 《일견》 a first look 〔glance, glimpse, sight〕. ¶ ～에 at first look 〔sight, glance〕; on sight / ～에 들다 be attracted at first sight / ～에 반하다 love 〔fall in love with〕 《*a person*》 at first sight; be struck 〔captivated〕 《by a woman》 at first glance.

**첫눈**[2] 《초설》 the first snow of the season.

**첫닭** the first cockcrow; the first crow of the cock. ¶ ～이 울다 crow; announce 〔greet〕 the dawn / ～이 울 때에 at cockcrow 〔cock crowing〕.

**첫더위** the first heat (of the season); the first spell of hot weather; the first hot spell 〔heat wave〕. ¶ ～가 시작되다 the first hot weather sets in.

**첫돌** ① 《아기의》 the first birthday of a baby. ② 《1주기》 the first anniversary 《of》. ¶ 창립 ～ 기념 행사를 갖다 observe the first anniversary of the opening 〔foundation〕 《of the firm》.

**첫딸** *one's* firstborn daughter. ¶ ～을 낳다 give birth to a girl at *one's* first childbirth / ～은 세간 밑천이다 When the first child is a daughter, that is a great help around the house.

**첫마디** an opening 〔initial〕 remark 〔word〕; the first word. ¶ ～를 꺼내다 be the first to speak; break the silence; break the ice by saying... (서먹함을 깨려고) / ～를 어떻게 꺼내야 할지 모르다 do not know how to broach 《a subject to *a person*》 / ～에 화를 내다 get angry at 《*a person's*》 first remark / ～부터 욕이었다 He abused me as soon as he opened his mouth. / 그의 ～는 나보고 왜 왔느냐는 것이었다 His first word to me was "Why did you come here?"

**첫머리** the beginning; the outset; the opening; the head 《of a column》; the top; the first (part). ¶ ～에서 끝까지 from first to last; from start to finish / 장(章)의 ～에 at the beginning of the chapter / 연설 ～에 성경의 한 구절을 인용하다 preface *one's* speech with a quotation from the Bible / 네 이름이 명단 ～에 나와 있다 Your name heads 〔tops〕 the list. *or* Your name is marked at the top of the list.

**첫무대**(一舞臺) *one's* first appearance (on the stage); *one's* debut. ¶ ～를 밟다 make *one's* debut (on the stage) / 그 배우는 1980년에 ～를 밟았다 The actor made his first appearance in 1980. / 그는 13세 때에 ～를 밟았다 He made his debut 〔made his first appearance on the stage〕 when he was thirteen.

**첫물** ① 《옷의》 new clothes that have yet to be laundered; new clothes worn for the first time; first wear(ing). ¶ ～옷 clothes that have never been laundered / 옷이 ～에 못 쓰게 되다 *one's* clothes are worn out before they got laundered. ② ⇨ 만물.

**첫발** the first step 《to, toward》; an initial step; 《발족》 a start. ¶ ～을 내딛다 take the first step; make 〔get〕 a start / ～을 잘못 디디다 make a false start; start in the wrong way.

**첫배** the first litter 〔hatch, brood〕. ¶ ～에 돼지가 새끼 세 마리를 낳다 have the first litter of three pigs. ◉ ～돼지 the first litter of pigs. ～병아리 the first hatch of chickens.

**첫봄** early spring; the beginning of spring. ¶ ～에 in (the) early spring; early in spring.

**첫사랑** *one's* first love; 《풋사랑》 calf love; 《사람》 *one's* first lover 〔sweetheart〕; the first girl 〔boy〕 *one* fell in love with. ¶ ～에 빠지다 fall in love for the first time / ～에 실패하다 lose *one's* first love; be disappointed 〔betrayed〕 in *one's* first love / ～을 모르다 have never experienced calf love.

**첫새벽** break of day; daybreak; early dawn 〔morning〕. ¶ ～에 before dawn; at daybreak; in the early dawn 〔morning〕; at the peep 〔crack〕 of day / ～에 일어나다 get up early in the morning.

**첫서리** the first frost (of the year). ¶～가 내리다 have the first frost of the year.

**첫선** 《등장》 the first public appearance; 《공개》 the first public exhibition 〔presentation〕. ¶ 전국에 ～을 뵐 신형 텔레비전 a TV set of a new model that is put for the first time on the nationwide sales network.

**첫소리** ① 〖음성〗 an initial sound; an initial consonant (in a Korean orthographic syllable). ② = 첫마디.

**첫손주**(—孫—) *one's* first grandchild.

**첫솜씨** a first try of *one's* skill; the first performance 〔attempt〕. ¶ ～치고는 잘 만들었다 You made it well for a green hand. / ～가 되어 잘 만들어질지 모르겠다 Since this is my first attempt, I don't know whether I can make it very well.

**첫술** the first spoonful of food (*one* takes at a meal). ¶ ～을 뜨다 take *one's* first spoonful of food at a meal / ～에 배부르랴 《속담》 You must not expect too much at your first attempt.

**첫아기** *one's* firstborn (child); the first child.

**첫아들** the firstborn son. ¶ ～을 낳다 give birth to a boy at *one's* first childbirth / ～을 보다 get a boy as *one's* first child.

**첫얼음** the first freeze (of the season).

**첫여름** early summer; the beginning of summer. ¶ ～에 early in summer.

**첫이레** the first week 〔the seventh day〕 after a childbirth.

**첫인상**(—印象) a first impression. ¶ ～이 좋다 make 〔give〕 a good 〔favorable〕 first impression 《on, upon》 / 좋지 않은 ～을 남기다 leave a bad 〔an unfavorable〕 first impression / 그의 ～이 좋지 않다 He impressed me unfavorably upon our first meeting.

**첫잠** ① 《초입의》 the first 〔early〕 stage of sleep; *one's* first sleep. ¶ ～에서 깨다 be aroused in *one's* first sleep; be awakened from *one's* first sleep / 애 우는 소리에 ～이 깨다 wake up at the cry of a baby soon after *one* has gone to sleep for the night. ② 《누에의》 the first dormant period of silkworms.

**첫정**(—情) a first attachment 〔affection, love〕. ¶ 서로 ～이 들다 fall in love with each other for the first time / ～을 못내 잊지 못하다 can't get over *one's* first attachment at all.

**첫째** the first; number one; No. 1; the top 〔first〕 place; the foremost. ¶ ～의 first; primary; foremost; leading / ～(로) first; firstly; in the first place; first of all; before everything; to begin with; at the outset / ～ 권 the book one; the first volume / ～ 목표 the prime target / ～가는 부자 the wealthiest person / 당대 ～가는 작가 the greatest writer of the day / ～로 오다 come first; be the first to come / ～를 하다 secure 〔take, win, get〕 (the) first place; stand 〔rank〕 first 《in, among》; be at the top 〔head, best〕 《of》; head 〔top〕 the list 《of》; finish 〔come in〕 first; come out first 〔top〕 / ～ 목적은 …이다 the primary object is... / 성공에는 건강이 ～다 Health is the first essential to success. / 그는 ～ 둘째를 다투는 부자다 He is one of the richest, if not richest man. / 그는 달리기에서 ～를 했다 He was (the) first in the race. / 우선 ～로 무엇을 해야 좋을까 What should we do first (of all)? / ～ 그는 부지런하다 Above all, he is diligent. / ～ 그 놈의 얼굴이 마음에 들지 않는다 To begin with 〔In the first place〕, I don't like his looks.

**첫추위** the first cold weather (of the season); the first spell of cold weather. ¶ ～가 들다 the first cold weather sets in.

**첫출발**(—出發) a start; a beginning. ¶ 인생의 ～ *one's* (first) start in life / 인생의 ～을 하는 청년 a young man on the threshold of life / ～이 좋다 〔나쁘다〕 make a good 〔wrong〕 start.

**첫출사**(—出仕) the beginning of *one's* official career; entering government service for the first time.

**첫판** the first round 〔game, bout〕; an initial round; the beginning. ¶ ～에 지다 get beaten in the first round 〔bout〕 《of》.

**첫판**(—版) the first edition. ⇨ 초판(初版).

**첫항해**(—航海) 《배의》 a maiden voyage; 《사람의》 *one's* first voyage. ¶ ～를 나서다 set out on her maiden voyage.

**첫해** the first year. ¶ 미국 간 ～ the first year *one* was in America.

◉ ～권농(勸農) being clumsy because of inexperience; a greenhorn.

**첫해산**(—解産) 《초산》 a woman's first delivery (of a child); *one's* first childbirth 〔confinement〕.

**첫행보**(一行步) ① 《처음 감》 *one's* first visit 〔errand〕. ¶ ～에 돈을 받아 오다 collect the money on *one's* first trip. ② 《첫 행상》 *one's* first ⌈venture at 〔trip of〕 peddling. ¶ ～에 상당한 이득을 보다 make a considerable profit on *one's* first peddling (trip).

**첫혼인**(一婚姻) *one's* first marriage.

**첫흥행**(一興行) the first public presentation of a play 〔performance〕.

**청** 《얇은 막》 a membrane; a film; a pellicle. ¶ 갈대청 the white membrane inside a reed / 귀청 the drum membrane; the eardrum / 목청 the vocal cords 〔bands〕.

**청**(青) blue (color); azure. ⇨ 청색.

**청**(請) a request; a favor; *one's* wishes; 《간청》 an entreaty; a solicitation. ⇨ 청하다. ¶ 간절한 청 an earnest request / 긴한 청 an urgent 〔important〕 request / …의 청에 따라 at *a person's* request; in compliance 〔accordance〕 with *a person's* request / 친구의 모처럼의 청으로 at the pressing request of a friend / 청을 넣다 make a request 《through *a person*》; ask a favor 《indirectly》/ 청을 들어주다 grant 〔comply with〕 《*a person's*》 request; do 《*a person*》 a favor / 청을 들어주지 않다 turn down 〔refuse, decline〕 《*a person's*》 request; refuse 《*a person*》 a favor; turn a deaf ear to a request / 청이 있다 have a favor to ask of 《*a person*》; wish to make 《*a person*》 a request; wish to ask a favor of 《*a person*》 / 청이 하나 있는데요 I have a favor to ask (of) you. *or* Will you do me a favor? / 청이라니 무슨 청인가요 What is your request? *or* What is that you would have me do? / 자네 청을 들어주겠네 You shall have your request. / 당신 청이야 안들어 줄 수 있나 How could I possibly refuse a request of yours?

**청**(廳) ① 《관청》 an office; an agency; a building. ¶ 청사 an office 〔a government〕 building / 시청 the City Hall. ② ⇨ 대청(大廳).

**청가**(請暇) application for leave. ～하다 apply for leave; apply for *one's* furlough.

**청가뢰**(青 —) 〖곤충〗 a green blister beetle; a Spanish fly; a cantharis.

**청각**(聽覺) (the sense of ) hearing; auditory sense. ¶ ～적으로 aurally / ～에 호소하는 힘 audio effects / ～ 신경을 곤두세우다 keep *one's* ears on the alert / ～에 호소하다 appeal to the ear / ～을 잃다 lose *one's* hearing / ～이 예민하다 have keen 〔acute〕 hearing; have a keen sense of hearing / 앞을 못 보는 사람들은 보통 ～이 좋은 법이다 People who cannot see usually have a fine sense of hearing.
◉ ～과민(증) hyperacusis. ～기관 a hearing 〔an auditory〕 organ. ～신경 the auditory 〔acoustic〕 nerve(s). ～심상(心象) an acoustic image. ～장애 hearing difficulties 〔impairments〕. ～중추 the auditory 〔hearing〕 centers 《of the brain》. ～형 《기억의》 the auditory type.

**청각채**(青角菜) 〖식물〗 a glue plant.

**청강**(聽講) attendance (at a lecture); auditing (a course). ～하다 attend (a lecture); listen to 《a lecture》; 《미》 audit 《a course at a university》. ¶ 국제법을 ～하다 audit "International Law" / ～을 허락하다 grant 《*a person*》 admission / ～무료 《게시》 Attendance 〔Admission〕 (is) free. / 윌슨 교수의 강의를 ～했다 I attended 〔audited〕 Professor Wilson's lectures.
◉ ～료 an admission fee. ～생 a special student; an auditor 《미》; an occasional student 《영》. ～증 an attendance 〔admission〕 ticket.

**청강자**(聽講者) an auditor; a listener; [총칭] audience; attendance. ¶ ～가 많다〔적다〕 have a large 〔small〕 attendance; there is a large 〔small〕 audience.

**청개구리**(青 —) 〖동물〗 a green frog; a ⌈tree frog; a hyla.

**청객**(請客) inviting guests. ～하다 invite a guest.

**청결**(清潔) cleanliness; neatness; purity. ～하다 (be) clean; neat; pure. ¶ ～하게 cleanly; neatly; purely / ～한 부엌 a clean kitchen / ～한 몸 a clean body / ～한 마음 a pure heart / ～하게 닦다 wipe 《*a thing*》 clean / ～히 하다 clean (up); make 〔keep〕 clean; cleanse; purify / ～히 해두다 keep 《*a thing*》 clean / 몸을 ～히 하다 keep *oneself* (neat and) clean.

**청경우독**(晴耕雨讀) ～하다 work in the field in fine weather and read at home in wet weather. ¶ 그 뒤로 그는 ～의 생활을 보냈다 Since then he led a life of (plowing and) working in the field in fine weather and stay at home reading when it is wet.

**청계** 〖민속〗 an evil spirit said to cause dire illness.

**청계**(淸溪) a clear 〔limpid, pellucid〕 stream 〔brook〕.

**청고**(淸高) ～하다 (be) pure and lofty. ¶ ～한 인격〔마음〕 a lofty and pure character 〔heart〕.

**청공**(青空) a blue 〔an azure〕 sky.

**청과**(青果) fruits and (green) vegetables. ◉ ～류 fruits; greens. ～상(商) 《사람》 a fruit and vegetable dealer; a greengrocer 《영》. ～시장 a 「fruit and vegetable 〔green-grocery〕 market. ～점 a greengrocery; a fruit and vegetable store.

**청관**(聽官) 〖해부〗 the auditory organs; 「the organs of hearing.

**청교도**(淸教徒) a Puritan. ¶ ～적인 puritanical; puritan. ◉ ～주의 Puritanism.

**청구**(請求) 《권한에 의한》 a demand; 《요청》 a request; 《당연한 권리로서의》 a claim; a call; an application. ～하다 ask 〔apply〕 for; request; demand; claim; call on 《*a person* to *do*》; 《대가·요금을》 charge. ¶ 손해 배상의 ～ a claim for damages / 지급의 ～ a demand for payment / ～할 수 있는 claimable / ～한 대로 as requested 〔demanded〕 / ～하는 대로 at *one's* request; on demand 〔request, application〕; in response to a claim / 지급을 ～하다 claim 〔demand〕 payment 《from *a person*》 / 견본을〔카탈로그를〕 ～하다 ask for a sample 〔catalog〕/ 손해배상을 ～하다 claim 〔make a claim for〕 damages.

청구에: ～에 응하다 meet 〔go along with, comply with, accede to〕 《*a person's*》 request 〔demand〕 / ～에 응하여〔따라〕 in compliance 〔conformity〕 with 《*a person's*》 request / …의 ～에 따라 on the request of….

청구를: ～를 받아들이다 concede a demand; grant a request / ～를 거절하다 deny 〔reject, refuse, decline, turn down〕 a request / ～를 철회하다 withdraw *one's* claim; take back *one's* demand.

¶ 그는 손해 배상을 ～해 왔다 He claimed payment from me for damages. / 그들은 손해 배상 ～에 응하지 않았다 They didn't comply with the claim for damages. / 목록은 ～가 있는 대로 무료로 보내 드립니다 Our catalog will be promptly sent 〔mailed〕 for free on request. / 지난달 산 책의 대금을 ～받았다 I was asked to pay 〔They sent me a bill〕 for the books I bought last month. / 이 어음은 ～가 있을 때 지급됩니다 This bill is payable on demand. / 그는 그의 차의 수리비로 400 달러를 나에게 ～했다 He charged me $400 for repairing his car.

◉ ～불 ⇨ 요구불. ～액 the amount asked 〔claimed〕. ～인〔자〕 a claimant; a demandant; an applicant: ～인 없는 은행 예금 an unclaimed 〔a dormant〕 bank account. 배상〔상환〕～ a claim for reimbursement.

**청구권**(請求權) a (right of) claim. ¶ 한국의 대일(對日) 재산 ～ Korea's property claims against Japan / ～을 포기하다 waive 〔relinquish, give up, abandon〕 *one's* claim 《for》; disclaim.

**청구멍**(請—) 《연줄》 a pull; connections; an in 《구어》. ¶ 좋은 ～ a good 〔the right〕 connections / ～이 있다 have a pull 《with the firm, on the president》; have an in 《with the police》 / 관청에 취직하려해도 ～이 없다 I want a job in the government but I don't know the right people.

**청구서**(請求書) 《손해 배상 등의》 a written claim; 《지급의》 a bill; an account; 《상점·식당 등의 계산서》 a check 《미》. ¶ ～를 내다 render 〔send in〕 an account; submit a bill 《to》 / ～를 쓰다 write 〔make〕 out a bill / 「～를 가져오세요」—「예, 알겠습니다」 《고급 식당 따위에서》 "Please bring me the bill." —"Yes, sir."

◉ 손해배상 ～ a written claim for damages. 지급～ a bill (for payment).

**청국**(淸國), **청나라**(淸—) Ch'ing; the Ch'ing Dynasty; China (under the Ch'ing Dynasty).

**청국장**(淸麴醬) (soup prepared with) fermented soybeans.

**청기와**(青—) a blue 〔green〕 tile. ◉ ～장수 one who keeps the trade secret of his special process 〔technique〕.

**청꾼**(請—) an influence peddler 〔middleman〕; a five percenter.

**청널**(廳—) a floor board [총칭] flooring.

**청년**(青年) a young man; a youth; [총칭] young people; the younger generation; the youth. ¶ 20세의 ～ a youth of twenty / ～신사 a young gentleman / 전도 유망한 ～ a promising youth / 혈기 왕성한 ～ [총칭] young blood(s); vigorous youth / 그녀의 아들은 훌륭한 ～이 되었다 Her son has grown into a fine young man.

◉ ～기(期) adolescence. ～단〔회〕 a young men's association. ～시대〔시절〕 *one's* younger days 〔years〕. ～운

동 a youth movement. ～회의소 the Junior Chamber. 「[chickpeas].
**청녹두**(青綠豆) 〖식물〗 tiny green peas
**청담**(清淡) ①《마음의》 purity and honesty; probity; uprightness; integrity; disinterestedness. ～하다 (be) honest; upright; clean-handed; disinterested. ②《맛·빛깔의》 simplicity《of color, taste》; plainness; lightness. ～하다 (be) simple; plain; light; mild.
**청담**(晴曇) clearness and cloudiness (of the sky).
**청대** 〖식물〗 a short-jointed variety of bamboo with white streaks on the stalk. 「green beans [peas].
**청대콩**(青—) beans not quite ripe;
**청동**(青銅) bronze. ¶ ～의 bronze / ～색의 bronzy. ◉ ～기(器) bronze ware; a bronze tool: ～기 시대 〖고고학〗 the Bronze Age. ～세공 bronze work; a bronze. ～주물 bronze casting. ～화로 a bronze brazier.
**청둥오리** 〖조류〗 a wild duck; a mallard (duck); a greenhead (수컷).
**청둥호박** a fully ripened pumpkin with hard skin. 「청사등롱.
**청등롱**(青燈籠) a blue-silk lantern. ⇨
**청등홍가**(青燈紅街) the gay quarters; a red-light district《미》.
**청딱따구리**(青—) 〖조류〗 a gray headed woodpecker; a black-naped green woodpecker.
**청란**(青鸞) 〖조류〗 an argus pheasant.
**청람**(晴嵐) shimmering of heated air; (a) haze in a fine day. ⇨ 아지랑이.
**청랑**(清朗) ～하다 (be) clear; fine; serene; bright. ¶ ～한 날씨 bright weather; a bright day / 날씨가 ～하다 The weather is fine. *or* It is a fine day.
**청량**(清涼) being clear and cool; being cool and refreshing; being crisp. ～하다 (be) clear and cool; cool and refreshing; crisp. ¶ ～한 날씨 nice cool weather. ◉ ～제(劑) a tonic; a refrigerant: 그녀의 부드러운 미소는 하나의 ～제였다 Her gentle smile was refreshing to me.
**청량음료**(清涼飮料) a cooling [refreshing] beverage; a soft [cold] drink《미》; a carbonated drink;《a bottle of》pop. ◉ ～점 a soft-drink stand; a soda fountain.
**청력**(聽力) (the power [sense] of) hearing; hearing ability; auditory capacity. ¶ ～이 좋다 have a keen sense of hearing / ～을 잃다 lose *one's* hearing / 나이 탓으로 ～이 쇠퇴했다 I lost my hearing with age. *or* My hearing got weaker with age. ◉ ～검사 a hearing test. ～계 an audiometer; a sonometer. ～측정 audiometry.
**청렴**(清廉) (unsullied) integrity; (strict) probity; uprightness; absolute honesty. ～하다 (be) clean-handed; upright; incorruptible. ¶ ～한 사람 a man of (stern) integrity; a man of pure heart and clean hands; an upright man / 모든 공직자의 ～도를 조사하다 conduct a survey of the degree of integrity of all government officials. ◉ ～정치 clean politics.
**청렴결백**(清廉潔白) absolute honesty. ＝청렴. ¶ 나는 그 일에 대해서 ～하다 I am innocent concerning that matter. *or* My hands are clean in regard to that matter. / 그는 ～한 사람이어서 출처가 분명치 않은 돈은 받지 않았다 As a man of high integrity, he did not think it right to accept money from questionable sources.
**청령**(聽令) heeding [obeying] an order. ～하다 heed [obey] an order.
**청록색**(青綠色) a bluish green color; bluish green; turquoise blue.
**청료**(青蓼) 〖식물〗 a kind of persicaria [smartweed].
**청룡**(青龍) a blue dragon. ◉ ～도 an old Chinese broadsword.
**청루**(青樓) a brothel; a house of ill-fame [ill-repute]; a whorehouse. ¶ ～에 드나들다 frequent brothels.
**청류**(清流) a (clear) limpid stream.
**청매**(青梅) a green [an unripe] plum.
**청맹과니**(青盲—)《눈》 an eye that is blind though it looks perfect; 〖의학〗 amaurosis;《사람》 an amaurotic [a bat-blind] person.
**청명**(清明) ①《맑음》 fineness; fairness; serenity; brightness. ～하다 (be) fine; clear; fair; bright. ¶ ～한 날씨 bright weather / ～한 하늘 a clear [crystalline] sky; an azure sky. ②《절후》 *ch'ŏngmyŏng,* one of the 24 seasonal divisions (＝about 5 April).
**청문**(聽聞) audience; audition. ～하다 listen《to》; hear.
◉ ～회 a (public) hearing;《미국 의회의》 the U.S. Congressional hearing: ～회를 열다 hold a hearing.
**청바지**(青—) (blue) jeans. ¶ ～를 입은《a boy》 in blue jeans; jeaned《teenager》/ ～를 입다 wear [have on, put on] jeans / 그녀는 ～를 입고 있었다 She was in [wearing] jeans. / 그들

은 모두 ～를 입고 나왔다 They came out, all in jeans.

**청백**(靑白) blue and white. ◉ ～전 a contest 〔tourney〕 between two groups 〔between the blue and white teams〕.

**청백**(淸白) ⇨ 청렴(淸廉). ¶ 그는 너무 ～하여 꺼림한 일은 않는다 He has too much integrity to get involved in shady deals. ◉ ～리(吏) a clean=handed 〔an uncorrupted〕 government officer.

**청병**(請兵) requesting (the dispatch of ) troops. ～하다 request (the dispatch of ) troops.

**청부**(請負) a contract 《for work》. ⇨ 도급(都給). ¶ ～로 by 〔under〕 contract / ～맡다 (have a) contract 《for the work》; receive a contract 《for the work from *a person*》/ ～를 주다 put 《the work》 out to contract; give out a contract 《for the work》. ◉ ～살인 murder by contract: ～ 살인자 a hired assassin 〔killer, murderer〕. ～전쟁 a proxy war.

**청빈**(淸貧) honest 〔honorable〕 poverty. ～하다 be poor but honest. ¶ ～한 생활을 하다 live 〔carry〕 a poor but honest life / ～을 예찬하다 make much of 〔praise, extoll〕 honest poverty.

**청사**(靑史) history; annals. ¶ 이름을 ～에 남기다 leave *one's* name in history / 이름이 ～에 빛나다 be famous in history; *one's* name is immortalized in history.

**청사**(靑絲) blue 〔green〕 yarn 〔thread〕.

**청사**(廳舍) a government office building.

**청사등롱**(靑紗燈籠) 《청사초롱》 a lantern covered with green silk in the middle and with red silk at both ends.

**청사진**(靑寫眞) a blueprint. ¶ ～을 만들다 make a blueprint of 《a plan》; blueprint 《a plan》/ 선진 조국의 ～을 제시하다 present a blueprint for the advanced fatherland / 아직 ～ 단계에 있다 be still in the blueprint stage.

**청산**(靑山) green 〔blue〕 mountains 〔hills〕. ¶ ～에 매 띄워 놓기다 rely on *one's* luck / 인간 도처 유～ (人間到處有靑山) *One's* fortune can be sought anywhere in the world. *or* Fortune awaits you everywhere.
◉ ～유수 eloquence; fluency: ～ 유수 같이 with great fluency 〔volubility〕; very fluently / 말이 ～ 유수다 be very eloquent; be a fluent speaker.

**청산**(靑酸) 〖화학〗 hydrocyanic 〔prussic〕 acid; hydrogen cyanide. ◉ ～가스 hydrocyanic acid gas. ～염(塩) a cyanide; a prussiate. ～중독 hydrocyanic poisoning.

**청산**(淸算) ① 《셈·채무 등의》 clearing off 〔up〕 《*one's* debts》; a settlement; clearance (무역의); 《회사 등의》 liquidation; winding up. ～하다 《지급의》 clear off 〔up〕 《*one's* debts》; square 〔settle, balance, fix 《속어》〕 《*one's* accounts》; 《회사 등이》 liquidate; wind up. ¶ (회사가) 부채를 ～하고 해산하다 [사람이 주어] liquidate 〔wind up〕 《a company》: [회사가 주어] go into liquidation / 그는 빚을 ～했다 He 「cleared off 〔paid back〕 his debt. / 가까스로 밀린 집세를 ～했다 I finally settled my back rent. / 부채를 ～하니 남는 것이 없었다 Nothing was left when we had cleared off our debts. ② 《죄·과거를》 ～하다 cleanse; become decent. ¶ 과거를 ～하(고 새출발하)다 liquidate 〔bury〕 the past (and start life again) / 악을〔죄를〕 ～하다 atone for *one's* crime 〔sin〕/ 죽음으로써 죄를 ～하다 commit suicide in atonement for *one's* crime; pay for *one's* sin with *one's* life / 그녀와의 관계를 ～하다 separate from 〔break up with〕 her.
◉ ～거래 a clearance contract; 〖증권〗 future transaction. ～계정 an open account: 남북한은 ～계정으로 물자거래를 하기로 원칙적인 합의를 보았다 South and North Korea agreed in principle to transact goods and materials on an open account. ～사무 liquidative affairs: ～ 사무소 a liquidation office. ～사원 liquidation partnership. ～서 a statement of liquidation; a balance sheet (결산서): 명세 ～서 an itemized account. ～액 an adjusted amount. ～인 a liquidator; a balancer (청산서를 작성하는). ～일 《주식 거래 등의》 a settlement 〔settling〕 day. ～회사 a company in liquidation. 강제～ forced liquidation.

**청산칼리**(靑酸―) potassium cyanide; cyanide of potassium. ¶ ～로 자살하다 commit a suicide by taking potassium cyanide.

**청상과부**(靑孀寡婦) a young widow.

**청상아리**(靑―) 〖어류〗 a bonito shark; a mako (shark).

**청새치**(靑―) 〖어류〗 a spearfish; a (blue) 「marlin.

**청색**(靑色) a blue color; blue. ¶ 짙은 ～

deep 〔dark〕 blue.
**청서**(青書) 《정부 간행물》 a blue book.
**청서**(清書) a fair 〔neat〕 copy. ～하다 make a fair copy 《of》; copy out neatly. ¶ 작문을 ～하다 make a fair copy of *one's* composition.
**청소**(清掃) cleaning; sweeping (쓸기); dusting (먼지떨기); mopping; scrubbing (걸레질); 《거리의》 street cleaning; scavenge. ～하다 clean; sweep; dust; scrub; mop; scavenge (길을). ¶ ～가 잘 된 clean; tidy / 깨끗이 ～하다 clean up 《a room》 / sweep 《a room》 clean / 집안을 ～하다 clean up a house; have 〔do〕 a house cleaning / 거리를 ～하다 clean 〔scavenge〕 a street; collect the garbage / 오물을 ～하다 collect 〔clear away〕 the night soil / 방을 깨끗이 ～해 두어라 Give this room a good cleaning 〔sweeping〕. / 모든 방이 ～가 잘되어 있다 All the rooms are kept clean and tidy. / 부엌을 깨끗이 ～할 생각이다 I'm going to have a good cleanup of the kitchen.
◉ ～당번 *one's* turn for doing the cleaning. ～도구 cleaning things; dusting 〔scrubbing〕 things. ～부(夫) a cleaner; a sweeper; a cleaning worker; 《도로의》 a street cleaner; a scavenger 《영》; 《쓰레기의》 a dustman 《영》; a garbage collector 〔man〕 《미》: 굴뚝 ～부 a chimney sweep(er). ～부(婦) a cleaning woman; a charwoman; a scrubwoman 《미》. ～주간 a cleanup week. ～차 《쓰레기 수집용의》 a garbage truck 〔wagon〕 《미》; a dust cart 《영》. 대～ 《do》 a general (house) cleaning. 도로～ street cleaning; scavengery; garbage disposal.
**청소기**(清掃機) a cleaner. ¶ 진공〔전기〕 ～ a vacuum cleaner / 양탄자를 진공 ～로 청소하다 run a vacuum cleaner over the carpet.
**청소년**(青少年) young people; teenagers; juveniles; youth; the younger generation. ¶ ～ 대상의 문학〔영화〕 literature 〔a film〕 for youngsters (and teenagers) / ～교육 juvenile education. ◉ ～범죄 juvenile delinquency 〔crimes〕: 요즘 흉악한 ～범죄가 급증하고 있다 The felonious juvenile crimes have been a sharp rise these days. ～보호위원회 the Commission on Youth Protection. ～선도위원회 the Juvenile Guidance Committee. ～층 the Pepsi generation 《미》. 세계 ～축구 대회 the World Youth Soccer Championship.
**청송**(青松) a green pine(tree).
**청수**(清水) clear water.
**청순**(清純) purity. ～하다 (be) pure (and innocent). ¶ ～한 처녀 a pure 〔an innocent〕 girl / 그녀는 아직 소녀의 ～함을 간직하고 있다 She still has the innocence of a young girl.
**청술레**(青—) 〖식물〗 a variety of early ripening greenish pear.
**청승** signs of a wretched fate; a pitiable 〔wretched〕 condition 〔look〕. ¶ ～ 떨다 act like fortune's orphan; try to work on 《another's》 compassion / ～궂다 ＝ 청승맞다. ◉ ～꾸러기 a person with bad luck written on his face; a sad-looking person. ～살 excess flesh afflicting a miserable old person.
**청승맞다** be suggestive of ill luck; be doomed to misery; 《애틋하다》 (be) plaintive; pitiful; ominously sorrowful; have the way of some thing plaintive. ¶ 청승맞은 곡 a plaintive tune / 청승맞게 울다 wail ominously 〔piteously〕 / 애기하는 투가 ～ have a plaintive way of speaking.
**청신**(清新) ～하다 (be) new and fresh. ¶ ～한 맛 freshness / ～한 시풍(詩風) a new and fresh style in poetry / ～한 맛이 없다 lack freshness; be stale / 그의 작품에는 ～한 맛이 하나도 없다 We find nothing new in his work.
**청신경**(聽神經) 〖해부〗 the auditory 〔acoustic〕 nerve.
**청신남**(清信男) a male Buddhist.
**청신녀**(清信女) a female Buddhist.
**청신호**(青信號) a green traffic signal; a green light; a go signal. ¶ ～가 켜졌다 The light is on for "Go."
**청실**(青—) blue 〔green〕 thread 〔yarn〕.
**청아**(清雅) elegance; refinement; clarity. ～하다 (be) elegant; refined; clear. ¶ ～한 목소리 a clear ringing voice / ～한 풍악 elegant music.
**청야**(清夜) a serene 〔clear〕 night.
**청약**(請約) subscription 《for stocks》. ～하다 subscribe 《for bonds, shares》; send a subscription. ¶ 그 회사의 주식을 100주 ～하다 subscribe for one hundred stocks of the company.
◉ ～금 subscription money. ～기한 a time limit for subscription. ～서 a written subscription; 《용지》 a subscription blank 《미》 〔form 《영》〕. ～순(順) the order of subscription received; the subscription order: ～순으로 in order of subscription; in the order of subscriptions received. ～자

a subscriber: ～자에 불리한 보험 약관 the insurance terms disadvantageous to the subscribers. ～처 a place for subscription.

**청어**(青魚) 〖어류〗 a herring.

**청옥**(青玉) 〖광물〗 sapphire.

**청올치** 《칡덩굴의 속껍질》 dried inner bark of arrowroot. ◉ ～끈 a string made of the inner bark of arrowroot.

**청와대**(青瓦臺) the Blue House; (the Korean) Presidential Mansion; the *Ch'ŏngwadae.*

**청요리**(清料理) Chinese cooking 〔food〕; 「a Chinese dish.

**청우**(晴雨) rain or shine; fair or rainy weather. ¶ ～에 관계 없이 rain or shine; wet or dry; whether it may rain or not; regardless of the weather. ◉ ～계 a barometer; a weatherglass: ～계가 올라가다〔내려가다〕 the barometer rises 〔falls, drops〕.

**청운**(青雲) ¶ ～의 뜻을 품다 aspire after greatness 〔distinction〕; have a high 〔great, lofty〕 ambition / ～의 뜻을 품은 청년 an aspiring 〔ambitious〕 youth 〔young man〕 / 그는 ～의 뜻을 품고 상경했다 He came to Seoul with high 〔great〕 ambitions. ◉ ～객 a person who 「aspires to 〔achieves〕 high offices; a man of great ambitions.

**청원**(請援) asking help; calling for aid 〔rescue〕. ～하다 ask 〔call〕 for help; call upon 《another》 for help; call in 《*a person's*》 aid; ask for 〔seek〕 《*a person's*》 assistance.

**청원**(請願) a petition 《for》; an application 《for》. ～하다 petition 《the government for》; present 〔submit, send in〕 a petition 《to》; file 〔lodge〕 《with the National Assembly》; apply 《for》. ¶ ～을 들어주다 grant a petition / ～을 기각하다 turn down 〔reject〕 a petition / 광업권을 ～하다 make petition for mining rights / 국회에 감세를 ～했다 We petitioned the National Assembly for a tax reduction.

◉ ～경찰 a policeman on special guard assignment; a security policeman 《of a bank》; a security 〔police〕 guard. ～권 《exercise》 the right of petition. ～법 the Petition Law. ～사항 petition matters. ～서 a (written) petition: 정부에 ～서를 제출하다 present a petition to the Government. ～심의위원회 a petition committee. ～자〔인〕 a petitioner.

**청유**(清遊) ～하다 go on a pleasure excursion 〔pleasant outing〕.

**청음**(清音) a clear voice 〔note〕; 〖음성〗 《무성음》 a voiceless consonant 〔sound〕.

**청음기**(聽音機) a sound detector 〔locator〕; 《수중의》 a hydrophone.

**청이불문**(聽而不聞) hearing and yet paying no attention 《to》; turning deaf ears 《to》. ～하다 turn a deaf ear 《to》; be deaf to 《a request》.

**청일**(淸日) Sino-Japanese; China=Japan. ◉ ～전쟁 the Sino-Japanese War (of 1894-95) (★ 두 나라 이름이 병렬되는 전쟁은 관습상 짧은 것을 먼저 씀).

**청일**(清逸) purity; loftiness. ～하다 (be) pure; lofty.

**청자**(青瓷) celadon (porcelain). ◉ ～색 celadon (green); jade green: ～색의 celadon. ～향로 an incense burner of celadon. 고려～ Koryŏ celadon (porcelain).

**청장**(廳長) a director (of a government office); the Administrator 《of the Supply Administration》.

**청전**(青田) green paddy fields; unripe rice fields.

**청정**(清淨) cleanness; purity. ～하다 (be) clean; pure. ¶ ～한 마음 a pure heart / ～한 공기 pure, fresh air.

◉ ～기(器) a purifier; 《공기청정기》 an air purifier. ～수역 the uncontaminated waters 〔seas〕. ～액(液) 〖사진〗 a cleaning solution. ～야채 clean 〔chemical-free〕 vegetables; vegetables grown chemicals free. ～재배 sanitary 〔germ-free〕 culture; hydroponics (수경법). ～제 a purifier; a detergent. 혈액～제 a blood purifier.

**청조**(青鳥) ① 《푸른 새》 a blue bird; a grosbeak (고지새). ② 《반가운 사자·편지》 a grace messenger 〔letter〕.

**청조**(清朝) 〖역사〗 the Ch'ing 〔Manchu〕 dynasty; the Manchu court. ¶ ～가 망하다 the Ch'ing dynasty ceases to exist / ～에 사신을 보내다 send an envoy to the Manchu court.

**청종**(聽從) obeying; listening 《to》; following. ～하다 obey; listen to 〔follow〕 《another's advice》; follow 《*a person*》 obediently; do as told submissively. ¶ 부모에게 ～하다 obey *one's* parents; mind what *one's* parents say / 아버지 말씀에 ～치 않다 defy *one's* father; will not listen to what father says.

**청주**(清酒) clear, refined rice wine. ¶ 특급～ special-grade rice wine.

**청죽**(青竹) a green bamboo; a newly

cut bamboo (갓 벤); unseasoned bamboo (마르지 않은).

**청중**(聽衆) an audience; hearers; an attendance. ¶ 많은〔적은〕 ~ a large 〔small〕 audience 〔attendance〕 / ~을 끌다 attract 〔draw〕 an audience 《of 5,000》 / ~을 열광시키다 arouse 〔move〕 *one's* audience to enthusiasm / ~이 꽉 차다 have a full attendance; have an overflow audience / 그의 연설에 ~이 많았다 His speech enjoyed a large audience. / ~이 점차 줄어들었다 The audience dropped off 〔thinned out〕. / ~의 우레와 같은 박수가 터져 나왔다 Thunderous applause arose among the audience. ◉ ~석 an audience seat; an auditorium.

**청지기**(廳—) a steward; an attendant to a high official; a chamberlain.

**청직**(淸直) integrity; honesty; probity. ~하다 (be) honest; upright; incorruptible; clean-handed.

**청진**(聽診) 〖의학〗 auscultation. ~하다 auscultate; (examine with a) stethoscope. ◉ ~기 a stethoscope: ~기를 대다 apply a stethoscope 《to》 / ~기로 진찰하다 examine with a stethoscope. ~법 auscultation; stethoscopy.

**청질**(請—) asking favors; currying favor; solicitation. ~하다 ask favors; court 《*a person's*》 influence 《on *one's* behalf》; solicit 《*a person*》 for *his* good offices. ¶ 밤낮 ~하며 돌아다니다 run around asking favors of people day and night.

**청참외**(青—) 〖식물〗 a green melon.

**청처짐하다** 《느리다》 (be) slow; sluggish; 《느슨하다》 (be) loose; slack. ¶ 청처짐한 걸음 a slow pace; a snail's pace.

**청천**(青天) the blue 〔azure〕 sky; the blue heaven.

**청천**(淸泉) a spring with clear clean water.

**청천**(晴天) a clear 〔cloudless〕 sky; fair 〔fine〕 weather. ¶ ~이 계속되다 have a (long) spell of fine weather; the fair weather continues 〔persists, lasts〕. ◉ ~기류 〖기상〗 the clear-air turbulance.

**청천백일**(青天白日) a bright blue sky. ¶ ~에 벼락이 내리다 be hit by a bolt from the blue; get a sudden and unexpected order 〔punishment〕 / ~의 몸이 되다 be cleared from 〔of〕 the charge (brought against *one*); have *one's* innocence proved 〔established〕. ◉ ~기(旗) a sun-in-the-blue-sky flag.

**청천벽력**(青天霹靂) a bolt from 〔out of〕 the blue; a thunderbolt from a clear sky; a sudden and unexpected blow 〔stroke〕. ¶ ~같이 out of the blue; like a bolt from the blue / 그것은 ~과도 같았다 It came like a bolt from the blue. / 그 소식은 나에겐 ~이었다 The news was a bolt out of the blue to me.

**청첩**(請牒) a letter of invitation; an invitation (card); an invite 《구어》. ¶ ~을 내다 send 〔issue〕 an invitation (card) 《to》 / ~을 받다 get 〔have, receive〕 an invitation 《from *a person*》; be invited. ◉ ~장 ⇨ 청첩: 결혼 ~(장) a wedding invitation (card).

**청청하다**(青青—) (be) bright green; nice 〔fresh〕 and green; verdant. ¶ 청청한 대나무 bright green bamboos / 산에 나무가 ~ a hill is nicely wooded.

**청초**(青—) a kite which is blue except at the top.

**청초**(青草) 《풀》 green grass; 《담배》 green tobacco.

**청초**(淸楚) neatness; tidiness; smartness. ~하다 (be) neat and clean; trim; tidy. ¶ ~한 꽃 a graceful flower / ~한 여자 a nice-looking girl / 옷차림이 ~하다 be neatly dressed.

**청추**(淸秋) ① 《가을》 a bright autumn 〔fall 《미》〕. ② 《음력 8월》 the eighth lunar month.

**청춘**(青春) youth; the springtime 〔prime〕 of life; the bloom 〔heyday〕 of youth. ¶ ~의 youthful; adolescent / 꽃다운 ~ the bloom of youth / ~의 고민 mental struggle of youth / ~의 꿈 a dream of youth / ~의 정열 the passion of youth; youthful ardor / ~의 피 *one's* young blood; the hot blood of youth / ~의 피가 끓다 burn with youthful ardor / ~을 즐기다 enjoy *one's* youth / ~의 피를 끓게 하다 [사물이 주어] stir up *one's* young 〔youthful〕 blood / 아까운 ~이 다 가다 *one's* precious young days are gone. ◉ ~기(期) adolescence; puberty. ~남녀 young boys and girls. ~시절 《in》 *one's* youth; *one's* youthful days 〔years〕.

**청출어람**(青出於藍) 《a disciple》 excel 〔outstrip, surpass〕 *one's* teacher 〔master〕 《in》.

**청취**(聽取) listening; hearing; 《라디오의》 listening-in; 《검열 등을 위한》 monitoring. ~하다 《듣다》 hear; listen to; 《라디오 등을》 listen (in) to 《the radio》. ¶ 라디오로 …을 ~하다 hear... on 〔over〕 the radio / 증언을 ~하다 hear 《*a person's*》 testimony; hold a hearing《on》/ 판사는 목격자의 증언을 ～했다 The judge heard the evidence of the eye-witness. / 라디오로 그녀의 연설을 ～했다 I「listened to 〔heard〕 her speech on 〔over〕 the radio. ◉ ～료 a radio license fee. ～율 program (listener) ratings. ～자 a (radio) listener; a wireless 〔broadcast〕 listener; a radio audience: BBC의 ～자 a listener to the BBC / ～자 참가 프로 a participation show. ～장치 a receiving set 〔apparatus〕; a radio receiver.

**청취테스트**(聽取―) an audition. ¶ ～를 하다 audition 《*a person*》; give an audition《to》/ ～를 받다 audition.

**청치**(青―) ① 《푸른 쌀》 green-tinged 〔less ripe〕 grains of rice. ② 《얼룩소》 a spotted bluish-gray cow.

**청칠**(青漆) green 〔blue〕 lacquer; green 〔blue〕 paint.

**청컨대**(請―) (if you) please; I pray; I beg; I hope 〔wish〕.

**청코너**(青―) 〖권투〗 the blue corner; the challenger's corner.

**청탁**(清濁) ① 《맑음과 흐림》 relative clearness (and muddiness); purity and impurity; 《옳음과 옳지 못함》 good and evil. ¶ 물의 ～ the purity 〔clarity〕 of water / ～을 가리다 discriminate good from bad / ～을 가리지 않다 be so broad-minded as to be tolerant of all sorts of men. ② 《소리의》 voiced and voiceless (consonants).

**청탁**(請託) 《부탁》 asking; begging; a request; a favor; a solicitation; entrusting. ～하다 beg 〔entreat, solicit, ask, request〕 《*a person*》 to exercise his influence 《in favor of》; entrust 《*a person* with a matter》. ¶ 긴한 ～ an urgent 〔important〕 request / 간절한 ～ an earnest request; entreaty; solicitation / 아무의 ～으로 at the request of *someone* / ～을 받다 be asked 〔requested〕 《to *do*》; receive a solicitation from *a person* 《to use *one's* good offices in *his* behalf》/ ～을 거절하다〔물리치다〕 reject 〔refuse, decline, turn down〕 《*a person's*》 request / ～을 들어주다「comply with 〔accede to〕 another's request; grant a request; do 《*a person*》 a favor / ～ 편지를 쓰다 write a letter asking a favor / 일자리를 하나 얻어 달라고 ～하다 ask 《*a person*》 to get a job for *one* / ～이 하나 있소 I have a favor to ask of you. / 내 ～ 좀 들어주지 않겠나 Will you do me a favor?

**청태**(青苔) 〖식물〗 ① 《이끼》 green moss 〔lichen〕. ¶ ～가 끼다 green moss gathers 〔grows〕. ② 《김》 green laver.

**청파**(青―) a green scallion.

**청편지**(請便紙) a letter asking favors; a letter of favor 〔intercession〕.

**청포**(青布) bluish hemp cloth.

**청포**(清泡) green-pea jelly.

**청풍**(清風) a fresh wind; a cool 〔refreshing〕 breeze. ◉ ～명월(明月) a fresh wind and a bright moon.

**청하다**(請―) ① 《요청·요구하다》 ask; beg; request; demand; call upon 《*a person*》 to 《*do*》; 《간청하다》 entreat; solicit; pray for; supplicate 《*a person* for pardon》. ¶ 청하는대로 at 《*a person's*》 request; as requested / 가르침을 ～ ask for instruction / 기부를 ～ ask 《*a person*》 for a subscription / 도움을 ～ ask 《*a person*》 for help; ask for 《*a person's*》 assistance; call for help / 면회를 ～ ask 《*a person*》 to see 《*one*》; ask for 〔request, seek, solicit〕 an interview 《with》/ 무엇을 (달라고) ～ ask 〔beg, solicit〕 《*a person*》 for *something;* apply 《*a person*》 for *something* / 연설을 ～ ask 〔call upon〕 《*a person*》 for 〔to make〕 a speech / 편지를 써달라고 ～ ask 《*a person*》 to write a letter / 허가를 ～ ask 《*a person's*》 permission; ask leave 《to *do*》/ 하룻밤 자고 가기를 ～ ask for a night's lodging / 청하지도 않았는데 돈을 빌려주겠다고 했다 He offered me a loan unasked 〔without my asking for it〕. ② 《부르다》 (***a***) 《초대하다》 invite 〔ask〕 《a person to dinner》; have 《*a person*》 in 《for dinner》. ¶ 청해서 at 〔by〕 《*a person's*》 invitation / 청한〔청하지 않은〕 손님 an invited 〔uninvited, uncalled-for〕 guest / 집으로 ～ ask 《*a person*》 to *one's* home; have 《*a person*》 over 〔in〕 / 자택으로 저녁 식사에 ～ invite 《*a person*》 home for dinner / 그 사람은 청하지도 않았는데 왔다 He came here uncalled. *or* He just asked himself to this house. (***b***) 《초빙하다》 engage 《a teacher》; call in; send for. ¶ 의사를 ～ send for 〔call in〕 a doctor / 전문가를 ～ engage the service of an expert. (***c***) 《초래하다》 bring 〔draw〕 upon 《*oneself*》; incur; cause; bring about 《a disaster》. ¶ 재앙을 ～ bring calamity upon *oneself;* court disaster / 스스로 청한 실책이니 어쩔 수 없다 He has none to blame but himself, for the blunder was of his own making. / 그것은 스스로 화를 청하는 짓이다 With that he is inviting disaster of his own accord. ③《잠을》¶ 잠을 ～ try to sleep.

**청향**(淸香) pure 〔noble〕 fragrance.

**청허**(聽許) permission; grant; approval; sanction. ～하다 accept; assent《to》; grant《*one's* request》; approve.

**청혼**(請婚) 「a proposal 〔an offer〕 of marriage; courtship; wooing. ～하다 propose (marriage)《to *a person*》; ask《*a person*》 to marry *one;* court; ask for《a lady's》 hand. ¶ 김씨 집에 ～하다 propose to the Kim's family / 돈을 노리고 ～하다 (남자가) seek a woman's hand for money / ～을 승낙〔거절〕하다 accept 〔decline〕《*a person's*》 proposal of marriage. ◉ ～장 a letter proposing a marriage.

**청혼**(請魂) 〘불교〙 invocation of the spirit of the dead. ～하다 invoke the spirit of the dead.

**청혼자**(請婚者) a suitor. ¶ ～가 많다 have many 「suitors 〔offers of marriage〕 / ～가 많은 처녀 a girl much in quest as a wife / 그녀에게는 ～가 없다 No man has asked for her hand.

**청홍**(靑紅) blue and red. ◉ ～실 blue and red threads. ～치마 blue and red skirts (worn by a bride).

**청훈**(請訓) a request for instructions. ¶ 본국 정부에 ～하다 ask *one's* home government for (further) instructions.

**체**[1]《체질하는》 a sieve; a sifter; a (mesh) strainer; a bolter; a screen (모래·석탄용의); a jig (선광용). ¶ 막체 a riddle / 체로 치다 put 〔pass, powder〕《*something*》 through a 「sieve 〔sifter〕; sift《flour》; sift; sieve; bolt; riddle. ⇨ 체질하다 / 모래를 체로 쳐서 자갈을 골라내다 sift out pebbles from sand.

**체**[2]《아니꼬울 때·탄식할 때》 Pshaw!; Tut!; Shucks; Phew! ¶ 체, 건방지게 Tut! Who do you think you are?

**체**[3]《짐짓 꾸밈》 pretense. ⇨ 체하다.

**체**(滯) 〘한의〙 indigestion; dyspepsia; stomach disorders. ⇨ 체하다.

**체**(體)《본보기·방식》 a style; a form. ¶ 체를 본받다 imitate a style / 체가 잡히다 take 〔get into〕 shape 〔form〕.

**-체**(體) ①《몸·조직》 the body; physique; build; frame; constitution. ¶ 건강체 a healthy body / 법인체 a corporate body. ②〘수학〙 a solid (body). ¶ 삼면체 a trihedron.

**체감**(遞減) (a) gradual decrease. ～하다 diminish successively; decrease in order. ◉ ～속도 (a) slowdown speed. 수익 ～의 법칙 the law of diminishing returns.

**체감**(體感) (a) bodily sensation; somesthesia. ◉ ～온도 〘의학〙 effective temperature; a wind-chill 「index 〔factor〕: 그 날은 산정의 ～온도가 영하 25도였다 That day the wind-chill on the top of the mountain was 25 degrees below zero. ～증 〘의학〙 cenesthopatie.

**체강**(體腔) 〘해부〙 the coelom (*pl.* ～s, -mata); the coelome; the body 〔somatic〕 cavity. ◉ ～벽 the body wall.

**체격**(體格) (a) physique; (physical) constitution 〔build〕; frame. ¶ 한국인의 ～ the 「physical build 〔physique〕 of the Korean / 가냘픈 ～ a slight build; a delicate physique / 무쇠 같은 ～ an iron constitution / 튼튼한〔단단한〕 ～ a 「strong 〔sturdy, compact, well-knit, well-set〕 frame / ～이 늠름한〔억센〕 of powerful physique / ～이 단단〔튼튼〕하다 be sturdy in build / ～이 단단한 사람 a person of sturdy build / ～이 좋다〔나쁘다〕 have a 「good 〔weak〕 constitution; be of 「strong 〔weak〕 build / 요즘 아이들은 ～이 좋다 Children today have good physique. / 그는 ～이 당당하다 He is 「very well built 〔a splendid physique〕. ◉ ～검사 a physical examination.

**체결**(締結) conclusion. ～하다 conclude《a treaty with》; enter into《a treaty with》; contract. ¶ 동맹 조약의 ～ the conclusion of a treaty of alliance / 조약을 ～하다 conclude 〔enter into〕 a treaty《with》/ 차관(借款)을 ～하다 contract a loan / 두 나라는 평화 조약을 ～하고 동맹국이 되었다 The two countries concluded a peace treaty and became allies.

**체경**(滯京) staying 「in the capital 〔in Seoul〕. ～하다 stay 〔remain〕 in the capital; make a stay in Seoul. ¶ ～중에 during *one's* 「stay 〔sojourn〕 in the capital; while in Seoul.

**체경**(體鏡) a full-length mirror; a large looking glass; a cheval glass.

**체계**(遞計) moneylending; usury. ◉ 체곗돈 money used for lending at interest. 체곗집 a money lender's; a loan office.

**체계**(體系) a system; an organization. ¶ ～적(인), ～있는 systematic / ～적으로 systematically / 사상～ a system of thought / ～가 있다 have system; be 「systematic 〔systematized〕 / ～가 없다

lack 〔have no〕 system / ～를 세우다 formulate 〔develop〕 a system 《of philosophy》/ ～를 이루다 form a 《complete》 system / 그것은 이론 ～가 뚜렷한 학설이다 It is a theory with a complete system. ◉ ～적 음소론 〖언어〗 systematic phonemics. ～화(化) systematization: ～화(化)하다 systematize / 학문 연구에는 모든 이론의 ～화가 필요하다 In pursuit of learning, it's necessary to systematize all the theories.

**체공**(滯空) staying 〔remaining〕 in the air. ～하다 stay 〔remain〕 in the air. ◉ ～기록 an endurance (flight) record. ～비행 an endurance flight. ～시간 the duration of a flight.

**체관**(諦觀) 《잘 봄》 seeing clearly; clear vision; 《체념》 resignation; being resigned. ～하다 see clearly; 《체념》 resign *oneself* 《to *one's* fate》; endure 《*one's* misfortune》 philosophically.

**체구**(體軀) 《몸》 the body; 《키》 height; stature; 《체격》 physique; physical constitution; build. ¶ ～가 건장하다 be of sturdy build / ～가 당당하다 have a 〔be a man of〕 magnificent physique / 당당한 ～의 여인 a woman of monumental build / ～가 우람하다 have a huge 〔gigantic〕 frame; be huge of limb / ～가 왜소하다 have a small frame; be tiny (of limb); be of slight build.

**체급**(體級) 〖스포츠〗 weight. ◉ ～제한 「weight limits.

**체기**(滯氣) an indication 〔a symptom, a touch〕 of indigestion 〔dyspepsia〕. ¶ ～가 있다 have an indication 〔a touch〕 of indigestion; suffer from slight indigestion / 피자를 먹으면 나는 늘 ～를 느낀다 Pizza always gives me indigestion. *or* Pizza always sits heavily on my stomach.

**체납**(滯納) arrears 《of rent, taxes》; delinquency in (making) payment. ～하다 fail to pay 《*one's* taxes》; default; be in arrear(s) with the payment; be delinquent in payment; let 《*one's* taxes》 fall into arrears. ¶ 독촉 후 20일간 ～할 때에는 upon delinquency of 20 days after call / 세금을 ～하다 fail to pay *one's* taxes / 회비를 ～하다 let *one's* membership dues fall into arrears / 나는 세금을 ～한 일이 없다 I have never let my taxes get in arrears. / 그는 전화 요금을 반년이나 ～했다 He hasn't paid the telephone charges for the past six months. *or* He is in arrears for six months' telephone charges. ◉ ～금 arrears; arrearage. ～상습자 a habitual delinquent. ～세금 taxes in arrears; back 〔delinquent〕 taxes. ～액 an amount in arrears. ～집세 the arrears of rent; back rent.

**체납자**(滯納者) a delinquent. ◉ ～명부 a delinquent list. 세금～ a tax delinquent; a delinquent taxpayer.

**체납처분**(滯納處分) disposition for 「failure to pay taxes 〔the recovery of taxes in arrears〕. ¶ 세금의 ～을 하다 institute a process against 《*a person*》 for the recovery of taxes in arrears; make an attachment on 《*a person's* property》 for unpaid taxes. ◉ ～비(費) the disposition fee for arrears.

**체내**(體內) the interior of the body. ¶ ～의〔에〕 in the body 〔system〕; internal 〔internally〕 / ～의 당분 body 〔tissue〕 sugar / 외과 의사는 그의 ～에서 총알을 빼내었다 The surgeon took out the bullet from his body. ◉ ～ 기생충 an endoparasite; an entozoon. ～수정(受精) internal 〔entosomatic〕 fertilization. ～시계 〖동물〗 a biological 〔an internal〕 clock. ～은닉 운반 《마약의》 body pack: ～ 은닉 운반을 하다 body-pack.

**체념**(諦念) ① 〖불교〗 apprehension of the truth; spiritual enlightenment. ～하다 apprehend the truth. ② 《단념》 abandonment; resignation; acceptance. ～하다 give up 《an idea》; abandon; resign 〔reconcile〕 *oneself* to 《*one's* fate》; get 〔be〕 resigned 〔reconciled〕 to 《*one's* loss》; accept the situation; make up *one's* mind 《to *something*》. ¶ 가망 없다〔틀렸다〕고 ～하다 give up 《*a thing*》 in dispair 〔as hopeless〕 / (환자를) 살아날 수 없는 것으로 ～하다 give over 《a patient》 for dead / 세상은 이런 것이려니 ～하다 take the world as it is / 실종〔사망〕한 것이라고 ～하다 give up 《*a person*》 for lost 〔dead〕 / 어쩔 수 없다고 ～하다 abide by 〔resign *oneself* to〕 the inevitable; submit to necessity / 이젠 마지막이라고 ～하다 give *oneself* up as 〔for〕 last; give up all hope of life / 죽음을 피할 수 없다고 ～하다 accept death with resignation / 운명이려니 하고 ～하다 resign *oneself* to *one's* fate 〔lot〕; accept *one's* fate philosophically / 그녀에게 프랑스행을 ～케 하기는

어렵다 It's difficult to「make her give up 〔dissuade her from〕 going to France.

**체능**(體能) physical fitness 〔aptitude〕. ◉ ～검사 a physical placement test.

**체대**(體大) being big in body 〔frame, build〕. ～하다 be of big build 〔frame〕; be large-limbed; have a huge body.

**체득**(體得) ① 《체험》 getting 〔realizing, learning〕 from 〔by〕 experience; experience. ～하다 get 〔learn, realize〕 from 〔by〕 experience; experience. ② 《습득》 mastery; comprehension. ～하다 master; comprehend; acquire. ¶ 기술의 비법을 ～하다 master the mysteries of the art.

**체량**(體量) weight. ⇨ 체중(體重).

**체력**(體力) physical 〔bodily〕 strength; bodily powers; physical stamina. ¶ ～을 검사하다 check up *one's* physical strength / ～을 기르다 develop 〔build up〕 *one's* physical strength / ～을 회복하다 recover *one's* strength / ～이 쇠약해지다 *one's* strength decline; grow weak / 힘든 노동을 할 ～이 없다 be not strong enough to do heavy labor / 그는 ～이 강하다 He is strong. *or* He is a man of great physical strength. / 요즘 나는 현저하게 ～이 떨어짐을 느낀다 I feel my strength decreasing markedly these days. ◉ ～검정〔테스트〕 an examination 〔a test〕 of physical strength. ～양성 development of physical strength; physical training. ～장(章) the physical charter; the physical strength measurement.

**체류**(滯留) stay; sojourn. ⇨ 체재(滯在). ～하다 stay; sojourn; stop (잠시). ¶ 미국에 ～중에 during *one's* stay in America; while *one* is in America / 오랫동안〔잠깐동안〕 ～하다 make a long 〔short〕 stay / 호텔에 ～하다 stay at a hotel; stop in a hotel / 우리는 사흘 밤을 그 호텔에 ～했다 We stayed three nights at that hotel. ◉ ～객 《여관의》 a (staying, resident) guest; 《일반 가정의》 a house guest; a sojourner; a stayer. ～기간 the length of *one's* stay. ～비 the (living) expenses during *one's* stay 〔visit, sojourn〕; 《숙박비》 the hotel expenses. ～지 the place one is staying 〔will stay〕.

**체맹**(締盟) conclusion of a treaty (of alliance). ～하다 conclude 〔sign〕 a treaty. ◉ ～국 a treaty power; a signatory (power) (조인국).

**체머리** a shaky head. ¶ ～를 흔들다 have a shaky head; 《진저리내다》 get sick and tired 《of》; be bored 《with》; 《구어》 be fed up 《with》.

**체메** a shameless 〔cheeky, audacious〕 person.

**체메다** fix a sieve net on its frame; make a sieve.

**체면**(體面) 《명예》 honor; 《명성》 (a) reputation; 《위엄》 dignity; prestige; 《면목》 face; 《겉모양》 appearances. ¶ ～상 for honor's 〔appearance'〕 sake; for the sake of appearances; (just) to save *one's* face 〔honor〕 / ～에 관계되다 concern 《*a person's*》 honor; affect 〔reflect on〕 *one's* honor 〔prestige〕; be compromising to *one's* reputation 〔fair name〕 / ～에 관계되는 문제 a matter of dignity; a question of "face" / ～에 구애되다 be face-conscious; be too much concerned about *one's* personal honor / ～이 깎이다 lose *one's* honor 〔face〕; dishonor *oneself* / ～이 서는 타협 a face-saving compromise; a compromise without (a) loss of face / ～을 세우다 save (*one's*) face 〔*one's* honor〕; 《세워주다》 save 《*a person's*》 honor 〔face〕; satisfy 《*a person's*》 honor; give 《*a person*》 face; keep 《*a person*》 in countenance / ～을 더럽히다 bring disgrace on *oneself;* disgrace *oneself* / ～을 돌보다 mind *one's* honor / ～을 돌보지 않다 have no regard to decency; take no account of the public eye / ～을 손상하다 hurt 〔wound〕 *one's* honor; impair the honor of 《*a person*》 / ～을 유지하다〔지키다〕 preserve *one's* honor; maintain *one's* dignity; save appearances; keep up 〔maintain〕 appearances; save the honor 〔face〕 of ... / ～을 잃다 lose (*one's*) face 〔honor〕; be put out of countenance; be in disgrace; come down a peg; lose face with the world / ～을 잃게 하다 put 《*a person*》 out of countenance; take 〔bring, let〕 《*a person*》 down a peg / ～을 중히 여기다 respect *one's* honor; make 〔think〕 much of *one's* honor 〔reputation〕 / ～을 차리다 save 〔keep up, patch up〕 appearances / ～을 차리기 위해 for decency's 〔appearance'〕 sake; to save appearances / 회사〔집단〕 ～을 손상시키다 throw 〔reflect〕 discredit upon *one's* firm 〔family〕 / 창피도 ～도 없다 be lost to all sense of decency; do not care what others will think / (…)하면 자네 ～에 관계되는

일이다 it will hurt your reputation if...; it will bring discredit on your name if... / 그것은 ~ 문제다 It is a matter of "face". *or* It is a point of honor with me. / 당신 ~에 그런 일을 할 수 없소 It would be beneath your dignity to do such a thing. / 무슨 ~으로 그에게 돈을 꾸어 달라겠나 Where would I get the face to ask him to lend me money?! / 이 돈은 ~상 받을 수가 없다 I cannot, in honor, accept this money. / 사람이 ~이 있어야지 You should have some sense of honor. / ~ 따위는 아무래도 좋다 I don't care a bit what people would say of me. *or* We cannot think of appearances now. / 자네는 지나치게 ~을 따지는군 You are too concerned 〔preoccupied〕 with appearance 〔your reputation〕. / 카터의 평양 방문은 북한에게 그들의 태도를 바꾸는데 필요한 하나의 ~치레의 구실을 주게 될것이다 Carter's Pyongyang visit could provide North Korea a face-saving excuse for a change in its attitude.

**체모**(體毛) body hair.

**체모**(體貌) = 체면(體面).

**체미**(滯美) stay(ing) in America 〔the United States〕. ~하다 stay 〔make a stay〕 in America. ¶ ~ 중에 while staying in America; during *one's* stay in the (United) States / ~중이다 be (staying) in America.

**체발**(剃髮) shaving *one's* head; tonsure. ~하다 take the tonsure; get 〔have〕 *one's* head shaved; become a Buddhist monk.

**체벌**(體罰) corporal 〔physical, bodily〕 punishment. ¶ ~을 가하다 inflict corporal punishment 《on *a person*》 / ~을 받다 get corporal punishment / 학교 선생님에 의한 ~은 법으로 규정되기에 앞서 사회 통념으로 보장되어야 할 문제다 The physical punishment by teachers is a matter to be guaranteed by common notion in society before it is legally defined.

**체불**(滯拂) a delay in payment; delayed payment 《of wages》. ~하다 fall into arrears; be left unpaid; be overdue; be back 《in, with》; be delayed. ¶ 급료가 열흘이나 ~되어 있다 The payment of wages is 10 days in arrears. ◉ ~금 an outstanding 〔unpaid〕 account. ~이자 accrued 〔outstanding〕 interest. ~임금 overdue wage; wage unpaid; 《pay》 wages in arrears; delayed pay: ~임금의 완전 청산을 요구하다 call for complete clearance of overdue wages.

**체비지**(替費地) an area of land secured by the authorities in recompense of development outlay.

**체색**(體色) 《동물의》 the color of the body.

**체선료**(滯船料) demurrage.

**체세포**(體細胞) 〖생물〗 a somatic 〔body〕 cell. ◉ ~분열 somatic (cell) division.

**체소**(體小) being small in body 〔frame, build〕. ~하다 (be) small; short; be small in body 〔frame, build〕. ¶ ~한 사람 a person of small build; a small person.

**체송**(遞送) conveyance; forwarding. ~하다 convey; send by post; forward.

**체스** 《서양 장기》 chess. ¶ ~의 말 a chessman. ◉ ~판 a chessboard.

**체신**(遞信) 《통신》 communication; 《우편》 postal services. ⇨ 통신. ◉ ~사무 postal and telegraphic service.

**체액**(體液) 〖생리〗 (a) body fluid; a secretion (분비액); semen (여성 체내에 남아 있는 남성의). ◉ ~병리학 humoral pathology.

**체약**(締約) the conclusion of a treaty; 《협정》 a treaty; a convention; an agreement. ~하다 conclude 《a treaty》.

**체언**(體言) 〖문법〗 indeclinable parts of speech in Korean grammar; a substantive.

**체열**(體熱) body heat; animal heat. ¶ ~을 발산하다 give off body heat.

**체온**(體溫) (body) temperature; body heat. ¶ ~의 오르내림 changes in *one's* temperature / ~을 재다 take the temperature 《of》 / ~을 유지하다 maintain 〔keep up〕 the body heat / ~이 높다〔낮다〕 have a high 〔low〕 temperature / ~이 오르다〔내리다〕 *one's* temperature rises 〔falls〕 / 환자의 ~은 섭씨 38.8도이다 The temperature of the patient is 38.8 degrees centigrade. / ~이 오르락 내리락 일정치 않다 My temperature fluctuates. / 그의 ~은 정상보다 좀 높다〔낮다〕 His temperature is a little above 〔below〕 normal. ◉ ~계 a (clinical) thermometer: 항내(肛內) ~계 a rectal thermometer / ~계를 흔들어 수은을 내리다 jerk down the mercury in the thermometer. ~곡선 a temperature curve. ~조절 regulation of body temperature. ~표 a fever 〔temperature〕 chart.

**체외**(體外) ¶ ~에〔로〕 outside the body / ~로 노폐물을 배출하다 discharge waste from the body.

◉ ～기생충 an epizoon (*pl.* -zoa). ～발생 ectogenesis. ～수정 external 〔in-vitro〕 fertilization; artificial insemination: ～ 수정 아기 a baby conceived out of the mother's body; an externally conceived baby / ～ 수정란 an egg fertilized in vitro.

**체위**(體位) 《체격》 physique; 《자세》 a posture; a position. ¶ ～의 physical / ～의 향상 improvement of physical condition / 국민 ～의 저하 deterioration in the national physique / ～가 저하되다 physical condition deteriorates; a physical standard goes down / 편안한 ～를 취하다 assume 〔take〕 a comfortable position 〔posture〕 / ～향상을 도모하다 try to improve the physique 《of young people》; try to elevate 〔raise〕 the physical standards 《of a nation》.

◉ ～저하 physical deterioration. ～적성 physical fitness. ～향상운동 a "keep fit" movement. 평균～ the physical average 《in the country》.

**체육**(體育) 《과목》 physical education (생략 P.E.); 《유동》 physical training (생략 P.T.) 《미구어》; athletics. ¶ ～의 날 Health-Sports Day / ～을 중시하다 stress 〔make much of〕 physical education; attach importance to physical education / ～을 장려하다 encourage physical culture.

◉ ～고등학교 a physical education high school. ～관 a gymnasium (*pl.* ～s, -sia); a gym 《미구어》: 잠실 ～관 Chamshil Gymnasium. ～교사 a physical education teacher; an athletics 〔a gymnastic〕 teacher. ～단체 an athletic organization. ～대회 an athletic meet(ing). ～부 《신문사의》 the department of athletics; 《학교의》 an athletic club. ～지도자 a physical director. ～특기생 a sports talent. ～학과 the course of physical education. ～회 an (amateur) athletic association: 대한 ～회 the Korea Amateur Sports Association. 한국～ 대학 the Hanguk College of Physical Education.

**체읍**(涕泣) weep. ～하다 weep and wail; shed tears.

**체인** a chain; 《자동차의》 a tire 〔skid〕 chain. ¶ 타이어에 ～을 채우다 put chains on *one's* car / 그 차는 ～을 채우고 있었다 The car had chains on.

◉ ～블록 a chain block. ～스모커 a chain smoker. ～점(店) a chain store 《미》; a multiple shop 《영》. ～톱 a chain saw.

**체인지** (a) change. ～하다 change. ¶ ～코트하다 change courts. ◉ ～오브 페이스 〖야구〗 a change of pace; a change-up.

**체장**(體長) 《동물의》 the (body) length. ¶ ～이 2미터이다 be two meters long / ～이 최대 3미터에 달하다 reach a maximum length of three meters.

**체재**(滯在) a stay; a sojourn. ⇨ 체류. ¶ 5일간 ～ 예정으로 서울에 도착하다 arrive in Seoul on a five-day visit 《to Korea》 / 그 손님은 1주일 전부터 이 곳에 ～ 중이십니다 The gentleman has been our guest since a week ago.

**체재**(體裁) 《일정한 형식》 (a) form; a style; a format; 《만듦새》 make-up; get-up. ¶ 동일 ～의 uniform; of the same pattern / 책의 ～ the format of a book / ～가 좋다 be of 〔in〕 good style / ～가 좋지 않다 be of 〔in〕 bad style / ～를 갖추다 have proper form 〔style〕 / 이 논문은 ～가 일정하다 This paper has a fixed format 〔form〕. / 그 책은 내용도 좋거니와 ～도 멋지다 The book has a fine format on top of the superior quality of its contents.

**체적**(體積) 《부피》 (cubic) volume; cubic content(s); capacity (용량). ¶ 물체의 ～ the volume of a body / 2입방 미터의 ～ a volume of 2 cubic meters / ～을 구하다 find the volume 《of》; cube. ◉ ～계 a stereometer. ～측정 stereometry. ～팽창 cubical expansion.

**체절**(體節) 〖동물〗 an arthromere; a metamere; a somite; a segment. ¶～의 arthromeric; metameric; somitic; somital; segmental. ◉ ～구성 segmentation. ～기관 a segmental organ.

**체제**(體制) 《조직》 (a) structure; a system; an organization; 《권력·정치 체제》 the Establishment. ¶ 경제 ～ an economic structure / 정치 ～ a political system; a regime / 신〔구〕～ a new 〔an old〕 order / 반～ 운동 an anti-establishment movement / 산업의 전시(戰時) ～ wartime industrial mobilization / 국내 ～를 강화하다 strengthen the internal structure of the nation / 군대의 편성 ～를 개혁하다 renovate the organization of an army.

◉ ～파 establishmentarians: ～파에 속하다 belong to the Establishment.

**체조**(體操) gymnastics; physical 〔gymnastic〕 exercises; gym work 〔exercises〕 《미》. ～하다 do 〔practice〕 gymnastics 〔gymnastic exercises〕. ¶ 기계 ～ apparatus 〔heavy〕 gymnastics / 맨손 ～ free gymnastics / ～를 하고 있다 be at gymnastics. ◉ ～경기 gymnastics (competition): 남자 단체 ～ 경기 the men's team gymnastics competition. ～교사 a gymnastic(s) teacher; a gymnast. ～기구 gymnastic appliances 〔apparatus, gear〕. ～선수 a gymnast. ～시간 a gymnastics hour 〔period〕. ～팀 a gymnastic team.

**체중**(體重) 《몸무게》 the weight (of *one's* body); *one's* (body) weight. ¶ ～의 증가 an increase in weight / ～의 감소 weight loss / ～을 달다 weigh *oneself* / ～을 줄이다 lose 〔reduce〕 weight; take off weight; 《구어》 reduce (감식 등으로); get *one's* weight down 《to 60kg》 / ～을 오른쪽 발에 싣다 rest 〔put〕 *one's* weight on *one's* right foot / ～이 늘다 put on 〔gain〕 weight / ～이 줄다 lose weight / ～이 60킬로그램 나가다 weigh 60 kilograms / ～이 1킬로그램 늘다〔줄다〕 make a gain 〔loss〕 of a kilogram in weight; gain 〔lose〕 a kilogram / ～이 얼마나 됩니까 How much do you weigh? *or* What is your weight? ◉ ～검사 〖스포츠〗 a weigh-in: ～검사를 받다 weigh in. ～계 a weighing machine; (the) scales.

**체증**(滯症) 《소화 기관의》 indigestion; dyspepsia; digestive disorders; 《교통의》 congestion. ¶ 교통 ～ traffic congestion / ～이 있다 suffer from indigestion. ◉ ～환자 a dyspeptic patient.

**체증**(遞增) gradual increase. ～하다 increase gradually.

**체질** sieving; screening; sifting. ～하다 sieve; screen 《coal, sand, gravel》; sift (out). ¶ ～하고 남은 무거리 screenings / ～한 자갈 screened gravel / 자갈을 ～하다 screen 〔riddle〕 gravel.

**체질**(體質) ① *one's* (physical) constitution; *one's* 《genetic》 make-up; 《소질》 predisposition 《to diabetes》. ¶ ～적(으로) constitutional(ly) / ～적인 결함 a constitutional defect / 병약한 ～ constitutional tendencies to disease / 암에 걸리기 쉬운 ～의 사람 a person constitutionally predisposed to cancer / ～에 맞다 agree with 〔suit〕 *one's* constitution / ～이 약하다 be of weak 〔delicate〕 constitution / 나는 감기에 걸리기 쉬운 ～이다 I'm apt to catch cold. / 그건 내 ～에 맞지 않는다 That doesn't suit my constitution. *or* That doesn't agree with me. ② 《기업·단체의》 innate characteristics; make-up; structure. ¶ 이 회사는 ～을 개선할 필요가 있다 This company needs improvements to its structure. ◉ ～개선 improving *one's* physical condition; 《기업 등의》 (radical) reform; revamping: 우리 경제의 ～ 개선을 하고 국제 경쟁력을 강화하다 improve the structure of our economy and raise our competitiveness in the world market. ～성 질환 constitutional disease.

**체취**(體臭) ① 《몸냄새》 body oder; 《구어》 B.O.; 《동물의》 body smell. ¶ ～가 나다 give out 〔send forth〕 a body odor / ～가 심하다 have strong body odor. ② 《분위기·특징》 《have》 a distinctive personality 〔aura〕. ¶ 이 작품에서는 저자의 ～가 느껴진다 This work reflects the distinctive personality of the author. *or* The novel emanates the strong personality of the author.

**체코** the Czech Republic. ¶ ～의 Czech. ◉ ～말 Czech. ～사람 a Czech.

**체크** ① 《대조·검사》 a check. ～하다 check; check 《*a thing*》 up; check up on 《*a thing*》; 《체크표를 하다》 tick 〔check〕 《*a thing*》 off; put a tick against 《*a thing*》; mark (off). ② 《수표》 a check 《미》; a cheque 《영》. ③ 《무늬》 a check; a chequer 《영》. ¶ ～무늬의 블라우스 a checked blouse. ◉ ～리스트 《대조표》 a checklist. ～아웃 (a) check-out: ～아웃하다 check out 《of》. ～오프 a checkoff. ～인 (a) check-in: ～인하다 check in 《at a hotel》.

**체통**(體統) 《체면》 《an official's》 decency; respectability; dignity; prestige; honor; face. ¶ ～이 서는 face-saving / ～에 관한 문제 a matter of dignity; a question of "face" / ～이 서다 save *one's* face / ～이 없다 be indecent 〔disrespectable, impudent〕 / ～ 없이 굴다 act improperly 〔disrespectably〕 / ～을 잃다 lose prestige; lose *one's* face.

**체팽창**(體膨脹) 〖물리〗 cubical expansion. ⇨ 체적 팽창. ◉ ～계수〔률〕 the coefficient of cubical expansion.

**체포**(逮捕) (an) arrest; apprehension; (a) capture. ～하다 arrest; apprehend; seize; catch; place under arrest; make an arrest. ¶ 몇 명을 ～하다 make several arrests / 살인 혐의로 ～하다 arrest 《*a person*》 for (alleged) murder / (아직) ~되지 않고 있다 be (still) at large / ~를 모면하다 escape arrest / ~에 순순히 응하다 surrender tamely; be arrested without resistance / 많은 사람이 ~되었다 A number of arrests were made. / 그녀에게는 ~령이 내려있다 There's warrant out for her arrest. ◉ ~영장 an arrest warrant; a warrant for 《*a person's*》 arrest: ~영장을 발부하다 issue 〔put out〕 a warrant for the arrest of 《*a person*》.

**체하다** pretend 《to》; affect; set *oneself* up as; feign; make believe; pose 《as》; make a pretense 〔feint, show〕 of 《*doing*》. ¶ 놀란 ~ feign surprise; affect wonder / 도망치는 ~ make as if one were going to run away / 들리지 않는 ~ pretend not to hear 《*a person*》 / 모른 ~ pretend 〔feign〕 ignorance 《about》; put on a show of ignorance; 《사람을 만났을 때》 look the other way; pretend not to recognize 《*a person*》 / 못 본 ~ pretend not to see; shut 〔close〕 *one's* eyes 《to》; wink 〔connive, blink〕 at 《a fault》/ 학자〔부자〕인 ~ pose as a scholar 〔richman〕 / 신사인 ~ affect a gentleman / 잘난 ~ put on airs 〔frills〕; give *oneself* airs; swagger / 잠자는 ~ sham 〔feign, simulate〕 sleep; pretend to be asleep / 잘난 체하지 마라 Don't pretend you're somebody. *or* Don't be conceited. / 그는 어리석은 체하고 사람을 속인다 He fools 〔deceives〕 people by pretending to be a fool. / 잠자는 체하자 Let's pretend to be asleep.

**체하다**(滯—) have a digestive upset; lie 〔sit〕 heavy on *one's* stomach. ¶ 먹은 음식이 ~ *one's* meal lies heavy on the stomach; suffer from indigestion; have an upset stomach.

**체한**(滯韓) stay(ing) in Korea. ~하다 stay in Korea. ¶ ~중에 while staying in Korea; during *one's* stay in Korea.

**체험**(體驗) (personal) experience. ~하다 experience (personally); go through; undergo. ¶ 직접 ~하다 gain *one's* experience at first hand / ~으로 알다 learn by 〔from〕 《direct, personal》 experience / ~을 말하다 relate 〔narrate, talk about〕 *one's* own experience(s) / ~을 살리다 make effective use of *one's* experience / 온갖 고생을 ~하다 undergo all sorts of hardships.
◉ ~담 the story of *one's* personal experiences.

**체현**(體現) (an) embodiment. ~하다 embody; impersonate; personificate. ¶ 그 상(像)은 조각가의 이상을 ~한 것이었다 The statue was the embodiment of the ideals of the sculptor.

**체형**(體刑) 《체벌》 corporal 〔physical, bodily〕 punishment; 《징역》 penal servitude; imprisonment with hard labor. ¶ ~을 과하다 inflict 〔impose〕 corporal punishment 《on *a person*》; sentence 《*a person*》 to 《three years'》 penal servitude.

**체형**(體型) *one's* figure; the shape of *one's* body. ¶ 표준 ~ standard proportions / 그녀의 새 드레스는 ~에 맞는다〔안맞는다〕 Her new dress is a good 〔poor〕 fit.

**체화**(滯貨) 《밀린 화물》 accumulation of undelivered goods 〔cargo〕; backlog; 《상품의》 accumulation of stocks; stockpiles of goods; piles of dead stock (팔다 남은 재고품). ~하다 accumulate. ¶ ~의 처리 disposal of stockpiles / ~를 처분하기 위한 세일 a sale to clear old stock; a clearance sale / ~를 일소하다 clear out the accumulated goods.

**첼로** 〖악기〗 a cello; a violoncello.
◉ ~연주자 a cello player; a cellist.

**쳇다리** a support on which a sieve is laid while in use; sieve-frame legs.

**쳇바퀴** the frame of a sieve. ¶ ~에 쳇불을 메우다 fix a sieve net on its frame / 다람쥐 ~ 돌 듯하다 go round and round; repeat the same thing endlessly.

**쳇불** a sieve net; the meshes of sieve.

**쳐가다** collect and take away 《garbage, *etc.*》; carry away; remove; clear. ¶ 변소를 ~ carry away the night soil from the stool pit.

**쳐내다** take away; remove; clean up; clear; 《준설하다》 clean (out) 《a well》; dredge 《a river》. ¶ 도랑을 ~ clean out a ditch / 돼지우리를 ~ clean up a pigsty 〔pigpen〕 / 뜰의 눈을 ~ clear the yard of snow; shovel away the snow from the yard / 외양간의 거름을 ~ clean a cowshed of manure.

**쳐다보다** 《위로》 look up 《at》; look upward; 《가만히》 look 〔gaze, stare〕 《at》. ¶ 얼굴을 ~ look up into 《*a person's*》 face; gaze 〔stare〕 《*a person*》 in the face / 하늘을 ~ look up to 〔into〕 the sky / 위를 쳐다보면 한이 없다 Don't compare yourself with those above you. *or* Don't aspire too high.

**쳐들다** ① 《들어 올리다》 lift (up); raise;

put 〔hold〕 up; heave; hoist. ¶ 고개를 ～ raise *one's* head / 무거운 돌을 ～ heave a heavy stone / 손을 번쩍 ～ raise 〔put up〕 *one's* hand high / 부끄러워 고개를 쳐들지 못하다 cannot hold up *one's* head for shame; cannot look 《*a person*》 in the face because of bad conscience / 반항심이 고개를 쳐들기 시작했다 Rebellion began to raise its head.
② 《초들다》 hold up; point out 〔to〕. ⇨ 초들다. ¶ 남의 결점을 ～ point to 〔out〕 another's defects; find fault with another.

**쳐들어가다** invade; penetrate 《into》; make an inroad into 〔on〕; 《집에》 break into 《a house》; raid 〔make a raid on〕 《*another's* house》. ¶ 적진으로 ～ make an inroad 〔a raid〕 on the enemy.

**쳐버리다** take 〔clear〕 away; remove; clean up; clear away. ¶ 길의 쇠똥을 ～ remove the cow dung from a road / 쓰레기를 ～ take refuse away; cart rubbish off.

**쳐주다** ① 《값을》 estimate 〔value, rate, assess〕 《*a thing*》 at; put 《*a thing*》 at. ¶ (물건을) 높이〔낮게〕 ～ rate 《*a thing*》 high 〔low〕; make much 〔little〕 of 《*a thing*》 / 집값을 3천만 원으로 ～ appraise a house at thirty million won / 그 책을 5천원 쳐 줄테니 나한테 팔아라 Sell the book to me, I'll pay 5,000 won for it.
② 《인정하다》 consider; acknowledge; regard 〔treat, look (up)on〕 《as》; 《알아주다》 recognize; appreciate; think highly of 《*a person*》; give 《*a person*》 a credit for. ¶ 세상에서 쳐주지 않는 작가 an obscure 〔unacknowledged〕 writer / 적임자로 ～ regard 《*a person*》 as suitable for the job / 지도자로 ～ acknowledge as leader / 정직한 사람으로 ～ give 《*a person*》 credit for being an honest man.
③ 《치워주다》 take away 〔remove〕 《*a thing*》 for 《*a person*》; clean 〔clear〕 up 《*a thing*》 for 《*a person*》.

**쳐죽이다** beat 〔strike, knock, club〕 《*a person*》 to death; strike 《*a person*》 dead. ¶ 몽둥이로 ～ club 《a dog》 to death.

**초** a candle; a taper (가는). ¶ 초의 심지 a candlewick / 초를 켜다〔끄다〕 light 〔put out〕 a candle / 초를 불어서 끄다 blow out a candle / 촛불로 책을 읽다 read a book by candlelight.

**초**(抄) 《초록》 an extract; an excerpt; a selection. ¶ 시초(詩抄) a selection of poems / 춘향전 초 excerpts from the "Story of *Ch'unhyang*".

**초**(秒) a second (of time). ¶ 천분의 1초 a millisecond / 백만분의 1초 a microsecond / 1초의 몇 분의 1까지 정확한 시계 a watch that can keep time to a split fraction of a second / 초시계 a stopwatch; a chronograph / 초를 다투는 문제다 There is no moment to lose.

**초**(草) ① 《초안》 a rough copy; a draft. ⇨ 초(草)하다. ¶ 법안의 초 a draft of a bill / 초(를) 잡다 write; (make a) draft 《of》. ② 《초서》 the cursive 〔running〕 style of writing Chinese characters; a cursive 〔running〕 hand.

**초**(醋) vinegar. ¶ 초간장 soy sauce mixed with vinegar / 초를 치다 flavor 〔season〕 《food》 with vinegar / 초에 버무리다 mix up with vinegar / 초에 절이다 pickle in vinegar.

**초-**(初) the beginning; (the) first; the early part; 《상순》 the first third of the month. ¶ 초가을 early autumn / 초하루 the first day 《of a month》.

**초-**(超) ultra-; super-; sur-; transcendental. ¶ 초현대적 ultramodern / 초자연적 supernatural / 초인간적 superhuman / 초경험적 transcendental; metempirical.

**초**(初) ① 《처음》 the beginning; (the) first; the early part. ¶ 1월 초 the beginning of January / 학기초 the beginning of the school term / 20세기 초에 in the early part 〔years〕 of the 20th century; early in the 20th century. ② 〖야구〗 ¶ 5회 초 the first half of the fifth inning.

**초가**(草家) a grass-roofed house; a (straw-)thatched cottage. ◉ ～삼간 a three-room thatched cottage; a small cottage. ～집 a thatched cottage.

**초가**(樵歌) a woodcutter's song.

**초가을**(初—) early autumn 〔fall 《미》〕; the beginning of autumn.

**초감각적**(超感覺的) extrasensory; supersensible; pretersensual.

**초강대국**(超强大國) a superpower; 〔총칭〕 the superpowers.

**초개**(草芥) bits of straw 〔grass〕; a worthless thing. ¶ ～ 같다 be worthless (as bits of straw) / ～ 같은 인생 a worthless life; a brief 〔transient〕 life; a humble life / 죽음을 ～ 같이 여기다 hold *one's* life as nothing; think nothing of *one's* life.

**초거성**(超巨星) a supergiant (star).
**초겨울**(初—) early winter; the beginning of winter.
**초견**(初見) the first view 〔sight〕. ~하다 see 《*something*》 for the first time.
**초경**(初更) the first watch of the night (=6-8 p.m.); early evening.
**초경**(初耕) 〖농업〗 the first tilling 〔plowing〕; a preliminary tilling. ~하다 till 〔plow〕 once; give a preliminary tilling.
**초경**(初經) 《첫월경》 menarche.
**초계**(哨戒) 〖군사〗 patrol(ling). ~하다 patrol. ¶ 연안 ~ coastal patrol / ~중이다 be on patrol / 해상 ~를 강화하다 strengthen 〔tighten〕 sea patrol. ◉ ~기 a patrol plane. ~선(線) a patrol line. ~정(艇) a patrol 〔picket〕 boat; a P.T. boat.
**초고**(草稿) a (rough) draft; a rough copy; notes; 《원고》 a manuscript (생략 MS, *pl.* Mss). ¶ 연설~ a draft for a speech / ~를 작성하다 make (out) a draft 《of》; draft 《a speech, an address》; prepare notes 《for a lecture》 / ~를 보면서 연설하다 speak from notes / ~ 없이 연설하다 speak without (referring to *one's*) notes; make a speech offhand.
**초고속**(超高速) superhigh 〔ultrahigh〕 speed. ¶ ~의 superspeed 《flight》. ◉ ~도로 a superhighway. ~도 촬영기 a superhigh-speed camera. ~열차 a superspeed 〔bullet〕 train. ~정보통신망 the Information Superhighway Network. ~컴퓨터 a supercomputer.
**초고주파**(超高周波) 〖통신〗 ultrahigh frequency (생략 UHF, u.h.f., uhf); superhigh frequency (생략 SHF, s.h.f.).
**초과**(超過) excess; 《잉여》 surplus. ~하다 exceed; be in excess 《of》; be over 〔above, more than〕. ¶ 인원 ~ an excessive number of people / 수입 ~ an excess of imports over exports / (화폐의) ~ 발행 excess issue; overissue / 견적보다 백만 원의 ~ an excess of 1,000,000 won over the estimate / 규정 중량을 ~하다 exceed the fixed weight; overweigh / 수요가 공급을 ~하다 the demand exceeds the supply / 정원을 ~하다 exceed the fixed number of people; exceed the number required / 제한 연령〔시간〕을 ~하다 exceed the age 〔time〕 limit / 연령〔체중〕 ~로 실격하다 be disqualified because of overage 〔overweight〕 / 지원자가 정원을 ~하다 applicants exceed the number required / 비용이 예산보다 많이 ~했다 The expense was well over the estimate. / 버스는 정원을 ~하고 있었다 The bus was overloaded. / 제한 시간을 ~했으니, 질문을 끝내 주십시오 You must finish your question immediately because you have already exceeded the time limit. ◉ ~(담보) 보험 excess insurance. ~소득 excess income. ~시간 extra time; overtime. ~액 a surplus; an excess 《of》. ~요금 excess fare(차의); excess baggage charge(수화물의). ~이득세 an extra profit duty 〔tax〕.
**초과근무**(超過勤務) overtime work 〔service〕; extra duties. ¶ ~(를) 하다 work overtime; do 《two hours'》 overtime / ~를 거부하다 refuse to do overtime. ◉ ~수당 overtime pay(ment); an overtime allowance: ~수당을 타다 be paid overtime.
**초교**(初校) 〖인쇄〗 the first proof (sheet). ¶ ~를 보다 read the first proof.
**초국가**(超國家) a superstate. ¶ ~적인 supernational; supranational. ◉ ~주의 ultranationalism: ~주의적 ultranationalistic / ~주의자 an ultranationalist.
**초군**(超群) preeminence. ~하다 (be) preeminent; [서술적] be preeminent above the rest 《for》; excel 《others in》. ¶ 그는 무예가 ~하다 His military 〔martial〕 arts stand out conspicuous.
**초균형예산**(超均衡豫算) surplus budget; budget with a revenue surplus.
**초근목피**(草根木皮) herb roots and tree bark; coarse and miserable food. ¶ ~로 연명하다 barely manage to keep alive with the aid of roots and bark.
**초급**(初級) a primary 〔an elementry〕 grade; the first 〔beginner's〕 class 《in English》; the junior course 《in French》. ¶ ~자 a beginner / ~용의 《books》 for beginners / 프랑스어의 ~코스 a beginner's course in French; elementary French / 나는 ~용 영어책을 원합니다 I want an English book for beginners. ◉ ~대학 a junior college. ~영어 elementary 〔beginner's〕 English.
**초급**(初給) an initial pay 〔salary〕. ⇨ 「초봉(初俸).
**초기**(初期) ① 《한 시대의》 the early days 〔years〕; the beginning. ¶ 고려 ~에 early in the Koryo era / 18세기 ~에 in the early years 〔part〕 of the 18th century; early in the 18th century. ② 《단계》 the first 〔initial,

incipient, early] stage; the primary stage. ¶ ～의 incipient; initial; early / 문명〔병〕의 ～ the early stage of civilization 〔of a disease〕/ 이 병은 ～에 치료하면 낫는다 The disease can be cured if treated in its early stages. ◉ ～결핵 early 〔incipient〕 T.B. ～작품 *one's* early works: 춘원의 ～ 작품 Ch'unwŏn's early works. ～침윤 〖의학〗 primary infiltration.

**초김치**(醋—) vegetables pickled in vinegar in early spring; vinegared kimchi.

**초꼬지** a small dried abalone.

**초나흗날, 초나흘**(初—) the 4th day of the month.

**초년**(初年) ①《인생의》 *one's* early years; the early part of *one's* life; *one's* young days. ¶ ～에 급제하다 pass the highest-level state examination 「in *one's* young days 〔early in *one's* life〕/ 운수가 ～에는 길하고 만년에는 흉하다 be destined to be lucky in early years but unlucky in later years. ②《첫해》 the first year; 《초기》 the early years. ◉ ～병 a new 〔raw〕 recruit. ～생 a mere beginner: 이 일에 나는 ～생이다 I'm a mere beginner in this business.

**초념**(初念) *one's* original mind 〔purpose, intention〕. ⇨ 초지(初志).

**초노급함**(超弩級艦) a superdreadnought.

**초능력**(超能力) a supernatural 〔preternatural〕 power; 《초감각》 extrasensory perception; 《염력》 psychokinesis. ¶ ～의 psychokinetic. ◉ ～자 a person with supernatural power; a person capable of extrasensory perception.

**초다짐**(初—) ～하다 eat a bit to take the edge off *one's* appetite before mealtime.

**초단**(初段) 《유도·바둑 등의》 the first grade. ¶ 바둑 ～자 a first-grade player of *paduk* / 유도 ～인 사람 a first-grader in *judo*.

**초단파**(超短波) 〖물리〗 ultrashort waves; very high frequency (생략 V.H.F., VHF, v.h.f., vhf). ¶ ～의 very-high-frequency. ◉ ～방송 ultrashort-wave broadcasting. ～수신기〔송신기〕 an ultrashort wave receiver 〔transmitter〕.

**초닷새**(初—) the 5th day of the month.

**초당**(草堂) a thatched cottage separated from the main building of a house.

**초당안보기구**(超黨安保機構) a suprapartisan 「organization 〔consultative body〕 for national security.

**초당파**(超黨派) ¶ ～의 suprapartisan; nonpartisan; 《미》 bipartisan. ¶ ～적으로 의안 통과에 합의했다 All the parties agreed to pass the bill through the National Assembly. ◉ ～내각 a suprapartisan 〔coalition〕 cabinet. ～외교 suprapartisan 〔nonpartisan〕 diplomacy: ～ 외교 정책 a suprapartisan foreign policy. ～정부 an all-party government.

**초대**(初—) 《풋내기》 a greenhorn; a green hand; a novice; a beginner. ¶ 그는 바둑에서는 아직 ～다 He is still just a beginner in *paduk*.

**초대**(初代) the first generation; 《사람》 the founder; the originator. ¶ ～의 the first. ◉ ～대통령 the first President. ～왕 the first king 〔the founder〕 of a dynasty.

**초대**(招待) (an) invitation; 《구어》 (an) invite. ～하다 invite; ask; extend an invitation 《to *a person*》. ¶ …의 ～로 at 〔on〕 the invitation of… / ～를 받다 receive 〔get〕 an invitation; be invited 《to dinner, by *a person*》; have an invitation 《from *a person*》/ 결혼식에 ～하다 invite 《*a person*》 to a wedding ceremony / 저녁 식사에 ～하다 invite 〔ask〕 《*a person*》 to dinner / ～에 응하다 accept an invitation / ～를 사절하다 decline an invitation; do not accept an invitation / ～가 쏟아져 들어오다 be flooded 〔inundated〕 with invitations / 선약이 있어서 ～에 응하지 못해 유감입니다 I regret that a previous engagement prevents me from accepting your kind invitation. ◉ ～객 an invited guest. ～권 an invitation card 〔ticket〕; a complimentary ticket. ～석 a seat reserved (for a guest). ～연 a dinner party: a feast; a banquet. ～일 《전시회 따위의》 a preview day. ～작가 the invited artist. ～장 a letter of invitation; an invitation (card): ～장을 내다 send 〔issue〕 an invitation (card) 《to》. ～전(展) a preview 《미》; a private view.

**초대면**(初對面) the first meeting 〔interview〕. ¶ ～인 사람 a stranger / ～의 인상 *one's* first impressions 《of》/ ～하다 meet 《*a person*》 for the first time / ～의 인사를 하다 introduce *oneself* 《to》.

**초대작**(超大作) a super-production; 《영화의》 a superfilm; a supra-feature film.

**초대형**(超大型) ¶ ～의 extra-large; outsize(d). ◉ ～여객기 a superliner: ～제트 여객기 a jumbo jet.
**초도**(初度) 《for》 the first time. ◉ ～순시 *one's* first tour 〔round〕 of inspection.
**초동**(初冬) the beginning of winter; 「early winter.
**초동**(樵童) a young firewood-gatherer; a young woodsman; a boy woodcutter.
**초동수사**(初動搜查) an initial investi- 「gation of the police.
**초두**(初頭) 《at》 the beginning; the outset; the first; the start. ¶ 회의 ～ the beginning of a meeting / 20세기 ～에 「early in 〔in the early part of〕 the 20th century.
**초들다** 《언급하다》 mention; refer to; 《열거하다》 enumerate; 《인용하다》 cite. ¶ 조상의 사적(事蹟)을 ～ refer to what *one's* forefathers had done / 남의 결점을 ～ mention 〔bring up〕 another's defects; find fault with another / 초들어 말할 만한 거리도 못 된다 It is not worth mentioning specially. / 그는 하나하나 그녀의 단점을 초들었다 He picked out her faults one by one.
**초등**(初等) a primary 〔an elementary〕 grade 〔class〕; the lowest class.
◉ ～과 an elementary course; a beginners' class. ～교육 elementary 〔primary〕 education: ～교육을 받다 go through the grades. ～반 a beginners' class. ～수학 elementary mathematics.
**초등학교**(初等學校) a primary 〔an elementary〕 school; a grade school 《미》. ¶ ～는 의무 교육이다 Elementary education is compulsory. / 낸시는 ～ 3년생이다 Nancy is a third grader. *or* Nancy is in the third grade. / 한국에서는 6세에 ～에 들어간다 In Korea children enter elementary school at the age of six. ◉ ～과정 an elementary school course of study. ～교사 an elementary 〔a primary〕 school teacher; a grade-school teacher 《미》. ～교육 elementary 〔primary〕 education. ～아동 a primary-school 〔grade=school〕 child; a pupil.
**초라니** 『민속』 one of the court performers of an exorcism ceremony who is disguised as a woman in colorful dress with a flag in her hand.
**초라떼다** 《창피당하다》 get snubbed 〔squelched〕; be humbled; get taken down a peg or two. ¶ 주제넘게 굴다가 ～ make a fool of *oneself* for being such a smart aleck.
**초라하다** ① 《모양·주제가》 (be) shabby; miserable; poor-〔wretched-〕looking; seedy; scruffy; beat-up (looking). ¶ 초라한 음식 coarse 〔plain〕 food / 초라한 옷 shabby clothes / 초라한 집 a shabby 〔poor, run-down〕 house; a humble cottage / 옷차림이 ～ be shabbily 〔poorly〕 dressed; be ill-clad / 행색이 ～ look poor; be of seedy appearance / 초라한 생활을 하다 live a miserable 〔wretched〕 life.
② 《행동이》 (be) mean; shabby; low; dirty; abject; dishonorable. ¶ 초라한 짓 a mean thing to *do* / 초라하게 굴다 behave shabbily 〔abjectly〕.
**초래**(招來) bringing about 〔on〕; incurring; inviting. ～하다 bring about 〔on〕; lead to; give rise to; produce; incur; cause.
¶ 뜻밖의 결과를 ～하다 produce 〔lead to〕 an unexpected result / 실패를 ～하다 cause 〔lead to〕 a failure; end 〔result〕 in failure / 위험을 ～하다 invite 〔bring on〕 danger / 죽음을 ～하다 cause *one's* death / 파멸을 ～하다 bring down ruin 《on *a person*》 / 화(禍)를 ～하다 bring calamity upon *oneself;* incur disaster / 인플레이션이 물가 상승을 ～했다 The inflation caused a rise in the prices of commodities. / 혁명이란 대개 많은 비참한 결과를 ～하는 것이다 Revolution generally conduces to much subsequent misery.
**초략**(抄略) 《노략질》 plunder; ravage; pillage; spoliation. ～하다 plunder; ravage; spoliate.
**초련** an early crop to be served until the regular harvest time.
**초련**(初戀) *one's* first love. ⇨ 첫사랑.
**초례**(醮禮) a wedding 〔marriage, nuptial〕 ceremony. ¶ ～를 지내다 perform 〔celebrate, hold〕 a marriage; celebrate a wedding.
◉ ～청 a wedding hall.
**초로**(初老) (the beginning of) middle age. ¶ ～의 elderly; middle-aged (★ middle-aged는 대체로 40·50대의 사람에 쓰이며, elderly는 이를 넘긴 사람에 쓰임) / ～의 신사 an elderly gentleman / ～기에 접어들다 enter upon middle age.
**초로**(草路) a path across a meadow 〔field of grass〕.
**초로**(草露) dew on the grass. ¶ 인생은 ～와 같다 Life is but a span. *or* The world is but a fleeting show. ◉ ～인

생 a transient 〔an ephemeral〕 life 〔existence〕.

**초록**(抄錄) an abstract; an extract; an excerpt; 《적요》 an epitome; a summary. ～하다 abstract; excerpt; extract; 《적요하다》 summarize; make a summary 〔an epitome〕 《of》. ¶ 연설을 ～하다 make an abstract of a speech / 이 구절은 그의 논문에서 ～했다 I excerpted this paragraph from his essay. ◉ ～자 《발췌자》 an abstracter; an excerpter; 《적요자》 an epitomist; a summarist.

**초록**(草綠) green; verdure (초목의). ¶ ～의 green; verdant; emerald / ～을 띤 greenish; greeny / ～으로 뒤덮인 산들 the mountains clad 〔covered〕 in fresh greenery 〔verdure〕 / ～을 칠하다 paint 《a door》 green / ～은 동색이다 《속담》 One devil knows another. *or* Like knows like.

**초롱** 《통》 a tin; a can 《미》; 《셀 때》 a bucketful; a containerful 《of liquid》. ¶ 물～ a water can 〔tin 《영》〕 / 석유 한 ～ a tin〔can〕 of kerosene / 물 두 ～ two pails of water.

**초롱**(―籠) a silk-covered lantern.

**초롱꽃** 〖식물〗 a bellflower; a Canterbury bell.

**초롱초롱하다** 《눈이》 (be) charmingly clear; limpid. ¶ 초롱초롱한 눈 limpid eyes.

**초름하다** ① 《몫이》 be small; be look smaller (than other shares). ② 《부족·미달하다》 be not enough; be hardly ample; be a bit short of.

**초립**(草笠) a straw hat worn by young married men (of below twenty). ◉ ～동〔둥이〕 a very young married man who wears a straw hat; a married lad wearing a straw hat.

**초막**(草幕) ① 《초가》 a straw-thatched cottage 〔hut〕. ② 《중의 집》 a Buddhist monk's hut 〔cell〕.

**초만원**(超滿員) being overfull of people; being filled to capacity. ¶ ～의 filled to overflowing; 《구어》 《a bus》 bursting at the seams / ～을 이루다 be filled 〔packed〕 to overflowing; be crowded beyond capacity / 강연회는 ～을 이루는 대성황이었다 The lecture meeting was a great success with the audience overjamming the auditorium.

**초매**(草昧) 《미개》 a primitive 〔uncivilized〕 state; primitiveness; 《혼돈》 chaos; confusion; disorder. ¶ ～한 primitive; uncivilized; unenlightened.

**초면**(初面) *one's* first meeting 〔interview〕 《with》; the first meeting 《between》. ⇨ 초대면(初對面). ¶ ～의 사람 a person met for the first time; a stranger / 그와는 그때가 ～이었다 That was the first time I had met him. *or* He had been a complete stranger to me until then. ◉ ～인사 greetings on the first meeting: ～인사를 하다 introduce *oneself* 《to》.

**초면**(炒麵) chow mein; Chinese fried noodles.

**초모**(醋母) mother-of-vinegar. ⇨ 아세트산균.

**초목**(草木) trees and plants; grass and trees; plant life; vegetation. ¶ 산천～ nature; natural scenery / 열대 지방의 ～ the vegetation of the tropics / 한 포기 ～도 볼 수 없는 산정(山頂) a mountaintop 「bare 〔absolutely denuded〕 of vegetation.

**초무침**(醋―) vegetables dressed with vinegar.

**초문**(初聞) hearing something for the first time; a news. ¶ 그것은 금시～이다 That's news to me. *or* It's the first time I've heard that.

**초미**(焦眉) ¶ ～의 urgent; pressing; impending / ～의 관심사 an issue of burning concern / ～의 문제 an urgent 〔a burning〕 question; a matter of urgent necessity. ◉ ～지급(之急) a burning 〔pressing〕 necessity; an urgent 〔a crying〕 need.

**초민**(焦悶) worry; distress; melancholy. ～하다 be agonized out of impatience; be worried 〔distressed〕; be sad at heart.

**초반**(初盤) the opening (part) 《of a game》; an early stage 《of a campaign》. ¶ 선거는 아직 ～전이다 The election campaign is still in its initial phase. / 그 시합의 승패는 ～에 결정되었다 The result of the game was decided in the early stages of it.

**초밥**(醋―) sushi; slightly vinegared rice ball topped with sliced raw fish, etc. on. ¶ ～집 a sushi shop 〔bar〕 / ～을 만들다 make hand-rolled sushi.

**초방**(初枋) 〖건축〗 the first cornice in the middle of a wall framed after setting up a pillar.

**초배**(初褙) underpapering (of a wall); underlining. ～하다 line 〔underline〕 《a wall》 with paper. ◉ ～지(紙) lining paper; a lining.

**초벌**(初―) the first; the primary; a

rough job. ¶ ~ 그림을 그리다 make a rough sketch ⟪of⟫. ◉ ~김 the first weeding. ~칠 (a) rough coating; the first 〔ground, primary〕 coat: ~칠 하다 give ⟪the door⟫ a first coat ⟪on⟫.

**초범**(初犯) ⟪죄⟫ the first offense 〔offence ⟪영⟫〕; ⟪범인⟫ a first offender.

**초범**(超凡) extraordinariness; being out of the common. ⇨ 비범. ~하다 (be) extraordinary; uncommon; be out of the common 〔ordinary〕.

**초벽**(初壁) a first 〔rough〕 coat of plaster ⟪on a wall⟫; roughcast; ⟪벽⟫ a rough-coated wall. ~하다 give ⟪the wall⟫ a first coat ⟪of plaster⟫; roughcast. ¶ ~을 치다 = ~하다.

**초병**(醋甁) a vinegar bottle. ◉ ~마개 [비유적] a person with repulsive and nauseous manners.

**초병**(哨兵) a sentry; a sentinel; a military guard. ¶ ~을 세우다 set up a sentry; post 〔station〕 a guard / ~을 교대하다 relieve a sentry. ◉ ~근무 sentry 〔guard〕 duty. ~선 a sentry line; a cordon.

**초보**(初步) the rudiments 〔elements〕 ⟪of⟫; the first stage; the ABC ⟪of⟫; a beginners' course ⟪in French⟫; the first step(s) ⟪to, in⟫.
¶ ~의 elementary; rudimentary / 영어 ~ an English primer / 산수의 ~ the elements 〔rudiments〕 of arithmetic; the ABC of arithmetic / ~를 가르치다 introduce ⟪*a person*⟫ into; give ⟪*a person*⟫ elementary lessons ⟪in⟫; teach ⟪*a person*⟫ the rudiments ⟪of⟫ / ~를 배우다 receive first lessons ⟪in French⟫ from ⟪*a person*⟫; take rudimentary lessons ⟪in English⟫ from ⟪*a person*⟫ / 영어를 ~부터 배우다 begin with the ABC of English / 영문법의 ~를 가르치다 initiate ⟪*a person*⟫ into the elements of English grammar / 그의 체스는 아직 ~다 He is still a green hand at chess. / 그는 영문법의 ~도 모른다 He doesn't know the first thing about English grammar. / 그의 연구는 아직도 ~ 단계이다 He is still in an early stage of his study. ◉ ~영어 elementary English. ~자 a beginner; a novice; a green hand; a greenhorn: ~자를 위한 for beginners. ~지식 a rudimentary 〔an elementary〕 knowledge ⟪of botany⟫.

**초복**(初伏) the first 10-day period of 「the dog days 〔summer doldrums〕. ¶ ~이 들다 the dog days begin 〔set in〕.

**초본**(抄本) an extract; an abstract; an abridged copy 〔transcript〕. ¶ 호적~ an abstract of *one's* family register.

**초본**(草本) 〖식물〗 a herb; [총칭] herbage. ¶ ~의 herbal; herbaceous.
◉ ~경(莖) 〖식물〗 a herbaceous stem. ~식물 a herbaceous plant.

**초봄**(初—) the beginning of spring; early spring. ¶ ~에 in (the) early spring; early in spring / 이 스웨터는 ~에 입기 좋다 This sweater is good to wear in early spring.

**초봉**(初俸) a starting 〔an initial〕 pay 〔salary〕. ¶ 나의 ~은 70만원이었다 I began 〔started〕 with a salary of 700,000 won a month.

**초부**(樵夫) a woodcutter; a woodman.

**초분**(初分) ⟪초년 운⟫ the forecast of *one's* luck for early in life. ¶ ~은 길하나 후분이 좋지 않다 You are lucky in your early days, but unlucky in later days.

**초비**(草肥) green manure. ⇨ 녹비(綠肥).

**초빙**(招聘) (an) invitation; a call. ~하다 invite; extend a call ⟪to⟫; call in; engage (고용); ⟪의뢰하다⟫ call on ⟪*a person* to *do*⟫. ¶ …의 ~으로 at the invitation ⟪of⟫ / ~에 응하다 accept a call ⟪from Mr. Kim⟫; accept the offer of a position; accept the appointment ⟪to the chair of chemistry⟫; accept the invitation ⟪to give a lecture⟫ / 우리 호텔은 그녀를 총지배인으로 ~했다 Our hotel engaged her as a general manager. / 우리는 전자 공학 전문가를 ~하고 싶다 We want to call in an electronics specialist. / 그는 버클리 대학의 한국문학 객원교수로 ~되었다 He was invited to give lectures on Korean literature as a visiting 〔guest〕 professor at Berkeley University.

**초사**(焦思) impatience; worry; anxiety. ~하다 be impatient ⟪to *do*⟫; be anxious ⟪for⟫; be in a fidget; ⟪마음 졸임⟫ worry (*oneself*) ⟪about⟫; trouble *oneself* ⟪about⟫; be anxious ⟪about⟫.

**초사흗날**(初—) the 3rd day of the month.

**초산**(初産) a woman's first delivery 〔childbirth, confinement〕. ¶ 그녀의 ~은 난산〔순산〕이었다 Her first delivery was 「a difficult 〔an easy〕 one. ◉ ~부(婦) a woman bearing 〔expecting〕 her first child; 〖의학〗 a primipara.

**초산**(硝酸) 〖화학〗 nitric acid. ⇨ 질산.

**초산**(醋酸) 〖화학〗 acetic acid. ⇨ 아세트

산.

**초상**(肖像) a portrait; a likeness. ⇨초상화. ¶ 등신대(等身大)의 ～ a life-size(d) portrait.

**초상**(初喪) (a period of) mourning. ¶～ 중이다 be in mourning《for》/ ～(이) 나다 a death occurs《in *a person's* family》/ ～을 당하다 have a death in *one's* family / ～을 치르다 observe mourning. ◉ ～집 a house 〔family〕 in mourning; a bereaved family.

**초상화**(肖像畫) a portrait; 《화법》 portrait painting. ¶～를 그리다 paint 〔draw〕 a portrait / ～를 그리게 하다 have 〔get〕 *one's* portrait 〔likeness〕 painted〔drawn, taken〕《by an artist》; sit to《a painter》 for *one's* portrait. ◉ ～가 a portrait painter. 유채～ a portrait in oils.

**초생**(初生) 《처음 생겨남》 (being) newborn. ◉ ～아 a newborn child.

**초서**(草書) 《서체》 a cursive style of writing Chinese characters; the grass 〔cursive〕 hand 〔style〕; 《글씨》 grass 〔cursive〕 characters. ¶～로 쓰다 write in a cursive hand / ～를 잘 쓰다 be good at writing in a cursive style. ◉ ～체 the "grasshand" 〔cursive〕 style.

**초석**(硝石) 〚화학〛 《질산칼륨》 potassium nitrate.

**초석**(礁石) a reef; a submerged rock.

**초석**(礎石) 《건물의》 a cornerstone; a foundation stone; a footstone; 《기초》 a foundation; a basis; 《희생》 a sacrifice. ¶ 나라의 ～ the pillar 〔mainstay〕 of the State / ～을 놓다 lay a foundation《for》; lay the cornerstone《of a building》/ ～이 되다 make a sacrifice of *oneself*《for》/ 그는 이 나라 민주 정치의 ～을 놓았다 He laid the foundations 〔cornerstone〕 of democracy in this country.

**초선**(初選) ¶～의 《당선》 newly-elected. ◉ ～의원 a newly-elected member of the National Assembly.

**초설**(初雪) the first snow(fall) (of the season).

**초성**(初聲) 〚음성〛 an initial sound 〔phoneme〕.

**초성**(焦性) 〚화학〛 ¶ ～주석산 pyrotartaric acid / ～몰식자산 pyrogallic acid; pyrogallol / ～황산 pyrosulfuric acid / ～황산염 a pyrosulfate.

**초소**(哨所) a guard 〔sentry〕 post; 《검문소》 a checkpoint.

**초소형**(超小型) ¶ ～카메라 a subminiature camera.

**초속**(秒速) the velocity 〔speed〕 per second. ¶～ 60미터로 at (a speed 〔velocity〕 of) 60 meters per 〔a〕 second.

**초속**(超俗) unworldliness. ¶～적(인) supermundane; unworldly; aloof from the world / ～적인 생활을 보내다 live a supermundane life.

**초속(도)**(初速(度)) 〚물리〛 initial velocity; 《탄환의》 muzzle velocity.

**초속도**(超速度) superhigh 〔ultrahigh〕 speed; super velocity.

**초순**(初旬) the first ten days of a month. ¶ 시월 ～에 early in October.

**초승**(初―) the first days of the month; the beginning of the month. ¶～에 at the beginning of the month; early in the month. ◉ ～달 a new 〔young〕 moon; a crescent (moon): ～달이 하늘에 떠 있다 The young moon hangs in the sky.

**초시계**(秒時計) a microchronometer; a stopwatch.

**초식**(草食) 《풀을 먹음》 eating grass; living on grass; 《채식》 eating vegetables; a vegetable diet. ～하다 eat grass; eat 〔live on〕 vegetables. ¶ ～의 plant-〔grass-〕eating; herbivorous. ◉ ～동물 a grass-eating 〔herbivorous〕 animal; a grazer; a herbivore.

**초신성**(超新星) 〚천문〛 a supernova.

**초실**(初室) 《새 집》 a newly built house; 《처음 아내》 *one's* first wife.

**초심**(初心) ① 《마음》 *one's* first 〔original〕 intention 〔aim, object, purpose〕. ¶ ～을 관철하다 accomplish 〔carry out〕 *one's* original intention. ② 《사람》 a beginner; a novice; a greenhorn. ⇨초보(初步). ◉ ～자: ～자를 위한 for beginners.

**초심**(初審) 《재판의》 the first hearing 〔trial〕. ⇨일심(一審).

**초아흐레**(初―) the ninth day of the month.

**초안**(草案) a (rough) draft. ¶ 연설～ a draft for a speech / 법안의 ～ a draft bill / ～을 작성〔기초〕하다 prepare 〔make out〕 a draft《for》; draft 〔draw up〕《a bill》. ◉ 민법～ a draft civil code.

**초야**(初夜) 《초경》 the first half part of the night; early evening; 《첫날밤》 the bridal 〔first〕 night. ◉ ～권 the right of first night; the *jus primae noctis* (L.).

**초야**(草野) the back 〔remote〕 country; an out-of-the-way place. ¶～에 묻혀 살다 lead a quiet country 〔retired〕 life; bury *oneself* 〔be buried〕 in the remote country.

**초여드레**(初―) the eighth day of the month.

**초여름** early summer; the beginning of summer. ¶ ～에 early in summer.

**초역**(抄譯) an abridged 〔an epitomized, a summarized〕 translation; a selected translation. ～하다 make an abridged 〔a summarized〕 translation 《of》; make a selected translation 《from》.

**초연**(初演) the first (public) performance 〔showing〕 《of》; the premiere (performance) 《of》. ～하다 give the first (public) performance 《of》; premiere 《a play》; stage 《a play》 for the first time.

**초연**(超然) aloofness; stand-offishness; transcendence. ～하다 (be) aloof; transcendental; stand-offish. ¶ ～히 〔한 태도로〕 with a disengaged 〔detached〕 air; with a stand-offish manner; aloof / …로부터 ～해 있다 「hold *oneself* 〔stand, keep〕 aloof from 《the world》; rise 〔stay, keep〕 above 《the world》 / 돈 문제에 ～하다 be above money matters / 속세를 버린 듯 ～히 살아가다 live like a hermit / ～한 입장을 취하다 maintain 〔take〕 a stand of aloofness 〔detachment〕; stand aloof 〔aside〕 / 그는 권력 다툼에서 ～해 있다 He holds himself aloof from the power struggles in the government. ◉ ～주의 a stand-off policy 〔attitude〕; (a principle of ) noninvolvement.

**초연**(硝煙) gunsmoke; smoke from the explosion of gunpowder. ¶ ～탄우(彈雨) 속에서 amid the smoke of powder and hail of bullets; in the thick of the fight / 경찰은 그의 의복에서 ～반응을 검출했다 The police detected traces of powder on his clothing.

**초연히**(悄然—) sadly; dejectedly; dispiritedly; with a heavy heart.

**초열지옥**(焦熱地獄) 〖불교〗 an inferno; a (burning) hell; Gehenna.

**초열흘(날)**(初—) the tenth day of the month.

**초엽**(初葉) the beginning; the early days 〔years〕; the initial phase. ¶ 20세기 ～에 in the early part of the 20th century.

**초엿새**(初—) the sixth day of the month.

**초오**(草烏) 〖식물〗 an aconite; a monkshood; a wolfsbane.

**초옥**(草屋) a thatched cottage. ⇨ 초가.

**초우라늄**(超—) transuranium. ◉ ～원소 a transuranic element.

**초원**(草原) a grass-covered plain; grassland(s); a prairie (북미의); pampas (남미의); a savanha(h) (열대·아열대의); a steppe (중앙 아시아의). ¶ ～동물 a grassland animal / ～의 집 a home 〔house〕 on a prairie.

**초월**(超越) transcendency. ～하다 transcend; rise above; stand aloof from 《the world》; excel; surpass. ¶ ～적인 transcendental; aloof / ～한 태도 a transcendental attitude / 돈문제를 ～하다 rise above money matters / 생사를 ～하다 disregard the peril of *one's* life / 이해를 ～하다 be disinterested / 현세(現世)를 ～하다 rise above the (mundane) world; stand aloof from the world / 자기를 ～하다 be above *oneself;* rise above self.
◉ ～수(數) 〖수학〗 a transcendental (number). ～신(神) a transcendental deity. ～주의 transcendentalism. ～철학 transcendental philosophy; transcendentalism. ～함수〔곡선〕 〖수학〗 a transcendental function 〔curve〕.

**초유**(初有) ¶ ～의 first; initial; original; unprecedented; unheard-of / 사상(史上) ～의 unprecedented in history / ～의 일 an unheard-of event.

**초유**(初乳) 〖의학〗 《산부의》 colostrum; foremilk; 《암소의》 beestings.

**초음속**(超音速) 〖물리〗 supersonic 〔hypersonic〕 speed. ¶ ～의 supersonic / ～으로 날다 fly at supersonic speed (★ hypersonic은 음속의 5배 이상의 속도).
◉～비행 《make》 a supersonic flight; supersonic aviation. ～여객기 a supersonic transport (생략 SST). ～제트기 a supersonic jet plane.

**초음파**(超音波) 〖물리〗 supersonic 〔ultrasonic〕 waves. ◉ ～발생기 an ultrasonic generator. ～위저상(僞底像) 〖해양〗 the deep scattering layer (생략 DSL). ～진단 an ultrasonography. ～진단 장치 an ultrasonograph. ～태아성감별 determination of a fetus' gender through ultrasound. ～학 supersonics; ultrasonics. ～화상 검사 an ultrasonic diagnostic.

**초이레**(初—) the seventh day of the month.

**초이틀**(初—) the second day of the month.

**초인**(超人) a superman. ¶ ～적(인) superhuman; preterhuman / ～적으로 superhumanly / 그녀는 세계 평화 유지를 위해 ～적인 노력을 했다 She made superhuman 〔herculean〕 efforts to maintain world peace. ◉ ～주의 supermanism.

**초인종**(招人鐘) a (call) bell; a doorbell; a buzzer. ¶ ～을 누르다 press 〔push〕

the button of a bell; press a buzzer / ～을 울리다 ring a (door)bell; ring the bell; buzz 《for》/ ～을 세 번 울리다 ring the bell three times / ～을 울려 하인을 부르다 ring for a servant / ～소리가 난다 There's the doorbell ringing. *or* There goes the bell! / 필요하실 땐 이 ～을 누르세요《게시》 Ring this bell 〔Press the bell button〕 when you want me.

**초일**(初日) the first day. ＝첫날.

**초읽기**(秒—) counting the second; 《로켓 발사시의》 a countdown; counting down; 《마지막 단계》《in》 the final stage. ～하다 count down. ¶ ～를 개시하다 start a countdown.

**초임**(初任) the first appointment. ⇨신임. ¶ ～ 인사를 하다 make an inaugural address. ◉ ～교원 a newly appointed teacher. ～급(給) the starting 〔initial〕 pay 〔salary〕.

**초입**(初入) 《어귀》 an entrance; an approach; a way in; 《처음 들어감》 the first entrance; entering for the first time. ¶ 길 ～ an entry to a road / 동네 ～ an entrance 〔approach〕 to a village; the outskirts of a village / 고속도로의 ～ the access 〔entrance〕 road to an expressway.

**초자**(硝子) glass. ⇨ 유리(琉璃).

**초자연**(超自然) supernaturalness. ¶ ～적(인) supernatural; preternatural. ◉ ～력 supernatural forces. ～주의 supernaturalism.

**초잡다**(草—) make a draft 《of》; draft. ¶ 연설을 ～ draft a speech.

**초장**(初章) the first of the 3 verses of a *shijo* poem; the first part of a song; 《음악의》 the first movement; 《글의》 the first chapter.

**초장**(初場) ① 《시장의》 the opening 〔morning〕 market 〔session, sale〕. ¶ ～부터 시세가 낮았다 The market opened lower. ② 《일의 첫머리 판》 the outset; the start; the beginning. ¶ ～에 at the start 〔outset〕/ ～부터 (right) from the beginning 〔start〕/ ～에는 회원이 단 3명이었다 We had only three members to start with.

**초장**(醋醬) 《초간장》 soy sauce mixed with vinegar.

**초장파**(超長波) 〖통신〗 a very low frequency (생략 V.L.F., VLF, v.l.f., vlf).

**초재**(草材) native medicinal herbs.

**초저녁**(初—) early (in the) evening 〔night〕. ¶ ～에 in evening; at dusk / ～잠이 들다 fall asleep early in the night.

**초적**(草笛) a reed 〔grass-blade〕 pipe.

**초전도**(超傳導) 〖물리〗 superconductivity. ◉ ～자석 a superconductive magnet. ～체〔물질〕 a superconductor; a superconductive substance.

**초절**(超絶) transcendence. ⇨ 초월. ～하다 transcend. ◉ ～론〔주의〕 transcendentalism.

**초점**(焦點) a focus (*pl.* ～es, foci); a focal point. ¶ 분쟁의 ～ the focus of trouble / ～이 없는 unfocused 《eyes》/ ～이 두 개 있는 bifocal / ～이 맞다〔맞지 않다〕 be in 〔out of〕 focus / ～을 맞추다 focus 《*one's* glasses on an object》; adjust the focus 《of a lens》/ …에 ～을 모으다 focus on 《an object》; bring 《an object》 to a focus / …에 ～을 두다 place the focus on 《a question》; focus on 《*a matter*》/ 공격의 ～이 되다 bear the brunt of an attack / 문제의 ～에 접근하다 go 〔get〕 to the heart of a matter / 말의 ～을 흐리다 evade the point / 그것이 바로 문제의 ～이다 That is the heart 〔the very point〕 of the matter. / 이 회의의 ～은 한일 양국의 무역 불균형을 어떻게 축소하느냐에 있다 The focal point of this conference is how to reduce the trade imbalance between Korea and Japan.
◉ ～거리 the focal distance 〔length〕: ～거리 측정기 a focimeter. ～면 a focal plane: ～면 개폐 장치 a focal plane shutter. ～심도 the depth of a focus. 고정～ a fixed focus. 자동～ self=focus(s)ing.

**초조**(初潮) menarche. ＝초경(初經).

**초조**(焦燥) fretfulness; impatience; irritation. ～하다 (be) fretful; impatient; irritated; anxious. ¶ ～한 마음 a feeling of impatience; a fretful state of mind / ～한 빛〔기색〕 a worried look / ～함을 느끼다 feel impatient 〔restless〕; fret; be in a fret / ～해 하다 fret; get irritated; eat *one's* heart out / ～해 하는 빛이 보이다 look worried / 시험 결과를 몰라 ～하다 be anxious to know the result of an examination / 빨리 집에 가고 싶어 ～해 하다 be impatient to go home soon / 그렇게 ～해 할 것 없다 You have nothing to fret about like that. / 일이 잘 풀리지 않아 ～감을 느꼈다 I「felt impatient 〔got irritated〕 because my work didn't go well.

**초종**(初終) the whole period of mourning (from beginning to end). ¶ ～이

끝나다 have gone through due formalities of mourning / ～을 치르다 go through due formalities of mourning. ◉ ～범절 customary procedure 〔due formalities〕 of mourning. ～장사〔장례〕 = 초종(初終).

**초주검되다**(初—) be more dead than alive; be all but dead; be half-dead; 《남에게》 be half-killed; be nearly 〔all but〕 killed.

**초지**(初志) *one's* first 〔original, initial〕 intention 〔aim, object, purpose, desire〕. ¶ ～를 굽히다 depart from 〔give up〕 *one's* original intention / ～를 관철하다 accomplish 〔carry out〕 *one's* original intention; attain *one's* original aim / ～를 이루다 realize 〔achieve〕 *one's* original desire / ～를 바꾸지 않다 stick to 〔abide by〕 *one's* original intention.

**초지**(草地) grassland; a grassy place; 《목초지》 a pasture; a green field.

**초지**(草紙) drafting paper.

**초지니**(初—) 〖조류〗 a yearling 〔2=year-old〕 falcon.

**초진**(初診) the first medical examination; the first visit (to a doctor). ¶ ～입니다 This is my first visit. *or* I am on my first visit. ◉ ～료 the fee charged for a patient's first visit; the fee for the first medical examination. ～환자 a new patient.

**초집**(抄集·抄輯) a collection of abstracts 〔extracts, excerpts〕. ～하다 make a collection of abstracts 〔extracts, excerpts〕. ¶ 법안～ extracts of bills; a copy of extracted bills.

**초집**(草集) a collection of manuscripts. ¶ 시문(詩文)～ a collection of manuscripts (of *one's* poems and prose).

**초창**(草創) beginning; initiation; inauguration; inception. ◉ ～기 an early stage; the pioneer days: 문명의 ～기 the beginning of civilization / 사업의 ～기 the pioneer days of an enterprise.

**초청**(招請) (an) invitation; a call. ～하다 invite; call (in). ⇨초대. ¶ 강사를 ～하다 invite 〔call in〕 a lecturer / 손님을 ～하다 invite a guest / 각국 대표를 평화 회의에 ～하다 call the representatives of each country to the Peace Conference. ◉ ～객 an invited guest. ～경기 an invitation game. ～국 a host nation 〔country〕: 피～국 an invited nation. ～연사 a guest speaker. ～외교 diplomacy by invitation; invitation diplomacy. ～장 a letter of invitation.

**초체**(草體) ⇨초서체(草書體). ¶ ～로 쓰다 write in cursive style; write a cursive hand.

**초추**(初秋) the beginning of autumn 〔fall 《미》〕; early autumn. ⇨초가을.

**초춘**(初春) the beginning of spring; early spring. ⇨초봄.

**초출**(抄出) extraction; selection; excerption. ～하다 extract 〔select〕 《from》; make an extract 《from》.

**초출**(初出) appearing for the first time; the first 《of the season》. ◉ ～참외 the first melon of the season.

**초출**(超出) excellence; remarkableness; prominence. ～하다 (be) excellent; remarkable; preeminent; prominent; outstanding; conspicuous.

**초췌**(憔悴) haggardness; emaciation. ～하다 (be) haggard; emaciated; gaunt; thin. ¶ ～한 얼굴 a haggard face 〔figure〕; a worn-out look / ～해지다 get 〔become〕 thin 〔emaciated, haggard〕; be worn out 〔exhausted〕; 《과로로》 be consumed 《with overwork》; 《근심으로》 be careworn.

**초취**(初娶) *one's* first 〔former〕 wife.

**초치**(招致) summons; invitation. ～하다 《불러오다》 summon; send for; invite; call; 《유치하다》 attract 《tourists》. ¶ 회의에 대표를 ～하다 call in conference delegates 《from》 / 올림픽 경기의 서울 ～운동을 벌이다 launch a drive to bring the Olympic Games to Seoul.

**초친놈**(醋—) a hopeless *roué* (F.); a rake of no promise; a worthless playboy.

**초친맛**(醋—) being out of taste; an insipid taste.

**초침**(秒針) the second hand 〔the sweep-second〕 (of a watch).

**초콜릿** (a) chocolate; a stick 〔bar〕 of chocolate. ¶ ～빛 chocolate; dark brown.

**초크** 《백묵》 《a piece of》 chalk. ¶ 색～ colored chalk; pastel / ～로 쓰다 write with 〔in〕 chalk / ～로 … 위에 쓰다 chalk 《*one's* name》 on … / ～로 잔뜩 판서를 해 놓은 칠판 a blackboard covered with scribbles in chalk.

**초탈**(超脫) transcendence. ⇨초월. ～하다 transcend; rise above; stand aloof 《from》. ¶ ～한 사람 a person who is above worldly things / ～한 태도 a disinterested attitude / 세속을 ～하다 rise above (the ways of ) the world; be free from the trammels of ordi-

nary life.
**초토**(焦土) 《불탄 흙》 scorched earth; burnt ground; 《불탄 자취》 the ruins of a fire. ¶ ∼가 되다, ∼화하다 get burnt 〔reduced〕 to ashes; be burnt to the ground / 아름다운 거리는 전쟁으로 ∼화되었다 War turned the beautiful streets into ruins. ◉ ∼전술 "scorched-land〔-earth〕" strategy 〔tactics〕.
**초특급**(超特急) a superexpress (train).
**초특작**(超特作) a super production; 《영화의》 a superfilm. ◉ ∼품 = 초특작.
**초파리**(醋—) a drosophila (*pl.* -lae); a vinegar fly.
**초판**(初—) 《기간·국면》 the first round 〔period, bout, scene〕; the start; the outset. ¶ ∼에 in the beginning; at the outset / ∼부터 from the beginning 〔start, first〕 / ∼부터 다시 시작하다 do all over again; begin afresh; make a 「new 〔fresh〕 start.
**초판**(初版) the first edition. ¶ ∼으로 5천부 찍다〔발행하다〕 print 〔issue, bring out〕 the first edition of 5,000 copies 《of a book》 / ∼은 일 주일도 안 되어 매진되었다 The first edition was exhausted 〔sold out〕 in less than a week. ◉ ∼본 a copy of the first edition; a "first-edition".
**초피**(貂皮) marten; sable.
**초하**(初夏) the beginning of summer; early summer. ¶ ∼에 early in summer.
**초하다**(抄—) 《뽑아적다》 abstract; extract; select. ¶ 시선집을 ∼ make a selection of poems.
**초하다**(草—) draft 〔draw up〕 《a bill》; make a draft 《of》; make a rough copy 《of》; write in rough form. ¶ 법안을 ∼ draft a bill.
**초하루**(初—) the first day of the month.
**초학**(初學) 《처음 배움》 first learning; elementary studies; 《초보》 rudimentary education 〔schooling〕. ¶ 아직 ∼이 되어서 별로 배운 것이 없다 I am just a beginner and haven't learned much yet. ◉ ∼자 a beginner; a novice.
**초한**(初寒) the first cold (of the season); the first spell of cold weather.
**초행**(初行) going for the first time; *one's* first trip 〔journey〕. ¶ ∼길 a road *one* has never been on before; *one's* first trip / 서울은 ∼이다 This is my first trip to Seoul.
**초현대적**(超現代的) ultramodern.
**초현실주의**(超現實主義) surrealism. ◉ ∼자 a surrealist.
**초호**(初號) ① 《창간호》 the first 〔initial, opening〕 number. ② 《활자》 No. 1 type. ◉ ∼활자 a 42-point type.
**초호**(礁湖) a lagoon.
**초혼**(初昏) the evening dusk; twilight. ⇨황혼(黃昏). ¶ ∼이 되다 dusk falls.
**초혼**(初婚) *one's* first marriage. ¶ 그녀는 ∼이다 This is her first marriage. / 그는 39세에 ∼을 했다 He married for the first time at thirty-nine.
**초혼**(招魂) invocation of the spirit of the dead 〔deceased〕. ∼하다 invoke (the spirit of the deceased). ◉ ∼제 a memorial service 〔rite〕 for the dead 〔deceased〕.
**초화**(草花) a flowering plant; a flower (of a herb).
**초회**(初回) the first round; the first time; 〖야구〗 the first inning. ◉ ∼(불입)금 《월부의》 the first installment; down payment: ∼불입금이 없는 월부 No money down.
**촉**(燭) ① 《촉광》 candle power (생략 c.p.). ¶ 60촉짜리 전구 a 60 candle-power bulb; a 60-watt (electric) bulb. ② 《촛불》 candlelight.
**촉**(鏃) 《화살촉》 an arrowhead; a steel point; 《뾰족한 끝》 a pointed part; a point; a tip; an end; a root (치아 등의). ¶ 펜촉 a pen point; a nib 《영》 / 만년필촉 the tip of a fountain pen / 이촉 a dental root.
**촉각**(觸角) 〖곤충〗 a feeler; an antenna (*pl.* -nae); a tentacle. ⇨더듬이[2]. ¶ 벌의 ∼ a feeler of a bee / 달팽이의 ∼ a horn of a snail / ∼을 뻗치다 put out 《*its*》 feelers. (★ put 〔throw〕 out feelers 는 관용적으로 타인의 의향 따위를 「타진하다」란 뜻으로도 쓰임). ◉ ∼선 an antennal gland.
**촉각**(觸覺) 〖생물〗 the sense of touch; (a) tactual sense; (a) tactile sensation. ¶ ∼의 tactile; tactual. ◉ ∼기관 a tactile 〔touch〕 organ. ∼마비 tactile anesthesia.
**촉감**(觸感) the (sense of) touch; the feel; tactile impression 〔sensation〕. ¶ ∼이 좋다 be agreeable 〔pleasant〕 to the touch 〔feel〕; feel smooth 〔soft〕; have a smooth feel / ∼이 좋지 않다〔나쁘다〕 be unpleasant to the touch; 《거칠다》 be rough to the touch; feel rough.
**촉관**(觸官) 〖생물〗 a touch 〔tactile〕 organ.
**촉광**(燭光) 《촛불 빛》 candlelight; 《밝기의 단위》 candle power (생략 c.p.). ¶

20～의 가스등 a gaslight of 20 candle power.

**촉구하다**(促求―) urge; press; demand 《a definite answer》; call upon 《*a person to do*》. ¶ 대답을 ～ press 《*a person*》 for an answer / 반성을 ～ call for grave reflection; demand 《*a person's*》 serious reflection / 주의를 ～ call 〔attract〕 《*a person's*》 attention to 《*a matter*》; urge 《a fact》 on 《*a person's*》 attention.

**촉규**(蜀葵) 『식물』 a rose mallow; a hollyhock. ⇨ 접시꽃. ◉ ～화＝촉규.

**촉노**(觸怒) touching off the anger of an elder. ～하다 touch off the anger of 《an elder》; offend 《an elder》; incur 《*a person's*》 anger.

**촉대**(燭臺) a candlestick. ＝촛대.

**촉더데**(鏃―) the knot of an arrowhead.

**촉돌이**(鏃―) a device used to insert or remove an arrowhead.

**촉루**(燭淚) droppings from a candle. ＝촛농.

**촉망**(囑望) expectation; hope. ～하다 fasten 〔hang, pin, put〕 *one's* hopes on 《*a person*》; expect much of 〔from〕 《*a person*》. ¶ ～되는 청년 a promising youth; a young man of much promise / 크게 ～하다 expect very much of 〔from〕 《*a person*》; entertain great expectations of 《*a person*》 / 그의 장래가 크게 ～된다 A great future 〔Much〕 is expected of him. / 그는 주변에서 ～을 받고 있다 He is the hope of those around him.

**촉매**(觸媒) 『화학』 a catalyst; a catalytic (agent). ¶ 한국 경제 활성화에 ～가 되다 act as the catalyst to stimulate 〔invigorate〕 the Korean economy.
◉ ～독 catalytic poison. ～반응 a catalytic reaction; catalysis. ～방지제 an anticatalyst. ～법 the contact 〔catalytic〕 process. ～작용 a catalytic action; 《cause》 catalysis.

**촉모**(觸毛) 『동물·해부』 a cirrus (*pl.* cirri); a tactile hair. ¶ ～가 있는 cirrate; cirrose.

**촉박**(促迫) urgency; imminence. ～하다 (be) urgent; imminent; pressing; impending; tense; acute; be near 〔close〕 at hand. ¶ 시간이 ～하다 be pressed 〔pushed〕 for time / 형세가 ～하다 a situation is tense 〔acute, urgent〕 / 기일이 ～하다 a set date is (near) at hand.

**촉발**(觸發) detonation by contact; contact detonation; 《감정의》 an excitement; being moved 〔stirred〕 《by》. ～하다 《기뢰 따위가》 detonate on 〔be detonated by〕 contact; 《사태를》 touch 〔spark, set〕 off; trigger (off); provoke 《a crises》. ¶ 지역 감정을 ～시키다 touch off the regional emotion 《of》 / 그 문제는 국제 분쟁을 ～할 위험이 있었다 The matter had the possibility of triggering an international dispute. ◉ ～장치 a contact-detonating device. ～지뢰 a contact mine.

**촉새** 『조류』 a (Korean black-faced) bunting.

**촉성**(促成) fostering 〔promoting, accelerating, quickening〕 the growth 《of》; promoting the completion 〔realization〕 《of》. ⇨ 촉진. ～하다 foster 〔promote, accelerate〕 the growth of; promote the completion 〔realization〕 of.

**촉성재배**(促成栽培) forcing culture. ～하다 force 《strawberries》. ¶ ～한 야채 forced vegetables / ～용 온상 a forcing house 〔bed〕; a hothouse.

**촉수**(觸手) ① 《손댐》 touching. ¶ ～ 엄금 《게시》 Hands off. ② 《더듬이》 an antenna (*pl.* -nae); a feeler; a tentacle. ¶ ～를 뻗치다 put out a feeler; [비유적] reach 《for》; try to get 〔hold of〕 《*something*》.

**촉수**(觸鬚) 『생물』 《하등 동물의》 a palp; a palpus (*pl.* -pi); 《물고기의》 a barbel.

**촉언**(囑言) dying words of entrusting 《another》 with *one's* future affairs. ～하다 ask 《*a person*》 to look after *one's* (future) affairs.

**촉진**(促進) promotion; acceleration; facilitation; quickening; hastening; furtherance. ～하다 promote; accelerate; expedite; quicken; further; speed 〔step, gear〕 up; facilitate; help 《a movement》 forward; give an impetus 〔a boost〕 《to》.
¶ …의 ～운동 a movement for the realization 〔furtherance〕 of …; a drive to press for 〔speed up〕… / 무역을 ～하다 encourage 〔promote〕 foreign trade / 식물의 성장을 ～하다 hasten 〔accelerate, force〕 the growth of a plant / 일을 ～하다 speed up a job; promote an undertaking / 식욕을 ～시키다 quicken 〔sharpen, stimulate〕 the appetite / 진보를 ～시키다 expedite 〔facilitate, further, speed up〕 the progress 《of》 / 판매를 ～하기 위해서는 광고에 더 많은 돈을 써야 한다 We need to spend more money on advertising to promote sales.

**촉진**(觸診) 〖의학〗 palpation. ～하다 palpate; examine 《*something*》 by feeling with the hand(s). ¶ 김 박사는 복부의 ～만으로 그 환자의 위에 이상이 있다는 것을 발견했다 Dr. Kim found that something was wrong with the patient's stomach simply by palpating her abdominal region.

**촉처봉패**(觸處逢敗) failure at every attempt.

**촉촉하다** (be) (slightly, moderately) wet; dampish; moist. ⇨ 축축하다. ¶ 이슬에 촉촉히 젖다 get moist 〔become wet〕 with dew; be bedewed.

**촉탁**(囑託) 《위촉》 commission; entrusting; charge; 《일》 part-time service 〔engagement〕; 《사람》 a part-time 〔temporal〕 employee; a nonregular member (of the staff). ～하다 entrust 〔charge〕 《*a person*》 with 《*a matter*》; give 《*a person*》 charge of; commission 《*a person* to *do*》. ¶ 관청의 ～ a part-time employee of a government office / 대학 교수에게 외교 문제 연구를 ～하다 commission a university professor to study diplomatic problems. ◉ ～교사 a part-time instructor 〔teacher〕. ～의(醫) a part-time 《school》 doctor.

**촌**(寸) ① = 치[1]. ② 《촌수》 a degree (of kinship 〔consanguinity〕). ¶ 삼촌 an uncle / 사촌 a cousin.

**촌**(村) ① 《마을》 a village; a hamlet (작은); a rural community. ¶ 빈민촌 a poor village. ② 《시골》 the country(side); a rural district. ¶ 촌 경치 rural scenery / 촌살림 country 〔rural, provincial〕 life / 촌에서는 보기 드문 rarely found in the country / 촌구석(에)서 살다 live in a remote country; live in an out-of-the-way place; live way back in the country 《미》.

**촌가**(寸暇) a moment's leisure; a spare moment; a little moment to spare. ¶ ～를 아껴서 독서하다 devote 〔give〕 every spare moment to reading / ～도 없다 have no time to spare at all; do not have a moment 〔minute〕 to call *one's* own / ～를 이용하다 make use 〔take advantage〕 of odd moments.

**촌가**(村家) a village 〔country〕 house; a rustic dwelling.

**촌각**(寸刻) a moment; a second. ¶ ～을 다투다 《병 등이》 require 〔call for〕 prompt treatment; 《문제 따위가》 need a speedy solution / ～을 다투어 …하다 lose no time in 《*do*ing》; 《*do*》 promptly 〔speedily〕.

**촌거**(村居) country 〔rural, rustic〕 life; rural living. ～하다 live 〔dwell〕 in the country; rusticate.

**촌극**(寸劇) a short (comic) play; a tabloid play; a little 〔short〕 dramatical performance; a little piece of side show; a skit.

**촌극**(寸隙) a short interval.

**촌길**(村—) a country lane 〔path, road〕.

**촌내**(寸內) a relative within the tenth degree; near relatives. ¶ 가까운 ～가 많다 have many near relatives.

**촌놈**(村—) a country fellow; a rustic; a rube; 《놀림조》 a country bumpkin; a boor; a yokel; a backwoodsman 《미》; a hillbilly. ¶ ～티가 나다 have the earmarks of a peasant / ～의 수작 마라 Don't make you a boor! / 나는 말하자면 서울 ～이다 I am, so to speak, a Seoul rustic.

**촌뜨기**(村—) a rustic; a bumpkin. ⇨ 촌놈. ¶ 시골에서 갓 올라온 ～ a man fresh from the country / 그는 영락없는 ～꼴이군 그래 He sure does look like a country bumpkin.

**촌락**(村落) a village; a hamlet. ◉ ～공동체 a village community.

**촌로**(村老) a village patriarch; [총칭] old folks of a village.

**촌묘**(寸描) a thumbnail 〔brief〕 sketch 《of the new principal》.

**촌민**(村民) a villager; [총칭] villagers; village folk 〔people〕; the inhabitants of a village.

**촌백성**(村百姓) country people 〔folk〕.

**촌보**(寸步) a few steps. ¶ ～도 양보하지 않다 do not yield 〔concede〕 a step 〔an inch〕 / ～도 옮길 수(가) 없다 be unable to move a step; cannot move *oneself* even an inch.

**촌부**(村婦) a country 〔village〕 woman.

**촌사람**(村—) a countryman; a rural dweller; countryfolk [총칭].

**촌샌님**(村—) an old country gentleman.

**촌수**(寸數) the degree of consanguinity 〔kinship〕; the distance of a blood relationship. ¶ 결혼 금지의 ～ the forbidden degree (of marriage) / ～가 멀다〔가깝다〕 be distant 〔near〕 in kinship / ～를 캐다〔따지다〕 trace the degree of kinship.

**촌스럽다**(村—) (be) countrified; (look) rustic; boorish; farmerish; hicky; [서술적] wear a rustic air; 《세련되지 않다》 (be) unfashionable; unrefined; unpolished; uncouth. ¶ 촌스러운 시골처녀 a cloddish country girl / 촌스럽게

차려 입다 be unfashionably 〔uncouth-ly〕 dressed.

**촌시**(寸時) = 촌음(寸陰).

**촌외**(寸外) a distant relative.

**촌음**(寸陰) the slightest space of time; a moment; a minute; an instant. ⇨ 촌각. ¶ ～을 아끼다 skimp on time; be careful of every minute; be jealous of every second; value each instant / ～을 아껴서 공부하다 use every available minute to study / ～을 아끼어 연구에 몰두하다 devote all *one's* time and energies to studies.

**촌장**(村長) a village chief 〔head〕.

**촌전척토**(寸田尺土) a small farm 〔field〕; a tiny strip 〔patch〕 of land.

**촌지**(寸地) an inch of land 〔territory〕.

**촌지**(寸志) a little token of *one's* gratitude 〔appreciation〕; a small present; 《봉투에 쓸 때》 With compliments. ¶ ～를 받아 주세요 This is just a token of my gratitude, please accept it.

**촌철**(寸鐵) ① 《작은 무기》 a small weapon. ¶ 몸에 ～도 지니지 않다 have not an inch of steel in *one's* possession; carry no weapons; be quite unarmed. ② 《경구(警句)》 a pithy 〔terse, witty, short sententious〕 saying; an epigram. ◉ ～살인 being pithy; being terse and to the point 〔quick〕.

**촌촌걸식**(村村乞食) ～하다 go (about) begging from village to village.

**촌충**(寸蟲) 〖기생충〗 a tapeworm; a taenia (*pl.* ～s, -niae). ◉ ～구제약 a taeniacide; a taeniafuge; a tapeworm remedy.

**촌탁**(忖度) guessing 〔surmising〕 《*another's*》 mind 〔feeling〕. ～하다 guess 〔sense〕 《*another's*》 feeling; conjecture; judge. ¶ 자기 나름대로 남의 마음을 ～하다 judge others in terms of *oneself;* project 《*a person's*》 feelings; measure other's corn by *one's* own bushel.

**촌토**(寸土) an inch of ground 〔land, territory〕; a small strip of land. ¶ ～도 양보하지 않다 do not cede an inch of ground; won't yield.

**촌티**(村—) rusticity; boorishness. ¶ ～(가) 나다 be boorish; look rustic; be countrified(-looking); have a rural appearance / 그 처녀는 아직 ～를 벗지 못하고 있다 The girl hasn't yet got the hayseed out of her hair.

**촌평**(寸評) a brief review 《of》; a brief comment 《on》. ¶ ～을 가하다 make a brief review 《of》.

**촐랑거리다** ① 《까불다》 act 〔be〕 frivolous 〔irresponsible, unserious, flippant〕; behave carelessly 〔rashly〕. ¶ 촐랑거리며 돌아다니다 gad 〔flit〕 about. ② 《물이》 lap. ⇨ 찰랑거리다.

**촐랑이** a frivolous 〔careless〕 person.

**촐랑촐랑** ① 《경박하게》 frivolously; flippantly; irresponsibly; unseriously. ② ⇨ 찰랑찰랑.

**촐싹거리다** ① 《경망스럽게 굴다》 act frivolously 〔irresponsibly, unseriously, flippantly〕. ② 《부추기다》 instigate; incite; stir up; urge; prod; needle. ¶ 촐싹거려 …하게 하다 set 〔needle〕 《*a person*》 to *do.*

**촐싹촐싹** ① 《촐랑촐랑》 frivolously; irresponsibly; unseriously; flippantly. ② 《들먹임》 inciting; instigating; disturbing.

**촐촐** with an empty stomach. ～하다 be somewhat 〔rather〕 hungry; feel a bit empty. ¶ ～(히) 굶다 go 〔get〕 hungry; starve / ～(히) 굶은 채(로) 《fall asleep》 on an empty stomach.

**촘촘하다** 《틈새 등이》 (be) close; thick; fine; dense. ¶ 나뭇결이 촘촘한 close=〔fine-〕grained / 촘촘한 박음새 close stitching; close stitches / 올이 촘촘한 천 cloth of (a) close texture / 쳇불이 촘촘한 체 a sieve of fine mesh / 모를 촘촘하게 심다 set rice seedlings close together.

**촛국**(醋—) an over-vinegared dish.

**촛농**(—膿) guttered candle(wax); melted wax running down a candlestick. ¶ ～이 앉다 a candle is guttered / ～이 흐르다 a candle gutters down / 책상 위에 ～을 흘려 그 위에 초를 세우다 stick a candle in its own wax on the desk / ～이 흐르고 있다 The candle is running.

**촛대**(—臺) a candlestick; a candlestand; a candle holder. ¶ ～에 초를 꽂다 fix a candle in a candlestick.

**촛불** candlelight. ¶ ～을 켜다 light a candle / ～을 (입으로) 불어서 끄다 blow out a candle / ～에 글을 읽다 read by candlelight / ～이 다 되어가다 The candle is burning low.

**총** 《말총》 the hairs of a horse's mane 「〔tail〕.

**총**(銃) 《총기》 a gun; a rifle (소총); [총칭] firearms; small arms. ¶ 22구경 총 a. 22-caliber gun; a. 22 gun / 총을 겨누다 point 〔level, aim〕 a gun 《at》; 《쏠 자세를 취하다》 hold *one's* gun at the ready / 총을 들이대고 납치하다 kidnap 《*a person*》 at gunpoint / 총을 메다 shoulder a gun

〔rifle〕/ 총을 쏘다 fire a「gun〔shot〕/ 받들어〔걸어〕 총하다 present〔pile, stack〕 arms / 총에 착검하다 fix a bayonet / 받들어 총《구령》 Present arms! / 세워 총《구령》 Order arms! / 걸어 총《구령》 Pile arms! / 총이 불을 뿜었다 The gun spat fire.

◉ 총개머리 the stock; the butt of a rifle. 총허리 the small of the butt.

따발총 a Russian automatic rifle. 단발총 a single-shot gun; a single-loader. 쌍발총 a double-barreled gun. 연발총 a magazine rifle; a repeater: 6 연발총 a six-shooter.

**총**(寵)《사랑》 favor. ⇨ 총애.

**총-**(總) all; whole; entire; general; overall; gross; total; full. ¶ 총소득 the gross income / 총본부 general headquarters; the center / 총예산 the total budget; the general estimate / 총대리점 a「sole〔general〕agency.

**총가**(銃架) an arm rack; a rifle stand; a gun「rest〔mounting〕.

**총각**(總角) an unmarried man; a bachelor; a celibate; a bach《미속어》. ◉ ~김치 pickled young radishes. ~처녀 young people (of both sexes); unmarried men and women.

**총감**(總監) an inspector general; a superintendent-general; a commissioner.

**총감독**(總監督)〖야구〗a general manager.

**총검**(銃劍) rifles and swords;《총끝에 꽂는》 a (sword) bayonet; side arms. ¶ ~을 꽂다〔떼다〕 fix〔unfix〕 a bayonet / ~으로 찌르다 bayonet《*a person*》; stab《*a person*》 with a bayonet / ~을 들이대고 at the「point〔end〕 of the bayonet. ◉ ~돌격 a bayonet charge. ~술 bayonet drill〔exercise, practice〕.

**총격**(銃擊) ~하다《소총으로》 shoot a rifle《at a target》;《몸을 숨기고》 snipe《at》;《기관총으로》 machine-gun《a building》;《전투기에서》 strafe. ¶ ~을 가하다 fire《at》; direct fire《toward》/ ~을 받다 be under fire; be shot (at); draw shots. ◉ ~전 an exchange of「shots〔fire〕; a gun battle; a gunfight: ~전을 벌이다 gunfight; fight a gun battle; exchange fire《with》.

**총결산**(總決算)〖경제〗final settlement of accounts; final balancing of books. ~하다 make final settlement of (accounts); settle〔balance〕 the accounts; close the books. ¶ 연말에 수입과 지출을 ~하다 balance the receipts and disbursements at the end of the year. ◉ 연말~ the year-end settlement (of the whole accounts).

**총경**(總警) a senior superintendent (생략 Sen. Supt.).

**총계**(總計) the total; the total「amount〔sum〕; the「sum〔grand, full〕total. ~하다 total; sum〔add〕up. ¶ ~하여 in all; in total; in toto; all told; in the aggregate《미》/ ~를 내다 total; sum up. ⇨~하다 / 손해를 ~하다 sum up the loss / ~50만 원이 되다 total〔work out at, make a total of, add up to, amount to〕500,000 won / ~가 얼마나 됩니까 What does the total come to? *or* What is the sum? *or* What do you make the sum? *or* How much is it altogether?

**총계정**(總計定) a final settlement.

**총고해**(總告解)〖가톨릭〗a general confession.

**총공격**(總攻擊) an all-out attack; a full-scale offensive. ~하다 make〔open, launch〕 an all-out attack《on, against》; attack《the enemy》in full force. ¶ 전 전선에서 ~하다 launch on a general offensive along the entire front / 미국 공군은 이라크 전차부대를 ~했다 The U.S. Air Force launched an all-out attack against the Iraqi tank forces.

**총괄**(總括)《개괄》generalization;《요약》summarization; recapitulation; summary. ~하다 generalize; summarize; sum up; recapitulate;《구어》recap. ¶ ~적인 general; summary; all-inclusive ⇨ 총괄적 / ~하여 in the「gross〔mass, lump〕; *en*「*masse*〔*bloc*〕(F.); collectively / ~해서 말하면 generally speaking; as a whole; to recapitulate; to sum up / 모든 문제를 ~하여 토의하다 discuss all the problems at one time. ◉ ~개념 a colligated concept (ion). ~보험 comprehensive〔blanket〕 insurance. ~운임 lump-sum freight. ~제어 시스템〖철도〗the multiple-unit control system. ~질문《국회 등에서의》 a general interpellation.

**총괄적**(總括的) all-inclusive; all-embracing; overall; blanket; lump-sum; omnibus. ¶ ~으로 in the gross〔mass, lump〕; collectively; *en*「*bloc*〔*masse*〕(F.). ◉ ~법안 an omnibus〔a blanket〕 bill. ~조항 a blanket clause. ~평가〖교육〗overall evaluation.

**총구**(銃口) the muzzle. ⇨ 총부리.

**총급**(怱急) ~하다 [서술적] be in a great hurry; be very urgent.

**총기**(銃器) [총칭] small arms; firearms. ¶ ~를 휴대한 강도 an armed robber. ◉ ~단속 gun control. ~사고 a firearm accident. ~실〔고〕 a gun room; an armory.

**총기**(聰氣) 《총명함》 brightness; sagacity; (spark of) intelligence; 《기억력》 a good memory; retentiveness. ¶ ~가 있다 be bright 〔intelligent〕/ ~가 없다 be dull 〔unintelligent〕/ ~가 좋다 have a good 〔retentive〕 memory.

**총냥이** a thin person with bulging eyes and a protruding mouth; a foxy person.

**총담요**(—毯—) a horsehair blanket.

**총대**(銃—) the barrel (of a gun); the gun barrel; 《총》 a gun; a rifle. ¶ ~를 메다 shoulder a rifle.

**총대리점**(總代理店) a general 〔sole〕 agency.

**총대우** a hat(-top) made of horsehair 〔oxhair〕.

**총대장**(總大將) 《총사령관》 a commander-in-chief; 《두목》 a leader; a boss.

**총독**(總督) a governor-general; a viceroy. ◉ ~부 the government-general; the Viceregal 《영》.

**총동원**(總動員) general 〔full〕 mobilization. ~하다 mobilize fully; make 〔effect〕 a general mobilization; mobilize all the resources 《of》. ¶ 온 가족이 ~하여 with the combined 〔united〕 efforts of the whole family / 산업계를 ~하다 mobilize all (of) the industrial world / 전학교가 ~하여 식목했다 All the teachers and students took part in planting trees. / 온 마을 사람들이 ~하여 산불 진화에 나섰다 All the villagers were mobilized to extinguish the forest fire. ◉ ~령 orders for the mobilization of the entire army: 국가~ national mobilization.

**총득점**(總得點) the total score; the total points made; the total runs 〔goals〕 scored (야구·축구 등의). ¶ ~ 10점을 얻다 score 10 in all.

**총람**(總覽) a conspectus; a general survey; 《서적》 a comprehensive bibliography.

**총람**(總攬) superintendence; (general) control. ~하다 superintend; oversee; preside over; control.

**총량**(總量) the total 〔aggregate〕 amount; the gross weight 〔volume〕.

**총력**(總力) all *one's* energy 〔strength〕; the aggregate power. ¶ ~을 다하여 《fight》 with all *one's* strength 〔might〕; with might and main; with concerted efforts / ~을 다하다〔기울이다〕 devote 〔direct〕 all *one's* might 〔strength〕 《to》/ 우리는 ~을 다해 이 난국을 타개해야 한다 We have to get over this difficulty 「using all our resources 〔with all our energies〕.
◉ ~안보(태세) 《strengthen》 an all-out national security (posture); a total security (posture). ~외교 total diplomacy. ~전 (a) total war; (an) all-out war: 내일 시합은 ~전이 될 것이다 We'll have to give it out all at the game tomorrow.

**총렵**(銃獵) shooting; hunting. ⇨ 총(銃) 사냥. ¶ ~을 금함 《게시》 Shooting Prohibited. ◉ ~가 a hunter; a huntsman; a sportsman. ~금지기 《미》 the closed 〔the close 《영》〕 season. ~기(期) the hunting 〔shooting〕 season; the open season. ~면허 a shooting license. ~세(稅) a shooting 〔hunting〕 tax.

**총론**(總論) general remarks; an outline 《of》; an introduction 《to》; a general summary. ¶ 민법~ an introduction to the study of civil law / ~에서 각론으로 들어가다 proceed from generalities into particulars; go 〔move〕 from the general to the particular.

**총론**(叢論) a collection of treatises 〔essays〕. ¶ 문학~ a collection of essays on literature.

**총리**(總理) ① 《내각의》 the Premier; the Prime Minister. ¶ 부~ the Deputy Prime Minister / 그는 3년간 ~ 자리를 지켜오고 있다 He has been holding the portfolio of Prime Minister for three years. ② 《총관리》 general overseeing 〔control〕. ~하다 preside over; oversee. ¶ 국무를 ~하다 「preside over 〔run〕 affairs of state. ◉ ~공관 the Prime Minister's official residence; the official residency of the Prime Minister. ~실 the Office of Premier. ~직 premiership.

**총림**(叢林) a dense wood 〔grove〕; 《덤불숲》 a bush; a thicket.

**총망**(怱忙) being very busy; great haste 〔hurry〕. ~하다 (be) very busy; hurried; rushed; flurried; [서술적] be in a hurry. ¶ ~히 in a great hurry; hurriedly / ~중에 in the midst of *one's* hurry 〔busyness〕.

**총명**(聰明) 《영민》 brightness; intelligence; sagacity; 《기억력》 a good

〔retentive〕 memory. ～하다 (be) bright; intelligent; sagacious; wise; 《기억력이》 have a good 〔sharp, retentive〕 memory. ¶ ～한 사람 a man of sagacity; an intelligent 〔a wise〕 person.

**총목록**(總目錄) the table of contents; a complete catalog(ue); a full list 《of》.

**총무**(總務) general affairs 〔business〕; 《사람》 a manager; a director. ¶ 원내 ～ 《미》 a floor leader; 《영》 a whipper-in; a whip. ◉ ～과〔국〕 the general affairs section 〔bureau〕. ～부 the general affairs department 〔division〕: ～부장 the chief of the general affairs department; a general manager.

**총민**(聰敏) cleverness and keenness; smartness and quickness. ～하다 (be) clever and keen; smart and quick.

**총반격**(總反擊) an all-out counterattack. ～하다 mount a general counterattack.

**총받이**(銃—) the firing 〔front, foremost〕 line; the forefront (of the battle).

**총보**(總譜) 〘음악〙 a full score.

**총복습**(總復習) a general review 〔revision 《영》〕 of *one's* lessons. ～하다 make a general review of *one's* lessons; go over all *one's* lessons.

**총본산**(總本山) the headquarters; 〘불교〙 the head temple 《of a sect》.

**총부리**(銃—) the muzzle 《of a rifle》. ¶～를 들이대다 point 〔level, aim〕 a gun at 《*a person*》; train *one's* gun 《on the enemy》/ ～를 들이대고 《threat *a person*》 at the point of a gun; at gunpoint 《미》.

**총사냥**(銃—) shooting; hunting; sporting 《주로 영》. ～하다 hunt with a gun; go shooting 〔hunting〕. ¶ ～을 금하다 prohibit hunting.

**총사령관**(總司令官) the supreme commander; the commander-in-chief (생략 C. in C.). ¶ 연합군 ～ the Supreme Commander for the Allied Powers.

**총사령부**(總司令部) the General Headquarters (생략 GHQ). ¶ 유엔군 ～ United Nations Command (생략 UNC).

**총사직**(總辭職) (a) general 〔mass〕 resignation; resignation in a body 〔*en masse, en bloc* (F.)〕. ～하다 resign in a body 〔*en masse*〕. ¶～을 요구하다 demand 《that the Cabinet》 resign *en* 「*masse* 〔*bloc*〕/ 그 수회 사건이 내각 ～의 도화선이 되었다 The bribery case triggered the resignation of the entire Cabinet.

**총살**(銃殺) shooting to death; 《처형》 execution by shooting 〔by a firing squad〕. ～하다 shoot 《*a person*》 dead 〔to death〕; execute 《a criminal》「by shooting 〔by a firing squad〕. ¶～당하다 be shot dead 〔to death〕; face 〔die before〕 a firing squad. ◉ ～대(隊) a firing squad. ～형 execution by a firing squad: ～형을 선고받다 be sentenced to face 〔die before〕 a firing squad.

**총상**(銃床) the stock 《of a rifle》; a 「gunstock.

**총상**(銃傷) a bullet 〔gunshot〕 wound. ¶ ～을 입다 suffer gunshot 《in *one's* right shoulder》.

**총생**(叢生) gregarious growth; growing in clusters; 〘식물〙 fasciculation. ～하다 grow dense 〔in clusters〕; 〘식물〙 be arranged in fascicles; form fascicles. ¶ ～하는〔의〕 arranged in fascicles; fasciculate; fascicular.
◉ ～식물 a social 〔gregarious〕 plant. ～엽 fascicled leaves.

**총서**(叢書) 《갖가지의》 a collection of books; a library; 《한 종류의》 a series 《of English literature》. ¶ ～로 출간되다 be published in a series.

**총선(거)**(總選(擧)) a general election. ～하다 hold 〔call〕 a general election; 《영》 go to the country. ¶～에서 승리하다 win the general election.
◉ ～일 the general election day.

**총설**(總說) = 총론(總論).

**총소리**(銃—) the report of a gun 〔rifle〕; (the sound of ) gunfire. ¶ ～가 울렸다 Bang went a gun. *or* There was the loud report of a gun. / 멀리서 ～가 한 방 들렸다 I heard a shot in the distance.

**총손질**(銃—) cleaning of a gun. ～하다 clean a gun. ◉ ～사고 a gun-cleaning accident.

**총수**(總帥) 《영도자》 the leader; 《총지휘관》 the commander-in-chief. ¶ K재벌의 ～ the head of the K Group.

**총수**(總數) the total 〔aggregate〕 (number); the whole sum; [부사적] in all 〔total〕; all told; altogether; in the aggregate. ¶ ～ 2백 a total of 200 / ～ 얼마나 되나 What does it amount to in all 〔in the aggregate〕? / ～ 2백이 된다 The total amounts to 200 (in all). *or* The total number is 200. *or* They number 200 in all.

**총수입**(總收入) the total income; the

gross revenue; gross earnings.
**총신**(銃身) the barrel《of a gun》.
**총신**(寵臣) *one's* favorite retainer 〔subject〕; a court favorite.
**총싸움**(銃—) a gun battle;《미》a gunfight;《미》a gunplay;《구어》《have》a shoot-out.
**총아**(寵兒)《사랑받는 아이》a beloved child;《시운을 탄 사람》a favorite; a popular person. ¶ 문단의 ～ a popular writer / 시대의 ～ a hero of the times / 운명의 ～ a Fortune's favorite.
**총안**(銃眼)《성벽의》a loophole; a port; a crenel(le). ¶ ～이 있는 crenellated / ～을 내다 crenellate.
**총알**(銃—) a (rifle) bullet; a shot. ¶ ～구멍 a bullet hole / ～로 꿰뚫다 send 〔fire〕 a bullet through《a wall》.
총알에: ～에 맞다 be hit by a bullet; get 〔receive〕 a bullet《in *one's* arm》/ ～에 맞아 죽다 be killed by a bullet; be shot dead.
총알을: ～을 다 쏘다 fire away all *one's* shots / ～을 뽑다 extract the bullet《from》; unload《a gun》/ ～을 재다 load《a gun》/ ～을 재어 발사 준비를 하다 load《a gun》ready for firing / ～을 재지 않은 총 an unloaded gun / 적에게 ～을 퍼붓다 rain bullets on the enemy; subject the enemy to fire.
총알이: ～이 뚫지 못하는 옷 a bulletproof jacket / ～이 미치는〔못 미치는〕곳에 within 〔out of〕 gunshot《of》/ ～이 무릎에 박이다 a bullet 〔lodges 〔gets embedded〕 in *one's* knee / ～이 벽을 꿰뚫다 a bullet goes through 〔penetrates〕 a wall / ～이 비오듯하다 bullets rain 〔shower like hail〕; bullets come thick and fast.
¶ ～은 다행히 스치기만 하고 명중하지 않았다 Luckily the bullet grazed and did not hit.
**총애**(寵愛) favor; good graces; love; affection; patronage. ～하다 favor; make a favorite of; receive《*a person*》into *one's* favor; love《*a person*》tenderly; patronize. ¶ ～하는 favorite; beloved; pet / ～를 받다 be a favorite with《*one's* master》; be in《*a person's*》favor 〔good graces〕; be the apple of《*a person's*》eye; be patronized / ～를 잃다 lose《*a person's*》favor; fall out of favor 〔into disfavor〕《with *a person*》/ ～를 얻다 win《*a person's*》favor.
**총액**(總額) the total; the total amount 〔sum〕; the sum total. ⇨ 총계(總計).
¶ 수출～ the total exports / 예산～ the total budget / ～ 5백만 원 ₩5,000,000 in total 〔in the aggregate〕/ ～ 50만 원이 되다 the total amounts to 500,000 won. 「gunbarrel.
**총열**(銃—) the barrel《of a gun》; the
**총영사**(總領事) a consul general (*pl.* consuls general, ～s). ¶ 김 싱가포르 ～ Consul-General Kim at Singapore.
◉ ～관 a consulate general: 카이로 주재 한국 ～관 Korean Consulate General in Cairo.
**총원**(總員) the entire strength; the whole personnel; all members; [부사적] in all; all told. ¶ 군대의 ～ the entire strength of an army / ～ 30명 thirty persons in all 〔all told〕.
**총의**(總意) the collective 〔general〕 will 〔opinion〕《of》; the consensus《of the people》. ¶ 국민의 ～ the general will of the nation; the consensus of the people / (총선거로) 국민의 ～를 묻다 appeal 〔go《영》〕 to the country.
**총이말**(驄—) a horse with bluish-gray hair.
**총자본금**(總資本金) gross capital;《공칭의》nominal 〔authorized〕 capital; the registered capital (등기필의).
**총잡이**(銃—) a gunman; a (professional) killer;《유명한》a gunfighter.
**총장**(總長) ①《대학의》the president《of a university》; a chancellor《영》;《사무 총장》the secretary-general. ¶ ～에 취임하다 assume the presidency《of a university》; take 〔occupy〕 the presidential chair《of》. ②《군대의》the chief《of an army, *etc.*》.
**총재**(總裁) a president;《은행·공기업 등의》a governor. ¶ 당～ the president of a party; a party chief / 부～ a vice-president / 명예～ an honorary president / ～가 되다 assume the presidency of.
**총점**(總點)《시험 등의》the total of *one's* marks;《경기의》the total score. ¶ 영어의 ～은 80점이었다 The total of marks in English was 80. 「tion〕.
**총좌**(銃座) a gun emplacement 〔posi-
**총중**(叢中) being amidst a crowd. ¶ 만록～의 홍일점 the only member of the fair sex present; the only lady in the assembly.
**총중량**(總重量) gross weight.
**총지배인**(總支配人) a general manager.
**총지출**(總支出) gross 〔total〕 expenditure.
**총지휘**(總指揮) the supreme command.

~하다 take the supreme command of 《an army》. ◉ ~관 = 총사령관.

**총질**(銃—) shooting; firing. ~하다 shoot 〔fire〕 《a gun》; fire at 《*a person*》.

**총집**(叢集) crowding around; swarming. ~하다 crowd; throng; swarm.

**총채** a 《horsehair》 duster. ¶ ~로 털다 dust 《the desk》.

**총첩**(寵妾) *one's* favorite mistress.

**총체**(總體) the whole; all. ¶ ~적으로 on the whole; all things considered; in general. ¶ 그의 연설은 ~적으로 평가하여야 한다 We have to appreciate his speech, considering it as a whole.

**총총**(怱怱) ~하다 (be) hasty; hurried; rushed. ¶ ~히 in haste; hastily; in a hurry 〔rush〕; hurriedly / ~히 떠나다 leave in haste / ~히 집에 돌아가다 hurry 〔scurry〕 home / ~히 다녀〔들러〕가다 make a hasty visit / ~ 이만 (줄이겠습니다) 《편지에서》 Yours in haste.

**총총걸음** (walking in) quick short steps; hurried walking. ~치다 walk in quick short steps; hurry along. ¶ ~으로 at a quick 〔brisk〕 pace; 《pass by》 with quick steps / ~으로 걸어 오다 come up 《the pavement》 with mincing steps.

**총총하다**(葱葱—) (be) thick; dense; close. ¶ 모를 총총하게 심다 plant young rice plants close together / 산에 나무가 총총하게 들어서다 a mountain is densely wooded.

**총총하다**(叢叢—) (be) dense; crowded; numerous. ¶ 총총히 densely; numerously; in large numbers / 별이 총총한 밤 a bright starry night / 하늘에 별이 ~ The sky is studded 〔crowded, strewn〕 with stars.

**총출동**(總出動) general mobilization. ~하다 have a general mobilization; be all mobilized 〔called out〕. ¶ 군대의 ~ the general mobilization of troops.

**총칙**(總則) general rules 〔provisions〕. ¶ 민법~ general provisions of the civil code.

**총칭**(總稱) a general 〔generic〕 term. ~하다 give a generic name 《to》; name generically. ¶ 이런 동물들을 ~하여 포유류라고 부른다 Mammalia is a general term for these animals. *or* These are known generally as Mammalia.

**총칼**(銃—) a gun and a sword; 《무력》 force of arms. ¶ ~로 다스리다 rule over 「with guns and swords 〔by force〕.

**총탄**(銃彈) a (rifle) bullet.

**총톤수**(總—數) gross tonnage. ¶ ~ 1만 톤의 배 a steamer of 10,000 tons gross / ~ 3만 5천 톤이다 have a gross tonnage of 35,000 tons; be 35,000 tons gross.

**총통**(總統) ① 《총괄》 presiding over. ② 《관직》 the President; the Generalissimo; the *Führer* (나치스의) (G.).

**총퇴각**(總退却) a general 〔full〕 retreat. ~하다 make a general retreat. ¶ ~중이다 be in full retreat.

**총파업**(總罷業) a general strike. ¶ ~에 들어가다 go on a general strike.

**총판**(總販) 《판매》 an exclusive sale; 《판매점》 the sole agency; 《사람》 the sole agent 〔distributor〕 《of books in Korea》. ~하다 make an exclusive sale 《of 》. ¶ ~ 특약을 맺다 enter into a special contract for the sole agency. ◉ ~계약 a contract for sole agency.

**총평**(總評) a general survey 〔review, critique〕. ¶ 문단~ a sweeping criticism 〔a general review〕 of the literary world.

**총포**(銃砲) guns; firearms; [총칭] gunnery. ◉ ~상 《상점》 a gun store 〔shop 《영》〕; 《상인》 a dealer in firearms. ~화약류 단속법 the Firearms & Explosive Control Law.

**총할**(總轄) general control 〔supervision〕. ~하다 supervise; superintend; have a general control 《over》.

**총합**(總合) gathering 〔collecting〕 together; the (sum) total; the total amount. ~하다 gather together; piece 〔put〕 together; sum 〔count〕 up; total.

**총화**(銃火) rifle fire; gunfire. ¶ 적의 ~를 무릅쓰고 defying 〔braving〕 the enemy's fire; under fire / ~를 받다 come 〔be〕 under fire / ~를 퍼붓다 rain shells 《on the enemy》; fire on 《the enemy》 / ~를 주고받다 exchange fire 《with the enemy》.

**총화**(總和) ¶ ~정치 politics of integration / 국민~ national harmony.

**총회**(總會) a general meeting 〔assembly〕; a plenary session 〔meeting〕. ¶ 정기〔임시〕~ an ordinary 〔extraordinary〕 general meeting / ~에 부치다 submit 《*a matter*》 to the general meeting for discussion. ◉ ~꾼 a professional troublemaker at stockholders' meetings; fixers of stockholders' meeting.

**총희**(寵姬) a favorite mistress.

**촬영**(撮影) photographing; taking a picture; 《영화》 filming; shooting 《a film》. ～하다 take a photograph 〔picture〕 of; photo; photograph; 《영화를》 film 〔shoot〕 《a scene》; make a film of 《a scene》. ¶ ～이 끝난 필름 an exposed film / 실내〔야간〕 ～ 《영화》 indoor 〔night〕 photographing / 영화를 ～하다 film 〔shoot〕 a moving picture / 사진을 ～하다 take a photograph 〔picture〕 of 《*a person*》; 《남이》 get 〔have〕 *one's* photograph taken / 그는 축구 시합을 영화로 ～했다 He filmed the soccer game. / 그 영화 ～은 7월 초에 개시될 예정이다 Shooting on the film is scheduled to start in early July. / ～금지 《게시》 No photos 〔photography〕.
◉ ～감독 a (movie) director. ～기 a (movie) camera. ～기사 a (movie) cameraman. ～기술 camera technique 〔work〕. ～대본 a continuity. ～소 a studio; a lot 《미》: 영화 ～소 a movie 〔film〕 studio. ～속도 crankspeed. ～시간 shooting time.

**최-**(最) the most; the extreme; the ultimate; the maximum; ultra(-). ¶ 최남단 the southernmost / 최첨단적(最尖端的)인 ultramodern.

**최강**(最强) ¶ ～의 the 「strongest 〔most powerful〕 《volleyball team in the world》.

**최고**(最高) the highest; the uppermost; the best. ¶ ～의 the highest; supreme; maximum; superlative; paramount; top-rate / 세계 ～의 산 the highest mountain in the world / 그의 혈압은～ 120, 최저 70이다 His blood pressure is one hundred and twenty over seventy. / 물가 지수는 ～에 달했다 The price index hit 〔reached〕 a new high. / 어제는 올여름 ～의 더위였다 Yesterday was the hottest day this summer. / 그는 차의 속도를 ～로 올렸다 He increased the speed of the car to the maximum. / 저희 회사 ～ 경영진에게 직접 말해 볼 기회를 주십시오 Please give me an opportunity to talk directly to our top management.
◉ ～가격 the highest 〔ceiling〕 price. ～간부 the executive. ～경영자 a CEO; a chief executive officer. ～고문 a supreme advisor. ～권 imperium; absolute 〔supreme〕 power. ～권위 the highest 〔supreme〕 authority. ～기관 the highest organization 〔organ, agency, institution〕. ～기온 the highest 〔maximum〕 temperature. ～사령관 the supreme commander; the commander in chief. ～사령부 the high command; the supreme headquarters. ～상 the highest 〔first〕 prize; a top-drawer award. ～속도 the maximum speed. ～수뇌 회의 a summit 〔top-level〕 conference. ～수준 the highest level. ～수훈 선수 〖야구〗 the most valuable player (생략 MVP). ～열도 the maximum heat. ～온도계 a maximum thermometer. ～음 〖음악〗 treble; soprano (여자의). ～임금제 the maximum wage system. ～법원 the Supreme Court. ～지도자 the top leader 〔executive〕. ～책임자〔수뇌자〕《정부 등의》 the highest 〔chief〕 executive. ～층 the uppermost stratum. ～품 the best stuff; top quality products. ～품질 top 〔the best〕 quality. ～학부 the highest seat of learning; the top educational institution. ～한도 the highest limit; the maximum: ～ 한도를 정하다 set an upper limit 《to》; put a ceiling 《on》 / 가격을 ～ 한도로 인상하다 raise the ceiling of the price. ～회의 the supreme council; the top-level meeting.

**최고**(催告) notice; demand; 《납입의》 a call. ～하다 notify; call upon 《*a person* to *do*》; demand payment 《of》.
◉ ～장 a call notice.

**최고급**(最高級) the highest 〔top〕 grade 〔class〕. ¶ ～의 of the highest grade 〔order〕; top-level〔-ranking〕; of the best 〔highest〕 quality; best; finest / 우리 회사의 제품은 ～에 끼인다 Our products are numbered 〔classed〕 among the best. ◉ ～품 an article of the highest quality; top quality products.

**최고기록**(最高記錄) the best record; an all-time 〔a new〕 high 《미》. ¶ 세계～ a world record / 자신의 ～ *one's* best record / ～을 내다 make 〔establish〕 the best record / ～을 깨뜨리다 break the best record.

**최고도**(最高度) the highest degree; the maximum; the climax. ¶～로 to the highest degree; to the utmost / ～로 활용하다 use 《*one's* talent》 to the highest degree; make the utmost use of 《*one's* ability》.

**최고득점**(最高得點) the highest point; 《시험의》 the highest 〔top〕 mark(s); 《경기의》 the highest score; 《투표의》 the largest vote. ¶ ～을 얻다 《시험에서》

get 〔gain, win〕 the highest mark(s) 《in》; 《경기에서》 make the highest score / ～으로 당선되다 be elected 《to the Assembly》 with the largest number of votes.

**최고봉**(最高峰) the highest peak 《of the Alps》; [비유적] the highest authority; the acme. ¶ 문단의 ～ the most prominent figure in the world of letters / 영시(英詩)의 ～ the high-water mark of English poetry / 화단(畫壇)의 ～ the greatest of all painters 《in Korea》 / 그 산은 세계의 ～이다 That mountain is the highest in the world. / 그 작품은 현대 문학의 ～이다 The work is a masterpiece of contemporary literature.

**최고위**(最高位) the highest rank; the top place. ¶ ～를 차지하다 hold (the) top place; rank first / 두 나라는 어제 첫번째 ～급 회담을 가졌다 Both countries held their first highest-level meeting yesterday.

**최고위원**(最高委員) a member of the supreme council; the supreme representative.

**최고조**(最高潮) the climax; the peak; the zenith. ¶ ～에 달하다 reach 〔come to〕 the climax / 해외 여행 붐은 이제 ～에 달했다 An overseas traveling boom has come to its peak. / 연극은 그 장면에서 ～에 달했다 The play reached the climax in that scene.

**최근**(最近) ① 《거리상의》 being the 「nearest 〔shortest〕. ¶ ～거리 the shortest distance. ② 《시간상의》 being the latest; the most recent. ¶ ～의 recent; the most recent; the latest; last (★ last와 latest는 둘 다 형용사 late의 최상급이지만 last는 「(순서적으로) 최후의」라는 뜻을 나타내고, latest는 「(시간적으로) 최근의」라는 뜻을 나타냄: the last page of a book 「책의 마지막 페이지」, the latest fashion 「최신의 유행」) / ～에 recently; lately; of late / 아주 ～에 most recently / ～까지 until a recent date; up to recently; till quite recently / 비교적 ～까지 until comparatively lately / ～의 유행 the latest 「fashion 〔mode〕 / ～ 3년 간 during 〔for, in〕 the last three years / ～호의 리더스 다이제스트 the latest number of the *Reader's Digest* / ～에 출판된 책 a book recently published / ～에 그를 전혀 만나 보지 못했다 I haven't seen anything of him lately. / ～에 언제 그를 만나셨나요 When did you see him last?

> **용법** **recently** 가까운 과거의 특정 시점을 뜻하는 경우에 흔히 쓰임. quite, only 따위의 부사와 함께 쓰이는 경우가 많음. 현재완료·과거형과 함께 쓰이며, 현재형과는 거의 쓰이지 않음. **lately** 현재의 시점을 포함하는 「최근」의 뜻으로, 현재완료의 문장, 의문문·부정문에 주로 쓰임. **of late** lately보다 격식 차린 말: My father has been very busy of late. 최근에 아버지는 매우 바쁘시다.

**최근세**(最近世) recent times; the modern period. ¶ 한국 ～사(史) a History of Modern Korea.

**최급하다**(最急—) be most 「urgent 〔pressing, demanding, vital, critical〕.

**최긴**(最緊) being most 「important 〔necessary, essential, indispensable, critical, vital〕. ～하다 be most important; be of vital importance; be most necessary; be quite essential. ¶ ～한 문제 the most important question / 살아가는 데 ～한 것은 돈이다 Money is the key to getting along in life.

**최다**(最多) being most numerous; the 「greatest 〔largest〕 in 「number 〔quantity〕; the most. ¶ 홈런의 ～기록 the record for the most home runs / ～승리 투수 『야구』 the pitcher with the greatest 〔largest〕 number of wins. ◉ ～량〔액〕 the 「greatest 〔largest〕 quantity 〔amount〕; the maximum.

**최다수**(最多數) the 「greatest 〔largest〕 number 《of》; the largest majority. ¶ ～의 인구 the largest population.

**최단**(最短) being the shortest. ¶ ～의 the shortest. ◉ ～거리〔코스〕 the shortest 「distance 〔course〕 《to》: ～코스를 취하다 take the shortest course 《to》. ～시일 the shortest time. ～작동시간 『컴퓨터』 the shortest operating time.

**최대**(最大) being the 「largest 〔greatest, biggest〕. ¶ ～의 the 「largest 〔greatest, biggest〕; (the) maximum (최대한의) / ～의 업적 the greatest achievement / 세계 ～의 유조선 the biggest tanker in the world / ～ 다수의 최대 행복 the greatest happiness of the greatest number / ～의 찬사를 보내다 bestow *one's* highest possible praise on 《*a person*》; praise 《*a person*》 to the skies / 우리들은 최소의 노력으로 ～의 능률을 올리려고 한다 We are trying to find the maximum of efficiency with

the minimum of labor.
◉ ～강우량 the maximum rainfall. ～공약수 〖수학〗 the greatest common measure (생략 G.C.M.); the greatest common divisor (생략 G.C.D.). ～량 the largest 〔maximum〕 quantity. ～순간 풍속 the maximum instantaneous wind speed. ～압력 the maximum pressure. ～장력(張力) the maximum tension. ～치(値) the maximum value.

**최대속력**(最大速力) the maximum speed. ¶ 시속 300마일의 ～을 내다 attain 〔reach〕 a maximum speed of 300 miles an hour.

**최대한(도)**(最大限(度)) the maximum. ¶ ～의 at its maximum / ～에 달하다 reach the maximum / ～의 능률을 내다 show 〔put out〕 the maximum efficiency / ～의 노력을 하다 do *one's* very best; make maximum efforts / 휴일을 ～으로 이용하라 Make the most of your holidays. / 건축비는 ～ 5천만 원이다 The building cost must not exceed fifty million won.

**최량**(最良) ¶ ～의 the best; the ideal / 경험은 ～의 교사다 Experience is the best teacher.

**최루**(催淚) causing tears. ◉ ～가스 tear gas; lachrymatory gas. ～총 a tear-gas gun. ～탄 a tear bomb; a tear-gas grenade 〔canister〕.

**최면**(催眠) inducement of sleep; hypnosis. ¶ ～의 sleep-inducing; hypnotic. ◉ ～요법 a hypnotic treatment; hypnotherapy. ～제 a sleep-inducing 〔sleeping〕 drug 〔pill〕; a hypnotic 〔soporific〕 (agent). ～학 hypnology. 자기～ self-hypnotism.

**최면상태**(催眠狀態) a hypnotic state; hypnosis; hypnotism; 〖심령술〗 a trance. ¶ ～에 있는 사람 a person in a hypnotic trance 〔state〕; a person under hypnosis / ～로 만들다 put 《*a person*》 into a state of hypnosis / ～에 빠지다 be hypnotized / ～에서 깨어나다 be dehypnotized; come out of hypnosis; break the hypnotic spell.

**최면술**(催眠術) mesmerism; hypnotism. ¶ ～의 hypnotic; mesmeric / ～을 걸다 mesmerize 〔hypnotize〕 《*a person*》; practice hypnotism / ～을 걸 대상자 a hypnotic subject / ～에 걸리다 be hypnotized 〔mesmerized〕; go into 〔fall under〕 hypnosis. ◉ ～사(師) a hypnotist; a mesmerist.

**최북**(最北) the northernmost. ◉ ～단 the northernmost tip 〔extremity〕.

**최상**(最上) ¶ ～의 the finest; the best; the highest 《quality》; supreme; of the first order / ～의 행복 the supreme happiness / ～의 컨디션이다 be in the best condition / ～의 방법은 선생님께 의논하는 것이다 The best way is to consult your teacher.
◉ ～등(等) the first order; the top 〔supreme〕 grade. ～위 숫자 〖컴퓨터〗 the most significant digit. ～층 the top floor; the uppermost story: ～층 계급 the uppermost stratum; the top class; the social elite; the upper crust. ～품 the best 〔finest〕 stuff; an article of the highest quality.

**최상급**(最上級) ① 《학급》 the highest grade; the top 〔highest〕 class. ¶ ～생 a senior (student). ② 〖문법〗 the superlative (degree). ¶ 'good'의 ～은 'best'이다 "Best" is the superlative (form) of "good."

**최선**(最善) the best; *one's* best. ¶ ～의 노력 the utmost 〔best〕 efforts; 《make》 all-out efforts / ～을 다하다 do *one's* best; do all *one* can; try *one's* utmost / 이것이 영어를 통달하는 ～의 방법이다 This is the best way to master English. / 이 경우엔 이게 ～을 다하는 일이라 생각한다 I think this is the best thing to do in this case. / 정직은 ～의 방책이다 Honesty is the best policy.

**최선두**(最先頭) the forefront; the head; the lead; the van. ¶ ～에 서다 be at the head 《of》; be in the forefront 《of a parade》; take 〔lead〕 the van / ～를 따라잡다 overtake the head 《of》.

**최성기**(最盛期) the peak period; the highest stage of development; the prime; the golden age 〔days〕; 《과일 등의 출회기》 the season; the best time 《for》. ¶ 문화의 ～에 달하다 reach the high watermark 〔zenith〕 of 《its》 culture / 사과는 지금이 ～다 Apples are in season now. *or* Apples are at their best now. / 로마는 아우구스투스 시대가 ～였다 Rome was in its prime during the age of Augustus.

**최소**(最小) ¶ ～의 the smallest; the least; (the) minimum; minimal / ～의 불편 the minimum of inconvenience / ～의 노력으로 최대의 효과를 올리다 achieve a maximum of efficiency at a minimum of effort. ◉ ～공배수 〖수학〗 the least 〔lowest〕 common multiple (생략 L.C.M.). ～ 공(통)분모 the least 〔lowest〕 common denominator (생략 L.C.D.). ~전류 a minimum current: ~전류 밀도 minimum current density / ~전류 차단기 a minimum current cutout switch. ~준비제도 『경제』 the minimum reserve system. ~치(値) the smallest value.

**최소**(最少) ① 《가장 적음》 ¶ ~의 the least 《amount》; the smallest 《group》; the lowest 《number》 / ~량 the minimum quantity / ~ 저항 the least resistance / 우리에겐 ~의 시간밖에 남지 않았다 We have the least time left. / 사고 건수는 과거 4년 중 ~였다 The number of accidents is the lowest in the 「past 〔last〕 four years. ② 《가장 젊음》 (being) the youngest.
◉ ~사용 빈도수 『컴퓨터』 the least frequently use (생략 LFU). ~시장접근〔개방〕 『경제』 Minimum Market Access 〔Opening〕.

**최소한(도)**(最小限(度)) the 〔a〕 minimum; [부사적] at a minimum; at (the) least; to say the least (of it). ¶ ~의 minimum / ~으로 하다 minimize / ~ 5년은 걸리다 take five years 「at least 〔at the minimum〕 / ~으로 줄이다 ruduce 《the expenses》 to the minimum; keep 〔hold〕 《the losses》 to a minimum / ~ 5백만 원의 자본이 필요하다 It requires a minimum capital of 5 million won. / 죄는 아닐지라도 ~ 비도덕적이다 It may not be criminal, but it is immoral, to say the least of it. / 그들은 피해를 ~도로 막았다 They 「confined 〔checked〕 the damage to 「the 〔a〕 minimum.

**최신**(最新) ¶ ~의 the newest 《model》; the latest; the most up-to-date 《method》; hot 《news》 / ~의 기술 the newest technology / ~이다 be the newest; be up-to-date; be ultramodern / 그 공장은 설비를 모두 ~의 것으로 바꿨다 The factory replaced all its equipment with the 「latest 〔up-to=date〕 machinery. / 「이것이 우리의 ~ 제품입니다」—「이전 제품과 어떤 점이 다른가요」 "This is our latest product." —"How does it differ from your previous products?"
◉ ~형 「a new 〔the latest〕 style 〔model, design〕 《of a machine》: ~형의 차 the latest-model car. ⇨ 최신식.

**최신식**(最新式) the 「latest 〔newest〕 fashion 〔style〕; the 「ultramodern 〔most up-to-date〕 style. ¶ ~의 of the 「latest 〔newest〕 style 〔model〕 / ~ 호텔 a hotel with the latest improvements / ~ 호텔을 짓다 build a hotel on the most up-to-date lines / 그것은 ~ 인쇄기다 It's a printing machine of the newest type.

**최신유행**(最新流行) the latest fashion; the newest style. ¶ ~의 latest-fashioned / ~의 모자 a new-look hat / ~의 구두를 신다 wear the latest thing in shoes / 그들은 모두 ~의 양장을 하고 있다 They are seen all dressed *à la mode.*

**최심**(最甚) ~하다 be 「most extreme 〔the worst〕. ¶ 피해가 ~하다 suffer the worst damage.

**최악**(最惡) the worst. ¶ ~의 경우에는 in the worst case; when 〔if〕 the worst comes to the worst / ~의 경우일지라도 at (the) worst / ~의 경우에 대비하다 prepare 〔provide〕 for the worst / ~의 사태를 극복하다 get the worst over.

**최우등**(最優等) being most excellent; the top grade; the highest class. ¶ ~으로 졸업하다 graduate with 「top honors 〔the greatest distinction, *summa cum laude* (L.)〕. ◉ ~생 a top student; a top-honors man.

**최우수**(最優秀) ¶ ~의 the most excellent; superior; first-rate; choice.
◉ ~상 the first prize. ~선수 the best player; 《야구의》 the most valuable player (of the year) (생략 MVP). ~품 a choicest article; A 1 goods.

**최음제**(催淫劑) an aphrodisiac (drug); a (love) philter.

**최장**(最長) ¶ ~의 the longest 《air route》 / ~ 다섯 자를 넘지 못하다 do not exceed five 「*ja* 〔feet〕 at the longest. ◉ ~거리 the longest 〔greatest〕 distance. ~교량 the longest bridge. ~부도(不倒)거리 『스키』 the day's longest successful jump.

**최저**(最低) ¶ ~의 the lowest; the lowermost; (the) minimum (최소의) / ~로 어림하다 give the lowest possible estimate; estimate 《a repair job》 at 《₩500,000》 at the minimum / 월급이 ~ 100만 원은 된다 The monthly salary is 1,000,000 won at the lowest. / 우리 가격은 ~입니다 Our prices are rock=bottom. 《미》 / 나는 ~ 10권의 책은 읽어야 한다 I have to read ten books at (the) least.
◉ ~가(격) the 「lowest 〔bottom〕 price; the floor price (제한 가격): 주가(株價)는 ~가를 기록했다 The stock prices 「hit a new low 〔dropped to an all=

time low]. ~기록 a record [new] low level; a new [an all-time] low《구어》. ~기온 the lowest [minimum] temperature: 오늘의 ~ 기온은 8도였다 Today's lowest (temperature) was 8 degrees centigrade. ~생활 the minimum standard of living: ~ 생활비 the minimum cost of living. ~액 the lowest estimate. ~연령 the minimum [lowest] age. ~온도계 a minimum thermometer. ~임금 the minimum wages: ~임금법 the Minimum Wages Act / ~임금제 the minimum wage system / ~임금 보장제 a minimum wage guarantee system. ~필요조건 the minimum requirements. ~혈압〖의학〗minimum blood pressure.

**최적**(最適) ~하다 (be) most suitable [agreeable]; ideal; the best suited; the fittest;《온도·습도 등이》(be) optimum. ¶ (기업 등의) ~ 규모 the optimum size / 그는 그 일에 ~의 인물이다 He is the only person for the job. / 이곳은 산책하기에 ~의 장소다 This is the most suitable place for walking.
◉ ~기준 the optimum standard: ~기준 임금 the optimum standard wages. ~속도 the optimum speed. ~온도[밀도] the optimum temperature [density (인구의)]. ~조건 the optimum (conditions).

**최전선**(最前線) the front line; the forefront. ¶ 우리는 적이 방어하는 ~을 돌파했다 We broke through the enemy's first line of defense.

**최종**(最終) ¶ ~의 the last《day, train》; the final《examination》; the closing《game》;《궁극의》ultimate《responsibility》/ ~적으로 lastly; finally; ultimately / 그 계획의 ~적인 비용은 최초의 것보다 적었다 The ultimate cost of the project was smaller than the original estimate.
◉ ~결과 an end result. ~결정 the final decision: 사장으로부터 ~ 결정이 내려졌다 The final decision was made by the president. ~기한 the deadline. ~목적 the ultimate object. ~목적지 the final destination. ~무기 an ultimate weapon. ~수요 final demand: ~수요자[소비자] an end user. ~시험 the final [last] examination. ~용도〖경제〗end use. ~일 the last day: 연극의 ~일 the last [closing] day of a play / ~일의 회의 the last-day session. ~제품 an end product. ~주자《계주에서》the anchor (man [woman]); the last runner. ~회(回)《경기의》the last round; the last inning(s).

**최종안**(最終案) the final program [plan]. ¶ ~에 동의하다 agree on the final blueprint / ~을 작성하다 formulate the final plan.

**최초**(最初) the beginning; the opening; the commencement;《발단》the start; the outset;《기원》the origin.
¶ ~의 the first《interpellator》; the initial《stages》; the opening《games》; the original《purpose》; the earliest《visitor》/ ~에 in the first place; at the start [outset, beginning] / ~부터 from the first [start, beginning, outset] / 일은 ~부터 잘 진행됐다 It went well from the start. / ~에는 그녀도 불쾌한 표정이었다 At first she looked displeased too. / 그가 ~로 왔다 He was the first to come. / ~에는 그럴 계획이 아니었다 It wasn't my original plan to do so. / ~에는 회원이 열밖에 없었다 We had only ten members to start with.

**최하**(最下) the lowest; the most inferior;《최악》the worst;《최저》the lowermost. ◉ ~가격 the lowest [minimum] price. ~등 the lowest grade [class]; the worst. ~연령 the minimum [lowest] age. ~층《건물의》the lowermost story; the ground floor;《사회의》the lowermost stratum《of society》; the lowermost class; the underworld. ~품 the worst stuff; an article of the lowest grade [quality].

**최하급**(最下級) the lowest grade [class]. ¶ ~의 of the lowest class; buck (군대 등에서의) / ~생 a first-year student;《미》a freshman (대학·고교의).

**최하위**(最下位) the lowest rank [position];《순위의》the tail end. ¶ ~의 팀 the tailender / ~에 있다 be the lowest in rank;《경기에서》be last;《구어》be in the cellar (리그전 등에서).

**최혜국**(最惠國) a most favored nation. ◉ ~대우 most-favored-nation treatment: ~대우를 하다 treat《Korea》as a most-favored-nation; give《Korea》most-favored-nation status. ~약관 the most-favored-nation clause (생략 MFNC): ~ 약관을 폐기하다 terminate the most-favored-nation provisions.

**최활** a flexible stick used as a cloth stretcher on a loom.

**최후**(最後) ① 《마지막》the last;《결말》the end.
최후의: ~의 last; final; ultimate (★

last는 연속되어 있는 것의 「마지막」 또 「이 앞의」란 뜻도 됨: last night. final은 「그것으로 완결됨」을 강조함. ultimate는 final과 대체로 뜻이 같지만, 도달되는 종극을 뜻함) / ~의 결정 the final 〔ultimate〕 decision / ~의 노력 final 〔last-spurt〕 effort / ~의 만찬 『기독교』 the Last Supper / ~의 승부 the closing 〔concluding〕 game / ~의 심판 the Last Judgment / ~의 5분간 the last five minutes in a crisis / ~의 일격 the last blow; a final blow / ~의 저항 a last-ditch resistance / ~의 점검 a last-minute checkup / ~의 한 사람까지 《fight》 to the last man / ~의 승리를 거두다 win the ultimate 〔final〕 victory / ~의 선을 넘다 《남녀가》 go the limit / …에 ~의 희망을 걸다 put *one's* last hope in….

최후까지: ~까지 to the last 〔end〕; to the last extremity / ~까지 반대하다 oppose to the last; be dead set against / 《연극·음악회 따위를》 ~까지 보다〔듣다〕 stay to the end of 《a play, a concert》; sit 《a play, a concert》 out / ~까지 싸우다 fight to the last 〔death〕; fight it out (★ 이 it 은 무의미한 형식상의 목적어: catch 〔get〕 it 「야단맞다」, lord it 「뽐내다」, have it out 「결말내다」 따위) / ~까지 의리를 지키다 remain faithful to the last / ~까지 저항하다 resist to the last (drop of *one's* blood) / 아무의 말을 ~까지 듣다 hear *a person* out / ~까지 읽다 read 《a book》 to the end.

최후로〔에〕: ~에〔로〕 lastly; in 〔at〕 the rear; at last; for the last time; in conclusion; 《결국》 eventually; in the end; in the long run / ~에〔로〕 나가다 go out 《of a theater》 after all the others; be the last to go out.

¶ ~에 누가 이길는지는 두고 볼 일이다 It is yet to be seen who will win in the end. / 말싸움이 ~에 가서는 주먹다짐이 되었다 The quarrel ended up in a fistfight. / 이것이 남편의 건강한 모습을 본 ~가 되었다 This was to be the last time I saw my husband alive. / ~에 웃는 자가 승리자다 He who laughs last laughs best. / ~로 나의 의견을 말하고 싶다 Lastly 〔In conclusion〕, I'd like to give my opinion.

② 《죽음》 *one's* last moment; *one's* death; *one's* end. ¶ ~의 말 *one's* dying words / (운이 다해) ~가 오다 come to *one's* account day / ~를 장식하다 be 〔bring〕 the last glory to *one's* life / ~를 지켜보다 watch 《*a person*》 die; see 《*a person's*》 last 〔end〕; be present at 《*a person's*》 deathbed / 비참한 ~를 마치다 meet (with) a tragic end; die a sad 〔pitiful〕 death / 훌륭한 ~를 마치다 meet *one's* fate like a brave man; die a heroic 〔glorious〕 death.

◉ ~수단 the 〔*one's*〕 last resort 〔resource〕; the ultimate 〔final〕 step; a drastic 〔radical〕 measure: ~수단을 취하다 take the ultimate step; resort to drastic measures. ~순간 the last 〔critical〕 moment: ~순간에 우리를 저버리다니 그 사람답다 It was like him to fail us at the last minute. ~운명 *one's* final destiny; *one's* ultimate fate. ~통첩 an ultimatum (*pl.* ~s, -ta): ~통첩을 보내다 send 〔deliver〕 an ultimatum.

**추**(錘) a (balance) weight; a poise. ¶ 시계추 a pendulum (weight) / 저울추 the weight of a balance / 낚시추 a (fishing) sinker / 낚시줄에 추를 달다 weight a line.

**추가**(追加) an addition; 《부가물·부록》 an addendum (*pl.* -da); an appendix (*pl.* -dices); 《보충》 supplement. ~하다 add 《A to B》; make an addition 《to》; supplement. ¶ ~의 additional; supplementary; supplemental / 예산에 ~하다 supplement a budget / 부록을 ~하다 add an appendix / 주문을 ~하다 add to *one's* order / 식사를 2인분 더 ~하다 order meals for two more / 또 ~하실 것 뭐 없습니까 Do you have anything to add? / 우리는 ~점을 3점 올려 승리를 확실케 했다 We made our victory sure by adding another three points.

◉ ~경정 예산(안) a revised supplementary budget (bill). ~비용 additional expenses. ~시험 a supplementary examination; 《성적 불량으로》 a make-up 《미》: ~시험을 치르다 make up an examination. ~신청 additional application. ~예산(안) an additional budget (bill). ~요금 an additional charge. ~조항 an added 〔an inserted, a supplementary〕 article. ~주문 《make》 an additional order: 맥주를 ~주문할까요 How about ordering some more beer? ~지출 a supplemental appropriation. ~징수(徵收) additional collection.

**추간**(追刊) additional publication. ~하다 publish in addition.

**추거**(推擧) = 추천(推薦).

**추격**(追擊) pursuit; chase; a follow-up

attack. ～하다 pursue; chase; run after; give chase《to》. ¶ ～을 중지하다 give up the chase《for》/ 적을 맹렬히 ～중이다 be in hot pursuit [chase] of the enemy; be pressing hard on the enemy / ～을 시작하다 start in pursuit [chase] of《the fleeting enemy》. ◉ ～기(機) a pursuit plane. ～전 a pursuit battle; a running fight (해상의).

**추경**(秋耕)《가을갈이》autumn plowing. ～하다, ～치다 plow in autumn; till a field in autumn; do the autumn [fall] plowing.

**추경**(秋景) autumn scene(s) [scenery].

**추계**(秋季) autumn; fall. ◉ ～운동회 an autumn ｢sports meet [athletic meeting].

**추계**(推計) estimating; estimation. ～하다 estimate. ¶ …으로 ～되다 be estimated at…. ◉ ～학 stochastics; inductive statistics.

**추고**(追考) reminiscence; recollection; retrospection; looking back. ～하다 recollect; reminisce [look back] on.

**추곡**(秋穀) autumn(-harvested) grains [rice]. ◉ ～수매 a purchase of autumn harvest grain (by the government): ～수매 가격 the government purchase price of rice.

**추골**(椎骨)〖해부〗a vertebra (*pl.* -brae). ¶ ～과 ～ 사이의 intervertebral.

**추골**(槌骨)〖해부〗a malleus (*pl.* mallei); a hammer.

**추괴**(醜怪) ugliness; disgracefulness. ～하다 (be) ugly; disgraceful.

**추교**(醜交) an illicit connection. ¶ ～를 맺다 have improper [scandalous] relations《with》.

**추구**(追求) pursuit; a chase. ～하다 pursue; seek [follow] after; chase. ¶ 행복의 ～ the pursuit of happiness; the search for happiness / …을 ～하여 in quest [pursuit, search] of... / 이익을 ～하여 in chase [pursuit] of profits / 목적[쾌락]을 ～하다 pursue an object [pleasures] / 행복을 ～하다 seek after happiness / 그는 지위와 권력을 ～하는 데 일생을 보냈다 He spent his whole life in pursuit of rank and power.

**추구**(追究) a thoroughgoing study; thorough investigation. ～하다 look closely《into》; investigate. ¶ 진리를 ～하다 seek truth / 문제를 ～하다 study a problem thoroughly / 인플레의 원인을 ～하다 investigate the causes of the《current》inflation.

**추궁**(追窮) close inquiry; (a) thorough investigation; cross-examination; pressing hard. ～하다 press《*a person*》hard《for an answer》; question《*a person*》; come down hard《on, upon》; cross-examine. ¶ 책임을 ～하다 call《*a person*》to account; take [call]《*a person*》to task《for》/ 나는 ～을 받고 대답에 궁했다 Pressed for an answer, I was at a loss how to reply. / 범인은 ～을 피하려고 거짓말을 했다 The offender told lies to take the heat off. / 우리는 그 행위에 대해 그의 책임을 ～할 것이다 We will press him to assume [take] responsibility for the action.

**추근추근** tenaciously; persistently; importunately; demandingly. ～하다 (be) tenacious; persistent; importunate; demanding. ¶ ～한 사람 a nuisance / ～한 외판원 a high-pressure salesman / ～하게 tenaciously; persistently; importunately; demandingly / ～ 묻다 pester [plague]《*a person*》with questions / ～ 조르다 ask《*a person*》importunately《for》; tease [pester, importune]《*a person* for *something*》/ 여자를 ～ 쫓아다니다 keep after [pester] a girl; dangle after [hang around] a girl with annoying persistence.

**추급**(追及) overtaking; catching up. ～하다 overtake; catch up《with》.

**추급**(追給) (a) supplementary pay [grant, allowance]. ～하다 pay in addition.

**추기**(秋氣) an indication of autumn (in the air); a sign of autumn; the early chill of autumn.

**추기**(秋期) autumn. ＝추계(秋季).

**추기**(追記) a postscript (생략 P.S.). ～하다 add a postscript《to》; add《to》.

**추기경**(樞機卿) a cardinal (of the Roman Catholic Church). ◉ ～회의 the Consistory.

**추기다**《달콤한 말로》cajole; wheedle;《충동하다》instigate; incite; stir up; egg《*a person*》on《to *do*》; put《*a person*》up《to (commit) a crime》;《꾀다》tempt《into》; entice; allure; seduce. ⇨부추기다. ¶ 아무를 추겨서 …시키다 tempt [set on] *a person* to *do* / 그들은 근로자들을 추겨서 파업을 일으키려 했다 They tried to instigate the workers to go on strike. *or* They tried to induce the workers to strike.

**추깃물** water from a rotting corpse.

**추남**(醜男) a bad-looking 〔an ugly〕 man.

**추납**(追納) supplementary payment. ~하다 pay in addition.

**추녀** 〖건축〗 the protruding corners of eaves.

**추녀**(醜女) an ugly 〔unsightly〕 woman.

**추념**(追念) ~하다 cherish the memory for the deceased; pay a tribute to the memory of 《*a person*》; mourn 《for the dead》. ◉ ~사 a memorial address 〔tribute〕.

**추다**[1] 《칭찬하다》 praise; talk up; speak highly 《of》; sing 〔sound〕 the praises 《of》; say pretty 〔nice〕 things 《to》; flatter. ⇨추어주다, 추어올리다.

**추다**[2] ① 《찾으려고 뒤지다》 ransack; rummage 《in》. ⇨ 뒤지다[1]. ② 《한쪽을 채어 올리다》 pull up; put up; lift up. ⇨추어올리다. ¶ 멍석 한구석을 ~ pull up 〔back〕 the end of a (rolled) mat.

**추다**[3] 《춤을》 dance. ¶ 장단〔피리〕에 맞추어 춤을 ~ dance to music 〔the flute〕/ 남의 장단에 춤을 ~ dance to *a person's* tune 〔pipe〕; be manipulated by another; be made a puppet by another / 함께 추실까요 May I have your next dance?

**추단**(推斷) 《추론》 (an) inference; (a) deduction; (a) conclusion. ~하다 infer 〔deduce〕 《from》; conclude; draw a conclusion. ¶ 이 사실에서 다음과 같이 ~할 수가 있다 From this fact we may safely infer as follows.

**추담**(醜談) a filthy 〔a foul, an obscene〕 talk; an indecent talk; a dirty 〔smutty〕 story. ⇨음담.

**추대**(推戴) ~하다 have 《*a person*》 as 《the president》 of; have 《*a person*》 over 《a society》; bring 《*a person*》 forward 《as boss》. ¶~식 an installation ceremony / 이 회는 남 박사를 총재로 ~하고 있다 This society is under the presidency of Dr. Nam.

**추도**(追悼) mourning. ~하다 mourn 《for the dead, over *a person's* death》; pay a 〔*one's*〕 tribute to the memory of 《*a person*》. ¶ ~식을〔회를〕 가지다 hold memorial services 〔a requiem〕 《for the late Mr. K》; hold a meeting in memory 《of *a person*》/ 이로써 고인에 대한 제 ~의 말을 마칩니다 With this I would end my parting address for the deceased. ◉ ~문 a memorial writing. ~사 a memorial address 〔tribute〕: ~사를 하다 give a memorial address 《of *a person*》.

**추돌**(追突) a rear-end collision. ~하다 bump into the rear of 《a truck》; collide with 〔run into〕 《a car》 from behind; strike the rear of 《a car》. ¶ ~하지 않도록 주의하시오 Drive (your car) carefully so as not to collide with another car from behind. / ~당하여 차가 대파되었다 Struck from behind, the car was damaged badly. / 눈길에 미끄러져 앞차와 ~했다 My car slipped on the snowy road and ran 〔rammed, smashed〕 into the rear of the car ahead. / 그는 너무 과속으로 달려 앞 차에 ~했다 He drove so fast (that) he crushed into the rear of a car. / 그녀는 ~을 당해 목에 충격상(傷)을 입었다 She got a whiplash injury when her car was run into from behind. (★ whiplash injury 는 자동차의 충돌·추돌 때 생기는 충격으로 목뼈를 다치는 부상).

**추락**(墜落) a fall; a drop; a crash (비행기의). ~하다 fall; drop; go down; crash. ¶ 바다로 ~하다 crash 〔go down〕 into the sea / 지면으로 거꾸로 ~하다 fall to the ground head over heels 《from》; fall 〔go down〕 headlong to the ground / 위신이 ~되다 lose *one's* prestige 〔authority〕/ 비행기가 들판에 ~했다 An airplane crashed in the field. / 그 비행기의 ~사고로 승객 및 승무원 전원이 사망했다 All the passengers and crew were killed in the plane 〔air〕 crash. / 버스 한 대가 호수로 ~했다 A bus plunged into the lake. ◉ ~사 death from a fall: ~사하다 be killed in a fall; be killed in a plane crash. ~사고 《비행기의》 a plane crash.

**추량**(秋涼) cool 〔chilly〕 autumnal weather. ¶ ~지절(之節) the cool season of autumn.

**추량**(推量) = 추측(推測).

**추레하다** (be) shabby; unclean; dirty; slovenly.

**추려내다** pick 〔sort, single〕 out; weed out. ⇨ 추리다. ¶ 나쁜 사과를 ~ single out the bad apples / 마을의 장정만을 ~ pick out only the able-bodied men of the village.

**추력**(推力) (a) thrust; impellent 〔driving〕 force.

**추렴** ① 《갹출금》 collection of money; the raising of money; a contribution. ~하다 collect 〔raise〕 money; collect contributions 〔subscriptions〕. ¶ ~으로 at the joint expense of / 소풍가는 비용을 ~하다 pool the expenses for a picnic; collect money for an outing /

돈을 ～해서 …를 사다 chip in 《*one's* share》 to buy…; raise money to buy… / 유족을 위해 100만 원을 ～하다 raise a million won for a bereaved family. ② 《각자 부담》 a Dutch treat; going Dutch; splitting 〔sharing〕 the bill. ～하다 have a Dutch treat; go Dutch; go fifty-fifty 《미구어》.

◉ 술～ a drinking party that goes Dutch.

**추렴새** ① = 추렴. ② 《갹출금》 a contribution; a subscription; a share. ¶ ～가 많다 a share is large.

**추록**(追錄) a postscript; a supplement; an addition. ～하다 supplement; add.

**추론**(推論) reasoning; (an) inference; a corollary (argument) (당연히 도출되는); induction (귀납); deduction (연역). ～하다 reason; infer 《from》; draw an inference 《from》; 《귀납하다》 induce; 《연역하다》 deduct. ¶ 그녀의 ～에는 다소 무리가 있는 것 같다 Her reasoning seems a little unnatural.

**추루**(醜陋) filthiness; being dirty and unsightly; foulness. ～하다 (be) filthy and ugly; unsightly.

**추리** 《쇠고기의》 beef flank.

**추리**(推理) reasoning (논리적 추리); ratiocination; (an) inference (추론). ～하다 reason; ratiocinate; infer 《from》. ¶ ～과정 a reasoning process / 결론을 ～하다 infer a conclusion / 하나하나 ～해 나가다 follow out a train of reasoning / 뛰어난 ～로 사건을 잇달아 해결하다 solve one case after another with *one's* brilliant reasoning.

◉ ～력 reasoning powers 〔faculties〕; deductive powers. ～소설 a detective 〔mystery〕 story; a mystery; a whodunit 《구어》 (★ who done 〔did〕 it?이 변형해서). ～작가 a detective story 〔mistery〕 writer. 귀납〔연역〕～ inductive 〔deductive〕 inference. 연결～ combined 〔compound〕 syllogism. 직접～ direct 〔immediate〕 inference.

**추리다** choose; select; pick 〔single〕 out; sort 〔screen〕 out; assort; 《체로》 sift out. ¶ 다 추리고 난 나머지 the leftovers after all the best ones have been picked out / 많은 것 중에서 ～ choose 〔select〕 《a book》 from among many / 우편물을 목적지 별로 ～ sort mail according to destinations / 추려서 말하다 give the outline 《of》; outline / 20명의 후보자 중에서 3명만 추렸다 Only three were selected from among twenty candidates.

**추맥**(秋麥) autumn-sown barley; the late barley.

**추명**(醜名) an ill name; notoriety; ill fame 〔repute〕; infamy; a scandal (추문). ⇨ 오명(汚名). ¶ ～을 사다 earn 〔fall into〕 bad repute; court a scandal; bring a bad name upon *oneself*.

**추모**(追慕) cherishing the memory of a deceased person. ～하다 cherish 〔respect〕 《*a person's*》 memory; look back upon the memory of 《a deceased person》 with reverence 〔affection〕. ¶ 선친을 ～하다 cherish the memory of *one's* late father / 은사를 ～하기 위하여 기념비를 세우다 set up a cenotaph to the memory of *one's* beloved teacher.

**추문**(醜聞) (a) scandal; ill fame. ¶ 놀라운 ～ a frightful scandal / ～을 일으키다 create 〔cause, make up〕 a scandal; give rise to (a) scandal / ～이 돌다 a scandal gets around 〔gets bruited about〕 / 한 여성과의 ～이 널리 퍼져 그는 많은 지지자를 잃었다 He lost a large number of supporters because a scandal over his relations with a woman got abroad. ◉ ～거리 a scandalous affair; a source of scandal. 성～ a sex scandal.

**추물**(醜物) 《물건》 an ugly 〔a dirty〕 object; 《사람》 an ugly 〔a dirty〕 person.

**추밀원**(樞密院) 《영국의》 the Privy Council.

**추방**(追放) ① 《일정 장소·조직 등에서》 expulsion; banishment; ouster 《미》; exile (귀양); deportation. ～하다 expel; banish; exile; deport; purge.

> 용법 **expel** 학교·모임 따위로부터의 제명(除名)처럼 개인 또는 작은 사회로부터의 추방. **banish** 사람을 국외로 추방한다는 뜻의 법률 용어. 역사적, 비유적으로도 쓰임. **exile** 태어난 나라로부터의 추방으로, 「유형시키다, 망명시키다」 등의 뜻. **deport** 외국인을 강제 송환, 국외 추방한다는 뜻. **purge** 공직에서 추방한다는 뜻.

¶ 빈곤의 ～ banishment of poverty / ～된 몸 a person in exile / 악서 ～운동 a campaign against harmful publications / ～을 당하다 get expelled 〔banished, exiled〕 / 국외로 ～하다 banish 〔deport〕 《*a person*》 from the land; put 〔drive〕 《*a person*》 out of the country / 학교에서 ～되다 be expelled from school / 직장에서 ～되다

be ousted from office / …의 ~을 선언하다 pronounce 《*a person's*》 exile / 이들 불법입국자를 국외로 ~하는 것이 국제법에 위반된다고 생각하십니까 Do you think it is against international law to deport those illegal aliens? ② 《공직에서의》 purge. ~하다 purge. ¶ 공직에서 ~하다 remove 〔oust〕 《*a person*》 from public office; purge 《*a person*》 from public life / ~을 해제하다 depurge; strike 《*a person's*》 name off the list of purgees / 그는 그 부정사건으로 공직에서 ~되었다 He was purged 〔removed〕 from public office because of that scandal.
◉ ~령 a deportation order; an expulsion decree. ~자 an exile; 《공직에서의》 a purgee: 국외 ~자 an exile; an expatriate. ~해제 depurge: ~해제자 a depurgee; the depurged [총칭].

**추백**(追白) = 추서(追書).

**추병**(追兵) soldiers in pursuit 〔chase〕; a pursuing party 〔force〕.

**추분(점)**(秋分(點)) the autumnal equinox.

**추비**(追肥) (applying of) additional fertilizer 〔manure〕.

**추산**(推算) calculation; computation; reckoning. ~하다 calculate; compute; reckon; 《추정하다》 estimate; put 《at》. ¶ 이익은 2,000만 원으로 ~했다 We estimated the profit at twenty million won.

**추삼삭**(秋三朔) the three autumn months.

**추상**(抽象) abstraction. ~하다 abstract 《from》. ¶ ~적(인) abstract; nonobjective; metaphysical / ~적으로 abstractly; in the abstract; in an abstract manner 〔way〕 / ~으로 말하다 speak in the abstract 〔in general terms〕.
◉ ~론 an abstract argument; generalities. ~명사 〖문법〗 an abstract noun. ~미 abstract beauty. ~예술〔미술〕 abstract art. ~적 관념 an abstract idea 〔notion〕; an abstraction. ~적 실재 an abstract entity. ~파 abstractionism: ~파 화가 an abstractionist. ~화(化) abstraction. ~화(畫) an abstract picture 〔painting〕: 반~화 a semiabstract painting.

**추상**(秋霜) ① 《서리》 autumn frost(s). ② 《엄격》 severity; sternness; mercilessness. ¶ ~ 같은 rigorous; severe; stern; relentless / ~ 같은 논고 《make》 a most relentless argument 《against》 / ~ 같은 명령 a stern order / ~ 같은 엄한 처벌 a severe punishment.

**추상**(追想) recollection; (a) retrospection; reminiscence. ~하다 look back on; recall (to *one's* memory); go over 《the past》 in *one's* mind; recollect; reflect. ¶ 과거를 ~하다 look back upon 〔to〕 the past; run back over the past / ~에 잠기다 lose *oneself* in (memories of) the past / 옛날을 ~케 하다 [사물이 주어] 「remind 《*a person*》 of 〔take 《*a person*》 back to〕 the old days; make 《*a person*》 remember the past. ◉ ~록(錄) (written) reminiscences; memoirs; recollections.

**추상**(推想) conjecture; guess; surmise; inference; imagination. ~하다 imagine; guess; conjecture; surmise; infer. ¶ 도저히 ~할 수 없다 It is past all conjecture.

**추색**(秋色) a sign 〔an indication〕 of autumn; autumn(al) colors 〔tint, scene(ry)〕. ¶ ~으로 물든 쓸쓸한 풍경 a desolate landscape enlivened by autumnal tints / ~이 완연하다 There is a definite sign of autumn in the air. *or* Autumn colors are in full glory. / ~이 깊어졌다 We are now in the midst of autumn.

**추서**(追書) a postscript (생략 P.S.). ⇨ 추신.

**추서**(追敍) posthumous honors. ~하다 honor posthumously; confer 〔give〕 posthumous honors on 《*a person*》. ⇨ 추증(追贈). ¶ 정부는 고인이 된 김박사에게 훈장을 ~하기로 결정했다 The government decided to award the late Dr. Kim a posthumous decoration.

**추서다** 《회복하다》 get strong 〔well〕 again; be *oneself* again; recover 〔regain〕 (*one's* health); come around. ¶ 일주일의 휴식으로 건강이 ~ regain *one's* health after a week's rest / 해산후에 몸이 좀처럼 추서지 않는다 She has been slow in coming around from having the child.

**추석**(秋夕) *Ch'usŏk*, the Korean Thanksgiving Day (which falls on the 15th of August by lunar calendar); the Full-moon Harvest Day. ¶ 한국 사람들에게는, ~이 여러 가지 축제 행사, 전통적인 놀이와 선물 교환 등이 어울려 행해지는 가장 명절 기분이 드는 축일이다 For Koreans, the *Ch'usŏk* is the most festive holiday with a variety of festivals, traditional games, and exchanges of gifts.
◉ ~선물 *Ch'usŏk* gifts: ~ 선물 시장 the *Ch'usŏk* gift market. ~성묘 a visit to *one's* ancestral graves on the occasion of *Ch'usŏk*: 우리는 ~ 성묘를 하기

위해 고향을 찾아간다 We make our way to hometowns to pay homage to our ancestors' graves on *Ch'usŏk.*

**추세**(趨勢) a tendency; a trend; a drift; a tide; a current; 《경과 과정》 the course 《of an event》. ¶ 시대의 ~ the current 〔trend〕 of the times / 여론의 ~ the trend 〔tendency〕 of public opinion / 일반적 ~ a general tendency / 자연의 ~ the course of nature / 현대 교육의 ~ present-day tendencies in education / 지금 ~로는 in the present state of things / 시대의 ~에 따르다〔를 거스르다〕 swim with 〔against〕 the stream 〔current〕 of the times / (자연의) ~에 맡기다 let 《*things*》 take their own course; leave 《*a matter*》 to take 〔run, follow〕 its own course; allow 《the situation》 to develop in its own way / 증가 ~에 있다 be on an increasing trend / 세상 ~에 역행하는 것은 현명치 않다 It is unwise to row against the current.
◉ 물가 ~a price trend.

**추소**(追訴) 〖법〗 a supplementary suit 〔action, indictment〕. ~하다 bring a supplementary suit 〔action〕 《against》; make a supplementary indictment.

**추속**(醜俗) unseemly 〔indecent〕 customs; ugly 〔foul〕 manners.

**추수**(秋收) (autumn) harvesting; gathering; (a) harvest. ~하다 harvest; gather in 《crops》; reap a harvest; crop. ¶ ~가 많다〔적다〕 get a good 〔poor〕 harvest 〔crop〕 / 3백석 ~ a harvest 〔crop〕 of 300 bags of rice / 파종에서 ~까지 from seedtime to harvest / ~에 바쁘다 be busy harvesting 〔gathering in *one's* crop〕. ◉ ~감사절 Thanksgiving (Day). ~기 harvest time.

**추스르다** ① 《매만져》 pick and trim; 《치켜올리다》 pick up and place in. ¶ 짚을 ~ pick straws and trim them / 업은 아이를 ~ jiggle the baby on *one's* back. ② 《일 등을》 set in order; put into shape; take care of; straighten up 〔out〕. ¶ 일을 ~ straighten matters out.

**추습**(醜習) a vice; unseemly 〔foul〕 habits; indecent practices.

**추시**(趨時) keeping pace with the times; keeping abreast of the times. ~하다 keep pace with the times; keep abreast of 〔keep up with〕 the times.

**추신**(抽身) ~하다 get *oneself* free 《from business》; disengage 〔disentangle〕 *oneself;* get away 〔absent *oneself*〕 from work. ¶ 잠시도 ~할 틈이 없다 be so busy that *one* can't get free for a moment.

**추신**(追伸) a postscript (생략 P.S.).

**추심**(推尋) 《돈의》 collection. ~하다 collect 《debts》; exact 《money from 〔of〕 a *person*》. ¶ 빚의 ~ exaction of debts.
◉ ~금 money (to be) collected; an exaction. ~료 a collection charge. ~어음 a bill for collection; a collection bill. ~위임 배서(背書) endorsement for collection. ~은행 a collection bank. ~인 a 《bill》 collector. ~장 a letter of collection. ~채무 a debt to be collected at the debtor's address.

**추썩거리다** keep shrugging 〔raising〕 《*one's* shoulders》; keep pulling up 《*one's* coat》. ¶ 어깨를 ~ keep raising 〔shrugging〕 *one's* shoulders / 옷을 ~ keep pulling up *one's* coat.

**추썩추썩** shrugging 《*one's* shoulders》 repeatedly; pulling up 《*one's* coat》 from time to time. ¶ 어깨를 ~하다 shrug *one's* shoulders from time to time.

**추악**(醜惡) ugliness; hideousness; abominableness. ~하다 《보기에》 (be) unsightly; ugly; hideous; disgusting; horrible; 《느낌·인상이》 abominable; repulsive; scandalous; monstrous. ¶ ~한 놈 a loathsome creature / ~한 짓 a dirty trick; mean conduct / ~한 인상(人相) ugly features / ~한 다툼 an abominable quarrel / ~한 사건〔소문〕 a scandalous affair 〔rumor〕 / ~하게 굴다 act 〔behave〕 vilely.

**추앙**(推仰) veneration; reverence; adoration; worship; respect. ~하다 revere; worship; adore; respect; look up to; hold 《*a person*》 in high esteem. ¶ 신(神)처럼 ~하다 deify 《*a person*》 / ~받다 be held in high esteem / 무인의 거울로 ~받다 be respected as a model soldier / 그는 일세의 사표(師表)로서 ~받았다 He was looked up to by his contemporaries as a paragon of virtue.

**추야**(秋夜) an autumn night. ¶ ~장 긴 긴 밤에 in the long nights of autumn; in autumn when the nights are long.

**추양**(秋陽) autumn sunshine; the autumn sun.

**추어**(鰍魚) 《미꾸라지》 a loach; a mud fish. ◉ ~탕 loach soup.

**추어내다** ⇨ 들추어내다.

**추어올리다** ① 《위로》 pull up; lift up; hoist. ¶ 치마를 ~ pull up *one's* skirt. ② 《치켜 세우다》 flatter; soft-soap. ¶ 그렇게 추어 올리지 말게 Don't flatter me like that.

**추어주다** praise; applaud; laud; extol; compliment; sing 〔sound〕 the praise 《of》; flatter. ¶ 일을 잘 했다고 ~ praise 《*a person*》 for doing a good job / 부하를 용감하다고 ~ applaud the bravery of *one's* men / 몹시 ~ talk up; praise 〔extol〕 《*a person*》 to the skies; speak very highly 《of 》/ 추어줄 만하다 be praiseworthy 〔laudable, commendable〕/ 그는 좀 추어주면 바로 혹한다 A little flattery will fetch him. / 추어주어 싫다는 사람은 없다 Nobody takes offense at a compliment.

**추억**(追憶) recollection; reminiscence; remembrance; retrospection; a retrospect; a reflection; a memory. ~하다 retrospect; recollect; reminisce; look back upon 〔to〕 《the past》; recall (to *one's* memory); go over 《the past》 in *one's* mind. ¶ 슬픈 ~ a sad memory / 즐거운 ~ pleasant 〔fragrant〕 memories / 어린 시절의 ~ *one's* reminiscence of childhood / ~을 더듬다 recall 〔recollect〕 the past / ~에 잠기다 indulge in retrospection / 지난 시절을 ~하게 하다 [사물이 주어] make 《*a person*》 reminiscent of the past; remind 《*a person*》 of the old days / 이것을 보니 어린 시절의 ~이 떠오른다 This reminds me of my childhood. / 이 공원은 우리의 ~을 간직하고 있다 This park has memories for us.
◉ ~거리 a remembrancer; a reminder; a memento. ~담 reminiscences; memoirs: 즐거웠던 옛 ~담을 이야기하다 talk 〔reminisce〕 about the good old days.

**추업**(醜業) a shameful 〔an immoral〕 calling; prostitution. ¶ ~에 종사하다 live a life of shame 〔prostitution〕; follow a shameful calling.

**추완**(追完) 〖법〗 subsequent completion. ~하다 complement; subsequently complete 《an act》; make subsequent completion.

**추요**(樞要) importance. ~하다 (be) important; vital; principal; chief; key; responsible (책임 있는).

**추우**(秋雨) an autumn rain.

**추운**(秋雲) an autumn cloud.

**추워지다** get 〔grow〕 cold(er); become 「chilly.

**추워하다** feel cold; be sensitive to the cold; complain of 〔about〕 the cold. ¶ 어린애가 추워한다, 담요를 더 덮어 주어라 The child complains of the cold, put another blanket over him. / 몹시 추워하는군 You are terribly susceptible to cold. *or* You get too cold.

**추월**(秋月) the autumn moon.

**추월**(追越) passing. ~하다 《차 따위가》 pass; 《경주 따위에서》 outstrip; 《따라잡다》 overtake; 《달려서》 outrun; 《앞서다》 get ahead of 《*a person*》; 《능가하다》 surpass; outdo; 《선박이》 outsail. ¶ 공업 생산에서 다른 모든 나라들을 ~하다 overtake 〔outstrip〕 all other nations in industrial production / 내 차는 트럭을 ~했다 My car 「got ahead of 〔overtook, passed〕 a truck. / 그녀는 선두에 있는 사람을 ~하여 맨 앞으로 나섰다 She has overtaken the leader and gone into the lead. / 우리나라는 자동차 생산에서 일본을 ~할 것이다 Our country will overtake 〔surpass〕 Japan in the production of cars. / 그는 여러 후배들에게 ~ 당했다 《진급·승급 등에서》 He has been outstripped by quite a few men younger than him. *or* He has seen a good many younger men promoted ahead of him.
◉ ~금지 《게시》 No passing. *or* Do not pass. *or* 《영》 Overtaking prohibited. *or* No overtaking. ~금지 구역 a no-passing 〔no-overtaking 《영》〕 zone. ~차선 a passing 〔an overtaking 《영》〕 lane.

**추위** coldness; (the) cold. ¶ 갑작스러운 ~ a cold snap / 심한 ~ the intense 〔bitter〕 cold / 살을 에는 듯한 ~ the biting 〔piercing〕 cold / ~로 떨다 shiver with cold; quiver from cold.
추위를: ~를 느끼다 feel (the) cold; 《오한이 나서》 have a chill / ~를 막다 keep off 〔out〕 the cold / ~를 견디다 stand 〔bear〕 the cold / ~를 타다 be sensitive 〔susceptible〕 to the cold / ~를 타는 체질 a cold 〔chilly〕 constitution / ~를 피하다 avoid 〔escape〕 the cold / ~를 이기려고 체조를 하다 do gymnastics to fight off the cold.
추위에: ~에 견디다 stand 〔bear〕 the cold / ~에 약하다 be oversensitive to cold; be easily affected by cold weather / ~에 익숙해지다 inure *oneself* 〔be accustomed〕 to the cold / ~에 지다 succumb to the cold.
¶ ~가 심하다 It is bitterly cold. / ~가 살을 에는 듯하다 It is biting cold. / 올

겨울 ～는 유별나다 The cold of this winter is quite unprecedented. / ～가 풀렸다 The cold has decreased in severity.

**추위**(皺胃) 《반추 동물의》 the abomasum (*pl.* -sa); the abomasus (*pl.* -si); the rennet (bag).

**추이**(推移) (a) change; (a) transition; (a) shift; development; the turn 〔course, trend〕 of affairs. ～하다 change; shift; undergo a change 〔transition〕. ¶ 시대의 ～ a shift 〔change〕 of the times / 시대의 ～와 더불어 with the change of times / 사태의 ～를 지켜보다 watch the development of events; see how things change / 어떻게 될지 ～를 두고 봅시다 Let's wait and see (what happens next).

**추인**(追認) ratification; confirmation. ～하다 ratify; confirm. ¶ ～을 받는 사람 a confirmee. ◉ ～자 a ratifier; a confirmor.

**추잠**(秋蠶) an autumn breed of silkworms. ¶ ～을 놓다 raise silkworms in autumn.

**추잡**(醜雜) filthiness; foulness; indecency; obscenity. ～하다, ～스럽다 (be) filthy; foul; indecent; obscene; vulgar; dirty; disgusting; sickening. ¶ ～한 관계 liaison; immoral intimacy / ～한 그림 an obscene 〔a filthy〕 picture / ～한 농담 a broad 〔blue〕 joke; a water-closet joke / ～한 말 a filthy 〔foul〕 talk; an indecent talk; a smutty talk / ～한 소설 an obscene 〔a hot〕 novel; a sensational 〔catching〕 novel / ～한 사람 a filthy 〔an indecent〕 person / ～한 잡지 a yellow journal 《미》 / ～한 짓 a dirty 〔an indecent〕 thing to do / ～한 소리를 하다 say improper 〔indecent〕 things / ～한 짓을 하다 take liberties with 《a woman》; commit obscene acts upon 《a girl》 / ～한 싸움을 하다 engage in mud-flinging at each other; fling 〔sling, throw〕 mud at each other.

**추장**(酋長) a chief(tain); a head.

**추장**(推奬) recommendation; commendation. ～하다 recommend; commend. ¶ ～할 만하다 be commendable 〔laudable〕; be worthy of commendation.

**추저분하다** (be) dirty and messy. ¶ 추저분한 곳 a messy place.

**추적**(追跡) chase; pursuit; tracking; 《진행·과정 등의》 (a) follow-up; tracing. ～하다 chase; pursue; give chase to; run 〔follow, be〕 after; trace; track. ¶ ～하고 있다 be in pursuit 〔chase〕 of 《the offender》; be on the track 〔trail〕 of 《a criminal》 / ～해 오다 come in pursuit / ～해 잡다 track down 《a thief》 / ～비행을 하다 fly chase 《on》 / ～시키다 send 《*a person*》 in pursuit of; put 《*a person*》 on the track of / 경관들은 곧 범인을 ～했다 The policemen were immediately 「in pursuit 〔on the track〕 of the offender. / 신문들은 정치자금의 흐름을 ～하고 있다 The papers are trying to trace the flow of money to politicians.

◉ ～권(權) 《국경을 넘어 추적할 수 있는》 the right of hot pursuit. ～기(機) a pursuit plane. ～기지〔장치〕 《인공위성 따위의》 a tracking station 〔device〕. ～원소 〖화학·생리〗 a tracer element. ～자 a pursuer; a chaser. ～조사 a follow-up 〔tracing〕 survey: ～조사를 하다 conduct a follow-up survey 《of, on》.

**추절**(秋節) 《미》 (the) fall; (the) autumn.

**추접스럽다** (be) dirty; mean; sordid; low-down. ¶ 추접스러운 놈 a dirty 〔low-down〕 guy / 추접스러운 생각 a mean 〔low-down〕 idea / 추접스럽게 굴다 behave in a mean 〔low-down〕 fashion.

**추접지근하다** (be) rather dirty and messy.

**추젓**(秋—) tiny shrimps salted in autumn.

**추정**(推定) an estimate; (a) presumption; (an) assumption; (an) inference; (an) illation; (an) estimation. ～하다 presume; assume; infer; estimate; draw a deduction. ¶ ～적(인) presumptive; assumed; constructive / 사실의 ～ presumption of fact / ～에 의하면 it is estimated that…. / 유죄로 ～하다 presume 《*a person*》 to be guilty / 그림을 어느 화가〔시대〕의 작품으로 ～하다 attribute a painting to 「an artist 〔a particular period〕 / 네가 말하는 것은 단지 ～에 불과하다 What you say amounts to a mere presumption. / 피해 총액은 약 5억원으로 ～됐다 The sum total of (the) damage is estimated at five hundred million won. / 그 사본의 연대는 8세기에서 10세기 사이라고 ～된다 The date of the manuscript is presumed somewhere between the eighth and tenth centuries.

◉ ～가격 the presumed 〔estimated〕

value 《of》. ~량 an estimated volume. ~매장량 an estimated 《bituminous》 deposit 《of》. ~범죄 a constructive crime. ~상속인 〖법〗 an heir presumptive (*pl.* heirs presumptive). ~연령 the「estimated 〔probable〕 age 《of the victim》:「그 사내의 나이를 얼마로 ~했습니까」—「20세 정도라고 생각합니다」 "How old would you estimate the man was?"—"I would say about 20 years old." ~위치 the estimated position 《of a plane》. ~전손(全損) 〖해상보험〗 constructive total loss. ~점유 constructive possession. ~증거 presumptive evidence.

**추종**(追從) following; 《모방》 imitation. ~하다 follow (in the footsteps of); follow suit; be servile to 《public opinion》. ¶ ~자들 followers; henchmen; hangers-on; *one's* admiring satellites / 타의 ~을 불허하다 be peerless; be without a peer; have no equal; be unrivaled 《by》; be second to none; outclass 〔outstrip〕 others / 그 나라의 외교 정책은 미국을 ~하고 있다 Regarding foreign policy, the country is closely following in America's footsteps. / 식물학자로서 그는 남의 ~을 불허한다 As a botanist, he is in a class by himself. / 그녀의 연기는 타의 ~을 불허한다 Her performance is second to none.

**추증**(追贈) posthumous conferment of honors. ~하다 confer 〔honor〕 posthumously.

**추지**(推知) (a) guess; (a) conjecture; (an) inference; (a) surmise. ~하다 guess; conjecture; surmise; infer 《from》; draw an inference 《from》; gather 《from》. 「걸레 a damp cloth.

**추지다** (be) damp; moist; wet. ¶ 추진

**추진**(推進) propulsion; drive. ~하다 propel; drive 〔push, thrust〕 forward; push ahead 《with, on》; expedite; step up; promote. ¶ 계획을 ~하다 go 〔move〕 ahead with a plan; carry forward a scheme / 자연 보호 운동을 ~하다 promote a (nature-)conservation movement / …을 위한 각종 시책들을 꾸준히 ~하다 steadily carry out various projects to… / 그들은 나의 충고를 무시하고 그 계획을 ~했다 They pushed「on 〔forward〕 with their plan in spite of my advice.

◉ ~기 a propeller; a screw (배의). ~력 (a) driving force; propelling power; propulsive force; a thrust: 백만 파운드의 ~력을 내다 generate 〔yield, develop〕 a thrust of a million pounds. ~모체 a nucleus. ~제〔용 연료〕 a propellant; a propellent: 일원(一元)~제 a monopropellant / 이원(二元)~제 a bipropellant.

**추징**(追徵) additional 〔supplementary〕 collection; supplementary charge. ~하다 collect in addition; make a supplementary charge; make an additional collection of; 《벌로서》 impose a penalty 《of 20,000 won》 on 《*a person*》. ¶ 그는 70만 원의 소득세를 ~당했다 《벌로서》 He was charged an additional seven hundred thousand won for income tax.

◉ ~금 money「collected 〔paid〕 in addition; an additional imposition; 《벌금》 a forfeit; a penalty. ~세 a penalty tax; tax penalty.

**추찰**(推察) (a) conjecture; a guess; (an) inference; (a) surmise. ~하다 conjecture; guess; infer; surmise; gather 《from》; guess. ¶ 남의 마음을 ~하다 read another's mind; enter into *a person's* feelings / 나의 ~이 맞는다면 … if I guess right…; if my guess is not wrong.

**추천**(推薦) recommendation. ~하다 recommend 《*a person* for a post》;「put in 〔say〕 a good word 《for *a person*》; propose(회원으로); sponsor(후원하다); nominate 《for, as》(지명하다).

¶ 유력한 ~ weighty recommendation / 아무의 ~으로 by 〔through〕 the recommendation of *a person;* on 〔at〕 the recommendation of *a person* / …을 회원으로〔어떤 자리에〕 ~하다 recommend 《*a person*》「for membership 〔for a position〕 / …을 간곡히 ~하다 give *one's* hearty recommendation to… / 후보자를 ~하다「put up 〔nominate〕 a candidate / 그분에게 잘 좀 ~해 주십시오 Please put in a good word for me with him. / 당신이라면 기꺼이〔안심하고〕 ~하겠소 I will「gladly 〔confidently〕 recommend you. / 저 사람은 ~할 수 없다 I don't have a good word to say for him. / 그녀는 교수 ~으로 교사로 취직했다 She got a position as a teacher through the recommendation of her professor.

◉ ~생 a recommended student. ~연설 《make》 a speech to recommend 《*a person*》 《for》. ~입학제 the system of admitting students into colleges on the recommendations of their high

school principals. ～자 a recommender; an introducer; a proposer; a sponsor: 피～자 a recommendee; a nominee. ～작가 a recommended writer. ～장〔서〕 a letter of recommendation; 《소개장》 a letter of introduction; an introductory letter. ～후보 a recommended candidate: 민주당 ～후보 a candidate recommended by the Democratic Party.
교육부 ～ 영화 a film recommended by the Ministry of Education.

**추첨**(抽籤) a lot; a draw; a lottery; a raffle (복권식의). ～하다 draw lots; hold a lottery. ¶～으로 by lottery; by drawing lots / ～으로 순번을 정하다 draw lots for turns / ～에 뽑히다 draw 〔have, get〕 a winning number (in a lottery); win (a prize) in a lottery / ～에 떨어지다 draw 〔have, get〕 a losing number; draw a blank / ～으로 정하다 draw lots to decide 《who does, whether...》; decide by drawing lots / 준결승의 대진～은 내일 행해진다 The draw for the semifinals will be made tomorrow. ◉ ～권〔기〕 a lottery「ticket 〔wheel (회전식)〕. ～번호 a lottery number. ～제 the lottery system: ～제 중학 입학 the lottery (and ward) system for middle school entrance.

**추축**(樞軸) 《기계의》 a pivot; an axle; an axis (*pl.* axes); 《중추》 a central point; the center 《of power》. ◉ ～국 《2차 대전 시의》 the Axis powers.

**추출**(抽出) abstraction; 〚화학〛 extraction; 《통계 조사에서》 sampling. ～하다 draw; extract; abstract; sample 《a population》. ¶무작위로 ～한 견본 a random sample / 사탕수수에서 설탕을 ～하다 extract sugar from sugar canes / 올리브의 열매에서 귀중한 기름이 ～된다 A valuable oil is extracted from olives. ◉ ～검사 a sampling inspection; a spot check. ～물 an extract: 증류 ～물 a distilled extract. ～법 a sampling process: 임의 ～법 a random sampling method; random sampling. ～용 용제(溶劑) 〚화학〛 an extractant. ～조사 a sample survey. ～표본 a sampling.

**추측**(推測) (a) guess; (a) surmise; (a) conjecture; (a) supposition; (a) presumption; (an) inference ～하다 guess; suppose; presume; gather 《from》; assume; infer 《from》; conjecture; speculate.

> (용법) **guess** 「추측하다」란 뜻으로 가장 흔히 쓰이는 일반적인 낱말. 충분한 증거나 확증이 없는 경우에 「…라고 짐작되다」란 막연한 추측을 나타냄. **suppose** guess와 대체로 뜻이 같으며, 추측해서 「…이 아닌가 생각하다」, 「…일지도 모른다고 생각하다」의 뜻. **presume** 확증은 없지만 느낌이나 경험에 의해 「추정하다」란 뜻. assume보다 뜻이 강하다. **gather** 들은 것, 행해진 것, 인상 따위에서 「추측하다」란 뜻. **assume** 증거도 없고, 의견 차이도 있지만 자기 생각에 「…일 것이라고 추측하다」의 뜻.

¶내 ～으로는 in my guess / ～으로「at a 〔by〕 guess; by inference / ～대로 as「conjectured 〔supposed〕 / 근거 있는 ～ a well-founded conjecture / ～이 맞다〔틀리다〕 guess「right 〔wrong〕; be「right 〔wrong〕 in *one's* conjecture / ～에 맡기다 leave 《*something*》 to 《*a person's*》 conjecture / ～에 지나지 않다 be mere guesswork; be a mere conjecture (and nothing more) / ～해서 말하다 speak from inference / 선거의 결과를 ～하다 guess the outcome of the election / 지원자가 천 명이 되리라고 ～하다 put the number of applicants at a thousand; estimate the applicants to number 1,000 / 어떤 사실에서 어떤 결과를 ～하다 infer a result from a certain fact / ～할 길이 없다 There is no guessing. *or* It is past (all) conjecture. / 그 밖엔 달리 ～할 수가 없다 I have no other conjecture to「offer 〔make〕 on it. / 내 ～은 틀리지 않았다 It was just as I had guessed. *or* I was right in my conjecture. / 내 ～으로는 그는 50세 가량이다 I should suppose him to be fifty. / 말씨로 ～건대 그는 외국 사람인 것 같다 I presume from his speech that he is a foreigner. ◉ ～기사 a speculative news「story 〔article〕. ～항법 〚해양·항공〛 dead reckoning.

**추켜들다** raise; hold up; lift (up); give 《a stone》 a lift; heave. ¶추켜들려고 하다 try to lift 《*something*》 / 어린아이를 ～ raise a boy aloft.

**추켜잡다** lift (up); hold up. ¶끌리는 치맛자락을 ～ hold up *one's* skirt to keep it from dragging.

**추키다** lift (up); hold up; hitch up. ¶바지를 ～ hitch up *one's* trousers.

**추탕**(鰍湯) loach soup.

**추태**(醜態) 《행동》 disgraceful behavior;

shameful 〔scandalous〕 conduct; 《외관》 an unseemly sight; 《상태》 a scandalous situation 〔state of affairs〕. ¶ ～를 부리다 act disgracefully; behave *oneself* disgracefully 〔in a shameful manner〕; make a (sorry) display of *oneself;* cut a sorry 〔a ridiculous, an unseemly〕 figure; make 〔create〕 an ugly scene / ～를 드러내다 reveal its scandalous nature 〔situation〕.

**추토**(追討) pursuing 《a routed army, a thief, *etc.*》 to subjugate. ～하다 hunt down and kill; track down and dispose of. ◉ ～군(軍) a punitive force. ～사(使) a general sent to chastise rebels.

**추파**(秋波) an amorous 〔a coquettish〕 glance; an ogle. ¶ ～를 던지다〔보내다〕 make (sheep's) eyes 《at》; ogle 《at》; cast 「an amorous 〔a coquettish〕 glance 《at》/ 그는 여자라면 누구에게나 ～를 던진다 He winks at every girl. *or* He makes sheep's eyes at every girl.

**추풍**(醜風) unseemly 〔indecent〕 cus-「toms.

**추풍**(秋風) an autumn wind 〔breeze〕. ◉ ～낙엽 falling leaves in the autumn wind: ～낙엽 같다 be like leaves falling in the autumn wind.

**추하다**(醜―) ① 《용모 등이》 (be) ugly; bad-looking; ugly-looking; plain; uncomely; 《미》 homely; ill-favored; unlovely. ¶ 추한 얼굴 an ugly face / 추한 여자 a plain 〔an ugly〕 woman / 그녀는 화상을 입어 얼굴이 추해졌다 Her face was disfigured by a burn.
② 《꼴사납다》 (be) unseemly; unsightly; indecent; unbecoming; 《수치스럽다》 (be) ignoble; ignominious; disgraceful; shameful; dishonorable; mean. ¶ 추한 관계 an improper relation; an illicit connection / 추한 짓 a dirty trick; indecent behavior; shameful conduct / 추한 관계를 맺다 have an 「illicit connection 〔evil relation〕 with / 추하게 굴다 behave in a shameful 〔low-down〕 fashion / (경기에서) 추하게 지다 be a bad loser; lose 《a game》 with (a) bad grace / 추하지 않은 복장을 하고 있다 be decently 〔respectably〕 dressed.

**추한**(醜漢) an ugly customer; a mean guy; a low-down type.

**추해당**(秋海棠) 〖식물〗 a begonia; an elephant's-ear.

**추행**(醜行) ugly 〔ignominious, shameful, scandalous〕 conduct; a misdeed; infamous 〔abominable, odious〕 conduct; an indecent act; a scandal. ¶ (여자에게) ～을 하다 commit obscene acts upon 《a woman》; make a sexual attack on 《a girl》 / ～을 들춰내다 bring a scandal to light; expose a scandal.

**추호**(秋毫) a bit; a whit; a hair; an atom. ¶ ～도 《not》 in the least; 《not》 at all; 《not》 a bit; 《not》 the slightest; 《not》 in any degree / 그런 일은 ～도 걱정 않는다 I don't care a straw about such a thing. / 남을 해칠 생각은 ～도 없었다 I didn't have the slightest intention to harm others. / 그런 짓을 하고도 그는 ～도 양심의 가책을 안 느꼈다 He never felt the slightest pang of remorse for such a deed. / 내 말에는 ～도 거짓이 없다 I mean everything I say. *or* Cross my heart, I'm not telling a lie. / 그에게는 양심 따위는 ～도 없다 He doesn't have 「a spark 〔an ounce, an atom〕 of conscience.

**추화**(秋花) an autumn flower.

**추확**(秋穫) harvest(ing) in autumn.

**추회**(追懷) recollection; reminiscence; retrospection. ⇨ 추억(追憶).

**추후**(追後) ¶ ～에 later (on); afterwards; 《이윽고》 by and by; in due (course of) time; in due course / ～ 통지가 있을 때까지 till further notice / 그것에 관해서는 ～에 논하기로 하자 We shall make mention of it later (on). / 정확한 정보는 ～ 우송한다 More exact information follows by mail.

**추흥**(秋興) pleasures 〔delights〕 of autumn; autumn fun.

**축**(丑) 〖민속〗 ① 《십이지의》 the Sign of the Ox (= the 2nd of 12 Earth's Branches). ② ⇨ 축방. ③ ⇨ 축시.

**축**(祝) a written prayer (offered at ancestor memorial service). ⇨ 축문.

**축**(逐) 《바둑》 being cornered always by one move.

**축**(軸) ① 《굴대》 an axis (*pl.* axes); an axle; 〖기계〗 an arbor; a spindle; a shaft; a pintle; 《추축》 a pivot. ¶ 수평축〔횡축〕 a horizontal 〔transverse〕 axis / 수직축 a vertical 〔longitudinal〕 axis / 지구는 그 축을 중심으로 24시간에 1회전한다 The earth turns on its axis once in 24 hours. ② 《지물의》 a roll; a ream. ¶ 종이 두 축 two rolls of paper.

**축**(縮) (a) lack; a deficit; deficiency; (a) shortage; shrinkage. ⇨ 축나다.

**축**[1] 《무리》 a group; a gang; a bunch 《of people, things》; a set.
¶ 한 축(one and) the same gang / 축에 들다〔끼이다〕《어울리다》 join 《a party》; mix *oneself* 《among》; 《부류에》 take *one's* place 《in, among》; be reckoned 〔numbered〕《among》/ 선진국 축에 끼이다 rank 〔be numbered〕 among the advanced nations / 축에도 못 들다 be insignificant; count for nothing 〔little〕; be of no account / 그이도 똑똑한 축에 든다 He is one of the clever ones. / 그 사람에 비하면 나 따위는 인간 축에도 못듭니다 I am a mere nothing before him. / 그래 뵈도 그 중에서는 그들이 가장 나은 축이라고 생각한다 They may not look like much but they're the best of the lot, I guess.

**축**[2] 《처진 모양》 drooping(ly); danglingly; limply. ¶ 축 늘어지다 hang loose 〔limply〕; dangle; 《지쳐서》 be dead tired; 《구어》 be dog-tired; be washed= out / 축 늘어진 귀 drooped 〔drooping, droopy〕 ears / 어깨가 축 늘어지다 *one's* shoulders droops; have drooping shoulders.

**축가**(祝歌) a song of congratulation 〔celebration〕; a festive song.
◉ 결혼 ～ a nuptial song.

**축가다**(縮—) 《수량이》 decrease; diminish; 《몸이》 lose weight. = 축나다.

**축감**(縮減) reduction; decrease; lessening. ～하다 be decreased 〔reduced, lessened〕; decrease; reduce; lessen.

**축객**(逐客) ～하다 turn a guest out; drive a visitor away. ¶ 문전 ～하다 refuse to see 《*a person*》; turn away a visitor at the door; shut the door on 〔to〕《*a person*》/ 문전 ～을 당하다 be turned away at the door; be refused admittance.

**축견**(畜犬) a kept 〔domestic〕 dog.

**축구**(蹴球) 《사커》 soccer; 《영》 (association) football (★ football이라고 하면 미국에서는 주로 미식 축구, 영국에서는 주로 럭비를 가리킴). ¶ 2002년(도) 월드컵 ～ the 2002 World Cup Soccer / ～를 하다 play soccer 〔football〕/ 그는 ～를 잘 한다 He is a good soccer player.
◉ ～경기〔시합〕 a soccer game. ～계 the world of soccer 〔football〕. ～공 a soccer ball. ～선수 a soccer 〔football〕 player; a soccerite; a footballer. ～장 a soccer 〔football〕 field. ～팀 a soccer 〔football〕 team; the eleven.
국제～연맹 the Fédération Internationale de Football Association (생략 FIFA). 대한 ～ 협회 the Korea Football Association.

**축나다**(縮—) 《수량이》 decrease; diminish; lessen; be deficient 〔lacking, missing〕; become 〔fall, come〕 short 《of 》; be found short 《of》; be reduced; 《몸이》 get 〔become〕 lean 〔thin〕; lose weight; lose flesh (병으로). ¶ 돈이 3백 원 ～ there is a deficit 〔shortage〕 of 300 won; 300 won is found missing / 벼가 말라서 한 섬에 두 되가 축났다 The rice has dried out and comes to 2 *toe* short of a *sŏm.* / 공부를 너무 하여 그는 몸이 좀 축났다 He lost some weight due to his hard study.

**축내다**(縮—) cause a loss 〔deficit〕; reduce a sum by 《a certain amount》; spend 《part of a sum》; take a bite of a sum; 《공금 등을》 defalcate; appropriate (도용하다). ¶ 은행돈을 약 백만 원 ～ appropriate about one million won of the bank's money 《for *one's* private use》/ 5천 원에서 천원을 ～ reduce the 5,000 won by 1,000; spend 1,000 of the 5,000 won; take 1,000 won from the 5,000.

**축년**(丑年) 〖민속〗 the Year of the Ox.

**축농증**(蓄膿症) 〖의학〗 ozena; empyema.

**축대**(築臺) an elevation; an embankment; a terrace. ¶ 위험 ～ an embankment in dangerous conditions / ～를 쌓다 build a ground up high / ～가 무너지다 an embankment collapses.

**축도**(祝禱) 〖기독교〗 (a) benediction; a blessing. ¶ ～를 하다 give a benediction; pronounce a benediction 《upon the congregation》.

**축도**(縮圖) a reduced drawing 〔copy〕; a miniature (copy); an epitome; a microcosm 《of 》. ¶ 사회〔미국〕의 ～ society 〔America〕 in miniature 〔microcosm〕/ 세계의 ～ the world in epitome / 인생〔현대 생활〕의 ～ an epitome of human 〔modern〕 life / ～를 그리다 make a miniature copy 《of 》; represent 〔draw〕《*a thing*》 on a smaller scale; scale down / 에머슨은 인간을 우주의 ～라고 생각했다 Emerson considered man (to be) the universe in microcosm. ◉ ～기(器) a pantograph; an eidograph.

**축록**(逐鹿) running for a high position; competition for a high office.

**축문**(祝文) a written prayer (offered at ancestor memorial service); a form of invocation. ¶ ～을 읽다 recite a written 〔ritual〕 prayer / ~을 쓰다 write 〔prepare〕 a prayer.

**축방**(丑方) 〖민속〗 the Direction of the Ox, northeast-by-north.

**축배**(祝杯) a toast; a celebratory drink. ¶ ~를 들다 drink a toast 《for, to》; drink 〔toast〕 (to) 《*a person's*》 health 〔success〕; drink in celebration of 《an event》 / 서로 ~를 들다 toast each other / 신랑 신부를 위해 ~를 들다 toast the bride and bridegroom / 김 군의 도미를 축하하여 ~를 들다 drink a toast for Kim to celebrate his going to America / ~합시다 Bottoms up! *or* Your health! *or* Here's to you! / 한 선생의 건강〔성공〕을 축하하며 ~를 드십시다 Let's drink to the health 〔success〕 of Mr. Han. / 그는 김 군을 위해 ~를 들자고 제의했다 He proposed a toast for 〔to〕 Mr. Kim.

**축복**(祝福) a blessing; (a) benediction. ~하다 bless; give 《*a person*》 *one's* blessing; give 〔pronounce〕 a benediction upon 《*a person*》. ¶ ~받은 나라 a blessed 〔God-favored〕 country / ~을 받다 be blessed; 「be given 〔receive〕 a benediction / 앞날을 ~하다 wish 《*a person*》 「good luck 〔a happy future〕 / 그대에게 ~이 있기를 (May) God bless you! / 두 사람은 양친과 친구들의 ~을 받으며 결혼했다 They got married with the blessings of their parents and friends. ◉ ~기도 《pronounce》 a benediction; a blessing.

**축사**(畜舍) a cattle shed 〔pen〕; a barn.

**축사**(祝辭) a congratulatory 〔complimentary〕 address 〔speech〕; (a message of) congratulations; felicitations. ¶ ~를 하다 deliver a congratulatory 〔felicitatory〕 address 《at a ceremony》; offer 〔tender, extend〕 *one's* congratulations 〔felicitations〕 《to *a person*》; congratulate 《*a person* on *his* success》 / ~를 낭독하다 read (aloud) a congratulatory address 〔message〕. ◉ 결혼~ wedding congratulations.

**축사**(縮寫) 《행위》 making a reduced copy; 《축사도》 a miniature 〔reduced〕 copy; a miniature reproduction. ~하다 draw 〔copy〕 《a map》 on a smaller scale; make a reduced copy 《of》. ¶ ~하여 in miniature / 지도를 1,000분의 1로 ~하다 draw a map on a scale of one to a thousand / 사진을 ~하다 reduce (the size of) a photograph / 실물의 5분의 1로 ~하다 reduce 《*a thing*》 to a scale of one fifth the natural size. ◉ ~도 = 축도(縮圖). ~사진 a reduced photograph.

**축산**(畜産) stock raising 〔farming〕; stockbreeding; livestock raising; animal husbandry. ⇨ 축산업.
◉ ~농가 a stock farmer. ~물 stock farm products. ~물 가공 처리법 the Livestock Processing Act. ~시험장 the Livestock Experiment Station. ~자금 (government) loans for livestock industry. ~장려 promotion 〔encouragement〕 of livestock farming. ~조합 a stock-raisers' association; a cooperative of livestock raisers. ~학 (the study of) animal husbandry; zootechny: ~학과 the department of animal husbandry.

**축산업**(畜産業) stockbreeding; stock raising; livestock raising 〔farming〕; the livestock industry.
◉ ~자 a livestock raiser 〔farmer〕; a stockbreeder. ~ 협동조합 중앙회 the National Livestock Cooperatives Federation.

**축생**(畜生) a dumb animal; a beast; a brute. ◉ ~도 〖불교〗 the tormenting purgatory; the World 〔Realm, Hell〕 of Beasts: ~도에 빠지다 degrade *oneself* to the level of the brute.

**축성**(祝聖) 〖가톨릭〗 consecration; sanctification. ~하다 consecrate; sanctify. ¶ ~된 consecrated; oblate.

**축성**(築城) castle construction 〔building〕; fortification. ~하다 build 〔construct〕 a castle; fortify 《a hill》. ¶ 야전~ field fortification. ◉ ~학〔술〕 (the science 〔art〕 of) fortification.

**축소**(縮小) (a) reduction; curtailment; retrenchment; abridg(e)ment; a cut; a scale-down; (a) contraction (단축). ~하다 reduce; curtail 《expenses》; retrench; abridge; cut 〔scale〕 down; 《단축하다》 contract. ¶ 군비의 ~ a reduction in armaments; a cutback in military strength / 예산의 ~ a reduction in revenue / 규모를 ~하여 on a reduced scale / 규모를 ~하다 reduce the plan 《of》; downscale / 군비를 ~하다 reduce 〔cut down〕 armaments / 인원을 ~하다 reduce 〔cut〕 the personnel 《of the factory》 / 그는 불경기 때문에 사업을 ~해야 했다 He had to make cutbacks in his business because of the depression. *or* The depression made him 「cut back 〔curtail〕 his business. ◉ ~판 = 축쇄

판. ~형 a miniature.

**축쇄**(縮刷) 〖인쇄〗 printing in smaller type 〔reduced size〕. ~하다 print in 「smaller type 〔reduced size〕; print a reduced-size edition 《of》. ◉ ~판(版) a reduced-〔smaller-〕size edition; a tabloid 〔pocket〕 edition: ~판으로 내다 publish 〔issue〕 in reduced size.

**축수**(祝手) ~하다 pray with *one's* hands pressed together; pray with joined 〔folded〕 hands; invoke by prayer. ¶ 병을 낫게 해 달라고 신에게 ~하다 pray to God for the recovery of *one's* health / 아무의 건강〔행운〕을 ~하다 wish *a person* good health 〔luck〕.

**축수**(祝壽) ~하다 wish 《*a person*》 a long life.

**축승**(祝勝) celebration of a victory; rejoicings over a victory. ¶ ~ 잔치를 하다〔베풀다〕 hold 〔give〕 a party in celebration of a victory; hold a victory celebration.

**축시**(丑時) 〖민속〗 the Watch of the Ox. ① the 2nd of the 12 double hours (= the period between 1 and 3 a.m.). ② the 3rd of the 24 hours (= 1:30-2:30 a.m.).

**축어**(逐語) ¶ ~적(으로) word for word; verbatim; literal(ly) / ~적으로 번역하다 translate 《a passage》 「word for word 〔verbatim〕. ◉ ~(번)역 literal 〔word-for-word, verbatim〕 translation 〔rendering〕.

**축연**(祝宴) a (congratulatory) banquet 〔feast〕 《given in honor of *a person*, held in celebration of an event》. ¶ ~을 베풀다 hold a feast in honor of 《*a person*》; hold a banquet in celebration of 《an event》.

**축우**(畜牛) a domestic cow 〔ox〕; [총칭] 「cattle.

**축원**(祝願) praying; a prayer; petition; (a) supplication. ~하다 pray 《for》; invoke; petition; supplicate; wish. ¶ 세계 평화를 ~하다 pray for the peace of the world / 신의 은총을 ~하다 pray to God for mercy / 아들의 성공을 ~하다 pray that *one's* son may succeed / 여행길이 무사하기를 ~하다 wish 《*a person*》 a good journey / 전승을 ~하다 pray for a victory in the war. ◉ ~문 a written prayer.

**축음기**(蓄音機) a gramophone; a phonograph 《주로 미》; a record player. ¶ 판이 자동적으로 바뀌는 ~ a phonograph with an automatic record changer / ~를 틀다 play 〔turn on〕 a phonograph; play 〔spin〕 a record; set a phonograph going / ~를 멈추다〔끄다〕 turn off a phonograph. ◉ ~바늘 (phonograph) needle; a stylus. ~음악 phonograph music; music on records 〔disks〕. ~판 a record; a disk.

**축의**(祝意) congratulations 《on》; *one's* good 〔best〕 wishes. ¶ ~를 표하여 in honor of 《*a person*》; in celebration of 《an event》 / ~를 표하다 extend 〔offer〕 *one's* congratulations 〔felicitations〕; express *one's* congratulations 〔good wishes〕; congratulate 〔felicitate〕 《*a person* on *his* success》 / 국기를 걸어 ~를 표하다 hoist the national flags to celebrate the day / 나는 그의 사업 성공에 ~를 표했다 I congratulated him on his success in business.

**축의**(祝儀) 《축하》 a celebration; a commemoration; 《정표》 a (congratulatory) gift; a present; 《돈》 a tip; a gratuity. ◉ ~금 《봉투에 넣은》 an envelope for presenting a gift of money.

**축이다** wet; moisten; damp(en); 《담그다》 dip. ¶ 목〔입술〕을 ~ moisten *one's* throat 〔lips〕 / 수건을 ~ wet 〔damp〕 a towel / 수건을 축여서 이마에 대다 apply a damped 〔moist〕 towel to *one's* forehead.

**축일**(祝日) a festival (day); a festive 〔festal〕 day; a fête 〔feast, gala〕 day; a public 〔legal〕 holiday; a red-letter day (★ 달력에 붉은 글씨로 표시한 일에 기인함); a flag day.

**축일**(逐一) 《하나씩》 one after another; one by one; 《상세히》 minutely; fully; in detail. ¶ ~ 보고하다 report in detail; make a detailed report.

**축일**(逐日) 《날마다》 day after 〔by〕 day; daily; every day. ¶ ~ 회의하다 confer 〔hold conferences〕 day after day.

**축장**(蓄藏) hoarding; storage; accumulation 《of》. ~하다 hoard; store; keep.

**축재**(蓄財) 《행위》 accumulation of wealth 〔riches〕; saving money; 《돈》 a store of money; amassed 〔accumulated, piled-up〕 wealth. ~하다 accumulate 〔amass〕 wealth. ¶ 그는 ~에 급급하고 있다 He is striving hard after wealth. *or* He is bent on moneymaking. / 정부는 부패 공무원의 부정 ~ 재산을 몰수하기 위해 국가의 권한을 강화하는 관련법 개정을 고려하고 있다 The government is considering revising relevant laws to empower the state to confiscate illegally gained assets of corrupt civil servants. ◉ ～자 a wealth accumulator; a moneymaker; a thrifty person; a moneygrubber. 부정～ illegal profiteering; property amassed by illegal means: 부정～자 an illicit fortune maker.

**축적**(蓄積) accumulation; storage; stockpiling. ～하다 accumulate; amass; store 〔hoard〕 up; stockpile. ¶ 자본〔부〕의 ～ accumulation of「capital 〔wealth〕/ 장기간에 걸친 농약의 체내 ～ a long term「accumulation 〔build=up〕 of agricultural chemicals in the body / 시량(柴糧)을 ～하다 lay in (a store of) rice and firewood / 재산을 ～하다 amass wealth; pile up a fortune / 지식을 ～하다 accumulate a store of knowledge / 에너지를 ～하다 store up energy / 우리는 ～효과를 알지 못하는 갖가지 화학물질을 음식물을 통해 체내로 흡수하고 있다 With our food we are taking in various chemical substances whose cumulative effects are unknown.
◉ ～배당 an accumulated dividend. ～이자 accumulated interest. 자본～론 the theory of capital accumulation.

**축전**(祝典) a celebration; a festival; festivities; 《기념제》 a commemoration. ¶ 25〔50, 60〕주년 ～ the「silver 〔golden, diamond〕 jubilee. ◉ 기념～ a commemoration festival: 50주년 기념 ～을 올리다 hold a celebration of the 50th anniversary 《of》.

**축전**(祝電) a「congratulatory 〔greetings〕 telegram; a (telegraphic) message of congratulations; a telegram of good wishes. ¶ ～을 치다〔보내다〕 send a congratulatory telegram 《to》; telegraph 〔wire, cable〕 *one's* congratulations 《to》; send 《*a person*》 *one's* congratulations by wire / ～이 잇따라 날아 들었다 Messages of congratulations came pouring in.

**축전**(蓄電) accumulation 〔storage〕 of electricity. ～하다 store electricity.
◉ ～기(器) a 〔an electric〕 condenser: 가변(可變)〔고정〕 ～기 a「variable 〔fixed〕 condenser. ～식 검전기(檢電器) a condensing electroscope. ～지(池) a storage「battery 〔cell〕; an accumulator.

**축전**(縮戰) deescalation of a war. ～하다 deescalate a war.

**축정**(築庭) landscape gardening. ～하다 garden; make a garden.

**축제**(築堤) (em)banking; embankment. ～하다 construct a riverbank; embank 〔dike〕 《a river》. ◉ ～공사 embanking; embankment works.

**축제**(祝祭) a festival; a fête; a gala. ¶ 노래와 춤의 ～ a song-and-dance festival / ～때에 on (the occasion of) a festival / ～ 기분이다 be in a festive mood / ～를 지내다 keep 〔observe, celebrate〕 a festival. ◉ ～일 a public holiday; a「fête 〔gala, festival〕 day.

**축조**(逐條) article by article; item by item; point by point; *seriatim* (L.). ◉ ～심의〔토의〕「an article-by-article 〔a clause-by-clause〕 discussion: ～심의하다 discuss 《a bill》 article by article; go through 《a plan》 item by item.

**축조**(築造) building; construction. ～하다 build; construct; erect. ◉ ～물 a building; a structure; an edifice.

**축중합**(縮重合) 〖화학〗 condensation polymerization.

**축지다**(縮―) ① 《사람 가치가》 discredit *oneself;* fall into discredit; bring discredit on *oneself.* ¶ 인기가 ～ lose *one's* popularity. ② 《몸이》 become weaker; lose weight; fail in health; get run down. ¶ 그는 앓아서 몸이 몹시 축졌다 He is terribly run down since his illness.

**축지법**(縮地法) a magic method of contracting space; "Seven-League Boots". ¶ ～을 쓰다 contract space by magic.

**축짓다**(軸―) 《추축을》 make a pivot; 《굴대를》 fix an axle; 《종이로》 roll paper into a roll.

**축차적**(逐次的) ¶ ～으로 《하나씩》 one by one; one after another 〔the other〕; point by point; 《차례로》 in order; 《연속적으로》 successively; in succession; 《서서히》 gradually.

**축척**(縮尺) 《a map on》 a reduced scale. ～하다 scale 《*a thing*》 down. ¶ ～ 천분의 1, the scale of one to a thousand; 《지도에서의 표기》 Scale: 1/1,000 / ～ 3만분의 1 지도 a map「drawn on 〔with〕 a scale of 1 to 30,000; a one=to-thirty-thousand map / ～ 7분의 1 모형 a one-seventh scale model 《of》/ 미국 잠수함 「노틸러스」의 실제 크기 98미터를 2미터로 ～한 모형 a model of U.S. submarine Nautilus scaled down to 2 meters from a real-life 98.
◉ ～도(圖) a map on a reduced scale.

**축첩**(蓄妾) keeping a「concubine 〔mistress〕; concubinage. ～하다 keep a mistress 〔concubine〕. ¶ ～공무원을 파면하다 fire a government official who has a concubine. ◉ ～제도 concubinage.

**축축** 《늘어진 모양》 all drooping 〔dangling〕 low; all sagging low; dingle=dangle; all limply. ¶ 나뭇가지가 ～ 늘어지다 the branches all droop low.

**축축하다** (be) slightly 〔moderately〕 wet; damp(ish); humid; moist; clammy; [서술적] feel damp. ¶ 축축한 공기 damp 〔humid〕 air / 축축한 날씨 damp 〔soft, sticky〕 weather; a damp 〔muggy〕 day / 축축한 바람 a damp 〔humid, moisture-laden〕 wind / 옷이 ～ my clothes feel wet / 등골에 땀이 ～ *one's* back is damp 〔clammy〕 with sweat / 땅이 비에 젖어 ～ the ground is wet from the rain / 밤이슬을 맞아 ～ be wet 〔damp〕 with night dew / 축축하고 퀴퀴하다 be damp and musty / 짚을 축축하게 축이다 moisten 〔dampen〕 straw / 축축해지다 become damp 〔moist, wet〕; moisten; dampen / 장마때에는 모든 것이 ～ During the rainy season the dampness penetrates everything.

**축출**(逐出) driving out; expulsion; dismissal; ejection; deportation; banishment. ～하다 drive 〔turn, send, get, put, force〕 《*a person*》 out; throw 〔kick〕 《*a person*》 out; 《지위·직책 등에서》 oust 〔expel, dislodge〕 《*a person* from a position》; hoof out; 《셋집·셋방 등에서》 evict 〔eject〕 《a tenant from the house》; put 《a tenant》 out. ¶ ～당하다 get driven 〔run, kicked〕 out; be expelled / 당(黨)에서 ～하다 oust 〔expel〕 《*a person*》 from the party / 집 밖으로 ～하다 turn 《*a person*》 out of the house; show 《*a person*》 the door / 사원을 회사에서 ～하다 fire an employee from the company / 선동자를 집회장에서 ～했다 We drove out an agitator from the meeting.

**축토**(築土) raising the ground level; 〖토목〗 banking. ～하다 lay earth on the ground; raise the ground level. ◉ ～지반 〖토목·건축〗 fill-up ground.

**축포**(祝砲) a cannon salute; a salute (of guns); 《육군의》 an artillery salute; a *feu de joie* (F.). ¶ 21발의 ～를 쏘다 give 〔fire〕 a twenty-one gun salute.

**축하**(祝賀) congratulations; (a) celebration; felicitations; *one's* good wishes. ～하다 congratulate 〔felicitate〕 《*a person* on *something*》; celebrate 《an event》; commemorate 《a wedding》. ¶ …을 ～하여 in celebration 〔commemoration〕 of…; congratulating…; in honor of… / ～의 말씀 congratulations; congratulatory remarks / ～할 일 a matter for congratulation / ～를 받다 receive congratulations 〔good wishes〕 《from》 / ～인사를 하다 offer 〔tender〕 《*a person*》 *one's* congratulations 《on an events》; make 〔deliver〕 a congratulatory address 《to》 / 생일을 ～하다 give 《*a person*》 birthday greetings / 전승을 ～하다 celebrate 〔greet〕 the war victory / 졸업을 ～하다 congratulate 《*a person*》 on *his* graduation / ～드립니다 I offer you my congratulations. *or* I wish you the joy of the occasion. / 한 군 ～하오 Congratulations, Mr. Han. / 합격을 ～합니다 I congratulate you upon your success in passing the examination. ◉ ～객 a congratulator; a well-wisher (결혼 등의). ～공연 a celebration public performance. ～선물 a congratulatory gift. ～연(宴) ⇨ 축하회. ～연설 a celebration address. ～장(狀) a letter of congratulation; a congratulatory note; greeting card. ～주(酒) a celebratory drink. ～퍼레이드 a celebration parade.

**축하다**(縮一) 《생기 없다》 (be) languid; inanimate; 《싱싱찮다》 (be) stale; [서술적] lack freshness.

**축하회**(祝賀會) a celebration; a party 〔banquet〕 held in celebration of 《an event》. ¶ ～를 열다 hold a celebration; give a party 〔hold a banquet〕 in celebration of 《an event》.

**축합**(縮合) 〖화학〗 condensation. ～하다 condense. ◉ ～물〔체〕 a condensate; a condensation product. ～반응 a condensation reaction. ～수지 condensation resin. ～제 a condensing agent. ～효소 a condensing enzyme.

**축항**(築港) harbor construction. ～하다 construct 〔improve〕 a harbor. ◉ ～공사 harbor work(s).

**춘경**(春耕) spring plowing. ～하다 plow 〔till a field〕 in (the) spring.

**춘경**(春景) 《봄경치》 spring scenery; a spring scene.

**춘계**(春季) spring; springtime; springtide. ◉ ～방학 the spring vacation. ～운동회 a spring athletic meet.

**춘곤**(春困) languor 〔lassitude〕 which

affects people in spring; "spring fever".

**춘광**(春光) spring 「scenes 〔scenery〕.

**춘궁**(春宮) 《동궁》 the Crown Prince.

**춘궁**(春窮) the spring austerity; spring poverty; spring shortage of food. ◉ ～기(期) the farm hardship period; the spring 「food-short 〔lean〕 season.

**춘기**(春期) spring(time). ⇨ 춘계(春季).

**춘기**(春機) sexual desire. ◉ ～발동 sexual awakening; puberty: ～발동기 the period of sexual awakening; (the age of ) puberty; adolescence / ～발동기의 남녀 boys and girls at puberty / ～발동기가 되다 arrive at puberty.

**춘난**(春暖) spring warmth; mild spring weather. ¶ ～지절 the 「mild 〔warm〕 season of spring.

**춘맥**(春麥) early 〔spring-sown〕 barley.

**춘면**(春眠) spring fever; drowsiness in the spring.

**춘몽**(春夢) spring dreams; visionary fancies; a springtime fantasy. ¶ 일장(의) ～ a scene in *one's* springtime dreams / 일장 ～으로 돌아가다 vanish like a 「vision 〔dream〕; end in an empty dream / 인생은 일장 ～이다 Life is but an empty dream.

**춘복**(春服) (a suit for) spring wear; a spring 「suit 〔clothes〕.

**춘부장**(春府丈) your honored father.

**춘분**(春分) the 「vernal 〔spring〕 equinox. ◉ ～날 Vernal Equinox Day.

**춘사**(春思) ① 《봄을 느끼는 마음》 feelings 〔sentiments〕 of spring; spring 「musing 〔meditation〕. ② 《색정》 spring fever; a surge of lust; thoughts of sex.

**춘사**(椿事) 《흉사》 a disaster; a disastrous accident; 《비극》 a tragedy. ¶ 일대 ～ a great accident / 철도의 ～ a terrible railroad accident / ～의 희생자 the victims of the accident / ～가 일어나다 an accident 「happens 〔occurs〕.

**춘산**(春山) mountains in springtime.

**춘삼월**(春三月) March 〔the last month of spring〕 in the lunar calendar. ¶ ～ 긴긴 해에 in springtime when days are long. ◉ ～호시절 the pleasant days of spring; the mild weather of spring.

**춘색**(春色) spring scenery; the vernal beauty of nature; a sign of spring. ¶ ～이 바야흐로 한창이다 The spring 「is now in full glory 〔is at its best〕. *or* Spring is bursting out all over.

**춘설**(春雪) spring snow.

**춘수**(春水) springtime 「water 〔stream〕; water scenes in the spring.

**춘수**(春愁) spring sadness; melancholy 〔nostalgia, anxiety〕 aroused in springtime.

**춘신**(春信) tidings of spring; signs 〔tokens〕 of spring; 《화신》 news of flowers.

**춘약**(春藥) an aphrodisiac (medicine); a sexual stimulant; a love-potion.

**춘양**(春陽) the spring sun(shine); 《봄철》 the springtime.

**춘우**(春雨) spring 「rain 〔drizzle〕.

**춘잠**(春蠶) a spring breed of silkworms. ¶ ～을 놓다 raise silkworms in spring.

**춘절**(春節) spring(time); the spring 「season.

**춘정**(春情) sexual 〔carnal〕 desire 〔passion〕; the sex 「urge 〔drive〕; lust; amorous thoughts; amour. ¶ ～을 느끼다 be seized with low passions; feel the sex urge / ～을 자극하다 in-flame 〔excite, arouse〕 *one's* 「sexual passion 〔carnal desire〕.

**춘초**(春初) early spring; the beginning 〔onset〕 of spring.

**춘추**(春秋) ① 《봄과 가을》 《in》 spring and autumn. ② 《나이》 *one's* honored age; years; winters 《시어》. ¶ ～ 80의 노인 a man of eighty winters / ～가 높다 be very old / ～가 기울다 decline in 「age 〔*one's* years〕 / 70의 ～를 누리다 attain the age of seventy; live to be seventy (years old) / ～가 어떻게 되십니까 How old are you? *or* Venerable sir, what may be your age? ③ 《오경(五經)의 하나》 the Chronicles of Lu (722-484 B.C.). ¶ ～의 필법 the guiding principle of Confucius in writing the Annals; moral criticism / ～의 필법을 빌면 as the ancient chroniclers of Lu would say.
◉ ～복 clothes 〔a suit〕 for spring or autumn; spring-and-autumn wear.

**춘파**(春播) ¶ ～한 sown in spring; spring(-sown) 《wheat》.

**춘풍**(春風) a spring 「wind 〔breeze〕; a 「balmy 〔mild〕 breeze of spring. ¶ ～에 돛단 듯하다 Everything goes 「all right 〔smoothly〕. ◉ ～추우(秋雨) 《지나간 세월》 the spring wind and the autumn rain; years come and gone: ～추우 십여 년이 지나갔다 More than ten years came and went. *or* Over ten years passed. ～화기(和氣) balmy spring weather.

**춘하추동**(春夏秋冬) spring, summer, autumn and winter; the four seasons; all the year round; always; throughout the year; the year long.

**춘한**(春寒) the lingering cold in spring. ◉ ～지절(之節) 《in》 early spring when the cold still lingers on.

**춘화**(春花) spring 〔vernal〕 flowers.

**춘화(도)**(春畫(圖)) an erotic 〔a pornographic〕 picture; [총칭] pornography.

**춘화처리**(春化處理) 〖농업〗 vernalization.

**춘흥**(春興) 《봄철의 흥취》 pleasures 〔delights〕 of spring; springtime fun. ¶ ～을 못 이기다 have spring fever.

**출가**(出家) 《가출》 leaving home; 《불문에 듦》 entering the priesthood. ～하다 leave home; renounce the world; enter the priesthood; take the tonsure; become a bonze.

**출가**(出嫁) a woman's being married (and leaving home). ～하다 be 〔get〕 married 《to *a person,* into a family》. ¶ ～한 married / 좋은 곳에 ～하다 make a good marriage; marry well / 딸을 ～시키다 marry *one's* daughter off; give *one's* daughter away in marriage / 김씨 가문으로 ～하다 be married to one of the Kims / ～외인(外人)이다 A married daughter is no better than a stranger.

**출가**(出稼) ～하다 work away from home; stay in another country for work.

**출간**(出刊) publication; issue. ～하다 publish; bring 〔put〕 out; issue.

**출감**(出監) release from prison. ～하다 be released 〔discharged〕 from prison; leave 〔come out of〕 prison. ◉ ～자 a released convict.

**출강**(出講) lecturing. ～하다 lecture; give lectures 《at》; teach 《at》; be a part-time teacher 〔lecturer〕 《at》. ¶ 나는 이 대학에 월요일에 ～한다 I teach at this university on Monday.

**출격**(出擊) a sally; a sortie. ～하다 sally (forth); make a sortie 〔sally〕. ¶ 백 회의 ～ 기록을 보유하다 have a record of 100 sorties / 미 해군의 함재기들이 USS 인디펜던스호 갑판 위에서 ～ 태세를 갖추고 있다 The US navy aircraft are on stand-by on the deck of the USS Independence. / 그는 제트기 조종사인데, 한국 전쟁 중 50회 이상의 ～을 하였다 He is a jet pilot, who flew more than fifty missions during the Korean war. ◉ ～명령 an order for a sally. ～준비 the preparation for a sally.

**출결**(出缺) attendance (and 〔or〕 absence). ¶ ～상태를 기록 유지하다 keep a record of 《students'》 attendance. ◉ ～기록 a record of 《student》 attendance.

**출경**(出京) ① 《서울을 떠남》 leaving the capital 〔Seoul〕; going to the country. ～하다 leave the capital 〔Seoul〕; go to the country. ② ＝상경(上京).

**출계하다**(出系—) get adopted 《into a family》; become an heir of another family (leaving *one's* own). ¶ 삼촌 집에 ～ be adopted by *one's* uncle.

**출고**(出庫) 「delivery of goods from 〔taking goods out of〕 a warehouse. ～하다 deliver 《goods》 from a warehouse; take 《goods》 out of a warehouse. ¶ 갓 ～된 소주 *soju* fresh from the distillery. ◉ ～가격 a factory 〔store〕 price. ～상품 goods delivered from the warehouse. ～전표 a shipping slip. ～지시(서) a delivery order.

**출관**(出棺) the departure of the hearse. ＝발인(發靷).

**출교**(黜敎) 《파문》 excommunication. ～하다 excommunicate.

**출구**(出口) ① 《나가는 어귀》 a way out; an exit; an outlet; a gateway; 《고속도로의》 an exit ramp. ¶ 극장의 ～ the exit of a theater / 종로 방면 ～ 《지하철에서》 the way out toward Chongno Street / 거리로 나가는 ～ a way out to the street; a street door / ～는 이쪽입니다 This (is the) way out. / ～를 모르겠다 I can't find my way out. / 그는 둘러보며 ～를 찾았다 He looked around for a way out. ② 《상품의》 sending 〔taking〕 out of a port; clearing a port. ～하다 send 〔take〕 out of a port. ◉ ～조사 《투표의》 an exit poll. 비상～ an emergency exit 〔door〕; a fire exit.

**출구**(出柩) taking 〔carrying〕 a coffin out of the house. ～하다 take 〔carry〕 a coffin out of the house.

**출국**(出國) departure from a country. ～하다 depart from a country; leave 〔go out of〕 a country. ◉ ～관리 departure control. ～기록카드 an embarkation card; a departure card. ～세(稅) exit tax: 대부분의 보도 매체들은 외국 관광을 떠나는 모든 한국인 여행객들로부터 ～세라는 명목으로 약 2만 원씩을 거둔다는 정부 계획에 반발했다 Most news media reacted against the government's plan to collect about 20,000 won in a kind of exit tax from every Korean citizen leaving on a foreign sightseeing tour. ～수속〔절차〕 departure 〔sailing〕 formalities 〔procedures〕: ～절차를 끝냈습니까 Have you gone through the departure procedures? ～허가(서) an exit 〔a departure〕 permit.

**출근**(出勤) attendance (at work); being on the job 〔on duty〕; going to work. ～하다 go 〔come〕 to (*one's*) office 〔work〕; leave home for work. ¶ ～이 이르다〔늦다〕 be early 〔late〕 at the office / ～해 있다 be at (*one's*) office; be present / 그는 오전 9시에 (사무실에) ～한다 He gets to the office at 9:00 a.m. *or* He is present at his office at nine in the morning. / 오늘은 오후 ～이다 I am on the afternoon shift today. / 나는 매일 버스로 ～한다 I take the bus daily to my work 〔office〕. /「너는 매일 아침 몇 시에 ～하느냐」—「8시 30분에」 "When 〔What time〕 do you 「leave home for 〔go to〕 work every morning?"—"At 8:30." ◉ ～부 an attendance book 〔record〕; a time book: ～부에 도장을 찍다 register 〔sign〕 *one's* name in the attendance book; punch the time clock. ～시간 the office(-going) hour; 《집을 나서는 시간》 the time *one* leaves home for the office; 《업무 개시 시간》 the start 〔beginning〕 of office 〔working〕 hours. ～율 (non-)absentee rate 〔ratio〕. ～일 *one's* workday; the office day; the day at the office: ～일수 the number of attendances. ～자 an attendant; [총칭] attendance.

**출근상태**(出勤狀態) the relative absenteeism; attendance state 〔figures〕. ¶ 그의 ～가 좋지 않다 His record of office attendance is unsatisfactory.

**출금**(出金) 《지출》 payment; defrayal; 《예금의》 drawing; a withdrawal 《of funds》. ～하다 《지출하다》 pay; defray; 《예금을》 make a withdrawal. ◉ ～전표 a paying-out 〔payment〕 slip.

**출납**(出納) receipts and disbursements 〔expenses〕; revenue and expenditure; incomings and outgoings. ～하다 take in and pay out; receive and disburse. ¶ 현금을 ～하다 handle the cash; be a cashier / 금전의 ～은 그 사람 혼자서 취급했다 He solely took charge of receipts and payments. ◉ ～계 the cashier('s section); the bursar('s office): ～계원 a cashier; a treasurer; 《은행의》 a (paying and receiving) teller / ～계를 보다 take charge of accounts. ～공무원 an official in charge of accounts; an accounting official. ～부 a cashbook; an account book. ～정산기(期) the settlement period.

**출동**(出動) going 〔starting, moving〕 out; getting 〔setting〕 in motion 〔action〕; 《군대의》 mobilization; marching; 《함대의》 sailing. ～하다 go 〔set, start, move〕 out; go into action; be mobilized 〔called out〕; 《군대가》 take the field; be sent out; 《함대가》 sail; put to sea; 《소방대가》 turn out. ¶ 군대의 ～ the mobilization 〔calling out〕 of troops / 함대의 ～ the moving out of a fleet / ～시키다 dispatch 《troops》; send; put 《jets》 in action / ～을 명령받다 be ordered to 《the front》; be called 〔ordered〕 out / ～준비를 명하다 order 《a troop》 to be ready to move; order to stand by; order standby mobilization / ～준비가 되어 있다 be ready to move / ～준비를 하다 hold itself in readiness for action; 《해군이》 be ready for sea / 폭도 진압을 위해 기동대가 ～했다 A riot squad was sent to suppress the mob. / 함대가 ～하다 a fleet moves out; a fleet is put to sea / 간밤의 큰 화재로 수십대의 소방차가 ～했다 Tens of fire engines turned out to fight the big fire last night. / 미국은 제7함대를 대만 해협에 ～시켰다 The United States moved the Seventh Fleet to the Straits of Taiwan. ◉ ～복 《진압 경찰의》 riot gear 〔garb〕; riot-police fatigues.

**출동명령**(出動命令) an order for moving 〔turning out〕. ¶ 육군의 ～ marching orders / 해군의 ～ sailing orders / 요격 ～ scramble order / ～을 내리다 give an order for moving 《on, out, in》 / ～을 받고 있다 《육군이》 be under orders for the front; 《해군이》 be under orders to proceed 《to》.

**출두**(出頭) appearance; presence; attendance. ～하다 appear 《at 〔before〕 the court》; attend; present *oneself* 《at》; make *one's* 〔put in an〕 appearance; turn 〔show〕 up; report *oneself* to. ¶ 자진 ～ voluntary appearance / 피고인 및 변호인의 ～ 없이 개정된 공판 a public trial held in the absence of the accused and his defense counsel / ～하지 않을 때에는 if *one* does 〔should〕 not attend; in case of nonattendance; in default of attendance / 몸소

～하다 appear in person / ～를 요구하다 request the attendance 〔presence〕 of 《*a person*》; ask 《*a person's*》 appearance / 임의 ～를 요구하다 ask 《*a person's*》 voluntary appearance / 법정에의 ～ 통지를 받다 be ordered to (appear in) court / ～하라고 통고하다 serve notice to appear; summon.

◉ ～명령 《issue》 an order requiring 《*a person*》 to report personally 《to a police station》; 《법정으로의》 《serve》 a subpoena 《on *a person*》; 《serve》 a summons 《on *a person*》 (to appear in court).

**출람**(出藍) ⇨ 청출어람(青出於藍). ～하다 《a disciple》 excel 〔outshine, outdistance, surpass, eclipse〕 *one's* master 《in》. ¶ ～지재(之材) a talented person who excels his teacher; a pupil greater than his master.

**출렁거리다** surge; roll; wave; waves rise; undulate; waves ripple.

**출력**(出力) ① 〖기계·전기〗 output; 《발전기의》 generating power; power 〔energy〕 output. ¶ ～ 50킬로와트의 라디오 방송국 a radio station with an output of 50 kW / ～ 8만 킬로와트의 수력 발전소 a hydroelectric power plant that generates 80,000 kilowatts of electricity / ～ 500마력의 모터 a motor that develops 〔has a capacity of〕 500 h.p. / ～이 작다〔크다〕 have a small 〔large〕 output / 이 엔진의 ～은 500마력이다 This is a 500 horsepower engine. ② 《돈을 냄》 capital investment; (an) outlay. ～하다 make a 《large, heavy》 outlay 《for》. ◉ ～계 an output meter. ～데이터 〖컴퓨터〗 output data. ～매체 〖컴퓨터〗 an output media. ～장치 an output device unit. ～터미널 〖컴퓨터〗 an output terminal.

**출렵**(出獵) ～하다 go hunting 〔shooting〕. ¶ ～나가 있다 be out hunting.

**출루**(出壘) ～하다 〖야구〗 go 〔get〕 to 《first》 base. ¶ 출루해 있다 [주자가 주어] be on 《the third》 base; [팀이 주어] have 《two》 on (base). ◉ ～율 〖야구〗 《a player's》 on-base percentage.

**출마**(出馬) 《말을 타고》 going out on horseback; 《입후보》 candidacy 《미》; candidature 《영》. ～하다 go out on horseback; 《입후보하다》 come 〔put *oneself*〕 forward as a candidate 《for》; run 〔stand 《영》〕 for 《the Assembly》. ¶ ～를 선언하다 declare *one's* candidacy 《for》 / 시장 선거에 ～하다 run 〔stand, be up〕 for mayor / ～를 포기하다 give up *one's* candidacy / 서울에서 ～하다 run as a candidate in Seoul / 대통령후보로 ～하다 run for the presidency / 이번 도지사 선거에 부디 ～해 주십시오 I beg you most earnestly to run in the coming gubernatorial election.

**출몰**(出沒) appearing frequently; frequent appearance; haunting. ～하다 appear frequently; make frequent appearances; frequent; haunt; infest. ¶ 해적〔잠수함〕이 ～하는 바다 a sea infested with pirates 〔submarines〕; pirate-〔submarine-〕infested seas / 그 곳에 호랑이가 ～한다 Tigers lurk there. / 적함이 자주 그 연안에 ～했다 A hostile vessel was often seen off the coast. / 그 산길에는 도둑이 ～한다 The mountain path is 「haunted by 〔infested with〕 robbers.

**출무성하다** ① 《굵기가》 have about the same thickness at the top and at the bottom. ② 《대가리가》 (be) even. ¶ 묘목들의 키가 ～ The young trees are of even height.

**출발**(出發) departure; leaving; starting; a start. ～하다 start 《from》; leave 《Seoul》; depart 《from》; take *one's* departure 《from》; set out 〔off〕 《from》; take off (비행기가); 《배로》 embark 〔set sail〕 《for America》.

> 용법 **start** 정지 상태에서 움직이기 시작하다, 대기 상태에서 여행이나 목적지로 출발하다의 뜻. 「동작」에 중점이 주어짐. stop의 반대어. **leave** 어떤 장소에서 떠나다. 열차·비행기 등 교통 기관이 일정한 시각에 출발·발차·출항하는 경우. **depart** 어떤 지점에서 출발하다의 뜻으로 격식차린 말. arrive의 반대어. **set out** 〔**off**〕 여행을 「떠나다」의 뜻. **take off** 비행기가 「이륙하다」의 뜻.

¶ ～에 즈음하여 at *one's* departure / ～ 직전에 just before departure / 하루 일찍 ～하다 start 〔depart〕 a day earlier / 일찌감치〔느지감치〕 ～하다 make an early 〔a late〕 start / ～준비를 하다 prepare for the start / ～을 그르치다 《경기에서》 make a false start; 《인생의》 make a wrong start in life / ～이 좋다 make a good start / 버스〔열차〕는 9시에 서울을 이미 ～했다 The bus 〔train〕 has already left Seoul at 9:00. / 열차는 3번 플랫폼에서 ～한다 The train leaves platform number 3. / 우리는 내

일 아침 파리로 ~한다 We are leaving 〔starting〕 for Paris tomorrow morning. / 비행기는 뉴욕을 향해 오전 9시에 ~한다 The plane takes off for New York at 9 a.m. / 그들은 신혼 여행을 ~했다 They set out on their honeymoon. / 우리 비행기는 안개로 인해 ~이 늦어졌다 Owing to the fog the departure of our plane was delayed. / 나는 금요일로 ~을 앞당겼다 I moved up my departure to Friday. / 그녀는 ~을 1주일간 늦췄다 She「put off 〔postponed〕 her departure for one week. / ~ 날짜가 임박하다 The day of my departure is near at hand.
◉ ~로비〔대기실〕《공항의》 a departure lounge. ~시간 the departure time: 이 버스의 ~시간은 몇시입니까 What is the departure time of the bus? ~신호 a starting 〔leaving〕 signal: ~신호원 《경기의》 a starter. ~역 a starting station. ~일 the date of *one's* departure; the departure day.

**출발점**(出發點) the starting point 〔place〕; 《의론 따위의》 a point of departure; 《육상 경기의》 the starting mark 〔line〕. ¶ ~에 서다 《육상 경기에서》 be on the 〔*one's*〕 mark.

**출범**(出帆) (a) sailing; (a) departure. ~하다 sail 《from》; set sail 《from》; leave 《Pusan for America》; put (out) to sea. ◉ ~기(旗) the Blue Peter. ~명령 sailing orders. ~시간 (ship's) sailing time. ~일 the sailing day.

**출병**(出兵) the dispatch of「troops 〔an expeditionary force〕 《to》; a military expedition. ~하다 dispatch 〔send〕 troops 《to》; send an expeditionary force 《to》. ¶ 월남 ~ the dispatch of troops to Vietnam.

**출분**(出奔) ~하다 run away 〔off〕 《from home》; abscond; decamp; 《구어》 clear out; 《구어》 make off; elope (남녀가 눈이 맞아).

**출비**(出費) expenses; expenditure; (an) outlay. ⇨ 지출(支出). ¶ ~를 억제하다 keep the expenses below; limit *one's* expenditure 《to》.

**출사**(出仕) ~하다 enter the service of government office; go into government service. 「office; go to work.

**출사**(出社) ~하다 go 〔come〕 to the

**출사**(出師) the dispatch of troops 《to》. ⇨ 출병(出兵). 「private house).

**출사**(出寫) a photographer's visit (to a

**출산**(出産) (a) childbirth; (a) birth; a delivery (분만). ~하다 have a baby; give birth to 《a child》; be delivered of 《a baby》. ¶ 첫 ~ *one's* first childbirth / 그녀는 사내아이를 ~했다 She gave birth to a baby boy. / 그녀는 ~이 머지 않다 She is going to have a baby pretty soon. / ~예정은 언제입니까 When is your baby due? / 그의 아내는 다음주 ~ 예정이다 His wife is expecting her baby next week.
◉ ~경력 *one's* parity. ~수당 (a) maternity benefit. ~예정일 the expected date of confinement. ~율 a birthrate. ~촉진제 a parturifacient. ~축하 a celebration of a birth; congratulations on a birth. ~휴가 a maternity leave. 「of the house.

**출상**(出喪) ~하다 carry the coffin out

**출생**(出生) (a) birth. ~하다 be born; come into being 〔existence〕. ¶ ~한 집 the house where *one* was born; the home of *one's* birth / 갓 ~한 아이 a newborn (baby) / 시골 ~ a rural birth; a country-born person / 가난한 집에 ~하다 be born of 〔to〕 a poor family / 양반 가문에 ~하다 be born to a noble 〔*yangban*〕 family / 달이 못 차서 ~하다 be born「prematurely 〔before its time, before the proper time〕 / 비천한 ~이다 be of low birth; be of humble origin / 한씨댁에 아들이 ~했다 A son was born to Mr. Han.
◉ ~률 the 〔a〕 birthrate. ~신고 a report 〔register〕 of a birth: ~ 신고하다 have 〔get〕 the birth 《of *one's* child》 registered. ~연월일 *one's* date of birth (생략 d.o.b.). ~증명서 a birth certificate. ~지 *one's* birthplace; *one's* place of birth.

**출생후**(出生後) (ever) since *one's* birth; in (all) *one's* days. ¶ ~처음으로 for the first time in *one's* life 〔since *one* was born〕 / ~ 병이라곤 앓아 본 적이 없다 I have never been ill a day of 〔in〕 my life.

**출석**(出席) attendance; presence. ~하다 attend 《a meeting》; be present 《at》; present *oneself* 《at》; take *one's* seat; 《얼굴을 내밀다》 make *one's* 〔put in an〕 appearance 《at》; show up.
¶ ~해 있다 be present 《at》 / ~을 부르다 call the roll; take the register (학교에서) / ~을 요청하다 request 〔ask for〕 《*a person's*》 attendance / ~ 부를 때 대신 대답하다 answer the roll for 《*a person*》 / ~이 고르지 않다 be irregular in attendance / ~하지 않다 absent *oneself* 〔stay away〕 《from school》 /

부디 ~해주시면 고맙겠습니다 Kindly give us the pleasure of your company. / 오늘 우리 반은 전원 ~이었다 Our class had perfect attendance today. / 자네 꼭 ~해 줘야겠네 I insist on your being present.
◉ ~률 the percentage of attendance. ~부 a roll (book). ~요구서 『법』 a summons. ~일수 the number of days 〔times〕 *one* has attended. ~정지 suspension of attendance. ~카드 《학생의》 an attendance card.

**출석자**(出席者) a person present; an attendee 《at》; [총칭] the attendance; those present. ¶ 많은 ~ a large attendance / 모임에는 ~가 많았다 The meeting had a large attendance. *or* The party was well attended. / ~가 줄었다 The attendance fell off. / 송별회에는 ~가 80명 이상이나 되었다 The farewell party was attended by more than 80 people.

**출세**(出世) ① 《입신》 rising in the world; success 〔advancement〕 in life; a successful career 〔life〕; 《승진》 promotion. ~하다 succeed in life; rise 〔go up, advance〕 in the world; make headway in life; get ahead in the 《business》; be promoted 《to the rank of manager》; make 〔win〕 a name for *oneself*. ¶ ~의 비결 secrets of success 〔a successful life〕 / ~한 사람 a successful man / ~할 기회를 놓치다 miss a chance to get ahead in life / ~가 빠르다 「mark a rapid rise 〔rise fast〕 in the world; make *one's* mark early in life; 《승진이》 win 〔get, obtain〕 rapid 〔quick〕 promotion / 장관으로 ~하다 rise to a (Cabinet-)Minister / ~의 계단을 오르다 climb the ladder of success / ~에 방해가 되다 《사물이》 stand in the way of *one's* advancement / 가난한 집에서 나서 크게 ~했다 Born of a poor family, he made his way in the world. / 재간만 있으면 어떠한 ~ 길도 열려 있다 All careers are open to talent. / 그는 아들이 ~하는 것을 보지 못하고 죽었다 He didn't live to see his son a great man. / 그는 동창생의 누구보다도 일찍 ~했다 He rose to a high position earlier than any of his classmates. / 나의 동창 중에는 ~한 사람이 많다 Many of my (former) schoolmates have risen to high positions.
② 《출가(出家)》 renouncing the secular world; entering the priesthood. ~하다 renounce the world; enter the priesthood; become a bonze.
◉ ~길 《take》 the road 〔highroad〕 to success 〔fame〕. ~욕 ambitions for success. ~제일주의 careerism.

**출세작**(出世作) 《작품》 the work which has won 〔earned〕 the author distinction 《as a novelist》; a work which has brought the author into prominence. ¶ 춘원의 ~은 "개척자"였다 Ch'unwŏn was first known for his work *Pioneers*. / 그 소설이 그의 ~이 되었다 That novel started him on the road to success.

**출소**(出所) 《출감》 release from prison. ~하다 be discharged 〔released〕 from prison; leave jail; come out of prison. ¶ ~가 허락되다 be released from prison; be let out of prison / ~시키다 release; set 《*a person*》 free from prison / 형기 만료로 ~하는 날을 기다리다 wait to be released upon the expiration of the term. ◉ ~자 a released convict.

**출소**(出訴) ~하다 institute a lawsuit 《against *a person*》. ⇨ 제소(提訴).

**출수**(出水) a flood; an inundation; a freshet (눈 따위가 녹아서 나는). ~하다 [강이 주어] overflow (its banks); [지역이 주어] be flooded; be inundated.

**출수**(出穗) coming out in ears. ~하다 be in (the) ear; come into ears; ear (up). ◉ ~기 the earing season.

**출신**(出身) 《신분》 a graduate (학교의); origin; birth. ¶ 군인 ~ a former military man / 대학 ~ a university man 〔graduate〕 / 공화당 ~의 장관 a minister from the Republican Party / …의 ~이다 《학교가》 be a graduate of 《Columbia University》; 《출신지가》 be a native of 《Kyŏngbuk》; come from 《Honam》 / 양반 ~이다 be of noble extraction; come of a noble family / ~이 비천하다 be of low birth; be of humble origin / 당신은 어디 ~입니까 Where do you come from? *or* Where are you from? / 우리 사장님은 농민 ~이다 The president of our company comes from a peasant family.
◉ ~교 the school 〔college〕 *one* graduated from; *one's* alma mater. ~자 《학교의》 a graduate; 《미》 an alumnus; 《여자》 an alumna. ~지 *one's* native place; *one's* birthplace; *one's* hometown 〔home〕.

**출아**(出芽) germination; sprouting; budding. ⇨발아(發芽). ～하다 germinate; sprout; bud; put forth〔out〕buds.

**출애굽기**(出一記)〖성서〗(The Book of) Exodus (생략 Exod.).

**출어**(出漁) going out fishing; sailing for fish. ～하다 sail〔go〕out fishing《in the high seas》. ¶ 제주도 앞바다에 ～중인 배 a boat〔vessel〕fishing off Chejudo. ◉ ～구역 a fishing area〔ground〕. ～권 the fishing right. ～기 the fishing season.

**출연**(出捐) donation; contribution; subscription. ～하다 donate; contribute. ¶ 자선 기금에 많은 돈을 ～하다 contribute a lot of money to the charity fund. ◉ ～금 a donation; a contribution. ～자 a donator.

**출연**(出演) *one's* appearance《on the stage》; a〔*one's*〕performance. ～하다 appear〔come〕on the stage; make *one's* appearance on the stage〔on television〕; take part in《a concert》; play; perform; sing(노래하다). ¶ 인기 스타 총 ～ an all-star cast / 춘향으로 ～하다「appear as〔play the part of〕*Ch'unhyang* / 처음 ～하다 make *one's*「début〔first appearance〕《on the stage, on television》/ 국립 극장에 ～하다 make *one's* appearance on the stage of the National Theater.
◉ ～계약 (a) booking. ～료 a performance fee; an actor's〔a singer's〕fee. ～자 an actor; a player; a performer; a singer; [총칭] the cast《of a play》.

**출영**(出迎) meeting;《요인 등의》reception. ～하다 go〔come〕(out) to meet《*a person*》on arrival; meet; greet; receive. ¶ (요인 등을) ～하는 사람들의 줄 a《diplomatic》receiving〔reception〕line / ～을 받다 be met〔received〕《at the airport, *etc.*》/ 마을 사람들의 ～을 받았다 I was met by the villagers.

**출옥**(出獄) release from prison. ⇨출소(出所). ¶ 가～ release on parole; provisional release.

**출원**(出願) (an) application. ～하다 make an application《to the government for an official sanction》; file an application《with the Patent Office for a patent》; apply《for》; put in《for》. ¶ 특허를 ～하다 apply (to the Patent Office) for a patent / 증명서〔여권〕의 교부를 ～하다 apply《to the authorities》for a certificate〔passport〕/ 특허 ～중《표시》Patent applied for. *or* Patent pending. ◉ ～기한〔마감〕the deadline〔time limit〕for application. ～번호 the application number. ～자 an applicant. ～절차 the procedure of application.

**출입**(出入) ①《드나듦》going in and out; comings and goings. ～하다 go〔come〕in and out; enter and leave; make *one's* entrance and exit《through a door》;《자주 다니다》visit; frequent《a place》. ¶ ～하는 배 incoming and outgoing vessels / 국회 ～ 기자 a newsman accredited to the House / 홍등가〔화류계〕에 ～하다 frequent the gay quarters; be a frequent visitor to the red-light districts / 사람의 ～이 많다 lots of people are coming and going / 선박의 ～이 잦다 have a lot of steady shipping / 관청 ～이 잦다 frequently visit government offices / 권문(權門)에 ～하다 frequent the houses of influential people / 도서관에 마음대로 ～하다 have free access to a library / 사람들이 항상 ～하다 people come and go all the time / ～을 허락하다 allow《*a person*》access to《*one's* house》; admit《*a person*》into《a place》/ ～을 금하다 declare《a place》off limits to《the students at the bar》;《막다》forbid《*a person*》the house / ～금지《게시》No trespassing. *or* Off limits. / 미성년자 ～금지《게시》No minors. / 미성년자는 그곳에 ～하지 못한다 The minors are not allowed to visit there. *or*《미》The place is off limits to the minors. / 그 집은 사람들 ～이 많다 The house has a large number of visitors. *or* The house is frequented by many visitors. / 그는 바깥 ～을 잘 안 한다 He is a family man. / 그런 자들은 ～시키지 마시오 Keep such men from the house.
②《나들이》going out for a visit. ～하다 go out for a visit. ¶ 주인은 ～하고 안 계십니다 The master has gone out and not come home yet.
③《물건의》taking〔putting〕in and out;《금전의》receipts and payments. ¶ 그는 금전 ～을 혼자 책임맡고 있었다 He solely took charge of receipts and payments.
④《단골 등의 관계》¶ ～하는 의사 *one's* family doctor / ～하는 상인 tradesmen who regularly〔usually〕come to *one's* house.
◉ ～구 an entrance (and exit); a doorway; a gateway. ～권 an admission ticket. ～증 a (gate) pass: ～증을 보이다 show *one's* pass to a guard.

～처《신문 기자의》a beat.

**출입국**(出入國) entry into and departure from the country; emigration and immigration. ◉ ～관리 immigration control〔management〕: ～ 관리국 the Exit and Entry Control Bureau; the Immigration Bureau / ～관리법 the Immigration Control Law. ～(기록)카드 an embarkation〔a disembarkation〕card.

**출자**(出資) (an) investment; financing. ～하다 invest〔sink, lay out〕money《in》; finance《an enterprise》; contribute money《to》. ¶ 개인 ～ 사업 a privately financed enterprise / 공동 ～ a joint contribution〔investment〕; joint capital (합병) / 주식에 ～하다 invest *one's* money in stocks / 광산에 ～하다 put *one's* money in mining / 그는 신규 사업에 많은 돈을 ～했다 He invested a lot of money in a new enterprise. ◉ ～ 관련회사 a capitally affiliated company. ～금 an investment; money invested; 《자본금》(a) capital. ～액 the amount (of money) invested; the amount of the investment. ～자 an investor; a financier; a contributor; a financial backer〔supporter〕.

**출자액**(出資額) the amount of the investment〔contribution〕; the amount (of money) invested. ¶ ～에 따라 이익을 분배하다 share the profit among us〔them〕according to our〔their〕investments.

**출장**(出張) an official trip〔tour〕; a business trip; a tour on duty. ～하다, ～가다 travel on (official) business《to》; make a business trip《to》; take〔go on〕an official〔a business〕trip《to》. ¶ ～을 보내다 send〔dispatch〕《*a person*》on business to《Japan》/ ～의 명을 받다 be ordered (to go) to《Pusan》on business / 공무로 지방에 ～가다 go to the country on official business / 상용으로 일본에 ～가다 go to Japan on business.

◉ ～명령 an order to go on an official〔a business〕trip. ～소 a branch〔local〕office; an agency; 《은행 등의》a (small) branch; 《영》a sub-branch. ～비 a travel(ing) allowance; travel(ing)〔trip〕expenses. ～여행 a business trip. ～원 a person dispatched on business〔official duties〕; an agent; a representative: 세관 ～원 a man sent from the custom house. ～지 the destination of *one's* business trip. ～지도 (giving) lessons at *one's* pupil's home. ～촬영 ⇨ 출사(出寫).

**출장**(出場)《어느 장소에》appearance《in a place》; 《참가》participation《in》; an entry《for》. ～하다 appear《in a place》; be present《to》; take part〔participate〕《in》; enter《for an event》; play《in》; 《경기에》take the field; compete《in》. ¶ 경기에 ～하다 take part in an athletic contest; enter a sporting〔sports〕event / ～을 취소하다 withdraw〔cancel〕*one's* entry《for》.

◉ ～선수 a participating athlete; an entrant; an entry. ～자 a participant; an entrant; a panelist (TV 퀴즈 프로의). ～자격 qualification《for the finals》: ～자격을 따다 qualify《for the finals》. ～정지 suspension: 그 선수는 ～정지를 당하고 있다 The player「is under suspension〔has been suspended〕.

**출전**(出典) the source; the authority. ¶ ～을 밝히다 indicate〔name〕the source《of》; give〔cite〕the authority《for》; 《정확히》give chapter and verse《for》/ 그 예문의 ～을 말해 주십시오 Please tell me the source of the illustrative sentence.

**출전**(出戰) ① 《전장으로》going to war. ⇨ 출정(出征). ② 《경기에》participation《in an athletic contest》. ⇨ 출장(出場). ～하다 participate〔take part〕《in athletic games》.

**출정**(出廷) 〖법〗a court appearance. ～하다 appear in court; present *oneself* at the court. ¶ ～하지 않을 때에는 in case of nonappearance; in default of attendance / ～해 있다 be in court.

◉ ～명령 an order to appear in court《as witness》; 《serve》a subpoena〔summons〕《on *a person*》: ～명령을 받다 be ordered to (appear in) court. ～일 the court day.

**출정**(出征) going to war〔the front〕; departure for the front; taking the field. ～하다 go to「war〔the front〕; depart for the front; take the field《against》. ¶ 지원병으로 ～하다 go to war as a volunteer / ～해 있다 be (away, in active service) at the front / ～을 전송하다 see《*a person*》off for the front. ◉ ～가족 the family of a soldier at the front. ～군 an army in the field; troops at the front: ～군인 a soldier going to the front; a soldier「at the front 〔in active service〕. ～기(記) a war account 〔journal, book〕.

**출제**(出題) making questions 《for an examination》. ～하다 set 《*a person*》 a problem 《in history》; make questions 《for an examination in English》 out of 《a textbook》; prepare an examination paper. ¶ 이번 시험은 교과서에서 ～될 것이다 The questions on the upcoming test will be taken from the textbook. / 선생님은 어려운 문제를 몇 개 ～하셨다 The teacher set us some difficult questions.
◉ ～경향 a tendency of questions: 나는 S대 입시의 ～ 경향을 조사해 보았다 I have studied the characteristics of the entrance examination questions for 〔of〕 S university. ～범위 the 〔a〕 range of possible questions. ～자 a person who makes questions for an examination: 영어의 입시 ～자는 남 교수님이라고 한다 I hear that the English paper in the entrance examination was set by Professor Nam.

**출중**(出衆) prominence; preeminence; excellence. ～하다, ～나다 (be) prominent; preeminent; excellent; conspicuous; outstanding; [서술적] tower high above 《others》; be out of the common 〔ordinary〕; stand out conspicuous 《among, from》; cut a prominent figure 《in, among》.
¶ ～하게 outstandingly; preeminently; by far (the best); far 〔out〕 and away; out of the common; extraordinarily / ～한 인물 a prominent figure / ～한 재간 extraordinary 〔outstanding〕 talent / ～한 재주가 있다 be of extraordinary talent / ～하게 공부를 잘하다 be by far the best student / 그는 ～한 재주를 가지고 있었다 He was endowed with rare gifts. / 이것은 ～한 작품이다 This is an excellent work.

**출진**(出陣) going to war 〔battle〕. ～하다 go to battle; take the field.

**출차**(出差) 〖천문〗 evection.

**출찰**(出札) issue of a ticket. ◉ ～계원 a ticket agent 〔clerk〕 《미》; a booking clerk 《영》. ～구 a ticket 〔booking 《영》〕 window 〔booth〕.

**출처**(出處) 《나온 곳》 the origin; the source. ¶ ～가 확실한 authentic 《news》; 《information》 drawn 〔collected〕 from a sure 〔reliable〕 source / 뉴스의 ～ the source of (the) news / ～가 확실하다 be from a reliable source; be authentic; be on good authority / ～가 분명치 않다 be of doubtful origin; be from an unreliable source / ～를 밝히다 《정보 등의》 disclose 〔indicate, name〕 the source 《of》 / 그 보도의 ～는 분명치 않다 The report rests on slender authority. *or* The report is from a doubtful source. / 이 구절의 ～는 성서다 The phrase is quoted from the Bible. / ～를 대라 Tell me where you got 〔found〕 it. / 그 운동자금의 ～를 모른다 I don't know who supplied the campaign funds. / 그 돈의 ～를 알고 싶다 I'd like to know where the money came from. / 경찰은 그 뉴스의 ～를 조사하고 있다 The police are looking for the source of the news.

**출초**(出超) 〖경제〗 an excess of exports (over imports); an exports surplus; a favorable balance (of trade).
¶ 30억 달러의 ～ an excess of exports amounting to 3 billion dollars / 일본은 한국과의 무역에서 큰 ～가 되지 않도록 노력하여야 한다 Japan must make efforts to see that she does not show a large export surplus in her trade with Korea.

**출출하다** be somewhat 〔rather〕 hungry; feel a bit empty.

**출타**(出他) leaving the house; going out 《on a visit》; an outing. ～하다 leave the house; go out 《on a visit》. ¶ ～하고 없다 have gone out and be not back yet; be out.

**출탄**(出炭) coal production; production of coal. ～하다 produce 〔yield〕 coal.
◉ ～량 output of coal 《from》; coal output.

**출토**(出土) 〖고고학〗 ～하다 [사물이 주어] be excavated 〔unearthed〕 《at a site, from the ruins of...》; be found 《at》; [장소가 주어] produce; yield.
◉ ～지 the site 〔location〕 at which 《an artifact》 was found 〔excavated〕; the find site. ～품 an artifact; an excavated 〔unearthed〕 article: 이들 ～품에 의해 이 지방의 유사(有史) 이전의 문화가 많이 밝혀지게 될 것이다 These new finds 〔discoveries〕 will throw considerable light on the prehistoric culture in this district.

**출판**(出版) (a) publication; publishing. ～하다 publish; issue; bring 《a book》 into the world; bring 〔put〕 out 《a book》. ¶ 예약 ～ publication by subscription / 한정 ～ limited publication / ～의 자유 freedom of the press / 책을 ～하다 publish 〔print〕 a book / 논문을 모아서 ～하다 publish (learned) papers in collected form / 자비로 ～하다 publish 《a book》 on *one's* own account / ～되다 be published (in book form); 「come out 〔appear〕 《in print》; see the light (of day) / 그 책은 벌써 ～되었다 The book is already out. / 그 책은 갓 ～된 것이다 The book is just off the press. / 서적의 ～은 자유다 The book press is free. / 아버지의 유고(遺稿)가 ～되게 되었다 My father's posthumous manuscripts have come to be published in book form.

◉ ～계(界) the publishing world; publishing circles. ～권 the right of publication; publication rights; a copyright. ～기금 publication fund. ～기념회 a party in honor 〔celebration〕 of the publication of 《*a person's*》 book; a publication party. ～목록 a catalog(ue) of publications. ～법 the Publication Law; the Press Law. ～부 a publication 〔publishing〕 department. ～부수 the number of issues; the number of copies printed 〔issued〕; the size of the edition; circulation. ～비 publishing costs. ～사 a publishing company 〔firm, house〕; a book concern 《미》. ～업 the publishing business: ～업자 a publisher / ～업을 시작하다 start in the publishing business. ～윤리 publishing ethics. ～인〔자〕 the publisher(s). ～조건 terms of publication. ～허가 a license to publish 《a book》; *imprimatur* (L.). ～협회 a publishers' association: 대한 ～문화 협회 the Korean Publishers' Association.

**출판물**(出版物) a publication. ¶ ～이 범람하다 have too many publications / ～을 단속하다 exercise control over publications.

**출품**(出品) exhibition; display; show. ～하다 exhibit; display; show; put 〔place〕 on exhibition 〔display, show, view〕; 《품평회에》 enter 《*one's* work in a competition》. ¶ 외국인의 ～ a foreigner's entry / 전람회에 ～하다 send 〔submit〕 《*one's* painting》 to an exhibition / ～돼 있다 be on display 〔show, exhibition〕 / 그가 ～한 그림은 모두 입상했다 He got prizes for all the pictures he sent to the exhibition.

◉ ～국 an exhibiting country. ～목록 a catalog(ue) of exhibits. ～물 an exhibit; an article on show 〔exhibition, display〕; things on exhibit; display items. ～자 an exhibitor. ～점수 the number of exhibits. ～품목 a list of exhibits; items for display.

**출하**(出荷) sending out goods; forwarding; shipping; shipment. ～하다 send out goods; forward; ship; 《상업 용어》 consign. ¶ 화물을 서울역에서 ～하다 ship goods from Seoul Station / 오늘은 야채의 ～량이 적었다 Vegetable shipments were scarce today. / 지난 달 항공편으로 생선 100상자를 ～했다 Last month we sent one hundred fish packs off by air. ◉ ～선(先)〔목적지〕 the destination. ～안내〔통지〕 an advice 〔a notice〕 of shipment; a shipping advice; a consignment note (철도편의). ～자 a shipper; a forwarder. ～지 the place of shipment.

**출항**(出航) sailing off; departure; 《항공기의》 a take-off. ～하다 start on a voyage; set sail 《from》; leave port 《at Inchŏn》; depart 《from》; put out to sea.

**출항**(出港) 《발항》 leaving port; departure from a port. ～하다 leave port; set sail 《from》; clear a port (통관 절차 등을 마치고); put out (to sea); steam 〔sail〕 out (of a harbor). ¶～준비를 하다 make ready for sailing / 부산을 ～하다 leave Pusan; set sail from Pusan / ～을 허가하다 give 《a ship》 clearance / 악천후로 그 배는 ～을 못하고 있다 Bad weather kept the boat in port.

◉ ～명령 an order for sailing 〔moving〕. ～서 a clearance paper. ～선 an outgoing 〔outward-bound〕 vessel. ～세 a clearance fee; clearance dues. ～수속 = ～절차. ～(예정)표 a sailing list. ～절차 clearance formalities: ～절차를 밟다 clear a ship 《at the customs house》. ～지 the outport; the clearance station. ～통지 a clearance notice. ～허가 《get》 clearance for leaving port: ～허가증 a clearance permit 〔certificate〕.

**출항정지**(出港停止) an embargo. ¶ ～를 하다 lay 〔put〕 an embargo on 《a ship》; lay 《a ship》 under an embargo / ～를 해제하다 lift 〔remove, take off〕 an embargo 《on a ship》 / ～중이다 be (placed) under an embargo.

**출행**(出行) ～하다 go out; 《원행》 make 〔go on〕 a journey 〔trip〕; take 〔go

money should be allotted for the relief of the destitute.

**충돌**(衝突) ① 《부딪침》 a collision; a crash; a smash-up 《미》; 《구어》 a bump; a pile up (여러 대의 차가). ～하다 collide 《with》; have a collision 《with》; run 〔bump, smash〕 《into》. ¶ 2중〔3중, 다중, 연쇄〕 ～ a「double 〔three-way, multiple, chain〕 collision / 정면 ～ a head-on collision / 바위에 ～하다 strike against 〔into〕 a rock / 전봇대에 ～하다 run 〔smash〕 into a telegraph pole / 두 대의 차가 서로 ～하다 two cars run into each other / 정면 ～하다 clash 〔collide〕 head=on 《with》 / ～ 사고로 죽다 be killed in a crash / 차 ～로 여덟 명이 사망했다 Eight people were killed in a car collision. / 짐수레에 트럭이 ～했다 The cart was run into by a motor truck. / 그의 차는 건널목에서 열차와 ～했다 His car「collided 〔was in collision〕 with a train at the level crossing. / 그 네거리에서 자동차의 4중 충돌이 있었다 There was a pileup of four cars at the cross roads.
② 《불화·불일치》 a conflict; a clash; a feud; a discord; a quarrel (말다툼); a falling-out. ～하다 《의견 등이》 conflict 〔clash〕 《with》; be in conflict 《with》; run counter 《to》; jar 《with》; 《불화하게 되다》 fall out 《with》; quarrel 《with》; be at strife 〔feud, variance, odds〕 《with》. ¶ 감정의 ～ an emotional 〔a temperamental〕 clash 《between, with》 / 신구 사상의 ～ the conflict between old ideas and new ideas / 의견의 ～ a clash of opinions; a conflict of views / 이해(利害)의 ～ a conflict 〔clash〕 of interests 《between》 / …일로 아무와 ～하다 clash 〔collide〕 with *a person* over … / ～을 피하다 avoid 〔ward off〕 friction 〔a collision〕 《with》 / 그는 아무와도 잘 ～한다 He is apt to fall out with anybody. / 그는 아버지와 ～했다 He quarreled with his father.
③ 《전투》 an encounter 《with》; a skirmish (소규모의). ～하다 clash with 《the enemy》; encounter 《an enemy aircraft》. ¶ 무력 ～ an armed conflict 《with, between》 / 국경에서의 양군의 ～ an encounter between two armies along the borderline.

**충동**(衝動) ① 《쑤석거림》 instigation; incitement; abetment. ～하다 《선동하다》 instigate; incite; abet; set 〔spur, egg〕 《*a person*》 on 《to *do*》; needle; 《유혹하다》 tempt; seduce; entice. ¶ …의 ～을 받아 at the instigation of…; abetted by… / 남을 ～(질)하여 …하게 하다 set 〔needle〕 *a person* to 《*do*》; abet *a person* in 《a crime》 / 둘이 싸우게 ～(질)하다 egg two persons on to fight with each other / 그는 그녀를 ～질해서 가출하게 했다 He enticed her away from home.
② 《강한 욕구》 an impulse; an impetus; an urge; 〖심리〗 a drive. ¶ 성적(性的) ～ the sex drive; a sexual drive 〔urge〕 / 여행하고 싶은 ～ the impulse to travel / (…하고 싶은) ～을 느끼다 feel an impulse to 《*do*》; have an urge to 《*do*》 / ～에 이끌리어 …하다 *do* on impulse; be driven by an impulse to *do* / 일시적 ～에 이끌리다「act on the spur 〔give way to the impulse〕 of the moment; act on impulse; have an urge 〔impulse〕 《to *do*》 / ～을 억제하다〔누르다〕 suppress 〔stifle〕 an impulse; inhibit 〔resist〕 an impulse 《to *do*》 / 나는 그녀를 때리고 싶은 ～을 느꼈다 I felt an「impulse 〔urge〕 to strike her.
◉ ～구매 impulse buying: ～ 구매자 an impulse buyer / ～ 구매를 하다 buy 《*something*》 on impulse.

**충동적**(衝動的) impulsive. ¶ ～인 사람 a man of impulse; an impulsive man / ～(인) 행동 an impulsive act / ～으로 《act》 impulsively; on 〔from〕 impulse; on the spur of the moment / 젊은이는 노인보다 더 ～이기 쉽다 The young are liable to be more impulsive than their elders.

**충량**(忠良) loyalty and honesty. ～하다 be loyal and honest 〔virtuous〕.

**충렬**(忠烈) unswerving loyalty; faithfulness.

**충령탑**(忠靈塔) a memorial to fallen heroes; a monument for the war dead; a war memorial.

**충류**(蟲類) insects and worms.

**충만**(充滿) repletion; fullness; abundance. ～하다 be full 《of》; be filled 〔replete〕 《with》. ¶ 원기 ～하다 be full of vitality; be all energy / 해학으로 ～해 있다 be「full of 〔replete with〕 humor / 유독 가스가 갱내에 ～해 있었다 The pit was filled with poisonous gas.

**충매**(蟲媒) 〖식물〗 entomophily; insect pollination. ◉ ～화(花) an entomophilous flower.

**충복**(忠僕) a faithful 〔devoted, dutiful〕 servant.

**충분**(充分) ～하다 《필요를 충족하다》 (be) enough; sufficient; 《많다》 (be) full; ample; plenty of; 《더할나위 없다》 good; 《완전하다》 (be) thorough; perfect; 《만족하다》 (be) satisfactory; 《알맞다》 (be) adequate.

> 용법 모두 「충분하다」의 뜻으로 쓰이지만, 내포된 미묘한 차이점을 크게 구별해 보면, **enough** 바람·희망을 채우기에, **sufficient** 필요를 채우기에, **adequate** 목적을 채우기에 「충분하다」란 뜻. **ample** 남아돌 정도로 「충분하다」.

¶ ～한 돈 enough money / ～한 보수 satisfactory pay / ～한 시간 plenty of time 《for》/ ～한 식량 sufficient provisions / ～한 식사 a good meal / ～한 음식의 공급 a sufficient 〔an ample〕 supply of food / ～한 이유 a good 〔an adequate〕 reasons / ～한 조사 a full 〔thorough〕 investigation / 살아가기에 ～한 수입 enough income to get along on / 그것이면 ～하다 That's enough. *or* That will do. / 그 일을 할 시간은 ～하다 We have time enough to complete (for) the work. / 그가 없어도 ～하다 We can do well without him. / 우선 만 원만 있으면 ～하다 Ten thousand won will 「suffice 〔do〕 for the present. / 그에게 그만큼 했으면 ～하다 You have done enough for him. / 이 식사는 두 사람 몫으로 ～하다 This meal is enough 〔adequate〕 for two.

**충분히**(充分一) enough; sufficiently; adequately; fairly; fully; in full; amply; plentifully; in plenty; satisfactorily; to *one's* satisfaction 〔heart's content〕; perfectly; thoroughly. ¶ ～ 먹다 eat enough; eat *one's* fill / ～ 보답하다 reward abundantly 〔amply〕/ ～설명하다 explain in full; explain at (full) length / ～ 쉬다 take 「*one's* fill of 〔a good〕 rest / ～ 알고 있다 know well enough / ～ 이해하다 understand perfectly / 영문학을 ～ 이해하고 있다 have a thorough understanding of English literature / ～ 성공할 가망이 있다 be in a fair way to succeed / ～ 표준에 달하다 be well up to the standard / …을 ～ 이용하다 take full advantage of… / 그 가치를 ～ 인정하다 come to a full appreciation of its value / 돈은 ～ 있다 have enough money 〔money enough〕/ 시간이 ～ 있다 have plenty of time 《for》/ 믿을 만한 이유가 ～ 있다 have good 〔every〕 reason to believe / 볼 만한 가치가 ～ 있다 be well worth seeing / 실력을 ～ 발휘하다 give full play to *one's* ability; make the most of what *one* has / 그 기회를 ～ 즐기다 enjoy the occasion to the full / ～라고까지는 할 수 없으나 though not 「sufficiently complete 〔wholly satisfactory〕/ 할 말은 ～ 했다 Enough has been said. / 성사될 가망이 ～ 있다 There is every promise of success. 「in flight.

**충빠지다** 《an arrow》 quiver 〔vibrate〕

**충사**(忠死) a loyal death. ～하다 die for *one's* loyalty.

**충색**(充塞) ～하다 《막다》 fill up; plug; stop (up); block; clog up; 《막히다》 be filled 〔stopped〕 up.

**충성**(忠誠) loyalty; faithfulness; devotion; fidelity; allegiance. ～스럽다 (be) loyal; faithful; devoted.

> 용법 **loyalty** 주로, 개인이나 국가에 대한 개인적인 충성. **fidelity** 약속·주의 따위에 대한 충성·성실을 뜻하며, 애착심보다는 의무감의 암시가 강함. **allegiance** 개인적인 감정보다는 국민으로서 국가에 대한 또는 단체의 구성원으로서 단체에 대한 충성·의무감을 뜻함. **devotion** 「…에 대한 헌신, 전념」이란 의미에서 「충성」의 뜻으로 새겨지는 말.

¶ ～스럽게 loyally; faithfully; devotedly / 국가에 대한 ～ allegiance to *one's* country / 팀에 대한 ～ loyalty to *one's* team / 과잉～ excessive loyalty / ～을 다짐〔맹세〕하다 pledge *one's* loyalty 〔allegiance〕 《to》; make a pledge of allegiance 《to the Queen》/ 나라에 ～하다 render devoted service to *one's* country; be loyal to *one's* country. ◉ ～선언 《공무원의》 a loyalty oath 《미》.

**충수**(蟲垂) 『해부』 the vermiform appendix. ◉ ～염(炎) appendicitis: ～염 절제(切除) (an) appendectomy.

**충순**(忠純) faithfulness and pureness; loyalty and sincerity. ～하다 (be) faithful and pure; honest and true.

**충순**(忠順) loyalty; fidelity; allegiance; devotion; obedience. ～하다 (be) loyal; dutiful; devoted; obedient.

**충신**(忠臣) a loyal 〔faithful〕 retainer 〔vassal〕; a loyal subject. ¶ ～ 노릇을 하다 serve loyally 〔faithfully〕/ ～은 두 임금을 섬기지 않는다 A faithful retainer will not serve two masters. / ~은 효자 가문에서 난다 A filial son makes a loyal subject.

**충신**(忠信) fidelity; loyalty; faithfulness; devotion.

**충실**(充實) 《실질이 있음》 substantiality; fullness; 《완비》 completeness; completion; perfection. ~하다 (be) full; replete 《with》; complete; rich; 《실질·내용이》 (be) substantial; solid. ¶ ~한 지식 full knowledge / 군비의 ~ military preparedness; completion 〔perfection〕 of preparation for war / ~한 생활 a full 〔fulfilling〕 life / 내용의 ~ richness in contents; substantiality / ~히 하다 enrich; make 《*a thing*》 satisfactory 〔complete〕; perfect; complete; bring 《facilities》 up to the mark / 국력의 ~을 꾀하다 carry out a plan to build up 〔consolidate〕 national power / 몸이 ~하다 be in perfect health; have a strong body / 벼알이 ~하다 rice grains are full / 지극히 ~한 생활을 하다 lead life to the fullest / 생활 내용을 ~히 하다 enrich *one's* experiences / 책의 내용이 ~하다 The book is substantial 〔very rich, meaty〕 in content. / 이 도서관은 장서가 ~하다 This library has a good collection of books. ◉ ~감 a sense of fulfillment: …에 어느 정도 ~감을 얻고 있다 find some fulfillment in 《*one's* work》.

**충실**(忠實) faithfulness; loyalty (국가·개인에 대한); fidelity (주의·신앙 등에 대한); devotion (헌신). ~하다 (be) faithful; true; loyal; devoted 《to》. ¶ ~한 벗 a faithful friend / 주인에게 ~한 개 a faithful dog to his master / 아내에 ~한 남편 a husband loyal to his wife / ~하게〔히〕 faithfully; loyally; devotedly; truly / 친구에게〔임무에〕 ~하다 be faithful to *one's* friend 〔duties〕 / 직무에 ~하다 be faithful 〔devoted〕 to *one's* duties / 원문에 ~하게 번역하다 be faithful 〔true〕 to the original in translation; make a faithful translation / 이 그림은 당시의 풍속을 ~하게 재현하고 있다 This picture faithfully reflects the manners and customs of those days. / 그는 주인에게 ~한 하인이다 He is a servant true to his master. / 직무에 ~치 않은 사람도 있다 Some persons are not faithful to their duties.
◉ ~도 『통신』 fidelity; 《텔레비전 영상의》 linearity: 고~도 수신기 a high-fidelity 〔hi-fi〕 receiver.

**충심**(忠心) faithfulness; loyalty; fidelity; allegiance.

**충심**(衷心) *one's* innermost heart; *one's* true heart. ¶ ~으로 heartily; cordially; deeply; from (the bottom of) *one's* heart; wholeheartedly / ~에서 우러나오는 동정 hearty 〔heartfelt〕 sympathy / ~에서 우러나오는 소리 *one's* sincere remark / ~으로 감사하다 thank 《*a person*》 from (the bottom of) *one's* heart / ~으로 환영하다 welcome 《*a person*》 heartily 〔cordially〕; give a hearty welcome / 귀하의 모친상에 즈음하여 ~으로 위로의 말씀을 드리는 바입니다 I would like to offer 〔express〕 my deepest condolences 〔sympathy〕 on the death of your mother.

**충심**(衝心) 『의학』 heart failure.

**충애**(忠愛) 《충성과 사랑》 loyalty and love; devoted affection; 《충군 애국》 loyalty and patriotism.

**충양**(蟲樣) =충수(蟲垂).

**충언**(忠言) (good, honest) advice; faithful counsel. ~하다 give 〔offer〕 good advice; advise. ¶ ~은 귀에 거슬린다 Good advice is 〔sounds〕 harsh to the ear. *or* Honest advice jars on the ear.

**충욕**(充慾) ~하다 gratify 〔satisfy〕 *one's* 「desire 〔appetite〕.

**충용**(充用) appropriation; application. ⇨충당. ~하다 appropriate 《to, for》; apply 《to》; earmark 《for》.

**충용**(忠勇) loyalty and valor 〔bravery〕. ¶ ~한 loyal and brave 〔courageous〕 《soldiers》.

**충원**(充員) 《인력의》 supplement of the personnel; 《군대의》 (army) reserves; recruits; drafts (of men). ~하다 supplement the personnel; call up 〔recruit〕 personnel. ¶ 결원은 곧 ~되어야 한다 We must fill up the vacancy right away. ◉ ~계획 a levy plan. ~소집 a general call-up 〔levy〕; calling out the reserves; a levy in mass.

**충의**(忠義) loyalty; fidelity; devotion. ~롭다 (be) loyal; faithful; devoted.

**충이다** ¶ 쌀 자루를 ~ shake a rice bag 「up and down 〔from side to side〕 《to pack rice to the full》; joggle 《rice in a bag》.

**충일**(充溢) overflowing; affluence; exuberance; abundance. ~하다 overflow; be full 《of energy》; be abundant 〔affluent, exuberant〕.

**충재**(蟲災) ⇨충해(蟲害).

**충적**(沖積) 〖지질〗 ◉ ～곡(谷) an alluvial valley. ～기(紀)〔세(世)〕 the alluvial「epoch〔period〕. ～물질 alluvial material. ～선상지(扇狀地) an alluvial fan. ～층 an alluvium; an alluvial bed. ～토 alluvial soil; alluvium. ～퇴적물 alluvial deposits. ～평야 an alluvial plain; a flood plain.

**충전**(充電) charge; charging. ～하다 charge《a battery》; give a charge of electricity to《a storage battery》; electrify. ¶ 그는 자동차 배터리를 ～케 했다 He got the car battery charged (with electricity). / 이 전기 자동차는 배터리를 1회 ～해서 90킬로미터를 달린다 This electric automobile will go 90 km on one battery charge.
◉ ～기 a (battery) charger. ～(용) 발전기 a charging dynamo. ～장치 charging equipment. ～전지〔전류〕 a charging「battery〔current〕. 과～ overcharge. 재～ recharging.

**충전**(充塡) filling「up〔in〕; stopping (up); plugging. ～하다 fill「up〔in〕; stop (up); plug. ¶ 치아를 ～하다 stop〔plug〕 a tooth; fill a tooth《with gold》. ◉ ～기 a plugger. ～물 a filling; a plug; a tamping. ～제(劑) fillers.

**충절**(忠節) loyalty; fidelity; allegiance; devotion. ¶ ～을 다하다 serve with loyalty; be「loyal〔devoted〕 to《*one's* lord》.

**충정**(衷情) *one's* inmost feelings; *one's* true〔inmost〕 heart. ¶ ～을 털어놓다 open *one's*「heart〔mind〕《to》; unbosom *oneself*《to》.

**충족**(充足) sufficiency; fulfillment. ～하다《채우다》 fill (up);《만족·충족 시키다》 satisfy《*a person's* need》; meet《the demand》; answer《the purpose》; fulfill《a condition》; gratify《*a person's* desire》;《보충하다》 make up《for》. ¶ ～되지 않은 욕구 an unfilled desire / 자기 ～적인 self-sufficient / 조건을 ～시키다 meet the requirements; satisfy the conditions / ～되지 않은 감이 들다 feel not quite satisfied; feel something is「wanting〔left out〕/ 이 강가를 산책하고 있노라면, 나는 언제나 마음의 ～감을 느낀다 When I take a stroll along this river, I never fail to feel contented in heart and mind.
◉ ～원리 〖철학〗 the principle of sufficient reason (충족이유율).

**충직**(忠直) faithfulness; uprightness; honesty. ～하다 (be) faithful; honest; upright. ¶ ～한 하인「an honest〔a faithful, a trusty〕 servant / ～한 마음 a true heart; an honest mind / ～하게 일하다 be faithful to *one's* duty.

**충천**(衝天) ～하다 rise〔soar〕 high up to the sky; go sky-high. ¶ 의기 ～하다 *one's* spirit soars《to the skies》; be in「high〔royal, towering, roaring〕 spirits.

**충충거리다** walk with quick steps; walk fast; walk at a quick pace.

**충충하다** ①《어둡다》 (be) dark; dull; gloomy; shady; dim; dusky; somber. ¶ 충충한 날씨 gloomy weather / 충충한 방 a「gloomy〔dimly-lit〕 room / 충충한 빛(깔) a「dark〔dull, somber〕 color / 충충하게 하다 darken; make dull / 이 방은 ～ This room is poorly lighted. ②《물이》 (be) full and deep. ¶ 우물에 물이 ～ The well has plenty of water in it.

**충치**(蟲齒) a「carious〔decayed, bad〕 tooth;《상태》 a dental caries. ¶ ～구멍 a cavity in a tooth / 치료를 하지 않은 ～ an untreated decayed tooth / ～가 먹다 get a decayed tooth; have a tooth decay / ～가 쑤시다 *one's* decayed tooth aches; have an ache in *one's* carious tooth / ～를 빼다 have a decayed tooth (pulled) out / ～를 치료하다 treat a decayed tooth / ～를 예방하다 prevent teeth from decaying; prevent tooth decay / ～에 봉을 박다 fill〔stop〕 a decayed tooth.

**충해**(蟲害) damage「from〔done by〕 insects; insect pests; vermin damage; a blight. ¶ ～를 입다 be damaged by insects; be blighted / ～에 의한 흉작 a crop failure due to an insect plague.

**충혈**(充血) 〖의학〗 congestion《of the brain》; hyperemia; afflux (of blood). ～하다 be congested; be〔become〕 engorged〔suffused〕 with blood;《눈이》 (be) bloodshot. ¶ ～성의 congestive / 동맥성 ～ arterial congestion / ～을 없애다 relieve《mucous membranes》 of congestion; decongest / ～시키다 congest; cause congestion / 그녀의 눈은 ～되어 있다 Her eyes are bloodshot. ◉ ～제거제 a decongestant. ～증상 congestive symptoms.

**충혼**(忠魂) ①《죽은》 a loyal soul;《죽은 이》 the「loyal〔war〕 dead. ¶ ～을 위로하다 propitiate the loyal dead. ②《충성심》 a「loyal〔faithful〕 spirit; loyalty. ◉ ～비 a monument to the「loyal〔war〕 dead.

**충효**(忠孝) loyalty and filial piety. ¶ ~ 겸전하다 be at once a loyal subject and a dutiful son / ~의 길은 둘이 아니요 하나다 Loyalty and filial duty are one and the same. ◉ ~사상 the thought of loyalty and filial piety.

**췌관**(膵管) 〖해부〗 a pancreatic duct.

**췌액**(膵液) 〖동물〗 pancreatic juice. ◉ ~소 〖생화학〗 pancreatin.

**췌언**(贅言) redundant 〔superfluous, unnecessary〕 words; (a) pleonasm; redundancy; tautology; idle 〔useless〕 remarks. ¶ 국방이 중요하다는 것은 ~을 요하지 않는다 There is no need to 「dwell upon 〔reiterate〕 the importance of our national defense.

**췌장**(膵藏) 〖해부〗 the pancreas. ¶ ~의 pancreatic. ◉ ~결석 a pancreatic calculus; a pancreatolith. ~염 pancreatitis. ~절개술 pancreatotomy.

**취** 〖식물〗 a fragrant edible wild aster.

**취**(嘴) 〖음악〗 a (woodwind) reed.

**취객**(醉客) a drunken man; a drunk「ard.

**취결**(就結) 《어음의》 drawing (of bills). ~하다 draw. ¶ …앞으로 어음을 ~하다 draw a bill upon 《*a person* for a sum》. ◉ 환어음~ a money-order exchange.

**취결례**(取潔禮) 〖가톨릭〗 purification. ◉ ~첨례(瞻禮) the Purification (of the Virgin Mary); Candlemas (Day).

**취관**(吹管) a blowpipe; a blast pipe. ◉ ~돌기 〖동물〗 a siphonal process. ~분석 〖화학〗 a blowpipe analysis.

**취광**(醉狂) 《취함》 a drunken frenzy; delirium tremens; 《사람》 a frenzied drunk.

**취급**(取扱) 《다룸》 ① 《사람의》 treatment; dealing; 《손님의》 service. ~하다 treat; deal with. ¶ 공평한 ~ a fair 〔square〕 deal / 남처럼 ~하다 treat 《*a person*》 as 〔like〕 a stranger / 어린애 ~을 하다 treat 《*a person*》 like a child; make a baby of 《*a person*》 / 무례한 ~을 받다 be ill-treated; 《구어》 get a raw deal / 사람을 공평하게 ~하다 deal justly 〔fairly〕 with *a person;* give *a person* a square deal / 저 가게는 손님 ~이 좋지 않다 Service in that store is bad 〔poor〕.
② 《물건의》 handling; manipulation; 《사물·일의》 treatment; dealing; management. ~하다 handle; manipulate; work 〔operate〕 《a machine》; 《처리하다》 deal with 《a problem》; manage; conduct; transact; take charge of (담당). ¶ ~하기 쉬운 manageable; easy to manage 〔handle〕 / ~하기 어려운 unmanageable; hard to handle 〔deal with〕 / ~이 편리하도록 for convenience in handling / 사회 문제를 ~한 소설 a novel that deals with social problems / 사무를 ~하다 conduct 〔carry on〕 business; manage affairs / 문제를 가볍게〔신중히〕 ~하다 deal with 〔handle〕 a matter lightly 〔carefully〕 / 조심스럽게 ~하다 handle with care / 거칠게 ~하다 handle roughly; give 《*a thing*》 rough handling / ~주의 《표시》 Handle with care. / 이건 정밀 기계니 조심해서 ~해라 As this is a delicate 〔precision〕 machine, you must handle it with care.
③ 《기타》 acceptance; dealing. ~하다 《받다》 accept; take in; 《매매하다》 deal 《in》; trade 《in》. ¶ 외환을 ~하다 deal in foreign exchange / 전보를 ~하다 accept 〔take in〕 telegrams / 저희는 그런 상품은 ~하지 않습니다 We are not dealing in 〔We don't sell〕 that kind 〔sort〕 of goods. / 전보 ~ 《게시》 Telegrams accepted.
◉ ~량 the volume of business; the total of dealings. ~설명서 《기계류 등의》 an instruction manual. ~소 an office; an agency (대리점): 화물 ~소 a freight agency 《미》; a forwarding agency 《영》. ~시간 service hour; hours of attendance. ~인〔자〕 an agent; a person in charge 《of》. ~점 a store dealing in 《a particular item》.

**취기**(臭氣) an offensive 〔odious〕 smell; a bad 〔foul, nasty, fetid, filthy〕 odor; a stench; a stink. ¶ ~가 있는 bad-smelling; malodorous; stinking / ~가 없는 inodorous; odorless / ~를 없애는 약 a deodorizer; a deodorant / ~를 발산하다 give 〔send〕 out an offensive smell; emit a foul 〔bad〕 odor / ~를 없애다 destroy the bad odor 《of》; deodorize / ~가 코를 찌르다 it stinks; be offensive to the nose.

**취기**(醉氣) (signs of) intoxication; tipsiness; inebriation. ¶ ~가 돌다 become 〔get, grow〕 drunk 〔tipsy〕; feel the effects of drink; feel 〔show〕 *one's* liquor; show signs of intoxication / ~가 깨다 become 〔get〕 sober; sober up; recover from *one's* intoxication / ~를 이기지 못하다 be overcome by the effects of the liquor; fall dead-drunk; pass out (drunk) / ~를 깨려고 물을 마시다 (take a cup of water to) cool 〔clear〕 *one's* coppers.

**취담**(醉談) talking under the influence of drink; drunken words; a remark made under the influence of alcohol. ～하다 talk under the influence of drink. ¶ ～이 진담이다 People tell the truth when they are drunk. / ～이니 나쁘게 생각지 마시오 Don't take me seriously — I'm drunk. *or* Don't mind his words — he's drunk.

**취대**(取貸) borrowing and lending; debt(s) and credit(s); loan(s). ～하다 borrow and lend.

**취도계**(醉度計) a drunkometer; a breathalyzer. ⇨ 음주 측정기.

**취득**(取得) (an) acquisition; 《사서 얻은》 (a) purchase. ～하다 acquire; get; obtain; gain; take possession of 《the new property》; purchase. ¶ 재산의 ～ the acquisition of property / 소유권을 ～하다 acquire the ownership 《of》 / 운전 면허를 ～하다 get 〔obtain〕 a driver's license. ◉ ～가격 acquisition cost. ～권 ownership: 선～권 『법』 the right of priority; a prior right. ～물 an acquisition; a find. ～세 an acquisition 〔sales〕 tax: 부동산 ～세 a real estate acquisition tax. ～시효 acquisitive 〔positive〕 prescription. ～자 an acquisitor.

**취락**(聚落) a settlement; a community; a village; a colony (생물의).

**취렴**(聚斂) exploitation; sweating; exaction; collecting heavy taxes. ～하다 exploit; exact; collect mercilessly.

**취로**(就勞) ～하다 set 〔go〕 to work; work; find work 〔employment〕. ¶ ～하고 있다 be at work. ◉ ～사업 a job-producing project. ～시간 working hours. ～일수 working days.

**취리**(取利) moneylending; usury. ～하다 lend money (out); run a moneylending business; practice usury. ¶ ～하여 돈을 모으다 make money by usury. ◉ ～업 moneylending business; usury: ～업자 a moneylender; an usurer.

**취목**(取木) layering. ⇨ 휘묻이.

**취미**(趣味) (a) taste; (an) interest; (a) liking; 《도락》 a hobby; pastime. ¶ 고상〔저속〕한 ～ a noble 〔vulgar, loud〕 taste / 세련된 ～ a refined taste / 다방면의 ～ varied 〔diversified, versatile, various〕 taste / 별난 ～ a taste for odd things; a bizarre taste / ～의 문제 a matter of taste / ～의 원예 horticulture 〔gardening〕 for pleasure.

> **용법** **taste** 「좋아하는 것」, 아름다움, 미술, 음악 등에 대한 감각적인 판단을 내릴 수 있는 능력, 즉 「심미안」 등을 뜻함. **interest** 주의·관심을 일으키는 힘·욕망이라는 뜻에서 「흥미·관심사 → 취미」라는 뜻이 된 말. **hobby** 정규의 일 이외로 지속적으로 무언가를 하는 것. 능동적으로 수준 향상을 위해 연구·수집·습득 따위를 하는 취미 행위. **pastime** 여가를 즐겁게 보내기 위해 일과성으로 행해지는 활동. 오락적인 뜻이 강한 낱말. 즉, 야구를 관전하는 것은 pastime 이고 야구를 하는 것은 hobby가 됨.

취미가: ～가 다양한 사람 a person with many interests 〔hobbies〕; a man of varied interests / ～가 없는 사람 a man of no taste / ～가 있다 have a taste 《for》; be interested 《in》 / ～가 없다 lack taste; have no taste 〔relish〕 《for》; be not interested 《in》 / ～가 좋다 [사람이 주어] have (a) good 〔well-cultivated〕 taste 《in clothes》; [사물이 주어] be in good taste / ～가 고상한 사람 a person of refined 〔well-cultivated〕 taste / 시에 ～가 없다 have no taste for poetry; have no interest in poetry.

취미에: ～에 맞다 suit 〔be congenial to〕 *one's* taste; be to *one's* liking 〔taste〕 / ～에 맞는 일 a job 〔an occupation〕 to *one's* liking / ～에 맞지 않다 be uncongenial to *one's* taste; be out of keeping with *one's* taste.

취미로: ～로 …을 하다 take delight 〔a pleasure〕 in *do*ing...; do 《*a thing*》 as a hobby 〔for mere pleasure, for fun〕 / ～로 그림을 그리다 dabble at 〔in〕 painting / ～로 사진에 손을 대다 dabble in photography as a hobby / ～로 우표를 모으다 collect stamps as a hobby / ～로 정원을 가꾸다 make a garden for pleasure.

취미를: …에 ～를 갖다 be interested 《in》; take an interest 《in》; have a taste 《for》; have a fondness 〔liking〕 《for》 / ～를 가지고 일하다 work with zest / ～를 기르다 cultivate a taste 《for music》 / ～를 붙이다 acquire 〔attain, develop〕 a taste 《for》; attain 〔acquire〕 an interest 《in》 / ～를 잃다 lose *one's* interest 《in》; lose *one's* taste 《for》.

¶ ～가 사람마다 다르다 Tastes differ. *or* There is no accounting for tastes. / 그들은 ～가 공통된 데가 많다 They have

many interests in common. / 그 부부는 ～가 서로 다르다 The couple have 〔has〕 different tastes. (★「부부」란 뜻의 couple은 단·복수 취급) / 그는 요즘 그림에 ～를 붙이기 시작했다 He has begun to get interested in painting. / 춤은 내 ～에 맞지 않는다 Dancing is not to my taste. *or* I don't care for dancing. / 이것이라면 모든 사람의 ～에 맞을 게다 This will please 〔suit〕 every taste 〔all tastes〕. / 너는 음악에 ～가 있는 것 같다 You seem to be of a musical turn.
◉ ～강좌 lectures on artistic topics. ～생활 a dilettante('s) life.
독서～ interest in reading; the pleasure of reading. 문학～ literary taste. 전원～ the pleasure of rural life.

**취사**(炊事) cooking; kitchen work 〔duty〕. ～하다 cook; do cooking. ¶ 그는 자신이 직접 ～한다 He cooks for himself. ◉ ～당번 『군사』 the cook's duty; 《사람》 a soldier on the cook's duty; [총칭] kitchen police. ～도구 cooking utensils; kitchenware. ～설비 cooking facilities. ～장 a kitchen; a cookhouse (별채의); a field kitchen (야영의); a galley (배의): 공동 ～장 a common 〔communal〕 kitchen.

**취사선택**(取捨選擇) choice; selection; selection or rejection; (an) option; sorting out. ～하다 choose; select; sort out; make *one's* choice. ¶ ～의 자유 freedom of choice / ～을 그르치다 make the wrong choice; make a mistake in the choice 《of》 / ～에 망설이다 be at a loss which to take 〔choose〕 《among》 / 너는 자유롭게 ～할 수 있다 You can have a free choice. ◉ ～권 a right of selection; an option.

**취산화서**(聚繖花序) 『식물』 centrifugal in= florescence; cyme. ¶ ～의 cymose; cymous.

**취색**(翠色) verdure; jade color(ed); 「green.

**취생몽사**(醉生夢死) leading a life of befuddled and dreamy indolence; idling *one's* life away. ～하다 live 「idly 〔to no purpose〕; slumber 〔sleep, idle〕 *one's* life away. ¶ ～하는 사람 idlers; lotus-eaters.

**취석**(臭石) 『광물』 stinkstone.

**취선옹**(醉仙翁) 『식물』 a rose campion.

**취소**(取消) (a) cancellation; (a) withdrawal; retraction (철회); (a) revocation 《of treaty》; a repeal (법률 등의); annulment (계약 따위의). ～하다 cancel; 《철회하다》 withdraw; 《발언을》 take back; retract; 《법률을》 repeal; 《명령·계약 따위를》 annul 《a contract》; revoke 《a command》. ¶ 면허(증)의 ～ the revocation of a license / 주문의 ～ cancellation of an order / ～할 수 있는 revocable; retractable; recallable / ～할 수 없는 irrevocable; beyond recall 〔revoke〕; irreversible / 앞서 한 말을 ～하다 withdraw 〔retract〕 *one's* statement; take back what one has said / 주문〔예약〕을 ～하다 cancel an order 〔a reservation〕 / 약혼을 ～하다 break off 〔end〕 *one's* engagement / 계약을 ～하다 cancel 〔break off〕 a contract / 그것은 ～할 수 있는〔없는〕 발언이다 It's a revocable 〔an irrevocable〕 statement. / 기사의 ～를 요구했다 I demanded a withdrawal of the statement in the newspaper. / 난 어제 한 약속을 ～하겠다 I'll take back the promise I made yesterday. / 다음 달 5일의 숙박 예약을 ～하고 싶습니다 I'd like to cancel my reservation for the night of the fifth of next month. / 그녀는 그 기사가 사실무근임을 주장하면서, 그 기사의 ～를 요구했다 She insisted that the statement was false and demanded its withdrawal. / 당일의 예약 ～에는 위약금이 부과됩니다 Cancellation of the reservation on the day will incur a cancellation charge.
◉ ～권 『법』 right of rescission; the right to rescind: ～권부 신용장 a revocable letter of credit. ～명령 a countermand (order). ～소송 an action for nullity.

**취소**(臭素) 『화학』 bromine.

**취소불능**(取消不能) ¶ ～의 irrevocable; irreversible; indefeasible. ◉ ～신용장 an irrevocable letter of credit.

**취안**(醉眼) drunken eyes; eyes dim 〔bleary〕 with drink. ¶ 몽롱한 ～으로 with glazed 〔drunken〕 eyes; with *one's* eyes 「blurred by 〔bleary from〕 drink; dazed by liquor / ～이 몽롱하다 *one's* eyes are blurred with drink; have drunken eyes.

**취안**(醉顔) a face flushed with liquor; a drunken look.

**취약**(脆弱) weakness; frailty; fragility; brittleness; flimsiness. ～하다 (be) weak; frail; fragile; delicate; flimsy; brittle. ¶ 우리 수출 산업의 구조적인 ～성을 시정하다 rectify any structural vulnerability of our export industries. ◉ ～지구〔지점〕 『군사』 a vulnerable area 〔point〕; the area vulnerable to the enemy's infiltration.

**취업**(就業) ①《일을 함》 working; beginning to work. ～하다 start 〔begin, set about〕 work. ¶ ～중이다 be at work; be on duty / ～중 면회 사절 《게시》 Interviews declined during working hours.

②《취직》 getting employment; taking a job. ～하다 find 〔get〕 work 〔employment〕; get 〔secure〕 a position 〔job, place〕《with a firm》. ⇨취직. ¶ 해외～ overseas employment / 미～자 구제계획 a program to help the unemployed / ～을 신청하다 apply for a position 〔job〕/ ～시키다 find 《*a person*》 a job / ～계약을 하다 sign on to work for 《a company》.

◉ ～규칙 office 〔shop〕 regulations. ～근로자 an employed worker 〔laborer〕. ～률 the percentage of employment. ～상태 the state of employment. ～시간 the working 〔business, office〕 hours. ～알선 job placement. ～연령 working age. ～인구 the working population: 여성의 직장 진출로 한국의 ～인구는 현저하게 증가되었다 With women entering the work force, the working population of Korea has increased remarkably. ～일수 days worked. ～제한 restriction on employment. ～지(地) the location 〔place〕 of employment.

**취역**(就役) ～하다 go 〔come〕 into commission 〔service〕; be placed 〔put〕 in 〔into〕 commission; be commissioned. ¶ 미국 항로에 ～하다 go into service on the American line / ～시키다 commission 《a ship》; place 〔put〕 《a ship》 in 〔into〕 commission / ～해 있다 be in commission / ～에서 해제하다 remove 《a ship》 from service; decommission 《a ship》.

◉ ～함 a commissioned ship.

**취옥**(翠玉) 〖광물〗《에메랄드》 an emerald; 《비취옥》 green jadeite; jade.

**취와**(醉臥) lying in a drunken stupor. ～하다 lie dead 〔blind〕 drunk.

**취음**(取音) a phonetic equivalent; transliteration. ～하다 borrow a phonetic equivalent; transliterate. ¶ 한자에서 ～한 말 a word transcribed in Chinese characters used phonetically. ◉ ～자(字) a Chinese transliteration of a Korean word.

**취의**(趣意) ＝취지(趣旨).

**취임**(就任) assumption of office; inauguration; installation. ～하다 take 〔assume〕 office 《as》; take (up) *one's* post 《with》; be inaugurated; be installed 《in an office》. ¶ ～을 발표하다 announce 《*a person's*》 assumption of office / ～을 수락하다 accept an appointment / ～을 거절하다 decline 〔turn down〕 an offer of a position / 공식으로 ～하다 take office formally / 교수로 ～하다 take up a professorship / 대통령으로 ～하다 take office as President; be inaugurated as President / ～선서를 하다 take the 〔*one's*〕 oath of office / 신임 교육부 장관은 내일 정식으로 ～한다 The new Education Minister will formally assume his office tomorrow. / 그는 선서하고 대통령으로 ～했다 He was sworn in as President. ◉ ～사〔연설〕 an inaugural (address). ～식 an inaugural ceremony; an inauguration: 대통령 ～식 날 Inauguration Day 《미》.

**취입**(吹入) recording. ～하다 record; put 《a song》 on a record 〔disk, tape〕; have 〔get〕 《*one's* speech, song》 recorded. ¶ 그녀는 바이올린 독주를 ～했다 She recorded her violin solo on a disk. ◉ ～소(所) a recording studio.

**취재**(取材) collection of (news) materials; news gathering; (news) coverage. ～하다 collect 〔gather〕 meterials 〔data〕 《on, for》; 《신문 기자가》 gather news; cover 《a meeting》. ¶ 사고를 현지 ～하다 cover an accident on the spot / ～여행을 떠나다 go on a material-gathering 〔fact-finding〕 tour for (writing) an article / 이 소설 내용은 한국 전쟁에서 ～하였다 This novel took its story from the Korean War.

◉ ～경쟁 competition in coverage. ～기자 a (news) reporter; 《미》 a legman. ～담당구역 *one's* newsbeat. ～원 a (news) source. ～활동 coverage activities; 《미구어》 legwork: 정치 관계의 ～활동 political legwork / ～활동 범위 the scope of news coverage activities.

**취조**(取調) questioning. ＝문초(問招).

**취종**(取種) gathering the seeds. ～하다 gather the seeds 〔breeds〕.

**취주**(吹奏) playing (wind instruments); blowing. ～하다 blow 《the trumpet》; play (on) 《the flute》. ◉ ～악 wind (-instrument) music: ～악단〔군악대〕 a brass 〔military〕 band. ～악기 a wind instrument. ～자 a player.

**취중**(醉中) ¶ ～의 싸움 a drunken

brawl 〔quarrel〕/ ～에 in a drunken state; under the influence of alcohol; in *one's* cups / ～에 실수하다 make a mistake while in *one's* cups; make a drunken slip / ～에 진담한다 One tells the truth when drunk.

**취지**(趣旨) 《뜻》 the meaning; 《요지》 the gist; the point; the purport; the effect; the tenor; 《목적》 an object; an aim; a purpose; intent (의도). ¶ 독립 선언서의 ～ the purport 〔gist〕 of the Declaration of Independence / 법의 ～ the intent of the law / 연설의 ～ the tenor 〔purport〕 of a speech / ～에 찬성하여 in support of its object / …라는 ～를 써 보내다 write to 《*a person*》 (to the effect) that… / 같은 ～의 말을 하다 speak to the same effect / 질문의 ～는 무엇입니까 What is the point of your question? / 이 운동의 ～를 설명하겠다 Let me explain the object of this movement. / 그 ～를 그에게 전하겠습니다 I will tell him to that effect. / ～는 좋습니다 It is a good idea. / ～를 알았습니다 I understand what you mean. / ～에 찬성하여 회원이 되었다 I joined the society in support of its object. / 본회의 설립 ～는 빈민 구제에 있다 The Society has been organized with the relief of the poor for its main object. / 그것은 법의 ～에 어긋나게 된다 That would run counter to the spirit of the law.

**취지서**(趣旨書) a prospectus. ¶ 학회 창립의 ～ a prospectus for the establishment of an academic society / ～에 씌어진 대로 as it is mentioned in the prospectus / ～를 작성하다 draw up 〔write out〕 a prospectus.

**취직**(就職) getting 〔finding〕 employment; taking a job. ～하다 find employment 〔work〕; secure 〔obtain, get〕 a position 《in, with》; get 〔find〕 a job 《with a firm》; enter (industrial) employment; 《구어》 sign on 《with a firm as a driver》. ¶ ～할 기회 employment 〔job〕 opportunities / ～을 부탁하다 ask 《*a person*》 for a job / ～을 신청〔지망〕하다 apply for a position 〔job〕; submit a job application 《to》 / ～을 알선하다 help 《*a person*》 get a job; find 〔get〕 《*a person*》 a job; put 《*a person*》 in the way of a job / ～시키다 get 《*a person*》 employed; place 《*a person*》 in a position; place 《*a person*》 in the service 《of a company》 / 신문사에 ～하다 get a job with a newspaper / 관청에 ～하다 enter government service / 그녀는 여행사에 ～해 있다 She is employed at a traveling agency.
◉ ～률 an employment rate. ～시험 an employment examination. ～신청 an application for a position. ～알선 (job) placement. ～정보지(誌) a job=placement journal 〔magazine〕. ～지망자 a job applicant 〔candidate〕; an applicant for a position. ～처(處) the place of employment.

**취직난**(就職難) the difficulty of finding employment 〔work〕; job shortage; scarcity of employment. ¶ ～이 심하다 it is very hard to find a job; jobs are very scarce / ～으로 곤란받다 have a hard time finding a job / ～을 완화하다 relieve the difficulty of finding employment.

**취직운동**(就職運動) job hunting; seeking employment. ¶ ～을 하다 seek employment; look 〔hunt〕 for a job 〔position〕; go around looking for work / 은행에 ～을 하다 seek employment at a bank / ～으로 바쁘다 be busy 「seeking employment 〔looking for a position〕.

**취직자리**(就職 —) a job; a position; a situation; an opening; a place. ¶ ～를 주선하다 assistant 《*a person*》 to a position; help 《*a person*》 (to) find a job / ～를 찾다 seek employment; look 〔hunt〕 for a position; 《찾아내다》 obtain employment; secure a position; get a job / ～를 찾아주다 find 〔get〕 《*a person*》 a job 〔place〕.

**취처**(娶妻) ～하다 take a wife; marry 〔espouse〕 《a woman》.

**취체**(取締) regulation. = 단속(團束).

**취침**(就寢) going to bed. ～하다 go to bed; turn in; retire (to rest, to bed, for the night). ¶ ～중 while (*one* is) asleep 〔sleeping〕; (while) in bed / ～전에 before retiring / 일찍 ～하다 retire early (to rest) / ～ 중 화재가 났다 A fire broke out while we were in bed.
◉ ～시간 (*one's*) bedtime: 내 ～ 시간은 11시이다 My bedtime is 11 o'clock.

**취태**(醉態) drunkenness; intoxication; drunken behavior. ¶ ～를 보이다 be seen drunk / ～를 부리다 put on a drunken display; be drunk and disorderly.

**취택**(取擇) picking out; choice; selection. ～하다 pick out; choose; select. ¶ ～하기 곤란하다 I am at a loss which to choose.

**취하**(取下) withdrawal; discontinuance. ～하다 withdraw; dismiss; drop; abandon. ¶ 신청을 ～하다 withdraw *one's* application / 소송을 ～하다 withdraw 〔call off, drop〕 a suit.

**취하다**(取―) ① 《채택하다》 adopt; assume; take. ¶ 공세를 ～ assume 〔take〕 the offensive / 방침을 ～ take 〔adopt, pursue〕 a course / 입장을 ～ take the stand 〔position〕 《that…》/ 조치를 ～ take a step 〔measure〕; make a move; take action / 강경한 태도를 ～ assume a firm 〔an unyielding〕 attitude / 서양 문물을 ～ adopt things Western / 그 설(說)은 취할 것이 못된다 The opinion is not worth serious consideration.
② 《선택하다》 prefer; choose; pick; take. ¶ 달리 취할 방도 the alternative / 많은 중에서 하나를 ～ choose 〔pick〕 one out of many / 제일 좋은 것을 ～ take the one *one* like best; take *one's* first choice / 어느 쪽을 취해야 할지 망설이다 be at a loss which to choose / 중용을 ～ go middle; take the (golden) mean 〔middle course〕/ B보다는 A를 취하겠다 I prefer A to B. *or* Preference is given to A over B.
③ 《얻다》 get; gain; take. ¶ 이(利)를 ～ derive benefit 《from》; profit 〔benefit〕 by 〔from〕 《*something*》; 《추구하다》 seek personal gain 〔interests〕; pursue 〔be bent upon〕 gain / 많은 이문을 ～ gain a fair margin of profit.
④ 《몸자세를》 get set 《to *do*》; assume a posture 《of》; pose; 《채비하다》 make 〔get〕 ready 《to *do*》; be 〔stand〕 ready 《for》. ¶ 싸우려는 자세를 ～ take a fighting stance; 《미》 square away 〔off〕 for a fight / 포즈를 ～ pose (*oneself*) 《as a model》; strike 〔get into〕 a pose; 《사진을 찍기 위해》 pose for *one's* picture; pose for a photography.
⑤ 《휴식·수면 등을》 take; have. ¶ 영양식을 ～ have some nourishment; take nourishing food / 휴식을 ～ have 〔take〕 a rest / 충분한 수면을 ～ take 〔have〕 a good sleep (한 번); get 〔have〕 enough 〔plenty of〕 sleep [일반적].
⑥ 《해석하다》 take; make out 《the meaning》; interpret 〔construe〕 《a passage》. ¶ 좋은〔나쁜〕 뜻으로 ～ take 《*a thing*》 well 〔badly〕; take 《*a thing*》「in good part 〔amiss〕/ 좋게도 나쁘게도 취할 수 있다 can be taken in either a good or a bad sense.
⑦ 《빼앗다》 get; take possession of; seize. ¶ 성을 ～ take a castle; carry 〔capture〕 a fortress.
⑧ 《꾸다》 borrow; lend. ¶ 돈을 ～ borrow money / 취해 주다 lend 《money》.

**취하다**(醉―) ① 《술에》 get 〔be〕 drunk 〔tipsy〕; become 〔be〕 intoxicated; be overcome with liquor; get 〔be〕 the worse for drink; be in *one's* cups.

> **용법** 「술에 취하다」의 가장 대표적인 표현은 **get 〔be〕 drunk. tipsy**는 「기분 좋을 정도로 취하다」란 뜻. **intoxicated**는 tipsy 보다는 취한 정도가 좀 센 느낌의 말. 문어적인 표현에 가깝다. 또 **drunk**는 서술적 용법에, **drunken**은 제한적 용법으로 쓰인다. intoxicated는 be intoxicated by the atmosphere 《of the party》 (분위기에 취하다)처럼 비유적으로 쓰이는 경우도 많다.

¶ 취한 drunk / 취하여 under the influence of liquor 〔drink〕/ 취한 체하고 pretending to be drunk / 맥주에 ～ get 〔be〕 drunk on beer / 거나하게 ～ be a bit tipsy; be in a cheerful mood with drink / 곤드레만드레 ～ drink *oneself* down; be drunk as a fish 〔tailor, fiddler〕; be dead 〔blind, beastly〕 drunk / 취해 쓰러지다 collapse under the influence of drink; fall dead drunk / 취해서 이성을 잃다 be dazed by liquor / 취해서 잠들다 drink *oneself* to sleep / 취해도 흐트러지지 않다 can take 〔hold〕 *one's* drink; can carry *one's* liquor (like a gentleman) / 취해 온다 The liquor「is creeping up on me 〔is beginning to take effect〕. *or* I'm starting to feel my drinks. / 인제 어지간히 취했다 I am already three sheets to the wind. / 그는 걸을 수 없도록 취했다 He was so intoxicated that he could not walk.
② 《도취하다》 be elated; be exalted 〔intoxicated〕. ¶ 성공에 ～ be elated with success / 음악에 ～ be lost in (the ecstasy of) the music; listen to music enchantedly / 행복〔환희〕에 ～ be ecstatically happy; be in an ecstasy of happiness; be intoxicated 〔inebriated〕 with delight / 일동은 취한 듯이 듣고 있었다 They all listened with rapt attention.
③ 《약물 등에》 be poisoned; get 〔be〕 intoxicated. ¶ 담배에 ～ smoke *oneself* ill 〔sick〕; become sick from smok-

ing / 마약에 ~ intoxicate *oneself* with drugs.

**취학**(就學) entering school. ~하다 enter 〔attend, go to〕 school. ¶ ~시키다 send 〔put〕 《a boy》 to school. ◉ ~률 the school attendance rate. ~아동 a schoolchild: 미~ 아동 a preschool child; a preschooler. ~연령 (the) school age: ~ 연령이 되다 attain 〔reach〕 the school age.

**취한**(取汗) 〖한의〗 inducing perspiration; diaphoresis; sweating. ~하다 induce perspiration; sweat out. ¶ ~하여 감기를 고치다 sweat out a cold. ◉ ~요법 sweating treatment.

**취한**(醉漢) a drunken fellow; a drunk; a drunkard.

**취항**(就航) commission; service. ~하다 enter service; put out to (sea); start on a voyage; be placed 〔put〕 into commission. ¶ 태평양 항로에 ~하다 be placed 〔put〕 on the Pacific line 〔run, service〕 / 여객기의 ~을 금지하다 inhibit the operation of 《North Korean》 airliners / ~시키다 place 《a ship》 in commission; commission 《a vessel》 in service. ◉ ~비행 an inaugural flight. ~선 vessels in commission.

**취향**(趣向) 《기호》 taste; liking; fondness; 《경향》 《follow *one's* artistic》 bent; inclination. ¶ 옷에 대한 ~ *one's* taste in dress / ~에 맞다 suit 〔be to〕 *one's* taste; please 〔suit, take〕 *one's* fancy / 고객들 ~에 맞도록 고심하다 studiously consult the tastes of *one's* customers.

**취화**(臭化) 〖화학〗 bromination. ⇨ 브롬화(化).

**취흥**(醉興) (drunken) merrymaking; the fun of being drunk. ¶ ~에 겨워 《go wild》 under the influence of wine; in *one's* exhilaration / ~이 도도하다 be merry 〔bubbly, sparkling〕 with wine; be bubbling over 〔excited, elated〕 under the influence of drink / ~에 겨워 춤을 추다 dance in drunken delight.

**-측**(側) a side. ¶ 좌측 the left 〔left=hand〕 side / 우측에 on the right side / 양측 both 〔the two〕 sides / 유엔측 the UN side / 노동자측 the labor side / 민주당측의 실책 a blunder on the part of the Democratic Party / 학생측의 요구 the demand on the part of the students / 잘못은 우리측에 있다 The fault is on our side. / 우리측에서는 아무 반대도 없다 There is no objection on our part. / 그것은 경영자측의 어리석은 행동이다 That is a foolish behavior on the part of the management.

**측각기**(測角器) an angle meter; a goniometer.

**측간**(測桿) a pole (used in land-surveying).

**측간**(厠間) a toilet shed; an outhouse.

**측거의**(測距儀) a range finder.

**측경기**(測徑器) calipers. ⇨ 캘리퍼스.

**측근**(側近) ① 《가까운 곁》 the surroundings; around 〔nearby〕 a person. ¶ ~에 모시다 stand by 《*a person's*》 side; attend 〔wait〕 on / ~에 아무도 없다 have nobody around *one;* be unattended 〔unaccompanied〕. ② ⇨ 측근자. ¶ 총리 ~ 소식통에 의하면 according to sources close to the Prime Minister.

**측근자**(側近者) a person around 〔close〕 to *one;* an aid 《미》; *one's* close staff members 〔associates〕; close attendants. ¶ 대통령 ~ those close to the President; a presidential aid.

**측도**(測度) measurement (of degree); gauging. ~하다 measure; gauge.

**측량**(測量) ① 〔일반적〕 measurement; measuring; 《토지의》 a survey; surveying; 《수심의》 sounding. ~하다 measure; survey; take 〔make〕 a measurement 〔survey〕 《of》; sound 《the sea》. ¶ 토지를 ~하다 survey land / 산의 높이〔바다의 깊이〕를 ~하다 measure the height of a mountain 〔the depth of the sea〕 / 항공 ~을 하다 make an aerial survey 《of》. ② 《헤아림》 estimation; guess; conjecture. ~하다 estimate; measure; guess; conjecture; fathom; sound. ◉ ~기 a surveying instrument: 수심 ~기 a depth-sounding apparatus. ~기사 a (land) surveyor; a surveying engineer. ~대 a leveling 〔range〕 pole; a ranging pole 〔rod〕. ~도 a survey map; an ordnance map 《영》. ~반 a surveying squad. ~선 a surveying ship. ~술 surveying (technique); mensuration.

**측면**(側面) 《물체의 옆면》 the side; 《옆》 the flank; 《한 면》 a side; an aspect; a profile (옆얼굴). ¶ ~의 side; flank; lateral / 건물의 ~ the side of a building / 기계의 좌우 양~ the right and left sides of a machine / ~을 방어하다 defend the flank 《of》; flank 《a troop》 / ~을 엄호하다 cover the flanks / (적의) ~을 공격하다 attack 《the enemy》 in the flank; launch

〔make〕 a flank attack《on, against》/ ～에서 돕다 give《*a person*》indirect aid; help《*a person*》indirectly / 적의 ～으로 돌다 get around the enemy's flank; outflank the enemy《on the right》/ 같은 것의 다른 ～이다 be different faces of the same thing / 기계의 왼쪽 ～을 벽에 고정시키다 fix the left side of the machine to the wall / 명랑한 ～만을 보이다 show only *one's* cheerful side / 사태를 다른 ～에서 보다 look at the situation from a different angle / 그에게 그런 진실된 ～이 있으리라고는 생각지 못했다 I hardly thought that he had such an serious side to him.

◉ ～공격《make》a flank attack. ～관(觀) a side 〔lateral〕 view. ～도(圖) a side 〔lateral〕 view. ～방어 a flank defense. ～우회 a flanking maneuver《of》. ～운동 a lateral movement. ～원조 indirect aid. ～종대 a column to a flank. ～행진 a flank march.

**측면**(測面) planimetry. ◉ ～기 a planimeter. ～법 a planimetric method; planimetry.

**측문**(仄聞) ～하다 hear casually; learn by hearsay. ¶ ～한 바에 의하면 from what I heard by chance; I hear 〔understand, am told〕 that....

**측백나무**(側柏—)〖식물〗a Chinese 〔an Oriental〕 arborvitae; a thuja.

**측벽**(側壁) a side wall.

**측보기**(測步器)《보수계》a pedometer.

**측사**(側射) a flanking fire.

**측사기**(測斜器)〖물리〗a clinometer.

**측산**(測算) calculation; estimation. ～하다 calculate; estimate.

**측선**(側線)《철도의》a siding;《미》a sidetrack;《어류의》the lateral lines《of a fish》;《경기장의》a sideline; a touchline (축구의). ¶ 열차를 ～에 넣다 sidetrack a train / (열차가) ～에서 대기하고 있다 be (waiting) on a siding.

**측실**(側室) a mistress. ⇨ 작은집.

**측심**(測深) (depth) sounding. ～하다 measure the depth《of》; sound; fathom; make soundings. ◉ ～기(器) a (depth) sounder; a depth finder; a bathymeter;《상표명》a Fathometer.

**측연**(惻然) ～하다 (be) sympathetic; compassionate. ¶ ～히 sympathetically; compassionately.

**측연**(測鉛)《cast》a sounding lead; a (lead) plummet; a plumb (bob). ¶ ～으로 깊이를 재다 plumb the depth《of the sea》. ◉ ～선 a plummet 〔lead〕 line; a sounding line. ～수(手) a leadsman.

**측열기**(測熱器) a calorimeter.

**측와**(側臥) ～하다 lie down on *one's* side.

**측우기**(測雨器) a rain gauge; a pluviometer; a udometer; a hyetometer.

**측원기**(測遠器) a range 〔position〕 finder; a telemeter.

**측은**(惻隱) ～하다 (be) sympathetic; compassionate. ¶ ～히 sympathetically; compassionately / ～지심(之心) natural sympathies / ～히 여기다 pity; commiserate 〔sympathize〕 with / ～한 마음이 들다 be overwhelmed with pity《for》; feel compassion 〔pity〕《for》; be touched with compassion; be moved to pity.

**측음**(側音) a sidetone;《설측음》a lateral (sound).

**측전기**(測電器) an electrometer.

**측점**(測點) a measuring point; a (surveying) station.

**측정**(測定) [일반적] measurement;《토지의》survey;《수심의》sounding. ～하다 measure; gauge; find. ¶ 거리를 ～하다 measure 〔find〕 the distance《to》/ 속력을 ～하다 determine the velocity《of》/ 태양의 높이를 ～하다 take the height of the sun / 정확히 ～하다 take an accurate measurement《of》/ ～을 잘못하다 measure《*something*》wrong(ly); make an error 〔a mistake〕 in measuring《the depth》.

◉ ～값 a measured value. ～기 a measuring instrument. ～기술 measurement techniques. ～장치 a measuring device.

**측정기**(測程器)《throw, heave》a log.

**측정법**(測定法) a method 〔way〕 of measurement;〖수학〗mensuration. ¶ 시간〔열량〕～ chronometry 〔calorimetry〕.

**측지**(測地) land surveying; a geodetic survey. ～하다 survey 〔measure〕 land. ◉ ～선 a geodetic 〔geodesic〕 line. ～위성 a geodetic 〔an earth-mapping〕 satellite. ～학 geodesy; geodetics: ～학의 geodetic(al); geodesic / ～학자 a geodesist.

**측천**(測天) (an) astronomical observation. ～하다 get 〔take〕 an astronomical observation; observe《the stars, the sun》.

**측판**(測板) a surveying table.

**측화산**(側火山)《기생 화산》a parasitic volcano.

**측후**(測候) a meteorological observation; meteorology. ～하다 make a meteorological observation《of》; observe (the weather).

**츱츱하다** (be) shameless; brazen-faced; dirty; mean. ¶ 그는 츱츱하게 남의 물건을 자꾸 달란다 He keeps asking me for things shamelessly.

**층**(層) ① 《계층·단계》 a class; stratum (*pl.* -ta); a level. ¶ 근로자층 the working class / 사회의 최하층 the lowest social stratum / 사회의 중간층 the middle layers of society; the middle classes / 지식층 the intellectual class / 고액〔저액〕 소득층 a higher-〔lower-〕 income group 〔bracket〕 / 갖가지 연령층의 사람들이 그 토론에 참가하였다 Different age groups took part in the discussion.

② 《지층 등의》 a layer; a stratum (*pl.* -ta); seam (광석 등의 엷은); a bed (석탄 등의). ¶ (석)탄층 a coal bed 〔seam〕 / 제3기층 the Tertiary formation / 중생층 the Mesozonic stratum / 층상(層狀)의 stratiform; stratified / 층이 두껍다 be thick-layered; 《인재의》 have a large stock 《of players》 to draw on; the 《skating》 population is large / 층을 이루다 be in layers 〔strata〕; be stratified.

③ 《건물 등의》 a floor; a story 《미》; a storey 《영》. ¶ 1층 the first 〔ground 《영》〕 floor; the first story / 2층 the 2nd 〔second〕 story 〔floor〕 《미》; the first floor 《영》; upstairs / 9층짜리 빌딩 《미》 a nine-storied〔-story〕 building / 지하 1〔2〕층 lower ground floor one 〔two〕 / 최상층의 방 a room on the top floor.

> 용법 **story, storey** 《영》「…층 빌딩」처럼 건물을 밖에서 보고 그 높이를 말할 때 주로 쓰임. **floor** 「1층, 2층, 3층…」처럼 건물 내부에 있는 각 층을 지칭할 때 씀. 《미》에서는 1층을 the first floor로 시작하여 2~3층을 the second 〔third〕 floor라고 하는데, 《영》에서는 1층이 the ground floor, 2층이 the first floor가 되어 《미》 《영》 사이에 1층씩 차이가 남.

¶「그 건물은 몇 층입니까」—「8층입니다」 "How high is the building ?"—"It is eight stories high 〔eight-storied〕." / 사무실은 몇 층에 있습니까 What floor is the office on ? / 2층과 3층에서는 (승강기가) 서지 않습니다 We don't stop at floors two and three.

④ 《정도》 ¶ 한층 더 furthermore; more; still more; all the more / 더 한층 노력하다 make greater efforts / 그건 한층 더 곤란하다 It is still more difficult.

⑤ 《등급》 a grade; a class. ¶ 갖가지 층의 인생 various kinds of life / 배우라고 해도 여러 층이 있다 There are various grades of actors.

**층각**(層閣) a many-storied〔-storeyed 《영》〕 building. ⇨ 층루(層樓).

**층계**(層階) stairs; 《손잡이가 있는》 a staircase; a stairway; 《입구 따위의》 steps; a flight of stairs (연속된 하나의 층계). ¶ ~위〔아래〕에서 at the head 〔bottom, foot〕 of the stairs / 마지막 ~ the top stairs / 가파른 ~ a steep staircase / 높은 ~ tall 〔long〕 stairs / ~를 오르다 ascend 〔go up〕 the stairs; go upstairs / ~를 내려가다 descend 〔go down〕 the stairs; go downstairs / ~를 헛디디다 miss *one's* footing on the stairs / ~에서 떨어지다 fall downstairs / ~를 급히 오르다〔내려가다〕 hurry upstairs 〔downstairs〕 / ~에서 미끄러지다 slip on the stairs / 그 ~는 몹시 가파르다 The stairs are very steep. / 그는 ~를 한 번에 두 단씩 뛰어 올라갔다 He flew up the steps, two at a time. ◉ ~참 a (mean) landing. 나선~ a spiral 〔corkscrew〕 staircase; a winding stair.

**층계송**(層階頌) 〚가톨릭〛 gradual; *Graduale* (L.).

**층나다**(層—) ① 《켜가》 be in layers 〔strata〕; be (formed) in seams; show 〔have〕 (a structure of ) layers. ② 《차이》 be uneven; show disparity 《in》. ¶ 연령이 ~ there is disparity in age / 이 반과 그 반은 성적이 크게 층난다 One class is far better 〔worse〕 than the other. *or* There is great disparity between the two classes in their marks.

**층널**(層—) a layer board.

**층대**(層臺) steps; a stairway; a terrace. ¶ 높은 ~ a long stairway; a high terrace / 가파른 ~ a steep stairway / ~를 올라가다〔내려가다〕 ascend 〔descend〕 the steps.

**층도리**(層—) 〚건축〛 a girth.

**층돌**(層—) 〚광업〛 a stone for assaying gold; a touchstone; a Lydian stone.

**층등**(層等) gradation; grade; difference. ¶ ~을 매기다 grade; graduate; discriminate.

**층루**(層樓) a many-storied〔-storeyed 《영》〕 building 〔turret〕; a building several stories high.

**층류**(層流) 〚물리〛 laminar 〔streamline〕 「flow.

**층리**(層理) 〚지질〛 stratification; bedding.

**층면**(層面) ①《쌓인 물건의》 the surface (of piled up things). ②〖지질〗 a stratification plane.

**층상**(層狀) being stratiform [stratified]. ¶ ~의 stratiform; stratified / ~을 이루다 be stratified; have a stratified formation; be in layers [strata]. ◉ ~격자(格子)〖물리〗 a layer lattice. ~암 a stratified rock. ~운 a stratiform cloud.

**층새**(層—)〖광업〗 the quality [grade] of gold. ¶ 금의 ~를 가리다 assay gold; grade gold. ◉ 층샛돌 ⇨ 층돌.

**층수**(層數) the number of layers [floors, stories, storeys《영》].

**층암절벽**(層岩絶壁) a rocky cliff; an overhanging [a perpendicular] cliff (piled up with rocks). ¶ ~을 기어 오르다 scale [clamber up] a rocky cliff.

**층애**(層崖)〖지질〗 an escarpment; a stratified precipice [cliff].

**층운**(層雲)〖기상〗 a stratus (*pl.* -ti).

**층적운**(層積雲)〖기상〗 a stratocumulus; a roll cumulus.

**층지다**(層—) = 층나다. ¶ 머리를 층지게 깎다 cut *one's* hair uneven.

**층집**(層—) a house [building] of more than one story [level, floor].

**층층다리**(層層—) a flight of steps; a staircase; stairs. ⇨ 층계.

**층층대**(層層臺) ⇨ 층대(層臺). ¶ ~를 올라가다[내려가다] go up [down] the stairs; ascend [descend] the steps.

**층층시하**(層層侍下) serving both parents and grandparents alive.

**층층이**(層層—) layer upon layer; one story [storey《영》] after another; pile after pile; in strata [layers, tiers]. ¶ ~ 쌓다 pile 《*something*》 in layers / 돌을 ~ 쌓아올리다 pile up stones / ~ 다 사람이 들었다 all the floors get occupied.

**층하**(層下) treating 《*a person*》 with less respect [favor] than others; disrespect; discrimination. ~하다 treat 《*a person*》 with less respect than others; discriminate against 《*a person, a thing*》; disrespect. ¶ 사람을 ~하다 discriminate against *a person;* treat *a person* with disrespect [discrimination]; make fish of one and flesh [fowl] of another / 사람 ~를 하지 않다 treat every person just and fair; treat all alike.

**치**(値)〖수학〗 numerical value. ⇨ 값.

**치**[1]《길이의 단위》 a Korean inch; a *ch'i;* one tenth of a *cha* (= 3.0303 cm).

**치**[2] ①《사람》 a fellow; a guy; a chap. ¶ 이[그, 저] 치 this [that] guy / 서울치 "one of those Seoul bastards" / 저 치가 그렇게 말했다 That guy told me so. ②《지정된 것》 a fixed quantity; a ration; a designated amount; 《몫·양》 a share; a part; a portion; 《음식의》 a helping; a serving. ¶ 하루치의 식량 a day's ration / 사흘치의 약 medicine for three days / 이달치 the fee [amount, charge, rent, *etc.*] for this month.

**치-** ¶ 치닫다 run up / 치솟다 go up; rise (high) / 눈을 치뜨다 turn up the eyes; cast an upward glance.

**치가**(治家) home management. ~하다 manage a household; regulate [order] a household.

**치가 떨리다**(齒—) ① 《분해서》 make [drive] 《*one*》 mad with vexation; be infuriated; be tense with indignation. ¶ 그의 말을 들으니 치가 떨린다 His remark makes me mad. / 우리 아이가 맞는 걸 보니 치가 떨린다 It gets my goat to see our boy whipped. ② 《지긋지긋해서》 be sick of; be disgusted with. ¶ 그 사람 생각만 해도 치가 떨린다 It makes me sick even to think of him.

**치감**(齒疳)〖한의〗 pyorrhea (alveolaris); Riggs' disease; bleeding gums.

**치감다** wind [bind, coil] upward 《around》.

**치경**(齒莖) the gums;〖의학〗 the gingiva; the teethridge. ¶ ~의 gingival.

**치고** 《예외 없이》 when it comes to; as for; 《…마다》 every; 《…(깐)으로는》 considering; seeing; for. ¶ 그것은 그렇다 ~ apart from that; be that as it may / 돈 있는 사람~ 돈 아끼지 않는 사람이 드물다 Most rich people are careful about spending money. / 한국 사람~ 누가 통일을 반대하랴 What [Surely no] Korean will object to the unification of Korea! / 나는 한국 명승지~ 안 가 본 데가 없다 I have been to every famous place in Korea. / 학교~ 체육관 없는 학교가 어디 있겠나 Who ever heard of a school without a gym?

**치고는** 《…에 비해서는》 considering; seeing; for. ¶ 여자~ for a woman; as women go / 일본인~ 한국어를 잘 한다 speak fluent Korean for a Japanese / 그는 나이~ 키가 크다 He is tall for his age. / 그녀는 40세~ 젊어 보인다 She looks young for 40. / 그는 처

음 하는 일～꽤 잘 했다 Seeing〔Considering〕 that he is new to the job, he has done very well.

**치골**(恥骨) 〚해부〛 the pubis (*pl.* pubes); the pubic bone.

**치골**(齒骨) 〚해부〛 (a) dentary bone.

**치과**(齒科) 〚의학〛 dental surgery; dentistry; 《병원》 a dentist's (office); a dental office 〔clinic〕. ¶ ～에 가다 go to (see) a dentist; go to the dentist's. ◉ ～교정학 orthodontics; orthodontia. ～기공 a dental technician. ～기구 dentists' tools; a dental 〔dentist's〕 instrument. ～대학 a dental college. ～용 드릴 a dental drill. ～위생 dental hygiene. ～의(사) a dentist; a dental surgeon; 《개업의》 a dental practitioner: ～ 의사의 진찰을 받다 consult 〔go and see〕 a dentist. ～의원 a dentist's (office); a dental clinic. ～치료 dental treatment. ～학 dentistry; odontology.

**치관**(齒冠) 〚해부〛 a crown (of a tooth).

**치국**(治國) governing 〔ruling〕 a country; statecraft. ～하다 govern 〔rule〕 a country.

**치근**(齒根) the root of a tooth.

**치근거리다** annoy; pester; bother; tease; make advance to (여자에게). ¶ 그녀에게 치근거리지 마라, 임자가 있는 몸이야 Don't make a pass at her, because she is taken.

**치근치근** teasingly; importunately. ～하다 = 치근거리다.

**치긋다** stroke upward; make an upward stroke (in writing). ¶ 획을 ～ make an upward stroke.

**치기**(稚氣) childishness; puerility. ¶ ～를 못 벗은 childish; puerile / ～를 벗다 get rid of childishness.

**-치기** (playing) a game. ¶ 딱지치기 a game of slap-match / 돈치기 a kind of coin-throwing game; chuck-〔pitch-〕 farthing.

**치다**[1] ① 《바람이》 blow violently 〔hard〕; sweep along 〔over〕; 《비가》 rain hard; 《눈이》 fall thick and fast. ¶ 바람이 세차게 치는 거리 a blustering street / 눈보라가 ～ [눈을 주어로] be driven by the wind / 바람으로 비가 들이쳤다 The wind drove the rain into the house. ② 《벼락이》 strike; hit; 《번개가》 lighten; 《천둥이》 thunder. ¶ 천둥 치는 소리 a peal 〔roar, roll〕 of thunder / 번개가 ～ lightning strikes 《a tree》; [장소가 주어] be struck by (a bolt of) lightning / 가까운 곳에 벼락이 쳤다 The thunderbolt fell close by. ③ 《물결이》 dash 《against》; roll; undulate; wave. ¶ 물결 치는 소리 the sound 〔roar〕 of the waves / 물결 치는 대로 《drift about》 at the mercy of the waves.

**치다**[2] ① 《때리다》 (***a***) 《손·물건 따위로》 hit; strike; beat; knock; slap; smack; thrash; punch; give 〔deal〕 a blow. ¶ 되치다 strike back / 공을 ～ strike 〔hit〕 a ball / 머리를 ～ hit 〔strike〕 《*a person*》 on the head / 볼기를 ～ flog 《*a person*》 on the buttocks / 손뼉을 ～ clap *one's* hands / 얼굴을 ～ strike 《*a person*》 in the face / 채찍으로 ～ lash; flog; whip 《*a person* on the leg》 / 타이프를 ～ tap (at) a typewriter; tap the keys of a typewriter / 사람을 치고 받고〔차고〕 하다 give *a person* cuffs and butts 〔kicks〕 / 녹초가 되도록 ～ beat 〔hit〕 up; pommel 《*a person*》 (to a jelly). (***b***) 《시계가》 strike. ¶ 세 시를 ～ strike three / 2시를 치자 on 〔at〕 the strike of two / 지금 몇 시를 쳤지 What did it 〔the clock〕 strike? (***c***) 《때려박다》 drive 〔knock〕 in(to); ram down 《a stake》. ¶ 못을 ～ drive 〔hammer〕 a nail into 《a wall》. (***d***) 《떡을》 pound 《rice》. ¶ 떡을 ～ pound steamed rice into dough; make rice-cake.

② 《공격하다》 (***a***) 《무력으로》 attack; assault; open 〔launch〕 an attack 《upon》; assail; 《쳐부수다》 destroy. ¶ 불시에 ～ make a surprise 〔sudden〕 attack on 《the enemy》; take 《the enemy》 unawares; take 〔attack〕 《the enemy》 by surprise / 성(城)을 ～ lay siege to a castle / 쳐서 빼앗다 take 《a fortress》 by storm 〔assault〕 / 쳐들어가다 invade; make an inroad 《on, into》; penetrate 《into》. (***b***) 《비난하다》 attack; charge; criticize; denounce; condemn. ¶ 신문에서 ～ write against 《*a person*》; attack 〔pound〕 《*a person*》 in the newspaper / 호되게 ～ denounce 《*a person*》 scathingly.

③ 《악기·종 따위를》 play (on); sound; beat; ring; clang 《a gong》. ¶ 북을 ～ beat 〔thump〕 a drum; play a 〔the〕 drum; pound on drums (세게) / 북을 쳐서 모으다 drum up; drum for 《customers》 / 종을 ～ strike 〔toll, ring〕 a bell / 피아노를 ～ play (on) the piano / 종 치는 소리가 들린다 I hear bells ringing 〔going〕.

④ 《게임·운동을 하다》 play 《a game》. ¶ 골프를 ～ play (at) golf; golf / 탁구

〔테니스〕를 ~ play ping-pong 〔tennis〕 / 헤엄을 ~ swim; have a swim / 헤엄을 쳐서 건너다 swim across 《a river》 / 카드를 ~ shuffle a pack of cards / 물장구를 ~ paddle *one's* feet in the water; make flutters 〔flutter kicks〕; swim with the thrash.

⑤ 《꼬리 등을》 wag; swish; 《날개 등을》 flap; clap; flutter; beat. ¶ 푸드득거리며 날개를 ~ flap 〔beat〕 (the) wings / 꼬리를 ~ wag 《its》 tail (개가); whisk 〔switch〕 《its》 tail (말이); swish 《its》 tail (소가).

⑥ 《가지 등을》 nip (off); snip; clip; trim off 〔away〕; snick. ¶ 가지를 ~ prune 〔trim〕 a tree; prune 〔trim〕 the branches off; lop off 〔down〕 trees / 곁가지를 ~ pinch out the side shoots / 순을 ~ nip the bud.

⑦ 《목을》 cut off. ¶ 목을 ~ cut off the head; behead 《*a person*》.

⑧ 《전보를》 send (a wire). ¶ 전보를 ~ send a telegram.

⑨ 《성공하다》 make a hit; win a success; be a hit. ¶ 히트를 친 노래 a hit song.

⑩ 《채치다》 cut 《a cucumber》 into fine strips. ¶ 채를 ~ shred vegetables.

⑪ 《밤을》 skin chestnuts.

**치다**[3] ① 《표시를》 ¶ 선을 ~ draw a line / 먹줄을 ~ stretch out an inking line / 밑줄을 ~ underline 《a word》; underscore 《a line》 / 밑줄 친 부분 an underlined 〔underscored〕 part / 점을 ~ mark with a dot 〔point〕; dot; point; spot.

② 《찍다》 seal; affix. ¶ 도장을 ~ seal 《a bond》; affix 〔stamp, put〕 *one's* seal 《to a bond》; stamp 《papers》 with *one's* seal.

③ 《점을》 ¶ 점을 ~ tell 《*a person's*》 fortune; 《점쳐 받다》 have *one's* fortune told; consult a fortuneteller / 길흉을 점~ tell 《*a person's*》 fortune; take auspices / 별로써 성격이나 운세를 점~ tell characters and fortunes by the stars.

④ 《시험을》 take; undergo. ¶ 시험을 ~ take 〔undergo, sit for〕 an examination; go 〔come〕 up for an examination; go in for an exam / 운전 면허 시험을 ~ take *one's* test for a driver's license.

⑤ 《셈을》 count; calculate; reckon; compute; work out; figure up; 《포함시키다》 count among; include; 《…로 잡다》 price; value 《at》; estimate 《at》. ¶ …까지 쳐서 including…; inclusive of… / …은 치지 않고 excluding…; exclusive of… / 이자까지 쳐서 20만 원 200,000 won inclusive of interest / 돈으로 ~ estimate in money / 셈을 쳐서 주다 tell down 〔out〕 money / 집 값을 5천만 원으로 ~ value the house at fifty million won / 잘못 ~ miscalculate; make a wrong estimate; make a mistake in reckoning.

⑥ 《…로 보다》 regard as; consider; think of 《as》; deem; reckon; count 《as, for》; look (up)on 《as》; take 《for》; 《가정하다》 suppose; presume. ¶ 그건 그렇다 치고 be that as it may / 그렇다 치더라도 but (still); and yet; nevertheless; however; still; all the same / 전방의 언덕을 적의 진지라고 치면 supposing that the hillock ahead is the enemy's position / 최유력자의 하나로 치고 있다 be rated among the most influential / 결석자는 불합격으로 친다 Those who absent themselves will be considered to have failed in the examination. / 그렇다 치더라도 사과를 하는 게 좋겠다 Still, you'd better apologize.

**치다**[4] ① 《넣다》 cover 《with》; put 《in (-to)》; sprinkle 《on, over, with》. ¶ 소금을 ~ put salt into 《food》; sprinkle salt on 《fish》; sprinkle 《fish》 with salt / 소금을 쳐서 먹다 eat with salt / 샐러드에 소스를 쳐서 먹다 put sauce on the salad / 고기에 후추를 ~ sprinkle 〔shake〕 pepper on 〔over〕 meat; sprinkle meat with pepper. ② 《기름을》 apply 《oil》; oil 《the wheel》. ¶ 기계에 기름을 ~ apply oil to a machine; grease a machine. ③ 《섞다》 mix; give; put 《in》. ¶ 음식에 독을 ~ put poison in the food. ④ 《체로》 sieve; sift. ¶ 가루를 체에 ~ put 〔pass〕 flour through a sieve 〔sifter〕.

**치다**[5] ① 《휘장·천막 등을》 put 〔set〕 up; hang (up); suspend; 《커튼 등을》 drop; draw; let fall 〔down〕 《the curtain》; 《그물·줄 등을》 pitch; stretch; extend. ¶ 그물을 ~ pitch 〔lay〕 a net; set 〔throw〕 a net / 모기장을 ~ put up 〔hang〕 a mosquito nets / 비상선을 ~ post 〔form, throw out〕 a (police) cordon / 줄을 ~ stretch a rope 《between》; 《둘러막다》 rope off 《a place》 / 천막을 ~ pitch 〔set up, put up〕 a tent / 문에 거적을 ~ cover a door with a straw mat / (거미가) 집을 ~ spin 〔weave〕 nets.

②《두르다》(***a***)《병풍·울타리 등을》set up; enclose《with, in》; surround《with, by》. ¶ 병풍을 ~ set up a screen (all around) / 울타리를 ~ make [put] a fence; enclose《a house》with a fence; fence round [about]《a house》. (***b***)《매다》tie; wear; put on; attach. ¶ 각반을 ~ wear gaiters; do up a puttee / 대님을 ~ wear cloth bands at the lower ends of trousers.

③《소리를》shout; cry; utter [give] a cry. ¶ 크게 소리(를) ~ cry [call] out; roar; howl / 호통을 ~ shout; yell; thunder; bark《at》; hurl words of thunder《at》/ 살려 달라고 소리 ~ scream [cry] for help.

④《기세 좋게 언동하다》¶ 활개를 치며 swinging *one's* arms; [비유적] with nothing to fear; with impunity / 공갈(을) ~ threaten; intimidate; blackmail; blackjack / 공갈을 쳐서 돈을 빼앗다 blackmail《*a person*》of his money; blackjack money out of《*a person*》/ 뺑소니를 ~ run away; flee; make *one's* escape / 큰소리(를) ~ talk big [tall]; brag; blow *one's* own trumpet.

⑤《진저리를》tremble; shudder《with terror》; give《*a person*》the (cold) creeps; make *one's* flesh creep; 《물려서》have (had) enough of《*something*》; become fed up《with》; get sick (to death)《of》. ¶ 생각만 해도 진저리가 쳐진다 The bare idea makes [turns] me sick. *or* The mere thought of it makes me tremble.

**치다**[6] ①《엮다》weave; make; braid《a rope》; plait《a straw mat》. ¶ 돗자리를 ~ weave a mat. ②《휘갑을》hem. ¶ 휘갑을 ~ hem the edges; bind the hem.

**치다**[7] ①《기르다》raise《sheep, hogs, silkworms》; rear《poultry》; keep《a dog》; 《먹이다》feed《cattle on hay》. ¶ 누에를 ~ rear [raise, breed] silkworms / 닭을 ~ keep [breed] hens [fowls]; raise [breed] chickens《미》/ 돼지를 ~ breed pigs; raise hogs / 벌을 ~ keep bees; engage in apiculture.

②《꿀을》store. ¶ 벌이 꿀을 ~ bees store honey.

③《가지를》spread; shoot out. ¶ 나무가 가지를 ~ a tree shoot out [spreads] branches; ramify.

④《새끼를》bring forth《its》young; reproduce《its》kind; litter; whelp; cub; pup (개가); kitten (고양이가); calf (소가); [비유적] yield [bear] interest. ¶ 개가 새끼를 ~ a dog whelps [pups].

⑤《손님을》keep a lodger [roomer]. ¶ 하숙을 ~ take in [keep] lodgers [boarders]; run [keep] a lodging house.

**치다**[8] ①《깨끗이 하다》clean; put in order; 《제거하다》take [clear] away; get rid of; remove; 《준설하다》clean (out). ⇨ 치우다. ¶ 길의 돌을 ~ remove a stone from the road / 눈을 ~ rake [shove, sweep] away snow; clear away [off] snow; clear《a road》of snow / 도랑[우물]을 ~ clean (out) a ditch [well] / 방을 ~ clean (up) a room; do a room; sweep a room clean / 변소를 ~ dip up night soil.

②《솎아내다》thin; weed out. ¶ 머리숱을 쳐내다 thin *one's* hair / 나뭇가지를 ~ thin the branches of a tree.

**치다**[9]《장난·걸음을》do; play. ¶ 어린애들이 장난을 ~ the children are playing [at play] / 못된 장난을 ~ play a prank [trick, practical joke]《on》; take liberties《with a girl》/ 가재 걸음(을) ~ walk [crawl] backward; make like a crayfish / 종종걸음을 ~ take short, quick steps; walk [run] with short steps; trip [trot] along.

**치다**[10]《차 따위가》run over《a man》; knock [run]《*a person*》down.

**치다꺼리** ①《치러냄》management; disposal; dealing《with》; tidying《up》; taking care of. ~하다 manage; dispose of; deal《with》; take care of; look after; attend《to》; tidy《up》. ¶ 손님 ~ entertaining guests / 살림 ~ management of a household; housekeeping; taking care of the housework / 손님 ~를 하다 take care of [entertain, attend to] a guest / 살림 ~를 하다 manage a house / 그 사건의 ~를 내가 맡았다 I was entrusted with the conduct [dealing] of the affairs.

②《바라지》help; aid; provision; supply(ing); taking care of; arranging; providing. ~하다 help; aid; look after; take care of; provide; supply; arrange. ¶ 아들의 살림 ~ helping out *one's* son (with household necessities) / 친구의 장례 ~ providing [arranging] a funeral for a friend; taking care of the arrangements for a friend's funeral / 친구의 혼인 잔치 ~를 하다 take care of [arrange] the wedding banquet for a friend / 아무개 일 ~를 하다 help *a person* to do *his* work; assist *a person*. 「upstairs.

**치닫다** go 〔run〕 up; run uphill; run

**치대다** ① 《위쪽으로 대다》 put 〔apply, place, stick, fix〕 on the upper side. ¶ 판자를 ~ fix a piece of board upward 《of a wall》 / 배를 좀더 치대시오 Moor the boat a bit farther up. ② 《문지르다》 knead; rub. ¶ 반죽을 ~ knead dough / 빨래를 ~ rub laundry.

**치도곤**(治盜棍) a club (for the lash). ¶ ~을 안기다 club 〔cudgel〕 《a criminal》; [비유적] teach 《*a person*》 a lesson; give 《*a person*》 a raw deal; give 《*a person*》 a hard time.

**치독**(治毒) treatment for poison; removal 〔neutralization〕 of poison; counteracting a poison; an antidote. ~하다 treat for poison; remove 〔neutralize, counteract〕 poison.

**치둔**(癡鈍) stupidity; dumbness; dullness. ~하다 (be) stupid; dumb; dull.

**치뜨다** raise; lift (*one's* eyes). ¶ 눈을 ~ cast an upward glance; lift up *one's* eyes; turn up the eyes.

**치뜨리다** toss up; throw up; pitch up. ¶ 볏단을 둑에 ~ toss sheaves of rice up on the levee.

**치뜰다** (be) mean; dirty; ugly; despicable. ¶ 치뜬 짓 a mean behavior 〔deed〕.

**치란**(治亂) 《태평과 어지러움》 peace reigns and 〔or〕 turbulent days; 《평정》 suppression of a rebellion. ~하다 suppress a rebellion; put down a revolt.

**치런치런** ① 《물이》 full; overflowing. ~하다 (be) full; overflowing. ¶ 우물에 물이 ~ 괴었다 The well is overflowing with water. ② 《스칠락말락》 long; dragging; trailing. ~하다 (be) long; dragging; be trailing (down). ¶ ~한 머리채 a long pigtail / 치맛자락을 ~ 늘어뜨리고 걷다 walk dragging *one's* skirt along.

**치렁거리다** ① 《드리운 것이》 drag; trail; hang down; droop. ¶ 버들가지가 ~ willow branches droop low / 치맛자락이 ~ *one's* skirt drags. ② 《시일이》 drag on; be prolonged 〔protracted〕.

**치렁치렁** 《늘어뜨림》 hanging (down); drooping; dragging. ¶ 치맛자락이 ~ 땅에 끌리다 *one's* skirt drags / 버들가지가 ~ 늘어지다 willow branches droop.

**치렁하다** (be) dragging; trailing; drooping; droopy. ¶ 버들가지가 ~ willow branches hang down droopingly / 치마가 ~ *one's* skirt is long and trailing.

**치레** embellishment; adornment; dressing-up; decorating. ~하다 embellish; adorn; decorate; deck 〔dress〕 up; smarten up. ¶ 겉~로만 for mere form's sake / 얼굴 ~를 하다 pretty *one's* face up; work on 〔paint, apply makeup to〕 *one's* face / 몸 ~를 하다 adorn *oneself*; dress up / 옷~를 하다 dress (*oneself*) up; attire *oneself* in *one's* best; be smartly dressed.

**치료**(治療) (medical) treatment; (medical) care; a cure; remedy. ~하다 cure 《*a person* of a disease》; remedy; treat. ¶ ~할 수 없는 병 an untreatable disease; a disease beyond medical treatment / 5일간의 ~를 요하는 화상(火傷) a burn requiring five days of treatment / ~를 받다 be treated; undergo (medical) treatment; receive medical attention / 이〔눈〕의 ~를 받다 have *one's* teeth 〔eyes〕 treated / 암 ~를 받다 be treated for cancer / ~중이다 be under (medical) treatment; be under the care of a doctor / ~하지 않고 내버려 두다 leave 《a decayed tooth》 untreated / ~받으러 가다 go to 《a doctor》 for treatment / 의사의 ~로 완쾌되다 recover completely under the treatment of a doctor / 상처를 ~하다 treat an injury / 응급 ~를 하다 give first aid / ~를 게을리하다 neglect to have proper medical care / ~중에 죽다 succumb under the treatment / 그 ~는 효과가 좋았다 The treatment worked well. / 그 병은 어떤 ~도 효과가 없었다 The case resisted all treatment. / 한 박사의 ~를 받고있다 I am under the treatment of Dr. Han. / 이 병은 빨리 ~하지 않으면 안 된다 This disease 「calls for 〔needs〕 prompt treatment. / 눈 ~에 3개월이 걸렸다 It took me three months to get my eye treated.

◉ ~대(臺) a treatment table. ~법 a (method of) medical treatment; a remedy; a cure: 확실한 ~법 a sure cure; a positive remedy; an infallible cure / 민간 ~법 a popular 〔folk〕 remedy / 암에는 아직 확실한 ~법이 없다 There is no certain cure for cancer yet. ~비 a doctor's fee 〔bill〕; a medical fee; smart money (배상조의). ~소 an infirmary; a clinic. ~자 a curer. ~학 therapeutics: ~학상의 therapeutic. ~효과 《a medicine with》 a curative effect; 《have》 therapeutic 〔remedial〕 value. 심리～ a psychical cure. 전기～ electrotherapy.

**치루**(痔瘻) 〖의학〗 an anal fistula (*pl.* -las, -lae); *fistula ani* (L.).

**치룽** a deep wicker basket without a lid. ◉ ～장수 a peddler who carries *one's* wares in a wicker basket.

**치룽구니** a stupid; a good-for-nothing fellow.

**치르다** ① 《지불하다》 pay; pay off 〔out〕; defray 《expenses》; clear 《*one's* debts》; settle 《*one's* accounts》. ¶ 어떤 대가를 치르더라도 at any price 〔cost〕 / 값을 ～ pay the price 《for》; pay for 《an article》 / 방세 9만원을 ～ pay 90,000 won for *one's* room 〔lodging〕 / 식사대를 신용카드로 치렀다 I paid for our meal by credit card.
② 《겪다》 undergo; go through; suffer; have. ¶ 감기를 ～ suffer a cold / 시험을 ～ have an examination / 형벌을 ～ undergo a punishment / 홍역을 ～ [비유적] have a hard time of it; have a bitter experience.
③ 《큰 일을》 carry out; go through; have; observe; put on (formalities). ¶ 손님을 ～ give 〔hold〕 a party; play host 《to》; entertain 《guests》 to 《dinner》 / 제사를 ～ observe the formalities of ancestor worship / 결혼식을 ～ have a wedding ceremony.

**치를 떨다**(齒—) ① 《분해서》 grind 〔gnash, grit〕 *one's* teeth 《with indignation》. ② 《인색하다》 grudge; be close-fisted; be awfully stingy. ¶ 돈이라면 치를 떤다 be niggardly of money; be close with *one's* money; spend money sparingly / 그는 한 푼에도 치를 떤다 He has a fit every time he has to spend a penny. *or* He pinches a penny till it hurts.

**치마** a skirt. ¶ ～의 주름 a pleat 〔gather〕 on a skirt / ～를 입다〔두르다〕 put on 〔wear〕 a skirt / ～를 벗다 remove 〔take off〕 *one's* skirt.
◉ ～끈 a girdle of a skirt. ～머리 a false hair used in making a full topknot. ～바지 (a pair of) culottes. ～상투 a topknot tied with false hair. ～양반(兩班) a man who has achieved social position by successive marriage with the nobility. ～폭 the width of a skirt: 어린애를 ～폭에 감싸다 tuck a child in a skirt. 치맛자락 the edge 〔end, hem〕 of a skirt; the trail: 치맛자락을 걷어 잡다 tuck up the skirt / 치맛자락을 끌다 trail *one's* skirt(s).

**치맛바람** 《입은 치맛자락의 서슬》 the swish of a skirt; 《설치는 여인의 서슬》 the influence of woman's power; 《학교에서의》 the frequent appearance of mothers on campus (where their sons and daughters are attending school); 《차림새》 woman's informal dress.

**치매**(癡呆) 〖의학〗 imbecility; dementia. ⇨ 치매증. ¶ 노인성 ～ senile dementia. ◉ ～노인 a dotard; an old man 〔woman〕 in *one's* dotage.

**치매기다** number in ascending order; start from the bottom in assigning numbers. ¶ 번지를 ～ number the houses in ascending order.

**치매증**(癡呆症) 〖의학〗 dementia. ◉ 마비성～ general paralysis 〔paresis〕; *dementia paralytica* (L.). 조발성～ *dementia praecox;* precocious dementia; schizophrenia.

**치먹이다** sell 《local products》 at the center of commerce; supply a city 〔town〕 with 《local products》.

**치먹히다** ① 《번호가》 be numbered upward. ¶ 번지가 ～ the houses are numbered upward. ② 《팔리다》 be sold to the center of commerce. ¶ 시골 물건이 서울로 ～ local products are ⌈sold to 〔in demand in〕 Seoul.

**치면하다** be nearly filled to the brim. ¶ 물이 그릇에 ～ a vessel is almost full of water.

**치명상**(致命傷) a mortal 〔fatal〕 wound. ¶ ～을 주다 give 《*a person*》 a mortal wound; do 《*a person*》 a deadly injury / ～을 입다 be fatally 〔mortally〕 wounded; suffer 〔receive〕 a mortal wound / 그 부상이 ～이 되었다 The wound proved fatal. / 그 실수가 회사에 ～을 입혔다 The error proved fatal to the company.

**치명적**(致命的) fatal; mortal; deadly; lethal. ¶ ～(인) 타격을 주다 deal 〔strike〕 《*a person*》 a fatal 〔mortal, deadly〕 blow / ～인 타격을 입다〔받다〕 suffer 〔receive〕 a deathblow / 나는 ～인 실수를 저질렀다 I made a fatal blunder. / 그녀의 한 마디가 나에겐 ～이었다 That one word from her put an end to all my hopes. / 그것은 한국의 해외 무역에 대한 ～인 타격이었다 It was a deathblow to Korea's foreign trade.

**치목**(治木) trimming 〔dressing〕 timber (for building purposes). ～하다 trim 《timber》.

**치목**(稚木) a young plant 〔tree〕; a sapling; a set.

**치민**(治民) governing the people. ～하다 govern (the people).

**치밀**(緻密) 《정밀》 minuteness; fineness; 《정교》 elaborateness; delicacy; 《정확》 precision; accuracy. ～하다 (be) elaborate; close; minute; fine; nice; delicate. ¶ ～한 precise; minute; elaborate; fine; close / 너무 ～한 overminute / ～하게 elaborately; minutely; closely; delicately / ～한 계획 a finely worked-out 〔a carefully thought-out〕 plan / ～한 관찰 a careful 〔close〕 observation / ～한 두뇌의 사람 a person capable of precise thinking / ～한 솜씨 elaborate 〔delicate〕 workmanship / ～한 추리 a close reasoning / ～하게 생각하다 think closely / ～하지 못하다 be lacking in precision / ～한 주의를 요하다 require a close attention / 그 조사는 ～하지 않다 The investigation lacks accuracy. / 그는 관찰이 ～하다 He is a minute 〔nice〕 observer. / ～하게 조사한 결과 그것은 복제(複製)임이 드러났다 Under close examination it was found to be a reproduction.

**치밀다** ① 《분노·욕심 따위가》 be filled 〔seized〕 with 《sorrow》; have a fit of 《anger》; fill *one's* heart with 《anger》; well up within *one.* ¶ 욕심이 ～ be seized with greed / 치미는 정욕을 누르다 mortify 〔control〕 *one's* passions; regulate *one's* desires / 뜨거운 눈물이 치밀어 올랐다 Hot tears welled up in my eyes. / 그녀 가슴에 분노가 치밀어 올랐다 A feeling of anger surged up in her. ② 《먹은 것이》 heave; rise; come up. ¶ 먹은 것이 ～ *one's* food comes back up. ③ 《위로 밀다》 push 〔shove, force〕 up; thrust up; raise (up). ¶ 죽순이 흙을 치밀고 올라 온다 Bamboo sprouts push up through the earth.

**치받다** butt up; push 〔thrust〕 up. ¶ 아무의 턱을 ～ give *a person* an uppercut on 〔to〕 the chin / 아무를 머리로 ～ give *a person* a butt of head; butt *a person* 《in the stomach》.

**치받이** ① 《비탈》 an upward 〔ascending〕 slope; an ascent; a climb; an upgrade; an uphill (road). ¶ 가파른 〔완만한〕 ～ a steep 〔gradual〕 ascent / 치받잇길 an uphill road / ～를 오르다 breast 〔struggle with〕 an ascent / 이 길은 줄곧 ～다 The road is uphill all the way. / 길은 이 곳에서부터 ～가 된다 The path ascends here. ② 〖건축〗 mud plastered on the ceiling. ～하다 plaster the ceiling.

**치받치다** ① 《버팀대로》 support; prop (up); bolster up; 《밀어올려》 push up. ¶ 토마토를 막대로 ～ support a tomato plant with a stick. ② 《연기·불길이》 rise; soar; flare. ¶ 연기가 ～ smoke rises / 불길이 ～ a flame flares 〔blazes, flames〕 up. ③ 《감정이》 surge; swell; well up. ¶ 분노가 ～ be seized with anger; flare up in anger. ④ 《먹은 것이》 heave; rise; come up. ¶ 먹은 것이 ～ *one's* food comes back up.

**치병**(治病) curing a disease. ～하다 cure 〔treat〕 a disease.

**치부**(恥部) 《남녀의》 the genitals; 《완곡하게》 the private parts; the intimate parts of the body; 《창피한 부분》 a disgrace; an embarrassment. ¶ 할렘 같은 지역은 뉴욕의 ～이다 The city of New York ought to be ashamed to have such a place as Harlem.

**치부**(致富) acquisition of wealth; making money. ～하다 make money; become rich; amass a fortune. ¶ 장사를 해서 크게 ～하다 make a great fortune by trade / 주식으로 ～하다 profit handsomely from stock speculation. ◉ ～꾼 one who makes money; a money-maker.

**치부**(置簿) 《기입함》 book-keeping; 《장부》 an account book; a ledger. ～하다 《장부에》 keep books; keep accounts; enter 《an item》 in a book; 《마음속에》 keep 〔bear〕 in mind; make a mental note of; engrave. ¶ …앞으로 ～하다 put 〔charge〕 《a sum》 to 《*a person's*》 account / 이 사실을 단단히 마음에 ～해 둬라 Be sure to bear this fact in mind. ◉ ～책 an account book; a ledger. 외상 ～ a credit account.

**치사**(致死) being fatal 〔mortal, deadly〕; killing. ¶ ～의 fatal; mortal; deadly; lethal; causing death / 상해～ (a) bodily injury resulting in death / 과실～죄 〖법〗 accidental homicide; 《commit》 involuntary manslaughter. ◉ ～량 《독극물의》 a fatal 〔lethal〕 dose: ～량의 수면제를 복용하다 take a fatal dose of sleeping pills. ～율 lethality.

**치사**(致謝) appreciation; extending thanks; gratitude. ～하다 extend thanks; appreciate; express *one's* gratitude 〔appreciation〕. ¶ 아무의 호

의를 ～하다 thank *a person* for *his* kindness.

**치사**(恥事) 《남부끄러움》 shame; disgrace; dishonor; infamy; ignominy; 《비열함》 meanness; dirtiness. ～하다〔스럽다〕 (be) shameful; dishonorable; disgraceful; ignominious; mean; dirty. ¶ ～한 행위 disgraceful behavior 〔conduct〕/ ～한 사람 a mean 〔shameless〕 fellow / ～스러운 꼴을 당하다 be put to shame; bring disgrace upon *oneself;* disgrace *oneself;* humiliate *oneself* / ～스러운 꼴을 보이다 expose *oneself* to shame; disgrace *oneself;* lay *oneself* open to scorn / ～스럽게 굴다 behave meanly 〔shamefully〕/ ～스럽게 여기다 be ashamed to 《*do*》; feel humiliated / ～스러운 줄을 모르다 know no shame; be shameless 〔brazenfaced〕/ ～스러운 것을 무릅쓰고 그에게 돈을 빌려 달라고 했다 Pocketing my pride, I asked him for a loan.

**치산**(治山) 《산소의》 keeping ancestral graves in order; 《산림의》 afforestation; forestry conservation. ～하다 keep ancestral graves in good shape; take good care of the forests; protect 〔conserve〕 the forests. ◉ ～치수 anti-flood 〔flood control〕 afforestation; conservation of rivers and forests: ～치수 사업 anti-erosion project.

**치산**(治産) management of *one's* property 〔estate〕. ～하다 manage *one's* property. ◉ 금～ 〖법〗 incompetency: 금～자 a person adjudged incompetent; an interdict. 한정～ quasi-incompetency.

**치살리다** 《추켜세우다》 praise 《*a person*》 to the skies; plaster 《*a person*》 with praise; give 《*a person*》 a boost; speak highly of; flatter.

**치상**(齒狀) dentiform; tooth-shape(d). ◉ ～구조 〖식물·동물〗 dentation.

**치상**(治喪) ～하다 take charge of 〔attend to〕 the funeral rites.

**치석**(治石) trimming 〔dressing〕 stone (for building purposes). ～하다 trim stone.

**치석**(齒石) tartar (on the teeth); dental calculus; odontolith. ¶ ～으로 더러워진 이 tartar-coated teeth / ～이 붙다 [이가 주어] be coated with tartar / ～을 제거하다 remove 〔scrape〕 tartar from 《*a person's*》 teeth; scale 《*a person's*》 teeth. ◉ ～제거 scaling (of the teeth): ～ 제거기 a scaler.

**치성**(致誠) 《정성을 다함》 devotion; loyal 〔faithful〕 service; 《신령·부처에의》 sacrificial service 《to spirits》; a devout prayer. ¶ ～을 드리다 offer a sacrifice 《to spirits》; offer a devout prayer.

**치세**(治世) a reign; a rule; a regime; 《태평시대》 peaceful times 〔ruling〕. ¶ …의 ～에 in 〔under, during〕 the reign of… / 영국은 엘리자베스 1세(世) ～에 해외로 대발전을 했다 England made a great overseas expansion in the reign of Queen Elizabeth I.

**치솟다** ① 《솟아오르다》 rise (suddenly); soar; skyrocket; shoot up; zoom (비행기가). ¶ 하늘 높이 ～ rise 〔soar〕 to the sky; shoot into the blue / 물가가 천정부지로 치솟고 있다 Prices are skyrocketing. / 불길이 치솟았다 Flames shoot up 〔rose higher〕. ② 《감정 등이》 be filled 〔seized〕 《with》; have a fit 《of》. ⇨ 치밀다 ①.

**치수**(一數) the number of *ch'i* 〔inches〕; measure; measurements; dimensions; size. ¶ ～대로 to measure; according to the measurements / ～를 재다 measure the length; take 《*a person's*》 measure(ments) 《for a new suit》; measure the size 〔dimension〕 《of》; take the size 《of》/ 자로 ～를 재다 take the measurements of 《a box》 with a rule / ～가 모자라다 be short (of measure); be wanting in length / ～를 틀리다〔잘못 재다〕 take a wrong measure; 《잘못 만들다》 make 《*a thing*》 to wrong measurements / 이 옷은 네 ～에 맞춰 만들었다 The clothes are made to your measure.
◉ ～금 《자의》 the ruler measure.

**치수**(治水) river improvement; river training; flood control. ～하다 regulate rivers 〔watercourses〕; control flood. ¶ ～는 정치의 가장 중요한 과제가 되어 왔다 Flood control has been a prime subject 〔duty〕 of government. ◉ ～계획 a water control project. ～공사 flood prevention works; river embanking. ～공학 hydraulic engineering.

**치수**(齒髓) 〖해부〗 the pulp (of a tooth); the dental pulp. ◉ ～강(腔) the pulp cavity. ～염 pulpitis.

**치수내다**(一數一) measure 《the length of》. ¶ 필목을 ～ measure the length of a piece of cotton.

**치술**(治術) ① 《치료술》 the medical 〔healing〕 art; medicine. ② 《정치술》 administrative skill; statecraft; statesmanship.

**치식**(齒式) 〚생물〛 a dental formula.

**치신** behaving 〔carrying〕 *oneself;* an act; 《위신》 prestige; dignity; authority; honor. ¶ ～을 잃다 lose 〔impair〕 *one's* dignity; lose authority 〔prestige〕; degrade *oneself;* compromise *one's* honor.

**치신경**(齒神經) 〚해부〛 the dental nerve.

**치신사납다** (be) shameful; indecent; disreputable; unsightly; outrageous. ¶ 치신사납게 굴다 behave outrageously 〔indecently, unseemly〕 / 그런 짓을 해서야 치신사나워 쓰겠느냐 It will bring a scandal upon you if you behave like that.

**치신없다** (be) undignified; ungentlemanly; unbecoming. ¶ 치신없는 짓 an undignified act 〔behavior〕 / 치신없는 사람 a person with no dignity / 치신없이 굴다 behave unseemly; act dishonorably.

**치아**(齒牙) the teeth. ⇨ 이[1] ①.

**치안**(治安) public peace (and order); (public) security. ¶ ～을 유지하다 maintain public peace and order / ～을 어지럽히다 disturb 〔break〕 public peace (and order) / 이 지역은 ～이 좋다〔나쁘다〕 This area is a safe 〔dangerous〕 place.
◉ ～감 Senior Superintendent General (생략 Sen. Supt. Gen.). ～경찰 the security police. ～당국 law enforcement authorities. ～문란 행위 disorderly conduct. ～방해 breach 〔disturbance〕 of public peace: ～방해자 a peacebreaker / 그들의 운동은～방해로 진압되었다 Their movement was suppressed as a breach of public peace. ～본부 the National Police Headquarters. ～유지 maintenance of (the) public peace: ～유지상 for security reasons / ～유지법 the Law for Maintenance of the Public Peace. ～재판 a summary trial. ～정감 Chief Superintendent General. ～총감 Commissioner General (of the National Police Agency). ～판사 a justice of the peace (생략 J.P.).

**치약**(齒藥) toothpaste; dental cream; [총칭] dentifrice.

**치어**(稚魚) a fry; a fingerling; [총칭] fry; the young of fish. ¶ 연어의 ～ salmon fry.

**치어리더** a cheerleader.

**치열**(治熱) 〚한의학〛 controlling 〔checking〕 a fever. ～하다 control 〔check〕 a fever. ¶ 이열(以熱)～ Like cures like.

**치열**(齒列) a set 〔row〕 of teeth; dentition. ¶ ～이 고르다〔고르지 않다〕 have a regular 〔an irregular〕 set of teeth.
◉ ～교정 correction of irregularities of the teeth; straightening of irregular teeth; 《기술》 orthodontics; orthodontia: ～교정기 a brace / ～교정의(醫) an orthodontist.

**치열**(熾烈) intensity; ferocity; fierceness; keenness; severity. ～하다 (be) intense; keen; severe; fierce. ¶ ～한 경쟁 (a) keen 〔sharp, fierce, hot, cutthroat〕 competition; hot 〔bitter〕 rivalry / ～한 논쟁 a heated 〔fiery〕 discussion; a hot argument / ～한 전투 a fierce battle 〔fight〕 / ～하게 싸우다 fight hard 〔furiously〕; have a fierce battle 〔engagement〕; engage in hot 〔harsh〕 fighting.

**치오르다** rise (up); go up. ¶ 하늘로 ～ soar 〔go up〕 in the air.

**치올리다** lift up; push 〔raise〕 up.

**치외법권**(治外法權) 〚법〛 extraterritoriality; extraterritorial rights; 《외교관의》 diplomatic immunity; 《영사 재판권》 consular jurisdiction. ¶ ～상의 extraterritorial / ～을 철폐하다 abolish 〔relinquish〕 extraterritoriality.

**치욕**(恥辱) disgrace; dishonor; shame; indignity; (a) humiliation. ¶ 심한 ～ a crying 〔burning〕 shame; a deep disgrace; a sore indignity / 국가의 ～ a disgrace to the nation; a national disgrace; a stain upon the national honor / ～을 당하다 be disgraced 〔dishonored, insulted〕; be subject to humiliation / ～을 주다 disgrace; dishonor; insult; humiliate; bring shame on 《*a person*》; make 《*a person*》 ashamed; put 《*a person*》 to shame; subject 《*a person*》 to humiliation / ～을 씻다 wipe away 〔off〕 a disgrace; clear *one's* reputation / ～을 초래하다〔가져오다〕 bring shame 〔disgrace〕 upon 「*one's* head 〔the name of *one's* family〕; suffer disgrace; disgrace *oneself* / ～을 참다 bear disgrace; pocket 〔book〕 an insult; eat humble pie 《영》; eat crow 《미》 / …을 ～으로 여기다 be ashamed of 《*doing*》; feel 〔think〕 it disgraceful 《to *do*》; feel shame 《to *do*》 / 나는 지금까지 이런 ～은 겪은 일이 없다 I have never been disgraced as much as this.

**치우**(癡愚) imbecility; stupidity.

**치우다** ① 《없애다·옮기다》 put 〔take, clear〕 away 〔off〕; work off; remove;

get 〔put〕 out of the way; 《챙기다》 keep; store; put 〔lay〕 《*a thing*》 away 〔up, by〕; put back (본디 있던 곳에); stow away; tuck away 《in a box》. ¶ 팔아치울 물건 goods for clearance sale / 거치적거리는 것을 ～ remove an obstacle; do away with a nuisance / 길의 돌을 ～ remove stones from the road / 밥상을 ～ clear the table; remove the dinner table / 의자를 ～ put the chairs back in their places / 읽던 책을 ～ put aside the book *one* is reading / 잡동사니를 ～ shift rubbish out of the way / 책을 책장에 ～ put the books away in the bookcase / 어린애가 장난 못하게 칼을 치워라 Put the knife away so that the child can't toy with it.
② 《정돈하다》 put 《*things*》 in order; put 〔set〕 《a room》 「to rights 〔straight〕; tidy up 《a room》; clean up; straighten up 《a room》; fix up 《미구어》. ¶ 어수선하게 늘어놓은 방을 ～ tidy (up) a disordered 〔cluttered〕 room / 부엌을 ～ straighten (out) the kitchen / 책상 위를 ～ clear up 〔out〕 *one's* desk / 하던 일을 ～ clean up unfinished work.
③ 《끝마치다》 finish; put an end to; bring to an end 〔a close〕; complete. ⇨ 해치우다. ¶ 먹어 ～ eat up all / 책 한 권을 읽어 ～ finish a book / 이 일을 되도록 빨리 해 치우자 Let's get through with this work as soon as we can.
④ 《딸을》 give 《*one's* daughter》 in marriage; marry 《*one's* daughter》 off. ⇨ 시집보내다.

**치우치다** ① 《쏠리다》 lean 《to, toward》; incline 《toward》; slant 《toward》. ¶ 약간 서쪽으로 치우친 곳에 a little to the west 《of》 / 벽이 동쪽으로 ～ a wall slants to the east. ② 《편파되다》 be biased 〔one-sided, prejudiced〕; be lopsided 〔unbalanced〕; be partial 《to》; have a partiality 《for, to》; 《도를 지나치다》 go to excess. ¶ 치우친 생각 a biased 〔one-sided, lopsided, partial, distorted〕 view; a prejudice / 감정에 ～ give way to 〔be carried away by〕 *one's* feelings / 막내 아들을 치우치게 사랑하다 be partial toward the youngest son / 치우치지 않다 be unbiased 〔impartial, unprejudiced, fair, equitable〕 / 그의 설은 너무 인도주의에 치우치고 있다 His theory makes too much of humanitarianism.

**치유**(治癒) healing; cure; recovery. ～하다 cure; heal; recover; be cured. ¶ ～할 수 있는〔없는〕 curable 〔incurable〕 / 병이 ～되다 be cured of a disease / 상처는 곧 ～될 것이다 The wound will soon heal up. ◉ ～기(期) convalescence. ～력 healing power; curative properties. ～율 a cure rate.

**치은**(齒齦) 〖해부〗 the gum(s); the gingiva (*pl.* -vae). ⇨ 잇몸. ◉ ～염 inflammation of the gums; gingivitis. ～절개술 gingivectomy. ～출혈 gingival bleeding.

**치음**(齒音) 〖언어〗 a dental (sound); a sibilant. ¶ ～화하다 dentalize.

**치의학과**(齒醫學科) the department of dentistry.

**치이다**[1] ① 《무거운 것에》 get hit; be crushed 〔squeezed〕; 《깔리다》 be pressed 〔held, caught〕 under. ¶ 손이 장도리에 ～ *one's* hand gets hit by a claw hammer / 손이 문틈에 ～ *one's* hand gets squeezed in the door / 무너지는 바위에 치여서 죽다 be crushed to death under the loosened rocks.
② 《차에》 get 〔be〕 run over 〔knocked down〕 《by》; be hit 《by》. ¶ 자동차〔기차〕에 ～ be run over by a car 〔train〕 / 차에 치여 크게 다치다 be seriously injured by a car.
③ 《덫에》 get trapped 〔entrapped〕; be caught in a trap. ¶ 곰이 덫에 ～ a bear is trapped.

**치이다**[2] 《피륙 올이》 lose 《its》 weave; 《솜 등이》 form into a lump; lump (up) to one side. ¶ 항라(亢羅)는 빨면 치인다 Silk gauze loses its weave when it is washed.

**치이다**[3] 《값이》 cost; amount to 《so much》; be priced 〔valued〕. ¶ 비싸게 ～ come 〔prove〕 expensive; run into (big) money / 싸게 ～ come cheap; cost little / 그렇게 하는 것이 싸게 치인다 It comes cheaper to do so. 「ton.

**치인**(癡人) an idiot; a fool; a simple-

**치자**(治者) a ruler; a sovereign; a person in power.

**치자**(梔子) 〖한의〗 a gardenia seed. ◉ ～나무 〖식물〗 a gardenia; a Cape jasmine. ～색 a reddish yellow color.

**치잡다** take 〔grab, snatch〕 up.

**치장**(治粧) 《꾸밈》 ornamentation; decoration; adornment; 《몸치장》 dress; (an) outfit 《for》; a turnout; preparation; 《화장》 makeup; *one's* toilet. ～하다 《꾸미다》 decorate; adorn; ornament (★ adorn은 주로 사람에 대해서, decorate나 ornament는 사물에 대해서 쓰

임); pretty up; 《몸치장을》 adorn *oneself* 《with jewels》; dress 〔attire, smarten〕 *oneself;* deck *oneself* out 〔up〕; spruce (*oneself*) up; 《화장을》 make *oneself* up; put on makeup; make *one's* toilet. ¶ 점포의 ~ shop decoration / 방을 그림으로 ~하다 decorate a room with pictures / 집을 ~하다 「pretty up 〔decorate〕 *one's* house / 잔뜩 ~하고 나서다 go out all dolled up.

**치적**(治績) *one's* administrative record(s) 〔achievements〕; (the results of an) administration. ¶ ~을 기념하여 비를 세우다 erect a monument in commemoration of 《*a person's*》 remarkable executive services / 그의 ~은 훌륭했다 His administration was a great success.

**치정**(癡情) a foolish passion; blind love; jealousy (질투). ¶ ~에 얽힌 범죄 a crime of passion / ~에 이끌리어 carried away by an amorous passion / ~에 빠지다〔눈이 멀다〕 be blinded with 〔by〕 amorous passion.
◉ ~관계 an amorous relationship: 두 사람 사이에 ~ 관계가 있었던 것 같다 It is suspected that there was 「a liaison 〔an amorous relationship〕 between the two. ~살인(사건) a sex murder (case).

**치조**(齒槽) 〖해부〗 an alveolus (*pl.* -li); an alveole; the socket of a tooth. ¶ ~의 alveolar. ◉ ~골막 alveolar periosteum. ~농루(膿漏) 〖의학〗 pyorrh(o)ea alveolaris. ~염 〖의학〗 alveolitis.

**치졸**(稚拙) crudity; artlessness. ~하다 (be) crude; naïve 〔naive〕; (awkwardly) artless. ¶ ~한 글씨로 with uncertain childish hand. ◉ ~미 the beauty of artlessness 〔naïveté〕.

**치죄**(治罪) punishment of crime. ~하다 punish 《*a person*》 for *his* crime; punish (a criminal).

**치중**(置重) attaching weight 〔importance〕 《to》. ~하다 attach weight 〔importance〕 to; lay 〔put〕 stress 〔emphasis〕 on 《grammar》; make much of; set 〔put〕 value on. ¶ 교육에 ~하다 attach importance to education; value 〔prize, make much of〕 education / 영어에 ~하다 stress 〔give weight to〕 English / 외모에 너무 ~해서는 안된다 You should not place too much emphasis on external appearances.

**치즈** cheese. ¶ ~덩어리 a chunk of cheese / ~를 얹은 빵 cheese and bread. ◉ ~버거 a cheeseburger. ~케이크 (a) cheesecake. ~크래커 cheese cracker.

**치지도외**(置之度外) 《도외시하여 내버려 둠》. ~하다 disregard; ignore; leave 《*a thing*》 out of 「account 〔consideration〕; take no account of 《*a thing*》; overlook. ¶ 그 책은 수익성을 ~하고 출판되었다 The book was published without regard for profit.

**치질**(痔疾) 〖의학〗 hemorrhoids; 《구어》 piles. ¶ 수〔암〕~ external 〔internal〕 hemorrhoids / ~이 있다 have 〔suffer from〕 piles / ~을 절제하다 excise a hemorrhoid tumor.
◉ ~수술 hemorrhoidectomy. ~환자 a victim of 〔a sufferer from〕 piles.

**치천하**(治天下) ~하다 rule over the whole nation; govern a country.

**치치다** ① 《올리어 긋다》 stroke 〔draw a line〕 upward. ¶ 획을 ~ make an upward stroke (in writing). ② 《치뜨리다》 raise; lift; toss 〔throw〕 up.

**치켜세우다** praise 《*a person*》 sky-high; loud 〔extoll〕 《*a person*》 to the skies; sing the praises 《of》; speak highly of; pay a tribute to. ¶ 교육에 공로가 많다고 ~ pay a tribute to 《*a person*》 for *his* many services to education.

**치크댄스** cheek-to-cheek dancing. ¶ ~를 추다 dance cheek-to-cheek 《with》.

**치키다** raise; lift (up); hoist; heave; boost; 《걷어 올리다》 tuck 〔gird, gather〕 up. ¶ 칼을 치켜들고 with a sword raised overhead / 눈을 치켜 뜨다 lift (up) 〔raise〕 *one's* eyes; cast an upward glance; turn up the eyes / 큰 돌을 치켜들다 heave up a large stone; give a large stone a lift / 와이셔츠 소매를 ~ hitch 〔roll〕 up the shirt sleeves / 치맛자락을 치켜 올리다 tuck up the skirt.

**치킨** chicken. ◉ ~라이스 chicken and rice fried. ~수프 chicken soup. ~커틀릿 chicken cutlets. ~프라이 fried chicken.

**치타** 〖동물〗 a cheetah.

**치태**(癡態) idiotic behavior; silliness; tomfoolery. ¶ ~를 부리다 make a fool of *oneself;* cut a ludicrous figure; make a disgraceful scene.

**치통**(齒痛) (a) toothache. ¶ ~이 심하다 have a bad toothache; suffer from a bad toothache / 주사를 맞았더니 ~이 좀 가라앉았다 The injection eased the toothache a little.

**치평**(治平) ～하다 govern so as to secure peace.

**치하**(治下) ¶ ～의 under the rule 〔reign〕《of》/ 입헌 ～의 under a constitutional government / 엘리자베스 여왕 ～의 영국 England under the reign of Queen Elizabeth / 영국 ～에 놓이다 come 〔fall〕 under British rule.

**치하**(致賀) a compliment; congratulation. ～하다 compliment; praise; congratulate 〔felicitate〕《*a person*》 on; celebrate; appreciate. ¶ ～하는 말 a congratulatory address; a congratulation / …을 ～하기 위하여 in honor 〔celebration〕 of... / 노고를 ～하다 thank 《*a person*》 for *his* trouble; show appreciation of 《*a person*》 for *his* services / 용기를 ～하다 compliment 〔praise〕《*a person*》 for *his* courage.

**치한**(癡漢) ① 《호색한》 a molester of women; 《구어》 a groper (혼잡한 차안의); 《속어》 a wolf. ¶ ～을 만나다 be molested 《in a crowded train》. ② 《치인》 a fool; an idiot. 「behavior.

**치행**(癡行) tomfoolery; silliness; idiotic

**치환**(置換) 〖화학〗 substitution; replacement; 〖수학〗 permutation; transposition. ～하다 substitute; replace; permute; transpose. ¶ X와 Y를 ～하다 replace X with Y; substitute Y for X.

**칙령**(勅令) a Royal decree 〔edict〕. ¶ ～으로 by Royal edict 〔ordinance〕/ ～을 내리다 issue a Royal decree 〔edict, ordinance〕.

**칙명**(勅命) a Royal order 〔command, commission, mandate〕. ¶ ～으로 by Royal order.

**칙사**(勅使) a Royal envoy 〔messenger〕.

**칙서**(勅書) a Royal letter 〔message〕.

**칙선**(勅選) a nomination by the King.

**칙어**(勅語) a Royal message.

**칙유**(勅諭) Royal instructions; a Royal mandate.

**칙임**(勅任) Royal appointment.

**칙재**(勅裁) Royal decision 〔sanction〕.

**칙지**(勅旨) a Royal order 〔wishes〕.

**칙칙폭폭** ① 《기차 소리》 chug-chug 〔chuff-chuff〕; puff-puff. ¶ ～ 소리를 내며 지나가다 chug 〔chuff〕 along. ② 《기차》 a choochoo 《소아어》.

**칙칙하다** (be) somber; dull; dark. ¶ 칙칙한 빛깔 a dark 〔somber〕 color / 칙칙한 청색 sordid blue / 칙칙해 보이다 look dark and dull. 「〔colored〕.

**-칙칙하다** (be) '-ish'; slightly tinged

**칙필**(勅筆) a Royal autograph; the King's own handwriting.

**칙허**(勅許) Royal permission 〔sanction, consent, grant〕.

**친-**(親) ① 《어버이》 parental. ② 《혈육》 *one's* own; *one's* blood; real; true. ¶ 친어머니 *one's* real mother / 친형제 *one's* blood brothers; brothers of the same venter 〔mother〕. ③ 《몸소》 by *oneself;* in person. ④ 《친밀》 pro; favoring. ¶ 친미〔일〕의 pro-American 〔=Japanese〕/ 친서방의 pro-Western / ～여 후보 a pro-government candidate.

**친가**(親家) *one's* old 〔parents'〕 home. ⇨친정(親庭). ¶ 아내는 시골에 있는 ～에 머물고 있다 My wife is staying with her parents in the country.

**친경**(親耕) royal plowing in person. ～하다 《the King》 plow in person.

**친고**(親告) 〖법〗 a victim's complaint; complaint from the victim.

◉ ～죄 〖법〗 an offense subject to prosecution only on complaint (from the victim).

**친고**(親故) relatives and friends.

**친교**(親交) (close) friendship; friendly relations; intimacy. ¶ ～(가) 있는 사람 a close 〔good〕 friend / …와 ～가 있다 be on close 〔friendly, good〕 terms 《with》; enjoy the friendship of; be good friends 《with》/ ～를 맺다 form 〔contract〕 a (close) friendship 《with》; make friends 《with》/ ～를 맺은 사이다 be on terms of friendship / ～를 끊다 break a (close) friendship 《with》/ ～를 도모하다 promote 〔develop〕 friendly 〔cordial〕 relations 《with》/ …와 ～를 지속하다 maintain friendly relations 《with》/ 30년간의 ～《maintain》 a friendship of thirty years' standing.

**친구**(親舊) a friend; a companion; a pal 《구어》; a chum 《구어》; a buddy 《구어》; [집합적] company. ¶ 내 ～ a friend of mine; one of my friends; my friend (★ a friend of mine은 「어떤 한 친구」, one of my friends는 「여러 친구 중의 한 친구」, my friend는 「상대방도 아는 내 친구」) / 여자～ a girlfriend / 남자～ a boyfriend / 술～ a drinking pal / 학교～ a schoolmate; a schoolfriend; a schoolfellow / 막역한 ～ a sworn 〔bosom〕 friend; *one's* best 〔trusted〕 friend / 미덥지 못한 ～ a fair-weather friend / 오랜 ～ an old friend; a friend of long standing / 참된 ～ a true 〔tried〕 friend / 친한 ～ a good 〔close, best〕 friend; a chum; a crony / 평생

의 ～ a lifelong friend; a companion for life / 고난을 함께 하는 ～ a companion of *one's* misery / ～를 고르다 choose a friend / ～를 사귀다 make a friend of; make friends with; associate with / 좋은〔나쁜〕 ～와 사귀다 keep good 〔bad〕 company; associate 〔mix〕 with a good 〔bad〕 friend / 서로 절친한 ～가 되다 become great friends / ～를 등한시하다 ignore 〔neglect〕 a friend / ～가 없다 have no friends; be friendless / 사람은 사귀는 ～를 보면 알 수 있다 You can judge a man by the company he keeps. / 이 세상에 믿을 ～란 많지 않다 Mighty few friends can be relied on in this world. / ～는 얻기보다 잃기가 쉽다 A friend is easier lost than found. / 어려울 때의 ～야 말로 참된 ～다 A friend in need is a friend indeed. / 그는 알고 지내는 사람은 많지만 ～는 별로 없다 He has many acquaintances but few friends.

**친권**(親權) 〖법〗 parental authority 〔prerogatives〕. ¶ ～을 행사하다 exercise parental power. ◉ ～자 a person in parental authority; a guardian (부모 이외의).

**친근**(親近) ～하다 (be) close; friendly; familiar; intimate. ¶ ～한 사이 close relationship; first-name basis / ～한 사이다 be intimate 《with》; be on friendly 〔familiar〕 terms 《with》 / 매우 ～하다 be thick 《with》; be hand in 〔and〕 glove 《with》 / (…와) ～해지다 make friends 《with》; get 〔become〕 familiar 〔friendly〕 《with》; come into close association 《with》.

> **참고** **intimate friend**의 뜻
> **intimate**란 형용사에는 크게 다섯가지 정도의 의미가 있는데, 이 중에서 friend를 앞에서 수식하는 경우는 「친한, 친밀한」이란 뜻과 「서로 관계가 밀접한, 마음을 서로 터놓는, 성적 관계가 있는」 따위 뜻이 있다. 「그는 나의 아내의 친한 친구다」를 He is my wife's intimate friend.라고 말한다면 듣는 사람은 아마 깜짝 놀랄 것이다. 왜냐하면 「그는 나의 아내와 동침하는 친구다」란 뜻도 되기 때문이다. 또 동성간에 「나는 그의 친한 친구다」를 I am his intimate friend. 라고 해서도 안 된다. 혹시 서로 「동성연애」를 하는 사이가 아닌가 하는 의심을 받기 때문이다. 이런 오해를 받지 않기 위해서는 intimate 대신에 close 〔best, good〕 friend 라고 하여야 한다.

**친근감**(親近感) affection; a sense 〔feeling〕 of affinity 〔closeness〕. ¶ 어버이와 자식간의 ～ affection between parent and child / ～을 느끼다 feel strong affinities 《with》; feel a sense of closeness 《with》; feel friendly 《toward》 / 같이 살면 ～도 생기는 법이다 Closeness develops among us as we go on living together. / 그녀의 행동에 ～을 느꼈다 I felt at ease with her behavior. / 처음 만났을 때부터 그녀에게 ～을 느꼈다 I've found something congenial in her since the day when we first met.

**친기**(親忌) the annual memorial service to *one's* departed parent.

**친남매**(親男妹) *one's* real 〔blood, own〕 brothers and sisters.

**친누이**(親—) *one's* real 〔blood, own〕 sister.

**친독**(親獨) ¶ ～의 pro-German. ◉ ～주의 pro-Germanism.

**친동기**(親同氣) *one's* real 〔blood, own〕 brother 〔sister〕.

**친동생**(親同生) ＝ 친아우.

**친등**(親等) the degree of kinship 〔consanguinity, relationship (by blood)〕.

**친딸**(親—) *one's* own 〔real〕 daughter.

**친러**(親—) ¶ ～의〔적인〕 pro-Russian. ◉ ～파 a pro-Russian party; the pro-Russians.

**친림**(親臨) the Royal presence; a Royal visit.

**친모**(親母) *one's* real 〔blood〕 mother.

**친목**(親睦) friendship; friendliness; fraternization; amity (단체·국가간의). ～하다 (be) friendly; 〔서술적〕 be on friendly terms; be in rapport 《with》. ¶ 상호의 ～을 꾀하다 cultivate 〔promote, enhance〕 mutual friendship / 이 파티의 주된 목적은 회원 상호간의 ～을 도모하는 데 있다 The main aim of this party is to 「promote 〔enhance〕 mutual friendship among the members of our club. ◉ ～단체 a friendly society. ～회 a social meeting 〔gathering〕; a convivial meeting; a get-together (meeting) 《미》: ～회를 열다 hold a social meeting.

**친미**(親美) ¶ ～의 pro-American; pro-United States. ◉ ～노선 the pro-American line. ～정책 pro-American policy. ～주의 pro-Americanism: ～주의자 a pro-American. ～파 a pro-American group 〔faction〕.

**친밀**(親密) intimacy; close friendship; close relationship. ～하다 (be) intimate; close; friendly. ¶ ～한 intimate; familiar; close / ～한 사이다 be on close 〔good〕 terms 《with》; be on terms of intimacy 《with》; be in friendly relations 《with》; be very good friends 《with》 / 서로 ～하게 사귀다 associate with each other closely; have a close friendship / 함께 ～하게 지내다 live a close life together / ～해지다 get on intimate terms 《with》; make 〔become〕 friends 《with》; develop 〔establish〕 a rapport 《with》 / 우리의 관계는 해마다 ～의 도를 더하여 갔다 Our relations have yearly gained in intimacy.

**친부**(親父) *one's* real 〔blood〕 father.

**친부모**(親父母) *one's* real 〔blood〕 parents. ¶ ～처럼 돌보아 주다 look after 《*a person*》 with parental affection 〔tenderest care〕; display a fatherly interest 《in》; bring up 《a child》 with motherly care / ～보다 양부모가 낫다 The foster parent is dearer to one than the real parent.

**친분**(親分) acquaintanceship; familiarity; (closeness of) friendship; intimacy. ¶ ～이 있다 be acquainted 〔familiar〕 《with》 / ～이 깊다 be intimate 《with》; be close 《to》; be on intimate terms 《with》; be in intimate relation 《with》 / ～이 없다 be not acquainted 《with》; be not close 《to》 / ～이 생기다 become acquainted 《with》 / ～이 두터워지다 get more closely acquainted / ～을 만들다 make an acquaintance; obtain access 《to》; make *one's* acquaintance.

**친불**(親佛) ¶ ～의 pro-French; Francophile. ◉ ～주의 Francophilia: ～주의자 a Francophile.

**친불친**(親不親) whether intimate or not; regardless of relationship; friends or not. ¶ ～간에 사람을 푸대접해서는 아니된다 You shouldn't go around slighting a person regardless of the terms you are on with him.

**친사돈**(親査頓) the parents of *one's* son=〔daughter-〕in-law.

**친산**(親山) *one's* parents' graves.

**친상**(親喪) mourning for *one's* parent; bereavement of *one's* parent. ¶ ～을 당하다 have *one's* parent die; mourn 〔be bereaved of〕 *one's* parent.

**친생자**(親生子) *one's* (real) child; a child of *one's* own.

**친서**(親書) 《자필의》 an autograph letter 〔message〕; 《대통령 등의》 a (personal) letter 〔message〕 《from President Clinton》. ～하다 write 《a letter, *etc.*》 in person. ¶ 특사는 대통령의 ～를 휴대했다 The special envoy carried a personal message of the President. / 그는 대통령에게 국왕의 친서를 전달했다 He handed an autographed letter from the King to the President.

**친서**(親署) a sign manual of the King 〔President〕; a Royal 〔Presidential〕 signature.

**친선**(親善) friendship; amity; friendly relations; goodwill. ¶ 주변 국가들과의 ～ amity with surrounding nations / 국제 ～에 기여하다 contribute to a better international understanding / 국제 ～을 도모하다 cultivate 〔promote〕 international friendship / 양국의 ～을 강화하다 strengthen the ties of friendship between the two nations. ◉ ～경기 a goodwill 〔friendly〕 match 〔game〕. ～관계 friendly 〔amicable〕 relations 《between, among》. ～방문 a 《four-day》 goodwill visit 《to a country》. ～사절 a goodwill envoy; 《사절단》 a goodwill mission: ～사절로 미국에 가다 go to the United States on a goodwill mission. ～여행 a goodwill tour. ～조약 a treaty of friendship 〔goodwill〕.

**친소**(親疎) (the relative degree of) intimacy 〔familiarity〕. ¶ ～를 가리다 discriminate among *one's* friends according to their intimacy with *one;* show favoritism; play favorites / ～를 가리지 않고 사귀다 associate 〔mix〕 with people whether they are intimate or not; mix with everybody without discrimination.

**친속**(親屬) ＝친족(親族).

**친손녀**(親孫女) a daughter of *one's* son; *one's* own granddaughter.

**친손자**(親孫子) a son of *one's* son; *one's* real 〔blood〕 grandson.

**친솔**(親率) the members of *one's* family; *one's* family.

**친수**(親授) giving 〔bestowing〕 《it》 in person. ～하다 give 〔bestow〕 《it》 in person.

**친수성**(親水性) 〖물리〗 hydrophile property.

**친숙**(親熟) familiarity; acquaintance. ～하다 be familiar 《with》; be well 〔thoroughly〕 acquainted 《with》. ¶ ～한 사람 an old acquaintance / ～해지다 get 〔become〕 familiar 《with》 / 아무와 ～한 사이다 be well acquainted with *a person*.

**친아들**(親―) *one's* true 〔real, own〕 son; *one's* son by blood.

**친아버지**(親―) *one's* real 〔blood〕 father. ¶ ～ 같은 사랑 a fatherly 〔paternal〕

love.

**친아우** *one's* real 〔blood〕 younger brother 〔sister〕.

**친애**(親愛) love; affection; intimacy. ～하다 love; feel affection for. ¶ ～하는 (my) dear; darling; beloved / ～하는 김 군 my dear (Mr.) Kim / ～의 정을 나타내다〔보이다〕 show affection《to》.

**친어머니**(親―) *one's* real 〔blood〕 mother.

**친언니**(親―) *one's* real 〔blood〕 elder sister.

**친여동생**(親女同生) *one's* true 〔real〕 (younger) sister; *one's* (younger) sister by blood.

**친영**(親英) ¶ ～의 pro-British.
◉ ～정책 a pro-British policy. ～주의 Anglophilia; Anglophilism: ～주의자 a pro-British; an Anglophil(e). ～파 the pro-British; sympathizers of Britain.

**친우**(親友) = 친구(親舊).

**친위대**(親衛隊) the Royal guards; the 《President's》 bodyguards.

**친의**(親誼) = 친분(親分).

**친일**(親日) ¶ ～의 pro-Japanese / ～적인 사람 a pro-Japanese; a Japanophile.
◉ ～파 a pro-Japanese (group).

**친자식**(親子息) *one's* real 〔blood〕 child 〔son, daughter〕. ¶ ～처럼 돌보다 look after 《*a person*》 with motherly care; display a fatherly interest 《in》.

**친전**(親展) Personal; Confidential; To be opened by addressee only (★ 편지 겉봉에 적는 말). ◉ ～서 a confidential 〔personal〕 letter.

**친절**(親切) kindness; goodness; friendliness; goodwill; a favor. ～하다 (be) kind; kindly; good; friendly; hospitable; obliging; kindhearted.

> 용법 **kind** 마음씨가 친절하다는 뜻의 가장 일반적인 말. **kindly** 원래 성격이 친절하여 그 호의가 겉으로 드러나는. **good** 도움을 준다는 뜻으로 친절한. **friendly** 친구로서 친절히 대하는. **hospitable** 손님이나 여행자 등에 대해서 친절한. **obliging** 남의 소원을 들어주거나 도움을 주어 친절하다는 뜻이 함축된 공손하며 격식차린 말.

¶ ～하게 kindly; obligingly; kindheartedly; with kindness / ～해 보이는 kindly-looking / ～한 말 kind words / ～한 사람 a kind person / ～한 행위 a kind act; an act 〔a piece〕 of kindness; a kindness / 조그만 ～ a small kindness 〔favor〕; a little act of kindness / ～한 마음에서 in 〔out of〕 kindness / ～을 가장하여 under the mask 〔show, pretense〕 of kindness / ～하게 굴다 act kindly 〔friendly〕; show kindness / ～하게도 …하다 be kind 〔good〕 enough to 《*do*》; be so kind as to 《*do*》; have the kindness to 《*do*》 / ～히 대하다〔을 베풀다〕 be kind 〔good〕 to 《*a person*》; show 《*a person*》 kindness; do 《*a person*》 a good turn; treat 《*a person*》 with kindness / ～에 보답하다 repay 《*a person's*》 kindness / ～을 거절하다 reject kindness / ～을 몰라보다 ignore 〔be unappreciative of〕 kindness / (남의) ～을 이용하다 take (mean) advantage of 《*a person's*》 kindness; avail *oneself* of 《*a person's*》 kind offer; impose on 《*a person's*》 kindness / ～하게 안내해 주셔서 고맙습니다 It is very kind of you to show me around. / 그는 원래가 ～하다 He is kindly by nature. *or* He was born a kind man. / ～하신 말씀 고맙습니다 It is very kind 〔sweet (여자에게)〕 of you to say so. / 그녀는 내게 ～을 베풀었다 She extended kindness to me. / 그녀는 나에게 여러 가지로 ～히 해 주었다 She did me a lot of kindnesses. *or* She was most obliging to me. (★ 여기서의 kindness는 보통명사화된 것) / ～을 베푼다고 한 노릇이 도리어 그에게 해가 되었다 What I had done out of kindness turned out detrimental to his interests.

**친정**(親政) royal governing in person. ～하다 《the King》 govern in person.

**친정**(親庭) a woman's parents' 〔old〕 home; *one's* maiden home. ¶ ～에 가다 go home to *one's* (real) parents.

**친족**(親族) a (blood) relative 〔relation〕 (of the same family name); a kinsman (남자); a kinswoman (여자); [총칭] kinsfolk; cousinage.
◉ ～관계 kinship (relation); relationship by blood and marriage. ～법 the Domestic Relations Law. ～회의 《hold》 a family council 〔conference〕.

**친지**(親知) a close acquaintance; an intimate friend. ¶ ～가 많다 have a wide 〔large〕 circle of acquaintances.

**친지간**(親知間) acquaintanceship; friendship. ¶ ～에 among 〔between〕 friends / ～에 서로 싸우다 quarrel among 〔between〕 friends.

**친척**(親戚) a relative; a relation; a kinsman (남); a kinswoman (여); [총칭] kinfolk. ¶ 일가 ～ *one's* relatives 「by blood and marriage 〔in blood and law]; *one's* kith and kin / 가까운[먼] ～ a near [distant] relative [relation] / 왕가의 ～이다 be akin to the royal family / …의 ～이라고 하다 claim kindred [kinship] with…; call cousin(s) with / 서로 ～사이처럼 지내다 associate with 《*a person*》 as if 《*they*》 were relatives; 《구어》 be just like family / 먼 ～보다 가까운 이웃이 낫다 A good neighbor is better than a relative afar off. / 그는 내 어머님 쪽으로 ～이 된다 He is related to me on my mother's side. ◉ ～관계 kinship; relationship.

**친친** coil upon coil; round and round. ¶ 밧줄을 ～ 동이다 wind a rope round 《*a thing*》 tight / 밧줄이 ～ 감기다 rope gets wound round and round tight.

**친친하다** (be, feel) cold and damp; clammy; [서술적] be unpleasantly damp and sticky. ¶ 등이 땀이 나 ～ *one's* back is clammy with perspiration.

**친칠라** 〖동물〗 a chinchilla.

**친탁하다**(親 —) take after *one's* father's [paternal] side.

**친필**(親筆) *one's* own handwriting; an autograph; 〖법〗 a holograph. ¶ ～의 autographic / ～ 편지 an autograph letter; a letter in *one's* own hand / 틀림없는 ～《*a person's*》 genuine autograph [handwriting].

**친하다**(親 —) ① 《가깝다》 (be) intimate; close; familiar; chummy; thick. ¶ 친하게 intimately; familiarly / 친한 친구 an intimate friend; a close [fast, bosom] friend / 친한 사이 intimate friendship / …와 ～ be on good [friendly] terms with; be friends [chums 《구어》] with; have a close [friendly] relation with; 《구어》 be chummy [thick, in] with / 친하게 굴다 behave familiarly toward 《*a person*》 / 서로 친한 사이다 be on intimate terms with each other; be friends [chums] 《with》 / 친해지다 make friends 《with》; become intimate [familiar] 《with》; get to know 《*a person*》 better; get thick 《with》 / 친한 사이에도 예절은 있어야 한다 The courtesies matter, even between friends. *or* Even among close friends courtesy should be maintained. / 우연한 기회에 친해졌다 A mere chance brought us into acquaintance. *or* I became acquainted with him by chance.

② 《가까이하다》 make friends 《with》; grow [become] intimate 《with》 (★ become intimate with a woman은 어떤 여성과 「불의의 관계를 맺다」의 뜻으로 되기 때문에 여성 앞으로 내는 편지에는 I want to become intimate with you.라고 쓰지 않도록 주의할 것). ¶ 친하기 쉬운 사람 a person easy to get acquainted with; a sociable person; a 「genial and accessible [friendly and approachable] person / 친하기 어려운 사람 a person hard to get acquainted with; an unfriendly and inaccessible [unapproachable] person / 친해지기 어려운 얼굴 a forbidding countenance / 자연과 친해지다 commune [hold communion] with nature / 그에겐 어딘가 친하기 어려운 데가 있다 There is something about him that discourages friendly advances.

**친할머니**(親—) *one's* real [blood] grand「mother.

**친할아버지**(親—) *one's* real [blood] grandfather.

**친형**(親兄) *one's* real [blood] elder 「brother [sister].

**친화**(親和) friendship; fraternity; intimacy; 《교우관계》 friendly relations 《with》; 《화학상의》 an affinity; an appetency. ～하다 be [make] friends [chums] 《with》; get on [along] 《with》; 〖화학〗 develop [have] an [a natural] affinity 《for》. ◉ ～력 〖화학〗 a chemical attraction; an affinity; an appetence.

**친환**(親患) *one's* parent's illness. ¶ ～이 있다 *one's* father [mother] is ill.

**친히**(親 —) ① 《친하게》 intimately; familiarly; in a friendly way. ¶ ～ 사귀다 be in close association 《with》; be intimate 《with》 / ～ 내왕하다 be in close contact 《with》; be close 《to》. ② 《몸소》 personally; in person; (for) *oneself*. ¶ ～ 방문하다 pay a visit in person; make a personal call 《on, at》 / ～ 보다 see 《*a thing*》 with *one's* own eyes; see 《*a thing*》 for *oneself*.

**칠**(七) seven. ¶ 제 7(의) the seventh.

**칠**(漆) ① 《옻칠》 lacquering. ⇨ 옻칠. ② 《도료》 paints; daubs; varnishes; 《바르기》 coating; painting; daubing; varnishing (니스의). ⇨ 칠하다. ¶ 물감칠 daubing colors 《on》 / 애벌칠 undercoating; an undercoat; the first [ground] coat / 페인트칠 painting; applying paint / 풀칠 pasting; applying paste / 칠을 다시 하다 repaint; recoat; paint afresh; give a new coat 《of paint》 to 《the door》 / 칠을 해서 지우다 paint out 《a signboard》; smear away 〔out〕/칠이 벗겨지다 the paint comes 〔peels〕 off / 칠 조심 《게시》 Wet 〔Fresh 《영》〕 Paint /칠이 군데군데 벗겨져 있다 The paint is off in places.

**칠각형**(七角形) a heptagon.

**칠거지악**(七去之惡) the seven valid grounds 〔causes〕 for divorce.

**칠기**(漆器) lacquer(ed) ware; lacquer; lacquerwork; a piece of lacquer(work).

**칠대양**(七大洋) the Seven Seas.

**칠독**(漆毒) lacquer poison(ing).

**칠떡거리다** trail; drag. ¶ 치마가 땅에 ~ *one's* skirt drags on the ground.

**칠떡칠떡** dragging; trailing; draggling. ¶ 치마가 진창에 ~ 끌리다 *one's* skirt drags in the mud.

**칠뜨기**(七一) ⇨ 칠삭둥이.

**칠럼거리다** overflow; slop 〔spill〕 over; brim over. ¶ 그녀가 걷는 대로 물통의 물이 칠럼거린다 The water slops over the brim of the bucket as she walks along with it.

**칠럼칠럼** overflowing; running 〔spilling, slopping〕 over; brimming over.

**칠렁거리다** be all overbrimming.

**칠렁칠렁** all splashing over; overbrimming; brimfully. ¶ 독마다 물이 ~차다 all the jars are full to the brim with water.

**칠레**《나라 이름》(the Republic of) Chile. ¶ ~의 Chilean; Chilian. ◉ ~사람 a Chilean; a Chilian. ~초석 〖광물〗 Chile saltpeter; sodium nitrate; cubic niter.

**칠령팔락**(七零八落) irregularity; unsortedness; unevenness; 《at》 sixes and sevens; scattered confusion. ~하다 (be) irregular; uneven; unsorted; [서술적] be in scattered confusion; be at sixes and sevens; be all messed up. ¶ 책이 ~으로 쌓여 있다 Books are piled up helter-skelter.

**칠면조**(七面鳥) ① 〖조류〗 a turkey. ¶ 수 ~ a male turkey; a turkey cock 《영》; a gobbler 《미》/ 암~ a turkey hen / ~가 울다 a turkey gobbles / 추수감사절에는 ~ 고기를 먹는다 On Thanksgiving Day we have turkey. ② 《사람》 a temperamental 〔capricious, unpredictable〕 person.

**칠목기**(漆木器) 《미》 wooden lacquerware.

**칠변형**(七邊形) 〖수학〗 a heptagon; a ｢septangle.

**칠보**(七寶) 〖불교〗 the Seven Treasures (*i.e.* gold, silver, lapis, crystal, coral, agate, and pearls). ◉ ~자기(瓷器) (F.) *cloisonné* (ware).

**칠보재**(七步才) 《문재(文才)》 outstanding literary talent; 《시재(詩才)》 eminent poetic genius 〔gift〕.

**칠분도미**(七分搗米) rice polished to a seven-percent loss (in grain weight).

**칠붓**(漆一) a lacquering brush.

**칠삭둥이**(七朔一) ① 《조산아》 a person born prematurely at the 7th month of pregnancy. ② 《바보》 a half-wit.

**칠색**(七色) seven colors; the primary 〔prismatic〕 colors. ¶ 무지개의 ~ the seven colors of the rainbow.

**칠서**(七書) 《사서삼경》 the Seven Books (of Ancient China).

**칠석**(七夕) the seventh evening of the seventh month of the lunar calendar; the Vega festival. ◉ ~물 the rainfall on the seventh day of the seventh lunar month: ~물 지다 have a rain on (lunar) 7 July. ~제 the Festival of the Vega 〔Weaver〕.

**칠성**(七星) the seven stars of the Great Bear 〔Ursa Major〕; the Big Dipper; the Plow 〔Plough 《영》〕. ◉ ~각〔당〕 〖불교〗 a Taoist shrine consecrated to the Big Dipper. ~판 the bottom lining board of a coffin: ~판을 지다 《죽다》 die; 《사지에 들다》 risk death; enter the jaws of death.

**칠성장어**(七星長魚) 〖어류〗 a lamprey; a rock sucker.

**칠소반**(漆小盤) a small lacquer(ed) ｢(dining) table.

**칠순**(七旬) ① 《날》 seventy days. ② 《나이》 seventy years (of age). ¶ ~ 노인 a septuagenarian / 나이 ~이 넘다 be over seventy years old.

**칠십**(七十) seventy; three score and ten. ¶ 제 ~(의) the seventieth / ~대의 노인 a septuagenarian.

**칠야**(漆夜) a pitch-dark〔-black〕 night.

**칠언**(七言) 〖문학〗 a composition in classical Chinese verse which has seven characters 〔syllables〕 in a line. ◉ ~절구(絕句) a quatrain with seven Chinese characters in each line 〔with seven-word lines〕.

**칠오조**(七五調) 〖문학〗 a verse of alternating seven-and-five-syllable meter.

**칠요**(七曜) "the Seven Luminaries"; the seven days of the week.

**칠월**(七月) July (생략 Jul.).

**칠일**(漆一) lacquering; lacquer work; painting (페인트칠).

**칠일장**(七日葬) a funeral held seven days after the death. ¶ ~을 지내다 hold a funeral seven days after the death.

**칠장이**(漆匠一) a lacquerer; a painter.

**칠전팔기**(七顚八起) indomitableness; inflexibility. ～하다 never give in to adversity; stand firm in difficult matters; "never-say-die"; being undaunted. ¶ ～의 정신 an indomitable spirit; fortitude of mind.

**칠전팔도**(七顚八倒) ～하다 writhe in agony; toss about in excruciating pain; go through 〔suffer〕 many hardships.

**칠정**(七情) the Seven Passions (*i.e.* joy, anger, sorrow, fear, love, hate, and lust).

**칠창**(漆瘡) inflammation 〔boils〕 of skin caused by lacquer poison.

**칠칠찮다** (be) slovenly; untidy; dowdy; sloppy; slipshod; messy; draggletailed; loose. ¶ 칠칠찮은 사내 a slouch.

**칠칠하다** ① 《길차다》 (be) exuberant; luxuriant; fresh and crisp. ¶ 배추가 ～ cabbages are fresh and crisp. ② 《행동이》 (be) decent; decorous; proper though young; be a little gentleman 〔lady〕. ¶ 칠칠치 못한 계집 a sluttish 〔slatternly, blowsy〕 woman; a draggletailed woman; a draggletail; a slut; a dowdy. ③ 《민첩하다》 (be) skillful; deft; dexterous; spry. ¶ 솜씨가 ～ have nimble hands / 그렇게 칠칠치 못한 사람은 아무 일에도 성공 못 한다 Such sluggard will not succeed in anything.

**칠판**(漆板) a blackboard; 《미》 a chalkboard. ¶ 분필로 ～에 쓰다 put down 《words》 on the board with chalk; chalk down 《words》〔chalk up 《a score》〕 on the blackboard / ～을 닦다 clean 〔erase 《미》〕 the blackboard. ◉ ～지우개 《미》 an (a blackboard) eraser; 《영》 a (black) board rubber.

**칠팔월**(七八月) July and 〔or〕 August. ¶ ～ 수숫잎 a person who is weak-minded and changes his mind often / ～ 은어 곯듯 한다 One has a hard time to make a living because of a sudden decrease of income.

**칠포**(漆布) 《칠을 한》 lacquered hemp cloth; 《관에 씌는》 a piece of cloth placed over a coffin.

**칠하다**(漆—) paint (그림물감·페인트를); varnish (니스를); lacquer (옻칠을); coat (그림물감·옻칠을); apply (페인트 따위를); enamel (에나멜을); plaster (회반죽을). ¶ 갓 칠한 freshly-painted / 다시 ～ repaint; recoat; paint afresh; give a new coat 《of paint》 to 《the door》 / 벽에 페인트를 ～ paint a wall; cover a wall with paint / 페인트를 고르게 ～ spread the paint evenly / 지도에 색을 ～ color a map / 새까맣게〔회색으로〕 ～ paint 《*a thing*》 jet-black 〔gray〕 / 처덕처덕 ～ daub 《a wall》 with 《mud》; bedaub / 가볍게 눌러 ～ dab 《paint on a canvass》 / 칠해서 지워버리다 paint out 《a signboard》; smear away / 색이 짙게 칠해져 있다 The color is thickly laid on. / 문에는 새로 니스가 칠해져 있었다 There was a fresh coat of varnish on the door.

**칠함**(漆函) a lacquered box 〔chest〕.

**칠현**(七賢) the Seven Sages (of Ancient China).

**칠현금**(七絃琴) 〚악기〛 a seven-stringed harp; a heptachord.

**칠화**(漆畫) a lacquer painting.

**칠흑**(漆黑) 《빛깔이》 jet-〔coal-〕black; 《어둠이》 pitch 〔dead〕 darkness. ¶ ～ 같은 《빛깔이》 《as》 black as ink 〔coal, eboy〕; jet-〔coal-〕black 《hair》; 《어둠 따위가》 pitch-dark; 《as》 dark as pitch / ～ 같은 밤 a jet-black 〔pitch-dark〕 night / ～ 같은 어둠 dead 〔total〕 darkness.

**칡** 〚식물〛 an arrowroot. ¶ 칡 가루 arrowroot starch / 칡덩굴 arrowroot vines 〔runners〕 / 칡덩굴에 엉키다 get entangled in arrowroot vines.

**칡범** a striped tiger; a real tiger (in contrast with a leopard).

**칡소** a striped ox 〔cow〕.

**침** saliva; spittle; spit. ¶ 침을 뱉다 salivate; spit 《at》 / 침을 삼키다 swallow *one's* saliva; 《조마조마해서》 catch 〔hold〕 *one's* breath; strain *one's* attention; 《욕심이 나서》 lust 《for》; gloat 《on, over》; be envious 《of》 / 침을 바르다 apply saliva to; moisten 《*a thing*》 with *one's* saliva; lubricate 《*a thing*》 with spittle / 입의 침이 마르다 *one's* mouth gets dry / (입의) 침이 마르도록 칭찬하다 be very loud in another's praises; speak in the highest terms 《of》 / 침이 튀다 sputter; splutter / 침을 튀기며 이야기하다 splutter 〔sputter〕 《the words》 out / 남의 얼굴에 침을 튀기다 spit 〔sputter〕 in 《*a person's*》 face 〔teeth〕 / 아무에게 침을 뱉다 spit at *a person;* spit in *a person's* 《face》 / 손가락에 침을 묻혀 책장을 넘기다 turn leaves with wet fingers 〔with fingers moistened〕 / 바닥에 침 뱉지 마시오 《게시》 No spitting on the floor.

**침**(針) ① 《가시》 a thorn; 《벌 등의》 a

sting(er); 《계기의》 pointer. ¶ 침으로 쏘다 sting. ② 《바늘》 a needle; 《시계의》 a hand 《on the clock》. ¶ 주사침 an injection syringe; a (hypodermic) needle. ¶ (주사)침을 찌르다 stick a needle 《in *a person's* arm》.

**침**(鍼) 《도구》 a needle (for acupuncture); 《침술》 acupuncture; acupuncturation. ⇨ 침술사. ¶ 침을 놓다 acupuncture; apply acupuncture 《on》; treat 《*a person*》 with acupuncture / 침을 맞다 get acupunctured; be treated with acupuncture / 삔 발에 침을 놓다 acupuncture a sprained ankle.

**침감**(沈—) a persimmon sweetened in salt water.

**침강**(沈降) sedimentation; precipitation. ~하다 precipitate; subside; settle (down). ◉ ~소(素) 《혈액중의》 precipitin. ~속도 〖의학〗 《혈액의》 a (blood) sedimentation rate. ~수갱(竪坑) a dropshaft. ~시험 《적혈구의》 a (blood) sedimentation test. ~장치 a sinking set.

**침골**(枕骨) 〖해부〗 the suboccipital bone.

**침공**(侵攻) (an) invasion; a raid; an inroad. ~하다 invade; make an invasion 《upon》; raid 《into》; make an inroad 《into, upon》. ¶ 그 해 북한군은 대거 남한 ~을 개시했다 In that year the North Korean armies began to invade the South Korea in full force.

**침구**(侵寇) (an) invasion. ~하다 invade.

**침구**(寢具) bedding; bedclothes. ¶ ~를 개다〔펴다〕 fold up 〔make〕 bedclothes 〔bedding〕 / ~를 치우다 put away bedclothes.

**침구**(鍼灸) acupuncture and moxibustion. ◉ ~술(術) (the art of) acupuncture and moxibustion. ~의(醫) an acupuncturist and moxa-cauterizer; a practitioner in acupuncture and moxibustion.

**침낭**(寢囊) a sleeping bag.

**침노하다**(侵擄—) invade; make an inroad upon 《a country》; come down upon 《a coast》; encroach 〔entrench〕 upon 《the territory of》. ¶ 변경을 ~ invade the frontier districts / 남의 권리를 ~ encroach upon another's rights / 이웃 나라를 ~ invade a neighboring country.

**침닉**(沈溺) 《주색·잡기에》 indulgence; addiction; infatuation. ~하다 indulge 《in gambling》; be addicted 〔given〕 《to》; give *oneself* up 《to liquor》; be infatuated with 《a woman》.

**침담그다**(沈—) cure 《a persimmon》 in salt water; remove the astringency 《of》.

**침대**(寢臺) a bed; a bedstead; a (sleeping) berth (열차·배의); a bunk (배의); a couch (휴식용); a cot (간이 침대). ¶ 접이식 ~ a folding(-type) bed; a rollaway bed / (침대차의) 상단〔하단〕의 ~ an upper 〔a lower〕 berth / ~겸용 소파 a sofa bed / ~를 예약하다 book a sleeping berth; reserve a berth 《for *one*》. ◉ ~권 a berth ticket; a pullman ticket. ~요금 a berth charge. ~차 a sleeping car 〔carriage〕; a sleeper 《구어》. ~커버 a bedcover; a bedspread.

**침독**(鍼毒) poison from acupuncture; poisoning caused by improper practice of acupuncture.

**침략**(侵掠) plunder; despoilment; pillage. ~하다 plunder; pillage; despoil.

**침략**(侵略) (an) aggression; (an) invasion; a raid; an incursion. ~하다 invade; aggress 《against》; raid; make a raid 《on》. ¶ ~적 aggressive / 영토~ territorial encroachment / 경제 ~ an economic invasion / 바다로부터의 ~ a seaborne invasion / 외부의 ~ external aggression / 이웃 나라를 ~하다 invade a neighboring country / 전체주의의 ~을 저지하다 halt totalitarian aggression / 무력에 의한 외국의 ~을 피하기는 매우 어려웠다 It was very difficult to keep away from other countries' armed aggression.
◉ ~국(國) an aggressor (nation). ~군 an invading army. ~자(者) an aggressor; an invader. ~전쟁 a war of aggression; an aggressive war. ~주의 a policy of aggression; an aggressive policy: ~주의자 a systematic aggressor; an advocate of aggressive policies. ~행위 an act of aggression; an aggressive act. 무력~ an armed aggression. 직접〔간접〕~ a direct 〔an indirect〕 aggression 〔invasion〕.

**침례**(浸禮) 〖기독교〗 baptism by immersion; immersion. ¶ ~를 베풀다 immerse; baptize immersion. ◉ ~교도 a Baptist. ~교회 the Baptist Church.

**침로**(針路) 《나침반의》 a course; 《항공기의》 a flight path. ¶ ~를 바꾸다〔돌리다〕 change 〔turn, shift, alter〕 *one's* course 《toward》 / ~를 잡다 direct 〔set〕 *one's* course 《toward, for》; 《배

가》 sail 〔head, make〕《for》/ ～를 북(北)으로 잡다 steer *one's* course northward; take 〔beat〕 a northerly course / ～를 잃다 lose *one's* course / ～를 정하다 fix *one's* course / ～에서 벗어나다 deviate 〔swerve〕 from *one's* course; go 〔stray〕 off (*one's*) course; be driven out of *one's* course《by a storm》/ ～에서 벗어나지 않고 있다 keep 〔stay, stand〕 on *one's* course / 우리는 섬 쪽으로 ～를 돌렸다 We directed our course towards the island. ◉ ～수정 course correction 〔adjustment〕.

**침마취**(鍼痲醉) anesthesia by acupuncture. ¶ ～를 시키다 anesthetize by acupuncture.

**침모**(針母) a seamstress; a needlewoman. ¶ 난～ a day 〔live-out〕 seamstress; a part-time seamstress / 든～ a resident 〔live-in〕 seamstress.

**침목**(枕木) a (railroad) tie《미》; a crosstie《미》; a (railway) sleeper《영》. ¶ ～을 갈다 renew the ties / ～을 괴다 support with a block.

**침몰**(沈沒) sinking; submersion; foundering (침수에 의한). ～하다 sink; go down; go 〔be sent〕 to the bottom; be submerged; founder (침수로). ¶ (사람이) 배와 함께 ～하다 go down with the ship / (배가) 승객 2백 명을 태운 채 ～하다 sink with two hundred passengers on board / ～시키다 sink《a ship》; send《a ship》to the bottom; submerge; put under water / (배에) 구멍을 뚫어 ～시키다 scuttle《a ship》. ◉ ～선 a sunken ship; a submerged vessel: ～선을 인양하다 salve 〔refloat〕 a sunken vessel / ～선 구조〔인양〕 작업 salvage.

**침묵**(沈默) silence; 《무언》 reticence; taciturnity. ～하다 hold *one's* tongue; be 〔keep〕 silent; become 〔go〕 silent; say nothing. ¶ 무거운 ～ an oppressive 〔a heavy〕 silence / ～을 지키다 keep silent; observe 〔keep, maintain, preserve〕 silence; remain silent 〔mute〕; keep *one's* tongue quiet; keep *one's* mouth shut; hold *one's* tongue / ～을 깨(뜨리)다 break *one's* 〔the〕 silence / 어색한 ～이 한동안 계속되다 an awkward silence hang《between them》for several minutes / ～시키다 silence; put 〔reduce〕《*a person*》to silence; talk《*a person*》down / 적의 포화를 ～시키다 silence the enemy's fire 〔guns〕/ 모두들 ～했다 Silence fell on the party. / ～은 승낙을 뜻할 때가 있다 Silence sometimes implies consent. / 그는 끝까지 ～을 지켰다 He held 〔preserved, kept〕 his silence to the last. / 나는 그의 ～을 무언의 승낙이라고 생각했다 I took his silence to be a tacit consent. / ～은 금이다 Silence is gold(en).

**침방**(寢房) a bedroom.

**침뱉다** salivate; spit; expectorate. ¶ 아무의 얼굴에 ～ spit in *a person's* face; spit at *a person;* [비유적] insult *a person* / 제 얼굴에 ～ disgrace *oneself* / 웃는 낯에 침 뱉으랴 《속담》 One can't behave rudely to a flattering person.

**침범**(侵犯) ① 《영토의》 (an) invasion; encroachment; intrusion; 《권리의》 violation; infringement. ～하다 invade; raid; make a raid upon; 《권리 등을》 violate; infringe on; (en)trench on; trespass on; encroach 〔intrude〕 on. ¶ 권한을 ～하다 infringe upon《*a person's*》authority / 사생활을 ～하다 violate 〔infringe upon〕《*a person's*》privacy / 인권을 ～하다 violate personal rights / 국적 불명의 항공기가 우리 영공을 ～했다 An unidentified aircraft violated our territorial airspace. ② 《병의》 an affection; an attack. ～하다 visit; affect; attack. ¶ 병이 ～하다 be attacked 〔stricken, seized, affected〕 with a disease; have an attack of illness. ◉ 국경～ a border 〔frontier〕 violation.

**침봉**(針峰) 《꽃꽂이의》 a frog.

**침불안석**(寢不安席) ～하다 cannot sleep well 〔at ease〕 because of anxieties.

**침사**(沈思) meditation; deep thought. ⇨심사숙고(深思熟考).

**침삼키다** swallow saliva; 《탐이 나서》 *one's* mouth waters《at》. ⇨침.

**침상**(針狀) ¶ ～의 needle-shaped; pointed; 〖식물〗 acerose. ◉ ～엽(葉) a needle (leaf). ～체 a spicule; 〖동물〗 a spiculum (*pl.* -la).

**침상**(寢牀) a couch; a bedstead; a bed.

**침소**(寢所) a sleeping place; a bedchamber; a bedroom.

**침소봉대**(針小棒大) (an) exaggeration. ～하다 exaggerate; overstate; color (too) highly; make a mountain (out) of a molehill. ¶ ～하여 with exaggeration; exaggeratedly / 위험을 ～하다 exaggerate 〔magnify〕 the peril / 그는 ～하여 말한다 He makes a mountain out of a molehill.

**침수**(浸水) inundation; flood; submersion (under water). ～하다 be flooded [inundated]; be submerged; be under water; 《배가》 (spring a) leak; make [take in] water. ¶ ～된 화물 wet [sea-damaged] goods / 배가 ～되어 침몰했다 The boat leaked [filled] and sank. / 500호 이상의 집이 마루까지 ～되었다 Over five hundred houses were flooded up to the floors. ◉ ～가옥 submerged [flooded] houses; houses under water. ～지역 the flooded [inundated] area; the area under water.

**침술**(鍼術) 『한의』 (the art of) acupuncture. ◉ ～사 an acupuncturist.

**침식**(浸蝕) 『지질』 erosion; corrosion. ～하다 erode 《the cliff》; corrode; wear [eat] away 《at the bank》; eat *its* way 《through solid rock》; 《물이》 wash out; 《바다가 육지를》 gain [encroach] on 《the land》. ¶ 토양 ～ soil erosion / 빙하의 ～ glacial erosion / 비[바람, 물]에 의한 ～ rain [wind, water] erosion / 바닷물이 육지를 ～하고 있다 The sea is eroding the land. / 비바람에 ～되어 그곳은 급사면이 되었다 Eroded by wind and rain, it formed a steep slope.
◉ ～대지(臺地)[분지] an eroded plateau [basin]. ～작용 erosion; erosive action: ～작용으로 by erosion; by the corrosive action 《of an acid》.

**침식**(寢食) sleep and food. ¶ ～을 같이하다 share board and room 《with》; live under the same roof 《for many years》 / ～을 잊고 간호하다 nurse 《a sick person》 devotedly / ～을 잊고 공부하다 be absorbed [buried] in *one's* study; devote *oneself* entirely to *one's* work / 급료는 ～ 제공에 월 80만 원이다 The pay is 800,000 won a month (and) all found. / 그녀는 ～을 잊고 빈민 구제에 진력했다 She denied herself all the comforts of life and worked for the relief of the poor and needy.
◉ ～불안 no comfort either in sleeping or in eating; constant anxiety: ～불안하다 be unable to eat and sleep comfortably; be under constant anxiety.

**침실**(寢室) a bedroom; a bedchamber; a sleeping room. ¶ ～겸 거실 《미》 a studio apartment; 《영》 a bed-sitting room.

**침염**(浸染) ① 《염색의》 dip-dyeing. ～하다 dip-dye 《cloth》; dye 《furs》 by completely immersing in the dye bath. ② 《감화·영향》 influence; a gradual addiction 《to》. ～하다 be influenced [inspired] with [by]; gradually become addicted [infected].

**침엽**(針葉) 『식물』 a needleshaped leaf; a needle (leaf). ◉ ～수 a conifer; a needle-leaf tree; a coniferous tree: ～수림 a coniferous forest.

**침울**(沈鬱) melancholy; depression; gloom. ～하다 (be) melancholy; dismal; gloomy; depressed. ¶ ～한 얼굴 a dismal look; a gloomy face / ～한 날씨 gloomy [depressing] weather / ～한 심정 a gloomy mind / ～한 얼굴을 하다 look blue [depressed]; wear a gloomy face.

**침윤**(浸潤) permeation; infiltration; saturation; seepage. ～하다 permeate 《through, in》; infiltrate [soak] 《into》; pervade; be soaked; be saturated.

**침입**(侵入) 《타국에의》 (an) invasion; a raid; inroads; (an) intrusion; 《남의 집에의》 (a) trespass. ～하다 enter forcibly 《into》; invade; make an invasion [a raid] 《on, into》; make inroads 《into enemy country》; 《남의 집 등에》 trespass 《on》; break [intrude] 《into》; force *one's* entry [way] 《into》; make a forcible entry 《into》. ¶ 가택 ～죄 unlawful entry / 남의 땅에 ～하다 trespass on *a person's* land / 적의 전차 부대가 동부 지방으로 ～했다 Enemy tank corps has invaded the eastern provinces. / 어젯밤 그녀의 집에 도둑이 ～했다 A burglar broke into her house last night.
◉ ～군 an invasion force. ～로 an invasion route. ～자 an invader; an intruder; a trespasser.

**침적**(沈積) deposition; sedimentation. ～하다 deposit; be deposited; settle. ◉ ～물 deposits; sludge.

**침전**(沈澱) precipitation; deposition; sedimentation. ～하다 settle (out); be precipitated; be deposited. ¶ 불순물을 ～시켜서 제거하다 precipitate [settle] impurities out of 《the water》 / 바닥에 찌끼가 ～됐다 Dregs are deposited at the bottom. ◉ ～기(器) 『물리·화학』 a precipitator. ～농도 precipitation density. ～물 a deposit; a sediment; a precipitate; dregs (술 따위의); lees (포도주의). ～반응 precipitation reaction. ～분석 precipitation analysis. ～제(劑) a precipitator; a precipitant. ～조(槽) a settling [precipitation] tank. ～지(池) a settling basin [pond].

～지시약 a precipitation indicator.

**침전**(寢殿) ① 《정자각》 a T-shaped building in front of a tomb. ② 《임금의》 the king's bedroom.

**침점**(侵占) encroaching; (invading and) occupying. ～하다 encroach on 《territory》; (invade and) occupy.

**침주다**(鍼—) acupuncture; apply 〔treat *a person* with〕 acupuncture.

**침중**(沈重) gravity; seriousness. ～하다 《사람됨이》 (be) grave; imposing; dignified; 《병세가》 (be) serious; critical; bad; [서술적] be in a critical condition.

**침지**(浸漬·沈漬) a soak; soakage. ～하다 soak; give a soak; immerse 〔steep〕 《in》; dip (잠깐).

**침질**(鍼—) 『한의』 acupuncturing. ～하다 (perform) acupuncture.

**침착**(沈着) composure; self-possession; presence of mind; calmness; coolness; staidness. ～하다 (be) composed; self-possessed; staid; calm; cool; 《구어》 unflappable; have presence of mind. ¶ ～하게〔히〕 calmly; coolly; composedly; 《act》 with composure 〔presence of mind〕 / ～한 사람 a calm person; a person with composure / ～한 성격 a staid character / ～한 태도 a calm attitude / ～한 태도를 보이다 bear *oneself* with coolness; show presence of mind / 몹시 ～하다 be (as) cool as cucumber / ～을 되찾다 recover *one's* composure; re-collect *oneself;* regain *one's* presence of mind / ～을 잃다 lose *one's* head 〔presence of mind, self-possession〕; become restless / 그들은 그녀의 ～함에 탄복했다 They were struck with admiration at her self-possession.

**침착성**(沈着性) composure. ⇨침착. ¶ ～을 잃다 lose *one's* head; become restless / ～을 잃지 않다 remain composed; be 〔remain〕 absolutely calm and self-possessed / ～을 되찾다 regain 〔recover〕 *one's* presence of mind; recover *one's* composure 〔self-possession〕.

**침체**(沈滯) stagnation; dullness; slackness; inactivity. ～하다 stagnate; get 〔become〕 stagnant 〔dull, slack, inactive〕. ¶ ～된 시장 a dull 〔slack〕 market / ～된 분위기 a dull 〔stagnant, depressed〕 atmosphere / ～되어 있다 be stagnant; be dull 〔inactive, depressed, slack〕 / (경기 등이) 아직도 ～의 늪에서 헤어나지 못하고 있다 be not yet out of a swamp of stagnation / 경기가 ～되어 있다 Business is stagnant 〔dull〕. *or* The market is depressed.

**침침하다**(沈沈—) ① 《어둡다》 (be) gloomy; dim; dimly-lit; 《날씨 등이》 (be) cloudy; dull. ¶ 침침한 방 a dimly-lit 〔an ill-lit〕 room / 침침한 곳에서 in the semidarkness 〔half dark〕; 《등불이》 in the poor 〔dim〕 light / 침침한 등불 밑에서 독서하다 read in the dim light of a lamp / 전등이 ～ The electric light is dim. *or* 《전압이 낮아져서》 The electric light is browned out. ② 《눈이》 (be) dim; obscure; misty; bleared. ¶ 눈이 ～ *one's* eyes glaze over 〔are dim〕; have dim eyes / 나이를 먹으면 눈이 침침해진다 Our sight grows dim with age.

**침탈**(侵奪) pillage; plunder; despoliation; spoliation; 『법』 disseisin; disseizin. ～하다 pillage; plunder; disseize. ◉ ～자 a disseisor; a disseizor: 피～자 a disseizee; a disseisee.

**침통**(鍼筒) a case 〔box〕 for acupuncture needles.

**침통하다**(沈痛—) (be) grave; pathetic; sad; mournful. ¶ 침통한 어조로 in a grave 〔sad, dismal, pathetic〕 tone / 침통한 얼굴로 with a sad look / 침통한 얼굴을 하다 look grave 〔sorrowful〕 / 왜 그리 침통한 얼굴을 하고 있는가 Why do you look so grave 〔sorrowful〕?

**침투**(浸透) permeation; infiltration; saturation; penetration; 『화학·생리』 osmosis. ～하다 permeate 《into》; infiltrate 〔penetrate〕 《into》; saturate; filter 《into》; percolate 《through》. ¶ 공산주의〔무장 간첩〕의 ～ the infiltration of communism 〔armed agents〕 《into a country》 / 정계에 ～하다 infiltrate into political circles / 고무에는 액체가 ～하지 못한다 Rubber is impervious to liquid. / 물은 모래에 ～한다 Water percolates through sand. / 그 새로운 사상이 사람들 마음에 ～했다 The new ideas filtered into the people's mind. ◉ ～계수 an osmotic coefficient. ～공작 infiltration conspiracy. ～분석 osmotic analysis; dialysis. ～성 permeability; osmosis. ～요법 osmotic treatment. ～작용 (an) osmotic action. ～작전 an infiltration operation.

**침투압**(浸透壓) osmotic pressure. ¶ ～을 측정하다 measure the osmotic pressure 《of》. ◉ ～측정 osmometry: ～측정으로 단백질의 분자량을 결정하다

determine the molecular weight of proteins by osmometry.

**침팬지** 〖동물〗 a chimpanzee.

**침하**(沈下) sinking; subsidence; settlement. ~하다 sink; subside; settle; submerge (수중으로). ¶ 지반이 ~하다 the ground sinks [subsides] / 이 지역의 지반은 작년 이래 약 3 센티미터 ~했다 The ground of this area has sunk about three centimeters since last year.

**침해**(侵害) infringement; encroachment; trespass; violation. ~하다 infringe (on); violate 《*a person's* right》; trespass [encroach] 《on *a person's* right》; intrude 《on, upon》.

> 용법 **infringe** 법·협정을 어기거나 남의 권리나 자유를 침해하다. **violate** 마땅히 지켜야 할 법이나 남의 자유 등을 침범하다. **trespass** 불법으로 남의 재산이나 권리를 침해하다. **encroach** 야금야금 파먹어 들어가듯이 남의 권리를 침해하다. **intrude** 요청이나 허락이 없음에도 불구하고 침입하듯이 남의 권리를 침해하다.

¶ 특허권~ an infringement of the patent / ~할 수 없는 inviolable / 프라이버시를 ~하다 violate 《*a person's*》 privacy / 그의 행위는 인권을 ~하는 것이다 His act violates human rights. / 나는 기득권을 ~당하고 싶지 않다 I don't want my vested interests to be trespassed upon. / 그것은 저작권 ~다 It is [constitutes] an infringement of copyright. ◉ ~자 an invader; a trespasser.

**침향**(沈香) 〖식물〗 an agalloch; aloes wood; agilawood.

**침흘리개** a slobberer; a slaverer; driveler; a drooler.

**침흘리다** salivate; drool; drivel; 《군침을》 *one's* mouth waters 《with desire》.

**칩** a chip. ◉ 감자칩 a potato chip. 컴퓨터칩 a computer chip.

**칩거**(蟄居) keeping indoors; staying in the house. ~하다 keep [stay] indoors; stay in [do not leave] the house; shut *oneself* up 《in a room》. ¶ 집 안에 ~하다 shut *oneself* up in *one's* house; remain indoors.
◉ ~생활 living in seclusion.

**칩룡**(蟄龍) 《숨은 용》 a hidden dragon; a dragon in concealment; 《숨은 영웅》 a hidden hero [talented man]; a giant in disguise.

**칩복**(蟄伏) 《동면》 hibernation. ~하다 hibernate.

**칩수**(蟄獸) hibernating animals; hibernants.

**칩충**(蟄蟲) hibernating [hibernant] insects.

**칫솔**(齒—) a toothbrush. ¶ 매식후마다 ~질 하시오 Brush your teeth after each meal.

**칭**(稱) ① 《명칭》 a name; a title; a designation; an appellation. ⇨ 칭하다. ② 《문법의》 person. ¶ 3인칭 단수 the third person singular (number).

**칭기즈칸** 《몽고 제국의 태조》 Genghis [Jinghis] Khan (1162-1227). ◉ ~요리 (a) Mongolian mutton barbecue.

**칭동**(秤動) 〖천문〗 libration.

**칭병**(稱病) 《행위》 malingering; 《꾀병》 (a) pretended [feigned, faked] illness. ~하다 pretend to be ill; feign illness; malinger. ¶ 그는 ~하여 회의에 참석하지 않았다 He did not attend the meeting, pretending that he was sick [ill].

**칭사**(稱辭) praise; a eulogy. ⇨ 찬사(讚辭).

**칭송**(稱頌) praise; eulogy; applause; admiration. ~하다 praise; laud; applaud; extol; admire; eulogize. ¶ 덕을 ~하다 extol 《*a person's*》 virtue / 그 고귀한 행동은 사람들로부터 ~을 받았다 The noble deed won him the admiration of the people.

**칭얼거리다** 《a baby》 fret; be peevish [fretful]; whine; whimper; cry peevishly. ¶ 아기는 잠이 오거나 배가 고프면 칭얼거린다 A baby gets fretful when he is sleepy or hungry.

**칭얼칭얼** peevishly; fretfully; whining; whimpering; fussing. ¶ 어린애가 ~울다 a baby cries peevishly.

**칭원**(稱寃) ~하다 say spiteful things 《of *a person*》; complain; blame. ¶ 계획이 잘못된 것을 ~하다 complain against 《*a person*》 for the falling through of a plan / 나를 ~하지 말라, 나는 잘못한 것 없다 Don't blame me; I have done nothing wrong to you.

**칭찬**(稱讚) praise; applause; extolment; admiration; commendation; laudation. ~하다 praise; applaud; admire; speak well [favorably, highly] of 《*a person*》; compliment; extol; eulogize; express praise of; bestow [shower] praise on.
¶ ~의 말 words of praise; a compliment; a praise; a eulogy / ~을 받다 get praised [applauded, extolled] 《by》; receive [win, enjoy] the admiration 《of》; draw praise 《from》; be well spoken of (★ speak well of의 수동

태는 be well spoken of 또는 be spoken well of의 두 가지를 쓸 수 있음) / 극구 ~하다 extol 〔laud〕 《*a person*》 sky-high 〔to the skies〕; bestow unstinted praise 《on》; be loud in 《*a person's*》 praises / ~할 만하다 merit 〔be worthy of 〕 praise; deserve admiration; be praiseworthy 〔laudable, admirable, commendable〕 / 그는 나를 매우 ~했다 He paid me a high compliment. / 그의 행위는 이루 다 ~할 수 없을 정도다 His deed is beyond all praise. / 우리는 그의 용기를 ~했다 We praised his courage. *or* We admired him for his courage.

> (용법) **praise** 사람·일에 대해서 진심으로 「칭찬하다」란 뜻의 가장 일반적인 말. **applaud** 박수 갈채하듯이 「칭찬하다」. **admire** 「탄복하다」「칭찬하다」의 뜻. 때로는 빈정대는 뜻으로 쓰이기도 함. **speak well of** 「칭찬하다」의 구어. speak ill of의 반대어. **compliment** praise나 admire와 같은 뜻의 일상어. 사교적인 경우에 흔히 쓰며, 사람을 목적어로 함. **extol** speak highly of (크게 칭찬하다)의 뜻으로 좀 딱딱한 말. **eulogize** 격식차린 말로 연설이나 글로 「칭송하다」의 뜻.

**칭탁**(稱託) an excuse; a pretext; a pretense 〔pretence 《영》〕; a plea; a feint; a make-believe. ~하다 make a pretense 〔pretext〕 of; make an excuse of; pretend 《to be ill》. ¶ …을 ~하여 under 〔on〕 the pretext 〔plea〕 of 《ill health》; under cover of; under the cloak 〔mask〕 of 《charity》 / 그는 병을 ~하여 일을 쉬고 싶어한다 He wants to be excused from his work under the pretext of ill health.

**칭탄**(稱歎) praise; admiration. ⇨ 찬탄.

**칭탈**(稱頉) an excuse; a pretext; a pretense 〔pretence 《영》〕; a plea. ~하다 find 〔give〕 a pretext; make 〔offer〕 an excuse; excuse *oneself;* make a plea 《of 》; make a pretense 《of 》. ¶ 쩍하면 ~하다 offer excuses at the drop of a hat.

**칭하다**(稱一) ① 《부르다》 call; name; style; designate; denominate; (en)title. ¶ 장비라 칭하는 사람 a man named 〔called〕 Changbi; a man by 〔giving〕 the name of Changbi / 소위 심리 소설이라 칭하는 것 what are called psychological novels / 동네 이름을 조양리라 ~ name the village 〔the village is called〕 Choyang-ni.
② 《일컫다》 say; claim; plead; 《사칭하다》 pretend; feign; 《주장하다》 claim. ¶ 병이라 ~ pretend to be ill; feign illness / 인구 백만이라 ~ the population is said to be one million; the population is given as a million / 친척이라 ~ claim to be a relative; introduce *oneself* as a relative / 스스로 대가(大家)라 ~ claim to be 〔represent *oneself* as〕 an authority.

**칭호**(稱號) a title; 《명칭》 a name; an appellation; a designation; 《학위》 a degree. ¶ 명예 교수의 ~ the title of professor emeritus / … ~를 주다 confer the title 〔degree〕 of… 《on *a person*》.

**카**[1] 《냄새·맛 등이 독할 때》 Phew (what a strong smell) !

**카**[2] a car. ◉ 카라디오 a car 〔an auto〕 radio. 카레이서 a (motor) racing driver. 카레이스 a motor race; motor racing. 카페리 a car 〔an automobile〕 ferry. 카포트 a carport. 카히터 a car heater. 오픈카 a car with the top lowered 〔folded back〕; a convertible.

**카나리아** 〖조류〗 a canary (bird). ¶ ～의 모이 canary seed.

**카나마이신** 〖약〗 kanamycine.

**카네기** 《미국의 강철왕》 Andrew Carnegie (1835-1919). ¶ ～홀 Carnegie Hall.

**카네이션** 〖식물〗 a carnation; a clove pink. ¶ 가슴에 다는 ～ 조화(造花) an artificial carnation corsage / 빨간 ～을 가슴에 달고 있다 wear a red carnation on *one's* breast.

**카누** a canoe. ¶ ～를 젓다 paddle a canoe / ～ 젓는 사람 a canoeist. ◉ ～ 경조(競漕) a canoe race; a canoeing event.

**카니발** a carnival.

**카덴차** 〖음악〗 *cadenza* (It.); cadence.

**카드** ① [일반적] a card; a slip (of paper) (종이 쪽지). ¶ 수강(受講) 등록 ～ a course registration card / 신청 ～ an application card / ～에 의한 분류 classification by cards / ～식으로 정리하다 arrange 《the data》 on a card system / ～를 철하다 file cards / ～에 적어 두다 note down 《*a matter*》 on a card. ② 《트럼프》 (playing) cards; a card game. ⇨ 카드놀이. ¶ ～ 한 벌 a pack 〔deck 《미》〕 of cards / ～를 도르다 deal the cards / ～를 섞어 치다〔떼다〕 shuffle 〔cut〕 the cards / ～로 재수를 점치다 tell *one's* fortune from cards / (점을 치기 위해) ～ 패를 늘어놓다 lay cards 《on the table》 / ～를 젖히다 turn over a card.
◉ ～검증기 〖컴퓨터〗 a card verifier. ～론 the loaning service provided by an ATM card; loan card service. ～목록 a card catalog 〔file〕. ～번호 a card number. ～색인 card-indexing (행위); a card index. ～서랍 a card tray 〔drawer〕; a catalog tray 〔drawer〕. ～식 the card system: ～식 목록 a card catalog / ～식 부기 bookkeeping on the card system / ～식 분류함 a sorting tray. ～판독기 〖컴퓨터〗 a card reader. ～편성 filing of cards. ～함 a card box 〔case〕; a card cabinet (서랍식의). 생일〔크리스마스〕～ a birthday 〔Christmas〕 card. 신용〔전화〕～ a credit 〔telephone〕 card. 출석～ an attendance slip.

**카드놀이** card playing; a game of cards; a card game. ¶ ～를 하다 play cards / ～ 하는 사람 a cardplayer / ～를 하고 있다 be at cards / ～에서 돈을 걸다 bet 〔gamble〕 at card; play cards for stakes / ～에서 속이다 cheat at cards / ～에 이기다〔지다〕 win 〔lose〕 at cards.

**카드뮴** 〖화학〗 cadmium (기호 Cd). ◉ ～옐로 cadmium yellow. ～오염 cadmium pollution. ～전지 a cadmium cell. ～중독 cadmium poisoning. 염화(塩化)～ cadmium chloride.

**카디건** 《스웨터》 a cardigan (jacket, sweater).

**카랑카랑하다** ① 《날씨가》 《the weather》 be clear and cold. ② 《음성이》 《a voice》 be clear and crisp 〔high-pitched〕.

**카레** curry; 《카레라이스》 curried pork 〔beef〕 stew with rice; curry and 〔with〕 rice. ¶ ～는 본래 인도 요리였으나 이제는 한국화되어 있다 Curry was originally an Indian dish, but it has been Koreanized. ◉ ～가루 curry powder. ～소스 curry sauce. ～요리 curried food; a curry.

**카로틴** 〖화학〗 carotin; carotene.

**카르** [<*Kar* (G.)] 〖지질〗 a cirque.

**카르노 사이클** 〖물리〗 Carnot cycle.

**카르바졸** 〖화학〗 carbazole.

**카르밤산**(一酸) 〖화학〗 carbamic acid.

**카르보닐** 〖화학〗 carbonyl.

**카르복시기**(一基) 〖화학〗 carboxyl group.

**카르스트** 〖지리〗 karst. ¶ ～ 지형의 karstic.

**카르타고** 《고대 도시 국가》 Carthage.

**카르테** [<*Karte* (G.)] 〖의학〗 a case history sheet; a (clinical) chart 《for a patient》; a patient's chart.

**카르텔** 〖경제〗 a cartel; a kartell; a trust. ¶ ~을 결성하다 cartelize; form a cartel / ~을 해체하다 decartelize; dissolve 〔break up〕 a cartel 《of steel companies》. ◉ ~협정 a cartel agreement: ~ 협정을 맺다 make 〔conclude〕 a cartel agreement. 불황(不況)~ a (business) recession cartel.

**카리브해**(一海) the Caribbean Sea.

**카리스마** 〖종교〗 (a) charisma (*pl.* -mata); (a) charism. ¶ ~적(인) charismatic / 그 정치가는 ~적인 데가 많다 The politician is very charismatic. *or* The politician possesses great charisma.

**카리에스** 〖의학〗 caries. ¶ ~에 걸린 아이 a carious child. ◉ 요추~ lumbar caries. 척추~ caries 〔tuberculous osteitis〕 of the vertebrae; spinal caries; Pott's disease.

**카메라** a camera. ¶ (…에) ~를 돌리다 〔들이대다〕 aim *one's* camera; level the camera 《at》 / ~를 찰깍 찍다 click a camera; snap a camera 《at》 / ~에 담다 photograph; take a photo 〔picture〕 of; film; 《속사》 take a snapshot of; snap 《*a person*》 / ~에 필름을 넣다 load a camera / ~ 플래시의 세례를 받다 be bathed in camera flashes / ~를 어깨에 메고 with a camera slung across *one's* shoulder / 그들은 손님들과 함께 ~ 앞에서 포즈를 취했다 They posed for the camera with their guests. ◉ ~맨 《영화·TV의》 a cameraman; 《사진사》 a photographer: 신문사의 ~맨 a press photographer. ~앵글 a camera angle. ~오퍼레이터 a camera operator. ~워크 a camera work. ~총 a camera gun. 필름 없는 디지털 ~ a "no film" digital camera.

**카메룬** 《나라 이름》 (the Republic of) Cameroon. ¶ ~의 Cameroonian. ◉ ~사람 a Cameroonian.

**카메오** 《가공 보석》 a cameo; 《영화 단역》 a cameo; a cameo role.

**카멜레온** 〖동물〗 a chameleon. ◉ ~자리 〖천문〗 the Chameleon. ~펀드 〖경제〗 a chameleon fund.

**카무플라주** a camouflage. ~하다 camouflage 《a war plant》; 《위장하다》 disguise 《*one's* real intention》; dissemble. ¶ 인간은 ~를 자연으로부터 배운다 Man borrowed the idea of camouflage from nature.

**카민** 〖화학〗 carmine; cochineal lake.

**카밀레** 〖식물〗 camomile.

**카바레** a cabaret. ¶ ~의 여급 a cabaret hostess.

**카바이드** 〖화학〗 (calcium) carbide.

**카보이** carboy; a wicker box or basket to keep large bottles in.

**카본** 〖화학〗 carbon. ◉ ~복사 a carbon copy. ~블랙 carbon black. ~인화법 carbon process. ~지 carbon paper; a carbon(한 장의). ~파이버 《탄소 섬유》 a carbon fiber.

**카뷰레터** 《자동차의》 a carburetor; a carbureter.

**카비네판**(一判) 〖사진〗 a cabinet size. ¶ ~ 사진 a cabinet (photograph).

**카빈총**(一銃) a carbine (rifle). ◉ 자동 ~ an automatic carbine.

**카세인** 〖화학〗 casein.

**카세트** a cassette. ¶ 나는 그 라디오 프로를 ~에 녹음했다 I taped 〔tape-recorded〕 the radio program on a cassette. ◉ ~녹음기 a cassette tape recorder. ~테이프 a cassette tape.

**카슈미르** 〖지리〗 Kashmir. ¶ ~(사람)의 Kashmirian 《children》. ◉ ~사람 a Kashmiri.

**카스텔라** a sponge cake. [< *pão de Castella* (Port.)]

**카스트** a caste. ⇨ 사성(四姓). ◉ ~제도 the caste system.

**카스피해**(一海) the Caspian Sea.

**카시오페이아자리** 〖천문〗 Cassiopeia.

**카약** a kayak.

**카오스** ① 《혼돈·혼란》 chaos. ② 〖그神〗 Chaos. ◉ ~이론 〖물리〗 a chaos theory.

**카우보이** a cowboy; 《미》 a wrangler; 《미구어》 a cowpuncher. ◉ ~영화 a cowboy picture; a western (film, movie); a horse opera.

**카운슬러** 《상담·조언자》 a counselor.

**카운슬링** 《상담·조언하는 일》 counseling.

**카운터** 《은행·상점 등의》 a (service) counter; a counting room; an account office; 《호텔의》 the office; the front desk; 《술집·다실 등의》 a bar. ¶ ~에 앉다 sit at the counter / 귀중품을 ~에 맡기다 check *one's* valuables at the front desk.

**카운터블로** 〖권투〗 a counterblow.

**카운트** a count; counting; the score. ~하다 count; take the count; keep score. ¶ ~ 아웃이 되다 be counted out / ~는 원 스리이다 The count is one-three. / 그는 ~ 8에서 일어섰다 《권투에서》 He got up at the count of eight. ◉ 풀~ a full count 《of three and two》 (★ 《미》에서는 three balls and two strikes라고 함).

**카운트다운** 《로켓 발사 등의》 a countdown. ～하다 count down. ¶ ～을 시작하다 begin the countdown.

**카이로** 《이집트의 수도》 Cairo. ◉ ～선언 the Cairo Declaration.

**카이스트** 《한국 과학 기술원》 KAIST. [<*K*orea *A*dvanced *I*nstitute of *S*cience and *T*echnology]

**카이저수염**(―鬚髯) a Kaiser 〔an upturned〕 mustache; a handlebar mustache.

**카자흐스탄** (the Republic of ) Kazakhstan. ¶ ～의 Kazakhstani. ◉ ～어 Kazakh.

**카지노** a casino.

**카카오** cacao. ◉ ～나무 a cacao tree. ～열매 cacao beans.

**카키** khaki (color). ¶ ～(색)의 khaki; olive-drab / ～복을 입고 in khaki (uniform).

**카타르** 〖의학〗 catarrh. ¶ ～성의 catarrhal 《pneumonia》. ◉ 비(鼻)～ nasal catarrh.

**카타르시스** 〖문학〗 catharsis (*pl.* -ses).

**카타스트로프** 《큰 재해》 a catastrophe.

**카타콤** 〖가톨릭〗 the Catacombs.

**카탈로그** a catalog(ue) 《of books》; a brochure (팜플릿식의). ¶ ～에 올리다 catalog(ue); place 〔put〕 《an item》 on 〔in〕 a catalog / 가격 표시 ～ a priced catalog / ～에 실려 있는 값 the list price / ～ 무료 증정 Catalog offered free.

**카턴** 《마분지》 carton; 《상자》 a carton 《of cigarettes》.

**카테고리** 〖철학〗 a category. ⇨ 범주. ¶ ～로 나누다 categorize 《as》; classify.

**카테터** [<*Katheter* (G.)] 〖의학〗 a catheter. ¶ ～를 넣다 insert 〔put〕 a catheter 《in》.

**카투사** KATUSA. [<*K*orean *A*ugmentation *T*roops to the *U*nited *S*tates *A*rmy] ¶ ～는 미군과 합동 근무를 한다 Katusas are on a joint duty with U.S. soldiers.

**카트리지** a cartridge. ¶ ～를 갈아 끼우다 put a new cartridge 《in》; replace the cartridge.

**카페** a café; a coffee shop; a coffeehouse; 《술집》 a bar; a cabaret; a saloon.

**카페인** 〖화학〗 caffein(e). ¶ ～을 함유하지 않은 noncaffein 《tea》; caffein-free 《coffee》 / ～을 제거하다 remove caffein from 《coffee》; decaffeinate / ～ 없는 것으로 주세요 《커피 따위를》 Make it decaf. ◉ ～제 a caffeine pill.

**카페테리아** a cafeteria; a self-service restaurant (셀프서비스의 간이 식당).

**카펫** 《양탄자》 a carpet; a rug (작은); [총칭] carpeting. ¶ ～을 깔다 spread 〔lay〕 a carpet; carpet 《a room, a floor》. ◉ ～청소기 a carpet sweeper.

**카폰** a car phone 〔telephone〕.

**카풀** a car pool. ¶ 우리 ～을 하는 게 어떨까, 하루는 내가 운전하고 다음 날은 자네가 하고 말이야 Why don't we form a car pool and I'll drive one day and you drive the next.

**카프르산**(―酸) 〖화학〗 capric acid; decanoic acid.

**카프리치오** 〖음악〗 a *capriccio* (It.); a caprice.

**카프릴산**(―酸) 〖화학〗 caprylic acid.

**카피** 《사본》 a copy. ¶ ～를 뜨다 take a copy 《of》; copy; duplicate / 이 서류를 두 장 ～해 주십시오 Please make two copies of this document. ◉ ～라이터 《광고 따위의》 a copywriter. ～라이트 《저작권》 a copyright.

**칵칵** with repeated coughs (to clear *one's* throat). ～하다 keep coughing away.

**칵칵거리다** keep coughing (to clear *one's* throat).

**칵테일** a cocktail. ¶ ～을 만들다 mix a cocktail / ～을 마시다 drink 〔have〕 a cocktail; cocktail. ◉ ～글라스 a cocktail glass. ～드레스 a cocktail dress; an afternoon dress. ～셰이커 a cocktail shaker. ～파티 a cocktail party.

**칸** ① 《칸살 넓이의 단위》 *k'an;* the unit of area 〔floor space〕; 《칸살·방을 세는 단위》 the unit of counting the number of *k'an* or rooms. ¶ 단칸집 a one-room house. ② 《칸막이》 a partition; a compartment. ¶ 칸을 막다 partition 《a room》 / 방의 일부를 칸을 막다 partition off a part of a room. ③ 《빈 곳》 (a) space; a blank (space). ¶ 알맞은 전치사를 써서 빈 칸을 채워라 Fill (in) the blanks with appropriate prepositions.

**칸** 《칭호》 a khan.

**칸나** 〖식물〗 a canna (flower).

**칸델라** 《광도의 단위》 a candela (생략 cd); 《등》 a metal hand lamp; a lantern. [<*candelaar* (Port.)]

**칸막이** 《막음》 partitioning; screening; 《막은 것》 a partition; a screen. ～하다 partition; screen off. ¶ 방을 ～해서 둘로 하다 partition 〔divide〕 a room into two parts 〔compartments〕. ◉ ～벽 a partition. ～판 a partition plate.

**칸살** ① 《면적》 the area 〔floor space〕 of one *k'an* (about 9 feet square). ¶ ～ 넓은〔좁은〕 방 a large 〔small〕 room / ～(을) 지르다 partition a room.

②《거리》 a space; an interval; distance.

**칸수**(一數) the number of *kan;* the floor space of a house.

**칸초네**〖음악〗 a *canzone* (It.).

**칸칸이**《방마다》(in) each〔every〕room; from room to room; room by room. ¶ ～ 사람이 들어 있다 Every room is occupied.

**칸타빌레**〖음악〗 cantabile.

**칸타타**〖음악〗 a cantata.

**칸트**《철학자》 Immanuel Kant (1724-1804). ¶ ～(철학, 학파)의 Kantian.

◉ ～철학 Kantianism; Kantism. ～학파 the Kantists: 신～ 학파 neo-Kantists; neo-Kantians.

**칼**[1] ①《썰거나 자르는》 a knife (*pl.* knives);《식칼》 a kitchen knife;《식탁용》 a table knife;《고기를 토막내는》 a cleaver; a meat chopper; a carving knife (푸주한 용);《생선용》 a fish knife;《접이칼》 a clasp knife; a jackknife;《과일 깎이용》 a fruit knife. ¶ 다목적 칼 an all-purpose utility knife / 면도칼 a razor / 주머니칼 a pocket knife / 날이 시퍼렇게 선 칼 a「well-sharpened〔sharply honed〕knife / 칼이 잘 들다〔안 들다〕 the knife「cuts well〔won't cut〕/ 칼로 베다 cut with a knife / 칼로 저미다 cut《the meat》in slices / 숫돌에 칼을 갈다 sharpen a knife on a whetstone / 칼 가는 사람 a knife「grinder〔sharpener〕/ 칼에 손가락을 베다 cut *one's* fingers on a knife.

②《무기용 검》 a sword; a saber (군도); a dagger (비수); a stiletto (단검). ¶ 서슬이 퍼런 칼 a gleaming「sword〔blade〕/ 칼을 들이대고《rob *a person* of *his* money》at the point of the sword / 칼로 찌르다 stab《*a person*》with a dagger; stab a dagger into《*a person*》/ 칼로 푹 찌르다 drive a「dagger〔sword〕home; run〔thrust〕a dagger《through the body》/ 칼을 뽑다 draw〔unsheathe〕a sword / 칼을 번쩍 들다 raise a sword / 칼을 휘두르다 brandish〔flourish〕a sword / 칼을 차고 있다 wear〔bear〕a「sword〔saber〕《at *one's* side》/ 칼을 품고 다니다 carry a dagger in *one's* bosom / 내리치는 칼을 맞다 suffer a sword-stroke / 내리치는 칼을 받아 넘기다 parry〔turn aside, ward off〕a sword thrust / 칼에 맞아 죽다 fall a victim to the dagger of《an assassin》; die「by〔beneath〕the sword《of an enemy》.

**칼**[2]〖고제도〗 a large wooden collar in which the neck of an offender is confined for punishment;《동양의》 a cang(ue);《서양의》 a pillory. ¶ 칼을 씌우다 put《*a person*》in the pillory / 칼을 쓰다 wear a cang(ue); be put in the pillory.

**칼감** a roughneck; a rowdy.

**칼국수** noodles cut out with a kitchen「knife.

**칼금** an incision; a notch; a nock. ¶ ～을 내다 notch; nick; snick.

**칼깃** a flight feather; a remex (*pl.* remiges); [총칭] the pinion.

**칼끝** the point of a「knife〔sword〕.

**칼날** the blade〔edge〕of a knife〔sword〕. ¶ ～을 세우다 put an edge《on》; give an edge《to》; edge; sharpen《a knife》/ ～이 서다 a knife takes an edge / ～이 무디다 the edge of a knife is「dull〔blunt〕/ ～ 위를 걷다 walk〔tread with bare feet on〕the edge of a sword.

**칼데라**〖지질〗 a caldera. ◉ ～호(수) a「crater lake.

**칼등** the back of a「knife〔sword〕.

**칼라**《옷깃》 a (shirt) collar. ◉ ～단추 a collar「button〔stud《영》〕. 소프트〔더블〕～ a「soft〔turn-down〕collar.

**칼러**《색깔》 (a) color. ¶「네 새 드레스는 무슨 ～지」―「붉은 ～야」 "What color is your new dress?"—"It's red."

**칼럼** a column.

**칼럼니스트** a (newspaper) columnist.

**칼로리** a「calorie〔calory〕(생략 cal). ¶ 저～의 low-caloric / 2,000 ～의 음식 a 2,000 caloric diet; 2,000 calories of food / ～가 많다〔적다〕 be「high〔low〕in calorific value; have a「high〔low〕caloric value / ～가 많은 음식 calorific food / 하루 평균 2,000 ～를 유지하다「maintain an average of 2,000 calories〔maintain as much as a 2,000 caloric diet〕per day / 하루 2,000 ～의 식사를 취하다 take a 2,000 caloric diet per day / 어른은 하루 최저 2,400 ～가 필요하다 Adults need 2,400 calories per day at the smallest quantity. ◉ ～가(價) calorific value. ～계산 calorie counting. ～섭취량 (a)「caloric〔calorie〕intake. ～식(食) a multipurpose meal. ～원(源) a calorie source. ～표 a caloric chart. ～함유량 caloric content. 킬로～ a kilogram calorie; a kilocalorie.

**칼로멜**〖화학〗 calomel. ◉ ～ 반전지(半電池) a calomel half cell. ～전극 a calomel electrode.

**칼륨**〖화학〗 potassium; kalium (기호

K). ◉ ~명반 potassium 〔potash〕 alum. ~염 potassic salt. ~유리 potash glass.

**칼리** 〖화학〗 kalium; potash. ⇨ 칼륨. ¶ ~의 potassic. ◉ ~비누 soft 〔potash〕 soap. ~비료 potassic fertilizer.

**칼리지** a college. ¶ ~보이 a college boy.

**칼리포르늄** 〖화학〗 californium (기호 Cf).

**칼립소** 〖음악〗 calypso (music).

**칼맞다** get stabbed; suffer a sword-stroke. ¶ 칼맞아 죽다 fall a victim to the dagger of 《an assassin》.

**칼뱅** 《종교 개혁가》 Jean Calvin (1509-64). ◉ ~주의 Calvinism. ~파 the Calvinists: ~파의 Calvinistic(al).

**칼부림** wielding a knife; stabbing 〔cutting〕 at 《*a person*》; 《유혈극》 bloodshed. ~하다 wield a knife; stab 〔cut〕 at 《*a person*》. ¶ 싸움 끝에 ~까지 하다 go so far as to stab at each other in a fight. ◉ ~사태 an affair of bloodshed: ~사태로 번지다 develop into bloodshed.

**칼붙이** an edge(d) tool; [총칭] cutlery.

**칼새** 〖조류〗 a kind of swift; a salangane; a chimney swift.

**칼슘** 〖화학〗 calcium (기호 Ca). ¶ ~을 함유하다 contain calcium.
◉ ~비누 calcium soap. ~시안아미드 calcium cyanamide; lime nitrogen. ~주사 an injection of calcium.

**칼시민** 《도료》 calcimine. ¶ ~을 칠하다 calcimine 《a wall》.

**칼자국** a scar from a knife 〔sword〕; a sword cut 〔wound〕. ¶ ~이 나다 get a blade scar / ~을 내다 《새김 눈을》 incise.

**칼자루** the handle 《of a knife》; the haft 《of a dagger》; the hilt 《of a sword》. ¶ ~를 쥐다 hold a sword by the hilt; [비유적] have the (final, last) say; have the whip hand.

**칼잡이** 《백장》 a butcher; a slaughterer; 《검객》 a swordman.

**칼질** cutting. ~하다 cut; chop; hash.

**칼집** a scabbard; a sheath; a case (단도의). ¶ 칼을 ~에서 뽑다 draw 〔unsheathe〕 *one's* sword / 칼을 ~에 꽂다 scabbard a knife; sheathe 〔put up〕 《*one's* sword》.

**칼춤** a sword dance. ¶ ~을 추다 dance 〔perform〕 a sword dance.

**칼침**(一鍼) the thrust of a knife 〔sword〕. ¶ ~을 주다 thrust a knife 〔sword〕; give 《*a person*》 a taste of the blade / ~을 맞다 get stabbed; be given a taste of the blade.

**칼칼하다** ⇨ 컬컬하다.

**칼코등이** a sword-guard.

**캄보디아** 《나라 이름》 (the State of) Cambodia; Kampuchea. ¶ ~의 Cambodian. ◉ ~사람 a Cambodian.

**캄브리아기**(一紀) 〖지질〗 the Cambrian period; the Cambrian.

**캄차카** Kamchatka. ¶ ~반도 the Kamchatka Peninsula.

**캄캄하다** ① 《어둡다》 (be) pitch-dark; 《as》 dark as pitch; 《as》 dark 〔black〕 as midnight; 《암담하다》 (be) dark; gloomy. ¶ 캄캄한 밤 a pitch-dark 〔jet-black〕 night / 캄캄한 앞날 gloomy prospects / 앞날이 ~ The future looks gloomy. *or* Things look black. / 방 속은 캄캄했다 It was pitch-dark within the room. / 캄캄해지기를 기다렸다 We waited for full darkness. ② 《알지 못하다》 [서술적] be ignorant 〔uninformed〕 of; be ill informed of; know nothing 《about》; have no idea of; be a stranger 《to》; be poorly 〔badly〕 informed. ¶ 세상 일에 ~ know nothing about 〔little of〕 the world; be ignorant of the ways of the world / 시국에 ~ be ignorant of the current situation / 주식 시장에 관해 전혀 ~ I 「know nothing 〔am quite in the dark〕 about the stock market.

**캄프리** 〖식물〗 a comfrey; a cumfrey.

**캅셀** [<*Kapsel* (G.)] 〖약〗 a capsule.

**캉캉** 《춤의 일종》 *cancan* (F.). ¶ ~을 추다 do the *cancan*.

**캐나다** Canada. ¶ ~의 Canadian. ◉ ~사람 a Canadian: 프랑스계 ~사람 a French Canadian.

**캐내다** ① 《발굴하다》 dig up 〔out〕; grub up; unearth. ⇨ 캐다. ¶ 나무 뿌리를 ~ grub up roots. ② 《비밀 등을》 worm 〔pry〕 《a secret》 out of 《*a person*》; ferret out 《a secret》; get 《*something*》 out of 《another》; get wind of 《*a matter*》; 《들춰내다》 reveal; disclose; find out. ¶ 넘겨짚어 정보를 ~ pump information out of 《*a person*》; pump 《*a person*》 for information / 힘들게 ~ sweat 《*a matter*》 out of 《*a person*》 / 진상(眞相)을 ~ find out the (real) truth of an affair; inquire into the true state of 《*a thing*》; go (down) to 〔get at〕 the root of 《a matter》.

**캐다** ① 《파내다》 dig up 〔out〕; grub up; unearth; 《식물을》 gather; pick; lift. ¶ 감자를 ~ dig out 〔up〕 potatoes; lift potatoes / 금을 ~ dig gold 《from a mine》/ 나물을 ~ dig up 〔gather〕 edible greens / 석탄을 ~ mine 〔dig out〕 coal / 약초를 ~ pick medicinal herbs / 풀뿌리를 ~ grub up grass roots. ②《알아내기 위해》 dig 〔pry, delve〕 into; poke and pry; inquire into; trace; probe. ¶ 근원을 ~ trace 《*a thing*》 to *its* source / 비밀을 ~ pry into a secret; probe 〔trace〕 a secret; 《캐내다》 ferret 〔worm〕 out a secret / 사건의 근본을 ~ go to the root of an affair; probe a matter to the bottom / 신원(身元)을 ~ inquire 〔look〕 into 《*a person's*》 antecedents; look into 《*a person's*》 family background; check up 《*a person's*》 record / 사건의 진상을 ~ inquire into the true state of things; go (down) to 〔get at〕 the root 〔bottom〕 of a matter / 철저히 ~ probe 《*a matter*》 to the bottom / 사건의 배후 관계를 ~ inquire into the hidden circumstances that led up to the case; investigate who is pulling the wires / 캐기 좋아하다 be fond of prying; be inquisitive.

**캐드** 〖컴퓨터〗 CAD. [< *C*omputer-*A*ided *D*esign]

**캐디** 〖골프〗 a caddie; a caddy. ¶ ~로 일하다 work as a caddie; caddie 〔caddy〕 《for a golfer》.

**캐딜락** 《고급 승용차의 상표》 a Cadillac (automobile).

**캐러멜** 《과자》 a caramel.

**캐러밴** 《사막의 대상·포장마차》 a caravan.

**캐럴** a (Christmas) carol.

**캐럿** a carat; a karat (★ karat은 carat의 이형(異形). 《미》에서는 보석은 carat, 금은 karat을 써서 구별하고 있음). ¶ 7 ~의 다이아몬드 a diamond of 7 carats; a 7-carat diamond / 18~의 금 gold 18-karats fine.

**캐리커처** 《풍자 만화》 a caricature.

**캐릭터** 《성격》 (a) character; 《중요 등장 인물》 a character. ◉ ~산업 character industry. ~상품 a product featuring a popular character.

**캐묻다** ask inquisitively; pry; be inquisitive 《about》; make a searching inquiry. ¶ 시시콜콜히 ~ inquire of 《*a person*》 about every detail of 《*a matter*》; ask 《*a person*》 prying questions; catechize 《*a person*》 to the last detail about 《*a matter*》/ 선생님은 말다툼의 이유를 꼬치꼬치 캐물으셨다 Our teacher strictly pressed us to tell the cause of the quarrel.

**캐미솔** 《여성용 옷》 a camisole.

**캐비닛** a 《steel》 cabinet; a console (라디오·TV의).

**캐비아** 〖요리〗 《철갑상어알 젓》 caviar(e).

**캐비지** 《양배추》 a cabbage. ◉ ~샐러드 coleslaw; coldslaw.

**캐빈** 《배·비행기의 객실·오두막》 a cabin.

**캐슈** 〖식물〗 a cashew. ◉ ~너트 a cashew nut. ~애플 a cashew apple.

**캐스터** 《방송국 등의》 a newscaster; an anchorman 《미》.

**캐스터네츠** 〖악기〗 (a pair of) castanets.

**캐스트** 《배역》 the cast (of characters); 《한 사람》 a member of the cast.

**캐스팅보트** the casting vote. ¶ 그 문제에 관해서 김의장이 ~를 던졌다 Mr. Kim used his casting vote over the issue. / 우리 당이 ~를 쥐고 있다 Our party holds the decisive vote.

**캐시미어** 《직물》 cashmere (cloth).

**캐시어** 《현금 출납계》 a cashier.

**캐시카드** 《현금 인출 카드》 a cash card; a bank card.

**캐주얼** 《평상복》 casuals. ◉ ~슈즈 casual shoes. ~웨어 casual wear 〔clothes, attire〕.

**캐처** 〖야구〗 a catcher 《on a team》. ¶ ~를 맡(아보)다 catch 《for the Yankees》; serve as catcher 《for》.

**캐치** catching; a catch. ~하다 catch 《a ball》; obtain 《information》. ◉ ~볼 playing catch: ~볼하다 play 〔have a〕 catch. 러닝~ a running catch.

**캐치프레이즈** 《표어》 a catch phrase.

**캐터펄트** 〖군사〗 《사출기》 a catapult. ¶ ~로 발사하다 catapult 《a deck plane》.

**캐터필러** 《무한궤도》 a caterpillar (tread); an endless (metal) belt 〔track〕; 《상표명》 Caterpillar.

**캐피털** 《자본》 capital; 《대문자》 capital (letter); 〖인쇄〗 an uppercase letter.

**캐피털리즘** 《자본주의》 capitalism.

**캑** with a cough or sputter (to get something out of *one's* throat). ~하다 cough; hack.

**캔** 《깡통》 a can. ◉ 캔맥주 a can of beer; a canned beer. 맥주캔 a beer can.

**캔디** 《사탕》 (a piece of) candy; 《영》 a sweet; a lollipop (막대 달린); [총칭] candies; 《영》 sweets.

**캔버스** 〖미술〗 canvas. ◉ ~틀 a (canvas) stretcher.

**캔슬** 《취소》 cancellation. ~하다 cancel.

**캔자스** 《미국의 주》 Kansas (생략 Kan., Kans., Kas.).

**캘리코** 《흰 무명》 calico.

**캘리퍼스** (a pair of) cal(l)ipers. ◉ 측미(測微)～ micrometer cal(l)ipers.

**캘리포니아** 《미국의 주(州)》 California (생략 Calif., Cal.).

**캘린더** a calendar. ◉ ～시계 a calendar watch. 벽〔탁상〕～ a wall 〔desk〕 calendar.

**캠** 〖기계〗 a cam. ◉ ～장치 cam mechanism.

**캠코더** a camcorder.

**캠퍼** 〖약〗 camphor. ◉ ～주사 (a) camphor injection; [비유적] a shot in the arm 《for morale》: ～ 주사를 놓다 give 〔administer〕 a camphor injection.

**캠퍼스** 《학원》 a campus. ¶ ～에서 on the campus / 대학 ～ a college campus.

**캠페인** a campaign; a drive. ¶ 에이즈 예방 ～ a campaign for the prevention of AIDS / ～을 벌이다 conduct 〔carry on〕 a campaign 《for, against》; campaign 《for, against》 / 판매 촉진 ～을 벌이다 conduct a campaign for sales promotion.

**캠프** a camp. ¶ ～를 치다 camp; build 〔make, set up〕 (*one's*) camp.
◉ ～생활 a camp life; camping(-out). ～용품 camp requisites; camping gear 〔outfit〕. ～장 a campground; a campsite. ～촌(村) a camping village. ～파이어 a campfire: ～ 파이어를 둘러싸고 앉다 sit around a campfire.

**캠핑** camping. ¶ ～ 가다 go (out) camping; leave for camping 《in》 / 그들은 산으로 ～을 갔다 They went camping in the mountains.
◉ ～시설 camping facilities; ～의자 a campstool. ～지역 a camping area; a caravan park. ～카 a camper; a motorized caravan 《영》; a motor home; a house trailer.

**캡** 《모자·뚜껑》 a cap. ¶ 캡을 쓰다 put a cap on / 캡을 벗기다〔떼다〕 remove a cap 《from a bottle》; open 《a bottle》.

**캡션** 《사진 설명·표제》 a caption.

**캡슐** 《약·인공 위성의》 a capsule. ¶ ～에 싼 capsulated / ～을 회수하다 recover a capsule. ◉ 우주～ a space capsule. 타임～ a time capsule.

**캡틴** the captain (of a team). ¶ 야구팀의 ～ the captain of the baseball team.

**캥거루** 〖동물〗 a kangaroo (*pl.* ～s, [총칭] -roo). ¶ 새끼 ～ a baby kangaroo; a joey / 작은 ～ a wallaby / 큰 ～ a giant kangaroo; a euro (*pl.* ～s); a wallaroo (*pl.* ～s).

**캥캥** 《강아지 따위의 소리》 yap, yap, yap; yelp, yelp, yelp. ¶ (강아지가) ～울다 yelp; yip; let out a yelp 〔yip〕.

**컁컁하다** (be) thin; lean; emaciated. ¶ 컁컁한 얼굴 a thin face.

**커녕** far from 《*doing*》; anything but; not at all; in no wise; instead of 《something expected》; 《말할 것도 없이》 not to mention; not to speak of; to say nothing of.
¶ 그렇기는～ far from it; on the contrary / 실망하기는～ far from being disappointed / 그는 내게 고마워하기는～ So far from thanking me, he... / 미인은～ 귀신 같다 She is far from beautiful, she is a fright. / 백 원은 ～ 십 원도 못 받겠다 One hundred won? —Why, we won't even get ten won! / 즐겁기는～ 불쾌하다 It is anything but pleasant. / 이 책은 유익하기는～ 매우 해롭다 So far from doing any good, this book does a good deal of harm. / 칭찬은～ 꾸지람만 들었다 In place of praise we heard scoldings. / 환영은～ 냉대를 받았다 Instead of open arms, we were given the cold shoulder. / 저축은～ 그날그날 살아가기도 힘들다 Far from saving money, I can hardly make my living. / 그는 영어는～ 우리말도 모른다 He doesn't know Korean, to say nothing of English.

**커닝** cribbing; cheating in an examination. ¶ ～을 하다 cheat 《in an examination, on a test》; do a dishonest trick; crib 《구어》 / ～을 하다(가) 들키다 be caught cribbing.
◉ ～페이퍼 a crib (sheet); a pony.

**커다랗다** (be) very big 〔large, great〕; huge; colossal; gigantic; enormous.
¶ 커다란 손실 a great 〔terrific〕 loss / 커다란 잘못 a big 〔huge〕 mistake / 커다랗게 (so that it is) very big; very large; on a large scale; hugely; colossally; enormously / 눈을 커다랗게 뜨고 with *one's* eyes wide open / 집을 커다랗게 짓다 build an enormous house / 사업을 커다랗게 시작하다 go into business on a big scale / 신문에 광고를 커다랗게 내다 place a large advertisement in a newspaper.

**커다래지다** become bigger 〔larger〕; gain 〔increase in〕 size; grow (up); become taller; be enlarged 〔magnified, expanded, extended〕. ¶ 눈이 ～ open *one's* eyes wide; be startled / 키가 ～ become taller; acquire 〔gain〕 height.

**커리큘럼** 〖교육〗 a curriculum (*pl.* ～s, -la); a course of study (한 과목의).

¶ 그 학교는 ～의 폭이 넓다 The school has a wide curriculum.

**커머셜** 《라디오·TV의》 a commercial 「message 〔announcement〕; a 《radio, TV》 commercial (광고 방송). ¶ ～시간 a commercial break. ◉ ～송 a commercial song (= C.M. song).

**커뮤니케이션** 《통신·소통》 communication(s). ¶ 매스～ mass communications; the press; journalism / 매스～ mass communication / ～의 단절 a breakdown in communication; a communication gap / 언어는 ～의 주요한 수단이다 Language is a chief means of communication.

**커미션** 《위탁 수수료》 a commission. ¶ 1할의 ～을 받다 receive a 10% commission 《on the sale of》/ ～을 떼다 take a commission 《of five percent》. ◉ ～브로커 a commission broker.

**커버** 《덮개》 a cover; a covering; 《책의》 a jacket; a dust 「cover 〔wrapper〕; 《덧양말의》 oversocks. ¶ 의자의 ～ a 「cover(-ing) 〔dust sheet〕 for a chair; a chair cover / ～를 씌우다 lay a cover; cover 《a chair with a cloth》; 《책에》 jacket / ～를 떼다 take off the cover 《from》. ◉ ～걸 《잡지 표지의》 a cover girl. ～유리 cover glass; deck glass.

**커버하다** ① 《경기에서》 cover 《3rd base》; back up; 《엄호하다》 cover 《*a person*》. ② 《보상·보충하다》 meet 《*a person's* expenses》; make up 《a loss》. ¶ 회사는 자산의 일부를 매각하여 손실을 커버하려고 했다 The company tried to make up its losses by selling some of its assets.

**커브** ① 《곡선》 a curve; a curved line. ¶ 상승 ～를 그리다 curve up / 상승 ～를 그리는 암 사망률 the up-curving cancer mortality. ② 《도로·철길의》 a curve; a bend. ¶ 급～ a 「steep 〔sharp〕 curve; a sharp 「bend 〔turn〕/ ～를 돌다 round a curve / 급～를 틀다 turn sharply; make a sharp turn 《at the intersection》/ ～길에서 고속으로 달리는 것은 위험하다 It is not safe to go round a bend at high speed. ③ 〖야구〗 a curve (ball). ¶ 날카로운 ～ a sharp-breaking curve / ～를 던지다 hurl 〔throw〕 a curve / ～로 타자를 애먹이다 throw a curve to dazzle the batter.

**커스터드** 《과자》 custard. ◉ ～푸딩 custard pudding.

**커지다** grow 「bigger 〔larger〕; increase in size; 《성장하다》 grow (up); become taller; 《증대하다》 swell; expand; be 「extended 〔expanded, enlarged〕; 《능력·업적 등으로》 attain greatness; 《중대해지다》 become 「serious 〔critical〕; 《악화되다》 aggravate; be made worse. ¶ 담이 ～ become emboldened / 부피가 ～ increase 〔grow〕 in volume; grow voluminous / 세력이 ～ increase in power; gain in influence / 문제가 커졌다 The problem has grown serious. / 이 마을은 최근에 커졌다 This village has grown big recently.

**커터** 《재단기》 a cutter; 《소형 범선》 a cutter. ◉ ～셔츠 a long-sleeved sport(s) shirt.

**커튼** a curtain 《at a window》; drapes (얇은 커튼 위에 덧씌우는). ¶ ～을 올리다 raise 〔draw up〕 a curtain / ～을 내리다 drop 〔lower〕 a curtain; draw 〔let, pull〕 down a curtain / ～을 치다 draw a curtain 《over》/ ～을 젖히다 draw aside a curtain; draw the curtain apart. ◉ ～레일〔로드〕 a curtain 「rail 〔rod〕. ～콜 a curtain call.

**커틀릿** 〖요리〗 a cutlet; a *côtelette* (F.). ◉ 포크～ a pork cutlet.

**커프스** cuffs. ◉ ～버튼 《꿰매 단》 cuff 〔sleeve 《영》〕 buttons; 《뗄 수 있는》 cuff 〔sleeve〕 links.

**커플** 《한 쌍》 a couple. ¶ 잘 어울리는～ a well-matched〔-mated〕 couple.

**커피** coffee. ¶ ～를 끓이다 brew coffee; make coffee (준비하다) / ～를 한 잔 마시다 drink a cup of coffee; have a coffee / ～를 블랙으로 마시다 drink coffee black; have black coffee / ～에 크림과 설탕을 타서 마시다 drink 〔have〕 coffee with cream and sugar. ◉ ～거르개 a coffee strainer. ～끓이개 a percolator; a coffee pot; 《드립식》 a dripolator. ～나무 a coffee tree 〔plant〕. ～세트 a coffee set. ～숍 a coffee shop. ～잔 a coffee cup. ～포트 a coffee pot. 블랙～ black coffee. 아이스～ ice 〔iced〕 coffee.

**컨덕터** 〖음악·전기〗 a conductor.

**컨덕턴스** 〖전기〗 conductance.

**컨디션** condition. ¶ (몸의) ～이 좋다 be 〔feel〕 well; be in good condition; 《운동 선수가》 be in 「fine 〔good〕 shape / ～이 나쁘다 be 〔feel〕 unwell; be out of 「condition 〔sorts, form〕; be in bad shape / (몸의) ～을 조절하다 adjust 〔fix〕 *one's* physical condition; tone up *one's* system / (훈련하여) ～을 유지하다 keep in training / (선수가) ～을 되찾다 regain *one's* form / (선수의) ～을 회복케 하다 get 《*a person*》 back into shape / (경기에서) ～은 최상이다 be in the best condition [form]; be in top form.

**컨베이어** 〚기계〛《자동운반장치》 a conveyor; a conveyer. ◉ ～시스템 a conveyer system.

**컨설턴트** 《상담역》 a consultant. ¶ 경영 ～ a management consultant.

**컨테이너** a container. ¶ ～ 트럭 a container truck / ～ 열차 a container train / ～선(船) a container ship [carrier]. ◉ ～부두 a container wharf; a container landing stage. ～수송[화] containerization.

**컨트롤** control. ¶ ～하다 control / ～이 좋다[나쁘다] 〚야구〛 have good [poor] (pitching) control / ～이 듣지 않다 〚야구〛 lose control 《of pitching》. ◉ ～룸 《관제실》 a control room. ～유닛 〚컴퓨터〛 a control unit. ～타워 《공항의》 a control tower (관제탑).

**컨트리** a country. ◉ ～뮤직 country music. ～클럽 a country club. ～하우스 《귀족·부호의 시골 저택》 a country house.

**컬** a curl (of hair). ¶ 머리를 컬하다 curl *one's* hair / 컬이 풀리다 go out of curl.

**컬러** (a) color. ◉ ～강철판 pre-tinged steel sheets; color steel sheets. ～방송 colorcasting; a colorcast. ～사진 a color photo(graph) [picture]. ～슬라이드 a color slide [transparency]. ～텔레비전 color television [TV]; 《수상기》 a color television set. ～필름 a color film. 로컬～ 《지방색》 local color.

**컬럼니스트** 《신문 등의 기고가》 a columnist.

**컬럼바이트** 〚광물〛 columbite.

**컬럼비아** 《미국의 도시》 Columbia. ◉ ～구 《워싱턴시》 the District of Columbia (생략 D.C.). ～ 대학 Columbia University.

**컬컬하다** be [feel] thirsty; 《술생각이 나서》 be thirsty for a drink. ¶ 목이 컬컬해 한 잔 했으면 좋겠다 I am thirsty and would like to have a drink.

**컴맹**(—盲) computer illiteracy. ¶ 요즈음 ～은 멸시 받아야 할 일로 여겨지게 되었다 Recently, computer illiteracy has been looked upon as something deserving of contempt.

**컴백** a comeback. ～하다 come back 《to *one's* former work》; make *one's* comeback. ¶ 전직책으로 ～하다 take up *one's* old position 《as》 / 영화계에 ～하다 find *one's* way back into the screen; make *one's* comeback on the screen.

**컴컴하다** ① 《어둡다》 (be) dark; somber; murky; gloomy. ¶ 아직 컴컴한 새벽에 in the gray of the morning. ② 《침침하다》 (be) dim. ③ 《마음이》 (be) dark; secretive; black-hearted; insidious. ¶속(이) 컴컴한 사람 a secretive [insidious] person; a person whose intention is hard to understand.

**컴퍼스** ① 《제도용》 (a pair of) compasses (한쪽 끝에 연필(심)을 끼우는 것); dividers (양쪽 끝에 침만 달린 것); 《나침반》 a mariner's compass. ¶ ～로 재다 measure with compasses. ② 《다리》 legs; locomotives 《영속어》. ¶ ～가 길다[짧다] have long [short] legs; be long-[short-]legged. ◉ ～오차 a compass error.

**컴퓨터** an (electronic) computer. ¶ ～로 제어[조종]되는 기계 a machine under computer control; a computer-controlled machine / 데이터를 ～에 입력하다 put [feed] data into a computer / 정보를 ～로 처리하다 process information with a computer / ～로 정보를 검색하다 obtain data from a computer; use a computer to search for data. ◉ ～게임 a computer game. ～공포증 computer allergy. ～그래픽스 computer graphics. ～기술 computer technology. ～바이러스 a computer virus. ～백신 a computer vaccin. ～범죄 a computer crime. ～시대 the computer age. ～언어 a computer language. ～정보처리 조직 an electronic data processing system (생략 EDPS). ～제어장치 a computer-control system. ～해커 a computer hacker (컴퓨터 프로그램의 불법 침입자). ～화 computerization: ～화하다 computerize / 이 부문을 하루속히 ～화해야 한다 We must computerize this department as soon as possible. 개인용 ～ a personal computer (생략 P.C.): 음성인식 개인용 ～ a voicerecognition P.C. 아날로그[디지털] ～ an analog(ue) [a digital] computer.

**컴프레서** 〚기계〛 a compressor.

**컴프리** 〚식물〛 a comfrey [cumfrey].

**컵** 《찻잔》 a cup; a teacup; a coffee cup; a demitasse (소형); a mug (대형); 《음료수용》 a glass; a drinking cup; 《우승배》 a cup; a trophy; 《계량용》 a measuring cup. ¶ 물 한 컵 a glass of water / 컵 하나 가득한 분량 a glassful 《of water》 / 여러 컵의 물을 마시다 drink many cups of water; have a cup of water after another / 우승컵

을 주다 honor 《a winner》 with a trophy / 우승컵을 타다 win the cup 〔trophy〕.

**컷** 《판화》 a (wood)cut; 《선화나 삽화》 a block; 《영화 등의》 cutting; a cut; 《테니스·탁구 등의》 a cut; 《머리의》 a haircut. ～하다 cut; 《삭제하다》 cross out; strike off; 《볼을》 cut; 《머리를》 get 〔have〕 a haircut; have *one's* haircut (short). ¶ 컷을 넣다 fill 《the space》 with a cut / 머리를 컷해주다 give 《*a person*》 a haircut. ◉ 컷 플레이 〖야구〗 cutoff play. 원컷 〖영화〗 one cut.

**컹컹** bowwow; barking. ～하다, ～거리다 keep barking. ¶ 개가 ～ 짖다 a dog barks 〔goes bowwow〕.

**케냐** 《나라 이름》 Kenya. ¶ ～의 Kenyan. ◉ ～사람 a Kenyan.

**케네디** 《미국의 제35대 대통령》 John Fitzgerald Kennedy (1917-63). ◉ ～국제 공항 Kennedy International Airport. ～라운드 the Kennedy round.

**케도** 《한반도 에너지 개발 기구》 KEDO. [<*K*orean Peninsula *E*nergy *D*evelopment *O*rganization]

**케라틴** 〖화학〗 ceratin; keratin. ¶ ～성의 keratinous. ◉ ～플라스틱 keratin plastic.

**케이맥** KMAG. [<*K*orean *M*ilitary *A*dvisory *G*roup]

**케이블** a cable. ◉ ～굴착기 a cable 〔tower〕 excavator. ～도표 a cable chart. ～부설 cable laying 〔placing〕: ～부설선(船) a cable layer. ～윈치 a cable winch. ～인양장치 cable hauling gear. ～잭 a cable jack. ～접속 cable splicing. ～철도 a cable 〔funicular〕 railway 〔tramway〕. ～카 a cable car; a funicular railway coach 《영》. ～크레인 a cable crane.

**참고** **컴퓨터 관련 용어**

1. 여러 형태의 컴퓨터 명칭

범용(汎用)컴퓨터 a general purpose computer. 개인용 컴퓨터 a personal computer (생략 PC). 슈퍼 컴퓨터 a supercomputer. 제5세대 컴퓨터 the fifth-generation computer. 미니 컴퓨터 a minicomputer. 슈퍼 미니 컴퓨터 a super minicomputer. 마이크로 컴퓨터 a microcomputer. 핸드헬드 컴퓨터 a handheld computer. 휴대형〔노트북〕 컴퓨터 a portable 〔notebook〕 computer. 랩톱 컴퓨터 a laptop computer (무릎에 올려놓고 쓰는). 워드프로세서 a word processor.

2. 컴퓨터의 주요 부품 명칭

◉ 콘솔 《조작용 탁자》 a console. 중앙처리장치 a *c*entral *p*rocessing *u*nit (생략 CPU). 자기테이프 장치 a magnetic tape unit 〔handler, storage〕. 자기디스크 장치 a magnetic disk unit 〔handler〕. 카드 판독 장치 a *c*ard *r*eader (생략 CR). 단말 장치 a terminal equipment. 라인프린터 a line printer. 광학식 문자 판독 장치 an *o*ptical *c*haracter *r*eader (생략 OCR). 광학식 마크 판독 장치 an *o*ptical *m*ark *r*eader (생략 OMR). 제어 장치 a control unit.

◉ 키보드 a keyboard. 본체 a main unit. 디스플레이 장치 a display unit. 액정 디스플레이 a liquid-cristal display. 플로피 디스크 장치 a floppy disk unit. 하드디스크 장치 a hard disk unit. 프린터 a printer. 플로터 a plotter. 마우스 a mouse. 스캐너 a scanner.

3. 컴퓨터의 주요 장치 및 기능 명칭

집적회로 an *i*ntegrated *c*ircuit (생략 IC). 대규모 집적회로 a *l*arge-*s*cale *i*ntegrated circuit (생략 LSI). 초대규모 집적회로 a *v*ery *l*arge-*s*cale *i*ntegrated circuit (생략 VLSI). 마이크로프로세서 a microprocessor. 램, 또는 랜덤액세스 기억장치 RAM; a *r*andom *a*ccess *m*emory. 롬, 판독 전용 기억 장치 ROM; a *r*ead *o*nly *m*emory. 바이트 a byte (정보의 기본 단위). 호스트 컴퓨터 a host computer. 워크스테이션 a workstation. 하드웨어 hardware. 소프트웨어 software.

4. 컴퓨터 운용에 관련되는 용어

운영 체제, 오퍼레이팅 시스템 OS; *o*perating *s*ystem. 제어 프로그램 a control program. 처리 프로그램 a processing program. 온라인 처리 on-line processing. 배치 처리 batch processing. 실시간 시스템 real time system. 시분할 시스템 TSS; *t*ime-*s*haring *s*ystem. 분산 처리 distributed processing. 네트워크 시스템 network system. 랜 LAN; *l*ocal *a*rea *n*etwork system. 도스 DOS; *d*isk *o*perating *s*ystem. 데이터 베이스 data base. 파일 a file. 순서도 a flowchart. 시스템 엔지니어 a system engineer. 프로그래머 a programmer. 오퍼레이터 an operator.

해저~ a submarine cable; an undersea cable: 광섬유 해저 ~ an undersea optical fiber cable.

**케이스** 《상자》 a case; 《사례》 a case. ¶ ~에 넣어 두다 keep 《glasses》 in a case / ~에 담다 pack 《wine bottles》 into a case; pack a case with 《wine bottles》 / ~ 바이 케이스로 case by case; on a case-by-case basis / 이것은 특수한 ~다 This is an unusual case. ◉ ~스터디 《사례 연구》 a case study. 담배~ a cigarette case.

**케이슨** 《수중 공사용 잠함》 a caisson. ◉ ~기초 《수중 공사의》 a caisson foundation. ~방파제 a concrete-caisson breakwater. ~병 〖의학〗 a caisson disease; compressed air sickness.

**케이에스** KS. [<*K*orean *S*tandards] ◉ ~마크 a KS mark. ~상품 KS goods.

**케이오** K.O. [<*k*nock-*o*ut] ¶ ~시키다 knock out; K.O. 《미구어》; kayo 《미구어》; count out; floor 《*a person*》 for a knockout / ~를 당하다 be knocked out; be KO'd 〔kayoed〕 《미구어》; be counted out / 3라운드에서 ~승을 거두다 score a third round knock-out victory.

**케이지비** 《구 소련의》 K.G.B. [<*K*omitet *G*osudarstvennoi *B*ezopasnosti (Russ.) = State Security Committee]

**케이크** a cake. ¶ ~를 자르다 knife a 《wedding》 cake. ◉ ~믹서 a cake mixer. 생일〔크리스마스〕~ a birthday 〔Christmas〕 cake.

**케이폭** 〖식물〗 kapok. ◉ ~유 kapok oil.

**케이프** a cape; a tippet. ¶ ~를 걸치다 wear a cape.

**케인스** 《경제학자》 John Maynard Keynes (1883-1946). ◉ ~ 학설 〖경제〗 Keynesianism.

**케임브리지** 《지명》 Cambridge. ◉ ~대학 Cambridge University: ~대학의 학생〔졸업생〕 a Cantabrigian.

**케첩** (tomato) ketchup; catchup; catsup 《미》.

**케케묵다** 《오래 되다》 (be) old (and stale); worm-eaten; rancid; musty; moldy; 《진부하다》 (be) timeworn; old-fashioned; antiquated; commonplace; worn-out; threadbare; hackneyed. ¶ 케케묵은 격언 a hackneyed saying; a copybook maxim / 케케묵은 규칙〔관습〕 a worm-eaten regulation 〔custom〕 / 케케묵은 생각〔사상〕 a moss-grown idea; an old-fashioned 〔out-of-date〕 idea / 케케묵은 쌀 stale rice / 케케묵은 이야기 an old story / 케케묵은 이론 a worn-out 〔threadbare〕 theory / 케케묵은 소리를 하다 make a commonplace 〔trite〕 remark.

**케페우스자리** 〖천문〗 Cepheus.

**켄타우루스자리** 〖천문〗 the Centaur; Centaurus.

**켄터키** 《미국의 주》 Kentucky (생략 Ky., Ken.).

**켄트지**(―紙) kent paper.

**켈로이드** 〖의학〗 keloid; cheloid. ¶ ~ 모양의 keloidal / ~ 모양의 화상 a keloid burn.

**켈트** 《켈트 사람》 a Celt; the Celts (켈트족). ◉ ~어 Celtic: ~어〔사람, 족〕의 Celtic.

**켕기다** ① (***a***) 《팽팽해지다》 be drawn 〔stretched〕 tightly; be tensed 〔strained, taut〕. ¶ 줄이 ~ a rope is stretched taut / 바지가 ~ *one's* trousers are tight / 힘줄이 ~ have a strain on the sinew; feel a sinew taut. (***b***) 《팽팽히 하다》 tighten 〔strain〕 《a rope》; stretch 《a rope》 tight; pull all the slack out of 《a rope》; make 《it》 taut. ¶ 너무 세게 켕기면 끊어진다 If you strain it too hard, it will break.
② 《마음이》 feel a strain; feel uneasy 〔compunction, guilty〕; feel ill at ease; feel timid 〔small〕; have something on *one's* conscience. ¶ 왜, 켕기나―대답을 못하게 Why don't you answer?―Something on your conscience? / 그렇게 말하니 좀 켕긴다 You have got me there.
③ 《마주 당기다》 pull each other.

**켜** a layer. ¶ 여러 켜를 쌓다 heap up in several layers / 켜를 이루다 be in layers.

**켜내다** 《실을》 reel silk off cocoons.

**켜다** ① 《불을》 light; kindle; burn; strike (a match); 《스위치를 돌려》 turn 〔switch〕 on. ¶ 가스를 ~ turn on the gas / 라디오를 ~ turn 〔switch〕 on the radio / 램프를 ~ light (up) a lamp; set a lamp alight / 라이터를 ~ strike a lighter; snap a lighter into 〔click a lighter to〕 flame / 불을 ~ make a light; light a light; light up 《a room》; 《전등을》 turn 〔put, switch〕 on the light / 성냥을 ~ light 〔strike, scrape〕 a match / 촛불을 ~ light a candle / 라디오를 켠 채 두다 keep the radio on / 전등이 켜져 있는 방 a room lighted by electricity; a room where an electric light is burning / 라이터가 켜지지 않는다 The cigarette lighter fails to work.

② 《들이켜다》 drink off; gulp down. ¶ 단숨에 ~ empty 《the glass》「at a draft 〔at one gulp〕/ 쭉 (들이) ~ take a long pull / 술 한 병을 다 ~ drink 〔drain〕 a bottle of wine to the dregs; crack a bottle of brandy 《속어》.
③ 《현악기 등을》 play (on); scrape (on) 《a fiddle》; sweep 《the strings》. ¶ 바이올린을 ~ play the violin; 《시끄럽게》 scrape on a fiddle / 바이올린 한 곡을 ~ play a tune on the violin.
④ 《톱으로》 saw 《wood》. ¶ 가로 켜는 톱 a crosscut saw / 세로 켜는 톱 a ripsaw / 널빤지를 ~ saw a board / 톱으로 ~ saw (off); cut with a saw / 통나무를 널빤지로 ~ saw a log into boards / 켜기 쉽다〔힘들다〕 saw easily 〔badly〕.
⑤ 《실을 뽑다》 spin off. ¶ (누에)고치를 ~ reel silk off cocoons.
⑥ 《기지개를》 stretch (*oneself*); stretch *one's* body with raised hands. ¶ 하품을 하며 기지개를 ~ stretch *oneself* with a yawn.
⑦ 《우레를》 give a mating call; imitate an animal call. ¶ 우레를 ~ imitate a pheasant call.

**켤레**[1] 〖수학〗 conjugation. ¶ ~ 직경〔각〕 a conjugate diameter 〔angle〕.

**켤레**[2] a pair. ¶ 구두 한 ~ a pair of shoes / 양말 두 ~ two pairs of socks / ~로 팔다 sell by the pair.

**켯속** the situation; the insides 《of a situation》; the secret 《of *a matter*》; the inside story 《of *a matter*》. ¶ 어떤 ~인지 모르다 be not in the know; be ignorant about things.

**코** ① [일반적] a nose; a trunk (코끼리의); a muzzle (개·말 따위의); a snout (돼지의). ¶ 들창코 a turned-up nose / 매부리코 a Roman nose; an aquiline 〔a hooked〕 nose / 사자코 a snub 〔pug〕 nose / 안장코 a short, flat nose; a blunt, fleshy nose / 뾰족코 a pointed nose / 주부코 a bulbous red nose; a whiskey nose / 우뚝한 코 a prominent nose; a shapely nose / 잘생긴 코 a shapely 〔well-cut〕 nose / 코먹은 소리 a nose voice; crooning (가수의) / 코먹은 소리를 하다 speak through the nose / 바로 코앞에서 under *one's* very nose; right before *one* / 코에서 단내가 나다 be dead tired; be fagged out; get tired 《of》.
코가: 코가 납작한 flat-nosed / 코가 찌그러진 사람 a person with a broken nose / 코가 납작해지다 [비유적] lose *one's* face; be humiliated; be taken down a peg / 코가 막히다 *one's* nose is stuffed 〔stopped, bunged〕 up / 코가 예민하다 have a good 〔keen, sharp〕 nose; have a good scent / 코가 예민한 《개 등의》 quick-scented / 코가 우뚝하다 [비유적] be elated 《over》; be puffed up 《with grid》.
코를: 코를 골다 snore; sleep audibly / 코를 납작하게 하다 [비유적] humble 《*a person's*》 pride; snub 《*a person*》; put 《*a person's*》 nose out of joint; take 《*a person*》 down a peg or two; crop 《*a person's*》 feathers / 코를 닦다 wipe *one's* nose / 코를 쥐다 pinch *one's* nose 〔nostrils〕; hold *one's* nose / (냄새가) 코를 찌르다 be offensive to the nose 〔smell〕; stink / 코를 킁킁거리다 sniff; whimper; whine (개 등이) / 코를 후비다 pick *one's* nose / 코를 잡아도 모르겠다 be as dark as pitch; be pitch=black. ¶ 나는 그와 매일 코를 맞대고 일한다 I work face-to-face with him every day. / 클레오파트라의 코가 조금만 낮았다면 세계의 역사는 바뀌었을 것이다 If Cleopatra's nose had been a little lower, the history of the world might have been different.
② 《콧물》 nasal mucus; snivel; snot 《비어》. ¶ 코를 닦다 wipe *one's* running nose / 코를 풀다 blow *one's* nose / 코를 흘리다 snivel; drivel; run at the nose / 코를 흘리는 아이 a child with a running nose / 코를 훌쩍이다 sniffle; snivel / 코 묻은 돈 a child's pocket money.
③ 《물건의》 the nose; the tip; the end; the toe. ¶ 신코 the toe 〔the front end〕 of a shoe / 버선코 the toe of a sock.
④ 《그물의》 the individual loops making up a net.

**코감기**(—感氣) a cold in the head 〔nose〕; coryza. ¶ ~에 걸려 있다 have a cold in the nose 〔head〕/ 코감기로 냄새를 못 맡는다 I cannot smell with a cold in the nose.

**코걸이** ① 《씨름에서》 a nose-grip; a nostril-grip. ② 《코에 거는》 a nose pendant 〔ring〕. ¶ 귀에 걸면 귀걸이, 코에 걸면 ~ differ with the circumstances.

**코골다** snore. ¶ 코고는 소리 snoring; a snore / 코고는 사람 a snorer / 드르렁드르렁 ~ snore loudly 〔terribly〕; blow 〔snore〕 like a grampus; "saw timber" / 코를 골기 시작하다 fall to snoring / 드러눕자 곧 코를 골다 plunge into a noisy sleep.

**코끝** the tip of a nose. ¶ 그는 나를 ~으로 부리려 한다 He turns up his nose at me.

**코끼리** an elephant. ¶ ~ 같은 elephantine; elephant-like / 흰~ a white 〔an albino〕 elephant / 수〔암〕~ a bull 〔cow〕 elephant / ~ 부리는 사람 an elephant trainer 〔driver〕; a mahout (인도의) / ~의 코 the trunk 〔proboscis〕 of an elephant. ◉ ~사냥 elephant hunting. 아프리카〔인도〕~ an African 〔Indian〕 elephant.

**코납작이** ①《코가 납작한》 a flat-nosed person. ②《기가 꺾인》 a person who has been taken down a peg (or two); a person frustrated by shame.

**코냑** 《브랜디》 cognac.

**코너** a corner; 《백화점 등의》 a special counter 〔section〕 《for children's wear》. ¶ ~를 찌르다 〖야구〗 clip the corner. ◉ ~워크 《투수의》 throwing strikes at the corners of the plate. ~킥 〖축구〗 a corner kick.

**코네티컷** 《미국의 주》 Connecticut (생략 Conn.).

**코넷** 〖악기〗 a cornet; a cornet-à-pistons. ¶ ~ 연주자 a cornet(t)ist.

**코높다** [비유적] (be) proud; "snooty" 《미구어》; [서술적] be elated 《over》; be puffed up 《with pride》; have *one's* nose in the air.

**코닌** 〖화학〗 conine(e); coniine.

**코다** 〖음악〗 a coda.

**코담배** snuff. ¶ 한 줌의 ~ a pinch of snuff / ~를 맡다 take (a pinch of) snuff.

**코대답**(—對答) an indifferent 〔a nonchalant〕 answer. ~하다 answer indifferently 〔nonchalantly, with no great enthusiasm〕.

**코데인** 〖화학〗 codeine.

**코도반** cordovan (leather); Spanish leather.

**코드** ①《줄》 a cord; 《전깃줄》 (an) electric cord; (a) flex. ②《암호》 a code. ◉ ~네임〔명〕 a code name. ~북 a code book. ~화 〖컴퓨터〗 coding. 오산검출(誤算檢出) ~ 〖컴퓨터〗 an error-detecting code. 자동검사~ 〖컴퓨터〗 a self checking code.

**코딱지** dried mucus from the nose; nose dirt; nose wax. ¶ ~가 생기다 nose wax gathers / ~를 후비다 pick *one's* nose.

**코떼다** get snubbed 〔humbled, spurned, rejected〕; get a snub; be put to shame. ¶ 돈 꾸어 달랬다가 ~ get turned down cold trying to borrow money / 월급을 올려 달랬다가 ~ have *one's* request for a raise flatly rejected.

**코뚜레** a nose ring. ¶ 쇠~ a cow's nose ring.

**코란** 〖종교〗《회교 경전》 the Koran. ¶ ~의 Koranic.

**코랄** 〖음악〗 a choral(e). ¶ 바흐의 ~ a Bach chorale.

**코러스** 〖음악〗《합창》 a chorus. ¶ ~를 하다 sing in chorus.

**코로나** 〖천문〗 a corona (*pl.* ~s, -nae). ¶ ~의 광망 coronal streamers. ◉ ~방전〔전압〕 corona discharge 〔voltage〕.

**코르덴** corduroy. ¶ ~바지 corduroy pants; (a pair of) corduroys / ~제품 corduroys.

**코르사코프병**(—病) 〖의학〗 Korsakoff's paychosis 〔syndrome〕.

**코르셋** a corset; corsets.

**코르크** cork; a cork (마개). ¶ ~제(製)의 cork 《sole》. ◉ ~나무 〖식물〗 a cork tree (황벽나무); a cork oak. ~마개 a cork stopper: ~ 마개를 한 병 a corked bottle / ~ 마개를 하다〔뽑다〕 cork (up) 〔uncork〕 《a bottle》. ~(마개)뽑이 a corkscrew. ~제품 corks. ~조직 〖식물〗 corky tissue. ~질(質) 〖생화〗 suberin(e): ~질화(化) 〖식물〗 suberization / ~질화하다 suberize. ~판 a cork board 〔sheet〕. ~피층(皮層) 〖식물〗 cork phellogen.

**코린트식**(—式) 〖건축〗 the Corinthian order. ¶ ~기둥 a Corinthian column.

**코막힘** nasal congestion.

**코만치족**(—族) a Comanche (*pl.* ~(s)).

**코맹맹이** a person who twangs; a person who speaks through the nose. ◉ ~소리 a nasal voice; a twang: ~ 소리하다 twang; speak through the nose.

**코머거리** a person with a stopped-up 〔congested〕 nose.

**코멘트** 《논평》 (a) comment. ¶ ~를 하다 make comment 《on》. ◉ 노~ No comment.

**코모로** (the Federal Islamic Republic of the) Comoros.

**코뮈니케** 《공식 성명》 a *communiqué* (F.). ¶ ~를 발표하다〔읽다〕 issue 〔read〕 a *communiqué*. ◉ 공동~ a joint *communiqué*.

**코뮌** 《행정구》 a commune. ¶ 파리 ~ the Paris Commune.

**코뮤니스트** a communist.

**코뮤니즘** 《공산주의》 communism.

**코미디** (a) comedy. ¶ 홈~ a sitcom [<*sit*uation *com*edy] / 나는 비극보다 ~

를 좋아한다 I prefer comedy to tragedy.
**코미디언** a comedian.
**코믹** a comic; 《신문 따위의 만화》 the comics 《미》; a comic strip. ¶ ~한 comic 《act》; comical.
**코민테른** the Comintern. [< *Com*munist *Intern*ational]
**코민포름** the Cominform. [< *Com*munist *Inform*ation Bureau]
**코밑** ¶ ~에 under the nose. ◉ ~수염 《wear》 a mustache.
**코바늘** a crochet「hook 〔needle〕.
**코발트** 〖화학〗 cobalt (기호 Co). ¶ ~빛의 cobaltic / ~를 함유하는 cobaltous. ◉ ~블루 cobalt blue; azure blue. ~색 cobalt. ~철 ferrocobalt. ~폭탄 a cobalt bomb; a C-bomb.
**코방귀** a pooh-pooh; a snort; pooh=poohing; snorting 《at》. ¶ ~ 뀌다 snort 〔sniff〕 at; turn up *one's* nose at; treat 《*a person*》 with「contempt 〔disdain〕.
**코방아찧다** fall flat on *one's* face.
**코볼** 〖컴퓨터〗 《사무용 프로그래밍 언어》 COBOL. [< *co*mmon *b*usiness *o*riented *l*anguage]
**코브라** 〖동물〗 a cobra.
**코빼기** ① 《비어》 = 코. ② 《얼굴》 a face. ¶ ~도 볼 수 없다 see nothing of 《*a person*》.
**코뼈** the nasal bone.
**코뿔소** 〖동물〗 a rhinoceros; a rhino 《구어》.
**코사인** 〖수학〗 cosine (생략 cos).
**코사크** Cossack. ◉ ~병(兵) a Cossack.
**코세다** (be) hardnosed; stiffnecked; stubborn; headstrong; self-assertive. ¶ 코센 사람 a self-assertive fellow; a「stubborn 〔hardnosed〕 person.
**코스** ① 《경로·여행 등의》 a course; 《경기장 등의》 a lane; a track; a route; 《골프의》 a golf course; a fairway. ¶ 제3 ~ Lane No. 3. / 남쪽〔북쪽〕 ~ the「southern 〔northern〕 route / 당일치기 ~ a one-day course 《of a trip》 / 하이킹 ~ a hiking trail / ~를 취하다 take a course / ~를 바꾸지 않다 hold 〔keep on〕 *one's* course / (골프에서) ~를 돌다 play a round / 전(全) ~를 완주하다 complete 〔finish〕 the course; stay the course 《in a marathon》; run the whole course / (로켓 등이) 제 ~에서 벗어나다〔벗어나지 않다〕 be「off 〔on〕 true course.
② 《학과 과정》 a course (of study). ¶ 박사 학위 ~ the doctor's course / 진학〔취직〕 ~ a「college 〔vocational〕 course / 프랑스어 ~를 택하다 take a course in French. ③ 《양식의》 ¶ 다섯 ~의 식사 a five-course dinner / 프랑스 요리의 풀코스 a full-course meal of French cuisine.
**코스닥** 〖증권〗 Korea Securities Dealers Automated Quotations (생략 KOSDAQ) (한국의 벤처 기업 육성을 위해 미국의 나스닥(NASDAQ)을 본떠 1996년에 설립된 주식 시장).
**코스모스** 〖식물〗 a cosmos.
**코스모트론** 〖물리〗 a cosmotron.
**코스타리카** 《중앙 아메리카의 공화국》 Costa Rica. ¶ ~의 Costa Rican. ◉ ~ 사람 a Costa Rican.
**코스튬** 《복장》 a costume; 《무대의상》 a theatrical costume.
**코스트** 《비용》 cost. ¶ 높은 ~ the high cost 《of an article》 / ~를 낮추다 reduce 〔cut down〕 the cost / 생산 ~의 절감을 꾀하다 try to reduce the cost of production / 우리는 생산 ~를 낮추었다 We lowered the cost of production. ◉ ~다운〔업〕「a reduction 〔an increase〕 in costs: 그 새로운 기술로 생산비가 ~ 다운〔업〕된다 The new technique will reduce 〔increase〕 the cost of production. ~(푸시)인플레이션 cost(-push) inflation.
**코스피** 《한국의 종합 주가지수》 KOSPI. [< the *Ko*rea *S*tock *P*rice *I*ndex]
**코싸쥐다** cover *one's* face for shame; hang *one's* head in shame.
**코안경**(一眼鏡) a *pince-nez* (F.).
**코알라** 〖동물〗 a koala (bear).
**코앞** ¶ ~에 right before *one*; under *one's* (very) nose; before *one's* eyes / ~에 닥치다 be「near 〔close〕 at hand; be imminent; be just ahead / ~에 닥친 impending; imminent 《danger》 / 단도를 ~에 들이대다 present a dagger under 《*a person's*》 nose / ~의 것을 못 보다 fail to see what is right under *one's* nose.
**코오디네이터** 《조정자》 a coordinator.
**코요테** 〖동물〗 a coyote.
**코웃음** a sneer; sneering. ~ 치다 sniff 《at》; sneer 《at》; laugh ironically.
**코인** 《화폐》 a coin. ◉ ~로커 a coin (-operated) locker.
**코일** 〖전기〗 a coil. ◉ 2차~ a secondary coil.
**코즈머폴리터니즘** 《세계주의》 cosmopolitanism.
**코즈머폴리턴** a cosmopolitan; a cosmopolite.
**코즈메틱** 《화장품》 《apply》 cosmetics.
**코찡찡이** a habitual「sniffer 〔sniffler〕.
**코청** 〖해부〗 the nasal septum.
**코치** 《행위》 coaching; training; 《사람》 a coach. ~하다 coach 《a team》. ¶ 야

구~ a baseball coach / 배팅 ~를 받다 be coached on batting / 야구팀을 ~하다 coach a baseball team.
◉ ~박스 〖야구〗 a coach's box.

**코침** tickling 《*a person's*》 nose. ~주다 tickle 《*a person's*》 nose.

**코카인** 〖화학〗 cocain(e). ◉ ~중독 cocainism; cocaine poisoning 〔addiction〕: ~ 중독자 a cocainist; a coke addict.

**코카콜라** 《상표명》 Coca-Cola; Coke. ¶ ~를 마시다 have a Coke.

**코카타르** 〖의학〗 nasal catarrh.

**코코넛** 〖식물〗 a coconut.

**코코아** 《음료》 cocoa; a cocoa tree (나무). ¶ ~를 마시다 drink 〔have〕 cocoa / ~를 홀짝거리다 sip cocoa.
◉ ~열매 a cocoa 〔cacao〕 bean; a cacao.

**코코야자**(一椰子) 〖식물〗 a coconut palm 〔tree〕; 《열매》 a coconut.

**코크스** 《연료》 coke. ¶ ~용 탄(炭) coking coal / ~를 때다 burn coke 《in a stove》 / ~를 연료로 하다 use coke for fuel. ◉ ~가마 a coking still. ~로(爐) a coke oven.

**코탄젠트** 〖수학〗 cotangent (생략 cot).

**코털** the hairs in 〔of〕 the nostrils; a vibrissa (*pl.* -rissae). ¶ ~을 뽑다 pull out the hairs out of the nostrils.

**코트**[1] 《양복의 상의》 a coat; a jacket; 《외투》 an overcoat. ¶ ~를 입다〔벗다〕 put on 〔take off〕 a coat / ~를 입고 있다 wear a coat.

**코트**[2] 《구기의》 a 《tennis》 court. ¶ ~를 만들다 lay out a court.

**코트디부아르** 《나라 이름》 (the Republic of) Côte d'Ivoire; the Ivory Coast.

**코트라** 《대한 무역투자 진흥공사》 KOTRA. [<*Ko*rea *Tra*de-Investment Promotion Agency]

**코튼** cotton. ◉ ~사(絲) machine cotton; cotton thread.

**코티손** 〖생화학〗 cortisone.

**코팅** 《천·렌즈 등의》 coating.

**코페르니쿠스** 《폴란드의 천문학자》 Nicolaus Copernicus (1473-1543). ¶ ~의 지동설 the Copernican theory (of the universe).

**코펜하겐** 《덴마크의 수도》 Copenhagen.

**코펠** a camp stove; *Kocher* (G).

**코풀다** blow the 〔*one's*〕 nose. ¶ 팽하고 ~ blow *one's* nose with a loud trumpeting noise.

**코프라** copra. ◉ ~유(油) copra oil.

**코피** blood from the nose; nosebleed(ing); nasal hemorrhage; 〖병리〗 epistaxis. ¶ ~가 나다〔를 쏟다〕 bleed at the nose; have a nosebleed 〔bloody nose〕; *one's* nose bleeds.

**코허리** the narrow part of the nose (at the base). ¶ ~가 시큰해지다 be almost moved to tears; be touched with compassion.

**코흘리개** a snotty(-nosed) kid; a snotnose; a sniveler.

**콕**[1] 〖기계〗 a cock; 《수도·가스의》 a tap; a faucet 《미》.

**콕**[2] ① 《찌르는 모양》 stinging; piercing; thrusting; poking; pricking; 《냄새·맛이》 biting; pungently. ¶ 바늘로 콕 찌르다 prick with a needle / 벌이 콕 쏘다 a bee stings abruptly 〔sharply〕 / 고추가 콕 쏘다 (red) pepper 「stings 〔bites〕 the tongue 〔is stinging hot〕 / 팔꿈치로 콕 찌르다 nudge 《*a person*》 with *one's* elbow / 아무의 옆구리를 콕 찌르다 poke 《*a person*》 in the ribs / 코를 콕 쏘다 assail *one's* nostrils.
② 《쪼다》 pecking; picking. ¶ 닭이 땅을 콕 쪼다 a hen pecks at ground.

**콕콕** ① 《쏘는 모양》 (***a***) 《찌르는 모양》 repeatedly stinging 〔piercing, thrusting, poking, pricking〕. ¶ 고추가 매워 ~쏘다 red pepper keeps *one's* tongue stinging / 바늘로 ~ 찌르다 keep pinpricking with a needle / 아무의 옆구리를 ~ 찌르다 keep poking 《*a person*》 in the ribs. (***b***) 《아픈 모양》 ¶ ~ 쏘는 통증 a smarting pain / ~ 쑤시다 sting; have a throbbing pain; 《상처가》 tingle 〔smart, throb〕 (with pain).
② 《쪼다》 repeatedly pecking; picking. ¶ 닭이 병아리를 ~ 쪼다 a hen keeps pecking away at a chick.

**콘** a 〔an ice-cream〕 cone.

**콘덴서** 〖전기〗 a condenser; a capacitor.

**콘덴스트밀크** condensed milk (농축우유).

**콘도르** 〖조류〗 a condor.

**콘도(미니엄)** a condominium (unit).

**콘돔** a condom; a (contraceptive) sheath; a rubber 《속어》.

**콘(드)비프** corn(ed) beef. ◉ ~통조림 a canned corn beef.

**콘사이스** concise. ¶ ~형 사전 a pocket(-sized) dictionary.

**콘서트** a concert. ¶ ~를 열다 give a concert. ◉ ~마스터 a concertmaster. ~홀 a concert hall.

**콘센서스** 《대다수의 의견》 a consensus. ¶ ~를 얻다 gain 〔win〕 a consensus.

**콘센트** 〖전기〗 a (wall) socket; a 〔an electric〕 point; 《미》 a wall 〔service, convenience〕 outlet; an outlet 《미》

(★ 콘센트는 한국식 영어). ¶ ~에 플러그를 꽂다 insert a plug in a wall outlet; plug in. 「*certo* (It.).

**콘체르토** 〖음악〗 a 《piano, violin》 *con-*

**콘체른** 《기업 합동》 a combine. [< *Konzern* (G.)]

**콘크리트** concrete. ¶ ~의 concrete / ~ 건물 a concrete building / 아직 굳지 않은 ~ fresh concrete / ~를 하다 concrete 《the pavement》; cover 〔lay, treat〕 《*something*》 with concrete. ◉ ~ 기초 공사 ground concrete work. ~노반(路盤) a concrete bed. ~믹서 a concrete mixer: ~ 믹서차 a cement mixer on wheels. ~바닥 a concrete floor. ~배송탑(配送塔) 〖토목〗 a concrete distributing tower. ~블록 a concrete block. ~포장 concrete pavement. 현장배합 ~ cast-in-place concrete.

**콘택트** 〖전기〗 contact; 〖사진〗 a contact print. ◉ ~ 렌즈 a contact lens: ~ 렌즈를 끼우다 wear contact lenses. ~송신 〖전자〗 contact sending. 「contest.

**콘테스트** a contest. ◉ 미인 ~ a beauty

**콘트라베이스** 〖악기〗 a double bass; a contrabass. ◉ ~연주자 a contrabassist; a bassist (댄스 밴드의).

**콘트라스트** 《대조·대비》 a contrast. ¶ ~를 이루다 (be in) contrast with.

**콘트랄토** 〖음악〗 a *contralto* (It.).

**콘티넨털** 《대륙의》 continental. ◉ ~탱고 the continental tango.

**콘티(뉴이티)** 〖영화〗 a continuity.

**콘플레이크** 《아침 식사용》 cornflakes.

**콜걸** 《전화 호출 매춘부》 a call girl.

**콜드게임** 〖야구〗 a called game 《미》. ¶ 폭우로 ~이 되었다 The game was called (off) because of a heavy rain.

**콜드크림** cold cream. 「《영》.

**콜드퍼머넌트** a cold wave; a cold perm

**콜라** 〖식물〗 a kola 〔cola〕 tree; a kola. ¶ ~ 열매 a kola 〔cola〕 nut; a kola.

**콜라주** 〖미술〗 collage.

**콜럼버스** 《이탈리아의 항해가》 Christopher Columbus (1451-1506). ¶ ~의 아메리카 발견 Columbus' discovery of America 〔the New World〕.

**콜레라** 〖의학〗 cholera. ¶ ~의 유행 an epidemic of cholera / ~가 발생〔만연, 유행〕하다 cholera breaks out 〔spreads, prevails〕 / ~에 걸리다 be infected with cholera / ~의 예방 주사를 하다 〔놓다〕 inoculate 《*a person*》 against cholera; 《본인이 맞다》 have a shot 《in the arm》 against cholera. ◉ ~균 a cholera germ 〔bacillus (*pl.* -cilli)〕; a comma (bacillus). ~방역 본부 Anti-cholera Headquarters. ~ 예방 주사 (an) anticholera injection: ~ 예방 주사액 the anticholera serum. ~ 오염 지역 the cholera afflicted areas. ~왁친〔백신〕 cholera vaccine. ~환자 a cholera patient; a case of cholera. 닭~ fowl 〔chicken〕 cholera. 돼지~ hog cholera. 의사(擬似)~ a suspected case of cholera; a quasi-cholera.

**콜레스테롤** 〖생화학〗 cholesterol. ¶ 낮은 〔높은〕~ 식품 low-〔high-〕cholesterol food / 그런 음식은 혈액 속의 ~치를 높인다 That sort of food will raise the cholesterol level in your blood.

**콜로라도** 《미국의 주》 Colorado (생략 Colo., Col.).

**콜로라투라** 〖음악〗 *coloratura* (It.); colorature. ◉ ~ 소프라노 *coloratura* soprano: ~ 소프라노 가수 a *coloratura* (soprano). 「um.

**콜로세움** 《원형 대경기장》 the Colosse-

**콜로이드** 〖화학〗 colloid. ¶ ~(성)의 colloidal. ◉ ~용액〔연료〕 colloidal solution 〔fuel〕. ~은(銀)〔금〕 colloidal silver 〔gold〕.

**콜로타이프** 〖인쇄〗 a collotype; a photogelatine process. ¶ ~로 인쇄하다 collotype; 《부탁해서》 have 《*a thing*》 collotyped. ◉ ~제판 the collotype 〔phototype〕 process. ~판(版) a collotype plate.

**콜록거리다** keep coughing 〔hacking〕.

**콜록쟁이** a person with a hacking cough; an asthmatic patient.

**콜록콜록** coughing 〔hacking〕 away. ¶ ~ 기침을 하다 keep coughing 〔hack-

**콜론**[1] a colon. ⌊ing〕.

**콜론**[2] 〖금융〗 a call loan; a demand loan.

**콜롬보** 《스리랑카의 수도》 Colombo. ◉ ~계획 the Colombo Plan.

**콜롬비아** 《남미의 공화국》 (the Republic of ) Colombia. ¶ ~의 Colombian. ◉ ~사람 a Colombian.

**콜리** 《개의 품종》 a collie.

**콜머니** 〖금융〗 call money.

**콜사인** 《전파 호출 부호》 a call sign 〔signal〕; call letters.

**콜콜** 《물이》 gushingly; 《잠을》 《sleep》 soundly; deeply; calmly. ⇨ 쿨쿨. ¶ (물이) ~ 샘솟다 gush up 〔out〕; well up / 잠을 ~ 자다 sleep soundly; sink into a heavy sleep.

**콜타르** 〖화학〗 coal-tar; tar. ¶ ~ 크레오소트〔피치〕 coal-tar creosote 〔pitch〕 / ~를 바르다 tar.

**콜택시** a call taxi.

**콜트** 《권총》 [<Samuel *Colt*] a Colt pistol.

**콜호스** 《구소련의 집단 농장》 a *kol*(*k*)*hos* (Russ.); colkhozs; a collective farm.

**콜히친** 〖약〗 colchicine. ◉ ~제제(製劑) 「colchicum.

**콤마** ① 《구두점의》 a comma. ¶ ~로 끊다 put 〔insert〕 a comma; punctuate with a comma. ② 〖수학〗 a decimal point. ¶ ~ 이하 below the decimal; [비유적] below the average / ~ 이하의 인간 a man below the average; a nobody.

**콤바인** 《농기계》 a combine harvester; 「a combine.

**콤비** combination. ¶ 명~ a 「good 〔happy〕 combination / …와 ~로 in combination with… / …와 ~가 되다 (form a) pair with… / …와 ~가 되어(서) 하다 join force with…; tie up with… / 그는 B씨와 ~다 His closest 「partner 〔associate〕 is Mr. B. ◉ ~블로 〖권투〗 a combination (blow).

**콤비나트** [< *kombinat* (Russ.)] an industrial complex. ¶ 석유 화학 ~ a petrochemical complex.

**콤비네이션** ⇨ 콤비.

**콤팩트** a compact. ◉ ~디스크 a compact disk (생략 CD).

**콤퍼지션** (a) composition.

**콤플렉스** 〖정신분석〗 complex (복합관념); 《열등 의식》 an inferiority complex. ¶ ~를 없애다 rid 《*a person*》 of *his* inferiority complex; dismiss a sense of inferiority (out of *one's* mind) / 그는 대학 출신자에게 ~를 느낀다 He feels inferior to university graduates.

**콧구멍** a nostril; the nostrils; the naris (*pl.* nares). ¶ ~을 벌름거리다 flare *one's* noses.

**콧김** the breath from the nose. ¶ ~을 쐬다 be exposed to the breath from the nose of 《*a person*》; [비유적] 《a woman》 be possessed by a man.

**콧날** the 「ridge 〔line〕 of the nose. ¶ ~이 서다 have a 「straight 〔high〕 nose.

**콧노래** crooning; humming through the nose. ~하다 croon; hum 〔sing〕 through the nose. ¶ ~를 부르며 일하다 do *one's* work humming a tune; hum songs at work.

**콧대** the bridge of the nose. ¶ ~가 높다 be 「proud 〔haughty, arrogant〕; be puffed up 《with pride》 / ~가 높은 사람 a high-hatted man; a high hat; a stuck-up person / ~가 세다 be self-assertive; be 「defiant 〔aggressive〕; be 「imperious 〔haughty〕 / ~가 센 사람 a self-assertive fellow; 「a defiant 〔an aggressive〕 person / ~를 꺾다 humble 《*a person's*》 pride; snub 《*a person*》 down; take 《*a person*》 down a peg; take the conceit out of 《*a person*》 / 한 밑천 생기자 그는 요즘 ~가 세어졌다 Having acquired a fortune he has grown quite arrogant lately.

**콧등** the ridge of the nose.

**콧마루** 「the ridge 〔the bridge〕 of the nose. ¶ ~가 높다 have a high-bridged nose.

**콧물** snivel; snot; nose 「runnings 〔drippings〕. ¶ ~을 닦다 wipe *one's* (running) nose / ~을 흘리다 snivel; drivel; run at the nose / ~을 훌쩍거리다 snivel; snuff; sniff.

**콧방울** the wings of the nose.

**콧병**(一病) ① 《코의 병》 nose 「trouble 〔ailment〕. ¶ ~을 앓다 have nose trouble. ② 《병아리의》 nasal congestion in chickens; croup.

**콧소리** ① 〖언어〗 a nasal (sound). ② 《코먹은 소리》 a nasal 「voice 〔tone, accent〕; a twang. ¶ ~로 말하다 speak through *one's* nose; nasalize the words; have a nasal 「tone 〔twang〕.

**콧수염**(一鬚髯) a moustache; a mustache 《미》. ¶ ~을 기르다 grow 〔cultivate〕 a mustache.

**콧숨** breathing through the nose. ¶ ~이 거칠다 breathe hard through the nose.

**콧잔등이** = 코허리.

**콩** a bean; beans; a soybean (대두); a pea (완두); a kidney bean (강낭콩). ¶ 검은콩 a black soybean / 커피콩 《roast》 coffee beans / 볶은 콩 parched beans / 땅콩 a peanut / 튀긴 콩 popped beans / 콩을 볶다 parch 〔roast〕 beans / 콩을 물에 담가(서) 불려 두다 keep beans 「steeped 〔soaked〕 in water / 콩밭에서 팥이 나랴 《속담》 An onion will not produce a rose. / 콩 심은 데 콩 나고 팥 심은 데 팥 난다 《속담》 Don't expect the extraordinary. *or* Like father, like son.

**콩가루** soybean flour.

**콩강정** a glutinous cake covered with roasted soybean.

**콩고** (the People's Republic of) Congo. ¶ ~의 Congolese. ◉ ~사람 a Congolese.

**콩고레드** 〖화학〗 Congo Red.

**콩고물** soybean flour. ◉ ~떡 rice cake coated with soybean flour.

**콩과**(一科) 〖식물〗 the pulse family;

*Leguminosae* (학명). ¶ ~ 식물 a leguminous [podded] plant.
**콩국** soybean soup. 「glomerate.
**콩글로머릿** 『경영』《복합 기업》 a con-
**콩기름** soy(bean) oil; (soya) bean oil; peanut oil (낙화생 기름).
**콩깍지** bean chaff; a bean hull [shuck]; peas(e)cod (완두의). ¶ ~를 까다 pod [hull] beans; shell peas.
**콩깻묵** bean cake; soybean (oil) meal.
**콩꼬투리** a bean [pea] pod; a legume.
**콩나물** bean sprouts.
◉ ~교실 an overcrowded classroom. ~국 bean-sprout soup. ~대가리 《음표》 a musical note. ~밥 rice cooked with bean sprouts. ~버스 an overloaded [a jam-packed] bus. ~시루 a jar for growing bean sprouts: ~ 시루 같다 be packed [jammed] like sardines; be jammed up.
**콩대** a beanstalk.
**콩댐** 《장판의》 waxing with ground beans. ~하다 wax 《the floor paper》 with ground beans. 「moth.
**콩독나방**(―毒―) 『곤충』 a yellow "bean"
**콩멍석** a straw mat spread out with beans. ¶ 빈대한테 물려 온몸이 ~이 되었다 I have swellings all over from bug bites.
**콩바구미** 『곤충』 a seed beetle.
**콩밥** boiled bean-mixed rice; 《죄수의 밥》 prison food [rations]. ¶ ~ 먹다 [비유적] serve a jail [prison] term; do [serve] time 《at》 / ~을 먹이다 send 《*a person*》 to prison; land [run] 《*a person*》 in jail.
**콩버무리** bean-mixed rice cake.
**콩볶듯하다** 《guns》 keep popping like beans being roasted; crack; crackle; rattle; snap. ¶ 총소리가 ~ guns keep peppering away / 콩볶듯하는 기관총 소리 the cracking [rattle] of machine guns.
**콩새** 『조류』 a (Korean) hawfinch.
**콩설기** layered bean-mixed rice cake.
**콩소메** 『요리』 *consommé* (F.); consomme; clear soup.
**콩알** a grain of beans. ¶ ~크기의 pea-sized / 간이 ~만해지다 be held [kept] in suspense; have *one's* heart in *one's* throat; be in great fear.
**콩엿** wheat-gluten mixed with popped beans.
**콩잎가뢰** 『곤충』 a bean-leaf bug.
**콩자반**(―佐飯) beans boiled in soy-sauce.
**콩장**(―醬) parched, seasoned beans.
**콩죽**(―粥) rice and bean porridge.
**콩짜개** split beans [peas].
**콩찰떡** a glutinous rice cake with beans in it.
**콩케팥케** a medley; a topsy-turvy; a pell-mell; a jumble; an utter confusion. ¶ ~가 되다 be at sixes and sevens; be mixed up (promiscuously); be jumbled up / ~ 쌓아 놓다 pile 《it》 up pell-mell.
**콩콩** ⇨ 쿵쿵.
**콩쿠르** [<*concours* (F.)] a contest; a competition. ¶ 사진[영화]~ a camera [movie] *concours;* a photo [movie] contest / 음악~ a musical contest.
**콩탕**(―湯) "bean broth"; a soup made from bean flour.
**콩튀듯(팥튀듯)하다** jump up with anger; be hopping mad. ¶ 성이 나서 ~ be [get] hopping mad; be carried away by anger; be wild with rage.
**콩트** 『문학』 a (short) short story; a *conte* (F.).
**콩팔칠팔** incoherently; ramblingly; pointlessly. ~하다 gibber; ramble; talk incoherently. ¶ ~ 지껄이다 say incoherent things; make a rambling [pointless] speech; talk wild.
**콩팥**[1] 《콩과 팥》 soybeans and redbeans.
**콩팥**[2] 《신장》 the kidney. ¶ ~이 나쁘다 have a kidney trouble.
**콩풀** a blister on pasted paper [cloth].
**콰르텟** 『음악』 a quartet(te). ¶ 스트링~ a string quartet.
**콰이어** 《성가대》 a choir.
**콱** ① 《세게》 strongly; hard; violently; pungently (냄새가); 《밀거나 당길 때》 with a jerk; 《단단히》 tightly; firmly; fast. ¶ 콱 밀다 push with a (sudden) jerk; push 《*a thing*》 with force / (냄새가) 코를 콱 찌르다 assail *one's* nostrils / 칼로 콱 찌르다 stab 《*a person*》 through; thrust a dagger home / 옆구리를 콱콱 쥐어박다 keep poking 《*a person*》 in the ribs / 화살이 나무에 콱 박혔다 Arrows are stuck fast in a tree. ② 《막히는 모양》 quite; strongly; stiflingly. ¶ (구멍·관 등이) 콱 막히다 be stopped [plugged] up; be [get] blocked; get clogged [stuffed, bunged]; be choked / 대답이 콱 막히다 be at a loss for an answer / 숨이 콱 막히다 be choked [suffocated]; be stifled / 코가 콱 막히다 *one's* nose is stopped [stuffed] up / 하수구가 콱 막혀 있다 The drain is completely bunged up.
**콴톰** 『물리』《양자》 a quantum (*pl.* -ta).

**콸콸** gushingly; in spouts; in profusion; in a steady stream. ～하다, ～거리다 spout; gush; gurgle.
¶～ 쏟아져 나오다 flow out steadily; gush out《of》/ 샘이 ～ 솟아 나오다 a spring「gushes〔wells〕up; a spring spouts forth / 피가 ～ 쏟아지다 bleed profusely〔badly〕; blood flows out.

**쾅**《터질 때》with a「boom〔roar〕; bang;《떨어질 때》with a「bump〔thud, thump〕. ～하다 go boom; boom; go bump; thud. ¶ 쾅 부딪다 bump against《a wall》; bump into《a man》/ 쾅(하고) 떨어지다 fall「heavily〔with a thump〕/ 쾅 소리가 나다 (go) bang; go off with a bang / 대포를 쾅 쏘다 boom a gun / 짐을 쾅 내려놓다 thump a bundle down / 쾅하고 대포 소리가 들렸다 Bang went the gun. / 그는 문을 쾅 닫았다 He「shut the door with a bang. / 문이 쾅하고 닫혔다 The door banged「shut〔back〕. *or* The door shut with a bang.

**쾅쾅거리다**《터질 때》keep「booming〔roaring〕;《떨어질 때》keep「bumping〔thumping, thudding〕; reverberate; resound. ¶ 대포가 ～ guns are booming away / 뜰에 짐 내려놓는 소리가 ～ bundles come bumping down into the yard / 마루를 쾅쾅거리며 걷다 stamp along the floor.

**쾌**《북어 셀 때》a string (of 20 dried pollacks). ¶ 북어 두 쾌 two strings of 20 dried pollacks.

**쾌감**(快感)「a pleasant〔an agreeable〕feeling〔sensation〕; a feeling of pleasure; ecstasy;《성교시의》(an) orgasm. ¶～을 느끼다 feel good; have a「good〔nice〕feeling;《구어》get a kick《out of driving a car at full speed》; feel pleasure. ◉ ～대(帶) a comfort zone〔line〕.

**쾌거**(快擧) a「brilliant〔remarkable, spectacular〕achievement〔feat, deed〕. ¶근래의 ～이다 be the most (heart-) stirring achievement in these days / 그녀는 3개의 큰 대회에 연속 우승하는 ～를 이루었다 She achieved the brilliant feat of winning three consecutive major tournaments.

**쾌남아**(快男兒) a「fine〔spirited, good〕fellow; a jolly (good) fellow; a regular fellow《미》.

**쾌도**(快刀) a sharp「knife〔sword〕. ¶～ 난마(亂麻)의 솜씨를 보이다 cut the Gordian knot; act decisively to solve a complicated problem.

**쾌락**(快樂) (a) pleasure. ¶ 인생의 ～ the「pleasures〔joys〕of life / 육체적〔관능적〕～ the pleasures of senses; sensual〔carnal〕pleasures / ～에 빠지다「be given〔give *oneself* up〕to pleasure / ～을 추구하다 seek〔pursue〕pleasure / 인생의 온갖 ～을 다하다 drain the cup of pleasure to the dregs / 온갖 인생의 ～을 버리다 cut off all comforts in life. ◉ ～주의〔설〕hedonism; epicureanism: ～주의자 a hedonist; an epicurean.

**쾌락**(快諾) a「ready〔willing〕consent. ～하다 consent〔agree〕readily; give *one's*「ready〔willing〕consent《to》; accept《an offer》readily. ¶～을 얻다 be given a「ready〔hearty〕consent / 그녀는 나의 요구를 ～했다 She readily agreed to my request.

**쾌마**(快馬) a swift horse; a fleet steed.

**쾌면**(快眠)《have》a good sleep.

**쾌미**(快味) a pleasant taste;「an agreeable〔a pleasant〕sensation〔feeling〕. ¶ 스키의 ～ the「delight〔pleasure〕of skiing.

**쾌변**(快辯) eloquence; fluent speech. ¶～을 토하다 make an eloquent「address〔speech〕.

**쾌보**(快報) good news; glad tidings; a joyful report. ¶～를 전하다 convey the good news《to》/ ～에 접하다 receive welcome news / ～로 전 시가(市街)가 들끓었다 The good news threw the whole city into a wild joy.

**쾌사**(快事) a pleasant「event〔matter〕; a joyful event; a delight; amenities (of life). ¶ 그것은 근래의 ～로 여겨졌다 It was regarded as one of the most delightful event of recent days.

**쾌속**(快速) a「high〔great〕speed. ¶～의 high-speed; fast; swift; speedy / ～을 내다 put on a high speed / 1시간 200 킬로의 ～으로 달리다 run at the high speed of 200 kilometers an hour. ◉ ～선 a fast sailing「ship〔boat〕. ～열차 a rapid(-service) train. ～정 a speedboat.

**쾌승**(快勝)「an overwhelming〔a sweeping, a decisive〕victory. ～하다 win「a sweeping〔an overwhelming〕victory《over》; win easily; come off with flying colors.

**쾌유**(快癒) recovery《from illness》. ⇨ 쾌차(快差). ¶～를 빕니다 I wish you quick recovery (from your illness).

**쾌재**(快哉) ¶～를 부르짖다 cry out "bravo"; yell〔shout〕for〔with〕delight

〔joy〕; utter yells of delight; shout with exultation.

**쾌적**(快適) ～하다 (be) agreeable; comfortable; pleasant. ¶ 따뜻하고 ～한 아담한 방 a warm and cozy little room / ～한 기차 여행 a pleasant train trip / 소풍에 ～한 날씨 agreeable 〔lovely〕 weather for picnic. ◉ ～온도〔조건〕 the optimum 「temperature 〔conditions〕.

**쾌조**(快調) a 「good 〔best, perfect, favorable〕 condition. ¶ (선수의 상태가) ～이다 be in 「the best 〔top〕 condition; be in good 「form 〔shape〕 / ～로 나아가다〔진척되다〕 make 「good 〔steady〕 headway; progress smoothly / 만사가 ～이다 Everything is going 「well 〔smoothly〕. *or* Everything is coming along.

**쾌주**(快走) fast 「sailing 〔running〕. ～하다 sail 〔run〕 fast 〔at an exhilarating speed〕; scud 《across the waves》. ¶ 자동차는 ～했다 The car ran beautifully.

**쾌차**(快差) complete recovery; restoration to health. ～하다 recover completely 《from》; make a complete recovery 《from》; be completely restored to health; get 〔be〕 perfectly well again. ¶ 중병에서 ～하다 recover completely from a serious illness.

**쾌척**(快擲) ～하다 generously throw out; make a generous contribution; contribute generously; give 《a fund》 willingly. ¶ 천만 원을 ～하다 generously give a donation of 10 million won 《to, toward》.

**쾌청**(快晴) fine 〔fair〕 weather; a 「bright 〔clear〕 sky. ～하다 (be) (very) fine; be nice and fine. ¶ ～한 날 a clear day / 다행히 그 날은 ～했다 Fortunately 〔Luckily〕 the weather turned out fine on that day.

**쾌쾌하다**(快快—) (be) liberal; generous; big-hearted; large-minded; great; be dashing and daring. ¶ 쾌쾌히 liberally; generously; willingly; gladly; happily / 쾌쾌히 허락하다 consent gladly; permit generously.

**쾌하다**(快—) ① 《기쁘다》 (be) happy; delightful; delighted. ¶ 쾌한 소식 a happy news. ② 《몸이》 be well again; (be) recovered. ¶ 몸이 이제 아주 ～I am perfectly well again.

**쾌한**(快漢) a jolly fellow; a nice man; a brick 《구어》; a regular guy 《미》.

**쾌활**(快活) ～하다 (be) cheerful; jolly; merry; jovial; lively; lighthearted. ¶ ～히 cheerfully; merrily; with a light heart / ～한 사람 a 「jolly 〔jovial〕 fellow; a 「cheerful 〔lively, merry, lighthearted〕 person; a person of 「cheerful 〔sunny〕 disposition.

**쾌히**(快—) ① 《기꺼이》 gladly; readily; willingly; with pleasure; with (a) good grace. ¶ ～ 승낙하다 agree 〔consent〕 readily 〔willingly〕 《to it》; give *one's* ready consent 《to》; readily accept 《an offer》 / 돈을 ～ 꾸어주다 lend money with (a) good grace / 부탁을 ～ 들어주다 be quite ready to comply with 《*a person's*》 request / 남의 충고를 ～ 받아들이다 take another's advice in good part. ② 《병이》 completely; nicely. ¶ 병이 ～ 낫다 be completely recovered from illness.

**쿠냥** [＜姑娘 (中)] a (Chinese) girl.

**쿠데타** 〖정치〗 a coup d'état (F.); a coup. ¶ 무혈～ a bloodless coup / ～를 일으키다 carry out a coup d'état; pull (off) a coup / ～를 모의하다 plot a coup d'état 《to overthrow the government》 / ～ 음모를 적발〔분쇄〕하다 uncover 〔foil〕 a coup plot.

**쿠렁쿠렁하다** (be) slack-filled; [서술적] be not full; be partly empty.

**쿠로시오** [＜黒潮(日)] the *Kuroshio* Current; the Japan Current 〔Stream〕; the Black Stream.

**쿠르드** ¶ ～의 Kurdish. ◉ ～말 Kurdish. ～사람 a Kurd. ～족 the Kurds.

**쿠릴** ¶ ～의 Kurilian. ◉ ～열도 the Kuril(e) Islands; the Kuriles. ～해류 the Kurilian Current.

**쿠바** (the Republic of) Cuba. ¶ ～의 Cuban. ◉ ～사람 a Cuban.

**쿠션** a cushion. ¶ 스리～ 〖당구〗 three-cushion 「billiards 〔carom〕; three cushions / ～이 좋은 의자 a soft, comfortable chair; a deep-cushioned seat / ～을 대다 cushion 《a seat》.

**쿠웨이트** 《중동의》 (the State of) Kuwait. ¶ ～의 Kuwaiti. ◉ ～사람 a Kuwaiti.

**쿠키** 《서양 비스킷》 a cookie 《미》; a cooky; 《영》 a biscuit.

**쿠페** 《소형 자동차》 a coupé; a coupe.

**쿠폰** a coupon; a voucher (식권·숙박권). ¶ (통신 판매 등의) 주문용 ～ an order coupon / ～으로 사다 purchase by means of coupon. ◉ ～제도 a coupon system.

**쿡**[1] 《요리사》 a 「cook; a chef. ◉ 쿡장 a head cook.

**쿡**[2] 《지르는 모양》 strongly; vigorously; hard. ⇨콕[2]. ¶ 단도로 쿡 찌르다 stab 《*a person*》 with a dagger; thrust a dagger home / 옆구리를 쿡 지르다 poke 〔nudge〕 《*a person*》 in the ribs.

**쿨러** 《냉각기》 cooler; 《냉방기》 an air conditioner. ¶ 카～ a 〔car cooler; a car air conditioner.

**쿨롬** 『전기』 a coulomb (생략 C). ¶ 10 ～ an abcoulomb. ◉ ～계 a coulomb meter; a coulometer.

**쿨리** [<苦力 (中)] a coolie; a cooly.

**쿨쿨**[1] 《물이》 gurgling. ～거리다[1] keep gurgling; gurgle and gurgle.

**쿨쿨**[2] 《잠을》 snoring; z-z-z. ～거리다[2] keep snoring. ¶ ～ 자다 sleep soundly 〔snoring〕; be fast asleep.

**쿵** plump; with a bang 〔bump, thud, thump〕; heavily. ¶ 쿵하고 떨어지다 fall plump 〔heavily, with a thud〕 / 쿵하고 부딪치다 bump against 《a wall》 / 쿵하고 짐을 바닥에 내려놓다 put down *one's* bundle on the floor with a thud / 쿵하고 쓰러지다 fall in 〔all of〕 a heap.

**쿵쾅거리다** keep banging 〔roaring, pounding〕; make a rattling sound; make 〔kick up〕 a racket. ¶ 쿵쾅거리는 포성 the roar of guns / 쿵쾅거리며 걷다 stamp along 《the floor》; walk along 《the passageway》 pit-a-pat 〔noisily〕 / 쿵쾅거리는 북소리가 들렸다 I heard a roll of drums.

**쿵쿵** ① 《떨어지는·부딪는 소리》 with thuds 〔thumps, plumps, flumps, bumps〕. ② 《북·포소리 등》 boom, boom; bang, bang. ¶ ～울리는 대포 소리 the booming sound of gun / 북을 ～ 울리다 rataplan; tomtom; beat loudly. ③ 《발소리》 stamping; treading noisily. ¶ 방안에서 ～거리며 거닐다 stamp about the room / ～거리며 계단을 오르다 stamp up the stairs / 마루 위를 ～거리며 달리다 《a child》 scamper around on the floor noisily. ④ 《찧는 소리》 pounding. ¶ ～ 방아를 찧다 pound 《grain》 with a pestle.

**쿵푸** [<工夫 (中)] kung fu; kung-fu.

**쿼츠** 《수정》 quartz. ◉ ～시계 a quartz watch 〔clock〕.

**쿼크** 『원자물리』 a quark.

**쿼터** ① 《4분의 1》 a 〔one〕 quarter. ¶ ～ 파이널 quarter final. ② 《할당》 quota; allotment. ¶ 수입 ～(량) an import (allotment) quota / ～를 삭감하다 cut the quota. ◉ ～량〔액〕 a quota; an allotment: 제조 ～량 production quotas. ～제 the quota system. ～제한 quota restrictions.

**쿼터백** 『미식 축구』 (a) quarterback (생략 q.b.). ¶ ～을 맡아보다 quarterback 《for a team》.

**쿼테이션** quotation. ◉ ～마크 quotation marks; inverted commas.

**쿼트** 《용량의 단위》 a quart.

**퀀셋** 『건축』 《상표명》 a Quonset hut 《미》; a Nissen hut.

**퀄퀄** gushing(ly); copiously; profusely. ⇨콸콸. ¶ ～ 쏟아져〔흘러〕 나오다 gush up 〔out〕; well up; spout forth; flow out steadily.

**퀑퀑** 《두드리는 소리》 rat(-a)-tat; 《총소리》 bang, bang; 《떨어지는 소리》 with thuds 〔thumps, plumps, bumps〕.

**퀘스천** a question. ◉ ～마크 a question mark; an interrogation mark 〔point〕: ～ 마크를 하다 put an interrogation mark.

**퀘이커** a Quaker; a Friend; a member of the Society of Friends.

**퀭하다** 《눈이》 (be) hollow; sunken; cavernous. ¶ 퀭한 눈 hollow eyes.

**퀴논** 『화학』 quinone.

**퀴놀린** 『화학』 quinoline.

**퀴륨** 『화학』 curium.

**퀴리** ① 《물리·화학자》 Marie Curie (1867-1934). ② 《물리학자·①의 남편》 Pierre Curie (1859-1906). ③ 《방사능 단위》 a curie (생략 Ci). ¶ 마이크로 ～ a microcurie / 밀리～ a millicurie.

**퀴즈** a quiz; a quiz game. ¶ 현상 ～쇼 《라디오·TV》 a giveaway show 〔program〕. ◉ ～프로 《라디오·TV》 a quiz program 〔show〕; a panel show: ～프로의 사회자 a quizmaster; 《영》 a question master / ～프로의 회답자 a contestant 〔competitor〕 (on a quiz show); a quiz panelist / 그녀는 TV의 ～프로에 나왔다 She appeared on the TV quiz program 〔show〕.

**퀴퀴하다** (be) fetid; stinking; foul-smelling; offensive; musty; moldy. ¶ 퀴퀴한 냄새 an offensive 〔a bad, a foul〕 smell / 생선이 썩어 ～ The fish is rotten and stinking.

**퀵** quick. ◉ 퀵모션 《with》 a quick motion. 퀵스텝 a quickstep. 퀵턴 a quick turn.

**퀸** a queen. ¶ 다이아몬드의 퀸 《카드놀이》 the queen of diamonds.

**퀸텟** 『음악』 a quintet(te).

**큐** ① 『당구』 a cue. ¶ 큐걸이 a cue rest 〔bridge〕 / 큐를 잡다 play billiards 《with》. ② 《신호》 a cue. ¶ 큐라이트 『TV』 cue light / 큐를 주다 cue; give 《*a person*》 a cue.

**큐비즘** 〖미술〗 cubism.
**큐시** 《품질 관리》 Q.C.; quality control.
**큐폴라** 〖화학〗 a cupola.
**큐피드** 〖로神〗 Cupid.
**크게** ① 《작지 않게》 large; big; greatly; in no small way; wide (넓게); extensively (광범하게); 《대규모로》 on a large scale; in a large 〔big〕 way.
¶ ∼ 되다 get bigger; grow larger; increase in size; 《중대화하다》 get 〔become〕 serious / ∼하다 make 《*a thing*》 larger; enlarge; magnify; extend (확장하다) / 사업을 ∼ 하다 carry on a business in a large way; carry on a large business / 사실을 ∼ 말하다 exaggerate 〔magnify〕 a fact / 일을 ∼ 만들다 aggravate a trouble; add fuel to the fire / 눈을 ∼ 뜨고 with *one's* eyes wide open / 가계에 영향을 ∼ 미치다 seriously affect *one's* household finances / 그 신문은 그 사건을 ∼ 다루었다 That paper 「played up the incident 〔gave the incident front page attention〕/ 그녀에게 ∼ 신세를 졌다 I owe her a great deal.
② 《매우》 very; much; far; greatly; largely; seriously; highly; remarkably; a great deal; to a great extent; in a large degree; to a considerable degree. ¶ ∼ 공헌하다 contribute largely toward; have an important role to play in; do much to 〔toward〕 / ∼ 기뻐하다 be very delighted; be highly pleased / ∼ 노염을 사다 give dire offense to 《*one's* master》 / ∼ 다르다 be widely different 《from》 / ∼ 도움이 되다 be very useful; be of great use 《to, for》 / ∼ 유행하다 have a great vogue; be much in vogue / ∼ 필요로 하다 be in great need; be needed badly / ∼ 환영하다 receive with open arms / ∼ 신세를 지고 있다 be deeply indebted to 《*a person*》 / 그 회사는 ∼ 적자를 내고 있다 The company 「is deeply in the red 〔has a large deficit〕.
**크기** 《사물의》 (a) size; dimensions (치수); magnitude (규모); volume (용적); bulk (부피); 《음량》 loudness; volume.
¶ ∼는 in size; in dimensions; in area (면적) / ∼에 따라서 according to size / 상당한 ∼의 fairly large-sized; good-sized; of reasonable dimensions / 중간 정도 ∼의 medium-〔moderate-〕sized / 그 방의 ∼ the dimensions of the room / 그 배의 ∼ the bulk of the ship / 그 수조의 ∼ the volume of the water tank / 개만한 ∼의 동물 a dog-sized animal / ∼가 다르다〔같다〕 differ 〔be equal〕 in size / ∼가 여러 가지로 다르다 vary in size / 같은 ∼이다 be of a 〔one〕 size / …쯤의 ∼이다 be about the size of…; be as large as… / 달걀의 절반〔갑절〕 ∼이다 be half 〔twice〕 the size of an egg / ∼는 나비 5미터 길이 6미터이다 《it》 measures 5 by 6 meters / 그것들은 대체로 같은 ∼이다 They are much of a size. / ∼는 어느 정도로 할까요 What size shall I make it? / 그것은 이 정도 ∼의 상자였다 《손짓을 하면서》 It was a box about this big. / 이 모형은 10분의 1 ∼로 만들어졌다 This model is made to a scale of 1/10 (★ 1/10 은 one-tenth로 읽음).
**크나큰** ever so big 〔large, great〕; as big 〔large, great〕 as can be; enormous; huge; colossal; gigantic. ¶ ∼ 건물 a massive building / ∼ 비용 an enormous expense; a huge cost / ∼ 잘못 a gross mistake; a grave 〔fatal〕 error.
**크낙새** 〖조류〗 a Korean redheaded woodpecker.
**크다**[1] ① 《형상이》 (be) big; large; great (★ big은 구체적 사물의 치수나 규모·범위가 크다는 뜻의 가장 구어적인 말. 또 정도를 나타내는 구어적 표현에도 쓰임: a big mistake. large는 big보다 덜 구어적, 수량이 많다는 뜻으로도 쓰임: a large population. great는 문어적인 말. 놀람·기쁨·노여움 따위의 감정이 수반됨. 정도를 뜻할 경우는 「위대한」이란 뜻이 암시됨: a great country).; grand; 《심하다》 (be) severe; heavy; 《거대하다》 (be) colossal; huge; gigantic; enormous; immense; 《광대하다》 (be) vast; extensive; spacious; 《부피가》 (be) bulky; massive; voluminous.
¶ 좀 큰 largish / 상당히 큰 of some size; good-sized; on the large side / 큰 인물 a man of great character 〔caliber〕 / 큰 잘못 a big 〔great, serious, gross〕 mistake; a grave error / 큰 것부터 작은 것의 순서로 늘어 놓다 arrange 《books》 in decreasing order of size / 야심이 ∼ have a great 〔high〕 ambition / 큰 기대를 걸다 expect great things from 《*a person, a thing*》 / 큰 의문으로 남다 remain a large question / A는 B보다 얼마나 큰가 How much larger is A than B? / 소년은 나이에 비해 ∼ The boy is big for his age.
② 《목소리가》 (be) loud; big. ¶ 큰 소

리 a big 〔loud〕 voice; a big sound 〔noise〕 (소음) / 큰 소리로 말할 수는 없지만 though this is not a thing to be openly 〔loudly〕 spoken about / 큰 소리쳐 미안하다 I'm sorry I yelled.
③ 《마음이》 (be) generous; liberal; magnanimous. ¶ 마음이 ～ be broad-minded 〔bighearted, generous, magnanimous〕; have a big heart / 손이 ～ have an open hand; be liberal 《of 〔with〕 *one's* money》; be generous 《with *one's* money》.

**크다**[2] 《자라다》 get 〔grow, become〕 big 〔taller〕; grow (up); fill out. ⇨ 커지다. ¶ 다 큰 아이 a grown-up child / 커서 옷을 못 입게 되다 outgrow *one's* clothes / 너 커서 무엇이 될래 What do you want to be when you grow up? / 전에 봤을 때보다 키가 컸구나 You have grown since I saw you last.

**크라운** 《왕관》 a crown. ◉ ～기어 a crown gear. ～유리 crown glass.

**크라이슬러** 《승용차 상표명》 a Chrysler. ¶ '95년도형 ～ the '95 model of the Chrysler.

**크라프트지**(—紙) kraft (paper).

**크래커** 《crunch》 a cracker. ◉ 소다～ a soda cracker.

**크랭크** a crank. ¶ ～업 하다 〖영화〗 finish filming / ～인 하다 〖영화〗 start filming. ◉ ～암 〖기계〗 a crank arm. ～축 〖기계〗 a crankshaft.

**크레디트** a credit. ¶ ～를 설정하다 establish 〔set up, open〕 a credit. ◉ ～타이틀 《영화 자막에 나오는 제작자·배우 등의 이름》 credit titles.

**크레디트카드** a credit card; a charge card; plastic (money) 《구어》: ～의 발행을 신청하다 apply for a credit card / ～로 지불하다〔사다〕 pay 〔buy 《*a thing*》〕 with *one's* credit card / 《상점 등에서》 ～를 사용할 수 있습니까 Do you accept credit cards?

> **참고 Cash or charge?**
> 미국의 슈퍼마켓에서는 계산을 할 때, 반드시 "Cash or charge?"라고 묻는다. 이 말은 「현금이세요? 아니면 카드세요?」라고 묻는 말이다.

**크레바스** 《빙하·설원의》 a crevasse.

**크레센도** 〖음악〗 crescendo (생략 cres., cresc.; 기호 <).

**크레오소트** creosote. ¶ ～의 creosotic; cresylic. ◉ ～유(油) creosote oil.

**크레용** (a) crayon. ¶ ～으로 그리다 draw 《a sketch》 with crayons 〔in crayon(s)〕. ◉ ～화 a drawing in crayon(s); a crayon drawing: ～화가 a crayonist.

**크레이터** 《분화구》 a 《lunar》 crater.

**크레이프** 《잔 주름이 진 직물》 crepe; *crepe* (F.); 《얇은 팬케이크》 a crepe. ◉ ～페이퍼 《포장·조화용》 crepe paper.

**크레인** 〖기계〗 a crane; a derrick (선박·부두의). ⇨ 기중기. ¶ ～으로 들어올리다 lift 〔hoist〕 《*a thing*》 with 〔by means of〕 a crane. ◉ ～선 a floating crane. ～운전사 a craneman; a crane operator. ～차 a crane truck.

**크레졸** cresol. ¶ ～의 cresylic. ◉ ～비누 cresol soap: ～비눗물 a saponated cresol solution. ～수 cresol water.

**크레틴병**(—病) 〖의학〗 cretinism. ◉ ～환자 a cretin.

**크레파스** a pastel crayon; a crayon pastel.

**크레펠린 검사**(—檢査) 〖심리〗 a Kraepelin census.

**크렘린** 《러시아 정부》 the Kremlin.

**크로노그래프** a chronograph.

**크로노미터** 《정밀 시계》 a chronometer.

**크로마뇽인**(—人) 〖인류〗 (a) Cro-Magnon man.

**크로마토그래프** 〖화학〗 a chromatograph.

**크로셰** ¶ ～ 뜨기 crochet work / ～ 바늘 a crochet hook 〔needle〕 / ～로 뜨다 crochet 《a shawl》.

**크로스** 《십자형》 a cross; 《교차하기》 crossing. ◉ ～레이트 〖경제〗 cross rates. ～바 a crossbar. ～스티치 《십자수》 (a) cross-stitch. ～오버 《입체 교차로·육교》 a crossover. ～워드 (퍼즐) a crossword puzzle: ～ 워드를 하다 do 〔work on〕 a crossword puzzle. ～카운터 〖권투〗 a cross (counter). ～컨트리 (레이스) a cross-country race; (a) cross-country.

**크로아티아** (the Republic of) Croatia ¶ ～의 Croatian / ～말 Croatian / ～사람 a Croatian.

**크로켓** 〖요리〗 a croquette (F.).

**크로키** 〖미술〗 a *croquis* (F.); a sketch; a rough draft.

**크롤**(**스트로크**) 〖수영〗 the crawl (stroke). ¶ ～로 헤엄치다 swim the crawl; crawl 《across a pool》 / ～을 배우다 learn the crawl.

**크롬** 〖화학〗 chrome; chromium (기호 Cr). ¶ 염화〔산화〕～ chrome chloride 〔oxide〕. ◉ ～강 chrome 〔chromium〕 steel. ～도금 chromium plating 〔plate〕: ～도금한 chrome-〔chromium-〕plated. ～명반 chrome alum. ～염료

a chrome dye. ～옐로 chrome yellow. ～처리 《염색에서》 chroming. ～철 ferrochrome. ～철광 chrome iron 〔ore〕; chromite.

**크루** 《배·비행기 등의 승무원》 a crew. ◉ ～컷 《짧게 깎은 머리》 a crew cut 〔haircut〕.

**크루즈미사일** 《순항 미사일》 a cruise missile.

**크리미아** 《우크라이나의 반도》 the Crimea. ◉ ～전쟁 the Crimean War.

**크리스마스** Christmas; Xmas 《구어》; 《당일》 Christmas Day. ¶ ～같은 〔분위기의〕 Christmasy; Christmassy / ～를 축하하다 keep 〔observe〕 Christmas / ～ 축하 인사를 하다 extend 〔offer〕 Christmas greetings 《to》 / ～ 쇼핑을 하다 do Christmas shopping / ～를 축하합니다 Merry Christmas! *or* A merry Christmas to you! ◉ ～선물 a Christmas present 〔gift〕. ～실 a Christmas seal. ～이브〔전야〕 《on》 Christmas Eve. ～캐럴 a Christmas carol. ～ 케이크 a Christmas cake. ～파티〔트리〕 a Christmas party 〔tree〕. ～휴가 the Christmas holidays 〔vacation〕.

**크리스마스카드** a Christmas card. ¶ ～를 받다 get a Christmas card 《from》 / ～를 보내다 send a Christmas card 《to》.

**크리스천** a Christian. ¶ ～답지 않은 unchristian. ◉ ～네임 a Christian name.

**크리스털** crystal. ◉ ～유리 crystal glass. ～정류기〔증폭기〕 a crystal rectifier 〔multiplier〕. ～제품 a crystal.

**크리켓** 〘스포츠〙 cricket. ¶ ～을 하다 play cricket. ◉ ～선수 a cricketer; a cricket player. ～팀 a cricket team; an eleven.

**크림** ① 《식품》 cream. ¶ ～ 그릇 a cream jug; a cream pitcher 《미》; a creamer 《미》 / 생～ fresh cream / ～ 모양의 creamy; creamlike / ～을 떠내다 skin off the cream 《from》 / (버터를 만들려고) ～을 휘젓다 churn cream. ② 《화장품》 《face, hand》 cream. ¶ 면도용～ shaving cream / 선탠～ suntan cream / ～을 바르다 cream 《*one's* face》; apply cream to 《*one's* hands》. ◉ ～빛 cream (color): ～ 빛의 cream-colored; cream 《curtains》; creamy. ～빵 a cream bun. ～소다 cream soda. ～소스 cream sauce. ～치즈 cream cheese.

**크립톤** 〘화학〙 krypton. ¶ ～ 86 krypton 86.

**크세논** 〘화학〙 xenon (기호 Xe).

**큰가시고기** 〘어류〙 a stickleback.

**큰개자리** 〘천문〙 the (Great) Dog; Canis Major.

**큰계집** *one's* legal wife (as opposed to *one's* concubine).

**큰고래** 〘동물〙 a razorback (whale); a finback; a rorqual.

**큰고랭이** 〘식물〙 a bulrush.

**큰골** 〘해부〙 the cerebrum.

**큰곰** 〘동물〙 a brown bear. ◉ ～자리 〘천문〙 the Great Bear; the Big Dipper; Ursa Major.

**큰기침** a big 'ahem'. ～하다 clear *one's* throat loudly (to draw attention); say a big 'ahem.' ¶ ～을 하고 방에 들어서다 go into the room with a big 'ahem'.

**큰길** a main 〔principal〕 street; 《영》 high street; a thoroughfare. ¶ ～을 활보하다 swagger along 〔strut on〕 the road.

**큰누이** *one's* eldest 〔oldest 《미》〕 sister.

**큰눈** a heavy (fall of) snow; a heavy snowfall. ¶ ～이 내렸다 It snowed heavily 〔hard〕.

**큰달** 《만월》 a full moon; 《긴달》 a 31-day month.

**큰대자**(一大字) ¶ ～로 눕다 lie at full length (with arms outstretched); lie spread-eagled 《on the grass》 / ～로 넘어지다 fall flat 〔full length〕.

**큰댁**(一宅) the head house. = 큰집.

**큰돈** a lot of money; a large 〔a big, an enormous〕 sum (of money); 《많은 비용》 a great cost. ¶ ～을 벌다 make a lot of money; realize a large profit; rake in money / ～을 투입하다 〔들이다〕 go to great expense; pay a big sum; 《투자하다》 invest a large sum 《in》 / ～을 써버리다 spend a great deal of money / ～이 들다 cost a great deal of money 〔a fortune〕 / ～을 들여서 짓다 build 《a hotel》 at a great 〔huge〕 cost / 나에겐 그런 ～이 나올 데가 없다 I don't know where I can get such a large sum.

**큰딸** *one's* eldest 〔oldest 《미》〕 daughter.

**큰마누라** *one's* wedded wife; a legal 〔lawful〕 wife.

**큰마음** ① 《대망》 (a) great ambition; great hopes 〔expectations〕; best wishes. ¶ ～을 품다 have 〔harbor〕 an ambition 《to *do*》 / …이 되려는 ～을 품다 be ambitious to become… / ～을 품고 미국으로 가다 go over to America with a great ambition. ② 《아량》 large-heartedness; broad-mindedness; generosity; liberality; openhandedness. ¶ ～ 쓰다 act generously / ～ 먹고 백만 원을 기부하다 donate

a million won generously / ～먹고 팁을 넉넉히 주다 tip 《a waiter》 generously.
③ 《눈 딱 감고》 treating *oneself* 《to》; going to the expense 《of》. ¶ ～ 먹고 비싼 컴퓨터를 사다 treat *oneself* to 〔splurge on〕 an expensive computer / ～ 먹고 새 옷 한 벌을 해 입다 indulge in a new suit / ～ 먹고 택시를 타다 take a taxi to the extent of bluing 《five thousand won》 / ～ 먹고 여비서를 쓰다 go to the expense of hiring a woman secretary.

**큰말** 〖언어〗 a "heavy isotope" of a word (in contrast with "light isotope").

**큰머리** a woman's formal hairdo.

**큰문잡다**(―門―) usher 《a distinguished guest》 in 〔to〕 the gate.

**큰물** a heavy flood; an inundation; a deluge; an overflow. ～지다〔나다〕 have a flood; get flooded; be in flood; be inundated. ¶ ～에 다리가 떠내려갔다 A bridge was swept away by the flood.

**큰바늘** 《시계의》 the long 〔minute〕 hand.

**큰바람** a fresh gale.

**큰박쥐** 〖동물〗 a flying fox; a fruit bat.

**큰부리고지새** 〖조류〗 a large-billed grosbeak.

**큰북** 〖악기〗 a big drum; 《오케스트라용》 a low 〔bass〕 drum.

**큰불** 《화재》 a big 〔large, great〕 fire; a disastrous 〔destructive〕 fire; a conflagration; 《총알》 game-hunting gunfire. ¶ ～이 나다 a big fire breaks out 〔takes place〕; be visited by a disastrous fire / ～ 놓다 set a big fire; 《사냥총을》 fire at a big game.

**큰비** a heavy 〔hard〕 rain; a torrential 〔copious, pelting〕 rain; a big 〔heavy〕 rainfall; a downpour 〔deluge〕 (of rain). ¶ ～가 오다 have a heavy rain; it pours; have a downpour; it rains heavily 〔cats and dogs〕; the rain fall in sheets.

**큰사람** ① 《키가》 a tall man. ② 《위대한》 a great man; an eminent person; a big gun. ¶ ～이 되다 attain greatness.

**큰사랑**(―舍廊) ① 《넓은》 a large guest room. ② 《웃어른의》 the living room of *one's* elders; the main guest room.

**큰사슴** 〖동물〗 a red deer; a wapiti (*pl.* ～(s)); an elk; a moose 《영》.

**큰사위** the husband of *one's* eldest 〔oldest 《미》〕 daughter; *one's* eldest son-in-law.

**큰살림** 《have》 a large 〔big〕 family; 《keep up》 a large establishment 〔household〕.

**큰상**(―床) 《잔치의》 a reception table offered bride or groom; 《귀빈의》 a formal table laden with food presented to the guest of honor. ¶ ～받다 be presented with a formal table.

**큰센바람** a strong gale.

**큰소리** ① 《음성》 a loud voice; a stentorian voice; a shout; a yell. ¶～로 in 〔with〕 a loud voice; loudly; at shouting pitch voice 〔throat〕 / ～로 말하다 speak 〔talk〕 loudly; shout / ～로 부르다 call in a loud voice; call out / ～로 외치다 yell; shout; cry in a loud voice; cry aloud 〔loudly〕 / ～로 을러대다 shout threats at 《*a person*》 / ～로 지시하다 shout instructions 〔*one's* orders〕 / ～로 도움을 청하다 scream 〔cry〕 for help / 그렇게 ～로 말하지 마라 Don't talk so loud. / 좀더 ～로 말해 주시오 Please speak a little louder. *or* Louder, please.
② 《야단치는 소리》 a shout; a yell; a roar; a bawl; a brawl. ¶ ～로 꾸짖다 shout 《at *a person*》; roar 〔thunder〕 《at》; browbeat 《*a person*》 into 《*doing*》 / ～ 한 번 못하다 be very submissive 〔docile〕; never raise *one's* voice / 나는 몹시 화가 나서 그녀에게 ～를 쳤다 I shouted at her in anger.
③ 《흰소리》 big 〔tall〕 talk; a loud 〔vainglorious〕 boast; bragging; high-sounding words; grandiloquence; magniloquence; highfalutin 《구어》; hot air 《속어》. ¶ ～치다 talk big 〔tall, boastfully, high and mighty〕; brag; make a great brag 〔boast〕 《of》; bluster; swagger 《about》; talk in large terms 《about》; use bombastic language; talk through *one's* hat 《구어》; be full of hot air; be a big talker / ～ 치는 사람 a braggart; a brag; a swaggerer; a person full of hot air; a ranter / ～만 탕탕 치다 be full of hot air / ～ 같지만 It may sound too big, but…. / ～ 좀 작작 해라 None of your hot air! / 그는 항상 ～치지만 아무도 믿지 않는다 He always talk big but no one believes it.

**큰손** 《증권 시장의》 a market maker; 《투기꾼》 a speculator.

**큰손녀**(―孫女) the eldest 〔oldest 《미》〕 granddaughter.

**큰손님** a distinguished 〔an important〕 guest; a guest of honor; 《많은 손님》 many 〔numerous〕 guests.

**큰손자**(一孫子) *one's* eldest 〔oldest 《미》〕 grandson.

**큰솥** a big pot 〔kettle〕; a caldron.

**큰아기** ① 《처녀》 an adolescent girl; a grown-up girl; a girl in her late teens. ② 《맏딸》 *one's* eldest 〔oldest 《미》〕 daughter.

**큰아들** *one's* eldest 〔oldest 《미》〕 son.

**큰아버지** an uncle (who is *one's* father's elder brother).

**큰어머니** an aunt (who is the wife of *one's* father's elder brother).

**큰언니** a boy's eldest 〔oldest 《미》〕 brother; a girl's eldest 〔oldest 《미》〕 sister.

**큰오빠** a girl's eldest 〔oldest 《미》〕 brother.

**큰옷** an outer robe worn on formal occasions.

**큰유리새**(一瑠璃一) 〖조류〗 a blue fly-catcher.

**큰이** ① 《남의 형제의 맏이》 the eldest of 《*a person's*》 children. ② 《남의 본처》 *a person's* legal 〔wedded〕 wife.

**큰일** ① 《큰 사업》 a great undertaking; a big 〔great〕 enterprise 〔task〕; a big business; a big plan. ¶ ~을 계획하다 plan a big enterprise / ~을 성취하다 do 〔achieve, accomplish〕 a great thing 〔work〕 / 장차 그는 틀림없이 ~을 할 거다 He is sure to do something big some day.
② 《중대한 일》 a matter of grave concern 〔great consequence, great importance〕; a serious 〔grave〕 affair 〔matter〕; a great trouble; a crisis (위기). ¶ ~(이) 나다 a serious thing happens; a serious problem pops 〔crops〕 up; face a matter of grave 〔serious〕 concern; get into trouble; be in a difficulty 〔fix, pickle〕 / ~이 되다 become 〔get, grow〕 serious; take a serious 〔grave〕 turn / ~났다고 떠들다 become alarmed 《at, over》; cry alarm / 이거 ~ 났구나 Good Heavens! *or* We really are in trouble! *or* We are in for it. *or* What a fine fix we're in! / ~을 저질렀군 Now you've done it! *or* See what you have done. / 다섯 식구를 먹여 살린다는 것은 ~이다 It is by no means easy to support a family of five. / (일이) 잘못되면 ~이다 A miss, and all is up 〔over〕. / 한 발짝만 헛디디면 ~난다 A single false step would be fatal. / 아버지가 아시게 되면 ~난다 If it comes to my father's ear, I shall get into an awful row. / 이것은 나라의 ~이다 This is a national crisis. / 틀림없이 어떤 ~이 일어났을 거라고 그는 말했다 He said he was sure that something very serious had taken place. / 「내기에서 이기지 못하면 백 만원의 손해를 보게 된단 말이야」 —「그거 ~이로군」 "I must win the bet, or I lose one million won."— "That is quite a situation to be in."
③ 《예식·잔치 등》 a great occasion; a big ceremony 〔banquet〕; a wedding; a funeral. ¶ ~을 치르다 go through 〔carry out〕 a wedding 〔funeral〕 / ~이 닥쳐오다 a big occasion draws near.

**큰절**[1] 《여자의》 a formal deep bow (made by a woman with her hands together before her forehead). ~하다 make a formal deep bow; bow low.

**큰절**[2] 《사찰》 the main 〔large〕 temple.

**큰집** ① 《크게 지은》 a big 〔large〕 house; a mansion (저택). ¶ ~ 쓰고 살다 live in a big house; be well-off. ② 《맏형의》 the house of *one's* eldest brother. ③ 《종가》 the house of the eldest son of a family; the head house; the main stock.

**큰처남**(一妻男) the eldest brother of *one's* wife.

**큰체하다** be proud 〔haughty〕; assume an air of importance; put on 〔give *oneself*〕 airs; swagger; hold *one's* head high; do the big 〔swell〕.

**큰춤** a full-dress dance; dancing in full dress 〔costume〕. ¶ ~추다 dance in full dress 〔costume〕.

**큰치마** a long trailing skirt.

**큰칼** 《형구》 a big cangue; a large pillory; 《칼》 a sword; a large knife.

**큰코다치다** have a bitter 〔terrible〕 experience; have a hard 〔rough〕 time (of it); [사물이 주어] cost 《*a person*》 dear; pay dearly 《for》; run into trouble. ¶ 믿지 못할 사람을 믿었다가 큰코다쳤다 I made the bitter mistake of putting my faith in someone who couldn't be trusted.

**큰톱** a pit saw; a 2-man ripsaw.

**큰판** 《도박의》 a high 〔deep〕 play 《at cards》.

**큰할아버지** the eldest brother of *one's* grandfather; a granduncle.

**큰형**(一兄) *one's* eldest brother 〔sister〕; 《호칭》 big brother.

**큰형수**(一兄嫂) the wife of *one's* eldest brother; *one's* eldest sister-in-law.

**클라리넷** 〖악기〗 a clarinet. ¶ ~을 불다 play on the clarinet. ◉ ~주자(奏者) a clarinet(t)ist; a clarinet player.

**클라리온** 〖악기〗 a clarion.

**클라이맥스** a 〔the〕 climax; the culmination 〔peak, maximum, apogee〕. ¶ ～에 달하다〔이르다〕 reach 〔come to〕 the climax 《of a story》; culminate 《in》/ 이 소설의 ～는 두 사람의 재회 장면이다 The climax in the novel is the scene in which the two meet again.

**클라인시험**(—試驗) 〖의학〗 a Kline test.

**클래스** 《학급》 a class; a division; 《등급》 a class. ¶ ～회 a class meeting / 영어 ～ an English class / 이코노미 ～ economy class / ～토론 a class discussion.

**클래스메이트** a classmate; a classfellow.

**클래식** a classic; [총칭] classics. ¶ ～한 classic; classical. ◉ ～음악 classical music.

**클랙슨** a Klaxon (상표명); a horn. ¶ ～을 울리다 sound the klaxon 〔horn〕; honk.

**클러치** 〖기계〗 a clutch. ¶ ～를 밟다 step on the clutch (pedal); press down on 〔push down〕 the clutch / ～를 넣다〔연결하다〕 put in the clutch / ～를 풀다 release 〔disengage〕 a clutch; declutch. ◉ ～페달 a clutch (pedal).

**클럽** ① 《동호 단체》 a club; a society; 《미국 대학생의》 a fraternity (남자의); a sorority (여자의). ¶ ～에 들다 join a club; become a member of a club / ～을 조직하다 organize a club. ② 《카드의》 《the ace of》 clubs. ③ 《골프채》 a (golf) club; a playclub. ◉ ～하우스 a clubhouse. ～활동 club 〔extracurricular〕 activities. ～회비 club dues. ～회원 a member of club; a clubman.

**클레오파트라** 《이집트의 여왕》 Cleopatra (69?-30 B.C.). ¶ ～의 코가 조금만 낮았더라면 세계의 역사는 달라졌을 게다 If Cleopatra's nose had been a little lower, the history of the world might have been different.

**클레이** ① 《점토》 clay. ② ⇨ ～사격, ～피전. ◉ ～사격 clay pigeon shooting. ～코트 a clay court. ～피전 《클레이 사격의 표적》 a clay pigeon.

**클레임** 〖경제〗 ① 《손해배상청구》 a claim (for damages). ¶ ～을 제기하다 advance a claim; make a claim on 《a company》; make 〔institute, bring forward, put in〕 a claim for compensation / ～에 응하다 meet a claim for damages. ② 《이의》 a complaint; an objection. ¶ ～을 제기하다 make a complaint; raise 〔lodge〕 an objection 《to》. (★ claim에는 「이의(異議)·고정(苦情)」이란 뜻이 없음).

**클렌징크림** cleansing cream.

**클로라민** 〖화학〗 chloramine.

**클로랄** 〖화학〗 chloral. ¶ ～로 처리하다 chloralize. ◉ ～중독 chloralism.

**클로람페니콜** 〖약〗 chloramphenicol.

**클로렐라** 〖식물〗 chlorella (algae).

**클로로다인** 《마취제》 chlorodyne.

**클로로마이세틴** 〖약〗 chloromycetin.

**클로로벤젠** 〖화학〗 chlorobenzene.

**클로로아세트산**(—酸) 〖화학〗 chloroacetic acid.

**클로로포름** 《마취제》 chloroform. ◉ ～중독 chloroformism.

**클로로필** 《엽록소》 chlorophyll.

**클로로필라아제** 〖생화학〗 chlorophyllase.

**클로르칼크** [<*Chlorkalk* (G.)] 《표백분》 chloride of lime.

**클로버** 〖식물〗 a clover. ¶ 네 잎 ～ a four-leaf(ed) clover.

**클로스** cloth; book(binder's) cloth. ◉ ～제본 cloth binding: ～로 제본하다 bind 《a book》 in cloth.

**클로즈게임** 《접전》 a close 〔seesaw〕 game.

**클로즈드 숍** 〖경제〗 《노동조합원만을 고용하는 사업소》 a closed shop.

**클로즈업** 〖영화〗 a close-up (생략 CU); a close shot; a close-up view 《of the moon》. ～하다 take a close-up 《of》; bring into a close-up. ¶ ～시킨 (영화의) 장면 a close-up shot 〔scene〕 (of a movie) / ～되다 be brought into a close-up; [비유적] be highlighted; be 〔come〕 in the lime-light 〔spotlight〕; be in the news 〔the public eye〕; came to the fore / ～하여 보여 주다 show 《a scene》 in close-up / 그 문제는 크게 ～되었다 The problem has been highlighted. ◉ ～사진 a close-up picture.

**클리닉** 《진료소》 a clinic.

**클리닝** cleaning; laundry. ¶ ～하러 보내다 send 《*one's* shirts》 to the wash 〔cleaner's〕.

**클린산업**(—産業) clean industry.

**클린업** 〖야구〗 cleanup. ◉ ～트리오 〖야구〗 numbers 3, 4 and 5 in the batting line-up; a trio of sluggers.

**클린치** 〖권투〗 a clinch; clinching. ～하다 clinch. ¶ ～를 하고 있다 be in a clinch.

**클린히트** 《야구》 a clean hit. ¶ ～를 치다 smash out a clean hit.

**클립** a clip; 《머리의》 a hairpin; a hair slide; 《컬용》 a curling pin; a curler. ¶ ～을 끼우는 넥타이 a clip-on tie / 서류를 ～으로 철하다 clasp 〔fasten〕 papers with a clip; clip papers / 머리에 ～을 하고 있다 *one's* hair is in curling pins.

**클링커** 〖기계·야금〗 clinker. ◉ ～냉각기

a clinker cooler. ~대(帶) a clinkering zone. ~벽돌 a clinker brick.

**큼직이** ① 《사물을》 (so that it is) big; large; greatly. ¶ 집을 ~ 짓다 build a house big / (옷을) 좀 ~ 해 주세요 Cut the coat 「rather full 〔with some allowance〕. ② 《도량을》 generously; liberally; magnanimously. ¶ 마음을 ~ 먹다 assume a generous attitude.

**큼직하다** ① 《사물이》 (be) quite 〔fairly〕 big 〔large〕; good-sized; [술어적] be on the large side. ¶ 큼직한 집 quite a big house / 큼직한 사람 quite a big person / 큼직한 글씨로 쓰다 write large / 일간신문에 큼직한 광고를 내다 put 〔run 《미》〕 a large ad in a daily paper. ② 《마음이》 (be) quite generous 〔liberal, magnanimous〕; [술어적] have a big heart.

**킁킁** snorting. ~하다〔거리다〕 keep snorting 〔sniffing〕. ¶ ~ 냄새를 맡다 sniff 《at》; give a sniff 《at》.

**키**[1] 《까부는》 a winnow; a winnowing basket; a winnowing-fan. ¶ 키로 까부르다, 키질하다 winnow 《chaff from grain》.

**키**[2] 《선박의》 a rudder (키 판); a helm (키자루); a (steering) wheel (타륜(舵輪)). ¶ 키잡이 a helmsman; a steersman; a man at the helm 〔wheel〕 / 키를 잡다 steer; be at the helm / 키를 돌리다 turn the helm.

**키**[3] 《신장》 stature; *one's* height; *one's* size. ¶ 키가 큰〔작은〕 사람 a man of great 〔small, low, short〕 stature; a tall 〔short〕 person / 중키의 사람 a person of mean 〔medium〕 stature 〔height〕 / 키가 크다〔작다〕 be high 〔low, short, small〕 in stature; be of great 〔small〕 stature; be tall 〔short〕 / 키가 자라다 grow 〔increase〕 in stature; become 〔grow〕 tall(er) / 키가 거의 같다 be nearly of the same height / 키가 모자라다 be under height / 키가 5피트이다 stand 〔measure〕 five feet (high); be five feet tall 〔in stature, in height〕 / 키가 장대 같이 크다 be as tall as a lamp-post / 키를 재다 measure 〔take〕 《*a person's*》 height / 키를 비교하다 measure *oneself* with 《*another*》 / 하이힐을 신어 키가 커 보이게 하다 wear high-heeled shoes to help *one's* height / 키 크고 속(이) 없다 be tall and lack insides / 키가 얼마나 되나 How tall are you? *or* How many feet do you stand? / 그는 키가 나보다 3센티미터나 크다〔작다〕 He is three centimeters taller 〔shorter〕 than I. / 그는 키가 작은 편이다 He is rather below the average height. / 키 크고 싱겁지 않은 사람 없다 There are no tall people who knows how to behave properly.

**키**[4] ① 《피아노·타자기 따위의》 a key. ¶ 키를 누르다 press down a key / 타자기의 키를 두드리다 pound 〔strike, tap〕 the keys of a type-writer / 전신기의 키를 치다 operate a telegraph key. ② 《열쇠》 a key. ¶ 마스터 ~ a master key / 자동차의 키 a car key; a key to *one's* car.
◉ 키보드 a keyboard. 키 스테이션 《미》 a key station. 키 워드 《해석상·색인 등의 주요어》 a key word.

**키내림** dropping to winnow. ~하다 drop 《grain》 to winnow it.

**키네마** 《영화》 a kinema; a cinema. ⇨ 「시네마.

**키니네** 《말라리아 특효약》 quinine.

**키다리** a tall, lanky 〔gangling〕 person.

**키드** 《가죽》 kid. ◉ ~구두 kid shoes. ~장갑 kid gloves; kids.

**키부츠** 《이스라엘의》 a kibbutz (*pl.* -im).

**키순**(—順) the order of stature 〔height〕. ¶ ~으로 in order of 〔according to〕 stature / ~으로 서다 line up 〔stand〕 (in a row) in order of height.

**키스** a kiss; a smack (쪽 소리 나는). ~하다 kiss 《a girl on the mouth》; give 《*a person*》 a kiss 〔smack〕; press *one's* lips against. ¶ 여자와 ~하다 kiss a girl / 사랑의 ~를 하다 kiss 《*a person*》 with love / 입술에 ~하다 kiss 《*a person*》 on the lips; press a kiss upon 《*a person's*》 lips / 이별의 ~를 하다 kiss 《*a person*》 good-by(e) / ~를 보내다 wave a kiss 《to》; blow 〔throw〕 a kiss 《to》 / ~를 빼앗다 steal a kiss from 《her》 / ~하지 않고 헤어지다 part with dry lips.

**키우다** ① 《양육하다》 bring up; raise; rear; foster; nurse; 《동식물을》 breed; raise; grow; rear.
¶ 어머니 손으로만 키운 《a child》 brought up exclusively by *his* mother / 아이를 우유〔모유〕로 ~ feed 〔raise〕 a child on the bottle 〔at the breast〕 / 아이를 훌륭히 ~ nurture a child the way a child should be brought up (바람직하게); breed a child a good boy 〔girl〕 (가정 교육이 좋게) / 손수 돌보아 ~ bring up 《a child》 under *one's* own care / 「금이야 옥이야」하고 키워지다 be reared 〔brought up〕 with the utmost care and affection.

> (용법) **bring up** (어린)아이가 성인이 될 때까지 보살펴가며 「키우다」「양육하다」라는 뜻으로 사람에게만 씀. **raise** 《미》 아이나 동물, 식물을 「키우다」, 「사육〔재배〕하다」라는 뜻. **rear** 격식을 차린 말로서 raise와 거의 같은 뜻으로 쓰임. **foster** 양자로서 「키우다」란 뜻. **nurse** 원래는 유아나 병자가 자립할 수 있게, 건강을 회복할 수 있게 「보살피다」라는 뜻이지만, 그것이 확대되어 약한 것, 불확실한 것을 「정성껏 키우다」란 뜻으로 쓰임. **breed** 가축이나 물고기를 교배를 통해서 「번식시키다」, 「사육하다」라는 뜻과 함께 사람이 아이를 「키우다」「성인이 되게하다」라는 뜻으로도 쓰임. **grow** 「자라다」, 「키우다」, 「성장하다」등의 뜻으로서, 사람·키·머리카락·손톱·초목·짐승 등이 자연의 이치에 따라 커지다, 성장하다라는 뜻.

② 《육성하다》 promote; support; protect; 《재질 등을》 develop; cultivate; 《훈련·교육하다》 educate; train; bring up. ¶ 법률가로 ～ bring up 《a boy》 to the legal profession / 외교관으로 ～ train 《*a person*》 for the diplomatic service / 담력을 ～ cultivate 〔foster, develop〕 courage / 국내 산업을 ～ promote domestic 〔home〕 industry / 재능을 ～ cultivate *one's* talent; develop 〔improve〕 *one's* ability / 인재를 ～ cultivate men of talent.
③ 《방치·조장하다》 neglect; leave 《a disease》 unattended to 〔uncared for〕; bolster 《up》. ¶ 병을 ～ neglect a disease; let a disease take its own course / 허영심을 ～ bolster up *one's* vanity.

**키위** ① 〖조류〗 a kiwi; an apteryx. ② 〖식물〗 《과일》 a kiwi (fruit 〔berry〕); a Chinese gooseberry.

**키인더스트리** 《기간 산업》 key industry.

**키질** winnowing. ～하다 winnow. ¶ 쌀을 ～하다 winnow rice.

**키친** a kitchen. ◉ ～싱크 《부엌의 싱크대》 a kitchen sink. ～웨어 《주방용품》 kitchenware.

**키퍼** 《축구 등의》 a keeper. ¶ 골 ～ a goalkeeper.

**키펀처** a keypuncher; a key-punch operator.

**키펀치** 〖컴퓨터〗 a key punch.

**키포인트** a main point. ¶ ～를 파악하다 get 〔catch〕 the point 〔the main idea〕 of 《a subject》 / 이것이 ～다 This is the most important point.

**키프로스** 《나라 이름》 Cyprus. ¶ ～(섬)의 Cypriot(e); Cyprian. ◉ ～사람 a Cypriot(e); a Cyprian.

**킥** 〖축구〗 a kick. ～하다 kick 《the ball》. ¶ ～을 잘하다 be good at kicking; be a good kicker.

**킥복싱** kick 〔Siamese〕 boxing.

**킥오프** 〖축구〗 a kickoff.

**킥킥** giggling; tittering; snickering. ～하다〔거리다〕 keep giggling 〔chuckling〕; titter; snicker; snigger 《영》; laugh in *one's* sleeve; laugh to *oneself* / ～거리며 쳐다보다 look at 《*a person*》 with furtive laughter.

**킥턴** 〖스키〗 a kick turn. ¶ ～을 하다 make a kick turn.

**킨키나 나무** 〖식물〗 a quinquina.

**킬로** a kilo; 《킬로미터》 a kilometer (생략 km); 《킬로그램》 a kilogram (생략 kg); 《킬로리터》 a kiloliter (생략 kl); 《킬로와트》 a kilowatt (생략 kw). ¶ 시속 2백 ～ a velocity of 200 km 〔kilometers〕 an hour. ◉ ～바이트 〖컴퓨터〗 a kilobyte. ～볼트 a kilovolt (생략 kv): ～ 볼트 암페어 a kilovolt-ampere (생략 kVA, kva). ～비트 〖컴퓨터〗 a kilobit. ～사이클 a kilocycle (생략 kc). ～암페어 a kiloampere. ～와트 a kilowatt (생략 kW, kw): ～ 와트시(時) a kilowatt-hour (생략 kWh, kwhr, K.W.H., kwh). ～칼로리 a kilocalorie. ～톤 a kiloton (생략 kt). ～헤르츠 a kilohertz (생략 kHz).

**킬로수**(一數) 《킬로미터의》 the number of kilometers 《used to express length of distance》; 《킬로그램의》 the number of kilograms 《used to express weight》; 《킬로와트의》 the number of kilowatts 《used to express electrical power》.

**킬킬** giggling; chuckling. ⇨ 킥킥.

**킷값** being worthy of *one's* height 〔stature〕; doing something well; being up to par. ～하다 be worthy of *one's* height; do it well; be up to par. ¶ ～도 못하다 be unworthy of *one's* stature.

**킹** a king.

**킹메이커** a kingmaker.

**킹사이즈** ¶ ～의 king-size(d).

**킹콩** King Kong.

**킹킹** whining; whimpering; peevishly. ～하다, ～거리다 keep whining 〔whimpering〕; be peevish 〔fractious〕. ¶ 아이가 몹시 ～거렸다 The child got very fractious.

**킹펭귄** 〖조류〗 a king penguin.

**킹피시** a kingfish.

**킹핀** 〖볼링〗 the kingpin (1번 또는 5번 핀).

**타**(他) other; the other; others; 《다른 것》 another thing; some others; the rest. ¶ 타도(他道) other provinces / 타의 추종을 불허하다 be「peerless〔unrivaled, matchless, unmatched〕; be without a peer; have no「equal〔parallel〕; outclass〔outdistance, outstrip〕others / 그녀는 골프에 있어서 타의 주종을 불허한다 She is second to none in golf.

**타**(打)《다스》 a dozen (생략 doz., dz.).

> **용법** dozen의 용법은 hundred, thousand의 용법에 준함. 다시 말해서 dozen 앞에 수사 및 a few, several, quite a few 등이 올 때에는 복수형 -s를 붙이지 않음. 생략형 doz., dz.는 단·복수 공용임.

¶ 여러 타의 dozens of... / 반 타 half a dozen / 맥주 다섯 타 five dozen bottles of beer / 한 타 얼마로 팔다 sell 《*a thing*》 by the dozen / 그것을 두 타 주십시오 I will take two dozen of them.

**타가**(他家) another「family〔house〕. ¶ ~에 양자로 들어가다 be adopted「into another family〔as *a person's* son〕.
◉ ~수정(受精)〖식물〗 allogamy; xenogamy: ~ 수정하다 cross-fertilize; cross-pollinate.

**타각증상**(他覺症狀) objective symptoms.

**타개**(打開) a break; a breakthrough; a new turn; a solution. ~하다 break 《the deadlock》; break through 《an obstacle》; tide over 《a difficult situation》; achieve a breakthrough; overcome; find a solution.
¶ 정국의 ~ a new turn of the political situation; introduction of a new situation in politics / 난국을 ~하다 find a way out of the difficulties; overcome〔get over, get out of〕difficulties / 막다른 국면을 ~하다 break (through) a deadlock; bring a deadlock to an end; resolve the situation / 우리는 어떻게 난국을 ~할 것인가를 의논했다 We discussed how to overcome difficulties.
◉ ~책 a way out; a remedy; a countermeasure; a plan for the way out; a solution to an impasse: (불황의) ~책을 강구하다 try to find a way out (of depression) / 정부는 지금의 금융 위기 ~책을 찾아내야만 한다 The government has to find a way out of the present financial crisis.

**타격**(打擊) ①《때려 침》 striking; a blow; a hit; a knock; a clout 《구어》; 《정신적인 충격》 a shock; a (mental) blow; 《손해》 a damage.
¶ 치명적인 ~ a「fatal〔mortal, deadly, smashing〕blow / ~을 가하다〔주다〕 strike a blow 《at, against》; give a blow 《to》; deal a 《fatal》 blow 《to, at》; shock / ~을 받다 get〔suffer〕a blow; be hit; be shocked 《at, by》/ 심한 ~을 받다 be hard hit 《by》; suffer a「severe〔telling〕blow / ~을 막아내다 fend off a blow / ~을 완화하다 soften a blow / 그의 사업은 그 화재로 큰 ~을 입었다 His business suffered serious damage from the fire. / 해운계는 전쟁으로 큰 ~을 받았다 The shipping world was hard hit by the war. / 그의 갑작스러운 죽음은 우리에게 큰 ~이었다 His sudden death was a great blow to us. *or* All of us were greatly shocked by his sudden death. / 그 사건으로 그의 좋은 평판은 큰 ~을 입었다 The trouble caused severe damage to his good reputation. / 수도권의 교통망은 태풍으로 큰 ~을 받았다 The transportation network in and around Seoul was severely hit by the typhoon.
②〖스포츠〗《야구의》 hitting; batting; a clout;〖권투〗 a punch; a sock; a clout; a smash. ¶ ~이 좋다〔나쁘다〕 hit「well〔badly〕; be「strong〔weak〕「in batting〔at bat〕/ 타자들은 ~이 좋았다〔부진했다〕 The batters played their parts well〔poorly〕.
◉ ~력〖야구〗 hitting〔batting〕power. ~률 the「batting〔hitting〕average. ⇨타율(打率). ~부진〖야구〗 shortage of hits; poor batting. ~상(賞) the batting award. ~순 the batting order. ~

연습 〖야구〗 batting practice. ~왕 the leading 〔top〕 hitter 《for this season》; the king 〔sultan〕 of swat. ~전 〖야구〗 a game with many hits.

**타견**(他見) 《남이 보는 바》 showing to others; exposure; 《남의 의견》 other's opinion 〔view〕. ¶ ~을 꺼리다 keep 《it》 secret; shun publicity / ~을 구하다 ask 〔seek, solicit, inquire〕 another's opinion 〔view(s)〕.

**타결**(妥結) a compromise settlement; an agreement. ~하다 = ~을 보다. ¶ ~을 보다 reach an agreement 《with》; make a compromise agreement 《with》; come to terms 《with》 / 원만하게 ~되다 come to an amicable 〔to a satisfactory〕 settlement / 정치적 ~을 모색하다 seek political compromise / 교섭은 원만하게 ~되었다 The negotiations reached a peaceful and satisfactory settlement. ◉ ~점 a point of agreement. ~조건 terms of agreement.

**타계**(他界) ① 《저승》 the other world; another world. ② 《죽음》 death; passing away; demise. ~하다 depart (from) this life; join 〔go over to〕 the majority; die; pass away; decease.

**타고나다** be born 《a musician》; be gifted 〔endowed〕 《with talent》. ¶ 타고난 innate 《characteristics》; inborn 《talent》; born 《artists》; natural 《gymnasts》; native 《wit》; inherent 《nature》 / 타고난 권리 *one's* birthright / 타고난 문장가(文章家) a natural-born stylist / 타고난 목소리 *one's* natural voice / 타고난 병 a congenital disease / 꼼꼼한 성격을 타고난 사람 a methodical person by nature / 타고난 시인 a born poet / 타고난 예술적 재질 an inborn talent of art / 배운 것이 아니라 타고난 재능 an art born in the man, not acquired / 타고난 교사이다 be designed 〔cut out〕 for a teacher / 타고난 장사꾼이다 be born a merchant; be a born merchant / 재간을 ~ be gifted with a talent / 좋은 팔자를〔복을〕 ~ be born under a lucky star; be born with a silver spoon in *one's* mouth / 타고난 악인은 없다 No man is born wicked. / 그녀는 타고난 허약 체질이다 She was born delicate. *or* She is delicate by birth. / 그녀는 미모와 지성을 함께 타고 났다 She's endowed with intelligence as well as good looks.

**타고을**(他—) an alien 〔a strange〕 county 〔province〕; another county 〔province〕.

**타고장**(他—) another place 〔province〕; a strange 〔an alien〕 place.

**타곳**(他—) a foreign 〔an alien〕 land; a strange place; another place. ¶ ~으로 이사 가다 move to a strange place. ◉ ~사람 a stranger.

**타관**(他官) 《타향》 a strange 〔an alien〕 land; a foreign country; a different part of the country. ¶ (멀리) ~에서 살다 live away from home / ~ 생활 십년이다 be absent from home for ten years.

**타구**(打毬) a kind of polo.

**타구**(打球) 〖야구〗 batting; 〖테니스〗 a stroke; 《친 공》 a batted ball. ◉ ~봉(棒)〔채〕 《골프》 a club; a driver.

**타구**(唾具) a spittoon; a cuspidor(e) 《미》.

**타국**(他國) a foreign country; an alien 〔a strange〕 land. ¶ ~의 foreign; alien / ~ 땅에서 죽다 die in a strange 〔foreign〕 land; die far from home. ◉ ~어 a foreign language; a strange tongue. ~인 a foreigner; a stranger; an alien.

**타기**(唾棄) casting away with contempt or hate; rejection. ~하다 throw away in disgust; detest; reject. ¶ ~할 detestable; disgusting; revolting; despicable / 그는 ~할 인물이다 He is a detestable 〔disgusting〕 fellow. / 그는 ~할 비열한 방법으로 그 돈을 손에 넣었다 He got the money by a despicably dirty trick.

**타기**(舵機) 〖항해〗 a steering gear; a helm. ⇨ 조타.

**타끈하다** (be) stingy; close-fisted; penny-pinching; [서술적] pinch and scrape; be a money-grubber 〔grasping rascal〕.

**타내다** get 《from *one's* elders》; obtain; get a grant. ¶ 어머니한테서 용돈을 ~ get pocket money from *one's* mother / 정부로부터 보조금을 ~ get a subsidy from the government / 그는 학비를 삼촌에게서 타낸다 He depends upon his uncle for his school expenses.

**타념**(他念) different 〔other〕 intention; other thoughts. ¶ ~ 없이 earnestly; intently; with undivided 〔absorbing〕 attention; whole-heartedly.

**타누르기** 〖씨름〗 pressing down 《*a person*》 with *one's* body.

**타닌** 〖화학〗 tannin. ◉ ~산 tannic acid; tannin: ~산염 tannate.

**타다**[1] ① 《불에》 (***a***) 《불이 붙어》 burn;

blaze; glow (석탄 따위가); be in flames.
¶ 벌겋게 타고 있는 석탄 glowing 〔live〕 coals / 활활 타고 있는 불 a blazing fire; roaring flames (소리를 내며) / 잘 ~ burn well; 《불붙기 쉽다》 be easy to burn; catch fire easily; be combustible 〔(in)flammable〕 / 잘 타지 않다 burn ill 〔dull(y), poorly, badly〕; do not burn (easily); be noncombustible; be non(in)flammable / 장작이 ~ firewood burns / 활활〔은근히〕 ~ burn briskly 〔quietly〕 / 불꽃을 내며 ~ burn with flame / 다 타버리다 be burnt up 〔off〕; burn completely up / 타고 있다 be burning; be on fire; be ablaze 〔aflame〕; be in flames / 이 장작은 타지 않는다 This wood will not 〔refuse to〕 burn.
(***b***) 《불이 나서》 burn; be burnt; be destroyed 〔consumed〕 by fire; be reduced to ashes; be gutted by fire.
¶ 불(에) 탄 산(山) a burnt hill; a hill devastated by fire / 불 탄 자리 the ruins 〔site〕 of a fire; a place burnt down by a (recent) fire; 《넓은 지역》 a fire-ravaged district 〔region〕; the area swept by the flames / 불에 타서 내려앉다〔무너져 내리다〕 be burnt down; burn and fall; be burnt to the ground; collapse in flames / 불(에) 타 없어지다 burn to nothing; be burnt away 〔out〕; burn itself out / 불에 타 죽다 be burnt to death; perish 「in the flames 〔by fire〕 / 불(에)타는 것을 면하다, 타지 않고 남다 remain unburnt; escape 〔survive〕 the fire; be saved from the flames / 그 화재로 많은 사람이 타 죽었다 Many persons were burnt to death in the fire. / 기적적으로 우리 집만 타지 않았다 My house alone miraculously escaped the fire.
(***c***) 《눋다》 scorch; burn; be 〔get〕 scorched 〔burned, charred〕.
¶ 타서 눌어 붙지 않는 프라이팬 a non-stick frying pan / 새까맣게 ~ be burnt 〔scorched〕 black 〔to a cinder〕; be charred; be blackened with fire / 밥이 ~ the rice is scorched 〔gets burned〕 / 밥이 타서 솥바닥에 눌어 붙었다 The rice got scorched and stuck to the bottom of the pot.
② 《햇볕에》 (***a***) 《살갗이》 be 〔get〕 sunburned 〔sunburnt〕; be suntanned 〔sunbaked〕; be browned 《with the sun》. ¶ (살이) 새까맣게 탄 deep-〔heavily-〕tanned / 햇볕에 탄 얼굴 a sunburnt 〔suntanned, sunbrowned〕 face / 바닷바람에 구릿빛으로 탄 어부 a fisherman browned by the briny air / 살갗이 타지 않도록 하다 keep 《*oneself*》 from getting sunburnt / 살갗이 타지 않게 하는 크림 anti-suntan 〔anti-sunburn, sunscreening〕 cream.
(***b***) 《바짝 마르다》 dry up; be dried up; parch; be parched. ¶ 바짝 탄 입술 parched lips / 비가 오지 않아서 밭의 보리가 탔다 The barley is parched from lack of rain.
③ 《목이》 have a dry throat. ¶ 목이 ~ be 〔feel〕 thirsty 〔dry〕; *one's* throat parches with thirst; be parched with thirst (몹시); 《술 마신 후에》 have 〔feel〕 a cobweb in the throat; have hot coppers / (술 마신 뒤에) 목이 타서 물을 켜다 cool *one's* coppers.
④ 《마음·정열 등이》 burn; glow; blaze; be aflame; 《애가》 be anxious; be anguished. ¶ 타오르는 정열〔사랑〕 burning passion 〔love〕 / 애가 ~ feel 〔be〕 uneasy 〔anxious〕 《about》; be worried 《about》; feel nervous; jitter; be in suspense / 청춘의 정열에 불~ burn with youthful ardor.
⑤ 《빛깔이》 ¶ (불)타는 듯한 주홍빛 blazing scarlet / 저녁놀로 벌겋게 (불)타는 하늘 the sky aglow with the setting sun / 온 산이 단풍으로 (불)타는 듯하다 The whole mountain is ablaze with autumn colors.

**타다**[2] ① 《탈것·짐승 등에》 ride 《a horse》; take 《a train, a bus, a plane》; take 〔have〕 a ride in 《a car》; ride in 《a cab》; 《올라타다》 get on 〔in(to)〕 《a train, a plane》; board 《a bus》; 《배에》 go 〔get〕 aboard 〔on board〕 《a ship》; embark on 〔in〕 《a ship》.
¶ 택시에〔마차를〕 ~ ride in a cab / 말을 ~ ride 〔mount, get on〕 a horse; ride horseback / 말을 타고 가다 go 〔travel〕 on horseback; ride 《to a place》 / 배를 ~ 《승선하다》 go 〔get〕 on board (a ship 〔boat〕); board 〔take〕 a ship; get into a boat; take ship; 《뱃사람이 되다》 go to sea; become a sailor / 비행기를 ~ have a ride 〔go up〕 in an airplane; take an airplane; 《오르다》 get into 〔get aboard〕 an airplane / 비행기를 타고 가다 fly 《to Hongkong》; go 〔travel〕 《to Hawaii》 by air 〔plane〕 (★ go by 뒤에 오는 명사는 무관사) / 열차를 타고 가다 travel 〔go〕 by rail 〔train〕; take a train 《to a place》 / 열차를 잘못 ~ take the wrong

train / (자동)차를 타고 가다 drive a motorcar; go by car / 타고 있다 be on 〔in〕 《a car》; be aboard 〔on board〕 《a ship》; 《말을》 be on horseback / 승강기를 타고 오르내리다 go up and down in an elevator / 갈아 ~ change 《planes at》; transfer 《to another car》; transship (배를) / 타지 못하고 놓치다 miss 〔lose〕 《*one's* train》; fail to catch 《*one's* train》; miss 《a bus》 / 버스가 만원이 되어 타지 못하다 fail to get in a crowded bus / 늘 타 버릇을 해서 익숙하다 get 〔be〕 used to riding 〔driving〕 / 나는 10시 30분발 부산행 특급을 탔다 I took the 10:30 limited express for Busan. / 그 여객기에는 한국인 관광객이 많이 타고 있었다 There were a lot of tourists from Korea on (board) the passenger plane. / 우체국까지 자전거를 타고 갔다 I rode a bicycle to the post office. / 그 관광버스에는 승객 30명과 승무원 2명이 타고 있었다 The sightseeing bus carried thirty passengers and a crew of two.

참고 「타다」의 여러 가지 표현
어떤 교통 기관을 이용하느냐를 말하려고 할 때, 열차·지하철·전동차·버스·택시·항공기 등을 타고 가는 것을 일반적으로 **take**라고 함. 교통 수단을 강조하려면 **go by** train; **come by** taxi; **arrive by** plane 따위로 말하면 됨. 다만 구어에서는 go by...보다 take ...쪽이 더 일반적임. 올라타는 동작을 말할 때는, 탈 것에 따라서 **get on** (a bus 〔train, plane〕); **get in** 〔**into**〕 (a car 〔taxi〕); **get** 「**on board** 〔**aboard**〕 (a ship 〔plane, train, bus〕) 또는 **board** (a ship 〔plane, train, bus〕)처럼 표현 방식이 다르다는 점에 유의해야 함. 어떤 교통 기관(항공기 포함)이라도 「올라타다」는 동작을 표현하는 말로 쓰이는 것이 **ride**. 택시 등을 잡는다는 뜻으로 쓰이는 말은 **get** 또는 **catch**임.

② 《산·나무·줄을》 climb 《a mountain, a tree; a rope》; go 〔step, walk〕 on. ¶ 무동〔목말〕을 ~ ride on 《*a person's*》 shoulders; ride piggyback 〔pickaback〕 《on *a person*》 / 산을 ~ climb (up) a mountain / 줄을 ~ haul 〔pull〕 *oneself* up by a rope; climb a rope; 《광대가》 walk (on) a tightrope; tightrope / 줄을 타고 내려오다 climb down a rope / 나무를 잘 타다 be a good climber; be good at climbing (trees) / 지붕을 ~ go from roof to roof; walk over the roofs / 네가 이 밧줄을 타면 아마 끊어질 것이다 This rope will probably break if you put your weight on it.

③ 《얼음을》 walk 〔slide〕 on 《the ice》. ¶ 스케이트를 타다 skate on the ice; do skating.

④ 《기회·틈을》 seize 《an opportunity》; take; get; 《기화로 삼다》 take advantage of 《*a thing*》; avail *oneself* of. ¶ 어둠을 타서〔타고〕 under cover of night 〔darkness〕; taking advantage of the darkness / 기회를 ~ get 〔seize〕 an opportunity; take advantage 〔avail *oneself*〕 of an opportunity / 틈을 ~ get time free; avail *oneself* of some free time; take the opportunity / 혼잡한 틈을 타 달아나다 take advantage of the confusion to run away.

⑤ 《기타》 ¶ 물결을 ~ ride on the waves; ride the surf (파도타기에서) / 인기의 물결을 ~ ride on the waves of popularity / 바람을 ~ be borne 〔wafted〕 by a breeze; be carried on a wind; 《불길이》 be fanned by a wind; [비유적] be apt to become the target of severe criticism; be an unrestful post / 전파를 ~ be broadcast (by radio); be 〔go, get〕 on the air (waves); take the air / 시대의 흐름을 ~ go with the tide of the times.

**타다**[3] 《넣다·섞다》 put in; add; mix; admix; dilute; water down; dissolve. ¶ 물감을 ~ dissolve dye 《in water》 / 물을 ~ add water; dilute 《a solution》 with water / 물을 탄 브랜디 brandy and water / 물을 타지 않은 브랜디 brandy straight / 우유에 물을 ~ adulterate milk with water / 포도주에 물을 ~ dash wine with water; water wine / 커피에 알코올을 조금 ~ lace coffee with spirits / 물에 소금을 ~ dissolve salt in water; salt the water / 설탕을 ~ put in sugar; sugar; sweeten with sugar / 술에 독을 ~ drop poison in the wine; poison the liquor / 음식에 독을 ~ put poison in the food / 위스키에 소다수를 타 주시오 Give me a glass of whisky and soda. / 홍차에 설탕을 탈까요 Do you take sugar in your tea?

**타다**[4] 《받다》 get; have; take; receive; obtain; be given; be awarded; be granted; be well received (인기를). ¶ 노벨상을 ~ be awarded a Nobel prize / 봉급〔월급〕을 ~ receive a salary; get paid / 월 200만 원의 월급을

~ draw 〔receive, get〕 a salary of two million won a month; draw a monthly pay of two million won 《from a firm》; get 〔make〕 2,000,000 won a month / 배급을 ~ draw *one's* rations / 상(금)을 ~ get 〔win, obtain〕 a prize / 상을 못 ~ miss 〔fail to win〕 a prize / 연금을 ~ receive 〔draw〕 a pension 〔an annuity〕 / 연금을 타는 사람 a recipient of a pension / 졸업장을 ~ receive a graduation certificate 〔diploma〕 / 아버지한테서 용돈을 ~ get pocket money from *one's* father / 그는 정년 퇴직으로 연금을 타게 되었다 He was 「pensioned off 〔retired on pension〕 at the age limit.

**타다**[5] ① 《가르다》 part; divide. ¶ 가르마를 ~ part 〔split〕 *one's* hair 《in the middle, at the side》. ② 《쪼개다》 split; divide; grind; saw. ¶ 탄 보리 ground 〔cracked〕 barley / 박을 ~ halve a gourd / 맷돌에 콩을 ~ split 〔grind〕 peas on a grindstone.

**타다**[6] ① 《악기를》 play (on). ¶ 가야금을 ~ play (on) a *kayagŭm* / 그 여자는 가야금을 잘 탄다 That woman is a good *kayagŭm* player. ② 《솜을》 beat 《cotton》 out; whip 〔willow〕 《cotton》.

**타다**[7] ① 《…하기 잘하다》 be apt to feel; be sensitive to; be tender; suffer (easily) from. ¶ 간지럼을 ~ be 〔feel〕 ticklish / 노염을 ~ be testy 〔touchy, irascible〕; be of an inflammable nature / 부끄럼을 ~ be 〔feel〕 shy; be bashful.
② 《…에 예민하다》 be susceptible 〔sensitive〕 to; be allergic to. ¶ 가뭄을 ~ be easily affected by dry weather / 더위를〔여름을〕 ~ be susceptible to the summer heat; lose flesh 〔weight〕 in summer; fall away in summer / 추위를 ~ be (over)sensitive to cold; be easily affected by cold weather / 옻을 ~ be allergic to lacquer 〔poison ivy〕 / 흰 옷은 더럼을 잘 탄다 White clothes pick up dirt easily.

**타닥거리다** ① 《걸음을》 plod on; walk with difficulty; trudge along 〔*one's* (weary) way〕; trudge on 《the street》; tread along 〔on〕. ¶ 타닥타닥 trudgingly; totteringly. ② 《살림을》 plod 〔scrape〕 along; barely manage to get along; make a bare living; eke out a scanty livelihood. ¶ 타닥타닥 barely; with difficulty. ③ 《빨래를》 beat pat=pat(-pat). ¶ 빨래를 방망이로 ~ paddle the laundry pat-pat-pat.

**타달–** ⇨ 터덜–.

**타당**(妥當) ~하다 (be) reasonable; sound; adequate; proper; appropriate; apposite; pertinent; right. ¶ ~한 의견 a right opinion / ~한 경영 방침 proper management policy / ~한 발언 an opportune 〔apposite〕 remark / ~치 않은 improper; inappropriate; inadequate; impertinent / ~하다고 인정하다 regard 《it》 as appropriate / 그건 ~한 방법이 못 된다 It's not an appropriate measure. / 그 정도가 ~할 것이다 That's about right.
◉ ~성(性) appropriateness; suitability; propriety; pertinence; validity: 그의 논리는 ~성이 결여되어 있다 His logic doesn't hold water. / 그의 주장에는 언제나 ~성이 있다 His argument is always valid. ~성 조사 a feasibility study.

**타도**(打倒) overthrow. ~하다 overthrow; overturn; strike down; topple 《*a person*》 from power. ¶ 정부를 ~하다 overthrow 〔topple〕 the government / 제국〔군국〕주의 ~ Down with imperialism 〔militarism〕!

**타도**(他道) another province; other 「provinces.

**타동**(他洞) another *dong* 〔village, community, block〕; other villages.

**타동**(他動) transitivity. ¶ ~의 transitive.
◉ ~사(詞) 〖문법〗 a transitive verb.

**타락**(墮落) depravity; (moral) corruption; degradation; fall; 《종교상의》 apostasy. ~하다 go to the bad; become depraved; degrade; be morally ruined; go wrong 〔astray〕; fall low (몸을); be corrupted; fall from grace (종교적으로). ¶ ~한 여자 a fallen 〔dissolute〕 woman / ~한 정치가 a corrupt politician / ~한 종교 a corrupted religion / ~한 학생 a depraved 〔degenerate〕 student; a student who has gone to the bad / ~한 생각〔도덕〕 depraved thoughts 〔morals〕 / 인격의 ~ degradation of character / ~시키다 corrupt; deprave; debase; lead 《*a person*》 astray / 아무를 ~에서 구하다 redeem 〔retrieve, save〕 *a person* from a depraved 〔delinquent〕 condition / 혼자 살면서부터 그는 ~했다 He has gone wrong since he began to live by himself. / 도박은 인간을 ~시킨다 Gambling leads man to ruin. / 그는 술로 인해서 ~했다 Drink led to his downfall. / 그녀가 그처럼 ~할 줄은 미처 생각 못 했다 I never thought she

would fall so low. / TV프로는 상업주의로 인해 ~되는 경향이 있다 TV programs are apt to be debased by commercialism.
◉ ~자 a degenerate; the fallen.

**타락줄** a rope made of human hair.

**타란텔라** 〖음악〗 the tarantella 〔tarentelle〕.

**타래** a bunch; a skein; a spiral; a coil. ¶ 실 한 ~ a skein of thread / 머리 꼭지한 ~ a lock 〔tuft, tress〕 of hair / 새끼 두 ~ two bunches 〔coils〕 of rope.

**타래과**(一菓) a kind of honey-cake.

**타래박** a long-handled well-dipper; a well bucket. ¶ ~으로 물을 푸다 dip up water; draw water 《from a well》 with a bucket.

**타래버선** children's quilted socks with decorations on them.

**타래송곳** ① 《병마개 빼는》 a corkscrew. ② 《나사 송곳》 a gimlet; an auger.

**타래쇠** a spiral metal door latch.

**타래타래** in coils 〔skeins〕; in spirals; round and round. ~하다 be in coils 〔spirals〕. ¶ 새끼를 ~ 감다〔사리다〕 coil the rope up.

**타력**(他力) the power of another; help from without; outside help; 《종교의》 salvation from outside. ¶ ~을 빌지 않고 with no outside help / 그는 무엇에나 ~에 의존한다 He always turns to others for help in everything. ◉ ~본원(本願) 〖불교〗 salvation by faith 〔through the benevolence of Amida Buddha〕. ~의존 reliance upon others.

**타력**(打力) 〖야구〗 batting 〔hitting〕 power. ¶ ~에서 앞서다 have better batters than; be superior to 《the opposing team》 in hitting power; outbat 〔outhit〕 《the other team》.

**타력**(惰力) (an) inertia; (a) momentum (*pl.* ~s, -ta); 《타성》 force of habit. ¶ ~으로 달리다 run by inertia / 자전거는 페달을 밟지 않아도 ~으로 얼마쯤은 달릴 수 있다 A bicycle can go some distance by inertia after you stop pedaling.

**타령**(打令) ① 《곡조의 하나》 a kind of tune; 《민요》 a ballad. ② 《뇌까림》 *one's* favorite 〔pet〕 phrase 〔saying〕. ¶ 그는 언제나 돈~이다 "Money" is a pet phrase of his.

**타륜**(舵輪) 〖항해〗 a steering wheel; a helm; the wheel. ¶ ~을 잡다 「be at 〔take〕 the wheel.

**타르** 〖화학〗 (coal) tar. ¶ ~계 화학 제품 a tar chemical / ~를 칠하다 tar / 이 담배는 ~ 성분이 적다 This cigarette contains little tar.

**타르머캐덤** 〖토목〗 tarmacadam.
◉ ~도로 a tarmacadam road; a tarmac. ~포장 tarmacadam (pavement).

**타르타르산**(一酸) 〖화학〗 tartaric acid.

**타르타르 소스** tartar sauce.

**타매**(唾罵) slander; calumination; insult; backbiting. ~하다 slander; calumninate; insult; backbite; abuse.

**타맥**(打麥) barley harvest. ~하다 harvest 〔thresh〕 the barley.

**타면**(他面) the other side 〔hand, phase, aspect〕. ¶ ~에서는 on the other hand; while; whereas / ~에서 생각해 보다 look at the other 〔reverse〕 side of the shield; view 《*a matter*》 from 「another 〔a different〕 angle.

**타면**(打綿) cotton beating. ~하다 beat cotton out; whip 〔willow〕 cotton.
◉ ~기(機) a cotton gin; a scutcher.

**타목** a thick husky voice.

**타문**(他聞) publicity; reaching others' ears. ¶ ~을 꺼리는 일 a confidential matter / ~을 꺼리다 [사람이 주어] be afraid of publicity; be anxious to keep 《*a matter*》 secret; [사물이 주어] be secret and confidential.

**타박** disparagement; finding fault 《with》; grumbling. ~하다 disparage; decry; find fault with; pick flaws with; grumble at. ¶ 음식을 ~하다 grumble 〔bitch 《속어》〕 at 〔about, over〕 the food / (옷이) 맞지 않는다고 ~하다 complain about the fit (of a garment). ◉ ~쟁이 a grumbler; a faultfinder. 음식~ grumbling at 〔about, over〕 the food.

**타박**(打撲) a blow; a stroke; a contusion.
◉ ~상(傷) a bruise; a contusion: ~상을 입다 get 〔sustain〕 a bruise 《on the leg》; be bruised 《all over》 / ~상을 입히다 bruise; contuse.

**타박타박**[1] 《걷는 모양》 ploddingly; totteringly; trudgingly. ¶ ~ 걷다 plod on *one's* way; trudge along 〔*one's* (weary) way〕; trudge on 《the street》; tread along 〔on〕; pad 〔jog〕 along.

**타박타박**[2] 《음식이》 being dry 〔not moist〕. ~하다 (be) dry; be not moist; be hard to chew. ¶ 떡이 ~해서 먹기 힘들다 The rice cake is so dry that it is hard to eat.

**타방면**(他方面) 《다른 방면》 another side 〔place, quarter〕; a different direction; 《다른 한 편》 the other side 〔hand〕.

**타봉**(打棒) 〖야구〗 batting. ¶ ～에 불이 붙다 pump out hits; pound (a pitcher) / ～을 봉쇄하다 throttle the bats 《of the opposing team》.

**타분하다** (be) stale; moldy; musty. ¶ 타분한 생선 stale fish / 타분한 생각 a musty idea.

**타블도트** 〖요리〗 a *table d'hôte* (F.).

**타블로** 〖미술〗 a tableau (*pl.* ～x, ～s).

**타블로이드** a tabloid. ¶ ～판 신문 a tabloid (newspaper) / ～형의 주간지 a weekly journal in tabloid form / ～판〔형〕으로 in tabloid form.

**타사**(他事) other matters. ¶ ～를 돌볼 겨를이 없다 have no time to think about other things; be too intent 《on *something*》 to think of anything else.

**타산**(打算) calculation; self-interest; money-mindedness. ～하다 calculate; reckon; consult *one's* own interest. ¶ ～적(인) calculating; selfish; mercenary; self-interested / 비～적인 disinterested; unselfish / ～적인 생각 a selfish 〔an egocentric〕 idea / ～적인 동기 a mercenary motive / ～적인 생각에서 from a self-centered viewpoint; in a spirit of calculation / 그녀는 ～적인 사람이다 She is a calculating woman. / 지독히도 ～적이군 How cold and calculating you are! / 그 자가 하는 일은 모두가 ～적이다 Everything he does is self-centered. *or* He is always consulting his own interests.

**타산지석**(他山之石) a 〔an object〕 lesson; an example *one* may profit by. ¶ ～으로 삼아라 Let this「be 〔serve as〕 a good (object) lesson to you. *or* A valuable lesson can be learned from it.

**타살**(他殺) murder; manslaughter (과실 따위에 의한); foul play (악질적인). ¶ ～의 혐의가〔흔적이〕 있다 There is a suspicion of「foul play 〔murder〕. / 아무래도 ～ 같다 There is every reason to believe that it is a murder. / 그의 시체가 발견되자 경찰은 ～로 단정했다 When he was found dead, the police concluded that it was (a case of) murder. ◉ ～시체 the body of a murder victim.

**타살**(打殺) beating 〔clubbing, striking〕 to death. ～하다 beat 〔club〕 《*a person*》 to death.

**타석**(打席) 〖야구〗 a batter's box (자리); a turn at bat (기회). ¶ ～에 서다〔들다〕 be at bat; take *one's* turn at the bat / 3～ 2안타 two hits three times up; two hits in three at bats / 첫 ～에서 홈런을 날리다 hit a homerun when *one* comes to bat the first time / 그는 4～ 3안타였다 He was at bat four times and scored three hits. ◉ 규정 ～수 the required minimum number of times at bat.

**타선**(打線) 〖야구〗 the (batting) line=up. ¶ ～이 작렬하다 make many hits; pump out hits / 상대 팀의 ～을 침묵시키다 keep the opposing team's bats silent.

**타선**(唾腺) 〖해부〗 a salivary gland. ◉ ～염색체 〖생물〗 a salivary chromosome.

**타성**(他性) 〖철학〗 otherness; differentness.

**타성**(他姓) another 〔a different〕 surname.

**타성**(惰性) 《타력》 inertia (관성); momentum (여세); 《습성》 force of habit. ¶ 지금까지의 ～으로 from (sheer) force of habit / ～으로 구르다 roll on by the force of momentum; roll by inertia / 그녀는 ～으로 그 일을 계속하고 있는 데 불과하다 She continues with work just「out of 〔by〕 habit.

**타수**(打手) a batter. ⇨ 타자(打者).

**타수**(打數) 〖야구〗 at-bats; times at bat; 〖골프〗 the number of strokes. ¶ 5～ five at bats / 5～ 3안타를 치다 make three hits in five at bats.

**타수**(舵手) a helmsman; a steersman; 《보트의》 a coxswain; a cox.

**타순**(打順) 〖야구〗 a batting order 〔line=up〕. ¶ ～을 바꾸다〔교체하다〕 reshuffle the batting order / ～을 정하다 decide the batting order / ～이 좋다〔나쁘다〕 The stronger 〔weaker〕 batters come to bat.

**타스** 《구 소련의 통신사》 Tass.

**타악기**(打樂器) a percussion instrument; the traps (경음악의). ¶ ～의 반주가 따르는 《a dance》 with percussion accompaniment. ◉ ～연주자 a percussionist.

**타액**(唾液) saliva; sputum. ¶ ～을 분비하다 salivate; secrete saliva. ◉ ～분비 salivation; flow of saliva. ～선 a salivary gland.

**타오르다** 《불이》 blaze up; flare up; burst into flames. ¶ 타오르게 하다 set afire 〔aflame, ablaze〕/ 기름 탱크에서 불길이 순식간에 타올랐다 The oil tank flared up in an instant. / 오랜만에 재회한 두 사람 사이에 사랑의 불길이 타올랐다 The flame of love flared up between them when they met after a long separation.

**타울거리다** struggle 〔strive〕 hard 《for, to *do*》; be overeager. ¶ 돈을 모으려고 ~ be overeager to make money; be money-mad.

**타워** a tower. ¶ 남산~ Namsan Tower. ◉ ~크레인 a tower crane.

**타원**(楕圓) an oval; an ellipse. ¶ ~(형)의 oval; elliptic(al) / ~으로 elliptically. ◉ ~궤도 an elliptical orbit. ~기둥 〖수학〗 a cylindroid; an elliptic cylinder. ~뿔 an elliptical cone. ~운동 elliptic motion. ~율 ellipticity. ~체 an oval figure; an ellipsoid: ~체의 ellipsoidal; spheroidal / 회전 ~체 an ellipsoid of revolution; a spheroid. ~컴퍼스 a trammel. ~형 an oval. ~회전자계(磁界) an elliptic rotating field.

**타월** a towel. ⇨ 수건. ¶ ~로 닦다 towel 《*oneself*》; wipe 〔dry〕 《*one's* hands》 with 〔on〕 a towel / ~을 던지다 《권투에서》 throw 〔toss〕 in the towel (패배를 인정함). ◉ ~걸이 a towel rail 〔rack, bar〕. ~담요 a blanket made of toweling. ~천 《a piece of》 toweling: ~천의 잠옷 a nightgown 〔pajamas〕 of toweling.

**타율**(他律) ① 《다른 규율》 another 〔a different〕 order 〔rule, discipline〕. ② 〖윤리〗 heteronomy. ¶ ~적인 행위 heteronomous behavior.

**타율**(打率) 〖야구〗 *one's* batting average (생략 bat. avg.). ¶ ~이 높다〔낮다〕 have a high 〔low〕 batting average / 그는 ~이 3할 5푼이다 He has a batting average of .350. (★ .350은 three-fifty; .400은 four hundred로 읽음).

**타의**(他意) 《남의 뜻》 another's will; 《딴 의도》 another 〔any other〕 intention; 《감춰진 의도》 an ulterior motive; a secret purpose; 《악의》 malice; ill will. ¶ ~가 없다 bear no hard feelings; have no other intention; have no grudge 《against》/ ~가 없음을 보이다 show that *one* has no other intention; make clear that *one* bears no malice 〔ill will〕/ 그의 외유는 ~에 의한 것이었다 He made the overseas tour not of his own will 〔accord〕. *or* He was compelled to make the overseas tour.

**타이**[1] 《태국》 (the Kingdom of) Thailand; Siam 《구칭》. ¶ ~의 Thai; Tai. ◉ ~말 Thai; Siamese. ~사람 a Thai; a Tai; a Thailander.

**타이**[2] ① 《동점》 a tie. ¶ ~로 끝나다 end in a 《3-3》 tie 《with》/ ~를 이루다 tie the score 《with a homer》/ 양팀은 ~가 되었다 The two teams tied. ② 《넥타이》 a necktie; a tie. ⇨ 넥타이. ◉ ~기록 an equal record: 세계 ~ 기록을 내다 equal 〔tie, match〕 the world mark 〔record〕. ~브레이크 〖테니스〗 a tie-break: ~ 브레이크로 이기다 win 《a set》 on the tie-break. ~스코어 a tie score: ~ 스코어가 되다 tie the score.

**타이가** 《아한대의 침엽수림》 a taiga.

**타이곤** 〖동물〗 a tigon. [< *tig*er+li*on*]

**타이르다** admonish 《*a person* for *his* fault》; remonstrate 《with *a person* about *his* behavior》; 《충고하다》 counsel 〔advise〕 《*a person* to *do*》; 《설득하다》 persuade 《*a person* to *do*》; 《도리로써》 reason 《with *a person* about *a thing*》. ¶ 공부 잘 하라고 ~ advise 《*a person*》 to study hard / 잘못을 ~ reason with 《*a person*》 on *his* mistake / 그릇된 행동을 ~ admonish 《*a person*》 for *his* misconduct / 타일러(서) …하게 하다 persuade 《*a person*》 to *do* 〔into *do*ing〕/ 타일렀으나 듣지 않았다 I have reasoned with him, but in vain. / 타일러서 그를 납득시켰다 I reasoned him into compliance. / 나는 그녀를 타일러 가출을 단념케 했다 I dissuaded her from running away from home. / 아무리 타일러도 막무가내다 All my advice falls flat upon him.

**타이머** a timer; a time switch; 《사진기의》 a (delay) timer. ¶ ~를 6시에 맞추다 set timer for six o'clock / 이 에어컨은 ~로 작동된다 This air conditioner works on a time switch.

**타이밍** timing. ¶ …와 정확히 ~을 맞추어 in exact timing with… / ~이 좋다〔나쁘다〕 be timely 〔untimely〕; be well 〔not well〕 timed / ~을 그르치게 하다 upset the 《opponent's》 timing / 그의 발언은 ~이 맞았다 His remark 「was quite timely 〔was timely on target〕. / 그는 공을 때리는 ~이 전혀 맞지 않는 군요 His timing in hitting the ball is hopeless, isn't it?

**타이어** a tire; a tyre 《영》. ¶ 닳아빠진 ~ a bald tire / 체인을 한 ~ a chained tire; a tire with a skid / ~자국 a tiremark; the imprint of a tire (tread) / ～가 펑크나다 [타이어가 주어] blow out; be 〔get〕 punctured; go flat; [사람·차가 주어] have a blowout; have 〔suffer〕 a flat tire; get a flat 《구어》/ ～를 갈다 change a tire; fix 〔fit〕 a new tire《on the wheel》/ 펑크난 ～를 갈다 change a flat tire / ～에 바람을 넣다 inflate 〔pump up〕 a tire / ～에 체인을 달다 chain 〔skid〕 tires. ◉ ～공장 a tire plant. 고무～ a rubber tire. 공기～ a pneumatic (tire). 예비～ a spare tire. 자동차～ an automobile tire.

**타이츠** tights; leotards. ¶ ～를 입은 여자 a woman in tights.

**타이트스커트** a tight skirt.

**타이틀** ①《선수권》 a title; a championship. ¶ ～을 다투다 play for the title / ～을 지키다 defend a title / ～을 빼앗다〔차지하다〕 gain a title; win a championship / ～을 잃다 lose a title / 그는 ～ 방어에 성공했다 He made good his title defense. ②《표제·직함》 a title. ¶ 책〔영화〕의 ～ the title of a book 〔movie〕/ 어마어마한 ～ a high=sounding title / ～이 없는 untitled; without any title. ◉ ～매치 『권투』 a title match: 논～ 매치 a nontitle match. ～보유자 the holder of the title; the champion. ～페이지 a title page.

**타이프** ① ⇨ 타입. ②《활자》 a type. ③《타자기》 a typewriter. ¶ ～의 연습 practice of typing / ～를 연습하다 practice typing / ～를 치다 typewrite; type (out) 《a letter》/ ～로 친 원고 a typed 〔typewritten〕 manuscript / 이 편지를 ～로 쳐 주시오 I want to have this letter typed. / ～를 1분에 몇 단어〔자〕 치십니까 How many words 〔letters〕 can you type a minute ? ◉ ～식 전신기 a telescripter; a teleprinter. ～용지 typewriter paper. ～인쇄물 a typescript.

**타이프라이터** a typewriter. ⇨ 타이프③. ◉ ～학원 a typing 〔typewriting〕 school. 영문～ an English-character typewriter. 한글～ a Korean-character typewriter. 휴대용～ a portable typewriter.

**타이피스트** a typist. ¶ 영문〔한글〕～ a typist in English 〔Korean〕.

**타인**(他人)《남》(*a*)《한 사람》 another person; 《전체》 (the) others; other people. ¶ ～ 앞에서 in the presence of others; before other people / ～은 어떤지 모르겠으되 as for myself; for my part; I don't know about others, but… / ～의 욕〔험담〕을 하다 speak ill 〔evil〕 of a person. (*b*)《무관계한 남》 an unrelated person; a stranger; an outsider (국외자). ¶ (마치) ～처럼 굴다 behave like a stranger; have a distant air / ～ 취급을 하다 treat 《*a person*》 like a stranger; make a stranger of 《*a person*》/ ～은 참견하지 마라 A third party should not thrust his nose into these matters. *or* It is none of your business.

**타인**(打印) punching. ◉ ～기 a punch; a punching machine.

**타일**(他日)《다른 날》 some 〔another〕 day; some other day 〔time〕; some day or other; 《일간》 one of these days; 《후일》 (at some time) in the future; at some future date. ¶ ～을 기약하고 헤어지다 part from 《*a person*》 deferring the matter to some future occasion / 방문을 ～로 미루다 make another date for a visit.

**타일** a tile. ¶ ～을 깔다〔붙이다〕 lay 〔set〕 tiles 《on》; face 〔cover〕 with tiles; tile 《a bathroom》/ ～을 깐 tiled 《bathroom》. ◉ ～공 a tiler; a tile=setter. ～공사 tiling; tiler's work; tile-setting. ～공장 a tilery. 도기(陶器)～ a ceramic tile.

**타임** ①《시간》 time; 《경기 중단 시간》 time-out. ¶ (경기 등에서) 2분 10초의 ～으로 in 〔with〕 a time of 2 minutes 10 seconds / ～을 재다 time; clock / ～을 청하다 take 〔call〕 a time-out (★ call은 심판이 선언할 경우) / …의 ～을 내다, ～은 …이다 clock 《10.4 seconds》; be clocked in 〔at〕 《2:33》; be timed (in) 《1.052》/ ～이 8초 떨어지다 lose eight seconds in *one's* timing / ～은 5분 8초다 He is timed 〔clocked〕 in 5 min. 8. / 내가 ～을 재 주마 I'll time you. ② 『사진』 time; exposure (노출 시간). ◉ ～래그 a time lag. ～리미트 《제한 시간》 a time limit; a deadline: ～리미트를 정하다 set 〔fix〕 a time limit 《for》; set a deadline 《for》. ～리코더 a time clock 〔recorder〕: 출퇴근 시각을 ～리코더로 기록하다 clock on and off at work; have *one's* arrival and departure times recorded by a time clock. ～머신 a time machine. ～셰어링 『컴퓨터』 time-sharing (시간 분할). ～스위치 a time switch; a timer. ～아웃 a time-out. ～업 Time's up. ～카드 a time card: ～카드를 눌러 찍다 《출근 때》 clock in 〔on〕; 《퇴근 때》 clock out 〔off〕. ～캡슐 a time capsule. ~키퍼 《시간 기록원〔기록기〕》 a timekeeper. ~테이블 《시각표》 a timetable; a train schedule (열차의). ~트라이얼 《자전거·자동차 경기 등의》 a time trial.

**타임스** 《신문》 *The Times* (of London).

**타입** 《형·유형》 (a) type; a pattern. ¶ 같은 ~의 사람 a person of the same type / 시대에 뒤진 ~의 사람 a person of old pattern; a man of old-fashioned type / 상인〔학자〕 ~의 사람 a man of a merchant 〔scholarly〕 type / 내가 좋아하는 ~의 여자 the kind 〔type〕 of girl I like / 그녀는 내가 좋아하는 ~이 아니다 She is not my type. / 난 저런 ~의 사내가 싫다 I don't like men of that type. *or* I don't like that type of men.

**타자**(打者) 『야구』 a batter; a batsman; a hitter. ¶ 다음 ~ the next batter / 왼손~ a left-handed hitter / 3할~ a .300 hitter (★ three hundred hitter로 읽음) / 1번~ the first batter; a leadoff (man). 「이터.

**타자기**(打字機) a typewriter. = 타이프라

**타자수**(打字手) a typist. = 타이피스트.

**타작**(打作) 《마당질》 thresh(ing). ~하다 thresh 〔thrash〕 《with a flail》; beat out; flail. ¶ 벼를 ~하다 thresh rice. ◉ ~마당 a threshing ground.

**타전**(打電) sending a telegram 〔wire〕; telegraphing. ~하다 telegraph; wire 《to》; send a telegram 〔wire〕 《to》; 《해저 전선으로》 cable; 《무선으로》 radio 《to》; send a radio 《to》; 《영》 wireless 《to》. ¶ 즉시 오라고 그에게 ~해라 Wire 〔Cable〕 him to come at once.

**타점**(他店) another store 〔firm〕. ¶ ~에서 사다 buy at some other store.

**타점**(打點) ① 《붓으로》 pointing; dotting; marking with a dot. ~하다 mark with a dot; dot. ② 《마음속으로》 marking a choice in *one's* heart. ~하다 choose in *one's* heart. ③ 『야구』 a run batted in (생략 R.B.I., r.b.i., rbi). ¶ 승리 ~ game winning runs batted in / ~을 올리다 drive 〔bat〕 in 《two》 runs.

**타조**(駝鳥) 『조류』 an ostrich.

**타종**(他宗) 『종교』 a different 〔another〕 sect; other sects; another religion.

**타종**(打鐘) striking 〔tolling〕 a bell. ~하다 strike 〔toll, ring〕 a bell.

**타죄**(他罪) another crime 〔offense〕; other crimes 〔offenses〕.

**타죽다** be burnt to death; perish in the flames 〔by fire〕. ¶ 그 화재로 많은 사람이 타 죽었다 Many persons were burnt to death in the fire.

**타지**(他地) 《다른 지방》 another province; a different part of the country; 《외국 땅》 a foreign country; an alien 〔a strange〕 land. ¶ ~ 사람 a stranger / ~에 살다 live away from home.

**타진**(打診) ① 『의학』 percussion; tapping. ~하다 sound; tap; examine by percussion. ¶ 의사는 환자의 가슴을 ~했다 The doctor sounded his patient's chest. ② 《남의 뜻을》 sounding; tapping. ~하다 sound (out) 《*a person* on *a matter*》; tap; feel out 《*a person* about *something*》. ¶ 남의 의견을 ~하다 tap 〔sound〕 another's opinion / 여론의 추세를 ~하다 gauge the trend of public opinion / 그 문제에 대해서 그의 의향을 ~해 볼 필요가 있다 We have to feel him out on the matter. / 그가 그 직책을 맡아주겠는지 어떨지 ~해 주겠느냐 Will you sound him out to see if he will accept the post? ◉ ~기 a plexor; a plessor. ~음 a percussion sound. ~판 a pleximeter.

**타짜**(꾼) a dishonest gambler; a card cheat; a cardsharp(er).

**타처**(他處) another place; other places. ¶ ~에(서) in 〔at〕 another 〔some other〕 place; elsewhere / ~에서 온 사람들 people from other places; out-of-town〔-village〕 people. ◉ ~지급 어음 『상업』 a domiciled bill.

**타천**(他薦) recommendation of other people. ¶ ~의 후보자 a candidate recommended by others / ~ 자천의 후보자가 많이 있었다 There were many candidates recommended either by other people or by themselves.

**타타르** 『역사』 Tartary; Tatary.

**타파**(打破) breaking; destruction; overthrow. ~하다 break down; do away with; abolish; overthrow 《bureaucracy》. ¶ 구습〔미신, 인습〕을 ~하다 do away with 〔break down〕 「the old practices 〔a superstition, conventionalities〕. ◉ 계급~ the abolition of class distinctions.

**타합**(打合) a previous arrangement; a consultation. ~하다 make (previous) arrangements 《as to time》; arrange 《*a matter* with *a person*》; prearrange. ¶ 만날 장소에 관해 ~하다 arrange where to meet / 그 일에 대해서는 그와 ~해 놓았다 I have made prior arrangements with him about that. / 그 건에 대하여 ~하고 싶습니다 I'd like to talk the case over with you.

**타향**(他鄕) another countryside; a place away from home; a foreign land; foreign parts. ¶～ 사람 a stranger; a foreigner / ～에서 away from home; in a strange land / ～에서 떠돌다 wander in a strange land; be an exile from home / ～에서 죽다 die in a strange land; die far from home / 10년이나 ～살이를 하다 be absent from home for 10 years.

**타협**(妥協) (a) compromise; (a) mutual concession; an understanding. ～하다 compromise; make 〔reach〕「a compromise 〔an agreement〕《with》; come to「terms 〔an understanding〕《with》. ¶～적인 태도 《assume》 a compromising attitude / ～적인 태도를 보이다〔보이지 않다〕 show「a 〔no〕 willingness to compromise / 비～적인 태도를 취하다 take an unyielding stand / ～하지 않는 사람 an uncompromising person; an intransigent (person) / (국제 문제 등의) ～에 의한 해결 a compromise solution / 양파간에 ～이 성립됐다 A compromise has been made between the contending parties. /「서로 조금씩 양보합시다」—「～의 여지가 없습니다」 "Let's meet each other halfway."— "There's no room for compromise."
◉ ～안 a compromise; a「compromise plan 〔proposal〕: ～안이 있는데 말씀드릴까요 May I suggest a compromise? ～자 a compromiser.

**타협점**(妥協點) a point of compromise 〔agreement〕; common 〔a meeting〕 ground. ¶～을 모색하다 seek mutually-agreeable compromise terms / ～을 발견하다〔찾아내다〕 find 〔work〕 out「a meeting point 〔common ground〕.

**타히티**(섬) 《남태평양의 섬》 Tahiti (Island). ◉ ～사람 a Tahitian.

**탁** ① 《부딪거나 터지는 소리》 with a「bump 〔clunk〕; with a crack; with a「pop 〔bang〕. ¶고무 풍선이 탁 터지다 a balloon「pops 〔bursts〕/ 머리를 탁 부딪다 bump 〔clunk〕 *one's* head against 《the doorframe》/ 문을 탁 닫다 slam 〔snap, bang〕 the door; shut the door with a bang / 상자 뚜껑을 탁 닫다 snap down the lid of the box / 책을 탁 덮다 shut a book with a「snap 〔clap〕.
② 《손으로 치는 소리》 with a slap 〔snap〕; with a crack. ¶탁 치다 slap 《*a person* in the face》; give 《*a person*》 a slap 《on the back》/ 무릎을 탁 치다 smack *one's* knee / 어깨를 탁 치다 pat 《*a person*》 on the shoulder.
③ 《끊어지거나 풀리는 소리》 with a snap; snappingly; with force. ¶(실따위가) 탁 끊어지다 snap (off, short) / 탁 부러지다 break with a snap / (감긴 것이) 탁 풀어지다 run down; come unwound; 《맨 것이》 come「untied 〔off〕/ 나뭇가지를 탁 꺾다 snap off a twig.
④ 《트이어 시원한 모양》 widely; extensively; vastly; 《가슴 속이》 refreshingly. ¶탁 트인 목초지 a wide open meadow / 탁 트인 전원 a wide spread of country / 시야가 탁 트이다 command extensive views.
⑤ 《숨막히는 모양》 stiflingly; chokingly. ¶숨이 탁 막힐 것 같은 먼지 a choking cloud of dust / 숨이 탁 막히는 더위였다 It was stifling hot.

**탁견**(卓見) 《명안》「a fine 〔an excellent〕 idea 〔view, opinion〕; 《통찰》 farsightedness; clear-sightedness; penetration. ¶～이 있다 have a long「head 〔view〕/ ～지사(之士) a man of farsight; a farsighted man / ～ 있는 clear-sighted; long-headed〔-sighted〕; farseeing.

**탁구**(卓球) table tennis; ping-pong. ¶～를 치다 play ping-pong. ◉ ～공 a ping-pong ball. ～대 a「ping-pong 〔table-tennis〕 table. ～선수 a「ping-pong 〔table-tennis〕 player. ～시합 a table-tennis tournament. 한국 ～협회 the Korea Table-tennis Association.

**탁론**(卓論) an outstanding theory 〔argument〕; a clever view.

**탁류**(濁流) a muddy stream; turbid waters 《of a river》. ¶～에 휩쓸리다 be swallowed up by the muddy stream / ～는 마을을 휩쓸었다 The muddy water rushed through the village.

**탁마**(琢磨) 《옥석의》 polishing (a gem); 《학문·덕행의》 improvement; cultivation. ～하다 polish; improve 《*one's* virtue》; cultivate 《*one's* mind》. ¶절차(切磋)～한 덕으로 by dint of hard work.

**탁목조**(啄木鳥) 〘조류〙 a woodpecker. ＝「딱따구리.

**탁발**(托鉢) religious mendicancy 《in Buddhism》. ～하다 go about asking for alms. ◉ ～승 a begging bonze; a mendicant monk.

**탁본**(拓本) ＝ 탑본(搨本).

**탁상**(卓上) ¶～의〔에〕 on the table 〔desk〕/ ～용의 desk 《dictionaries》. ◉ ～계획 a「desk 〔paper〕 plan. ～공

론 a desk 〔mere〕 theory; an impracticable proposition: ～공론가 an armchair theorist. ～시계 a table clock. ～연설 an after-dinner speech; a speech (made) at a dinner 〔luncheon〕: 간단한 ～ 연설을 하다 make a little after-dinner speech. ～일기〔캘린더〕 a desk diary 〔calendar〕. ～전화 a desk telephone.

**탁선**(託宣) an oracle; a divine revelation 〔message〕.

**탁설**(卓說) an excellent 〔remarkable〕 opinion; a far-sighted 〔sound and sensible〕 view.

**탁성**(濁聲) a thick voice.

**탁세**(濁世) 《혼탁한 세상》 the 〔this〕 corrupt 〔vice-ridden, degenerate〕 world; 《속세》 this world; the sublunary world.

**탁송**(託送) consignment. ～하다 consign 《goods to a forwarding agency》; send 《*a thing*》 by 〔through, under the care of〕 《*a person*》. ¶ 공항에서 짐들을 운송업자에게 ～시켰다 At the airport I sent my baggage on through a forwarding agency. ◉ ～품 a consignment.

**탁아소**(託兒所) a day 〔public〕 nursery; a day-care center 《미》; a crèche 《영》; a child-care center. ¶ 요즈음 아이들을 ～에 맡기고 직장에 나가는 젊은 부부들이 늘고 있다 Nowadays there are an increasing number of young parents who go to work leaving their children at day-care centers.

**탁엽**(托葉) 〖식물〗 a stipule. ＝턱잎.

**탁월**(卓越) excellence; superiority; preeminence; eminence; prominence. ～하다 (be) excellent; eminent; prominent; distinguished; surpass 《in》. ¶ ～한 수완 superior ability / ～한 인물 a person of outstanding stature 〔greatness〕 / ～한 학자 a prominent scholar / 인물, 역량이 모두 ～하다 surpass others both in character and ability.

**탁음**(濁音) 〖음성〗 a voiced sound 〔consonant〕; a sonant. ¶ ～의 sonant.

**탁자**(卓子) a table. ¶ 둥근 ～ a round table / 4인용의 ～ a table for four / ～를 끼고 마주 앉다 [두 사람이 주어] sit across a table; [한 쪽이 주어] sit across from 《*a person*》 at a table / ～에 둘러앉다 sit (a)round a table / ～에 놓다 put 《*a thing*》 on the table. ◉ ～손 a wooden 〔metal〕 support under a shelf 〔table〕.

**탁주**(濁酒) raw 〔unrefined〕 rice wine; *makkŏlli*. ＝막걸리.

**탁탁** ①《일을 해치우는 모양》 promptly; quickly; speedily; with (brisk) dispatch. ¶ 일을 ～ 해치우다 finish *one's* business with dispatch; do a thing quickly; be prompt in *one's* work; make short 〔quick〕 work of *one's* business.
②《픽픽 쓰러지는 모양》《fall》 in rapid 〔quick〕 succession; 《come down》 one after another. ¶ 적탄에 병사들이 ～ 쓰러졌다 The soldiers fell thick and fast under the enemy's fire.
③《소리나는 모양》 with cracks 〔pops〕; flapping; clattering; rattling. ¶ 고무풍선이 ～ 터지다 balloons burst with pops / 날개를 ～ 치다 flap 〔flutter〕 《its》 wings / 먼지를 ～ 털다 beat the dust off 《*one's* trousers》; 《총채로》 dust bustlingly with a duster / 손뼉을 ～ 치다 clap *one's* hands / 장작이 ～ 소리를 내며 타다 firewood 「burns crackling 〔burns with a cracking〕.
④《침 뱉는 모양》 spitting hard or in rapid succession. ¶ 침을 ～뱉다 spit and spit 《at》; go spit-spit-spit.
⑤《숨이 막히는 모양》 stifling; short of 〔out of〕 breath; gasping. ¶ 숨이 ～ 막히다 be stifled; be gasping for breath; lose *one's* breath.

**탁탁하다** ①《피륙이》 (be) close-woven; thick and strong. ⇨톡톡하다②. ②《살림이》 (be) abundant; plentiful. ¶ 살림이 ～ be well 〔comfortably〕 off.

**탁하다**(濁—) ①《물 따위가》 (be) muddy; turbid; dull; thick; 《불순하다》 (be) impure; foul. ¶ 탁한 공기 impure 〔foul〕 air / 탁한 물 muddy water / 탁한 세상 the corrupt world / 마음이 탁한 사람 a person with dark designs; an inscrutable 〔untrustworthy〕 person / 탁해지다 become muddy 〔turbid, impure, thick〕; become cloudy (술 따위가) / 가스는 방안 공기를 탁하게 한다 Gas spoils 〔poisons〕 the air of a room. / 우물이 탁해졌다 The well has got muddy.
②《음성 따위가》 (be) thick; 《안색이》 (be) dark; gloomy (우울하다). ¶ 탁한 목소리 a thick voice / 탁한 표정을 짓고 있다 wear 〔put on〕 a gloomy expression.

**탄**(炭) ⇨석탄, 연탄.

**탄갱**(炭坑) 〖광산〗 a coal mine; 《갱도》 a (coal) pit. ¶ ～을 파다 work a coal mine. ◉ ～침수 a mine flood.

**탄고**(炭庫) a coal cellar 〔bin, bunker〕.

**탄광**(炭鑛) 〖광산〗 a coal mine; a colliery. ◉ ～근로자 a coal miner; a collier. ～업 the coal-mining industry: ～업자 a coal-mine operator. ～주 a coal-mine owner; a colliery proprietor. ～지대 a coal-mining region 〔area〕. ～회사 a colliery 〔mining〕 company.

**탄내** a burnt smell. ¶ 무슨 ～가 난다 There's a smell of something burning 〔smoldering〕.

**탄내**(炭―) (char)coal fumes; 《연탄 가스》 briquet gas. ¶ ～를 맡다 get poisoned by briquet gas.

**탄대**(彈帶) a cartridge belt. ⇨ 탄띠.

**탄도**(彈道) a trajectory; a line of fire; the path of a projectile. ¶ 곡사〔직사〕～ a curved 〔flat〕 trajectory / ～를 그리며 날다 follow a ballistic course. ◉ ～계수 the coefficient of a trajectory. ～곡선 a ballistic curve. ～비행 a trajectory 〔suborbital〕 flight. ～탄 a ballistic missile: 대륙간 ～탄 an intercontinental ballistic missile (생략 ICBM). ～학 ballistics.

**탄두**(彈頭) a warhead (포탄의). ¶ 미사일 ～ a missile warhead / 핵～ a nuclear warhead.

**탄띠**(彈―) a bandolier 〔bandoleer〕; a cartridge 〔an ammunition〕 belt.

**탄력**(彈力) ① 〖물리〗 elasticity; resilience; spring; bounce; give. ¶ ～ 있는 elastic; springy; resilient / ～ 없는 inelastic; nonelastic; of no bounce / 이 낡은 고무줄은 ～이 없다 There is no spring left in these old rubber bands. ② 《융통성》 flexibility. ¶ ～적인 태도를 취하다 take a flexible attitude / 실제적인 운용에 있어서는 이들 규칙이 ～적으로 적용되어야 한다 In actual use, these rules should be applied flexibly. ◉ ～계 an elastometer. ～성 elasticity; resilience; flexibility; adaptability: ～성이 없는 계획 an inflexible program. ～세율 elastic tax rates. ～소 〖생화학〗 elastin. ～시험 an elasticity test.

**탄로**(綻露) disclosure; revelation; exposure; divulgence; detection. ～나다 get found out 〔detected, divulged, exposed, disclosed〕; be revealed 〔laid bare〕; come 〔be brought〕 to light; come out. ¶ ～날까봐 (두려워서) for fear of detection / 그것은 틀림없이 ～날 것이다 It is bound to come out. / 음모는 ～나고 말았다 The plot has been laid bare. / 비밀이 ～났다 The secret leaked 〔got〕 out. / 과거가 ～난 후 아무도 그를 존경하지 않았다 After his past was raked up, no one respected him.

**탄막**(彈幕) a 〔an artillery〕 barrage. ¶ 엄호～ a covering barrage / ～을 치다 put up a barrage. ◉ ～포화 covering fire; a curtain fire.

**탄말**(炭末) charcoal dust.

**탄맥**(炭脈) a coal seam 〔vein〕.

**탄명스럽다** (be) fuzzy-minded; vague; ambiguous.

**탄미**(歎美) admiration; adoration; appreciation. ～하다 admire; be filled with admiration; appreciate; adore; praise; laud. ¶ ～할 만한 admirable. ◉ ～자 an admirer; an adorer.

**탄복**(歎服) ～하다 admire; be struck 〔moved〕 with admiration; feel admiration 《for》; be deeply impressed 《with, by》. ¶ ～할 만한 admirable; praiseworthy; worthy of admiration / ～케 하다 evoke admiration from 《*a person*》; impress 《*a person*》 favorably / 그녀의 재능에 ～했다 I was struck by her ability.

**탄사**(歎辭) 《감탄의 말》 admiration; 《탄식하는 말》 lamentation.

**탄산**(炭酸) 〖화학〗 carbonic acid. ¶ ～의 carbonic / ～을 없애다 decarbonate. ◉ ～가스 carbonic acid gas; carbon dioxide. ～결핍증 〖의학〗 acapnia. ～공(孔) 〖지질〗 a *mof(f)ette* (F.). ～나트륨 sodium carbonate; carbonate of soda: 천연 ～나트륨 natron. ～납 lead carbonate. ～동화작용 assimilation of carbonicacid gas 〔carbon dioxide〕; 《광합성》 photosynthesis. ～석회 calcium carbonate; carbonate of lime. ～소다 ⇨ ～나트륨. ～수 carbonated 〔aerated〕 water; soda (water). ～수소나트륨 bicarbonate of soda; sodium bicarbonate. ～암모늄 ammonium carbonate; *sal volatile* (L.). ～암모니아수 salt of hartshorn; *sal volatile.* ～염 a carbonate. ～음료 a carbonated drink; soda (pop) 《미》; a fizzy drink 《구어》. ～천(泉) a carburetted 〔carbonated〕 spring. ～칼륨 potassium carbonate; carbonate of potash; pearl ash (조제의). ～칼슘 calcium carbonate.

**탄산증**(呑酸症) 〖의학〗 pyrosis; heartburn.

**탄산지**(炭酸紙) carbon paper. ¶ ～로 복사하다 take copies with carbon paper / ～로 복사한 카피 a carbon copy.

**탄상**(炭床) a coal bed. ⇨ 탄층(炭層).

**탄상**(歎賞) admiration; praise. ＝ 탄미.

**탄생**(誕生) (a) birth; 《그리스도의》 the Nativity. ～하다 be born; come into ｢the world 〔existence〕. ¶ 새로운 클럽의 ～ the birth of a new club / ～을 축하하다 celebrate 《*a person's*》 birth. ◉ ～석 a birthstone. ～일 a birthday. ⇨ 생일. ～지 *one's* birthplace.

**탄성**(彈性) 〖물리〗 elasticity. ¶ ～이 있는 elastic; springy; buoyant; resilient / ～이 없는 inelastic; nonelastic.
◉ ～고무 elastic gum; gum elastic; (India) rubber. ～공학 elasticity engineering. ～률 the modulus 〔coefficient〕 of elasticity. ～설계 〖건축〗 an elastic design. ～체 an elastic body.

**탄성**(歎聲) 《탄식의》 a sigh (of grief); 《감탄의》 a sigh of admiration; an exclamation. ¶ ～을 발하다 sigh 《over》; heave 〔breathe, utter〕 a sigh of grief; deplore; grieve 〔lament〕 《for, over》; utter 〔let out〕 a cry of admiration / 장엄한 폭포의 광경에 저절로 ～이 터져 나왔다 At the sight of the magnificent waterfall, we let out a cry of wonder in spite of ourselves.

**탄소**(炭素) 〖화학〗 carbon. ¶ ～질의〔를 함유한〕 carbonaceous; carbonous / ～를 제거하다 decarbonize / ～와 화합시키다 carburet; carbonize / ～화하다 carbonate. ◉ ～강 carbon steel. ～봉 a carbon point. ～선 a carbon filament. ～섬유 a carbon fiber. ～제거 decarbonization.

**탄수**(炭水) ① 《석탄과 물》 coal and water. ② 《탄소와 수소》 carbon and hydrogen.

**탄수화물**(炭水化物) 〖화학〗 a carbohydrate. ¶ ～이 적은 식사 a low-carbohydrate diet; a diet low in carbohydrates.

**탄식**(歎息) a sigh; 《비탄》 lamentation; grief. ～하다 sigh 《over》; heave 〔draw〕 a sigh (of grief); sigh for grief; grieve 《for, about》; lament; deplore. ¶ 자신의 불운을 ～하다 lament (over) *one's* misfortune / 정계의 부패를 ～하다 deplore the corruption of political circles / ～으로 날을 보내다 sigh away *one's* days.

**탄신**(誕辰) a (royal) birthday; the king's birthday; the birthday of a sage 〔saint〕. ¶ 제84회 ～ the 84th birthday.

**탄알**(彈—) a bullet (소총탄); a shot (산탄); a shell (포탄). ¶ ～ 자국 a bullet hole / ～에 맞다 be hit by a bullet; get 〔receive〕 a bullet 《in *one's* arm》 / ～에 맞아 죽다 be killed by a bullet; be shot dead / ～을 재다 load 《a gun》; charge 《a gun》 / 총에서 ～을 뽑(아내)다 unload a gun / ～이 넓적다리에 박히다 a bullet is lodged 〔embedded〕 in *one's* thigh / ～이 비오듯하다 bullets fall thick and fast / 비오듯하는 ～ 속을 전진하다 advance under a shower of bullets.

**탄압**(彈壓) 《압제》 oppression; pressure; suppression 《of》; a crackdown 《on》. ～하다 oppress 《the people》; suppress 《the movement》; repress; crack down on 《political activity, students》. ¶ ～적(인) oppressive; high-handed; coercive (강제적인) / ～적인 수단 coercive method / ～을 가하다 bring pressure on; subject 《*a person*》 to pressure; clamp down on 《the minority group》 / ～을 받다 be suppressed; be subjected to pressure 〔suppression〕 / 언론의 자유를 ～하다 suppress freedom of speech; place a gag on the freedom of speech / 그 운동은 치안 방해로 ～을 받았다 The movement was suppressed as a breach of the public peace. / 자유는 결코 ～되어서는 안 된다 Freedom should never be suppressed.
◉ ～정책 an oppressive 〔a repressive〕 measure.

**탄약**(彈藥) ammunition; munitions; ammo 《구어》. ¶ ～ 50발 fifty rounds of ammunition.
◉ ～고 a magazine. ～상자 an ammunition box 〔chest〕; a cartridge box. ～제조소 an ammunition factory; ammunition works. ～집적소〔저장소〕 an ammunition dump 〔area〕. ～차 an ammunition car; an ammo carrier. ～창(廠) an ammunition depot. ～통 a cartridge.

**탄우**(彈雨) a shower 〔rain, hail〕 of bullets 〔shells〕. ¶ ～ 속에〔을〕 《advance》 under a rain of shells; amid a hail of bullets.

**탄원**(歎願) (a) petition; (an) entreaty; (a) supplication; (an) appeal. ～하다 implore; petition 《the government》; appeal 《to》; entreat 《*a person* for money》; supplicate. ¶ ～하는 표정으로 with an imploring look / ～을 받아들이다 listen 〔lend an ear〕 to 《*a person's*》 entreaties; grant a petition 〔an entreaty〕 / 정부에 구조를 ～하다 petition the government for relief / ～을 받아들이지 않다 reject an entreaty;

turn a deaf ear to 《*a person's*》 entreaties; turn down a petition / 그는 마을 사람들의 ~으로 석방되었다 He was released on the petition of the villagers.
◉ ~자 a supplicant; a petitioner.

**탄원서**(歎願書) a (written) petition. ¶ ~를 내다 present 〔send in, deliver, submit〕 a (written) petition 《to》; file a petition with 《the government》 / 많은 사람들이 그 ~에 서명했다 Many people signed the petition.

**탄일**(誕日) a birthday. ⇨ 탄신(誕辰).

**탄자니아**《나라 이름》 Tanzania. ¶ ~의 Tanzanian. ◉ ~사람 a Tanzanian.

**탄저**(炭疽) ◉ ~균 the bacteria of anthrax; *Bacillus anthracis.* ~병 《동물의》 (an) anthrax; 《식물의》 anthracnose.

**탄전**(炭田) 〖광산〗 a coalfield.

**탄젠트** 〖수학〗 a tangent (생략 tan).

**탄주**(彈奏) play; performance. ~하다 play (on) 《the piano》; perform; pluck 〔touch〕 《the strings of》. ◉ ~법 touch. ~자 a player; a performer.

**탄지** burnt tobacco left over in a pipe.

**탄진**(炭塵) coal dust.
◉ ~폭발 an explosion of coal dust.

**탄질**(炭質) the quality of coal. ¶ ~이 좋다〔나쁘다〕 The coal is of good 〔poor〕 quality.

**탄차**(炭車) a coal waggon; a coal truck 《영》.

**탄착**(彈着) the hit 〔impact, fall〕 of a shot 〔bullet, shell〕. ◉ ~거리 the range of a gun; 《within》 gunshot: ~거리 200m의 소총 a rifle with a range of 200 meters. ~관측 spotting: ~관측기(機) a spotter plane. ~점 point of the impact 《of a shell》. ~지역 〖군사〗 the area within 《rifle, mortar, etc.》 range; the possible target area 《of a missile》.

**탄창**(彈倉) 〖군사〗 a magazine 《of a machine gun》.

**탄체**(彈體) 《유도탄의》 the airframe.

**탄층**(炭層) 〖지질〗 a coal seam 〔bed〕. ¶ ~이 깊은 탄갱 a colliery with a thick 〔deep〕 bed.

**탄탄대로**(坦坦大路) a broad level highway; a royal road.

**탄탄하다** (be) strong; solid; firm; stout; strongly-built; 《몸이》 (be) robust; tough; sinewy. ¶ 탄탄한 집 a solidly-built house / 탄탄한 체격의 남자 a powerfully-built man; a man of solid build / 탄탄하게 만들어져 있다 be strongly built 〔made〕 / 모양은 어떻든 탄탄하게만 되어 있다 It is made for strength and not for appearance.

**탄탄하다**(坦坦—) (be) level; even; smooth; flat. ¶ 탄탄한 길 a smooth road.

**탄탈** 〖화학〗 tantalum (기호 Ta).

**탄편**(彈片) a shell splinter; a fragment of shell.

**탄폐**(炭肺) black lung (disease); a lung disease due to coal dust.

**탄피**(彈皮) an empty cartridge.

**탄하다** ① 《참견하다》 make uncalled-for remarks; poke 〔put, stick〕 *one's* nose into 《another's affair》; be nosy. ② 《시비조로》 give 《*a person*》 a retort 〔back talk〕; cavil 〔rail〕 at; find fault with 《a remark》; criticize; pick a quarrel 《with》. ¶ 아무의 말을 ~ cavil at what *a person* has said / 남의 일을 ~ criticize another's affairs.

**탄핵**(彈劾) impeachment; denunciation; accusation; censure. ~하다 impeach 《*a person* of 〔with〕 a crime》; denounce; accuse 《*a person* of misdemeanor》; censure. ¶ 판사는 뇌물을 먹고 ~을 받았다 The judge was impeached for taking bribes.
◉ ~연설 an impeachment address. ~자 an impeacher; a denunciator. ~재판소 a Court of Impeachment.

**탄핵안**(彈劾案) an impeachment motion 〔resolution〕. ¶ 정부 ~을 제출하다 introduce a motion of impeachment against the Government.

**탄화**(炭化) 〖화학〗 carbonization. ~하다 carbonize; char; carburet. ◉ ~규소 silicon carbide. ~물 a carbide. ~법 (means of) carbonization. ~수소 hydrocarbon. ~철 cementite. ~칼슘 calcium carbide. ~플루오르 fluorocarbon.

**탄환**(彈丸) 《산탄》 a shot; 《총탄》 a bullet; 《포탄》 a shell; a (cannon) ball; shrapnel (유산탄). ⇨ 탄알. ¶ ~이 뚫지 못하는 bulletproof; shellproof / ~에 의한 부상 a gunshot wound / ~이 다 떨어지다 fire away all *one's* shots / 빗발치는 ~ 속을 나아가다 advance under a shower 〔hail, rain, storm〕 of bullets / 적에게 ~을 퍼붓다 rain 〔shower〕 shells upon the enemy / 한 발의 ~이 그녀의 목숨을 앗았다 A bullet killed her. ◉ ~열차 a bullet train. ~저장실 a magazine; a depot.

**탄회**(坦懷) ~하다 (be) openhearted; candid. ⇨ 허심탄회.

**탄흔**(彈痕) a bullet mark 〔hole〕; a shot hole. ¶ ~ 투성이의 벽 a bullet-pocked wall / ~이 남아 있는 대문 a bullet-holed gate.

**탈**《가면》 a mask. ¶ 탈을 쓰다 wear 〔put on〕 a mask; mask *one's* face; use a mask; cover *one's* face with a mask;《위선의》dissemble; play the hypocrite / 위선의 탈을 쓴 사람 a hypocrite; a wolf in sheep's clothing 〔in a lamb's skin〕/ …의 탈을 쓰고 under the mask 〔cloak〕 of 《friendship, charity》; in 〔under〕 the semblance of 《a sage》; under the color of 《religion》/ 탈을 벗다 take 〔throw〕 off *one's* mask 〔disguise〕; unmask; show *one's* true colors (정체를 드러내다) / …의 탈을 벗기다 unmask 〔take off the mask of〕 《a hypocrite》; debunk 《an imposter》.

**탈**(頉) ① 《사고》 an accident; an incident; an untoward event; 《장애》 a hitch; a snag; a failure; a trouble; a mishap; 《지장》 a hindrance; an impediment; interruption. ¶ 별 탈이 없는 한 if nothing interferes / 탈 없이 without a hitch 〔trouble〕; 《순조로이》 smoothly; well; all along; 《무사히》 safely; in safety; safe and sound; 《건강하게》 in good health / 탈 없이 진행되다 go on without hitch 〔trouble〕; keep going in good shape; go all right 〔well〕; run smoothly / 일에 탈이 생기다 have trouble with the affair / 술담배를 조금 하는 것쯤은 탈 없을 테지 A little wine and tobacco will do you no harm. / 애, 큰 탈이 났다 Good heavens, we're in real trouble!
② 《병》 sickness; illness 《영》; a disease; a trouble; a disorder; 《고장》 something wrong; breakdown. ¶ 과식하여 탈이 나다 make *oneself* ill by overeating; overeat *oneself* ill / 기계가 탈이 나다 a machine breaks down; something goes wrong with a machine; have 〔run into〕 trouble with the machine / 몸에 탈이 나다 get ill 〔sick〕; have (health) difficulties / 배탈이 나다 have a stomach trouble; suffer from indigestion / 무리를 한 것이 탈이 된 겁니다 This comes of the strain of work. *or* The strain has begun to tell on me.
③ 《흠》 a fault; a defect; a flaw; 《트집》 faultfinding. ¶ 탈을 잡다 find fault with; pick flaws with; haggle 《about》; cavil at; 《시비를》 accuse 《*a person*》 falsely; make a false charge 《against》/ 그 친구는 게으른 것이 탈이다 The bad thing about him is his laziness.

**탈각**(脫却) a breakaway. ～하다 get rid 〔clear〕 of; rid 〔extricate〕 *oneself* of; slough off; shake *oneself* free from; free *oneself* from; emerge from. ¶ 그들은 아직도 구습에서 ～못 하고 있다 They cannot get rid of 〔free themselves from〕 the old custom yet.

**탈각**(脫殼) 〖동물〗 exuviation. ～하다 exuviate; cast off a shell 〔skin〕; slough.

**탈거**(奪去) ～하다 take away; carry off.

**탈것** 《육상의》 a vehicle; 《수상의》 a vessel; 《교통기관》 a (public) conveyance; (a means of) transport.

**탈격**(奪格) 〖문법〗 the ablative case.

**탈고**(脫稿) completion of a manuscript. ～하다 finish writing; complete 《a novel》; [원고가 주어] be completed. ¶ 그가 집필중인 소설은 곧 ～한다 The novel he is writing is near completion. / 그 저작은 이미 ～되었다 The work is already complete in manuscript.

**탈곡**(脫穀) threshing (grain); thrashing. ～하다 thresh 〔thrash〕 《wheat》; do the threshing. ◉ ～기 a threshing machine; a thresher.

**탈교**(脫教) renegation. ⇨ 배교(背教).

**탈구**(脫臼) 〖의학〗 dislocation. ～하다 get 〔be〕 dislocated; slip 〔be put〕 out of joint. ¶ 그의 왼팔이 ～되었다 He has had his left arm dislocated. *or* His left arm is out of joint. ◉ ～교정 extension. ～부전(不全) incomplete dislocation.

**탈나다**(頉―) ⇨ 탈(頉). ① 《병나다》 become 〔get, fall〕 ill; be taken ill. ② 《고장나다》 break down; get out of order. ¶ 시계가 ～ a watch breaks down / 일이 ～ a plan is ruined. ③ 《사고나다》 have a hitch 〔mishap, trouble〕; run into trouble. ¶ 그녀에게 뭔가 탈난 게 틀림없어 Some mishap must have happened to her.

**탈놀음** a masque; a masque 〔mask〕 play.

**탈당**(脫黨) secession 〔withdrawal〕 from a party; defection; bolting 《미》. ～하다 secede (from a party); withdraw 〔defect, bolt〕 from a party; desert 〔leave, abandon〕 a party. ¶ 그는 민주당을 ～했다 He resigned his membership of the Democratic Party. ◉ ～성명(서) a (written) statement of *one's* secession from a party. ～신고(서) a written report of *one's* secession from the party. ～자 a defector; a seceder;

a bolter: ~자가 속출했다 One member after another left the party.

**탈락**(脫落) ① 《빠짐》 (***a***) 《붙은 것이》 falling 〔coming〕 off. ~하다 fall 〔slip〕 off; shed. (***b***) 《누락》 an omission. ~하다 be omitted; be left out; be excluded 〔eliminated〕. ¶ 공천에서 ~되다 be left out of the public nomination / 예선에서 ~하다 be eliminated 《from the tournament》; be rejected in an elimination round / 문장 중에 ~이 있다 There are omissions in the sentence. ② 《이탈》 defection; dropping away (낙오). ~하다 fall away 《from》; 《낙오하다》 fall 〔drop〕 behind; drop out. ¶ (대학생의) 중도 ~ the expulsion before 〔prior to〕 graduation / 많은 선수들이 레이스에서 ~했다 Many runners dropped out of the race. ◉ ~자 a 《high school》 dropout.

**탈력**(脫力) lassitude; enervation; listlessness. ¶ ~감 a feeling of lassitude 〔enervation, listlessness〕 / ~감을 느끼다 feel listless 〔washed-out, enervated〕.

**탈루**(脫漏) an omission; being left out; missing. ~하다 get omitted; be left out; be missing.

**탈륨** 〖화학〗 thallium (기호 Tl).

**탈리도마이드** 〖약〗 thalidomide. ◉ ~장애아 a thalidomide baby 〔child〕.

**탈린**(脫燐) 〖화학〗 dephosphorization. ~하다 dephosphorize.

**탈모**(脫毛) 《빠짐》 loss 〔falling out〕 of hair; 《뽑음》 depilation. ~하다 《*one's* hair》 fall out 〔off〕; lose hair; bald; 《동물이》 molt. ¶ 이 로션은 ~를 방지한다 This lotion stops the hair from falling out. ◉ ~제 a depilatory (agent); a hair remover. ~증 〖의학〗 alopecia; depilatory disease: 원형 ~증 alopecia areata. ~크림 depilatory cream.

**탈모**(脫帽) doffing *one's* hat 〔cap〕; 《구령》 Hats off! ~하다 take 〔pull〕 off *one's* hat 〔cap〕; remove *one's* hat 〔cap〕; uncover 〔bare〕 *one's* head.

**탈무드** 〖유대교〗 the Talmud. ◉ ~학자 a Talmudic scholar; a Talmudist.

**탈바가지** a mask (made from a calabash 〔gourd〕).

**탈바꿈** (a) transformation; (a) metamorphosis. ~하다 change (the shape of); assume another 〔a different〕 shape; metamorphose; transform.

**탈바닥** splashing; spattering. ~거리다 keep splashing 〔spattering〕; splash about in 《the water》.

**탈박** dabbling; splashing. ~거리다 keep dabbling in the water.

**탈법행위**(脫法行爲) an evasion of the law; a slip from the grip of the law. ¶ 그건 분명히 ~가 된다 That constitutes a clear evasion of the law.

**탈복**(脫服) expiration of the period of mourning. ⇨ 탈상(脫喪).

**탈북**(脫北) 《북한으로부터의》 defection from North Korea. ◉ ~자 a North Korean defector; a defector from North Korea: 현재 많은 ~자가 남한에 살고 있다 Currently, many North Korean defectors are residing in South Korea.

**탈산**(脫酸) 〖화학〗 deoxidization; deoxidation. ~하다 deoxidize.

**탈삼진**(奪三振) 〖야구〗 a strike-out. ¶ 그는 ~ 24개로 시즌 12승째를 올렸다 He scored his 12th win of the season, with 24 strike-outs. ◉ ~기록 the strike-out record. ~왕 the (season's) record holder in 〔for〕 the most strike-outs.

**탈상**(脫喪) expiration of the period of mourning; the end of mourning. ~하다 finish 〔come out of〕 mourning; leave off 〔get over〕 mourning.

**탈색**(脫色) decoloration; decolorization; bleaching. ~하다 decolor; decolorize; bleach; blanch. ◉ ~제 a decolorant; a decolorizer; a bleaching agent.

**탈선**(脫船) desertion from a ship. ~하다 desert a ship; run away from a ship. ◉ ~자 a deserter (from a ship); a run-away sailor.

**탈선**(脫線) ① 《열차 등의》 derailment. ~하다 be 〔get〕 derailed; derail; run off the track 〔rails〕; leave the rails; jump 〔leave〕 the track 《미》. ¶ 열차가 ~했다 The train derailed 〔ran off the rails〕. ② 《행동 등의》 deviation; aberration; departure; divergence; 《이야기 등의》 a ramble; (a) digression; an excursion; side-tracking. ~하다 《행동이》 deviate 〔go away〕 from the right path; get on the loose; go astray 〔wild〕; be erratic 〔eccentric〕; 《이야기 등이》 digress 〔go adrift〕 《from the subject》; make a digression; get sidetracked; be off the subject; talk (away) 〔wander, stray〕 from the subject 〔point〕; get off the point. ¶ 의론이 ~하다 argue beside the point / 이야기가 ~했다 The talk digressed from the subject. *or* The talk got sidetracked. / 그 선생님은 수업 중에 자주 ~한다 The teacher often gets sidetracked in class. ◉ ~경관 a policeman (who indulges) in an escapade. ~학생 an erratic student.

**탈세**(脫稅) evasion of taxes; tax evasion 〔dodging〕. ~하다 evade 〔dodge〕 a tax; defraud the revenue (수입을 속여서). ¶ ~의 수단 a tax dodge / ~혐의로 수사하다 investigate《*a person*》 on suspicion of tax evasion / ~를 묵인해 주고 돈을 받다 pocket money after conniving at the tax dodgings / ~를 적발하다 accuse《*a person*》 of tax evasion / 그 회사는 ~의 혐의가 있다 The firm has fallen under suspicion of tax-dodging. / 대기업의 ~실태는 명확히 밝혀져야 한다 The facts should be brought to light concerning tax evasion on the part of big business.
◉ ~액 the amount of the tax evasion. ~자 an evader of taxes; a tax dodger 〔evader〕. ~품 smuggled goods (밀수품); undeclared goods (on which the tax has been circumvented).

**탈속**(脫俗) unworldliness; absence of vulgarity. ~하다 be above worldly things; detach from worldly things; rise above the world; be free from conventionality 〔vulgarity〕; be "liberated". ¶ 그 화가는 ~적인 화풍으로 알려져 있다 The artist is known for her unworldly style of painting.

**탈수**(脫水) dehydration; 《세탁기의》 spin-drying. ~하다 dehydrate; desiccate; 《세탁기에서》 spin-dry《laundry》; spin 《clothes》 dry. ◉ ~기(機) a dehydrator; 《세탁기의》 a (spin) drier; dryer. ~작용 dehydration. ~제 a dehydrating agent; a desiccant. ~증상〔상태〕《인체의》 dehydration: ~ 상태가 되어 있다 be dehydrated.

**탈수소**(脫水素) 〖화학〗 dehydrogenation.

**탈습**(脫濕) dehumidification. ◉ ~기(器) a dehumidifier.

**탈싹** with a plop; with a thud 〔flump〕. ⇨ 털썩. ~하다 make a plop 〔thud〕. ¶ ~ 떨어뜨리다 drop《a plate》 with a thud; bump《*a thing*》 down / ~ 쓰러지다 fall in 〔all of〕 a heap; fall with a thud / 짐을 바닥에 ~ 내려 놓다 put down *one's* bundle on the floor with a thud / 책상에 ~ 주저앉다 flop down before 〔at〕 *one's* desk.

**탈싹거리다** keep plopping 〔thudding〕; keep bobbing; jolting. ¶ 궁둥이를 ~ move *one's* bottom up and down / 탈싹거리며 걷다 jolt 〔bob〕 along.

**탈쓰다**[1] ① 《얼굴에》 wear a mask; mask *one's* face. ¶ …의 탈을 쓰고 under the mask 〔cloak〕 of 《friendship, charity》. ② 《위선 등의》 dissemble; play the hypocrite; pretend; feign; assume. ¶ 종교의 탈을 쓰다 assume the mask of religion / 그때까지 그는 자비심 많은 신사의 탈을 쓰고 있었다 Until then he played the charitable gentleman.

**탈쓰다**[2] 《닮다》 be just 〔exactly〕 like 《*a person*》; be a look-alike for 《*a person*》.

**탈염**(脫塩) desalinization; 〖화학〗 desalting; demineralization. ~하다 desalt; desalinate; desalinize. ◉ ~공장 《바닷물의》 a desalination plant. ~수(水) desalted 〔demineralized〕 water.

**탈영**(脫營) desertion from barracks; decampment; being AWOL (★ AWOL [éiwɑl] = *a*bsent *w*ith*o*ut *l*eave). ~하다 desert from 〔break out of〕 barracks; desert *one's* colors; go over the hill 《미》; go AWOL. ◉ ~병 a deserter; a runaway soldier.

**탈옥**(脫獄) prison breach; prison 〔jail〕 breaking; a jailbreak. ~하다 escape (from) prison; break (out of) prison. ¶ ~을 기도하다 plan 〔attempt〕 an escape from jail; try to break prison / 그는 ~했다 He escaped from the prison. ◉ ~수 a prison breaker; an escaped prisoner 〔convict〕.

**탈의**(脫衣) divestiture; divestment; disrobing. ~하다 disrobe; get undressed; undress *oneself;* take off *one's* clothes. ◉ ~실 a dressing 〔changing〕 room; a locker room. ~장 《해수욕장의》 a bathhouse; bathing booth.

**탈자**(脫字) 《빠진 글자》 an omitted word 〔letter〕; a missing word 〔letter〕. ¶ ~가 많다 Many words are left out. ◉ ~기호 a caret (★ 보통 ∧로 표시함).

**탈잡다**(頉—) find fault 〔pick flaws〕 with; cavil at; blame; charge; accuse; make a pretext of. ⇨ 탈(頉). ¶ 늦게 왔다고 ~ blame 《*a person*》 for coming late; accuse 《*a person*》 of arriving late / 이러니저러니 탈잡다 criticize 《*a person*》 for one thing or another / 과일이 상했다고 탈잡아 값을 깎다 cut 〔slash〕 the price of fruit claiming that it is spoiled.

**탈장**(脫腸) 〖의학〗 rupture; (abdominal) hernia (*pl.* ~s, -ae). ¶ ~이 되다 be affected with hernia; have a hernia. ◉ ~대(帶) a hernia belt; a truss. ~수술 herniotomy. ~증 hernia. ⌈tion.

**탈저**(脫疽) 〖한의〗 gangrene; sphacela-

**탈적**(脫籍) ~하다 have *one's* name removed 〔deleted〕 from the 《family, military, school, party》 register. ¶ ~절차를 끝마치다 go through the procedure of canceling *one's* name in the register.

**탈주**(脫走) (an) escape; (a) flight; abscondence; decampment; a break (-away); (a) desertion. ~하다 escape; flee; abscond; decamp; run 〔make〕 away; make off (with *oneself*); break loose 〔away〕; bolt; desert 《barracks, a ship》; fly the coop 《미속어》. ¶ ~를 기도하다 plan 〔attempt〕 an escape. ◉ ~계획 an escape plan. ~병 a deserter; a fugitive 〔runaway〕 soldier. ~자 an absconder; a runaway; a refugee; an escapee; a bolter; a fugitive; a deserter; a defector.

**탈지**(脫脂) removal of fat 〔grease〕; [형용사적] fat-removed; non-fat. ~하다 remove fat 〔grease〕 《from》. ¶ ~하지 않은 양털 grease wool; wool in the grease. ◉ ~면(綿) absorbent 〔sanitary〕 cotton; cotton wool 〔batting 《미》〕. ~유(乳) skim 〔non-fat〕 milk.

**탈진**(脫盡) exhaustion. ~하다 get exhausted 〔worn out, utterly fatigued〕. ¶ 오랜 병 끝이라 그는 ~감을 느꼈다 After his long illness he felt physically and mentally drained 〔washed-out〕.

**탈출**(脫出) (an) escape; extrication; 《낙하산으로》 bailing out 《of a plane》. ~하다 escape from 《a prison》; flee from; extricate *oneself* from 《danger》; get away 《from a place》; get out of; bail out. ¶ 적국을 ~하다 escape from the enemy land / 비행기에서 낙하산으로 ~하다 make a parachute jump 〔bail out〕 from a plane / 집단으로 ~하다 stage a mass breakout 《from a reformatory》. ◉ ~속도 《인력에서의》 escape velocity; breakaway speed: 우주선은 ~ 속도까지 가속되었다 The spaceship was boosted to escape velocity.

**탈춤** a masque 〔masked〕 dance. ¶ 봉산 ~ the traditional Korean Pongsan masked dance.

**탈취**(脫臭) deodorization. ~하다 deodorize; remove 〔kill, take away〕 the odor 《of》. ◉ ~제 a deodorant; a deodorizer; a deodorizing agent.

**탈취**(奪取) capture; seizure; wresting. ~하다 capture; carry off; grab; seize; wrest; 《권력·지위 등을》 usurp. ¶ 남의 소유물을 ~하다 take another's property / 왕위를 ~하다 usurp the throne / 요새를 ~하다 carry 〔take〕 a fortress / 군사적 수단으로 권력을 ~한 자는 같은 수단으로 그 지위에서 쫓겨나기 쉽다 Those who capture power by military means are apt to be unseated by the same means.

**탈타리** ① 《사람》 a man who is flat broke 〔penniless〕. ⇨ 빈털터리. ② ⇨ 탈탈이.

**탈탈** with a rattling 〔clattering〕 noise. ⇨ 털털. ~거리다 rattle; clatter; shake; be shaky 〔bumpy〕; 《차 등이》 jolt. ¶ 차가 몹시 ~거렸다 I had a bumpy ride. ◉ ~이 《구어》 a jalopy; a rattletrap bus.

**탈퇴**(脫退) secession; withdrawal. ~하다 secede 〔withdraw〕 from; break (away) from; bolt from; leave; disconnect *oneself* from. ¶ ~서를 내다 submit a written notice-to-quit 《to an association》 / 그는 노조에서 ~했다 He withdrew from the union. / 그는 그 협회를 ~하기로 작정했다 He has decided to secede 〔withdraw〕 from the association. / 나는 그 협회에서 ~하고 싶다 I want to leave the association. ◉ ~자 a seceder; a bolter 《미》.

**탈피**(脫皮) ① 《동물의》 molting; (a) molt. ~하다 shed 〔slough, cast (off)〕 *its* skin; molt 《into an adult》. ¶ 누에는 ~할 때마다 자란다 A silkworm grows every time it casts off the skin. ② [비유적] self-renewal. ~하다 grow out of; outgrow. ¶ 구태에서 ~하다 break with convention; grow out of 〔outgrow〕 *one's* former self.

**탈하다**(頉—) plead; make a pretext of; make an excuse of; make a plea of.

**탈함**(脫艦) desertion from a warship. ~하다 desert a warship. ◉ ~자 a naval deserter.

**탈항**(脫肛) 〖의학〗 prolapse of the anus; *prolapsus ani* (L.). ~하다 suffer from prolapse of the anus.

**탈환**(奪還) recapture; retaking; recovery; forcible recovery. ~하다 take back by force; win back; retake; recapture; recover; regain; reconquer. ¶ 진지를 ~하다 take back 〔reoccupy〕 a fort 〔position〕.

**탈황**(脫黃) 〖화학〗 desulfurization; desulfuration; purification. ~하다 desulfurize; desulfurate; desulfur; purify; devulcanize. ◉ ~기(器) a desulfurizer; a purifier. ~제 a desulfurizing a 〔devulcanizing〕 agent. 배연(排煙)~ desulfurization from exhaust gas. 중유~ desulfurization from fuel oil.

**탈회**(脫會) secession 〔withdrawal〕 《from a society》; defection. ~하다 withdraw 〔secede, resign〕 from 《an association》; break away from 〔leave〕 《a society》; drop out 《of an organization》; drop 〔give up〕 *one's* membership; cease to be a member 《of》. ¶ ~시키다 expel 《*a person*》 from 《a club》; force 《*a person*》 to resign from 《an association》. ◉ ~신고 a report of secession. ~자 a seceder.

**탈회**(奪回) retaking; recovery; recapture. ⇨ 탈환(奪還).

**탐검**(探檢) probe; investigation; examination. ~하다 probe; investigate; examine.

**탐관오리**(貪官汚吏) a corrupt official; a graft-happy official.

**탐광**(探鑛) 〖광산〗 prospecting. ~하다 prospect 《a region for gold》.
◉ ~자 a prospector.

**탐구**(探究) 《조사》 (an) investigation; (an) inquiry; 《연구》 research; (a) study. ~하다 investigate; do research 《in, on》; make researches in; inquire into; explore; delve 《into》. ¶ 과학의 ~ a study of science / 암의 원인을 ~하다 investigate the possible causes of cancer / 과학적 ~에는 상상력이 불가결하다 Imagination is indispensable for scientific research.
◉ ~심 the spirit of inquiry. ~자 an investigator; an inquirer; a researcher.

**탐구**(探求) a quest; search; pursuit. ~하다 search for; pursue 《truth》. ¶ 지식의 자유로운 ~ free quest for knowledge / 진리의 ~ pursuit of truth / 진리를 ~하다 seek (after) truth / 그는 진지한 진리의 ~자이다 He is an earnest seeker after truth.

**탐나다**(貪—) [대상이 주어] be desirable; be appetizing; be tempting; [사람이 주어] be desirous 〔covetous〕 of; be envious of; desire; lust after 〔for〕. ¶ 탐나는 여자 a desirable 〔lust=arousing〕 woman / 탐나는 음식 appetizing 〔mouthwatering〕 food / 돈이 ~ be covetous of money / 권력이 탐난다 I am covetous of power. *or* I lust for power. / 친구의 사진기를 봤을 때, 나는 그것이 몹시 탐났다 When I saw my friend's camera, I wanted very much to get it.

**탐내다**(貪—) desire; want; covet; lust 《for, after》; have a desire 〔lust, yen〕 for; be greedy 《after》; be covetous 〔envious〕 of; be mad after; be dying for. ¶ 돈을 ~ be greedy for money; be money-mad / 남의 것을 ~ covet what belongs to others / 남의 재산을 ~ be covetous of another's property / …을 탐내는 눈으로 보다 cast covetous 〔greedy〕 eyes (up)on / 그는 명예를〔돈을〕 탐내지 않는다 He has no desire for fame 〔wealth〕. / 남의 것을 탐내지 마라 You should not covet 「what 〔anything which〕 belongs to others.

**탐닉**(耽溺) 《빠짐》 ① 《몰두》 immersion 《in study》; be immersed in; be 「absorbed 〔lost, engrossed〕 in; be devoted to. ¶ 서양 문학 연구에 ~하다 be immersed in the study of Western literature. ② 《주색 따위에》 indulgence; addiction. ~하다 indulge in; be addicted to; give *oneself* up to. ¶ 주색에 ~하다 indulge in liquor and sex / 쾌락에 ~하다 indulge in 〔give *oneself* up to〕 pleasure.
◉ ~생활 a fast 〔riotous〕 life; a life of follies 〔debauchery〕; a life given to riotous pleasures: ~생활을 하다 live fast; lead a fast 〔riotous, dissolute〕 life. ~자 an addict; a fast liver; a loose man; a libertine; a debauchee.

**탐독**(耽讀) indulgence in reading; avid reading. ~하다 read avidly 〔with avidity〕; be absorbed 〔engrossed〕 in reading; steep *oneself* 《in》; pore over; be immersed in 《a book》; devour; have *one's* nose buried in 《a book》. ¶ 소설을 ~하다 「be fond of 〔have a passion for〕 novels; be a great novel reader / 그는 고서를 ~하고 있다 He is poring over an old book.
◉ ~자 an inveterate reader.

**탐리**(貪吏) a greedy 〔grasping〕 official.

**탐리**(貪利) love of undue gain; greed; avarice; covetousness; cupidity. ~하다 be greedy 〔avaricious, covetous〕 of gain 〔undue profits〕.

**탐문**(探問) indirect inquiry; roundabout investigation. ~하다 inquire 〔find out〕 about indirectly; sound (out) by indirect inquiry.

**탐문**(探聞) information (obtained by

inquiry); a tip 《on》; a pickup; a wrinkle 《구어》. ~하다 [사람이 주어] obtain information (by inquiry); learn; get wind of (우연히); [사물이 주어] reach 〔come to〕 *one's* ear(s); come to *one's* knowledge. ¶ ~한 바에 의하면 according to what we have learned / ~ 수사를 하다 snoop for information; 《구어》 keep 〔go〕 on with the legwork.

**탐미**(耽美) a fondness for 〔an obsession with〕 works of art and beautifu

◉ ~주의 (a)estheticism: ~주의자 an (a)esthete. ~파 the (a)esthetic school; 《단체》 the (a)esthetes.

**탐방**(探訪) (private) inquiry; a visit; an interview. ~하다 visit; (visit a place and) inquire 〔make inquiries〕 into 《*something*》; interview.

◉ ~기 a report of inquiries. ~기사 a report; a reportorial piece: ~기사를 쓰다 report 《for a newspaper》; write by the leg 《미》; have an interview 《with》. ~기자 a (newspaper) reporter; an interviewer; a legman; a leg writer. 사회~ reporting; reportorial sleuthing. 카메라~ a photographic interview.

**탐사**(探査) inquiry; investigation; probing. ~하다 make inquiries; investigate; inquire 〔look〕 into. ¶ 심해(深海) ~용 선박 a vessel designed for deep sea probes / 고적을 ~하다 visit a place of historical interest / 내정을 ~하다 inquire into the real state / 석유를 ~하다 explore for oil / 철저히 ~하다 make a thorough 〔rigid〕 inquiry.

◉ ~기(機) a 《space》 probe: 월면 ~기 a lunar probe.

**탐상**(探賞) sightseeing; a sightseeing excursion 〔trip〕; exploration of beauties. ~하다 go to see; explore and admire the scenery 《of》.

**탐색**(探索) ① 《수색》 a search; a hunt; a quest. ~하다 search 《for》; make a search for; look 〔quest〕 for; delve into; hunt up; probe. ¶ 단서를 따라 ~하다 follow up a clue / 범인의 행방을 ~하다 inquire into 〔look for〕 the whereabouts of the culprit / 경찰은 범인을 ~중이다 The police are 「searching 〔looking, making a search〕 for the criminal.

② 《조사》 (an) inquiry; (an) investigation; (a) research. ~하다 inquire 〔make inquiries〕 into; investigate; probe.

◉ ~기구(氣球) an observation 〔a sounding〕 balloon. ~자 an investigator. ~전 an engagement in reconnaissance; a reconnoitering skirmish. 달 ~용 로켓 a lunar probe.

**탐스럽다**(貪—) (be) desirable; appetizing; attractive; tempting; charming; very nice; lovely. ¶ 탐스러운 과일 appetizing fruit / 탐스러운 꽃 a very beautiful flower / 탐스러운 여인 a charming woman / 이게 제일 ~ This suits my taste best.

**탐승**(探勝) sightseeing; a sightseeing excursion 〔trip〕. ~하다 see the sights; explore the scenery 《of》; visit scenic spots; go sightseeing. ¶ ~길을 떠나다 go on a trip to explore the beauties of; go on a sightseeing trip.

◉ ~객 a sightseer; visitors to scenic spots.

**탐식**(貪食) voracity; edacity; gluttony. ~하다 eat greedily 〔voraciously, avidly〕; wolf *one's* food; be gluttonous; gormandize. ¶ ~하는 사람 a voracious person; a glutton; a gormandizer.

**탐심**(貪心) avarice; greed; cupidity.

**탐욕**(貪慾) avarice; greed; rapacity; covetousness; cupidity. ~스럽다 (be) avaricious; greedy; rapacious; covetous, hoggish; wolfish; insatiable. ¶ ~스럽게 avariciously; rapaciously; greedily; hoggishly; wolfishly / ~의 화신 《be》 avarice itself; 《be》 the incarnation of avarice.

◉ ~한(漢) a greedy 〔grasping〕 fellow; a shark; a harpy.

**탐재**(貪財) love of money; avarice; desire for wealth; greed. ~하다 lust after; be avaricious 〔greedy, money=mad〕; covet for property.

**탐정**(探情) ~하다 sound (out) 〔feel〕 《*a person* on *a matter*》; throw 〔put〕 out a feeler; probe 〔try to find out〕 《*a person's*》 intention.

**탐정**(探偵) ① 《일》 detective service 〔work〕; secret investigation; espionage; espial. ~하다 spy 《on *a person*, into a secret》; inquire into 〔investigate〕 《*a matter*》; search 《for》; ferret 〔trace, track〕 out; detect; do detective work. ② 《사람》 a detective; a criminal agent; an investigator 《미》; a spy; a plainclothesman (사복형사); a sleuth 《미》; a gumshoe 《미속어》; a hawkshaw 《미구어》. ¶ ~에게

뒤밟히다 be shadowed by a detective / ～을 도중에 따돌리다 give a detective the slip on the way; shake off a detective. ◉ ～소설 a detective 〔crime〕 story; a whodunit 《미구어》; a mystery story. 사설～ a private detective; a private eye 《미속어》: 사설〔사립〕 ～사 a private detective agency 〔firm〕.

**탐조**(探照) throwing 〔beaming〕 a searchlight. ～하다 throw 〔beam〕 a searchlight 《on》. ¶ 해상을 ～하다 flash over the sea. ◉ ～등 a searchlight; 《대공용》 an anti-aircraft searchlight: ～등으로 비추다 turn 〔play〕 a searchlight on 《a plane》; sweep 《the sea》 with a searchlight / ～등을 켜다 switch on a searchlight.

**탐지**(探知) detection; finding out by indirect inquiry; ascertaining. ～하다 detect; search 〔spy, worm, pump〕 out 《a secret》; trace 〔ferret, smell〕 out 《a plot》; get 〔have〕 wind of 《an affair》; learn 〔find out〕 《a fact》 by inquiry. ¶ 비밀을 ～하다 smell out a secret / 음모를 ～하다 scent 〔trace〕 out a plot; smell out treachery.
◉ ～기 a detector; a locator; a 《people》 sniffer: 거짓말 ～기 a lie detector / 전파 ～기 (a) radar; a radar set; a locator 《미》. ～기지 a detection station. ～소(所) 《핵실험의》 a monitoring station. ～장치 detection equipment; a monitoring device; a detection 〔detecting〕 device: 레이더 및 기타의 ～ 장치 radar and other sensing devices.

**탐측**(探測) sounding; probing.
◉ ～기 a probe; a prober: 화성 ～기 a Mars 〔Martian〕 probe. ～기구(氣球) a pilot balloon. ～로켓 a sounding rocket.

**탐침**(探針) 〖의학〗 a probe; an explorer. ¶ ～을 넣다 probe 《a wound》; plunge a probe 《into》.

**탐탁스럽다, 탐탁하다** (be) desirable; agreeable; nice; welcome; likable; pleasing; 《사물이》 (be) solid; substantial; [서술적] be to *one's* satisfaction.
¶ 탐탁한 여자 a woman after *one's* heart / 탐탁스러운 물건 an article to *one's* liking / 탐탁지 않은 undesirable; unlikable; unsatisfactory; disagreeable; unpleasing / 탐탁지 않은 손님 an unlooked-for guest; an unwelcome visitor / 탐탁지 않은 인물 an undesirable person / 탐탁지 않은 인상 an unfavorable 〔unpleasant〕 impression / 탐탁지 않은 청혼자 an ineligible suitor; a detrimental 《속어》 / 탐탁지 않은 평판 an unsavory reputation / 탐탁스럽게 굴다 act kindly 〔friendly〕 / 탐탁스러워하다 find satisfactory; be pleased with; like / 양식은 별로 탐탁스럽지 않다 I don't much care for western food. / 빛깔이 탐탁하지 않다 The color is not much to my fancy. / 그와의 동행은 별로 탐탁스럽지 않다 I am rather disinclined to go with him.

**탐탐**(耽耽) 《watch》 vigilantly 《for a chance》; 《look for a position》 eagerly.

**탐탐** 《타악기》 a tam-tam. ⌊⇨ 호시탐탐.

**탐폰** 〖의학〗 a tampon.

**탐하다**(貪一) covet 《fame》; be greedy 《of, for》; be covetous 《of》. ¶ 명리(名利)를 ～ covet 〔thirst after〕 fame and gain / 안일을 ～ live in idleness; pass *one's* days in indolence; idle away *one's* time / 폭리를 ～ make an excessive 〔undue〕 profit; profiteer.

**탐해등**(探海燈) a searchlight (that sweeps the sea); a flashlight. ¶ ～으로 해면을 탐조하다 sweep the sea with a searchlight / ～을 비추다 turn 〔play〕 searchlights 《upon *something*》.

**탐해법**(探海法) 〖항해〗 creeping.

**탐험**(探險) exploration; expedition. ～하다 explore; make an exploration. ¶ 미～ 지방 unexplored regions / 북극～ 길에 나서다 go on an Arctic expedition / 무인도를 ～하다 explore an uninhabited island / 심해(深海) ～은 매우 흥미롭다 The exploration of the ocean depth is very interesting.
◉ ～가 an explorer. ～기(記) an account of an expedition 《to Africa》. ～비행 an exploratory flight 《over the Antarctic continent》. ～선 a research 〔an expedition〕 ship. ～여행 an expedition; an exploration. 우주～ space exploration.

**탐험대**(探險隊) an expeditionary 〔exploration〕 party. ¶ ～장 the leader 〔chief〕 of an expedition / ～를 조직〔지휘〕하다 organize 〔lead, command〕 an expedition / ～를 파견하다 dispatch an expeditionary 〔exploration〕 party 〔force〕.

**탐호**(貪好) fanatic love; devotion; indulgence. ～하다 be very fond of; be a fanatic lover of; have a great liking for; indulge in; take much delight in.

**탐혹**(耽惑) addiction; infatuation;

immersion; spooniness. ～하다 get addicted to; get infatuated with; immerse *oneself* in. ¶ 여자에게 ～하다 be infatuated 〔taken〕 with a woman; be smitten with 〔by〕 a woman's charms.

**탑**(塔) a tower; a pagoda (절의); a monument (기념탑). ¶ 돌탑 a stone monument / 뾰족탑 a steeple / 오층탑 a five-storied pagoda / 화재 감시탑 a fire tower / 탑을 세우다 build 〔erect, put up〕 a tower / 공(功)든 탑이 무너지랴 《속담》 Hard work is never wasted.

**탑본**(搨本) a rubbed copy; a 〔an ink〕 rubbing. ～하다 take a rubbing 《of》. ¶ ～을 뜨다 make a rubbing 《of》.

**탑비**(塔碑) a tower and a monument (at a tomb).

**탑삭** with a snap 〔snatch〕; 《날쌔게》 suddenly; with a dash. ¶ ～ 움켜쥐다 snatch 〔grasp, clutch〕 at / (물고기가) 미끼를 ～ 물다 rise to 〔snap at〕 the bait.

**탑삭나룻** a short bristly beard.

**탑삭부리** a man with a short bristly beard.

**탑새기주다** disturb; interrupt; intrude (*oneself*) 《upon》; thwart; hinder 《*a person* from 〔in〕 *doing*》; spoil. ¶ 남의 일에 ～ throw a monkey wrench into someone else's project; put 〔thrust〕 a spoke in *a person's* wheel / 남의 계획에 ～ counteract 〔cross, thwart〕 *a person's* plan.

**탑손** the hand that holds the lower part of a plow 〔plough 《영》〕.

**탑승**(搭乘) embarkation; boarding; riding 《a ship, a plane》. ～하다 get into; board; 《비행기에》 get on 《a plane》; 《함선에》 embark on 〔go on board〕 a ship. ¶ 비행기에 ～하다 have a ride 〔go up〕 in an airplane; get into 〔get aboard〕 an airplane / ～시키다 embark 〔enplane, entrain〕 《troops》 / 대한항공에 ～해 주셔서 감사합니다 《기내 방송》 "Thank you for flying on board Korean Air."
◉ ～구 a boarding gate. ～권(券) a boarding card 〔pass〕. ～원 《비행기 등의》 a crew-man; a crew member; a (flight) crew (전원). ～자〔객〕 a passenger: ～자 명단 a (passenger) manifest. ～절차 boarding procedures: 「～절차가 시작됐습니까」—「아뇨, 아직입니다. 10분만 더 기다려 주십시오」 "Has boarding started already?"—"No, sir. Will you wait another ten minutes, please?"

**탑재**(搭載) loading; embarkation; entrainment. ～하다 load; embark; entrain; take in. ¶ ～되어 있다 be loaded 《with goods》; have 《rocket guns》 on board / 기차에 군수품을 ～하다 entrain military supplies / 배에 화물을 ～하다 load a ship with goods; get 〔take〕 goods on board / 그 군함은 12인치 포 10문을 ～하고 있다 The warship carries 〔mounts〕 ten 12-inch guns. ◉ ～량 burden; burthen; 《have》 a carrying capacity 《of 5,000 tons》. ～중량 weight on board.

**탑전**(榻前) 《임금의 앞》 the presence of a king. ¶ ～에 나가다 come into the Royal presence.

**탑파**(塔婆) 〖불교〗 a stupa; a pagoda.

**탓** ① 《잘못》 fault; blame; responsibility; 《결과》 consequences; a result; 《영향》 influence; an effect. ¶ 마음의 탓 a trick of senses 〔of the imagination〕 / …탓이다 be *one's* fault; be to blame; be due to…; be attributable to…; be caused by…; be the result of… / …탓으로 돌리다 put 《*a matter*》 down to…; lay 〔pin〕 the blame on 《*a person*》; lay the fault at 《*a person's*》 door / 실패를 불운한 탓으로 돌리다 attribute 〔ascribe, impute〕 *one's* failure to bad luck; set *one's* failure down to bad luck / 열이 있는 탓인지 어지럽다 I feel giddy, I suppose it is the effect of fever. / 모두 네 탓이니 할 수 없다 You have no one but yourself to blame. / 네 탓 내 탓 할 것 없다 We shouldn't blame each other. *or* Let's not worry about who's to blame. *or* It's no more your fault than mine. / 네 탓에 나까지 욕먹었다 I got scolded, too, and all because of your fault.
② 《이유》 (a) reason; ground(s). ¶ 나이 탓으로 because of 〔owing to〕 *one's* age / 나이 탓으로 허리가 굽다 be bent with age / 무슨 탓으로 늦었느냐 Why are you late? / 출석자가 적은 것은 날씨 탓이다 The bad weather is responsible for the small attendance.

**탓하다** put 〔lay〕 blame on; lay the fault to; attach blame to; blame 〔reproach, rebuke〕 《*a person* for *something*》; censure; reprove. ¶ 자신을 ～ reproach *oneself* 《for》 / 하늘을 ～ quarrel with Providence / 네가 잘못하고 왜 남을 탓하느냐 Why do you try to shift the blame on me when all the time you are to blame? / 나만 잘못한다고

탓하지 마시오 Don't lay the blame on me alone. *or* Don't make me the scapegoat.

**탕** 《소리》 bang; boom; with a bump. ⇨ 탕하다. ¶ 주먹으로 탁자를 탕 하고 치다 bang *one's* fist on the table / 문을 탕 하고 닫다 bang a door; slam the door shut; shut a door with a bang / 탕소리를 내며 터지다 go off with a bang / 탕 하고 총소리가 났다 Bang! went the gun.

**탕**(湯) ① 《국》 soup; broth. ② 《탕약》 a medicinal decoction; an infusion. ③ 《목욕간》 a (hot) bath. ¶ 남탕 a bath for men; the men's section / 여탕 the ladies' section / 탕에 들어가다 get into a bathtub; have a dip in the bath (-tub) / 탕에 들어가 있다 soak in the bath(tub).

**탕가니카** Tanganyika. ◉ ~사람 a Tanganyikan. ~호(湖) Lake Tanganyika.

**탕감**(蕩減) (a) write-off 《debts》; cancellation. ~하다 write off 《debts》; cancel (out); cross off 《accounts》. ¶ 빚을 ~해 주다 forgive 《*a person*》 a debt; cancel 〔write off〕 a debt.

**탕개** a clamp; a fastener. ¶ ~를 먹이다 clamp; tighten up. ◉ ~목 a piece of wooden peg for tightening up a fastening rope. ~붙임 fastening (to) a block of wood with a guy (line). ~줄 a guy (line); a fastening rope: ~줄이 끊어지다 a guy is broken; a rope is gone.

**탕객**(蕩客) a fast liver; a libertine; a prodigal.

**탕거리**(湯—) soup makings; ingredients for soup; soup stock.

**탕건**(宕巾) a horsehair skullcap formerly worn by officials under their hats. ¶ ~ 바람으로 with *one's* skullcap exposed; with *one's* (outer) hat off / ~집 the case of a horsehair skullcap.

**탕관**(湯罐) a pipkin.

**탕기**(湯器) a soup bowl.

**탕메**(湯—) soup and rice (offered at ancestor-memorial services).

**탕면**(湯麵) noodle soup; noodles in broth.

**탕반**(湯飯) rice in broth 〔soup〕; rice soup.

**탕부**(蕩婦) a lewd 〔wanton, loose〕 woman; a woman of easy virtue 〔of loose morals〕; a slut; 《속어》 a bitch.

**탕산하다**(蕩産—) squander 〔dissipate, ruin〕 *one's* fortune; run 〔go〕 through *one's* fortune.

**탕솥**(湯—) a soup kettle.

**탕수**(湯水) hot 〔boiling〕 water; hot-spring water. ◉ ~통 a hot-water tank.

**탕수육**(糖水肉) 〖요리〗 deep-fried pork 〔beef〕 covered with sweet and sour starchy sauce.

**탕심**(蕩心) a lewd mind; loose morals; salacious thinking.

**탕아**(蕩兒) a prodigal; a libertine; a debauchee.

**탕약**(湯藥) a medicinal decoction; an infusion; herb 〔herbal〕 tea.

**탕자**(蕩子) a prodigal 〔profligate〕 son.

**탕전**(帑錢) the privy purse.

**탕진**(蕩盡) squandering. ~하다 squander; dissipate 《a fortune》; run 〔go〕 through 《*one's* fortune》; run 〔give〕 out of. ¶ 돈을 ~하다 run through all *one's* money / 가산을 ~하다 squander 〔dissipate, fritter away〕 *one's* fortune / 정력을 ~하다 be drained of *one's* energy.

**탕제**(湯劑) ＝탕약(湯藥).

**탕치**(湯治) a hot-spring cure. ~하다 cure 《an illness》 by hot baths; take a hot-spring cure; take the baths for medical purposes. ¶ 온양에 ~하러 가다 go to *Onyang* for a hot-spring cure. ◉ ~객 a person staying at a spa to cure a disease. ~요법 spa treatment; a hot-spring cure. ~장 a spa; hot springs; a watering place.

**탕치다**(蕩—) ① 《재산을》 squander *one's* fortune. ⇨ 탕진하다. ¶ 노름으로 ~ gamble away *one's* fortune. ② 《탕감하다》 write off; let off. ¶ 빚을 ~ write off a debt; let 《*a person*》 off *his* debt.

**탕탕**[1] 《빈 모양》 ¶ ~ 비다 be all emptied; be quite deserted; be quite 〔nearly〕 empty.

**탕탕**[2] 《쏘거나 치는 소리》 booming 〔banging〕 repeatedly; 《두드리는 소리》 rapping 〔pounding〕 repeatedly; 《큰소리치는 모양》 big; with big words; with hot air. ¶ ~ 총을 쏘다 fire a gun in rapid succession; blaze away / 총소리가 ~ 나다 a gun is banging away; guns are banging / 문을 ~ 두드리다 rap 〔pound〕 at the door / 참석자들의 정숙을 요구하며 테이블을 ~ 치다 rap a table to call a meeting to order / ~ 큰소리치다 talk big; brag; be full of hot air 《속어》; talk through *one's* hat 《구어》.

**탕탕거리다** 《총소리가》 keep banging 〔booming〕; 《두드리다》 keep rapping 〔pounding〕; 《큰소리치다》 keep talking big.

**탕파**(湯婆) a foot warmer; a hot-water bag 〔bottle〕; a warming pan. ¶ 잠자

리에 ~를 넣다 put a hot-water bottle in the bed.

**탕평채**(蕩平菜) 《묵청포》 *tangpyungchae;* mung-bean jelly curd.

**탕하다** 《소리가》 go bang 〔boom〕; go off with a bang; bark; boom. ¶ 탕하고 부딪다 bump against 《a wall》; bump into.

**탕화**(湯花) incrustations 〔deposits〕 of hot-spring water; flowers of sulphur; geyserite.

**태**[1] 《금》 a crack; a fissure. ¶ 태간 그릇 a cracked ware; a crackle / 태가 가다 crack; be cracked / 이 잔은 태가 갔다 There is a crack in this cup.

**태**[2] 《새 쫓는》 a cracking whip.

**태**(胎) 〖해부〗 the amnion 〔caul〕 and the placenta; 《후산의》 the afterbirth. ¶ 태를 가르다 cut the navel cord / 그는 태를 길렀다 [비유적] He is stupid 〔defective〕.

**태**(態) ① 《모양·맵시》 a form; a figure; a shape; 《외양》 appearances; 《태도》 an air; bearing; carriage. ¶ 고운 태 a certain fairness 〔gracefulness〕 about *one* / 태가 없다 be modest 〔unassuming, unaffected〕. ② 《문법의》 voice. ¶ 능동〔수동〕태 the active 〔passive〕 voice.

**태가**(駄價) portage (인부의); carriage; cartage (짐수레의); freightage; freight (charges). ¶ ~를 치르다 pay carriage.

**태가다** crack; be cracked; be crackled; have a crack. ⇨ 태[1].

**태고**(太古) ancient times; remote ages 〔antiquity〕. ¶ ~의 ancient; primeval; of immemorial antiquity / ~부터 from 〔since〕 time immemorial; from remote antiquity / 태곳적 사람들 ancient 〔primeval〕 people. ◉ ~대 〖지질〗 the Archean Era. ~사 ancient history.

**태과하다**(太過―) (be) much excessive; too much.

**태교**(胎教) antenatal training; prenatal care of an unborn child through the attention of a pregnant woman to her own mental health; fetal education. ¶ ~에 좋다〔나쁘다〕 have a good 〔bad〕 prenatal influence 〔effect〕 on 《*one's* child》. 「= 타이[1].

**태국**(泰國) (the Kingdom of ) Thailand.

**태권도**(跆拳道) the Korean martial art of empty-handed self-defense; *t'aekwondo.* ◉ 세계 ~ 연맹 the World *T'aekwondo* Federation (생략 WTF).

**태그** 〖야구〗 a tag. ~하다 tag; touch 《a runner with the ball》. ◉ ~레슬링 a tag wrestle. ~매치 a tag match. ~팀 a tag team.

**태극**(太極) the Great Absolute (in Chinese philosophy)—the source of the dual principle of Yin and Yang. ◉ ~선(扇) a fan with a *T'aegŭk* symbol 〔design〕; a yin-yang fan.

**태극기**(太極旗) the national flag of Korea; *T'aegŭkgi.*

**태기**(胎氣) signs 〔indications〕 of pregnancy; a feeling that *one* is pregnant.

**태깔** ① 《태와 빛깔》 form and color. ② 《교만한 태도》 a haughty attitude. ~스럽다 (be) haughty; arrogant.

**태껸** the kicking and tripping art (as a sport).

**태나다**(態―) look nice.

**태낭**(胎囊) 〖동물〗 an embryonic sac.

**태내**(胎內) the interior of the womb; [부사적] in the womb. ¶ ~의 아이 a child in the womb; an unborn child; a fetus / ~에서 죽다 die while in the womb. ◉ ~전염 prenatal 〔antenatal〕 infection.

**태내다**(態―) strike an attitude; give *oneself* airs; put on 〔assume〕 airs; high-hat 《*a person*》.

**태다수**(太多數) a great 〔large〕 number 《of 》; a great many 《of 》; a large 〔great〕 majority.

**태도**(態度) an attitude; 《거동》 a manner; behavior; bearing; demeanor; deportment; (a) mien; an air. ¶ 강경한 ~ a firm attitude 《toward》; a strong stand 《against the U.S.》 / 심적 ~a mental attitude / ~에 나타내다 betray 《*one's* displeasure》 in *one's* look 〔manner〕; express 《*one's* emotion》 by outward signs.

태도가: ~가 부드럽다〔점잖다〕 move 〔bear *oneself* 〕 gracefully; be of gentle manners / 말하는 ~가 조심스럽다 be modest in *one's* speech.

태도로: 결연〔단호〕한 ~로 in a determined attitude 〔manner〕; with a determined air / 깜짝 놀란 ~로 with an air 〔a look〕 of surprise; as if in surprise / 좀 놀란 ~로 with some little show of astonishment 〔alarm〕 / 우호적인 ~로 in a friendly manner / 강한 ~로 나오다 show a bold 〔unyielding〕 front; go strong; take the high hand with 《*a person*》.

태도를: ~를 고치다 revise 〔modify〕 *one's* attitude; improve *one's* behavior; mend *one's* ways / ~를 바꾸다 change *one's* attitude 〔tune〕; alter *one's* stand / ～를 정하다 determine *one's* attitude 《toward a problem》; decide 《on *do*ing, on peace》 / ～를 밝히다 define 〔clarify〕 *one's* attitude; make *one's* attitude clear / ～를 밝히지 않다 do not commit *oneself;* be noncommittal 〔uncommitted〕 《on an issue》 / 강경한 ～를 취하다 assume 〔take〕 a firm attitude 《toward》; take a strong stand 《against *a person*, on an issue》 / 명백한 ～를 취하다 take a clear stand 《on a problem》 / 모호〔애매〕한 ～를 취하다 assume 〔maintain〕 an ambiguous 〔a dubious〕 attitude 《toward a problem》; sit on the fence / 연약한 ～를 취하다 take a soft stand 《toward the country》 / 오만한 ～를 취하다 strike a haughty attitude. ¶ 그는 ～가 거만하다 He has a haughty bearing. / 그는 ～가 아주 훌륭하였다 He was wholly respectable in bearing. / 너는 선생에게 대하는 ～가 나쁘다 You do not know how to behave to your teacher. / 요즘 그 사람 ～가 이상하다 He is「not his usual self 〔not quite himself〕 these days. / 그의 ～가 좀 이상하다 His behavior is rather strange. *or* 《수상하다》 There is something suspicious about him. / 윗사람에게는 언제나 공손한 ～로 대해야 한다 You should always bear yourself modestly toward your superiors.

**태독**(胎毒) 〖의학〗 the baby's eczema traceable to congenital syphilis.

**태동**(胎動) 《태아의》 quickening (최초의); fetal movement; the movements of the fetus; 《징후》 signs 〔indications〕 《of forthcoming activities》. ～하다 quicken; show signs 《of》. ¶ 민주화의 ～이 보인다 There is a quickening of democratization.

◉ ～기 the quickening period.

**태두**(泰斗) an authority; a leading light 〔expert, specialist〕; a luminary; a star. ¶ 경제학의 ～ a great authority on economics / 한국 의학계의 ～ a luminary in the medical profession of Korea.

**태령**(泰嶺·太嶺) a steep high pass; a 「sharp divide.

**태류**(苔類) 〖식물〗 the liverworts.

**태막**(胎膜) a fetal 〔an embryonic〕 membrane.

**태만**(怠慢) ① 《게을리함》 negligence; neglect; 《직무의》 (a) default; dereliction; delinquency; 《부주의》 inattention; carelessness. ～하다 (be) negligent; delinquent; inattentive; careless; inadvertent; remiss. ¶ 정부의 ～ the supineness of the government / 당국의 ～을 공격하다 attack the authorities concerned for neglect of duty / 직무에 ～하다 be negligent 〔remiss〕 in *one's* duties; be neglectful of *one's* duties ⇨ 직무태만 / ～히 하다 neglect 〔shirk〕 《*one's* duties》; slight; leave 《*a thing*》 to take care of itself / 직무를 ～히 하다 neglect *one's* duties; be negligent of 〔be unmindful of〕 *one's* duties; be derelict in *one's* duties 〔work〕 / 이 재해는 주지사의 ～에서 일어났다 This evil has happened through the governor's default.

② 《불이행》 default; failure; omission; nonfulfillment. ¶ ～죄 a sin of omission; criminal neglect.

**태몽**(胎夢) a dream that *one* is going to get pregnant.

**태무**(殆無) ～하다 (be) very scarce; very few 〔rare〕; virtually nonexistent. ¶ 소득이 ～했다 I scarcely gained anything. / 성공의 가능성이 ～하다 There is not the remotest chance of success. / 교통 사고 없는 날이 ～하다 Scarcely a day passes without a traffic accident.

**태반**(太半) 《양적으로》 the greater 〔best, most〕 part; the great 〔large〕 portion; 《숫적으로》 the (great) majority; the bulk. ¶ ～은 mostly; for the most part; in large part; generally; nearly all / ～의 경우 in the majority of cases / 일이 ～ 끝났다 The work is nearly completed. *or* We are almost through with the work. / ～의 학생은 그 운동에 무관심했다 The majority of the students were indifferent to the movement. / 그는 생애의 ～을 외국에서 보냈다 He lived abroad for the greater part of his life.

**태반**(胎盤) 〖해부〗 the placenta (*pl.* ～s, -tae). ¶ ～의 placental / ～이 있는〔없는〕 placental 〔implacental〕.

◉ ～염 placentitis (*pl.* -titides). ～음 a placental souffle. ～형성 placentation. 유～ 포유 동물 placental animals 〔mammals〕; placentalia.

**태백성**(太白星) 〖천문〗 Venus; the evening 「star.

**태벌**(笞罰) ＝태형(笞刑).

**태변**(胎便) a meconium; the first fecal discharges of a new-born child.

**태부리다**(態―) ＝태내다.

**태부족**(太不足) a great want 〔shortage, dearth, lack〕. ～하다 be in great shortage; be greatly wanted; be much lacking.

**태산**(泰山) a high mountain; a tremendous thing. ¶할 일이 ～ 같다 have ever so many things to do / ～같이 믿다 place great reliance 《upon, in》; put *one's* utmost confidence 《in》 / ～같이 까딱도 안 하다 be firm 〔steady〕 as a rock / ～같이 쌓여 있다 be piled up (mountain-)high; lie in heaps / 갈수록 ～이다 One misfortune follows close on the heels of another. *or* Out of the frying-pan into the fire. / ～ 명동에 서일필(鼠一匹) 《속담》 The mountains have brought forth a mouse.
◉ ～준령 high and steep mountains.

**태상왕**(太上王) an abdicated king; the ex-King.

**태상황**(太上皇) an abdicated emperor; the ex-Emperor.

**태생**(胎生) ① 〖생물〗 viviparity. ¶～의 viviparous / 반～의 semioviparous. ② 《출생》 birth; origin. ¶미국 ～의 한국인 an American-born Korean / ～이 비천한 of humble 〔low〕 origin 〔birth〕 / 비천한 ～이다 be of low birth; be of humble origin / 외국 ～이다 be of foreign birth; be foreign born / 그는 서울 ～이다 He comes 〔hails〕 from Seoul. / 어디 ～이오 Where were you born? *or* What is your birthplace?
◉ ～동물 a viviparous animal. ～지 *one's* birthplace; *one's* place of birth; *one's* native place. ～학 〖의학〗 embryology: ～학자 an embryologist.

**태서**(泰西) the Occident; the West; the Western countries 〔nations〕. ¶～의 of the West; Western; Occidental.
◉ ～문물 Occidental civilization; things Western 〔European〕. ～제국(諸國) the Western countries.

**태선**(苔癬) 〖의학〗 lichen. ¶～의 lichenous.

**태세**(態勢) 《태도》 an attitude; setup; 《준비》 preparedness; 《상태》 a condition. ¶…할 ～에 있다 be 〔stand〕 ready 〔prepared, poised〕 《for, to *do*》; be in fit shape 《to *do*》 / ～를 갖추다 complete arrangements 《for, to *do*》; get fully prepared 《for, against》; make *one's* preparations 《to *do*》; be groomed 《to *do*》 / 전투 ～를 갖추고 있다 be in combat readiness; be combat-ready; stand poised for action / 전투 ～를 취하다 hold battle position / 반격 ～를 갖추다 prepare to counterattack / 받아들일 ～를 갖추다 make preparations to receive 《new members》 / 방어 ～를 취하다 assume a posture of defense / 철통같은 방위 ～를 견지하다 maintain an iron-tight defense posture.

**태수**(太守) a governor; a viceroy.

**태심하다**(太甚―) (be) exceedingly severe; extreme.

**태아**(胎兒) 《임신 3개월까지의》 an embryo; 《3개월 이후의》 a fetus; [일반적] an unborn child 〔baby〕. ¶～의 embryonic; fetal / ～의 성감별 fetal sexidentification / ～의 성감별을 하다 identify the sex of embryos.
◉ ～교육 antenatal training 〔puericulture〕. ～기 the fetal 〔prenatal〕 life: ～기의 감염 prenatal infection. ～생활 fetal life. ～절개 embryotomy. ～절제술 embryectomy.

**태아**(胎芽) 〖식물〗 a propagule; a bulbil.

**태양**(太陽) the sun. ¶～의 solar; heliacal / ～의 표면 the sun's surface / ～표면의 대폭발 a solar flare; a chromospheric eruption / (북극 등에서의) 한밤중의 ～ the midnight sun.
◉ ～경(鏡) a solar eyepiece. ～계 the solar system. ～관측 solar observation: ～ 관측기 a helioscope / ～ 관측위성 an orbiting solar observatory (생략 OSO). ～광선 the rays of the sun; sunrays; sunbeams: 인공 ～ 광선 artificial sunrays. ～년 a solar year. ～력 the solar calendar. ～로 a solar furnace. ～복사 solar radiation. ～사진 a solar print. ～순환기 〖천문〗 the solar cycle. ～숭배 heliolatry; sun worship 〔cult〕. ～신(神) the sun god 〔goddess〕; 〖그神〗 Helios; 〖로神〗 Sol. ～신경총(叢) 〖해부〗 the solar plexus. ～신화 a solar 〔sun〕 myth: ～신화설 solarism. ～에너지 solar energy. ～연구〔학〕 heliology. ～열량계 a heliothermometer. ～의(儀) 〖천문〗 a heliometer: ～의 측정 heliometry. ～일 a solar day: 평균 ～일 a mean solar day. ～전지 a solar cell 〔battery〕. ～전파 a solar noise; solar radio-frequency radiation. ～중심설 the Copernican system 〔theory〕; heliocentricism. ～증류기 a solar still. ～충 〖동물〗 a heliozoan. ～풍 (the) solar wind. ～흑점 a sunspot; a solar spot: ～흑점설 the sunspot theory.

**태양**(態様) a mode.

**태양등**(太陽燈) a sunlamp; a sunray 〔heat〕 lamp. ¶～을 쐬다 treat 《a patient》 with a sunlamp / ～ 치료를

받다 receive 〔undergo〕 a sunray treatment; take artificial sunlight treatment; lie under a sunlamp 〔heat lamp〕.

**태양열**(太陽熱) solar heat; the heat of the sun's rays. ¶ ~을 이용하다 utilize 〔make use of〕 the heat of the sun / ~을 이용한 온수 수영장 a solar-heated swimming pool. ◉ ~주택 a solar (=heated) house. ~집열기(集熱器) a solar collector.

**태어나다** be born; come into being 〔existence, the world〕; see the light. ¶ 태어난 곳〔고향〕 *one's* birthplace; the place of *one's* birth; *one's* native place; *one's* (old) home / 태어난 집 the house where *one* was born; the home of *one's* birth / 태어난 환경 *one's* natal environment / 갓 태어난 아기 a newborn (baby) / (곧) 태어날 아이 the coming 〔expected〕 child / 아직 태어나지 않은 아이 an unborn child / 태어날 때부터 from birth / 내가 태어난 이래 ever since my birth 〔I was born〕; in (all) my born days; in my life / 태어나서 처음(으로) for the first time 「in *one's* life 〔since *one* was born〕 / 맏아들로 ~ be born the eldest son / 부자로 ~ be born rich; be born with a silver spoon in *one's* mouth / 가난하게 ~ be born poor / 가난한 집에 ~ be born of a poor family / 시각 장애인으로 ~ be born blind / 팔자좋게 ~ be born under a lucky star / 1975년 9월 20일에 태어났다 I was born on September 20, 1975. / 한씨 댁에 사내아이가 태어났다 A baby boy was born to Mr. Han.

**태업**(怠業) a work stoppage; a slowdown 《미》; a go-slow. ~하다 start a slowdown 〔go-slow〕; go on a slowdown strike.

**태없다**(態—) 《뽐내지 않다》 never strike an attitude; never give *oneself* airs; never put on 〔assume〕 airs; (be) modest; unassuming; unaffected. ¶ 태없이 modestly; unassumingly; unaffectedly / 태없는 사람 a democratic person; a man of plebeian habits / 그는 정말 태없는 사람이다 He never puts on 〔assumes〕 airs.

**태연자약**(泰然自若) imperturbability; composure; self-possession; presence of mind. ⇨ 태연하다. ~하다 remain composed; (be) perfectly calm; cool and collected; calm and self-possessed. ¶ 그는 어떠한 위험에 부닥쳐도 ~했다 His courage was equal to any danger.

**태연하다**(泰然—) (be) calm; cool; collected; composed; self-possessed; undisturbed. ¶ 태연한 태도 a calm attitude / 태연히 coolly; calmly; with composure; in a self-possessed manner / 태연히 죽음에 임하다 face death calmly 〔with perfect composure〕; meet death with fortitude / 아무 일도 없던 것 같이 태연히 앉아 있다 be sitting calmly as if nothing had happened / 그는 그 비보를 듣고도 태연하였다 He kept his countenance at the sad news.

**태열**(胎熱) 〖의학〗 congenital fever.

**태엽**(胎葉) a (coil 〔spiral〕) spring. ¶ 시계~ a watch spring / 실~ a hairspring / 큰 ~ the main spring / ~풀린 시계 a run-down clock / ~을 감다 wind a spring / ~이 풀리다 a spring unwinds; a spring runs down. ◉ ~장치 clockwork: 이 장난감은 ~ 장치로 움직인다 This toy moves 〔works〕 by clockwork 〔by a spring〕.

**태우다**[1] ① 《불에》 burn 《*a thing*》; commit to the flames; put 〔throw〕 into the fire; incinerate; cremate (시체를); 《화재로》 have 〔get〕 《*one's* house》 burnt down. ¶ 시체를 ~ burn a dead body to ashes; cremate / 쓰레기를 ~ burn rubbish / 집을 ~ have *one's* house burnt down / 불에 태워 죽이다 burn 《*a person*》 to death; burn 《*a person*》 alive / 태워 재가 되게 하다 reduce to ashes / 나는 그 편지를 태워버렸다 I burned that letter.

② 《눌리다》 burn; scorch 《*a thing*》; singe; char (새까맣게). ¶ 새까맣게 ~ char; burn to a cinder / 옷을 ~ burn *one's* clothes; get *one's* clothes singed / 다리미질 하다가 셔츠를 ~ scorch a shirt in ironing / 밥을 ~ burn 〔scorch〕 the rice.

③ 《담배를》 smoke; have 〔take〕 a smoke; puff 《a cigar》. ¶ 나는 담배를 태우지 않는다 I don't smoke. *or* I am a nonsmoker.

④ 《속을》 burn 《*one's* soul》; agonize. ¶ 속을 ~ be worried 〔anxious, agonized, anguished〕; burn with anguish 〔anxiety〕 / 아무의 속을 ~ make 《*a person*》 worry; make 《*a person*》 awfully anxious / 사랑으로 가슴을 ~ burn with love 《for》 / 애를 ~ worry *oneself*.

**태우다**[2] ① 《탈것 등에》 carry; take in;

take 《*a person*》 on board; place 《*a person*》 in a train; let ride; give a ride; pick up (도중에서); 《수용하다》 accommodate.
¶ 군인을 태운 차 a car 〔train〕 carrying soldiers / 백 명을 태우는 차 a car that can accomodate 100 persons; a car with a hundred-passenger capacity / 손님을 ∼ take passengers on board (배에); take in passengers; 《도중에》 pick up passengers / 어린애를 목말 ∼ carry a child on *one's* shoulders / 태워 주다 give 《*a person*》 a lift 〔ride〕 《in *one's* car》; give 《*a person*》 (a) passage 《on *one's* boat》; 《거들어서》 help 《*a person*》 into 《a car》 / 차에 손님을 ∼ take on 〔pick up, load〕 passengers / 버스가 도중에서 손님을 ∼ a bus picks up passengers on the way / 말(에) ∼ set 《*a person*》 on a horse; help 《*a person*》 mount / 어린애를 기차에 태워 주다 help a child on the train / 자동차에 나를 좀 태워주시오 Give me a ride 〔lift〕 in your car, please. / 그 유람선은 여객 1,000명을 태울 수 있다 The cruise ship can accommodate a thousand passengers. / 그녀를 집까지 태워주었다 I gave her a lift home. *or* I drove her home. / 거기까지 오토바이에 태워 드리지 I will take 〔run〕 you there on my motorcycle. / 그를 광주행 열차에 태워 주었다 I placed him on a train for Kwangju.
② [비유적] ¶ 비행기를 ∼ flatter to the skies; plaster 《*a person*》 with praise / 비행기 태우지 마시오 None of your flattery now!
③ 《내기에 돈을》 put 《money》 down on the table as a wager; 《상금을》 award. ¶ 돈을 ∼ lay a wager 《on the table》.

**태우다**[4] ① 《가르마를》 have 《*one's* hair》 parted. ¶ 가르마를 한가운데 ∼ have *one's* hair parted in the middle.
② 《맷돌에》 have 《*something*》 ground 〔split〕. ¶ 맷돌에 콩을 ∼ have 《*a person*》 split peas on the grindstone.
③ 《갈라주다》 divide 《*a thing* among》; portion out; apportion. ¶ 재산을 아들들에게 ∼ divide *one's* property among *one's* sons; settle *one's* property on *one's* sons.

**태우다**[4] 《연줄·그네를》 pull 〔let〕 in and out. ¶ 연줄을 ∼ let the string of a kite in and out / 그네를 ∼ let the swing go back and forth.

**태위**(胎位) 『의학』 presentation (of the fetus in labor).

**태음**(太陰) the moon. ◉ ∼관측〔거리〕 lunar observation 〔distance〕. ∼력 the lunar calendar. ∼순환기 the lunar cycle. ∼숭배 moon worship. ∼시 the lunar time. ∼일〔월, 년〕 a lunar day 〔month, year〕. ∼표 lunar tables. ∼학자 a selenologist; a lunarian.

**태의**(胎衣) 『해부』 the mucosa of the placenta.

**태자**(太子) the crown prince; the Heir Apparent. ¶ 마의 ∼ Prince Maŭi. ◉ ∼궁 the crown prince's palace. ∼비 the crown princess.

**태작**(駄作) a poor work 〔piece of writing〕; poor 〔worthless〕 stuff; trash.

**태장**(笞杖) 《대막대》 a bamboo paddle (used for punishment); 《볼기침》 beating (on the buttocks); flogging; flagellation.

**태점**(胎占) predicting the sex of an unborn child by divination.

**태조**(太祖) the first King 《of the dynasty》; the founder 《of a dynasty》.

**태좌**(胎座) 『식물』 a placenta.

**태죄**(笞罪) a crime punishable by flogging.

**태주** 『민속』 *t'aeju;* the spirit of a little girl who died of smallpox. ◉ ∼할미 a woman possessed by a *t'aeju.*

**태중**(胎中) ¶ ∼에 in pregnancy / 둘째 아들이 ∼이었다 I was pregnant with my second son.

**태질** ① 《타작》 threshing 《grain》; flailing. ∼하다, ∼치다 thresh; flail. ¶ 벼를 ∼하다 thresh the rice grains out / ∼하듯 하다 keep flailing 〔beating〕 hard. ② 《메어침》 throwing 〔casting〕 down. ∼하다, ∼치다 throw 〔cast, fling〕 《*a person*》 down. ¶ 책을 마룻바닥에 ∼치다 fling a book down on the floor / 사람을 ∼치다 throw *a person* down.

**태초**(太初) the beginning of the world. ¶ ∼에 in the beginning.

**태코그래프** a tachograph.

**태코미터** 『기계』 a tachometer.

**태클** 『스포츠』 a tackle. ∼하다 tackle 《*a person*》. ¶ 플라잉 ∼을 하다 make a flying tackle.

**태평**(泰平·太平) ① 《세상의》 (perfect) peace; tranquility; undisturbed peace. ∼하다 (be) peaceful; quiet; tranquil. ¶ ∼한 세상에 in time of peace; in peaceful times / ∼을 구가하다 enjoy the blessing of peace / 천하가 ∼하다 Peace reigns over the land. *or* All

the world is at peace. / 전란이 끝난후 백성들은 오래도록 ∼시대를 누렸다 After the war the people enjoyed a long period of peace and tranquility.
② 《마음의》 easygoingness; optimism. ∼하다 (be) easy(going); happy-go=lucky; 《걱정없다》 (be) carefree; insouciant; [서술적] be free from care; 《낙천적이다》 (be) optimistic; leisurely. ¶ 무사 ∼한 얼굴 a carefree face / ∼한 사람 an easygoing person; a happy-go-lucky person / 천하 ∼한 생활 《lead》 a free and easy mode of life; easy living / ∼스러운 소리를 하다 talk happy-go-lucky nonsense / 그는 만사에 ∼이다 He takes things easy. ◉ ∼가(歌) a song of peace. ∼무드 a mood of tranquility and satisfaction. ∼성대 a peaceful reign; a reign of peace. ∼천하 a peaceful world; a world at peace.

**태평양**(太平洋) the Pacific (Ocean). ¶ ∼의 Pacific / ∼시대 《the opening of》 a (great) Pacific era; the Era of the Pacific / 동북 아시아 국가들로부터 온 전문가들은 지역적인 경제 협력의 증진과 신 ∼ 공동체에 대처하기 위한 방안들을 토의하였다 Experts from Northeast Asian countries discussed ways to enhance regional economic cooperation and cope with the New Pacific Community. ◉ ∼경제협의회 the Pacific Basin Economic Council (생략 PBEC). ∼연안 the Pacific coast: ∼ 연안국가 the Pacific Basin countries 〔nations〕. ∼전쟁 the Pacific War. ∼지역 the Pacific area. ∼함대 the Pacific fleet. ∼항로 service on the Pacific: ∼항로에 취항하다 go into service on the Pacific. ∼ 횡단비행 a transpacific flight. 범∼회의 the Pan-Pacific Conference. 환(環)∼국가 the Pacific rim nations.

**태풍**(颱風) a typhoon. ¶∼의 눈 the eye of a typhoon; the typhonic center / ∼이 북상하다 a typhoon comes up north / ∼이 맹위를 떨치다 a typhoon rages / ∼의 습격을 받다 be hit 〔struck〕 by a typhoon / ∼이 발생했다 A typhoon formed 〔was born〕. ∼이 급속히 발달했다 The typhoon developed quickly. / ∼이 제주도에 접근하고 있다 A typhoon is 「approaching 〔coming nearer to〕 Cheju Island. / ∼은 남해안에 상륙할 것이다 The typhoon will strike 〔hit〕 the southern coast of Korea. ◉ ∼경보 《issue》 a typhoon warning. ∼권 the typhoon area: ∼권내에 있다 be within the typhoon area. ∼주의보 a typhoon alert.

**태형**(笞刑) (punishment by) flogging; whipping. ¶ ∼을 가하다 punish 《*a person*》 by flogging.

**태환**(兌換) 〖경제〗 (financial) conversion. ∼하다 convert; redeem. ¶∼할 수 있는〔없는〕 convertible 〔inconvertible〕. ◉ ∼권 a convertible note: ∼권을 발행하다 issue convertible notes. ∼성 convertibility. ∼은행 a bank of issue. ∼정지 suspension of specie payment. ∼제도 the conversion system. ∼준비 specie reserve. ∼지폐 = ∼권.

**태후**(太后) ⇨ 황태후.

**택배**(宅配) a home delivery (service). ∼하다 deliver 《*a thing*》 to *a person's* house. ¶ 소화물을 ∼로 보내다 send a parcel by home delivery service / 이 소포를 주소지에 ∼해 주십시오 Please have 〔get〕 this parcel delivered to the addressee's house. / ∼해 준다면, 이것을 사겠다 If you can deliver this, I'll take it. ◉ ∼사업 a home delivery business. ∼취급소 a home delivery service agency. ∼편 (a parcel 〔goods〕 sent through) a home 〔door-to-door〕 delivery; a home delivery service.

**택시** a taxi; a taxicab; a cab. ¶ 개인∼ an owner-driven taxi; a driver-owned taxi / 손님을 찾아 다니는 ∼ a cruising taxi / ∼로 가다 go by taxi 〔in a taxi〕; taxi 《to》 / ∼를 타다 take 〔hire〕 a taxi / (손을 들어) ∼를 멈춰 세우다 halt a taxi / (소리를 질러) ∼를 부르다 hail a taxi; 《전화로》 call a taxi / ∼를 잡다 take a taxi; pick up a taxi / 요금을 내고 ∼를 내리다 pay off a taxi / ∼ 영업을 하다 operate a taxi service / ∼를 불러 주시오 Call me a taxi. *or* Call a taxi for me. ◉ ∼강도 a taxi robber; 《행위》 taxi holdup. ∼미터 a taximeter. ∼승차장 a taxi stand 《미》; a cabstand 《미》; a taxi rank 《영》. ∼요금 cab-fare; taxi fare: ∼ 요금 병산제 the taxi fare system adding time element to distance. ∼운전사 a taxi driver; a cabman; a cabdriver; a cabby 〔cabbie〕 《구어》; taximan 《영》; 《여자》 a cabette; a woman cabdriver. ∼회사 a taxi 〔taxicab〕 company.

**택일**(擇日) choice of an auspicious day. ∼하다 choose an auspicious day.

**택일적**(擇一的) alternative. ¶ ～으로 in an alternative way.

**택지**(宅地) land for housing; a housing site; a house [building] lot (보통 한 채분의); 《이미 집이 들어선》 a residential land. ¶ ～를 조성하다 prepare a housing site; turn 《the land》 into housing lots; develop land for housing. ◉ ～개발 housing land development. ～분양 sale of building lots: ～분양업자 an agent who sells building lots. ～조성 residential development. 「a good land [lot].

**택지**(擇地) selecting land. ～하다 select

**택진**(宅診) office consultation; seeing 《a patient》 at *one's* office. ¶ 오전 ～ 오후 왕진 "Hours of Consultation: before noon, at office; afternoon for calls." ◉ ～시간 the office hours.

**택하다**(擇—) choose 《between two things》; pick 《*something*》 out of 《from》; prefer 《A to B》; elect 《to *do*》; select.
¶ 길일을 ～ choose [fix upon] an auspicious day / 셋 가운데 하나를 ～ choose [single out] one 「from [out of] the three / 그의 작품 중에서 최고의 것을 ～ select [choose] the best of his works / 허(虛)를 버리고 실(實)을 ～ discard the shadow for the substance / 불명예보다 차라리 죽음을～ choose death before dishonor; 《I》 would rather die than be disgraced; prefer death to the loss of honor / 좋은 물건을 택하셨습니다 You've made a good choice. / 목사는 성경에서 한 구절을 택했다 The pastor selected a passage from the Bible. / 「어느 것을 택하시겠습니까」—「저기 있는 붉은 것으로 하겠습니다」 "Which one would you like to choose ?"—"That red on over there."

**탤런트** 《재능 있는》 a person of 《theatrical》 talent; a 《TV》 personality; [총칭] 《young》 talent. ¶ 프로듀서는 새로운 ～를 찾고 있다 The producer is on the lookout for new talent. ◉ 텔레비전 ～ a television personality; [총칭] TV talent: 그녀는 유명한 TV ～이다 She is a well-known TV personality.

**탤컴파우더** 《주로, 땀띠용》 talcum powder.

**탬버린** 〖악기〗 a tambourine.

**탭댄서** a tap dancer.

**탭댄스** a tap dance. ¶ ～를 추다 tap=dance. 「grain.

**탯자리개** ropes for binding sheaves of

**탯줄**(胎—) 〖생리〗 the umbilical cord; the navel string. ¶ ～ 잡듯 하다 hold very tight [fast]; take fast hold of.

**탱고** 〖음악〗 the tango. ¶ ～를 추다 dance the tango. 「daisy.

**탱알** 〖식물〗 an aster; a Michaelmas

**탱자** 《열매》 a fruit of the trifoliate orange. ◉ ～나무 〖식물〗 a trifoliate orange tree.

**탱커** a tanker (boat); an oiler (유조선). ◉ 오일 ～ an oil tanker. 초대형～ a supertanker.

**탱크** ① 〖군사〗 a tank. ⇨ 전차(戰車). ② 《통》 a tank; 《수조》 a water tank; a cistern. ¶ 가스[석유, 기름] ～ a gas [an oil] tank / 고압 ～ a (high-)pressure tank [vessel] / 구형(球形)의 ～ a spherical tank. ◉ ～로리 a tanker; a tank truck 《미》; a tank lorry 《영》. ～선 ＝탱커. ～용량[저장량] tankage; the capacity of a tank. ～차 《철도의》 a tank car. ～톱 a tank top (수영복형 여성용 웃옷).

**탱탱하다** 《팽팽하다》 (be) taut; tight; distended; 《부어서》 (be) swollen; puffy; tumid; [서술적] be hard and taut. ¶ 줄이 ～ a line is tight [taut] / 종기가 탱탱하게 붓다 a boil is swollen up taut.

**탱화**(幀畫) 〖불교〗 a picture of Buddha to hang on the wall.

**터**[1] ① 《장소》 a site; a place; a lot; a ground; 《공간》 space; room; 《일이 벌어지는》 an arena; a theater. ¶ 빈터 vacant land; a vacant [an empty] lot; an open space [field] / 빨래터 a wash place; a place for doing the laundry (at the streamside) / 싸움터 the seat [theater] of war; a battlefield / 쓰레기터 a garbage pit; a rubbish dump [tip] / 일터 *one's* place of work; *one's* jobsite; *one's* office / 장터 a marketplace / 절터 a temple site / 집터 a house site; a building lot / 터를 돋우다 build up [fill in, raise] the land 《for》 / 터를 차지하다 occupy much space; take up much room.
② 《기초》 the foundation; the ground; footing; foothold; groundwork; spadework. ¶ 터를 닦다 prepare the ground 《for》; pave the way 《for》; establish the foundation 《of》 / 터가 잡히다 have a firm foothold; be well-grounded / 성공할 수 있는 터를 쌓다 lay the 「groundwork [basis] of success / 그는 인제 장사터가 잡혔다 He has his business well on its way.

**터**[2] 《예정》 a plan; a schedule; 《예기》

an expectation; an anticipation; hope; 《의도》 an intention; a design.
¶ …할 터이다〔테다〕 be going to 《*do*》; plan to; be expected to; be supposed to; 《의도》 intend to 《*do*》 / …ㄹ테지 be likely; must be / 내일은 무엇을 할 테요 What are you going to do tomorrow? / 그가 내일이면 올 터이다 He is expected (to come) tomorrow. / 오늘은 손님이 있을 텐데 I expect visitors today. (★「…텐데」는 「…터인데」의 준말) / 지금쯤은 그이가 병원에서 나왔을 텐데 He must have been discharged from the hospital by now (but I haven't seen him). / 무엇을 할 텐가 What do you intend to do? / 오늘 가는 것이 좋을 테지요 It will be better to go today, you know. / 설마 자네 혼자 가는 것은 아닐 테지 Surely you are not going alone? / 「그 사람 또 실패했다더군」—「그럴 테지」 "He made another failure, I'm told."—"Quite likely." / 그렇게 했으면 성공했을 텐데 If he had done so, he might have succeeded.

**터널** 《굴》 a (railway) tunnel. ¶ 죽령(竹嶺) ~ the Chungnyŏng Tunnel / 해저〔하저〕~ an undersea 〔a riverbed〕 tunnel / ~을 뚫다〔파다〕 build 〔bore, cut, dig, excavate〕 a tunnel 《through a mountain》; tunnel 《a hill》 / ~로 들어가다 go into a tunnel / ~에서 나오다 come out of a tunnel / ~을 지나(가)다 go through a tunnel / 500미터 전방 ~ 《게시》 Tunnel 500 m ahead. ◉ ~개통 the opening of a tunnel. ~공사 tunneling work. ~효과(效果) 〖물리〗 a tunnel effect.

**터놓다** ① 《막힌 것을》 open 《it》 up; lay 〔make〕 open; let 《it》 go 〔out〕; release; unstop; undam 《a river》; clear; 《방따위를》 throw 《rooms》 into 《one》. ¶ 두 방을 하나로 ~ throw 〔knock〕 two rooms into one / 물꼬를 ~ open a paddy sluice / 둑을 ~ break 〔burst〕 a dam 《on a river》.
② 《금했던 것을》 remove 《a prohibition》; lift 《a ban》. ¶ 봉쇄를 ~ raise a blockade / 통제를 ~ remove control 《on》; decontrol.
③ 《마음을》 unbosom *oneself* 《to》; speak *one's* mind 《to》; open *one's* heart 《to》; lay *one's* heart bare; take 《*a person*》 into *one's* confidence; disclose *one's* innermost intention 《to》. ⇨ 털어놓다 ②. ¶ 흉금을 터놓고 이야기하다 talk without reserve; have a heart-to-heart talk 《with》 / 그녀는 누구하고나 터놓고 이야기한다 She talks quite frankly 〔freely〕. / 그는 마음을 터놓을 수 있는 친구다 He is the kind of person I can open myself up to.

**터닝포인트** 《전환점》 a turning point.

**터다지다** harden the ground 〔earth〕 by pounding; level the ground 《for》; consolidate 〔solidify〕 the foundation 《of a building》.

**터닦다** ① 《집터를》 build up a site 《for》; prepare the ground 《for》; clear the foundation 《of》; level 〔smooth〕 the ground. ② 《토대를》 consolidate the foundation. ⇨ 닦다 ⑤.

**터덕거리다** ① 《걸음을》 walk wearily; walk heavily over 〔along〕; plod 《on, along》. ② 《살림이》 make a bare living. ③ 《일을》 struggle with hard work.

**터덜거리다** ① 《걸음을》 walk 〔plod〕 wearily 《along》; trudge along *one's* weary way. ② 《바퀴소리가》 jolt; rattle along 《a stony road》. ¶ 고물 택시가 터덜거리며 울퉁불퉁한 언덕길을 내려갔다 An old-fashioned taxi rattled along down the uneven hillside road.

**터덜터덜** ⇨ 터덜거리다. ① 《걷는 모양》 trudging; plodding. ¶ 그는 ~ 집을 향해 걸어갔다 He went home with heavy 〔weary〕 feet. ② 《소리》 rattling; clattering.

**터득**(攄得) 《이해》 understanding; comprehension; grasp (파악); mastery (숙달). ~하다 understand; grasp; comprehend; acquire 《a skill》 master 《the art of...》; learn 《from experience》. ¶ ~하기 어려운 hard to understand 〔learn〕; incomprehensible; puzzling / ~하기 쉬운 easy to understand 〔learn〕 / 요령을 ~하다 learn the knack 《of a trade》; get the hang 《of the job》 / 진리를 ~하다 understand 〔perceive〕 a truth / 장사하는 요령을 ~하기란 쉬운 일이 아니다 It is not easy to learn how to handle business.

**터뜨리다** ① 《파열시키다》 break 〔burst, tear〕 《*a thing*》; have 《*a thing*》 break 〔burst, tear〕. ¶ 종기를 ~ break *one's* boil; have *one's* boil break / 둑을 ~ have a dike collapse; break 〔burst〕 a dike / 풍선을 ~ break a balloon.
② 《폭발시키다》 explode; blast; blow up. ¶ 노여움을 ~ vent *one's* anger 《on》; let loose *one's* anger / 다이너마이트를 ~ set 〔touch〕 off a dynamite / 울분을 ~ give vent to *one's* pent-up

anger; let loose *one's* indignation / 샴페인을 ~ pop open a champagne bottle / 울음을 ~ burst 〔break〕 into tears; burst 〔fall to〕 crying / 웃음을 ~ burst 〔errupt, go off〕 into laughter; burst out laughing; roar with laughter.

**터럭** hair. ⇨ 털.

**터리풀** 〖식물〗 meadowsweet; dropwort.

**터릿선반**(―旋盤) 〖기계〗 a turret lathe.

**터무니없다** 《근거 없다》 (be) unfounded; baseless; groundless; [서술적] have no foundation; 《엉뚱하다·당치않다》 (be) extraordinary; outrageous; wild; absurd; fabulous; preposterous; exorbitant; ridiculous; unreasonable. ¶ 터무니없는 값 an exorbitant 〔an incredible, a fabulous〕 price / 터무니없는 거짓말 a damned 〔whopping〕 lie; a whopper / 터무니없는 계획 a wild 〔an absurd〕 project; a wildcat scheme / 터무니없는 생각 a wild idea; a fantastic notion / 터무니없는 야심 an intemperate 〔inordinate〕 ambition / 터무니없는 요구 an excessive 〔unreasonable, inordinate〕 demand / 터무니없는 소문 a groundless 〔a wild〕 rumor; an unfounded gossip / 터무니없는 말을 퍼뜨리다 spread a false report / 터무니없는 소리를 하다 say extraordinary 〔absurd〕 things; talk wild / 터무니없는 의심을 받다 be suspected when *one* is innocent; incur groundless suspicion; be falsely suspected 《of theft》 / 나는 그녀에게 터무니없는 짓을 저질렀다 I've done a terrible thing to her. / 터무니없는 소리 그만 두게 Don't talk nonsense. *or* Don't be absurd.

**터무니없이** 《근거 없이》 without any foundation; groundlessly; 《가당찮게·엉뚱하게》 absurdly; enormously; exorbitantly; fabulously; unreasonably; incredibly; ridiculously. ¶ ~ 비싼 ridiculously 〔fabulously〕 high / ~ 싸다 be ridiculously cheap; be dirt cheap / ~ 비싸게 샀다 I got it at an absurdly high price. / ~ 오랜 시간이 걸렸다 It took an incredibly long time.

**터미널** a 《bus》 terminal; 《종착역》 a terminus (*pl.* -ni, ~es); 《컴퓨터의 단말장치》 a terminal. ¶ 버스 ~에 있는 백화점 a department store at a bus terminal / ~ 빌딩 《철도역의》 a building containing a railroad terminal; 《공항의》 a terminal (building). ◉ ~호텔 《철도의》 a hotel at 〔above, near〕 a railroad terminal. 버스~ a bus terminal.

**터벅거리다** plod on; trudge along 〔*one's* (weary) way〕; totter.

**터벅터벅** ploddingly; trudgingly; totteringly. ¶ 빗속을 ~ 걸어가다 plod 〔tread, trudge〕 on in the rain.

**터번** 《wear》 a turban; a pugree (인도인이 쓰는 가벼운). ¶ ~을 두른 turbaned.

**터보건** 《썰매의 일종》 a toboggan.

**터보제트** a turbojet (engine). ◉ ~기 a turbojet. ~ 헬리콥터 a turbojet helicopter.

**터보프롭** 《엔진》 《프로펠러가 달린 터보제트》 a turboprop; a turbopropeller engine; a turboprop(-jet) engine; a propeller turbine engine; a propjet (engine). ◉ ~기 a turboprop (plane).

**터부** (a) taboo; (a) tabu. ¶ ~시(視)하다 taboo; put 〔place〕 (a) taboo on 《*something*》; put 《*something*》 under taboo / 그 부족에서는 수렵 중에 말하는 것이 ~로 되어 있다 Among those tribesmen speech is taboo while hunting.

**터부룩-** ⇨ 더부룩-.

**터분하다** ① 《맛이》 (be) unpleasant-tasting; muddy-tasting. ¶ 터분한 음식 untasty food; dull fare / 입이 ~ have a muddy 〔brown〕 taste in *one's* mouth. ② 《사람됨이》 (be) sloppy; untidy; messy. ¶ 터분한 사람 an untidy person.

**터빈** a turbine (engine). ◉ ~기관차 a turbine locomotive. ~발전기 a turbine generator. ~엔진 a turbine engine. 가스〔압력, 반동〕~ a gas 〔pressure, reaction〕 turbine. 증기〔공기, 충격, 수력〕~ a steam 〔an air, an action, a water〕 turbine.

**터세다** 《a site》 (be) ill-omened 〔unlucky, ill-fated〕; [서술적] have an unfortunate aspect.

**터수** ① 《처지》 *one's* status 〔place〕; financial 〔social〕 standing. ¶ 자신의 ~를 알다 know *one's* place in life / 우리는 호화주택에 살 ~가 못 된다 We aren't rich enough to live in a palatial mansion. ② 《관계》 relationship; friendship; terms. ¶ 그와는 아주 친한 ~다 I am on very close terms with him. / 둘이는 서로 너나들이 하는 ~다 They are on 「a first-name basis 〔thee-and-thou terms〕 with each other.

**터알** a vegetable garden within the fence of *one's* house.

**터울** the age gap (among siblings); the disparity of ages between siblings. ¶ 한 살 ～의 아이 a child born within a year of another; children born in two successive years / ～이 잦다 be frequent in having a baby / 그 집 형제들은 모두 세 살 ～이다 The boys 〔brothers〕 in that family are spaced three years apart.

**터울거리다** be all eagerness 《to》; be bent on 《*do*ing》; make desperate 〔frantic〕 efforts.

**터잡다** pick out 〔select, secure〕 a site 〔lot, spot〕; 《기초를》 establish the foundation 《of》.

**터전** a (residential) site; a lot; the grounds; a base. ¶ 넓은 ～ a large lot / ～을 잡다 occupy 〔pick up〕 a lot / 이것이 우리 생활 ～이 되어 있다 This forms the basis of our livelihood.

**터주**(―主) 〖민속〗 the tutelary spirit of a house site. ◉ 터줏대감 a senior 〔an old〕 member; an old-timer 《구어》; an old-stager 《영구어》.

**터주다** leave 《a way》 open; give leave 〔permission〕; lift 〔remove〕 the ban 《on》; clear 《*a thing*》 out of *a person's* way. ¶ 길을 ～ clear 〔open〕 the way 〔track〕 《for *a person*》; make way 《for *a person*》; open out (군중이 좌우로 갈라져서) / 외상을 ～ let 《*a person*》 open a credit 〔charge〕 account; open a charge account 《for *a person*》 / 자활(自活)의 길을 ～ put 《*a person*》 in the way of getting in independent living / 후진들을 위해 길을 ～ give the young people a chance; open the way for the promotion of *one's* juniors.

**터지다** ① 《싸움·사건 등이》 break 〔burst〕 out; take place. ¶ 전쟁이 ～ a war breaks out / 중대한 사건이 ～ a serious matter pops up.
② 《파열하다》 (***a***) 《갈라지거나 찢어져서》 burst 〔break〕 (open); crack 〔split〕 open; be 〔get〕 torn; tear; rip (open); 《종기 등이》 burst; break; collapse; 《피부가 얼어서》 chap; get chapped 〔cracked〕. ¶ 터진 손 chapped hands / 터진 데 《옷 등의》 a rip; a rent 《in a sleeve》; a tear; an open seam; 《양말의》 a run / 가슴이 터질 것 같은 heart-rending〔-breaking〕 / 봉투가 ～ an envelope gets ripped / 옷솔기가 ～ be unsewn; be rent 〔ripped, split〕 up the seams; come open 〔apart〕 at the seams / 수도관이 얼어 ～ a water pipe freezes up and breaks / 종기가 곪아 ～ a boil breaks / 입술이 ～ *one's* lips crack / 상의(上衣)의 터진 데를 깁다 mend a rent 〔tear〕 in *one's* coat / 밤송이가 터졌다 The chestnuts burst open. (***b***) 《무너지다》 break (down); burst; collapse; give way. ¶ 둑이 ～ a dike collapses 〔gives way〕 / 홍수로 댐이 터졌다 The flood burst the dam.
③ 《폭발하다》 explode; burst (up); blow up; go up 〔off〕; detonate; 《화산이》 erupt; burst into eruption; burst 〔break〕 out 〔forth〕. ¶ 울화통이 ～ [사람이 주어] fly into a passion; burst into a rage / 화약이 ～ gunpowder explodes / 굉장한 소리를 내며 ～ blow up 〔go off〕 with a terrific explosion / 쌓이고 쌓인 울분이 터졌다 Their smoldering resentment burst into flame 〔flared up〕.
④ 《탄로나다》 come 〔be〕 out; get exposed; be disclosed 〔revealed〕; be found out; be laid bare; come 〔be brought〕 to light. ¶ 비밀이 터졌다 The secret came out 〔leaked out〕.
⑤ 《샘·피 따위가》 spout 《out》; spurt 《out, up》; gush out. ¶ 코피가 ～ bleed at the nose; have bloody nose.
⑥ 《얻어맞다》 get a blow; be struck 〔beaten〕; get licked 《구어》. ¶ 그는 멍이 들도록 그들에게 얻어터졌다 He was beaten black and blue by them.

**터치** ① 《스포츠》 a touch. ¶ 주자에 ～하다 《야구에서》 touch a runner (with the ball) / 네트에 ～하다 《배구에서》 touch the net / 골에 ～하다 《수영에서》 touch the finish wall / ～의 차로 이기다 《수영에서》 defeat 《*one's* opponent》 by a touch; touch 《another swimmer》 out.
② 《필치·피아노 따위의》 a touch. ¶ 그녀는 가벼운 ～로 피아노를 쳤다 She played the piano with a light touch.
③ 《관계》 ～하다 take part in; touch on; concern *oneself* 〔be concerned〕 《in, with》; have a hand 《in》. ¶ 나는 그 문제에 ～하고 싶지 않다 I don't want to be concerned with the matter. / 그 건에 대해서는 일체 ～하지 마라 You should not have any thing to do with the affair.
◉ ～다운 〖럭비〗 《make, score》 a touchdown. ～라인 〖축구〗 a touch line. ～아웃 〖야구〗 touching 〔tagging〕 《a runner》 out: ～ 아웃시키다〔되다〕 touch 〔be tagged〕 out.

**터키** ① 《칠면조》 a turkey. ② 《나라 이름》 Turkey. ¶ ～의 Turkish; Ottoman.

◉ ~말 Turkish. ~모(帽) a tarboosh; a fez. ~ 사람 a Turk; an Osmanli. ~ 황제 the Sultan (of Turkey).

**터틀넥** a turtleneck. ¶ ~의 스웨터 a turtleneck sweater.

**터프** tough. ~하다 (be) tough; hardy; firm. ◉ ~가이 a tough guy.

**턱**[1] the jaw; 〖해부〗 maxilla (*pl.* -lae); 《아래턱의 앞부분》 the chin; the chops; the mandible (포유 동물·어류 등의). ¶ 위〔아래〕~ the upper 〔lower〕 jaw / ~이 나온〔늘어진〕 with prominent 〔drooping〕 jaw / 이중턱 a double chin / 턱이 빠지다 dislocate *one's* jaw / 턱을 쓰다듬다 rub *one's* chin / 턱을 내밀다 stick out *one's* chin / 턱을 당기다 draw in *one's* chin / 턱을 치켜들다 turn up *one's* nose / (사람을) 턱으로 부리다 have 《*a person*》 at *one's* beck (and call); order 《*a person*》 about / 턱으로 가리키다 indicate 《*a thing*》 with *one's* chin / 손으로 턱을 괴다 rest *one's* chin 〔cheeks〕 on 〔in〕 *one's* hand / 턱을 받치고 이야기를 듣다 listen to a speech with *one's* chin on *one's* hands / 턱을 당기고 가슴을 펴라 Chin down, chest out! ◉ ~뼈 a jawbone.

**턱**[2] 《높은 데》 a projection; a prominence; an elevated place; a raised spot; a rise; a sill. ¶ 문턱 a door 〔window〕 sill / 고개 턱 the top of a pass 〔slope〕 / 턱(이)지다 rise; swell.

**턱**[3] 《음식 대접》 a treat; a feast; a good meal. ¶ 한턱 내다 give 《*a person*》 a treat; treat 《*a person*》 to 《*something*》; stand treat 《for *one's* friend》; stand 《*a person* dinner》 / 술을 한턱 내다 treat 〔stand, buy〕 《*a person*》 a drink / 돌아가며 한턱 내다 treat 《friends》 by turns / 오늘은 내가 한턱 낸다 It is my treat today.

**턱**[4] ① 《까닭》 (a) reason; grounds. ¶ …할〔일〕 턱이 없다 there is no reason for…; it cannot be…; it is impossible 〔hardly possible〕 that…; *one* cannot believe that… / 내가 알 턱이 있나 How should I know that? / 그가 알고 있을 턱이 없다 How can he know it? ② 《정도》 extent; (a) degree. ¶ 아직 그턱이다 be still the same; It's still much the same. / 「사업이 어떤가」—「그저 그턱이지」 "How's business?"—"Just so-so." / 환자는 그저 그턱이다 The patient is no better than before. ③ 《능력》 *one's* ability 〔power〕. ¶ 턱도 안 닿다 be beyond *one's* reach 〔power〕.

**턱**[5] ① 《의젓이 구는 모양》 with a grand air; in a dignified manner; composedly; without hesitation. ¶ 돈을 턱 내다 show *one's* generosity with *one's* money; generously pay the money / 의자에 턱 앉다 sit at ease in a chair / 손을 턱 내밀다 ask for 《*something*》 with no hesitation. ② 《긴장을 푸는 모양》 at complete ease. ¶ 마음을 턱 놓다 put 〔set〕 *one's* mind at complete ease; feel quite relieved. ③ 《붙잡는 모양》 ¶ 손을 턱 잡다 hold 《*a person's*》 hand passionately 〔affectionately〕.

**턱걸이** ① 《철봉의》 chinning exercises; a chin-up. ~하다 chin *oneself* (up); do a chin-up 〔chinning exercises〕. ¶ ~ 몇 번이나 할 수 있니 How many times can you chin youself up? ② 《싸움·씨름 때의》 hitting 〔catching *a person* by〕 the chin; a chin blow 〔catch〕. ~하다 hit on 〔catch by〕 the chin; topple with a chin blow 〔catch〕. ③ 《얹혀지냄》 parasitism; sponging off 《others》. ~하다 sponge 《upon others》; be a parasite 〔hanger-on〕; lead a parasitic 〔dependent〕 existence.

**턱까불다** 《죽을 때의》 give a death rattle; breathe *one's* last; expire.

**턱끈** 《모자의》 a chin strap. ¶ ~을 걸다 have 《*one's* cap》 strapped to *one's* chin.

**턱끼움** 〖건축〗 fitting; a dovetail; dovetailed work.

**턱밀이** 《씨름》 a kind of hand-to-jaw wrestling. ~하다 wrestle hand-to-jaw.

**턱밑** ① 《턱의 끝》 the tip of the chin. ② 《가까운 곳》 beneath *one's* chin; right under *one's* nose. ¶ ~에 두고 보지 못하다 can't see 〔fail to find〕 what is right under *one's* nose.

**턱받이** a bib; a pinafore; a feeder 《영》.

**턱뼈** 〖해부〗 a jawbone; a maxillary bone.

**턱살** the lower jaw; the chin.

**턱솔** 〖건축〗 the overlap where two pieces of wood are joined.

**턱수염**(—鬚髥) a beard. ¶ ~을 기르다 grow 〔have, wear〕 a beard.

**턱시도** a tuxedo (*pl.* ~es); a tuxedo jacket; a dinner jacket 〔coat 《영》〕.

**턱없다** ① 《터무니없다》 (***a***) 《근거·이유 없다》 (be) groundless; unfounded; without reason; unreasonable. ¶ 턱없는 소문 a groundless rumor; an unfounded gossip / 턱없이 때리다 knock 《*a person*》 on no provocation / 턱(도) 없이 욕하다 abuse 《*a person*》 without rhyme or reason. (***b***) 《지나치다》 (be) immoderate; extreme; excessive; 《당

치 않다》 (be) extraordinary; exorbitant; absurd; wild; preposterous; darned《미속어》. ¶ 턱없는 값 an exorbitant 〔a fancy〕 price / 턱없는 계획 a wild 〔an absurd〕 project; a wildcat scheme / 턱없는 요구 an extravagant 〔unreasonable〕 demand; a wholly unacceptable demand / 턱없이 돈을 쓰다 fool *one's* money away; make extravagant expenditures / 턱(도)없이 비싸다 be exorbitantly dear; be ridiculously high / 턱(도)없이 키가 크다 be extremely tall / 턱(도)없는 소리를 하다 say extraordinary 〔absurd〕 things; talk nonsense 〔wild〕.
② 《신분에 맞지 않다》 be not suitable to *one's* means; 《능력 밖이다》 be beyond *one's* reach 〔power〕. ¶ 턱도 없는 생각을 갖다 have ideas above *one's* station / 그런 사치는 나에겐 턱도 없다 Such a luxury is beyond my reach.

**턱잎** 〖식물〗 a stipule.

**턱주가리** the lower jaw.

**턱짓** moving *one's* chin as a gesture; pointing with *one's* chin. ~하다 make a gesture by moving *one's* chin; point with *one's* chin.

**턱찌끼** the remnants 〔leavings〕 of a meal; the leftovers. ¶ ~의 half-eaten; remaining 《food》.

**턱촌목** a marking gauge.

**턱턱** ⇨ 탁탁.

**턴** 《수영 등의》 a turn. ~하다 turn; make a 《quick》 turn; tip off the wall (풀에서). ¶ 그는 턴을 잘 한다 He makes a good turn.
◉ 턴테이블 a turntable.

**턴키** 〖경제〗 turnkey (base system).

**턴파이크** 《유료 고속도로》 a turnpike (생략 tpk, tpke).

**털** ① 《사람의》 (a) hair; down (솜털). ¶ 털 같은 hairy / 털이 있는 haired; hairy / 털이 없는 hairless; bald / 털이 많은 hairy; thick-haired / 겨드랑이 털 underarm 〔armpit〕 hair / 곱슬곱슬한 털 curly 〔crisp〕 hair / 부드러운 털 soft hair / 빳빳한 털 coarse 〔bristly〕 hair / 센 털 gray hair / 털 나는 약 a hair-grower〔-restorer〕 / 털을 뽑다 pull out a hair; unhair / 머리털을 지지다 frizzle 〔friz〕 and curl hair; have *one's* hair frizzled and curled / 털이 나다 hair grows 〔appears, comes out〕 / 털이 많다 be hairy 〔thickly-haired〕 / 털이 성기다 be thinly-〔sparsely-〕haired / 털이 빠지다 hair 「falls out 〔comes off〕; [사람이 주어] lose *one's* hair / 머리털을 쥐어뜯다 tear 〔rend〕 *one's* hair / 털이 좀 빠졌다 A few hairs 「fell out 〔came off〕. / 그의 다리에 털이 나기 시작했다 Hair began to grow on his legs.
② 《짐승의》 fur; wool (양털); 《거센 털》 bristle (돼지 따위의); 《새털》 feathers (깃털). ¶ 털셔츠 a woolen shirt / 털양말 woolen socks 〔stockings〕 / 털옷 woolen clothing / 털외투 a fur 〔woolen〕 (over)coat / 닭의 털을 뜯다 pluck (the feathers of) a chicken / 제 털 뽑아 제 구멍에 박다 [비유적] be rigid 〔inflexible〕; be strait-laced 〔hidebound〕; lack resourcefulness 〔flexibility〕 / 털도 안 뜯고 먹으려 한다 be hasty 〔impatient〕; be out to get all 《*a person's*》 possessions.
③ 《보풀》 nap; shag; fuzz; fluff. ¶ ~이 일다 get 〔be〕 fuzzy 〔fluffy〕.

**털가죽** a fur; a fell; a pelt (생가죽); a flix (토끼·비버 등의). ¶ ~ 제품 a fur piece; [총칭] furs.

**털갈다** 《깃털을》 molt; 《짐승이》 shed 《its》 hair 〔coats〕. ¶ 털가는 시기 the molting season; the molt.

**털갈이** 《새의》 molting; 《짐승의》 coat-shedding; shedding hair.

**털게** 〖동물〗 a hairy crab.

**털구멍** pores (of the skin).

**털끝** ① 《털의 끝》 the end of a hair; the tips of hair; hair tips. ② 《조금》 a bit; a jot; a whit. ¶ ~만큼도 《not》 in the least; 《not》 at all; 《not》 a bit 〔whit〕; 《not》 in the slightest degree; in no degree / ~만큼도 개의치 않다 don't care at all; don't care a straw; don't give a damn / ~만큼도 의심할 여지가 없다 There isn't the faintest shadow of doubt about it. / 그것을 할 생각은 ~만큼도 없다 I don't have the slightest intention of doing it. / 그에게는 양심이라고는 ~만큼도 없다 He has not an atom of conscience in him. / 그의 말에는 진실이 ~만큼도 없다 There is not an ounce of truth in what he says.

**털내의**(一內衣) (knitted) woolen underwear.

**털다** ① 《붙은 것을》 shake off 〔down〕; knock 〔beat〕 off; 《먼지 따위를》 dust 《*a thing*》; clear (away, out); sweep (away, off) 《dust》; brush off. ¶ 그을음을 ~ sweep away 〔off〕 soot / (발을 굴러서) 눈을 ~ stamp the snow from 《*one's* boots》 / 솔로 먼지를 ~ brush away dust; brush 《a hat》 / 구둣솔의

모래를 ～ shake the sand from *one's* shoes / 뿌리의 흙을 ～ shake the earth away from the roots / 옷에 묻은 눈을 ～ wipe the snow from *one's* clothes / 옷에 묻은 먼지를 ～ shake the dust off *one's* clothes / 담뱃재를 ～ knock 〔tap〕 the ash off *one's* cigarette. ②《금품을》(***a***)《가진 것을 전부》empty. ¶ 돈지갑을〔주머니를〕 ～ empty *one's* purse (to the last penny); clear *one's* purse out / 가진 돈을 몽땅 ～ give all the money *one* has in hand / 주머니를 털어 그에게 만원을 주었다 I gave him ten thousand won, all that I happened to have with me. / 그는 가진 재산을 다 털어 먹었다 He ran through his fortunes. (***b***)《도둑이》rob《*a person*》of; strip《*a person*》of; steal《*a thing* from *a person*》; pilfer 〔filch〕《articles from a shop》. ¶ 금고를 ～ rob a safe / 은행을 ～ break into 〔burglarize, burgle《속어》〕 a bank;《강도가》rob a bank / 소매치기가 주머니를 ～ a pickpocket picks《*a person's*》pocket.

**털럭거리다**《늘어진 것이》keep slapping 〔slupping, slipping〕; flap; flop. ¶ 신 뒤축이 떨어져 ～ the heel of *one's* shoe gets loose and keeps slapping / 열어 놓은 창문에서 커튼이 털럭거리고 있다 The curtains are flapping at the open window.

**털럭털럭** swingingly; with slaps.

**털리다**[1] ①《붙은 것·묻은 것이》get shaken 〔knocked, beaten〕 off;《먼지가》get dusted 〔brushed〕 off. ¶ 옷의 먼지가 잘 ～ *one's* clothes are easily dusted / 담뱃재가 좀체 털리지 않는다 The ashes just won't knock out of the pipe. ②《전부 비우게 되다》get emptied. ¶ 그는 노름에서 몽땅 털렸다 He was cleaned out in gambling. ③《도둑에게》get robbed《of》. ¶ 금고를 ～ have *one's* safe robbed / (소매치기에게) 주머니를 ～ have *one's* pocket picked《of a purse》/ 우리가 집을 비운 사이에 털렸다 We had our house robbed in our absence. *or* Our house was robbed while we were away.

**털리다**[2]《털게 하다》have《*a person*》shake 〔knock, beat, dust, brush〕《*it*》off.

**털모자**(—帽子) a fur hat (모피의); a woolen cap (털실로 짠).

**털목**(—木) coarsely woven cotton (cloth).

**털목도리** a comforter (털실로 짠); a boa (모피제); a woolen muffler.

**털방석**(—方席) a fur cushion.

**털배자**(—褙子) a women's fur vest 〔waistcoat〕.

**털버덕거리다** keep splashing 〔slopping〕.

**털버덕털버덕** with splashes.

**털벙** with a plop; with a splash.

**털보** a hairy 〔shaggy〕 person.

**털복사, 털복숭아** a fuzzy peach.

**털복숭이** a hairy person 〔thing〕. ¶ ～의 hairy; shaggy《dog》.

**털붓** a (writing 〔painting〕) brush; a hair pencil (수채화용).

**털붙이**《털가죽》furs;《털 물건》fur pieces; fur goods; [총칭] furs;《털옷》fur clothes;《털실로 만든》woolen goods 〔stuff〕.

**털빛** the color of the hair 〔fur〕.

**털셔츠** (knitted) woolen underwear.

**털수세** a thick bristling beard.

**털스웨터** a jersey; a sweater《미》.

**털신** arctic boots 〔shoes〕.

**털실** wool(l)en yarn; worsted (yarn); wool; knitting wool. ¶ ～로 스웨터를 짜다 knit wool into a sweater; knit a sweater out of wool. ◉ ～가게 a wool shop. ～뭉치 a knitting ball.

**털쌘구름** 〖기상〗 a cirrocumulus (*pl.* -li).

**털썩** with a thud 〔plump, thump, flump〕; heavily. ¶ 의자에 ～ 앉다 flop 〔plunk *oneself* down〕 in a chair; plump 〔flop〕 down into a chair; drop into a chair / 땅바닥에 ～ 주저앉다 sit flat 〔flop〕 on the ground; squat down on the ground / ～ 떨어지다 fall plump 〔heavily〕 / ～ 떨어뜨리다 flump 〔flop〕 down / 짐을 바닥에 ～ 내려 놓다 put down *one's* bundle on the floor with a thud.

**털썩거리다** keep plopping 〔thudding〕.

**털양말**(—洋襪) worsted 〔woolen〕 stockings 〔socks〕.

**털어놓다** ①《속엣 것을》empty (out); shake out. ¶ 상자 속의 물건을 ～ shake out the contents of a box / 호주머니를 ～ empty *one's* pockets. ②《마음 속을》open *one's* heart; take《*a person*》into *one's* confidence; confide in《*a person*》; disclose; reveal; lay bare; confess; tell 〔talk〕 frankly 〔without reserve〕. ⇨ 터놓다③. ¶ 털어놓고 말하면 to be frank 〔candid〕 with you; frankly speaking / 마음 속을 ～ open 〔bare, unlock〕 *one's* heart《to》; unbosom 〔unburden〕 *oneself*《to》; speak (out) *one's* mind / 모든 것을 ～ confess everything; make a clean breast of《*a matter*》/ 비밀을

~ confide 〔reveal, disclose〕 a secret to《*a person*》/ 사실을 ~ lay bare the facts / 털어놓고 이야기하다 talk straight; talk without hiding anything / 자 모두 털어놓아라 Now! Out with the whole story! *or* Give it to me straight. / 이 일은 아무에게도 털어놓지 않았다 I have kept this matter secret.

**털어먹다** spend the last cent; run through; eat《*a person, oneself*》out of house and home; eat《*a person, oneself*》up. ⇨ 떨어먹다. ¶ 재산을 ~ squander 〔go 〔run〕 through〕 *one's* fortune / 이러다가 그는 집이건 땅이건 다 털어먹을 게다 At this rate he will soon eat himself out of house and land.

**털옷** a fur 〔woolen〕 robe. 「overcoat.

**털외투**(—外套) a fur coat; a fur-lined

**털장갑**(—掌甲) fur 〔woolen〕 gloves.

**털찝** a waster; a squanderer; a libertine; a prodigal; a dissipater; a debauchee; 《봉》 a dupe; an easy mark; 《구어》 a sucker.

**털층구름** 〖기상〗 a cirrostratus (*pl.* -ti).

**털터리** a man who is clean broke; a man with empty pockets; a penniless person. ⇨ 빈털터리.

**털털** ① 《걷는 모양》 plodding; trudging(ly). ② 《소리》 with dull clinks; with clatter. ¶ ~ 소리가 나다 make a rattling sound.

**털털거리다** ① 《걸음을》 plod 〔trudge〕 along 〔on〕. ② 《소리를》 keep clattering 〔rattling〕. ¶ 털털거리는 고물차 a rattling old car; a flivver 《미속어》; a jalopy 《구어》 / 마차의 털털거리는 소리 the rattling of a cart / 자동차가 털털거리며 지나가다 A motorcar rattles 〔rumbles〕 along the road.

**털털이** ① 《탈것》 a rattling thing; a rattletrap; a jalopy 《구어》; a (junk) flivver 《미속어》. ② 《사람》 a sloven; a slouch. 「and easy.

**털털하다** 《사람이》 (be) unaffected; free

**털토시** fur-lined wristlets. ¶ ~를 끼다 wear 〔put on〕 fur-lined wristlets / ~를 끼고 게구멍을 쑤시어도 제 재미라 《속담》 One can do as one pleases. *or* Every man to his taste.

**텀벙** with a plop 〔splash〕. ~하다 splash; plop. ¶ 물에 ~ 떨어지다 drop into the water with a plop 〔splash〕; fall plop into the water; flop into the water / 탕(湯)에 ~ 들어가다 plump into the bath / 물속에 ~ 뛰어 들다 jump into the water with a splash; plop 〔splash〕 into the water / ~ 소리를 내다 make a splash.

**텀벙거리다** keep splashing 〔plopping〕; splash about. ¶ 물속에서 ~ splash about in the water.

**텀블러스위치** a tumbler 〔link〕 switch.

**텀블링** 《공중제비》 tumbling.

**텁석** with a snatch; with a snap; greedily. ¶ ~ 물다 snap 〔bite〕 at / (물고기가) 미끼를 ~ 물다 snap at 〔rise to〕 the bait / ~ 받아먹다 snap 《it》 up / ~ 움켜쥐다 snatch; grasp greedily. 「beard.

**텁석나룻** a bushy 〔shaggy, heavy〕

**텁석부리** a man with bushy whiskers.

**텁석텁석** with snatches; with snaps; greedily. ¶ ~ 받아먹다 keep snapping at 《it》.

**텁수룩하다** (be) thick; shaggy; bushy. ¶ 텁수룩한 머리 long unkempt hair; a mop of hair / 수염이 ~ have a thick 〔bushy〕 beard; be heavily bearded 《apparently unshaved for weeks》/ 구레나룻이 텁수룩하게 나다 have a shaggy growth of whiskers.

**텁텁이** a broad-minded 〔casual〕 person; a person in free and easy manner.

**텁텁하다** ① 《입맛이》 (be) thick and tasteless; unpleasant-tasting; [서술적] have a muddy taste; be rough and unpleasant to the palate. ¶ 텁텁한 된장국 thick and tasteless bean=paste soup / 입이 ~ have a muddy 〔brown〕 taste in *one's* mouth. ② 《성미가》 (be) free and easy; broad=minded; careless. ¶ 성미가 텁텁해서 누구나 가리지 않고 잘 사귀다 be so broad-minded as to associate with men of all shades. ③ 《눈이》 (be) dim; blear(y); blurred.

**텃고사**(—告祀) offering a sacrifice to the tutelary spirit of a house site.

**텃구실** the site tax; a duty on site.

**텃도지**(—賭地) site 〔lot〕 rent.

**텃마당** the threshing ground of a community.

**텃밭** a vegetable 〔kitchen〕 garden. ¶ ~가꾸기 vegetable gardening for *one's* family / ~을 가꾸다 grow vegetables for 「the house 〔*one's* family〕.

**텃새** 〖조류〗 a resident (bird); a permanent resident.

**텃세**(—貰) rent for a (house) site.

**텃세하다**(—勢—) take advantage of being on *one's* own ground to act high-handedly; put on a proprietary air; play the cock-of-the-walk; lord it over a newcomer.

**텅** ¶ 텅 빈 empty; vacant; bare; void; hollow; deserted / (속이) 텅 빈 나무 a hollowed tree / 텅 빈 느낌 a sense of emptiness; a hollow feeling (inside of *one*); hollowness / 방이 텅 비다 a room is empty / 호주머니가 텅 비다 *one's* purse does not contain a farthing / 집은 텅 비어 있었다 The house was found empty 〔deserted〕.

**텅스텐** 〖화학〗 tungsten; wolfram (기호 W). ¶ ~의 tungstic; tungstenic. ◉ ~강(鋼) tungsten steel. ~산(酸) tungstic acid: ~ 산염 tungstate. ~전구 a tungsten lamp 〔bulb〕. ~철 ferrotungsten. 산화 ~ tungsten oxide.

**텅텅** all hollow. ¶ ~ 비다 be quite empty / 그 방은 ~ 비어 있다 The room is all empty. / 모든 방들이 ~ 비어 있다 All the rooms are empty.

**테**[1] ① 《둘러 메우는》 a hoop. ¶ 테를 메우다〔두르다〕 hoop 《a barrel》; bind with hoops; put a hoop on 《a tub》/ 테가 느슨해지다〔벗겨지다〕 a hoop gets loose 〔comes off〕/ 테를 벗기다 unhoop 《a barrel》; take off the hoops. ② 《안경 등의》 a rim; a frame. ¶ 무테 안경 rimless glasses / 금테〔검은 테〕 안경 gold-〔black-〕rimmed spectacles. ③ 《모자 띠》 a band; a stripe; 《언저리》 a brim; a rim. ¶ 금테 두른 모자 a cap banded with gold stripes / 테가 넓은 모자 a broad-brimmed hat. ④ ⇨ 테두리.

**테**[2] 《실묶음》 a reel; a skein; a bunch. ¶ 실 한 테 a skein of thread.

**테너** 〖음악〗 《음역》 tenor; 《사람》 a tenor (singer). ¶ ~로 부르다 sing tenor.

**테네시** 《미국의 주》 Tennessee (생략 Tenn.).

**테니스** (lawn) tennis. ¶ ~볼 a tennis ball / ~라켓 a tennis racket / ~를 치다 play tennis. ◉ ~경기〔대회〕 a tennis match 〔tournament〕. ~선수 a tennis player; a netter 《미구어》. ~코트 a tennis court. ~화 tennis shoes; sneakers 《미》. 단식〔복식〕~ a tennis match 〔game〕 of singles 〔doubles〕.

**테두리** ① 《가장자리》 the border; the edge; 《테》 the brim; the rim; the frame. ¶ 검은 ~ black borders 〔edges〕; 《부고 등의》 mourning borders / ~를 두르다 put a border on; rim; border; margin; frame. ② 《윤곽》 an outline; an overall picture; a rough sketch. ¶ 계획의 ~ an outline of a scheme. ③ 《범위》 a limit; a framework; the confines 《of》. ¶ ~ 밖에(서) outside 〔beyond〕 the limit 《of》/ ~ 안에(서) within the limit 〔framework〕 《of》/ 법의 ~ 안에서 within the legal limit; without infringement of the law / ~를 넘어서다 exceed 〔go beyond〕 the limit / ~를 정하다 fix the limit; set limits 〔bounds〕 《to》; set framework 《for》/ 통제의 ~를 넓히다〔좁히다〕 widen 〔narrow〕 the sphere of control / 법의 ~를 벗어나다 pass 〔overstep〕 the bounds of legality; commit a trespass.

**테라마이신** 〖약〗 《상표명》 Terramycin.

**테라스** a terrace. ¶ ~에(서) on the terrace. ◉ ~하우스 a terrace(d) house.

**테라코타** 《붉은 점토의 설구이》 terra-cotta. ¶ ~의 terra-cotta 《figurine》 (공예품·건축용).

**테러** terror; terrorism. ~하다 terrorize. ¶ ~ 습격 a terroristic raid; a terror raid / ~의 희생이 되다 fall a victim to terrorism. ◉ ~단 a gang of terrorists; the terrorists. ~분자 a terrorist element. ~사건 a case of terrorism; a terrorist outrage. ~전술 terrorist(ic) tactics. ~조직 a terrorist organization. ~집단 a terrorist group. ~행위 (an act of) terrorism: ~ 행위자 a terrorist.

**테러리스트** a terrorist.

**테러리즘** terrorism.

**테레빈유**(—油) turpentine; 《구어》 turps. ¶ ~를 바르다 turpentine.

**테르븀** 〖화학〗 terbium. ¶ ~의 terbic. ◉ 산화~ terbia.

**테르펜** 〖화학〗 terpene.

**테리어** 〖동물〗 a terrier (사냥개·애완용의 작은 개).

**테마** 《논제·주제》 [< *Thema* (G.)] a theme; subject matter. ¶ 연구~ a subject of study 〔research〕/ 음악의 ~ the theme of a music / 삼각 관계를 ~로 소설을 쓰다 write a novel with a love triangle as its theme / 자네 졸업 논문의 ~는 무엇이지 What is the subject of your graduation thesis? ◉ ~공원 a theme park. ~뮤직 theme music; 《방송 개시·종료의》 a signature (tune). ~소설 a novel with a purpose. ~송 a theme 〔title〕 song.

**테메(우)다** hoop; bind with hoops; put a hoop on. ¶ 통을 ~ hoop a barrel; put a hoop on a barrel.

**테밖** outside the circle 〔sphere, bounds〕 《of politics》.

**테석테석** rough(ly); coarse(ly). ～하다 (be) rough; coarse. ¶ ～하게 구운 도기(陶器) unglazed pottery; bisque; biscuit (ware).
**테스터** 〖전기〗 a (circuit) tester.
**테스토스테론** 〖생화학〗 testosterone (남성 호르몬).
**테스트** a test; testing; a workout 《미》; a quiz; 《배우·가수의》 an audition; a tryout. ～하다 test. ¶ 학력 ～ an achievement test / 성능 ～ a performance 〔an efficiency〕 test / 실력 ～ an ability test / 지능 ～ an intelligence test / 음성을 ～하다 test *one's* voice / ～를 받다 take 〔undergo〕 a test; 《가수 등이》 get an audition / ～에 패스하다 pass a test / 그들은 팔기 전에 차를 ～한다 They will try out 〔test-drive〕 the car before they put it on sale. ◉ ～분석 test analysis. ～케이스 a test case. ～코스 a test course. ～파일럿 a test pilot. ～패턴 《TV》 a test pattern.
**테이블** a table (★ 서랍 없는 책상, 식탁, 작업대 등을 뜻하며 desk와 구별됨). ¶ ～에 둘러 앉다 sit around a table / ～을 사이에 두고 앉다 [두 사람이 주어] sit across a table; [한 쪽이 주어] sit across from 《*a person*》 at a table / 여러분 ～로 나와 앉으세요. 식사 준비가 다 됐습니다 Please be seated at the table, every body. The dinner is ready. ◉ ～매너 table manners. ～보 a table cover; a tablecloth (식탁의). ～센터 《중앙의 그릇받침》 a doily. ～차지 《지정좌석료》 a cover charge.
**테이블스피치** an after-dinner speech; a speech (made) at a dinner 〔luncheon〕. ¶ 간단한 ～를 하다 make a little after-dinner speech.
**테이프** ① 《종이·헝겊·비닐 등의》 (a) tape; 《축하용》 a paper streamer; a colored tape ribbon; 《녹음 테이프》 a (sound recording) tape. ¶ 골인 지점의 ～ 《육상 경기의》 the finish tape / ～ 한 권 a reel 〔spool〕 of tape / ～를 끊다 《경주에서》 breast the tape; 《개통식 등에서》 cut the tape 《for》; cut a ribbon 《on a new office building》 / ～를 던지다 fling 〔throw〕 a paper streamer 《across, to》; shower with streamers / ～에 녹음하다 record 《music》 on tape; put 《the conversation》 on tape; tape-record; tape / 모든 데이터는 ～에 기록되어 기억장치에 저장된다 All data goes on tape for storage. ② 《줄자》 a tape measure; the tape. ◉ ～녹음 tape recording. ～덱 a tape deck. 스테레오～ a stereo tape: 스테레오 ～ 재생 장치 a stereophonic tape player. 자기～ a magnetic tape.
**테이프리코더** a (magnetic) tape recorder. ¶ ～로 녹음하다 record on a tape recorder / ～를 작동시키다 set a tape recorder in operation.
**테일라이트** 《자동차의 미등》 a taillight; 「a tail lamp.
**테일러** 《양복장이》 a tailor.
**테일러 시스템** 〖경영〗 the Taylor system.
**테제** [< *These* (G.)] 〖철학〗 a thesis (*pl.* theses).
**테크네튬** 〖화학〗 technetium.
**테크노스트레스** 《기술 환경에서 생기는 스트레스》 techno-stress.
**테크노크라시** 《기술주의》 technocracy.
**테크노크라트** 《기술 관료》 a technocrat.
**테크노폴리스** 《기술 산업 도시》 a technopolis.
**테크놀로지** 《과학 기술》 technology. ¶ 하이～ high technology / ～아트 technology art.
**테크니션** 《기술자》 a technician.
**테크니컬 녹아웃** 〖권투〗 a technical knockout; a T.K.O.
**테크니컬러** 《상표명》 Technicolor; 〖영화〗 technicolor. ¶ ～로 in technicolor.
**테크니컬 파울** 〖농구〗 a technical foul.
**테크닉** 《기교》 (a) technique. ¶ 연주의 ～ a playing technique 《on the piano》 / ～이 뛰어나다 be superior in technique; show 〔display〕 an excellent technique.
**테토론** Tetoron (폴리에스테르 섬유의 상표명).
**테트라포드** 《호안(護岸)용 블록》 a tetrapod.
**테플론** 《상표명》 Teflon. ¶ ～ 프라이팬 a Teflon frying pan.
**텍사스** 《미국의 주》 Texas (생략 Tex.). ¶ ～의 Texan. ◉ ～사람 a Texan. ～히트 〖야구〗 a Texas leaguer; a blooper.
**텍스트** ① 《교과서》 a textbook. ¶ 영어 ～ an English textbook / ～ 24 페이지를 펴시오 Open the text at 〔Turn to 《미》〕 p. 24. ② 《원문·본문》 a text. ¶ ～대로의 인용 a textual quotation. ◉ ～끝 〖컴퓨터〗 an end of text (생략 ETX). ～대입호출 〖컴퓨터〗 a call by text. ～북 a textbook. ～시스템 〖컴퓨터〗 a text system. ～시작 〖컴퓨터〗 a start of text (생략 STX). ～에디팅〔편집〕 〖컴퓨터〗 text editing. ～윈도 〖컴퓨터〗 a text window. ～처리 〖컴퓨터〗 text processing. ～파일 〖컴퓨터〗 a text file. ～편집기 〖컴퓨터〗 a text editor.
**텐스** 〖문법〗 《시제》 the tense.

**텐트** a tent; [총칭] tentage. ⇨ 천막.
**텔레그래프** 《전신》 telegraph.
**텔레마케팅** 〖경제〗《전화에 의한 판매 방식》 a telemarketing.
**텔레마크** 《스키》 telemark (position, turn). ~하다 telemark.
**텔레미터** 《원격 계측기》 a telemeter. ¶ ~의 신호 telemetry signals / (측정치 따위를) ~로 전송(電送)하다 telemeter / ~로 반송하다 telemeter back. ◉ ~스테이션 a telemetering station. ~장치 a telemeteric system.
**텔레비전** television (생략 TV); 《영구어》 (the) telly; 《미속어》 a boob tube; 《수상기》 a television 〔TV〕 set. ¶ ~의 televisionary; televisional / ~ 취재반 a television crew / 19인치 ~ a TV set with a 19 in. wide screen / ~을 장시간 보는 사람 a heavy TV watcher / ~을 보다 watch 〔look at, view, see〕 television / ~을 켜다〔끄다〕 turn on 〔off〕 television 〔a TV set〕 / ~에 나오다 make a television appearance; make an appearance on TV; appear 〔go〕 on television; get on television 〔TV〕 / ~에 출연하다 appear on a television show; do a television program / ~ 생방송에 나오다 go on live television / ~ 앞에서 떠날 줄 모르다 glue *oneself* to a television set; be planted in front of a TV set / ~으로 on television 〔TV〕; on the telly 《영속어》 / ~으로 보다 teleview; see 《*a person*》 on television; watch 《a soccer game》 on TV / ~의 화상(畵像)을 보내다 radio TV pictures 《to》 / ~에서 지금 무엇을 하느냐 What's on TV now? ◉ ~광(狂) a television fanatic; a vidiot 《미속어》. ~기사 a television technician. ~기자 a TV reporter. ~뉴스 telenews; TV news. ~드라마 a teledrama; a television 〔TV〕 drama. ~ (방송)국 a television 〔TV〕 station. ~송신기 a television transmitter; a televisor. ~수상기 a television (set); a TV set. ~수상면 a telescreen; a video screen. ~시청률 an audience rating. ~시청자 a televiewer; a viewer; the TV audience [집합적]. ~연속(방송)극 a television serial drama; a soap opera 《미》. ~영상(映像) a TV image. ~영화 a telefilm; a TV movie. ~전화 a television telephone; a TV phone. ~카메라 a television 〔TV〕 camera; a telecamera. ~탑 a television tower. ~토론회 a TV 〔televised〕 debate. ~프로 a television program; a TV show: 어린이용 ~ 프로 a kid program on television; a kidvid. ~회의 a teleconference. 고화질 ~ a high-definition television (생략 HDTV). 컬러 ~ a color television. 폐쇄 회로 ~ a closed-circuit television (생략 CCTV).
**텔레비전 방송**(一放送) a television 〔TV〕 broadcast; a telecast. ¶ ~을 하다 telecast; televise; make a telecast / ~을 하고 있는 축구 a televised 〔telecast〕 soccer. ◉ ~자 a telecaster.
**텔레커뮤팅** 《재택근무》 a telecommuting.
**텔레타이프** a teletype(writer); a teletype printing system; a teleprinter. ¶ ~를 치다〔로 송신하다〕 teletype; send 《a message》 by teletype / ~로 보낸 통신 a teletype (message).
**텔레텍스** 〖컴퓨터〗 a teletex.
**텔레텍스트** 《문자 다중방송》 a teletext.
**텔레파시** 《정신 감응》 telepathy. ¶ ~의 telepathic / ~로 전하다 communicate by telepathy; telepath / ~를 행하다 telepathize.
**텔레팩스** 《전송사진》 telefacsimile; telefax.
**텔레포트** 〖통신〗《통신 위성과 연결되는 지상 통신 센터》 a teleport.
**텔렉스** 《시스템》 telex; 《통신문》 a telex; 《상표 이름》 Telex. [< *tel*egraph *ex*change] ¶ ~로 정보를 교환하다 exchange information by telex / 지금 LA에서 ~가 들어왔다 A telex has just arrived from LA. ◉ ~ 타자원 a telex operator.
**텔롭** 《TV》《화면 송출 방식의 하나》 a TELOP. [< *tel*evision *o*paque *p*rojector]
**텔루륨** 〖화학〗 tellurium (기호 Te). ¶ ~과 화합시키다 tellurize. ◉ ~ 금은광(鑛) petzite. ~ 니켈광(鑛) melonite. ~산(酸) telluric acid: ~ 산염 tellurate. 아(亞)~산 tellurous acid: 아~산염 tellurite.
**텔스타** 《미국 통신 위성》 Telstar.
**텔오토그래프** 《통신인쇄》 a telautograph.
**텝** 《수량》 as many 〔much〕 as; 《거리》 as far as; 《시간》 as long as. ¶ 한 섬 텝이나 먹다 eat a whole bag of rice / 두 달 텝이나 걸린다니 You say it takes two whole months?
**템페라** 〖미술〗 (a) tempera (painting); a painting in distemper. ◉ ~화가 a tempera artist.
**템포** 《속도》 tempo; speed. ¶ 소설의 ~ the tempo 〔pace〕 of a story / ~가 빠른〔느린〕 곡 a tune with quick 〔slow〕 tempo / 빠른〔느린〕 ~로 at quick 〔slow〕 tempo; rapidly 〔slowly〕 / ~에

맞추다 keep pace with the tempo《of modern life》/ ～가 맞지 않다 be out of tempo / ～가 빠르다〔느리다〕 be「quick〔slow〕of moving; be「fast=moving〔slow-moving〕; be「quick〔slow〕in tempo / 생산 ～를 빨리하다〔느리게 하다〕「step up〔slow down〕the tempo of production.

**텡쇠**《허약자》 a person who looks strong but is actually quite weak; a hollow shell of a person.

**토**[1] ①《한문 구절 끝에 붙이는》 Korean letters added to the end of Chinese phrase to show the syntactical relationship. ¶ 토를 달다 add *Hangeul* suffixes to Chinese texts. ②《한자음을 표시하는》 *Hangeul* letters of the Korean phonetic syllabary「printed〔written〕at the side of Chinese characters. ③《토씨》 a particle; a postposition.

**토**[2]《간장 찌꺼기》 the「scum〔sediment, dregs〕of soysauce.

**토건업**(土建業) civil engineering and construction business. ◉ ～자 a civil engineering and building constructor; a construction contractor; a builder.

**토관**(土管) an earthen pipe〔tube〕; a clay pipe; a (drainage) tile (하수의).

**토굴**(土—) 〖조개류〗 mud oysters.

**토굴**(土窟) a dugout; a large cave. ¶ ～에서 사는 사람 a cave dweller.

**토글스위치** 〖전기〗 a toggle switch.

**토기**(土器) an earthen vessel; earthenware [총칭]. ¶ ～의 파편《유적에서 나오는》 a potsherd; a sherd. ◉ ～장이 an earthenware maker; a potter. ～점 an earthenware shop.

**토끼** a (house) rabbit (집토끼); a hare (산토끼). ¶ ～ 둘을 잡으려다가 하나도 못 잡는다 be defeated by *one's* own greed;《속담》 Grasp all, lose all. / ～를 다 잡으면 사냥개를 잡는다 ⇨ 토사구팽. ◉ ～고기 hare meat. ～굴 a rabbit「hole〔burrow〕. ～그물 a net for catching rabbits; a rabbit net. ～사냥《go》 hare〔rabbit〕hunting. ～사육장 a (rabbit) warren; a rabbitry. ～자리 〖천문〗 the Hare; Lepus. ～장 a rabbit hutch. ～해 〖민속〗 the Year of the Hare.

**토끼뜀** ～하다 jump along in a squatting position.

**토끼잠** a light sleep. ¶ ～ 자다 have a poor sleep; sleep「lightly〔badly〕; be wakeful.

**토끼풀** 〖식물〗 a white Dutch clover; a white Dutch. ¶ 네 잎 ～ a four-leaf(-ed) clover.

**토너먼트** a tournament; a tourney. ¶ ～에서 1위가 되다 take first place in a tournament / 테니스 ～에서 (끝까지) 이겨남다 remain a winner in the tennis tournament.

**토네이도** 〖기상〗 a tornado (*pl.* -does, -dos); a twister《미구어》.

**토농**(이)(土農(—)) a native farmer; a settled farmer.

**토닉**《강장제》 a tonic.

**토닥거리다** keep「patting〔tapping, knocking, rapping〕. ¶ 고기를 다지느라고 ～ be chopping meat on the kitchen board / 토닥거리며 아기를 잠재우다 let a baby fall into sleep by patting.

**토닥토닥** knocking〔rapping, patting〕repeatedly. ¶ 문을 ～ 두드리다 be rapping on the door.

**토단**(土壇) a dirt platform; a terrace of earth.

**토담**(土—) an earthen wall; a mud〔dirt〕wall; an adobe wall. ◉ ～장이 a mud-wall builder. ～집 a mud-wall hut; an adobe hut.

**토대**(土臺) ①《토단》 a terrace of earth. ②《건축의》 a foundation. ¶ ～를 앉히다〔다지다〕 lay the「foundation〔cornerstone〕《of》/ ～를 굳히다 solidify the foundation / ～를 쌓다 build up the foundation / 집의 ～가 든든하다 a house is built on a firm foundation; the house has a firm foundation. ③《(사물의) 기초》 a foundation; groundwork; a base; a basis (*pl.* bases); a cornerstone. ¶ …을 ～로 한 based upon... / …을 ～로하여 on the basis of... / ～를 이루다 form the basis《of》/ ～가 마련되다 the groundwork is done; the way is paved《for》; a cornerstone is laid / ～를 쌓다 pave the way for《*one's* success》; lay the groundwork《for》/ 실지 체험을 ～로 소설을 쓰다 write a novel based on *one's* actual experience / 적은 자본을 ～로 장사를 시작하다 start a business on small capital / 종교는 신앙을 ～로 한다 Religion is based on faith. / 초등 교육은 인간의 ～를 쌓는 교육이다 Primary education forms the groundwork for building up a man's character.

**토댄스**《발레의》 toe-dancing; toe dance. ¶ ～를 하다 toe-dance.

**토라지다** ①《성이 나서》 be(come)「sulky〔peevish〕; go into the sulks; pout; sulk; be in the sulks. ¶ 토라진 소리를 하다 say spiteful things / 토라져서 잠자리에서 일어나지 않다 stay in bed sulkily 〔out of spite〕/ 돈을 빌려 주지 않는다고 ~ sulk over a rebuff on borrowing money / 그는 그 말에 또 토라졌다 He turned sulky again at the words. ② 《음식이》 lie heavy on *one's* stomach; "repeat"; keep tasting. ¶ 먹은 것이 ~ food "repeats"; *one* keeps tasting what *one* has eaten.

**토란**(土卵) 〖식물〗 a taro (*pl.* ~s). ◉ ~국 soup with taro in it; taro soup.

**토렴** pouring hot broth over rice 〔noodles〕 a little at a time to heat them up. ~하다 heat up 《rice》 by pouring hot broth over a little at a time.

**토로**(吐露) exposing 〔revealing〕 *one's* thoughts. ~하다 express 〔put〕 《*one's* view》; set forth 《*one's* opinion》; lay bare 〔pour out〕 《*one's* heart》; speak 《*one's* mind》; give vent to 《*one's* feelings》; disclose 〔reveal〕 《a secret to *a person*》. ¶ 기탄없이 의견을 ~하다 express *one's* opinion freely / 어머니에게 부친 편지에는 그녀의 진정이 ~되어 있었다 She expressed her true feelings in her letter she sent to her mother.

**토록** ① 《하도록》 to the point where it does 〔say, is〕. ② 《정도》 as much as; to the extent of. ¶ 종일~ all day (long); throughout the day / 그~ 많은가 Is there that much?

**토론**(討論) (a) debate; (a) discussion. ~하다 debate 《on》; discuss 《a subject with *a person*》; dispute 《about》; hold a debate 《on a subject》; talk up 《미》.
¶ 무익한 ~ a sterile discussion / 활발한 ~ a lively discussion; a hot debate / ~의 광장 the forum of debate / ~의 명수 a good debater; a master of fence / 많은 ~ 끝에 after much discussion / ~중의 under discussion / ~에 들어가다 enter upon 〔open〕 a debate; go into a discussion 《on, concerning》/ ~에 부치다 put 《a question》 to debate; bring 《a question》 up for debate / ~에 참가하다 join the debate; take the floor / 평화에 관해 ~하다 debate on peace / ~을 시작하다 open the debate / ~을 끝내다〔종결짓다〕 close 〔wind up, closure〕 a discussion 〔debate〕; apply the closure to the debate / ~ 종결의 동의를 제출하다 《의회에서》 bring a motion for closure.
◉ ~술 dialectics. ~자 a debater; a panelist. ~종결 closure (of debate). ~회 a debate; a forum; 《공개의》 a panel discussion: 공개 ~회 an open forum / TV ~회 a TV debate / 대통령 후보의 ~회 a Presidential debate. 대체~ 《전반적》 general debate; 《예비적》 preliminary discussion; 《안건의》 first reading. 자유〔집단〕~ free 〔group〕 discussion.

**토룡**(土龍) an earthworm. ⇨지렁이.

**토류**(土類) 〖화학〗 earths. ¶ ~의 earthy. ◉ ~ 금속 an earth metal.

**토륨** 〖화학〗 thorium (기호 Th). ◉ ~텅스텐 thoriated tungsten. 산화~ thoria.

**토르소** 〖미술〗 a torso (*pl.* ~s, -si).

**토리**[1] 《실뭉치》 a spool of thread. ◉ ~실 thread in spools.

**토리**[2] 《쇠고리》 an iron ring fixed on the end of the shaft of an arrow.

**토리**(土理) fertility of soil; soil conditions.

**토마루**(土—) a mud floor.

**토마토** 〖식물〗 a tomato (*pl.* ~es); a love apple. ◉ ~소스 tomato sauce. ~주스 tomato juice. ~케첩 tomato ketchup 〔catchup, catsup〕.

**토마호크** 《순항 미사일》 a Tomahawk; 《북미 인디언의 도끼》 a tomahawk.

**토막** a piece; a block; a bit; a fragment; a slice; a scrap (끄트러기). ~나다 be broken into pieces. ~내다〔치다〕 cut 〔chop〕 into pieces; cut 《*a thing*》 in slices; cut 〔hack〕 to pieces; slice; fillet (생선 등을). ¶ 고등어 한 ~ a slice 〔cut, fillet〕 of mackerel / 나무 한 ~ a piece 〔block〕 of wood / 역사의 한 ~ a page 〔scene〕 of history / 엿 한 ~ a piece 〔bar〕 of taffy / ~ 살인 사건 a case of torso murder / ~ 시체 a mangled 〔dismembered〕 body.
◉ ~극 a little dramatical performance; a short play; a skit. ~나무 a piece 〔block, chip, splinter〕 of wood; wood in blocks.

**토막**(土幕) a mud hut; a dugout.

**토막토막** (in)to pieces; piece by piece. ¶ ~ 자른 무 thick slices of radish / 생선을 ~ 자르다 chop fish into pieces / 나무를 ~ 베다 saw wood into pieces.

**토멸**(討滅) conquest; extermination; annihilation. ~하다 conquer; exterminate; annihilate. ¶ 적을 ~하다 destroy the enemy.

**토목**(土木) 《공사》 engineering 〔public〕 works. ¶ ~ (사업)을 일으키다 undertake public works.
◉ ~건축(업) the civil engineering and construction (industry). ~ 공사

civil engineering works; public works. ～공이 a boor; a yokel; a dumbbell《미속어》. ～공학 civil engineering. ～과〔국〕 the public works section〔bureau〕. ～기계 civil engineering machinery [총칭]. ～기사 a civil engineer. ～도급업자(都給業者) a public works contractor. ～인부 a construction worker.

**토미사일**《대전차 유도 미사일》 a TOW missile. [< *t*ube-launched, *o*ptically tracked, *w*ire-guided missile]

**토민**(土民) the natives; the aborigines.

**토박이**(土—) natives; aborigines. ¶ ～의 native-born; trueborn; born and bred. ◉ 서울～ a Seoulite to the backbone; a truebred〔trueborn〕 Seoulite.

**토박하다**(土薄—)《땅이》 (be) infertile; meager; sterile; barren; unproductive; sick. ¶ 토박한 땅 unproductive land / 이 곳은 땅이 ～ The soil here is poor.

**토방**(土房) an earth-floored〔a dirt=floored〕 room.

**토벌**(討伐) conquest; subjugation; suppression. ～하다 conquer; subjugate; suppress; put down; subdue. ¶ 공비를 ～하다 liquidate〔subdue〕 red guerrillas / 반란군을 ～하다 suppress a rebellion. ◉ ～군〔대〕 a punitive force: ～군을 보내다 send a punitive force〔expedition〕《against》. ～전 a punitive expedition.

**토벽**(土壁) a mud wall.

**토병**(土兵) local troops.

**토비**(土匪) local rebels; rebellious natives; native insurgents.

**토비**(討匪) suppression of bandits. ～하다 suppress〔put down〕 bandits.

**토사**(土砂) earth and sand. ◉ ～붕괴 a landslide; a soil avalanche: ～붕괴로 집 세 채가 흙더미에 묻혔다 Three houses collapsed and were buried under a landslide.

**토사**(吐瀉) vomiting and diarrhea. ～하다 suffer from vomiting fits and diarrhea; vomit and run off at the bowels. ◉ ～곽란 『한의』 acute gastroenteritis; vomiting and diarrhea. ～물 vomit and excreta; the matter vomited.

**토사구팽**(兎死狗烹) A thing is cherished only so long as it is useful. *or* When cunning hares are all caught it is the turn of the faithful hound to be killed for meat.

**토산**(土山) a mountain without rocks.

**토산물**(土産物) products of the district〔place〕; local〔native〕 produce; regional products.

**토산불알** 『한의』 a testicle swollen with elephantiasis.

**토색**(討索) (an) extortion; blackmail(ing). ～하다 extort《money from *a person*》; blackmail《*a person*》 for; practice extortion.

**토설**(吐說) ＝실토(實吐).

**토성**(土星) 『천문』 Saturn. ¶ ～의 고리 Saturn's rings; the belts of Saturn.

**토성**(土城) a wall of earth; a mud wall; mud fortifications.

**토속**(土俗) local customs; folkways. ◉ ～신앙 (a) folk belief. ～음악 a folk music. ～학 folklore: ～학자 a folklorist.

**토순**(兎脣) a harelip; a split lip. ⇨ 언청이.

**토스** a toss; tossing. ～하다 toss《a ball》. ◉ ～배팅 『야구』 a pepper game.

**토스터** a toaster; an electric toaster. ¶ ～로 빵을 굽다 make toast in a toaster. ◉ 자동～ a pop-up〔an automatic〕 toaster.

**토스트** toast. ¶ 버터를 바른〔안 바른〕～ buttered〔dry〕 toast / ～를 굽다 make toast; toast / ～에 버터를 바르다 butter toast; spread toast with butter; spread butter on toast. ◉ ～샌드위치 a club sandwich. 프렌치 ～ French toast.

**토시** 《wear, put on》 wristlets (to protect against the cold).

**토신**(土神) 『민속』 a deity of the soil.

**토실토실** ～하다 (be) plump; chubby; rotund; tubby; fat. ¶ ～한 볼 chubby cheeks / ～한 아기 a chubby baby / ～한 얼굴 a full face / ～ 살이 찌다 be plump〔chubby〕.

**토심스럽다**(吐心—) (be) disgusting; unpleasant; feel bad. ¶ 거지에 동냥주듯하니 토심스러워 못 받겠다 I can't accept it without feeling bad because he gives it to me as if it were alms for a beggar.

**토씨** 『문법』 a postposition; a postpositional word. ＝조사(助詞).

**토악질**(吐—) ①《구토》 an attack〔a fit〕 of vomiting. ～하다 vomit; fetch〔bring, throw〕 up; spew out the vomit. ¶ 먹은 것을 ～하다 throw up what *one* has eaten. ②《부정 소득의》 coughing up〔repaying, refunding, replacing〕 ill-gotten money. ～하다 cough up〔repay, refund, replace〕 ill-gotten money; disgorge. ¶ 먹었던 돈을 ～하다 repay what *one* has embezzled / 그는 먹은 돈 2백 만 원을

~했다 He has disgorged the embezzled two-million won.

**토양**(土壤) soil. ¶ 메마른〔비옥한〕 ~ poor 〔rich, good, fertile〕 soil / 벼농사에 적합한 ~ the soil suitable for growing rice. ◉ ~개량제 a soil conditioner. ~미생물 soil microbes. ~오염 soil pollution 〔contamination〕. ~조사 an agronomical survey. ~침식 soil erosion. ~학 pedology; soil science: ~학자 a pedologist; a soil scientist / 응용~학 agrology.

**토어**(土語) a native language; a local tongue.

**토역**(土役) mud work; earth work. ~하다 do mud work; plaster with mud. ◉ ~꾼 a navvy; a construction worker.

**토옥**(土屋) a mud hut.

**토요일**(土曜日) Saturday (생략 Sat.).

**토욕질**(土浴—) a dust bath; 《a hen, horse》 wallowing in mud 〔dirt〕; dusting. ~하다 have 〔take〕 a dust bath; wallow in mud 〔dirt〕.

**토우**(土雨) a dust storm; a rain of dust.

**토우**(土偶) a clay figure 〔doll〕; a clay figurine (작은 것).

**토의**(討議) (a) discussion; (a) debate; (a) deliberation. ~하다 discuss 《politics, a social problem》; hold a discussion 《with another》; deliberate upon 〔over〕 《*a matter*》; debate on 〔about〕 《a question, a problem》. ¶ ~를 끝내다〔종결하다〕 close a discussion / ~에 들어가다 open a debate; enter into a discussion / ~에 부치다 submit 《a subject》 to debate; bring up 《*a matter*》 for discussion; bring 《*a matter*》 for deliberation; bring 《a bill》 to the floor for debate / ~에 오르다 come 〔be brought〕 up for discussion / ~중이다 be under discussion 〔debate〕; be on the carpet 〔tapis〕 / ~중의 문제 questions under deliberation 〔yet in debate〕 / 열띤 ~를 벌이고 있다 be under heavy 〔intense〕 debate / 철저히 ~하다 discuss 《*a matter*》 thoroughly 〔exhaustively, fully〕; talk 〔thrash〕 《*a matter*》 out / 우리는 영어 교육의 문제들에 관해 오랜 시간 ~하였다 We discussed the problems of teaching English for a long time. *or* We had a long discussion about the problems of teaching English. ◉ ~사항 items on the agenda. ~안(案) a subject for debate 〔discussion〕. 긴급~ an urgent consultation.

**토익** 《국제 커뮤니케이션 영어 능력 테스트》 TOEIC. 〔< *T*est *o*f *E*nglish for *I*nternational *C*ommunication〕

**토인**(土人) a native; an aboriginal; aborigines [총칭].

**토일릿** a toilet; a toilet room 《미》. ⇨ 화장실. ¶ ~에 물을 내리다 flush the toilet.

**토장**(土葬) interment; inhumation; burial. ~하다 inter; inhume; bury in the ground.

**토장**(土醬) soybean paste.

**토적**(土賊) local bandits 〔thieves〕; local rebels 〔insurgents〕.

**토적**(討賊) ~하다 attack 〔subdue〕 thieves 〔the rebels〕.

**토제**(吐劑) 〖약〗 an emetic (medicine); a vomitory.

**토족**(土族) (relatives of) native gentry.

**토종**(土種) 《재래종》 a native kind 〔species〕; a local 〔home〕 breed. ¶ ~의 native; indigenous / ~딸기 native strawberries / ~닭 a native chicken / 한국 ~의 동식물 the plants and animals indigenous to Korea.

**토주**(土酒) the *sul* 〔wine〕 of the place 〔district〕; (*sul* of) local brew.

**토지**(土地) 《땅》 ① 《지면》 land; ground; a piece 〔tract〕 of land (한 구획의); 《소유지》 a lot 〔plot〕; an estate; (a piece of) real estate (부동산). ¶ 넓은 ~ broad acres / 작은 ~ a patch of land / 50평의 ~ a lot of 50 *p'yŏng* / ~를 갖고 있다 own 〔hold, have, possess〕 land / ~를 놀려 두다 keep land idle / ~를 매매하다 deal in real estate / ~를 사다〔팔다〕 buy 〔sell〕 (a piece of) land; buy 〔sell〕 a lot / ~를 빌다 lease 〔rent〕 land 〔a lot〕 / ~에 투자하다 invest in real estate / 그는 집을 지을 양으로 그 ~를 샀다 He bought the land for the purpose of building on it. / 그는 오하이오에 광대한 ~를 소유하고 있다 He owns a large tract of land in Ohio. / 나는 서울 근교에 200평방미터의 ~를 샀다 I bought a 200 squaremeter lot in the suburbs of Seoul. ② 《토양·흙》 soil; land. ¶ 기름진 ~ fertile land 〔soil〕; rich land / 메마른 ~ poor 〔barren〕 soil; barren 〔sterile〕 land / ~를 갈다 cultivate land; till the soil 〔ground〕 / ~를 비옥하게 하다 enrich the soil. ◉ ~가격 the price 〔value〕 of land. ~가옥 real estate; land and houses. ~개량 land improvement: ~ 개량법 the Land Improvement Act / ~ 개량사업 land improvement enterprises. ~개발 estate 〔land〕 development: 한국 ~ 개발 공사 Korea Land Development

Corporation (생략 KLDC). ～개혁 land reform. ～거래 dealings in real estate: ～ 거래 신고제 the land deal reporting system; the land transaction notification system. ～건물 premises. ～관리인 a land steward; a land agent. ～구획정리 land 「(re)-adjustment 〔reallocation〕: ～ 구획정리 사업 a land 「adjustment 〔reallocation〕 work. ～균분론(均分論) agrarianism: ～ 균분론자 an agrarianist. ～대장〔등기부〕 a land register; a terrier; a cadastre: ～ 과세대장 the land tax ledger. ～매매 =～거래. ～면적(面積) land area. ～몰수 〖법〗 escheat. ～불법점거자 a squatter. ～브로커〔중개인〕 a real estate agent; a land agent 《미》; a realtor 《미》. ～사기꾼 a land swindler; a fake land broker. ～ 세제(稅制) a land taxation system. ～수용 expropriation of land; eminent domain: ～ 수용권(權) (the right of) eminent domain / ～ 수용법 the Compulsory Purchase of Land Act. ～전매(轉賣) selling land repeatedly from one person to another; land rolling. ～제도 the land system. ～초과 이득세 a land profit tax; a tax for the excessively increased value of land. ～측량 land surveying.

**토지소유**(土地所有) landholding. ◉ ～권(權) landownership; 〖법〗 a (possessory) title to land: ～권 이전 등기 registration of the transfer of the ownership of the land. ～자 a landowner; a landholder; a landed proprietor; a territorial owner; [총칭] the landed interest.

**토질**(土疾) an endemic disease; a local disease; 《폐디스토마》 pulmonary distoma; pulmonary distomatosis.

**토질**(土質) the nature of the soil 〔ground〕; the soil. ¶ 부드러운〔단단한〕 ～ soft 〔hard〕 soil. ◉ ～분석 soil analysis. ～시험 a soil test. ～역학 〖토목〗 soil mechanics.

**토찌끼** dregs of soysauce.

**토착**(土着) aboriginality; settling (new territory). ～하다 settle (in a new territory). ¶ ～의 native(-born); aboriginal; indigenous / ～ 인디언 a native=born Indian / 담배는 한국 ～ 식물이 아니다 Tobacco is not a plant indigenous to the soil of Korea. ◉ ～동식물 aborigines; autochthon(e)s. ～민 a native; the natives [총칭].

**토치** a torch. ¶ 금속 절단용 ～ a metal=cutting torch. ◉ ～램프 a (blow-) torch; a blowlamp.

**토치카** [<*tochka* (Russ.)] 〖군사〗 a pillbox. ◉ ～진지 a *touchka* position; a cluster of pillboxes.

**토코페롤** 〖생화학〗 tocopherol.

**토크 쇼** a talk show; a chat show 《영》. ◉ ～사회자 a talk show 「host 〔interviewer〕.

**토큰** a token (coin). ◉ 버스～ a bus 「token.

**토키** 〖영화〗 a talkie; a talking picture 〔film〕; a sound film; talkies [총칭]. ◉ ～대본 a talkie script. ～만화 an animated cartoon. ～작가 a script 「writer.

**토킥** 〖축구〗 a toe kick.

**토탄**(土炭) peat; turf. ¶ ～ 같은 peaty. ◉ ～지 a peat 「bog 〔moor〕; a turbary. ～층 peat deposits.

**토털** a total; the total 「amount 〔sum〕. ◉ ～스코어 total score.

**토테미즘** 〖사회〗 totemism.

**토템** 〖사회〗 a totem. ¶ ～ (신앙)의 totemic; totemistic / ～ 연구가 a totemist. ◉ ～숭배 totemism. ～폴 a totem pole 〔post〕.

**토플** 《외국어로서의 영어 능력 검정시험》 TOEFL. [<Test of English as a Foreign Language]

**토플리스** 《수영복의 일종》 a topless suit. ◉ ～ 댄서 a topless dancer.

**토픽** 《화제》 a topic; a subject 《of conversation》. ¶ 오늘의 ～ current topics; the topics 「of the day 〔today〕.

**토하다**(吐—) ① 《게우다》 vomit; throw up; bring 〔fetch, cough〕 up; spew 〔spit〕 out; disgorge. ¶ 먹은 것을 ～ throw 〔bring〕 up what *one* has eaten / 피를 ～ spit 〔vomit, cough up〕 blood / 토하기 위해 목구멍에 손가락을 넣다 put *one's* fingers down *his* throat to make *himself* vomit / 토할 것 같다 feel 「sick 〔nausea〕; feel like throwing up / 토하게 하다 induce 《*a person*》 to vomit 〔throw up〕 / 그 환자는 먹기만 하면 토한다 What the patient eats comes back. *or* The patient cannot 「hold food on his stomach 〔hold down any food〕. / 그는 전부 토해 버렸다 He emptied his stomach. / 그는 먹은 돈 2백만 원을 토해냈다 He has disgorged the embezzled 2 million won.

② 《토로하다》 express 《*one's* view》; give vent 《to》; utter; deliver; speak out 《*one's* mind》. ¶ 본심을 ～ disclose *one's* real 〔true〕 intention; 「lay bare 〔pour out〕 *one's* heart.

③ 《내뿜다》 emit; puff out 《smoke》; breathe out (숨을); belch forth; send forth 〔up, out〕 (연기 등을). ¶ 연기를 토하는 굴뚝 a chimney emitting 〔sending forth〕 smoke / 크게 숨을 ~ exhale 〔breathe out〕 deeply / 저 화산은 끊임없이 검은 연기를 토하고 있다 The volcano is constantly emitting clouds of black smoke.
④ 《기타》 ¶ 기염을 ~ wag *one's* tongue 〔jaw〕; give full rein to *one's* tongue; argue furiously 〔vehemently〕; 《흰소리를》 talk big; spread *oneself* / 열변을 ~ speak with fervor 〔heat〕; make an eloquent speech.

**토현삼**(土玄蔘) 〖식물〗 a figwort.

**토혈**(吐血) vomiting 〔spitting〕 of blood; hematemesis; hemorrhage of the stomach. ~하다 vomit 〔spit〕 blood. ◉ ~증 〖의학〗 hematemesis.

**토호**(土豪) a landed proprietor; a wealthy landowner; 《호족》 a powerful local family 〔clan〕. ◉ ~질 《practice》 tyranny; oppression.

**토후**(土侯) an emir; a sheik.
◉ ~국 an emirate; a sheikdom.

**톡** ① 《불거진 모양》 protruding; protuberant; bulging; 《비어져 나온 모양》 popping 〔peeping〕 out. ¶ 두툼한 지갑으로 인해 톡 불거져 나온 주머니 a pocket bulging with an overstuffed pocketbook / 눈알이 톡 불거지다 have protruding 〔bulging〕 eyes; be a pop-eyed 〔lobster-eyed〕. ② 《끊어지거나 부러지는 소리》 with a snap. ¶ (실 따위가) 톡 끊어지다 snap short 〔off〕 / 바늘을 톡 부러뜨리다 snap a needle / 잔가지를 톡 꺾다 snap off a twig / 연필심이 톡 부러지다 the lead of a pencil 「snaps 〔breaks with a snap〕. ③ 《쏘는 모양》 sharply; prickingly; spicily. ¶ 맛이 톡 쏘다 taste hot; have a burning taste; be pungent; bite / 톡 쏘아 붙이다 make cutting remark; make a biting retort / 고추는 혀를 톡 쏜다 Red pepper bites 〔burns〕 the tongue. ④ 《부딪는 소리》 with a pat 〔rap, thud, bump〕. ¶ 어깨를 톡 치다 give 《*a person*》 a pat on the shoulder / 잉크병이 마루에 톡 떨어지다 an ink bottle falls on the floor with a thud. ⑤ 《기타》 ¶ 손톱으로 톡 튀기다 fillip; flip / 벼룩이 톡 튀다 a flea hops.

**톡탁** tapping; rapping; knocking; dabbing. ~하다 = 톡탁거리다.

**톡탁거리다** tap 〔rap, knock〕 on 《a desk》.

**톡톡** ① 《불거진 모양》 protruding 〔bulging〕 in several places.
¶ 게 눈이 ~ 불거지다 crabs pop their eyes out.
② 《부러지는 모양》 with snaps; 《별안간》 suddenly; abruptly; 《말을》 sharply. ¶ 연필심이 ~ 부러지다 the lead of a pencil breaks easily / 아무의 말을 ~ 쏘아 주다 give a series of sharp rejoinders; make one biting retort after another.
③ 《두들기거나 부딪는 소리》 with pats 〔raps, knocks〕. ¶ 어깨를 ~ 치다 keep patting 《*a person*》 on the shoulder / 문을 ~ 두드리다 knock on 〔at〕 the door; tap 〔rap〕 on 〔at〕 the door / 문을 ~ 두드리는 소리가 났다 There was a rap 〔knock〕 on the door.

**톡톡하다** ① 《국이》 (be) thick; rich. ② 《피륙이》 (be) thick; close; close-woven. ¶ 톡톡한 천 cloth of a close texture.

**톡톡히** ① 《엄하게》 severely; harshly; scathingly. ¶ ~ 꾸짖다 scold 〔berate 《미》〕 《*a person*》 scathingly; give 《*a person*》 a good scolding / ~ 책망 듣다 get severely scolded; be given a good scolding; get a round rating / ~ 때려주다 give 《*a person*》 a sound thrashing / 홍수를 만나서 ~ 혼났다 We had a terrible experience on account of the flood. ② 《많이》 much; quite a lot; loads of. ¶ ~ 벌다 earn 〔make〕 a lot of money; make a pot 〔pots〕 of money / 이문을 ~ 남기다 make a big profit. ③ 《배게》 close; thick. ¶ 베를 ~ 짜다 weave cloth thick. ④ 《진하게》 thick; rich. ¶ 국을 ~ 끓이다 prepare soup thick.

**톤** a ton; tonnage (톤수).
¶ 톤당(當) per ton / 톤세(稅) tonnage dues / 미(美)〔작은〕 톤 an American 〔a short〕 ton; a ton of 2,000 *lb*s. / 영(英)〔큰〕 톤 a British 〔long〕 ton; a ton of 2,240 *lb*s. / 미터 톤 a metric ton; a ton of 1,000 kilograms / 석탄 두 톤 two ton(s) of coal / 적재량 10톤의 배 a ten-tonner / 3천 톤의 기선 a steamer of 3,000 tons / 5톤 적재 화차 a five-ton freight car 《미》; a five-ton waggon 《영》.
◉ 광산톤 a smelter's 〔Cornish mining〕 ton; a ton of 2,352 *lb*s. 등록톤 a register ton. 배수톤 a displacement ton. 용적톤 a measurement 〔volume, freight〕 ton. 적재톤 a shipping ton. 총톤 a gross ton.

> 참고 **ton**의 종류 및 그 차이: 미터법의 톤은 metric ton (미터 톤)이라고 하며, 1,000kg. 《미》 톤은 2,000파운드, 약 907kg이며 short ton 또는 American ton이라 함. 《영》 톤은 2,240파운드, 약 1,016kg이며 보통 gross ton 또는 long ton이라 함.

**톤수**(―數) tonnage; (number of) tons; burden. ¶ 이 배의 ~는 얼마입니까 What is the tonnage of this ship? / 이 배의 ~는 3천 톤이다 This steamer is 3,000 tons burden. *or* This ship displaces 3,000 tons.
◉ ~증서 〖조선〗 a tonnage certificate. 등록〔순〕~ registered 〔net〕 tonnage. 재화(載貨) 중량~ deadweight capacity 〔tonnage〕.

**톨** a grain; a nut. ¶ 밤 한 톨 a chestnut / 쌀이 한 톨도 없다 We don't have a grain of rice.

**톨게이트** 《통행료 받는》 a tollgate.

**톨루산**(―酸) 〖화학〗 toluic acid.
◉ ~염 toluate.

**톨루엔** 〖화학〗 toluene; toluol.

**톨스토이** 《소설가》 Leo Nikolaevich Tolstoi (1828-1910). ◉ ~이즘 Tolstoyism.

**톱**[1] 《켜는》 a saw. ¶ 내릴톱 a ripsaw / 대톱 a large saw; a pit saw (둘이 켜는) / 양날 톱 a double-edged saw / 외날 톱 a single-edged saw; a handsaw / 활톱 a hacksaw / 실톱 a coping saw / 쥐꼬리톱 a compass saw / 체인톱 a chain saw / 동가리톱 a crosscut saw / 둥근톱 a circular 〔buzz 《미》〕 saw / 톱으로 켜다 cut with a ripsaw; saw 《wood》.

**톱**[2] top. ¶ 톱과 꼴찌 the top and the bottom / 한 반의 톱 the top student of a class; the head of the class / 톱을 끊다 lead; take the initiative 〔lead〕 《in》; top 〔lead off〕 the list 《of》; be at the top 〔head〕 《of》; be the first 《to *do*》; come to the top.

**톱기사**(―記事) a front-page 〔lead〕 story; the top 〔leading〕 article in a newspaper; a lead.

**톱날** ⇨ 톱니.

**톱뉴스** top news; big news; the front=pager. ¶ ~로 다루다 take 《an article》 as top news.

**톱니** the teeth of a saw; a saw tooth. ¶ ~ 모양의 sawlike; saw-toothed; lacerated; jagged; serrated / ~ 세우는 기계 a saw sharpener; a sharpening machine / ~를 세우다 set (the teeth of) a saw.

**톱니바퀴** a toothed wheel. ¶ ~의 이 a cog; a tooth / ~가 (맞)물리다 gear 《into, with》; be in gear 《with》; gather in upon; mesh 《with》 / ~가 안 물리다 be out of gear; do not mesh / 두 개의 ~가 맞물다 the two cogwheels engage each other.
◉ ~구동〔전동〕 a gear drive. ~장치 gear(ing); toothed (wheel) gearing; a train of gears.

**톱매니지먼트** top management.

**톱밥** sawdust.

**톱상어**(―魚) 〖어류〗 a saw shark.

**톱손** a saw handle. 「a sawyer.

**톱질** sawing. ~하다 saw. ¶ ~하는 사람

**톱클래스** ¶ ~의 leading; foremost; topflight; top-notch 《구어》.

**톱타자**(―打者) 〖야구〗 a lead-off (man) (팀의); the first batter (그 회의).

**톱톱하다** 《국물이》 (be) thick; rich; heavy.

**톱풀** 〖식물〗 a milfoil; a yarrow.

**톳** a 100-sheet bundle 《of laver》.

**톳나무** a large 〔big〕 tree; a gigantic 〔towering〕 tree.

**통**[1] ① 《부피·몸집》 the bulk 《of a cabbage head》; the body 《of a gourd》. ¶ 배추 통이 크다 the cabbage has a large head. ② 《세는 말》 a head of cabbage; a gourd. ¶ 박 한 통 a gourd / 배추 세 통 three heads of cabbage. ③ 《피륙의》 a roll: 광목 7~ seven rolls of calico. ④ 《노름의》 10 or 20 points obtained from 3 cards.

**통**[2] ① 《바지의》 the width of a crotch part of a trouser; 《넓이》 breadth; girth (둘레). ¶ 소매통 a sleeve opening / 소매통이 좁다 a sleeve is tight. ② 《광맥의》 the breadth of a vein (of ore).

**통**(統) ① 〖고제도〗 a census unit of five houses. ② 《행정 구역》 a *t'ong* (=a subdivision of a *dong,* a small section of a city).

**통**(桶) a tub; a cask; a barrel; a pail; a bucket; a can; a canister; a box; a bowl. ¶ 대통 the bowl of a pipe / 똥통 a "honey bucket"; a manure pail / 물통 a water bucket / 술통 a wine barrel 〔cask〕; 《큰》 a butt / 석유통 a kerosene can 〔tin〕; an oil can / 성냥 한 통 a box of matches / 작은 나무통 a keg / 통에 넣다 put 《*a thing*》 in a barrel; barrel / 통을 메우다 hoop a tub. ◉ 통널 a stave; a lag. 통메장

이 a cooper; a hooper. 통받침 a gantry; a stilling (맥주통의). 통장이=통메장이. 통주둥이 a tap; a bunghole.

**통**(筒) ① 《관·파이프 등》 a tube; a pipe; a gun barrel (총신); a sleeve (기계의); 《깡통 따위》 a tin 《영》; a can 《미》. ¶ 대통 a bamboo tube / 마분지통 a cardboard tube. ② [비유적] caliber; scale 《of doing *things*》 (도량); relative bigness 〔boldness〕 of character (대담성). ¶ 통이 큰 사람 a man who does things in a big way / 사람의 통이 작다 be a person of small caliber.

**통**[3] ① 《복잡한 상황·사이·동안》 ¶ 충돌하는 통에 by the force of impact / 북새통에 한몫 보다 fish in troubled waters; gain an advantage from the confused state of affairs / 싸움 통에 휩쓸리다 be involved in the turmoil of a fight / 떠드는 통에 정신을 차릴 수 없다 be unable to collect *oneself* amid the noise and uproar / 이사 통에 접시를 깨뜨렸다 Dishes were broken in the confusion of moving. / 전쟁 통에 사람이 많이 죽다 Many lives are lost in the ravages of war. ② 《동아리》 a gang; a group; a junto 〔junta〕; cahoots. ¶ 한통이 되다 be in cahoots with; be in collusion 〔league〕 with / 한통이 되어 음모를 꾸미다 plot together in cahoots.

**통**(通) 《문서》 a document; a paper; 《증서》 a bond; 《편지》 a letter; a note. ¶ 편지 두 통 two letters / 계약서 2통 two copies of the contract / 호적등본 3통 three complete copies of *one's* family register / (서류) 2〔3, 4, 5〕통을 작성하다 make out 《a document》 in duplicate 〔triplicate, quadruplicate, quintuplicate〕; draw up two 〔three, four, five〕 copies 《of》 / 정부(正副) 2통을 제출하다 present in duplicate.

**통** [부사적] ① ⇨ 온통. ② 《전연》 entirely; utterly; completely; quite. ③ 《전연 … 않다》 (not) at all; (not) in the least. ¶ 통 모르겠다 cannot make head or tail of 《*something*》 / 그는 요즘 통 오지 않는다 He doesn't come here at all these days. / 그 일은 통 잊어버리고 있었다 I had forgotten about it completely. / 요즘 통 그를 못 만난다 I have seen nothing of him of late.

**-통**(通) 《정통한 사람》 an authority 《on a subject》; an expert 《in, at》; a well-informed person; 《미술품 등의》 a connoisseur 《of antiques》. ¶ 법률통 an authority on law; a legal expert / 소식통 informed sources / 재정통 an expert on financial affairs; a financial expert / 정계의 소식통 a man conversant with political affairs; a political wiseacre / 중국통 an authority on Chinese affairs / …통이다 be an authority 《on》; be conversant 《with》; be expert 《in, at》; be well informed 《of, about, on》; be well up 《on, in》 / …통인 체하다 pretend to know everything 《about》 / …통임을 과시하다 make a show 〔display〕 of *one's* knowledge 《of 》; parade *one's* expertise 《about, on》.

**통가리**(桶—) 《곡식 더미》 a heap 〔stack〕 of grain put in a straw rain-shelter.

**통가죽** ① 《가죽》 the whole skin 《of an animal》. ② 《한복》 a garment made so it can be laundered without the usual removal of seams.

**통각**(痛覺) a sense 〔sensation〕 of pain. ¶ 무(無)～의 analgesic. ◉ ～계(計) an algometer; an algesimeter. ～공포증 algophobia. ～과민(증) hyperalgesia. ～상실증 『병리』 analgesia.

**통감**(統監) ① 《지휘·감독》 supervision. ～하다 supervise; superintend; take supreme command of. ¶ 연습을 ～하다 supervise the manoeuvers. ② 《관직》 the Resident-General. ◉ ～대리 an acting Resident-General. ～부(府) the Residency-General.

**통감**(痛感) ～하다 feel keenly 〔acutely, deeply〕; fully 〔keenly〕 realize; take 《*something*》 to heart. ¶ 어학의 필요성을 ～하다 keenly feel the necessity of linguistic knowledge / ～케 하다 impress on *one;* drive home on *one* / 사람들은 환경 보호의 필요성을 ～하기 시작하였다 People are beginning to feel keenly the necessity to protect the environment.

**통거리** the whole; all the stuff. ¶ ～로 by the lump 〔heap, lot〕 / 땅을 ～로 사다 buy up the whole lot of land.

**통겨주다** let 《*a person*》 know stealthly; disclose; let out (a secret).

**통겨지다** ⇨ 퉁겨지다.

**통격**(通格) 『문법』 the common case.

**통격**(痛擊) a severe 〔hard, bitter〕 blow; a severe attack. ～하다 attack severely; make a bitter attack on 《*a person*》. ¶ ～을 가하다 attack 《*a person*》 severely; deal a hard blow to 《*a person*》; 《비판》 criticize 《*a person*》 scathingly.

**통계**(統計) statistics; a numerical statement. ¶ ~의 statistical / ~상(으로) statistically; in the statistics / ~가 나타내는 바에 의하면 (statistics) figures show 〔teach us, disclose〕 that...; according to statistics / ~를 잡다〔내다〕 collect 〔gather〕 statistics 《of》; take 〔get〕 the statistics; prepare 〔compile〕 statistics 《of》/ ~를 표로 나타내다 tabulate statistics / ~를 (비교)대조하다 collate statistics / ~적 숫자를 들다 give statistical figures / ~에 의하면 여자는 남자보다 오래 산다 Statistics show that women live longer than men.
◉ ~도표 a statistical chart 〔graph〕. ~보고 a statistical report. ~분석 a statistical analysis (*pl.* -ses). ~역학 statistical mechanics. ~연감 a statistical yearbook. ~자료 statistical data. ~전문가 a statistician; a statist; a statistical expert. ~조사 (a) statistical research 〔investigation〕; statistics and research. ~지도 a statistical map; a cartogram. ~청 the National Statistical Office. ~치(値) 〖수학〗 statistics. ~표 a statistical table. ~학 (the science of ) statistics: ~학자 a statistician; a statist; a man of figures. 사망〔출산〕~ statistics of mortality 〔birth〕. 인구~ a census; statistics of population: 인구 동태 ~ vital statistics.

**통고**(通告) notice; notification; announcement; (a) warning. ~하다 notify 《*a person* of, that...》; give 《*a person*》 notice 《of, that...》; send word 《that...》; warn 《*a person* of》; 〖법〗 garnish.
¶ 일방적인 ~ a one-sided 〔unilateral〕 notice / 사전에 ~하다 give 《*a person*》 previous notice / 5일 전에 ~하다 give five day's notice / 임박해서 ~하다 give 《*a person*》 very short notice 《of》/ ~를 발하다 issue a notification / ~ 없이 불참하다 absent *oneself* without notice / ...라는 ~를 받고 있다 be in receipt of the notice that...; be on notice that ... / 경찰서에 출두하라는 ~를 받다 be served with a notice to appear at the police station / 하루 전 ~를 요하다 A day's notice is required.
◉ ~서 a (written) notice. ~처분 a noticed disposition.

**통곡**(痛哭·慟哭) wailing; keening. ~하다 weep loudly 〔bitterly〕; wail. ¶ 그녀는 아이를 잃고 ~하고 있었다 She was wailing for her lost child.

**통과**(通過) (a) passage 《미》; passing 《영》; transit. ~하다 pass (through); go 〔get〕 through; be carried (의안의). ¶ 세관을 ~하다 go 〔pass〕 through the customs / 시험에 ~하다 pass an examination / 시내를 ~하다 pass through the city / 서울 상공을 ~하다 pass over 〔fly over〕 Seoul / 영국을 ~하다〔~해 가다〕 pass through 〔go by way of 〕 England / 의안〔법안〕을 ~시키다 carry 〔pass〕 a bill; pass 〔get〕 a bill through / 법안의 ~를 지연시키다 stall a bill / (법안이) 만장일치로 국회를 ~하다 《a bill》 pass 〔be carried in〕 the Assembly by a unanimous vote / 기차는 서지 않고 역을 ~했다 The train passed the station without stopping. / 그녀는 제1차 심사를 ~했다 She passed the first screening.
◉ ~무역 transit trade. ~사증(査證) a transit visa. ~세 transit duty 〔dues〕; tolls (운하·교량 등의). ~여객 a transit 〔through〕 passenger 〔traveler〕. ~역 a nonstop station. ~의례 a rite of passage; an initiation ceremony. ~화물 transit goods; 《포장 표지》 "Transit".

**통관**(通關) customs clearance 《of goods》; clearance 《of goods》 through the customs. ~하다 clear 〔pass〕 the customs; clear 《goods》 through (the) customs; enter 〔clear〕 《a ship》.
◉ ~사무소 a custom-clearance office. ~세 a clearance 〔customs〕 fee; a custom charge. ~수수료 a clearance 〔customs〕 fee. ~신고서 a bill of entry. ~필 cleared: 수입〔수출〕 ~필 cleared inwards 〔outwards〕. ~항 a port of entry. ~허가증 an entry 〔a goods clearance〕 permit.

**통관절차**(通關節次) customs formalities 〔procedure〕; clearance; customs entry. ¶ ~를 위해 for customs purposes / ~를 마치다〔밟다〕 go through the customs formalities; clear 〔go through〕 customs; pass customs entry.

**통괄**(統括) summary; generalization. ~하다 summarize; generalize.

**통권**(通卷) the consecutive number of volumes. ¶ 제5권 제2호(~10호) Vol. 5 No. 2 (Serial Number 10).

**통근**(通勤) attending office; 《탈것으로》 commutation 《미》; commuting 《미》; 《입주 근무에 대하여》 living out. ~하다 attend 〔go to〕 (*one's*, the) office; commute 《from, to》; go 〔come〕 to

work. ¶ 매일 열차로 ∼하다 go to the office daily 〔every day〕 by train; take the train daily to work / 오토바이로 ∼하다 ride a bike (back and forth) to work / 그는 인천에서 서울로 ∼한다 He commutes to Seoul from Inch'ŏn. / 회사는 ∼하기에 편한 거리에 있다 The company is within easy commuting distance.
◉ ∼객 (열차의) a commutation passenger 《미》; a season-ticket passenger 《영》. ∼거리 commuting distance. ∼비 transit expenses to and from *one's* place of work. ∼수당 commutation 〔commuting〕 allowance. ∼시간 《소요 시간》 time required to get to the office; 《시간대》 commuter time; 《at》 rush hours. ∼열차 a commuter 〔commuting〕 train 《미》; a train for commuters. ∼자 a commuter 《미》; a living-out employee; a commutation passenger. ∼정기(定期) 승차권 a commutation ticket; a season ticket 《영》. ∼제(制) a living-out system. ∼증명서 a commutation certificate. ∼지옥 commuters' hell; commuting hell; a commuter-stampede: ∼지옥을 완화하기 위해 전철의 운행 횟수를 늘린다고 한다 I hear they are going to run more trains to ease the present commuters' hell.

**통금** ① 《몰아친 값》 the total price. ② 《도매값》 a wholesale price.

**통금**(通禁) 《야간의》 a curfew. ⇨ 통행금지(通行禁止). ¶ ∼을 실시하다 impose 〔order〕 a curfew. ◉ ∼사이렌 a curfew siren. ∼시간 curfew hour. ∼위반 a curfew violation: ∼위반자 a curfew violator. ∼해제 the removal 〔lifting〕 of curfew: ∼해제 구역 a curfew-lifted area.

**통기**(通氣) ventilation; draught; draft; 《공기 쐬기》 airing. ⇨ 통풍(通風).

**통기공**(通氣孔) a breathing hole; a vent (hole); a ventilator; 〖기계〗 an air hole 〔vent〕.

**통김치** Kimchi 〔pickles〕 made of whole cabbages. ◉ ∼쌈 pickled cabbage leaves stuffed with rice.

**통나무** a log; unsplit wood. ¶ ∼를 널로 켜다 saw a log into boards / ∼를 뗏목을 만들어 강 하류로 보내다 raft logs down the river. ◉ ∼다리 a log bridge. ∼배 a dugout 〔canoe〕. ∼집 a log cabin.

**통념**(通念) a common idea 〔notion〕; a generally 〔commonly〕 accepted idea. ¶ 사회∼ a socially accepted idea; a social common notion / 그 생각은 일반적인 ∼이다 The idea is generally 〔commonly〕 accepted.

**통달**(通達) mastery; expertise; conversance. ∼하다 be well 〔deeply〕 versed 《in》; have a thorough knowledge 《of》; be thoroughly 〔well〕 acquainted 《with》; be familiar 《with》; be well posted 《on》; be at home 《in》; be conversant 《with》. ¶ 고고학에 ∼하다 be well versed in archeology / 역사에 ∼하다 be conversant with history / 영어에 ∼해 있다 be versed 〔well up〕 in English; be conversant with English; have a (great) command of English / 맡은 일에 ∼하기란 쉽지가 않다 It is not easy to be a master of *one's* work.

**통닭** a whole chicken; 《통닭구이》 a chicken roasted whole; a roast chicken.

**통대구**(―大口) a dried whole codfish.

**통독**(通讀) reading 《a book》 from beginning to end. ∼하다 read 〔go, get〕 through 《a book》; read 《a book》 from cover to cover. ¶ 그 책은 ∼할 가치가 있다 The book is worth (while) reading through.

**통돌다** 《알려짐》 be generally known 〔announced〕; be generally agreed upon; be widely circulated.

**통람**(通覽) a survey; a general 〔an overall〕 survey; an overview. ∼하다 survey; look over; glance (*one's* eyes) over; take a (general) survey of; 《통독하다》 read through. ¶ 보고서를 ∼하다 look over 〔read through〕 a report.

**통렬**(痛烈) severity; sharpness; fierceness; ferocity. ∼하다 (be) severe; sharp; fierce; bitter. ¶ ∼히 severely; sharply; fiercely; bitterly / ∼한 일격 a knockdown 〔telling, terrible〕 blow / ∼한 비난 severe reproval / ∼히 비판하다 criticize severely 〔cuttingly〕.

**통례**(通例) a common 〔an ordinary〕 practice. ¶ ∼의 usual; customary; common; ordinary; general / ∼로 as an ordinary practice; ordinarily; as a rule; customarily; usually; commonly; generally; on the whole / 백화점은 오전 10시에 개점하는 것이 ∼이다 Ordinarily department stores open at 10 A.M. *or* It is usual for department stores to open at 10 A.M.

**통로**(通路) a passage; a passageway; a way; a pathway; an alley (좁은); 《극

장·객차 내 따위의》 an aisle; a walkway (공원 따위의); 《짐승의》 a track. ¶ ～측의 좌석 an aisle seat / ～를 가로막다 stand in 〔block〕 《*a person's*》 way / ～를 트다〔내다〕 clear the passage; open a passage 《through》 / ～에 서 있지 마시오 Don't keep standing in the path. / ～에도 사람이 가득했다 Even the aisles were crowded with people. / ～ 없음 《게시》 Dead end.
◉ 비밀～ a secret passage; an underground passage.

**통론**(通論) an outline 《of》; an introduction 《to》. ◉ 문학～ an introduction to literature. 법학～ an outline of law.

**통마늘** a whole bulb of garlic.

**통말**(桶—) a bucket-shaped measure.

**통메(우)다**(桶—) ① 《테를 끼다》 ⇨ 테메(우)다. ② 《빽빽이 들어서다》 be closely packed; be crowded; be packed like sardines; be jammed 《in》.

**통모**(通謀) ～하다 conspire with; work 〔act〕 in concert 〔collusion, league〕. ¶ ～하여 in conspiracy; in collusion.

**통문**(通文) a circular (letter). ¶ ～을 돌리다 send (out) 〔issue, address〕 a circular (letter); circularize.

**통밀다** regard all as the same; dispose of all collectively. ¶ 통밀어 on the average / 크기에 상관없이 통밀어 하나에 백 원씩 치다 value each at one hundred won regardless of the size.

**통발** 〖식물〗 a bladderwort.

**통발**(筒—) 《고기 잡는》 a weir (made of willow 〔bamboo〕); a fish trap.

**통방이** a rattrap.

**통법**(通法) ① 《통칙》 a universal law. ② 〖수학〗 reduction to a single unit.

**통변**(通辯) ＝통역(通譯).

**통보**(通報) reporting; information; a report. ～하다 report; notify; inform 《of》. ¶ 경찰에 ～하다 notify the police 《about *a matter*》.
◉ ～기관 an information agency.

**통보**(通寶) "currency" (inscription on the head of ancient coins); ... coin (of olden days).

**통보리** uncracked grains of barley.

**통분**(通分) 〖수학〗 reduction 《of fractions》 to a common denominator. ～하다 reduce 《fractions》 to a common denominator. ◉ ～모(母) ⇨ 공통분모.

**통분**(痛憤·痛忿) great indignation. ～하다 (be) highly indignant.

**통비**(通比) 〖수학〗 a common ratio.

**통사정**(通事情) ① 《사정을 알아줌》 having sympathetic understanding; having an understanding heart. ～하다 have sympathetic understanding; have an understanding heart; understand. ② 《사정함》 an appeal; a complaint; unbosoming *oneself;* speaking *one's* mind. ～하다 make an appeal 《to》; complain 《of》; unbosom *oneself* 《of》; divulge; get 《it》 off *one's* chest; speak *one's* mind 〔tell frankly〕 《about》. ¶ 곤란한 사정을 친구에게 ～하다 tell a friend quite frankly about *one's* difficulties.

**통산**(通算) summing up; the aggregate; the sum total. ～하다 sum 〔add〕 up; aggregate; total; 《포함시키다》 include. ¶ ～하여 in the aggregate / ～하면 《개괄해서》 to sum up; taken altogether / 미결 40일 ～ 1년의 금고 one year's imprisonment with credit for forty days service as an unconvicted prisoner / ～하여 20년 이상의 for the total period of twenty years or more / ～하면 …이 되다 amount to; add up to; in all; total to / 미결을 ～하다 《재판의》 include the number of the days in the detention house / 미결일수 30일을 ～한다 The term of imprisonment will include thirty days of unconvicted detention.

**통상**(通常) [부사적] ordinarily; usually; normally; commonly; generally; under normal conditions; as a general rule. ◉ ～복(服) everyday clothes; a business suit. ～우편 ordinary post; ordinary mail: ～우편물 ordinary mail 〔postal〕 matter. ～회원 an ordinary 〔a regular〕 member.

**통상**(通商) commerce; trade; commercial intercourse 〔relations〕. ～하다 trade 《with a country》. ¶ ～의 편의 commercial facilities / ～을 시작하다 open trade 《with a country》 / 한국은 많은 국가와 ～한다 Korea trades with many countries. / 전쟁으로 두 나라의 ～은 단절되었다 The war interrupted the flow of commerce between the two countries.
◉ ～관계 trade relations. ～국(局) the Board of Trade. ～로(路) a trade 〔trading〕 route; a channel of trade. ～무역 trade and commerce. ～사절단 a trade mission 〔delegation〕. ～위원 a trade commissioner. ～촉진 acceleration of trade transaction. ～ 항해 조약 a treaty of commerce and navigation; a commerce and navigation

treaty.

**통상**(筒狀) cylinder-shape. ¶ ～의 cylindrical; tubiform; tubular.

**통상조약**(通商條約) a commercial treaty; a trade agreement; a treaty of commerce. ¶ ～을 맺다 conclude 〔sign〕 a commercial treaty; enter into a treaty of commerce 《with》.

**통석**(痛惜) deep regret. ～하다 regret deeply; deplore; grieve 〔lament〕 《at》; feel grieved 《at》.

**통설**(通說) a commonly accepted theory; a 「common 〔prevalent, widely held〕 view; a 「popular 〔prevailing〕 opinion.

**통성**(通性) ① 《공통의 성질》 a common 「property 〔quality〕; generality. ¶ 녹이 잘 스는 것은 모든 금속 ～이다 To rust easily is a property of all metals. ② 〖문법〗 the common gender.

**통성명**(通姓名) exchanging names. ～하다 exchange names; introduce 《themselves》 to each other.

**통소**(洞簫) a bamboo flute. ⇨통소.

**통속** 《단체》 a gang; a cabal; 《협잡꾼의》 a decoy; a shrill 《미》; 《경매 때의》 a by-bidder; a puffer; 《음모》 a cabal; a secret 「agreement 〔plot, intrigue〕. ¶ 한 ～이 되다 plot together; conspire 《with》; act 〔be〕 in 「collusion 〔league〕 《with》; 《속어》 be in cahoots 《with》/ …과 한 ～이 되어서 in 「league 〔conspiracy, collusion〕 with…; 《속어》 in cahoots with… / 한 ～이 되어 남을 속이다 conspire 「together 〔with someone〕 to cheat *a person* / 그들은 한 ～이다 They are in cahoots with each other. / 그놈의 ～을 누가 알 수 있나 Who can tell what secret agreement they've made? *or* I can't guess what secret game they've made.

**통속**(通俗) ① 《풍속》 a common custom. ② 《일》 popularity; conventionality. ¶ ～적〔의〕 popular; common; commonplace; conventional / ～적으로 popularly; 《explain》 in plain language; 《write》 in a popular style / ～적인 기사 an unscientific 〔a non=technical〕 account / ～적으로 말하면 to use plain language; in common parlance / 이 책은 ～적으로 재미있게 쓰여 있다 This book is written in an interesting, non-technical way.
◉ ～문학 light 〔popular〕 literature. ～소설 a 「popular 〔lowbrow〕 novel. ～어 popular 〔familiar, colloquial〕 language; (a) colloquialism. ～음악 popular music. ～체 a 「colloquial 〔familiar〕 style.

**통속화**(通俗化) popularization. ～하다 popularize.

**통솔**(統率) command; leadership. ～하다 command; lead; direct; take 〔assume〕 the leadership of; be 「in command 〔at the head〕 of 《an army》. ¶ …의 ～하에 있다 be under the command 〔leadership〕 of.
◉ ～권 (the right of) command. ～력 leadership; ability to command. ～자 a leader; a commander: ～자가 되다 take the lead of; stand at the head of; be in command of 《an army》.

**통송곳** a drill with a crescent blade.

**통수**(統帥) the (prerogative of) supreme command. ～하다 command; have the command of. ◉ ～권(權) the prerogative of supreme command. ～부 the high command.

**통신**(通信) ① 《편지 왕래》 correspondence; 《연락》 communication. ～하다 correspond 《with》; communicate 《with》; report 《for a paper》. ¶ ～을 시작하다〔계속하다〕 「get into 〔keep in〕 communication 《with》/ 지금 그 지방과의 ～은 불가능하다 Communication with those parts is impossible at present.
② 《보도》 news; a report; 《정보》 information. ¶ 런던에서의 ～에 의하면 according to a dispatch from London; a London dispatch says (that…).
◉ ～공학 telecommunication engineering. ～과 the communications division. ～기관 communications media; 「an organ 〔a medium, a means〕 of communication. ～기술 the technology of communications. ～대 a signal corps. ～대학 a home study college. ⇨방송 통신 대학. ～두절 communication blackout. ～란(欄) a correspondence column; 《신문·잡지의》 the "letter-to-the-editor" columns; 《그림 엽서의》 space for a message. ～망 newsgathering 「facilities 〔organization〕; a communications 「network 〔system〕. ～방해 communication jamming; blanketing: ～ 방해를 하다 jam communication. ～병(兵) a signalman 《미》; a signal corpsman; a telegraphist 《영》. ～보도 기관 vehicles of news. ～비 communication expenses; postage. ～사(士) 《유선의》 a telegraph operator; 《무선의》 a 「wireless 〔radio〕 operator. ～사업 communication 「service 〔enterprise〕. ～선(線) a line of

communication(s); a communications line. ~선로공 a cablesetting worker. ~수단 a means of communication. ~시설 the communication facilities 〔system, setup〕. ~위성 a communication 〔relay〕 satellite: 국제 전신 ~ 위성 the International Telecommunications Satellite (생략 INTELSAT). ~장비 (tele)communications equipment. ~통(筒) a message tube; a communication tube 〔cylinder〕. ~학교 《통신 교육 기관》 a correspondence school.

긴급~ urgent correspondence. 국제 전신 ~ 연합 the (United Nations) International Telecommunication Union (생략 ITU). 정보 ~부 the Ministry of Information & Communication: 정보 ~부 장관 the Minister of Information & Communication. 한국 ~ the Korea Telecom.

**통신강좌**(通信講座) instruction 〔giving lessons〕 by correspondence; a correspondence course 〔lesson〕; a postal course of tuition 《영》; a postal training course. ¶ ~를 하다〔받다〕 give 〔take〕 correspondence lessons 《in English》.

**통신교육**(通信教育) education by correspondence; a correspondence course of 《high school》 education. ¶ ~을 하다 teach by correspondence / ~을 받다 take 〔do〕 a correspondence course 《in economics》.

**통신사**(通信社) a news agency 〔wire service 《미》〕. ¶ 미국 합동 국제 ~ the United Press International (생략 U.P.I.) / 연합 ~ The Yonhap News Agency (한국); the Associated Press (생략 A.P.) (미국) / 이타르·타스 ~ the ITAR-TASS News Agency (러시아) / 프랑스 ~ Agence France-Presse (생략 A.F.P.) / 신화 ~ Xinhua News Agency (중국).

**통신사무**(通信事務) a post and telegraph service; communication business 〔affairs〕. ¶ ~를 취급하는 관서 a government office transacting communication business.

**통신원**(通信員) 《신문사 등의》 a correspondent; a reporter; 《회사의 통신계원》 a correspondence clerk. ¶ 신문의 ~으로 일하다 report 〔correspond〕 for a newspaper / 본사 뉴욕 ~ our correspondent in New York. ◉ 특파〔종군〕~ a special 〔war〕 correspondent.

**통신정보수집**(通信情報蒐集) 『군사』 Comint; COMINT. [< *com*munications *int*elligence]

**통신판매**(通信販賣) mail order; mail-order business. ¶ ~로 by 〔through〕 mail order / ~를 하다 run a mail-order business / ~로 팔다 sell 《goods》 by mail; sell 《*something*》 to a mail-order customer / ~로 사다 buy 《clothes》 from a mail-order house. ◉ ~회사〔점〕 a mail-order firm 〔house, store〕.

**통약**(通約) 『수학』 reduction to a common measure. ⇨ 약분(約分).

**통어**(統御) 《지배》 rule; 《제어》 control; 《다룸》 management. ~하다 rule; govern; control; hold 〔bring〕 under *one's* control 〔girdle〕; manage; administrate 《미》. ¶ 부하를 ~하다 control *one's* subordinates / ~를 잘 하다 control 《*one's* subordinates》 properly / 학생을 잘 ~하다 have the students well in hand / ~할 수 없게 되다 get beyond 〔out of〕 control; get out of hand.

**통역**(通譯) 《일》 interpreting; (an) interpretation; 《사람》 an interpreter. ~하다 interpret. ¶ ~을 통해서〔없이〕 이야기하다 speak through 〔without〕 an interpreter / ~ 일을 보다 act as interpreter; interpret 《for *a person*》 / ~을 좀 해주게 Will you please interprete for me? ◉ ~관 an official interpreter; a secretary-interpreter.

**통용**(通用) popular 〔common〕 use; circulation; currency. ~하다 pass 《for》; circulate; be in common use; be 〔pass, go, run〕 current; 《용인되다》 be accepted; be 〔hold〕 true 〔good〕; 《유효하다》 be available; be good 〔valid〕; be honored; 《규칙 따위가》 hold good 〔true〕. ¶ 세상에 ~되다 pass current with the world / 국제간에 ~되다 have international currency / (가짜돈 따위를) ~시키다 pass; give currency to / ~되지 않게 되다 lose currency / 영어가 ~됩니다 《게시》 English spoken here. / 달러는 어디서나 ~된다 Dollars go 〔can be used, pass current〕 anywhere. / 여기서 영어는 ~되지 않는다 English is not spoken here.

◉ ~기간 the term of validity; the valid period 《of a ticket》: ~ 기간 당일 한 《표의 표기》 Good 〔Available, Valid〕 for the day of issue only. ~문(門) a gate for the general public; a side gate. ~어 a current word; a word in current use; a popular usage. ~화폐 currency; a current coin; a circulating medium.

**통운**(通運) transportation; forwarding; shipping. ~하다 transport; forward; ship. ◉ ~회사 a transportation company; a forwarding agent 〔agency〕; an express company 〔agency〕《미》; shippers.

**통원**(通院) going to hospital. ~하다 go to hospital regularly; attend a hospital (as an outpatient); visit a hospital for treatment. ◉ ~환자 an outpatient. ⇨ 외래 환자.

**통유**(通有) commonness; a common trait. ~하다 be common 《to》; be a common characteristic 《of》. ◉ ~성(性) 《성격의》 a common trait; 《물질의》 common properties of matter; a property common to all kinds of matter.

**통으로** all; wholly; collectively; in the lump; in the gross 〔mass〕; in one lot; *en bloc* (F.). ¶ ~ 삼키다 swallow 《*a thing*》 down 〔up〕 (without chewing); swallow 《it》 whole / ~ 팔다 sell by the lump; sell wholesale.

**통음**(痛飮) hard 〔heavy〕 drinking; a carousal. ~하다 drink 〔imbibe〕 heavily 〔hard, deep〕; drink a great deal; carouse. ¶ 밤을 새워 ~하다 keep drinking all night; make a night of it / 지난 밤, 나는 자포자기한 기분으로 ~했다 Last night I drank heavily, in a mood of desperation.

**통일**(統一) ① 《통합》 unity; unification; coordination; uniformity; 《표준화》 standardization. ~하다 unify; coordinate; consolidate; 《표준화하다》 standardize. ¶ ~된 unified; uniform; systematic; homogeneous / ~적인 unific(ative) / 가격을 ~하다 standardize the prices / 나라를 ~하다 unify a nation; bring a country under a single authority 〔one sway〕 / 철자법을 ~하다 standardize spelling rules / ~이 안 돼 있다 lack unity 〔coordination〕; be without coordination; be incoherent / 다양성 속에서 ~을 찾아내다 find unity in diversity / 재(再)~하다 reunify 〔reunite〕 《Korea》 / ~의 길은 아직도 멀다 The unification is still a long way off. / 많은 당파를 ~하는 것은 불가능하다 It is impossible to unify a lot of parties.
② 《장악》 rule; sway; dominance. ~하다 rule; dominate. ¶ 그는 중국 전토를 ~했다 He united the whole land of China under his sway.
③ 《집중》 concentration. ~하다 concentrate; centralize. ¶ 정신을 ~하다 concentrate *one's* attention 《on》.
◉ ~견해〔의견〕 a united 〔collective〕 view 〔opinion〕. ~국가 a unified nation. ~교(敎) (Moon's) Unification Church. ~방식 a unification formula. ~벼 *'Tongil'* breed rice. ~부 the Ministry of Unification: ~부 장관 the Minister of Unification. ~성 unity. ~안보 정책 조정 회의 the Unification and Security Policy Coordination Council. ~전선 《form》 a united front. ~정부 a unified government. ~천하 unification 〔domination〕 of the whole world. ~체 a unified body; a unity; a whole. ~행동 united action. 국내~ unification of the country; national unity 〔unification〕.

**통장**(通帳) 《은행의》 a bankbook; a passbook.

**통장**(統長) the head of a *t'ong*, subdivision of a city's district.

**통장수**(桶―) ① 《통 파는》 a tub seller; a cooper. ② 《젓갈 파는》 a peddler who carries pickled seafood in a tub.

**통장작**(―長斫) log firewood; unsplit firewood.

**통절**(痛切) ~하다 (be) urgent; keen; poignant; acute. ¶ ~히 keenly; poignantly; acutely; severely / ~히 느끼다 feel 〔realize〕 keenly 〔acutely〕; take 《*something*》 to heart / 건강의 고마움을 그 때 ~히 느꼈다 At that time I keenly felt what a blessing it is to be healthy.

**통점**(痛點) 『생리』 a pain spot.

**통정**(通情) ① 《통사정》 having sympathetic understanding; unbosoming *oneself*; 《통심정》 rapport. ~하다 =통사정하다. ② 《간통》 adultery. ~하다 carry on with 《a woman, a man》; have a liaison 〔an intrigue〕 with 《*a person*》.

**통젖**(桶―) the handles of a tub.

**통제**(統制) control; regulation; regimentation. ~하다 control; exercise control over 〔on〕; hold under control; place 《*a thing*》 under (government) control; regulate; govern.
¶ ~가 없는 uncontrolled; noncontrolled / 정부의 ~ government control / 산업을 ~하다 regulate 〔regiment〕 industries / 엄격한 ~를 실시하다 exercise strict 〔close〕 control 《over》 / ~를 강화하다 tighten 〔strengthen〕

the control 《of, over》/ ～를 완화하다 alleviate 〔ease〕 (the) control / ～를 풀다〔해제하다〕 lift 〔remove〕 the control(s) 《over》/ 그것은 정부 ～하에 있다 It is under government control. / 전체 학생이 ～가 잘 되어 있다 The student body is well under control.
◉ ～가격 controlled prices. ～경제 controlled 〔managed, planned〕 economy; controlled economics. ～구역 a restricted area; a control zone. ～기관 a control agency 〔instrument, organ〕; an organ for control. ～무역 controlled trade. ～범위 『경영』 the span of control; the limitation of control. ～철폐 decontrol. ～품(品) controlled goods 〔articles〕; goods under government control. 물가～ price control: 물가 ～령 the Price Control Ordinance / 물가 ～ 조치 the price control measure.

**통제부**(統制府) 《해군의》 a naval yard; a naval station; an admiralty port.

**통조림**(桶—) 《제조》 packing; canning 《미》; tinning 《영》; 《제품》 canned 〔tinned 《영》〕 food 〔goods〕. ～하다 ⇨ ～으로 하다. ¶ ～으로 한 canned; tinned 《영》/ ～을 따다 open a can 〔tin 《영》〕; saw out the top of a can 〔tin 《영》〕/ ～으로 하다 pack 《meat》 in a can 〔tin 《영》〕; 《미》 can; 《영》 tin.
◉ ～공 a packer; a canner; 《영》 a tinner. ～공선(工船) a canning factory ship. ～공업 the packing 〔canning 《미》, tinning 《영》〕 industry. ～공장 a packing house; 《미》 a cannery; a canning plant; 《영》 a tinning works. ～밀크 evaporated milk. ～식품 canned provision; canned 〔tinned 《영》〕 food. ～업자 a packer; a canner 《미》; a tinner 《영》: 식육 ～업자 a meat packer. ～제조법 canning; tinning 《영》. 고기～ canned 〔tinned 《영》〕 meat. 쇠고기～ canned 〔tinned 《영》〕 beef; 《조미한》 corned beef. 연어〔생선〕～ canned 〔tinned 《영》〕 salmon 〔fish〕.

**통줄** 《연줄》 the string let out by turning the kite-reel endways. ～주다 let the string out fast by turning the kite-reel endways.

**통줄**(筒—) 《쓰는》 a round 〔cylindrical〕 rasp.

**통증**(痛症) (a) pain; 《부분적인》 an ache; 《갑작스러운》 a pang; 《쑤시는》 a twinge; 《욱신거리는》 a smart; 《따끔따끔한》 a prickle; a sore (눈·목의).
¶ 격심한 ～ a severe 〔a sharp, an acute〕 pain / 따끔따끔 쑤시는 ～ a prickling pain; a prickle / 상처의 ～ a smart of a wound / 옆구리의 ～ a pain 〔stitch〕 in *one's* side / ～을 느끼다 feel 〔have, suffer〕 a pain / ～을 멎게 하다 stop (the) pain / ～을 없애다 remove 〔banish, kill〕 (the) pain / ～을 완화시키다〔가라앉히다〕 allay 〔alleviate, mitigate, ease, relieve〕 the pain; make the pain easier / ～을 참다 stand 〔bear, endure〕 the pain / ～이 더하다〔덜하다〕 the pain increases 〔abates〕/ ～이 멎다 the pain stops / ～이 심하다 feel a bad 〔severe〕 pain 《in *one's* teeth》.

**통지**(通知) 《통고》 (a) notice; (a) notification; 《알림》 information; 《통신》 communication; 《상업상의》 an advice. ～하다 notify 《*a person* that, of》; inform 《*a person* that, of》; let 《*a person*》 know 《that, of》; communicate 《news to, with *a person*》; advise 〔apprise〕 《*a person* that, of》; 《해약·해고 등의 예고》 give 《*a person*》 notice 《that, of》.
¶ ～가 있는 대로 at a minute's notice; immediately on receipt of *a person's* notice / ～대로 as per advice / 추후 ～가 있을 때까지 till further notice 〔advice〕/ ～를 받다〔가 있다〕 be informed 《of, that...》; have 〔receive〕 notice 《of, that...》; be notified 〔advised〕 《of, that...》; receive advices / ～를 기다리다 await word / 미리 ～하다 give 《*a person*》 previous notice; send word beforehand / …라는 ～가 있었다 word has reached 《this office》 that...; word was received 《at the headquarters》 that... / …라는 ～에 접했다 advice has been to the effect that... / …을 ～해 드리는 바입니다 I beg to inform 〔tell〕 you that.... / 그 일에 관해서 자세히 ～해 주십시오 Give me a detailed account of the matter. / 시험 결과는 7일 이내에 우편으로 ～해 드립니다 We will inform 〔notify〕 you of the results of the examination by mail within seven days.
◉ ～서 a notice. ～예금 a deposit at call; a deposit of notice. ～인 an informer. ～표 an advice slip. 계약 만기 ～ a notice of expiration of contract. 어음 부도〔집회〕 ～ a notice of dishonor 〔meeting〕. 착화(着貨)〔이전, 해약〕～ a notice of arrival 〔removal, cancellation〕. 생활～표 《학교 성적표》 a school report (card).

**통짜** the whole mass〔lump〕. ¶ ∼로 ⇨ 통째(로).

**통짜다**[1] 《한 동아리로서》 pledge *oneself* to become a member of a gang〔cabal〕; form a gang〔group〕. ¶ 통짜고 음모하다 form a gang to plot / 서로 ∼ make a secret pact; be in cahoots with one another; form a group〔gang〕/ 통짜고 남을 속이려 하다 conspire together to cheat *a person*.

**통짜다**[2] 《하나로》 put〔fit, piece〕together; frame; assemble.

**통째(로)** all; whole; altogether; bodily; entirely; in 《its》 entirety. ¶ ∼ 굽다 roast 《a chicken》 whole / ∼ 먹다 eat 《*something*》 whole; 《재물·이익 등을》 take all to *oneself*; get the exclusive possession of / 생선을 ∼ 먹다 eat a fish whole; eat a fish, bones and all / 뱀은 먹이를 ∼ 삼킨다 Snakes swallow their victims whole.

**통찰**(洞察) discernment; penetration; insight. ∼하다 discern; penetrate 《into》; read 《*a person's* heart》; see through; see into 《*something* hidden》.

**통찰력**(洞察力) an insight; penetration; vision. ¶ ∼이 있는 discerning; penetrative; penetrating; perceptive / ∼이 있다 have an insight 《into》/ 그는 예리한 ∼이 있는 사람이다 He is a man of keen insight.

**통첩**(通牒) a note; a notification; a circular; instruction. ∼하다 notify 《*a person* of, that…》; give notice 《to》; communicate; instruct. ¶ 최후 ∼《send, deliver》 an ultimatum / ∼을 발하다 issue〔send〕a notification / 황급히 ∼을 내다 send a message posthaste to…. ◉ 외교∼ a diplomatic note.

**통촉**(洞燭) seeing; understanding; judgment; discernment. ∼하다 deign to see; see; realize; understand; judge; discern.

**통치**(通治) curing all kinds of disease. ∼하다 cure all kinds of disease; be (medically) effective on a broad spectrum. ¶ 만병∼약 a cure-all; a panacea.

**통치**(統治) rule; reign; government. ∼하다 rule〔reign〕over 《a country》; govern; administer; dominate.
¶ 국가의 ∼ the administration of the state / …의 ∼하에 있다 be under the rule of… / 왕은 그 나라를 20년간 ∼했다 The king ruled the country for twenty years. / 영국왕은 군림하지만 ∼하지 않는다 The English sovereign reigns, but does not rule〔govern〕.

> 용법 **rule** 권력을 행사해서 독재적·전제적으로 「통치하다」라는 뜻. 엄격히 말한다면 선거를 통해서 선출된 사람이나 단체에 대해서는 쓰지 아니함. 다만 쉬운 말이어서 govern대신 곧잘 쓰임. **reign** 실제의 정치에는 참여하지 않고 「군림하다」라는 뜻. **govern** 나라나 국민을 「통치하다」「다스리다」라는 뜻. 입헌·독재·세습 등의 형태와는 상관없이 잘 다스려지고 있다는 뜻으로 쓰임. **administer** 규칙을 지키면서 「행정에 관여하다」「관리·운영하다」라는 뜻. **dominate** 우세한 힘을 가지고 「지배하다」라는 뜻으로서 달갑지 않다는 뉘앙스를 내포함.

◉ ∼권 《exercise *one's*》 sovereign〔supreme〕power; sovereignty. ∼기관 government organs〔machinery〕. ∼자 the ruler; the sovereign. ∼제도 a ruling system. ∼행위 an act of the state; an act of government.

**통치마** a seamless one-piece skirt.

**통칙**(通則) a general〔common〕rule〔principle〕. ¶ ∼으로서 as a general rule.

**통칭**(通稱) a common〔popular〕name; an alias. ¶ 존스, ∼ 탐 Jones, who「is commonly called〔goes by the name of〕'Tom' / 그는 ∼ 짐이라고 부른다 He goes by the name of Jim. *or* He is commonly called Jim. / 이 거리는 ∼ 「장미꽃 거리」라고 불리운다 This street is commonly known〔called〕as 'Rose (of the Valley) Street.'

**통쾌**(痛快) a great〔keen〕pleasure. ∼하다 (be) most pleasant; extremely delightful; 《가슴 설렘》 (be) exciting; thrilling; 《통렬》 (be) incisive; trenchant. ¶ ∼한 문장 an incisive style / ∼한 모험 이야기 a thrilling adventure story / 우승을 해서 매우 ∼한 기분이었다 It was extremely delightful for us to win the trophy. / 그의 연설은 ∼했다 He made a marvelous〔stunning〕speech. / 나는 그날밤 ∼히 마셨다 That night I drank to my heart's content. / 그거 참 ∼하다 How delightful and gratifying! ◉ ∼감 smart〔thrilling〕feelings.

**통탄**(痛歎) deep lamentation; bitter grief; deep regret. ∼하다 grieve〔lament〕deeply〔bitterly〕; deplore. ¶ ∼할 deplorable; lamentable; regrettable / 아주 ∼스러운 일 a matter of great regret / …은 ∼할 일이다 It is 「deplorable〔much to be regretted〕 that ... should....

**통통**[1] 《굵은 모양》 plumply; full. ～하다 (be) plump; chubby; full. ¶ ～한 볼 chubby cheeks / ～한 얼굴 a full face / ～한 젖가슴 a full 〔rich, well-rounded〕 breast / ～하게 살찌다 plump (up, out); become rounded / 울어서 눈이 ～ 붓다 have *one's* eyes swollen with weeping; *one's* eyes are all swollen 〔puffed up〕 with crying / 몸이 ～하다 look chubby.

**통통**[2] 《내는 소리》 beating; pounding; resounding; 《발동기의》 chug-chug. ～거리다 pound; resound. ¶ ～배 a motor-powered launch / 마루가 ～거리다 a floor resounds / 마루를 ～ 구르다 pound on the floor / 문을 ～ 두드리다 tap 〔pound〕 at the door / (배가) ～거리며 나아가다 chug off / 어린애가 마루를 ～거리며 돌아다니다 a child scampers around on the floor / ～거리며 계단을 오르다 stamp upstairs.
◉ ～걸음 walking with pounding 〔quick〕 steps.

**통틀다** take 《it》 all and put 《it》 together (in one lump).

**통틀어** taking all (things) together; all put together; in all; (in) all told; altogether; all inclusive; *en bloc* (F.); in a gross. ¶ ～ 만 원, 10,000 won 「for the whole lot 〔in all told〕 / ～ 말하면 taking all (things) together; to sum up / ～ 얼마냐 How much (is it) all together? *or* What do you charge for them all?

**통팥** whole 〔unsplit〕 red beans.

**통폐**(通弊) a common abuse 〔evil, weakness〕; a prevailing fault. ¶ 이것들은 현대 사회의 ～이다 These are evils common to all the classes in this society. / 남의 성공을 시새우는 것은 인간의 ～이다 It is a common weakness of human nature to envy others for their success. / 증수회는 우리나라 정계의 ～이다 Bribery is an evil practice prevalent in our political circles.

**통폐합**(統廢合) 《conduct》 the merger and abolition 《of》.

**통풍**(通風) ventilation (방 따위의); a draft (보일러의). ～하다 let air in; circulate air. ¶ 이 방은 ～이 잘 된다〔되지 않는다〕 This room is well 〔badly〕 ventilated. ◉ ～갱 《광산의》 an air pit. ～관 an air pipe; a vent pipe. ～구 a draft 〔ventilating〕 hole; a ventilation opening. ～기 a ventilator. ～장치 a ventilation device 〔apparatus〕. ～창 a ventilating window. ～통 a ventiduct; an air duct. 자연〔인공〕 ～ a natural 〔an artificial〕 draft.

**통풍**(痛風) 〚의학〛 gout; podagra. ¶ ～에 걸리다 be afflicted with gout; be gouty.

**통하다**(通—) ① 《교통·차편이》 pass; run; 《개통하다》 be opened 《to traffic》; 《길 따위가 …로》 lead 《to, into》; open 〔give〕 《into a room, upon a corridor, garden》; communicate 《with》. ¶ 해안으로 통하는 길 a road leading 〔going〕 to the seashore / 안뜰로 통하는 작은 문 a small gate leading 〔giving〕 into the court / 머지않아 우리 고향으로 통하는 철도가 놓인다 A railroad will soon be laid to our hometown. / 여기서 진주까지 통하는 철도가 있다 A railroad runs 〔extends〕 from here to Chinju. / 이 마을에서 무주까지 통하는 버스가 있다 There is a bus service between this village and Muju. / 이 방의 한 쪽은 별실로 통해 있다 One end of this room communicates with another room.
② 《유통·소통하다》 (***a***) 《전기 따위가》 circulate; transmit; 《공기 따위가》 go 〔pass〕 through; circulate; ventilate; flow. ¶ 전기가 통하고 있는 전선 a live wire; an electrified wire / 공기가 통하지 않는 방 an unaired room / 전기가 ～ be charged with electricity / 전류를 ～ charge 《*a thing*》 with electricity; electrify 《a wire》; turn on electricity; send 〔apply〕 an electric current 《to》 / 공기가 잘 ～ be well ventilated; have good ventilation / 금속류는 전기가 통한다 Metals transmit electricity. (***b***) 《물·연기 따위가 빠지다》 draw; drain; run through. ¶ 토관에 물이 (잘) 통하게 하다 make water run through earthen pipes / 하수관에 물이 잘 통한다 The sewer runs well. / 이 굴뚝은 연기가 잘 통하지 않는다 This chimney does not draw well. (***c***) 《전화가》 go 〔put, get〕 through; get connected 《with》; 《a line》 be on. ¶ 전화가 ～ a phone call is put 〔goes, gets〕 through; be on the line / 전화가 통하지 않다 a call fails to go 〔get〕 through; the phone 〔wire〕 is dead; the line is out / B씨에게 전화를 했으나 통하지 않았다 I could not get Mr. B on the phone. *or* I couldn't get through to Mr. B. (***d***) 《대소변이》 ¶ 대변〔소변〕이 ～ have regular bowel

movements 〔urination〕/ 대변이 잘 통하게 하다 keep the bowels loose / 대소변이 통하지 않다 have excretory difficulties; have trouble passing excrements.

③ 《뜻·말·의사가〔를〕》 be understood; be comprehended; be spoken (언어가); 《알리다》 inform 《*a person* of a fact》; communicate 《*a matter* to *a person*》; 《서로 마음이》 enjoy (mutual) understanding; understand (each other); be conveyed 〔communicated〕 《to》; be of a mind. ¶ 이야기가 통하는 사람 a man of sense; a sensible 〔an intelligent〕 person / 뜻을〔의사를〕 ~ make *oneself* understood; make known *one's* intention; get across the idea 〔meaning〕/ 생각이 상대에게 ~ have *one's* ideas communicated to another; get *one's* ideas across / 서로 마음이 ~ understand each other's sentiments / 말이 서로 통하지 않다 be unable to communicate with each other because of the language barrier / 내 영어로는 의사가 통하지 않았다 I couldn't make myself understood with my English. / 내 의사가 통했을까 Did I make myself clear? / 이 나라에서는 영어가 통하지 않는다 English is not spoken in this country. / 귀띔을 해주었지만 그에겐 통하지 않았다 My hint was lost upon him.

④ 《글의 뜻이》 make sense. ¶ 글의 뜻이 통하지 않다 a sentence doesn't make sense / 이 부분의 뜻이 잘 통하지 않는다 I can't catch meaning of this passage. *or* This passage is unintelligible.

⑤ 《용납되다》 pass; get by; be admissible. ¶ 그런 구실은 통하지 않는다 That sort of excuse won't get by. / 그런 변명은 해 보았자 통하지 않는다 Such excuses will not do. / 네 의견이 그들에겐 통할 것 같지 않다 Your opinion will not go down with them. / "법을 몰라서"란 말은 통하지 않는다 Ignorance of the law excuses no one.

⑥ 《알려지다》 (***a***) 《일반에게 …로》 pass 《for, as》; figure as; be known as; pass current. ¶ …란 이름으로 ~ pass under the name of; go 〔be known〕 by the name of... / …의 권위자로 ~ be reputed 〔acknowledged〕 as an authority / 진짜로 ~ pass for 〔as〕 genuine. (***b***) 《얼굴이》 ¶ 얼굴이 널리 ~ be widely known; have a wide 〔large circle of〕 acquaintance; get around 《미구어》; have influence 《with, in》.

⑦ 《훤히 알다》 know well 《about》; be well 〔deeply〕 versed 《in》; be well informed 《of, about, as to》; be familiar 〔conversant〕 《with》; be at home 《in, on》; be thoroughly 〔well〕 acquainted 《with》; be an expert 《in, on》. ¶ 고금의 학문에 ~ be versed in lore, ancient as well as modern / 내부 사정에 ~ be well up on the inside story; be well informed of the inside facts; be in the know / 천문에 ~ know a lot about astronomy / 그는 중국 사정에 속속들이 잘 통한다 He knows a lot about Chinese affairs. *or* He is well informed about Chinese affairs.

⑧ 《은밀히》 (***a***) 《남녀가》 become intimate 《with》; have relations 〔an affair〕 《with》; form a liaison 《with》. ¶ 정을 ~ have an illicit intercourse 《with》; carry on with 《a man, a woman》; have a liaison 〔an intrigue〕 with 《*a person*》. (***b***) 《내통하다》 communicate secretly 〔intrigue〕 《with the enemy》; betray; be in touch with 《the other party》. ¶ 기맥을 ~ keep 〔be〕 in touch 《with》; be in secret communication 《with》; have a tacit understanding 《with》/ 적과 ~ prostitute *oneself* to the enemy.

⑨ 《친히 사귀다》 keep company 《with》; hold 〔have〕 intercourse 《with》.

⑩ 《투과하다》 penetrate; pierce; permeate. ¶ 빛을 통하는 pervious 〔penetrable〕 to light / 물이 ~ be pervious to water; let in water / 물이 통하지 않다 impervious to 〔proof against〕 water; do not let in water; be waterproof 〔watertight〕/ 유리는 빛이나 열을 통한다 Glass is pervious to 〔transmits〕 light and heat.

⑪ 《유효하다》 pass; circulate; hold good; be good; be valid. ¶ 규칙이 ~ a regulation holds (good) / 이 돈은 어디서나 통한다 This money passes 〔can be used〕 freely everywhere.

⑫ 《경유·부탁하다》 go 〔pass〕 through; get through. ¶ 아무를 통해서 through *a person;* be the agency 〔medium, good offices〕 of *a person* / 중매인을 통해서 청혼하다 propose to 《a girl》 through a go-between / 시내를 통해 가다 go through the city / 아무를 통해서 소식을 전하다 send news through *a person* / 아무를 통해서 취직 운동을 하다 try to get a job through the good offices of *a person.*

⑬《시간·공간에 걸치다》¶ 1년을 통하여 all the year around〔round〕; throughout the year / 전국을 통하여 throughout〔all over〕the country / 일년을 통해서 편지 한 장 보내지 않다 let the whole year go by without writing a single letter.
⑭《유관하다》be concerned〔connected〕《with》. ¶ 문학과 음악은 서로 통한다 There is an interrelation between literature and music.

**통학**(通學) attending school. ～하다 attend〔go to〕school〔classes〕. ¶ 도보로 ～하다 attend school on foot / 자택에서 ～하다 attend school from *one's* home / 그는 줄곧 열차로 ～하고 있다 He goes to school, all train-ride. / 나는 매일 버스로～하고 있다 I go to school「by bus〔on the bus〕every day. ◉ ～구역 a school district. ～생《기숙 학교의》a day student. ～차 a school bus〔train〕.

**통한**(痛恨) great sorrow〔regret〕; deep〔bitter〕regret. ～하다 grieve bitterly; regret deeply. ¶ ～의 눈물 tears of bitterness / 일생 일대의 ～사 (a matter of) the greatest regret of *one's* life.

**통할**(統轄) (general) control; supervision. ～하다 control; exercise control《over》; govern; supervise; be in charge of. ¶ 그는 새로운 프로젝트를 ～하고 있다 He is in charge of the new project. ◉ ～구역 the area under the direct control. ～자 the person in charge.

**통합**(統合) integration; unification; unity; merger; synthesis. ～하다 integrate; unify; combine; put〔bring〕together; make into one. ¶ ～적(인) unified; synthetic / 국민 ～의 상징 the symbol of the unity of the people / 여러가지 의견들을 ～하다 integrate various opinions / 지금 두 개의 도시를 ～하려는 계획이 진행 중이다 They are planning to unify two towns now.
◉ ～계획 a plan for integrating《the police》. ～참모본부《미국의》the Joint Chiefs of Staff (생략 J.C.S.).

**통항**(通航) navigation; sailing. ～하다 navigate; sail; ply《between two places》. ¶ 파나마 운하를 ～하는 배가 많아졌다 There has been an increase in navigation through the Panama Canal.

**통행**(通行)《다님》passing; passage; transit; traffic. ～하다 pass《through》; go past; go through〔along〕. ¶ ～할 수 있는 passable / ～할 수 없는 산길 an impassable〔impracticable〕mountain road / ～을 막다 close a road; close the street to traffic / ～을 방해하다 obstruct〔impede〕(the) traffic; bar the way; stand〔get〕in《*a person's*》way; block《*a person's*》passage / ～이 막혀 있다 Traffic is blocked. *or* Traffic is held〔tied〕up. / 일방 ～《게시》One way (only). / 우측 ～《게시》Keep (to the) right. / 이 거리는 일방 ～이다 This is a one-way street. / 전방 ～ 불가《게시》Blocked further on. / 이 거리는 ～량이 많다〔적다〕There is「a lot of〔not much〕traffic in this street. / 이 도로는 좁아서 차가 ～하지 못한다 This road is so narrow that cars cannot go through.
◉ ～권(券)〔증〕a pass;《적국·피점령지의》a safe-conduct (pass); a safeguard. ～권(權) the right of way〔passing〕. ～료 passage money; a toll: ～료 받는 곳 a tollhouse; a toll station / 혼잡 ～료 congestion fees / 통과하는 모든 차량으로부터 ～료를 받다 collect toll from every passing vehicle. ～세 a traveling tax; transit duty〔tax〕(화물의);《통행료》a toll. ～우선권 the right of way. ～인 a passersby (*pl.* passerby); a pedestrian (보행자).

**통행금지**(通行禁止) suspension of traffic;《야간 외출 금지》a curfew;《게시》Road closed. *or* Closed to traffic. *or* No thoroughfare. *or* Blocked. ¶ 도로를 ～시키다 close (up) a road; seal a street to traffic; block a street / 야간 ～를 실시하다 impose a curfew / 제차(諸車) ～《게시》No thoroughfare for vehicles. *or* Closed to all vehicles.
◉ ～구역 a no passing zone. ～시간 curfew hour.

**통혈**(通穴) a draft〔ventilating〕hole; a ventilation opening; a vent; a funnel;《광산의》an air-shaft;《터널의》an air pit. ～하다 open ventilation.

**통혼**(通婚) ～하다 make a proposal of marriage《to *someone*》; enter into matrimony.

**통화**(通貨)〚경제〛currency; (current) money; a circulating medium. ¶ ～의 안정 stabilization of the currency / ～의 안정을 방해하다 disturb the stability of the currency / ～의 절하〔절상〕devaluation〔revaluation〕(of the currency) /「러시아의 ～가 무엇인지 아느냐」―「루블이지. 그 정도는 나도 안다」“Do you know what Russian curren-

cy is ?"—"Sure, Ruble ! I'm not stupid, you know."
◉ ～가치 currency value. ～개혁 monetary 〔currency〕 reform. ～공급량 a (total) money supply. ～공급 인플레이션 money supply inflation. ～관리 currency management. ～단위 a currency unit. ～발행고 amount of currency in issue. ～수축 deflation. ～시장 currency market. ～안정 증권 monetary stabilization bond. ～안정책 measures to stabilize a currency. ～위기 a monetary crisis. ～위조 counterfeiting of currency. ～유출〔유입〕 the efflux 〔influx, inflow〕 of currency. ～유통 currency circulation: ～유통량 the total amount of money in circulation. ～재조정 currency realignment. ～재팽창 reflation. ～정책 a monetary policy; fiscal 〔currency, credit〕 policy. ～제도 a currency 〔monetary〕 system. ～증발(增發) increased issue of currency. ～축소〔수축〕 deflation 〔contraction〕 of currency. ～통제 currency control(s). ～팽창 currency inflation 〔expansion〕; inflation 〔overissue〕 of currency: ～팽창론 inflationism. ～표시 currency denomination.
관리～ the managed 〔controlled〕 currency: 관리 ～ 제도 the managed currency 〔monetary〕 system. 봉쇄～ blocked currency. 성장～ growth currency. 준비～ reserve currency. 총～공급 증가율 the total money supply increase rate.

**통화**(通話) a (telephone) call; telephone conversation. ～하다 speak 〔talk〕 over 〔upon〕 the telephone; speak by telephone. ¶ 세 ～ three (telephone) calls / 시내〔시외〕～ a city 〔long-distance〕 call / 지명 ～ a person-to-person call / ～중이다 be talking over 〔be on〕 the telephone; 《전화가》 the line is busy / 한 ～ 3분간의 요금은 300원이다 The charge 〔fee〕 is 300 won for each call of 3 minutes. / ～중 Line, busy 《미》. *or* Number, engaged. / ～중일 때는 조금 후에 다시 거십시오 If the line is busy, please try later. / 한 ～가 되었습니다 Your three minutes are up. / 몇 ～였습니까 How many minutes did we speak?
◉ ～량 telephone traffic. ～료 the fee 〔charge〕 for a telephone call; the call charge: 시외 ～료 the distance-call charge. ～신호 a busy signal. ～회로 a talking 〔speaking〕 circuit.

**통화횟수**(通話回數) the number of telephone calls. ◉ ～계 a phonemeter; a message 〔service〕 register. ～제 the message rate 〔call〕 system.

**통회**(痛悔) 『가톨릭』 contrition. ～하다 be contrite.

**통효**(通曉) ① 《통달》 mastery; conversance; (a) thorough knowledge. ～하다 be well acquainted with; be versed in; have a thorough knowledge. ② ＝철야(徹夜).

**퇴다** ① 《샅샅이》 search everywhere for; leave no stone unturned. ② 《삼을》 soften and spread hemp tufts.

**퇴각**(退却) (a) retreat; (a) withdrawal; retirement; falling back; backdown. ～하다 retreat 《from, to》; beat 〔make〕 a retreat; withdraw; retire; fall back. ¶ ～중인 적군 retreating enemy troops / ～을 엄호하다 cover a retreating army; protect the retreat / 예정된 ～을 하다 make a prearranged retreat 〔withdrawal〕; retreat as prearranged / 무사히 ～하다 make good *one's* retreat / 전(全)전선에서 ～하다 retreat along the whole line / 정연히〔대오를 흩뜨리고〕 ～하다 retreat in good order 〔in disorder〕 / 허둥지둥 ～하다 beat a hasty retreat. ◉ ～군 an army in retreat; a retreating army. ～로 a route of retreat; a withdrawal route: ～로를 차단하다 cut off 〔intercept〕 a retreat. ～명령 an order 〔a signal〕 to retreat. ～선 a line of retreat. 총～ a full 〔general〕 retreat: 총～하다 be in full retreat.

**퇴거**(退去) leaving; evacuation; withdrawal; removal. ～하다 leave; depart 《from》; quit; evacuate; withdraw 〔go away〕 《from a place》. ¶ ～를 명하다 order 《a place》 out of 《*a person*》 〔to quit 《a place》〕 / ～시키다 expel 〔evict〕 《*a person*》 from 《a place》 / ～를 통보하다 give 《*a person*》 notice to quit / 수비대를 진지에서 ～시키다 evacuate a garrison from a post. ◉ ～명령 an order of removal; an expulsion order: ～ 명령을 받다 be ordered to quit 《a place》. ～보상금 compensation for removal. ～신고 a removal report.

**퇴고**(推敲) polish; elaboration; improvement. ～하다 polish; elaborate (on); improve; work on *one's* manuscript 〔composition〕 to improve 〔revise〕 the wording. ¶ ～를 거듭하다

work 〔do〕 《*one's* composition》 over again and again; spend much time in the choice of diction / ～할 여지가 있다 admit of further polish 〔elaboration〕.

**퇴골**(腿骨) a leg 〔thigh〕 bone.

**퇴관**(退官) retirement from office 〔service〕; resignation of *one's* post 〔commission〕. ～하다 retire from office 〔service〕; resign. ¶ ～하여 연금 생활을 하다 retire and be pensioned off.

**퇴교**(退校) ① 《퇴학》 dismissal 〔expulsion〕 from school; 《자퇴》 withdrawal from school; leaving school. ～하다 leave 〔give up〕 school. ¶ ～ 처분을 받다 be dismissed 〔expelled〕 from school / (부모가) ～시키다 remove 《*one's* son》 from school. ② 《하교》 the closing of school; coming home from school. ～하다 school gets out; leave school; go 〔come〕 home from school. ¶ ～ 후에 after school (is over); after the school hours.

**퇴군**(退軍) withdrawal; retreat. ⇨ 퇴각(退却). ～하다 withdraw; retreat.

**퇴근**(退勤) leaving *one's* office 〔desk, work〕; going home. ～하다 leave the office; finish *one's* work (for the day) and leave; go home from work. ¶ ～길에 on *one's* way home from the office / 여섯시 ～이다 The office close at six (o'clock). / 「～합시다. 정말 피곤하군요」—「하지만 5시밖에 안 됐는걸요」 "Let's call it a day. I'm really tired." —"But it's only 5 o'clock." ◉ ～ 시간 the closing hour 〔time〕.

**퇴기**(退妓) a retired *kisaeng;* an ex-*kisaeng.*

**퇴김** jerking (a kite string). ～주다 jerk (a kite string).

**퇴내다**(退—) be satiated 《with》; be glutted 《with》; surfeit *oneself* 《with》; have had enough 《of》.

**퇴락**(頹落) dilapidation. ～하다 dilapidate; go to ruin; fall into decay 〔ruin〕.

**퇴로**(退路) the path of retreat. ¶ ～를 끊다 intercept 〔cut off〕 the 《enemy's》 retreat; block the way of retreat; cut the line of retreat.

**퇴맞다**(退—) ⇨ 퇴박맞다.

**퇴물**(退物) ① 《물려 받은 것》 things handed down 《from *one's* older brother》; a hand-me-down 《from》 《구어》; reach-me-down 《from》 《영구어》; a used article. ② 《퇴박맞은 것》 a thing rejected; rejected goods. ③ a retired person. ¶ 기생 ～ an ex-*kisaeng.*

**퇴박맞다**(退—) get rejected; be refused 〔rebuffed〕; be sent back; get turned down. ¶ 면허 신청이 ～ an application for a license is turned down / 제품이 규격에 맞지 않아 ～ manufactured goods are rejected for failure to meet specifications.

**퇴박하다**(退—) reject; repulse; refuse; rebuff; decline; turn down.

**퇴보**(退步) a step backward; retrogression; a backward step; a setback. ～하다 go 〔move〕 backward; slip back; retrogress; retrograde; deteriorate. ¶ ～적(인) retrogressive; backward / 문명의 ～ the retrogression of civilization; a backward step 〔movement〕 in civilization / 모든 일이 ～하고 있다 Things are going backward.

**퇴비**(堆肥) compost; barnyard 〔farmyard〕 manure. ¶ ～더미 a compost pile 〔heap〕; a manure heap / ～를 주다 compost 《the land》.

**퇴사**(退社) 《퇴직》 retirement 〔withdrawal〕 from a company; 《퇴근》 leaving the office (for the day). ～하다 《퇴직하다》 leave 〔retire from〕 《the company》; 《퇴근하다》 leave work 〔the office〕. ¶ ～ 시각에 at closing time / ～ 길에 on *one's* way back from the office / 일신상의 사정으로 ～하다 resign for personal reasons / 사원은 오후 6시에 ～한다 Workers clock out 〔off〕 at 6:00 p.m. *or* Workers punch out at 6:00 p.m. 《미구어》 (★ 타임리코더로 퇴근 시간을 카드에 찍는 행위에서 유래).

**퇴산**(退散) dispersal; dismissal; discharge; breaking up. ～하다 disperse; break up. ¶ ～시키다 disperse; expel; drive away / 군중을 ～시키다 disperse the crowd / 적을 ～시키다 put the enemy to flight.

**퇴색**(退色·褪色) fading; faded color (색깔). ～하다 fade; lose color; go off. ¶ ～한 faded; discolored / ～하기 쉬운 fugitive 〔fading〕 《color》 / ～하지 않는 fadeless; fadeproof; fast; standing / ～하지 않는 빛깔 a fast 〔fadeless〕 color / 당(黨)의 군색채를 ～시키다 discolor the military image of the party / 이 색은 세탁을 해도 ～하지 않는다 This color will stand washing. / 이 넥타이는 햇빛으로 ～했다 This tie has been discolored by the sun.

**퇴석**(退席) ～하다 leave *one's* seat; retire; withdraw. ¶ ～을 명하다 order 《*a person*》 to leave 《the room》.

**퇴석**(堆石) ① 《돌더미》 a pile of stones.

② 〚지질〛 a moraine.

**퇴세**(頹勢) *one's* declining fortunes; a downward tendency; decay; decline. ¶ ~를 만회하다 retrieve 〔restore〕 the declining fortunes《of》; recover from the downward tendency; rally.

**퇴속**(退俗) 〚불교〛 retiring from the Buddhist priesthood. ~하다 retire from the Buddhist priesthood; return to the laity.

**퇴역**(退役) retirement (from service). ~하다 retire (from service); leave office 〔the army〕. ¶ ~ 육군 소령 김일동 retired Army Major Kim Il-Tong / ~시키다 decommission; put 〔place〕《an officer》 on the retired list; mothball《a ship》/ 그는 54세에 ~했다 He「retired from service 〔left the army〕 at the age of fifty-four.

◉ ~ 군인 an ex-serviceman; a veteran《미》. ~연금 a retiring pension. ~ 장교 a retired officer; an (army) officer on the retired list. ~함(艦) a warship out of commission.

**퇴영**(退嬰) retrogression; conservatism. ~하다 retrograde; retrogress. ¶ ~적인 retrogressive; conservative.

**퇴원**(退院) leaving (the) hospital; *one's* discharge from (the) hospital. ~하다 leave (the) hospital; be discharged 〔released〕 from (the) hospital. ¶ ~을 명하다 order《a patient》 out of (the) hospital / ~해도 좋다〔하기에는 이르다〕 be 〔be not〕 well enough to leave (the) hospital / ~이 허가되다 be given permission to leave (the) hospital / ~해 있다 be out of hospital / 그는 곧 ~할 것입니다 He will soon be out of hospital. ◉ ~환자 a discharged patient.

**퇴위**(退位) (an) abdication. ~하다 abdicate (the throne); step down from the throne《in favor of *one's* son》. ¶ ~시키다 depose 〔dethrone〕《a king》/ 황제는 황태자에게 자리를 물려주고 ~했다 The emperor abdicated (from) the throne in favor of the crown prince.

**퇴일보**(退一步) ~하다 take a step backward; shrink back; flinch.

**퇴임**(退任) retirement《from *one's* office》. ⇨ 퇴직. ~하다 retire 〔resign〕 from *one's* office 〔post〕. ¶ 임기 만료로 ~하다 resign from office upon completing *one's* term of office / 그녀는 건강상의 이유로 ~했다 She resigned from her post on the grounds of ill=health.

**퇴장**(退場) ①《회의·식장·경기장 따위에서》 leaving. ~하다 leave《the hall》; go away《from》. ¶ 모두 ~할 때까지 until everyone leaves / ~을 명하다 order《*a person*》 out of the room 〔hall〕; order《*a person*》 out / ~당하다 be banished from the room; be ordered away from the hall / 심판은 선수에게 ~을 명했다 The umpire 〔referee〕 ordered the player out of the ground. / 그는 반칙으로 ~당했다 He fouled out of the game.

②《무대에서》 exit (한 사람이); exeunt (두 사람 이상이). ~하다 make *one's* exit; leave the scene. ¶ 맥베스 ~《극본의 지시》 "Exit Macbeth" / 배우가 ~했다 The actor made his exit.

③《의회 등에서》 a walkout. ~하다 walk out of the chamber; walk out on the debate. ¶ 총~하다 walk out *en masse*《from》/ 야당 의원들은 이른바 국무총리의 답변이 불성실하고 불충분하다는 것에 항의하여 국회 본회의에서 ~했다 The opposition members walked out of the House plenary session in protest over what they called "insincere and insufficient answers" by Premier. ◉ 총~ a general walkout.

**퇴장**(退藏) hoarding; dead storage. ~하다 hoard《goods》; store《*something*》 away《in a back room》; put 〔keep〕《*something*》 in dead storage. ¶ 재고품의 ~ inventory hoarding. ◉ ~물자 hoarded (and concealed) goods. ~품 an article kept in dead storage.

**퇴적**(堆積) (an) accumulation; a heap; a pile; a build-up. ~하다 accumulate; be piled up; be heaped up. ¶ ~한 accumulative / 열차 불통으로 정거장에는 화물이 ~해 있다 Owing to the interruption of railway traffic, there are mountains of freight piled up at the station. / 토사가 ~하여 삼각주를 이룬다 Sand and gravel accumulate and make a delta. ◉ ~물 deposits; sediment(s). ~암 (a) sedimentary rock. ~층 a sedimentary layer 〔stratum〕; a layer of sediment: 하안(河岸) ~층 a river drift.

**퇴정**(退廷) ~하다 ①《조정에서》 leave (the royal) court. ②《법정에서》 leave the court 〔courtroom〕. ¶ 판사는 그에게 ~을 명했다 The judge ordered him to leave the courtroom.

**퇴조**(退潮) ①《썰물》 the ebb 〔low〕 tide; the ebbing 〔falling〕 tide. ¶ ~시

에 at low water. ②《쇠퇴》 decline; a downward trend〔tendency〕. ¶ (사물이) ~를 보이다 be declining; be on the decline; be on the ebb / 철강 산업에도 ~의 기미가 보이기 시작했다 There are some signs that the steel industry is heading for a downturn.
◉ ~기(期) a period of ebb.

**퇴주**(退酒) sacrificial wine emptied from the cup (in order to refill it with fresh wine). ◉ ~기(器), 퇴줏그릇 a vessel for emptied wine.

**퇴직**(退職) 《정년의》 retirement; 《사직》 resignation. ~하다 retire; resign 《*one's* position》; leave〔retire from〕office 《at the age of 65, because of illness》; go out of office. ¶ ~을 명하다 retire 《*a person*》; place 《*a person*》 on the retired list / 연금을 주어 ~시키다 pension off 《*a person*》 / 일신상의 사정으로 ~하다 resign from *one's* job for personal reasons / 그는 ~ 권고를 받았다 He was advised to resign. / 그는 무능하다는 이유로 강제 ~당했다 He was compulsorily retired as incompetent. / 그 회사는 인원 삭감을 위하여 60세 이상의 직원에게 연금을 주어 ~시켰다 The company cut back on staff by pensioning off employees aged over 60.
◉ ~공무원 a retired official. ~수당 ⇨ 퇴직금. ~연금 a retirement annuity〔pension〕; an old-age pension. ~연령 the retirement age. ~연한(年限) the age limit (for retirement). ~원(願) *one's* resignation: ~원을 제출하다 hand in *one's* resignation. ~자 a retired person〔employee〕; a retiree 《미》. ~적립금 a reserve (fund) for retirement allowance; 자원〔명예〕~ voluntary retirement〔resignation〕.

**퇴직금**(退職金) 《정년에 의한》 a retirement allowance〔grant〕; retirement pay〔benefit〕; 《해고시의》 a discharge〔severance〕 allowance; 《영》 redundancy pay. ◉ 일시~ a lump sum retirement allowance; a retirement lump sum grant.

**퇴진**(退陣) decampment; [비유적] retirement. ~하다 decamp; withdraw; [비유적] retire 《from a position》; give up *one's* position; step down; resign; go out of office. ¶ 곧 ~하는 총리 the outgoing premier / 내각의 총~을 요구하다 ask the Cabinet to resign *en bloc* / 그는 이미 일선에서 ~해 있다 He is now relieved of a responsible position. / 그의 ~이 가깝다 He is on the way out.

**퇴짜**(退—) rejection; refusal; a turndown; a setdown; rebuff; a reject. ~놓다 reject; refuse; rebuff; turn down. ¶ 여자에게 ~ 맞은 남자 a jilted lover / ~맞다 be rejected; meet with refusal; meet a rebuff; be turned down / 여지없이 ~ 놓다 give a flat refusal; refuse point-blank; squarely reject / 월급을 올려 달랬다가 ~ 맞았다 I asked for a raise (in pay) but got turned down. / 그가 청혼했을 때 그녀는 ~를 놓았다 She refused him when he begged her to marry him. / 회사측은 노조의 임금 인상 요구를 ~ 놨다 The management flatly「rejected〔turned down〕 the union's demand for higher wages.

**퇴청**(退廳) ~하다 leave the (government) office for the day. ◉ ~ 시간 the closing hour〔time〕《of a government office》.

**퇴출**(退出) leaving; withdrawal. ~하다 leave 《*one's* office》; retire〔withdraw〕《from》.

**퇴치**(退治) ①《정복》 conquest; subjugation; suppression. ~하다 conquer; subdue; suppress; subjugate. ¶ 괴물을 ~하다 slay〔kill〕 a monster / 폭력배를 ~하다 subjugate gangsters. ②《박멸》 extirpation; extermination; wiping〔stamping〕 out. ~하다 wipe〔stamp, root〕 out; clean up; exterminate; extirpate; eradicate; eliminate; get rid of; destroy. ¶ 쥐를 ~하다 exterminate rats; rid 《a house》 of rats / 말라리아를 ~하다 eliminate〔stamp out〕 malaria / 가난과 질병을 ~하다 wipe〔stamp〕 out disease and poverty / 부엌에서 바퀴벌레를 ~하려면 어떻게 하죠 What can I do to rid the kitchen of cockroaches?
◉ 문맹~ a crusade against illiteracy.

**퇴침**(退枕) a "box pillow"; a kind of wooden pillow with drawers in it. ¶ ~을 베다 rest *one's* head on a "box pillow".

**퇴폐**(頹廢) 《도덕·풍기의》 corruption; degeneration; demoralization; decadence. ~하다 degenerate; decay; decline; be corrupted; be demoralized. ¶ ~한, ~적인 decadent; declining / 도의의 ~ decadence; moral decay / ~한 세상 the decadent world / ~적인 영화 a decadent film / ~(적인) 문학 decadent literature / 도의의 ~가

오늘날과 같이 심한 때는 없었다 Never have public morals been more deplorably corrupt.
◉ ~기(期) a period of decadence. ~영업 a decadent entertainment business. ~(유흥)업소 a decadent business 〔entertainment〕 establishment. ~이용업소 barbershops providing lewd services to customers. ~주의 decadence: ~주의자 a decadent. ~풍조 decadent (and degenerating) trend: ~풍조 퇴치 운동 an anti-decadence drive.

**퇴하다**(退―) 《물리치다》 reject; turn down; send back; refuse to accept 〔receive〕. ¶ 뇌물을 ~ reject the bribe / 선물을 ~ refuse to accept a present / 혼담을 ~ turn down a proposal of marriage.

**퇴학**(退學) ① 《스스로》 leaving school (before graduation); (a) withdrawal from school. ~하다 leave 〔quit, withdraw from〕 school 〔college〕. ¶ 중도 ~하다 leave school halfway; leave 《university》 before graduation; drop out (of school) / 유급이 되어 ~하다 flunk out of 《a university》 / 가정 형편으로 ~하다 leave school 「for family reasons 〔owing to family circumstances〕 / ~시키다 《학부형이》 remove 〔withdraw〕 《*one's* son》 from school; take 《*one's* son》 out of school / 그는 병 때문에 대학을 중도에서 ~했다 「Owing to 〔On account of〕 illness he left university before graduation.
② 《학교가》 expulsion from school. ¶ ~시키다 expel 〔dismiss〕 《a student》 from school; take 《a student》 out of school / ~(을) 당하다 be expelled 〔dismissed〕 from school.
◉ ~생 a dropout; an expelled student. ~신고 a notice of quitting 〔leaving〕 school. ~처분 expulsion of a student from a school.

**퇴행**(退行) ① ⇨ 퇴화. ② 〖심리·천문〗 regression.

**퇴혼하다**(退婚―) decline a proposal of marriage; break off an engagement.

**퇴화**(退化) 〖생물·의학〗 retrogression; degeneration; 《기관 등의》 atrophy. ~하다 degenerate; retrograde; deteriorate; 《기관 등이》 atrophy; be atrophied. ¶ ~된 degraded; degenerate(d); atrophied / ~시키다 degenerate; degrade / 문명을 ~시키다 set back civilization / 고래는 뒷발이 ~돼 있다 The whale has its hind legs degenerated. / 사용하지 않는 기관은 ~한다 An unused organ will atrophy.
◉ ~기관(器官) 〖생물〗 a rudiment; a rudimentary organ. ~동물 a degenerate (animal). ~작용 the process of degeneration.

**퇴회**(退會) withdrawal 《from a party, from membership》. ~하다 withdraw 《from》; leave 《a society》; resign *one's* membership.

**툇도리**(退―) 〖건축〗 the beams of 「a verandah 〔an anteroom〕.

**툇마루**(退―) the floor of a Korean verandah.

**투**(套) ① 《버릇》 a habitual way; a habit; a way; a manner. ¶ 말투 *one's* way of talking; the way *one* talks / 독특한 말투 *one's* peculiar way of speaking; *one's* peculiarity in speech / 그는 말투가 이상하다 He has a quaint way of speaking. / 그의 일하는 투가 마음에 안 든다 I am disgusted with his way of doing things. *or* I don't like the way he does things.
② 《법식》 a form; a style. ¶ 편지투 the forms of letter writing / 옛투 an old style; a conventional form / 춘원(春園)투의 소설 a novel written in the style of Ch'unwon's.

**투견**(鬪犬) 《싸움》 a dogfight; 《개》 a fighting dog.

**투계**(鬪鷄) 《쌈닭》 a fighting cock; a gamecock; a game fowl; 《닭쌈》 cockfighting; a cockfight. ◉ ~장 a cockpit.

**투고**(投稿) a contribution. ~하다 contribute 《(an article) to a periodical》; write 《for a magazine》. ¶ ~ 환영 All contributions are welcome. *or* Open to all contributors. / 그는 종종 이 잡지에 ~한다 He is a frequent contributor to this magazine. / 본지(本誌)에의 ~를 환영합니다 You are cordially asked to write for our magazine.
◉ ~란(欄) a readers 〔contributors'〕 columns. ~자 a contributor.

**투과**(透過) penetration; permeation. ~하다 transmit; penetrate; permeate 《through》; filter 《out》. ¶ 방사능은 철판도 ~한다 Radioactivity can even penetrate an iron plate. ◉ ~성 permeability: ~성의 막(膜) a permeable membrane.

**투광기**(投光器) a floodlight; a light projector (장치).

**투구** a (war) helmet; a headpiece; a headgear. ¶ ~를 쓰다 wear a helmet / ~를 벗다 take *one's* helmet off.
◉ ~끈 a helmet cord.

**투구**(投球) 〖야구〗 《야수의》 throwing; a throw; 《투수의》 pitching; a pitch; delivery. ～하다 pitch 〔throw, hurl〕 a ball; make a throw 《to》. ¶ 왼손～ left-handed pitching / 멋진 ～ fine delivery; neat pitching / 첫～는 폭투(暴投)가 되었다 The first pitch went wild. / 그는 두번째 ～를 왼쪽 스탠드로 쳐냈다 He whacked the second delivery into the left field stands.
◉ ～동작 a windup. ～연습 a warming up for pitching.

**투구벌레** 〖곤충〗 a beetle; a coleopteron (*pl.* -ra).

**투그리다** snarl 〔howl, growl〕 ready to 「fight.

**투기**(投棄) abandonment. ～하다 throw 〔cast〕 《*something*》 away; dump 《waste into a river》. ¶ 쓰레기를 노상에 불법 ～하다 throw away the rubbish illegally on the road.

**투기**(投機) (a) speculation; a flier 《미구어》; a venture. ～하다 speculate 《in》; make a venture; gamble 《in》.
¶ ～적인 speculative; risky / ～ 억제 대책 the anti-speculation measures / ～에 성공하다 make a hit in a speculation / ～에 손을 대다 dabble in speculation / ～에 실패하다 fail in speculation / 주식〔토지〕에 ～하다 speculate in stocks 〔land〕 / ～로 벌다〔손해보다〕 「make money 〔be hard hit〕 in speculation / ～에 손을 대어 큰 손해를 보다 lose heavily in speculation / ～목적으로 사다 buy 《a house》 on speculation / 부동산은 더 이상 ～적인 매매의 대상이 안 된다 Real estate will no longer be subject to speculative hoarding and selling.
◉ ～꾼〔업자〕 a (professional) speculator; 《주식》 a stockjobber. ～매매 sales by speculation; speculative trading 〔sales〕. ～매입 a speculative buying. ～방지법 the Antiprofiteering Law. ～사업 a speculative venture 〔business〕. ～시장 a speculative market. ～심 a speculative streak 〔disposition〕; a gambling spirit: ～심을 일으키다 be tempted to speculate. ～심리 speculative psychology. ～열 a craze 〔mania〕 for speculation; speculative enthusiasm 〔craze〕. ～자본 〖경제〗 《미》 venture capital; 《영》 risk capital. ～주(株) a speculative stock.
부동산～ speculation in real estate: 전국적으로 부동산 ～가 다시 일어날 조짐 signs of recurrence of speculative investment in real estate across the country.

**투기**(妬忌) jealousy; green envy; heartburning ～하다 be 〔feel〕 jealous 《of, over》; envy 《*a person*》. ¶ ～심 많은 jealous; envious / ～로 애태우다 be consumed with jealousy.

**투기**(鬪技) a contest; a match; a bout.
◉ ～자 a contestant; a competitor. ～장 an arena; a ring.

**투깔스럽다** (be) coarse; rough; crude.

**투덜거리다** grumble 《at, about》; complain 《of》; mutter 《about》; murmur (with discontent); 《미》 gripe 《at, about》. ¶ 투덜거리는 사람 a grumbler / 대우가 나쁘다고 ～ complain of ill treatment; 《봉급의 경우》 complain that *one* is not paid well / 투덜거리지 마라 Never grumble so! / 무엇이 못마땅한지 그는 밤낮 투덜거리기만 한다 I don't know what is biting him, but he keeps bitching all the time. / 그는 혼자 투덜거리며 가버렸다 He went away muttering to himself. 「ble.

**투레질** (a baby's) burbling. ～하다 bur-

**투망**(投網) a cast(ing) net. ～하다 cast a net; throw a cast-net. ¶ ～의 호적지 a good cast / ～하러 가다 go cast=netting.

**투매**(投賣) a sacrifice sale; 《재고 정리》 a clearance sale; 《해외 시장의》 dumping. ～하다 sell 《*something*》 at a loss 〔sacrifice〕; sacrifice 《goods》; dump 《goods abroad》. ¶ 그들은 재고품을 해외 시장에서 ～했다 They sold their stock at a sacrifice on the overseas market. / 그들은 해외 시장에서 잉여 물자를 ～하려고 한다 They are trying to dump surplus goods on the overseas market. ◉ ～가격 a bargain 〔sacrifice〕 price. ～시장 a dumping field. ～품 sacrifice goods. 출혈～ a distress 〔slaughter〕 sale.

**투명**(透明) transparency; pellucidity; clarity. ～하다 (be) transparent; pellucid; limpid; clear; lucid. ¶ 불～한 opaque; milky; turbid; cloudy / 반～의 semitransparent; translucent; translucid / 무색 ～한 colorless and transparent / ～한 물 clear 〔crystal〕 water / ～해지다 become transparent; clarify.
◉ ～기수(機首) 〖공군〗 《폭격기 등의》 transparent nose; plexiglas nose. ～도 transparency; the degree of clearness: 호수의 ～도를 재다 measure the clarity of the water in the lake. ～유리 plain (plate) glass. ～인간 an invisible man. ～전구 a clear bulb.

～지(紙) tracing paper. ～질(質) 〖생물〗 hyaloplasm. ～체 a transparent body. ～캐비닛 a see-through cabinet.

**투묘**(投錨) anchoring; anchorage. ～하다 anchor; drop 〔cast〕 anchor; come to anchor. ¶ ～되어 있다 lie 〔be〕 at anchor. ◉ ～지 an anchorage.

**투미하다** (be) dull; stupid; stolid.

**투밀이** 〖건축〗 ～하다 round off the edges of (lattice strips).

**투박스럽다, 투박하다** ① 《사람이》 (be) clumsy; gawky; awkward; vulgar; crude; uncouth; boorish; uncivilized. ② 《물건이》 (be) crude; coarse; unshapely; ungraceful; awkward-looking. ¶ 투박스러운 구두 heavy unshapely shoes; clodhoppers / 투박스러운 그릇 crudely made dishes; crockery / 투박한 손 rough hands / 투박스러운 천 thick coarse fabric.

**투베르쿨린** 〖의학〗 tuberculin. ¶ ～ 검사를 한 tuberculin-tested (생략 T.T.) / ～ 검사를 받다 be tuberculin-tested. ◉ ～반응 a tuberculin reaction: ～ 반응 검사 a tuberculin test / 음성〔양성〕 ～ 반응 a negative 〔positive〕 reaction of a tuberculin test / ～ 반응을 보다 examine the responsive effect of tuberculin. ～요법 tuberculin treatment. ～주사액 tuberculin.

**투병**(鬪病) a struggle 〔fight〕 against a disease. ¶ 그는 ～ 생활 10년이 된다 He has lived ten years of his life under medical treatment. *or* He has struggled 〔fought〕 against the disease for ten years. ◉ ～생활 *one's* life under medical treatment.

**투사**(投射) 〖수학·심리〗 projecting; 〖전자〗 projection; 〖물리〗 incidence. ～하다 project 《on》. ¶ …에 광선을 ～하다 project a beam of light on to. ◉ ～각 an angle of incidence 〔projection〕. ～광 transmitted light. ～면 a plane of incidence. ～물 a projectile. ～법 〖심리〗 projective technique. ～선 an incident ray. ～영(影) a (picture) projection.

**투사**(透寫) tracing. ～하다 trace (out) 《a writing, a drawing》. ◉ ～지 《a sheet of》 tracing paper.

**투사**(鬪士) a fighter; a combatant; a champion. ¶ 노동 운동의 ～ a fighter for labor; a labor agitator / 자유의 ～ a fighter for freedom; a champion of liberty / 독립～ a leader of national independence movement / 혁명～ a champion of revolution.

◉ ～형(型) 〖심리〗 the athletic (type).

**투서**(投書) 《밀고》 an anonymous notice 〔letter〕; 《투고》 a contribution; a letter from a reader (to the editor) (독자의). ～하다 send 《a note》 anonymously; 《투고》 contribute; send a contribution 《to a magazine, *etc.*》; write (a letter) to 《the *Tong-a*》. ¶ ～ 환영 Contributions are cordially invited. / "타임지에 ～하겠다"고 하는 것이 영국인의 상투적인 협박 문구이다 "I will write to the Times" is a favorite threat of Britons. / 귀지(貴紙)에 ～를 게재하여 주시기를 부탁드립니다 I venture to ask you for the hospitality of your columns. ◉ ～란(欄) the contributors' 〔readers'〕 column: ～란 편집자 a letter(s) editor. ～인 a (letter) contributor; a correspondent. ～함 a box for receiving unsigned complaints; a complaints 〔suggestion〕 box.

**투석**(投石) stone-throwing〔-hurling〕. ～하다 throw 〔cast, hurl〕 a stone 〔rock〕 《at》. ◉ ～기(器) a catapult. ～전(戰) a fight with stone missiles.

**-투성이** 《…로 덮인》 covered 〔smeared〕 all over with; 《…이 많은》 full of; filled with. ¶ 오자(誤字) 투성이의 책 a book full of misprints / 흙투성이의 차 a car splashed all over with mud / 땀투성이다 be all of 〔in〕 a sweat / (온통) 빚투성이다 have many debts / 피투성이가 되다 be smeared 〔covered〕 with blood; be bathed in blood / 옷이 흙투성이가 되다 *one's* clothes get all covered with mud; get *one's* clothes splattered with mud / 그 여자의 이야기는 모두 거짓말투성이였다 Her whole story was a tissue of lies.

**투수**(投手) 〖야구〗 a pitcher; a hurler; a twirler 《구어》; a moundsman. ¶ 승리〔패전〕～ a winning 〔losing〕 pitcher / 구원～ a relief pitcher / 선발～ a starting pitcher / 완투～ a thorough going pitcher / 10승 ～ a 10-game winner / 궁지에 몰린 ～ a pitcher in the hole 《미》 / ～를 하다 pitch 〔hurl〕 《for *one's* team》; take the mound / ～를 교체하다 change 〔shift〕 the pitcher. ◉ ～전 a pitchers' battle; a hurling 〔pitching, mound〕 duel. ～진 the pitching 〔mound〕 staff; the hill staff. ～판 a pitcher's plate 〔box〕; the mound; the rubber 《미구어》. 우완～ a right-handed pitcher; a right-hander. 좌완～ a left-handed pitcher; a left-hander; a southpaw (pitcher). 주전～ an ace (pitcher).

**투숙**(投宿) putting up 〔registering〕《at a hotel》; stopping 〔staying〕 at 《a hotel》. ～하다 stop 〔put up〕 at 《a hotel》; lodge 《at a hotel》; check into 《a hotel》. ¶ 함께 ～하다 stay at the same hotel; 《한 방에》 share a room 《with》. ◉ ～객 a guest (registered at hotel); a lodger. 장기 ～ 호텔 a residential hotel; a long-term lodging hotel.

**투시**(透視) ① 《비추어 봄》 seeing through. ～하다 see through. ② 《X선의》 fluoroscopy; roentgenoscopy; examination by fluoroscopy. ～하다 examine by fluoroscopy; look at 《*a person's* chest》 through the fluoroscope. ③ 《천리안》 clairvoyance; second sight. ～하다 divine; see through; sense (psychically, through telepathy).
◉ ～검사 《X선의》 fluoroscopy. ～경(鏡) a fluoroscope. ～도 a perspective drawing 〔view〕; an opened-up view 《of a factory》 showing the interior. ～도법 perspective (representation): ～도법으로 그리다 draw in perspective. ～력 《광학 기계의》 penetration; 《꿰뚫어 보는》 clairvoyant 〔psychic〕 power. ～화법 ＝～도법.

**투신하다**(投身—) ① 《종사·진출하다》 engage 《in》; plunge 〔launch〕 into 《politics》; embark in 〔launch forth on〕 《an enterprise》. ¶ 사업에 ～ launch out 〔forth〕 on an enterprise; embark in 〔upon〕 an enterprise / 정계에 ～ enter the political world; enter 〔launch〕 into politics; take up politics as a career / 정당에 ～ join 〔cast *one's* lot with〕 a party / 그는 실업계에 투신하고 있다 He is engaged in the business world.
② 《몸던져 자살하다》 drown *oneself* (in the water); throw *oneself* into the water 〔river〕; "jump off the bridge"; kill *oneself* by throwing *oneself* in front of a running train. ¶ 투신한 시체를 건져 올리다 pull a body from a watery grave / 어젯밤에 한강에 투신자살한 사람이 있었다 Last night someone drowned himself in the Han River.

**투실투실** ⇨ 토실토실.

**투심**(妬心) jealousy; envy.

**투약**(投藥) medication; prescription (of medicine); dosage. ～하다 give 〔administer〕 (a dose of) medicine to 《a patient》; 《처방을 내주다》 prescribe (a medicine) for 《a disease》. ¶ 과잉～ excessive dosing 〔medication〕; overdosing; overdosage / 환자에게 ～하다 prescribe for a patient; dose a patient. ◉ ～대(代) medication cost. ～량 dosage; a dose. ～창구(窓口) a medicine window; a pharmacist office (약국의).

**투어리스트** 《여행자·관광객》 a tourist. ◉ ～클래스 《여객기·여객선의 2등칸》 tourist class. ～홈 《민박 가능한 집》 a tourist home.

**투여**(投與) medication. ⇨ 투약. ¶ 약을 ～하다 give medication 〔a drug, medicine〕 《to a patient》.

**투열**(透熱) 〖물리〗 ¶ ～의 diathermanous; diathermic. ◉ ～계 a diathermometer. ～성(性) diathermancy: ～성의 diathermanous. ～요법 diathermy; diathermic treatment.

**투영**(投影) ① 《그림자》 a (cast) shadow. ～하다 project; reflect; cast a reflection 《on, in》; throw an image on. ¶ ～시키다 shed light 《on》.
② 〖수학·심리·미술〗 projection. ～하다 project 《an article》.
◉ ～기(機) a projector. ～도〔화〕 a projection chart 〔drawing〕; a raised plan; 〖기하학〗 a projected figure: ～도법〔화법〕 the method of projections. ～면 a projected plane; a plane 〔surface〕 of projection. ～법 〖심리〗 projective technique. 구면 ～법 《지도의》 globular projection.

**투옥**(投獄) imprisonment; confinement; jailing. ～하다 cast 〔throw〕 《*a person*》 into prison; put 《*a person*》 in jail 〔prison, behind bars〕; imprison; jail; commit 《*a person*》 to prison; run in 《구어》. ¶ ～되어 있는 behind bars 《구어》 / ～당하다 be put in jail; be taken 〔sent〕 to jail; be flung into jail; be consigned to prison.

**투우**(鬪牛) 《소》 a fighting bull; 《싸움》 a bullfight; bullfighting; blood sports. ～하다 fight a bull; have a bullfight; have bulls fight (each other). ◉ ～사 a bullfighter; a matador; a toreador (마상의). ～장 a bullring.

**투원반**(投圓盤) 〖스포츠〗 the discus (throw). ～하다 throw a discus.
◉ ～선수〔경기자〕 a discus thrower.

**투입**(投入) ① 《던져 넣음》 throwing 〔putting〕 in(to). ～하다 throw 〔cast〕 in(to); put in(to); 《인원 등을》 order 《troops》 in; commit to; 〖화학〗 project 《into, on》. ¶ ～병력 commitment /

대량 ~ a massive commitment《of manpower》/ 그것을 위해 ~된 노력 the work that has been put into it / 공격에 ~하다 throw《battalion》into attack / 전선(戰線)에 재~하다 recommit《a regiment》to battle / 미국은 그 전투에 2개 보병 사단을 ~했다 The U.S. committed two infantry divisions in the battle.
② 《자금 등의》 investment. ~하다 invest《capital in》; lay out〔sink〕《capital in some venture》; spend〔expend〕《money on anything》. ¶ 비료의 ~량 the input of manure / 5천만 원을 ~해서 지은 집 a house built at a cost of fifty million won / 회사 주식에 가진 돈을 몽땅 ~하다 invest all *one's* money in a company's stock.
◉ ~량 an input (자본재나 용역의). ~용량〖전기〗making capacity. ~자본 an investment. 동전~구《자동 판매기 등의》a slot. 우편물~구 a letter drop.

**투자**(投資) (an) investment. ~하다 invest in; make an investment in; lay〔put〕out《*one's* money》in;《가망 없는 사업에》sink《money, capital》in. ¶ ~ 및 기타의 자산 합계〖경영〗total investment and other assets / 확실〔유리〕한 ~ a sound〔good〕investment / 부차적 ~ a side investment / 토지에 ~하다 invest〔sink〕*one's* money in land; put *one's* money into land / 광산에 거액의 ~를 하다 invest heavily in a mine / 가진 돈을 가장 유리하게 ~하다 place *one's* money to the best advantage / (이익을) 다시 그 사업에 ~하다 plow back《the profits》into the enterprise / 재산을 한 사업에 몽땅 ~하다 put all *one's* eggs in one basket / ~로 다액의 수익을 얻다 get a good return on an investment / 국내 시장을 외국의 직접 ~가 가능하도록 개방하다 open the domestic market to foreign direct investment.
◉ ~가〔자〕an investor: 기관 ~가 an institutional investor / 일반 ~가 the investing public; general investors. ~감세(減稅) an investment tax credit. ~계획 an investment program〔plan〕; investment planning. ~상담소 an investment counsel office. ~성향(性向) readiness to invest: 기업의 ~성향은 계속 높아가고 있다 Industry's readiness to invest continues to rise. ~수익률 rate of return on common stocks〔on investment〕. ~순위 investment priority. ~시장 an investment market. ~신탁 (an) investment trust: ~ 신탁 회사 an investment trust company / ~ 신탁에 돈을 맡기다 have *one's* money trusted with an investment company. ~액 an amount invested. ~유인(誘因) an investment incentive. ~은행 an investment bank. ~의욕(意慾) willingness to risk money. ~자본 invested capital. ~주식〔증권, 채권〕an investment stock〔security, bond〕. ~환경 (an) investment climate〔environment〕: 국내의 외국 ~ 환경을 개선하다 improve the nation's foreign investment environment. ~회사 an investment company. 개인~ an individual investment. 공공~ public investment. 민간~ private investment. 국민 ~ 기금 the National Investment Fund. 국제 ~ 보증 기구 MIGA. [<*M*ultilateral *I*nvestment *G*uarantee *A*gency] 한국 ~ 개발 공사 the Korea Investment Development Corporation. 한국 ~ 금융 회사 the Korea Investment and Finance Corporation.

**투쟁**(鬪爭) a fight; (a) combat; a struggle; a conflict; strife;《파업》a strike. ~하다 fight《for, against》; struggle. ¶ 노사간의 ~ strife between capital and labor / 인종간의 ~ racial strife〔conflicts〕/ ~적인 combative / 인간은 선사시대 이래 자연과 ~해 왔다 Man has been struggling against nature since prehistoric times. ◉ ~방침 a struggle policy. ~본능 fighting instinct(s). ~본부 the strikers' headquarters. ~심 a combative spirit. ~위원회 a strike committee. ~의식 strife consciousness. ~자금 a strike fund. ~전술 struggle tactics. ~태세 a struggle set-up. ~파 the militants.

**투전**(投錢) = 돈치기.

**투전**(鬪牋) 《패(牌)》 Korean playing cards;《놀이》a game of cards; gambling; gaming. ~하다 play cards; gamble. ¶ ~판에서 재산을 날리다 lose *one's* fortune at the gambling den〔place〕. ◉ ~꾼 a cardplayer; a gambler.

**투정** complaining; grumbling; growling. ~하다 grumble for《*something*》; complain《about, of》; growl. ¶ 시계 사 달라고 ~하다 grumble after《*a person*》to buy *one* a watch / 돈 달라고 ~하다 press importunately《*a person*》for money / 과자를 달라고 ~하다 clamor for candy. ◉ ~질 =투정. 밥~ grumbling over〔at〕*one's* food. 잠~

growling when *one* wakes up.

**투조**(透彫) 〖미술〗 openwork. ¶ ～의 open-worked.

**투지**(鬪志) fighting 〔combative〕 spirit. ¶ ～를 보이다 show fight / ～ 만만하다 have a great deal of fight (in *one*); be full of fight / ～를 잃다 lose fighting spirit / ～에 불타다 burn with combativeness; be full of fight.

**투창**(投槍) 〖스포츠〗 javelin (throw). ～하다 throw a javelin. ◉ ～선수 a javelin thrower.

**투척**(投擲) throwing; a throw. ～하다 throw. ¶ 수류탄을 ～하다 throw a hand grenade. ◉ ～경기 a throwing event.

**투철**(透徹) penetration; thoroughness. ～하다 (be) penetrating; lucid; limpid; clear; thorough; thoroughgoing. ¶ ～한 이론 intelligible theory / ～한 두뇌 clear brains / ～한 민족주의자 a nationalist to the bone.

**투포환**(投砲丸) 〖스포츠〗 shot-put(ting). ～하다 put a shot. ◉ ～선수 a shot-putter.

**투표**(投票) 《표결》 vote; suffrage; 《투표를 하기》 poll; ballot; voting; balloting. ～하다 ballot 《for》; cast a ballot; vote 《미》; cast a 〔*one's*〕 vote 《for》; poll; 《실시하다》 take 〔hold〕 a ballot; take a vote 《for...》. ¶ ～의 결과 the voting results / ～하러 가다 go to the poll 〔the polls 《미》〕 / 보수당 후보에게 ～하다 vote the Conservative ticket / P씨에 ～하다「give *one's* vote to 〔vote for〕 Mr. P / …에게 ～하도록 간청하다 ask 《*a person*》 to vote for...; solicit votes for; canvass for....

투표에: ～에 부치다 put 《the question, a bill》 to the 〔a〕 vote; put 《a proposition》 on the ballot; submit 《a bill》 to a ballot; take a ballot 《on a question》 / ～에 이기다 beat 《another》 at the poll; outvote 《another》; win a ballot / ～에 지다 be outvoted.

투표로: 무～로 without vote 〔voting〕 / ～로 결정하다 determine 〔decide, settle〕 by ballot 〔vote, poll〕 / ～로 부결하다 vote down 《a measure》 / ～로 뽑다〔선거하다〕 elect by vote; vote by ballot.

투표를: …에 찬성 ～를 하다 vote for 〔in favor of〕...; ballot for... / …에 반대 ～를 하다 vote against 〔in opposition to〕...; ballot against ... / 재～를 요구하다 demand a new ballot.

¶ ～ 결과는 찬성 20, 반대 10표였다 The vote stood at twenty ayes and ten noes. / 그 당은 ～수의 4분의 1을 얻었을 뿐이었다 The party only polled a quarter of the votes cast. / 나는 K씨에게 ～했다 I gave my vote to Mr. K. / 몇몇 회원은 그에게 반대 ～했다 Some members of the club blackballed him.

◉ ～계표원 a tally clerk. ～구 a voting 〔polling〕 district. ～기 a voting machine. ～마감 closing of the poll 〔vote〕. ～소 a polling place 〔station〕; a polling 〔voting〕 booth; the polls 《미》. ～수 the votes cast. ～(용)지 a ballot 〔voting〕 paper; a ballot. ～율 the voting rate 《of women》. ～일 a voting day. ～자 a voter. ～참관인 an official observer at polling station; a voting witness. ～함(函) a ballot box: 투표가 끝나면 ～함은 봉인된다 After voting is over, the ballot box is sealed.

부정～ an illegal 〔unjust〕 ballot. 신임～ a vote of confidence. 직접～ 《put it to》 a direct (popular) vote; 《elected by》 direct vote of the people.

**투표권**(投票權) the (right to) vote; *one's* voting power. ¶ ～을 행사하다 exercise *one's* voting power / ～을 주다 qualify 《*a person*》 as voter / ～을 빼앗다 deprive 《*a person*》 of the right to vote / ～을 잃다 lose *one's* vote.

**투피스** a two-piece suit 〔dress〕.

**투하**(投下) throwing down; dropping; 《자본을》 invest 《in》. ～하다 《높은 데서》 throw down; drop; 《자본을》 invest 〔sink〕 《in》. ¶ 폭탄을 ～하다 drop bombs 《upon》 / 의료품을 ～하다 (air-) drop medical supplies / 주식에 자본을 ～하다 invest *one's* money in stocks. ◉ ～자본 invested capital. ～탄 a dropped bomb.

**투하**(投荷) 〖보험〗 《난파선 등에서 짐을 던짐》 jettison; 《그 화물》 jetsam; jettisoned goods 〔cargo〕. ～하다 jettison cargo; cast cargo overboard.

**투함**(投函) ～하다 drop 《it》 in a box; put 《a letter》 into a mailbox; 《미》 mail; 《영》 post. ¶ 투표지를 투표함에 ～하다 deposit a ballot in the ballot box.

**투항**(投降) (a) surrender. ～하다 surrender 《to the enemy》; lay down *one's* arms. ¶ 조건부로 ～하다 surrender on stated conditions / 우리는 결코 ～하지 않겠다 We shall never surrender. / 납치범들은 곧 경찰에 ～했다 The hijackers soon surrendered to the police. ◉ ~자 one who surrenders.

**투해머**(投—) 〖스포츠〗 the hammer throw(ing). ~하다 throw a hammer. ◉ ~선수 a hammer thrower.

**투혼**(鬪魂) fighting 〔combative〕 spirit.

**툭, 툭탁, 툭툭** ⇨ 톡, 톡탁, 톡톡.

**툭하면** at the slightest provocation; at the drop of a hat; without any reason; always; be apt to; ready to. ¶ ~ …하다 be apt 〔liable, prone〕 to 《*do*》/ ~ 사람을 치다 ready to punch a person; punch a person at the slightest provocation / ~ 싸우다 pick a fight at the slightest provocation / 너는 ~ 나를 욕한다 You choose every opportunity to insult me.

**툰드라** tundra. ◉ ~지대 a tundra area.

**툴륨** 〖화학〗 thulium.

**툴툴거리다** complain angrily; grumble; growl. ¶ 월급이 적다고 ~ complain about the salary / 사진기를 사 주지 않는다고 아버지에게 ~ grumble at his father for not buying him a camera.

**툽상스럽다** ① 《사람이》 (be) clumsy; gawky; awkward; vulgar; crude; uncouth; boorish; uncivilized. ② 《사물이》 (be) crude; coarse; unshapely; unwieldy; ungraceful; awkward-looking.

**퉁**[1] 《놋쇠》 inferior 〔cheap〕 brass.

**퉁**[2] 《소리》 booming; with a boom. ¶ 북을 퉁 울리다 boom a drum; beat a drum / 대포를 퉁 쏘다 boom a gun; fire a gun with a boom.

**퉁가리** 〖어류〗 a kind of freshwater catfish.

**퉁겨지다** ① 《꼭 짜여 있던 것이》 be off; come apart; get out of place; 《뼈마디 등이》 be put out of joint; be dislocated 〔disjointed〕; be disconnected. ¶ 책상 다리가 ~ the leg of a table gets disjointed. ② 《일이》 get disclosed; be revealed; come 〔be〕 out; be laid bare; come 〔be brought〕 to light. ¶ 비밀이 ~ a secret is disclosed.

**퉁구스** a Tungus (*pl.* ~(es)); a Tunguz (*pl.* ~(es)). ◉ ~어 Tungus.

**퉁기다** ① 《버틴 것을》 loosen 《it》; take 《it》 apart; get 《it》 out of place. ¶ 기둥 받침을 ~ slip a pillar stay. ② 《현악기를》 pluck the strings 《of a *kayagŭm*》; thrum (on); strum (on). ¶ 기타 줄을 ~ pick 〔thrum (on)〕 a guitar. ③ 《기회를》 miss; let go. ¶ 기회를 ~ miss 〔let go, let slip〕 a chance. ④ 《뼈를》 put 《it》 out of joint; dislocate. ¶ 뼈를 ~ dislocate a bone.

**퉁맞다** ⇨ 퉁바리맞다.

**퉁명스럽다** (be) blunt; brusque; gruff; curt; unaffable. ¶ 퉁명스럽게 curtly; brusquely; bluntly / 퉁명스러운 사람 a blunt 〔gruffish〕 person / 퉁명스럽게 대답하다 give a curt 〔blunt〕 answer; reply brusquely 〔snappishly〕 / 퉁명스럽게 말하다 talk bluntly; speak stiffly; be blunt of speech / 그녀는 언제나 나에게 퉁명스럽게 군다 She is always brusque 〔curt〕 with me.

**퉁바리** a woman's rice-bowl made of cheap brass. ~맞다 get rudely rebuffed; suffer 〔meet with〕 a rebuff.

**퉁방울** ① 《방울》 a brass bell. ② 《눈》 large protruding eyes; goggle 〔pop, lobster〕 eyes. ◉ ~이 a pop-〔lobster-〕eyed person; a pop-eye.

**퉁부처** a brass statue of Buddha.

**퉁소** a bamboo flute. ¶ ~를 불다 play 〔blow on〕 the bamboo flute.

**퉁어리적다** (be) senseless; reckless (in behavior).

**퉁주발**(—周鉢) a cheap brass rice-bowl.

**퉁탕거리다** ① 《구르는 소리》 keep beating 〔pounding, pattering〕. ¶ 어린애가 퉁탕거리며 마루 위를 뛰어다닌다 A child is scampering around on the floor. ② 《총소리》 keep banging away. ¶ 총 소리가 ~ a gun is 〔guns are〕 banging away.

**퉁탕퉁탕** ① 《구르는 소리》 beating 〔pounding, pattering〕 repeatedly. ② 《총소리》 banging repeatedly 〔confusedly〕. ¶ 총소리가 ~ 나다 guns are banging.

**퉤** spitting. ¶ 퉤퉤 spit-spit!

**튀각** flakes of kelp 〔tangle〕 deep-fried; deep-fried kelp 〔tangle〕.

**튀기** ① 《탁맥(駝驘)》 a hybrid between a male donkey and a cow. ② 《잡종·혼혈아》 a half-breed; a half-blood; a hybrid; a cross; a crossbreed. ¶ ~ 소녀 a half-breed girl / 한국 사람과 일본 사람의 ~ a person of mixed Korean and Japanese parentage / 백인과 흑인의 ~ a mulatto (*pl.* ~(e)s) / 노새는 말과 당나귀의 ~이다 A mule is a cross between a horse and an ass.

**튀기다**[1] ① 《손톱·손가락으로》 fillip; flip; snap; flick. ¶ 손가락으로 ~ flip 《*a thing*》 away with *one's* finger / 주판알을 ~ work the beads (on an 〔*one's*〕 abacus); [비유적] consult *one's* own interests.
② 《물 따위를》 splash 〔spatter〕 《*one's*

clothes with mud, mud on *one's* clothes》; dabble. ¶ 발로 물을 ~ splash the water with *one's* foot / 흙탕물(을) ~ splash mud about 〔over, on〕; 《사람에게》 splash 《*a person*》 with muddy water / 흙탕물을 튀기며 걸어가다 drabble along / 침을 튀기며 이야기하다 talk with *one's* spittle flying.
③ 《놀라게 하다》 start; scare away. ¶ 꿩을 ~ start a pheasant / 토끼를 굴에서 ~ start a hare from its burrow.
④ 《건드려 달아나게 하다》 send 《*a thing*》 flying; send 《*a thing*》 off.

**튀기다²** 《기름에》 fry; 《튀밥 등을》 pop. ¶ 닭을 기름에 ~ fry chicken in oil / 쌀을 ~ pop rice.

**튀김** 《음식》 (deep-)fried food; a fried dish; a fry; fritters; 《일》 frying. ¶ 굴 ~ fried oysters / ~ 기름 frying oil / ~ 덮밥 a bowl of rice topped with fries.

**튀니지** 《나라 이름》 Tunisia. ¶ ~의 Tunisian. ◉ ~ 사람 a Tunisian.

**튀다** ① 《탄력으로》 spring; bound; rebound; bounce.

> **용법** **spring** 정지 상태에서 갑자기 튀는 움직임. **bound** 계속해서 통통 튀면서 이동하는 움직임. **bounce** 공 따위가 표면에 부딪쳤다가 다시 튀어 오르는 움직임.

¶ (공이) 잘 ~ bound well / 쥐덫이 ~ a rattrap springs. ② 《터지는 힘으로》 snap; crack; crackle; pop (open); 《불똥 등이》 spark; sputter. ¶ 불똥이 ~ spark; emit 〔give off〕 sparks; sparks shoot up in the air / 숯불의 불꽃이 ~ the burning charcoal sputters / 장작이 타면서 ~ the firewood crackles as it burns. ③ 《침·물이》 spatter; splash; splatter; get spattered; be splashed. ¶ 얼굴에 침이 ~ *one's* face is spattered with saliva / 옷에 흙물이 ~ *one's* clothes are splashed 〔splattered〕 with muddy water. ④ 《달아나다》 fly (away); run away; make off; take to flight; flee. ¶ 도둑이 ~ a robber takes to flight.

**튀밥** popped rice.

**튀어나오다** ① 《돌출하다》 project; protrude; jut (out); strike 〔stick〕 out; stand out. ¶ 튀어나온 projecting; protruding; prominent; outthrust; 〖해부·동물〗 extensile / 담장 밖으로 튀어나온 소나무 a pine tree jutting beyond the walls / 정원 위로 튀어나와 있다 《the balcony》 jut out over the garden.
② 《밖으로》 run out; rush 〔burst〕 out; spring out; 《껑충》 jump 〔leap, bounce〕 out. ¶ 거리로 ~ rush out into the street / 방에서 ~ rush 〔run, dash, dart〕 out of the room; 《분연히》 fling away 《in a rage》 / 집을 ~ dart 〔rush〕 out of a house; 《가출하다》 run away from home; fly from *one's* home / 잠자리에서 ~ spring 〔nip 《영속어》〕 out of bed / 우리 속에서 ~ break out of a cage; break loose.

**튀하다** scald (in order to remove the hair from animals or the feathers from birds). ¶ 돼지를 더운 물로 ~ scald a pig in hot water.

**튜너** 《라디오·텔레비전의》 a tuner.

**튜바** 〖악기〗 a tuba.

**튜브** a tube; 《타이어 속의》 an inner (air)tube. ¶ ~에 든 그림물감 tube colors / ~에 든 치약 a tube of toothpaste / ~의 그림물감을 짜내다 squeeze paint from a tube.

**튜턴** Teuton. ¶ ~의 Teuton(ic). ◉ ~인종 the Teutonic race 〔peoples〕. ~족(族) the Teutons: ~족의 사람 a Teuton.

**튤립** 〖식물〗 a tulip.

**트다¹** ① 《싹이》 sprout; bud out; spring 〔come〕 up. ¶ 싹〔움〕이 ~ sprout; put forth 〔shoot out〕 buds; come into bud; bud out / 뽕나무가 파릇파릇 싹이 트기 시작했다 The mulberry trees have put forth their young green leaves.
② 《피부가》 crack; chap. ¶ 튼 손 chapped hands / 손이 ~ *one's* hands chap 〔get chapped〕; [사람이 주어] get chapped hands / 추우면 살갗이 잘 튼다 Cold weather chaps the skin. *or* The skin often chaps in cold weather.
③ 《동이》 break; break open; dawn. ¶ 동이 ~ dawn; the day breaks; the eastern sky turns gray / 먼동이 터온다 The eastern sky is gradually turning gray. *or* The dawn breaks.

**트다²** ① 《통하게 하다》 break 《it》 open; slit 《it》 open; open 《it》. ¶ 구멍을 ~ make a hole 《in》 / 길을 ~ break 〔build, open up〕 a road; break trail / 칸막이를 ~ take off a partition / 아귀를 ~ make a side slit 〔opening〕 / 두 방을 터서 하나로 하다 throw 〔knock〕 two room into one. ② 《개시하다》 open 《it》; begin 《it》; initiate 《it》. ¶ 거래를 ~ enter into a connection 〔business

relation] with; open 「correspondence [an account] with / 외상을 ~ open a charge account / 은행과 거래를 ~ open an account 「with [at] a bank.
**트라이** 『럭비』 a try. ¶ ~로 4점을 얻다 score four points with a try / ~를 성공시키다 score a try; make a successful try. 「period.
**트라이아스기**(一紀) 『지질』 the Triassic
**트라이애슬론** 《철인 경기》 a triathlon.
**트라이앵글** 『악기』 a triangle.
**트라코마, 트라홈** 『의학』 trachoma. ¶ ~에 걸린 trachomatous / ~에 걸리다 「suffer from [be afflicted with] trachoma.
**트라피스트** 『가톨릭』 a Trappist. ◉ ~ 수도원 a Trappist monastery (남); a Trappist convent (여). 「verse.
**트래버스** 『등산』 a traverse. ~하다 tra-
**트래지코미디** 『연극』 a tragicomedy.
**트랙** a track. ¶ ~과 필드 track and field. ◉ ~경기 track 「events [athletics]; running events: ~경기회 a track 「meet [meeting].
**트랙터** a tractor. ¶ 경작용 ~ a farm tractor; an agrimotor.
**트랜스** 『전기』 a (power) transformer. ¶ ~가 탔다 The transformer burned
**트랜스시버** 『무선』 a transceiver. 「out.
**트랜싯** 『측량』 a transit.
**트랜지스터** a transistor. ¶ 휴대용 ~ 수신기 a portable transistor set. ◉ ~ 라디오[TV] a transistor 「radio [television]. 광(光)~ a photo-transistor.
**트램폴린** 『스포츠』 a trampoline.
**트랩** a movable flight of steps; 《배의》 a gangway (ladder); 《비행기의》 a (plane) ramp; landing steps; traps. ¶ ~을 오르다[내리다] go [step] up [down] the 「ladder [ramp].
**트랭퀼라이저** 『약』 《안정제》 a tranquilizer; a tranquilizing pill (알약).
**트러블** a trouble. ¶ 가정의 ~ a family trouble / ~을 일으키다 make [stir up, cause] trouble; raise hell / …와 ~이 생기다 get into trouble with 《the police》. ◉ ~메이커 a troublemaker.
**트러스** 『건축·토목』 a truss. ◉ ~교(橋) a truss bridge: 나무 ~교 a wooden [timber] truss bridge.
**트러스트** 『경제』 a (business) trust. ¶ ~를 만들다[조직하다] organize a trust. ◉ ~금지법 an antitrust law. ~발기인 a trust promotor. ~조직 a trust system.
**트럭** a truck 《미》; an autotruck; a lorry 《영》. ¶ ~ 5 대분의 화물 five truckloads of goods / 장거리 운행 ~ a long-haul truck / ~으로 운반하다 carry in a truck; haul by truck. ◉ ~운송 trucking; truck transport: ~운송업자 a trucker. ~운전사 a truck driver. 군용~ a military truck.
**트럼펫** 『음악』 a trumpet. ◉ ~주자(奏者) a trumpeter; a trumpet player.
**트럼프** (playing) cards; trump card. ¶ 한 벌의 ~ a pack of cards; a deck of cards 《미》 / ~로 점을 치다 tell *one's* fortune from cards / ~를 치다 play [be at] cards / ~의 패를 떼다[도르다] cut [deal] the cards.
**트렁크** ① 《가방》 a (cabin) trunk; 《손에 드는》 a portmanteau (*pl.* ~s, ~x); a suitcase 《미》. ¶ ~를 가득 채운 옷 a trunkful of dress. ② 《자동차 짐칸》 the trunk (compartment); the luggage compartment; the foot. ¶ ~ 뚜껑 the trunk lid.
**트레머리** a swept-back hair with the chignon. ~하다 have a chignon; do (up) *one's* hair in a "swept-back" style with the chignon.
**트레몰로** 『음악』 *tremolo* (It.).
**트레바리** a perverse person; a cross-patch (심술꾸러기).
**트레슬** 『토목』 a trestle; a tressle; trestlework. ◉ ~교(橋) a trestle bridge.
**트레이너** 《사람》 a trainer; 《옷》 a sweat suit; track suit 《영》.
**트레이닝** 《훈련·연습》 training. ¶ ~을 하고 있다 be in training 《for the game》 / ~을 받고 있다 be under training 《for the coming Olympics》.
◉ ~셔츠 a training jacket. ~캠프 a training camp. ~팬츠 《미》 sweat pants; 《영》 track-suit trousers (★ training pants라고 하면 유아용 바지를 뜻함). 하드~ hard training.
**트레이드** 《무역·상업·거래》 trade; 『야구』 《선수교환》 trading of players. ~하다 trade 《a player》 for 《another》; 《영》 transfer 《a soccer player》. ◉ ~네임 trade name. ~마크 a trademark. ~머니 money paid for a 《baseball》 player.
**트레이서** 『화학·전자』 a tracer.
◉ 방사성~ a radioactive tracer.
**트레이싱페이퍼** tracing paper.
**트레일러** a trailer. ◉ ~버스 a trailer bus. ~하우스 a trailer house; a house
**트렌치코트** a trench coat. 「trailer.
**트로이** 《옛 도시》 Troy. ¶ ~의 Trojan / ~의 목마 the Trojan Horse. ◉ ~전쟁 the Trojan War.
**트로이카** a troika. ¶ (구소련 외교의) ~

방식 the "troika" plan 〔principle〕.

**트로피** 《win》 a trophy.

**트롤** 《저인망》 a trawl. ¶ ~로 잡다 trawl 《for》. ◉ ~망(網) a trawl(net); a ground net. ~선(船) a trawlboat; a trawler. ~어업 trawl fishery; trawling.

**트롤리** 《일반 노면을 달리는 전차》 a trolley (car). ◉ ~버스 a trolley bus 〔coach〕.

**트롬본** 〖악기〗 a trombone. ◉ ~ 주자(奏者) a trombonist.

**트롯** 〖무용〗 a trot.

**트리밍** 〖복식〗 trimming(s); 〖사진〗 trimming. ~하다 trim. ¶ 모피 ~을 단 코트 a coat with fur trimmings / 확대할 때에 ~을 해서 오른쪽 끝 사람은 빼주세요 In enlarging, please trim the picture and leave out the person at extreme right in the negative.

**트리오** a trio (*pl.* ~s). ¶ ~로 노래하다 sing in trio / ~를 연주하다 play a trio. ◉ 보컬~ a vocal trio.

**트리코마이신** 〖약〗 trichomycine.

**트리콧** 《옷감》 *tricot.* ◉ ~기 a tricot loom. ~자켓 a tricot jacket.

**트리튬** 〖화학〗 tritium.

**트리플** 《3중〔배〕의》 triple; 〖야구〗 《3루타》 a triple. ◉ ~보기 〖골프〗 a triple bogey. ~크라운 《삼관왕》 a Triple Crown: ~ 크라운의 triple-crowned 《players》. ~플레이 〖야구〗 a triple play.

**트릭** 《속임수》 a trick; a catch; bunko 《미구어》. ¶ 영화의 ~ 제작 the fabrication of faked pictures / ~을 쓰다 resort to tricks / 감쪽같이 ~에 걸려들다 be nicely tricked 〔taken in〕 / ~을 써서 …하게 하다 trick 《*a person*》 into *do*ing. ◉ ~사진 a trick 〔fake〕 picture; 《사진술》 fake photography. ~영화 a trick picture 〔film〕. ~촬영 trick shot 〔work〕. ~플레이 a trick play.

**트릴** 〖음악〗 《가늘게 떠는 발성법》 a trill; a trillo (*pl.* -li, ~es). ¶ ~로 노래하다 trill; sing in a tremulous voice.

**트릴레마** 《삼중고(三重苦)》 trilemma.

**트림** belching; a belch; burp 《구어》. ~하다 belch; burp. ¶ ~이 나(오)다 = ~하다 / 아기를 ~하게 하다 burp a baby.

**트립신** 〖생화학〗 trypsin.

**트립토판** 〖생화학〗 tryptophan(e).

**트릿하다** ① 《속이》 feel heavy on the stomach; 〔서술적〕 be not easily digested. ¶ 속이 ~ sit 〔lie〕 heavy on *one's* stomach. ② 《사람이》 (be) dull; dubious; vague; lukewarm.

**트위드** 《옷감》 tweed (스카치 직물); 《옷》 tweeds. ¶ ~를 입은 남자 a man in 〔wearing〕 tweeds / 밤색 ~ 양복을 입은 dressed in a brown tweed suit.

**트위스트** 《댄스의》 the twist. ¶ ~를 추다 twist; dance 〔do〕 the twist.

**트이다** ① 《막혔던 것이》 get cleared; be open(ed); be cut (길 등이); 《운이》 be in the ascendant. ¶ 탁 트인 목장 a wide open meadow / 탁 트인 전원 a wide spread of country / 길이 ~ a road is cleared 〔opened up〕 / 눈이 ~ come 〔be brought〕 to *one's* senses; awake from an illusion / 하늘이 ~ the sky clears up / 막혔던 가슴이 ~ feel refreshed 〔relieved〕 (at heart) / 운이 ~ be in luck's way; fortune turns in *one's* favor; fortune begins to smile on 《*a person*》 / 운이 트이기를 바라며 살다 live in hopes of better fortune / 자꾸 올라감에 따라 굉장한 경치가 눈 앞에 트였다 As we climbed higher, a wonderful view opened out before us. ② 《마음이》 be liberal; be open-hearted〔-minded〕. ¶ 속이 트인 사람 a man of the world; a sensible man; a person of a liberal turn of mind / 탁 트인 성격의 남자 a jolly open-hearted fellow / 사람의 속이 ~ be liberal 〔open-hearted, big-hearted〕; have a liberal 〔generous〕 mind.

**트적지근하다** feel uncomfortable in the stomach; be belch. ¶ 너무 먹어 속이 ~ have eaten too much and feel uncomfortable in the stomach.

**트집** ① 《까탈》 strain; bend; warp; a hitch; 《틈새》 a crack; a break; a fissure. ¶ ~(이) 나다 get cracked; have a hitch; have a split / 우정에 ~이 가다 cause a strain in the friendship / 계획에 ~이 생기다 have a hitch in the plan / 찻잔에 ~이 생겼다 There is a crack in this teacup. ② 《탈》 a fault; blemish; a false charge. ¶ ~을 잡다 make a false charge 《against》; find fault with; pick flaws 〔holes〕 with 〔in〕; cavil at / 말을 ~잡다 find fault with 《*a person's*》 remark / 사소한 일에도 ~을 잡다 trump up charges on the slightest pretext / ~잡아 싸움을 걸다 pick a quarrel with 《*a person*》 / 그는 ~을 잡아 아내를 내쫓았다 He made false accusations against his wife and threw her out. ◉ ~쟁이 a faultfinder; a nit-picker; a caviler.

**특가**(特價) a special 〔bargain〕 price; a specially reduced price. ¶ ~의 bargain-priced / ~로 팔다 sell 《*a thing*》 at a 「special 〔reduced, bargain〕

price; sell at sacrifice; 《팔다 남은 책을》 remainder. ◉ ～본 a book reduced in price; a bargain-priced book. ～제공 a special offer. ～판매 sale at a「special〔reduced〕price; a bargain sale. ～품 an article offered at「special〔specially reduced〕prices; bargain-priced articles: ～품 판매장 a bargain counter.

**특검법**(特檢法) 《특별 검사(제)》 the「independent〔special〕counsel bill (to investigate the scandals).

**특공**(特功) a great achievement; distinguished service; special merit. ¶ ～을 세우다 gain〔win, get〕a great achievement; render distinguished service.

**특공대**(特攻隊) a special attack corps; a suicide squad; a commando; a ranger corps 《미》. ¶ 인질들을 구출하기 위해 ～를 파견하다 send the commandos to rescue the hostages.

**특과**(特科) a special course; 〖군사〗 a technical corps. ◉ ～병 a soldier other than infantry; a technical soldier.

**특권**(特權) a privilege; a special〔an exclusive〕right; a prerogative. ¶ ～이 있는〔부여된〕privileged / 국회 의원의 ～ the privilege of Parliament / 여성의 ～ a woman's prerogative / 외교관의 ～ diplomatic privileges (and immunities) / ～을 부여하다 grant〔accord〕a privilege 《to *a person*》; confer a privilege 《on *a person*》 / ～을 가지다〔누리다〕possess a special right; hold〔enjoy〕a privilege / …을 전유(專有)하는 ～을 누리다 enjoy an exclusive prerogative of... / ～을 잃다 be deprived of a privilege / ～을 행사하다 exercise a privilege / 그렇게 하는 것은 우리의 ～이다 It is our prerogative to do so. / 우리에게는 도서관을 이용하는 ～이 주어졌다 We were given the special right to use the library. ◉ ～남용 the abuse of privilege. ～상실 lapse〔loss〕of privileges. ～의식 the sense of privilege. ～침해 breach of privilege.

**특권계급**(特權階級) the privileged classes. ¶ 법을 잘 알고 있는 어떤 사람들은 자신들을 ～에 속하는 사람으로 보기 때문에 이를 지키지 않는 경향이 있다 Some people, who are aware of the law, are inclined not to observe it because they regard themselves as persons of the privileged classes. ◉ 소수～ a privileged minority; the privileged few.

**특근**(特勤) special「service〔duty〕; extra duty; overtime work. ～하다 do extra work; work overtime. ¶ 근로자들은 ～을 거부하고 있다 The workers are refusing to do overtime. ◉ ～수당 overtime「pay〔allowance〕.

**특급**(特急) a「special〔limited〕express (train); a super-express; a cannonball 《구어》. ¶ ～을 타다 take〔board〕a limited express. ◉ ～권 a limited express ticket. ～ 열차 = 특급.

**특급**(特級) special grade; 《특등》 superior quality. ◉ ～주(酒) the「highest〔best〕quality wine. ～품 a special grade article;「an extra fine〔a superfine〕brand. ～호텔 a five-star hotel.

**특기**(特技) special ability〔talent, skill〕; speciality. ¶ 마술이 나의 ～중 하나이다 Magic is one of my specialities. ◉ 군사～ military occupational speciality (생략 MOS).

**특기**(特記) special mention. ～하다 mention〔write, refer to〕specially; make special mention of; 《신문 등의》 give (special) prominence to; lay special stress on. ¶ ～할 만한 remarkable; striking; noteworthy / ～할 만하다 be worth〔deserve〕special mention / 그것은 ～할 만한 업적이다 That's a noteworthy achievement.

**특대**(特大) an outsize. ¶ ～의 outsize(d); oversize; extra-big〔-large〕; king=size(d). ◉ ～호 《잡지》 a special enlarged issue; an enlarged special edition.

**특대**(特待) (a) special treatment〔courtesy〕; distinction. ～하다 give a special treatment; show special courtesy toward; treat 《*a person*》 with distinction. ¶ ～ 받다 be treated with distinction. ◉ ～권 a complimentary ticket. ～생 a scholarship student: ～생 제도 the system of exempting honor students from paying tuition.

**특등**(特等) a special grade〔class〕; the top grade. ◉ ～석 a special seat; a box (seat) (극장의). ～실 a special (=class) room; 《배의》 a stateroom; a cabin deluxe. ～품 an article of special quality; an「extra-fine〔super=fine〕article〔brand〕; a choice article.

**특례**(特例) a special「case〔example〕; a particular instance; 《예외》 an exception. ¶ ～로(서) as an exception / ～에 따라서 in accordance with the exception provided for / ～를 만들다

make an exception to the rule; 《선례를》 provide 〔create〕 a precedent / 그를 위해 ～가 만들어졌다 They made an exception in his favor. ◉ ～법 an 〔a special〕 exemption law. 전시(戰時)～ a wartime exception.

**특매**(特賣) a special 〔bargain〕 sale; sale at a special price. ～하다 sell at a special 〔specially reduced〕 price; conduct a special sale. ¶ 대할인 가격으로 ～하다 make a special offer at greatly reduced prices / 연 2회의 서적 ～가 행해진다 Special sale of books is conducted twice a year. / 그 가게에서 지금 양복을 ～중입니다 The store is having a sale on suits. / 정가 5,000원, ～ 가격 2,000원 《게시》 Regular price ₩ 5,000, sale price ₩ 2,000. ◉ ～가격 a sale price. ～기간 the period for special sale. ～일 a (special) bargain day. ～장 a bargain counter; a bargain floor; a bargain basement (지하층의). ～품 articles for bargain 〔special〕 sale; an article offered at a bargain (price); 《표시》 Bargains: ～품은 반환하거나 교환하지 않습니다 No returns or exchanges on sale items.

**특명**(特命) ① 《명령》 a special command 〔order〕; a special appointment 〔assignment〕; 〚군사〛 a mission. ～하다 order 〔command, appoint〕 specially. ¶ ～의 extraordinary / ～을 띠고 with a special mission. ② 《특지》 special consideration 〔grace〕. ⇨ 특지(特旨). ◉ ～전권 공사 〔대사〕 a minister 〔an ambassador〕 extraordinary and plenipotentiary.

**특무**(特務) special duty 〔service〕. ¶ ～를 띠고 on special duty; with a special commission.
◉ ～공작원 a secret agency. ～기관 the Special Service Agency 〔Organization〕; the secret (military) agency 〔service〕: 한때 ～ 기관에 있던 사람 a one-time secret service man. ～대 the Counter Intelligence Corps (생략 C.I.C.). ～함 〚해군〛 an auxiliary vessel. ～함정 〚해군〛 an auxiliary service ship.

**특배**(特配) special distribution; a special 〔an extra〕 ration; 《배당》 a special 〔a bonus〕 dividend. ～하다 distribute exceptionally 〔specially〕; ration specially.

**특별**(特別) being special. ～하다 (be) special; especial; express; particular (특정의); peculiar (고유의); extraordinary (비범한); extra (여분의); exceptional (예외의).
¶ ～히 specially; especially; particularly; in particular; extraordinarily; exceptionally / ～히 좋은 extra-fine; superfine; choice / ～한 것 a special thing; a special; a specific / 우리와 ～한 관계에 있는 분들 those with whom we have a special connection / ～한 이유 a particular 〔special〕 reason / ～한 호의로 by special grace / ～히 이렇다 할 이유도 없이 for no particular reason / ～히 주의하다 pay special attention 《to》; exercise special care / ～한 취급을 하다 give 《*a person*》 special treatment / ～히 정한 경우를 제외하고(는) unless otherwise provided for / 그 사람만은 ～이다 He is an exception. *or* He is different. *or* He is a special case.
◉ ～계약 a special contract. ～공채 a special loan. ～권한 《재판의》 special jurisdiction. ～규정 an express provision. ～급부 a fringe benefit. ～기(機) a special plane: ～기로 미국에 가다 go to the United States by special plane. ～기획 a special project. ～당좌예금 a special current account. ～대우 special treatment. ～명령 〚군사〛 special order. ～배달 special delivery. ～법 a special 〔particular〕 law. ～변호인 (a) special counsel. ～보조금 a special grant. ～보좌관 《대통령의》 President's Special Adviser; Special Assistant 《for the Foreign Affairs》 to the President. ～비 extra cost. ～사면 ⇨ 특사(特赦). ～상(賞) a special prize 《for outstanding performance》. ～상여금 a special bonus. ～석 a reserved 〔special〕 seat; a box (극장의). ～세 a special tax. ～ 소비세 special excise tax. ～손실 〚경영〛 extraordinary expense 〔loss〕. ～시 a special city 〔municipality〕. ～열차 a special train. ～예산 a special 〔an extraordinary〕 budget. ～운임 a special fare 〔rate〕. ～위원 an extraordinary member 《of a committee》. ～위원회 〚정치〛 a special 〔an interim〕 committee. ～의회 an extraordinary 〔a special〕 session of the Assembly. ～이익 〚경영〛 extraordinary income. ～인출권 〚금융〛 《IMF를 통해 창출된 준비 자산》 special drawing rights (생략 SDR). ～임무 a special mission; (a) special duty 〔service〕. ～입장권 a complimentary ticket. ～재판소〔법정〕 an extraordinary

tribunal. ～전보 a special telegram. ～조사위원회 〖정치〗 a select committee. ～조처〔조치〕 special measures. ～주문 a special order. ～지출 a special grant. ～직 a special position in Government service. ～치료 special treatment. ～프로 a special 〔feature〕 program; 《인기프로》 an attraction. ～항고(抗告) a special complaint. ～해상경보 special marine warning. ～호 《잡지 따위의》 a special 〔an extra〕 number 〔issue〕; a special. ～회계 special accounts. ～회원 a special member. ～훈련 special training.

**특별검사**(特別檢事) an independent special prosecutor. ¶ 그들은 1979년의 군사 반란을 조사하기 위해 정치적으로 중립인 ～가 임명되어야 한다고 요구하였다 They demanded that special prosecutors, who are politically neutral, be appointed to probe the military mutiny of 1979.

**특별배당**(特別配當) an extra 〔a special〕 dividend; a plum (많은 액수의). ～하다 issue extra dividends. ◉ ～금 《유가증권의》 a bonus dividend.

**특별수당**(特別手當) a special 〔an extra〕 allowance; a bonus; an allotment (미군사). ¶ ～을 타다 be paid extra / ～이 연(年) 2백만 원이다 I collect 2,000,000 won a year in bonuses.

**특별요금**(特別料金) 《가외의》 an extra fee 〔charge〕; 《할인의》 a specially reduced fee. ¶ 가외 ～을 물다 pay extra.

**특별임용**(特別任用) special appointment. ¶ 총영사로 ～되다 be specially appointed Consul General.

**특별취급**(特別取扱) special 〔preferential〕 treatment 〔handling〕. ¶ ～을 하다 make discrimination 〔an exception〕 in 《*a person's*》 favor; give 〔accord〕 《*a person*》 special 〔preferential〕 treatment / ～을 하지 않다 make no exception.

**특보**(特報) a special report; special news; a (news) flash. ～하다 give a special report on; flash 《the news of》. ¶ 개표 결과를 ～하다 flash the ballot-counting results. ◉ 뉴스～ a news flash.

**특사**(特使) a special envoy; an emissary; a special 〔an express〕 messenger. ¶ ～를 파견하다 dispatch a special envoy 《to》. ◉ 대통령～ a presidential envoy.

**특사**(特赦) (an) amnesty; a special pardon (개인의). ～하다 grant 〔give〕 an amnesty 《to》. ¶ 정치범을 ～하다 grant an amnesty to political prisoners / ～로 출감하다 be released from prison 「under an amnesty 〔on a special pardon〕 / ～에서 빠지다 be excluded from the amnesty / ～의 범위를 확대하다 extend amnesties 《to》 / 광복절을 축하하여, ～가 발표될 예정이다 A general amnesty is to be declared in celebration of the National Liberation Day. ◉ ～권 the prerogative of mercy. ～령 an amnesty; a decree of amnesty 〔oblivion〕.

**특사**(特賜) a special grant (from king). ～하다 give as a special grant; grant specially.

**특산**(特産) a special product; an indigenous product; a speciality. ◉ ～물〔품〕 a special 〔an indigenous〕 product; a (local) speciality: 이 지방의 주요 ～물 the principal products of this district / 인삼은 개성의 ～물이다 Ginseng is a speciality of Kaesŏng. ～종 an endemic species. ～지 special production localities.

**특상**(特上) ¶ ～의 superfine; the finest 〔choicest, best〕. ◉ ～품 choice goods.

**특상**(特賞) a special prize.

**특색**(特色) a specific character; a characteristic; a peculiarity; a distinctive feature; a distinguishing quality; 《작품·지방 등의》 color; a trait (성격상의). ¶ ～ 있는 special; characteristic; peculiar; distinctive / ～ 없는 indistinctive; featureless; colorless; common / …이 ～이다 be characterized by / (―이) …의 ～을 나타내다〔이루다〕 be characteristic of; characterize; feature; mark; stamp; be typical of / ～을 발휘하다 display *one's* characteristic feature / ～을 살리다 make the best of 《its》 characteristic traits / ～ 지우다〔짓다〕 characterize; mark; distinguish; color / 그 이야기는 지방적 ～이 많다 The story has much local color. / 의지가 강한 것이 그의 ～이다 Strong-mindedness is his outstanding characteristic. / 이 지방에는 이렇다 할 ～이 없다 This country has no special characteristics worthy of mention. / 이 작품에는 시대적 ～이 잘 나타나 있다 This work clearly reveals the features characteristic of the period. / 이것이 우리 시대의 ～이다 This is a unique feature of our time. / 그의 문체는 명료함이 ～이다 His style is characterized by clarity.

**특선**(特選) (a) special choice 〔selection, approval〕; (a) recognition; 《특상》 special prize; the highest honors. ～하다 choose 〔select〕 specially. ¶ 전람회에서 ～이 되다 「be specially selected 〔win a special recognition, win the highest honors〕 at an art exhibition. ◉ ～미(米) choice rice. ～품 choice goods: ～품 매장 the choice 〔deluxe〕 article counter.

**특설**(特設) special establishment 〔installment, accommodation〕. ～하다 set up 〔establish, install〕 specially. ¶ 이 국제회의를 위해 구내에 우체국이 ～되었다 A special post office was set up on the premises to serve this international congress.

◉ ～도로 an accommodation road. ～링 a specially prepared ring. ～전화 a specially installed telephone. ～학급 a special class. ～회장(會場) a site 〔room, place, *etc.*〕 especially prepared for a meeting 〔an event, *etc.*〕: 그는 새로운 기획을 위해 ～ 회장을 준비했다 He prepared a special place for the new project.

**특성**(特性) a special 〔distinctive〕 quality; a specific 〔special, peculiar〕 character 〔characteristic〕; a peculiarity; a (special) property; a feature; 《개인의》 a trait of character; individuality; an idiosyncrasy; 〖생물〗 a diagnosis.

¶ 국민적 ～ a national trait / ～을 갖다 possess the characteristics 《of》/ ～을 나타내다 show 〔exhibit〕 a special quality 〔character〕/ (어떤 일이) …의 ～을 나타내다 characterize; mark; be characteristic of / ～을 살리다 make the most of 《its》 characteristics / 탄력은 고무의 ～이다 Elasticity is a property of India rubber. / 비누는 때를 없애는 ～이 있다 Soap has the property of removing dirt. / 애국심은 이 국민의 현저한 ～이다 Patriotism is a marked characteristic of this nation.

**특수**(特殊) ～하다 (be) special; specific; particular; peculiar; characteristic; distinct; individual; unique.

¶ ～한 목적 a particular object; a special purpose / ～한 성질 *one's* own nature; 《개성》 an individuality; an idiosyncrasy / ～한 예 a special example / ～한 원인 a specific cause / ～한 방법으로 in a particular way / 그녀는 정계에서 ～한 지위를 점하고 있다 She holds a unique position in the political world. / 이 쪽의 ～한 사정을 이해하여 주십시오 Please take our particular situation into consideration.

◉ ～강(鋼) special steel. ～ 공작 요원 a commando 〔saboteur〕 《of north Korea》. ～교육 special education; education for the handicapped 〔retarded〕. ～근무 special service 〔work〕; a special duty: ～근무 수당 a special service 〔work, duty〕 allowance. ～무기 a special 〔super〕 weapon. ～배임(背任) aggravated breach of trust. ～법인 a corporation 〔juridical person〕 having special status. ～부대 〖군사〗 special forces. ～사항 special matters 〔items〕; specifics. ～성 (a) peculiarity; special characteristics. ～은행 a chartered 〔special〕 bank. ～촬영 《영화의》 shooting for special effect(s); trick shooting. ～층 a privileged class. ～학급 《정신·지체 장애자를 위한》 special classes for the education of physically or mentally handicapped children. ～합판 special plywood. ～회사 a chartered company 《영》. ～효과 〖영화·TV〗 special effect(s). ～훈련 special training.

**특수**(特需) special procurements; emergency 〔special procurement〕 demands 〔orders〕 《due to the outbreak of war》. ◉ ～경기 a special procurement boom. ～수출품 special demand exports.

**특수사정**(特殊事情) special circumstances 〔necessities〕. ¶ 지방의 ～ special necessities of the regions.

**특수취급**(特殊取扱) special treatment 〔handling〕. ～하다 make discrimination in 《*a person's*》 favor; give 《*a person*》 special treatment.

◉ ～우편 mail for special handling.

**특수화**(特殊化) specialization; specification. ～하다 specialize; specify; differentiate.

**특실**(特室) a special chamber; 《열차의》 a parlor car; a special coach.

**특약**(特約) a special contract 〔agreement〕. ～하다 make a special contract; contract specially. ¶ (한 회사의 술만을 파는) ～주점 a tied house / A.P. ～ under a special contract with A.P. / …와 ～이 있다 be under a special contract with... / …와 ～을 맺다 make 〔enter into〕 a special contract 〔agreement〕 with.... ◉ ～조항 《보험의》 a clause containing special policy conditions. ～(판매)점 a special agent; a chain store (미국식의): 우리는 이 회사의 ~점이 되었다 We have acquired a franchise [special agents] to sell this company's goods.

**특용**(特用) a special use. ~하다 use specially; use 《*a thing*》 for a special purpose. ◉ ~작물 a crop for a special use; cash [lucrative] crops.

**특유**(特有) peculiarity. ~하다 (be) peculiar 《to》; characteristic 《of》; special 《to》; unique. ¶ ~한 맛 a peculiar flavor / ~한 아름다움 beauty of 《its》 own; a unique beauty / 이 지방 ~의 풍습 a custom peculiar to this district / 한국 ~의 미술 Korea's characteristic arts / 그 사람 ~의 서체 his special style of calligraphy / 이런 표현법은 영어 ~의 것이다 These expressions are peculiar to English. / 오렌지에는 그 자체의 ~한 향기가 있다 The orange has a scent all [of] its own. ◉ ~성 a peculiarity; uniqueness.

**특이**(特異) ~하다 (be) singular; peculiar; unique. ¶ ~한 예 a peculiar case / ~한 현상 《전례 없는》 an unprecedented phenomenon / ~한 재능의 소유자 a person of [with a] unique talent / 그녀는 ~한 복장을 하고 있었다 She was dressed in singular fashion. ◉ ~성 (a) peculiarity; singularity; uniqueness. ~세포 〖식물〗 an idioblast. ~체질 an idiosyncrasy; 〖의학〗 diathesis (*pl.* -ses); 《이상 민감증》 an allergy 《to》: 그는 항생 물질에 민감한 ~체질이다 He is allergic to antibiotic substances.

**특작**(特作) a special production; 《영화의》 a special film. ◉ ~품 《영화의》 a feature (film). 초~ a super production; 《영화의》 a super picture.

**특장**(特長) a strong point; a merit; a forte. ¶ 이 사전의 ~ strong points of this dictionary / 이 신형차의 최대 ~은 경쾌한 주행성이다 The strongest point of this new model is its smooth running.

**특전**(特典) 《특혜》 a special favor; a benefit; 《특권》 a privilege; 《편리·이익》 advantage. ¶ 본회 회원의 ~ advantages of membership in this society / 세금 면제의 ~ the privilege of exemption from taxation / ~을 주다 privilege; grant a special privilege [favor] 《to》 / …의 ~을 취소하다 revoke the privilege of... / 수영장 수시 사용의 ~이 있다 enjoy free use of the swimming pool / 노인들에게는 공공 교통 수단에 무료 승차할 수 있는 ~이 있다 Old people enjoy [are granted] the privilege of traveling on public vehicles free of charge.

**특전**(特電) a special telegram [cable, dispatch]. ◉ 로이터~ Reuter's special (service).

**특전단**(特戰團) a ranger-commando force.

**특점**(特點) a distinctive [distinguishing, characteristic] mark; a characteristic; a special [distinctive] feature [character]; peculiarity.

**특정**(特定) identification. ~하다 specify; identify. ¶ ~의[한] specific; specified; special; particular / ~ 행위의 금지 prohibition of specific acts / ~한 죄에 대한 감형 individually specified commutation of punishment / 그 돈은 ~ 목적[분야]에 쓰이게 되어 있다 The money is to be used for 「a specific purpose [specific areas].
◉ ~계약 a specified contract. ~명제 〖논리〗 a subaltern proposition. ~물(物) a specific thing. ~범죄 가중처벌법 《violation of》 the Additional Punishment Law on Specific Crimes. ~승계인 a singular successor. ~업종 specially designated industries. ~외래품 《수입이 금지된》 specially banned [prohibited] import goods. ~요금 a specified [a special, an exceptional] fare [rate]. ~운임 special freight rates. ~유증 a specific testamentary gift; a specific property devised. ~인 a specific [specified] person; a designated person. ~자본 special capital. ~재산 specific [particular] property. ~지역 a specific region; 《투기 억제의》 the special (tax) zones. ~(투기)주식 designated speculative stocks.

**특제**(特製) special make [manufacture]. ~하다 make [manufacture] specially. ¶ ~의 specially made [manufactured]; of special make; 《제본(製本)에서》 specially bound; 《호화로운》 deluxe. ◉ ~본(本) a specially bound book. ~품 a specially made article; specialties.

**특종**(特種) ① 《종류》 a special kind. ② 《뉴스》 exclusive news; an exclusive; a scoop; a news beat 《미》. ¶ ~을[~ 기사를] 내다[싣다] publish an exclusive [exclusive news] 《on》 / ~을 잡다 get a scoop; scoop / 타사(他社)에 앞서 ~을 내다 scoop the rival paper; get a scoop [beat] on other papers.

**특지**(特志) ①《의사》 special intention; special interest. ②《특지가》 a volunteer; a person interested.

**특진**(特進) a special promotion of rank. ¶ 2계급 ~하다 be specially promoted two ranks《after *one's* death in the line of duty》.

**특질**(特質) a characteristic; a special quality; a specific character. ⇨ 특성(特性). ¶ 웃음은 인간만의 ~인가 Is laughter a quality of man only?

**특집**(特輯) a special edition; a supplement. ~하다 prepare a special number; make up a special edition. ¶ 우리는 주택 문제의 ~을 기획하고 있다 We are planning a supplement on housing problems. ◉ ~기사 feature articles; a feature story《미》. ~호 a special number〔issue〕. 뉴스~ a special news program. 신년 ~호 a January number with New Year features; a special January issue. 일요 ~판 Sunday features. 임시 ~호 an extra special issue.

**특징**(特徵) a special〔distinctive〕feature; a (distinguishing) characteristic; a peculiarity (특이점); a trait; individuality (개성). ¶ ~적인 characteristic; distinctive; peculiar; remarkable / 성격의 두드러진 ~ the salient traits of *one's* character / ~ 있는 목소리 a distinguished voice / ~ 있는 얼굴 a face with a distinctive〔noticeable〕feature / ~(이) 없는 featureless; characterless; common / ~ 없는 얼굴 a face「without (any) character〔lacking in character〕/ ~ 짓다〔지우다〕 characterize; distinguish; mark; give《*something*》a distinction / 캘리포니아의 ~은 기후와 풍경이다 The main features of California are the climate and the scenery. / 이 마을 사람들은 소박하고 겸손한 것이 ~이다 The villagers are characterized by simplicity and modesty. / 그의 목소리에는 ~이 있다 There is an individuality in his voice.

**특채**(特採) special appointment〔employment〕. ~하다 employ specially; take《*a person*》into service specially.

**특청**(特請) (a) special request. ~하다 request specially; make a special request.

**특출**(特出) ~하다 (be) outstanding; prominent; [서술적] stand out〔conspicuous〕; be by far the best; tower above《others》; distinguish *oneself.* ¶ ~하게 out〔far〕and away; by far; exceptionally; matchlessly / ~한 인물 an outstanding〔a great〕figure / 그는 전교에서 성적이 ~하게 좋다 He is by far the best student in the whole school.

**특칭**(特稱) special designation; a special name; 〖논리〗 a particular. ~하다 give a special name to; designate in particular; particularize. ◉ ~명제〖논리〗 a particular〔subaltern〕proposition.

**특파**(特派) dispatch; special assignment. ~하다 dispatch〔send〕specially. ¶ 지방~ a local dispatch / 사원을 런던에 ~하다 dispatch〔send〕a member of the staff to London for special purposes. ◉ ~사절 a special envoy〔mission〕. ~(전권)대사 an ambassador extraordinary〔on special mission〕.

**특파원**(特派員) a mission; a delegate; 《신문·통신사의》 a (special) correspondent. ¶ AP (서울) ~ an AP correspondent (in Seoul) / 타임스지(紙)의 극동~ a special correspondent of *the Times* on a mission to the Far East.

**특품**(特品) top-grade merchandise; an article of special quality.

**특필**(特筆) special writing〔mention〕. ~하다 write〔mention, refer to〕specially; make special mention《of》; 《신문 따위가》 give (special) prominence to; lay special stress on / ~할 만한 deserving〔worthy of〕special mention; (highly) important; remarkable; striking / ~할 만한 사건 a big〔capital〕event / 대서~하다 write in large〔golden〕letters / 그것은 역사상 ~할 만한 사건이었다 It was a historically important event.

**특허**(特許) ①《특별한 허락》 a special permission〔license〕. ~하다 grant《*a person*》a special permission〔license〕; license《*a person*》to《*do*》. ②《정부가 은행·회사에 주는》 a charter; a concession (채굴·부설권 등의). ~하다 charter《a company to *do*》. ¶ 버스 영업에 대한 ~ a franchise for a bus service. ③〖법〗《고안품의》 a patent. ~하다 patent. ¶ ~를 출원하다 apply for a patent / ~를 얻다〔따다〕 obtain〔get, secure, take out〕a patent《for〔on〕an invention》; patent《an invention》; have《an article》patented / ~를 얻은 발명 a patented〔patent〕invention /

신안 ~를 받다 take out a patent for 〔on〕 a new invention / ~가 나오다 A patent is granted 《for》. / ~ 출원중 《표기》 Patent pending. *or* Patent applied for. / ~ 출원중이다 We are now applying for a patent.

◉ ~계약 a licensing deal. ~기간 the term of license. ~대리인 a patent agent 〔attorney〕. ~명세서〔목록〕 a patent specification 〔roll〕. ~법 (a) patent law; the Patent Act. ~변리사 사무소 a patent attorney's office. ~보상 patent compensation. ~사용료 (a) patent royalty. ~소유자 a patentee. ~심판〔심사〕 patent judgement 〔examination〕. ~장 a charter; a special license. ~청 The Industrial Property Office (한국); the Patent Office 〔Agency〕 (미국). ~출원 a patent application: ~ 출원료 a patent fee / ~출원인 an applicant for a patent. ~품 a patented article; a patent.

**특허권**(特許權) a patent (right); the right to a patent. ¶ ~을 보유하다〔얻다〕 hold 〔obtain〕 a patent right / ~을 침해하다 infringe (on) 「a patent right 〔the patent〕 / 그건 ~ 침해가 된다 It constitutes an infringement of patent. ◉ ~사용료 (a) royalty. ~수여자 a patentor. ~자 a patentee. ~침해 a patent infringement: ~ 침해로 말썽이 안 나도록 조심해야 하겠습니다 Let's make sure that there will be no trouble with patent-right infringements.

**특혜**(特惠) special favor 〔benefit〕; preference; special 〔preferential〕 treatment. ¶ ~의 preferential / ~를 받다 receive preferential treatment / ~ 세율의 적용을 받다 enjoy a tariff preference 《of 6%》.

◉ ~관세〔세율〕 preferential tariff 〔duties〕. ~금리 a preferential interest rate. ~금융 preferential financing. ~대우 preferential treatment. ~융자 a privileged 〔preferential〕 loan. ~주의 preferentialism. 세제(稅制)~ a tax favor; tax privileges.

**특화**(特化) ⇨ 특수화, 전문화.

**특효**(特效) (a) special 〔miraculous〕 virtue 〔efficacy〕 《for》. ¶ ~가 있다 be specially efficacious 〔good〕 for 《a disease》 / 신경통에 ~가 있다 have a special virtue for curing neuralgia; be specially good for neuralgia / 이 약은 다음 여러 병에 ~가 있다 This medicine is effective for the following diseases. ◉ ~약 a specific (medicine) 《against, for》; a sovereign remedy 《for malaria》; a wonder drug.

**특히**(特一) specially; expressly; especially; particularly; in particular; above all; first of all; before everything (else); 《부정》 least of all.

> **용법** **specially** 어떤 하나의 목적·용도 등을 강조하는 「특히」란 뜻, generally 와 상대되는 낱말: This book was written *specially* for beginners. (이 책은 특히 초보자를 위해 씌여졌다). **especially** 다른 것과 비교하였을 때 「비교적 그 정도가 높게」란 뜻이며, ordinarily와 상대되는 낱말: The second chapter of this book is *especially* interesting. (이 책의 제2장은 다른 장에 비해 특히 재미있다). **particularly** 「같은 종류의 것들 중에서 특별히 지적한다면 이것」이란 뜻을 나타내는 낱말. specially나 especially와 대용할 수 있다: He is good at sports in general, but (he is) *particularly* good at baseball. (그는 스포츠 만능이지만, 특히 야구를 잘 한다.)

¶ ~ 중대한 일 a matter of especial importance / ~ 그의 희망으로 at his special request / ~ 말해 두겠는데… let it be emphatically said that... / ~ 그날에 한해서 on that particular day / ~이렇다 할 이유도 없이 for no particular reason / ~ 막내 아들을 사랑하다 especially love *one's* youngest son / ~ 주의하다 pay particular attention 《to》 / 이것이 ~ 중요하다 This is 「specially important 〔of special importance〕. / 외국어, ~ 영어의 지식은 필수적이다 Some knowledge of foreign languages, of English in particular, is essential. / 나는 ~ 마늘을 싫어한다 I dislike garlic most of all. / 이 습관은 남성, ~ 교육을 받은 남성에게서 볼 수 있다 This custom is observed among men, more particularly among educated men. / ~이 사실에 주목해 주시기 바랍니다 I wish to call your particular attention to this fact. / 나는 그녀의 가족, ~ 그녀의 모친이 마음에 안 든다 I don't like her family, and least of all her mother. / 이 한영 사전은 ~ 사업하는 사람들에게 쓸모가 있다 This Korean-English dictionary is particularly useful for businessmen.

**튼실하다** (be) strong and firm; solid and full; tightly packed.

**튼튼하다** 《건강하다》 (be) healthy;

strong; strong and healthy; sound; robust; 《단단하다》 (be) strong; solid; stout; firm; sound; sturdy; substantial; durable (마디다).
¶ 튼튼한 기초 a strong 〔firm, sound〕 foundation / 튼튼한 몸 a healthy 〔sound〕 body / 튼튼한 사람 a strong person; 《체격이》 a man of solid 〔sturdy〕 build 〔physique〕; a powerfully-〔strongly-〕built man / 튼튼한 자본 substantial capital / 튼튼한 집〔구조〕 a solid house 〔structure〕 / 튼튼한 천〔줄〕 stout cloth 〔cords〕 / 튼튼히〔하게〕 strongly; stoutly; solidly; sturdily; firmly / 국방을 튼튼히 하다 strengthen the national defense / 몸을 튼튼히 하다 improve 〔build up〕 *one's* health / 튼튼해지다 become healthy; grow strong; gain 〔improve〕 in health; 《회복되다》 be all right again; be well again / 짐을 튼튼히 묶다 pack securely / 토대가 ~ The foundation is secure 〔solid, firm〕. / 이 양말은 특히 뒤꿈치가 튼튼합니다 These socks are reinforced at the heels. / 모양새는 어쨌든 튼튼하게만 되어 있다 It is made for strength and not for appearance. / 튼튼한 것은 보증하겠습니다 I will answer for its durability.

**틀** ① 《테》 a frame; framework. ¶ 사진틀 the frame of a picture; a picture frame / 수틀 an embroidery frame; a tambour / 창틀 a window frame; a sash / 틀에 끼우다 frame 《a picture》; set 〔put〕 《a picture》 in frame.
② 《골·판》 a mold; a cast; a matrix; 〚기계〛 《형을 뜨는 데 쓰이는》 a die. ¶ 틀을 뜨다 make a model 《of》; model 《a tooth in wax》 / 틀에 부어 뜨다 cast in a mold.
③ 《형식화》 formality; a formula (*pl.* ~s, -lae); 《일정 모형》 a model; pattern. ¶ 틀에 박히다 get 〔fall into〕 a groove; harden into a set formula; get into a rut; be conventional / 틀에 박힌 grooved; conventional; stereotyped; hackneyed; manneristic / 틀에 박힌 말 a set (form of ) phrase; a set formula; the routine of phrases / 틀에 박히지 않은 unconventional; offbeat; 《자유로운》 free / 틀에 박히지 않은 소설 an offbeat novel / 틀에 박다 [비유적] squeeze 《an individual》 into a pattern; regiment; standardize.
④ 《형태화》 a shape; a form. ¶ 틀을 잡다 get 〔lick〕 《*a matter*》 into shape; give shape to 《*a matter*》 / 틀이 잡히다 take 〔be in〕 shape; take a concrete 〔definite〕 form; materialize.
⑤ 《기계》 a machine; a device; a gadget. ¶ 재봉틀 a sewing machine / 솜틀 a cotton gin; a gin; a saw gin; a willow (machine).
⑥ 《인간의》 caliber 〔calibre 《영》〕; capacity; degree of ability. ¶ 사람의 틀이 크다〔작다〕 be a person of large 〔small〕 caliber.

**틀거지** dignity; an imposing manner 〔attitude〕. ¶ ~가 있다 be dignified / ~가 없다 lack dignity.

**틀국수** machine-made noodles.

**틀누비** machine-quilting.

**틀니** an artificial 〔a false〕 tooth (*pl.* teeth); a denture. ¶ ~를 끼우다〔빼다〕 put in 〔take out〕 *one's* false teeth / ~를 해박다 have a false 〔an artificial〕 tooth put in.

**틀다** ① 《돌리다》 (***a***) 《비틀다》 twist; wrench; screw; wring; give 《a rope》 a twist. ¶ 나사못을 ~ screw; drive 〔turn, put on〕 a screw / 밧줄을 홱 ~ give a violent twist to a rope. (***b***) 《작동시키다》 turn 《the stopcock》; switch on; put 〔play〕 《a record on a phonograph》; wind (감다). ¶ 가스를 ~ turn on the gas / 꼭지를 ~ turn the tap on / 라디오를 ~ turn 〔switch〕 on the radio / 전축을 ~ play 〔turn on〕 an (electric) record player. (***c***) 《머리를》 tie 〔do〕 up (*one's* hair). ¶ 상투를 ~ tie up a topknot; wear a topknot / 머리를 틀어 올리다 do 〔put〕 *one's* hair up. (***d***) 《방향을》 change; shift; turn. ¶ 방향을 ~ change 〔shift〕 *one's* course; 《배가》 alter the course; fleet / 핸들을 왼쪽으로 ~ turn a handle to the left; wheel left. ② 《일을》 thwart; cross; work against; put a spoke in 《another's》 wheel. ¶ 계획〔일〕을 ~ counteract 〔thwart〕 《*a person's*》 plan 〔design〕; throw in a monkey wrench. ③ 《솜을》 gin (out) 〔willow〕 (cotton).

**틀리다**[1] ① 《돌아가다》 get turned 〔wound〕; wind; turn. ¶ 나사가 ~ a screw turns / 태엽이 ~ a spring is wound up. ② 《비틀리다》 get twisted 〔wrenched, warped〕; warp. ③ 《상투·머리가》 get tied; tie. ¶ 상투가 잘 틀리지 않다 a topknot won't tie properly. ④ 《솜이》 get ginned 〔willowed〕. ¶ 솜이 ~ cotton is willowed.

**틀리다**[2] ① 《잘못되다》 be mistaken 《in》; become 〔be〕 wrong 〔erroneous, incorrect〕; be false; 《잘못하다》 mis-

take; make a mistake《in》; err; commit 〔make〕 an error 《in calculation》. ¶ 틀린 생각 a「wrong 〔false〕 idea; a mistaken notion / 틀린 판단 misjudgment; miscalculation / 계산이 ~ miscalculate; miscount; make「a mistake 〔an error〕 in (*one's*) calculation / 해답이 ~ answer wrong / 판단이 ~ judge wrongly; err 〔make an error〕 in judgment; misjudge / 맞춤법이 ~ the spelling is wrong; be misspelled / 틀리지 않다 be right; be correct / 틀리지 않고 하다 go through without stumbling / 틀린 것이 있으면 고치시오 Correct errors, if any. / 그에 대한 자네 생각은 틀렸네 You are mistaken about him. / 네 계산은 모두 틀렸다 You have got all your sums wrong. / 일기 예보가 또 틀렸다 The weather forecast was wrong again. / 내 추측은 틀리지 않았다 I was right in my conjecture. / 편지의 주소가 틀렸다 The letter was wrongly addressed.
② 《사이가》 fall out 《with》; be at odds 《with》; get estranged 《from》; get on bad terms 《with》. ¶ 서로 틀려 말을 하지 않다 have fallen out with each other and aren't on speaking terms / 서로 틀려서 얼굴도 대하지 않다 don't see eye to eye with each other.
③ 《나쁘다》 become 〔be〕 bad 〔evil, wrong, immoral, perverse〕. ¶ 틀린 생각 an evil intention; a bad idea / 틀린 사람 a bad person / 틀린 짓 an evil deed; a misdeed; evildoing.
④ 《심사가》 get 〔become〕 twisted 〔warped, crooked〕. ¶ 심사가 ~ have a perverse mind; be in a crooked temper.
⑤ 《다르다》 be different 《from》; differ 《from》; be unlike; vary 《from》. ¶ 성격이 ~ be different 〔dissimilar〕 in character / 이 물건과 그 물건은 값이 틀린다 The prices of the two articles are different. *or* There is a discrepancy in price between the two.
⑥ 《일이》 go「wrong 〔amiss, awry〕; be done for; be ruined; fail; end in failure; be spoilt. ¶ 일은 다 틀렸다 The「game 〔jig〕 is up. *or* All's lost. / 그 자는 이제 틀렸다 He is done for. / 이 사업도 이젠 틀렸다 It is all up with this business. / 환자는 이제 틀렸다 The patient has little chance to pull through. *or* The patient is hopeless.

**틀림** ① 《잘못》 being wrong; a mistake; an error; a fault; a discrepancy; 《믿을 수 없음》 unreliability. ¶ ~이 없도록 to prevent mistakes; so that everything is all right / 내 기억에 ~이 없다면 if I remember「right(ly) 〔correctly〕 / 그의 말에 ~이 없다 What he says is「right 〔correct〕. / 계산에 ~이 있다 There is a mistake in the「calculation 〔bill〕. / 그 사람은 ~이 없다 He is quite a reliable person. *or* You can count on him. / 내 눈에는 ~이 없다 I have an unerring eye.
② 《다름》 being not the same; being different. ¶ ~없도록 to make sure (of it); for caution's sake / 네가 말하는 사람이 내 친구임에 ~이 없다 The man that you are talking about is none other than my friend. / 값에는 ~이 없으나 품질에는 차이가 있다 There isn't any difference in the price, but there is a difference in the quality.

**틀림없다** ① 《정확·확실하다》 (be) correct; exact; right; be free from mistakes; 《확신·신뢰할 만하다》 (be) sure; certain; unfailing; infallible; reliable; trustworthy. ¶ 틀림없는 계산 a correct calculation / 틀림없는 사람 a「reliable 〔trustworthy〕 person / 사격 솜씨가 ~ be a reliable shot / 그의 판단에 맡겨 두면 틀림없을 게다 It may safely be left to his judgement. / 그는 틀림없는 사람인가 Can he be「trusted 〔relied upon〕? / 그 사람 말이 맞는다고 보아 ~ We have every reason to believe in his words.
②《바로 …이다》 be no other than; be the very one; there is no doubt that (it is...). ¶ 자넨 그 사실을 들었음에 ~ You must have heard of it. (★「…했음에 틀림없다」의 뜻일 때는 must have + p.p.의 형태를 취함.「…임에 틀림없다」에 대한 부정「…일 리가 없다」는 cannot (be), cannot have+p.p.로 나타냄) / 이상과 같이 틀림없음 I affirm the above statement to be correct「in every respect 〔to the best of my knowledge〕. / 이 책은 선생님이 사라는 책임에 ~ This must be the book the teacher told us to get. / 그 소문은 정말임에 ~ The rumor must be true. / 곧 비가 올 것임에 ~ It must rain soon. / 그는 무죄임에 ~ He must be innocent. *or* I am sure「of his innocence 〔that he is innocent〕.

**틀림없이** 《정확히》 correctly; rightly; errorlessly; 《확실히》 certainly; surely; beyond 〔no, without〕 doubt; 《분명히》 evidently; 《꼭·반드시》 without fail.

¶ ~ …라고 생각하다 take (it) for granted that…; conclude that… / ~ …하다 do not fail to *do* / 돈을 ~ 돌려 주다 return the money without fail / 일을 ~ 하다 make a plan sure; see that a plan works out all right; 《꼭》 do a job without fail / ~ 내가 잃은 시계다 It is the same 〔very〕 watch that I lost. / ~ 아버지의 필적이다 It is my father's handwriting beyond doubt. *or* There is no doubt that this is my father's handwriting. / ~ 이렇게 되리라고 생각했지 This is just what I expected. *or* I thought just as much. / ~ 그런 이야기였습니다 It is so, if I am correctly informed. / ~ 나와 주실 테죠 May I count on your coming?

**틀수하다** (be) generous; liberal; magnanimous; lenient; broad-minded.

**틀스럽다** (be) dignified; commanding.

**틀어넣다** push 〔thrust, force〕 《*a thing*》 in; squeeze 《*a thing*》 in; crowd 〔jam, stuff, tuck〕 《*a thing*》 into. ¶ 옷을 장에 ~ jam *one's* clothes into a chest / 돈을 주머니에 ~ stuff 〔shove〕 money into *one's* pocket.

**틀어막다** ① 《구멍을》 stop 〔block〕 up 《a hole》; stuff; fill; plug. ¶ 구멍을 흙으로 ~ fill 〔plug up〕 a hole with earth / 귀를 ~ wad 〔fill, stop〕 *one's* ears 《with cotton》 / 새는 데를 찾아 구멍을 ~ find and stop leaks. ② 《억제·저지하다》 curb; stop; check; put a stop to. ¶ 입을 ~ stop *one's* mouth; put a gag on 《*a person*》; bind 《*a person*》 to secrecy; gag / 돈으로 입을 ~ buy 《*a person's*》 silence; put a gold muzzle 《on newspapers》.

**틀어박다** ① ⇨틀어넣다. ② 《사장하다》 hoard (up); keep 《*a thing*》 in dead storage.

**틀어박히다** confine *oneself* to 〔in〕 《a room》; stay in 〔indoors, at home〕; closet *oneself* in 《*one's* office》; shut *oneself* up; be confined 〔closeted〕 in 《*one's* room》. ¶ 집에만 틀어박혀 있는 사람 a home immured person; a stay-at-home; a home-body 《미속어》 / 서재에 ~ be confined in *one's* study / 시골에 틀어박혀 살다 live in rural retirement 〔seclusion〕 / 온종일 방에만 ~ keep (to) *one's* room all day long.

**틀어지다** ① 《빗나가다》 swerve; turn aside; go astray; 《뒤틀려 휘다》 warp; be warped; be curved. ¶ 공이 왼쪽으로 ~ a ball flies off to the left 〔to left field〕.
② 《두 사람 사이가》 get twisted; be distorted; go awry; get a kink in 《it》; kink. ¶ 둘의 사이가 ~ fall out with each other; be estranged from each other / 두 친구는 중상 때문에 한때 사이가 틀어졌다 The two old friends were separated for a time by spiteful gossip.
③ 《일·계획 등이》 be upset; go wrong 〔amiss〕; miscarry; break down; fall through; fail; be a fiasco. ¶ 계약이 ~ a contract 「goes wrong 〔doesn't work out the way it should〕 / 교섭〔협상〕이 ~ negotiations break down / 예상이 ~ [일이 주어] fall short of 〔belie〕 *one's* expectations; [사람이 주어] be disappointed of *one's* expectations / 일이 ~ a plan 「goes wrong 〔is a fiasco〕 / 그로 인해 모든 것이 틀어졌다 Everything went wrong because of him. / 그렇게 되면 모든 예정이 틀어지고 만다 It would upset the whole schedule.
④ 《꼬이다》 get 〔be〕 twisted; be distorted; go 〔be〕 awry; kink.

**틀지다** (be) dignified; have dignity. ¶ 사람이 틀지어 믿을 만하다 be dignified and reliable.

**틀톱** a pit 〔frame〕 saw.

**틈** ① 《벌어진》 an opening; an aperture; a gap; a crack; a chink; a crevice; 《불화》 an estrangement; a breach of friendship. ¶ 창틈 a chink in the window / 문틈 a crack in the door / 바위틈 a crack in a rock / 틈으로 엿보다 peep through the opening / 틈이 벌어지다 have a crevice; be cracked; have a break 《in *one's* friendship》 / 둘 사이에 틈이 생기다 be estranged from each other.
② 《공간》 room; space; 《간격》 interval; 《시간》 time. ¶ 어느 틈에 before *one* knows / 집을 비운 틈에 while *one* is out 〔away from home〕 / 한 사람도 들어갈 틈이 없다 There is no room left for a single person.
③ 《여가·짬》 spare 〔leisure〕 time; time to spare; leisure (hours). ¶ 틈이 있다 have time to spare; be free / 틈이 없다 have no time (to spare); be busy; be pressed for time / 갈 틈이 없다 cannot find time to go / 틈이 나다 get free; come to have time / 틈을 내다 find time; make time 《to *do*》 / 틈 있을 때 when *one* is at leisure; in 〔at〕 *one's* leisure hours; when *one*

finds the time / 책 읽을 틈이 없다 have no time to read / 그는 놀 틈이 거의 없다 He has very little time for amusements. / 오후엔 틈이 좀 있습니다 I have some leisure from my work in the afternoon. / 틈 보아 놀러 오시오 Come and see me when you have time (to spare). / 그는 틈 있는 대로 공부를 한다 He spends every free moment studying.
④《기회》 an opportunity; a chance; an occasion. ¶ 틈이 있을 때마다 at every opportunity; whenever the opportunity arises / 틈을 보다 wait for a chance 《to *do*》/ 틈을 노리다 watch for a chance / 도망칠 틈이 없다 have 〔see〕 no chance to escape / 그는 틈을 타서 문 있는 쪽으로 도망쳤다 He saw his opportunity and made for the door.

**틈나다** ①《벌어지다》 open; get a crack 《in》. ②《겨를이 생기다》 become free; come to have time; get leisure. ¶ 며칠 있어야 틈이 나겠다 I shall not have time for several days. / 틈나는 대로 찾아가겠다 I'll go and see as soon as I find time.

**틈바구니** ①《깨진 틈》 a gap; a crack; a crevice; a chink. ⇨틈①.
②《벌어진 사이》 a narrow space 《between, among》. ¶ 두 사람 ~에 끼이다 be「squeezed 〔pinned〕 in between two people / 의리와 인정의 ~에 끼어 진퇴유곡이다 be in a dilemma between *one's* sense of duty and *one's* feelings / 나는 양쪽의 ~에 끼어서 입장이 매우 난처하다 I am in an awkward position, caught between the two interested parties.

**틈새** a gap; an opening. ◉ ~시장 a niche market.

**틈새기** ⇨틈바구니②.

**틈입**(闖入) intrusion; breaking in(to). ~하다 intrude; break in(to).

**틈타다** take advantage of; avail *oneself* of; seize an opportunity; make the most of a chance. ¶ 혼란을 틈타 taking advantage of the confusion / 적은 어둠을 틈타 전진했다 The enemy advanced under cover of night.

**틈틈이** ①《깨진 틈마다》 at each gap. ②《짬짬이》 at each moment of leisure; at spare moments; in odd minutes; in the intervals 《of *one's* work》. ¶ ~ 꽃을 가꾸다 raise flowers in *one's* spare moments / ~ 공부하다 turn every odd moment to account for *one's* studies / 이것은 ~ 해서 될 일이 아니다 This isn't a job which can be done in your spare time.

**티**[1] ①《이질물》 a mote; a particle; a grit; a foreign element. ¶ 눈에 티가 들다 have「*something* 〔a mote〕 in *one's* eye / 김에서 티를 골라 내다 pick the grits out of the laver. ②《흠》 a flaw; a speck; a spot. ¶ 옥에 티 a flaw in a gem; a fly in the ointment; a scratch on the mirror / 그는 우유부단한 것이 옥에 티다 [비유적] Irresolution is a defect in his otherwise perfect character. ③《기색·작태》「a spot 〔a touch, a smack, a taste, an air〕 of...; something of.... ¶ 군인 티가 나는 soldierly; soldier-like; martial / 부자 티를 내다 give *oneself* the air of a millionaire / 양반 티가 있다 have something of the gentleman about *one* / 시골 티가 나다 have a bit of the country about *one;* be countryfied; have hayseed in *one's* hair / 그는 학자 티가 난다 He has something of a scholar about him.

**티**[2] ①《글자》 the letter "T". ②《차》 tea. ③《골프의》 a (golf) tee.
◉ ~형(型) T-shape.

**티격나다** break up 《with》; quarrel 〔fall out〕 《with》; split; be at odds 《with》. ¶ 아무와 ~ be at odds with 《*a person*》; be on bad terms with 《*a person*》/ 서로 ~ fall out with each other; be at odds.

**티격태격** disputing; wrangling; quarrelling. ~하다 dispute 〔quarrel, wrangle〕 《with》; bicker with each other.

**티끌** ①《먼지》 dust; a mote. ¶ ~이 앉다 dust accumulates; be covered with dust / ~을 털다 shake off the dust; dust 《furniture》/ ~ 모아 태산 《속담》 Many a little makes a mickle. / 집안에는 ~ 하나 떨어져 있지 않다 There is not a speck of dust in the whole house.
②《조금》 《not》「a bit 〔a particle, an atom, a jot, a fig, an ounce, etc.〕. ¶ ~만큼의 값어치도 없다 It is not worth「a snap 〔of *one's* fingers〕. / 양심이라곤 ~만큼도 없다 He doesn't have an ounce of conscience in him. / 그녀는 ~만큼의 상식도 없다 She has not a bit of common sense.
◉ ~세상 this filthy world; this world full of woes and cares.

**티눈** 《발의》 a corn. ¶ ~이 생긴 발가락 a toe with a callosity / 발에 ~이 박이

다 have a corn on *one's* foot.
◉ ～약 a corn plaster.

**티뜯다** ① 《흠잡다》 pick a hole 〔flaw〕 in; carp 〔cavil〕 at; find fault with; pick on; nag. ¶ 아무를 ～ pick on *a person* / 아무의 글을 ～ pick a hole in what *a person* has written. ② 《이질 물을》 remove a foreign element; clean. ¶ 김을 ～ clean laver (of grits).

**티베트** Tibet. ¶ ～의 Tibetan.
◉ ～말 Tibetan. ～사람 a Tibetan.

**티보다** see 〔examine to see〕 whether there is any flaw in 《it》; find a flaw in 《it》; 《티뜯다》 try to find a fault.

**티본 스테이크** (a) T-bone steak.

**티브이** TV. 〔< *te*le*v*ision〕

**티비** 〖의학〗 T.B.; TB; t.b.; tb.; tuberculosis. 〔< *t*ubercle *b*acillus〕

**티석티석** unevenly; irregularly; coarsely. ～하다 (be) uneven; irregular; coarse. ¶ ～한 천 coarse cloth.

**티셔츠** a T-shirt; a tee shirt.

**티슈페이퍼** tissue paper; 《화장용》 facial tissues.

**티스푼** 《찻숟갈》 a teaspoon. ¶ ～ 하나의 설탕 a teaspoonful of sugar.

**티시** 《여행자 수표》 a TC. 〔< *t*raveler's *c*heck〕

**티엔티** T.N.T.; TNT. 〔< *t*ri*n*itro*t*oluene〕

**티자** a T square.

**티오** 《인원 편성표》 T.O.; TO. 〔< *t*able of *o*rganization〕

**티적거리다** keep picking on 〔"riding"〕; keep carping at; keep teasing 〔needling〕; pick a quarrel. ¶ 아무를 못 살게 ～ "ride" *a person* to death.

**티커** 《주식 가격 표시기》 a (stock) ticker; 《영》 a tape machine.

**티처** a teacher.

**티케이오** 〖권투〗 T.K.O.; TKO. 〔< *t*echnical *k*nock*o*ut〕

**티켓** a ticket.

**티크** 《나무》 a teak; 《목재》 teak (wood).
◉ ～재(材) teakwood; teak.

**티타늄** 〖화학〗 titanium. ◉ ～강(鋼) titanium steel.

**티티새** 〖조류〗 a dusky thrush.

**티파티** 《다과회》 a tea party; tea. ¶ ～를 열다 give 〔hold, have〕 a tea party.

**티푸스** 〖의학〗 《장티푸스》 typhoid fever; 《발진티푸스》 typhus (fever). ¶ 악성 발진 ～ malignant typhus.

**티피컬** 《전형적인》 typical. ～하다 (be) typical. ¶ ～한 영국 신사 a typical English gentleman.

**틴에이저** a teenager; a boy 〔girl〕 in his 〔her〕 teens.

**틴에이지** teenage. ¶ ～의 소년들 teenage(d) boys.

**팀** a team. ¶ 홈～ the home team / 팀을 짜다 make up a team / 팀에 들어 있다 be a member of a team; be on the 《baseball》 team / 팀 강화를 위해 젊은 선수를 많이 기용하다 employ many younger players to reinforce *one's* team / 우리들은 같은 팀이다 We are in the same team. *or* We are teammates. / 그는 자네 팀(선수)인가 Is he on your team? ◉ ～메이트 a teammate. ～타율 〖야구〗 a team batting average. ～플레이 team play; the play for *one's* team.

**팀스피리트 (군사훈련)** the Team Spirit; the annual South Korea-U.S. military exercise.

**팀워크** teamwork. ¶ ～가 좋다〔나쁘다〕 have fine 〔be poor in〕 teamwork / 훌륭한 ～로 성공하다 succeed by means of good teamwork.

**팀파니** 〖악기〗 timpani; a set of kettledrums. ¶ ～ 연주자 a timpanist.

**팁** ① 《행하·정표》 a tip; a gratuity.
¶ 팁 제도 the tipping system / 많은 팁 a good 〔large〕 tip / 적은 팁 a small tip / 팁을 후하게 주는 손님 a high-tipping customer; a good 〔generous〕 tipper / 팁을 받다 receive 〔accept〕 a tip / 팁을 기대하다 expect a tip / 팁을 주다 give a tip; tip 《a waitress》 / 팁 3천 원을 주다 tip 《*a person*》 3,000 won / 팁을 넉넉히 주다 tip generously 〔handsomely〕; give a generous tip / 팁을 적게 주다 undertip / 팁을 주어 …시키다 tip 《a waitress》 into 《*doing something*》 / 거스름돈은 자네 팁으로 받아 두게 Keep the change as a tip to you. / 팁 일체 사절(謝絶) 《게시》 No tips accepted. *or* Tips declined. / 팁·세금 포함 《표시》 Service charge and tax are included. / 이것은 자네에게 주는 팁일세 This is for your trouble. / 「그녀에게 얼마나 팁을 주지」—「2달러면 충분할 거야」 "How much should I give her as a tip?"—"Two dollar will be enough."
② 〖야구〗 a tip.

**팅크** a tincture. ¶ 요오드～ tincture of iodine / 캠퍼～ tincture of camphor.

**파**[1] 〖식물〗 a leek; a Welsh 〔spring〕 onion; a green onion. ◉ 파강회 green onion bundles.

**파**[2] 〖음악〗 fa. ¶ 파음 F; f.

**파**(派) ① 《그룹·패거리》 a group; a coterie; 《파벌》 a clique; a faction. ¶ 교장파 the supporters of the principal / 소장파 a young group / 전전〔전후〕파 the prewar 〔postwar〕 generation / 관학(官學)파와 사학(私學)파 the government and the private school factions.
② 《당파》 a party; a faction. ¶ 강경파 the hard-line faction / 온건파 the moderate faction; the moderates / 좌〔우〕파 the left-〔right-〕wing faction; leftists 〔rightists〕 / 주류파 the mainstream faction; the mainstreamers / 비주류파 the nonmainstreamers / 중도파 the middle-of-the-road faction; the middle-of-the roaders / 혁신파 the reformists / 두 파로 갈라지다〔나뉘다〕 be divided into two factions 〔schools, camps〕.
③ 《학파·유파》 a school. ¶ (문학·예술상의) 고전파 〔낭만파〕 the classical 〔romantic〕 school.
④ 《종파》 a sect; a denomination; 《족벌》 a branch of a family 〔clan〕. ¶ 감리교파 the Methodist communion / 개신교의 여러 파 Protestant denominations. ⇨ 파나다.

**파**(破) damage; injury; breakage; break-down.

**파격**(破格) breaking the rules; an exception; an irregularity; 〖문법〗 a solecism. ~하다 break (the rules); make an exception; make a solecism; commit an offense against grammar. ¶ ~적인 exceptional; unprecedented; extraordinary; special; 《변칙의》 abnormal; irregular; broken / ~적 승진 an exceptional promotion / ~적인 대우를 받다 enjoy exceptionally good treatment / ~적인 값으로 팔다〔제공하다〕 sell 《*a thing*》 at an absurdly low price; offer 《goods》 at a great bargain / 그건 ~이다 It is a break with tradition. ◉ ~구문 〖문법〗 an anacoluthon (*pl.* -tha).

**파견**(派遣) dispatch; despatch; detachment. ~하다 dispatch; despatch; send; detach; 《대사를》 accredit. ¶ 군대〔함대〕를 ~하다 dispatch an army 〔a fleet〕 《to》 / 대사를 ~하다 accredit an ambassador 《to》 / 대표를 ~하다 delegate 〔send〕 a representative / 사절을 ~하다 dispatch 〔send〕 an envoy 《to》 / 우리는 현지에 조사단을 ~ 했다 We sent 〔dispatched〕 a research group to the spot / 통상 문제를 논의하기 위하여 정부는 미국에 특별 사절을 ~했다 The Government dispatched a special envoy to the United States to talk over the trade issue.
◉ ~군 an expeditionary force 〔army〕. ~단 a delegation. ~대 a detachment; a contingent.

**파경**(破鏡) 《거울》 a broken mirror; 《이혼》 (a) divorce; separation. ¶ 그 부부는 마침내 ~에 이르렀다 The couple were finally divorced.

**파계**(破戒) violation 〔transgression〕 of the 《Buddhist》 commandments; apostasy. ~하다 violate 〔break〕 the Buddhist commandments; transgress; apostatize. ◉ ~승(僧) an apostate 〔a depraved〕 monk; a fallen 〔sinful〕 priest. ~자 a transgressor.

**파고**(波高) the height of a wave; wave height.

**파고다** a pagoda. ◉ ~공원 Pagoda Park.

**파고들다** 《조사·검토하다》 dig 〔delve, probe〕 into 《a problem》; investigate; make a thorough investigation; 《침식·침투하다》 eat into; gnaw 《at *one's* heart》; burn into 《*one's* mind》; cut into. ¶ 남의 (선거) 기반에 ~ encroach upon another's「constituency 〔sphere of influence〕 / 마음 속에 ~ eat into *one's* heart / 외국 시장에 ~ make an inroad into 〔(up)on〕 a foreign market / 두 손을 묶은 밧줄이 살에 파고 들었다 The rope with which his hands were tied cut into the flesh.

**파곳** 〖음악〗 a faggot; a *faggoto* (It.); a bassoon. ◉ ~주자(奏者) a bassoonist; a *faggoto* player.

**파괴**(破壞) destruction; demolition;

ㅍ

breakdown. ～하다 break (down); destroy; 《건물 등을 허물다》 demolish; pull [take, tear] down; 《산산조각으로》 break [take] … 「to pieces [into fragments]; break up; smash; shatter; 《손상하다》 damage.

> (용법) **break** 「부수다, 파괴하다」란 뜻의 가장 일반적인 말. 부분이 떨어져 나가는 것을 뜻함. **destroy** 회복이 불가능할 정도로 부서지든가, 물체를 허물어뜨리는 것. **pull** [**take**, **tear**] **down** 건물 같이 인공적으로 만들어진 물체를 허무는 것. **demolish** 위의 말과 거의 동의어로 쓰이지만 「완전히 파괴하다」라는 강한 의미가 내포됨. **break** [**take**] **… to pieces** [**into fragments**]; **break up** 산산조각으로 부순다는 뜻. **smash** 보통 의도적으로, 또는 힘을 주어 순간적으로 소리를 내어 산산조각 내는 것. **shatter** 유리·거울 등 깨지기 쉬운 것을 산산조각 내는 것. **damage** 흠집을 내거나 일부를 부서뜨려 손상을 입히는 것.

¶ ～적인 destructive; ruinous; subversive; wasteful 《war》/ ～되다 be broken (down); be destroyed [smashed, demolished, wrecked] / 가정의 평화와 행복을 ～하다 destroy the peace and happiness of families / 한 마을을 완전히 ～하다 raze a village to the ground / 다리는 완전히 ～되었다 The bridge was completely wrecked. / 태풍으로 많은 가옥이 ～되었다 Many houses were demolished by the typhoon / 토네이도로 마을의 집들이 수십 채 ～되었다 Dozens of houses in the town were destroyed by the tornado.

◉ ～계수(係數) a modulus of rupture. ～공작 subversive activities. ～력 destructive power. ～병기 destructive weapons: 대량 ～ 병기 a weapon of mass destruction. ～분자 a subversive (element); a disrupter: ～ 분자를 색출하다 ferret out subversive elements. ～시험 a breaking [rupture] test. ～자 a destroyer; a disrupter; a devastator; a desolator. ～작용 《세포의》 destructive metabolism. ～주의 destructionism; vandalism: ～ 주의자 a destructionist. ～활동[행위] subversive activities: ～ 활동 방지법 the Anti-Subversive Activities Act.

**파국**(破局) collapse; catastrophe; an end(파멸). ¶ ～적인 catastrophic / ～에 직면하다 be in the face of ruin / ～으로 몰고 가다 drive into catastrophe / 우리들의 결혼은 6년만에 ～을 맞았다 Our marriage collapsed [broke down] in the sixth year. / 그의 경영 관리 실패는 회사를 ～으로 몰고 갔다 His failure in management caused the collapse of the company.

**파급**(波及) spreading; extending. ～하다 spread [extend] 《to, over》; reach; 《영향을》 influence; have repercussions; affect (바람직하지 않은 방향으로). ¶ 전국에 ～하다 extend all over the country; raise [create] a nationwide stir / 정계에 ～하다 affect [have repercussions in] the political world / 전쟁은 아시아에까지 ～되었다 The war was carried into Asia. / 그 격렬한 학생 집회는 한국 각지의 대학으로 ～되었다 The violent student's rally spread to other universities throughout Korea. / 그 스캔들은 각료들에게까지 ～ 되었다 The scandal spread to the ministers.

◉ ～효과 a ripple effect 《on》; pervasive effect: 소득세 감세는 경기 동향에 ～효과가 클 것이다 Income tax reductions will have no small ripple effect on the volume of business transactions.

**파기**(破棄) 《폐기》 destruction; 《무효화》 annulment; cancellation (취소); breach (약속의); abrogation (조약의); reversal (판결의); revocation (판결·계약의). ～하다 tear 《*a thing*》 to pieces and throw 《it》 away; destroy; 《무효로 하다》 annul 《a decision》; cancel 《a contract》; break 《a promise》; abrogate [quash] 《a lease》; scrap 《a treaty》; reverse 《a sentence》. ¶ 문서의 ～ the destruction [tearing up] of documents / 조약의 ～ abrogation of a treaty / 원심을 ～하다 annul the original decision; quash [reverse] the original judgment [decision] / 그는 약혼을 일방적으로 ～했다 He broke off [cancelled] our engagement without consulting me. / 그 통상 조약은 일방적으로 ～되었다 The commercial treaty was abrogated one-sidedly.

**파김치** pickled scallion [leek]. ¶ ～가 되다 [비유적] get dead tired; be worn-out; wilt (with exhaustion); 《구어》 be dog-tired.

**파나다**(破—) get broken [damaged]; become defective; acquire a flaw (보석·그릇 등의). ¶ 그릇이 ～ a dish gets damaged / 파난 그릇 a broken dish; a dish with a flaw in it.

**파나마** 《나라 이름》 (the Republic of) Panama. ¶ ∼의 Panamanian.
◉ ∼모자 a Panama (hat). ∼분쟁 the Panamanian dispute ∼사람 a Panamanian. ∼운하 the Panama Canal: ∼ 운하 지대 the Panama (Canal) Zone. ∼지협 the Isthmus of Panama.

**파나물** scallion salad.

**파내다** dig up 〔out〕; dig open; unearth 《a buried treasure》; excavate; disinter 〔exhume〕 《a dead body》. ¶ 땅에서 ∼ dig *something* from 〔out of〕 the ground / 광산에서 금을 ∼ dig gold from a mine / 감자를 ∼ dig (up) potatoes / 나무 뿌리를 ∼ dig 〔grub〕 up the roots of a tree / 무덤을 ∼ dig a grave open / 석탄을 ∼ mine 〔dig out〕 coal.

**파내다**(破—) have 《*a thing*》 broken 「〔damaged〕.

**파노라마** a panorama. ¶ ∼ 같은 풍경 a panoramic 〔panorama-like〕 view.
◉ ∼ 사진기 a panoramic 〔pantoscopic〕 camera; a pantoscope.

**파다** ① 《땅·구멍을》 dig; delve; bore 《a hole in a board》; drive 《a tunnel》; 《바위를》 cave 《a rock》; 《파서 뚫다》 excavate 《a canal》; 《후벼서》 scoop out. ¶ 구멍을 ∼ excavate 〔make〕 a hole 《in》 / 굴을 ∼ drive 〔excavate〕 a tunnel 《through》 / 참호를 ∼ excavate a trench / 땅을 ∼ delve 〔dig in〕 the ground; till the soil (경작하다) / 모래를 ∼ dig up the sand / 우물〔연못〕을 ∼ dig a well 〔pond〕.
② 《이치·문제 등을》 make a search 〔inquiry〕 《into, for》; investigate 〔study〕 thoroughly; delve 〔probe〕 into 《a problem》; dig into. ¶ 깊은 학리(學理)를 ∼ explore an abstruse theory / 진상을 ∼ inquire into the true state of things; go (down) to 〔get at〕 the bottom of a matter.
③ 《새기다》 carve 《in, on, out of》; engrave; chisel (정으로); sculpt (조각하다); cut; inscribe (새겨넣다). ¶ 묘비에 이름을 ∼ engrave 《*a person's*》 name on the tomb stone / 도장을 ∼ engrave a seal; 《남을 시켜》 have *one's* seal engraved.
④ 《공부를》 study 〔work〕 hard; drudge; grind 《구어》; bone up on. ¶ 공부만 파는 학생 a dig 《미구어》; a plugger 《미구어》; a grinder 《구어》 / 영어를 들이 ∼ study English in earnest; grind away at English.

**파다하다**(頗多—) 《매우 많다》 (be) numerous; abundant; large in number; have a good many; 《빈번하다》 be quite frequent. ¶ 그러한 예가 ∼ We have a good many such examples. *or* That sort of thing happens quite often.

**파다하다**(播多—) (be) widely rumored; be spread widely; [서술적] be widely known; be rife. ¶ 그가 이혼했다는 소문이 ∼ It is widely rumored that he has divorced his wife. / 그가 자살했다는 소문이 ∼ The news of his suicide is noised abroad. / 사장이 곧 사직하리라는 소문이 ∼ The air is filled with rumors that the president of the company will soon resign his post.

**파닥거리다** ⇨ 퍼덕거리다.

**파담**(破談) breaking off; cancellation; rejection. ∼하다 break off 《an engagement》; be cancelled.

**파도**(波濤) waves; billows (큰 물결); surges (굽이치는); a beachcomber (밀려 오는); a surf (밀려와 부서지는); a breaker (부서지는); a ripple (작은); rough 〔heavy, high〕 seas (거친).
¶ 큰 ∼ a great wave; a billow / ∼ 소리 the sound 〔roar〕 of the waves / ∼ 모양의 wave-like / ∼가 잔잔한 calm; smooth / ∼ 치다 wave; undulate; roll / ∼ 치는 대로 《drift about》 at the mercy of the waves / ∼가 일다 swell; surge; the sea rises high / ∼가 자다 the sea goes down; the waves subside / ∼가 거칠다 have a rough sea; The waves are high. / (배가) ∼를 뒤집어 쓰다 ship a wave; be washed by the sea 〔waves〕 / ∼를 타다 ride on the waves / ∼를 헤치고 나아가다 cut through high seas; plow 〔cleave〕 through the waves / ∼에 표류하다 drift 〔float〕 on the waves / ∼에 까불리다〔시달리다〕 be tossed about by the waves / ∼에 휘말리다 be swallowed up by the waves / ∼에 휩쓸리다 be washed 〔carried〕 away by the waves / ∼와 싸우다 buffet the waves / ∼처럼 밀려오다 attack in a surging mass; surge 〔rush〕 upon / ∼가 바닷가로 밀려온다 The waves beat upon the seashore. / ∼가 높다 The waves are high. *or* The seas are running high.

**파도타기**(波濤—) surfboard-riding; surfing. ∼하다 surf; ride the surf. ¶ ∼하는 사람 a surfer; a surf rider.

**파동**(波動) a wave 〔an undulatory〕 motion; undulation; 『의학』 fluctuation. ∼하다 fluctuate; undulate; move in waves. ◉ ~계 a cymograph; a kymograph. ~설 《빛의》 the wave 〔undulatory〕 theory (of light). ~역학 wave mechanics. 가격~ fluctuations in prices. 경제~ an economic crisis. 정치~ a political upheaval. 증권~ a stock market crisis; wild fluctuations of the stock market.

**파두**(巴豆) 〖식물〗 a croton (plant).

**파라과이** (the Republic of) Paraguay. ¶ ~의 Paraguayan. ◉ ~사람 a Paraguayan.

**파라다이스** 《천국》 Paradise; 《에덴 동산》 the Garden of Eden; 《낙원》 a paradise.

**파라솔** a parasol; a sunshade. ¶ ~을 받다 put 〔hold〕 up a parasol.

**파라슈트** a parachute; a chute. ⇨ 낙하산. ¶ ~를 펴다〔의 끈을 당기다〕 pull the rip cord of *one's* parachute.

**파라오** 《고대 이집트의》 a Pharaoh.

**파라티온** 《농약》 parathion (insecticide). ◉ ~중독 parathion poisoning.

**파라티푸스** 〖의학〗 paratyphoid (fever); paratyphus (G.). ◉ ~균 a paratyphoid bacillus.

**파라핀** 〖화학〗 《미》 paraffin; 《영》 (paraffin) wax. ◉ ~연고 paraffin ointment. ~유 paraffin 〔coal〕 oil. ~지 paraffin 〔wax(ed)〕 paper. ~합성물 paraffinoid.

**파란**(波瀾) 《물결》 waves; surges; 《소란》 (a) trouble; (a) disturbance; commotion; 《성쇠》 ups and downs; vicissitudes. ¶ 가정의 ~ family 〔domestic〕 trouble / ~ 많은 생애 a checkered career; an eventful life / ~을 일으키다 cause trouble; raise a disturbance / 그는 ~만장한 생애를 보냈다 He has had many vicissitudes. *or* His life was full of ups and downs. / 정계는 일대 ~이 일듯한 형세다 There are indications of rather stormy political season.

**파랑** blue. ¶ 초록빛을 띤 ~ Nile blue; robin's-egg blue. ◉ ~쐐기나방 〖곤충〗 an oriental moth.

**파랑**(波浪) 《물결》 waves; 《큰 파도》 a billow; a surge. ◉ ~ 주의보 a high sea warning: 지방 기상대는 오늘 아침 ~주의보를 내렸다 The local meteorological station issued a high sea warning this morning.

**파랑새** 〖조류〗 a broad-billed roller; 《행복의 상징으로서의》 a blue bird.

**파랑이** a blue one 〔thing〕; blue stuff.

**파랗다** ① 《색깔이》 (be) blue; azure; green (녹색의). ¶ 파란 하늘 a blue sky / 파란 풀 green grass / 파란 눈의 소녀 a blue eyed girl / 파랗게 칠하다 〔물들이다〕 paint 〔dye〕 blue.
② 《창백하다》 (be) pale; pallid. ¶ 파랗게 질린 얼굴빛 a pale complexion / 놀라서 파랗게 질리어 pale with fright / 얼굴이 파랗게 질리다 *one's* face turns ashen 〔deadly pale 〔white〕 as a sheet〕; lose *one's* color; turn pale.

**파래** 〖식물〗 green laver; sea lettuce.

**파래박** a gourd vessel used for bailing water out of a boat.

**파래지다** 《하늘·나뭇잎이》 become 〔turn〕 blue 〔green〕; 《얼굴이》 turn 〔go〕 pale 〔pallid, white〕; lose color. ¶ 나뭇잎이 ~ leaves of trees turn green / 얼굴이 ~ *one's* face turns pale / 파래졌다 빨개졌다 하다 turn alternately pale and red.

**파렴치**(破廉恥) shamelessness; infamy; ignominy; impudence; brazenness. ~하다 (be) shameless; infamous; ignominious; brazen(-faced); [서술적] be dead 〔lost〕 to all (sense of) shame. ¶ ~한 거짓말쟁이 a shameless liar / 그는 ~하다 He has no sense of decency. / 그는 ~한 행위로 해고당했다 He was discharged for his shameful conduct. ◉ ~범 an infamous criminal. ~죄 an infamous offense 〔crime〕. ~한 a shameless fellow; a knave.

**파르대대하다** (be) bluish 〔greenish〕. ⇨ 「파르스름하다.

**파르르** ¶ ~ 끓다 be hissing hot / ~ 화를 내다 simmer with rage / 두려움으로 ~떨다 tremble with fear / 입술이 ~ 떨렸다 My lips quivered.

**파르스름하다** 《빛깔이》 (be) bluish; greenish; [서술적] be tinged with blue 〔green〕; have a bluish 〔greenish〕 tint; 《얼굴이》 (be) rather pale 〔pallid〕.

**파르족족하다** = 파르스름하다.

**파르테논** 《그리스의 신전》 the Parthenon.

**파릇파릇** all spotted green 〔blue〕; green 〔blue〕 here and there. ~하다 (be) freshly blue; vividly green; verdant. ¶ ~한 신록의 계절 the season of fresh verdure / 싹이 ~ 돋아나다 the buds come out all green / 나뭇잎이 ~ 돋아난다 The leaves come out on the trees all fresh and green.

**파리**[1] 〖곤충〗 a fly. ¶ ~를 쫓다 fan 〔drive, scare〕 flies away / ~를 날리다 [비유적] 《*one's* business》 be slack 〔dull〕 / ~를 잡다 catch flies; 《파리채 등으로》 flap 〔swat〕 a fly / ~가 쉬를 슬다 a fly blows / …에 ~가 꾀다 flies swarm 《round, about》/ ~가 윙윙거린다 Flies are buzzing around. / 여름에는 장사가 안 돼 ~를 날린다 [비유적] Business is slack 〔dull〕 in summer. ◉ ~똥〔자국〕 a flyspeck. ~목숨 a mean 〔cheap〕 life; an ephemeral 〔insignificant〕 existence. ~약 fly poison; 《물약》 fly water. ~잡이 《기구》 a flycatcher: ~잡이 끈끈이 flypaper / ~잡이통 a flytrap; a fly bottle. ~채 a fly flap 〔swatter〕; a flapper.

**파리**[2] 《프랑스 수도》 Paris. ¶ ~의 Parisian. ◉ ~사람 a Parisian; 《여자》 a Parisienne. ~제 (祭) the Fourteenth of July; *le qua-torze juillet* (F.).

**파리하다** 《창백하다》 (be) pale; pallid; 《여위다》 (be) thin; lean; 《해쓱하다》 gaunt; emaciated. ¶ 파리한 사람 a lean 〔gaunt〕 person / 파리한 얼굴 a thin 〔drawn〕 face / 파리해지다 become thin; lose *one's* weight; lose flesh; fall off / 앓고 나서 파리해 보이다 look thin after an illness.

**파마** a permanent (wave); a perm 《구어》. ⇨ 퍼머(넌트). ~하다 have *one's* hair permed 〔permanently waved〕; have 〔get〕 a perm(anent). ¶ ~하러 미장원에 가다 go to the beauty parlor for a permanent.

**파먹다** ① 《파서 먹다》 dig 《*a thing*》 out and eat 《it》; 《먹어 들어가다》 eat into 〔away, out〕; bore 〔gouge〕 into (벌레 따위가). ¶ 벌레가 파먹은 목재 worm-eaten timber / 수박을 ~ scoop 〔dig〕 a watermelon out and eat it / 감자를 ~ dig potatoes up and eat them / 땅을 ~ [비유적] live by farming / 벌레가 ~ a worm bores into 《the apple》.
② 《무위도식하다》 eat idle bread; live in idleness.
③ 《재산 따위를》 eat away what *one* has.

**파면**(罷免) dismissal; discharge. ~하다 dismiss; discharge; relieve 《*a person*》 of his post; remove 《*a person*》 from office; fire 《미구어》. ¶ ~당하다 be dismissed 〔discharged, fired〕; be relieved of *one's* post / 그는 부정행위로 ~당했다 He was discharged 〔dismissed〕 for doing something dishonest. ◉ ~권 the right of dismissal; the right to remove 《*a person*》 from office.

**파멸**(破滅) ruin; destruction; wreck; collapse; downfall; fall. ~하다 be ruined 〔wrecked〕; be done for; go 〔fall〕 crash; go to (rack and) ruin. ¶ ~에 직면하다 be on the brink 〔verge〕 of ruin / ~의 원인이 되다 cause 〔become the cause of〕 *one's* ruin / ~을 초래하다 bring (down) ruin 《upon *oneself*》; ruin *oneself* / 아무를 ~시키다 bring *a person* to ruin / 술이 그의 ~을 가져왔다 Drinking was the ruin of him.

**파문**(破紋) 《물결》 a ripple; a water ring; a (wave) ring on the water; 《영향》 a stir; a sensation; repercussions. ¶ ~을 그리다 ripple; ripple out (in waves) / ~을 던지다 cause 〔create, make〕 a sensation 《in》; create a stir 《in》/ 정계에 ~을 던지다 create a stir 〔an uproar〕 in the political world; cause a sensation 〔ripple〕 in the political world / 그 보도는 온 나라 안에 큰 파문을 일으켰다 The news created a great stir in the country.

**파문**(破門) 《종교상의》 excommunication; 《사제지간의》 expulsion. ~하다 excommunicate 《from》; expel 《*one's* pupil》. ¶ ~을 당하다 be excommunicated; be expelled / 그는 가톨릭 교회에서 ~당했다 He was excommunicated from the Catholic Church.

**파묻다**[1] ① 《…속에》 bury 《in, under》; 《매장하다》 entomb; inter; inhume; plant 《미속어》. ¶ 파묻은 불씨 a banked fire 〔charcoal〕; an ash fire; buried embers / 땅 속에 깊이 ~ bury *something* deeply in the ground / 시체를 ~ bury a dead body; commit a body to the earth / 두 손에 얼굴을 파묻고 with *one's* face buried in *one's* hands / 손수건에 얼굴을 파묻고 울다 weep into *one's* handkerchief. ② 《마음 속에》 keep 〔bear〕 《*a matter*》 in mind. ¶ 가슴 속 깊이 파묻어 두다 keep 《a *matter*》 all to *oneself*. ③ 《일·사건을》 smother 〔cover, hush〕 up. ¶ 사건을 쉬쉬 ~ hush 〔cover〕 up the scandal 〔matter〕.

**파묻다**[2] 《꼬치꼬치 묻다》 ask inquisitively 〔closely〕; dig for information; quiz. ¶ 글 뜻을 ~ press 《*a person*》 for the precise meaning of a sentence / 남의 계획을 ~ quiz *a person* about *his* plan.

**파묻히다** be 〔get〕 buried 《in, under》; be interred (시체가); be hidden; 《세상에》 be buried in oblivion; live in obscurity. ¶ 눈에 ~ be buried under 〔in〕 the snow; be snowed under / 세상에 ~ be kept from the public eye; live in obscurity / 시골 구석에 ~ bury

〔live〕 *oneself* in the country; live an obscure life in the country / 일에 ～ be up to the neck in work / 그 사건은 어둠 속에 파묻혔다 The matter has been covered 〔hushed〕 up.

**파물**(破物) a damaged 〔defective〕 article; damaged goods. ¶ ～로 만들다 damage; spoil; crack.

**파미르** Pamir. ◉ ～고원 the Pamirs.

**파발**(擺撥) 〖고제도〗 a post station; a stage. ◉ ～꾼 an express messenger. ～마(馬) a post horse: ～마를 띄우다 dispatch a messenger on a post horse.

**파방치다**(罷榜—) break up 《*one's* home》 to move; shut up 《*one's* house》; wind up 《*one's* family affairs》.

**파방판**(罷榜—) an end; a close; the final scene; the breaking-up time. ¶ ～이 되다 come to an end; get finished.

**파벌**(派閥) a clique; a faction; a coterie. ¶ ～을 없애다 eliminate the factionalism / 여러 ～로 갈라지다 split into petty factions / 어느 정당에나 ～이 많다 All the political parties are faction=ridden. / 이 난국을 타개하는 데는 ～을 초월한 협력이 요청된다 Non-factional cooperation is required to tide over this crisis. ◉ ～다툼〔싸움〕 a factional 〔an interfactional〕 strife 〔dispute〕; rivalry between factions. ～심 a sectarian mind. ～주의 factionalism. ～해소 elimination of factionalism.

**파병**(派兵) the dispatch of forces 〔troops〕. ～하다 dispatch 〔send〕 troops 《to》; send an army 《against》. ¶ 해외로 ～하다 send troops overseas.

**파브르** 《프랑스 곤충학자》 Jean Henri Fabre (1823-1915). ◉ ～ 곤충기 Fabre's *Souvenirs entomologiques.*

**파삭거리다, 파삭하다** (be) crisp; crumbly; friable 《rock》; [서술적] be dry and crumbling; be rot away.

**파삭파삭** ⇨ 푸석푸석. ¶ ～한 과자 a crisp cake / ～한 흙 crumbly soil.

**파산**(破産) insolvency; bankruptcy; (financial) failure. ～하다 go 〔become〕 bankrupt 〔insolvent〕; go into bankruptcy; 《구어》 go bust; fail. ¶ ～한 bankrupt; failed / ～ 상태에 있다 be in (virtual) bankruptcy / ～을 선고하다 adjudicate 〔declare〕 《*a person*》 insolvent 〔bankrupt〕 / ～지경에 이르다 be on the verge 〔brink〕 of bankruptcy / ～ 직전에 몰리다 be driven to the verge of bankruptcy / ～시키다 make 《*a person*》 bankrupt / 그는 사업에 실패하여 ～했다 He failed in his business and went bankrupt.

◉ ～관재인 a receiver; a trustee in bankruptcy. ～법 the Bankruptcy Act. ～선고 an adjudication of bankruptcy: ～ 선고를 받다 be declared bankrupt. ～신청 a petition for bankruptcy: ～신청을 하다 file for bankruptcy. ～자 a bankrupt; an insolvent: 도덕적 ～자 a moral bankrupt. ～절차 bankruptcy procedure 〔proceedings〕. ～채권 claims provable in bankruptcy. ～채무 debts provable in bankruptcy. ～청산인 an assignee in bankruptcy; a liquidator in bankruptcy. ～행위 an act of bankruptcy.

**파산적**(—散炙) beef-and-green onion shish kebab.

**파상**(波狀) wave; undulation. ¶ ～적인 wavelike; wavy; undulating; 〖식물〗 gyrose; wave-edged / ～적인 파업 a piston strike.

**파상공격**(波狀攻擊) an attack in waves. ¶ 폭격기에 의한 ～ an air 〔aerial〕 raid in waves; wave bombing / ～을 가하다 launch 〔make〕 a series of attacks 《on, upon》.

**파상풍**(破傷風) 〖의학〗 tetanus; lockjaw; 《말의》 stag evil. ¶ ～의 tetanic. ◉ ～균 a tetanus bacillus (*pl.* bacilli). ～항독소 혈청 an antitetanic serum (*pl.* ～s, -ra).

**파생**(派生) derivation. ～하다 derive 〔be derived〕 《from》; stem 《from》; originate 《in》; give rise to (사건이). ¶～적인 derivative; secondary (이차적인) / ～적인 사건 a matter incidental to a main issue / 명사에서 ～한 형용사 an adjective derived from a noun / 그것은 ～적인 문제에 지나지 않는다 It's purely a secondary matter. / 뜻밖의 사태가 ～했다 An unexpected situation developed (from it). ◉ ～어 a derivative (word). ～어미 a derivational suffix. ～형 a derived form.

**파선**(波線) a wave; a wavelike 〔wavy〕 line.

**파선**(破船) 《조난》 shipwreck; wreck; 《배》 a ship in distress; a wrecked vessel. ～하다 be shipwrecked; be wrecked. ¶ ～현장 the scene of the wreck 〔disaster〕 / 암초에 걸려 ～한 배 a ship wrecked on the rocks / ～한 배를 구하다 save a ship from wreck; salvage a ship in distress.

**파선**(破線) a broken 〔dashed〕 line.

**파손**(破損) damage; injury; breakage;

breakdown. ～하다 be damaged; be broken (down); be destroyed; 《…을》 damage; break; spoil; destroy. ¶ ～된 damaged; broken / ～되기 쉬운 easy to break; fragile / 심하게 ～된 옛 성 a dilapidated old castle / ～되어 있다 be broken; be out of repair / ～을 면하다 be 〔remain〕 intact / ～된 곳을 수리하다 repair the damages / ～이 크다〔경미하다〕 suffer a heavy 〔slight〕 damage / 태풍으로 가옥들의 ～이 컸다 The typhoon caused heavy damage to houses. ◉ ～물〔품〕 damaged goods. ～부분 a damaged 〔broken〕 part 〔section〕; 《제방 따위의》 a breach.

**파쇄**(破碎) crush(ing); smash; breaking 〔cracking〕 to pieces; fragmentation. ～하다 crush; smash; shatter; break 〔crack〕 to piece; break up. ◉ ～기 a disintegrator; a crusher.

**파쇠**(破—) scrap iron; iron scraps.

**파쇼** [<*fascio* (It.)] 《주의》 Fascism; 《사람》 a fascist. ◉ ～사상 Fascism; fascist(ic) ideas. ～화 fascistization: ～화하다 fascistize.

**파수**(把守) watch; lookout; guard; vigilance; surveillance. ～보다 watch; guard; stand watch 〔guard〕; keep (a) watch 〔a lookout〕; be on the lookout 〔watch, guard〕. ◉ ～꾼 a watchman; a guard; a lookout; a keeper; a picket: ～꾼을 두다 place a guard 《at》; set 〔post〕 a lookout 《for》. ～막 a watch 〔sentry〕 box; a watchhouse; a lookout. ～병 a sentry; a guard; a sentinel.

**파스** 〖약〗 PAS. [<*P*ara-*A*mino-*S*alicylic Acid]

**파스칼** ① 《컴퓨터 프로그램 언어》 Pascal; PASCAL. ② 《압력의 단위》 a pascal (생략 Pa).

**파스텔** pastel. ◉ ～컬러 pastel shades 〔colors〕. ～화(畵) a pastel (drawing); a drawing in pastel. ～화가 a pastelist.

**파슬리** 〖식물〗 a parsley.

**파슬파슬** crumbling. ～하다 (be) crumbly. ¶ 과자가 ～ 부스러지다 the cake crumbles.

**파시스트** a fascist.

**파시즘** Fascism.

**파악**(把握) 《잡아 쥠》 grasping; seizing; grabbing; 《이해》 understanding; grasping 《the situation, the meaning, *etc.*》. ～하다 grasp; seize; understand; catch hold of. ¶ 요점을 ～하다 grasp the point / 문장의 뜻을 ～하다 grasp the meaning of a sentence / 한국 문화의 본질을 명확히 ～하다 have 「a clear 〔an accurate〕 grasp of the essence of Korean culture / 그는 사태를 잘 ～하지 못한 것 같다 It seems that he has but a poor 〔feeble〕 grip of the situation.

**파안**(破顔) (breaking into) a broad smile. ¶ ～ 대소하다 give 〔show〕 a broad smile; smile broadly; burst into laughter.

**파약**(破約) (a) cancellation of a contract 〔promise〕. ～하다 cancel a contract 〔an agreement〕; break *one's* word 〔promise〕.

**파업**(罷業) ① 《폐업》 giving up *one's* business; closing up *one's* business; closing out (of business); closing up shop. ～하다 give up *one's* business; close *one's* business up 〔out〕; close out; close up shop.
② 《동맹 파업》 a strike; a walkout 《미》. ～하다 strike; turn out; go 〔come out〕 on strike; have 〔conduct〕 a strike; walk out 《미》. ¶ ～ 중지 명령 a stop-strike order / ～에 들어가다 go (out) on strike; go on a strike / ～중이다 be on (a) strike / ～을 중지하다 halt 〔call off〕 a strike / 직공들은 노임 인상을 요구하여 24시간 ～했다 The workmen walked out on a 24-hour strike for higher wages / ～은 중지〔해제〕되었다 The strike was 「halted 〔called off〕.
◉ ～권 the right to strike: ～권을 행사하다 exercise *one's* right to strike. ～기금 a strike fund. ～수당 《노조가 지급하는》 strike pay. ～자 a striker. ～지령 a strike call 〔order〕: ～ 지령을 내리다 call a strike; instruct the workers to go on strike. ～파괴자 a strike-breaker; a scab; a blackleg 《영》; a rat 《속어》. 동정～ a sympathetic strike. 시한～ a strike for a limited number of hours. 총～ a general strike.

**파열**(破裂) explosion; bursting; rupture; puncture. ～하다 explode; burst; rupture; puncture.

> 용법 **explode** 화약 따위가 폭발하거나, 갑자기 박살이 나서 사방으로 흩어지는 것. **burst** 안으로부터의 압력에 의해 터지면서 갈라지는 것. **rupture** 혈관이 터지거나, 교유관계·담판 따위가 결렬되는 것. **puncture** 바늘·못 따위에 찔려서 타이어 따위가 「펑크」나는 것.

¶ 보일러〔수도관〕의 ～ bursting of a boiler 〔waterpipe〕 / 심장〔혈관〕의 ～

rupture of the heart 〔a blood vessel〕/ ~직전이다 be on the brink of explosion / 보일러의 ~로 두 사람이 다쳤다 The boiler burst, injuring two people. ◉ ~음 〖음성〗 a plosive (sound); 《폭탄의》 the crump(ing). ~탄 an explosive; a bomb; a shell.

**파옥**(破獄) (a) breach of prison; prison-breaking; a jailbreak. ⇨ 탈옥(脫獄). ~하다 escape (from a) prison; break jail; break out of prison. ◉ ~도주 breaking out of jail; escaping from prison.

**파우더** 《가루·분·화약》 powder.

**파운데이션** 《화장품》 foundation; 《속옷》 a foundation garment. ◉ ~크림 foundation cream.

**파운드** 《화폐 단위》 a pound (기호 £); a pound sterling (영국 화폐); a quid 《영구어》; 《무게》 a pound (기호 lb. (*pl.* lbs.)). ¶ 5 ~ 지폐 a five pound note / ~로 팔다 sell by the pound / ~를 평가 절하하다 devaluate the sterling / 몸무게가 몇 ~입니까 How many pounds do you weigh? ◉ ~지역 the sterling area. ~환(換) the pound exchange.

**파운드케이크** (a) pound cake.

**파울** 〖스포츠〗 (a) foul play; a foul. ¶ ~의 foul; against the rules / ~을 하다 violate 〔act against〕 the rules; play foul; commit a foul / ~로 퇴장당하다 foul out of the game / 상대의 ~을 주장하다 lodge a foul against 《a rival》; claim a foul / (야구에서) ~(볼)을 치다 foul; hit a foul ball. ◉ ~그라운드 〖야구〗 a foul territory. ~라인 a foul line. ~볼 a foul ball. ~팁 a foul tip. ~플라이 a foul fly.

**파워** power. ◉ ~게임 power game: ~게임의 무대 the stage of power game. ~브레이크 power brakes. ~셔블 a power shovel. ~스티어링 power steering. ~포지션 〖골프〗 a power position. ~폴리틱스 《무력 외교》 power politics. ~플랜트〔하우스〕《발전소》 a power plant 〔a powerhouse〕. 블랙~ 《흑인 해방 운동》 Black Power 《미》.

**파이**[1] 《양과자》 a pie; 《미》 a potpie (주로 고기의). ¶ ~껍질 (a) piecrust; the shell of a pie. ◉ 건포도~ a raisin pie. 고기~ a meat pie. 복숭아〔애플〕~ a peach 〔an apple〕 pie. 크림~ a cream pie. 호박~ a pumpkin pie.

**파이**[2] 〖수학〗 pi (*pl.* ~s); $\pi$. ◉ ~중간자 〖원자물리〗 a $\pi$-meson.

**파이버** 《섬유》 fiber; fibre 《영》. ◉ ~관(管) a fiber pipe. ~글라스 fiberglass; fibrous 〔spun〕 glass; Fiberglas (상표명). ~보드 fiber board. 광(光)~ optical fiber. 카본~ carbon fiber.

**파이트** 《경쟁》 a fight; a contest; 《투지》 fight; fighting spirit. ◉ ~머니 a fighter's purse; fight money.

**파이프** ① 《관》 a pipe; a tube. ¶ 수도~ a water pipe / ~로 물을 끌어오다 draw 〔lead〕 water through a pipe / ~를 통해 집안으로 물이 들어온다 Water is piped into the house. ② 《담뱃대》 a (tobacco) pipe (대담배용); a cigarette holder (궐련용). ¶ ~를 물고 with a pipe in *one's* mouth; with a pipe between *one's* teeth / ~가 막혀 있다 the pipe is clogged / ~에 불을 댕기다 light *one's* pipe / ~를 피우다 pull at a pipe / ~의 재를 떨다 tap *one's* pipe out; knock the ashes from *one's* pipe / ~에 담배를 재다 fill 〔load〕 *one's* pipe (with tocacco) / ~를 청소하다 clean a pipe / ~에 궐련을 끼우다 fit a cigarette into the holder. ◉ ~라인 《도관》 a pipeline. ~렌치 〖기계〗 a pipe wrench. ~오르간 a pipe organ.

**파인** fine. ◉ ~세라믹스 fine ceramics. ~케미컬 〖화학〗 fine chemical.

**파인더** 《망원경의》 a finder; 《사진기의》 a (view)finder. ◉ 자동조절 직시~ an iconometer.

**파인애플** 〖식물〗 a pineapple.

**파인트** 《건량·액량 단위》 a pint (생략 pt.).

**파인플레이** 〖스포츠〗 a fine play. ¶ ~를 하다 make a fine play.

**파일**(八日) 〖불교〗 the anniversary of the birth of Buddha; Buddha's birthday (festival); the eighth of April of the lunar calendar. ◉ ~등(燈) lanterns burned on Buddha's birthday.

**파일**[1] 《서류철》 a file. ◉ ~캐비닛 a file cabinet.

**파일**[2] ① 《원자로》 a 〔an atomic〕 pile. ② 《기초 공사용 말뚝》 a pile. ③ 〖방직〗 《부드러운 털·면모》 pile. ◉ ~천 cloth 〔fabric〕 with pile.

**파일럿**[1] a pilot. ¶ 테스트 ~ a test pilot. ◉ ~램프 a pilot lamp 〔light〕. ~숍 a pilot shop; an antenna shop. ~팜 《실험 농장》 a pilot farm. ~플랜트 a pilot plant.

**파일럿**[2] 〖컴퓨터〗 PILOT. [<*P*rogrammed *I*nquiry, *L*earning *O*r *T*eaching]

**파임내다** break an agreement.

**파자마** pajamas 《미》; pyjamas 《영》. ¶ 타월천의 ~ pajamas made of towel cloth / ~ 바람으로 in *one's* pajamas. ◉ ~아랫도리 a pajama bottom; pajama trousers. ~윗도리 a pajama top; a pajama coat.

**파장**(波長) (a) wavelength. ¶ ~이 다르다 be on a different wavelength 《from》/ ~을 맞추다 tune in to 《the first program of KBS》 ◉ ~계 a cymometer; a wavemeter. ~정조기(整調器) a tuner.

**파장**(罷場) 《과거장의》 the conclusion of state examinations; 《시장의》 the close of a marketplace. ~하다 state examinations come to a close; a marketplace closes 《at》. ◉ ~시세 the closing 「quotation 〔price〕.

**파적**(破寂) killing time; diversion for idle moments; beguiling the tedium. ~하다 kill 〔beguile〕 time; divert *oneself* from idle moments. ◉ ~거리 a kill-time; a timekiller.

**파종**(播種) sowing; seeding. ~하다 sow; sow seed; scatter (seed). ¶ 봄에 ~하다 sow seed in spring / 밭에 ~하다 scatter the fields with seed / 밭에 밀을 ~하다 sow a field with wheat. ◉ ~기(期) the seedtime; the sowing season. ~기(機) a seeder; a 「sowing 〔seeding〕 machine.

**파죽지세**(破竹之勢) irresistible force; crushing 〔overwhelming〕 power. ¶ ~로 나아가다 march in great force; carry everything before *one;* advance 「unresisted 〔unopposed〕.

**파지**(破紙) a 「defective 〔tattered〕 sheet of paper; remnants of paper; waste-paper.

**파직**(罷職) dismissal 〔removal〕 from office; discharge; deprivation of office. ~하다 dismiss 《*a person*》 from office; discharge 《*a person*》 from 《*his*》 duties; remove 《*a person*》 from office; fire 《미구어》.

**파찰음**(破擦音) 〖음성〗 an affricate.

**파천**(播遷) royal flight from the palace 〔capital〕. ~하다 flee from the royal palace 〔capital〕.

**파천황**(破天荒) unprecedentedness. ¶ ~의 record-breaking; unprecedented; unheard-of.

**파철**(破鐵) =파쇠.

**파초**(芭蕉) 〖식물〗 a banana plant; a 「plantain.

**파출**(派出) dispatch(ing); derivation. ~하다 dispatch; send 「out 〔off〕. ◉ ~부(婦) a visiting housekeeper 〔maid〕; a charwoman 《영》. ~소 branch office; 《경찰의》 a police 「box 〔stand〕: ~소에 신고하다 report to a policeman at the police stand; 《습득물 따위를》 take 〔carry〕 《*a thing*》 to a police box.

**파충류**(爬蟲類) the reptiles; creeping things; Reptilia. ¶ ~의 reptilian / ~의 동물 a reptile / ~를 먹고 사는 reptilivorous. ◉ ~시대 〖지질〗 the reptilian age. ~학 herpetology.

**파치**(破—) broken 〔damaged〕 articles; defective goods.

**파카** 《옷》 a parka. ◉ 오리털~ a duck 「down parka.

**파크 앤드 라이드 방식** park-(and-)ride system (전철역이나 버스 터미널에 주차시키고 통근하는 방식).

**파키스탄** (the Islamic Republic of) Pakistan. ¶ ~의 Pakistani. ◉ ~사람 a Pakistani.

**파킨슨법칙**(—法則) 〖사회〗 Parkinson's 「law.

**파킨슨병**(—病) 〖의학〗 Parkinsonism; Parkinson's disease; paralysis agitans.

**파킹** parking. ◉ ~랏 《주차장》 a parking lot. ~미터 a parking meter. ~티켓 《주차 위반 딱지》 a parking ticket.

**파탄**(破綻) ① 《실패》 failure; 《결렬》 a rupture; a breakdown. ~하다 fail; break down; come to a rupture. ¶ 우리의 화평 시도는 ~이 났다 Our attempt to make peace 「failed 〔ended in failure〕. / 교섭은 ~되었다 The negotiation came to rupture.
② 《파산》 bankruptcy. ~하다 become 〔go〕 bankrupt; be ruined; break down. ¶ 은행의 ~ a bank failure.
③ 《파괴》 breaking. ¶ 인격의 ~을 가져오다 break up *one's* personality; lead to the bankruptcy of *one's* character.

**파토스** pathos. ⇨ 페이소스.

**파트** ① 《부분·맡겨진 일》 a part. ¶ 자네는 자네의 ~를 맡게, 나머지는 내가 하겠네 You do your part and I shall do the rest. ② 《코러스 따위의》 a part. ¶ 소프라노 ~ the soprano part. ③ 《부서》 a section. ¶ 수출~ the export section.

**파트너** a partner. ¶ 댄스 ~ a dancing partner / 나는 이따금 그녀의 ~가 되어 춤을 췄다 I happened to be partners with her in dancing.

**파트타이머** a part-timer.

**파트타임** a part-time. ¶ ~으로 일하다 work part-time.

**파티** a party; a meeting; social gathering. ¶ ~에 잘 나가는 사람 a partygoer / 남성〔여성〕만의 ~ a 「stag 〔hen〕 party / ~를 열다 give 〔hold, have〕 a party. ◉ 깜짝~ a surprise party. 디너~ a dinner party.

**파파노인**(皤皤老人) a very old person;

a gray-haired old person.

**파파라치** 《유명인을 좇아다니는 사진 기자》 paparazzi (*sing.* -zzo) (It.).

**파파야** 〖식물〗 a papaya.

**파파인** 〖화학〗 papain.

**파편**(破片) a broken piece; a fragment; a splinter; 《도자기 따위의》 a shard; a potsherd. ¶ 포탄의 ~ a shell splinter / 깨진 꽃병의 ~ the fragments of a broken vase / 발에 ~이 박혔다 I've got a splinter in my foot. ◉ 유리~ pieces 〔bits〕 of broken glass.

**파피루스** 〖식물〗 a papyrus (*pl.* -ri); a paper reed 〔rush〕.

**파하다**(罷—) end; stop; discontinue; break off; bring to an end; be over 〔out〕; give up; quit. ¶ 학교가 파한 후에 after school (is over) / 회의를 ~ end a meeting; bring the meeting to a close / 일을 ~ stop work; leave off work / 공부를 중도에서 ~ give up studying halfway through; leave school in midterm / 혼담을 ~ break off marriage talks / 학교는 4시에 파한다 We are through school at four. / 나는 늘 연회가 파하기 전에 나온다 I make it a rule to leave banquets before they are over.

**파하다**(破—) 《쳐부수다》 beat; defeat; smash; (put to) rout. ¶ 적을 ~ smash the enemy / 적진을 ~ break through the enemy line.

**파행**(爬行) creeping; crawling. ~하다 creep; crawl. ◉ ~동물 a reptile.

**파행**(跛行) limping. ~하다 limp (along). ¶ ~적 운영 the crippled operation 《of》 / 경기는 당분간 ~ 상태가 계속될 것이다 The economy will be limping along for the time being. ◉ ~국회 《normalize》 the crippled operation of the National Assembly; the limping 〔crippled〕 House operation.

**파헤치다** 《땅을》 dig 〔turn〕 up 《the soil》; dig 《the ground》 over; tear up 《a road》; [비유적] rake up 《an old scandal》; 《깊이 생각·검토하다》 investigate; delve 〔probe〕 into 《a problem》. ¶ 문제를 근본부터 ~ attack a problem at the grass-roots / 도로가 몇 군데 파헤쳐져 있다 The road is torn up at several places.

**파혼**(破婚) breaking off a marriage engagement; (a) breach of promise of marriage. ~하다 break the engagement; break (off) engagement 《with》.

**파훼**(破毁) destruction; demolition; 〖법〗 annulment; breach. ~하다 destroy; demolish; annul; break; scrap; quash.

**파흥**(破興) a chill over 〔on〕 the 「pleasant party 〔feast〕. ~하다 spoil 〔put a damper on〕 the fun 〔pleasure〕 《of》; dampen 〔cool down〕 《*a person*'s》 enthusiasm; throw a wet blanket 《on》; wet-blanket. ¶ ~하는 사람〔것〕 a skeleton at the feast 〔banquet〕; a killjoy; a wet blanket.

**팍, 팍팍** ⇨ 퍽[1].

**팍삭** flopping 〔plopping〕 down; sinking. ~하다 《주저앉음》 get flopped down; get deflated; go down; 《깨짐》 give a fizz; fizz.

**팍삭거리다** all get deflated; get all deflated 〔flopped down〕.

**판** 《벌어진 곳》 a place; a spot; a site; a scene; 《판국》 (the) state of affairs; (the aspect, the phase of) the situation; circumstances; 《때》 the moment; 《경우》 the occasion; the case; 《횟수(回數)》 a game; a round; a bout; a match. ¶ 노름판 a gambling place / 싸움판 a fighting scene / 씨름 한 판 a round of wrestling / 단판 씨름 a single-round wrestling / 이러한 판에 at this juncture; in the present 〔critical〕 juncture of things / 위급한 판에 in the moment of danger; at critical moment / 막판에 at the last moment / …할 판이다 be going to; be about to *do;* be on the point of *do*ing / 두 판 이기다〔지다〕 win 〔lose〕 two games / 바둑 한 판 두다 play a game of *paduk;* have a game of *paduk* with 《*a person*》 / 카드놀이 한 판 벌여볼까 How about a round of cards?

**판**(板) a board; a plank; a plate; a disk 〔disc〕 (원반). ¶ 목판 a wooden board / 철판 an iron 〔a steel〕 plate; a sheet (of) iron / 장기판 a chessboard.

**판**(版·判) ① 《판목》 a (printing) block; 《도판》 a plate; a cast. ¶ 판본 a printed book / 판화 a print; a woodcut / 판에 박은〔박힌〕 말 a set 〔conventional, hackneyed, stereotyped〕 phrase / 판에 박힌 인사말을 하다 give a conventionally worded address.

② 《판수》 printing; print; an edition; an impression. ¶ 신판 a new edition / 개정판 a revised edition / 초판 the first print 〔edition〕 / 제3판 the third edition 〔printing〕 / 시내판 the city edition / 지방판 the local 〔provincial〕 edition / 판을 짜다 compose; set (in type) / 판을 개정하다 publish a new edition / 판을 거듭하다 go through 〔run into〕 several editions / 그 책은 6판이 되었다 The book 「reached its sixth edition 〔ran into six editions〕. ③《판형》 size; format. ¶ 사륙판 duodecimo; crown octavo / (사진의) 명함판 the size of a visiting card / 이 책은 그것과 같은 판이다 This book is the same size as that.

**판**(瓣) 《기기(器機)의》 a valve; 《화판》 a petal. ¶ 4판화(花) a flower of four petals; a four-petal(l)ed flower / 가스〔증기〕판 a gas 〔steam〕 valve / 안전판 a safety 〔relief〕 valve; an escape 〔a pop-off〕 valve.

**판가름** judging sides (which side is right and which side is wrong); a showdown; decision. ～하다 judge 《a competition, fight, *etc.*》; decide; sit in judgment 《on》; have a final showdown 《미구어》. ¶ 싸움을 ～하다 judge which of the two fighting parties is right and which is wrong / ～나다 be decided 〔settled〕; turn out 〔prove〕 to be...; come to a conclusion / 두 사람 사이의 다툼은 아직 ～이 나지 않았다 The quarrel between them has not been settled yet.

**판각**(板刻) engraving (on woodblocks); woodcutting; 《판각한 것》 a wood engraving; a woodcut. ～하다 engrave 《designs, letters》 on wood; make a print from a woodblock. ◉ ～본 a woodblock-printed book. ～사(師) a woodcutter; a wood engraver; a block cutter; xylographer. ～술 xylography. ～자(字) a block letter. ～화 a woodcut; a woodblock print; xylograph.

**판검사**(判檢事) judges and public prosecutors; judicial officers; [총칭] the bench.

**판결**(判決) (a) judgment; 〖법〗 a judicial decision; a decision (of the court); a ruling; adjudication. ～하다 judge; decide 《on a case》; give decision 〔pass judgment〕 《on a case》; adjudicate 《on an action》; sentence 《*a person*》 to 《death》.

판결의: ～의 번복 reversal of a decision / ～의 집행 execution of judgment / ～의 집행을 정지하다 suspend a judgment.

판결에: ～에 승복하다 accept a decision / ～에 불복하다 protest against a decision; demur to 〔at〕 a judgment.

판결을: ～을 내리다 give a decision 《upon》; adjudicate 《on a case》; rule 《that...》; judge / 사형 ～을 내리다 sentence 《*a person*》 to death / 아무에게〔사건에〕 ～을 내리다 pass sentence 〔judgment〕 upon *a person* 〔case〕 / 불리한 ～을 내리다 decide 〔rule〕 against 《*a person*》 / ～을 선고하다 deliver judgment 《on *a person*》; hand down a decision / ～을 번복하다 reverse a decision / ～을 유예〔연기〕하다 reserve 〔suspend〕 judgment / ～을 지지하다 sustain a decision / ～을 취소하다 set aside a decision / 사형 ～을 받다 receive a death sentence / 유죄〔무죄〕 ～을 받다 receive a verdict 〔be given a decision〕 of "guilty" 〔"not guilty"〕.

¶ ～은 원고의 패소〔승소〕로 돌아갔다 The case was decided against 〔in favor of〕 the plaintiff.

◉ ～문 the decision: ～문을 읽다 read the ruling; read out the decision. ～서 a written judgment. ～유예 reserving 〔suspending〕 judgment. ～이유 reasons for decision 〔the judgment〕. ～주문(主文) the text of a decision; formal adjudication. 최종～ the final decree.

**판공비**(辦公費) expediency fund; 《접대비》 expense account; 《예비비》 extra-expenses; 《기밀비》 confidential money 〔expenses〕.

**판관**(判官) 《재판관》 a judge; a justice.

**판관사령**(判官使令) a henpecked husband; a man tied to his wife's apron strings.

**판구조론**(板構造論) 〖지질〗 plate tectonics.

**판국**(一局) a situation; the position 〔state〕 of affairs; the state of things; the aspect of affairs. ¶ 험한 ～ a tricky 〔touchy, perilous〕 situation / 수습할 수 없는 ～ an uncontrollable situation / ～을 관망하다 watch the situation; watch how things develop; see how the wind blows; see which way the cat will jump / 새로운 ～으로 접어들다 take a new turn; take on a new aspect; enter upon a new phase.

**판권**(版權) copyright; literary property. ⇨ 저작권(著作權). ¶ ～ 기한이 지난 out of copyright / ～을 얻다 copyright 《a book》; acquire 〔obtain〕 a copyright 《for a book》 / ～을 소유하다 hold 〔own〕 the copyright in 〔of〕 《a book》 / ～을 침해하다 infringe the copyright 《of》; pirate / 1958년 맥밀런사(社) ～ 획득 Copyright, 1958, by The Macmillan Company / 그의 저작에는 아직 ～이 살아 있다 His works are

still copyright.
◉ ～소유 ownership of copyright; 《표시》 Copyrighted. *or* All rights reserved. ～소유자 a copyrighter; a copyright holder. ～양도 transfer of copyright. ～장(張) the copyright page; a colophon; an imprint. ～침해 an infringement of copyright; a copyright infringement; (literary) piracy.

**판금**(板金) a (metal) plate; sheet metal. ¶ ～공 a sheet metal worker.

**판나다** ① 《끝나다》 get finished; come to an end 〔a close, a conclusion〕; be over. ¶ 싸움이 ～ a fight is over; the winner is decided. ② 《다하다》 be all gone; run out; be exhausted. ¶ 떡이 ～ the rice cake is all gone / 양식이 판났다 Our provisions are running out. ③ 《파멸하다》 be ruined; go 〔fall〕 crash; go bankrupt. ¶ 회사가 ～ a company is bankrupt / 살림이 ～ a family is ruined.

**판다** 〖동물〗 a panda; a bearcat; a cat bear.

**판다르다** be entirely different; be quite another thing; be poles apart. ⇨판이하다.

**판단**(判斷) 《단정》 (a) judg(e)ment; (an) adjudication; (a) decision; 《결론》 conclusion; 《추산》 estimation; 《추단》 (an) inference; 《재량》 discretion; 《해석》 (an) interpretation. ～하다 judge; decide; conclude; infer; 《해석》 interpret; 《이해》 understand; 《꿈을》 interpret; read; 《점을》 divine.
¶ 나의 ～으로는 in my judgment; as I take it / 자기 ～으로 on *one's* judgment / 네 말로 미루어 ～하면 judging from what you say / 운수를 ～하다 tell 《*a person's*》 fortune / (공정한) ～을 내리다 pass a (fair) judgment 《on》 / ～을 그르치다 judge wrongly; make an error of 〔err in *one's*〕 judgment / 경험으로 미루어 ～을 내리다 form conclusions from experiences / 겉모양을 보고 ～하다 judge by 〔from〕 appearances / 자네 ～에 맡기겠네 I will leave (it to) you to judge for yourself. / 나의 ～으로는 그는 아주 정직한 사람이다 I judge him to be a very honest man.
◉ ～기준 a yardstick for judgment; a standard of judgment. 종합～ (a) synthetic judgment.

**판단력**(判斷力) judgment; discrimination; discernment; perception. ¶ ～이 건전한〔부족한〕 사람 a man of sound 〔poor〕 judgment / ～이 좋다 have good judgment / ～이 없다 be lacking 〔wanting〕 in judgment / ～을 잃다 lose *one's* judgment.

**판도**(版圖) (a) territory; a dominion; a domain. ¶ ～를 넓히다 extend 〔expand〕 《*one's*》 territory; enlarge the scope of *one's* influence.

**판도라** 〖그神〗 Pandora. ¶ ～의 상자 Pandora's box.

**판독**(判讀) reading; 《암호 따위의》 decoding; decipherment. ～하다 decode; decipher; read; make 《a text》 out. ¶ ～하기 힘든 illigible; hard to make out; undecipherable / 고문서를 ～하다 decipher an old manuscript / 그 문서는 ～할 수 없다 The writing cannot be made out.

**판돈** money set upon the gambling table; stakes. ¶ ～을 맡는 사람 stakeholder / ～을 쓸다 rake in the stakes; sweep the board; take the pool / ～을 떼다 divide up the stakes 〔the money on the board〕.

**판들다** run 〔go〕 through *one's* fortune; go bankrupt; be ruined; be broke.

**판례**(判例) a (judicial) precedent; a leading case. ¶ ～를 인용하다 cite 〔refer to〕 a precedent 〔case〕 / 새로운 ～를 만들다 set 〔establish〕 a new precedent. ◉ ～법 case law; the judge-made law. ～위반 a contravention to judicial precedents. ～집 a (judicial) report; law reports.

**판로**(販路) a market 《for goods》; an outlet. ¶ ～가 없다 be not demanded; there is no market 《for》 / ～가 열리다 a market opens 《for》 / ～를 개척하다 open (up) 〔find〕 a market 《for》; pioneer markets / ～를 구축하다 build (up) a market 《for》 / ～를 막다 clog marketing channels / ～를 찾다 look for a market / ～를 잃다 lose *one's* market / ～를 확장하다 extend 〔enlarge〕 the market / 이 물건은 ～가 넓다 〔좁다〕 There is a good market 〔small demand〕 for these articles. /그것은 어디에 내 놓아도 ～는 있다 We can find a market for it everywhere.
◉ 수출～ an export outlet.

**판막**(瓣膜) 〖해부〗 a valve (of the body). ◉ ～염 valvulitis. ～증 valvular disease; mitral disease. 호흡～ pulmonary valves.

**판매**(販賣) (a) sale; selling; merchandising; marketing. ～하다 sell; merchandise; market; deal in; handle. ¶ ～되고 있다 be on sale; be on the market / 아침 6시 이후에는 벨데스크와 커피숍에서도 담배를 ～합니다 《게시》

Cigarettes also on sale after 6 a.m. at bell desk and coffee shop. / 이 상품은 수주(受注)〔예약〕~하게 되어 있다 This product is sold by order 〔subscription〕. / 그는 빵을 제조 ~하고 있다 He both bakes and sells bread.
◉ ~가격 the selling price: ~ 가격의 1할 할인으로 사다 buy 《goods》 at 10 per cent discount off the price. ~과〔부〕 a sales department. ~대리점 a selling agent; a distributor. ~루트 a distribution channel; a marketing route. ~망 a sales network. ~분석 sales analysis. ~비 the distribution cost; selling expenses. ~소〔점〕 a store; 《영》 a shop. ~수단 sales tactics. ~수입 circulation income (신문의). ~술 salesmanship. ~업자 a distributor. ~원(元) a selling agency. ~원(員) a salesperson; a salesman; a saleswoman; a salesclerk 《미》; a shop assistant 《영》. ~인 a seller; a merchandiser; a marketer; an agent. ~전 a sales war. ~정책 a sales policy. ~조건 the condition of sale. ~조합 a marketing cooperative. ~촉진 sales promotion. ~확장 expansion of circulation (신문의). 신용~ selling on credit.

**판명**(判明) becoming clear. ~되다 《분명해지다》 become clear 〔plain〕; 《확인되다》 be ascertained; be confirmed; 《알려지다》 be known; 《…라는 것이》 prove 〔turn out〕 to be 《false》; be proved to be; 《신원 등이》 be identified as 《Mr. K》. ¶ 신원이 ~되지 않다 *one's* identity is unclear; *one* is unidentified / 그는 첩자로 ~되었다 He is identified as an agent. / 그 서류는 위조임이 ~ 되었다 The document was proved to be false. / 그 소문은 헛소문이었음이 ~되었다 The rumor turned out (to be) false. / 그의 소재는 아직 ~되지 않았다 His whereabouts is 〔are〕 still unknown. / 원인이 ~되지 않는 한 우리는 속수무책이다 Until we know the cause, there's nothing we can do about it.

**판목**(版木) a wood block; a wooden printing block.

**판몰이** winning all the money that there is around a gambling place; walking off with the stakes. ~하다 win all (the money); walk off with the stakes.

**판무관**(辦務官) a commissioner.

**판무식**(判無識) being utterly ignorant 〔illiterate〕. ◉ ~쟁이 an utterly ignorant person; a total ignoramus.

**판문점**(板門店) P'anmunjŏm; the P'anmunjŏm truce village. ◉ ~ 공동 경비구역 the Joint Security Area at P'anmunjŏm. ~ 군사 정전위원회 (제10차) 회의 the (10th) Military Armistice Commission Meeting (held) at P'anmunjŏm. ~중립국 감시위원회 the Neutral Nations Supervisory Commission at P'anmunjŏm. ~회담 P'anmunjŏm Talks.

**판박이**(版—) 《책》 a printed book; 《그림》 a decalcomania; 《틀에 박힌 것》 a fixed 〔stereotyped, conventional〕 thing. ◉ ~소리 a *cliché* (F.); a trite remark; a hackneyed 〔stereotyped〕 expression.

**판별**(判別) distinction; discrimination. ~하다 distinguish 《between A and B》; tell 《A》 from 《B》; discriminate 《between A and B, one from the other》; mark 〔notice〕 the difference 《between》. ¶ ~할 수 있는〔없는〕 distinguishable 〔indistinguishable〕 / ~할 수 없을 정도로 indistinguishably / ~할 수 없다 cannot tell 《A from B》; cannot discriminate 〔distinguish〕 《A from B》 / 시비곡직을 ~하다 discriminate between right and wrong / 진짜와 가짜를 ~하다 distinguish the real thing from imitations 〔false ones〕.

**판본**(版本) a woodblock-printed book; a block 〔xylographic〕 book.

**판사**(判事) a judge; a justice; [총칭] the judiciary; the bench. ¶ 예심〔배석〕~ a preliminary court 〔an associate〕 judge / 재판은 K~ 주재로 개정되었다 The court was opened, presided over by Justice K. ◉ ~석 a judge's seat; the bench. ~직 judgeship; the bench. 부장~ a senior judge; a chief judge 《of the district court》. 주심~ a presiding judge.

**판상**(辦償) compensation. ⇨ 배상, 변상.

**판새류**(瓣鰓類) 〖동물〗 bivalve mollusca.

**판서**(判書) 〖고제도〗 the chief of any one of the *yukcho* (=Six Boards) of the Government; a minister.

**판서**(板書) ~하다 write on the blackboard.

**판설다** (be) unfamiliar 《with the scene 〔situation〕》; be unaccustomed 《to》.

**판세**(—勢) 《노름판의》 the drift of a game; 《사물의 형세》 the situation; the state 〔condition〕 of affairs 〔things〕; 《전망》 the prospects. ¶ ~가 유리하게 되다 things take favorable turn / ～를 관망하다 watch the situation; watch the development of affairs; see how the wind blows; 《구어》 (wait and) see which way the cat will jump / ～가 어떤가 What is the situation? *or* What are the chances? (승부의) / ～가 좋다〔나쁘다〕 The prospects are「bright〔gloomy〕. / ～가 점점 불리하다 Things are going from bad to worse. / ～가 일변하여 우리 편이 유리〔불리〕해졌다 The tide turned「in our favor〔against us〕.

**판소리** a traditional Korean narrative song; a narrative musical form unique to Korea; *pansori*. ～하다 recite *pansori*. ¶ ～는 1인극〔모노 드라마〕 비슷한 한국 특유의 한 예술 형태이다 *Pansori* is a unique Korean art form similar to monodrama.

**판수** 《점쟁이 소경》 a blind fortuneteller; 《소경》 a blind person.

**판시**(判示) judgment; (a) decision; a ruling. ～하다 decide 《on a case》; give (a) decision 《on a case》; rule 《that... should...》. ¶ 판사는 그에겐 그런 돈을 청구할 권리가 없다고 ～했다 The judge ruled that he had no right to claim such a sum.

**판연**(判然) ～하다 (be) clear; plain; distinct; definite; evident. ¶ ～히 clearly; plainly; definitely / 둘 사이에는 ～한 차이가 있다 There is a distinct difference between the two.

**판유리**(板琉璃) sheet glass (얇은); plate glass (두꺼운); flat glass; 《한 장》 a glass plate; a pane.

**판이**(判異) ～하다 [서술적] be entirely 〔quite, widely〕 different 《from》; be diametrically opposed 《to》; differ entirely 《from》. ¶ 이 두 물질은 서로 ～한 성질을 갖고 있다 These two materials have quite different properties.

**판자**(板子) a (wooden) board; a plank (두꺼운); [총칭] boarding. ¶ ～ 조각 a small piece of a board / ～로 막다〔두르다〕 board「up〔in〕; enclose with boarding / ～를 대다〔깔다〕 board; plank 《a house, a floor》; lay boards on 《a floor》 / (재목을) ～로 켜다 saw into planks. ◉ ～문 a wooden door. ～벽 a board wall. ～울타리 a board fence. ～지붕 a shingle roof. 판잣집 a board-framed house; a makeshift hut; a shack; a barrack; a shanty.

**판장**(板牆) a wooden wall; a board fence. ¶ ～으로 둘러치다 enclose with a board fence.

**판재**(板材) ① 《널빤지》 a board; a plank. ② 《관널》 boards for a coffin.

**판정**(判定) (a) decision; (a) judgment. ～하다 decide; judge. ¶ ～을 내리다 pass judgment 《on》; give a decision 《against, for, in favor of》 / ～을 뒤엎다 reverse the 《umpire's》 decision / ～을 그르치다 misjudge / ～으로 이기다 《경기에서》 win「on points〔on a decision〕; defeat 《*one's* opponent》「on points〔by a decision〕 / ～으로 지다 lose a decision 《to》; lose 《a match》「on points〔by a decision〕 / 그 건물은 기준에 맞다고 ～되었다 The building was judged to be up to standard. / 그는 심판의 ～에 따랐다 He accepted the「umpire's〔referee's〕 decision.

**판정승**(判定勝) a win「by a decision〔on points〕. ～하다 win「by a decision〔on points〕. ¶ 김 선수에게 ～을 주다 give the game to Kim / 10회전에서 김 선수는 한 선수에게 ～을 거두었다 In a 10 round bout Kim won by decision over Han. / 그는 심판 전원 일치의 ～을 거두었다 He won the match by a unanimous decision.

**판정패**(判定敗) a lose「by a decision〔on points〕. ～하다 lose 《a match》 on points; be defeated 〔beaten〕 by a decision; lose a decision 《to》.

**판지**(板紙) pasteboard; cardboard; paperboard; carton.

**판차리다** get a place ready for 《gambling》.

**판촉**(販促) sales promotion. ～하다 promote sales. ¶ ～을 위해서는 광고에 더 많은 돈을 써야 한다 We need to spend more money on advertising to promote sales.

**판치다** have a great deal of influence 《with, over》; be influential; lord it over; exercise great influence 《over》; stand「unchallanged〔unrivaled〕. ¶ 동네에서 ～ have a great deal of influence with the villagers / 그는 정계에서 판치는 실력자다 He is a man of influence in the political world.

**판크레아틴** 〖생화학〗 pancreatin.

**판타스틱** 《멋진·공상적인》 fantastic.

**판타지** 〖음악〗 《환상곡》 a fantasia; a fantasy.

**판탈롱** 《여성 바지》 pantaloons.

**판판이** at every round; every time; all the time; always. ¶ ～ 지다 get defeated「every time〔at every turn〕/ ～ 거짓말만 하다 lie all the time.

**판판하다** (be) even; smooth; level; flat. ¶ 판판히 smoothly; evenly / 판판한 땅

even 〔level, flat〕 ground / 땅을 판판히 고르다 level 〔roll〕 the ground.

**판형**(判型) a format.

**판화**(版畫) 《목판화》 a (woodblock) print; a woodcut; 《동판화》 a copperplate engraving; an etching (부식 동판의); 《석판화》 a lithograph. ◉ ~가 a printmaker; 《목판의》 a woodblock artist; 《동판의》 a copperplate engraver; an etcher (부식 동판의); 《석판의》 a lithographer. ~술 (pictorial) wood(block) printing.

**판히**(判—) clearly; plainly; distinctly; obviously. ¶ ~ 보이면서 멀다 be far away although it can be seen distinctly in the distance / ~ 들여다보이다 be seen through clearly; be patently transparent.

**팔** an arm; the forearm (팔꿈치에서 팔목); the upper arm (어깨에서 팔꿈치). ¶ 오른〔왼〕팔 the right 〔left〕 arm.
팔로: 팔로 끌어안다 hug 〔embrace, take〕 in *one's* arms / 두 팔로 들다〔잡다〕 hold 《*a thing*》 with both arms.
팔에: 팔에 기장(記章)을 달고 with a badge on *one's* arm / 팔에 완장을 두르고 with an armband round *one's* arm / 팔에 기대다 lean on 《*a person's*》 arm (for support) / 팔에 보퉁이를 끼다〔들다〕 hold a parcel under *one's* arm / 팔에 매달리다 cling to 〔hang on〕 《*a person's*》 sleeve / 팔에 부상을 입다 be wounded in the arm / 팔에 안고 있다 have 《a baby》 in *one's* arms.
팔을: 팔을 걷어 올리다〔붙이다〕 roll 〔turn, tuck〕 *one's* sleeves up; bare *one's* arm / 팔을 끼다 《남과》 lock arm in arm with 《*a person*》 / 팔을 내밀다 extend 〔hold out〕 *one's* arm; stretch *one's* arm 《toward》 / 팔을 굽히다 bend 〔hunch〕 *one's* arm / 팔을 비틀다 screw 〔twist〕 《*a person's*》 arm hard / 팔을 (들어)올리다 raise *one's* arm / 팔을 잡다 hold 〔take〕 《*a person*》 by the arm; hold 〔take〕 《*a person's*》 arm; 《붙잡다》 grab 〔seize〕 《*a person*》 by the arm / 팔을 젓다 swing *one's* arms.
팔이: 팔이 없는 armless / 팔이 부러지다 break *one's* arm; have *one's* arm broken / 팔이 들먹거리다 [비유적] be itching for action; *one's* fingers itch 《to *do*, for *something*》.
¶ 팔이 들이굽지 내굽지 않는다 《속담》 Blood is thicker than water. / 그녀는 애인의 한 쪽 팔을 끼고 들어왔다 She came in on her boyfriend's arm.

**팔**(八) eight. ¶ 제8 the eighth / 8분의 1 one-eighth.

**팔각**(八角) eight angles; [형용사적] octagonal. ◉ ~당〔정〕 《건축물》 an octagonal building 〔pavilion〕; an octagon. ~형 an octagon.

**팔걸이** an armrest; an elbow rest. ◉ ~의자 an armchair; an elbowchair.

**팔괘**(八卦) the Eight Trigrams for divination.

**팔굽혀펴기** 『체조』 《미》 a push-up; 《영》 a press-up. ¶ 그는 매일 아침 ~를 20번 한다 He does 20 push-ups every morning.

**팔꿈치** an elbow. ¶ ~의 관절 an elbow joint / ~로 쿡 지르다 jog 〔jostle, nudge〕 with *one's* elbow / ~를 펴다 square 〔spread out〕 *one's* elbow / ~로 사람들을 헤치며 나아가다 elbow *one's* way through / 그의 코트는 ~가 해졌다 His coat is out at the elbow.

**팔난봉** 《사람》 a fast liver; a debauchee; a profligate; 《행위》 all kinds of debauchery. ¶ ~ 다 부리다 indulge in all kinds of debauchery.

**팔다** ① 《판매하다》 sell; offer 《*a thing*》 for sale; put 〔place〕 《articles》 「on sale 〔on the market〕; deal in 《goods》; 《처분하다》 dispose of. ¶ 팔 수 있는 salable; marketable / 팔 수 없는 unsalable; unmarketable / 팔 물건〔집〕 an article 〔a house〕 for sale / 팔아 치우다 sell (off, out); dispose of / 팔고 다니다 carry 《fish》 about for sale; hawk; peddle / 가재를 다 ~ dispose of all the household goods / 노예로 ~ sell 《*a person*》 for a slave / 몸을 ~ prostitute *oneself;* sell *oneself* for money / 소를 ~ sell a cow / 비싸게 ~ sell dear 〔high, expensively〕; sell at a high price / 싸게 ~ sell cheap; sell at a low price / 시가(時價)로〔에〕 ~ sell at the current market price / 외상으로 ~ sell on credit 〔time〕 / 밑지고 ~ sell at a loss 〔sacrifice〕; sell under 〔at less than〕 cost; sacrifice / 절개를 ~ sell 〔prostitute〕 *one's* honor 〔chastity〕 (for money) / 만원에 ~ sell 《*a thing*》 for ten thousand won / 한 개 5백 원씩에 ~ sell at 500 won a piece / 다스로 ~ sell by the dozen / 집을 팔아 넘기다 sell *one's* house over 《to *a person*》 / 그것은 그 백화점에서 판다 You can buy 〔get〕 it at the department store. /「나 차를 팔려고 해」―「얼마에 팔려고 그래」 "I'm thinking of selling the car."―"How much are you asking for it?"

② 《이름 등을》 take advantage of 《*one's* name》; trade on. ¶ 이름을 ～ 《자신의》 trade on *one's* 「name 〔reputation〕; 《남의》 assume 《*a person's*》 name; make a fraudulent use of 《*a person's*》 name / 아버지의 이름을 팔아 장사하다 do business by taking advantage of *one's* father's reputation / 그런 일에 내 이름을 팔지 말아 다오 I don't want my name to be given in such a connection.

③ 《배반하다》 betray; sell out. ¶ 나라를 ～ betray 〔sell〕 *one's* country; turn traitor to *one's* country / 반역자는 적에게 조국을 팔았다 The traitor betrayed *one's* country to the enemy.

④ 《곡식을》 buy 《grain》. ¶ 쌀을 ～ buy 〔purchase〕 rice.

⑤ 《주의를 흩뜨리다》 turn 「away 〔aside〕; divert. ¶ 한눈을 ～ look 「away 〔aside, off〕; take *one's* eyes off 《*a thing*》 / 책을 보지 않고 한눈을 ～ look away from *one's* book / 정신을 ～ divert 〔dis-tract〕 *one's* attention 《from》 / 한눈팔지 않고 공부하다 be devoted heart and soul to *one's* studies; apply *oneself* closely to *one's* studies / 운전하면서 한눈팔지 마라 Don't divert your attention from driving a car.

**팔다리** the legs and arms; the limbs. ¶ ～가 없는 limbless / ～를 벌리고 《lie》 spread-eagled / ～를 쓰지 못하게 되다 lose the use of *one's* limbs.

**팔도강산**(八道江山) the land of Korea; the scenery of all parts of Korea.

**팔등신**(八等身) well-proportioned figure. ¶ ～의 미인 a 「well-proportioned 〔well-shaped〕 beautiful woman.

**팔딱거리다** ① 《박동치다》 palpitate; pulsate; throb; beat. ¶ 맥이 ～ *one's* pulse 「pulsates 〔beats〕 (rapidly) / 가슴이 ～ *one's* heart 「throbs 〔palpitates, beats〕 / 그 광경을 보고 가슴이 심하게 팔딱거렸다 My heart beat fast at the scene. ② 《뛰다》 jump; hop; spring (up); leap; bound.

**팔딱팔딱** ① 《박동》 palpitating; throbbing; pulsating. ¶ 맥이 ～ 뛰다 *one's* pulse pulsates; have a pulse / 가슴이 ～ 뛰다 *one's* heart 「palpitates 〔throbs〕. ② 《뛰는 모양》 hopping; leaping; jumping. ¶ ～ 뛰다 《a frog》 jump; 《버둥질》 struggle to get free.

**팔뚝** the forearm; the wrist area (above the wrist joint). ◉ ～시계 ⇨ 손목시계.

**팔라듐** 〖화학〗 palladium (기호 Pd).

**팔랑개비** ① 《바람개비》 a pinwheel. ¶ 바람에 뱅뱅 도는 ～ a pinwheel whirling in the wind. ② 《사람》 a 「careless 〔hasty, frivolous〕 person.

**팔레스타인** Palestine. ◉ ～게릴라 Palestinian guerillas. ～해방기구 Palestine Liberation Organization (생략 PLO).

**팔레트** 〖미술〗 a palette. ◉ ～나이프 a palette knife.

**팔리다** ① 《상품이》 sell; be sold; be in demand; 《시장성이 있다》 be marketable; be salable. ¶ 잘 팔리는 물품 a 「good 〔quick〕 seller / 팔리지 않는 물품 unsalable goods; dead stocks / 잘 ～ sell well; have 〔enjoy〕 a 「good 〔large〕 sale; be in great demand; there is a good demand; outsell (다른 것보다) / 잘 팔리지 않다 do not sell well; be 「in poor 〔not in much〕 demand; have a poor sale / 날개 돋친 듯 〔불티나게〕 ～ sell like hot 「cakes 〔wildfire, fun〕 / 제일 잘 ～ be the 「best 〔top〕 seller / 금방 ～ sell right away; find a 「quick 〔ready〕 sale; meet ready sale / 좋은 값에 ～ fetch 〔go for〕 a good price; sell at good price; sell dear / 팔린 물건 《표시》 Sold. / 이런 상품은 절대로 팔리지 않는다 Goods of this kind will never sell. / 그것은 값이 싸서 잘 팔렸다 It had a good sale because of its low price. / 이런 종류의 책은 우리 나라에서 틀림없이 잘 팔릴 것이다 A book of this kind would have an assured sale in our country. / 우리 학교 졸업생은 아주 잘 팔린다 [비유적] There is a great demand for our graduates. / 그 집은 경매에서 5천만 원에 팔렸다 The house went for 50 million won at the auction.

② 《얼굴·이름이》 become 「well-known 〔famous, popular〕. ¶ 잘 팔리는 사람 a popular person; a man of great popularity / 얼굴이 팔려 있다 be widely known.

③ 《주의력·정신이》 have *one's* attention caught 《by》; be 「distracted 〔preoccupied〕 《by》; 《열중하다》 be absorbed 《in》; be intent 《on》. ¶ 눈이 딴 데 ～ *one's* eyes 「stray 〔wander off〕; look at something else / 다른 일에 정신이 팔려 있다 be preoccupied with something else / 마음이 여자한테 ～ be attracted by a woman / 노는 데 정신이 팔려 공부는 뒷전이다 be too much absorbed in play to think of *one's* study / 이야기하는 데 정신이 팔려 시간 가는 줄 몰랐다 Absorbed in chatting, I was unaware of the passage of time.

**팔림새** sale(s); demand. ¶ ~가 좋다〔나쁘다〕 sell 〔do not sell〕 well; be a good 〔poor〕 seller; be in 〔not in much〕 demand; there is a good 〔poor〕 demand 《for》 / ~가 빠르다〔더디다〕 be quick-〔slow-〕selling.

**팔만대장경**(八萬大藏經) the *Tripitaka* Koreana.

**팔매** throwing (stones). ¶ 돌~ stone throwing / ~질하다 throw; sling; hurl; fling 《a stone at》.

**팔면**(八面) eight sides; 《여러 방면》 all sides; [형용사적] 8-sided. ◉ ~부지 a complete stranger. ~체 an octahedron.

**팔면육비**(八面六臂) ¶ ~의 versatile; all=around / ~의 활약을 하다 play a very active part in many fields.

**팔모**(八—) eight angles. ¶ ~의 octagonal. ◉ ~꼴 an octagon. ~살 octagonal lattice(work).

**팔목** the wrist. ⇨ 손목. ¶ 남의 ~을 잡다 take 〔seize〕 *a person* by the wrist.

**팔미틴** 〖화학〗 palmitin. ◉ ~산 palmitic acid: ~산염〔에스테르〕 palmitate.

**팔방**(八方) ¶ (사면)~으로〔에〕 in all directions; on all sides; all around / (사면)~으로부터〔에서〕 from all directions 〔sides〕; from every side; from all around / …하기 위해 ~으로 손을 쓰다 leave no stone unturned to *do* / ~으로 찾아보았으나 그것을 찾아내지 못했다 We did everything possible to find it, but 「with no success 〔to no avail〕.

**팔방미인**(八方美人) a beauty in every respect; a person who is nice to everybody; everybody's friend. ¶ 그는 ~이다 He tries to please everybody. ◉ ~주의 a please-all policy; flunkyism.

**팔베개** ¶ ~를 베다 rest *one's* head on *one's* elbow 〔arm〕; make a pillow of *one's* arm / ~를 하고 자다 sleep with *one's* head (pillowed) on *one's* arm.

**팔분쉼표**(八分—標) 〖음악〗 an eighth rest.

**팔분음표**(八分音標) 〖음악〗 a quaver; an 「eighth note.

**팔분의**(八分儀) an octant.

**팔불출**(八不出) a dull 〔stupid〕 fellow; 「a fool.

**팔삭둥이**(八朔—) 《조산아》 a baby born prematurely in the eighth month of pregnancy; 《얼뜨기》 an idiot; a stupid; a half-witted person. ¶ ~를 낳다 give birth to a baby two months premature.

**팔세토** 〖음악〗 falsetto. ¶ ~로 in falsetto. ◉ ~가수 a falsetto (singer).

**팔손이나무** 〖식물〗 an evergreen shrub of the family *Araliaceae.*

**팔순**(八旬) eighty years; four score years. ¶ ~ 노인 an octogenarian.

**팔시간**(八時間) eight hours. ◉ ~노동 eight-hour labor. ~제 the eight-hour day (system).

**팔심** the strength of *one's* arm. ¶ ~이 세다 have strong 〔brawny〕 arms.

**팔십**(八十) eighty; a fourscore. ¶ ~ 노인 an octogenarian; an 80-year-old man 〔woman〕.

**팔씨름** arm 〔Indian〕 wrestling. ¶ ~을 하다 wrestle with *one's* arms; arm-wrestle 《with》.

**팔아먹다** ① 《매각하다》 sell; sell off 〔out〕; dispose of. ¶ 지식을 ~ peddle *one's* knowledge / 헐값으로 ~ sell 《an article》 for a mere song / 가산을 팔아먹고 살다 live 〔make *one's* living〕 by selling *one's* property / 명예를 ~ sell *one's* honor (for money). ② 《정신을 빼앗기다》 lose *one's* heart 《to》; be 「carried away 〔fascinated〕 《by》; engross *one's* mind.

**팔아치우다** sell off 〔out〕; trade away. ¶ 그들은 오래된 재고품을 싼값으로 팔아치웠다 They sold off the old stock at discount prices.

**팔오금** the bend 〔crook〕 of the arm.

**팔월**(八月) August (생략 Aug.). ◉ ~ 한가위 the 15th day of the 8th month of the lunar calendar; the midautumn 〔harvest-moon〕 festival.

**–팔이** a peddler; a hawker. ¶ 신문~ a newsboy.

**팔인교**(八人轎) an 8-porter sedan chair.

**팔일오**(八一五) the Liberation Day of Korea; August 15th, 1945. ¶ ~ 54주년 (기념식) (the ceremony of) the 54th anniversary of Korea's Liberation.

**팔자**(八字) ① 《운명·숙명》 (a) destiny; (a) fate; *one's* (fated) lot; 《불교에서》 Karma; 《운수》 *one's* star 〔fortune〕; luck. ¶ ~가 좋다 be fortunate; be blessed with good fortune / ~가 사납다 be unfortunate; be ill-fated / ~를 잘〔잘못〕 타고 나다 be born under a lucky 〔an unlucky〕 star / ~를 고치다 《재가하다》《a woman》 marry again; 《출세하다》 rise suddenly in the world; 《벼락 부자가 되다》 gain sudden wealth / ~로 알고 체념하다, ~ 소관으로 돌리다 resign *oneself* to *one's* fate; be reconciled to *one's* fate; accept 《*something*》 as fate / …할 ~다 be

fated 〔destined〕 to *do* / 불행을 ~로 돌리다 ascribe *one's* ill luck to fate / 큰 사람 될 ~다 be destined to become a great man / 일찍 죽을 ~다 be fated to die young / 모두가 내 ~다 It is all due to the stars I was born under. / 사람 ~ 알 수 없다 No one can foretell his destiny.
② 《한자(漢字)의 八자》 the Chinese character 八(=eight). ¶ 이마에 ~를 그리다 frown; knit *one's* brows.
◉ ~걸음 a splay-footed 〔toe-out〕 walk; [비유적] a dignified gait: ~걸음하다 walk with the toes turned out (-ward).

**팔자땜**(八字—) struggling to compensate for an unlucky destiny; working to ward off the evil that fate has in store for *one*. ~하다 suffer a minor misfortune in compensation for *one's* predestined ill fate.

**팔재간**(—才幹) 〖씨름〗 techniques with 「*one's* arms.

**팔절판**(八切判) 〖사진〗 octavo (size).

**팔죽지** the upper arm.

**팔짓** swinging 〔waving〕 *one's* arms; gesturing with *one's* arms; arm gestures. ~하다 swing 〔wave〕 *one's* arms; make gestures with *one's* arms.

**팔짝-** ⇨ 펄쩍-.

**팔짱** folding *one's* arms. ¶ ~을 끼다 《자신의》 fold *one's* arms (across *one's* chest); 《남과》 put *one's* arms through another's; link arms with 《*a person*》 / ~을 끼고 《자기의》 with *one's* arms folded; with folded arms / …와 ~을 끼고 걷다 walk arm in arm with… / ~을 끼고 방관하다 look on 「with folded arms 〔with *one's* hands in *one's* pockets〕; stand idle / 지금은 ~ 끼고 방관할 때가 아니다 This is not a time for us to remain idle.

**팔찌** 《팔가락지》 a bracelet; a bangle; an armlet; 《활 쏠 때의》 an armband to hold up *one's* sleeves (used by archers); a bracer. ¶ ~를 끼다 wear a bracelet.

**팔촌**(八寸) ① 《촌수》 a third cousin. ¶ 사돈의 ~ a cousin 40 times removed; an unrelated person; a stranger. ② 《여덟 치》 8 inches.

**팔팔하다** 《성질이》 (be) short-〔quick-〕tempered; violent; impatient; 《기운이》 (be) lively; animated; active; sprightly. ¶ 팔팔한 젊은이 a lively youth / 그는 나이는 많으나 아직 ~ He may be old but he's still quite spry.

**팔푼이**(八—) a fool; a simpleton; a dullard; a half-wit.

**팡파르** [<*fanfarer*(F.)] a fanfare; a flourish (of trumpets); a tucket. ¶ ~를 울리다 sound 〔play〕 a fanfare.

**팡파지다** ⇨ 펑퍼지다.

**팥** a red-bean; an adzuki bean; an Indian bean. ◉ 팥고물 mashed red-bean (used to coat rice cake). 팥꼬투리 a red-bean pod. 팥꽃나무 〖식물〗 the lilac daphne. 팥단자(—團子) red-bean dumplings. 팥떡 rice cake coated with mashed red-beans. 팥물 water in which red-beans were boiled. 팥밥 rice cooked with red-beans. 팥빙수(—氷水) adzuki bean sherbet. 팥소 bean jam.

**팥죽**(—粥) red-bean 〔adzuki-bean〕 porridge; thick red-bean 〔red adzuki bean〕 soup with rice cake. ¶ 동지에 ~을 먹는 것은 우리가 지켜 온 관습이다 It has been our tradition to eat red adzuki bean porridge on *Tongji* 〔winter solstice〕. / ~ 한 그릇에 장자의 명분을 팔다 〖성서〗 sell *one's* birthright for a mess of pottage.

**패**(牌) ① 《푯조각》 a tablet; a tag; a plate; a tally. ¶ 명패 a nameplate / 금패 수령자 a gold medalist / 나무패를 붙이다 fasten 〔tie〕 《a package》 with a wooden tag. ② 《무리》 a group; a company; a gang; a clique; a circle; a set. ¶ 우리 패 our group; our team / 젊은 패 young folks / 패를 짓다 form a gang / 그런 패들과는 어울리지 마라 Don't mix with such a set. ③ 《마작의》 a tile; a (mah-jong) piece; 《화투 등의》 a (playing) card. ¶ 패가 좋다〔나쁘다〕 have a good 〔bad〕 hand / 패를 떼다 cut the cards / 패를 도르다 deal the cards. 「uation.

**패**(覇) 〖바둑〗 an alternate-capture sit-

**패가**(敗家) ~하다 ruin *one's* family; a family goes bankrupt 〔to ruin〕.
◉ ~망신 ruining both *oneself* and *one's* family: 그는 노름으로 ~망신했다 He gambled himself out of house and home.

**패각**(貝殼) a shell. ¶ ~ 모양의 shell-shaped; conchoidal. ◉ ~세공(細工) shellwork.

**패거리**(牌—) a lot 〔set〕; a party; a bunch. ¶ 못된 ~ a gang of punks.

**패검**(佩劍) 《칼을 참》 wearing 〔carrying〕 a sword 〔saber〕; 《찬 칼》 a sword worn. ~하다 wear 〔carry〕 a saber 《at *one's* side》.

**패군**(敗軍) a defeated army. ¶ ~지장은

병법을 말하지 않는다 A defeated general should not talk of battles. *or* It is not for the loser to talk about tactics.

**패권**(覇權) ①《지배권》 supremacy; dominance; mastery; leadership; 《타국에 대한》 hegemony. ¶ ~을 쥐다 hold supremacy《in over》; gain the hegemony《of》/ ~을 다투다 struggle for supremacy / 해상의 ~을 쥐다 dominate 〔rule〕 the sea / 강대국들은 세계의 ~을 놓고 다투고 있었다 The great powers were struggling 〔striving〕 for the supremacy 〔hegemony〕 of the world. ②《선수권》 a championship. ¶ ~을 쥐다 win a championship.
◉ ~주의 hegemonism. 반~조항 the antihegemony clause.

**패기**(覇氣)《의기》 spirit; vigor; drive (적극성); 《야심》 ambition; aspiration. ¶ ~ 있는 사람 an ambitious person; a man of spirit / ~가 만만하다 「be full of 〔be bursting with〕 ambition / 그는 ~가 있다 He has great spirit 〔drive〕. / 그는 ~가 없다 He lacks spirit. / 그는 지나치게 신중해서 ~가 없다 He is too cautious and lacks ambition.

**패널** 〚건축〛 a panel; 《토론 참가자단》 a panel. ◉ ~디스커션 a panel discussion. ~쇼 《TV 퀴즈 프로그램》 a panel show. ~조명 panel lighting. ~히터 an oil-filled electric radiator.

**패널리스트** 《토론자》 a panelist.

**패다**[1] ① 《쪼개다》 break 《wood》 to pieces; split; chop (up) (잘게). ¶ 장작을 ~ split firewood; split 〔chop〕 wood. ② 《때리다》 beat 〔strike〕 hard; give 〔deal, deliver〕 《*a person*》 a blow; thrash; hit; assault. ¶ 몹시 ~ give 《*a person*》 a sound beating; beat 《*a person*》 to a jelly 〔mummy〕 / 멍이 들도록 ~ beat 《*a person*》 black and blue.

**패다**[2] ① 《파게 하다》 have 〔let〕 《*a person*》 dig 《the ground》. ② 《파이다》 get dug; be hollowed out. ¶ 볼이 우묵히 팬 사람 a person with hollow cheeks; a hollow-〔sunken-〕cheeked person / 비에 땅이 팼다 The ground is hollowed out by the rain. / 땅이 굳어 패지 않는다 The ground is so hard that it won't dig.

**패다**[3] 《이삭이》 come out. ¶ 이삭이 ~ come into ears; be in (the) ear / 이삼일만 있으면 벼이삭이 모두 팰 것이다 The rice plants will all come into ears in a few days.

**패담**(悖談) an unreasonable remark; perverse talk(s). ~하다 say unreasonable thing; talk indecency.

**패덕**(悖德) immorality; demoralization; corruption; a lapse from virtue.
◉ ~한(漢) an immoral 〔a depraved〕 man; a scoundrel. ~행위 immoral conduct: an immoral act.

**패도**(覇道) ruling by force; military rule; the rule of might.

**패드** 〚양재〛 a pad; falsies 《구어》. ¶ ~를 두껍게 넣은 heavily padded 《shoulders》 / 어깨의 ~ a shoulder pad.

**패랭이** ① 《옛날 모자》 a rough bamboo-hat worn by mourners 〔lowly persons〕. ② ⇨ 패랭이꽃. 「wild pink.

**패랭이꽃** 〚식물〛 a (fringed) pink; a

**패러그래프** a paragraph.

**패러글라이더** a paraglider.

**패러다임** 《이론적인 틀》 a paradigm.

**패러데이** 《전기량의 단위》 a faraday (생략 F). ¶ ~의 법칙 Faraday's Law.
◉ ~관(管) a Faraday's tube.

**패러독스** 《모순》 a paradox. ¶ ~한 paradoxical.

**패럿** 〚電〛 a farad (생략 F). ¶ 백만 ~ a megafarad / 100 만분의 1 ~ a microfarad.

**패류**(貝類) shellfish. ◉ ~학 conchology: ~학자 a conchologist.

**패륜**(悖倫) immorality. ¶ ~의 immoral.
◉ ~아 an immoral person. ~행위 immoral conduct; immorality.

**패리티** 〚경제〛 《동등·균등》 parity. ◉ ~가격 a parity price. ~계산 a parity account 〔computation〕.

**패망**(敗亡) (a) defeat; ruin; wreck. ~하다 get defeated 〔ruined, annihilated〕; go 〔fall, come〕 to ruin. ¶ 그 나라는 사치풍조에 빠져 ~했다 The country was ruined by rolling in luxurious habits 〔lavishing upon its pleasures〕.

**패멸**(敗滅) destruction; ruin; annihilation; demolition. ~하다 get destroyed 〔ruined, annihilated〕; be demolished.

**패모**(貝母) 〚식물〛 a checkered lily; a crown imperial.

**패물**(貝物) shell goods; shellware; things made of coral 〔amber, crystal, tortoiseshell〕.

**패물**(佩物) personal ornaments 〔adornment〕; accessories.

**패밀리** a family. ◉ ~닥터 a family doctor. ~맨 《가정적인 사람》 a family man.

**패배**(敗北) (a) defeat; a loss; (a) rout

(패주). ～하다 be defeated 〔beaten〕; lose a battle 〔game〕; suffer a defeat. ¶～로 끝나다 end in defeat / ～를 인정하다 admit defeat / ～를 당하다 meet 〔suffer〕 a 《severe》 defeat (at the hands of…) / 총선거에서 ～하다 lose 〔be defeated in〕 the general election / 적은 완전히 ～했다 The enemy was defeated completely. / 우리 팀은 3점 차이로 B교에 ～했다 Our team 「was defeated by 〔lost the game to〕 B school by three points. ◉ ～주의 defeatism: ～주의자 a defeatist.

**패보**(敗報) the news of defeat.

**패사**(稗史) an unofficial history; a private narrative history.

**패색**(敗色) signs of defeat; unfavorable signs in battle. ¶～이 짙다 Most likely we will lose this game. *or* Defeat seems certain. *or* The odds are against our team. (★ odds는 「승산」의 뜻).

**패석**(貝石) fossil shells.

**패설**(悖說) ＝패담.

**패세**(敗勢) a losing situation; the reverse tide of a war; signs of defeat; unfavorable signs in battle.

**패션** 《유행》 (a) fashion. ¶최신～ the latest fashion / ～을 따르다 follow the fashion / ～을 만들어내다 set a 〔the〕 fashion. ◉ ～디자이너 a fashion designer. ～모델 a fashion model; a clotheshorse. ～산업 the fashion industry. ～쇼 a fashion show. ～잡지 a fashion journal.

**패소**(敗訴) losing a lawsuit; a lost case. ～하다 lose a suit 〔case〕; fail in an action. ¶원고〔피고〕～의 판결이 나왔다 Judgment was given 〔passed〕 against the plaintiff 〔defendant〕.

**패스** ① 《무료 입장권·승차권》 a pass; a free ticket 〔pass〕; 《정기권》 a commutation ticket 《미》; a season ticket 《영》. ② 《합격·통과》 passing. ～하다 pass. ¶시험에 ～하다 pass 〔succeed in〕 an examination 〔a test〕 / (물건이) 검사에 ～하다 pass muster; stand the test. ③ 《구기에서의》 a pass; passwork. ～하다 pass 《a ball to another》. ¶～에 의한 공격 a passing attack / (럭비에서) 빠른 ～로 트라이를 성공시키다 score a try on fast passwork. ④ 《카드놀이》 a pass. ～하다 pass (기권하다).
◉ ～포트 a passport: ～포트를 신청〔교부〕하다 apply for 〔issue〕 a passport. 통근～ a season ticket for workers; a commutation ticket.

**패스트볼** 〖야구〗 a passed ball. ¶～로 득점하다 score on a passed ball.

**패스트푸드** 《햄버거·프라이드 치킨 따위》 fast food. ¶～체인 a fast-food chain / ～식당 a fast-food restaurant.

**패싸움**(牌—) a gang fight. ～하다 have a gang fight; fight in groups.

**패쓰다**(覇—) 《바둑에서》 make a no-man's point.

**패악**(悖惡) wickedness; perverseness. ～하다 (be) wicked; perverse.

**패업**(覇業) achievements of a conqueror; domination; hegemony. ¶～을 이룩하다 establish *oneself* as ruler of a country.

**패용**(佩用) wearing 《a decoration》. ～하다 wear. ¶구내 출입증 ～《게시》 Always wear your pass while on the premises.

**패운**(敗運) ruinous luck; being fated to lose; *one's* 「declining fortune 〔waning star〕.

**패인**(敗因) the cause of defeat. ¶연습 부족이 그의 ～이었다 His lack of training was the cause of his defeat in the match. / 이번의 주된 ～은 상대를 얕잡아 본 데 있다 Our defeat this time was chiefly caused by our overoptimistic estimate of the opponent's ability.

**패자**(敗者) a loser; a defeated person 〔player〕; the defeated; the vanquished. ◉ ～부활전 《경기의》 a consolation 〔revival〕 match 〔round, race〕.

**패자**(覇者) a supreme ruler; 《경기의》 a champion (of a game); a winner; a titleholder.

**패잔**(敗殘) survival after defeat. ◉ ～병 remnants of a defeated army 〔troop〕; stragglers: 소탕 작전에서 3백 명의 ～병이 사살되거나 붙잡혔다 Three hundred stragglers were either killed or captured in the mopping-up operation.

**패잡다**(牌—) get the deal; become 〔have *one's* turn as〕 "the house" in a gambling game.

**패장**(敗將) a defeated 〔vanquished〕 general.

**패전**(敗戰) (a) defeat; a lost battle. ～하다 lose a battle 〔war〕; get defeated 〔vanquished〕. ¶～의 혼란속에서 in the chaos following the war defeat. ◉ ～국 a defeated 〔vanquished〕 nation. ～투수 〖야구〗 a losing pitcher.

**패주**(敗走) (a) rout; flight; *débâcle* (F.). ～하다 get routed; be put to rout;

take to flight; flee. ¶ 적을 ~케 하다 put the enemy to rout; set an enemy flying.

**패총**(貝塚) a shell mound [heap].

**패키지** a package. ◉ ~딜 《일괄 거래·교섭》 a package deal. ~상품 package goods. ~투어 《여행업자 주관의》 a package tour.

**패킹** 《포장》 packing. ¶ 짐을 ~하다 do one's packing.

**패턴** 《모범·견본·양식·형》 a pattern. ¶ 새로운 ~의 차 a car of a new pattern. ◉ ~인식 pattern recognition.

**패퇴**(敗退) defeat; retreat (퇴각). ~하다 《퇴각하다》 retreat; 《패배하다》 be defeated; be beaten.

**패트런** a patron(남); a patroness(여).

**패트롤** a patrol. ~하다 go on patrol (duty); patrol 《an area》. ¶ ~중인 경찰관 a policeman on patrol. ◉ ~카 a (police) patrol car; 《미》 a squad [cruise, prowl] car.

**패트리어트미사일** 《대미사일용 미사일》 a Patriot missile.

**패하다**(敗—) ① 《지다》 get defeated 《in》; be beaten 《in》; lose 《a game, a battle》; suffer [sustain] a defeat. ¶ 경기에 ~ lose a game [match, bout] / 선거전에 ~ suffer a defeat [be beaten] in an election campaign / 체스에 ~ be beaten in a game of chess / 전쟁에 ~ be defeated in a war; lose a war / 1대 5로 ~ be defeated [lose the game] by a score of 1 to 5. ② 《거덜나다》 get ruined; go broke; go to ruin. ¶ 집안이 ~ a family goes to ruin.

**패혈증**(敗血症) 〖의학〗 blood poisoning; septicemia. ¶ ~의 septicemic / 출혈성 ~ 〖수의〗 hemorrhagic septicemia.

**팩스, 팩시밀리** 《전송사진》 a fax; a facsimile. ¶ ~로 보내다 fax 《a letter》 to 《*a person*》.

**팩터리 숍** 《직매장》 a factory shop.

**팩터링제도**(—制度) 〖경제〗 factoring system.

**팬**[1] 《애호자》 a fan; an enthusiast. ¶ 야구팬 a baseball fan / 영화팬 a movie fan / Y의 열렬한 팬 an enthusiastic [a fanatical] admirer of Y. ◉ ~레터 fan mail 《미》; fan letters.

**팬**[2] 《선풍기·송풍기의》 a fan. ◉ ~히터 a fan heater.

**팬시산업**(—産業) fancy industry.

**팬지** 〖식물〗 a pansy; a heartsease. ¶ 야생 ~ a kiss-me-quick.

**팬츠** 《짧고 꼭 끼는 것》 briefs; 《쇼트 팬츠형》 shorts 《미》; 《선수용》 athletic shorts; 《러닝용》 running shorts; 《복싱·수영용》 trunks; 《남성용 속옷》 underpants; 《여성·어린이용》 panties; 《바지》 pants (★ 《미》에서 pants는 평상복의 바지). ◉ 핫~ hot pants.

**팬케이크** a pancake; a griddlecake; a flapjack 《미》; 《화장품》 pancake.

**팬터마임** 《무언극》 a pantomime; a dumb show. ¶ ~을 하다 pantomime 《an act》; represent 《*something*》 by dumb show / ~을 하는 사람 a pantomimist.

**팬텀** 《도깨비》 phantom; 《전폭기》 a Phantom (F-4의 별칭).

**팬티** panties. ◉ ~거들 a panty girdle. ~스타킹 《미》 (a pair of) panty hose; 《영》 (a pair of ) tights.

**팸플릿** a pamphlet; a leaflet; a brochure. ¶ ~을 배포하다 distribute pamphlets. ◉ 선전~ a propaganda pamphlet.

**팻말**(牌—) a bulletin [notice 《영》] board.

**팽** 《한 바퀴 도는 모양》 (a)round; circling; 《아찔한 모양》 reelingly. ¶ 동네를 한 바퀴 팽 돌다 go round the village 《on a bicycle》 / 소문이 팽 돌다 a rumor spreads [gets around] fast / 술이 팽 돌다 the alcohol goes to *one's* head / 눈이 팽 돈다 My eyes swim. *or* I feel dizzy.

**팽개치다** 《내던지다》 ① 《물건을》 throw [cast, fling] 《at, out, away》. ¶ 창 밖으로 ~ throw 《*a thing*》 out of the window / 책을 책상 위에 ~ slam a book on the desk / 책가방을 바닥에 ~ throw [fling] *one's* satchel down on the floor. ② 《포기하다》 give [throw] up; abandon; quit 《*one's* job》; renounce 《*one's* title》; lay down 《*one's* life》; 《버려두다》 neglect; fling [cast, lay] aside 《*one's* work》; leave [let] 《*a thing*》 alone [unattended, untouched]. ¶ 하던 일을 ~ leave *one's* work unfinished / 직위를 ~ throw up [resign from] *one's* office [position] / 그는 3년 전에 목사직을 팽개치고 작가가 되었다 He left [gave up] the ministry and became a writer three years ago. / 그 문제를 그대로 팽개쳐 두어서는 안 된다 You must not leave the matter unsettled.

**팽그르르** 《spinning, whirling, revolving, turning》 around smoothly. ¶ ~ 돌다 turn (round); revolve.

**팽글팽글** 《turning, spinning, revolving》 round and round smoothly; in a circle. ¶ 팽이가 ~ 돌다 A top spins [goes, turns] round and round.

**팽나무** 《식물》 a (Chinese) nettle tree.

**팽대**(膨大) swelling; expansion; tumefaction. ~하다 swell; expand; become bulky.

**팽만**(膨滿) inflation. ~하다 be inflated. ¶ 복부~ abdominal inflation.

**팽배**(澎湃) overflowing; surging. ~하다 overflow; surge; rise like a flood tide. ¶ ~하는 민주주의 사상 the flood tide of democracy.

**팽압**(膨壓) 〖식물〗 turgor pressure.

**팽이** a top. ¶ ~채 the whipcord of a top / ~를 돌리다 spin a top / ~가 서다 a top sleeps.

**팽창**(膨脹) ① 《부풀어 오름》 expansion; swelling. ~하다 expand; swell. ¶ 열에 의한 ~ thermal expansion / 금속은 열을 가하면 ~한다 Metals expand when they are heated. / 가스가 열을 받아 ~했다 The gas expanded with heat. ② 《증대》 (an) increase; growth. ~하다 increase; grow. ¶ 도시의 ~ urban growth / 예산의 ~ an increase in the budget / 인구의 급격한 ~ a rapid increase in population / 국고의 세출은 해마다 ~해 가고 있다 State expenditure increases year by year. / 서울은 교외로 급속히 ~해 나가고 있다 Seoul is expanding 〔spreading〕 rapidly into the surrounding countryside.
◉ ~계 〖물리〗 a dilatometer. ~계수 the coefficient of expansion. ~균열 《요업에서》 cracking due to expansion. ~력 expansive force 〔power〕. ~률 the rate of expansion. ~성 expansibility; extensibility. ~정책 expansionist policies. ~주의 expansionism: ~주의자 an expansionist. 선(線)~ 〖물리〗 a linear expansion. 체(體)~ 〖물리〗 a cubical expansion. 통화 ~ inflation of currency.

**팽팽** ⇨핑핑. ¶ 팽이가 ~ 돌다 a top spins round and round.

**팽팽하다** ① 《켕기다》 (be) tight; taut. ¶ 팽팽하게 tightly; closely; tensely / 팽팽하게 하다 strain; stretch / 줄을 팽팽히 당기다 stretch a rope tight; tighten a rope / 줄이 ~ a rope is taut.
② 《팍하다》 (be) narrow-minded (편협); touchy; testy; hidebound; rigid; strait-laced; illiberal. ¶ 성질이 팽팽한 사람 a narrow-minded 〔testy〕 person.
③ 《대등하다》 (be) very close; equal; even. ¶팽팽한 경기 a close contest; an even match / 양진영이 팽팽하게 맞서다 two parties are in bitter tug-of-war 《over》. 「just right.

**팽하다** be neither more nor less; (be)

**팍하다**(愎—) (be) testy; quick-tempered; peppery; waspish; snappish; snippy; petulant.

**퍼내다** draw 〔dip〕 up; bail 〔ladle〕 out 〔up〕; take out 〔up〕; scoop out 〔up〕; pump out 〔up〕. ¶ 독의 쌀을 ~ take dry rice out of a jar / 분뇨를 ~ dip up night soil / 배의 물을 ~ bail water out of a boat / 삽으로 모래를 ~ dip out sand with a shovel / 스푼으로 ~ spoon out / 솥에서 국을 ~ ladle soup out of a kettle / 우물물을 ~ draw water from a well.

**퍼덕거리다** ① 《새·돛·깃발 등이》 flap; flutter. ¶ 새가 날개를 ~ a bird flaps 〔flutters〕 its wings / 돛이 바람에 ~ a sail flutters in the wind / 커튼〔깃발〕이 ~ a curtain 〔flag〕 flaps in the wind. ② 《물고기가》 leap; flop; flounder; jump; splash. ¶ 고기가 ~ a fish flops 〔shakes its tail (꼬리를)〕.

**퍼덕퍼덕** 《새·돛 따위가》 flapping; fluttering; 《물고기가》 flopping; leaping; splashing.

**퍼들링** 〖야금〗 a puddling.

**퍼뜨리다** 《종교·사상 등을》 spread; disseminate; diffuse; propagate; make popular; 《소문 등을》 set 《a rumor》 afloat; start 〔circulate, spread〕 《a rumor》; let it be known 《that ...》; make 《*a thing*》 known. ¶ 정보를 ~ spread 〔disseminate〕 information / 불교를 ~ propagate Buddhism / 헛소문을〔유언비어를〕~ spread 〔circulate〕 a false rumor; set a false rumor afloat / 있는 말 없는 말 퍼뜨리고 다니다 spread scandal about 《*a person*》 blending truth with fiction / 그녀가 소문을 퍼뜨린 것 같다 She seems to have spread the rumor. / 그녀가 그 얘기를 온 동네 방네에 퍼뜨릴 게다 She will trumpet that story all over the village.

**퍼뜩** 《occurring》 suddenly; in a flash. ¶ ~ 생각나다 suddenly occur to *one;* flash across *one's* mind / ~ 어떤 생각이 그의 머리를 스쳤다 An idea flashed across 〔on〕 his mind. / 혹시 그들이 자객일지도 모른다는 생각이 ~ 들었다 The suspicion flashed across him that they might be assassins.

**퍼렇다** (be) blue; azure. ⇨파랗다.

**퍼레이드** a parade. ¶ 자동차 ~ a motorcade / ~를 펼치다 hold a parade.

**퍼머**(**넌트**) a permanent (wave); a perm 《구어》. ~하다 get a permanent; have *one's* hair permed 〔set〕; give a permanent.

**퍼먹다** ①《퍼서 먹다》 scoop 〔dip, ladle〕 and eat. ¶ 밥을 숟가락으로 ～ scoop rice with a spoon and eat it; eat rice with a spoon / 국을 냄비에서 ～ ladle soup out of a pan and eat it. ②《급하게 많이 먹다》 shovel down 〔in〕; eat greedily. ¶ 밥을 ～ shovel the rice down.

**퍼붓다** ①《퍼서 붓다》 dip 〔scoop, ladle〕 (up) and pour. ¶ 독의 물을 솥에 ～ dip water from a jar and pour it into a kettle. ②《끼얹다》 pour 〔throw〕 《water》 upon 〔over〕; douse 《*a person*》 with water; dash 《water》 over; play 《a stream of water》 on. ③《폭언·비난 등을》 heap 〔shower, rain〕 《abuses》 upon; asperse 《*a person*》 with bitter reproaches; lay 〔fix〕 《blame》 on; 《포화를》 subject 《the enemy》 to 《fire》. ¶ (야구에서) 맹타를 ～ shower hits 《on the opposing team》 / 온갖 욕설을 ～ shout all kinds of abuses 《at》 / 입정사납게 욕설을 ～ abuse 《*a person*》 in foul language / 질문을 ～ bombard 《*a person*》 with questions; rain questions on 《*a person*》. ④ [자동사] 《쏟아지다》 pour on; rain hard on; 《눈이》 fall thick and fast. ¶ (억수같이) 퍼붓는 비 pouring 〔heavy, pelting〕 rain / 내리 퍼붓는 눈보라 속을 달리다 run in a heavy snowstorm / 비가 (억수같이) 퍼붓는다 It is raining in torrents 〔(in) buckets〕. *or* It's raining cats and dogs.

**퍼석(퍼석)하다** (be) dry; friable; crumbly; [서술적] be dry and crumbling. ¶ 날씨가 가물어서 땅이 퍼석퍼석했다 The weather had been dry and the ground was crumbly.

**퍼센트** percent; per cent(기호 %, 생략 p.c., per ct.). ¶ 20～의 할인 a 20 percent discount / 6～의 증가 an increase by six percent / 지원자의 30～, 30% of the applicants / 백 ～의 능률을 올리다 secure one-hundred percent efficiency / 5 ～의 이익을 남기다 get 5% interest; get interest at 5 percent / 취직률은 100 ～였다 The employment rate was 100 percent. / 문맹자는 인구의 몇 ～나 되나 What percent of the population is illiterate?

**퍼센티지** (a) percentage.

**퍼스낼리티** 《인품·개성》 personality.

**퍼스널 컴퓨터** a personal computer (생략 PC).

**퍼스트** 《제1의》 first; 〖야구〗 《1루》 first base; 《1루수》 a first baseman. ◉ ～클래스 the first class: ～클래스로 여행하다 travel 〔go〕 first-class. ～레이디 the first lady (★ 종종 the First Lady).

**퍼올리다** draw up; scoop 〔dip〕 up; pump up. ¶ 우물에서 물을 ～ pump water from a well.

**퍼즐** a puzzle. ¶ 크로스워드 ～ a crossword puzzle / 그 여자는 ～을 하고 있다 She is at a puzzle now.

**퍼지** 《이론이 유연성이 있는》 fuzzy. ◉ ～공학 fuzzy engineering. ～논리 fuzzy logic. ～이론 the fuzzy theory. ～집합 〖수학〗 fuzzy set.

**퍼지다** ①《벌어지다》 spread out; widen; broaden; get broader. ¶ 퍼진 어깨 broad shoulders / 끝이 ～ the tip spreads out.
②《삶은 것이》 《boiled stuff》 get thicker and softer; become sodden. ¶ 떡밥이 잘 ～ rice for cake gets nice and soft.
③《널리》 (***a***) 《번지다》 spread (out); extend; stretch; 《초목이》 grow thick 〔rank〕; ramble; run (out); 《술·약 기운이》 take effect. ¶ 퍼진 나뭇가지 spreading branches / 가지가 ～ branches spread / 뿌리가 ～ roots spread / 햇살이 ～ the sun begins to shine broad and wide; the sun is high in the sky / 술기운이 ～ be well under the influence of liquor / 독이 그의 온몸에 퍼졌다 The poison has passed into his system. / 가지가 퍼져 있다 The branches are growing rank. / 불길이 끊임없이 퍼졌다 The flames have steadily spread. (***b***) 《전파·보급되다》 spread; be diffused 〔propagated〕; pervade; be circulated; 《소문 등이》 spread; get abroad 〔about, around〕; go the rounds; get 〔take〕 air; get 〔take〕 wind. ¶ 소문이 ～ a rumor spreads; a rumor is abroad 〔current, in circulation〕 《about》 / 이 노래는 학생들 간에 널리 퍼져 있다 This song is 「much in vogue 〔very popular〕 with the students. / 그 소식은 삽시간에 퍼졌다 The news spread like wildfire. / 냄새가 온 집안에 퍼졌다 The odor penetrated the whole house. / 그의 새 학설이 널리 퍼졌다 His new theory gained ground. (***c***) 《병 따위가》 spread; prevail; be prevalent; be widespread. ¶ 콜레라가 퍼지는 것을 막다 prevent 〔check〕 the spread of cholera / 그 전염병은 순식간에 마을에 퍼졌다 The epidemic prevailed quickly in the village.

④ 《자손·씨가》 breed; propagate; flourish; multiply / 자손이 ～ have numerous descendants; have a flourishing progeny / 파리는 무섭게 퍼진다 Flies multiply (themselves) enormously.
⑤ 《구김살이》 get smoothed; smooth out. ¶ 천이 잘 ～ a cloth irons well.
⑥ 《칠·분 따위가 먹다》 spread. ¶ 잘 ～ spread well.

**퍼컬레이터** 《커피 끓이는 기구》 a percolator.

**퍼트** 〖골프〗 a putt. ¶ ～연습을 하다 practice putting.

**퍼티** 《유리 끼울 때 쓰는 접합제》 putty. ¶ 유리 ～ glazier's putty.

**퍼펙트게임** 〖야구〗 a perfect game.

**퍼프** a (powder) puff.

**퍽**[1] ① 《찌르는 모양》 with a thrust; 《thrusting》 hard. ¶ 칼로 퍽 찌르다 thrust with a knife. ② 《쓰러지는 모양》 with a thud; 《collapsing》 feebly. ¶ ～ 쓰러지다 fall with a flump / 총에 맞아 그 자리에 퍽 쓰러지다 be shot and collapse on the spot.

**퍽**[2] 《매우》 very much; quite; terribly; awfully; badly. ¶ 퍽 크다 be very big / 퍽 재미 있다 be right interesting / 퍽 기뻐하다 be very glad; be much pleased / 퍽 피곤하시겠습니다 You must be very tired. / 퍽 기쁘시겠습니다 How glad you must be ! / 퍽 컸구나 What a big boy you've grown ! / 비가 퍽 많이 왔다 A fair amount of rain has fallen. / 그의 몸이 퍽 좋아졌다 His health has been very much improved.

**퍽석** limply; with a flump. ¶ 의자에 ～ 주저앉다 slump down onto 〔into〕 a chair; sit limply in a chair.

**편둥거리다** lead an idle life; idle 〔dawdle〕 *one's* time away. ⇨ 빈둥거리다.

**펀드** 〖경제〗 fund. ◉ ～매니저 《투자 운용 담당자》 a fund manager.

**펀들거리다** idle *one's* time away. ⇨ 빈둥거리다.

**펀뜻** =언뜻.

**펀치** ① 《타인기》 a punch; 《a pair of》 cancels. ¶ ～카드 a punch(ed) card / ～로 찍다 punch 《a ticket》. ② 《음료》 punch. ③ 〖권투〗 a punch. ¶ ～를 먹이다 land a punch 《on》; punch 《*a person* on the chin》 / ～를 얻어맞다 get a punch 《on the nose》 / 강한 ～를 도전자 몸통에 먹이다 land powerful punches on the challenger's body.

**펀칭백** 〖권투〗 a punching bag.

**펀칭볼** 〖권투〗 a punching ball.

**펀펀하다** (be) even; level; flat. ⇨ 반반하다 ①. ¶ 펀펀한 땅 even 〔flat〕 ground.

**펀하다** (be) wide; broad; vast; boundless. ¶ 펀한 들 a wide plain / 펀히 widely; broadly; vastly; boundlessly.

**펄** ① 《개펄》 a tideland; a tidal flat. ② 《들판》 a wide expanse of land; a vast plain; a prairie.

**펄떡–** ⇨ 팔딱–.

**펄럭거리다** flutter; whip; stream; flicker; flap; wave. ¶ 바람에 ～ flutter 〔whip〕 in the wind / 펄럭거리는 깃발 a streaming flag / 바람에 펄럭거리는 머리 hair streaming in wind / 깃발〔돛〕이 바람에 ～ a flag 〔sail〕 flaps 〔flutters, waves〕 in the wind.

**펄럭펄럭** with a flutter 〔flap, wave〕; fluttering; flapping; waving. ¶ 깃발이 바람에 ～ 나부끼다 a flag flaps in the wind / 나뭇잎이 바람에 ～ 흔들리다 the leaves (of a tree) flutter in the wind.

**펄렁거리다** ⇨ 펄럭거리다.

**펄스** 〖전기〗 a pulse; an electric pulse. ¶ ～를 발생시키다 pulse 《a transmitter》. ◉ ～동작시간 pulse operating time. ～반복수 a pulse repetition 〔recurrence〕 rate. ～변조(變調) pulse modulation: ～ 위상〔밀도, 진폭, 주파수〕 변조 pulse phase 〔number, amplitude, frequency〕 modulation. ～폭(幅) pulse width 〔length〕.

**펄썩** ① 《먼지·연기 등이 나는 모양》 rising lightly. ¶ 먼지가 ～ 나다 a great cloud of dust rises lightly. ② 《주저앉는 모양》 collapsing; flopping. ¶ ～ 주저앉다 collapse; drop on *one's* knees / 땅 위에 ～ 주저앉다 flop down on the ground / ～ 의자에 주저앉다 drop heavily into a chair; plump 〔sink〕 into a chair.

**펄쩍** ① 《여는 모양》 suddenly; abruptly. ② 《뛰는 모양》 nimbly; lightly. ¶ ～ 뛰다 make a sudden leap; jump 〔start, spring〕 to *one's* feet / 그는 놀라서 ～ 뛰었다 He was startled into a jump / 성나서 ～ 뛰다 leap up with anger; fly into rage; start up with anger.

**펄쩍펄쩍** jumping 〔leaping, springing〕 up and down. ¶ ～ 뛰다 jump up and down / 성이 나서 ～ 뛰다 bounce with anger.

**펄펄** ① 《끓는 모양》 boiling (hard); simmering; seething. ¶ 물을 ～ 끓이다 keep water at a simmer / 물이 ～ 끓다 water is boiling hard. ② 《뜨겁게 다는 모양》 feverish (신열이); broiling; scorching. ¶ 몸이 ～ 끓다 have a high fever; be burning up with fever. ③ 《날거나 나부끼는 모양》 fluttering; flapping; in flakes (눈 따위가). ¶ 새가 ~ 날다 a bird flies flapping its wings; a bird wings its way swiftly / 눈이 ~ 날리다 snow flutters about / 깃발이 바람에 ~ 날리고 있다 The flag is fluttering in the wind.

**펄펄하다** ⇨ 팔팔하다.

**펄프** (wood) pulp. ¶ ~로 만들다 reduce 《wood》 to pulp; pulp. ◉ ~공장 a pulp mill. ~재 pulpwood. 대용~ substitute for wood pulp. 목재~ wood pulp. 인견~ rayon pulp.

**펌블** 〖야구〗 fumbling; a fumble. ~하다 fumble 《a grounder》; boot 《a ball》.

**펌프** a pump. ¶ ~의 자루〔손잡이〕 a pump handle 〔brake〕 / ~를 틀다 work a pump / ~로 물을 퍼내다 pump the water out 《of》 / ~로 우물물을 퍼올리다 pump water up 〔out〕 from a well / ~로 물을 탱크에 넣다 pump water into a tank / ~로 자전거 타이어에 공기를 넣다 pump up *one's* bicycle tires. ◉ ~실 a pump room 〔house〕. ~우물 a pump well. ~장치 a pumping plant. 순환〔송수〕~ a circulating pump. 압력~ a pressure pump. 자전거~ a bicycle pump. 증기~ a steam pump. 회전~ a rotary pump.

**펑** pop; bang; plop. ⇨ 펑하다.

**펑퍼지다** get well-developed 〔well-rounded〕.

**펑퍼짐하다** (be) flat and round; broad and roundish. ¶ 펑퍼짐한 언덕 a gently sloping hill / 펑퍼짐한 엉덩이 well-rounded hips.

**펑펑** ① 《폭음 소리》 with explosion after explosion; popping and popping. ¶ ~ 불꽃이 하늘로 올랐다 Bang! Bang! Up went the fireworks.
② 《쏟아지는 모양》 gurgling and gurgling; bubbling and bubbling; gushing; spouting; 《눈이》 falling thick and fast; in a whirl. ¶ ~ 솟는 샘 a gushing fountain / (물이) ~ 흐르다 flow in streams; gush out; stream down / 눈물을 ~ 쏟다 shed copious 〔a flood of〕 tears / 피가 ~ 나오다 bleed profusely; blood streams down / 샘이 ~ 솟다 a spring bubbles up / 눈이 ~ 쏟아진다 The snow falls 「thick and fast 〔in a whirl〕. / 상처에서 피가 ~ 내솟았다 Blood spouted from his wound.

**펑하다** pop; bang; plop; cloop. ¶ 펑하고 with a pop 〔bang〕 / 펑하고 폭발하다 go off with a bang / 펑하며 마개가 빠졌다 The cork came out with a pop.

**페가수스자리** 〖천문〗 the Winged Horse; Pegasus.

**페그마타이트** 〖광물〗 pegmatite.

**페넌트** a pennant. ¶ ~를 교환하다 exchange the pennants. ◉ ~레이스 a pennant race.

**페널티** 〖스포츠〗 《반칙에 대한 벌》 a penalty. ◉ ~골 〖축구〗 a penalty goal. ~에어리어 〖축구〗 a penalty area. ~킥 〖축구〗 a penalty kick.

**페노바르비탈** 〖약〗 phenobarbital; luminal (진통 수면제).

**페놀** 〖화학〗 phenol; carbolic acid. ◉ ~산〔수지〕 phenolic acid 〔resin〕.

**페놀프탈레인** 〖화학〗 phenolphtalein.

**페니** 《화폐 단위》 a penny (*pl.* -nies, pence). ⇨ 펜스[1]. ¶ 반 ~ a halfpenny [héipni] / 1 ~ 반 three halfpence [héipəns].

**페니스** 〖해부〗 a penis. (*pl.* -nes, ~es).

**페니실린** 〖약〗 penicillin. ¶ ~을 주사하다 give 《*a person*》 a penicillin injection 〔an injection of penicillin〕 / 10만 단위의 ~(을 주사하다) (give *a person* an injection of) 100,000 units of penicillin. ◉ ~쇼크 《a case of》 a penicillin shock. ~연고 a penicillin ointment. ~주사 a penicillin shot 〔injection〕.

**페니키아** Phoenicia; Phenicia. ¶ ~ (사람·말)의 Phoenician. ◉ ~말 Phoenician. ~사람 a Phoenician.

**페닐기**(―基) 〖화학〗 phenyl.

**페닐렌기**(―基) 〖화학〗 phenylene.

**페달** a pedal. ¶ ~을 밟다 pedal 《a bicycle》.

**페더급**(―級) 〖권투〗 the featherweight. ◉ ~선수 a featherweight (boxer).

**페디큐어** 《발톱 손질》 (a) pedicure. ¶ ~를 하다 give 《oneself》 pedicure.

**페로시안화**(―化) 〖화학〗 ◉ ~나트륨 sodium ferrocyanide; yellow prussiate of soda. ~물 ferrocyanide; prussiate. ~칼륨 potassium ferrocyanide; yellow prussiate of potash.

**페루** 《남미의 공화국》 (the Republic of) Peru. ¶ ~의 Peruvian. ◉ ~사람 a Peruvian.

**페르시아** Persia. ¶ ~의 Persian. ◉ ~고양이 a Persian cat. ~만 the Persian Gulf. ~말 Persian. ~사람 a Persian. ~양탄자 a Persian rug 〔carpet〕.

**페르미** 〖물리〗 a fermi (10조분의 1cm).

**페리(보트)** 《연락선》 a ferry(boat).

**페미니스트** 《여권론자》 a feminist.

**페미니즘** 《여권주의》 feminism.

**페미컨**《말린 쇠고기》pem(m)ican.
**페서리**《피임구》a pessary.
**페소**《중남미·필리핀 등지의 화폐 단위》a peso (기호 P).
**페스트**〖의학〗(the) pest; the bubonic 〔black〕 plague; (a) pestilence. ◉ ~균 a plague bacillus.
**페스티벌**《축제》a festival.
**페시미스트**《비관론자》a pessimist.
**페시미즘**《비관주의》pessimism (염세주의).
**페어플레이** fair play. ¶ ~를 하자 Let's play fair.
**페이**《봉급》pay. ◉ ~데이 a payday《미》; a wage day《영》.
**페이드아웃**〖영화·TV〗(a) fade-out.
**페이드인**〖영화·TV〗(a) fade-in.
**페이브먼트**《포장도로》pavement.
**페이소스**《비애》pathos. ¶ ~가 넘치는 full of pathos / 그의 작품에는 일말의 ~가 감돌고 있다 There is a touch of pathos in his works.
**페이스**《보조·속도》(a) pace. ¶ 자기 ~로 at *one's* own pace / ~를 지키다 go 〔proceed〕 at *one's* own pace; keep within *one's* speed / 상대의 ~를 흐트러뜨리다 put *one's* opponent off 〔out of〕 *his* stride; disturb *one's* rival's rhythm.
**페이지** a page; a leaf (★ a page는 한 쪽, a leaf는 앞뒷쪽 즉 한 장을 말함). ¶ 반대 ~ the opposite page / 오른쪽 ~ the right-hand page; the recto / 왼쪽 ~ the left-hand page; the verso / ~당 자수 the number of characters per page / 500 ~의 책 a book of five hundred pages / 제7 ~에 in the seven page / 5 내지 10 ~에 on pages 5-10 / ~를 넘기다 turn (over) the leaves《of a book》; turn 〔leaf〕 the pages《of》; leaf through《a book》/ ~를 매기다 page《a book》; paginate / ~를 채우다 fill pages / …의 역사에 새로운 한 ~를 장식하다 add a new page to the history of... / 25 ~에 계속《지시》Continued on page 25. / 5 ~를 펴시오 Open (your book) at page 5.
**페이퍼**《종이》paper;《사포》sandpaper; emery paper;《논문》a paper. ¶ ~로 문지르다 sandpaper《a plank》. ◉ ~나이프 a paper knife. ~백《책의 장정》a book in paperback (format); a paperback (book); a softcover.
**페인트** ①《도료》paint. ¶ ~칠한 벽 a painted wall / ~를 칠하다 paint《a room white》/ ~ 주의〔조심〕《게시》Wet paint!《미》; Fresh paint!《영》/ 곳곳에 ~가 벗겨졌다 The paint has peeled off in places. ②〖스포츠〗《시늉》a feint. ¶ ~ 모션 a feint motion ◉ ~가게 a paint store 〔shop〕. ~장이 a (house) painter. 수성~ water paint.
**페치카** [<*pechka* (Russ.)] a Russian 〔Manchurian〕 stove.
**페티코트**《스커트 밑에 입는 속치마》a petticoat.
**페팅**《남녀의》petting. ◉ 소프트~ soft petting; necking. 헤비~ heavy petting.
**페퍼민트**《박하》peppermint.
**페하**〖화학〗pH. [<*p*otential of *h*ydrogen] ◉ ~가 pH value. ~계 a pH meter.
**펙틴**〖생화학〗pectin. ◉ ~산 pectic acid: ~산염 pectate.
**펜** a pen.
¶ 펜촉 a nib;《미》a pen point / 펜대 a penholder / 펜글씨 pen writing / 가는〔굵은〕 펜 a fine 〔broad〕 pen / 펜을 들다 pick 〔take〕 up *one's* pen / 펜을 놓다 put down *one's* pen / ~을 꺾다《저술을 그만두다》give up writing 〔*one's* pen〕 / 펜으로 쓰다 write with 〔in〕 pen and ink / ~은 칼보다 강하다 The pen is mightier than the sword.
◉ 펜네임 a pen name: K라는 펜네임으로 under the pen name of K.

> **참고** 펜의 종류
> 만년필 fountain pen, 볼펜 ballpoint pen, 샤프펜(슬) mechanical pencil, 사인펜《끝이 부드러운》felt-tip 〔felt-tipped〕 pen (★《미》에서는 보통 felt pen이라고 함), 깃털펜 quill (pen).

**펜더**《자동차의 흙받기》《미》a fender; a bumper;《영》a wing; a mud guard;《선박의》(a) fender (방현재).
**펜던트**《wear》a pendant.
**펜맨십**《펜습자》penmanship;《공책》a copybook.
**펜스**[1] pence. ⇨ 페니. ¶ 2 ~《금액》twopence[tʌ́pəns];《주화》a twopenny [tʌ́pni] / 2 ~의 twopenny.
**펜스**[2]《야구장 등의》a fence. ¶ 타구가 ~를 넘어갔다 The batted ball went over the fence.
**펜실베이니아**《미국의 주》Pennsylvania (생략 Pa., Penn., Penna.).
**펜싱** fencing. ¶ ~칼 a (fencing) foil / ~연습을 하다 practice fencing. ◉ ~교사 a fencing master. ~교습소〔도장〕 a fencing school. ~선수 a fencer; a foilsman.
**펜치** pinchers; pliers.
**펜클럽** the P.E.N. Club (★ the International Association of Poets, Play-

wrights, Editors, Essayists, and Novelists의 약칭).

**펜타곤** 《미국 국방부》 the Pentagon.

**펜타퀸** 〖약〗 pentaquin(e).

**펜토오스핵산**(一核酸) 〖생화학〗 pentose nucleic acid (생략 PNA).

**펜팔** a pen pal; 《영》 a pen friend. ¶ ~과 편지 왕래를 하다 correspond 〔exchange letters〕 with a pen pal.

**펜화**(一畫) an ink 〔a pen-and-ink〕 drawing; a pen sketch 〔portrait〕.

**펠리컨** 〖조류〗 a pelican (사다새).

**펠트** felt. ◉ ~모자 a (soft) felt hat.

**펨프** 《뚜쟁이》 a pimp; a procurer.

**펩신** 〖화학〗 pepsin.

**펩톤** 〖화학〗 peptone.

**펭귄** 〖조류〗 a penguin.

**펴내다** 《발행하다》 publish; issue. ¶ 펴낸이 a publisher.

**펴놓다** unfold; unroll; spread; lay spread 〔open〕. ¶ 자리를 ~ spread a mat / 이부자리를 ~ spread the bedclothes; make 〔prepare〕 a bed / 책을 ~ open a book.

**펴다** ① 《펼치다》 《접힌 것 등을》 spread; unfold 《a newspaper》; open 《a book》; unroll 《a scroll》; lay (out). ¶ 날개를 ~ spread the wings / 담요를 ~ spread 〔lay out〕 a blanket / 3페이지를 ~ open 《the book》 at 〔to〕 page 3 / (쥐었던) 손바닥을 ~ open *one's* palm / 이부자리를 ~ make 〔make up, prepare, fix〕 a bed; spread *one's* quilts / 지도를 ~ spread a map.
② 《굽은 것 등을》 straighten; stretch; uncoil (말린 것을); 《쇠붙이를 때려서》 planish; roll; beat out; 《구김·주름살 등을》 smooth out 《creases》; iron out (다리미로). ¶ 구겨진 종이를 ~ smooth out crumpled paper / 구부러진 철사를 ~ straighten out a crooked wire / 바지의 구김살을 ~ take creases out of the trousers; smooth 〔press〕 out wrinkles from 〔in〕 the trousers.
③ 《몸을》 stretch; straighten; hold out; stick 〔throw〕 out 《*one's* chest》. ¶ 가슴을 펴고 걷다 walk with *one's* chest out / 몸을〔허리를〕 ~ stretch 〔straighten, unbend〕 *oneself* / 어깨를 ~ open *one's* shoulders / 팔을 ~ stretch 〔hold out〕 *one's* arm 《to》; reach 〔put〕 out *one's* hand 《for》.
④ 《재능을》 cultivate 《*one's* abilities》; develop 〔display〕 《*one's* talent》; 《뜻을》 realize. ¶ 뜻을 ~ have *one's* will; realize *one's* desire / 천부적 재능을 ~ develop 〔display, give full play to〕 *one's* natural abilities.
⑤ 《세력을》 establish 《*one's* influence》; extend 〔expand〕 《*one's* power 〔influence〕》; 《경계·수사 등을》 form; set up; spread. ¶ 경계망을 ~ throw 〔form〕 a police cordon 《around the area》 / 수사를 ~ institute 〔make〕 a search 《for》; conduct 〔make〕 an investigation 《into, of》 / 수사망을 ~ spread 〔drop, set up〕 the dragnet.
⑥ 《법률·정치를》 promulgate; rule. ¶ 법령을 ~ put a law into force 〔effect〕 / 계엄령을 ~ place 〔put〕 《a city》 under martial law; impose martial law 《on the country》 / 선정(善政)을 ~ govern 〔rule〕 well 〔wisely〕.
⑦ 《기를》 ease 《*one's* mind》; relieve. ¶ 선생이 엄해서 아이들이 기를 못 편다 The teacher is so strict that the children are ill at ease.
⑧ 《살림을》 ease; alleviate; improve. ¶ 옹색한 살림을 ~ improve *one's* meager livelihood.

**펴이다** ① 《펴지다》 get unfolded 〔straightened, smoothed〕. ② 《형편이》 get better; improve; be eased. ¶ 셈이 ~ become better off / 재정적 곤란이 ~ financial difficulties are eased; straightened / 형편이 ~ circumstances improve / 금년에는 형편이 펴이시길 빕니다 I hope you'll be better off this year. ③ 《일 따위가》 get straightened out; be smoothed 《down, over》. ¶ 일이 ~ a matter gets straightened out; an affair is smoothed down.

**펴지다** ① 《펼쳐지다》 get unfolded 〔unrolled, spread〕; spread (out). ¶ 두루마리가 ~ a roll of paper unrolls / 자리가 ~ a mat is unfolded 〔spread〕.
② 《주름이》 get smoothed; be flattened; become smooth. ¶ 옷의 주름이 ~ wrinkle in cloth smooth out / 이마의 주름이 ~ wrinkles on *one's* brow are gone; be relieved of *one's*.
③ 《굽은 것이》 get straightened; straighten (out, up); stretch (out). ¶ 굽은 철사가 ~ a bent wire is straightened out / 굽은 허리가 ~ *one's* bent waist straightens up.
④ 《접힌 것이》 open; be laid open. ¶ 책이 ~ a book lies open.

**편**(便) ① 《쪽》 a side; 《방향》 a direction; a way. ¶ 이〔저〕편 this 〔that〕 way / 왼편〔오른편〕에 on the left 〔right〕 side / 동〔서〕편 the east 〔west〕 side / 서편으로 산맥이 보인다 A mountain range is seen to the west.

② 《한패》 a party; a faction; a side; a part. ¶ 우리 편 our side; our party 〔team〕; our friends 〔supporters〕; we; us / 저 편 the other side; the opposite party 〔team〕/ 근로자 편의 요구 the demands on the part of the workers / 편을 짓다 form a faction 〔clique〕; band together / 자기 편으로 끌어들이다 win 〔get, gain〕 《*a person*》 over to *one's* side / 상대편에 붙다 go over to the opposite party / 그는 언제나 우리 편을 들어 준다 He is always on our side 〔friend〕.
③ ⇨인편. ¶ 친구 편에 보내다 send 《*a thing*》 through a friend.
④ 《교통편》 service; facilities; 《편의》 convenience; 《우편》 mail 《미》; post 《영》. ¶ 철도〔버스〕편 a railroad 〔bus〕 service / 항공편으로 부치다 send 《a letter》 by air mail / 당신은 무슨 편으로 갑니까 By what means 〔How〕 are you going? / 기차편으로 갑니다 I'm going by train. / 그 섬으로 가는 배편이 있습니까 Is there any steamer service to the island? / 이곳은 교통편이 좋다 There are good transportation facilities here. / 우리집은 지하철편이 좋은〔나쁜〕 곳에 있다 My house is conveniently 〔inconveniently〕 located for the subway.
⑤ 《…하는 쪽》 ¶ 그는 잔인한 편이다 He tends to cruelty. / 물가는 자꾸 올라가는 편이다 Prices are soaring. / 너는 즉시 가는 편이 좋겠다 You had better go at once. / 그 분은 좀 엄한 편이라고 생각지 않습니까 Don't you think that he is a little on the strict side? / 그는 나이에 비해 늙은 편이다 He is rather old for his age.

**편**(編) 《편찬》 compilation; compiling; editing. ¶ 김 박사 편(의) compiled 〔edited〕 by Dr. Kim.

**편**(篇) ① 《권》 a book; a volume. ¶ 상편〔하편〕 the first 〔second〕 volume; Book I 〔II〕. ② 《장·절》 a chapter; a section; a part; 《작품 수》 a piece. ¶ 제2편 the second chapter / 한 편의 시 a piece of poetry; a poem.

**편가르다**(便―) divide 〔separate〕 into two groups 〔teams〕. ¶ 편갈라서 싸우다 divide into two groups and fight.

**편각**(偏角) 〖측량〗 declination; angle of deviation; 〖수학〗 amplitude; 〖항공〗 variation. ◉ ～계 a declinometer. 자기(磁氣) ～ magnetic declination.

**편강**(片薑) sliced dried ginger.

**편견**(偏見) a biased 〔distorted, prejudiced〕 view; (a) prejudice; (a) bias. ¶ 인종적 ～ racial prejudice; racism / 개인적 ～ a personal bias / ～적인 prejudiced; biased; partial / ～없는 unprejudiced; unbiased; impartial; fair / ～을 가지다 〔품다〕 hold 〔harbor〕 a biased view 《of》; be prejudiced 〔biased〕 against 《*a person*》; have a prejudice 〔bias〕 against 《*a thing*》/ ～을 버리다 cast 〔put〕 away a prejudice; divest 《*one's* mind》 of prejudice; get over *one's* prejudice / 그렇게 생각하는 것은 너의 ～이다 You are biased to think so. / 그는 외국인에 대하여 ～을 가지고 있다 He has a prejudice against foreigners.

**편곡**(編曲) 〖음악〗 (an) arrangement. ～하다 arrange; 《관현악으로》 orchestrate. ¶ Y씨 ～의 곡 a piece arranged by Mr. Y / 피아노용으로 ～하다 arrange 《a piece of music》 for the piano / 이 바이올린곡은 피아노곡으로도 ～되어 있다 This music for the violin is also arranged for the piano.
◉ ～자 an arranger; an adapter.

**편광**(偏光) 〖물리〗 polarized light; 《빛의 쏠림》 polarization (of light).
◉ ～각 a polarizing angle; an angle of polarization. ～경 a polarimeter; a polariscope. ～계 a polarimeter. ～렌즈 a polarizing lens. ～면 a plane of polarization. ～자〔프리즘〕 a polarizer. ～측정 polarimetry. ～탄성(학) photoelasticity: ～ 탄성의 photoelastic. ～판 a polarizing plate: 인조 ～판 a polaroid. ～필터 a polarizing filter. ～현미경 a polarization microscope.

**편년사**(編年史) a chronicle; annals.

**편년체**(編年體) a chronological form 〔order〕. ¶ ～로 《arrange》 in a chronological order; chronologically.

**편뇌**(片腦) 〖한의〗 (refined) camphor.
◉ ～유 camphor oil.

**편달**(鞭撻) ① 《때림》 whipping; lashing. ～하다 whip; lash. ② 《격려》 encouragement; urging. ～하다 encourage 〔urge〕 《*a person* to *do*》; spur 《*a person*》 on 《to *do*》. ¶ 가일층 ～해 주십시오 I must seek your further advice 〔assistance〕 and encouragement. / 저의 성공은 당신의 지도 ～ 덕분입니다 I owe my success to your guidance and encouragement.

**편대**(編隊) (a) formation. ¶ 3기 ～로 in a three-plane formation / 폭격기의 대～ a large formation of bombers / ～를 짓다 fly into formation; formate.

◉ ～장 a flight leader.

**편대비행**(編隊飛行) formation flying; a formation flight. ¶ ～을 하다 fly in formation; make a formation flight.

**편도**(片道) one way. ¶ ～ 5천원 five thousand won one way / 목포까지 ～ 한 장 주십시오 A one-way ticket to Mokp'o, please. ◉ ～승차권 a one-way ticket 《미》; a single (ticket) 《영》. ～요금 a one-way fare 《미》; a single fare 《영》.

**편도**(扁桃) 〖식물〗 an almond tree; 《열매》 an almond. ◉ ～유 almond oil.

**편도선**(扁桃腺) 〖해부〗 the tonsils; the amygdalae (*sing.* -la). ¶ ～이 붓다 have swollen tonsils / 그녀는 어제 ～을 떼어 냈다 She had her tonsils removed yesterday. ◉ ～비대 tonsillar hypertrophy; swollen 〔enlarged〕 tonsils. ～수술 tonsillectomy: ～ 수술을 하다 tonsillectomize 《*a person*》. ～염 tonsillitis: 화농성 ～염 septic tonsillitis.

**편두통**(偏頭痛) 〖의학〗 (a) migraine; (a) megrim; a sick 〔migraine〕 headache. ¶ ～이 나다 have 〔suffer from〕 a migraine.

**편들다**(便―) side 〔take sides〕 with; take 《*a person's*》 part 〔side〕; support; back up. ¶ 아들을 ～ side with *one's* son / 가난한 사람들을 ～ take part with 〔take up the cause of〕 the poor.

**편람**(便覽) a handbook 《to, of》; a manual 《of》. ¶ 영문법 ～ a handbook of English Grammar / 대학 ～ a college catalog 〔prospectus〕.

**편력**(遍歷) ① 《이곳저곳의》 wandering; a travel; a tour; a pilgrimage. ～하다 wander 〔travel, tour〕 about; make a tour of 《the country》. ¶ 각국을〔국내 각지를〕 ～하다 travel through many countries 〔parts of country〕. ② 《여러가지 경험》 ¶ 그의 파란 많은 인생～도 종말에 가까워지고 있다 He is nearing the end of his checkered life. / 수많은 여성 ～끝에 그는 마침내 결혼했다 He finally got married after having been involved with many women. ◉ ～자 an itinerant; a pilgrim; a rover.

**편류**(偏流) 〖항공〗 (a) drift; (a) deflection; 〖포술〗 windage. ◉ ～각 a drift angle. ～계 a drift meter.

**편리**(便利) convenience; expediency; handiness (다루기); facilities (설비). ～하다 (be) convenient; expedient; handy; serviceable; useful. ¶ ～상 for the sake of convenience / ～한 기구 a useful instrument; a handy gadget / ～한 곳에 있다 be conveniently located / ～하게 하다 facilitate / 공공의 ～를 도모하다 promote the benefit of the public / 아무의 ～를 도모하다 serve 〔suit〕 *a person's* convenience / 교통이 ～하다 be convenient for transportation / 수영하기에 ～하다 be handy for swimming / 이것은 호주머니에 넣고 다니기에 ～한 사전이다 This is a handy dictionary to carry in the pocket. / 지하철을 이용하면 ～하다 It is convenient if you use the subway. / 아이들의 교육에 ～한 곳이다 It is a convenient 〔good〕 place for the education of our children. / 도로가 좁은 도시에서는 자동차보다 자전거가 ～하다 Bicycles are more convenient 〔useful〕 than car in cities where the roads are narrow.

**편린**(片鱗) 《비늘》 a small piece of fish scale; 《일면》 a part; a portion; a glimpse. ¶ 이로써 그의 성격의 ～을 엿볼 수 있다 It enables us to get a glimpse of his personality. / 그 에세이에서 당시 사람들의 생활의 ～을 엿볼 수 있다 From the essay you can get a glimpse of the way people lived then.

**편마암**(片麻岩) 〖지질〗 a gneiss.

**편면**(片面) one side. ◉ ～레코드 a single faced record 〔disk〕. ～인쇄기 a single-side (printing) machine.

**편모**(偏母) *one's* widowed 〔lone〕 mother. ◉ ～슬하 having only *one's* mother to serve: ～ 슬하에 있다 live with *one's* widowed mother.

**편모**(鞭毛) 〖생물〗 a flagellum. ◉ ～충 〖동물〗 a flagellate (*pl.* -lata).

**편무**(片務) a unilateral duty 〔obligation, responsibility〕. ¶ ～적 unilateral. ◉ ～계약 a unilateral 〔an independent, a one-sided〕 contract.

**편무역**(片貿易) one-side 〔one-way〕 trade.

**편물**(編物) 《뜨개질》 knitting; crochet; 《짠것》 knitted goods; knitwear. ～하다 knit crochet; do knitting. ¶ 파랑과 초록 털실을 섞어 ～하다 knit the blue with the green wool. ◉ ～기계 a knitting machine 〔frame〕; a knitter.

**편발**(編髮) plaiting the hair; braided hair. ⇨ 변발(辮髮).

**편법**(便法) 《try to find》 an easier method; a handy way; a short cut; 《devise》 an expedient; a convenient mode. ¶ 일시적 ～ a temporary expedient / ～을 쓰다 adopt 〔resort to〕 an expedient / 우리는 이 어려운 고비를 넘길 수 있는 어떤 ～을 강구해야 한다 We've got to devise some expedient to tide us over this crisis.

**편벽**(偏僻) 《치우침》 one-sidedness; partiality; bias. ~하다, ~되다 (be) eccentric; partial; biased; one-sided. ¶ ~한 사람 an eccentric person / ~된 생각〔관점〕 a biased view.

**편복**(便服) casual wear; everyday 〔ordinary〕 clothes; an everyday suit; a housedress. ¶ ~으로 외출하다 go out in *one's* casual wear / 이 옷은 ~으로 하기엔 너무 좋다 This dress is too good for everyday wear.

**편상화**(編上靴) lace-up boots.

**편서풍**(偏西風) 〖기상〗 the prevailing westerlies.

**편성**(編成) organization; formation; composition. ~하다 form 《a class》; organize 《a corps》; compile 〔make up〕 《a budget》; draw up 《a program》; compose 《a train》. ¶ …으로 ~되어 있다 consist of…; be composed 〔made up〕 of… / 새로 ~된 사단 newly organized division / 12량 ~의 열차 a train of twelve cars 〔carriages〕 / 초보자를 위한 반을 ~하다 form a class for beginners / 추가 경정 예산을 ~하다 make up 〔draw up〕 a revised supplementary budget / 한 학급은 40명으로 ~되어 있다 A class consists of forty pupils. / 회계 연도가 시작되는 1월부터 방송 프로의 ~이 바뀔 예정이다 The broadcasting stations are planning new programs for the financial year starting in January. ◉ 프로그램~ program(m)ing.

**편수**(編修) editing; compilation. ~하다 edit; compile. ◉ ~관 an editorial officer; an (official) editor. ~국 the Textbook Compilation Bureau. ~부 an editorial department.

**편승하다**(便乘—) ① 《탈 것에》 get a lift in 《*a person's* car》; take passage in 《a steamer》; hitchhike 《to a place》 《미》. ¶ 한 친구가 인천까지 그의 차에 편승시켜 주었다 A friend gave me a lift in his car as far as Inch'ŏn. ② 《기회에》 take advantage of 《the trend of public opinion》; avail *oneself* of 《an opportunity》; 《구어》 jump on the bandwagon. ¶ 업자들은 철도 운임의 인상에 편승하여 가격을 올렸다 Manufacturers took advantage of the rise in railroad fares to raise prices.

**편식**(偏食) an unbalanced diet. ~하다 have an unbalanced diet. ¶ ~하는 아이 a child who eats only what he likes / 건강한 사람은 ~하지 않는다 Healthy people eat balanced meals.

**편심**(偏心) 《사람의》 a one-sided mind; a partial disposition; 〖기계〗 eccentricity. ◉ ~륜 an eccentric (wheel). ~봉 an eccentric rod. ~ 톱니바퀴 an eccentric gear.

**편쌈**(便—) a gang fight. ~하다 have a gang fight; fight in groups. ◉ ~꾼 a gang fighter.

**편안**(便安) 《무사》 safety; security; 《평온》 peace; tranquility; 《편함》 ease; comfort; 《건강》 good health. ~하다 (be) well; peaceful; tranquil; calm; comfortable; easy; safe; secure; carefree. ¶ ~한 생활 a quiet 〔peaceful〕 life / ~한 잠 a calm 〔peaceful〕 sleep / 마음이 ~하다 have *one's* mind at rest; feel at ease; be free from care / 마음이 ~할 때가 없다 have no moment of ease / 이 의자는 ~하다 This is a comfortable chair. / 이제 좀 ~해졌습니까 Do you feel better now? / 이 약을 먹으면 곧 ~해질 거다 This medicine will give you immediate relief.

**편안히**(便安—) 《안전하게》 safely; in safety; 《평온하게》 in peace; peacefully; calmly; quietly; 《안락하게》 comfortably; in comfort; at (*one's*) ease; at rest; 《탈없이》 safe and sound; well. ¶ ~ 지내다 live in peace; live 〔lead〕 a quiet life; 《안락하게》 live in comfort; be comfortably 〔well〕 off; 《탈없이》 get along well / ~ 앉으십시오 Please sit at ease. / 그들은 연금으로 ~ 살고 있다 They lead a comfortable life on a pension. / ~ 잠드소서 《조사·묘비에서》 Rest 〔May he rest〕 in peace.

**편암**(片岩) 〖광물〗 schist (rock).

**편애**(偏愛) (a) partiality 《of affection》; special fondness 《for, to》; favoritism. ~하다 love with partiality; show favoritism toward; dote on 《*one's* youngest child》 to the exclusion of 《the others》. ¶ 어머니는 그를 ~했다 The mother was partial to him. / 막내 아들에 대한 그녀의 ~는 그를 응석받이로 만들었다 Her partiality to the youngest son made him selfish.

**편액**(扁額) a tablet; a plaque.

**편영**(片影) a shadow; a speck; a sign.

**편육**(片肉) sliced boiled meat; boiled beef slices.

**편의**(便衣) = 편복(便服). ◉ ~대 plain-clothes soldiers; a partisan; snipers; irregular troops.

**편의**(便宜) convenience; facilities; bene-

fit; advantage; expediency.
¶ ～상 for convenience' sake (★ convenience 어미에는 '(어포스트러피)만을 붙이고, s는 안 붙임. for goodness' sake 등도 같음); as a matter of convenience / 외국인 관광객〔학생, 여행자〕의 ～를 도모하여 for the convenience 〔advantage〕 of foreign tourists 〔students, travelers〕 / ～를 도모하다 consult 〔administer to〕 《*a person's*》 convenience; consider 《*a person's*》 advantage / 모든 ～를 제공하다 accord 〔afford〕 every facility 《for》; give 《*a person*》 every convenience / 사용자의 ～를 위하여 상세한 설명서가 첨부되어 있다 Detailed instructions are attached for the convenience of users. / 그가 도움을 청하자 경찰은 ～를 봐 주었다 When he asked for help, the police accomodated him. / 가능한 모든 ～를 제공해 드리겠습니다 I will give you every convenience 〔facility, assistance〕 for it. *or* I'll do what I can do for you. / 사서는 ～상 갖가지 약어를 사용한다 Dictionaries use a lot of abbreviations for the sake of convenience. ◉ ～점 a convenience store. ～주의 opportunism; expediency: ～주의자 an opportunist; a timeserver. ～치적선(置籍船) a ship sailing under a flag of convenience.

**편이하다**(便易―) (be) handy; easy; convenient; serviceable; useful.

**편익**(便益) 《편리》 convenience; facility; 《이익》 benefit; advantage. ¶ ～을 주다 provide facility; give advantage.

**편입**(編入) ① 《짜넣음》 weaving 《in》. ～하다 weave 《in》.
② 《집어넣음》 entry; admission; incorporation (합병); 〖군사〗 enlistment; enrol(l)ment 《in》; posting (배속). ～하다 《집어넣다》 class 《with, among》; include 《in》; 《예산에》 insert; 《학급에》 admit 〔put〕 《into》; enrol(l) 《into》; be placed 《in a grade》; 《군대에》 assign 《to the infantry》; enrol(l) 〔incorporate〕 《into》; 《예비역에》 transfer 《to the reserve》. ¶ 포병에 ～되다 be assigned to the artillery / 그 마을은 B시(市)에 ～되었다 The village was incorporated 〔absorbed〕 into B city. / 그는 전문 대학에서 4년제 대학으로 ～했다 He transferred 〔switched 《구어》〕 from a two-year college to a university. ◉ ～생 an enrolled student; a transfer student; an enrol(l)ee: 대학의 ～생 모집 the recruitment of transfer students by institutions of higher learning. ～시험 a transfer admission test; an examination for special admission 《into a school, into a class》: 그는 3학년 ～시험에 합격했다 He has been admitted through examination into the third year class.

**편자** 《말굽의》 a horseshoe; a shoe. ¶ ～를 박다 shoe a horse.

**편자**(編者) an editor; a compiler.

**편재**(偏在) maldistribution 《of wealth》; uneven 〔unfair〕 distribution. ～하다 《materials, funds, commodities》 be maldistributed. ¶ 부의 ～ the maldistribution 〔uneven distribution〕 of wealth / 물자가 ～해 있다 Materials are maldistributed. / 우리 사회가 해결해야 할 문제의 하나는 부의 ～이다 One of the problems that our society has yet to solve is the maldistribution of wealth.

**편재**(遍在) omnipresence; ubiquity. ～하다 (be) omnipresent; ubiquitous; widespread. ¶ 이 기묘한 풍습은 국내 도처에 ～해 있다 This strange practice is found through the length and breadth of the country.

**편저**(編著) compilation; redaction. ～하다 compile; redact. ◉ ～자 the author and compiler 《of a dictionary》.

**편전**(便殿) a royal palace 《to live in》; the Imperial resting house; the king's private quarters 〔living room〕.

**편제**(編制) ＝편성(編成). ◉ ～표 《군대의》 a table of organization.

**편주**(扁舟) a small 〔light〕 boat; a bark.

**편죽**(片竹) a piece 〔chip〕 of bamboo.

**편중**(偏重) ～하다 attach 〔give〕 too much importance 《to》; overemphasize 《intellectual training》; make too much of; lay disproportionate emphasis 《on》. ¶ 이 회사는 학력 ～을 피하고 능력주의를 취하고 있다 This company does not make too much of school careers but takes merit 〔ability〕 system.

**편지**(片紙·便紙) a letter; a message; a note; [총칭] mail; correspondence. ～하다 write 〔send〕 a letter.
¶ 17일자 ～ a letter dated 〔of, under date of〕 the 17th / ～의 사연 the contents 〔purport, text〕 of a letter / ～를 쓰다 write a letter 《to》; write 《*a person*》 a letter / ～를 써 놓고 가다 leave a letter for 《*a person*》 / ～의 답장을 하다 answer a letter / ～로 신청하다 apply by letter / ～를 주고받다

correspond with each other; exchange letters / ～를 써주다 write a letter for 《*a person*》/ ～를 부치다 mail 〔post 《영》〕 a letter / ～를 받다 receive 〔get, have〕 a letter from / ～를 봉하다 seal a letter / ～를 뜯다 open 〔unseal〕 a letter; cut a letter open / ～에 이름과 주소를 쓰다 put name and address on a letter / 나에게 편지 온 것이 있습니까 Is there any mail for me? / 귀하의 ～ 잘 받았습니다 Your letter has been received with thanks. *or* Thank you very much for your kind letter. / 도착하시면 ～(를 해) 주십시오 Please write me a letter when you arrive there. / 주소가 잘못되어(서) ～가 가지 않았다 The letter miscarried, because it was wrongly addressed. / 매월 말일은 ～ 쓰는 날입니다 《게시》 The last day of month is Letter Writing Day.

◉ ～봉투 an envelope. ～지 letter 〔writing〕 paper; notepaper. ～통 a letter case; a mailbox 《미》; a letter box 《영》. ～틀 letter-writing conventions; a letter-writing model. 사례～ a thank=you letter 〔note〕; a letter of thanks; 《대접받은 데 대한》 a bread-and-butter letter. 안부～ a letter enquiring after *one's* health. 연애～ a love letter. 인사～ (a letter of) greetings.

> 참고 편지의 맺음말
> 회사나 단체 앞으로 보내는 편지의 경우, 《미》에서는 Sincerely 또는 Cordially, 《영》에서는 Yours faithfully. 개인 앞으로의 사무적인 편지에서는 《미》는 Sincerely 또는 Sincerely yours, 《영》은 Yours sincerely를 씀. 가족에 대해서는 《미》《영》이 모두 예외 없이 쓰는 것이 Love. 친한 사이에서는 Take care, Bye for now, Yours, Take care, Love (★ 주로 여성이 사용) 따위가 쓰인다. Affectionately yours, Yours affectionately 따위도 쓰이나 이들은 남성간에는 쓰지 않는 것이 일반적이다. 남성간의 서신에서는 All the best, Best wishes, Regards 따위도 쓰인다.

**편집**(偏執) bias; obstinacy; bigotry. ～하다 stick to 《*one's* prejudice》; show bias. ◉ ～광 《상태》 monomania; 《사람》 a monomaniac. ～병 paranoia: ～환자 a paranoiac; a paranoid.

**편집**(編輯) editing; compilation; 《영화 필름의》 cutting. ～하다 edit 《a magazine》; compile 《a dictionary》. ¶ ～을 맡다 take on the editorship 《of》/ 이 책은 저명한 학자 4사람이 ～했다 Four famous scholars edited this book. / 그녀는 대학 신문을 ～하고 있다 She is editing a campus newspaper.

◉ ～마감 the editorial deadline. ～방침 an editorial policy. ～부 the editorial department. ～실 《신문사의》 the desk; the editorial room. ～원 a member of the editorial staff. ～자 an editor; a compiler; a (film) cutter (영화 필름의). ～장 the chief 〔managing〕 editor; 《신문사의》 the copy chief 《미》; the general editor (간행물의). ～주간 an editor in chief. ～회의 《hold》 an editorial conference. ～후기(後記) an editorial note. 한국～기자회 The Korea Copy Editors Association.

**편짓다**(片—) 《목재를》 sort 《lumber》 according to use; 《인삼을》 arrange 《ginseng》 to make a fixed number of pound lots.

**편짜다**(便—) form 〔make up〕 a team 〔party〕; team up; 《편을 가르다》 separate into groups. ¶ …와 ～ take part with; team up with; tie up with 《미》/ 셋이 ～ three band together to form a team 〔side〕/ 편을 짜서 화투놀이를 하다 play cards in teams.

**편짝**(便—) a side; one side. ¶ 이〔저〕～ this 〔the other〕 side / 우리〔저〕～ our 〔the other〕 side 〔party〕/ 한 ～으로 기울다 lean to one side; be one=sided / 한 ～ 말만 듣다 hear only one side of the story.

**편차**(偏差) 〖물리·공업〗 (a) deflection; 〖생물·통계〗 (a) deviation; 〖측량〗 (a) declination; 〖자기〗 (a) variation; 〖항공·해양〗 (a) drift; driftage; 〖포술〗 windage. ◉ ～값 the deviation (value). ～계(計) 〖측량〗 a declinometer. 자기～ magnetic declination. 표준～ 〖통계〗 the standard deviation.

**편찬**(編纂) compilation; editing. ～하다 compile; edit. ¶ 이 책은 잘 ～되어 있다 This book is excellently got up. / 사전은 널리 타인의 저작을 모아 ～된 것이다 A dictionary is largely a compilation from the works of others. / 그 사전은 지금 ～중에 있다 The dictionary is in course of compilation. ◉ ～위원 a compilation committee: 국사 ～ 위원회 the National History Compilation Committee. ～자(者) a compiler; an editor.

**편찮다**(便—) 《불편하다》 (be) inconvenient; uncomfortable; 《병으로》 (be) ill; sick; unwell; upset; distressed. ¶ 몸이 ~ feel unwell 《with a cold》; be out of sorts / 몸이 편찮아서 on account of illness / 속이 ~ have something wrong with *one's* inside; *one's* stomach is out of order / 마음이 ~ feel uneasy 《at, about》; feel sorry for; be painful 〔regrettable〕 / 어디 편찮으십니까 Is there anything wrong with you? / 그것을 생각하면 마음이 ~ It pains me to think of it.

**편충**(鞭蟲) 《기생충의 하나》 a whipworm.

**편취**(騙取) a fraud; a swindle; an imposture; a cheat. ~하다 obtain by fraud; defraud 《*a person*》 of 《*a thing*》; cheat 《*a person*》 out of 《*a thing*》. ¶ 돈을 ~하다 swindle money 《out of》. ◉ ~자 a swindler; an impostor; a cheat.

**편측**(片側) one side.

**편층운**(片層雲) a fractostratus (*pl.* -ti).

**편친**(偏親) one parent. ¶ ~ 가족 a single-parent 〔one-parent〕 family / ~을 가진 아이 a child with only one parent living; a motherless 〔fatherless〕 child.

**편토**(片土) a small piece of land; a small plot of ground.

**편파**(偏頗) partiality; favoritism; (unfair) discrimination; 《일방적》 one-sidedness; 《불공평》 unfairness. ~하다 (be) partial; one-sided; biased; unfair. ¶ ~적으로 partially; unfairly / ~적인 판정 one-sided judgment / ~적인 짓을 하다 deal unfairly 《with》; be unfair in *one's* dealing 《with》; discriminate 《against》.

**편편이**(便便—) by each messenger 〔mail〕.

**편편하다**(便便—) (be) free from care; comfortable. ¶ 편편히 지내다 lead a comfortable life.

**편평족**(扁平足) 〚병리〛 flatfoot; splayfoot; 《발》 a flatfoot (*pl.* -feet); a splayfoot (*pl.* -feet). ¶ ~이다 be flat-footed; have flatfeet.

**편평하다**(扁平—) (be) flat; level; even; horizontal.

**편하다**(便—) ① 《편리하다》 (be) convenient; handy; expedient. ¶ 편한 물건 a handy thing; a convenience / 편한 방도 an expedient measure; an expediency / 교통이 ~ have (good) facilities of communication / 쓰기에 ~ be convenient of use; be easy 〔handy〕 to use / 그 책은 작아 주머니에 넣기에 ~ The book is small and handy for the pocket.

② 《편안하다》 (be) comfortable; easy; untroubled; undistressed; free from care (걱정 없다). ¶ 편히 comfortably; at *one's* ease; in comfort / 발이 편한 신 comfortable shoes to wear; shoes easy to walk in / 편히 살다 live in comfort 〔ease〕; lead an easy 〔a comfortable〕 life / 마음이 ~ be carefree; feel at ease; have a clear conscience; have nothing to worry about / 속이 ~ feel comfortable in the stomach / 잠시도 마음 편할 때가 없다 have no moment of ease / 마음을 편하게 먹다 ease *one's* mind; take things easy / 부모를 편히 모시다 let *one's* parents lead a comfortable life.

③ 《수월하다》 (be) easy; light; simple; unburdensome. ¶ 편한 일 an easy 〔a soft〕 job; light work 〔labor〕 / 편하지 않은 일 no slight labor; no easy work 〔job〕 / 편하게 easily; with ease; without difficulty 〔trouble〕 / 제일 편한 방법을 취하다 follow 〔take〕 the line of least resistance / 편하지 않다 be difficult; be hard.

**편향**(偏向) a propensity 《for》; a tendency 《toward, to》; an inclination 《to》; a leaning 《toward》; (a) deviation 《from》; 〚물리〛 (a) deflection. ~하다 tend 《toward, to》; be inclined; be slanted; be biased 《toward》; deflect; be deflected. ¶ ~된 biased; prejudiced. ◉ ~교육 ideologically prejudiced education; politically biased education. ~판〔코일〕 《브라운관의》 a deflecting plate 〔coil〕.

**편협하다**(偏狹—) (be) narrow-minded; illiberal; intolerant; hidebound. ¶ 편협한 생각을 갖고 있다 have a narrow (=minded) view 《of》 / 그의 태도는 ~ He is exclusive in manner.

**편형동물**(扁形動物) a flatworm.

**펼치다** spread; extend; expand; unfold 〔unroll, open〕 《it》; lay out 《*one's* clothes》. ⇨ 펴다. ¶ 자리를 ~ spread a mat / 지도를 ~ spread (out) a map / 손을 ~ open *one's* hand / 책을 ~ open a book / 새가 날개를 펼쳤다 The bird expanded its wings.

**폄론**(貶論) adverse criticism; disparagement. ~하다 disparage; censure.

**폄하다**(貶—) disparage; speak ill 〔evil〕 of; speak slightingly of; despise; depreciated 《*a person's* abilities》; disparage; abuse; throw mud at 《*a person*》. ¶ 아무를 ~ speak ill of *a person;* run *a person* down / 몹시 ~ denounce scathingly 〔roundly〕; get

〔have〕 *one's* knife into 《*a person*》.

**평**(坪) a *p'yŏng*. ① 《지적의》 a unit of area (=3.954 sq. yds.); 《입체의》 a unit of volume (=7.9 cub. yds.). ¶ 그 건물은 건평이 40평이다 The building has a floor space of 40 *p'yŏng*. / 「이 땅은 몇 평이나 됩니까」—「80평입니다」 "What size is this lot in *p'yŏng*?" —"This lot is 80 *p'yŏng*." ② 《유리·헝겊·벽의》 a square *cha* of cloth, glass or wall (=0.11 sq. yds). ③ 《조각·동판의》 a square *ch'i* of engraving or copperplate (=1.04 sq. inches).

**평**(評) 《비평》 (a) criticism; a critical essay; 《논평》 (a) comment; 《신간 서적의》 a review; a note (단평). ⇨ 평하다. ¶ 신문평 a newspaper 〔press〕 comment / 영화평 a review of movies / 평이 좋다〔나쁘다〕 be favorably 〔unfavorably〕 received; have a good 〔bad〕 reputation.

**평-**(平) common; ordinary; plain; mere. ¶ 평교사 a common teacher / 평당원 a rank-and-file member / 평사원 a mere clerk.

**평가**(平價) 〖경제〗 par; parity. ¶ ~로 at par / ~ 이상〔이하〕이다 be above 〔below〕 par. ◉ ~절상 (upward) revaluation; upvaluation: ~절상하다 revaluate 〔revalue, upvalue〕 《the currency, the dollar》 / 일본엔(円)은 20% ~ 절상되었다 The yen was upvalued by 20%. ~절하 devaluation: ~절하하다 devaluate 〔devalue〕 《the currency》. 금~ gold parity.

**평가**(評價) appraisal; valuation; assessment (과세를 위한); estimation (견적); appreciation; rating; 〖교육〗 evaluation. ~하다 appraise; value 《*a thing* at $15》; assess; estimate; appreciate; rate; evaluate; 《등급별로》 grade.

> **용법** **value** 물건이나 물품을 「돈으로 평가하다」, 또는 건강·명예 등을 「중히 여기다」라는 뜻. **assess** 「과세액을 책정하기 위해 평가〔사정〕하다」라는 뜻. **estimate** 주관적으로 「어림하다」라는 뜻으로서, 문득 생각이 나서 하건, 심사숙고 끝에 하건 간에 결과는 같음. **appreciate** 「(예술적 가치를) 음미하다, 감상하다」라는 뜻과 「가치를 인정하다」 「높이 평가하다」라는 뜻이 있음. **rate** 「(단계를 지어) 평가하다」라는 뜻. **grade** 품질·가치·지위·진보 등을 「등급별로 나누다」, 《미》에서는 「성적을 매기다」라는 뜻으로도 씀.

¶ 아무리 높이 ~해도 at the highest estimate; at most / 높게〔낮게〕 ~하다 rate 《*a thing*》 high 〔low〕; place 〔set〕 high 〔low〕 value on 《*a thing*》; make much 〔little〕 of 《*a thing*》 / 과대 ~하다 overestimate; overrate; overvalue; think too highly of; think 〔make〕 too much of; put 〔set〕 too high a valuation 《on》 / 손해를 ~하다 estimate the damage / 재산을 …로 ~하다 appraise property at… / 사람을 겉모양으로 ~하다 judge 〔estimate〕 a person by appearance / 아무의 능력을 높이 ~하다 set a high value on *a person's* abilities / 자신의 기준으로 남을 ~하다 measure others by *one's* own standard / 나는 시인으로서 키츠를 바이런 이상으로 ~한다 I put Keats above Byron as a poet. / 교사는 학생들의 능력을 정확히 ~하여야 한다 Teachers must evaluate 〔estimate〕 their students' ability accurately. / 나의 집은 1억 원으로 ~되었다 My house was valued 〔assessed〕 at one hundred million won. / 성적은 다섯 단계로 ~된다 The grades are rated on five levels. ◉ ~교수단 a group of professors assigned to evaluate the government policies. ~기준 a valuation basis; an appraisal standard. ~액 the estimated 〔appraised〕 value; an assessment: ~액 100만원의 그림 a painting with a value of one million won. ~이익〔손실〕 a valuation profit 〔loss〕. ~자 an appraiser; a valuer. ~전 a tryout match.

**평각**(平角) 〖수학〗 a straight angle.

**평결**(評決) a decision; a verdict (배심원의). ~하다 decide; render a verdict on. ¶ 비밀 ~ a privy 〔sealed〕 verdict / ~을 내리다 bring in 〔give, deliver, return〕 a verdict 《of》 / 원고에게 유리한 ~ a verdict for the plaintiff.

> **참고** 배심원의 평결: 미·영의 배심제 재판에서는 일반 사람 중에서 선출된 배심원단(jury)의 심판에 의해 유죄 (guilty) 또는 무죄(not guilty)가 결정됨. 이 결정을 평결(verdict)이라 하는데, 재판장은 이에 따라서 판결(sentence)을 내림.

**평고대**(平高臺) 〖건축〗 laths.

**평교**(平交) friends of about the same age. ◉ ~간(間) friendship among people of comparable age.

**평균**(平均) ① 《고름》 an average; 〖수

학] the (arithmetical) mean. ～하다 average; take the mean of. ¶～의 average; mean / 한 사람 ～ per head; *per capita* (L.) / 연〔월〕 ～ the yearly 〔monthly〕 mean / 한 달의 ～ 강수량 the average monthly rainfall / ～하여 on an 〔the〕 average / ～ 이상〔이하〕이다 be above 〔below〕 the average; be above 〔below〕 par / ～을 내다〔잡다〕 find 〔strike, take〕 an average / 하루 ～ 열 시간 일하다 average 10 hours' work a day; work 10 hours a day on average / 이 나라의 인구 밀도는 1평방 마일에 ～5명이다 In the country there are, on an average, five persons to the square mile. / 이 반 학생들의 ～ 신장은 167 센티미터이다 The average height of the pupils of this class is 167 centimeters.
② 《균형》 equilibrium; balance. ⇨균형, 평형. ¶ 한 발로 몸의 ～을 유지하다 balance *oneself* on one leg.
◉ ～거리 the mean distance. ～기온 the mean air 〔atmospheric〕 temperature. ～대 〖스포츠〗 a balance beam. ～수 the mean number. ～수명 the average life span: 그 나라 ～ 수명은 56세이다 The average length of life in that country is fifty-six. ～여명(餘命) 〖보험〗 average future lifetime; life expectancy. ～연령 the average age. ～오차 the mean error. ～온도 the mean temperature. ～운동 〖스포츠〗 balance. ～원가(原價) the average cost. ～율(律) 〖음악〗 equal temparament; meantone tuning. ～율(率) the average rate. ～점 the average mark 〔grade, score〕. ～치 the mean value; the mean (number). ～타율 《야구》 a batting average. ～(태양)시 the mean (solar) time.
기하～ the geometric mean. 조화～ the harmonic average.

**평기와**(平—) a plain roof tile.

**평년**(平年) 《예년》 a normal 〔an average〕 year; 《윤년이 아닌》 a common 〔civil〕 year; a non-leap year. ¶ 기온은 ～과 같다 We have average temperature. / 올해는 ～보다 덥다 It is hotter this year than usual. ◉ ～작 a normal crop 〔harvest〕; an average crop: ～작 이상〔이하〕이다 be above 〔below〕 the average crop / 올해의 벼농사는 ～작을 웃돌〔밑돌〕 전망이다 This year's rice crop is expected 「to be better than 〔to fall short of〕 the average.

**평다리치다**(平—) sit with *one's* legs stretched 〔sprawling〕 out.

**평등**(平等) 《균등》 equality; 《공평》 impartiality. ～하다 (be) equal; even; impartial. ¶～히 《고르게》 equally; evenly; 《차별 없이》 impartially; without discrimination / ～한 권리 an equal right / ～한 대우 equal treatment; parity of treatment / ～하게 하다 equalize 《one with another》; even; level; place 《all》 on a footing of equality / ～한 입장에서 on an equal 〔one〕 footing / ～하게 분배하다 divide equally / 사람을 ～하게 대(우)하다 treat persons without discrimination; 〖성서〗 be no respecter of persons / 만민은 법 앞에 ～하다 Men are all equal before 〔in the eye of〕 the law. / 신은 모든 인간을 ～하게 만드셨다 All men were created equal by God.
◉ ～주의 the principle of equality; egalitarianism: ～주의자 an egalitarian. ～화 equalization; equaling out. 기회 ～ equality of opportunity. 민족 ～ racial equality.

**평론**(評論) 《비평》 (a) criticism; a critique; 《시사평》 a review; a comment; an editorial comment. ～하다 criticize; review; comment on. ¶ 영문학 ～ a criticism of English literature / 시국을 ～하다 comment on the current situation / 영화를 ～하다 make a critical remark on the movie. ◉ ～가 a reviewer; a commentator; a critic. ～문 a critical essay. ～잡지 a review.

**평말**(平—) an even measure (of grain).

**평맥**(平脈) the normal 〔regular〕 pulse. ¶ 맥박(脈搏)이 ～이 되다 The pulse becomes normal.

**평면**(平面) a plane (surface); a level. ¶～의 plane; level; flat / 동일 ～상에 있다 be on the same level 《with》; be in one plane; be flush 《with》.
◉ ～각 a plane angle. ～경(鏡) a plane mirror. ～교차 〖철도〗 grade crossing 《미》; level crossing 《영》: ～교차점 a grade 〔level 《영》〕 crossing. ～기하(학) plane geometry. ～도 a plane figure; a ground plan. ～도법 ichnography. ～묘사 a plane delineation; an objective description. ～삼각법 plane trigonometry. ～지도 a map on Mercator's 〔mercator〕 projection; a Mercator 〔mercator〕 chart. ～항법 plane sailing.

**평미레**(平—) a grain leveler (used in measuring grain); a leveling stick.

◉ ～질 strickling: ～질하다 strickle; strike the measure; level with a grain leveller.

**평미리치다**(平—) 《말질》 level 《grain》; measure by an even measure; 《평등(平等)》 level off; even; equalize; make even 〔uniform〕.

**평민**(平民) a commoner; a man of the people; [총칭] the commons; the common people. ¶ ～적인 democratic / ～으로 태어나다 be a commoner by birth. ◉ ～재상 a commoner premier. ～주의 democratism; democracy: ～주의자 a democrat.

**평반자**(平—) a level ceiling (made of a wooden frame pasted across with paper).

**평방**(平方) the square (of a number). ⇨제곱. ¶ 2마일 ～ two miles square / 2 ～마일 two square miles. ◉ ～근 『수학』 a square root (of a number).

**평범**(平凡) commonness; commonplaceness. ～하다 (be) common; ordinary; commonplace; humdrum; mediocre; 《단조롭다》 (be) dull; flat; monotonous; 《특색 없다》 (be) featureless. ¶ ～한 얼굴 ordinary personal appearance; a face without any character / ～한 사람 a mediocrity; an ordinary man; the man in the street / ～한 생활을 하다 live a humdrum life / ～한 일 a commonplace; an everyday life / 그 이야기는 ～하였다 The story fell flat. / 그는 아주 ～한 화가에 지나지 않는다 He is but the commonest kind of painter. / 그는 ～한 작가가 아니다 He is no ordinary writer. / 그의 얼굴은 ～하다 His face lacks distinction.

**평복**(平服) 《일상복》 clothes for everyday wear; ordinary clothes; informal dress; 《경찰관의 제복 등에 대하여》 plain clothes; 《군복에 대하여》 civilian clothes; 《군속어》 civies; mufti. ～하다 wear plain clothes. ¶ ～으로 in plain clothes.

**평분**(平分) equal division. ～하다 divide equally; divide into two equal parts. ◉ ～선 a bisecting line. 주야 ～시 『천문』 equinox.

**평사원**(平社員) a mere 〔plain〕 clerk 〔employee〕 《of a company》; the rank and file. ¶ 여전히 ～으로 지내다 remain 〔live the humdrum life of〕 a mere clerk.

**평상**(平床) a flat bench; a wooden bed.

**평상**(平常) ⇨평상시. ¶ ～의 ordinary; usual; everyday / ～상태 normal conditions / ～으로 돌아가다 return 〔be restored〕 to normal 〔normality〕; resume 《its》 normal conditions / 업무는 ～대로 (한다) Business (is) as usual. ◉ ～복 = 평복(平服).

**평상시**(平常時) normal 〔ordinary〕 times; 《평화시》 peace time; [부사적] normally; usually; as a usual thing; commonly; customarily. ¶ ～보다 일찍 일어나다 get up earlier than usual.

**평생**(平生) *one's* whole life. ⇨일생. ¶ ～의 한(恨) a lifelong regret / 한 ～ *one's* lifetime; *one's* whole life; a (single) life / 암 연구에 ～을 바치다 devote *one's* lifetime to the study of cancer / ～을 독신으로 지내다 stay 〔remain〕 single 〔unmarried〕 all *one's* life; live and die a bachelor (남자); live and die a spinster (여자) / 은혜는 ～ 잊지 않겠습니다 I shall never forget your kindness for the rest of my life. ◉ ～교육 lifelong education; continuing education. ～소원 a lifelong desire; a desire cherished for life. ～학습 lifelong study.

**평서문**(平敍文) 『문법』 a declarative sentence; an assertive sentence.

**평석**(評釋) explanatory (and critical) notes; (an) annotation. ～하다 annotate 《a book》; supply 《a book》 with explanatory (and critical) notes.

**평소**(平素) ordinary times. ¶ ～에 in ordinary days 〔times〕; usually; ordinarily; as a regular 〔usual〕 thing; always / ～와 같이 as usual / ～의 소망이 이루어지다 *one's* long=cherished desire is realized / 그에게는 ～와 다른 점이 없었다 There was nothing unusual 〔strange〕 about him. / ～ 아버지로부터 그렇게 들어왔다 I have been constantly told so by my father.

**평수**(坪數) the number of *p'yŏng;* acreage; area; 《건평》 floor space 〔area〕. ¶ ～ 20평이다 cover 20 *p'yŏng.*

**평시**(平時) normal 〔ordinary〕 times; 《평화시》 peace time. ¶ ～의 in peace time; peacetime / ～에는 ordinarily; usually; in time of peace. ◉ ～국제법 international law in time of peace. ～산업 peacetime industry. ～정원(定員) peace establishment. ～편제 peace organization 〔establishment, footing〕.

**평신도**(平信徒) a lay believer; 《남자》 a layman; 《여자》 a laywoman; [총칭] the lay believers.

**평안**(平安) well-being; peace; tranquil(l)ity; calmness; quietness. ～하다 (be) well; peaceful; tranquil; quiet; calm. ¶ ～히 in peace; peacefully / 부모님이 ～하시냐 How are your parents —are they well?

**평야**(平野) a plain; an open field.

**평열**(平熱) the normal temperature. ¶ 내 체온은 ～이 되었다 My temperature has become normal. / 나의 ～은 36.5 도이다 My normal temperature is 36.5 degrees. (★ thirtysix point five로 읽음).

**평영**(平泳) the breaststroke. ～하다 swim 〔do〕 (the) breaststroke.
◉ ～선수 a breaststroker.

**평온**(平溫) 《평상 온도》 normal temperature; 《평균 온도》 an average 〔a mean〕 temperature; 《평상 기온》 the normal air 〔atmospheric〕 temperature.

**평온**(平穩) calmness; quiet(ness); quietude; tranquil(l)ity; serenity. ～하다 (be) calm; quiet; tranquil; peaceful. ¶ ～무사하게 《live》 in peace and quiet / ～해지다 become quiet; quiet 〔quieten 《영》〕 down / 이내 ～을 되찾았다 It was not long before peace was restored. / 그날은 ～무사히 넘겼다 The day passed uneventfully.

**평원**(平原) a plain; 《미국의》 a prairie (대초원). ¶ ～ 광야 a wide plain; a vast moorland.

**평의**(評議) consultation; conference; discussion; deliberation. ～하다 confer; discuss; deliberate on; hold a conference; consult together; take counsel 《with》. ¶ ～에 부치다 submit 《*a matter*》 to discussion; have a conference on 《*a matter*》.
◉ ～원 a councilor; a trustee (재단의). ～회 a council; a conference; 《재단 따위의》 a meeting of the board of trustees.

**평이**(平易) easiness; simplicity; plainness. ～하다 (be) easy; simple; plain. ¶ ～하게 easily; plainly; simply / ～한 문체 a simple style / ～하게 말하면 to use simple 〔plain〕 language / ～하게 말하다 explain simply / ～하게 하다 simplify / ～한 말로 써 있다 be written in plain 〔untechnical〕 language.

**평일**(平日) 《일요일이 아닌》 a weekday; 《평상일》 ordinary days. ¶ ～에는 on weekdays; on ordinary days / ～처럼 as usual.

**평자**(評者) 《비평하는 사람》 a critic; a commentator; 《책·연극의》 a reviewer.

**평작**(平作) a normal 〔an average〕 crop. ¶ ～ 이상〔이하〕이다 be above 〔below〕 the normal 〔average〕 crop.

**평전**(評傳) a critical biography.

**평점**(評點) 《학력의》 marks (점수); a grade; grading (평가점) (★ 《미》에서는 점수도 평가점도 모두 grades라고 하지만, 《영》에서는 A, B, C의 평가점은 grades, 점수는 marks라고 함); 《가치의》 evaluation marks.

**평정**(平定) suppression; repression; subjugation. ～하다 suppress; repress; subdue; subjugate; put down; crush; tranquilize. ¶ 반란을 ～하다 suppress a revolt.

**평정**(平靜) calm; serenity; tranquility; equability; equanimity. ～하다 (be) calm; tranquil; serene; peaceful; equable. ¶ 마음의 ～ *one's* presence 〔peace〕 of mind; composure / 마음의 ～을 유지하다 keep *one's* calmness 〔head〕; remain calm / 마음의 ～을 잃다 lose *one's* composure 〔presence of mind〕 / ～을 되찾다 recover composure; restore to tranquility; quiet down / ～을 가장하다 feign calmness.

**평정**(評定) evaluation; rating. ～하다 rate; evaluate; put a value on.

**평준**(平準) 《수준》 level; 《평균》 equality.
◉ ～점 a level point. ～화 equalization; leveling (off): ～화하다 level 《the various classes》; equalize.

**평지** 〖식물〗 a kind of rape(-weed).

**평지**(平地) flatland; level ground; flat country; even land. ¶ ～풍파 raising of unnecessary troubles; an unexpected disturbance 〔trouble〕; a storm in a teacup / ～ 풍파를 일으키다 raise 〔make, kick up〕 unnecessary trouble; provoke a storm in a dead calm / ～ 낙상하다 fall down and get hurt on the level ground; have an unexpected disaster 〔accident〕.

**평직**(平織) plain fabrics.

**평집**(平—) 〖건축〗 a small house (with but three or four crossbeams).

**평찌** an arrow flying low and level.

**평탄**(平坦) 《지면이》 evenness; flatness; 《일생이》 calmness; composure; tranquility; peace of mind. ～하다 (be) even; level; flat; smooth; calm; composed; peaceful. ¶ ～한 길 a level 〔flat〕 road / ～한 인생 《lead》 an uneventful life / 길을 ～하게 하다 level a road / 그의 일생은 ～했다 His life ran in the groove.

**평토**(平土) leveling ground after

burial. ～하다 level off《a grave》. ◉ ～장(葬) burying without making a mound on the grave.

**평판**(平板) a flat board; a slat.

**평판**(評判)《명성》fame; (a) reputation; (a) repute; a name;《세평》the world's opinion; popularity; a report; a rumor; sensation.

> 용법 **fame** 어떤 행위나 공적 때문에 좋은 뜻에서 유명하다는 뜻. **reputation** 일반적으로, 어떤 사실을 인정하는 사람들이 내리는 평가. **popularity** 일반 대중에게 받아들여져 인기가 있는 것. **rumor** 이야기에 꼬리가 붙어 널리 퍼져 나가는 소문. **sensation** 특히 굉장한 소문이 나서 한바탕 큰 소란을 피우게 되는 경우.

¶ ～이 좋다 be well [highly] spoken of; have a good reputation [name, character]; be in high [good] repute; be popular / ～이 나쁘다 be ill [poorly] spoken of; have a bad name [reputation]; be unpopular / ～이 나다 get a reputation; be rumored; be talked of; create a sensation; become popular / 그 영화는 ～이 좋았다 The film was the talk of the town. / 그는 여성들 사이에서 ～이 좋다 He is popular among [with] women.

**평판인쇄**(平版印刷) lithography; lithoprinting《미》. ～하다 lithograph; lithoprint. ◉ ～공 a lithoprinter. ～소 a lithographer; a lithoprinter.

**평평하다**(平平—)《판판함》(be) flat; level; even; horizontal;《평범함》(be) ordinary; commonplace; run-of-the-mill.

**평하다**(評—) criticize; comment on. ⇨ 비평하다.

**평행**(平行)〖수학〗parallel; parallelism. ～하다 run [be] parallel《to, with》. ¶ ～의 parallel《to》/ …와 ～으로 선을 긋다 draw a line parallel to… / 길이 철도와 ～하게 나 있다 The road runs parallel to the railroad. / 전주가 선로와 ～하게 서 있다 A line of telegraph-poles stands parallel with the railroad. ◉ ～력〖물리〗parallel forces. ～봉 parallel bars;《종목》the parallel bars: 2단 ～봉 uneven bars. ～사변형 a parallelogram. ～선 parallel lines. ～운동 a parallel motion. ～육면체 a parallelepiped. ～이동〖수학〗translation. ～자 a parallel ruler. ～좌표 parallel [Cartesian] coordinates.

**평형**(平衡) equilibrium; balance; counterbalance; counterpoise. ～하다 be balanced [poised]; be in equilibrium. ¶ ～을 유지하다 equilibrate; maintain balance; keep *one's* balance / ～을 잡다 balance; poise; balance *oneself* / ～을 잃다 lose balance. ◉ ～감각 the [*one's*] sense of equilibrium. ～교부금 an equalization subsidy [grant-in-aid]《to a local government》. ～력〖물리〗counter balance. ～상태 (a state of) equilibrium. ～수준기 a balance level. ～시험 a balancing test. ～타(舵) a balanced rudder. 안정[불안정]～ stable [unstable] equilibrium.

**평화**(平和) peace;《화합》harmony. ～스럽다, ～롭다 (be) peaceful; tranquil; harmonious. ¶ ～적인 peaceful《citizens》; peaceable《people》/ ～적으로 peacefully;《전쟁없이》at peace;《평온하게》in peace / ～롭게 peacefully; in peace;《사이좋게》harmoniously / 세계의 ～ the peace of the world; world peace / 마음의 ～ peace of mind / ～적(인) 정권 교체 peaceful power transfer; peaceful government change / ～롭게 수습하다 settle《*a matter*》in an amicable way; bring《*a matter*》to an amicable settlement / ～롭게 살다 live in peace; lead a peaceful life; enjoy a life of peace / ～를 깨뜨리다 break [disturb] the peace / ～를 유지하다 keep [maintain] the peace / ～를 회복하다 restore peace / ～를 위해 애쓰다 labor for peace / 영원한 ～를 확립하다 establish [secure] a permanent peace / ～적 통일을 모색하다 explore ways toward peaceful unification / 국제간의 ～를 촉진하는 것이 우리들의 사명이다 Our mission is to promote peace among the nations. ◉ ～감시자 a peacekeeper. ～공세 a peace offensive. ～공존 peaceful coexistence. ～교란자 a peacebreaker. ～교섭[회담] peace talks. ～국가 a peaceful nation. ～기념일《제1차대전의》Armistice Day. ～론자 a pacifist;《경멸적》a peacemonger. ～봉사단 the Peace Corps (volunteers): ～ 봉사단원 a Peace Corpsman. ～부대 the Peace Corps. ～사절 a peace envoy. ～산업 the peacetime industry. ～애호국민 a peace-loving nation. ～운동 a peace [pacifist] movement. ～유지군《유엔의》the Peace Keeping Force (생략 PKF): 다국적 ～ 유지군 the multi-national peace-keeping force. ～유지활동《유엔

의》 the Peace Keeping Operations (생략 PKO). ~이용 peaceful uses《of atomic energy》. ~정책 policy of universal peace. ~조약《conclude》a peace treaty. ~주의 pacifism: ~주의자 a pacifist. ~통일 peaceful unification: ~통일 방안 《Seoul-initiated》 peaceful unification formulas / ~통일 정책 자문 위원회 the Advisory Council on Peaceful Unification Policy (생략 ACPUP). ~혁명 a bloodless revolution. ~협정 a peace agreement. ~회의 a peace conference. 집단~ collective peace.

**평활**(平—) an archery practice bow.

**평활**(平滑) ~하다 (be) level; even; smooth. ◉ ~근(筋) 『해부』 a smooth muscle: ~근종(腫) 『의학』 a leiomyoma (*pl.* -mata).

**평활**(平闊) levelness and broadness. ~하다 (be) level and broad.

**폐**(肺) the lungs. ¶ 폐가 약하다〔나쁘다〕 have a 「weak 〔bad〕 chest / 폐를 앓다 have lung trouble / 그는 오른쪽 폐가 나쁘다 His right lung is affected. ◉ 폐경변(硬變) 『의학』 pulmonary cirrhosis; pneumonocirrhosis. 폐경화 『의학』 induration of the lung.

**폐**(弊) ①《폐단》 an evil; a vice; a bad custom; a corrupt practice. ¶ 음주의 폐 the evil of drink; the bad habit of drinking; the vice of intemperance / 관습의 폐 the evil of convention. ②《남에 대한 누》 (a) trouble; a bother; an annoyance; an inconvenience. ¶ 폐가 안 된다면 if it is not inconvenient to you / (…에게) 폐를 끼치다 trouble 《*a person*》; cause 〔give〕 《*a person*》 trouble; get 《*a person*》 into 「trouble 〔mischief〕; put 《*a person*》 to trouble; annoy; bother; be 〔make *oneself*〕 a nuisance 《to》; cause annoyance 《to》; put 《*a person*》 to inconvenience; 《시간상》 take up much of 《*a person's*》 time / 폐를 끼쳐 미안합니다 I am sorry to have caused you so much trouble. / 폐 많이 끼쳤습니다 Thank you for all your trouble. *or* I am afraid I have put you to much trouble. *or* 《시간을 빼앗은 때》 I'm afraid I have taken up much of your time. / 남한테 폐 끼칠 것 없다 There's no need to trouble others. / 남에게 폐가 되지 않도록 주의해야 한다 We must take care not to make ourselves a nuisance to others.

**폐**-(弊) 《저희》 my 〔our〕 humble…. ¶ ~가(家) my (humble) house / ~사(社) our (humble) company 〔firm〕.

**폐가**(廢家) 《낡은 집》 a ruined house; a deserted house; 『법』 ending a house 〔family〕; 《상속자 없는》 a family that has come to an end. ~하다 the house comes to an end.

**폐간**(廢刊) discontinuance 《of a publication》. ~하다 cease to publish; discontinue 《issuing》; go out of existence; 《구어》 fold. ¶ ~된 잡지 a defunct magazine / ~이 되다 be discontinued; go out of print; cease to be published. / 그 잡지는 1년만에 ~되었다 The magazine only 「lasted 〔survived〕 for a year.

**폐갱**(廢坑) an abandoned 〔unworked〕 mine; a dead pit. ⇨ 폐광(廢鑛).

**폐결핵**(肺結核) 『의학』 phthisis; (pulmonary) tuberculosis (생략 T.B.); consumption. ¶ ~에 걸리다 suffer from tuberculosis of the lungs. ◉ ~환자 a 「tuberculosis 〔TB〕 patient; a consumptive (patient).

**폐경기**(閉經期) 『생리』 the climacteric; the (time of ) menopause.

**폐관**(閉館) closing 《its doors》. ~하다 《a building》 close; be closed. ¶ ~시각 the closing 「time 〔hour〕.

**폐광**(廢鑛) 《폐기한》 an abandoned 〔unworked〕 mine; 《바닥이 난》 an exhausted mine. ~하다 abandon 〔disuse〕 a mine.

**폐교**(廢校·閉校) abolition 〔closing〕 of a school. ~하다 abolish 〔close〕 a school.

**폐기**(廢棄) 《법률 등의》 abrogation; repeal; 《불용의 것을》 abolition; abandonment. ~하다 do away with; 《폐품 따위를》 abolish; abandon; scrap; disuse; junk; discard (습관을); 《조약·법규 따위의》 abrogate 《a treaty》; annul; repeal 《a law》; scrap 《a plan》. ¶ 오래된 서류를 ~하다 scrap old documents / 조약을 ~하다 annul 〔abrogate〕 a treaty / 이런 낡은 것들은 이제 모두 ~할 시기이다 It's about time all these old things were done away with. ◉ ~자료 『컴퓨터』 a junk.

**폐기물**(廢棄物) scrapped material; waste(s). ¶ 공장 ~ factory waste / 플라스틱 ~ waste plastic material(s) / ~을 바다에 실어다 버리다 tow garbage out to sea and dump it. ◉ ~처리 《원자로의》 disposal of (radioactive) waste; waste disposal: 방사성 ~ 처리는 지금 커다란 사회 문제가 되어 있다 How to

dispose of radioactive waste is now a big social problem. ~처리장 garbage 〔refuse〕 dump.
**폐기종**(肺氣腫) 〖의학〗 emphysema of the lungs; pulmonary 〔vesicular〕 emphysema.
**폐낭**(肺囊) 〖동물〗 a lung 〔pulmonary〕 「sac.
**폐농**(廢農) giving up farming; failure in farming. ~하다 stop 〔give up〕 farming; fail 「in 〔at〕 farming.
**폐단**(弊端) an abuse; an evil; evil practices; corrupt practices. ¶ ~을 없애다 〔고치다〕 remedy 〔correct〕 an abuse / 남에게 의지하려는 ~이 있다 have a bad habit of relying on other people / 거기에는 여러 가지 ~이 따른다 It is attened by 〔with〕 many evils.
**폐동맥**(肺動脈) 〖해부〗 the pulmonary artery.
**폐디스토마**(肺—) pulmonary distoma; distoma pulmona; lungdistoma.
**폐렴**(肺炎) 〖의학〗 pneumonia; inflammation of the lungs.
**폐롭다**(弊—) ① 《귀찮다》 (be) bothersome; troublesome. ¶ 폐롭게 굴다 cause trouble / 손님이 ~ a guest is bothersome. ② 《성미가》 (be) particular; fussy; fastidious; picayune; odd; queer. ¶ 폐로운 사람 a 「fussy 〔queer〕 person; a fussbudget; an odd 「fish 〔duck〕.
**폐막**(閉幕) 《무대의》 (the falling of) the curtain; 《일이 끝남》 the end 《of an event》. ~하다 bring the curtain down on; close the curtain on; end; bring to an end. ¶ 공연은 9시에 ~된다 The performance 「ends 〔closes〕 at nine. ◉ ~식 the closing ceremony.
**폐문**(肺門) 〖해부〗 the hilum of the lung; the pulmonary hilum. ◉ ~림프선염 tuberculous adenitis of the hilum of the 《right 〔left〕》 lung.
**폐문**(閉門) closing the gate; 《게시》 Door closed; Closed. ~하다 close (the gate); bar the gate; close up. ◉ ~시간 (the) closing time.
**폐물**(廢物) a useless thing; waste 〔discarded〕 material 〔products〕; waste; 《찌끼·쓰레기》 refuse; trash 《미》; rubbish 《영》. ¶ ~이 되다 become useless. ◉ ~이용 the 「utilization 〔reuse〕 of 「waste materials 〔discarded articles〕.
**폐방**(廢房) a 「disused 〔deserted〕 room. ~하다 stop using a room; shut off a room.
**폐백**(幣帛) *pyebaek;* presents (of silk); 《신부의》 a bride's presents to her parents-in-law; 《의식》 a traditional ceremony to pay respect to the bridegroom's family by the newly=wedded couple right after their wedding.
**폐병**(肺病) 〖의학〗 a 「lung 〔chest〕 trouble; a lung disease; (pulmonary) consumption; tuberculosis (생략 T.B.). ¶ ~으로 죽다 die of 〔be down with〕 consumption; die from the white plague / ~을 앓다 suffer from consumption; have a lung trouble / 그는 ~에 걸렸다 He got his lungs affected. ◉ ~환자 a T.B. patient; a lung case; a consumptive (patient); 《구어》 a lunger.
**폐병**(廢兵) a 「disabled 〔broken〕 soldier.
**폐부**(肺腑) 《허파》 the lungs; 《마음 속》 the bottom of *one's* heart; *one's* inmost heart; 《급소》 a vital point; a critical area. ¶ ~를 찌르다 sting *one* to the quick; come 〔be brought〕 home to *one;* touch *one's* heart deeply; 《비평 따위가》 appeal 〔go〕 to the heart / ~를 찌르는 듯한 penetrating; heartbreaking / ~에서 우러나오다 come from the heart.
**폐비**(廢妃) 《폐하는 일》 deposal of a queen; 《사람》 a deposed queen. ~하다 depose (a queen).
**폐사**(廢寺) a ruined temple.
**폐색**(閉塞) (a) blockade; blocking(-up); stoppage; 〖의학〗 occlusion. ~하다 block 《a harbor *etc.*》; blockade; bottle up. ¶ 항구를 ~하다 block up 〔blockade〕 a harbor. ◉ ~구간〔신호〕 〖철도〗 a block 「section 〔signal〕. ~선(船) a blockader. ~음 an occlusive. ~전선 〖기상〗 an occluded front. 장(腸) ~ 〖의학〗 intestinal obstruction; ileus.
**폐석**(廢石) 〖광산〗 muck; debris; goaf.
**폐선**(廢船) a scrapped 「ship 〔vessel〕; a ship that is out of service. ~하다 scrap a vessel.
**폐소공포증**(閉所恐怖症) 〖심리〗 claustro- 「phobia.
**폐쇄**(閉鎖) ① 《닫음》 closing; 《내쫓음》 a lockout. ~하다 shut (down); close (down); 《내쫓다》 lock 《the employees》 out. ¶ 공장을 ~하다 close down a factory / 독감 때문에 임시로 학교를 ~하다 close classes temporarily because of the flu epidemic. ② 《외부와의 단절》 ¶ ~적인 《자폐적인》 uncommunicative; unsociable; 《배타적인》 exclusive; cliquish. ◉ ~기(機) breech mecha-

nism. ～사회 a closed 〔close(ly)-knit〕 society. ～음 a stop(sound); an implosive. ～회로 a closed circuit: ～회로 텔레비전 closed-circuit television (생략 CCTV). ～회사 a close(d) corporation.

**폐수**(廢水) waste water. ¶ 공장 ～ liquid waste from a factory / 생활 ～ domestic wastewater / 축산 ～ 처리 정화조 wastewater treatment facilities for livestock farms / 공장 ～에 의한 환경 오염 environmental pollution caused by liquid waste from factories / 저비용의 축산 ～ 정화 시스템이 성공적으로 상업화되었다 A system to purify livestock waste water at low cost has been successfully commercialized. ◉ ～방출 discharging waste water; dumping 〔draining〕 wastewater. ～처리 liquid waste treatment; disposal of waste water. ～처리장(치) a waste water disposal plant. ～ 처리 장치에는 막대한 비용이 든다 A wastewater disposal plant costs lots of money. 불법〔무단〕～배출 illegal discharging of waste water.

**폐수종**(肺水腫) 〖의학〗 an edema of the lungs; a pulmonary edema.

**폐스럽다**(弊—) (be) troublesome; worrisome; bothersome; annoying; cumbersome.

**폐습**(弊習) evil 〔corrupt〕 customs; evils; an evil practice; a bad customs. ¶ 방치할 수 없는 ～ crying abuse / ～을 없애다 break down evil customs; do away with evil practices / ～을 고치다 remedy 〔put a stop to〕 abuses.

**폐안**(廢案) a rejected bill 〔project〕; a draft withdrawn.

**폐암**(肺癌) cancer of the lungs; lung cancer.

**폐어**(肺魚) 〖어류〗 a lungfish; a dipnoan (fish).

**폐어**(廢語) an obsolete 〔a disused〕 word.

**폐업**(廢業) closing〔quitting〕 *one's* business; discontinuance 〔abolishment〕 of business. ～하다 《장사를 그만두다》 close 〔give up〕 *one's* business; [가게·공장 등이 주어] close down; 《의사·변호사가》 give up *one's* practice; 《은퇴하다》 retire from business. ¶ 부근에 큰 슈퍼마켓이 생겨서 많은 소매점들이 ～하지 않을 수 없게 되었다 Because a big supermarket opened in the neighborhood, a lot of retail stores 「had to close 〔were driven out of business〕. ◉ ～신고 a report of cessation of business: ～신고를 하다 report the cessation of business.

**폐엽**(肺葉) a lobe of the lung. ◉ ～절제 lobectomy.

**폐옥**(廢屋) 《버려진 집》 a deserted house; 《황폐한 집》 a ruined house.

**폐원**(閉院) the closing 〔recess〕 of the Assembly 〔Parliament〕. ～하다 close 〔recess〕 the Assembly 〔Parliament〕. ◉ ～식 the closing ceremony of the Assembly.

**폐위**(廢位) dethronement. ～하다 dethrone; depose 《a sovereign》; take the crown from 《a king》.

**폐유**(廢油) waste oil; 《덩어리진》 waste oil clot.

**폐인**(廢人) a disabled person; a person who is maimed 〔crippled〕 for life. ¶ ～이나 다름없이 되다 become as good as a living dead / 그의 아들은 전쟁에서 ～이 되었다 His son was maimed in the war.

**폐일언하고**(蔽一言—) in a word…; to sum up; in short 〔brief〕. ¶ ～ 네가 잘못했다 In short, you are to blame.

**폐장**(肺臟) 〖해부〗 the lungs.

**폐장**(閉場) (the) closing of a place. ～하다 《a place》 close; be closed; close 《a place》.

**폐적**(廢嫡) 〖법〗 disinheritance. ～하다 disinherit.

**폐절제**(肺切除) 〖의학〗 pneumonectomy; pneumectomy.

**폐점**(閉店) ～하다 《영업 시간이 지나》 close (the) shop 〔*one's* doors〕; 《폐업하다》 shut up shop; wind up *one's* business. ◉ ～시간 the closing time. ～ (염가) 대매출 《게시》 Clearance sale for closing business. *or* Going-out-of-business sale. *or* Final bargain sale before closing.

**폐정**(閉廷) 〖법〗 dismissing the court. ～하다 dismiss 〔adjourn〕 the court. ¶ 재판장은 화요일까지 ～ 선언했다 The presiding judge adjourned court till Tuesday.

**폐정맥**(肺靜脈) the pulmonary veins.

**폐지**(閉止) stoppage. ～하다 stop; cease; close. ◉ 월경 ～기 the climacteric; the turn 〔change〕 of life: 월경 ～기의 여성 a woman at the menopause.

**폐지**(廢止) 《풍속·제도의》 abolition; disuse; discontinuance; 《법률·조약의》 repeal; abrogation; 《취소》 annulment; nullification. ～하다 abolish; disuse; do away with; discontinue; phase out (단계적으로); 《법령 등을》 abrogate; repeal; annul; cancel. ¶ ～되다 be abolished; go out of use 〔existence〕; fall into disuse 〔desuetude〕/그 법률은 1년 전에 ~되었다 The law was repealed one year ago./허례를 ~하기란 그렇게 간단한 것이 아니다 It is not so simple as it seems to do away with formalities.

**폐질**(廢疾) an incurable 〔a fatal〕 disease. ¶~이 되다 be disabled; be crippled for life. ◉ ~보험 disability insurance. ~자 a disabled person.

**폐질환**(肺疾患) pulmonary complaints 〔diseases〕.

**폐차**(廢車) a scrapped vehicle 〔car〕; a car out of service; a disused car. ~하다 scrap a car; put a car out of service. ¶저 망가진 차는 ~되었다 That wrecked car was scrapped.
◉ ~장 an auto junkyard.

**폐창**(廢娼) abolition of licensed prostitution; abolition of white slavery. ~하다 abolish licensed prostitution.

**폐첨**(肺尖) 〚해부〛 the apex of a lung. ◉ ~카타르 the catarrh of the apex; pulmonary apicitis.

**폐출혈**(肺出血) 〚의학〛 lung hemorrhage; pneumo(no)rrhagia.

**폐충혈**(肺充血) 〚의학〛 hyperemia 〔congestion〕 of the lungs; pneumonemia.

**폐침윤**(肺浸潤) 〚의학〛 (amyloid) infiltration of the lungs.

**폐포**(肺胞) 〚해부〛 an alveolus (*pl.* -li); pulmonary alveoli. ◉ ~음(音) 〚의학〛 a vesicular murmur.

**폐품**(廢品) abandoned 〔waste〕 articles; useless 〔thrown-away〕 things; junk; refuse. ¶~ 처리 disposal of waste articles/~을 회수하다 collect waste articles/~이 되다 become useless/우리 구(區)에는 ~ 수집차가 10대 있다 Our district has 10 trucks for collecting waste.
◉ ~수집〔회수〕 collection 〔reclamation〕 of waste articles 〔materials〕; recovery of scrap: ~ 회수〔수집〕 업자 a ragman; a junk dealer. ~이용 the utilization of waste materials; the reuse of discarded articles. ~재생 recycling of waste articles: ~재생 공장 a recycling plant.

**폐풍**(弊風) an evil practice. ⇨ 폐습(弊習).

**폐하**(陛下) 《3인칭》 His 〔Her〕 Majesty (생략 H.M.); 《2인칭》 Your Majesty 〔Majesties〕; 《양(兩)폐하》 Their Majesties. ¶황제~ H.M. the Emperor; His Majesty/황후 ~ H.M. the Empress; Her Majesty.

**폐하다**(廢—) 《풍속·제도 따위를》 discontinue; abolish; shut down; abandon; do away with; 《법률·조약 따위를》 repeal; abrogate. ¶노예 제도를 ~ abolish slavery/법률을 ~ repeal a law/허례를 ~ do away with formalities. 「abandon study.

**폐학**(廢學) ~하다 give up *one's* studies;

**폐함**(廢艦) a decommissioned warship; a ship out of commission; a scrapped warship. ¶~ 처분하다 put 《a warship》 out of commission; decommission; scrap a warship.

**폐합**(廢合) abolition and amalgamation. ~하다 abolish and amalgamate; reorganize; consolidate. ¶국과(局課)의 ~ rearrangement of bureaus and sections. ◉ ~정리 reorganization; rearrangement.

**폐해**(弊害) an evil; an abuse; a vice; evil practices; 《악영향》 an evil 〔a harmful, a baneful〕 influence; an evil effect. ¶~를 고치다 correct 〔remedy〕 an abuse/~가 따르다 [사물이 주어] be attended by evils/~를 끼치다, ~가 있다 exert an evil influence upon 《children》; have an injurious effect upon 《society》; give 〔cause〕 trouble/그는 흡연의 ~를 강조했다 He emphasized the bad effect of smoking.

**폐허**(廢墟) the ruins 《of a castle》; the remains 《of a temple》. ¶~로 변한 성 a castle in ruins/~가 되다 be ruined; fall into ruins; 《되어 있다》 be 〔lie〕 in ruins/고도(古都)는 ~가 되어 있다 The ancient city lay in ruins.

**폐환**(肺患) a lung 〔chest〕 trouble; a lung disease.

**폐활량**(肺活量) the air capacity of the lungs; lung 〔breathing〕 capacity.
◉ ~계(計) a pneumatometer; a pulmometer; a spirometer. ~측정 pulmometry; spirometry.

**폐회**(閉會) the closing 《of a meeting 〔the House〕》; a close. ~하다 close 《a meeting》; adjourn. ¶~되다 be closed; come to a close/~를 선언하다 declare the meeting 〔sitting〕 closed/~중이다 be out of session.
◉ ~사 《give》 a closing address. ~식 the closing ceremony.

**폐회로**(閉回路) 〚전기〛 a closed circuit. ¶~로 방송하다 broadcast by closed circuit. ◉ ~ 텔레비전 closed-circuit television (생략 CCTV).

**포**(砲) 《대포》 a cannon; a gun; a howitzer (곡사포); an artillery piece; a fieldpiece (야포); [총칭] gunnery;

ordnance. ¶ 박격포 a mortar / 12인치 포 a 12-inch gun / 포 5문 five guns / 자주포 a mobile gun / 함포 a naval gun / 해안포 a coastal gun.

**포**(苞) 〖식물〗 a bract. ⇨ 포엽.

**포**(脯) dried slices of meat seasoned with spices. ¶ 육포 dried slices of beef / 포를 뜨다 slice meat (for the purpose of seasoning and drying it).

**포** 〖인쇄〗 point (type). ¶ 9포 활자 (a) 9-point type.

**-포** a period (of time). ¶ 달포 a month.

**포가**(砲架) 〖군사〗 a gun carriage; a naval gun mount (군함의). ¶ ~를 세우다 set a gun carriage / ~에서 내리다 dismount 《a gun》.

**포개다** pile 〔heap〕 up; put 〔lay〕 《*one thing*》 on (top of) 《another》; put 《*a thing*》 upon 《another》. ¶ 포개 놓은 쟁반 stacked trays; a stack of trays / 포개 놓은 석장의 베니어판 three layers of plywood / 담요를 여러 장 포개서 덮고 자다 sleep under several layers of blankets / 포개서 쌓지 마시오 《게시》 Do not stack. *or* Not to be stowed below another.

**포격**(砲擊) shelling; (an) (artillery) bombardment; a cannonade; an artillery firing; a gunshot. ~하다 shell; bombard; fire; cannonade. ¶ 오랜~ 끝에 after a long bombardment / ~을 받다 be under fire; be shelled 〔bombarded〕 《by》 / ~을 개시하다 open fire 《on a fort》 / 적의 참호를 ~하다 shell the enemy's trenches / 적의 전함을 겨냥하여 ~하다 fire at an enemy battleship.

**포경**(包莖) 〖의학〗 phimosis. ◉ ~수술 an operation for phimosis; phimosiectomy.

**포경**(捕鯨) whaling; whale fishing 〔hunting〕. ~하다 whale; hunt whales. ¶ 국제~ 규제 조약 the International Whale Fishing Control Treaty / 국제~ 협정 the International Whaling Convention (생략 IWC). ◉ ~금지 a moratorium on whale hunting: ~ 금지 운동 an antiwhaling campaign. ~기지 a whaling station. ~모선 a whale factory ship. ~선 a whaling vessel 〔ship〕; a whaler: ~선단 a fleet of whalers / ~ 선원 a whaling man. ~업 the whaling industry. ~장 a whaling ground; a whale fishery. ~포 a whaling 〔harpoon〕 gun: ~포수 a harpoon gunner. ~회사 a whaling company.

**포고**(布告) proclamation; declaration. ~하다 proclaim; declare; announce (발표하다). ¶ 선전~ a declaration of war / ~ 제1 호 the initial proclamation / ~를 내다 issue 〔make〕 proclamation / 그 나라는 이웃 나라에 대해 선전~했다 The country declared war against its neighbor. ◉ ~령 a decree; an edict. ~문 a declaration; a decree.

**포괄**(包括) complete 〔blanket〕 coverage; inclusion; comprehension. ~하다 include; comprehend; comprise; take in; contain; cover. ¶ ~적(으로) inclusive(ly); comprehensive(ly) / ~적 핵실험 금지 조약 the Comprehensive Test Ban Treaty (생략 CTBT) / ~ 군축 협상 comprehensive disarmament negotiation / ~적 군축 계획 the comprehensive program of disarmament / 주택 문제에 관한 ~적 연구 a comprehensive study of housing problems / 이들 문제에 관한 ~적인 의견을 요청한다 We require a general opinion of these problems. ◉ ~범위 the coverage 《of an agreement》. ~보험 blanket insurance: ~ 보험 증권 a blanket policy. ~사증(査證) a blanket visa. ~승계인 a general successor. ~안(案) a package plan. ~요금 an inclusive charge. ~유증(遺贈) a universal legacy. ~조항 a blanket clause.

**포교**(布敎) missionary work; propagation 《of religion》. ~하다 propagate 〔spread〕 《a religion》; propagandize; preach 《Buddhism》. ¶ ~에 종사하다 be engaged in missionary work. ◉ ~사업 missionary work. ~자 a propagator; a missionary. ~지(구) a mission (field).

**포구**(砲口) the muzzle of a gun. ¶ …에 ~를 향하다 direct 〔train〕 a gun 《on》. ◉ ~장전식 포 a muzzle loading gun.

**포구**(浦口) an inlet; a port; a boat landing.

**포근하다** ① 《폭신하다》 (be) soft and comfortable; downy; fluffy. ¶ 포근한 방석 a nice soft cushion / 포근한 이부자리 a soft, comfortable bedding; downy bedclothes.
② 《따뜻하다》 (***a***) 《아늑하다》 (be) comfortably warm; cozy; snug. ¶ 어머니의 포근한 가슴 mother's warm breast. (***b***) 《겨울 날씨가》 (be) mild; genial; warm. ¶ 포근한 겨울 a soft 〔mild, green〕 winter / 포근한 날씨 a mild 〔moderate, temperate〕 climate.
③ 《마음이》 (be) relaxed; warm-heart-

ed; [서술적] feel good 〔comfortable〕; be warm and comfortable. ¶ 그에게는 인간적인 포근함이 있다 There is a lot of human warmth in him.

**포근히** ① 《잠을》 sound; deep; heavy; fast. ¶ ~ 잠들다 fall fast asleep. ② 《아늑히》 warmly; comfortably; softly; snugly.

**포금**(砲金) gun metal.

**포기** 《풀·야채 등의》 a head; a plant; a root. ¶ 풀 한 ~ one plant / 배추 두~ two heads of cabbage / 배추 ~가 크다 a cabbage has a large head (on it); be a large head of cabbage.

**포기**(抛棄) giving up; abandonment; renunciation; renouncement (권리의); relinquishment (요구의). ~하다 give up; desert (버리다); abandon (계획의); 《요구·권리 등의》 renounce; surrender; relinquish.
¶ ~한 시합 a forfeited game / 전쟁의 ~ renunciation of war / 계획을 ~하다 abandon 〔give up〕 *one's* attempt / 권리를 ~하다 give up 〔relinquish〕 *one's* right; renounce *one's* claim / 직장을 ~하다 desert *one's* job / 지위를 ~하다 throw up *one's* position 〔post〕 / 첫날에 시험을 ~하다 give up the examination on the first day / 상속권을 ~하다 renounce the right of succession / 그녀는 재산권을 ~했다 She renounced her claim to the property. / 그녀는 자진해서 그 권리를 ~하기로 서약했다 She willingly swore to give up the right. / 그는 병 때문에 학업을 ~하지 않을 수 없었다 He could not help but lay aside his studies because of illness. / 우리는 결코 자유를 ~하지 않을 것이다 We shall never surrender our liberty.

**포대**(布袋) a burlap 〔cloth〕 bag; a sack; a gunnysack.

**포대**(砲臺) 〖군사〗 a battery; a casemate; 《요새》 a fortress; a fort. ¶ ~를 구축하다 build a fort.

**포대기** a quilt for little children; a wadded baby wrapper.

**포도**(葡萄) 《열매》 a grape; 《나무》 a (grape)vine. ¶ ~한 송이 a bunch 〔cluster〕 of grapes / ~수확 a vintage / ~의 풍작〔흉작〕 an abundant 〔a poor〕 vintage / ~를 재배하다 raise 〔grow〕 grapes.
◉ ~당(糖) grape sugar; 〖화학〗 glucose; dextrose. ~덩굴 a grapevine. ~밭 a vineyard; a vinery. ~산(酸) racemic acid. ~상구균(狀球菌) a staphylococcus (*pl.* -cocci). ~색 dark purple; (a) wine color. ~씨 a grapestone. ~재배 vine culture; viticulture; vine 〔grape〕 growing: ~ 재배자 a vine grower; a viniculturalist. ~종(腫) 〖의학〗 a staphyloma (*pl.* -mata). ~즙 grape juice.

**포도**(鋪道) a paved street 〔road〕; a pavement.

**포도대장**(捕盜大將) 〖고제도〗 a police chief.

**포도주**(葡萄酒) (grape) wine; vinous liquor. ¶ 백~ white wine; Rhenish wine; hock; sherry; *vin blanc*(F.) / 적(赤)~ red 〔purple〕 wine; claret; Bordeaux. ◉ ~양조장 a vineyard; an estate; a chateau (프랑스의); 《미》 a winery.

**포도청**(捕盜廳) 〖고제도〗 the police bureau.

**포동포동하다** (be) chubby; fat; plump; full. ¶ 얼굴이 포동포동한 full-cheeked / 포동포동한 얼굴 a chubby face / 살이 포동포동하게 찌다 be plump.

**포드** 《미국의 자동차왕》 Henry Ford (1863-1947); 《자동차》 a Ford (car).
◉ ~재단 the Ford Foundation.

**포란**(抱卵) incubation.¶ ~하다 incubate; 《물고기의》 spawn. ◉ ~기(期) 《새의》 sitting.

**포로**(捕虜) ① 《전쟁 등에서의》 a prisoner of war (생략 POW, P.O.W.); a war prisoner; a captive. ¶ ~가 되다 be taken prisoner 〔captive〕 《by the enemy》 (★주어가 복수일 때도 prisoners로 하지 않음) / ~로 하다 capture; take 〔make〕 《*a person*》 prisoner / ~를 수용하다 intern a prisoner / ~를 교환하다 exchange prisoners. ② [비유적] a slave; a victim. ¶ ~로 하다 captivate; charm; enthrall / ~가 되다 fall (a) victim 〔be a slave〕 《to her charms》; be enslaved 〔enthralled, captivated〕 《by her beauty》.
◉ ~교환 an exchange of prisoners of war: ~ 교환 협정 the Prisoners of War Exchange Pact. ~송환 the repatriation of prisoners of war: ~ 송환 관리 repatriation and custody of prisoners of war. ~수용소 a prison 〔prisoner-of-war, POW〕 camp. ~인도 the delivery of prisoners. ~학대 POW atrocities.

**포르노** pornography; 《구어》 porn(o). ¶ ~의 pornographic / ~ 여배우 a porno actress 〔queen〕. ◉ ~사진 a pornographic picture. ~숍 a porno shop. ~영화 a porn(ographic) 〔blue〕 film; 《구어》 a skin flick. ~작가 a pornographer. ~잡지 a pornographic magazine.

**포르르** ①《끓어오르는 모양》 bubbling; seething; boiling. ∼하다 bubble 〔boil〕 up; seethe. ②《타는 모양》《burn》 crisply. ∼하다 burn up in no time. ③《떠는 모양》 trembling; quivering. ∼하다 quiver; tremble. ④《갑자기 나는 모양》 ¶ ∼ 날다 flush.

**포르말린** 〖화학〗 formalin. ¶ ∼소독 formalin disinfection / ∼으로 소독하다 disinfect 《*a thing*》 in formalin.

**포르테** 〖음악〗 a forte (It.) (생략 f.).

**포르투갈** (the Republic of) Portugal. ¶ ∼의 Portuguese. ◉ ∼말 Portuguese. ∼ 사람 a Portuguese; the Portuguese [총칭].

**포르티시모** 〖음악〗 a fortissimo (It.) (생략 ff.).

**포르피린** 〖생화학〗 porphyrin.

**포르핀** 〖화학〗 porphin(e).

**포름산**(―酸) 〖화학〗 formic acid.

**포마드** pomade; pomatum; hair grease. ¶ ∼를 바르다 pomade; apply pomade 《to the hair》.

**포만**(飽滿) satiety; satiation. ∼하다 be 「satiated 〔full〕 《with》.

**포말**(泡沫) a bubble; foam; froth. ¶ ∼같은 bubbly; foamy / ∼같은 명성 「a short-lived 〔an ephemeral〕 reputation / ∼ 몽환(夢幻)의 세상 a transient life. ◉ ∼경기(景氣) an ephemeral boom. ∼회사 a bubble company; a fly-by-night concern.

**포목**(布木) linen and cotton; dry goods 《미》; drapery 《영》. ◉ ∼상 《장수》 a draper; a dry-goods dealer 《미》. ∼전(廛) a dry goods store; a draper's.

**포문**(砲門) 《포구(砲口)》 the muzzle of a gun; 《군함의》 a porthole; 《성벽의》 an embrasure. ¶ ∼을 열다 open fire 《on》; [비유적] broach a discussion.

**포물선**(抛物線) 〖수학〗 a parabola. ¶ ∼을 그리다 describe a parabola / ∼을 그리며 날다 pass 《overhead》 describing a parabola. ◉ ∼운동 a parabolic motion 「(of a cannon).

**포미**(砲尾) the gun breech; the breech

**포박**(捕縛) (a) arrest (and binding); capture. ⇨ 체포. ∼하다 arrest (and tie up); apprehend; catch; seize.

**포병**(砲兵) 《병사》 an artilleryman; 《부대》 the artillery. ¶ ∼전 artillery 「fighting 〔duel〕. ◉ ∼기지 an artillery base. ∼대〔단〕 an artillery unit 〔corps〕. ∼대대 an artillery battalion 《미》; an artillery brigade 《영》. ∼사령관 an artillery commander. ∼중대 a battery. ∼진지 「an artillery 〔a gun〕 position. ∼학교 the Artillery School. 사단〔군단〕∼ division 〔corps〕 artillery. 중(重)∼ heavy artillery.

**포복**(匍匐) creeping (and crawling). ∼하다 creep 〔crawl〕 flat on the ground; go on all fours. ¶ 적의 참호에 ∼하여 접근하다 approach to the enemy trench by crawling and creeping. ◉ ∼경(莖) 〖식물〗 a creeping 「stem 〔shoot〕. ∼식물 a creeper (plant); a vine.

**포복절도**(抱腹絶倒) convulsions of laughter. ∼하다 hold *one's* sides with laughter; be convulsed with laughter; roll about with laughter. ¶ 그는 모든 청중들을 ∼케 했다 He set the whole audience roaring with laughter. / 그의 이야기가 너무 우스워서 모두 ∼했다 His story was so funny that we were all in convulsions.

**포부**(抱負) 《큰 뜻》 an ambition; an aspiration; 《희망》 *one's* hopes; 《계획》 *one's* plan. ¶ ∼가 있는 ambitious; aspiring / ∼를 말하다 express *one's* 「wishes 〔hopes〕; speak of *one's* aspiration(s) / 그는 큰 ∼를 가지고 있다 He has great ambitions. / 새 시장은 기자회견에서 그의 ∼를 이야기했다 At the press conference the new mayor outlined his ambitious program.

**포비슴** 〖미술〗《야수파》 Fauvism. ◉ ∼화가 a Fauvist.

**포살**(捕殺) catching and killing. ∼하다 catch and kill.

**포상**(砲床) a gun 「platform 〔emplacement〕.

**포상**(褒賞) a prize; a reward; an award. ∼하다 give an award; award a prize. ¶ ∼을 받다 win a prize / 그는 시의 발전에 이바지했다는 이유로 ∼을 받았다 He received an award for his contribution to the development of the city. ◉ ∼수령자 a prize winner. ∼수여 prize-giving.

**포석**(布石) 《바둑》 the strategic placing of stones (in a game of *baduk*); [비유적] preparatory steps 《for *doing*》; the groundwork 《for》; paving the way for the future. ∼하다 《바둑에서》 make a strategic move; place stones in strategic positions; [비유적] take preparatory steps 《for》; pave the way for the future. ¶ 장래의 발전을 위해 ∼하다 lay the foundations for future development / 당원을 정부 기관의 요소 요소에 ∼하다 place party members in all the important government positions.

**포석**(鋪石) a paving stone.
**포섭**(包攝) ① 〚논리〛 connotation; subsumption. ~하다 connote; subsume. ② 《동조자로 끌어들임》 ~하다 win 〔gain〕 《*a person*》 over to *one's* side; bring 《*a person*》 around. ¶ ~공작을 하다 contrive to win 《*a person*》 over to *one's* side / 뇌물로 남을 ~하다 fix 〔bring around〕 *a person* by bribery.
**포성**(砲聲) the boom 〔roaring〕 of the sound of gunfire. ¶ 멀리서 ~이 들렸다 We heard the distant boom of guns. / ~이 천지를 진동했다 The cannon's roar rent the air.
**포수**(砲手) 《사냥꾼》 a hunter; 《대포의》 a gunner; an artilleryman.
**포수**(捕手) 〚야구〛 a catcher. ¶ 그는 5년 동안 자이언트 팀의 ~를 했다 He sat behind the plate for the Giants for five years.
**포술**(砲術) gunnery; artillery (skills). ◉ ~교관 a gunnery instructor. ~장(長) a chief gunner; a gunnery lieutenant.
**포스겐** 〚화학〛 phosgene. ◉ ~가스 phosgene gas; carbonyl chrolide.
**포스아웃** 〚야구〛 a force-out. ¶ ~시키다 force 《a runner》 out.
**포스터** a poster; a placard; a bill. ¶ 영화〔광고〕~ a movie 〔an ad〕 poster / 선전~ publicity posters / ~를 붙이다 put up a poster; post a bill; placard 《a wall》 / ~를 떼어내다 tear off a poster; clear 《a pole》 of bills / ~로 선전하다 advertize with posters. ◉ ~광고 billing. ~컬러 a poster color.
**포스트** 《지위·자리》 a position; a post. ¶ ~가 비기를 기다리다 wait for a vacant post.
**포승**(捕繩) a rope to bind a criminal with. ¶ ~에 묶이다 be bound with a rope / ~을 풀다 unbind 〔untie〕 《*a person*》 / 순순히 ~을 받다 suffer *oneself* to be bound 〔arrested〕; be arrested without resistance.
**포식**(捕食) predation. ~하다 prey upon 《birds》. ◉ ~동물 a predator; a predatory animal.
**포식**(飽食) eating *one's* fill; satiation; gluttony. ~하다 eat 〔have, take〕 *one's* fill; satiate 〔glut〕 *oneself* 《with》; eat to *one's* heart's content; be satiated 《with food》. ¶ 난의(暖衣) ~하다 be well-fed and well-clad; eat well and dress well; live in luxury.
**포신**(砲身) a gun barrel; the barrel of a gun 〔cannon〕.
**포악**(暴惡) violence; outrage (난폭); ruthlessness; cruelty (무자비); atrocity (잔학); barbarity. ~하다 (be) atrocious; ruthless; outrageous; barbarous. ¶ ~무도한 살인범 a ruthless 〔diabolical〕 murderer / ~한 짓을 하다 commit 〔perpetrate〕 atrocities 〔outrages〕.
**포안**(砲眼) 《성벽의》 an embrasure; a gun hole.
**포연**(砲煙) the smoke of cannon; artillery smoke; battle smoke.
**포열**(砲列) a battery (line); a train of artillery. ¶ ~을 배치하다 lay 〔arrange, position〕 a field battery; place guns in position.
**포엽**(苞葉) 〚식물〛 a bract. ¶ ~의 bracteal / ~이 있는 bracteate.
**포옹**(抱擁) an embrace; a hug. ~하다 embrace; hug; cuddle; hold 《*a person*》 to *one's* breast 〔in *one's* arms〕. ¶ 서로 ~하다 embrace each other.
**포용**(包容) inclusion; tolerance. ~하다 include; tolerate. ¶ 갖가지 다른 의견들을 ~하다 tolerate different opinions / 사람을 ~할 아량이 있다 have the capacity for tolerance.
◉ ~력 broad-mindedness; tolerance: ~력이 있는 사람 a broad-minded 〔magnanimous〕 person (도량이 넓은); a liberal and tolerant person (관대한) / ~력이 크다 possess a capacious mind; be so broad-minded as to admit men of all shades. ~정책 《북한에 대한 한국의》 the engagement policy; the "sunshine policy" of engagement with the North.
**포워드** 〚스포츠〛 a forward (생략 F.W.).
**포위**(包圍) encirclement; envelopment; a siege; besiegement. ~하다 close in; surround; encircle; besiege; 《경찰이》 throw a cordon around 《a place》. ¶ 적을 ~하다 lay siege to the enemy / ~를 풀다 raise 〔lift〕 the siege 《of a town》 / 겹겹이 ~되다 be closely surrounded 《by》; be closely besieged / 적의 ~를 뚫다 break through the besieging enemy forces / 그들은 3면에서 적군을 ~했다 They surrounded the enemy from three sides. / 경찰은 그들의 은신처를 ~했다 The police closed in on their hideout.
◉ ~공격 an enveloping attack. ~군 a besieging army. ~망 an encircling net. ~사격 enveloping fire. ~작전 an encircling 〔enveloping〕 operation. ~전 a siege warfare; a battle of encirclement. ~태세 an encircling formation: ~태세를 취하다 get into encir-

cling formation.

**포유**(哺乳) lactation; suckling; nursing. ~하다 suckle; give suck to; nurse 《*one's* baby》. ◉ ~동물 a mammal; a mammalian; a suckler: ~ 동물학 mammalogy / ~ 동물학자 a mammalogist. ~류 〖동물〗 Mammalia.

**포육**(脯肉) 《미》 jerked meat; (beef) jerky; dried meat.

**포의**(布衣) a scholar without a government position; a commoner.

**포인터** 《개》 a pointer.

**포인트** 《경기의 득점》 a score; a point; 《전철기》 a (railroad) switch; points; a point switch; 《활자의》 point; 《소수점》 a decimal point; 《요점》 the point 《of a story》. ¶ 6 ~ 활자 6-point type / ~에서 벗어나다 be beside 〔off〕 the point / ~를 올리다〔따다〕 gain 〔score, get, win〕 a point / ~를 잃다 lose a point / ~에서 이기다 outpoint 《*a person*》 / 나는 그의 설명의 ~를 잡지 못했다 I didn't get the point of his explanation. ◉ ~게터 a scorer, a point getter.

**포자**(胞子) 〖생물〗 a spore. ◉ ~낭(囊) a sporocyst. ~생식 reproduction by spore; sporogenesis; sporogony.

**포장**(布帳) a linen awning 〔screen〕; a curtain; 《마차의》 a roof; a hood; 《자동차의》 a (convertable) top. ¶ ~을 씌우다〔걷다〕 pull up 〔let down〕 the hood.

**포장**(包裝) packing; packaging; wrapping. ~하다 pack; package 《미》; wrap 《it》 (up). ¶ ~ 상자 무료 제공 《게시》 Case free. *or* Packaging free. *or* No charge for case. / 상자로 ~하다 pack 《*a thing*》 in a box / ~을 풀다 unwrap 《a package》; unpack 《a box》 / ~이 잘 되어 있다〔나쁘다〕 be well 〔badly, defectively〕 packed / ~은 될 수 있는 대로 잘 해야 한다 Packing must be done with the greatest possible care. / 이 라디오를 선물용으로 ~해 주세요 Please gift-wrap this radio. / 과잉 ~은 천연 자원의 낭비이다 Overpackaging wastes natural resources.
◉ ~기계 a packing machine; a packer. ~물 a package. ~비 a packing charge. ~육(肉) packaged meat. ~재료 packing materials. ~지 packing 〔wrapping〕 paper.

**포장**(褒章) a medal 《for merit》.

**포장**(鋪裝) paving; pavement. ~하다 pave 《a road with asphalt》. ¶ 훌륭하게 ~된 도로 a well-paved road / 갓 ~된 도로 a newly paved road / 콘크리트로 ~하다 pave a road with concrete. ◉ ~공사 pavement work(s); paving (operation). ~도로 a paved road; a pavement: 아스팔트 ~도로 an asphalt pavement; an asphalt-surfaced road. ~재료 paving materials.

**포장마차**(布帳馬車) ① a covered carriage 〔wagon 《미》〕; a (horse and) buggy (소형의); 〖미국 역사〗 a prairie schooner 〔wagon〕. ② 《술 파는》 a movable bar on a covered cart in which liquor and some simple side dishes are served; a covered cart bar; a small wheeled snack bar with a tent; a *pojangmacha*.

**포전**(砲戰) 《engage in》 an artillery fight.

**포졸**(捕卒) 〖고제도〗 a raiding constable; a thieftaker 《영》.

**포좌**(砲座) a gun platform; a gun rest 〔mount〕.

**포주**(抱主) the master 〔mistress, keeper〕 of a brothel; a whoremonger; a pimp.

**포즈** a pose. ¶ ~를 취하다 pose (*oneself*) 《as a model》; strike 〔get into〕 a pose; take *one's* pose / ~를 바꾸다 change *one's* pose; enter into a new pose / 사진을 찍기 위해 ~를 취하다 pose for *one's* picture; pose for a photograph / ~를 취하게 하다 pose 《*a person*》.

**포지션** a position. ¶ ~을 맡다 take 〔assume〕 a position / 자기 ~을 지키다 stand 〔guard〕 *one's* position / ~이 바뀌다 be changed in *one's* position.

**포지티브** 《적극적인·양성의》 positive; 〖사진〗 a photographic positive.

**포진**(布陣) the lineup 《of》; lines. ~하다 line up; take up *one's* position; 《군대를》 array troops for battle. ¶ 경찰 기동대는 바리케이드 앞에 ~했다 The riot police took up their position in front of the barricade.

**포진**(疱疹) 〖의학〗 herpes. ¶ 입언저리 ~ cold sores; fever blisters 〔sores〕 / 단순 ~ herpes simplex / 대상(帶狀) ~ *herpes zoster* (L.); shingles.

**포차**(砲車) a gun carriage.

**포착**(捕捉) 《붙잡음》 capture; 《이해》 apprehension. ~하다 catch; seize (and hold); take 〔catch〕 hold of; pick up; 《이해하다》 understand. ¶ ~하기 어려운 elusive; intangible; hard 〔difficult〕 to understand / 기회를 ~하다 seize an opportunity / 뜻을 ~하기 어렵다 can hardly grasp the meaning / 레이더가 국적불명의 비행기를 ~했

다 The radar picked up a plane of unknown nationality.

**포충망**(捕蟲網) 「an insect 〔a butterfly〕 net.

**포충엽**(捕蟲葉) 〖식물〗 an insectivorous leaf.

**포츠담** 《독일의 도시》 Potsdam. ◉ ~선언 the Potsdam Declaration (of 1945). ~협정 the Potsdam Agreement.

**포츠머스** 《미국 항구 이름》 Portsmouth. ◉ ~조약 the Portsmouth Peace Treaty (1905).

**포커** 《카드놀이》 poker. ¶ ~를 치다 play poker. ◉ ~페이스 《wear》 a poker face: ~ 페이스의 poker-faced.

**포켓** 《웃저고리의》 a pocket; an inside pocket (안의); a breast pocket (가슴의); a side pocket (양 옆의); 《바지의》 a trouser pocket; a hip pocket (뒤의). ¶ ~이 없는 바지 pocketless trousers / ~에 양손을 지르고 with *one's* hands in *one's* pockets / ~에 넣다 pocket; put 《*a thing*》 in(to) *one's* pocket / ~에서 꺼내다 take 《a letter》 out of *one's* pocket / ~을 달다 sew up a pocket 《on a coat》 / ~을 뒤지다 search *one's* pocket; fish 〔feel〕 in *one's* pocket 《for》 / ~이 불룩하다 Your pockets are bagging. ◉ ~머니 pocket money. ~북 a pocket(-sized) book. ~판 a pocket edition: ~판 사전 a pocket dictionary. ~형 a pocket-size.

**포크**[1] 《식사용》 a fork. ¶ 한 벌의 나이프와 ~ a knife and fork. ◉ ~볼 〖야구〗 a fork ball. 디저트용 ~ a dessert fork. 샐러드용 ~ a salad fork. 식사용 〔식탁용〕 ~ a 「dinner 〔table〕 fork.

**포크**[2] 《돼지고기》 pork. ◉ ~소테 pork *sauté*. ~촙 pork chop. ~커틀릿 a pork cutlet.

**포크댄스** a folk dance; folk dancing.

**포크리프트** 《지게차》 a forklift.

**포크송** a folk song. ◉ ~가수 a folk singer.

**포타슘** 〖화학〗 potassium.

**포타주** 《진한 수프》 thick 〔cream〕 soup; *potage* (F.).

**포탄**(砲彈) a shell; an artillery shell; a cannonball. ¶ ~의 연기 shell smoke / 적에게 ~을 퍼붓다 fire shells over the enemy; rain artillery fire on the enemy / 빗발치는 ~ 속을 전진하다 advance under a rain of shells.

**포탈**(逋脫) 《세금의》 tax evasion. ~하다 evade 〔dodge〕 a tax; defraud the revenue. ◉ 세금 ~액 the amount of the tax evasion. 세금 ~자 a tax evader.

**포탑**(砲塔) a (gun) turret; a cupola; 《군함의》 a barbette.

**포태**(胞胎) conception; pregnancy. ~하다 conceive; get pregnant.

**포터** a (luggage) porter 《영》; a redcap 《미》; 《공항의》 a skycap.

**포터블** portable. ¶ ~라디오 a portable radio / ~컴퓨터 a laptop computer.

**포토** 《사진》 a photo. ◉ ~스튜디오 a photo studio. ~콘테스트 a photo contest.

**포트와인** 《포도주》 port wine.

**포트폴리오** 《장관의 직》 portfolio; 《서류가방·명세표》 a portfolio.

**포파이** 《만화 주인공》 Popeye.

**포퓰러** popular(ity). ¶ ~한 popular; well-known. ◉ ~뮤직 popular 〔pop〕 music. ~송 a 「popular 〔pop〕 song.

**포플러** 〖식물〗 a poplar.

**포플린** poplin; broadcloth 《미》.

**포피**(包皮) 〖해부〗 the foreskin; the prepuce. ¶ ~의 preputial.

**포학**(暴虐) tyranny; outrage; atrocity. ~하다 (be) tyrannical; outrageous; atrocious. ¶ ~한 군주 a tyrant; a 「cruel 〔bloody〕 ruler / 온갖 ~한 짓을 다하다 commit every sort of atrocity. ◉ ~무도 tyranny and injustice.

**포함**(包含) inclusion; comprehension; implication. ~하다 include; contain; comprehend; 《뜻을》 imply. ¶ …을 ~해서 including…; inclusive of… / 모든 비용을 ~해서 including all expenses 《of》; all charges included / …을 ~하지 않고 excluding…; exclusive of… / 다량의 탄산가스를 ~한 공기 air loaded with carbonic acid gas / …에 ~되다 〔~되어 있다〕 be 「comprised 〔included〕 in / ~시키다 include; count 《in, among》 / 신축 비용은 세금을 ~해서 총액 5천만 원이 된다 The building expenses amount to fifty million won including the tax. / 그들 속에는 여자가 셋 ~되어 있었다 Three women were included among them. / 이 술은 알코올이 15% ~되어 있다 This liquor contains 15% of alcohol. / 민주주의란 말에는 어떤 뜻이 ~되어 있는가 What is implied by the word democracy? ◉ ~량 the (amount of) content. ~률 the percentage of content. 세금~ 〖상업〗 duty paid. 운임~ 〖상업〗 freight prepaid 《미》; carriage paid 《영》.

**포함**(砲艦) 〖해군〗 a gunboat. ¶ ~ 외교 gunboat diplomacy.

**포핸드** 〖테니스·탁구〗 a forehand.

**포화**(砲火) (a) gunfire; (a) shellfire; (an) artillery fire. ¶ ~의 섬광 a gun-flash / ～(의 세례)를 받다 be under heavy fire / ～를 퍼붓다 rain fire 《on the enemy》; bring 《the enemy》 under fire / 서로 ～를 주고 받다 exchange fire / ～를 집중시키다 concentrate fire 《on》.

**포화**(飽和) 〖화학·물리〗 saturation. ～하다 get 〔be〕 saturated; be in saturation. ¶ ～시키다 saturate 〔charge〕 《with》. ◉ ～곡선 a saturation curve. ～기 a saturator. ～도 a degree of saturation. ～액 a saturated liquid. ～온도 saturation temperature. ～용액 a saturated solution. ～전류 a saturation current. ～점 the saturation point. ～증기 saturated vapor 〔steam〕. ～화합물 〖화학〗 a saturated compound.

**포화상태**(飽和狀態) (a state of ) saturation. ¶ ～에 있다 be in saturation; be saturated / 서울의 교통 사정은 ～에 있다 The streets of Seoul are completely choked 〔extremely congested〕 with traffic. / 한국의 인구는 ～에 있다 Korea cannot stand any further increase of its population.

**포환**(砲丸) 〖스포츠〗 a shot; a weight; 《포탄》 a cannonball. ¶ ～을 던지다 put a shot. ◉ ～던지기 the shot-put: ～던지기 선수 a shot-putter.

**포획**(捕獲) capture; (a) seizure. ～하다 capture; seize; catch. ¶ 적선을 세 척 ～하다 capture 〔seize, make prize of 〕 three enemy ships. ◉ ～량 a catch 《of whales》. ～물 a prize; a booty. ～선 a captured ship. ～자 a captor.

**포효**(咆哮) 《맹수의》 roaring; 《개·늑대의》 howling. ～하다 roar; howl. ¶ 호랑이의 ～ the roars of a tiger / ～하는 파도 소리 the roar of the sea.

**폭**(幅) ① 《너비》 width; breadth. ¶ 폭(이) 넓은 wide; broad / 폭이 좁은 narrow / 폭을 넓히다 widen; broaden / 이 강의 ～은 얼마인가 How wide is this river? / 폭이 15미터이다 It is fifteen meters wide 〔across〕. ② 《도량·포용성》 generosity; broad-mindedness; caliber; 《범위》 range; 《여지》 latitude. ¶ 지식의 폭을 넓히다 enlarge the range of *one's* knowledge / 폭이 넓은 사람 a man of large 〔great〕 caliber / 폭넓은 의견을 수렴하다 collect extensive opinions from the people / 그녀는 요즘 연기의 폭이 넓어졌다 Her performances have gained in depth 〔breadth〕. / 방침 결정에서 선택의 폭을 다소 주다 allow 《*a person*》 some latitude in determining the course of action. ③ 《영향력·세력》 influence; power. ¶ 그는 이 부근에서는 폭넓은 영향력이 있다 He has great influence over 〔on〕 the people around here. ④ 《값의 차이》 ¶ 값의 폭이 크다 The price range is large. ⑤ 《그림 따위의》 a piece 《of picture》; a scroll. ¶ 그림 한 폭 a scroll (picture) / 두 폭 병풍 a double-folded screen / 그 경치는 마치 한 폭의 그림을 펼쳐 놓은 것 같다 The scene looks like a picture scroll spread out.

**폭** ① 《또래》 of the same age group. ¶ 그들은 내 어린 동생 폭밖에 안 된다 They must be of the same age group as my little brother. ② 《정도》 approximately; about; 《비율》 rate; ratio. ¶ 천 명에 하나 폭으로 in the ratio of one to a thousand persons / 하루 만 원 폭으로 at the rate of 10,000 won a day / 열 시간 폭이 된다 It's about 10 hours. ③ 《셈》 supposition; accounting 《for》; (to all) appearances; seeming. ¶ 잘 되긴 잘 된 폭이지 Still, it turned out all right, I guess (but...).

**폭거**(暴擧) (an act of ) violence; a rash 〔reckless〕 act 〔attempt〕; outrage; violence; a riot (폭동). ¶ ～로 나오다 resort to 〔use〕 violence; make a reckless attempt / 인간의 존엄을 침해하는 ～ an outrage against human dignity.

**폭격**(爆擊) (aerial) bombing 〔bombardment〕; a bombing attack 〔raid〕. ～하다 bomb; bombard; make a bombing raid. ¶ 도시를 무차별 ～하다 bomb city indiscriminately / 그 도시는 바다와 공중에서 ～당했다 The city was bombarded from sea and air. ◉ ～대 a bombing squadron; an air strike force. ～목표 a bombing target. ～수 a bombardier. ～조준기 a bombsight.

**폭격기**(爆擊機) a 《heavy, light》 bomber. ¶ 전투～ a fighter-bomber / B-52 장거리～ a B-52 long-range bomber. ◉ ～대 a squadron of bombers; a bomber 〔bombing〕 fleet.

**폭군**(暴君) a tyrant; 《전제 군주》 a despot. ¶ 남편은 집에 있을 때 종종 ～이 되곤 한다 My husband often bosses myself and children in the house.

**폭도**(暴徒) a mob; mobsters; rioters. ¶ ～를 진압하다 put down a mob / ～의 습격을 받다 be mobbed / ～화하다 turn into a mob / ～들은 거리를 휩쓸었다 The mob stormed through the street.

**폭동**(暴動) a riot; a disturbance; an uprising. ¶ ~을 일으키다 start 〔raise〕 a riot; create a disturbance / ~을 진압하다 suppress 〔put down〕 a riot / 교도소 안에서 ~이 일어났다 A riot broke out in the jail. ◉ ~자 a rioter; a rebel; 《군대의》 a mutineer. ~죄 (a charge of) sedition. ~ 진압 경찰 riot police; a riot squad.

**폭등**(暴騰) a sudden 〔sharp〕 rise; a boom 《미》; a jump. ~하다 rise steeply; jump; soar; go up sharply; skyrocket; boom. ¶ ~하는 물가 soaring prices; boom prices 《미》 / 5백 원에서 천 원으로 ~하다 jump from 500 to 1,000 won / 인플레로 물가가 ~하고 있다 Prices are soaring 〔skyrocketing〕 owing to the inflation. / 물가가 ~했다 Prices have taken a jump. *or* There has been a sudden rise in prices.

**폭락**(暴落) a sudden 〔heavy〕 fall; a slump; a crash; a sharp 〔steep〕 decline. ~하다 drop 〔fall, decline〕 sharply; decline heavily; nose-dive; plummet; plunge. ¶ 주가의 ~ a heavy fall 〔steep decline〕 in stock prices / 주식 시장의 ~ a slump 〔plunge〕 in stockmarket / 인기가 ~되다 have a sudden fall in *one's* popularity / 은행주가 크게 ~했다 Bank stocks showed a big drop. / 그녀는 주식의 ~으로 2천만원의 손실을 보았다 She lost twenty million won in a slump in stocks.

**폭력**(暴力) violence; force; brute force. ¶ 가정내 ~ domestic 〔family〕 violence / ~으로 by force 〔violence〕; by recourse to violence / ~을 가하다 cause 〔offer〕 violence 《to》; commit violence 《toward》 / ~을 휘두르다〔행사하다〕 use 〔employ, resort to〕 violence; use *one's* fist; do violence to 《*a person*》 / ~으로 강제〔강요〕하다 coerce 《*a person* to *do* it》 by violence; bulldoze 《*a person* to *do* it》 / ~에 호소하다 appeal 〔resort〕 to force; use force; have recourse to violence / ~이 난무하다 an act of violence prevails 《on》 / ~으로 돈을 빼앗다 take money by force / 하나의 ~은 다른 폭력을 가져오고 그것은 또 다른 폭력을 불러일으킨다 An assault would lead to another violence, and would give rise to a third one.
◉ ~교실 a classroom ruled by violence. ~단 a strong-arm gang; a gang of toughs: ~단원 a gangster / ~단 일제 검거〔소탕〕 a rounding-up of gangsters. ~배 hooligans; street-toughs: 학교 주변의 ~배 hooligans lurking around schools / ~배의 단속을 강화하다 tighten control on hooligans. ~범죄 a crime of violence. ~정치 terrorism in politics; strong-arm politics. ~조직 an organized group of gangsters. ~지배〔주의〕 club law. ~행사 use of violence 〔force〕. ~행위 use 〔an act〕 of violence; gangsterism: ~ 행위 등 처벌에 관한 법률 《violate》 the Law on Punishment of Violent Acts. ~혁명 a violent 〔an armed〕 revolution. 조직 ~ violence committed by a criminal organization; organized crime. 집단 ~ organized violence.

**폭로**(暴露) exposure; disclosure; *exposé*(F.). ~하다 expose; disclose; reveal; divulge; bring 《*a matter*》 to light; 《구어》 rake (up) the muck 《about》. ¶ ~되다 be exposed; be discovered; be betrayed; come 〔be brought〕 to light; be disclosed / ~하겠다고 위협하여 under threat of exposure / 비밀을 ~하다 divulge 《*a person's*》 secret; reveal 〔expose〕 a secret / 사회에 ~하다 make a public disclosure of 《*a matter*》 / 아무의 정체를 ~하다 show *a person* in *his* true color / 자기의 무지를 ~하다 betray *one's* ignorance. ◉ ~기사 an *exposé*. ~소설 a telltale story. ~전술 exposure 〔muckraking 《미구어》〕 tactics.

**폭뢰**(爆雷) a depth charge 〔bomb〕; an antisubmarine bomb.

**폭리**(暴利) excessive profits; exorbitant interest; unfair profits 〔profiteering〕 (부당한); usury (고리의). ¶ ~를 취하는 사람 a profiteer / ~를 취하다 profiteer 《in》; make undue 〔excessive〕 profits 《on》 / ~를 단속하다 control profiteering.

**폭명**(爆鳴) detonation. ◉ ~가스 detonating gas.

**폭민**(暴民) rioters; a mob. ◉ ~정치 mob rule; mobocracy; ochlocracy.

**폭발**(爆發) (an) explosion; detonation; blasting; blowing up; 《화산의》 (an) eruption. ~하다 explode; burst out; blow up; go off; erupt (화산이).
¶ 가스의 ~ explosion of gas / 전후의 인구 ~ the population explosion after the war / ~시키다 explode; burst (up); detonate; blow up; set 《a dynamite》 off / ~ 직전에 있다 be close to (the) explosion point / 보일러가 ~했다

A boiler exploded. / 화약통이 ～했다 The barrel of gunpowder blew up. / 그의 노여움이 ～했다 His anger exploded. *or* He exploded with rage. / 평소의 울분이 ～했다 Their smoldering resentment burst into flame. / 화학약품 공장에서 ～이 일어났다「An explosion occurred 〔There was an explosion〕 at a chemical factory. / 유엔 평화 유지군은 세계 도처의 ～ 직전에 있는 지역에서 활동 중이다 U.N. peacekeeping forces are in action in flash=points around the world.
◉ ～가스 explosive gas. ～력 explosive power. ～물 an explosive: ～물 처리반 a bomb disposal unit. ～방지 장치《보일러의》 a hydrostat. ～성 explosiveness: ～성의 explosive《compounds, substances》. ～신관 a detonating fuse. ～약 blasting 〔detonating〕 powder; an explosive. ～음 a blast; an explosion. ～지점 the point of explosion. ～탄 an explosive shell; a bombshell; a bomb.

**폭발적**(爆發的) explosive. ¶ ～으로 explosively / ～인 인기《win, enjoy》 tremendous popularity / ～인 인구 증가 a population explosion / ～으로 팔리다 sell like hot cakes / 젊은이들 사이에는 요즘 비디오 게임이 ～인 인기다 Enthusiasm for video games is now raging among young people.

**폭사**(爆死) death by explosion. ～하다 be killed by a bomb; die in an explosion.

**폭삭** entirely; wholly; completely. ¶ 건물이 ～ 주저앉았다 The building collapsed completely.

**폭서**(暴暑) intense 〔severe, torrid〕 heat (of summer).

**폭설**(暴雪) a heavy (fall of) snow; a heavy snowfall. ¶ ～ 지역 an area of high snowfall / ～에 파묻히다 be buried 〔stalled〕 in a snowdrift; be snowed under.

**폭소**(爆笑) a burst 〔roar〕 of laughter; an explosive laugh 〔laughter〕; uproarious laughter. ～하다 roar with laughter; burst into laughter; burst out laughing. ¶ 청중을 ～케 하다 set *one's* audience into a roar of laughter / ～가 터졌다 There was a burst of laughter.

**폭스테리어**《개》 a fox terrier.

**폭스트롯**《dance》 a fox-trot.

**폭식**(暴食) overeating; gluttony; gorging. ～하다 overeat; eat too much; gorge; make a pig of *oneself*.
◉ ～가 an excessive eater; a glutton.

**폭심(지)**(爆心(地)) the center of an explosion;《원폭의》 the hypocenter; ground zero.

**폭압**(暴壓) oppression; coercion; repression; subduing.

**폭약**(爆藥) an explosive; blasting powder. ¶ 고성능 ～ high explosives / ～을 장치하다 lay 〔set〕 an explosive / ～에 점화하다 set off the blasting powder.

**폭언**(暴言)《난폭한 말》 violent 〔harsh, intemperate〕 language;《욕지거리》 abusive words;《부당한 말》 an unreasonable statement. ～하다 use offensive 〔abusive, crude, violent〕 language; talk rudely 〔abusively〕.

**폭염**(暴炎) scorching heat wave; the scorching 〔intense〕 heat of summer.

**폭우**(暴雨) a heavy 〔violent〕 rain; a (heavy, great) downpour; a torrential rain. ¶ ～로 피해를 입다 be damaged by a heavy rain.

**폭위**(暴威) tyranny; violence; abuse of power. ¶ ～를 떨치다 tyrannize《over》; act tyrannically; play havoc《with》.

**폭음**(暴飮) drinking too much; heavy 〔excessive〕 drinking. ～하다 drink too much 〔to excess〕; be intemperate. ◉ ～폭식 excessive drinking and eating: ～폭식하다 overeat and overdrink; eat and drink to excess 〔immoderately〕.

**폭음**(爆音)《폭발음》 an explosion; an explosive 〔a bursting〕 sound;《엔진 등의》 a roar; roaring. ¶ 제트기 ～에 괴롭힘을 당하다 be annoyed by the noisy roar of jet planes / ～은 1마일 밖에서도 들렸다 The explosion was heard a mile away.

**폭정**(暴政) tyranny; despotism; despotic rule; tyrannical government. ¶ ～을 펴다 tyrannize (over a country) / ～에 시달리다 groan under tyranny.

**폭주**(暴走)〖야구〗a reckless run;《자동차 등의》 reckless driving; speeding. ～하다 run 〔drive〕 recklessly. ¶ 그는 차를 ～했다 He drove his car recklessly. ◉ ～열차〔택시〕 a runaway train 〔taxi〕. ～운전 reckless driving. ～족 crazy 〔reckless〕 drivers; a motorcycle gang; hell's angels; bikers《구어》: 그는 ～족이다 He belongs to a motorcycle gang. *or* He's a motorcycle gang member.

**폭주**(暴酒) ＝폭음(暴飮). ◉ ～가 a hard drinker; a wine bibber; a soaker.

**폭주**(輻輳) (over)crowding; congestion《of traffic》; pressure《of business, orders》; influx 《of people》. ～하다 be (over)crowded; be congested 《with》. ¶ 교통의 ～ a traffic jam 〔congestion〕/ 화물의〔우편물의〕 ～ a congestion of goods 〔mail matter〕/ 주문의 ～ pressure 〔a flood〕 of orders / ～를 완화하다 relieve the congestion 《of》/ 도심의 교통 ～로 늦어지다 be delayed by the congestion of traffic in town.

**폭죽**(爆竹) a (fire)cracker; a petard; a flip-flap; a squib 《미》. ¶ ～을 터뜨리다 fire squibs; set 〔shoot〕 off firecrackers / 중국인은 악령을 쫓는데 ～을 사용한다 The Chinese use crackers to frighten away evil spirits.

**폭침**(爆沈) blowing up; sinking by an explosion. ～하다 blow up; sink by an explosion.

**폭탄**(爆彈) a bomb; a bombshell. ¶ ～을 투하하다 bomb; drop a bomb 《on a city》/ 시한 ～을 설치하다 set a time bomb. ◉ ～선언 a bombshell declaration; a thunderbolt-like declaration: ～ 선언을 하다 make a bombshell announcement. ～적재량 bomb carrying capacity. ～투하 bombing; bomb-dropping: ～ 투하기 a bomb-release. 고성능～ a TNT 〔high explosive〕 bomb.

**폭탄주**(爆彈酒) *poktanju;* 《미》 boilermaker; a glass of beer with a smaller glass of whiskey submerged in it (and a participant is forced to drink it like a shot).

**폭투**(暴投) 〖야구〗《투수의》 a wild pitch; 《선수의》 a wild throw; a throwing error. ～하다 《투수가》 pitch wild 《to a batter》; throw a wild ball; throw wild (to first base).

**폭파**(爆破) blasting; blowing up; explosion. ～하다 blast; blow up; explode. ¶ 다이너마이트로 암석을 ～하다 blast a rock with dynamite / 다리를 ～하다 blow up a bridge. ◉ ～작업 blasting operations.

**폭포**(瀑布) a waterfall; falls; a cascade (갈라진); a cataract (큰). ¶ 나이아가라 ～ (the) Niagara Falls / 여러 단계를 이루어 떨어지는 ～ a waterfall dropping down a series of cascades / ～처럼 쏟아지다 fall 〔come down〕 in cataracts 〔torrents〕.

**폭풍**(暴風) a wild 〔violent〕 wind; a windstorm; a storm. ¶ ～의 진로 a storm lane / ～의 중심 a storm center; the eye of a storm / ～을 만나다 encounter a storm; be overtaken by a storm / ～이 지나갔다 The storm is over 〔gone〕. / ～이 일었다〔잠잠해졌다〕 A storm rose 〔abated〕. ◉ ～경보〔주의보〕 a storm warning 〔alert〕. ～권 a storm area 〔zone〕: ～권 안에 있다 be within the storm zone. ～설 a snow-storm; a blizzard. ～피해 storm damage; havoc wrought by storms.

**폭풍**(爆風) a bombshell 〔detonation〕 blast.

**폭풍우**(暴風雨) a storm; a rainstorm; a tempest; a hurricane (서인도 제도의); a typhoon (태풍). ¶ ～의 stormy / ～로 파괴된 damaged by storms / ～로 고립된 마을 a stormbound village / ～가 맹위를 떨쳤다 The storm ran riot. / ～가 그쳤다 The storm passed off 〔blew out〕. / ～의 뒤끝은 고요했다 The storm was followed by a great calm. / 일기 예보에서 ～가 있을 것이라고 한다 The forecast says there will be storms.

**폭한**(暴寒) severe 〔intense〕 cold.

**폭한**(暴漢) a ruffian; a rowdy; a thug; a tough 《미》. ¶ ～에게 습격당하다 be assaulted by a thug.

**폭행**(暴行) (an act of ) violence; riotous conduct; an outrage; an assault; 《부녀자에 대한》 a rape. ～하다 make an assault upon 《*a person*》; behave violently; rape 《a woman》; commit an outrage. ¶ ～을 가하다 assault; attack; do 〔use〕 violence to 《*a person*》/ 시체에는 ～의 흔적이 보이지 않았다 The body bore no marks of violence. / 그는 아내에게 ～을 가해 이혼당했다 He was divorced for being violent toward his wife. ◉ ～자 an outrager; an assaulter; a violator; a rapist (부녀자에 대한).

**폰** 〖물리〗《음의 크기 단위》 a phon. ¶ 신형 항공기용 엔진의 소음은 120폰이었다 The noise level of the new air-plane engine registered 120 phons.

**폴** 〖레슬링〗 a fall. ¶ 폴승 a victory by a fall / 폴로 이기다 win by a fall; beat 〔defeat〕 《*one's* opponent》 by a fall.

**폴라로이드** 《인조 편광판》 a polaroid. ◉ ～ 카메라 《상표명》 a Polaroid (Land) camera.

**폴라리스** 《미사일 무기》 a Polaris (missile). ◉ ～ 잠수함 a Polaris(-armed) submarine: ～형 잠수함 a submarine of the Polaris type.

**폴란드** Poland. ¶ ～의 Polish. ◉ ～말 Polish. ～인 a Pole; the Poles [총칭].

**폴로** 〖스포츠〗 polo. ¶ ～ 볼 a polo ball. ◉ ～경기자 a poloist; a polo player. ～스틱 a polo stick.

**폴로네즈** 〖음악·무용〗 (a) polonaise. ¶ ~를 추다 dance the polonaise; polonaise.
**폴로늄** 〖화학〗 polonium (기호 Po).
**폴로셔츠** a polo shirt.
**폴리네시아** 《대양주 동부의》 Polynesia. ¶ ~의 Polynesian.
**폴리에스테르** 〖화학〗 polyester.
**폴리에틸렌** 〖화학〗 polyethylene. ◉ ~글리콜 polyethylene glycol.
**폴리오** ① 〖의학〗 《소아마비》 polio. ② 〖인쇄〗 a folio.
**폴리우레탄** 〖화학〗 polyurethan(e).
**폴리텐** 《합성수지》 polythene.
**폴리펩티드** 〖화학〗 a polypeptide.
**폴리프로필렌** 〖화학〗 polypropylene. ◉ ~옥시드 polypropylene oxide.
**폴카** 《춤》 (a) polka. ¶ ~를 추다 dance the polka; polka.
**폴트** 《테니스의》 a fault (서브의 실패).
**폼** 《모양·형태》 form; carriage; way of holding *oneself*. ¶ ~이 좋다 have a nice form; have a smart carriage.
**폼페이** 《이탈리아의 옛 도시》 Pompeii.
**퐁당** with a 「splash 〔plop〕. ¶ (물에) ~ 빠지다 fall plop into 《the water》; drop into 《the water》 with a splash; flop into 《the water》 / (물에) ~ 뛰어들다 jump into 《the water》 with a splash; plunge with a splash.
**퐁당거리다** keep 「splashing 〔plunging〕. ¶ 물 가운데서 ~ splash about in the water.
**퐁당퐁당** with splashes; with splash after splash. ¶ 물에 ~ 뛰어들다 jump into the water splash-splash-splash; plunge into the water / ~ 헤엄치다 swim splashing the water.
**퐁퐁** ① 《방귀를》 《flatulating》 in poops; with a poop-poop-poop! ② 《구멍이》 breaking open repeatedly. ③ 《샘솟다》 bubbling; gurgling.
**표**(表) ① 《일람표·목록 따위》 a table; a tabular statement; a schedule (예정표); a diagram; a chart; a list (목록). ¶ 시간표 a time table; 《학교의》 a schedule / 표에(서) 보인 바와 같이 as shown in the table / 표로 만들다 tabulate; put into tabular form; make into a table; make a list of; list. ② 《표지·표시》 a sign; a token; a souvenir. ⇨ 표지·표시. ③ 《상서》 a memorial to the Throne. ¶ 표를 올리다 memorialize the King 《on》; appeal to the Emperor 《for》.
**표**(票) ① 《돈으로 사는 권(券)》 a ticket; a coupon (ticket). ¶ 표 파는 곳 a ticket 「office 〔cage, counter〕; a booking 「office 〔window〕 《영》; a box office (극장의) / 왕복표 a round-trip ticket 《미》; a return (ticket) / 입장표 an admission 〔entrance〕 ticket / 점심 식사표 a 「ticket 〔coupon〕 for lunch / 당일 유효표 a day ticket; a ticket available on the day of issue only / 표를 끊다〔사다〕 get 〔buy, take〕 a ticket; book 《for Busan》 / 표를 검사하다 examine a ticket / 표를 찍다 punch 〔clip〕 a ticket / 광주까지의 2등표를 하나 주시오 (Please give me) a second=class (ticket) to Gwangju.
② 《쪽지·딱지》 a card; a label (병·짐 등에 붙이는); a tag (꼬리표·짐표); 《보관표》 a receipt; a check; a chit (영수증·전표 등). ¶ 번호표 a number check / 이름표 a name 「card 〔plate〕 / 짐표 a baggage check / (짐에) 꼬리표를 달다 fasten 〔attach, fix 《미》〕 a 「label 〔tag〕 to 《a trunk》; tag 〔label〕 《*one's* luggage》 / 표를 붙이다 paste a 「card 〔label〕; label 《a package, a bottle》; put a tag 《on an article》.
③ 《투표의》 a vote; a ballot (paper). ¶ 깨끗한 한 표 an honest vote / 표를 얻다〔모으다〕 win 〔get, draw, gather, round up〕 votes / (깨끗한) 한 표를 던지다 cast a (clean) 「vote 〔ballot〕 《for *a person*》 / 500표 중 215표를 얻다 poll 〔win〕 215 votes of 500 cast / 동의는 45표 대 23표로 부결되었다 The motion was rejected by a vote of 45 to 23. / 그는 상대를 5백 표 리드하고 있었다 He led his opponent by 500 votes.
◉ 고정표 solid 〔an assured, a safe〕 vote; solid 〔assured〕 support (전체): 그는 종교 단체의 고정표로 당선됐다 He is elected on loyal support from religious organizations. 농촌표 farm vote(s): 농촌표는 여당의 것이다 The farm vote belongs to the Government party. 동정표 sympathy votes. 부동표 floating 〔shifting, uncommitted〕 votes: 그는 부동표 획득에 애를 썼다 He tried hard to attract floating votes. 여성표 women's votes. 조직표 organized votes. 지지표 (votes cast in) support.
**표**(標) ① 《부호·푯말》 a mark; a sign. ¶ 별표 an asterisk; a star / 물음표 a note of interrogation / 표를 하다 mark; put a mark 《on》. ② 《휘장》 a badge; a mark. ¶ 모자표 a badge on *one's* cap / 회원표 a membership badge / 표를 달다 wear a badge. ③ 《증거·증》 a written statement; a bond;

a deed; a proof; a testimony. ¶ 돈표 a voucher; a check. ④《표적》a token; a sign; a manifestation. ¶ 감사하다는 표로 in token of *one's* gratitude; as a mark of *one's* appreciation.

**표결**(表決) =의결(議決)

**표결**(票決) a vote; voting; a decision by vote. ~하다 take a vote《on》. ¶ 아슬아슬한 ~《by》a close vote《of 100 to 99》/ ~에 들어가다 come to a vote / ~에 부치다 put 〔submit〕《a bill》to a vote 〔ballot〕/ ~을 요구하다 call for a division《on *a matter*》.

**표고**《버섯》a *p'yogo* (mushroom); *Lentimus edodes* (학명).

**표고**(標高) (an) altitude. ⇨ 해발(海拔).

**표구**(表具) mounting; papering. ~하다 mount《a picture》; paper;《시켜서》have《a picture》mounted. ◉ ~사 a picture framer; a paper hanger.

**표기**(表記) ①《겉에 씀》inscription on the outside《of a package》. ¶ ~의 inscribed on the face; marked on the outside / ~금액 the sum inscribed on the face / ~ 주소 the address mentioned on the outside; the above address.
②《내용을 나타내어 적기》declaration. ~하다 declare; insure. ¶ ~의 declared; insured / 가격 ~의 우편물 mail with value declared; insured mail.
③《철자》spelling; transcription (음성기호로). ~하다 spell; transcribe; write. ¶ 한글을 로마자로 ~하다 Romanize Korean 〔Hangŭl〕. ◉ ~가격 a list price; declared value. ~법《문자의》orthography;《숫자·기호의》a notational system 〔convention〕; (a system of ) notation.

**표기**(標記) marking; a mark; a sign. ~하다 mark.

**표나다**(表—)《두드러지다》stand out; be striking 〔conspicuous〕;《겉에 드러나다》show signs 〔a trace〕; give evidence《of》; be shown clearly. ¶ 표(가) 나게 conspicuously; noticeably; strikingly; remarkably / 도둑맞은 표가 나다 show signs of having been stolen; show signs of having had part of it stolen / 표나게 예쁘다 be strikingly beautiful / 회색은 먼지가 묻어도 표나지 않는다 Gray does not show the dust.

**표독**(慓毒) fierceness; ferocity; savageness. ~하다〔스럽다〕(be) fierce; ferocious; savage. ¶ ~스러운 얼굴로 with a look of venom / ~하게 말하다 speak daggers to《*a person*》.

**표류**(漂流) drift; drifting. ~하다 drift about 〔out (to sea)〕; be adrift《on the sea》. ¶ 물결 치는 대로 ~하다 be 〔drift about〕 at the mercy of the waves / 배는 바람과 파도에 운명을 내맡긴 채 ~하고 있었다 The ship went drifting at the mercy of the wind and waves. ◉ ~물 floating wreckage; flotsam; floatage. ~선 a drifting ship; a derelict ship (버려진). ~자 a castaway《on an island》; a person adrift on the sea.

**표리**(表裏)《겉과 속》inside and outside; the front and (the) back; two sides《of *a thing*》;《두 마음》duplicity. ¶ ~가 없다 be single-hearted〔-minded〕/ ~가 있다 be double-dealing 〔two-faced, treacherous〕/ ~없이 single-heartedly; faithfully / ~가 있는 사람 a double-dealer. ◉ ~부동 treacherousness; deceptiveness; being two-faced. ~일체 two sides of the same coin: 형제는 ~ 일체가 되어서 일했다 The brothers worked in close cooperation.

**표면**(表面) the surface; the face;《외면》the outside; the exterior;《외관》the external appearance. ¶ ~의〔적인〕superficial; apparent; ostensible; seeming; external; outward / 거울의 ~ the surface of the mirror / 건물의 ~ the outside of a building / ~상의 이유 an ostensible reason / ~에 on the outside 〔face, surface〕/ ~(적)으로는 outwardly; on the surface; apparently; seemingly; on the face of it / ~에 나타나다 get shown on the face; appear 〔be〕 in the public eye; be in the limelight / 그의 친절은 ~뿐이다 His kindness is only on the surface. / 그녀는 ~에 나서기를 싫어한다 She wants to stay in the background. / 사건의 진상은 겉으로 나타난 ~만을 보아서는 알 수 없다 One cannot tell the true state of affairs simply from appearances.
◉ ~경화《강철의》case 〔surface〕 hardening. ~계수〖물리〗surface coefficient. ~금리〖경제〗a coupon rate. ~기호〖물리〗surface symbol. ~마찰 surface friction. ~마취〖의학〗surface 〔permeation〕 anesthesia. ~수〖농업〗surface water. ~장력〖물리〗surface tension: ~ 장력계 a tensiometer. ~전하〖물리〗surface charge. ~파 a surface wave. ~ 활성제〖화학〗a surface-active agent; a surfactant.

**표면적**(表面積) the surface 〔superficial〕 area.
**표면화**(表面化) ～하다 come to the fore 〔surface〕; come into 〔out in〕 the open. ¶ 사건이 ～되었다 The affair came to be noticed by the public. / 우리들의 견해 차이가 ～되기 시작했다 Our differences in opinion began to surface.
**표명**(表明) (an) expression; (a) manifestation. ～하다 express; make an expression 《of》; demonstrate; show; manifest; give voice to; declare; state. ¶ 사의(辭意)～ announcement of *one's* intention to resign / 반대의사를 ～하다 express *one's* opposition; declare 〔express *oneself*〕 against / 의안에 찬성임을 ～하다 declare for a bill / 소신을 ～하다 express *one's* belief / 대통령께서는 한미간의 경제 문제에 관해 소신을 ～하였다 The President expressed his opinion on the economic problems between Korea and the United States.
**표방**(標榜) ～하다 《공언하다》 profess 《*oneself* to be》; 《내걸다》 adopt a platform 〔slogan, motto (*pl.* ～(e)s) 《of》; 《주장하다》 advocate 〔champion, espouse〕 《the cause of Democracy》; 《지지하다》 stand for. ¶ 정의를 ～하다 be professedly for justice; champion the cause of justice; be clothed with righteousness / 인도주의를 ～하다 claim to stand for humanitarian principles; advocate the cause of humanitarianism.
**표밭**(票—) a favorable voters' district; a reliable source of votes; an area of strong electoral support 《for》.
**표백**(漂白) bleaching; decoloration. ～하다 bleach; decolor(ize). ◉ ～분 bleaching powder; chloride of lime. ～액 a bleaching solution. ～제 a bleaching agent; a bleach; a decolorant. ～조(槽) a kier.
**표범**(豹—) 〖동물〗 a leopard; a panther; 《암컷》 a leopardess; a pantheress. ◉ ～나비 a fritillary. 미국～ an American leopard. 흑～ a black panther.
**표변**(豹變) a sudden change; a volte=face; an about-face. ～하다 change suddenly; do a complete turnaround; do 「a 180 degree turn 〔an about-turn〕; 《변절하다》 turn *one's* coat. ¶ 거절했더니 그녀는 태도를 ～했다 When I said no, she changed her tune 〔attitude〕「unexpectedly 〔suddenly〕.
**표본**(標本) 《실물 견본》 a specimen; 《견본》 a sample; 《전형》 a type; a model; an example; 〖통계〗 a sample. ¶ 무작위 ～ 〖통계〗 a random sample / 알코올에 담아 놓은～ a specimen preserved in alchol / 진열용의 ～ a museum specimen / 곤충의 ～을 만들다 make specimen of insects / 그는 근면의 ～이다 He is a model of industry. / 그는 미국 애국자의 훌륭한 ～이었다 He was a fine type of the American patriot. ◉ ～분포 〖통계〗 sample distribution. ～실 a specimen room; 《식물의》 a herbarium (*pl.* ～s, -ia). ～조사 a sample survey. ～진열장 a specimen room 〔gallery〕. ～추출 sampling. 동물〔식물〕～ a zoological 〔botanical〕 specimen. 박제～ a stuffed specimen.
**표상**(表象) 〖심리〗 an image; (a) representation; 〖철학〗 an idea; 《상징》 a symbol; an emblem. ～하다 represent; symbolize; stand for; be symbolic 〔emblematic〕 of. ◉ ～설 representation. ～주의 presentationism. 부분～ a partial idea.
**표석**(漂石) 〖지질〗 an erratic block; a 「(traveled) boulder.
**표석**(標石) a stone landmark; a boundary stone; a milestone (이정표).
**표수**(票數) the number of votes.
**표시**(表示) ① 《나타냄》 (an) indication; (an) expression; (a) manifestation; (a) demonstration. ～하다 indicate; show; manifest; express; make known. ¶ 의사～ expression of *one's* intention / 온도계는 온도를 ～한다 The thermometer indicates temperature. / 포장지에는 상품의 제조 월일과 장소가 ～되어 있다 The wrapper tells you when and where the article was produced. ② 《표적》 a sign; a token; a mark. ¶ 감사〔경의〕의 ～로 as a mark of *one's* appreciation 〔esteem〕. ◉ ～기 an indicator; an annunciator (승강기 등의). ～등 a pilot lamp. ～장치 a display.
**표어**(標語) a slogan; a motto (*pl.* ～(e)s); a catchword; a watchword; a rallying word; a cry. ¶ 교통 안전～ a traffic safety slogan / ～를 모집하다 offer a prize for the best slogan 〔motto〕.
**표연**(飄然) ¶ ～히 《정처없이》 aimlessly; 《훌쩍》 casually; abruptly / 그는 ～히 집을 나섰다 He left home aimlessly.
**표음**(表音) phonetic representation. ～하다 represent 〔write〕 phonetically. ◉ ～문자 a phonetic symbol; phonetics. ～주의 phoneticism: ～주의자 a

phoneticist.

**표의**(表意) ideographic representation. ◉ ～문자 an ideogram; an ideograph; pictographs.

**표장**(標章) an emblem; an ensign; a mark; a badge.

**표저**(瘭疽) 〚의학〛 whitlow; felon; paronychia.

**표적**(表迹) a sign; a mark; a token; a manifestation; a certificate; a proof; a testimony; a memento; a souvenir. ¶ 감사의 ～ a token of *one's* gratitude / 잘못한 ～ a proof that *one* is to blame / 하와이에 다녀온 ～으로 as a souvenir of *one's* visit to Hawaii / ～을 남기지 않다 leave no trace behind.

**표적**(標的) a target; a mark. ¶ ～을 맞히다〔맞히지 못하다〕 hit 〔miss〕 the mark. ◉ ～사격 target 「practice 〔shooting〕. ～장(場) a target range. ～지역 《미사일 실험의》 a target area. ～함(艦) a target ship.

**표절**(剽竊) plagiarism; (literary) piracy. ～하다 plagiarize; pirate; crib 《구어》. ◉ ～물 a plagiarized article. ～자 a plagiarist; a (literary) pirate.

**표정**(表情) (a) (facial) expression; a look (얼굴·눈의). ¶ ～이 풍부한 expressive / ～없는 얼굴 a 「wooden 〔poker〕 face; a dead pan / ～이 없다 be 「expressionless 〔inexpressive, immobile, wooden, flat〕 / ～을 짓다 make a facial expression; show a look of; express 《*one's* feelings》 facially / ～을 살피다 study the pleasure of 《*a person*》; read 《*a person's*》 face / ～에 나타나다 betray 《*one's* emotions》; look; show / ～이 굳어지다 harden *one's* face.

**표제**(表題·標題) 《책의》 a (book) title; 《논설의》 a heading; a head (title); 《사진·만화 등의》 a caption 《미》. ¶ …라는 ～로 under the head of / ～를 달다 give a 「title 〔headline〕 to; put a caption on 《a cartoon》. ◉ ～어 《사전의》 a main entry; a head word; 《용어 해설 사전의》 a lemma (*pl.* ～s, -mata): 난외 ～어 a catchword. ～음악 program music. 부～ a subtitle.

**표주박** a small gourd vessel; a dipper.

**표준**(標準) a standard; a level (사회적·정신적); a norm (작업량의); a criterion (*pl.* ～s, -ria) (척도); a measure (판정의); 《평균》 the average.
¶ ～의〔적인〕 standard; normal; average (평균의) / 일정한 ～ a fixed standard / 높은〔낮은〕 ～ a 「high 〔low〕 standard 《of education》 / 비교의 ～ a standard of comparison / ～ 이상〔이하〕의 above 〔below〕 standard 〔average〕 / ～을 높이다〔낮추다〕 raise 〔lower〕 the standard; level 「up 〔down〕 / ～이 높아지다 rise to a higher level / ～을 정하다 fix 〔set up〕 the standard; standardize / 사람마다 사물을 판단하는 ～이 다르다 People judge things by different standards. / 그 물건은 ～ 미달이다 The goods 「are not 〔have not come〕 up to the standard. *or* The article fall short of the standard. / 이 학생들은 ～ 이하〔이상〕이다 These students are 「below 〔above〕 the average. / 그녀는 당시의 ～으로는 키가 큰 편이었다 She was rather tall according to the standard of her time.
◉ ～가격 the standard price. ～건물가격 the building standard cost. ～규격 the standard: ～규격에 합격하다〔맞다〕 meet 〔satisfy〕 the standard; qualify for the standard. ～기록 the standard record; 《예선 통과의》 the qualifying standard 〔time, distance〕. ～도량형 standard weights and measures. ～상태 a normal state. ～생활비 the standard cost of living. ～시계 a standard clock. ～어〔말〕 the standard language. ～영어 standard English; King's 〔Queen's〕 English 《영》. ～오차 〚통계〛 the standard deviation. ～형 a standard type; 《치수》 standard size. ～화 standardization: 자동차의 부품을 ～화하다 standardize the parts of an automobile. 한국 ～ 연구소 the Korea Standards Research Institute. 한국 ～ 협회 The Korean Standards Association (생략 KSA).

**표준시**(標準時) standard time; Greenwich (Mean) Time (생략 G.M.T.); 《협정 세계시》 Universal Time Coordinated (생략 UTC). ◉ 한국～ Korean Standard Time (생략 KST).

**표지**(表紙) a (book) cover; a binding. ¶ 책에 ～를 달다 cover a book; put the covers on a book. ◉ ～도안 a cover design. ～커버 a (book) jacket. 앞〔뒤〕 ～ a 「front 〔back〕 cover. 종이〔천, 가죽〕～ a 「paper 〔cloth, leather〕 cover: 종이 ～의 책 a book (bound) in paper covers; a paperback / 가죽 ～의 책 a book bound in leather; a leatherbound book / 천 ～의 책 a book with cloth-binding.

**표지**(標識) a mark; a sign; a signal; a beacon (항로의). ¶ 교통 ～ a traffic sign / 「진입금지」의 ～ a "No Entry" sign; a sign saying "No Entry." ◉ ～

등 a beacon light. ～물 a signal. ～조(鳥) a bird marked with a band 〔ring《영》〕; a banded 〔ringed《영》〕 bird. 지상～ a ground mark.

**표징**(表徵) a sign; a symbol; an indication.

**표차**(表差) 〚수학〛 difference table; tabular difference.

**표착**(漂着) drifting ashore. ～하다 drift ashore; be cast 〔thrown, washed〕 ashore. ◉ ～물 flotsam; articles washed ashore; 《유목》 drift-wood.

**표창**(表彰) (official) commendation; honoring. ～하다 recognize 《*a person's* contribution》 publicly; honor 《*a person*》 with testimonial commending 《*his* achievements》; make a public recognition of 《*a person's* services》. ¶ ～받다 win official commendation; be cited《for》/ 뛰어난 봉사로 ～을 받다 be given a citation for 《*one's* 〔its〕》 excellent service 《to》. ◉ ～대(臺) 《경기의》 a winners' podium; a victory stand. ～식 a commendation ceremony; a ceremony of awarding an honor. ～장 a letter of commendation; a testimonial; a citation: 대통령 ～장 a presidential citation.

**표창**(鏢槍) a dart; a javelin.

**표출**(表出) expression. ～하다 express. ¶ 감정을 ～하다 express *one's* feelings.

**표층**(表層) the outer(most) layer 〔stratum〕; the surface 〔top〕 layer. ¶ 지구의 ～ the crust of the earth. ◉ ～붕괴 a surface avalanche.

**표토**(表土) topsoil; regolith.

**표피**(表皮) 〚해부〛 the outer(most) layer of the skin; the cuticle; the epidermis. ¶ ～의 epidermal. ◉ ～세포 an epidermal cell. ～조직 the epidermal tissue.

**표하다**(表―) express; show; indicate; manifest 《*one's* feeling》; exhibit; bespeak; offer 《*one's* congratulations》; 《증명하다》 demonstrate; prove. ¶ 사의(謝意)를 ～ express 〔show, voice〕 *one's* gratitude; tender *one's* thanks / 조의를 ～ present *one's* condolences 《to》/ 유감의 뜻을 ～ express 〔show〕 *one's* regret / 그녀는 명백히 불만을 표했다 She manifested dissatisfaction.

**표하다**(標―) mark; put 〔place〕 a mark on 《*a thing*》. ¶ 읽은 곳을 ～ mark the place that *one* has read (up to) / 옷에 이름을 써서 ～ mark *one's* name on *one's* clothes.

**표현**(表現) 《주로 말로》 (an) expression; 《구체적인 형태로》 (a) representation; 《서술》 description. ～하다 express; give expression 《to》; be expressive 〔representative〕 of; represent. ¶ ～상의 expressional / ～적인 expressive / ～이 풍부한 full of expression / 교묘〔적절〕한 ～ a happy 〔an adequate, an apt〕 expression / 예술적 ～ artistic presentation / ～의 자유 freedom of expression / 무어라고 ～할 수가 없다 cannot put it in words; be inexpressible / 그 경치는 말로 ～할 수 없을 만큼 아름다웠다 The scenery was beautiful beyond expression 〔words〕. ◉ ～력 *one's* power of expression; expressiveness: ～력이 풍부한 말 an expressive word 〔phrase〕. ～주의 expressionism. ～파 《유파》 the expressionist school; 《사람》 the expressionists. ～형식 forms of expression.

**푯대**(標―) a signpost; a mark(ing) post; a (signal) post; a pillar.

**푯돌**(標―) a stone marker; a marker stone; a landmark 〔boundary〕 stone; a milestone. ¶ ～을 세우다 set up a landmark stone.

**푯말**(標―) a post; a signpost. ¶ ～을 세우다 set up a signpost.

**푸** ① 《내뿜는 소리》 with a "whew"; with a light whistle. ② 《방귀소리》 with a light "poop".

**푸가** 〚음악〛 a (musical) fugue. ¶ ～풍의 곡 a fugate.

**푸근―** ⇨ 포근―.

**푸나무서리** a place luxuriant 〔overgrown〕 with vegetation; a thicket.

**푸네기** *one's* near relatives.

**푸념** 《무당의》 the ravings of a shaman (transmitting the rage of spirits while in a trance); 《불평》 an idle 〔a doleful〕 complaint; a grumble; a grievance. ～하다 rave; complain 《of, about》; grumble 《at》; dwell on grievances.

**푸다** ① 《물·가루 등을》 draw 〔dip, scoop〕 up; ladle (국자로); drain; bail out; spoon up (스푼으로). ¶ 두레박으로 물을 ～ draw water 《from a well》 with a bucket / 삽으로 ～ shovel; take up with a shovel / 양동이로 모래를 퍼 올리다 dip 〔take〕 up sand with a bucket / 뱃바닥의 물을 퍼내다 bail water out of a boat. ② 《밥·곡식 등을》 scoop out; take out. ¶ 솥에서 밥을 ～ scoop rice out of a pot / 독에서 쌀을 ～ take rice out of a jar / 그릇에 밥을 퍼담다 serve rice in a bowl; serve out rice; fill a bowl with rice / 제손으

로 밥을 퍼먹다 help *oneself* to rice.

**푸닥거리** a service 〔ceremony〕 of exorcism; an exorcism. ~하다 perform an exorcism; exorcize.

**푸대접**(—待接) unkind 〔uncivil〕 treatment; a cold 〔frigid〕 reception; inhospitality. ~하다 treat 《*a person*》 unkindly 〔coldly, inhospitably〕; receive 《*a person*》 with indifference; give a cold reception to; be inhospitable to; give 〔turn, show〕 the cold shoulder to. ¶ ~을 받다 receive unkind treatment; be treated inhospitably / ~을 감수하다 submit to 〔brook, swallow, stomach〕 cold treatment.

**푸두둥거리다** flitter and flitter; flutter and flutter. ¶ 푸두둥거리며 날아가다 flitter 〔flutter〕 away.

**푸(드)덕거리다** ⇨ 퍼(드)덕거리다.

**푸드득** ① 《푸드덕》 flap; flutter; flop; flounder. ② 《부드득》 grind; creak.

**푸들** 《개》 a poodle (dog).

**푸딩** 《죽 모양의 서양 요리》 pudding.

**푸뜩푸뜩** all occurring 〔appearing〕 suddenly; now and then; intermittently. ~하다 (be) intermittent. ¶ 생각이 ~ 나다 ideas pop up; an idea occurs to *one* now and then / 눈이 ~ 내리다 snow comes down in intermittent flurries.

**푸르께하다** (be) bluish; greenish.

**푸르다** ① 《색이》 (be) blue; azure; green. ¶ 푸른 하늘 a blue sky; the blue heavens / 푸른 대 a green bamboo / 신록의 푸른 산들 the mountains in fresh verdure. ② 《서슬이》 (be) sharp(edged). ¶ 서슬이 ~ 《칼날이》 have a sharp edge; 《세력이》 be high and mighty.

**푸르데데하다** 《푸르다》 (be) sordidly bluish 〔greenish〕; 《창백하다》 (be) rather pale 〔pallid〕.

**푸르디푸르다** be blue as blue can be; be green as green can be; be ever so blue 〔green〕.

**푸르락붉으락** ⇨ 붉으락푸르락.

**푸르르** 《끓는 모양》 bubbling; seething; 《타는 모양》 in a burst of flame; in a huff; 《떠는 모양》 trembling.

**푸르스름하다** (be) bluish 〔greenish〕; be tinged with blue.

**푸르죽죽하다** =푸르데데하다.

**푸른곰팡이** 〖식물〗 green mold; a penicillium (*pl.* -lia).

**푸릇푸릇** all spotted green 〔blue〕; green 〔blue〕 here and there. ~하다 be all spotted green 〔blue〕; be green 〔blue〕 here and there. ¶ 풀이 ~ 돋아나다 grass sprouts out all green here and there / 얼굴에 ~ 멍이 들다 *one's* face is bruised dark here and there.

**푸만하다** feel stuffy from overeating.

**푸새**[1] 《풀을 먹임》 starching. ~하다 starch 《clothes》.

**푸새**[2] 《풀》 grasses; plants; pasturage.

**푸석돌** 〖광물〗 a crumbly 〔soft〕 stone.

**푸석이** 《물건》 a crumbly thing; fragile stuff; 《사람》 a fragile 〔frail〕 person.

**푸석푸석** all crisp 〔crumbly, rotting away〕. ~하다 be all crisp 〔crumbly, rotting away〕; (be) fragile; brittle; breakable. ¶ ~ 부서지다 crumble; break into crumbs.

**푸석하다** (be) crisp; crumbly; be rotting away.

**푸성귀** greens; green vegetables; greenstuff.

**푸솜** raw cotton.

**푸에르토리코** 《서인도 제도의 섬》 Puerto Rico. ¶ ~의 Puerto Rican. ◉ ~ 사람 a Puerto Rican.

**푸접없다** 《붙임성 없다》 (be) unfriendly; unsociable; 《쌀쌀하다》 (be) cold; icy; frigid; cool. ¶ 푸접없는 대답을 하다 reply snappishly; give a curt reply.

**푸주**(—廚) a meat 〔butcher〕 shop; a butcher's 《영》. ◉ ~한(漢) a butcher; a meatman.

**푸줏간** ⇨ 푸주.

**푸지다** (be) abundant; profuse; liberal; generous. ¶ 푸진 음식 abundant food; generous portion / 푸진 대접 liberal treatment / 푸지게 abundantly; profusely; much; plenty / 푸지게 먹다 eat plenty / 푸지게 대접하다 treat 《*a person*》 liberally.

**푸짐하다** (be) abundant; plentiful; profuse; generous.

**푸집개** a cover for weapons.

**푸푸** puffing; in puffs. ¶ ~ 불다 puff and blow.

**푸하다** (be) untidy; loose; puffy. ¶ 푸한 머리 untidy hair / 푸한 짐 a loose bundle / 머리가 푸하게 일어서다 *one's* hair bristles up untidily.

**푹** ① 《깊이》 (***a***) 《속에 빠져드는 모양》 deep(ly); sinking in. ¶ 수렁에 푹 빠지다 《발 등이》 stick in the mud; get stuck in the mud / 푹 가라앉다 sink deep / 뜨거운 목욕물에 몸을 푹 담그다 ease into a hot bath. (***b***) 《덮거나 싸는 모양》 completely; entirely; with no gaps. ¶ 푹 싸다 wrap 《it》 all up carefully / 모자를 푹 눌러 쓰다 pull 〔draw, slouch〕 *one's* hat (well) over *one's* eyes; wear *one's* hat low over *one's* eyes / 이불을 푹 덮다 tuck the

bedding up snug / 이불을 푹 뒤집어 쓰다 pull the bedclothes over *one's* head. (***c***) 《잠을》 well; sound(ly); deep. ¶ 푹 자다 sleep soundly; have a good sleep; pass 〔have〕 a good night. (***d***) 《찌르는 모양》 thrusting hard. ¶ 단도로 푹 찌르다 stab 《*a person*》 with a dagger; plunge a dagger into 《*a person's* heart》; thrust a dagger home. (***e***) 《파거나 패인 모양》 deep(ly). ¶ 푹 파다 dig deep(ly) / 비가 와서 땅이 푹 패였다 The raindrops have hollowed out the ground.
② 《쉬는 모양》 enough; sufficiently. ¶ 푹 쉬다 rest up; take *one's* fill of rest; take a good rest / 하룻밤 푹 쉬다 have a good night's rest.
③ 《흠씬》 well; completely; thoroughly; all over. ¶ 푹 끓이다 boil well / (고기를) 푹 삶다 do (meat) well 〔thoroughly〕; boil 《meat》 to a pulp (흐물흐물하게) / 푹 젖다 get wet through 〔all over〕; 《옷이》 get dripping wet.
④ 《갑자기 줄어드는 모양》 sharply. ¶ 푹 줄다 decrease 〔decline, fall off〕 sharply 〔remarkably〕 / 인기가 갑자기 푹 떨어지다 have a sudden fall in *one's* popularity.
⑤ 《쓰러지는 모양》 flop; with a thud. ¶ 푹 쓰러지다 fall with a flop.
⑥ 《내뿜는 모양》 puffing; in a puff.
⑦ 《폭삭》 rotting away. ¶ (나무가) 푹 썩다 become crumbly; undergo rot.
⑧ 《고개를》 ¶ 고개를 푹 숙이다 hang *one's* head; bow *one's* head far down; sink *one's* head on *one's* chest 〔breast〕 / 고개를 푹 숙이고 with *one's* head drooped 〔down〕.

**푹신푹신** all soft 〔fluffy, spongy, downy, flossy, yielding, springy〕. ~하다 (be) all soft, *etc.* ¶ ~한 소파 a soft, comfortable sofa.

**푹신하다** (be) soft; fluffy; downy; spongy; yielding. ¶ 나는 푹신한 침대가 좋다 I like a soft bed.

**푹푹** ① 《찌르다》 piercing 〔pricking〕 repeatedly. ¶ 바늘로 ~ 찌르다 keep pricking with a needle. ② 《쑤시다》 piercing(ly); extreme(ly). ¶ 곪은 손가락이 ~쑤시다 A festered finger is tingling. ③ 《사정없이》 blunt(ly); sharp(ly). ④ 《아낌없이》 freely; liberally; lavishly. ¶ 돈을 ~ 쓰다 spend money freely; be lavish 〔liberal〕 of *one's* money. ⑤ 《삶다》 《boiling》 completely; thoroughly; well. ¶ ~ 삶다 boil thoroughly. ⑥ 《더위가》 ¶ ~ 찌는 sultry; muggy; (damp and) close / 날이 ~ 찌다 it is steaming hot 〔sultry〕. ⑦ 《썩다》 rotting rapidly 〔completely〕. ¶ 날이 더워 고기가 ~ 썩다 meat rots fast because of the hot weather / 속이 ~ 썩다 get sick at heart. ⑧ 《빠지다》 sinking deep(ly). ¶ 발이 눈에 ~ 빠지다 *one's* feet sink deep in the snow.

**푹하다** (be) unseasonably warm; mild.

**푼** ① 《돈 한 닢》 a *pun*; an old coin; a Korean penny(=1 / 10 *ton*). ¶ 몇 푼어치 안되는 지식 small knowledge / 돈 한 푼 없다 haven't a penny 〔a red cent 《구어》〕 《with *one*》; be utterly 〔dead, flat〕 broke; be stony(-broke) 《속어》 / 돈 한 푼 없이 내쫓겼다 I was driven out penniless. / 한 푼도 깎을 수 없습니다 I wouldn't come down a cent. *or* I can't take a penny off. / 그런 일〔것〕에는 한 푼도 낼 수 없다 I wouldn't give a penny for that. / 한 푼의 가치도 없다 It isn't worth a farthing.
② 《백분율》 (a) percentage; percent 〔%〕. ¶ 1할 5푼 fifteen percent / 3푼 이자 three percent interest.
③ 《길이 단위》 a measure of length; a tenth of a Korean inch (=*ch'i*).
④ 《무게 단위》 a Korean penny-weight 《0.01323 ounce, 0.375 gram》.

**푼끌** a small narrow chisel.

**푼내기** 《조그마한 노름》 penny-gambling; penny ante. ◉ ~흥정 small-time 〔"penny-ante"〕 business; business in a small way 〔on a small scale〕.

**푼더분하다** ① 《얼굴이》 (be) plump; well-rounded; full. ② 《씀씀이·대접 등이》 (be) ample; plentiful. ¶ 푼더분한 주안(酒案) ample food and drinks / 푼더분하게 대접하다 treat 《*a person*》 liberally.

**푼돈** a small 〔paltry〕 sum (of money); an odd sum of money; loose 〔broken〕 money; pennies; chicken feed 《속어》. ¶ 천 원, 2천 원의 ~ a paltry sum of one or two thousand won / ~을 모으다 save money little by little; save *one's* pocket money / ~을 아끼다 be chary of pennies; be penny-wise / ~도 없어 쩔쩔매다 don't know where *one's* next cent is coming from.

**푼사**(―絲) a kind of untwisted silk thread used in embroidery.

**푼수**(―數) ① 《율》 rate; 《비》 ratio; percentage; 《정도》 degree; extent. ¶ 이 ~로 나간다면 (if things go on) at this rate / 두 사람 ～를 일하다 do two men's work. ② 《사람》「a thoughtless 〔an indiscreet, an imprudent〕 person.

**푼어치** a pennyworth; a penny's worth; penny merchandise.

**푼주** an earthenware bowl with a wide brim and a narrow base.

**푼치** a small difference; a bit. ¶ ～도 틀림이 없다 be exactly alike / ～도 양보하지 않다 make no concession at all; don't yield a fraction of an inch.

**푼푼이** penny by penny. ¶ ～ 모은 돈 money saved「penny by penny 〔little by little〕.

**푼푼하다** ① 《넉넉하다》 (be) ample; sufficient; abundant. ¶ 푼푼한 돈〔음식〕 abundant「money 〔food〕. ② 《활수하다》 (be) liberal; generous.

**푼푼히** 《넉넉히》 amply; abundantly; sufficiently; 《활수하게》 liberally; generously.

**풀**[1] grass; a plant; a herb (약초); a weed (잡초); pasture (목초).
¶ 풀 한 포기〔잎〕 a single plant; a blade of grass / 풀이 난 땅 grass-grown land; a「grassy 〔weedy〕 place / 풀을 베다 mow 〔cut〕 grass / 잔디풀을 베다 cut the grass on a lawn / 뜰의 풀을 뽑다 weed a garden / 풀을 (뜯어) 먹다 《a cow》 feed on grass; graze / 소에게 풀을 먹이다 graze a cow / 풀이 우거지다 be overrun with grass / 나는 풀 위에 드러누웠다 I threw myself on the grass.

**풀**[2] ① 《붙이는》 paste; starch (녹말풀); glue (아교풀); gum; mucilage (고무풀). ¶ 풀이 잘 먹은 well-starched 《cloth》; starchy 《shirt》 / 종이에 풀을 바르다 paste paper / 옷에 풀을 먹이다 starch clothes / 풀로 붙이다 paste; stick 《*a thing*》 with paste / 풀을 개다 temper starch with water / 풀을 쑤다 make paste / 풀의 응어리를 없애다 bring paste to a smooth consistence. ② 《활기》 spirit; vigor. ⇨ 풀기 ②.

**풀**[3] ① 《수영장》 a swimming pool; a swimming bath 《영》. ¶ 실내 ～ an indoor (swimming) pool. ② 《공동 출자·이용》 a pool. ～하다 pool 《money》. ¶ 자력〔정보, 인력〕을 ～제(制)로 하다 pool (*one's*) resources 〔information, staff〕. ◉ 풀 강의제(講義制) a faculty pool system. 모터 풀 《배차용 차량 대기장》 a motor pool. 카 풀 《자가용 공동 이용》 a car pool 《미》.

**풀가사리, 풀가시** 〚식물〛 a glue plant.

**풀기**(一氣) ① 《빳빳함》 stiffness; starch (-iness). ¶ ～가 있다 be starchy 〔starched, stiff〕 / ～가 없다 be not starched; be「unstarched 〔unstiffened〕. ② 《활기》 stamina; energy; vigor; vitality; spirit. ¶ ～가 없다 be lacking「spirit 〔life〕.

**풀다** ① 《맨 것·묶은 것·엉킨 것을》 untie 《a string》; undo 《a bundle》; unbind 《a bandage》; loosen 〔let down〕 《*one's* hair》; unpack 《a package》; unfasten 《a rope》; unravel 《a thread》; disentangle 《a knot》; unknit (편물을); 《꼰 것을》 untwist; untwine. ¶ 밧줄을 ～ untie a rope / 개를 ～ loose a dog / 구두끈을 ～ untie *one's* shoestrings; unlace *one's* shoes / 꾸러미〔보따리〕를 ～ undo 〔unwrap〕 a package; unpack / 단추를 ～ undo 〔unfasten〕 buttons; button off; unbutton 《a coat》 / 엉킨 매듭을 ～ disentangle a knot / 여장을 ～ take off *one's* traveling attire; 《숙박하다》 stop 〔put up〕 at an inn / 짐을 ～ unload 《a cart, a ship》; unpack; [배가 주어] discharge「cargo 〔freight〕. / 소를 목장에 풀어 내놓다 turn cattle out to graze.
② 《해제하다》 remove; cancel; rescind; dissolve; lift; release; disengage; absolve; free; 《구속을》 unbind. ¶ 금지령을 ～ lift a ban; remove a prohibition / 봉쇄를 ～ remove 〔raise, lift〕 a blockade / 자금의 동결을 ～ thaw the frozen assets / 제재를 ～ lift *one's* sanctions 《against》 / 포위를 ～ raise a siege / 교도소에서 풀어 주다 release 《a man》 from prison / 마침내 그들은 인질을 풀어 주었다 At last they released the hostages.
③ 《용해하다》 dissolve; melt. ¶ 물에 소금을 ～ dissolve salt in water / 물감을 ～ dissolve a dye.
④ 《논을》 turn land into 《a paddy》; create 《a paddy》 out of land. ¶ 개펄에 논을 ～ turn shoreland into paddies.
⑤ 《피로를》 relieve; banish; rid of; ease. ¶ 몸을 ～ relieve *one's* fatigue; 《준비운동으로》 warm 〔limber〕 up; 《해산하다》 deliver a child; give birth to a child / 여행의 피로를 ～「take a rest 〔refresh *oneself*〕 after a fatiguing journey / 잠을 자서 피로를 ～ sleep off *one's* fatigue.
⑥ 《없애어 시원하게 하다》 (***a***) 《감정·의혹 등을》 dispel 《doubts》; dissipate; remove; clear away 〔up〕. ¶ (울적한) 기분을 ～ dispel 〔dissipate〕 the gloom;

distract *oneself* 〔*one's* mind〕 (from cares); recreate 〔divert〕 *oneself* / 의심을 ~ dispel 〔remove, dissolve, clear up〕 《*a person's*》 doubts / 오해를 ~ remove 〔dispel, correct〕 the misunderstanding / 혐의를 ~ clear *oneself* 「from suspicion 〔of the charge〕; dispel 〔disarm, clear away〕 suspicion. (***b***) 《원한 등을》 vent; let out; work off; revenge *oneself.* ¶ 원한을 ~ vent *one's* spite; work off 〔satisfy〕 *one's* grudge; pay 〔wipe〕 off old scores 《with *a person*》.

⑦ 《소원을 이루다》 realize; satisfy; gratify. ¶ 소원을 ~ realize *one's* desire; gratify *one's* wishes; have *one's* wish fulfilled.

⑧ 《문제 따위를》 solve; answer; work out; puzzle out; unravel; 《해몽하다》 interpret; clear up 《the meaning》. ¶ 꿈을 ~ interpret a dream / 방정식을 ~ solve 〔reduce〕 an equation / 수수께끼를 ~ solve 〔guess, undo, find out〕 a riddle; answer 〔solve, make out〕 a puzzle; solve a mystery / 암호문을 ~ decipher a code; decode / 어려운 문제를 ~ solve 〔work out〕 a hard problem; 《비상 수단으로》 cut the Gordian knot / 점괘를 ~ interpret 〔expound〕 *one's* divination sign.

⑨ 《진정시키다》 calm; pacify; 《갈증 등을》 appease; quench. ¶ 노염을 ~ appease 〔calm〕 *one's* anger / 갈증을 ~ quench 〔appease〕 thirst.

⑩ 《설명·해석하다》 state; expound. ¶ 교리를 ~ expound a doctrine / 자세히 ~ explain 《a question》 in details.

⑪ 《사람을》 send out; call out. ¶ 사람을 풀어 범인을 찾다 send out men in search of a criminal / 증원 부대를 ~ send out fresh troops.

⑫ 《코를》 ¶ 코를 ~ blow *one's* nose.

**풀대님** wearing *one's* breeches without tying their ends up at the ankle. ¶ ~하고 sloppily dressed; in untidy attire.

**풀등** a grassy sandbank.

**풀떡** lightly; nimbly; quickly. ¶ ~ 뛰어내리다 swing *oneself* down 《from》 / 말 위에 ~ 뛰어 오르다 spring on the horse; rise a horse with a swing / 개울을 ~ 뛰어넘다 clear a brook in one vault.

**풀떼기** a thick gruel of grain flour.

**풀리다** ① 《매듭이》 《it》 untie; come 〔get〕 loose 〔untied, undone, unbound, unfastened〕; 《짐이》 come 〔get〕 unpacked; 《얽힌 것이》 come 〔get〕 disentangled 〔unraveled〕; 《구두끈이》 become unlaced; loosen; come 〔get〕 loose; 《꼰 것이》 become untwisted; 《편물이》 come 〔get〕 unweaved; 《천의 가장자리가》 fray; become frayed. ¶ 구두끈이 ~ *one's* shoestrings get loose; *one's* shoes 「come untied 〔become unlaced〕 / 머리가 ~ *one's* hair gets loose / 엉킨 매듭이 ~ a knot is disentangled.

② 《제거·해제되다》 get removed; be dissolved; be lifted; get relieved; be disengaged; be absolved; be freed. ¶ 금지령이 ~ a ban is lifted; a prohibition is removed / 봉쇄가 ~ a blockade is lifted 〔raised〕 / 이제까지의 수입 금지 또는 수입제한 리스트에서 ~ be freed from the hitherto import embargo or restriction list / 포위가 풀렸다 The siege was raised 〔lifted〕.

③ 《방면되다》 become free; get released; be set free. ¶ 갇혔던 몸이 ~ be released 《from prison》.

④ 《유통되다》 get circulated; be released; go into circulation. ¶ 새 화폐가 ~ the new currency goes into circulation / 은행돈이 ~ money in the bank is released.

⑤ 《용해되다》 《it》 dissolve; melt. ¶ 설탕이 잘 ~ sugar dissolves nicely / 언 땅이 곧 풀릴 것이다 The ground will thaw soon.

⑥ 《원한이》 get vented; be taken out; be revenged. ¶ 원한이 ~ a grudge is satisfied; be revenged 《upon *a person*》.

⑦ 《소원이》 get realized; be satisfied; be fulfilled. ¶ 소원이 ~ *one's* desire is realized; *one's* wishes are gratified; *one's* wish is fulfilled; *one's* will is carried out.

⑧ 《누그러지다》 (***a***) 《감정·노여움이》 get disarmed; be calmed 〔pacified, appeased〕; be allayed; [사람이 주어] relent 《toward》; be dispelled. ¶ 노여움이 ~ *one's* anger is pacified 〔gone, appeased〕; relent toward 《*a person*》 / 우리들의 감정 대립은 좀처럼 풀리지 않았다 Our emotional entanglement would not melt. (***b***) 《날씨·몸 등이》 warm up; become mild; be mitigated; moderate; go down. ¶ 얼었던 몸이 ~ *one* becomes warm; *one* thaws out (from the cold) / 추위가 풀렸다 The cold has decreased 〔relaxed〕 in severity. / 그의 기분이 이제 풀렸다

His feeling relaxed now.
⑨ 《긴장이》 relax; slacken; abate; flag; become remiss; remit. ¶ 마음이 ～ *one's* mind relaxes; become 〔go, get〕 off *one's* guard / 학생들의 규율이 풀린 것 같다 Discipline seems relaxed among the students. / 바짝 긴장되었던 그의 마음이 일시에 풀렸다 His strained nerves relaxed at once.
⑩ 《문제·수수께끼가》 get solved; be worked out; be unraveled; meet with solution 〔disentanglement〕. ¶ 풀리지 않은 문제 an unsolved problem / …의 실마리가 ～ find a 〔the〕 clue to / 문제 〔수수께끼〕가 ～ A problem 〔puzzle〕 is solved.
⑪ 《의혹·오해가》 get resolved; be dispelled; be removed; be cleared away. ¶ 의혹이 ～ a doubt is dispelled / 오해가 ～ a misunderstanding is removed / 혐의가 ～ be cleared of charge / 그에 대한 의심은 아직도 풀리지 않고 있다 My suspicions about him have not yet cleared up.
⑫ 《피로 등이》 recover from; get over; feel easy. ¶ 피로가 ～ recover from 〔get over〕 *one's* fatigue; be relieved of *one's* fatigue / 뻐근한 어깨가 ～ *one's* stiff shoulders feel easy.

**풀매** a small hand mill (used to grind rice for starch).

**풀매듭** a knot that is easily untied; a knot that unties itself.

**풀머리** loosened 〔undressed, unkempt, let-down〕 hair. ～하다 let 〔wear〕 *one's* hair down.

**풀먹이다** starch 《*one's* clothes》.

**풀멸구** 〖곤충〗 a leafhopper.

**풀무** (a pair of ) bellows; a blower (송풍기). ◉ ～질 using bellows: ～질하다 blow with the bellows.

**풀무치** 〖곤충〗 a migratory locust.

**풀밭** a grass field; a meadow; a lawn; a green; a weedy field. ¶ ～에 누워 뒹굴다 lie down on the grass / ～에 누워 자다 sleep on a bed of grass.

**풀백** 〖축구〗 a fullback (생략 f.b., fb).

**풀베이스** 〖야구〗 ¶ ～의 bases-loaded / ～로 with the bases loaded. ⇨ 만루.

**풀뿌리** grass roots. ◉ ～민주주의 grass=roots democracy. ～운동 a grass=roots movement (일반 대중의 운동).

**풀빛** (light) green; yellowish green; grass green.

**풀세트** 〖테니스〗 a full set. ◉ ～게임 a full-set game 〔match〕.

**풀솜** silk wool; floss (silk). ◉ ～나물 cottonweed. ～할머니 a maternal grandmother.

**풀숲** the grass; a brake; a thicket.

**풀스피드** full speed. ¶ ～로 달리다 run (at) full speed.

**풀쌀** rice for making rice-paste.

**풀썩** ① 《먼지·연기 등이》 rising lightly. ¶ 먼지가 ～ 나다 a great cloud of dust rises lightly. ② 《주저앉는 모양》 collapsing. ¶ 집이 ～ 내려앉다 a house collapses completely / 땅 위에 ～ 주저앉다 flop down on the ground.

**풀썩풀썩** 《dust, smoke》 lightly rising. ¶ 먼지가 ～ 나다 dust keeps rising lightly.

**풀쐐기** 〖곤충〗 a hairy caterpillar.

**풀쑤다** ① 《풀을》 prepare 〔make〕 starch 〔paste〕. ② 《재산을》 toss away 《*one's* fortune》; squander 〔dissipate〕 (*one's* property).

**풀어내다** ① 《엉킨 것을》 unravel; disentangle. ¶ 엉킨 실을 ～ disentangle tangled threads. ② 《문제를》 solve; unravel; work out. ¶ 힘든 문제를 ～ solve 〔"crack"〕 a difficult problem / 수수께끼를 ～ solve 〔figure out〕 a puzzle.

**풀어놓다** ① 《끌러 놓다》 untie; unfasten; undo; get 〔leave〕 《*a thing*》 untied 〔unfastend, undone〕; loosen; get 〔leave〕 《*a thing*》 loosened. ¶ 짐을 ～ undo a bundle; leave a bundle undone / 개를 ～ loose a dog. ② 《제거·해제하다》 remove; lift; leave 《*a thing*》 removed 〔lifted〕; release; disengage. ③ 《논을》 turn land into 《a paddy》 and leave it that way.

**풀어먹이다** ① 《사람에게》 distribute 《food》 among the people. ② 《귀신에게》 perform an exorcism with sacrificial food to drive out evil spirits.

**풀어주다** set 《*a person*》 free; liberate 《*a person*》.

**풀어지다** ① ＝ 풀리다 ①,⑤,⑥,⑧,⑨,⑩,⑪,⑫. ② 《국수·죽이》 become soft. ¶ 죽이〔국수가〕 ～ gruel 〔noodles〕 turn(s) soft. ③ 《눈이》 become bleared; get 〔go〕 bleary. ¶ 눈이 ～ *one's* eyes get bleared; have bleary eyes.

**풀이** ① 《설명》 (an) explanation; (an) interpretation; elucidation. ⇨ 해석(解釋). ～하다 explain; interpret; construe; elucidate. ② 〔접미사〕 《무당의》 exorcising; a shamanistic rite. ～하다 exorcise.

**풀잎** a blade of grass; a leaf (of grass). ◉ ～ 피리 a grass harp.

**풀잠자리** 『곤충』 a (green) lacewing; a lacewing(ed) fly.

**풀죽다** ① 《옷이》 lose its starch; come unstarched; get limp. ¶ 옷이 ~ clothes lose their starch. ② 《사람이》 be dejected; be cast down; be dispirited; lose *one's* heart. ¶ 풀죽은 얼굴을 하다 look blue 〔downcast〕.

**풀질** applying paste 〔glue〕. ~하다 apply paste 〔glue〕.

**풀쩍** 《문을》 opening 〔closing〕 the door suddenly; 《몸 따위를》 lightly leaping 〔jumping〕. ~하다 open 〔close〕 《the door》 suddenly; lightly leap 〔jump〕.

**풀쩍거리다** keep opening and closing 《the door》; come in and go out all the time; keep coming in and going out.

**풀쳐생각** unburdening *one's* mind; putting *one's* mind at ease; relaxing; taking it easy. ~하다 get 《trouble》 off *one's* mind; unburden *one's* mind of; put *one's* mind at ease about; relax; take it easy. ¶ ~하고 너무 걱정 마시오 Don't worry, forget about it!

**풀치** 『어류』 a young hairtail; a scabbard fish. ⇨갈치.

**풀치다** release; free from (troublesome thoughts). ¶ 생각을 ~ put *one's* mind at ease.

**풀칠** 《풀칠》 applying paste; 《끼니를 이음》 living hand-to-mouth. ~하다 apply paste 《to》; live hand-to-mouth. ¶ 입에 ~하다 make *one's* bare living; eke out a living / 입에 ~조차 할 수 없다 cannot keep body and soul together.

**풀카운트** 『야구』 a full count 《of three two》.

**풀칼** a wooden paper-knife used to spread paste.

**풀타임** full time. ¶ ~ 교사 a full time teacher / ~임금 full-time wages / ~으로 일하다 work full time.

**풀풀** ① 《새가》 flapping. ¶ 새가 ~ 날다 a bird flies 「flapping its wings 〔beating the air〕. ② 《동작이》 (being) energetic 〔spirited〕; moving fast; flying 〔running〕 swiftly 〔nimbly〕. ③ 《괄괄함》 (being) spirited 〔fiery, impetuous, hot-tempered〕.

**풀풀하다** (be) irascible; short-tempered; petulant.

**풀피리** ⇨풀잎피리.

**품**[1] ① 《옷의》 width 《of a coat》. ¶ 앞품 the breast width / 뒤품 the shoulder width / 품이 넓다 〔좁다〕 be (of) broad 〔narrow〕 width. ② 《가슴》 the bosom; the breast. ¶ 자연의 품에 안기어 in the bosom of nature / 지갑을 품에 넣다 tuck 〔put〕 a wallet into *one's* bosom / 어린애를 품에 안고 가다 carry a baby in *one's* bosom.

**품**[2] 《일》 labor; work ¶ 하루 품 a day's work / 품을 팔다 work for wages; work as a day laborer / 품이 들다 require (much) labor; be troublesome / 품을 덜다 save labor / 품을 들이다 put in work / 품을 갚다 work in return.

**품**[3] 《외양》 appearance; looks; 《모양》 way (*one* looks or behaves). ¶ 사람된 품 *one's* nature; *one's* character / 사람 생긴 품 *one's* looks 〔appearance〕 / 날뛰는 품 the way *one* gambols about; the wild 〔arrogant〕 way *one* behaves.

**품**(品) ① 《물품》 an article; an item. ¶ 국산~ homemade〔domestic〕 goods / 외제~ foreign-made articles / 수입~ imported articles 〔goods〕. ② 《품질》 quality. ¶ 고급~ high-quality articles; goods of higher grade / 저질~ goods of inferior quality. ③ 《품계》 정〔종〕 2~ the senior 〔junior〕 grade of the second (court) rank. ⇨품삯.

**품값** wages; pay (usually for odd jobs).

**품갚음** returning work for work; working in return; exchange labor. ~하다 return work for work; work in return; exchange labor.

**품격**(品格) (a) grace; dignity; character. ¶ ~이 있다 be elegant 〔refined, dignified〕.

**품계**(品階) 『고제도』 《벼슬의》 a (court) rank.

**품귀**(品貴) (a) shortage 〔scarcity〕 of goods 〔stock, supply〕. ¶ ~ 상태이다 be scarce; The stock is small 〔low〕. *or* The stocks are in short supply. / ~ 상태가 되다 [사람·상점이 주어] run short 《of an item》; [상품이 주어] be in short supply; run short; get 〔become〕 scarce / 콩이 ~다 We are low in 〔on〕 soybeans. / 생선이 ~로 값이 올랐다 Fishes went up in price because of the short supply. ◉ ~주(株) stocks (which are) in short supply; stocks in which the market is tight.

**품다** ① 《가슴에》 embrace; hug; take 〔hold〕 in *one's* bosom. ¶ 가슴에 비수를 ~ carry 〔wear〕 a dagger in *one's* bosom / 어린애를 가슴에 ~ hold a baby in *one's* bosom. ② 《생각을》 cherish 《the illusion that》; entertain 《doubts》; have; bear 〔hold, keep〕 in mind; 《의혹·악의를》 harbor 《suspicion》; bear 《malice》. ¶ 희망을 ~ entertain hope / 야망을 ~ have an ambition / 원한을 ~ harbor a grudge 《against》; nurse resentment / 의심을 품을 여지가 없다 There is no room for suspicion. ③ 《알을》 sit; brood. ¶ 알을 ~ sit 〔brood〕 on eggs / 암탉에게 알을 품게 하다 set a hen on eggs.

**품돈** (a day laborer's) wages; pay.

**품등**(品等) 《등급》 (a) grade; rating; 《품질》 quality.

**품명**(品名) the name of an article.

**품목**(品目) a list of articles 〔items〕. ¶ ~별로 item by item / 주요 제조〔수출〕 ~ the chief items of manufacture 〔export〕. ◉ 영업 ~ business items; items of business.

**품사**(品詞) 〖문법〗 a part of speech; a word class. ◉ 팔(八)~ the eight parts of speech 《in English》.

**품삯** (a day laborer's) wages; pay. ¶ ~을 주다 pay wages; pay for labor / ~받고 일하다 work by the day; hire out.

**품성**(品性) (a) character; (a) nature. ¶ ~이 좋은〔나쁜〕 사람 a man of noble 〔mean〕 character / ~을 도야하다 cultivate 〔build〕 (up) *one's* character / ~이 저열〔훌륭〕하다 be of low 〔fine〕 character.

**품성**(稟性) nature; a natural gift.

**품속** (inside) the bosom. ¶ 어린애를 ~에 안다 hold 〔carry〕 a baby in *one's* bosom.

**품안** = 품속.

**품앗이** exchange of services 〔labor〕; working in turn for one another. ~하다 exchange services; work in turn for each other.

**품위**(品位) ① 《존엄성》 grace; dignity. ¶ ~가 있다 (be) dignified; elegant; graceful / ~를 높이다 ennoble 《*a person*》 / ~를 떨어뜨리다 lose *one's* dignity; degrade 〔disgrace〕 *oneself* / ~를 지키다 maintain 〔keep〕 *one's* dignity / 학문은 사람의 ~를 높인다 Learning ennobles a man. / 그는 ~ 있는 신사이다 He is a dignified man. / 그런 일은 너의 ~를 떨어뜨린다 That would be a disgrace to you. ② 《계급》 a (court) rank; position. ¶ ~가 높은 사람 a person of high rank. ③ 《품등》 grade; 《품질》 quality; 《금은》 a carat; 《순도》 fineness. ¶ ~가 낮은 광석 a low-grade ore / ~가 낮다 be low in quality 〔grade〕.

**품의**(稟議) consultation 《with a superior》; conferring 《with a superior》; the process of obtaining sanction 《from senior executives》 for a plan by circulating a draft proposal. ~하다 consult 〔confer〕 《with a superior》. ◉ ~서 a round robin; a draft prepared and circulated by *a person* in charge to obtain the sanction to a plan.

**품절**(品切) absence from stock; [부사적] out of stock; 《게시》 Sold out; Out of stock. ¶ ~이 되다 run 〔be〕 out of stock; be sold out / 물건이 ~되어 미안합니다 I am sorry to say the article is out of stock.

**품종**(品種) a sort; a kind; a species; a description; 《변종》 a variety; 《가축의》 a breed; 《품등》 a grade. ¶ 개량된 새 ~의 토마토를 생산하다 produce a new improved variety of tomatoes / 이 상점에는 여러 ~의 백합이 있다 This store has various kinds of lilies. ◉ ~ 개량 《가축의》 breed improvement; cattle breeding; 《식물의》 plant breeding; selective breeding 《of cattle 〔rice plants〕》.

**품질**(品質) (a) quality. ¶ ~이 좋다〔나쁘다〕 be good 〔bad, poor〕 in quality; be of good 〔inferior〕 quality 《of 》/ ~을 개량하다 improve the quality / …에 비하여 ~이 떨어지다 be inferior to 《*a thing*》 in quality. ◉ ~관리 quality control (생략 QC). ~규격 specifications. ~보증 a warranty 〔guarantee〕 of quality 《of goods》; 《게시》 Quality Guaranteed: ~보증 제도 a quality certification system. ~본위 《게시》 Quality first: ~ 저하 deterioration. ~증명 a hallmark.

**품팔다** work for (daily) wages; work as a day laborer.

**품팔이** being a day laborer; a wageworker; doing day labor. ~하다 work for (daily) wages; hire out as a day laborer. ◉ ~꾼 a day laborer; a wageworker; a pieceworker.

**품평**(品評) estimation; evaluation; judgment; criticism 《of goods, *etc.*》. ~하다 estimate; evaluate; judge; criticize. ◉ ~회 a competitive 〔prize〕 show; an exhibition; a fair 《미》: 꽃〔개〕 ~회 a flower 〔dog〕 show / 농산물 ~회 an agricultural fair.

**품하다**(稟—) proffer 《*something*》 to a superior for approval; submit 《a plan》 to a superior.

**품행**(品行) conduct; behavior; demeanor; deportment; moral character. ¶ ~이

단정한 사람 a person of good conduct. ~이 단정하다 be well-behaved; be 《*a person*》 of good conduct / ~이 나쁘다 be poorly behaved; be ill-mannered 〔ill-conducted〕; be 《*a person*》 of loose conduct / 그는 ~이 단정하다 His conduct is exemplary 〔perfect〕.

**풋—** 《덜 익음》 green; unripe; 《미숙함》 novice; inexperienced; 《새로 나옴》 new; fresh.

**풋감** an unripe 〔a green〕 persimmon.

**풋거름** green manure. ⇨ 녹비(綠肥).

**풋것** the first product 《of fruits, vegetables》 of the season.

**풋게** early-autumn crab.

**풋고추** an unripe 〔a green〕 pepper.

**풋곡식**(—穀—) new grain.

**풋과실**(—果實) green fruits; newly picked fruit which is not quite ripe.

**풋김치** kimchi prepared with young vegetables.

**풋나물** 《a dish of》 seasoned young herbs. ¶ ~ 먹듯하다 eat with avidity.

**풋내** smell of fresh young greens. ¶ ~나다 smell of greens; [비유적] be green 〔unfledged, inexperienced〕.

**풋내기** ① 《무경험자》 an inexperienced person; an amateur; a green 〔new, raw〕 hand; a greenhorn; a fledgling 《미》; a beginner; a fresher 《영》; a cub; a novice; a tyro; a squirt 《구어》. ¶ ~의 new, green, raw / ~ 야구선수 a rookie / ~ 기자 a cub reporter. ② 《들뜬 사람》 a restless 〔fidgety〕 person.

**풋노트** a footnote(각주).

**풋담배** green tobacco; pipe tobacco prepared from green leaves.

**풋돈냥** a trivial amount of money; a petty fortune which has come into *one's* hand suddenly. ¶ ~이나 모았다 lately saved up a bit of money.

**풋라이트** footlight(각광).

**풋마늘** a young 〔an unripe〕 garlic.

**풋머리** the time for the first product of the season to appear.

**풋바심** harvesting grain before it is ripe. ~하다 harvest grain while it is still unripe.

**풋밤** an unripe chestnut.

**풋배** an unripe pear.

**풋벼** unripe rice. ◉ ~바심 harvesting unripe rice.

**풋볼** ① 《공》 a football. ② 《경기》 (the game of) football.

**풋사랑** puppy 〔calf〕 love.

**풋솜씨** lack of skill; undeveloped 〔imperfect〕 skill.

**풋워크** 〖스포츠·권투〗 footwork. ¶ ~가 좋다〔나쁘다〕 *one's* footwork is good 〔poor〕 / ~가 어지러워지다 lose *one's* footwork.

**풋잠** a light sleep; a doze.

**풋장** grass 〔branch〕 fuel (cut and dried in autumn).

**풋장기**(—將棋) unskilled chess 〔*changgi*〕; a green hand at chess; an amateur's chess.

**풋콩** an unripe bean 〔pea〕.

**풍** ① 《방귀가》 (flatulating) with a poop! ¶ 방귀를 풍 뀌다 break wind noisily; break wind "poop"! ② 《구멍이》 breaking open. ¶ 땅에 구멍이 풍 뚫어지다 a big hole is made 〔gapes〕 in the ground.

**풍**(風) ① 《바람》 (the) wind. ¶ 동풍 the east wind / 강풍 a strong wind. ② 《허풍》 a boast; a brag; exaggeration; tall 〔big〕 talk; bluster; bravado. ¶ 풍을 치다〔떨다〕 boast; brag; exaggerate; talk big 〔tall〕; "be full of hot air"; "be an old windbag" / 그 놈은 밤낮 풍만 떨고 다닌다 He is full of brag. / 그 사람 얘기는 약간 풍이 섞였어 His statement is rather exaggerated. / 풍을 쳐도 분수가 있지 That's about enough of your hot air. ③ 《풍병》 palsy; paralysis. ¶ 풍에 걸리다 have a stroke of 〔be taken with〕 paralysis; suffer from nerve troubles. ④ [접미사] 《양식·풍습》 a mode; a style; an air; a manner; a fashion; a custom. ¶ 도회풍 town manners; urbanity / 미국풍 an American style 〔fashion〕; American manners / 한국풍의 집 a Korean-style house.

**풍각쟁이**(風角—) a street 〔strolling〕 singer 〔musician〕.

**풍격**(風格) 《풍채》 appearance; 《품격》 character; personality. ¶ 왕자의 ~ 《have》 a regal presence / ~이 있는 인물 a man with a distinctive 〔remarkable〕 character / ~이 있는 문장 style of a distinctive quality.

**풍경**(風景) 《경치》 scenery; a landscape; 《전망》 a scene; 《조망》 a view.

> 용법 **scenery** 한 지방 또는 한 나라의 풍경. **landscape** 어느 한 시점(視點)에서 볼 수 있는 육지의 풍경. **scene** 한정된 한 장면의 풍경. **view** 「조망, 광경」을 뜻하는 일반적인 말.

¶ 거리의 ~ a street scene / 산의 ~ mountain scenery / 갑자기 눈앞에 ~이 펼쳐지다 suddenly a scene opens up before *one's* eyes / 이 근처는 ~이 좋다

The neighborhood has [presents] a very fine view. ◉ ～화 a landscape (painting); 《바다의》 a seascape; a seapiece: ～화가 a landscape painter.

**풍경**(風磬) a wind-bell; a brass bell with a "fish" clapper. ◉ ～소리 the tinkling of a wind-bell.

**풍경치다**(風磬―) keep going in and out busily.

**풍광**(風光) (beautiful) scenery; natural [scenic] beauty. ◉ ～명미(明媚) great scenic beauty: 그곳은 ～명미하다 The scenery there is really beautiful [picturesque].

**풍구**(風―) 《농기구》 a kind of grain blower; 《풀무》 (a pair of) bellows.

**풍금**(風琴) an organ; a harmonium; a reed organ; ⇨ 오르간. ¶ ～을 치다 play (on the organ). ◉ ～ 연주가 an organist; an organ grinder. 전기 ～ an electric organ.

**풍기**(風紀) 《규율》 discipline; 《사회적》 public morality [morals]. ¶ 학교의 ～ school discipline / ～가 나쁘다 be under loose discipline / ～를 해치다 injure [corrupt] public morals; have a harmful effect upon public morality / ～가 문란하다 have lax public morals / ～를 단속하다 enforce discipline 《among》; control public morals / 요즈음 ～가 문란해졌다 Public decency has recently become corrupt [loose]. ◉ ～문란 demoralization; the decay of public morality. ～위원회 a disciplinary committee.

**풍기다** ①《냄새를》 spread odor in the air; scent; perfume; give off 《an odor》; 《냄새가》 spread; hang in [fill] the air; smell 《of》; have an odor; 《악취가》 stink; reek; 《향기가》 be fragrant. ¶ 좋은[나쁜] 냄새를 ～ smell sweet [bad]; give off a sweet [bad] smell / 주위에 향기를 ～ 《꽃따위가》 scent the air / 장미의 향기가 ～ the fragrance of roses hangs in the air / 그녀는 싸구려 향수 냄새를 풍겼다 She reeked with cheap perfume. / 하수도가 악취를 풍긴다 The ditch stinks (offensively). ② 《기미를》 smack [savor] of. ¶ 관리 티를 잔뜩 ～ smack [savor] strongly of the bureaucrat / 그는 어제 사직할지도 모른다는 인상을 풍겼다 He dropped me a hint that he might resign. ③ 《까불다》 rid grain of chaff and grit. ④ 《날짐승을》 scatter birds; 《날짐승이》 birds scatter.

**풍년**(豊年) a year of abundance; a fruitful [rich, plenteous, bumper] year; a banner year for crops; 《풍작》 a good harvest. ¶ ～을 축하하다 celebrate a good harvest / 금년은 ～이 들 것이다 We will have a good harvest this year. / 눈이 많이 오면 ～이 든다 A snow year, a rich year. ◉ ～거지 one who gets nothing at a time when everyone else gains. ～축제 the celebration of a good harvest; a harvest festival.

**풍덩** with a splash. ¶ 물에 ～ 뛰어들다 jump into the water with a splash; plunge in.

**풍덩거리다** keep splashing [plunging].

**풍덩풍덩** with splashes; with splash after splash. ¶ 물에 ～ 뛰어들다 jump into the water splash-splash-splash; plunge into the water.

**풍뎅이** 『곤충』 a scarabaeid (beetle); a scarab.

**풍도**(風度) attitude; appearance; mien. ¶ 대인(大人)의 ～ the attitude [bearing] of a gentleman.

**풍동**(風洞) a wind tunnel. ◉ ～시험 a wind tunnel test.

**풍떨다** ⇨ 풍(風) ②.

**풍랑**(風浪) wind and waves; heavy seas. ¶ ～이 심하다 have high [heavy] seas / ～에 시달리다 be buffeted by the wind and waves / ～과 싸우다 battle with [struggle against] the wind and waves.

**풍량계**(風量計) an airflow meter.

**풍력**(風力) the force [velocity] of the wind; 《동력으로서의》 wind power. ◉ ～계 a wind gauge; an anemometer. ～계급 a wind scale; a scale of winds. ～발전소 a wind power plant [station]. 자동 ～기록계 an anemograph.

**풍로**(風爐) a cooking brazier (with an air vent below); a portable (clay) cooking stove.

**풍로**(風露) wind and dew.

**풍류**(風流) ①《음악》 (wind) music. ②《멋·아치》 elegance; taste; refinement. ¶ ～적인 refined; elegant; tasteful; poetical / ～를 알다 have an eye for the picturesque; have a love of the poetical / ～를 모르다 be out of taste / ～를 일삼다 indulge in romantic pursuits.

◉ ～랑(郞) an elegant young man; a gay blade; a young dandy; a man-about-town. ～인(人) a man of refined taste.

**풍만**(豊滿) 《풍족》 abundance; opulence; plenty; 《살이 찐》 plumpness; corpulence; stoutness. ～하다 (be) abundant; plentiful; fleshy; plump; buxom; stout. ¶ ~한 가슴 a full 〔an ample〕 bosom / 육체가 ~한 미인 a plump voluptuous beauty.

**풍매**(風媒) 〖식물〗 wind-fertilization; anemophily. ¶ ~의 anemophilous; wind-fertilized. ◉ ~식물 an anemophile; an anemophilous plant. ~화(花) an anemophilous flower.

**풍모**(風貌) 《풍채》 *one's* personal appearance; mien; 《용모》 looks; features. ¶ ~가 당당한 사람 a man of dignified presence.

**풍문**(風聞) a (current) rumor; hearsay; a report. ¶ ~을 퍼뜨리다 set a rumor afloat; spread 〔start, circulate〕 a rumor / …이라는 ~이다 There is a rumor that…. *or* It is said that…. / 이것은 단지 ~에 지나지 않는다 This is mere hearsay.

**풍물**(風物) ① 《경치》 scenery; a landscape; nature. ② 《풍속과 사물》 institution and customs. ¶ 영국의 ~ the institution and customs of Britain; things English / 화이트씨는 특히 한국의 ~에 관심이 있다 Mr. White is especially interested in things Korean. ③ 《악기》 instruments for folk music. ◉ ~시 a poem concerning a landscape; natural poetry.

**풍미**(風味) (a) flavor; (a) savor; (a) taste; (a) relish. ¶ ~가 있는 delicious; savory; tasty / ~가 없는 flavorless; tasteless; insipid / ~를 내다 season; flavor; give a flavor 《to》 / ~를 더하게 하다 improve 〔enhance〕 the flavor 《of》 / 이 술에는 독특한 ~가 있다 The wine has a characteristic flavor 〔taste〕 all of its own.

**풍미하다**(風靡—) sway; sweep; dominate; predominate; overwhelm. ¶ 천하를 ~ rule 〔sway〕 the (whole) world; take the world by storm.

**풍병**(風病) ① 〖한의학〗 《풍기》 nervous disorders believed to be caused by wind; palsy; epilepsy; paralysis. ② 《문둥병》 leprosy.

**풍부**(豊富) (an) abundance; (a) plenty; (an) affluence; wealth; richness. ~하다 (be) abundant; plentiful; affluent; rich; ample. ¶ 내용이 ~한 substantial; of rich contents / ~한 수산 자원 an abundant supply of water / 비타민 C가 ~한 오렌지 an orange rich in vitamin C / ~한 물의 공급 an abundant 〔a plentiful〕 supply of water / 경험이 ~하다 have much experience 《in》 / ~하게 하다 enrich 《the contents》 / ~하게 갖춰 놓다 have a variety 《of goods》 in stock / 천연 자원이 ~하다 be rich in natural resources / 지식이 ~하다 have a great wealth of knowledge / 쿠웨이트는 석유가 ~하다 Kuwait abounds in oil. *or* Kuwait is an oil-rich country. / 그는 교사로서의 경험이 ~하다 He has a lot of experience as a teacher.

**풍비박산하다**(風飛雹散—) ① 《흩어짐》 scatter (like the wind and hail); get scattered; be wasted. ② 《흩음》 scatter 《*a thing*》; waste; squander.

**풍상**(風霜) ① 《바람과 서리》 wind and frost. ② 《시련》 hardships. ¶ 10년 ~ ten years of hardship / ~을 겪다 suffer hardships.

**풍선**(風船) a (toy) balloon. ¶ 실을 맨 ~ a toy balloon on a string / ~을 불다 inflate a balloon / ~을 띄우다 fly 〔send up〕 a balloon / ~을 터뜨리다 break a balloon / ~이 터졌다 The balloon burst. ◉ ~껌 《a piece of》 bubble gum. ~폭탄 a balloon bomb.

**풍설**(風說) a rumor; an unfounded report; speculation; hearsay. ¶ 항간의 ~ the talk of the town / …에 관해 여러 가지 ~이 분분하다 Much speculation is rife concerning….

**풍설**(風雪) wind and snow; wind-driven snow; a snowstorm.

**풍성**(風成) 〖지질〗 ¶ ~의 aeolian. ◉ ~암〔분지, 층〕 an aeolian rock 〔basin, deposit〕.

**풍성**(豊盛) abundance; plenitude; affluence; richness. ~하다 (be) abundant; plentiful; affluent; rich; ample. ¶ ~한 수확 an abundant crop 〔harvest〕 《of rice》 / 풍성한 사회 an affluent society / 풍성한 검은 머리 abundant black hair.

**풍세**(風勢) the force 〔velocity〕 of the wind; wind force. ¶ ~를 이용하다 take advantage of the wind.

**풍속**(風俗) manners; customs; public morals (풍기). ¶ ~을 어지럽히다 corrupt 〔be an offense against, offend (against)〕 public morals 〔decency〕; destroy good manners / 남의 나라에 가면 그 나라 ~을 따라야 한다 When at 〔in〕 Rome, do as the Romans do. ◉ ~경찰 moral police. ~문학 *genre* literature. ~사범 《행위》 a violation of public morals; an indecent offense; 《사람》 violaters of public morals. ~소설 a novel of manners. ~습관 manners and customs. ～영업 the entertainment and amusement trades (such as bars, restaurants, etc.). ～화〔도〕 a *genre* picture 〔painting〕.

**풍속**(風速) wind velocity 〔speed〕; the velocity 〔speed〕 of the wind. ¶ ～ 50 미터의 태풍 a typhoon blowing 50 meters per second. ◉ ～계 an anemometer; a wind gauge. 순간최대 ～ the maximum instantaneous wind speed.

**풍수**(風水) 〖민속〗 ① the geomantic system of topography used in choosing auspicious sites for graves and houses. ② 《지관》 a geomancer. ◉ ～설 the theory of geomancy. ～학 geomancy; geomantic studies of topography.

**풍수해**(風水害) damage caused by storm and flood; storm and flood damage. ◉ ～대책 measures against damage from storm and flood.

**풍습**(風習) (manners and) customs; practices. ¶ ～에 따르다 observe a custom / 이 지방에는 아직 옛날 ～이 남아 있다 Some old customs still obtain in this part of the country. / 나는 이 고장 ～에 익숙지 못하다 I am not accustomed to the manners and customs here.

**풍식**(風蝕) wind erosion; weathering.

**풍신**(風神) 《풍백》 the god of wind; 《풍채》 mien; appearance; countenance; air. ¶ ～이 좋다 have a fine appearance 〔presence〕.

**풍아**(風雅) elegance; grace; refinement. ～하다 (be) elegant; graceful; refined; tasteful.

**풍악**(風樂) (Korean) music. ¶ ～을 잡히다 have music played.

**풍압**(風壓) 〖기상〗 wind pressure; 〖항해·항공〗 leeway. ◉ ～계 a pressure anemometer.

**풍어**(豊漁) a large 〔good〕 catch; a good haul (of fish). ¶ 꽁치의 대～ a big catch 〔haul〕 of mackerel pike.

**풍요**(豊饒) richness; wealth; abundance. ～하다 (be) rich; abundant; bountiful. ¶ ～로운 사회 an affluent society / ～한 땅 〖성서〗 a land flowing with milk and honey.

**풍우**(風雨) wind and rain; 《폭풍우》 a rainstorm; tempest. ¶ ～를 무릅쓰고 가다 go 「in spite 〔in the teeth〕 of the raging storm / ～ 대작(大作)하다 have a driving rainstorm.

**풍운**(風雲) 《바람과 구름》 winds and clouds; 《형세》 the state of affairs; the situation. ¶ ～의 뜻 a great ambition / ～의 뜻을 품다 cherish an ambition; have an adventurous spirit. ◉ ～아 a hero 〔an adventurer〕 of the troubled times. ～조화 mysteries of wind and cloud; exercise of supernatural power.

**풍월**(風月) 《자연의 미》 beauties of nature; 《시》 poetry. ¶ 들은 ～ a smattering (of knowledge) / ～을 즐기다 enjoy nature / ～을 벗삼다 commune with nature / ～을 짓다 compose a poem / 서당 개 3년에 풍월 읊는다 《속담》 A saint's maid quotes Latin. *or* The sparrow near the school sings the primer. ◉ ～객 a person who dabbles in poetry; a poet.

**풍위**(風位) the direction of the wind. ¶ ～를 측정하다 define the direction of the wind.

**풍자**(諷刺) (a) satire; (a) sarcasm; (an) innuendo; (an) irony; a lampoon (가벼운) (★ 풍자적 행동을 말할 때는 관사가 있음). ～하다 satirize; 《시나 글로》 lampoon. ¶ ～적인 satirical; sarcastic; ironical / 사회에 대한 통렬한 ～ a bitter 〔keen, scathing〕 satire on society. ◉ ～가 a satirist; a lampooner. ～문 a lampoon. ～문학 a satire; satirical literature. ～소설 a satirical novel 〔story〕. ～시 a satirical poem; a satire; a lampoon; a pasquinade. ～화 a caricature. 해학 ～극 a burlesque.

**풍작**(豊作) a good 〔a rich, an abundant〕 harvest; a bumper 〔heavy〕 crop. ¶ ～의 해 a year of plenty; 《과일 따위의》 a fruitful 〔good〕 year; 《곡식의》 a bumper crop year / 쌀은 ～이 확실시된다 There is every prospect of a large rice crop. / 올해는 대체로 ～이었다 The crop was generally abundant this year.

**풍장**(風葬) burial 〔disposal of a body〕 by exposure to the elements; aerial sepulture 〔burial〕.

**풍재**(風災) damage from wind; a disaster caused by wind; crop loss 〔blight〕 caused by wind.

**풍전등화**(風前燈火) a candle flickering in the wind; [비유적] a precarious situation to be in. ¶ 국운이 ～이다 The fate of the nation 「hangs by 〔on〕 a thread 〔is in an extremely precarious position〕.

**풍정**(風情) elegance; refinement; fineness; tasteful appearance; an artistic air.

**풍조**(風鳥) 〖조류〗 a bird-of-paradise.

**풍조**(風潮) 《조수》 the lee(ward) tide; 《세태》 a tendency; a trend; a drift; the tide; the current; the stream; the fashion. ¶ 세상 ~ the trend 〔drift〕 of the times; the tone of society; the fashion of the world / ~를 따르다 swim with the stream; follow the tide.

**풍족**(豊足) (an) abundance; (a) plenty; (an) ampleness. ~하다 (be) abundant; plentiful; ample. ¶ ~하게 살다 be well 〔comfortably〕 off; live in plenty 〔clover, abundance〕 / 재정이 ~하다 be financially well off.

**풍진**(風疹) 〖의학〗 rubella; German measles.

**풍진**(風塵) wind-blown dust; 《속세의》 troubles 〔cares〕 of life; worldly affairs. ¶ ~을 피하다 seclude *oneself* from the world; live in seclusion; lead a sequestered life. ◉ ~세상 this world of woe and tumult. 세상~ troubles of life 〔of the world〕.

**풍차**(風車) ① 《풍차》 a windmill. ② = 풍구(風—). ③ =팔랑개비. ◉ ~발전기 a fan-driven generator. ~펌프 a wind pump.

**풍채**(風采) *one's* (personal) appearance; (an) air; presence; mien. ¶ ~가 당당한 사람 a man of imposing appearance 〔fine presence〕 / ~가 초라한 사람 a man of meager appearance; a plain-looking man / ~가 당당하다 have a commanding presence; have a lofty bearing 〔imposing appearance〕; be stately in mien / ~가 좋다 have a fine presence; look fine.

**풍치**(風致) ① 《우아》 taste; elegance. ¶ ~가 있다 be elegant 〔tasteful, charming〕. ② 《경치》 scenic beauty; the charm of scenery. ¶ ~가 좋다 have beautiful scenery / ~를 더해 주다 improve 〔add charm to〕 the view; improve 〔enhance〕 the beauty of the scenery / ~를 해치다 spoil 〔impair〕 the view 〔beauty〕 of the scenery. ◉ ~림 an ornamental forest plantation; a forest grown for scenic beauty. ~지구 a scenic area 〔zone〕; nature preservation area; the area where unauthorized alteration of the landscape is forbidden by law.

**풍치다**(風—) ⇨풍(風) ②.

**풍침**(風枕) an air cushion; a pneumatic pillow.

**풍토**(風土) natural features 《of a region》; climate; a clime. ¶ ~의 climatic; endemic (지방 특유의) / 한국의 문화〔정신〕적 ~ the cultural 〔spiritual〕 climate of Korea / ~에 익숙해지다 be 〔get〕 acclimatized 〔acclimated 《미》〕. ◉ ~기(記) a topography. ~병 an endemic disease; a locally prevalent ailment. ~순화 acclimatization; acclimation. ~학 climatology: ~학자 a climatologist.

**풍파**(風波) ① 《바람과 물결》 the wind and waves; a storm; a tempest; rough seas. ¶ ~를 만나다 be caught by a storm / ~가 일다〔자다〕 the wind and sea rise 〔go down〕 / ~를 무릅쓰고 in the face 〔teeth〕 of wind and waves. ② 《어려움》 hardships; a storm. ¶ ~를 겪다 suffer 〔undergo〕 hardships. ③ 《분란》 a trouble; a disturbance; discord; a quarrel. ¶ ~를 일으키다 create 〔raise〕 a disturbance; cause trouble; kick up a row / 평지 ~를 일으키다 cause trouble where there is no cause; provoke a storm in a dead calm; raise unnecessary trouble / 저 가정에는 ~가 끊일 사이가 없다 There are constant troubles in that family. ◉ 가정~ family troubles; domestic discord. 세상~ the storms 〔rough and tumble〕 of life.

**풍편**(風便) rumor; hearsay. ¶ ~에 듣다 hear of; know by hearsay.

**풍해**(風害) =풍재(風災).

**풍향**(風向) (the direction of ) the wind. ¶ ~이 바뀌다 the wind shifts; the direction of the wind changes. ◉ ~계(計)〔기(旗)〕 a weathercock; a wind vane.

**풍화**(風化) 〖지질〗 weathering; efflorescence. ~하다 weather; effloresce. ¶ 비바람으로 ~된 바위 rocks weathered by wind and water / ~된 석회 air=slaked lime. ◉ ~물 efflorescence. ~작용 weathering; the action of natural forces. ~토(土) soil of weathered rock.

**풍흉**(豊凶) good and bad harvests; good years and bad.

**퓨리턴** 《청교도》 a Puritan; 《엄격한 사람》 a puritan; 《주의》 Puritanism.

**퓨마** 〖동물〗 a puma.

**퓨즈** 〖전기〗 a fuse. ¶ ~가 끊어지다 a fuse is burnt out / ~를 넣다 fit 〔put〕 a fuse 《to》 / ~를 갈다 replace a fuse; put in a new fuse. ◉ 안전~ a safety fuse.

**퓰리처상**(—賞) the Pulitzer Prize 《for

drama》. ◉ ～ 수상자 a Pulitzer Prize winner; a Pulitzer laureate. ～ 수상작(품) a Pulitzer Prize work.
**프라이** 〖요리〗 a fry; something fried. ¶ ～로 하다 fry / ～한 fried. ◉ ～팬 a frying pan; a skillet. 새우～ fried lobster 〔prawns〕. 에그～ fried eggs.
**프라이드** 《자존심》 pride ¶ ～가 높은 proud; self-respecting / …하는 것은 ～가 용납치 않다 be too proud to *do*; be above *do*ing.
**프라이버시** privacy. ¶ 남의 ～를 침해하다 infringe upon *a person's* privacy.
**프라임 레이트** 〖경제〗 the prime rate.
**프라하** 《체코의 수도》 Praha; Prague. ◉ ～ 시민 a Praguer.
**프락치** a fraction; 《러》 *fraktsiya*. ◉ ～활동 fraction activities.
**프랑** 《프랑스의 화폐》 a franc (기호 fr.).
**프랑스** France. ¶ ～의 French. ◉ ～말 French; the French language. ～사람 a Frenchman; a Frenchwoman; the French [총칭]. ～요리 French dishes; 《요리법》 French cuisine. ～혁명 the French Revolution.
**프랑크푸르트** 《독일의 도시》 Frankfurt.
**프래그머티즘** 〖철학〗 pragmatism.
**프랜차이즈** 〖야구〗 franchise.
**프러시아** 《독일 북부의 옛 왕국》 Prussia.
**프러포즈** 《청혼》 a proposal of marriage 《to a girl》. ～하다 propose 《to a girl》.
**프런트** 《호텔의》 the front 〔reception〕 desk. ◉ ～유리 《자동차의》 a windshield.
**프런티어 정신**(—精神) 《개척자 정신》 the frontier spirit.
**프레스** ① 《다림질》 press. ¶ ～가 잘 된 바지 a well pressed trousers. ② 《역도의》 press. ¶ ～에서 135킬로를 들다 lift 135 kilos in press. ③ 《신문》 the press. ◉ ～박스 the press box. ～센터 the press center. ～ 캠페인 a press campaign. ～코드 the press code.
**프레스코** fresco. ◉ ～화(畫) a fresco: ～화가 a frescoer.
**프레스토** 〖음악〗 presto (It.).
**프레스티시모** 〖음악〗 *prestissimo* (It.).
**프레시** fresh. ¶ ～하게 느껴지다 feel fresh; find something fresh and clean 《in a picture》.
**프레올림픽** the Pre-Olympics; the Pre-Olympic Games.
**프레이즈** 《성구》 a phrase. ◉ 캐치 ～ a catch phrase.
**프레이즈반**(—盤) 〔<fraise〕 a milling machine.
**프레젠트** 《선물》 a present; a gift. ～하다 give 〔make〕 a present 《to *a person*》; make 《*a person*》 a present of.
**프렌치** French. ◉ ～드레싱 〖요리〗 French dressing. ～ 어니언 수프 French onion soup. ～ 토스트 French toast. ～ 호른 〖음악〗 a French horn.
**프렐류드** 〖음악〗 a prelude.
**프로** ① 《프롤레타리아》 the proletariat(e); a proletarian. ② = 프로그램. ③ 《직업적》 pro; professional. ¶ ～로 전향하다 turn professional 〔pro〕. ④ 《퍼센트》 per cent. ◉ ～레슬링 pro(fessional) wrestling. ～문학 proletarian literature. ～복싱 pro boxing 《구어》: ～ 복싱 선수 a pro boxer; a ring pro; a pugilist. ～선수 a pro(fessional) player. ～야구 pro(fessional) baseball; 《구단》 a professional baseball-team; a proball team: ～ 야구 선수 a professional baseball player; a proball player. ～의식 the pride of a professional. ～축구 a pro football. ～팀 a professional team. 대북 방송 ～ a program beamed at North Korea.
**프로그래머** 《컴퓨터의》 a (computer) programmer.
**프로그래밍** 《컴퓨터의》 program(m)ing.
**프로그램** a program. ¶ ～을 진행시키다 proceed with a program; go on with a program / ～대로 진행되다 proceed according to the program; go on as scheduled / 컴퓨터의 ～을 만들다 write a program for a computer / ～을 컴퓨터에 넣다 program a comuter; program 《a problem》 into a computer. ◉ ～제어 〖전기〗 program control. ～학습 program(m)ed learning.
**프로그맨** 《잠수부·공작 요원》 a frogman (*pl.* -men).
**프로덕션** 《제작·생산》 production; 《영화 제작소》 a movie studio 〔lot〕; 《예능 프로덕션》 a theatrical agency.
**프로듀서** 〖연극·영화〗 a producer.
**프로메테우스** 〖그神〗 Prometheus.
**프로메튬** 〖화학〗 promethium (기호 Pm).
**프로모터** 《창립자·후원자·흥행주》 a promoter.
**프로세스** 《과정·진행》 a process.
**프로이트** Freud. ◉ ～학설〔주의〕 Freudianism.
**프로젝트** a project.
**프로카인** 〖약〗 procain.
**프로테스탄트** 〖기독교〗 Protestant; 《주의》 Protestantism; 《신자》 a Protestant.
**프로텍터** 《방호구》 a 《chest》 protector; a 《face》 guard.
**프로토콜** 〖컴퓨터〗 《통신 규약》 a protocol.
**프로토타입** 《시험 제작 원형》 a prototype.
**프로톤** 〖화학·물리〗 a proton.
**프로튬** 〖화학〗 protium (기호 $H^1$).
**프로파간다** 《선전》 propaganda (work);

publicity.
**프로판** 〖화학〗 propane. ◉ ~가스 propane 〔liquefied petroleum〕 gas (생략 LPG); LP gas; propane.
**프로페서** 《교수》 a professor (★ 성명 앞에서는 흔히 Prof.로 생략 (*Prof.* John Smith). 단 성에만 붙일 경우는 생략치 않음 (*professor* Smith)).
**프로페셔널** ① 《직업적·전문적》 professional 《team》. ② 《선수》 a professional player; a pro (*pl.* ~s).
**프로펠러** a propeller. ¶ ~를 돌리다 spin a propeller. ◉ ~기(機) a propeller(=driven) plane. ~소리 the whir 〔burr, roar〕 of a propeller.
**프로피온산**(一酸) 〖화학〗 propionic acid.
**프로필**[1] 《옆 얼굴·윤곽》 a profile; 《인물 단평》 a brief character sketch. ¶ 한 선생의 ~ a sketch of Mr. Han's career and personality.
**프로필**[2] 〖화학〗 ◉ ~기(基) propyl. ~ 알코올 propyl alcohol.
**프로필렌** 〖화학〗 propylene. ◉ ~ 글리콜 propylene glycol.
**프록코트** 《19세기 신사 정복》 a frock coat.
**프롤라민** 〖생화학〗 prolamin(e).
**프롤락틴** 〖생화학〗 prolactin; lactogenic hormone.
**프롤레타리아** 《사람》 a proletarian; 《계급》 the proletariat; the working class. ◉ ~독재 dictatorship of the proletariat. ~문학 = 프로 문학. ~혁명 a proletarian revolution.
**프롤로그**[1] 《서언·서막》 a prolog(ue).
**프롤로그**[2] 〖컴퓨터〗 《프로그래밍 언어》 PROLOG. [< *pro*gramming in *log*ic]
**프롤린** 〖생화학〗 proline.
**프롬프터** 〖연극〗 a (theater) prompter.
**프롭제트** 〖기계〗 a propjet; turboprop.
**프루트** 《과일》 fruit (집합 명사); fruits (각종의). ◉ ~주스 fruit juice. ~펀치 〔칵테일, 샐러드〕 a fruit cup 〔coktail, salad〕.
**프리깃함**(一艦) 《소형 구축함》 a frigate.
**프리다이얼** 《미》 a toll-free (telephone) number; a toll-free call.
**프리랜서** a free lance; a free-lancer. ¶ ~로서 활약〔집필〕하다 act 〔write〕 as a free lance; free-lance / 그는 ~로 일하기 위해 정규직을 버렸다 He gave up his regular job in order to do free=lance work.
**프리마돈나** 《가극의》 a prima donna (*pl.* ~s, prime donne). ¶ 가극의 ~ the prima donna in an opera.
**프리미엄** a premium (*pl.* ~s). ¶ ~을 붙이다 put a premium 《on》 / 2할의 ~으로 팔리다 be sold at a premium of 20 percent.
**프리배팅** 〖야구〗 free batting; batting practice.
**프리사이즈** 《표시》 One Size Fits All.
**프리스로** 〖농구〗 a free throw. ¶ ~를 넣다 sink a free throw.
**프리스타일** 〖수영·레슬링〗 the freestyle; 〖레슬링〗 freestyle 〔all-in〕 wrestling.
**프리에이전트** 〖스포츠〗 《미》 free agent (자유 계약 선수).
**프리웨이** 《다차선식 고속도로》 a freeway.
**프리저** 《냉동 장치》 a freezer. ¶ 아이스크림 ~ an ice-cream freezer.
**프리즘** 〖물리〗 a prism. ¶ ~의 굴절 prismatic refraction. ◉ ~쌍안경 prismatic binoculars. 직각 ~ a right=angled prism.
**프리지어** 〖식물〗 a freesia.
**프리토킹** free 〔unstructured〕 conversation.
**프리킥** 〖축구〗 a free kick.
**프리패브** prefabrication. ◉ ~주택 a prefabricated house; a prefab.
**프리패스** a free pass; a free ticket; a pass admitting a person free.
**프린세스** 《공주》 a princess.
**프린스** 《왕자》 a prince.
**프린트** 《옷감》 print; 《인쇄》 printing; 《인쇄물》 a printed 〔mimeographed〕 copy. ¶ ~로 하다 print; mimeograph. ◉ ~배선 a printed circuit. ~장이 a (mimeograph) printer. 강의~ a printed lecture; a printed synopsis of a lecture.
**프릴** 〖양재〗 a frill.
**프토마인** 〖화학〗 ptomaine. ◉ ~ 중독 ptomaine poisoning.
**프티부르주아** 《사람》 a petty 〔*petit*〕 *bourgeois*; 《계급》 petty 〔*petite*〕 *bourgeoisie*.
**플라네타륨** 〖천문〗 a planetarium.
**플라멩코** 《집시춤의 하나》 flamenco. ¶ ~를 추다 dance the flamenco.
**플라밍고** 〖조류〗 a flamingo (*pl.* ~(e)s).
**플라스마** 〖물리·생리〗 plasma.
**플라스크** a flask; a flasket (소형의).
**플라스터** 〖건축〗 plaster.
**플라스틱** (a) plastic; [총칭] plastics. ◉ ~산업 the plastics industry. ~제품 a plastic; plastic goods. ~주민(등록)증 a plastic ID card.
**플라시보 효과** 〖의·약〗 placebo effect.
**플라이** ① 〖야구〗 a fly (ball). ¶ 라이트 ~를 날리다 fly into right field. ② 《체중의》 flyweight. ¶ ~급의 flyweight. ◉ ~급 선수 a flyweight. 외야 ~ an outfield fly.
**플라잉** 《경주에서》 a premature start; 《미》 a breakaway. ~하다 make a premature start; break away; jump

〔beat〕 the gun.
**플라즈마** 〖생리〗 plasma.
**플라타너스** 〖식물〗 a plane (tree); a platan(e); a sycamore.
**플라토닉** 《정신적인》 Platonic; spiritual. ◉ ~ 러브 Platonic love.
**플라톤** 《그리스의 철학자》 Plato (427-347 B.C.). ◉ ~ 철학〔주의〕 Platonism. ~학파 a Platonist.
**플란넬** flannel. ◉ ~ 제품 flannels.
**플랑크톤** 〖생물〗 plankton. ¶ 동물성 ~ zooplankton; animal plankton / 식물성 ~ phytoplankton; plant plankton / ~을 먹이로 하는 물고기 a planktivorous 〔plankton-feeding〕 fish. ◉ ~학(學) planktology.
**플래시** a flash; 《회중 전등》 an electric torch; a flashlight 《미》. ¶ ~를 켜다〔비추다〕 flash *one's* torch / ~를 터뜨리다 light a flash bulb; snap a flashlight / ~를 터뜨려 사진을 찍다 take a photograph with a blare of flashlight / ~(세례)를 받다 be in a flood 〔flares〕 of flashlights. ◉ ~ 파우더 flash(light) powder.
**플래시백** 〖영화〗 a flashback. ~하다 flash back 《to the original scene》.
**플래카드** a placard. ¶ ~를 들고 행진하다 march with placards lifted up.
**플래티나** platinum (기호 Pt). ⇨ 백금.
**플랜** a plan. ¶ ~을 세우다 make 〔form, map out〕 a plan 《for》.
**플랜트** 《공장설비》 a plant. ◉ ~ 수출 export of (industrial) plants; plant export.
**플랩** 〖항공〗 a flap(보조익).
**플랫** ① 〖음악〗 a flat (기호 ♭). ② 《경주에서》 ¶ 9초 ~ flat at nine seconds; nine seconds flat.
**플랫폼** 《승강장》 a 《train》 platform; a track. ¶ ~에서 on the platform / 2번 ~ platform No. 2; Track Two / ~의 역명(驛名) 표시판 a station-name sign at a platform.
**플러그** 〖전기〗 a plug. ¶ ~를 꽂다 put the plug in 《the socket》; plug (in). ◉ ~앤드 플레이 〖컴퓨터〗 plug and play. ~ 퓨즈 a plug fuse. 단로(斷路) ~ a disconnecting plug. 연결~ an attaching plug.
**플러스** plus; addition; adding; 《이익》 a gain 《to *one's* happiness》; an advantage; an asset. ~하다 add 《two》 to 《six》; 《기여하다》 contribute 《to》; do 《much》 for. ¶ ~ 요소 a plus factor / 조금이라도 ~가 된다면 if there is any gain / ~ 여부를 헤아려〔따져〕 보다 weigh the plus and minus 《of》 / 마이너스보다 ~되는 면이 많다 The pluses outweight the minuses. / 그건 ~ 마이너스 제로다 That would mean no gain 《for you》. / ~는 커녕 도리어 마이너스가 되었다 Far from being a gain, it proved (to be) a loss. / 3 ~ 4는 7, Three plus four is 〔makes, equals〕 seven. *or* Three and four are 〔make, equal〕 seven. ◉ ~기호 a plus (sign). ~알파 plus something.
**플레어스커트** a flared skirt.
**플레오마이신** 《항생 물질》 phleomycin.
**플레이** a play. ◉ 파인 ~ a fine play.
**플레이백** 《녹음·녹화의》 (a) playback. ~하다 play back.
**플레이볼** 〖스포츠〗 play ball.
**플레이스킥** 〖축구〗 a place-kick; a placement kick. ~하다 make a place-kick; place-kick 《a ball》.
**플레이어** 《사람》 a player; 《축음기》 a record player.
**플레이오프** a play-off.
**플레이트** a plate; 〖야구〗 《투수》 a pitcher's plate; 《홈》 the home plate. ¶ ~를 밟다 take the plate 〔mound〕 / ~를 물러나다 give up the mound 《for another pitcher》. ◉ ~전류 plate current.
**플렉스타임** 《자유 근무 시간제》 flextime 〔flexitime 《영》〕; flextimer 〔flexitimer 《영》〕; flexible time.
**플로렌스** Florence.
**플로리다** 《미국의 주》 Florida (생략 Fla., Flor.).
**플로어** a floor. ◉ ~ 매니저 a floor manager. ~쇼 a floor show. ~ 시프트 a floor-mounted gear shift.
**플로어링** 〖건축〗 flooring.
**플롯** a plot. ¶ 소설의 ~ the plot of a story.
**플루오르** 〖화학〗 fluorine(생략 F). ¶ ~(중독)증 〖의학〗 fluorosis / ~ 처리 fluorination; fluoridization. ◉ ~산 fluoric acid: ~산염 fluorate.
**플루오르화**(一化) 〖화학〗 fluoridation. ◉ ~물 a fluorid(e). ~수소 hydrogen fluoride: ~ 수소산 hydofluoric acid. ~암모늄〔칼슘〕 ammonium 〔calcium〕 fluoride.
**플루토늄** 〖화학〗 plutonium (기호 Pu).
**플루트** 〖음악〗 a flute. ¶ ~를 불다 play the flute. ◉ ~주자 a flutist; a flute player.
**피**[1] ① 《혈액》 blood. ¶ 피투성이의 bloody; smeared with blood; blood-soaked / 피 묻은 stained with blood; bloodstained / 피바다 a pool 〔sea〕 of blood / 피의 순환 blood circulation / 엉긴 피 clotted blood; a clot of blood / 피 묻은 손수건 a bloodstained 〔blood=

smeared〕 handkerchief / 피가 나다 bleed 《from the nose》 / 피가 묻다 become tainted with blood / 피를 묻히다 smear with blood / 피를 흘리다 spill〔shed, let〕 blood / 피를 토하다 《객혈》 spit 〔eject〕 blood; cough out blood; 《토혈》 vomit blood / 피를 빼다 draw 〔let〕 blood / 피를 빨다 suck up blood / 피를 멎게 하다 stop bleeding; stanch〔arrest〕 the flow of blood / 전쟁터는 피바다를 이루었다 The battlefield was flooded with blood. / 그 사건은 끝내 피를 보고야 말았다 The affair「resulted 〔ended up〕 in (a) bloodshed. *or* The affair had a violent outcome.

② 《혈통》 blood (relation) (혈연); consanguinity (혈족); lineage (가계). ¶ 피를 나눈 형제 a blood brother; a brother by blood / 피를 이어받다 descend 《from》 / (아무와) 피가 섞이다 be related to 《*a person*》 by blood / 피는 못 속인다 Blood will tell. / 피는 물보다 진하다 《속담》 Blood is thicker than water. / 그에게는 프랑스인의 피가 섞여 있다 He has some French blood (in his veins).

③ [비유적] ¶ 피도 눈물도 없는 cold-blooded; stonehearted; insusceptible to pity / 두 국민간의 피로써 다져진 우의(友誼) the friendship sealed in blood between the two peoples / 피가 끓다 *one's* blood「boils 〔tingles〕 / 피가 끓게 하다 put fire into 《*a person's*》 blood; inflame the「blood 〔ardor〕 《of》; stir 《*a person's*》 blood / 피에 주리다 thirst for blood; be bloodthirsty / 정의를 위해 피를 흘리다 bleed for a righteous cause / 그들은 마치 피에 굶주린 늑대처럼 행동했다 They acted like bloodthirsty wolves. / 젊은 시절의 면학은 후일 너의 피와 살이 된다 What you have seriously learned in your youth will enrich your body and soul in your later life.

**피**[2] 〖식물〗 a Decan grass; a barnyard「grass 〔millet〕.

**피검**(被檢) being arrested. ¶ 그는 선거법 위반으로 ~되었다 He was arrested for violations of the election law. ◉ ~자 the arrested; a person in custody.

**피겨스케이팅** figure skating. ¶ ~을 하다 skate figures 《on the ice》. ◉ ~선수 a figurer.

**피격**(被擊) suffering 〔being under〕 attack. ¶ ~되다 be attacked 〔assaulted〕 《by》.

**피고**(被告) 《민사》 a defendant; 《형사》 an accused person; the accused. ◉ ~대리인 the defendant's representative. ~변호인 (the) counsel for the「defense 〔accused (형사의)〕. ~석 the dock; the bar.

**피고름** bloody pus.

**피고용인**(被雇傭人) an「employee 〔employe〕; the employed [총칭].

**피곤**(疲困) tiredness; weariness; exhaustion; fatigue. ⇨ 피로. ~하다 (be) tired; weary; fatigued; exhausted. ¶ ~한 느낌 tired feeling; the feeling of「tiredness 〔languidness〕 / 서 있어서 ~하다 be tired from standing.

**피골**(皮骨) skin and bones. ¶ ~이 상접하다 be reduced to (mere) skeleton; be all skin and bones; be worn to a shadow.

**피그미족**(一族) a Pygmy; a Pigmy.

**피근피근** refusing to listen; stubbornly. ~하다 (be) stubborn; contrary. ¶ ~ 말을 듣지 않다 stubbornly refuse to listen; insist on having *one's* own way.

**피나다** ① bleed. ⇨ 피[1]. ¶ 코에서 피가 나다 bleed at the nose. ② 《고생하다》 ¶ 피나는 노력 blood-and-tears endeavor.

**피나무** 〖식물〗 a「linden 〔lime〕 (tree); a bass(wood).

**피난**(避難) refuge; shelter. ~하다 take 〔seek〕 refuge 《in, from》; take 〔find〕 shelter 《in, from》; flee 《to a place》 for safety; go out of the danger. ¶ 그들은 우리집으로 ~을 왔다 They sought shelter at my house. / 우리는 아이들을 시골로 ~시켰다 We evacuated the children to the country. / 홍수 때문에 그들은 근처 초등학교 건물로 ~했다 They took refuge from the flood in the primary school building nearby. ◉ ~경로 an evacuation route. ~명령 an evacuation order. ~민 a refugee; an evacuee; displaced people: 다수의 ~민이 이웃나라로 ~하였다 Lots of refugees took refuge in the neighboring countries. ~살이 refugee life. ~소〔처〕 a (place of) refuge; a (safe) shelter; a haven.

**피날레** 〖음악〗 a finale; 《극·오페라 따위의》 the end; a grand final.

**피낭**(被囊) 〖생물〗 a cyst; 〖해부〗 a capsule; a tunic.

**피넛**《땅콩》 peanuts. ◉ ~버터 peanut「butter.

**피눈물** bitter tears; tears of agony. ¶ ~나게 번 돈 money earned by the sweat of *one's* brows / ~을 흘리다 weep 〔shed〕「bitter tears 〔tears of blood〕.

**피니시** 《마무리》 a finish; 《체조의》 the landing (착지).

**피닉스** 《불사조》 the ph(o)enix.

**피다** ① 《반듯해지다》 be straightened (곧게); be flattened (평평하게); become smooth (주름 따위가); 《it》 spread 〔straighten, smooth〕 out. ⇨ 펴다. ② 《꽃이》 bloom; open; come 〔be〕 out; [나무가 주어] blossom; flower; come into flower. ¶ 갓 핀 new-blown 《roses》 / 봄에 피는 화초 plants 「blooming 〔flowering〕 in spring / 복숭아꽃이 필 때에 in the peach-blossom time / 피어 있다 be in 「bloom 〔blossom〕; be flowering; be out / 피기 시작하다 start flowering; come into blossom / 활짝 피다 be in full bloom; be at *its* best; be all 「open 〔out〕 / 피게 하다 make a flower bloom / 빨갛게 ~ bloom red. ③ 《불이》 burn; be kindled. ¶ 불이 ~ a fire burns / 잘 피지 않다 《장작불이》 burn poorly. ④ 《얼굴이》 look better; bloom; 《경제 사정이》 ease (financially); take a turn for the better; improve; 《살림이》 be well-off. ¶ 얼굴이 ~ *one's* complexion blooms; gain color; look better / 금전적인 사정이 ~ *one's* financial condition 「eases 〔improves, looks up〕 / 그는 이제 살림이 피었다 He is well-off now.

**피담보인**(被擔保人) a warrantee.

**피대**(皮帶) a (leather) belt.

**피동**(被動) passivity; passiveness. ¶ ~적(으로) passive(ly). ◉ ~사(詞) 〖문법〗 a passive verb. ~형 the passive form.

**피둥피둥** ① 《뚱뚱한 모양》 ~하다 (be) fat; corpulent; plump. ¶ ~ 살찐 사람 a 「plump 〔fat〕 person; a fatty. ② 《피근피근》 refusing to listen; stubbornly; contrarily. ¶ ~ 말을 듣지 않다 refuse to listen 《to *a person*》; insist on having *one's* own way.

**피드백** 〖전기·컴퓨터〗 feedback. ¶ 정보를 ~하다 feed back information. ◉ ~ 시스템 the feedback system. ~증폭기 a feedback amplifier.

**피딱지**[1] 《혈액의》 a layer of coagulated blood; a blood clot. ¶ ~가 앉다 get 〔have〕 a blood clot.

**피딱지**[2] 《종이》 poor-quality paper made of mulberry bark.

**피땀** blood and sweat; greasy sweat. ¶ ~ 흘려 번 돈 money earned by the sweat of *one's* brows / ~ 흘리며 일하다 toil and moil.

**피똥** bloody stools; excrement mixed 「with blood.

**피라미** 〖어류〗 a dace (fish); a minnow.

**피라미드** a pyramid. ¶ ~ 모양의 pyramidal; pyramidic(al) / 계단식 ~ a step pyramid / ~식 조직 a pyramid organization / 역(逆)~ an inverted pyramid. ◉ ~식 판매방식 a multilevel marketing 〔sales〕 system.

**피란**(避亂) fleeing from a war; refuge; shelter. ⇨ 피난(避難). ~하다 flee from a war; take 〔seek〕 refuge; get out of the danger.

**피력**(披瀝) ~하다 express 《*one's* opinion》; lay bare 《*one's* heart》; reveal 《*one's* intentions》. ¶ 흉중을 ~하다 open *one's* heart 《to》; unbosom *oneself* 《to》; confess / 수상은 그의 정견을 ~했다 The premier set forth his political views.

**피로**(披露) announcement (발표); introduction (소개); advertisement (광고). ~하다 announce; introduce; advertise. ◉ ~연 a reception; a banquet; a dinner for making an announcement: 결혼 ~연 《give》 a wedding reception; a wedding dinner 《미》.

**피로**(疲勞) fatigue; tiredness; exhaustion. ~하다 be 「tired 〔weary, fatigued〕. ¶ 육체적〔정신적〕 ~ physical 〔mental〕 fatigue / 눈의 ~ eye strain / ~를 모르는 tireless; inexhaustible / 몹시 ~하다 be tired to death; be exhausted; be dead-〔dog-〕tired / ~를 느끼다 feel 「tired 〔weary〕 / ~가 쌓이다 get more and more tired / ~한 기색이 보이다 show signs of fatigue / 일을 해서 ~하다 get tired 「with 〔from〕 *one's* work (★ tired of는 「싫증이 나다」란 뜻) / ~가 풀리다 recover from *one's* fatigue / 오랜 여행의 ~ the exhaustion of a long journey / 오래 걸어 나는 ~했다 The long walk tired me out. *or* I was tired out by the long walk. / 두서너 시간 잠을 잤더니 ~가 풀렸다 A few hours of sleep relieved my fatigue. / 나는 3분만 걸어도 ~해진다 I get tired even if I walk for only three minutes. / ~해서 먹기도 싫다 I'm too tired to eat. ◉ ~감 tired feeling. ~강도 fatigue strength. ~물질 〖의학〗 fatigue stuff. ~상태 a fatigued condition.

**피로인산**(—燐酸) 〖화학〗 pyrophosphoric acid. ◉ ~염(塩) pyrophosphate; diphosphate.

**피로톡신** 〖생화학〗 pyrotoxin.

**피로황산**(—黃酸) 〖화학〗 pyrosulfuric acid. ◉ ~염 pyrosulfate.

**피뢰침**(避雷針) a lightning rod [conductor].

**피륙** dress goods; textiles; dry goods 《미》. ◉ ～장수 a dealer in textile fabrics; a draper 《영》.

**피리** 《가로로 부는》 a flute; a fife (군악대용); 《세로로 부는》 a pipe; an oboe. ¶ ～를 불다 play 《a tune》 on the flute; play [blow on] the flute. ◉ ～구멍 a stop [fingerhole] of a flute. ～소리 the sound of a flute; piping (sound). ～혀 a reed. 풀～ a reed.

**피리새** 〖조류〗 a bullfinch.

**피리어드** 《종지부》 a period; a full stop. ¶ ～를 찍다 put a period [an end] 《to》.

**피마자**(蓖麻子) 〖식물〗 a castor-oil plant; a castor bean. ◉ ～기름 castor oil.

**피막**(皮膜) 〖해부〗 a membrane; a film; a tapetum (*pl.* -ta). ◉ ～조직 〖해부〗 epithelium.

**피막**(被膜) 〖해부〗 a tunic.

**피막이풀** 〖식물〗 a marsh pennywort.

**피망** 〖식물〗 a pim(i)ento; a green [bell] pepper.

**피맺히다** extravasate; get bruised.

**피명**(被命) commission. ¶ ～되다 receive an (official) order; be ordered [appointed].

**피밥** cooked barnyard millet.

**피배서인**(被背書人) an endorsee [indorsee].

**피병원**(避病院) a hospital for contagious disease; a quarantine; an isolation hospital.

**피보증인**(被保證人) the principal debtor; a warrantee.

**피보험물**(被保險物) an insured article; insured property.

**피보험자**(被保險者) an insured person; the insured.

**피보호국**(被保護國) a dependency; a dependent state.

**피보호자**(被保護者) a ward; a *protégé(e)* (F.).

**피복**(被服) clothes; clothing. ◉ ～비 clothing expenses. ～상 a clothier('s). ～수당 a clothing allowance. ～창 a clothing depot.

**피복**(被覆) covering; coating. ～하다 cover; coat. ◉ ～선(線) coated [insulated] wire. ～재료 covering material.

**피봉**(皮封) an envelope; the outside cover.

**피부**(皮膚) the skin. ¶ ～의 cutaneous / ～가 희다[거무스름하다] have a fair [dark] skin / ～가 거칠다[약하다] have a rough [delicate] skin / ～가 매끄럽다[튼튼하다] have a smooth [strong] skin / 사람은 ～색으로 차별되어서는 안 된다 People should not be discriminated against due to their skin color. ◉ ～감각 skin sensation. ～건조증 xeroderma. ～경화증(硬化症) sclerema; scleroderma. ～과 dermatology: ～과 의사 a dermatologist; a skin doctor [specialist]. ～병 a skin [cutaneous] disease: ～병학 dermatology. ～색소 결핍증 alphodermia. ～성형술 dermatoplasty. ～신경 cutaneous nerves. ～암 cutaneous cancer; cancer of the skin. ～염 dermatitis. ～이식 skin grafting; a skin transplant. ～테스트 〖의학〗 skin test. ～호흡 skin respiration: ～ 호흡을 못해서 죽다 die of skin suffocation.

**피브리노겐** 〖생리〗 fibrinogen.

**피브린** 〖생리〗 fibrin.

**피비린내** ¶ ～ 나는 bloody; sanguinary; bloodstained / ～ 나는 싸움 a sanguinary battle / ～ 나는 광경 a bloody sight.

**피사** 《이탈리아의 도시》 Pisa. ¶ ～의 사탑 the Leaning Tower of Pisa.

**피사리** weeding. ～하다 pick out [pluck] weeds; weed 《a rice field》.

**피사체**(被寫體) a subject; an object (of shooting). ¶ 카메라에서 ～까지의 거리 camera-to-object distance.

**피살**(被殺) being killed. ¶ ～되다 be killed [murdered]. ◉ ～자 a murderee; the victim of a murderer. ～체 the body of a murdered person.

**피상**(皮相) 《표면》 the surface; 《겉모양》 an outward look [appearance]. ¶ ～적인 《표면적인》 superficial; 《천박한》 shallow / ～적인 견해 a superficial view / ～적인 논의[입씨름] a shallow argument / 사태를 ～적으로만 보지 마라 Don't look only at the surface of things. / 그의 상황 분석은 너무 ～적이다 His analysis of the situation is too superficial [shallow].

**피상속인**(被相續人) 〖법〗 an ancestor; predecessor; an inheritee.

**피새** a quick temper. ¶ ～(를) 내다 lose *one's* temper easily / ～(가) 여물다 be quick-tempered.

**피서**(避暑) getting away (out of town) for the summer; avoiding the heat of summer; summering. ～하다, ～ 가다 avoid [get away from] the summer heat; summer; go for the summer 《at, in》; go to a summer resort. ¶ 설악산으로 ～ 가다 go to Mt. Sŏrak for the summer [summering]; summer at Mt. Sŏrak. ◉ ～객 a summer visitor [vacationer]. ～지 a summer resort.

**피선**(被選) being elected. ¶ ～되다 be

elected 〔chosen〕/ 나는 의장에 ~되었다 I was elected chairman.

**피선거권**(被選擧權) eligibility for election. ¶ 국회의원의 ~이 있다 be eligible for election as a member of the National Assembly; be qualified to run for the National Assembly.

**피선거인**(被選擧人) a person eligible 「for elective office 〔for election〕. ¶ ~ 명부 a list of those eligible for an elective office.

**피스톤** 《기계의》 a piston. ¶ 평형 ~ a balance piston. ◉ ~로드 a piston 〔connecting〕 rod. ~링 a piston ring.

**피스톨** 《권총》 a pistol; a revolver.

**피습**(被襲) ¶ ~당하다 get attacked 〔assaulted〕/ 그는 노상에서 강도에게 ~당했다 He was attacked by a robber on the road.

**피승수**(被乘數) 〖수학〗 a multiplicand.

**피시** 《개인용 컴퓨터》 a PC. 〔<*p*ersonal *c*omputer〕「polychlorinated biphenyl.

**피시비** 〖화학〗 PCB; polychlorobiphenyl;

**피시에스** 《개인 휴대 통신》 personal communication system (생략 PCS).

**피신**(避身) (secret) escape; flight. ~하다 escape secretly; flee unawares; hide *oneself*. ¶ 목숨을 부지하여 간신히 ~하다 barely escape with *one's* life / ~하여 몸의 안전을 도모하다 seek safety in flight.

**피아**(彼我) he and I; they and we. ¶ ~의 우열을 논하다 discuss 〔argue about〕 the advantages and disadvantages of both sides / ~의 세력이 백중하다 Both sides are nearly equal in strength. / ~의 사고방식에는 커다란 차이가 있다 There's a great difference between his thinking and mine.

**피아노** a piano. ¶ ~를 치다 play (on) the piano / ~레슨을 받다 take piano lessons 《from *a person*》/ ~를 연습하다 practice (on) the piano / ~에 맞춰 노래하다〔춤추다〕 sing 〔dance〕 to the piano / ~로 쇼팽의 곡을 치다 play a Chopin on the piano. ◉ ~교사 a piano teacher. ~독주곡 a piano solo (*pl.* ~s, -li). ~독주(회) a piano recital. ~사(四)중주곡 a piano quartet(te). ~삼(三)중주곡 a piano trio. ~용 의자 a piano stool. ~조율사 a pianotuner. ~협주곡 a piano concerto. 수형(竪型)~ an upright piano.

**피아니스트** a pianist; a piano player.

**피아니시모** 〖음악〗 pianissimo (생략 pp.).

**피아르** 《홍보》 P.R. 〔<*p*ublic *r*elations〕 ~하다 publicize; advertise; give publicity 《to》. ¶ ~가 잘 돼 있다 be well publicized / 신제품의 ~를 하다 advertise a new product / 우리 회사는 ~에 힘을 쏟고 있다 Our company is putting a lot of effort into public relations. ◉ ~계원 public relations man; a PR man. ~영화 a PR film. ~카 a public relations car. ~활동 public relations (activities); publicity activities.

**피안**(彼岸) ① 《저쪽 물가》 the other shore. ② 《내세》 the other world; the promised land; Paradise; 〖불교〗 Pāramita.

**피압박**(被壓迫) ◉ ~민족〔계급〕 the oppressed people 〔class〕; the oppressed (★ 복수 취급): ~민족 해방(운동) (the campaign for) liberation of the oppressed people 〔nation〕.

**피앙세** 《약혼자》 a *fiancé* (F.) (남); a *fiancée* (F.) (여).

**피어나다** ① 《불이》 burn again; blaze up (again); rekindle (itself). ¶ 불이 ~ a fire rekindles / 장작이 ~ firewood starts to burn again. ② 《형편이》 get better; improve; begin to prosper 〔flourish〕. ③ 《소생하다》 revive; come to *oneself* 〔life again〕. ④ 《꽃이》 come into bloom; blossom.

**피에로** 〖연극〗 a pierrot; a clown.

**피엑스** 〖미군사〗 a post exchange; a PX (*pl.* PXs).

**피엘오** 《팔레스타인 해방기구》 PLO. 〔<the *P*alestine *L*iberation *O*rganization〕

**피우다** ① 《재주·계교를》 use; do; play; bring into play; resort to. ¶ 재주를 ~ do 〔play〕 tricks / 계교를 ~ play (nasty) tricks on 《others》; resort to wiles. ② 《불을》 burn; kindle; make a fire. ¶ 숯불을 ~ make fire with charcoal / 난로에 불을 ~ make a fire in the stove / 장작을 ~ burn firewood. ③ 《담배·향을》 smoke; puff 《at a pipe》; fumigate; burn 《incense》. ¶ 담배를 ~ smoke 《tobacco》; have a cigarette; smoke a pipe / 향을 ~ burn incense / 훈약을 ~ fumigate / 나는 담배를 피우지 않는다 I don't smoke. ④ 《냄새를》 emit 《a scent》; give out 〔off〕 《an odor》; scent; perfume. ¶ 장미꽃 냄새를 피우는 상자 a box perfumed with roses / 그는 마늘 냄새를 피우고 있었다 He reeked of garlic. ⑤ 《부리다·떨다》 do; display; perform. ¶ 익살을 ~ make clever jokes; jest / 소란을 ~ make 〔create〕 a commotion / 바람을 ~ have an affair 《with》. ⑥ 《꽃을》 bloom; blossom.

**피원조국**(被援助國) a recipient country; an aid recipient.

**피의자**(被疑者) a suspected person; a (criminal) suspect; a person under suspicion. ¶ 살인 사건의 ～ a suspect in a murder; a suspected murderer / ～의 사진 the photograph of a criminal suspect.

**피임**(被任) being named 〔appointed〕. ～되다 be appointed 〔named, designated, elected〕. ¶ ～된 관리 an appointed official. ◉ ～자 an appointee; a person nominated 《as chairperson》.

**피임**(避姙) contraception; 《산아 제한》 birth control. ～하다 prevent pregnancy 〔conception〕; practice contraception 〔birth control〕; 《경구 피임약으로》 be on the pill. ¶ ～의 contraceptive. ◉ ～기구〔용구〕 a contraceptive (appliance, device): ～용구를 사용하다 use a contraceptive. ～링 《wear》 an intrauterine (contraceptive) device (생략 IU(C)D). ～법 a contraceptive measure 〔device, method〕: ～법에 관한 지식 contraceptive information. ～수술 a contraceptive operation. ～약 a birth control pill; contraceptive (pill): 경구 ～약을 먹다 take oral contraceptives.

**피자** 〖요리〗 pizza; (a) pizza pie. ¶ ～점 a pizza parlor; a pizzeria.

**피자식물**(被子植物) an angiosperm.

**피장파장** evenness; a tie; equality; (being) much the same. ¶ 이제는 ～이다 Now we are all square. *or* Now we are quits. / 그래서 ～이다 It is an even thing.

**피제수**(被除數) 〖수학〗 the dividend; the number to be divided.

**피조개** an ark shell.

**피조물**(被造物) a created thing; a creature; creation [총칭].

**피죽**(—粥) gruel made of barnyard millet.

**피지**(皮脂) sebum; sebaceous matter. ◉ ～선(腺) 〖해부〗 sebaceous glands.

**피지급인**(被支給人) a payee.

**피진**(皮疹) 〖의학〗 efflorescence; exanthema.

**피질**(皮質) 〖의학〗 the cortex (*pl.* -tices); the bark. ¶ ～의 cortical. ◉ ～회백질 the gray matter of the cortex.

**피차**(彼此) ① 《이것과 저것》 this and that. ② 《서로》 you and I; both (sides); each other. ¶ ～ 사랑하다 love each other / ～의 구별을 할 수 없다 be unable to tell friend from foe / ～ 다툴 것이 없다 There's no need for quarrelling back and forth.

**피차간**(彼此間) between you and me; between both sides 〔parties〕; both of us; each other. ¶ ～에 서로 돕다 help each other 〔one another〕 / 잘못은 ～에 마찬가지다 Both of us are to blame. *or* The blame is on 「both sides 〔you and me〕.

**피차일반**(彼此一般) both the same; no difference between them 〔us, him and me〕. ¶ ～이다 be mutually equal 〔the same〕; It works both ways. / 가난하기는 ～이다 You are not rich, nor am I (either). *or* When it comes to being poor, we're in the same boat. / 날 보고 비겁하다니, ～이 아닌가 If I am a coward, you're another. / 「나는 수학이 골칫거리다」—「～이다」 "I'm not good at math."—"Neither am I."

**피처** 〖야구〗 a (baseball) pitcher. ¶ ～노릇을 하다 pitch; play as a pitcher / 타이거즈의 ～로서 완투하다 「pitch the whole game 〔go the distance〕 for the Tigers. ◉ ～ 플레이트 the pitcher's plate; the mound.

**피천하다**(被薦—) get recommended 《for a position》.

**피천 한 잎 없다** be penniless; haven't a red cent.

**피청구인**(被請求人) a claimee; a demandee.

**피초청국**(被招請國) an invited country. ◉ ～ 대표 a visiting delegate.

**피츠버그** 《미국의 도시》 Pittsburg.

**피층**(皮層) 〖식물〗 cortex. ¶ ～의 cortical.

**피치** 《아스팔트》 pitch; 〖야구〗 a pitch; 〖음악〗 a pitch; 《배의》 a plunging by bow and stern; 《고조》 peak; top; 《속도·능률》 pace. ¶ 급～로 at high speed; rapidly / ～를 올리다〔떨어뜨리다〕 quicken 〔slacken〕 the pace; get up 〔slow down〕 the speed / 나는 ～를 올려 일을 끝냈다 I finished my work at high speed.

**피치자**(被治者) the governed; the ruled. ¶ 치자(治者)와 ～ the ruler and the ruled.

**피치카토** 〖음악〗 pizzicato.

**피침**(被侵) suffering invasion; being raided; being violated. ～하다 be invaded; be violated.

**피칭** 〖야구〗 pitching. ¶ ～ 연습을 하다 practice pitching. ◉ ～머신 a pitching machine.

**피켈** 〖등산〗 a pickel.

**피켓** a picket; picketing. ¶ ～을 치다 put 〔place, post〕 a picket 《in front of a factory》; picket 《a place of work》. ◉ ～라인 a picket line: ～ 라인을 돌파하다 cross 〔break through〕 a picket line.

**피코** 《$10^{-12}$를 나타내는 수의 단위》 pico-. ◉ ～그램 a picogram. ～초 a picosecond (생략 Ps).

**피콜로** 〖악기〗 a piccolo (*pl.* ~s); an octave flute. ◉ ~주자(奏者) a piccoloist.

**피크** 《정점》 the peak. ¶ 교통 혼잡의 상태가 ~인 때 the peak hours of traffic / 그녀의 인기는 ~에 달했다 Her popularity has reached its peak.

**피크닉** a picnic. ¶ ~가다 go (out) on a picnic; go picnicking 《in》; have a picnic / 숲속으로 ~가다 picnic in the woods / 공원으로 ~이나 가자 Let's go picnicking in the park.

**피크린산**(一酸) 〖화학〗 picric acid.

**피클** 《절인 것》 pickles.

**피타고라스** 《그리스의 수학자》 Pythagoras. (582?-500? B.C.). ¶ ~의 정리 the Pythagorean theorem.

**피탈**(被奪) suffering robbery; having something taken away. ~되다 be robbed of 《*a thing*》; have 《*a thing*》 taken away.

**피통치**(被統治) being subject 《to》; being governed 〔ruled〕 《by》. ◉ ~국 a subject state.

**피투성이** ¶ ~의 bloodstained; bloody; gory / ~가 되다 be covered 〔smeared〕 with blood; be bloodied / 그는 얼굴이 ~가 되어 병원으로 실려갔다 He was carried into the hospital, his face a mass of bleeding flesh. / 그녀는 ~가 되어 쓰러져 있었다 She lay in blood. *or* She lay bleeding all over her body.

**피트** feet (생략 ft.) (*sing.* a foot). ¶ 5 ~ 3인치 five feet three inches; 5ft. 3in.; 5′ 3″ / 2 ~자 a two-foot rule / 그는 키가 5 ~ 6인치다 He stands five feet six inches high.

**피티에이** 《특히 미국의 사친회》 a PTA. [< *P*arent-*T*eacher *A*ssociation]

**피펫** 〖화학〗 a pipet(te). ◉ 흡수~ an absorption pipet.

**피폐**(疲弊) impoverishment; exhaustion. ~하다 be(come) impoverished 〔exhausted〕. ¶ 농촌의 ~ the impoverished conditions of rural communities / 재정의 ~ financial exhaustion / ~시키다 impoverish; exhaust / ~되어 있다 be in an exhausted 〔impoverished〕 condition.

**피폭**(被爆) being bombed. ~되다 be bombed; suffer from bombing. ¶ 원폭의 ~자 an atomic bomb 〔A-bomb〕 victim. ◉ ~도시 an air-raided city; a city which has suffered from bombing. ~지구 a bombed-out area.

**피피엠** ppm; p.p.m.; P.P.M. [< *p*arts *p*er *m*illion]

**피하**(皮下) ¶ ~의 under the skin; 〖의학〗 hypodermic; subcutaneous. ◉ ~기종(氣腫) subcutaneous emphysema; aerodermectasis. ~선(腺) 〖동물〗 a hypodermal gland. ~일혈(溢血) subcutaneous extravasation of blood; (an) ecchymosis (*pl.* -ses). ~조직 subcutaneous tissue. ~주사 (a) hypodermic 〔subcutaneous〕 injection: ~주사기 a hypodermic syringe / ~주사를 놓다 inject 《a medicine》 under the skin. ~지방 subcutaneous fat. ~출혈 hypodermal bleeding. ~층 〖식물〗 the hypoderm; the hypoderma. ~투약 hypodermic medication.

**피하다**(避一) ① 《도피하다》 get away; run away 〔off〕; flee; take to flight; escape; hide *oneself* (은신하다). ¶ 난을 ~ flee from the war; take refuge; go 《to a place》 for safety / 더위를 ~ get away from the heat; go to a summer resort / 남모르게 ~ sneak away; slip off 〔away〕 / 국외로 ~ flee abroad / 피해서 몸의 안전을 기하다 seek safety in flight.

② 《비키다》 avoid; avert; ward off 《danger》; duck away 《from the ball》; dodge 《a blow》; 《가까이 않다》 keep out 《of》; keep 〔stay〕 away 《from》; keep 〔stay〕 clear of; keep aloof 《from》. ¶ 길을 ~ get out of the way / 날아오는 돌을 ~ duck away from a stone thrown at *one* / 남의 눈을 ~ avoid the eyes of others; avert people's eyes; shun the public eye / 사람을 ~ avoid *a person;* keep away from *a person;* 《만나는 것을》 avoid meeting *a person* / 암초를 ~ steer clear of a rock 〔reef〕 / 위험을 ~ avoid 〔avert〕 danger; keep away from danger / 주먹을 ~ dodge 〔elude〕 a blow / 자동차를 ~ dodge a car; 「get out of the way of 〔step aside from〕 a car / 햇볕을 ~ shelter *oneself* from the sun / 요즘 그는 나를 피하고 있다 He has been 「giving me a wide berth 〔keeping out of my way〕 recently.

③ 《모면하다》 escape; get off 〔free〕; get away 《from》; get out of; be saved 《from》. ¶ 재난을 ~ escape a disaster 〔mishap〕 / 위험을 ~ escape danger / 죽음을 ~ escape death; be saved from death / 추격자로부터 ~ shake off 〔escape〕 *one's* pursuers.

④ 《회피하다》 evade 《punishment》;

shirk; sidestep; shun; get around. ¶ 피하기 어려운 책임 unshirkable responsibility / 책임을 ~ shirk *one's* responsibility / 확답을 ~ take care not to commit *oneself;* steer clear of a definitive commitment / 법망을 ~ evade 〔dodge, get around〕 the law; get out of the clutches of the law.

**피한**(避寒) wintering; hibernation (동면). ~하다 winter 《at, in》; pass the winter 《at, in》; go to a winter resort; go 《to a place》 for the winter; hibernate. ◉ ~지 a winter resort; winter quarters.

**피해**(被害) 《손해》 damage; harm; loss; 《상해》 injury; casualty (사상). ¶ ~가 크다〔많다〕 be badly damaged 《by》; suffer heavily 《from》; be hard hit 《by》 / ~가 적다 suffer lightly 《from》 / ~를 입다 suffer damage 《from a flood》; be damaged 《by a storm》; be injured 《by》 / ~를 모면하다 be undamaged; 《물건이》 be intact; 《사람이》 escape injury / ~를 주다 damage; do damage 《to》; 《사람에 대한 정신적·육체적 피해; 물건에 대한 피해》 harm; do harm 《to》; 《상해》 injure 《*a person*》 / 태풍으로 쌀농사는 큰 ~를 입었다 The typhoon did great damage to the rice crop. *or* The rice crop was badly damaged by the typhoon. / 지진은 그 도시에 큰 ~를 입혔다 The earthquake caused great damage to the city. / 태풍의 ~는 광범위했다 The typhoon caused extensive 〔widespread〕 damage. / 인적 ~는 없는 것으로 보도되었다 No personal injury was reported. ◉ ~망상(妄想) 〖병〗 persecution mania; the delusion of persecution; paranoia (통속적): ~ 망상자 a persecution maniac; a person suffering from persecution mania 〔paronoia〕. ~액 the amount 〔extent〕 of damage; the damage. ~의식 the feeling of being victimized. ~자 《천재(天災) 따위의》 a sufferer; 《도난·재해의》 a victim; 《부상자》 the injured person 〔party〕: 홍수 ~자 the victims of the flood. ~지 the damaged 〔affected〕 area 〔district〕.

**피험자**(被驗者) 《실험의》 a (test) subject; a testee.

**피혁**(皮革) hides; leather (무두질한). ◉ ~공업 the leather industry. ~상 a dealer in hides; a tanner; a pelterer. ~제품 leather articles 〔goods〕. 모조 ~ leatherette. 인조〔합성〕~ artificial 〔synthetic〕 leather.

**피후견인**(被後見人) 〖법〗 a ward.

**픽**[1] ① 《쓰러지는 모양》 weakly; feebly. ¶ 픽 쓰러지다 fall down feebly; fall senseless to the floor. ② 《웃는 모양》 smiling 〔laughing〕 listlessly. ¶ 픽 웃다 grin; smile listlessly; give an aimless smile. ③ 《바람 빠지는 소리》 a hissing sound; a hiss; a whoosh. ¶ 바람이 픽 빠지다 lose what little air it has / 픽하며 풍선의 바람이 빠졌다 The balloon got deflated with a whoosh.

**픽**[2] 《악기의》 a pick; a (bone) plectrum.

**픽션** 《소설·허구》 (a) fiction.

**픽업** ① 《전축의》 a 《phonograph》 pickup; a cartridge. ② 《차량》 a pickup (truck).

**픽픽** ① 《쓰러짐》 all weakly; feebly. ¶ ~ 쓰러지다 several fall down feebly; fall down feebly again and again. ② 《웃음》 all smiling 〔laughing〕 aimlessly. ¶ ~ 웃다 several laugh listlessly; keep laughing listlessly; give listless smiles. ③ 《바람 빠짐》 ⇨ 픽[1] ③.

**핀** a pin. ¶ 넥타이핀 a tiepin; a stick pin / 머리핀 a hairpin / 안전핀 a safety pin / 압핀 a thumbtack / 골프〔볼링〕핀 a pin / 핀을 지르다 〔꽂다〕 pin up 《a garment》; fasten with a pin; pin 《*a thing*》 on 〔to〕...; get 《*something*》 fixed with a pin / 머리에 핀을 꽂다 fix the hair with pins.

**핀란드** Finland. ¶ ~의 Finnish. ◉ ~말 Finnish. ~ 사람 a Finn.

**핀볼** pinball; a pinball game.

**핀셋** a *pincette* (F.); 《a pair of》 tweezers. ¶ ~으로 집다 hold 〔pick up〕 《*a thing*》 with tweezers; tweeze.

**핀잔** a rebuke; a reprimand; upbraiding; scolding; (a) personal reproof. ~주다, ~하다 rebuke; reprimand 《*a person*》 personally; reprove 《*a person*》 to *his* face; give a rebuff 《to *a person*》. ¶ ~맞다 get rebuked 〔reprimanded, upbraided, scolded〕; meet with 〔get, suffer〕 a rebuff.

**핀치** 〖야구〗 a pinch. ¶ ~에 몰리다, ~를 맞이하다 be thrown into a pinch 〔fix〕 / ~를 벗어나다 tide over a crisis / 그는 타자를 3진으로 잡아 ~에서 벗어났다 He worked himself out of a jam by striking out the batter. ◉ ~러너 a pinch runner. ~히터 a pinch hitter; a substitute batter: 그는 ~히터로 나가 홈런을 쳤다 He pinch=hit a homer.

**핀트** 〔< *punt* (D.)〕 《촛점》 focus; 《요점》 the point. ¶ ~가 맞다 be 〔get〕 in focus / ~가 안 맞다 be out of focus /

～를 맞추다 get《*a thing*》in focus; adjust〔take〕the focus; focus《*one's* camera》/ 얼굴에 ～를 맞추다 focus on the face / 그의 말은 ～가 안 맞는다 His remarks are off the point.

**필**(匹) ①《피륙의》a roll. ②《마소의》a head. ¶ 말 세 필 three horses / 두 필의 소 two head of cows.

**필**(疋) a roll of cloth. ¶ 무명 두 필 two rolls of cotton cloth / 필로 팔다 sell《cloth》by the roll.

**-필**(畢) finishing; completing; finished; done; completed. ¶ 지급필《기재 사항》Paid / 검사필 Examined.

**필가**(筆架) a pen-rack; a writing-brush rack.

**필갑**(筆匣) a writing-brush case; a pen case.

**필견**(必見) ¶ 학생 ～의 영화 a movie that students should not miss / ～의 명화다 The film is a 'must'.

**필경**(筆耕) copying; stencil-paper writing. ～하다 copy; write; stencil. ◉ ～료 a copying fee. ～자 a copyist; a scribe; a stenciler (등사판의).

**필경**(畢竟) after all; in the end; in the last〔final〕analysis. ¶ ～ 그는 오지 않을 것이다 He will not come after all.

**필공**(筆工) a writing-brush maker.

**필기**(筆記) note-taking;《필기한 것》notes. ～하다 take〔make〕notes of; write〔note, put〕down. ¶ 강의를 ～하다 make〔take〕notes of a lecture / 흑판의 낱말들을 ～하라 Write down the words on the blackboard.
◉ ～구 writing materials; pen and pencils. ～시험 a written examination〔exam〕. ～자 a copyist. ～장 a notebook; a memo book. ～체 cursive script: ～체로 쓰다 write in script〔in cursive letters〕.

**필담**(筆談) conversation by writing. ～하다 carry on a conversation by means of writing; chat by letter〔note〕.

**필답**(筆答) answering in writing; a written answer〔reply〕. ～하다 answer in writing. ◉ ～시험 a written examination.

**필독**(必讀) required reading. ¶ 학생 ～의 책 a book which every student must〔should〕read; a must book for students.

**필두**(筆頭)《붓끝》the tip of a writing brush;《첫머리》the first on the list. ¶ …의 ～에 at the head of… / 사장을 ～로 with the president at the head of the list; from the president down / 그의 이름은 그 대회 우승 후보로 ～에 올라 있다 His name is the first on the list as the favorite in the tournament.

**필드**〖스포츠〗the field. ◉ ～경기 field sports. ～워크 fieldwork. ～종목 a field event.

**필딩**〖야구〗fielding.

**필라델피아**《미국의 도시》Philadelphia.

**필라멘트**〖전기〗a filament.

**필력**(筆力)《운필의 기세》the power〔strength〕of the〔*one's*〕brush stroke(s);《문장력》the ability to write. ¶ ～이 있다 have a forceful touch in *one's* handwriting.

**필로카르핀**〖약〗pilocarpine.

**필름** film. ¶ 한 통의 ～ a reel〔spool〕of film / ～에 담다 film《a scene》/ 사진기에 ～이 들어 있느냐 Is there any film in your camera? ◉ ～편집 cutting. 네가〔포지〕～ (a) negative〔positive〕film. 컬러〔흑백〕～ (a) color〔black-and-white〕film.

**필리버스터**〖정치〗《의사 진행 방해(자)》(a) filibuster.

**필리핀** (the Republic of) the Philippines. ¶ ～의 Philippine; Filipino. ◉ ～사람 a Filipino (남); a Filipina (여). ～제도 the Philippine Islands.

**필마**(匹馬) a single horse. ◉ ～단기(單騎) riding alone without servants〔retinue〕. ～단창(單槍) fighting alone.

**필멸**(必滅) being fated to perish. ¶ 생자 ～이다 All living things must die.

**필명**(筆名)《예명》a name as a calligrapher;《펜 네임》a pen name; a *nom de plume* (F.). ¶ …의 ～으로 under the pen name of… / ～이 높다 be a famous calligrapher〔writer〕.

**필묵**(筆墨) brush and Chinese ink; pen and ink.

**필법**(筆法)《운필법》a style of penmanship; the technique of calligraphy;《문체》a style of writing. ¶ 힘찬 ～ a powerful stroke of the brush.

**필봉**(筆鋒) ①《붓끝》the tip of a brush. ②《붓의 위세》the power of the pen. ¶ ～이 날카롭다 have a sharp style of writing; be sharp in *one's* argument.

**필부**(匹夫) ①《한 남자》an individual; a man. ②《신분 낮은 사내》a man of humble position. ◉ ～지용(之勇) foolhardiness. ～필부(匹婦) humble men and women; common people; (every) Jack and Jill.

**필사**(必死)《꼭 죽음》certain〔inevitable〕death;《사력을 다함》desperation. ¶ ～적(인) desperate; frantic / ～적으로

frantically; desperately; for *one's* life (목숨걸고) / ~의 각오로 with a firm resolve to lay down *one's* life 《for》/ ~적으로 일하다 work for *one's* life / ~적으로 도망치다 run dead away; run for dear life / ~적이 되다 become desperate; be driven to desperation / ~적으로 노력하다 make desperate 〔frantic〕 efforts; turn at bay.

**필사**(筆寫) copying; transcription. ~하다 copy; transcribe.

**필산**(筆算) arithmetic worked on paper; calculation with figures written down on paper. ~하다 do the sums on a piece of paper.

**필살**(必殺) ¶ ~의 일격을 가하다 deliver a deadly blow 〔a death blow〕.

**필생**(畢生) ¶ ~의 lifelong / ~의 노력 lifelong efforts / ~의 대작 *one's* masterpiece / ~의 사업 *one's* lifework.

**필생**(筆生) a copyist; an amanuensis.

**필설**(筆舌) brush and tongue; writing and speech. ¶ ~로 다 할 수 없다 be beyond description; beggar (all) description; words 「cannot 〔fail to〕 describe 《the beauty of...》/ 눈 앞에 펼쳐진 광경은 ~로 다 할 수 없을 정도로 아름다웠다 The scene spreading before us was too beautiful for words.

**필세**(筆勢) *one's* stroke of the brush 〔pen〕; penmanship. ⇨ 필력(筆力).

**필수**(必須) ¶ ~의 indispensable 《to》; essential 《to》; necessary; requisite; compulsory (꼭 배워야 하는) / 이 일을 완성하려면 너의 도움이 ~적이다 Your help is indispensable to finish this work. / 건강은 성공에 ~적이다 Good health is essential to success in life. / 의식주는 생활의 ~이다 Food, clothing and shelter are necessities 〔necessaries〕 of life. ◉ ~과목〔학과〕 a compulsory 〔required〕 subject 〔course〕. ~ 아미노산 essential amino acids. ~조건 a necessary 〔an indispensable, an essential〕 condition; a *sine qua non* (L.); a prerequisite: 병역을 마쳐야 함은 취직에 ~ 조건이다 The completion of military service is a prerequisite to employment. ~조항 a mandatory clause.

**필수품**(必需品) necessaries; necessities; necessary articles. ¶ 생활 ~ the necessities 〔necessaries〕 of life / 장기 여행의 ~ the necessary articles for a long journey / TV는 현대 가정의 ~이다 A television set is a necessity 〔must〕 in the modern home.

**필순**(筆順) the stroke order 《of a Chinese character》. ¶ ~을 틀리다 write 《a character》 with strokes in the wrong order.

**필승**(必勝) certain 〔sure, unfailing〕 victory. ¶ ~의 신념 faith in certain victory; the conviction of sure victory / ~을 기하다 《자신을 갖다》 be confident of winning 〔victory〕; 《결심하다》 resolve to secure a victory at any cost / ~의 신념을 가지고 싸우다 fight confident that *one* will win in the end / 그것은 나의 새로운 ~ 전략이다 It's my new win-win strategy.

**필시**(必是) certainly; surely; definitely; without doubt. ¶ 그녀는 ~ 기뻐할 거야 She'll be very pleased, I'm sure.

**필연**(必然) being in the natural order of events; the natural outcome 《of what has taken place》. ¶ 논리적〔물리적〕 ~ logical 〔physical〕 necessity / ~적인 inevitable; necessary / ~적으로 certainly; surely; definitely; without doubt; necessarily; inevitably / ~의 결과로서 by a natural process 《of cause and effect》; as a logical consequence / 그것은 역사의 ~이다 That is one of the inevitabilities of history. / 인구가 늘면 ~적인 결과로 식량이 부족해진다 If the population increases, the food supply decreases as a necessary result.
◉ ~성 necessity; inevitability.

**필연**(筆硯) pen and ink(-stone); 《문필》 literary work. ¶ ~을 벗삼다 be engaged in literary work.

**필요**(必要) necessity; need. ~하다 be necessary; be in need 《of》; (be) needed. ¶ ~한 necessary; needed; required; 《불가결한》 essential; indispensable / ~할 때는 in case of need; if 〔when〕 necessary; if need be / ~에 따라서 as the occasion demands; as the need arises; as needed / ~에 의해서 out of (sheer) necessity; driven by necessity; under the pressure of necessity / …할 ~가 있다 it is necessary 《to *do*》; have got to 《*do*》; have to 《*do*》; must 《*do*》; need to 《*do*》; there is a necessity for *do*ing / …할 ~가 없다 there is no necessity 〔call〕 for 《*do*ing》; need not 〔don't have to〕 《*do*》; there is no need to 《*do*》; 《무익》 there is no use in 《*do*ing》/ …을 ~로 하다 need; be 〔stand〕 in need of; call for; require; want; have use for / 이 구두는 수선할 ~가 있다 These

shoes「want repairing〔need repairs〕./ 할 ~가 없는데 했다 I needn't have done it. / 할 ~가 없어서 안 했다 I didn't need to do it. / 이런 일에는 용기가 ~하다 It takes courage to do this kind of work. / 아무래도 5,000원은 ~하다 I must have five thousand won. *or* I'm awfully in need of 5,000 won. / 이 경우 냉정하게 생각할 ~가 있다 The occasion calls for a cool head. / 내가 그런 일을 할 ~가 있을까 What need have I to do so? *or* What should I do it for? / 말할 ~가 없다 It is needless to say (that...). / 그는 언제나 ~ 이상으로 돈을 많이 갖고 있다 He always has more money than he needs. / 자네가 돈이 ~할 때는 내 얼마든지 줌세 I will go to any expense whenever you need it. / ~는 발명의 어머니 Necessity is the mother of invention. / 서두를 ~는 없다 There is no need to hurry. *or* You don't have to hurry. / 그런 시설의 ~는 절실했다 The need for such an institution is keenly felt. / 난 그 문제를 속히 해결할 ~가 있다고 생각한다 I feel a need to solve the problem quickly.
◉ ~경비 necessary expenses. ~성 necessity. ~악 a necessary evil: 막대한 선거 비용을 민주 정치의 한 ~악으로 보는 정치가도 있다 Some politicians see huge campaign spending as a necessary evil in a democracy. ~전제 조건 a prerequisite 《for》. ~조건 a necessary condition; a *sine qua non* (L.); a requirement; a requisite. ~품 an indispensable〔a necessary〕article; a necessity; a requisite.

**필유곡절**(必有曲折) There's a reason for everything.

**필자**(筆者) 《글의》 the writer; the author; 《글씨의》 the calligrapher. ¶ 이 글의 ~《필자 자신을 말할 때》 the present writer / 이 소설의 ~는 젊은 여성이다 This novel was written by a young lady.

**필적**(匹敵) a rival; a match; an equal. ~하다 equal; rival; be a match 《for》; be equal 《to》; compare 《with》; stand comparison 《with》; rank 《with》 《지위 따위가》. ¶ ~할 만한 것이 없다 have no equal〔match〕《in experience》; be unequaled〔unrivaled〕《in cooking》/ 그와 ~할 만한 인물은 이제 없을 것이다 We shall never see his match. / 이 대학은 미국의 일류 대학에 ~할 만하다 This university「is the equal of〔ranks with〕the best universities in the United States.

**필적**(筆跡) ① 《글씨 형적》 a specimen of handwriting; a calligraphic specimen; a holograph. ② 《글 솜씨》 *one's* handwriting; *one's* hand; *one's* style of handwriting. ¶ 남자〔여자〕의 ~ a masculine〔feminine〕hand / ~을 감정하다 analyze handwriting / ~이 좋다〔나쁘다〕 write a good〔bad〕hand / 편지는 그의 ~이다 The letter is written in his hand. / 이 ~은 나의 것이 아니다 This handwriting is not mine.
◉ ~감정 handwriting analysis: ~감정인 a handwriting analyst. ~학〔관상법〕 graphology.

**필전**(筆戰) a war of the pen; paper warfare; controversies on the printed page.

**필주**(筆誅) ¶ ~를 가하다 denounce 《*a person*》 with the pen〔in writing〕.

**필중**(必中) ~하다 never fail to hit the target. ¶ 일발 ~을 기하다 aim carefully so as to hit the target with the first shot.

**필지**(必至) inevitability. ~하다 be sure to come; be inevitable; be unavoidable; be destined 《to fail》.

**필지**(必知) a must to know; indispensable information.

**필지**(筆地) a lot〔plot, piece〕(of land).
◉ ~조사〔측량〕 "field by field" land surveying.

**필진**(筆陣) the writing〔editorial〕staff; 《필전(筆戰)의》 a maneuver in a battle by pen. ¶ ~을 펴다 set〔put〕out〔forth〕an argument 《for, against》.

**필첩**(筆帖) ① 《필적집》 specimens of handwriting. ② 《공책》 a notebook.

**필치**(筆致) ① 《필세》 a stroke of the brush; 《서화의》 a touch. ¶ 가벼운 ~로 with a light touch. ② 《문체》 a literary style. ¶ 경묘하고 원숙한 ~ an easy and well-mellowed style.

**필터** 《여과기》 a filter; a strainer; 《카메라》 a (color) filter; 《담배의》 a filter tip. ¶ ~가 달린〔안 달린〕 담배 a filter-tipped〔plain, non-filter〕cigarette.
◉ 자외선〔적외선〕 ~ an ultraviolet〔infrared〕filter.

**필통**(筆筒) 《필갑》 a pencil case; 《붓통》 a writing-brush stand.

**필하다**(畢―) finish; complete; end; achieve; be〔get〕through. ¶ 대학원 과정을 ~ complete the postgraduate course.

**필하모닉** 《음악회》 philharmonic; 《교향

악단》 a Philharmonic. ¶ 서울 ~ 오케스트라 the Seoul Philharmonic Orchestra.

**필화**(筆禍) a trouble brought on by a slip of the pen. ¶ ~를 입다 be indicted 〔prosecuted〕 for *one's* writings / ~를 입게 되다 get into trouble because of *one's* article 《in a magazine》. ◉ ~사건 an affair brought on by *one's* article 《in a magazine》.

**필휴**(必携) indispensableness; 《안내서》 a handbook; a manual. ¶ 학생 ~의 책 a book indispensable to students.

**필히**(必―) by all means; surely; certainly; without fail. ¶ ~ …하다 be sure to *do;* never fail to *do; do* without fail / ~ 오너라 Be sure to come. / ~ 그 편지를 부칠 것 Be sure to mail the letter.

**핌피** a pimfy; a PIMFY. 〔<*p*lease *i*n *m*y *f*ront *y*ard〕 (★ nimby 또는 NIMBY의 상대 개념으로, 지역 발전에 유리한 편의 시설을 인근에 끌어들이려는 지역 이기주의.)

**핍박**(逼迫) ① 《재정의》 pressure 《for money》; tightness 《of money》. ~하다 be tight; get stringent. ¶ 재정의 ~ tight financial conditions / 금융 시장의 ~ tightness of the money market / 금융이 ~해 있다 The money-market is stringent. *or* Money is tight. ② 《정세의》 ~하다 be strained; grow tense. ¶ ~한 impending / 정세가 ~하다 The situation is pressing.

**핏기**(―氣) the color of the face; *one's* complexion. ¶ ~없는 얼굴 a pale face; a face as white as a sheet / ~가 없다 have a bad complexion; look pale 〔sallow, unwell〕 / ~가 가시다 become 〔turn〕 pale / 그녀는 병으로 얼굴에 ~가 없다 Her cheeks are pale with sickness.

**핏대** (blue) veins. ¶ ~(를) 올리다〔세우다〕 get angry; boil 〔turn purple〕 with rage.

**핏덩어리, 핏덩이** ① 《피의 덩어리》 a clot of blood; clotted blood; gore. ② 《갓난아이》 a newborn baby.

**핏발** being bloodshot; a bloodshot condition; 〖의학〗 congestion(충혈). ¶ ~이 선 눈 bloodshot eyes / ~이 서다 get congested 〔bloodshot〕 / ~이 삭다 congestion 〔bloodshot condition〕 clears up.

**핏빛** blood red. ¶ ~으로 물들다 be dyed in blood red.

**핏자국** a bloodstain; a mark of blood. ¶ ~이 있는 bloodstained.

**핏줄** ① 《혈관》 a blood vessel; a vein. ② 《혈족》 ties of blood; blood relationship; consanguinity; 《혈통》 descent; lineage; stock. ¶ ~이 같다 be related 《to *a person*》 by blood; be of the same blood / 그들은 ~을 나눈 형제다 They are of the same blood. *or* They are blood brothers. / 그는 양반의 ~을 물려 받았다 He「comes of 〔is descended from〕 noble stock. / ~이란 속일 수 없는 것이다 Blood will tell.

**핑** ① 《돌다》 round; circling; quickly. ¶ 학교를 한 바퀴 핑 돌다 walk all round the school. ② 《어지러움》 dizzy; giddy. ¶ 머리가 핑 돌다 get dizzy 〔giddy〕 / 술이 핑 돌다 the alcohol goes to *one's* head.

**핑거볼** 《식탁에서 손 씻는 그릇》 a finger bowl. ¶ ~에 손을 씻다 rinse *one's* finger tips in a finger bowl.

**핑계** an excuse; a pretext; a pretense. ¶ 그럴듯한 ~ a plausible excuse; a specious pretense / 서투른 ~ a poor 〔flumsy, weak〕 excuse / ~를 만들다 make 〔find〕 an excuse 〔a pretext〕 《for being late》 / …하다는 ~로 on the pretext of…; with the excuse that… / 병을 ~하다 plead illness; find an excuse in *one's* illness / 그것은 ~에 지나지 않는다 That's a mere excuse. / 그는 요리조리 ~를 대고 일을 게을리 한다 He shirks his work on some pretext or other. / ~ 말고 모임에 출석해라 Come to the meeting without making any excuses. / ~ 없는 무덤 없다 《속담》 A pretext is never wanting.

**핑그르르** (spinning, whirling, revolving, turning) around smoothly. ¶ 공을 ~ 돌리다 spin a ball round.

**핑글핑글** (turning, spinning, revolving) round and round smoothly.

**핑크** 《분홍색》 pink. ◉ ~무드 an amorous mood.

**핑퐁** 《탁구》 ping-pong; table tennis. ¶ ~을 치다 play ping-pong. ◉ ~대 a ping-pong table.

**핑핑** round and round; quickly. ¶ 머리가 ~ 돌다 feel dizzy.

**핑핑하다** ① 《켕기다》 (be) tight; taut. ② 《어슷비슷하다》 be even 《with》; be on a par 《with》; be equal 《to》. ¶ 둘의 힘이 서로 ~ The two are evenly matched with respect to strength. ③ 《팽창하다》 be swollen hard; (be) bulging; bursting. ¶ 살쪄서 핑핑한 bulging / 소가 너무 먹어서 배가 ~ a cow eats till its belly bursts.

**하**(下) ① 《하급》 the low class 〔grade〕. ¶ 하의 하 the lowest (of the low); the poorest; the worst. ② [부사적] below; under; underneath. ¶ 아무의 감독〔지휘〕 하에 under the supervision 〔command, direction〕 of *a person*. ③ 《책의》 the last volume. ¶ 하권 the last volume (of a series of 3 books).

**하**[1] 《하도》 very; too (much); extremely; hard. ¶ 하 비싸다 be very expensive / 하 졸라대다 tease hard 《for *something*》 / 하 무서운 통에 소리도 못질렀다 I was too scared to let out a sound.

**하**[2] 《입김으로》 with a hot wet breath; [감탄사] Ha !; Huh !; Oh ! ¶ 하, 네가 국회의원이 된단 말이지 Ha ! You mean to be an M.P. !

**하가**(何暇) what spare time ?; what leisure ?; what chance ? ¶ 어느 ～에 책을 읽나 When 〔Where〕 would I ever find the time to read a book ?

**하감**(下疳) 〚한의〛 chancre.

**하감**(下瞰) looking down 《at》. ～하다 look down 《at》; overlook; command a bird's-eye view 《of》.

**하강**(下降) descent; falling; dropping; a fall; a drop; 《경기의》 a decline; a downturn. ～하다 descend; drop; fall. ¶ 기온의 ～ a drop in temperature / 경기가 ～하고 있다 Business is taking a downturn 〔downswing〕. *or* The economy 〔market〕 is on the decline 〔downturn〕. / 비행기가 서서히 ～하고 있다 The airplane is gradually descending 〔coming down〕.
◉ ～기류 a descending air current. ～선: ～선을 나타내다 《도표 따위가》 show a downward curve / ～선을 그리다 be on a downhill run; be on the decline 〔wane〕.

**하객**(賀客) a well-wisher; a congratulator. ¶ 신년～ a New Year's caller 〔visitor〕.

**하게하다** 《말을 놓다》 use familiar-style speech forms 《with》.

**…하게 하다** 《억지로》 make 《*a person do*》; cause 《*a person* to *do*》; force 〔compel〕 《*a person* to *do*》; induce 《*a person* to *do*》; 《허락·방임하여》 let 《*a person do*》; allow 《*a person* to *do*》; 《부탁해서》 get 〔have〕 《*a person* to *do*》; have 〔get〕 《*a thing*》 *done* 《by *a person*》. ¶ 남이 간섭 못～ restrain *a person* from interference 〔interfering〕 / 그녀가 돌아오면 전화하게 할까요 Shall I have her call you back when she gets home ?

**하계**(下界) ① 《이 세상》 the lower world; this world; 《지상》 the earth. ¶ ～의 earthly; sublunary; mundane; temporal / 이 ～에서 here below / ～를 굽어보다 look down on the earth.
② 《낮은 곳》 a lower place 〔region〕.

**하계**(下計) the worst plan 〔scheme〕.

**하계**(河系) a river system.

**하계**(夏季) summer; summertime; the summer season. ¶ ～용의 for summer use. ◉ ～강좌 a summer lecture course. ～학교〔강습회〕 a summer school 〔course〕; summer lectures. ～휴가 the summer vacation 〔holidays〕.

**하고** with; and; like; 《…와 함께》 along 〔together〕 with. ¶ 너～ 나 you and I / 그 사람～ 가다 go with him / 친구～ 싸워서는 안된다 You shouldn't fight with your friends. / 가족～ 상의해 보죠 Let me talk it over with my family.

**하고많다** (be) plenty; plentiful; abundant; innumerable; numerous. ¶ 그는 하고많은 재산을 당대에 다 탕진했다 He squandered a tremendous fortune in his lifetime.

**하곡**(夏穀) summer crops; wheat and barley. ◉ ～수매가(收買價) the government purchase price of barley.

**…하곤 하다** make a habit 〔practice, regular thing〕 of 《*do*ing》; *do* from time to time. …하곤 했다 used to *do*; did *do*; would *do*. (★ would는 과거의 우연, 불규칙적 습관, 개인적 흥미를 포함한 반복적 행위를 나타냄. used to는 과거의 규칙적인 습관, 지속적인 상태 따위를 나타내며 특히 과거와 현재를 대조시키는 경우에 씀). ¶ 공원에 가서 놀곤 했다 We used to go to the park and play. / 바다에서 헤엄치곤 했다 We would swim in the ocean (from time to time). / 그는 젊었을 때 그 곳에 잘 가곤 했었지 He would (often) go there when he was young.

**하관**(下官) a lower 〔subordinate〕 official. 「the grave; inter.

**하관**(下棺) ∼하다 lower a coffin into

**하관**(下觀) the lower part of the face; the jaw (area). ¶∼(이) 빨다 have a pointed jaw.

**하교**(下敎) 《전교》 an order from the king; a royal command; 《명령·지시》 an instruction 〔order〕 from a superior. ∼하다 instruct; give 〔issue〕 orders. ¶∼를 충실히 지키다 be obedient to the orders of.

**하구**(河口) the mouth of a river; a river mouth; an estuary. ◉ ∼둑 공사 the construction of estuary dyke. ∼항 an estuary harbor.

**하권**(下卷) the 2nd 〔3rd〕 volume of a book; the last volume.

**하극상**(下剋上) the lower dominating the upper; a revolt against seniors. ¶∼의 시대 the period characterized by inferiors overthrowing their superiors.

**하급**(下級) a low(er) class 〔grade〕. ¶ ∼의 lower-grade; junior; 《officials》 in the lower echelons; inferior.
◉ ∼관리〔공무원〕 lower-level officials; a petty 〔minor, junior〕 official; minor government official. ∼관청 a subordinate office. ∼노동자 a low-class laborer. ∼반 a lower class; an underclass. ∼법원 a lower 〔an inferior〕 court: ∼법원에서 in the court below. ∼생 a lower-class student 〔boy, girl〕; an underclassman 《미》. ∼선원 petty crewmen; sailors and stokers. ∼자 a subordinate; the lower-grade personnel; (*one's*) inferior; the inferior ranks. ∼장교 a junior officer; [총칭] officers at the junior level. ∼직(職) a subordinate official post; a lower post: ∼직원 the lower-grade personnel of a government 〔public〕 office. ∼품 lower-grade goods.

**하기**(下記) what is stated below. ¶∼의 the following; the undermentioned; 《the men》 mentioned below / ∼사항 the following items / ∼학생 the following students / ∼와 같이 as follow; as in the following / ∼ 통계 참조 See the statistics below / 합격자의 명단은 ∼와 같다 The names of the successful applicants are as follows: ….

**하기**(夏期) the summer period; summer(time). ⇨ 하계(夏季).

**하기는** ① 《…하는 것은》 as for *do*ing 〔being〕. ¶ ∼ 하지만 *do* all right but; *do* it but; be all right but; be indeed but. ② 《실상은》 in fact; in truth; indeed. ¶ ∼ 그것이 틀림없다 Really it must be so. / ∼그래〔그렇군〕 It's a fact. *or* Yes, you are right. *or* Well, you may put it that way. / ∼ 그렇게 돼야 할 것이야 Indeed it has got to be that way. ③ 《그러나》 but; however; though; only; 《…이기는 하나 그러나》 (It is) true, but…. ¶∼ 예외도 있지 There are, indeed, some exceptions to this. / ∼ 대수로운 일은 아니지만 It does not count much, though. (★ 구어에서는 앞의 예에서처럼 though를 나중에 말할 때가 많다. 「하기는, 돈이 많이 들지도 모르지만」 It may cost you a lot, though.) / 이 꽃은 매우 곱다, ∼ 향기는 없지만 This flower is very lovely, only 〔though〕 it has no scent.

**하기식**(下旗式) a flag-lowering ceremony; 〖군사〗 a retreat. ◉ ∼나팔 a retreat.

**하기야** indeed; definitely. ¶ ∼ 세상 만사는 돈이면 다니까 It is safe to bet that money is everything nowadays.

**하나** ① 《일》 one. ¶∼에서 열까지 from beginning to end; in everything; in every particular / ∼를 보고 열을 알다 be quick to understand; have a very intelligent mind / ∼만 알고 둘은 모른다 judge everything by one thing he knows.
② 《한 개》 one; one thing; the one…; the other one; 《한 사람》 one person; one man. ¶ 3인조 강도의 ∼ one of the gang of three robbers / ∼씩 one by one; one at a time; piece by piece; 《개별적으로》 individually; separately / (사람이) ∼ 둘씩 by ones and twos / ∼ 남김없이 without exception; to the (very) last; 《사람》 (one and) all; all together; every one (of them); to the last man; 《모두》 all (of) / 이것은 ∼에 50원이다 It is fifty won each 〔a piece〕. / 그녀는 수학 문제를 ∼씩 풀었다 She solved math problems one by one. / 방이 ∼ 더 있었으면 한다 We'd like to have one more room. / 그 중 ∼가 검고 나머지는 희다 One (of them) is black and the others are white. / 이 서류는 ∼도 틀린 데가 없다 There is not a single mistake in this document.
③ 《유일》 (the) only one. ¶∼의 single;

only; sole; unique / 단 ～뿐인 친구 *one's* 〔the〕 one and only friend / 그녀의 단 ～의 꿈 her one and only dream / 나는 아우가 ～뿐이다 I have an only brother. / 이 책을 읽은 사람은 너 ～뿐이다 You are the only one that has read this book. / 모든 것이 자네 생각 ～에 달려 있네 Everything depends on「you 〔your decision〕.
④ 《동일》 (one and) the same. ¶ 그들은 모두 ～의 종류에 속한다 They are one and the same kind. / 우리 생각은 ～다 Our ideas are the same.
⑤ 《일체》 one body; a unity. ¶ ～되어서 (행동하다) (act) in a body 〔as one man〕 / ～가 되다 become one; be (-come) united; unite (together) / ～가 되어서 싸우다 fight as one body / 전국민이 ～가 되었다 All the nation is united. / 양측은 ～가 되어 난문제를 해결했다 The two parties worked together to solve the difficult problem.
⑥ 《한편》 ¶ ～는 가족을 위해, 또 ～는 나라를 위해 partly for *one's* family, and partly for *one's* country.
⑦ 《조차》 not even; not so much as. ¶ 그는 편지 ～ 제대로 쓰지 못한다 He cannot so much as write a letter in a proper way. / 그 정치인은 연설 ～ 제대로 못 한다 The politician cannot even speak in public properly.

**하나**[2] 《…하지만》 do 〔say, think, be, *etc.*〕 but; 《그러하나》 however; but; yet.

**하나님** ⇨ 하느님.

**하나하나** one after another; one by one; one at a time; piece by piece; 《개별적으로》 individually; separately; 《상세히》 minutely; in all particulars; fully; in detail; 《생략 없이》 without omission. ¶ 법안을 ～ 토의하다 discuss the bills one by one / ～보고하다 report in detail; make a detailed 〔circumstantial〕 report.

**하녀**(下女) a maid(servant); a housemaid; a woman servant (*pl.* women servants). ¶ ～를 두다 keep a maid.

**하념**(下念) gracious consideration. ～하다 give gracious consideration to; deign to be considerate about. ¶ ～하여 주셔서 감사합니다 Thank you for your「kind 〔gracious〕 consideration.

**하느님** God; the Lord; the King of Heaven; the Almighty; the Supreme Being; the Creator; the Divinity. ¶ ～의 가호 divine protection / ～의 말씀 the word of God; the word of the Spirit; the Word / ～의 심판 the justice of Heaven; divine judgment / ～의 은총 the blessing 〔grace〕 of God; divine blessing 〔grace〕 / ～을 공경하다 revere God; be pious / ～께 맹세하다 swear before 〔by〕 Heaven / ～을 믿다 believe in God / ～께 빌다 pray to God / ～ 만이 아신다 God only knows 《that, when, where, why》 / ～맙소사 Heaven forbid! / ～ 살려 주시옵소서 God save me!

**하느작거리다** flutter; quiver; swing; sway; tremble. ¶ 바람에 하느작거리는 갈대 reeds swaying in the breeze.

**하는 수 없이** unavoidably; inevitably; unwillingly. ¶ ～…하다 be forced 〔compelled, obliged〕 to *do* / 아버지의 파산으로 ～ 대학을 중퇴했다 Father went bankrupt, so I was「obliged 〔forced〕 to drop out of college.

**하늄** 〖화학〗 《인공 방사성 원소》 hahnium (기호 Ha) (원자번호 105).

**하늘** ① 《천공》 the sky; the blue; the heavens; 《상공》 the skies; 《공중》 the air. (★ the sky가 일상 쓰는 일반적인 용법이며 문어·시어 및 일기에 관해서 말할 때는 종종 the skies의 꼴도 쓰임. 또 시에서는 heaven도 쓰임). ¶ ～을 찌를 듯한 sky-scraping 《building》 / ～ 높이 high up in the sky / 푸른〔맑은, 잿빛, 흐린〕 ～ the blue 〔clear, gray, cloudy〕 sky / 가을 ～에 in the autumn air; in 〔under〕 the autumn sky / 차가운 ～에 빛나는 별 stars in the frosty sky / ～의 별따기 (it is as difficult as) plucking a star out of the heavens; (be) not easier than picking a star out of the sky / ～을 날다 fly in the air / ～을 쳐다보다 look (up) at the sky / ～로 날아오르다 soar up to the sky / ～에 애드벌룬이 떠 있다 An advertizing balloon is floating in the sky. / ～에 무지개가 섰다 A rainbow appeared across 〔in〕 the sky. / ～이 무너져도 솟아날 구멍이 있다 《속담》 There is a way out of every situation, however bad.
② 《종교에서》 heaven; Heaven; God. ¶ ～ 무서운 줄 모르는 말 a blasphemous remark / ～에 계신 우리 아버지 our Father which art in Heaven (★ art는 고어) / ～은 스스로 돕는 자를 돕는다 《속담》 Heaven helps those who help themselves. *or* Aid yourself, and heaven will aid you. ◉ ～나라 (the kingdom of) Heaven; Paradise; Elysium (천당). ～빛 sky blue; sky-blue color; azure: ～빛의 sky-blue; azure.

**하늘가재** 〖곤충〗 an earwig.
**하늘거리다** sway; tremble; waver; quiver; 《불꽃이》 flicker; flare. ¶ 하늘거리는 불꽃 wavy flames / (나뭇잎 따위가) 바람에 ~ tremble in the breeze; sway to the wind.
**하늘다람쥐** 〖동물〗 a flying squirrel.
**하늘소** 〖곤충〗 a long-horned beetle; a longicorn (beetle).
**하늘지기** 〖식물〗 a kind of sedge.
**하늘하늘** 《가볍게》 lightly; buoyantly. ¶ ~한 천 light and flimsy cloth / 종잇조각이 하늘로 ~ 올라갔다 A piece of paper rose buoyantly in the air.
**하늬(바람)** a west wind.
**하다**[1] ① 《행하다》 do; perform; undertake; make; act; 《시도하다》 try; attempt; 《실행하다》 carry out; practice; 《역할을》 act 〔serve〕 as; 《종사하다》 engage 〔be engaged〕 in; 《착수하다》 set about; go in for. ¶ 하고 있는 일 the work in hand / 하면 할 수 있다는 정신 a "can-do" spirit / 하는 일마다 everything 〔whatever〕 *one* 「does 〔tries〕 / …하기 위해, …하려고 in order 「to 〔that… may〕 《*do*》; (so) that… 「may 〔can〕; so as to 《*do*》; for; for the purpose of; with the intention of / …할 수 있다〔없다〕 be 「able 〔unable〕 to 《*do*》 / …하기 일쑤다 be apt 〔be liable〕 to 《*do*》 / …하게 되다 learn to 《*do*》; come to 《*do*》 / …을 하기에까지 이르다 go the length of 《*do*ing》 / …하기로 하고 있다 make it a 「rule 〔practice〕 to 《*do*》; make a point of 《*do*ing》 / 할 일이 없다〔많다〕 have 「nothing 〔a lot, much〕 to do / 하라는 대로 ~ do as 《*a person*》 says 〔likes, wishes〕; do what *one* is told to 《*do*》 / …할 마음이 있다 have a mind to 《*do*》; be willing to 《*do*》 / …하고 싶은 마음이 들다 feel inclined to *do* 《*something*》; feel like 《*do*ing, a walk》; feel moved to 《*do*》 / …하고 싶은 마음이 없다 do not feel like 《*do*ing》; be in no mood 〔humor〕 《for, to *do*》 / 해보다 try to *do;* have 〔make〕 a try 《at *a thing*》 / 할 수 있는 데까지 해보다 try 「everything that could be done 〔all that is (humanly) possible〕; try 〔do〕 *one's* best / 하는 일 없이 지내다 idle away *one's* time; live 「an idle life 〔a life of ease〕; eat the bread of idleness / 공무원(노릇)을 ~ work as a public official / 사업을 ~ run a business / 일을 ~ do a job; work / 전쟁을 ~ wage a war / 중매 노릇을 ~ act as go-between; arrange a match 《between A and B》 / 징역살이를 ~ serve a prison term; do 〔serve〕 time 《at》 / 못된 짓을 ~ do an evil deed; commit a crime / 그는 전에 교장을 했었다 He used to be a principal. / 좋을 대로 해라 You may do as you please. / 할 바를 모르겠다 I 「don't know 〔am at a loss〕 「what to do 〔how to act〕. / 동생은 무엇이든 언니가 하는 대로 했다 The younger sister 「behaved 〔did everything〕 just as her older sister did. / 하는 일마다 (잘) 되지가 않아서 그는 자포자기해 있었다 He was kind of desperate because everything he did went wrong. / 걷기도 전에 뛰려고 하지 마라 Don't try to run before you can walk.
② 《…로 하다》 make; make 《a musician》 of 《*a person*》. ¶ 아무를 미치게 ~ drive 《*a person*》 mad; send 《*a person*》 crazy 〔out of his wits〕 / 그 여인을 아내로 맞이~ make the woman *one's* wife / 아무를 행복하게 ~ make 《*a person*》 happy / 아들을 의사가 되게 ~ make a physician of *one's* son; bring up *one's* boy for the medical profession.
③ 《부르다》 call; name. ¶ F라고 하는 사나이 a man 「named 〔called〕 F / 나는 김이라고 합니다 My name is Kim. / 이 곳은 공원이라 할 만한 곳이 없다 There is no park 「worth mentioning 〔worthy of the name〕 here.
④ 《소문에 듣다》 they 〔people〕 say; it is said; I hear. ¶ 그렇다고 하더군 So I understand. / 그는 사직했다고 하던데 The story goes that he resigned his post.
⑤ 《알다》 know; 《배우다》 study. ¶ 영어를 꽤 ~ be pretty good at English; have a good command of English.
⑥ 《경험하다》 experience; go through. ¶ 고생을 ~ go through hardships and privations; undergo hardships.
⑦ 《값이》 cost 《10,000 won》; be worth; be valued. ¶ 2억 원 하는 집 a house that costs two hundred million won / 사과 한 개에 천 원 한다 The apples are one thousand won each.
⑧ 《몸에 걸치다》 wear. ¶ 귀덮개를 ~ wear earmuffs.
⑨ 《…하려고 하다》 ¶ …하려고 in an 「effort 〔endeavor〕 to *do;* by way of *do*ing / 이제 막〔바야흐로〕 …하려고 ~ be 「about 〔going〕 to *do;* be on the 「point 〔verge, brink〕 of *do*ing / 그는 막 등불을 끄려고 했다 He was about

to turn off the light.
⑩《먹다》 eat; 《마시다》 drink; 《피우다》 smoke. ¶ 점심을 ～ lunch; take 〔have〕 lunch(eon) / 한 잔 ～ have a drink / 한 잔 더 하시겠습니까 Will you have another glass? / 나는 담배를 못 합니다 I don't smoke. *or* I am not in the habit of smoking. / 술을 못 합니다 I am of a sober habit.
⑪《말하다》 say; speak; talk; remark. ¶ 남이 뭐라고 하든 whatever others may say 《about, of》 / 영어로 ～ speak in English / 자네 지금 무어라 했나 What did you say just now? / 영어로 그것을 뭐라고 합니까 How 〔What〕 do you 「say 〔put, call〕 it in English?
⑫《…라고 한다면》 ¶ 만약 내일 비가 온다고 하면 … If it is rainy tomorrow, … / 지금, y가 $x^3$과 같다고 하자 Let $y$ equal $x^3$ 〔x cubic〕.

> 참고 **make, have, get, do** 따위의 동사 용법: 이런 동사는 명사와 결부되어 「…을 하다」의 형태로 관용적인 표현을 만드는 일이 많다. 이러한 표현은 흔히 동사 하나로 바꾸는 것이 가능하다. 보기: 대답을 하다 make an answer=answer / 휴식을 취하다 have a rest=rest.

**하다²** 《매우》 be quite; be indeed. ¶ 좋기도 ～ be quite nice / 빠르기도 ～ be speedy indeed / 참 이상하기도 ～ How strange!
**하다못하다** fail to do 〔make, finish〕; try to do but do not. ¶ 일을 ～ fail to finish a job / 일을 하다 못해 남기다 leave a job unfinished / 하다 못하면 백 원에라도 팔아야겠다 I'll have to sell it for 100 won if that's all I can get for it.
**하다못해** 《적어도》 at least; at most; at best; 《심지어》 《go》 as 〔so〕 far as to; even; 《종국에는》 at the extreme 〔end, limit〕; at the worst; in the end; finally. ¶ 못된 짓을 ～ 나중에는 도둑질까지 했다 He went so far as to commit theft in the end. / ～ 백 원이라도 주었으면 좋겠다 At least you can let me have 100 won. / 의사를 청하려면 ～ 택시비라도 있어야 되겠다 If you're going for the doctor, at least you'll have to cab fare. / ～ 하인들까지도 주인을 멸시했다 Even his servants despised him.
**하단**(下段) ① 《글의》 a lower column. ② 《계단의》 a lower step 〔tier〕; 《침대차의》 the lower berth; the latter 〔lower〕 part.
**하단**(下端) the lower end 《of a pole》; 《페이지의》 the tail. 「platform.
**하단**(下壇) ～하다 leave 〔go down〕 the
**하달**(下達) notice 〔notification〕 to an inferior. ～하다 notify (to) an inferior; convey to the people. ¶ 대통령의 뜻을 ～하다 convey the wishes of the president. ◉ 상의(上意)～ conveying the will and ideas of those in authority to their subordinates; communication from the top down: 상의～하다 transmit 《policy decisions》 down 「the hierarchy 〔the chain of command〕; pass the word down 《구어》.
**하대**(下待) ① 《대우》 disrespectful treatment 〔reception〕; inhospitability. ～하다 treat 〔receive〕 with disrespect; be inhospitable 《towards》. ② 《말을 낮춤》 ～하다 use low form of speech 《to》; do not mister 《*a person*》.
**하도** very much indeed; ever so hard. ¶ ～ 기뻐서 in the excess of *one's* joy / ～ 보고 싶어서 in *one's* eagerness to see it / ～ 바빠서 잠도 제대로 잘 수 없다 be too busy to get enough sleep / 길을 ～ 걸어 다리가 아프다 walked so hard that *one's* legs ache / 세월이 ～ 빨리 가다 time flies ever so fast.
**하도급**(下都給) subcontracting; a subcontract. ～하다 subcontract. ¶ ～을 주다 subcontract 《*something*》 to 《*a person*》; sublet / ～을 맡다 take on 《a job》 as subcontractor; be a subcontractor 《on the construction work》. ◉ ～부조리 《공사의》 a malpractice associated with construction subcontracting. ～업자 a subcontractor; a subcontract firm (업체).
**하도롱지**(一紙) brown (wrapping) paper; sulfate paper; kraft paper.
**하드보드** 『건축』 hardboard.
**하드보일드** 《비정한》 hard-boiled. ¶ ～한 문체 a hard-boiled style.
**하드웨어** 『컴퓨터』 hardware. ◉ ～기술자 a hardware specialist. ～키 a hardware key. ～호환성 hard-ware compatibility.
**하등**(下等) a low(er) class 〔grade〕; inferiority; vulgarity. ¶ ～의 《열등한》 inferior; low; mean; 《조야한》 coarse; vulgar (상스러운). ◉ ～동물 lower animals; the animals of a lower order. ～미(米) low-grade rice; rice of inferior quality. ～사회 the lower classes; the lower order of society.

～선객(船客) a steerage passenger. ～식물 lower plants; the plants of a lower order. ～인간 a mean(-spirited) fellow; a person of low character. ～품 an inferior article; an article of inferior quality.

**하등**(何等) (not) any; little; (nothing) whatever; (not) in any way; (not) at all. ¶ ～의 이유도 없이 without any reason; for nothing / ～의 관계도 없다 have no connection 〔relation〕 whatever 《with》; have nothing to do 《with》; be not in any way related 《with》 / ～의 이상도 없다 Nothing is wrong 〔the matter〕. *or* Everything is all right. / ～의 이상할 것도 없다 There is nothing strange about it. / 어머니는 치료를 받았으나 ～의 효험이 없었다 The treatment had no effect on my mother at all.

**하락**(下落) 《가격·가치의》 a fall 〔drop, decline〕 《in price》; depreciation; a slump (폭락). ～하다 fall (off); decline; come 〔go〕 down. ¶ 물가의 ～ a decline 〔fall〕 in prices / 연료 가격의～ a fall 〔decline〕 in the price of fuel 〔oil〕 / ～시키다 depreciate; lower; bring down 《prices》; degrade / 급격한 ～ a sharp 〔precipitate〕 drop / 인기가 ～하다 lose *one's* popularity; fall in popularity / 설탕값이 20퍼센트나 ～했다 The price of sugar has fallen (by) 20 percent. / 주가가 ～하고 있다 Stock prices are on the decline. / 풍작으로 쌀값이 ～했다 The good harvest brought down the price of rice. / 원화에 대한 달러값이 꾸준히 ～하고 있다 The value of the dollar is falling steadily against the won.
◉ ～세〔경향〕 《show》 a declining tendency; 《take》 a downward trend; a downtrend: 물가는 ～세에 있다 Prices are tending to fall. ～시세 『증권』 a bear 〔bearish〕 market.

**하략**(下略) omitted below; the rest omitted; omission from here on; "etc. etc."; "…". ～하다 omit the rest.

**하량하다**(下諒—) condescend to take note of; consider; look upon 〔understand〕 with symphathy. ¶ 곤란한 사정을 ～ condescend to take 《*a person's*》 difficult circumstances into consideration / 사정이 이러하오니 하량하소서 Such being the case, I beg you will kindly excuse me.

**-하러** to; for; in order to; for the purpose of. ¶ 산책～ 나가다 go (out) for a walk / 백화점에 쇼핑～ 가다 go shopping at a department store.

**하렘** 《이슬람의》 a harem; 《처첩》 concubines; 《규중》 women's quarters.

**하려**(下慮) gracious consideration. ⇨ 하념(下念).

**하례**(賀禮) 《식》 a congratulatory ceremony; a celebration; 《축하》 congratulation. ～하다 hold a congratulatory ceremony; celebrate; congratulate. ¶ ～를 받다 accept 《*a person's*》 felicitation. ◉ 신년～ the New Year's ceremony.

**하롱거리다** act rashly 〔carelessly〕; be flippant.

**하롱하롱** rashly; carelessly; flippantly. ¶ ～ 까불다 behave flippantly.

**하루** ① 《초하루》 the first day (of a month). ② 《날수》 a (single) day; one day. ¶ 꼬박～ a whole day / ～의 일 a day's work / ～ 세 끼의 밥 three meals a day / ～ 세 번 three times a day / ～ 걸러 every other 〔second〕 day; on alternate days / ～에 《비율》 per 〔a〕 day; 《동안에》 (in) a day / ～이틀에 in a day or two; in one or two days / ～도 어기지 않고 to a day / 십년을 ～같이 for ten years as one day / ～ 종일 all day (long); all through the day; the whole day; throughout the day; (a)round the clock / ～종일 걸리다 take a whole day / ～얼마(씩)에 일하다 work by the day / ～걸러 배달하다 deliver 《the mail》 every other day / ～가 다르게〔날이 갈수록〕 좋아지다 get better every day 〔day by day〕 / 어제는 ～ 종일 너를 기다렸다 I waited for you all day long yesterday. / 단～도 그가 실험실에 나가지 않는 날은 없었다 Not a day passed 「that he did not go 〔without his going〕 to the laboratory. ③ 《어느 날》 one day. ¶ ～는 one day / ～는 그가 산책을 나갔다 One day he went out for a walk.

**하루갈이** the (size of) field 〔paddy〕 that takes a day's plowing.

**하루거리** 『의학』 tertian ague; malarial 〔intermittent〕 fever. ¶ ～에 걸리다 be taken with tertian ague.

**하루바삐** as soon as possible; without a day's delay. ¶ ～ 하다 lose no time in doing 《*a thing*》 / ～ 회복하시기를 빕니다 I wish you earliest possible recovery.

**하루살이** 『곤충』 a dayfly; a mayfly; 《영》 a green drake; a drake (fly); an ephemera (*pl.* ～s, -erae). ¶ ～ 같은 ephemeral; transient; evanescent;

short-lived / ～ 같은 인생 an ephemeral life 〔existence〕.

**하루아침** one morning. ¶ ～에 in a morning; overnight; in a (single) day; in a short time; in a brief space of time / ～에 유명해지다 leap 〔flash〕 into fame / ～에 부자가 되다 wake up to find *oneself* suddenly rich / 로마는 ～에 이루어진 것이 아니다 《속담》 Rome was not built in a day.

**하루치** one day's portion; a ration (식량의). ¶ ～의 배급량 a day's ration.

**하루하루** every day; daily; from day to day; day after 〔by〕 day; one day after another. ¶ ～의 생활 everyday 〔day-to-day〕 life; *one's* daily life / (정해진) ～의 일 routine work 〔duties〕; the daily round (of life) / ～ 나아지다 get better day by day / ～ 미루다 put 《*a matter*》 off from day to day; put 《*a matter*》 off and off / ～ 추워진다 It is growing colder day by day.

**하룻강아지** a (one-day-old) puppy. ¶ ～ 날뛰듯 하다 act naughtily; misbehave / ～ 범 무서운 줄 모른다 《속담》 Fools rush in where angels fear to tread. *or* An ignorant person doesn't stand in awe of the great.

**하룻날** 《초하룻날》 the first of a month.

**하룻밤** a 〔one〕 night; 《온 밤》 all night. ¶ ～ 사이에 in one 〔a single〕 night; overnight / ～을 묵다 put up for a night; stop 〔stay〕 overnight / ～ 묵어 가기를 청하다 ask for a night's lodging 〔shelter〕 / ～을 뜬 눈으로 새우다 sit 〔stay〕 up all night; be wide awake all night; pass a sleepless night / ～을 이야기로 지새우다 talk a night over / ～을 자도 만리성을 쌓는다 strike up a deep friendship quickly.

**하류**(下流) ① 《하천의》 the downstream; the lower reaches 〔course〕 of a stream. ¶ ～에〔쪽으로〕 downstream; down the river / 한강 ～에 on the lower Han River / 여기서 5마일 ～에 마을이 있다 There is a village five miles down the river 〔downstream〕 from here. ② 《사회의》 the lower classes; low-class people. ¶ ～의 lower-class. ◉ ～계급 the lower classes. ～배 low-class people. ～사회 the lower classes; the lower order 〔strata〕 of society: ～사회의 말 the language of the gutter. ～생활 (a) low life.

**하륙**(下陸) landing; disembarkation; unloading. ～하다 land; disembark; unload 〔discharge〕 《a ship, cargo from a ship》. ¶ 그 배는 짐을 ～중이다 The ship is unloading. / 세관 검사가 끝나는 대로 짐을 ～하겠습니다 We will start unloading soon after the customs inspection. ◉ ～항 a port of discharge.

**하르르하다** (be) flimsy; thin; filmy 「《cloth》.

**하릅** a one-year-old horse 〔ox〕; a yearling. ◉ ～송아지 a one-year-old calf.

**하리**(下吏) a low 〔petty〕 official.

**하리놀다** calumniate; slander.

**하리다** 《사치를 부리다》 indulge in luxury; be addicted to extravagance; be given to luxury.

**하리들다** have 〔run into〕 a hitch; get thwarted 〔frustrated〕; be crossed. ¶ 계획에 ～ get thwarted in *one's* project; have a hitch in *one's* plan.

**하리쟁이** a slanderer; a calumniator.

**하릴없다** (be) unavoidable; inevitable; helpless; cannot be helped; there is no help for it; nothing can be done about it. ¶ 바보라는 말을 들어도 ～ I can't help being called a fool.

**하릴없이** 《어쩔 수 없이》 against *one's* will; unwillingly; 《불가피하게》 unavoidably; inevitably; without choice 〔alternative〕; for lack of an alternative; helplessly; with no other course. ¶ ～ 복종하다 be obliged to obey / ～ 자네에게서 비난을 듣게 됐다 I knew I deserve your reproaches.

**하마**(下馬) dismounting (from a horse); getting off a horse. ～하다 dismount (from a horse); get off a horse; alight from a horse. ◉ ～비(碑) a notice stone requiring riders to dismount. ～석 a horse block; a step(-stone).

**하마**(河馬) 〖동물〗 a hippopotamus (*pl.* ～es, -mi); a hippo (*pl.* ～s) 《구어》.

**하마터면** almost; nearly; by a close shave; by a hair's breadth; by the skin of *one's* teeth; on the verge 〔brink〕 of. ¶ ～ 죽을 것을 살았다 I was saved from death by a hair's breadth. / ～ 죽을 뻔했다 I came within an inch of being killed. *or* I had a close call 〔shave〕. *or* I nearly 〔almost〕 died. (★ I was nearly 〔almost〕 died.는 「나는 거의 죽어 있었다」란 뜻) / ～ 빠져 죽을 뻔했다 I was on the verge of drowning. / ～ 치일 뻔했다 I narrowly 〔just〕 missed being run over 《by a lorry》. / ～ 실수할 뻔했다 I nearly made a mistake. / ～ 회사가 파산할 상태였다 The firm was teetering on the edge 〔verge〕 of bankruptcy.

**하마평**(下馬評) an appointment widely rumored among the public; common gossip; an outsider's irresponsible talk; a rumor. ¶ ～에 의하면 …라고들 한다 It is rumored [There is speculation] that…; Rumor has it that … / 보궐 선거를 앞두고 많은 이름이 ～에 오르고 있다 Many people are speculated [rumored] to stand for the by-election.

**하명**(下命) 《명령》 a command; 《주문》 an order. ～하다 order; command; give an order [a command]; issue a command. ¶ ～을 바랍니다 We solicit your orders. / 무엇이든 ～만 하십시오 We are entirely at your service. *or* We are ready to meet any request of yours.

**하모니** 《조화》 harmony. ¶ 카펫 색깔이 벽과 ～를 이루고 있다 The color of the carpet is in harmony with the wall.

**하모니카** 〖악기〗 a harmonica. ¶ ～를 불다 play the harmonica.

**하묘**(下錨) anchoring; mooring; dropping an anchor. ～하다 (drop an) anchor; lower an anchor; moor.

**하문**(下門) 〖해부〗 the vulva; the vagina.

**하문하다**(下問—) condescend to inquire of an inferior. ¶ 불치(不恥) ～ be not ashamed to seek counsel of an inferior.

**하물**(荷物) 《수화물》 baggage 《미》; luggage 《영》; freight; cargo. ⇨ 화물.

**하물며** 《더더군다나 …하다》 much [still] more; 《더더군다나 …아니다》 much [still] less; 《말할 것도 없다》 not to mention [speak of]; to say nothing of; let alone. ¶ 이웃도 도와야 하거늘 ～ 부모를 돌보지 않아 되겠느냐 If you should help your neighbors, how much more should you help your parents! / 쌀 살 돈도 없는데 ～ 옷 살 돈이 있으랴 I don't have any money for rice, much less for clothes. / 그는 영어도 모르거늘 ～ 불어를 할 수 있으랴 He knows no English, let alone [not to speak of] French. / 개조차 저렇듯 주인에게 충실하거늘 ～ 우리 인간에게 있어서랴 If a dog is as faithful as that to its master, how much more so should we human beings be! / 선생님조차 저토록 공부를 해야 하거늘～학생에 있어서랴 《학생은 말할 나위도 없다》 If the teacher has to work so hard, how much more must the students!

**하박**(下膊) 〖해부〗 the forearm; the antebrachium. ◉ ～골 forearm bones.

**하반**(下半) the lower half; the latter half. ◉ ～기 the latter [second] half of the year. ～신 the lower half of *one's* body.

**하번**(下番) relief from [going off] duty [guard].

**하복**(下腹) 〖해부〗 the abdomen; the underbelly. ◉ ～부 the abdominal [hypogastric] region; the hypogastrium (*pl.* -tria): ～부의 hypogastric.

**하복**(夏服) a summer suit [uniform]; summer clothes; a garment [dress] for summer wear. ¶ 이것은 ～으로 좋다 This is good for summer wear.

**하부**(下部) the lower part.
◉ ～구조 the understructure; the substructure. ～기관 subordinate offices [agencies]. ～여백 《도서의》 a bottom [tail] margin. ～조직 a lower branch 《of an organization》; the infrastructure; a subordinate [subsidiary] organization.

**하사**(下士) 〖육군·공군·해병〗 a staff sergeant; 〖해군〗 a petty officer second class.

**하사**(下賜) a Royal gift [grant]. ～하다 grant; give; bestow; confer. ¶ 금일봉을 ～하다 grant [give] 《*a person*》 money 《in appreciation of *his* services》.
◉ ～금 an Imperial [a Royal] grant [bounty]. ～품 an Imperial [a Royal] gift.

**하사**(何事) anything; everything; something; what matter. ¶ 정신 일도(精神一到) ～불성(不成) Nothing is impossible to a determined mind. *or* Where there is a will, there is a way.

**하사관**(下士官) 〖해군〗 a petty officer; 〖육군〗 a noncommissioned officer (생략 NCO, N.C.O.); a noncom.

**하산**(下山) descending a mountain. ～하다 go down [climb down, descend] a mountain; bring 《it》 down the mountain; 《절에서》 leave a temple.

**하상**(河床) the riverbed.

**하선**(下船) leaving a ship; getting off a ship. ～하다 leave a ship; get off a ship; disembark; go [come] ashore (상륙하다). ¶ (승무원을) ～시키다 discharge; land.

**하선**(下線) an underline; an underscore. ¶ ～을 긋다[치다] underline 《a word》; underscore 《a line》 / ～친 부분 an underlined [underscored] part.

**하세**(下世) 《별세》 passing away; death; 《세상을 멀리함》 seclusion from society.

**하소**(煆燒) 〖화학〗 calcination; calcining.

～하다 calcine. ◉ ～기 a calciner; a calcinatory. ～로(爐) a calcinatory.

**하소연하다** complain of; mutter; appeal《to》. ¶ 서러운 사정을 ～ plead *one's* sorry situation / 억울하다고 ～ complain of an injustice / 동정해 달라고 ～ appeal to《*a person*》for *his* sympathy.

**하수**(下水)《오수》sewage; waste 〔foul〕 water;《설비》a sewerage (system); drainage; a drain; a sewer.

> **용법** **sewage** 배출되는「하수, 오수」란 뜻으로 격식차린 말. **waste water**「폐수, 하수, 오수」를 뜻하는 sewage보다 넓은 뜻의 일반적인 말. **sewerage** 배수를 위한 파이프·도랑이나 수채 따위 하수 처리를 위한 설비 상황에 중점을 둔 말. **drainage** 배수의 방법이나 시스템에 중점을 둔 말. 그러나「하수〔배수〕 설비」의 뜻으로 sewerage와 drainage를 공용하는 경우가 많음.「하수」와 관련이 있는 **drain, sewer**는 둘 다「배수구, 배수관」을 뜻하나, sewer는 지하에 있는 것을 뜻함.

¶ ～가 넘치다 the drains overflow / ～가 막히다 the drain is 〔drains are〕 blocked 〔stopped up〕 / 정화 처리를 하지 않은 ～ raw sewage / 이 시(市)는 ～ 설비가 잘 되어 있다 This city has a very adequate sewerage system.

◉ ～공사 laying sewers; sewer construction; drainage 〔sewerage〕 works. ～관(管) a drainpipe; a cesspipe; a sewer pipe. ～구 a sewer; a gutter; a ditch; a drain: ～구를 청소하다 clear 〔scour〕 a drain. ～도 a sewer; a sewerage: ～도 사용료〔세〕 sew(er)age charges 〔tax〕. ～조(槽) a cesspool. ～처리 sewerage; sewage disposal: ～처리장 a sewage (treatment) plant.

**하수**[1](下手)《서툰 솜씨》lack of talent; unskillfulness;《사람》a poor hand.

**하수**[2](下手) ①《살인》murder; laying (murderous) hands on. ～하다 murder. ② ⇨ 착수(着手).

**하수**(下垂) drooping; hanging down.
◉ ～증(症)〖의학〗ptosis. 위～ gastroptosis.

**하수인**(下手人)《살인자》the perpetrator《of the murder》; the murderer; the slayer. ¶ ～은 누구라고 생각하나 Who do you think was the murderer?

**하숙**(下宿)《숙박하기》boarding; lodging; board and lodging; board and room (식사 제공);《하숙집》(*one's*) lodging(s); a boardinghouse. ⇨ ～집. ～하다 board 〔lodge, room〕《at *a person's*, with *a person*》; take up *one's* quarters 〔lodgings〕. ¶ 고급 ～ a high-class boardinghouse / 여염(집) ～ a private boardinghouse; a private house taking in boarders / 식사 없는 ～ lodging without board / ～(집)을 하다〔치다〕 run 〔keep, operate〕 a lodging house; take in 〔keep〕 lodgers 〔boarders〕 / ～생활을 하다 live in lodgings 〔a lodging house〕 / ～을 바꾸다 change *one's* lodgings / ～을 찾고 있다 be on a hunt for lodgings / 그녀는 김선생님 댁에 ～하고 있다 She is rooming「at Mr. Kim's 〔with Mr. Kim〕. / 나는 학교 부근에 ～하고 있다 I have taken a room near the school.

◉ ～방 a rented room; a room for rent. ～비 the charge for (board and) lodging; board charge: 나의 ～비는 식비까지 합해서 월 30만원입니다 I pay 300,000 won a month for room and board. ～생 a student boarder. ～인《식사 제공이 없는》a roomer《미》; a lodger《영》;《식사 제공을 받는》a boarder; a paying guest (★ 하숙집이 단지 장삿속으로 하는 것은 아니라고 인식시키기 위한 완곡한 표현). ～집 a boardinghouse; rooming 〔lodging〕 house.

**하순**(下旬) the third 〔the last 10 days〕 of a month; the latter part of the month. ¶ 5월 ～에 toward the end of May; in the latter part of May; late in May / 7월 ～중에 during the last ten days of July.

**하시**(下視)《내려다봄》looking down;《멸시》despising; contempt; looking down on《*a person*》. ～하다《내려다보다》look down (from a height);《멸시하다》despise; look down on《*a person*》; look down *one's* nose at《*a person*》; hold《*a person*》in contempt.

**하악**(下顎)〖해부〗the submaxilla (*pl.* -lae); the lower 〔under〕 jaw. ◉ ～골〖해부〗the (lower) jawbone; the submaxillary bone.

**하안**(河岸) a riverside; a riverbank; a waterfront.

**하야**(下野) retirement (from public life); getting out of office. ～하다 go out of office 〔power〕; resign 〔step down〕 from *one's* public post; get out of office. ¶ 총리는 ～를 결심했다 The Premier made up his mind to「resign 〔leave〕 office.

**하얗다** (be) white; very white; pure white; snow-white. ¶ 하얗게 칠하다

paint white / 그녀의 머리가 ~ Her hair is snow-white. / 일어나 보니 눈이 하얗게 쌓여 있었다 I awoke to find the ground silvery white with snow.

**하얘지다** get (very) white; become (snow-)white; 《머리가》 turn gray 〔white〕. ¶ 머리가 ~ *one's* hair turns white 〔gray〕.

**하여간**(何如間) anyhow. ⇨ 하여튼.

**하여금** letting; making; forcing. ¶ 그로 ~ 편지를 쓰게 하다 make him write a letter / 나로 ~ 회를 대표하게 하라 Let me represent the association. / 부모로 ~ 어렵게 사시게 할 수는 없다 I can't leave my parents in needy circumstances. / 그로 ~ 싫든 좋든 사직하지 않을 수 없게 만들었다 He was forced 〔compelled〕 to resign.

**하여튼**(何如―) anyhow; anyway; at any rate; in any case 〔event, circumstances〕; at all events; somehow or other; all in all; one way or the other. ⇨ 어쨌든. ¶ 그것은 ~(간에) be that as it may; be the matter what it may / …은 ~《…은 제쳐두고》 setting aside; aside 〔apart〕 from…; let alone…; not to speak of / ~ 그렇게 하죠 I will do so, anyway. / ~ 나하고 같이 가자 In any case, let's go together. / ~ 돈은 빌려 주겠네 I will lend you the money in any event. / ~ 너는 해 보는 게 좋겠다 At all events you had better try. / ~ 사실이다 Believe it or not, it's a fact. / ~ 준비만은 해 두지 In any case 〔At all events〕, I will make preparations for it. / 할 수 있을지 어떨지 ~ 해보지 Whether it's possible or not, I want to give it a try. / ~ 오기는 하는 거냐 You are coming anyway? / ~ 자넨 죄를 면할 수가 없네 You are guilty one way or the other. / ~ 알려 드리겠습니다 Let me give you the information for what it may be worth. / ~ 이 계획을 포기할 수는 없다 I must stick to this plan whatever「happens 〔may happen〕.

**하역**(荷役) loading and unloading; cargo work; stevedoring. ~하다 load and unload; do the cargo working. ¶ 석탄 ~을 하다 load 〔unload〕 coal.
◉ ~계원 a tallyman; a tally clerk. ~기계 a cargo-handling machine. ~사무소 a tally office. ~시설 loading facilities. ~윈치 a cargo winch. ~인부 a longshoreman 《미》; a stevedore. ~장치 a cargo gear.

**하연**(賀宴) a party in honor of the occasion; a celebration banquet; a congratulatory feast. ¶ ~을 베풀다 hold a banquet (in honor of the occasion).

**하염없다** ① 《생각이 없다》 (be) absent-minded; blank; idle. ¶ 하염없는 나날 idle days. ② 《그침이 없다》 (be) endless; ceaseless. ¶ 하염없는 눈물을 어찌할 수 없었다 Try as I might, I could not hold 〔keep〕 back my tears.

**하염없이** ① 《생각없이》 blankly; vacantly; idly. ¶ ~ 세월을 보내다 pass time doing nothing; idle *one's* time away / 그는 ~ 뜰의 소나무만 바라보고 있었다 He kept gazing blankly at a pine tree in the yard. ② 《그침없이》 endlessly; ceaselessly; unceasingly. ¶ ~ 눈물을 흘리다 give free vent to *one's* tears; be dissolved in tears.

**하염직하다** be worth doing 〔trying〕. ¶ 하염직한 일이다 It is a job worth doing.

**하오**(下午) afternoon. ¶ ~에 in the afternoon / ~ 4시에 at four in the afternoon; at 4 p.m. / ~ 늦게 in the late afternoon.

**하옥**(下獄) imprisonment; confinement. ~하다 put in jail; cast into prison; send to jail; imprison; lock up.

**하와이** Hawaii. ¶ ~의 Hawaiian.
◉ ~말 Hawaiian. ~사람 a Hawaiian. ~제도 the Hawaiian Islands.

**하와이안** Hawaiian. ◉ ~기타 a Hawaiian guitar. ~음악 Hawaiian music.

**하원**(下院) the Lower House 〔Chamber〕; the House of Commons (영국 및 캐나다의); the House of Representatives (미국의). ◉ ~의원 《미국의》 a member of the House of Representatives; a Representative; a Congressman; a Congresswoman; a Congressperson (남녀공통); 《영국의》 a member of the House of Commons; a Member of Parliament (생략 M.P.): ~의원이다 be in the House; be a member of the House of Representatives 〔Commons〕 / ~의원 스미스씨 *Rep.* Smith 《미》; Mr. Smith, M.P. ~의장 the Speaker of the House 《미》; the Speaker (of the House of Commons) 《영》.

**하위**(下位) a low(er) rank; a subordinate 〔junior〕 position; a low(er) grade. ¶ ~의 junior; low(er)-ranking; subordinate / ~이다 be below 〔inferior to〕 《another》 in rank; occupy 〔hold〕 a subordinate position 《to》;

be placed under 《another》; be inferior 《to》/ ～로 떨어지다 sink in the scale. ◉ ～개념 〖논리〗 a subordinate concept. ～구분 (a) subdivision: ～구분하다 subdivide. ～타자 〖야구〗 a batter at the bottom end of the order. ～팀 low-ranking teams.

**하의**(下衣) 《a pair of》 trousers; pants.

**하의**(下意) 「the will and ideas 〔the wishes〕 of the lower-grade personnel; 《민의》 the will of the people; the popular opinion.

**하이** high. ◉ ～다이빙 high diving: ～다이빙 선수 a high diver. ～볼 a highball 《미》; (a) whisky and soda 《영》. ～템포 a fast 〔high〕 tempo. ～허들 〖스포츠〗 the high hurdle(s). ～힐 high-heeled shoes; 《wear》 high heels.

**하이드라지드** 〖약〗 hydrazide (of isonicotinic acid).

**하이드라진** 〖화학〗 hydrazine.

**하이드로설파이트** 〖화학〗 hydrosulfite.

**하이드로스키** 〖화학〗 a hydro-ski.

**하이드로퀴논** 〖화학〗 a hydroquinone.

**하이라이트** a highlight. ¶ 오늘 뉴스의 ～ the highlights of today's news / 다음은 스포츠 뉴스의 ～입니다 Coming next are the sports highlights.

**하이에나** 〖동물〗 a hyena.

**하이잭** hijacking; skyjacking (특히 비행기의). ～하다 hijak 《an airplane》. ¶ ～방지를 위해 사용되는 여러 가지 방책 several devices in use to prevent hijacking / ～사건 a hijack / 그 비행기는 권총에 위협당해 ～되었다 The plane was hijacked at gunpoint. ◉ ～범인 a hijacker.

**하이칼라** ① 《유행을 따름》 stylishness; dandyism; smartness; chic; 《멋쟁이》 a smartly dressed person; a person of fashion; a dandy; a swell; a fop. ¶ ～옷 a smart dress / ～색시 a chic girl. ② 《이발》 *one's* hair in foreign style. ¶ ～(머리)를 하다 cut 〔wear, dress〕 *one's* hair in foreign style.

**하이커** 《도보여행자》 a hiker.

**하이킹** 《도보여행》 (a) hiking; a hike. ～가다〔하다〕 go on a hike; go hiking 《in the country》; hike 《to》. ◉ ～코스 a hiking trail.

**하이테크** 《고도 첨단 기술》 high-tech; high technology. ¶ 근년에 한국의 ～ 산업은 놀라운 진전을 이룩했다 Korea's high-tech industry has made great progress in recent years. ◉ ～기업 a high-tech company. ～산업 a high-tech industry. ～제품 high-technology products.

**하이틴** *one's* late teens. ¶ ～의 소년 a boy in his late teens. (★ high-teen, low-teen은 우리식 표현).

**하이파이** 《고충실도 재생》 high fidelity. ¶ ～의 high-fidelity; hi-fi 《구어》/ ～비디오 a hi-fi video. ◉ ～녹음 a hi-fi recording. ～재생 장치 a high-fidelity sound reproduction system; a hi-fi set. ～플레이어 a hi-fi record player.

**하이퍼-** 《초(超)-, 과도의》 hyper-. ◉ ～마켓 《교외에 있는 초대형 슈퍼마켓》 a hypermarket. ～미디어 〖컴퓨터〗 《복수의 미디어를 유기적으로 결합시킨 것》 hypermedia. ～소닉 《극초음속의》 hypersonic (음속의 5배 이상). ～텍스트 〖컴퓨터〗 《비순차적인 내용 검색이 가능한 텍스트》 a hypertext. ～텐션 《과도의 긴장·고혈압》 hypertension.

**하이픈** a hyphen. ¶ ～을 넣다〔으로 잇다〕 hyphen; hyphenate 《two words》.

**하인**(下人) a (male) servant; a manservant; a domestic (servant). ¶ ～을 두다 keep a servant; have a servant in *one's* service. ◉ ～배(輩) servants; menials; a lowly fellow; low classes.

**하인**(何人) what(ever) person; everyone; every person; all. ¶ ～을 막론하고 whoever it may be; irrespective of who it may be / ～이고 들여서는 안 된다 You shouldn't let anybody in, whoever it may be.

**하인방**(下引枋) 〖건축〗 the lower lintel (of a door, window); the baseboard (of a room); skirting.

**하자**(瑕疵) a flaw; a blemish; a blur; a defect. ¶ ～ 없는 flawless; immaculate; all-perfect.

**하잘것없다** (be) insignificant; negligible; trifling; trivial; [서술적] be beneath notice; be unworthy of attention 〔serious consideration〕. ⇨하찮다. ¶ 하잘것없는 인간 a person of no importance 〔account〕; a nobody / 하잘것없는 일〔것〕 triflers / 하잘것없는 작품 a work of low 〔small〕 merit / 하잘것없는 일에 법석을 떨다 make a fuss about trifles / 하잘것없는 일로 다투었다 We quarreled 〔We had a quarrel〕 over a trifle. / 나같이 하잘것없는 사람이 어찌 이런 일을 할 수 있겠습니까 How is it possible for such an insignificant being as myself to do this work?

**하잠**(夏蠶) summer silkworms.

**하장**(賀狀) a message of congratulation; a congratulatory letter; a greeting card.

**하저**(河底) the bed 〔bottom〕 of a river; a riverbed (하상). ◉ ~터널 a riverbed tunnel.

**하전**(荷電) 〖물리〗 electric charge. ◉ ~입자 a charged particle.

**하절**(夏節) summer; the summer season.

**하정**(賀正) New Year's greetings; 《연하장의 문구》 a Happy New Year!

**하제**(下劑) 〖약〗 a laxative (완화제); a purgative; a cathartic. ¶ ~를 먹다 take a laxative; use a purgative.

**하종가**(下終價) 〖증권〗 《hit》 the daily permissible bottom.

**하주**(荷主) the owner of baggage (임자); a shipper (선적인); a consignor (하송인).

**하중**(荷重) load. ◉ ~시험 a load test. 동~ live 〔mobile, dynamic〕 load. 마력~ 〖항공〗 weight per horsepower loading. 안전~ safe load. 유료~ pay load. 정〔부동〕~ dead 〔static〕 load. 제한~ proof load.

**하지**(下肢) the lower limbs; the legs.

**하지**(夏至) the summer solstice. ◉ ~선 the Tropic of Cancer.

**하지만** however; but; still; (and) yet; nevertheless; though; although. ¶ 그렇기는 ~ It is true…, but / ~ 그건 너무 심한 요구가 아닌가 But it is asking too much, isn't it? / 그는 부자이긴 ~ 행복하지는 않다 He is rich but not happy. / 읽기는 ~ 쓰지는 못 한다 I can read, but I can't write. / 모두가 그럴듯~ 나로서는 찬성 못 하겠다 That's all very well, but I do not agree.

**-하지 않도록** lest…; for fear (that)…; (so as) not to…; (so) that… may not…. (★ lest, for fear는 문어적. 또한 lest, for fear의 절에는 《영》에서는 should를 쓰며 《미》에서는 동사의 원형을 씀: He tried his best *lest* 〔for fear (that)〕 he (should) ruin his own reputation). ¶ 취하지 않도록 해라 See that you do not get drunk. / 그녀에겐 말하지 않도록 해라 Take care not to tell her.

**-하지 않을 수 없다** cannot but *do;* cannot help but *do;* cannot help *do*ing; have to *do;* have not choice but to *do;* be compelled 〔forced, obliged〕 to *do.* ¶ 웃지 않을 수 없다 I cannot help laughing. / 그의 말을 신용하지 않을 수 없다 I cannot but believe him. / 그녀를 동정하지 않을 수 없다 I cannot help but feel sorry for her. / 나는 동의하지 않을 수 없었다 I could not withhold consent. / 긴급한 일이 있다고 해서 곧 가지 않을 수 없었다 I had to go straightaway because they said it was urgent.

**하지하**(下之下) the lowest of its kind; the worst 〔poorest〕 of all. ¶ ~의 the lowest; the worst.

**하직**(下直) leave-taking; (saying) good=by(e); a parting call. ~하다 take *one's* leave; take leave 〔farewell〕 《of》; say good-bye 《to》; bid farewell 《to》. ¶ 웃어른에게 ~하다 take leave of *one's* elders / 고향을 ~하다 leave *one's* native place / 이 세상을 ~하다 leave this world; die / …에게 ~하러 가다 make 〔pay〕 a farewell call 《on *a person*》; pay a farewell visit 《to *a person*》.

**하차**(下車) alighting; getting off 《a train, *etc.*》. ~하다 alight 〔get down〕 《from a car》; get off 〔leave〕 《the train》; get out 《of a car》. ¶ 그는 대전에서 ~했다 He got off at Taejŏn. ◉ ~구 the exit; the way out. ~역 the station where *one* gets off 《the train》; a detraining point. 도중~ a stopover 《station》: 도중 ~하다 stop over 《at》 / 도중~ 무효 《표시》 No stopover (allowed) on this ticket.

**하찮다** 《시시하다》 (be) insignificant; unimportant; [서술적] be beneath notice; be of little importance; be of no account 〔consequence〕; 《사소하다》 (be) trifling; trivial; 《무가치하다》 (be) worthless; valueless; unworthy; 《쓸모없다》 (be) useless. ⇨ 하잘것없다. ¶ 하찮은 선물 a trifling gift / 하찮은 녀석 a worthless fellow; a good-for=nothing; a small fry; a nobody / 하찮은 일 a poor job (하는 일); unattractive work (재미없는); a matter of no importance 〔weight, account〕; a trifling thing; a trivial 〔trifling〕 affair 〔matter〕; a trifle / 하찮게 여기다 make 〔think〕 nothing of / 하찮은 녀석들로 보다 reckon 《them》 as very small fry / 하찮은 일을 크게 떠벌리다 make much of a trifling matter; make a mountain of molehill; make a fuss about trifles / 하찮은 것에 돈을 낭비하다 spend *one's* money ⌈on worthless things 〔to no purpose〕; waste 〔fritter away〕 *one's* money / 이건 하찮은 것입니다만 《무엇을 선물할 때》 Here's a small present for you. *or* Here's something I thought you might like.

**하책**(下策) the worst policy 〔plan〕.

**하천**(河川) 《강》 a river; a watercourse (수로); 《개울》 a brook; a rivulet;

stream (흐름). ⇨강. ¶ ~의 유역 a river basin; a riverside; a valley (큰 강의). ◉ ~개수 river improvement. ~계(系) a river system. ~공사 river (conservation) works. ~공학 riparian 〔river〕 engineering. ~부지 a (dry) riverbed: ~부지 사용 허가 a permit to use a dry riverbed. ~수질 기준치 criteria for measuring river water quality. ~오염 the river contamination 〔pollution〕: 공장 폐수로 인한 ~오염 the river pollution caused by liquid waste from factories. ~학 potamology.

**하청**(下請) a subcontract. ~하다 subcontract. ¶ ~을 맡다 take on 《a job》 as subcontractor; be a subcontractor 《on the construction work》/ ~을 주다 subcontract 《*something*》 to 《*a person*》; sublet / 우리는 그 회사의 ~공사를 맡고 있다 We get subcontracted work from the company. / 그 건축가는 그 일을 그에게 ~주었다 The architect sublet the work to him.
◉ ~공사〔일〕 (a) subcontracted work. ~공장 a subcontract factory 〔plant〕. ~인〔업자〕 a subcontractor.

**하체**(下體) ① 《아랫도리》 the lower part of the body; the nether limbs. ② 《음부》 privy parts.

**하층**(下層) ① 《아래의 켜》 a lower 〔an underlying〕 layer 〔stratum〕. ② 《사회의》 a lower social stratum. ¶ 최~의 사람들 the dregs of society.
◉ ~계급 the lower classes: ~계급이다 be lower-class. ~대기(大氣) lower atmosphere. ~류(流) an undercurrent; 《반대방향으로 흐르는》 an underset; an undertow. ~민 the people of the lower classes; the (great) unwashed; the masses. ~사회 the lower strata of society: ~사회의 말 the language of the gutter. ~생활 (a) low life. ~운(雲) lower clouds.

**하치**(下—) a low 〔poor〕 grade of stuff 〔goods〕; an inferior article; an article of inferior 〔poor〕 quality. ¶ 이 물건은 ~이다 This article is of inferior quality.

**하치장**(荷置場) a yard; a storage space; a depository; a repository. ¶ 노천 석탄~ an open storage yard for coal.

**하키** 〖스포츠〗 hockey. ¶ ~를 하다 play hockey. ◉ ~선수 a hockey player. ~스틱 a hockey stick.

**하퇴**(下腿) the (lower) leg; 〖해부〗 the crus (*pl.* crura). ◉ ~골 the leg bones (=fibula and tibia). ~동맥 the crural artery. ~절단 the amputation of a lower leg.

**하트** heart; 《카드놀이의》 a heart. ¶ ~의 퀸〔에이스, 잭〕 the queen 〔ace, knave〕 of hearts. ◉ ~형 a heart shape; a heart: ~형의 heart-shaped.

**하편**(下篇) the last volume. = 하권(下卷).

**하품** yawning; a yawn (한 번 하는). ~하다 yawn; gape; give a 《big》 yawn. ¶ (따분해서) ~이 나는 boring; dull; tedious / ~을 참다 suppress 〔stifle, smother〕 a yawn; choke down a yawn; bite off a yawn / 자꾸 ~을 하다 have the gapes / ~하며 기지개를 켜다 stretch *oneself* with a yawn / 큰 ~을 하다 yawn a big long yawn / 손으로 ~을 가리다 hide a yawn behind *one's* hand / ~을 하며 말하다 yawn out 《*something*》 / 신문을 읽으며 ~하다 yawn over the papers / ~은 옮는다 Yawning is catching 〔infectious〕. / 그분의 강의는 ~이 나온다 His lectures are 「boring 〔as dull as ditchwater〕.

**하품**(下品) poor 〔low〕 grade. ⇨하치.

**하프** 〖악기〗 a harp. ¶ ~를 연주하다 play the harp. ◉ ~주자(奏者) a harpist.

**하프백** 〖축구〗 a halfback; 〖럭비〗 a scrum half. ¶ ~을 맡다 play (at) halfback.

**하프시코드** 〖악기〗 a harpsichord.

**하프타임** 〖스포츠〗 half time.

**하필**(何必) ¶ ~(이면) of all things 〔places, occasions〕; of all others 〔people〕 / ~이면 오늘 today of all days / ~이면 그날에 on that day of 「all days 〔all others〕 / ~(이면) 그 사람이 he of all men / ~(이면) 그런 곳에서 그녀를 만나다니 How surprising that I should come across her there of all places! / ~ 그런 싸구려를 살게 뭐람 Why did you buy such a cheap thing, of all things? / ~이면 왜 제가 가야만 합니까 Why should I go of all things? / ~ 오늘 가야 맛이냐 Why do you have to choose to go today necessarily? / ~이면 그런 남자와 결혼하다니 Just imagine 〔Fancy〕 her marrying such a man of all 「men 〔others〕!

**하하** Ha ha! ~하다〔거리다〕 laugh 《with joy》.

**하하다** 《숨을》 blow upon; breathe upon 《*a thing* to dampen 〔warm〕 it》; go ha! ¶ 거울에 입김을 하하고 내뿜다 breathe on a glass.

**하학**(下學) ending of the school day. ～하다 school gets 〔lets〕 out; school ends for the day; leave school (at the end of the day). ¶ ～후(에) after school / 3시면 ～한다 School finishes 〔is over〕 at three. ◉ ～시간 the time *one* gets out of school; the time school is over 〔out〕; dismissal time. ～종 the dismissal bell.

**하항**(河港) a river port; an inland port.

**하해**(河海) rivers and seas. ¶ ～ 같은 은혜 unlimited grace.

**하행**(下行) going down; going away from Seoul. ～하다 go down; go away from Seoul. ◉ ～선 a down line: ～선 승강장 a down platform. ～열차 a down train; an outbound train: 다음 ～열차는 몇 시에 있습니까 What time is the next down train?

**하향**(下向) looking 〔bending, facing〕 downward; a downward look; 《시세의》 a downward trend. ◉ ～세〔경향〕 a downward 〔declining〕 tendency; a downturn: ～세가 되다 《증권이》 begin to「decline 〔go down〕; show a「downward tendency 〔downturn〕. ～조정 a downward adjustment.

**하향**(下鄕) going to *one's* country home. ～하다 go to *one's* country home.

**하현**(下弦) the last phase 〔quarter〕 of the moon. ◉ ～달 a waning 〔an old〕 moon.

**하혈**(下血) discharging blood; a bloody flux 〔discharge〕; 〖의학〗 mel(a)ena. ～하다 discharge blood through the vulva 〔anus〕; flux.

**하회**(下回) the next time; the next chapter 《of a novel》; the reply 《to a letter》. ¶ ～를 기다리다 await 《*a person's*》 reply.

**하회하다**(下廻—) be less 〔lower〕 than ...; be below 《the average》. ⇨ 밑돌다.

**학**(學) 《학문》 learning; 《연학(硏學)》 study; 《학업》 studies; 《학술》 science; scholarship; erudition. ¶ 사회학 sociology.

**학**(鶴) 〖조류〗 a crane.

**학감**(學監) a school superintendent 〔overseer〕; a dean (대학의).

**학계**(學界) academic circles; the academic 〔learned〕 world. ¶ ～의 권위 an authority of the academic world; a prominent figure in the learned world / ～의 인정을 받다 gain academic recognition 《as...》 / ～에서 특출한 존재가 되다 cut a prominent figure in the academic circles.

**학과**(學科) 《과목》 a school subject; a subject of study (on a school curriculum); 《과정》 a course of study; a school course; 《전공의》 department. ¶ 영문～ an English literature course / 네 전공이 무슨 ～냐 Which department「do you belong to 〔are you in〕? ◉ ～목 subjects on a school curriculum. ～시험 examinations in academic subjects; an achievement test. ～증설 《permit》 establishment of new departments.

**학과**(學課) a lesson; schoolwork. ¶ ～를 복습하다 review *one's* lessons / ～를 예습하다 prepare *one's* lessons. ◉ ～시간표 a schedule (of class hours).

**학관**(學館) an institute; a private educational institution; a school; an academy. ¶ 영어～ an English-language institute.

**학교**(學校) a school; [총칭적] an educational establishment 〔institution〕; an institution of learning. ¶ ～가 파한 후 after school (is over).

학교의: ～의 성적 *one's* school record 〔achievement〕 / ～의 성적이 좋다〔나쁘다〕 do well 〔badly〕 at school; have a good 〔bad, poor〕 school record.

학교에: ～에 가다 leave 《home》 for school / ～에 다니다 attend 〔go to〕 school / ～에 다닐 때 while a student at school; when (*one* was) at 〔in〕 school (★ in은 《미》, at는 《영》); in *one's* school days / (잊고) ～에 두고 오다 leave 《an umbrella》 at school / ～에 들어가다 enter a school; go「to 〔into〕 school / ～에 보내다〔넣다〕 send 〔put〕 《a boy》 to school; get 《a boy》 into a 《good》 school.

학교에서: ～에서 in 〔at〕 school (★ school은 「교사(敎舍)」를 뜻할 때 외에는 관사를 안 붙임) / (교사가) ～에서 가르치다 teach (a) school / ～에서 돌아오다 come 〔return〕 home from school / ～에서 점심을 먹다 take *one's* lunch at school / ～에서 제적하다 strike 《*a person's*》 name off the school register / ～에서 제적되다 be expelled from (the) school; be removed from the school register.

학교를: ～를 그만두다〔중퇴하다〕 leave 〔stop〕 school; give up 〔quit 《미》〕 school / ～를 그만두게 하다 make 《a boy》 leave school / ～를 나오다 graduate from 《a university》; leave school; step 〔get〕 out of a school. ⇨ ～를 졸업하다 / ～를 빼먹다 play truant

〔hookey《미구어》〕《from school》; cut school / ～를 설립하다 establish 〔found, start, set up〕 a school / ～를 쉬다 stay away from school; 「absent *oneself* 〔be absent〕 from school / ～를 쉬게 하다 keep《a boy》out of school / ～를 운영하다 keep 〔conduct, run〕 a school / ～를 조퇴하다 leave school early; leave the class before it is dismissed; come away before school is out / ～를 졸업하다 leave 〔finish〕 school; complete the school course; graduate from school《미》(★ graduate는《영》에서는 「대학을 졸업하다」의 경우에만 사용됨).
¶ 그는 ～를 갓 나왔다 He is 「fresh from 〔just out of 〕 school. / ～는 6시에 파한다 School ends 〔is over〕 at six. *or* Classes are dismissed at six. / 「～는 몇 시에 시작되나」—「9시에 시작한다」 "What time does school begin?"—"School begins at nine." / 어느 ～에 다니나 What school do you 「go to 〔attend〕? *or* Where do you go to school? / 어느 ～에 가겠느냐 Which school are you going to enter? / ～는 내일부터 여름방학이다 School breaks up tomorrow for the summer vacation. / 내일은 ～ 수업이 없다〔～를 쉰다〕 We have no school tomorrow. / 그는 ～선생을 하고 있다 He teaches (in a) school *or* He is a schoolteacher. / 나는 매일 아침 7시에 집을 나와 ～에 간다 I leave home for school at seven every morning. / 학교에 우산을 두고 왔다 I've left my umbrella at school. / ～앞 — 서행《게시》 School — Go slow.
◉ ～가방《어깨에 걸치거나 메는》 a school satchel. ～경영 school management. ～급식 school lunch. ～문법 school grammar. ～방송《TV·라디오》 a school broadcast; broadcasting programs for schools. ～법인 an incorporated educational institution; an educational foundation. ～보건법 the School Health Law. ～생활 school 〔college〕 life. ～선생 a schoolteacher. ～신문 a school paper. ～요람 a school prospectus 〔catalog《미》〕. ～위생 school hygiene. ～의(醫) a school doctor 〔physician〕. ～장(長) the principal 〔headmaster〕 of a school. ～장(葬) school funeral. ～차(差) (a) disparity (in academic standards) among schools: ～차를 없애다 diminish the scholastic disparity among schools. ～친구 a schoolfellow; a schoolmate.

> **참고** 미국의 (초·중등) 학교 교육
> (1) 교육 감독 기관 — 교육의 모든 권한은 각 주정부(州政府)에 위임되어 있어서, 연방 정부(the Federal Government)의 역할은 한국과 비교하면 매우 작다. 예를 들면, 우리 나라의 교육부 (The Education Ministry)와 같은 전국적 통제 기관이 미국에는 없다. 군(郡)이나 시(市)의 지방 교육위원회 (board of education)가 학교 교육의 모든 문제를 다룬다. 교과서의 검인정 제도(screening of textbooks by the Education Ministry)가 없으며, 각 주가 가르쳐야 할 내용을 규정한 가이드라인이 있을 뿐이다. 또 의무교육(compulsory education) 기간과 학교 제도 등도 주(州)에 따라 다른 경우가 많다.
> (2) 학교 제도 — 6-3-3제 (an elementary school — a junior high school — a senior high school): 8-4제(an elementary school — a high school) 따위가 주된 제도이나, 6-6제 (an elementary school — a combined high school): 유치원 2년을 포함한 6-4-4제 따위도 행해지고 있다.
> (3) 우리 나라 학교의 영어 표현.
> 초등학교 an elementary school / 중〔고등〕학교 a junior 〔senior〕 high school / 기술〔전문〕학교 a technical school / 공립〔사립〕학교 a public 〔private〕 school.

**학교교육**(學校敎育) school education; schooling. ¶ ～을 받다 have school education; have schooling. ◉ 정규～ regular 〔formal〕 schooling.

**학구**(學究) ① 《학문 탐구》 study; learning; 《학도》 a scholar; a student. ¶ ～적(인) academic; scholarly; scholastic / ～적 저작 a scholarly work / ～적 정신 a scholastic 〔scholarly〕 spirit / 그는 ～적인 기질이다 He's the 〔an〕 academic type. ② 《글방 선생》 a villageschool teacher. ◉ ～(적) 생활 an academic 〔a scholarly〕 life; a life of learning: ～(적) 생활에 들어가다 take up a student's life; enter into a scholarly life.

**학구**(學區) a school district. ◉ ～제(도) school district 〔zone〕 system.

**학군**(學群) a school group. ◉ ～제(도) the school group system.

**학군단**(學軍團) ⇨ 학생 군사 교육단.

**학급**(學級) a (school) class; a grade 《미》. ¶ ～을 편성하다 organize a class / 두 ～으로 나누다 divide《pupils》

into two classes / ～에서 몇 째나 하나 How do you stand in your class ?
◉ ～담임 a class teacher; a homeroom teacher. ～문고 a classroom library. ～위원 a class representative. ～임시 폐쇄 temporary closing of classes.

**학기**(學期) a (school) term; a session《미》; 《2학기제의》 a semester 《미》. ¶ ～중 during (the) term; in term.
◉ ～말《at》 the「end 〔close〕 of a (school) term: ～말의 terminal; term end / ～말에 at the end of the term / ～말 시험 a「term 〔terminal, semester〕 examination; a final (examination) / ～말 방학 term-end holidays. ～초《at》 the beginning of a term. 제1～ the first term; 《2학기제의》 the first semester.

**학내**(學內) ¶～의 in the university; within the campus; on (the) campus《미》.

**학년**(學年)「a school 〔an academic〕 year; 《학급》 a class; a grade《미》; a form《영》; 《대학의》 a year. ¶ 제1～ the first grade《미》; the first form《영》(★《미》에서는 초등학교에서 고등학교까지를 연속된 학년으로 세기 때문에, 최종 학년은 the twelfth grade가 됨) / 1〔2, 3, 4〕～생 a first-〔second-, third-, fourth-〕 year student; a first 〔second, third, fourth〕 grader《미》; 《고교 이상》 a「freshman 〔sophomore, junior, se-nior〕 / 3～ A반, 3 A class / 오는 3월에 2～이 된다 I shall be in the second「year 〔grade〕 next March. /「너는 몇 ～이냐」―「3학년입니다」"What「grade 〔year〕 are you in ?" ―"I'm in the third「grade 〔year〕." / 그는 중학교 2～에 재학중이다 He is in the second grade of the junior high school. *or* He is a second grade junior high school boy.
◉ ～말 the end of a school year: ～말 시험 an end-of-year examination; 「an annual 〔a final〕 examination / ～말의 휴가 holidays after an annual examination.

**학당**(學堂) 《글방》 a village school; 《학교》 a school.

**학대**(虐待) mistreatment; maltreatment; ill-treatment; cruelty. ～하다 treat《*a person*》 cruelly 〔badly, ill〕; use《*a person*》 ill; be cruel to《*a person,* an animal》; ill-treat; maltreat; mistreat《미》; abuse (어린이 등을 혹사하거나 괴롭히는). ¶ 정신적 ～ mental cruelty / 약자를 ～하다 oppress 〔bully〕 the weak / 동물을 ～하다 be cruel to animals / 아내를 ～하다 treat *one's* wife cruelly; abuse *one's* wife / ～받다 be ill-treated; be maltreated; be subjected to harsh usage / ～에 견디다 못해 being unable to「endure 〔bear〕 the severity of the treatment / 네가 ～받고 있는 걸 보고 가만히 있을 수 없다 I can't allow you to be ill-treated. / 모든 포로들은 여러 형태로 ～를 받았다 All the prisoners of war suffered several kinds of cruelty.
◉ ～음란증 sadism: ～성 음란증자 a sadist / 피(被)～음란증 masochism. 동물 ～ 방지 협회 the Society for Prevention of Cruelty to Animals (생략 S.P.C.A.).

**학덕**(學德) learning and virtue. ¶～을 겸비하다 be eminent in both learning and virtue.

**학도**(學徒) =학생(學生). ◉ ～병 a student soldier. ～호국단 the Student Defense Corps (생략 SDC).

**학동**(學童) a schoolboy; schoolchildren.

**학력**(學力) attainments in scholarship; scholastic 〔literary〕 ability; scholarly 〔academic〕 attainments. ¶～이 뛰어난 excellent in scholarship / ～이 뛰어난 사람 a person of great scholastic ability; a person excellent in scholarship / 전문대학 졸업 이상의 ～이 있는 자 a person with at least a junior college education / ～이 있다 〔없다〕 be a「good 〔poor〕 scholar; have 〔have no〕 scholarly competence / ～이 우수하다 be an excellent scholar / 대학을 나온 이상의 ～이 있다 have a higher level of academic ability than the average university graduate; surpass college graduates in scholarly attainments / 그 시험을 치르기에는 아직 ～이 모자란다 My「attainment 〔academic ability〕 is not yet up to the standard of the examination. *or* I have not scholarship enough to take the examination. / 요즘 대학생들의 ～이 눈에 띄게 저하되었다고 한다 It is said that there has recently been a remarkable decline in the level of academic achievement of university students.
◉ ～고사 a scholastic achievement test; an examination in academic subjects: 대입 ～고사 the state test for college entrance; the state-run Scholastic Ability Achievement Test (생략 SAT) for college entrance.

**학력**(學歷) *one's* schooling; *one's*「academic 〔school〕 career; *one's* education-

al background; formal schooling. ¶ ～을 불문하고 regardless of *one's* school career; irrespective of the academic background / 고졸 또는 동등 이상의 ～이 있는 자 those who possess attainments equal to or higher than those of upper secondary school graduates / ～이 없다 have no regular schooling / ～이 없는 사람 a person without 「any school education 〔any academic background〕/ ～이 별로 없다 have little regular schooling; have had little in the way of formal schooling.
◉ ～사회 a society in which *one's* schooling counts. ～편중(偏重) excessive valuing of academic background; putting undue emphasis on educational background: ～편중 사회 an academic background oriented society; a society which sets excessive value on the academic background than his real ability.

**학령**(學齡) school age. ¶ ～ 미달의 아이 a preschool child / ～에 달하다〔달하지 않다〕 reach 〔be under〕 school age.
◉ ～아동 a child of school age; school-aged children.

**학료**(學寮) a dormitory.

**학리**(學理) (a) theory; a scientific principle. ¶ ～적인〔상의〕 theoretical / ～적(인) 연구 theoretical study 《of》/ ～의 응용 the practical application of scientific principles / ～를 연구하다 study the principles of a science / ～를 실지로 응용하다 put (a) theory into practice / 사회의 변화를 ～적으로 연구하다 study social changes theoretically.

**학명**(學名) a scientific name; a technical term. ¶ ～을 붙이다 give a scientific name 《to》. ◉ 동물～ a zoological name. 식물～ a botanical name.

**학무**(學務) school affairs; educational matters; (the business of) education.
◉ ～과 the section of educational 〔school〕 affairs. ～국 the education and management bureau. ～국장 the Chief of the Educational Bureau.

**학문**(學問) 《학문 추구》 (the pursuit of) learning; (the prosecution of) studies; 《학력·학식》 learning; scholarly attainments; 《지식》 knowledge; information; education; schooling; 《학술》 a science (분야).
¶ ～적(으로) scientific(ally) / ～이 있는 learned; 《교육을 받은》 educated / ～이 없는 사람 an uneducated man; 《무학자》 an illiterate / ～의 자유 academic freedom / ～을 위한 학문 learning for its own sake / ～을 하다 learn; study; pursue *one's* learning 〔studies〕; engage in studies / ～을 하게 하다 give 《*a person*》 an education / ～을 과시〔자랑〕하다 parade 〔display〕 *one's* learning 〔scholarship〕; 「brag about 〔boast of〕 *one's* learning / ～을 좋아하다 like 〔be fond of〕 learning / ～의 길을 걷다 tread the path of learning / ～이 있다 be learned 〔educated〕 / ～이 깊다 be erudite; be a man of deep learning / ～이 넓고도 깊다 possess learning both broad and deep / ～이 진보하다 make progress 〔improve〕 in *one's* studies; go ahead with *one's* studies / ～만으로 교사가 될 수는 없다 Mere scholarship does not qualify a person for a teacher. / 사회학은 사회 현상을 다루는 ～이다 Sociology is a science which deals with social phenomena.

**학벌**(學閥) an academic clique 〔group〕; academical sectarianism 〔factionalism, cliquism〕; school ties. ¶ 옥스포드 대학의 ～ an Oxford clique / ～의 폐해 the evils of an academic clique / ～을 짓다 form a clique 〔faction〕 of graduates of the same school / ～을 타파하다 break down academic cliques.
◉ ～싸움 rivalry between school factions.

**학병**(學兵) a student soldier.

**학보**(學報) a gazette; a school bulletin.

**학부**(學府) a seat of learning; an academic center; an educational institution. ◉ 최고～ the highest seat of learning; the highest educational institution.

**학부**(學部) a school 〔department〕 (of a university); a faculty 《영》 (★ 《미》에서는 faculty하면 「교원 전체」의 뜻으로도 쓰이므로 「학부」를 a department라고 할 때가 많음). ◉ ～장 the dean of a faculty. 문〔공, 교양, 이(理), 의, 농, 경제, 정치, 법〕～ the Faculty of Literature 〔Engineering, Liberal Arts, Physical Science, Medicine, Agriculture, Economics, Political Science, Law〕 (★ 다음처럼 부르는 「학부」도 있다: 의～ the college of Medicine / 법 ～ the Law School; the School of Law (「대학원」일 때도 있음) / 사(史)～ the Department of History).

**학부모**(學父母) parents of students. ¶ 일부 ～들의 지나친 정도의 교육열 the

exceptional zeal for education among parents. ◉ ~회 a parent's association.

**학부형**(學父兄) parents (and brothers) of students.

**학비**(學費) school(ing) 〔educational〕 expenses. ¶ ~를 대주다 pay 《*a person's*》 〔help 《*a person*》 with〕 educational 〔school〕 expenses; supply 〔provide〕 《*a person*》 with *his* school expenses / ~를 벌다 earn *one's* school expenses by working; work for *one's* education / ~를 조달하다 obtain money for school expenses / ~에 곤란을 받다 be hard up for school expenses; be unable to pay *one's* own way through school / ~ 면제의 특전을 누리고 있다 「be granted 〔enjoy〕 the priviledge of free tuition fees; be exempted from paying school fees / ~는 숙부가 대고 있다 I depend upon my uncle for my school expenses.

**학사**(學士) 《대학 졸업생》 a university graduate; a university man; 《학위》 a bachelor. ◉ ~등록제 the bachelor registration system; the college graduate registry system. ~학위 a bachelor's degree. ~회관 The University Graduates' Club. 문~ 《학위》 Bachelor of Arts (생략 B.A.); 《사람》 a bachelor of arts.

**학사**(學事) school affairs; education(al) matters. ◉ ~보고 a report of education(al) matters. ~시찰 (an) educational inspection. ~징계 disciplinary measures taken by school authorities; a scholastic warning.

**학살**(虐殺) (a) massacre; (a) slaughter; butchery. ~하다 massacre; slaughter; slay. ¶ 집단~ mass slaughter; genocide / 수백 명의 주민들이 ~당했다 Hundreds of the residents were slaughtered. ◉ ~자 a slaughterer; a slayer. 대량~ a large-scale massacre; a holocaust.

**학생**(學生) ① 《학교의》 a student; a pupil. (★ 《미》에서는 중학생 이상을 student라 하고 초등학생은 pupil이라고 한다. 《영》에서는 대학생만이 student, 기타는 모두 pupil이라고 함). ¶ ~용(의) (intended) for (the use of ) students / ~의 날 Students' Day (= 3 November, date of the Kwangju Student Incident of 1929) / 법과 ~ a law student; a student of law / K대학의 ~ a student at K University; a K University student / ~ 1만 명의 대학교 a university with a student enrollment of 10,000 / 학교를 빼먹는 ~ a hook(e)y player 《미구어》 / ~다운 태도 bearing like a student; manner proper to a student; behavior worthy of a student / ~들에게 인기가 있다 be popular with 〔among〕 the students / 이 대학은 ~이 많다 This university has a large student body. ② 《생전에 벼슬 못 한》 a deceased scholar who lacks official rank.

◉ ~가(街) the students' quarter. ~과 《대학의》 the student affairs section. ~군사 교육단 Reserve Officer's Training Corps (생략 ROTC). ~기질 the spirit of a student; the students' way of thinking. ~보도(補導) student guidance. ~복 a school uniform. ~생활 student life; college life. ~소요 a student disturbance. ~시절 《in》 *one's* school days. ~운동 a student movement 〔activity〕. ~자치 기구〔회〕 an autonomous student body. ~증 a student(s) identification card. ~처 the office of student affairs: ~처장 the dean of student affairs. ~할인 a fare reduction for students; a student discount: ~할인증 a certificate of qualification for the fare reduction for students. ~활동 student activities. ~회 a students' association: ~회 회장 the president of the student council / 총~회 the General Students Association. ~회관 a students' hall; a student center; the student union building. 전국~총연합회 the National Federation of Student Association.

**학생감**(學生監) ⇨ 학감(學監).

**학설**(學說) a theory; a doctrine. ¶ 새~을 세우다 set up 〔formulate, construct, advance〕 a new theory.

**학수**(鶴壽) a long life.

**학수고대**(鶴首苦待) ~하다 wait impatiently 〔expectantly〕 《for》; wait for 〔look forward to〕 《*a thing*》 with impatience; wait for 《news》 on tiptoe; be on the tiptoe of expectation. ¶ 당신이 오기를 ~하고 있다 We are eagerly looking forward to your visit.

**학술**(學術) 《학문과 예술》 art and science; 《과학》 science; 《학문》 learning; scholarship (★ 영어로 「학술」에 딱 맞아떨어지는 말은 없음). ¶ ~의〔적인〕 scientific; scholastic; academic / ~적〔상의〕 연구 scientific research.

◉ ~강연 a scientific lecture 《meeting》. ~교환 academic exchange. ~논

문 a scientific treatise; an academic essay 〔thesis〕. ~단체 an academic society. ~서(書) a scientific 〔learned〕 book 〔work〕. ~(용)어 a technical 〔scientific〕 term. ~잡지 a scientific 〔learned〕 journal. ~조사 a scientific investigation.

**학술원**(學術院) an academy; the National Academy of Sciences. ¶~회원 a member of the National Academy of Sciences. ◉ 미국~ the American Council of Learned Societies.

**학습**(學習) 《배워 익힘》 studying; drilling; 《공부》 learning; study. ~하다 study; drill; learn (★ study에는 특수한 문제를 연구하거나 노력하여 지식을 구한다는 뜻이 있으므로, 아이들이 학습할 경우는 learn을 씀). ◉ ~능력 learning ability. ~사전 a learner's 〔learners'〕 dictionary. ~서 a study book; a handbook for students. ~이론 a learning theory. ~자 a learner. ~장 a workbook; a drill book; a notebook. ~장애〔불능〕a learning disability (생략 LD). ~지도 요령 a course of study; the government curriculum guidelines.

**학승**(學僧) a learned priest.

**학식**(學識) scholarship; learning; knowledge; erudition (심원한). ¶~ 있는 learned; erudite / ~과 경험이 있는 사람 a man of learning and experience / 심원한 ~ profound knowledge 〔learning〕; erudition / ~과 덕망이 있는 사람 a learned and virtuous man / ~이 많다 be learned 〔erudite〕; be a man of scholarly attainments / ~이 없다 be unlettered 〔ignorant, uneducated, untutored〕; lack scholarship.

**학업**(學業) *one's* studies; *one's* schoolwork; 《면학》 learning; study 《of》; 《학문》 scholarship. ¶~을 게을리하다 neglect *one's* schoolwork / ~을 마치다 complete *one's* studies / ~을 폐하다 give up 〔abandon〕 *one's* studies; leave off *one's* scholastic studies / ~에 열중하다〔힘쓰다〕 work hard (at *one's* lessons); attend to *one's* studies with diligence; apply *oneself* closely to *one's* studies / ~에 더욱 힘쓰도록 해라 Give more time and energy to your work. ◉ ~성적 a school record; scholastic performance: ~성적이 좋다 be a good scholar; do well 〔be clever〕 at school.

**학연**(學緣) school ties. ¶~이 있는 사람들 those related by school ties 〔bonds〕; *one's* school ties / 우리 사회에서 ~은 정치인에게 때때로 귀중한 자산이 된다 School ties would sometimes be a valuable asset to a politician in our society.

**학예**(學藝) art(s) and letter(s); 《학문·예술의 소양》 literary and artistic accomplishments; 《문화·교양》 culture. ◉ ~란 the literary column(s). ~면 the literary 〔culture〕 page. ~부 the department of Liberal Arts; the fine arts and literature department (신문사의). ~품 student work(s). ~회 a school arts festival; a school's annual arts day; literary exercises.

**학용품**(學用品) school supplies 〔things〕.

**학우**(學友) a schoolmate; a schoolfellow; a fellow student; a classmate. ◉ ~회 《재학생의》 a students' society 〔association〕; 《졸업생의》 a graduates' 〔an alumni〕 association.

**학원**(學院) an (educational) institute; an academy; a school; 《단기 주입식의》 a cram school. ◉ 외국어~ a foreign language institute.

**학원**(學園) a campus; a school. ¶~의 자유 academic 〔campus〕 freedom. ◉~도시 a college 〔university〕 town. ~분쟁 a campus dispute. ~사찰 inspection on campus activities. ~생활 school 〔campus〕 life; student life. ~소요 campus unrest 〔disturbances〕. ~자율화 campus liberalization; campus autonomy; autonomy of universities.

**학위**(學位) a 〔an academic〕 degree; a doctorate (박사). ¶문학사〔이학사〕의~ the degree of Bachelor of Arts 〔Science〕 / 의학박사〔문학석사〕의~ the degree of Doctor of Medicine 〔Master of Arts〕 / ~를 주다 grant 〔award〕 《*a person*》 a degree; confer a degree 《on *a person*》 / ~를 받다 be granted 〔awarded〕 a degree / ~를 얻다〔따다〕 take 〔get, obtain, receive, win, secure〕 a degree 《from Y University, in engineering at Cambridge》; commence 《M.A.》 / ~를 갖고 있다 hold 〔bear, have〕 a degree / 논문을 제출하여 ~를 청구하다 apply for a degree by presenting a thesis / ~를 따기 위해 공부하다 study 〔work〕 for a degree 《in economics》 / 그는 작년에 K대에서 문학박사 ~를 땄다 He took his degree of Lit. D. from K University last Year. / 그의 철학 박사 ~는 런던대학에서 취득한 것이다 He got his Ph.D. from London

University. ◉ ～논문 a thesis for a degree; 《석사의》 a master's thesis; 《박사의》 a doctoral 〔doctor's〕 thesis 〔dissertation〕. ～수여식 the (ceremony of) conferment of a degree.

**학자**(學者) a scholar; a learned man; a man of learning; 《대학자》 an erudite; a savant; a pundit; 《연구자》 a student; 《미구어》 a brain; a double-dome. ¶ ～적인〔기질의〕 scholarly; academic / ～다운 scholarlike; scholarly / 탁월한 스페인어 ～ an eminent Spanish scholar; a notable scholar of Spanish / ～연하다 assume the air of a scholar; set up for a scholar; be pedantic / 그는 ～기질이다 He is of a scholarly turn of mind. / 그는 ～다운 데가 있다〔조금도 없다〕 He has something 〔nothing〕 of the scholar about him. ◉ ～고문단 《대통령의》 a brain trust 《미》.

**학자**(學資) ＝ 학비(學費). ◉ ～금 school expenses; an education fund. ～보험 educational endowment insurance.

**학장**(學長) a dean; a president; a rector. ◉ ～회의 the council of deans. 총～회의 a meeting of the heads 〔deans and presidents〕 of colleges and universities.

**학적**(學籍) a school 〔college〕 register. ◉ ～부 a school 〔college〕 register: ～부에 올리다〔에서 빼다〕 「put 《*a person's*》 name on 〔strike 《*a person's*》 name off〕 the school register / ～부에 올라있는 학생 총수는 1만 명이다 The total registration of students is ten thousand.

**학점**(學點) a unit; a point; a credit 《미》. ¶ 2～짜리 불어 강의를 수강하다 take a French course for 2 credits 〔points〕 / 영어에서 8 ～ 따다 take 〔earn〕 eight credits in English. / ～이 모자라다 do not have sufficient credits 《to graduate》 / 1주에 2시간씩 30주 동안 강의로 4～을 주다 give four credits for 〔to〕 a lecture of two hours per week for a term of thirty weeks / 졸업에 필요한 ～을 따지 못하다 fail to earn 〔obtain, acquire〕 enough credits 「to graduate 〔for graduation〕 / 어학 강좌는 어느 것이건 모두 2～이다 Each of the language courses carries two credits. ◉ ～교환제 cross registration system. ～제도 the credit 〔unit〕 system.

**학정**(虐政) tyranny; despotism (독재). ¶ ～을 하다 tyrannize 《over》; rule cruelly (with a rod of iron) / ～에 신음하다 groan under (ruthless) tyranny.

**학제**(學制) an educational 〔a school〕 system. ¶ ～를 개혁하다 reform the educational 〔school〕 system. ◉ ～개혁〔개편〕 (a) reform 〔reorganization〕 of the educational 〔school〕 system: ～개혁안 the proposed educational system reform.

**학질**(瘧疾) ague; malaria; malarial fever; paludism. ¶ ～에 걸리다 be taken with malaria. ◉ ～모기 〖곤충〗 an anopheles; a malaria mosquito.

**학질떼다**(瘧疾—) be cured of malaria; [비유적] get rid of a nuisance; rid *oneself* of a nuisance.

**학창**(學窓) a school; a campus. ¶ ～을 떠나다 leave school. ◉ ～생활 school life. ～시절 *one's* school days.

**학춤**(鶴—) ① 《학의 춤》 the dance of a crane. ② 《사람이 추는》 a dance in the costume of a crane.

**학칙**(學則) school regulations. ¶ ～을 지키다〔어기다〕 observe 〔break〕 school 〔college〕 regulations / 금후 학원 질서를 어지럽히는 학생들에게 ～이 엄격히 적용될 것이다 School regulations will hereafter be strictly applied to the students who disturb the campus order. ◉ ～변경 the revision of school regulations.

**학통**(學統) a scholastic mantle.

**학파**(學派) a school; a sect; a doctrinal faction. ¶ 한 ～를 세우다 found a school / 두 ～로 갈라지다 be divided into two different schools. ◉ 에피쿠로스～ the school of Epicurus. 헤겔～ the Hegelian school.

**학풍**(學風) 《교풍》 academic traditions 〔features, atmosphere〕; school character (학교의 기풍); 《연구의 방법》 a method of study. ¶ ～을 세우다 set up the character of a school; establish a school tradition.

**학해**(學海) the world of 「knowledge 〔literature and science〕; the vast field of learning; the academic world.

**학행**(學行) scholarship and virtue.

**학형**(學兄) ① 《학우간에》 you. ② 《편지에서》 Mr. ¶ 김인수 ～ Mr. Kim Insu.

**학회**(學會) a learned 〔scientific〕 society; an institute; an academy; 《모임》 an academic meeting. ¶ ～에 참석하다 attend a meeting 《of the Korean Cancer Society》 / 물리～에서 연구를 발표하다 read a paper at a meeting of the Physical Society. ◉ 한국 영어영문

～ the English Literary Society of Korea. 한글～ the Korean Language (Research) Society.

**한**(恨) 《원한》 a grudge; resentment; a bitter feeling; spite; hatred; rancor; 《한탄》 a mixed feeling of sorrow and regret (unique to Korean); an unsatisfied desire. ¶ 한 많은 regrettable; hateful / 한되는 일 a grudge; grievances / 천추의 한 a lasting regret / 한이 없다 have nothing to regret / 한을 품다 bear 〔cherish, nurse〕 《*a person*》 a grudge; have a 「grudge 〔spite〕 《against *a person*》; harbor enmity 《toward》 / 한을 풀다 revenge *oneself* 《on *a person*》; vent 〔wreak, work off〕 *one's* grudge 《on *a person*》 / 한 많은 일생을 보내다 lead a life full of tears and regrets / …에 대한 한이 맺히다 have a deep-rooted grudge 〔regret〕 against 《*a person, a thing*》.

**한**(限) ① 《한계》 a limit; limits; a bound; bounds. ¶ 한이 있다 be 「limited 〔restricted, finite〕; have a limit / 한이 없다 be 「unlimited 〔boundless, endless, infinite, eternal〕 / 허욕에는 한이 없는 것 같다 There seems to be no end to avarice. / 그의 야망은 한이 없다 There are no bounds to his ambition. / 위를 보면 한이 없다 Don't compare yourself with those above you. *or* Learn to be satisfied.

② 《기한》 a term; a period; a time limit; time. ¶ 열흘을 한하고 돈을 취해 주다 lend money on the condition that it be returned within ten days / 수업료는 이달 25일한 납부할 것 The tuition fees shall be paid not later than the 25th of this month.

③ 《…하는 한·조건》 so 〔as〕 far as; to the limit that…; unless. ¶ 가능한 한 as 「far 〔much〕 as possible; as much as *one* can; to the best of ability / …을 하는 한 (for) as long as *one* 「*does* 〔continues to *do*〕 / …하지 않는 한 unless 〔until〕 *one does* / 내가 아는 〔알고 있는〕 한 so far as I know; to the best of my knowledge / 목숨이 (붙어) 있는 한 as long as *one* lives / 사정이 허락하는 한 as 〔so〕 far as circumstances permit / 따로 규정이 없는 한 unless otherwise provided / 사정이 허락하는 한 빨리 돌아오겠다 I'll come back as soon as the situation permits. / 될 수 있는 한 하겠습니다 I will do 「my utmost 〔everything in my power, all I can〕. / 될 수 있는 한 돈을 많이 취해 주오 Lend me as much money as possible. / 내가 살아 있는 한 네 마음대로 하지 못한다 So long as I live, I won't let you have your way. / 네가 가지 않는 한 나도 가지 않겠다 Unless you go, I won't go either.

**한**(漢) 《중국의》 Han; the Han dynasty. ¶ 전한(前漢) the 「Earlier 〔Western〕 Han / 후한(後漢) the 「Later 〔Eastern〕 Han.

**한** ① 《하나》 a; one. ¶ 한 개 one; a piece / 한 사람 a 〔one〕 man / 한 마디 a 〔one〕 word / 한 광주리의 복숭아 a basket of peaches / 밥 한 그릇 a bowl of boiled-rice / 한 집 걸러 next door but one. ② 《같은》 the same. ¶ 한 방을 쓰다 share the same room 《with》 / 한 하숙에 기숙하다 board and lodge in the same boarding house / 둘은 한 집에서 산다 The two live in the same house. ③ 《온·전》 the whole; the entire. ¶ 한 고을을 차지하다 possess the whole county / 한 여름을 낚시질로 보내다 spend all the summer in fishing. ④ 《가장·한창》 the peak; the extreme; the most; the very. ¶ 한가운데 the (very) middle / 한겨울 《in》 the depth 〔deep, dead〕 of winter; 《in》 midwinter / 한여름 midsummer; high 〔full〕 summer / 한낮 high noon; midday / 한밤중에 in the middle of the night; at dead of night; at midnight. ⑤ 《대략》 about; approximately. ¶ 한 열흘 about 10 days / 한 5백 원 about 500 won / 한 20명이 행방 불명이다 An estimated twenty persons are missing.

**한가**(閑暇) spare 〔leisure〕 time; leisure; time to spare. ～하다 ＝한가롭다. ¶ ～히, ～로이 in a leisurely way; with leisure / ～한 때 when *one* is free 〔at leisure〕; in *one's* leisure hours; at *one's* leisure / ～한 몸이 되다 become a man of leisure / ～한 생활을 즐기다 enjoy a life of leisure / ～한 때를 어떻게 보내십니까 How do you fill your leisure? / 이것은 ～할 때 할 일이다 This is for leisure hours. / ～하게 놀고 있을 때가 아니다 It's no time to remain idle. / 그런 ～한 소리를 하고 있을 때가 아니다 This is no time to be talking so complacently.

**한가닥** ¶ ～ 희망 a 「ray 〔gleam〕 of hope / ～의 희망마저 잃다〔끊기다〕 lose *one's* last hope; deprive 《*one*》 of the 「last 〔sole remaining〕 hope / 환자는 아직 ～의 희망은 있다 There is still a ray of hope of the patient's recovery. / 그

의 이야기에는 ～의 진실도 없다 There is not a shred of truth in his story.

**한가롭다**(閑暇—) have spare time; have leisure; (be) leisured; be at leisure; (be) idle. ¶ 한가로운 때 *one's* leisure hour; spare time / 한가로운 사람 a person of 〔at〕 leisure / 한가롭게 거닐다 walk to and fro leisurely.

**한가운데** the very middle; the center; the heart. ¶ 방 ～ 눕다 lie right in the middle of a room / 머리 ～를 가르다 part *one's* hair in the middle / 강 ～ 배를 띄우다 sail a boat in the middle of a river / 과녁 ～를 맞히다 hit the target right in the center / 서울 ～에 가게를 내다 set up a store right in the heart of Seoul.

**한가위** August 15th of the lunar calendar; the Harvest Moon festival.

**한가을** ① 《중추》 midautumn; the middle of autunm; the depth of autumn; 《추수기》 the busy harvesting season; the busy harvest time. ② 《가을 내내》 the whole autumn 〔fall〕; all the autumn through. ¶ ～ 아무것도 않고 놀다 idle away the whole fall.

**한가지** ① 《한 종류》 one 〔a〕 kind. ¶ 벼는 풀의 ～다 The rice plant is a kind of grass. / 이 ～로 그의 소행을 알 수 있다 This one instance is enough to show his everyday conduct. / 이 ～로 백 가지 그의 행동을 미루어 알 수 있다 This case will show all the rest of him.

② 《같음》 (one and) the same; being much 〔almost〕 the same. ¶ ～로 equally; without discrimination; as in the same way as / 모든 사람을 ～로 대우하다 treat all people equally / 새것이나 ～다 be as good as new / 죽은 것이나 ～다 be practically 〔virtually as good as〕 dead / 이 둘은 품질이 ～다 These two are of the same quality. / 영과 혼은 요컨대 ～다 The spirit and the soul are one and the same after all. / 달이 찼다 기우는 것과 ～로 나라도 한번 성하면 쇠한다 There are ups and downs in a nation just as moon waxes and wanes. / 언니는 고양이를 싫어하는데 나도 ～다 My sister doesn't like cats, and I don't either. / 그 점, 나도 ～다 That goes for me, too. *or* The same thing can be said of me. / 나도 너와 ～로 무경험이다 I have no more experience than you. / 자네도 술을 못하는군. 나도 ～야 You don't drink ? Neither do I.

**한갓** only; alone. ¶ ～ 시간의 문제 merely a question of time / ～ 빵만으로는 살지 못한다 We cannot live on bread alone. / 게으른 것이 그의 ～ 결점이다 The only drawback is that he is lazy. / 그것은 ～ 핑계에 불과하다 That is simply an excuse, and nothing more.

**한갓지다** (be) unhurried and quiet; peaceful and leisurely; secluded; out=of-the-way; remote. ¶ 한갓진 촌에 살다 live in an out-of-the-way village.

**한강**(漢江) the Han River. ¶ ～의 기적 Miracle on the Han River / ～ 상수원 관리 체계 정립을 위한 심포지엄 a symposium for establishing a system of managing the tap-water resources of the Han River. ◉ ～대교 the Grand Han River Bridge. ～종합개발계획 the integrated Han River development project.

**한 개**(一箇) one; a piece; a unit. ¶ ～씩 one by one / ～ 50원 fifty won apiece 〔each〕 / 비누 ～ a cake of soap / 각설탕 ～ a lump of sugar / ～ 얼마씩 팔다 sell 《*a thing*》 at so much each 〔apiece〕 (★ sell watermelons by the piece라고 하면 수박을 한쪽씩 쪼개어 판다는 뜻이 됨). / 이 사과는 ～ 2천원 합니다 These apples cost two thousand won each 〔apiece〕.

**한거**(閑居) a retired 〔quiet, secluded〕 life; 「a leisurely 〔an idle〕 life. ～하다 live 〔dwell〕 seclusion 〔retirement〕; lead a sequestered 〔secluded, cloistered〕 life; lead a leisurely life. ¶ 소인이 ～하면 나쁜 짓을 한다 The devil finds mischief for idle hands to do. *or* Idleness is the parent of all vice.

**한걱정** a big worry; a great anxiety; a great headache. ¶ ～ 생기다 have a great headache / ～놓다 be relieved of a great anxiety.

**한걸음** a 〔one〕 step; a pace; 《한달음》 a run. ¶ ～으로 at 〔in〕 a stride / ～한 걸음 step by step / ～ 앞서가다 go a step ahead 《of *a person*》; leave a bit earlier / ～ 뒤져가다 go a step behind 《*a person*》; leave a bit later / ～ 앞으로 나아가다 take 〔make〕 a step forward / ～ 뒤로 물러나다 take a step backward; retrace a step / ～ 더 나아가다 go a step farther / 천릿길도 ～부터 《속담》 A journey of a thousand miles begins with one step.

**한걸음에** at a stretch; without stopping (on the way). ¶ ～ 서울까지 가다 go to Seoul in one stretch / ～에 달려가

가져오겠습니다 I will run down for it.

**한겨울** midwinter; the depth of winter.

**한결** 《눈에 띄게》 conspicuously; remarkably; 《한층》 much more; still more; 《특히》 especially; particularly. ¶ ～ 두드러지다 be conspicuous 《among》; stand out conspicuously / 비를 맞은 단풍이 ～ 아름답다 Rain adds a special charm to the red-tinted autumnal leaves. / 고독감이 ～ 더해진다 My sense of isolation becomes doubly acute. / 이것이 그것보다 ～ 더 크다 This is much bigger than that. / 고치니까 ～ 보기가 낫다 The change makes it look much nicer. / 드레스를 입은 그녀는 ～ 더 매력적이다 Her dress makes her all the more attractive.

**한결같다** (be) constant; never-changing; consistent; uniform. ¶ 한결같은 사랑 constant love / 한결같은 우정 unfailing 〔unwavering〕 friendship / 한결같은 태도 a consistent attitude / 나의 의견은 ～ I am still of the same opinion.

**한결같이** 《변함없이》 constantly; consistently; invariably; uniformly; as ever; 《동등하게》 equally; 《같게》 alike. ¶ ～ 사랑하다 love 《*a person*》 as ever / 차별 철폐를 ～ 주장하다 consistently advocate abolishing discrimination / ～ 부지런히 공부하다 study hard as ever / 모두 복장을 ～입고 있다 All are dressed alike.

**한겻** a quarter of a day. ◉ ～일 a job that will take a few hours; a quarter-day's work.

**한겻지다** ⇨ 한갓지다.

**한계**(限界) 《경계선을 갖는》 bounds; 《더는 넘을 수 없는 한도》 limits; a limit; limitations (능력 따위의). ¶ 인간 능력의 ～ the limitations of human faculty / ～를 두다〔정하다〕 set limits 〔a limit, bounds〕 《to》; limit / ～를 넘다 pass 〔exceed, overstep〕 the limit 《of》; cross the line 《of》 / 능력〔안전성〕의 ～를 넘다 be beyond *one's* ability 〔the margin of safety〕 / ～를 느끼다 realize the limitations 《of parliamentary democracy》 / 힘의 ～를 넘어서다 overpass *one's* strength / 자기 능력의 ～를 알다 learn the limits of *one's* ability; know *one's* limitations / (체력의) ～에 도전하다 try *one's* 《physical》 limits / 체력의 ～를 알아야 한다 We must recognize our physical limitation. / 모든 것에는 ～가 있다 There is a limit to everything. ◉ ～가격 《최고의》 a ceiling price. ～개념 a concept of limitation. ～능률 marginal efficiency. ～생산력 marginal productivity. ～생산비 marginal cost of production. ～선(線) a boundary line; 〖물리〗 a limiting line. ～소비성향 〖경제〗 a marginal propensity to consume. ～속도 critical speed. ～수심(水深) critical depth. ～온도 critical temperature. ～원가 marginal cost. ～이익 marginal profits 〔income〕. ～효용 〖경제〗 marginal utility: ～효용 체감의 법칙 the law of diminishing marginal utility.

**한계점**(限界點) the critical point; the uppermost limit. ¶ ～에 달하다 reach 〔be at〕 the top 〔uppermost limit〕.

**한고비** 《위기》 the crucial 〔critical〕 moment; the crisis (*pl.* crises); 《전환점》 the turning point 《of an illness》; the height; the peak. ¶ 병의 ～ the crucial stage of an illness / ～ 넘(기)다 the crisis 〔worst〕 is over; pass the critical point 〔stage〕; be over the hump 《구어》 / 열은 지금이 ～다 The fever has reached its height. / 앞으로 24시간이 ～일 겁니다 《의사의 말》 The next twenty-four hours will be critical. *or* We shall know one way or the other in the next 24 hours.

**한곡**(一曲) a piece of music; a tune; a melody. ¶ ～ 연주하다 play a tune / 플루트를 ～들려주다 play 《*a person*》 a tune on the flute.

**한교**(韓僑) Korean residents abroad; overseas Koreans.

**한구석** one 〔a〕 corner; a nook; a secluded place. ¶ ～에 앉다 sit in a corner / ～에 놓다 put 《*a thing*》 in a corner 《of a room》 / 마을 ～에 살다 live in an obscure nook of a town 〔village〕 / 시골 ～에 박히다 live in a secluded village.

**한국**(寒菊) 〖식물〗 a winter chrysanthemum.

**한국**(韓國) Korea; the Republic of Korea (생략 R.O.K.). ¶ ～의 Korean / ～사정에 밝다 be well-informed on Korean affairs / ～화하다 Koreanize. ◉ ～관(館) 《국제 박람회 등의》 Korean Pavilion. ～국민 the Korean (people). ～말〔어〕 Korean; the Korean language: ～말로 무어라 합니까 What do you call it in Korean ? *or* What is the Korean for 《flower》? ～사람 a Korean. ～요리 Korean dishes. ～육군 the Republic of Korea Army (생략 R.O.K.A.). ～전쟁 the Korean War: ～

전쟁과 같은 또다른 비극의 재발을 막다 prevent the recurrence of another tragedy such as the Korean War. ～학 Korean studies; Koreanology. ～형 경수로 the South Korean-type〔-model〕 light water (nuclear) reactor.

**한국계**(韓國系) [형용사적] of Korean ancestry. ◉ ～미국인 a Korean-American; an American of Korean descent: ～3세(世) 미국인 a third-generation American of Korean descent.

**한국무역협회**(韓國貿易協會) the Korea International Trade Association (생략 KITA). ¶ ～는 이미지 재정립과 21세기에 대비하기 위해, 영문 명칭을 종전의 KFTA에서 KITA로 바꾼다고 공표했다 To reestablish its image and prepare for the 21st century, the Korea Foreign Trade Association (KFTA) declared that it will change its English name from KFTA to the Korea International Trade Association (KITA).

**한국은행**(韓國銀行) the Bank of Korea. ◉ ～권 a Bank of Korea note. ～법 〖법〗 the Bank of Korea Act. ～총재 the Governor of the Bank of Korea.

**한군데** ① 《한 곳》 one place. ¶ 책을 ～에 쌓다 pile the books up in one spot / 그 책 파는 데가 ～ 있다 There is one store where the book is sold. ② 《같은 장소》 the same place. ¶ 형제가 ～ 산다 The brothers live in the same place. / 그들은 모두 ～서 왔다 All of them came from the same part of the country.

**한그루** 〖농업〗 raising a single crop 《of rice》 a year; single-crop farming.

**한근심** = 한걱정.

**한글** the Korean alphabet; Hangŭl. ◉ ～날 Hangŭl Proclamation Day. ～맞춤법 Hangŭl orthography; the rules 〔system〕 of spelling of Hangŭl. ～전용 exclusive use of Hangŭl.

**한기**(寒氣) ① 《추위》 cold weather. ② 《오한》 a chill; chilliness; a cold fit. ¶ ～가 나다 feel a chill; feel chilly; have a chill 〔a cold fit〕.

**한길**[1] 《큰 길》 a mainroad; a high road; a (through) street; a thoroughfare; a main 〔principal〕 street; an avenue 《미》 (★ 미국의 대도시에서는 avenue와 street를 세로·가로의 도로로 구분해서 쓰고 있는 일이 있음. 가령 뉴욕에서는 Avenue는 남북, Street는 동서로 뻗은 대로에 씀). ¶ ～복판에서 in the middle of the street / ～을 막다 block the road / (집이 없어) ～에 나앉게 되다 become 〔be rendered〕 homeless; be thrown out on the street.

**한길**[2] 《깊이의》 one 〔a〕 fathom. ¶ 깊이가 ～이다 be a fathom deep.

**한꺼번에** 《한 번에》 at once; at a 〔one〕 time; 《일거에》 at a stretch 〔sitting, stroke, breath〕; 《동시에》 at the same time; simultaneously; 《여럿이 함께》 all together; 《한목에》 in the 〔a〕 lump; in the gross. ¶ 과자를 ～ 다 먹어버리다 eat all the cakes up at one sitting / 사람이 ～ 몰려오다 people crowd in 〔on〕 all at the same time / 한달치의 식량을 ～ 사다 buy food in bulk for the whole month / 3개월치의 봉급을 ～ 타다 receive three months' pay in a lump / ～ 오지 말고 한 사람씩 오너라 Don't come all together, but one by one. / ～ 두 가지 일을 하지 마라 Do not attempt to do two things at a time. / ～ 그런 많은 지출을 하면 생활에 영향을 미친다 Such an expenditure in one lot will affect the safety of living.

**한껏**(限—) ① 《한도까지》 to the (very) limit; the utmost; 《마음껏》 to *one's* satisfaction; to *one's* heart's content; as much as *one* likes 〔wishes〕; to the full; to the fullest measure. ¶ ～ 먹다〔마시다〕 eat 〔drink〕 *one's* fill / ～ 싸게 팔다 sell at the lowest possible price; sell dirt-cheap 《구어》 / ～ 울다 weep *oneself* out; cry 〔weep〕 *one's* fill; have a good cry; have *one's* cry out / ～ 즐기다 enjoy *oneself* to *one's* heart's content / 인생을 ～ 즐기다 enjoy life to the full. ② 《힘껏》 to the best of *one's* ability; with all *one's* might; to the top of *one's* form 〔bent〕. ¶ ～ 일하다 work to the best of *one's* ability; work as hard as *one* can / ～ 힘을 내다 put out 〔forth〕 all *one's* strength / ～ 잡아당기다 pull with all *one's* strength.

**한끝** ① 《일단》 one end; one side. ¶ 줄 ～에 돌을 달다 tie a stone to the end of a rope. ② 《맨끝》 an end; the very end; the tail-end. ¶ 하늘 ～ the (farthest) end of the sky / 줄 ～에 서다 stand at the end of a row.

**한끼** a 〔one〕 meal. ¶ ～는 국수를 먹다 eat noodles for a meal / ～를 거르다 miss a meal / 하루에 ～밖에 못 먹다 have only one meal a day.

**한나라**(漢—) 《중국의》 Han; the Han dynasty. ⇨ 한(漢).

**한나절** half a day. ¶ ～이나 잠자다 sleep for the whole morning 〔afternoon〕.

◉ ～일 half-a-day's work.

**한낮** 《정오》 noon; noontide; 《at》 high noon; midday; 《백주》 《in》 broad daylight; 《in》 the daytime. ¶ ～의 햇살을 받으며 걷다 walk in the daytime sun.

**한낱** only; mere(ly); sheer; nothing but. ¶ ～ 서생(書生) a mere student / ～ 핑계 a mere excuse / 나는 ～ 고학생에 불과하다 I am「nothing but 〔no more than〕 a self-supporting student. / 그는 ～ 허풍선이에 지나지 않는다 He is nothing but a「boaster 〔braggart〕.

**한내**(限內) ① 《기한 안》 within「a time limit 〔a definite period of time〕. ② 《경계 안쪽》 within a boundary. ③ 《규정 등의》 within a「limitation 〔rule〕.

**한눈** ① 《한쪽 눈》 one eye. ¶ ～이 안 보인다 be blind「of 〔in〕 one eye / ～으로 겨냥하다 aim 《at *something*》 with one eye. ② 《한 번 보기》 a look; a glance; a glimpse. ¶ ～에 at a「look 〔glance〕; on 〔at〕 sight / ～에 반하다 fall in love 《with a girl》 at first sight; be captivated 《by a girl》 at first glance; take a fancy 《to *a person*》 at first meeting / 그 언덕에서는 도시 전체가 ～에 내려다 보인다 From that hill you can get a view of the whole city. ③ 《곁눈》 looking aside. ⇨한눈 팔다.

**한눈팔다** look「away 〔off, aside〕; take *one's* eyes off 《*a thing*》; wander *one's* eyes. ¶ 한눈팔며 운전하기 inattentive driving / 책을 보지 않고 ～「take *one's* eyes off 〔look off〕 *one's* book / 한눈팔며 걷다 walk along gazing around / 한눈팔지 않고 공부에 열중하다 be devoted heart and soul to *one's* studies; apply *oneself* closely to *one's* studies / 한눈팔며 운전하지 마시오 Don't take your eyes「off the road 〔look aside〕 while driving a car.

**한다한** distinguished; eminent; influential; respectable; decent. ¶ ～ 선비 an eminent scholar / ～ 사람 (a) somebody; a person of some note or importance / ～ 집안 a「respectable 〔distinguished〕 family / ～ 대학 a university of high reputation; a prestige university.

**한닥거리다, 한닥이다** move; sway; wobble; shake. ¶ 이가 ～ a tooth loosens 〔becomes loose〕.

**한닥한닥** moving 〔swaying, shaking, wobbling〕 repeatedly. ¶ ～하는 의자 a rickety 〔an unsteady〕 chair / 책상 다리가 ～ 놀다 the legs of a table are「wobbly 〔rickety〕.

**한달음에** straight through; without a pause for breath; at a run. ¶ ～ 갔다 오다 take a run to 《the town》.

**한담**(閑談) a chat; an idle talk; a confab 《구어》; a gossip. ～하다 chat 《with》; have a「chat 〔confab〕 《with》; have a「gossip 〔rambling talk〕 《with》. ¶ ～으로 시간을 보내다 chat the time away / 나는 그와 오랫동안 ～을 나누었다 I had a long chat with him. / ～으로 시간 가는 줄 몰랐다 While chatting we took no note of time. ◉ ～설화 a chat; a leisurely conversation.

**한대**(寒帶) 〖지리〗 the Frigid Zones. ◉ ～기후 a polar climate. ～동물〔식물〕「a polar 〔an arctic〕 animal 〔plant〕. ～지방 《in》 the cold latitudes. 남〔북〕 ～ the「South 〔North〕 Frigid Zone; the Antarctic 〔Arctic〕 Zone 〔Region〕.

**한댕거리다, 한댕이다** move 〔sway, swing, shake, wobble〕 a little. ¶ 한댕한댕 shaking; swinging.

**한더위** great heat; the hot season; the midsummer heat. ¶ ～가 물러가다 the hot season gets over.

**한데** ① 《문밖》 outdoors; out of doors; 《노천》 the open. ¶ ～의 open-air; outdoor / ～에서 in the open (air); out of doors; outdoors / ～서 자다 sleep 〔pass the night〕 in the open (air); sleep「on the bed of grass 〔under the open sky〕. ② 《규정 지역 밖》 outside (of a fixed area); the wrong place. ¶ 자동차가 ～로 달리다 a car runs off the road. ◉ ～우물 a well outside the house enclosure. 한뎃뒷간 an outside privy; an outhouse.

**한도**(限度) a limit; limits; bounds; a ceiling. ¶ ～ 안에서 within the limit 《of》 / 5만원을 ～로 하여 within the limits of 50,000 won / ～를 넘다 go「beyond 〔exceed, overstep〕 the「limits 〔bounds〕; go too far / ～를 넘지 않도록 하다 keep within bounds 〔the limits〕 / ～를 정하다 fix the limit(s); set a「limit 〔limits〕; put a ceiling 《on》 / ～에 이르다 reach the「limit 〔ceiling〕; be stretched to the limit(s) / 만원을 ～로 빌려주다 lend money within a 10,000 won limit / 100만원 ～ 내에서 생활하다 live within the framework of one million won / 만사에는 ～가 있다 There is a limit to everything. *or* Everything has its limits. / 농담에도 ～가 있지「You are talking 〔Don't take〕 your joke too

far. / 인내에도 ～가 있다 Human patience has its limits. / 이것이 내 능력의 ～다 This is all I can do.
◉ 신용～ a credit limit. 최대〔최고〕～ the maximum 〔uppermost〕 limit. 최소〔최저〕～ the minimum 〔bottommost〕 limit: 최저 ～의 생활 the minimum standard of living / 최소～의 비용으로 at a minimum of expense.

**한독**(韓獨) Korea and Germany; [형용사적] Korean-German.

**한돌림** ①《차례의》 one 〔a〕 round. ¶ 술이 ～ 돌다 the liquor is passed around once; have a round of drinks. ②《원둘레의》 one circumference.

**한동기**(—同氣) full 〔whole〕 brothers 〔sisters〕; brothers 〔sisters〕 of the same parents. ¶ ～끼리 싸우다 brothers 〔sisters〕 quarrel (among themselves).

**한동생**(—同生) a full 〔whole〕 brother 〔sister〕. ⇨ 한동기.

**한동안** [부사적] for (quite) a time 〔while〕; for a short time; for some time. ¶ ～ 머물다 stay quite a while / ～ 번영하다 flourish for a while / 이만 돈이면 ～은 넘길 수 있다 This sum will tide me over the crisis. / ～ 지나서야 그 일을 알아챘다 It was not for some time that I noticed it. / ～ 쇠고기 값은 내리지 않을 게다 It will be some time before the price of beef comes down.

**한되다**(恨—) regret 《that...》; feel regret 《at》; be 〔feel〕 sorry 《about, for, that...》; be a matter for regret; be mortified 《by, at》; It is a pity 《that ...》. ¶ 젊어서 공부 못 한 것이 ～ regret that *one* couldn't study while young / 한되는 일은 하나도 없다 I have nothing to repent of.

**한두** one or two. ¶ ～ 번 once or twice / ～ 사람 one or two persons / ～ 해 one 〔a〕 year or two / ～ 번이 아닌 not once or twice; again and again; repeatedly / ～ 가지 일 a thing or two; one or two things.

**한둘** one or two. ¶ 사과 ～ one or two apples.

**한드랑거리다** move to and fro; sway. ¶ 나뭇가지가 바람에 ～ branches are swaying in the wind.

**한드랑한드랑** moving to and fro; swaying.

**한들거리다** shake; tremble; sway. ¶ 나뭇잎이 바람에 ～ leaves are trembling in the wind / 치마가 바람에 ～ a skirt sways in the wind.

**한들한들** shaking; trembling; swaying.

**한때** 《일시》 (at) one time; 《전에》 once; sometime. ¶ ～의 lasting for a short time; passing; transient; ephemeral; momentary; temporary / ～의 인기 an ephemeral popularity / 아침의 분주한 ～ a busy part of 〔spell in〕 the morning / 가족의 단란한 ～ a happy time at home / ～뿐이다 be transient 〔transitory, temporary, passing〕; be short-lived / ～ 번영하다 flourish for a while / 즐거운 ～를 보내다 have a pleasant 〔good〕 time (of it) / 미모도 ～다 Beauty is evanescent 〔lasts only for a time〕. / 그도 ～는 좋은 세월을 구가했었다 He was prosperous in his day. *or* He has seen better days. / 그 모자는 ～ 유행했다 The hat was once in fashion. / 그는 ～ 거지나 다름없었다 He was as good as a beggar at one time. / 그의 소설은 ～ 꽤 인기가 있었다 At one time his novels attained great popularity.

**한란**(寒暖) heat and cold; temperature. ◉ ～계 a thermometer; the mercury.

**한랭**(寒冷) cold; coldness; chillness. ～하다 (be) cold; chilly. ◉ ～전선 〖기상〗 a cold front: ～전선이 남하했다 The cold front pushed southward.

**한량**(限量) 《분량》 a limited 〔fixed〕 quantity; 《한정》 a limit; limits; bounds; an end. ¶ ～없다 be immeasurable 〔limitless, boundless, endless〕; there is no limit 〔end〕 to ...; know no end 〔limits, bounds〕 of... / ～없는 감사 unbounded gratitude / ～없이 unlimitedly; limitlessly; boundlessly; without limit; immensely; endlessly; 《매우》 extremely / ～없이 귀중한 교훈 a lesson of incalculable value / 욕심엔 ～이 없다 There is no limit to man's desire. *or* Avarice knows no bounds 〔limits〕. / 이처럼 잘 대우해 주시니 영광스럽기 ～없습니다 It is the utmost honor for me to be treated like this.

**한량**(閑良) 〖고제도〗 one of the military officer class who has not passed the State Examination; 《헙헙한 사람》 an open-handed man; 《난봉꾼》 a prodigal; a fast liver; a playboy.

**한러**(韓—) Korea and Russia; [형용사적] Korean-Russian. ◉ ～관계 Korean=Russian relations. ～국경 the Korean=Russian border.

**한련**(旱蓮) 〖식물〗 a nasturtium; a tropaeolum.

**한류**(寒流) a cold current.

**한류**(韓流) "Korean Wave", the ongoing frenzy of Korean pop culture that is sweeping across the vast regions of

East Asia.

**한림**(翰林) the Royal Academy; 《벼슬》 a Royal archivist 〔chronicler〕. ◉ ∼원 an academy; an institute.

**한마디** a (single) word. ∼하다 「speak briefly 〔say a word〕 《about》; say a (good) word 《for *a person*》; make a 「remark 〔comment〕 《on》. ¶ ∼(만) 더 one more word; one word more / ∼로 말하면 in a word; in short; to sum up (the story) / 끝으로 ∼ 《I should like to say》 just a word in conclusion / ∼ 감사의 뜻을 표하다 add a word of gratitude 《to him for ...》 / ∼로 그렇게 말할 수만은 없다 cannot say so sweepingly / ∼할 게 있다 I must say a word to you. / 그는 ∼ 인사도 없이 떠났다 He left us without having the politeness to say good-by. / 집사람은 영어를 ∼도 못합니다 My wife cannot speak a single word of English. / ∼ 인사 말씀 드리겠습니다 Ladies and gentlemen, may I just say a few words by way of greeting. / 회의석상에서 그는 ∼도 발언하지 않았다 He did not utter a word throughout the conference.

**한마음** one mind. ¶ ∼으로 with one accord / ∼한 뜻 everyone being 「of the same mind 〔in accord〕 / ∼이 되다 become one mind; become united / ∼이 되어 일하다 act in concert 《with》; work together in perfect accord; work in close cooperation / 그들은 ∼이다 They have one mind 「between 〔among〕 them.

**한명**(限命) the appointed limit of life; the destined duration of life.

**한모금** a drop; a draft 《미》; a draught 《영》; a sip (차·술의). ¶ ∼에 at 「a 〔one〕 draft / ∼의 물 a draught of water / ∼마시다 take a sip 《of wine》.

**한목** 《일거에》 all at once; 《한꺼번에》 all together; in a 「mass 〔lot〕; in bulk; in a lump. ¶ 물건을 ∼에 보내다 send things all together / 일년치 봉급을 ∼(에) 타다 receive a year's pay in a lump / 한 달치 식량을 ∼에 사다 buy food in bulk for the whole month.

**한몫** a 〔one〕 share; *one's* 「lot 〔portion, quota〕; a cut 《구어》. ¶ ∼ 끼다〔타다〕 take 〔get〕 *one's* share 《in》; receive *one's* quota / …의 계획에 ∼ 끼다 take a share in 《*a person's*》 project / ∼ 내다 pay *one's* share; take 〔bear〕 *one's* share of expense / 이익의 ∼을 받다 have a share in the profit; share in the profit / ∼을 요구하다 claim *one's* share 《in 〔of〕 the profits》 / ∼ 주다 give a share 《to》 / 내게도 ∼ 주시오 Please give me my share, too.

**한무릎공부**(一工夫) concentrated study over a fairly long period.

**한문**(漢文) Chinese writing. ¶ ∼으로 써 있는 책 a book written in classical Chinese. ◉ ∼자 Chinese characters. ∼학 Chinese 「literature 〔classics〕: ∼학자 a scholar of Chinese classics.

**한물** 《채소·어류 등의》 the season; the best time 《for》; 《최성기》 the prime. ¶ ∼지나다〔가다〕 be past 《its》 season / 꽃이 ∼지다 flowers are at their best / 오이가 ∼ 지다 cucumbers come in season / ∼가다 《유행 따위가》 go out of 「fashion 〔vogue, style〕; be 「outmoded 〔outdated〕 / 딸기는 지금 ∼이다 Strawberries are now in season. / 그 여자도 이제 ∼ 갔다 She has seen her best days. *or* She is past her prime.

**한미**(韓美) Korea and America; [형용사적] Korean-American. ¶ ∼ 21세기 위원회 the Korea-U.S. 21st Century Council / ∼간의 문제 an issue between Korea and the United States; a Korean-American question.
◉ ∼경제 협력 위원회 the Korea-U.S. Economic Cooperation Committee (생략 ECC). ∼관계 Korean-American relations. ∼무역 마찰 Korea-U.S. trade dispute. ∼상호 방위 협정 the ROK=U.S. Mutual Defense Agreement. ∼안보 학술 회의 Korea-U.S. security seminar. ∼안보 협의회 the Korea-U.S. Security Consultative Meeting. ∼우호 협회 the Korean-American Friendship Association. ∼재계 회의 the Korea-U.S. Business Conference. ∼재단 the American-Korean Foundation (생략 A.K.F.). ∼주둔군 지위 협정 the ROK-U.S. Agreement on Status=of-Forces in Korea; the ROK-U.S. Status of forces Agreement (생략 SOFA). ∼합동 연습 Korea-U.S. joint maneuvers. ∼합동 해상 훈련 a (South) Korea-U.S. joint naval exercise. ∼행정협정 the ROK-U.S. Administrative Agreement. ∼협회 the Korean-American Association. ∼환율 won-dollar rate.

**한미연합**(韓美聯合) the union of ROK=U.S. ◉ ∼군 the ROK-U.S. Combined Forces: ∼군 사령부 the ROK-U.S. Combined Forces Command (생략 CFC) / ∼군 사령관 《General R.》 Commander-in-chief of the ROK-U.S. Combined Forces Command. ～야전군 the ROK-U.S. Combined Field Army.

**한민족**(漢民族) the Han race; the Chinese. ⇨ 한족(漢族).

**한밑천** a sizable amount of capital. ¶ ～ 장만하다〔잡다〕 amass 〔make〕 a sizable fortune.

**한바닥** the center; the heart; the main point. ¶ 시장 ～ 《in》 the「center 〔heart〕 of a market (place) / 도시의 ～을 폭격하다 bomb the heart of the city.

**한바퀴** a round; a turn; a lap (운동장의). ¶ ～ 돌다 take a turn 《round the garden》; go round; make the rounds 《of a pool》; make a tour 《of》; 《담당 구역을》 go *one's* rounds / 공원 주위를 ～ 돌다 take a walk「through 〔around〕 the park / 연못을 ～ 돌다 go round a pond / 세계를 ～ 돌다 travel round the world / 그라운드 상공을 ～ 돌다 circle over the ground.

**한바탕** a scene; a round; a bout. ¶ ～의 씨름 a「round 〔bout〕 of wrestling / ～ 부는 사나운 바람 a sudden puff 〔a gust〕 of wind / ～ 싸우다 make a scene 《with *a person*》 / ～ 울다 cry for a spell / ～ 연설을 하다 make a (big) speech / ～ 야단치다 give 《*a person*》 a good scolding / ～ 소나기가 쏟아지더니 그쳤다 After a short shower it cleared up. / 우리는 그것 때문에 ～ 웃었다 We had a good laugh over it.

**한반도**(韓半島) the Korean Peninsula. ¶ ～에서의 평화와 안정의 유지 the maintenance of peace and stability on the Korean Peninsula / ～에서의 긴장을 완화하다 defuse tension on the Korean Peninsula / ～에서의 유일한 합법적인 국가 the sole legitimate state on the Korean Peninsula / 중국은 ～ 핵화를 반대하는 종래 입장을 고수한다고 그는 말했다 He said that China remains firm on its position opposing the nuclearization of the Korean Peninsula. ◉ ～에너지개발기구 the Korean (Peninsula) Energy Development Organization (생략 KEDO).

**한발**(旱魃) a (long) drought; a (long spell of) dry weather; a dry spell; lack of rain. ¶ ～이 계속되다 have a long drought / ～을 겪고 있다 be suffering from want of rain / 금년 벼농사는 ～로 인해서 막대한 피해를 입었다 The rice crop (of) this year has sustained heavy damage from a drought. ◉ ～대책 measures against drought; counter drought measures. ～지역 a drought-stricken area. ～피해 damage from a drought; drought damage.

**한발** a 〔one〕 step. ¶ ～ 한 발 step by step; 《서서히》 gradually; by degrees; inch by inch; bit by bit / ～ 늦다 fall a step behind 《*a person*》 / ～ (앞으로) 나오다 take 〔make〕 a step forward / ～ 두 발 물러서다 step backward a pace or two / ～ 먼저 떠나다 start a little before 《*a person*》 / ～ 늦어 기차를 놓치다 miss the train by a second / ～ 양보하다 yield a step; concede a point / ～도 양보 않다 do not「yield 〔budge〕「a step 〔an inch〕; hold 〔stand〕 *one's* ground / ～ 차로 그를 못 만났다 I missed him by a second. *or* I just missed「meeting 〔seeing〕 him.

**한발짝** a 〔one〕 step. ⇨ 한발. ¶ ～도 밖에 안 나가다 keep indoors; keep the house / 지쳐서 이제 ～도 움직일 수 없다 I am too tired to walk another step.

**한밤(중)**(―(中)) 《at》 midnight; 《in》 the「middle 〔dead〕 of the night. ¶ ～까지 far into the night; until the middle of the night; till late at night / 모두 잠든 ～에「at dead of night 〔at midnight〕 when all is silent / ～에 전화가 잘못 걸려온다는 것은 매우 짜증나는 일이지 It's most annoying to get a wrong number at this time of night, you know ! *or* How would you like being woken up by a wrong number in the middle of the night ! / ～에 소방차의 요란한 사이렌 소리에 잠이 깼다 In the middle of the night I was awaken by a fire engine with its siren screaming.

**한밥** 《제 끼니 아닌》 a meal made outside regular mealtimes. ¶ ～ 차리지 않게 제때 오시오 Please come at the regular mealtime, for it will be troublesome to set up a separate table later.

**한방**(一房) a 〔one〕 room; 《같은 방》 the same room; 《온 방》 the whole room. ¶ ～을 쓰다, ～에 거처하다 live in the same room with 《*a person*》; share a room with; room with.

**한방**(一放) a (single) shot; a round. ¶ ～의 총소리 the report of a gun (-shot) / ～ 쏘다 fire a shot / ～도 쏘지 않고 without firing a shot / ～에 쏘아잡다 kill 《a bird》「at a shot 〔at the first fire〕.

**한방**(韓方·漢方) traditional「Oriental 〔Chinese, herb〕 medicine. ◉ ～약 ⇨

한약. ~의(醫) a herbal (medical) doctor. ~의원 an Oriental medicine clinic. ~치료 Oriental medical treatment.

**한방울** a drop. ⇨ 방울 ②. ¶ 눈물~ a tear(drop) / ~씩 drop by drop / 그때 그녀는 눈물 ~ 흘리지 않았다 She did not shed a single tear at that time.

**한배** ① 《동물의》 a litter; a brood 〔hatch〕. ¶ ~ 강아지 a litter of puppies; puppies of the same litter / ~의 병아리 a brood of chickens. ② 《사람》 a womb; a venter; a belly. ¶ ~형제 brothers of the same womb.

**한번**(一番) a 〔one〕 time; once; one round. ¶ ~에 《단번에》 all at once; at a stroke; 《함께》 all together; 《한번에》 at a time; at a stretch (계속해서); 《동시에》 at the same time; 《한번의 시도로》 at one try; on the 〔*one's*〕 first try; at a 〔one〕 go / 다시 ~, ~ 더 once more 〔again〕; again; yet again 〔once〕 / 단 ~ once (and) for all / ~만 once only; for once / 닷새에 ~ once every five days / 한 달에 ~ once a month / 5년에 ~ once in five years / ~에 하나〔둘〕씩 《deal with》 one 〔two〕 at a time / ~도 결석 않고 without a single absence; without missing a single lesson / ~뿐이 아니라 more than once; once and again; again and again; repeatedly / 다시 ~ 해보다 make another 〔a second〕 attempt / 책을 ~읽다 read a book once / 씨름을 ~하다 have a round of wrestling / ~도 …않다 never *do;* do not *do* once / ~보면 그만이다 One look is enough. / 그 이야기는 ~만 들어도 결코 잊히지 않을 것이다 Once you hear the story, you will never forget it. (★ 이 once는 접속사=if once, when once) / 나는 일주일에 ~ 영화를 보러 간다 I go to the movies once a week. / 그런 일은 ~도 해본 적이 없다 I have never done such a thing. / ~에 두 가지 일을 하지 말라 「Do not attempt 〔Stop trying〕 to do two things at a time. / 언제 ~ 놀러 오십시오 Please drop in at my house someday. / ~쯤 가볼만한 곳이다 The place is worth a visit. / 내가 ~ 해 보죠 Let me have a try. / ~쯤 유럽 여행을 하고 싶다 I'd like to go on a tour of Europe once at least. / ~가도 화냥, 두 번 가도 화냥 《속담》 Once one has done a wicked deed, one does not hesitate to do anything far more wicked. / 어디 ~ 봅시다 Let's have a look at it.

**한벌** a suit 《of clothes》; 《가구·도구 따위》 a set; a suite. ¶ 가구 ~ a set 〔suite〕 of furniture / 여름옷 ~ a summer suit; a suit of summer clothes / 찻잔〔식기〕 ~ a tea 〔dinner〕 set.

**한복**(韓服) (traditional) Korean clothes 〔costume, dress〕. ¶ ~을 입은 《a girl》 in Korean dress 〔clothes〕 / ~을 입고 있다 be in Korean clothes; have Korean clothes on / 대량 생산되는 서구식 기성복 시대인 오늘날, 거리에서 ~을 보기란 매우 드물다 In this age of mass=produced Western-style ready-to=wear garments, "*hanbok*", traditional Korean dresses, are rarely seen on the street.

**한복판** the (very) middle; the center 〔centre 《영》〕; the heart. ¶ ~의 middle; central / ~에 right 〔just〕 in the middle 〔center〕 《of》; midmost 《of》 / 그라운드의 ~에(서) (right) in the middle of the ground / 적(敵)의 ~에 in the midst of the enemy / 서울 ~ the heart of Seoul / 과녁 ~을 맞히다 hit the target right 〔fairly〕 in the center / 길의 ~을 걷다 walk in 〔keep to〕 the middle of the road / 바로 이마 ~에 맞았다 It struck him full in the forehead. / 그는 길 ~에 쓰러졌다 He fell on the middle of the road.

**한불**(韓佛) Korea and France; [형용사적] Korean-French. ◉ ~사전 a Korean-French dictionary.

**한사**(寒士) a penniless 〔poor〕 scholar.

**한 사람** one person. ¶ 내 친구의 ~ a friend of mine / ~이서 alone; by *oneself* (단신으로); for *oneself* (혼자힘으로) / ~ 두 사람씩 by ones and twos / 한 사람, ~씩 one by one; one at a time; one after another in turn (차례로); individually / ~ 한 사람씩 방을 나갔다 They left the room one by one 〔one after another〕. / 나도 그것을 믿지 않는 ~이다 I, for one, do not believe it. / 그는 평의원의 ~이다 He is one of the councilors. / 한 사람 ~ 물어 보았다 I asked them one after another. / 합격자는 12명, 나도 그 중의 ~이다 Twelve passed the examination, including myself. / ~에 두 개씩 주시오 Give them two apiece.

**한사리** 《조수의》 the flood 〔spring〕 tide(s); the spring(s).

**한사코**(限死—) to the death; at the risk of *one's* life; with 〔for〕 all *one's* life; 《기를 쓰고·완강히》 desperately;

frantically; like hell 《구어》; persistently; relentlessly. ¶ ~ 반대하다 persist in *one's* opposition; be dead set against; oppose stoutly / ~ 싸우다 fight at the risk of *one's* life / 그는 ~ 가겠다고 고집했다 He insisted on going in person. / 웨이터는 ~ 팁을 받지 않았다 The waiter absolutely refused to accept the tip.

**한산**(閑散) 《상거래의》 inactivity; dullness; slackness; 《한적함》 leisure; quiet(ness). ~하다 (be) inactive; dull; slack; stagnant; 《한적함》 (be) leisurely; quiet; have leisure. ¶ ~한 시장 a「dull 〔flat〕 market / 이 시간에는 거리가 ~하다 The traffic is light about this time. / 거래가 아주 ~했다 Deals were exceedingly light.
◉ ~기「a slack 〔an off 〕 season.

**한살** ① 《나이》 one year of age. ② 《한몸·결합》 one flesh; the same flesh. ¶ (남녀가) ~(이) 되다 (they) stick together (and become one); share a bed 《with》; become man and wife.

**한삼덩굴** 〖식물〗 a Japanese hop.

**한색**(寒色) 〖미술〗 a cold color.

**한생전**(限生前) *one's* whole life; a lifetime.

**한서**(寒暑) cold「and 〔or〕 heat; temperature (온도). ¶ ~의 차가 적다 the heat and cold are moderate / 그 나라는 ~의 차가 심하다 The country is marked by a wide range of temperature between the hottest and coldest periods of the year.

**한서**(漢書) Chinese books; Chinese「literature 〔classics〕; 《한문의》 a book in Chinese.

**한선**(汗腺) 〖해부〗 a「sweat 〔perspiratory〕 gland. ◉ ~염 hidradenitis.

**한세상**(一世上) ① 《한평생》 a lifetime; *one's* whole life. ¶ ~을 편안히 살다 live comfortably throughout *one's* life / ~이란 잠깐이다 Life is short. *or* Our life is but a span. / 이렇게 살아도 ~이요 저렇게 살아도 ~이다 Life is one and the same no matter how you spend it. ② 《좋았던 때》 the best time in *one's* life; the heyday of *one's* life. ③ [부사적] all *one's* life; throughout *one's* life; through life; to the end of *one's* life; as long as one lives.

**한속** 《한마음》 one mind. ¶ ~이다 be of「one 〔a〕 mind; 《한통속》 be 〔act〕 in「collusion 〔concert, league, cahoots〕 《with》 / ~이 되다 conspire 《with》; go (into) cahoots 《with》 / …와 ~이 되어 in「collusion 〔league, conspiracy, secret understanding〕 with….

**한손** one 〔a single〕 hand; each hand. ¶ ~의 one-〔single-〕handed / ~에 하나씩 one to each hand / ~에는 우산 한 손에는 보퉁이를 들고 with an umbrella in one hand and a package in the other / ~으로 헤엄치다 swim one=handed / ~을 호주머니에 찔러 넣다 thrust *one's* hand into *one's* pocket / 그는 ~에 지팡이를 짚고 갔다 He went away a stick in hand (★ a stick in hand는 with 〔holding〕 his stick in his hand의 뜻. hand에 관사·소유대명사 따위가 안 붙음에 주의: pipe in mouth).

**한손놓다** 《일이》 come to an end for the moment; bring 《the job》 to a pause for the present; 《한 장면이》 be completed. ¶ 일은 이것으로 한손놓았다 With this I've got the hard part of the work done.

**한솥밥** the same mess. ¶ ~을 먹다 break bread 《with *a person*》; live under the same roof as 《*a person*》 / 그와는 3년 동안이나 ~을 먹은 사이다 I lived under the same roof with him for three years.

**한수**(一手) 《바둑·장기 등의》 a move. ¶ ~ 두다 make a move; 《한 판》 play a game of 《chess》 / ~ 높다〔위다〕 be a cut above 《*a person*》; be one up on 《*a person*》; be superior 《to》; surpass; excell / 그가 너보다 ~ 위다 He is a cut above you. / 이 ~로 승부가 결판나다 This one move decides the game.

**한순**(一巡) one round of shooting 5 arrows. ¶ 우리들은 활을 ~씩 쏘았다 Each of us had a round of shooting five arrows.

**한순배**(一巡杯) a round of drink. ¶ 술을 ~ 돌리다 pass the liquor around once; have a round of drinks.

**한술** a「spoonful 〔bite, morsel〕 of food. ¶ ~ 뜨다 take a spoonful of food; have a bite / ~ 더 뜨다 [비유적] be「not 〔hardly〕 less「wicked 〔vicious, severe, harsh〕 than…; outdo; outwit; browbeat.

**한숨** ① 《숨》 a breath; 《휴식》 a pause; a rest; a relief. ¶ ~ 돌리다 take breath; pause for breath; take 〔have〕 a「rest 〔breather〕 / ~ 돌릴 여유를 찾다 seek a breather 《in the cold war》 / ~ 자다 take a nap; sleep a wink or two; catch forty winks / ~ 돌릴 틈도 없이 바쁘다 We are too busy to find time

for breath. / ~ 돌리고 합시다 Let's have a little rest, and start again.
② 《탄식》 a sigh; a 「deep 〔heavy〕 breath. ¶ ~짓다〔쉬다〕 sigh; heave 〔draw, fetch〕 a sigh; draw a 「deep 〔long〕 breath / ~을 지으며 with a sigh; sighing(ly) / 깊이 ~을 쉬다 take a deep breath / ~쉬며 말하다 say 《*a thing*》 with sighs.
③ 《단숨》 ¶ ~에 at 「a 〔one〕 stretch / ~에 들이켜다 down 《a bowl of water》 at one draft; drink 《*one's* wine》 down 〔up〕 in a single 「draft 〔gulp〕 / 언덕 위로 ~에 뛰어오르다 run up a hill at a dash.

**한시**(漢詩) a Chinese poem; Chinese 「poetry [총칭].

**한시도**(一時一) even for a moment. ¶ ~ 잊지 않다 keep 〔bear〕 《*something*》 in mind all the time; never 〔do not〕 forget 《it》 even for a moment / ~몸에서 떼지 않다 always 「carry 〔keep〕 《it》 about 〔on〕 *one* / ~ 당신을 잊은 적이 없습니다 You are always present in my 「thoughts 〔mind〕.

**한시름** a big worry; a great anxiety; 《구어》 a great headache. ¶ ~ 놓다 feel relieved; be relieved of a great anxiety / 모두들 ~ 놓았다 Every one gave a sigh of relief. / 자네 말을 듣고 ~ 놓았네 What you told me made me feel relieved.

**한식**(寒食) 〖민속〗 the 105th day after the winter solstice (on which sacrificial food is offered at the ancestral tombs).

**한식**(韓式) Korean style. ◉ ~집 a Korean-style house.

**한식**(韓食) Korean-style food; a Korean 「meal.

**한심**(寒心) a pity; a regret; deplorableness; hopelessness; dejectedness. ~하다, ~스럽다 《가엾다》 be a pity; 《한탄스럽다》 (be) deplorable; regrettable; lamentable; 《실망스럽다》 (be) disheartening; discouraging; hopeless; 《부끄럽다》 (be) shameful; 《비참하다》 (be) miserable; unhappy; wretched. ¶ ~한 일, ~사(事) a matter for regret; a 「source 〔cause〕 of disappointment; a 「disheartening 〔discouraging〕 thing / ~한 사람 a wretch; a hopeless fellow / ~한 죽음을 하다 die a disgraceful 〔an ignominious〕 death / 나 자신을 ~하게 여기다 be ashamed of *oneself* (for what *one* has *done*) / 내 신세가 ~스럽구나 Ah me! How miserable I am! / 나라 일이 날로 어지러워 가니 ~하다 It is deplorable that the affairs of the nation should get messed up worse and worse. / 애가 저렇게 지각이 없으니 장차 무엇이 될는지 ~하다 Since the boy hasn't any sense at all, I am deeply concerned over his future. / 뭐 커닝을 했다고. 정 말이지 ~한 녀석이다 You cheated in the examination? I'm ashamed of you.

**한쌍**(一雙) a pair; a couple. ¶ 좋은 ~ a good pair / ~의 a 「pair 〔couple〕 of / 잘 어울리는 ~의 부부 a well-matched couple.

**한아름** an armful. ¶ ~의 마른 풀 an 「armful of hay.

**한약**(韓藥·漢藥) (an) Oriental 〔Chinese, herb〕 medicine; a herbal 「medicine 〔remedy〕; herbs. ◉ ~국〔방〕 an Oriental medical establishment; a dispensary of 「Oriental 〔Chinese〕 medicine; a herb shop. ~재(材) medicinal herbs: ~재상(材商) a dealer in Oriental medicines; a herb dealer. ~재시장〔약령시(藥令市)〕 a medicinal herb market; an Oriental medicinal market.

**한양**(韓洋) [형용사적] Korean and European 〔foreign〕; semi-Western style. ◉ ~식 절충 a compromise between Korean and European styles: ~식절충의 집 a house 「of 〔in〕 semi-Western style / ~식 절충의 요리 semi-Western cooking.

**한어**(漢語) the Chinese language; a Chinese word.

**한어**(韓語) Korean (language); a Korean 「word.

**한 없다**(恨一) be gratified; have nothing to be 「regretted 〔desired〕; be perfectly happy. ¶ 한 칠십 살았으니 인제 죽어도 ~ Since I have lived to be seventy, I shall have no regret if I die now. / 내집이라고 한 번 쓰고 살아봤으면 한 없겠다 I should be very happy if I could ever own a house of my own.

**한없다**(限一) (be) limitless; unlimited; endless; boundless; infinite. ¶ 한없이 endlessly; unlimitedly; boundlessly; without 「end 〔limit〕; infinitely; extremely; immensely / 한없는 바다 a boundless (expanse of the) ocean / 한없는 가능성을 내포하다 have boundless potentialities 《for》 / 아들을 한없이 사랑하다 love *one's* son 「no end 〔ever so much〕 / 욕심은 ~ Avarice 〔Desire〕 knows no bounds.

**한여름** ① 《한창 더위》 midsummer; the 「middle 〔height〕 of summer; high 〔full〕 summer. ¶ ~에 in the middle of (the) summer; in 〔at〕 the height of summer; in full summer / ～ 더위 the midsummer heat / 산 중의 절에서 ～을 보내다 spend 〔pass〕 midsummer at a temple in the mountains. ② 《온 여름》 the whole summer; all the summer (long). ¶ ～도 잠깐 가다 the summer passes away quickly.

**한역**(漢譯) a「translation 〔version〕 in classical Chinese; a Chinese translation. ～하다 translate 〔put, turn〕 into classical Chinese.

**한역**(韓譯) translation into Korean; 《역문(譯文)》 the Korean「rendering 〔version〕. ～하다 translate 〔put, render〕 into Korean. ¶ 햄릿 ～판 a Korean「translation 〔version〕 of *Hamlet*. ◉ 영문～ English-(to-)Korean translation: 영문 ～법 how to translate English into Korean.

**한열**(寒熱) heat and cold; chillness and fever.

**한영**(韓英) Korea and Britain; [형용사적] Korean-English. ◉ ～사전 a Korean-English dictionary.

**한옆** one「side 〔flank〕. ¶ ～에 on 〔to〕 one side; aside; by the side 《of》; 《한구석》 in a corner / ～에 비켜놓다 draw to *one's* side; put 《*things*》 aside / ～으로 밀다 push aside / ～으로 비키다 step 〔stand〕 aside; go to one side.

**한오금** the large crook of an archer bow.

**한옥**(韓屋) a (traditional) Korean-style house.

**한외**(限外) out of bounds; beyond the limit. ◉ ～발행 excess issue; overissue; an extra issue. ～원심기(遠心機) an ultracentrifuge. ～현미경 an ultramicroscope.

**한우**(寒雨) a cold rain.

**한우**(韓牛) Korean 〔homebred〕 beef cattle.

**한운**(閑雲) wandering clouds; leisurely clouds. ◉ ～야학(野鶴) wandering clouds and wild cranes: ～야학을 벗 삼다 lead a leisurely life; lead a life free from worldly care in the bosom of nature.

**한움큼** a handful 《of sugar》; a grasp; a fistful. ¶ ～의 쌀 a handful of rice / ～쥐다 make one grip of.

**한월**(寒月) a「winter 〔wintry〕 moon.

**한유**(閑遊) idling; loafting. ～하다 idle; loaf; amuse *oneself*.

**한음**(漢音) the pronunciation of Chinese characters.

**한의**(韓醫·漢醫) a herb doctor. ⇨ 한방(韓方). ◉ ～사 an Oriental 〔a herbal〕 (medical) doctor; a herb doctor. ～원(院) an Oriental medicine clinic; a herb clinic. ～학 Oriental medicine: ～학과 the department of Oriental medicine.

**한의과대학**(韓醫科大學) a college of Oriental medicine. ◉ K대 ～ the K University, College of Oriental Medicine.

**한이**(韓伊) Korea and Italy; [형용사적] Korean-Italian.

**한인**(閑人) an idle person; a man of leisure; a loafer. ¶ ～물입(勿入) 《게시》 No admittance except on business. ◉ ～한담(閑談) idle talks of an idle fellow.

**한인**(漢人) a Chinese.

**한인**(韓人) a Korean; Korean people.

**한인**(韓印) Korea and India; [형용사적] Korean-Indian.

**한일**(韓日) Korea and Japan; [형용사적] Korea(n)-Japan(ese). ¶ ～ 무역의 불균형 the trade imbalance between Korea and Japan; Korea-Japan trade imbalance / 대통령께서는 「나는 귀하의 취임이 ～간의 미래 지향적인 관계 설립에 새로운 전기를 마련하게 되기를 바랍니다」 라고 말씀하셨다 The President said, "I hope your inauguration will provide for a new momentum in building up a future-oriented relationship between Korea and Japan." ◉ ～민간합동 경제위원회 the Joint Conference of Korea-Japan & Japan-Korea Economic Committees. ～사전 a Korean-Japanese dictionary. ～의원연맹 the Korea-Japan Parliamentarians League. ～회담 the Korean-Japanese Conference; the Korea-Japan talks: ～ 각료 회담 the Korea-Japan Ministerial Conference / ～무역 회담 the Korea-Japan trade conference.

**한일월**(閑日月) leisure; spare time. ¶ ～을 보내다 live a「quiet 〔retired〕 life.

**한일자**(一一字) ¶ ～로 in a straight「line 〔beeline〕; straight / ～로 꽉 다문 입술 tightly drawn lips / 입을 ～로 다물다 close *one's* lips firmly.

**한입** a mouthful; a bite. ¶ ～에 at a mouthful / 사과를 ～먹다 take a bite out of an apple / 볼이 미어지도록 ～에 처넣다 cram 《*something*》 into *one's* mouth; take a big mouthful 《of》.

**한자**(漢字) a Chinese「character 〔ideograph〕. ¶ 상용(常用)～ the Chinese characters for common use / ～로 쓰다 write in Chinese character / 중고교 한문 교육용 기초 ～ basic Chinese characters to be taught at middle and high schools. ◉ ～어 a word written in Chinese characters. ~제한 limitation in 〔restriction on〕 the use of Chinese characters. ~철폐 abolition of Chinese characters. ⌈League.

**한자동맹**(—同盟) 〖역사〗 the Hanseatic

**한자릿수**(—數) a single digit; a single-figure number. ¶ 소비자 물가의 상승률은 여름이 끝날 때까지는 ~로 둔화될 것이 거의 확실하다 Consumer price increases will almost certainly slow to single digits by late summer.

**한잔**(—盞) 《분량》 a cup 《of tea》; a glass 《of beer》; a cupful 〔glassful〕 《of water》; 《음주》 a drink 《of liquor》; a swig; a spot (of drink) 《영구어》. ~하다 have 〔take〕 a drink; take a drop. ¶ …을 ~ 더 another cup 〔glass〕 of… / 차 ~ a cup of tea / ~ 내다 treat 《*a person*》 to drinks / ~ 권하다 offer 《*a person*》 a glass of liquor / 앉아서 ~하다 sit over *one's* whisky 〔drink〕 / 그는 ~만 마셔도 얼굴이 빨개진다 A single cup of wine makes him flushed. / 가끔 ~합니다 I enjoy a glass now and then. / 우리는 ~하면서 그 문제를 이야기했다 We discussed the matter over a drink. / 오늘밤 ~하세 Let's have a drink tonight. *or* How about having a drink tonight? / 맥주 ~ 더 하시겠습니까 Would you like another glass of beer? / 맥주라도 ~ 하면서 이야기 하자 Let's talk over a glass of beer. / 그는 ~하고 얼큰한 기분으로 귀가했다 He came home in high spirits after (having) a drink.

**한잠** a sleep; a nap; a deep 〔sound〕 sleep. ¶ ~ 자다 get a sleep; 《잠시 졸다》 sleep 〔have〕 a wink; take a nap / ~ 청하다 try and get a sleep / ~ 푹 자다 have a sound 〔deep〕 sleep / ~ 들다 fall into a deep sleep / ~도 못 자다 can't get a wink of sleep; have a sleepless night.

**한재**(旱災) (a) drought; (a) drought disaster. ¶ ~를 입다 suffer from a drought.

**한저녁** a late supper.

**한적**(閑寂) quiet(ness). ~하다 (be) quiet; sequestered; retired; secluded. ¶ ~한 곳 a retired 〔quiet〕 place; a secluded spot / ~하게 살다 live a retired 〔lonely〕 life.

**한절**(寒節) a cold season.

**한점**(—點) a point; a speck (조금); a dot (작은); 《바둑의》 a stone; 《조각》 a piece 《of》. ¶ 고기 ~ a piece of 《roast》 meat / ~을 얻다 《경기에서》 score a point; score a run (야구에서) / ~을 놓다 《바둑에서》 put a stone in advance / 하늘에는 구름 ~ 없다 There is not a speck of cloud in the sky.

**한정**(限定) limitation; (a) restriction. ~하다 limit; restrict; set limits 〔a limit〕 to; 《의미 따위를》 qualify. ¶ ~적(인) limitative; qualifying; defining / ~된 지면 limited space / …에 ~되다 be limited to… / 그들의 활동은 좁은 범위에 ~돼 있다 Their activities are restricted within narrow limits. / 연설은 7분 동안으로 ~돼 있다 Speeches are limited to 7 minutes. / 우리 클럽의 회원 총수는 20명으로 ~되어 있다 Our club membership is restricted to twenty. ◉ ~가격 the ceiling price. ~사(詞) 〖문법〗 a definitive (word); a determiner; 〖논리〗 a determinant. ~상속 qualified acceptance of heritage. ~전쟁 (a) limited war. ~출판 limited publication. ~치산(治産) quasi-incompetence: ~치산자 a quasi-incompetent (person). ~판 a limited edition 《of 500 copies》: 400부 ~판 a limited edition 〔publication〕 of 400 copies

**한제**(韓製) Korean make; [형용사적] made in Korea. ¶ ~의 Korean-made; of Korean make; 《국산의》 home-made.

**한조각** a piece 《of》; a bit; a fragment; a scrap. ¶ 고기 ~ a piece of meat / 빵 ~ a piece 〔slice〕 of bread / 깨진 유리 ~ a piece of broken glass / ~의 양심도 없다 have not a glimmer of conscience / ~의 양심도 없는 사내 a man without even a trace of conscience.

**한족**(漢族) the Han race; the Chinese.

**한족**(韓族) the Korean race.

**한종일**(限終日) all day (long).

**한줄기** ① 《한 가닥》 a streak; a ray. ¶ ~빛 a streak 〔ray〕 of light / ~희망 a ray 〔gleam〕 of hope / ~의 눈물 a trickle of tears. ② 《한바탕》 a spell; a period; [부사적] for a while. ¶ 소나기가 ~ 쏟아지다 have a (spell of) shower.

**한줌** a handful; a lock 《of grass》. ¶ ~의 쌀 a handful of rice.

**한중**(寒中) midwinter. ¶ ~에 during the cold season; in (the depth of) winter. ◉ ~수영 midwinter swimming. ~훈련 midwinter training; winter exercises.

**한중**(韓中) Korea and China; [형용사적] Korean-Chinese; Sino-Korean. ¶

～관계 Sino-Korean relations; relations between Korea and China / ～수교 4주년 기념 조찬회 a breakfast meeting to mark the fourth anniversary of full diplomatic ties between Korea and China.
◉ ～국교 정상화 restoration of diplomatic ties between Korea and China; normalization of Sino-Korean diplomatic relations. ～무역「Korean-Chinese〔Sino-Korean〕trade; trade between Korea and China. ～사전(辭典) a Korean-Chinese dictionary. ～합작영화 Korean-and-Chinese-made film; a film jointly made by Koreans and Chinese.

**한즉** 《그러면》 if so; then. ¶ ～, 인제 어떻게 하는 것이 좋을까 Then, what should we do now?

**한증**(汗蒸) a「steam〔sweating〕bath. ～하다 take a「steam〔sweating〕bath. ◉ ～막 a sweating bathroom: ～막 같다 be sweltering(ly) hot.

**한지**(韓紙) *Hanji,* Korean paper handmade from mulberry trees. ¶ ～는 주로 전통적인 붓글씨와 묵화용으로 쓰인다 *Hanji,* Korean paper is mainly used for traditional calligraphy and painting.

**한직**(閑職) a sinecure; an「easy〔unimportant〕office〔post〕. ¶ ～에 있다 occupy a post of leisure / ～에 있는 사람 a sinecurist / ～이 아니다 be hardly a sinecure; be「no〔not a〕sinecure / ～으로 쫓겨나다 be downgraded to a trifling job; be relegated to a less important post.

**한진**(汗疹) 〚한의〛 prickly heat; (a) heat rash. ⇨ 땀띠.

**한집** 《한 채》 a house; 《같은 집》 the same house. ¶ ～에 살다 live under the same roof; share〔live in〕the same house 《with》 / ～ 따다〔잃다〕 《바둑에서》 gain〔lose〕a point.

**한집안** ① 《한 가족》 *one's* family〔people, folk〕. ¶ ～식구 (the people in) *one's* family; *one's* folk / ～이나 다름없다 be in close relation with each other / ～ 식구처럼 대하다 treat 《*a person*》 as a member of *one's* family; give 《*a person*》 family comforts. ② 《친척》 *one's* relatives; *one's* kinsfolk; a clan; the same「family〔clan〕.

**한짝** ① 《외짝》 one odd (unmatched member of a pair); one of a pair; the「pair〔mate, fellow〕《to, of》; the other one. ¶ 구두 ～ an odd shoe / 장갑 ～이 어디 갔을까 Where is the mate to this glove? ② ＝한쪽.

**한쪽** 《방향》 a quarter; 《양쪽 중의》 one side; the other one; 《다른 쪽》 the other「side〔hand〕; 《당사자의》 a party; the other party; 《길의》 one way. ¶ ～끝 an edge; one end / ～날의 면도 칼 a single-edged blade / ～ 눈〔귀, 손〕「an eye〔an ear, a hand〕; *one's* other「eye〔ear, hand〕/ ～만의 unilateral; one-sided; lopsided / ～으로 치우치다〔기울다〕 lean to one side; 《불공평》 favor one side at the expense of the other; be impartial; show partiality to one side 《over the other》 / ～에〔으로〕 치우쳐 있다 be one-sided / 길의 ～을 걷다 keep to one side of the road / ～의 주장〔말〕만을 듣다 hear〔listen to〕only one side of the story / 계약의 ～당사자 a party to the contract / ～귀가 안들리다 be deaf「of〔in〕one ear / ～에서만 투시되는 창문 a one-way window / ～은 평면, 다른 한쪽은 원뿔 모양으로 되어 있다 It is plane one side and conical on the other. / ～말만 믿지 마라 One must not believe only one side of the story.

**한차례**(一次例) one round; once; a time; a turn; 《잠시》 for some time; for a「time〔while, spell〕. ¶ ～의 비 a short shower / (담당 구역을) ～ 돌다 go *one's* rounds / ～ 쉬다 take〔have〕a (short) rest; take〔have〕a breather; rest for a moment / ～ 씨름을 하다 have a round of wrestling / 소나기가 ～ 퍼부었다 There was a shower for some time.

**한참** ① 《노정》 the distance from one「stage〔stopping place〕to another; a distance; an interval. ¶ ～ 가다 집이 하나씩 있다 houses are quite far apart. ② 《한 차례》 a pause; a spell; a period (between breaks); one「time〔stretch, sitting〕. ¶ ～의 일 a spell of work. ③ 《얼마 동안》 for a「time〔while, spell〕. ¶ ～ 만〔후〕에, ～ 있다가 after a good while / ～ 있다가 대답하다 answer after a spell / ～ 만일세 It is a long time since「we met〔I saw you last〕.

**한창** ① 《절정》 the height; the peak; the zenith; 《in》 prime〔flower, bloom〕. ¶ ～때 《인생의》 the prime of *one's* life; 《in》 *one's* prime;「the best days〔the heyday〕of *one's* life; 《계절의》 the best season / ～ 일할 나이의 젊은이들 youth of working age / ～ 젊었을 때에 in the prime of (*one's*) youth; in *one's* days (★ in *one's* days는「한창 활약하던 때에」라는 뜻도 있음) / (꽃이) ~이다 be in full bloom 〔glory, flush, swing〕; be at 《their》 best / ~때를 지나다 be past *one's* 〔its〕 prime 〔best〕; be on the decline 〔wane〕 / 요사이는 딸기가 ~이다 Strawberries are in (season) now. / 봄이 ~이다 Spring is far 〔well〕 advanced. / 지금이 ~ 여름이다 It is the height of summer now. / 그는 지금 ~때이다 He is just at the prime of life. / ~ 먹을 나이다 A boy has a keen appetite at his age. / 서울의 벚꽃은 4월 중순이 ~이다 The cherry blossoms in Seoul are best at the middle of April. (★ 형용사의 최상급은 순수하게 서술적으로 쓰일 때에는 정관사가 붙지 않음: The lake is the deepest around here. 「이 호수는 이곳에서 제일 깊다」 The lake is deepest around here. 「이 호수는 여기가 제일 깊다」 전자는 the deepest one의 생략이며 한정용법 (attributive use)임). ② 《…하는 중·최고조》 in the midst 〔middle〕 of; at the height of; in the thick of 《a battle》. ¶ ~이다 be at its height; be in full swing; be going (at) full blast 《구어》 / ~전쟁 중에 in the midst of war / 낮의 ~ 더울 때에 in the heat of the day; in the hottest part of the day / ~ 비가 쏟아지는 때 《come》 in the midst of a heavy rain / 싸움이 ~일 때(에) in the thick 〔midst〕 of the battle; in the heat of an action / 폭풍우가 ~ 휘몰아칠 때 at the height of the storm / ~ 더운 때에 비가 오지 않다 have no rain at the height of the hot season / ~ 공부하고 있는데 친구가 찾아오다 a friend calls on me while I am (in the middle of ) studying / 연회가 ~ 무르녹았다 The banquet is at its height 〔peak〕 now. / 그것에 대해서 지금 ~ 논의중이다 Discussion is now in full swing on that subject. / ~ 행복에 젖어 있을 때 뜻하지 않은 병마가 그를 덮쳤다 At the very height of his happiness 〔Just when everything was going so well for him〕, he was afflicted by an unexpected illness.

**한천**(旱天) dry weather; a (spell of) drought.

**한천**(寒天) ① 《날씨》 cold weather. ② 《우무》 agar(-agar); Chinese gelatin(e). ¶ ~질〔모양〕의 gelatinous; jellylike. ◉ ~배양기(培養基) an agar culture medium.

**한철** one season.

**한촌**(寒村) a poor 〔an impoverished, a lonely, a deserted〕 village.

**한추위** ① 《한차례의 추위》 a spell of cold weather; a cold snap. ② 《큰 추위》 very cold weather; intense cold.

**한층**(―層) ① 《한 층계》 one story 〔floor, level〕. ② 《더욱》 more; still 〔much〕 more; (all) the more. ¶ ~ 힘드는 일 (much) harder work / ~ (더) 노력하다 make greater efforts / ~ 높다 be still higher / ~ 더 조심하다 take all the more care / 그는 막내라서 ~ 더 귀엽다 I love him the more because he is my youngest child. / 고독감이 ~ 더 심해졌다 My sense of isolation became doubly acute.

**한치** an inch. ⇨ 치¹. ¶ ~ 앞도 안 보이다 cannot see an inch ahead (of *one*) / ~ 앞도 볼 수 없는 눈보라 a blinding blizzard 〔snowstorm〕 / ~ 앞도 내다볼 수 없는 세상이다 Nobody knows what may happen tomorrow. / ~의 땅도 양보할 수 없다 We shall never cede an inch of ground.

**한칸** a 〔one〕 *kan*. ◉ ~방 a room one *kan* in area; a small room.

**한칼** ① 《칼질》 a single stroke of the sword. ¶ ~에 목을 베다 cut off 〔down〕 《*a person's*》 head with 〔at〕 one 〔a single〕 stroke of the sword. ② 《고기의》 a slice 《of meat》. ¶ 고기 ~ 살 수 없다 can't afford to buy a single slice of meat.

**한탄**(恨歎) lamentation; deploring; sighing; regret. ~하다 lament; deplore; sigh at; regret. ¶ ~할 deplorable; regrettable; lamentable / ~할 일 a matter for regret / ~할 만한 사태 a deplorable 〔sad〕 situation / 일신의 불행을 ~하다 bewail *one's* misfortune / 자식 없음을 ~하다 regret that *one* is childless / 정계의 부패를 ~하다 deplore the corruption of political circles / 친구의 죽음을 ~하다 lament over 〔for〕 a friend's death / …은 ~할 노릇이다 It is to be regretted that… / 책임 있는 자리에 있는 사람이 그런 짓을 했다니 ~할 일이다 It is regrettable 〔deplorable〕 that a man such a responsible position should have done such a thing. / 자신의 불행을 ~해 보았자 소용없다 It's no use lamenting one's misfortune.

**한턱** a treat; an entertainment; a feast; hospitability. ~하다〔내다〕 treat 《*a person*》 to 《a dinner》; give *a person* 《*something*》 as a treat; entertain 《*a person*》. ¶ ~거리 something to make a treat out of / ~먹다 have a feast / ~ 얻어먹다 be treated; get a treat /

술을 ～내다 treat《*a person*》to a drink / 저녁을 ～하다 give a dinner《for *a person*》; entertain《*a person*》with a dinner; have《*a person*》for dinner / 돌아가며 ～내다 provide a round of entertainment / 내가 ～낼 차례다 It is my treat now.

**한통(속)**《한패거리》a companion; a group; a party; a circle; a gang (악당의); a colleague;《공모자》a confederate; an accomplice; a fellow conspirator. ¶ ～이 되어 in conspiracy [collusion, cahoots]《with》/ ～이 되다 conspire《with》; act in collusion《with》; plot together;《미》go (into) cahoots《with》/ ～이 되어 사람을 속이다 go in cahoots to swindle《*a person*》/ 그는 그 무리와 ～이 되어 은행 강도짓을 하려고 했다 He was in cahoots with the gang in their attempt to rob the bank.

**한통치다** group them [lump things] together. ¶ 한통쳐서 (lumping) all together; as a group; in the gross; in one lot / 모두 한통쳐서 도둑놈으로 생각하다 regard the lot of them as robbers.

**한파**(寒波) a cold wave. ¶ 전국에 ～가 내습하다 a cold wave hits [grips, seizes] the whole country.

**한판** a round; one game; a session. ¶ 씨름을 ～하다 have a round of wrestling / 바둑을 ～ 두다 play a game of *paduk*. ◉ **～승부** a contest of single round.

**한팔**《한쪽 팔》one arm. ¶ 그가 없으니 ～을 잃은 것만 같다 I miss his service keenly.

**한패**(一牌) one of the (same) party [group, set]; fellows; a confederate. ¶ ～가 되다 join《others in *something*》; participate [take part] in《*something*》; mix *oneself*《among》/ 그도 ～임에 틀림없다 He must be one of the party. / 그는 그 일당과 ～였다 He was one [a member] of the group. *or* He was a party to the plot. / 그들은 모두 그 놈과 ～다 They are none of them [None of them are] any different from him.

**한편**(一便) ①《한쪽》one side; one way; one direction. ¶ ～에 on one side / 길의 ～을 걷다 keep to one side of the street / ～에 치우치다《불공평》be one=sided; be partial《to》. ②《자기편》a friend;《동맹자》an ally;《지지자》a supporter; *one's* side. ¶ ～이 되다 side with《*a person*》; stand by《*a person*》; support /《게임에서》partner《with》; pair (off)《with》/ …을 ～으로 끌어들이다 win《*a person*》over to *one's* side / 나는 너와 ～이다 I stand your friend. ③《…한 외에》in addition to《*doing*》; in the meantime; on the one hand; meanwhile; besides; while; but (at the same time). ¶ 산업이 개발되는 ～ 원시적인 씨족 사회는 무너지게 되었다 Industry started to develop, while the primitive clan society began to collapse. / 그의 이야기는 슬픈 ～ 우스웠다 His tale was sad but at the same time funny. / 그는 회사에 나가는 ～ 집에서 영어도 가르치고 있다 Besides [While] working at the business firm, he gives private lessons in English at home. ④《한편 … 또 한편 …》on the one hand… on the other (hand); partly… and partly…. ¶ 그를 나는 한편 힘으로 또 ～으로는 설득으로 내 제의를 수락하게 했다 I made him agree to my proposal partly by force and partly by persuation.

**한평생**(一平生) *one's* whole life; a lifetime; [부사적] for life; all life long; throughout *one's* life. ¶ ～ 편히 지내다 live comfortably to the end of *one's* life / ～ 독신으로 지내다 remain single [a bachelor (남), a spinster (여)] all *one's* life / 나는 ～ 그날을 잊지 못하리라 I shall never forget that day as long as I live.

**한푼** a [one] penny; a coin; a copper. ¶ 동전 ～《even》a (single) penny / ～ 없는 penniless / ～의 값어치도 없다 be not worth a farthing / ～ 없는 빈털터리가 되다 go (clean) broke《구어》; become penniless; be reduced to the last penny / ～도 깎을 수 없습니다 I can't take a penny off. / 그 때 돈이라고는 ～도 없었다 I had not even a penny at that time.

**한풀꺾이다, 한풀죽다** lose heart; be disheartened [dejected]; be in low spirits; be dispirited; be taken down a peg (or two); be crestfallen; be in blues [dumps]《구어》. ¶ 한풀꺾이어 in low spirits; dejectedly; crestfallen / 그 소식을 듣고 그는 한풀죽었다 His spirits fell at the news. / 그는 나한테 져서 한풀꺾였다 It took some of the starch out of him when he got defeated by me. / 추위도 한풀꺾인 것 같다 The cold seems to have decreased in severity. / 첫번에 실패하자 그의 열의는

한풀꺾였다 The initial failure daunted 〔chilled〕 his ardor.

**한풀다**(恨—) realize *one's* desire; attain an ambition; gratify *one's* wishes; have *one's* cherished desire realized. ¶ 한(을) 풀어 주다 fulfill《*a person's*》 desire; gratify 〔satisfy〕《*another's*》 desire / 갖고 싶던 사진기를 가져 한을 풀다 satisfy a yen for a camera / 그의 한을 모두 풀어 줄 수는 없었다 It was impossible to satisfy all his desires.

**한풀이하다**(恨—) vent *one's* spite《over》; satisfy a grudge; revenge *oneself* for; pay off old scores《with》; take out《*one's* anger》.

**한풍**(寒風) a cold 〔chilly, bleak〕 wind.

**한하다**(限—) limit; restrict. ¶ 어른에 한한 영화 a film for adults only / 그때에 한하여 on that particular occasion for that once / 이번에 한하여 for this time only; for this once / 그사람에 한해서 그런 짓은 결코 하지 않는다 He is the last man to do such a thing. / 지불은 현금에 한합니다 Cash only. / 1인 1매에 한함《표시》 Admission for one person only. / 통용 기한은 발행 당일에 한함《표시》 Available on the day of issue only. / 학생에 한해서 입장을 허가함《게시》 Admission to students only. / 일요일에 한해서 입장 무료다 Admission is free on Sundays only.

**한학**(漢學) Chinese literature; Chinese classics. ¶ ～의 대가 an authority on Chinese classics. ◉ ～자 a scholar of Chinese classics.

**한한사전**(漢韓辭典) a dictionary of classical Chinese explained in Korean.

**한해**(旱害) drought damage; a drought disaster. ¶ ～를 입다 suffer from a drought / 올해의 벼농사는 전국적으로 많은 ～를 입었다 The rice crop this year has suffered a lot from the drought in most of the country.
◉ ～지구 a drought-stricken area. ～상습 지역 areas vulnerable to drought; a chronically drought-stricken area.

**한해**(寒害) cold-weather damage; damage from 〔caused by〕 cold weather. ¶ ～로 부터 농작물을 지키다 protect crops from being damaged by cold weather.

**한해살이** 〖식물〗 an annual plant; annuals.

**한호**(韓濠) Korea and Australia; 〔형용사적〕 Korean-Australian.

**한화**(閑話) chatting; gossip; idle talk. ～하다 talk idly; chat; gossip.

**한화**(韓貨)《돈》 Korean money;《화물》 Korean goods.

**할**(割) percentage; percent (기호 %). ¶ 연 1할 2푼의 이자 an interest of 12 percent per annum / 3할 할인해 팔다 sell at 30% discount / 그는 수입의 몇 할을 소득세로 내느냐 What percentage of his income is paid income tax?

**할거**(割據) ～하다 hold *one's* own ground; each holds *his* own sphere of influence; maintain sectional authority. ¶ 군웅～의 시대 the age of rival chiefs 〔warlords〕. ⇨ 군웅할거.

**할근거리다** gasp; pant; wheeze; rattle; breathe hard. ¶ 숨을 ～ gasp; breathe hard.

**할기족족** with a displeased look from the corner of *one's* eyes. ～하다 look displeased 〔discontented〕. ¶ ～ 쳐다보다 glare; look daggers《at》; scowl from the corner of *one's* eyes.

**할깃-** ⇨ 흘깃-.

**할당**(割當)《행위》(an) assignment; (an) allotment; (an) allocation (자금의); a quota; a ration《of food》(배급). ～하다 assign; allot; allocate; apportion; parcel out; give a quota; ration (배급하다). ¶ ～된 일 allotted 〔assigned〕 work / 각자에게 몫을 ～하다 allot a share to each / 방을 ～하다 assign a room《to *a person*》/ 일을 ～하다 assign a task《to *a person*》; assign《*a person*》 for a task / 주(株)를 ～하다 allot shares / 한 사람 앞에 5천 원을 ～하다 allot 5,000 won per head / (배우에게) 배역을 ～하다 assign a role《to each actor》; cast the parts《to the actors》/ 예산의 15퍼센트를 그 기획에 ～했다 We allocated fifteen percent of our budget to the project. / 금년도의 이민 ～ 인원은 이미 찼다 The quota of immigrants for this year has already been filled.
◉ ～금 allotment;《부과금》 assessment. ～량〔액〕 a quota; an allotment; a stint (일의): 전력의 ～량 an allocated amount of power / ～량을 이행하다 fulfill *one's* quota / ～량을 삭감하다 cut the quota / 모든 일에 ～량이 정해졌다 Quotas were laid down for all work. ～배급 quota delivery; rationing. ～제 the quota system: 수출～제 the export quota system. ～제한 quota restrictions. ～통지 an allotment letter 〔notice〕; a letter of allotment. ～표 an allotment chart.

**할듯할듯** looking as if *one* were going to《*do*》; always being on the point

〔verge〕 of 《doing》. ¶ 일을 ～하면서 아니 하다 look about to do the work but never do it / 그는 대답을 ～하다가 말았다 He kept looking as if he were going to come up with an answer but then he never did.

**할딱거리다, 할딱이다** pant; gasp (for breathing); breathe hard 〔with difficulty〕; be out 〔short〕 of breath; be panting 〔gasping〕 for breath.

**할딱할딱** panting; puffing; breathing heavily. ¶ ～ 달리다 run along panting.

**할똥말똥하다** hesitate to 《do》; waver over 《doing》; be half-hearted.

**할렐루야** Halleluiah; Allelujah.

**할례**(割禮) 〖종교〗 circumcision (ceremony). ¶ ～를 행하다 circumcise 《*a person*》.

**할로겐** 〖화학〗 halogen. ¶ ～의 halogenous / ～화(化) halogenation.
◉ ～계 the halogen series. ～화물(化物) a halide; a halogenide.

**할리우드** Hollywood. ¶ ～(영화계)의 Hollywoodian.

**할말** 《하고 싶은·해야 할》 what *one* has 〔wants〕 to say; *one's* say; 《주장》 *one's* claim 〔point, case〕; 《불평》 something to say 《against》; a complaint; a grievance; 《이의》 an objection.
¶ 양쪽의 ～을 듣다 hear both sides (of the story); listen to the cause of either party / 네게〔그것에 관해〕 ～이 있다 I have something 「to tell you 〔to say about that〕. / 너에게 ～이 많다 《듣기 싫은 소리》 I have a bone to pick with you. / ～은 해야 한다 You should say what you have to say. / ～이 있으면 해라 Say your say. *or* Tell me what you have to say. / ～은 서슴지 말고 해라 Don't be afraid. Say anything you want to say. *or* Don't hesitate. Speak out. / 거기 대해서는 나도 ～이 있다 I have a say in the matter, too. / 별로 ～이 없다 I have nothing special to say for myself. / 뭐 ～이 있는가 Have you anything to complain of 〔about〕? / ～은 다 했다 I have had my say.

**할머니** ① 《조모》 a grandmother; a grandma; a granny 《소아어》. ② 《친척의》 a related woman of *one's* grandmother's generation. ③ 《노부인》 an old woman 〔lady〕; a granny 《구어》.

**할멈** an old woman; a granny; 《하녀》 an old maid.

**할미** ⇨ 할머니.

**할미꽃** 〖식물〗 a pasqueflower; a windflower.

**할미새** 〖조류〗 a wagtail.

**할복**(割腹) disembowelment; *harakiri*. ～하다 disembowel *oneself*; commit disembowelment 〔*harakiri*〕; rip *oneself* up. ◉ ～자살 suicide by disembowelment.

**할부**(割賦) 《분할 지급》 payment in 〔by〕 installments. ¶ ～로 사다 buy 《a TV set》 on the installment 〔easy payment〕 plan / ～(제)로 팔다 sell 《a refrigerator》 on the installment plan / 차를 ～로 사다 buy a car on the installment plan; buy a car on time 《미》 / 텔레비전 대금을 다달이 ～로 내고 있다 We're paying for the television by monthly installment. ◉ ～납입금 an installment (money). ～상환 amortization. ～제(制) the installment plan 〔system〕 《미》. ～판매 selling on an installment basis.

**할선**(割線) 〖수학〗 a secant; a secant line.

**할쑥하다** 《얼굴이》 (be) thin and pale; drawn; lean; emaciated. ¶ 할쑥한 얼굴 a haggard 〔worn〕 face.

**할아버지** ① 《조부》 a grandfather; a grandpa. ② 《친척의》 a related man of *one's* grandfather's generation. ③ 《노인》 an old man.

**할아범** an old 〔aged〕 man(servant).

**할애하다**(割愛—) 《내주다》 share willingly 〔generously〕; part with 《*something*》; 《양보해 나누다》 spare 《*something*》 for 《*a person*》. ¶ 지면을 ～ allow space 《for》 / (남에게) 식량을 ～ spare part of the provisions 《for another》 / 바쁜 중에도 시간을 ～ take time off *one's* busy work.

**할양**(割讓) (a) cession; alienation. ～하다 cede 《a part of *its* territory to another country》; alienate 《*a thing*》 to. ¶ 토지를 …에게 ～하다 alienate lands to 《*a person*》.

**할인**(割引) (a) discount; (a) reduction; (a) rebate. ～하다 discount; make 〔give, allow〕 a discount 《on an article, off the price》; take 〔cut〕 《30 percent》 off; 《어음을》 discount 《a bill》. ¶ 50%의 단체～ a fifty percent group discount / 왕복권 1할 ～, 10% off for a round trip ticket / 값을 1할 ～하다 make 〔allow〕 a discount of 10% 〔10% discount〕 off the price; reduce the price by 10% / 5% ～해서 팔다〔사다〕 sell 〔buy〕 《*a thing*》 at a discount 〔reduction〕 of 5 percent / 대량 주문에는 ～해 드립니다 We make a reduction on a big order. / 사업자 및 단체객을 위한 ～요금 있음 《게시》 Commercial and group rates available. / 현금이면 얼마나 ～됩니까 Do you allow any discount for cash? *or* Do you make any allowance for cash payment? / 저희 상점에서는 모든 상품을 3할 ～해서 팔고 있습니다 We sell all the articles at「a discount of 30 percent 〔reduced prices by 30 percent〕 at our store.

◉ ～가격 a bargain price; a reduced price: ～가격으로 at a reduced price; at a discount; at a cut rate 《미》. ～권 a discount coupon 〔ticket〕; a reduced-rate 〔cut-rate〕 ticket. ～국채 a discount government bond. ～금융채(債) a discount bank debenture. ～기간 the term of discount. ～소매점 a discount (retail) store. ～수수료 a discount 〔reduced〕 rate; a discount commission 〔charge〕. ～승차권 a reduced fare ticket. ～시간 reduced fare hours. ～액 a discount. ～어음 a discount(ed) bill; a bill discounted. ～율 a discount rate. ～채권 a discount bond. 동업자(간) ～ (a) trade discount. 현금～ a discount for cash; (a) cash discount. 조조(早朝) ～영화 《see》 a morning movie at reduced admission.

**할인**(割印) a tally impression; affixing a seal over two edges. ¶ ～을 찍다 put 〔affix〕 a seal at the joining of two papers / ～을 찍은 서류 documents with a tally impression.

**할일** things to do. ¶ ～이 많다 have lots to do; be busy / ～(이) 없다 have nothing to do.

**할주**(割註) an inserted note.

**할증**(割增) a premium; a bonus; an extra 《charge, fare, dividend》. ～하다 give 〔pay〕 an extra 〔a premium〕. ¶ ～부(附)로 판매하다 be selling at a premium / 오후 10시 이후는 3할의 심야 ～요금이 된다 After 10 p.m. you pay 30% (in) extra as late hour premium.

◉ ～금 a premium; a bonus 《on a loan》: ～금부 채권 a premium bond; a premium-bearing debenture. ～배당금 an extra dividend; a bonus. ～요금 an extra fare 〔charge〕; a surcharge. ～임금 extra 〔premium〕 wages; extra 〔premium〕 pay.

**할짝거리다** keep licking; keep lapping. ¶ 개가 우유를 할짝거리고 있다 The dog is lapping milk.

**할쭉하다** ＝할쑥하다.

**할퀴다** ① 《손톱으로》 scratch; claw (고양이 따위가). ¶ 할퀸 상처 a scratch; a nail mark / 전쟁이 할퀸 자국 traces of the ravages of war / 손톱으로 얼굴을 ～ scratch 《*a person's*》 face with *one's* fingernails / 고양이가 사람을 ～ a cat claws a person. ② 《훔치다》 filch; pilfer; swipe.

**핥다** lick; lap; taste. ¶ 핥은 듯 깨끗이 먹다 lick 《the bowl》 clean / 그는 숟가락을 깨끗이 핥았다 He licked the spoon clean. / 고양이는 제 발을 핥고 있었다 The cat was licking its paws.

**핥아먹다** ① 《혀로》 lick 《up》; lap 《up》. ¶ 고양이가 우유를 ～ a cat laps milk up. ② 《속여 뺏다》 swindle 《*a person*》; acquire 《*a person's things*》 by fraud.

**핥아세다** acquire by fraud; defraud 〔hoax, mulct〕 《*a person*》 of 《*something*》. ¶ 남의 재물을 ～ cheat *a person* out of *his* property.

**핥이다** 《혀로》 get licked 〔lapped〕; have 《*something*》 licked 〔lapped〕; have 《*a person*》 lick 《it》. ¶ 개에게 손을 ～ have *one's* hand licked by a dog; have a dog lick *one's* hand.

**함**(函) a box; a case; a chest. ¶ 옷함 a clothes chest / 서류(정리)함 a filing cabinet / 사서함 a post-office box (생략 P.O.B.).

**함교**(艦橋) 〖군사〗 the bridge (of a warship). ¶ ～에 서다 stand on the bridge of a warship. ◉ ～갑판 the bridge deck. 전〔후〕～ the fore 〔after〕 bridge.

**함구**(緘口) holding *one's* tongue; keeping *one's* mouth shut. ～하다 keep *one's* mouth shut; hold *one's* tongue; keep *one's* lips tight; keep silent. ¶ ～무언하다 keep *one's* mouth shut (and remain silent) / 그는 ～무언이었다 He would not open his mouth. *or* He remained silent to the last.

◉ ～령 a gag law 〔rule〕: ～령을 내리다 give an order to keep silence; prohibit free expression of opinion.

**함기**(艦旗) an ensign.

**함께** ① 《같이》 together. ¶ …와 ～ 《더불어》 (along 〔together〕) with…; in company with…; 《포함하여》 including…; inclusive of… / 모두 ～ all together / ～ 지내다〔살다〕 live together 〔under the same roof〕; live with 《*a person*》 / ～일하다 work together; work with 《*a person*》 / ～ 가다 go together; go with 《*a person*》; accompany 《*a person*》 / 대중과 ～행동하다 act in common with the people / ～ 노래하다 sing in chorus; sing in unison / ～ 섞다 put together; mix up / 나도 아이

들과 ～ 놀았다 I joined the children's sports. / 그와 ～ 있는 것을 보이고 싶지 않다 I don't like to be seen in his company.
② 《양쪽 모두》 both; neither (부정); 《똑같이》 alike; equally. ¶ 형제가 ～ both (the) brothers / 부부가 ～ 열심히 일한다 Both husband and wife work hard. / 그 두 학생은 ～ 내게 친절히 대해 줬다 Both the two pupils were kind to me. ⇨ 함께하다.
③ 《…함에 따라》 as; with. ¶ 나이가 듦과 ～ as *one* grows older; with *one's* increasing 〔advancing〕 years / 나이를 먹음과 ～ 그녀의 매력이 더해졌다 She has become more charming with age.

**함께하다** share 《*something*》 with; participate 〔take part〕 in 《*something*》; partake of 《*something*》. ¶ 기쁨을 ～ share in each other's joy / 식사를 ～ eat at the same table; have 《lunch》 together / 침식을 ～ live together / 고락(苦樂)을 ～ be partner of 《*a person's*》 joys and sorrows; share joys and sorrows with 《*a person*》 / 한평생을 ～ share 《our, your, their》 lives; be partners for life / …와 운명을 ～ cast 〔throw〕 in *one's* lot with 〔among〕; share *one's* fate with 《*a person*》; be in the same boat / 우리는 이해(利害)를 함께하고 있다 We have common interests.

**함닉**(陷溺) ～하다 《빠지다》 ① 《물속에》 drown; sink. ② 《주색·사물에》 indulge 《in》; be addicted 〔given〕 《to》; give *oneself* up 《to》; abandon *oneself* 《to》.

**함대**(艦隊) 《큰》 a fleet; 《작은》 a flotilla; a squadron; a division. (★ fleet는 함대 사령관이 있는 규모가 큰 함대. squadron은 fleet의 한 분대에 해당되는 작은 규모의 함대로 특수 임무를 가진 것. division은 4, 5척 정도의 매우 작은 함대).
◉ ～기지 a fleet base. ～사령관 the commander of a fleet.

**함락**(陷落) 《적진의》 fall; surrender. ～하다 fall; surrender. ⇨ 함몰. ¶ 요새를 ～시키다 take a fortress / 로마는 ～되었다 Rome has fallen!

**함량**(含量) content. ¶ 광석의 우라늄 ～ the uranium content of the ore / 주철(鑄鐵)은 탄소의 ～이 많다 Cast iron has a high carbon content. / 지방～이 많은 것을 먹지 마라 Don't eat food with a high fat content. ◉ 알코올〔비타민〕 ～ alcohol 〔vitamin〕 content.

**함령**(艦齡) the age 〔life〕 of a warship. ¶ ～ 초과의 overage 《warships》.

**함몰**(陷沒) 《두려빠짐》 (a) subsidence; a cave-in; (a) collapse; sinking; 《멸망》 total destruction. ～하다 《두려빠지다》 cave 〔fall〕 in; sink; give in inwardly; collapse; 《멸망하다》 get destroyed altogether; get annihilated. ¶ 도로의 ～(장소) a cave-in in the road / 지진으로 도로가 ～했다 The road sank 〔caved in〕 by the earthquake. ◉ ～지진 a fallen 〔cave-in〕 earthquake. ～해 an ingression sea. ～호 a cave-in lake.

**함미**(艦尾) the stern of a warship. ¶ ～에 astern. ◉ ～닻〔묘(錨)〕 the stern anchor. ～포(砲) a stern chaser.

**함박** ① 《함지박》 a scooped wooden dish. ② ⇨ 함박꽃.

**함박꽃** 〖식물〗 a peony (flower).
◉ ～나무 *Magnolia Sieboldii* (학명).

**함박눈** large flakes of snow; large snowflakes. ¶ ～이 내린다 It snows in large flakes. *or* Snow is coming down in large flakes.

**함부로** ① 《무차별로》 indiscriminately; 《되는대로》 at random; blindly (목표 없이); 《무모하게》 recklessly; rashly; indiscreetly (신중치 못하게); 《생각 없이》 thoughtlessly; 《과도하게》 excessively; to 〔in〕 excess; immoderately; 《불필요하게》 more than is necessary; needlessly; unnecessarily; 《부당하게》 unreasonably; unduly. ¶ (남의 말을) ～ 믿다 believe 《what people say》 too readily; be credulous / ～ 돈을 쓰다 spend money recklessly; make extravagant expenditures / ～ 때리다 hit 《*a person*》 without reason; beat 《*a person*》 mercilessly / 말을 ～ 하다 talk at random; be rough 〔rude, short〕 in *one's* speech; talk wild; say whatever 〔the first thing that〕 comes into *one's* head / 종이를 ～ 쓰다 waste paper / 일을 ～ 하다 scamp *one's* work; do a slapdash job; do a job in a rough 〔slapdash〕 fashion / 아무데나 ～ 침을 뱉다 don't care where *one* spits; spit all over the place indiscriminately / 나는 약속을 ～ 하지는 않는다 I do not make rash promises. / 일단 직업을 택했으면 ～ 바꾸지 말아야 한다 You shouldn't lightly change your job once you have chosen it. / 행동을 ～ 해서는 안 된다 Don't act thoughtlessly 〔rashly〕. / ～ 친구에게 돈을 빌려서는 안 된다 You shouldn't borrow money from your friends rashly.
② 《허가 없이》 without permission

〔leave〕. ¶ ～ 내 방에 들어오지 마라 Don't enter my room without permission. / ～ 들어오지 말 것 《게시》 No entry 〔admittance〕 「without permission 〔except on business〕. *or* 《미군사》 Off limits to unauthorized personnel.

**함빡** ¶ ～ 젖다 be all wet; be wet to the skin; get soaked 〔wet〕 through; be drenched 〔soaked〕 with rain; be drenched to the skin; get wet all over; 《특히 옷이》 get dripping wet / 술에 ～ 취하다 get quite 〔dead〕 drunk / 옷이 이슬에 ～ 젖다 *one's* clothes are all wet with dew / 얼굴에 웃음을 ～ 띠고 방안으로 들어오다 come into the room with *one's* face beaming with big smiles.

**함상**(艦上) ¶ ～의〔에〕 aboard; on board.

**함석** zinc; tin; galvanized iron. ¶ ～을 입히다 zinc / ～으로 지붕을 이다 roof with galvanized iron sheets.
◉ ～지붕 a zinc 〔tin〕 roof: ～지붕의 tin-roofed. ～집 a house with 「a zinc roof 〔galvanized iron roofing〕. ～판 sheet zinc; galvanized iron sheet.

**함선**(艦船) warships and other ships; naval vessels.

**함성**(喊聲) a great outcry; a war 〔battle〕 cry; shouting; a war whoop. ¶ 승리의 ～ a shout of victory 〔triumph〕 / ～을 올리다〔지르다〕 raise 〔give〕 a war 〔battle〕 cry; raise a great war whoop; give a shout of triumph.

**함수**(含水) 〖화학〗 ¶ ～의 hydrous; hydrated. ◉ ～량 water content. ～탄소 carbohydrate. ～화(합)물 a hydrated compound; a hydrate.

**함수**(函數) 〖수학〗 a (mathematical) function. ¶ ～의 functional / ～적으로 functionally. ◉ ～공간 functional space. ～관계 functional relation. ～기호 a functional symbol. ～론 the theory of functions. ～방정식 a functional equation. ～식 a functional formula. 대수〔삼각〕～ an algebraic 〔a trigonometrical〕 function.

**함수**(鹹水) salt water; sea water; brine.
◉ ～어 〖어류〗 a salt-water fish. ～호 a salt(-water) lake; a lagoon.

**함수**(艦首) the bow(s) (of a warship).
◉ ～포 a bow gun 〔chaser〕.

**함수초**(含羞草) 〖식물〗 a mimosa.

**함실** a smooth-bottom fireplace. ◉ ～방(房) a room with a hypocaust heated by a smooth-bottom fireplace.

**함실함실** ⇨ 흠실흠실.

**함씨**(咸氏) an honored nephew; your nephew.

**함양**(涵養) fostering; cultivation; culture. ～하다 foster; cultivate 《a love of nature》; develop 《a taste for fine arts》; build up 《character》. ¶ 덕성을 ～하다 cultivate moral character.

**함열**(艦列) a column of warships.

**함원**(含怨) ～하다 harbor 〔nurse〕 a grudge; have a grievance; bear 〔cherish〕 ill will.

**함유**(含有) ～하다 contain; include; have 《in》; hold. ¶ 금을 ～하다 contain gold.
◉ ～량(量) content: 광석의 은 ～량 the silver content of an ore / 지방 ～량 fat content / 알코올 ～량이 많다 contain a high percentage of alcohol. ～성분 an ingredient; a component. ～율 content by percentage.

**함입**(陷入) subsidence; sinking. ～하다 subside; sink; cave 〔fall〕 in; collapse.

**함자**(銜字) an honored name; your 〔his〕 name. ¶ 선생님의 ～가 어떻게 됩니까 What is your name, sir?

**함장**(艦長) the captain 〔commander〕 (of a warship); 《기함의》 the flag captain. ◉ ～실 the captain's cabin.

**함재**(艦載) ～하다 carry aboard a warship; load a warship. ◉ ～기 a ship 〔deck 《미》〕 plane; 《항공 모함의》 a carrier-borne 〔carrier-based〕 aircraft [총칭]. ～보트 《land by》 a ship's boat. ～수뢰정 a torpedo launch.

**함적**(艦籍) the Navy list 《of ships》. ¶ ～에서 빼다 strike 《a ship》 off the Navy list.

**함정**(陷穽) ① 《만들어 놓은》 a pitfall; a pit; a trap; 《짐승을 잡기 위한》 a game pit; a deadfall. ¶ ～에 빠뜨리다 ensnare; entrap; catch 《an animal》 in a trap / ～에 빠지다 fall 〔walk〕 into a pit(fall); get 〔be〕 caught in a trap; be entrapped 〔ensnared〕. ② 《음모·계략》 a trap; a snare; a pitfall. ¶ ～이 있는 문제 a catch question 《in an examination》 / ～에 빠지다 be caught in a snare 〔trap〕 《set by *a person*》; be (en)trapped; be ensnared; fall victim to a plot / ～을 놓다〔파다〕 lay 〔set〕 a trap 《for》 / 자신이 만든 ～에 빠지다 be caught in *one's* own snare.
◉ ～수사 a sting operation; a criminal investigation using a decoy; entrapment.

**함정**(艦艇) a naval 〔war〕 vessel; warships.

**함종**(艦種) a category 〔class〕 of warships; a warship category 〔class〕.

**함지** ① 《나무 그릇》 a large scooped

wooden bowl. ② 〚광산〛 a pan for gold panning. ③ 《함지박》 a scooped wooden dish.

**함지**(陷地) sunken land; a hollow.

**함진아비**(函—) male friends of the would-be bridegroom carrying a box of presents from the groom to the bride's family on the day before the wedding.

**함체**(艦體) the hull of a warship.

**함축**(含蓄) implication; significance; overtones. ～하다 imply; signify; suggest. ¶ ～성이 있는 significant; meaningful; pregnant with meaning / ～성이 있는 말 a phrase pregnant with 〔hidden〕 meaning; an expression full of overtones / 이 말에 ～되어 있는 뜻을 잘 생각해라 Think carefully about what this expression implies. / 그의 말에는 ～성이 있다 What he says is full of suggestions 〔significance〕.

**함치르르** ⇨ 흠치르르.

**함포**(艦砲) 〚군사〛 the guns of a warship; a naval gun. ◉ ～사격 bombardment from naval guns; shelling from a warship: ～사격을 하다 bombard 《a city》 from 「the sea 〔a warship〕; shell 《a fort》 by war vessels.

**함함하다** (be) soft and gleaming. ¶ 고슴도치도 제 새끼는 ～고 한다 《속담》 Everyman's goose is a gander.

**함형**(艦型) a type of warship.

**함호**(鹹湖) ⇨ 함수호.

**함흥차사**(咸興差使) a messenger sent out on an errand who never returns. ¶ 그는 한번 가더니 ～다 He has gone and never returned.

**합**(合) ① 《합계》 the sum; the total (amount 〔sum〕). ¶ 합해서 in total; in the aggregate; altogether; in all; all told / 합을 구하다 do 〔figure out〕 the sum 《of》 / 2와 2의 합은 4, Two and two make 〔are〕 four. ② 《겨루기의》 a bout. ¶ 20여합을 싸우다 fight more than twenty bouts 《each other》. ③ 〚논리〛 synthesis. ④ 〚천문〛 (astronomical) conjunction; conjuncture.

**합**(盒) a brass bowl with a lid.

**합격**(合格) success in an examination; passing an exam. ～하다 《수험생이》 pass an exam; get through 《a test》; succeed in 《an examination》; 《표준에》 come up to the standard 〔mark〕; stand the test; pass inspection; make the grade 《as》; 《채용에》 be found eligible 〔qualified〕 《for a post》; be accepted. ¶ 전과목에 ～하다 pass every subject / 신체 검사에 갑종으로 ～하다 pass as A on *one's* physical examination / 시험 성적은 나빴지만 그는 간신히 ～했다 He didn't do well in the exam, but he got by. / 대학 ～을 축하한다 Congratulation on passing the college entrance examination.
◉ ～라인 the passing mark 〔grade〕; ～라인에 달하다 make the passing mark. ～률 the ratio of successful applicants; the (examination) pass rate. ～여부 success or failure. ～자 a successful candidate 〔applicant〕. ～점 《물건의》 standard marks; a passing mark; 《사람의》 the qualifying marks 〔score〕. ～증(證) a certificate; 《미》 a credit (어떤 과목의). ～통지 a notice of success. ～품 goods found acceptable; tested goods.

**합계**(合計) the (sum) total; the total amount 〔sum〕; an aggregate 《of》. ～하다 add 〔sum〕 up; add together; total. ¶ ～하여 in total; altogether; in all; all told / ～ …이 되다 total...; add 〔make〕 up to...; make a total of... / ～를 내(보)다 figure out a sum / 비용은 ～해서 3만 원이 되었다 The expenses totaled 〔amounted to, ran up to〕 30,000 won. *or* The expenses reached a total of 30,000 won. / ～가 얼마 나옵니까 What does the total come to?

**합금**(合金) 〚화학〛 an alloy; a compound metal; amalgam (수은과 타금속의). ～하다 alloy 《metals, silver with copper》; make an alloy of 《copper and tin》. ◉ ～강(鋼) alloy(ed) steel.

**합기도**(合氣道) *hapkido,* an art of self=defense (a kind of combined form derived from *judo* and *t'aekwondo*).

**합내**(閤內) an honored family; your family. ◉ ～제절 all your family.

**합당**(合當) fitness; suitability; appropriateness. ～하다 (be) fit; suitable; proper; befitting; adequate; appropriate; reasonable. ¶ ～한 사람 a competent 〔suitable〕 person; a person qualified 《for the task》 / ～한 지위 a suitable position / 그 경우에 ～한 예〔조처〕 an example 〔measures〕 appropriate to the case 〔the occasion〕 / ～한 가격으로 at a reasonable price / ～한 조건으로 on fair 〔reasonable〕 terms / ～하지 않다 be improper 〔unsuitable, inappropriate〕.

**합당**(合黨) a party merger. ～하다 parties merge; merge the parties.

**합동**(合同) (a) combination; (a) union;

《기업·조직 따위의》 amalgamation; merger; 〖수학〗 congruence (도형의). ~하다 join; combine; unite 《in (to) one body, with others》; amalgamate 《with》; merge. ¶ ~의 united; joint (합작); incorporated; 〖수학〗 congruent 《triangles》 / ~하여 in combination; jointly / ~하여 사업을 하다 join (hands) 《with *someone*》 in an enterprise / 우리는 ~해서 사태 수습에 임했다 We made a joint effort to save the situation.

◉ ~결혼(식) a mass 〔group〕 wedding. ~관리〔경영〕 a joint control 〔management〕. ~군사훈련 the 《Korean=U.S.》 joint military exercise. ~사업 a joint undertaking 〔venture〕. ~삼각형 〖수학〗 congruent triangles. ~선거 연설 a joint election campaign. ~연설회 a joint stumping 〔speech〕 rally; a joint session for election speech. ~위령제 a joint service for the 《war》 dead; a joint memorial service. ~위원회 a joint committee 《of both Houses》. ~작전 joint 〔concerted, united, combined〕 operations. ~장(葬) a joint funeral: ~국민장 the joint national funeral service. ~조사반 《수사의》 a joint investigation team. ~회의 a joint session 〔convention, meeting〕.

**합동참모회의**(合同參謀會議) the Conference of the Joint Chiefs of Staff. ¶ ~의장 the Chairman of the Chiefs of Staff; the JCS chairman.

**합력**(合力) 《힘을 합침》 joint efforts; combined strength; working together; cooperation; 〖물리〗 a resultant (force). ~하다 join forces; make a united effort; unite *one's* efforts with; work together; cooperate with.

**합류**(合流) ① 《모임》 (***a***) 《강의》 a confluence; a junction 〔meeting〕 《of two rivers》. ~하다 join; flow 〔run〕 together; flow into each other. ¶ 두 강이 ~하는 곳에 at the junction of two rivers / 그 강은 한강과 ~한다 The river joins the Han river. / 두 개의 강이 이 지점에서 ~한다 Two rivers meet one another at this point. / 강이 어느 지점에서 ~하는가 At what point do the rivers join 〔meet〕? (***b***) 《사람의》 meeting; gathering. ~하다 gather; come together; meet; join. ¶ 우리들은 중도에서 동료 일행과 ~했다 We joined the party on the way.

② 《합동》 joining; linking; union. ~하다 join 《a party》; unite 〔link up〕 《with》; be merged 《into one group》. ¶ 공화당에 ~하다 join the Republican; join forces with the Republican / 운동에 ~하다 join in a movement.

◉ ~점(點) the junction 〔confluence〕 of two rivers; the meeting place 《of two civilization》.

**합리**(合理) rationality; reasonableness. ¶ ~적(인) rational; reasonable; logical / ~적으로 rationally; logically; in a rational manner / 그녀의 사고 방식은 ~적이다 Her way of thinking is logical. ◉ ~론〔주의〕 〖철학〗 rationalism: ~주의자 a rationalist; a practical=minded person; a pragmatist. ~성 rationality.

**합리화**(合理化) rationalization. ~하다 rationalize; make 《it》 more rational 〔reasonable〕. ¶ 경영의 ~ the rationalization of management / 산업의 ~ industrial rationalization / 자기 행위를 ~하다 rationalize *one's* behavior / 경영을 ~하다 streamline the management / 그 TV공장에서는 조립 공정의 ~로 대폭적인 원가 절감을 실현했다 A major cost reduction was realized at the TV plant through rationalization of the assembly process.

**합명회사**(合名會社) an unlimited partnership. ¶ ~한일 상사 Hanil & Co.

**합반**(合班) a combined class. ~하다 combine 《two》 classes. ¶ ~수업 combined classwork 〔teaching〕.

**합방**(合邦) 《병합》 (an) annexation (of a country); 《통합》 unification of 《two》 countries. ~하다 annex; get annexed. ¶ ~되다 be annexed 《to》 / 미국은 텍사스를 1845년에 ~했다 The U.S. annexed Texas in 1845.

**합법**(合法) lawfulness; legality; legitimacy. ¶ ~적(인) lawful; legal; legitimate / ~적 정부 a legitimate government / ~적 투쟁 a law-abiding struggle / 나는 ~적 수단으로 그에게 대항하겠다 I will challenge him by lawful means. / 그 파업은 ~적이다 The strike is legal 〔lawful〕. / 자네가 그렇게 하는 것은 ~적이다 It is lawful for you to do so. / 그 행위가 ~적임은 이론(異論)의 여지가 없다 The legality of the act cannot be disputed. ◉ ~성 lawfulness; legality: 그는 그 절차의 ~성을 문제 삼았다 He questioned the legitimacy of the proceedings. ~주의 legitimacy; legalism.

**합법화**(合法化) legalization. ~하다 legalize. ¶ 주류 판매를 ~하다 legalize the sale of alcoholic drinks.

**합병**(合倂) (a) merger; (a) combination; (an) amalgamation; (a) consolidation. ～하다 merge; combine; consolidate; amalgamate; affiliate.

> 용법 회사·기업의 「합병」이라고 할 때, 가장 일반적으로 쓰이는 영어는 merger이고, 격식을 차린 딱딱한 문맥에서는 amalgamation이 쓰임. amalgamation은 회사·기업의 「합병」 이외의 경우에도 쓰이지만, merger는 「합병」의 경우에만 쓰인다. 여기에서의 「합병」이란 여러 개 회사가 대등한 입장에서 새로운 하나의 회사·기업으로 변신하는 경우이고, 하나의 회사에 다른 회사가 흡수되는 경우는 absorption이 된다.

¶ 인수 ～《기업의》 mergers and acquisitions (생략 M&A) / (큰 것에) ～되다 be merged 〔absorbed〕 into; be affiliated to / A와 B를 ～하다 combine A with B / 단과대학을 종합 대학교에 ～하다 affiliate a college with 〔to〕 a university / H사와 M사는 작년에 ～했다 Company H and Company M merged last year. / A, B 두 회사는 ～하여 C사(社)가 되었다 A and B Companies (were) merged 〔amalgamated〕 to form C Company. / 몇 개의 작은 상사가 ～하여 규모가 큰 조직이 되었다 Some small business firms were merged 〔combined〕 into a large scale organization. / A사는 B사에 (흡수) ～되었다 A Company was merged into B Company. ◉ ～절차〔조건〕 amalgamation procedure 〔condition〕. ～증 『의학』 a complication: ～증이 생기다 develop a complication; a complication arises 〔sets in〕

**합보시기**(盒—) a small bowl with a lid.

**합본**(合本) 《책의》 copies 《of a magazine》 bound together in one volume. ～하다 bind copies together in one volume. ¶ 일년분의 ～ the annual volume 《of a magazine》.

**합사**(合絲) twisting threads together; a twisted 〔plaited〕 thread.

**합사하다**(合祀—) enshrine together; dedicate 《a shrine》 to several deities.

**합삭**(合朔) 『천문』 the conjunction of the moon and the sun.

**합산**(合算) adding up. ～하다 add up 〔together〕; sum (up). ¶ 잡비를 ～하면 총지출은 10만 원 이상이 된다 The total expenditure will amount to over a hundred thousand won when we add up sundries. ◉ ～신고 joint returns. ～액 total (amount).

**합살머리** honeycomb tripe (beef from the reticulum).

**합석**(合席) sitting 〔meeting, consulting〕 together. ～하다 sit 〔meet, consult〕 together; sit with 《*a person*》; sit in company 《with *a person*》. ¶ 식당에서 남과 ～하다 share a table with another at a restaurant / 나도 ～했다 I was among the company.

**합선**(合線) 『전기』 a short (circuit). ～하다 make a short circuit; short-circuit.

**합섬**(合纖) ⇨합성 섬유. ◉ 한일～회사 the Hanil Synthetic Fiber Co.

**합성**(合成) 『물리』 composition 《of forces》; 『화학』 synthesis. ～하다 compose; compound; synthesize. ¶ ～의 compound; synthetic / 석유를 ～하여 고무를 만들다 produce rubber from petroleum by synthesis.
◉ ～고무 synthetic rubber: ～고무 원료 material for synthetic rubber. ～금 an alloy; synthetic gold. ～력 a resultant force. ～물 a compound; a complex; a composite (thing); a synthetic 〔synthesized〕 product: 식염은 나트륨과 염소의 ～물이다 Common salt is a compound of sodium and chlorine. ～물질 a synthetic substance: 현대는 ～물질의 시대이다 This is the age of synthetics. ～분(分) a component (part). ～비료 compound fertilizer. ～사진 a composite photograph 〔picture〕. ～섬유 synthetic 〔chemical〕 fiber. ～세제 a synthetic detergent. ～수 『수학』 a composite number. ～수지 plastics; synthetic resins. ～어 a compound word. ～연료 synfuel. 〔<*synthetic fuel*〕 ～염료(染料) synthetic dyestuff. ～운동 『물리』 resultant motion. ～원유 syncrude. ～유전자 a synthesized gene. ～음 a synthetic sound. ～음성 『컴퓨터』 a synthetic speech. ～음악 synthetic music. ～주(酒) compound 〔synthetic〕 liquor. ～피혁(皮革) synthetic leather. ～화학 synthetic chemistry.

**합세**(合勢) joining forces. ～하다 join forces; form an alliance 《with》. ¶ 반정부 운동에 ～하다 join in the anti-government campaign.

**합수**(合水) a confluence; joining 〔meeting〕 of two streams. ～하다 flow together; join; meet. ¶ 세 강이 이 지점에서 ～한다 Three rivers meet one another at this point.

**합숙**(合宿) ～하다 lodge 〔board〕 together; 《합숙 훈련의》 stay together in a camp 《for training》. ¶ (선수가) ～ 중에 있다 stay in a training camp / 야구부는 제주도에서 1주간 ～한다 The baseball club will have 〔hold〕 a training camp on Cheju island for a week. ◉ ～소 a boarding 〔lodging〕 house; 《운동 선수의》 a training camp. ～훈련 camp training: ～ 훈련을 하다 live together in a training camp.

**합승**(合乘) riding together; sharing a vehicle; 《차》 a jitney (cab) 《속어》; an omnibus. ～하다 ride together; share the car 《with》; ride 〔go 《to a place》〕 in the same car 《with *a person*》. ¶ 택시를 ～하다 share a taxi 《with *a person*》. ◉ ～객 a fellow passenger.

**합심**(合心) unison; accord; concert. ～하다 be united; be of one accord 〔one mind〕. ¶ ～하여 with one accord / 서로 ～해서 하자 Let's work in unison.

**합의**(合意) (mutual) agreement; mutual 〔common〕 consent. ～하다 agree; consent; come to 〔reach〕 an agreement; be agreed 〔accorded〕. ¶ 국민의 〔보편적인〕 ～ a national 〔general〕 consensus / 쌍방의 ～ 아래 by mutual consent; under a mutual agreement / ～ 아래 별거하다 live apart by mutual consent / 양자는 ～에 이르렀다 The two sides「came to 〔arrived at, reached〕 an agreement. *or* An agreement was reached between the two. ◉ ～문서 a written agreement; a statement of mutual agreement. ～이혼 a divorce by mutual agreement.

**합의**(合議) consultation; conference; counsel. ～하다 consult together 《about》; confer 《with》; hold a conference; go into counsel; talk over 《*a matter*》 together. ¶ ～에 따라 after consultation; by mutual consent. ◉ ～사항 items of understanding. ～재판 a collegiate judgment. ～제(制) a representative 〔parliamentary, council〕 system: ～제 법원 a collegiate court.

**합일**(合一) union; unity; oneness. ～하다 unite; consolidate; get 〔be〕 united.

**합자**(合字) a ligature; a double letter.

**합자**(合資) joint stock; partnership. ～하다 join 《stock》; enter into partnership 《with》; unite in a joint-stock company. ◉ ～회사 a joint-stock company; a limited partnership: Y ～회사 Y & Co., Ltd.

**합작**(合作) collaboration; joint work (작품의). ～하다 collaborate 〔cooperate〕 《with *a person* on *a thing*》; team up 《with》; 《저술을》 write 《a book》 jointly 《with *a person*》; coauthor 《a book》. ¶ 그 영화는 그들 부자의 ～이다 He collaborated with his father on the movie. ◉ ～물 a joint work 〔production〕. ～자 a collaborator; 《저술의》 a joint author; a coauthor. ～투자 joint venture: ～투자 회사 a joint-venture company. ～회사 a joint corporation. 영불 ～영화 a British-French joint-product film.

**합장**(合掌) ～하다 join *one's* hands 〔press *one's* hands together〕 in prayer. ¶ ～을 하고 with *one's* hands clasped in prayer. ◉ ～배례(拜禮) worshipping with the palms of the hands together.

**합장**(合葬) burying 〔inter〕 together. ～하다 bury together. ¶ 부부를 ～하다 bury the wife together with her husband.

**합재떨이**(盒―) an ashtray with a lid.

**합제**(合劑) a medical mixture; a compound.

**합주**(合酒) home-brewed alcoholic liquor (made from glutinous rice and used as a summer drink).

**합주**(合奏) 〚음악〛 a concert; an *ensemble* (F.). ～하다 play in concert. ¶ 2〔3, 4, 5〕부 ～ a duet 〔trio, quartet, quintet〕. ◉ ～곡 an *ensemble* (piece). ～단 a (musical) *ensemble;* a concert group.

**합죽거리다** mumble with (a toothless mouth); keep mumbling with *one's* toothless mouth.

**합죽선**(合竹扇) a folding fan (with spokes made of double slips of bamboo).

**합죽이** a toothless person (with pursed lips).

**합죽하다** (be) toothless and puckered.

**합죽할미** a toothless old woman.

**합죽합죽** mumbling; toothlessly mouthing.

**합중국**(合衆國) a federation; a federal 〔united〕 states. ◉ 아메리카〔미〕～ the United States (of America).

**합지**(合紙) pasteboard.

**합참**(合參) ⇨ 합동 참모 회의.

**합창**(合唱) a chorus. ～하다 sing together 〔in chorus〕; chant in unison (불경 따위를). ¶ 남성〔여성〕～ a men's 〔women's〕 chorus / 혼성 ～ a mixed chorus / 2〔3, 4〕부 ～ a duet 〔trio, quartet〕. ◉ ～곡 a chorus; a choral; a part-song. ～대〔단〕 a chorus; 《교회의》 a choir: ～대〔단〕원 a chorus

〔choir〕 member; a chorus「boy 〔girl〕; a chorist; a choir singer / ～대장 a chorus master. ～자 a chorist; a chorister. 국립～단 the National Chorus. 빈 소년 ～단 the Vienna Boys' Choir.

**합창**(合瘡) healing up 《of a boil》. ～하다 《a boil》 heal up.

**합체**(合體) union; incorporation, combination. ～하다 unite 〔be united〕 《with》; combine 〔be combined〕 (into one); be incorporated 《into a larger town》.

**합치**(合致) agreement; concurrence. ⇨ 일치. ～하다 coincide; agree 〔accord〕 with. ¶ 우리의 희망에 ～하는 제안 the offer which wholly「gratifies 〔meets with〕 our wishes.

**합치다**(合—) ① 《하나로》 join (together) 《into one》; combine 《with》; unite; merge; meet; put 〔bring〕 together. ¶ 두 반을 ～ combine two classes / 합쳐서 하나로 되다 be「united 〔merged〕 into one / 방 셋을 합쳐서 하나로 하다 throw 〔knock〕 three rooms into one / 세 회사를 하나로 ～ merge three companies into one / 종이를 두 장 ～ put two sheets of paper together / 각 파벌을 합쳐서 하나의 당(黨)으로 하다 combine the factions into a party / 두 개의 길은 거기서 합친다 The two roads「join 〔meet〕 there. / 힘을 합쳐 일하자 Let us unite our efforts. / 그들은 힘을 합쳐서 일했다 They worked「together 〔with combined efforts〕. / 그 나라는 독일과 프랑스를 합친 것만큼 크다 The country is as large as Germany and France put together.
② 《한데 섞다》 mix; admix; compound; combine; put together. ¶ 물과 술을 ～ mix liquor with water / 큰것 작은 것을 한데 합쳐서 팔다 sell big ones and small ones all mixed together.
③ 《셈을》 add up; sum up; total; 《이것 저것》 put together. ¶ 모두 합쳐서 taking all together; in all; all told; altogether / 3과 5를 ～ add three to five / 그것은 둘을 합친 것보다 무겁다 It is heavier than two put together.

**합판**(合版) joint publication. ～하다 publish jointly.

**합판**(合板) a sheet of plywood; a plywood board; a veneer board; plywood [총칭]. ◉ 프린트 ～ printed plywood.

**합판**(合辦) joint management. ⇨ 합작. ¶ ～의 joint. ◉ ～사업 joint venture 〔project〕.

**합판화**(合瓣花) 〖식물〗 a「compound 〔gamopetalous〕 flower.

**합평**(合評) a joint「review 〔cirticism〕. ～하다 jointly criticize. ◉ ～회 a meeting for joint criticism.

**합하다**(合—) ① 《합치다》 put 〔bring〕 together; unite. ¶ 힘을 ～ cooperate; join「forces 〔hands〕 / 힘을 합해서 어려움을 이겨내자 Let's join forces to overcome the difficulties. ② 《합쳐지다》 be united; be made into one; be「put 〔joined〕 together; be combined. ③ 《만나다》 meet; join; gather; come together. ④ 《합당하다》 fit; suit; 《의견이》 agree; harmonize with; be in tune with.

**합헌**(合憲) ¶ ～의, ～적인 constitutional. ◉ ～성 constitutionality.

**합환주**(合歡酒) the drink by which the bride and bridegroom pledge their troth; the wedding drink. ¶ ～를 나누다 exchange nuptial cups.

**핫-** ① 《솜을 둔》 padded with cotton wool. ¶ 핫두루마기 an outer-coat padded with cotton / 핫이불 cotton-padded bedclothes. ② 《배우자를 가진》 having a spouse. ¶ 핫아비 a man with a wife / 핫어미 a woman with a husband.

**핫것** cotton-padded「clothes 〔bedding〕.

**핫길**(下—) the lowest grade; the「poorest 〔most inferior〕 stuff; a low-grade article; (an article of ) inferior quality.

**핫뉴스** hot news.

**핫도그** a hot dog 《미》.

**핫라인** a hot line. ¶ 나는 대통령과 ～으로 연결되어 있다 I have a hot line to the President. *or* I have hot-line access to the President.

**핫머니** 〖경제〗 《고금리 단기 자금》 hot money.

**핫바지** ① 《솜바지》 (a pair of ) cotton-padded trousers. ② 《촌뜨기》 a bumpkin; 《바보》 an ignorant fool.

**핫워** hot war.

**핫케이크** a hot cake; a pancake; a griddlecake.

**핫퉁이** ① 《통통한》 clothes padded thick with cotton wool. ② 《철지난》 cotton-padded clothes worn out of season.

**항**(項) ① 《항목·조항》 a clause; a paragraph; an item (예산표 따위의). ¶ 항(項)으로 가르다 paragraph; itemize / 제1조 제2항에 해당되다 come under「Clause 2, Article 1 〔Subsection 2, Section 1〕. ② 《수학의》 a term. ¶ 방정식의 1항 a「term 〔member〕 of an equation / 2〔3, 다(多)〕～식 a「binomial 〔trinomial, polynomial〕 expression.

**-항**(港) a port; a harbor.

> 용법 **port**는 항구와 그 도시를 포함한 「항구」의 뜻. **harbor**는 부두 시설을 갖춘 항구 그 자체만을 가리키며, 비유적으로 「피난처」의 뜻으로도 쓰임.

¶ 부산항 Pusan harbor; the port of Pusan / 자유항 a free port.

**항간**(巷間) 《on》 the street; 《about》 the town. ¶ ~에 떠도는 얘기 a topic widely talked about; the talk of the town / ~에 떠도는 이야기〔소문〕에 의하면 a rumor has it that…; according to what people say; it is rumored (in the town) that… / ~에 소문이 돌다 a rumor is going around town.

**항거**(抗拒) resistance. ~하다 resist 《to》; defy; disobey; oppose; rebel 〔revolt〕 《against》. ¶ 독재 정치에 ~하다 resist 〔rise against〕 dictatorial governement / 권위에 ~하다 revolt against authority / 여론에 ~하다 defy 〔challenge〕 public opinion / 완강히 ~하다 make a strong stand 《against》; offer (a) stubborn 〔tenacious〕 resistance 《to》. ◉ ~죄 an offense of resisting lawful order.

**항고**(抗告) 〖법〗 a complaint; an appeal; a protest. ~하다 complain 《against a decision》; appeal 《from a decision》; file a protest 《against》. ¶ 피고는 그 판결에 대해 즉시 ~했다 The defendant made an immediate appeal against the sentence. ◉ ~기간 the term for complaint. ~심(審) hearing of complaint. ~인 a complainer. ~장(狀) a bill of complaint. ~재판 an appeal trial. 즉시~ 《lodge, make》 an immediate complaint 〔appeal〕 《against》.

**항공**(航空) aviation; flying; 《항공회사》 airline, air; airway 《영》. ¶ ~의 aeronautic; aerial / 민간~ civil aviation / 국제〔국내〕~ international 〔domestic〕 aviation / 대한 ~ Korean Air / 영국 ~ British Airways.

◉ ~가 an airman; an aviator; a birdman; 《여자》 an aviatress; an aviatrix. ~계 the aerial world; aviation circles. ~계기 aeronautical 〔aircraft〕 instruments. ~공학 aeronautical engineering. ~(교통)관제 air-traffic control (생략 A.T.C.): ~관제관 an air-traffic controller / ~관제탑 a control tower. ~권 an airline ticket. ~기록기 a flight recorder. ~기사 an aeronautical engineer. ~기상학 aeronautical meteorology; aerology. ~기지 an air base. ~대 the air force; a flying 〔an air, an aviation〕 corps. ~등 a navigation light. ~등대 an aerial beacon 〔lighthouse〕. ~로 an airline 〔air route〕; an airway; an air lane; a skyway 《미》: ~로를 열다 establish 〔open〕 an air route 〔line〕. ~모함 an aircraft carrier; a flattop 《미구어》. ~물리학 aerophysics. ~방위 구상 〖군사〗 (the) Air Defence Initiative (생략 ADI). ~병(兵) an airman. ~병(病) aviation sickness. ~보험 flight 〔aerial, aviation〕 insurance. ~복 aviation garment. ~ 봉함엽서 an aerogramme. ~부대 an air force 〔corps〕. ~사 an aerial navigator. ~사업 air transportation business; air service. ~사진 an air 〔aerial〕 photograph: ~사진술 aerophotography. ~수송 air transportation; air service; an airlift: ~수송 화물 airborn 〔airlift〕 goods; an air freight 〔cargo〕 / 국내 ~수송 internal 〔domestic〕 air transportation. ~술 aeronautics; airmanship; aviation. ~시대 the air age. ~시설 air service; airline facilities. ~심리학 aviation psychology. ~역학 aeromechanics; flight dynamics. ~연구소 an aeronautical research institute. ~요금〔운임〕 an air fare. ~우편 airmail; airpost 《영》: ~우편물 airmail matter / ~등기 우편 registered airmail / ~우편으로 편지를 보내다 send a letter 《to L.A.》 by airmail; airmail a letter. ~우표 an airmail stamp. ~의학 aeromedicine; aeronautic medicine. ~일지 an air log(book). ~전자공학 avionics. ~조약 an air treaty. ~중대 an air squadron. ~중이염 〖의학〗 aerootitis media; the aviator's ear. ~지도 an airmap; an aerial chart. ~지원 an air cover. ~측량 an aerial survey. ~통신위성 an aerial communications satellite. ~편 《send a letter by》 airmail. ~학 aeronautics. ~학교 an aviation school. ~학회 a society for aeronautical and space science. ~협정 an aviation accord; an air agreement. ~화물 an air cargo. ~회사 an airline (company); an aviation company. (★ 회사명으로는 … Airlines 또는 … Airways라고 하는 경우가 많음).

국제 민간~기구 the International Civil Aviation Organization. 내(耐)~성 airworthiness. 민간~규제 the Civil Air Regulation. 한국~대학 the Hanguk Aviation College.

**항공기**(航空機) a flying machine; an aeroplane; an airplane; a plane; aircraft [총칭] ⇨ 비행기. ¶ ～ 사고 a plane accident / ～ 운항 안전법 the Law on Aircraft Safety / ～ 연료 aircraft fuel / ～ 납치 an aircraft hijack. ◉ ～대피소 an aircraft shelter. ～산업 (an) aircraft (manufacturing) industry. ～승무원 an aircrew; a flight crew; an aircrewman. ～정비사 an aircraft maintenance person. ～조종사 a pilot: ～부조종사 a copilot. ～조종술 (aircraft) pilotage; airmanship.

**항공우주국**(航空宇宙局) 《미국의》 the National Aeronautics and Space Administration (생략 NASA).

**항공우주산업**(航空宇宙産業) the aerospace industry.

**항공표지**(航空標識) a radio [an aerial, an air(way)] beacon. ◉ ～소 an aeronautical radio beacon station; a radio beacon 《미》.

**항구**(恒久) permanency; perpetuity; eternity. ～하다 (be) permanent; perpetual; lasting; eternal. ¶ ～적(인) permanent 《measures》; perpetual; (ever)lasting; eternal / ～적 평화 《establish》 permanent peace. ◉ ～성 permanency; imperishability 《of the universe》. ～화 perpetuation: ～화하다 perpetuate 《the world's peace》.

**항구**(港口) a port; a harbor. ¶ ～를 떠나다 clear a port; leave (a) port; sail from a port / ～에 들어가다 enter [make] (a) port; come [put, get] into port / ～에 있는 배 vessels in port / ～에 도착하다 reach port; enter in harbor / ～에 들르다 call [touch] at a port / ～에 들르지 않다 make no port. ◉ ～도시 a port city [town].

**항균성**(抗菌性) antibiosis. ¶ ～의 antibiotic; antibacterial. ◉ ～물질 antibiotics.

**항내**(港內) (the inside of) a harbor. ¶ ～에 within [in] the harbor; in port / ～가 깊어서 큰 배도 정박할 수 있다 The deep harbor affords an excellent anchorage for big ships. ◉ ～설비 harbor [port] facilities.

**항다반사**(恒茶飯事) a common [an every-day, a run-of-the-mill] occurrence [event, affair].

**항도**(港都) a port (town).

**항독성**(抗毒性) ¶ ～의 antitoxic.

**항독소**(抗毒素) 〖의학〗 an antitoxin; an antivenom. ¶ ～를 주사하다 inject an antitoxin (serum). ◉ ～요법 antitoxin treatment.

**항등식**(恒等式) 〖수학〗 an identical equation; an identity.

**항라**(亢羅) a kind of silk gauze; sheer silk. ◉ 저(紵)～ sheer cambric.

**항렬**(行列) 《혈족간의》 degree [distance] of kin relationship. ¶ 같은 ～이다 be a collateral relative; be in the same generation of the clan. ◉ ～자(字) a generation character; *one's* generation name.

**항례**(恒例) = 상례(常例).

**항로**(航路) a sea [sailing] route; a course; a sea lane; 《정기편의》 a line; a service; 《항공로》 an air [aerial] route [line]; an airway. ¶ 정기～ a regular line [service] / 부산 홍콩～ the Pusan Hongkong run / 유럽～의 배 a European liner; a ship on the European line [run, service] / ～를 바꾸다 change *one's* course / ～를 열다 launch [open, inaugurate] a regular service 《between two ports》 / ～를 정하다[잡다] lay a course; shape *one's* course / ～를 잘못 잡다 take a wrong course; mistake *one's* course / ～를 남쪽으로 잡다 steer south. ◉ ～도 a track chart. ～변경 a shift in course (with the same destination). ～부표 a fairway buoy. ～신호 a marine signal; plying signals. ～이탈 《항공기의》 deviation from the 《international》 flight route: ～ 이탈을 하다 veer off course. ～표지 a beacon; a channel mark; a seamark. 국내[국제]～ a domestic [an international] line [course]: 국내 ～선(船) a steamer on the domestic line. 안전～ a fairway. 외국～ an ocean lane [route, service]: 외국 ～선(船) an ocean liner. 유럽～ a European (steamship) line [service, run]: 유럽 ～에 취항시키다 put 《a ship》 on the European service. 자유～ free service. 정기[부정기]～ a regular [an irregular] service [line].

**항론**(抗論) refutation; contradiction; confutation. ～하다 refute 《an argument》; confute.

**항만**(港灣) harbors. ◉ ～개량 harbor improvement. ～검역소 a quarantine station in port. ～공사 harbor construction work. ～노동자 a dock worker; a stevedore (하역인); a longshoreman 《미》; a docker 《영》. ～사업 harbor works. ～시설 port [harbor] facilities. ～운송 transportation service in harbors; harbor express service. ～하역(荷役) harbor loading and unloading. 국제～협회 the International Association of Ports and Harbors (생략 IAPH).

**항명**(抗命) disobedience; insubordination. ～하다 disobey 《*a person's*》 order. ¶ 국무총리는 교육부에서 ～행위를 주도한 사람들에 대해 엄벌을 내리라고 지시했다 The prime minster ordered strict disciplinary action against those who led an insubordination at the Education Ministry. ◉ ～죄 mutiny: 하극상의 장교를 ～죄로 다스리다 discipline a 「mutinous 〔rebellious〕 officer for disobedient conduct.

**항목**(項目) an item; a point; a head; a heading; 《조항》 a clause; a provision. ¶ 9개 ～의 요구 a nine-point demand / ～으로 나누다 itemize / 문제를 3개 ～으로 나누다 devide the problem under three headings / 카탈로그의 ～에 번호를 매기다 number the items in a catalogue / 문제를 ～별로 검토하다 examine the problems item by item / 그것은 이 ～에 들어간다 It belongs 「in 〔to〕 this category. *or* It comes under this heading. ◉ ～별 표 an itemized list 《of》. ～화 itemization; specification.

**항무**(港務) harbor affairs; port business; harbor 〔port〕 service.

**항문**(肛門) 『해부』 the anus; the fundament; 《동물의》 the vent; 《완곡한 표현》 the back passage. ¶ ～의 anal 《disease》. ◉ ～경(鏡) an anoscope; a proctoscope. ～과 proctology: ～과 의사 a proctologist / ～과 병원 an anal disease hospital. ～괄약근(括約筋) the anal sphincters. ～병 an 「anal 〔rectal〕 disease; piles. ～부 the anal region. ～주위염 inflammation of the anus; periproctitis.

**항법**(航法) navigation. ¶ 계기(에 의한) ～ instrumental navigation / 천문(에 의한) ～ celestial navigation. ◉ ～사(士) a navigator. 극지～ polar navigation.

**항변**(抗辯) 《반박》 a protest; 『법』 (a) refutation; confutation; 《피고의》 a plea; (a) defense. ～하다 《반론하다》 protest; refute 《the accusation》; 《피고가》 make a plea; defend *oneself;* 《항의하다》 file a protest 《with *a person,* against》. ¶ 사실 부인의 ～ a plea of the general issue / 상관에게 ～하다 remonstrate with *one's* superior / 소송에 ～하지 않기로 했다 We have decided to file no answer to the suit. ◉ 방소(妨訴)～ a plea in abatement.

**항병**(降兵) a surrendered soldier.

**항복**(降伏) (a) surrender; capitulation. ～하다 surrender 《to》; capitulate 《to the enemy》; give in 《to *one's* rival》; hang out the white flag. ¶ ～의 제의 offer to surrender / ～을 권하다 invite 〔call on〕 《the enemy》 to surrender; summon 〔urge〕 《the enemy》 to surrender / …라는 조건으로 ～하다 capitulate under the condition that… / ～시키다 make 《the enemy》 surrender; bring 《*a person*》 to *his* knees / 「～이다」고 하다 《상대에게》 admit (*one's*) defeat; cry uncle 《미구어》 / 너에겐 ～이다 I give in to you. / 자, ～해라 Give up. ◉ ～권고(서) a summons to surrender. ～기 a white flag; a flag of surrender. ～문서 an instrument of surrender. ～조건 terms of capitulation: ～조건을 정하다 capitulate. 무조건〔조건부〕～ 「an unconditional 〔a conditional〕 surrender: 무조건 ～을 요구하다 demand an unconditional surrender / 무조건 ～하다 surrender unconditionally; surrender at discretion.

**항산**(恒産) 《일정한 재산》 fixed property; 《일정한 생업》 fixed occupation. ¶ ～이 있는 사람 a person of fixed property; a man of property / ～이 없으면 항심(恒心)도 없는 법이다 A real property, a real purpose. *or* Competency is for constancy of mind.

**항산성**(抗酸性) ¶ ～의 acid-fast〔-proof〕. ◉ ～균 an acid-fast bacterium (*pl.* -ria).

**항상**(恒常) always; at all times; all the time; constantly; 《보통》 as a rule (대개); ordinarily; usually; 《상습적으로》 habitually; customarily. ¶ 아침이면 ～ 산책을 나가다 be in the habit of going for a walk in the morning / 그는 ～ 그렇게 말을 했다 He used to say so. / 나는 ～ 다섯시면 일어나기로 하고 있다 I make it a 「rule 〔point〕 to get up at five. / 그는 ～ 부모에게 걱정만 끼친다 He is a constant source of anxiety to his parents. / 우리들은 ～ 만일의 경우에 대비하고 있어야 한다 We must always be prepared for the worst. ◉ ～성 『생리』 homeostasis.

**항생**(抗生) 『식물』 《균류의》 antibiosis. ¶ ～의 antibiotic / 제4세대 ～제 the 4th-generation antibiotic; a fourth-generation of antibiotic. ◉ ～물질 an antibiotic (substance): ～물질학 antibiotics. ～학 antibiotics (★ 단수 취급).

**항서**(降書) 《서신》 a capitulatory letter; 《문서》 a written surrender.

**항설**(巷說) gossip 〔(a) rumor〕 in the streets; a town talk; a talk of the town; a hearsay. ¶ ～에 의하면 a rumor has it that… / ～이 분분하다 Wild rumors are in circulation.

**항성**(恒性) constancy; permanency. ¶ ～의 constant.

**항성**(恒星) 〚천문〛 a fixed 〔permanent〕 star; a sun. ¶ ～의 sidereal. ◉ ～시〔일, 년〕 sidereal time 〔day, year〕. ～주기 a sidereal revolution. 「세.

**항세**(港稅) port 〔harbor〕 dues. ⇨ 입항

**항소**(抗訴) 〚법〛 an appeal 《to a higher court》; an intermediate appeal. ～하다 appeal 《against a decision, from a lower to a higher court》; bring an appeal 《in a higher court》; enter 〔lodge, file〕 an intermediate appeal 《against》. ¶ ～를 기각하다 dismiss 〔turn down〕 an appeal / ～를 철회하다 withdraw an appeal / 판결에 불복하여 ～하다 appeal against the decision / 그는 서울 고등 법원에 ～했다 He appealed to the Seoul High 〔Appellate〕 Court. ◉ ～권 the right of appeal. ～기각 the dismissal of an appeal. ～법원 a court of appeal(s); an appellate court. ～심 a hearing of an appeal; a trial on an appeal case. ～이유 the grounds of an appeal. ～인 an appellant. ～장 a petition of appeal. ～(제기)기간 the time for appeal; the term allowed for appeal.

**항속**(航續) 《배의》 cruising; 《항공기의》 flight. ¶ 이 비행기는 ～ 10시간이 됐다 This plane remained in the air for 10 hours. ◉ ～거리 a (flying 〔cruising〕) range 〔radius〕 《of 1,800 km》: 이 비행기는 ～거리가 길다 This plane has a long range. ～력 a cruising 〔flying〕 power 〔capacity〕. ～시간 the duration of a cruise 〔flight〕; endurance: ～시간 기록 an endurance record. 「les.

**항쇄족쇄**(項鎖足鎖) a pillory and shack-

**항습**(恒習) a usual 〔regular, steady, customary〕 habit.

**항시**(恒時) always. = 항상(恒常).

**항심**(恒心) a constant 〔steady〕 mind; constancy; steadiness.

**항아리**(缸―) a jar; a pot. ◉ ～손님 〚한의〛 parotitis; mumps (★ 단수 취급). 꿀～ a honey jar. 물～ a water jar.

**항암**(抗癌) ¶ ～의 anticancer. ◉ ～제 an anticancer medicine 〔drug〕; a cancer-inhibiting drug.

**항언**(抗言) protestation; a protest; a retort. ～하다 protest; make a protest.

**항오**(行伍) the ranks; the files; an array; a formation. ¶ ～ 정연하다 be in regular rank; be in perfect order / ～를 흩뜨리다 break the line 〔ranks, column〕.

**항외**(港外) ¶ ～의〔에(서)〕 outside the port 〔harbor〕 / ～에 정박하다 lie at anchor off the harbor / 배가 ～로 나오다 sail out of a harbor. ◉ ～정박지 a roadstead.

**항용**(恒用) ① 《보통임·흔함》 (being) ordinary; ordinariness; a commonplace; [부사적] usually; commonly. ¶ ～ 있는 일 a common 〔an everyday〕 affair / 학생에게 ～ 있는 일로서 as is usual 〔often the case〕 with students; as students will. ② 《항상》 always; at all times; constantly.

**항원**(抗元·抗原) 〚의학〛 an antigen.

**항의**(抗議) protestation; a protest; a remonstrance (가벼운); an objection (반대); an exception (이의); a complaint; 〚법〛 a demur. ～하다 protest 〔make a protest〕 《to *a person* against》; offer 〔raise〕 an objection 《to》; object 《to》; take exception 《to》; complain.

> **용법** 「…에 반대하여 항의하다」는 protest against 《the war》가 《미》·《영》에서 쓰이는 일반적 형태지만, 《미》에서는 protest 《the war》도 흔히 쓰임.

¶ ～를 제기하다 make 〔lodge, enter〕 a protest 《with *a person* against *something*》 / 그들은 무기 사용에 대하여 그에게 강력히 ～하였다 They made a strong protest to him against the use of arms. (★ protest에 against를 붙이지 않고 다음처럼 쓰면 「주장하다」란 뜻도 됨: He protested the boy's innocence. (그는 소년의 무죄를 주장했다)) / 우리는 심판의 판정에 ～했다 We lodged a protest against the referee's decision. / 그들은 발전소 건설에 ～하고 있다 They are protesting against the building of the power plant.

◉ ～데모 《stage》 a protest demonstration 〔march, parade〕. ～서〔문〕 a (written) protest; a note of protest: ～문을 전달하다 hand a protest note 《to》. ～운동 a protest movement. ～집회 a protest meeting 〔rally〕. ～파업 a protest strike 《against》. 엄중～ a strong protest: 엄중～를 제기하다 lodge a strong 〔stiff〕 ptotest 《with the government against…》. 집단~ a mass protest.

**항일**(抗日) anti-Japan; resistance to Japan; [형용사적] anti-Japanese. ◉ ~사상 anti-Japanese sentiments. ~운동 a resist-Japanese movement. ~투쟁 an anti-Japanese struggle.

**항쟁**(抗爭) (a) contention《with each other, for power》; contending; (a) dispute; strife; 《투쟁》(a) struggle; 《저항》 resistance. ~하다 contend 〔strive〕《with, for, against》; dispute 《against *a person*, with》; resist; struggle《with, against》; 《저항하다》 resist; offer resistance.

**항적**(航跡) a wake (behind a sailing ship); a furrow; a track; 〖항공〗 a flight path; 《비행운》 a vapor trail; a condensation trail; a contrail. ¶ ~을 남기다 leave a wake / 다른 배의 ~을 따라가다 steer in the wake of another vessel. ◉ ~도 a track chart.

**항전**(抗戰) fighting《against》; (armed) resistance. ~하다 fight《against》; resist; offer 〔make, put up〕 armed resistance《to, against》. ¶ 필사적으로 ~하다 make 〔offer〕 a do-or-die resistance. ◉ ~력 power of resistance. 대게릴러~ resistance to guerrilla.

**항정**《개·돼지의 목덜미》 the back neck of a dog 〔pig〕; 《쇠고기》 chuck beef.

**항정**(航程) ① 《배의》 the run 〔passage〕 (of a ship); the distance covered (by a ship); 《항해》 a sail; a voyage. ¶ 하루의~ a day's sail《from, between》. ② 《항공기의》 a flight; a lap; a leg (장거리 여행의 1행정). ¶ 전~을 날다 fly 〔cover〕 the whole distance / 비행기는 그곳에서 목적지까지의 최후 ~에 들어갔다 The plane set out on its last leg from there. ◉ ~지시기 a distance recorder. ~표《비행기의》 a logbook.

**항주**(航走) sailing; steaming; run. ~하다 sail; steam; run. ¶ 25 노트의 속력으로 ~하다 run at (a speed of) twenty=five knots. ◉ ~속도 curising speed. 수면~ a surface run.

**항진**(亢進) (a) rise; (an) acceleration; 〖의학〗 exasperation. ~하다 rise; accelerate; exasperate; 《병세의》 grow worse. ¶ 심계(心悸)~ 〖의학〗 palpitation; heart acceleration.

**항진**(航進) sailing; steaming. ~하다 sail; steam; proceed. ¶ 그 배는 30 노트로 ~할 수 있다 The ship can sail 30 knots an hour.

**항차** 《긍정》 much 〔still〕 more; 《부정》 much 〔still〕 less. ⇨ 황차, 하물며.

**항체**(抗體) 〖생리〗 an antibody.

**항풍**(恒風) a constant wind.

**항해**(航海) navigation; a (sea) voyage; (a) sailing; 《순항》 a cruise. ~하다 《배·사람이》 sail; navigate; make a voyage《over, to》; 《사람이》 take (a) passage《on (board) the Queen Elizabeth》; 《순항하다》 cruise. ¶ ~길에 오르다 《사람이》 start 〔go〕 on a 《first》 voyage; 《사람·배가》 set sail; 《배가》 put out to sea / ~에 견디다〔견디지 못하다〕 《배가》 be seaworthy 〔unseaworthy〕; 《사람이》 be a good 〔bad〕 sailor / ~중이다 《사람이》 be on a voyage; 《사람·배가》 be (out) at sea / ~중에 during the voyage / ~ 중인 배 a ship at sea / ~ 중의 무사를 빌다 wish 《*a person*》 *bon voyage* 〔a pleasant trip, a safe voyage〕 / ~ 중에 병이 나다 fall ill while on a voyage 〔at sea, aboard a liner〕 / ~를 계속하다 《사람이》 continue the voyage; 《배가》 keep the sea; hold on her course / 시험 ~에 나서다 sail on a sea trial / 유쾌한 ~를 하다 enjoy a pleasant sea trip 〔voyage〕 / 태평양을 ~하다 sail the Pacific / 그는 지금 ~ 중에 있다 He is now 「on a voyage 〔at sea〕. / 대단히 평온한 ~였다 We had a very smooth 〔calm〕 passage. / 그는 내년 세계 일주 ~에 나선다 He is going to start 〔set out〕 on a voyage around the world next year. ◉ ~계기 a nautical instrument. ~권 the right of navigation. ~근무 sea service; service afloat. ~도 a (navigator's) chart. ~등 a navigation light. ~사 a mate; a navigation officer: 1등 ~사 the chief 〔first〕 mate 〔officer〕 / 2〔3〕 등 ~사 the second 〔third〕 mate. ~상태 service condition. ~성능 sea going qualities. ~속도 sea 〔service〕 speed. ~수당 a sea allowance. ~술 (the art of) navigation; seamanship. ~용선(傭船) a voyage charter; a trip charter. ~위성 a navigation satellite. ~자 a mariner; a seaman; a navigator. ~장 a navigating officer. ~적성 검사 〖항해〗 《배의》 a test of seaworthiness. 연습~ a training voyage.

**항해일지**(航海日誌) a (voyage) log; a logbook; a ship's journal 〔log〕. ¶ ~를 쓰다 keep a logbook / ~에 써넣다 enter 《events》 in a logbook; log 《the miles run》.

**항행**(航行) navigation; sailing; cruising; a cruise. (⇨ 항해). ~하다 navigate;

sail; cruise; steam. ¶ ～의 자유 freedom of navigation 〔passage〕/ ～이 가능한〔불가능한〕 강 a navigable 〔an unnavigable〕 river / ～중인 선박 a steamer 〔ship〕 under way / 공해에서 ～의 자유를 인정하다 recognize freedom of navigation on the 「high seas 〔open sea〕/ 해안을 따라 ～하다 follow the shoreline. ◉ ～구역 a navigation area. ～권 the right of navigation.

**항혈청**(抗血淸) an antiserum (*pl.* ～s, 「-ra).

**항히스타민제**(抗一劑) an antihistaminic agent 〔medicine〕; an antihistamine.

**해**[1] ①《태양》 the sun; 《일광》 sunlight. ⇨햇볕. ¶ 해가 지기〔저물기〕 전에 before the sun sets; before (it gets) dark; while it is still light / 해를 향해〔등지고〕 heliotropically 〔apheliotropically〕/ 해가 뜨다〔돋다〕 the sun rises 〔comes up, goes up〕/ 해가 지다 the sun sets 〔goes down, sinks〕/ 해가 저물다 night falls; it gets dark / 해가 저문 뒤에 after dark; with the sun down / 해가 저물 때 돌아오다 return at sunset / 해가 구름에 가리우다 the sun is clouded over / 해가 중천에 떠 있다 The sun is high. / 해는 동쪽에서 떠서 서쪽으로 진다 The sun rises in the east and sets in the west. / 해는 지고 갈 길은 멀다 The night is falling, and the way is long.
② 《낮》 daytime (when the sun is up). ¶ 하루 해를 보내다 pass 〔send〕 a day / 해가 짧다 the daytime is short / 해가 짧아지다 the days grow shorter / 해가 길어지다 the days grow longer; the days are getting longer.

**해**[2] ① 《년》 a year. ¶ 올해 this year / 지난 해 last year / 여덟 해 eight years / 해마다 every year; year after year / 해가 지남에 따라 as (the) years go 〔pass〕 by; with each year that goes by; with (the passing of) the years / 해가 가기〔해를 넘기기〕 전에 before the year is out; within the year / 해마다 한 번 once a 〔every〕 year / 해를 넘기다 enter a new year; 《식물 따위가》 keep over the winter / 새해를 맞이하다 welcome 〔greet, hail〕 the New Year / (묵은) 해를 보내다 see the old year out; ring out the old year / 해가 다 가다 be at the end of the year / 해가 바뀌다 the year changes; the New Year comes round. ② [접두어] of the current year; new; fresh. ¶ 해콩 ⇨햇콩.

**해**[3] 《웃는 모양》 with a light giggle; tee=hee! ¶ 해 웃다 give a light giggle.

**해**(亥) 〖민속〗 ① 《십이지의》 the Sign of the Boar (=the 12th of the 12 Earth's Branches). ② ⇨해방(亥方). ③ ⇨해시(亥時).

**해**(害) 《위해》 injury; harm; hurt; 《손상》 damage; 《해독》 evil; injury; an evil 〔baneful〕 influence; evil 〔harmful, injurious〕 effects. ⇨해(害)하다.

> 용법 **injury** 「해」를 나타내는 가장 넓은 뜻의 말, 신체·감정·권리 등이 상처·침해됨을 강조, 반드시 고의적임을 뜻하지 않음: Such a remark was an injury to my feeling. (그러한 말은 나의 감정을 해치는 것이었다) **harm** injure 한〔당한〕 결과 생기는 물질적·정신적·도의적인 손해에 사용됨: The hail did a lot of harm to the spring vegetables. (우박은 봄 채소에 커다란 해를 끼쳤다) **damage** 가치·명예·재산 따위가 소실(消失)됨을 강조함: The typhoon caused widespread damage. (태풍이 광범한 손해를 가져왔다)

¶ 해가 되는 harmful; hurtful; injurious; noxious / 해가 없는 harmless; unharmful; innocuous; innoxious / 음주와 흡연의 해 the bad 〔ill, harmful〕 effects of drinking and smoking / …에 해가 되다 do 《*a person*》 harm; do harm 〔cause, damage〕《to》; be injurious 〔harmful〕《to》; be bad for / 건강에 해롭다 be 「bad for 〔injurious to〕 (the) health / 해를 입다 suffer damage; be damaged 《by》; 《해독을》 suffer from evil effects; be badly affected 《by》/ 해를 입히다 inflict injury 〔damage〕 upon; do wrong 〔injury, damage〕《to》; cause damage 〔loss〕/ 그것은 너에게 아무 해도 없을 게다 It will make 〔do〕 you no harm. / 나는 너에게 해가 되는 말은 안 한다 I say nothing to your disadvantage. / 담배는 백해무익하다고 그는 믿고있다 He believes that smoking does nothing but harm.

**해-**(該) that; the said; the person 〔matter〕 in question. ¶ 해인물 the said person; the person in question.

**-해**(海) ¶ 동해 the East Sea / 사해(死海) the Dead Sea.

**해갈**(解渴) ～하다 appease 〔quench, slake, relieve〕 *one's* thirst; 《가뭄의》 wet dry weather; be relieved from drought; bring the end of drought.

**해감** water sediment; silt. ¶ ～내가 나다 smell of mud.

**해거름** nightfall; sunset; sundown;

dusk. ¶ ~에 at about sunset.

**해거리** every other 〔second〕 year; 《in》 alternate years.

**해결**(解決) (a) solution; (a) settlement; a way out (해결책). ~하다 solve 《a question》; resolve 《a difficulty》; settle 《an argument》; bring 《*a matter*》 to a settlement.
¶ 원만한〔만족스러운, 평화적〕 ~ an amicable 〔a satisfactory, a peaceful〕 settlement / 조속히 ~해야 할 문제 a problem that must be solved as soon as possible / 분쟁을 ~하다 settle a dispute 〔grievance〕; settle 《a family》 trouble / 원만하게 ~하다 bring 《*a matter*》 to a peaceful 〔amicable〕 settlement / ~을 짓다 bring a solution 《to》 / 협상으로 ~하다 negotiate a settlement 《of a problem with *a person*》 / ~되다 be solved 〔settled〕; come 〔be brought〕 to a settlement 〔decision〕; reach 〔arrive at〕 a solution / 국제분쟁을 외교로 ~하다 settle an international dispute by diplomacy / 문제는 원만히 ~되었다 The matter 「has been settled amicably 〔has been brought to an amicable settlement〕. / 너희들끼리 ~해라 Settle it between you. / 문제는 드디어 ~되었다 The question is finally settled. / 시간이 ~한다 Time will solve the matter. / 그건 내 자신이 ~할 일이다 That's something I must work out for myself. / 경찰은 마침내 그 살인 사건을 ~했다 The police have finally cracked that murder case. / 그 문제는 여전히 미~인 채로 남아 있다 It remains an unsolved problem. *or* The matter still remains unsolved.
◉ ~조건 terms of settlement. ~책 a solution 《to a problem》; find a way out of 《the difficulty》 / 나는 지금 ~책을 모색 중이다 I am considering how to settle the matter.

**해결사**(解決士) a trouble-solving broker.

**해경**(海景) a (sea-)coast landscape; a seascape; a marine view; a view from the seashore. ◉ ~화 a seapiece.

**해고**(解雇) (a) discharge; (a) dismissal; 《미》 a lay-off (일시적인). ~하다 discharge; dismiss; fire; sack 《구어》; give 《*a person*》 the shake 《영구어》; lay 《*a person*》 off (일시적인). ¶ 종업원을 ~하다 dismiss an employee / 급료를 주어 ~하다 pay 《*a person*》 off / 즉석에서 ~하다 send 〔turn, put〕 《*a person*》 to the rightabout(s) / ~되다〔당하다〕 be 〔get〕 discharged 〔dismissed〕; get 〔be〕 fired 〔sacked 《구어》〕; get 〔be given〕 the sack 《영구어》; be laid off / 즉각 ~당하다 receive prompt dismissal / 일거리가 부족해서 직원의 반이 ~되었다 Because of a shortage of work, half the staff were discharged. / 노조는 그의 ~에 대해 항의하고 있다 The union is protesting against his dismissal.
◉ ~권 the right of dismissal. ~기준 criteria for personnel dismissal. ~수당 a dismissal allowance; severance pay 《영》; a redundancy payment 《영》. ~장 a notice of discharge; a dismissal notice. ~통지 a dismissal notice: 한 달 전에 ~ 통지를 하다 give 《*a person*》 one month's notice (of dismissal). 집단~ a mass dismissal.

**해골**(骸骨) a skeleton; skeletal bones. ¶ ~ 처럼 마른 사람 a walking skeleton / ~처럼 수척하다 be reduced to skeleton; be all skin and bone.

**해공전**(海空戰) an air-and-sea battle.

**해괴**(駭怪) strangeness; outrageousness; scandalousness; monstrousness. ~하다 (be) strange; outrageous; monstrous; scandalous. ¶ ~한 소문 a wild rumor / ~망측하다 be extremely outrageous 〔scandalous, monstrous, shameful, disgraceful〕.

**해구**(海狗) 〖동물〗 a fur seal; a sea bear. ◉ ~신(腎) the penis of a sea bear.

**해구**(海寇) pirates; sea marauders.

**해구**(海溝) 〖지질〗 a 〔an ocean〕 deep; a (sea) trench.

**해국**(海菊) 〖식물〗 a kind of aster.

**해군**(海軍) the navy (★ 단·복수 취급); the naval forces; 《군인》 a navy 〔naval〕 man; 《수병》 a sailor; 《사관》 a naval officer; [집합적] naval personnel; the Navy [총칭]. ¶ ~의 naval; navy / 미국~ the United States Navy (생략 USN) / 영국~ the Royal Navy (생략 RN).
◉ ~공창 a naval arsenal 〔dockyard〕; a navy yard 《미》. ~군악대 the Marine band. ~기(機) a navy plane. ~기(旗) the navy flag. ~기지 a naval base. ~대학 the Naval Staff College. ~력 naval strength 〔power〕; sea 〔maritime〕 power. ~무관 a naval *attaché*. ~병원 a naval hospital. ~복 a seaman's uniform. ~본부 the Navy Headquarters. ~부대 naval forces. ~사관〔장교〕 a naval officer: ~사관 학교 the Naval Academy / ~ 사관 생도 a

naval cadet; a midshipman. ~성 《미국의》 the Department of the Navy; the Navy. ~장관 《미》 the Secretary of the Navy; 《영》 the First Lord of the Admiralty. ~차관 the Vice-Minister of the Navy. ~참모총장 the Chief of Naval Operations (생략 C.N.O.). ~헌병 the shore patrol (생략 S.P.).

**해굽성**(一性) 『식물』 (positive) heliotropism.

**해금**(奚琴) 『악기』 a Korean fiddle.

**해금**(解禁) lifting 〔removal〕 of a ban 〔an embargo〕; 《수렵 등의》 the opening of the shooting 〔fishing〕 season. ~하다 remove 〔take off, lift〕 the embargo 《(up)on the export of coal》; lift 〔remove〕 the ban 《on gold》. ¶ 연어잡이가 다음 주 ~된다 The salmon season opens next week. / 그 사건의 기사는 어제 ~되었다 The press ban on the case was removed yesterday. / 석유 수출 금지령은 곧 ~될 것이다 The oil embargo 〔The embargo on oil〕 is expected to be lifted soon.
◉ ~기 《사냥의》 the open season; the opening of the shooting season. 정치활동~ lifting (of) the ban on political activities 《of former politicians》. 추가~ additional lifting of the 《political》 ban 《imposed on old-school politicians》.

**해기**(海技) seamanship. ◉ ~사 면허증 a certificate of competency in seamanship; a seamen's competency certificate.

**해껏** 《온종일》 all day long; until sunset; till dark. ¶ ~ 일하다 work till dark.

**해끄무레하다** (be) nice and whitish. ¶ 해끄무레한 얼굴 a clean and whitish face.

**해끄스름하다, 해끔하다** (be) whitish.

**해낙낙하다** (be) satisfied; pleased; content(ed).

**해난**(海難) a disaster at sea; a shipwreck. ¶ ~을 당하다 《배가》 meet with a disaster at sea; be wrecked; 《사람이》 be shipwrecked.
◉ ~구제소 a life saving station; a house of refuge 《미》. ~구조 sea rescue (work); salvage; 《항공기까지 동원된》 air-sea rescue (생략 A.S.R.): ~구조선 a salvage boat / ~구조원 a lifesaver; [총칭] the Lifesaving Service / ~구조 작업 salvage work 〔operation〕. ~사고 a marine accident. ~신호 《radio》 an SOS; 《flash》 a distress signal; a mayday 〔Mayday〕 call 〔signal〕. ~심판 a marine accident inquiry: ~심판법 the Sea Accident Inquiry Law / ~심판소 the Maritime Distress Inquiry Agency / ~심판 위원회 the Martime Accident Inquiry Committee / 중앙 ~심판원 the Central Office of Marine Accidents Inquiry.

**해납작하다** (be) white and broad 〔flat〕.

**해내다** ① 《이겨내다》 beat; defeat; get 〔gain〕 the better of 《*a person*》; vanquish; 《찍소리 못 하게》 talk 〔argue〕 《*a person*》 down; put 《*a person*》 to silence; corner 《*a person*》 in argument. ¶ 나는 논쟁에서 그를 찍소리 못 하게 해냈다 I drove him into a corner. / 많은 사람 앞에서 그 녀석을 찍소리 못하도록 마구 해냈다 I put him down in front of everybody. ② 《수행·성취하다》 carry 「out 〔through〕; complete; achieve; accomplish; pull 《a scheme》 off; see 〔put〕 《*a thing*》 through; bring 《*one's* work》 to completion. ¶ 일을 혼자서 ~ complete the task by *oneself* / 계획한 바를 ~ carry through an undertaking / 잘 ~ do well; make a success of; acquit *oneself* to *one's* credit / 우리는 해냈다 We made it! / 나는 그것을 해내겠다고 결심했다 I made up my mind to 「go through with it 〔carry it out〕.

**해넘이** nightfall; sunset; sundown 《미》. ¶ ~ 무렵 (at) about sunset; toward nightfall / ~ 전에 before (it gets) dark / ~에서 해돋이까지 from sunset till sunrise; from sundown to sunup.

**해녀**(海女) a woman diver 《for abalones, *etc.*》. ¶ 제주도는 ~로 유명하다 Chejudo is famous for woman divers.

**해년**(亥年) 『민속』 the Year of the Boar.

**해단**(解團) disbanding. ~하다 disband 《an athletic team》. ◉ ~식 the ceremony of disbanding.

**해달**(海獺) 『동물』 a sea otter. ¶ ~의 모피 a sea-otter fur.

**해답**(解答) a solution 《to 〔of〕 a problem》; an answer 《to a question》. ~하다 solve 《a problem》; answer 《a question》. ¶ 시험 문제의 ~ answers 〔a key〕 to examination questions / ~이 달린 문제집 a collection of questions with answers attached / 바른〔틀린〕 ~을 내다 give a correct 〔wrong〕 answer; answer correctly 〔incorrectly〕 / 나는 첫 문제의 ~을 못했습니다 I failed to answer the first question.
◉ ~란 the answer column 〔section〕: ~은 소정 ~란에 기입하시오 Write your answer in the appropriate place. ~

용지 an answer sheet. ∼자 a solver; an answerer.

**해당**(解黨) dissolution (of a party). ∼하다 dissolve (a party). ¶ 군사 정권의 탄압은 모든 정당을 ∼하지 않을 수 없도록 하였다 The oppression by the military regime drove all the political parties to dissolution.

**해당**(該當) ∼하다 《조항 따위에》 come 〔fall〕 under 《Article 3》; come 〔fall〕 within the purview of; be applicable to (조항 등이 적용할 수 있다); correspond 《to》 (맞먹다); 《조건을 충족시키다》 fulfill. ¶ 그것에 ∼하는 예 a case in point / 석 달 월급에 ∼하는 보너스 a bonus equivalent to three months' pay / 조건에 ∼하다 fit 〔meet, satisfy〕 the requirements; fulfill the conditions / ∼ 항목을 보다 turn to the appropriate heading / ∼ 항목을 참조하다 refer to the appropriate heading / 그것은 형법 제37조에 ∼된다 It comes under Article 37 of the Criminal Code. *or* Article 37 of the Criminal Code applies 〔is applicable〕. / 이 규정은 너의 경우에는 ∼되지 않는다 This rule is not applicable to your case. / 그 학교는 우리 나라의 중학교에 ∼한다 The school corresponds to our junior high school. / 조건에 ∼하는 응모자는 한 사람도 없었다 No applicant satisfied the requirements. / 한국말로 「세배」에 딱 ∼되는 영어는 없다 There is no English exactly equivalent to *sebae*. ◉ ∼사항 pertinent 〔relevant〕 data.

**해당화**(海棠花) 〚식물〛 a sweetbrier.

**해대다** fall 〔turn〕 upon 《*a person*》; go at 《*a person*》; turn 〔round〕 on 《*a person*》; fly 〔lash out〕 at 《*a person*》; defy. ¶ 약속을 어겼다고 한바탕 ∼ fly at 《*a person*》 for breaking *his* promise / 그것을 듣자 그는 주인에게 해댔다 Hearing that, he turned 〔fell〕 upon his master.

**해도**(海圖) a (marine) chart; a hydrographic(al) chart. ¶ ∼에 기재되어 있지 않은 uncharted; not marked on the chart / 그 섬은 ∼에 나와 있지 않다 That island is not charted. ◉ ∼실 a chart room. ∼학 chartology; c(h)artography.

**해도** even though *one* does 〔thinks, granting〕; if; even if 〔though〕; though; granting 〔supposing〕 that…. ¶ 그것이 사실이라 ∼ granting 〔supposing〕 it to be true; granted it is true / 설령 네가 옳다고 ∼ even if you are in the right / 비록 그가 취해 있었다 ∼ granting that he was drunk / 설사 이번에 실패한다 ∼ 기회가 한 번 더 있다 You have another chance even if you fail this time.

**해독**(害毒) harm; evil; poison; an evil 〔a baneful〕 influence; blight; canker. ¶ 기계 문명의 ∼ the blight of mechanical civilization / 청소년에게 ∼이 되는 잡지 a magazine harmful to youth / ∼이 없는 제초제 harmless weed killer / ∼을 끼치다 cause damage 《to》; exert a baneful 〔harmful〕 influence 《on society》.

**해독**(解毒) 〚의학〛 counteracting 〔neutralizing〕 poison; detoxification; detoxication. ∼하다 counteract 〔neutralize〕 the poison; remove the (effect of) poison 《from》; detoxify; detoxicate.

**해독**(解讀) decoding; decipherment; making out 《the meaning, *etc.*》. ∼하다 break 〔crack〕 《the enemy's code》; decipher; decode.

> 용법 암호를 「해독하다」에는 (a) 「암호의 비밀을 풀다」와 (b) 「암호문(文)을 보통문으로 고치다」의 뜻이 있는데 break는 (a)의 뜻만을 가짐. 또 decipher, decode는 어느쪽의 의미로도 쓰이지만, (b)의 뜻일 때가 많음.

¶ ∼하기 어려운 indecipherable / ∼할 수 있는 decipherable / 암호 전보를 ∼하다 decipher a (coded) telegram / 마야의 그림 문자는 아직 ∼되어 있지 않다 Mayan hieroglyphics have yet to be deciphered. / 난필이라 ∼하는 데 애먹었다 I found it hard to read the scrawl. ◉ ∼자 《암호의》 a decoder. 사진∼ photographic interpretation. 암호∼기 〔장치〕 a decoder.

**해독제**(解毒劑) a remedy against poison; an antidote for 〔to〕 poison; a detoxicant. ¶ ∼를 먹이다 administer an antidote 《to》 / ∼를 쓰다 apply an antidote 《to a disease》 / 우유는 어떤 종류의 독에 대해서는 ∼ 구실을 한다고 한다 Milk is said to be an antidote for some poisons.

**해돋이** (the) sunrise; sunup 《미》. ¶ ∼에 at sunrise / ∼ 전에 before dawn / ∼를 구경하다 see the sunrise 《from》 / ∼에 일어나다 get up 〔rise〕 with the sun.

**해동**(解凍) thawing; a thaw. ∼하다 thaw 〔defrost〕 《frozen meat》. ¶ 냉동식품을 요리하기 전에 ∼시키다 leave frozen food to thaw before cooking / ∼

으로 길이 질퍽거린다 The roads are bad 〔muddy〕 because of the thaw.

**해동갑**(—同甲) coinciding with the sunset; [부사적] until sunset; all day long. ~하다 do 《*something*》 until sunset; coincide with the sunset. ¶ ~하여 밭일을 하다 work in the fields until sunset.

**해동청**(海東青) 《송골매》 a peregrine falcon; a duck hawk.

**해득**(解得) understanding; comprehension. ~하다 understand; comprehend; grasp (the meaning of). ¶ ~이 빠른〔느린〕 quick 〔slow〕 of apprehension; quick-〔slow-〕witted / ~이 쉬운〔어려운〕 easy 〔hard〕 to understand 〔learn〕.

**해뜨리다** wear out. ⇨ 해어뜨리다.

**해뜩거리다** ⇨ 희뜩거리다.

**해라하다** use the low forms of speech 《to *one's* inferior(s) 〔junior(s)〕》; use the plain style of speech.

**해란초**(海蘭草) 〖식물〗 a kind of toadflax.

**해로**(海路) a sea route; a seaway. ¶ ~로 부산에 가다 go to Pusan by sea 〔ship〕; take a sea route to Pusan.

**해로**(偕老) 《a married couple》 growing old together. ~하다 grow old together. ¶ 백년~ 《husband and wife》 sharing the years happily together / 백년~의 가약을 맺다 be united as man and wife (for weal or woe); swear to become one flesh.

**해로동혈**(偕老洞穴) ① 《부부의》 growing old together and sharing a common grave. ~하다 grow old together and are buried in the same grave. ② 〖동물〗 a Venus's-flower-basket.

**해롭다**(害—) (be) harmful; injurious; detrimental; noxious; [서술적] be bad 《for》. ¶ 건강에 해로운 detrimental 〔injurious〕 to health / 농작물에 해로운 harmful to the crops / 몸에 ~ affect 〔tell on〕 *one's* health; be bad for the health / 심신에 ~ be harmful both to mind and body / 눈에 ~ be bad for 〔injurious to〕 the eyes / 해롭지도 이롭지도 않다 do neither harm nor good / 술은 건강에 ~ Drinking is injurious to one's health. / 그렇게 하면 네게 ~ If you do that, you will be sorry. / 나는 그렇게 해도 해롭진 않을 것으로 여긴다 I see no harm in doing so. / 나는 흡연이 ~고 믿는다 I believe that smoking does nothing but harm. / 지나친 운동은 ~ Too much exercise will (only) do you harm.

**해롱-** ⇨ 희롱-.

**해류**(海流) 〖지학〗 an ocean 〔a sea〕 current; a (marine) current. ¶ ~를 타다 ride an ocean current. ◉ ~도 a current chart. ~병(瓶) an ocean current bottle.

**해륙**(海陸) land and sea. ¶ ~공으로 by land, sea and air / ~공의 입체전 three-dimensional warfare. ◉ ~양면작전 amphibious operations. ~양서(兩棲) 동물 an amphibious animal; an amphibian. ~양용 비행기〔전차〕 an amphibious plane 〔tank〕.

**해리**(海里) a nautical 〔sea〕 mile; a knot (★ 1해리는 약 1852미터).

**해리**(海狸) 〖동물〗 a beaver; a castor. ◉ ~향 castor 《the secretion from a beaver's groin》.

**해리**(解離) 〖화학〗 dissociation. ~하다 dissociate. ◉ ~곡선 a dissociation curve. ~압(壓) dissociation pressure. ~열 heat of dissociation.

**해마**(海馬) ① 〖어류〗 a sea horse; a hippocampus. ② 〖동물〗 a walrus. ③ = 해상(海象).

**해마**(海魔) a spirit of the sea; a sailor's devil.

**해마다** every year; each year; yearly; annually; from year to year; year by 〔after〕 year. ¶ 수입은 ~ 증가한다 The imports show a yearly increase. / ~ 이맘때면 눈이 오기 시작한다 It always begins to snow at this time of (the) year.

**해만**(海灣) ① 《만》 a bay (작은); a gulf (큰); an inlet; an arm of the sea (후미). ② 《바다와 만》 sea and bay.

**해말갛다** ⇨ 희멀겋다.

**해말쑥하다** (be) fair and clean. ⇨ 희멀쑥하다.

**해맑다** (be) white and clean.

**해망쩍다** (be) slow-witted; dull; stupid.

**해머** a hammer. ◉ ~던지기 hammer throwing: ~던지기 선수 a hammer thrower. 공기~ an air hammer; a pneumatic (power) hammer. 증기~ a steam hammer.

**해먹** a hammock; a swinging couch. ¶ ~에서 자다 sleep in a hammock / ~을 치다〔걸다〕 sling 〔lash〕 a hammock.

**해먹다** 《음식을》 cook 〔make〕 and eat; 《횡령하다》 take unjust possession of 《*something*》; pocket; peculate; embezzle; appropriate (to *oneself*); misappropriate; divert 《public money》 into *one's* own pocket; 《생활 방편으로》 earn a living 《by》; 《하다》 do. ¶ 점심을 ~ prepare lunch and eat; get lunch ready and have it / 공금을 ~ embezzle 〔appropriate〕 government 〔public〕 money / 일이 힘들어 해먹을 수가 없다 The work is too damn much trouble to do. / 이 더위라니 정말이지 해먹을 수가 없다 I really can't stand this heat. *or* The heat is really unbearable.

**해면**(海面) the surface of the sea; 《표준 해면》 the sea level. ¶ ~에 떠오르다 float up to the surface of the sea; surface / 거울 같이 잔잔한 ~에 두 척의 요트가 떠 있었다 Two yachts were afloat on a glassy sea. ◉ ~기압 the pressure of the atmosphere at sea-level; sea-level (atmospheric) pressure. ~온도 (a) sea-surface temperature.

**해면**(海綿) a (natural) sponge. ¶ ~모양〔질〕의 spongy; 〖해부〗 cancellous / ~으로 빨아들이다 sponge up 〔off〕 《spilled ink》. ◉ ~고무 sponge rubber. ~동물 a sponge. ~조직 spongy tissue. ~질 sponge matter; sponginess. ~체 a spongy body. 목욕용~ a bath sponge.

**해면**(解免) release; exoneration 《from duty, obligation》; acquittal; discharge; firing 《from a job》. ~하다 be released from; be exonerated 〔acquitted〕 of; be discharged from.

**해명**(解明) elucidation; explication; explanation. ~하다 make 《a mystery》 clear; elucidate 《the meaning》; explicate 《a theory》; throw 〔shed〕 light (up)on; clarify. ¶ 진상의 ~ investigation into 〔of〕 the truth 《about》 / ~을 요구하다 demand an explanation 《of *a person*》 / 발언 내용을 ~하다 clarify the statement 《*one* made on the assembly floor》 / 진상 ~에 나서다 set about uncovering the truth / 그 사건의 수수께끼는 아직 ~되지 않고 있다 The mystery of that incident hasn't been solved yet. ◉ ~서 a letter of explanation; a written explanation.

**해몽**(解夢) interpretation of dreams. ~하다 interpret 〔read〕 a dream. ◉ ~가 a dream reader; an oneirocritic; an oneiroscopist.

**해무**(海務) maritime 〔marine, sea〕 affairs. ◉ ~협회 the marine association.

**해무**(海霧) a sea fog; a fog on the sea.

**해묵다** 《물건이》 get a year old; age a year; 《일이》 drag on for a year (without getting finished). ¶ 해묵은 쌀 《전년도의》 rice of the previous year's crop; 《오래된》 old rice; long-stored rice / 해묵은 논쟁 a long-pending 〔an outstanding〕 dispute.

**해묵히다** 《일을》 let work drag on for a year without getting finished; 《물건을》 let 《*a thing*》 get to be a year old.

**해물**(海物) marine products. ◉ ~상 a dealer in marine products. ~탕면 noodle soup with mixed seafoods.

**해미** a thick sea fog; a heavy fog on the sea. ¶ 바다에 ~가 끼다 the sea is covered with heavy fog.

**해미**(海味) tasty dishes from the sea; seafood.

**해바라기** 〖식물〗 a sunflower. ¶ ~기름 sunflower oil.

**해박**(該博) erudition; profundity. ~하다 (be) extensive; erudite; profound. ¶ ~한 지식 profound learning; a wide 〔an extensive〕 knowledge 《of》; erudition / 그는 ~한 지식의 소유자다 He is a man of 「great learning 〔immense erudition〕.

**해반드르르하다** (be) fair and lustrous. ⇨ 희번드르르하다.

**해반지르르하다** (be) neat and fair.

**해발**(海拔) above the sea; above (the) sea level. ¶ 그 산은 ~ 3천 미터이다 The mountain is 3,000 meters above the sea (level).

**해발쭉하다** (be) wide open. ⇨ 헤벌쭉하다.

**해방**(亥方) 〖민속〗 the Direction of the Boar (=northwest-by-north).

**해방**(解放) ① 《감금·속박·억압으로부터》 release; liberation; emancipation 《of slave》. ~하다 release; liberate 《*a person* from》; emancipate; free 《*a person*》 from. ¶ 인민〔민족〕 ~전선 the National Liberation Front / 노예를 ~하다 free 〔liberate, emancipate〕 a slave / 여성을 부엌에서 ~시키다 liberate women from (the drudgery of) the kitchen / 그는 인간의 정신을 돈에 대한 예속으로부터 ~시켰다 He liberated the human soul from its slavery to money. ② 《책임 따위로부터》 ~하다 free 〔release〕 《*a person* from responsibility》. ¶ 빈곤으로부터의 ~ freedom from poverty / 죄의식에서 ~되다 be released from a sense of guilt / 빈곤으로부터 ~시키다 liberate people from poverty / 나는 마침내 일에서 ~되었다 At last I was released 〔freed〕 from my work.
◉ ~군 a liberation army 〔forces〕. ~자 a liberator; an emancipator. ~운동 a liberation campaign; lib 《구어》: 여성 ~운동 women's liberation movement; women's lib. ~전쟁 a war of liberation: 민족 ~ 전쟁 a national liberation war. ~지구 a liberated area

〔district〕.

**해방감**(解放感) a sense 〔feeling〕 of freedom 〔liberation〕. ¶ 온갖 의무에서 벗어난 ～ a feeling of release from all kinds of obligation.

**해법**(解法) a solution; a clue 〔key〕 to 「solution.

**해변**(海邊) the beach; the seashore; the seaside; the coast. ¶ ～의 도시 a seacoast 〔coast〕 town; a town along the coast / ～으로 나가다 go 〔come〕 「down to 〔out on〕 the beach / ～으로 끌어 올리다 haul 《a boat》 ashore / ～을 산책하다 take a walk along the beach; stroll about the beach.

**해병**(海兵) a marine. ¶ 귀신 잡는 ～ a hard-hearted 〔lion-hearted, fearless, dauntless〕 marine. ◉ ～대 a marine corps; 《미》 the Marines; the (U.S.) Marine Corps; 《영》 the Royal Marines: ～대원 a marine; a leatherneck 《구어》 / ～대 사령관 the Marine Corps Commandant.

**해보다** ① 《시도하다》 try *doing*; try to *do;* give it a try 〔trial〕; do 《*something*》 on trial; attempt; have a try 〔a go, a shot〕 《at》; make an attempt 《at, to *do*》; take chances. ¶ 처음 ～ try 《shooting》 for the first time / 일을 ～ try a job; try work / 저항을 ～ offer 〔put up〕 resistance / 돈을 모으려고 ～ attempt to make money / 달아나려고 ～ make an attempt to run away / 또 한 번 ～ make another attempt; try again / 역량을 시험～ try *one's* strength / 되든 안 되든 ～ run the task; try 〔take〕 *one's* chance / 시험삼아 사용～ try *a person* 〔*a thing*〕 out; 《구어》 give *something* 〔*a person*〕 a try; employ 《*a person*》 on trial / 할 수 있거든 해보라 I would like to see you try it. *or* Do it if you can. *or* 《반어적으로》 Try and do it. / 해보았자 소용없다 It's 〔There is〕 no use trying.
② 《겪다》 experience; know; try; have a chance to try. ¶ 고생을 ～ know hardship / 사랑을 ～ experience love / 그녀와는 말해 본 일이 없다 I have never spoken to her.
③ 《싸우다》 pit *one's* strength; fight; fight it out; contend with; stand against. ¶ 해볼테면 해보자 If you want to fight, let's fight then. / 그 놈과는 끝까지 해보겠다 I'll fight him to the bitter end.

**해부**(解剖) ① 《의학상의》 dissection; 《사인(死因) 조사의》 a postmortem (examination); an autopsy. ～하다 dissect; anatomise; hold an autopsy 〔a postmortem (examination)〕 《on》. ¶ 생체 ～ vivisection / 병리～ pathological anatomy / ～토록 하다 have 《a body》 dissected; submit 《a dead body》 for an autopsy / 시체 ～결과 타살로 판명되었다 The postmortem examination showed that it was a case of murder.
② [비유적] (an) analysis (분석); parsing (문장의). ～하다 analyze; parse. ¶ 문제를 면밀히 ～하다 analyze a problem / 아무의 심리를 ～하다 analyze *a person's* psychology.
◉ ～대〔실〕 a dissecting table 〔room〕. ～도(刀) a dissecting knife; a scalpel. ～도(圖) an anatomical 〔anatomy〕 chart; a chart of anatomy. ～도구〔용구〕 dissecting tools. ～모형 an anatomical specimen 〔model〕. ～용 시체 a subject for dissection. ～자 a dissector; a prosector (표본 담당의). ～체 an anatomy.

**해부학**(解剖學) (the study or science of) anatomy. ¶ 동물〔인체〕 ～ animal 〔human〕 anatomy / ～ (상)의 anatomical / ～상〔적으로〕 anatomically / ～적 특징 a anatomical feature. ◉ ～자 an anatomist.

**해빙**(海氷) sea ice.

**해빙**(解氷) ① 《얼음의》 thawing of ice; a break-up of ice. ～하다 thaw; break up; defrost 《frozen food》. ¶ 압록강은 ～되었다 The Yalu is now free from ice. / 남부 지방에서 ～이 시작되었다 The ice has begun to melt in the southern districts. ② 《국제간 긴장의》 détente; the easing 〔relief〕 (of international tension).
◉ ～기 《얼음의》 the thawing season: ～기가 되었다 The thawing season has set in.

**해사**(海事) maritime affairs 〔matters〕. ¶ ～의 maritime. ◉ ～법 maritime law. ～심판소 the Maritime 〔Admiralty〕 Court. ～협회 a marine association.

**해사하다** (be) clean and fair; fair-complexioned.

**해산**(海山) 〚지학〛 a seamount; a sea-mountain; an undersea mountaion.

**해산**(海産) marine products. ⇨ 해산물. ◉ ～식품 seafood. ～업 the marine products industry.

**해산**(解産) (a) childbirth; a delivery; parturition. ～하다 give birth to 《a child》; have a baby; be delivered of 《a baby》. ¶ ～ 구완을 하다 assist at a childbirth / ～기가 있다 labor starts; [사람이 주어] begin 〔go into〕 labor;

have 〔begin to feel〕 labor pains / 그녀는 다음달에 ～할 예정이다 She expects to be confined next month. ◉ ～기(期) *one's* time; period 〔term〕 of delivery. ～달 the expected month of *one's* childbirth. ～미역 seaweed for soup fed to a woman just out of childbirth. ～비(費) childbirth expenses. ～어미 a woman just out of childbirth. 첫～ *one's* first confinement.

**해산**(解散) ① 《모임의》 breakup; dispersion. ～하다 break up; disperse. ¶ 집회를 ～하다 break up a meeting / 군중을 ～시키다 disperse a crowd / ～을 명하다 order 《a crowd》 to 「disperse 〔break up〕 / 그 데모는 경찰에 의해서 ～되었다 The demonstration was dispersed by the police. / ～ 《구령》 Dismiss!
② 《회사·조직 등의》 dissolution 《of a company》; disorganization (단체의); liquidation (회사 따위의); disbandment (군대의). ～하다 dissolve 《partnership》; disorganize; wind up; 《해산이 되다》 be dissolved; be disorganized; be liquidated; go into liquidation; be disbanded. ¶ ～을 명하다 order 《an organization》 to be disbanded / 그 정당은 ～ 명령을 받았다 That party was ordered to be dissolved.
③ 《국회의》 dissolution (of the Assembly). ～하다 dissolve 《the House》; 《해산이 되다》 be dissolved. ¶ 국회를 ～하겠다고 으르다 threaten to dissolve the National Assembly / 국회는 ～되었다 The Assembly has been dissolved.
◉ ～권 the right to dissolve 《the House》. 강제～ compulsory winding-up. 임의～ voluntary winding-up.

**해산물**(海産物) marine 〔sea〕 products. ¶ ～이 풍부하다 be rich in marine products. ◉ ～가공품 processed maritime products. ～상(인) a dealer in 「marine products 〔seafoods〕.

**해삼**(海蔘) 〖동물〗 a sea 「slug 〔cucumber〕; a trepang. ◉ ～탕(湯) braised sea cucumber.

**해상**(海上) the sea. ¶ ～의 《accidents》 at sea; 《ship》 on the sea; maritime; marine / ～에서 《float》 on the sea; at sea; during the voyage (항해중) / ～으로 《travel》 by sea / ～에 있다 《항해중》 be at sea / ～에서 생활하다 live on the sea / ～에서 폭풍을 만나다 be overtaken by a storm at sea.
◉ ～공원 a marine park: 국립～공원 a national sea park. ～권 maritime 〔sea〕 power; the command of the sea: ～권을 장악하다 rule the sea; have the command of the sea. ～근무 sea 「service 〔duty〕; service afloat. ～무역 maritime 〔sea〕 trade; overseas trade. ～발사 미사일 a sea-based 〔sealaunched, sea-〔ship-〕borne〕 missile. ～법 the 「maritime 〔marine〕 law. ～보급로 a maritime supply route. ～보안과 a maritime security division. ～봉쇄 a blockade at sea. ～비행 an 「ocean 〔overseas〕 flight. ～생활 a 「seafaring 〔sailor's〕 life; ocean life; life 「afloat 〔at sea〕: ～생활을 하다 go to sea; follow the sea. ～수송〔운송〕 transport by sea; marine transport (ation): ～수송로 marine transportation routes / ～운송 협정 an agreement on maritime transport(ation). ～시운전 a sea trial. ～여행 a voyage on the sea; traveling by sea; seafaring: ～여행자 a traveler by sea; a sea traveler; a seafarer / ～여행을 하다 travel by sea; journey over (the) sea. ～자위대 《일본의》 the Maritime Self-Defense Force. ～정찰기 a maritime patrol aircraft (생략 MPA). ～호텔 a floating hotel. ～화재 a fire at sea; a fire 「on 〔in〕 a ship.

**해상**(海床) 〖지질〗 the 「bottom 〔bed〕 of the sea; the 「sea 〔ocean〕 floor.

**해상**(海商) 《장사》 marine commerce; 《사람》 a sea trader.

**해상**(海象) 〖동물〗 《바다코끼리》 an elephant seal.

**해상력**(解像力) 〖사진〗 resolution; resolving power. ¶ ～이 높은 렌즈 a high resolution lens.

**해상보험**(海上保險) marine insurance. ¶ ～에 들다 insure 《the cargo》 against sea perils; effect 〔take out〕 marine insurance. ◉ ～ 대리업자 a marine insurance agent. ～업자 an underwriter. ～증권 a marine insurance policy. ～회사 a marine insurance company.

**해생동물**(海生動物) a maritime animal.

**해서**(楷書) the regular "square-hand" style of writing Chinese characters; the printed style of writing. ¶ ～로 쓰다 write in the 「square 〔printed〕 style.

**해석**(解析) analysis; analytical study. ～하다 analyze; analyse 《영》. ◉ ～기하학 analytic(al) geometry. ～학 analytics; analysis. ～함수 an analytic function.

**해석**(解釋) 《풀어 밝힘》 (an) interpretation; construction (법의); 《설명》 (an)

explanation; (an) elucidation (해설); (an) explication (문학작품 등의). ～하다 interpret; construe (말·행위·문장·구성 등에 관한 해석); 《설명하다》 explain; explicate; elucidate; illustrate (★ explain은 가장 일반적인 말. explicate는 문어체. elucidate는 이유 등을 분명히 한다는 뜻의 격식차린 말. illustrate는 보기나 그림으로써 해석을 제시한다는 뜻).
¶ ～의 차이 a discrepancy in interpretation / 일방적인 ～ a one-sided interpretation / 법의 ～ the construction 〔interpretation〕 of law / …을 잘못 ～하다 take 〔interprete〕 《*a thing*》 wrongly; misinterpret; misconstrue; put a wrong construction on 《*a thing*》 / 선의〔악의〕로 ～하다 take 《*a person's* words》 in good 〔bad〕 part; interpret 《*a person's* action》 favorably 〔unfavorably〕; put a good 〔bad〕 construction 〔interpretation〕 on what 《*a person*》 has said / 바른〔틀린〕 ～을 내리다 give 〔put〕 a correct 〔wrong〕 interpretation / 여러 가지로 ～되다 admit of various interpretations / 그의 침묵은 찬성의 뜻으로 ～되었다 His silence was construed as approval. / 그녀는 나의 말을 나쁘게 ～했다 She took my words in the wrong sense. / 그의 연설은 정부에 대한 공격으로 ～되었다 His speech was construed as an attack on the government. / 그녀는 영어의 ～력이 부족하다 She is poor at reading English. *or* She is not very good at making sense out of a passage of English. ◉ 영문 ～법《책이름》 *How to Translate English Correctly.*

**해설**(解說) 《설명》 (an) explanation; (an) interpretation; a commentary. ～하다 explain; interpret; comment on 《the world affairs》. ¶ 뉴스 ～ a news commentary / 축구 경기에 대한 방송 ～ a broadcast commentary on a football match / 어려운 구절을 ～하다 explain the difficult passage / 그는 국제 정세에 관해서 자세히 ～했다 He commented on the international situation. ◉ ～기사 a commentary. ～서 a manual; a handbook 《of roadsigns》; a how-to book (제법 따위의); a guide (안내서); a reference book (참고서). ～자 a 《news》 commentator; 《라디오·TV뉴스의》 a newscaster.

**해성**(海成) [형용사적] sea-formerd.
◉ ～단계 〖지질〗 a sea terrace. ～층 〖지질〗 the sea layer. ～토 〖지질〗 earth formed by the sea.

**해소**(解消) ① 《해약》 annulment; (a) cancellation; obliteration. ～하다 cancel 《a contract》; annul; break (off) 《a marriage》; 《해소되다》 be cancelled; be annuled; be dissolved. ¶ 계약을 ～하다 cancel 〔annul〕 a contract / 혼약을 ～하다 break 〔call off〕 the 〔*one's*〕 engagement.
② 《고뇌·어려움 등의》 solution; settlement. ～하다 get solved 〔settled〕; be cleared up; get rid of 《*something*》. ¶ 골치아픈 문제의 ～ clearing up a difficult problem / (…의) 부족을 ～하다 supply 〔cover, fill up, remedy〕 shortage 《of》 / 주택난을 ～하다 solve the housing problem / 스트레스를 ～하다 get rid of stress / 교통 체증을 ～하다 solve the (problem of) traffic congestion 《in Seoul》; clear a traffic jam / 어려움은 곧 ～될 것이다 The difficulty will soon ravel out. / 정계의 불안은 ～되었다 The political unrest died down. / 그는 밤에 오토바이를 달려서 욕구불만을 ～했다 He worked his frustration off by riding his motorcycle at night.

**해소수** a little over a year.

**해소일**(—消日) idling away「*one's* time 〔the days of *one's* years〕; leading an idle life. ～하다 idle 〔loaf, dawdle〕 away the days of *one's* years.

**해손**(海損) sea damage; marine losses; 〖보험〗 an average (loss). ¶ 공동〔단독〕～a general 〔particular〕 average. ◉ ～계약〔조항〕 an average agreement 〔clause〕: ～계약 증서 an average bond. ～공탁금 an average deposit. ～담보 with average (생략 W. A.): ～부담보(不擔保) free of all average (생략 f.a.a.). ～정산 average adjustment: ～정산서 an average statement / ～정산인(精算人) an averager; an average adjuster. ～화물 sea-damaged goods.

**해송**(海松) 〖식물〗 ① 《곰솔》 a black pine. ② 《잣나무》 a Korean pine. ③ 《해변솔》 any (sea)shore pine.

**해수**(咳嗽) 〖의학〗 a cough; coughing. ◉ ～약 a cough「medicine 〔remedy〕; a remedy for cough; cough syrup.

**해수**(海水) seawater; saltwater; brine. ¶ ～가 들어오는 것을 막다 hold back the seawater. ◉ ～어(魚) a saltwater fish. ～오염 seawater pollution 〔contamination〕. ～온도 seawater temperature. ～증류〔담수화〕공장 a seawater distillation 〔desalinization〕 plant.

**해수**(海獸) a sea 〔marine〕 animal.

**해수욕**(海水浴) sea bathing; a saltwater bath. ¶ ～을 하다 bathe in the sea; have 〔take〕 a dip 〔bathe《영》〕 in the sea / ～하러 가다 go sea-bathing; go swimming (in the sea) / 속초로 ～을 가다 go swimming 〔bathing〕 at Sokch'o. ◉ ～객 a sea bather. ～복 a bathing suit; a swimsuit. ～장 a swimming beach; a (sea) bathing resort.

**해시**(亥時) 〖민속〗 the Watch of the Boar: ① the last of the 12 double-hours (=the period between 9 and 11 p.m.). ② the 23rd of the 24 hours (=9:30-10:30 p.m.).

**해시계**(一時計) a sundial.

**해시라이스** 《양식》 rice with hashed meat (and potatoes).

**해식**(解式) 〖수학〗 a solution 《of, to》; a key 《to》.

**해식**(海蝕) 〖지질〗 coastal 〔wave〕 erosion; erosion 〔corrosion〕 by seawater. ◉ ～동굴 a marine cave. ～작용 abrasion. ～지형 marine topography.

**해신**(海神) the sea god; 〖로神〗 Neptune; 〖그神〗 Poseidon.

**해심**(害心) malicious intent; an evil intention; malice; ill will.

**해심**(海深) sea depth; the depth of the sea. ¶ ～을 재다 sound 〔plumb〕 the sea; take soundings.

**해쓱하다** (be) pale; pallid; wan. ¶ 해쓱해지다 turn 〔go〕 pale 〔white〕 / 몹시 ～ be ashy pale / 죽은 사람처럼 ～ look ghastly.

**해씨**(該氏) the said gentleman; that person.

**해악**(害惡) evil; harm; mischief; 《악영향》 an evil influence 〔effect〕. ¶ 사회에 큰 ～을 끼치다 exert an evil influence on society; inflict great mischief on the community.

**해안**(海岸) the seashore; the (sea-)coast (연안); the seaside (★ 특히 《영》에서는 행락지로서의 해안); the beach; 《시어》 a strand. ¶ ～의 coastal 《defense》; seashore; seaside 《town》 / ～의 별장 a seaside villa; a villa by the sea 〔seaside〕 / ～에(서) on the shore 〔beach〕; by the sea; at the seaside / (배에서) ～쪽으로 coastwards / ～을 끼고〔따라〕 along the shore 〔coast〕; coastwise / ～ 가까이 inshore / ～을 산책하다 take 〔have〕 a walk along the beach; promenade along the beach 《at East Sea》 / ～을 끼고 항행하다 sail coastwise 〔along the coast〕 / ～으로 파도가 밀려오다 be washed ashore / 그는 ～에 별장을 가지고 있다 He has a villa at the seaside. / 그들은 ～에 수영하러 갔다 They went to the beach for a swim. / 여름 휴가 때는 ～으로 가자 Let's go to the seaside for our summer vacation. / 젊은이들은 ～에서 배구를 하고 있었다 The young people were playing volleyball on the beach.

◉ ～거리 a sea 〔coast(al)〕 road; the waterfront street. ～경비 coast(al) defense: ～경비대 the coast guard. ～경찰 the shore patrol. ～상륙〔양륙〕 beach landing. ～선 the coastline 〔shoreline〕; 《철도》 a coastal railroad: 들쭉날쭉한 ～선 a rugged coastline / ～선을 기선(基線)으로 영해 범위가 결정된다 Territorial limits on the sea are determined on the basis of coastlines. ～제방 a coastal levee; a sea bank 〔embankment〕. ～지방 a seaside district. ～지역 the coastal area. ～침식 coastal 〔beach〕 erosion. ～평야 a coastal plain. ～포대(砲臺) a coast-battery〔-fort〕.

> **용법** **seashore** 해변의 땅·지면을 가리키는 가장 일반적인 말. **coast** 육지에서 본, 바다와 육지가 접하는 곳으로 「해안·연안 지역」이란 뜻. **shore** 바다에서 본, 육지와 바다의 접촉 지역인 「해변의 땅」. 바다뿐만 아니라 만·호수·강 따위의 연안을 나타내기도 한다. **seaside** 피서·피한·해수욕 따위를 할 수 있는 휴양지로서의 「해안」. **beach** 「파도치는 물가, 둔치」를 뜻하는 평탄한 모래 땅. 흔히 해수욕장으로 쓰이는 곳.

**-해야하다** must (*do*); have (got) to (*do*); need to (*do*); ought to (*do*); should (*do*). ¶ 집을 수리해야 한다 The house must be repaired. / 항상 열심히 일해야 한다 I always have to work hard. / 이웃을 사랑해야 한다 You should love your neighbor.

**해약**(解約) cancellation 〔annulment, dissolution〕 (of a contract). ～하다 cancel 〔break, void, annul〕 a contract 〔an agreement〕. ¶ 예약을 ～하다 cancel a reservation / 정기 예금을 ～하다 cancel a time deposit; close a fixed deposit account / 보험을 ～하다 cancel an insurance contract; surrender an insurance policy. ◉ ～금 a cancellation fee. ～반환금 〖보험〗 cancel returns; premium surrendered (생명 보험의).

**해양**(海洋) the sea(s); the ocean. ¶～

의 자유 freedom of the seas.

◉ ～개발 ocean development. ～경찰청 the National Maritime Police Agency. ～과학 ocean science; oceanography. ～관측선 a marine research ship; a surveying ship 〔raft〕. ～국 a maritime country 〔power, nation〕. ～국민 a maritime 〔seagoing, seafaring〕 people. ～기상대 a marine meteorological observatory. ～대학 the Maritime College: 한국～대학교 Korea Maritime University. ～동물학 marine zoology. ～목장 a marine ranch. ～문학 sea literature. ～물리학 oceanophysics. ～박람회 an ocean(ic) 〔a marine〕 exposition. ～박물관 a marine archeological museum: 국립～박물관 the National Maritime Museum. ～법 law of the sea; the sea laws. ～생물 a marine organism; oceanic life: ～생물학 marine biology. ～석유 offshore oil. ～성 기후 an oceanic climate. ～소년단 the Sea Scouts. ～소설 a sea story. ～수산부 the Ministry of Oceans and Fisheries. ～식물 an oceanophyte; a sea plant. ～연구소 the Ocean Research and Development Institute. ～오염 sea contamination; contamination of sea water: ～오염 방지 조약 Convention on the Prevention of Marine Pollution (by Dumping of Wastes and Other Matters). ～오염 방지법 the Sea Pollution Prevention Law 〔Act〕. ～온도차 발전 (power generation by) ocean thermal energy conversion; OTEC power generation. ～자원 resources of the sea; marine resources. ～지리학 ocean geography. ～측량 marine surveying. ～투기(投棄) deep-sea disposal; disposal at sea. ～학 oceanography: ～학자 an oceanographer.

**해어**(海魚) a sea fish.

**해어**(海語) nautical 〔sea〕 terms. ◉ ～사전 a dictionary of nautical terms.

**해(어)뜨리다** wear 《it》 out 〔away, down〕. ¶ 옷을 ～ wear out *one's* clothes / 구두를 ～ wear *one's* shoes out 〔into holes〕.

**해(어)지다** get worn out 〔away, down〕; get tattered. ¶ 해어진 ragged; worn=out; threadbare; frayed / 가장자리가 해어진 칼라 a frayed collar / 여기저기 해어져 실밥이 드러난 상의(上衣) a coat threadbare in spots / 너덜너덜 ～ be reduced to 〔fall into〕 tatters; tatter; be worn to rags / 구두의 뒤축이 닳아 해졌다 The heels of my shoes have worn down. / 저고리를 여러 해 입었더니 소매가 해어졌다 My coat is frayed in the edges of its sleeves with the use of years. / 옷장 안에는 그녀가 오래 입어 해어진 낡은 옷만 있었다 The ward=robe contained only clothes she had worn out.

**해역**(海域) a sea 〔an ocean〕 area; waters. ¶ 지중해 ～ the Mediterranean waters.

**해연**(海淵) the lowest depth of an ocean; the deep; the abyss.

**해연풍**(海軟風) a sea breeze.

**해열**(解熱) removal 〔alleviation〕 of fever. ～하다 alleviate (a) fever; bring down 《*a person's*》 fever; reduce 〔lower〕 《*a person's*》 temperature. ◉ ～제 a fever remedy; a febrifuge; an antipyretic; medicine to bring down fever.

**해오라기** 『조류』 a white heron; a snowy egret.

**해오라기난초**(一蘭草) 『식물』 a fringed orchis 〔orchid〕.

**해왕성**(海王星) 『천문』 Neptune.

**해외**(海外) foreign 〔overseas〕 countries. ¶ ～의 oversea(s); foreign / ～로〔에〕 abroad; oversea(s); beyond 〔over〕 the seas; across the ocean / ～에서 from beyond the sea(s); from over the sea; 《import》 from abroad / ～로 가다 go abroad / ～로 수출하다 export 《goods》 abroad / ～로 여행하다 go on 〔make〕 a trip abroad; travel abroad / ～에 이름을 떨치다 obtain an international reputation / ～에서 돌아오다 return from abroad 〔overseas〕 / 군대를 ～에 파견하다 send an army abroad 〔overseas〕 / 그는 다년간 ～에서 생활했다 For many years he lived beyond the seas. *or* He lived abroad for many years. / 우리 회사는 각종 전자 제품을 ～로 수출하고 있다 Our company exports various electronic appliances. / 그 회사는 ～에서 원료를 수입한다 The company gets raw material from abroad.

◉ ～건설공사 overseas construction projects. ～건설업체 the construction companies engaged in overseas projects; an overseas construction company 〔firm〕. ～경제〔군사〕 원조 overseas economic 〔military〕 aid. ～경제협력기금 the Overseas Economic Cooperation Fund. ～공관 a diplomatic office in the foreign country. ～관광 an overseas sightseeing tour. ～귀환

자 repatriates from overseas. ～무역 foreign 〔overseas〕 trade. ～문학 foreign literature. ～발전 overseas expansion. ～방송 overseas 〔international〕 broadcasting; overseas radio (casting) service; an overseas radio broadcast: ～방송을 듣다 listen to《music》 on an overseas radio broadcast. ～사업부 the overseas「operations 〔projects, business〕 division 〔department〕. ～수주(受注) winning overseas contracts. ～시장「an oversea(s) 〔a foreign〕 market: ～시장 조사 foreign market research. ～시찰 a tour of inspection abroad: ～시찰 여행에서 돌아오다 return from a tour of inspection abroad. ～여행 an overseas「trip 〔tour〕; overseas 〔foreign〕 travel: ～여행을 자유화하다 liberalize the overseas trips / ～여행을 하다 travel 〔tour〕 abroad. ～영토 overseas possessions. ～유학 a study abroad: ～유학 알선업체 the overseas study brokerage companies. ～이민 emigration; *emigrés* (F.). ～이주 emigration. ～자녀교육 education of children living overseas. ～전보 a cable (message); a cablegram. ～정보 information from abroad; knowledge on foreign affairs: ～정보를 직접 얻기 위하여 with a view to getting firsthand information abroad. ～진출 the advance《of Korean exports》 into overseas markets; starting up overseas activities《by Korean firms》; overseas expansion: 한국 상품의 ～진출 appearance of Korean merchandize on foreign markets; export of Korean commodities. ～통신 news from abroad; transoceanic communication. ～투자 overseas 〔foreign〕 investment. ～특파원 overseas 〔foreign〕 correspondents. ～파병 overseas「dispatch 〔deployment〕 of armed forces. ～판(版) an overseas edition. ～협력위원회《경제의》International Economic Policy Council: ～협력 위원회 기획단 the International Economic Policy Council (at the Economic Planning Board). ～홍보활동 an overseas information activity.

**해외근무**(海外勤務) overseas service. ¶ ～의 명을 받다 be transferred abroad; be transferred to overseas service. ◉ ～수당 overseas service allowance.

**해외사정**(海外事情) information from abroad; (knowledge of) foreign affairs. ¶ ～에 어둡기 때문에 for lack of overseas information available.

**해우**(海牛)〖동물〗a sea cow; a manatee; a dugong. ◉ ～류 Sirenia.

**해운**(海運) sea 〔marine, ocean〕 transport(ation); shipping. ¶ 그 지역은 ～상으로 많은 자연의 이점을 지니고 있다 That area has many natural facilities for seaborne traffic.
◉ ～계 the shipping world; shipping circles. ～관리 control of marine transportation. ～국(國) a maritime power. ～국(局) the Maritime Transportation Bureau. ～동맹 a shipping 〔steamship, freight〕 conference. ～업 marine transportation business; maritime trade; the shipping「industry 〔business, trade〕: ～업자 a shipping agent 〔agency (회사)〕; shipping interests [총칭]. ～정책 a shipping policy. ～협정 an agreement on maritime transport. ～화물 seaborne goods.

**해웃값** money paid a *gisaeng* for her favors 〔services〕.

**해원**(海員) a seaman; a mariner; a sailor; a seafarer; a crewman; a crew [총칭]. ¶ ～이 되다 become a seaman; go to sea. ◉ ～명부 a crew list. ～생활 a seafaring life; a sailor's life. ～숙박소 a sailor's home. ～양성소 a seamen's training school. ～용어 a nautical term. ～조합 a seamen's「union 〔association〕.

**해읍스름하다** (be) whitish; [서술적] be not quite white; be not white 〔clean〕 enough.

**해의**(害意) malicious intent; malice; ill will; murderous intent (살의). ¶ ～를 품다 bear《*a person*》 malice; mean mischief.

**해이**(解弛) relaxation; slackening; looseness; laxity. ～하다 slacken up; relax; grow lax. ¶ 도덕심의 ～ a laxity of moral fiber / 기강이 ～하다 discipline「slackens 〔grows lax〕/ 마음이 ～하다 *one's* attention relaxes; *one's* mind becomes remiss / 공직자들의 ～된 기강에서 발생하다 result from slackened discipline among public officials.

**해인초**(海人草)〖식물〗Corsican weed.

**해일**(亥日)〖민속〗the Day of the Boar.

**해일**(海溢) a tidal wave; a seismic sea wave; a *tsunami.* ¶ ～을 일으키다 cause 〔set up〕 tidal waves / ～이 덮치다 be「struck 〔hit, swept〕 by a tidal wave / ～에 휩쓸리다 be washed away by a tidal wave / 지진이 있을 때면 흔히 ～이 일어난다 Earthquakes often cause

tidal waves. / 남해안에 ～이 덮쳤다 A tidal wave struck 〔visited, swept along〕 the south coast.
◉ ～경보 a tidal wave warning.

**해임**(解任) release from office; dismissal; discharge. ⇨ 해직. ～하다 release 〔remove〕《*a person*》 from *his* office; relieve《*a person*》 of *his* post; dismiss; discharge; recall. ¶ ～되다 be released from 〔relieved of 〕 *one's* office; be dismissed from service / 대통령은 교육부 장관을 ～했다 The President dismissed the Education Minister. ◉ ～장(狀) a letter of dismissal; walking papers《구어》.

**해자**(垓子) a moat; a fosse. ¶ ～를 두른 성(城) a moated castle / ～를 파다 dig a moat.

**해자**(楷字) a Chinese character written in the regular "square-hand" 〔printed〕 style; a clearly written character.

**해작질** toying with *one's* food 〔drink〕. ～하다 toy with *one's* food 〔drink〕; pick at *one's* food.

**해장** drinking to relieve a hangover. ～하다 chase a hangover with a drink. ◉ ～국 a broth to chase a hangover; *haejangguk,* a soup containing coagulated cow's blood, beef and vegetables: ～국은 한국 사람들이 즐겨 찾는, 특히 숙취에서 깨어나려는 술꾼들에게 인기 있는 국이다 *Haejangguk* is a popular soup among Koreans, particularly drinkers who are trying to recover from hangovers. ～술 alcohol used as a hangover-chaser; a hair of the dog《구어》: ～술을 마시다 take a hair of the dog that bit *one.*

**해장**(海葬) a burial at sea 〔in the sea〕. ～하다 bury at sea; consign《*a person's* body》 to a watery grave. ⇨ 수장(水葬).

**해저**(海底) the bottom 〔bed〕 of the sea; the sea bottom; the seabed; the ocean floor. ¶ ～의 submarine; undersea / ～의 개발 sea-floor development / ～에 가라앉다 sink 〔go down〕 to the bottom of the sea / 그 배는 ～에 침몰했다 The ship sank to the bottom of the sea.
◉ ～광물자원 mineral resources at the sea bottom; offshore minerals. ～군사이용금지조약 Treaty on the Prohibition of the Emplacement of Nuclear Weapons and Other Weapons of Mass Destruction on the Seabed and the Ocean Floor and in the Subsoil Thereof. ～동식물 the benthos; submarine 〔sea-bottom〕 life. ～릉(陵) an underwater tomb. ～유전 a submarine oil field; an offshore oil field. ～유정굴착기 an offshore (oil) drilling rig; an offshore rig; a floating rig. ～유층(油層)〔유맥(油脈)〕 an offshore 〔undersea〕 oil layer 〔deposit, reserve〕. ～자원 seabed 〔undersea, offshore〕 resources; sea 〔ocean〕 bottom resources. ～전선《lay》 a submarine cable (line). ～전신 cable (service); submarine telegraph: ～전신으로 by cable. ～조사 a submarine survey. ～지진 a submarine earthquake. ～침적물 a submarine deposit. ～탄전 a submarine coal field. ～탐색기 a (remote-control) "deep drone" underwater explorer. ～탐험 an undersea exploration: ～탐험가 an aquanaut. ～터널 a submarine 〔an undersea〕 tunnel. ～화산 a submarine 〔submerged〕 volcano.

**해저드**〖골프〗 a hazard; a water hazard.

**해적**(海賊) a pirate; a sea robber; a corsair. ¶ ～질을 하다 commit piracy; pirate《a ship》; rob at sea / ～이 설치는 바다 a sea infested with pirates; pirate-infested waters. ◉ ～기 a pirate flag; a black flag; the Jolly Roger. ～선 a pirate ship; a sea rover 〔marauder〕. ～판 a pirate(d) edition 〔version〕: 음반〔비디오 테이프〕의 ～판 a pirated (version of a) record 〔video tape〕. ～행위 (an act of ) piracy.

**해전**(一前) before sunset.

**해전**(海戰) a sea fight 〔battle〕; a naval battle 〔engagement〕; 〔총칭〕 naval warfare. ¶ 미드웨이 ～ the Sea Battle off the Midway Islands. ◉ 트라팔가르 ～ the Battle of Trafalgar.

**해제**(解除) ① 《취소》 cancellation; dissolution; 《해금》 lifting; removal《of a ban》. ～하다 《계약 등을》 cancel; 《금지를》 lift《a ban, a restriction》; call off 《an alert》; remove《control》. ¶ 무장 ～ disarmament / 경보를 ～하다 call off an alert; 《공습의》 sound the all-clear / 계약을 ～하다 cancel 〔annul〕 a contract / 금령(禁令)을 ～하다 lift 〔remove〕 a ban《on》/ 통제를 ～하다 remove the control(s)《on》; decontrol 《prices》/ 금지가 ～되다 obtain the annulment of the ban / 쌀의 가격 통제를 ～하다 remove price control over rice / 게릴라들의 무장을 ～하다 disarm a guerrilla band / 공습 경보는 ～되었다

The air-raid alarm is cleared. / 석탄은 3월 1일부터 통제를 ~한다 Coal will be decontrolled as from 1st March. ② 《해방》 release; absolution; discharge; acquittal; exoneration. ~하다 release; free; absolve; exonerate 《*a person* from an obligation》. ◉ ~조항〔조건〕 a resolutive clause 〔condition〕. 계약~ revocation 〔rescission, cancellation〕 of a contract. 폭풍 경보 ~ lifting of a storm warning; "all clear".

**해제**(解題) a bibliographical explanation 〔introduction〕 《of, to》; a bibliographical essay 《on》. ~하다 give a bibliographical explanation 《of》; annotate bibliographically. ◉ ~목록〔서목〕 an annotated catalogue 〔bibliography〕. ~자 a bibliographer. 한서(漢書)~ bibliographical notes on Chinese literature.

**해조**(害鳥) an injurious 〔a harmful〕 bird; a bird that does harm 《to the rice crop》; vermin [총칭].

**해조**(海鳥) a sea bird; a seafowl. ◉ ~분(糞) guano (*pl.* ~s).

**해조**(海藻) 『식물』 seaweeds; marine algae 〔plants〕; seaware (비료용). ◉ ~분(粉) kelp meal. ~회(灰) kelp (ash).

**해조**(諧調) melody; harmony; euphony.

**해조음**(海潮音) the sound 〔boom〕 of the sea 〔waves〕.

**해주다** do 《*something*》 for 《another》; help 《with》; do as a favor. ¶ 편지 번역을 ~ translate a letter 《for *a person*》 / 심부름을 ~ run an errand 《for *a person*》 / 새옷을 ~ make 《*a person*》 new clothes / 그녀는 거의 언제나 아들의 숙제를 해주는 모양이다 I hear she almost always does her boy's homework for him.

**해죽**– ⇨ 히죽–.

**해중**(海中) the middle of the sea; the bottom of the sea. ¶ ~에 《fall》 in 〔into〕 the sea; 《sink》 under 〔beneath〕 the sea. ◉ ~공원 an underwater 〔a submarine〕 park. ~생물 sea life. ~화산 a submarine volcano.

**해지**(解止) cancellation of a contract; 『법』 rescission. ~하다 cancel a contract; surrender 《an insurance policy》. ⇨ 해약.

**해지다**[1] ⇨ 해(어)지다.

**해지다**[2] 《저물다》 the sun sets.

**해직**(解職) release from office; dismissal; discharge. ~하다 release 《*a person*》 from *his* office; relieve 《*a person*》 of *his* post; dismiss; discharge; fire. ⇨ 해임(解任). ¶ ~되다 be relieved of *one's* post; be released from *one's* office 〔position〕; be dismissed / 그는 수회죄로 ~되었다 He was fired for having taken a bribe. ◉ ~수당 dismissal 〔severance〕 pay; a discharge allowance. ~통고 《hand》 a dismissal notice.

**해질녘** 《at》 sunset; 《toward》 sundown. ¶ ~에 toward nightfall 〔evening〕.

**해질성**(一性) 『식물』 negative heliotropism; apheliotropism. ¶ ~의 apheliotropic.

**해찰** 《버릇없음》 brashness; rudeness; inconsiderateness; 《경망함》 flippancy; frivolousness; lack of seriousness. ~하다 treat inconsiderately 〔brashly, rudely〕; behave flippantly 〔frivolously, in a helter-skelter fashion〕; spoil things. ~궂다〔스럽다〕 《버릇없다》 (be) brash; rude; unmannerly; inconsiderate; 《경망하다》 (be) flippant; frivolous; unserious; slapdash.

**해체**(解體) ① 《분해》 taking 《a machine》 apart 〔to pieces〕; dismantling. ~하다 disjoint 《a machine》; take 〔pull〕 《a machine》 apart 〔to pieces〕; dismantle 《an engine, a factory》; break up 〔scrap〕 《a ship》; pull down 《a building》. ¶ 기계를 ~하다 take a machine to pieces; disjoint 〔knock down〕 a machine / 기계를 ~해서 운반하다 convey a machine in sections / 낡은 배를 ~하다 break up 〔scrap〕 an old ship / 그 건물은 ~되었다 The building was pulled down. ② 《해산》 (a) dissolution; disorganization; dismemberment. ~하다 dissolve; disorganize; liquidate; break up. ¶ 조직의 ~ the dissolution of an organization / 재벌을 ~하다 dissolve 〔break up〕 a *chaebŏl* / 발전적으로 ~하다 be dissolved to form better organization. ③ 《해부》 dissection. ⇨ 해부. ◉ 선박~업자 a ship breaker.

**해초**(海草) seaweeds. = 해조(海藻).

**해춘**(解春) thawing; the beginning of spring; the spring thaw. ~하다 it thaws; spring begins; the spring thaw sets in.

**해충**(害蟲) a harmful 〔a noxious, an injurious〕 insect; vermin [총칭]. ¶ ~의 피해 insect plague / ~을 구제하다 get rid of harmful insects; exterminate vermin 〔noxious insects〕; debug. ◉ ~구제(驅除) extermination of vermin: ~구제자(者) an (insect) exterminator.

**해치** 『항해』 a hatch. ¶ ~의 뚜껑 a hatch cover.

**해치다**(害—) injure; harm; (cause) damage; hurt; impair; spoil; do《*a person*》harm; mar; kill (죽이다). ¶ 국가 발전을 해치는 요인 an element detrimental to national development / 아무를 ∼ do harm to [injure, kill] *a person* / 건강을 ∼ injure *one's* health; *one's* health fails / 과로로 건강을 ∼ damage *one's* health with overwork / 감정을 ∼ hurt [injure]《*a person's*》feeling / 공익을 ∼ be detrimental to the public interest / 미관을 ∼ mar [spoil, injure] the beauty《of》; disfigure《the scenery》/ 위(胃)를 ∼ get *one's* stomach out of order / 풍치를 ∼ destroy the scenic beauty《of a place》/ 과로는 건강을 해친다 Overwork [Working too hard] will injure your health. / 그는 남의 감정을 해치는 것을 아무렇지도 않게 여긴다 He thinks nothing of hurting other people's feelings. / 정부는 한미간의 기존 우호 관계를 해치지 않는 선에서 사태의 해결을 모색할 것이다 The government will seek to solve the incident in such a way as not to hamper the friendly relations between Korea and the United States.

**해치우다** finish up; get through《a task, with *one's* work》; do completely; get《it》done; make an end of《*one's* task》;《죽이다》kill; do [make] away with; do for;《패배시키다》defeat; beat; knock《*a person*》over; floor. ¶ 일을 다 ∼ get a job finished / (상대를) 간단히 ∼ defeat《an opponent》with one hand [a single blow] / 내일 외출을 위해서는 이 일을 오늘 해치워야 한다 I have to finish this work today so that I will be free to go out tomorrow.

**해커**《컴퓨터의》a hacker.

**해탈**(解脫) deliverance (of *one's* soul); (Buddhistic) emancipation《from worldly attachments》. ∼하다 be delivered from《passions, worldly bonds》. ¶ 사바[번뇌]에서 ∼하다 be delivered from worldly existence; get freed from the ties of this world; be cut loose from the ties of the earth.

**해태** the unicorn-lion; an omniscient mythical beast.

**해태**(海苔) laver. = 김[1].

**해태**(懈怠) laziness. = 나태(懶怠).

**해토**(解土) thawing of the ground. ∼하다 the ground thaws (out). ◉ ∼머리 the beginning of the thaw.

**해트트릭**〘축구·크리켓〙a hat trick.

**해파리**〘동물〙a jellyfish; a sea jelly; a medusa (*pl.* ∼s, -sae). ¶ ∼의 medusan / ∼모양의 medusoid.

**해판**(解版)〘인쇄〙distribution of printing type. ∼하다 distribute the type; decompose.

**해포석**(海泡石)〘광물〙meerschaum; sepiolite.

**해표**(海豹) = 바다표범.

**해풍**(海風) a sea wind [breeze].

**해피엔딩** a happy ending. ¶ ∼으로 끝나다 come to [have] a happy ending; end happily.

**해하다**(害—) injure《*one's* health》; damage; harm; do harm《to》; hurt《*a person's* feelings》; spoil; mar; impair. ¶ 해할 뜻[마음] malicious intent; malice; murderous intent (죽일) / 사람을 ∼「do harm to [injure, kill] a person / 해할 뜻을 품다 bear《*a person*》malice; mean mischief.

**해학**(諧謔) a jest; a joke; humor; good-humored banter; (a) pleasantry; a wisecrack. ¶ ∼적인 humorous; jocular; witty / ∼의 멋을 알다[모르다] have a [no] sense of humor / ∼의 멋을 아는 사람 a man with a sense of humor / ∼을 섞은 이야기 conversation seasoned with humor / ∼을 농(弄)하다 crack [tell, let off] jokes; make a joke / ∼을 섞어서 말하다 speak humorously [in a humorous vein] / 그에게는 ∼이 통하지 않았다 My joke「was lost [fell flat] on him.

◉ ∼가 a humorist; a humorous person; a man of humor; a joker; a jokester; a jester. ∼곡 a scherzo (*pl.* -s, scherzi) (It.). ∼극 a farce; a burlesque; a comedy (희극). ∼문학 humorous literature. ∼미 a spice of humor. ∼소설 a humorous story.

**해항**(海港) a seaport.

**해해거리다** keep laughing playfully [in fun]; frolic.

**해협**(海峽)〘지리〙a strait; a channel; narrows; a sound《미》. ¶ ∼을 건너다 cross a strait [channel] / 대한∼ the Straits of Korea.

**해화석**(海化石)〘동물〙star coral.

**해후**(邂逅) a chance [casual] meeting; a fortuitous [an unexpected] meeting; an encounter《with》. ∼하다 meet (again) by chance; happen [chance] to meet; come [fall] across《*a person*》; be reunited《with》; encounter. ¶ 그녀는 마침내 40세 되는 생일에 꿈에 그리던 남자와 ∼했다 She finally met the man of her dreams on her fortieth birthday. ◉ ∼상봉 = 해후.

**핵**(核) 《원자·세포 따위의》 a nucleus (*pl.* -clei); 《과실의》 a core; a kernel; a stone; 《중심》 a core; a nucleus (조직 따위의). ¶ 핵의 nuclear / 핵개발 nuclear development / 핵경쟁 a nuclear race / 세포핵 a cell nucleus / 원자핵 the nucleus of an atom; an atomic nucleus / 핵안전 협정 the nuclear safeguard accord / 핵섬광 a nuclear [fission] flash / 핵이 있는 nucleate / 핵의 재처리 nuclear reprocessing / 시민권 운동의 핵 the nucleus of the civil rights movement.

**핵가족**(核家族) a two-generation [nuclear] family. ¶ 두드러진 ～추세 the conspicuous trend toward nuclear families.

**핵공격**(核攻擊) a nuclear attack. ¶ ～을 가하다 launch [make] a nuclear attack 《on》.

**핵과**(核果) 『식물』 a stone-fruit; a drupe.

**핵막**(核膜) 『생물』 the nuclear membrane.

**핵망**(核網) 『생물』 a nuclear network [reticulum (*pl.* -la)].

**핵무기**(核武器) 『군사』 a nuclear weapon; [총칭] nuclear arms [weaponry]. ¶ 소형 ～ a low-power nuclear weapon / ～의 개발 nuclear-weapons development / ～에 의한 파괴[보복] nuclear destruction [retaliation] / (한나라의) ～ 보유 가능성 nuclear capability / (한나라의) ～ 보유수 nuclear capacity / ～공장 nuclear facilities. ◉ ～보유국 a nuclear power: ～비보유국 a non-nuclear power. ～운반로켓 a nuclear carrying rocket. ～폐기 total destruction [abolition] of nuclear weapons. ～확산(擴散) ⇨ 핵확산.

**핵무장**(核武裝) nuclear armament(s). ～하다 arm *itself* [be armed] with nuclear weapons; go nuclear 《구어》. ¶ ～의 철폐 nuclear disarmament / ～을 금지하다 denuclearize 《a country》. ◉ ～경쟁 a nuclear arms race. ～국 a nuclear-armed country; a nuclear power. ～금지[비～]지역 a denuclearized [nuclear-free] zone. 비～화 denuclearization.

**핵물리학**(核物理學) nuclear physics. ◉ ～자 a nuclear physicist.

**핵미사일**(核—) nuclear missiles.

**핵반응**(核反應) (a) nuclear reaction.

**핵발전소**(核發電所) a nuclear power plant.

**핵병기**(核兵器) = 핵무기.

**핵보유국**(核保有國) ⇨ 핵무기 보유국. ¶ 인도는 ～이 되었다 India has become a nuclear power. *or* India has gone nuclear.

**핵분열**(核分裂) 『물리』 nuclear fission; splitting of an atomic nucleus; 『생물』 nuclear division [fission]. ¶ ～을 일으키다 cause nuclear fission / ～을 지속시키다 sustain nuclear fission. ◉ ～물질 fissionable materials [minerals]. ～생성물 a fission product. ～연쇄반응 fission chain reaction. ～폭탄 a (nuclear) fission bomb.

**핵붕괴**(核崩壞) disintegration of a cell nucleus; karyoclasis.

**핵산**(核酸) 『생화학』 nucleic acid. ◉ 디옥시리보～ deoxyribonucleic acid (생략 DNA). 리보～ ribonucleic acid (생략 RNA).

**핵시대**(核時代) the atomic [nuclear] age.

**핵시설**(核施設) nuclear facilities. ¶ 북한은 혐의를 받고 있는 ～에 대한 국제적인 사찰을 받아야 한다 North Korea should accept international inspection of its suspected nuclear facilities.

**핵실험**(核實驗) nuclear (weapons) testing; a nuclear test (1회의). ¶ ～의 금지 a nuclear test ban / ～의 중지[재개] a suspension [resumption] of nuclear test / ～을 하다 carry out a nuclear test / ～을 재개하다 resume nuclear testing. ◉ ～경쟁 nuclear testing competition. ～금지협정 a nuclear test ban agreement. ～장 a nuclear testing ground. 고공(高空)～ a high altitude nuclear test. 대기권～ a nuclear test in the air [atmosphere]; an atmospheric nuclear test. 지하～ an underground nuclear test.

**핵심**(核心) the (hard) core; the kernel; 《요점(要點)》 the point; the nub; guts 《속어》. ¶ 문제의～ the heart [kernel, nub] of a question; the very core of a subject / 문제의 ～을 언급하다[찌르다] touch the core 《of a subject》; come [get] to the point; get down to the nitty-gritty 《속어》 / 문제의 ～을 파악하다 go [get] to the heart of a matter; get at the real gist; get at the heart 《of *a matter*》 / 그의 말은 ～에서 벗어나 있다 His argument is beside the point. / 그는 문제의 ～을 찌르는 질문을 했다 He asked the questions which got to the heart of the matter. / 문제의 ～이 분명하지 않다 The real root of the problem isn't clear. ◉ ～부 nucleus.

**핵알레르기**(核—) (a) nuclear allergy.

**핵에너지** nuclear energy [power]. ¶ ～의 이용은 종종 많은 논쟁을 불러 일으키곤 한다 The use of nuclear energy often gives rise to a lot of controversy.

**핵연료**(核燃料) nuclear fuel. ¶ 사용된 ~의 재처리 the reprocessing of spent nuclear fuel. ◉ ~사이클 a nuclear fuel cycle. ~재처리공장 a nuclear fuel reprocessing plant. ~집합체 a (nuclear) fuel assembly.

**핵우산**(核雨傘) the《American》nuclear umbrella.

**핵원형질**(核原形質) 〖생물〗 nucleoplasm.

**핵융합**(核融合) 〖물리〗 nuclear fusion. ◉ ~폭탄 a (nuclear) fusion bomb.

**핵인**(核仁) 〖생물〗 a nucleolus (*pl.* -li).

**핵(입)자**(核(粒)子) 〖물리〗 a nucleon. ◉ 중~ a hyperon.

**핵자기공명**(核磁氣共鳴) NMR. 〔< *n*uclear *m*agnetic *r*esonance〕

**핵잠수함**(核潛水艦) a nuclear-powered submarine.

**핵장비**(核裝備) ¶ ~(를) 하다 nuclearize《a submarine》/ ~할 수 있는 nuclear-capable《aircraft》/ 이 부대는 ~를 하고 있다 This unit has nuclear capability. *or* This unit is nuclear-capable.

**핵전력**(核戰力) nuclear capability.

**핵전쟁**(核戰爭) (a) nuclear war. ¶ ~의 위협 a nuclear threat / ~의 위협을 줄이다 reduce the threat of a nuclear war / 인류를 ~에 의한 절멸에서 구하다 save mankind from nuclear extinction 〔annihilation〕.

**핵질**(核質) 〖생물〗 nucleoplasm; nuclear substance; karyoplasm; karyotin.

**핵클럽**(核—) the Nuclear 〔Atomic〕 Club.

**핵탄두**(核彈頭) a nuclear warhead. ◉ ~미사일 a nuclear missile; nuclear tipped missile; missile with a nuclear warhead. 전략~ a strategic nuclear warhead.

**핵투명성**(核透明性) the nuclear transparency. ¶ 북한의 ~ 보장에 관한 문제를 제기하다 raise the question of guaranteeing North Korean nuclear transparency.

**핵폐기물**(核廢棄物) nuclear waste(s); radio active waste(s). ¶ ~처리 nuclear waste disposal / ~처리장 a nuclear waste dump site / 러시아는 바다에 ~ 투기(投棄)를 재개할 것이라고 예고했다 Russia warned that it would resume dumping nuclear waste in the sea.

**핵폭발**(核爆發) a nuclear explosion. ◉ ~장치〔실험〕 a nuclear device 〔test〕.

**핵폭탄**(核爆彈) a nuclear bomb; an N-bomb.

**핵학**(核學) 〖생물〗 karyology.

**핵항공모함**(核航空母艦) a nuclear-powered aircraft carrier.

**핵화학**(核化學) nuclear chemistry. ◉ ~자 a nuclear chemist.

**핵확산**(核擴散) nuclear proliferation; spread of nuclear arms 〔weapons〕. ¶ ~을 방지하다 prevent nuclear proliferation. ◉ ~금지조약 the Nuclear Nonproliferation Treaty (생략 NPT).

**핸드드릴** a hand drill.

**핸드백** a handbag; a purse.

**핸드볼** 〖스포츠〗 handball. ~하다 play handball.

**핸드폰** a cellphone; a cellular 〔cell, portable〕 phone; a mobile phone.

**핸들** 《손잡이》 a handle; 《자전거의》 handlebars; 《자동차의》 a (steering) wheel; 《도어의》 a knob. ¶ ~을 잡다 《차의》 sit at the wheel / ~을 우〔좌〕로 꺾다 wheel right 〔left〕.

**핸들링** 〖축구〗 handling.

**핸디캡** a handicap. ¶ ~을 주다 give 《*a person*》 a handicap / 약한 것이 ~이 되다 be handicapped by *one's* weakness / 그는 학력이 없는 것이 ~이다 He is handicapped by his lack of formal education.

**핸섬** handsome. ¶ ~한 남자 a handsome 〔good-looking〕 man.

**핼리** 《천문학자》 Edmund Halley (1656-1742). ◉ ~혜성 Halley's comet.

**핼쑥하다** have a bad complexion; look pale 〔sallow, unwell〕. ¶ 핼쑥한 얼굴 a pallid 〔wan〕 face / 송장처럼 ~ look ghastly / 몹시 핼쑥해지다 turn ghastly 〔deadly〕 pale.

**햄**[1] ham. ¶ 훈제〔스모크〕햄 smoked ham. ◉ 햄샌드위치 ham-sandwiches. 햄샐러드 ham and salad. 햄에그 ham and eggs.

**햄**[2] 《아마추어 무선사》 a (radio) ham.

**햄버거** a hamburger. ◉ ~스테이크 a hamburg(er) steak.

**햅쌀** new rice; the first crop of rice for the year. ◉ ~밥 boiled new rice; rice cooked from the new crop.

**햇-** new; of the year. ¶ 햇감자 a new crop of potatoes.

**햇것** a new crop; the year's crop.

**햇곡식**(—穀食) a new crop of the year.

**햇귀** early morning sunshine; the first rays of the sun; the sun's rays; a sunny spot.

**햇덧** a short autumn day.

**햇무리** the halo of the sun; a ring. ~하다 the sun has a ring around it.

**햇무리구름** 〖기상〗 a cirrostratus cloud.

**햇물** ① ⇨햇무리. ② 《샘물》 a spring that gushes forth only after the year's rainy season.

**햇발** ⇨ 햇살.

**햇병아리** 《병아리》 a chicken; a chick; 《풋내기》 a fledgling; a greenhorn; a「new 〔green〕 hand; a novice; a tenderfoot. ¶ 대학을 갓 나온 ～ a new-fledged university man. ◉ ～기자 a cub (reporter) 《on the *Dong-A*》. ～순경「a fledgling 〔an inexperienced〕 policeman; a newly-fledged policeman.

**햇볕** the「warmth 〔heat〕 of the「sunbeams 〔sunlight〕; the sun. ⇨ 볕. ¶ ～에 in the sun / ～이 잘 드는 sunny 《room》 / 따갑게 내리쬐는 ～ the「glaring 〔burning, scorching〕 sun / ～이 들다 shine in / 방에 ～이 들다 the sun「shines 〔comes〕 into the room / ～이 쬐는〔드는〕 곳에 in a sunny place; in the sun / ～이 안 쬐는〔드는〕 곳에 in a「sunless 〔shady〕 place; in the shade; out of the sun / ～을 쬐다 take the sun; bask 〔bathe〕 in the sun / ～에 쬐다 expose 《*a thing*》 to the sun / ～을 받지 않도록 하다 protect 〔screen〕 《*a thing*》 from the sun; keep 《*something*》「out of the sun 〔in the shade〕 / (살갗이) ～에 타다 be 〔get〕 sunburnt; be「sunbaked 〔(sun)tanned〕; be browned 《with the sun》 / ～에 탄 얼굴 a「sunburnt 〔suntanned〕 face / ～에 타지 않도록 하다 keep 《*oneself*》 from getting sunburnt / ～을 들이다 let in the sunlight / ～에 내놓아 두다 keep 《*a thing*》 in the sun / ～에 말리다 dry 《*a thing*》 in the sun / 곡식을 ～에 널다 spread grain out beneath the sun / 우리집 마당엔 ～이 잘든다 Our garden gets a lot of「sunlight 〔sunshine〕. / 그 집은 남향이라 겨울에도 ～이 잘 든다 As it faces south, the house catches the sun even in winter.

**햇빛** sunshine; sunlight; sunbeams. ¶ 강렬한 ～ glaring 〔hard〕 sunlight / ～에 쬐다 sun; expose 《*a thing*》 to the sun / ～을 들이다 let the sun in / ～을 가리다 screen 〔shade〕 《*a thing*》 from the sun / ～을 보다 see the light of day; 《실현되다》 be realized; materialize; 《세상에 알려지다》 come 〔be brought〕 to light; become known / ～을 보지 못하다 keep indoors; 《식물·장소 등이》 be sunless; have no sunshine; 《알려지지 않다》 remain「obscure 〔unknown〕; 《법안 따위가》 be「shelved 〔tabled, stifled〕 / 그 책은 결국 ～을 보지 못했다 [비유적] The book did not see the light after all.

**햇살** sunbeams; the rays of the sun; sunlight. ¶ 부드러운 ～ soft sunlight; soft 〔gentle〕 rays of the sun / 나뭇가지 사이로 비치는 ～ sunbeams shining through branches of trees / ～이 퍼지다 the sun「spreads its beams 〔shines broad〕 / ～을 받다 be in the sun;「bask 〔bathe〕 in the sun.

**햇수**(—數) the number of years. ¶ 여기에 온 지 ～로 3년이다 It is my third year here.

**햇콩** new beans; the year's new crop「of beans.

**햇팥** new red beans; the year's new crop of red beans.

**행**(行) ① 《줄》 a line; a row 《of written, printed characters》. ¶ 한 행 걸러 《write》 on every other line / 밑에서 10행째 the tenth line from the bottom / 행을 바꾸다 begin a new「line 〔paragraph〕. ② 〖불교〗 religious asceticism; *Samskāra* (Sans.). ③ 《시의》 a line (of verse); a verse.

**행**(幸) happiness; good「luck 〔fortune〕. ¶ 행인지 불행인지 for good or for evil; luckily or unluckily.

**-행**(行) (bound) for; destination. ¶ 부산행 열차〔차표〕 a「train 〔ticket〕 for 〔to〕 Busan / 그 배는 부산행이다 The ship is bound for Busan.

**행각**(行脚) ① 《돌아다님》 traveling on foot; a walking tour. ～하다 travel on foot; go on a walking tour. ¶ 사기～을 하다 commit a fraud 《on》; practice a deception. ② 〖불교〗 a pilgrimage. ～하다「go on 〔make〕 a pilgrimage. ◉ ～승 a priest on a pilgrimage; an itinerant monk.

**행간**(行姦) committing adultery. ⇨ 간음「(姦淫).

**행간**(行間) space between the lines; line spacing. ¶ ～의 여백 interlinear space / ～을 떼다 leave space between (the) lines; space out / ～에 숨겨진 뜻을 읽다 read between the lines.

**행객**(行客) a traveler; a wayfarer.

**행군**(行軍) a (military) march; marching. ～하다 march. ¶ ～코스 a march route / ～중이다 be on the march. ◉ ～대형 a march formation. ～명령 marching orders. ～서열 an order of march. ～속도 a rate of march. ～종대 a marching column. 강～ a forced march. 눈속～ a march through the snow. 철야～ an overnight march.

**행궁**(行宮) a temporary palace.

**행글라이더** 〖스포츠〗 a hang glider. ¶ ～비행 hang gliding. 「《영》.

**행낭**(行囊) a mailbag 《미》; a postbag

**행내기** ⇨ 보통내기.

**행년**(行年) *one's* age〔years〕.

**행동**(行動) action; an act; conduct; behavior; a movement; a move; 〖군사〗 operations. ～하다 act; behave (*oneself*); conduct *oneself;* take action; move. ¶ ～적인 사람 an active person; a man of action / 단체로 ～하다 act as a group; act together / 단독으로 ～하다 act separately 《from》; act independently 《of》; go *one's* own way / 자주적으로 ～하다 do *one's* own will; go *one's* own way / 신중히 ～하다 take a cautious action; play safe / 제멋대로 ～하다 have *one's* (own) way 《in everything》; carve for *oneself.*

행동의: ～의 자유가 허용되다 be allowed freedom of action〔movement〕; be allowed to go *one's* own way / ～의 자유를 속박하다 restrain 《*a person's*》 freedom of action; tie 《*a person's*》 hands; pin〔tie〕 《*a person*》 down 《to a contract》.

행동을: ～을 개시하다 start action; set to work; make a move / ～을 삼가다〔조심하다〕 be prudent in *one's* conduct / ～을 일으키다 go〔get, move〕 into action / ～을 주시하다 watch 《*a person's*》 movement / ～을 취하다 act; behave; take action 《against》 / 독자적 ～을 취하다 act in *one's* own way / …에 대하여 직접 군사 ～을 취하다 take direct military action against... / ～을 감시하다 watch〔keep an eye on〕 《*a person's*》 movement / …와 ～을 같이〔함께〕 하다 act〔go along 《구어》〕 with 《*a person*》; act together; cooperate 《with》; cast in *one's* lot 《with》; move in harmony 《with》; act in concert〔line〕 《with》 / 자유 ～을 취하다 act for *oneself;* do as *one* pleases; take free action.

행동에, 행동으로: ～에 나타내다 show in *one's* manner / ～에 들어가다 go〔get〕 into action / (생각 따위를) ～에〔으로〕 옮기다 translate 《an idea》〔put 《*one's* idea》〕 into action; carry out〔execute〕 《a resolution》.

행동이: ～이 기민하다 be prompt〔quick〕 in action / ～이 대담하다 be bold in action; act boldly / ～이 수상하다 act〔behave〕 suspiciously.

¶ 박군은 한번 결심하면 곧 ～으로 옮기는 사람이다 Mr. Park acts immediately when he makes a decision. / 단체여행 중에는 자기 멋대로 ～을 해서는 안된다 You must not do your own way in a group tour. / 그의 행동은 신사적이었다 He behaved like a gentleman. / 단독 ～은 삼가주십시오 Don't act independently〔on your own〕.

◉ ～강령 a code of conduct. ～거지 (conduct and) behavior; deportment; manners; bearing; demeanor. ～과학 behavioral science. ～권 《생태계의》 the〔*its*〕 home range. ～대 an action group〔corps〕. ～력 *a person's* ability to act. ～미술 action painting: ～미술가 an action painter. ～반경 an action radius; a cruising〔an operation〕 radius. ～방침 the course of action. ～방향 a line of action. ～범위 a sphere of action; elbowroom. ～양식 〖사회〗 a behavior pattern. ～인 a man of action. ～주의 〖심리〗 behaviorism: ～주의 심리학자 a behaviorist. ～특성 a behavioral characteristic. ～파 〖철학〗 《능동주의》 activism. 한국 ～과학 연구소 the Korean Institute for Research in the Behavioral Science.

**행동개시**(行動開始) 〖군사〗 deployment. ～하다 deploy 《an army, a troop》. ◉ ～시간 (the) H-hour; (the) zero hour. ～(예정)일 the deployment day; D-day.

**행동통일**(行動統一) action in concert 《with》; united action. ～하다 act in concert 《with》. ¶ 파업자들끼리 ～이 안되고 있다 There is lack of unity among the strikers.

**행락**(行樂) pleasure-making; holiday-making; a good time; a pleasure trip; an outing. ～하다 have a good time; go on「an outing〔an excursion, a pleasure trip〕. ¶ 봄철의 ～ pleasures of spring time; 《나들이》 a spring outing. ◉ ～객 a vacationer 《미》; a holiday-maker 《영》. ～지 a pleasure〔holiday〕 resort: 설악산은 서울 사람들에게 ～지로 잘 알려져 있다 Mt. Sŏrak is well-known as a resort for people from Seoul.

**행랑**(行廊) rooms on both sides of the main gate where servants live; servants quarters. ◉ ～것 servants; menials. ～살이 《lead, live》 the life of a resident servant. ～아범〔어멈〕 a man〔woman〕 servant who lives in. ～채 ＝행랑.

**행려**(行旅) travel; 《사람》 a traveler. ◉ ～병사자 one who has sickened and died unidentified by the roadside. ～병자 a person fallen sick on the road; an ill wayfarer.

**행렬**(行列) ① 《줄지은 것》 a procession;

《차례를 기다리는》 a line; a queue. ¶ 자동차의 ~ an array of cars / ~을 짓다 《쇼핑 등의》 form a line 〔queue 《영》〕; stand in line; line up; queue (up) 《영》 / ~을 지어 in procession; in a line; in a queue / ~에 끼어 들다 break into a line 《of waiting people》; jump a queue. ② 《행진》 (a) procession; (a) parade; (a) march; 『수학』 a matrix (*pl.* -trices, ~es). ¶ ~의 선두〔후미〕 the head 〔tail〕 of a procession / ~을 지어가다 march in procession; parade / ~이 거리를 누비다 processions parade the streets. ◉ 가장~ a fancy-dress parade.

**행로**(行路) 《길》 a road; a path; a course; 《여로》 a journey; a career. ¶ ~지인(之人) a complete outsider; an utter stranger. ◉ 인생~ the 《thorny》 path 〔course〕 of life; life's journey 〔pilgrimage〕: 인생~는 험난하다 Life is full of troubles 〔rubs〕.

**행리**(行李) 《여행할 때의》 a (wicker) portmanteau 〔suit case〕; a trunk; a baggage 《미》 〔luggage 《영》〕. ¶ ~에 챙겨 넣다 pack in a trunk; pack a trunk 《with clothes》.

**행망쩍다** (be) careless; inattentive.

**행방**(行方) the place where *a person* has gone; *one's* whereabouts 〔traces〕. ¶ ~이 묘연한 missing; lost / 오랫동안 ~을 몰랐던 long-lost 《sister》 / ~을 감추다 disappear; cover *one's* traces 〔tracks〕; conceal *oneself;* hide out; run away / ~을 찾다 trace; search 〔hunt, look〕 for 《*a person*》; search 《a city》 for the traces 《of a lost child》 / ~을 알아내다 locate 《*a person*》; discover the trace of 《a missing man》; find out 《*a person's*》 whereabouts 〔hiding place〕; track down 《a criminal》 / 그녀를 찾아 보았지만 ~이 묘연했다 We failed to 〔We didn't〕 find any trace of her. / 나는 그녀의 ~을 알고 싶다 I want to know her whereabouts. / 경찰은 그녀의 ~을 찾고 있다 The police are searching 〔looking〕 for her. / 아직도 세사람의 ~은알 수 없다 Three people are still unaccounted 〔not accounted〕 for.

**행방불명**(行方不明) "whereabouts unknown"; missing. ¶ ~이다 be missing 〔lost〕; *a person's* whereabouts is unknown / ~이 되다 be 〔get〕 lost; be lost sight of; stray out of contact; 《소식없다》 be heard of no more; nothing more is heard of 《*a person*》 / 승무원 중 7명은 ~으로 보도되었다 Seven of the crew were reported (as) missing. / 그 전투에서 ~된 병사는 5명이었다 In that battle the number of soldiers missing in action was 5. ◉ ~자 a missing person; 《전투 중 행방 불명》 an MIA 〔<*m*issing *i*n *a*ction〕: 사상자와 ~자 the killed, wounded and missing / ~자 중에는 그의 이름도 있었다 He was among the missing.

**행보**(行步) walking; going on foot. ~하다 walk; go on foot. ¶ 인생의 ~ *one's* walk of life / ~를 멈추다 stop walking / 발길이 향하는 대로 ~를 옮기다 be always on the move as the mood takes *one*.

**행복**(幸福) happiness; bliss; blessedness; good fortune. ~하다〔스럽다〕 (be) happy; blessed; blissful; fortunate. ¶ ~하게 happily; in happiness / ~의 절정 《at》 the seventh heaven / ~의 추구 pursuit 〔quest〕 of happiness / 인생의 ~ human happiness; happiness of life / ~을 누리다 enjoy happiness / ~하게 살다 live happily; lead 〔live〕 a happy life / ~을 빌다 wish 《*a person*》 every happiness; wish 《*a person*》 well 〔(good) luck〕 / ~을 깨뜨리다 wreck 〔ruin〕 《*a person*》 happiness of life / 남의 ~을 부러워하다 covet 〔envy, feel envious of〕 the happiness of others / 더할나위 없이 ~하다 be as happy as *one* can be / ~에의 길은 하나가 아니다 There are different ways to happiness. / 건강한 몸으로일할 수 있는 것보다 ~한 것은 없다 There is nothing happier than to work in good health. / 그 당시의 나는 ~의 절정에 있었다 That was the happiest time of my life. ◉ ~감 a feeling of happiness; a sense of well=being; 『심리』 euphoria. ~론 『철학』 eud(a)emonics. ~설 『철학』 eud(a)emonism.

**행불행**(幸不幸) happiness or misery; weal or woe; good or ill fortune; good or bad luck. ¶ 인생의 ~ the lights and shadows 〔the ups and downs〕 of life / ~은 생각하기 나름이다 Luck is a matter of attitude. / 나는 그의 ~에 개의치 않는다 I never mind the weal or woe of him.

**행사**(行使) use; exercise. ~하다 use; make use of; employ 《*one's* privilege》; exercise 《*one's* rights》. ¶ 권력을〔권리를〕 ~하다 exercise *one's* power 〔right〕 / 무력을 ~하다 appeal 〔resort, go〕 to arms; use force / 묵비권을 ~하다 use *one's* right to keep silent / 투표〔선거〕권을 ~하다 exercise *one's* right to vote; cast *one's* vote / 실력을 ~하다 use 〔employ〕 force; appeal to arms; 《경찰 등이》 resort to forced measures / 특권을 ~하다 employ *one's* privilege / 그들은 마침내 실력 ~로 나왔다 They finally resorted to force.

**행사**(行事) an event; a function. ¶ 다채로운 ~ colorful events / 학교의 ~ 계획 a schedule for the activities of the school year / 경축 ~의 하나 《as》 one of the celebration program / 이것은 우리 학교의 가장 큰 ~중 하나이다 This is one of the biggest events held by our school. ◉ 국제적 ~ an international event. 연중~ 〔총칭〕 the year's regular functions; the chief events of the year; 《하나의》 an annual function; a regular annual event.

**행상**(行商) ① 《장사》 peddling; hawking; an itinerant trade. ~하다 peddle; hawk; engage in an itinerant trade. ¶ 시골로 다니며 ~하다 peddle goods about the country / (지방으로) ~나가다 go on a peddling tour / ~사절 《게시》 No solicitors allowed! *or* No hawkers! ② 《행상인》 a peddler; a hawker; 《구어》 a huckster; a bell-ringer.

**행상**(行賞) awarding 《*a person*》 (with a) prize. ~하다 award a prize 《to *a person*》; reward 《*a person* for *his* service》.

**행색**(行色) ① 《차림새》 *one's* appearance (in traveling outfit). ¶ ~이 초라하다 look shabby. ② 《태도》 demeanor; attitude.

**행서**(行書) the "running-hand" 〔semi-cursive〕 style of Chinese penmanship.

**행선지**(行先地) 《목적지》 *one's* destination; the end of *one's* journey; the place where *one* 「is going 〔has gone〕; 《소재》 *one's* whereabouts (★ 단·복수 취급). ¶ ~를 알려 주시오 Kindly tell me where you are going. / 나는 그녀의 ~를 모른다 I don't know where she has gone.

**행성**(行星) 〖천문〗 a planet; a globe; a primary. ¶ ~의 planetary.
◉ ~광행차(光行差)〔세차(歲差)〕 planetary aberration 〔precession〕. ~상(狀)성운 a planetary nebula. ~운동〔환류〕 planetary 「motion 〔circulation〕. ~의 a planetarium. 내~ an 「inferior 〔interior〕 planet. 대~ a major planet. 소~ a minor planet; an asteroid; a planetoid. 외~ 「an exterior 〔an outer, a superior〕 planet.

> **참고** 행성의 종류
> 「수성」 Mercury, 「금성」 Venus, 「화성」 Mars, 「목성」 Jupiter, 「토성」 Saturn, 「천왕성」 Uranus, 「해왕성」 Neptune, 「명왕성」 Pluto.

**행성간탐사기**(行星間探査機) an interplanetary probe.

**행세**(行世) 《처세》 *one's* way of living (through the world); 《태도》 *one's* behavior 〔bearing, manners〕; 《가장》 (false) show; pretense. ~하다 《행동하다》 conduct *oneself;* behave; 《가장하다》 pass *oneself* off 《as》; pretend; assume an air 《of a millionaire》. ¶ ~를 잘못하다 misconduct *oneself;* misbehave / … ~를 하다 successfully impersonate 《a detective》; pose as; set *oneself* up as 《a poet》; pass *oneself* off as 《a lawyer》; assume the air of / 남편 ~를 하다 pose as husband / 교수 ~를 하다 set *oneself* up as a professor / 주인 ~를 하다 assume 〔put on〕 a proprietary air.

**행세**(行勢) seizing 〔assuming〕 《political》 power 〔influence〕. ~하다 wield 〔exercise〕 *one's* power 〔influence〕 《over》. ¶ ~하는 집안 「a distinguished 〔an influential〕 family / 그는 재계에서 크게 ~한다 He has great influence over the financial world. *or* He is powerful in the financial world.

**행수**(行首) the 「head 〔leader〕 of a group; a boss.

**행수**(行數) the number of lines.

**행실**(行實) conduct; behavior; demeanor. ¶ 좋은〔훌륭한〕~ good 〔honorable〕 conduct / 나쁜〔못된〕 ~ misconduct; misbehavior / ~이 좋은 well-behaved 〔-conducted〕 / ~이 좋다 be well-behaved; show good deportment 〔conduct〕 / ~이 나쁘다 misbehave 〔misconduct〕 *oneself;* behave badly / ~이 나쁜 사람 a person of bad conduct 〔behavior, loose morals〕; a badly-behaved person; a bad character 《구어》 / ~을 고치다 (a)mend *one's* ways 〔conduct〕 《구어》; turn over a new leaf / ~을 조심하다 be careful 〔prudent, discreet〕 in *one's* conduct.

**행악**(行惡) violence; wickedness; perverseness. ~하다 practice 〔practise 《영》〕 wickedness; do violence; give vent to *one's* spite.

**행여(나)**(幸—) by (any) chance; possibly; by some chance (or other). ¶ ～하고 on the chance 《of finding you》; 《요행을 바라고》 on the off-chance / ～…하지나 않을까 하고 for fear of; for fear that… may… / ～ 꿈이 아닌가 몸을 꼬집어 보다 pinch *oneself* to make sure that *one* is not dreaming / ～나 있을세라 우려했던 일이 사실로 되었다 My (worst) fear has come true. / ～댁에 계실까 해서 찾아 왔습니다 I came on the (off) chance of finding you at home. / ～ 오지 않을까하여 기다렸다 I have waited in case you might drop by.

**행운**(幸運) good luck; good fortune; lucky break. ¶ ～의 fortunate; lucky; happy / ～의 여신 the Goddess of Fortune / ～의 연속 repeated strokes of luck / ～의 편지 a chain letter / ～을 빌다 wish 《*a person*》 good luck / (요행히도) …할 ～을 만나다 be lucky enough to *do;* have the (good) fortune to *do* / ～의 절정에 있다 be at the top of fortune's wheel / ～을 얻다 have good luck / ～을 타고 나다 be born under a lucky star / 자기의 ～을 감사하다 thank *one's* lucky stars / ～이 돌아왔다 Good luck has come round to my door. / ～을 빕니다 I wish you good luck. / ～의 전조다 It will bring good fortune. / 이 무슨 ～이냐 What a stroke of luck! / ～에게 버림 받았다 My luck ran out. *or* Luck deserted me.

◉ ～아 a lucky fellow 〔person〕; a fortune's favorite; a child of fortune.

**행운유수**(行雲流水) going smoothly 〔swimmingly〕; being free and easy.

**행원**(行員) a bank employee 〔clerk〕.

**행위**(行爲) 《행동》 an act; an action; a deed; 《행실》 conduct; behavior; 《소행》 a work; 《*one's*》 doing.

> **용법** **act** 하나하나의 행위, 또는 일시적인 행위. **action** 어떤 행위의 과정 전체, 또는 어떤 기간에 걸쳐 행해진 여러 차례의 행위 전체. **deed** 의도적인 행위를 나타내는 말로, 종종 눈에 띄는 훌륭한 행위. **behavior** 어떤 상황·경우에 나타나는 사람의 행동·처신 따위를 나타내는 말. **conduct** 도덕적인 관점에서 본 행동.

¶ 영웅적 ～ a heroic deed; a heroism / 정당한 ～ a justifiable 〔legitimate〕 act / 친절한 ～ an act of kindness / 잔학 ～ an act of cruelty; an atrocity / ～를 하다 act; take steps; perform an act / 공무원의 부정～를 조사하다 investigate irregularities of government officials / 말이 아닌 ～로써 의중을 보이다 show *one's* intention not by words but by deeds / 그의 ～는 꼭 미친 사람 같다 He behaves himself exactly like a madman. / 그는 용감한 ～로 표창받았다 He was rewarded for his brave deed.

◉ ～능력 (legal) capacity: ～무능력 (legal) incompetence. ～세 the service 〔act〕 tax. ～자 a doer; a transactor; a performer 《of a deed》. ～지 the place of an act. 도덕(적) ～ a moral act.

**행음**(行淫) committing adultery. ～하다 commit adultery.

**행인**(行人) a passerby (*pl.* passersby); a foot passenger; a wayfarer (나그네). ¶ ～의 발길이 끊어졌다 The street was deserted. *or* There is not a soul to be seen on the street.

**행인**(杏仁) an apricot stone.

**행자**(行者) 『불교』 a layman engaged in performing religious 〔Buddhistic〕 austerities; an ascetic (devotee).

**행장**(行狀) ① 《죽은 이의》 records of a deceased person's life; records of *one's* doings during *one's* lifetime; a necrology. ② 《수감자의》 (a record of) *one's* behavior; conduct.

**행장**(行裝) travel gear; a traveler's equipment; a traveling outfit 〔kit, suit〕. ¶ ～을 차리다 prepare 〔equip, outfit〕 *oneself* for a journey / ～을 풀다 take off *one's* traveling attire; 《숙박하다》 check in at a hotel 《미》.

**행적**(行蹟) the achievements of *one's* lifetime; *one's* work 〔contributions〕.

**행전**(行纏) leggings; puttees; gaiters. ¶ ～을 치고 with gaitered legs / ～을 치다 wrap *one's* legs with puttees.

**행정**(行政) administration 《of government》. ¶ ～적인〔상의〕 executive; administrative / ～적 수완이 있다 have administrative ability 〔talent〕 / ～의 능률화를 도모하다 streamline the administration / 현재의 시장은 ～적인 수완이 없다 The present mayor 「is an incompetent administrator 〔has no administrative ability〕.

◉ ～각부 administrative branches. ～감독 administrative control 〔management〕. ～감사 administrative inspection 〔audit〕. ～개혁 a reform of the administrative structure; (an) administrative reform: ~개혁 위원회 the Administration「Reform〔Renovation〕 Commission / ~ 개혁 조사 위원회 the Administrative Improvement Research Commission / ~개혁을 행하다 carry out an administrative reform; reform the administration. ~경찰 the administrative police. ~관 an executive〔administrative〕 official; the executive [총칭]. ~관청「a government〔an administrative〕 office〔agency〕. ~구획〔구역〕 an administrative district〔division, section〕; (area of ) jurisdiction: ~ 구역 개편 the revision of administrative districts. ~권 administrative「right〔power, authority〕. ~기관 an administrative「organ〔body, machinery〕; an executive agency. ~대학원 a graduate school of public administration. ~명령 an administrative「〔executive〕 order. ~법〔정리(整理)〕 administrative「law〔readjustment, reorganization〕. ~법령 an administrative decree. ~부 the Executive; the Administration: ~부 수반 the Chief Executive. ~사무 administrative affairs. ~서사 an administrative scrivener. ~소송 administrative litigation. ~수도 an administrative capital city. ~수완 administrative「ability〔capacity〕: ~수완이 부족하다 have no administrative ability; be an incompetent administrator. ~원《중국의》 the Executive Council. ~자치부 the Ministry of Government Affairs and Home Affairs. ~정리 administrative「adjustment〔reorganization〕. ~조처 an administrative「measure〔action〕: ~조처를 취하다 take administrative action《against》; enforce administrative measures. ~지도 administrative guidance. ~질서범 those charged with violating minor administrative codes. ~처벌 the administrative punishment. ~처분 an administrative disposition. ~학 public administration. ~협정 an administrative agreement; 《주한 미군과의》 a status-of-forces agreement.

**행정**(行程) ① 《거리》 (a) road distance; 《여정》 a distance to cover; a journey; 《행군의》 a march; 《일정》 an itinerary. ¶ 하루의 ~ a day's journey / 일행은 하루 평균 ~ 10마일의 속도로 나아갔다 The party covered ten miles a day on average. / 열흘간의 ~을 무사히 끝내고 돌아왔다 I returned safe after a journey of ten days. ② 〖기계〗 a stroke; a travel; an excursion. ¶ 4 ~의 four-stroke 《engine》.

**행정기구**(行政機構) administrative organization; an administrative structure. ¶ 현존 ~를 간소화〔정리〕하다 simplify〔streamline〕 the government structure in existence.

**행정조직**(行政組織) = 행정기구.

**행주** a dishcloth 《영》; a dishrag 《미》; a dish towel 《미》. ¶ ~ (를) 치다 wipe with a dishcloth. ◉ ~질 wiping with a dishcloth. ~치마 an apron.

**행중**(行中) 《일행》 a company; a party; a troop; a troupe. ¶ ~에 끼다 join the company.

**행진**(行進) marching; a march; a parade. ~하다 march; proceed; parade. ¶ 평화의 ~ a peace march / 거리를 ~하다 march「through〔down〕 the street / 의기양양하게 ~하다 march「in triumph〔triumphantly〕. ◉ ~곡 a march: 군대 ~곡 a military march / 결혼〔장송〕 ~곡 a「wedding〔funeral〕 march.

**행짜** mischief. ⇨ 행티.

**행차**(行次) an honored「going〔coming〕; a visit; a trip; traveling. ~하다 go; come; visit; go on a trip. ¶ ~ 뒤에 나팔 [비유적] a day after the fair; the doctor after death.

**행커치프** a handkerchief (*pl.* ~s, 「-chieves).

**행티** ill-willed behavior. ¶ ~ 사납다 be「peevish〔mean〕/ ~ 부리다 show ill will; do mean things.

**행패**(行悖) misconduct; misbehavior. ~하다 do violence 《to》; misbehave *oneself.* ¶ ~를 부리다 resort to violence; commit an outrage 《on》; play havoc 《with, among》/ 그는 온갖 ~를 부렸다 He absolutely ran amuck.

**행포**(行暴) violence; lawless acts; doing violence; committing lawless acts. ~하다 do violence 《to》, commit lawless acts; perpetrate an outrage. ¶ 갖은 ~를 다 부리다 commit all sorts of excesses.

**행하**(行下) 《하인에게 주는》 a gift of money from a master to his servant; 《놀음차》 a tip; a gratuity. ¶ ~를 주다 tip; give a gratuity 《to》.

**행하다**(行—) ① 《행위를 하다》 do; act; work; 《행동하다》 behave (*oneself*); conduct〔carry〕 *oneself.* ¶ 기적을 ~ work a miracle / 나쁜 짓을 ~ do wrong; commit an evil act.
② 《실행하다》 do; practice〔practise 《영》〕 《asceticism》; put 《a theory》 into practice; carry out 《a plan》; act

upon 《*one's* principle》; 《이행하다》 perform; discharge 《*one's* duty》. ¶ 의무를 ~ perform 〔discharge〕 *one's* duty / 과감한 개혁을 ~ carry out a drastic reform / 생각한 것을 실제로 ~ put an idea into practice / 말은 쉬워도 행하기는 어렵다 Theory is one thing, practice is another. *or* Easier said than done. ③ 《실시하다》 conduct 《education, investigation》; exercise 《control, administration》; 《법률 등을》 put in force; enforce; put in operation; 《행사하다》 exercise 《authority》. ¶ 정의를 ~ dispense justice. ④ 《거행하다》 hold 《a funeral》; give 《an examination》; observe 《a festival》; perform 《a ceremony》; celebrate; solemnize 《a wedding》. ¶ (의)식을 ~ perform 〔hold, administer〕 a ceremony / 혼례를 ~ hold 〔perform, solemnize〕 a「marriage 〔wedding〕.

**행해지다**(行—) be done; be put into practice; be carried out; 《실시되다》「come into 〔be put in〕 force; take effect; become effective; 《거행되다》 take place; be held; come off. ¶ 이 의식은 지금도 행해지고 있다 The rite is still in force. / 이 지방에서는 여러가지 옛풍습이 지금도 행해지고 있다 A number of ancient customs「still exist 〔are still maintained〕 in this part of the country.

**행형**(行刑) 〖법〗 the execution of a sentence; execution; decapitation. ~하다 execute; decapitate. ◉ ~학 penology.

**향**(向) ① 《방향》 a direction; a quarter; 《방위》 a compass direction; a situation. ¶ 서향의 facing west; in the western direction / 풍향 the direction of the wind; the quarter from which the wind blows. ② 《집의》 an exposure; an aspect. ¶ 남향집 a house「facing (the) south 〔exposed to the south〕 / 서향이다 《집이》 look to the west; 《창이》 open to the west / 우향우 《구령》 Right turn 〔face〕!

**향**(香) (a) perfume; (an) incense. ¶ 향을 피우다 burn incense.

**향가**(鄕歌) native songs; old Korean「folksongs 〔ballads〕.

**향갑**(香匣) an incense case.

**향관**(鄕關) *one's* native province; *one's* home 〔native〕 land.

**향교**(鄕校) a local old-time school belonging to the Confucian shrine.

**향군**(鄕軍) 《재향 군인》 a veteran; an ex-serviceman; an ex-soldier; reservists; 《부대》 veterans troops. ¶ 백만 ~을 무장시키다 provide 〔furnish, supply〕 one million veterans with arms.

**향긋하다** (be) somewhat fragrant; have a faint sweet scent.

**향기**(香氣) (a) fragrance; (a) perfume; an aroma; a sweet「odor 〔smell〕; scent. ¶ 꽃 ~ the fragrance of a flower / 장미 ~ the smell of roses / 문학의 ~가 높은 of high literary merit; rich in literary flavor / (좋은) ~가 나다 smell sweet; give a nice smell / ~가 좋다 be「fragrant 〔aromatic〕; be sweet-smelling〔-scented〕 / ~가 좋은 sweet-smelling; fragrant; sweet-scented; aromatic / ~를 내다〔풍기다〕 give out a smell; emit 〔send forth〕 fragrance / ~ 짙은 향수를 쓰다 use「powerful 〔strong〕 scent 〔perfume〕 / 방안에는 꽃 ~가 감돌고 있었다 Flowers perfumed the room. / 새로 끓인 커피 ~가 온 방안에 가득하였다 The aroma of the freshly-brewed coffee wafted through the room.

**향기롭다**(香氣—) (be) fragrant; sweet; aromatic; sweet-smelling; sweet=scented; odoriferous. ¶ 향기로운 냄새 a「sweet 〔fragrant〕 smell / 향기로운 꽃 a fragrant flower.

**향꽂이**(香—) an incense「holder 〔burner〕.

**향나무**(香—) 〖식물〗 aromatic trees; a Chinese juniper.

**향낭**(香囊) an incense「pouch 〔bag〕; a sachet.

**향내, 향냄새**(香—) = 향기(香氣).

**향년**(享年) *one's* age at death. ¶ ~ 칠십세다 He died at (the age of) seventy.

**향당**(鄕黨) *one's* native village community; a village community.

**향도**(嚮導) guidance; guiding; leading; conducting; 《사람》 a guide; a leader. ~하다 guide; conduct; lead. ◉ ~기 a leader plane. ~함 a (flotilla) leader; a guide (ship).

**향락**(享樂) enjoyment. ~하다 enjoy 《the pleasures of the senses》; seek pleasure 《in》. ¶ ~적인 pleasure seeking; given up to pleasure; merry-making; self-indulgent / ~생활을 보내다 lead a gay life; live a life of pleasure; enjoy life / ~에 빠지다 abandon *oneself* to pleasure. ◉ ~업소 a pleasure-seeking business establishment. ~주의 epicurism; hedonism; 《문예상의》 dilettantism: ~ 주의자 an epicure; a hedonist.

**향로**(香爐) an incense burner; a censer. ◉ ~석 the stone before a tomb that the incense burner is put on.

**향료**(香料) 《식품의》 spice(s); spicery; 《화장품 등의》 (a) perfume; aromatic essence. ◉ ~식물 aromatic plants.

**향리**(鄕里) *one's* hometown; *one's* native village 〔town〕.

**향미**(香味) flavor; smack. ◉ ~료 flavorings; spices; condiments.

**향방**(向方) a direction; bearings; a course; a destination; an aspect. ¶ ~을 모르다 do not know the direction; have no sense at all; don't know which way is up.

**향배**(向背) for or against; pro or con; where *one* stands or leans (on an issue). ¶ ~를 정하다〔분명히 하다〕 define 〔clarify〕 *one's* attitude 《toward》; decide definitely whether *one* is for or against 《a policy》 / ~를 분명히 하지 않다 sit on the fence; be noncommittal.

**향불**(香―) an incense fire; burning incense. ¶ ~을 피우다 burn incense.

**향사**(向斜) 〖지질〗 a syncline; a synclinal (fold). ¶ ~곡(谷) a synclinal valley.

**향상**(向上) elevation; rise; 《개선》 improvement; uplift; 《진보》 (self-) advancement; progress. ~하다 rise; get 〔be〕 elevated; progress; improve; better *oneself;* advance. ¶ 지위의 ~ a rise in position / 교육 수준의 ~ the elevation of education standards / 여성의 지위 ~ the rise in women's social status / 국민 체위의 ~ the improvement of the national physique / 생활 수준의 ~ the improvement of living standards / ~시키다 raise; elevate; improve; better / 학문이 ~하다 improve 〔advance〕 in *one's* studies / 노인 복지를 ~시키다 promote welfare for the old people / ~하도록 노력하다 struggle for betterment / 노동자의 지위 ~을 도모하다 try to raise laborers' social status / 생활의 ~을 꾀하다 try to improve *one's* living condition; try to get 〔gain〕 a better life (for *oneself*) / 그의 영어 실력은 크게 ~했다 He has remarkably improved in his ability of English. ◉ ~심(心) aspiration; ambition; a desire to improve *oneself.*

**향선**(香腺) 〖동물〗 a scent bag 〔gland〕.

**향속**(鄕俗) country 〔rural〕 ways; local customs.

**향수**(享受) enjoyment; fruition. ~하다 enjoy; have; be given.

**향수**(享壽) enjoying longevity. ~하다 enjoy old age; live to a ripe old age.

**향수**(香水) a (liquid) perfume; a scent; perfumed 〔scented〕 water; *eau-de-Cologne* (F.); toilet water; [총칭] perfumery. ¶ ~를 뿌리다 perfume 〔scent〕 《a handkerchief》; spray perfume 《on, over》; put on 〔wear, use〕 perfume / ~내가 너무 진하다 be excessively perfumed / 그는 그녀가 사용한 ~를 정확히 알아맞췄다 He accurately guessed the perfume she was wearing. ◉ ~병(甁) a perfume 〔scent〕 bottle. ~뿌리개 an 〔a perfume〕 atomizer; a scent spray(er).

**향수**(鄕愁) homesickness; nostalgia 《for》. ¶ ~를 느끼다 feel homesick; feel nostalgia 〔nostalgic〕 《for》; long 〔yearn〕 for *one's* home / ~에 젖다 be nostalgic 《for》 / ~에 젖게 하다 make 《*a person*》 homesick; make 《*a person*》 pine 〔sick〕 for home / 이 노래는 나를 ~에 젖게 한다 This song makes me homesick 〔nostalgic〕.

**향습성**(向濕性) 〖식물〗 positive hydrotropism.

**향신료**(香辛料) spice(s).

**향심력**(向心力) = 구심력(求心力).

**향악**(鄕樂) Korean music (as contrasted with *Tang-ak,* Chinese music).

**향연**(香煙) ① 《연기》 the smoke of incense burning. ② 《담배》 fragrant tobacco.

**향연**(饗宴) a feast; a banquet; a dinner. ¶ ~을 베풀다 hold 〔give〕 a banquet.

**향열성**(向熱性) 〖생물〗 positive thermotropism.

**향유**(享有) enjoyment; possession. ~하다 enjoy; possess *oneself* 〔be possessed〕 of. ⇨ 누리다[2]. ¶ 인권의 ~ the enjoyment of personal right / 국민은 모든 기본적 인권의 ~를 방해받지 않는다 The people shall not be prevented from enjoying any of the fundamental human rights.

**향유**(香油) fragrant 〔perfumed, aromatic〕 oil; 《참기름》 sesame oil. ◉~고래 〖동물〗 a sperm whale.

**향응**(響應) ① 《메아리》 resonance; echo; reverberation; response; respondence. ~하다 resonate; echo; reverberate; respond. ② 《맞장구》 following suit; chiming. ~하다 follow suit; chime 《in》.

**향응**(饗應) 《대접》 an entertainment; a treat; 《연회》 a banquet; a dinner; a feast. ~하다 entertain 《*a person*》 at dinner; treat 《*a person*》 to a dinner 《by way of bribing *him*》; give 〔hold〕 a party 〔banquet〕 《for *a person*》. ¶ ~을 받다 be treated 《to a dinner》; be entertained 〔regaled〕 《with refreshments》/ 후보자는 유권자들에게 호화로운 ～을 베풀었다 The candidate treated the voters to a sumptuous bash.

**향의**(向意) intention; inclination. ～하다 intend to; be inclined to.

**향일**(向日) turning toward the sunlight. ◉ ～성(性) 〖식물〗 positive heliotropism. ～화(花) = 해바라기.

**향전**(香奠) = 부의(賻儀).

**향점**(向點) 〖천문〗 the apex. ◉ 태양～ the solar apex.

**향정신성**(向精神性) ¶ ～의약품 psychotropic (medicine) (정신 안정제·환각제 따위).

**향지성**(向地性) 〖식물〗 (positive) geotropism.

**향초**(香草) ① 《풀》 fragrant grass; an aromatic plant; herbs. ② 《담배》 fragrant tobacco.

**향촉**(香燭) incense and candles (used in traditional rites).

**향촌**(鄕村) the country; a country village; country districts.

**향취**(香臭) = 향기(香氣).

**향토**(鄕土) *one's* native place 〔province〕; *one's* birthplace 〔hometown〕. ¶ ～의 자랑 the pride of *one's* hometown 〔province〕/ ～물산 traditional folk products / 그는 우리 ～의 자랑이다 He is the pride of our hometown.

◉ ～무용 a folk dance. ～문학 folk literature. ～민요 a folk song. ～사(史) (a) local history: ～사가(史家) a student of local history. ～색 local color: ～색 짙은 rich in local color; of rich local color. ～애 local patriotism; love for 〔of〕 *one's* home province. ～연예 a performing art peculiar to a locality; a folk entertainment. ～예비군 the homeland 〔local〕 reserve forces. ～예술 folk art; local crafts. ～완구 a folk toy. ～요리 local 〔country〕 dishes; a style of cooking peculiar to a certain locality. ～음식 《offer》 native local foods. ～음악 folk 〔local〕 music. ～인형 a local doll. ～지(誌) a chronicle of a province; (a) local history.

**향하다**(向—) ① 《얼굴을》 turn (*one's* head) 《toward》; turn 〔set〕 *one's* face 《to, toward》. ¶ …을 향해서 오른쪽으로 on the right as *one* faces 《it》; on *one's* right / 향하여 왼쪽으로 세번째 사람 the third person from the left / 위를〔밑을〕 ～ look up(ward) 〔down(ward)〕/ 서로 마주 ～ be opposite 《to》; face each other / 서로 마주 향하여 서다 stand face to face 〔vis-à-vis〕/ 벽쪽을 향하여 서다 stand with *one's* face turned toward a wall; stand face to a wall / 거울을 향해 서다 stand before 〔look in〕 a mirror / 책상을 향해 앉다 sit at *one's* desk / 뒤쪽을〔오른쪽을, 반대쪽을〕 향해서 보아라 Look back 〔to the right, the other way〕. / 그녀는 식탁을 사이에 두고 남편과 마주 향해 앉았다 She sat down at the table across from her husband.

② 《면하다》 face (on); front (on); look out 《on》. ¶ 집이 숲쪽〔큰길쪽〕을 향해있다 The house looks toward the woods 〔faces on the highway〕. / 창문은 뜰을 향해 있다 The windows looks out on the garden. / 내 방은 뜰을 향해 있다 My room 「looks out into 〔opens into, opens out on〕 the garden.

③ 《지향하다》 (***a***) 《마음이》 grow; get; tend 〔trend〕 toward. ¶ 마음은 고향을 ～ *one's* mind goes off to *one's* home; yearn for home / 민심이 향하는 바를 살피다 see 〔watch〕 the trend of popular feelings. (***b***) 《겨냥하다》 point 〔present〕 《*a thing*》 at; aim 《*one's* revolver》 at 〔on〕; turn 〔train〕 《*one's* rifle》 on; direct 《a gun》 against. ¶ …을 향해 권총을 발사하다 fire a pistol at… / 경찰은 하늘을 향해 권총을 쏘았다 The police fired a shot into the air. / 그의 말은 나를 향한 것이었다 His remarks were directed at me. (***c***) 《가리키다》 point 《to》. ¶ 자침(磁針)이 북(北)을 향하고 있다 The magnetic needle points to the north. (***d***) 《가다》 proceed 《to》; go 《to, toward》; start 〔leave〕 《for》; make 《for》; take *one's* way 《toward》; direct *one's* steps 《toward》. ¶ …을 향해 가다 be going 《toward》; be headed 《for, toward》; be on the way 《toward》/ 서울을 향하여 가다 go toward Seoul; leave for Seoul / 미국을 향해 떠나다 leave 〔sail〕 for America; head on to America (비행기로) / 육지를 향해 항해하다 sail toward 〔steer for〕 the land / 적을 향해 돌격하다 make a raid on the enemy / 발길이 향하는 대로 어디든지 간다 I go wherever my feet takes me. / 승리를 향하여 전진하자 Let's go ahead to victory.

**향학심**(向學心) love of learning; a desire to learn; a scholarly bent; intellectual appetite. ¶ ～에 불타다 burn with the desire for learning; aspire after further knowledge; be eager to learn / ～에 불타는 사람 an ardent lover of learning.

**향합**(香盒) an incense box 〔jar〕.

**향후**(向後) hereafter; hence (forth). ¶ ～ 수주일〔수개월〕간 for a few weeks 〔months〕 ahead 〔from now〕.

**허**(虛) an unguarded position 〔moment〕; unpreparedness. ¶ 허를 찌르다 catch 《*a person*》 off *his* guard; attack 《*one's* adversary》 on the unguarded side; take 《the enemy》 unawares; take advantage of 《*a person's*》 unpreparedness / 계략의 허를 찌르다 baffle 〔discomfit〕 《*a person's*》 design / 허를 찔리다 be thrown 〔caught〕 off *one's* guard; be caught napping / 허를 보이다 lay *oneself* open to attack; be off *one's* guard / 허를 찌른 질문에 나는 답을 할 수 없었다 The question caught me off my guard and I couldn't think of an answer.

**허** Oh!; Alas! ¶ 허, 실수했구나 Oh dear! I have made a mistake. / 허, 또 당했군 Gosh, I've lost again. / 허, 일다 틀렸다 Alas! All is over.

**허가**(許可) ① 《허락함》 permission; leave. ～하다 permit; give 《*a person*》 leave 《to *do*》. ¶ 입국 ～ entry permit / 건축 ～ a building 〔construction〕 permit / 상륙 ～ 《grant a sailor》 shore leave / ～ 없이 without permission 〔leave〕 / ～가 나다 be permitted.
허가를: ～를 얻다 be permitted; obtain 〔be granted〕 permission; get a permit / ～를 얻어 by permission 《of the authorities》; with 《*a person's*》 permission / 외출 ～를 얻다 be permitted 〔get permission〕 to go out / ～를 청하다 ask for permission; apply for a permit / ～를 취소하다 cancel permission.
¶ 선생님의 ～를 얻고나서 그렇게 해라 Ask permission from your teacher to do that. *or* Ask your teacher for permission to do it. / 이 곳에서 사진을 찍으려면 당국의 ～를 얻어야 한다 You must apply to the authorities for permission to take photographs here. / ～ 없이 출입을 금함 《게시》 Off limits to unauthorized person.
② 《승인》 approval; sanction; 《미구어》 an O.K. 〔OK, okay〕 (*pl.* O.K.'s). ～하다 sanction; approve 《of》; give *one's* approval 《to》; O.K. 〔OK, okay〕. ¶ 정부는 두 대학의 신설을 ～했다 The government has sanctioned the establishment of two new universities. / 마침내 ～가 나왔다 At last the approval came through.
③ 《면허》 license; 《인가》 authorization; go-ahead 《미》. ～하다 《면허하다》 license; grant 〔give〕 a license; 《인가하다》 authorize; give the go-ahead. ¶ ～료 a license fee / ～되다〔나다〕 be licensed 〔authorized〕; get a license.
허가를: …할 ～를 얻다 be authorized to 《*do*》 / ～를 얻어 영업하다 do business under license / ～를 신청하다 apply for a license / 공채 발행의 ～를 신청하다 apply for authority to issue a loan.
¶ 그 식당은 식중독을 일으킨 이유로 영업 ～를 취소당했다 The restaurant had its business license revoked for causing food poisoning.
④ 《입학·입장의》 admission. ～하다 《입장을》 give admittance; admit; 《입학을》 admit; matriculate (대학에의). ¶ 나는 A대학에 입학이 ～되었다 I've received admission to A university. *or* I've been admitted to A university. ◉ ～제 a license system: 사냥은 ～제이다 Hunting is on a license system. ～증 a permit; a written permission; 《면허》 a license: 주류 판매 ～증 the liquor license; a license to sell alcoholic beverages.

**허겁**(虛怯) foolish fear; funk. ◉ ～쟁이 a scaredy-cat; a coward.

**허겁지겁** in a hurry 〔flurry〕; hastily; hurriedly; confusedly; hurry-scurry; helter-skelter. ⇨허둥지둥. ¶ ～ 달아나다 run off helter-skelter 〔hurry-scurry〕; run away with the tail between the legs / ～ 물러가다 make 〔beat〕 a hasty retreat; sneak off.

**허공**(虛空) the (empty) sky 〔air〕; (empty) space; an empty void. ¶ ～에 in the air 〔sky〕 / ～에 뜨다 float in the air; 《무(無)가 되다》 come 〔be brought〕 to nothing; end (up) in failure / ～을 응시하다 stare into space / ～에 매달리다 hang 〔be suspended〕 in midair; dangle in space.

**허구**(虛構) a fabrication; (a) fiction; a concoction; an 〔a complete〕 invention. ～하다 fabricate; invent; make up; concoct; misrepresent. ¶ ～적인 made-up; invented; fictitious; false; fake / 순전한 ～ a pure 〔an out-and-out〕 fabrication; a perfect fake / 그 이야기는 순전히 ～이다 The story is a pure fiction.

**허구렁**(虛―) an empty hole; a pit. ¶ ～에 빠지다 fall into a pit.

**허구리** the sides of *one's* waist; the flank.

**허구하다**(許久—) be a very long time; (be) very long. ¶ 허구한 날 day in (and) day out; so many days / 허구한 세월을 덧없이 보내다 spend many long years in vain.

**허근**(虛根) 〖수학〗 an imaginary root.

**허기**(虛飢) an empty stomach; hunger. ¶ ～를 느끼다 feel hungry 〔empty〕 / ～를 달래다 appease 〔alleviate〕 *one's* hunger 《with scanty food》 / …을 먹고 ～를 면하다 satisfy *one's* hunger on 〔by eating〕…. ◉ ～증 a hungry feeling; a gnawing hunger: ～증이 나다 be 〔feel〕 hungry.

**허기지다**(虛飢—) ① 《배고파》 be famished; be exhausted with hunger. ② 《욕망으로》 hunger 《for》; thirst 《after》.

**허깨비** ① 《헛것》 a hallucination; a phantom; vision. ¶ ～를 보다 see visions 〔a phantom〕. ② 《귀신·도깨비》 a spook; a (hob)goblin.

**허니문** a honeymoon. ¶ 「～은 어디로 가니」—「제주도로 간다」 "Where are you going on 〔for〕 your honeymoon?"—"We're going to Chejudo."

**허다하다**(許多—) (be) numerous; innumerable; frequent; common. ¶ 허다한 일 a common 〔familiar〕 affair; not an uncommon case / 허다한 학생 중에 among so many students / 그런 예가 ～ We have a number of examples of that sort. / 그런 일은 ～ That sort of thing happens quite often.

**허닥하다** begin to take out what is stored away; get 〔eat〕 into the stores; nibble on what has been set aside. ¶ 저장해 둔 쌀을 ～ nibble on the rice which has been set aside.

**허덕거리다** ① 《숨이 차서》 pant; gasp (for breath); breathe hard 〔heavily〕; get 〔be〕 out of breath; get 〔become〕 short of breath; be breathless; 《지쳐서》 be exhausted; be tired out. ¶ 숨이 차서 ～ gasp for breath; be short 〔out〕 of breath / 지쳐서 ～ be dog-tired; walk *one's* legs off / 무거운 짐을 지고 ～ pant under a heavy load. ② 《애쓰느라고》 toil and moil; fight hard 《with poverty》; make frantic efforts; strive wildly; work madly. ¶ 돈을 좀 모으려고 ～ make frantic efforts to get some money together / 기일까지 일을 끝내려고 ～ work madly to get the job done by the deadline date.

**허덕이다** ① 《숨을》 ⇨ 허덕거리다 ①. ② 《고난에》 languish; be tormented 《by》. ¶ 빈곤에 허덕이는 사람 a poverty-stricken person / 가난〔생활고〕에 ～ suffer dire poverty; be poverty-stricken; be pressed 〔tormented〕 by poverty; languish in poverty / 중소기업들은 불황에 허덕이고 있다 The small and medium industries are suffering from a depression. / 그 회사는 경영난에 허덕이고 있다 The firm is having a hard time carrying on as a going concern.

**허덕지덕**, **허덕허덕** 《숨이 차서》 panting; gasping for breath; 《지쳐서》 dog-tired; 《애쓰느라고》 striving madly; desperately. ～하다 make desperate efforts.

**허두**(虛頭) opening words 〔remarks〕; the beginning; the opening.

**허둥거리다** get 〔be〕 flustered; be in a flurry; rush about madly. ¶ 어쩔 줄 몰라 ～ be so flustered that *one* does not know what to do.

**허둥지둥** in a flurry 〔fluster, hurry〕; madly; hurry-scurry; helter-skelter. ～하다 get 〔be〕 all flustered. ¶ ～ 달아나다 run away with bare life 〔in a flurry〕; run off helter-skelter 〔hurry-scurry〕 / ～ 밖으로 뛰어 나가다 hurry out; go out hurriedly / 그는 ～ 정거장으로 달려갔다 He rushed madly to the station.

**허드레** odds and ends; trash. ◉ ～꾼 an odd-job man; an odd-jobber; a handyman. 허드렛물 water for sundry uses. 허드렛일 odd jobs; a trifling job.

**허드재비** odds and ends; odd bits; odd jobs; a trifling job.

**허든거리다** flounder; reel 《about》; be unsteady 《on *one's* feet》; have trouble with *one's* legs.

**허들** 《장애물》 a hurdle; 《경기》 a hurdle race; (the) hurdles (★ 단수 취급). ¶ ～을 뛰어넘다 jump 〔leap〕 over a hurdle; clear a hurdle; hurdle / ～에서 1위를 차지하다 come first 〔win first place〕 in the hurdles. ◉ ～선수 a hurdler; a hurdle skipper 〔topper〕.

**허락**(許諾) ① 《승낙》 consent; agreement; assent; approval; acceptance; permission. ～하다 consent 〔agree, assent〕 《to》; accept; comply 《with》; say yes 《to》; 《허가하다》 admit; allow 〔permit, grant〕 《*a person* to *do*》. ¶ ～을 언어 with 《*a person's*》 permission / ～ 없이 without 《*a person's*》 permission 〔consent〕 / ～할 수 있는 permissible / ～할 수 없는 unallowable; impermissible / 법이 ～하는 범위 내에

서 within the law; as far as the law permits / 시간이 ~하는 한 so far as time permits / 사정이 ~하면 so far as circumstances permit; if possible / 지면이 ~하는 한 to the limit of space / 요청을 ~하다 grant 〔allow〕 a request / 결혼을 ~하다 give 《*a person*》 permission to marry; consent to 《*a person's*》 marriage / 외출을 ~하다 give 《*a person*》 leave to go out; let 《*a person*》 go out / 그들은 인근 사람들의 ~을 받고 공사를 시작했다 They started the construction with the neighbors' consent. / 사태는 일각의 지체도 ~지 않는다 The situation does not admit of a moment's delay. / 사치한 생활은 나의 재정이 ~지 않는다 I cannot afford to live in luxury. *or* My income doesn't allow me to live extravagantly. ② 《여자가 몸을》 ~하다 give 〔submit〕 *oneself* (up) to 《a man》; allow 《a man》 to take liberties with *one*. ¶ 여자가 몸을 ~하다 surrender *one's* chastity 〔body〕 to a man; give *oneself* to a man's embrace.

**허랑방탕**(虛浪放蕩) dissoluteness; profligacy; loose and profligate living. ~하다 (be) loose; dissolute; dissipated. ¶ ~한 생활을 하다 lead a dissipated life; indulge in dissipation.

**허례**(虛禮) dead forms; empty 〔hollow, useless〕 formalities. ¶ ~적인 언사 empty 〔vain〕 words / ~를 없애다 dispense with empty forms; abolish 〔do away with〕 useless formalities / ~에 빠지다 lapse into an empty formality / ~에 흐르다 run into empty forms. ◉ ~허식 empty formalities and vanity.

**허룩하다** (be) almost empty. ¶ 쌀자루가 ~ a rice bag is almost empty; be down to the bottom of the rice bag.

**허름하다** ① 《낡아서》 (be) old; shabby. ¶ 허름한 옷 shabby clothes / 허름한 집 a shedlike house. ② 《값이》 (be) cheap; low.

**허릅숭이** an unreliable person; a careless 〔reckless〕 fellow.

**허리** ① 《몸의》 the waist; 《짐승의》 the haunch. ¶ ~가 가는 slim-〔slender-〕waisted / ~가 굽다 *one's* back is doubled over; be bent (in the back) / ~가 굽은 할머니 a stooped old woman / ~가 굵은 thick in the waist / ~가 가는 여인 a slender-waisted woman; a woman with a wasp waist / ~가 날씬하다 have a supple 〔slim, slender〕 waist / ~가 아프다 have (a) backache; *one's* back hurts 〔is sore, is stiff〕 / ~가 절구통 같다 have no waist / ~를 굽히다〔구부리다〕 bend the body; stoop (down); bend *oneself* low / ~를 굽혀 인사하다 greet with a deep bow / ~를 삐다 have *one's* waist dislocated / ~를 펴다 stretch 〔straighten〕 *oneself* / 이야기의 ~를 끊다〔꺾다〕 interrupt 《*a person*》 (while *he* is speaking); damp 〔choke〕 the rising tone 〔spirit〕 of the conversation; spoil a story / ~에 칼을 차다 wear a sword on *one's* side / ~를 재다 measure *one's* waist / 그는 나이 먹어 ~가 굽었다 He is bent with age. / 물은 내 ~까지 찼다 The water was up to my waist. ② 《옷 따위의》 the waist. ¶ 치마 ~를 달다 attach the waist part of a skirt. ◉ ~둘레 *one's* waist 〔hip (여)〕 measurement: ~둘레를 재다 take *a person's* hip measurement; measure *a person's* hips / 그녀의 ~둘레는 90센티미터이다 Her waist is ninety centimeters around. ~뼈 the hipbone; the hucklebone. 허릿매 the shape of *one's* waist: 허릿매가 곱다〔밉다〕 have a shapely 〔an unshapely〕 waist.

**허리띠**, **허리끈** a waistband; a belt; a girdle; a sash (여성용). ¶ 허리띠를 매다 tie a belt / 허리띠를 풀다 untie a belt; ungirdle *oneself* / 허리띠를 졸라 매다 tie up *one's* belt tightly.

**허리질러** 《run》 across the middle 《of》.

**허리춤** inside the waist of *one's* trousers; *one's* trousers-tops 〔waist-tops〕. ¶ ~에 감추다 slip 《*something*》 in the waist of *one's* trousers / 지갑을 ~에 넣다 carry a wallet in the waist of *one's* trousers.

**허리치기** 〖유도〗 a hip throw; 〖레슬링〗 a cross-buttock. ¶ ~를 하다 have 〔get, take〕 《*a person*》 on the hip.

**허리케인** 《서인도 제도·멕시코만에서 발생하는 폭풍우》 a hurricane.

**허리통** the measurement 〔girth〕 of *one's* waist. ¶ ~이 굵다 have a big 〔stout〕 waist / ~이 굵어지다 grow fat round the middle / ~이 절구통 같다 have a very stout waist.

**허릿심** ① 《허리의》 the stamina of *one's* waist. ¶ ~이 세다 have a strong back. ② 《화살의》 the resilience of the middle of an arrow.

**허망**(虛妄) untruth; falsity. ~하다 (be) vain; untrue; false; unreliable; groundless. ¶ ~지설(之說) a falsehood; a groundless 〔an unreliable〕 story.

**허명**(虛名) an empty name; a vain 〔spurious, false, undeserved〕 reputation. ¶ ~을 좇는 사람 a publicity-seeker / ~무실하다 be vain 〔empty, unsubstantial〕 / ~을 좇다 court publicity; be hungry for fame.

**허무**(虛無) nothingness; nihility; *nihil* (L.); futility. ~하다 (be) nonexistent; nil; null; futile; vain; empty. ¶ ~적인 nihilistic / ~하게 in vain; to no purpose 〔end〕; futilely / 인생은 ~한 것이다 All is vanity in life. *or* Life is but an empty dream. ◉ ~감 a sense of futility. ~주의 nihilism: ~주의자 a nihilist.

**허무맹랑하다**(虛無孟浪―) be fabulous 〔empty, groundless, wild, unreliable〕. ¶ 허무맹랑한 소문 a groundless rumor / 허무맹랑한 소리를 하다 say extraordinary 〔absurd〕 thing; talk wild.

**허물**[1] 《꺼풀·껍질》 a skin; a cast-off skin; a covering; an ecdysis (*pl.* -ses); exuviae. ¶ 매미의 ~ the cast-off shell of a cicada; a cicada's shell / 뱀의 ~ the cast-off skin of a snake; a slough / ~을 벗다 《a snake》 cast off its skin; slough 〔shed〕 its skin; exuviate / ~이 벗겨지다 have the skin scraped; skin peels off / 햇볕에 너무 노출되어 등의 ~이 벗겨졌다 I was out in the sun so much that (the skin on) my back peeled.

**허물**[2] 《과실》 a fault; a mistake; an error; a misdeed; a misstep; a blame. (★ fault는 성격·습관·도덕상의 잘못, mistake는 착각에서 오는 잘못, error는 악의 없는 판단의 잘못, blame은 과실의 책임을 말함). ¶ ~을 깨닫다 realize a fault; be convinced of *one's* fault / ~을 눈감아주다 overlook 〔pass over〕 《*a person's*》 mistake; wink 〔connive〕 at 《*a person's*》 misdeed / ~을 (뒤집어) 씌우다 put 〔lay〕 the blame upon; attach blame to; lay *one's* fault on 《*a person*》 / ~을 용서하다 forgive 《*a person*》 for *his* fault / 내게는 ~이 없다 I am not to blame. / ~ 없는 사람은 없다 Every man is liable to error. *or* To err is human.

**허물다** pull 〔take, tear〕 down; break up 〔down〕; destroy 《a house》; demolish. ¶ 돌담을 ~ demolish a stonewall / 집을 ~ pull down a house.

**허물벗다**[1] cast (off ) the skin; shed the skin. ⇨ 허물[1].

**허물벗다**[2] 《누명벗다》 clear *oneself* of a false charge; have *one's* innocence established; be cleared from the charge; exculpate *oneself.* ¶ 그가 억울한 허물을 벗는 데 10년 걸렸다 It took him ten years 「to clear himself of the false charge 〔to prove his innocence〕.

**허물어지다** crumble; collapse; fall 〔break〕 down; give way. ¶ 허물어져 가는 crumbling; rickety; half-ruined / 집이 ~ a house collapses / 터널이 허물어져 노무자 10명이 생매장되었다 Ten workmen were buried alive in a cave-in of the tunnel.

**허물없다** be on familiar 〔friendly〕 terms; (be) unceremonious; don't have to stand on ceremony. ¶ 허물없는 친구 a candid friend; a friend on frank terms / 허물없이 without reserve / 허물없이 말하다 talk in a familiar way; have a confidential talk; have a free chat; talk without reserve / 우리는 허물없는 사이다 We are on familiar terms with each other. / 서로 허물없는 사이기에 이런 말을 하네 I inform this to you because we are friends of quite open.

**허발** voracity. ~하다 (be) voracious.

**허방** a hole; a hollow; a sunken place; a depression. ¶ ~을 디디다 step in a hollow; make a false step / ~에 빠지다 fall into a hole.

**허방다리** a pit(fall); a trap. ⇨ 함정(陷穽).

**허방짚다** miscalculate; shoot at the wrong mark; make a wrong guess; misjudge; miss; bring *one's* eggs 〔hogs〕 to a bad 〔the wrong〕 market.

**허방치다** miss *one's* aim 〔object〕; make a wrong guess. ⇨ 허방짚다.

**허벅다리** a thigh. ¶ ~를 드러내다 bare 〔expose〕 *one's* thighs.

**허벅살** 《사람의》 the flesh of the thigh; 《소의》 a round; 《돼지의》 ham.

**허벅지** the fleshy inside of the thigh.

**허벅허벅** very soft; all flabby. ~하다 (be) very soft; be all flabby.

**허보**(虛報) a false report. ¶ 그것은 ~였다 The report has proved false.

**허분허분** soft and juicy. ~하다 (be) soft and juicy. ¶ 사과가 ~ 씹히다 an apple is soft and juicy to *one's* teeth.

**허비**(虛費) useless expenses; (a) waste. ~하다 waste 《*one's* money on trifles》. ¶ 시간의 ~ waste of time / 돈을 ~하다 spend money wastefully; waste money 《on》; fool away *one's* money / 시간을 ~하다 waste 〔idle away〕 *one's* time /

결국 시간의 ～로 끝났다 It resulted in 〔ended up as〕 a waste of (my) time.

**허비다, 허비적–** ⇨ 후비다, 후비적–.

**허사**(虛事) a vain attempt; a failure. ¶ (일이) ～로 돌아가다, ～가 되다 end in failure; come to naught 〔nothing〕; be in vain; prove futile 〔all in vain〕/ 그에게 탄원했지만 ～였다 I implored him, but no soap. / 그의 노력이 ～가 되었다 His efforts went by the board. / 나의 모든 노력은 ～로 돌아갔다 All my efforts have gone to nothing. *or* Nothing has resulted from my efforts. / 그는 일자리를 찾으려고 1년 이상 애썼으나 모두 ～였다 He tried to find a job for more than a year all in vain.

**허사**(虛辭) ① 〚문법〛 an expletive. ② a lie. ⇨ 허언(虛言).

**허상**(虛像) 〚물리〛 a virtual image; [일반적] a ghost 〔false〕 image. ¶ 뇌물 사건으로 그 정치가의 명성이 단지 ～에 지나지 않았음이 입증되었다 The bribery scandal proved that the politician's fame was only a false image.

**허섭스레기** odd ends; odd bits; trash.

**허세**(虛勢) a false show of power 〔strength, courage, influence〕; a bluff; bluster. ¶ 취중의 ～ pot-valor; Dutch courage / ～를 부리는 사람 a bluffer; a swaggerer / ～를 부리다 show off; make a false show (of power); bluff; bluster; show 〔put on〕 a bold 〔brave〕 front / 저건 단지 ～야, 사실인즉슨 그는 자신이 없거든 It's mere bravado. Actually, he's not confident at all. / 그는 뻐기고 있지만, 실은 ～에 지나지 않는다 Although he is throwing his weight around, it's only bluff.

**허송**(虛送) wasting time; passing time idly. ～하다 waste time; idle *one's* time away; pass *one's* time idly. ◉ ～세월 = 허송.

**허수**(虛數) 〚수학〛 an imaginary (number).

**허수아비** 《set up》 a scarecrow; [비유적] a puppet; a figurehead; a dummy. ¶ ～ 노릇을 하다 be a puppet / 그는 회장이라 해도 ～나 마찬가지다 He is a dummy 〔nominal〕 president. *or* He is a president only in name. / 사장은 그저 ～에 지나지 않는다 The president is only a dummy. *or* The president has practically no authority. ◉ ～ 사장 a dummy boss; a nominal boss.

**허술하다** ① 《초라하다》 (be) very old; shabby; worn-out. ¶ 허술한 옷 shabby clothes / 옷차림이 ～ be shabbily dressed. ② 《허점이 있다》 (be) lax; loose; careless. ¶ 허술한 방어 a loose defense / 허술한 금융 정책 a profligate 〔lax〕 financial policy / 허술한 틈을 노리다 try to catch 《*a person*》 off *his* guard / 돈을 허술하게 다뤄서는 안 된다 Don't handle money carelessly. / 대통령은 경비가 허술해서 저격당했다 The President was shot because he was inadequately guarded.

**허스키** husky. ◉ ～보이스 a husky 〔harsh, throaty〕 voice.

**허식**(虛式) 〚수학〛 an imaginary expression.

**허식**(虛飾) (an) affectation; ostentation; (a) show; display; overdressing. ～하다 affect; overdress; show off. ¶ ～적인 showy; ostentatious; flashy / ～이 없는 plain; unaffected / ～이 없는 말 words without trimming / 그는 모든 ～을 싫어한다 He dislikes all ostentation. / 그의 연설은 ～에 차 있었다 His speech was full of show and display. ◉ ～가 a fop; a dandy; a dude; a show-off.

**허실**(虛實) truth (or falsehood); the true and the false. ¶ ～을 밝히다 ascertain the truth 《of》/ 적의 ～을 탐지하다 discover the strong and weak points of the enemy.

**허심**(虛心) a disinterested mind; an open mind; freedom from prejudice.

**허심탄회**(虛心坦懷) frankness; open-mindedness; candor. ～하다 (be) open-minded; frank; candid. ¶ ～하게 frankly; candidly; open-mindedly; with an open mind; without reserve; 《편견 없이》 without prejudice / ～하게 이야기하다 speak frankly; have a heart-to-heart talk 《with》/ 이 문제에 관해서는 모두가 ～하게 논의하는 것이 필요하다 It is necessary for everyone to discuss this matter with an open mind 〔with open minds〕.

**허심하다**(許心—) confide 《in》; trust; admit 〔take〕 《*a person*》 into *one's* confidence; make a confident 《of *a person*》.

**허약**(虛弱) weakness; feebleness; delicateness; infirmity. ～하다 (be) weak; feeble; delicate; infirm; frail; 《병약하다》 (be) sickly. ¶ ～한 사람 a weakly 〔an infirm〕 person; [총칭] the feeble / 몸이 ～하다 have a weak 〔delicate〕 constitution; be in poor health / ～체질로 태어나다 be born delicate 〔weak〕. ◉ ～아 a weak 〔frail, delicate〕 child; (physically) weak children. ～체질 a weak constitution.

**허언**(虛言) a lie; a falsehood; an untruth; a fabrication. ～하다 (tell a) lie.

**허여멀겋다** (be) nice and fair.

**허여멀쑥하다** (be) clean and fair. ¶ 얼굴이 ～ have a fair [light] complexion.

**허열**(虛熱) 〖한의〗 consumptive fever.

**허영**(虛榮) vanity; vainglory. ¶ ～의 vain; vainglorious / ～ 때문에 for vanity's sake / 여자의 ～ feminine vanity / ～에 차다 be full of [filled with] vanity.

**허영거리다** totter; falter; be shaky. ¶ 허영거리는 걸음 faltering [tottering] steps / 앓고 나서 ～ be shaky after *one's* illness.

**허영심**(虛榮心) vanity. ¶ ～이 강한 vain; full of vanity; vainglorious / ～에 이끌리어 driven by vanity; out of vanity / ～을 만족시키다 satisfy *one's* vanity / ～을 버리다 give up *one's* vanity; rise above vanity / ～을 자아내다[부채질하다] inflate [excite, stimulate, appeal to] *one's* vanity / 여자는 대개 ～이 강하다 Women are generally vain creatures. / 아들을 유명 대학에 넣고 싶어하는 것은 부모의 ～일지 모른다 It is perhaps out of vanity that parents try to send their sons to famous universities.

**허영허영** tottering; faltering.

**허옇다** (be) very white; pure [snow] white; quite [ash] pale. ¶ 허연 이빨을 드러내다 show *one's* white teeth / 안색이 ～ look very pale. 「gray [white].

**허예지다** get [become] pure white; turn

**허욕**(虛慾) vain ambitions; false desires; avarice; greed(iness). ¶ ～이 많은 사람 a grasping person / ～이 너무 많다 have too much to wish.

**허용**(許容) 《허가》 permission; allowance; approval; sanction; tolerance. ～하다 permit; allow; approve; grant; tolerate. ¶ 체납을 ～하지 않다 admit of no default of payment / 이것은 관용으로 ～되어 있다 This is sanctioned by usage. ◉ ～량 a permissible [tolerable] amount; an acceptable limit: (방사능의) 최대 ～량 the maximum permissible dose of radiation. ～범위 a permissible range. ～시간 allowed time. ～오차 《기계·통계에서의》 an allowable [a permissible] error; a tolerance 《of 5 microns》. ～온도 allowable [permissible] temperature. ～한계[한도] a tolerance limit: 방사능의 노출 ～ 한도 the maximum permissible exposure to radiation.

**허우대** a (fine) tall figure; build; physique. ¶ ～가 당당한 신사 a gentleman of imposing stature / ～가 좋다 have a fine tall figure; be of large [stout] build.

**허우룩하다** feel a certain emptiness; miss; (be) lonely; lonesome.

**허우적거리다** struggle; paw the air. ¶ 물에서 헤어나려고 ～ paw the air to get out of the water / 물에 빠져 ～ be almost drowned and struggle / 고양이가 강물에 빠져 허우적거리고 있었다 A cat fell in the river and was struggling to get out.

**허우적허우적** struggling; pawing the air. ¶ ～ 걷다 walk swinging *one's* arms.

**허울** 《a nice》 appearance; exterior. ¶ ～만은 outwardly; in appearance; apparently; seemingly / ～뿐이다 be not so good as it looks; be deceptive / ～이 좋다 have a good-looking appearance / ～ 좋은 도둑놈 a wolf in sheep's clothing / ～ 좋은 하눌타리 a person [thing] only superficially attractive / ～을 잘 쓰고 나다 be born with a nice look / ～만 좋았지 (속은) 별것 아니었다 It was not so good as it looked. / 그가 대학 교수라고, 사람은 ～만으로 판단할 수가 없지 He is a professor? You can't judge people by their appearance, can you?

**허위**(虛僞) (a) falsehood; 〖논리〗 fallacy. ¶ ～의 false; untrue; sham; fictitious / ～ 기재를 하다 make a false description / 그의 진술은 ～였다 His statement proved false. ◉ ～신고 a false return. ～진단서 a false diagnosis; 《the issuance of》 a wrongful medical examination [check-up] certificate. ～진술 a false representaton; (a) misrepresentation: ～ 진술하다 make a false statement 《of *something*, that ...》; 《증인이》 give false evidence [testimony]; bear false witness.

**허위넘다** go over panting and heaving. ¶ 고개를 ～ go over a (mountain) pass panting and heaving.

**허위단심** struggling with all *one's* might; laboriously. ¶ 아들을 보려고 ～ 먼 곳을 찾아가다 struggle a long distance to see *one's* son.

**허장성세**(虛張聲勢) bravado and bluster; swashbuckling; (a) bluff. ～하다 indulge in bravado and bluster; swashbuckle; bluff. ⇨ 허세.

**허적거리다** scatter; disperse; ransack; rummage. ¶ 서랍 속을 ～ ransack a

drawer; rummage 〔rout〕 in a drawer / 닭들이 건초더미를 ~ chickens scatter a bunch of hay. ┌ter along.
**허전거리다** totter; falter. ¶ 다리가 ~ tot-
**허전하다** feel empty; feel a vacuum; miss 《*something*》; feel lonesome; miss 《*a person*》. ¶ 호주머니가 ~ have a light 〔lean, slender〕 purse / 친구가 가고나니 ~ My friend has gone and I am lonely. / 이방엔 가구가 없어서 ~ This room looks bare 〔empty〕 without furniture. / 책상이 없어지니 방이 ~ Now that the table has been taken away, the room seems empty to me.
**허점**(虛點) a blind point 〔spot〕; a loophole. ¶ 법의 ~ a loophole 〔blind spot〕 in the law / 법의 ~을 찌르다 make an illicit use of law; impose upon a blind spot in the law / 법의 ~을 발견하다 find a loophole in the law / 범인은 경찰의 경비 ~을 틈타 도망쳤다 The criminal escaped through the blind point of the police guard.
**허정** deceptive appearance; emptiness. ~하다 be not as good as it looks.
**허정거리다** stagger 〔totter, reel〕 along 〔on〕; lose *one's* legs. ¶ 허정거리며 with tottering steps; with an unsteady walk / 무거운 짐을 지고 ~ stagger under a heavy load.
**허줏굿** 〖민속〗 a shaman's initiatory dance to invoke the spirit.
**허청대고** blindly; plunging right in; recklessly; at random; happy-go=lucky. ¶ 일을 ~ 시작하다 plunge into a deal recklessly.
**허초점**(虛焦點) 〖물리〗 a virtual focus.
**허출하다** (be) empty; hungry. ¶ 속이 ~ have an empty stomach; be hungry.
**허탈**(虛脫) 〖의학〗 (physical) collapse; prostration; 《무기력》 lethargy; 《무관심》 apathy. ~하다 (be) prostrated; [서술적] be in a state of lethargy. ◉ ~감 despondency: …생각에 그녀는 심한 ~감을 느꼈다 She became very despondent at the thought that….
**허탈상태**(虛脫狀態) 《무기력》 a state of lethargy 〔stupor〕; 《망연》 absent-mindedness. ¶ ~에 있다 《무기력하다》 be in a state of lethargy; 《무관심하다》 be sunk in apathy; 《멍해 있다》 be utterly absent-minded; be in a state of absolute bewilderment.
**허탕** wasted 〔fruitless, vain〕 labor 〔effort〕. ¶ ~치다 *one's* labor is lost; *one's* undertaking comes to nothing; come to 〔go for〕 nothing; prove fruitless / 만나러 갔다 ~치다 go on an empty errand; go in vain; make a fruitless call / ~짚다 make vain 〔futile〕 efforts; exert *oneself* to no purpose; waste time and labor / 그는 친구를 보러 갔다 ~치고 돌아왔다 He wasted a trip trying to see his friend. / 우리들의 모든 노력은 ~으로 끝났다 All our efforts ┌came to nothing 〔were wasted〕. ┌simulation.
**허투**(虛套) feigning; sham; pretense;
**허투루** carelessly; negligently; roughly; in a slovenly way; in a perfunctory manner. ¶ ~ 보다 hold 《*a person, a matter*》 cheap; make light 〔nothing〕 of; think little 〔nothing〕 of; belittle; slight; treat 《*a person*》 with contempt / ~볼 수 없는 사나이 a crafty 〔tricky〕 fellow; a sly dog / 물건을 ~ 다루다 handle things roughly / 일을 ~하다 do a rough 〔slapdash〕 job / 저 사람은 ~ 볼 수 없는 친구다 He is not a man to be trifled with. *or* He is a man deserving 〔worthy〕 of due consideration.
**허튼계집** a wanton 〔loose〕 woman; a slut; a woman of loose morals 〔easy virtue〕.
**허튼고래** a hypocaust with the support stones distributed so as to circulate the hot air.
**허튼맹세**(—盟誓) an idle 〔a shaky〕 pledge; an idle vow. ¶ ~를 하다 make an idle 〔a shaky, a shifty〕 vow.
**허튼모** scatter-planted rice plants (as contrasted with row-planted).
**허튼소리** idle talk; nonsense; absurd remarks; random speech. ~하다 talk nonsense 〔rot, rubbish〕; talk at random; make irresponsible remarks. ¶ ~로 시간을 보내다 pass time in idle talk / 그 녀석의 말은 ~다 He does not mean what he says. / ~ 좀 작작 해라 Away with your lies! *or* Don't say such utter silly talk. / 너의 ~는 신물이 나도록 들었다 I'm fed up with your silly talk.
**허튼수작**(—酬酌) idle remarks; idle talk. ⇨ 허튼소리. ¶ ~을 하다 say silly things; talk rot 〔rubbish〕.
**허튼톱** a saw that can be used as either a crosscut saw or a ripsaw.
**허파** the lungs; 《소·양 따위의》 lights. ¶ ~에 바람이 들다 be giggly 〔gigglesome, giddy〕 / 허팟줄이 끊어지다 lose control and burst into laughter.

**허풍**(虛風) exaggeration; a tall 〔big〕 talk; a tall tale; bragging; hot air 《미구어》. ¶ ～ 떨다〔치다〕 exaggerate; brag; boast; talk big 〔tall〕; 《자화자찬》 blow *one's* own horn 《미구어》 〔trumpet 《영구어》〕; color 《a story》 too highly; make too much of 《*a matter*》 / 그는 ～만 떤다 He is full of brag. / 그가 한 말에는 ～이 많다 What he has told us is a lot of hot air. / ～을 떨어도 분수가 있지 You brag too much. *or* That's enough of your boasting. ◉ ～선(이) a (vain) boaster; a gasbag; a braggart.

**허하다**(虛—) ① 《속이 비다》 (be) hollow; empty; vacant; vacuous; inane. ¶ 속이 ～ be hollow inside; be inane. ② 《약하다》 (be) weak; sickly; feeble; delicate; frail. ¶ 몸이 ～ be weak in body; be delicate in health; have a weak constitution / 기가 ～ lack vitality; be unenergetic.

**허하다**(許—) 《허락》 permit; give 《*a person*》 permission 〔leave〕; allow; 《원하는 바를》 grant; admit; approve; 《경제력이》 can afford. ¶ 시간〔사정〕이 허하는 한 so far as time permits 〔circumstances permit〕 / 결혼을 ～ give 《*a person*》 permission to marry; consent to 《*a person's*》 marriage / 수입이 허하는 한 몸가축을 잘 하다 dress *oneself* as well as *one* can afford upon *one's* income.

**허한**(虛汗) night sweat(s) (★ sweat는 보통 단수형, 병 따위로 몸에 이상이 있어 땀이 날 때에는 흔히 복수형). ¶ ～을 흘리다 sweat at night.

**허행**(虛行) a visit made in vain. ～하다 go 〔visit〕 in vain; make a visit 《on *a person*》 in vain 〔to no purpose〕; make a fruitless call 《on *a person*》.

**허허** Ha ha!; with a laugh. ～거리다 keep laughing. ¶ ～ 웃다 laugh aloud / ～ 웃으면서 《answer》 with a (high) laugh.

**허허바다** a boundless ocean; a vast expanse of sea.

**허허벌판** a vast empty plain; a vast expanse of field.

**허허실실**(虛虛實實) a heated controversy. ¶ ～로 regarding truth as truth and falsehood as falsehood; accepting failure as failure and success as success; recognizing reality / ～의 싸움 a match between equally shrewd people; 《it is》 diamond cut diamond / ～의 싸움이다 Both contestants are full of wiles and tricks. *or* It is a game 〔match〕 of shrewdness.

**허혼**(許婚) accepting *one's* hand in marriage; betrothal. ～하다 accept in marriage; betroth 《*one's* daughter to》; consent to a marriage.

**허화**(虛華) empty 〔outward〕 show; superficial glamour.

**허황하다, 허황되다**(虛荒—) (be) false; absurd; wild; ungrounded; unreliable; preposterous. ¶ 허황된 계획 a wild-goose chase; a chimerical project; a visionary scheme / 허황된 생각 a fantastic idea 〔notion〕; a wild idea / 허황된 이야기 an absurd 〔an incredible, a vague〕 story; sheer 〔clotted〕 nonsense; a cloud of words; a wild dream / 허황된 소리를 하다 talk nonsense; talk something incredible 〔fantastic, absurd〕.

**헌** ① 《낡은》 old; shabby; worn-out; used; secondhand; cast-off. ¶ 헌 옷 old clothes; secondhand 〔used〕 clothing / 헌 차 a used 〔secondhand〕 car / 헌 책 a secondhand 〔used〕 book. ② 《부스럼이 난》 with a boil on it. ¶ 헌데 a boil.

**헌거롭다**(軒擧—) ① 《의기가》 (be) high-spirited; triumphant; elated; exultant. ② 《도량이》 (be) generous; bighearted; be liberal 《with money》. ③ 《풍채가》 (be) manly; imposing; [술어적] have a fine presence; look fine; have a lofty bearing.

**헌걸스럽다** (be) elated; high-spirited; 《풍채가》 (be) manly; imposing.

**헌걸차다** be full of elation; (be) elated.

**헌것** old 〔worn-out, secondhand, used〕 things.

**헌계집** "an old bag"; a deflowered girl; a worn-out woman; a divorcee (이혼녀).

**헌금**(獻金) 《행위》 giving money; (the) contribution 〔donation〕 of money; 《돈》 a contribution; a donation; 《교회 등에서의》 《take》 a collection; an offering. ～하다 contribute 〔donate〕 money 《to》; subscribe to 《a fund》. ¶ ～을 모으다 collect contributions 《from》; make 〔take〕 a collection 《for the relief fund》 / 3만 원을 ～하다 make a contribution of 30,000 won 《to a fund》. ◉ ～자 a contributor; a donor. ～함(函) a collection 〔contribution〕 box; 《교회의》 an offertory box.

**헌납**(獻納) presentation; offering; contribution; donation. ～하다 present 《an airplane to the army》; offer; contribute; donate. ◉ ～식 a dedication 〔presentation〕 ceremony. ～자 a contributor; a donor. ～품 an offering; a present.

**헌당**(獻堂) the dedication of a temple 〔church〕; consecration. ～하다 consecrate a church. ◉ ～식 a dedication ceremony.

**헌데** 《부스럼》 a boil; an abscess. ¶ ～가 나다 have a boil / ～가 도지다 a boil gets bad again / ～를 건드리듯 (조심조심하여) very cautiously 〔gingerly〕; with great caution.

**헌등**(獻燈) a votive lantern.

**헌법**(憲法) the constitution; the constitutional law. ¶ ～상(의) constitutional / ～상으로 constitutionally / ～규정에 위반하여 contrary to the constitutional provision / 민주주의에 의거한 ～ a constitution based on democracy; democratic nation's constitution / ～에 보장된 권리 *one's* constitutional rights / ～을 개정하다 amend 〔revise〕 the constitution / ～을 기초하다 draft a constitution / ～을 발포하다 promulgate the constitution / ～을 시행하다 enforce the constitution / ～을 수호하다 safeguard the constitution / ～을 제정하다 establish 〔frame〕 the constitution / ～의 개정안을 제출하다 initiate a constitutional amendment / ～ 제 7조 Article 7 〔the seventh article〕 of the constitution / 영장 없는 구속은 ～ 위반이다 Making an arrest without a warrant is unconstitutional. / 표현의 자유는 ～에 보장되어 있다 Freedom of expression is guaranteed under the constitution.

◉ ～개정 revision 〔amendment〕 of the constitution; 《하나의》 an amendment to the constitution; a constitutional amendment. ～기관 a constitutional institution. ～발포 the promulgation of the constitution. ～옹호〔수호〕 운동 a movement for protection of the constitution. ～위반 a breach of the constitution: ～ 위반의 unconstitutional. ～재판소 the Constitutional Court. ～정신 the spirit of the constitution; constitutional principles. ～정치 constitutional government; constitutionalism. ～제도 a constitutional regime. ～제정 enactment of a constitution: ～ 제정권 constituent power. ～학자 a scholar of 〔an expert in〕 constitutional law; a constitutional scholar 〔lawyer〕. 대한민국 ～ the Constitution of the Republic of Korea. 성문〔불문〕～ a written 〔an unwritten〕 constitution.

**헌병**(憲兵) 〖육군〗 a military policeman; an MP; the military police [총칭]; 〖해군〗 a shore patrol(man); an SP; the shore patrol [총칭]. ◉ ～대 〖육군〗 the military police 〔MP〕; 〖해군〗 the shore patrol 〔SP〕; the provost guard. ～사령관 a provost marshal. ～사령부 the provost marshal headquarters. ～장교 a provost officer. ～파견대 a detachment of the military police; a provost guard.

**헌사**(獻辭) a dedication; a dedicatory letter.

**헌상**(獻上) a humble presentation; an offering to a superior. ～하다 (humbly) present 《*a thing* to *a person, a person* with *a thing*》; offer 《to a superior》; make 《*a person*》 a present of 《*a thing*》. ◉ ～품 a (humble) offering 〔present〕; a gift 〔token〕.

**헌쇠** old iron; scrap iron.

**헌수**(獻壽) a toast to 《*a person's*》 longevity. ～하다 offer a toast to 《*a person's*》 longevity.

**헌시**(獻詩) a dedicated poem. ～하다 present 〔dedicate〕 a poem 《to》.

**헌신**(獻身) self-sacrifice; devotion; dedication. ～하다 devote 〔dedicate〕 *oneself* 《to》; sacrifice *oneself* 《to》. ¶ ～적인 devoted; self-sacrificing / ～적으로 devotedly / 사업에 ～하다 dedicate *one's* time 〔*one's* life, *oneself*〕 to business / 그녀는 평생을 빈민 구제에 ～했다 She devoted her whole life to helping the poor. / 그는 그 지역의 발전을 위해 ～적인 노력을 했다 He devoted himself to the development of the area.

**헌신짝** a worn-out shoe; an old shoe. ¶ ～같이 버리다 throw 《*a thing*》 away like an old shoe; cast 《*a thing*》 as worthless / 지위를 ～같이 버리다 throw up *one's* office just as *one* would throw away an old hat.

**헌옷** old 〔used, worn-out〕 clothes; secondhand 〔used〕 clothing. ¶ ～ 가게 a secondhand clothes 〔clothing〕 store / ～ 장수 an old-clothes dealer; a wardrobe dealer 〔man〕.

**헌작**(獻爵) offering a cup of wine (to souls in a traditional rite). ～하다 offer a cup of wine 〔drink〕.

**헌장**(憲章) a charter; a written constitution; articles of constitution. ¶ 어린이 ～ the Children's Charter / 유엔 ～ the United Nation's Charter.

**헌정**(憲政) constitutional government; constitutionalism. ¶ ～의 위기 a constitutional crisis / ～의 정도(正道) the regular procedures of constitutional government / ～을 실시하다 adopt constitutional government / ～의 실효를 거두다 act up to the principles of constitutional government; realize constitutional government. ◉ ～ 옹호 defense 〔safeguard〕 of the constitution: ～ 옹호 운동 a campaign for safeguarding 〔defending〕 constitutionalism. ～질서 constitutional order.

**헌정**(獻呈) offering; presentation (to a superior). ～하다 present 《a copy》 to 《*a person*》. ◉ ～본(本) a presentation 〔complimentary〕 copy. ～판(版) an author's copy.

**헌짚신** worn-out straw sandals. ¶ ～도 짝이 있다 《속담》 Every Jack has his Gill 〔Jill〕.

**헌책**(一冊) a secondhand 〔used〕 book; an old book. ◉ ～방 a secondhand bookstore; a used-book store.

**헌책**(獻策) (a) suggestion; (a piece of) advice. ～하다 suggest 《that...》; submit a plan 《to》; make a suggestion; advise 《the president on his policy-making》.

**헌칠민틋하다** (be) *svelte* (F.); have a 「dashing figure.

**헌칠하다** have a well-proportioned figure; have a smart 〔dashing, pleasantly-shaped〕 figure.

**헌털뱅이** ＝헌것.

**헌팅캡** a cloth 〔tweed, flat〕 cap; a hunting cap (수렵용 모자).

**헌헌장부**(軒軒丈夫) a manly man.

**헌혈**(獻血) blood donation; donating blood. ～하다 donate 〔give〕 *one's* blood 《to》. ◉ ～운동 a blood (donation) drive 〔campaign〕. ～자 a (blood) donor. ～차 a mobile van where blood is collected from donors. ～카드 a blood donor's official registration card. 집단 ～ group blood donation.

**헌화**(獻花) 《꽃을 바침》 a floral tribute; an offering of flowers; wreath-laying. ～하다 offer flowers; lay wreaths 《at》. ¶ 고인의 영전에 ～하다 offer flowers to the soul of the deceased / …의 무덤에 ～하다 lay a wreath on the tomb of.... ◉ ～식 a wreath-laying ceremony.

**헐값**(歇一) a dirt-cheap price. ¶ ～에〔으로〕 《갯값에》 at a giveaway price; far below cost; for a song / ～에 팔다 sell at a low 〔slaughter〕 price; sell 《*a thing*》 dirt-cheap; sell for an old song / ～에 사다 have 〔buy〕 a dead bargain; get 《*a thing*》 dog-cheap.

**헐겁다** (be) loose; 〔술어적〕 be not tight. ¶ 헐거운 구두 easy-fitting shoes; loose(-fitting) shoes / 헐겁게 매다 tie loosely / 나사가 좀 ～ The screw is a little too loose. / 장갑이 손에 ～ Gloves are loose 〔loose-fitting〕 on the hand. / 살이 빠져서 이 스커트가 헐거워졌다 I've lost weight, and now this skirt is loose on me 〔too loose for me〕.

**헐근거리다** ⇨ 할근거리다.

**헐다**[1] ① 《낡다》 get old; become shabby; wear out; be worn-out. ¶ 옷이 ～ *one's* clothes wear out. ② 《부스럼》 get 〔have〕 a boil 《on》; develop a boil; be sore 〔inflamed〕. ¶ 얼굴이 ～ have a boil on *one's* face / 상처가 헐었다 The wound became inflamed.

**헐다**[2] ① 《허물다》 pull 〔tear, take, knock〕 down; destroy; demolish. ¶ 집을 ～ pull a house down. ② 《돈을》 break; change. ¶ 만원 짜리를 ～ break 〔change〕 a 10,000-won note (into small money). ③ 《헐뜯다》 slander; defame; speak ill of. ¶ 아무를 헐어 말하다 speak ill of *a person.*

**헐떡거리다, 헐떡이다** ① 《숨이》 pant; gasp (for breath); puff (and blow); breathe hard 〔heavily〕; be short of breath. ¶ 헐떡거리며 gasping(ly); panting(ly); between gasps; out of breath / 헐떡이며 말하다 speak panting; gasp 〔puff, pant〕 out / 무거운 짐을 지고 ～ pant under a heavy load / 그 여자 아이는 숨을 헐떡이며 말했다 The little girl gasped out her words. ② 《헐거워서》 be easy(-fitting); be loose.

**헐떡하다** ① 《얼굴이》 (be) pale; pallid; drawn; worn. ② 《눈이》 (be) hollow; sunken.

**헐뜯다** slander; libel; disparage; calumniate; malign; run 《*a person*》 down; pick on 《*a person*》. ¶ 아무를 ～ pick on *a person;* cry 〔run〕 down *a person* / 아무의 성공을 ～ belittle *a person's* success / 뒤에서 남을 ～ backbite *a person;* speak ill of *a person* behind *his* back / 뒤에서 남을 헐뜯는 짓을 그만둬라 Don't 「run people down 〔speak ill of others〕 behind their backs.

**헐렁거리다** ① 《헐거워》 get 〔fit〕 loose; be loose(-fitting); be baggy; be too big 〔large〕 《for》. ¶ 신이 ～ *one's* shoes fit 〔feel〕 loose / 구멍이 커서 쐐기가 ～

the hole is too big and the wedge is loose in it. ②《행동이》 act 〔behave〕 frivolously 〔imprudently〕.

**헐렁이** a frivolous 〔an imprudent〕 person; an unstable 〔untrust-worthy〕 person.

**헐렁하다** (be) very loose.

**헐렁헐렁** ①《헐거워》 loose; too big; 《바지가》 baggy. ～하다 (be) all loose; awfully loose. ¶그의 코트는 ～하다 His coat is too big. ②《행동이》 frivolously; imprudently. ～하다 (be) all unstable; terribly unstable. ¶사람이 ～하다 He is very unstable.

**헐레벌떡** panting and puffing. ～하다, ～거리다 pant and puff; breathe hard; be out 〔short〕 of breath. ¶～ 달려가다 run along panting and puffing / 그녀는 ～거리며 말을 끊었다 She stopped talking, quite out of breath. *or* She stopped talking for lack of breath.

**헐레이션** 〖사진〗 halation.

**헐리다** get pulled 〔torn, taken〕 down; be destroyed 〔demolished〕; be torn to pieces. ¶집이 ～ a house is pulled down / 그 낡은 건물은 흔적도 없이 헐렸다 The old building was completely demolished 〔was razed to the ground〕.

**헐벗다** 《사람이》 be in need 〔want〕 of clothes; be poorly 〔shabbily〕 clothed; 《나무가》 be bared 〔stripped〕 of leaves. ¶헐벗은 산 a bare 〔bald〕 mountain / 헐벗은 아이들 children in rags.

**헐변**(歇邊) low interest; a low rate of interest.

**헐수할 수 없다** be quite hopeless 〔impossible〕; be at *one's* wit's end; be at the end of *one's* tether. ¶헐수할 수 없이 as there is no help; driven at a tight corner; at a pinch.

**헐쑥하다** (be) thin and pale; drawn; lean; emaciated. ⇨ 핼쑥하다.

**헐하다**(歇—) ①《값이》 (be) cheap; inexpensive; be low in price (★ cheap는 「싸구려」, 「조악한 물건」이라는 느낌을 수반하므로 자사(自社)의 상품 등에 관해서는 이것을 피해 inexpensive라고 할 때가 많음. 또 남의 물건에 대해서 cheap라고 하면 실례가 되는 때도 있음). ¶헐한 물건 low-priced goods; a (good) bargain / 헐하게 cheap; cheaply; at a low 〔moderate〕 price / 헐하게 팔다 sell cheap; sell at a low price 〔rate, figure〕 / 값을 헐하게 하다 make 《*a thing*》 cheap(er); put 〔get〕 the price down; reduce 〔cut, drop〕 the price 《of》. ②《가볍다》 (be) light; lenient. ¶헐한 벌 a light 〔lenient〕 punishment. ③《쉽다》 (be) easy; light; simple. ¶헐한 일 light work.

**헐후하다**(歇后—) (be) insignificant; trivial; shabby; poor; worthless.

**험객**(險客) ①《성질이 험악한》 a roughneck; a tough 〔sinister, dangerous〕 character. ②《험구가》 a foul-mouthed person; a slanderer.

**험구**(險口) 《험담》 an evil tongue; slander; abuse; 《사람》 a foul-mouthed person; a slanderer; a knocker; a carper. ～하다 slander; abuse; speak ill of; "knock".

**험난**(險難) danger; difficulty; roughness; toughness. ～하다 (be) rough and difficult; be full of danger; (be) rugged; perilous; 《정세가》 (be) depressing; bleak. ¶～한 길 a thorny path; the way of the Cross; 《산길》 a steep 〔rugged, treacherous〕 mountain road / (등산의) ～한 코스 a dangerous trail 〔course〕 / 앞길이 ～하다 There is a rocky going ahead. *or* [비유적] The prospects are dark. / 이 회사의 앞길은 ～하다 This company's prospects look rather bleak.

**험담**(險談) (a) slander; abuse; calumny. ～하다 slander; say bad things about 《*a person*》; speak ill of 《*a person*》; speak against; talk scandal 《about》. ¶～ 잘 하는 사람 a scandalmonger; backbiter.

**험로**(險路) a rough 〔rugged〕 road; a steep path; a breakneck 〔dangerous〕 road.

**험상**(險狀) grimness; sinisterness; dangerousness.

**험상궂다, 험상스럽다**(險狀—) (be) grim; rough; terrible; savage-looking. ¶험상궂은 얼굴 a grim face; a sinister countenance; a stern expression / 험상궂은 얼굴을 하다 look sternly 〔severely〕 《at》; scowl 《at》.

**험악하다**(險惡—) 《위험》 (be) dangerous; perilous; 《길이》 (be) steep; rugged; 《사태가》 (be) serious; critical; grave; tense; 《날씨가》 (be) threatening; stormy. ¶험악한 산길 rugged 〔steep〕 mountain path / 험악한 날씨 foul 〔stormy, rough〕 weather / 험악한 분위기 an awkward atmosphere / 험악한 얼굴 a threatening 〔menacing〕 look; an angry look / 험악한 태도 an abrupt manner / 날씨가 험악해서 owing to the severity of the weather; under stress of weather / 험악한 얼굴로 보다 look darkly at 《*a person*》; survey 《*a person*》 with a stern look / 형세가 날로 험악해지고 있다 The situation is getting uglier every day. / 날씨가 몹시 험악하군 The sky looks very threatening.

**험준**(險峻) steepness; precipitousness; ruggedness. ～하다 (be) steep; precipitous; rugged; rough. ¶ ～한 산맥 a rugged mountain range.

**험하다**(險—) ① 《산길 등이》 (be) rugged; rough; steep; dangerous; perilous; precipitous. ¶ 험한 산길 a rugged 〔sheer〕 mountain road. ② 《날씨 등이》 (be) foul; stormy; rough; threatening. ¶ 험한 날씨 foul 〔rough〕 weather. ③ 《얼굴·표정》 (be) sinister; grim; savage-looking; fierce.

**헙수룩하다** ① 《머리털이》 (be) untidy; untrimmed; disheveled. ② 《주제가》 (be) shabby; poor-looking; seedy; run-down. ¶ 헙수룩한 옷 shabby clothes / 차림새가 ～ be shabbily 〔poorly〕 dressed.

**헙헙하다** ① 《사람됨이》 (be) easy-going; be not firm. ② 《손쓰는 품이》 (be) liberal; generous; lavish. ¶ 돈씀씀이가 ～ be generous 〔liberal, free〕 with *one's* money; be open-handed; spend 〔use〕 (*one's*) money freely.

**헛가게** a booth; a stall.

**헛간**(—間) a storeroom with an open front; an open shed; a barn.

**헛걸음** a visit 〔trip〕 in vain; a fruitless 〔frustrating〕 journey. ～하다 make a visit 《on *a person*》 in vain; make a fruitless call 《on *a person*》; pay 《*a person*》 a visit 〔visit *a person*〕 to no purpose. ¶ 아무를 ～시키다 send *a person* on a fool's errand / 그가 집에 없을는지 모르지만 ～할 셈치고 가보는 것도 좋을테지 He may not be at home, but you might go just on chance.

**헛것** a phantom; an apparition.

**헛구역**(—嘔逆) 〖의학〗 vomiturition; a queasy feeling. ¶ ～질하다 have a queasy feeling; be queasy.

**헛글** fruitless 〔wasted〕 learning. ¶ ～(을) 배우다 waste *one's* schooling; learn nothing.

**헛기운** 《make》 a show of courage; 《show》 Dutch courage (술취한 때의).

**헛기침** clearing *one's* throat to attract another's attention; ahemming. ～하다 clear *one's* throat to attract another's attention; ahem.

**헛김** an air leak; a leak. ～나다 get a leak; spring a leak; leak; 《맥빠짐》 get frustrated; lose heart; be dispirited.

**헛노릇** vain efforts; wasted labor. ～하다 labor in vain; do useless work.

**헛다리짚다** make a false 〔wrong〕 step; [비유적] 「fall short of 〔don't come up to〕 *one's* expectation; guess wrong; make a wrong guess 〔estimate〕; shoot at a wrong mark; be wide of the mark. ¶ 나에게서 돈을 빌리겠다니, 헛다리짚지 마 If you expect to borrow money from me, you are barking up the wrong tree.

**헛돌다** 《바퀴·기계 등이》 run idle; race.

**헛되다** ① 《보람없다》 (be) idle; vain; futile; empty; [서술적] be in vain; be of no use 〔avail〕. ¶ 헛된 노력 vain efforts / 헛된 세상 the futile world / 헛된 시도 a wild-goose chase 〔race〕 / 헛된 이름 an empty name 〔title〕; a false 〔bubble〕 reputation / 헛된 죽음을 하다 die in vain 〔to no purpose〕 / 헛되지 않다 be worthwhile 《to *do*》; be worth 《*doing*》 / 더이상 기다려 보았자 헛된 일이다 There is no point in waiting any longer. / 그녀의 노력은 헛되고 말았다 Her efforts bore no fruit. / 그에게 기부 좀 하라고 해보았자 헛된 일이다 To ask him for a subscription is like beating the air. / 그녀를 보고 빙긋 웃어보였지만 헛된 일이었다 My smile was lost on her. / 내 노력은 헛되지 않았다 I have not labored in vain. ② 《사실이 아님》 (be) untrue; false; empty; [서술적] be devoid of truth. ¶ 헛된 소문 a groundless rumor.

**헛되이** uselessly; in vain; vainly; 《무익하게》 to no purpose; fruitlessly (성과없이); 《목적도 없이》 aimlessly; 《아무것도 안 하고》 idly. ¶ ～ 저항하다 resist in vain / 세월을 ～ 보내다 idle *one's* time away; live in idleness / 돈을 ～ 쓰다 spend (*one's*) money uselessly; waste 〔throw away〕 *one's* money / ～ 일생을 보내다 pass a life in idleness / 자넨 모처럼의 기회를 ～ 할 작정인가 Are you going to pass up such a good opportunity ?

**헛된말** idle 〔empty〕 words; unbelievable words. ¶ ～을 하다 say useless 〔pointless〕 things; say something incredible.

**헛듣다** 《잘못 듣다》 hear 《it, him》 wrong 〔amiss〕; mishear; 《흘려 버리다》 take no notice 《of》; pay no attention 《to》; give no heed 《to》. ¶ 말을 ～ mishear 《*a person's*》 remark; misunderstand 《*a person*》 / 헛들은 것이나 아닌가 하고 내 귀를 의심했다 I could hardly believe my ears.

**헛디디다** lose 〔miss〕 *one's* footing; miss *one's* step; make 〔take〕 a false step; let《*one's* foot》slip. ¶ 벼랑을 헛디뎌 바다로 떨어지다 step over the cliff into the sea / 발을 헛디뎌 계단에서 굴러떨어졌다 I lost my footing and fell down the stairs. / 한발짝만 헛디뎠으면 밑의 바위에 떨어져서 목숨을 잃었을 것이다「A single misstep 〔One false step〕 and I should have been hurled to my death on the rocks below.

**헛맹세**「an idle 〔a false〕 pledge 〔vow〕. ～하다 make「an idle 〔a false〕 vow.

**헛물켜다** make vain efforts; exert *oneself* to no purpose; get nothing for *one's* pains; labor for nothing; waste time and labor; plow the「sand(s) 〔air〕; catch at shadows. ¶ 그런 사람을 믿었다가 헛물만 켰다 I made a fool of myself counting on such a person. / 고생만하고 헛물만 켰다 It was 〔turned out〕 a mere waste of labor. *or* I gained nothing for all my trouble.

**헛발** ¶ ～ 디디다 make a false step; tread on air.

**헛방**(一放)《헛총질》a miss shot; a poor shot; a shot wide of the mark;《공탄》a blank「shot 〔cartridge〕;《헛된 말》empty talk; "gas"; "hot air". ¶ ～ 놓다 shoot and miss; miss a shot;《헛된 말을》talk through *one's* hat; "shoot the breeze".

**헛방**(一房) a room not in use (and available for storage space).

**헛방귀** a silent odorless fart.

**헛배부르다** ①《먹지 않고도》have a false sense of satiety. ②《가스가 차서》get bloated up (with gas); feel bloated;《실속없이》be bloated up《with pride》.

**헛보다** mistake 〔take〕《A for B》; get the wrong view《of》; fail to see (properly). ¶ 신호를 ～ mistake 〔misread〕 a signal; fail to「see 〔recognize〕 a signal.

**헛보이다** get improperly seen; be misviewed; get mistaken.

**헛불** a「miss 〔poor〕 shot; a shot wide of the mark. ¶ ～ 놓다《총을》shoot and miss;《말을》talk big; brag.

**헛소동**(一騷動) much ado about nothing; (a case of) much cry and little wool. ¶ ～을 부리다〔하다〕 make a fuss about nothing.

**헛소리** ①《잠꼬대》(***a***)《잠결에 하는》talking in sleep; sleep talking. ¶ ～(를) 하다 talk in *one's* sleep. (***b***)《허튼 소리》idle words; silly talk; nonsense; gibberish; rubbish; bunk《미속어》. ¶ ～(를) 하다 talk nonsense 〔rot, rubbish〕; say silly things / 무슨 ～를 하는 거냐 What are you talking about? ②《고열에 시달려 나오는》talking in delirium; delirious utterances. ¶ ～(를) 하다 talk「deliriously 〔in (a) delirium〕; utter ravings / 그는 높은 열에 시달려 뜻모를 ～를 하고 있었다 During his high fever he became delirious and said strange things.

**헛소문**(一所聞) a groundless rumor; a false rumor; idle gossip. ¶ ～을 퍼뜨리다 set a false rumor afloat.

**헛손질** pawing the air; a mishit. ～하다 paw 〔beat〕 the air.

**헛수**(一手)〖바둑·장기〗「a wrong 〔an ineffective〕 move. ¶ ～를 두다 make「a wrong 〔an ineffective〕 move.

**헛수고** useless 〔fruitless, vain, wasted〕 efforts; waste of labor; useless 〔fruitless〕 labor. ～하다 make vain efforts; work in vain; get nothing for *one's* pains; labor in vain. ¶ ～가 되다 end in (mere) waste of labor; be in vain; prove fruitless / ～로 돌아가다 *one's* labor comes to「nothing 〔naught〕; *one's* efforts prove「fruitless 〔unavailing〕 / ～만 했다 I gained nothing for all my trouble. / 공연한 ～하지 말게 Don't look for a needle in a haystack. / 우리의 노력은 모두 ～였다 All our efforts were vain.

**헛심** wasted strength; useless effort.

**헛애** a「useless 〔fruitless〕 efforts. =헛수고. ¶ ～를 쓰다 make vain effort; waste *one's* time and labor.

**헛웃음** a「feigned 〔pretended〕 smile; a simper. ¶ ～(을) 치다 feign 〔force, affect〕 a「laugh 〔smile〕; put on a diplomatic smile.

**헛일** useless work; vain effort; lost 〔fruitless〕 labor. ～하다, ～되다 do useless work; labor in vain; *one's* work comes to nauxght; *one's* labor is lost. ¶ ～이다 be (of) no use; be of no avail; be useless; be in vain; be no good.

**헛잠** sham 〔feigned, pretended〕 sleep; a simulation of sleep;《선잠》a nap; a catnap. ¶ ～을 자다 sham 〔feign〕 sleep; pretend to be asleep; play possum;《선잠을》take 〔have〕 a nap.

**헛잡다** ①《잘못 고르다》pick up wrongly; fail to pick up the right one. ¶ 제비를 ～ pick a losing number in lottery. ②《도둑을》arrest by mistake. ¶ 도둑을 ～ arrest the wrong person for a robber. ③《잘못 쥐다》 fail to catch 〔grasp〕; miss *one's* hold; let slip (through *one's* fingers). ¶ 찻잔을 헛잡아 떨어뜨리다 let a cup slip and drop.

**헛장** pretended defiance; a bluff; a bold front. ¶ ~ 치다 bluff; hurl pretended defiance 《at *a person*》.

**헛짚다** ⇨ 헛다리짚다

**헛청**(―廳) a shed; a barn.

**헛총**(―銃) a blank cartridge; a blank shot. ¶ ~ 놓다 fire 〔discharge〕 a blank cartridge. ◉ ~질 firing a blank: ~질하다 fire a blank.

**헛치다** fail to hit; miss 《*one's* aim》; strike at the air; 《구어》 whiff (야구에서); 《권투에서》 swish the air; 《골프》 foozle.

**헛코골다** pretend to snore.

**헛턱** 《빈 턱》 an unrealized entertainment; a Barmecide's feast.

**헛헛증**(―症) hungriness; a chronic hunger. ¶ ~이 있다 suffer from chronic hunger.

**헛헛하다** feel hungry; (be) hungry.

**헝가리** 《나라 이름》 Hungary. ¶ ~의 Hungarian. ◉ ~말 Hungarian. ~사람 a Hungarian.

**헝거스트라이크** a hunger strike. ¶ ~를 하다 go on a hunger strike.

**헝겁(지겁)** in elation 〔delight〕; transported with joy; leaping out of *one's* skin.

**헝겊** a piece of cloth; a rag; a scrap. ◉ ~신 cloth 〔canvas〕 shoes. ~조각 a scrap of cloth.

**헝클다** ⇨ 엉클다.

**헝클어지다** get (en)tangled; be in a tangle; be matted. ¶ 헝클어진 머리 matted 〔tangled, disheveled〕 hair / 헝클어진 것을 풀다 disentangle; unravel 《a complicated matter》.

**헤** agape; wide open. ¶ 입을 헤 벌리다 open *one's* mouth wide; gape / 헤하고 웃다 laugh with *one's* mouth wide open.

**헤게모니** 《지배권》 hegemony. ¶ ~싸움 strife over hegemony / ~를 잡다 hold hegemony.

**헤근거리다** shake; wobble; be loose.

**헤근헤근** shaking; loose. ¶ 사개가 ~ 놀다 dovetails wobble.

**헤다**[1] ①《헤엄치다》 swim; take 〔have〕 a swim. ②《고비를》 try to escape from; struggle to wriggle out of difficulty.

**헤다**[2] 《멋대로 하다》 act 〔behave〕 as *one* likes; do what *one* wants to; 《난척하다》 be stuck up; be puffed up; assume airs 〔an air of importance〕; give *oneself* airs.

**헤대다** move about busily; hustle 〔bustle〕 about.

**헤덤비다** rush about.

**헤드라이트** a headlight. ¶ ~를 켜다〔끄다〕 turn on 〔off〕 the headlight.

**헤드록** 〖레슬링〗 a headlock.

**헤드폰** a headphone.

**헤딩** heading 《a soccer ball》. ~하다 head 《the ball》. ¶ ~으로 슛을 성공시키다 head the ball into the opponent's net.

**헤뜨리다** scatter; strew; disperse. ¶ 닭이 모이를 ~ chickens scatter their feed / 군중을 ~ disperse a crowd / 방에 지스러기를 ~ litter a room with scraps.

**헤로인**[1] 〖약〗《마취제》 heroin. ◉ ~중독 heroinism.

**헤로인**[2] 《여주인공》 a heroine.

**헤르니아** 〖의학〗《탈장》 hernia.

**헤르츠** 《주파수의 단위》 a hertz (생략 Hz). ◉ ~파 a hertzian wave.

**헤르쿨레스자리** 〖천문〗 Hercules.

**헤매다** ①《이리저리》 wander 〔roam, knock, ramble〕 about; walk around; stray about; kick around 《구어》; rove. ¶ 들판을 ~ wander over 〔roam about〕 the field / 숲속을 정처 없이 ~ stray aimlessly through the wood / 아무를 찾아 산중을 ~ comb the mountains for *a person* / 생사지경을 ~ hover 〔linger〕 between life and death / 할 일이 없이 종일 거리를 ~ wander about the town all day long with nothing to do. ②《마음이》 be embarrassed 〔perplexed〕; be at a loss. ¶ 어쩔 줄 몰라 ~ be at a loss what to do.

**헤먹다** get loose; become loose-fitting.

**헤모글로빈** 《혈색소》 hemoglobin.

**헤무르다** (be) feeble; flaccid; unstrung; falling apart. ¶ 헤무른 사람 a feeble 〔sapless〕 person / 헤무른 살 flaccid 〔flabby〕 flesh.

**헤묽다** (be) watery; flabby; sloppy; thin.

**헤번드르르** ⇨ 번드르르.

**헤벌어지다** (be) very wide; too spacious.

**헤벌쭉** wide open. ~하다 (be) wide open. ¶ ~웃다 smile a broad smile.

**헤브라이** 〖역사〗 the Hebrews. ⇨ 히브리. ◉ ~사람 a Hebrew. ~어(語) Hebrew.

**헤브라이즘** Hebraism.

**헤비급**(―級) 〖권투〗 the heavyweight (class). ◉ ~선수 a heavyweight (boxer).

**헤살** 《훼방함》 slander(ing); hindrance;

interference; disturbance. ¶ ～놓다〔부리다〕 engage in slander 〔backbiting〕; interfere with; talk against; obstruct; stand in one's way; thwart / 계획을 ～놓다 thwart 《*a person's*》 plan / ～놓지 마라 Don't stand in my way. *or* Don't disturb 〔interrupt〕 me.
◉ ～꾼 a slanderer; an obstructionist.

**헤식다** 《무르다》 (be) soft; weak; brittle; feeble; flabby; fragile; crumbly; sluggish. ¶ 헤식은 쌀 soft rice / 헤식은 사람 a person of weak constitution; a person who lacks vitality.

**헤실바실** frittering away; inadvertently running out of. ¶ 돈을 ～ 다 써 버리다 fritter away all the money *one* has / ～ 쌀이 다 없어지다 the rice runs out before *one* is aware of it.

**헤싱헤싱하다** (be) loose; slack.

**헤아리다** ① 《요량하다》 consider; weigh; ponder. ¶ 일을 잘 헤아려 하다 undertake a plan with due consideration. ② 《가늠·짐작하다》 fathom; sound; plumb; surmise; conjecture. ¶ 마음을〔가슴속을〕 ～ fathom 《*a person*》; figure 《*a person*》 out; enter into 《*a person's*》 feelings; read 《*a person's*》 mind 〔thoughts〕; sympathize with 《*a person*》 / 하늘의 뜻은 헤아릴 수 없다 The ways of Heaven are inscrutable. / 고마운 마음 이루 헤아릴 수 없다 You can't guess 〔I can't tell you〕 how grateful I am to you. ③ 《세다》 count; calculate; estimate. ¶ 수(數)를 ～ count 〔estimate〕 the number / 헤아릴 수 없다 be incalculable; be innumerable / 그러한 예는 헤아릴 수 없이 많다 There are countless 〔numerous〕 instances like that.

**헤어나다** get out of 《a difficulty》; escape from 《danger》; extricate *oneself* from 《difficulties》; free *oneself* of 〔from〕 《a bondage》; find 〔cut〕 *one's* way through. ¶ 헤어날 길 없다 have no way out / 난관〔어려움〕에서 ～ get out of trouble; find *one's* way out of difficulty 〔a scrape〕; tide over a difficulty / 슬럼프에서 ～ pull *oneself* out of the slump.

**헤어네트** a hairnet.

**헤어브러시** a hairbrush.

**헤어스타일** a hairstyle.

**헤어지다** ① 《흩어지다》 get scattered 〔strewn, dispersed〕. ¶ 졸업생이 각처로 ～ the graduates are scattered in all directions / 삼삼오오 헤어지다 disperse by twos and threes. ② 《이별하다》 break up; separate; part 《from, with》; part company 《with》; 《부부가》 be separated; divorce *oneself* 《from》. ¶ 헤어진 아내 a separated 〔divorced〕 wife / 동무와 ～ part from a friend / 서로 헤어져 살다 live separately; live apart from each other / 드디어 헤어질 날이 왔다 At last there came a parting day. / 서로 헤어질 생각을 하고 있다 They are considering divorce. / 헤어진 지 10년이나 됩니다 It has been ten years since I saw you last.

**헤어토닉** a hair tonic.

**헤어핀** a hairpin.

**헤엄** swimming; a swim. ～치다 swim; have a swim. ¶ ～ 잘 치는 사람 a good swimmer / ～쳐 건너다 swim across 《a river》 / ～치러 가다 go swimming 《in a river》; go 《to a lake》 for a swim / 옆으로 ～치다 swim on *one's* side / ～을 잘 치다 swim well; be a good swimmer; be good at swimming / ～을 잘 못 치다 be a poor swimmer / 건너편 둑으로 ～ 쳐 가다 swim to the opposite bank / 내를 ～쳐 올라〔내려〕가다 swim against 〔down〕 the stream / 나는 조금도 ～칠 줄 모른다 I can't swim a stroke. / ～치는 법을 좀 가르쳐 다오 Teach 〔Show〕 me how to swim. ◉ 개～ the dog paddle.

**헤적이다** rummage; ransack; scatter; disperse. ¶ 서류를 ～ rummage among papers / 공을 찾느라 수풀을 ～ rummage the thicket to search a ball.

**헤죽거리다** walk briskly swinging *one's* arms.

**헤죽헤죽** walking briskly swinging *one's* arms.

**헤집다** tear up; turn up; dig up and scatter. ¶ 닭이 흙을 ～ a chicken scratches the dirt up.

**헤치다** ① 《파헤치다》 dig up 《earth》; turn up. ¶ 무덤을 ～ open 〔violate〕 a grave; dig 〔lay〕 a grave open. ② 《흩뜨리다》 scatter; disperse; break up. ¶ 모인 사람을 ～ disperse a crowd. ③ 《좌우로》 push aside; make *one's* way 《through》; push 〔elbow〕 *one's* way 《through》. ¶ 군중을 헤치고 나아가다 elbow 〔push〕 *one's* way through a crowd / 배가 물결을 헤치고 나아갔다 The boat plowed through the waves.

**헤프다** ① 《쓰기에》 be not durable; be easy to wear out; be soon used up; go fast. ¶ 요새 돈이 ～ Money doesn't go far these days. / 이 비누는 ～ This soap doesn't last long. ② 《씀씀이가》 (be) wasteful; uneconomical. ¶ 돈을

헤프게 쓰다 be too free with *one's* money; be wasteful of money. ③《말이》(be) voluble; talkative; glib (=tongued). ¶ 그녀는 말이 너무 ~ She speaks too much. ④《몸가짐이》(be) loose; dissipated; dissolute. ¶ 몸가짐이 헤픈 여자 a loose woman.

**헤피** wastefully; uneconomically. ¶ 돈을 ~ 쓰다 waste 〔squander〕 money.

**헤하다** beam with joy; grin (broadly).

**헤헤** ¶ ~ 웃다 laugh foolishly.

**헥타르** 《면적의 단위》 a hectare (10,000 m²).

**헥토-** 《미터법의》 hecto-. ◉ ~그램 a hectogram. ~리터 a hectoliter. ~미터 a hectometer.

**헥토파스칼** 《기압의 단위》 hectopascal.

**헬레니즘** 〖역사〗 Hellenism.

**헬륨** 〖화학〗 helium (기호 He).

**헬리오스탯** 〖광학〗 a heliostat.

**헬리오트로프** 〖식물〗 a heliotrope.

**헬리콥터** a helicopter; a copter 《구어》; a chopper 《미구어》; an eggbeater 《미속어》. ¶ ~로 가다 helicopter (off ) 《to》/ ~로 운반되다 be transported by helicopter; be helicoptered 《to》. ◉ ~모함(母艦) a helicopter carrier. ~발착장 a heliport; a helipad.

**헬리포트** 《빌딩 옥상 따위의》 a heliport.

**헬멧** a helmet; 《작업장의》 a hard hat; 《오토바이 운전자의》 a crash helmet. ¶ ~을 쓴 남자 a helmeted man.

**헬스클럽** a health club. ¶ 「무료 초대권」이란 미끼에 걸려 지독히 비싼 ~에 들게 되었다 I was lured into a very high-priced health club by a "free guest pass."

**헷갈리다** ① 《마음이》 be confused; *one's* attention is distracted; *one's* thoughts are scattered. ¶ 머리가 헷갈린다 I'm getting confused. / 아이들이 떠들어서 정신이 ~ The children are too noisy for me to concentrate. ② 《뜻이》 be confused 〔tangled〕; be hard to distinguish; 《길 따위가》 be hard to find 〔see, make out〕. ¶ 두 글자의 뜻이 ~ the two words are confused in meaning.

**헹가래** tossing. ¶ ~치다 toss 《*a person*》 into the air.

**헹구다** wash out; rinse out 〔away〕; give 《*a thing*》 a rinse 〔swill〕. ¶ 빨래를 ~ rinse out the wash.

**헹글헹글** loose-fitting; baggy. ~하다 (be) loose-fitting; baggy.

**혀** ① a tongue. ¶ 혀가 잘 돌아가다 have a glib tongue; be oily-tongued / 혀가 돌아가지 않다 be tongue-tied; be unable to speak distinctly; *one's* speech is slurred (술취해서); have an impediment in *one's* speech (언어 장애) / 혀를 내밀다 《사람이》 put 〔thrust〕 *one's* tongue out 《at》; 《개 따위가》 loll (out) *its* tongue / 혀를 차다 click 〔clack〕 *one's* tongue; cluck; go tsk's / 혀를 내두르다 marvel 《at》; be astounded / 혀를 깨물다 bite *one's* (own) tongue / 혀가 꼬부라지도록 술을 마시다 drink till *one's* tongue trips / 고추가 매워 혀가 얼얼하다 Hot pepper burns my tongue. ② 《악기의》 a reed (of a wind instrument).

**혀꼬부랑이** a person with a speech impediment.

**혀끝** the tip of the tongue.

**혀밑샘** 〖생물〗 the sublingual gland.

**혀뿌리** 〖해부〗 the root of the tongue; the lingual radix.

**혀짜래기** ⇨ 혀짤배기.

**혀짤배기** a tongue-tied person; a person whose speech is impeded by a short tongue.

**혁대**(革帶) a leather belt. ¶ ~를 졸라매다〔늦추다〕 tighten 〔loosen〕 *one's* belt. ◉ ~고리 a buckle; a clasp.

**혁명**(革命) a revolution; a revolutionary upheaval 〔outbreak〕. ~하다 start 〔carry out〕 a revolution; revolutionize. ¶ ~적 revolutionary 《ideas》/ 잡지계의 일대 ~ a great revolution 〔an epoch-making reform〕 in the magazine world / ~적인 기술의 진보 revolutionary improvements in technology / ~을 진압하다 foil a revolution / 정치에서 ~ 보다 점진을 택하다 prefer evolution to revolution in politics / 그 나라에 ~이 일어났다 A revolution broke out in the country. / 오토메이션은 산업계에 ~을 가져왔다 Automation has revolutionized the industrial world. / 컴퓨터는 우리의 일상 생활에 ~적인 변화를 가져왔다 The computer has brought a revolutionary change in our daily life. ◉ ~가(家) a revolutionist; a revolutionary. ~가(歌) a revolutionary song. ~군 a revolutionary army. ~당 a revolutionary party. ~사상 revolutionary ideas 〔thoughts〕. ~사업 (the) revolutionary tasks. ~시대 an epoch of revolution. ~아(兒) a man of revolutionary temperament. ~운동 a revolutionary movement. ~위원회 《쿠데타후의》 a junta. ~전쟁 a revolutionary war. ~정부 a revolutionary government. 반(反)~ a counterrevolution: 반～의 counterrevolutionary.

**혁신**(革新) (a) reform; (a) renovation; (an) innovation(쇄신). ～하다 reform; renovate; innovate; make a reform ⟪in⟫. ¶ ～적인 innovative; innovating; progressive / 교육의 ～ an educational renovation / 정치의 ～ a political reform 〔renovation〕/ 낡은 제도를 ～하다 reform an old system / ～적인 사상을 품다 have progressive 〔innovative〕 ideas / 회사는 많은 기술을 ～했다 The company has put through many technical improvements. ◉ ～세력 the progressive force; the progressive political group. ～운동 a reform movement. ～자 a reformer; an innovator. ～정권 reformist 〔renovationist, progressive〕 government. ～정당 a progressive party; a reformist (political) party. ～파 the reformist; a reformist group 〔party〕. 자기～ self-reform: 자기 ～ 운동 the self-reform drive.

**혁지**(革砥) a (razor) strop 〔strap〕. ¶ ～에 갈다 strop 〔strap〕 ⟪a razor⟫; sharpen ⟪a razor⟫ on a strop.

**혁혁하다**(赫赫—) (be) bright; brilliant; beaming; radiant; distinguished; glorious. ¶ 혁혁한 공적 a glorious exploit / 혁혁한 명성〔승리〕 a brilliant reputation 〔victory〕.

**현**(弦) ① ⟪활시위⟫ a bowstring. ② 〖수학〗 a chord; a subtense; a hypotenuse. ③ 〖천문〗 a quarter (moon).

**현**(現) present; existing; actual; current. ¶ 현내각 the present Cabinet / 현대통령 the President in office.

**현**(絃) ① ⟪악기의⟫ a string; a chord. ② ⇨ 현악기.

**현가**(現價) the present 〔current〕 price.

**현격**(懸隔) a (wide) difference; a disparity; a discrepancy; a gap. ～하다 (be) (widely) different ⟪from⟫; far 〔wide〕 apart ⟪from⟫. ¶ ～한 차이 a wide difference 〔gap〕/ 이상과 현실 사이에는 ～한 차가 있다 There is a great gap between our ideal and the reality. / 빈부의 차가 ～하지 않다 The gulf between rich and poor is not very wide.

**현관**(玄關) ⟪입구⟫ the (front) door 〔entrance〕; the porch; ⟪현관홀⟫ the entrance 〔front〕 hall; the entry hall ⟪미⟫. ¶ ～으로 들어가다 「enter at 〔go in by〕 the front door / 손님을 ～까지 배웅하다 see a visitor to the door / (손님을) 맞이하러 ～으로 나가다 answer the door / 자동차를 ～에 대다 drive a motorcar up to the door / 김포 공항은 한국의 ～이다 Kimpo Airport is the gateway to Korea.

**현군**(賢君) a wise king.

**현금**(玄琴) 〖악기〗 a kind of harp.

**현금**(現今) the present time 〔day〕; these days; now; nowadays. ¶ ～의 present(-day); current; of today / ～의 형세 the existing 〔present, prevailing〕 state of things / ～에 이르기까지 until 〔up to〕 the present / ～의 경제 상황 the present 〔current〕 economic situation.

**현금**(現金) ⟪현찰⟫ cash; ⟪현재 있는 돈⟫ actual 〔ready〕 money; ⟪맞돈⟫ prompt 〔spot〕 cash; ready funds.
¶ ～으로 거래하다 deal in cash; conduct business on a cash basis / (수표를) ～으로 바꾸다 cash ⟪a check⟫; have 〔get〕 ⟪a check⟫ cashed; convert ⟪a bond⟫ / ～으로 사다〔팔다〕 buy 〔sell〕 ⟪*a thing*⟫ for cash / ～으로 지급〔지불〕하다 pay in cash; present ready money; pay down ⟪미⟫ / ～이 달리다 be 〔run〕 short of cash / ～이 없다 be out of cash / ～의 경우는 1할을 깎아 주다 take 10 percent off for cash / ～으로 사시면 5프로 할인해 드립니다 Goods are subject to 5 percent discount when paid in cash. / ～만 받습니다 ⟪게시⟫ We accept cash only. / ～ 대신 수표론 안되겠습니까 May I give you a check instead of paying you in cash ? / 그녀는 대가의 일부를 ～으로 지불했다 She paid part of the price in cash. / 우리는 많은 ～이 필요하다 We need a lot of ready money now.
◉ ～가격 a cash 〔spot〕 price. ～거래〔매매〕 cash transactions. ～계정 a cash account. ～구매 cash purchase; purchase with cash. ～급여액 cash wages. ～등록기 a cash register. ～보유고 ⇨ ～시재액. ～분개장 a cash journal. ～비율 cash ratio. ～상환(相換) cash on delivery (생략 c.o.d.). ～상환(償還) cash redemption. ～선불 advance payment in cash; an advance of cash 〔money〕. ～수송차 an armored car ⟪미⟫; a car 〔van〕 used for transporting cash; a security vehicle. ～수요 the demand for cash. ～수입 (a) cash 〔money〕 income. ～시재액(時在額) cash on 〔in〕 hand. ～인출 카드 a cash card. ～입출기 an automated teller machine (생략

ATM). ～자동 지급기 a cash dispenser. ～자산 cash assets. ～정가 a cash price. ～주의 a pay-as-you-go policy; no-credit policy. ～지불 cash payment; down payment《미》: ～ 지불 주문 cash with order (생략 C.W.O., c.w.o.) / ～지불 할인 cash discount; cash rebates. ～차관(借款) cash loan; loans in cash. ～출납계원 a cashier. ～출납부《소액의》a (petty) cashbook. ～판매 cash〔spot〕sales; selling for cash: ～ 판매주의 cash and carry 《미》. ～할인 a cash discount.

**현금화**(現金化) encashment. ～하다《수표 따위를》encash; cash (in)《a check》; convert《a bond》(into cash); 《증권을》realize; liquidate《*one's* securities》. ¶ ～할 수 있는 liquid; quick 《미》.

**현기증**(眩氣症) dizziness; giddiness; the whirl of the brain; 〖의학〗(a) vertigo. ¶ ～이 나는 높이에서 at a giddy〔dizzy〕height《from the ground》/ ～이 나다, ～을 느끼다 be〔feel〕dizzy; get〔feel〕giddy; *one's* head swims / 때때로 ～이 나다 have frequent dizzy spells; be subject to attacks of vertigo / 일어설 때 ～이 나다 feel〔get〕dizzy〔giddy〕on standing up. ◉ 산후～ puerperal vertigo.

**현대**(現代) the present age〔time, day〕; modern times; today; our own day. ¶ ～의 contemporary; present-day; current; of our own time / ～에 (있어서) in our time; at the present day; in these modern days / ～의 한국 modern〔contemporary〕Korea; (the) present-day Korea; Korea (of) today / ～의 과학자 the scientists of the time / ～ 일류의 화가 one of the foremost artists of our time / ～는 정보화 사회이다 Today is the age of the information-oriented society / ～의학으로도 고치지 못하는 병이 많다 There are many diseases that cannot be cured even by modern medical science.

◉ ～교육 modern education. ～극 a modern play〔drama〕; a drama of present-day life. ～문 contemporary writings; 《문체》current style. ～문학 current〔contemporary〕literature. ～사(史) contemporary history. ～사상 modern ideas; contemporary thought. ～사조 current thought; 《시대 정신》the spirit of the times. ～생활 present-day life. ～성(性) modernity. ～식 a modern style〔fashion〕: ～식 건물 a building in modern style. ～어 a living〔modern〕language. ～영어 present-day〔current〕English. ～인 a man of today〔the present age〕; the moderns [총칭]. ～작가 a contemporary writer. ～전(戰) modern war(fare). ～판(版) a modern edition〔version〕《of》.

**현대적**(現代的) modern(-type); modernistic; up-to-date; up-to-the-minute; contemporary. ¶ ～인 건물 a building in modern style / ～으로 in a modern style; along〔on〕modern lines / 그녀의 의상 디자인에는 ～인 감각이 넘쳐흐르고 있다 Her dress design is full of modern perceptivity.

**현대풍**(現代風) the present〔latest, up-to-date〕fashion; the modern style〔fashion〕; modernism. ¶ ～의 of the modern style; up-to-date / ～으로 in the present fashion〔style〕.

**현대화**(現代化) modernization; updating. ～하다 modernize; update; 《현대풍으로 되다》be modernized. ¶ 완전히 ～하다 be completely modernized / ～하지 않으면 사업은 손해를 보게 된다 The business will lose money if it doesn't modernize.

**현등**(舷燈) 《선박의》a side〔running〕light; 《항공기의》a position light.

**현란**(絢爛) gorgeousness; brilliancy; splendor. ～하다 (be) gorgeous; brilliant; splendid; dazzling; gaudy. ¶ ～한 의상 a gorgeous costume / ～한 색채 brilliant〔dazzling〕colors / ～한 문체(文體) a flowery〔ornate〕style.

**현량하다**(賢良―) (be) wise and good〔virtuous〕.

**현명**(賢明) wisdom; sagacity; perspicacity; 《분별》prudence; 《양식》good sense; 《상책》advisability. ～하다 (be) wise; sensible; intelligent; sagacious; prudent; judicious; discreet; advisable; well-advised. ¶ ～한 방책 a wise policy / ～한 사람 a wise man; an intelligent person / ～한 판단 a sound judgment / ～하게 처신하다 act wisely〔sensibly〕/ ～치 못한 ill-considered; injudicious; inadvisable; unwise / ～한 조치를 취하다 adopt a wise policy; act wisely / 그렇게 하는 것이 과연 ～할까 몰라 I can't help wondering if we are wise to do so. / 어두워지면 이 거리를 거닐지 않는 것이 ～하다 It is sensible〔prudent〕not to walk along this street after dark.

**현모양처**(賢母良妻) a wise mother and good wife.

**현몽하다**(現夢―) appear 〔come to *one*〕 in a dream.

**현묘하다**(玄妙―) (be) abstruse; occult; arcane; recondite; deep; esoteric. ¶ 현묘한 사상 a profound idea.

**현무암**(玄武岩) 〖지질〗 basalt; whin (-stone); trap(rock).

**현문**(舷門) 《뱃전에 걸쳐 놓은 출입구》 a gangway.

**현물**(現物) the (actual) goods 〔article, thing〕; the real thing; 《상품 거래의》 spots; spot goods. ¶ ～을 보지 않고 《buy an article》 without seeing the goods / ～로 지급하다 pay in kind / ～을 보지 않고는 무어라고 말할 수 없다 I cannot say either way before I inspect the article. / 대금은 ～ 인수와 동시에 지급해 주십시오 Please pay on receipt of the goods. *or* The goods must be paid for on delivery.
◉ ～ 가격 spot prices. ～거래〔매매〕 spot trading 〔transaction〕; over-the-counter business. ～급여 the truck (system); (a) payment 〔an allowance〕 in kind. ～배상 reparations in kind. ～소득 income in kind. ～시장 the spot market; the spots; the over-the-counter market. ～인도 delivery of the goods. ～중매인 a spot broker. ～출자 investment in kind: ～출자하다 make investment in kind; invest with goods.

**현미**(玄米) uncleaned 〔unpolished, unmilled〕 rice; brown 〔rough〕 rice.
◉ ～빵 unmilled-〔whole-〕rice bread.

**현미경**(顯微鏡) a microscope. ¶ 배율 백배의 ～ a microscope of 100 magnifications / 고배율의 ～ a powerful 〔high-powered〕 microscope / ～적인 microscopic / ～으로 검사하다 examine 《*a thing*》 with a 〔the〕 microscope; inspect 《*a thing*》 microscopically / ～(적)으로 연구하다 make a microscopic study 《of》 / ～으로 보다 see 〔look at〕 《*a thing*》 through 〔under〕 a microscope / ～의 초점을 맞추다 focus a microscope 《on, upon》.
◉ ～검사 a microscopic examination 〔test〕. ～관찰 fractography. ～분석 microscopic analysis. ～사진 a microphotograph; a photomicrograph; ～ 사진 장치 a microphotographic 〔photomicrographic〕 apparatus / ～사진기 a photomicroscope / ～사진술 microphotography; photomicrography. ～자리 〖천문〗 the Microscope; Microscopium.

**현미분광기**(顯微分光器) a microspectroscope.

**현미해부**(顯微解剖) 〖생물〗 microdissection.

**현부**(賢婦) a virtuous wife; a wise woman.

**현부인**(賢夫人) a wise woman; a lady of wisdom; your (honored) wife.

**현사**(賢士) a wise scholar; a sage.

**현삼**(玄蔘) 〖식물〗 *Scrophularia buergeriana* (학명).

**현상**(現狀) the present state 〔situation〕; the actual state 〔condition〕; the existing state of things; the existing condition 〔circumstances〕; the *status quo* (L.). ¶ 경제계의 ～ the present 〔prevailing〕 economic situation 〔condition〕 / 한국의 ～ the present state of affairs in Korea; Korea as she is 〔stands〕 / ～으로는 in 〔under〕 the existing circumstances; as affairs 〔things, matters〕 now stand; as things stand 〔are〕 today; under the present conditions / ～ 그대로 in *status quo;* as 《it》 is / ～에 만족하다 be content with things as they are / ～을 유지하다 maintain 〔preserve〕 the *status quo;* keep things in *status quo;* leave the matter as it is / ～을 타파하다 break the situation; do away with the present state of things / 농촌의 ～을 개선하다 better farming village conditions / 우리는 이 공정하지 못한 ～을 옳게 고쳐야 한다 We have to correct this unfair state of affairs. ◉ ～유지 maintenance of the *status quo:* ～유지 협정 a standstill 〔status quo〕 agreement. ～타파 destruction of the *status quo.*

**현상**(現象) a phenomenon (*pl.* -mena); an appearance 《in the sky》. ¶ 자연 ～ a natural phenomenon / 사회 발달에 있어서의 일시적 ～ a passing phase in the development of society / 기(奇)～을 나타내다 present an extraordinary phenomenon / 이상한 ～이 일어났다 A strange phenomenon presented itself.
◉ ～계 〖철학〗 the phenomenal world. ～과학 a phenomenal science. ～론 phenomenalism. ～학 phenomenology. 물리적～ physical phenomenon. 언어～ phenomena of language.

**현상**(現像) 〖사진〗 (film) developing; development. ～하다 develop 《(a) film》. ¶ 너무〔덜〕 ～된 overdeveloped 〔underdeveloped〕 / 필름을 ～시켰다 I had my film developed. ◉ ～과다

overdevelopment. ~부족 underdevelopment. ~액 a developing solution; a developer. ~지 developing-out paper (생략 D.O.P.). ~촉진제 an accelerator. ~탱크 a developing tank. 사진~실 a D.P. & E. room. 자동~실 an automatic development room.

**현상**(懸賞) a prize contest 〔competition〕; 《그 상품·상금》 a prize; a reward. ¶ 소설의 ~ 모집 a prize novel competition / ~ 붙은 with a prize offered / ~을 걸다 offer a prize 〔reward〕 《for》; set 〔put〕 a prize 《on the offender's head》 / ~에 응모하다 participate in 〔enter〕 a prize competition.

◉ ~광고 an advertisement for a prize contest; a prize ad. ~금 prize money; a prize; a reward: 범인 체포에 ~금 2백만 원을 걸다 offer a reward of two million won for the capture of the criminal / ~금을 타다 win 〔carry off〕 a prize 《in a contest》. ~논문〔소설〕 a prize essay 〔novel〕: ~ 소설을 모집하다 invite 《*a person*》 to enter the novel competition. ~당선자 a prize winner. ~문제〔과제〕 a problem 〔subject〕 for a prize contest.

**현상태**(現狀態) the present state of things; the present circumstances 〔situation〕; the existing condition. ¶ ~로는 as matters stand (now); as the case stands at present; under the present conditions; judging by the present situation.

**현선**(絃線) (cat)gut; a chord; a string.

**현세**(現世) this world 〔life〕; the present age. ¶ ~의〔적인〕 worldly; earthly; mundane; secular / ~와 내세 this world and the next / ~에서는 in this world; in life / ~의 쾌락 wordly pleasure. ◉ ~주의 secularism.

**현세기**(現世紀) the present century; this century.

**현손**(玄孫) descendants of the fourth generation; a grandson's grandson.

**현송**(現送) sending in cash; sending the actual thing; a shipment of gold. ~하다 transport cash 《to》; send the (actual) goods; make a shipment of gold.

**현수교**(懸垂橋) a suspension bridge. ¶ ~를 놓다 construct a suspension bridge 《over a river》; suspend a bridge 《over a river》; span 《a river》 with a suspension bridge.

**현수근**(懸垂筋) 〖해부〗 a suspensory muscle.

**현수막**(懸垂幕) 《방 따위의》 a hanging screen; a curtain; 《극장의》 a drop curtain; 《플래카드》 a placard. ¶ ~을 내걸다 put up a placard.

**현수선**(懸垂線) 〖수학〗 a catenary.

**현숙**(賢淑) womanly wisdom and virtue. ~하다 (be) wise and virtuous.

**현시**(現時) the present time; today.

**현시**(顯示) (a) revelation; (a) manifestation; show; display. ~하다 show; display; unfold; reveal.

**현시대**(現時代) the present age; modern times.

**현신**(賢臣) a wise retainer; a loyal vassal.

**현신하다**(現身—) present *oneself* before a superior; put in *one's* appearance; appear.

**현실**(玄室) the inside of tumulus.

**현실**(現實) (an) actuality; (a) reality. ¶ 엄한 인생의 ~ the stern 〔hard, harsh〕 realities of life / ~의 actual; real / ~적(인) realistic; practical; down-to-earth / ~로 actually; in actuality; practically / ~적으로 《think》 realistically; actually / ~의 문제로서 in actuality; as a matter of fact / ~에서 유리되다 be out of touch with reality / ~로 되다 become reality / ~에 맞는 계획을 세우다 plan realistically 〔on a realistic basis〕 / ~에 맞는 생각을 하다 base *one's* ideas on the real conditions / ~에 맞지 않다 do not fit in with the reality; be at variance with the reality 〔real conditions, actual state of things〕 / 이상을 추구하고 ~을 망각하다 be absorbed in the ideal and neglect the actual / ~에서 도피하다 escape from reality / ~을 직시하다 face up to reality / 이상과 ~을 혼동해서는 안 된다 Don't confuse the ideal with the real. / 여당은 좀더 ~ 감각이 있는 정치를 배워야 한다 The ruling party have to learn more about practical 〔realistic〕 politics.

◉ ~감 the sense for the real. ~계 the real 〔actual〕 world. ~도피 escapism. ~론 a bread-and-butter theory; realism. ~성 actuality; reality: 네 계획에는 ~성이 없다 Your plan is not practical. ~주의 actualism; realism: ~주의자 a realist / ~주의적인 realistic; down-to-earth.

**현실화**(現實化) actualization; realization; materialization. ~하다 actualize; realize; materialize; 《금리·환율 따위의》 readjust to a realistic level. ¶ 환율을

～하다 readjust the won-dollar exchange rate to a realistic level.

**현악**(絃樂) 〖음악〗 string music. ◉ ～기 a stringed instrument; the strings [총칭]. ～단 a string band. ～사중주(단) a string quartet(te). ～삼중주(단) a string trio. ～오중주(단) a string quintet(te). ～합주 a string ensemble: ～합주단 a string orchestra.

**현안**(懸案) a pending bill 〔question, problem〕; a longstanding 〔an outstanding〕 question. ¶ 다년간의 ～ a long-pending〔-standing〕 question 〔problem〕/ 양국간의 ～ 문제 a question pending between the two countries / ～으로 남겨 두다 leave 《*a matter*》 in abeyance; leave 《a question》 for future settlement; leave 《a question》 undecided; table 《a bill》 for further discussion / 그 문제는 아직 ～으로 남아 있다 The question is still unsettled.

**현애**(懸崖) an overhanging cliff; a precipice.

**현양하다**(顯揚—) gain fame; become famous; be widely known.

**현업**(現業) site 〔shop-floor〕 operations. ◉ ～관청 a government enterprise (engaged in manufacture or processing); a nonclerical government department (철도청 따위). ～원(員) a nonclerical 〔blue-collar〕 worker.

**현역**(現役) 〖군사〗 active service; 《휴직에 대하여》 service on full pay. ¶ ～의 《군대》 on the active list; 《군함》 in commission; commissioned / ～ 복무 중이다 be in active service; be on service; be on the active list / ～에 취역하다〔에서 물러나다〕 enter 〔retire from〕 active service / 2개월의 훈련 후 ～에 편입되다 be activated after two months of training / 그는 아직 ～이다 He is still in the active service. ◉ ～군인 a soldier on service; a serviceman on active duty. ～명부 the active list. ～선수 a player on the active list. ～장교 an officer in active service 〔on the active list〕. ～편입 activation. ～함 a warship in commission; a warship on 〔in〕 active service.

**현우**(賢友) a wise friend.

**현우**(賢愚) wisdom or folly; the wise and the foolish.

**현월**(弦月) ⇨ 초승달.

**현유**(現有) ¶ ～의 present; current; existing; on hand / ～석유 비축량 the current oil stock; 《Korea's》 current stocks of oil. ◉ ～금액 cash on hand. ～물품 goods in stock. ～세력 current strength; present resources. ～의석(議席) seats currently held by a party.

**현인**(賢人) a wise man; a sage. ¶ ～회의 a conference of wise men.

**현임**(現任) the present office 〔post〕; the present holder of the office. ◉ ～자 the present holder of the office.

**현자**(賢者) ＝현인. ¶ ～와 우자 the wise and the foolish.

**현장**(現場) the spot; the scene 《of a murder》; 《건축 따위의》 a site; 《야외 조사 따위의》 the field. ¶ ～에서 on the spot; in the act of 《stealing》/ 사고〔조난〕 ～ the scene of the accident 〔disaster〕/ ～에서 얻은 지식 knowledge gained in the field / ～에 도착하다〔달려가다〕 arrive at 〔rush to〕 the scene 《of the accident》/ 사고 ～을 목격하다 be an eyewitness of the accident / 우연히 ～을 목격하게 되다 happen to come across the scene 《of the accident》/ ～에서 잡히다 be arrested on the spot 〔in the very act〕; be caught in the act 《of stealing》/ 사고 ～을 조사하다 investigate the scene of the accident / 이곳이 범행 ～이다 This is the spot where the crime was committed. / 충돌한 차의 운전자는 ～에서 즉사했다 The driver of the crashed car was killed on the spot. / 군중이 사고 ～에 몰려왔다 A crowd of people swarmed to the place where the accident had happened. / 그들은 ～에서 일하고 있다 They work in the field. ◉ ～감독 a field overseer; a site foreman. ～거래 spot trading. ～검증 an inspection of the scene. ～관리 field supervision. ～근무 field service. ～도〔매매〕 spot delivery 〔sale〕: ～도 가격 a loco price. ～보고 a field report. ～부재증명 an alibi. ～사무소 a field office. ～시찰 a spot inspection; 《conduct》 an on-the-spot inspection. ～연수 on-the-job training 〔experience〕. ～재연 《범행 등의》 a reconstruction of the scene. ～조사 an on-the-spot probe 〔survey〕. ～주임 a foreman. ～중계 TV coverage of the scene; remote hookup. ～취재 newsgathering at the scene 《of the accident》: 열차 사고를 ～ 취재하다 cover a train accident at the scene. ～확인 an on-the-spot inspection.

**현재**(現在) ① the present time; [부사적] at present; at the present time; currently; 《미》 presently; (here and) now. ¶ ～의 present; existing; current / ～까지 up to now; until today; to date / ～의 상태 the present 〔existing〕 state of 《the Middle East》 / ～로는 at present; at this time; as of now; for the time being (당분간); as things are; under existing circumstances / ～(의) 회원수 the actual membership; the number 《of...》 extant / 4월 ～의 학생수 the number of students as of April / ～ 있는 장소 the place where *one* is 「at present 〔now〕 / ～대로 두다 leave 《*a matter*》 as it is / 나는 ～의 일에 만족하고 있다 I'm content with my present job. / 이것이 나의 ～ 주소이다 This is my present address. / ～의 상황하에서 그것은 불가능하다 It is impossible under the present circumstances. / ～ 우리에겐 그 이상의 자세한 정보가 입수되어 있지 않다 We haven't got any further information at present. / 이 일에 관해서는 ～까지 아무 것도 알려져 있지 않다 Nothing has been known about this to date. ② 〖문법〗 the present tense. ◉ ～시제 〖문법〗 the present (tense). ～완료 〖문법〗 the present perfect (tense). ～(인)원 the present members on the list. ～진행형 〖문법〗 the present progressive.

**현재**(賢才) distinguished ability 〔talent〕; a man of talent; a wise man.

**현저하다**(顯著—) 《두드러지다》 (be) notable; conspicuous; marked; remarkable; distinguished; striking; prominent; outstanding; 《명백하다》 (be) obvious. ¶ 현저히 remarkably; markedly; strikingly; conspicuously / 현저한 공적 distinguished services 《to》 / 현저한 사실 an obvious fact / 현저한 차이 a sharp 〔striking〕 difference 《in》 / 현저한 대조 a striking contrast / 현저히 다른 substantially different / 인구의 현저한 증가 a marked increase in population / 현저하게 발달하다 make marked 〔remarkable, conspicuous〕 progress.

**현정부**(現政府) the present 〔existing〕 Government 〔Administration〕.

**현제**(舷梯) an accommodation 〔a gangway〕 ladder.

**현존**(現存) ～하다 exist (actually); be in existence; be extant; subsist. ¶ ～의〔하는〕 existing; actual; extant; living / 그는 현존하는 피해자 중 최연장자이다 He is the oldest of the living victims. / 이 절은 우리 나라에 ～하는 가장 오래된 목조 건축물의 하나이다 This temple is one of the oldest wooden structures existing in our country. ◉ ～작가 living writers.

**현주**(現住) actual residence. ～하다 dwell 〔reside, live〕 at present. ◉ ～민 a native; natives. ～소 *one's* present address 〔domicile, abode, residence〕. ～자 a current occupant.

**현지**(現地) the very spot; the (actual) locale; the field. ¶ ～에서 on the spot 〔scene〕; locally / ～의 (in-the-)field; (on-the-)spot / ～에서 찍은 photographed on the actual location / ～의 사람들 local people / 핵 발전소 건설에 대한 ～ 주민들의 저항 the resistance of the local communities to the construction of a nuclear power plant / 분쟁을 ～에 한정케 하다 keep the conflict local; localize the conflict / 그는 ～에서 고용되었다 He was locally employed. ◉ ～기관 a field organization. ～로케이션 〖영화〗 an on-the-spot location. ～르포〔보고〕 a spot 〔a field, an on-the-spot〕 report; a report from the spot; 〔집합적〕 *reportage* (F.). ～방송 an on-the-spot broadcast. ～법인 a local subsidiary. ～사찰(査察) an on-site inspection. ～생산 local production (국산 T.V. 등의). ～시간 local time: ～ 시간으로 오후 3시(한국 시간으로 일요일 새벽 4시) at 3 p.m. local time (04:00 KST Sunday). ～시찰 여행 a fact-finding tour. ～인 the natives. ～제대 the discharge in *one's* service area. ～조달 self-subsistence〔-sufficiency〕 on the spot: ～ 조달률 domestic content. ～지도원 a field supervisor. ～채용 《일》 local employment: ～ 채용한 사무원 a clerk employed by the local office. ～통화 local currency. ～특파원 a correspondent on the scene 〔in the field〕.

**현지조사**(現地調査) an on-the-spot 〔a field〕 survey 〔investigation, inquiry〕; investigation on the scene. ¶ ～를 하다 study 《the question》 on the spot 〔scene〕; conduct a spot investigation. ◉ ～반 a field (investigation) party; a fact-finding team.

**현지처**(現地妻) *one's* mistress kept in a place 〔country〕 he frequents on business.

**현직**(現職) the present office 〔post〕; 《현직자》 an incumbent; 〔형용사적〕 incumbent. ¶ ～의 serving 《officials》;

《a policeman》 on the active list 〔in active service〕; incumbent / ～의 국회의원 an incumbent National Assembly member / ～의 이점 an advantage of being an incumbent / ～에 머물다 remain in *one's* present post; stay on the job / ～에서 물러나다 resign from *one's* post. ◉ ～대통령 the incumbent president. ～후보 incumbent (candidate): 미국 대통령 선거에서는 ～ 후보는 도전자보다 훨씬 유리하다 In America's presidential election, the incumbent has a formidable edge over the challenger.

**현찰**(現札) (hard) cash; actual 〔ready〕 money. ⇨현금. ¶ ～로 사다 buy 《an article》 for cash / ～을 쥐어 주다 give 《*a person*》 cash / ～로 지급하다 pay in cash; present ready money / 수표를 ～로 바꾸다 cash a check; have 〔get〕 a check cashed.

**현창**(舷窓) a porthole; a side light.

**현책**(賢策) a wise policy. ¶ …하는 것이 ～이다 it is well-advised 〔advisable〕 to *do.*

**현처**(賢妻) a wise 〔virtuous〕 wife.

**현철**(賢哲) a sage; the wise. ～하다 (be) wise; sagacious; intelligent.

**현충일**(顯忠日) the Memorial Day.

**현충탑**(顯忠塔) a memorial monument.

**현측**(舷側) the (ship's) side. ¶ ～에 《bring a boat》 alongside a ship. ◉ ～인도 free alongside (ship) (생략 FAS., f.a.s.).

**현탁액**(懸濁液) 〖화학〗 suspension; a suspension 《of silt》 in 《water》.

**현판**(懸板) a hanging board (with a picture or some calligraphy on it). ¶ ～식 a plate-〔board-〕hanging ceremony.

**현품**(現品) the article in question; this article 《on display》; goods 〔items〕 in stock (재고품); the (actual) goods. ¶ ～을 조사해 보다 check up on the number of articles / ～을 보지 않고는 뭐라 말할 수 없다 I cannot say either way before I inspect the article. / ～상환으로 대금을 지급하겠습니다 I'll pay the charge on delivery. ◉ ～급여 wages in kind. ～대장 a stock ledger. ～상환지급 cash 〔collect 《미》〕 on delivery (생략 C.O.D.). ～선도(先渡) goods promptly delivered.

**현하**(現下) the present time; now. ¶ ～의 present; at the present; current; of today / ～의 극동 정세 the present 〔current〕 of the Far East.

**현학**(衒學) pedantry. ¶ ～적(인) pedantic. ◉ ～자 a pedant.

**현행**(現行) [형용사적] present; existing; current; now in use; in force.

> 용법 **present** 시간적인 면에 중점을 두고, 현시점의 상황 따위를 문제로 할 때 쓰임. **existing, current** 제도나 상황 따위의 존재를 문제의 중심으로 삼고, 그것이 지금 행해지고 있느냐 아니냐를 말할 때 쓰임. 존재 여부에 중점을 둘 때는 existing을, 상황이나 동작이 진행 중임을 강조할 때는 current를 씀. **now in use** 어떤 사물 따위가 현재 사용되고 있다는 뜻일 때 쓰임. **in force** 법률·규칙 따위처럼 정부나 권력자가 시행하고 있음을 나타내는 뜻일 때 쓰임.

¶ ～대로 the same as at present / ～교통법규 the current traffic regulations / ～가격 the going 〔current〕 price / ～ 임금률은 너무 낮다 The ruling rates of wages are too low. / 지하철의 운임은 ～대로이다 There will be no change to the subway fare. ◉ ～교과서 the textbooks now in use. ～규정 the regulations in force; the standing rules. ～맞춤법 the current spelling system. ～법 the existing 〔operative〕 law; the law in force / ～법에 의하면 according to the law now in force / ～법의 적용을 받다 be subject to the existing laws. ～제도 the present system: ～ 제도로는 under the present system.

**현행범**(現行犯) a crime committed in the presense of a policeman; 《사람》 a criminal caught red-handed 〔in the (very) act〕; a criminal taken in an act of crime; 〖법〗 a flagrant delictor 〔offender〕. ¶ ～을 잡다 catch 《*a person*》 in the act of 《committing a theft》; catch 《a thief》 red-handed / ～으로 잡히다 be caught 〔taken〕 in the (very) act; be caught red-handed; be apprehended while committing a crime.

**현혹**(眩惑) dazzlement; bewilderment; a daze. ～하다 dazzle; bewilder; blind; mesmerize; enchant; take 《*a person*》 in (속이다). ¶ ～되다 get dazzled 〔bewildered〕 《by riches, money》; be blinded / 돈에 ～되다 be blinded by the lure of lucre / ～적인 enchanting / ～시켜 …하게 하다 dazzle 〔mislead〕 《*a person*》 into *doing* / 달콤한 말에 ～되지 마라 Don't be taken in by seductive words.

**현화식물**(顯花植物) = 꽃식물.

**현황**(現況) the present state 〔situation〕; a state of affairs; the *status quo* (L). ⇨ 현상(現狀). ¶ 중국의 ~ the present state of things 〔affairs〕 in China / 우선, 우리 제품의 각 생산 라인의 ~을 알고 싶다 To start with, I'd be interested in knowing where each of our product lines stands.

**현훈**(眩暈) dizziness; giddiness; the whirl of the brain. ◉ ~증 vertigo.

**혈**(穴) 《구멍》 a hole; 《풍수지리상의》 a spot where influences to *one's* fortune converge; 《침의》 a region for acupuncture.

**혈거**(穴居) cave dwelling; troglodytism. ~하다 live 〔dwell〕 in a cave; be a cave dweller. ¶ ~하는 cave-dwelling; troglodytic. ◉ ~생활 cave dwelling. ~시대 the cave age. ~인 a caveman; a cave dweller.

**혈관**(血管) a blood vessel; a vascular tract; a vein. ¶ 피는 ~을 통해 체내를 흐른다 Blood flows in the body through blood vessels. ◉ ~경련 an angiospasm; a vascular spasm. ~경화 hardening 〔sclerosis〕 of the blood vessels. ~반사 a vascular reflex. ~신경 vasomotor nerves. ~압박기 a compressor. ~압축 thlipsis. ~이식 a vascular transplant. ~접합 inosculation. ~파열 the rupture 〔bursting〕 of a blood vessel. ~학 angiology. ~협착〔폐색〕 angiostenosis. ~확장 신경 a vasodilator. ~확장제 a vasodilator.

**혈괴**(血塊) 〖한의〗 a clot of blood; gore.

**혈구**(血球) a blood corpuscle 〔cell〕. ◉ ~계수 the blood count. ~세포 결핍 the deficiency of red corpuscles; oligocythemia; aglobulism. ~소 hemoglobin.

**혈기**(血氣) 《기운》 vitality; strength; 《격하기 쉬운》 animal spirits; hot blood; 《젊음의》 youthful ardor 〔vigor〕. ¶ ~왕성한 청년 a sanguine youth / ~가 왕성하다 be full of youthful vigor; be in the prime of health; be a hot-blooded youth / ~ 차다 be spirited 〔vigorous, hot-blooded〕 / ~에 이끌리다 be driven 〔carried away〕 by youthful ardor.

**혈농**(血膿) bloody pus 〔matter〕.

**혈뇨**(血尿) 〖의학〗 bloody urine; hematuria. ◉ ~병 〖수의〗 red water.

**혈담**(血痰) blood(y) phlegm.

**혈당**(血糖) 〖생리〗 blood sugar; sugar in the blood. ¶ ~치 the blood-sugar level / ~검사를 받다 receive a blood sugar test.

**혈로**(血路) a perilous way out; a difficult escape-route; a hard way of getting along. ¶ ~를 찾다〔뚫다〕《어려움을 극복하다》 find a way out 《of the difficulties》; 《적의 포위를 뚫다》 cut 〔fight〕 *one's* way (through the enemy line) / 불경기를 극복하기 위해 수출에서 ~를 찾았다 We looked 〔turned〕 to export to provide us with a way out of the recession.

**혈루**(血淚) tears of blood; bitter tears. ¶ ~를 흘리다 shed bitter tears.

**혈류**(血瘤) 〖의학〗 a hematocele.

**혈리**(血痢) 〖의학〗 bloody diarrhea.

**혈맥**(血脈) ① 《혈관》 a blood vessel; an artery (동맥); a vein (정맥). ② 《혈통》 lineage; (a) pedigree. ◉ ~상통(相通) consanguinity; blood relationship.

**혈맹**(血盟) a blood pledge 〔alliance〕. ¶ ~으로 다져진 맹방 a "blood-tied" alliance.

**혈반**(血斑) 〖의학〗 a blood spot.

**혈변**(血便) bloody stool 〔excrement, feces〕; hemafecia. 「of blood.

**혈병**(血餠) 〖생리〗 a blood clot; a clot

**혈색**(血色) (a) complexion; color. ¶ 썩 좋은 ~ a high color / ~이 좋은 사람 a person of healthy complexion / ~이 좋은 얼굴 a sanguine face / ~이 좋다 be high in color; look well; have a good 〔ruddy, healthy〕 complexion; look rosy 《미》 / ~이 나쁘다 look pale 〔unwell〕; have a pale 〔wan, sallow〕 complexion; have no color / ~이 좋아〔나빠〕지다 gain 〔lose〕 color / 그녀는 곧 ~도 좋아지고 체중도 늘어났다 Her color soon improved, and she started to put on weight.

**혈색소**(血色素) hemoglobin.

**혈서**(血書) a writing in blood; something written in blood. ¶ ~를 쓰다 write 《a petition》 in *one's* own blood / ~로 탄원〔맹세〕하다 petition 〔seal〕 in blood.

**혈석**(血石) 〖광물〗 bloodstone; heliotrope.

**혈세**(血稅) a tax paid by the sweat of *one's* brow; a blood tax. ¶ ~를 물리다 tax 《people》 to the bone / ~를 낭비하다 waste the tax-payers' precious money.

**혈소판**(血小板) 〖의학〗 a thrombocyte; a blood platelet; a plaque. ¶ ~ 활성 인자 a platelet activating factor (생략 PAF).

**혈속**(血屬) blood relatives.

**혈손**(血孫) 《자손》 direct descendants; *one's* own flesh and blood.

**혈안**(血眼) a bloodshot eye. ¶ ～이 되다 feel mad; get hot 〔wild〕; get excited / ～이 되어서 madly; desperately; frantically / ～이 되어 찾다 make a desperate effort to find; look for 《*a thing*》 frantically 〔in a frenzy〕; make a frantic search for 《*a thing*》 / …에 ～이 되다 be trying frantically to; make a frantic attempt to; be mad about 《making money》; be hellbent on *doing*.

**혈암**(頁岩) shale. ◉ ～유〔타르〕 shale 「oil 〔tar〕.

**혈압**(血壓) blood pressure. ¶ ～이 높다〔낮다〕 have (a) high 〔low〕 blood pressure / ～이 정상인〔높은〕 사람 a person with normal 〔high〕 blood pressure; a normotensive 〔hypertensive〕 / ～을 낮추다 reduce *one's* blood pressure; bring down the blood pressure / ～을 높이다 raise 《*a person's*》 blood pressure / ～을 재다 《남의》 take 〔measure〕 《*a person's*》 blood pressure; 《자기의》 have 〔get〕 *one's* blood pressure measured 〔taken〕 / ～이 오르다 *one's* blood pressure goes up / 너의 ～은 120에 80이다 Your blood pressure is 120 over 80. / 이 약을 복용하면 ～이 내려갈 겁니다 This medicine will lower your blood pressure. / 그렇게 애를 태우면 ～이 올라간다 A lot of worrying like that will send your blood pressure up. ◉ ～강하제 a hypotensive drug; a depressor. ～계 a blood pressure gauge; a tonometer; 《특히 동맥용》 a sphygmomanometer; a hemadynamometer; a hemomanometer. ～측정 sphygmomanometry. ～항진제 a hypertensive drug. 정상～ normal blood pressure; normotension: 정상～의 normotensive. 최저〔최고〕～ minimum 〔maximum〕 blood pressure. 고～(증) high blood pressure; hypertension: 고～의 hypertensive. 저～(증) low blood pressure; hypotension: 저～의 hypotensive.

**혈액**(血液) blood. ¶ ～의 hematal; hematic; hemal / ～ 같은 hematoid / AB형의 ～ blood of the AB type / ～은 체내를 순환한다 Blood circulates through the body. / O형의 ～은 누구에게나 수혈해줄 수 있다 O-group blood may be transfused into people of all groups.
◉ ～검사(檢査) a blood test: ～검사를 받다 have *one's* blood examined / ～검사를 하다 examine the blood. ～순환 the circulation of the blood: 운동을 하면 ～ 순환이 잘 된다 Exercise improves the circulation of the blood. ～암 leukemia(백혈병). ～은행〔원〕 a blood bank. ～응고 blood coagulation; the clotting of blood. ～제공자 a blood donor. ～투석(透析) hemodialysis: ～투석기 a hemodialyzer. ～형 a blood type 〔group〕: RH식 ～형 an Rh blood group / ～형을 검사하다 examine the type of *one's* blood / ～형을 맞추다 《수혈·수술 등에서》 match 《a patient's》 blood group / 너의 ～형은 무슨형이냐 What is your blood group 〔type〕? / 나의 ～형은 O형이다 I have type O blood. *or* My blood group is O.

**혈연**(血緣) blood ties; a blood relation; kinship; family connection(s). ◉ ～관계 consanguinity; blood relationship; the ties of blood: ～관계에 있다 be related by birth. ～단체 a kinship society. ～사회 blood society.

**혈온**(血溫) 〖의학〗 blood heat; the temperature of blood. ◉ ～점(點) the blood-heat point.

**혈우병**(血友病) h(a)emophilia; bleeder's disease. ¶ ～의〔에 걸린〕 hemophilic. ◉ ～환자 a h(a)emophiliac; a bleeder.

**혈육**(血肉) 《소생의 자녀》 *one's* flesh and blood; *one's* offspring. ¶ 슬하에 일점 ～이 없다 be (in a sheer) childless. ◉ ～상쟁(相爭) domestic discord 〔trouble〕.

**혈장**(血漿) 〖생리〗 (blood) plasma; (a) serum (*pl.* ～s, sera).
◉ 건조～ dried plasma. 인공～ a plasma substitute; dextran.

**혈전**(血栓) 〖의학〗 a blood clot; a thrombus (*pl.* -bi). ◉ ～증(症) 〖의학〗 thrombosis: ～증의 thrombotic. 관상동맥～증 coronary thrombosis. 뇌～증 cerebral thrombosis.

**혈전**(血戰) a desperate 〔bloody〕 fight; a bloody battle. ～하다 fight a bloody battle; fight desperately. ◉ ～지 a scene of desperately-fought battle.

**혈족**(血族) *one's* blood relative; *one's* (kith and) kin; a relative by blood; *one's* flesh and blood. ◉ ～결혼 marriage within the blood; a consanguineous marriage; (an) intermarriage; endogamy: 대대로 ～결혼을 하고 있는 가족 an inbred family. ～관계 (a) blood relationship; ties of blood; kinship.

**혈종**(血腫) 〖의학〗 a hematoma (*pl.* ～s, -mata).

**혈청**(血淸) 〖의학〗 (a) (blood) serum (*pl.* ～s, -ra). ◉ ～간염 serum hepatitis. ～검사 《conduct》 serum test. ～반응 (a) serum reaction; (a) seroreaction. ～병 a serum disease; serum sickness. ～요법〔치료〕 serum treatment 〔therapy〕; serotherapy. ～주사 (a) serum injection. ～진단 serum diagnosis; serodiagnosis. ～학 serology.

**혈침**(血沈) 〖의학〗 a blood 〔an erythrocyte〕 sedimentation rate (적혈구 침강 속도). ¶ ～13, precipitation thirteen milimeters / ～을 재다 measure the precipitation of 《*a person's*》 blood. ◉ ～검사 an erythrocyte sedimentation test.

**혈통**(血統) blood; lineage; (a) pedigree; a family line; descent; stock. ¶ 아버지〔어머니〕쪽의 ～ the paternal 〔maternal〕 line / ～이 좋은 개 a breedy dog; a pedigreed dog (혈통서가 있는) / ～을 조사하다 inquire into 《*a person's*》 lineage; trace 《*a person's*》 descent 《to》; trace back 《*a person's*》 family line / ～이 좋다 《동물이》 have a good pedigree; be of good stock 〔a good line〕; 《사람이》 come from a good family; be of good stock 〔family〕 / 왕의 ～을 받다 be of royal descent 〔extraction〕; come from royal blood / ～은 속일 수가 없다 Blood will tell. / 그 ～은 지금 끊어져 버렸다 The (family) line has died out. / 그의 집안은 단명한〔장수하는〕 ～이다 He comes from 〔of〕 a short-〔long-〕lived family. / 저 집안은 음악가의 ～이다 The blood of musicians runs in that family. ◉ ～서 《개 따위의》 a pedigree (registration certificate); a certificate of breed: ～서가 있는 말 a pedigreed horse. ～주의 〖법〗 《국적 취득의》 *jus sanguinis* (L.).

**혈투**(血鬪) a bloody fight; a desperate struggle 〔fight〕. ⇨ 혈전(血戰). ¶ ～를 벌이다 fight desperately 〔a bloody fight〕; engage in a life-and-death struggle.

**혈판**(血判) ～하다 seal 《a written pledge》 with (*one's*) blood. ◉ ～서 a document 〔petition, pact〕 sealed with blood.

**혈한**(血汗) = 피땀.

**혈행**(血行) blood circulation; the circulation (of the blood). ¶ ～을 돕다 quicken 〔improve〕 the circulation 〔flow〕 of the blood. ◉ ～계(計) a tachometer. ～기(관) circulatory organs. ～장애 (an) interruption in blood circulation.

**혈혈단신**(孑孑單身) all alone in the world. ¶ ～이다 be all alone.

**혈흔**(血痕) a bloodstain; a mark 〔spot, trace, smear〕 of blood. ¶ ～이 있는 bloodstained. ◉ ～검사 the examination of bloodstains.

**혐기**(嫌忌) aversion; abhorrence. ～하다 feel aversion 《to, toward》; abhor.

**혐기**(嫌氣) 〖생물〗 ¶ ～성의 anaerobic. ◉ ～균(菌) anaerobic bacteria; anaerobes. ～성 생물 an anaerobe.

**혐연권**(嫌煙權) non-smoker's rights; the right to refuse exposure to tobacco smoke; the right to avoid passive smoking.

**혐오**(嫌惡) disgust; (a) hatred; (an) aversion; repugnance; (a) dislike. ～하다 hate; dislike; abhor; detest; loathe; be disgusted 《with》. ¶ ～할 hateful; disgusting; detestable; loathsome / ～의 빛 a repugnant look; a loathsome 〔sickening〕 countenance / ～감을 품다 have a hatred 《for》; have 〔feel〕 an aversion 《to》; feel hatred 《against *a person*》 / 그는 그 광경을 ～의 눈으로 보았다 He viewed the scene with loathing 〔repugnance, distaste〕. / 나는 그의 간사한 태도에 ～감을 느꼈다 I felt a strong hatred 〔dislike〕 for his cunning behavior.

**혐의**(嫌疑) ① 《의심》 (a) suspicion; charge; an accusation. ～스럽다, ～쩍다 (be) suspicious; doubtful; questionable. ¶ 절도 ～로 on a charge 〔under accusation〕 of theft / 살인 ～로 구속되다 be arrested on 〔under〕 suspicion 〔charges〕 of being the murderer.

혐의를: ～를 두다 cast 〔throw〕 suspicion 《on》; attach suspicion 《to》; fix *one's* suspicion 《upon》 / ～를 받다 incur suspicion; be suspected of 《a crime》; fall 〔come〕 under suspicion 《of theft》 / ～를 불러일으키다 arouse suspicion 《in *a person's* mind》; rouse 〔arouse〕 *a person's* suspicion / ～를 받을 만한 상황에 under suspicious circumstances / 터무니 없는 ～를 받다 be suspected without cause 〔when *one* is innocent〕; incur groundless suspicion / ～를 품다 have a suspicion 《that...》; be suspicious 《of》; suspect 《*a person* of murder》 / ～를 풀다 dispel 〔clear away〕 suspicion; clear *oneself*

of suspicion / 그는 강도들 중의 하나로 ~를 받고 있다 He is under suspicion as one of the robbers.
② 《싫어함》 dislike; aversion.
◉ ~자 a suspected person; a suspect; a criminal suspect. 「끼인각.

**협각**(夾角) 〖수학〗 an included angle. ⇨

**협객**(俠客) a chivalrous person; a man of chivalrous spirit; a selfstyled humanitarian. ¶ ~ 기질의 chivalrous; of chivalrous spirit.

**협곡**(峽谷) 〖지리〗 a gorge (절벽 사이의); a ravine (급류의 침식에 의한); a glen (스코틀랜드 등의); a canyon 《미》 (대협곡). 「zygomatic bone.

**협골**(頰骨) 〖해부〗 the cheekbone; the

**협공**(挾攻) an attack on both sides 〔flanks〕; a pincer 〔scissors〕 attack. ~하다 attack 《the enemy》 on 〔from〕 both flanks 〔sides〕; scissor 〔pinch〕 in. ¶ ~당하다〔을 받다〕 be attacked on both sides; find *oneself* between two fires. ◉ ~작전 pincers; a pincer operation 〔movement〕; pincer tactics: ~작전으로 서서히 적을 죄어들어 가고 있다 The pincers are gradually closing in on the enemy.

**협궤**(狹軌) 〖철도〗 a narrow gauge.
◉ ~철도 a narrow-gauge railway.

**협기**(俠氣) a chivalrous spirit; chivalry. ¶ ~ 있는 manly; chivalrous; gallant / ~ 부리다 act the man.

**협낭**(頰囊) 〖동물〗 a cheek pouch.

**협도**(俠盜) a generous 〔chivalrous〕 robber; a Robin Hood.

**협동**(協同) cooperation; collaboration; partnership; united efforts; joint endeavor. ⇨공동(共同). ~하다 cooperate; collaborate; unite; join forces 《with》; team up 《with》. ¶ ~의 communal; joint; concerted; united / ~으로 in partnership 《with》; jointly; communally / ~하여 in cooperation 〔collaboration, concert, association, participation〕 《with》; jointly.
◉ ~기업(企業) a cooperative 〔joint〕 enterprise. ~농장 a collective farm; 《구소련의》 a *kolkhoz;* 《이스라엘의》 a kibbutz. ~작업 group work. ~작전 joint warfare; combined operations. ~정신 cooperative spirit.

**협동조합**(協同組合) a cooperative association 〔society〕; a cooperative; a co-op 《구어》. ¶ ~ 상점 a cooperative store / ~에 가입하다 join a co-op.
◉ ~원 a copartner. 생산자~ a producer's cooperative (society). 소비자~ a consumer's cooperative (society).

**협동체**(協同體) a community; a communal society. ⇨공동체. ◉ 촌락~ a rural 〔village〕 community.

**협량**(狹量) narrow-mindedness. ~하다 (be) narrow-minded; ungenerous; intolerant.

**협력**(協力) cooperation; collaboration; working together. ~하다 cooperate 《with》; work 〔pull〕 together; collaborate 《with》; unite *one's* efforts 《with》; make united efforts; join forces 〔hands〕 《with》; team up 《with》; make common cause 《with》.
¶ 정신적〔물질적〕~ spiritual 〔material〕 cooperation / 긴밀한 ~ close cooperation; intimate collaboration; 《미》 a tie-up 《with》 / ~적인〔으로〕 cooperative 〔cooperatively〕 / …와 ~해서 in cooperation 〔partnership, collaboration, concert〕 《with》 / 긴밀히 ~해서 하다 work in close cooperation 〔shoulder to shoulder〕 / …의 ~을 얻다 obtain cooperation from…; win 〔secure〕 the cooperation of…; get 《*a person*》 into line / ~을 구하다〔요청하다〕 ask 〔appeal to〕 《*a person*》 for help 〔assistance〕 / 아무의 일에 ~하다 have a share in *a person's* business / ~ 관계를 더욱 강화하다 further strengthen *our* cooperative relations 《in》 / 당신의 ~에 감사드립니다 I appreciate your cooperation. / 귀하의 ~을 부탁드리고자 합니다 I would like to ask for your cooperation. / 많은 사람들의 ~으로 공사가 완성되었다 The construction work was completed by the united efforts of a great number of people. ◉ ~자(者) a cooperator; a collaborator; a co-worker. 경제~ economic cooperation. 기술~ technical cooperation. 상호~ mutual coop- 「eration.

**협로**(夾路) a branch road.

**협로**(峽路) a mountain road.

**협로**(狹路) a narrow road; a bypath.

**협만**(峽灣) a fjord; a fiord.

**협문**(夾門) a small side gate 〔door〕.

**협박**(脅迫) a threat; (a) menace; intimidation (위협); blackmail (갈취); extortion; 〖법〗 duress. ~하다 threaten; intimidate; menace; extort; blackmail.
¶ ~적(인) treatening; menacing / ~하여 by intimidation 〔threats〕 / ~당하여〔받아〕 under threat 〔menace, duress(e)〕 / ~에 의한 자백 confes-

sion under threat 〔duress〕/ 권총으로 ~하다 threaten 《*a person*》 with a revolver / ~을 받아 …하다 be threatened to *do* / ~하여 …하게 하다 intimidate 〔force〕《*a person*》 into 《*do*ing, confession》/ 죽인다고 ~하다 threaten 《*a person*》 with death; threaten to kill / 그는 나를 ~하여 10만 원을 갈취했다 He blackmailed me out of 100,000 won. / 그들은 고소하겠다고 나를 ~했다 They threatened me with a lawsuit. *or* They threatened to take me to court. / 그는 ~당하여 회사의 기밀을 훔쳤다 He was intimidate 〔blackmailed〕 into stealing the company's secrets.

> 용법 **threaten** 상대방에게 어떤 행동을 하라고 말로써 협박하는 것. **intimidate** 상대방의 약점을 잡아 자기 뜻대로 시키는 것. **manace** 상대방이 공포심을 느낄 수 있는 수단을 써서 위협하는 것. **extort, blackmail** 금품을 갈취할 목적으로 협박하는 것으로서 전자가 더 격식 차린 말.

◉ ~사건 extortion case. ~자 an intimidator; a blackmailer. ~장 a threatening 〔blackmail〕 letter. ~전화 《receive》 a threatening (telephone) call. ~죄 intimidation.

**협살**(挾殺) 〖야구〗 a rundown. ~하다 run down 〔touch out〕 《a runner》.

**협상**(協商) 《교섭》 negotiation; 《협정》 an agreement; 《외교》 an *entente* (F.). ~하다 negotiate 《with》. ¶ ~을 맺다 conclude an *entente* 《with》/ ~중이다 be in 〔under〕 negotiations / ~을 시작하다 open 〔start〕 negotiations 《with》/ ~을 재개하다 put negotiations back on track / ~은 결렬됐다 The negotiations fell through.

◉ ~가 a negotiator. ~가격 a negotiated price. ~국(國) a party to an *entente;* an *entente.* ~조약 an *entente* (*cordiale*) (F.); an agreement; an understanding; a convention. 비밀〔비공개〕~ a closed-door negotiation. 삼국~ the Triple *Entente.* 평화~ peace negotiations.

**협소**(狹小) narrowness. ~하다 《면적이 작다》 (be) small; 《폭이 좁다》 narrow; 《좁고 답답하다》 confined; 《한정되다》 limited. ¶ ~한 곳 a confined place / ~한 방 a small room.

**협실**(夾室) a side room.

**협심**(協心) unison; concert; cooperation. ~하다 unite; be in union 《with》. ¶ ~해서 일하다 work in unison.

**협심증**(狹心症) 〖의학〗 stricture of the heart; angina pectoris 〔cordis〕; a heart attack (심장 발작). ¶ ~으로 죽다 die of 〔from〕 heart attack.

**협애**(狹隘) narrowness; smallness; limitedness. ~하다 (be) narrow; small; limited; confined; cramped. ¶ 지역이 ~하다 be limited in area.

**협약**(協約) an agreement; a convention; a pact; an *entente* (*cordiale*) (F.); an understanding. ⇨ 협정. ~하다 enter into an agreement; agree on. ¶ 구두 ~ a verbal agreement / ~을 맺다 conclude 〔enter into〕 an agreement 《with》. ◉ ~국 a party to an agreement 〔*entente* (F.)〕. ~서 a written agreement 〔understanding〕. 노동~ a labor agreement 〔pack〕: 조합은 회사와 노동 ~을 맺었다 The union concluded 〔entered into〕 a labor agreement with the company. 단체~ a collective agreement. 신사~ a gentleman's agreement. 통상~ a commercial *entente.*

**협업**(協業) cooperation; cooperative work. ~하다 cooperate; work in cooperation.

**협의**(協議) conference; council; consultation; deliberation; discussion. ~하다 confer 〔consult〕 《with》; deliberate 《on *a matter*》; discuss 《*a matter*》; talk 《with *a person*》 over 《*a matter*》; hold a conference (★ discuss는 that이 이끄는 명사절을 받지 않음). ¶ ~하에 by mutual agreement 〔consent〕; upon deliberation 《with》/ ~중이다 [일이 주어] be under consideration 〔deliberation, discussion〕; [사람이 주어] be in conference / ~를 보다 come to 〔arrive at, reach〕 an agreement / ~에 부치다 bring 《*one's* plan》 up at a meeting; send 〔refer〕 《*a matter*》 to conference / 충분히 ~하다 talk over 《*a matter*》 fully / 다음 사항들이 ~결과 결정되었다 The following decisions were made as a result of the conference. / 이 문제는 내일 회의에서 ~될 것이다 This problem is to be discussed 〔talked about〕 at the meeting tomorrow.

◉ ~사항 a subject 〔topic〕 of discussion (토론의 주제); a matter for consultation; an item on the agenda (개별적인). ~이혼 a divorce by agreement 〔(mutual) consent〕: ~이혼하다

divorce 〔be divorced from〕《one's wife》 by agreement. ～회 a conference; a council: ～회원 a conferee.

**협의**(狹義) a narrow sense; a restricted meaning. ¶ ～의 in a narrow sense / ～의 교육 education in the narrow sense (of the word) / ～로 해석되다 take 《a word》 in a narrow sense; interpret 〔construe〕 in a narrow sense.

**협잡**(挾雜) cheating; fraud; trickery; swindle; jugglery. ～하다 cheat; swindle; embezzle; commit a fraud; fake; juggle. ¶ ～의 tricky; fake; sham; bogus; false; spurious / ～에 걸리다 fall a victim to a fraud; be taken in / ～질로 살다 live on fraudulent practices / 도박에서 ～해먹다 cheat in gambling / 회사 돈을 ～해먹다 embezzle the money of a firm. ◉ ～꾼〔배〕 an impostor; a swindler; a crook; a fraud; a trickster; a cheat. ～물 a fake; a sham; an adulteration; an adulterated thing; a fraud.

**협장**(脇杖) a crutch. ⇨ 목다리.

**협정**(協定) an agreement; an arrangement; a convention; a pact. ～하다 agree upon 《the price》; arrange 《with》; make arrangements 《with》; make 〔conclude, arrive at, enter into〕 an agreement 《with》.

¶ ～의 conventional / ～에 의하여 by agreement; under an agreement made 《with》 / ～을 맺다 conclude a convention 《with》; conclude 〔pass〕 an agreement 《with》 / ～에 조인하다 sign an agreement / ～을 깨다〔폐기하다〕 break 〔abrogate〕 an agreement / ～을 지키다 fulfill 〔carry out, live up to, act up to〕 an agreement / ～이 이루어지다 reach 〔come to〕 an agreement 《with》 / 가격을 ～하다 make an agreement on prices / 한미간에 군사 ～이 성립되었다 A military convention was reached between Korea and America.

◉ ～가격 an agreed price. ～가맹국 a signatory; a contracting member. ～관세율 a conventional tariff. ～서 a written agreement; a protocol: ～서를 작성하다 prepare an agreement / ～서를 교환하다 exchange copies of an agreement 《with》. ～안(案) a draft agreement. ～위반 a breach of an agreement. ～임금 wages agreed upon; agreed wages.

국제～ an international agreement; an accord. 상호～ a bilateral agreement. 어업～ a fisheries agreement. 운임～ a freight convention. 잠정～ a *modus vivendi* (L.); provisional agreement. 정보 기술～ the Information Technology Agreement (생략 ITA). 정보 통신～ the Information and Telecommunication Agreement (생략 ITA). 통상～ a trade agreement 〔pact〕; an agreement on commerce. 편무(片務)～ a unilateral agreement. 핵실험 금지～ the Nuclear Test-ban Accord.

**협조**(協調) cooperation; 《국제적》 concord; 《조화》 harmony; 《타협》 conciliation. ～하다 cooperate with; act in harmony 〔concert〕 with.

¶ ～적 (being) cooperative; conciliatory; harmonious / ～적 태도〔정신〕 a cooperative 〔conciliative〕 attitude 〔spirit〕 / 국제간의 ～ international cooperation / 보다 긴밀한 ～ 체제 closer cooperation systems / ～하여 in cooperation 《with》 / ～적이 아닌, ～가 결여된 lacking in cooperation; incooperative; uncooperative / ～적(인) 정신으로써 in a spirit of cooperation; cooperatively / ～케 하다 make 《*a person*》 act in concert 〔alignment〕 《with》; bring 《dissidents》 into line / ～를 유지하다〔잃다〕 maintain 〔lack〕 harmony / 이 문제의 해결에는 노사간의 ～가 불가결하다 Conciliation between labor and management is essential to solve this problem. ◉ ～심 a spirit of cooperation. ～자 a cooperator; a helper; a supporter.

**협주곡**(協奏曲) 〚음악〛 a concerto (*pl.* ～s). ¶ 바이올린 ～ a violin concerto.

**협죽도**(夾竹桃) 〚식물〛 an oleander; a rosebay.

**협착**(狹窄) narrowness; 〚의학〛 stricture; strangulation; stenosis (*pl.* -noses). ～하다 (be) narrow; confined; limited; cramped; constricted.

◉ ～부 an isthmus (*pl.* -muses, -mi). ～사격 miniature cartridge practice; morris-tube practice. ～탄 a miniature cartridge 〔munition〕. 직장 ～ 〚의학〛 stricture of the rectum.

**협찬**(協贊) 《찬성》 approval; 《지지》 support; 《협력》 cooperation; 《주최·후원》 cosponsorship. ～하다 《찬성하다》 approve of 《a plan》; give *one's* approval 《to》; 《지지하다》 support; give *one's* support; 《협력하다》 cooperate 《with》; join hands 《with》; 《주최·후원하다》 cosponsor. ¶ 교육부의 ～을 얻다 be approved by the Education Ministry / 문화 단체 주최의 연주회에 ~하다 support a musical concert sponsored by a cultural society / 자선 바자회는 L사 주최, H사 ~으로 열렸다 The charity bazzar was sponsored by company L with the cooperation of company H.

**협화**(協和) harmony; concord; concert; (musical) consonance. ~하다 be in harmony 〔concord〕 《with》; act in concert 《with》; 《음향이》 be consonant 《with》. ◉ ~음 a consonance; a concord. ~음정 a consonant interval.

**협회**(協會) a society; an association; an institution; a league. ¶ ~를 조직하다 organize 〔form〕 an association. ◉ 농구~ the Basketball League. 대한출판 문화~ the Korean Publisher's Association. 동물 애호~ the Society for the Prevention of Cruelty to Animals (생략 S.P.C.A.). 아시아~ the Asiatic Society. 저작가~ the Authors' League. 한국 문인〔여류 문인〕 ~ the Korean Literary Men's 〔Women's〕 Association.

**혓바늘** fur (on *one's* tongue). ¶ ~이 돋은 혀 a coated 〔furred〕 tongue / ~이 돋다 get「fur on the tongue 〔a coated tongue〕 《from inflammation》.

**혓바닥** the flat of the tongue. ¶ ~의 glossal / ~ 모양의 tongue-like / ~으로 핥다 lap with the tongue / ~을 내밀다 put 〔stick, poke, thrust〕 out *one's* tongue 《at》.

**혓소리** 〖언어〗 a lingual (sound).

**형**(兄) ① 《남자끼리의》 an elder 〔older 《미》〕 brother; a big brother 《구어》. ¶ 맏〔제일 작은〕형 *one's* eldest 〔youngest elder〕 brother / 매〔자〕형 a brother-in-law / 형수 *one's* sister-in-law; *one's* elder brother's wife / 형인 톰 Tom, elder of the brothers / 형 행세를 하다 pose 〔give *oneself* airs〕 as 《*a person's*》 senior / 형 만한 아우 없다 《속담》 "The younger sibling is never the equal of the older." ② 《친구간》 you; Mr. …. ¶ 김형 Mr. Kim.

> 참고 영어에서는 연령의 상하 관계를 분명히 해야 할 특별한 경우를 제외하고는, 대개의 경우 형제자매를 말할 때 older, younger를 붙이지 않고, 그냥 *one's* brother, *one's* sister로 부름. 형제자매간 서로의 호칭도 「형, 누나」 대신 John, Mary 처럼 직접 이름을 부르는 것이 일반적임.

**형**(刑) a punishment; a penalty; a sentence (선고). ¶ 형의 집행 the execution of a sentence / 형의 적용 the application of a punishment / 형에 복역하다 serve 〔submit to〕 *one's* sentence / 형을 내리다 inflict a punishment 《on》 / 형을 받다 get convicted; be sentenced 《to》 / 형을 면하다 escape punishment 〔justice〕 / 형을 감(減)하다 reduce 〔commute〕 a sentence / 형을 선고하다 pass 〔pronounce〕 a sentence 《on》 / 형의 집행을 유예하다 suspend (the execution of) a sentence / 징역 5년형에 처하다 sentence 〔condemn〕 《*a prisoner*》 to five years at 〔with 《영》〕 hard labor. ◉ 형집행정지 the stay of execution of the sentence. 재산형 a pecuniary punishment. 종신형 a life sentence; imprisonment for life.

**형**(形) 《형상》 (a) shape; 《형식》 (a) form; (a) pattern; 《대소》 a size; 《책의》 a format; 《컴퓨터》 a type. ¶ V자형의 V-shaped / 대〔소〕형의 large= 〔small-〕sized 《car》 / 포켓형의 사전 a dictionary of pocket size; a pocket= size(d) dictionary.

**형**(型) ① 《모형》 a model; 《주물(鑄物)》 a mold; a matrix (*pl.* ~es, -trices). ② 《양식》 (a) style; (a) type; a mode; a pattern; a make. ¶ 신형 자동차 a new model car / 군인형의 사람 a man of soldierly type / 남성형의 여자 a woman of masculine type / 새로운 형의 모자 a new-look hat / 형이 다르다 be of another type / 요즈음 이런 형의 코트가 유행하고 있다 This style of coat is now in fashion.

**형**(桁) 《건물의》 a beam; a crossbeam; 《교량의》 a girder; [총칭] girderage.

**형강**(形鋼) section 〔shape〕 steel. ◉ ~압연기 a rolling mill for section steel.

**형광**(螢光) 〖물리〗 fluorescence. ¶ ~을 발하다 fluoresce; be fluorescent; generate fluorescence.

◉ ~도료 (a) fluorescent paint. ~등 a fluorescent light 〔tube, lamp〕. ~물질〔재료〕 a fluorescent material. ~성 fluorescence; fluorescent. ~안료 a fluorescent pigment. ~염료(染料) (a) fluorescent dye. ~조명 fluorescent lighting. ~체 a fluorescent body. ~투시경 a fluoroscope. ~판(板)〔막, 면〕 a fluorescent plate 〔screen〕. ~표백 fluorescent bleaching: ~표백제 a fluorescent bleaching agent.

**형교**(桁橋) a girder bridge.

**형구**(刑具) an implement of punishment 〔torture〕.

**형국**(形局) ①《형세》 a situation. ②《관상·풍수 지리의》 aspect; appearance.

**형극**(荊棘) thorns; brambles. ¶ ～의 길 a thorny path; a brambly way; the way of the Cross / 그 후 그의 일생은 ～의 길이었다 His life thereafter was full of trials and tribulations.

**형기**(刑期) a prison term; a term of imprisonment; a hitch 《미구어》; *one's* time 《to serve in prison》. ¶ ～를 마치다 serve out *one's* sentence 〔term, time〕 / ～를 치르다 serve *one's* term of imprisonment; 《구어》 do time 《in Suwon Prison》 / ～가 만료되어 출소하다 leave prison 〔be set free〕 at the expiration of *one's* term.

**형명**(刑名) the name 〔designation〕 of a penalty.

**형무**(刑務) prison affairs.

**형무소**(刑務所) ＝교도소.

**형벌**(刑罰) a punishment; a penalty; punitive 〔vindication〕 sanction. ⇨형(刑). ¶ ～을 가하다, ～에 처하다 punish, inflict a punishment 〔penalty〕 on 《a culprit》 / ～을 받다 receive a punishment 〔penalty〕 / ～을 면제해 주다 let 《*a person*》 off a penalty.

**형법**(刑法) 〖법〗 [총칭] criminal 〔penal〕 law; 《좁은 뜻의》 the Criminal Law 〔Act〕; 《형법전》 the Criminal 〔Penal〕 Code. ¶ ～상의 criminal; penal 《offense》 / ～상의 범죄 a penal 〔criminal〕 offense / ～상의 죄인 a penal offender; a cirminal / ～에 따라 다스리다 deal with 《*a person*》 according to the provisions of the cirminal code. ◉ ～위반 a penal offense. ～학 criminal jurisprudence: ～학자 「a scholar of 〔an authority on〕 the criminal code; a specialist in criminal law. 국제～ the international criminal law.

**형부**(兄夫) a girl's elder sister's husband; a girl's brother-in-law.

**형사**(刑事) ①《사건》 a criminal 〔penal〕 case. ¶ ～상의 criminal; penal. ②《사람》 a (police) detective; 《미》 an operative; 《미구어》 a gumshoe; a dick; 《사상 담당》 a secret service man; 《수사 담당》 an investigator. ¶ 그 살인 사건 담당 ～ a detective on the murder case / 사복 ～ a plain=clothes policeman / ～를 배치하다 place a stakeout 《on a house》; assign a detective to stake out 《*a person's* house》 / ～가 나를 미행하고 있다 A detective is tailing me. ◉ ～과 the detective division. ～기동대 a police task-force squad. ～문제 a criminal case. ～범 《사람》 a criminal; a convict (즉결의); 《범죄》 a criminal 〔penal〕 offense; an indictable offense. ～법원 a criminal court. ～보상 criminal indemnity 〔compensation〕: ～보상법 the Criminal Indemnity Act. ～사건 a criminal case; a penal offense: ～ 사건 전문 변호사 a criminal lawyer 〔attorney 《미》〕. ～사법공조조약 《국제간의》 a treaty for mutual assitance in criminal matters. ～실 detectives' quarters; a detective squad room. ～재판 a criminal trial: ～ 재판 관할권 criminal jurisdiction. ～ 책임 criminal liability: ～ 책임을 묻다 hold *a person* liable 《for a case》. ～ 처분 《suffer》 a criminal punishment. ～피고인 the accused (★ 단수 취급): ～피고인석 a dock. ～학 criminology; penology.

**형사소송**(刑事訴訟) a criminal action 〔suit, prosecution〕. ¶ ...을 상대로 ～을 제기하다 proceed against 《*a person*》 criminally. ◉ ～법 the Criminal Procedure Code 〔Law〕. ～절차 criminal proceedings.

**형삭반**(形削盤) 〖기계〗 a shaping machine; a shaper.

**형상**(形狀·形相) 《형태》 form; shape; configuration; 《모습·모양》 a figure; an appearance. ¶ ～이 가지가지다 be various 〔vary〕 in form 〔shape〕; be of varied forms 〔shape〕 / 무시무시한 ～을 하고 with a fierce look.

**형상**(形象) a shape; a figure; a phenomenon; (a) figuration. ⇨형상(形狀).

**형색**(形色) form and color; 《용모·안색》 general looks; appearance; a 〔*one's*〕 complexion.

**형석**(螢石) 〖광물〗 fluor(ite); fluorspar.

**형설**(螢雪) diligent study. ¶ ～지공(之功) diligent study; fruits of diligent study / ～의 공을 쌓다 apply *oneself* to *one's* studies diligently; devote *oneself* to *one's* studies.

**형성**(形成) formation; making; molding; 《천체의》 evolution. ～하다 (take) form; shape; make; compose; mold; constitute; build up. ¶ ～적 평가 〖교육〗 formative evaluation / ～되다 be formed 〔shaped, constituted〕 / ～중이다 be in the making / 그녀의 성격을 ～케 한 것은 그녀가 어린 시절을 보낸 그 환경이었다 Her character has been molded 〔shaped〕 by the environment in which she passed her girlhood. ◉ ～기(期) the formative period 《of a nation》; the formative years 《of an individual》. ～물질 『동물』 a formative substance. ～세포 a formative cell. ～소(素) a plastic material; formation stuff. ～층(層) 『식물』 cambium. 인격～ the formation of character; character building: 인격～기 the formative period 《in the life of a man》.

**형세**(形勢) 《정세》 the situation; the state of affairs 〔things〕; the tide; how the land lies; the trend 〔run〕 of events; 《전망》 the prospects; the outlook; the chances; appearances; 《형편》 circumstances; 《풍수의》 the 「geomantic topography 〔auspiciousness〕 of the situation.
¶ 세계의 ～ the world situation; the position 〔state〕 of world affairs / 현재의 ～로는 as matters stand; as things are 〔stand〕 / ～가 불리한 때에는 when *one* finds *oneself* on unfavorable ground / ～의 역전 a reversal of the situation / ～가 유리〔불리〕하다 the situation is favorable 〔unfavorable〕 / ～를 관망하다 sit on the fence; watch the development of affairs / ～를 지켜보다 watch the situation; wait for a turn of events / ～를 파악하다 take in 〔realize, grasp〕 the situation / ～를 일변시키다 change the tide 《in the East》; turn the tide 〔the tables〕 《against, in *one's* favor》 / ～는 어떤가 What is the situation? *or* Which way is the wind blowing? *or* 《승부 따위가》 What are the chances? / ～는 점점 불리하다 Things are going from bad to worse. / ～는 일변하여 우리에게 불리〔유리〕하게 되었다 The tide turned 「against us 〔in our favor〕.

**형수**(兄嫂) *one's* elder brother's wife; *one's* sister-in-law.

**형식**(形式) (a) form; (a) formality.
¶ ～적 formal; coventional. ⇨ 형식적 / 복잡한 ～ a complicated form / ～을 차리지 않고 without ceremony 〔formality〕 / 논문 ～으로 in the form of a treatise / 어떤 ～으로든지 in any shape or form / ～에 구애되다〔사로잡히다〕 《절차·문서 따위에서》 insist on 〔stick to, be fussy about, 《구어》 be sticky about〕 the proper forms 〔procedure(s), formalities〕; 《예의상》 be too formal; stand on ceremony / ～에 따르다 follow the formalities 〔the conventions〕 (특히 문학이나 예술의) / ～에 중점을 두다 attach importance to form / 정당한 ～을 밟다 go through 〔observe〕 the proper 〔due〕 formalities / ～을 버리다 do away with all formalities / ～을 차리다 observe forms; be ceremonious; be formal / ～을 중시하다 respect the formalities 〔convention〕 / ～을 갖추다 complete the formal requirements / 그는 지나치게 ～을 따진다 He sticks too much to forms 〔formalities〕. / 지나치게 ～을 따지면 근본을 망각하게 된다 Excessive adherence to form can render a work lifeless.
◉ ～논리 formal logic. ～도야 『교육』 formal building of character. ～미(美) the beauty of form. ～법 formal law. ～주어〔목적어〕 『문법』 a formal subject 〔object〕. ～주의〔론〕 formalism; 《관청의》 red-tapism: ～주의자 a formalist.

**형식연도**(型式年度) 《자동차 따위》 a model year.

**형식적**(形式的) ¶ ～인 formal; superficial; perfunctory 《inspection》 / ～으로 formally; perfunctorily; for form's sake; for the sake of formality; as a matter of form / ～인 일 a matter of form / ～의례 formality 《at a wedding 〔funeral〕》 / ～인 표현 a formal expression / 우리 ～인 일이 아닌 실질적인 문제를 이야기합시다 Let's cut through the red-tape and talk about essential matters.

**형안**(炯眼) ① 《날카롭게 빛나는 눈》 a piercing and shining eye. ② 《통찰력》 insight; penetration; acumen.

**형언**(形言) description; expression. ～하다 describe; express. ¶ ～할 수 없다 be beyond description 〔words〕; baffle 〔beggar〕 description / 너무 아름다워서 ～할 수 없다 be too beautiful for words / 뭐라고 ～할 수 없는 공포를 느끼다 feel a nameless fear / 그 참상은 이루 ～할 수가 없었다 Their misery was beyond description 〔expression〕.

**형용**(形容) 《생긴 모양》 form; shape; figure; appearance; 《표현》 description; qualification; modification; 《비유》 a metaphor; a figure of speech; a figurative expression. ～하다 describe; modify; explain with 〔put into〕 words; verbalize; express figuratively. ¶ ～할 말이 없다 [사물이 주어] baffle 〔beggar, defy, be beyond〕 description; be too 《beautiful》 for words.

**형용사**(形容詞) 〖문법〗 an adjective; 《일반적으로》 an epithet. ¶ ～적인 adjectival / 명사적 용법의 ～ an adnoun. ◉ ～구〔절〕 an adjective phrase 〔clause〕. 서술적～ a predicative adjective. 제한적～ a limiting adjective.

**형이상**(形而上) ¶ ～의 metaphysical; abstract; immaterial / ～의 문제 a metaphysical matter; an abstract matter. ◉ ～학 metaphysics; metaphysical philosophy: ～학자 a metaphysician / ～학적 유심론〔결정론〕 metaphysical idealism 〔determinism〕.

**형이하**(形而下) ¶ ～의 physical; concrete; corporeal; material. ◉ ～학 a concrete 〔physical〕 science.

**형장**(兄丈) you.

**형장**(刑場) a place of execution; 《처형대》 a scaffold. ¶ ～의 이슬로 사라지다 die on the scaffold; be executed; end *one's* life on the gallows.

**형적**(形迹·形跡) 《흔적》 traces; vestiges; marks; 《증거》 indications; signs; evidence(s). ¶ ～도 없이 without leaving any trace / ～을 감추다 remove all traces 《of》; cover (up) *one's* traces; destroy all evidence / 조금도 ～을 남기지 않다 leave no trace behind / 이 집엔 사람이 들었던 ～이 없다 This house gives no evidence of having been lived in. / 지금은 그 무덤이 ～도 없이 사라졌다 No traces of the grave remain now. *or* All traces of the grave 「have been obliterated 〔are gone〕.

**형정**(刑政) penal administration.

**형제**(兄弟) 《육친의》 a brother; a sister; 《동포》 brethren; 〖사회·인류〗 a sibling (남녀). ¶ ～의 《남》 brotherhood; fraternity; 《여》 sisterly / ～의 우애 brotherly 〔sisterly〕 love 〔affection〕; fraternal love 〔affection〕 / ～의 의를 맺다 form a fraternal friendship 《with》 / ～가 몇이 되느냐 How many brothers and sisters do you have? (★ 한국어에서는 5형제인 경우, 자기를 포함시켜 Five.라고 대답하는 것이 일반적이지만, 영어에서는 자기를 포함시키지 않고 Four. 또는 Two brothers and two sisters.라고 대답하는 것이 보통이다). ◉ ～간 brotherhood; brotherly ties; fraternity. ～싸움 a quarrel 〔trouble〕 between brothers 〔sisters〕. ～자매 brothers and sisters. 사촌～ cousins. 의～ plighted brothers. 이복〔배다른〕～ a half brother; a brother of the half blood. 이부～ half brothers; uterine brothers; brothers on the mother's 〔maternal〕 side. 젖～ a foster brother 〔sister〕. 친(親)～ a full 〔whole〕 brother 〔sister〕.

**형조**(刑曹) 〖고제도〗 the Ministry of Justice ◉ ～판서 the Minister of Justice.

**형지**(型紙) a paper 〔dress〕 pattern 《for a dress》. ⇨ 본.

**형질**(形質) ① 《형태와 성질》 characteristic form and nature 〔quality〕. ② 《유전적인》 a character; characteristics. ◉ ～세포 a plasma cell. ～인류학 physical anthropology. ～전환 〖유전〗 transformation.

**형체**(形體) (a) form; (a) shape; the body. ¶ ～를 알아볼 수 없게 beyond 〔out of〕 recognition / ～를 갖추다 be given a form; be embodied / ～를 부여하다 embody. ◉ ～미(美) physical beauty; the beauty of form.

**형태**(形態) (a) form; a shape; 〖심리〗 a *Gestalt* (G.); 《언어의》 morphology. ¶ ～를 바꾸다 transform; transfigure / … 의 ～를 취하다 assume the form of ... / 얼음·눈·수증기는 모두 물의 다른 ～다 Ice, snow and steam are different forms of water. / 민주주의는 정치의 한 ～이다 Democracy is a form of government. ◉ ～론(論) 〖언어〗 morphology; morphemics; accidence: ～론적 구조 morphologic construction. ～발생 〖생물〗 morphogenesis. ～변화 〖언어〗 modification. ～소(素) a morpheme: ～소론 morphemics. ～심리학 *Gestalt* 〔form〕 psychology; configurationism. ～음소론〖언어〗 morphophonemics. ～학 〖생물〗 morphology: ～학자 morphologist / 사회 ～학 social morphology. ～효용 form utility.

**형통하다**(亨通—) go well; turn out well; prove successful; be realized; be fulfilled. ¶ 만사가 ～ everything goes well.

**형틀**(刑—) a chair in which a criminal is fastened to be interrogated.

**형편**(形便) ① 《상태》 (**a**) 《경과》 the course 《of events》; the development 《of an affair》; 《추이》 the turn 《of events》; 《결과》 the issue 《of a war》; the consequences 《of *one's doing*》. ¶ 일 되어가는 ～ the course 〔run, development〕 of events 〔affairs〕; the turn of events / 일이 되어가는 ～을 지켜보다 watch the development 〔course〕 of events; wait for the turn of events; wait and see how things will turn

out; watch which way the cat jumps; see which way the wind blows / 되어가는 ～을 보아 결정하세 Let us see how things turn out before we decide. (***b***) 《사정》 circumstances; conditions; reasons; 《형세》 the situation; the state of affairs 〔things〕; the condition of affairs. ¶ ～상 in view of circumstances / ～이 그러하므로 such being the case; under those circumstances / 가정 ～으로 on account of family affairs; for family reasons / 일의 ～으로 for reasons of *one's* work / 부득이한 ～ 때문에 through 〔owing to〕 unavoidable circumstances / 일신상의 ～으로 for personal reasons / ～에 의해 for certain 〔private〕 reasons; for reasons of *one's* own; owing to circumstances; in view of changed circumstances / 지금 ～으로는 under the present circumstances; in the present state of things 〔affairs〕; as the matters 〔things〕 stand now / ～이 허락하면 가겠다 I will come if circumstances permit.
② 《살림의》 *one's* family circumstances; *one's* family fortune; *one's* financial situation. ¶ ～이 넉넉하다 be well off; be amply provided for / 가정 ～으로 학교를 그만두다 quit school for family reasons / ～이 아주 말이 아니다 be badly off / 그는 가난하여 밥도 제대로 먹지 못할 ～이다 He is so poor that he cannot feed himself.
③ 《편익》 convenience. ¶ ～상 for convenience's sake / ～이 닿으시면 if (it is) convenient (to you); if it suits your convenience / ～이 닿는 대로 at the first opportunity; at *one's* first 〔earliest〕 convenience / 시간의 ～도 있고 해서 for consideration of time requirements / ～에 따라서(는) according to circumstances; if occasion requires / ～이 좋다〔나쁘다〕 be convenient 〔inconvenient〕 / ～이 좋아〔나빠〕 지다 become convenient 〔inconvenient〕; make a good 〔an evil〕 case for....

**형편없다**(形便—) 《비참하다》 (be) miserable; be wretched; 《시시하다》 (be) trivial; trifling; poor; unworthy; useless; 《망쳐지다》 be spoilt; be ruined; 《지독하다》 (be) terrible; dreadful; awful. ¶ 형편없는 근시안 a dreadful near-sighted person / 형편없는 놈 an impossible fellow; a good-for-nothing / 형편없는 바보 an absolute fool / 형편없는 선물 a trifling gift / 형편없는 악당 an accomplished villain / 형편없는 시〔오두막〕 a wretched poem 〔hovel〕 / 형편없는 책 a book of no value / 불경기로 사업이 ～ The depression has ruined our business. / 그 때문에 교사로서의 내 권위가 형편없어졌다 It set my authority over my students at defiance.

**형편없이**(形便—) 《몹시》 severely; terribly; harshly; 《가차없이》 unsparingly; mercilessly; roundly; 《아주》 thoroughly; utterly; completely. ¶ ～ 고생하다 suffer terribly 〔a great deal〕 《from》; go through many hardships / ～ 지다 be beaten all hollow / 비 때문에 꽃이 ～ 되었다 The rain has wrought havoc with the flowers.

**형평**(衡平) balance; equilibrium; equipoise. ¶ ～의 원칙을 무시하다 ignore the principle of equity. ◉ ～법 『영미법』 equity: ～법 재판소 a court of equity; an equity court; 《미》 a (court of) chancery. ～운동 the social equality movement; the leveling movement. ～원칙 the principle of equity 〔equilibrium〕: ～ 원칙에 어긋나다 be against the principle of equity.

**형해**(形骸) 《골조》 a frame(work); a skeleton; 《잔해》 a ruin; a wreck. ¶ ～만 남기다 be reduced to an empty shell / 그 절은 이제 ～조차 남아 있지 않다 Nothing remains of the temple now. / 그 성문(城門)은 지금 ～만이 남아 있다 All that remains of the castle gate is its frame.

**형형색색**(形形色色) ¶ ～의 various; all sorts of; of different 〔all〕 kinds 〔sorts〕; various kinds of / ～의 물건 articles of different sorts and kinds; a great variety of things / ～으로 variously; in many ways; diversely / ～의 책들이 선반 위에 꽂혀 있었다 There were various books arranged on the shelf.

**형형하다**(炯炯—) (be) glaring; piercing; penetrating. ¶ 안광이 ～ have glittering 〔penetrating〕 eyes; be sharp= 〔eagle-〕eyed

**혜고**(惠顧) 《왕림》 a gracious 《your, his》 visit; 《돌봐줌》 (your, his) kind regards 〔attention〕. ～하다 kindly visit; regard with kindness; treat with benevolence.

**혜람하다**(惠覽—) deign to read; kindly read 〔peruse〕.

**혜림**(惠臨) 《your, his》 gracious visit.

~하다 graciously 〔kindly〕 visit 〔come〕. ¶ 부디 모임에 ~하여 주시기 바랍니다 We request the honor of your presence at the meeting.

**혜사하다**(惠賜—) bestow; graciously give; kindly grant.

**혜서**(惠書) your kind 〔gracious〕 letter. ¶ ~는 받아보았습니다 Your letter has been noted with thanks.

**혜성**(彗星) 〖천문〗 a comet; [비유적] sudden prominence; a meteoric rise; a star. ¶ 핼리~ Halley's comet / 정계의 ~ dark horse in politics; a political meteor / ~과 같이 나타나다 be brought into sudden prominence; make a sudden 〔meteoric〕 rise from obscurity. ◉ ~군(群) a comet group.

**혜시**(惠示) your kind instruction 〔information〕. ~하다 kindly show 〔instruct, inform〕.

**혜안**(慧眼) a keen 〔sharp〕 eye; 《a man of》 keen insight; (good) judgment; acumen. ¶ ~의 keen〔sharp〕-eyed; quick-sighted; insightful 《comments》; perceptive; discerning.

**혜존**(惠存) 《증정본에》 "With the compliments 《of the author》"; 《사진 따위에》 "To 〔Presented to〕 Mr. … with best wishes from —".

**혜택**(惠澤) 《은혜·호의》 a favor; (a) blessing; (a) kindness; 《이익》 benefit; 《자애》 benevolence; mercy. ¶ 문명의 ~ the benefits of civilization / 자연의 ~ the blessings of nature / 신께서 내리신 ~으로 by the grace of God; with God's blessing / ~을 입다 be benefited; receive a favor from 《*a person*》 / ~을 주다 bestow a favor 《on》 / 전국민이 고루 문화 ~을 누릴 수 있도록 하다 enable all citizens to receive cultural benefits equally. ◉ ~자 a beneficiary.

**혜한**(惠翰) =혜서(惠書).

**호**(戶) a house; a door; a family (가구). ¶ 50호 되는 작은 마을 a hamlet of 50 houses.

**호**(弧) an arc.

**호**(湖) ⇨ 호수(湖水). ¶ 미시간 호 Lake Michigan.

**호**(號) ① 《번호》 a number; an issue (잡지·신문의); 《크기》 size; 《실의 굵기》 count. ¶ 제2호 number two (생략 No. 2; 2); the second number / 다음호 the next number 〔issue〕 / 14호실 Room No. 14 / 「신여성」 3월호 the March issue of *Shin-yŏsŏng* / 50호짜리 풍경화 a landscape about 32 (inches) by 46 inches / 서울 중구 정동 1의 48 호, 1-48 Chŏng-dong, Chung-gu, Seoul Korea / 이하 다음호에 To be continued. / 다음호에서 완결 To be concluded (in the next number). ② 《이름》 a title; 《아호》 a pen name; a pseudonym; 《배 이름》 the…. ¶ 마산호 the S.S. Masan.

**호**(壕) 《참호》 a trench; 《방공호》 an underground air-raid shelter; a dugout. ¶ ~를 파다 dig a trench.

**호-**(好) good. ¶ 호시절 the 〔*one's*〕 time; due time / 호적수 a good rival 〔match〕.

**호가**(呼價) 《부르는 값》 a nominal price 〔quotation〕; the price asked; a bid; a price offered (살 사람이 부르는). ~하다 《살 사람이》 name a price; bid; make a bid; 《팔 사람이》 demand 〔ask〕 a price. ¶ 엄청나게 ~하다 ask 〔name, demand〕 an extravagant price 《for》.

**호가호위**(狐假虎威) An ass in lion's skin.

**호각**(互角) equality; evenness; par; a good match. ¶ ~의 equal; even; evenly-〔well-〕matched / ~의 경기 a close 〔well-matched〕 game; an even match; an equal contest 〔fight〕 / 경기가 ~을 이루다 match 《each other》; be equal 《to》, be even 《with》; play an even game; run a dead heat.

**호각**(號角) a (signal) whistle. ¶ ~을 불다 blow a whistle.

**호감**(好感) (a) good feeling; goodwill; a favorable 〔good〕 impression. ¶ ~이 가는 amiable; affable; attractive; pleasing / ~이 가지 않는 unaffable; unattractive; repulsive / ~을 사다 win 《*a person's*》 favor 〔goodwill〕 / ~을 주다 give 〔make〕 a good impression; impress *one* favorably / ~을 가지다 have 〔entertain〕 a friendly feeling toward 《*a person*》; be favorably 〔kindly〕 disposed toward 《*a person*》 / 나는 그녀에게 ~을 가지고 있다 I have a good 〔friendly〕 feeling toward her. / 그녀가 취한 행동은 모두에게 ~을 주었다 The way she acted gave a good 〔favorable〕 impression to all. / 그는 내게 ~을 주었다 He impressed me favorably.

**호강** comfort; luxury; extravagance; sumptuosness. ~하다 live in 「luxury 〔comfort, clover, grand style〕. ~스럽다 (be) easy and comfortable; cozy; luxurious. ¶ ~스러운 생활 a luxurious 〔an extravagant〕 life.

**호객**(呼客) 《행위》 touting. ~하다 tout

(for customers); solicit custom.
◉ ～꾼 a tout(er); 《미》 a (hotel) runner; 《구경거리의》 a barker; a spieler; 《속어》 《매춘의》 a pander; a pimp.

**호걸**(豪傑) a hero; an outstanding 〔extraordinary〕 man 〔character〕; a larger-than-life figure; ～스럽다 (be) heroic; gallant; intrepid; brave. ¶ ～풍의 웃음 a broad 〔hearty〕 laugh / 그에겐 ～다운 데가 있다 He wears a heroic air. / 그는 ～풍의 사나이다 He is something of a hero.

**호격**(呼格) 『문법』 the vocative case.

**호경기**(好景氣) (a wave of ) prosperity; good times; a boom (갑작스런); robust 〔vigorous〕 economy. ¶ 전쟁으로 인한 ～ a war boom / ～의 흐름을 타다 take advantage of a boom; ride on the upswing of the market / 주식 시장은 ～다 The stock market is quite lively 〔booming〕. ◉ ～시대 prosperous times; good times; a boom period.

**호곡**(號哭) wailing; weeping aloud. ～하다 wail; weep aloud; bewail.

**호광**(弧光) an arc light. ◉ ～등 an arc lamp. ～로(爐) an arc furnace. ～전압 arcing voltage.

**호구**(戶口) the number of houses and families; population. ◉ ～조사 census taking; a census: ～조사원 a census taker / ～ 조사 기록부 a census register / ～ 조사를 하다 take the census.

**호구**(好球) 『야구』 a nice ball. ¶ ～를 놓치다 miss a nice ball.

**호구**(虎口) ① 《위험》 a tiger's mouth; the jaws of death; danger. ¶ ～를 벗어나다 escape from the jaws of death; get out of danger / ～에 들어가다 get into a perilous place. ② 《바둑의》 an area on the *paduk* checkerboard that is surrounded by three white 〔black〕 stones.

**호구**(糊口) a meager living; a bare livelihood 〔subsistence〕. ～하다 eke out a living; keep the pot boiling; keep body and soul together; make *one's* bare living; gain a bare livelihood; live from hand to mouth. ¶ ～지책(之策) a means of livelihood; a way to make ends meet / 그는 아르바이트로 겨우 ～하고 있다 He gets a bare livelihood on the income from his part-time job.

**호국**(護國) defense of *one's* fatherland. ¶ ～정신 the spirit for defending *one's* country 《against enemies》 / ～의 꽃으로 산화하다 die a glorious death on the battle field.

**호기**(好期) a good 〔favorable〕 season; a good 〔right〕 time 《of *one's* life》.

**호기**(好機) a good 〔favorable, golden〕 opportunity; a good chance; a good time 〔occasion〕. ¶ 천재일우의 ～ the chance of lifetime / ～를 기다리다 wait and see a good opportunity / ～를 놓치다 miss 〔lose〕 a good 「opportunity 〔chance〕; let a chance go 〔slip〕 / ～를 포착하다 seize 〔take〕 an opportunity; the forelock; avail *oneself* of 「an 〔a perfect〕 opportunity / 이런 ～는 다시는 오지 않을 게다 A chance like this will never come again. / 너무 오래 망설이면이 ～를 놓치게 될 것이다 If you hesitate too long, you will miss this golden opportunity. / ～를 놓치지 마라 Seize the opportunity while you can.

**호기**(豪氣) heroism; bravery; an intrepid spirit; a stout heart; bravado. ～롭다 (be) heroic; brave; gallant; daring; intrepid; stout-hearted. ¶ ～를 부리다 display bravery; swagger / ～있게 큰 돈을 내다 fork out a big sum / ～있게 팁을 주다 give a generous tip.

**호기성**(好氣性) 『식물』 aerotropism. ¶ ～의 aerotropic; aerobic. ◉ ～생물 an aerobe; an aerobium (*pl.* -bia). ～세균 aerobic bacteria (*sing.* -rium).

**호기심**(好奇心) curiosity; inquisitiveness. ¶ ～이 강한 사람 an inquisitive 〔a curious〕 person / ～에 이끌리어 prompted 〔impelled〕 by curiosity; from 〔out of 〕 curiosity / ～이 강한〔많은〕 curious; full of curiosity; inquisitive / ～을 일으키다 arouse 〔stimulate〕 *one's* curiosity / ～을 만족시키다 satisfy 〔gratify〕 *one's* curiosity / ～에서 가 보았다 I went there out of curiosity / 아이들은 ～이 많다 Children are full of curiosity.

**호깨나무** 『식물』 a raisin tree.

**호남**(湖南) 《지방》 the Honam district 〔area〕; the Chŏlla-do provinces.
◉ ～고속도로 the Honam Expressway. ～선 the Honam 〔Taejŏn-Mokp'ŏ〕 (Railroad) Line. ～평야 the Honam Plains.

**호남아**(好男兒) 《미남자》 a handsome man; a good-〔fine-〕looking man; an Adonis; 《멋진 사내》 a fine 〔nice〕 fellow; 《미구어》 a regular guy.

**호농**(豪農) a wealthy 〔rich〕 farmer; a gentleman farmer.

**호다** broad-stitch. ¶ 솔기를 ~ broad-stitch the seams 《of clothes》.

**호담**(豪膽) intrepidity; fearlessness; boldness; dauntlessness; a stout heart. ~하다 (be) intrepid; fearless; dauntless; daring; have「iron nerves 〔nerves of steel〕; be stout of heart. ¶ 그는 ~하다 He has iron nerves.

**호도**(糊塗) ~하다 gloss over; varnish; temporize; patch up. ¶ ~지책 an expedient / 일시적으로 ~하다 temporize; patch up 《*things*》 for the moment; make shift 《with》; gloss over 《*one's* mistake》/ 그는 결코 사실을 ~할 사람이 아니다 He is the last man to gloss over the matter.

**호도깝스럽다** (be) rash; reckless; unstable.

**호도애** 〚조류〛 a turtledove.

**호되다** (be) severe; hard; harsh. ¶ 호된 더위〔추위〕 intense heat 〔cold〕/ 호된 비평 (a) scathing 〔harsh〕 criticism / 호된 일 hard 〔heavy〕 work / 호된 형벌 a severe punishment / 호되게 severely; harshly; violently / 호되게 꾸짖다 scold severely / 호되게 재촉하다 press hard for 《*a thing*》/ 이런 호된 추위는 처음이다 I have never experienced such a severe cold before.

**호두**(胡―) 〚식물〛 a walnut (tree). ¶ ~까기 (a pair of ) nutcrackers / ~를 까다 crack a walnut. ◉ ~까기 《도구》 (a pair of ) nutcrackers. ~껍질 a walnut shell. ~속 the kernel of a walnut; 《미궁(迷宮)》 a maze; a labyrinth: ~속 같다 [비유적] be so complicated that *one* can't tell 《A from B》. ~잠(潛) a jade hairpin with a walnut-shaped top.

**호드기** a reed pipe.

**호드득거리다** ① 《소리》 crackle; pop; snap. ¶ 숯불이 ~ the burning charcoal keeps snapping. ②《방정떨다》 act rashly; be imprudent 〔frivolous〕.

**호드득호드득** ① 《소리》 popping; crackling; snapping. ¶ 옥수수가 ~ 튀다 corn keeps popping. ② 《방정》 rashly; imprudently.

**호들갑떨다** be extravagant 〔over-excited〕 in speech; be bubbling over.

**호들갑스럽다** (be) abrupt and frivolous; flippant; rash; imprudent. ⇨ 호들갑떨다. ¶ 호들갑스런 수작 flippant remarks / 호들갑스럽게 웃다 laugh in a flippant manner / 호들갑스럽게 굴다 act hastily; take a rash step.

**호등**(弧燈) an arc lamp 〔light〕.

**호떡**(胡―) a Chinese stuffed pancake.

**호락질** single-handed farming; a family farming. ~하다 raise crops single-handed(ly).

**호락호락** 《수월하게》 easily; without ado; readily; 《만만한》 yielding; easy-going. ~하다 (be) ready; easily manageable; tractable; easy-going. ¶ ~ 계략에 걸려들다 fall an easy victim to a scheme / ~ 속아 넘어가다 be deceived easily.

**호랑나비**(虎狼―) 〚곤충〛 a swallowtail (butterfly).

**호랑이**(虎狼―) ① 〚동물〛 a tiger; a tigress (암컷). ¶ ~ 담배 먹던 시절에 long, long ago / ~에게 고기 달란다 ask when *one* should expect to be asked of / ~꼬리를 밟다 tread on a tiger's tail; take a great risk / ~도 제 말하면 온다 《속담》 Talk of the devil, and he is sure to appear. / ~는 죽어서 가죽을 남기고, 사람은 죽어서 이름을 남긴다 《속담》 Tigers leave only their skins when they die, but through his achievements a man's name lives on. / ~굴에 가야 ~ 새끼를 잡는다 《속담》 Nothing venture, nothing have. ② [비유적] a formidable person; a tiger.

**호래아들**, **호래자식** a boor; an ill-mannered 〔a rude〕 person.

**호렴**(胡―) Chinese salt; rough salt.

**호령**(號令) a (word of ) command; an order; 《큰소리》 a yell; a shout. ~하다 command; (give an) order; dictate; give 〔shout〕 a command; yell (at); shout. ¶ 부하를 ~하다 yell at *one's* subordinate / 천하를 ~하다 dictate to the whole world; hold sway over the whole country.

**호로**(葫蘆) 〚식물〛 a gourd.

**호롱** the base of a kerosene lamp. ◉ ~불 a small kerosene lamp.

**호루라기** a whistle.

**호르르** ①《타는 모양》《burning》 rapidly 〔lightly〕. ¶ ~ 타버리다 burn rapidly. ② 《날갯소리》 《birds》 flapping; fluttering. ¶ (새가) ~ 날아가다 《birds》 fly with a flap of the wings. ③《호각소리》 piping; whistling. ¶ ~ 불다 whistle; pipe.

**호르몬** (a) hormone. ¶ ~의 hormonal; hormonic / ~의 불균형 a hormone imbalance / 남성〔여성〕 ~ a male 〔female〕 sex hormone. ◉ ~결핍증 hormone deficiency. ~요법 hormone therapy. ~장애 a hormonal disturbance. ~제(劑) a hormone drug 〔preparation〕.

**호른** 〚악기〛 a horn. ◉ ～연주자 a horn player; a hornist.

**호리** 〚농업〛 a one-ox plow 〔plough《영》〕. ◉ ～질 one-ox plowing: ～질하다 plow with a one-ox plow.

**호리다** 《유혹하다》 seduce; allure; tempt; entice; 《매혹하다》 fascinate; bewitch; charm; captivate; 《혼란케 하다》 confuse 《the people》; 《속이다》 deceive; lead 《*a person*》 astray. ¶ 돈으로 여자를 ～ tempt 〔allure〕 a girl with money / 사내는 소녀를 달콤한 말로 호렸다 The man seduced the girl with honeyed words.

**호리병**(葫―甁) a gourd bottle; a calabash. ¶ ～ 모양의 gourd-shaped. ◉ ～박 〚식물〛 a (bottle) gourd.

**호리호리하다** (be) tall and willowy 〔slender〕; slim; slimly-built; slight. ¶ 호리호리한 여자 a slim girl; a woman with a slender figure.

**호마**(胡馬) a Manchurian horse.

**호마**(胡麻) 《참깨》 sesame (plant).

**호매하다**(豪邁―) (be) intrepid; bold; dauntless; indomitable; undaunted. ¶ 호매한 기상 an indomitable spirit.

**호머** 〚야구〛 a homer; a home run. ◉ 결승～ a home run to end the game; a clinching homer.

**호면**(湖面) the surface of a lake. ¶ ～에는 바람 한 점 없었다 Not a breeze stirred the lake.

**호명**(呼名) calling 《*a person*》 by name; (a) roll call (점호). ～하다 call 《*a person*》 by name; call the roll. ◉ ～자 a caller.

**호모** 《남자 동성애》 homosexuality; 《동성애자》 a homosexual; a gay; 《속어》 a homo.

**호모사피엔스** 〚인류〛 *Homo sapiens* (L.).

**호미** 〚농업〛 a weeding hoe (with a short handle). ¶ ～로 막을 것을 가래로 막는다 《속담》 A stitch in time saves nine.

**호미씻이** 《논매기 끝낸 뒤의》 a farmer's feast after the final weeding of rice paddies. ～하다 have 〔enjoy〕 a "hoe-washing" holiday.

**호미자락** the depth of the tip of a hoe. ¶ 비가 ～만큼 오다 have a rain that soaks the earth an inch deep.

**호밀**(胡―) 〚식물〛 rye. ◉ ～빵 rye bread.

**호바늘꽃**(胡―) 〚식물〛 a Manchurian willow-weed.

**호박** 〚식물〛 a pumpkin; 《미》 a squash; 《애호박》 a zucchini 《미》. ¶ ～ 같은 얼굴 a fat pumpkin-like face; a plain face / ～에 침주기 plow the sand(s); have no effect 《on》 / ～이 굴렀다〔넝쿨째로 굴러 떨어졌다〕 receive a windfall; have a stroke of unexpected good luck 〔fortune〕. ◉ ～고지 dried slices of young pumpkin. ～밭 a pumpkin plantation 〔patch〕. ～씨 a pumpkin seed. ～엿 pumpkin taffy. ～전 pan-fried zucchini slices. ～죽 squash porridge.

**호박**(琥珀) 〚광물〛 amber; succinite. ¶ ～의 succinic / ～색의 amber-colored / ～속에 든 동물〔식물〕 amber fauna 〔flora〕. ◉ ～단(緞) 《직물》 taffeta; taffety. ～산(酸) 〚화학〛 succinic acid. ～색 amber (color); lime. ～잠(簪) an amber hairpin. 인조～ artificial amber; amberoid.

**호박개** 〚동물〛 a large hairy dog.

**호박벌** 〚곤충〛 a carpenter bee.

**호반**(虎班) 〚고제도〛 the military nobility. ⇨ 무반(武班).

**호반**(湖畔) a lakeside; the shores of a lake. ¶ ～에 on 〔by〕 a lake / ～의 lakeside / ～의 집 a house by the lake; a lakeside cottage / ～을 거닐다 ramble along the shores of lake. ◉ ～도시 a lake city. ～시인 the Lake Poets. ～(시인)파 the Lake school.

**호반새**(湖畔―) 〚조류〛 a kingfisher.

**호방하다**(豪放―) (be) free-hearted; large-minded; (manly and) open-hearted; open; vigorous; virile; unrestrained. ¶ 호방한 사람 an open-hearted man / 호방한 필치 a vigorous 〔soul-packed〕 touch 〔penmanship〕.

**호배추**(胡―) 〚식물〛 a Chinese cabbage; a pe-tsai.

**호버크라프트** 《수륙 양용 보트》 a Hovercraft (상표명).

**호범꼬리**(胡―) 〚식물〛 the Manchurian histort.

**호법**(護法) 《국법의》 the defense of the constitution; 《종교의》 the defense of a religion.

**호별**(戶別) each house. ¶ ～로 (from) house to house 〔door to door〕; at each house / ～로 권유하다 canvass from door to door. ◉ ～방문 《판매》 house-to-house 〔door-to-door〕 sales; 《선거에서》 house-to-house 〔door-to-door〕 canvassing (for voters): ～방문 외판원 a door-to-door salesman / ～방문을 하다 visit from door to door; 《선거에서》 make a house-to-house canvass / 그는 ～ 방문으로 회비를 모았다 He made house-to-house visits to collect the (membership) fees. ～세 a house rate 〔tax〕. ～조사 a house-

to-house investigation 〔census〕.
**호복**(胡服) a Chinese garment 〔gown〕.
**호봉**(號俸) a serial 〔pay〕 step; a salary class. ¶ 5 ~, the fifth-class salary / 그는 ~ 조정 외에는 공무원 봉급이 동결될 것이라고 했다 He noted that the wages of government officials would be frozen except in the case of promotion in the salary step.
**호부**(好否) good and 〔or〕 bad; likes and 〔or〕 dislikes. ¶ ~간에 whether *one* likes it or not.
**호부**(豪富) a man of great wealth and power; a plutocrat.
**호부**(護符) =부적(符籍).
**호비다** pick 《*one's* nose 〔teeth〕》; 《파다》 dig up; grub. ⇨후비다. ¶ 귓속을 ~ clean *one's* ears. 「bushclover.
**호비수리**(胡—) 〖식물〗 the Manchurian
**호비칼** a gouge; a router.
**호사**(豪奢) luxury; extravagance; sumptuousness. ~하다 live in clover; luxuriate in. ~스럽다 (be) extravagant; luxurious; magnificent; grand; sumptuous. ¶ ~스러운 생활을 하다 live in luxury 〔grand style〕; live like a prince. 「a hustler.
**호사가**(好事家) a busybody; a go-getter;
**호사다마**(好事多魔) There's many a slip between the cup and the lip. 「fop.
**호사바치**(豪奢—) a dandy; a gallant; a
**호산성**(好酸性) 〖의학〗 ¶ ~의 acidophilic; acidophile; acidophil. ◉ ~균 an acidophilic bacterium (*pl.* -ria).
**호상**(好喪) a propitious mourning (of a person dying old and rich).
**호상**(弧狀) ¶ ~의 arc(-shaped). ◉ ~열도(列島) a crescent-shaped 〔an arcuate〕 archipelago.
**호상**(湖上) ¶ ~의〔에서〕 on 〔in〕 the lake / ~의 일몰 sunset on the lake. ◉ ~가옥 a lake dwelling. ~생활시대 the lacustrine age 〔period〕. ~생활자 a lake dweller.
**호상**(豪商) a wealthy merchant 〔businessman〕; a merchant prince; a business magnate; a baron.
**호상**(護床) 〖토목〗 an apron. ◉ ~댐 a counterdam; a secondary weir.
**호상**(護喪) 「taking charge of 〔directing〕 a funeral (ceremony). ~하다 「take charge of 〔oversee, direct〕 a funeral. ◉ ~소 the office in charge of a funeral; the funeral director's. ~차지(次知) the funeral director.
**호색**(好色) lasciviousness; sensuality; amorousness; lewdness; lust; eroticism. ~하다 be fond of sex; be sensual 〔lascivious, lewd〕. ¶ ~의 lustful; lewd; sensual; erotic; dirty-minded 《구어》. ◉ ~꾼 a lewd 〔lascivious〕 man; a sensualist; a satyr; a Don Juan. ~문학 obscene 〔pornographic, erotic〕 literature. ~증 〖병리〗 erotomania. ~한(漢) = 호색꾼.
**호생**(互生) 〖식물〗 growing in alternation. ¶ ~의 alternate. ◉ ~엽(葉) alternate leaves (on a plant).
**호생지덕**(互生之德) the grace of sparing a life by pardoning a condemned person.
**호선**(互先) 《바둑》 alternative moving. ¶ ~으로 두다 have the first move in alternate games; play on an equal footing.
**호선**(互選) mutual election 〔vote〕; co-option; co-optation. ~하다 co-opt; elect by mutual vote; elect from among 《themselves》. ¶ 위원회는 위원장을 ~한다 The committee elects a chairman from its own members. / 사장은 임원들간의 ~으로 선출된다 The president is elected by mutual vote among members of the board.
◉ ~투표 mutual vote.
**호선**(弧線) an arc (of a circle); a crescent-shaped line.
**호성적**(好成績) good results 〔marks〕. ¶ ~을 올리다 obtain 〔gain, attain〕 good 〔excellent〕 results; do an excellent job; make a good 〔fine〕 record; do well.
**호세아서**(—書) 〖성서〗 (The Book of) Hosea (생략 Hos.).
**호소**(呼訴) 《불평·고충 등의》 a complaint; 《정의·법 등에》 an appeal; a petition. ~하다 complain of; appeal to 《a sense of justice》; appeal 〔resort〕 to 《arms》; have recourse to 《violence》. ¶ 국민에게 ~하다 appeal to the people 〔nation〕 / 이성〔정의감〕에 ~하다 appeal to *one's* reason 〔sense of justice〕 / 아무의 판단에 ~하다 appeal to *a person* to judge / ~할 곳 없다 have no place to appeal to; have no court of appeal.
**호소**(湖沼) lakes and marshes. ¶ ~의 lacustrine. ◉ ~학 limnology: ~학자 a limnologist.
**호송**(護送) (a) escort; (a) convoy. ~하다 escort; convoy; send 《*a person*》 under guard. ¶ 군대의 ~을 받다 be under the convoy of troops; be sent under convoy of troops / 수송선을 ~

하다 convoy transports / 죄인을 ～하다 send a prisoner under guard / 범인은 열차로 서울까지 ～되었다 The culprit traveled to Seoul by rail, under police escort. ◉ ～선(단) a (escorted) convoy; an armed convoy. ～차 a prison van 《영》; a patrol [paddy] wagon 《미》; 《구어》 a Black Maria.

**호수**(戶數) the number of houses [families].

**호수**(好手) 《바둑·장기의》 a good move.

**호수**(湖水) a lake. ¶ ～의 lacustrine / 호숫가 the lakeside / 산정 ～ Lake *Sanjŏng* (★ 관사 없음. the Lake of *Sanjŏng* 의 경우는 정관사가 붙음) / 호숫가에 있는 호텔 a hotel on the lake; a lakeside hotel.

**호수**(號數) number; a register [serial] number. ¶ 집～ the number of a house / ～를 거듭하다「go through [run into] several editions.

**호스** a hose; a hosepipe. ¶ ～로 물을 뿌리다 hose water 《over, on》; water 《the garden》 with a hose. ◉ 소방～ a fire hose.

**호스텔** a hostel. ◉ 유스～ a youth hostel.

**호스트** a host. ◉ ～ 프로그램 〖컴퓨터〗 a host program.

**호스티스** a hostess; a barmaid (술집의). ◉ 에어～ an air stewardess.

**호스피스** 《말기 환자의 간호 요양시설》 a hospice.

**호승지벽**(好勝之癖) love of beating others; a competitive spirit.

**호시기**(好時機) ⇨ 호기(好機).

**호시절**(好時節) a nice season [time]; a favorable season.

**호시탐탐**(虎視眈眈) [부사적] with vigilant hostility. ～하다 watch vigilantly for 《a chance》; seek for 《a position》 eagerly; look enviously 《at》; cast covetous eyes 《on *a thing*》. ¶ 그들은 ～ 공격의 기회를 노리고 있다 They are watching for an opportunity to attack you.

**호신**(護身) self-protection; self-defense [defence 《영》]; self-preservation. ～하다 protect *oneself;* defend *oneself.* ¶ ～용의[으로] for self-protection; for use in self-defense. ◉ ～부(符) an amulet (carried on *oneself*); a talisman 《against traffic accidents》. ～술 the art of self-defense: ～술을 알고 있다 know how to defend [protect] *oneself.*

**호심**(湖心) the heart [center] of a lake.

**호심경**(護心鏡) a (copper) breastplate put on the chest of *one's* armor (to protect the heart).

**호안**(好顔) a happy face.

**호안**(護岸) shore [bank] protection; 《강의》 a river wall; 《해안의》 a seawall; a sea bank. ◉ ～공사 shore [bank] protection works: ～ 공사를 하다 execute [carry out] the work of bank protection. ～제방 an embankment; a dyke [《미》 dike].

**호안석**(虎眼石) 〖광석〗 a tigereye; a tiger's eye.

**호양**(互讓) mutual concession; compromise; give and take. ～하다 make a mutual concession 《on *a matter*》; compromise [give and take] 《on, with》. ¶ ～의 정신으로 in a compromising [give-and-take, conciliatory] spirit / ～ 정신에 의거하여 based on the spirit of compromise / ～ 정신으로 문제를 해결하다 settle a matter by mutual concessions.

**호언**(好言) kind words; nice words.

**호언**(豪言) big [tall] talk; boasting; bombast; bragging; a loud boast. ～하다 talk big; talk bombastically; brag; boast. ◉ ～장담 = 호언(豪言): ～장담하는 사람 a braggart; a boaster.

**호연**(好演) 《연극 따위의》 good [excellent] acting; 《연기·연주 따위의》 a good performance. ～하다 act [perform] well; put up a good show.

**호연하다**(皓然―) 《썩 희다》 be snow white; 《명백하다》 (be) clear; patent.

**호연지기**(浩然之氣) a vast-flowing spirit; a great morale; a refreshed feeling. ¶ ～를 기르다 revive *one's* exhausted [spent] energy; refresh [recreate] *oneself* 《with》; enliven [nourish] *one's* spirits.

**호열자**(虎列剌) = 콜레라.

**호염**(好塩) ¶ ～성의 halophilic; halophilous; halophile; halophil. ◉ ～균(菌) halophilic bacteria; halophiles.

**호오**(好惡) *one's* likes and dislikes; partiality.

**호외**(戶外) the open air; outdoors. ¶ ～의 out-of-door; open-air.

**호외**(號外) 《신문·잡지의》 an extra (edition) 《of a newspaper》; a special; 《일정 수 밖의》 an extra number; a supernumerary. ¶ ～로 보도하다 announce 《an event》 in an extra / ～를 내다[발행하다] issue [put out, publish] an extra / ～요, ～ 《외치는 소리》 "Extra, Extra!"

**호우**(豪雨) a heavy rain(fall); a downpour; a torrential [hard] rain. ¶ 집중

～localized heavy rain; a (local) downpour / ～로 강이 범람하다 the heavy rain causes rivers to overflow. ◉ ～주의보 torrential 〔heavy〕 rain warning.

**호운**(好運) (a stroke of) good fortune; (good) luck; propitious fate; a lucky break《미》. ⇨ 행운(幸運). ¶ ～이 계속되다 have「a chain of lucky breaks 〔repeated strokes of luck〕.

**호위**(護衛) a guard; a bodyguard; an escort; 《집단》 guard; escort. ～하다 guard; escort. ¶ 구축함으로 ～된 상선단 a convoy of merchant ships with a destroyer escort / 경찰의 ～ 아래 under police escort / ～를 붙이다 place 《*a person*》 under escort 〔guard〕. ◉ ～경관 a police guard. ～대(隊) a security squad. ～병 a guard. ～전투기 an escort fighter. ～함(艦) an escort ship 〔vessel〕; a naval escort: ～함대 a fleet escort force.

**호유**(豪遊) extravagant merrymaking; a spree; an orgy. ～하다 go on an extravagant spree; spend money in a royal style; paint the town (red) 《구어》.

**호음**(豪飮) heavy 〔deep〕 drinking; a carouse. ～하다 drink deep 〔hard〕; swill; soak《미구어》; carouse.

**호읍**(號泣) wailing; loud lamentation; moaning. ～하다 wail; weep 〔cry〕 bitterly; lament aloud; moan.

**호응**(呼應) ① 《부름에 응함》 hailing (to) each other. ～하다 hail (to) 〔call to〕 each other. ② 《기맥상통》 response; acting in concert. ～하다 respond 《to a request》; act in concert 〔unison〕 《with》. ¶ …에 ～하여 in cooperation 〔concert, unison〕 with…; in response to… / 서로 ～해서 적을 공격하다 attack the enemy in concert. ③ 〖문법〗 concord (수·격·성·인칭의 일치); agreement. ¶ 시제(時制)의 ～ sequence of tenses / 술어 동사는 주어의 인칭과 수에 ～한다 A predicative verb agrees with its subject in number and person.

**호의**(好意) (a) goodwill; good wishes; 《친절》 favor; kindness; 《우호》 friendliness; 《알선》 good offices; courtesy. ¶ ～적인 kind; friendly; well-disposed / ～적인 사람 a well-wisher / ～로, ～적으로 out of kindness 〔goodwill〕; in a friendly way / ～적인 충고 well-meant advice / ～적인 대답 a favorable answer / …의 ～로 through the kindness 〔good offices〕 of; by the courtesy of… / ～적으로 보다 see 《*a thing*》 with a favorable eye; view 《*a thing*》 in a favorable light / 아무리 ～적으로 보아도 even when considered in a most favorable light; to say the most of it; at best / ～로써 with good intentions / ～에 보답하다 return 《*a person's*》 favor 《by》 / ～를 갖다 feel 〔entertain〕 good will 《toward》; be friendly 〔warm〕 《to》; be favorably disposed 《toward》; mean well 〔kindly〕 《to, by》; regard 《*a person*》 kindly; be sympathetic 《toward》; have a liking 《for》 / …에게 ～를 보이다 show a friendly feeling for…; show a feeling of amity toward… / ～를 저버리다 fail to return 〔respond to〕 《*a person's*》 kindness; 《무시하다》 disregard 〔ignore〕 《*a person's*》 goodwill / 그의 ～에서 나온 충고는 도리어 악의로 해석되었다 His well-meant advice was taken amiss. / 친구의 ～로 이 직업을 얻었다 I got this job through the kindness 〔good offices〕 of my friend. / 이 사진은 리처드 스미스씨의 ～로 게재되었습니다 These photographs are reproduced by courtesy of Mr. Richard Smith. / 보여주신 ～만으로도 족합니다 I will take the will for the deed.

**호의**(好誼) good 〔warm, close〕 friendship.

**호의호식**(好衣好食) living in clover. ～하다 dress well and fare richly; live well 〔in clover〕.

**호인**(好人) a good-natured person; a good and honest person. ¶ 그는 ～이지만 소심한 사람이다 He is kindhearted but timid person.

**호인**(胡人) a Manchurian.

**호장**(豪壯) ① 《호화웅장함》 grandeur; splendor; magnificence. ～하다 (be) grand; splendid; magnificent; 《저택 따위》 (be) palatial; imposing. ② 《씩씩함》 vigorousness. ～하다 (be) vigorous; brave.

**호장**(虎杖) 〖식물〗 a knotweed.

**호재(료)**(好材(料)) good material; excellent data; 〖증권〗 bullish 〔encouraging〕 factors.

**호저**(湖底) the bottom of a lake.

**호저**(豪豬) 〖동물〗 a porcupine; a hedgehog 《미》.

**호적**(戶籍) census registration; 《호적부》 a family register. ¶ ～에 올리다 put 〔enter〕 《*a person's* name》 in a family register: have 《a *person's* name》 listed 〔entered〕 in the family regis-

ter / ~에서 빼다 remove 《*a person's* name》 from a family register; have 《*a person's* name》 deleted from the family register / ~을 조사하다 inquire into 《*a person's*》 family register / 그는 ~에 양자로 되어 있다 He is registered as an adopted son.
◉ ~계원 a registrar. ~등본〔초본〕 a copy 〔an abstract〕 of *one's* family register. ~법 the Family Registration Act.

**호적**(好適) ~하다 (be) suitable; fit; good; best; ideal. ¶ 피서지로 ~하다 be ideal 〔suitable〕 for a summer resort. ◉ ~지(地) an ideal place 《for》.

**호적**(胡笛) = 날라리.

**호적**(號笛) a siren; a horn; a whistle; a hooter. ¶ ~을 불다 hoot; whistle.

**호적수**(好敵手) a good match 〔rival〕; a worthy opponent; a lively competitor. ¶ ~가 나타났다 a noticeable rival came up 《in our line of business》/ 두 팀은 ~이다 The two teams are well matched.

**호전**(好戰) bellicosity; jingoism; a pro-war inclination. ¶ ~적 jingoistic; bellicose; warlike; pro-war; militant / ~적인 국민 a warlike 〔bellicose〕 people / ~적인 사람 a trigger-happy man / ~적인 국민이라는 딱지가 붙다 be branded as a warlike nation 〔people〕/ ~적인 언사를 쓰다 employ warlike language. ◉ ~국 a warlike country.

**호전**(好轉) a turn 〔change〕 for the better; a favorable turn 〔move〕; improvement. ~하다 take a favorable turn; change 〔take a turn〕 for the better; improve; 《구어》 pick 〔look〕 up (시장경기 따위가). ¶ 식량 사정의~ improvement in the food situation / 경기가 ~하고 있다 Business is looking up. / 국면은 ~되고 있다 The tide is turning in our favor. / 그녀의 병세는 ~되었다 Her condition has improved considerably. *or* Her illness took a turn for the better.

**호접**(胡蝶) a butterfly. = 나비[1].

**호젓하다** (be) still; silent; hushed; lonely; solitary; desolate. ¶ 호젓한 거리 a deserted street / 호젓한 산길 a lonely mountain path / 호젓한 살림 a lonely life.

**호정**(糊精) 〖화학〗 dextrine.

**호조**(戶曹) 〖고제도〗 the Ministry of Finance.

**호조**(好調) a favorable 〔satisfactory〕 tone. ¶ ~의 favorable; satisfactory; 《선수 등이》 in good condition 〔shape〕; in form / ~를 보이다 progress favorably; go on smoothly; go 〔get on〕 well 《with *one's* work》/ 차츰 ~를 보이다 take a favorable turn; turn for the better; show a favorable tendency / 만사 ~를 보이고 있다 Everything is fine 〔going well〕. /「이 달의 매출은 꽤 ~롭군요」—「이대로 계속되면 좋겠는데 말이에요」 "Sales are pretty good this month, aren't they ?"—"Let's hope it continues."

**호족**(豪族) a powerful family 〔clan〕.

**호졸근하다** ⇨ 후줄근하다.

**호종**(扈從) 《거가(車駕)의》 attendance. ~하다 attend on 《a dignitary》; be in attendance on 《the king》. ¶ …을 ~하여 in attendance on 《a lord》; attending on 《*one's* master》.

**호주**(戶主) the head of a family 〔household〕; the master of a house; a householder. ¶ ~와의 관계 *one's* relation to the head of the family. ◉ ~권 the headship of a family; the leadership of a household. ~상속권 the right of succeeding 《*a person*》 as the head of a family. ~상속인 the heir(ess). ~제 the head of family system.

**호주**(好酒) love of drink. ◉ ~가〔객〕 a person who likes his drink; a hard 〔heavy〕 drinker.

**호주**(濠洲) (the Commonwealth of) Australia. ⇨ 오스트레일리아.

**호주머니** a pocket; a kick 《속어》. ¶ 뚜껑달린 ~ a flap pocket / 상의 ~ a coat pocket / 안 ~ an inside pocket / 바지 뒷~ a hip 〔back〕 pocket / 스커트의 ~ a placket / ~가 없는 pocketless 《trousers》/ ~에 들어갈 수 있는 pocketable; pocket(-size(d)) 《dictionary》/ ~를 뒤지다 search *one's* pocket; feel 〔fumble, dip〕 in *one's* pocket for 《*something*》; fish in *one's* pocket 《for》/ ~에 넣다 pocket; put 〔drop〕 《*a thing*》 in(to) *one's* pocket / ~에서 꺼내다 take 《a letter》 out of *one's* pocket; draw 《*a* newspaper》 from *one's* pocket / ~에 처〔쑤셔〕 넣다 cram 〔stuff〕 *one's* pocket 《with》/ 네 ~가 불룩하다 Your pockets are bagging. / ~가 두둑하다 [비유적] have a heavy 〔plump, well-filled〕 purse; have a fat pocketbook 〔purse〕; be flush with money / ~가 거의 비다 [비유적] have a scanty supply of money; have a light 〔an empty〕 purse / 만 원 지폐

한장을 ~에 넣고 나가다 go out with a 10,000-won bill 〔note〕 in *one's* pocket / 그는 두 손을 ~에 찌른 채 서 있었다 He stood there with his hands stuffed tight into his pocket.

◉ ~사정 *one's* financial 〔pecuniary〕 position 〔circumstances〕; *one's* finances 〔funds〕: ~ 사정이 나쁘다 be short of money; have a light purse.

**호초**(胡椒) black pepper. ⇨ 후추.

**호출**(呼出) 《불러냄》 a call; calling out; 《소환》 a summons; a subpoena. ~하다 call 《*a person*》 (out); 《법정으로》 summon; cite; subpoena; 《전화로》 call 〔ring〕 《*a person*》 up (on the phone); call 《*a person*》 to the phone. ¶ 원고〔피고〕를 ~하다 cite the plaintiff 〔defendant〕 《before the judge》 / 법정에 ~되다 be summoned to the court / (경찰 등의) ~에 응하다〔응하지 않다〕 answer 〔ignore〕 a summons / 그녀를 전화로 ~하여 그의 말을 전해 주었다 I rang her up on the phone and gave her his message.

◉ ~부호 〖통신〗 a call sign; call letters. ~신호 a call signal. ~장 a (writ of ) summons; a subpoena (벌칙을 첨가한): ~장을 보내다 serve a subpoena on 《*a person*》; serve 《*a person*》 with a summons. 자동~ an automatic calling. 무선 ~(수신)기 a beeper; a (radio) pager.

**호치**(皓齒) clean white 〔pearly〕 teeth.

**호치키스** a stapler; a stapling machine; 〖상표명〗 a Hotchikiss.

**호칭**(互稱) the name 〔title〕 that each calls the other; mutual designations.

**호칭**(呼稱) a name; a title; a designation; an appellation. ~하다 call; name; designate. ¶ 홍콩 A형이라고 ~된 유행성 감기 the influenza that is referred to as Hong Kong A.

**호콩**(胡—) a peanut. = 땅콩.

**호쾌**(豪快) ~하다 exciting; stirring; animating; heroic; dynamic; superb. ¶ ~한 인물 a large-hearted man / 그는 ~하게 웃었다 He gave a hearty laugh.

**호크** a hook. = 훅[2].

**호타**(好打) 〖야구〗 a good hit. ~하다 make a good hit; get a timely hit.

◉ ~순(順) the best part of the batting order. ~자 a good 〔nice〕 hitter; 《강타자》 a slugger.

**호탕**(豪宕) vigor and valor; a heroic temper; intrepidity. ~하다 (be) vigorous and valiant; stalwart; intrepid. ¶ ~한 웃음 a hearty 〔broad〕 laugh.

**호탕하다**(浩蕩—) (be) vast; boundless; immense.

**호텔** a hotel. ¶ ~의 로비 a hotel lobby; a lounge / ~ 생활을 하다 make *one's* home in a hotel / ~ 생활을 하는 사람 a hotel resident / ~에 묵다 put up 〔stay〕 at a hotel; check in 《미》/ ~을 경영하다 run 〔keep〕 a hotel / ~ 예약을 해 놓았습니다 I've arranged your hotel accommodation. / 그녀는 화요일에 ~에 들어가, 목요일 아침에 떠났다 She checked in at the hotel on Tuesday and checked out Thursday morning. / 나는 ~ 예약을 마쳤다 I have reserved a room in 〔at〕 a hotel. / 어느 ~에 묵고 계십니까 What hotel are you staying at 〔in〕? ◉ ~ 경영자〔지배인〕 a hotelkeeper; a hotelier. ~보이 a bellboy 《미》; a page boy 《영》. ~종업원 a hotel employee; 《사무원》 a hotel clerk; 《객실담당자》 a room clerk.

**호통** a yell; a shout; a roar. ~치다 yell; shout; roar 《at》. ¶ 일을 빨리 하라고 ~ 치다 yell 《for *a person*》 to get the job done fast / 주인의 ~바람에 혼이 나다 be startled at the yell of *one's* master / 상사가 갑자기 나에게 ~쳤다 My boss suddenly started to yell at me.

**호투**(好投) 〖야구〗 clean 〔fine, good〕 pitching. ~하다 pitch well 〔expertly〕. ¶ ~를 계속하다 keep up the good pitching / ~를 보이다 do some nice pitching.

**호패**(號牌) 〖고제도〗 an identity tag.

**호평**(好評) a favorable comment 〔reception, opinion, notice〕; public favor 〔approval〕; popularity. ¶ ~의 of good repute; well-received; popular / ~을 듣다 hear excellent accounts 《of》/ ~을 받다 be given a favorable reception; win 〔gain〕 popularity; meet with public approval; gain public 〔popular〕 favor / 신문의 ~을 받다 be favorably noticed by the press / ~이다 be popular 《with》; be highly 〔favorably〕 spoken of; enjoy (general) popularity / 그의 연설은 ~을 받았다 His speech was well received. / 이 영화는 학생간에 ~이다 This film is popular with 〔among〕 students.

◉ 대~ great public favor.

**호포**(號砲) a signal gun. ¶ ~를 쏘다 fire a signal gun.

**호프** a hope; a youth of promise. ¶ 우리 학교의 ~ the hope of our school.

**호프만방식**(一方式) 《보상금 산출의》 the Hoffmann method.

**호피**(虎皮) a tiger skin. ◉ ～ 방석 a tiger-skin cushion.

**호학**(好學) (a) love of learning; an intellectual appetite. ～하다 be fond of learning; be studious. ¶ ～의 선비 a lover of learning.

**호한**(好漢) a good 〔nice〕 fellow; a nice guy; a regular guy 《미구어》.

**호헌**(護憲) protection of 〔safeguarding〕 the Constitution. ◉ ～운동 a movement for the defense of the Constitution; a movement opposing revision of the Constitution.

**호혈**(虎穴) a tiger's den; [비유적] the jaws of death. ¶ ～에 들어가다 put 〔poke〕 *one's* head into the tiger's den 〔lion's mouth〕 / ～을 벗어나다 escape from the jaws of death.

**호협**(豪俠) chivalrousness; gallantry; bravery. ～하다 (be) chivalrous; gallant; brave; valiant. ¶ ～한 기상 chivalrous disposition; gallantry.

**호형**(弧形) an arc (shape).

**호형호제**(呼兄呼弟) close friendship. ～하다 call each other brother; be intimate with each other; be good friends.

**호혜**(互惠) mutual benefits; reciprocity. ¶ ～의 reciprocal / ～ 평등의 원칙 the principle of equality and reciprocity. ◉ ～관세율 a reciprocal tariff. ～무역 reciprocal trading: ～ 무역협정 a fair 〔reciprocal〕 trade agreement. ～조약 a reciprocal treaty. ～주의 the principle 〔spirit〕 of reciprocity. ～ 통상 조약 a reciprocal-trade pact.

**호호**[1] 《입김을》 blowing and blowing; puff-puff. ¶ 추워서 손을 ～ 불다 warm *one's* hands with *one's* breath; blow on *one's* hands to keep them warm.

**호호**[2] 《웃음》 Hee-hee!; ha-ha!; with giggles. ～하다, ～거리다 giggle and giggle. 「호호.

**호호**(戶戶) every 〔each〕 house. ⇨ 가가

**호호백발**(皓皓白髮) hoary 〔snow-white〕 hair; 《사람》 a white-haired old man.

**호화**(豪華) splendor; gorgeousness; pomp; luxury; extravagance. ～롭다 (be) splendid; gorgeous; grand (장대한); magnificent (장려한); pompous; luxurious (사치스러운); elegant; deluxe. ¶ ～ 생활 an extravagant life / ～롭게 살다 live in 「luxury 〔grand style〕 / 어젯밤의 파티는 ～판이었다 We had a big 〔grand〕 party yesterday evening. / 국

---

**참고** 호텔에 관한 영어

1. 호텔 종류
일반 호텔 a hotel / 단기 체류용의 호텔 a transient hotel / 장기 체류용의 호텔 a resident 〔residential〕 hotel / 자동차 여행자를 위한 간이 호텔 a motel; a motor hotel / 유스 호스텔 a youth hostel (자전거·도보 여행자를 위한 값싼 숙박소) / 일류 호텔 a first-rate〔-class〕 hotel / 호화 호텔 a deluxe hotel / 최고급 호텔 a five-star hotel.

2. 객실과 내부 구조
1인용 객실 a single; a single(-bedded) room / 2인용 객실 a twin(-bedded) room / 3인용 객실 a triple(=bedded) room / 스위트 a suite (두 칸으로 되어 있는 특별실) / 욕실이 딸린〔안 딸린〕 객실 a room with 〔without〕 a private bathroom.

3. 요금
객실 요금 room charges 〔rates〕; 《객실 요금만 받는 경우》 European Plan (생략 EP) / 《일박 2식의 경우》 Modified American Plan (생략 MAP) / 《일박 3식의 경우》 American Plan (생략 AP); full-pension 〔board〕 / 《간단한 아침 식사만 제공되는 경우》 Continental Plan (생략 CP) / 서비스 요금 service charge / 《단체 여행 중의》 개인별 계산 personal account / 잡부금 miscellaneous 〔incidental〕 charges.

4. 담당 부서·사람·장소
프런트 the front desk; the reception (desk) / 프런트 담당자 a front desk clerk / 예약 담당자 a reservation clerk / 회계 담당자 the cashier / 포터 a porter / 보이 a bellboy; a bellhop; a page boy 《영》 / 《식당의》 웨이터 a waiter (남자); a waitress (여자) / 객실 담당 종업원 (a) room service; a chambermaid (여자) / 전화 교환수 an operator / 로비 lobby / 식당 dining room; a restaurant / 간이 식당 a coffee shop / 연회실 a banquet hall.

5. 절차
예약 (a hotel) reservation / 예약 재확인 reconfirmation / 예약 상황(狀況) reservation status / 예약 취소 (요금) cancel (charge); cancellation / 체크인(절차) 《숙박을 위한》 the check-in (procedure) / 체크아웃 (절차) 《퇴숙할 때의》 the check-out (procedure) / 숙박 카드 a registration card.

세청은 정당한 수입원이 없이 ～ 생활을 하는 사람들에게 추가적인 무거운 소득세를 부과했다 The Office of National Tax Administration has imposed additional heavy income taxes on persons who enjoy 'extravagant' life without due income sources. ◉ ～선(船) a luxury liner. ～주택 a palatial mansion. ～판(版) (a) deluxe edition.

**호화찬란**(豪華燦爛) ～하다 (be) gorgeous; brilliant; gaudy; dazzling; sumptuous. ¶ ～한 신부 의상 an absolutely gorgeous 「bridal 〔wedding〕 costume.

**호환**(虎患) disaster caused by tigers; the ravages of tigers.

**호황**(好況) a prosperous condition; prosperity; a boom; a brisk market. ¶ ～의 prosperous; favorable / ～의 산업계 the industrial world under boom conditions / ～과 불황의 순환 the cycle of boom and bust / ～이다 be prosperous; be in a prosperous condition; be 「booming 〔flourishing〕/ ～을 누리다 enjoy a favorable business 「climate 〔conditions〕 / ～의 조짐을 보이다 show signs of prosperity; present a favorable aspect / 한국의 자동차 산업은 ～이다 The Korean car industry is 「flourishing 〔thriving, booming〕. (★ flourishing은 최고의 번성기, thriving은 유리한 조건하에서의 번영, booming은 일시적인 경기 상승) / 전자 산업은 ～에 접어들고 있다 Electronic industry is 「picking up 〔taking a turn for the better〕.
◉ ～국면(局面) a booming stage: ～ 국면에 접어들다 enter a booming stage. ～산업 a boom(ing) industry. ～시대 prosperous 「days 〔times〕; boom days 《미》; flush times.

**호흡**(呼吸) ① 《숨》 a breath; breathing; respiration. ～하다 breathe; respire. ¶ 심〔복식〕～ deep 〔abdominal〕 breathing / 인공～ artificial respiration / ～할 때마다 at every inhale of *one's* breath / ～이 곤란하다 have difficulty in breathing; breathe 「hard 〔with difficulty〕 / 심～을 하다 breathe deeply; take a deep breath / 코로 ～하다 breathe through the nose / ～이 거칠다 breathe hard; pant for breath / 이제 ～하기가 많이 편해졌다 I'm breathing more easily now. / 그의 ～이 멎었다 He stopped breathing.
② 《일의 장단》 time; rhythm; tune. ¶ ～이 맞다 be in rhythm; be in harmony 《with》; work in perfect harmony / ～을 맞추다 keep 「step 〔time〕 《with》; act in concert 《with》 / 그 사람과는 ～이 잘 맞지 않는다 I don't get along very well with him. / 두 사람은 ～이 잘 맞아서 일이 순조롭게 진행되었다 The two (men) worked together in harmony, and the work proceeded smoothly.
◉ ～곤란 difficulty in breathing; difficult breathing; laboring breath: ～ 곤란에 빠지다 lapse into dyspnea; become unable to breathe. ～기(器) 《기관》 (the) respiratory organs; 《계통》 the respiratory system: ～기 (계통의) 질환 respiratory ailments; pulmonary disease / 급성 ～기 질환 acute respiratory disease (생략 ARD). ～기능 the respiratory function. ～력(力) inhaling capacity. ～보조기 a breathing apparatus; a breathing aid; a respirator (장치). ～수(數) a breath rate. ～운동 breathing exercise: ～ 운동 기록기 a spirograph; a pneumograph; a pneumatograph. ～작용 『동·식물』 respiration. ～정지 『의학』 apn(o)ea. ～중추 《뇌의》 the respiratory center. ～촉박(促迫) gasping; being broken-winded. 정상～ 『의학』 eupn(o)ea.

**혹**[1] 《병적인》 a lump; a swelling; a wen (특히 머리 부분의); 《군살》 an excrescence; an outgrowth; 『의학』 vegetation; 《부딪쳐서 생긴》 a bump; an abscess; 《나무의》 a 「knot 〔knob〕 on a tree; a gnarl; 《낙타의》 a hump.
¶ 얼굴 오른쪽에 혹이 있다 have a wen on the right side of *one's* face / 혹투성이 나무 a 「knotty 〔gnarled〕 tree / 혹 떼러 갔다 혹 붙여 오다 try to get rid of trouble and end up with twice as much; go for wool and come home shorn / 혹이 가라 앉았다 The bump has gone down.

**혹**[2] 《마시는 소리》 with a 「breath 〔gulp〕; 《부는 소리》 《blowing》 with a puff.

**혹**(或) ① 《혹간》 sometimes; at times; rarely; occasionally; now and then.
¶ 혹 내가 그를 찾아가기도 하고 혹 그가 찾아 오기도 한다 Sometimes I go to see him, and sometimes he comes to see me. / 혹 틈이 있으면 책을 읽는다 I read books once in a while when I have time. ② 《어쩌면》 maybe; perhaps; possibly; by 「any 〔some〕 chance. ¶ 혹 그의 말이 옳을는지도 모른다 Maybe what he says is right. ③ 《또는》 or; or else; either... or. ¶ 이달 혹은 내달에 either this month or next / A 혹은 B

를 취할 수 있다 We can take A or B, either one.

**혹간**(或間) sometimes; once in a while; rarely. ¶ ～ 영화 구경을 가다 go to the movies once in a while 〔rarely〕.

**혹독**(酷毒) severity; harshness; cruelty. ～하다 (be) severe; harsh; cruel; stern; merciless. ¶ ～한 사람 a harsh person / ～한 추위 severe 〔intense, bitter〕 cold; biting 〔severely〕 cold weather / ～한 비평 a severe criticism / ～한 처사를 하다 do《*a person*》 a bad turn; treat《*a person*》 badly.

**혹부리** a person who has a wen 〔growth〕 (on his face).

**혹사**(酷使) exploitation; harsh 〔rough〕 treatment; driving 〔working〕《*a person*》 hard. ～하다 work 〔drive〕《*a person*》 hard; sweat《*one's* workers》; be a hard master. ¶ ～당하는 노동자 down trodden workers / ～하는 사람 a hard master 〔mistress〕 / 육체〔두뇌〕의 ～ an immoderate use of *one's* physical 〔mental〕 power; abuse of *one's* body 〔brain〕 / 두뇌를 ～하다 overstrain 〔overtax〕 *one's* brains / 몸을 ～하다 overwork 〔overdrive〕 *oneself;* work too much / 눈을 ～하다 overwork *one's* eyes; use *one's* eyes too much / (물건이) ～에 견디다 「stand (up to) 〔withstand〕 rough use / 그 회사는 싼 임금으로 근로자를 ～한다 That company underpays and overworks 〔sweats〕 its employees.

**혹서**(酷暑) brutal 〔intense, severe, torrid, withering, wilting〕 heat. ¶ ～의 계절 the hot season; the hottest weather / ～에 견디다 stand the heat of summer / ～에 몸조심하십시오 Please take good care of yourself in this terrible heat. / 그는 도시의 ～를 피해서 동해안으로 갔다 He went to East Shore to escape the intense heat of the city.

**혹설**(或說) one opinion; a certain view 「(put forward).

**혹성**(惑星) 〚천문〛 a planet. ＝행성(行星).

**혹세무민**(惑世誣民) ～하다 delude the world and deceive the people.

**혹시**(或是)《행여나》 if; in case《of》;《걱정하여》 lest... should...;《어쩌면》 maybe; perhaps; possibly; by any chance 〔possibility〕. ¶ ～ 비가 오면 if it rains; in case of rain / ～ …하지나 않을까 하여 for fear of... 〔that... may ...〕 / ～ 하고 걱정했던 일이 사실이 되었다 My fear has come true. *or* The worst that we feared has happened. / ～ 김군을 아십니까 Do you happen to know Mr. Kim (by any chance)? / ～ 그가 올지도 모르겠다 He may possibly come. / ～ 못 오시는거나 아닌가 걱정했습니다 I was just becoming nervous lest you should disappoint us. / ～ 그를 만날 수 있을까 해서 역에서 기다렸다 I waited at the station on the chance of meeting him. / ～ 댁에 계시지나 않나 해서 들러 보았습니다 I came on the (off=) chance 「of finding you at home 〔that I might find you at home〕. / ～ K씨의 주소를 아시는지요 Don't you happen to know Mr. K's address? / ～ 낸시가 아닌가요 Are you Nancy by any chance?

**혹심**(酷甚) being extreme 〔severe〕. ～하다 (be) extreme; severe. ¶ ～하게 extremely; severely / ～한 더위 severe 〔intense〕 heat / ～한 피해를 입다 suffer heavy losses.

**혹염**(酷炎) ＝혹서(酷暑). 「rumen.

**혹위**(―胃)《소 따위의》 a paunch; a

**혹자**(或者)《어떤 사람》 some(one); a certain person. ¶ ～는 그렇게들 말한다 Some people say so.

**혹평**(酷評) (a) severe 〔harsh, bitter, scathing, sharp〕 criticism; strictures; a cruel remark. ～하다 criticize severely; pass harsh 〔incisive〕 criticism 《on》; pass strictures《on》; castigate. ¶ 그의 최근 소설은 ～을 받았다 His latest novel was subjected to severe 〔harsh〕 critisism. ◉ ～가 a severe critic; a hypercritic.

**혹하다**(惑―) ①《반하다》 be madly in love《with》; lose *one's* heart to; be taken《with her, by her beauty》;《빠지다》 get 〔be〕 infatuated with《a woman》; be captivated 〔fascinated〕 by《a woman's beauty》; fall a victim to《a woman's charm》.
②《미혹되다》 be deluded 〔misled, led into error, trapped〕. ¶ 무당의 말에 ～ be deluded by a shaman's predictions.

**혹한**(酷寒) brutal 〔severe, intense, bitter, extreme〕 cold; a hard 〔severe〕 winter. ¶ ～지절에 in this coldest season; in these days of midwinter / ～에 견디다 endure 〔stand〕 the intense cold.

**혹형**(酷刑) a severe 〔cruel, extreme〕 punishment 〔penalty〕. ¶ ～을 과하다 punish severely; inflict a severe punishment《on》.

**혹혹**《마시는 모양》 with gulp after gulp;

sipping noisily; 《부는 모양》 puffing and puffing. ¶ ～ 불다 puff and blow.

**혼**(魂) a soul; a spirit; 《귀신》 a ghost. ¶ 혼이 담긴 soulful 《poem》 / 혼을 담다 give life to; put life into; breathe life into / 혼을 부르다 call back the spirit of a deceased person / 혼이 나가다 the spirit 〔soul〕 departs the body; 《멍하다》 be absent-minded / 죽음은 육체와 혼을 갈라 놓는다 Death separates the soul from the body.

**혼가**(婚家) the family that has a wedding.

**혼겁**(魂怯) extreme astonishment; funk. ～하다 be astonished; be startled 〔appalled〕; be all broken up 《by》.

**혼곤**(昏困) ～하다 (be) drowsy; lethargic.

**혼구**(婚具) utensils used in a wedding ceremony; wedding equipment.

**혼구멍내다**(魂—) ＝혼내다.

**혼기**(婚期) (the) marriageable age; nubility. ¶ ～가 되다 be of marriageable age; reach a marriageable age / ～가 된 딸 a marriageable daughter / ～를 놓치다 lose 〔miss〕 a chance of marriage; be past (the) marriageable age; become an old maid.

**혼나다**(魂—) ① 《놀라다》 get frightened out of *one's* wits; be startled 〔horrified, scared〕. ¶ 개한테 ～ get frightened by a dog. ② 《호된 경험을 하다》 have bitter experience; have an awful 〔a hell of a〕 time; have 〔get〕 the worst of it; be hard put to it; have a hard 〔bad〕 time (of it) 《with *a person*》 (★ 이 it는 뜻이 없는 관용적 표현임). ¶ 경관한테 ～ get 「roughed up 〔grilled〕 by a policeman / 시험치르느라 ～ sweat out an exam / 아버지한테 ～ catch 〔get〕 hell from *one's* father; be severely scolded by *one's* father / 아버지가 알게 되면 혼날 게다 「It will go hard with him 〔He'll catch hot〕 if his father learns about it.

**혼내다**(魂—) ① 《놀래주다》 frighten 《*a person*》 out of *his* wits; startle; horrify; scare. ¶ 여기 숨었다가 그 애가 지나가면 혼내 주자 Let's hide here and give him a start when he comes by. ② 《맛을 보이다》 make 《*a person*》 smart; make 《*a person*》 pay dear 〔for〕; give 《*a person*》 a hard time; give 《*a person*》 an awful 〔"a hell of a"〕 time; do 〔serve〕 《*a person*》 a bad 〔an ill〕 turn; teach 《*a person*》 a lesson. ¶ 돈을 받으려면 그를 한번 혼을 내야 한다 We will have to teach him a good lesson if we want to get our money back. / 이 녀석을 단단히 혼내줘야지 I'll bring him to cry mercy. *or* He shall smart for this.

**혼담**(婚談) a marriage proposal; an offer of marriage; a proposal to introduce prospective marriage partners (중매의). ¶ ～을 꺼내다 propose (marriage) 《to》; make a proposal of marriage; bring word of a prospective marriage partner / ～을 깨다 wreck 〔break up〕 the plans for a marriage / ～을 거절하다 refuse 〔decline〕 an offer of marriage / ～이 있다 have an offer of marriage / ～이 쏟아져 들어오다 be flooded with offers of marriage.

**혼도**(昏倒) a faint; a swoon. ～하다 faint (away); fall unconscious; fall into a swoon; have a fainting fit.

**혼돈**(混沌) chaos; nebulosity; confusion; disorder. ～하다 (be) chaotic; nebulous; confused; disorderly. ¶ ～상태에 빠뜨리다 reduce to a chaotic state; throw into confusion / ～ 상태에 있다 be in chaos 〔confusion, a chaotic condition〕.

**혼동**(混同) mixing; confusion. ～하다 confuse 〔confound, mix up〕 《*one thing* with *another*》; mistake 《A》 for 《B》. ¶ ～하여 indiscriminately; confusedly / 공사를 ～하다 confuse 〔mix up〕 public and private matters / 남의 이름을 ～하다 confuse 〔mix up〕 names / 목적과 수단을 ～하다 confound 〔confuse〕 the means with the end; confuse means and ends / 자유와 방종을 ～하다 confuse liberty with license; take license for liberty.

**혼뜨다**(魂—) be amazed 〔astounded〕; be frightened out of *one's* wits; be terrified out of *one's* senses; be stupefied with amazement; be in a state of abstraction.

**혼란**(混亂) confusion; disorder; commotion; chaos; a mix-up 《구어》. ～하다 (be) confused; disorderly; chaotic; [서술적] be thrown into confusion 〔disorder〕; be in confusion; be a mess. ¶ 정치적 ～ political chaos / ～을 틈타 taking advantage of the confusion / ～시키다 confuse; disorder; throw into confusion / ～통에 한 몫 벌다 fish in troubled waters / (일대) ～을 일으키다〔가져오다〕 give rise to 〔lead to, result in〕 (great) confusion / 사회적 ～을 조장하다 foment social disorder / 온 도시가 ～에 빠져

있다 The whole city is plunged in confusion. *or* The whole city is 「turned upside down 〔in utter confusion〕. / 한때 큰 ～을 보였다 There was a great confusion for a time. / 국민 경제는 인플레로 ～해졌다 The national economy was dislocated by inflation. ◉ ～상태 a state of confusion: ～ 상태에 빠지다 be thrown into confusion 〔disarray〕 / ～ 상태에 있다 be in (a state of ) disorder 〔confusion〕.

**혼령**(魂靈) the spirit (of the dead); 《*a person's*》 departed soul; the soul.

**혼례**(婚禮) a marriage 〔wedding, nuptial〕 ceremony; a wedding; nuptials. ¶ ～의 선물 a wedding 〔marriage〕 present 〔gift〕 / ～를 치르다 solemnize a marriage / ～에 초대받다〔참석하다〕 be invited to 〔present at〕 a wedding.

**혼매**(昏昧) stupidity; idiocy; ignorance. ～하다 (be) ignorant; silly; stupid.

**혼문**(混文) 〖문법〗 a mixed sentence; a compound-complex sentence.

**혼미**(昏迷) stupefaction; (bewildering) confusion; 〖의학〗 stupor. ～하다 (be) stupefied; confused. ¶ ～ 상태에 in a fuddled state / ～ 상태에 빠지다 be thrown into confusion / ～해지다 lose *one's* consciousness / ～케 하다 confuse; bewilder; stupefy / 정계는 매우 심한 ～ 상태에 있다 The political circles are in wild confusion.

**혼방**(混紡) mixed 〔blended〕 spinning. ¶ ～의 mixed(-spun) 《fabrics》 / 화학섬유 30퍼센트 ～의 with 30% chemical fiber mixed / 면 20%의 ～ 모직물 woolen stuff with 20% cotton mixed / 이 코트는 모와 화학섬유의 ～이다 This coat is of wool and chemical fiber. ◉ ～사(糸) mixed 〔blended〕 yarn.

**혼백**(魂帛) a silk spirit-tablet. ◉ ～상자 a case in which the spirit-tablet is kept.

**혼백**(魂魄) the soul; the spirit; the ghost. ¶ 그의 ～은 아직도 이승을 떠돌고 있다 His spirit is still haunting this world.

**혼비백산**(魂飛魄散) ～하다 get frightened out of *one's* senses; be scared out of *one's* wits.

**혼사**(婚事) a marital 〔matrimonial〕 matter.

**혼색**(混色) a mixed 〔compound〕 color; a color blend; a color mixture.

**혼서**(婚書) a marriage letter sent to the bride's family from the bridegroom's family.

**혼선**(混線) ① 《전신·전화의》 cross; entanglement of wires; 〖전기〗 contact. ～하다 get entangled 〔mixed up〕; get 〔have〕 a crossed line (전화가). ¶ ～이 돼 있다 《전화가》 The wires 〔lines〕 are mixed. *or* The lines are crossed. *or* 《라디오가》 The radio signals are jammed up. / ～으로 그와 통화가 되지 않는다 The wires are crossed, and I can't get him. ② 《혼란》 confusion. ～하다 confuse. ¶ 그의 이야기는 자주 ～이 된다 His talks often get mixed up. ◉ ～상태 confusion; a mess. 간헐～ 〖전기〗 intermittent contact.

**혼성**(混成) mixture; composition; 〖영화〗 mixing; 〖언어〗 blending; contamination; hybridization. ～하다 mix; mingle; compound. ¶ ～의 mixed; compound; composite. ◉ ～곡 a medley. ～물 《혼합물》 a mixture; 《합성물》 a compound; a medley. ～어 a hybrid (word); a blend; a portmanteau word. ～여단 a mixed 〔composite〕 brigade. ～열차 a composite train. ～주 a mixed drink; a cocktail. ～재배 ⇨ 혼작(混作). ～팀 a combined team: 연세·고려대의 ～팀 the Yŏnsei-Korea combined team.

**혼성**(混聲) 〖음악〗 《a work for》 mixed voices. ◉ ～(4부)합창 a mixed chorus (in four voice parts).

**혼솔** broad-stitched seams.

**혼수**(昏睡) a coma; a trance; stupor; sinking; lethargic sleep; 〖의학〗 lethargy. ¶ ～의 comatose; lethargic(al). ◉ ～상태 a comatose state; a lethargic condition: ～ 상태에 빠지다 become unconscious; fall 〔slip〕 into a comatose state; lapse into a coma / ～ 상태에 있다 be in a state of coma / 그는 벌써 3일 동안이나 깊은 ～상태에 있다 He has been in a deep coma for three days.

**혼수**(婚需) articles 〔expenses〕 essential to a marriage.

**혼식**(混食) ～하다 《주식과 부식의》 have rice together with various side dishes (for a nutricious diet); 《쌀과 잡곡의》 eat (boiled) rice with other cereals.

**혼신**(混信) 〖전기〗 jamming; (an) interference; a cross tone; crosstalk.

**혼신**(渾身) the whole body. ¶ ～의 힘을 다하여 with all *one's* might; with might and main; by using all *one's* strength / ～의 힘을 내다 put forth every ounce of *one's* energies; put *one's* energy into 《*one's* work》.

**혼약**(婚約) an engagement. ＝약혼(約婚).

**혼연**(渾然) wholly; in perfect harmony. ¶ ~ 일체가 되다 be united 〔jointed〕 together; form 〔constitute〕 a perfect 〔complete, harmonious〕 whole.

**혼영**(混泳) a medley (race). ¶ 400m 개인 ~ 《win》 the individual 400-meter medley (race).

**혼외**(婚外) ¶ ~의 extramarital; extra-matrimonial. ◉ ~정사 extramarital sex 〔(sexual) relations〕.

**혼욕**(混浴) mixed bathing. ~하다 《men and women》 bathe together.

**혼용**(混用) ~하다 use 《*one thing*》 together with 《*another*》; mix 《A and B》. ¶ 한글과 한자를 ~하다 use *Hangŭl* at the same time with Chinese characters / 미국 영어와 영국 영어의 ~은 바람직하지 않다 It is not advisable to mix American English and British English.

**혼인**(婚姻) marriage. ⇨ 결혼. ¶ ~을 빙자한 간음 행위 the behavior of inducing women into sexual relations under the pretext of marriage / ~시키다 marry 《*one's* daughter to a rich man》; give 《*one's* daughter》 away (in marriage) 《to》 / 그 ~은 파탄이 났다 The marrige broke up. ◉ ~미사 a nuptial mass. ~신고 a report of marriage; a marriage registration: ~신고하다 register *one's* marriage. ~잔치 a wedding reception. ~집 a house 〔family〕 with a wedding occuring.

**혼입**(混入) ~하다 《섞다》 mix 《A with B, A and B》; mingle; 《섞어지다》 get mixed 《with》.

**혼자** 《한 사람》 one person; 《홀몸》 a single person; [부사적] alone; by *oneself* (혼자서); for *oneself* (혼자 힘으로). ¶ ~의 single; sole; only / ~ 걷다 go alone 〔all by *oneself*〕 / ~ 결정하다 decide by *oneself* / ~ 결정해서 하다 do 《it》 on *one's* own authority / ~ 남다 be left alone 〔to *oneself*〕 / ~ 떠맡다 undertake alone 〔single-handed〕 / ~ 이익을 차지하다 get all the benefits without division; monopolize the profit / ~ (몸이) 되다 be left alone; be left to *oneself;* 《의지할 데 없이》 be thrown on *one's* own resources 〔devices〕; have no one to care for / ~ 살다 live alone 〔by *oneself*〕; lead a solitary life; 《배우자 없이》 live 〔remain〕 single; live a single 〔a bachelor('s), a spinster('s)〕 life / ~ 식사하다 eat by *oneself;* sit down to dinner all by *oneself* / ~ 웃다 smile 〔chuckle〕 to *oneself* / ~ 있기를 좋아하다 love solitude; adore *one's* own company / ~ 여행(을)하다 travel 「alone 〔by *oneself,* without a companion〕; make a solitary journey / 일을 ~ 하다 work alone; do all the work by *oneself* / ~ 중얼거리다 mutter 〔mumble〕 to *oneself* / ~ 차지하다 have 《a large room》 to *oneself* / (남에게 의지하지 않고) ~(서) 해나가다 be independent; paddle *one's* own canoe 〔boat〕 / ~ 왔습니다 I have come all by myself. / 공부는 ~하지 않으면 안 된다 You must study (by) yourself. / 그는 낡은 오두막에 ~ 살고 있다 He lives by himself in an old cottage. / 이 아기는 이제 ~ 걸을 수 있다 This child can now walk by itself. / 그렇게 늦은 밤에 여자 ~ 외출하는 것은 위험하다 It is dangerous for a woman to go out 「by herself 〔alone〕 so late at night.

**혼작**(混作) 『농업』 (growing) mixed crops; mixed cultivation; crop-mixing. ~하다 grow as mixed crops; raise 〔cultivate〕 together.

**혼잡**(混雜) 《혼란》 confusion; disorder; 《붐빔》 a crush; crowdedness; congestion; bustle. ~스럽다, ~하다 be in confusion 〔disorder, a bustle〕; (be) confused; disordered; be at sixes and sevens; (be) crowded; congested; bustling; be jammed up (with people). ¶ 아침〔저녁〕의 ~한 시간 the morning 〔evening〕 rush hours / ~을 틈타 in the confusion of the moment; taking advantage of the confusion / ~ 속에서 in the confusion / ~ 속을 헤치고 나아가다 push *one's* way through a crowd / ~ 속에 휩쓸리다 be lost in the crowd / 교통의 ~을 완화하다 relieve traffic congestion 〔jam〕 / 큰 도시의 ~을 피하다 get away from the hustle and bustle of a big city / 도시의 거리는 ~하다 The streets of cities are congested. / 매일 아침 서울로 이어지는 모든 도로는 차로 ~하다 Every morning automobiles congest all the roads leading to 〔into〕 Seoul. ◉ ~통행료 《교통의》 congestion fees.

**혼잣말** talking to *oneself;* a soliloquy; a monolog(ue). ~하다 talk 〔speak, mutter〕 to *oneself;* think aloud; soliloquize. (★ say to *oneself*라고 하면 「마음 속으로 생각하다」란 뜻이 되며, 소리를 내어 말하는 뜻으로 쓰이지 않는 것이 보통임). ¶ 중얼중얼 ~을 하다 mutter 〔mumble〕 to *oneself* / 그녀는 자주 ~을 한다 She often talks to herself.

**혼잣손** a single hand; single-handedness. ¶ ～으로 by *one's* own effort / ～으로 일하다 work single-handed; do 《*a thing*》 single-handed.

**혼전**(婚前) ¶ ～의 premarital / ～에 before marriage. ◉ ～성관계 premarital sex; premarital (sexual) relations 《with》.

**혼전**(混戰) a mixed-up 〔confused, tangled〕 fight; a melee; a scuffle; an imbroglio; a free-for-all (fight). ～하다 fight in confusion; have a free=for-all; get into a tangle 〔an imbroglio〕. ¶ 금년의 우승기 쟁탈전은 ～이었다 This year's pennant race has been in confusion.

**혼절**(昏絶) fainting; a swoon. ～하다 faint; swoon; fall unconscious.

**혼종**(混種) ¶ ～의 half-breed〔-bred〕; half-blood(ed) 《sheep》.

**혼쭐나다**(魂—) ① 《혼나다》 get scared 〔startled〕; be struck dumb; have a hard 〔rough〕 time (of it) 《with *a person*》. ⇨ 혼나다 ①②. ② 《황홀감으로》 be transported 〔entranced〕; be fascinated.

**혼처**(婚處) a marriageable family or person.

**혼천의**(渾天儀) 〖천문〗 an armillary sphere; an astrolabe.

**혼취**(昏醉) dead-drunkenness; inebriation; intoxication. ～하다 get dead drunk; be intoxicated 〔boozy〕.

**혼탁**(混濁·溷濁) muddiness; impurity; turbidity. ～하다 (be) muddy; turbid; thick; cloudy; dull. ¶ ～한 공기 foul air / ～한 세상 the corrupt world / ～하지 않은 마음 pure heart / 물을 ～하게 하다 muddle water.

**혼합**(混合) mixing; mixture; admixture; intermixture. ～하다 mix; mingle; blend; compound; intermix; commingle. ¶ ～하기 쉬운 mixible; easy to mix / ～하기 어려운 unmixible / 물과 술을 ～하다 mingle wine and water / 색깔이 잘 ～되지 않는다 The colors don't mingle well. / 물과 기름은 ～되지 않는다 Oil and water will not blend 〔mix〕. ◉ ～경기 a mixed competition 〔race〕; a medley. ～경제 mixed economy. ～기 a mixer. ～교육 mixed education; coeducation. ～물 a mixture; a blend; a medley; a compound; an amalgam; alloy. ～비 the mixture ratio. ～비료 compost; compound manure; mixed fertilizer. ～색 a mixed color. ～세 mixed (tax=) duties. ～양식 〖건축〗 the composite order. ～주 blended liquor; mixed spirits; a mixed drink; a cocktail.

**혼행**(婚行) a marriage procession. ～하다 go to the house of *one's* bride 〔bridegroom〕 to perform the wedding.

**혼혈**(混血) mixed blood 〔breed〕; racial mixture. ¶ ～의 《*a person*》 of mixed blood 〔race〕; half-breed / 그는 황인종과 흑인종의 ～이다 He was born of mongoloid and negroid parentage. ◉ ～아 a child of mixed race 〔parentage〕; a mixed-blood; a half-breed 〔=blood〕; a half-caste; a Eurasian (동·서양인의); an Amerasian (미국·아시아인의); a mulatto (흑·백인의): ～아 문제 the problem of mixed blood / 한국인과 미국인의 ～아 a half-Korean half=American child 〔boy, girl〕. ～종 ⇨ 잡종.

**혼혼하다**(昏昏—) (be) confused; muddled; unconscious; dark; be in a stupor.

**혼화**(混化) compound; blend. ～하다 be made into a compound; compound 《with》; blend into.

**혼화**(混和) mixture; mingling; blend. ～하다 mix; blend; compound; mingle.

**혼효**(混淆) mixing; mixture; confusion; a medley; a jumble; a mess; a tangle. ～하다 mix up; mingle; confuse; jumble 〔huddle〕 together; be confused 〔jumbled, tangled〕; be mixed 〔messed〕 up.

**홀**(笏) a (flat) baton; a scepter 〔sceptre 《영》〕.

**홀**[1] 《큰 방·로비》 a hall. ¶ 댄스～ a dance hall / 콘서트～ a concert hall.

**홀**[2] 〖골프〗 a hole; a cup. ¶ 공을 홀에 넣다 hole a ball. ◉ 홀인원 《get, make》 a hole in one.

**홀-** 《짝 없음》 single. ¶ 홀몸 a single man 〔woman〕.

**홀가분하다** (be) light; free and easy; unencumbered. ¶ 홀가분한 행장 a light traveling outfit / 홀가분한 살림 an unencumbered life / 홀가분한 기분으로 with a light heart / 몸차림이 ～ be lightly dressed / 몸〔마음〕이 ～ be unencumbered; feel free and easy / 홀아비여서 홀가분한 몸이다 I'm a widower and have no one dependent on me. / 시험이 끝나 마음이 홀가분했다 I felt a load off my mind when the examination was over.

**홀꽃노루발** 〖식물〗 a singleblossom pyrola.

**홀대**(忽待) inhospitable 〔unkind〕 treatment; neglecting; slighting. ～하다 treat 《*a person*》 unkindly 〔inhospitably〕; neglect 〔slight〕 《*a person*》.

¶ 손님을 ~하다 treat a guest unkindly; neglect a guest.

**홀딩** 《배구·축구·권투 따위에서》 holding.

**홀딱** ① 《벗는 모양》 《removing *a thing*》 completely; nakedly. ¶ ~ 벗고 《go》 stark-naked; with nothing on; in *one's* bare skin / 옷을 ~ 벗다 take *one's* clothes off completely; strip *oneself* bare 〔stark-naked〕; become stark-naked; strip *oneself* completely; slip off *one's* clothes / 머리가 ~ 벗어지다 *one's* head is as bald as an egg. ② 《뒤집는 모양》 《turning *a thing*》 inside out. ¶ 저고리를 ~ 뒤집다 turn *one's* coat inside out / 바람에 ~ 뒤집힌 우산 an umbrella blown inside 〔wrong side〕 out by the wind. ③ 《반하는 모양》 deeply; madly; up to the neck. ¶ ~ 반하다 be deeply 〔madly〕 in love 《with》; lose *one's* heart 《to》; be over (head and) ears in love 《with》; be up to the ears in love 《with》 / 그는 그녀에게 ~ 반했다 He is awfully struck on her. *or* He is dead gone on her. ④ 《속은 모양》 successfully; fairly; nicely; completely. ¶ ~ 속아 넘어가다 be nicely 〔fairly〕 taken in; fall an easy victim to 《*another's*》 trick.

**홀란드** Holland. ⇨ 네덜란드.

**홀랑** ① 《죄다 드러나는 모양》 all naked. ¶ 옷을 ~ 벗다 strip *oneself* all naked / 가슴이 ~ 드러나다 *one's* breasts are exposed naked. ② 《헐겁게 들어가는 모양》 loosely; easily. ¶ ~ 들어가다 slip into place.

**홀랑거리다** ⇨ 훌렁거리다.

**홀로** single; alone; by *oneself;* single-handed. ⇨ 혼자. ¶ ~되다 become 〔be left〕 a widows/ ~살다 live alone; remain single / ~ 싸우다 fight alone 〔single-handed〕 / ~ 외출하다 go out by *oneself.*

**홀로그래피** 《입체 사진술》 holography.

**홀로그램** 《입체 화상》 a hologram.

**홀리다** ① 《귀신·악마 등에》 get possessed 《by, with》; be obsessed 《by》; be bewitched 《by》; be devil-possessed. ¶ 귀신에게 ~ be possessed by a demon / 여우에 ~ be bewitched 〔befooled〕 by a fox / 마치 무엇에 홀린 사람처럼 as if possessed by some devil or other. ② 《이성에게》 get infatuated 〔captivated, bewitched〕. ¶ 여자한테 ~ get infatuated with a woman; be gone on a woman. ③ 《현혹되다》 get tempted; be deluded 〔tricked, deceived, seduced〕. ¶ 돈에 홀려 나쁜 짓을 하다 be tempted by money to do wrong.

**홀맺다** tie 〔knot〕 《*a thing*》 securely.

**홀몸** 《단신》 a single person; 《독신》 an unmarried person; a bachelor (남자); a spinster (여자); a bachelor girl. ¶ 평생을 ~으로 지내다 remain single all *one's* life.

**홀보드르르하다, 홀보들하다** be delicate and soft.

**홀소리** 〚언어〛 a vowel. ⇨ 모음(母音).

**홀수**(一數) an odd 〔uneven〕 number.

**홀스타인** 《젖소 품종》 a Holstein (cow).

**홀시**(忽視) contempt; neglect; negligence. ~하다 despise; make light of; slight; treat lightly; snub.

**홀씨** 〚식물〛 a spore. ⇨ 포자(胞子).

**홀아비** a widower. ¶ ~는 이가 서 말 A widower cannot 「look after himself properly 〔keep the house clean and tidy〕. ◉ ~살림 the life of a widower; a single life; a bachelor life.

**홀아비김치** kimchi made solely of radish or cabbage.

**홀아비꽃대** 〚식물〛 a piperaceous plant.

**홀알** an unfertilized egg.

**홀앗이살림** a household with no encumbrances; a small family.

**홀어미** a widow.

**홀연**(忽然) suddenly; all of a sudden; unexpectedly; in an instant; in a flash; in a moment 〔twinkling〕. ¶ ~(히) 나타나다 appear suddenly / ~(히) 사라지다 vanish 〔disappear〕 as if by magic / ~히 왔다(가) 홀연히 사라지다 disappear as suddenly as *one* appears / 그는 ~히 안개 속으로 사라졌다 He faded in a flash into fog.

**홀짝거리다** ① 《국물을》 keep sipping 〔supping, slurping, sucking〕. ¶ 국을 ~ sip 〔slurp up〕 soup. ② 《콧물을》 keep sniffling 〔snivelling〕. ③ 《우는 모양》 weep 〔cry〕 with sniffling. ¶ 어린애가 ~ a child cries and sniffles.

**홀짝홀짝** ① 《콧물을》 sniffling 〔snivelling〕 repeatedly. ¶ 코를 ~들이마시다 keep sniffling. ② 《우는 모양》 weeping and sniffling away. ¶ ~ 울다 weep and sniffle away. ③ 《국물을》 with sip after sip 〔slurp after slurp〕; sucking away. ¶ ~들이마시다 keep sipping 〔slurping up〕 《soup》; drink 《liquor》 by sips 〔in little sips〕; sip (at) 《liquor》. ④ 《가볍게 뛰는 모양》 at a bound; at a jump. ¶ ~ 뛰다 leap lightly / 새가 ~ 날아 오르다 a bird suddenly takes wing.

**홀쭉이** a lanky person.

**홀쭉하다** ① 《몸피가》 (be) lanky; spindly; slender; slim. ¶ 홀쭉한 사나이 a lanky man / 홀쭉한 아가씨 a slim girl. ② 《앓거나 지쳐서》 (be) haggard; gaunt; skinny; emaciated. ¶ 홀쭉한 사람 a 「skinny 〔scrawny〕 person; 《구어》 a bag of bones / 홀쭉해지다 grow 〔become〕 thin; lose flesh / 근심으로 홀쭉해지다 become thin from worries. ③ 《끝이》 (be) pointed; tapering. ¶ 꼬리가 ~ have a 「pointed 〔slim〕 tail / 나무 끝이 ~ a tree has a tapering top.

**홀쳐매다** tie 〔knot〕 securely. ⇨ 홀맺다.

**홀치기** 《염색》 variegation; dapple; 《천》 tie-dyed fabrics. ¶ ~ 염색의 variegated.

**홀태** ① 《생선》 a slim fish without spawn. ② 《물건》 a slim thing.

**홀태바지** skin-tight trousers.

**홀태버선** (a pair of) tight socks.

**홀태부리** the 「nose 〔front end〕 of a pointed object.

**홀태질** stripping 〔threshing〕 grain from the ear on a threshing machine. ~하다 thresh.

**홀하다** (忽—) ① 《경솔·소홀하다》 (be) careless; inconsiderate; negligent; hasty; rash; thoughtless; 《거칠다》 (be) rough; harsh. ¶ 대접이 ~ be 「careless 〔inhospitable〕 in treating 《*a person*》 / 행동이 ~ act 〔behave〕 rashly. ② 《대수롭지 않다》 be of little importance; be of no 「account 〔value〕; (be) worthless insignificant.

**훌훌** ① 《타는 모양》 in flames; briskly. ¶ 마른 잎이 ~ 타다 dry leaves burn briskly. ② 《뛰는 모양》 with leaps and bounds. ¶ 여우가 ~ 재를 넘어가다 a fox leaps and bounds over a hill. ③ 《나는 모양》 flying; fluttering. ¶ 새가 ~ 날아가다 a bird flutters away. ④ 《마시는 모양》 with slurps. ¶ 죽을 ~ 마시다 slurp *one's* porridge. ⑤ 《던지는 모양》 tossing and tossing 《light things away》. ⑥ 《벗는 모양》 ¶ 옷을 ~ 벗다 slip off *one's* clothes.

**홈**[1] a groove; 《기둥의》 a flute; 《쇠시리》 a quirk. ¶ 홈을 파다 groove; cut 〔hollow out〕 a groove.

**홈**[2] ① 《가정》 *one's* home. ② 《정거장의》 a platform. ¶ (열차가) ~에 들어오다 〔을 나가다〕 come into 〔go out of〕 the platform; pull in 〔out〕. ③ 『야구』 home 「base 〔plate〕. ¶ ~인하다 get home. ④ 《고향》 *one's* hometown. ◉ 홈드레스 a housedress; a house frock. 홈룸 『교육』 a homeroom. 홈뱅킹 《집에서 받는 은행 서비스》 home banking. 홈베이스〔플레이트〕 『야구』 a home 「base 〔plate〕. 홈비디오 《가정용 비디오 장치》 home video. 홈쇼핑 home shopping.

**홈걸이** 《홈통 받치는》 a gutter hook.

**홈그라운드** home ground. ¶ ~에서 경기를 하다 play at home 「ground 〔park〕; play as 「host 〔franchise team〕.

**홈런** 『야구』 a home run; a homer. ¶ ~을 치다 hit 〔slam〕 a home run 《over the left field fence》. ◉ ~더비 a home-run derby. ~왕 a home-run 「king 〔leader〕. 굿바이~ a home run to end the game; a game-ending homer. 장외~ an out-of-the-park homer.

**홈메이드** 《자가제·국산의》 ¶ ~의 home-made 《cake》; domestic 《articles》.

**홈스트레치** 『스포츠』 《미》 《come into》 the homestretch; 《영》 the home-straight.

**홈스펀** 《손으로 짠 직물》 homespun.

**홈식** nostalgia; homesickness. ¶ ~에 걸린 사람 a homesick person / ~에 걸리다 get 〔become〕 homesick.

**홈인** 『야구』 ~하다 get 〔reach〕 home; cross the home plate.

**홈질** broad-stitching. ~하다 broad-stitch.

**홈착거리다** ① 《뒤지다》 search; fumble. ¶ 주머니를 ~ search 〔fumble in〕 *one's* pocket. ② 《씻다》 wipe away (tears). ¶ 눈물을 ~ keep wiping tears from *one's* eyes.

**홈쳐때리다** give 《*a person*》 a good whaling; dust 〔thrash〕 《*a person's*》 jacket.

**홈치다** ⇨ 훔치다.

**홈치작거리다** search 〔fumble〕 leisurely. ¶ 주머니를 ~ search 〔fumble around in〕 *one's* pocket leisurely.

**홈켜잡다** grip 《*a thing*》 with force; clutch.

**홈켜쥐다** hold 《*a thing*》 tight in *one's* hand; grasp tightly; take 「fast 〔firm〕 hold 《of》.

**홈타기** a fork; a crotch. ¶ ~진 forked / 나무~ the crotch of a tree / 바지 ~ the crotch of trousers.

**홈통** (—桶) ① 《물을 끄는》 a 〔an open〕 water pipe; a conduit; an aqueduct; 《수평의》 a gutter; 《세로》 a drainpipe; a rainwater pipe; a 「downspout 〔downpipe 《영》〕. ¶ ~으로 물을 끌다 draw water by (means of) a pipe / 지붕에 ~을 달다 gutter a roof. ② 《창틀·장지 따위의》 a groove on a window frame

〔doorsill〕.
**홈팀** 《자기 고장의 팀》 the home team.
**홈파다** groove; cut 〔hollow out〕 a groove 《in》. ¶ 탁상 가장자리에 홈을 파다 cut a groove along the edges of a table.
**홈패다** get grooved; be dug out. ¶ 비로 길에 홈(이) 패다 a road is dug out by the rain.
**홈 페이지** 〖컴퓨터〗 《인터넷에 마련된 자기만의 공간》 a home page.
**홈홈하다** wear a look of satisfaction.
**홉** 〖식물〗 a hop (plant); hops (열매). ¶ 홉을 따다 gather 〔pick〕 hops / 홉으로 (맥주의) 맛을 내다 hop. ◉ 홉 건조기 an oast. 홉 건조실 an oast house. 홉밭 a hopfield; a hopyard.
**홉**(合) *a hop:* a unit of measure (= 1/10 *toe,* 0.18*l* (부피), 0.33 $m^2$ (넓이)).
**홉뜨다** turn up the whites of *one's* eyes.
**홋홋이** without encumbrances; with no ties 〔dependents〕. ¶ 그 부부는 딸린 것 없이 둘이 ～ 산다 The couple leads a carefree life with no one to worry about except themselves.
**홋홋하다** have no encumbrances 〔ties, dependents〕; (be) unencumbered; carefree. ¶ 홋홋한 살림 a household with no encumbrances; a carefree household with few dependents to worry about.
**홍**(紅) red; a red color.
**홍기**(紅旗) a red flag; 《공산당 등의》 the Red Flag.
**홍꼭지**(紅—) a kite with a round piece of red paper at its top.
**홍당무**(紅唐—) a red radish; a carrot. ¶ 얼굴이 ～가 되다 turn as red as a turkey cock; blush (to the roots of *one's* hair); be flushed 《with shame》;
**홍도**(紅桃) 〖식물〗 a peach tree which puts out red blossoms (나무); a red peach blossom (꽃).
**홍두**(紅荳) 〖식물〗 an Indian licorice; a jequirity; a jequirity bean (열매).
**홍두깨** ① 《다듬이질의》 a wooden roller used for smoothing cloth (by wrapping and beating it on it). ¶ 아닌 밤중에 ～ 〔비유적〕 a bolt from 〔out of〕 the blue; a thunderbolt from a clear sky. ② 〖농업〗 soil which an inexpert plowman has neglected.
◉ ～살 rump. ～생갈이 plowing the spots neglected by an inexpert plowman. ～질 smooth cloth on a wooden roller.
**홍등가**(紅燈街) gay quarters; a red-light district 《미》; a brothel area.
**홍련**(紅蓮) a red lotus (blossom).
◉ ～지옥 《불교》 one of the Eight Icy Hells, where cold winds turn *one's* skin the color of red lotus.
**홍루**(紅淚) 《미인의 눈물》 tears of a fair; 《피눈물》 bloody tears.
**홍매**(紅梅) a plum with red blossoms.
**홍모**(鴻毛) wild-goose down 〔feather〕. ¶ 목숨을 ～같이 여기다 〔비유적〕 make 〔think〕 nothing of *one's* life; hold *one's* life as nothing.
**홍문**(紅門) ① 《정문(旌門)》 a red gate erected in honor of a loyal retainer, a filial son or a virtuous woman. ② ⇨ 홍살문.
**홍방울새**(紅—) 〖조류〗 a mealy redpoll.
**홍백**(紅白) red and white. ◉ ～전 a contest between red and white camps 〔teams〕. ⇨ 청백전.
**홍보**(弘報) (public) information; publicity; public relations (생략 P.R.).
◉ ～과(課) a public relations department 〔section, office〕. ～관(官) a public relations 〔affairs〕 officer. ～ 조사연구소 the Office of Information Research. ～지(誌) a PR brochure 〔pamphlet〕 (소책자); a public relations magazine (잡지).
**홍보석**(紅寶石) a ruby.
**홍보활동**(弘報活動) public relations (생략 P.R.); publicity activities. ¶ ～을 더욱 강화하다 further 〔strengthen, step up〕 publicity activities 《on》. ◉ 해외 ～ the (government's) overseas publicity activities.
**홍살문**(紅—門) a red gate with spiked top.
**홍삼**(紅蔘) ginseng steamed red.
◉ ～근(根) a red ginseng. ～정〔차〕 red ginseng extract 〔tea〕.
**홍색**(紅色) 《붉은 색》 red; a red color. ¶ ～을 띤 reddish; pinkish. ◉ ～짜리 a new bride (dressed in her red skirt).
**홍소**(哄笑) loud laughter; a roar of laughter; a guffaw. ～하다 laugh loud(ly); roar with laughter; guffaw. ¶ ～를 터뜨리다 roar with laughter; burst into laughter.
**홍수**(洪水) a flood; an inundation; a deluge (대홍수).

> 용법 **flood** 하천이 범람하는 상태. **inundation** 하천의 범람으로 인하여 광범위한 토지가 침수된 상태. **deluge** 호우에 의한 극심한 홍수.

¶ 노아의 ～ Noah's Flood; the Deluge; the Flood / 우편물의 ～ 〔비유적〕 a flood 〔deluge〕 of letters / 자동차의 ～

[비유적] a torrent of automobiles / ~와 가뭄이 없는 비옥한 땅 fertile land free of flood and drought / ~가 나다 have a flood; get flooded; be 「flooded 〔under water〕; be inundated / ~로 유실되다 be 「carried 〔washed〕 away by a flood / ~ 피해를 입다 《사람이》 suffer from a flood; 《집·논밭이》 be flooded; be under water / ~로 집의 2층까지 침수됐다 Flood reached the second floor of the house. / 경기 북부 지방을 엄습한 폭우로 ~가 나서 많은 사람이 생명을 잃었다 A lot of people have been killed as a result of floods by torrential rain that hit northern Gyeonggi provinces.
◉ ~경보 a flood warning. ~보험 flood insurance. ~예보 a flood forecast. ~조절 flood control. ~지역 「a flooded 〔an inundated〕 area 〔district〕. ~피해자 floods victims. 대~ a 「great 〔disastrous, heavy〕 flood.

**홍수**(紅樹) 『식물』 a mangrove tree.
◉ ~림 a mangrove forest.

**홍수막이**(洪水—) damming against floods. ~하다 dam 《up》.

**홍순**(紅脣) ① 《여인의 입술》 red 〔rosy〕 lips; rouged lips (입술 연지를 칠한). ② 《꽃송이》 a half-open flower.

**홍시**(紅柿) a mellowed persimmon.

**홍실**(紅—) red thread(s).

**홍안**(紅顔) a 「ruddy 〔rosy〕 face; peachy 〔pink〕 cheeks. ¶ ~의 rosy=cheeked; ruddy-faced / ~의 미소년 a handsome rosy-cheeked youth; a 「fair 〔handsome〕 youth; an Adonis.

**홍어**(洪魚) 『어류』 a skate; a thornback.

**홍업**(洪業·鴻業) a glorious achievement; great 「work 〔exploit〕.

**홍역**(紅疫) 『의학』 the measles; rubeola. ¶ ~을 하다 catch 〔have〕 the measles / ~을 치르다 [비유적] have a hard time (of it); have bitter experiences / ~은 두번 걸리지는 않는다 You'll have no second go of measles.

**홍연광**(紅鉛鑛) 『광물』 crocoite; red lead 「ore.

**홍염**(紅焰) ① 《불꽃》 red 「blazes 〔flares〕 of flame. ② 『천문』 a solar prominence 〔protuberance〕.

**홍엽**(紅葉) 《단풍이 든》 red leaves (of autumn); autumnal 「colors 〔tints〕; 《단풍나무의》 red maple foliage. ¶ ~으로 물들다 turn red; be tinged with red / 만산은 ~으로 불타고 있었다 All mountains were 「ablaze 〔aflame〕 with autumnal tints.

**홍예**(虹霓) 《무지개》 a rainbow; 《아치》 an arch. ¶ ~틀다 build as an arch; arch 《a gate》. ◉ ~다리 an arched bridge. ~문 the arch of a gate; an arched gate.

**홍옥**(紅玉) 《보석》 ruby; carbuncle; 《사과의 일종》 a Jonathan (apple).

**홍위병**(紅衛兵) 《중국의》 the Red Guards.

**홍은**(鴻恩) great 「favor 〔benevolence〕.

**홍익인간**(弘益人間) devotion to the welfare of mankind.

**홍인종**(紅人種) the 「red 〔American 「Indian〕 race.

**홍일점**(紅一點) 《여자》 the only member of the fair sex 《among》; the only woman in the 「company 〔group〕; 《이채로움》 standing out; surpassing; excelling (others). ¶ 그녀는 참석한 회원 중 ~이다 She is the only woman present among the members.

**홍적세**(洪積世) 『지질』 the Pleistocene 「epoch.

**홍적층**(洪積層) 『지질』 a diluvium (*pl.* ~s, -via); a diluvial formation. ◉ ~토(土) diluvium; diluvial 「soil 〔deposits〕.

**홍조**(紅潮) 《얼굴의》 flushing; a glow; 《바다》 reflections of the morning sun on the sea; 《월경》 menses; menstruation periods; monthlies. ¶ 소모성의 ~ 《폐결핵 환자의》 hectic flush / 두 뺨에 ~를 띠고 with a blush on *one's* cheeks / ~를 띠다 《얼굴이》 be flushed; ⌊blush.

**홍조류**(紅藻類) red algae.

**홍진**(紅疹) = 홍역(紅疫).

**홍진**(紅塵) 《흙먼지》 dust in the air; thick dust; 『기상』 a dust storm; 《세속》 the troublesome affairs of the mundane world. ¶ ~을 피하다 keep away from the din and bustle of the world.
◉ ~만장 《raise》 a cloud of dust. ~세계 the dusty world.

**홍차**(紅茶) black tea; 《a cup of》 tea. ¶ 설탕을 넣은 ~ tea with sugar.

**홍채**(紅彩) 『해부』 the iris (of the eye).
◉ ~염(炎) iritis. ~절제(술) 『의학』 iridectomy.

**홍초**(紅—) 《초》 a red candle; 《연》 a paper kite that is all red except for ⌊the tail.

**홍치마**(紅—) a red skirt.

**홍코너**(紅—) 《권투》 the champion's 〔defender's〕 corner.

**홍콩** Hong Kong; Hongkong.
◉ ~달러 Hongkong dollar.

**홍하**(紅蝦) 『동물』 a (spiny) lobster.

**홍학**(紅鶴) 『조류』 a flamingo (*pl.* -(e)s).

**홍합**(紅蛤) 『조개류』 a (hard-shelled) ⌊mussel.

**홍해**(紅海) the Red Sea.

**홑** 《한겹》 single; one-ply; single layer. ¶ 홑이다 be single-layered; be one sheet; be one-ply.

**홑겹** a single layer.
**홑눈** 〖동물〗 a stemma (*pl.* -mata, ~s); an ocellus (*pl.* -lli). ¶ ~의 ocellar.
**홑담** a single-layered wall.
**홑대패** a single-edged plane.
**홑몸** ① 《독신자》 a single person; a bachelor; a spinster (여자); bachelorhood; spinsterhood. ¶ ~으로 살다 live single; lead a bachelor's 〔spinster's〕 life. ② 《혼자서》 ¶ ~으로 여행하다 travel alone / ~으로 적진에 뛰어들다 penetrate the enemy position single-handed. ③ 《임신 않은》 a woman who is not pregnant; 《홋홋한》 a person without encumbrances.
**홑바지** unlined trousers 《women's undergarment》.
**홑반** a single layer of cotton wool. ◉ ~뿌리 a garment with a single layer of cotton padding.
**홑벌** ① ⇨ 단벌. ② 《한 겹》 single-ply; a single-ply 〔one-layered〕 thing. ◉ ~바지 unlined trousers. ~옷 the only clothes *one* has.
**홑(벌)사람** a shallow-minded 〔mean〕 person.
**홑벽**(一壁) a single partition; a thin wall.
**홑소리** 〖언어〗 a single sound; a monosyllabic sound. ⇨ 단음(單音).
**홑실** a single-ply thread; singles.
**홑옷** unlined clothes.
**홑으로** ① 《한 겹으로》 as a single ply; out of a single sheet. ¶ ~ 되다 be made of a single sheet. ② 《적은 수효로》 merely; only; no more than. ¶ ~ 서너 개 만이 아니다 It isn't just a mere three or four of them.
**홑이불** a single-layer quilt; a (bed) sheet.
**홑지다** (be) simple; uncomplicated; plain.
**홑집** 〖건축〗 a single-wing house; a shack.
**홑창**(一窓) 〖건축〗 a sliding window without an inner one.
**홑치마** ① 《한 겹의》 an unlined skirt. ② 《속치마 없이 입는》 a skirt worn without an underskirt.
**화**(火) ① 《성》 resentment; anger; rage; wrath. ¶ 홧김에 in a fit of anger 〔temper〕; exasperatedly / 화를 잘 내는 hot-〔quick-, short-〕tempered; irritable / 화를 잘 내는 사람 a person with an explosive temper; a hot-〔short-〕tempered person / 화가 치밀었다 I 「had a fit of anger 〔got into a rage〕. / 그는 아내에게 화를 터뜨렸다 He vented his anger on his wife. / 그녀는 홧김에 남편에게 대들었다 In a fit of anger 〔rage〕, she flew out at her husband. ② 《오행의》 "Fire"—one of the five primary elements (*i.e.* Metal, Wood, Water, Fire and Earth). ③ 《화요일》 Tuesday.
**화**(禍) (an) evil; trouble(s); 《불행》 (a) misfortune; a mishap; 《재난》 a disaster; a calamity; a woe. ¶ 화가 되다 be injurious 《to》; be the ruin 《of》; bring evil 《to》; prove a curse 《to》 / 화를 당하다 meet with (a) disaster 〔calamity, misfortune〕; 《죽음을》 get killed / 화를 면하다 be saved from disaster / 화를 자초하다 bring (an) evil upon *oneself;* ask for trouble; invite disaster 《by *one's* misconduct》 / 남에게 화를 끼치다 get 《*a person*》 into trouble / 화를 피하다 keep off a misfortune / 입은 화의 근원 《속담》 Out of the mouth comes evil. *or* Confine your tongue, lest it (should) confine you.
**-화**(化) ~하다 "-ize". ¶ 기계화 mechanization / 도시화 urbanization / 합리화 rationalization / 기계화하다 mechanize / 미국화하다 Americanize / 서양화하다 Westernize; Europeanize / 한국화하다 Koreanize.
**-화**(畫) a picture; a painting; a drawing. ¶ 동양화 an Oriental painting / 서양화 a Western painting / 풍경화 a landscape (painting).
**-화**(靴) shoes; boots. ¶ 등산화 mountain-climbing boots / 스키화 ski boots.
**화가**(畫架) 〖미술〗 an easel.
**화가**(畫家) a painter; an artist; 《우스개》 a knight of the brush. ¶ 같은 ~의 그림 a picture from the same brush / ~가 되다 enter upon a painting career / ~를 그만두다 abandon the palette. ◉ 인물~ a portrait painter.
**화간**(和姦) 〖법〗 fornication; adultery with consent. ~하다 fornicate 《with a woman》.
**화강암**(花崗岩) granite.
**화객선**(貨客船) a cargo-passenger ship.
**화경**(火鏡) a sunglass; a burning glass.
**화경**(花梗) a flower stalk; a peduncle. ⇨ 꽃자루.
**화공**(火攻) attacking with fire. ~하다 attack with fire.
**화공**(畫工) a painter; an artist; a master of the brush.
**화공과**(化工科) 《대학의》 the Department of Chemical Engineering.
**화관**(花冠) ① 《관》 a woman's ceremonial coronet. ¶ ~무 a flower crown dance. ② = 꽃부리.
**화광**(火光) the light of fire 〔flames〕.

¶ ～이 충천하다 「flames light〔a pillar of flames〕soar up the sky.

**화교**(華僑) Chinese emigrants; Chinese resident abroad; overseas Chinese merchants.

**화구**(火口) ①《아궁이》a fuel intake. ②《화산의》a crater. ◉ ～곡(谷)〖지질〗a crater valley. ～구(丘) a volcanic cone. ～벽(壁) a crater wall. ～원(原) a crater basin. ～호(湖) a crater lake.

**화구**(畵具)《도구》painting materials.

**화근**(禍根) the root of evil; the source(s) of trouble. ¶ ～이 되다 be *one's* ruin / ～을 없애다 eliminate the root of the evil; remove the source(s) of (the) trouble / ～을 남기다 turn a blind eye to future trouble〔evil〕/ ～을 내포하다 be fraught with evil / 장래의 ～이 되다 form a source for future trouble / ～이 뿌리 깊다 The cause of the trouble lies deep-seated. / 친절이 도리어 ～이 되었다 My kind intentions became the cause of my〔his〕ruin. ◉ ～거리 a source of future misfortune; something that will make trouble.

**화급**(火急) urgency; exigency; emergency. ～하다 (be) urgent; pressing; exigent; imminent; be an emergency. ¶ ～한 경우에는 in case of emergency; in an emergency.

**화기**(火氣) ①《답답증》a stifling sensation in the chest. ②《노여움》anger; ire. ③《불기》heat of fire. ¶ ～엄금《게시》No Fire. *or* Caution: Inflammable. / ～ 주의《게시》Watch out for fire hazards. / ～가 있는 데서 사용하지 마시오《게시》Do not use near fire or flame.

**화기**(火器) ①〖군사〗firearms; hardware《구어》. ②《불담는》a fire container. ◉ 경(輕)～ light firearms. 소～ small arms. 중(重)～ heavy firearms.

**화기**(和氣)《날씨》mild weather; beautiful warmweather;《기색》peacefulness; harmony. ¶ ～애애하다 be peaceful; be harmonious / ～애애하게 full of harmony; harmoniously; peacefully / ～애애한 가정 a home where peace and happiness prevail〔reign〕; a happy home.

**화끈** with a sudden flash of heat; with a throb〔glow, flush〕. ～하다 get a hot flash; suddenly throb with heat; get a glow〔flush〕.

**화끈거리다** feel hot; burn; glow; flush; throb with heat. ¶ 화끈거리는 얼굴로 with a flushed face / 신열로〔술을 먹어〕얼굴이 ～ *one's* face is flushed with fever〔drink〕/ 더운 열기로 뺨이 ～ *one's* cheeks glow with the hot air; the hot air makes the cheeks glow / 온몸이 ～ *one's* body is 「all aglow〔all of a glow〕/ 나는 부끄러워서 얼굴이 화끈거렸다 My face〔ears〕burned in embarrassment.

**화끈달다** get enraged; be infuriated; be maddened; "burn".

**화나다**(火―) get angry《at *a matter*, with *a person*》; become enraged〔indignant〕《at an insult, with *a person*》; be offended〔provoked〕《by》; get mad《미구어》. ¶ 화나게 하다 enrage; exasperate; provoke; offend; displease; make《*a person*》angry〔mad〕/ 이런 하찮은 일들이 때로 사람을 화나게 한다 Such trifles occasionally ruffle tempers.

**화난**(禍難) a disaster; a misfortune; a mishap.

**화내다**(火―) get〔become〕angry《with *a person*, at *a matter*》; fly into a passion; get into a rage; lose *one's* temper; get mad《at》《미구어》; blow *one's* top. ¶ 벌컥 ～ flare up; fly into a rage / 걸핏하면 ～ easily take offense / 그는 내가 그렇게 말했더니 더욱 화냈다 When I said so, he grew doubly angry. / 자네가 화내는 것도 당연하다 You may well be angry〔offended〕at it.

**화냥년** a wanton〔dissolute〕woman; an adulterous wife; a whore.

**화냥질** adultery. ⇨서방질.

**화농**(化膿)〖의학〗suppuration; the formation〔discharge〕of pus. ～하다 suppurate;《상처가》fester;《종기 따위가》come to a head. ¶ ～성(性)의 suppurative; festering / ～성 염증 purulent inflammation. ◉ ～균(菌) suppurative〔pyogenic〕microorganism. ～열 a suppurative fever. ～작용 pyogenesis. ～제 a maturative.

**화닥닥** ⇨후닥닥.

**화단**(花壇) a flower bed〔garden〕.

**화단**(畵壇) the artist world; painting〔artistic〕circles.

**화답**(和答) a response. ～하다 respond《in singing, reciting or verse》.

**화대**(花代) a charge for *kisaeng's* services; a *kisaeng's* fee. ⇨팁.

**화덕**(火―) ①《화로》a (charcoal) brazier. ②《솥 거는》a (cooking) stove.

**화독**(火毒) inflammation caused by a burn. ◉ ～내 the smell of burnt food; scorching smell of food.

**화동**(和同) unison; harmony. ～하다 get in unison; be in harmony.

**화두**(話頭) a「topic〔subject〕of conversation. ¶ ～를 돌리다 change「the topic〔*one's* subject〕; shift the conversation.

**화드득** 《쏟아지는 소리》 with a slush 〔slosh〕; 《터지는 소리》 with a bang; crackle or whiz; 《경망스런 태도》《acting》 foolishly; rashly; silly. ～거리다 keep going slush; keep「banging 〔crackling, whizzing〕.

**화딱지**(火—) a「hot〔quick〕temper; a spasm of temper; a fit of anger; a dander 《미구어》. ¶ ～가 나다 have a (fit of) spasm; be offended 《at, by》; take offense 《at》.

**화라지** a long spread-out branch; a bough; a limb (*esp.* as firewood).

**화락**(和樂) harmony; unity; peace. ～하다 be harmonious; be at peace with each other; dwell in「unity〔harmony〕. ¶ 그의 집안은 ～하다 Perfect peace reigns in his family. *or* His family live in perfect harmony.

**화랑**(花郞) an elite youth in Silla Dynasty (who excelled in beauty, bravery and military arts). ◉ ～도(徒) = 화랑.

**화랑**(畫廊) a (picture) gallery; an art「gallery.

**화랑이**(花郞—) 〖민속〗 a kind of theatrical performer.

**화려**(華麗) splendor; magnificence; gorgeousness; brilliance. ～하다 (be) splendid; magnificent; gorgeous; brilliant. ¶ ～하게 brilliantly; gaudily; gorgeously / ～한 도안 a colorful design / ～한 문체 florid〔flowery〕style / ～한 색깔 a「gay〔gorgeous〕color / ～한 생애 a brilliant career / ～한 옷 gala dress; gay〔gorgeous〕garments / ～한 생활(을 하다) (lead) a gay life / 눈부시게 ～하다 dazzle 《*a person*》 with「brilliance〔splendor〕/ ～한 복장을 하다 be「flashly〔gaily, gorgeously, gaudily〕dressed / ～한 것을 좋아하다 be fond of「show〔display〕/ 체조선수는 우리에게 ～한 연기를 보여 주었다 The gymnast gave us a splendid performance.

**화력**(火力) 《불의 힘》 heating〔thermal〕power; 〖군사〗 firepower; firing power 《of troops》. ¶ ～이 세다〔약하다〕 have「strong〔weak〕calorific force / ～을 줄이다 damp down 《a furnace》 / ～에 견디다 resist the action of fire / ～이 우세하다 surpass 《the enemy》 in firepower; outgun 《the enemy》 / 적의 ～을 제압하다 silence〔neutralize〕enemy firepower. ◉ ～증강 increase「in〔of〕firepower. ～지원 fire support.

**화력발전**(火力發電) thermal power generation. ◉ ～소 a thermal power plant 〔station〕.

**화로**(火爐) a (charcoal) brazier; a fire pot. ¶ 화롯불을 쬐다 warm *oneself* at a brazier; warm *one's* hands over a brazier.

**화룡점정**(畫龍點睛) completing the eyes of a painted dragon; the finishing「touch〔stroke〕.

**화류계**(花柳界) the gay quarters; the world of the *gisaeng;* a red-light district 《미》; the *demimonde* (F.). ¶ ～여자 a woman of gay world; a *gisaeng;* a prostitute; a *demimondaine* (F.).

**화류병**(花柳病) a venereal disease (생략 VD, V.D.).

**화면**(畫面) a scene; 《영화·TV의》 a screen; a picture; 《그림의》 a canvas; 〖수학〗 a picture plane. ¶ 《영화·TV에서》 ～에 들어오다 enter〔get into〕the picture / ～에서 사라지다 go〔get〕out of the picture / ～이 바뀌다 the scene「changes〔shifts〕/ (TV의) ～이 어둡다 The picture is not bright enough. ◉ ～구성 the composition of a picture. ～비(比) 〖TV〗 picture ratio. 분할(分割)～ 〖영화·TV〗 a split screen.

**화목**(火木) firewood.

**화목**(花木) a flower plant; a flowering plant; a flowering tree.

**화목**(和睦) peace; harmony; concord. ～하다 be at peace with each other; be in「harmony〔concord〕; dwell in「unity〔harmony〕. ¶ ～하게 harmoniously; in「harmony〔peace〕; affectionately / ～하게 살다 live happily together; live in perfect「harmony 〔concord〕; be happy with 《*one's* wife》 / 그 부부는 무척 ～하다 There is perfect conjugal harmony between them. / 그의 집안은 아주 ～하다 Perfect peace reigns in his family. *or* His family live in perfect harmony.

**화무십일홍**(花無十日紅) Every flower has its ebb. *or* Pride「goes〔comes〕before a fall. *or* All that's fair must fade.

**화문**(花紋) flower patterns; a floral design; figures of flowers. ◉ ～석(席) a mat woven with flower designs.

**화물**(貨物) 《운송 화물》 freight 《미》; goods 《영》; 《배의》 cargo. ¶ ～을 나르다 carry freight / 철도의 파업으로 역에는 많은 ～이 쌓여 있다 Because of the

rail strike, a lot of freight is piled up in the station.
◉ ～계(係) a freight section: ～계원 a freightman; a freight clerk. ～보관증 a warrant; a warehouse receipt 〔certificate〕. ～상〔인〕환증 a consignment sheet; a bill 〔waybill〕 of loading 《미》; a receipt note 《영》. ～선 a cargo boat 〔ship〕; a freight vessel; a freighter. ～송장 a manifest. ～수송 a freight traffic 〔transportation〕; freight (age); shipment. ～수송기 a cargo plane; an (air) freighter. ～승강기 a freight elevator. ～실 《비행기의》 a hold. ～역(驛) a (railroad) freight terminal; a freight depot 《미》; a goods station 《영》. ～열차 a freight (train) 《미》; a goods train 《영》: ～ 열차로 한 열차분 an entire freight train load 《of coffee》. ～운송 freight(age); forwarding (탁송); shipment. ～운임 goods rates 《영》; freight (rates) 《미》; 《수상의》 freightage; 《육상의》 carriage; 《철도의》 railway freight charges. ～인수 receipt of goods. ～자동차 a (motor) truck 《미》; a (motor) lorry 《영》. ～적재량 cargo capacity. ～차 《열차》 a freight car 《미》; a goods van 〔wagon〕 《영》; 《무개 화차》 a flatcar 《미》; an open goods wagon 《영》; 《유개 화차》 a boxcar 《미》; closed goods wagon. ～취급 forwarding; transportation 《미》; transport 《영》: ～ 취급인 a freighter; a freight 〔goods, forwarding〕 agent; an expressman 《미》 / ～ 취급소 a freight 〔goods〕 office; a forwarding agency. ～칸 《열차의》 a goods car; 《항공기의》 a hold; a cargo compartment. ～통지서〔수송장〕 a waybill. ～폭주 congestion of freight traffic. ～환신용장 a documentary (letter of) credit. ～환어음 《draw》 a documentary draft 〔bill〕.

**화미하다**(華美—) (be) splendid; gorgeous; pompous; showy; gaudy; luxurious; extravagant.

**화밀**(花蜜) 〖식물〗 (floral) necta.

**화반**(花盤) ① 〖건축〗 a board put on top of the *ch'obang* (=first cornice on a pillar) to hold the *chang-yŏ* (=beam support). ② 《꽃 담는》 a flowerpot shaped like a flower.

**화반석**(花班石) red marble.

**화방**(畫房) 《화실》 a studio; an *atelier* (F.); 《화랑》 a gallery; 《재료점》 an art store.

**화방수**(—水) a whirl (pool); an eddy.

**화백**(畫伯) an artist; a (master) painter; a great 〔distinguished〕 artist.

**화법**(話法) 〖문법〗 narration; speech.

**화법**(畫法) the art of drawing. ¶ 산수 ～ landscape painting / ～에 맞다〔어긋나다〕 be in 〔out of〕 drawing.

**화변**(禍變) a great disaster 〔calamity〕.

**화병**(火病) hypochondria; an ailment supposedly caused by *one's* pent-up resentment.

**화병**(花甁) a (flower) vase. ⇨꽃병.

**화보**(花譜) an album 〔a catalog〕 of flowers; a horticultural guide.

**화보**(畫報) a pictorial; a graphic; an illustrated magazine; 《보도를 겸한》 pictorial 〔illustrated〕 news; a picture report. ◉ 시사～ news in pictures; a pictorial record of current events.

**화보**(畫譜) a picture album 〔book〕.

**화복**(禍福) weal and 〔or〕 woe; fortune and 〔or〕 misfortune; happiness and 〔or〕 misery; prosperity and 〔or〕 adversity; good and 〔or〕 evil. ¶ 인생의 ～ the haps and mishaps 〔vicissitudes, ups and downs〕 of life; the happiness and misery of life. 「on.

**화본**(畫本) silk 〔paper〕 used to paint

**화본과**(禾本科) 〖식물〗 Gramineae. ¶ ～식물 (true) grasses. ⇨볏과식물.

**화부**(火夫) 《기관의》 a stoker; a fireman 《미》; 《난방의》 a boilerman; 《화장터의》 a cremator; a corpse man.

**화분**(花盆) a flowerpot; a jardiniere (장식용). ¶ ～에 심은 화초 a potted flowers.

**화분**(花粉) ＝꽃가루. ◉ ～열(熱) hay fever; pollinosis. 「come single.

**화불단행**(禍不單行) Misfortunes never

**화사**(華奢) luxury; pomposity; splendor. ～하다 (be) luxurious; pompous; splendid; flamboyant. ¶ ～한 옷차림을 하고 있다 be flamboyant 〔gaily〕 dressed.

**화사첨족**(畫蛇添足) a superfluity; a redundancy. ⇨사족(蛇足).

**화산**(火山) a volcano (*pl.* ～(e)s). ¶ ～의 활동 volcanic activity / ～의 폭발 the eruption of a volcano; a volcanic eruption / ～이 폭발하다 a volcano bursts into eruption. ◉ ～관측소 a volcanological observatory. ～국 a volcanic country. ～군(群) a volcanic group. ～니(泥) volcanic mud; moya. ～대(帶) a volcanic zone. ～도(島) a volcanic island. ～맥(脈) a volcanic chain 〔range〕. ～분출물 volcanic product 〔ejecta〕. ～사(砂) volcanic sand. ～석 volcanic rock. ～암(岩) 《a piece of》 volcanic 〔igneous〕 rock; lava (용암). ～암맥 a volcanic dike. ～열도 a chain of volcanic islands. ～작용 volcanism; volcanic action. ～지대 a volcanic「region 〔zone〕. ～지진 a volcanic earthquake. ～탄(彈) volcanic bomb. ～토(土) trass. ～학 volcanology; vulcanology: ～학자 a volcanologist. ～현상 a volcanic phenomenon; volcanism. ～활동 volcanic activity. ～회(灰) volcanic ash; pozzolana.

**화살** an arrow; a shaft; a bolt (굵은). ¶ 비오듯 쏟아지는 ～ a shower of arrow / ～이 나는 소리 the「humming 〔whizzing〕 (sound) of an arrow / ～을 쏘다 shoot 〔send, discharge, let off〕 an arrow《at》/ 시위에 ～을 메기다 fix 〔notch〕 an arrow to the bowstring / ～이 과녁을 맞히다 an arrow hits the「mark 〔target〕/ ～처럼 빠르다 be as swift as an arrow / 질문의 ～을 던지다 fire questions《at *a person*》; discharge 〔fire off〕 a「volley 〔barrage〕 of questions《at *a person*》/ ～은 과녁 한복판에 맞았다 The arrow hit the target right in the center. / ～이 그의 어깨에 박혔다 An arrow lodged in his shoulder. / ～은 이미 시위를 떠났다 [비유적] The result is out of our hands now. ◉ ～깃 the feathers of an arrow. ～대 an arrow shaft. ～자리〖천문〗the Arrow; Sagitta. ～촉 an arrowhead; the「barb 〔point〕 of an arrow; a gad. ～통 a quiver. ～표 an arrow: 이 ～표 방향으로 가시오《게시》Please follow this arrow.

**화살나무**〖식물〗a winged euonymus.

**화상**(火床) a fire (place) grate;《보일러의》a firebed.

**화상**(火傷) a (skin) burn (불에 의한); a scald (열탕에 의한). ¶ 제1〔2, 3, 4〕도 ～ a first-〔second-, third-, fourth-〕degree burn / ～자국 a scar of a「burn 〔scald〕/ 손의 ～ a burn on *one's* hand / ～을 입다 get 〔be〕 burned 〔scalded〕; have 〔suffer〕 a burn; be 〔get〕 scorched (부젓가락 따위에) / 큰〔중〕～을 입다 be badly burned; suffer heavy burns / ～으로 물집이 생기다 blister; be covered with blisters.

**화상**(和尙)〖불교〗a Buddhist priest.

**화상**(華商) a Chinese merchant (residing abroad).

**화상**(畫商) a picture dealer; a dealer in paintings.

**화상**(畫像) a portrait (초상); a picture;〖TV〗an image;〖영화〗a picture on the screen. ¶ 흐릿한 ～〖TV〗a blurred image; a picture out of focus / 선명한 ～ a clear picture / ～이 일그러지다 the picture is「distorted 〔fuzzy〕. ◉ ～면적〖TV〗a picture area. ～신호 video signals.

**화색**(和色)《온화한》a「peaceful 〔serene〕 countenance; a「happy 〔genial〕 expression;《건강한》a healthy complexion.

**화생**(化生)〖동물〗metaplasia;〖불교〗transformation;〖군사〗biochemical. ～하다 transform. ¶ ～전(戰) biochemical warfare.

**화생방전**(化生放戰)〖군사〗chemical, biological and radiological warfare; CBR warfare.

**화서**(花序) ＝꽃차례. 「(Sp.).

**화서지몽**(華胥之夢) a midday nap; *siesta*

**화석**(化石)《돌》a fossil;〖고생물〗fossil remains;《작용》fossilization; petrifaction. ¶ 동물〔물고기〕의 ～ a fossil「animal 〔fish〕/ 살아있는 ～ a living fossil / ～화(化)하다 fossilize; petrify / ～을 찾아다니다 hunt for fossils. ◉ ～연료 fossil fuels. ～인류 fossil men. ～층(層) a fossiliferous stratum. ～학 fossilology: ～학자 a fossilologist.

**화선지**(畫宣紙) Chinese drawing paper.

**화섬**(化纖)《화학섬유》chemical 〔synthetic〕 fiber.

**화성**(化成) transformation; change;〖화학〗chemical synthesis. ～하다 transform; change. ◉ ～공업 the chemical (and synthetic) industry. ～비료 a「compound 〔complex〕 fertilizer.

**화성**(火成)〖지질〗¶ ～의 igneous; pyrogenous; pyrogenic. ◉ ～광물 a pyrogenetic mineral. ～광상 igneous (ore) deposits. ～설(說) the vulcanian theory. ～암 igneous 〔eruptive〕 rock: 심성(深成) ～암 Plutonic rock.

**화성**(火星)〖천문〗Mars. ¶ ～의 Martian / ～중심의 areocentric. ◉ ～인 a Martian; an inhabitant of Mars.

**화성**(和聲)〖음악〗《현상》harmony; concord;《음》a chord. ¶ ～적 harmonic. ◉ ～법 the law of harmony. ～학(學) harmonics. 「painter.

**화성**(畫聖) a great artist; a master

**화성**(化性)〖생물〗voltinism. ¶ ～일(一)〔이(二)〕～의 univoltine 〔bivoltine〕《silkworms》.

**화세**(火勢) the force of the「fire 〔flames〕.

**화솥** a「hat-shaped 〔wide-brimmed〕 ket-tle. 「wealth.

**화수분** an inexhaustible fountain of

**화수회**(花樹會) a convivial party of the

members of a clan; a family reunion.
**화술**(話術) the art of「conversation 〔narration, talking〕; the storyteller's art. ¶ ～에 능하다 be a good「conversationalist 〔storyteller, talker〕/ ～에 능한 사람 a good「conversationalist 〔storyteller, talker〕; a master storyteller; 《대화에》 a brilliant conversationalist.
**화승**(火繩) a fuse; a matchlock (cord). ◉ ～총 a matchlock (gun); a firelock.
**화식**(火食) (eating) cooked food. ～하다 eat 《fish》 cooked; make a diet of cooked food.
**화식**(和食) = 왜식(倭食). 「of a flower.
**화식도**(花式圖) a (botanical) diagram
**화식조**(火食鳥) 〖조류〗 a cassowary.
**화신**(化身) (the) incarnation; (the) personification; (the) embodiment 《of courage》. ¶ 부처님의 ～ Buddha incarnate / 신의 ～ god incarnate; a manifestation of a god / 악마의 ～ the「incarnation 〔embodiment〕 of evil; the devil incarnate / 탐욕의 ～ a perfect picture of avarice / 그녀는 미덕의 ～이다 She is the incarnation of virtue. *or* She is virtue itself.
**화신**(花信) tidings of flowers; news about flowers coming in bloom. ◉ ～풍(風) spring breezes (presaging blossome). 「*lier* (F.).
**화실**(畫室) an (artist's) studio; an *ate-*
**화심**(花心) ① 《꽃술 부분》 the「heart 〔central part〕 of a flower. ② 《미인의 마음》 the「heart of a beautiful woman.
**화심**(禍心) malicious 〔evil〕 intention; a perfidious「heart 〔mind〕.
**화씨**(華氏) 〖물리〗 Fahrenheit (생략 Fahr., F.). ¶ ～ 50도, 50 degrees (by) Fahrenheit; 50°F. ◉ ～온도계 a Fahrenheit (thermometer).
**화압**(花押) a signature.
**화약**(火藥) gunpowder; powder. ¶ ～의 폭발 a powder explosion / ～을 폭발시키다「blow up 〔explode〕 explosives 〔gunpowder〕/ ～을 지고 불로 들어가다 invite danger; be a case of insect flying into a flame to death.
◉ ～고 a (powder) magazine; an explosives warehouse. ～공장 a powder(-manufacturng) factory 〔plant〕; an explosives「plant 〔factory〕. ～류(類) explosives: ～류 단속법 the Explosives Control Act. ～ 취급 면허장 a gunpowder license. ～취급인 a「dealer in 〔handler of〕 gunpowder. ～통 a powder flask. 무연～ smokeless gun=powder. 흑색～ black powder.
**화엄경**(華嚴經) 〖불교〗 the *Avatamska Sutra.*
**화연**(花宴) a banquet celebrating *one's* sixtieth birthday.
**화열**(火熱) caloric heat.
**화염**(火焰) a flame; a blaze. ¶ ～에 싸이다 be「wrapped 〔enveloped〕 in flames; be in a blaze. ◉ ～방사기 〖군사〗 a flamethrower. ～병 a「gasoline 〔petrol〕 bomb; a Molotov cocktail. ～용접 flame welding.
**화엽**(花葉) 〖식물〗 ① a floral leaf. ⇨ 꽃잎. ② 《꽃과 잎》 blossoms and leaves.
**화예**(花蘂) 〖식물〗 a pistil and a stamen. ⇨ 꽃술.
**화요일**(火曜日) Tuesday (생략 Tues.).
**화용월태**(花容月態) a lovely face and graceful carriage.
**화운**(和韻) composing a verse in response (following the rimes used by another).
**화원**(花園) a flower garden.
**화음**(和音) 〖음악〗 a chord; an accord. ¶ ～의 chordal. ◉ ～계 a harmonometer. 기초～ a fundamental chord. 변화～ an altered chord. 으뜸～ a primitive 〔tonic〕 chord. 5도～ the fifth (chord).
**화의**(和議) ① 《평화 교섭》 negotiations for peace; a peace conference; 《화해》 reconciliation. ～하다 negotiate for peace; make reconciliation 《with》. ¶ ～를 맺다 make 〔conclude〕 peace 《with》; make a reconciliation 《with》/ ～를 제의하다 sue for peace; make overtures「for 〔of〕 peace. ② 〖법〗 (a) composition. ～하다 make a composition 《with》. ¶ 채권자와 ～가 성립되다 make a composition with *one's* creditors. ◉ ～법 the Composition Law. ～사건 a composition matter; a case of composition. ～신청 application 〔petition〕 for composition. ～절차 composition proceedings (상법의); procedures of composition (화의법의).
**화이트소스** 《요리》 white sauce.
**화이트칼라** a white-collar worker; an office worker. ¶ ～의 white-collar(ed).
**화이트하우스** 《백악관》 the White House.
**화인**(火因) the「origin 〔cause〕 of a fire. ¶ ～ 불명의 화재 a fire of unknown origin / ～을 조사하다 inquire into the cause of the fire. 「jewels.
**화잠**(花簪) a bridal hairpin inlaid with
**화장**(一長) the sleeve length. ◉ ～걸음 leisurely steps; a gentlemanly gait.
**화장**(火葬) cremation. ～하다 cremate 《the remains》; burn 《a dead body》 to ashes. ◉ ～인부 a cremator; a

burner at a crematory. ～장〔터〕 a crematory《미》; a crematorium (*pl.* ～s, -ria)《영》; a cremation ground. ～허가증 a certificate permitting cremation. 전기～ electric cremation.

**화장**(化粧) (a) makeup; (a) toilet; beauty care; dressing. ～하다 make up (*one's* face); put on (*one's*) makeup; make *one's* toilet; make *oneself* up; paint 〔powder, embellish〕 *one's* face; dress *oneself;* apply makeup. ¶ ～용의 for toilet 「use 〔purposes〕; cosmetic / 짙은〔엷은〕 ～ an 「thick 〔thin〕 toilet; a 「heavy 〔light〕 makeup / ～ 안 한 얼굴 an unpowdered face / 짙은 ～을 하다 paint *one's* face thick; make a heavy toilet; wear heavy makeup; put on thick paint / ～을 고치다 touch up 〔fix〕 *one's* makeup; rearrange *one's* face / ～을 마치다 finish 〔fix〕 up *one's* toilet; complete *one's* makeup / ～을 지우다 remove 〔take off〕 *one's* makeup / 거의 ～을 안 하다 wear 「little 〔hardly any〕 makeup / ～중이다 be at *one's* toilet / ～을 공들여 하다 give much time and care to *one's* toilet / 눈물로 ～이 지워졌다 Her tears washed away the paint from her face. / 나의 아내는 ～을 안 해도 아름답다 My wife is beautiful with no makeup on.
◉ ～대(臺) a dressing table; a toilet= stand; a dresser《미》. ～도구 a make= up set; a dressing equipage (케이스에 든). ～복 a bathrobe; a dressing gown. ～비〔료〕 beauty expenses. ～비누《a cake of》toilet soap; bathroom soap. ～상자 a 「dressing 〔toilet〕 case;《휴대용》 a vanity (case, box). 기초～ makeup base; a foundation: 기초 ～으로 크림을 바르다 use some cream as a makeup base. 「water 〔lotion〕.

**화장수**(化粧水) (beauty) wash; toilet

**화장실**(化粧室)《변소》 toilet; water closet (생략 W.C.); lavatory (*pl.* -ies);《가정의》 bathroom; washroom; restroom;《남성용》 men's room; gentlemen;《여성용》 ladies' room; ladies. ¶ 지금 ～은 비어 있습니다〔사용중입니다〕 The closet is now 「vacant 〔occupied〕. / ～이 어디 있습니까 Where can I wash my hands? *or* Where is the restroom? / 「미안합니다만 ～ 좀 써야겠습니다」—「좋습니다. 복도로 나가면 왼쪽에 있습니다」—「감사합니다」 "Excuse me, but nature calls."—"OK. The restroom is out in the hallway to your left."—"Thank you."

> **용법** **toilet, water closet** 가장 일반적인 말. water closet은 수세식 변소를 가리키며 주로 《영》에서 쓰임. **lavatory** toilet, water closet을 피하기 위한 완곡한 말씨. **bathroom, washroom** 원래 「욕실」「세면실」의 뜻이지만 미국이나 영국의 가정에서는 욕실과 변소가 함께 있기 때문에 완곡하게 말할 때 쓰임. **rest room** 호텔·레스토랑 등의 변소를 가리킴. 이 대신으로 washroom, lavatory도 쓰임. **men's room** 「남성용」, **ladies' room** 「여성용」을 의미하는 말. **gentlemen, ladies** 「남성용」, 「여성용」의 의미이지만 주로 화장실 입구의 게시용으로 쓰임.

**화장지**(化粧紙) toilet 〔lavatory〕 paper 〔tissue〕;《두루마리》 a toilet roll.

**화장품**(化粧品)《한가지》 a cosmetic; [총체적] cosmetics; toiletries (★ 비누·치약 등도 포함). ¶ 남성용 ～ men's toiletries / 외제 ～ a foreign brand cosmetic.
◉ ～류 toiletries; cosmetics. ～매장(賣場)《백화점의》 a cosmetic(s) 〔beauty〕 counter. ～상자 a beauty kit. ～점(店) a cosmetic store (★《미》에서는 보통 a drugstore). ～회사 a cosmetic firm.

**화재**(火災) a fire; a conflagration (대화재). ¶ 누전으로 인한 ～ a fire caused by the short circuit / 원인 불명의 ～ a fire of unknown origin / 자동 ～ 탐지 및 경보 장치 automatic fire detection and alarm system / ～가 나다 a fire 「breaks out 〔occurs, takes place〕/ ～를 내다 have 〔let〕 a fire break out; cause 〔start〕 a fire / ～를 당하다 suffer from a fire; be caught in a fire / ～를 당한 사람들 sufferers from a fire; burnt-out people / ～로 타다 be burnt in a fire; be destroyed by fire / (건물이) ～로 전소되다 burn 〔be burnt〕 down / ～ 현장에서 빠져 나갈 데를 잃다 be trapped in a fire; be cut off by a fire / ～ 원인은 누전이었다 A leakage of electricity caused the fire. / 과열이 ～의 원인으로 보고 있다 Overheating is supposed to have started the fire. / ～로 책들을 몽땅 불태웠다 I had all my books burnt in the fire. / ～ 발생시는 비상 계단을 사용하시오《게시》 In case of fire, use exit stairs only. / 어제 저녁 ～로 11명이 소사했다 The fire last evening claimed eleven lives. ◉ ～대피구〔로〕 a fire escape. ～대피훈련 a fire drill. ～방지주간 Fire Prevention Week. ～ 예방조

례 a fire prevention ordinance. ～현장 the scene of a fire: ～현장의 도둑 a thief at a fire; a looter / ～ 현장에서 도둑질을 하다 loot 〔steal *something*〕 at a fire.

**화재**(畫才) an artistic talent; the artist's skill.

**화재경보**(火災警報) an alarm of fire. ¶ ～를 울리다 sound a fire alarm. ◉ ～기 a fire alarm (box); 《ring》 a signal box; pull a firebox alarm. ～장치 fire-warning facilities.

**화재보험**(火災保險) fire insurance. ¶～에 들다 insure 《a house》 against fire; get 〔have〕 《*one's* house》 insured against fire / 그 집은 5천만원짜리 ～에 들어 있다 The house is insured against fire for 50,000,000 won. ◉ ～료(料) a fire-insurance premium. ～업자 a fire underwriter. ～회사〔계약, 증서〕 a fire insurance company 〔contract, policy〕.

**화적**(火賊) ＝불한당(不汗黨).

**화전**(火田) 〖농업〗 land made arable by the slash-and-burn method; a slash=and-burn field; fields cleared for cultivation by burning. ◉ ～농법 slash-and-burn farming; the slash=and-burn method (of agriculture). ～민 'fire-field' 〔slash-and-burn〕 farmers.

**화전**(火箭) a fiery dart; an incendiary arrow; a rocket (signal).

**화전**(花煎) ① 《꽃전》 a cake made in the shape of a flower. ② 《부꾸미》 fried-flower cookies.

**화전**(和戰) ① 《전쟁과 평화》 war and 〔or〕 peace. ¶ ～ 양면에 대비하다 be prepared both for war and peace. ② 《강화》 making 〔concluding〕 peace 《with》. ◉ ～ 양면정책 stick-and-carrot strategy. ～ 조약 a peace treaty.

**화젓가락**(火―) ⇨부젓가락.

**화제**(話題) a topic 〔subject〕 (of conversation); a talk (화젯거리). ¶ ～의 인물 the man in the news / 오늘의 ～ the topics of the day; current topics / 일상의 ～ an everyday topic 《on》; a topic everybody's lips / ～에 오르다 become the subject of a conversation; be brought into conversation; be talked about; be brought up / 항간의 화젯거리가 되다 be the talk of the town / ～가 풍부하다 have a large 〔an ample〕 stock of topics / ～가 떨어지다 〔막히다〕 run out of anything 〔have nothing more〕 to talk about / ～를 돌리다 change the subject; shift the conversation / 전직 시장의 수회 사건이 세간의 ～가 되었다 The bribery case involving a former mayor has become the topic in the world.

**화제**(畫題) 《그림 제목》 the title 〔subject, motif〕 of a picture 〔painting〕; 《그림 위의》 a composition written on a picture to explain it.

**화조**(花鳥) ① 《꽃과 새》 flowers and birds. ¶ ～풍월(風月)을 벗삼다 lead the life of a nature lover; live a life amid nature's glories. ② 《그림·조각》 a painting 〔sculpture〕 of flowers and birds. ◉ ～화첩(畫帖) an album of flowers and birds.

**화족**(華族) a peer; a noble(man); [총칭] the peerage; the nobility.

**화주**(火酒) strong liquor; (ardent) spirits; firewater 《미》.

**화주**(花柱) a style. ＝암술대.

**화주**(貨主) a shipper; a consignor; the owner of goods.

**화중군자**(花中君子) the lotus flower.

**화중왕**(花中王) the peony.

**화중지병**(畫中之餠) 《그림의 떡》 a desirable but unattainable object; a prize beyond *one's* reach.

**화증**(火症) (pent-up) fury 〔rage, wrath〕; anger; ire; (a) passion. ¶ ～이 나다 get angry 〔mad〕; fly into temper 〔a rage〕; flare up; blow *one's* top.

**화집**(畫集) a book of paintings. ¶ 렘브란트 ～ 《책 이름》 Collected paintings of Rembrandt.

**화차**(貨車) a freight car 《미》; a goods wagon 〔van〕 《영》. ¶ ～1대분 a carload 《of freight》 《미》; a wagonload 《of goods》 《영》 / ～로 by freight 《미》; by goods 《영》 / 가축용 ～ a cattle car.

**화창**(和暢) balminess; brightness. ～하다 (be) balmy; bright; genial; sunny. ¶ ～한 날씨 balmy 〔bright〕 weather / ～한 봄날 a balmy spring day.

**화채**(花菜) honeyed juice mixed with fruits as a punch.

**화첩**(畫帖) a picture album 〔book〕.

**화초**(花草) flowering plants; flowers. ¶ ～를 가꾸다 cultivate 〔grow〕 flowering plants / ～를 화분에 심다 pot up flowers; plant flowers in a pot. ◉ ～기생 just a pretty-pretty singsong girl. ～말 a beautiful horse. ～밭 a flower garden. ～재배 floriculture; cultivation of flowers. ～장이 a florist; a floriculturist; a flower man. ～전시회 a flower show. ～집 a flower 〔florist's〕 shop.

**화촉**(華燭) ①《초》 a colored candle. ②《혼인》 a wedding; a marriage ceremony. ¶ ~지전(之典) =화촉② / ~을 밝히다 celebrate a wedding; hold 〔solemnize〕 a marriage ceremony.
◉ ~동방(洞房) the bridal room for the wedding night.

**화축**(花軸) a flower stalk. =꽃대.

**화치다** 《a ship》 roll (from side to side).

**화친**(和親) friendly relations; amity. ~하다 make peace 《with》; enter into friendly relations 《with》. ◉ ~조약 a peace treaty. ~협상(協商) an *entente cordiale* (F.).

**화침**(火針) a red-hot needle (used in breaking a boil). ¶ ~질하다 break 〔open, lance〕 a boil with a red-hot needle.

**화탁**(花托) a receptacle. =꽃턱.

**화톳불** a bonfire. ¶ ~을 놓다 make a bonfire.

**화통** 〖건축〗 a crose groove at the top of a pillar.

**화통**(火筒) a smokestack; a funnel.

**화투**(花鬪) Korean playing cards; "flower cards". ~하다〔치다〕 play 〔shuffle〕 "flower cards". ◉ ~놀이 playing "flower cards"; card playing.

**화판**(花瓣) a petal. =꽃잎.

**화판**(畫板) a drawing board.

**화편**(花片) fallen petals.

**화평**(和平) peace; harmony; placidity. ~하다 (be) peaceful; placid; harmonious. ¶ ~을 제의하다 make a proposal for peace / ~을 주장하다 advocate peace 《with》. ◉ ~공작 a peace move. ~교섭 peace negotiation.

**화폐**(貨幣) 《통화》 money; currency; 《경화》 a coin; coinage [총칭]. ¶ ~의 구매력 purchasing power of money / ~의 앞면〔뒷면〕 the head 〔tail〕 of a coin / ~의 발행 the issue of coinage / ~의 절상〔절하〕 revalue 〔devalue〕 《the won》 / ~의 대내〔대외〕적 가치 domestic 〔foreign〕 value of money / ~를 주조〔발행〕하다 mint 〔issue〕 coins / 어떤 단위의 ~로 드릴까요 《은행 창구 등에서》 In what denominations would you like it?
◉ ~가격 money price. ~가치 the value of money; monetary 〔currency〕 value: ~ 가치가 오르다〔내리다〕 increase 〔decrease〕 in monetary value. ~개혁 currency reform; 《평가절하》 devaluation. ~경제 (a) monetary economy. ~교환 가치 the exchange value of currency. ~교환소 an exchange house 〔shop〕; a money change booth. ~단위 a monetary unit 〔currency〕. ~본위 a monetary standard. ~소득 a monetary income. ~위조 coining; counterfeiting: ~ 위조자 a coiner; a counterfeiter. ~유통량 the amount 〔volume〕 of coins in circulation; the amount of currency. ~제도 the monetary system. ~주조 coinage; mintage. ~착각 money illusion (화폐액면가의 대소가 실질 구매력의 대소라고 착각 하는 것). 대용~ token money 〔coin〕. 위조~ counterfeit money; an imitaion coin.

**화포**(火砲) a gun; a firearm.

**화포**(花布) 〖식물〗 a bract.

**화포**(畫布) a canvas (for a painting). ◉ ~틀 a canvas stretcher.

**화폭**(畫幅) a picture; a drawing; a painting.

**화풀이**(火—) satisfying resentment; venting *one's* wrath. ~하다 satisfy *one's* resentment 〔grudge〕; take *one's* anger out 《on》; vent *one's* wrath 〔spite〕 《on》; wreak *one's* anger 〔wrath〕 《on *a person*》. ¶ 엉뚱한 사람에게 ~하다 snarl at a wrong person; vent *one's* anger without reason upon a person / 나한테 ~할 것 없다 You shouldn't take your anger out on me. / 그는 아내한테 ~를 했다 He vented his anger on his wife.

**화품**(畫品) artistic merit of a picture 〔drawing〕.

**화풍**(和風) a balmy wind; a gentle 〔mild〕 breeze.

**화풍**(畫風) a style of painting 〔drawing〕. ¶ 터너의 ~ the brush 〔school〕 of Turner; Turner's brushwork.

**화피**(花被) 〖식물〗 a floral envelope; a perianth; a perigone. ⇨ 꽃덮이.

**화필**(畫筆) a paint brush; a painter's 〔an artist's〕 brush.

**화하다**(化—) change 〔turn〕 《to, into》; convert 《into, to》; be transformed; be turned. ¶ 돌로 ~ change 〔turn〕 into (a) stone; petrify / 불타서 재로 ~ burn to ashes / 죽어서 흙으로 ~ die and decompose into earth / 죽어서 나비로 ~ turn 〔metamorphose〕 into a butterfly after *one's* death.

**화학**(化學) chemistry. ¶ ~적(으로) chemical(ly) / ~적 광도 측정 actinometry / ~적 성질 chemical property / ~적으로 추출하다 chemically extract 〔recover〕.
◉ ~결합 chemical combination; a chemical bond. ~공업 chemical industry. ~공장 a chemical factory 〔plant, works〕. ~공학 chemical engineering. ~광량계 an actinometer. ~구조 the chemical structure 《of a drug》. ~기

구〔기기〕 chemical instruments 〔appliances, implements〕. ～기호 a chemical sign 〔symbol〕: ～ 기호법 chemical notation. ～무기〔병기〕 chemical weapons 〔arms〕: ～ 무기 금지 기구 the Organization for the Prevention of Chemical Weapon (생략 OPCW) / ～무기 금지 조약 the Chemical Weapons Convention (생략 CWC). ～물질 chemical substances; chemicals. ～반응 a chemical reaction. ～방정식 a chemical equation. ～변화 a chemical change. ～분석 (a) a chemical analysis. ～비료 (a) chemical fertilizer. ～선 actinic rays. ～섬유 a synthetic 〔chemical〕 fiber. ～소방차 a chemical fire engine. ～시약(試藥) a chemical reagent. ～식(式) a chemical formula. ～실험 a chemical experiment: ～ 실험실 a chemical laboratory. ～약품 pharmaceuticals; pharmaceutical products. ～에너지 chemical energy. ～역학(力學) chemical dynamics. ～연구소 the Institute for Chemical Research. ～요법 〖의학〗 chemotherapy: ～ 요법의(醫) a chemotherapist / ～ 요법제(劑) a chemotherapeutic agent; a chemotherapeutant. ～자 a chemist. ～작용 (a) chemical action: ～ 작용으로 chemically / ～ 작용을 일으키지 않는 inert; neutral. ～전(戰) chemical warfare: 생～전 biochemical warfare ～정련 chemical scouring. ～제(劑) chemicals. ～제품 chemical goods 〔products〕. ～조미료 a synthetic seasoning (agent); [일반적] monosodium glutamate (글루타민산모노나트륨; 생략 MSG). ～조성 chemical composition. ～처리 (a) chemical treatment: ～ 처리공장 a chemical processing plant. ～천칭 a chemical 〔analytical〕 balance. ～친화력 chemical affinity. ～펄프 chemical pulp. ～합성 chemosynthesis. 무기〔유기〕～ inorganic chemistry. 실용～ practical chemistry. 이론 ～ theoretical chemistry. 한국 ～연구소 the Korea Research Institute of Chemical Technology.

**화학적 산소 요구량**(化學的酸素要求量) 〖환경〗 a chemical oxygen demand (생략 COD). (★ 생화학적 산소 요구량 BOD (biochemical oxygen demand)와 마찬가지로 물의 오염도를 나타내며 단위는 ppm.)

**화합**(化合) 〖화학〗 (chemical) combination. ～하다 (chemically) combine 《with》. ¶ 수소와 산소는 ～해서 물이 된다 Hydrogen combines with oxygen to form water. ◉ ～력 combining power; chemical affinity. ～물 a (chemical) compound 《of A and B》: ～물 반도체 〖컴퓨터〗 a compound semiconductor. ～열(熱) the heat of combination.

**화합**(和合) harmony; concord; unity; union; peace(평화). ～하다 harmonize 《with》; live in harmony 〔peace〕 《with》; agree 《with each other》; be in accord 《with》; get along well 〔amicably〕 《with》. ¶ 부부의 ～ conjugal harmony / 국민의 ～과 단결 national reconciliation and unity / 일가의 ～ a harmonious family life / ～하여 살다 live in peace 〔harmony〕 / 부부 ～의 비결을 너에게 가르쳐 주겠다 I'll teach you the secret of harmonizing as man and wife. ◉ ～일치 unity; unanimity.

**화해**(和解) an amicable settlement; (a) reconciliation; an accommodation; 《타협》 (a) compromise; composition; 〖법〗 out-of-court settlement. ～하다 make up 《with》; make peace 《with》; be 〔become〕 reconciled 《with, to each other》; come to terms 《with》; settle *one's* differences 《with》; reach 〔arrive at〕 an amicable settlement 《with》; 《타협하다》 compromise 《with》; be settled out of court. ¶ ～할 수 없는 irreconcilable / ～시키다 reconcile 《persons to each other, A to 〔with〕 B》; make peace 《between》; settle (a dispute) peacefully 〔amicably〕 / 서로 ～해서 다시 친구가 됩시다 Let us become reconciled and be friends again. / 왜 그녀와 ～하지 않나 Why don't you make it up with her? / 그는 나를 그녀와 ～시켰다 He reconciled me with 〔to〕 her. / 그는 A와 B를 ～시키는 데 성공했다 He succeeded in making peace between A and B.

**화현**(和絃) 〖음악〗 a chord; a concord.

**화협**(和協) consultation 〔conference〕 in a chatty 〔familiar〕 tone. ～하다 consult 〔confer〕 (quite) freely 《with *a person*》.

**화형**(火刑) burning at the stake. ～하다 burn 《*a person*》 (to death) at the stake. ¶ ～을 당하다〔에 처해지다〕 be burnt at the stake; be burned alive 〔to death〕.

**화호불성**(畫虎不成) failing to succeed in imitating *another's* achievement.

**화환**(花環) a (floral) wreath; a garland (of flowers); 《하와이의》 a lei. ¶ ～을 바치다 place 〔lay〕 a wreath 《at the tomb, before the monument》; place a floral tribute 《on the grave of》.

**화환신용장**(貨換信用狀) ⇨ 화물환신용장.

**화환어음**(貨換―) 〖경제〗《draw》 a documentary「bill 〔draft〕. ⇨ 화물환어음.

**화훼**(花卉) a flowering plant. ◉ ～산업 floricultural industry. ～원예 floriculture: ～ 원예가 a floriculturist. ～품평회 a flower show; a floricultural show.

**확**[1] 《절구의 구멍》 the hollow of a grain mortar; 《절구》 a mortar. ¶ 절구 확이 넓다 a mortar has a large bowl.

**확**[2] ①《부는 모양》 blowing hard; with a great puff; with a gust. ⇨ 확하다. ¶ 촛불을 확 불어 끄다 blow out a candlelight / 바람이 확 불다 a gust of wind blows. ②《일어나는 모양》 flaring up; with a flame; with a burst. ⇨ 확하다. ¶ 불이 확 일어나다 a flame flares up / 확 타오르다 burst into flame(s); flare 〔flame〕 up / 불이 확 종이에 당기다 paper catches fire. ③《달려드는 모양》 going 〔lunging〕 suddenly at; attacking. ⇨ 확하다. ¶ 개가 확 달려들다 a dog suddenly springs 《at *a person*》. ④《갑자기》 rapidly; suddenly; in a flash; 《힘차게 하는 모양》 with force; with a jerk. ¶ 확 당기다〔밀다〕 pull 〔push〕 with a (sudden) jerk; give 《it》 a vigorous「pull 〔push〕.

**확견**(確見) a definite「idea 〔view〕.

**확고**(確固) firmness; determination. ～하다 (be) firm; definite; resolute; fixed; steady; determined. ¶ ～하게, ～히 firmly; determinedly; adamantly; unswervingly; resolutely / ～부동한 indefatigable; invincible; unshakable; unyielding; unwavering; adamantine / ～한 신념 a firm faith / ～한 의지 an「iron 〔adamant〕 will / ～한 정책 a rock-ribbed policy / 그의 결심은 ～부동하다 He stands firm in his resolution. / ～한 증거가 있다 There is indisputable evidence (for it). / 미국의 한국에 대한 지지는 ～하다 The United States is steadfast in its support of the Republic of Korea.

**확답**(確答) a definite answer 〔reply〕. ～하다 answer 〔reply〕 definitely; give a definite「answer 〔reply〕. ¶ ～을 안 주다 give no definite answer; be noncommittal / ～을 얻다 secure 〔gain〕 a definite answer / ～을 요구하다 press 《*a person*》 for a definite answer; insist on a definite answer from 《*a person*》 / ～을 피하다 be noncommittal in *one's* answer; avoid committing *oneself* in *one's* answer.

**확대**(擴大) 《수량·규모의》 extension; (an) increase; 《사이즈의》 magnification; enlargement; 《단계적인》 escalation. ～하다 《수량·규모가》 expand; extend; increase; 《사이즈가》 magnify; scale up; enlarge; 《번지다》 spread; expand. ¶ 2배로 ～한 사진 a twice enlarged photograph / ～축소가 가능한 복사기 a copying machine capable of enlargement and reduction / 수입〔수출〕의 ～ the expansion of「imports 〔exports〕 / ～되고 있는 소프트웨어 시장 the expanding market for software / 사진을 ～하다 enlarge a photograph / 생산을 ～하다 increase 〔boost〕 the production 《of》 / …의 크기로 ～하다 magnify to the size of... / 양국 간의 경제 분야의 협력을 ～하다 expand bilateral partnership in the areas of economy / 문제가 ～되다 a problem「spreads 〔grows〕 / 사업을 60퍼센트 ～하다 expand business by sixty percent / 반란이 전국으로 ～되었다 The revolt spread throughout the country. / 그 국지 전쟁은 자칫 잘못하면 세계전으로 ～될 위험성이 있다 The local war is likely to escalate into a global war.
◉ ～경 a magnifying「glass 〔lens〕; a magnifier; 《현미경의》 an amplifier. ～균형 〖경제〗 expanded equilibrium. ～기(器) an enlarger. ～사진 an enlarged photo. ～위원회 《a meeting of》 a committee with enlarged membership: ～ 투쟁위원회 an expanded struggle committee. ～율 magnifying power; 〖사진〗 an enlargement ratio; the scale of enlargement. ～재생산 enlarged reproduction; reproduction on an enlarged scale. ～해석 a broad interpretation: ～해석하다 stretch the meaning of 《the law》 / 법을 자신에게 유리하게 ～ 해석하다 stretch the law in *one's* favor. ～행렬 〖컴퓨터〗 an augmented matrix. ～화면 〖컴퓨터〗 fat bits. ～회담〔회의〕 《hold》 an「expanded 〔extended〕 meeting.

**확론**(確論) an infallible argument; an「incontrovertible 〔indisputable〕 opinion; an established theory. ～하다 discuss 〔argue〕 definitely.

**확률**(確率) 〖수학〗 probability. ¶ ～의 법칙 the laws of probability / 눈이 올 ～은 20퍼센트이다 The probability that it will snow is 20 percent. / 이 사업이 성공할 ～은 높다〔낮다〕 There is「much 〔little〕 probability of our success in this business. ◉ ～곡선 〖통계〗 a probability curve. ～변수 a random 〔stochastic〕 variable. ～분포 probability distribution. ～예보 『기상』 probability forecast 《of rainfall》. ～오차 『통계』 a probable error. ～진폭 probability amplitude. ～편차 『경제』 probable deviation. ～표본 a probability 〔random〕 sample. ～함수 『수학』 a probability function.

**확립**(確立) establishment; settlement. ～하다 establish; build up; fix; settle. ¶ ～된 definite; established; settled / 평화의 ～ the establishment of peace / 명성을 ～하다 establish *one's* reputation / 방침을 ～하다 put the policy on a firm footing / 여성의 지위를 ～하다 establish women's status / …라는 사실이 ～되었다 It has been very clearly established that…. / 기초를 ～하다 set up a foundation / 이 이론은 아직 학문적으로 ～되어 있지 않다 This theory is not yet scientifically established.

**확보**(確保) security; insurance; guarantee. ～하다 secure; ensure 〔insure 《미》〕 《*one's* life》; assure 《*one's* comfort》; make sure of 《a copy of a book, *one's* position》; guarantee; maintain 《place and order》. ¶ 교두보를 ～하다 secure 〔establish〕 a bridgehead / 식량을 ～하다 secure foodstuffs / 좌석을 ～하다 secure a seat / 영원한 평화를 ～하다 ensure a firm and everlasting peace / 역사상 불후의 지위를 ～하다 vindicate *oneself* a permanent place in history / 안전성을 ～하다 ensure against risks / 인재를 ～하다 collect talented people / 당선에 필요한 표를 ～하다 secure enough votes to be elected / 학위가 있으니까 문제없이 직장이 ～될 게다 Your degree will insure you a job. / 그 일 덕분에 생활에 충분한 수입이 ～되었다 The job secured me a decent salary.

**확보**(確報) a definite 〔sure, confirmed〕 report; a reliable communication; authentic news. ～하다 give a definite report. ¶ 이 보도에는 ～가 없다 This report needs confirmation. / 아직 ～에 접하지 못하고 있다 The report has not yet been confirmed.

**확산**(擴散) spread(ing); dissemination; 《핵병기 따위의》 proliferation; 『물리·화학』 diffusion 《of light, gas》. ～하다 spread; disseminate; proliferate; 『물리·화학』 diffuse. ¶ 가스의 ～ the diffusion of gases / 핵무기의 ～을 막다 check the spread 〔proliferation〕 of nuclear weapons; prevent nuclear proliferation. ◉ ～광(光) a diffused light. ～능(能) diffusing power. ～반사 diffuse(d) reflection. ～벽 a diffusion wall. ～속도계 a diffusionmeter. ～율 a diffusion coefficient. ～음 a diffused sound. ～재(材) a dispersing agent. ～전류 a diffusion current. ～전위(電位) diffusion potential. ～제(劑) a dispersing agent. ～체 a diffuser; 『원자물리』 a diffusate. ～펌프 a diffusion pump. 핵～방지조약〔협정〕 a nuclear (weapons) non-proliferation treaty 〔agreement〕.

**확성기**(擴聲器) a (loud)speaker; 《휴대용》 《미》 a bullhorn; 《영》 loudhailer; a megaphone (전기의); 《장내·기내의 방송 장치》 a public address 〔PA, P.A., p.a.〕 system. ¶ ～로 말하다 speak over a loudspeaker / ～로 (소리를) 높이다 amplify 《the voice》 over a loudspeaker / ～로 아무를 부르다 page 《*a person*》 over the loudspeaker.

**확쇠** 『건축』 an iron saucer on which a door pivots.

**확수**(確守) = 고수(固守).

**확신**(確信) (a) conviction; a firm belief; confidence (자신); assurance. ～하다 believe firmly; be 〔feel〕 convinced 《of, that》; convince *oneself* 《of》; be sure 〔certain, convinced, confident〕 《that…, of *something*》. ¶ ～을 가지고 with confidence; in the firm belief 《that…》; confidently / ～을 갖다 have confidence 《that》; feel sure 《of, that》 / ～을 얻다 gain confidence / ～을 주다 carry conviction 《to》 / 성공할 ～이 없다 be not confident of success / 우리 팀이 이길 것을 ～한다 I feel confident that our team will win. / 변호사는 그 죄수의 결백을 ～하고 있다 The lawyer is convinced 〔assured〕 of the innocence of the prisoner. / 그는 신의 존재를 ～하고 있다 He is positive as to the existence of God. / 날이 감에 따라 점점 ～을 굳혔다 I was confirmed in my belief with the lapse of time. / 나는 이길 수 있다는 강한 ～을 가지고 있었다 I had a strong conviction that I would win.

**확실**(確實) ① 《틀림없음》 certainty; sureness; authenticity. ～하다 (be) certain; sure; positive; definite; authentic. ¶ ～히 certainly; surely; for certain; no doubt; beyond doubt / ～한 근거 solid 〔sure〕 grounds 《for belief》 / ～한 방법 a sure 〔safe, valid〕 method / ～한 사실 a certain fact / ～한 증거

positive evidence 〔proof〕/ ～한 보도 accurate information / …이 ～하다고 생각하다 be confident 〔sure〕 of《success》/ ～하게 하다 ensure; secure; make sure of / ～히는 모르다 don't know for certain / ～히 그는 오게 되어 있다 He is bound to come. / ～한 것은 말할 수 없다 I cannot say for certain. / ～치 않은 것을 단정해서 말하지 마라 Don't say so positively what you don't know for certain. / 자네가 성공할 것은 ～하다 You are sure to succeed. *or* I'm sure that you will succeed. (★ You are sure of success. 또는 You are sure that you will succeed. 이면 「너는 성공할 자신이 있다」란 뜻이 됨) / 그녀는 ～히 이상한 여자다 She is a funny girl, and that's the truth.
② 《믿을 만함》 reliability; trustworthiness; soundness. ～하다 (be) reliable; trustworthy; secure; 《재정적으로》 (be) sound; solid; safe (무난하다). ¶ ～한 담보 a gilt-edged 〔good〕 security / ～한 물건 a sound 〔reliable〕 article / ～한 보증인 a reliable surety / ～한 사람 a reliable 〔trustworthy〕 man / ～한 사업 a secure business; a safe 〔sound〕 business / ～한 투자 a secure 〔solid, sound〕 investment / 저 사람 ～한가요 Is he to be trusted?
◉ ～성 certainty; reliability; validity: ～성이 있다 be (most) probable.

**확약**(確約) a strict 〔definite〕 promise. ～하다 promise positively 〔definitely〕; give 〔make〕 a definite promise; give 《*a person*》 *one's* word 《to *do*》; commit *oneself* 《to *do*》. ¶ ～을 얻다〔받다〕 get a definite promise / ～은 할 수 없다 I cannot make a definite promise.

**확언**(確言) a definite 〔positive〕 statement; assurance; assertion; affirmation. ～하다 state 〔say〕 definitely 〔positively〕; assert; assure; affirm; commit *oneself*. ¶ 그 점은 ～하기 어렵다 I am not positive about the point. / 그가 거기 있었다고 ～할 수 있다 I can affirm that he was there.

**확연하다**(確然―) (be) definite; positive; sure; clear; certain. ¶ 확연히 definitely; positively; surely; certainly; assuredly; clearly.

**확인**(確因) a definite cause 〔reason〕.

**확인**(確認) confirmation; verification; 《신원의》 identification; 《법률상의》 corroboration. ～하다 confirm; check; verify; ascertain; identify (신원을); corroborate (법적으로). ¶ ～되지 않은 unconfirmed; naked 《confession》/ …의 사실을 ～하다 ascertain the truth of… / 시체의 신원을 ～하다 identify a corpse / 보도를〔풍문을〕 ～하다 confirm a report 〔rumor〕/ 사실 여부를 ～하다 ascertain whether 〔if〕 it is true / 계약을 ～하다 confirm a contract / 신원을 ～하다 check 〔verify〕 *one's* identity / 나의 호텔 예약을 ～하고 싶습니다 I want to confirm my reservation at your hotel. / 그 이야기는 ～해 볼 필요가 있다 The story requires confirmation. / 그의 죽음은〔이 보도는〕 아직 ～되지 않고 있다 His death 〔This report〕 is not yet confirmed. ◉ ～반응 confirmatory reaction. ～사항 items to be confirmed 〔verified〕. ～서 a (written) confirmation; a confirmation document. ～신용장 a confirmed L.C. ～통지서 a confirmation note. ～판결 a declaratory judgment.

**확장**(擴張) extension; expansion; enlargement; aggrandizement; increment; dilation. ～하다 extend; expand; enlarge; aggrandize; increase; dilate. ¶ 거리를 ～하다 widen a street / 교사(校舍)〔점포〕를 ～하다 enlarge 〔expand〕 the school-buildings 〔shop〕/ 운동장을 ～하다 enlarge the playground / 사업을 ～하다 extend 〔expand〕 *one's* business 〔trade〕; branch out *one's* business / 현재의 4차선에서 6차선으로 ～되다 be expanded to six lanes from the present four lanes / 판로를 ～하다 extend the market 《for》. ◉ ～공사 extension work. ～근(筋) 『해부』 a dilator; a dilatator. ～기(器) a dilator. ～명제 『논리』 an ampliative proposition. ～정책 a policy of expansion; expansionism (영토 따위의); an expansionist policy. 영토～ territorial expansion: 영토 ～론 (territorial) expansionism / 영토 ～정책 a policy of territorial expansion. 도로～계획 a street-widening project.

**확전**(擴戰) (war) escalation.

**확정**(確定) 《결정》 decision; conclusion (귀결); settlement; 《확인》 confirmation; corroboration; ascertainment (판명). ～하다 《정하다》 make a definite decision; decide upon 《*a matter*》; settle; fix (날짜 따위를); confirm; corroborate; 《법률 따위를》 establish. ～되다 be 〔get〕 decided 《upon》; be settled; be fixed (upon); become final 〔definite, certain〕; come to a definite decision; 《판명되다》 be ascertained.

¶ ～적인 fixed; decided; definite; established; final / ～적(으로) definite(ly); final(ly); decided(ly); certain(ly) / ～된 사실 an established fact / (형이) 아직 ～돼 있지 않다 be not irrevocably settled yet / 이건 ～된 사실이다 This is an established fact. / 취해야 할 조처는 아직 ～을 못보았다 The step to be taken is not yet decided upon. / 그가 그 일을 떠맡으리란 것은 ～적이다 It is definite that he will take the job. / 재판은 피고의 승소〔패소〕로 ～되었다 The case has been decided in favor of 〔against〕 the defendant. / 그의 해외 여행은 ～됐다 It is decided that he shall be sent abroad. / 날짜가 ～되면 알려 주겠다 I'll let you know when the date is fixed. ◉ ～공채 fixed bonds. ～금액 a definite amount. ～기한 〖법〗 a certain time. ～사항 a definitely settled matter. ～신고 《소득세의》 a 〔*one's*〕 final income tax return 《for the year》: ～ 신고를 하다 file a 〔*one's*〕 final return 《for the year》. ～안(案) a final draft. ～의무〔채무〕 a determinate obligation. ～일자 a fixed 〔an inconvertible〕 date. ～판결 a final and conclusive judgment.

**확증**(確證) a sure 〔decisive, convincing, corroborative, positive〕 proof; conclusive evidence; corroboration; confirmation. ～하다 prove 〔show〕 positively; give positive 〔convincing〕 proof of; corroborate; confirm.
¶ ～적(인) corroborative; confirmatory / ～이 따르지 않는 uncorroborated 《confession》 / …의 ～을 잡다 secure 〔obtain〕 positive evidence of… / 그의 소행이라는 ～이라도 있단 말인가 Do you have any positive proof that he did it? / 그녀가 거기에 있었다는 ～은 없다 There is no positive proof that she was there.

**확집**(確執) adherence to *one's* own opinion 〔view〕. ～하다 adhere 〔stick, cling〕 to *one's* own opinion.

**확충**(擴充) (an) expansion; (an) amplification; 〖논리〗 distribution. ～하다 expand 《productivity》; amplify; distribute. ¶ 생산(력)의 ～ the expansion of production 〔productivity〕 / 시설을 ～하다 expand and improve the facilities / 조직의 ～을 기하다 attempt to expand an organization.

**확하다** ① 《부는 모양》 blow hard. ② 《일어나는 모양》 flare up. ③ 《달려드는 모양》 lunge 《at》.

**확호**(確乎) firmly; determinedly. ～하다 (be) firm; determined.

**확확** ① 《바람이》 with great puffs; with gusts; blowing and blowing; huffing and puffing. ¶ 바람이 ～ 불다 have gust after gust of wind. ② 《불길이》 flaring up incessantly; with flame after flame; with burst after burst. ¶ 불길이 ～ 일어나다 a fire is flaming up / 불이 솜에 ～ 당기다 cotton flames up. ③ 《기타》 ¶ (볼이나 얼굴이) ～ 달아오르다 flush up (hotly); feel 《*one's* face》 burning 《with shame》 / ～ 잡아당기다 tug; pull 〔drag〕 《a rope》 with jerks.

**환**[1] 《줄》 a kind of file 〔rasp〕; a serrated iron piece. ¶ 환 쓸다 file; rasp.

**환**[2] 《그림》 a rough drawing; a sketch. ¶ 환을 치다 draw 〔make〕 a sketch.

**환**(丸) a pill. ¶ 청심환 pills that clear *one's* chest / 대보환(大補丸) tonic pills.

**환**(換) 〖경제〗 a money order; exchange; 〖상업〗 transfer.
¶ 환거래 exchange transactions / 환관리 exchange control 〔regulation〕; restrictions on exchange / 환수취인 the payee / 환시세, 환율 the (foreign) exchange rate; the rate of exchange / 환(시세)변동 foreign exchange fluctuations; changes in the exchange rate / 환어음 a bill of exchange (생략 B.E., B/E, b.e.); a draft / 환취결 통지서 an advice of drawing / 환평가(平價) parity 〔par value〕 of exchange / 내국〔외국〕환 domestic 〔foreign〕 exchange / 달러〔원〕환 dollar 〔won〕 exchange / 소액환 a postal note / 외국환 시세표 exchange quotations / 우편환 a postal money order / 전신환 a telegraphic remittance / 환을 취결하다 draw a money order 《on *a person* for 5,000 won》 / 환을 현금으로 바꾸다 have a money order cashed / 환으로 송금하다 remit 〔send〕 《3,000 won》 by money order / 1만 원짜리 우편환을 한 장 끊어 주시오 Give me a postal money order for ten thousand won.
◉ 환리스크 exchange risk. 환브로커 an exchange 〔a bill〕 broker. 환시장 an exchange market. 환은행 an exchange bank. 환차손(換差損) an exchange loss. 환차손익 the profit or loss on a foreign exchange. 환차익(換差益) a foreign exchange profit. 환투기 an exchange speculation. 환평형조작 an exchange equalization operation.

**환**(環) a ring.

**환가**(換價) conversion (into money); realization. ～하다 convert into money; cash; sell; realize. ¶ 재산을 ～하다 realize property. ◉ ～ 불능자산 unrealizable assets. ～성 marketability; market value. ～율 a conversion rate.

**환각**(幻覺) 《작용》 hallucination; 《환상으로 보이는 것》 a hallucination; a hallucinatory image. ¶ ～을 일으키다 hallucinate; see things / ～에 시달리다 suffer from hallucinations / 주정꾼들은 이따금 ～을 일으킨다 Drunken men are sometimes subject to hallucinations. ◉ ～제 a hallucinogen; a hallucinogenic 〔psychedelic〕 drug; acid 《속어》: ～제 상용자 a psychedelic. ～증(상) hallucinosis; a hallucination.

**환갑**(還甲) *one's* 60 th birthday (anniversary). ¶ 어머님은 금년에 ～을 맞으셨다 My mother reached the age of sixty this year. ◉ ～노인 an old person of sixty; a sexagenarian. ～잔치 《give》 a banquet on *one's* 60th birthday.

**환경**(環境) (an) environment; surroundings; a *milieu*(F.); circumstances. ¶ ～의 변화 a change in *one's* circumstances / 사회적〔자연적〕 ～ social 〔physical〕 environment / 한국의 지리적 ～ the geographic setting of Korea / ～의 영향 the influence of environment / (근처) ～이 좋다〔나쁘다〕 be in a decent 〔an undesirable〕 neighborhood / ～에 지배〔좌우〕되다 be influenced 〔conditioned〕 by *one's* environment 〔surroundings〕 / ～에 순응하다 adjust *oneself* to *one's* environment / 좋은 ～에서 자라다 be raised in a satisfactory 〔favorable〕 environment / 아이들 교육에는 ～이 중요하다 Environment is the first consideration in the education of children. *or* A child's schooling is greatly influenced by his home environment. / 그것은 ～탓이다 The surroundings are to blame for it. / 산업 폐기물의 불법 투기 때문에 ～이 파괴되고 있다 The unregulated disposal of industrial effluent 〔waste〕 despoils the environment. / 사람은 ～의 산물이다 Man is the product of circumstances. *or* Man is the creature of his environment.

◉ ～공학 environmental engineering. ～관리 environment management. ～교육 education from *one's* environment. ～권 the right to protect 〔preserve〕 *one's* environment; the right of entitlement to a good environment; the environment right. ～기준 the environmental standard 《for》. ～난민 environmental refugee 《by the drought》. ～디자인 environmental design. ～문제 an environmental problem 〔issue〕. ～미화원 a street cleaner; a scavenger; a garbage man. ～보전(保全) environmental preservation: ～보전법 the Environmental Preservation Law. ～보호 the protection of environment: ～보호법 the environmental protection law / ～보호론자 an environmentalist. ～부 the Ministry of Environment: ～부 장관 the Minister of Environment. ～순응자 a person who can adapt himself to the environment 〔situation〕. ～예술 environmental art. ～오염 environmental pollution 〔contamination〕. ～요인 a habitat factor. ～위생 environment(al) sanitation 〔hygiene〕: ～위생학 environmental hygienics. ～음악 ambient music. ～의 날 the (World) Environment Day. ～의학 environmental medicine. ～테러 environmental terror. ～파괴 environmental disruption. ～평가 environmental assessment.

교육～ school surroundings; educational environment. 국립 ～ 연구소 the National Environmental Protection Institute. 중앙 ～ 분쟁 조정위원회 the Central Environmental Disputes Coordination Commission. 한국 ～ 운동 연합 the Korean Federation for Environmental Movement (생략 KFEM).

**환곡**(換穀) exchanging grain. ～하다 exchange grain.

**환골탈태**(換骨奪胎) adaptation; modification; recasting. ～하다 adapt; modify; recast 《writing》.

**환관**(宦官) a eunuch.

**환국**(還國) homecoming. ＝귀국(歸國).

**환군**(還軍) withdrawal of「an army 〔troops〕; a troop withdrawal. ～하다 withdraw troops.

**환궁**(還宮) return(ing) to the Royal Palace. ～하다 return to the Royal Palace.

**환금**(換金) ① 《환전》 an exchange (of money). ～하다 exchange. ¶ 10만원을 달러로 ～하다 exchange 100,000 won into dollars. ② 〖상업〗 realization; conversion 《of goods》 into money. ～하다 realize 《*one's* securities, property》;

convert 〔turn〕《goods》 into money; 《수표 따위를》 cash 《a check》; have 〔get〕 《a check》 cashed. ◉ ~작물 a cash crop.

**환급**(還給) return; restoration; restitution; retrocession. ~하다 return; restore; retrocede; refund. ¶ 생각지도 않았는데 세금의 일부가 ~되었다 To my pleasant surprise, part of the tax I paid was refunded. ◉ ~금 refund.

**환기**(喚起) awakening; evocation. ~하다 awaken 《*one's* sympathy》; rouse; arouse; call 〔draw〕 《*a person's* attention》; evoke; excite 《attention, curiosity》; stir up. ¶ 여론을 ~하다 arouse 〔excite, stir up〕 public opinion / 환경 오염에 세인의 주의를 ~하다 draw people's attention to enviromental pollution / 이 환경 문제에 여러분의 주의를 ~하고자 합니다 I'd like to call your attention to this environmental issue.

**환기**(換氣) ventilation; changing air. ~하다 ventilate 《a room by opening windows》; air. ¶ ~가 잘 되다〔안 되다〕 be well 〔badly〕 ventilated / ~를 위해 창문을 열다 open the windows to let fresh air in / 이 방은 ~가 나쁘다 This room is stuffy. ◉ ~갱 a ventilating shaft. ~공 a ventilating hole; a ventilating opening. ~공사 ventilation work. ~장치 ventilation facilities 〔equipment, arrangement〕; a ventilator; a ventilating device: 완전한 ~장치가 돼 있다 have the most thorough ventilation. ~창 a vent; a window for ventilation. ~통 a ventilator; a ventilation funnel.

**환난**(患難) hardships; distress; misfortune. ¶ ~을 겪다 go through hardships; 《구어》 have a rough time / ~을 견디다 endure hardships.

**환납**(還納) returning 《public goods》. ~하다 return 《public goods》.

**환담**(歡談) a pleasant chat 〔talk〕. ~하다 have a pleasant chat 〔talk〕 《with》; confabulate 《with》. ¶ 그와 차를 마시면서 꽤 오랫동안 ~을 나누었다 I had a nice long chat with him over a cup of tea.

**환대**(歡待) a (hearty) welcome; a warm 〔cordial〕 reception; hospitality. ~하다 give 《*a person*》 a cordial reception 〔hearty welcome〕; entertain 〔receive〕 《*a person*》 warmly; welcome. ¶ ~를 받다 be warmly received; be accorded a warm welcome; be received cordially / 그녀는 가는 곳마다 ~를 받았다 She was warmly received wherever she went. / 그는 김씨 부부의 ~를 받았다 He enjoyed the hospitality of Mr. and Mrs. Kim.

**환도**(環刀) a sword; a saber. ◉ ~뼈 〖해부〗 the hipbone. ~상어 〖어류〗 a thresher (shark).

**환등**(幻燈) a magic lantern (예전의); a filmslide; a color slide (천연색의). ◉ ~기 a slide projector. ~필름 a filmstrip. ~화 a slide.

**환락**(歡樂) pleasure(s); merriment; mirth; merrymaking; gaieties. ~하다 enjoy *oneself;* have fun. ¶ ~의 생활 a path strewn with roses / ~을 좇다 pursue 〔seek〕 pleasure; go the primrose path; gather (life's) roses / ~에 도취하다 be steeped in the sweet pleasures of life / ~에 빠지다 indulge in 〔give *oneself* up to〕 pleasure / ~의 꿈에서 깨어나다 awake 〔sober down〕 from a dream of pleasure. ◉ ~가 an entertainment district (of a town); an amusement area; 《매춘 등의》 gay quarters; a red-light district.

**환롱질**(幻弄—) cheating 《*a person*》 by switching objects. ~하다〔치다〕 cheat 《*a person*》 by switching 《objects》; switch 《objects》 while 《*a person*》 is unaware; pull a switch-act (behind *a person's* back).

**환류**(還流) a return current; a back flow 〔current〕; 〖기상〗 convection; 〖화학〗 reflux. ~하다 return 《to normal circulation》; flow back; have a reflux. ¶ 자금의 ~ the reflux of capital. ◉ ~냉각기 a reflux condenser. ~식 분무기 a still burner 〔control〕 atomizer.

**환매**(換買) barter. ~하다 barter.

**환매**(還買) repurchase; redemption; 〖증권〗 short covering. ~하다 buy 《*a thing*》 back; repurchase; redeem; cover short. ◉ ~계약 a repurchase agreement. ~권 the right of repurchase; the redemptive right.

**환멸**(幻滅) disillusion(ment); disenchantment. ¶ ~의 비애 a sad disillusionment; the sorrow of disillusionment / ~을 느끼다 be 〔get, become〕 disillusioned 〔disenchanted〕 / 정치에 ~을 느끼는 사람들이 많다 There are a lot of people who are disillusioned with politics.

**환몽**(幻夢) an empty 〔a vain〕 dream.

**환문**(喚問) 〖법〗 a summons (*pl.* ~es). ~하다 summon 《*a person*》 for examination. ¶ ~되다〔받다〕 be summoned;

「be served with 〔receive〕 a summons.

**환물**(換物) conversion of money into goods. ～하다 convert money into goods.

**환부**(患部) the affected 〔diseased〕 part; the seat of a disease. ¶ ～를 식히다 〔따뜻이하다, 절개하다〕 cold (down) 〔warm (up), cut out〕 the affected part / ～를 치료하다 dress an affected part / ～에 약을 바르다 apply medicine to the affected part.

**환부**(還付) return. ⇨ 환급(還給).

**환불**(還拂) (a) refundment; (a) refund; (a) drawback; (a) repayment. ～하다 pay back; repay; refund; reimburse; rebate. ¶ 관세를 ～하다 draw back the duties paid / 대금을 ～하다 return the price paid. ◉ ～금 a refund; a repayment.

**환산**(換算) conversion; change. ～하다 convert 《into》; change 《into》. ¶ 미터로 ～하여 calculated in terms of meters / 달러를 원으로 ～하다 convert dollars into won / 에이커를 평방 킬로미터로 ～하다 turn acres into square kilometers / 총액을 한국 화폐로 ～하면 약 50,000원이 된다 The sum will come to about fifty thousand won in Korean currency 〔money〕. ◉ ～계수 a conversion factor. ～식 a conversion formula. ～율 a conversion ratio; an exchange rate (외국환의): 1달러 1,200원의 ～율로 at the conversion rate of ₩1,200 to the dollar. ～표 a conversion 〔an exchange〕 table.

**환상**(幻想) a fantasy (공상); an illusion (환각); a vision (시각적인); a (day-) dream (몽상); a reverie. ¶ ～적(인) dreamy; visionary; fantastic / ～적인 분위기 an air of fantasy; a dreamy atmosphere / ～을 품다 have an illusion; fantasize; dream 《of, that》 / 깨어진 ～ a shattered illusion / 즐거운 ～ a sweet illusion / ～에서 깨어나다 wake from *one's* reverie / 우리는 더이상 정부 공약에 ～을 갖지 않는다 We no longer have any illusions about what the government promised to do. ◉ ～가 a dreamer; a visionary; a fantast. ～곡 a fantasia; a (musical) fantasy.

**환상**(幻像) a phantom; a phantasm; an apparition; an illusion; a vision. ¶ ～을 좇다 pursue phantoms / ～을 보다 see a vision.

**환상**(環狀) a ring shape; annulation. ¶ ～의 ring-shaped; loop; circular / ～8호선 Loop 8. ◉ ～근 〖생물〗 a circular muscle. ～녹지 a ring green. ～도로 a loop 〔circular, ring〕 road; a loop 〔belt〕 highway; a beltline avenue (도시의). ～방전 a ring discharge. ～선 《철도의》 a loop 〔belt〕 line. ～성운 〖천문〗 the Ring Nebula. ～연골 〖해부〗 the ring 〔cricoid〕 cartilage. ～열석(列石) 〖고고학〗 a stone circle. ～전류 ring current.

**환생**(還生) reincarnation; rebirth; transmigration; metempsychosis (윤회). ～하다 be reincarnated; be born again; come back to life; transmigrate.

**환성**(歡聲) a shout of joy 〔jubilation〕; a hurrah; a cheer. ¶ ～을 지르다 shout 〔cry〕 for joy; give 〔send up, raise〕 a cheer; raise a shout (of joy); cry "Hurrah" / (와) ～을 지르며 with vociferous cheers / 그의 모습이 보이자 군중은 ～을 질렀다 The crowd cheered wildly when he came in sight.

**환속**(還俗) return to secular life 〔to the laity〕. ～하다 return to secular life; leave 〔quit〕 the priesthood.

**환송**(還送) sending back 〔home〕; repatriation. ⇨ 송환(送還). ～하다 send back; send home (본국으로); repatriate.

**환송**(歡送) a farewell; sending off; a send-off. ～하다 bid farewell to; send 〔see〕 《*a person*》 off; give 《*a person*》 a good 〔hearty〕 send-off. ¶ 성대한 ～을 받다 「be given 〔receive〕 a good send-off / 그들 모두가 그를 ～했다 They all gave him a hearty send-off. ◉ ～식 a farewell 〔send-off〕 ceremony. ～회 a farewell party 《in honor of》.

**환시**(幻視) a visual hallucination.

**환시**(環視) ¶ 중인 ～리에 in public; in company; in the presence of the whole company; with all eyes fixed (up)on 《*one*》 / 중인 ～의 대상이 되다 become the object 〔focus, center〕 of public attention / 중인 ～리에 창피를 당했다 I was put to shame in public. *or* I was publicly disgraced.

**환심**(歡心) good graces; favor. ¶ ～을 사다 court 《*a person's*》 good graces; curry favor 《with *a person*》; win 《*a person's*》 favor; ingratiate *oneself* 《with *a person*》; insinuate *oneself* into 《*a person's*》 favor; 《여자의》 win a girl's heart / ～을 사려고 하다 try to win 《*a person's*》 favor.

**환약**(丸藥) a (medical) pill; a globule. ¶ ～을 짓다 make a pill; pill.

**환어음**(換—) a bill of exchange (생략 B.E., B / E, b.e.); a draft. ¶ A은행 앞으로 발행한 ~ a draft on A Bank / 3천 달러의 ~을 발행하다 draw a bill of exchange 《on *a person*》 for 3,000 dollars. ◉ ~발행인 the drawer 〔payer, sender〕. ~인수인〔지급인〕 the payee. 기명식 ~ a special bill. 무기명식 ~ a bill to bearer. 부도~ a dishonored 〔bad〕 bill. 외국〔내국〕~ a foreign 〔a domestic 《미》, an inland 《영》〕 bill (of exchange). 요구불 ~ a draft on demand; a demand draft 〔bill〕. 일람불 ~ a bill at sight; a sight bill 〔draft〕. 장기〔단기〕~ a long 〔short〕 bill.

**환언하다**(換言—) say 〔put〕 in other words. ¶ 환언하면 in other words; that is (to say); namely.

**환영**(幻影) a phantom; a vision; an illusion; a phantasm. ¶ ~을 좇다 pursue phantoms; be lured by 〔under〕 an illusion / ~을 보다 see *something* in a vision.

**환영**(歡迎) (a) welcome; (a) reception; an ovation. ~하다 welcome; give a welcome 《to *a person*》; bid 《*a person*》 welcome; receive warmly 〔favorably〕; give a reception 〔ovation〕 《to》; like. ¶ 대~ a hearty welcome 〔reception〕; an enthusiastic ovation / 성대한 ~ red carpet (welcomes) 《미》 / ~받는〔받지 못하는〕 손님 a welcomed 〔an unwelcomed〕 guest / ~을 받다 be received favorably; be welcomed; be warmly received; be given 「a welcome 〔a warm reception〕 / 가는 곳마다 ~(을) 받다 be welcomed wherever *one* goes; be warmly received everywhere / ~을 받지 못하다 be not welcomed / 쌍수로 ~하다 welcome 〔receive〕 《*a person*》 with open arms / 대대적으로 ~하다 stage a festive welcome 《for》 / 박수로 ~하다 welcome 〔greet〕 《*a person*》 with a clapping of hands / 열렬히 ~받다 be enthusiastically received 〔welcomed〕; get 〔receive〕 an enthusiastic 〔a rousing〕 welcome 〔reception〕 / ~의 뜻을 표하다 say welcome to 《*a person*》; bid 《*a person*》 welcome / ~의 손을 내밀다 extend the glad hand of welcome 《to *a person*》 / 언제든지 ~하겠습니다 You shall always be welcomed. / 독자의 투고를 ~합니다 Contributions from readers are cordially invited. / 그런 사람은 어디를 가나 ~받는다 Such a man is sure to be welcomed wherever he may go. / 그 보도는 특히 우리 나라 중공업계에서 ~할 만한 것이었다 The news was, in particular, most welcome to our heavy industries.
◉ ~대회 the welcoming rally 《for》. ~만찬회 a reception dinner: ~ 만찬회를 열다 give 〔hold〕 a dinner party to welcome 《*a person*》. ~사 《give》 an address of welcome. ~식 the welcoming ceremony. ~아치 a welcome arch. ~위원회 a reception committee.

**환영회**(歡迎會) a welcome meeting 〔party〕; a reception. ¶ ~를 열다 give 〔hold〕 a welcome party; give a reception (dinner); host a welcoming party.

**환원**(還元) ① 《되돌림》 restoration. ~하다 restore 《to its original state》; be restored to 《the former condition》. ¶ 이익을 사회에 ~하다 return 《the company's》 profits to society / 국민이 낸 세금은 어떤 형태로 (국민에게) ~되는가 In what form will the taxes paid by the people be returned to them?
② 〖화학〗 reduction; resolution (분해); deoxidization (산화물의). ~하다 reduce 《to its components》; be reduced 《to》; 《원소로》 resolve 《into its elements》; 《산화물을》 deoxidize; 《금속 등을》 revive. ¶ ~된 reduced / (본디의 상태로) ~시키다 〖화학〗 revivify / 화합물은 그 본래의 원소로 ~된다 The compound resolves itself into its elements.
◉ ~당(糖) reducing sugar. ~법 reductionism. ~작용 a reducing process. ~장치 a reductor. ~제 a reducing 〔deoxidating〕 agent; a reducer; a reductant. ~철 reduced iron.

**환유**(換喩) [수사적] metonymy.

**환율**(換率) the (foreign) exchange rate; the rate of exchange. ¶ 1달러 1,200원의 ~로 at the (exchange) rate of 1,200 won to the U.S. dollar / ~을 안정시키다 stabilize exchange rates / ~은 매일 변동된다 Exchange rate is subject to daily fluctuation. ◉ ~변경 exchange (rate) fluctuations. ~인상 a raise in exchange rates. 대미~ the (exchange) rate on America; the U.S. dollar rate. 고정 ~제 a fixed 〔pegged〕 exchange rate system. 변동 ~제 the fluctuating 〔floating〕 exchange rate system.

**환자**(患者) a patient; a sufferer 《from a cold》; a case 《of cholera》; a subject 《of operation》. ¶ 절망적인 ~ a hopeless 〔fatal〕 case / ~가 많은 계절

a sickly season / 소화불량 ～ a patient suffering from indigestion / ～를 진찰하다 see 〔examine〕 a patient / 새 ～가 속출하고 있다 New cases are reported one after another. / ～는 경과가 좋다 The patient is progressing favorably. / 서울에 장티푸스 ～가 3명 발생했다 There broke out in Seoul three cases of typhoid fever. / 저 의사는 ～가 많다 The doctor has a large practice. ◉ ～명부 a sick list; a list of inpatients (입원 환자의). ～운반차 an ambulance. 외과～ a surgical subject. 동상～ a frostbite victim. 무료～ a charity-patient; a free patient. 새～ a new 〔fresh〕 case. 수술～ a subject to be operated on; a surgical patient; a surgery case.

**환장**(換腸) ～하다 《정신나가다》 go crazy 〔mad〕; lose 〔be out of〕 *one's* mind; 《병적으로 열중하다》 be blind with love 《for》; be madly in love 《with》; be crazy 《about》. ¶ 도박에 ～하다 have a mania for gambling / 여자에게 ～하다 be infatuated with a woman / 난 그 일로 ～할 지경이야 It's enough to drive me crazy.

**환쟁이** a dauber; a (wretched) painter.

**환전**(換錢) exchange (of money); money changing. ～하다 exchange 《dollar into won》; change 《a 10,000-won note》. ¶ 1만원권을 천원짜리 지폐 10장으로 ～하다 change a 10,000-won bill into ten 1,000-won bills / 공항에서 달러를 파운드로 ～했다 I changed some dollars into pounds at the airport.
◉ ～기 a money-changing machine. ～상 《사람》 an (authorized) exchanger; an exchange broker; 《가게》 an exchange house. ～수수료 a commission 〔charge〕 for exchanging money.

**환절**(換節) a change of seasons. ◉ ～기 a change of season; the turning point of the season.

**환절**(環節) 『동물』 segment; 《환절로 되어 있음》 annulation.

**환지**(一紙) sketching 〔drawing〕 paper.

**환지**(換地) replotting; a piece of land substituted 《for》; 《토지》 a substitute lot 《for》. ◉ ～예정지 the reserved land for replotting. ～처분 the disposal of replotting.

**환짓다**(丸一) make a pill; pill.

**환청**(幻聽) auditory hallucination. ¶ ～으로 시달리다 suffer from auditory hallucinations. 「an atoll.

**환초**(環礁) a (ring-shaped) coral island;

**환치다** sketch; paint; draw a rough sketch 《of》; daub. ¶ 대나무를 ～ sketch a bamboo.

**환태평양**(環太平洋) the Pacific rim. ¶ ～국가들 the Pacific basin 〔rim〕 countries / ～조산대(造山帶) the circum-Pacific orogenic zone / ～지진대 the circum-Pacific earthquake belt.

**환표**(換票) 《선거에서》 ballot switching; voting irregularities. ～하다 switch ballots; commit voting irregularities.

**환품**(換品) exchange of goods 〔articles〕. ～하다 exchange goods.

**환풍기**(換風機) a ventilation 〔ventilating〕 fan.

**환하다** ① 《탁 트이다》 (be) open; clear; unobstructed. ¶ 환히 트인 길 clear passage; an open road / 길이 ～ a road is wide open; a road is clear / 환히 보이다 get an unobstructed view; be open to the eye.
② 《밝다》 (***a***) 《어둡지 않다》 (be) light; bright. ¶ 환한 방 a well-lighted room; 《볕이 잘 들어》 a sunny room / 달빛이 환한 밤 a bright moonlit night / 환한 곳에서 in the light / 날이 환하게 밝다 the day dawns bright / 환하게 하다 brighten; lighten; light up; make brighter / 환해지다 lighten; grow 〔get〕 light; light up / 밖은 아직도 ～ It is still light (enough) outside. (***b***) 《표정이》 (be) bright; radiant; sunny; [서술적] look happy. ¶ 환한 미소 a sunny smile / 환한 표정 a bright look; a radiant 〔beaming〕 face. (***c***) 《전망 등이》 (be) bright; rosy. ¶ 환한 미래 a bright 〔rosy〕 future. (***d***) 《정통·소상하다》 [서술적] know well 《about China》; be familiar 《with》; be versed 《in》; be learned 〔well up〕 《in》; be conversant 《with》; be well acquainted 《with》; be well informed on 《sportsdom》. ¶ 문학에 ～ be well read in literature / 미국어법에 ～ have a good knowledge of Americanisms / 사무에 ～ be well versed in business methods / 시세에 ～ be conversant with the market prices / (그 곳) 지리에 ～ be familiar 〔well acquainted〕 with 《a place》; know *one's* way about 《in the town》 / 네 속을 환히 알 수 있다 I can see through your mind 〔intention〕 clearly.
③ 《얼굴이》 be big and open; (be) fine-looking; handsome. ¶ 환한 얼굴 a big open face; a handsome face; clear-cut figures.
④ 《명백하다》 (be) clear; distinct; plain; evident; obvious; patent; explicit. ¶ 환

한 사실 a plain truth; an obvious fact / 불을 보는 것 만큼이나 ~ be as clear as day; be as plain as the sun.

**환향**(還鄕) return to *one's* native place 〔hometown〕. ~하다 return to *one's* native place; go back home. ◉ 금의 ~ returning home loaded with honors; returning home in glory.

**환형**(環形) a ring shape. ¶ ~의 looped; ringshaped. ◉ ~동물 an annelid; a round 〔segmented〕 worm; Annelida.

**환호**(歡呼) a cheer; an ovation; an acclamation; a hurrah. ~하다 cheer; give cheers; shout for joy; acclaim; jubilate. ¶ ~ 속에 amid (hearty) cheers; amidst of the loud acclamations 《of》 / 아무에게 ~를 보내다 give *a person* hearty cheers 〔an ovation〕 / ~로(써) 맞이하다 hail 《*a person*》 with acclamation(s); greet 《*a person*》 with hearty cheers / ~로써 보내다 send off 《*a person*》 with a roar of applause / 귀청이 터질 듯한 ~ 속에 비행기는 김포 공항을 떠났다 The plane left the Kimpo Airport amid deafening cheers. ◉ ~성 a shout of joy; a cheer: ~성을 올리다 give a shout of joy; shout for joy; send up rousing cheers.

**환후**(患候) the sickness 〔illness〕 of a person honored.

**환희**(歡喜) (great) joy; delight; gladness; jubilation; ecstasy. ~하다 be glad; be in delight; be happy 〔ecstatic〕; rejoice. ¶ ~의 눈물을 흘리다 shed tears of joy.

**활** ① 《쏘는 무기》 a bow; archery (궁술). ¶ 활쏘기 an archery practice / 활의 명수 an expert 〔a master〕 archer / 활을 메우다 string a bow / 활을 쏘다 shoot a bow 〔an arrow〕 / 활을 (잔뜩) 당기다 draw *one's* bow to its full extent / 활에 화살을 메기다 fix 〔put〕 an arrow to *one's* bow. ② 《무명활》 a bow and string for beating cotton wool. ¶ 활로 솜을 타다 beat 〔willow〕 cotton with a bow and string. ③ 《현악기의》 a bow. ¶ 활을 쥐는 손 the bow hand.

**활강**(滑降) 『스키』 a descent. ◉ ~경기 downhill competition; a downhill race.

**활개** ① 《사람의》 *one's* arms; *one's* limbs. ¶ 네 ~ *one's* arms and legs / ~치다 swing *one's* arms / ~(를) 치며 swinging *one's* arms; [비유적] with nothing to fear; triumphantly / ~치며 걷다 walk swinging *one's* arms / 네 ~치다 walk with a swaggering gait; strut; swagger about. ② 《새의》 the wings of a bird. ¶ ~치다 flap 〔beat〕 the wings; flutter.

**활갯짓** swinging *one's* arms in walking; strutting; swaggering. ~하다 swing *one's* arms; strut; swagger 《about》.

**활고자** the tips of a bow (to which the string is attached).

**활공**(滑空) 『항공』 gliding; a glide; volplane. ~하다 glide; volplane. ◉ ~각 the angle of glide. ~거리 a gliding distance. ~기 a glider; a sailplane; an aerodone.

**활극**(活劇) 《장면》 a fighting scene; 《영화》 an action film 〔movie〕; 《난투》 a scuffle. ¶ ~을 벌이다 《연기로》 play 〔act out, enact〕 a fighting scene; 《맞붙어 싸우다》 fight 《with》; scuffle 《with》.

**활기**(活氣) vigor; spirit; energy; liveliness; animation; vitality; briskness; activity. ¶ ~찬〔있는〕 animated 《talk》; vital 《person》; active 《market》; brisk 《trade》; energetic 《way of *do*ing》; spirited 《debate》; lively 《scene》; vigorous 《style》; full of life / ~ 없는 spiritless; lifeless; dull; inert; inanimate; dead-alive.

활기가: ~가 있다 be full of life 〔vigor〕; be all astir; be full of beans 《영구어》 / ~가 없다 be lifeless 〔inert, inactive, dead, unresponsive〕; be spiritless 〔dull, sluggish, tired, unanimated, passive, torpid〕; be wanting in spirit 〔life〕.

활기를: ~를 띠다 be(come) animated 〔enlivened〕; become active 〔brisk, lively〕; grow lively; show liveliness 〔life〕 / ~를 띠게 하다 give life to; animate; stimulate; inspire; activate; enliven; invigorate; put (new) life into 《*a person, a thing*》; pop up 《미구어》 / ~를 보이다 present an animated 〔active, brisk, lively〕 appearance; show liveliness 〔life〕.

활기에: ~에 차다〔넘치다〕 be full of spirit 〔life〕; be full of pep 《미구어》 / ~에 찬 도시 a city vibrant with life and energy.

¶ 경제계는 ~를 띠었다 The economic world showed signs of life. / 온 거리는 ~를 띠고 있었다 All the town was up. / 시장은 때가 감에 따라 ~를 띠게 되었다 The market place has become active 〔shown life〕 as time goes on.

**활달**(豁達) liberality; generosity; indulgence; magnanimity; large-〔big-〕heartedness; broad-mindedness. ~하다 (be) liberal; generous; magnanimous; large-〔big-〕hearted; open-hearted; broad-minded. ¶ ～한 태도 free and open manners; a big-hearted 〔broad-minded〕 nature.

**활대** a (sail) yard; the cross-stick at the top of a sail.

**활동**(活動) 《활약》 activity; action; operations; 《기능》 function; working 《of the bodily organs》. ～하다 《활약하다》 be active; lead a stirring 〔an active〕 life; play 〔take〕 an active part 〔role〕 《in》; be on the go 《속어》; show activity; 《바삐 돌아다님》 canvass; campaign; 《기능을 하다》 function; work. ¶ 클럽〔과외〕～ club 〔extracurricular〕 activities / 구조～ a rescue operation / ～적(인) active; energetic; dynamic; go-getting 《미구어》 / 다방면의 ～ *one's* multifarious 〔innumerable〕 activities / ～적인 생활 an active life / ～을 개시하다 get into action; come into play; 《조직·단체가》 come into operation; become operative; 《화산이》 burst into activity; 《군대가》 begin operations / ～을 무디게 하다 hamper *one's* activity / ～시키다 bring 《*a thing*》 into play; call 《*a thing*》 into action; set 《*a thing*》 into motion / …을 마음껏 ～케 하다 give free play 〔scope〕 to… / 한창 ～중이다 be in full activity 〔swing〕; be up and doing / 정계에서 ～하다 「be active 〔play an active part〕 in politics. ◉ ～가(家) an active 〔energetic〕 person; a man of action; an activist (정치적인). ～력 activity; vitality; energy. ～무대 *one's* field 〔stage〕 of action 〔activity〕: ～무대가 넓다 have a wide sphere of action. ～범위〔분야〕 *one's* scope 〔sphere〕 of activity 〔action〕. ～전류 《세포 조직의》 an action current. ～주의 activism; energism. 교내～ school activities. 정신～ mental activity; the activity of *one's* mind.

**활등** the back of a bow. ◉ ～코 a high-bridged nose.

**활딱** ① 《벗는·벗어진 모양》 all; completely; entirely. ¶ 머리가 ～ 벗어지다 get all bald and shiny on top; be bald as an egg 〔a billiard ball〕 / 옷을 ～ 벗다 strip *oneself* of all *one's* clothes; strip *oneself* bare 〔stark-naked〕. ② 《끓어 넘치는 모양》 boiling over.

**활량** ① 《활 쏘는 사람》 an archer; a bow-and-arrow man. ② 《무위도식자》 an idler; a drone; 《헙헙한 사람》 an openhanded man; a liberal giver; 《난봉꾼》 a fast liver; a playboy.

**활력**(活力) energy; vitality; vital power 〔force〕; 《구어》 《plenty of》 go; zip; pep. ¶ ～이 넘치는 도시 a city full of vitality / ～ 있는 vital; animated; in blood / ～을 주다 vitalize; invigorate / 침체된 수출에 참신한 ～을 불어넣다 inject fresh vigor to the stagnant exports / 그녀는 ～이 넘쳐흐르고 있었다 She was full of vitality 〔go〕. ◉ ～설 〖철학〗 vitalism. ～소 a tonic; a vitamin. ～위축 〖의학〗 abiotrophy. ～회복 revitalization.

**활로**(活路) a way out 《of the difficulty》; a means of escape. ¶ ～를 찾다〔열다〕 find a way out (of the difficulty); cut *one's* way 《through the enemy》; find a means of survival / 그들은 예상치 못했던 분야에서 하나의 ～를 찾아냈다 They found a means of escape in an unexpected quarter.

**활머리** the top plait of false hair formerly worn by a bride at her wedding ceremony.

**활무대**(活舞臺) a sphere 〔field〕 of activity; the field 〔stage〕 of action; an arena. ¶ ～에 나오다 come upon the stage of action.

**활물**(活物) a living being 〔creature〕. ◉ ～기생(寄生) 〖생물〗 a parasitism on living things.

**활물질**(活物質) 〖전기〗 an active material.

**활발**(活潑) liveliness; briskness; sprightliness; activity. ～하다 (be) lively; brisk; vivacious; sprightly; vigorous; active; be full of life. ¶ ～히 actively; lively; briskly; vivaciously; vigorously / ～한 기상 a vigorous spirit / ～한 사람 an active 〔a lively〕 person / (거래가) ～한 시장 a brisk 〔lively, booming〕 market / ～하게 움직이다 move lively 〔briskly〕 / 동작이 ～하다 be quick in action; be brisk in *one's* movement / ～하게 하다 make 《a chemical reaction》 active; activate 《a chemical reaction》 / 토론을 ～히 전개하다 have lively 〔animated〕 discussion 《on *a matter,* with *a person*》 / 사내아이는 여자아이보다 ～하다 A boy is more active than a girl. / 시황(市況)은 오전중 ～했다 The tone of the market was brisk 〔active〕 in the morning.

**활보**(闊步) a swaggering pace; strutting. ～하다 stride; stalk; strut; swagger (about); walk with a swaggering gait; walk with great strides. ¶ 거리를 ～하다 strut 〔stride along〕 a street;

stalk (along) the streets.

**활불**(活佛) a living Buddha; an incarnation of Buddha; 《라마교의》 the grand Lama; 《사람》 a benevolent person.

**활비비** a bowstring drill.

**활빈당**(活貧黨) outlaws who rob in order to help the poor; (a band of) Robin Hoods.

**활빙**(滑氷) (ice-)skating. ∼하다 (ice=)skate.

**활살**(活殺) life and / or death. ¶ ∼을 마음대로 하다 have another's life in *one's* hands; have an absolute power 《over *a person*》.

**활새머리** a hair cut short along the edges and long at top.

**활석**(滑石) 〚광물〛 talc; talcum; steatite. ¶ ∼(모양)의 talcoid / ∼질〔성〕의 talcky. ◉ ∼분(粉) talcum powder.

**활선어**(活鮮魚) fresh 〔raw〕 fish. ◉ ∼운반선 a fresh fish carrier.

**활성**(活性) 《사업·경제 등의》 vitality; 〚화학〛 activity. ¶ ∼의 active; activated / 비(非)∼의 inert. ◉ ∼가스 activated gas. ∼비타민제 an activated vitamin preparation. ∼탄 activated carbon 〔charcoal〕. ∼탄소 active carbon. 계면(界面) ∼제 a surface active agent.

**활성화**(活性化) 〚화학〛 activation. ∼하다 〚화학〛 activate; (re)vitalize 《the economy》. ¶ 증권 시장의 ∼ revitalization of the securities market / 지방 경제의 ∼를 도모하는 계획들 the projects to revigorate local economics / 세계 경제를 ∼하다 revitalize the global economy.

**활수**(滑手) generosity; liberality. ∼하다 (be) liberal; generous; openhanded. ¶ ∼하게 돈을 쓰다 be free 〔generous〕 with *one's* money; lavish *one's* money 《on》.

**활시위** a bowstring. ¶ ∼를 메우다〔풀다〕 string 〔unstring〕 a bow.

**활안**(活眼) a quick eye; open 〔observant, alive, active, wide-awake〕 eyes; penetrating 〔piercing〕 eyes; insight.

**활액**(滑液) 〚해부〛 synovia. ◉ ∼낭 a bursa (*pl.* ∼s, -sae): ∼ 낭염 bursitis.

**활약**(活躍) (great) activity; action. ∼하다 be active 《in》; display 〔show〕 activity; take 〔play〕 an active part 〔important role〕 《in》; participate actively 《in》. ¶ 정계에서 ∼하다 play an active part in politics / 그 시합에서 대∼을 하다 do a very good job in the game; be the outstanding player in the game / 그의 ∼ 시대는 지나갔다 The time for his activity has passed.

**활어**(活魚) live fish. ◉ ∼선(船) a live-fish transport (ship). ∼조(槽) a fish preserve; a fish-tank (횟집의); a live-box; a (live) well (어선의).

**활연**(豁然) ∼하다 (be) wide; open; extensive. ¶ ∼히 with a sudden flash; in a flash; all of a sudden / ∼히 깨닫다 be awakened with a sudden flash (of realization); 《a truth》 burst upon *one* / ∼히 큰 들이 눈앞에 전개되다 a wide plain suddenly spreads out before *one's* eyes.

**활엽수**(闊葉樹) a broadleaf 〔broad=leaved〕 tree.

**활용**(活用) ① 《응용》 practical use; application. ∼하다 put 〔turn〕 《knowledge》 to practical use; apply; utilize 《*one's* experience》; make the good use of 《*one's* abilities in a job》. ¶ 최대한으로 ∼하다 make the best 〔most〕 use of 《*a thing*》/ 완전히 모두 ∼하다 make full use of 《*a thing*》/ 인재를 잘 ∼하다 use the right man in the right place / 자본을 ∼하다 make efficient use of funds / 휴가를 ∼하다 spend a vacation wisely / 과학적인 발견을 산업 생산에 ∼하다 apply scientific discoveries to industrial production / 이 2일간의 연휴를 가능한 한 잘 ∼하고 싶다 I should 〔would〕 like to make the most of these two straight holidays.

② 〚문법〛 《어미 변화》 inflection; 《영》 inflexion; 《동사의》 conjugation; 《격변화》 declension. ∼하다 inflect; conjugate; decline.

◉ ∼례 an inflectional paradigm. ∼어 inflected 〔inflective〕 words. ∼형 an inflectional form; a conjugated form.

**활유어**(蛞蝓魚) 〚동물〛 a lancelet; an amphioxus (*pl.* -oxi, -oxuses).

**활인화**(活人畫) a living picture; a *tableau vivant* (F.).

**활자**(活字) 〚인쇄〛 a printing 〔movable〕 type; type [총칭]. ¶ 5호 ∼ No. 5 type / 7호 ∼ No. 7 type; ruby type 《미》; brilliant type 《영》/ 6호 ∼ No. 6 type; brevier / 큰〔작은〕 ∼ 《print in》 large 〔small〕 type / ∼의 오식 a typographical error; a misprint / 큰 ∼의 표제 a headline in large type / ∼로 인쇄하다 print in type / ∼로 짜다 set up 《manuscripts》 (for printing); put 《manuscripts》 in type / 이름을 ∼체로 쓰다 write *one's* name in block letters; print *one's* name / 작은 ∼는 눈에 해롭다 Small print 「is bad for eyes 〔hurts your eyes〕.

◉ ～금 type metal. ～면 typeface. ～본 a printed book. ～인쇄 type-printing; typography. ～주조 type-founding 〔=casting〕: ～ 주조소 a type foundry. ～체 print. ～판(版) a printed edition. ～화(化) printing; putting 《a manuscript》 into print; typesetting: ～화되다 get 〔find 《its》 way〕 into print; see 〔appear in〕 print; see the light of day (출판되다). 고딕～ Gothic types. 악보～ a font of music type. 포인트～ point types. 표음～ a phonetic sign; a phonotype.

**활주**(―柱) 〖건축〗 a crooked post used as a support.

**활주**(滑走) 《비행기의》 《start》 the roll; a taking-off 〔landing〕 run (이착륙); volplaning; gliding (공중); 《얼음판·눈위의》 sliding. ～하다 roll; run; volplane. ¶ …의 고공에서 훌륭한 공중 ～를 하다 make a splendid volplane from a height of… / 비행기가 물 위를 ～한다 A plane slides over the water. / 비행기가 ～해서 이륙했다 The airplane taxied and took off. ◉ ～각 a gliding angle. ～로 a runway; an airstrip; a runfield: ～로 위치 표시등 an airstrip beacon / ～로 위를 지나쳐 달리다 overshoot the runway. ～륜(輪) landing 〔alighting〕 wheels. ～속도 planing speed. ～지시 〖항공〗 taxiing instruction.

**활죽** the prop-stick of a sail.

**활줌통** the handle of a bow.

**활집** a bow case.

**활짝** ① 《시원하게》 wide(ly); clear(ly); extensively. ¶ ～ 개다 clear up / ～ 갠 하늘 a clear 〔cloudless〕 sky / ～ 트인 들판 an open field / ～ 열다 open wide 〔up〕; fling 〔throw〕 open; leave 〔keep〕 《a door》 open (열어 두다). ② 《꽃·웃음 등이》 brightly; beamingly; radiantly. ¶ ～ 핀 장미 a full-blown rose; a rose in full bloom / (꽃이) ～ 피어 있다 be in full bloom 〔flower〕; be in all 《its》 glory / ～ 웃다 beam 《upon, at》; smile a broad smile; grin from ear to ear.

**활짱** the body of a bow. ◉ ～묶음 〖인쇄〗 braces; pointed parentheses ({ }).

**활차**(滑車) a pulley; a block; a tackle. ¶ ～에 줄을 꿰다 lead a rope through a pulley. ◉ ～ 장치 tackling; (a) tackle; a whip; a pulley block. 가동〔고정〕 ～ a movable 〔fixed〕 pulley. 변속 ～ a speed pulley; a speeder. 복(複)～ a compound pulley.

**활착**(活着) taking 〔striking〕 root; rooting; rootage. ～하다 take 〔strike〕 root.

**활촉**(―鏃) an arrowhead; the barb 〔point〕 of an arrow.

**활터** an archery field 〔range〕.

**활톱** a hack saw.

**활판**(活版) 〖인쇄〗 type-printing; typography (활판술). ¶ ～으로 인쇄하다 print with type / ～으로 하다 put into type / ～을 짜다 set type; compose. ◉ ～본 a printed book. ～소(所) a printing shop 〔office〕; a printer (사람). ～인쇄 letterpress; letterpress printing (인쇄물).

**활하다**(滑―) ① 《미끄럽다》 (be) smooth; sleek; slippery. ② 《헐겁다》 (be) loose; ③ 《대변이》 (be) soft; easy.

**활화**(活畫) picturesque scene(ry).

**활화산**(活火山) an active 〔a live〕 volcano. ◉ ～대(帶) an active volcano belt.

**활활** 《불타는 모양》 in great 〔tall〕 flames; vigorously. ¶ 장작이 ～ 타다 firewood burns vigorously / ～ 부채질하다 fan *oneself* briskly.

**활황**(活況) activity 《in business》; briskness; prosperity. ¶ ～을 띠다 become 〔be〕 active; look brisk 〔animated〕; show (signs of) activity; present animated 〔brisk, lively〕 appearance; boom; 《상점 따위가》 do brisk business. ◉ ～산업 the expanding industry.

**홧김**(火―) ¶ ～에 under the influence of anger; in a fit 〔moment〕 of anger 〔rage, temper, pique〕; in the heat of passion; exasperatedly / ～에 치다 strike 《*a person*》 in anger / ～에 술을 마시다 drink liquor in anger.

**홧술**(火―) liquor drunk in anger.

**홧홧** hot(ly); fierily; feverishly. ～하다 feel hot 〔warm〕; (be) hot; fiery; feverish. ¶ 몸이 ～ 달다 be feverish / 숯불이 ～하다 charcoal burns hot / 술을 먹어 얼굴이 ～하다 feel *one's* face burning from the drink; *one's* cheeks are flushed with wine.

**황**(黃) ① 《황색》 yellow (color). ② 《석유황》 orpiment; 〖화학〗 sulfur 〔sulphur 《영》〕 (기호 S). ③ 《보리·밀의 병해》 blight. ¶ 황내리다, 황들다 get blighted.

**황갈색**(黃褐色) yellowish brown.

**황감**(惶感) deep 〔reverent〕 gratitude. ～하다 (be) exceedingly 〔deeply, reverently〕 grateful. ¶ ～하게도 graciously.

**황겁**(惶怯) (a) fear; awe. ～하다 (be) afraid; awed; awe-struck〔-stricken〕; fearful; [서술적] be filled with fear.

**황경**(黃經) 〖천문〗 (celestial, ecliptic) longitude.

**황경나무**(黃―) 〖식물〗 an Amur cork tree.

**황계**(黃鷄) a yellow hen 〔cock〕.
**황고**(皇考) *one's* deceased father.
**황고집**(黃固執) obstinacy; stubbornness; 《사람》 a bullheaded 〔pig-headed〕 person; a headstrong person.
**황공**(惶恐) being awe-stricken; fear(fulness). ∼하다 (be) gracious; august; awful; awe-stricken; awe-inspiring. ¶ ∼하게도 graciously; (The King) deigned 《to *do*》 / ∼무지하다 be extremely awe-stricken.
**황구**(黃口) 《새새끼》 a fledgling with a yellow bill; 《어린이》 a child.
**황구**(黃狗) a yellow dog. ◉ ∼신(腎) the penis of a yellow dog. ∼피(皮) the skin of a yellow dog.
**황국**(黃菊) a yellow chrysanthemum.
**황금**(黃金) 《금》 gold; 《돈》 money; 《재물》 wealth. ¶ ∼의 gold; made of gold; golden / ∼의 나라 a rich country; an El Dorado / ∼(의) 알을 낳는 거위 《kill》 the goose that lays the golden eggs; the golden goose / ∼은 만능이다 A golden key will open most locks. *or* Money makes the mare to go. ◉ ∼률 the golden rule. ∼분할(分割) 〖수학〗 the golden section. ∼빛 a gold(en) color; golden yellow. ∼숭배 plutolatry; mammon-worship; mammonism. ∼시대 the golden age; 《전성기》 《in》 *one's* palmy days. ∼정략 a bribing policy.
**황금**(黃芩) 〖식물〗 a kind of skullcap plant.
**황금만능**(黃金萬能) ¶ ∼의 devoted to the pursuit of wealth; worldly; mammonistic / ∼시대 a mammonish age / ∼주의 the almighty dollar principle; mammonism / ∼주의자 a mammonist; a mammonite.
**황급**(遑急) extreme urgency 〔haste〕. ∼하다 (be) urgent; pressed and agitated. ¶ ∼히 hastily; in hot haste; in a flurry / ∼히 달아나다 run away in a flurry; bundle off 〔away〕; beat a hasty retreat.
**황기**(黃旗) a yellow flag.
**황기** (皇芪·皇耆) 〖식물〗 a kind of milk vetch; 《그 뿌리》 milk vetch root.
**황기끼다**(一氣一) be seized with fear; get intimidated 〔cowed, awe-struck〕; be overcome with fright.
**황녀**(皇女) an Imperial 〔a Royal〕 princess.
**황년**(荒年) ＝흉년.
**황달**(黃疸) 〖의학〗 jaundice; the yellows (동물의); icterus. ◉ ∼ 환자 an icteric (-al). 신생아 ∼ jaundice of the newborn; yellow gum 《영》.
**황답**(荒沓) a barren 〔devastated〕 paddy=field.
**황당**(荒唐) absurdity; nonsense. ∼하다 (be) absurd; preposterous; wild; nonsensical. ¶ 그 무슨 ∼한 소리야 What an absurd suggestion! ◉ ∼객 a windbag; a wild talker; a braggart; an unreliable person.
**황당무계**(荒唐無稽) ⇨황당. ∼하다 (be) absurd; wild; incoherent; nonsensical; fantastical; preposterous; fabulous. ¶ ∼한 이야기 an absurd story; sheer 〔clotted〕 nonsense; lies; a fabrication; a cock-and-bull story / ∼한 소리를 하다 talk nonsense; talk something incredible 〔fantastic, absurd〕 / ∼한 풍설을 퍼뜨리다 set wild rumors afloat.
**황대구**(黃大口) a dried codfish with its belly cut open.
**황도**(皇都) the capital of an empire.
**황도**(黃道) 〖천문〗 the ecliptic; the girdle. ◉ ∼광(光) the zodiacal light. ∼대(帶) the zodiac. ∼면 the plane of the ecliptic.
**황동**(黃銅) brass. ◉ ∼광(鑛) copper pyrites; chalcopyrite. ∼색 brass yellow. ∼전(錢) brass coins.
**황랍**(黃蠟) yellow beeswax. ◉ ∼촉(燭) a yellow-beeswax candle.
**황량**(荒凉) desolateness; dreariness. ∼하다 (be) desolate (and forlorn); dreary; bleak; deserted; ruined; wild; lonesome. ¶ ∼한 벌판 a desolate plain; wilderness / ∼하고 바람이 휘몰아치는 황무지 a desolate, wind-swept moorland area.
**황록색**(黃綠色) yellow(ish) 〔pea〕 green; olive color. ◉ 담(淡)∼ pistachio.
**황룡**(黃龍) a yellow dragon. ◉ ∼수(鬚) a variety of chrysanthemum.
**황률**(黃栗) ＝황밤.
**황릉**(皇陵) an Imperial mausoleum (*pl.* -lea); an Emperor's tomb.
**황린**(黃燐) 〖화학〗 yellow phosphor; white phosphorus. ◉ ∼ 성냥 a lucifer 〔yellow phosphorus〕 match.
**황림**(荒林) a deserted woods; a neglected 〔an overgrown〕 grove.
**황마**(黃麻) 〖식물〗 a jute. ◉ ∼ 부대 a jute 〔gunny〕 bag.
**황막**(荒漠) wildness; vastness. ∼하다 (be) wild; waste; 《광막하다》 (be) vast; extensive; wide; boundless; limitless. ¶ ∼한 벌판 a vast wilderness; a vast wasteland.
**황망**(慌忙) being in a flurry; being in haste; being agitated. ∼하다 (be) hur-

ried; flurried; agitated. ¶ ∼히 in a flurry; helter-skelter.
**황망**(遑忙) busyness. ∼하다 (be) very busy.
**황매**(黃梅) a yellow plum (tree).
**황명**(皇命) an Imperial 「order 〔command, mandate〕.
**황모**(黃毛) hair from a weasel's tail. ◉ ∼필 a writing brush made of weasel-tail hair.
**황무**(荒蕪) wilderness; barrenness; desolation. ∼하다 (be) wild; waste; barren; uncultivated.
**황무지**(荒蕪地) waste 〔barren, wild, uncultivated〕 land; a barren tract; a wilderness; a waste. ¶ ∼를 개간하다 reclaim 〔break up〕 wild land; clear waste land / 그 땅의 대부분이 아직 ∼이다 The greater part of the land still lies waste.
**황민**(荒民) famine-stricken people; famine sufferers.
**황바리** 〖동물〗 a kind of crab with two long feelers.
**황밤**(黃—) a dried shelled chestnut.
**황백**(黃白) 《금과 은》 gold and silver; 《돈》 money.
**황봉**(黃蜂) = 참벌.
**황비**(皇妃) a queen consort; an empress; a queen.
**황사**(黃砂) yellow sand; the floating yellow dusts stemmed from a spring air stream ascending with fine dirt of Gobi Desert in northern China. ¶ ∼를 싣고 오는 바람 winds carrying yellow sand; the yellow-sand winds (from China). ◉ ∼현상 atmospheric phenomena of the wind carrying yellow 「dusts 〔sand〕; the floating yellow-sand phenomena.
**황사**(黃絲) yellow thread.
**황사등롱**(黃紗燈籠) 〖고제도〗 a yellow-gauze lantern (carried by low-ranking officials).
**황산**(黃酸) 〖화학〗 sulfuric 〔sulphuric 《영》〕 acid; (oil of) vitriol. ¶ ∼의 vitriolic / 묽은 ∼ dilute sulfuric acid / ∼을 끼얹다〔뿌리다〕 throw vitriol 《at, on, over》; throw acid 《at, on》. ◉ ∼구리 copper 「sulfate 〔sulphate 《영》〕; sulfate of copper; blue vitriol. ∼나트륨 sodium sulfate. ∼납 lead sulfate. ∼아연 sulfate of zinc. ∼암모늄 ammonium sulfate. ∼염(塩) a sulfate; salt of sulfuric acid; vitriol. ∼제일〔제이〕철 ferrous 〔ferric〕 sulfide. ∼지(紙) parchment 〔sulfate〕 paper; vegetable parchment. ∼철 sulfate of iron. ∼ 칼륨〔마그네슘〕 potassium 〔magnesium〕 sulfate. ∼ 코발트 cobalt sulfate.
**황상**(皇上) the present Emperor; His Majesty.
**황새** 〖조류〗 a white stork. ¶ 뱁새가 ∼를 따라가려 하다 [비유적] try to do what is beyond *one's* capacity.
**황새걸음** the gait of a stork; a long stride. ¶ ∼(을) 하다 take 〔walk with〕 long 〔big〕 strides.
**황새냉이** 〖식물〗 《겨잣과의》 a lady's-smock; a lady smock.
**황새치**(黃—) 〖어류〗 a swordfish; a broadbill (swordfish). ◉ ∼자리 〖천문〗 the Swordfish; Dorado.
**황색**(黃色) yellow; yellow color. ◉ ∼신문 a yellow journal 〔paper, rag, sheet〕; the yellow press [총칭].
**황석**(黃石) 〖광물〗 yellow calcite.
**황설**(荒說) an absurd story; nonsense; tommyrot; balderdash; a lie; a hoax.
**황성**(皇城) the Imperial city; the Capital.
**황성**(荒城) a ruined castle.
**황소** a bull. ¶ ∼처럼 일하다 work like a bull. ◉ ∼자리 〖천문〗 the Bull; Taurus.
**황소걸음** 《황소의》 the gait of a bull; 《느린》 a slow step; a leisurely pace. ¶ ∼하다 walk 「slowly 〔leisurely〕.
**황소바람** a heavy draft (of air); a big blow. ¶ 바늘구멍으로 ∼ 들어온다 《속담》 "The small hole made with a needle lets in a big blow."
**황손**(皇孫) an Imperial grandson; the grandson of an Emperor.
**황송하다**(皇悚—) 《황공(惶恐)하다》 (be) awe-stricken; 《죄송(罪悚)하다》 (be) indebted; obliged; grateful; 《분에 넘치다》 be too good for *one;* be unworthy of. ¶ 황송하게도 obligingly; graciously / 말씀드리기(가) 황송합니다만… May I humbly inform you that…. / 그건 너무나 황송합니다 That would be too much trespassing on your 「hospitality 〔kindness〕, I fear.
**황수정**(黃水晶) 〖광물〗 citrine.
**황숙하다**(黃熟—) ripen yellow.
**황실**(皇室) the 「Imperial 〔Royal〕 Household 〔House, Family〕; the reigning line. ◉ ∼비(費) the Imperial Household 「expenses 〔allowances〕; the civil list 《영》. ∼ 소유지 an Imperial estate; Crown lands. ∼ 재산 the Imperial 「estate 〔property〕.
**황아**(荒—) variety goods; notions; small items; sundries; dime-store merchandise. ◉ ∼장수 a peddler of sundries. ∼전(廛) a 「notions 〔variety〕 store; a dime store.

황야(荒野) a wilderness; the wilds; a waste; wasteland. ¶ ～를 헤매다 wander 〔roam〕 in the wilderness.
황어(黃魚) 〖어류〗 a dace; a chub.
황연(晃然) brightly; clearly; well. ¶ ～ 대각(大覺)하다 understand perfectly; see through clearly; attain spiritual enlightenment.
황연(黃鉛) chrome yellow. ｢jack〕.
황열(병)(黃熱(病)) 〖의학〗 yellow ｢fever
황오리(黃—) 〖조류〗 a sheldrake.
황옥(黃玉) 〖광물〗 yellow jade; topaz.
황운(皇運) the ｢luck 〔fortunes〕 of an Emperor.
황위(皇位) the (Imperial) Throne. ¶ ～를 잇다〔에 오르다〕 ｢succeed to 〔accede to, ascend〕 the Throne.
황위(皇威) Imperial ｢prestige 〔power, influence, dignity〕. ｢itude.
황위(黃緯) 〖천문〗 celestial 〔ecliptic〕 lat-
황은(皇恩) Imperial ｢favor 〔grace〕.
황음(荒淫) carnal excesses; sexual indulgence; dissipation. ¶ ～ 무도하다 be dissipated and depraved.
황인종(黃人種) the yellow race.
황자(皇子) an Imperial prince.
황작(黃雀) ① 《꾀꼬리》 a golden oriole. ② 《참새》 a sparrow.
황잡(荒雜) incoherence; desultoriness; looseness. ～하다 (be) incoherent; desultory; loose; slipshod; careless; unorganized; unsystematic. ¶ ～한 논의 an incoherent argument / ～한 사고 방식 a loose way of thinking / ～한 지식 unsystematic knowledge.
황적색(黃赤色) yellowish red.
황전(荒田) uncultivated 〔unopened〕 fields; ｢a deserted 〔a neglected, an overgrown〕 field; overgrown land.
황제(皇帝) an emperor. ¶ ～의 imperial / ～의 지위에 오르다〔를 물러나다〕 accede to 〔abdicate〕 the throne. ◉ ～폐하 His 〔Your〕 Majesty the Emperor. 신성 로마 ～ the Roman Emperor.
황조(皇祖) ① 《황제의》 imperial ancestors. ② 《할아버지》 *one's* own revered dead grandfather.
황조(黃鳥) 〖조류〗 a golden oriole.
황조근정훈장(黃條勤政勳章) the Order of Service merit, Yellow Stripes.
황조롱이 〖조류〗 a kestrel; 《영》 a windhover.
황족(皇族) the ｢Imperial 〔Royal〕 family; royalty; 《일원》 ｢an Imperial 〔a Royal〕 prince 〔princess〕; a member of the Imperial family. ¶ ～의 Imperial; Royal; of Royal blood. ◉ ～회의 the Imperial Family Council.
황지(荒地) waste 〔barren〕 land; desert 〔desolate〕 land; a waste; a desolation; a wilderness; wild(s).
황진(黃塵) ① 《흙먼지》 dust in the air; airborne dust; 〖기상〗 a dust storm. ¶ 만장(萬丈)의 ～ a cloud of dust / ～ 만장의 도시 a dust-swept city. ② 《속진》 the troublesome affairs of the mundane world.
황차(況且) much 〔still〕 more; much 〔still〕 less. ⇨ 하물며. ｢ber.
황채(黃菜) a dish of sliced ripe cucum-
황천(皇天) ① 《하늘》 High Heaven; Heaven of High; God's Heaven. ② 《하느님》 God. ¶ ～은 굽어 살피소서 God 〔Heaven〕 be my witness! *or* So help me heaven. ◉ ～후토(后土) the gods of heaven and earth.
황천(荒天) stormy 〔rough〕 weather. ¶ ～을 무릅쓰고 출항하다 sail in the stormy weather; set sail into the rough sea.
황천(黃泉) (the "yellow spring" of) Hades; the ｢region 〔land〕 of the dead. ◉ ～길 the ｢way 〔road〕 to Hades; a journey to the other world; death: ～길을 떠나다 go to *one's* ｢long 〔last〕 home; go on *one's* last journey.
황천객(黃泉客) a dead person. ¶ ～이 되다 go down to the shades; go on a journey whence no traveler returns; join the great majority; depart (from) this life; pass away; die.
황철광(黃鐵鑛) 〖광물〗 (iron) pyrites; fool's gold. ｢quality).
황청(黃淸) yellow honey (of superior
황체(黃體) 〖해부〗 《난소의》 a corpus luteum (*pl.* corpora lutea). ◉ ～ 호르몬 progesterone; progestin.
황촉(黃燭) 《밀초》 a beeswax candle.
황촉규(黃蜀葵) 〖식물〗 a kind of hibiscus.
황촌(荒村) a ｢deserted 〔desolate〕 village; a ghost town.
황충(蝗蟲) 〖곤충〗 a locust.
황치마(黃—) a kite which is white in the upper half and yellow in the lower half. ｢mandate〕.
황칙(皇勅) an Imperial decree 〔edict,
황칠(黃漆) a yellow dye from Jeju Island. ◉ ～나무 〖식물〗 *Textoria morbifera* (학명).
황태손(皇太孫) the eldest grandson of an Emperor.
황태자(皇太子) the Crown Prince; the

Prince Imperial; the Heir Apparent (to the Throne); 《영국의》 the Prince of Wales. ¶ ~를 책봉하다 proclaim the Heir Apparent to the Throne. ◉ ~비(妃) the Crown Princess. ~전하 His Imperial Highness the Crown Prince.

**황태후**(皇太后) the Empress Dowager; the Queen Mother. ◉ ~폐하 (Her Imperial Majesty) the Empress Dowager.

**황토**(荒土) barren land; wasteland; 《전쟁에 의한》 war-devastated〔-battered〕 land; a bombed area.

**황토**(黃土) yellow soil; (yellow) ocher; loess. ◉ ~색 mud yellow.

**황통**(皇統) the Imperial line(age). ¶ ~을 잇다 accede to the Throne.

**황파**(黃—) ⇨ 움파.

**황파**(荒波) rough seas; raging「waves〔waters〕; a「heavy〔high〕 sea.

**황폐**(荒廢) 《토지·가옥 등이》 waste; ruin; devastation; 《도덕·정신 등이》 moral「decay〔decline〕; desolation of the spirit. ~하다 be devastated; go〔fall into〕 to ruin; be laid waste. ¶ ~한 ruined; devastated / 전쟁으로 ~된 지역 war-devastated areas / ~케 하다 lay 《the land》 waste; devastate 《land》 / ~되어 있다 lie in ruins; be laid waste; be in a state of desolation; be out of repair (건물이) / 내전으로 그 지역은 ~화되었다 That area went to ruin by the civil war. / 지나친 입시 경쟁은 학생들의 마음을 ~케 했다 Excessive competition in entrance examination has devastated students' moral fiber. ◉ ~지 waste land; a devastated region. 산림 ~ forest denudation.

**황포**(黃袍) the Imperial robe.

**황하**(黃河) 《중국의 강》 the Yellow River; the Hwang Ho.

**황해**(黃海) the Yellow Sea.

**황혼**(黃昏) dusk; twilight; 《시어》 gloaming; crepuscule. ¶ ~에 in the dusk of the evening; at「dusk〔sundown〕; in the gathering「dusk〔darkness〕/ ~이 지다〔깃들다〕 dusk falls / 인생의 ~기에 in the twilight years of *one's* life; in〔at〕 the evening of *one's* life.

**황홀**(恍惚·恍惚) 《무아경》 rapture; ecstasy; trance. ~하다 be in「ecstasies〔raptures〕; (be) enraptured; entranced; charmed; enchanted. ¶ ~하여 in an ecstasy; in raptures; in a trance; with rapture / ~해지다 be in「raptures〔ecstasies〕 《over》; be「enraptured〔entranced, charmed, enchanted, spellbound〕 《by, with, at, over》; be carried away 《by》; fall into a trance / ~케 하다 charm; enrapture; enchant; fascinate; spellbind / 음악에 ~해지다 be carried away by the music; be enraptured in listening to the music / 그녀는 ~해졌다 She was thrown into ecstasy. / 그는 그녀를 ~하게 바라보았다 He gazed upon her with rapture. *or* He was struck by her charms.

**황화**(黃化) 〖화학〗 sulfuration〔sulphuration 《영》〕; sulfurization. ~하다 sulfurate; sulfurize. ◉ ~ 고무 vulcanized India rubber. ~ 구리 copper sulfide. ~나트륨 sodium sulfide. ~물 a sulfide; a hydrosulfide. ~물감 sulfide「dyes〔dyestuff〕; sulfur color. ~ 석회 sulfurated lime. ~수소 sulfureted hydrogen; hydrogen sulfide. ~아연(亞鉛) blende. ~ 알릴 allyl sulfide. ~ 암모니아 ammonium sulfide. ~은(銀) silver sulfide. ~철 iron sulfide. ~ 칼륨 sulfurated potash. ~탄소 carbon sulfide.

**황화**(黃花) a yellow chrysanthemum.

**황화**(黃禍) the Yellow Peril.

**황화병**(黃化病) 〖식물〗 icterus; yellows.

**황후**(皇后) an empress; a queen;「an empress〔a queen〕 consort. ◉ ~폐하 Her (Imperial) Majesty the Empress.

**홰**[1] 《횃불의》 a torch; a flambeau; a firebrand. ¶ 홰에 불을 붙이다 kindle〔light〕 a torch / 홰를 들다 carry a torch in *one's* hand.

**홰**[2] ① 《닭장의》 a perch; a roost. ¶ 《닭이》 홰에 오르다 《a hen》 go to roost; be on the perch. ② 《새벽 닭 우는 소리》 a〔the〕 crow. ¶ 닭이 두 홰 울다 the cock crows twice.

**홰나무** 〖식물〗 a pagoda tree; a Chinese scholar tree. ⇨ 회화나무.

**홰치다** flap the wings; flutter. ¶ 닭이 ~ a hen flaps its wings.

**홰홰** 《내두르는 모양》 round and round. ¶ 횃불을 ~ 휘두르다 swing a torch about; fling a torch around / 단장을 ~ 휘두르다 brandish a stick 《at *a person*》.

**홱** ① 《갑자기》 suddenly; with a bang; 《잽싸게》 quickly; with dispatch; nimbly. ¶ 홱 지나가다 pass quickly; flit 《across the sky》 / 뒤를 홱 돌아보다 turn right round; wheel about; turn face about / 몸을 홱 비키다 dodge *oneself;* dodge 《a blow》 nimbly / 웃옷을 홱 벗다 whip off *one's* coat / 얼굴을 홱

붉히다 blush all of a sudden / 창밖으로 얼굴을 홱 내밀다 pop *one's* head out of the window / 문이 홱 열렸다 The door swung 〔sprang, flew〕 open. / 바람이 홱 불었다 There was a gust of wind.
② 《힘차게》 vigorously; with a jerk; with a shove; with a whack 〔swish〕. ¶ 홱 당기다〔밀다〕 pull 〔push〕 with a (sudden) jerk; give 《it》 a vigorous 〔quick〕 pull 〔push〕 / 홱 던지다 throw 〔fling, hurl〕 《*a thing*》 at 《*a person*》 / (문 따위를) 홱 열다 fling 〔throw〕 《a window》 open / 홱 뿌리치다 jerk 《*one's* arm》 loose; shake *oneself* loose 〔free〕 from 《*a person's* grasp》 / 홱 뿌리치고 달아나다 tear *oneself* away from 《*another's* grasp》; break free of 《*a person*》 / 채찍으로 홱 갈기다 whack 〔give a whack〕 with a whip.

**홱홱** ① 《날쌔게》 snap-snap; with dispatch; quickly. ¶ 일을 ~ 해치우다 finish *one's* job quickly. ② 《갑자기》 swish=swish; whoosh-whoosh; speedily; fast. ¶ 자동차가 ~ 지나가다 cars zoom by. ③ 《던지다》 flinging repeatedly; bang-bang(-bang). ¶ ~ 책을 던지다 bang books away. ④ 《뿌리치다》 with shove after shove; with jerk after jerk. ¶ ~ 팔을 뿌리치다 keep jerking *one's* arm loose; keep shoving 《*a person*》 away with *one's* arm. ⑤ 《때리다》 with whack after whack. ¶ 채찍으로 ~ 갈기다 keep whacking with a whip; keep whipping 《*a person*》.

**횃대** a clothes rack; a clotheshorse; a coat hanger.

**횃댓보** a clothes protector put over a clothes rack.

**횃불** a torchlight; a torch; a flambeau (*pl.* ~s, -beaux); 《봉화》 a signal fire. ¶ ~을 들다 carry a torch in *one's* hand / ~을 켜다 kindle (burn) a torch / ~로 앞길을 비추다 light *one's* way with a torch. ◉ ~ 행렬 《have》 a torchlight procession 〔parade〕.

**횃줄** a clothesline.

**횅댕그렁하다** (be) hollow; empty; deserted; [서술적] feel hollow; look bare 〔empty, hollow〕. ¶ 횅댕그렁한 방 an empty room / 손님이 다 떠나서 방이 ~ The room feels empty now that all the guests have left.

**횅하다** ① 《통달하다》 be familiar 《with》; be well acquainted 《with》; be well 〔deeply〕 versed 《in》; be well posted 《in》; be at home 《in》. ¶ 이 곳 지리에 ~ know the lay of the land around here / 문학에 ~ be well versed in literature / 길을 횅하게 알다 know the road well / 그는 그 일에는 ~ He has the business at his finger's tips.
② 《공허하다》 (be) vacant; empty; deserted; void. ¶ 집이 ~ a house is empty / 거리가 ~ a street is deserted.

**회**(回) 《횟수》 a time; (★ 보통 ... times는 3회 이상에 쓰임: 1회 once; 2회 twice; 3회 three times; 4〔수〕회 four 〔several〕 times); 《카드놀이·권투·경기 등의》 a round; a bout, a game (한 판 승부); 《야구의》 (an) inning.
¶ 제1회전 《야구의》 the first inning; 《권투 따위의》 the first round / 2회초〔말〕 《야구의》 the first 〔second〕 half of the second inning; the top 〔bottom〕 of the 2nd inning / 3회 승부 a three=game contest; a match of three games / 10회전 《권투 등의》 a bout of ten rounds / 회를 거듭하다 do 〔hold〕 it several times / 회를 거듭함에 따라 as the game advances 〔progresses〕 / 회를 거듭할수록 잘 하다 get better each time / 회를 채우다 play the full game; finish the round / 학급회는 연 2회 열린다 The class meeting is to be held twice a year. / 경기는 연장 16회전에 이르렀다 The game went to 16 inning. / 경기의 첫 회가 벌어지고 있다 The first bout is taking place. / 그는 토너먼트 3회까지 진출했다 He went on to the third round of the tournament.

**회**(灰) ① ⇨ 석회(石灰). ¶ 회를 바르다 plaster; stucco. ② [통속적] calcium oxide. ◉ 회반죽 plaster; mortar.

**회**(蛔) a mawworm; an ascarid. ⇨ 거위[2]. ¶ 회가 동하다 [비유적] be appetizing; be tempting 〔attractive〕; make *one's* mouth water; have an itch 〔a desire〕 《for, to *do*》; have a 《great》 mind 《to *do*》.

**회**(會) ① 《모임》 a meeting; a gathering; a get-together; a conference; a convention; a party; a function.
¶ 회를 소집하다 call a meeting / 회를 열다 hold 〔open〕 a meeting; give a party / 회에 출석하다 attend 〔be present at〕 a meeting / 회에 불참하다 fail to attend 〔be absent from〕 a party 〔meeting〕 / 회는 4시에 해산했다 The meeting broke up at four o'clock. / 회는 유회(流會)되었다 The meeting fell through. / 회는 연 2회 회장이 소집한다 The meeting shall be called by the president twice a year.

> **용법** **meeting** 가장 일반적이며 폭넓은 뜻으로 쓰이는 낱말. 모든 회합을 가리키는데 쓸 수 있음. **gathering** 허물없는 분위기의 모임을 가리키는 말. **get=together** gathering과 거의 비슷한 뜻을 나타내지만, 보다 구어적인 표현. **conference** 전문적인 문제를 협의하기 위해 모인 회합. **convention** 대규모적인 연차 대회 따위. **party** 사교상의 목적으로 모이는 모임. **function** 규모가 크거나 어떤 것을 기념하기 위해 모인 집회.

②《조직》 a society; an association (협회); a club (클럽); a circle.

> **용법** **society**, **association** 공통의 관심사에 대한 상호간의 이해를 보다 깊게 하기 위해 조직된 단체. 다만 전자가 후자보다 목적·회원 자격·활동면 등에 있어서 보다 제한적인 성격을 띠고 있음. **club** 회원 자격·회비·회합 시간 등이 명확히 정해져 있는 규모가 작은 모임. **circle** 공통의 관심사를 가지고 즐기기 위해 모이는 작은 그룹.

¶ 금주회(禁酒會) a teetotal party 〔society〕/ 문학회 a literary club 〔society〕/ 회를 조직하다 form 〔organize〕 a society / 회에 가입하다 join a society; associate *oneself* with a society / 회에서 탈퇴하다 leave 〔resign from〕 a society.

**회**(膾) 《육회》 minced raw meat; 《생선회》 sliced raw fish; slices of raw fish. ¶ 다랑어회 slices of raw tuna; sliced tuna / 생선회를 치다 prepare a dish of sliced raw fish; slice raw fish / 회로 먹다 eat 《it》 raw.

**회갑**(回甲) *one's* 60th birthday (anniversary). ⇨ 환갑(還甲). ◉ ~연(宴) 《give》 a banquet on *one's* 60th birthday.

**회개**(悔改) repentance 《for *one's* sins》; remorse; penitence. ~하다 repent (of); be(come) repentant 〔penitent〕 over 〔for〕; reform *oneself;* turn over a new leaf. ¶ ~하면 죄를 용서받는다 Repentance wipes out sin.

**회견**(會見) an interview; a meeting. ~하다 have an interview 〔a talk〕 《with》; see; interview; meet 〔meet with 《미》〕 《*a person*》; give an interview to 《the pressmen》. ¶ …와의 ~에서 in an interview with / ~을 청하다 ask for 〔request〕 an interview 《with *a person*》/ ~을 허락하다 grant 〔give〕 an interview 《to a journalist》.

◉ ~기(記) a record 〔an account〕 of an 〔*one's*〕 interview. ~담 an (oral) interview. ~자 an interviewer; a visitor. 공식~ a formal interview. 기자~ a press 〔news〕 conference 〔interview〕: 기자 ~을 거절하다 refuse to be interviewed by newsmen / 기자 ~을 하다 meet the press; hold 〔host〕 a press conference. 단독~ a single interview; an exclusive interview 《with》: 단독 ~을 청하다 ask for an exclusive interview with. 비공식~ an informal interview.

**회계**(會計) ①《계산》 the account; the reckoning; accounting; 《재정》 finance; 《계산서》 a bill; 《미》 a check; 《지급》 payment. ~하다 account; count; reckon; pay 〔foot〕 a bill. ¶ 오늘 모임의 ~는 A씨가 맡아 본다 Mr. A will take charge of the fiscal side of today's meeting. / 그는 클럽의 ~를 맡고 있다 He keeps the club's accounts. ②《사람》 an accountant; a treasurer (단체의 회계 간사); a cashier (출납계); a paymaster.

◉ ~과 the accounts 〔accounting〕 section: ~ 과장 an accountant general. ~기 『컴퓨터』 a billing machine. ~단위 the unit of accounting. ~법 『법』 the Public Account Law; 《방식》 an account system. ~법규 fiscal laws and regulations. ~보고 a financial 〔an accounts, a treasurer's〕 report. ~사 an accountant: 공인~사 《미》 a certified public accountant (생략 C.P.A., CPA); 《영》 a chartered accountant (생략 C.A.). ~서류 financial documents. ~원 an accountant; an accounting clerk; 《출납계》 a cashier; 《단체 등의》 a treasurer. ~장부 an account book; a ledger. ~정보 시스템 『컴퓨터』 an AIS. [<*a*ccounting *i*nformation *s*ystem] ~학 accounting; accountancy. 일반〔특별〕~ the general 〔special〕 account: 일반 ~에서 양곡 특별 ~로의 대체 transfer (of fund) from the general account to the food special account.

**회계감사**(會計監査) an audit; auditing. ¶ ~를 하다 examine accounts officially; audit. ◉ ~관 an auditor; commissioners of audit 《영》.

**회계연도**(會計年度) a fiscal 〔financial 《영》〕 year. ¶ 2000 ~, 2000 fiscal year; fiscal 2000.

**회고**(回顧) recollection; reminiscence;

retrospect; retrospection; review. ～하다 recollect; reminisce 《about》; retrospect; look back 《upon, on, over, at》; think back 《across two decades》; recall; review 《*one's* past life》; pass 《*one's* life》 in review; run 《*one's* mind》 back over. ¶ ～적(인) retrospective / ～와 전망 retrospect and prospect / 지난날을 ～하면 on looking back 「upon 〔into〕 the past / 학창시절을 ～하다 look back upon *one's* student days / 1985년을 ～하다 review 1985 in retrospect. ◉ ～담(談) recollections. ～록(錄) reminiscences; memoirs. ～장면 《영화의》 a retrospective shot. ～전(展) the retrospective(s) 《of *a person's* art works》.

**회고**(懷古) nostalgia; yearning for the old days; retrospection; cherishing thoughts of the past. ～하다 recollect 〔look back upon〕 the past; recall the 「past 〔old days〕 to *one's* mind. ¶ ～의 정에 젖게 하다 carry *one* back to the 「happy 〔good〕 old days / ～의 정을 못 이기다 [장소가 주어] bring back 《to *one*》 dear memories of the past / 나이가 들면 ～하는 버릇이 많게 마련이다 The older we get, the more fondly we think of the past. ◉ ～담 reminiscences; recollections; *one's* past stories: ～담을 하다 talk over old times. ～시 a reminiscent poem.

**회공** being 「hollow 〔empty〕 inside. ～하다, ～되다 become hollow; get empty.

**회과**(悔過) repentance; penitence. ～하다 regret 《to have *done,* having *done*》; repent 《of 》; be repentant 〔penitent〕 《for》; be sorry for. ¶ ～ 자책(自責)하다 repent *one's* sins and reproaches *oneself.*

**회관**(會館) a hall; an assembly 「hall 〔house〕; a club-house. ◉ 기독교 청년 ～ the 「Young Men's Christian Association 〔Y.M.C.A.〕 Hall.

**회교**(回敎) Islam. ⇨ 이슬람.

**회군**(回軍) withdrawal of an army 〔of troops〕; a troop withdrawal. ～하다 《an army》 withdraw.

**회귀**(回歸) a revolution; recurrence; (one) complete revolution; 〖수학·통계〗 regression. ～하다 recur; revolve; make one full revolution; occur periodically. ◉ ～계수 a regression coefficient. ～곡선 〖수학〗 a regression curve. ～년 〖천체〗 a tropical year. ～대(帶) 〖지질〗 the tropical zone. ～동맥 〖해부〗 a recurrent artery. ～ 무풍대 〖지질〗 the calm zone of the tropics. ～선(線) the tropics: 남북 ～선 the tropic of 「Capricorn 〔Cancer〕. ～성 recurrence; a tendency to recur. ～신경 a recurrent nerve. ～열(熱) 〖의학〗 recurrent 〔relapsing〕 fever; typhinia.

**회규**(會規) ＝ 회칙(會則).

**회기**(回忌) an anniversary of 《*a person's*》 death.

**회기**(會期) 《국회·회의》 (the duration of) a session; a sitting; 《기간》 a term; a period. ¶ 국회 ～ 중에 during 「the Assembly session 〔the session of the Assembly〕; while the Assembly 「is sitting 〔in session〕 / ～를 연장하다 extend the session / 20일간의 ～로 임시 국회가 열렸다 The extraordinary Assembly opened for a 20-day extraordinary session. ◉ ～연장 「a prolongation 〔an extension〕 of a session.

**회나무** 〖식물〗 a Korean spindle tree.

**회담**(會談) a talk; talks; a conference; a meeting. ～하다 talk 〔speak〕 together; have 〔conduct〕 a talk 《with》; confer 《with》; have a conference 《with》. ¶ 비공식 ～ an informal get-together; a conversation (외교상의) / 전화 ～ a telephone conference / 한미 서울 ～ the ROK-U.S. talks in Seoul / ～을 중단하다〔끝내다〕 「cut off 〔wind up〕 talk / 장시간 ～하다 have a long talk 《with *a person*》 / ～은 현재 진행 중이다 Talks are now 「underway 〔in progress〕. / 대통령은 야당 당수들과 ～하셨다 The President had a talk with the Opposition party leaders.
◉ 4자～ a four-party meeting; four-way 《Korea》 talks: 남북한간의 항구적인 평화를 확보하기 위한 제6차 4자～이 8월 5일 제네바에서 재개된다고 보도되었다 It is reported that four-way talks aimed at securing a lasting peace between North and South Korea will reconvene for a sixth session on Aug. 5 in Geneva. 3자〔국〕～ a tripartite conference. 여야(중진)～ bipartisan conference (of key leaders).

**회답**(回答) a reply; an answer; a response. ～하다 reply 《to》; answer; respond 《to》; give 「a reply 〔an answer〕. ¶ …의 ～으로(서) in 「answer 〔reply〕 to / ～을 회피하다 evade an answer / 편지 ～을 하다 answer 〔reply to〕 the letter; reply by letter / 아무에게서 ～이 있다〔없다〕 get 「an 〔no〕 answer from *a person* / 아무 ～도 없다 hear nothing in reply; fail to get any response / 내 전갈에 대해서 그로부터 한 마디의 ～도 없었다 No word has come from him in answer 〔reply〕 to my message. / ～을 기다리겠습니다 I hope to hear from you soon. *or* I am looking forward to your letter. / ～이 늦어서 죄송합니다 I must apologize for not answering you sooner. / 곧 ～을 주시면 감사하겠습니다 I should be very happy if you would answer my letter soon. / ～을 부탁합니다 *Répondez, s'il vous plaît* (F.) (생략 R.S.V.P.) (=Reply, if you please.). ◉ ～자〔인〕 an answerer; 《퀴즈 프로그램의》 a panelist; 《앙케이트의》 a respondent.

**회당**(會堂) 《예배당》 a church; 《공회당》 a public 〔town〕 hall; a civic auditorium (*pl.* ～s, -ria); 《집회장》 an assembly hall. ¶ 청중이 ～에 꽉 차 있었다 The hall was crowded with audience.

**회독**(回讀) reading 《a book》 in turn; circulation 《a book》 to be read. ～하다 read 《a book》 in turn; circulate reading material.

**회동**(會同) meeting 〔gathering〕 together; a meeting; an assembly; a gathering. ～하다 meet 〔gather〕 together; assemble; get together; have a meeting.

**회동그랗다** ① 《눈이》 be wide-opened= eyed with surprise. ② 《거리낄 것 없다》 (be) carefree; [서술적] be free from bothers. ③ 《완결하다》 (be) completely finished; completed. ¶ 남은 일을 회동그랗게 해치우다 clean up unfinished work.

**회두리** the end; the finish; the last turn 〔round〕. ◉ ～씨름 the last round of a *ssirŭm* match. ～판 = 회두리.

**회람**(回覽) circulation. ～하다 pass 《a circular notice》 on 《to *a person*》; send 《a circular》 round 《to all the members》; read 《a magazine》 in turn. ¶ 이 통지문을 읽고 ～시켜 주시오 Please read this notice and pass it on. ◉ ～문고 a circulating library. ～잡지 a circulating magazine.

**회람판**(回覽板) a circulating bulletin; a circular notice. ¶ ～을 돌리다 pass on a circular notice.

**회랑**(回廊) a corridor; a gallery; an ambulatory; a veranda. ◉ 공중～ an air corridor 《to Berlin》.

**회례**(回禮) returning a courtesy; a return visit 〔present〕. ～하다 return a courtesy 〔compliment, call〕; give 〔send, make〕 a present in return. ¶ ～로 in return for.

**회례**(廻禮) a round of social visits. ～하다 pay social visits; go around making calls; go a round of complimentary visits 〔calls〕. ¶ 신년 ～를 하다 make (a round of) New Year's calls.

**회로**(回路) ① 《돌아오는 길》 a return trip; the return way; the road back. ¶ ～에 on *one's* way back 〔home〕. ② 〖전기〗 a 〔an electric〕 circuit. ¶ ～를 열다〔닫다〕 open 〔close〕 a circuit. ◉ ～도 a circuit diagram. ～망(網) an electric network; circuitry. ～시험기 a circuit tester. ～접속기 〖전기〗 a circuit closer. ～제어기 a circuit controller. ～차단기 a circuit breaker. 진공관～ a vacuum tube circuit. 집적～ an integrated circuit.

**회로**(懷爐) a (portable) body warmer; a pocket heater; a hand-warmer. ¶ ～를 지니다 use a body warmer; carry 〔have〕 a pocket heater 《with *one*》.

**회록**(會錄) assembly records; the minutes; proceedings.

**회뢰**(賄賂) 《금품》 a bribe; palm oil 《속어》; grease 《속어》; 《행위》 bribery. ⇨ 뇌물.

**회류**(會流) confluence; conflux. ～하다 join; flow together; merge 《into》. ◉ ～점 a point of confluence; a junction.

**회맹**(會盟) a league; a covenant. ～하다 league 〔band〕 together; form a league; enter into a covenant.

**회명**(會名) the name of a society 〔an association〕.

**회모**(懷慕) longing; yearning; deep attachment. ～하다 long 〔yearn〕 for; love dearly.

**회무**(會務) affairs 〔business〕 of a society. ¶ ～를 총괄하다 preside over the business of an association.

**회문**(回文) ① 《회장》 a circular (letter); a round robin. ¶ ～을 돌리다 send (out) 〔issue, address〕 a circular; circulate a letter. ② 《한시체의》 a reversible poem that can be read both ways; a palindrome.

**회반죽**(灰—) mortar; plaster; stucco. ¶ ～을 바르다 plaster; stucco.

**회백색**(灰白色) light gray 〔grey 《영》〕; ash color. ¶ ～의 ash-colored; ashen.

**회백수염**(灰白髓炎) 〖의학〗 poliomyelitis.

**회백질**(灰白質) 〖해부〗 gray matter.

**회벽**(灰壁) a (lime-)plastered wall.

**회보**(回報) ① 《회신》 a reply; an answer. ～하다 give a reply; send an answer. ② 《복명》 reporting when *one* returns.

~하다 report「when *one* returns〔on *one's* return〕.

**회보**(會報) assembly〔association〕reports; a bulletin; the transactions (of a society). ¶ 동창회 ~를 내다 issue an alumni〔alumnae (여성의)〕bulletin / 협회는 연 2회 ~를 내기로 되어 있다 The society is to issue a bulletin twice a year.

**회복**(回復·恢復) ① 《본디 상태로》 recovery; restoration; retrieval; rehabilitation; 《시세의》 recovery; reaction. ~하다 get back; recover 《strength》; regain 《*one's* reputation》; restore 《peace》; rehabilitate 《*one's* character》; retrieve 《*one's* honor, position》; get over 《a loss》; repair 《*one's* exhausted energies》; 《실지 등을》 win back; 『법』《소송에 의해》 replevy; be restored to 《*one's* honor》. ¶ 국토를 ~하다 rehabilitate a country; regain a lost territory / 사회질서를 ~하다 restore public order / 평화의 ~을 바라다 desire to restore peace / 국가 경제의 안정을 ~하다 restore stability to the country's economy / 명예를〔신용을〕~하다 retrieve〔redeem〕*one's* honor〔credit〕/ 시장 경기가 ~되었다 The market has revived. / 경기 ~의 징후가 있다 There are signs of a business recovery. / 우리 나라의 경제는 ~되어 가고 있다 The economy of our country is「picking up〔improving〕.
② 《건강의》 recovery 《from illness》; recuperation 《after an illness》. ~하다 recover (from illness); get well again; be restored to health; recover〔regain〕《*one's* health》; get over 《a disease》; get better.
¶ 건강 ~을 위해 in order to regain *one's* health; to find *one's* health / 시력〔청력〕을 ~하다 recover *one's* sight〔hearing〕/ 의식을 ~하다 regain consciousness / 원기를 ~하다 recover *one's* spirits / ~의 조짐이 없다 show no progress toward recovery / ~이 더디다 be slow in recovery; show little progress toward recovery / ~을 더디게 하다 retard *one's* recovery / 그는 ~할 가망이 없다 There is no hope of his recovery. / 그는 건강이 거의 ~되었다 He has almost recovered his health. / 부디 빨리 ~되십시오 I hope you will soon be all right〔get well〕again. / 나는 감기에 걸리면 ~이 늦다 I am slow in recovering when I catch cold. / 환자는 곧 ~될 것이다 The patient will soon come round. / 피로 ~에는 잠을 잘 자는 것이 제일이다 The best way to recover from *one's* fatigue is to sleep well.
◉ ~력 《질병 등의》 recuperative power. ~실 《병원의》 a recovery room; a convalescent ward. 권리~ recovery of rights.

**회복기**(回復期) (a period of) convalescence; a convalescent stage. ¶ ~의 환자 a convalescent〔recovering〕patient; a convalescent / ~의 경제 reflationary〔recovering, resurgent〕economy / ~에 있다 be in the convalescent stage; be convalescing; be getting better.

**회복통**(蛔腹痛) 『한의』 a stomachache caused by worms.

**회부**(回附) transmission; 『법』 return. ~하다 transmit 《to》; refer 《to》; send (over) 《to》; forward 《to》; pass on 《to》. ¶ (의안이) 위원회에 ~되다 be submitted to a committee / 그 사건은 하급 법원으로 ~되었다 The case was remitted to a lower court. / 이 문서를 총무부에 ~해 주십시오 Please「send this paper〔pass this paper on〕to the general affairs department. / 법안은 국회에 ~되었다 The bill was (amended and) sent back to the Assembly.

**회비**(會費) 《회원의》 a (membership) fee; dues (of a member); 《회합의》 the subscription 《for a meet(ing)》. ¶ 클럽 ~ club dues; *one's* club subscription 《영》/ 파티~ contribution fee; *one's* share of party expenses / 연(年)~ annual dues〔fees〕/ ~를 거두다 collect dues / ~를 내다 pay *one's* membership fee〔club dues〕/ ~는 1년에 2만원이다 Membership fees are 20,000 won a year. / ~ 만 원 당일 납부할 것 You are requested to pay a fee of ten thousand won on that day. / 그는 ~를 미납했다 He has not yet paid the membership fee.
◉ ~미납자 one who「is in arrear(s) in〔has not paid〕the membership fee.

**회사**(回謝) a present in token of *one's* gratitude; a return present. ~하다 send 《a present》 in token of *one's* gratitude; send as a return present.

**회사**(會社) a company (생략 Co.); a corporation 《미》; 《상사》 a (business) firm; an office (사무소). ⇨ 참고 p. 2567.
¶ ~에 나가다〔출근하다〕go to work; 《사무직 사람이》 go to the office / ~에 다니다〔근무하다〕serve in〔work for, be

an employ of〕「an office〔a firm, a company〕/ ～에 들어가다〔채용되다〕join a company; enter (the service of) a corporation / ～를 그만두다〔사임하다〕quit〔leave, retire from (정년으로)〕the company / ～를 조직〔설립〕하다 organize〔establish〕a company / ～를 해산하다 dissolve〔liquidate, wind up〕a company / ～ 조직으로 하다 incorporate; (re)organize into a company / 어느 ～에 근무하십니까 Which〔What〕company do you work for? / 이 건은 ～에 가서 나의 상사와 의논해 보겠습니다 I'll discuss this with my superiors back at the office.

> (용법) **company**「회사」를 나타내는 가장 일반적인 말. 규모나 내용에 상관치 않고 일상적인 뜻의「회사」를 뜻함. **corporation** 법인으로 인정된「유한 회사」란 뜻으로 미국에서 쓰임. **firm** 두 사람 이상의 합자(合資)로 설립한 회사란 뜻. company와 같은 뜻으로도 쓰임. **office**「일하는 장소」로서 회사를 지칭하는 말로, go to the office「회사에 가다〔다니다〕」처럼 관용적으로 쓰임.
> ▶ 구체적인 회사명의 표기는 다음과 같음. 브라운 주식회사《미》Brown Co. Inc. 또는 Brown Inc.;《영》Brown Co. Ltd. (★ Inc.는 Incorporated의 생략형). / 주식회사 a joint-stock company; a joint-stock corporation《미》(생략 Co.) / 유한책임회사《미》an incorporated company (생략 Inc.); a limited liability company《영》(생략 Ltd.).

◉ ～내규 company「bylaws〔regulations〕. ～법 company law《영》; corporation law《미》. ～사장 the president of a company. ～업무 company affairs; the「business〔affairs〕of a corporation. ～임원 a board member. ～정관 the articles of association; the memorandum and articles of association. ～조직 company system. ～조합 a company(-based) union. ～중역〔이사〕a company executive; a member of the directory.

**회사원**(會社員) an office worker;《특정 회사의》「an employee of〔a clerk in〕a《trading》company; an office man; a white-collar worker《미》.

**회사채**(會社債) a「company〔corporation〕bond; a (company) debenture. ¶ ～를 발행하다 issue bonds / 2천만 원의 ～를 모집하다 issue debentures amounting to 20 million won.
◉ ～권 a (debenture) bond. ～권자(權者) a debenture holder. ～발행 debenture「floatation〔issue〕: ～ 발행액 the debentures issued; the issue amount of debentures / ～ 발행 한도 the issue limit of debentures. ～상환 debenture redemption. ～유통 시장 debenture trading market. ～이자 debenture interests. 담보〔무담보〕～「a secured〔an unsecured〕debenture. 보증～ a guaranteed debenture bond. 정리～ an adjustment bond.

**회상**(回想) recollection; retrospection; reflection; reminiscence. ～하다 look back「on〔over〕《the past》; recollect; recall《*something*》to *one's* mind; reminisce《about》. ¶ 어린 시절의 ～ the memories of childhood / ～에 잠기다 indulge〔be lost〕in reminiscences / 과거를 ～하다 review the past; reflect on the past (days);「run back over〔look back into〕the past / 노인들은 종종 ～을 즐겨 한다 Old people often enjoy retrospection. ◉ ～기〔록〕reminiscences; memoirs: 그는 제2차대전 ～록을 출판했다 He published his memoirs of World War II. ～장면〖영화〗a flashback; a retrospect sequence.

**회색**(灰色) an ash color; gray〔grey《영》〕color. ¶ ～의 ash-colored; gray; ashen / ～빛이 도는 grayish; ashy / 그녀는 ～ 옷을 입고 있었다 She was dressed in gray. ◉ ～분자 a wobbler. ～차일구름 altostratus (생략 As).

**회생**(回生) a return to life; resurrection; resuscitation. ～하다 come to life again; return to life; rise from the dead; revive; resuscitate《from apparent death》; be restored to life again. ¶ 기사 ～의 묘약 a wonder drug to「raise the dead〔restore the dead to life〕; a magic drug to resurrect the dead; a wonderworking medicine.

**회서**(回書) a written reply; a letter of reply.

**회석**(會席) a meeting-place;《참석》the presence of the members of a meeting;《모임》a meeting.

**회선**(回船)《돌아가는 배》a return boat; the boat back;《배를 돌림》turning a boat around. ～하다 turn《a boat》around;《a boat》turn around.

**회선**(回線)〖전기〗a circuit. ◉ 개방〔국부〕～「an open〔a local〕circuit. 단(短)〔일차, 폐색〕～ a「short〔primary, closed〕

참고 **우리 나라의 회사 조직과 직위의 영어명**

부서명·직위명 등을 실제로 표기할 때는 정관사 **the**를 붙인다. 부서명은 고유명사적으로 생각하여 단어의 첫자를 대문자로 쓰는 것이 일반적이다.

1. 회사의 조직·부서명: 회사 조직은 업종·규모·형태 등에 따라 다양하다. 이사회(board of directors),—사업본부(division),—부(department),—실(office),—과(section),—계(subsection) 등으로 나뉜다. 그러나 본부 제도가 없는 회사에서는 division(부), —department(과),—section(계)이 된다. 또 본사와 지사가 있는 경우, 동일 부서의 표기 구분은 본사의 것을 corporate *accounts* department처럼 corporate를 붙인다. 아래에 쓰인 d.는 department 또는 division의 약자임.

감사부 internal auditing d. / 경리부 general accounting d.; accounts d.; budget & accounting d. / 관재부(管財部) properties administration d. / 구매부 purchasing d. / 기술부 engineering d.; technical development d. / 기자재부 machinery & materials d. / 기획부 planning d. / 노무부 labor relations d. / 무역부 import & export d. / 복지 후생부 welfare d. / 사업부 enterprises d. / 상품개발부 product development d. / 상품관리부 product administration d. / 생산관리부 production control d. / 생산부 production d. / 서무부 general affairs d. / 선전〔광고〕부 advertising d. / 섭외부 foreign 〔public〕 relations d. / 수입부 import d. / 수출부 export d. / 시장 개발 기술 서비스부 marketing & technical services d. / 업무부 sales administration d. / 연구 개발부 R & D d. (Research and Development) / 영업부 sales d.; marketing d. / 인사부 personnel d. / 자금부 finance processing d. / 자재부 materials d. / 재무부 finance d. / 전자계산부 electronic information system d. / 조사부 business research d.; information & research d. / 증권부 securities d. / 총무부 administration d.; general affairs d. / 통신부 communications d. / 특허부 patent d. / 판매관리부 sales administration d. / 판매부 sales d. / 판매촉진부 sales promotion d. / 해외부 overseas d.; international d. / 해외사업부 overseas operations d. / 홍보부 public relations d.; publicity d. / 기획실 corporate planning office / 비서실 secretariat / 사사실(社史室) corporate history office.

2. 회사의 직위명: 직위명은 직무 권한에 따라 갖가지 호칭이 있을 수 있다.

회장 chairman; chairman of the board (of directors); board chairman; 《실권을 쥔 최고경영자》 CEO (=Chief Executive Officer) 《미》 / 부회장 vice-chairman / 사장 president; managing director 《영》; 《실권을 쥔 사장》 chief executive (officer) (★ 회장이 CEO인 경우는 chief operating officer가 됨) / 부사장 executive vice-president / 대표이사 representative director; managing director 《영》 / 전무(이사) executive (managing) director / 상무(이사) managing director / 이사 director; member of the board (★ 비상근이사 outside director; 상근이사 inside 〔fulltime〕 director) / 감사역 auditor / 고문, 상담역 (senior) corporate adviser; counselor / 비서 secretary / 본부장 division director; general manager / 국장 director; general manager / 부장 (general) manager; director; division 〔department〕 head / 차장 deputy 〔assistant (to)〕 general manager; deputy director; 《부장대리》 acting 〔assistant (to)〕 general manager / 과장 (section) manager; section chief 〔head〕 / 대리 assistant (to) manager; acting manager / 계장 subsection head 〔chief〕; senior staff; assistant to manager / 과원, 부원 staff / 평사원 rank-and-file employee 〔worker〕; [집합적] the ranks; the rank and file. 지점장 branch 〔district, general〕 manager / 지점차장 deputy branch manager; assistant district 〔regional〕 manager / 공장장 plant manager / 반장 foreman.

3. 기타: 명함이나 서류 따위에 이름과 직함을 표기할 때는 아래와 같이 쓴다.

(명함) Chang-jin Chun
General Manager, Export Department

(서류) Chang-jin Chun
General Manager,
Export Department

circuit. 전화~ a telephone circuit.

**회선**(迴旋·回旋) rotation; revolution; 《식물 따위의》 winding; involution. ~하다 rotate; revolve; turn 〔spin〕 round. ◉ ~곡(曲) 〖음악〗 a rondo. ~교 a swivel bridge. ⇨ 선개교(旋開橋). ~기중기 a rotary crane. ~동맥 circumflex artery. ~포(砲) a swivel gun. ~포탑 a (rotating) turret.

**회송**(回送) =환송(還送). ¶ 승객을 태우지 않고 버스를 차고에 ~하다 drive a bus without passengers to the shed.
◉ ~차 an out-of-service car 〔train〕; a deadhead 《미》; 《고장차》 a car being returned for repairs.

**회수**(回收) (a) withdrawal; (a) collection; recovery; retrieval; recall; revulsion; call-back (판 물건의); drawing in (은행권 등의). ~하다 withdraw 《coins, books》 from circulation; collect 《waste materials》; recall 《a defective product》; withdraw; draw back; call in. ¶ 자본의 ~ the revulsion of capital 《from an industry》 / 폐품〔빈병〕을 ~하다 collect 「waste articles 〔empty bottles〕 / 대출금을 ~하다 withdraw 〔draw in〕 loans; collect 〔call in〕 debts / 외상값을 ~하다 collect bills / 헌 천원권 지폐를 ~하다 withdraw old 1,000-won notes from circulation / 착수(着水)한 우주선을 ~하다 recover a spacecraft after splashdown / 잡지를 ~하다 withdraw magazines from circulation / 제조회사는 하자품의 ~를 개시했다 The manufacturer began to recall the defective goods. ◉ ~금 recovery. 통화~ the withdrawal of notes in circulation.

**회수권**(回數券) 《구매용》 a coupon ticket; 《통근용》 a commuter's 〔commutation〕 ticket 《미》; a book of tickets 《영》. ¶ 20회의 ~ a ticket of 20 coupons; a twenty-trip ticket book.
◉ 철도~ a railroad commuter's ticket.

**회식**(會食) dining together; 《군인의》 mess. ~하다 have 〔take〕 a meal together; dine together; dine 《with》; mess 《with, together》. ¶ 오늘 저녁에는 친구들과 ~ 약속이 있다 I have a dinner engagement with my friends this evening. *or* I have an engagement to dine with my friends this evening.

**회신**(回信) a reply; an answer. ~하다 answer 〔reply to〕 a letter; send a reply 《to》. ¶ 우표를 첨부하고 주소를 쓴 ~용 봉투 a stamped, self-addressed envelope.

**회신**(灰燼) ashes; embers. ¶ ~으로 화(化)하다 be reduced 〔burnt〕 to ashes; be consumed 〔destroyed〕 by fire; 《건물이》 be burnt to the ground; be burnt down.

**회신료**(回信料) postage for a reply; return postage. ¶ ~로서 170원 우표를 동봉하다 enclose a 170 won stamp for return postage 〔for a reply〕.
◉ ~선납 reply 〔answer〕 paid: ~선납 전보 a reply-paid telegram.

**회심**(會心) congeniality; complacency. ¶ ~의 작품 a (piece of) work after *one's* (own) heart; a satisfactory (piece of) work / ~지우(之友) a friend after *one's* (own) heart 〔bosom〕 / ~의 미소를 짓다 give 〔smile〕 a smile of satisfaction; smile complacently; grin with satisfaction. ◉ ~처 what *one* is happy about; the source of *one's* complacency 〔satisfaction〕.

**회양목**(—楊木) a box(wood) tree; 《재목》 boxwood. ◉ ~과(科) *Busaceae* (학명).

**회오**(悔悟) repentance 《for》; remorse 《for》; contrition 《for》; regret 《at》. ~하다 repent (of); be sorry 《for》; feel remorse 《for》; regret. ¶ ~의 눈물을 흘리다 shed tears of repentance 〔remorse〕 / ~의 빛을 보이다 show repentance / 저지른 죄에 대한 ~에 휩싸이다 be filled 〔overcome〕 with remorse for *one's* crime.

**회오리바람** a whirlwind; a cyclone; a tornado; a twister 《미》; an eddy-wind.

**회우**(會友) 《동료 회원》 a fellow member.

**회원**(會員) a member 《of a society 〔an association〕》; membership [총칭].
¶ ~의 자격 (qualifications for) membership / ~의 특전 privileges of membership / ~(이) 아닌 사람 non-members / ~을 그만두다 retire from membership 《to》 / ~을 모집하다 collect 〔raise, seek〕 members; invite a membership / ~이 되다 become a member 《of the tennis club》; enroll *oneself* as a member; join 《a society》 / ~이 되어 있다 hold membership 《in the club》; keep *one's* name 「on the list of membership 〔on the books〕 / ~을 …명으로 제한하다 limit the membership to / ~으로(서) 명부에 올리다 enroll 《*a person*》 on the list of membership / ~의 자격이 있다 be eligible for membership; be entitled to the membership 《of》 / ~의 자격을 잃다

〔되찾다〕 lose 〔regain〕 *one's* membership / ～으로 하다 enroll 《*a person*》 in a society / ～이 많다〔적다〕 have a large 〔small〕 membership; have a large number of 〔do not have many〕 members / 본회는 ～이 500명이다 The society has a membership of 500. / 현재 ～ 모집 중 《게시》 Applications for membership are now being accepted.
◉ ～국 a member nation. ～권 a membership card; a member's ticket (할인권 따위). ～명부 a list of membership; a membership list. ～배지 a membership badge. ～제 the membership system: ～제의 클럽 a club for members only / 이 골프장은 ～제로 되어 있다 This golf course is open to members only. *or* This golf links is not open to non-members. ～증 a membership card. 보통～ an ordinary member. 찬조～ a supporting 〔patronage〕 member.

**회유**(回遊·回游) a round 〔circular〕 trip 〔tour〕; an excursion; 《물고기의》 migration. ～하다 go on an excursion; make a cruise 〔an excursion, a circular〕 tour; 《물고기가》 wander 〔move〕 about 《the open seas》; make (seasonal) migrations. ◉ ～선〔열차〕 an excursion boat 〔train〕. ～어(魚) a migratory 〔wandering〕 fish. ～운임 excursion fare.

**회유**(懷柔) appeasement; pacification; conciliation. ～하다 《달래다》 appease; pacify; conciliate; placate; 《포섭하다》 win 《*a person's*》 heart; gain 〔win〕 《*a person*》 over 《to *one's* side》; draw 〔bring〕 over 《*a person*》 to *one's* side. ¶ 그들은 우리를 ～하려고 갖은 술책을 다 썼다 They took every measure to win us over.

**회유책**(懷柔策) 《유화책》 an appeasement policy; a conciliatory policy 〔measure〕; 《포섭책》 a measure to win 《*a person*》 over to *one's* side. ¶ ～을 쓰다 work out 〔devise〕 an appeasement 〔a conciliatory〕 measure.

**회음**(會飮) drinking together; compotation; carousing. ～하다 drink together; have a drinking party; carouse. ◉ ～자 a compotator.

**회음**(會陰) 〖해부〗 the perineum. ◉ ～근(筋) the perineal muscle. ～부(部) the perineal region.

**회의**(懷疑) (a) doubt; skepticism; incredulity; unbelief; disbelief. ～하다 doubt; be skeptical 《about》. ¶ ～적인 skeptic(al); incredulous / ～적으로 보다 take a skeptical 〔dim〕 view 《of》 / 인생에 대한 ～로 고민하다 be tormented by *one's* doubts about life.
◉ ～론〔설〕 (the argument of) skepticism: ～론자 a skeptic / 순수 ～론 absolute 〔Pyrrhonic〕 skepticism; Pyrrhonism. ～주의 (the principle of) skepticism. ～파(派) the skeptic school; the skeptics.

**회의**(會議) a conference; a meeting; a council; a convention (대회).

> [용법] **conference** 전부터 계획된 공식적인 것으로서 「국제회의(international conference)」나 「평화회의(peace conference)」처럼 각 방면의 대표자가 모여 어떤 문제에 관해 협의하여 결론을 도출해 내는 회의. **meeting** 가장 일반적인 말로서 의논·타협·토론 따위를 위해 모이는 2, 3명의 회사원으로 행하는 소규모 회의나 국회의 위원회처럼 규모가 큰 회의 따위에 폭넓게 쓰임. **council** 상설 「자문기관」적인 성격의 소규모 회의. **convention** 정기적으로 행해지는 대규모의 「대회」「연차회의(annual convention)」 따위를 가리킴.

¶ ～의 참석자 a conferee / ～를 소집하다 call 〔assemble〕 a conference 〔a council〕; convene 〔convoke〕 a convention / ～를 열다〔개최하다〕 hold 〔call〕 a council 〔conference, session〕; sit in 〔go into〕 conference; sit in council together / ～를 조종하다 manipulate a convention / ～에 부치다 refer 〔submit, send〕 《*a matter*》 to conference; lay 〔bring〕 《a question》 before the council; put 〔refer〕 《*a matter*》 to a meeting / ～에 소집되다 be summoned to council / ～에 참가하다 join 〔take part in, participate in〕 a conference / ～에 참석하다 attend a conference; meet in conference 〔convention〕 / ～중이다 be in conference 《with》 / ～에서 문제를 토론하다 discuss 〔talk about〕 a problem at the meeting / ～중 《게시》 Now in session. *or* Conference now in session. / 그 문제에 관해서 지금 ～중이다 They are now discussing that question.
◉ ～록 assembly 〔conference〕 records; the minutes; proceedings. ～사항 an order of the day; an agenda: ～사항을 변경하다 make a change in the agenda. ～실 a conference 〔a

council, an assembly] room. ～장 a meeting [an assembly] hall; a conference place: ～장은 어딥니까 Where is the meeting to be held? 가족～ a family meeting [conference]. 국무～ the Cabinet council [meeting]. 국제～ an international conference. 긴급～ 《hold, convoke》 an urgent conference [meeting]. 「ideogram.

**회의문자**(會意文字) an ideograph; an

**회의안**(回議案) a circular bill.

**회임**(懷妊) = 임신(妊娠).

**회자**(膾炙) ～하다[되다] be well-known; be in everyone's mouth; be on everybody's lips. ¶ 뭇 사람 입에 ～되다 be in everybody's mouth; be on everyman's lips; be a household word; be well known to everybody.

**회자수**(劊子手) a head cutter; an executioner.

**회자정리**(會者定離) We meet only to part. *or* We never meet but we part.

**회장**(回章) a circular. = 회문.

**회장**(回裝) ① 《족자 따위의》 the border edging 《of a screen [scroll, map]》. ② 《저고리의》 the ornamental edgings of a woman's coat.

**회장**(回腸) 〖해부〗 the ileum. ◉ ～염(炎) ileitis. ～절개(술) ileostomy.

**회장**(會長) the president 《of a society》; the chairman 《of a committee [board], of an assembly》; a grand 《of a club》. ¶ ～의 직[직위] presidency; chairmanship / ～이 되다 be elected chairman; become chairman / ～ 노릇을 하다 preside at [over] a meeting; take the chair / ～으로 떠받들다 set 《*a person*》 up as chairman; have 《*a person*》 as president / 언어학회는 ～으로 K박사를 추대하고 있다 The philological society has Dr. K for president. *or* The philological society is under the presidency of Dr. K. ◉ ～석 the chair. 이사회～ 《회사의》 the chairman of the board of directors.

**회장**(會場) the place 《for the meeting, where the party is to be held》; 《개최지》 a venue; the grounds.

**회장**(會葬) attendance at a funeral. ～하다 attend a funeral. ◉ ～자 the mourners; persons attending a funeral: ～자(者)의 열(列) a procession of mourners / 그 장례식엔 많은 ～자가 있었다 Many people attended the funeral service.

**회장석**(灰長石) 〖광물〗 anorthite.

**회저**(壞疽) 〖의학〗 gangrene; necrosis. ¶ ～가 생기다, ～에 걸리다 gangrene (sets in); necrotize; be affected by mortification. 「wire.

**회전**(回電) a reply telegram; a return

**회전**(回轉) turning; (a) revolution; (a) rotation; 《선회》 (a) gyration. ～하다 revolve; rotate; gyrate; turn [go, move, spin] round; run (기계가). ¶ 180도 ～하다 rotate in a 180-degree arc / 1～하다 make one revolution [rotation, full turn]; turn full circle; 《공중 제비로》 somersault; turn a somersault; 《위를 아래로》 turn upside down; turn bottom over top; turn over / ～시키다 turn 《*a thing*》 round; turn 《a wheel》 / 프로펠러를 ～시키다 swing the propeller / 볼을 ～시키다 〖야구〗 give a ball a spin [spinning motion]; put spin on a ball / 자금～을 촉진하다 quicken the turnover of the fund / 매분 100～의 속도로 at 100 revolutions per minute (생략 100 r.p.m.) / 좌[우]～금지 《게시》 No left [right] turn. / 차바퀴는 축(軸)을 중심으로 ～한다 A wheel turns [works] on its axle [axis]. / 지구는 태양의 주위를 ～한다 The earth turns [goes, moves] round the sun. / 그는 머리(의) ～이 빠르다 He is quick on the uptake. *or* He is sharp-witted. / 스크루가 굉장한 속력으로 ～했다 The screw went round at a very great speed. ◉ ～건조기 a drying tumbler. ～경기 《스키의》 slalom. ～계(計) a revolution-indicator; a trochometer; an odometer. ～근(筋) 〖해부〗 the rotator. ～기관 〖기계〗 a rotary engine. ～기중기 a rotary crane. ～나침반 a gyrocompass. ～단면도 a revolved section. ～등 a revolving light; a flashlight (등대용). ～력 turning force; rotary power. ～로(爐) 〖기계〗 a revolving furnace; a rotary oven. ～마찰 〖물리〗 rolling friction. ～목마 a merry-go-round; a car(r)ousel; roundabout 《영》. ～무대 a revolving stage. ～문 a turnstile; a revolving door. ～반(盤) 《전축의》 a turntable; a rotating [turning] disk; a rotary table; 〖전기〗 a finger plate. ～반지름 a radius of gyration; a turning radius. ～밸브 a rotary valve. ～분산 〖물리〗 rotatory dispersion. ～서가 a revolving bookstand. ～속도 speed of revolution: ～속도계[기록계] a tachograph. ～수 the number of rotations [revolution]: 엔진의 ～수를

올리다 rev up an engine. ～압축기 a rotary compressor. ～운동 a rotary 〔rotatory〕 motion 〔movement〕. ～율 《자금 따위의》 the rate of turnover 《of capital》. ～의(儀) a gyroscope; a gyrostat. ～의자 a swivel 〔pivot, revolving〕 chair. ～익(翼) 《헬리콥터의》 a rotor(blade); 《송〔선〕풍기 따위의》 the blade(s) 《of a fan》. ～자(子) a rotor. ～자금 a revolving fund 〔capital〕. ～질량 gyrating mass. ～착암기 a rotary rock drill. ～창 a pivoted 〔swivel(ing)〕 window. ～체 a body of revolution 〔rotation〕. ～축(軸) the axis 〔pivot〕 of rotation 〔gyration〕. ～탑 《유원지 등에 있는》 《swing on》 a ring pole. ～플레이너 rotary planer. ～항로 표지 a rotating (radio) beacon.

**회전**(會戰) a engagement; a battle; an encounter. ～하다 fight with 〔engage〕 the enemy.

**회절**(回折) 〖물리〗 diffraction. ～하다 diffract 《rays》; be diffracted.
◉ ～각 the angle of diffraction. ～격자(格子) a diffraction grating. ～계(計) 〖물리〗 a diffractometer. ～대(帶) a diffraction zone. ～무늬 a diffraction pattern. ～산란(散亂) diffraction scattering ～상(像) a diffraction figure 〔image〕. ～손실 〖전기〗 a diffraction loss. ～스펙트럼 a diffraction spectrum. ～음 a diffracted sound. ～파〔광〕 a diffracted wave 〔ray〕. ～현상 〖물리〗 a diffraction phenomenon. ～환(環) 〖천문〗 a diffraction ring. ～효과 a diffraction effect.

**회정**(回程) a return trip; the return way; the way back. ～하다 return; retrace 《*one's* step》; start on *one's* way back. ¶ ～에 오르다 start on *one's* way back.

**회조**(回漕) sea 〔marine〕 transportation; shipping. ～하다 transport 《goods》 by sea; ship. ⇨ 해운.

**회죄**(悔罪) repentance (of *one's* sin); penitence. ～하다 repent of *one's* sin; be penitent of *one's* sin.

**회주**(會主) the promoter 〔sponsor〕 of a meeting; the host of a party.

**회중**(會衆) an audience; people gathered together; a congregation (특히 교회의); an attendance (회중의 수). ¶ 많은 ～ a large attendance / ～은 그의 웅변에 깊이 감동했다 The audience were deeply moved by his eloquence.

**회중**(懷中) 《품 속》 (inside) *one's* pocket; 《마음 속》 (inside) *one's* mind. ¶ ～경 a pocket mirror / ～물〔품〕 a pocketbook 《미》; a purse; a wallet / ～품 조심 《게시》 Beware of pickpockets.
◉ ～시계 a (pocket) watch; a ticker 《속어》. ～전등 a flashlight 《미》; an electric torch 《영》; a torch lamp: ～전등을 켜다〔끄다〕 turn 「on 〔off〕 a flashlight / ～전등으로 비추다 shine 〔put the light from〕 a flashlight on 《an object》; shine the light around.

**회지**(會誌) a bulletin. ¶ 동창～ an alumni bulletin.

**회진**(回診) (a doctor's) round of visits. ～하다 go the rounds (of *one's* patients); do 〔make〕 *one's* rounds. ¶ 의사 선생님이 곧 ～하러 오신다 The doctor will soon come round to see you.

**회집**(會集) a gathering; an assemblage; a crowd. ～하다 gather; assemble; get together.

**회천**(回天) 《왕의 뜻을 돌림》 bringing the king's will around (to a different point of view); 《세력 회복》 restoration of the national prestige. ～하다 make a king change his heart; rehabilitate 《a nation》. ¶ ～지업(之業) a great undertaking to restore the national prestige; a great work to save a nation on the verge of ruin.

**회청색**(灰青色) grayish blue ¶ 푸른 기가 도는 ～ pearl blue.

**회초간**(晦初間) about 〔toward〕 the end of one month and the beginning of the following month.

**회초리** a whip; a rod; a switch; a cane (등·대나무 따위의) ¶ 버들 ～ a switch from a willow tree / ～로 때리다 whip 〔lash, flog〕 《*a person*》 with a switch; give 《*a person*》 a caning / ～를 맞다 be whipped; be caned 〔lashed〕; get the cane.

**회춘**(回春) 《봄이》 the return of spring; 《몸·건강이》 recovery 《from a serious illness》; restoration to health; 《되젊어짐》 rejuvenation. ～하다 spring returns; recover; regain *one's* health; be restored to health; be rejuvenated. ◉ ～기(期) 《노년의》 Indian summer. ～약〔제〕 a rejuvenating drug 〔medicine〕. ～하천 〖지질〗 a rejuvenated river.

**회충**(蛔蟲) a roundworm; a mawworm; an ascarid; a belly worm 《속어》. ¶ ～이 생기다 get roundworms. ◉ ～약 a medicine for expelling mawworms; a vermifuge; an anthelmint(h)ic (drug). ～증 〖의학〗 ascariasis.

**회치다**(膾—) 《육회》 make 〔prepare〕 ground 〔minced〕 raw meat; 《생선회》 slice 〔make sliced〕 raw fish. ¶다랑어〔참치〕를 ～ slice tuna to prepare a dish of 「raw fish 〔*sashimi*〕.

**회칙**(回勅) 《로마교황의》 an encyclical (letter); an encyclic.

**회칙**(會則) the rules 〔regulations〕 of a society; the bylaws of an assembly. ¶～의 일부를 개정하다 make a partial amendment of the rules of the society.

**회태**(懷胎) conception; gestation. ⇨ 임신(妊娠). ◉ ～기간 a gestation period. ～연령 conception age.

**회판** the end; the last round; the finals.

**회편**(回便) a return messenger 〔envoy〕; 「return post 〔mail〕.

**회포**(懷抱) *one's* bosom; *one's* heart; *one's* inmost thoughts. ¶ 슬픈 ～ sad thoughts / ～를 풀다 unburden 〔unbosom〕 *oneself* 《to *a person*》.

**회피**(回避) evasion; avoidance. ～하다 evade; avoid; shirk; shun; sidestep; dodge; elude 《payment》; get around 《the difficulty》. ¶ 언급을 ～하다 decline 〔evade〕 to comment 《on》 / 책임을 ～하다 evade 〔shirk〕 *one's* responsibility; flee from responsibility / 전쟁을 ～하다 avoid war / 파업을 ～하다 head off a strike / ～하는 태도를 취하다 keep aloof from 《*a matter*》 / 기자의 질문을 ～하다 sidestep 〔evade〕 the reporter's questions / 문제에 대한 결정을 ～하다 avoid making a decision of the issue / 타국의 분쟁에 말려드는 것을 ～하다 avoid 〔steer clear of〕 involvement in conflicts between other powers / 최근 그는 의식적으로 나를 ～하고 있다 He has intentionally been shunning me of late. ◉ ～전술 dodging 〔evasive〕 tactics.

**회한**(悔恨) remorse; (a) regret; (a) repentance; contrition. ¶ 뼈저린 ～ poignant regret / 그는 ～의 눈물에 젖어 있었다 He was in bitter tears of remorse.

**회합**(會合) a meeting; a gathering; an assembly; 《구어》 a get together (친한 사람들끼리의 모임). ～하다 meet; gather; assemble; 《구어》 get together. ¶～장소 a meeting place; a rendezvous; a venue 《구어》 / 정치적 ～의 참석자 the attendance at a political meeting / ～의 날짜를 정하다 fix the day for the meeting / ～의 약속을 지키다〔어기다〕 keep 〔break〕 an appointment / 그들은 1년에 한 번 ～한다 They meet together once a year.

**회항**(回航) 《항해》 navigation; cruise; sailing about; 《되돌아옴》 a return cruise; sailing back. ～하다 navigate; sail about; return from a cruise; reverse a ship; sail back. ¶ 배를 ～시키다 bring 〔take〕 a ship 《to Pusan, home》 / 그 배는 인천으로 ～되었다 The ship was taken 〔brought〕 to Inch'ŏn.

**회향**(回向) 〖불교〗 a Buddhist memorial (for the dead); a mass (for the repose of a soul); good deeds with hope that the merit will accrue to others. ～하다 hold a memorial service 《for》; say prayers for the repose of 《*a person's*》 soul.

**회향**(茴香) 〖식물〗 a (common) fennel. ◉ ～유〔풀〕 fennel oil 〔plant〕.

**회향**(懷鄕) longing for home; nostalgic reminiscence. ～하다 long for home; be homesick; be nostalgic. ⇨ 향수.

**회혼**(回婚) the 60th wedding anniversary; the diamond wedding. ◉ ～례 a feast celebrating the 60th wedding anniversary.

**회화**(會話) (a) conversation; a talk. ～하다 speak 〔talk〕 《with *a person*》; have a conversation 〔talk〕 《with》. ¶～실력 *one's* speaking ability / 아무와 영어로 ～하다 talk 〔converse〕 in English with *a person*. ◉ ～문 colloquial literature. ～술 conversation techniques; the art of conversation. ～책 a conversation book. ～체 colloquialism; colloquial style: ～체의 colloquial 〔spoken〕 《English》 / ～체로 (쓰다) (write) in a colloquial style. 영어 ～ a conversation in English: 영어 ～를 잘하다 be good at English (conversation); be a good speaker of English / 영어 ～를 연습하다 practice English conversation 《by listening to the radio》.

**회화**(繪畫) [일반적] pictures; 《펜·크레용·연필의》 drawings; 《그림물감의》 paintings. ¶ ～적인 pictorial; graphic / 시의 ～적인 아름다움 the pictorial beauty of a poem. ◉ ～전시회 an exhibition 〔a showing〕 of pictures; an art 〔a painting〕 exhibition; a picture show.

**회화나무** a pagoda tree; a Chinese scholar tree. = 홰나무.

**회환**(回還) return; coming back. ～하다 return; come back.

**회회청**(回回靑) blue dye used for glazing porcelain.

**회회하다**(恢恢—) (be) vast; immense; roomy.

**회훈**(回訓) 〖정치〗 instructions (from *one's* home government in response to a request). ～하다 give 〔send〕 return instructions; reply with instructions.

**획**(畫) a stroke (in a Chinese character); a stroke (of the brush); a dash. ¶ 획수 the number of strokes; the stroke count / 삼획으로 된 글자 a character made in three strokes; a 3=stroke character / 획을 긋다 make a stroke / 획을 내리긋다 make a vertical 〔downward〕 stroke / 획을 가로 긋다 make a horizontal 〔side〕 stroke.

**획** ① 《빨리 도는 모양》 with a swerve; with a whirl; speedily; fast; 《힘차게 당기거나 미는 모양》 with a jerk. ¶ 뒤로 획 돌다 turn right round; wheel round; pivot quickly / 획 당기다〔밀다〕 pull 〔push〕 with a (sudden) jerk; give 《it》 a vigorous pull 〔push〕. ② 《세게 부는 모양》 with a whiff; in a gust. ¶ 촛불을 획 불어 끄다 whiff out a candle / 남포를 획 불어 끄다 blow out a lamp with a puff / 바람이 획 불다 have a gust of wind.

**획기적**(劃期的) (being) epoch-making; epochal. ¶ ～인 기록 an epoch-making record / ～인 일〔발견〕 an epoch-making event 〔discovery〕 / ～인 시대 a great epoch in (history) / 역사상 ～인 사건 the landmarks of history.

**획득**(獲得) acquisition; acquirement; possesion; gain; taking. ～하다 get; gain; win; obtain; secure; acquire.

> 용법 **get** 「손에 넣다→획득하다」란 뜻의 가장 일반적인 말. **gain** 무언가 자신에게 유리한 것을 애를 써 「손에 넣다」란 뜻의 말. **win** 경기 따위로 남과 겨루어 「손에 넣다」란 뜻. **obtain** 바라고 있던 것을 「손에 넣다」란 뜻의 격식차린 말: obtain a post. **secure** 손에 넣기도 어렵고 유지하기도 어려운 것을 「손에 넣다」란 뜻. **acquire** 오랜 시일이 걸려 힘들게 「손에 넣다」란 뜻.

¶ 권리를 ～하다 acquire 〔secure〕 right / 재산을 ～하다 acquire property / 지위를 ～하다 obtain an appointment 〔a position〕 / 금메달을 ～하다 win a gold medal / 언론의 자유를 ～하다 obtain freedom of speech / 부정한 수단으로 부를 ～하다 obtain 〔acquire〕 wealth dishonestly 〔by illegal means〕. ◉ ～면역성 acquired immunity. ～물 an acquisition. ～형질 〖생물〗 an acquired character.

**획력**(畫力) the power of a stroke (in painting or calligraphy).

**획법**(畫法) the canons of brushing strokes (in painting or calligraphy).

**획수**(畫數) the number of strokes (in a Chinese character).

**획순**(畫順) the stroke order (in writing a Chinese character).

**획연**(劃然) ～하다 (be) distinct; clear. ¶ ～히 distinctly; clearly / 양자간의 ～한 구별 a clear distinction between the two.

**획인**(畫引) an index arranged according to the total number of strokes in each Chinese character.

**획일**(劃一) uniformity; standardization. ¶ ～적인 uniform; standardized / ～적으로 uniformly / ～적 교육 uniform education / ～하게 하다 make 《*a thing*》 uniform; standardize / 고도로 전시 체제화된 ～적인 사회에 혼란을 주지 않으면서 경제와 대외 관계를 개선하다 improve economy and external relations without disturbing highly mobilized and monolithic society. ◉ ～화〔주의〕 standardization: 교육 제도의 ～화 the regimentation of educational system / 자동차 부품을 ～화하다 standardize the automobile parts.

**획정**(劃定) delimitation: demarcation. ～하다 demarcate; delimit; mark out; draw a boundary (line). ¶ 경계를〔국경을〕 ～하다 mark out 〔fix, delimit, demarcate〕 a boundary 〔frontier〕 line.

**획책**(劃策) planning; scheming; a plan; a scheme; a stratagem. ～하다 plan; scheme; project; form 〔lay〕 a plan; map 〔work〕 out a plan; concoct 〔cook up〕 a scheme; formulate 〔frame〕 a program(me); 《책동하다》 maneuver; manoeuvre 《영》; use artifice; frame (up). ¶ 그는 그 자리를 차지하려고 ～했다 He schemed for the position / 그는 뒤에서 여러 가지로 ～하고 있다 He is working behind the scene.

**획획** ① 《연해 도는 모양》 with swerve after swerve; with repeated jerks; whirling and whirling; speedily; fast. ¶ 자동차 바퀴가 ～ 돌아가다 the wheels of a car keep whizzing / 시계 바늘을 ～돌리다 keep whirling the hands of a clock around. ② 《잇달아 부는 모양》

in gusts. ¶ 바람이 ~ 불다 the wind blows in gusts.

**횟가루**(灰—) lime powder; powdered ｢lime.

**횟감**(膾—) ingredients for making a raw (fish, meat) dish.

**횟돌**(灰—) limestone. ｢mass of lime.

**횟반**(灰—) a ｢hardened 〔condensed〕

**횟수**(回數) the number of times; frequency; the oftenness. ¶ ~를 거듭하다 repeat 《so many times》/ ~를 거듭함에 따라 《경기가》 as the game ｢advances 〔progresses〕/ 그는 요즘 결석 ~가 잦아졌다 He has been more frequently absent lately. ◉ ~곡선 〖통계〗 a frequency curve.

**횟잎나무** 〖식물〗 a small spindle tree.

**횟집**(膾—) a restaurant specializing in ｢sliced raw fish 〔*sashimi*〕.

**횡**(橫) = 가로.

**횡갱**(橫坑) 〖광산〗 a drift; a driftway; an adit.

**횡격막**(橫隔膜) 〖해부〗 the diaphragm; the midriff. ¶ ~의 phrenic.

**횡관**(橫貫) running 〔cutting〕 across. ~하다 run 〔cut〕 across. ◉ ~철도 a railroad running across (the country).

**횡단**(橫斷) crossing; cutting across; traversing. ~하다 cross; traverse; go 〔walk, run, sail, travel, swim, fly, *etc.*〕 across. ¶ 비행기로 대서양을 ~하다 fly across the Atlantic Ocean / 도로를 ~하여 건너편으로 가다 cross the road to the other side / 선로(線路)를 ~하다 go across a track / ~ 금지 《게시》 No crossing. *or* No jay-walking. ◉ ~로 a crosscut (road); a transverse. ~면 a ｢cross 〔transverse〕 section; a transection. ~보도 《미》 a crosswalk; a pedestrian crossing. ~지하도 an underpass. 대륙~철도 a transcontinental railroad. 태평양~비행 a transpacific flight; a flight across the Pacific.

**횡대**(橫隊) a rank; a line; a line abreast (함대의). ¶ ~로 in line / 2열 ~로 정렬하다 form 〔be drawn up in〕 a double line / 4열 ~로 서다 form (up) four deep / ~로 섯 《구령》 Line up facing the front! ◉ ~비행 flying in line abreast: ~비행을 하다 fly in line abreast. ~행진 marching in a line.

**횡도**(橫道) 《부정》 unrighteous ways; injustice; wickedness; iniquity; 《옆길》 a side road; a by-road; a byway.

**횡득**(橫得) an unexpected gain; a windfall. ~하다 gain unexpectedly; have a windfall 《of》.

**횡듣다**(橫—) hear 《it, him》 wrong 〔amiss〕; mishear; misunderstand (오해하다). ¶ 아무의 말을 ~ mishear *a person* / 자네가 내말을 횡들은 것 같군 You must have misheard me. *or* You haven't heard me rightly 〔correctly〕.

**횡렬**(橫列) a rank; a line. ¶ ~을 짓다 stand abreast in a ｢rank 〔line〕.

**횡령**(橫領) usurpation; seizure; dispossession; 《공금 따위의》 embezzlement; (a) misappropriation. ~하다 usurp; seize upon 《*a person's* property》; embezzle 《money from a company》; appropriate 《government money》; misappropriate 《public money》. ¶ 은행〔남〕의 돈을 ~하다 embezzle money from ｢a bank 〔a person〕/ 정부 재산을 ~하다 appropriate a government property to *oneself*. ◉ ~자 a usurper; a dispossessor; an embezzler. ~죄 embezzlement: 그는 ~죄로 기소되었다 He was accused on a charge of embezzlement.

**횡류**(橫流) ~하다 put 《controlled goods》 on the black market; sell 《controlled goods》 through illegal channels. ~되다 《goods》 flow into illicit channels; flow into the black market.

**횡목**(橫木) a crosspiece; 《빗장 따위》 a (cross)bar; 《울짱 따위》 a (cross)rail.

**횡문근**(橫紋筋) 〖해부〗 a ｢striated 〔striped〕 muscle. ◉ ~섬유 〖해부〗 a striated muscle fiber. ~종(腫) 〖의학〗 a rhab-domyoma (*pl.* ~s, -mata).

**횡보**(橫步) ~하다 walk sideways; sidle 《through the crowed》; edge along.

**횡보다**(橫—) see wrongly; misjudge; be deceived; make a wrong estimation 《of》. ¶ 신호를 ~ mistake 〔misread〕 a signal.

**횡사**(橫死) ｢a violent 〔an unnatural, an accidental, an untimely, a suspicious〕 death; death by violence; 《참사》 a tragic death. ~하다 die ｢an unnatural 〔a violent〕 death; die by violence; meet (with) a violent death 〔end〕; meet an untimely death. ¶ 그녀는 18세에 ~했다 She died a violent death at the age of eighteen.

**횡서**(橫書) writing ｢horizontally 〔in a lateral line, sideways〕; horizontal writing. ~하다 write ｢laterally 〔in lateral lines, sideways〕; write from left to right.

**횡선**(橫線) a horizontal line; a cross line; a line across. ¶ ~을 (북북) 긋다

cross (roughtly) / 글자 아래에 ～을 긋다 underline a word. ◉ ～수표 a crossed check.

**횡설수설**(橫說竪說) random talk; idle talk; contradictory 〔outlandish, absurd〕 remarks; jargon; nonsense. ～하다 talk at random; talk wild(ly); "talk applesause 〔baloney, sleep-dip, bull〕"; jargon; speak contradictorily. ¶ ～하는 대답 a roaming reply / 네 말은 ～이라 이해할 수 없다 What you say is「all Greek 〔double Dutch〕 to me.

**횡수**(橫數) a chance 〔an accidental〕 hit; a lucky shot 〔hit〕; unlooked-for fortune 〔misfortune〕; a stroke of good 〔bad〕 luck; a fluke. ¶ ～에 돈을 모으다 make money by sheer good luck / ～로 이기다 win by a fluke.

**횡수막이**(橫數—) 〖민속〗 an exorcism held at the beginning of the year to dispel evils for the year.

**횡액**(橫厄) unexpected bad luck; an unexpected disaster; unforeseen calamity; misfortune; a mishap. ¶ ～에 걸리다 have an accident; suffer an unexpected misfortune.

**횡영**(橫泳) sidestroke. ⇨사이드스트로크. ～하다 do 〔swim〕 sidestroke.

**횡위분만**(橫位分娩) 〖의학〗 crossbirth.

**횡의**(橫議) irrelevant discussions; a digression; a sidetracked argument.

**횡일**(橫溢) ～하다 flow out of its ordinary channel; overflow.

**횡일성**(橫日性) 〖식물〗 diaheliotropism.

**횡재**(橫財) unexpected fortune 〔gains, profit〕; a windfall. ～하다 make a lucky find; come into unexpected fortune; have a windfall; make a good buy. ¶ 그 가격이라면 ～나 다름없다 That's a real bargain at that price, isn't it?

**횡전**(橫轉) a lateral turn(ing); rolling sideways; a (barrel) roll (by an airplane). ～하다 turn laterally; roll sideways; make 〔do〕 a roll (비행기가).

**횡지성**(橫地性) 〖식물〗 transverse geotropism.

**횡진**(橫陣) a line abreast; a rank.

**횡철**(橫綴) ① 《글자의》 lateral spelling. ～하다 spell laterally; spell from left to right. ② 《책의》 oblong bookbinding. ～하다 bind 〔sew, stitch〕 《a book》 sideways.

**횡축**(橫軸) ① a cross 〔transverse〕 axle; 〖기계〗 a horizontal shaft; 〖수학〗 the horizontal axis; the x-axis. ② 《가로 거는 족자》 a wide hanging roll.

**횡탈**(橫奪) seizure by force; unlawful seizure. ～하다 seize by force; usurp.

**횡파**(橫波) 〖물리〗 a transverse wave.

**횡포**(橫暴) violence (폭력); oppression (압제); tyranny (포학); high-handedness (고압적). ～하다 (be) oppressive; tyrannical; despotic; 《고압적인》 overbearing; high-handed; 《부당한》 unreasonable. ¶ 군부의 ～ the despotism of the military / ～를 부리다 tyrannize 《over》; carry matters with a high hand; behave very high-handedly.

**횡행**(橫行) rampancy; prevalency. ～하다 《모로 가다》 go sidewise; walk sideways; 《뽐내며 걷다》 stride; strut; 《설치다》 be rampant 〔prevalent〕; be overrun with; be infested with 《robbers》 (장소가). ¶ 건달들이 ～하는 거리 a hooligan-infested street; a town infested 〔overrun〕 with hooligans / 큰 도시에는 범죄가 ～한다 Crime is rampant in the big city. / 공직자 사이에 부정이 ～하고 있다 Bribery 〔Corruption〕 is rampant among the officials.

**효**(孝) filial piety 〔devotion〕; being dutiful to *one's* parents. ¶ 부모에게 효를 다하다 show *one's* parents every attention; be「dutiful to 〔thoughtful about〕 *one's* parents; be a good son 〔daughter〕.

**효**(效) efficacy; benefit; good; virtue (약 따위의) 《성과》 an effect; a result; fruits. ¶ 효가 있다 be efficacious; be 〔prove〕 effective; work well 《on》; take effect; be good 《for》; be beneficial 《to, in》 / 효가 없다 have no effect 《on》; do no good; be of no use; avail nothing; yield no results. ¶ 그녀의 설득도 효가 없었다 Her persuasion「did not work 〔was futile〕.

**효경**(孝經) the Book of Filial Piety.

**효과**(效果) (an) effect; effectiveness; efficacy (약 따위의); 《결과》 a result; fruit. ¶ (예술품 등의) 전체적 ～ the general effect; the *tout ensemble* (F.) / 열이 금속에 미치는 ～ the effect of heat upon metals.

효과가: ～가 있다 be effective 〔effectual〕; take effect; have an effect 《on》; do 《*a person*》 good; prove fruitful 〔successful〕; be efficacious (약 따위) / ～가 없다 be ineffective; be ineffectual; be fruitless; be (of) no good 〔use〕; 《약 따위가》 be inefficacious; have 〔produce〕 no effect 《on》 / ～가 빠르다 be quick in 《its》 effect; bring an immediate result on 《*a person*》; have an instant effect on 《a headache》; 《약이》 work 〔take effect〕 instantly / ～가 적다 have little effect 《on》/ …하는 ～가 있다 have the effect of …ing / 고혈압 방지에 ～가 있다 be effective for the prevention of high blood pressure.

효과를: ～를 거두기 위해서 to be effective; in order to reap the fruits; 《일이》 to produce satisfactory results / ～를 거두다 get 〔obtain〕 good results; 《사항이》 produce satisfactory results / 충분히 ～를 올리다 bear 《its》 full fruit / 극적 ～를 높이다 heighten the dramatic effect.

¶ ～는 만점이었다 It has gone quite for. / 이 약은 차멀미에 즉각적인 ～가 있다 This medicine has an immediate effect on carsickness. / 여러 번 시도해 보았지만 그다지 ～가 없었다 Repeated attempts have been made「without any noticeable result 〔only to bring poor result〕. / 어떤 실제적인 ～는 생기지 않을 게다 It will not lead to any practical result. / 처벌도 그에겐 아무 ～가 없었다 Punishment had very little effect on him.

**효과적**(效果的) ¶ ～인 effective; effectual; successful; efficacious (약 등이) / ～인 교수법 efficient methods of teaching / 질병에 대한 ～인 치료법 an efficacious cure for a disease / ～으로 effectively; with effect / 가장 ～인 영어 공부는 어떻게 하면 됩니까 How can I learn English most effectively?

**효녀**(孝女) a filial 〔dutiful〕 daughter.

**효능**(效能) (an) effect; efficacy; virtue; benefit; good; use. ¶ 약의 ～ the efficacy of a remedy / 심장병에 ～이 있는 efficacious for heart disease / ～이 있다 be effective 〔efficacious, effectual〕; do 《*a person*》 good; be good 《for colds》/ ～이 없다 be ineffective 〔inefficacious〕; be (of) no good; be useless / ～이 나타나다 《약의》 take effect; prove efficacious / 이 약은 치통에 놀라운 ～이 있다 This medicine works wonders on a toothache. / 그 약은 어떤 ～이 있느냐 What is the medicine good for? / 이 온천은 신경통에 ～이 있다 This hot spring is good for rheumatism.

◉ ～서 《약의》 a statement of virtues.

**효도**(孝道) filial duty 〔piety, devotion〕. ～하다 be dutiful 〔devoted, obedient〕 to *one's* parents; be a good son 〔daughter〕. ¶ ～하는 아들 a dutiful son; a son who is devoted to his parents / ～를 하고 싶어 할 때는 이미 부모가 안 계시다 When *one* would be filial, *one's* parents are gone. *or* A son never thinks of his parents until it is too late.

**효력**(效力) force; effect; 《약 따위의》 (an) effect; efficacy; (healing) virtue; 《법률상의》 validity.

¶ ～이 있다 be effective; be efficacious; do good; have effect 《on》; 《법적으로》 be in force 〔effect〕; be valid / ～이 없다 be ineffective; be inefficacious; 《법률·계약 등이》 be null and void / ～을 잃다 lose effect 〔validity〕; become invalid 〔null and void〕/ ～을 발생하다 come into force 〔effect, operation, play〕; take effect 《on》; become 〔be〕 effective 〔operative〕/ 법률과 동일한 ～을 갖다 have the full force and effect of a law / 비준을 거치고 ～을 발생하다 take effect on ratification / 그 계약은 5년간 ～이 있다 The contract「holds good 〔is valid〕 for five years. / 이 계약은 이미 ～을 잃었다 This contract has already expired. *or* This contract has already ceased to be binding. / 이 규칙은 아직 ～이 있다 This rule is still in effect 〔force〕.

◉ ～발생 effectivation.

**효모**(酵母) yeast; ferment; barm; leaven. ¶ …에 ～를 넣다 leaven; add yeast to. ◉ ～균 a yeast fungus (*pl.* ～es, -gi); yeast.

**효부**(孝婦) a faithful 〔dutiful〕 daughter-in-law.

**효성**(孝誠) filial piety 〔devotion〕; love for *one's* parents. ～스럽다 (be) filial; [서술적] be dutiful 〔devoted, obedient, considerate〕 to *one's* parents.

¶ ～이 지극하다 be devoted to *one's* parents / ～이 지극한 사람 one who loves *one's* parents / 부모에게 ～을 다하다 discharge *one's* duties to *one's* parents.

**효소**(酵素) 〖화학〗 an enzyme; a 〔an unorganized〕 ferment. ¶ ～의 enzymatic 《action》. ◉ ～공학 enzyme engineering. ～세제 enzyme detergent. ～학 enzymology.

**효수**(梟首) hanging up the head of a decapitated criminal on a pole. ～하다 hang up the head of a decapitated criminal; gibbet a head. ¶ ～경중(警衆) 하다 display the criminals' heads as a warning to the people.

◉ ～대 a gibbet; a stock.

**효순**(孝順) filial obedience 〔piety〕. ～하다 (be) filial; [서술적] be obedient to *one's* parents.

**효시**(嚆矢) the beginning; the first; the first person 《to *do*》; a pioneer 《in》; a trailblazer; the first instance. ¶ 이로써 …의 ～로 한다 this was the first instance of… / 미국 유학은 그를 ～로 한다 He was the first one to go to America for study.

**효심**(孝心) a filial heart; (feelings of) filial piety. ¶ ～이 깊은 dutiful; filial; devoted.

**효양**(孝養) dutiful service to *one's* parents. ¶ ～을 다하다 「take good care of 〔be dutiful to〕 *one's* parents.

**효용**(效用) 《용도》 use; 《유용성》 usefulness; utility; 《효능》 (an) effect; benefit; good; virtue. ¶ 비～ disutility / 한계 ～ marginal utility / ～이 있다 be useful; be of use; be effective / 이 백신은 작년에 유행한 독감에 ～이 있었다 This vaccine was effective against the influenza prevalent last year. ◉ ～가치 effective value; utility value. ～체감의 법칙 〖경제〗 the law of diminishing utility. 자연〔최종, 잉여〕～ gratuitous 〔final, surplus〕 utility.

**효율**(效率) the utility factor; 〖물리〗 efficiency. ¶ 높은 ～ a high degree of efficiency / 기계의 ～ mechanical efficiency / ～이 낮은 일 inefficient work / ～을 높이다 promote efficiency / 생산 ～을 높이다 raise the efficiency of production / 이런 추위에서는 일의 ～이 떨어진다 We cannot work efficiently in this cold wave. ◉ ～곡선 an efficiency curve. ～평가 merit rating. 열 ～ thermal efficiency. 종합～ overall efficiency.

**효자**(孝子) a dutiful 〔filial〕 son; a devoted son; a good son.

**효행**(孝行) 《효도》 filial piety 〔devotion, duty〕; 《행위》 filial conduct. ～하다 be dutiful to *one's* parents. ◉ ～상 a prize for filial conduct.

**효험**(效驗) (an) effect; efficacy; (a) virtue 《of a medicine》. ⇨ 효능(效能). ¶ ～이 뚜렷한 wonderfully efficacious; of miraculous efficacy / ～이 뛰어난 약 a wonder drug / ～보다 get results 《from》 / ～이 있다 be efficacious; be effective; do 《*a person*》 good; take effect / ～이 없다 be inefficacious; be ineffective; do 《*a person*》 no good; have no effect.

**후**(后) 《황후》 an empress; 《왕비》 a queen.

**후**(後) [부사적] ① 《나중에》 afterward(s); after; later (on); in future. ¶ 한 이틀 후에 《지금부터》 in a couple of days; 《그 때부터》 a couple of days after 〔later〕 / 도착하고 2, 3일 후에 a few days after *one* arrived / 지금부터 10년 후에 in ten years; ten years from now / 흐린 후 맑음 《일기예보》 Cloudy, fine later. / 후에 가겠다 I will come later (on). / 잠시 후에 다시 생각해보니 내 잘못이었다 On second thought, I have found I was to blame. / 그는 후에 후회할 것이다 He will repent later. ② 《…한 뒤에》 after 《*do*ing》; next to; behind; following. ¶ 그 후에 after that; subsequently / 점심 먹은 후에 떠나자 Let's start off after lunch. / 그가 떠난 후로 통 소식이 없다 I haven't heard anything from him since he left here.

**후** blowing; with a puff 〔whiff〕. ¶ 후 불다 whiff; puff / 촛불을 후 불어 끄다 blow out a candle-light with a puff.

**후각**(嗅覺) the sense of smell; the olfactory sense. ¶ ～이 예민하다 have a keen nose; have a good 〔an acute〕 sense of smell / 미각과 ～은 밀접한 관계가 있다 Taste and smell are closely connected. / 개의 ～은 사람보다 민감하다 Smell is more acute in dogs than in men. ◉ ～계 an olfactometer. ～과민〔감퇴〕 hyperosmia 〔hyposmia〕. ～기관 an organ of smell; an olfactory organ. ～동물 an osmatic animal. ～신경 the olfactory nerve. ～작용 olfaction.

**후갑판**(後甲板) the quarterdeck; the afterdeck.

**후견**(後見) guardianship; wardship; tutelage; tutorage; 《원조》 assistance. ～하다 act as (a) guardian 《for》; look after 《children》. ¶ ～을 받다 be (placed) under the guardianship 《of》; be in ward 《to》.

**후견인**(後見人) 〖법〗 a guardian; a tutor; a curator; 《연기자의》 a prompter. ¶ 유언으로 ～을 지정하다 designate a guardian by will / ～이 되다 act as (a) guardian; take charge of the tutelage of 《*a person*》 / 그는 조카의 ～이 되었다 He became a guardian for his nephew.

**후계**(後繼) succession. ～하다 succeed to; succeed 《*a person* in *his* office》. ¶ ～ 내각 the incoming Cabinet; the succeeding government.

**후계자**(後繼者) a successor; an inheritor; 《남자》 an heir; 《여자》 an heiress.

¶ A씨의 ～로서의 주필 the editor as a successor to Mr. A / ～가 되다 step into《*a person's*》shoes / 누가 당신의 ～가 됩니까 Who will「succeed to your post〔take over your position〕? / 사장은 부장 ～를 물색중이다 The boss is looking for a man who is capable of stepping into a director's shoes.

**후고**(後顧) looking behind〔back〕; the future outlook (for people or things left behind). ～하다 look behind; worry over the future; worry about the family left behind. ¶ ～의 염려《장래》anxiety about *one's* future;《가정》anxiety about *one's* home; worrying about the family left behind / ～의 염려를 없애다 free《*a person*》from anxiety about *his* family; free《*a person*》from solicitude〔anxiety〕about the future / 현부(賢婦)는 남편에게 ～의 근심이 없도록 한다 A wise wife will free her man from family cares.

**후골**(喉骨) the Adam's apple.

**후광**(後光)《광륜》a halo (*pl.* ～(e)s); a nimbus (*pl.* ～es, -bi); an aureole. ¶ ～으로 둘러싸인 그리스도의 그림 a painting of Christ with his head surrounded by a halo / ～이 비치다 a halo shines (about *one's* head); a nimbus envelopes〔appears round〕*one's* head; *one's* head is surmounted by an aureole. ◉ ～효과 halo effect.

**후군**(後軍)〖군사〗the rear of an army; the rear guard. ¶ ～이 되다 bring〔close〕up the rear.

**후굴**(後屈)〖의학〗retroflexion. ◉ 자궁 ～증 retroflexion of the uterus.

**후궁**(後宮) a royal harem〔concubine〕.

**후기**(後記) a postscript (생략 P.S., p.s.); an afternote. ¶ 편집～ the editor's postscript〔notes〕.

**후기**(後期)《시기》the latter term〔period〕; the last〔second〕half year; the second semester《미》(2학기제 학교의). ¶ ～에 latterly / 18세기 ～에 in the later〔latter part of the〕eighteenth century / 전쟁의 ～ the last period〔stage〕of a war. / 이 토기는 신라 시대 ～의 것이다 This earthenware was made during the latter part of the *Shilla* period. ◉ ～결산 the settlement of accounts for the second half. ～그리스어 late Greek. ～대학 universities〔colleges〕in the second (screening) group: ～ 대학입시 entrance exam for the second-group colleges and universities. ～배당 a dividend for the second half. ～시험 the second〔final〕examination.

**후기인상파**(後期印象派) the Postimpressionism. ¶ ～화가 a Postimpressionist.

**후끈–** ⇨ 화끈–.

**후년**(後年)《다음다음해》the year after next;《장래》in years to come; in the future;《그 후》later; afterward; in later years. ¶ 내～, 후～ three years from now / ～에 가서 in future years; in years to come; at a later date.

**후뇌**(後腦)〖해부〗the hindbrain.

**후뇌**(嗅腦)〖해부〗the rhinencephalon (*pl.* -la). ¶ ～의 rhinencephalic.

**후닥닥** ①《갑자기》with a jump〔start〕; suddenly;《열쌔게》quickly; nimbly. ¶ 개천을 ～ 건너 뛰다 leap over a ditch with a jump / ～ 뛰어가다 break into a run / ～ 일어나다 start〔spring〕to *one's* feet; get up with a jump;《잠자리에서》jump〔start, spring〕out of bed / 옷을 ～ 벗다 whip off *one's* clothes / ～ 방에서 뛰쳐 나오다 rush〔dart, bounce〕out of the room / ～ 날아가다 fly away in surprise. ②《서둘러》hurriedly; with a rush; in a「flurry〔hurry〕; in haste. ¶ ～후닥닥 in a great hurry; with all haste; hurry-scurry / 밥을 ～ 먹다 take a hurried〔hasty〕meal.

**후닥닥거리다** ①《열쌔게 행동하다》keep jumping; scamper; act quickly. ¶ 사방으로 후닥닥거리며 도망가다 scamper off in all directions / 닭이 기적 소리에 놀라서 ～ chickens scamper at the sound of a train whistle. ②《급히 서두르다》hurry up; rush; make haste. ¶ 일을 빨리 끝내려고 ～ rush to get a job done in a hurry.

**후당**(後堂) a separate house in the rear.

**후대**(後代) future〔coming〕generations; posterity; after〔coming〕ages. ¶ 창립자의 정신을 ～에 전하다 hand down the founder's spirit to future generations / 그의 이름은 ～에 남을 것이다 His name will go down in history.

**후대**(厚待) a warm〔hearty, cordial〕reception; hospitable〔kind〕treatment; hospitality. ～하다 treat hospitably〔kindly〕; give a warm〔hearty〕reception《to》; receive warmly. ¶ ～를 받다 be given「hospitable treatment〔a cordial reception〕/ 체류시에 ～를 베풀어 주시어 감사합니다 I thank you for your hospitality shown to me during my stay.

**후더침**(後—) complications arising from childbirth.

**후덕**(厚德) liberality; liberal favor; great virtue. ∼하다 (be) liberal; generous; virtuous. ¶ 그는 ∼한 사람으로 지역사회의 유지였다 He was a virtuous man and a leader in the community. ◉ ∼군자 a liberal 〔virtuous〕 gentleman.

**후두**(後頭) 〖해부〗 the occiput (*pl.* ∼s, -pita); the back of the head. ◉ ∼결절 the occipital protuberance. ∼골 the occipital (bone). ∼엽 the occipital lobe.

**후두**(喉頭) 〖해부〗 the larynx (*pl.* ∼es, larynges). ¶ ∼의 laryngeal; laryngal. ◉ ∼개(蓋) the epiglottis. ∼결핵 tuberculosis of the larynx; laryngeal tuberculosis. ∼경(鏡) a laryngoscope: ∼경 검사 laryngoscopy. ∼낭(囊) a laryngeal「pouch 〔sac〕. ∼삽관법(揷管法) 〖외과〗 intubation of the larynx. ∼암 laryngeal cancer; cancer of the larynx. ∼염 laryngitis. ∼음 〖음성〗 a laryngeal「voice 〔sound〕; a guttural (sound). ∼인대(靭帶) the laryngeal ligament. ∼절개술 laryngotomy. ∼카타르 laryngeal catarrh.

**후두두** with a「clatter 〔patter〕; scatteringly. ¶ 비가 ∼ 내리고 있다 The rain is falling in drops. *or* Raindrops are pattering.

**후두부**(後頭部) 〖해부〗 the occipital region; the occiput (*pl.* ∼s, -pita); the back (part) of the head. ¶ ∼를 때리다 strike 《*a person*》 on the back of *his* head.

**후둥이**(後—) the later born of twins; the younger twin.

**후들거리다** tremble; shake; quiver; shiver 《with cold》. ¶ 무서워서 다리가 ∼ *one's* legs are trembling with fear.

**후들후들** trembling; shaking; shivering. ¶ ∼ 떨다 tremble all over; be all of a tremble; quiver / 다리가 ∼떨리다 *one's* legs are trembling / 추워서 ∼ 떨다 shiver 〔shake〕 with cold.

**후등**(後燈) rear-light; 《미등》 a taillight.

**후딱** quickly; quick as「thought 〔lightning, wink〕; speedily; at once; promptly; immediately; instantly; in「an instant 〔a moment, a jiffy〕. ¶ 일을 ∼ 해치우다 get a job done in a jiffy / 자리에서 ∼ 일어나다 stand up quickly; spring to *one's* feet / 심부름을 ∼ 다녀오다 do an errand in no time at all.

**후딱후딱** all 〔one after another〕 quickly 〔speedily, with dispatch, in a jiffy〕. ¶ 일을 ∼ 해치우다 get the jobs done one right after another / 그는 무엇이나 ∼ 잘한다 He does things with efficient dispatch.

**후래삼배**(後來三杯) the late-comer has to drink three cups of wine in a row; "making up for lost time"; catching up with the drinking.

**후략**(後略) omission of what follows; the rest omitted.

**후레아들** an「ill-bred 〔ill-mannered〕 fellow.

**후레이** 《응원의》 Hurray!; Hurrah!

**후려갈기다, 후려치다** hit; beat; thump; punch; strike; knock; give 〔deal〕 《*a person*》 a blow; slap (손바닥으로); lash (채찍으로). ¶ 얼굴을 ∼ strike 《*a person*》 across 〔in〕 the face; punch 《*a person*》 in the nose / 머리를 ∼ strike 〔beat〕 《*a person*》 on the head / 실컷 ∼ give 《*a person*》 a good beating / 주먹으로 ∼ smash 《*a person*》 with the fist / 채찍으로 ∼ lash 《*a person*》 with a whip; whip 《*a person*》.

**후련하다** feel relieved; feel unburdened; feel refreshed (much) better. ¶ 후련토록 울다 weep *one's* fill / 토하고 나니 속이 ∼ feel better after throwing up / 하고 싶은 말을 하니 속이 ∼ Now that I have had my say, I feel much better (for it). / 빚을 다 갚아서 ∼ The load is off my mind now that I have cleared off my debts.「a burden.

**후렴**(後斂) 《노래의》 a (musical) refrain;

**후루루** ① 《호각 부는 소리》 whistling; blowing. ∼하다 whistle; blow. ¶ 호각을 ∼ 불다 whistle; blow a whistle. ② 《타버리는 모양》 burning up with a flicker. ∼하다 burn up with a flicker; go up in flames. ③ =후루룩.

**후루룩** 《날개 치는 소리》 with a flutter; 《마시는 소리》 《drinking》 with a slurp. ¶ 죽을 ∼ 들이마시다 slurp down *one's* porridge / 새가 ∼ 날아가다 a bird flutters away.

**후루룩거리다** 《새가》 keep fluttering; fly; 《마시다》 keep slurping.

**후륜**(後輪) a「rear 〔back〕 wheel. ◉ ∼구동 rear-wheel drive.

**후리다** ① 《몰다》 hunt「up 〔out〕; round up; net 《fish, birds》 (그물로). ¶ 그물로 물고기를 ∼ chase 〔catch〕 fish with a net / 멧돼지를 ∼ hunt out wild boars. ② 《모난 곳을》 shave 〔plane〕 off; cut 〔round〕 off the edges. ③ 《낚아채다》 snatch (away) 《from, off》;

wrest 《from》; catch away. ¶ 여자의 손에서 핸드백을 ~ snatch 〔hook〕 a handbag from a lady's hand. ④ 《유혹하다》 captivate; seduce; coax; cajole. ¶ 남자를 ~ captivate a man with wiles.

**후리질** 《후려들임》 fishing with a net 〔seine〕; seining. ~하다 fish with a (large) net; seine.

**후리후리하다** (be) high in stature; (be) tall and slender. ¶ 후리후리한 남자 a tall lank man; a gangling fellow 《미》 / 후리후리한 미녀 a beautiful girl, slender as a lily.

**후림** 《유혹·꾐》 seduction; a seductive trick; a wile. ¶ ~ 비둘기 a decoy pigeon / ~을 당하다 be seduced; be tricked / ~에 넘어가다 be caught by trick; be taken in.

**후림대수작**(一酬酌) seductive words.

**후림불** 《서슬·걸려듦》 entanglement; involvement; a by-blow. ¶ ~에 걸려들다 get entangled 〔involved〕 in; get mixed up 《in a trouble》; suffer a by-blow.

**후릿고삐** a halter (long enough to whip the animal with its end).

**후릿그물** a dragnet; a seine.

**후면**(後面) the back side; the reverse (side); the rear. ¶ 학교 ~에 in the rear 〔at the back〕 of the school.

**후무리다** make 《*something*》 *one's* own surreptitiously; embezzle; pocket; possess *oneself* 《of》. ¶ 그는 사무실의 공금을 후무려 도망쳤다 He fled away embezzling a lot of public money from the office.

**후문**(後門) a back 〔rear〕 gate 〔door〕.

**후문**(後聞) an after-talk.

**후물거리다** mumble; chew with toothless gums.

**후물림**(後—) 《물려받음》 handing down; a thing handed down; 《구어》 a hand=me-down. ¶ 형의 ~옷 clothes handed down from *one's* brother.

**후물후물** 《입 안에서》 mumbling; chewing with toothless gums.

**후미** a bend of the water; a cove; an inlet (강의); a bay (바다의).

**후미**(後尾) the rear; the tail (end); 《배의》 the stern. ¶ ~의 rear; back; aft (선미의) / ~에 at the rear 《of》 / 행렬의 ~에 따라붙다 join the tail of the procession. ◉ ~경호 the rear guard. ~등 a taillight.

**후미지다** ① 《물굽이가》 (get a) bend in; form an inlet; 《an arm of the sea》 run deep into the land. ¶ 후미진 곳 a deep spot 《in the water》. ② 《으슥하고 호젓하다》 get deep; (be) retired; secluded. ¶ 후미진 곳 a secluded spot; an out-of-the-way place; a recess; a nook. ◉ 후밋길 a mountain path 〔road〕 with a bend in it.

**후박**(厚薄) 《두께가》 thick and/or thin; relative thickness 〔thinness〕; 《후함과 박함》 liberal and/or stingy; much and/or little partiality. ¶ ~이 없다 be impartial 〔equitable, fair〕.

**후박나무**(厚朴—) 『식물』 ① 《목련과의》 a silver magnolia. ② 《녹나뭇과의》 *Machilus Thunbergii* (학명).

**후반**(後半) the latter 〔second〕 half. ¶ 18세기 ~에 in the latter half of the 18th century; late in the 18th century / 그는 일생의 ~을 고향마을에서 지냈다 He lived the latter part of his life in his native village.

◉ ~기 the latter half of the year. ~생(生) the later half 〔part〕 of *one's* life: 그의 ~생은 참으로 비참한 것이었다 The latter half of his life was a miserable one indeed. ~전(戰) the second half of the game: ~전에 들어가다 advance 〔get〕 into the second 〔latter〕 half 《of a game》.

**후발**(後發) ¶ ~(개발)도상국 least developed among developing countries (생략 LDDC) / ~ 중소기업체들 a group of small and medium-sized enterprises that got into the business later / 불경기 기간 중, ~ 제조업들은 고전을 면치 못하고 있다 During the period of depression, those manufacturers who are latecomers in the market are forced to be under great disadvantage.

**후방**(後方) the rear; 《전선에 대해》 the home 〔civilian〕 front; rear service.

¶ ~에 backward; in 〔at〕 the rear; behind / 적의 ~을 습격하다 attack the enemy in the rear / 우리들은 ~ 부대이다 We are the rear guards 〔units〕. / 차 운전시는 전방뿐만 아니라 ~도 잘 살펴라 When driving a car, observe the movement of traffic not only ahead of you but (also) behind you.

◉ ~경계 레이더 a tail warning radar. ~근무 rear service (at the base); duties 「in the rear 〔on the home front〕: ~ 근무로 배치되다 be assigned to the base. ~기지 a rear base. ~난기류 『항공』 wake turbulence. ~부대 troops in rear. ~사령부 headquarters in the rear. ～지역 the communications zone. ～진지 〖군사〗 a fallback position.

**후배**(後輩) *one's* junior; younger men. ¶～를 돌보다 patronize *one's* juniors / 그는 우리보다 훨씬 ～다 He is many years our junior 《in service, in graduation》. / 그는 나보다 3년 ～다 He is three years behind me 《in school》. ◉ 학교～ *one's* junior in school.

**후배주**(後配株) 〖증권〗 a deferred stock.

**후배지**(後背地) 〖지리〗 the hinterland.

**후번**(後番) next time; next round; next game.

**후벼내기** a tool used for digging out chisel dust.

**후보**(後報) a later report; later 〔further〕 news; further information. ¶～를 기다리고 있다 We are expecting further details.

**후보**(候補) ① 《입후보》 candidacy; 《영》 candidature. ⇨후보자. ¶～로 나서다 be a candidate for 《the next Presidency》; come forward as a candidate 《for an election, for Presidency》; run 〔be up〕 for 《Presidency》 《미》; stand for 《Parliament》 《영》 / 입상 ～의 작품 works being considered for prize / ～로 세우다 put up 〔forward〕 《*a person*》 as a candidate / ～를 사퇴하다 withdraw *one's* candidacy / 박씨는 차기 총장의 가장 유력한 ～이다 Mr. Park is the most likely candidate for the next presidency. ② 《운동팀의》 substitution. ¶～선수 a substitute (player). ◉ ～지 a proposed site; a most suitable place 《for》; a first choice 《for》: 새로운 종합 병원의 ～지 a site proposed for a new general hospital.

**후보자**(候補者) a candidate; an applicant. ¶～ 경력 공보 the candidates' career bulletin / ～ 명부 a list of (eligible) candidates; 《정당의》 《미》 a slate; a ticket / ～ 지명 nomination of a candidate / ～를 세우다 field 〔ticket〕 a candidate; put ... on the (party) ticket / ～의 난립을 막다 check random candidacy / 의석 하나를 놓고 15명의 ～가 난립하고 있다 There is a crowded field of 15 candidates for one seat. *or* Fifteen candidates are crowding each other out for one seat. ◉ 공인〔비공인〕 ～ an official 〔unofficial〕 candidate. 낙선～ a defeated candidate.

**후부**(後夫) *one's* second husband.

**후부**(後部) the rear; the back 〔hind〕 part; 《배의》 the stern. ¶～의 back; rear; hind; posterior / ～에 at 〔in〕 the rear. ◉ ～좌석 the rear 〔back〕 seat.

**후분**(後分) *one's* luck 〔fortune〕 in later years. ¶～이 좋다 be lucky later in life.

**후불**(後拂) deferred payment; later payment. ¶～로 하다 pay later; pay 《for the goods》 on delivery; pay when *one* collects 《the clothes from the cleaner's》 / 물건을 ～로 사다 buy goods on credit 〔deferred terms〕 / 대금 ～로 이 물건을 배달해 주십시오 Please send this as a deferred payment.

**후비**(后妃) an empress; a queen.

**후비다** ① 《파내다》 dig in 〔up〕; scoop out; gouge. ¶ 땅을 후벼파다 dig in the ground. ② 《코·귀를》 pick. ¶ 코〔귀, 이〕를 ～ pick *one's* nose 〔ears, teeth〕. ③ 《일의 속내를》 examine closely; pick at 《the inside facts》.

**후비적거리다** keep gouging; keep scooping 〔scraping〕 out; 《귀·코 따위를》 keep picking. ¶ 귀〔코〕를 ～ keep picking *one's* ears 〔nose〕.

**후비적후비적** 《후벼파내는 모양》 gouging; scooping 〔scraping, digging〕 out; 《후비는 모양》 picking. ¶ 귀를 ～ 후비다 keep picking *one's* ears.

**후사**(後事) 《장래의》 future 〔later〕 affairs; 《죽은 뒤의》 *one's* affairs after *one's* death. ¶～를 부탁하다 entrust 《*a person*》 with future affairs; ask 《*a person*》 to look after *one's* affairs 「when *one* is gone 〔while *one* is away〕 / ～를 딸에게 맡기다 entrust the future affairs to *one's* daughter.

**후사**(後嗣) 《후계자》 a successor; 《상속인》 an heir 〔heiress (여자)〕. ¶～가 없다 have no descendants / ～가 끊어지다 a family become extinct; a family line breaks.

**후사**(厚謝) warm 〔hearty〕 thanks; handsome recompense; a liberal reward. ～하다 recompense handsomely; thank heartily; reward warmly.

**후산**(後産) (bearing) the afterbirth. ～하다 bear the afterbirth.

**후살이**(後—) remarriage; a second marriage (of a woman).

**후생**(後生) 《후진》 juniors; younger students 〔scholars〕; younger fellows; 〖불교〗 the life to come; the future life 〔existence〕. ¶～이 가외(可畏)라 Youth should be regarded with respect.

**후생**(厚生) the welfare 〔well-being〕 of

people; public 〔social〕 welfare. ¶ 정부의 ~ 지출 government spending on welfare; government's welfare spending. ◉ ~과 the welfare section. ~사업 (public) welfare enterprise; welfare 〔social〕 work. ~시설 welfare facilities 〔institution〕. ~연금 a welfare pension 〔annuity〕: ~ 연금 보험 welfare pension 〔annuity〕 insurance.

**후서방**(後書房) *one's* second husband. ¶ ~을 얻다 marry again; remarry.

**후세**(後世) the future; coming 〔after〕 ages; 《사람》 future generations; posterity.
¶ ~에 전하다 hand down to posterity / ~에 전해지다 go down 〔be handed down〕 to posterity / ~를 위해 쓰다 write for posterity / 이름을 ~에 남기다 earn *one's* place in history; hand *one's* name down to posterity; immortalize *one's* fame; be remembered forever / 사건의 판단은 ~로 넘기다 leave the judgment on 《*a matter*》 to posterity / 옳고 그름을 ~에 묻다 let posterity judge for itself / 그의 충성스러움은 ~의 귀감이 될 것이다 His loyalty will afford a model to coming generations.

**후속**(後續) succession; succeeding; following. ~하다 succeed; follow. ¶ ~의 following; succeeding / 이 열차는 만원이므로, ~열차를 이용해 주십시오 This train is full; please wait for the next one. ◉ ~부대 《후위》 rear guard; a rear party (육군); 《증원 부대》 reinforcements; 《해군》 a unit next astern. ~조치 《take》 follow-up measures.

**후손**(後孫) descendants; [총칭] posterity; offspring; progeny. ¶ ~에게 전하다 〔전해지다〕 hand 〔go〕 down to *one's* posterity / ~을 남기다 《survive and》 leave offspring / …의 ~이다 be a descendant of…; be descended from….

**후송**(後送) sending back 《from the front》; evacuation 《to the rear》. ~하다 send back 《to the rear》; evacuate 《to the rear》. ¶ (군인이) 부상〔질병〕으로 본국으로 ~되다 be sent home as an invalid / 포로들은 ~되었다 The prisoners of war were sent to the rear. / 수화물은 ~하겠습니다 We will send your baggage to you later. ◉ ~병원 an evacuation hospital. ~환자 an evacuated casualty.

**후수**(後手) ① 《선수에 대해》 ¶ ~가 되다 be forestalled 〔outmaneuvered〕. ② 《바둑 등에서》 playing as second mover.

**후술**(後述) ~하다 say 〔mention, describe, touch upon〕 later. ¶ 상세한 것은 ~ 참조 See below for further details.

**후식**(後食) (a) dessert. ¶ ~으로 나온 아이스크림 the icecream served for dessert.

**후신**(後身) 《다시 태어난 몸》 *one's* later self; *one's* future being; *one's* new existence after rebirth; 《이전의 형태에서 변한 것》 a transformation. ¶ 이 대학은 구제 직업학교의 ~이다 This college used to be a vocational school in the old system.

**후신경**(嗅神經) 〖해부〗 an olfactory nerve.

**후실**(後室) *one's* second wife. ◉ ~자식 a child born of the second wife.

**후안**(厚顔) a brazen face; impudence; effrontery; shamelessness; cheek. ◉ ~무치(無恥) shamelessness; brazen impudence: ~무치하다 (be) impudent; unabashed; shameless; thick=skinned / ~무치한 사람 a shameless 〔brazen〕 fellow; a saucy 〔cheeky, brazen-faced〕 person.

**후열**(後列) the rear (rank, row); the back row. ¶ ~ 오른쪽에서 3번째 the third from right in the back row.

**후예**(後裔) a descendant; a scion; offspring. ¶ 명문의 ~ a scion of an illustrious family / …의 ~이다 be descended from…; be a descendant of…; trace *one's* ancestry from… / 6대째의 ~ *one's* descendant in the sixth generation.

**후원**(後苑·後園) a backyard; a rear garden.

**후원**(後援) support; backing; patronage; assistance; sponsorship (자금 등의); help; aid. ~하다 support; give 〔lend〕 support 《to》; back (up); be 〔stand〕 behind 《a movement》; give backing 《to》; help; aid; stand by; sponsor. ¶ ~ 없는 unbacked; without backing / …의 ~하에 with the support 〔help〕 of…; supported 〔aided〕 by…; 《행사 따위》 under the auspices 〔patronage〕 of…; through the sponsorship of…; sponsored by… / 국민의 ~이 있다 have the people behind *one's* back / 경제적으로 ~하다 support 《*a person*》 financially; give financial support 《to *a person*》 / 정부의 ~을 얻다 have government support / ~을 바랍니다 I hope to have your support. / 그 전람회는 H신문사의 ~으로 개최되었다 The exhibition was held under the sponsorship of the H newspaper. ◉ ～군 (armed) support; reinforcements. ～단체 a supporters' organization.

**후원자**(後援者) a supporter; a sponsor; a patron; a booster 《미》. ¶ 그에게는 존슨이라는 ～가 있다 He has a supporter in the personage of Johnson.

**후원회**(後援會) an aid association; a backers' 〔supporters'〕 association. ¶ ～를 만들다〔조직하다〕 organize a society for the support 《of》.

**후위**(後衛) ① 〖군사〗 the rear (guard). ¶ ～를 맡다 fight a rear guard action. ② 《테니스》 the back player; 《축구》 a back; a fullback. ¶ ～를 보다 play the back.

**후유** 《한숨 소리》 with a sigh; whew! ¶ ～하고 한숨 돌리다 give 〔breathe〕 a sigh of relief. / ～하고 짐을 내려놓다 let *one's* burden down with a "whew!".

**후유증**(後遺症) an aftereffect 《of a disease, of an injury》; [비유적] aftermath; 〖의학〗 a sequela (*pl.* ～e). ¶ 선거의 ～ the aftermath of elections / 그의 부상은 완쾌되었으나 추워지면 ～으로 동통이 온다 Although the wound has healed, he still has attacks of pain as aftereffect when it is cold. / ～이 있을지도 모른다 I am afraid there may be an aftereffect.

**후은**(厚恩) 《베풀어 준》 great favor 〔kindness〕; 《갚아야 할》 great obligations; great debts of gratitude. ¶ ～을 입다 be under great obligations to 《*a person*》; owe 《*a person*》 great debts of gratitude / ～을 베풀다 do 《*a person*》 great favor; do great favor for 《*a person*》 / ～은 잊지 않겠습니다 I shall always consider myself indebted to you. *or* I will never forget ｢your kindness 〔what you have done for me〕.

**후음**(喉音) a guttural sound; gutturals. ¶ ～화하다 gutturalize.

**후의**(厚意) great kindness; kind intentions; goodwill; good wishes; favor. ¶ 아무의 ～로 through the kindness 〔good offices〕 of *a person* / ～를 감사하다 thank 《*a person*》 for *his* kindness; appreciate 《*a person's*》 help / ～를 거절하다 decline 《*a person's*》 kind offer / 베풀어 주신 ～에 깊이 감사합니다 I am deeply indebted to you for your kindness. *or* Thank you very much for your kindness.

**후의**(厚誼) close 〔warm, fast, deep〕 friendship; (your) favor 〔kindness〕. ¶ ～에 보답하다 repay 《*a person*》 for *his* kindness; do something for 《*a person's*》 favor / 재직중의 ～에 감사드립니다 Thank you for your favor 〔kindness〕 during my years of service here. *or* I am grateful for the kindness you showed me during my term of office.

**후인**(後人) future generations; posterity.

**후일**(後日) later days; the future; another day. ¶ ～에 in (the) future; later (on); some (other) day / ～을 위하여 《훈계》 as a warning for the future; 《참고로》 for future reference; 《증거로》 as a future proof / ～에 화근을 남기다 leave evils to spring up in the future; sow seed of trouble for the future / ～ 또 만나자 I'll see you again. ◉ ～담(譚) reminiscences; remembrance; recollection; subsequent events: 사건의 ～담 a sequence 〔sequel〕 to the event.

**후임**(後任) 《사람》 a successor 《to a post》; an incomer; 《임무》 a duty left over by the person formerly in charge. ¶ ～ 교장 선생님 the incoming principal / …의 ～으로 in succession to…; as (the) successor to…; to succeed… / ～이 되다 succeed 《*a person* in *his* post, to *a person's* post》; take 《*a person's*》 place; fill 〔step into〕 《*a person's*》 shoes / ～으로 뽑히다〔지명되다〕 be elected 〔designated〕 to a vacancy / ～이 결정될 때까지 대리를 보다 act during a vacancy / ～으로 앉히다 put 〔install〕 《*a person*》 in 《another's》 place / A씨의 ～으로 B씨가 음악을 담당한다 Mr. B is Mr. A's successor as the music teacher. / ～을 찾을 때까지 그대로 있어 주기 바랍니다 Please wait till we find another to take your place. / 그의 ～은 누구일까 Who will take his place? *or* Who will succeed him? ◉ ～자 a successor.

**후입**(後入) 〖컴퓨터〗 last in. ◉ ～선출 〖컴퓨터〗 last in-first out (생략 LIFO): ～선출 교체 방식 last in-first out replacement policy / ～ 선출 기억 장치 last in-first out memory. ～후출 last in=last out (생략 LILO).

**후자**(後者) the latter; the other. ¶ 전자와 ～ the former and the latter / ～의 경우에는 in the latter case / 전자는 …, ～는 … the one 〔former〕 … while the other 〔latter〕… / 전자가 ～보다 낫

다 the former is better than the latter / ~의 경우, 사태는 우리에게 상당히 불리해질 것이다 In the latter case, things will become pretty unfavorable for us.

**후작**(侯爵) a marquis; a marquess. ◉ ~부인 a marchioness; 《영국 이외의》 a *marquise* (F.).

**후장**(後場) 〖증권〗 the afternoon session.

**후장**(後裝) breech-loading. ◉ ~총 a breech-loading gun 〔rifle〕.

**후제**(後—) another day; some other day 〔time〕; [부사적] later (on); afterward(s). ¶ ~ 또 찾아올게 I will call on you later on.

**후조**(候鳥) a migratory bird. ＝철새. ¶ ~의 이동 the migration of birds.

**후주곡**(後奏曲) 〖음악〗 a postlude.

**후줄근하다** (be) limp; wilted; droop; flag; be a little soggy; be wet enough to lose starch. ¶ 옷이 이슬에 젖어 ~ *one's* clothes get wet with dew and lose their starch.

**후중**(後重) being constipated 〔costive〕. ~하다 (be) constipated; costive.

**후진**(後陣) the rear guard; the rear echelon.

**후진**(後進) ① 《후배》 a junior; a younger man 〔fellow〕; the younger generation [총칭]; 《예술·문학의》 an epigone. ¶ ~을 돌보다 「look after 〔be helpful to〕 *one's* juniors / ~을 위한 길을 열어 주기 위해 (in order) to facilitate the promotion of younger men; to open the way for *one's* juniors / ~을 위하여 길을 열다 give younger men a chance; make room for *one's* juniors / ~을 위해 용퇴하다 resign in favor of *one's* juniors; resign to open the way for the promotion of *one's* juniors.
② 《미발달》 underdevelopment; backwardness; lagging behind. ¶ ~의 backward; underdeveloped; less advanced / ~적인 사회 상태 a backward state of society.
③ 《후퇴》 backward motion; sternway (선박의). ~하다 back (away from); reverse; slip backward; 《선박이》 go 〔move〕 astern; make sternway. ¶ ~ 금지 《게시》 No backing.
④ 〖컴퓨터〗 backspace (생략 BS).
◉ ~국 a backward country 〔nation〕; an underdeveloped country. ~등 《자동차의》 a backup light; a reversing light. ~성 backwardness; laggardliness: ~성을 탈피하다 emerge from backwardness. ~지역 underdeveloped areas; 《새로 개발되는》 a newly-developing area. ~키 〖컴퓨터〗 the backspace key.

**후처**(後妻) a second wife. ¶ ~를 맞다 〔얻다〕 marry 〔take〕 a second wife; get remarried 《to》 / ~로 맞다 take 《a woman》 for 〔as〕 a second wife.

**후천성**(後天性) ¶ ~의 postnatal; acquired. ◉ ~ 면역결핍 증후군 〖의학〗 acquired immune deficiency syndrome (생략 AIDS).

**후천적**(後天的) *a posteriori* (L.); postnatal; acquired. ¶ ~ 면역 acquired immunity / ~으로 *a posteriori* / 성격은 ~으로 형성된다 You can form your own personal character in the course of your lifetime. *or* Personality is largely acquired through experience. / 그의 낙천적인 성격은 ~인 것이다 He was not born an optimist.

**후추** pepper; black pepper. ¶ ~를 치다 sprinkle pepper 《on》; pepper / ~는 작아도 맵다 Small he may be, but he is not a man to be trifled with.
◉ 후춧가루 ground pepper: 후춧가루병 a pepper caster 〔castor, duster〕.

**후취**(後娶) remarriage; a second marriage; (taking) a second wife. ¶ ~를 얻다 take a second wife; remarry.

**후치사**(後置詞) 〖문법〗 a postposition.

**후탈**(後頉) 《병의》 later complications of a disease; 《산후의》 complications from childbirth; 《뒤탈》 trouble ensuing after the disposal of a matter; (troublesome) aftermath; repercussions; an aftereffect. ¶ ~ 없게 일을 잘 처리하다 handle things so that there will be no trouble later on.

**후터분하다** (be) a bit sultry; stuffy. ¶ 후터분한 날씨 rather sultry weather.

**후텁지근하다** (be) sultry; sticky; stuffy.

**후퇴**(後退) ① 《뒤로 물러섬》 (a) retreat; retrogression; regression. ~하다 go 〔move, fall〕 back; back (away); recede; retreat; 《배가》 go astern. ¶ 전략적〔작전상〕 ~ a strategic retreat / 1보 ~하면 반드시 2보 전진하기로 하자 Let's make it a rule never to take one step back without taking two (steps) forward. ② 《경기의 후퇴》 (a) recession. ¶ 경기가 ~하다 Business 「fell off 〔is dull〕. / 경기 ~를 극복하다 overcome the recession.
◉ ~각 〖항공〗 a sweepback (angle). ~군 an army in retreat; a retreating army. ~명령 an order to retreat. ~이동 retrograde movement. ~익(翼)

〖공군〗 a swept-back wing; a back-swept wing.

**후편**(後便) 《나중 인편》 a later messenger; 《나중 편지》 *one's* next 〔later〕 letter; 《미》 the 〔*one's*〕 next 〔later〕 mail 〔post〕; 《뒷기회》 a later opportunity; 《뒤쪽》 the back side.

**후편**(後篇) 《후반》 the latter part 《of a book》; the concluding part; 《전편(前篇)에 대해》 the second 〔last〕 volume; 《속편》 a sequel 《to》.

**후하다**(厚—) 《두껍다》 (be) thick; 《인심·인정이》 (be) kind; kindhearted; cordial; warm; hospitable; benevolent; nice; friendly; 《보수·대우 등이》 (be) generous; lenient; liberal. ¶ 후한 대접 liberal entertainment; a hospitable reception; warm hospitality / 후한 보수 a generous reward / 금전에 ～ be generous with *one's* money / 점수가 ～ be generous with *one's* marks; be generous 〔liberal〕 in marking 〔grading〕; be a good marker / 시골은 도시보다 인심이 ～ People are friendlier in the country than in the city.

**후학**(後學) 《후진학자》 younger students 〔scholars〕; *one's* junior(s); 《후일의 참고》 future information 〔reference〕. ¶ ～을 위하여 for *one's* future information; for future use 〔benefit〕.

**후항**(後項) 《다음 조항》 the succeeding 〔following〕 clause; a later item; 〖수학〗 the consequent; the latter term.

**후행**(後行) 《동반》 escorting a bride 〔bridegroom〕; 《사람》 an escort of a bride 〔bridegroom〕. ～하다 escort 〔accompany〕 the bride 〔bridegroom〕.

**후형질**(後形質) 〖생물〗 metaplasm.

**후환**(後患) 《뒷근심》 later 〔future〕 trouble; an evil consequence; (later) complications. ¶ ～을 두려워하여 for fear of future troubles / ～이 없도록 so as to prevent any trouble that might occur later; so there will be no future trouble / ～을 남기다 sow seeds of trouble / ～을 없애다 「get rid of 〔remove〕 the source of evils.

**후회**(後悔) 《회개하는 마음》 repentance; 《유감스러움》 (a) regret; 《자책의 마음》 remorse. ～하다 repent 《of what I've done》; regret; be sorry 〔penitent〕 《for》; feel remorse 《for *one's* crime》. ¶ 경거망동을 ～하다 regret *one's* rash action / 게을렀음을 ～하다 repent (of) *one's* idleness / 죄를 ～하다 repent (of) *one's* sin / 그런 짓 한 것을 ～하다 regret having 〔to have〕 done such a thing / 일을 저질러 놓고 보니 ～가 막심합니다 I feel awfully sorry for what I have done. / ～막급(莫及), ～해 봤자 소용없다 《속담》 It is no use crying over spilt milk. *or* It is too late for regret. / 자네 나중에 ～할 거다 You'll be sorry (for it).

**후후** 《소리》 with puff after puff; blowing and blowing. ¶ ～ 불다 keep puffing / 촛불을 ～ 불어 끄다 blow out the candle.

**후후년**(後後年) three years from now.

**훅**[1] 〖권투〗 a hook. ¶ 상대의 턱에 레프트 훅을 먹이다 deliver 〔let go〕 a left hook to the opponent's jaw.

**훅**[2] 《고리 단추》 a hook; a snap hook; a hook and eye. ¶ 등에서 훅으로 채우게 된 옷 a dress that hooks at the back / 훅을 채우다 hook (up) 《a dress》 / 훅을 벗기다 unhook; undo a hook and eye.

**훅**[3] 《마시는 소리》 with a sip 〔slurp〕; with a gulp; 《부는 소리》 with a whiff 〔puff〕. ¶ 국을 훅 들이마시다 slurp up soup; gulp soup down / 촛불을 훅 불어 끄다 puff out a candle(light).

**훅하다** go at eagerly; jump 〔dart〕 at; spring 〔fly〕 at; be eager to. ¶ 그는 과자라면 훅한다 He always jumps at cakes. / 그는 돈벌이라면 훅한다 He is eager to make money.

**훅훅** 《마시는 모양·소리》 with sip after sip 〔slurp after slurp〕; sucking away. ¶ 국을 ～ 들이 마시다 slurp away at the soup.

**훈감하다** (be) rich and savory 〔flavorful〕; tasteful; delicious; tasty.

**훈계**(訓戒) admonition; exhortation; a lecture; warning. ～하다 counsel; admonish 〔exhort〕; exhort 《*a person* to *do something*》; caution; warn. ¶ 엄하게 ～하다 utter a strong warning / 학생의 부주의를 ～하다 admonish a student for his carelessness. ◉ ～방면(放免) release with a warning.

**훈고**(訓詁) exposition; a commentary; exegesis (성서·경전의); scholia (*sing.* -lium). ◉ ～학 exegetics; exegetical studies: ～학자 a scholiast.

**훈공**(勳功) distinguished 〔meritorious〕 service(s); merits; exploits (of war). ¶ 혁혁한 ～ a brilliant exploits / ～에 의하여 in recognition of *one's* (distinguished) services / ～을 세우다 render distinguished 〔meritorious〕 services 《to the state》; distinguish *oneself* 《in》; gain 〔win, get〕 distinction / 그

의 ～에 대해 훈장이 수여됐다 A medal was awarded (him) for his meritorious services.
**훈기**(勳記) diploma (of merit, decoration).
**훈기**(薰氣) warm air; heat. ¶ ～ 있는 방 a warm room.
**훈김**(薰—) 《훈기》 warm fumes 〔vapor, steam〕; 《세력》 influence; power. ¶ 아버지 ～으로 출세하다 rise in the world through *one's* father's influence.
**훈독**(訓讀) the Korean reading 〔rendering translation〕 of a Chinese character.
**훈등**(勳等) the order of merit.
**훈련**(訓鍊) training; (a) drill; practice; (training) exercise; (a) discipline. ～하다 train; drill; exercise; discipline. ¶ 맹～ hard 〔intensive〕 training / 잘 ～된 well-trained〔-disciplined〕 / ～ 부족인 ill-trained / ～을 강화하다 intensify training / ～을 받다 be trained 〔disciplined〕 《in》; undergo training 〔discipline〕; get training / ～중이다 be under 〔in〕 training / ～이 잘 되어 있다 be well trained 〔drilled〕; be highly disciplined; be under perfect discipline / 병사들은 한동안 사격 ～을 받아야만 했다 The soldiers had to go through some rifle drills. / 전문가로서의 기술을 몸에 익히려면 여러 해에 걸친 ～이 필요하다 It takes you years of practice to acquire the skill of an expert.
◉ ～교관 a drillmaster; a drill instructor (생략 DI). ～교본 a drill book; a training manual. ～법 a way of training. ～비행 a training flight. ～사 《개의》 a dog trainer; a handler. ～생 a trainee. ～소집 점검 a roll call for mobilization drill. ～장(場) a training camp 〔ground〕; a drill field. ～지원함 a training support ship.
**훈련소**(訓練所) a training school 〔institute, center〕. ¶ 육군 신병 ～ an army recruit training center.
**훈령**(訓令) instructions; an (official) order; a directive. ～하다 instruct; direct; give 〔issue〕 instructions. ¶ 정부의 ～에 의하여 by instructions from the Government / ～을 내리다〔발하다〕 give 〔issue〕 instructions 〔an order〕 / 본국 정부에 ～을 요청하다 ask for instructions from the home Government / 다음 ～이 있을 때까지 대기하다 wait (for) further instructions.
◉ ～전보 a telegraphic instruction.
**훈민정음**(訓民正音) the Korean script. ⇨한글.
**훈방**(訓放) ～하다 dismiss 《*a person*》 with a caution; release 《*a person*》 with warning. ¶ ～되다 be freed after admonition / 죄질이 가벼워 ～되다 be released with only warning due to a light charge.
**훈수**(訓手) 《바둑·장기의》 help from an outsider; a hint; a tip. ～하다 suggest what move to make; help from the side 《with》; give a hint 〔tip〕 《on》; kibitz. ¶ 장기를 ～하다 help 《*a person*》 with a move in chess / ～없기다 No helping from the outsiders!
**훈시**(訓示) 《훈계》 instruction; admonition; counsel; 《훈사》 an admonitory speech; (an address of) instructions; 《공무상의》 official instruction 〔announcements〕; a directive. ～하다 instruct; admonish; give counsel; give 〔issue〕 (an address of) instructions; make an admonitory speech; give a directive; give out official announcements. ¶ 졸업식날 교장 선생님의 ～ the principal's address on a commencement day / 부하들에게 아침 ～를 하다 give a morning address to *one's* men.
**훈신**(勳臣) a meritorious subject 〔retainer〕; a vassal 〔statesman〕 of merit.
**훈약**(薰藥) 〖한의〗 errhine; a medicinal snuff. ¶ ～을 쐬다 apply errhine.
**훈위**(勳位) the order of merit.
**훈육**(訓育) (moral) education; educative instruction; discipline; character building. ～하다 instruct; train; discipline. ◉ ～주임 a teacher in charge of moral training.
**훈장**(訓長) a (village) schoolmaster; a teacher.
**훈장**(勳章) a medal; a decoration; an order. ¶ ～을 달다 wear a decoration / ～을 타다 be decorated; have an order conferred upon 《*one*》 / ～을 주다〔수여하다〕 decorate 《*a person*》 (with an order); confer 〔award〕 a decoration 〔an order〕 《on *a person*》 / …의 가슴에 ～을 달아주다 pin a decoration upon the breast of 《*a person*》.
◉ 국민～ the Order of National Service Merit. 금탑산업 ～ the Gold Tower Order of Industrial Service Merit. 문화～ the Order of Culture.
**훈전**(訓電) telegraphic instructions. ～하다 send instructions by wire.
**훈제**(燻製) smoking 《of meat》; smoke=

drying. ¶ ～의 smoked; smoke-dried / ～연어 smoked salmon / ～로 하다 smoke; kipper; bloat (생선을); dry 《fish》 in the smoke. ◉ ～실(室) a smokehouse. ～품 smoked 「meat 〔fish〕.

**훈족**(一族) 〖역사〗 the Hun tribes.

**훈증**(燻蒸) fumigation. ～하다 fumigate; smoke. ¶ 유황으로 ～하다 sulfur; sulfurize; fumigate 《a room》 with sulfur; smoke out 《a sickroom》. ◉ ～소독(법) fumigation. ～제 a fumigant.

**훈풍**(薰風) a balmy wind; a warm breeze. ¶ ～이 부는 5월 May, with its warm breezes / ～에 흔들리는 꽃들 flowers waving in the warm breeze.

**훈화**(訓話) a moral discourse; an admonitory lecture.

**훈훈하다**(薰薰—) be comfortably warm; nice and warm; 《인정이》 (be) warm-hearted; kindhearted. ¶ 훈훈한 마음 a 「warm 〔kindly〕 heart / 훈훈해지다 get 〔grow〕 warm(er) / 방이 ～ the room is comfortably warm / 봄햇살이 ～ I feel comfortably warm in the spring sun.

**훌닦다** 《몹시 나무라다》 nag 〔snarl〕 《at》; berate; abuse 〔criticize, rebuke〕 《*a person*》 severely; call 〔take〕 《*a person*》 to task. ¶ 훌닦아 세우다 give 《*a person*》 snuff.

**훌닦이다** get 「nagged 〔picked on, berated, fussed at〕.

**훌떡** ① 《벗어진 또는 뒤집히는 모양》 all quite; utterly; completely. ¶ ～ 뒤집힌 우산 an umbrella blown inside out 《by the wind》 / 신을 ～ 벗다 slip off *one's* shoes / 옷을 ～ 벗다 strip *oneself* of all *one's* clothes; strip *oneself* 「bare 〔stark-naked〕 / ～ 벗어지다 become bald all over; 《이마가》 be bald as a coot. ② 《뛰어넘는 모양》 at a 「bound 〔jump〕; lightly (and nimbly); quickly. ¶ 울타리를 ～ 뛰어넘다 jump clean over the fence.

**훌떡거리다** be apt to slip out; 《*one's* shoes》 slip all the time.

**훌떡훌떡** loosely; slipperily. ¶ 신이 ～ 벗어지다 *one's* shoes keep slipping all the time.

**훌라댄서** a hula dancer.

**훌라댄스** hula(-hula). ¶ ～를 추다 dance 「the hula.

**훌라후프** a hula hoop; hula-hooping.

**훌렁** ⇨ 훌랑.

**훌렁거리다** slip in and out loosely; fit in loosely; be loose. ¶ 옷이 훌렁거린다 The clothes hang loose on me.

**훌렁이질** 《쑤셔댐》 hand-threshing back and forth; 《훑음》 shucking back and forth; 《문지름》 scrubbing the inside of an object clean; 《드나듦》 letting in and out. ～치다 《쑤심》 keep hand-threshing back and forth; 《훑음》 keep shucking; keep removing (what is on the outside of an object); 《문지름》 keep scrubbing the inside of an object clean; 《드나듦》 keep letting 《*someone, something*》 in and out.

**훌륭하다** ① 《멋지다》 (be) nice; fine; handsome; excellent; splendid; superb; magnificent; grand; 《당당하다》 (be) stately; imposing; commanding. ¶ 훌륭히 finely; nicely; excellently; superbly; splendidly; brilliantly; magnificently / 훌륭한 번역 an excellent translation / 훌륭한 선물 a 「handsome 〔nice〕 present 〔gift〕 / 훌륭한 솜씨 great 〔remarkable, wonderful〕 skill / 훌륭한 저택 a 「magnificent 〔fine〕 mansion / 훌륭한 풍채 commanding presence; imposing appearance / 훌륭히 성공하다 achieve brilliant success / 훌륭히 해내다 come off with 「flying colors 〔with colors flying〕.
② 《존경할 만하다》 (be) honorable; respectable; 《값 있다》 (be) worthy; 《떳떳하다》 (be) decent; presentable; commendable. ¶ 훌륭히 respectably; decently / 훌륭한 뜻 an honorable intention / 훌륭한 목적〔업적〕 a 「worthy end 〔achievement〕 / 훌륭한 인물 a respectable person / 훌륭한 직업 a respectable occupation / 훌륭한 일생을 보내다 lead a 「worthy 〔reputable〕 life / 훌륭히 생활하다 make a decent living / 어떤 일이든 훌륭히 해내다 be quite equal to anything / 그는 어디에 내놓아도 훌륭한 청년이다 He is a very presentable young man.
③ 《칭찬할 만하다》 (be) admirable; praiseworthy; creditable; commendable. ¶ 훌륭히 admirably; creditably / 훌륭한 저작 admirable writing / 훌륭한 행동 a commendable act / 훌륭히 해내다 acquit 「*oneself* creditably 〔to *one's* credit〕 / 그가 자신의 잘못을 인정했다는 것은 훌륭한 일이다 It is to his credit that he has acknowledged his error.
④ 《고상하다》 (be) noble; lofty; high. ¶ 훌륭한 목적 a noble 「end 〔aim〕 / 훌륭한 생각 a lofty idea / 훌륭한 정신 a noble spirit / 훌륭한 인격의 사람 a person of good character / 자네의 동기는 훌륭한 것이다 You have acted from high motives.
⑤ 《위대하다》 (be) great; prominent;

eminent. ¶ 훌륭한 학자 an eminent 〔a great〕 scholar / 훌륭해지다 become great 〔prominent〕; attain greatness; 《출세하다》 get on in life; rise in the world / 이 아이는 훌륭한 사람이 될 게다 This child will do well 〔get on in life〕.
⑥ 《공명 정대하다》 (be) fair; square; honest. ¶ 훌륭한 승부 fair play / 훌륭히 fairly; squarely / 훌륭한 조치 a square deal / 훌륭히 싸우다 fight 〔play〕 fair / 훌륭히 이기다 win a fair victory. ⑦ 《충분하다》 (be) sufficient; good enough; justifiable; worthy. ¶ 훌륭한 증거 sufficient evidence / 이 집은 내가 살기에 ~ This house is good enough for me to live in.

**훌부드르르하다, 훌부들하다** (be) nice and soft; [서술적] be agreeable to the touch; feel soft.

**훌부시다** ① 《씻다》 rinse out; wash clean; wash off 〔out〕 well. ¶ 병을 ~ rinse out a bottle. ② 《먹다》 eat up; eat 《*a thing*》 clean; clean 《the board》.

**훌뿌리다** shake off 《*a person*》 with contempt; refuse 《*a person's* request》 point-blank; give a flat denial.

**훌쩍** ① 《날음·뜀》 with a jump 〔bound〕; suddenly; swiftly; nimbly. ¶ 말에〔에서〕 ~ 올라타다〔내리다〕 swing into 〔down〕 the saddle; spring on 〔off〕 the horse / 새가 ~ 날아가다 a bird suddenly flies 〔wings〕 off / 개천을 ~ 건너 뛰다 leap over a ditch with a jump. ② 《코를》 sniffling; snivelling. ¶ 코를 ~ 들이마시다 sniffle; snivel. ③ 《울다》 weeping and sniffling away. ¶ ~훌쩍 울다 weep and sniffle away. ④ 《들이마시다》 sipping; supping; slurping; at a gulp. ¶ 국을 ~ 들이마시다 slurp up 〔gulp down〕 soup. ⑤ 《떠나다》 aimlessly. ¶ 그는 ~ 집을 떠났다 He left home 「aimlessly 〔like a wind〕.

**훌쩍거리다** ① 《액체를》 sip 《hot coffee》; slurp 《*one's* soup》; suck in 《*one's* noodles》. ¶ 그는 훌쩍거리면서 커피를 마셨다 He drank his coffee with a sip. / 수프를 훌쩍거리면서 먹지 마라 Don't slurp your soup! ② 《콧물을》 snivel 〔sniff〕 repeatedly. ¶ 시끄럽게 코를 ~ sniff noisily. ③ 《울다》 sob; weep silently. ¶ 그녀는 훌쩍거리며 대답했다 She answered with a sob.

**훌쭉하다** ⇨ 홀쭉하다. ¶ 볼이 ~ have hollow cheeks / 훌쭉해지다 lose much flesh; grow very thin.

**훨훨** ① 《불타다》 in flames. ¶ (장작이) ~ 타다 《firewood》 go up in flames. ② 《뛰다》 with leaps and bounds. ¶ 사슴이 ~ 재를 넘어가다 a deer leaps and bounds over a hill. ③ 《날다》 flying; fluttering. ¶ 새가 ~ 날아가다 A bird flutters away. ④ 《던지다》 hurling 〔throwing〕 with ease. ¶ 짐짝을 ~ 던지다 hurl baggages with ease. ⑤ 《벗어 부치다》 slipping off 《*one's* clothes》. ¶ 옷을 ~ 벗다 slip off *one's* clothes. ⑥ 《떨어버리다》 dusting actively. ¶ 옷의 먼지를 ~ 털다 shake dust off *one's* clothes.

**훨훨하다** (be) soft; watery; washy; thin; weak; wishy-washy.

**훑다** ① 《벼·삼 따위》 thresh; hackle; strip. ¶ 벼를 ~ thresh rice / 버들잎을 ~ strip off the leaves of a willow. ② 《겉을》 remove (what is on the outside of an object). ¶ 버들가지의 껍질을 ~ scrub away the bark of willow twig. ③ 《속을》 scrub out; remove (what is on the inside of an object). ¶ 오징어 속을 훑어내다 clean 〔remove the entrails of〕 a squid. ④ ＝훑어보다.

**훑어보다** ① 《사람을》 give a searching glance 《at》; look 《*a person*》 up and down; scrutinize; 《*a person's* face》. ¶ 아무를 위아래로 ~ stare *a person* up and down; survey *a person* from head to foot. ② 《죽 살피다》 look 「over 〔through〕 《the page》; pass an eye over 《the manuscript》; scan 《a newspaper》. ¶ 서류를 대충 ~ 「read hastily 〔go〕 through the document / 편지를 대강 ~ glance over a letter; skim through a letter.

**훑이** a tool for threshing 〔stripping, shucking〕.

**훑이다** ① 《벼 따위가》 get threshed 〔hackled, stripped, shucked〕. ¶ 벼가 잘 훑이지 않다 the rice is hard to thresh. ② 《물건 겉이》 get removed; get scrubbed off. ③ 《물건 속이》 get removed; get scrubbed out. ④ 《줄다》 contract; shrink; shrivel. ¶ 설사로 몸이 ~ get thin after a siege of diarrhea.

**훔쳐내다** 《닦아내다》 mop 〔wipe〕 up 《a soil, water》; wipe 〔swab〕 off 《the dust》; 《도둑질》 steal; pilfer; purloin; 《더듬다》 fumble 《for, after》; grope 《for》. ¶ 먼지를 ~ wipe off the dust / 걸레로 물을 훔쳐내라 Wipe up the water with a cloth.

**훔쳐때리다** beat up; thrash; wallop; 〔lick.

**훔쳐먹다** 《먹다》 eat by stealth; 《훔치다》 embezzle (착복하다); steal; swipe 《구어》. ¶ 회사돈을 ~ embezzle the money of a firm.

**훔쳐보다** steal a glance 《at》; look 〔glance〕 furtively 《at》; cast 〔throw〕 a furtive 〔surreptitious〕 glance 《at》. ¶ 얼굴을 슬쩍 ~ steal a glance at 《*a person's*》 face / 그는 옆에 앉은 학생의 답안지를 훔쳐보았다 He looked furtively at the answer sheet of the student sitting next to him.

**훔치개질** 《도둑질》 swiping; stealing; larceny; 《닦음질》 wiping. ~하다 steal; pilfer; sneak; snitch 《구어》; swipe; 《닦음질하다》 wipe (off).

**훔치다** ① steal 《*a thing* from *a person*》; rob 《*a person* of *a thing*》; pilfer 《*a thing* from a shop》; lift; plagiarize; snatch; rustle.

> **용법** **steal** 「훔치다」라는 뜻의 가장 일반적인 말로, 「몰래 훔치다」의 뜻. **rob** 「강탈하다」「빼앗다」의 뜻으로 폭력이나 협박, 사기 행위에 의하여 훔친다는 뜻. **pilfer** 「좀도둑질하다」의 뜻. **lift** 《구어》 「남의 물건을 슬그머니 후므리다」의 뜻. **plagiarize** 남의 문장이나 작품 따위를 「도용하다」「표절하다」의 뜻. **snatch** 남이 가지고 있는 물건을 「낚아채다」「후려채다」의 뜻. **rustle** 《미구어》 방목하는 가축이나 말을 「훔치다」의 뜻.

¶ 훔친 물건 stolen goods / …을 훔쳐 달아나다 run away 〔make off〕 with…; walk off 〔away〕 with… / 상점의 물건을 ~ lift articles in a store / 그는 노인의 돈을 훔쳤다 He stole money from an old man. *or* He robbed an old man of his money. / 남의 아이디어를 훔치는 것은 좋지 않다 It's not good to steal someone else's ideas. / 누군가 내 만년필을 훔쳤어 Somebody has swiped my fountain pen. / 간밤에 도둑이 들어서 돈을 훔쳐 갔다 A thief stole into my house last night, and took away some money.
② 《닦다》 wipe; mop (up); swab. ¶ 걸레로 ~ wipe 《the floor》 with a cloth / 행주로 ~ dry 《a dish》 with a cloth / 엎지른 물을 ~ mop up spilt water.
③ 《더듬다》 fumble 《for》; grope 《for》.
④ 《때리다》 beat up; thrash; slap.

**훔켜잡다** grasp 〔grab, seize, catch, snatch〕 firmly; hold on to; lay a tight hold of. ⇨ 움켜잡다.

**훔훔하다** wear a look of satisfaction.

**훗날**(後—) the future; another day. ⇨ 뒷날. ¶ ~에 in (the) future; later (on); some (other) day / ~에 화근을 남기다 leave evils to spring up in the future; sow seed of trouble for the future.

**훗달**(後—) next 〔the following〕 month.

**훗배앓이**(後—) complications following childbirth; afterpains.

**훗보름**(後—) the latter half of a month.

**훗훗하다** (be) uncomfortably warm; very warm 〔hot〕.

**훙서**(薨逝) a royal death; demise. ~하다 《a king, a prince》 die; pass away.

**훤칠하다** (be) strapping; tall and slender; [서술적] be high in stature. ¶ 그는 ~ He is slim and tall.

**훤하다** ① 《탁 트이다》 (be) wide; open; extensive. ¶ 훤히 트인 broad and wide / 훤히 트인 전망 an open view.
② 《흐리게 밝다》 (be) dimly white; light. ¶ 훤한 하늘 a light sky; a dawning sky / 훤해지다 lighten; grow 〔get〕 light; light up / 훤하게 동이 튼다 The dawn begins to whiten the sky.
③ 《얼굴이》 (be) good looking; fair; handsome. ¶ 얼굴이 훤하게 생기다 have a nice fair face.
④ 《정통하다》 be familiar 《with》; be well versed 《in》; be conversant 《with》; be well acquainted 《with》; be well up 《in》. ¶ 광산업에 훤한 사람 a mining expert / 법률에 ~ be learned in the law / 업무에 ~ be well versed in *one's* business 〔work〕.

**훨씬** 《정도》 much 《bigger》; by far; far (and) away; very much; a great deal; considerably. ¶ ~ 좋은 물건 a much 〔far〕 better article / ~ 저쪽에 in the distance; far ahead / ~ 이전에 a long time ago / 그보다 ~ 전에 long 〔a long time〕 before that / ~ 뒤에 와서 long afterward(s) / 무엇보다도 ~ 뛰어나다 be far and away 〔by far〕 the best of all / 이것이 저것보다 ~ 크다 This is lots 〔far〕 bigger than that. / 이 편이 ~ 좋다 This is far 〔much〕 better. *or* This is far and away 〔out and out〕 the best. / 그녀는 언니보다 ~ 미인이다 She is far more beautiful than her elder sister.

**훨쩍** 《훨찐》 widely; broadly; far apart; 《시원스레》 very; exceedingly (wide). ¶ 문을 ~ 열어 놓다 leave the door wide open / 어깨가 ~ 벌어지다 have broad shoulders / ~ 넓다 be very wide.

**훨훨** ①《불이 타는 모양》in great flames; with a bright flame. ¶ (불이) ∼ 타오르다 burst into flames; go up in flames; flare up. ②《부채질하는 모양》(fanning) briskly; vigorously. ¶ ∼ 부채질하다 fan *oneself* briskly. ③《옷을 벗는 모양》doffing briskly. ¶ 옷을 ∼ 벗다 take off *one's* clothes briskly; whip off *one's* clothes. ④《날아가는 모양》flying with great flaps of wings.

**훼방**(毁謗) ①《비방》slander; calumny; defamation; vilification. ∼하다 slander; defame; vilify; backbite; speak ill of. ②《방해》interference; interruption; obstruction. ∼하다 disturb; interfere《with》; interrupt; thwart. ¶ 작업을 ∼놓다 hinder《*a person*》in *his* work; interfere with《*a person's*》work.

**훼살** interferences; obstruction. ∼하다 interfere; obstruct; throw an obstacle in《*a person's*》path.

**훼손**(毁損)《명예》defamation (of character); libel (문서에 의한); slander (구두에 의한);《사물》damage; injury. ∼하다 defame; damage; injure; impair; spoil; mutilate. ¶ 태풍에 의한 ∼ damage caused by a typhoon / 발행자를 명예∼으로 고발하다 accuse a publisher of libel / 새 고속도로가 그 지방(경관)을 ∼시켰다 The countryside has been spoiled by the new freeway. ◉ ∼본(本) a damaged book.

**휑뎅그렁하다** ⇨ 횅댕그렁하다.

**휑하다** ⇨ 횅하다.

**휘**(諱)《죽은 이의 이름》a posthumous designation〔name, title〕.

**휘** ①《바람 소리》whistling; with a puff〔whiff〕. ¶ 바람이 휘 불다 A wind blows and puffs / 바람이 솔밭을 휘 불고 지나가다 The wind whistles through the pine trees. ②《숨소리》sighing; with a sigh. ¶ 휘 한숨을 쉬다 heave a sigh / 휘 숨을 내쉬다 let out a long breath.

**휘갈기다**《채찍 등을》whip〔lash〕《*a person*》; trail *one's* whip《across the horse》;《글씨를》write hastily; scribble; scrawl. ¶ 두서너 줄 휘갈겨 쓰다 scrawl〔scribble〕a few lines《on a sheet of paper》.

**휘감기다** ①《휘말리다》get wound (round); coil〔wind, twine〕*itself* round. ¶ 담쟁이에 휘감긴 나무 a tree entwined with an ivy / 컨베이어 벨트에 휘감겨 들어가다 be「caught by〔entangled in〕the conveyer belt of a machine. ②《휘둘리다》be distracted〔confused〕. ¶ 사람들 외치는 소리에 정신이 ∼ be confused by the shouts of people.

**휘감다** coil〔wind, twine〕around; fasten〔tie〕round. ¶ 뱀이 사람을 ∼ a snake winds itself round a person / 기둥에 밧줄을 둘둘 ∼ round〔wind〕a rope around a pillar. / 부러진 다리에 붕대를 ∼ bandage〔bind〕up a broken leg.

**휘갑치다** ①《뒷일 없게》settle〔dispose of〕《*a matter*》; fix《up》; finish; wind〔clear〕up. ¶ 일을 ∼ settle a matter; get a matter settled / 집안 일을 ∼ clear up *one's* household affairs. ②《가장자리가 풀리지 않게》hem (up); border; stitch up. ¶ 멍석 가장자리를 ∼ hem the edges of a straw mat.

**휘날리다**《바람에》flap; fly; wave〔stream〕(in the wind); flutter;《이름이》《*one's* name》resound; become famous〔reknown, well-known〕. ¶ 바람에 ∼ flutter〔wave, fly〕in the wind / 바람에 휘날리는 깃발 a flag streaming in the wind / 명성을 천하에 ∼ make a noise in the world; win〔enjoy〕a worldwide reputation.

**휘늘어지다**《가지 따위가》hang down; droop;《처지다》hang; dangle. ¶ 허리까지 휘늘어진 검은 머리 black hair falling〔cascading〕down to *one's* waist / 가지가 휘늘어진 버들 a drooping〔weeping〕willow.

**휘다** ①《휘어지다》bend; be〔get〕bent; curve; swerve;《뒤둥그러져》warp; be warped;《압력으로》yield; give. ¶ 가지가 휘도록 열매가 달린 with branches heavily laden with fruit / 나이를 먹어 허리가 ∼ be bowed with years; be bent with age / 마룻바닥이 피아노 무게로 ∼ The floor gives (in) under the weight of the piano. / 볕을 받아 판자널이 휘어졌다 The sun has warped the boards. ②《휘게 하다》bend〔curve, crook〕《*a thing*》. ¶ 철근을 ∼ bend〔curve〕a steel bar. ③《휘어잡다》bend《*a person*》to *one's* will; force《*a person*》to give in; control《*a person*》.

**휘도**(輝度)〖물리〗brightness.

**휘돌다**《it》whirl; turn; spin; rotate; revolve; race〔speed, tear, rush, fly〕around. ¶ 곶을 ∼ go round a cape.

**휘돌리다** whirl〔rotate, turn, spin, revolve〕《*a thing*》.

**휘동광**(輝銅鑛)〖광물〗chalcocite; copper glance; vitreous copper.

**휘두르다** ① 《손에 쥐고》 whirl 〔swing〕 《*a thing*》 around; brandish; flourish; wield; wave (about); throw about; 《과시하다》 display; show off; 《남용하다》 abuse 《*one's* authority》. ¶ 권력을 ~ exercise 〔exert, wield〕 *one's* authority 〔power〕 《over》 / 팔을 ~ throw *one's* arms about / 단도를 ~ brandish a dagger / 단장을 ~ swish a cane 〔*one's* stick〕 / 팔을 붙잡고 ~ swing 《*a person*》 round holding him by the arms / 주먹을 휘두르며 을러대다 shake *one's* fist 《at *a person,* in *a person's* face》 / 헛 ~ 〖야구〗 swing at the ball and miss; fan 〔strike at〕 the air; swing wide / 붓을 ~ wield *one's* (writing) brush 〔pen〕. ② 《얼을 빼다》 confuse; bewilder. ③ 《제 뜻대로》 make a puppet 《of *a person*》; have 《*a person*》 under perfect control. ¶ 아무한테 휘둘리다 be swayed by *a person;* be wrapped around *a person's* finger; be at *one's* beck and call / 그는 아내한테 휘둘려 지낸다 He is under apron strings.

**휘둥그래지다** open 《*one's* eyes》 wide; be surprised 〔be startled〕 《at》. ¶ 눈이 휘둥그레져서 with *one's* eyes wide open; with saucer eyes / (놀라서) 눈이 ~ goggle *one's* eyes; *one's* eyes grow round.

**휘둥그렇다** 《눈이》 be wide-eyed 《with 「surprise》.

**휘뚜루** for various uses; in various ways; for general 〔all〕 purposes. ¶ ~ 쓰이다 have various 〔many〕 uses; be used 〔serviceable〕「in various ways 〔for various purposes〕.

**휘뚝거리다** ① 《사물이》 totter; wobble; shake; be unsteady. ¶ 뾰족 구두를 신고 ~ totter on high-heels / 책상다리가 ~ the legs of the table are wobbling 〔wobbly〕. ② 《마음이》 feel nervous 〔jittery〕; be worried 〔upset〕.

**휘뚝휘뚝** tottering; wobbling; unsteadily. ¶ 뾰족 구두를 신고 ~ 걷다 totter along on high heels / 사다리가 ~ 넘어갈 것 같다 the ladder is wobbly and may fall at any moment.

**휘뚤휘뚤** windingly; meanderingly. ~하다 (be) winding; meandering; serpentine. ¶ 길이 ~하다 The road is winding.

**휘말다** ① 《적셔서 더럽히다》 make wet and dirty; spoil. ¶ 옷을 ~ get *one's* clothes wet and dirty. ② 《마구 휘감다》 wind around carelessly.

**휘말리다** be rolled 〔wrapped, engulfed〕 《in》; be dragged 《into》; be caught 《in a machine》; be involved 〔entangled〕 《in a war》; get mixed up 《in a trouble》. ¶ 권력 싸움에 ~ be caught up in a power struggle / 전쟁에 ~ be involved in a war; be drawn 〔dragged〕 into a war / 전쟁에 휘말리지 않도록 하다 keep 〔stay〕 out of a war.

**휘몰다** ① 《말·차 따위를》 drive hard; urge on; hasten; hurry. ¶ 말을 ~ urge on a horse / 차를 ~ drive a car fast; step on the gas / 자동차를 휘몰아 현장으로 급행하다 rush 〔hasten〕 to the scene in a car. ② 《가축·사냥감 등을》 drive; chase 《a fox》; round up; run 《a hare》 (down); rattle 《foxes》. ¶ 가축을 휘몰아 들이다 drive in cattle. ③ 《억지로 …하게 하다》 drive 〔press〕 hard; urge on; spur on. ¶ 국민을〔나라를〕 전쟁으로 ~「drive the people 〔urge the nation〕 to war.

**휘몰아치다** 《바람이》 blow violently 〔boisterously〕; blow hard (and strong); sweep over 〔along〕; 《눈이》 fall in whirls; fall thick and fast. ¶ 휘몰아치는 비바람을 무릅쓰고 그는 출발했다 He set out in spite of a violent wind and rain. / 그 일대는 온종일 강풍이 휘몰아쳤다 The strong wind swept over the region all day long.

**휘몰이** ① 《말·차 따위의》 driving hard; urging on; hastening; hurrying. ② 《가축·사냥감 등의》 chasing 《into *a place*》; rounding up; running; driving. ~하다 chase 《into *a place*》; round up; run; drive. ¶ 물고기를 ~하다 run fish. ◉ ~판 the scene 〔occasion〕 of chasing; a roundup.

**휘묻이** layering; a layer. ~하다 lay; layer 《a tree》.

**휘발**(揮發) volatilization. ~하다 volatilize. ◉ ~기(器) a carburetter; a vaporizer. ~물 a volatile substance 〔matter〕. ~성 volatility: ~성의 volatile / ~성 니스 spirit varnish / ~성 용제(溶劑) a volatile solvent.

**휘발유**(揮發油) volatile oil(s); benzine; naphtha; gasoline; gas 《구어》. ¶ 가짜 ~ adulterated 〔fake, false〕 gasoline.

**휘보**(彙報) 《보고집》 an itemized collection of reports; 《잡지 따위》 a bulletin; a magazine.

**휘석**(輝石) 〖광물〗 pyroxene; augite.

**휘선**(輝線) 〖물리〗 a bright line (of a gaseous element in spectrum). ◉ ~스펙트럼 a line spectrum.

**휘슬** a whistle. ¶ ～을 불다 blow a whistle.

**휘안광**(輝安鑛) 『광물』 stibnite; antimony glance.

**휘암**(輝岩) 『광물』 pyroxenite.

**휘어넘어가다** fall for another's wiles 〔words〕; be taken in by 《*a person's*》 honeyed words; play into the hands of 《*someone*》.

**휘어대다** force 〔squeeze, push〕 in.

**휘어들다** get forced 〔squeezed, pushed〕 in.

**휘어박다** ① 《넘어뜨리다》 bring down; throw down. ② 《굴복시키다》 bring 《*a person*》 to *his* knees; break 《*a person's*》 will; force 《*a person*》 to give in.

**휘어박히다** ① 《넘어지다》 get brought down; be thrown down. ② 《굴복하다》 yield; give in; submit; surrender; bow to; succumb to.

**휘어잡다** ① 《손에》 hold 《*a thing*》 supple 〔bent, doubled up〕 in *one's* hand; grasp. ¶ 버들가지를 ～ hold willow branches in *one's* hand. ② 《사람을》 have 《*a person*》 under *one's* control 〔in *one's* grasp〕; keep 《*a person*》 under control; keep a firm grip 《on *a person*》; get 《*a person*》 under *one's* thumb; lead 《*a person*》 by the nose. ¶ 휘어잡을 수가 없다 have no check over 《*a person*》; have little control 〔weight〕; be beyond *one's* control.

**휘어지다** get bent; be crooked; be curved; bend; curve; warp. ¶ 철사가 ～ a wire gets bent 〔bends〕 / 판자가 ～ a board warps.

**휘영청** 《shine》 bright(ly). ¶ 달이 ～ 밝다 The moon beams down.

**휘우듬하다** (be) slightly bent 〔curved〕.

**휘우뚱** off balance. ～하다 lose *one's* balance. ¶ ～ 넘어가다 be thrown off balance.

**휘은광**(輝銀鑛) 『광물』 argentite; silver glance.

**휘장**(揮帳) a curtain; a curtain screen; a hanging; hangings.

**휘장**(徽章) a badge (모표·회원 표지 등); an emblem (표상); (an) insignia (소매·깃의); an ensign; a mark. ¶ ～을 달다 put on insignia / ～을 달고 있다 wear 〔put on〕 a badge.

**휘적거리다** swing 《*one's* arms》. ¶ 팔을 휘적거리며 걷다 walk with a swagger.

**휘적휘적** swinging *one's* arms. ¶ ～걷다 swagger.

**휘젓다** ① 《뒤섞다》 stir 〔mix〕 (up); whip 《eggs》; give 《the porridge》 a stir; churn 《milk》; beat up 《cream》. ¶ 커피에 설탕을 넣어 ～ stir sugar into *one's* coffee / 달걀을 잘 휘저어야 한다 You must beat 〔whip〕 up an egg. ② 《찾느라고》 ransack; rummage 〔rout〕 《in a drawer》. ¶ 서랍속을 ～ ransack 〔rummage in〕 a drawer. ③ 《팔을》 swing 《*one's* arms》. ¶ 팔을 휘저으며 걷다 walk swinging *one's* arms. ④ 《어지럽게》 upset; disarrange; disturb. ¶ 아무의 마음을 ～ disturb *a person's* mind; upset *a person*. ⑤ 《마음대로 하다》 throw 《the company's affair》 into confusion.

**휘정거리다** stir up 《the sediments in water》; make 《water》 muddy 〔turbid〕; muddy 《a well》; muddle.

**휘주근하다** ① ＝후줄근하다. ② 《몹시 지쳐》 (be) tired out; dead tired; [서술적] droop; be limp with exhaustion; be worn out; be all in 《미구어》. ¶ 피로로 몸이 ～ be tired out; droop with fatigue.

**휘지다** get worn out; be exhausted.

**휘지르다** soil 〔spoil〕 《clothes》. ¶ 바지를 온통 휘질렀다 I have got my pants all dirty.

**휘지비지**(諱之祕之) ⇨ 흐지부지.

**휘집**(彙集) collection; assortment. ～하다 collect; assort.

**휘철광**(輝鐵鑛) 『광물』 specular iron ore.

**휘청거리다** 《휘어지다》 yield; give; flex; bend; 《낭창거리다》 be flexible 〔pliant, resilient〕; sway gently; 《발걸음 등이》 be unsteady; totter; stagger; reel; falter (경영 등의). ¶ 휘청거리는 낚싯대 a whippy fish pole / 휘청거리는 회사 a faltering firm / 회초리가 ～ a whip is flexible / 강타를 얻어맞고 ～ reel under a heavy blow.

**휘청휘청** 《휘어져 흔들리는 모양》 yielding; flexibly; pliantly; resiliently; 《몸을 가누지 못하는 모양》 tottering; staggering; reeling.

**휘추리** a twig; a sprig; a spray.

**휘파람** a whistle; 《여자의 주의를 끌려는》 a wolf whistle. ¶ ～을 불다 whistle; give a whistle; whistle on with fingers (손가락을 넣어서) / ～을 불어 알리다 whistle by way of a signal / …을 ～으로 부르다 whistle for 《a taxi》.

**휘필**(揮筆) ＝휘호(揮毫).

**휘하**(麾下) (troops) under *one's* command. ¶ ～의 under *one's* command; under the banner 《of》 / ～에 모이다 rally round 《*a person*》; join 〔follow〕 the banner 《of》; enlist in the banner 《of》.

**휘하다**(諱―) shun; avoid the use of;

put a taboo on. ¶ 임금의 이름을 ~ avoid「using〔mentioning〕a king's name.

**휘호**(揮毫)《글씨》(hand)writing;《그림》painting; drawing《a picture》; "wielding a brush". ~하다 write; draw; paint; wield a brush. ¶ ~를 부탁하다 ask for a specimen of《*a person's*》handwriting. ◉ ~료「a fee〔an honorarium〕for a「writing〔painting〕.

**휘황찬란**(輝煌燦爛) ~하다《눈부시다》(be) resplendent; brilliant; iridescent. ¶ 거리는 네온 사인으로 ~했다 The street was blazing with (varicolored) neon signs. / 객실에는 등불이 ~했다 The drawing room was brilliantly lighted.

**휘휘** round and round (about); in circles. ¶ ~ 감다 wind《a rope》round《*a thing*》/ 실을 ~ 감다 wind threads on a reel round and round / 단장을 ~ 휘두르다 brandish〔wield〕*one's* stick.

**휘휘하다** (be) dreary; desolate; forlorn. ¶ 혼자 가기에는 ~ be too desolate to go alone.

**휙** ①《돌아가는 모양》with a swerve; with a jerk; with a whirl;《갑자기》suddenly;《빨리》quickly; speedily; fast. ¶ 휙 뒤돌아 보다 turn right round; look round / 휙 열리다 fling〔throw〕open / 시곗바늘을 휙 돌리다 whirl the clock hands around. ②《바람 등이》with a whiff; in a gust. ¶ 바람이 휙 불다 have a gust of wind / 화살이 휙 날아갔다 An arrow whizzed past. ③《던지는 모양》light and nimbly. ¶ 사자를 향해서 창을 휙 던지다 dart a spear at the lion.

**휠체어** a wheel chair.

**휩싸다** ①《휘둘러 싸다》wrap《up, in》; lap《in》; tuck up《in》. ¶ 아기를 담요로 ~ wrap a baby in a blanket / 종이〔거적대기〕로 ~ wrap〔roll〕《*a thing*》up in「paper〔a mat〕/ 망토로 몸을 ~「wrap *oneself*〔be wrapped〕up in a cloak. ②《비호하다》protect; shield; take《*a person*》under *one's* wing. ③《덮어 가리다》cover《with》; mantle《in》; envelop《in》; veil《in》; shroud《in》.

**휩싸이다** ①《둘러싸이다》be bundled〔swaddled〕《in》; get〔be〕wrapped up《in》; tuck *oneself* up《in》. ¶ 담요에 ~「be wrapped〔tuck *oneself*〕up in a blanket; envelop〔roll〕*oneself* in a rug. ②《덮여 가려지다》get〔be〕covered〔mantled, enveloped, veiled, shrouded〕《in》. ¶ 안개에 휩싸인 탑 a tower enveloped in mist / 불길에 ~ be enveloped in flames / 신비에 ~ be shrouded in mystery; be wrapped in a shroud of mystery.

**휩쓸다** ①《모조리》sweep away〔up, off, over〕; carry everything before *one;*《화재 등이》make a clean sweep《of》;《풍미하다》overwhelm; sway; sweep. ¶ 승리를 ~ walk〔go〕away with all the victories of the games; win a sweeping victory《over》/ 판돈을 ~「sweep away〔rake up〕the money on the gambling table / 유럽 전토를 ~ sweep over the whole of Europe / 인기를 ~ win sweeping popularity; monopolize popularity / 홍수가 온 들판을 휩쓸었다 The flood swept the field away. ②《설치다》overrun; rampage. ¶ 부랑배가 시내를 휩쓸고 다니다 hoodlums tear the town up.

**휩쓸리다** ①《모조리》be swept《away, up, off, over》. ¶ 공황에 ~ be seized with a panic / 군중에 ~ be swept along in the crowd / 물결에 ~ be「swept away〔swallowed up〕by the waves / 전쟁에 ~ be involved in a war; be「dragged〔drawn〕into a war. ②《설치는 힘에》be overrun; suffer a rampage.

**휴가**(休暇) a holiday; holidays; a vacation; time off; (a) leave (of absence);《미국 대학의》a《summer》recess;《군인 등의》(a) furlough. ★ 보통 holidays는 a vacation과 같으나《미》에서는 vacation을 많이 씀.《영》에서는 초등·중학교의 휴가에는 holidays를, vacation은 대학 등에 씀. leave는 공무원·군인의 휴가.

¶ ~ 때에 in vacation time / ~중이다 be on leave / ~기한을 넘기다 outstay *one's* leave (of absence).

휴가로: ~로 여행 중이다 be away on「vacation〔holiday(s)〕/ ~로 해변에 가 있다 be「vacationing〔holidaying《영》〕at the seaside.

휴가를: ~를 얻다 take a vacation; get〔obtain, secure〕a leave of absence; have a furlough; take *one's* day off《미》; take a holiday / 사흘 ~를 얻다 take〔have〕three days off; take a three days' vacation; have〔get〕a three days' furlough / ~를 주다 grant《*a person*》a leave of「absence〔furlough〕; give《*a person*》some days off / ~를 보내다 spend *one's* holiday〔leave〕《in the country》/ ~를 마치고

돌아오다 come back from holiday / 일주간의 ～를 얻어 귀향하다 go home on a week's leave.

¶ 내일부터 ～다 Our vacation begins tomorrow. / 그는 ～중이라 없다 He is away on his vacation. / 그는 ～로 고향에 내려가 있다 He is at home on vacation. / 일주일의 ～를 주십시오 I should [would] like to get a week's leave. / 언제 여름 ～가 시작됩니까 When are you to break up for the summer? / ～에는 어디로 가십니까 Where are you going 「for your holidays [to spend your vacation]? / 그는 ～로 어디론가 가고 없었다 I found him away on vacation. / ～동안 즐겁게 보냈다 I have had a pleasant holiday.

◉ ～여행 a holiday trip; a vacation tour [trip] 《미》. ～원(願) 《ask for》 a leave of absence; a leave application. 겨울[여름]～ the winter [summer] vacation [holidays]. 특별～ a special leave: 일 년 동안의 특별～를 받다 be given a special one-year leave.

**휴간**(休刊) suspension [discontinuation] of publication. ～하다 suspend [discontinue] publication; stop issuing 《a newspaper》. ¶ 연중 무～이다 be issued all the year round; be issued daily throughout the year / 내일은 ～입니다 There will be no issue of the paper tomorrow.

◉ ～일 《신문의》 a 'no-issue' day.

**휴강**(休講) ～하다 cancel *one's* lecture(s) [class(es)]; do not attend school; cannot meet *one's* class. ¶ 김(金)교수 오늘 ～《게시》 Prof. Kim's lectures [classes] for today are canceled. *or* No class (today)—Prof. Kim.

**휴게**(休憩) (a) rest; a (rest) break; (a) recess; 《막간》 an intermission; 《영》 an interval. ～하다 rest; take a rest [recess, break]. ¶ 일을 중지하고 ～시간을 가지다 rest [take a rest] from (*one's*) work / (장거리 버스의) ～ 시간을 갖기 위한 정차 a rest stop. ◉ ～소 a resting place; 《극장 등의》 a lobby. ～시간 a recess; 《영화관 등의》 an intermission; 《영》 interval. ～실 a resting room; 《호텔 따위의》 a lounge; 《극장의》 a *foyer* (F.).

**휴관**(休館) ～하다 《영화관 등이》 close 《the theater》; be closed 《for the day》. ¶ 금일 ～《게시》 Closed for today.

**휴교**(休校) temporary closure of a school. ～하다 close 《the school》 for the time being. ¶ 학교는 당분간 ～한다 School is closed 「for some while ahead [for the time being].

**휴대**(携帶) ～하다 carry (along with *one*); take [bring, have] 《*a thing*》 with *one*. ¶ ～용(의) portable 《radios》; hand 《cameras》; pocket 《dictionaries》 / ～용 무선기(無線機) a portable radiophone; a walkie-talkie; a walky=talky / ～용 스테레오 카세트 테이프 플레이어 a portable stereo cassette tape player / 무기를 ～하다 carry a weapon / 여행에 안내서를 ～하다 provide *oneself* with a guidebook to *one's* trip / 이 사전은 ～가 편리하다 This dictionary is easy [handy] to carry about. / 운전자는 면허증의 ～가 의무적이다 Any driver is required [obliged] to carry a driver's license with him.

◉ ～검전기(檢電器) a lineman's detector. ～식량 provisions; 《비상용》 emergency rations; 《군용의》 field [combat] rations. ～수화물 hand baggage [luggage 《영》]. ～연료 a gas cylinder; 《미》 《상표명》 Sterno; 《영》 solid camping fuel. ～전화[폰] a portable telephone; a cellular phone.

**휴대품**(携帶品) *one's* personal effects [belongings]; hand baggage [luggage 《영》]. ◉ ～보관소 a cloakroom 《영》; a checkroom 《미》; a parcels room. ～신고대 《공항의》 a declaration counter. ～유치창고 《공항의》 the dutiable goods custody area.

**휴등**(休燈) giving up the use of a lamp. ～하다 cease to use a lamp.

**휴머니스트** 《인간주의자》 a humanist; 《인도주의자》 a humanitarian.

**휴머니즘** humanism; humanitarianism.

**휴머니티** humanity; humaneness.

**휴면**(休眠) 〖생물〗 dormancy; quiescence. ¶ ～중의 〖식물〗 dormant; resting. ◉ ～기 a period of dormancy; a resting stage. ～아(芽)[포자] a dormant [resting] bud [spore].

**휴식**(休息) (a) rest; repose; a respite; relaxation; (a) recess (학교 등의 휴게 시간). ～하다 rest (*oneself*); take a rest [respite, breather]; repose; relax. ¶ 5분간(의) ～ a five minutes' recess / 잠깐 ～하다 rest a while; take a blow [short rest] / 충분히 ～하다 rest quite a long while; take a long [good] rest / 한 시간 ～하다 rest for an hour; have an hour's break [intermission].

◉ ～시간 a recess; a breathing time; a breather; a break: 우리 학교는 정오에 한 시간의 ～ 시간이 있다 Our school has an hour's recess at noon.

**휴양**(休養) (a) rest; repose; relaxation; recreation; recuperation (병후의); lay off《미속어》. ～하다 rest; take a rest; relax; enjoy *oneself;* repose; give *oneself* a respite;《병후에》recuperate. ¶ (병으로) 일 년간 ～하다 have a year's holiday to recruit《at》/ 낸시, 1주일간 집에서 (푹) ～해라 Take a week's rest at home, Nancy. ◉ ～생활《병후의》a life of recuperation. ～시설 vacation 〔rest and recreation〕 facilities; recuperation facilities (병후의). ～여행 a trip of recreation. ～지 a recreation center; a rest area.

**휴업**(休業)《점포 등의》closing down; suspension of「business 〔operations〕; closure;《회사·공장의》a shutdown. ～하다《점포 등이》be closed (to business); suspend「business 〔operations〕; close down《a plant》. ¶ 임시 ～(일)「a special 〔an extra〕 holiday;《게시》Temporarily closed. / ～중의 공장 an idle factory / 당일 은행은 ～이다 Banks are closed for the day. / 저 공장은 원료 부족으로 아직껏 ～하고 있다 The factory still remains idle owing to want of raw materials. / 개점 ～ 상태다 The door is opened, but practically no business is done within. / 금일～《게시》Closed for the day. *or* Closed today. / 당분간 ～합니다《게시》Closed until further notice. / 첫째, 셋째 일요일은 ～《게시》Not open on first and third Sundays. ◉ ～일 a (business) holiday;《은행의》a bank holiday.

**휴연**(休演) no performance. ～하다 suspend 〔cancel〕 the performance《of a play》;《배우가》「do not 〔fail to〕 appear (on the stage); do not perform 〔give a performance〕《that night》. ¶ 금일 ～《게시》Today's performance「cancelled 〔suspended〕.

**휴일**(休日) a holiday; a day off, a rest day. ¶ ～ 기분으로 in a holiday「mood 〔spirit, vein, atmosphere〕/ ～을 즐기는 사람 a holiday-maker; a holidayer / 매주 일 회 ～을 주다 give a day off every week / ～을 이용하여 여행하다 go away for a holiday; go vacationing / 해안에서 ～을 보내다 spend a holiday at (the) seaside; spend a seaside holiday / 우리는 멋진 ～을 보냈다 We had a splendid holiday.
◉ ～근무 holiday work. ～수당 non=duty allowance. ～여행 a holiday trip;《주말의》a weekend trip; a vacation trip《미》.

**휴장**(休場)《사람의》(an) absence (from the stage);《극장 등의》closure. ～하다 close 〔shut〕《a theater》(temporarily);《사람이》absent *oneself* from (the stage).

**휴전**(休電) suspension of power supply. ◉ ～일(日) a no-power day;《게시》No power supply day.

**휴전**(休戰) a cease-fire; truce; (a) suspension 〔cessation〕 of hostilities; an armistice (화평 교섭을 위하여). ～하다 stop fighting (temporarily); make a truce《with》; suspend 〔call off〕 hostilities; conclude an armistice《with》. ¶ ～ 후의 한국 부흥 post-truce rehabilitation of Korea / ～을 요구하다 ask for a「truce 〔cease-fire〕/ ～ 상태를 유지하다 maintain a cease-fire / 전 전선에 걸쳐 ～이 명령되었다 A cease-fire has been ordered on all fronts. / 3건의 ～ 위반이 있었다 There were three cases of truce violation. *or* Three incidents marred the cease-fire.
◉ ～교섭〔협상〕 truce 〔cease-fire〕 negotiations. ～기(旗) a flag of truce. ～기념일《제1차 대전의》Armistice Day. ～명령 a cease-fire; orders to suspend hostilities. ～선(線) a truce line;「a cease-fire 〔an armistice〕 line. ～조약《conclude》a treaty of「truce 〔armistice〕《with》. ～협정 a cease-fire agreement; the Armistice Agreement: 중대한 ～협정 위반 a serious violation of the Armistice Agreement / ～협정을 맺다 reach 〔arrive at, come to〕 a cease-fire agreement《with》. ～회담 a truce 〔an armistice, a cease-fire〕 talks 〔conferences〕. 전면～ a general truce. 중립국 ～ 감시단 the Neutral Nations Supervisory Commission for Armistice.

**휴정**(休廷) ～하다 the court does not sit; [사람이 주어] hold no court; adjourn the court《until》. ¶ 토요일은 ～입니다 No court will be held on Saturday. / 월요일까지 ～했다 The court was adjourned till Monday. ◉ ～일 a non-judicial day; a *dies non* (*juridicus*) (L.).

**휴지**(休止) a pause; a standstill; suspension; (a) rest; stoppage; discontinuance; a halt a letup《구어》. ～하다 cease; pause; stop; halt; suspend; discontinue; come to a standstill. ◉ ～기(期)〖생물〗a period of dormancy; a resting stage. ～부〖음

악〗 a rest; a pause; 〖언어〗《구두점》 a stop; a period: ～부를 찍다 put a period 《to》. ～상태 a standstill; a deadlock.

**휴지**(休紙) 《허드렛종이》 wastepaper; a scrap of paper; paper scraps; 《화장지》 toilet 〔lavatory〕 paper 〔tissue〕; a toilet roll (두루마리); tissue paper (코 푸는). ¶ ～를 줍다 pick up wastepaper / ～화하다 become wastepaper; become null (and void); make a "scrap of paper" of 《a treaty》; be invalidated / 약속을 ～화하다 go back on *one's* pledge / ～ 조각이나 다름 없다 be as good as wastepaper; be a mere scrap of paper / ～를 버리지 마시오 《게시》 No littering 〔dumping〕. / 공채는 인플레이션으로 ～가 되었다 The bonds became mere scraps of paper as a result of the inflation.

**휴지통**(休紙桶) a wastebasket 《미》; a wastepaper basket 〔bin 《영》〕. ¶ ～에 넣다 throw in(to) a wastebasket.

**휴직**(休職) suspension 〔leave of absence (본인이 희망하는)〕 from work; a layoff. ～하다 temporarily rest 〔retire〕 from *one's* office. ¶ ～이 되다 be suspended from *one's* job 〔duties〕; get placed on the reserve list; be (temporarily) laid off / 1년간 ～하다 have 〔be given〕 one year's leave of absence / 그의 회사는 그가 박사 과정을 끝낼 수 있도록 ～을 허락했다 His company granted him a leave of absence so that he could complete his doctorate. / 그 자동차 공장에서는 100명 이상의 근로자들이 ～되었다 More than 100 workers were laid off in the car factory. ◉ ～급(給) 《군인 등의》 half pay.

**휴진**(休診) 《a physician's》 not seeing patients; suspension of medical examination. ～하다 accept no patients; close the office 〔surgery 《영》〕 《for the day》; do not hold office 〔consultation〕 hours. ¶ 금일 ～ 《게시》 Closed today. *or* No consultations 〔appointments〕 today. *or* 《영》 No surgery today. ◉ ～일 a non-consultation day.

**휴학**(休學) 《a year's》 leave of absence 《from school》. ～하다 withdraw 〔absent *oneself*〕 from school temporarily 〔for a time〕; have leave of 《one year's》 absence from school. ¶ 오랫동안 ～하고 있다 be long absent from school / 3개월 간의 ～원을 내다 apply for three months' leave of absence. ◉ ～생 a student who stays out of school temporarily.

**휴한지**(休閑地) ① 《묵히는》 land in fallow; idle 〔fallow〕 land; a fallow (field). ¶ ～를 이용하다 make use of idle land. ② ＝ 공지(空地).

**휴항**(休航) suspension of sailing 〔flying〕. ～하다 suspend the sailing 〔flying〕 《on a line》; 《배가》 be laid up.

**휴행**(携行) ～하다 take 〔carry〕 《a lunch》 with *one;* take 《*a thing*》 along.

**휴화산**(休火山) an inactive 〔a dormant, a sleeping〕 volcano.

**휴회**(休會) adjournment; a recess. ～하다 adjourn; (go into) recess; take a recess. ¶ ～중 《be》 in recess; in adjournment; out of 〔not in〕 session / ～에 들어가다 《the Assembly》 recess / ～를 선포하다 call a recess; declare adjournment. ◉ 자동～ automatic adjournment.

**휼계**(譎計) a trick; a wile; a deceitful scheme; skulduggery. ¶ ～를 쓰다 resort to skulduggery / ～에 넘어가다 fall for a scheme; get tricked 〔cheated, victimized〕.

**휼미**(恤米) relief grain.

**휼민**(恤民) relief of the people. ～하다 relieve 〔give relief to〕 the people.

**휼병**(恤兵) aid for the troops; the relief of soldiers. ～하다 give relief 〔aid, comfort〕 to the troops. ◉ ～금 a war relief fund. ～사업 war charities; war relief work.

**휼전**(恤典) charity relief from the government for the victims 《of》.

**흄관**(―管) a Hume concrete pipe.

**흉** ① 《흉터》 a scar. ¶ 흉이 있는 얼굴 a scarred face; a face with a scar / 흉이 없어지다 the scar dies away; the scar leaves no trace. ② 《흠》 a fault; a defect; a drawback; a flaw; a blemish. ¶ 흉을 잡다 find fault with; pick out 《*a person's*》 defects / 흉없는 사람은 없다 Nobody is perfect.

**흉가**(凶家) a house of ill omen; a haunted house.

**흉강**(胸腔) 〖해부〗 the thoracic 〔chest〕 cavity; the thorax (*pl.* ～es, -races). ◉ ～경 a thoracoscope.

**흉격**(胸隔) 〖해부〗 the lower chest.

**흉계**(凶計) a wicked 〔an evil〕 design; wiles; an intrigue; a sinister plot; a reprehensible project. ¶ ～를 꾸미다 devise a sinister plot; form a wicked design 《on》.

**흉골**(胸骨) 〚해부〛 the sternum (*pl.* ～s, -na); the breastbone. ¶ ～의 sternal / ～ 밑의 substernal. ◉ ～통 sternalgia; sternodynia.

**흉곽**(胸廓) the chest; the thorax (*pl.* ～es, -races). ¶ ～의 thoracic; thoracal / ～이 넓다〔좁다〕 have a broad 〔narrow〕 chest. ◉ ～내시경 a thoracoscope. ～성형술 〚의학〛 thoracoplasty. ～외과 chest 〔thoracic〕 surgery.

**흉금**(胸襟) the bosom; the heart; the inner mind. ¶ ～을 털어놓다 unbosom *oneself* 《of》; open 〔lay bare〕 *one's* heart 《to》; take 《*a person*》 into *one's* confidence 《in》; disclose *one's* innermost intention 《to》 / ～을 터놓고 이야기하다 have a heart-to-heart talk 《with》; talk without reserve; have a frank chat 《with》.

**흉기**(凶器) an offensive 〔a dangerous, a deadly, a lethal〕 weapon. ¶ ～를 지니다 carry a deadly weapon / 자동차는 때때로 달리는 ～라고도 한다 Cars are sometimes called deadly weapons on wheels.

**흉내** (an) imitation; mimicry; a take-off 《구어》; 《태도·소리 따위의》 impersonation. ～내다 imitate; copy; take off; 《사람의》 mimic; mock; monkey; ape; follow 《*a person's*》 example; do 〔give〕 an imitation 《of》; do a takeoff 《of》; make like 《another》.

> 용법 **imitate** 「흉내내다」의 일반적인 말. **copy** 될 수 있는 대로 충실히 묘사·재생하는 것을 말함: She always copies my hairdo.(그녀는 언제나 내 머리 스타일을 흉내내고 있다). **mimic** 동작·말투 따위를 조롱하면서 흉내내는 것을 말함 : The comedian mimicked some politicians.(희극 배우가 일부 정치가들의 흉내를 내면서 조롱했다). **mock** mimic보다 경멸하는 뉘앙스가 짙게 풍기는 말: He mocked the way she spoke.(그는 그녀의 말버릇을 비웃으며 흉내냈다). **ape** 가치 있다고 여겨지는 것을 생각 없이 덮어놓고 흉내내는 것을 말함: The new rich began to ape the manners of fashionable society. (졸부들이 상류 사회의 풍습을 흉내내기 시작했다).

¶ 앵무새는 사람의 말을 ～낸다 Parrots imitate human speech. / 그녀의 단점이 아니라 장점을 ～내라 You should copy her good points, not her bad points. ◉ ～말 an onomatopoeia; an onomatopoetic word; an echoword. ～쟁이 a (clever) mimic; a copycat; an imitator.

**흉년**(凶年) a bad 〔lean〕 year; a year of bad 〔poor〕 harvest; a year of famine. ¶ ～에 윤달 [비유적] one disaster following on the heels of another / ～으로 인해 owing to the year of bad crops / ～이 들다 be a bad year for 《the rice crop》; have a short crop of 《rice》. ◉ ～거지 a beggar in a lean year.

**흉노**(匈奴) 〚역사〛 the Huns.

**흉도**(凶徒) rioters; outlaws; rebels.

**흉막**(胸膜) 〚해부〛 the pleura (*pl.* ～s, -rae). = 늑막. ◉ ～염 pleurisy.

**흉몽**(凶夢) a bad dream; a dream of ill omen; a nightmare.

**흉물**(凶物) an evil person; a villain. ～스럽다 (be) villainous; infamous; wicked.

**흉배**(胸背) ① 《가슴과 등》 breast and back. ② 《옛 관복의》 embroidered patches of the breast and on the back of official uniforms.

**흉벽**(胸壁) ① 《가슴의》 walls of the chest. ② 《성벽의》 a breastwork 〔parapet〕. = 흉장(胸牆).

**흉변**(凶變) a disastrous occurrence; a calamity; a disaster; a tragic accident; 《암살》 (an) assassination; 《살인》 murder. ¶ ～을 당하다 suffer a calamity; get assassinated 〔murdered〕.

**흉보**(凶報) bad 〔ill〕 news; evil tidings; news of death. ¶ 유족에게 ～를 전하다 break sad news to the family.

**흉보다** speak ill 〔evil〕 of; disparage; condemn; run 〔call〕 down; criticize. ¶ 안 듣는 데서 ～ backbite 《*a person*》; speak ill of 《*a person*》 behind *his* back.

**흉복**(胸腹) the midriff area (between chest and abdomen). ◉ ～통 a pain in the midriff.

**흉부**(胸部) the breast; the chest; 《곤충 따위의》 the thorax (*pl.* ～es, -races). ¶ ～에 통증을 느끼다 feel a sharp pain in the chest / 그는 ～에 관통상을 입었다 He was shot through the breast. ◉ ～내시경 a thoracoscope. ～대동맥 a thoracic aorta. ～성형술 〚의학〛 thoracoplasty. ～엑스선 검사 a chest X-ray (examination). ～외과 chest 〔thoracic〕 surgery. ～질환 a chest trouble 〔disease〕.

**흉사**(凶事) an event of ill omen; an

unlucky affair; an untoward event; a misfortune; a disaster; a calamity; ⌊death.

**흉상**(凶狀) a vile attitude.

**흉상**(凶相) ① 《관상술의》 a physiognomy that presages bad luck. ② 《흉한 외모》 an ugly face; an unseemly appearance.

**흉상**(胸像) 〖미술〗 a (sculpture) bust.

**흉선**(胸腺) 〖해부〗 the thymus (gland); 〖요리〗 the (neck, throat) sweetbread. ◉ ～염(炎) thymitis.

**흉수**(凶手) ¶ ～에 걸리다〔쓰러지다〕 fall a victim to the dagger of an assassin; meet *one's* death through foul play.

**흉수**(胸水) 〖의학〗 fluid in the thoracic cavity; water on the chest.

**흉악**(凶惡) 《성질의》 wickedness; heinousness; villainousness; 《생김새》 crudeness; ugliness. ～하다 (be) bad; wicked; heinous; fiendish; atrocious; brutal; crude; ugly; unseemly. ¶ ～한 짓 a felon deed; an atrocious act. ◉ ～범(犯) 《범죄》 a vicious 〔heinous〕 crime; 《범인》 a vicious criminal. ～성 brutality; atrocity; heinousness: ～성을 띠다 have a touch of brutality; be something of a villain.

**흉악망측**(凶惡罔測) 《성질이》 extreme wickedness 〔heinousness, villainousness〕; 《생김새가》 extreme crudeness 〔ugliness〕. ～하다 (be) extremely wicked 〔bad, crude, ugly〕.

**흉어**(凶漁) a poor catch (of fish). ¶ 잇따른 ～로 어부들은 죽을 지경이다 Fishermen are hard hit by the prolonged scarcity of fish.

**흉위**(胸圍) *one's* chest measurement; 《여자의》 *one's* bust measurement; the girth of the chest. ¶ ～를 재다 take 《*a person's*》 chest measurement; measure (the girth of) 《*a person's*》 chest / ～가 90센티미터다 I measure ninety centimeters around the chest. / ～가 얼마나 되는가 What is your chest measurement?

**흉인**(凶刃) an assassin's dagger 〔blade〕. ¶ ～에 쓰러지다 be assassinated 《by》; fall a victim to an assassin's dagger.

**흉일**(凶日) a bad 〔black〕 day; an ill-starred 〔unlucky〕 day.

**흉작**(凶作) a bad (poor, lean) crop 〔harvest〕; a crop 〔harvest〕 failure. ¶ ～이 든 해 a lean 〔bad〕 year 《for the rice crop》 / 보리는 ～이었다 We had a small crop of wheat. / 올해 쌀 농사는 10년래의 ～이다 The rice crop this year is the worst that we have had for the last 〔past〕 ten years.

**흉잡다** find fault with; point out 《*a person's*》 defects; pick at; pick holes 《in》.

**흉잡히다** be found fault with; be spoken ill of; be picked on. ¶ 귀먹은 것을 ～ *one's* deafness is regarded as a drawback.

**흉장**(胸牆) a breastwork; a parapet.

**흉조**(凶兆) a bad 〔an evil〕 omen; a sign of evil. ¶ ～의〔인〕 ill-boding / ～이다 bode ill 〔evil〕 《to, for》.

**흉중**(胸中) *one's* bosom 〔heart, mind, feelings, thoughts, intentions〕. ¶ ～에 in *one's* heart 〔mind〕 / ～을 살피다〔헤아리다〕 read 《*a person's*》 mind; feel for 《*a person*》; 《동정하다》 sympathize with 《*a person*》 / ～을 밝히다 unbosom *oneself;* speak *one's* bosom 《to》; open 〔lay bare〕 *one's* heart / ～에 떠오르다 enter 〔come across〕 *one's* mind; occur to *one;* [사람이 주어] think of; hit upon 《a plan》 / ～에 간직해 두다 keep 《*something*》 to *oneself;* bury 《*a matter*》 in *one's* bosom.

**흉증**(凶證) ① 《음흉함》 slyness; sneakiness; underhandedness; insidiousness; treachery. ～부리다 act in a sly 〔sneaky, treacherous〕 way. ～스럽다 (be) sly; sneaky; snaky; underhanded; two-faced; double-dealing; insidious; treacherous. ② 《흉조》 ill omen.

**흉추**(胸椎) 〖해부〗 the thoracic verte- ⌊brae.

**흉측스럽다**(凶測―) ⇨ 흉측하다.

**흉측하다**(凶測―) 《성질이》 (be) terribly heinous 〔wicked, villainous〕; 《얼굴이》 (be) very ugly 〔crude〕.

**흉탄**(凶彈) a bullet shot by a villain 〔an assassin〕; an assassin's bullet. ¶ ～에 쓰러지다 be shot (to death) by an assassin; be killed 〔felled〕 by an assassin's bullet.

**흉터** a scar. ¶ 그의 뺨에 ～가 있다 There is a scar on his cheek. / 상처는 나아도 ～는 남을 것이다 Even after the wound heals, the scar will remain.

**흉통**(胸痛) a pain in the chest; a chest pain; pleurodynia. ¶ ～을 느끼다 have 〔feel〕 a pain in the chest. ◉ 전염성 ～증 〖의학〗 epidemic pleurodynia.

**흉포**(凶暴) atrocity; ferocity; brutality. ～하다 (be) atrocious; ferocious; brutal. ¶ ～한 살인자 a fierce 〔violent〕 killer / ～성을 드러내다 show 〔display, exhibit〕 *one's* brutality; go berserk / 도주 중인 범인은 ～한 자로서 흉기를 소지하고 있다 The criminal on the run is a brutal one, carrying a leathal weapon.

**흉하다**(凶—) ① 《모습이》 (be) ugly; bad-〔ugly-〕looking; 《보기에》 (be) unseemly; unsightly; ungainly; indecent. ¶ 흉한 얼굴 an ugly face / 보기 ~ be ugly to look at / 보기 흉하지 않은 복장을 하다 be decently 〔respectably〕 dressed / 배가 나와서 그는 보기 ~ He looks awful with that potbelly. / 그의 얼굴에는 흉한 상처가 있다 His face is disfigured with a scar. ② 《불길하다》 (be) ill; evil; ill-omened; unlucky; portentous; bad. ¶ 흉한 꿈 an unlucky 〔ominous〕 dream / 흉한 날 an ill-omened day; a black-letter day / 흉한 예감 ominous presentiment / 흉한 소리를 하다 croak; forebode evil. ③ 《성질이》 (be) wicked; vicious; malicious. ¶ 흉한 놈 a wicked man; a rascal / 흉한 짓 a wicked 〔bad〕 act.

**흉한**(凶漢) 《악인》 a villain; a ruffian; 《공격자》 an assailant; 《살인자》 a murderer; a killer. ¶ ~의 손에 쓰러지다 fall a victim to an assassin; be killed by an assassin; be murdered.

**흉행**(凶行) (an act of) violence; (an) outrage; 《범죄》 a crime; 《살인》 murder; 《암살》 (an) assassination. ¶ ~의 현장 a scene of crime 〔murder, outrage〕 / ~을 저지르다 do violence to 《*a person*》; commit a crime 〔an atrocity〕; 《살해하다》 commit murder.

**흉허물** a defect; a flaw; faults (for each other to pick at).

**흉허물없다** be intimate enough to overlook each other's faults. ¶ 흉허물없는 친구 friends intimate enough to overlook each other's faults; a friend on frank terms / …와 흉허물 없는 사이다 be on intimate 〔familiar〕 terms with 《*a person*》; be hand in glove with 《*a person*》.

**흉헙다** (be) ugly; unseemly; awful; terrible. ¶ 보기 ~ be awful to look at / 색깔이 ~ The color is dreadful.

**흉흉하다**(洶洶—) ① 《물결이》 rage; (be) high. ② 《인심이》 be filled with alarm; (be) panic-stricken; [서술적] be in great alarm 〔fear〕. ¶ 전쟁이 나서 인심이 ~ People are panic-stricken with the outbreak of war.

**흐너뜨리다** pull 〔take〕 down; demolish; 「destroy.

**흐너지다** fall down; get pulled down; collapse.

**흐놀다** long 《for》; sigh 《for》; yearn 《after》. ¶ 고향을 ~ long for home.

**흐느끼다** sob; blubber; weep softly; whimper. ¶ 흐느껴 울다 be choked with 〔drowned in〕 tears / 흐느껴 울며 말하다 sob out; say between sobs / 유족들 사이에서 흐느끼는 소리가 들렸다 There were sobbings among the bereaved.

**흐느적거리다** flutter; sway gently; wave. ¶ 잎이 바람에 ~ leaves flutter in the breeze / 버들이 바람에 ~ the willow is swaying to the wind.

**흐늘거리다** ① 《놀고 지내다》 idle 〔dawdle〕 *one's* time away; loaf away *one's* time. ② 《흐물거리다》 be soft 〔mushy, flabby, squashy〕. ③ 《흔들거리다》 hang loosely; dangle; sway gently. ¶ 풍경(風磬)이 ~ a wind-bell is swaying gently in the breeze.

**흐늘어지다** hang loosely; dangle; droop (heavily). ¶ 버들 가지가 ~ willow branches droop heavily.

**흐늘쩍거리다** move around slowly 〔sluggishly, idly〕. ¶ 흐늘쩍거리며 걷다 walk slowly; poke along; have a ramble.

**흐늘쩍흐늘쩍** slowly; sluggishly; idly. ¶ ~걷다 loiter; stroll; poke along.

**흐늘흐늘** ① 《놀고 지내는 모양》 idly; lazily. ¶ ~ 놀고 있다 loaf 〔dawdle〕 about / ~걷다 walk lazily. ② 《흐물거리는 모양》 softly; mushily; flabbily; squashily. ¶ ~하게 삶다 boil 「softly 〔to pulp〕. ③ 《매달린 것이》 dangling; swaying gently 〔easily〕. ¶ 깃발이 바람에 ~ 움직이고 있다 The flag is streaming 〔flappering〕 gently in the wind.

**흐드러지다** ① 《썩 탐스럽다》 become splendid; (be) splendid; fetching. ¶ 꽃이 흐드러지게 피다 flowers come out splendidly. ② 《무르익어서》 get overripe 〔too soft〕.

**흐들갑스럽다** be exaggerated 〔overexcited〕 in speech; be bubbling over; be bombastic; flippant. ¶ 흐들갑스럽게 말하다 describe 《an event》 in exaggerated terms; give an overdrawn description 《of》.

**흐려지다** ① 《날씨가》 become cloudy 〔overcast〕; cloud (over); cloud up. ¶ 하늘이 갑자기 흐려졌다 The sky was suddenly overcast. / 하늘이 흐려지더니 비가 내리기 시작했다. The sky clouded over and it started to rain. ② 《투명한 것이》 (***a***) 《눈이》 get bleary; grow dim. ¶ 나이 먹음에 따라 눈이 ~ *one's* eyes grow dim as *one* gets old / 눈물로 눈이 ~ be blurred with tears; tears blur *one's* eyes. (***b***) 《부

옇게 되다》 become dim; be clouded; become smoked (up) (램프의 등피가); get fogged 〔misted〕 (유리 따위가 수증기로); 《광택이》 be tarnished; be dull; be milky. ¶ 욕실의 거울이 수증기로 흐려졌다 The bathroom mirror got all steamy. / 입김에 안경이 흐려졌다 My breath fogged my glasses.
③ 《얼굴·마음이》 cloud; be clouded. ¶ 그녀의 안색이 흐려졌다 Her face clouded over.

**흐르다** ① 《액체가》 (***a***) 《유동하다》 flow; run; stream; course; trickle (졸졸). ¶ 호수에서 흘러 나오는 강(江) a river which proceeds from the lake / 강이 ~ a river flows / (강물이) 굽이쳐 ~ meander / (강이) 바다로 흘러가다 find its way to the sea / 한강은 도심을 흐른다 The Han river flows through the city. / 물이 흐르지 않는다 The water 「stands still 〔is stagnant〕. (***b***) 《흘러내리다》 flow 〔stream〕 down; run down. ¶ 눈물이 흐르는 눈 eyes streaming with tears / 땀이 쏟아져 ~ [사람이 주어] run 〔be streaming〕 with sweat / 얼굴에 땀이 ~ sweat runs down *one's* face / 피가 콸콸 ~ blood streams 〔rains〕 down / 눈물이 그 여자의 뺨을 흘러내렸다 Tears streamed 〔rolled〕 down her cheeks. (***c***) 《쏟아지다》 spill; be spilt; slop over. ¶ 국이 마루에 ~ soup is spilt on the floor / 식탁에 국물이 흘렀다 There are some slops on the table.
② 《넘치다》 run over; overflow; brim over 《with》. ¶ 세면기의 물이 넘쳐 흐르고 있다 The water is overflowing the basin. / 컵에 너무 많이 따르면 넘쳐 흐른다 Never fill the cup too full, or it will brim over.
③ 《세월이》 pass (away); flow by; elapse. ¶ 세월이 흐름에 따라 with the passage 〔lapse〕 of time 〔years〕; in the course of years; as time passes on / 그로부터 10년이 흘렀다 Ten years have passed since then. / 세월이 흘러 그 일은 잊혀졌다 With 「the lapse of time 〔the passage of years〕 the event was forgotten.
④ 《떠다니듯 이동하다》 float; drift; wander. ¶ 하늘에 구름이 흘러간다 Clouds are drifting in the sky. / 참석자들 사이에 우호적인 분위기가 흘렀다 A friendly atmosphere prevailed among those present. / 그는 이곳저곳을 정처없이 흘러다녔다 He wandered from one place to another. / 고기 굽는 냄새가 흘러왔다 The smell of roasted meat came drifting through the air.
⑤ 《쏠리다》 incline 〔run〕 《to》; lapse 〔fall〕 《into》; be 「carried away 〔swayed〕 《by》. ¶ 감정에 ~ be swayed by sentiment / 극단으로 ~ run to extremes; go to excess / 사치에 ~ lapse into luxury; become extravagant.
⑥ 《윤기·기름기 따위가》 ¶ 윤기가 흐르는 검은 머리 glossy 〔sleek〕 black hair 《hung down to *one's* waist》 / 얼굴에 기름기가 ~ grease exudes on 〔oozes out of〕 *one's* face; *one's* face is sleek; have a well-fed look.

**흐르르하다** (be) flimsy; flabby; squashy; flaccid; limp. ¶ 종이가 얇고 ~ the paper is thin and flimsy / 이 풀먹인 칼라는 더운 날에는 흐르르해진다 This starched collar soon gets limp in hot weather.

**흐름** ① 《물의》 flowing; a flow; a stream; a current; a watercourse; 〖컴퓨터〗 a flow. ¶ 물〔공기〕의 ~ the flow 〔flowing〕 of water 〔air〕 / ~을 따라〔거슬러〕 헤엄치다 swim with 〔against〕 the current / ~이 빠른〔느린〕 강 a fast=flowing 〔slow-moving〕 river. ② 《흐르듯 움직이는 것》 ¶ 의식의 ~ the stream of consciousness / 차의 ~ the flow of traffic / 시간의 ~ the passage 〔lapse〕 of time / 시대〔역사〕의 ~을 거역하다 go against 「the current of the times 〔the flow of history〕 / 나는 사람들의 ~에 밀려 나아갔다 I was pushed along by the stream of people. ◉ ~도 〖컴퓨터〗 a flow diagram; a flowchart: ~도 기호 〖컴퓨터〗 a flow-charting symbol / ~도 작성 자 〖컴퓨터〗 a flowchart template. ~선 〖컴퓨터〗 a flowline. ~제어 〖컴퓨터〗 a flow control. ~주성(走性) 〖생물〗 rheotaxis.

**흐리다**[1] ① 《날씨가》 (be) cloudy; clouded; overcast. ¶ 흐린 날씨 cloudy weather / 흐린 날 a cloudy day / 날이 ~ it is cloudy / 하늘이 아주 ~ The sky 「is overcast 〔has clouded up〕.
② 《희미하다》 (be) dim; clouded; blurred; smoked. ¶ 등불이 ~ a light is dim / 인쇄가 ~ printing is blurred / 등피가 ~ a lamp chimney is smoked.
③ 《눈이》 (be) dull; dim; bleared; bleary. ¶ 눈이 ~ have bleary eyes.
④ 《탁하다》 (be) muddy; turbid. ¶ 흐린 물 muddy water / 장마철의 흐린 강물 the turbid waters in the rainy season.

⑤《불분명하다》 be not clear; (be) indistinct; vague; hazy; fuzzy; obscure; ambiguous; equivocal. ¶ 셈이 ～ be hazy about the accounts; be unpunctual in *one's* payment / 정신이 ～ have a vague memory.

**흐리다**[2] ① 《흔적을》 blot out; efface. ¶ 오징어가 먹물로 자취를 ～ an inkfish blots out its traces with its ink. ② 《혼탁하게 하다》 make 《water》 muddy 〔turbid, cloudy〕; muddy 《a well》. ③ 《불분명케 하다》 make indistinct 〔vague, obscure, ambiguous〕; equivocate. ¶ 대답을 ～ equivocate in replying; give a vague 〔a noncommittal, an evasive〕 answer / 말 끝을 ～ leave *one's* statement vague; give a noncommittal answer / 셈을 ～ leave accounts hazy / 요점을 ～ evade the point. ④ 《명예를 더럽히다》 blemish; stain. ¶ 가문의 명성을 ～ stain the good name of *one's* family.

**흐리마리하다** ① 《거취 따위가》 (be) undecided; indefinite; uncertain; vague; ambiguous. ¶ 거취가 ～ have an undecided attitude / 대답이 ～ be vague in *one's* answer; answer ambiguously; beat around the bush. ② 《생각·기억이》 (be) hazy; misty; nebulous. ¶ 생각이 흐리마리하여 분명치 않다 have (only) a hazy idea.

**흐리멍덩하다** ① 《기억이》 (be) indistinct; dim; vague; faint; hazy; nebulous. ¶ 흐리멍덩하게 vaguely; dimly; indistinctly; obscurely / 흐리멍덩한 눈 clouded 〔glazed〕 eyes / 기억이 ～ *one's* memory is dim 〔hazy, fuzzy〕. ② 《명확하지 못하다》 (be) confused; muddled; indecisive, uncertain; dubious. ¶ 흐리멍덩한 셈 muddled accounts / 대답이 ～ an answer is indecisive / 생각이 ～ an idea is confused 〔muddled〕 / 태도가 ～ *one's* attitude is ambiguous / 머리가 ～ feel *one's* brains muddled. ③ 《우둔하다》 (be) dim; dull. ¶ 귀가 ～ be hard of hearing.

**흐리터분하다** ① 《사물이》 (be) cloudy; hazy; indistinct; obscure. ¶ 흐리터분한 날씨 a cloudy 〔gloomy〕 weather / 셈이 ～ be hazy about the accounts. ② 《사람이》 (be) dark-minded; dull; sluggish, slovenly; be not open. ¶ 흐리터분한 사람 a slovenly person.

**흐릿하다** ① 《날이》 (be) rather cloudy 〔overcast〕. ¶ 흐릿한 날씨 rather cloudy 〔gray〕 weather. ② 《침침하다》 (be) rather dim 〔clouded, blurred, smoked〕. ¶ 안개 속에 등불이 ～ Lights are burning dimly in the fog. / 집이 안개 속에 흐릿하게 보인다 The house looms through the mist. ③ 《눈이》 (be) rather dull 〔bleary〕. ¶ 흐릿한 눈 glazed 〔glassy〕 eyes; clouded 〔lackluster, fishy〕 eyes / 나이를 먹으면 눈이 흐릿해진다 Our sight grows dim with age. ④ 《혼탁하다》 (be) rather muddy 〔turbid〕. ⑤ 《희미하다》 (be) indistinct; vague; dim; obscure; faint. ¶ 그 소리는 멀어지면서 차츰 흐릿해졌다 The sound grew fainter and fainter in the distance. / 당시의 일은 그저 흐릿하게 기억날 뿐이다 I remember those days only vaguely.

**흐무러지다** ① 《익어서》 get 〔be〕 overripe 〔overmature〕. ② 《물에 불어서》 (be) sodden; swollen; soaked. ¶ 쌀이 물에 불어 ～ rice gets very soft soaking up water.

**흐무뭇하다** (be) quite pleasing 〔gratifying, satisfactory〕; (be) greatly pleased 〔gratified, satisfied〕.

**흐물흐물하다** (be) overripe; very soft; flabby; pulpy. ¶ 흐물흐물하게 삶다〔곯이다〕 boil 《*something*》 to a pulp; boil long 〔to a jelly〕 / 흐물흐물해지다 be reduced to pulp 〔jelly〕.

**흐뭇이** pleasingly; satisfactorily; sufficiently.

**흐뭇하다** 《만족스럽다》 (be) gratifying; satisfying; heartwarming; 《유쾌하다》 (be) pleasing; pleasant; 《기쁘다》 (be) joyful; delightful. ¶ 마음이 흐뭇해지는 이야기 a heartwarming story; a nice story to hear / 부모는 아들의 성공에 흐뭇해 한다 The parents are pleased with their son's success. / 그것은 보기에 흐뭇한 광경이었다 It was a lovely sight to see.

**흐벅지다** (be) plump; full. ¶ 흐벅진 젖가슴 full breasts; a plump bosom / 흐벅진 넓적다리 살 plump flesh of the thigh.

**흐슬부슬** crumbling. ～하다 (be) crumbling; unglutinous. ¶ 과자가 ～ 부스러지다 cakes crumble / 이 밥은 ～하다 The boiled-rice is poor in gluten.

**흐지부지** ① 《어물어물 넘기는 모양》 hushing up; in secret. ¶ ～ 끝나다 end in smoke; come to nothing / 독직 사건을 ～해 버리다 hush up a case of bribery; stifle a corruption scandal / 우리의 계획은 모두 ～되고 말았다 All our plans have 「fizzled out 〔come to nothing〕. ② 《없애거나 없어지는 모양》 wasting; to no purpose. ¶ 돈을 ～

다 쓰다 waste 〔throw away〕 all the money / 쌀이 ~ 다 없어지다 rice is used up wastefully.

**흐트러뜨리다** ① 《여기저기》 scatter 《*things*》; strew; 《군중 따위를》 disperse; scatter; break up; dispel. ¶ 닭이 모이를 ~ a hen scatters its feed / 정신을 ~ distract 〔divert〕 *one's* attention / 바람이 길에 낙엽을 흐트러뜨렸다 The wind strewed 〔scattered〕 the road with leaves. ② 《머리를》 dishevel; mess up 《*one's* hair》. ¶ 머리를 흐트러뜨리고 with disheveled hair / 머리를 ~ get *one's* hair disheveled.

**흐트러지다** ① 《흩어지다》 scatter (about); be dispersed; be scattered; 《정신이》 be distracted. ¶ 쌀이 ~ rice is scattered. ② 《머리카락·복장 등이》 be disheveled 〔messed up〕. ¶ 머리가 ~ *one's* hair gets disheveled; become loose / 흐트러진 머리를 빗어 올리다 comb up loose hair / 열(列)이 ~ the lines fall into disorder.

**흐흐** 《웃음 소리》 Huh-huh!

**흑**(黑) 《흑색》 black; a black color; 《바둑돌》 a black stone. ⇨ 흑색. ¶ 흑을 백이라고 우기다 talk black into white.

**흑** 《흐느낌》 with a sob.

**흑갈색**(黑褐色) dark brown.

**흑고니**(黑―) 〖조류〗 a black swan.

**흑고래**(黑―) 〖동물〗 a black whale.

**흑내장**(黑內障) 〖의학〗 black cataract; amaurosis.

**흑다이아**(黑―) 《보석》 a black diamond; 「《석탄》 coal.

**흑단**(黑檀) 〖식물〗 an ebony; blackwood. ¶ ~(제(製))의 ebony 《desk》.

**흑당**(黑糖) ① muscovado. ⇨ 흑설탕. ② 《엿》 black rice-candy.

**흑대두**(黑大豆) black soybeans.

**흑두**(黑豆) black beans.

**흑두루미**(黑―) 〖조류〗 a hooded crane.

**흑두재상**(黑頭宰相) a young prime minister.

**흑룡강**(黑龍江) the Amur River.

**흑막**(黑幕) ① 《검은 장막》 a black curtain. ② 《음흉한 내막》 concealed circumstances; the inside; something fishy. ¶ ~을 캐내다 try to uncover suspected irregularities / ~을 폭로하다 expose a secret 《of》 / 그 일에는 ~이 있다 There is something fishy about the matter. ◉ ~외교 secret 〔behind-the-scenes〕 diplomacy; diplomacy curtained off from the public.

**흑맥주**(黑麥酒) black beer; porter's ale; 「stout.

**흑미**(黑米) 〖식물〗 wild rice; water rice.

**흑반**(黑斑) a black spot; 〖의학〗 melasma. ¶ 밀의 ~병 black leaf spots on wheat.

**흑발**(黑髮) black hair. ¶ ~의 여인 a black-haired woman.

**흑백**(黑白) 《흑과 백》 black and 〔or〕 white; 《옳고 그름》 good and 〔or〕 bad (선악); right and 〔or〕 wrong. ¶ ~불분(不分) black and white (are) all mixed up; (there is) no clear distinction between good and bad / ~을 가리다 discriminate between good and bad 〔right and wrong〕; tell good from bad; decide which is right / ~을 다투다 contend as to which is right; dispute on the right and wrong of a case / 사람은 ~ 논리로 사건을 판단하려는 경향이 있다 One tends to judge events in terms of black and white. ◉ ~사진 a black-and-white photograph; a photograph in black-and-white. ~영화 a black-and-white picture; a monochrome film. ~텔레비전 《방송·프로》 black-and-white 〔B/W〕 television; 《수상기》 a black-and-white television set; a monochrome television set. ~페이지 〖출판〗 a 「black-and-white 〔B/W〕 page.

**흑빵**(黑―) brown 〔rye〕 bread; dark 「〔black〕 bread.

**흑사병**(黑死病) 〖의학〗 the (black, bubonic) plague; the pest; black death (중세의).

**흑삼릉**(黑三稜) 〖식물〗 a bur reed.

**흑색**(黑色) a black color; black. ◉ ~인종 the black race. ~화약 black gunpowder; blasting powder.

**흑색선전**(黑色宣傳) a malicious (false) propaganda; a covert propaganda. ¶ 그들의 ~은 남한에서의 사회 혼란 야기를 노린 것임이 분명하다 Their malicious propaganda is no doubt aimed at causing social confusion in South Korea.

**흑설탕**(黑雪糖) muscovado; unrefined 「〔raw〕 sugar.

**흑셔츠**(黑―) a black shirt; 〖역사〗 the Black Shirts; the Fascists. ◉ ~당 《파시스트당》 the Blackshirts; the Italian Fascist Party: ~당원 a Blackshirt.

**흑수병**(黑穗病) smut; dustbrand; bunt (밀의). ¶ ~에 걸리다 smut; become smutted; become affected by smut.

**흑수정**(黑水晶) 〖광물〗 morion; dark cairngorm; smoky quartz.

**흑심**(黑心) a black heart; evil intentions; dark designs. ¶ ~을 품다 harbor an evil heart; cherish a dark design / ~을 품은 evil-minded; black-hearted; wicked; crafty.

**흑연**(黑鉛) 『광물』 black lead; graphite; plumbago. ¶ ～을 바르다, ～으로 닦다 black-lead. ◉ ～광(鑛) a graphite deposit. ～로(爐) a graphite 〔carbon〕 reactor. ～화(化) graphitization: ～화탄소 graphitized carbon.

**흑연**(黑煙) ① 《연기》 black 〔murky〕 smoke. ¶ 자욱한 ～ a dense cloud of black smoke. ② 《먹줄》 a painter's ink-line.

**흑요석**(黑曜石) 『광물』 obsidian; volcanic 「glass.

**흑운모**(黑雲母) 『광물』 biotite.

**흑의**(黑衣) black clothes; a black dress. ¶ ～를 입다 wear black (clothes); dress 〔be clad〕 in black.

**흑인**(黑人) a black; a colored 〔black〕 person; a Negro; [총칭] colored people; the colored.

¶ ～을 차별하다 segregate 「the colored 〔colored〕 people」 / ～가수〔과학자〕 a black singer 〔scientist〕.

◉ ～거주지구 a black neighborhood; a black ghetto. ～문제 the colored problem 〔question〕. ～분리반대 anti-segregation 《movement》. ～분리 정책 the segregation policy. ～영가(靈歌) a Negro spiritual. ～옹호 negrophilism: ～옹호자 a negrophil. ～음악 Negro music. ～종 the colored 〔black, Negro, African〕 race. ～지대 the Black Belt. ～차별대우 segregation 《미》; 《남아프리카》 apartheid: ～차별 대우 폐지론자 《경멸적》 a nigger lover. ～차별철폐 《미국의》 integration; desegregation. ～학교 a colored school.

> 참고 「흑인」을 가리키는 **black**이란 말이 옛날에는 경멸적인 뉘앙스를 가졌으나, 현재는 가장 흔히 쓰이는 말이 되었다. 반대로 Negro는 옛날에는 감정적인 색채가 없는 말이었으나, 현재 미국에서는 차별적인 개념이 풍기는 말이 되어서 사용하지 않는 것이 좋다. 미국의 흑인은 African-American 또는 Afro=American이라고 부르기도 한다.

**흑자**(黑字) ① 《글자》 black characters 〔letters, figures〕. ② 《고딕 글자》 blackface; boldface; Gothic (type). ③ 『경제』 figures in black ink 〔in the credit column〕; a black-ink balance. ¶ 국제수지 ～국 a balance-of-payments surplus country / ～를 내다 go into the black / ～이다 be in (the) black / ～를 유지하다 keep the balance in the black / 우리 사업은 지금 ～다 Our business is now in the black. / 우리는 10억원이 ～다 We are one billion won in the black. ◉ ～예산 a black=ink budget. ～재정 balanced budget financing.

**흑점**(黑點) a black 〔dark〕 spot; 《태양의》 a sunspot; a macula (*pl.* -lae). ¶ ～의 분해 sunspot disintegration / 태양 ～의 활동이 가장 활발한 시기 a period of maximum sunspot activity. ◉ ～주기 a sunspot cycle.

**흑조**(黑潮) the Black 〔Japan〕 current.

**흑지**(黑—) black stones used in *paduk;* black checkers.

**흑체**(黑體) 『물리』 a black body. ◉ ～방사 black body radiation.

**흑칠**(黑漆) black lacquer. ¶ ～한 black=painted.

**흑탄**(黑炭) 『광물』 black 〔bituminous〕 「coal.

**흑토**(黑土) 『지질』 black soil 〔earth〕. ◉ ～대(帶) a black earth district 〔zone〕; the black belt.

**흑판**(黑板) a blackboard. ＝ 칠판(漆板).

**흑해**(黑海) the Black Sea; the Euxine Sea.

**흑흑** ① 《우는 소리》 sobbing. ～하다 sob; whimper (어린애가). ¶ ～ 느껴울다 sob. ② 《추위에》 shuddering with cold. ～하다 shudder with cold.

**흔들거리다** keep swaying 〔shaking, swinging, rocking〕; flicker (불꽃 따위가). ¶ 초롱이 바람에 흔들거린다 The lantern is swinging in the wind.

**흔들다** ① 《물체를》 shake; swing; wave; rock; wag; roll.

> 용법 **shake** 반대나 거부의 표시로 고개를 옆으로 흔드는 것. 또는 세이커·약병 등을 상하·좌우로 가볍게 흔드는 것. **swing** 배트·라켓·팔 등을 한 점을 축으로 하여 크게 반원을 그리며 흔드는 것. **wave** 깃발·모자 등을 신호나 인사의 표시로서 천천히 흔드는 것. **rock** 흔들의자나 요람을 가볍게 흔드는 것. **wag** 개가 반가워서 꼬리를 흔드는 것. **roll** 옆으로 흔들어 대는 것을 나타냄.

¶ 깃발을 ～ wave a flag / 꼬리를 ～ wag its tail (개가); whisk 〔switch〕 its tail (말이) / 나무를 ～ shake the tree 《for fruit》 / 머리를 ～ shake *one's* head; say "no" / 몸을 ～ shake 〔sway〕 *oneself* / 손을 ～ wave *one's* hand; give a wave of *one's* hand / 어깨를 잡아 ～ shake 《*a person*》 by the shoulders / 흔들어 깨우다 shake 《*a person*》 out of *his* sleep; wake by shaking / 흔들어 떨어뜨리다 shake down / 어린애를 흔들어

재우다 rock a baby to sleep.
② 《마음·분위기 따위를》 stir up; disturb; agitate; upset; move. ¶ 결심을 ~ shake *one's* resolution; stagger 《*a person's*》 resolution / 민심을 ~ inflame 〔stir up〕 the popular passion / 그 오직(汚職)사건은 정치가에 대한 국민의 신뢰를 뿌리째 흔들어 놓았다 That corruption scandal shook the people's confidence in politicians to its very foundations.

**흔들리다** ① 《물체가》 shake; be shaken; quake; waver; wave; swing; sway; rock; vibrate; rattle; 《배가》 roll (옆으로); pitch (앞뒤로); toss 〔heave〕 (아래위로); 《매달린 것이》 swing; oscillate; 《차가》 joggle; jolt (덜컹); 《불이》 flicker; flare (불꽃이).
¶ 바람에 흔들리는 나무들 trees nodding in the wind / 바람에 흔들리는 불꽃 wavy flames in the wind / 바람에 ~ be swayed by the wind; sway (about) to the wind; tremble in the breeze / 좌우로 ~ rock from side to side / 앞뒤로 ~ rock back and forth / 창문이 바람에 ~ a window is rattled by the wind / 전후 좌우로 ~ 《배가》 roll and pitch / 이가 ~ a tooth is loose; have a loose tooth / 토대까지 ~ be「shaken 〔reeled〕 to 《its》 foundations / 집이 흔들리는 것을 느끼다 feel the house shake / 기차가 지나갈 때 다리가 흔들렸다 The bridge swayed as the train passed over it.
② 《마음·분위기 따위가》 disturbed; agitated; moved. ¶ 결심이 ~ *one's* resolution shakes; waver 〔be shaken〕 in *one's* resolution / 신념이 ~ be shaken in *one's* belief / 자신감이 ~ *one's* confidence is unsettled / 흔들리는 정치 형세 unsettled political conditions / 흔들리는 세계 경제 an unstable world economy / 아들을 믿는 아버지의 마음은 흔들리지 않았다 The father's trust in his son was unshaken.

**흔들목마**(—木馬) a rocking horse; a cockhorse; a hobbyhorse.

**흔들의자**(—椅子) a rocking chair; a rocker.

**흔들이** a pendulum; a bob.

**흔들흔들** swingingly; wavingly; swayingly; rockingly; shakily. ~하다 sway; swing; rock.

**흔연하다**(欣然—) (be) happy; cheerful; willing.

**흔연히**(欣然—) gladly; happily; joyfully; cheerfully; with「pleasure 〔delight〕; willingly; with good grace. ¶ ~ 맞다 give 《*a person*》 a warm welcome / ~ 승낙하다 accept willingly; be glad to accept.

**흔적**(痕迹) 《자취》 traces; marks; a track (발자취); 《징후》 a sign; indications (형적(形跡)); vestiges (유적).
¶ ~도 없이 without leaving any trace / 옛 성곽의 ~ Vestiges of an ancient castle / …(의) ~이 있다 bear the marks of... / …(의) ~을 남기다 leave traces of... / (전혀) ~을 남기지 않다 leave no「traces 〔marks〕 of 《*something*》 / ~을 감추다 cover up *one's* traces / ~을 발견하다 find traces 《of》 / ~을 없애다 remove all traces 《of》 / 도둑이 창으로 들어온 ~이 있다 There are evidences of the burglar having entered by the window. / 그는 교살된 ~이 있다 There are evidences of his having been strangled. / 그의 얼굴에는 고생한 ~이 엿보였다 His features wore the stamp of hardships. / 다리는 떠내려가서 ~도 없다 The bridge has been completely「carried 〔washed〕 away. ◉ ~기관 〖생물〗 a「vestigial 〔rudimentary〕 organ.

**흔전거리다** live on easy street; be well off.

**흔전만전** in「plenty 〔abundance〕; amply; abundantly; in profusion. ~하다 (be) plentiful; profuse; abundant; ample; rich. ¶ 돈을 ~ 쓰다 《낭비》 spend money in profusion; waste 〔throw away〕 *one's* money.

**흔쾌**(欣快) pleasure; delight. ~하다 (be) pleasant; happy; delightful; open-handed; generous. ¶ 그는 흔쾌히 많은 돈을 공동모금에 기부했다 He generously contributed large sum of money to the community chest.

**흔하다** ① 《많다》 (be) plenty; plentiful; rife; common; be met with everywhere. ¶ 흔하지 않은 uncommon; extraordinary / 흔해 빠진 이름 a common name / 흔해빠진 이야기「an old 〔a well-known〕 story; a twice-told tale / 흔해빠진 일 a commonplace「affair 〔event〕; an everyday affair / 돈이 ~ Money is in plentiful supply. / 이 병은 젖먹이에게 ~ Babies are subject to this disease. / 흔한 것이 여자다 If there's one thing we have enough of, it's women. / 그런 물건은 흔하지 않다 Such things are by no means common.
② 《구하기 쉽다》 (be) easily obtainable; readily available. ¶ 흔한 책 a book that can easily be had.

**흔히** commonly; frequently; ordinarily;

generally; often; usually. ¶ ～ 쓰이는 말 a frequently used word / ～ 일어나는 일 an affair of common occurrence / ～ …하다 be liable to *do;* be apt to *do;* be natural (that...) / 이런 일은 ～ 있는 일이다 Such things are apt to happen. / 허약한 사람은 ～ 감기가 든다 The weak is susceptible to a cold. / 이 병은 ～ 아이들에게 잘 걸린다 This disease prevails much among children. / 그런 실수는 ～ 젊은이들이 범한다 Young people are liable to commit such errors. / 상사에게 야단을 맞았다구─그런일은 ～ 있는 일이야, 심각해 하지 말라구 The boss got mad at you? It could happen to anyone. No hard feelings.

**흘게늦다** ①《매듭·사개 따위가》 (be) loose; loose-jointed; loose-hinged. ②《하는 짓이》 (be) loose; lax; slovenly. ¶ 그는 ～ He wants screwing up.

**흘겨보다** look at sideways; look out the corner of *one's* eye(s); look askance《at》; glare《at》. ¶ 그는 화가 나서 나를 흘겨 보았다 He glared at me with resentment.

**흘근거리다** ①《걸음을》 walk slowly 〔lazily〕. ②《늑장부리다》 dawdle; linger; tarry; be slow(-moving); be tardy in *do*ing《*a thing*》.

**흘근흘근** walking slowly 〔lazily〕. ¶ ～ 걷다 walk slowly.

**흘금거리다** keep looking sideways; keep leering 〔ogling, eyeing〕.

**흘금흘금** looking sideways over and over again; leering and leering; ogling and ogling. ¶ ～보다 keep eyeing.

**흘긋** ⇨흘끗.

**흘기다** leer (with *one's* eyes); look askance; glare《at》; scowl; look angrily 〔sharply〕; look daggers《at》. ¶ 무섭게 ～ glare fiercely《at》; look sharply《at》; scowl《at》/ 그녀는 나를 무섭게 흘겼다 She gave me a fierce sidelong scowl. / 그녀는 샘이 나서 나에게 눈을 흘겼다 She shot an envious, sidelong glance at me.

**흘기죽죽** with a displeased look from the corner of *one's* eyes. ～하다 look displeased 〔discontented〕.

**흘깃거리다** keep glaring 〔scowling〕; keep looking angrily 〔sharply〕《at》.

**흘깃흘깃** glaring and glaring; scowling and scowling. ¶ ～ 보다 keep glaring.

**흘끔하다** 《눈이》 (be) sunken; be hollow《with tiredness, *etc.*》. ¶ 흘끔하게 패인 볼 hollow 〔sunken〕 cheeks / 그녀는 피곤해서 눈이 흘끔했다 Her eyes were sunken from exhaustion.

**흘끗** 《한번 얼씬》 catching a glimpse; 《곁눈질》 casting a sidelong glance. ～하다 catch a glimpse; glance to one side. ¶ ～ 보다 glance 〔cast a glance〕《at》; get 〔catch〕 a glimpse《of》; take a brief look《at》/ 자동차 지나가는 것이 ～눈에 뜨이다 catch a glimpse of a car passing by / 그녀의 뒷모습이 ～보였다 I caught a glimpse of her back.

**흘끗거리다** keep glancing sideways.

**흘끗흘끗** glancing sideways over and over again. ¶ ～ 보다 keep glancing to one side.

**흘떼기** the sinewy 〔membraneous〕 parts of meat; a tough piece 〔part〕.

**흘러가다** flow; run; 《시간이》 fly; pass. ¶ (강이) 바다로 ～ find its way to the sea / 그 때로부터 20년이라는 세월이 흘러갔다 Twenty years have passed since then.

**흘러나오다** flow out; run out; effuse; stream out; ooze out (고름 따위가). ¶ 상처에서 피가 흘러나왔다 The blood flowed out from the wound.

**흘러내리다** ①《떨어지다》 fall; drop; run 〔stream, pour〕 down. ¶ 눈물이 그녀의 볼을 (줄줄) 흘러내렸다 Tears ran 〔trickled〕 down her cheeks. ②《옷 따위가》 slip 〔slide, glide〕 down; work down.

**흘러보다** sound (out); tap. ¶ 아무의 속을 ～ sound *a person* out / 아무의 의견을 ～ seek 〔sound, fathom〕 *a person's* opinion; feel *a person's* pulse.

**흘레** copulation; coupling; pairing. ～하다 copulate; mate; pair. ¶ ～붙이다 make copulate; mate together / 개를 ～붙이다 mate dogs together.

**흘리다** ①《액체를》 let 《water》 flow 〔run out〕; 《쏟아뜨리다》 spill; drop; 《피·눈물을》 shed. ¶ 국을 ～ spill soup / 눈물을 ～ shed tears; be in tears / 피눈물을 ～ weep bitter tears / 땀을 ～ sweat / 콧물을 ～ run at the nose; snivel / 코피를 ～ bleed at the nose / 전쟁에 이기고자 많은 피를 흘렸다 Tons of blood were shed to win the war. / 누군가 잉크를 흘렸다 Someone has upset the inkstand. ②《잃어버리다》 drop; lose. ¶ 돈을 ～ drop money / 지갑을 ～ lose *one's* wallet. ③《조금씩》 give《it》 out piecemeal; give《it》 in little driblets. ④《글씨를》 write in a cursive hand; scribble. ¶ 편지를 흘려 쓰다 scribble a letter. ⑤《귓전으로》

take no notice of; pay no attention to; let《a question》by. ¶ 그는 나의 충고를 한귀로 듣고 한귀로 흘려 버렸다 In his case, my advice went in one ear and out of the other.

**흘림** writing in a cursive hand; the cursive 〔"flowing"〕 style of penmanship. ¶ ～으로 쓰다 write in a cursive hand; scribble busily.

**흘림흘림** (by) piecemeal; little by little; bit by bit; in little driblets. ¶ ～주다 dribble out; give by 〔in〕 driblets / 돈을 ～ 갚다 return money in small sums.

**흘립**(屹立) ～하다 tower (high); soar; rise. ¶ 그 산은 다른 산봉우리 위에 ～하고 있다 The mountain soars high above all its rivals.

**흘미죽죽** sluggishly; in a slovenly way. ～하다 (be) sluggish; slovenly.

**흘수**(吃水) draft; draught. ¶ ～가 깊은〔얕은〕배 a deep-〔light-, shallow-〕 draft ship / ～18피트의 배 a vessel of 18 feet draft / ～를 재다 take the draft《of a ship》/ 이 배는 ～가 얕다〔깊다〕 This ship draws shallow 〔deep〕 draft. ◉ ～계 a draft gauge. ～선 the water-line; the draft (line): 만재 ～선 the load line 〔waterline〕. ～제한선 a vessel with freeboard. ～표 the draft mark. 선미～ after draft. 선수～ forward 〔fore〕 draft. 적재 ～량 load drafts. 중앙〔평균, 경하(輕荷)〕～ midship 〔mean, light〕 draft.

**흘쩍거리다** dawdle 〔loaf〕 at; idle along; delay. ¶ 일을 ～ dawdle at *one's* work; loaf on the job. 「delaying.

**흘쩍흘쩍** dawdling; loafing; idling;

**흙**《토양》earth; soil;《진흙》mud; clay (찰흙);《지면》the ground. ¶ 흙으로 만든 earthen; clay / 흙을 파다 dig up earth; till the soil; do farming; dig in the ground / 내 눈에 흙이 들어가기 전에는 [비유적] so long as I live / 흙을 덮다 heap up earth; cover with earth; earth up / ～에 묻다 bury《*a thing*》in the ground / 이국땅의 흙이 되다 die in a strange 〔foreign〕 land; find *one's* grave in a far-off foreign land / 흙으로 돌아가다 return 〔fall back〕 to dust; turn to clay; die / …의 흙을 밟다 set 〔plant〕 foot on《foreign》soil; tread《British》soil / 사람은 한 줌 흙에 지나지 않는다 Man is but a lump of clay.

**흙감태기** being covered all over with mud. ¶ ～가 되다 be covered all over with mud 〔dirt〕; be besmeared 〔soiled〕 with mud; get muddy; muddy *oneself*. 「ground.

**흙구덩이** a hole 〔hollow, cavity〕 in the

**흙내** earth-smelling; (an) earthy smell. ¶ ～(를) 맡다 take a sniff at earth;《초목이》take 〔strike〕 root. 「paved.

**흙다리** a wooden bridge with mud

**흙담** ＝토담.

**흙더미** a heap of earth; a ball of mud.

**흙더버기** 《covered with》caked mud splashes; all mud-splashed〔-splattered〕.

**흙덩어리** a lump of earth; a clod.

**흙돋우기** raising the ground level; filling-up;〖토목〗banking. ～하다 lay earth on the ground; raise the ground level.

**흙먼지** dust; a cloud of dust. ¶ ～를 일으키다 raise a cloud of dust.

**흙무더기** a heap 〔pile〕 of earth.

**흙뭉치** a ball 〔lump〕 of earth 〔mud, clay〕. 「clay〕.

**흙뭉텅이** a large lump of earth 〔mud,

**흙받기** ①《미장이의》a (plasterer's) mortarboard; a hawk. ②《자동차 바퀴의》a mudguard; a splashboard; a fender; a wing《영》.

**흙밥**《삽·괭이의》a spadeful 〔hoeful〕 of earth;《쟁기의》the earth turned over by a plow.

**흙방**(—房) a naked room with a mud floor and mud walls.

**흙벽**(—壁) a mud-plastered wall.

**흙벽돌**(—壁—) a block of dried mud; adobe; a sun-dried brick. ¶ ～집 an adobe house.

**흙비** a dust storm; a sandstorm.

**흙빛** the color of the earth; (an) earthlike color. ¶ (얼굴 따위가) ～인 deadly 〔ghastly〕 pale; ashy / ～이 되다《얼굴이》go 〔turn〕 ghastly 〔deadly〕 pale; go 〔turn〕 as pale as ashes.

**흙빨래** soiling *one's* clothes with muddy water.

**흙손** a (plasterer's) trowel: a float. ¶ ～으로 바르다 trowel; lay on《plaster》with a trowel. ◉ ～끝 a trowel-shaped chisel used for finishing gutters.

**흙손질** trowelling; plastering with a trowel. ～하다 trowel; plaster with a trowel.

**흙일**《토역》earthwork(s);《미장이 일》plastering. ～하다 do earthwork 〔the plastering〕. ¶ ～하는 사람 a navvy.

**흙장난** ～하다 play with the soil.

**흙질** mud-plastering. ～하다 mud-plaster; do the「mud〔plastering〕work.
**흙창**(一窓) a window papered on both inside and outside.
**흙칠** ～하다 daub with mud. ¶ 얼굴에 ～하다 daub *one's* face with mud.
**흙탕** ① ＝흙탕물. ②《질퍽한 곳》a muddy spot. ¶ ～에서 놀다 play in the mud. ◉ ～길 a muddy road.
**흙탕물** muddy water. ¶ ～을 튀기다 splash〔spatter〕mud / ～을 뒤집어 쓰다 be spattered with mud.
**흙투성이** being「covered〔daubed〕all over with earth. ¶ ～가 되다 be covered with「mud〔earth〕.
**흠**(欠) ①《상처》a scar; a cicatrix (*pl.* -trices). ¶ 얼굴에 흠이 지다 get〔have, bear〕a scar on *one's* face.
②《물건의》a flaw; a crack; a speck; a scratch; a disfigurement;《과일의》bruise. ¶ 꽃병에 흠이 가다 a vase has a crack / 흠이 있다 be「scratched〔cracked, disfigured〕; have a flaw《in》/ 흠이 없다 be without flaw; be「flawless〔perfect〕/ 흠이 있으니 값을 좀 싸게 해 드리죠 It has some flaws, so I will lower it a little in price.
③《인간의 결점》a fault; a defect; a flaw; a blemish; a mar; a stain; a blur. ¶ 게으른 것이 그의 흠이다 The bad thing about him is his laziness. / 흠없는 사람은 없다 Nobody is perfect. / 성급한 것이 그의 흠이다 Rashness is his defect. *or* He is lacking in steadiness. / 그 사람의 흠이라면 단지 술마시는 것뿐이다 Drinking is one flaw in his otherwise perfect character. / 나의 비서는 너무 유능해서 흠을 잡을 데가 없다 My secretary is so efficient, I can't find fault with anything she does.
**흠**《비웃는 소리》Hum!; Hm!; Hmph!; Humph! ¶ 흠하고 웃다 laugh sardonically; laugh with a sniff; humph.
**흠구덕**(欠一) backbiting; (a) slander; aspersions. ～하다 backbite; slander; cast aspersions on《*a person*》;「talk about〔speak ill of〕《*a person*》behind *his* back.
**흠나다**(欠一) ＝흠지다.
**흠내다**(欠一) ①《얼굴에》scar; make a scar. ¶ 얼굴에 ～ scar *one's* face. ②《물건에》mar; crack; scratch; make a「flaw〔crack, scratch〕.
**흠뜯다**(欠一) slander; speak「ill〔evil〕of; run down; backbite. ¶ 남을 잘 흠뜯는 사람 a scandalmonger; a scandalbearer / 아무를 ～ run *a person* down.
**흠모**(欽慕) admiration; adoration; high regard. ～하다 admire; adore; esteem; be deeply attached to; make an idol of. ¶ 그는 아직(까지) 고향 사람들의 ～를 받고 있다 He is still the idol of his countrymen.
**흠빨다** suck hard. ¶ 흠빨며 감빨다 suck 《it》 up greedily.
**흠뻑** very much; plenty; fully; all; completely;《마음껏》to *one's* heart's content; to *one's* satisfaction;《젖은 꼴이》to the skin. ¶ ～ 젖다 be soaked to the skin; be wet through; be soaked with rain / 비가 ～ 오다 have much rain / ～ 기뻐하다 be greatly pleased; be much delighted / 취할 때까지 ～마시다 drink till all is blue / 땀을 ～흘리다 be all in sweat.
**흠실흠실** ～하다 (be) soft; overboiled; be boiled soft. ¶ 고기를 ～ 삶다 boil meat tender.
**흠씬** enough; sufficiently; greatly; to the fullest measure; thoroughly; utterly; completely. ¶ 고기를 ～삶다 boil meat「to a pulp〔soft enough〕/ ～먹다 eat *one's* fill / 비가 ～오다 have sufficient rain.
**흠앙**(欽仰) adoration; reverence; high esteem. ～하다 adore; revere; look up to with reverence; esteem highly.
**흠잡다**(欠一) find fault with; pick at; pick holes in《*a thing*》; cavil〔carp〕at; complain about. ¶ 방이 좁은 것을 ～ find fault with a room because it is so small / 흠잡을 데가 없다 be faultless; leave nothing to be desired / 남의 흠잡기를 좋아하다 be fond of finding fault with others / 아무도 흠잡히기를 좋아하지 않는다 Nobody likes to be found fault with.
**흠정**(欽定) ¶ ～의 authorized〔established〕by the king; compiled by royal order. ◉ ～역성서「the Authorized〔the King James〕Version (of the Bible). ～헌법 a constitution granted by the king.
**흠지다**(欠一) ①《얼굴에》get scarred; have〔leave〕a scar. ¶ 아문 상처가 ～ heal to a scar / 이마에 ～ get〔have〕a scar on *one's* forehead. ②《물건 등에》get「marred〔cracked, scratched〕; get〔have〕a「flaw〔crack, scratch, speck〕.
**흠지러기** stringy ends of meat.
**흠집**(欠一) a scar; a cicatrix (*pl.* -trices). ¶ ～이 있는 flawed; cracked;

disfigured; bruised / ～ 있는 손 a scarred hand / ～이 생기다 flaw; crack (금이 감); 《과일이》 bruise 《easily》.

**흠축**(欠縮) shortage; deficiency; want; deficit. ¶ ～ 나다 be 〔fall, run〕 short; be insufficient; be shy 《of》 / ～ 내다 cause a shortage 《of》; make a deficit 《of》.

**흠치르르** ～하다 (be) sleek; glossy. ¶ ～ 윤이 흐르다 be smooth and glossy; be sleek.

**흠칫** recoiling 〔shrinking〕 with a fright 〔surprise〕. ～하다 recoil; shrink; pull back 《*one's* head, neck, shoulders》 in surprise 〔fright〕. ¶ ～ 놀라다 be startled 《at》.

**흡광**(吸光) 〖물리〗 extinction.

**흡기**(吸氣) 《마심》 inhalation of air 〔breath〕; inspiration; 《공기》 air breathed in. ～하다 inhale; breathe 〔suck〕 in. ◉ ～공 《제트 엔진의》 an intake. ～기 an aspirator.

**흡력**(吸力) absorption 〔sucking〕 power. ⇨ 흡인력.

**흡반**(吸盤) a sucker. ⇨ 빨판.

**흡사**(恰似) a close resemblance; [부사] like; as; just as; as if 〔though〕; as it were. ～하다 be alike; be just as; resemble closely; be closely akin 《to》; be much 〔about〕 the same. ¶ 아주 ～ 하다 be as like as two peas 〔eggs〕; be exactly alike; be a replica; be a copy 《of》 / ～ 죽은 사람과 같다 look as if dead; be more dead than alive / ～ 지옥과 같다 It is a veritable hell. / 용모가 아버지와 ～하다 He looks like his father very much. *or* He is the perfect image of his father. / ～ 달이 뜬 것처럼 밝다 It is as bright as if the moon had risen.

**흡상**(吸上) suction. ～하다 suck 〔draw, pump〕 up.

**흡수**(吸水) suction of water; water absorption. ～하다 draw water by sucking; suck water; absorb water 《from》. ◉ ～관 a siphon; a suction pipe. ～시험 a water absorption test. ～펌프 a suction pump.

**흡수**(吸收) absorption; suction; 《열의》 decalescence; 《빛의》 extinction; 《동화》 assimilation. ～하다 absorb; suck 〔take〕 in; imbibe; assimilate (동화하다). ¶ 영양의 ～ absorption of nourishment / 공기로부터 수분을 ～하다 absorb moisture from the air / 서양 문명을 ～하다 assimilate Western civilization / 실업자를 ～ 하다 absorb the jobless into work; mobilize labor 《for public work》 / 혈액내에 ～되다 be absorbed into the blood / 피부를 통해 체내로 ～되다 be absorbed into the system through the skin / 스폰지는 물을 ～한다 A sponge absorbs water. / 이 나라는 동서 문화 ～에 바빴다 This country was busy in assimilating both Occidental and Oriental civilization.
◉ ～계수〔율〕 an absorption coefficient 〔factor〕; absorptivity. ～관 an absorption tube. ～구(口) a suctorial mouth. ～기 an absorber. ～력 absorption force; absorbing power; 《청소기 등의》 sucking power; 《이해력》 receptivity: ～력이 있는 absorbent; absorptive. ～성 absorptiveness: ～성의 absorbent; absorptive. ～스펙트럼 an absorption spectrum. ～열 heat of absorption. ～작용 《a process of》 absorption. ～제 an absorbent. ～조직 an absorptive tissue. ～합병 《기업 따위의》 merger.

**흡습**(吸濕) moisture absorption. ¶ ～성 hygroscopic property; hygroscopicity / ～성의 hygroscopic / ～성이 강하다 be highly hygroscopic. ◉ ～제 a desiccant; a moisture absorbent.

**흡연**(吸煙) smoking. ～하다 smoke (tobacco, a cigarette, a pipe); have a smoke. ¶ 여기서는 ～을 금하고 있다 No smoking is allowed here. *or* Smoking is prohibited here. / ～ 절대 금지 《게시》 Absolutely no smoking. / ～을 많이 하면 성대가 나빠지는 경향이 있다 Much smoking tends to injure the voice. / ～은 당신 건강에 해롭다 Smoking is hazardous to your health.
◉ ～실 a smoking 〔smoke 《주로 영》〕 room; 《배의》 a smoking saloon. ～자 a smoker. ～장소 a smoking area 〔corner〕.

**흡열**(吸熱) ¶ ～의 endothermic; endoergic. ◉ ～반응 〖화학〗 (an) endothermic 〔endoergic〕 reaction. ～화합물 an endothermic 〔endoergic〕 compound.

**흡음**(吸音) sound absorption. ◉ ～력〔재〕 sound-absorbing power 〔materials〕. ～률 acoustic absorptivity.

**흡인**(吸引) absorption; suction; imbibition; attraction. ～하다 absorb; suck (in, up); imbibe; attract; draw in (by suction). ◉ ～기 an aspirator. ～력 sucking force. ～병 a suction bottle. ～작용 the process of absorption.

**흡입**(吸入) inhalation; indraft; imbibition. ～하다 inhale; intake; suck in; breathe 〔draw〕 in. ◉ ～관 a suction 〔an incurrent〕 pipe. ～밸브 a sucking 〔a suction, an admission〕 valve. ～요법 inhalation treatment; inhalational therapy.

**흡입기**(吸入器) an inhaler; an inhalator; an inspirator. ¶ 산소 ～ an oxygen inhaler 〔inspirator〕/ (환자에게) ～를 대주다 treat 《a patient》 with an inspirator; give 《a patient》 inhalation treatment; give 《a patient》 oxygen.

**흡족**(洽足) sufficiency; ampleness. ～하다 (be) sufficient; ample. ¶ ～히 enough; sufficiently; fully; to the full; in plenty; 《만족히》 to *one's* heart's content / ～히 물을 주다 give a good watering / ～한 얼굴을 하다 look satisfied.

**흡지**(吸枝) 〖식물〗 a sucker.

**흡착**(吸着) adsorption; adhesion. ～하다 stick fast to; adsorb. ◉ ～기 an adsorber. ～열 heat of adsorption. ～제 an adsorbent.

**흡출**(吸出) suction; sucking. ～하다 suck 〔draw〕 out. ◉ ～관 a draft tube. ～송풍기 an induced draft fan.

**흡혈**(吸血) bloodsucking; sucking blood. ◉ ～귀 a vampire; a bloodsucker. ～동물 a bloodsucker. ～박쥐 a vampire bat.

**흣대** a potter's (shaping) stick.

**흥**(興) fun; mirth; pleasure; merriment; joy; excitement. ¶ 흥이 나면 when fancy leads *one* / 흥에 겨워(서) in the excess of mirth; driven by *one's* enthusiasm / 흥이 나다 get 〔became〕 absorbed 〔more and more interested〕 《in》; warm (up) 《to *one's* work》 / 흥을 깨다 spoil 《*a person's*》 pleasure 〔fun〕; kill the joy; put 〔throw〕 a wet blanket on / 흥을 깨는 사람 a killjoy; a spoilsport; a skeleton at the feast 〔banquet〕 / 흥이 깨지다 find *one's* fun spoiled; the spell is broken / 흥을 돋우다 give 〔add〕 a zest to; add to the amusement 〔pleasure〕 《of》 / 좌석의 흥이 깨지지 않도록 하다 keep the ball rolling; keep up the ball / 흥에 못 이기다 be overwhelmed with fun / 그는 언제나 좌석의 흥을 깨뜨린다 He is a wet blanket in every company. / 그의 말로 좌석의 흥이 깨졌다 His remark cast a chill over the whole company. *or* Their fun was spoiled by his remark.

**흥**[1] [부사] ¶ 코를 흥 하고 풀다 blow *one's* nose with hissing sound / 《아이에게》 흥 해 Blow, honey!

**흥**[2] [감탄사] Hum!; H'm! Hmph! ¶ 흥 하고 코 웃음을 치다 turn up *one's* nose at 《*a person*》.

**흥감** exaggeration; grandiosity; bombast. ～부리다 exaggerate; stretch. ～스럽다 be given to exaggeration; (be) bombastic; high-flown. ¶ ～스럽게 exaggeratedly; pompously / ～스럽게 떠들어 대다 make a fuss too much.

**흥건하다** ① 《물 따위가》 be full of water. ¶ 웅덩이에 빗물이 흥건하게 괴었다 A puddle is full of rainwater. / 그의 등에는 땀이 흥건했다 His back was clammy with perspiration. ② 《국물이》 have too much liquid in it.

**흥겹다**(興—) be full of fun; (be) delightful; fun; exciting. ¶ 흥겹게 gaily; merrily; joyously; pleasantly / 흥겨운 김에 in the excess of mirth / 한참 흥겨운 판에 in the midst of *one's* merriment / 흥겨운 하루 a day full of fun; a fun-packed day; an exciting day / 흥겨워하다 amuse 〔disport〕 *oneself;* have fun; be amused / 흥겹게 놀다 make merry; have fun 《at》.

**흥글방망이놀다** interfere 《with》; meddle 《in》; thwart; frustrate.

**흥나다**(興—) get merry; grow excited; have fun. ¶ 흥이 나서 춤추다 dance in *one's* mirth / 흥이 나면 시를 읊는다 When I am in the mood, I recite poems.

**흥덩흥덩** having too much water in it. ～하다 have too much water in it. ¶ ～국물뿐이구나 The soup is all water with no meat in!

**흥뚱새** 〖조류〗 a tree-pipit.

**흥뚱항뚱** carelessly; heedlessly; recklessly. ¶ ～ 듣다 listen to 《*a person*》 in an absent sort of way; pay little 〔no〕 attention to / 일을 ～하다 do a job carelessly.

**흥륭**(興隆) prosperity; rise. ～하다 prosper; rise; flourish. ¶ 국가의 ～ the rise of the nation / 문화의 ～ the flourishing of culture.

**흥망**(興亡) rise and fall; ups and downs; vicissitudes (영고성쇠); existence (존망). ¶ 로마 제국의 ～ the rise and fall of the Roman Empire / 이 나라의 ～은 …에 걸려 있다 The fate of this country depends upon… / 이것은 국가의 ～이 걸려 있는 중대한 문제이다 This is a grave problem upon which the destiny of the nation depends. / 나는 ～을 걸고 이 사업을 해 보겠습니다. I will try my luck with this business. / 그것은 나라의 ～을 건 한 판 싸움이었다 It was a battle on which the fate of the country hung.

**흥미**(興味) (an) interest; zest. ¶ 대단한 ～ great 〔deep, intense, active, high〕 interest / ～있는 interesting; amusing; exciting / ～없는 uninteresting; dull; of no interest.

흥미가: ～(가) 있다 be interesting 〔attractive, amusing〕 / 다소 ～(가) 있는 이야기 a subject of some interest / ～(가) 없다 be uninteresting 〔dull, insipid〕; be of no interest.

흥미를: 다양한 ～를 가진 사람 a man of many interests; a person with multiple interests / 대단히 ～를 자아내는 뉴스 a most intriguing piece of news / ～를 가지다〔느끼다〕 take 〔feel〕 (an) interest《in》; be interested《in》/ …에 큰 ～를 갖다 take a strong interest in… / 깊은 ～를 갖고 with a keen 〔deep〕 interest / ～를 더하다 add zest to《*something*》/ ～를 보이다 show (an) interest《in》/ ～를 끌다 attract 〔engage〕《*a person's*》 interest / ～를 잃다 lose (an) interest《in》/ ～를 잃게 하다 spoil《a *person's*》 interest / ～를 일으키다 [사물이 주어] rouse 〔arouse; awaken, excite〕 *one's* interest《in》.

¶ 그러한 제안은 나로서는 ～가 없다 Such a suggestion does not appeal to me. / 그런 것들은 나에게 아무 ～도 없다 Such things have no interest for me. / 그는 새로운 ～를 가지고 그 책의 연구를 시작했다 He began to study the book with new interest. / 그 영화는 매우 ～ 있었다 I've got a lot of fun out of 〔from〕 the picture. *or* The picture thrilled 〔excited〕 me a great deal.

**흥미본위**(興味本位) ¶ ～의 aimed chiefly at amusing 〔entertaining〕《the readers》/ ～의 주간지 a sensational weekly magazine / ～의 문학 popular literature / ～의 읽을거리 amusing 〔light〕 reading / ～로 out of mere curiosity / 이 책은 ～로 씌어져 있다 This book is intended for popular 〔mass〕 consumption. *or* This book is meant for the lowbrows. / 나는 그 책을 ～로 읽고 있다 I am reading the book for amusement.

**흥미진진**(興味津津) ～하다 be very 〔intensely〕 interesting; be of great 〔absorbing〕 interest; be full of interest; be of immense interest《to *one*》; be absorbing. ¶ 그가 다음에 무엇을 할지를 지켜보는 것은 ～한 일이다 It will be very interesting to see what he will do next.

**흥분**(興奮) excitement; agitation; stimulation. ～하다 be 〔get〕 excited 〔agitated〕; be aroused《to activity》; be stimulated《into action》; be worked up《over》; work *oneself* up《into a passion》; get warm 〔hot〕. ¶ ～하여 in excitement; excitedly; in an excited state of mind / ～하기 쉽다 be easily excited 〔agitated〕; be excitable 〔passionate, jumpy〕 / ～시키다 excite; stimulate; get《*a person*》 excited 〔worked up〕 / ～하지 않고 있다 keep calm / 그 사건으로 ～해 있다 be in a state of excitement about the affair / ～을 가라앉히다 allay 〔calm down〕《*a person's*》 excitement; cool down《*a person's* hot temper》/ 그는 ～ 상태에 있다 His nerves are on edge. *or* He is in a wrought-up state. / 그 뉴스는 사람들을 크게 ～ 시키고 있다 The news causes great excitement among people. / 지금 그녀의 ～을 가라 앉히려 해도 헛수고다 It's no use trying to calm her down. / 환자를 ～시켜서는 안 된다 The patient must not be excited. / ～하지 마라 Don't be upset. *or* Calm down. *or* Take it easy. / 그는 ～한 나머지 심장 마비로 쓰러졌다 Overexcited, he collapsed and died from a heart attack. ◉ ～상태 an excited condition 〔state〕. ～성 excitability; irritability; sensitiveness. ～음료 an exhilarating drink; a pick-me-up. 신경성 ～ 『생리』 erethism.

**흥분제**(興奮劑) a stimulant; an excitant 〔exciter〕; an incitant 〔invigorator〕; 《구어》 a pep pill; 《속어》 an upper. ¶ ～를 복용하다〔복용시키다〕 take 〔administer〕 a stimulant.

**흥성**(興盛) prosperity. ～하다 grow in prosperity; become prosperous; prosper; thrive.

**흥성흥성**(興盛興盛) thriving; flourishing; roaring; booming. ～하다 (be) prosperous; thriving; roaring; booming. ¶ 장사가〔사업이〕 ～하다 The business is booming.

**흥신소**(興信所) a (private) detective agency《미》; an inquiry agency 〔office〕. ¶ 상업 ～ a credit bureau; a commercial (inquiry) agency / ～의 직원 a private detective 〔investigator〕《미》; an inquiry agent《영》.

**흥얼거리다** 《노래를》 hum 《a tune》; croon 《a song》; sing to *oneself*; 《중얼거리다》 murmur; mutter.

**흥얼흥얼** humming; crooning. ¶ ～ 혼자 노래하다 croon to *oneself*.

**흥업**(興業) promotion of industry; inauguration of a new industrial enterprise. ～하다 promote industries; undertake an industrial enterprise.

**흥이야항이야** meddling; prying; interfering. ～하다 intermeddle in 《other people's affairs》; thrust 〔put, stick, poke〕 *one's* nose into 《another's affair》. ¶ 남의 일에 ～하다 poke 〔stick〕 *one's* nose into another person's business.

**흥정** 《매매》 buying and selling; purchase and sale; 《거래》 a bargain; trade; dealing; (a) transaction; business. ～하다 buy and sell; deal 〔trade〕 《in cotton with》; do business 《with》; have dealings 《with》; make a deal 《with》. ¶ 술자리에서의 ～ a Dutch 〔wet〕 bargain / 정치적 ～ political compromise / 정당간의 ～ a deal between the political parties / 값을 ～하다 bargain 〔haggle〕 with 《*a person*》 over the price 《of an article》 / ～이 많다 have lots of business / ～이 없다 make few sales; do little business / ～을 붙이다 act as broker 〔go-between, intermediary〕 / ～은 붙이고 싸움을 말리랬다 One should help bargaining and stop quarrels. / ～이 끝났으니 한잔 내겠네 The bargain is concluded, and I'll treat you to drinks.
◉ ～거리 merchandise. ～꾼 《중개인》 a mediator; a go-between; a middleman; a broker; 《사고 파는 사람》 buyers and 〔or〕 sellers; a dealer; a trader. ～솜씨 the tricks of trade.

**흥진비래**(興盡悲來) After fun comes sorrow. *or* After joy come tears.

**흥청거리다** ① 《홍에 겨워 거드럭거리다》 indulge in riotous fun; make merry; be on a spree; exult; be highly elated; be in high spirits. ¶ 술집을 드나들며 만판 ～ paint the town red / 흥청거리며 살다 live in a racket of enjoyment; live in great style. ② 《돈을 마구 쓰다》 lavish 〔squander〕 *one's* money 《on》; spend money lavishly 《on》.

**흥청망청** ① 《즐기는 모양》 merrily; gaily; with elation. ¶ ～ 놀고 마시다 be 〔go〕 on a drinking spree. ② 《흔전만전》 in profusion; lavishly. ¶ ～돈을 쓰다 spend money in profusion; be lavish with *one's* money.

**흥취**(興趣) interest; taste; (a) charm; elegance; grace. ¶ ～있는 tasteful; elegant; attractive / ～가 있다 be interesting 〔fun〕; be of absorbing interest / 겨울철 쓸쓸한 경치도 또한 ～가 있다 A desolate winter scene has a charm of its own. / 오래 된 물방아는 그 정원의 ～를 더했다 An old water wheel graced the garden.

**흥타령**(―打令) a kind of folksong with a "hum" at the end of each line.

**흥패**(興敗) rise and fall 〔decline〕. ⇨흥망. ¶ 국가의 ～가 달려 있는 싸움 a battle which decides the fate of a country.

**흥하다**(興―) ① 《일어나다》 rise; be in the ascendant. ¶ 나라가 ～ a country rises. ② 《번영하다》 thrive; flourish; prosper; boom. ¶ 흥하는 집안 a thriving family / 장사가 ～ business booms 〔flourishes, prospers〕 / 흥하든 망하든 해 보겠다 I will try, sink or swim 〔fail or succeed〕.

**흥행**(興行) 《1회의》 a performance; a show; a run; 《사업》 show business; the entertainment industry. ～하다 perform; give a performance; produce 《a play》; put on 《a show》; show 〔run〕 《a play》. ¶ ～을 목적으로 for business 〔commercial〕 purposes / 하룻밤만의 ～ a one-night stand 《미》 / 지방에서 ～하고 있다 be on the road 《미》 / 하루 3회 ～이 있다 There are three performances a day. *or* They give three shows a day. / 그 연극은 장장 100일간 ～되었다 The play had a run of 100 days.
◉ ～가치 audience value; box-office value: ～ 가치가 있는 영화 a picture of proven box-office power; a film with audience appeal / 이 쇼는 ～ 가치가 충분하다 This show will be good box-office. ～계(界) the entertainment world; the show business circles. ～계통 a circuit; a chain. ～권(權) performance 〔production〕 rights; 《연극의》 stage 〔dramatic〕 right. ～단 a (theatrical) company; a troupe; a circus (서커스의). ～물 a (public) performance; a show; an exhibition. ～사 a show proprietor 〔manager〕. ～성적 a box-office record: ～ 성적은 썩 좋았다 It was a great box-office success. ～

세(稅) an entertainment tax. ～수익 box-office profits. ～장 a show place. ～주(主) a promotor; a show manager; a showman; an impresario; 〖영화〗 a film producer (제작자). 단기～ a short run. 야간～ a night performance. 자선～ a charity performance 〔show〕. 주간～ a matinée. 지방～ a road 〔traveling〕 show.

**흥행화**(興行化) adaptation for performance 〔the stage〕. ～하다 adapt 《a story》 for performance; 〖연극〗 put on a stage; stage 《a play》; 〖영화〗 filmize 〔film, screen〕 《a story》.

**흥흥** Hum hum!; Hmph hmph!

**흥흥거리다** ① 《흥겨워서》 hum; croon; sing to *oneself;* hum a tune. ¶ 흥흥거리며 일하다 do *one's* work humming a tune. ② 《아이가》 grumble; complain; whine; whimper.

**흩날리다** send off flying (in all directions); scatter; blow 《*something*》 off 〔away〕. ¶ 바람이 꽃을 ～ the wind sends blossoms flying.

**흩다** scatter (about); strew; disperse; 《머리털 따위를》 loosen; dishevel.

**흩뜨리다** scatter (about); disperse; 《머리 따위를》 dishevel. ¶ 머리를 흩뜨리고 with *one's* hair shaken loose; with disheveled 〔disordered〕 hair / 휴지 조각을 ～ scatter bits of waste paper / 흩뜨려 놓다 leave 《*things*》 scattered 〔lying〕 about.

**흩뿌리다** scatter (about); strew; sprinkle. ¶ 씨를 ～ distribute seed over 《a field》 / 얼어붙은 길에 모래를 ～ sprinkle sands on the icy road / 전단을 ～ distribute bills; broadcast leaflets.

**흩어지다** ① 《헤어지다》 scatter; get scattered. ¶ 꽃이 바람에 ～ blossoms are scattered in the wind. ② 《뿔뿔이》 disperse; break up; scatter. ¶ 가족이 사방으로 ～ a family scatters in all directions / 유대 민족은 온 세계에 흩어져 있다 The Jewish race is spread all over the world. / 길에 광고지가 흩어져 있다 The streets are littered with handbills. / 땅 위에 낙엽이 흩어져 있다 The ground is strewn 〔scattered〕 with fallen leaves. ③ 《정신이》 be distracted.

**흩이다** get 〔be〕 scattered 〔dispersed〕. ¶ 꽃이 바람에 ～ blossoms are scattered by the wind.

**희가극**(喜歌劇) (a) comic opera; an operetta.

**희가스**(稀―) 〖화학〗 rare 〔noble〕 gases. ◉ ～류 원소 rare-gas elements.

**희곡**(戲曲) (a) drama; a play. ¶ ～적(인) dramatic(al). ◉ ～작가 a dramatist; a playwriter; a playwright. ～작법 dramaturgy. ～집 a collection of plays.

**희곡화**(戲曲化) dramatization. ～하다 dramatize; make a dramatic version 《of a novel》.

**희구**(希求) desire; want; aspiration. ～하다 desire 《to *do*》; want; aspire 《to, after》; seek; ask 〔long〕 for 《*a thing*》. ¶ 쌍방이 다 평화를 ～하고 있다 Both sides are longing for peace.

**희귀**(稀貴) rarity; rareness. ～하다 (be) rare. ¶ ～한 물건 a rarity; a curiosity; a black swan; a white crow / ～한 새 a rare bird / ～한 식물 an out-of-the-way plant / ～한 현상 a singular 〔striking〕 phenomenon. ◉ ～본(本) a rare book. ～종(種) a rare variety; a rarity.

**희극**(喜劇) (a) comedy; (a) farce (소극(笑劇)); a funny show 《미》. ¶ ～적(인) comic(al); farcical / ～을 벌이다 [비유적] play the fool; create a comic scene / ～을 연출하다 perform a comedy / 한 바탕 ～이 벌어졌다 A comic scene was enacted (on the spot). ◉ ～문학 comic literature. ～배우 a comedian; 《남》 a comic 〔comedy〕 actor; 《여》 a comic 〔comedy〕 actress. ～영화 a comic film 〔picture〕. ～작가 a writer of comedies; a comedy 〔comic〕 writer.

**희극**(戲劇) ① 〖연극〗 a farce. ② 《행동》 a farcical act.

**희금속**(稀金屬) 〖화학〗 rare metals.

**희기**(喜氣) a happy frame of mind; a mood of cheerfulness; gay spirits; a happy feeling; good humor.

**희끄무레하다** (be) whitish; rather fair. ¶ 희끄무레한 얼굴 a rather fair face.

**희끄스름하다** (be) whitish.

**희끈거리다** get dizzy 〔giddy〕; become shaky.

**희끈희끈** dizzily; giddily; shakily.

**희끔하다** (be) whitish.

**희끗거리다** ＝희뜩거리다.

**희끗희끗하다** be streaked 〔shot〕 with gray (머리가); (be) grizzled; 《옷감 따위가》 (be) pepper-and-salt. ¶ 머리가 희끗희끗한 사람 a grizzle-haired man / 머리가 희끗희끗해지다 [머리가 주어] show white streaks; be shot 〔streaked〕 with gray; become grizzled 〔grizzly〕 / 그의 머리가 희끗희끗해지기 시작한다 His hair is beginning to frost a little.

**희나리** wet firewood.

**희넓적하다** (be) white and broad.

**희년**(稀年) seventy years of age.

**희다** ①《색이》(be) white;《살이》(be) fair;《머리가》(be) gray; hoary. ¶ 백설같이 흰 snow-white / 흰 얼굴 a fair 〔white〕 face / 흰 머리 gray hair / 살빛이 ~ have a fair 〔light〕 complexion / (머리가) 희어지다 become white; turn white; turn gray / 희게 하다 make《*a thing*》white; whiten;《탈색》blanch; bleach (무명 따위를); refine (가루 등을) / 흰 머리를 검게 물들이다 dye *one's* (gray) hair black / 양털 같은 흰 구름이 창공에 떠 있었다 Fleecy clouds floated in the blue sky. ②《희떱다》(be) showy; snobbish. ⇨ 희떱다.

**희담**(戲談) a joke; a jest; fun; banter; a pleasantry; a witticism.

**희대**(稀代) uncommonness; uniqueness; rarity. ¶ ~의 uncommon; rare; extraordinary; unheard-of;《비길 데 없는》peerless; matchless; unique / ~의 영웅 a unique 〔peerless〕 hero; a hero for the century; an extraordinary hero / ~의 악당 a notorious villain.

**희디희다** (be) very white; snow-white; immaculately white; be as white as snow.

**희떱다** ①《허영》(be) showy; vain; vainglorious. ②《씀씀이가》be generous though penniless. ③《언행이》(be) snobbish; conceited; pretentious.

**희뜩거리다** get very dizzy 〔giddy, shaky〕;《*one's* head》swim. 「er.

**희뜩머룩이** a spendthrift; a free spend-

**희뜩희뜩하다** ①《현기증으로》be very dizzy; get very giddy. ⇨ 희뜩거리다. ②《흰색이》be dotted with white;《머리털이》(be) grizzly. ¶ 머리가 희뜩희뜩한 gray-haired; grizzled; grizzle-haired.

**희락**(喜樂) joy and pleasure; felicity; happiness.

**희랍**(希臘) Greece. ⇨ 그리스.

**희로**(喜怒) joy and 〔or〕 anger; emotion; feelings.

**희로애락**(喜怒哀樂) joy, anger, sorrow and pleasure;《감정》feelings; emotions. ¶ ~의 정 feelings of joy and anger 〔humor and pathos〕/ ~을 얼굴에 나타내지 않다 do not betray *one's* feelings 〔emotions〕.

**희롱**(戲弄) ridiculing; jesting; banter; raillery; chaff; a joke. ~하다 banter; chaff; tease《*a person* with *his* cowardice, *a person* with jest》; poke fun《at》; make fun 〔sport, game, a fool〕 of; make a jest of; make a mock of; ridicule; toy 〔play〕《with》; trifle 〔fool〕《with》. ¶ ~조로 in a mocking tone / ~조로 말하다 say《*a thing*》in 〔for〕 sport / 운명에 ~당하다 be at the mercy of fate / 여자를 ~하다 sport 〔toy〕 with a woman. ◉ 성~ sexual harassment.

**희롱거리다** jest; play pranks; frolic; horse around; cut capers; act 〔play〕 the giddy goat.

**희롱해롱** playing pranks; frolicking; joking; horsing around; cutting capers.

**희맑다** (be) white and clean.

**희망**(希望)《바라는 마음》(a) hope;《소망》(a) wish; (a) desire;《포부》(an) ambition; (an) aspiration;《기대》expectation(s);《요구》(a) request; a demand. ~하다 hope《to *do,* that...》; hope for《*something*》; wish《to *do, a person* to *do*》; desire《*something,* to *do*》; aspire to 〔after〕《*something*》;《기대하다》expect.

> 용법 **hope** 적어도 주관적으로는 실현 가능하다고 생각되는 사항에, 기대를 걸고 바라는 경우에 씀. **wish** 일의 가능성 여부와는 관계없이 또 실현 불가능하다고 생각되는 것일지라도, 그렇게 되었으면 좋겠다고 생각할 때 씀. **desire** wish 보다 강한 욕구를 나타내는 말.

¶ 간절한 ~ an ardent desire; an earnest wish; *one's* dearest ambition / 연래(年來)의 〔오랜〕 ~ *one's* long-cherished desire / ~대로《자기의》as *one* wishes;《상대의》as requested; at《*a person's*》request / 일루의 ~ a ray of hope / ~의 서광 the dawn of hope / 헛된 ~ an empty hope.

희망에: ~에 빛나는 얼굴 a face beamed with hopes / ~에 찬 젊은이 young hopefuls / ~에 찬 말 hopeful words / ~에 따라 at *one's* request; by *one's* desire; in compliance with *one's* request 〔order〕/ ~에 반(反)하여 against 〔contrary to〕 *one's* wishes 〔expectations〕/ Y씨의 ~에 따라 at Mr. Y's wish 〔request〕/ ~에 살다 live in hope(s) / ~에 차 있다 be hopeful; be full of hope.

희망을: …의 ~을 가지고 in hopes of...; in the hope that...; with the hope 〔desire〕 of... / 인생에 새로운 ~을 가지고 with a new hope in life / (…에) ~을 걸다 anchor *one's* hope《in, on》; attach *one's* hope《to》; pin 〔hang, lay〕 *one's* hope on《*a person, a*

*thing*》/ ～을 달성하다 realize 〔gratify, get〕 *one's* wishes; attain *one's* desires / ～을 들어주다 fulfill 〔meet〕《*a person's*》 wishes; gratify 〔satisfy〕《another's》 desire / ～을 말하다 lay *one's* wish before 《another》; express the hope 《that…》/ ～을 묻다 ask 《*a person's*》 wishes / ～을 버리다 despair 《of *do*ing》; give up 《all》 hope 《of *do*ing》/ (가망이 없는데도) ～을 버리지 않다 hope against hope / ～을 꺾다 blast 〔stifle, blight〕 hopes 《for negotiation》/ ～을 잃다 lose hope / ～을 주다 arouse 〔awaken, encourage〕 a hope; raise hopes / ～을 품다〔가지다〕 hope; cherish a desire; cherish 〔entertain, foster〕 a hope 《that…》/ ～을 가질 수가 없다 see no hope 《of success》; be past all hope; there is no hope 《for》.
희망이: …의 ～이 있다〔없다〕 there is a 〔no〕 hope of… / ～이 끊어지다 lose 〔be disappointed in〕 *one's* hopes / …에 대한 ～이 높아지다 hopes rise for…. ¶ 앞날에 ～이 없다 The future looks gray. / 그녀의 ～은 배우가 되는 것이다 She hopes to become an actress. *or* It is her hope to be an actress. / 나의 모든 ～이 수포로 돌아갔다 All my hopes have been crushed to pieces. / 그는 아들의 장래에 ～을 걸고 있다 He expects much of his son in future. / 그는 어떻게 하면 환자에게 회복할 수 있다는 ～을 줄 수 있을까 하고 고심했다 He was quite at a loss as to how to give his patient some hope of recovery.
◉ ～교 the school that *one* most wants to get into. ～소매가격 《생산자의》 a manufacturer's recommended price (생략 MRP). ～음악회 《라디오 따위의》 a request concert. ～조건 the terms 〔conditions〕 desired. ～퇴직 voluntary resignation; voluntary retirement (before the retirement age).

**희망봉**(喜望峯) 《아프리카의 곶》 the Cape of Good Hope.

**희망자**(希望者) a person who wants 〔wishes, desires〕 《to *do*》; 《지원자》 an applicant; a candidate. ¶ 입회～ an applicant 〔candidate〕 for membership.

**희망적 관측**(希望的觀測) *one's* wishful thinking. ¶ ～과 냉엄한 현실을 혼동하다 confuse wishful thinking with grim reality / 그들은 금년에는 경기가 좋아질 것이라고 하지만, 그것은 ～에 지나지 않는다 They say business will recover this year, but I think that's just wishful thinking.

**희멀겋다** (be) nice and fair.

**희멀쑥하다** (be) fair and clean. ¶ 희멀쑥한 얼굴 a fair-and-clean face.

**희묵**(戲墨) 《글씨》 my (humble) writing; 《그림》 my (unworthy) drawing.

**희문**(戲文) nonsense literature; a burlesque; a literary parody; humorous writing. ◉ ～작가 a humorist.

**희묽다** (be) white and flabby.

**희미**(稀微) dimness; faintness; 《불분명함》 vagueness; indistinctness; mistiness. ～하다 《미약하다》 (be) dim; faint; vague; indistinct; misty; hazy. ¶ ～하게 faintly; dimly; vaguely; indistinctly / ～한 광선 dim 〔feeble〕 light / ～하게 보이다 be seen dimly; be dimly visible 《in the distance》/ ～하게 빛나다 shine dimly / ～하게 기억하고 있다 have a dim memory 《of》; remember dimly / ～해지다 become dim 〔faint〕 / ～한 태도를 취하다 assume an ambiguous attitude 《to, toward》/ 빛이 멀리서 ～하게 보인다 A light glimmers in the distance. / 그 시절의 일은 그저 ～하게 기억날 뿐이다 I remember those days only vaguely. *or* I have only a faint memory of those days. / 날이 밝아지면서 별빛이 차차 ～해졌다 The stars faded before the approaching day. / 멀리서 종소리가 ～하게 들려왔다 A distant sound of a bell was faintly heard.

**희박**(稀薄) thinness; rarity; rarefaction; diluteness. ～하다 《엷다》 (be) thin; weak; 《액체 농도가》 dilute(d); 《기체가》 rarefied; 《밀도 등이》 sparse. ¶ ～한 공기 thin 〔rarefied〕 air / 인구가 ～하다 be thinly 〔sparsely〕 populated / ～하게 하다 thin 《a liquid》; rarefy 《a gas》; dilute 《a solution》; attenuate 《a liquid》/ 높은 산꼭대기에는 공기가 ～하다 The air is thin at the top of the high mountain.

**희번덕거리다** keep goggling 〔rolling〕 *one's* eyes 《from excitement 〔anger〕》; turn *one's* eyes up and down. ¶ 괴로워서 눈을 ～ turn *one's* eyes up and down in agony / 희번덕거리며 둘러보다 look around 〔about〕 with *one's* eyes rolling.

**희번덕희번덕** goggling 〔rolling〕 *one's* 「eyes.

**희번드르르하다** ① 《얼굴이》 (be) fair and radiant 〔lustrous〕. ② 《거죽이》 (be) showy; garish. ¶ 그는 희번드르르하게 옷만 잘 입었지 보잘것 없는 사람이다 He wears showy clothes but there is not much of a person beneath them. ③ 《말이》 (be) specious. ¶ 그는 희번드르르하게 말은 그럴듯이 하나 실속이 없다 What he says sounds good, but he is unreliable.

**희번들하다** ⇨ 희번드르르하다.

**희번지르르하다** (be) neat and fair.

**희번하다** (be) dimly white; dawn gray 〔grey《영》〕. ¶ 동녘 하늘이 희번해졌다 The dawn whitened the eastern sky.

**희보**(喜報) good news; glad tidings.

**희불그레하다** (be) pinkish.

**희붐하다** (be) faintly light; dimly white. ¶ 희붐히 동이 틀 무렵 at peep of day; at the first gray of dawn / 희붐해지다 grow light; turn gray / 동녘하늘이 희붐히 밝아왔다 The first streaks of light began to glimmer in the eastern sky.

**희비**(喜悲) joy and sorrow. ¶ ～가 엇갈리다 have mingled feelings of joy and sorrow. ◉ ～극 a tragicomedy. ～쌍곡선 mingled feelings of joy and sorrow.

**희사**(喜事) a joyful event; a happy accident; a matter for congratulation.

**희사**(喜捨) charity; almsgiving; (a) donation; (a) contribution. ～하다 give alms; give (money to) charity; donate. ¶ ～를 받다 receive alms 〔donations〕 / ～를 요청하다 beg for donations; make a collection 《for》; pass 〔send〕 the hat round 《for》 / 응분의 ～를 하다 contribute *one's* mite 〔due share〕. ◉ ～금 a gift of money; money given in charity; alms; donations. ～함 an offertory chest 〔box〕.

**희색**(喜色) a glad countenance; a joyful look; a happy 〔pleased〕 look. ¶ ～이 만면하다 brighten up with joy; beam with joy; be all smiles.

**희생**(犧牲) a sacrifice; 《자기 희생》 self-sacrifice; self-immolation; 《피해자》 a victim; 《대신 바치는》 a scapegoat. ～하다 sacrifice; victimize; make a scapegoat 〔victim〕 of 《*a person*》. ¶ ～적(인) self-sacrificing / ～적 봉사(가격)의 offered almost at cost price / …을 ～하여 at the sacrifice 〔expense, price, cost〕 of... / 어떠한 ～을 치르더라도 at all costs; at any cost 〔price, sacrifice〕 / ～을 치르다 make sacrifices 《for》 / 많은 ～을 치르다 pay dearly 〔a heavy price〕 《for》 / …의 ～이 되다 get 〔be〕 sacrificed to...; victimized; fall a victim 〔sacrifice, prey〕 to... / 몸을 ～하다 sacrifice *oneself;* make a martyr of (*one's*) *self* / 나는 어떤 ～을 치르더라도 그것을 해낼 생각이다 I am determined to see it through to the bitter end. *or* I will get my way at any cost. / 그는 음모의 ～이 되었다 He fell a victim to the plot. / 많은 ～을 치르고〔치르지 않고〕 승리했다 The victory was bought dearly 〔cheaply〕. / 그녀는 그이를 위하여 자신의 행복을 ～했다 She sacrificed her happiness for him. / 그는 건강을 ～해 가면서 그 연구를 완성했다 He completed his research at the expense of his health. ◉ ～물 an object of sacrifice; a victim. ～번트〔플라이〕 〖야구〗 a sacrifice bunt 〔fly〕. ～적 정신 the spirit of self-sacrifice: ～정신이 강한 사람 a self-sacrificing person. ～타 〖야구〗 a sacrifice (hit); sacrifice batting: ～타로 2루에 보내다 sacrifice 《a runner》 to second.

**희생자**(犧牲者) a victim; a prey; 《사고 따위의》 a casualty. ¶ ～들의 유가족 the families of victims / 호텔 화재로 많은 ～가 생겼다 The fire in the hotel took a heavy toll of lives.

**희서**(稀書) a rare book.

**희석**(稀釋) 〖화학〗 dilution; attenuation. ～하다 dilute; attenuate. ¶ ～한 dilute; diluted. ◉ ～도(度) dilution. ～액 diluted 〔weak〕 solution. ～열 the heat of dilution. ～제 a diluent.

**희세**(稀世) being rare 〔extraordinary, phenomenal〕. ¶ ～의 uncommon; rare; extraordinary; unique; phenomenal / ～의 영웅 a unique 〔peerless〕 hero; a hero for the century; a hero of extraordinary caliber / ～지재(之才) a phenomenal talent.

**희소**(稀少) scarcity; rarity. ～하다 (be) scarce; rare. ◉ ～가치 scarcity 〔rarity〕 value. ～물자 scarce materials 〔goods〕. ～성 scarcity.

**희소**(喜笑) ～하다 laugh for 〔with〕 joy; have a laugh of joy.

**희소식**(喜消息) good news; glad tidings. ¶ ～에 그는 미칠 듯이 기뻐했다 At the glad tidings he was beside himself with joy. / 너에게 전해 줄 ～이 있다 I have some (very) good news for you. / 무소식이 ～《속담》 No news is good news.

**희수**(稀壽) seventy years of age. ◉ ～연(宴) the celebration of *one's* seventieth birthday.

**희수**(喜壽) seventy-seven years of age.

**희아리** dried red pepper spoiled with white spots.

**희언**(戲言) = 희담(戲談).

**희열**(喜悅) joy; gladness; delight; ecstasy; rapture. ¶ ～의 소리를 지르다 cry out for joy.

**희염산**(稀塩酸) 〖화학〗 dilute(d) hydrochloric acid.

**희우**(喜雨) a welcome rain; an overdue rain; a rain after drought.

**희원**(希願) (a) hope; (a) wish; (a) desire. ～하다 hope; wish; desire.

**희유**(稀有) ～하다 (be) rare; uncommon; unusual; 《전례가 없는》 (be) unprecedented; unheard-of. ⇨ 희귀. ¶ ～의 호우(豪雨) unprecedented rainfall / ～한 사건 a rare 〔an uncommon〕 incident 〔case〕.

**희읍스름하다** (be) whitish; be not quite white; be not white 〔clean〕 enough.

**희종**(稀種) a rare variety.

**희질산**(稀窒酸) 〖화학〗 dilute nitric acid.

**희짓다**(戲―) interfere; obstruct; set up a block.

**희치희치** 《피륙·종이가》 worn out here and there; out of shape here and there; 《벗어지다》 peeling 〔coming〕 off here and there. ～하다 be worn 〔out of shape, peeling off〕 here and there. ¶ 베가 ～하다 the weaves of cloth are out of shape here and there / 테이블의 칠이 ～ 벗어지다 varnish comes off a table here and there.

**희토류원소**(稀土類元素) 〖화학〗 a rare-earth element.

**희필**(戲筆) my (humble) writing; my (unworthy) drawing.

**희학**(戲謔) a joke; a jest; kidding; a pleasantry. ～하다 joke; jest; make fun 《of》; kid. ◉ ～질 joking; jesting.

**희한**(稀罕) rarity; singularity; being uncommon. ～하다 (be) rare; curious; uncommon; singular; odd. ¶ ～한 물건 a rarity; a curiosity / ～한 사람 a rare person / ～한 경험 an unusual experience / 간밤에는 ～한 꿈을 꾸었어 I had a strange dream last night. / ～한 일도 다 있군 How can a thing like that happen.

**희화**(戲畫) a caricature; a cartoon; a comic picture. ¶ ～화(化)하다 make a caricature 《of》; caricature.

**희황산**(稀黃酸) 〖화학〗 dilute sulphuric acid.

**희희**(嘻嘻) tittering; laughing aloud. ¶ ～웃다 titter; laugh aloud.

**희희낙락**(喜喜樂樂) rejoicing; jubilation. ～하다 rejoice; jubilate; be in delight; be very joyful. ¶ ～하여 merrily; joyfully; cheerfully.

**흰개미** 〖곤충〗 a white ant; a termite.

**흰골무**(떡) finger-sized rice cakes without spice covering.

**흰곰** 〖동물〗 a white 〔polar〕 bear.

**흰깨** white sesame.

**흰꼬리수리** 〖조류〗 a white-tailed sea eagle.

**흰나비** 《흰나비류》 a white (butterfly); 《배추흰나비》 a cabbage butterfly; a small 〔cabbage〕 white.

**흰누룩** malt made of flour and glutinous rice.

**흰눈썹뜸부기** 〖조류〗 a waterrail; a clapper rail; a mud hen.

**흰담비** 〖동물〗 an ermine.

**흰독말풀**(―毒―) 〖식물〗 a datura; a thorn apple.

**흰둥이** 《병적인》 an albino; 《백인》 a white man; a white 《구어》.

**흰떡** rice cakes.

**흰말** a white horse.

**흰머리** gray 〔grey 《영》〕 hair (반백); white hair (전백). ¶ ～가 섞인 머리 hair streaked with gray 〔grizzled〕 hair / ～를 뽑다 pull 〔pluck〕 out a white hair / ～를 염색하다 dye *one's* hair; have *one's* hair dyed / 갑자기 ～가 늘었다 My hair has rapidly turned gray 《with age》. / 조금씩 ～가 생기기 시작한다 My hair is beginning to go gray 〔to show white streaks〕.

**흰멧새** 〖조류〗 a snow bunting; a snowflake.

**흰무리** rice cakes steamed without shaping.

**흰물떼새** 〖조류〗 a Kentish plover.

**흰바곳** 〖식물〗 an aconite; a wolfsbane.

**흰밥** plain white rice (cooked with nothing mixed in).

**흰배지빠귀** 〖조류〗 a pale thrush.

**흰불나방** 〖곤충〗 a fall webworm.

**흰뺨검둥오리** 〖조류〗 a spotbill duck.

**흰뺨오리** 〖조류〗 a goldeneye.

**흰소리** 《희떠운 소리》 a snobbish 〔pretentious〕 remark; a saucy 〔fresh〕 thing to say; 《허풍》 a loud boast; high 〔tall〕 talk; bragging. ¶ ～치다 talk big 〔tall〕; brag; boast 《of, about》; swagger 《about》; talk in large terms 《about》; talk through *one's* hat 《구어》. ◉ ～꾼 a vain 〔an empty〕 boaster; a braggart; a boaster.

**흰신** white shoes.

**흰쌀** polished rice; white rice.

**흰여우** 〖동물〗 a white 〔silver〕 fox; a blue 〔an Arctic〕 fox (북극 여우).

**흰엿** white rice candy.

**흰옷** white clothes.

**흰자** ⇨ 흰자위. ◉ ~가루 powdered white. ~질 protein; albumin. ⇨ 단백질.
**흰자위** ① 《계란의》 the white (of an egg); albumin. ② 《눈알의》 the white of the eye.
**흰죽**(一粥) rice gruel [porridge]. ¶ ~을 끓이다 boil rice into 《thick, thin》 gruel / ~을 먹다 eat gruel / 어린애에게 ~을 먹이다 feed rice gruel to a little child.
**흰줄** a white stripe [line].
**흰쥐** 〚동물〛 a white rat; an albino rat.
**흰털** white hair [fur, wool].
**흰털바늘꽃** 〚식물〛 a kind of willowweed.
**흰털제비꽃** 〚식물〛 a viola; a kind of violet.
**흰토끼** a white rabbit.
**흰팥** small white adzuki beans.
**흰포도주**(一葡萄酒) white wine; Rhine wine.
**횡하다** (be) dazed; stupefied; stunned; feel *one's* head turning [whirling, swimming]. ¶ 머리가 ~ *one's* head turns [whirls] / 정신이 ~ be stupefied [stunned].
**횡허케** fast; swiftly. ¶ ~ 가버리다 go away like the wind.
**히드라** 〚동물〛 a hydra (*pl.* ~s, -drae).
**히드라스틴** 〚화학〛 hydrastin(e).
**히드로아황산염**(一亞黃酸塩) 〚화학〛 hydrosulfite; hydrosulphite.
**히로뽕** Philopon (상표 이름에서); hiroppon. ◉ ~ 밀매자 a philopon trafficker. ~상습자 a philopon addict.
**히말라야** Himalaya(s). ¶ ~의 Himalayan. ◉ ~ 산맥 the Himalayas; the Himalaya Mountains.
**히브리** Hebrew. ¶ ~의 Hebraic; Hebrew. ◉ ~말 Hebrew. ~사람 a Hebrew. ~서(書) 〚성서〛 the Epistle of St. Paul (the Apostle) to the Hebrews; 《약칭》 Hebrews (생략 Heb.).
**히스타민** 〚화학〛 histamine. ¶ 항(抗)~의 antihistaminic.
**히스테리** 〚의학〛 hysteria; hysterics (발작). ¶ ~의 hysteric(al) / ~적으로 hysterically / ~를 일으키다 go [fall] into hysterics; have an attack of hysteria; get [become] hysterical.
**히아신스** 〚식물〛 a hyacinth.
**히어로** a hero.
**히어링** hearing. ◉ ~ 연습[훈련] a drill in hearing.
**히죽거리다** 《이를 드러내고》 grin 《at》; 《얼빠진 것처럼》 simper 《at》; 《약간 득의만만하여》 smirk. ¶ 도대체 무엇 때문에 히죽거리는거냐 What on earth are you grinning at? / 히죽거리지 마라 Wipe that silly smile off your face.
**히죽이** with a grin; with a sweet smile. ¶ ~ 웃다 grin at 《*a person*》; smile sweetly / 그는 자기도 모르게 ~ 웃었다 An unconscious smile beamed over his countenance.
**히죽히죽** grinningly; with a broad grin. ¶ ~ 웃다 grin (broadly) 《at》.
**히치하이크** a hitchhike; 《go on》 hitchhiking.
**히터** a heater. ¶ ~를 켜다[끄다] turn on [off] a heater.
**히트** ① 〚야구〛 a hit; a single (hit) (단타); a safe [base] hit. ¶ ~를 치다 hit; make [get] a hit / 세 개의 ~를 허용하다 allow three hits; pitch a three-hitter / 투수에게서 ~ 다섯을 빼앗다 collect five hits off the pitcher / ~를 하나도 주지 않다 pitch [hurl] a no-hitter / ~ 네 개로 2점을 따내다 score two runs on four hits / ~ 세 개로 막다 limit 《the opposing team》 to three hits; pitch [hurl] a three-hitter / 노~노런을 달성하다 pitch a no-hit, no-run game. ② 《성공》 a hit; a great (box-office) success. ~하다 《일이》 make [be] a (big) hit; 《사람이》 win a success. ¶ 그 영화는 예상 밖에 크게 ~했다 The movie was unexpectedly a big hit. / 이 노래는 지금 한창 ~중이다 This song is high in the charts. ◉ ~송 a hit song. ~앤드런 〚야구〛 hit-and-run play. ~앨범 a hit album. ~차트 the hit chart.
**히트바이피치** 〚야구〛 a pitch which hits the batter. ¶ ~를 맞다 be hit by a pitch [pitched ball] / ~로 일루에 나가다 get to [take] first hit by a pitched ball.
**히포콘드리** 〚의학〛 《심기증》 hypochondria. ¶ ~의 hypochondriac.
**히피** a hippie; a flower child; [총칭] hippies. ◉ ~족 (the) hippies. ~촌 a hippie commune.
**히히거리다** ⇨ 해해거리다.
**힌두** ¶ ~의 Hindu; Hindoo. ◉ ~교(敎) Hinduism. ~교도 a Hindu; a Hindoo. ~어(語) Hindustani; Hindostani.
**힌트** a hint; a clue. ¶ ~를 주다 give [drop] 《*a person*》 a hint / ~를 얻다 get [take] a hint 《from》; pick up an idea / 실제의 범죄에서 ~를 얻은 소설 a novel suggested by an actual crime.
**힐기죽거리다** sway *one's* body [hips] (in walking).
**힐기죽힐기죽** swaying *one's* body [hips].
**힐끗** ⇨ 흘끗.
**힐난**(詰難) blame; censure; reproach. ~하다 blame; censure; reproach; take [call] 《*a person*》 to task 《for *something*, over *something*》.

**힐문**(詰問) cross-examination; cross-questioning; close questioning; a rigid 〔searching〕 inquiry; grilling. ～하다 examine 〔question〕 《*a person*》 closely; demand 《an explanation》 from 〔of〕 《*a person*》; cross-examine 《*a person*》. ¶ …의 실패를 ～하다 needle 《*a person*》 over the failure of... / 그리 ～조로 묻지 마시오 Stop questioning 〔cross-examining〕 me like that.

**힐책**(詰責) rebuke; reprimand; reproof; reproach; censure. ～하다 rebuke 《*a person* for *something*》; reprimand; reprove; reproach; censure. ¶ 직무 태만을 ～하다 rebuke 《*a person*》 for *his* neglect of duty / 그는 감독 불충분으로 ～당했다 He was reprimanded for insufficient control.

**힘** ① 《체력》 (physical) strength; energy; force; power; might.

> 용법 **strength** 사람의 체력, 군대의 병력 등. **energy** 정력·원기라는 의미로서의 힘. **force** 힘(power)을 드러내 보이기도 하고, 이를 실제로 행사하여 사람이나 사물을 움직이는 경우에 씀. **power** 능력으로서의 힘. **might** 문어로서 초인적인 강력한 힘을 가리킴.

¶ 힘만으로 by sheer strength / 힘있는 strong; mighty / 힘없는 weak; of little strength; powerless; feeble / 힘으로 by force; through force; by dint of strength; by sheer 〔main〕 strength; by using *one's* fist / 힘세다 be strong 〔mighty〕 / 힘자랑을 하다 make a boast of *one's* strength.

힘이: 힘이 있다 be strong 〔mighty〕 / 힘이 없다 be weak; be feeble; do not have much strength / 힘이 늘다〔줄다〕 gain 〔diminish〕 in strength / 힘이 다하다〔빠지다〕 lose (all) *one's* strength; [사람이 주어] be exhausted; be spent up; be wrung out / 힘이 붙다 gain strength / 힘이 장사다 have the strength of a horse 〔lion〕; be a Hercules.

힘을: 힘을 겨루다 have a strength contest; measure 〔match〕 *one's* strength 《with》 / 힘을 내다 put forth 〔out〕 *one's* strength / 힘을 시험하다 try *one's* strength 《against, with》 / 힘을 잃다 lose strength / 힘을 집중하다 concentrate *one's* energy 〔strength〕 upon / 힘을 회복하다 regain 〔renew〕 strength / 온 몸의 힘을 양팔에 주다 throw all the strength of *one's* body into *one's* arms / 어깨의 힘을 빼다 relax *one's* shoulders.

¶ 힘이 정의다 "Might is right." / 그녀는 너무 쇠약해서 걸을 힘이 없었다 She was so weak that she had not got the strength to walk.

② 《물리적 힘》 force; power; energy. ¶ 열의 힘 energy of heat; caloric force / 자석의 힘 the virtue of the magnet / 증기의 힘 the power of steam / 힘이 강한 엔진 a high-powered engine / 나는 항상 자연의 힘이 얼마나 위대한가를 명심하고 있다 I am always reminded how great the forces of nature are.

③ 《작용》 agency; action. ¶ 눈에 보이지 않는 힘 an invisible agency / 하느님의 힘 agency of Providence.

④ 《능력》 ability; power; strength; faculty; capacity; capability. ¶ 듣는 힘 the faculty of hearing / 힘의 부족 want of ability / 힘이 모자라는 incapable; incompetent / 힘이 자라는 한 as far 〔hard, much〕 as *one* can; to the best 〔utmost〕 of *one's* ability 〔power〕; to the top of *one's* bent / 힘을 기르다 acquire the power of 〔ability to *do*〕...; cultivate the faculty of... / 힘을 발휘하다 display 〔show, exhibit〕 *one's* ability / 힘이 미치지 못하다 be beyond *one's* power; be above *one's* ability; be not in 〔be out of〕 *one's* power; be more than *one* can do / 힘을 다하다 do *one's* best; strain *one's* powers to the limit / 그에게는 사람을 잘 통솔할 힘이 있다 He has good leadership.

⑤ 《권력·세력·위력》 power; force; authority; sway; influence; weight. ¶ 부모의 힘으로 through the influence of *one's* parents / 수(數)의 힘으로 by force of numbers / 경찰의 힘 the power 〔authority〕 of the police / 여론의 힘 the force of public opinion / 전통의 힘 the weight of tradition / 힘의 정치 power politics; rule by might / 힘의 균형 balance of power; power balance / 힘을 행사하다 exercise a force; exert 〔exercise〕 *one's* influence 《over》 / 힘의 우위를 유지하다 maintain the superiority in strength 《over》; maintain the upper hand in power 《over》 / 그의 말에는 힘이 있다 He speaks with authority.

⑥ 《공헌》 contribution; service. ¶ …하는 데 힘이 크다 contribute greatly to; make 〔do〕 much for; be instrumental in 《*do*ing, a work》; have a share in 《*do*ing, a work》/ 새 학교를 세우는 데는 그의 힘이 컸다 He has contributed much in establishing the new school. / 근대 과학의 힘으로 공업이 크게 진보했다 Great industrial progress has been made through modern science.

⑦ 《도움》 help; aid; assistance; support; service. ¶ …의 힘으로 by [with] the aid [help] of…; through 《*a person's*》 aid / 힘을 빌다 get 《*a person's*》 help; enlist the help [aid] 《of *a person*》/ 남의 힘을 빌지 않고 하다 do 《*something*》 without help (from another); work alone [all by *oneself* ] / 힘을 빌리러 가다 go to 《another》 for help / 남의 힘을 기대하다 count on [figure on] another (for help); look to another for help / 힘을 빌려주다 help; aid; give assistance; extend help to; lend a helping hand to; lend *one's* influence 《to》/ 힘이 되다 (be a) help; be of help [service] 《to》; give assistance [aid] to / 언제건 힘이 되어 드리겠습니다 You will always find a friend in me. / 힘이 되어 주는 친구는 자네뿐일세 You are the only friend I can turn to for help.

⑧ 《기운·용기》 energy; vigor; courage; heart; nerve; pep; ginger. ¶ 힘없는 소리로 in a weak voice / 힘을 잃다 lose heart [courage]; get dejected [dispirited, disheartened] / …에 힘을 얻다 be encouraged by…; be cheered up by…; be comforted by…; take comfort [heart] from… / 힘을 북돋우다 cheer 《*a person*》 up; give vigor to 《*a person*》/ 힘을 쏟다 throw energy 《into》/ 힘이 나다 cheer up; take heart; become heightened in spirits; pull *oneself* together; get encouraged / 힘이 없다 lack vigor; be in low [poor] spirits; be out of spirits [energy]; be in the blues.

⑨ 《강세》 force; stress; emphasis. ¶ 힘찬 연설 an effective [a powerful] speech / 힘있는 문장 a forceful sentence; a forcible style / 힘을 주다 stress; emphasize; accentuate / 힘을 주어 말하다 lay stress [emphasis] on *one's* words.

⑩ 《노력》 labor; effort; exertion; endeavors. ¶ 자기 힘으로 by *one's* own efforts / 힘을 합하여 《work》 in cooperation 《with》; by united effort / 힘을 합치다 《협력하다》 cooperate 《with》; unite [combine, join] efforts; join forces 《with》/ 힘을 다하다 make every effort; exert *oneself;* use *one's* endeavor.

⑪ 《효과·효력》 efficacy; effectiveness; effect; efficiency. ¶ 약의 힘 the efficacy [virtue] of drug / 과학의 힘으로 through science / 그의 연설은 군중을 진정시키는 큰 힘이 있었다 His speech was very effective in calming the crowd. / 이 약의 힘으로 기침이 나았다 I got rid of my cough with this medicine.

⑫ 《자력(資力)》 means; resources. ¶ 그는 돈의 힘만으로 정계에 진출했다 He got into politics by the sheer force of money. / 나한테는 자식들을 대학에 보낼 힘이 없다 I don't have the means to send my sons to college. / 나에겐 집을 가질 만한 힘이 없다 I can't afford to have a house of my own.

⑬ 《폭력》 violence; force. ¶ 힘으로 by (main) force; through force; by a strong-arm method 《미》/ 힘에 호소하다 appeal [resort, have recourse] to force.

**힘겨룸** a contest of strength. ～하다 have a strength contest; have a trial of strength. ¶ ～을 해보자 Let's see who is the stronger, you or I. *or* Let's see which of us is the strongest.

**힘겹다** ＝힘부치다.

**힘껏** with all *one's* strength [might]; with might and main; to the best of *one's* ability [power]. ¶ ～하다 do *one's* best [utmost]; do everything 「in *one's* power [as *one* can] / ～ 당기다 pull with all *one's* force [strength]; pull with might and main / ～ 싸우다 fight for all *one* is worth / ～ 일하다 work with all *one's* strength; work 「at [up to] capacity / ～ 돕다 do *one's* best [utmost] to help 《*a person*》.

**힘꼴** brawn; muscle; muscular [physical] strength. ¶ ～이나 쓰는 brawny; 《a man》 with muscle.

**힘들다** ① 《벅차다》 be laborious [arduous, strenuous, toilsome, troublesome, tough, painful]. ¶ 힘든 일 a hard [painstaking, back-breaking, laborious] job; an uphill task / 농사가 잘 안 되어서 살기 ～ be pinched (economically) because of a bad harvest. ② 《어렵다》 be hard [difficult, hard going, tough sledding]. ¶ 힘든 문제 a difficult problem / 더워서 일하기가 ～ be so hot that it is hard to work / 몸

을 굽히기가 ~ have trouble in bending *oneself* / 일자리를 구하기가 ~ have difficulty in finding a job / 그 일이 그에게는 좀 힘들었던 것 같다 The work seems to have been a little too hard for him. / 마침내 가장 힘드는 고비는 넘어섰다 At last we have broken the back of the work. /자 이제부터가 ~ Here comes the hardest part of the work. / 그 일을 하는 데는 별로 힘들지 않았다 I had little difficulty [trouble] (in) doing the work. / 산꼭대기까지 올라가는 것은 무척 힘드는 일이었다 It was a hard strain to reach the mountain top.

**힘들이다** ① 《체력·노력을》 put in *one's* strength [labor, efforts]; make efforts; exert *oneself;* endeavor. ¶ 일에 ~ throw *oneself* into *one's* work / 힘들여 운반하다 carry the load laboriously / 힘들인 보람이 있었다 My efforts were rewarded. ② 《애쓰다》 take pains; elaborate 《on》; render services 《to》. ¶ 힘들여서 laboriously; with (much) trouble; with (great) efforts / 조금도 힘들이지 않고 without taking the least pains; without any effort; easily / 일껏 힘들였는데도 after much trouble; after all *one's* efforts / 책상을 힘들여 만들다 make a desk elaborately / 힘들여 계획하다 elaborate on a plan.

**힘부치다** be more than *one* can do; be not strong [capable] enough 《to *do*》; be beyond *one's* ability [power, reach]. ¶ 그와 씨름하기엔 내 힘이 부친다 I am not strong enough to wrestle with him. / 그 일은 내 힘에 부치는 일이다 The job is beyond my ability.

**힘빼물다** pretend to strength; boast of *one's* prowess; act mighty.

**힘세다** (be) powerful; strong; mighty. ¶ 그이는 대단히 힘이 세다 He is of great [Herculean] strength. *or* He is as strong as a horse.

**힘쓰다** ① 《체력을》 put forth [out] *one's* strength 《to lift a stone》.
② 《노력하다》 endeavor; do *one's* best; strive; exert *oneself;* make efforts; exert *one's* energies 《in a work》; busy *oneself* 《with *one's* work》. ¶ 힘써 공부하다 study hard / 학업에 ~ attend to *one's* studies with diligence / 목적을 달성하려고 ~ strive after [for] *one's* object / 문제를 해결하려고 ~ set *oneself* to solve a problem / 출세하려고 ~ do *one's* best to succeed in life / 어학 연구에 특히 ~ lay special emphasis (up)on the study of languages.
③ 《애쓰다》 labor; toil; take (much) pains. ¶ 힘써 글을 짓다 struggle through a composition / 힘쓴 보람이 있다[없다] I labored to some [no] purpose. / 힘써 모은 돈이다 The money has been saved by the sweat of my brow.
④ 《돕다》 help; aid; assist; give a (helping) hand; lend *one's* help. ¶ 친구의 취직을 위해서 ~ help a friend land a job / 한 군이 힘써 주어서 through Mr. Han's aid; by the kind assistance of Mr. Han / 자네 이외에 나를 위하여 힘써 줄 사람은 없네 I have no one to turn to for aid but you. / 될 수 있는 한 힘쓰지요 I will do what I can for you. (★ what = all that).

**힘없이** feebly; droopingly; dejectedly; 《힘없는 목소리로》 in a feeble voice. ¶ 그는 질문에 ~ 대답했다 He answered the question helplessly [weakly].

**힘입다** owe; be indebted (for). ¶ 아무에게 ~ be indebted to *a person;* enjoy *a person's* favor / 나의 성공은 그의 조력에 힘입은 바 크다 I owe my success chiefly to his help. / 일본의 문명은 처음에는 중국과 한국, 뒤에는 서양 제국에 힘입은 바 크다 Japan is much indebted for her civilization to China and Korea first and then to the Western countries.

**힘있다** ① 《힘이 세다》 (be) strong; have strength. ② 《문장·어조가》 (be) forceful; powerful; heavy. ¶ 힘있는 문장 powerful sentences / 힘있는 어조 a heavy accent. ③ 《지위·권력으로 보아》 (be) influential; carry weight; have power. ¶ 힘있는 사람 an influential person; a person who carries some weight / 일을 이루게 하는 데 힘이 있다 carry enough weight to see a plan through.

**힘자랑** boast of *one's* strength. ~하다 boast [be proud] of *one's* strength.

**힘주다** 《힘을 쓰다》 devote *one's* strength 《to》; concentrate 《upon》; 《강조하다》 put stress 《on》; emphasize.

**힘줄** ① 《근육》 a muscle; 《건(腱)》 a tendon; a sinew. ¶ ~투성이의 sinewy / ~이 굵은 팔 sinewy arm / ~이 당기다 have a strain in muscle. ② 《혈맥·혈관》 a vein. ③ 《섬유질의》 a fiber [fibre 《영》]; a string. ¶ ~이 많은 stringy; fibrous / ~이 많은 고기 tough meat;

stringy meat. ◉ 고기～ strings in the meat.

**힘줌말** an intensive 〔emphatic〕 word.

**힘차다** ①《박력·정력이 넘치다》 be full of strength; (be) powerful; energetic; forceful. ¶ 힘찬 연설 a powerful speech. ②《벅차다》 (be) laborious; tough; hard; difficult. ¶ 힘찬 일 a laborious task; a tough job.

**힙** the hip.

**힝** 《코푸는 소리》 with a hissing sound; 《비웃는 소리》 pshaw. ¶ 코를 힝 풀다 blow *one's* nose with a hissing sound.

**힝그럭** an arrowhead in the shape of a willow leaf.

**힝힝** with hissing sounds. ¶ 코를 ～ 풀다 blow *one's* nose repeatedly.

# 엣센스 한영 사전 부록

## 차 례

# (1) 미·영 중요 어구 비교

| Korean | American | British |
|---|---|---|
| 정 치 관 계 (POLITICS) | | |
| 정부 | Administration | Government |
| 연립내각 | fusion administration | coalition government |
| 장관 | Secretary | Minister |
| 각료 | cabinet officer; cabinet member | cabinet minister; member of the cabinet |
| 국무부(《영》 외무성) | State Department | Foreign Office |
| 의회 | Congress | Parliament |
| 의원 휴게실 | cloakroom | lobby |
| 의안의 통과 | passage of a bill | passing of a bill |
| …출신 국회 의원 | representative from ...; the gentleman from ... | member for ... |
| 공천 후보자 명단 | ticket | list of candidates |
| 입후보; 출마 | candidacy | candidature |
| 국회의원에 출마하다 | run for Congress | stand for Parliament |
| 보궐 선거 | special election | by-election |
| 절대 다수 | majority | clear majority |
| 선거 운동 | campaign | canvass |
| 투표수 점검자 | canvasser | scrutineer |
| 정당 강령 | party platform | party programme |
| 정당 연합 | party fusion | party coalition |
| 공무원 | officeholder | civil servant |
| 지방세 | local taxes | local rates |
| 재판·경찰·범죄·소방 관계 (POLICE, etc.) | | |
| 사법권 | judiciary | judicature |
| 검사 | district attorney | public prosecutor |
| 배심원 | venireman | juryman |
| 변호사 | trial lawyer | advocate |
| 변호사의 자격을《미》〔면허를《영》〕 얻다 | be admitted to the bar | be called to the bar |
| (법정의) 속기사 | stenographer | shorthand writer |
| 증인을 서다 | take the (witness) stand | enter the witness box |
| 교도소 | jail | gaol [dʒeil] |
| 교도관; 간수 | prison guard | warder; prison officer |
| 교도소장 | the warden of the prison | the governor of the prison |
| 경찰서 | station house | police station |
| 경찰서장 | chief of police | chief constable |
| 형사 | investigator | detective |
| 경관; 순경 | patrolman | constable |
| 경찰봉 | policeman's billy | policeman's truncheon |

| Korean | American | British |
|---|---|---|
| 유치장 | calaboose《속어》 | lock-up |
| 소방서 | fire department | fire(-brigade) station |
| 소방 비상선 | fire line | fire cordon |
| 소년원 | workhouse | house of correction |
| 양로원 | almshouse | workhouse |
| 노상 강도《행위》 | oldup | highway robbery |
| 노상 강도《사람》 | holdup man | highwayman |
| 좀도둑 | porch climber | cat burglar |
| 방화 범인 | firebug《속어》 | incendiary |
| 곁쇠 | a passkey | a skeleton key |

## 교 통 관 계 (TRANSPORTATION)

| Korean | American | British |
|---|---|---|
| 철도 | railroad | railway |
| 고가 철도 | elevated railroad; the L《구어》 | overhead railway |
| 지하철 | subway | tube; underground |
| 레일 | track; tracks | lines; metals |
| 탈선하다 | jump the track | run off the line; jump the metals |
| 침목(枕木) | tie; crosstie | sleeper |
| 보통 열차; 완행 열차 | accommodation train | slow train |
| 정거장; 역 | railroad depot | railway station |
| 플랫폼 | track | platform |
| 서울행 열차는 10번 플랫폼입니다 | You will find the train for Seoul on Track 10. | You will find the train for Seoul at Platform 10. |
| 종착역 | terminal | terminus |
| 역장 | station agent | station master |
| 이 표로 도중 하차를 할 수 있습니까 | Does this ticket allow me to stop over [off]? | Does this ticket allow me to break journey? |
| 기관차 | locomotive | engine |
| 기관사 | engineer | engine driver; driver |
| 화물 열차 | freight train | goods train |
| 화차 | freight car | goods waggon; goods van |
| 객차 | passenger car | passenger coach |
| 식당차 | diner | dining carriage |
| 유개 화차 | boxcar | goods-waggon |
| 열차 차장; 여객 전무 | conductor | guard |
| 건널목지기 | gate tender | gatekeeper |
| 보선공 | tracklayer | platelayer |
| 정지 신호 | stop light | red light |
| 편도표(片道票) | one-way ticket | single ticket |
| 왕복표 | round-trip ticket | return ticket |
| 회수권; 정기권 | commutation ticket | season ticket |
| 매표소 | ticket office | booking office |
| 매표계(원) | ticket agent | booking clerk |

| Korean | American | British |
|---|---|---|
| 안내소 | bureau of information; information bureau | inquiry office |
| 휴대품 보관소 | baggage room; checkroom | cloakroom |
| 수화물(手貨物) | baggage | luggage |
| 수화물을 맡기다 | check a baggage | register a luggage |
| 포터 | redcap | station-porter |
| 신문 · 잡지 판매소 | news stand | bookstall |
| 시간표 | schedule | timetable |
| 기차 시간에 대다 | catch a train | be in time for a train |
| 전원 승차하여 주십시오 | All aboard ! | Take your seats ! |
| 전원 갈아타십시오 | All out ! | All change ! |
| 갈아타다 | transfer | change cars |
| 비행기 | airplane | aeroplane |
| 비행장 | airdrome | aerodrome |
| 자동차 | automobile; auto | motorcar; car |
| 가솔린 | gasoline | petrol |
| 화물 자동차 | truck | lorry |
| 관광 버스 | sightseeing bus | charabanc |
| 살수차(撒水車) | sprinkling wagon | water cart |
| 주차장 | parking lot | car park |
| 시내 전차 | streetcar | tramcar |
| 보도; 인도 | sidewalk | footpath; pavement |
| 큰거리; 큰길 | main street | high street |
| 차도; 포장 도로 | pavement | roadway |
| 지하도 | underpass | subway |

## 체신(遞信) 관계 (POST AND TELEGRAPHIC SERVICES)

| Korean | American | British |
|---|---|---|
| 우편(으로) | (by) mail | (by) post |
| 국내 우편물 | domestic mail | inland mail |
| 관제 엽서 | postal card | postcard |
| 등기 우편료 | registry fee | registration fee |
| 속달편 | special delivery | express delivery |
| 우체국 사무원 | mail clerk | postal clerk |
| 우편 집배원 | mail carrier; mailman | postman |
| 포스트; 우체통 | mailbox | pillar box; letter box |
| 소포 | package | parcel |
| 전신 기사 | telegrapher | telegraphist |
| 전화 번호부 | telephone book | telephone directory |
| 전화 교환국 | central office | exchange |
| 공중 전화 | telephone booth | telephone box; call box |
| 장거리 전화 | long distance call | trunk call |
| 《전화에서》 통화가 끝났습니까 | Are you through? | Have you finished? |
| 《전화에서》 나왔습니다. 말씀하세요 | You are connected. / Go ahead. | You are through. |

| Korean | American | British |
|---|---|---|
| 《전화에서》 통화중입니다 | Line's busy! | Number's engaged! |
| 전보 용지 | telegram blank | telegram form |
| 라디오 | radio | wireless |
| 진공관 | tube | valve |

## 저널리즘 관계 (JOURNALISM)

| Korean | American | British |
|---|---|---|
| 인쇄소 | printery | printing office |
| 논문; 사설 | editorial | leader; leading article |
| 신문 기자 | newspaperman | pressman; journalist |
| 논설 위원 | editorial writer | leader writer |
| (신문·잡지 따위의) 부주필 (副主筆) | copyreader | subeditor |
| 탐방 기자 | paragrapher | paragraphist |
| 특종(特種) 기사 | beat | scoop |
| 신문〔잡지〕 판매원 | news agent | newsdealer |
| 스트라이크를 하다 | walk out | strike |
| 연좌 데모; 농성 데모 | sit-down strike | stay-in strike |
| 삼문 소설(三文小說) | dime novel | shilling shocker; cheap novel; yellow-back |

## 학 교 관 계 (SCHOOL)

| Korean | American | British |
|---|---|---|
| (대학의) 교직원 | faculty | college staff |
| 대학생 | college student | undergraduate |
| 대학 1년생 | freshman | first-year man |
| 대학 2년생 | sophomore | second-year man |
| 대학 3년생 | junior | third-year man |
| 대학 4년생 | senior | fourth-year man |
| …을 전공하다 | major in… | specialize in… |
| 시험에 떨어지다 | flunk in an examination | fail in an examination |
| 졸업생 | alumnus | graduate; old boys |
| 동창회 | alumni association | graduates' association |
| 졸업식 | commencement | speech day |
| 졸업 증서 | sheepskin | diploma |
| 졸업하다 | graduate from | graduate at |
| (남녀 공학의) 여학생 | coed | woman student |
| 초등 학교 교사 | grade teacher | elementary school teacher |
| 여선생 | schoolma'am | school mistress |
| 공립 학교 | public school | council school |
| 사립 학교 | private school | public school |
| 필수 과목 | required subject | compulsory subject |
| 선택 과목 | elective subject | optional subject |
| 교실 | recitation room | classroom |
| 강당 | auditorium | assembly hall; hall |
| 교정 | campus | school grounds |
| 휴게 시간 | intermission | break |

| Korean | American | British |
|---|---|---|
| 기숙사 | dormitory | hall of residence; hostel |
| 통신 교수 | correspondence course | post course of tuition |
| 가정용품 · 가구 · 의복 관계 (FURNITURE, etc.) | | |
| 지갑 | pocketbook | purse |
| 양품상 《사람》 | notion counter | haberdasher |
| 회중 전등 | flashlight | electric torch |
| 도시락 | dinner pail | lunchbox |
| 깡통 | can | tin |
| 주전자 | kettle | teakettle |
| 물따르개 | pitcher | jug |
| 스튜 냄비 | kettle | stewpan |
| 알루미늄 | aluminum | aluminium |
| 철물상 | hardware store | ironmonger's |
| 축음기 | phonograph | gramophone |
| 펜촉 | pen point | nib |
| 단화(短靴) | low shoes; oxfords | shoes |
| 덧신 | rubbers | galoshes |
| 편상화(編上靴) | shoes | boots |
| 유모차; 동차(童車) | baby carriage | perambulator; pram |
| 휴지통 | wastebasket | wastepaper basket |
| 쓰레기 | trash | rubbish |
| 쓰레기통 | ashcan; garbage can | dustbin |
| 정원; 뜰 | yard | garden |
| 정원사 | landscape architect | landscape gardener |
| 셋집 | house for rent | house to let |
| 하녀; 식모 | waitress; chambermaid | parlourmaid; housemaid |
| 가구 | furnishings | upholstery |
| 화장대 | bureau; dresser | dressing table |
| 긴의자 | davenport | settee |
| 베란다 | porch; piazza (미남부) | verandah |
| 차양(遮陽)《창문의》 | window shades | (window) blinds |
| 계단 | stairway | staircase |
| 거실(居室) | living room | sitting room |
| 응접실 | parlor | drawing room |
| 세면소 | washroom; toilet | lavatory; closet |
| 세면기 | washbowl | wash-hand basin |
| 중산모(帽) | derby (hat) | bowler (hat) |
| 신사복 | business suit | lounge suit |
| 프록코트 《남자용 예복》 | Prince Albert | frock coat |
| 턱시도 《남자의 야회복》 | tuxedo (coat) | dinner jacket |
| 조끼 | vest | waistcoat |
| 넥타이핀 | stickpin | breastpin |
| 바지 멜빵 | suspenders | braces |
| 양말 대님 | garters | suspenders |

| Korean | American | British |
|---|---|---|
| 브로치 | breastpin | brooch |
| 레인코트 | raincoat | mackintosh; waterproof coat |
| 먼지막이 외투 | duster | dust-cloak; covert coat |
| 나들이옷 | glad rags | dress togs; Sunday clothes |
| 세놓는 의상 | costumes to rent | costumes on hire |
| 포목점 | dry goods store | draper's (shop) |
| 양복점 | tailor shop | tailor's (shop) |
| 기성복 | store clothes | ready-made clothes |
| 사라사 | calico | print |
| 내의(內衣); 속셔츠 | undershirt | vest; singlet |

## 음식물 관계 (FOOD, etc.)

| Korean | American | British |
|---|---|---|
| 과자 가게 | candy store | sweetshop |
| 사탕 | candy | sweets |
| 비스킷 | cracker | biscuit |
| 제과점 《빵 · 생과자 따위의》 | bakery | baker's shop |
| 아이스크림 | ice cream | ice |
| 담배 가게 | cigar store | tobacconist's (shop) |
| 과일 가게 | fruit seller 〔dealer〕 | fruiterer |
| 디저트 | dessert; desserts | sweet course; sweets |
| 식료품점 | grocer shop; grocery | grocer's (shop) |
| 곡물(穀物) | grain | corn |
| 오트밀 | cereal | porridge |
| 옥수수 | corn | maize; Indian corn |
| 땅콩 | peanuts | monkey-nuts; earth-nuts |
| 생선 가게 | fish dealer | fishmonger |

## 백화점·호텔·회사 관계 (BUSINESS)

| Korean | American | British |
|---|---|---|
| 백화점 | department store | the stores |
| 판매 감독 | floorwalker | shopwalker |
| 월부 판매 | installment plan | hire-purchase (system) |
| 연쇄점 | chain store | multiple shop |
| 상점; 가게 | store | shop |
| 상점에 근무하다 | be clerking in a store | be serving behind the counter |
| 점원; 판매원 | salesclerk | shop assistant |
| 상점 주인 | storekeeper | shopkeeper |
| 1층 | first floor | ground floor |
| 2층 | second floor | first floor |
| 재고품 총정리 판매; 떨이 판매 | unloading sale | clearance sale |
| 흑자; 이익 | black | profit |
| 적자; 결손; 부채 | red | loss |
| 외무 판매원; 외판 사원 | traveling salesman | commercial traveller |
| 수금원; 빚쟁이 | bill collector | debt collector |
| 사무원 | white-collar worker | black-coat worker |
| 승급 | boost 〔raise〕 in pay | rise in salary |

| Korean | American | British |
|---|---|---|
| 직업 소개소 | employment bureau | registry office |
| 게시판 | billboard | hoarding |
| 인부 | laborer | navvy (철도·도로 공사 등의) |
| 잡역부(婦); 여자 허드렛일꾼 | scrubwoman | charwoman |
| 구두닦기 | bootblack | shoeblack |
| 상업 회의소 | board of trade | chamber of commerce |
| 경영하다 | operate 《a factory》 | run 《a factory》 |
| 주(株) | stock | share |
| 주주(株主) | stockholder | shareholder |
| (주식)회사 | (business) corporation | (business) company |
| 증권 거래소 | stock market | stock exchange |
| 사장 | president of a corporation | chairman of a company |
| 중역; 이사 | member of the directory | member of the directorate |
| 지폐; 어음 | bill | note |
| 휴일 | legal 〔public〕 holiday | bank holiday |
| 엘리베이터 | elevator | lift |
| (호텔의) 보이 | bellboy | hotel page |
| 문지기 | janitor | porter |
| 화장실; 변소 | toilet | lavatory |
| 아파트 | apartment | flat |
| 관리인 | janitor | caretaker |

## 운동·사교·오락 관계 (SPORTS, etc.)

| Korean | American | British |
|---|---|---|
| 운동 기구 | sporting goods | sports requisites |
| 수렵(狩獵) | hunting | shooting |
| 권투 선수 | boxer | bruiser (프로복서) |
| 영화 | movies; cinema | pictures; cinema |
| 톱 스타 《배우》 | headliner | star; topliner |
| 첫날; 개연일(開演日) | opening night | first night |
| 막간(幕間) | intermission | interval; break |
| 댄스홀 | dance hall | dancing saloon |
| 원유회(園遊會) | lawn fete | garden party |
| 시소대(臺) | teeterboard | seesaw |
| 회전 목마 | carousel | merry-go-round |
| 썰매 | sled | sledge |

## 시간의 표현법 (TIME)

| Korean | American | British |
|---|---|---|
| 몇 시입니까 | Do you have the time?<br>What time do you have? | Can you tell me the time?<br>What time do you make it?<br>What is the time by you? |
| 8시 15분 전 | a quarter of eight | a quarter to eight |
| 8시 30분 | half after eight; eight-thirty | half past eight |
| 반 시간 후 | a half hour later | half an hour later |
| 2주간 | two weeks | a fortnight |

| Korean | American | British |
|---|---|---|
| 수주간 | in weeks | for weeks |
| 신년; 새해 | New Year's | New Year's Day; New Year |
| 주초(週初) | the first of the week | early in the week |
| 주말(週末)경에 돌아옵니다 | I shall return around the last of the week. | I shall return about the end of the week. |
| 내주의 화요일 | a week from Tuesday | Tuesday week |
| 4개월 이내 | inside of four months | within four months |
| 11월 5일부터 12월 4일까지 | November 5 through December 4 | from November 5 to December 4 inclusive |

## 기 타 (OTHERS)

| | | |
|---|---|---|
| 기상대 | National Weather Service | Meteorological Office |
| 가을 | fall | autumn |
| 서머타임 | daylight-saving time | summer time |
| 병 | sickness | illness |
| 약제사 | druggist | chemist |
| 약국 | drugstore | chemist's (shop) |
| 장의사 | funeral director | undertaker |
| 이발소 | barber shop | barber's (shop) |
| 마구간 | barn | stable |
| 양계장 | chicken yard | fowl-run |
| 돼지우리 | hog pen | piggery; pigsty |
| 수탉 | rooster | cock |
| 곤충 | bug | insect |
| 성(姓) | family name; last name | surname |
| 명함 | calling card | visiting card |
| 백년잔치; 백년제(祭) | centennial | centenary |
| 1조(兆) | a trillion | a billion |
| 10억(億) | a billion | a thousand millions; a milliard |
| 재목 | lumber | timber |
| 권총 | rod; gun | pistol; revolver |
| 반반의 | fifty-fifty | half-and-half |
| 좋아 | O.K. | all right |

# (2) 영작문에 도움이 되는 예문과 용법

## 여러 가지 주어

(1) *We* are prohibited from smoking in the car.
*Smoking* in the car is prohibited.
(차 안에서는 금연) [대명사·명사]

(2) *To err* is human; *to forgive*, divine.
(잘못은 인간의 상사(常事)요, 용서는 신의 본성이다) [부정사]

(3) *Losing his fortune* drove him mad.
(재산을 잃고 그는 실성했다) [동명사]

(4) *That we shall succeed* is pretty certain.
(우리가 성공하리라는 것은 거의 틀림없다) [명사절]

(5) *From the gate to the porch* was no great distance.(대문에서 현관까지는 그리

먼 거리는 아니었다) [전치사구]

(6) Is *it* really impossible for you *to come to us?*(정말 저희들 집에는 오실 수가 없습니까) [형식주어 it]

(7) *It* rains hard.(비가 몹시 내린다) [비인칭동사의 주어]

(8) *There* has been another *car accident.* (또 자동차 사고가 일어났다) [There ~]

(9) *Care* killed the cat.(걱정은 명을 줄인다) [무생물이 주어]

## 다섯 가지 기본적 문형(文型)

**S**... **S**ubject **V**... **V**erb
**C**... **C**omplement **O**... **O**bject
**IO**... **I**ndirect **O**bject
**DO**... **D**irect **O**bject

(1) 주어(…는)+완전자동사(…하다) **(S+V)**

*Birds sing.* (새들은 노래한다)
*He smiled.* (그는 웃었다)
*John lives* near the park. (존은 공원 부근에 산다)
*I went* to the city last month. (나는 지난 달 그 도시에 갔었다)
The *sun rises* in the east. (태양은 동쪽에서 뜬다)
*She got up* at seven. (그녀는 7시에 일어났다)

【주의】 이탤릭체 이외의 부분은 modifiers (수식어구)로서 문법상으로는 문장의 principal element (주요소)가 아니다. 의미상으로는 설령 중요하더라도 이러한 modifiers는 문장의 subordinate element(종요소)라 부른다.

(2) 주어(…는)+불완전자동사(…이다)+보어 **(S+V+C)**

*She is pretty.* (그녀는 아름답다)
*He has grown old.* (그는 나이를 먹었다)
Your *father looks young* for his age. (네 부친은 나이에 비해 젊어 보이신다)
*He kept silent.* (그는 침묵을 지켰다)

(3) 주어(…는)+완전타동사(…하다)+목적어(…을) **(S+V+O)**

*I know him.* (나는 그를 안다)
*Have you had* your *breakfast?* (아침을 먹었느냐)
*You must read* the *book* by the end of this month. (이 달 말까지 그 책을 다 읽으셔야 합니다)

(4) 주어(…는)+동사(여격 동사)(…하다)+간접목적어(…에게)+직접목적어(…을) **(S+V+IO+DO)**

*Mr. Smith gave me a book.* (스미스 씨는 나에게 책을 한 권 주셨다)

【주의】 직접목적어를 앞에 내놓으면, 제3 형식이 된다. *Mr. Smith gave a book* to me. 이 경우 to me는 부사구.

The *maid brought me* a cup of *tea.* (하녀는 차를 한 잔 갖고 왔다)
*Give me it* again.

【주의】 직접목적어가 it나 them인 경우, 영국에서는 그것을 간접목적어 앞에 내놓는 경우가 많다. *I showed it you* the other day. (미국에서는 보통, *I showed it to you* the other day.라 함.)

*He asked me my opinion.* (그는 나의 의견을 물었다)

(5) 주어(…는)+불완전타동사(…하다)+목적어(…을)+보어(…하게) **(S+V+O+C)**

The *sun keeps us warm.* (태양은 우리를 따뜻하게 해준다)
*We heard her sing.* (우리들은 그녀가 노래하는 것을 들었다)
*Don't leave* the *door open.* (문을 열어 놓지 마라)

【주의】 They *made* him king. She *called* him a fool. Please *paint* the door green. 에서처럼 목적어를 「…으로[하게] 만들다, …하게[라고] 하다」로 나타내는 동사를 작위동사(作爲動詞) (factitive verb)라 한다. *He was made king* by them. 처럼 수동형으로 하면 제2의 문형이 된다.

## 시제(Tense)의 표현법

**A.** 현재 (**Present Tense**)

I *like* baseball. (나는 야구를 좋아한다) [현재의 동작 상태] / The earth *goes* round the sun once a year. (지구는 일 년에 한 번 태양의 둘레를 돈다) [불변의 진리] / I *leave* home for school at seven. (나는 7

시에 학교로 떠난다) [현재의 습관] / He *starts* tomorrow morning. (그는 내일 아침 출발한다) [미래의 대용] / He *shouts*, he *groans* in pain.(그는 소리치며, 고통에 신음한다) [역사적 현재] / I will go if it *is* fine tomorrow. (내일 날씨가 좋으면 가겠다) [조건이나 때를 보이는 부사절 중에서]

**B.** 과거 (**Past Tense**)

She *was* once a teacher. (그녀는 한때 교사였다) [과거의 사실] / I *rose* every day at six. (나는 매일 6시에 일어났다) [과거의 습관]

【주의】 과거의 습관을 강조하는 데는 used to(규칙적), would(불규칙적)를 사용한다.

**C.** 미래 (**Future Tense**)

(1) 단순미래(무의지(無意志) 미래)

*I will* [*shall* 《영》] be free tomorrow. (내일은 여가가 있습니다) [1인칭] / *You will* be able to go to college. (너는 대학에 진학할 수 있을 게다) [2인칭] / *His uncle will* probably leave everything to him. (그의 삼촌은 아마 그에게 모든 재산을 남겨 줄 것이다) [3인칭]

(2) 의지미래

*I will* study hard. (열심히 공부하겠다) [1인칭] / *You shall die.* (=I will kill you.) (죽일 테다) [말하는 이의 의지] / *The finder shall* receive a reward. (=I will give a reward to the finder.) (발견자에게 사례함) [말하는 이의 의지]

【주의】 미국에서는 모든 인칭에 will을 쓰거나 (will을 세게 발음함) want to, have to 따위를 쓴다.

(3) 단순미래의 의문문

*Shall I* get there in time if I take the 2:30 train? (2시 30분 기차를 탄다면 시간 안에 거기 닿을 수 있을까) [1인칭] / *Shall you* get there in time if you take the 4:30 train? [2인칭]

【주의】 미국에서는 Will I...? Will you...?의 형식으로 단순미래의 의문문을 만드는 경우가 많다.

*Will he* recover from his disease? (그의 병은 회복될까요) [3인칭]

(4) 의지미래의 의문문

*Shall I* open the window? (창문을 열까요) [상대방의 의향을 물음] / Which book *will you* take? (어느 책을 가지시겠습니까) [상대방의 의향을 물음] / *Will you* tell me your name? (이름을 말씀해 주십시오) [의뢰] / *Will your father* consent to go with you? (너의 아버지께서는 너와 함께 가는 것을 승낙하실까) [제3자의 의사를 상대에게 물음] / *Shall the servant* call for the doctor? (하인을 시켜 의사를 부르게 할까요) [상대의 의향을 물음]

**D.** 현재완료 (**Present Perfect Tense**)

I *have* just *finished* writing the letter. (방금 그 편지를 다 썼다) [동작의 완료] / Winter is over and spring *has come.* (겨울이 가고 봄이 왔다—지금은 봄이다) [과거 동작에서 현재 상태로의 추이] / *Have* you ever *read* this story? (이 소설을 읽은 적이 있느냐) [현재까지 경험] / I *have been waiting* for him more than an hour. (나는 1시간 이상이나 그를 기다리는 중이다) [현재까지 동작의 계속] / We *have lived* here for three years. (우리는 3년간 이곳에 살고 있다) [현재까지 상태의 계속] / Please return the book as soon as you *have done* with it. (그 책을 다 읽으시면 곧 돌려주십시오) [부사절 중에서 미래완료의 대용]

**E.** 과거완료 (**Past Perfect Tense**)

When I reached the station, (I found) the train *had* already *started.* (내가 역에 도착하였을 때 기차는 이미 떠나고 없었다) [과거의 어떤 때까지 동작의 완료] / I met Mr. Nam yesterday. I *had* not *seen* him for two years. (나는 어제 남선생을 만났다. 2년 동안 서로 만나지 못했다) [과거 어떤 때까지의 경험] / She was thirty years old, and *had been married* five years. (그녀는 당시 30세로서 이미 5년 전부터 결혼 생활을 하고 있었다) [과거 어떤 때까지 상태의 계속]

**F.** 미래완료 (**Future Perfect Tense**)

He *will have reached* Seoul by eight this evening. (그는 오늘밤 8시까지는 서울에 도착해 있을 것이다) [미래의 동작의 완료] / I am going to climb Mt. Halla this summer. Then I *shall have been* there three times. (이번 여름 한라산에 오르려고 한다. 그러면 세 번 등반한 것이 된다) [미래의 어떤 때까지 경험] / It *will have been raining* for ten days tomorrow. (내일로 열흘이나 계속 비가 내린 것이 된다) [미래의 어떤 때까지 동작의 계속] / I *shall have lived* here for two years next April. (오는 4월로 2년 동안 이곳에 사는 것이 된다) [미래의 어떤 때까지 상태의 계속]

## 가정(假定)의 표현법

**A.** 현재〔장차〕 만일 …이면〔하다면〕

What shall we do *if it rain(s)?* (만일 비가 오면 어떻게 할까)

【주의】 가정법현재형은 다음과 같은 경우에 쓰인다.

I asked that he *come*(=should come) to my office. (그에게 내 사무실로 오라고 부탁했다) / My employer insists that I *be*(=should be) prompt. (빨리 하라고 고용주는 나에게 말한다)

**B.** 현재 만일 …라고 한다면

*If* I *were* you, I *would buy* this house. (만일 내가 자네라면, 이 집을 살 텐데) [현재의 사실에 반대하는 가상] / *If* he *were* here, I *could consult* him about this business. (만일 그가 이곳에 있다면, 이 사업에 관해서 의논할 수 있을 텐데) [현재의 사실에 반대하는 가상]

**C.** 현재 만일 …이 없다면〔…이 아니라면〕

*If* he *had not* that bad habit, I *would recommend* him. (그가 그 나쁜 버릇만 없다면, 그를 추천할 텐데) / *If it were not for* the sun, nothing *could live.* (만일 태양이 없다면, 아무 것도 생존할 수 없을 것이다) / *But for*(=*If it were not for*) your help, I *should fail.* (만일 당신 도움이 없다면, 나는 실패할 것이다)

**D.** 장차 만일 …라 한다면(미래에 관한 실현성이 희박한 사실에 대한 가상)

*If* some one *were to give* you a million dollars, what *would* you *do?* (만일 누가 100만 달러를 준다면, 어찌 하겠는가) / *If* the sun *were* to *rise* in the west, I *would not break* my promise. (설령 태양이 서쪽에서 뜨는 일이 있더라도 나는 약속을 어기지 않겠다)

**E.** 장차 만일 …이라면〔…이 아니라면〕(미래에 대한 강한 의문을 나타냄)

*If* it *should rain* tomorrow, I *shall* 〔*will*〕 not *go* there. (만일 내일 비가 온다면, 나는 거기에 가지 않을 것이다) / *If* he *should not arrive* by five, I *shall have to go* there by myself. (만일 그가 5시까지 오지 않는다면, 나 혼자라도 가야만 될 거다)

**F.** 과거에 만일 …이었다면

*If* Mr. Han *had been alive,* he *would have treated* me kindly. (한 선생님이 살아 계셨다면, 나에게 친절히 대하여 주셨을 텐데) / *If* I *had known* your address, I *would have called* on you. (댁의 주소를 알고 있었다면, 찾아 뵈었을 텐데) / *Had he tried* once more, he *might have succeeded* in it. (그는 한번 더 해 보았더라면, 성공했을지도 모른다)

**G.** 과거에 만일 …이 아니었다면

*If it had not been for* (=*But for*) your kind advice, *he would not have given up* smoking. (친절하신 충고가 없었던들, 그는 금연을 하지 않았을 겁니다) / I *should have been* Prime Minister by now *if it hadn't been for* it. (그런 일만 없었던들, 나는 지금쯤 총리가 되어 있을 텐데)

## 부정(否定)을 나타내기

**A. not**을 사용하여

John *isn't* here. (존은 여기 없다)

I *don't* have enough money to buy it.
I *haven't* enough money to buy it.
I *haven't* got enough money to buy it.
(나는 그것을 살 만한 돈이 없다)

The concert *didn't* begin at 7:30. (연주회는 7시 30분에 시작하지 않았다) / She will *not* go to church tomorrow. (그녀는 내일 교회에 가지 않을 게다) / He could *not* even write his name. (그는 자기 이름조차 쓰지 못했다) / I'm afraid I'm *not* going to pass the examination. (나는 시험에 합격할 것 같지 않다) / *Don't* be late for school! (학교에 늦지 마라) / Smoking is *not* allowed. (금연) / Cars must *not* be parked in front of the entrance. (현관 앞에 주차 금지) / I *won't* do it. (그것을 하지 않겠다) / He *wouldn't* answer any questions. (그는 어떤 질문에도 대답하려 하

지 않았다) / I *didn't* need to hurry. (나는 서둘 필요가 없었다) / You *needn't* have hurried. (너는 서두르지 않아도 좋았을 텐데) / You *don't* have to go to school today. (너는 오늘 학교에 가지 않아도 된다) / You *haven't* got to answer all the questions in the examination paper. (시험지의 문제에 다 답할 필요는 없다) / You had better *not* be late for class. (수업엔 늦지 않는 게 좋다)

**B. no**를 사용하여

There is *no* one. (아무도 없다) / I've got *no* money. (돈을 갖고 있지 않다) / That is *no* easy task. (그것은 쉬운 일이 아니다) / This fountainpen is *no* good. (이 만년필은 좋지 않다) / It is *no* use crying over spilt milk. (지난 일은 후회해도 소용없다) / There is *no* use in trying to do such a thing. (그런 일은 해보았자 헛일이다) / *No* one came. (아무도 안 왔다) / There is *no* telling who will win the race. (누가 경주에 이길지 아무도 모른다) / *No* parking. (주차 금지)

**C.** 부분 부정(部分否定)과 전체 부정

*All* that sparkles is *not* diamond. (반짝이는 것이라고 다 다이아몬드는 아니다) [부분 부정] / *Both* my parents are *not* living. (양친이 다 생존해 계신 것은 아니다) [부분 부정] / I know *neither* of them. (나는 그들의 어느 쪽도 알지 못한다) [전체 부정] / *Every* man can *not* be a poet. (아무나 다 시인이 될 수 있는 것은 아니다) [부분 부정] / *Nobody* knows the truth. (아무도 그 진상을 모른다) [전체 부정] / *No one* has seen the wind. (바람을 본 사람은 아무도 없다) [전체 부정] / "Do you know *either* of them?" "No, I do *not* know *either* of them." (「너는 그들 중 어느 한 쪽을 아느냐」 「아니, 아무도 모른다」) [전체 부정] / You *cannot* be *always* happy. (항상 행복할 수만은 없다) [부분 부정] / I'm *not absolutely* sure. (나는 절대적으로 확신을 갖고 있는 것은 아니다) [부분 부정] / It was *not altogether* his fault. (그건 완전히 그의 죄만은 아니었다) [부분 부정] / It was *not at all* his fault. (그것은 전혀 그의 잘못이 아니었다) [전체 부정]

**D.** 이중 부정(二重否定)

He is *not un*happy. (그는 불행하지는 않다) / He did *not* say that he would *not* come. (그는 오지 않겠다고는 안 했다) / They *never* meet *without* quarreling. (그들은 만나기만 하면 꼭 싸운다) / There is *no* rule *but* has some exceptions. (예외 없는 규칙은 없다) / In fact, I was *not unaware* of his presence. (실은 나는 그가 와 있음을 알고 있었다) / He *never failed to* keep his promise. (그는 약속을 어긴 적이 없다—꼭 지켰다)

**E.** 부정적인 말을 사용하여

He has but *few* chances of success. (그가 성공할 가망은 거의 없다) / I saw *few* people there. (거기서 나는 거의 아무도 보지 못했다) / She knows *little*, but talks a lot. (그녀는 아는 것이라곤 거의 없으나, 잘 지껄인다)

【주의】 few, little은 부정적인 뜻을 가지나, 여기에 부정관사가 붙어서 a few, a little이 되면 "약간은 있다"라는 긍정적인 뜻을 갖게 된다

She *rarely* writes to me. (그녀는 좀처럼 나에게 편지를 안 한다) / I can *scarcely* hear you. (나는 네 말이 거의 들리지 않는다) / *Hardly* a leaf is left on the tree. (거의 하나의 잎도 나무에 달려 있지 않다) / It *seldom* snows in these regions. (이 지방에는 거의 눈이 내리지 않는다) / Employment is now very *scarce.* (요즘은 취직 자리가 거의 없다) / It is *impossible* to tell when he will come. (그가 언제 올는지 모른다) / He was the *only* doctor in the village. (이 마을에는 그 사람 말고는 의사가 하나도 없었다)

**F.** 강한 부정

I am *not at all* sorry. (=I am *by no means* sorry.) (나는 전혀 섭섭하지 않다) / He is *far from being* bright. (그의 머리는 좋기는 커녕 아주 나쁘다) / I *cannot possibly* allow you to do that. (도저히 자네에게 그것을 하게 할 수는 없네) / He didn't under-stand *a single* word of it. (그는 그것의 한 마디도 이해하지 못했다) / *None* of your absence! (바보 소리 하지 마라) / He is *not a bit* ashamed. (그는 조금도 부끄럽게 여기지 않는다) / He is *absolutely* useless. (그는 조금도 쓸모가 없다) / I did not go *any farther.* (나는 조금

도 나아가지 않았다) / Your shadow hasn't grown *any less.* (자넨 조금도 여위지 않았네 그려)

**G.** 부정어를 사용치 않는 부정의 표현

It is *too* hot *to* work. (더워서 일할 수가 없다) / Make haste, *or* you will miss the train. (서둘지 않으면 기차를 놓친다) / We started *before* the sun rose. (우리는 해가 뜨기 전에 출발하였다) / *Who knows?* (= *God only knows.*) (누가 알겠는가—아무도 모른다) / *Who could have foreseen* it?(= *No one could have foreseen* it.) (누가 그것을 예견할 수 있었을 것인가—아무도 예견할 수 없었다) [반어적] / This is *the happiest* day I have ever had in my life. (오늘처럼 즐거웠던 날은 없다) / It is *one thing* to know and *another* to do. (안다는 것과 실행한다는 것은 별개 문제이다) / She was *the last* person I expected to see in such a place. (설마 이런 곳에서 그녀와 만날 줄은 생각도 못 했다) / I wonder why that beautiful lady *remains* single. (저런 미인이 어째서 미혼으로 남아 있을까)

## 수동을 나타내기

**1. be** [**get, become**] + 과거분사

He *gave* her a vase. (그는 그녀에게 꽃병을 주었다)→She *was given* a vase *by* him.

【주의】 위와 같이 수동의 문장이 능동의 문장의 동사를 그대로 취하고, 전치사도 by로 족한 경우가 많으나, 그렇지 않은 경우도 많다.

Heavy clouds *hid* the sun. (검은 구름이 태양을 가렸다)→The sun *was obscured by* heavy clouds.

They *made us work* very hard. (그들은 우리를 매우 혹사했다)→We *were made to work* very hard.

The hunter *perceived a bear* approach the river. (사냥꾼은 곰이 강으로 접근해 오는 것을 보았다)→*A bear was perceived to* approach the river by the hunter.

We *allowed each speaker* ten minutes. (우리는 각 연사에게 10분간씩 말할 것을 허용했다)→*Each speaker was allowed* ten minutes.

Every member of our club *knows his name.* (우리 회원은 누구나 그의 이름을 알고 있다)→His name *is known to* every member of our club.

Wine *is made from* grapes. (포도주는 포도로 만든다) / This house *is built of* wood. (이 집은 목조이다) / He *got* [*became, grew*] *accustomed to* such a mode of life. (그는 그런 생활 양식에 익숙해졌다) / The window *got broken* by somebody. (누군가에 의해서 창문이 부서졌다) / That problem *is being discussed by* the commitee now. (그 문제는 현재 위원회에서 토의되고 있다)

**2. have** [**get**] + 목적어 + 과거분사 [부정사]

I *had* my purse *stolen.* (나는 지갑을 도둑맞았다) [경험의 수동형] / She *had* [*got*] her house *burnt* down in the fire. (그녀는 화재로 집을 몽땅 태웠다) / He *had* his wife *die.* (그는 부인을 잃었다) / I don't like to *have* him *go.* (나는 그를 보내는 건 싫다) / She *get* her finger *caught* in the car door. (그녀는 자동차 문에 손가락이 끼었다)

【주의】 위에 든 보기에서처럼 조동사 be를 사용하지 않고 수동의 뜻을 나타내는 경우가 있는 반면, 형식상 수동형이면서 우리말로는 능동의 뜻을 나타내는 경우와 그 반대의 경우도 있다.

I *am acquainted* with him. (나는 그와 아는 사이다) / He *was seated* at the table. (그는 자리에 앉아 있었다) / She *was* much *pleased* to hear that. (그녀는 그것을 듣고 매우 기뻐했다)

Do it at once. (곧 그것을 해라)
*Let it be done* at once. [명령의 수동형]

**3.** 동사 자체가 수동적

My hat *blew* into the river. (나의 모자는 강으로 날려갔다) / This book *sells* well. (이 책은 잘 팔린다) / A large house *is building* on the hill. (=A large house *is being built* on the hill.) (언덕 위에 큰 집이 건축 중이다)

## 의문 · 명령 · 감탄을 나타내기

**A.** 의문을 나타내기

1. 의문부사의 내용

*When* shall we start? (↷) (언제 출발할까) / *Where* does he live now? (그는 지금 어

디에 살고 있지) / *Why* do you think so? (왜 그렇게 생각하지) / *How* old are you? (몇 살이냐) / *How* about a drink? (한 잔 들겠나)

2. 의문대명사의 사용

*Who* is he?(↘) He is my brother. (그는 누구지—그는 나의 형[동생]이다) [이름·혈족 관계] / *What* is he? He is a student. (그는 무엇을 하지—학생이야) [직업·신분] / *Who* do you think did this? (누가 이것을 하였다고 너는 생각하지) / *Who* [*Whom*] do you want to see? (누구를 면회하려는 거지) / *Who* [*Whom*] is the letter from? (이 편지는 누구에게서 온 것이지) / *Which* of you are going ? (너희들 중 누가 가는 거지) / In *which* room are they staying? (그들은 어느 방에 묵고 있지) / *Whose* friend is Smith? (스미스는 누구의 친구지) / *Whose* is this? (이것은 누구 것이지) / *What* can I do for you? (무엇을 드릴까요) 《점원이 손님에게》 / *What* color is the flag? (그 기는 무슨 색이지) / *What* for? (무엇 때문이지)

3. 의문부사[대명사]를 쓰지 않는 경우

*Is* he your friend? (↗) (그는 너의 친구냐) [도치] / *Are* you happy now? (너는 지금 행복한가) / *Do* you remember him? (그를 기억하고 있느냐)

*Have* you any money?
*Do* you have any money?
*Have* you got money? (돈을 갖고 있느냐)

*Have* you ever seen a white snake? (흰 뱀을 본 적이 있느냐) / *Shall* I go (there) at once? (곧 갈까요) / *May* I ask a question? (질문을 해도 좋습니까) / *Would* the coming Friday suit you? (다음 금요일은 형편이 닿겠느냐) / *Can* this dress be cleaned today? (이 옷을 오늘 세탁할 수 있겠나) / The light is very bad here. *Is* this dress *blue, or black?* (↘) (이곳은 매우 어둡군. 이 옷은 청색인가 검정인가) / *Do* you like to play *basketball or baseball?* (↗)—Yes, I like both these sports. (농구나 야구를 좋아하는가—네 둘 다 좋아합니다)

4. 의문 형식을 취하지 않는 의문문 《문장 끝이 올림조(↗)가 된다》

*You are leaving so soon?* (그렇게 빨리 떠나십니까) / *John is married?* I didn't know that. (존이 결혼했다고, 나는 몰랐는데) / *You are going?* (가시는 겁니까)

【주의】 부가 의문

Today is Monday, *isn't it?* (오늘은 월요일이지요) / English isn't difficult, *is it?* (영어는 어렵지 않지요) / That's funny, *isn't it?* (그것 참 재미있지) / I suppose I should get my hair cut, *shouldn't I?* (나 머리를 깎아야 하겠지)

【주의】 수사(修辭) 의문(형식은 의문문이나, 실질적으로 평서문과 같음)

*What* is the use? (=Of course, there is no use at all.) (무슨 소용이 있담—전혀 소용이 없다) / *Who* do you think I am? (나를 누구라고 생각하느냐—이런 대접을 하다니) / *Isn't* that beautiful? (아 참 예쁘다)

**B.** 명령을 나타내기

1. 명령형을 취한다

*Go* straight. (곧바로 가라) / *Be careful* with fire. (불조심해라) / *Mind* your own business! (남의 일에 간섭하지 마라) / *Never mention* it again! (그건 두 번 다시 말하지 말게) / *Don't talk* so fast. (그렇게 빨리 말하지 말게) / *Don't let* the bird fly away. (그 새를 놓치지 마라) / *Let* this *be* a lesson to you. (이 일을 교훈으로 삼아라) / *Do come* again. (꼭 또 오십시오) [강조적] / *Do stop* making that noise. (그런 시끄러운 소리 좀 내지 말게) [강조적] / *Pass* me the salt, please. (소금을 이리 건네 주십시오) / *Won't* you come in? (=Come in, *won't* you?) (들어오시지 않겠소) [가벼운 명령] / *Do not* fear. (무서워하지 마) [부정적 명령] / *Let* me *do* it. (=Permit me to do it.) (그것은 제가 하죠) [제1인칭의 명령] / *Let* young men *bear* this in mind. (청년은 이 일을 명심해야 할 것이다) [제3인칭의 명령]

2. 명령형을 취하지 않는다

You carry the table into the room, George. (조지, 자넨 그 테이블을 방으로 운반해 주게) / Mary, you're going to bed early tonight! (메리, 오늘 밤에는 일찍 자는 거다) / You will pack and leave this house. (짐을 싸 이 집을 나가주게) / You shall go tomorrow. (내일 가도록 해라) / She shall come here whether she wants or not. (완력을 써서라도 그녀를 이리 오도록 하게) / You are to be up at five! (너는 5시에 일어나는 거다) / You must not tell him. (그에게 말하면 안 된다) / You can't play baseball in the garden! (뜰에서 야구를 하면 안 된다)

3. 게시(揭示)

No parking here. (주차 금지) / No scribbling (allowed) on the wall. (낙서 금지) / No admission except on business. (무용자 출입 금지) / Keep off. (출입 금지) / Off limits. (출입 금지)

**C.** 감탄을 나타내기

Wonderful! (훌륭하다; 멋지다) / How delicious! (정말 맛있다) / How the star twinkles! (야 그 별, 참 잘도 반짝이네) / How pretty this rose is! (이 장미는 참 예쁘기도 하군) / How annoying having to stand all the way home on the bus! (귀가하는 버스에서 내내 서 있어야 한다는 것은 얼마나 괴로운 일인가) / What a large building it is! (이것 참 큰 빌딩이군) / What a fine view! (얼마나 멋진 경치인가) / What impudence! (정말이지 뻔뻔스럽군) / Who would have thought it! (누가 그것을 생각인들 하였으랴) / Just think of it! (생각만 하여도 견딜 수 없다) / Oh! If I had only known! (아 내가 그것을 알기만 했다면) / We have had such a pleasant time! (매우 재미있었다) / It simply cannot be done! (도저히 그런 일은 할 수가 없다) / Ouch! It hurts. (아야, 아프다) / Why, it's Mary! (어머나, 메리 아냐) / Poor thing! (가엾어라)

## 간접 화법으로 나타내기

**A.** 평서문의 경우

The lady said to me, "I *will* sing my favorite song." (그 부인은 나에게 '내가 즐겨 부르는 노래를 하겠어요' 라고 말하였다) → The lady told me (that) she *would* sing her favorite song.

You said to me, "You *shall* have my knife."(자네는 나에게 '나이프를 주겠다' 고 했네) → You told me (that) I *should* have your knife.

You said to me, "I *shall* certainly succeed." (자네는 '꼭 성공한다' 고 나에게 말했네) → You told me (that) you *would* certainly succeed.

Mr. Brown said to me, "I *have broken* your telescope." (브라운씨는 나에게 '자네 망원경을 깨뜨렸네' 라고 말했다) → Mr. Brown told me (that) he *had broken* my telescope.

John said, "Mary *arrived* an hour ago." (존은 '메리가 1시간 전에 도착했다' 고 말했다) → John said that Mary (*had*) *arrived* an hour before.

**B.** 의문문의 경우

(1) 의문사가 있을 때 (의문사는 연결어가 됨)

He said to me, "*Why* did you strike my brother?" (그는 나에게 '왜 내 동생을 때렸느냐' 고 물었다) → He asked me *why* I had struck his brother.

He said to her, "*What* is the matter?" (그는 그녀에게 '무슨 일이냐' 고 물었다) → He asked her *what* was the matter.

(2) 의문사가 없을 때 (if, whether를 연결어로 한다)

He said to her, "Have you had your breakfast?" (그는 그녀에게 '아침 식사를 하였느냐' 고 물었다) → He asked her *if* she had had her breakfast.

**C.** 명령문의 경우

He said to me, "Wait a minute." (그는 나에게 '잠깐 기다려 주게' 라고 말했다) → He *told* me *to wait* a minute.

He said to me, "Please wait a minute." (그는 나에게 '잠시 기다려 주세요' 라고 말했다) → He *asked* me *to wait* a minute.

I said to him, "Don't be idle."(나는 그에게 '게으름 피우지 말라' 고 했다) → I *told* him *not to be* idle.

She said, "Let's start early."(그녀는 '일찍 떠납시다' 라고 말했다) → She *suggested that we should* start early.

**D.** 감탄문의 경우(평서문으로 고친다)

He said, "Hurrah! I have won!" (그는, '만세, 이겼다' 고 소리쳤다) → He exclaimed with delight that he had won.

He said, "Oh my! How foolish I have been!" (그는 '아 참, 정말로 바보짓을 했네' 라고 말했다) → He confessed with regret that he had been very foolish.

【주의】 He remarked how foolish he had been.과 같은 표현도 할 수 있다.

## It의 용법

**A.** 날씨·시간·거리 따위(**Impersonal *It***)

*It* rains a great deal in these districts in the winter. (이 지방에서는 겨울에 많은 비가 내린다) / *It's* time to go now. (이제 떠나야 할 시간이다) / *It* is six years since we moved here. (이곳으로 이사온 지 6년이 된다) / *It* is (a) five minutes' walk. (걸어서 5분이면 갈 수 있는 곳이다)

**B.** 형식적인 주어 또는 목적어(**Preparatory *It***)

*It* is difficult *to beat him.* (그를 이기는 것은 어렵다) / *It* was easy for me *to understand his state of mind.* (그의 마음 상태를 알기란 나에게는 쉬운 일이었다) / I think *it* wrong *to value money more than time.* (돈을 시간보다 소중히 여기는 것은 잘못된 일이라 생각한다) / *It's* no good *hoping for their help.* (그들의 원조를 기대해 봤자 헛일이다) / *It* was a pity (*that*) *you couldn't come.* (자네가 오지 못한 것은 정말 유감이었네) / *It* matters little *who has done it.* (누가 했는가는 문제가 안 된다) / You must see to *it that no harm comes to her.* (그녀에게 해가 미치지 않도록 돌보지 않으면 안 된다) / *It* was *yesterday* that I saw her in the park. (내가 공원에서 그녀를 만난 것은 어제였다)

**C.** 환경이나 부정(不定)을 나타낸다

"Who is *it?*"—"*It's* me." (누구십니까—접니다) / In the dance, *it* is grace. (춤에서는 우아함이 가장 중요하다) / We must fight *it* out. (일이란 끝까지 해내야 한다)

## 부정사의 용법

**A. to**없는 부정사

Let's all *go* to the cinema. (모두 영화 구경 가자) / Let him *come.* (그를 오게 하여라) / I heard her *play* the piano. (나는 그녀가 피아노 치는 것을 들었다) / I saw him *cross* the street. (나는 그가 거리를 횡단하는 것을 보았다—처음부터 끝까지 보았다) / *cf.* I saw him *crossing* the street. (나는 그가 거리를 횡단중인 것을 보았다) / I will have the porter *carry* your baggage for you. (포터에게 짐을 운반시키겠다) / Will you help me (to) *clean* the car? (자동차 닦는 것을 거들어 주겠느냐)

【주의】 미어(美語)에서는 help의 뒤에 to 없는 부정사를 쓰는 경우가 많다.

I will have him *translate* the book. (그에게 이 책을 번역시키겠다)

**B. to** 있는 부정사

He seems *to be* rich. (그는 부자인 것 같다) / *To love* and *to be loved* is the greatest happiness on earth. (사랑을 하고 사랑을 받는다는 것은 이 세상에서 가장 큰 행복이다) [주어] / *To see* you is always a great pleasure. (당신을 뵙는다는 것은 언제나 큰 즐거움입니다) [주어] / He wants *to learn* English. (그는 영어를 배우고 싶어한다) [목적어] / What I like is *to swim* in the sea and then *to lie* on the warm sand. (내가 좋아하는 것은 바다에서 헤엄을 치고 따뜻한 모래에 누워있는 것이다) [보어] / That is not the way *to speak* to your uncle. (그러한 말투로 너의 아저씨에게 말하는 법이 아니다) [형용사적] / This water is good *to drink.* (이 물은 먹을 수 있다) [형용사를 수식] / There is nothing *to be feared.* (두려워할 것은 아무 것도 없다) [명사를 수식] / He is working late *to make up* for his absence yesterday. (그는 어제의 결석을 메꾸기 위해 늦게까지 공부하고 있다) [목적] / He was lucky enough *to win* the prize. (그는 다행히 상을 탔다) [결과] / I was very glad *to see* you. (만나 보게 되어 대단히 기뻤다) [원인] / We *are to meet* at five. (우리는 5시에 만나기로 되어 있다) [be to] / *To tell you the truth,* I don't know what the answer is. (사실을 말하면, 답이 무엇인지 모릅니다) / *To think* he knew about it all the time! (항상 그가 그것에 관해 알고 있었다니, 설마)

## ~ing의 용법

**A.** 분사구문(**Participial Construction**)
The girls marched on, *singing* merrily. (소녀들은 즐겁게 노래하며 행진하여 갔다) [동시] / *Hearing* a noise, I jumped out of bed. (시끄러운 소리에 나는 침대에서 뛰어 나왔다) [때를 나타냄] / *Having finished* my work, I went out for a walk. (일을 마치고 나는 산책을 나갔다) [때－완료－를 나타냄] / *Having* no money with me, I could not buy it. (돈이 없어서 살 수 없었다) [이유] / Weather *permitting*, we shall start tomorrow. (날씨가 좋으면 내일 떠나겠습니다) [조건] / *Turning* to the left, you will find the place you want. (좌측으로 돌면, 찾으시는 곳이 나옵니다) [조건] / *Admitting* your principle to be right, how could you put it into practice? (자네의 원리는 옳다 치더라도 대체 어떻게 실용으로 옮길 수가 있는가) [양보]

**B.** 동명사(**Gerund**)를 포함하는 몇몇 관용구
It is no use *crying* over spilt milk. (돌이킬 수 없는 일 한탄해야 소용없다) [It는 crying이라는 gerund를 받는다] / I cannot help *laughing* at his foolish idea. (그의 어리석은 생각에 웃지 않을 수가 없다) / There is no *knowing* what he is thinking about. (그가 무엇을 생각하고 있는지 전혀 알 수 없다) (=It is impossible to know what he is thinking about.) / On *receiving* the telegram, he turned pale. (전보를 받자마자, 그는 창백해졌다) (=As soon as he received the telegram, he turned pale.) / When I heard the news, I felt like *crying*. (그 소식을 듣고 나는 울고 싶은 심정이었다) [crying은 like라는 형용사(전치사)의 목적어] *Talking* (=While we are on the subject) of Johnson, what has become of his wife? (존슨의 이야기가 되었습니다만, 그의 부인은 어찌 되었습니까)

## 비교를 나타내기(Comparison)

**1.** 비교의 표현은 대체로 다음 세 형식으로 표현된다.

**A.** 비교급을 사용한다
The lion is *stronger than* the tiger. (사자는 호랑이보다 더 강하다) / He is much *better* today *than* he was yesterday. (오늘 그는 어제보다 훨씬 기분이 좋다)

**B.** 최상급을 사용한다
He is *the tallest* boy in this class. (그는 이 반에서 가장 키가 크다) / Spring is *the best* of all season. (봄은 모든 계절 중에서 가장 좋다)

**C.** 기타(관용적인 어구의 사용)
I *prefer* the city *to* the country. (나는 시골보다 도시가 좋다) / He is *as* tall *as* she. (그는 그녀와 키가 같다)

**2.** 비교의 표현을 그 사용되는 뜻에 따라 구분하면 다음과 같다.

**A.** **A**는 **B**보다 (더) …이다〔하다〕
You are *taller than* I. (너는 나보다 키가 더 크다)
【주의】 than은 접속사. than me로 하지 않도록 주의할 것.
He is *more* diligent *than* his brother. (그는 동생보다 더 부지런하다) / "Which do you like *better*, tea or coffee?" "I like coffee *better*." ('홍차와 커피 중 어느 쪽을 더 좋아하십니까' '커피를 더 좋아합니다') / This pen is *much better than* that. (이 펜이 저것보다 훨씬 더 좋다) / He *prefers* skiing *to* swimming. (그는 수영보다 스키를 더 좋아한다) / He is *two years older than* I. (그는 나보다 두 살 위이다) (=He is *two years senior to* me. *or* He is *older than* I *by two years*.) / He is *the older of* the two. (그 두 사람중에서는 그가 손위이다)

**B.** …보다 …하게
This morning I got up ten minutes *earlier than* usual. (오늘 아침 나는 여느때보다 10분 일찍 일어났다) / I went there five minutes *ahead* of the appointed time. (나는 약속 시간보다도 5분 일찍 거기

에 갔다) / He came home much *earlier than* we expected. (그는 우리가 예상했던 것보다 일찍 귀가하였다)

**C.** …하면 할수록
*The more* one has, *the more* one wants. (가지면 가질수록 욕심이 더 난다) / *The more, the merrier.* (사람이 많으면 많을수록 그만큼 더 재미있다) / Hear him out, and you will understand him *the better.* (그가 말하는 것을 끝까지 들으세요. 그러면 그만큼 잘 이해할 수 있을 것입니다)
【주의】 이 항의 the는 부사임.

**D.** 점차 …하게 되다
It is *growing colder and colder.* (점점 추워진다) / He *becomes less and less diligent.* (그는 점점 게을러진다) / The story *becomes more and more interesting.* (이야기는 점점 재미있어진다)

**E. A**는 **B**정도로〔만큼〕 …이다〔하다〕, …만큼 …은 아니다〔…하지 않다〕
John is *as* young *as* my brother. (존은 나의 동생만큼 어리다) / He is *not so* handsome *as* Mr. Smith. (그는 스미스씨만큼 잘생기지는 못했다) / She *cannot* sing *so* well *as* you. (그녀는 노래를 너만큼 못한다)

**F. A**는 **B**의 …배나 …이다〔하다〕
Your father has *three times as* many books *as* my brother. (너의 부친께서는 우리 형의 세 배나 책을 가지고 계신다) / This box is *twice as* heavy *as* that one. (이 상자는 저 상자의 배나 무겁다) / He works *twice as* hard *as* others. (그는 다른 이의 두 배나 열심히 일을 한다)

**G.** 가장〔무엇보다도〕 …하다
Mt. Paektu is *the highest* mountain in Korea. (백두산은 한국에서 가장 높은 산이다) / Mt. Paektu is *higher than any other* mountain in Korea. (백두산은 한국의 다른 어느 산보다도 높다) / This is *the most* interesting story that I have ever read. (이것은 내가 지금까지 읽은 것 중 가장 재미있는 책이다) [ever는 최상급을 강조] / *Nothing* is *more* precious *than* one's life. *or Nothing* is *so* precious *as* one's life. (사람의 생명처럼 존귀한 것은 없다) / I like *nothing better than* this. (이것보다 더 좋아하는 것은 없다) / The river is *deepest* here. (강은 이곳이 가장 깊다) [the를 붙이지 않음] / This is *much the most* difficult. (이것은 아주 대단히 어렵다) / There is *no* place *like* home. (고향처럼 좋은 곳은 없다) (=*No* place is *so* good *as* home.) / This boy is *as* clever *as any* in the class. (이 소년은 반의 어느 학생 못지않게 영리하다)

**H.** 될 수 있는 한…
Please go there *as* soon *as you can.* (될 수 있는 대로 빨리 거기에 가 주시오) / You ought to be *as* careful *as possible.* (가급적 주의하지 않으면 안 된다)

**I.** …보다는 오히려…
He is *not so much* a novelist *as* a poet. (그는 소설가라기보다는 오히려 시인이다) / He is a scholar *rather than* a teacher. (그는 교사라기보다는 오히려 학자다) / She was *more* shy *than* unsocial. (그녀는 비사교적이라기보다는 수줍음을 탔다) / I *would rather* (=*sooner*) die *than* suffer disgrace. (수치를 당하느니 차라리 죽음을 택하겠다)

**J. than** ~ 따위의 생략
You will soon get *better.* (곧 나을 겁니다) / I like summer *best.* (나는 여름이 제일 좋다)

## 관사의 용법

### 정관사의 용법

**A.** 보통명사에 붙는 정관사
(1) 전술한 명사를 반복하는 경우
I bought *an* interesting *book* yesterday. I have read *the book* through.
(2) 문맥이나 상황으로 판단될 경우
Will you shut *the door?*
Send for *the doctor.*
(3) the best, the proper, the real 따위의 뜻을 나타낸다. 이 경우 발음은 강형(強形)이 된다
She is *the* [ði:] *pianist* of the day. (그녀야말로 당대 일류의 피아니스트다) / He is

quite *the* [ðiː] *gentleman.* (그야말로 정말 신사다)

(4) 영어 특유의 표현

He looked *me* full in *the* face. (그는 내 얼굴을 뚫어지게 보았다) / I grasped *him* by *the* sleeve. (나는 그의 소매를 잡아당겼다)

(5) 우리 일상의 경험 범위 내에서 하나밖에 없다고 생각되는 사물을 가리킨다.

Long live *the king.*

*the sun; the moon; the earth;* etc.

(6) 보통명사가 대문자로 시작되어 고유의 (또는 유일한) 것을 나타내는 경우

*the Lord* (=God); *the Savior; the Book* (=Bible); etc.

(7) 방위명(方位名), 자연 현상의 경우

*the east; the west; the south; the north; the wind; the storm; the weather;* etc.

(8) 자연의 사물에 대한 평범한 묘사의 경우

*the green* (초원); *the plain; the country; the meadow; the wild* (황야); *the field(s)* (밭); etc.

(9) 배분적 용법의 경우. 이 경우 per의 뜻이 되고, 전치사 by를 수반하여 도량(度量)의 단위를 나타낸다.

This cloth is sold by *the yard.* (이 옷감은 야드 단위로 판다)

by *the pound;* by *the hour;* by *the day;* by *the gallon;* by *the inch;* by *the dozen;* etc.

(10) such와 같은 뜻으로 쓰이는 경우

He is not *the man* to tell a lie. (=He is not such a man as will tell a lie.) (그는 거짓말을 할 사람이 아니다)

(11) 보통명사의 단수형을 수반하여 추상적인 관념을 나타내는 경우

*The pen* is mightier than *the sword.* (문(文)은 무(武)보다 강하다) / True poetry touches *the heart.* (진정한 시는 심금을 울린다)

**B.** 고유명사에 붙는 정관사

고유명사는 원칙적으로 정관사를 필요로 하지 않으나, 다음 경우는 정관사를 붙인다

(1) 국명(國名)

*the United States of America; the United Kingdom;* etc.

(2) 도시, 지방명

*the Hague; the Lake District* (영국의 호반 지방); *the Tyrol;* etc.

(3) 도로, 가로명

*the Dover Road; the Thames Embankment; the High Street;* etc.

(4) 호텔, 극장, 학교, 박물관, 동물원 이름

*the Hotel Cecil; the Globe Theatre; the University of Oxford; the British Museum;* etc.

(5) 철도, 운하, 선박 이름

*the Great Central Railway; the Suez Canal; the Mayflower;* etc.

(6) 서적, 잡지, 신문 이름

*the Concise Oxford Dictionary; the Youth's Companion; the Reader's Digest; the Korea Times;* etc.

(7) 해양, 하천, 고개, 반도, 해협 이름

*the Atlantic; the Rhine; the Kirkstone Pass; the Malay Peninsula; the English Channel;* etc.

【주의】 다음과 같은 경우는 정관사를 붙이지 않는다
Hyde Park; Lake Sanjŏng (=the Lake of Sanjŏng); Mount Everest; President Lincoln; Oxford University; Seoul Station; etc.

**C.** 형용사에 붙는 정관사

(1) the+형용사=보통명사의 복수, 또는 집합명사

*the dead*(죽은 사람들); *the rich; the poor; the needy*(생활 곤궁자); etc.

(2) the+현재분사=집합명사

*the sleeping; the dying;* etc.

(3) the+과거분사=보통명사의 복수

*the learned*[lə́ːrnid](학식 있는 사람); *the wounded; the bereaved*(유족); etc.

단수의 경우는

*the deceased* [disíːst] (고인); *the accused* [əkjúːzd] (피고인); *the betrothed* [bitróuðd] (약혼자); etc.

(4) the+형용사=추상명사

*the true* (진실된 것); *the sublime*(숭고한 것); *the beautiful*(=beauty); *the good*(선행); etc.

(5) the+형용사가 어떤 사물의 부분을 나타내는 경우

*the middle* of the river(중류(中流)); *the yellow* of an egg(달걀의 노른자위); *the thick* of the wood(숲이 우거진 곳); etc.

(6) 정관사+형용사[부사]의 비교급

*The more* one gets, *the more* one wants. (얻으면 얻을수록 더 갖고 싶어진다) / *The more the better.* (많으면 많을수록 좋다) / I love him none *the less* for his faults. (결점은 있지만 그래도 그가 좋다) / We respect him all *the more* because of it. (그것 때문에 더욱 더 그를 존경한다)

**D.** 불완전 한정(限定)의 관사

(1) *the man* in the moon; *the view* from the upper story; *the book* (that) you lent me ~; etc.

(2) Necessity is *the mother* of invention. (필요는 발명의 어머니)

Ulsan is *the Manchester* of Korea.

(3) *the famous* Napoleon; *the ambitious* Caesar; etc.

(4) *the lower* class(하층 계급); *the greater* part of land; etc.

(5) *the first* ~; *the second* ~; etc.

(6) He is *the very* picture of his father. (그는 부친을 빼쏘았다)

(7) The boy is *the cleverest* of all. / Here in California I like spring *the best.* 《미어》

부정관사의 용법

(1) a, an =one

Rome wasn't built in *a day.*

(2) the same

Birds of *a feather* flock together. (같은 것끼리 모이게 마련이다)

(3) some, certain

In *a sense* it is true. (어떤 뜻으로는 정말이다)

(4) 계량 또는 정도 따위를 나타내는 경우

*a* great *deal* of ~; *a lot* of ~; *many a* ~; *a little; a few;* etc.

(5) 수량을 나타내는 특수한 표현의 경우

*a dozen* of sheep; *a host* of daffodils (수선화의 무리); *a school* 〔*shoal*〕 of fish(es); etc.

(6) per의 뜻을 나타내는 경우

I write home twice *a month.* / He walks at the rate of four miles *an hour.*

(7) 「…와 같은」의 뜻을 나타내는 경우

We need *a Washington.*

She is *a rose* in June.

【주의】 이 용례는 고유명사에 많다.

(8) 추상명사에 붙는 경우

It is *a pity* that he failed in the examination.

(9) 물질명사에 붙는 경우 (종류를 나타냄)

They sell *an* excellent *coffee* at that shop.

(10) 형용사와 함께 보통명사의 단수화(單數化)를 나타내는 경우

*a white*(백인); *a native; a noble; a handful* of sand(한 줌의 모래); etc.

(11) 대표적으로 쓰이는 경우

A tiger(=Any tiger) is a fierce animal. (호랑이는 맹수이다)

총칭 관사의 용법

*The owl* cannot see well in the daytime.
*Owls* cannot see in the daytime.
*An owl* cannot see well in the daytime. (올빼미는 낮에는 잘 보지 못한다)

【주의】 위 문장 중에서 복수형이 가장 많이 쓰임.

(1) the+단수 보통명사

*The child* is father of *the man.*

*The* early *bird* catches *the worm.*

(2) the+복수 보통명사

*The owls* have large eyes and soft plumage. / *the Americans; the Brothers* Grimm (그림 형제); the *whites; the Koreans; the Chinese; the English;* etc.

(3) the+집합 명사

*the nobility*(귀족); *the world*(세계의 사람들); *the cattle*(소); etc.

(4) 총칭적으로 쓰이는 악기 이름의 경우

He plays *the piano* 〔*the violin,* etc.〕.

무관사의 경우의 일반적 원칙

(1) 총칭적으로 쓰인 보통명사의 복수

*Dogs* are faithful animals.

(2) 일반적으로 추상명사, 물질명사, 고유명사의 경우

*Honor* must be our only guide.

*Iron* is heavier than *wood.*

*Shakespeare* is a great dramatist.

*Deer* like the thick woods.

(3) 가정 용어의 경우

*father; mother; papa; mama;* etc.

*breakfast; lunch(eon); dinner;* etc.

We had *supper* at six.

(4) 관직명, 칭호 따위를 나타내는 경우

*President* Kennedy; *Queen* Elizabeth Ⅱ; *Professor* Moulton; etc. / Mr. Eisenhower, *President;* Mr. Kim, *Premier* 《동격》 / Elizabath Ⅱ, *Queen* of England; Darwin, *author* of the *Origin of Species.*

(5) 자격을 나타내기 위하여 주격보어로서 사용되는 경우

He was appointed *principal* of our school.

(6) 「~의 자격으로」

He entered the bank *as manager.* / Tennyson succeeded Wordsworth *as poet laureate.* (테니슨은 계관 시인으로서 워즈워

스의 뒤를 이었다)

(7) *Strong man as he was,* he could not bear the pain. / *Woman though she was,* she dared to say so.

(8) *Boys,* be ambitious!; *Poor thing!; Good God!;* etc.

(9) 접속사 또는 전치사에 의해 밀접하게 결합되어 대조나 연립(聯立)을 나타내는 경우

*rich* and *poor*(부자나 가난한 사람이나); *young* and *old*(젊은이나 노인이나); *weak* and *strong*(약자나 강자나); *pipe* in *mouth*(입에 파이프를 물고); *arm* in *arm; side* by *side; little* by *little; day* after *day;* from *flower* to *flower;* from *head* to *foot;* from *hand* to *mouth*(입에 풀칠이나 하며); from *door* to *door*(이 집 저 집으로); *bread* and *butter*(버터를 바른 빵); etc.

(10) 나란히 나열되어, 하나의 정리된 뜻을 갖는 경우, 뒤의 명사는 무관사.

*a watch* and *chain*(시곗줄이 달린 시계); *a cup* and *saucer*(접시에 놓인 컵); *a needle* and *thread*(실을 꿴 바늘); *a poet* and *statesman*(시인이며 정치가); *the bread* and *butter*(버터를 바른 빵); etc.

(11) 표제, 게시, 광고 따위의 경우

*Contents*(차례); *Index*(색인); *Entrance*(입구); *Way out*(출구); *Wicket*(개찰구); *Admission free*(무료 입장); *Not for sale*(비매품); etc.

(12) What is the English for the Korean "*ch'aek*"? It is "*book.*"

(13) He died of *consumption.*

【주의】 단, My father has got *the gout.* (부친은 통풍에 걸렸다) She has *a headache* 〔*a cold, a fever,* etc.〕 She has *the measles.* (그녀는 홍역을 앓고 있다)

(14) 운동이나 게임의 명칭

Let's play *baseball* 〔*football, tennis,* etc.〕. / Let's play *billiards.*

(15) 학과명(學科名)

Next Monday we are to have an examination in *mathematics.* (이번 월요일에는 수학 시험이 있다)

(16) 책의 표제명

*Paradise Lost*('실락원(失樂園)'); *Robinson Crusoe;* etc.

(17) 달, 요일명 따위의 경우

*January; February; Sunday;* ... etc.

(18) 시간의 한 때를 나타내는 경우

at *dawn;* at *noon;* at *dusk*(저녁 무렵에); at *twilight*(황혼에); etc. / *Night* was falling.

(19) last(지난), next(오는)를 week, month, year 따위와 함께 쓰는 경우

I saw him *last year.*

【주의】 단, '이듬, 이튿, 다음의' 따위의 뜻을 나타내는 경우는 정관사를 취한다.

He went there *the next morning.*

I shall see there *the* day *after* tomorrow.

(20) It is *a kind of bird.*

A gig is *a kind of carriage.*

【주의】 단, I do know *what kind of a man* he is.

(21) *Man* is mortal.

*Man* with the head, *woman* with the heart. (남자는 두뇌, 여자는 정(情))

Men die, but *man* is immortal. ((개개의) 사람은 죽지만, 인간은 불멸이다)

(22) I see *horses* coming. (*cf.* see *a horse* coming); There are *pictures* on the wall. (*cf.* There is *a picture* on the wall.)

(23) I go *to school* (every day). (현재의 습관을 나타낸다); I am going *to market.* I go *to bed* at ten. I go *to church* every Sunday. I must go *to hospital.* (입원하지 않으면 안 된다); away from *school*(학교를 결석하여); etc.

【주의】 학교나 교회의 건물 그 자체를 뜻하는 경우는 정관사를 취한다. *The school is near the church.*

또 다음 연어(連語)에 주의할 것.

| | | | |
|---|---|---|---|
| be | *at school*(수업 중)<br>*at church*(설교 중)<br>*at table*(식사 중)<br>*at breakfast*<br>*at home* | be | *in prison*(수감 중)<br>*in bed*(취침 중)<br>*in market*(물건사러 장 보는 중)<br>*in hospital* |

(24) Last night a great earthquake *took place.* (간밤에 큰 지진이 일어났다)

I have *caught cold.* (감기가 들었다); *make haste*(서두르다); *make room* for an old man(노인에게 자리를 양보하다); *give birth*(낳다); *lose sight* of(시야에서 놓쳐버리다); *cast anchor*(닻을 내리다); *set sail* from(출범하다); *send word*(말을 전하다); *keep house*(집안일을 하다); etc.

(25) be *of use*(=useful); be *of value*(=valuable); be *of importance*(=important); be *of opinion* ~ (=believe); be *in use; Out of sight, out of mind.* (떨어져 있으면 정도 멀어진다); etc.

(26) 관용구(Idiomatic Phrases)의 경우

| | | | |
|---|---|---|---|
| *by*<br>(탈것) | *train, car*<br>*ship, tram(car)*<br>*bus, plane* | *by*<br>(우편물) | *letter, air mail*<br>*postcard, parcel*<br>*post; mail* 《미》 |

by { land(육로로) / sea(해로로) / water(〃) / air(공로로) }  on { foot(도보로) / horseback(말로) / fire(화재로) / board(승선하여) }

관사의 위치

(1) *all the* boys here; *Both the* brothers are diligent.

(2) He gave me *half the* money that he had with him. I paid *double the* price. He is *twice the* man he was. (그는 과거의 그보다 배나 컸다)

(3) I am not so foolish as to do *such a* thing.

(4) *What a glorious* sunset it is! *How old a* man he is!

(5) *However dark a* night is may be, I will go there. / This is *too good an* opportunity. / He is *so honest a* man. / We had *as good a* time *as* you had the other day.

(6) *Many a* day he wandered about in the country. / They stayed there *half an* hour.

(7) It was *rather* a fine day yesterday. (어제는 비교적 날씨가 좋았다)

It's *only a* trifling[tráifliŋ] joke. (그것은 하찮은 농담에 지나지 않는다)

## 조동사(Auxiliary Verbs)의 용법

**A. Cannot**(…일 리가 없다)

He may be a good teacher, but he *cannot be* a great scholar. (그는 훌륭한 교사일지는 모르나 위대한 학자는 아니다) / He *cannot have done* such a thing. (그가 그런 일을 했을 리가 만무하다)

【주의】 능력(…할 수 있다)을 나타내는 can의 미래는 be able to의 형을 쓴다. 과거형의 경우도 could를 사용하는 것은 가급적 피하여, I was able to climb the mountain.이라든가 I managed to get the book.와 같이 하는 것이 좋다.

**B. Must**(…임에 틀림없다)

He *must be* a fool to do such a thing. (그런 일을 하다니 그는 바보임에 틀림없다) / I *must have left* it at home. (나는 집에 그것을 놓고 왔음에 틀림없다)

【주의】 의무, 필요(…하지 않으면 안 되다)의 뜻을 나타내는 must의 미래나 과거는 have to를 쓴다.

**C. May**가 쓰이는 관용구

He works hard (*so*) *that* he *may* succeed. (그는 성공하려고, 열심히 공부한다) / You *may well* say so. (자네가 그렇게 말하는 것도 당연하다) / You *may as well* begin at once. (자네, 지금 곧 시작하는 편이 좋겠네) / He *may not have arrived* there yet. (그는 아직 거기에 도착하지 못했을지도 모른다) 《과거사실에 대한 현재의 가능한 추측》

**D. Ought to**

We *ought to* call on him. (그를 방문하지 않으면 안 된다)

【주의】 도의상의 의무 · 당연함을 나타내는 ought to는 should보다 뜻이 강하다든가 약하다는 여러 주장이 있으나 특별한 차이가 없다고 보는 것이 좋겠다. 구어에서는 ought to가 더 많이 사용된다.

The ship *ought to* arrive at noon, if there is no accident. (사고만 없다면 그 배는 정오에 도착할 것이다) [당연함의 뜻] / The ship *ought to* have arrived there by this time. (그 배는 지금쯤은 이미 그 곳에 도착해 있어야 한다)

**E. Dare, Need**(의문문 및 부정문에서는 보통 조동사로 취급된다)

"Must I read this book today?" "No, you *need not*." (「이 책을 오늘 읽지 않으면 안 되나요」「아니, 그럴 필요는 없어」) / *Need* you ask your father's consent? (자네 부친의 승낙을 얻어야 하나)

【주의】 필요가 없었다(없을 것이다)의 뜻으로는 I *did not have to* ask my father's consent. 또는 You *will not have to* do so.와 같이 말한다.

【주의】 주동사(主動詞)로서는 You *do not need to* buy this book.

I *dare say* (=Parhaps) it is a lie.(아마 그것은 거짓말일 거요) / He *dare not come* to see me again. (그는 감히 나를 다시 만나러 오지 못할 것이다)

【주의】 주동사(主動詞)로서는 He *dares to do* what he knows to be dangerous.(그는 위험하다고 알고 있는 일을 망설이지 않고 거침없이 해낸다)

**F. Be to**의 형

The meeting *was to* be on Sunday. (그 모임은 일요일에 있을 예정이었다) [예정] / What *am* I *to* do next ? (다음에는 무엇을 하여야 됩니까) [의무] / He *was* never *to* see his native country again. (그는 두 번 다시 고국을 보지 못할 운명이었다) [운명] / Beer like that *is* not *to* be had outside of Germany. (그러한 맥주는 독일 이외에서는 구할 수 없다) [가능]

**G.** 습관을 나타내는 **Would**와 **Used to**

There *used to* be a house here. (이곳에는 이전에 집이 한 채 있었다)

He *used to* go fishing in that river. (그는 언제나 그 강에 고기를 낚으러 가곤 하였다)

He *would* often go fishing in that river. (그는 가끔 그 강에 낚시를 가곤 하였다)

【주의】 would는 used to보다 불규칙적인 과거의 습관을 나타내는 경우가 많다.

**H. Should**의 특수 용법(당연함, 기쁨, 노여움, 놀람 따위의 감정을 포함하는 절(節) 안에서)

It is quite proper that we *should* know it. (그것을 우리가 알고 있는 것은 당연하다)

It is remarkable that he *should* have said nothing of it. (그가 그 일에 대하여 한 마디도 하지 않은 것은 주목할 만한 일이다)

【주의】 단지 사실로서 말하는 경우는 should를 쓰지 않아도 된다.

It is strange that she *married* such an old man. (그녀가 그런 노인과 결혼한 것은 이상하다)

**I. Lest... should**(…하지 않도록, …하면 아니 되므로)

Work hard *lest* you *should* fail. (실패하지 않도록 열심히 공부하여라)

## 전치사의 용법

| 전치사의 용법 일람표 | | | |
|---|---|---|---|
| 장소·운동·방향 | at, in; on, over, above; to, for, toward, from; into, out of, inside, within, without; before, behind, after, along, across, through; around, round, about; among, between, amid; against, beneath, beside, beyond, by, down, for, near, off, up | | |
| 때·시간 | at, in, on; within, after; till, by; for, during, through; since, from; to, past; about; behind, toward, with | | |
| 재료·원료 | of, from, into, in | 원인·이유 | from, through, for, of, at, with |
| 행위자·수단·도구 | by, through, with, on | 목적·목표 | at, for, after, on |
| 소유·부속 | of, with | 결과 | to, in |
| 내용 | of | 출신·가계 | from, of |
| 표준·비율 | by, at | 방법·모양 | in, by, after |
| 교환·가격 | for, at | 상태·종사 | in, into, under, on, at |
| 우열·비교 | above, below, to, with | 제외 | except, but |
| 관계 | on, of, about | 부가 | besides |
| 성질 | of | 조건·양보 | with, but, for |

**A.** 장소·방향·운동의 전치사

(1) **at, in**

He lives *at* Chongno *in* Seoul. (서울의 종로에) / He lives *at* No. 102, Hongje=dong. (홍제동 102번지에) / We spent our holidays *at* Haeundae. (해운대에서) / They landed *at* the foot of Hallasan. (한라산 기슭에) / Come in *at* the window. (창으로) / He drank *at* a brook. (시냇물에서) / My uncle lives *in* England [London]. (영국[런던]에)

【주의】 at school(수업 중), at church(예배 중), at home(재가 중), at court(궁정에서), at sea(항해 중), stay at Kim's(=stay with

Kim) (김군의 집에 머물다), in court(법정에서); in school(재학 중), in(=on) the sea(바다에서), in(=on) the street(노상에서)

(2) **on, over, above**

The dews *on* the lawn look like pearls. (잔디 위의 이슬－위에 접착) / There is a picture *on* the wall. (벽에는－측면에 접착) / He fell *on* his face. (쓰러졌다－땅과 접촉하여 이면(裡面)) / an inn *on* the lake (호반의 여인숙－접근) / The sun shines *on* the earth. (지면을－표면으로의 방향) / The lamp is hanging *over* the table. (테이블 바로 위에－떨어져서 바로 위) / There is a signboard *over* the door. (문 위에－부착된 위) / We spread a tablecloth *over* the table. (테이블 위에－덮어서) / Let's go *over* the hill. (언덕을 넘어－운동) / The water came *above* my knees. (무릎 위 까지－접촉하여 초과) / We looked at the moon *above* us (= over us, =over our head).(떨어져서 위)

【주의】 on land(육상에), on the coast(해안에서), off the coast(난바다에서).

(3) **to, for, toward, from**

I went *to* Seoul. (서울로－방향 및 도착지점) / I went *toward* the window. (창문 쪽으로－도착을 포함치 않고 운동의 방향을 나타냄) / My house stood *toward* the lake. (호수에 면하여－서 있는 위치의 방향) / She has left *for* Boston. (보스턴으로－목적지를 나타냄)

【주의】 for는 동사 depart, leave, sail, start, be bound 따위의 다음에 쓰인다.

I went *to* Pusan *from* Seoul. (서울에서－출발점)

(4) **into, out of, inside, outside, within**

He went *into* the room just when I came *out of* it. (방 안으로, 방 안에서－드나드는 동작을 나타냄) / He is standing just *inside* the door. (문안 쪽에－위치를 나타냄) / There is an old oak tree just *outside* the room. (방 밖에－위치를 나타냄) / Our school stands *within* a few miles of Seoul. (서울에서 수마일 이내에－범위)

(5) **before, behind, after**

He sits *before*(=in front of) me. (…의 앞에－위치) / He sits *behind*(=at the back of) me. (…의 뒤에－위치) / In English the verb comes *before* the object. (목적어에 앞섬－순서) / In English the object comes *after* the verb. (동사에 계속됨－순서)

(6) **along, across, through**

We walked *along* the river. (…을 따라서－외측을 따라서의 운동) / We sailed *along* the river. (…을 따라서－내측을 따라서의 운동) / Many new-built houses were scattered *along* the lake. (호수를 따라－서 있음) / He succeeded in swimming *across* the river. (횡단하여) / The Hangang flows *through* Seoul. (관통하여)

(7) **around, round, about**

She wore a necklace *around* her neck. (…의 주위에－위치) / I walked *round* the pond. (…의 둘레－운동) / Her hair hung *about* her neck. (…의 주변에 위치) / I walked *about* the wood. (돌아다니다－운동)

(8) **among, between, amid**

The birds are flying about *among* the trees. (나무들 사이를－셋 이상의 사이) / The Pacific lies *between* Korea and America. (한미간에－양자간)

(9) **against, beneath, beside, beyond, by, down, for, near, off, up**

*against* the wall(기대어, 의지하여) / *beneath* the top of the hill (…의 바로 밑에－떨어져서 아래) / a pillow *beneath* my head(머리 밑의－접촉한 밑) / *beside*(=by the side of) me (옆에) / *beyond* the seas (해외에) / *by* the post office (…가까이에) / *by* the window (…옆에) / I went to Berlin *by* (=by way of) Siberia. (시베리아 경유로) / *down* the river(강을 내려가－아래 방향으로의 운동) / I went *down*(=along) the street. (도로를 따라서) / *for* a mile(1마일의 구간－거리) / Keep *off* the grass. (잔디밭에 들어가지 말 것－떨어져 있는 상태) / *near* the church (…곁에) / *up* the hill (…의 위로－위로의 운동)

**B.** 때의 전치사

(1) **at, in, on**

*at* three o'clock(세 시에), *at* noon (정오에)

【주의】 at는 때의 한 점을 나타낸다. at the beginning of last month 〔week〕, at the middle of July, at the end of next week 〔month〕, at the middle(중간), in the middle(한가운데), at the age of thirty-one (31세 때에), in old age(노년 시대에), at present

*in* summer(여름에); *in* August(8월에); *in* 1999(1999년에) / *in* the day 〔daytime〕(낮에는); *in* the night(밤중에); *in* the days of old(왕년); *in* all one's life(이

나이를 먹기까지, 지금까지); *on* Sunday(일요일에); *on* the 9th day(9일에); *on* Friday morning(금요일 아침에); *on* the night of May 5th(5월 5일 밤에); *on* the day(그 날에)

【주의】'월요일에' 라고 할 때 on Monday 외에 다음과 같은 표현이 가능하다. on Mondays, on a Monday, of a Monday. 일반적으로 '월요일에는' 이라는 표현에는 on Mondays를 쓰는 편이 좋다. on Monday는 문장의 뜻에 따라 '다음 월요일' 또는 '지난 월요일' 의 뜻이 된다.

(2) **in, within, after**

My father will come back *in* a week. (1주일이면—경과) / I want you to return *within* two hours. (2시간 이내에—범위) / He came back to Pusan *after* a week. (1주일 뒤에—경과)

(3) **till, by**

We worked hard *till* sunset. (일몰까지) / *By* this time next year the work will have been completed. (내년 이맘때까지는) / till now(지금까지); till then(그 때까지); by the evening(저녁때까지는); by the beginning of the year(금년초 까지는)

【주의】till은 계속의 뜻으로 '까지', by는 기한을 말하며 '까지는' 의 뜻을 나타낸다.

(4) **for, during, through**

I have not seen him just *for* a year. (만 1년 동안) / He visited many scenic spots *during* his stay. (그의 체재 중) / He stayed at home *through* the summer. (한 여름 내내) / *for* long(오랫동안); *for* a while(잠시 동안); *for* ever(영원히); *during* one's absence (결석 중); *during* the day= in the daytime(낮에)

(5) **since, from**

He has been in Korea *since* 1949. (1949년 이래) / He stayed in Korea *from* 1948 *till* 1949. (1948년부터 1949년까지) / I have known him *from* a child(=*since* his childhood).

(6) **to, past**

It is a quarter *to* ten. (10시 15분 전) / It is half *past* three. (3시 반)

(7) **about, behind, toward, with**

*about* three o'clock(3시경) / He came to Seoul *about* 1944. (1944년경) / He came here an hour *behind* time. (1시간 늦어서) / He came home *toward* evening. (저녁 무렵에) / He rises *with* the sun. (해 뜨는 시간에—동시) / *With* these words he went out of the room. (이 말을 남기고 바로—직후)

**C.** 재료·원료 : **from, of, into, in**

The wardrobes are made of wood. (나무로—원료의 형태가 변화하지 않는 경우) / Wine is made *from* grapes. (포도로—원료의 형태가 변화하는 경우) / Grapes are made *into* wine. (포도주로—원료가 변하여 제품이 된 결과) / You must not write it *in* red ink. (붉은 잉크로) / She is dressed *in* black. (검은 옷을 입고)

【주의】① in은 carve *in* wood, cast *in* silver, paint *in* oil, speak *in* English, write *in* ink 따위의 동사 뒤에 오는 경우가 많다.

② 음식물에는 on을 사용한다. live *on* rice, dine *on* curried rice, feast *on* wine.

**D.** 행위자·수단·도구 : **by, through, with, on**

He was killed *with* a sword *by* a burglar. (칼로, 강도에 의해) / The city was destroyed *by* the air raid. (공습으로)

【주의】by는 행위자, with는 도구에 쓰인다. 행위자는 반드시 인간에게만 한정되는 것은 아님.

*By*(=*Through*) your help, I could succeed. (원조로) / He went to Boston *by* train. (기차로)

【주의】운수·교통 기관의 수단은 by로 나타낸다. *by* land, *by* sea, *by* air, *by* train, *by* bus, *by* ship, *by* plane, *by*(=on) bicycle. *cf.* *on* foot, *on* horseback.

I heard the symphony *on* the radio. (라디오로) / play *on* the piano [violin] (피아노를 치다[바이올린을 켜다])

**E.** 소유·부속 : **of, with**

the legs *of* a table(테이블의 다리) / the cover *of* a book(책의 표지) / a man *with* a red face(붉은 얼굴의 사람)

**F.** 내용 : **of**

a cup *of* coffee(한 잔의 커피) / a glass *of* wine(한 잔 가득한 술) / a spoonful *of* sugar(한 숟가락의 설탕)

**G.** 원인·이유 : **from, through, for, of, at, with**

I refused his offer *from* private reasons. (개인적 이유로) / He died *from* worries. (노심초사로) / *From* your silence, I fear you are wrong. (잠자코 있는 것으로 보아—from은 직접적 원인을 나타냄) /

*Through* wine they had a quarrel with each other. (술로 인해—through는 간접적 원인을 나타냄) / This calamity happend *through* your negligence. (너의 태만으로) / *For* this reason I recommend you to read this book. (이런 이유로) / Chinhae is noted 〔famous, well-known〕 *for* its cherries. (벚꽃으로 이름이 높다)

【주의】 for는 reason의 앞, 또는 noted, famous, celebrated, well-known 따위의 뒤에 쓰는 것이 보통이다.

He died *of* consumption. (폐병으로) / I shall be glad *of* your company. (동석해 주신다면) / She fainted *at* (the) sight of the battlefield. (…을 보고) / I was surprised *at* the news. (…을 듣고)

【주의】 be surprised, be astonished, be amazed, be frightened, be alarmed 따위 뒤에서는 at로 그 감정의 원인을 나타낸다

I am pleased *at* his punctuality 〔*with* the boy〕. (그의 정확함에〔그 소년에게〕)

【주의】 유쾌 · 불쾌를 나타낼 때에는 at 또는 with가 잇따른다. angry, delighted, amused, displeased, offended, disgusted 따위는 이 전치사를 취한다.

**H.** 목적·목표 : **at, for, after, on**

Everybody laughed *at* him. (그를) / Some toil *for* fame, while some toil *for* money. (명성을 위해, 돈을 위해) / We provide *for* our children. (아이들을 기르기 위해) *cf.* We provide *against* misfortune. (불운에 대비하여) / The police ran *after* the burglar. (강도를 뒤좇아) / He went to Pusan *on* business. (상용으로)

【주의】 *on* a visit(방문차), *on* a journey(=tour) (여행으로), *on* an embassy(사절로서)

**I.** 결과 : **to, in**

*To* our surprise he failed again. (놀랍게도 그는 또 실패했다) / His attempt ended *in* a failure. (그의 시도는 실패로 끝났다)

**J.** 출신지·가계 : **from, of**

He comes *from* New York. (뉴욕 출신) / He comes *of* a noble family. (귀족 출신) / Plants grow out *of* the earth. (땅에서)

**K.** 표준·비율 : **by, at**

Sugar is sold *by* the pound. (파운드 단위로); *by* my watch(내 시계로는); *by* his looks(겉모양으로는); *by* rule(규칙에 따라서) / The train was running *at* full speed. (전속력으로) / *at* the rate of 32 miles an hour(시속 32마일로); *at* that rate (그 비율로); *at* 15° (15도에서)

**L.** 교환·가격 : **for, at**

I have exchanged my old bicycle *for* a new one. (새것과) / This book can be bought *for* two dollars. (2달러로) / I bought the sugar *at* fourpence a pound. (1파운드에 4펜스로)

【주의】 for와 at는 종종 혼동되기 쉬운데 for는 순전한 가격을 나타내고, at는 항상 비율을 나타내는 말이 붙음.

*cf.* I bought it *for* 500 won. (500원에)
I bought it *at* 500 won apiece.(1개 500원씩에)

**M.** 우열·비교 : **above, below, to, with, against**

Health is *above* wealth. (…보다 낫다) / Brutes are *below* man. (…만 못하다) *cf.* Brutes are *beneath* man. = Brutes are far *below* man. / I prefer English *to* algebra. (대수보다 영어가 좋다) / He is two years junior *to* me. (그는 나보다 두 살 아래이다) / You must compare the translation *with* the original. (비교하다) / You can compare life *to* a voyage. (비유하다) / Twelve is *to* four what (=as) three is *to* one. (12 : 4 = 3 : 1) / We were then only two, *against* ten of them. (그들 10명에 비하여, 우리는 겨우 두 사람이었다)

**N.** 관계 : **on, of, about, in**

His lecture *on* atomic energy was very fine. (원자력에 관한) / Have you heard *about* her? (그녀에 관한 소문) / Have you heard *of* Mr. Son? (손 선생에 관하여—유무를 묻는 점에서 전자와 다름) / Seoul has greatly increased *in* population. (인구에 있어서)

**O.** 성질 : **of**

I have been looking for a man *of* your character. (당신 같은 성격의 사람) / a man *of* courage (용기가 있는 사람)

**P.** 방법·식·모양 : **in, by, after**

He read the poem *in* this manner. (이런 식으로) / I committed an outrage upon you *by* mistake. (과오로) / She would speak *with* calmness. (조용히) / The place was named *after* the first president. (초대 대통령을 따라)

**Q.** 상태·종사 : **in, into, under, on, off, at**

I never fail to take an hour's walk *in* good weather. (날씨가 좋은 때에는) / A friend *in* need is a friend indeed. (어려운 때의 친구) / At last he ran *into* debt. (빚을 진) / I could never speak a word *under* 〔*in*〕 the circumstance. (이런 사정에서는) / Even on Sunday I am *on* duty. (일이 있는) *cf. off* duty (비번인) / When the firemen came, the house was already *on* fire. (타고 있었다) / When will you be *at* home tomorrow? (집에 있음—상태) / When will you be *at* work tomorrow? (작업 중—종사)

【주의】 상태 : *at* leisure(여가가 있는), *at* peace (평화롭게). 종사 : *at* play(놀고), *at* church(예배중)

**R.** 제외 : **except, but**

Read the last page *but* one. (맨 뒤에서 2페이지째) / The war brought nothing *but* misery. (불행을 제외하고는, 불행밖에는)

**S.** 부가(付加) : **Besides**

*Besides* being a politician, he is a pianist. (정치가인 것 이외에 또) / I earn nothing *besides*(=except) my salary. *cf.* I earn special income *besides* (=in addition to) my salary.(봉급 외에 가외로)

**T.** 조건·양보 : **with, but for**

*With* your help I could have succeeded. (너의 도움이 있었다면, 나는 성공할 수 있었을 텐데) / *But for* his aid I could not have succeeded. (그의 도움이 없었다면 나는 성공할 수 없었을 게다) / *With* all his merits he was modest. (그는 장점이 있는데다 또한 겸허했다)

**U.** 격(格)의 관계

(1) 동격 : **of**

The Continent *of* Asia is larger than that *of* Europe. (아시아 대륙) / the Republic *of* France (프랑스 공화국) / the title *of* Knight (기사라는 칭호) / the city *of* Rome (로마시)

(2) 주격 : **for, of, with**

It is necessary *for* you to go at once. (네가 가는 것) / It is kind *of* you to say so. (당신이 그렇게 말하여 주는 것) / How is it *with* him? (=How is he?) (그는 어떻게 지냅니까)

(3) 소유격(E. 소유·부속 참조)

(4) 목적격 : **to, for, of**

He gave an apple *to* me. (나에게) / He bought an apple *for* me. (나에게) / He asked a question *of* me. (나에게) *cf.* write a letter *to* her. (그녀에게 편지를 쓰다); write a letter *for* her. (그녀에게〔그녀를 대신해서〕 편지를 써 주다)

**V.** 기 타

(1) 근접 : **with, to**

It is necessary to connect atomic science *to* industry. (연결시키다) / I'm closely associated *with* him. (그와 밀접한 관계가 있다) / This story is related *to* an old Korean legend. (옛날 한국의 전설과)

(2) 분리 : **from, of**

The corn is separated *from* the chaff. (왕겨로부터) / She was relieved *from*(=*of*) danger. (위험에서) *cf.* I am free *from* business. (일이 없다) / I cannot break myself *of* the habit. (습관을 깨다) / This cigarette is free *of* tax. (무세(無稅)로)

(3) 일치 : **with**

I cannot agree *with* you. (일치하다) / Burns and Shelley were *with* us. (우리들의 동지였다) / I sympathize *with* you. (동정하다)

(4) 적응(適應) : **to, for, after**

This wine is *to* my taste. (입에 맞다) /It is good *for* the health to keep early hours. (건강에 좋다) / We must live *after* the fashion of the time. (시대 조류에 따라서)

## 관계사 · 접속사의 용법

특수한 관계대명사

**A. As**

*Such* men *as* (=Those who) heard his speech praised him. (그의 연설을 들은 사

람들은 그를 칭찬했다) / This is *the same* watch *as* I lost yesterday. (이것은 어제 내가 잃은 것과 같은 모양의 시계다)

【주의】 잃어버린 바로 그 시계라면 *the same* watch *that* I lost.

He was a Russian, *as* (=which fact) they could tell by his accent. (그는 러시아 사람이었는데, 그것은 그의 말의 악센트로 알았다)

**B. Than**

You have more money *than* is needed. (너는 필요 이상의 돈을 갖고 있다)

**C. But**(=that... not)

There is no one *but* knows that. (그것을 모르는 자는 없다) / Who is there *but* commits errors? (과오를 범하지 않는 사람이란 있을 수 없다)

특수한 접속사

**A.** 상관접속사

*Both* he *and* his brothers are doctors. (그나 그의 형제도 다 의사다) / This box is *at once* cheap *and* strong. (이 상자는 값이 싸고도 튼튼하다) / His knowledge is *not only* wide *but* (*also*) deep. (=His knowledge is deep *as well as* wide.) (그의 지식은 넓을 뿐 아니라 깊다) / *Either* you *or* I must go there. (너나 나 둘 중 하나가 가야만 한다) / *Neither* the road *nor* the path is safe. (도로도 작은 길도 모두 안전치 못하다)

【주의】 위 예문의 상관접속사 뒤에는 동일 품사를 사용하지 않으면 안 된다.

He was *so* ill *that* he could scarcely speak. (그의 병 증세가 매우 심해서 거의 말도 하지 못했다) [결과] / He is *such* an honest man *that* everybody trusts him. (그는 정직한 사람이므로 모두가 그를 신용한다) [결과] / *No sooner* had he seen me *than* he left the room. = *Scarcely* (= *Hardly*) had he seen me *when* (= *before*) he left the room. (그는 나를 보자마자 방을 나갔다) [때] / He must do it *whether* he likes it *or* not. (그는 좋든 싫든 그것을 하지 않으면 안 된다) [양보] / *As* rust eats iron, *so* care eats the heart. (녹이 쇠를 부식시키는 것처럼, 근심은 사람의 마음을 좀먹는다) [비교] / She is *as* clever *as* her brother. (그녀도 그녀의 오빠만큼 영리하다) [비교] / It is *so* hot *that* I cannot sleep. (잠을 잘 수 없을 만큼 덥다) [정도] / Betty is not *so* pretty *as* her sister. (베티는 그녀의 동생만큼 예쁘지 않다) [비교]

**B.** 구접속사(句接續詞)

One must do one's duty *as long as* one lives. (사람은 살아 있는 한 그의 의무를 다하여야 한다) [시간] /I will read the book *so long as* it is instructive. (이롭기만 하다면 나는 그 책을 읽을 생각이다) [조건] /She hurried *so that*(=*in order that*) she might catch the train. (기차 시간에 대기위해 그녀는 서둘렀다) [목적] /He works hard *for fear* (*that*) he should fail. (그는 실패하지 않도록 열심히 공부했다) [목적]/ Take an umbrella with you *in case* it should rain. (비가 올지도 모르니 우산을 갖고 가거라) [조건] / He talks *as if* (=*as though*) he knew everything. (그는 마치 모르는 것이 없는 것처럼 말을 한다) [양상] / *Even if* I were rich, I would work. (비록 부자라 할지라도 나는 일하겠다) [양보] / *Now that* you have finished your work, you are free to go and play. (너는 일을 끝마쳤으니, 마음대로 나가 놀아도 좋다) [한정]

## (3) 영문 일기 쓰는 법

적어도 하루에 한 번은 자기의 생활을 조용히 반성해 보는 것이 바람직한 일이다. 어떤 경험도, 마음의 눈으로 곰곰히 생각하는 과정을 통해 비로소 선(善)한 방향으로 자기의 인격을 높이며, 내일의 비약을 약속하여 준다. 자기나라 글로 일기를 쓰는 것은 "자기 반성의 기회"를 갖는다는 것에 커다란 의의를 찾을 수 있으나, 영문으로 일기를 쓰는 경우는 이러한 것보다는 "영어와의 친숙과 숙달"이라는 영어 학습상의 목적이 더 크다고 할 수 있겠다. 옛부터 Practice makes perfect.라는 격언도 있듯이, 영문 일기도 매일 계속해서 씀으로써 영어 실력을 향상시킬 수 있다. 무리하게 처음부터 좋은 문장의 글을 쓰려고 애를 태울 것이 아니라 자기가 잘 알고 있는 영어로 가벼운 기분으로 일상의 체험 따위를 계속해서 쓰는 것이 긴요한 것이다. 다음에 주의하여야 할 몇 가지 점을 간추려 말하겠다.

(1) 매일 계속해서 쓸 것—설사 1, 2행이라도 빠지지 않고 계속해서 쓰면 영어 실력 함양에 도움이 된다.

(2) 정확한 문장을 쓰도록 노력할 것—배우지 않은 자기류의 문장이나 단어 따위를 쓰면 영어 실력이 늘지 않는 것은 말할 것도 없고 오히려 나쁜 습관이 들어 마이너스가 된다. 사전을 항시 옆에 놓고 불확실한 점은 몇 번이고 찾아서 옳게 적는다

(3) 단순한 문형(文型)이나 쉬운 단어를 사용할 것—처음부터 고상한 사상 따위를 명문으로 쓰고자 애를 쓰면 쓸수록 써 나갈 수가 없게 된다. 딱딱한 문장은 쓰지 않는 편이 좋다.

(4) **Thinking in English**—처음 우리말로 글을 짓고 그것을 영역하는 것은, 우리 글에 이끌리게 되어 좋은 영문을 쓸 수가 없게 된다. 처음부터 영어로 생각하여 쓰는 습관을 붙이자.

일기란 순전히 개인적인 것이므로 형식에 있어서 이렇다할 엄밀한 규칙이 있는 것은 아니다. 많은 사람들이 쓰고 있는 대체로 일정한 형식이 있을 뿐이다. 아래에 이를 요약하여 영문 일기 쓰기의 참고로 제공한다.

## 1. 날 짜 쓰 기(Date)

일기의 처음은 날짜, 요일로 시작되는 것이 일반적이다. 보기를 '11월 3일 수요일'로 하면 다음과 같은 여러 형의 쓰는 식이 있다.

(1) Wednesday, November 3.
(2) November 3rd, Wednesday.
(3) November 3, Wednesday.
(4) Wednesday, November 3rd.
(5) Wed., Nov. 3.
(6) Nov. 3rd, Wed.

특히 연호를 기록하는 경우에는
Wednesday, November 3, 1999

특히 축제일을 기록하는 경우는
Wed., Nov. 3. Culture Day.

특히 체류 사실을 기록하는 경우는
Washington, November 3.
November 3rd, Washington.

주일명이나 월명을 생략하여 쓰는 경우는 다음과 같다.

주일명 : Sun., Mon., Tues., Wed., Thurs., Fri., Sat.

월명 : Jan., Feb., Mar., Apr., Aug., Sept., Oct., Nov., Dec. (May, June, July는 보통 약자를 쓰지 않는다. 단, July는 Jul., Jy., 또 June은 Jun., Je. 따위로 생략하는 경우가 간혹 있다).

## 2. 날 씨(Weather)

날씨는, 날짜 다음에 계속해서 쓰는 것이 보통이나, 상세하게 쓸 경우는 본문에 넣는다. 사용되는 용어에는 다음과 같은 것들이 있다.

맑음 : fine, fair, clear, beautiful, bright, cloudless, sunny, favorable, ideal
흐림 : cloudy, overcast, gloomy, dull
비 : rainy, wet, a light [heavy, torrential, streaming] rain, occasional [intermittent] rain, a shower, a drizzle
눈 : snowy, a light [heavy] snow
바람 : foul, windy, stormy, nasty
추움·더움 : cold, chilly, cool, warm, hot, sultry
기타 : misty, foggy, frosty, sleety

또한 이상의 용어를 접속사로 맺어서 fine and warm(맑고 따뜻함), cold but beautiful(추우나 맑음) 따위로 쓰거나, 부사를 사용하여 subtly mild(훈훈하다), scorchingly hot(매우 덥다), refreshingly cool(서늘하다) 따위로 할 수도 있다. 또 날씨의 변화가 있는 경우에는 fine, cloudy later(맑은 후 흐림), fine, shower in the evening(맑음, 저녁 때 소나기) 따위로도 한다.

## 3. 본 문(Body)

**1.** 생 략

일기는 매일 쓰는 것이므로, 문장은 간결한 것이 가장 좋다. 그러기 위해서 항상 분명한 주어(필자 자신을 나타내는 I, 시간·날씨 따위를 나타내는 It)나 동사, 없어도 뜻의 혼란을 야기하지 않는 어구 따위는 생략하는 경우가 많다.

〈보기〉 6시 기상
(I) Got up at 6.
11시 취침
(I) (Went to [To]) Bed at 11.
하루 종일 비
(It) Rained all day.

내일모레

(the) day after tomorrow

**2.** 시제(時制)

현재형·과거형 어느 것을 사용해도 좋으나 그날의 단순한 경험의 기술(記述)로서는 과거형을 쓰는 것이 일반적이다. 그러나 일상의 습관적 행위, 일반적 진리 또는 필자 자신의 심경 따위를 말하는 경우는 현재형이 쓰인다.

〈보기〉 오후 대준군이 왔다.

Taejun came to see me in the afternoon.

날씨가 나날이 따뜻해진다.

It is getting warmer day by day.

## 4. 본문의 보기

1월 1일 수요일

맑은 하늘, 고요한 정월 초하루가 밝았다.

읍내 삼촌댁에 누이동생과 함께 세배드리러 갔다. 정오쯤 급우들로부터 많은 연하장이 날라왔다. 어느 것이나 새해의 기쁨과 연초의 새로운 결심을 말하고 있다.

나의 고교생활도 앞으로 1년 남짓하다. 올해야말로 후회하지 않도록 열심히 최선을 다해 공부하자.

Wed., Jan. 1.

A serene New Year's Day blessed with fine weather.

Paid a visit of respect on New Year's Day to the uncle's in the town with my sister. About noon, I was almost swamped with greeting cards from my classmates, each wishing me a happy New Year, and reminding me of his new resolutions.

My high school life will end in just over a year's time. I am firmly resolved to do my best in my studies this year, so as to have no regrets in the future.

2월 11일 목 흐린 후 맑음

오늘은 나의 17번째 생일이다. 대준이와 황원이를 나의 간소한 생일 파티에 초청하였다.

요즈음 나는 행복이란 것에 관해 생각한 바가 있는데, 나는 그것을 우정이라는 형태로 여기고 싶다. 사람과 사람간의 진실한 마음이 오고 감—거기에는 가장 순수한 기쁨이 있을 것 같다. 또한 우정을 키우기 위해서는 서로가 어떠한 경우에 있어서도 성실하지 않으면 안된다고 나는 생각한다.

Thurs., Feb. 11. Cloudy first, later fine.

Today is my 17th birthday. Invited Taejun and Hwangwon to my small birthday party.

Recently, I often think about the true meaning of happiness, which, I think, consists in friendship. The direct contact of a sincere heart with another—undoubtedly this is the purest of joys. In order to cultivate real friendship, I hold it essential for us to be faithful to one another at all times.

3월 5일 월 맑고 쌀쌀함

입춘이 지난 지 한 달이 된다. 어쩐지 좀 쓸쓸하다. 바람은 아직 쌀쌀하나 새들의 지저귀는 노래 소리는 봄을 예고하는 듯하다. 오후에는 뚝으로 산책을 나갔다. 벌써 따뜻한 양지에는 새싹이 파릇파릇 돋아나와 있었다.

Mon., Mar. 5. Fine but pretty cold.

It is a month since the 'Onset of Spring' is over, and I feel myself somewhat incomplete. The wind is still cold, but the singing of birds seems to foretell the coming of spring. In the afternoon, I went for a stroll along the river bank. Some sunny, warm spots had fresh young grass coming up already.

4월 8일 토 흐린 후 맑음

봄이다! 만물이 생기에 넘친다. 벚꽃도 벌써 만발하였다. 내일은 일요일이니 창경궁은 꽃구경하는 사람들로 법석일 게다.

저녁에 내 친구 검둥이를 데리고 한강변으로 놀러갔다. 넓은 곳이 좋았던지 이리 뛰고 저리 뛰며 매우 기뻐했다.

Sat., Apr. 8. Cloudy, later clear.

It is spring. All nature is full of life. Cherry blossoms are at their best now. Tomorrow being Sunday, Ch'anggyŏng-kung will be jammed with people who have come to see the flowers.

Went to the Hangang bank with my pet dog "Blacky" in the evening. Finding himself in the open, Blacky jumped about overjoyed.

5월 2일 수 맑음

녹음이 짙어졌다. 또한 오늘은 구름 한 점 없는 맑은 날씨다. 내일은 인호와 북한산에 하이킹을 간다. 준비를 갖춘 후 일찍 자다.

Wed., May 2. Fine.

The world is now clad in green foliage. It is really fine, with not a speck of cloud in the sky. Will go hiking tomorrow to Puk'ansan with Inho. Made preparations, went to bed earlier than usual.

6월 17일 금 비

장마가 들고부터 매일 비만 내린다. 우울하고 모든 것이 곰팡이 투성이어서 책을 읽을 기분도 나지 않아 상봉이의 집에 가서 바둑을 두었다.

Fri., June 17. Rain.

Rain every day since the wet season has set in. Felt so depressed and mold is on everything that I couldn't even read. I called on Sangbong and we played *paduk*.

8월 5일 일 맑음

찌는 듯이 덥다. 2주일 동안이나 비 한 방울 뿌리지 않는다. 뜰 안의 나무들도 축 늘어져 있다. 해질 무렵에 바싹 마른 마당에 물을 뿌리고서 기분이 조금은 상쾌했다. 밤에는 시원한 바람을 쐬러 바닷가로 나갔다.

Sun., Aug. 5. Fine.

A scorching hot day! Not a drop of rain for almost two weeks. The garden plants are drooping. Toward sundown, I watered my parched garden and felt a little refreshed. In the evening, went out to enjoy the cool breeze on the beach.

9월 19일 수 맑음

어제까지의 사납게 불던 태풍은 멎고, 오늘 밤의 둥근 달은 유달리 아름답다. 길가 수풀 속에서 (이름 모를) 벌레들이 흥겹게 울고 있다. 아—가을이다.

Wed., Sept. 19. Fair.

The typhoon which raged till yesterday has passed. Tonight, the harvest moon is especially beautiful. By the road insects are chirping and singing merrily in the bush. Autumn is here!

10월 20일 토 맑음

여느 때보다 1시간 일찍 일어남. 운동 대회에는 더할 나위 없는 맑은 날씨다. 7시에 등교. 100미터 경주에서는 2등. 집에 돌아오니 녹초가 됨. 식사 후 바로 취침.

Sat., Oct. 20. Fair.

Got up an hour earlier than usual. Our athletic meeting was favored by ideal weather. Arrived at school at seven. I got the second prize in the 100-meter dash. When I got home, I was dog-tired and went to bed soon after dinner.

11월 7일 수 맑음

첫서리가 내렸다. 요즈음은 아침 저녁으로 제법 쌀쌀하게 느껴진다. 등화가친의 계절이다. 나의 공부도 제법 궤도에 들어선 것 같다. 이제까지의 나의 태만을 벌충해야겠다.

Wed., Nov. 7. Fair.

Had the year's first frost this morning. The morning and evening air has grown pretty cold recently. A good season for reading! I'm really getting into the mood for study. I will try to make up for my past idleness.

12월 31일 월 맑음

1년도 지나고 보니 너무 짧은 것 같다. 결심했던 일을 제대로 실행했는가 생각해 보니 의심스럽다. 그러나 내딴에는 무척 노력했다고 생각된다. 다가오는 새해에는 커다란 희망을 안고 제야의 종소리에 아쉬운 이 1999년을 보내기로 하겠다.

Fri., Dec. 31. Clear.

The year is almost over, but I feel that it was altogether too short. Did I fulfill all my resolutions? I am not sure of that. But at least I made an effort. Embracing greater hopes for the coming new year, I will bid farewell to the year 1999 with the bell ringing out the old year.

~~~~~~~~~~~~~~~~~~~

다음에 어떤 고교생의 미국 여행기의 한 부분을 실어 참고 자료로 제공한다.

*July 27. Cloudy. In Washington.*

Unlike New York City. Washington is a political center and is more quiet. The highest place from which I could view the city was not a skyscraper but the Washington Monument.

The Washington Monument, dedicated to George Washington, the first President of the United States is of white marble and a little more than 555 feet high.

The Capitol is a majestic building. A Capitol guide showed us around, and we saw and heard about the rotunda with its many wonderful paintings, including those showing the scenes of Columbus' landing and the signing of the Declaration of Independence.

Close by the Capitol there is the Library of Congress, which, the guide told us, is the finest library building in the
~~~~~~~~~~~~~~~~~~~

world.

The Lincoln Memorial stands in the northern part of Potomac Park. Inside there is a big marble statue of Abraham Lincoln facing the Washington Monument and the Capitol across a rectangular pool.

7월 27일 흐림 워싱턴에서

워싱턴은 뉴욕시와 달리 정치의 중심지로 뉴욕보다 조용하다. 시가를 내려다볼 수 있는 가장 높은 곳은 마천루(摩天樓)가 아니라 워싱턴 기념비였다.

워싱턴 기념비는 합중국의 초대 대통령, 조지 워싱턴을 기념하기 위한 것으로 흰 대리석으로 만들어졌고 높이는 555ft 남짓하다.

의사당은 큰 건축물이다. 의사당의 안내원을 따라 아름다운 그림이 많이 걸려 있는 회랑(回廊)을 보고, 설명을 들으면서 돌았다. 이 그림들 중에는 콜럼버스의 상륙이나 독립 선언서의 서명 광경이 있었다.

의사당 바로 옆에는 국회 도서관이 있는데 그것은 안내원 말에 의하면 세계에서 가장 뛰어난 도서관이라고 한다.

링컨 기념관은 포토맥 공원 안 북쪽에 서 있다. 내부에는 큰 대리석의 아브라함 링컨의 상이 있다. 그것은 직사각형의 연못을 사이에 두고 워싱턴 기념비와 의사당을 마주 보고 있다.

# (4) 영문 편지 쓰는 법

한 마디로 영문 편지라 해도 여러 가지 종류가 있다. 즉, 일반 사람들이 주고 받는 사교문(Social Letters), 상업 거래에 쓰이는 상용문(Business Letters), 나라나 관청간에 오고 가는 공용문(Official Letters) 등 그 종류는 많으며 형식도 또한 서로 각각 다르다. 그러나 편지 쓰는 법에 관해서는 양(洋)의 동서를 불문하고 공통된 요령과 고유의 특이한 요령이 있다. 전자는 (1) 예의, (2) 간결, (3) 정확, (4) 명료 따위의 여러 성질이고, 후자는 주로 형식과 구성의 면이다. 따라서, 여기서는 후자에 중점을 두게 되는 것은 당연한 일이나, 우선 전자의 편에 서서 영문 편지의 특질상에서 생기는 면을 몇 개 말하고자 한다.

(1) 예의 영문 편지에 관한 거의 모든 책이 "Your attitude"라는 말을 들고 있다. 이것은 영문 편지의 하나의 특질이다. "Your attitude"라는 것은 편지는 상대방을 존중하며 상대의 입장에 서서 자기가 말하고자 하는 바를 말하는 태도를 가리키는 것이다. 즉, 하나에서 열까지 I로 시작하여 I로 끝나는 1인칭 중심이 되어서는 안 된다는 말이다.

다음으로 type된 편지를 받는 경우가 있다. handwriting과 typewriting을 예의라는 점에서 보면 어떻게 구분되겠는가? 일반적으로 friendly letter는 type하지 않은 handwriting이, business letter는 그 반대로 type된 것이 예의에 맞는다. 그러나 최근에는 friendly letter도 typewriting의 것으로 바뀌어져 가고 있다.

(2) 간결 편지란 이쪽의 의사를 상대방에게 전하는 것이므로, 될수록 상대가 쉽게 이해할 수 있도록 배려하지 않으면 안 된다. 인사말과 끝맺음 말이 너무 길어서, 가장 필요로 하는 요점이 흐릿해지는 편지쓰기는 피하여야 한다. 또, 사용하는 어구의 면에서도 난해한 말이나 아리송한 표현을 쓰지 않도록 주의하여야 한다. 특히, 우연히 알게 된 Idiom 따위를 충분히 소화도 못 시킨 채 쓰게 되면, 마치 상투머리에 양복 입은 것처럼 어색한 감을 주기 쉬우므로 이러한 경향은 신중을 기해야 한다.

(3) 정확 모든 문장이 문법적으로 정확함을 요구하는 것처럼 편지의 글도 문법적인 정확성이 요구된다. 학교 문법을 잘 활용할 것이며, 조금이라도 의심되는 점이 있으면 잘 확인해서 문장을 작성하는 습관을 길러야 한다. 특히, 관사·전치사 등 우리말에 없는 말의 용법이나 동사의 변화 따위에는 세심한 주의를 기울여야 한다.

(4) 명료 이것은 특별한 설명을 필요로 하는 것은 아니나, 요건의 하나이므로, 특히 명료성을 잃기 쉬운 경우의 보기를 들어 설명하겠다. 문법상이나 내용상의 경우는 말할 필요도 없고, 수(數)에 관한 잘못이 불명료함을 초래하는 경우도 적지 않다. 1,000,000을 잘못하여 10,00,000라고 comma(,)를 잘못 찍으면 상대방은 0을 빠뜨린 것이 아닌가 하고 오해를 하기 쉽다. 또 수사(數詞)를 포함하는 명사의 경우는 한층 더 주의하지 않으면 안 된다. 8-day clock는 '태엽을 한 번 감으면 8일 동안 가는 시계'라는 뜻인데 이 시계 1개라고 쓰는 것을 1 8-day clock라 쓰게 되면 '18일 간'이라고 오독하기가 쉽다. 따라서 수사를 포함하는 명사의 경우는 정확하게 an 8-day clock, seven 4-room houses(4칸의 집 7동)라고 쓰지 않으면 안 된다. 요는 읽는 사람의 입장에 서서 명료하게 쓰도록 주의해야 한다.

# 1. 영문 편지의 형식

사교문의 편지는 다음 부분으로 이루어진다.

ⓐ 두서(頭書) (Heading)
ⓑ 서부(序部) 또는 상대방 주소(Introduction *or* Inside Address)
ⓒ 허두(Salutation *or* Greeting)
ⓓ 본문(Body) ⓔ 맺음말(Complimentary Close *or* Subscription)
ⓕ 서명(Signature) ⓖ 추신(Postscript)

(**Social Letter**의 형식)

ⓐ *Correspondent's address*
*Date*

*Name*
*Address* ⓑ

ⓒ *Salutation*
ⓓ *Body*

ⓔ *Complimentary Close*
ⓕ *Signature*

ⓖ *P. S.*

추신은 필요에 따라서 쓰는 것이며, 반드시 써야 하는 것은 아니다. P.S.라 생략하여 쓴다.

ⓐ 120 Tangju-dong
Chongno-gu, Seoul
January 15, 1999

ⓑ Mr. Ch'angjin Chŏn
312 Hongje-dong
Sŏdaemun-gu, Seoul
ⓒ Dear Mr. Chŏn
ⓓ You know I am leaving for home soon and shall not have a chance to see you again. So, before I go, I am giving a little party at my house to all my friends. Please come on the 21st inst. at 7 p.m.

ⓔ *Yours sincerely,*

ⓕ *Andrew Smith*

ⓖ P.S. Would you mind giving me a picture of yourself?

(**a**) 두서(Heading)에는 발신인의 주소와 날짜를 쓴다. 발신인의 주소를 잘 알고 있는 사람에 대해서는 날짜만을 쓰기도 한다. 주소는 우리말의 경우와는 반대로 좁은 구역부터 넓은 구역의 순서로 쓴다.

보기 : ① 320 Namsan-dong
Chung-gu, Seoul
Feb. 5, 1999
② 35-2 Tongshin-dong,
Tongdaemun-gu, Seoul.
March 3, 1999.

①처럼 각 행(行)의 머리를 일직선으로 하는 식을 Block Form(수직식)이라 하며, 타이프된 편지는 이런 형이 보통이다. 또 ②의 경우처럼 각 행의 머리가 사선(斜線)을 이루고 있는 경우를 Indented Form(사선식)이라 한다.

①처럼 주소와 날짜의 행 끝에 피리어드를 찍지 않은 것을 Open Style(개식), ②처럼 피리어드를 찍은 것을 Closed Style(폐식)이라 한다. 대체로 ①은 미국식, ②는 영국식이다. 또한 번지 앞에는 No. (number의 뜻인 라틴어 *numero*의 약자)를 붙이는 경우도 있고, 그 대신 #을 쓰는 경우도 있다.

(**b**) 서부(序部)(Introduction)에는 수신인의 주소·성명을 기입하나 가능한 한 3행으로 간추린다. 첫째 행에는 수신인의 성명, 둘째 행에는 번지, 동의 이름, 셋째 행은 구, 시, 도명을 쓴다. 외국으로 보내는 편지는 국명도 쓴다. 그러나 이 서부는 친밀한 사이의 Social Letter의 경우는 보통 생략된다. Business Letter의 경우에는 편지의 끝 좌측 밑에 쓰는 경우도 있으며 오히려 이것이 정중한 형식이다. 이 수신인의 성명을 쓸 때 존칭을 잘못 쓰면 큰 실례가 되므로 아래에 그 용법을 약술한다.

1) Mr.: Mister의 생략으로 특정한 직함을 갖지 않은 남자에게 쓴다.

2) Esq. : Esquire의 생략으로 특히 변호사 · 검사 · 저명한 인사에게 쓴다. 단, 이것은 성명 앞에 붙이지 않고 뒤에 붙인다.
(보기) : Wŏnu Nam, Esq.

3) Miss : 미혼의 여자에게 쓴다.

4) Mrs. : 기혼의 부인에게 쓴다. 단, 이 용법에 관하여는 서명 · 명함의 설명을 참조하라.

5) Master : 상대가 소년인 경우에 쓴다.

6) Messrs.[mèsəz] : 두 사람 이상 연명(連名)의 경우 또는 회사, 상점에 보내는 경우.

7) Misses : Miss의 복수. 용법은 위와 동일.

8) Mesdames[méidæm] : Mrs.의 복수. 용

법은 위와 동일.

9) Rev. : Reverend[révərənd]의 생략으로 목사·신부·승려 등 성직자의 경우에 쓴다. 반드시 The를 붙여 쓴다.

(보기) : The Rev. Charles Robinson; The Rev. Mr. Robinson; The Rev. Dr. Robinson

10) Hon. : Honorable의 생략으로 판사 · 검사 · 각료 · 국회의원 기타 고급 관리에게 쓴다.

11) Dr. : Doctor의 생략으로 박사 학위를 가진 사람에게 붙이는 칭호.

12) Prof. : Professor의 생략으로 대학 교수에게 붙이는 칭호.

13) 육·해·공군의 장교는 그 계급명을 머리에 붙인다.

(보기) : Major William Richardson.

(**c**) 허두(Salutation) 본문에 들어가기 전의 호칭으로서 우리말 편지의 "근계(謹啓)…전상서(前上書)" 따위에 해당되는 말이다. 이것은 편지의 종류·상대의 위치에 따라 달라진다. 또 맺음말과도 서로 어울리지 않으면 안 된다. 맺음말과 허두의 일반적인 상관 관계는 다음과 같다.

| | 허 두 | 맺 음 말 |
|---|---|---|
| 사교문 | My dear Sir [Madam], [:] | Yours sincerely, Yours truly, |
| | My dear Mr. [Mrs., Miss]__, | Yours sincerely, |
| | Dear John, | Yours sincerely, |
| | Dear Father, Dear Mother, | Yours affectionately, Your loving daughter [son], |
| | Dear Mr. [Mrs., Miss]__, | Yours sincerely, |

Sir 한 단어만 쓰는 경우는 공식적인 경우에만 한한다. 극히 친한 친구 사이에는 Christian Name(이름)이나 애칭을 쓰며, Family Name(성)은 쓰지 않는다. 동료간에는 Dear Mr.— 라 쓴다. 일반적으로 최초의 단어와 최후의 단어는 대문자로 하는 것이 좋다. 즉, Dear old Dad; My dear Mr. Smith 따위처럼 한다. 또 허두의 다음에는 극히 격식을 갖춘 경우는 콜론( : )을 붙이고, 비공식적인 경우는 콤마(,)를 붙이는 것이 보통이다. 기타 콜론과 대시를 겸용( : —)하는 경우도 있다.

(**d**) 본문(Body)은 패러그래프마다 최초의 행(行)을 5자 정도 안으로 들여서 쓰기 시작하며 각 패러그래프의 머리를 가지런히 맞춘다. 타이프로 치는 경우 행간은 single spacing으로 하고 패러그래프가 바뀔 적에는 double spacing으로 하는 것이 일반적이다. 짧은 편지인 경우는 모두를 double spacing으로 하여도 좋다. 내용은 우리 글의 의례적인 표현이나 인사는 불필요하며, 될 수 있는 한 구어적인 표현으로 요건부터 쓰기 시작한다.

(**e**) 맺음말(Complimentary Close)은 본문에서 2행 정도 띄어서 페이지의 중간 정도에서부터 쓰기 시작한다. 이는 우리말의 여불비례(餘不備禮) · 근배(謹拜) · 경백(敬白) 따위에 해당되는 말로 가장 널리 사용되는 것은 "Yours sincerely"나 "Truly yours"이다. 친밀한 사이인 경우는 간단히 "Yours"나 "Truly", "Sincerely" 따위로 쓴다. 맺음말의 최초의 글자는 대문자로 쓰고 끝에는 콤마로 끝맺음하는 것이 보통이나, 허두 끝에 콤마를 붙이지 않은 경우에는 맺음말의 끝에도 콤마를 붙이지 않는다.

(**f**) 서명(Signature)은 소위 말하는 '사인'으로 맺음말로부터 2행 밑 약간 우측으로 들어가서 쓰는 것이 보통이다. 편지를 타자로 찍은 경우라도 최후의 서명만은 반드시 자필로 쓰며, 처음 대하는 상대에 대해서는 알아보기 쉽도록 서명 밑에 다시 타자로 이를 명시하는 경우도 있다.

영미인의 서명을 보면, Wallace Lee Wilson이라고 Full name을 쓴 것, 또는 W. L. Wilson, 혹은 Wallace L. Wilson이라 약기한 것 따위가 있으나 어느 것이나 다 옳다. W. L. Wilson이 영국식, Wallace L. Wilson으로 쓰는 것이 미국식이다. 서명에 있어서 우리가 가장 범하기 쉬운 잘못은 기혼 부인의 경우이다. 남편이 생존해 있는 경우는 Mary Smith (Mrs. John E. Smith)라 하는 것이 Formal 한 형식이다. 즉, 자기 이름을 쓰고 다음에 ( )안에 남편의 이름을 덧붙인다. Mrs. Mary Smith라 하면 미망인임을 나타내는 것이 되므로 주의하여야 한다. 또 수신인의 성명을 기재할 때도 이 점에 대해서 각별한 주의가 필요하다. 즉, 상대가 기혼 부인으로 남편이 생존중인 경우는 Mrs. John E. Smith와 같이 남편의 성명에 Mrs.를 붙인다. 또 서명을 할 경우에 있어서 부인의 성(姓)을 써야 할 필요가 있는 경우는 Mary Taylor Smith라 쓴다.

다음으로 미혼녀의 경우는 Miss Chimi Kim 또는 (Miss) Chimi Kim이라 서명하는 것이 일반적이다. 요는 여자인 경우는 Mrs. 또는 Miss를 빠뜨리지 않고 정확히 써야 한다.

(**g**) 추신(追伸)(Postscript)은 본문에서 빠뜨려 쓴 내용을 첨기하는 것으로 그 위치는 서명 다음에 2~3행 띄어서 행(行)의 중앙에서 약간 좌측으로 들어가서 P.S.라 쓰고 필요한

사항을 기록한다. 우리말의 추신(追伸)·추백(追白) 따위에 해당되며 너무 길지 않도록 주의해야 한다. 또한 동봉한 서류 따위가 있는 경우는 편지 좌측 밑에 2 enclosures처럼 쓰면 된다.

## 2. 봉투 쓰는 법

봉투쓰기는 ⓐ 수신인의 성명·주소, ⓑ 발신인의 성명·주소, ⓒ 보충적인 지정 사항 따위이다.

수신자의 성명에 경칭을 붙여 봉투 중앙에 쓰고 그 밑에 주소를 쓴다. 봉투에 쓰는 수신자·발신자의 주소·성명은 위에 든 Block Form이나 Indented Form중 하나로 통일시켜야 한다. ⓒ는 지정난으로 Confidential, Private, Personal(친전), Urgent, Immediate(지급), c/o Postmaster(국유치 우편), Photo(사진재중), Kindness of Mr. Nam (남씨 전교(轉交)), Air Mail(항공편) 등을 봉투의 좌측 하단에 기입하고 밑줄을 친다. 영문 편지에서는 봉투에 자기의 주소·성명을 쓰지 않는 경우가 있으나 내부에는 반드시 써야 한다. 또는 봉투 이면에 발신자의 주소를 쓸 경우는 다음과 같이 한다. 우리가 흔히 봉하는 부분에 쓰는 '封', '緘' 따위를 써서는 안 된다.

(1) **Indented Style**

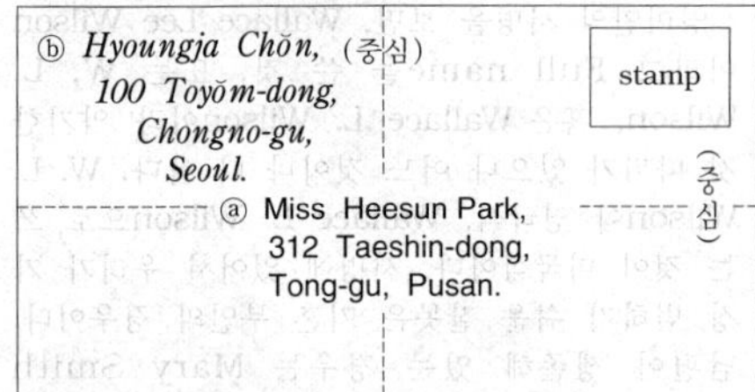


(2) **Block Style**

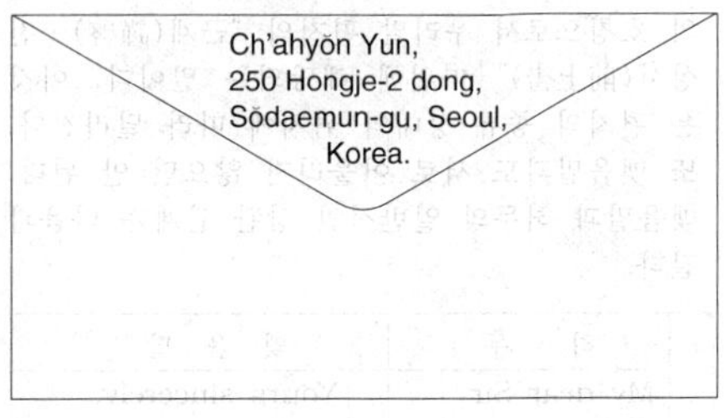


## 3. 엽서 쓰기

보통 엽서의 겉면 쓰기는 봉투와 같은 형식으로 쓴다. Aerogram은 Air Letter라고도 하며 항공 봉함 엽서로 편지지와 봉투를 겸한 편리한 엽서의 하나인데 이는 인쇄된 형식에 따라 해당란에 내용을 기재하면 된다. 지정란은 보통의 편지 형식에 따라 쓴다.

그림엽서는 보통 통신문을 좌측 반, 수신인 성명을 우측 반 부분에 쓰는 규정이 있다.

## 4. 여러 가지 편지의 실례(實例)

(1) 개인 편지(Personal Letters)

우선, Scotland의 한 여고 학생이 한국의 한 친구에게 보낸 편지를 참고로 하겠다.

20 King's Road,
Rosyth, Tife, Scotland.
15th October, 1999.

My dear Kyŏngho,

Thank you very much for your most welcome letter. I've been very busy these days, with studies and fitting in dancing and drama. My week seems to fly like an arrow.

Scotland is quite beautiful, especially up in the Highlands, either in summer when the heather is covering the hills or in winter when snow covers the hills. The only thing to complain about is the weather, because, when winter comes, it is very cold. But it does not worry me so much now.

I look forward to the snow, as I can

go sledging on the small hills, not very far from where I live.

Perhaps you are fond of films. I am very fond of them, and usually go when there is a good film. The one I enjoyed most was "Lawrence of Arabia." My favourite actress is Hayley Mills.

I hope you are keeping well.

Your loving friend,

Jane

내 친구 경호에게

편지 고맙다. 최근 나는 공부에다가 댄스·연극 준비 따위로 몹시 바쁘단다. 한 주일이 화살처럼 빠르게 날아가버리는 것 같은 기분이란다.

스코틀랜드는 대단히 아름다운 곳이란다. 특히 고지대에 오르면 히스가 무성하게 산을 덮는 여름, 하얀 눈이 산을 덮는 겨울, 어느 것이나 다 멋지단다. 다만, 한 가지 흠은 기후이어서, 겨울이 오면 몹시 추운 것이지. 그러나 그것은 이제 내게 그리 염려스러운 것은 아니란다.

나는 눈이 내리기를 고대하고 있다. 집에서 멀지 않은 조그마한 언덕으로 썰매를 타러 갈 수가 있기 때문이지.

너도 영화 관람을 좋아하겠지. 나는 매우 좋아해서 좋은 영화가 들어오면 거의 빼놓지 않고 구경을 간단다. 가장 좋았던 것은 '아라비아의 로렌스'였고, 좋아하는 배우로는 헤일리 밀스를 들 수 있다.

내내 건강하기를 빌면서

다정한 친구

1999. 10. 15. 제인

(2) 상업용 편지(Business Letters)

상업문의 형식도 사교문과 대체로 일치하고 있다. 다만, 약식의 형식은 피하는 것이 좋다. 대체로 business letter는 발신인의 회사명, 주소 따위가 인쇄된 편지지를 사용하므로 날짜만을 쓰면 좋도록 되어 있다. 무게 있는 당당한 형식과 외관을 지닌 편지지는 실물의 편지에서 발신자의 위신을 은연 중에 나타내며, 수신자에게 회사의 이미지를 강하게 어필하는 것이므로 용지, 외관, 형식을 선택함에 신중해야 한다. 또 우송하는 경우와 전송하는 경우 즉 fax나 e-mail의 두 경우도 고려에 넣어야 한다.

용지는 괘선이 없는 상질의 백지가 좋으며, 사이즈는 A4 규격(210mm×297mm)이 일반적이다. 또 가장 중요한 것은 편지를 면밀히 검토하여 무결함의 서신을 보내도록 하는 것이다.

다음 편지의 좌측 밑에 있는 SY/sc(또는 SY: sc)는 각기 편지의 발신인과 타이프를 친 사람 이름의 머리 글자를 나타낸다. 즉, SY는 발신인 임 성재의 머리 글자이고 sc는 타이프를 친 사람, 예를 들면 최숙자의 머리 글자이다.

**HANJIN MOTOR CO., LTD.**
**15 Taeshin-dong, Tong-gu, Seoul, Korea**

November 20, 1999

Messrs. New Asia Motor Corporation
2060 Queen's Road
Rangoon Burma

Dear Sirs,

We take much pleasure in announcing that we are ready to supply you with any quantity of our 1998 model of Hanjin vehicles which surpass all the former models in their higher horse power, greater efficiency, better dependability as well as more attractive appearance.

The detailed explanation of each item of the outstanding merits of these vehicles is given in the catalogs, pamphlets and literatures that we are sending to you under separate cover. Special mention should further be made that the repeated rationalization in the productive operation and equipments has made it possible for our products to be competitive with other foreign made vehicles in the overseas markets both in prices and in superior performances.

We anticipate your utmost efforts in promoting the sales of our products in your territory so that you may find satisfactory profit from handling them. The customers would, we believe, also appreciate your endeavors.

Trusting in your energetic cooperation, we look forward to mutual good business.

Yours very truly,
HANJIN MOTOR CO., LTD.
*Sungjae Yim*
Sungjae Yim
Export Manager

SY/sc

**JOHN L. JONES, INC.**
**1728 West 48th Street**
**New York 38, New York**

January 6, 1999

Mr. James L. Johnson
2839 Allston Road
Chicago 26, Illinois
Dear Mr. Johnson:

Several weeks ago you asked me to let you know when it would be convenient for me to see you in New York about your firm's account.

I find that I shall be free all day on Thursday, January 11, and will be delighted to meet you in your New York office at whatever time may be convenient to you.

I look forward with pleasure to meeting you.

Sincerely yours,
*George R. Smith*
George R. Smith
Sales Manager

GRS: hn

(3) 만찬에의 정식 초대장(Invitation)

(A) 초대장

Mr. and Mrs. James Mason
request the pleasure of
Mr. Kimun Song
company at dinner
on Tuesday evening, August the first
at seven o'clock
at the Lotte Hotel

R.S.V.P.

【주의】 R.S.V.P.는 프랑스어 Répondez, s'il vous plaît(=Reply, if you please.)의 생략으로 '회신을 바랍니다'의 뜻. 초대장의 말미에 첨기함.

(B) 위 초대장에 대한 회신

Mr. Kimun Song accepts with pleasure the kind invitation of Mr. and Mrs. James Mason to dinner on Tuesday evening, August the first at seven o'clock at the Lotte Hotel.

(4) 생일 축하 선물에 대한 인사
(Greetings for Present)

Dear Tom,

You cannot imagine how surprised and delighted I was that you remembered my birthday. The beautiful wrist watch you sent will always remind me of your kindness.

Gratefully yours,

(5) 새 취임을 축하하는 서신
(Congratulation)

Dear George,

Congratulations on your new appointment. You're a lucky man, but no one deserves it more. It sounds like a job that is exactly suited to you, and you are sure to do well in it. All my best wishes for your future.

Sincerely yours,

(6) 친구를 소개하는 서신(Introduction)

Dear Mr. Smith,

I would like to introduce my friend, Mr. Jones, who is going to Paris next month for a rather long stay. As he will be a stranger in a strange city, any little courtesy you can show him will be very much appreciated.

Yours truly,

(7) 이전(移轉)의 통지(Notice of Removal)

Dear Mr. Han,

Allow me to inform you that we moved a few days ago to 152, Hongŭn-dong, Sŏdaemun-gu. Please feel free to visit us when you happen to come this way.

Yours sincerely,

(8) 호텔의 예약(Reservation)

Gentlemen:

I would like to reserve a double room with bath for the period from April 24 to May 5.

Please confirm this reservation by wire today, since we plan to leave the city by Wednesday. We expect to arrive about 8 p.m. on April 25.

Truly yours,

(9) 개점 통지(Announcement)

Gentlemen:

We take much pleasure in announcing that we have this day opened a business firm at the above address under the style of

HAN-JIN TRADING CO., LTD.

as commission agents for the purpose of conducting import and export business.

We trust that our knowledge and experience of commission business in general, particularly of American business, enables us to gain your confidence.

For the necessary information regarding our financial position, we refer you by permission to the Bank of America, Pusan branch.

We hope that we may have the pleasure of serving you.

⑽ 취직 원서

(Application for Employment)

〔1〕

Gentlemen,

I have seen your advertisement in today's Korea Times requiring the services of a business assistant, and I have a desire to apply for that position.

I am now twenty-five years and six months old and a graduate of Seoul National University, College of Commerce. I have been two years in the employ of Tong-il Trading Co., Ltd., Seoul.

I enclose a letter of recommendation from Mr. Han, the president of the said firm, and a sheet of my personal record.

I shall be most grateful if you give me an opportunity of meeting you personally for further information.

〔2〕

Dear Sirs,

I should like to have you consider my application for the position you advertised in the April 1st issue of the Korea Times.

I am a graduate of Korea University, 1999, majoring in four years' course of political economy. The details of my education are given on the enclosed sheet.

Although I have had as yet a poor experience, I have a great desire to get into the employ of a trading concern and to learn how to handle actual business in that line. Should you think favorable of my application, kindly grant me a personal interview.

⑾ 추천장

(Introduction & Recommendation)

Han-Jin Trading Co., Ltd.

320, 4-ga Ch'ungjŏngno Sŏdaemun-gu, Seoul

Call: (735) 1984~85

March 3, 1999

To whom It may Concern:

Miss Youngsook Lee has been my private secretary for the past two years, and has in every way showed herself to be efficient and useful. She is what we call a ready worker, always willing to work for me and sparing no efforts. I feel confident that she will prove an invaluable help to anyone who may be fortunate enough to secure her services.

Yours very truly,

*Ch'ahyŏn Yun*

President

⑿ 영수증(Receipt)

May 5th, 1999

Received from Mr. Kim the sum of ₩50,000 in part payment of a "Minsŏng" brand electronic calculator.

Minsŏng Electric Co., Ltd.

## (5) 영문 이력서 쓰는 법

현재 우리 나라에서 행하여지고 있는 영문 이력서의 형식은, 한국 사람과 영미인 모두에게 만족이 될 수 있도록 우리 나라식의 이력서에 영미식을 가미한 형식이라고도 할 수 있다. 작성시 일반적인 주의 사항은 다음과 같다.

1. 손으로 쓴 것은 판독하기가 어려우므로 컴퓨터나 타자로 작성할 것.

2. 용지의 상부 중앙에 Personal History 또는 라틴어의 Curriculum Vitae[kəríkjuləm váiti:]라 쓴다.

3. 주어 I는 원칙적으로 생략. 단, 부사나 부사구가 선행하는 경우는 생략하지 않는다.

4. 본문은 원칙적으로 과거형을 쓴다. 단, 특별한 뜻을 나타내고자 하는 경우는 이에 상응한 시제를 쓴다.

5. 수동형·분사구문을 사용한 경우는 주어 I와 함께 이에 따르는 be 동사를 생략한다.

6. 본문에는 couldn't, didn't, hadn't, wasn't 따위의 생략형은 사용치 않는다.

7. 사진을 붙이는 장소는 용지의 좌측 상단이나 우측 상단이 좋다. 전체로 보아 균형이 맞는 곳이 좋다.

8. 우리 나라에서는 신장은 미터, 체중은 킬로로 나타내나, 영미에서는 신장은 foot 또는 inch, 체중은 pound를 단위로 나타낸다.

9. Signature는 항상 펜으로 쓰고, 그 밑에 반드시 활자체로 다시 한 번 성명을 적는다.

10. 보통, Social rank 또는 최후의 Pledge(선서) 따위는 기록하지 않는 대신, 본인의 Special study; Major subjects(전공 과목), Reference(조회처) 따위를 첨가한다.

CURRICULUM VITAE

Name in Full : Wonjoon Han
Date of Birth : September 20, 1975(Age : 24)
Permanent Domicile : 78 Majang-dong, Sŏngdong-gu, Seoul.
Present Address :
140 Hannam-dong, Yongsan-gu, Seoul.
Education :

Entered the Namsan Junior High School, March, 1988; finished the three=year course of the same, February, 1991.

Entered the Paemun Senior High School, March, 1991; finished the three=year course of the same, February, 1994.

Admitted to the Korea College of Engineering, March, 1994; graduated from the same, February 1998, taking the B.E. (Bachelor of Engineering) degree.

Major Subjects : Mechanical Engineering, Theoretical Physics, Factory Management.

Activities in College :
Auto Club membership
Baseball Club membership

Occupation :

Employed by the Shinjin Motorcar Co., Ltd., March, 1998, and have since been in the service of the same company.

Special acquirements:

Typewriting (50 words a minute) and English conversation.

Reward and Punishment : None.
Referential Data:
1. Physical : Height, 5.42 ft.; Weight, 121 lbs.
2. Hobbies : Photography and classical music.
3. Sports : Swimming and basketball.

References:
1. Prof : Wonu Nam of the Korea College of Engineering.
20 Tonam-dong, Sŏngbuk-gu, Seoul.
2. Mr. Hansŏng Yu, director of the Personnel Bureau, Shinjin Motorcar Co., Ltd.
33 Hannam-dong, Yongsan-gu, Seoul.

I hereby certify the above statement to be true and correct in every detail.

(*Signature*)
Wonjoon Han

July 11, 1999

# (6) 영문 명함 만들기와 그 사용법

## 1. 명함 만들기

명함은 방문용(Visiting Card)은 필기체, 사무용(Business Card)은 활자체의 것을 사용한다. 크기는 남자용이 7.5×4cm, 여자용은 9×7cm 정도가 보통이다.

(1) 성명만 기입한 명함

*Myungsub Jang*

남자의 경우 Mr.를 붙이지 않는 것이 보통, 기혼 부인은 남편 이름 앞에 Mrs.를 붙인다. 미망인인 경우는 자기 이름 앞에 Mrs.를 붙인다.

(2) 주소를 기입한 명함

**Miss Heesun Park**

35 T'ONGŬI-DONG
CHONGNO-GU, SEOUL
TEL. (735) 1984-9

주소는 좌측 아래 구석에 기입하거나 또는 이름 바로 아래에 기입한다.

(3) 신분·직함을 기입한 명함

TEL. (735) 1984-9

**HANJIN MOTOR CO., LTD.**
**MANUFACTURING DEPT.**

SUNGJAE YIM
CHIEF OF PRODUCTION
CONTROL

5 NAMSAN-DONG
CHUNG-GU SEOUL

개인의 이름을 중앙에 쓰고 회사명을 그 밑에 기입하는 경우도 있으며, 근무처와 자택의 주소를 다 기입하는 경우도 있다. 학생의 경우는 학교명을 이름 바로 밑에 기입하기도 한다.

(4) 공동 명함

*Mr & Mrs Changjin Chŏn*

*10 Donam-dong*
*Songbuk-gu, Seoul*

주로 부부가 함께 사람을 방문하는 경우 쓰인다.

(5) 간단한 어구를 넣은 명함

관직명은 넣더라도 될수록 간략히 한다.

*A Happy New Year*

**Yunpyo Lee**

21 Namsan-dong, Chung-gu

## 2. 명함의 사용법

(1) 방문시

사람을 방문했을 때는 명함을 놓고 오는 것이 예의이다. 상대가 없을 때는 방문 목적에 따라 명함의 한 귀를 접든가 또는 프랑스어로 각기 알맞은 곳에 기호를 쓰든가 한다.

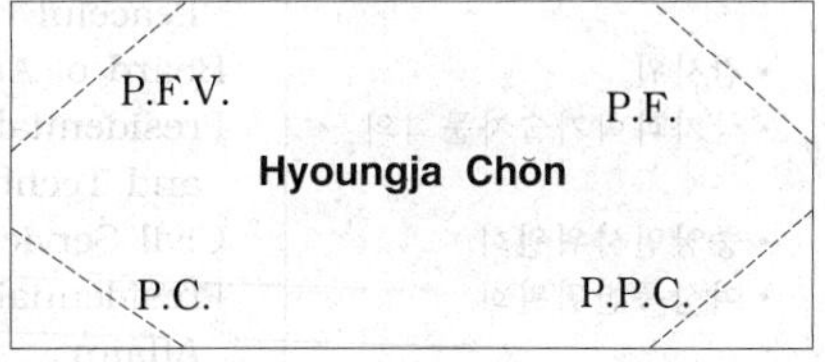


P.F.V.는 make a call(단순한 방문), P.F.는 congratulate(축하), P.C.는 condole(조의(弔意)), P.P.C.는 take leave(작별)의 뜻을 나타낸다.

(2) 소개의 명함

명함으로 소개장을 대용하는 경우는 친밀한 사이에 한하므로 형식에 있어서도 여러 가지가 있다. 명함 뒷면에 소개의 말을 간략하게 기입하는 방법도 흔히 쓰인다.

**CHŎNGNAM KIM**

Introducing
Mr. Jonghan Lee
to
Mr. Gyuhyŏn Hwang

소개 명함의 뒷면

*I have much pleasure in introducing to you my friend, Mr. Jonghan Lee, who is the professor of Korea University.*

*C.K.*

(3) 문병 및 그 사례의 명함

문병을 갔다가 상대가 중태로 면회할 수 없는 경우는 좌측 상단에 To inquire.라 써서 시중드는 사람에게 주고 온다. 병자가 완쾌된 후의 인사로서는, With thanks for your kind inquiry.라 써서 보낸다.

# (7) 우리 나라 정부 기구명

다음에 수록된 행정 · 입법 · 사법부의 직제와 직위 및 이의 영문 번역은 행정자치부 · 국회사무처 등에서 제공한 1999년도 기구표 및 자료에 의거한 것임.

## 1. 중 앙 관 청

| 우 리 말 | 영 문 용 어 | 비 고 |
|---|---|---|
| 1. 조 직 | | |
| (1) 행정부 | **Executive Branch** | |
| 1) 대통령직속기관 | | |
| • 대통령비서실 | Office of the President | |
| • 대통령경호실 | Presidential Security Service | |
| • 국가정보원 | National Intelligence Service | |
| • 국가안전보장회의 | National Security Council | |
| • 민주평화통일자문회의 | Advisory Council on Democratic and Peaceful Unification | |
| • 감사원 | Board of Audit and Inspection | |
| • 국가과학기술자문회의 | Presidential Advisory Council for Science and Technology | |
| • 중앙인사위원회 | Civil Service Commission | |
| • 여성특별위원회 | Presidential Commission on Women's Affairs | |
| • 중소기업특별위원회 | Presidential Commission on Small and Medium Business | |
| 2) 국무총리직속기관 | | |
| • 국무총리비서실 | Prime Minister's Secretariat | |
| • 국무조정실 | Office for Government Policy Coordination | |
| • 비상기획위원회 | Emergency Planning Commission | |
| • 공정거래위원회 | Fair Trade Commission | |
| • 금융감독위원회 | Financial Supervisory Commission | |
| • 국민고충처리위원회 | Ombudsman of Korea | |
| • 청소년보호위원회 | Commission on Youth Protection | |
| 3) 기획예산처 | Ministry of Planning and Budget | |
| • 기획관리실 | Planning and Management Office | |
| • 정부개혁실 | Government Reform Office | |
| • 예산실 | Budget Office | |
| • 재정기획국 | Fiscal Planning Bureau | |
| • 예산관리국 | Budget Management Bureau | |
| 4) 법제처 | Government Legislation Agency | |
| • 법제기획관 | Director General for Legislation Planning | |
| • 행정법제국 | Legislation Bureau of Administration Affairs | |
| • 경제법제국 | Legislation Bureau of Economic Affairs | |
| • 사회문화법제국 | Legislation Bureau of Social and Cultural Affairs | |
| • 행정심판관리국 | Bureau of Administrative Appeals Management | |
| 5) 국정홍보처 | Government Information Agency | |
| • 홍보기획국 | Planning Bureau | |

| 우 리 말 | 영 문 용 어 | 비 고 |
|---|---|---|
| • 국정홍보국 | Coordination Bureau | |
| • 분석국 | News Analysis Bureau | |
| 6) 국가보훈처 | Patriots and Veterans Administration Agency | |
| • 기획관리관 | Planning and Management Officer | |
| • 보훈관리국 | Benefits Bureau | |
| • 보훈선양국 | Commemoration Bureau | |
| • 복지사업국 | Welfare Services Bureau | |
| 7) 재정경제부 | Ministry of Finance and Economy | |
| • 기획관리실 | Planning and Management Office | |
| • 세제국 | Tax and Customs Office | |
| • 경제정책국 | Economic Policy Bureau | |
| • 국고국 | Treasury Bureau | |
| • 금융정책국 | Financial Policy Bureau | |
| • 국제금융국 | International Finance Bureau | |
| • 경제협력국 | Economic Cooperation Bureau | |
| • 국민생활국 | Welfare and Consumer Policy Bureau | |
| 8) 국세청 | National Tax Service | |
| • 기획관리관 | Assistant Commissioner for Planning and Management | |
| • 납세지원국 | Taxpayer Service Bureau | |
| • 법무심사국 | Legal Affairs and Appeals Bureau | |
| • 개인납세국 | Individual Taxation Bureau | |
| • 법인납세국 | Corporate Taxation Bureau | |
| • 조사국 | Investigation Bureau | |
| 9) 관세청 | Customs Service | |
| • 기획관리관 | Planning and Management Officer | |
| • 통관국 | Customs Clearance Bureau | |
| • 감시국 | Inspection and Control Bureau | |
| • 조사국 | Investigation Bureau | |
| • 정보협력국 | Information and International Affairs Bureau | |
| 10) 조달청 | Supply Administration | |
| • 기획관리관 | Planning and Management Officer | |
| • 물자비축국 | Property and Stockpile Bureau | |
| • 구매국 | Procurement Bureau | |
| • 시설국 | Construction Contract Bureau | |
| 11) 통계청 | National Statistical Office | |
| • 통계기획국 | Statistical Planning and Management Bureau | |
| • 경제통계국 | Economic Statistics Bureau | |
| • 사회통계국 | Population and Social Statistics Bureau | |
| • 통계정보국 | Statistical Information and Data Management Bureau | |
| 12) 통일부 | Ministry of Unification | |
| • 기획관리실 | Planning and Management Office | |
| • 통일정책실 | Unification Policy Office | |
| • 정보분석국 | Information Analysis Bureau | |
| • 교류협력국 | Intra-Korean Exchanges and Cooperation Bureau | |

| 우 리 말 | 영 문 용 어 | 비 고 |
|---|---|---|
| • 인도지원국 | Humanitarian Affairs Bureau | |
| 13) 외교통상부 | Ministry of Foreign Affairs and Trade | |
| • 기획관리실 | Planning and Management Office | |
| • 외교정책실 | Policy Planning and International Organizations Office | |
| • 아시아태평양국 | Asian and Pacific Affairs Bureau | |
| • 북미국 | North American Affairs Bureau | |
| • 중남미국 | Latin American and Caribbean Affairs Bureau | |
| • 구주국 | European Affairs Bureau | |
| • 아중동국 | Middle East and African Affairs Bureau | |
| • 조약국 | Treaties Bureau | |
| • 문화외교국 | Cultural Affairs Bureau | |
| • 재외국민영사국 | Overseas Residents and Consular Affairs Bureau | |
| • 통상교섭본부 | Office of the Minister for Trade | |
| 14) 법무부 | Ministry of Justice | |
| • 기획관리실 | Planning and Management Office | |
| • 법무실 | Legal Affairs Office | |
| • 검찰국 | Prosecution Bureau | |
| • 보호국 | Social Protection and Rehabilitation Bureau | |
| • 교정국 | Correction Bureau | |
| • 출입국관리국 | Immigration Bureau | |
| 15) 검찰청 | Public Prosecutor's Office | |
| • 사무국 | Administration Bureau | |
| • 총무부 | General Affairs Department | |
| • 중앙수사부 | Central Investigation Department | |
| • 형사부 | Criminal Department | |
| • 강력부 | Violent Crime Department | |
| • 공안부 | Public Security Department | |
| • 공판송무부 | Criminal Trial and Civil Litigation Department | |
| • 감찰부 | Inspection Department | |
| 16) 국방부 | Ministry of National Defense | |
| • 기획관리실 | Planning and Management Office | |
| • 획득실 | Acquisition Office | |
| • 정책기획국 | Policy Planning Bureau | |
| • 인사복지국 | Personnel and Welfare Bureau | |
| • 동원국 | Mobilization Bureau | |
| • 군사시설국 | Military Installations Bureau | |
| 17) 병무청 | Military Manpower Administration | |
| • 기획관리관 | Planning and Management Officer | |
| • 징모국 | Conscription Bureau | |
| • 동원소집국 | Mobilization and Call Bureau | |
| 18) 행정자치부 | Ministry of Government Administration and Home Affairs | |
| • 기획관리실 | Planning and Management Office | |
| • 인사국 | Personnel Bureau | |

| 우 리 말 | 영 문 용 어 | 비 고 |
|---|---|---|
| • 행정관리국 | Administrative Management Bureau | |
| • 자치행정국 | Local Autonomy Administration Bureau | |
| • 지방재정세제국 | Local Finance and Local Tax Bureau | |
| • 민방위재난통제본부 | Headquarters of Civil Defense and Disaster Management | |
| 19) 경찰청 | National Police Agency | |
| • 경무기획국 | Police Administration and Planning Bureau | |
| • 방범국 | Crime Prevention Bureau | |
| • 수사국 | Criminal Investigation Bureau | |
| • 경비교통국 | Public Security and Traffic Bureau | |
| • 정보국 | Intelligence Bureau | |
| • 보안국 | National Security Bureau | |
| 20) 교육인적자원부 | Ministry of Education and Human Resources Development | |
| • 기획관리실 | Planning and Management Office | |
| • 학교정책실 | School Policy Office | |
| • 평생교육국 | Lifelong Education Bureau | |
| • 고등교육지원국 | Higher Education Bureau | |
| • 교육자치지원국 | Local Education Support Bureau | |
| 21) 과학기술부 | Ministry of Science and Technology | |
| • 기획관리실 | Planning and Management Office | |
| • 과학기술정책실 | Science and Technology Policy Office | |
| • 연구개발국 | Research and Development Bureau | |
| • 원자력국 | Nuclear Energy Bureau | |
| • 기초과학인력국 | Basic Science and Manpower Bureau | |
| • 과학기술협력국 | Science and Technology Cooperation Bureau | |
| 22) 기상청 | Meteorological Administration | |
| • 기획국 | Planning Bureau | |
| • 예보국 | Forecast Bureau | |
| • 응용기상국 | Applied Meteorology Bureau | |
| 23) 문화관광부 | Ministry of Culture and Tourism | |
| • 기획관리실 | Planning and Management Office | |
| • 종무실 | Religious Affairs Office | |
| • 문화정책국 | Cultural Policy Bureau | |
| • 예술국 | Arts Bureau | |
| • 문화산업국 | Culture Industry Bureau | |
| • 관광국 | Tourism Bureau | |
| • 체육국 | Sports Bureau | |
| 24) 문화재청 | Cultural Properties Administration | |
| • 문화재기획국 | Cultural Properties Planning Bureau | |
| • 문화유산국 | Cultural Heritage Bureau | |
| 25) 농림부 | Ministry of Agriculture and Forestry | |
| • 기획관리실 | Planning and Management Office | |
| • 농업정책국 | Agricultural Policy Bureau | |
| • 국제농업국 | International Agriculture Bureau | |
| • 식량생산국 | Foodgrain Policy and Agricultural Production Bureau | |
| • 농산물유통국 | Agricultural Marketing Policy Bureau | |

| 우리말 | 영문용어 | 비고 |
|---|---|---|
| • 축산국 | Livestock Bureau | |
| • 농촌개발국 | Rural Development Bureau | |
| 26) 농촌진흥청 | Rural Development Administration | |
| • 기획관리관 | Planning and Management Officer | |
| • 연구관리국 | Research Management Bureau | |
| • 기술지원국 | Extension Bureau | |
| 27) 산림청 | Forest Service | |
| • 기획관리관 | Planning and Management Officer | |
| • 임업정책국 | Forestry Policy Bureau | |
| • 국유림관리국 | National Forest Administration Bureau | |
| • 사유림지원국 | Private Forest Assistance Bureau | |
| 28) 산업자원부 | Ministry of Commerce, Industry and Energy | |
| • 기획관리실 | Planning and Management Office | |
| • 무역투자실 | Trade and Investment Policy Office | |
| • 자원정책실 | Energy and Resources Policy Office | |
| • 산업정책국 | Industrial Policy Bureau | |
| • 산업기술국 | Technology Policy Bureau | |
| • 자본재산업국 | Capital Goods Industries Bureau | |
| • 생활산업국 | Electronics, Textile and Chemical Industries Bureau | |
| 29) 중소기업청 | Small and Medium Business Administration | |
| • 기획관리관 | Planning and Management Officer | |
| • 중소기업정책국 | Small and Medium Business Policy Bureau | |
| • 경영지원국 | Management Assistant Bureau | |
| • 벤처기업국 | Venture Business Bureau | |
| • 기술지원국 | Technology Promotion Bureau | |
| 30) 특허청 | Industrial Property Office | |
| • 기획관리관 | Planning and Management Officer | |
| • 관리국 | Administration Bureau | |
| • 심사1국 | Examination Bureau 1 | |
| • 심사2국 | Examination Bureau 2 | |
| • 심사3국 | Examination Bureau 3 | |
| • 심사4국 | Examination Bureau 4 | |
| 31) 정보통신부 | Ministry of Information and Communication | |
| • 기획관리실 | Planning and Management Office | |
| • 정보화기획실 | Informatization Planning Office | |
| • 정보통신정책국 | Information and Communication Policy Bureau | |
| • 정보통신지원국 | Telecommunication Business Promotion Bureau | |
| • 전파방송관리국 | Radio and Broadcasting Bureau | |
| • 우정국 | Posts Bureau | |
| • 체신금융국 | Postal Savings, Insurance and Finance Bureau | |
| 32) 보건복지부 | Ministry of Health and Welfare | |
| • 기획관리실 | Planning and Management Office | |
| • 사회복지정책실 | Social Welfare Policy Office | |

| 우 리 말 | 영 문 용 어 | 비 고 |
|---|---|---|
| • 보건정책국 | Health Policy Bureau | |
| • 보건증진국 | Health Promotion Bureau | |
| • 연금보험국 | Pension and Health Insurance Bureau | |
| 33) 식품의약품안전청 | Food and Drug Administration | |
| • 기획관리관 | Planning and Management Officer | |
| • 식품안전국 | Food Safety Bureau | |
| • 의약품안전국 | Pharmaceutical Safety Bureau | |
| • 안전평가관 | Safety Evaluation Officer | |
| 34) 환경부 | Ministry of Environment | |
| • 기획관리실 | Planning and Management Office | |
| • 환경정책국 | Environmental Policy Bureau | |
| • 자연보전국 | Nature Conservation Bureau | |
| • 대기보전국 | Air Quality Management Bureau | |
| • 수질보전국 | Water Quality Management Bureau | |
| • 상하수도국 | Water Supply and Sewage Treatment Bureau | |
| • 폐기물자원국 | Waste Management and Recycling Bureau | |
| 35) 노동부 | Ministry of Labor | |
| • 기획관리실 | Planning and Management Office | |
| • 고용정책실 | Employment Policy Office | |
| • 노정국 | Labor Policy Bureau | |
| • 근무기준국 | Labor Standards Bureau | |
| • 산업안전국 | Industrial Safety and Health Bureau | |
| • 근로여성정책국 | Women Workers' Bureau | |
| 36) 건설교통부 | Ministry of Construction and Transportation | |
| • 기획관리실 | Planning and Management Office | |
| • 수송정책실 | Transport Policy Office | |
| • 국토정책국 | National Development Policy Bureau | |
| • 토지국 | Land Bureau | |
| • 주택도시국 | Housing and Urban Affairs Bureau | |
| • 육상교통국 | Surface Transportation Bureau | |
| • 건설경제국 | Construction Economy Bureau | |
| • 기술안전국 | Technology and Safety Bureau | |
| • 도로국 | Road Bureau | |
| • 수자원국 | Water Resources Bureau | |
| • 항공국 | Civil Aviation Bureau | |
| 37) 철도청 | National Railroad Administration | |
| • 기획관리관 | Planning and Management Officer | |
| • 영업국 | Transportation Business Bureau | |
| • 시설국 | Civil Engineering Bureau | |
| • 전기국 | Electrical Engineering Bureau | |
| • 재무관리국 | Finance Management Bureau | |
| • 차량본부 | Rolling Stock Headquarters | |
| 38) 해양수산부 | Ministry of Maritime Affairs and Fisheries | |
| • 기획관리실 | Planning and Management Office | |
| • 해양정책국 | Marine Policy Bureau | |
| • 해운물류국 | Shipping and Logistics Bureau | |
| • 항만국 | Ports and Harbors Bureau | |
| • 수산정책국 | Fisheries Policy Bureau | |

| 우 리 말 | 영 문 용 어 | 비 고 |
|---|---|---|
| • 어업자원국 | Fishery Resources Bureau | |
| 39) 해양경찰청 | National Maritime Police Agency | |
| • 경무국 | Police Administration Bureau | |
| • 경비구난국 | Guard and Rescue Bureau | |
| • 정보수사국 | Intelligence and Investigation Bureau | |
| • 해양오염관리국 | Marine Pollution Control Bureau | |
| 40) 여성부 | Ministry of Gender Equality | |
| (2) 입법부 | **Legislative Branch** | |
| 1) 국회 | the National Assembly | |
| • 의장비서실 | Office of the Speaker | |
| • 상임위원회 | Standing Committee | |
| • 특별위원회 | Special Committee | |
| • 국회운영위원회 | House Steering Committee | |
| • 법제사법위원회 | Legislation and Judiciary Committee | |
| • 정무위원회 | National Policy Committee | |
| • 재정경제위원회 | Finance and Economy Committee | |
| • 통일외교통상위원회 | Unification, Foreign Affairs and Trade Committee | |
| • 행정자치위원회 | Government Administration and Local Autonomy Committee | |
| • 국방위원회 | National Defense Committee | |
| • 교육위원회 | Education Committee | |
| • 과학기술정보통신위원회 | Science, Technology, Information and Telecommunications Committee | |
| • 문화관광위원회 | Culture and Tourism Committee | |
| • 농림해양수산위원회 | Agriculture, Forestry, Maritime Affairs and Fisheries Committee | |
| • 산업자원위원회 | Commerce, Industry and Energy Committee | |
| • 보건복지위원회 | Health and Welfare Committee | |
| • 환경노동위원회 | Environment and Labor Committee | |
| • 건설교통위원회 | Construction and Transportation Committee | |
| • 정보위원회 | Intelligence Committee | |
| • 예산결산특별위원회 | Special Committee on Budget and Accounts | |
| • 윤리특별위원회 | Special Committee on Ethics | |
| • 여성특별위원회 | Special Committee on Women's Affairs | |
| • 국제 경기대회 지원특별 위원회 | Special Committee on International Games | |
| • 국제 경쟁력 강화 및 경제제도 개혁에 관한 특별위원회 | Special Committee on International Competitiveness Advancement and Economic System Reform | |
| • 재해대책 특별위원회 | Special Committee on Disaster Prevention and Management | |
| 2) 국회사무처 | National Assembly Secretariat | |
| • 사무총장 | Secretary-General | |
| • 사무차장 | Deputy Secretary-General for Administrative Affairs | |

| 우 리 말 | 영 문 용 어 | 비 고 |
|---|---|---|
| • 입법차장 | Deputy Secretary-General for Legislative Affairs | |
| • 기획조정실 | Planning and Coordination Office | |
| • 관리국 | Management and Maintenance Bureau | |
| • 국제국 | Inter-Parliamentary Affairs Bureau | |
| • 공보국 | Public Information Bureau | |
| • 비상계획관 | Emergency Planning Officer | |
| • 총무과 | General Services Division | |
| • 법제예산실 | Legislative and Budgetary Counseling Office | |
| • 의사국 | Proceedings Bureau | |
| • 기록편찬국 | Records and Publication Bureau | |
| 3) 국회도서관 | National Assembly Library | |
| • 입법조사분석실 | Legislative Research and Analysis Office | |
| • 수서정리국 | Acquisition and Processing Bureau | |
| • 참고봉사국 | Reference Service Bureau | |
| • 정보처리국 | Information Technology Management Bureau | |
| (3) 사법부 | **Judicial Branch** | |
| 1) 대법원 | the Supreme Court | |
| • 대법원장비서실 | Secretariat Office | |
| 2) 법원행정처 | Ministry of Court Administration | |
| • 기획조정실 | Planning and Coordination Office | |
| • 비상계획관 | Emergency Planning Officer | |
| • 감사관 | Inspector General | |
| • 사법정책연구실 | Judicial System Research Office | |
| • 공보관 | Public Information Officer | |
| • 총무국 | General Affairs Bureau | |
| • 조사국 | Judicial Information Bureau | |
| • 법정국 | Registry Bureau | |
| • 송무국 | Litigation Bureau | |
| • 사법연수원 | Judicial Research & Training Institute | |
| • 법원공무원연수원 | Court Clerks Training Institute | |
| 3) 고등법원 | High Court | |
| • 사무국 | Secretariat Bureau | |
| 4) 지방법원 | District Court | |
| • 사무국 | Secretariat Bureau | |
| 5) 가정법원 | Family Court | |
| • 사무국 | Secretariat Bureau | |
| 6) 지방법원지원 | Branch Court | |
| • 사무국 | Secretariat Bureau | |
| (4) 기타헌법기관 | **Other Constitutional Organs** | |
| 1) 헌법재판소 | Constitutional Court | |
| • 소장사무처장 | President Secretary General | |
| • 사무처 | Secretariat | |
| • 심판사무국 | Judgment Affairs Bureau | |
| 2) 중앙선거관리위원회 | Central Election Management Committee | |

| 우 리 말 | 영 문 용 어 | 비 고 |
|---|---|---|
| • 위원장 | Chairman | |
| • 사무총장 | Secretary General | |
| • 사무차장 | Deputy Secretary General | |
| • 기획관리관 | Planning and Management Officer | |
| • 선거관리실 | Election Management Office | |
| • 정당국 | Political Party Bureau | |
| 2. 직 위 | | |
| (1) 행정부 | **Executive Branch** | |
| • 장관 | Minister | |
| • 청장 | Administrator or Commissioner | |
| • 차관 | Vice Minister | |
| • 차장 | Deputy Administrator or Commissioner | |
| • 차관보, 실장 | Assistant Minister (for ○○○) | |
| • 국장, 부장 | Director General or Officer | |
| • 심의관(GR 2~3) | Director General or Officer | |
| • 심의관(GR 3) | Deputy Director General or Officer | |
| • 과장 | Director | |
| • 계장 | Deputy Director | |
| (2) 입법부 | **Legislative Branch** | |
| • 의장 | Speaker | |
| • 부의장 | Vice Speaker | |
| • 위원장 | Chairperson / Chairman, Chairwoman | |
| • 사무 총장 | Secretary-General | |
| • 사무 차장 | Deputy Secretary-General | |
| • 도서관장 | Chief Librarian | |
| (3) 사법부 | **Judicial Branch** | |
| • 대법원장 | Chief of Justice | |
| • 대법관 | Justice | |
| • 법원장 | Chief of Judge | |
| • 부장판사 | Senior Judge | |
| • 판사 | Judge | |
| • 처장 | Minister | |
| • 차장 | Vice Minister | |

## 2. 지 방 관 청

| 우 리 말 | 영 문 용 어 | 비 고 |
|---|---|---|
| 1. 조 직 | | |
| (1) 서울특별시 | **Seoul Metropolitan City** | |
| • 공보관 | Public Information Officer | |
| • 기획 관리실 | Planning and Management Office | |
| • 투자 관리 담당관 | Investment Management Officer | |
| • 기술 심사 담당관 | Engineering Review Officer | |
| • 감사관 | Inspector General | |
| • 내무국 | Internal Affairs Bureau | |
| • 재무국 | Finance Bureau | |

| 우리말 | 영문용어 | 비고 |
|---|---|---|
| • 보건 사회국 | Health and Social Affairs Bureau | |
| • 문화국 | Culture Bureau | |
| • 주택국 | Housing Bureau | |
| • 도시계획국 | City Planning Bureau | |
| • 도로국 | Public Roads Bureau | |
| • 하수국 | Sewerage Bureau | |
| • 가정복지국 | Family Welfare Bureau | |
| • 소방본부 | Fire Fighting Headquarters | |
| (2) 광역시 | **Metropolitan City** | |
| • 기획관리실 | Planning and Management Office | |
| • 감사실 | Inspection Office | |
| • 내무국 | Internal Affairs Bureau | |
| • 재무국 | Finance Bureau | |
| • 보건사회국 | Health and Social Affairs Bureau | |
| • 도시계획국 | Urban Planning Bureau | |
| • 건설국 | Construction Bureau | |
| • 소방본부 | Fire Fighting Headquarters | |
| (3) 도 | **Province** | |
| • 기획관리실 | Planning and Management Office | |
| • 내무국 | Internal Affairs Bureau | |
| • 보사환경국 | Health and Environment Affairs Bureau | |
| • 산림국 | Forestry Bureau | |
| • 건설도시국 | Construction Bureau | |
| • 민방위국 | Civil Defense Bureau | |
| 【행정 구역】 | | |
| • 시 | Shi (City) | |
| • 구 | Gu (District) | |
| • 동 | Dong (Sub-District) | |
| • 도 | Do (Province) | |
| • 군 | Gun (County) | |
| • 읍·면 | Ŭp (Town) and Myŏn | |
| 2. 직 위 | | |
| • 시장 | Mayor | |
| • 부시장 | Deputy Mayor | |
| • 도지사 | Governor | |
| • 부지사 | Vice Governor | |

# (8) 미·영의 정부 기구명

## 1. 미 국 정 부

| 우리말 | 영문용어 | 비고 |
|---|---|---|
| 대통령 | President | |
| 부통령 | Vice President | |
| 국무부 | Department of State | |
| 국무장관 | Secretary of State | |

| 우 리 말 | 영 문 용 어 | 비 고 |
|---|---|---|
| 국무차관 | Deputy Secretary of State | |
| 정무담당차관 | Under Secretary for Political Affairs | |
| 국무차관보 | Assistant Secretary of State | |
| 재무부 | Department of the Treasury | |
| 재무장관 | Secretary of the Treasury | |
| 재무차관 | Deputy Secretary of the Treasury | |
| 국방부 | Department of Defense | |
| 국방장관 | Secretary of Defense | |
| 국방차관 | Deputy Secretary of Defense | |
| 육군성 | Department of the Army | |
| 해군성 | Department of the Navy | |
| 공군성 | Department of the Air Force | |
| 합동참모본부 | Joint Chiefs of Staff | |
| 법무부 | Department of Justice | |
| 법무장관 | Attorney General | |
| 법무차관 | Deputy Attorney General | |
| 내무부 | Department of the Interior | |
| 내무장관 | Secretary of the Interior | |
| 내무차관 | Under Secretary of the Interior | |
| 농무부 | Department of Agriculture | |
| 농무장관 | Secretary of Agriculture | |
| 농무차관 | Deputy Secretary of Agriculture | |
| 상무부 | Department of Commerce | |
| 상무장관 | Secretary of Commerce | |
| 상무차관 | Under Secretary of Commerce | |
| 노동부 | Department of Labor | |
| 노동장관 | Secretary of Labor | |
| 노동차관 | Under Secretary of Labor | |
| 보건사회 복지부 | Department of Health and Human Services | |
| 보건사회복지장관 | Secretary of Health and Human Services | |
| 보건사회복지차관 | Under Secretary of Health and Human Services | |
| 주택도시개발부 | Department of Housing and Urban Development | |
| 주택도시개발부장관 | Secretary of Housing and Urban Development | |
| 주택도시개발차관 | Under Secretary of Housing and Urban Development | |
| 교통부 | Department of Transportation | |
| 교통장관 | Secretary of Transportation | |
| 교통차관 | Deputy Secretary of Transportation | |
| 에너지부 | Department of Energy | |
| 에너지장관 | Secretary of Energy | |
| 에너지차관 | Deputy Secretary of Energy | |
| 교육부 | Department of Education | |
| 교육장관 | Secretary of Education | |
| 재향군인원호부 | Department of Veterans Affairs | |
| 재향군인원호장관 | Secretary of Veterans Affairs | |
| 재향군인원호차관 | Deputy Secretary of Veterans Affairs | |

## 2. 영국정부

| 우리말 | 영문용어 | 비고 |
|---|---|---|
| 내각(內閣) | the Cabinet | ※ 영국 정부 기구에서 부서의 장을 모두 장관으로 표기하였으나, Secretary는 기존의 장관, Minister는 신설된 부서의 장관을 칭하는 경우가 많음. |
| 수상 | Prime Minister | |
| 재무성 | the Exchequer | |
| 재무장관 | the Chancellor of the Exchequer | |
| 대법원 | Lord Chancellor's Department | |
| 대법관 | Lord Chancellor | |
| 농어식량성(農漁食糧省) | Ministry of Agriculture, Fisheries & Food | |
| 농어식량장관 | Minister of Agriculture, Fisheries & Food | |
| 외무연방성 | Foreign and Commonwealth Office (생략 Foreign Office) | |
| 외무연방장관 | Secretary of State for Foreign and Commonwealth Office(생략 Foreign Secretary) | |
| 국방성 | Ministry of Defence | |
| 국방장관 | Secretary of State for Defence | |
| 내무성 | Home Office [Department] | |
| 내무장관 | Secretary of State for the Home Department (생략 Home Secretary) | |
| 교통성 | Department of Transport | |
| 교통장관 | Secretary of State for Transport | |
| 교육고용성 | Department of Education & Employment | |
| 교육고용장관 | Secretary of State for Education & Employment | |
| 사회보장성 | Department of Social Security | |
| 사회보장장관 | Secretary of State for Social Security | |
| 환경성 | Department of the Environment | |
| 환경장관 | Secretary of State for the Environment | |
| 보건성(保健省) | Department of Health | |
| 보건장관 | Secretary of State for Health | |
| 통상산업성 | Department of Trade and Industry | |
| 통상산업장관 | Secretary of State for Trade and Industry | |
| 랭커스터성 | the Duchy of Lancaster | |
| 랭커스터 장관 | Chancellor of the Duchy of Lancaster | |
| 웨일스성 | the Welsh Office | |
| 웨일스 장관 | Secretary of State for Wales | |
| 스코틀랜드성 | the Scottish Office | |
| 스코틀랜드장관 | Secretary of State for Scotland | |
| 북아일랜드성 | the Northern Ireland Office | |
| 북아일랜드장관 | Secretary of State for Northern Ireland | |
| 법무성 | Law Officer's Department | |
| 법무성장관 | Attorny General | |
| 해외개발성 | Overseas Development Administration | |
| 해외개발장관 | Minister of State for Overseas Development Administration | |
| 행정처 | Office of Public [Civil] Service | |
| 행정처장관 | Minister for the Civil Service | |
| 국새상서(國璽尙書)부 | Privy Council Office | |
| 국새상서부장관 | Lord Privy Seal and Leader of the House of Lords | |
| 내셔널 헤러티지성 | Department of National Heritage | |
| 내셔널 헤러티지장관 | Secretary of State for National Heritage | |

# (9) 미·영의 주(州) 및 주요 도시명

## 1. 미국의 주(州)

네바다 Nevada (Nev., NV)
네브래스카 Nebraska (Neb., Nebr., NE)
노스다코타 North Dakota (N.D., N.Dak., ND)
노스캐롤라이나 North Carolina (N.C., NC)
뉴멕시코 New Mexico (N.M., N.Mex., NM)
뉴욕 New York (N.Y., NY)
뉴저지 New Jersey (N.J., NJ)
뉴햄프셔 New Hampshire (N.H., NH)
델라웨어 Delaware (Del., DE)
로드아일랜드 Rhode Island (R.I., RI)
루이지애나 Louisiana (La., LA)
매사추세츠 Massachusetts (Mass., MA)
메릴랜드 Maryland (Md., MD)
메인 Maine (Me., ME)
몬태나 Montana (Mont., MT)
미네소타 Minnesota (Minn., MN)
미시간 Michigan (Mich., MI)
미시시피 Mississippi (Miss., MS)
미주리 Missouri (Mo., MO)
버몬트 Vermont (Vt., VT)
버지니아 Virginia (Va., VA)
사우스다코타 South Dakota (S.D., S.Dak., SD)
사우스캐롤라이나 South Carolina (S.C., SC)
아이다호 Idaho (Id., Ida., ID)
아이오와 Iowa (Ia., IA)
아칸소 Arkansas (Ark., AR)
알래스카 Alaska (Alas., AK)
애리조나 Arizona (Ariz., AZ)
앨라배마 Alabama (Ala., AL)
오리건 Oregon (Ore., Oreg., OR)
오클라호마 Oklahoma (Okla., Ok)
오하이오 Ohio (O., OH)
와이오밍 Wyoming (Wyo., Wy., WY)
워싱턴 Washington (Wash., WA)
웨스트버지니아 West Virginia (W.Va., WV)
위스콘신 Wisconsin (Wis., Wisc., WI)
유타 Utah (Ut., UT)
인디애나 Indiana (Ind., IN)
일리노이 Illinois (Ill., IL)
조지아 Georgia (Ga., GA)
캔자스 Kansas (Kan., Kans., KS)
캘리포니아 California (Calif., Cal., CA)
켄터키 Kentucky (Ky., Ken., KY)
코네티컷 Connecticut (Conn., CT)
콜로라도 Colorado (Colo., Co)
테네시 Tennessee (Tenn., TN)
텍사스 Texas (Tex., TX)
펜실베이니아 Pennsylvania (Pa., Penn., Penna., PA)
플로리다 Florida (Fla., FL)
하와이 Hawaii (Hi., HI)

## 2. 미국의 주요 도시

내슈빌 Nashville (Tenn.)
노퍽 Norfolk (Va.)
뉴어크 Newark (N.J.)
뉴올리언스 New Orleans (La.)
뉴욕 New York (N.Y.)
뉴헤이븐 New Haven (Conn.)
댈러스 Dallas (Tex.)
덴버 Denver (Colo.)
디트로이트 Detroit (Mich.)
라스베이거스 Las Vegas (Nev.)
로스앤젤레스 Los Angeles (Calif.)
로체스터 Rochester (N.Y.)
롱비치 Long Beach (Calif.)
마이애미 Miami (Fla.)
멤피스 Memphis (Tenn.)
모빌 Mobile (Ala.)
미니애폴리스 Minneapolis (Minn.)
밀워키 Milwaukee (Wis.)
버밍햄 Birmingham (Ala.)
버펄로 Buffalo (N.Y.)
보스턴 Boston (Mass.)
볼티모어 Baltimore (Md.)
샌디에이고 San Diego (Calif.)
샌안토니오 San Antonio (Tex.)
샌프란시스코 San Francisco (Calif.)
세인트루이스 St. Louis (Mo.)
세인트폴 St. Paul (Minn.)
세인트피터즈버그 St. Petersburg (Fla.)
솔트레이크시티 Salt Lake City (Ut.)
스프링필드 Springfield (Mass.)
시애틀 Seattle (Wash.)
시카고 Chicago (Ill.)
신시내티 Cincinnati (O.)
애크런 Akron (O.)
애틀랜타 Atlanta (Ga.)
앨버커키 Albuquerque (N.Mex.)
앵커리지 Anchorage (Alas.)
엘패소 El Paso (Tex.)
오마하 Omaha (Nebr.)
오클랜드 Oakland (Calif.)
워싱턴 Washington (D.C.)

인디애나폴리스 Indianapolis (Ind.)
잭슨 Jackson (Miss.)
잭슨빌 Jacksonville (Fla.)
컬럼버스 Columbus (O.)
캔자스시티 Kansas City (Kans.)
클리블랜드 Cleveland (O.)
탬파 Tampa (Fla.)
포트워스 Fort Worth (Tex.)
포틀랜드 Portland (Oreg.)
피닉스 Phoenix (Ariz.)
피츠버그 Pittsburgh (Penn.)
필라델피아 Philadelphia (Penn.)
호놀룰루 Honolulu (Hi.)
휴스턴 Houston (Tex.)

### 3. 영국의 주요 주(州)

#### 잉글랜드(England)

그레이터맨체스터 Greater Manchester
글로스터셔 Gloucestershire
노샘프턴셔 Northamptonshire
노섬벌랜드 Northumberland
노스요크셔 North Yorkshire
노팅엄셔 Nottinghamshire
노퍽 Norfolk
더럼 Durham
더비셔 Derbyshire
데번 Devon
도싯 Dorset
랭커셔 Lancashire
런던 Greater London
레스터셔 Leicestershire
링컨셔 Lincolnshire
머지사이드 Merseyside
버크셔 Berkshire
버킹엄셔 Buckinghamshire
베드퍼드셔 Bedfordshire
사우스요크셔 South Yorkshire
서리 Surrey
서머싯 Somerset
서퍽 Suffolk
셀럽 Salop
스태퍼드셔 Staffordshire
아일오브와이트 Isle of Wight
에식스 Essex
에이번 Avon
옥스퍼드셔 Oxfordshire
워릭셔 Warwickshire
웨스트미들랜드 West Midlands
웨스트서식스 West Sussex
웨스트요크셔 West Yorkshire
윌트셔 Wiltshire
이스트서식스 East Sussex
체셔 Cheshire
컴브리아 Cumbria
케임브리지셔 Cambridgeshire
켄트 Kent
콘월 Cornwall
클리블랜드 Cleveland
타인 위어 Tyne and Wear
헤리퍼드 우스터 Hereford and Worcester
하트퍼드셔 Hertfordshire
햄프셔 Hampshire
험버사이드 Humberside

#### 스코틀랜드 (Scotland)

그램피언 Grampian
덤프리스 갤러웨이 Dumfries and Galloway
로디언 Lothian
보더스 Borders
센트럴 Central
셰틀랜드 Shetland
스트래스클라이드 Strathclyde
오크니 Orkney
웨스턴 아일스 Western Isles
테이사이드 Tayside
파이프 Fife
하일랜드 Highland

#### 웨일스(Wales)

궨트 Gwent
디퍼드 Dyfed
미드글러모건 Mid-Glamorgan
사우스글러모건 South Glamorgan
웨스트글러모건 West Glamorgan
클루이드 Clwyd
귀네드 Gwynedd
포이스 Powys

#### 북아일랜드(Northern Ireland)

노스다운 버로 North Down Borough
뉴리 몬 Newry and Mourne
뉴튼애비 Newtownabbey
다운 Down
단개넌 Dungannon
란 버로 Larne Borough
러머배디 Limavady
런던데리 시티 Londonderry City
리즈번 버로 Lisburn Borough
마러펠트 Magherafelt
모이얼 Moyle
밸리머니 Ballymoney
밸리미나 버로 Ballymena Borough
베인브리지 Banbridge
벨파스트 시티 Belfast City
스트러밴 Strabane
아마 Armagh

아즈 버로 Ards Borough
앤트림 Antrim
오모 Omagh
캐릭퍼거스 Carrickfergus
캐슬레이 Castlereagh
콜레인 버로 Coleraine Borough
쿡스타운 Cookstown
크레이개번 Craigavon
퍼매너 Fermanagh

4. 영국의 주요 도시

글래스고 Glasgow Scot.
노리치 Norwich Eng.
노샘프턴 Northampton Eng.
노팅엄 Nottingham Eng.
뉴캐슬어폰타인 Newcastle-upon-Tyne Eng.
더비 Derby Eng.
던디 Dundee Scot.
런던 London Eng.
런던데리 Londonderry N.Ire.
레스터 Leicester Eng.
리버풀 Liverpool Eng.
리즈 Leeds Eng.
맨체스터 Manchester Eng.
버밍엄 Birmingham Eng.
벨파스트 Belfast N.Ire.
본머스 Bournemouth Eng.
볼튼 Bolton Eng.
브라이튼 Brighton Eng.
브래드포드 Bradford Eng.
브리스톨 Bristol Eng.
블랙풀 Blackpool Eng.
사우샘프턴 Southampton Eng.
셰필드 Sheffield Eng.
스완지 Swansea Wales
애버딘 Aberdeen Scot.
에든버러 Edinburgh Scot.
옥스퍼드 Oxford Eng.
요크 York Eng.
윈체스터 Winchester Eng.
입스위치 Ipswich Eng.
카디프 Cardiff Wales
캔터베리 Canterbury Eng.
케임브리지 Cambridge Eng.
코번트리 Coventry Eng.
포츠머스 Portsmouth Eng.
플리머스 Plymouth Eng.
헬리팩스 Halifax Eng.
헐 Hull Eng.

## (10) 주요국 통화 일람

| 국 명 | | 통 화 단 위 | 약 호 |
|---|---|---|---|
| 그리스 | (Greece) | Drachma=100 Lepta | Dr |
| 남아프리카 공화국 | (South Africa) | Rand=100 Cents | R |
| 네덜란드 | (Netherlands) | Guilder=100 Cents | D.GI |
| 노르웨이 | (Norway) | Krone=100 Öre | NKr |
| 뉴질랜드 | (New Zealand) | Dollar=100 Cents | NZ $ |
| 덴마크 | (Denmark) | Krone=100 Öre | DKr |
| 독일 | (Germany) | Mark=100 Pfennigs | DM |
| 라오스 | (Laos) | Kip=100 Ats | K |
| 러시아 | (Russia) | Ruble=100 Kopecks | R |
| 말레이시아 | (Malaysia) | Ringgit=100 Sen | M$ |
| 멕시코 | (Mexico) | Peso=100 Centavos | P |
| 미얀마 | (Myanmar) | Kyat=100 Pyas | K |
| 미합중국 | (United States) | Dollar=100 Cents | $ |
| 베트남 | (Viet Nam) | Dong=10 Hao | D |
| 브라질 | (Brazil) | Cruzeiro=100 Centavos | Cr $ |
| 사우디아라비아 | (Saudi Arabia) | Riyal=100 halalas | SRI |
| 스웨덴 | (Sweden) | Krona=100 Öre | SKr |
| 스위스 | (Switzerland) | Franc=100 Centimes | SFr |
| 스페인 | (Spain) | Peseta=100 Centimos | Pta |
| 영국 | (United Kingdom) | Pound=100 Pence | £ |
| 오스트레일리아 | (Australia) | Dollar=100 Cents | A$ |
| 이라크 | (Iraq) | Dinar=1,000 Fils | ID |
| 이란 | (Iran) | Rial=100 Dinars | R |

| 국 명 | | 통 화 단 위 | 약 호 |
|---|---|---|---|
| 이집트 | (Egypt) | Pound=100 Piasters<br>=1,000 Milliemes | £E |
| 이탈리아 | (Italy) | Lira=100 Centesimi | L |
| 인도 | (India) | Rupee=100 Paise | Re |
| 인도네시아 | (Indonesia) | Rupiah=100 Sen | Rp |
| 일본 | (Japan) | 円, Yen'=10 錢 Sen | ¥ |
| 중국 | (China) | 元, Yuan=10 角 Chiao<br>=100 分 Fen | Y |
| 캐나다 | (Canada) | Dollar=100 Cents | Can $ |
| 쿠웨이트 | (Kuwait) | Dinar=1,000 Fils | KD |
| 타이 | (Thailand) | Baht=100 Satang | B |
| 터키 | (Turkey) | Lira=100 Kurus | LT |
| 파키스탄 | (Pakistan) | Rupee=100 Paisa | P.Re |
| 포르투갈 | (Portugal) | Escudo=100 Centavos | Esc |
| 프랑스 | (France) | Franc=100 Centimes | Fr |
| 필리핀 | (Philippines) | Peso=100 Centavos | P |

## (11) 세계 주요 도시 표준시 대조표

※ 하루를 24시간으로 표시

| 런던·GMT (A) | 베를린·파리 (B) | 카이로·아테네 (C) | 바그다드 (D) | 카라치 (E) | 방콕 (F) | 홍콩 (G) | 서울 (H) | 시드니 (I) | 호놀룰루 (J) | 샌프란시스코 (K) | 시카고·달라스 (L) | 뉴욕 (M) | 리우데자네이루 (N) |
|---|---|---|---|---|---|---|---|---|---|---|---|---|---|
| 15 | 16 | 17 | 18 | 20 | 22 | 23 | 0 | 1 | 5 | 7 | 9 | 10 | 12 |
| 16 | 17 | 18 | 19 | 21 | 23 | 24 | 1 | 2 | 6 | 8 | 10 | 11 | 13 |
| 17 | 18 | 19 | 20 | 22 | 24 | 1 | 2 | 3 | 7 | 9 | 11 | 12 | 14 |
| 18 | 19 | 20 | 21 | 23 | 1 | 2 | 3 | 4 | 8 | 10 | 12 | 13 | 15 |
| 19 | 20 | 21 | 22 | 24 | 2 | 3 | 4 | 5 | 9 | 11 | 13 | 14 | 16 |
| 20 | 21 | 22 | 23 | 1 | 3 | 4 | 5 | 6 | 10 | 12 | 14 | 15 | 17 |
| 21 | 22 | 23 | 24 | 2 | 4 | 5 | 6 | 7 | 11 | 13 | 15 | 16 | 18 |
| 22 | 23 | 24 | 1 | 3 | 5 | 6 | 7 | 8 | 12 | 14 | 16 | 17 | 19 |
| 23 | 24 | 1 | 2 | 4 | 6 | 7 | 8 | 9 | 13 | 15 | 17 | 18 | 20 |
| 24 | 1 | 2 | 3 | 5 | 7 | 8 | 9 | 10 | 14 | 16 | 18 | 19 | 21 |
| 1 | 2 | 3 | 4 | 6 | 8 | 9 | 10 | 11 | 15 | 17 | 19 | 20 | 22 |
| 2 | 3 | 4 | 5 | 7 | 9 | 10 | 11 | 12 | 16 | 18 | 20 | 21 | 23 |
| 3 | 4 | 5 | 6 | 8 | 10 | 11 | 12 | 13 | 17 | 19 | 21 | 22 | 24 |
| 4 | 5 | 6 | 7 | 9 | 11 | 12 | 13 | 14 | 18 | 20 | 22 | 23 | 1 |
| 5 | 6 | 7 | 8 | 10 | 12 | 13 | 14 | 15 | 19 | 21 | 23 | 24 | 2 |
| 6 | 7 | 8 | 9 | 11 | 13 | 14 | 15 | 16 | 20 | 22 | 24 | 1 | 3 |
| 7 | 8 | 9 | 10 | 12 | 14 | 15 | 16 | 17 | 21 | 23 | 1 | 2 | 4 |
| 8 | 9 | 10 | 11 | 13 | 15 | 16 | 17 | 18 | 22 | 24 | 2 | 3 | 5 |
| 9 | 10 | 11 | 12 | 14 | 16 | 17 | 18 | 19 | 23 | 1 | 3 | 4 | 6 |
| 10 | 11 | 12 | 13 | 15 | 17 | 18 | 19 | 20 | 24 | 2 | 4 | 5 | 7 |
| 11 | 12 | 13 | 14 | 16 | 18 | 19 | 20 | 21 | 1 | 3 | 5 | 6 | 8 |
| 12 | 13 | 14 | 15 | 17 | 19 | 20 | 21 | 22 | 2 | 4 | 6 | 7 | 9 |
| 13 | 14 | 15 | 16 | 18 | 20 | 21 | 22 | 23 | 3 | 5 | 7 | 8 | 10 |
| 14 | 15 | 16 | 17 | 19 | 21 | 22 | 23 | 24 | 4 | 6 | 8 | 9 | 11 |

(1) 위 표 안의 숫자는 서울(한국 표준시)을 기준으로 한, 각지의 동일 날짜의 시간; 고딕체 숫자는 하루 전 날짜의 시간을 나타낸다. GMT는 그리니치 표준시.

(2) 여름에는 나라에 따라 서머타임을 실시하는 곳이 있으므로 요주의.

(3) 위 표에 없는 도시는 아래 지명을 참조. ( )의 알파벳은 위 표 상단에 명시된 지명과 같다는 뜻. +30, +60은 해당 숫자에 30분 또는 60분을 더한 시간, −30은 30분을 뺀 시간을 나타낸다.

나이로비(D)
뉴델리(E)+30
뉴올리언스(L)
도쿄/동경(H)
디트로이트(M)
로마(B)
로스앤젤레스(K)
리스본(A)
마닐라(G)
마드리드(B)
마이애미(M)
멕시코시티(L)
모스크바(D)
몬트리올(M)
베를린(B)
베이루트(C)

베이징(G)
벤쿠버(K)
보스턴(M)
봄베이(E)+30
부다페스트(B)
부에노스아이레스(N)
브뤼셀(B)
빈(B)
상파울루(N)
상하이(G)
세인트피터즈버그(D)
스톡홀름(B)
시애틀(K)
싱가포르(G)
암스텔담(B)
앙카라(C)

앵커리지(J)+60
양곤(F)−30
오슬로(B)
오타와(M)
와르소(B)
워싱턴(디씨)(M)
자카르타(F)
캔버러(I)
캘커타(E)+30
코펜하겐(B)
콜롬보(E)+30
프라하(B)
하노이(F)
헬싱키(C)

## (12) 지방 행정 단위의 영어 표기

행정자치부 1995.2

| 지방 행정 단위명 | 사 용 구 분 | 영 어 표 기 | 비 고 |
|---|---|---|---|
| 서울 특별시 | 주소로 사용시 | Seoul City(서울 시티) | |
| | 기관 명칭 | Seoul Metropolitan City<br>(서울 메트로폴리탄 시티) | |
| ○○광역시 | 주소로 사용시 | ○○ City (○○ 시티) | |
| | 기관 명칭 | ○○ Metropolitan City<br>(○○ 메트로폴리탄 시티) | |
| ○○도 | | ○○ Province (○○ 프라빈스) | |
| ○○시 | | ○○ City (○○ 시티) | |
| ○○군 | | ○○ County (○○ 카운티) | |
| ○○구 | 주소로 사용시<br>※특별시·광역시 구별 없이 | ○○ District (○○ 디스트릭트) | |
| | 기관 명칭<br>• 자치구<br>• 일반구 | ○○ Metropolitan District<br>○○ District | |

# (13) 한국 전통 식품의 영어명 표기 방법

농림부 1994. 12

| 부류 | 식 품 명 | 영 어 표 기 | 비 고 |
|---|---|---|---|
| 김치 | 깍두기김치 | Kimchi (Cubed radish kimchi) | 김치류는 Kimchi로 표기 통일하고 ( ) 안에 품목명을 영어로 병기 |
| | 나박김치 | Kimchi (Watery kimchi) | |
| | 동치미김치 | Kimchi (Watery radish kimchi) | |
| | 배추김치 | Kimchi (Cabbage kimchi) | |
| | 무청김치 | Kimchi (Radish leaf kimchi) | |
| | 유채김치 | Kimchi (Rape leaf kimchi) | |
| | 갓잎김치 | Kimchi (Mustard leaf kimchi) | |
| | 갓줄기김치 | Kimchi (Mustard stem kimchi) | |
| 장 | 고추장 | Korean hot pepper paste(Kochujang) | 외국의 hot sauce, chilli sauce와 구별표기 |
| | 간장 | Soy sauce | ( )에 품목명을 소리나는 대로 영어로 표기 |
| | 된장 | Soybean paste (Toenjang) | |
| | 청국장 | Soybean paste (Ch'ŏnggugjang) | |
| 죽 | 호박죽 | Pumpkin soup powder | 분말죽류: soup powder 죽(물이 포함된 것): soup |
| | 들깨죽 | Perilla soup powder | |
| | 쌀죽 | Rice soup powder | |
| | 현미죽 | Brown rice soup powder | |
| | 찹쌀죽 | Sweet rice soup powder | |
| | 율무죽 | Job's tears soup powder | |
| | 단팥죽 | Red bean soup powder | |
| 국수 | 즉석면(라면) | Instant noodles | Noodle로 표기 통일하고 메밀냉면만 vermicelli로 구별 표기 |
| | 쑥국수 | Mugwort noodles | |
| | 칡국수 | Arrowroot noodles | |
| | 도토리국수 | Acorn noodles | |
| | 메밀국수 | Buckwheat noodles | |
| | 쌀국수 | Rice noodles | |
| | 감자국수 | Potato noodles | |
| | 메밀냉면 | Buckwheat vermicelli | |
| 묵 | 메밀묵 | Buckwheat curd | 묵류는 curd로 통일 표기 |
| | 도토리묵 | Acorn curd | |
| 미숫가루 | 쌀미숫가루 | Parched rice powder | Parched+품목명+powder로 통일 표기 |
| | 찹쌀 〃 | Parched sweet rice powder | |
| | 보리 〃 | Parched barley powder | |
| | 쌀보리〃 | Parched naked barley powder | |
| | 수수 〃 | Parched sorghum powder | |
| | 조 〃 | Parched millet powder | |
| 건채류 | 무말랭이 | Dried radish slice | Dried+품목명+slice로 통일 표기 |
| | 호박고지 | Dried squash/pumpkin slice | |
| | 가지말랭이 | Dried eggplant slice | |
| | 박고지 | Dried gourd slice | |
| | 토란말랭이 | Dried taro stem slice | |
| | 도라지말랭이 | Dried bellflower root slice | |
| | 산채나물 | Edible greens | |
| | 실고추 | Shredded red pepper | |

| 부류 | 식 품 명 | 영 어 표 기 | 비 고 |
|---|---|---|---|
| 절임 | 단무지 | Radish pickle | 품목+pickle로 통일 표기 |
| | 오이지 | Cucumber pickle | |
| | 염교 | Scallion pickle | |
| | 달래지 | Wild garlic pickle | |
| | 깻잎지 | Perilla leaf pickle | |
| 음료 | 식혜 | Rice nectar (Shikhye) | 쌀알이 포함되어 nectar로 표기 |
| | 수정과 | Sweet cinnamon punch | |
| | 소주 | Soju | 수정과는 건물이 포함되지 않으므로 punch로 표기 |
| | 약주 | Rice wine (clear) | |
| | 탁주 | Rice wine (cloudy) | |
| 차류 | 계피차 | Cinnamon tea | 품목명+tea로 통일 표기 |
| | 구기자차 | Boxthron tea | |
| | 치커리차 | Chicory tea | |
| | 컴프리차 | Comfry tea | |
| | 유자차 | Citron tea | |
| | 인삼차 | Korean ginseng tea | 한국 인삼을 강조 표기 |
| | 녹차 | Green tea | |
| | 감잎차 | Persimmon leaf tea | |
| | 홍차 | Black tea | |
| | 옥수수차 | Corn tea | |
| 해조류 | 말린김 | Dried laver | 돌김은 양식이 아닌 자연산 김이므로 stone보다는 natural이 적합 |
| | 조미김 | Seasoned, roasted laver | |
| | 돌김 | Natural laver | |
| | 미역 | Sea mustard | |
| | 염장미역 | Salted sea mustard | |
| | 미역튀각 | Fried sea mustard | fried+품목명으로 통일 표기 |
| | 다시마튀각 | Fried sea tangle | |
| | 건파래 | Dried sea lettuce | |
| | 말린다시마 | Dried sea tangle | |
| | 다시마말이 | Rolled sea tangle | |
| 젓갈류 | 새우젓 | Salted shrimp | 젓갈류에는 fermented란 표기없이 Salted+품목명으로 통일 표기 |
| | 멸치젓 | Salted anchovy | |
| | 명란젓 | Salted pollack egg | |
| | 창난젓 | Salted viscera | |
| | 밴댕이젓 | Salted shad | |
| | 황새기젓 | Salted sword fish | |
| | 굴젓 | Salted oyster | |
| | 전복젓 | Salted abalone | |
| | 조개젓 | Salted clam | |
| | 게젓 | Salted crab | 액젓의 경우 품목명+sauce로 통일 표기 |
| | 멸치액젓 | Anchovy sauce | |
| 한과류 | 강정 | Korean cracker(Kangjŏng) | |
| | 유과 | Korean cracker(Yugwa) | |
| | 약과 | Korean cracker(Yakgwa) | |
| | 전병 | Korean cracker(Chŏnbyŏng) | |
| | 산자 | Korean cracker(Sanja) | |
| | 야채만두 | Vegetable dumpling | Dumpling으로 표기하되 내용물의 영어명을 그 앞에 |
| | 쇠고기만두 | Beef dumpling | |

| 부류 | 식 품 명 | 영 어 표 기 | 비 고 |
|---|---|---|---|
| 만두류 | 돼지고기만두 | Pork dumpling | 표기 |
| | 꿩만두 | Pheasant dumpling | |
| | 김치만두 | Kimchi dumpling | |
| 기타 | 감식초 | Persimmon vinegar | |
| | 죽염 | Salt roasted in bamboo | |
| | 물엿 | Dextrose syrup | |
| | 삼계탕 | Chicken stew with ginseng | |
| | 엿기름 | Malt | |
| | 누룽지 | Nurungji(Roasted cooking rice) | |

## (14) 잘못된 우리식 영어 표현들

우리식으로 꾸며 만들어진 영어의 낱말들을 순수한 영어로 잘못 알고 사용하는 경우가 많다. 대표적인 몇 가지를 열거해 본다.

| 우리말 표현 | 우리식 영어 표현 | 올바른 영어 표현 |
|---|---|---|
| 가솔린 스탠드 | gasoline+stand | filling station; gas station; 《영》 petrol station |
| 골든 아워 | golden+hour | prime (television) time |
| 골인 | goal+in | reach the finish (line); get 〔make, score〕 a goal; get married |
| 덤프카 | dump+car | dump truck; 《영》 dump lorry |
| 모닝 서비스 | morning+service | special rate in the morning |
| 백미러 | back+mirror | rearview mirror; 《영》 driving mirror |
| 샐러리맨 | salary+man | office 〔white-collar〕 worker |
| 애프터 서비스 | after+service | after-sales service; repair service |
| 오더 메이드 | order+made | made-to-order; custom-made |
| 오피스 레이디 | office+lady | (woman) office worker |
| 올드 미스 | old+Miss | old maid; unmarried woman |
| 팬티 스타킹 | panty+stocking | (a pair of ) panty hose |
| 테이블 스피치 | table+speech | (after-dinner) speech |

## (15) 무역 용어 및 약어표

| Korean(국어) | English(영어) | Abbreviation(약어) |
|---|---|---|
| 가격 | price; quotation; value | pr.; quotn.; val. |
| 가격할인 | reduction | redn.; redu. |
| 각서장(覺書狀) | memorandum book | M.B. |
| 감정(鑑定) | surveying | surv. |
| 감정인(人) | surveyor | surv. |
| 같은 곳〔책, 페이지, 장〕에서 | ibidem《Latin》—from the same source | Ibid.; Ib. |
| 같이, 동(同) | idem《Latin》—the same | id. |
| 개량(改良) | Improvement | Imp. |
| 개인계정(計定) | Private account | P/A; p.a. |
| 거래 | transaction(s) | trans. |

| Korean(국어) | English(영어) | Abbreviation(약어) |
|---|---|---|
| 검사필(畢) | Examined | Exd. |
| 검증(檢證) | verification | verif. |
| 견본 | pattern | patt. |
| 견적 | estimate | Est. |
| 경유(經由) | through | thro. |
| 경제개발위원회《미》 | Committee for Economic Development | CED |
| 경제자문위원회《미》 | Council of Economic Advisers | CEA |
| 경제재정위원회 | Economic and Finance Committee | E.F.C. |
| 경제협력국《미》 | Economic Cooperation Administration | E.C.A. |
| 계상필(計上畢) | Figured | figd. |
| 계약 | contract | Cont.; Contr. |
| 계약서 | Agreement | Agmt. |
| 계정(計定) | account | ac; a/c; acct. |
| 계정서(書) | Statement of account | S/a |
| 계정지급필(畢) | account paid | A/P |
| 곤포(梱包) | bales | B.; B/ |
| 공동계산; 조합계산 | Joint Account | J/A; J.A.; Jt. a/c |
| 공동해손(共同海損)《保險》 | General Average | G/A; G.A.; g.a. |
| 공동해손부담보(不擔保)《保險》 | Free of General Average | F.G.A.; f.g.a. |
| 공매(公賣) | public sale | P/S. |
| 공문서류 | official documents | O.D. |
| 공시(公示); 게시; 보고 | bulletin | bul. |
| 공인생명보험회사 | Chartered Life Underwriter | C.L.U. |
| 공인회계사 | Certified Public Accountant | C.P.A. |
| 공장 | manufactory | manuf. |
| 공증인(公證人) | notary public | N.P. |
| 공하(空荷)운임 | Dead Freight | D.F.; D/f; D.Frt. |
| 관세 및 무역에 관한 일반협정 | General Agreement on Tariff & Trade | G.A.T.T. |
| 광고 | advertisement(s) | ad.; advts. |
| 교환 | exchange | Ex; ex.; exch. |
| 구(舊)용선(傭船)계약 | old charter | O/C; o.c. |
| 구(舊)조건 | old terms | O/T; O.t. |
| 구입필(購入畢) | bought | Bght. |
| 구조화물차인잔고 (救助貨物差引殘高) | salvage loss | S.L. |
| 국(局) | bureau | bur. |
| 국제결제은행 | Bank for International Settlements | B.I.S. |
| 국제무역기관 | International Trade Organization | I.T.O. |
| 그램 | gram(me); Gram(me) | gr.; Grm. |
| 그레인(=0.064g) | grains (weight) | gr. |
| 그로스《12타(打)》; 대(大) 그로스《12그로스》 | gross; Great Gross | gr.; grs.; G.Gr. |
| 그리니치 표준시 | Greenwich Mean Time | G.M.T. |
| 극상(極上) | best quality | XXXX. |
| 극상등《棉花》 | Fully good | F.g.; f.g. |
| 극상등 | superfine | super. |
| 극상의 보통품《棉花》 | Fully good ordinary | F.g.o.; f.g.o. |
| 극상의 중(中)《棉花》 | Fully good middling | F.g.m.; f.g.m. |
| 극상품 | superfine | sup. |

| Korean(국어) | English(영어) | Abbreviation(약어) |
|---|---|---|
| 금년에 | hoc anno《Latin》—in this year | h.a. |
| 금속화폐 | metallic currency | M/C; m.c. |
| 금액 | amount | amt. |
| 급(級) | Class | Cl. |
| 급행 | express | Exp.; exp.; X |
| 기간연장조항《保險》 | Continuance clause | C.c. |
| 기성(旣成)의 | ready-made | r.m. |
| 기업조합 | syndicate | synd. |
| 기입필(畢) | Entered | Entd. |
| 나포부담보(拿捕不擔保) | Free of Capture and Seizure | F.C. & S.; F.C.S.; f.c.s. |
| 낙찰 | knocked down | Kd. |
| 난(欄) | Column | Col. |
| 내외통상국(內外通商局)《미》 | Bureau of Foreign and Domestic Commerce | B.F.D.C. |
| 내용 | Content | Cont. |
| 노동조합 | trade union | t.u. |
| 높이 | Height; height | H.; ht. |
| 누손(漏損) | ullage | ull. |
| 단기(短期)어음 | Short bill | S.b. |
| 단독해손(海損) | Particular average | P.A.; P/a; p.a. |
| 단독해손담보 | subject to particular average; with average; with particular average | s.p.a.; W.A.; w.a,; W.P.A. |
| 단독해손부담보(不擔保)《保險》 | Free from Particular Average | F.P.A.; f.p.a. |
| 담보차입증; 예금증명서 | memorandum of deposit | M.D. |
| 당기(當期)중등품 | fair average quality of the season | F.a.q.s. |
| 당좌계정(當座計定) | Account Current; Current Account | A/C; Curt. Acct. |
| 대리권(權) | agency | agcy. |
| 대리영사 | Deputy Consul | D.C. |
| 대리인; 대변인 | attorney | atty. |
| 대리점(店) | agent; agency | Agt.; agcy. |
| 대변(貸邊) | Credit; Creditor | Cr. |
| 대변표 | Credit Note | C/N; C.N. |
| 대차대조표 | Balance Sheet | B/S; b/s |
| 도(度) | Degree | D. |
| 도난, 불착의 위험《保險》 | Theft, Pilferage & Non-delivery | T.P.N.D. |
| 도매(都賣) | wholesale | wh.; whol.; whsle. |
| 도착 | arrival | arr. |
| 도착예정시간 | estimated time of arrival | ETA |
| 도착필(畢) | arrived | arr. |
| 독일 화폐 | Reichsmark | R.m.; R. |
| 독점(獨占) | exclusive | excl. |
| 동등한 | equal; equivalent | eq. |
| 동봉물 | Enclosure; Enclosures | Enc(s); Encl(s); Encs. |
| 동부표준시《미》 | Eastern Standard Time | EST |
| 동시 신용장(信用狀) 개설 계정(計定) | Back-to-Back account | B.B. |
| 등록필(畢) | registered | reg.; regd. |

| Korean(국어) | English(영어) | Abbreviation(약어) |
|---|---|---|
| 마대(麻袋)《棉花》 | bale(s) | Bl(s) |
| 마력(馬力) | horse power | H.P.; h.p. |
| 만국전신암어 (萬國電信暗語)사용 | International Code Used | I.C.U. |
| 매물(賣物) | on sale | o/s |
| 매방(買方)선택 | Buyer's option | B.O. |
| 매상(賣上)계산서 | account sales | A/S; a/s |
| 매약필(賣約畢) | sold | sld. |
| 매우 양질 | very good quality | XXX. |
| 매입필(買入畢) | bought | Bt. |
| 매입자(買入者) | purchaser | pch.; pchsr. |
| 메모 | Memorandum | Mem; Memo. |
| 명기무(明記無) | not specified | n.s. |
| 무(無)배달 | no delivery | n/d; n.d. |
| 무(無)조건용선계약 | open charter | O/C; o.c. |
| 무역 | trading | trdg. |
| 무일부(無日附) | no date | n/d; n.d. |
| 무임(無賃)발송 | Free dispatch | f.d. |
| 미불(未拂) | outstanding | o/s |
| 미완(未完) | continued | Contd. |
| 바구니 | basket | Bkt. |
| 박리다매 | small profits and quick returns | S.P.Q.R. |
| 반 | Half | Hf. |
| 반환필(畢) | returned | red.; ret.; retd. |
| 받을어음 | Bills Receivable | B/R; B'REC |
| 발명자 | inventor | inv. |
| 발췌 | abstract statement; extract | Abs. Sta.; ext. |
| 발행 | Issue | I.; Iss. |
| 발행인(人)《어음》 | drawers | Dr(s). |
| 발행일결제거래 | when issued | w.i. |
| 배당금 | Dividend | D.; Div. |
| 백(百) | Centum; centum | C.; c. |
| 범선 | brig | br. |
| 법인조직; 회사《미》 | Incorporated | Inc. |
| 별송(別送) | extra | ext. |
| 보고(報告) | report | rpt. |
| 보세창고 | Bonded Warehouse | B.W. |
| 보증부(保證付) | Guaranteed; warranted | Gu.; wd. |
| 보통 | ordinary | ord.; ordy. |
| 보통품 | Common | Com. |
| 보험 | insurance | ins.; insce. |
| 보험계정(計定) | underwriting account | U/A; u.a. |
| 보험료 | premium | pm. |
| 보험업자 | underwriter | u/w |
| 본선(本船)수취증 | mate's receipt | M/R; M.R. |
| 본선도(本船渡) | Free on Board | F.O.B.; f.o.b. |
| 본점(本店) | Head Office | H.O. |
| 부(部); 과(課) | Department | Dept. |
| 부기 | book-keeping | B.K. |

| Korean(국어) | English(영어) | Abbreviation(약어) |
|---|---|---|
| 부당(不當)주문; 불량주문 | bad order | b.o. |
| 부동산 | estate | Est. |
| 부두도(埠頭渡) | Free on Quay | F.O.Q. |
| 부본(副本) | duplicate | Dup; dupl. |
| 부불(賦拂) | installment | inst. |
| 부셸 | bushel 《《미》2,150.41입방인치; 2,219.36입방인치》 | bush; bsh.; bu. |
| 부족 | shortage | shtg. |
| 분개장(分介帳)《簿記》 | Journal | J.; Jr. |
| 분배 | Division | Div. |
| 분손(分損)《保險》 | partial loss | p.l. |
| 불량 | no good | N.G.; n.g. |
| 비용 | expense | Exp.; exp |
| 비용무료 | Free of Charge | F.O.C.; f.o.c. |
| 비율 | rate | rt. |
| 사량(死量) | Dead Load | D.L. |
| 사본 | carbon copy; duplicate | C.C.; c.c.; Dup; Dupl. |
| 사본(寫本)배부처 | carbon copy | C.C.; c.c. |
| 사중(死重) | Dead Weight | D.W.; D/W |
| 사채(社債) | bond; Debenture | bd.; Deb. |
| 사채권(券) | Debenture | D. |
| 산업별노동조합회의 | Congress of Industrial Organization | CIO |
| 상공회의소 | Chamber of Commerce | C.C; C/c; C.of C. |
| 상기(上記) | supra (above) | sup. |
| 상등《棉花》 | Fully good | F.g.f; f.g.f. |
| 상선(商船) | mercantile marine | m.m. |
| 상선조약 | Merchant Shipping Act | M.S.A. |
| 상업; 통상 | Commerce | Com.; Comm. |
| 상업의 | Commercial | Cml. |
| 상자《박스》 | cases; Case; case | c/-; C.; c. |
| 상자《複數》 | Cases | C/S |
| 상표조례 | Merchandise Marks Act | M.M.A. |
| 상품 | goods; Merchandise | gds.; Mds.; Mdse. |
| 상품매상장(賣上帳) | sales book | S.B. |
| 상품목록 | catalog; catalogs | Cat.; Cats. |
| 상환 | reimbursement | rembt. |
| 생명보험증권 | Life Insurance Policy | L.I.P. |
| 서류 | documents | Doc.; doc.; doct. |
| 서류첨부 | Document(s) attached | Doc./attache |
| 서명 | signature; signed | sg.; sgd.; sig. |
| 선거인도(船渠引渡) | Free Docks | F/D; F.D. |
| 선명미상(船名未詳)보험증서《保險》 | Floating Policy | F/P; F.P. |
| 선물(先物) | Forward Delivery; futures | F/D; Fut. |
| 선박 및 적하(積荷) | ship and goods | S.G. |
| 선복인도(船腹引渡) | Free from alongside | F.f.a. |
| 선불필(畢) | prepaid | ppd. |
| 선서서(宣誓書) | affidavit | afft. |

| Korean(국어) | English(영어) | Abbreviation(약어) |
|---|---|---|
| 선적(船積); 적송품(積送品) | shipment | ship.; shipmt.; shipt. |
| 선적불(船積拂) | Cash on Shipment | C.O.S. |
| 선적전(前) 현금불(拂) | Cash before delivery | C.B.D. |
| 선적지시서 | shipping order | S.O.; s.o. |
| 선측인도 | Free alongside ship | F.A.S.; f.a.s. |
| 선하(船荷)증권 | Bill of Lading | B/L; B/Ldg. |
| 선하증권첨부 일람출급어음 | Sight draft, bill of lading attached | S.D.B.L. |
| 설립필(畢) | established | Estd.; Estab. |
| 세(稅) | tax | tx. |
| 세계산업노동자 | Industrial Workers of the World | I.W.W. |
| 세관 | Customs House | C.H. |
| 세금지급필(支給畢) | Duty Paid | D.P. |
| 세금환불 | Drawback | Dbk. |
| 센트 《미화폐》 | Cent; cent | C.; c. |
| 소포 | parcel | pcl. |
| 속(束); 묶음; 포(包) | bundle; bundles | bdl.; bdl/s |
| 속달 | express | Exp.; exp. |
| 손익(損益) | profit and loss | P.& L. |
| 손해면제 | Free of damage | f.o.d. |
| 송금 | remittance | rem.; remit.; remt. |
| 송장(送狀) | invoice | inv. |
| 수금인(收金人) | Collector | Colr. |
| 수량 | quantity | qty. |
| 수수료 | Commission | Com.; Comm. |
| 수수료포함 본선도(本船渡) | Free on board and Commission | F.O.B. & C. |
| 수입(輸入) | Import | Imp.; Impt. |
| 수입(收入) | income; revenue | in.; rev. |
| 수정한 | corrected | Cor. |
| 수출 | export | Exp.; exp. |
| 수출금융공사 | Export Finance Cooperation | E.F.C. |
| 수출상(商) | exporter | Exp.; exp. |
| 수취(受取) | receipt | rect.; recpt.; rept. |
| 수취계정(計定) | Accounts Receivable | A/cs Rec/ |
| 수취필(畢) | received | red.; recd.; rec'd. |
| 수표 | cheque; check; draft; giro 《Spanish》 | Chq.; Cheq.; dft.; g/ |
| 수하물 | luggage | lugg. |
| 순(純)중량 | net weight | n.wt. |
| 순익(純益) | net gain | N.G.; n.g. |
| 숫자 | figure | Fig. |
| 승인(承認) | acknowledgement; approval | ackgt.; ackmt.; appro. |
| 시(時); 시간 | hour; hours | h.; hr.; hrs. |
| 시가표(時價表) | price current | P/C |
| 시험필(試驗畢) | examined | Ex.; ex. |
| 신계정(新計定) | Compte Nouveau 《French》 | C.n. |

| Korean(국어) | English(영어) | Abbreviation(약어) |
|---|---|---|
| 신용장(信用狀) | Letter of Credit | L/C |
| 신주(新株) | new bond | N/B; N.B. |
| 실제중량 | actual weight | A/W |
| 아시아 극동 경제위원회 | Economic Commission for Asia and Far East | E.C.A.F.E. |
| 액면(額面) | face value | f.v. |
| 약(約) | about | abt. |
| 약속어음 | promissory note | P/N; p.n. |
| 약자(略字) | abbreviation | Abbr. |
| 약정(約定)의 | stipulated | stp. |
| 양질 | good quality | XX. |
| 양질의 | good | gd. |
| 양하비(揚荷費)선주(船主) 무(無)부담 | free out | f.o. |
| 양호품 | Good Merchantable Quality | G.M.Q. |
| 어음매입수권서(授權書) | Letter of Authority | L/A |
| 어음인수; 수주(受注) | acceptance | acpt. |
| 어음인수도(渡) | Documents against Acceptance | D/A |
| 어음장 | bill book | B.B. |
| 억류조항《保險》 | Detention Clause | D.C. |
| …에 대해서 | Against | C. |
| 연기(延期) | Deferred; extension | De.; Def.; ext. |
| 연기한 | extended | Ext. |
| 연방곡물보험회사《미》 | Federal Crop Insurance Corporation | F.C.I.C. |
| 연방준비은행《미》 | Federal Reserve Bank | F.R.B. |
| 열외(列外) | exception | exc. |
| 영국 세관 | Her Majesty's Customs | H.M.C. |
| 영국 톤; 대(大)톤《2,240lbs》 | Gross Ton | Grs.T. |
| 영사송장(領事送狀) | Consular Invoice | Con.Inv. |
| 영수증 | receipt | recpt.; rect.; rept. |
| 예(例) | example | Ex.; ex. |
| 예금계정(計定) | Deposit Account | D/A |
| 예금증서 | Deposit Receipt | D.R. |
| 예정(豫定)보험증권 | Open Policy | O.P. |
| 외국의 | foreign | F.O.R.; f.o.r. |
| 외국포획부담보(不擔保)《保險》 | Free from Foreign Capture | F.f.c. |
| 외국환(換) 어음 | Foreign Bill of Exchange | F.B.E. |
| 외지지급(外地支給)어음 | Foreign Domicile Bill | F.D.B. |
| 요구불《어음》 | Demand Draft | D/D; D.D.; d/Dft. |
| 요구불(要求拂) | on demand | o/d |
| 용선(傭船)계약 | Charter Party | C/p; C.Py. |
| 우등 | superior | sup. |
| 우선(優先) | preference; preferred | pr.; pref. |
| 우편요금 지급필(畢) | postage paid | p.p.; p.pd. |
| 우편료선불 | postpaid | ppd. |
| 우편사서함 | post office box | P.O.B. |
| 우편송금환 | Postal Money Order | P.M.O. |
| 우편환(換) | money order; postal order; post office order | m.o.; P.O.; p.o.o. |

| Korean(국어) | English(영어) | Abbreviation(약어) |
|---|---|---|
| 운송 | transportation | transp. |
| 운송비 | carriage | Carr. |
| 운송중(中) | in transit | in trans.; I.T. |
| 운임 | Freight | Frt.; frt.; fgt. |
| 운임, 보험료, 수수료 및 이자 포함가격 | Cost, Insurance, Freight, Commission and Interest | C.I.F.C. & I |
| 운임, 보험료, 수수료 포함 가격 | Cost, insurance, Freight, and Commission | C.I.F. & C |
| 운임, 보험료, 이자 및 환비용 포함가격 | Cost, insurance, freight, interest, and exchange | c.i.f.i. & e |
| 운임, 보험료 포함가격 | Cost, Insurance and Freight | C.I.F.; c.i.f. |
| 운임선급(先給) | Freight prepaid | Frt.ppd. |
| 운임선불(運賃先拂)로 | Carriage paid | Cge. pd.; Carr.pd. |
| 운임청구서 | Freight Bill | F.B. |
| 운임포함가격 | Cost and Freight | C. & F.; C & F |
| 원산국(原産國) | Country of Origin | C/O; C.O. |
| 원산지증명서 | Certificate of Origin | C/O; C.O. |
| 원장(元帳)《簿記》 | Ledger | L.; Led. |
| 원지도(原地渡) | Delivery on Field | D.O.F. |
| 원천과세주의 | pay as you earn; pay as you enter | P.A.Y.E. |
| 위임장 | Power of Attorney | P.A.; P/A; p.a. |
| 위탁품; 위탁판매품 | Consignment | Consgt.; Con'st |
| 위험(危險)담보 | against risk | a.r. |
| 위험회사부담 | Company's risk | C/R |
| 유한회사 | Limited | Ld.; Limd.; Lmd.; Ltd. |
| 은행 | bank | B.K.; Bnk. |
| 은행업무 | banking | bkg. |
| 은행통장 | bank book | B.B. |
| 은행할인 | Bank Discount | B/D |
| 은행환(換)어음 | Bank Draft | B/D |
| 응모(應募)자본금 | subscribed capital | subs. cap. |
| …의 계정(計定) | account of | A/O; A.O. |
| 의무; 채무 | obligation | ob. |
| …의 지시로[명령으로] | im Auftrag《German》—by order of | i.A. |
| 이류(二流); 이급선 | second class | B/ |
| 이배; 이중 | double | dbl. |
| 이월(移越) | brought down; Brought forward; Brought over; carried over | B/D; Bt.fwd.; B/o; c/o |
| 이자(利子) | interest | int. |
| 이자무(無)포함 | Not including Interest | Ex. INT. |
| 이중강도 | all of double strength | XX. |
| 이체필(移替畢) | transferred | transf'd |
| 익명의 | anonymous | anon. |
| 인도(引渡)《海運》 | delivery | Dely.; D/y |
| 인도부두 | Delivered docks | D/D |
| 인도시(時)지급 | pay on delivery | P.O.D. |
| 인도지시서《倉庫》 | Delivery Order | D/O; D.O. |
| 인도필(畢) | Delivered | Deld.; de'd |

| Korean(국어) | English(영어) | Abbreviation(약어) |
|---|---|---|
| 인도한 | delivered | D/d |
| 인수(引受)어음 | acceptance | acc. |
| 인수장(帳) | receipt book | R.B. |
| 인수필(畢)《어음의》 | Honored | Hon'd |
| 인수필(畢) | accepted | acc. |
| 인수후(後) …일《어음》 | days after acceptance | D.A.; d.a. |
| 일광절약시 | daylight-saving-time | d.s.t. |
| 일기장《簿記》 | Day Book | D.B. |
| 일등품 | A one; first class | A1 |
| 일람(一覽)출급어음 | sight draft | S/D; st.dft. |
| 일람불(一覽拂) | at sight | A/S; a/s |
| 일람후불(後拂) | After Sight | A/S; a/s |
| 일부후《어음》 | after date | A/D; a/d |
| 일하구량미달(一荷口量未達) | Less than carload lots | L.C.L.; l.c.l |
| 임명; 약속; 임무 | appointment | apmt. |
| 입항계(入港屆) | Bill of Entry | B/E; B.E. |
| 자금이 없음 | no funds | N/F; n/f |
| 자본; 자본주(株) | Capital stock | C.S. |
| 자본계정(計定) | Capital Account | C/A |
| 자본금 | capital | Cap. |
| 자산과 부채 | resources and liabilities | res'ces & lia'ties |
| 자산상태(資産狀態) | Financial Standing | Fin. Stng. |
| 자유무역부두(埠頭) | Free trade wharf | F.T.W. |
| 잔고(殘高) | balance | Bal.; B/ce |
| 잡비; 잡화(雜貨); 잡제품 | sundries | sdy.; sund.; sunds. |
| 장거리 전화 | long-distance telephone | L.D.Tel. |
| 재(再)보험 | reinsurance | R.I. |
| 재산목록; 재고품 | inventory | inv't.; invt. |
| 재항본선도(在港本船渡) | Free on Board, harbor | f.b.h. |
| 저당(抵當) | mortgage | mge.; mtg. |
| 적출(積出)통지서 | Shipping Note | S/N; S.N. |
| 적하비(積荷費) 선주(船主) 무(無)부담 | free in | f.i. |
| 전(全)위험담보《保險》 | Against All Risks (marine) | A.A.R. |
| 전(全)해손부담보(不擔保)《海上保險》 | Free of all average | F.A.A.; f.a.a. |
| 전기이월(前期移越) | brought forward | b/f |
| 전로수로(全路水路) 수송의 | all water | A/W |
| 전매특허 | patent | pat. |
| 전보 | telegram | Tgm. |
| 전부지급필(畢) | all paid | o.pa. |
| 전손(全損) | total loss | T.L. |
| 전손담보(擔保)《保險》 | All Risk | A.R. |
| 전손담보조건《海上保險》 | total loss only | T.L.O. |
| 전시(戰時)담보 | war risk | W/R; W.R. |
| 전신환(電信換) | telegraphic money order | T.M.O. |
| 전액불입필(全額拂入畢) | Fully Paid | F.Pd.; f.pd. |
| 전액지급필(畢) | fully paid | Fy.pd.; fy.pd. |

| Korean(국어) | English(영어) | Abbreviation(약어) |
|---|---|---|
| 정부 | Government | Govt. |
| 제일의; 최상의 | Prime | IA.; Ia. |
| 제조 | manufacture | manuf. |
| 제조업 | manufacturing | manuf.; mfr. |
| 제조자 | manufacturer | manuf. |
| 조수; 보조자 | assistant | asst. |
| 조직 | system | syst. |
| 조합 | partnership | ptn'rship |
| 조항 | Clause; Article | Cl.; Art. |
| 조회선(照會先) | reference | refce. |
| 좋은 상표 | a good brand | a.g.b. |
| 주문 | Order | O.; o. |
| 주문기장부(記帳簿) | order book | O.B. |
| 주문번호 | Order number | O/no.; ord.No. |
| 주소 | address | Add. |
| 주식 | share | sh.; shr. |
| 주식거래소 | Board; Stock Exchange | bd.; St.Ex. |
| 중개수수료 | brokerage | Brkage. |
| 중등(中等)《棉花》 | middle | mid. |
| 중등의 하(下)《棉花》 | low middling | l.mid.; l.m. |
| 중등품《棉花》 | middling | mid. |
| 중등품 | Fair average quality | F.a.q. |
| 중량 | weight | wgt. |
| 즉(卽) | id est《Latin》—that is | i.e. |
| 증가 | increase | Inc. |
| 증명 | certificate | Cert. |
| 증명필(畢) | certified | Cert. |
| 증명필송장(送狀) | Certified Invoice | Cert. inv. |
| 증표(證票) | voucher | vr. |
| 지국(支局) | sub office | S.O.; s.o. |
| 지급 | payment | pmt.; paymt.; paym't.; payt. |
| 지급거절《어음》 | non-payment | n/p |
| 지급도(支給渡)《어음》 | Documents against payment | D/P |
| 지급수취필(畢) | payment received | pr. |
| 지급어음 | Bills Payable | B/P; B.P.; B'PAY |
| 지급필(畢) | paid | pd. |
| 지불계정(計定) | Accounts Payable | A/cs Pay. |
| 지불도 일람불(支拂渡一覽拂) 어음 | Sight draft documents against payment | S/D D/P |
| 추심은행(推尋銀行) 지시서류도(指示書類渡) | Documents Against Discretion of Collecting Bank | D.A.D. |
| 지점 | branch | br. |
| 직선항(港) | direct port | d.p. |
| 진형(珍型); 변형 | Fancy | F'cy. |
| 차기(次期)이월 | Carried forward | C.F.; C/f; Carr; Fwd. |
| 차변(借邊) | debit; debtor | Debt.; dbt.; dt. |
| 차변표 | Debit Note | D/N |

| Korean(국어) | English(영어) | Abbreviation(약어) |
|---|---|---|
| 차용증 | I owe you | IOU |
| 착선인도(着船引渡) | free overside | f.o. |
| 참조 | Attention; Reference | Att.; Attn.; Ref. |
| 참조필(畢) | Referred | Ref. |
| 참조하다 | compare to; refer | cf. |
| 창고간(間)약관 | warehouse to warehouse | W/W; W.W. |
| 창고료 | storage | stge; stor. |
| 창고증권 《埠頭》 | Dock Warrant | D/W |
| 창고증권 | warehouse receipt; Warehouse Warrant | whs.rec.; W/R; W.R.; W/W; W.W. |
| 채권 | bond | bd. |
| 채무자 | debtor(s) | Dr(s). |
| 척도(尺度) | Gauge | G. |
| 철물(鐵物) | Hardware | Hawe. |
| 첨부서류 | Document attached | D/A; D.A.; d/a; d.a. |
| 청동(青銅) | bronze | br. |
| 초과정박; 체선료(滯船料) | demurrage | dem. |
| 초과지급 | overpaid | o.pd.; o/pd. |
| 초과청구; 적하(積荷)초과 | overcharge | o/c |
| 초과 통신료 지불필(畢) | extra message paid | X.M.P. |
| 총중량 | gross-weight | gr. wt. |
| 최대량 | maximum | max. |
| 추가(하다) | supplement | sup.; supp.; suppl. |
| 추미(追尾); 속행; 뒤따르는 | Follow up | F.up. |
| 추정전손(推定全損) | Constructive Total Loss | C.T.L. |
| 출납(현금)계(係) | cashier | Cash. |
| 출납계회계; 재무관; 경리부장 | treasurer | treas.; treasr. |
| 콜대부(貸付)(Call loan) | Demand Loan | D/L |
| 쿠폰무(無) | without coupon | ex. cp. |
| 탄창(炭倉)인도 | Free in bunker | f.i.b. |
| 통 | cask | c. |
| 통관(通關)하다 | Cleared | Cld. |
| 통상; 일반 | general | gen. |
| 통지 | advice | adv. |
| 통화 | Currency | cur.; Cy. |
| 특허청 | Patent Office | Pat.Off. |
| 판매서 | bill of sale | B/S; b/s |
| 표(俵); 곤(梱) | bales | B/; B. |
| 표준 | standard | std. |
| 품절 | out of stock | o/s |
| 품질 | quality | qlty. |
| 하등의 중 《棉花》 | Fully low middling | F.l.m.; f.l.m. |
| 하마차임(荷馬車賃) | Cartage | Cart. |
| 하물 | package | pkg.; pkge. |
| 하위의 | Junior | Jr.; jun.; junr.; jur. |
| 하주(荷主)위험 | Owner's risk | O/R; O.r.; o.r. |
| 하환(荷換)어음 | Documentary Draft | D/D; D.D. |
| 할인 | discount | D/C; dis; Disc.; Disct. |

| Korean(국어) | English(영어) | Abbreviation(약어) |
|---|---|---|
| 항(港) | harbor | h.; Hbr. |
| 항공선하(航空船荷)증권 | Airway Bill | A/B |
| 항로변경약관 | Deviation Clause | D/C |
| 항목; 품목 | item | it. |
| 항의서; 거절증서; 이의(異意) 제기; 해난보고서 | a protester; for protest | a.p. |
| 항해 | voyage | voy. |
| 해난(海難)신호 | Save our ship; Save our souls; Suspend other service | S.O.S. |
| 해상보험증권 | Marine Insurance Policy | M.I.P. |
| 해손(海損); 평균 | average | Av. |
| 헥타(면적) | hectare | ha. |
| 현금(지급) | ready money | r.m. |
| 현금(現金) | Cash | C. |
| 현금불(現金拂)주문 | Cash with Order | C.W.O. |
| 현금상환(相換)인도 | Cash on Delivery | C.O.D. |
| 현금어음 | cash order | c/o |
| 현금출납장(帳) | cash book | C/B |
| 현물매매조건 | Full out terms | F/O; F.O. |
| 현품(現品)인수 | Receipt of goods | R.O.G. |
| 협회 | association | Assn.; Asso. |
| 형제 | brother | br. |
| 형제 《商會名》 | brother; brothers | Bro.; Bros. |
| 혼합 | assortment | assmt. |
| 혼합한 | assorted | asstd. |
| 화물상환불(相換拂) | payable on receipt | P.O.R. |
| 화물운송장(狀) | way bill | W/B; W.B. |
| 화물인도 | Free on Truck | F.O.T.; f.o.t. |
| 화재보험증서 《保險》 | Fire Policy | F/P |
| 화차도(貨車渡) | Free on wagons | f.o.w. |
| 확정오퍼 | Firm offer | F.O. |
| 환(換) | exchange | Ex.; ex. |
| 환어음 | Bill of Exchange; Bills of Exchange; draft | B/E; B.E.; Bs/E; dft. |
| 회(會) | meeting | mtg. |
| 회계 | account | ac; a/c; acct. |
| 회계보고(報告) | Financial Statement | Fin. Stat. |
| 회답; 회답필 | answer; answered | ans. |
| 회사 | Company; Corporation 《미》 | Co.; Coy; Corp. |
| 회사연도 | Financial Year | Fin.Yer. |
| 회신 | return of post | R/P; R.P. |
| 회신료전납(全納) | reply paid | R/P; R.P. |
| 후(後) | after | aft. |

# (16) 불규칙 변화표

## 1. 형용사·부사

| 원 급 | 비 교 급 | 최 상 급 |
|---|---|---|
| bad 나쁜 | worse | worst |
| badly 나쁘게 | worse | worst |
| evil 사악한 | worse | worst |
| far 먼 (거리) | farther | farthest |
| far 먼 (정도) | further | furthest |
| good 좋은 | better | best |
| ill 나쁜 | worse | worst |
| late 늦은 (시간) | later | latest |
| late 늦은 (순서) | latter | last |
| little 적은 | less<br>lesser (적은 쪽의) | least |
| many 수가 많은 | more | most |
| much 양이 많은 | more | most |
| old 늙은 (노약·신구) | older | oldest |
| old 늙은 (형제·자매) | elder, older 《미》 | eldest, oldest 《미》 |
| well 잘 | better | best |

## 2. 동 사

현대 미국어 용법에 의한 변화를 주체로 보였다.
고딕은 중요한 단어.

| 현 재 | 과 거 | 과 거 분 사 | 현재분사 |
|---|---|---|---|
| **A** abide 머물다, 살다 | abode, abided | abode, abided | |
| **arise** 일어나다, 생기다 | **arose** | **arisen** [ərízn] | |
| **awake** 눈을 뜨다 | **awoke**, **awaked** | **awaked**, **awoke** | |
| **B** backbite 험구를 하다 | backbit | backbitten, backbit | |
| backslide 뒷걸음질 치다 | backslid | backslidden, backslid | |
| **be** (**am**, **is**, **are**)…이다 | **was**, **were** | **been** | |
| **bear**[1] 견디다, 나르다 | **bore** | **borne** | |
| **bear**[2] 낳다 | **bore** | **borne**, 《수동》 be **born**, be **borne** by | |
| **beat** 치다 | **beat** | **beaten** | |
| **become** …이 되다 | **became** | **become** | |
| befall 일어나다, 생기다 | befell | befallen | |
| beget 생기게 하다, 초래하다 | begot | begotten, begot | -tting |
| **begin** 시작하다, 시작되다 | **began** | **begun** | **-nning** |
| begird 둘러싸다, 에두르다 | begirt, begirded | begirt, begirded | |
| behold 보다, 바라보다 | beheld | beheld | |
| **bend** 구부리다, 구부러지다 | **bent** | **bent** | |
| bereave 빼앗다, 잃게 하다 | bereaved, bereft | bereaved, bereft | |
| beseech 청하다, 구하다 | besought | besought | |
| beset 포위하다, 둘러싸다 | beset | beset | -tting |
| bespeak 미리 요구하다 | bespoke | bespoken, bespoke | |
| bespread 전면에 퍼지게 하다 | bespread | bespread | |
| bestrew 흩뿌리다 | bestrewed | bestrewed, bestrewn | |
| bestride 걸터 타다 | bestrode | bestridden, bestrid | |

| 현 재 | 과 거 | 과 거 분 사 | 현재분사 |
|---|---|---|---|
| bet 걸다, 내기를 하다 | bet, betted | bet, betted | -tting |
| betake …로 향하다, 가다, 의지하다 | betook | betaken | |
| bethink 숙고하다 | bethought | bethought | |
| **bid** 명하다 | **bade**, **bid**, bad 《고》 | **bidden**, **bid** | **-dding** |
| **bind** 묶다, 동이다 | **bound** | **bound** | |
| **bite** 물다, 물어 뜯다 | **bit** | **bitten**, **bit** | |
| bleed 피가 나오다 | bled | bled | |
| blend 혼합하다 | blended, 《고》 blent | blended, 《고》 blent | |
| **bless** 은총을 내리다 | **blessed**, **blest** [blest] | **blessed**, **blest** [blest] | |
| **blow** 바람이 불다, 꽃이 피다 | **blew** | **blown** | |
| **break** 깨뜨리다, 부서지다 | **broke** | **broken**, broke 《고》 | |
| breed 새끼를 낳다 | bred | bred | |
| **bring** 갖고 오다 | **brought** | **brought** | |
| broadcast 방송하다 | -casted | -casted, broadcast 《고》 | |
| **build** 세우다, 조립하다 | **built** | **built** | |
| **burn** 타다, 태우다 | **burnt**, **burned** | **burnt**, **burned** | |
| **burst** 터지다, 터지게 하다 | **burst** | **burst** | |
| **buy** 사다 | **bought** | **bought** | |
| **C can** …할 수 있다 | **could** [kud] | —— | |
| **cast** 던지다 | **cast** | **cast** | |
| **catch** 잡다 | **caught** [kɔːt] | **caught** [kɔːt] | |
| chide 꾸짖다 | chided, chid | chided, chid, chidden | |
| **choose** 가리다, 선택하다 | **chose** | **chosen** | |
| cleave 쪼개(지)다, 갈라지다 | cleft, cleaved, clove | cleft, cleaved, cloven | |
| cling 달라붙다 | clung | clung | |
| **clothe** 옷을 입다 | **clothed**, 《고》 clad | **clothed**, 《고》 clad | |
| **come** 오다 | **came** | **come** | |
| **cost** 비용이 들다 | **cost** | **cost** | |
| **creep** 기다 | **crept** | **crept** | |
| crow (수탉이) 울다 | crowed, crew | crowed | |
| curse 저주하다 | cursed, curst | cursed, curst | |
| **cut** 자르다, 베다 | **cut** | **cut** | **-tting** |
| **D dare** 감히 …하다 | **dared**, 《고》 durst | **dared** | |
| deal 다루다, 관계하다 | dealt | dealt | |
| **dig** 파다 | **dug** | **dug** | **-gging** |
| **do, does** 하다, 행하다 | **did** | **done** | |
| **draw** 긋다, 그리다 | **drew** | **drawn** | |
| **dream** 꿈꾸다 | **dreamed**, **dreamt** [dremt] | **dreamed**, **dreamt** [dremt] | |
| **drink** 마시다 | **drank** | **drunk** | |
| **drive** 쫓다, 차를 몰다 | **drove** | **driven** [drívn] | |
| dwell 살다 | dwelt, dwelled | dwelt, dwelled | |
| **E eat** 먹다 | **ate** [미 eit/영 et] | **eaten** | |
| **F fall** 떨어지다 | **fell** | **fallen** | |
| **feed** 음식을 주다 | **fed** | **fed** | |
| **feel** 느끼다 | **felt** | **felt** | |
| **fight** 싸우다 | **fought** | **fought** | |
| **find** 발견하다 | **found** | **found** | |
| flee 도망치다 | fled | fled | |

| 현 재 | 과 거 | 과거분사 | 현재분사 |
|---|---|---|---|
| fling 내던지다 | flung | flung | |
| **fly** 날다 | **flew** | **flown** | |
| forbear 억제하다, 삼가다 | forbore | forborne | |
| **forbid** 금하다 | **forbade**, **forbad** | **forbidden** | **-dding** |
| forecast 예측하다 | forecast, forecasted | forecast, forecasted | |
| forego 버리다, 그만두다 | forewent | foregone | |
| foreknow 미리 알다 | foreknew | foreknown | |
| foresee 예견하다 | foresaw | foreseen | |
| foretell 예고하다 | foretold | foretold | |
| **forget** 잊다 | **forgot** | **forgotten**, **forgot** | **-tting** |
| forgive 용서하다 | forgave | forgiven | |
| forsake 저버리다 | forsook | forsaken | |
| forswear 맹세코 그만두다 | forswore | forsworn | |
| freeze 얼다, 얼리다 | froze | frozen | |
| G gainsay 반박하다 | gainsaid | gainsaid | |
| **get** 얻다 | **got** | **got**, **gotten** | -tting |
| gild 금박을 입히다 | gilded, gilt | gilded, gilt | |
| gird 허리를 띠 따위로 두르다 | girt, girded | girt, girded | |
| **give** 주다 | **gave** | **given** | |
| **go** 가다 | **went** | **gone** | |
| grave (모양을) 새기다 | graved | graven, graved | |
| **grind** (갈아서) 가루로 만들다 | **ground** | **ground** | |
| **grow** 성장하다 | **grew** | **grown** | |
| H hamstring 절름발이를 만들다 | -strung, 《고》 | -strung, 《고》 | |
| **hang** 걸다, 매달다 | **hung** └-stringed | **hung** └-stringed | |
| **have**, **has** 갖다 | **had** | **had** | |
| **hear** 듣다 | **heard** | **heard** | |
| heave 《항해》 감아 올리다, 던 | hove | hove | |
| hew 베어 넘기다 └지다 | hewed | hewn, hewed | |
| **hide** 숨기다, 숨다 | **hid** | **hidden**, **hid** | |
| **hit** 맞히다, 때리다 | **hit** | **hit** | **-tting** |
| **hold** 잡다, 유지하다 | **held** | **held** | |
| **hurt** 상처내다 | **hurt** | **hurt** | |
| I inlay 박아 넣다 | inlaid | inlaid | |
| inset 끼워넣다 | inset | inset | -tting |
| K **keep** 유지하다 | **kept** | **kept** | |
| kneel [ni:l] 무릎을 꿇다 | knelt [nelt], kneeled | knelt [nelt], kneeled | |
| knit 짜다 | knitted, knit | knitted, knit | -tting |
| **know** 알다 | **knew** | **known** | |
| L lade 짐을 싣다 | laded | laden, laded | |
| **lay** 놓다, 눕히다 | **laid** | **laid** | |
| **lead** 이끌다 | **led** | **led** | |
| **lean** 기대다 | **leaned**, **leant** [lent] | **leaned**, **leant** [lent] | |
| **leap** (껑충) 뛰다 | **leaped**, **leapt** | **leaped**, **leapt** | |
| | [《미》 li:pt/《영》 lept] | [《미》 li:pt/《영》 lept] | |
| **learn** 배우다, 알다 | **learned**, **learnt** | **learned**, **learnt** | |
| **leave** 떠나다 | **left** | **left** | |
| **lend** 빌리다 | **lent** | **lent** | |
| **let** …시키다 | **let** | **let** | **-tting** |

| | 현 재 | 과 거 | 과 거 분 사 | 현재분사 |
|---|---|---|---|---|
| | **lie** 드러눕다, 가로놓이다 | **lay** | **lain** | **lying** |
| | **light** 빛나다, 내리다 | **lighted, lit** | **lighted, lit** | |
| | **lose** 잃다 | **lost** | **lost** | |
| M | **make** 만들다 | **made** | **made** | |
| | **may** …일지도 모르다 | **might** | — | |
| | **mean** 의미를 갖다 | **meant** [ment] | **meant** [ment] | |
| | **meet** 만나다 | **met** | **met** | |
| | methinks …라 생각되다 | methought | — | |
| | misgive 염려케 하다 | misgave | misgiven | |
| | mislay 잘못 놓다 | mislaid | mislaid | |
| | mislead 그릇 판단케 하다 | misled | misled | |
| | misread 잘못 읽다 | misread [misréd] | misread [misréd] | |
| | misspell 잘못 쓰다 | misspelled, misspelt | misspelled, misspelt | |
| | **mistake** 틀리다 | **mistook** | **mistaken** | |
| | misunderstand 오해하다 | misunderstood | misunderstood | |
| | mow 베다 | mowed | mowed, mown | |
| | **must**[1] …하지 않으면 안 되다 | **had to, must** | **have had to** | |
| | **must**[2] …에 틀림없다 | **must have**+*p.p* | — | |
| O | **ought to** …하여야 한다 | **ought to have**+*p.p.* | — | |
| | outbid 비싼 값을 매기다 | outbade, outbid | outbidden, outbid | -dding |
| | outdo …보다 낫다 | outdid | outdone | |
| | outgo …보다 빨리 가다 | outwent | outgone | |
| | outgrow …보다 크게 되다 | outgrew | outgrown | |
| | outlay 소비하다, 쓰다 | outlaid | outlaid | |
| | outride …보다 빨리 타고 가다, 앞지르다 | outrode | outridden | |
| | outrun …보다 빨리 달리다 | outran | outrun | -nning |
| | outshine …보다 빛나다 | outshone | outshone | |
| | outspread 펼치다, 퍼지다 | outspread | outspread | |
| | outwear …보다 오래가다〔견디다〕 | outwore | outworn | |
| | overbear 압도하다 | overbore | overborne | |
| | overblow 날려 버리다 | overblew | overblown | |
| | overcast 어둡게 하다 | overcast | overcast | |
| | overcome 정복하다 | overcame | overcome | |
| | overdo 도를 지나치다 | overdid | overdone | |
| | overdraw 과장하여 말하다 | overdrew | overdrawn | |
| | overdrink 과음하다 | overdrank | overdrunk | |
| | overeat 과식하다 | overate | overeaten | |
| | overgrow 전면에 자라다 《잡초 따위가》 | overgrew | overgrown | |
| | overhang …위에 걸치다 | overhung | overhung | |
| | overhear 언뜻〔귓결에〕 듣다 | overheard | overheard | |
| | overlay 들씌우다 | overlaid | overlaid | |
| | overleap 뛰어 넘다 | overleaped, overleapt | overleaped, overleapt | |
| | overlie …위에 눕다 | overlay | overlain | -lying |
| | overpay 더 많이 지불하다 | overpaid | overpaid | |
| | override 짓밟다 | overrode | overridden | |
| | overrun 침략하다 | overran | overrun | -nning |
| | oversee 감독하다 | oversaw | overseen | |

| | 현 재 | 과 거 | 과 거 분 사 | 현재분사 |
|---|---|---|---|---|
| | oversell 너무 팔다 | oversold | oversold | |
| | overset …을 뒤엎다 | overset | overset | -tting |
| | overshoot 지나치다 | overshot | overshot | |
| | oversleep 너무 오래 자다 | overslept | overslept | |
| | overspend 낭비하다 | overspent | overspent | |
| | overspread 온면에 덮다 | overspread | overspread | |
| | overtake 따라 붙다 | overtook | overtaken | |
| | overthrow 뒤집어 엎다 | overthrew | overthrown | |
| | overwork 지나치게 일하다 | -worked, overwrought | -worked, overwrought | |
| | overwrite 너무 쓰다 | overwrote | overwritten | |
| P | partake (얼마큼) 마시다, 먹다 | partook | partaken | |
| | **pass** 통과하다, 통과시키다 | **passed** | **passed**, 《고》 *past* | |
| | **pay** 지급하다 | **paid** | **paid** | |
| | pen 가두다 | penned, pent | penned, pent | -nning |
| | prove 증명하다 | proved | proved, proven | |
| | **put** 놓다 | **put** | **put** | **-tting** |
| Q | quit 포기하다, 그만두다 | quitted, quit | quitted, quit | -tting |
| R | radiocast 라디오로 방송하다 | radiocast, radiocasted | radiocast, radiocasted | |
| | **read** [riːd] 읽다 | **read** [red] | **read** [red] | |
| | reave 약탈하다 | reaved, reft | reaved, reft | |
| | rebuild [ribíld] 재건하다 | rebuilt | rebuilt | |
| | recast [rikɑ́ːst] 고쳐 만들다 | recast | recast | |
| | relay 교체시키다 | relaid | relaid | |
| | rend 찢다, 분열시키다 | rent | rent | |
| | repay 환급하다, 보답하다 | repaid | repaid | |
| | reread [riríːd] 다시 읽다 | reread [-réd] | reread [-réd] | |
| | resell [risél] 전매하다 | resold | resold | |
| | retake [ritéik] 회복하다 | retook | retaken | |
| | rewrite [riráit] 다시 쓰다 | rewrote | rewritten | |
| | rid 면하게 하다 | rid, ridded | rid, ridded | -dding |
| | **ride** 말 따위를 타다 | **rode** | **ridden** | |
| | **ring** 울리다 | **rang** [ræŋ] | **rung** [rʌŋ] | |
| | **rise** 올리다, 올라가다 | **rose** | **risen** [rizn] | |
| | rive [raiv] 잡아 뜯다 | rived | rived, riven [rívn] | |
| | roughcast [rʌ́f-] 초벽을 치다, …의 대강 줄거리를 세우다 | roughcast | roughcast | |
| | **run** [rʌn] 달리다 | **ran** [ræn] | **run** [rʌn] | **-nning** |
| S | saw 톱으로 켜다 | sawed | sawed, sawn | |
| | **say** 말하다 | **said** [sed] | **said** [sed] | |
| | **see** 보다 | **saw** | **seen** | |
| | **seek** …을 구하다 | **sought** [sɔːt] | **sought** [sɔːt] | |
| | **sell** 팔다 | **sold** | **sold** | |
| | **send** 보내다 | **sent** | **sent** | |
| | **set** 배치하다, 설치하다 | **set** | **set** | **-tting** |
| | **sew** [sou] 꿰매다 | **sewed** | **sewed**, **sewn** | |
| | **shake** 떨다, 흔들다 | **shook** [ʃuk] | **shaken** | |
| | **shall** …일 것이다 | **should** [ʃud] | — | |
| | shave 면도하다 | shaved | shaved, shaven | |
| | shear 양 따위의 털을 깎다 | sheared | sheared, shorn | |

| 현 재 | 과 거 | 과 거 분 사 | 현재분사 |
|---|---|---|---|
| **shed** 흘리다 | **shed** | **shed** | **-dding** |
| **shine** 반짝이다 | **shone** | **shone** | |
| shoe 말에 편자를 박다 | shod | shod, shodden | |
| **shoot** 쏘다, 발사하다 | **shot** | **shot** | |
| **show** 보이다, 증명하다 | **showed** | **shown**, **showed** | |
| shred 조각을 내다 | shredded, shred | shredded, shred | -dding |
| shrink 오그라들다, 움츠리다 | shrank, shrunk | shrunk, shrunken | |
| **shut** 닫다 | **shut** | **shut** | **-tting** |
| **sing** 노래하다 | **sang**, sung [sæŋ, sʌŋ] | **sung** [sʌŋ] | |
| **sink** 가라앉다, 가라앉히다 | **sank**, sunk | **sunk**, sunken | |
| **sit** 앉다 | **sat** | **sat** | **-tting** |
| slay 죽이다, 살해하다 | slew | slain | |
| **sleep** 자다 | **slept** | **slept** | |
| slide 미끄러지다〔뜨리다〕 | slid | slid, slidden | |
| sling 던지다 | slung | slung | |
| slink 살금살금 걷다 | slunk | slunk | |
| slit 가늘게 베다, 찢다 | slit | slit | -tting |
| **smell** 냄새를 맡다, 냄새 나다 | **smelled**, **smelt** | **smelled**, **smelt** | |
| smite 세게 치다 | smote | smitten, smit, smote | |
| **sow** 종자를 뿌리다 | **sowed** | **sown**, **sowed** | |
| **speak** 말하다 | **spoke** | **spoken** | |
| **speed** 급히 가다, 서둘게 하다 | **sped**, **speeded** | **sped**, **speeded** | |
| **spell** 철자하다 | **spelled**, **spelt** | **spelled**, **spelt** | |
| spellbind 마술을 걸다 | spellbound | spellbound | |
| **spend** 소비하다, 쓰다 | **spent** | **spent** | |
| spill 흘리다, 흐르다 | spilled, spilt | spilled, spilt | |
| spin 실을 잣다 | spun | spun | -nning |
| spit 침을 뱉다 | spat, spit | spat, spit | -tting |
| split 찢다, 갈라지다 | split | split | -tting |
| **spoil** 망쳐놓다, 망치다 | **spoiled**, **spoilt** | **spoild**, **spoilt** | |
| **spread** 펴다, 펼치다 | **spread** | **spread** | |
| **spring** 튀다, 튀게 하다 | **sprang**, **sprung** | **sprung** | |
| squat 웅크리다 | squatted, squat | squatted, squat | -tting |
| **stand** 서다, 세우다 | **stood** | **stood** | |
| stave 통널을 떼내다 | staved, stove | staved, stove | |
| **steal** 훔치다 | **stole** | **stolen** | |
| stick 찌르다, 고집하다 | stuck | stuck | |
| sting 찌르다, 자극하다 | stung | stung | |
| stink 악취를 풍기다 | stank, stunk | stunk | |
| strew 흩뿌리다, 뿌리다 | strewed | strewed, strewn | |
| stride 활보하다 | strode | stridden, 《고》 strid | |
| **strike** 치다 | **struck** | **struck**, stricken | |
| string 실로 꿰다 | strung | strung | |
| strive 노력하다 | strove | striven [strívn] | |
| sunburn 볕에 태우다 | sunburned, sunburnt | sunburned, sunburnt | |
| **swear** 신명에게 맹세하다 | **swore** | **sworn** | |
| sweat [swet] 땀을 흘리다 | sweat, sweated | sweat, sweated | |
| **sweep** 쓸다, 청소하다 | **swept** | **swept** | |
| **swell** 부풀다, 부풀리다 | **swelled** | **swelled**, **swollen** | |

| 현 재 | 과 거 | 과 거 분 사 | 현재분사 |
|---|---|---|---|
| **swim** 수영하다 | **swam** | **swum** | **-mming** |
| **swing** 흔들리다, 흔들다 | **swung** | **swung** | |
| **T take** 취하다, 타다, 먹다, 마시다 | **took** | **taken** | |
| **teach** 가르치다, 교육하다 | **taught** | **taught** | |
| **tear** [tɛər] 찢다, 잡아찢다 | **tore** | **torn** | |
| telecast 텔레비전 방송을 하다 | telecast, telecasted | telecast, telecasted | |
| **tell** 말하다, 알리다 | **told** | **told** | |
| **think** 생각하다, …라 여기다 | **thought** | **thought** | |
| thrive 번창하다, 무성하다 | throve, thrived | thriven [θrívn], thrived | |
| **throw** 던지다 | **threw** | **thrown** | |
| thrust 밀다 | thrust | thrust | |
| tread 걷다, 밟다 | trod | trodden, trod | |
| **U** unbend 똑바로 펴다 | unbent | unbent | |
| unbind (매듭을) 풀다 | unbound | unbound | |
| underbid …보다 싸게 하다 | underbid | underbid, underbidden | |
| undergo 경험하다 | underwent | undergone | |
| underlay …의 밑에 깔다 | underlaid | underlaid | |
| underlie …의 밑에 있다, 눕다 | underlay | underlain | -lying |
| undersell …보다 싼 값에 팔다 | undersold | undersold | |
| **understand** 이해하다 | **understood** | **understood** | |
| undertake 인수하다, 떠맡다 | undertook | undertaken | |
| underwrite 밑에 기명하다 | underwrote | underwritten | |
| undo 원상태로 하다 | undid | undone | |
| ungird …의 띠를 끄르다 | ungirt, ungirded | ungirt, ungirded | |
| unlay 꼬인 것을 바로잡다 | unlaid | unlaid | |
| upset 뒤집어 엎다 | upset | upset | -tting |
| **W wake** (잠을 깨다, 깨우다) | **waked**, **woke** | **waked**, woken, 《고》 **woke** | |
| waylay 매복하다 | waylaid | waylaid | |
| **wear** 몸에 지니고〔입고〕 있다 | **wore** | **worn** | |
| weave 베를 짜다, 엮다 | wove | woven, wove | |
| wed …와 결혼하다 | wedded | wedded, 《고》 wed | -dding |
| **weep** 울다 | **wept** | **wept** | |
| **will** …할 것이다 | **would** [wud] | —— | |
| **win** 이기다, 얻다 | **won** [wʌn] | **won** [wʌn] | **-nning** |
| **wind** [waind] 감다 | **wound** [waund] | **wound** [waund] | |
| withdraw 움츠리다 | withdrew | withdrawn | |
| withhold 보류하다 | withheld | withheld | |
| withstand 저항하다, 반항하다 | withstood | withstood | |
| **work** 일하다, 공부하다 | **worked**, 《고》 **wrought** [rɔːt] | **worked**, 《고》 **wrought** [rɔːt] | |
| wrap 싸다, 감싸다 | wrapped, wrapt | wrapped, wrapt | -pping |
| wring 짜다, 짜내다 | wrung | wrung | |
| **write** 쓰다 | **wrote** | **written** | |

# (17) 우리 나라 행정 구역의 로마자 표기(도·시·구·군·읍)
## Names of Administrative Units

※문화관광부고시 제2000-8호, 2000.7.7.국어의 로마자 표기법에 의거.
※지면 관계로 반복되는 동일한 구명(區名) 및 군명(郡名)과 읍명이 같은 것은 생략하였음.

| 한글(한자) Hangeul(Chinese Characters) | 로마자 표기 Romanization |
|---|---|
| 서울특별시(서울特別市) | Seoul-teukbyeolsi |
| 종로구(鍾路區) | Chongno-gu |
| 중구(中區) | Chung-gu |
| 용산구(龍山區) | Yongsan-gu |
| 성동구(城東區) | Seongdong-gu |
| 광진구(廣津區) | Gwangjin-gu |
| 동대문구(東大門區) | Dongdaemun-gu |
| 중랑구(中浪區) | Jungnang-gu |
| 성북구(城北區) | Seongbuk-gu |
| 강북구(江北區) | Gangbuk-gu |
| 도봉구(道峰區) | Dobong-gu |
| 노원구(蘆原區) | Nowon-gu |
| 은평구(恩平區) | Eunpyeong-gu |
| 서대문구(西大門區) | Seodaemun-gu |
| 마포구(麻浦區) | Mapo-gu |
| 강서구(江西區) | Gangseo-gu |
| 양천구(陽川區) | Yangcheon-gu |
| 구로구(九老區) | Guro-gu |
| 금천구(衿川區) | Geumcheon-gu |
| 영등포구(永登浦區) | Yeongdeungpo-gu |
| 동작구(銅雀區) | Dongjak-gu |
| 관악구(冠岳區) | Gwanak-gu |
| 강남구(江南區) | Gangnam-gu |
| 서초구(瑞草區) | Seocho-gu |
| 강동구(江東區) | Gangdong-gu |
| 송파구(松坡區) | Songpa-gu |
| 부산광역시(釜山廣域市) | Busan-gwangyeoksi |
| 중구(中區) | Jung-gu |
| 동구(東區) | Dong-gu |
| 서구(西區) | Seo-gu |
| 남구(南區) | Nam-gu |
| 북구(北區) | Buk-gu |
| 영도구(影島區) | Yeongdo-gu |
| 부산진구(釜山鎭區) | Busanjin-gu |
| 동래구(東萊區) | Dongnae-gu |
| 해운대구(海雲臺區) | Haeundae-gu |
| 금정구(金井區) | Geumjeong-gu |
| 사하구(沙下區) | Saha-gu |
| 강서구(江西區) | Gangseo-gu |
| 연제구(蓮堤區) | Yeonje-gu |
| 수영구(水營區) | Suyeong-gu |

| 한글(한자) Hangeul(Chinese Characters) | 로마자 표기 Romanization |
|---|---|
| 사상구(沙上區) | Sasang-gu |
| 기장군(機張郡) | Gijang-gun |
| 대구광역시(大邱廣域市) | Daegu-gwangyeoksi |
| 달서구(達西區) | Dalseo-gu |
| 수성구(壽城區) | Suseong-gu |
| 달성군(達城郡) | Dalseong-gun |
| 인천광역시(仁川廣域市) | Incheon-gwangyeoksi |
| 연수구(延壽區) | Yeonsu-gu |
| 계양구(桂陽區) | Gyeyang-gu |
| 부평구(富平區) | Bupyeong-gu |
| 남동구(南洞區) | Namdong-gu |
| 강화군(江華郡) | Ganghwa-gun |
| 옹진군(甕津郡) | Ongjin-gun |
| 광주광역시(光州廣域市) | Gwangju-gwangyeoksi |
| 광산구(光山區) | Gwangsan-gu |
| 대전광역시(大田廣域市) | Daejeon-gwangyeoksi |
| 유성구(儒城區) | Yuseong-gu |
| 대덕구(大德區) | Daedeok-gu |
| 울산광역시(蔚山廣域市) | Ulsan-gwangyeoksi |
| 울주구(蔚州區) | Ulju-gu |
| 경기도(京畿道) | Gyeonggi-do |
| 수원시(水原市) | Suwon-si |
| 성남시(城南市) | Seongnam-si |
| 의정부시(議政府市) | Uijeongbu-si |
| 안양시(安養市) | Anyang-si |
| 부천시(富川市) | Bucheon-si |
| 광명시(光明市) | Gwangmyeong-si |
| 고양시(高陽市) | Goyang-si |
| 동두천시(東豆川市) | Dongducheon-si |
| 안산시(安山市) | Ansan-si |
| 과천시(果川市) | Gwacheon-si |
| 평택시(平澤市) | Pyeongtaek-si |
| 오산시(烏山市) | Osan-si |
| 시흥시(始興市) | Siheung-si |
| 군포시(軍浦市) | Gunpo-si |
| 의왕시(儀旺市) | Uiwang-si |
| 구리시(九里市) | Guri-si |
| 용인시(龍仁市) | Yongin-si |

| 한글(한자) Hangeul(Chinese Characters) | 로마자 표기 Romanization | 한글(한자) Hangeul(Chinese Characters) | 로마자 표기 Romanization |
|---|---|---|---|
| 상주시(尙州市) | Sangju-si | 양산시(梁山市) | Yangsan-si |
| 함창읍(咸昌邑) | Hamchang-eup | 웅상읍(熊上邑) | Ungsang-eup |
| 문경시(聞慶市) | Mungyeong-si | 물금읍(勿禁邑) | Mulgeum-eup |
| 가은읍(加恩邑) | Gaeun-eup | 김해시(金海市) | Gimhae-si |
| 경산시(慶山市) | Gyeongsan-si | 진영읍(進永邑) | Jinyeong-eup |
| 하양읍(河陽邑) | Hayang-eup | 밀양시(密陽市) | Miryang-si |
| 군위군(軍威郡) | Gunwi-gun | 삼랑진읍(三浪津邑) | Samnangjin-eup |
| 의성군(義城郡) | Uiseong-gun | 하남읍(下南邑) | Hanam-eup |
| 청송군(靑松郡) | Cheongsong-gun | 거제시(巨濟市) | Geoje-si |
| 영양군(英陽郡) | Yeongyang-gun | 신현읍(新縣邑) | Sinhyeon-eup |
| 영덕군(盈德郡) | Yeongdeok-gun | 의령군(宜寧郡) | Uiryeong-gun |
| 청도군(淸道郡) | Cheongdo-gun | 함안군(咸安郡) | Haman-gun |
| 화양읍(華陽邑) | Hwayang-eup | 가야읍(伽倻邑) | Gaya-eup |
| 고령군(高靈郡) | Goryeong-gun | 창녕군(昌寧郡) | Changnyeong-gun |
| 성주군(星州郡) | Seongju-gun | 남지읍(南旨邑) | Namji-eup |
| 칠곡군(漆谷郡) | Chilgok-gun | 고성군(固城郡) | Goseong-gun |
| 왜관읍(倭館邑) | Waegwan-eup | 남해군(南海郡) | Namhae-gun |
| 예천군(醴泉郡) | Yecheon-gun | 하동군(河東郡) | Hadong-gun |
| 봉화군(奉化郡) | Bonghwa-gun | 산청군(山淸郡) | Sancheong-gun |
| 울진군(蔚珍郡) | Uljin-gun | 함양군(咸陽郡) | Hamyang-gun |
| 평해읍(平海邑) | Pyeonghae-eup | 거창군(居昌郡) | Geochang-gun |
| 울릉군(鬱陵郡) | Ulleung-gun | 합천군(陜川郡) | Hapcheon-gun |
| 경상남도(慶尙南道) | Gyeongsangnam-do | 제주도(濟州道) | Jeju-do |
| 마산시(馬山市) | Masan-si | 제주시(濟州市) | Jeju-si |
| 합포구(合浦區) | Happo-gu | 서귀포시(西歸浦市) | Seogwipo-si |
| 회원구(會原區) | Hoewon-gu | 북제주군(北濟州郡) | Bukjeju-gun |
| 내서읍(內西邑) | Naeseo-eup | 한림읍(翰林邑) | Hallim-eup |
| 진주시(晋州市) | Jinju-si | 애월읍(涯月邑) | Aewol-eup |
| 문산읍(文山邑) | Munsan-eup | 구좌읍(舊左邑) | Gujwa-eup |
| 창원시(昌原市) | Changwon-si | 조천읍(朝天邑) | Jocheon-eup |
| 동읍(東邑) | Dong-eup | 남제주군(南濟州郡) | Namjeju-gun |
| 진해시(鎭海市) | Jinhae-si | 대정읍(大靜邑) | Daejeong-eup |
| 통영시(統營市) | Tongyeong-si | 남원읍(南元邑) | Namwon-eup |
| 산양읍(山陽邑) | Sanyang-eup | 성산읍(城山邑) | Seongsan-eup |
| 사천시(泗川市) | Sacheon-si | | |